South America
Central America
and the
Caribbean
2015

South America Central America and the Caribbean 2015

23rd Edition

Routledge
Taylor & Francis Group

LONDON AND NEW YORK

23rd edition published 2014
by Routledge
2 Park Square, Milton Park, Abingdon, Oxon, OX14 4RN

and by Routledge
711 Third Avenue, New York, NY 10017

Routledge is an imprint of the Taylor & Francis Group, an Informa business

First published 1985

ISBN: 978-1-85743-733-1
ISSN 0258-0661

Regional Editor Jackie West

Regional Organizations Editor Helen Canton

Senior Editor, Statistics Philip McIntyre

Senior Editor, Directory Iain Frame

Statistics Researchers Varun Wadhawan (Team Manager), Mohd Khalid Ansari (Senior Research and Training Associate),
Meghal Arora, Swati Gambhir, Nirbachita Sarkar

Directory Editorial Researchers Arijit Khasnobis (Team Manager), Rima Kar (Deputy Team Leader),
Bhawna Chauhan, Swati Chopra, Anveshi Gupta

Contributing Editors (Commodities) Gareth Wyn Jones, Gareth Vaughan

Contributing Editor (Regional Organizations) Catriona Holman

Senior Editor Juliet Love

Typeset in New Century Schoolbook
by Data Standards Limited, Frome, Somerset

Printed and bound in the United States of America by
Edwards Brothers Malloy on sustainably sourced paper

FOREWORD

The 23rd edition of SOUTH AMERICA, CENTRAL AMERICA AND THE CARIBBEAN provides a survey of the political and economic life both of the region and of the more than 50 countries and territories within it. The volume contains three distinct, though complementary, areas. Part One consists of seven introductory articles, covering a variety of subjects of regional significance, including an analysis of changes in Latin American politics; the moves towards autonomy in the Caribbean Overseas Territories; reform of drugs policy in Latin America; the continuing violence and domestic insecurity in Mexico; and natural hazards in the Caribbean. New for this edition is an examination of the growing influence of the People's Republic of China in Latin America, as well as an assessment of the geopolitics of energy in the Caribbean. In Part Two the main political and economic events in each of the 54 countries and territories in the region are examined in detail. In addition, all statistical and directory material has been extensively updated. Comprehensive coverage of international organizations active in Latin America and the Caribbean is included in Part Three, as are research institutes, books and periodicals relevant to the region. Extensive background information on the region's major primary commodities is also provided.

There was much change in many of the countries of the region in the year under review. Changes of government took place in Chile, Honduras, El Salvador, Costa Rica, Panama, Antigua and Barbuda, Sint Maarten and Montserrat. Presidential elections were also due before the end of 2014 in Brazil, Bolivia and Uruguay. In Brazil, President Dilma Rousseff was campaigning to secure a second term in office and an unprecedented fourth consecutive term for her Partido dos Trabalhadores, while in Bolivia another left-wing head of state, Evo Morales, was aiming for re-election. Similarly, in Uruguay, the left-leaning Frente Amplio was hoping for a third presidential term. In Haiti, progress was made towards the holding of much-overdue legislative elections before the end of the year, with the conclusion of the 'El Rancho' accord in January and the appointment of a new electoral council in May. President Juan Manuel Santos won another term in office in Colombia in June; the victory was seen as endorsement of his ongoing negotiations with the Fuerzas Armadas Revolucionarias de Colombia (FARC) rebels in an attempt to end the long-running civil war.

In various parts of the region, there was economic and political upheaval. In mid-2014 a US ruling in favour of foreign creditors (the so-called 'vulture' funds) who had refused rescheduled repayment terms pushed Argentina into a technical default and the Argentine economy towards an uncertain future. In Mexico, Enrique Peña Nieto's administration succeeded in gaining legislative approval for wide-ranging economic reforms that were expected to revolutionize the country's energy and telecommunications sectors. Meanwhile, in Venezuela, the Government of Nicolás Maduro struggled to contend with social unrest caused, *inter alia*, by rising prices and shortages of basic goods. The continuing gloomy economic outlook in Venezuela threatened the future of its Petrocaribe initiative, on which many Caribbean countries, already under economic pressure, depended for cheap oil supplies.

The entire content of the print edition of SOUTH AMERICA, CENTRAL AMERICA AND THE CARIBBEAN is available online at www.europaworld.com. This prestigious resource incorporates sophisticated search and browse functions as well as specially commissioned visual and statistical content. An ongoing programme of updates of key areas of information ensures currency of content, and enhances the richness of the coverage.

The Editors are grateful to all the contributors for their articles and advice, and to the numerous governments and organizations that provided statistical and other information.

September 2014

HEALTH AND WELFARE STATISTICS: SOURCES AND DEFINITIONS

Total fertility rate Source: WHO Global Health Observatory. The number of children that would be born per woman, assuming no female mortality at child-bearing ages and the age-specific fertility rates of a specified country and reference period.

Under-5 mortality rate Source: WHO Global Health Observatory. Defined by WHO as the probability of a child born in a specific year or period dying before reaching the age of five, if subject to the age-specific mortality rates of that year or period.

HIV/AIDS Source: UNAIDS. Estimated percentage of adults aged 15 to 49 years living with HIV/AIDS. < indicates 'fewer than'.

Health expenditure Source: WHO Global Health Observatory.
US $ per head (PPP)
International dollar estimates, derived by dividing local currency units by an estimate of their purchasing-power parity (PPP) compared with the US dollar. PPPs are the rates of currency conversion that equalize the purchasing power of different currencies by eliminating the differences in price levels between countries.
% of GDP
GDP levels for OECD countries follow the most recent UN System of National Accounts. For non-OECD countries a value was estimated by utilizing existing UN, IMF and World Bank data.
Public expenditure
Government health-related outlays plus expenditure by social schemes compulsorily affiliated with a sizeable share of the population, and extrabudgetary funds allocated to health services. Figures include grants or loans provided by international agencies, other national authorities, and sometimes commercial banks.

Access to water and sanitation Source: WHO/UNICEF Joint Monitoring Programme on Water Supply and Sanitation (JMP) (Progress on Drinking Water and Sanitation, 2013 Update). Defined in terms of the percentage of the population using improved facilities in terms of the type of technology and levels of service afforded. For water, this includes house connections, public standpipes, boreholes with handpumps, protected dug wells, protected spring and rainwater collection; allowance is also made for other locally defined technologies. Sanitation is defined to include connection to a sewer or septic tank system, pour-flush latrine, simple pit or ventilated improved pit latrine, again with allowance for acceptable local technologies. Access to water and sanitation does not imply that the level of service or quality of water is 'adequate' or 'safe'.

Carbon dioxide emissions Source: World Bank, World Development Indicators database, citing the Carbon Dioxide Information Analysis Center (sponsored by the US Department of Energy). Emissions comprise those resulting from the burning of fossil fuels (including those produced during consumption of solid, liquid and gas fuels and from gas flaring) and from the manufacture of cement.

Human Development Index (HDI) Source: UNDP, *Human Development Report* (2014). A summary of human development measured by three basic dimensions: prospects for a long and healthy life, measured by life expectancy at birth; access to knowledge, measured by a combination of mean years of schooling and expected years of schooling; and standard of living, measured by GNI per head (PPP US $). The index value obtained lies between zero and one. A value above 0.796 indicates very high human development, between 0.710 and 0.796 high human development, between 0.534 and 0.710 medium human development, and below 0.534 low human development. A centralized data source for all three dimensions was not available for all countries. In some cases other data sources were used to calculate a substitute value; however, this was excluded from the ranking. Other countries, including non-UNDP members, were excluded from the HDI altogether. In total, 187 countries were ranked for 2013.

ACKNOWLEDGEMENTS

The editors gratefully acknowledge the co-operation, interest and enthusiasm of all the authors who have contributed to the volume. We are also indebted to the many organizations connected with the region, particularly the national statistical offices. We owe special thanks to a number of embassies and ministries. We are also grateful to the University of Southampton Cartographic Unit for supplying the maps included in the Geography sections.

We are most grateful for permission to make extensive use of material from the following sources: the United Nations' statistical databases and *Demographic Yearbook*, *Statistical Yearbook*, *Monthly Bulletin of Statistics*, *Industrial Commodity Statistics Yearbook* and *International Trade Statistics Yearbook*; the United Nations Educational, Scientific and Cultural Organization's *Statistical Yearbook* and Institute for Statistics database; the *Human Development Report* of the United Nations Development Programme; the Food and Agriculture Organization of the United Nations' statistical database; the statistical databases of the World Health Organization; the statistical databases of the UNCTAD/WTO International Trade Centre; the International Labour Office's statistical database and *Yearbook of Labour Statistics*; the World Bank's *World Bank Atlas*, *Global Development Finance*, *World Development Report* and World Development Indicators database; the International Monetary Fund's statistical database, *International Financial Statistics* and *Government Finance Statistics Yearbook*; the World Tourism Organization's *Compendium* and *Yearbook of Tourism Statistics*; the UN Economic Commission for Latin America and the Caribbean's Statistical Yearbook; the US Geological Survey; the International Telecommunication Union; the International Road Federation's *World Road Statistics*; Lloyd's List; and *The Military Balance 2014*, a publication of the International Institute for Strategic Studies, Arundel House, 13–15 Arundel Street, London WC2R 3DX.

CONTENTS

THE CONTRIBUTORS

Charles Arthur. Freelance journalist specializing in Caribbean politics and economics.

Dr Ame Bergés. Associate Fellow of the Institute of Latin American Studies, University of London, United Kingdom, and freelance writer specializing in Latin American economic development.

Dr Roland O. B. van den Bergh. Economist at Curconsult NV, Curaçao.

Dr Julia Buxton. Professor of Comparative Politics in the School of Public Policy at the Central European University, Budapest, Hungary.

Jessica Byron. Senior Lecturer in the Department of Government at the University of the West Indies, Mona Campus, Kingston, Jamaica.

Prof. Peter A. R. Calvert. Emeritus Professor of Comparative and International Politics at the University of Southampton, United Kingdom.

Dr Peter Clegg. Senior Lecturer in the Department of History, Philosophy and Politics at the University of the West of England, Bristol, United Kingdom.

Dr John Crabtree. Research Associate at the Latin American Centre at the University of Oxford, United Kingdom.

Dr David Díaz Arias. Associate Professor of History and Director of Graduate Studies in the Department of History at the University of Costa Rica.

Prof. David Fleischer. Professor of Political Science at the Instituto Sociedade, População e Natureza at the University of Brasília, Brazil.

Prof. Francisco E. González. Riordan Roett Senior Associate Professor of Latin American Studies at the School of Advanced International Studies at Johns Hopkins University, Washington, DC, USA.

Thomas Grisaffi. Leverhulme Early Career Research Fellow at the Institute of Latin American Studies, University of London, United Kingdom.

Dr David Howard. Lecturer in Sustainable Urban Development at the University of Oxford, United Kingdom.

Dr Gareth A. Jones. Professor of Urban Geography in the Department of Geography at the London School of Economics and Political Science, United Kingdom.

Prof. Antoni Kapcia. Professor of Latin American History and Director of the Centre for Research on Cuba at the University of Nottingham, United Kingdom.

Prof. Colin M. Lewis. Professor Emeritus of Latin American Economic History at the London School of Economics and Political Science, United Kingdom.

Prof. Robert E. Looney. Professor of National Security Affairs and Associate Chair of Instruction in the Department of National Security Affairs at the Naval Postgraduate School, Monterey, CA, USA.

Sandy Markwick. Writer and researcher specializing in Latin American affairs.

Dr Emily Morris. Research Associate and Lecturer in the Economic Development of Latin America and the Caribbean at University College London's Institute of the Americas, United Kingdom.

Sir Keith Morris. Former British Ambassador to Colombia.

Pablo Navarrete. Freelance writer and researcher on Latin America.

Dr Keron Niles. Renewable energy and energy efficiency specialist.

Dr Francisco Panizza. Associate Professor of Latin American Politics at the London School of Economics and Political Science, United Kingdom.

Daniel Sachs. Political Analyst for Control Risks, London, United Kingdom, specializing in Mexico, Central America and the Caribbean.

Dr Diego Sánchez-Ancochea. Lecturer in the Political Economy of Latin America at the University of Oxford, United Kingdom.

Dr Hans Steinmüller. Assistant Professor in the Department of Anthropology at the London School of Economics and Political Science, United Kingdom.

Jeremy Thorp. Former British Ambassador to Colombia.

Dr Ronny Viales-Hurtado. Professor of Economic History in the Graduate Programme of the University of Costa Rica.

Nicholas Watson. Director of Latin America Analysis at Teneo Intelligence, New York, USA.

Dr Peter Watt. Lecturer in the Department of Hispanic Studies at the University of Sheffield, United Kingdom.

Phillip Wearne. Writer and researcher specializing in Latin American affairs.

Mark Wilson. Writer and researcher specializing in Caribbean affairs.

ABBREVIATIONS

Abog.	Abogado	Confed.	Confederation	
AC	Acre	Cont.	Contador	
Acad.	Academician; Academy	Corpn	Corporation	
Adm.	Admiral	CP	Case Postale; Caixa Postal (Post Box)	
admin.	administration	C por A	Compañía por Acciones (Joint Stock Company)	
AG	Aktiengesellschaft (Joint Stock Company)	Cres.	Crescent	
Ags	Aguascalientes	CSTAL	Confederación Sindical de los Trabajadores de América Latina	
a.i.	ad interim			
AID	(US) Agency for International Development	CT	Connecticut	
AIDS	acquired immunodeficiency syndrome	CTCA	Confederación de Trabajadores Centroamericanos	
AK	Alaska	Cttee	Committee	
AL	Alabama, Alagoas	cu	cubic	
ALADI	Asociación Latino-Americana de Integración	cwt	hundredweight	
Alt.	Alternate			
AM	Amazonas; Amplitude Modulation	DC	District of Columbia, Distrito Central	
amalg.	amalgamated	DE	Delaware, Departamento Estatal	
AP	Amapá	Dec.	December	
Apdo	Apartado (Post Box)	Del.	Delegación	
approx.	approximately	Dem.	Democratic; Democrat	
Apt	Apartment	Dep.	Deputy	
Apto	Apartamento	dep.	deposits	
AR	Arkansas	Dept	Department	
asscn	association	devt	development	
assoc.	associate	DF	Distrito Federal	
asst	assistant	Dgo	Durango	
Aug.	August	Diag.	Diagonal	
auth.	authorized	Dir	Director	
Ave	Avenue	Div.	Division	
Av., Avda	Avenida (Avenue)	DN	Distrito Nacional	
AZ	Arizona	dpto	departamento	
		Dr(a)	Doctor(a)	
BA	Bahia	Dr.	Drive	
BCN	Baja California Norte	DR-CAFTA	Dominican Republic-Central American Free Trade Agreement	
BCS	Baja California Sur			
Bd	Board	dwt	dead weight tons	
Blvd, Blvr	Boulevard			
b/d	barrels per day	E	East, Eastern	
Bldg	Building	EC	Eastern Caribbean; European Community	
BP	Boîte Postale (Post Box)	ECCB	Eastern Caribbean Central Bank	
br.(s)	branch(es)	ECLAC	(United Nations) Economic Commission for Latin America and the Caribbean	
Brig.	Brigadier			
BSE	bovine spongiform encephalopathy	Econ.	Economist	
BTN	Brussels Tariff Nomenclature	ECOSOC	(United Nations) Economic and Social Council	
		ECU	European Currency Unit	
C	Centigrade	Ed.(s)	Editor(s)	
c.	circa; cuadra(s) (block(s))	Edif.	Edificio (building)	
CA	California; Compañía Anónima	edn	edition	
CACM	Central American Common Market	EEC	European Economic Community	
Camp.	Campeche	EFTA	European Free Trade Association	
cap.	capital	e.g.	exempli gratia (for example)	
Capt.	Captain	eKv	electron kilovolt	
CARICOM	Caribbean Community and Common Market	eMv	electron megavolt	
CCL	Caribbean Congress of Labour	Eng.	Engineer; Engineering	
Cdre	Commodore	Ens.	Ensanche (suburb)	
CE	Ceará	ES	Espírito Santo	
Cen.	Central	Esc.	Escuela; Escudos; Escritorio	
CEO	Chief Executive Officer	esq.	esquina (corner)	
CET	Common External Tariff	est.	established; estimate, estimated	
cf.	confer (compare)	etc.	et cetera	
Chair.	Chairman	eV	eingetragener Verein	
Chih.	Chihuahua	EU	European Union	
Chis	Chiapas	excl.	excluding	
Cia, Cía	Companhia, Compañía	exec.	executive	
Cie	Compagnie	Ext.	Extension	
c.i.f.	cost, insurance and freight			
C-in-C	Commander-in-Chief	F	Fahrenheit	
circ.	circulation	f.	founded	
CIS	Commonwealth of Independent States	FAO	Food and Agriculture Organization	
cm	centimetre(s)	FDI	foreign direct investment	
CMEA	Council for Mutual Economic Assistance	Feb.	February	
Cnr	Corner	Fed.	Federation; Federal	
CO	Colorado	FL	Florida	
Co	Company	FM	frequency modulation	
Coah.	Coahuila	Fri.	Friday	
Col	Colonel	fmrly	formerly	
Col.	Colima, Colonia	f.o.b.	free on board	
Comm.	Commission	Fr	Father	
Commdr	Commander	Fr.	Franc	
Commdt	Commandant	ft	foot (feet)	
Commr	Commissioner	FTA	free trade agreement	

g	gram(s)		m	metre(s)
GA	Georgia		m.	million
GATT	General Agreement on Tariffs and Trade		MA	Maranhão; Massachusetts
GDP	gross domestic product		Maj.	Major
Gen.	General		Man.	Manager; managing
GM	genetically modified		MD	Maryland
GmbH	Gesellschaft mit beschränkter Haftung (Limited Liability Company)		MDG	Millennium Development Goal
			ME	Maine
GMT	Greenwich Mean Time		mem.	member
GNP	gross national product		MEV	mega electron volt
GO	Goiás		Méx.	México
Gov.	Governor		mfrs	manufacturers
Govt	Government		MG	Minas Gerais
Gro	Guerrero		Mgr	Monseigneur; Monsignor
grt	gross registered tons		MHz	megahertz
GSP	Global Social Product		MI	Michigan
Gto	Guanajuato		Mich.	Michoacán
GWh	gigawatt hours		Mlle	Mademoiselle
			mm	millimetre(s)
ha	hectares		Mme	Madame
HDI	Human Development Index		MN	Minnesota
HE	His (or Her) Eminence; His (or Her) Excellency		MO	Missouri
hg	hectogram(s)		Mon.	Monday
HGV	Heavy goods vehicle		Mor.	Morelos
HI	Hawaii		MOU	Memorandum of Understanding
HIPC	heavily indebted poor country		movt	movement
HIV	human immunodeficiency virus		MP	Member of Parliament
hl	hectolitre(s)		MS	Mato Grosso do Sul; Mississippi
HLTF	High Level Task Force		MSS	Manuscripts
HM	His (or Her) Majesty		MT	Montana
Hon.	Honorary (or Honourable)		MW	megawatt(s); medium wave
HQ	Headquarters		MWh	megawatt hour(s)
HRH	His (or Her) Royal Highness			
HS	Harmonized System		N	North, Northern
			n.a.	not available
IA	Iowa		NAFTA	North American Free Trade Agreement
ibid.	ibidem (in the same place)		Nat.	National
IBRD	International Bank for Reconstruction and Development (World Bank)		NATO	North Atlantic Treaty Organization
			Nay.	Nayarit
ICC	International Chamber of Commerce		NC	North Carolina
ID	Idaho		NCO	Non-Commissioned Officer
IDA	International Development Association		ND	North Dakota
IDB	Inter-American Development Bank		NE	Nebraska
i.e.	id est (that is to say)		NGO	Non-governmental organization
IGAD	Intergovernmental Authority on Development		NH	New Hampshire
IL	Illinois		NJ	New Jersey
ILO	International Labour Organization		NL	Nuevo León
IMF	International Monetary Fund		NM	New Mexico
IN	Indiana		NMP	net material product
in (ins)	inch (inches)		No(.)	number, número
Inc	Incorporated		Nov.	November
incl.	including		nr	near
Ind.	Independent		nrt	net registered tons
Ing.	Engineer		NV	Naamloze Vennootschap (Limited Company); Nevada
Insp.	Inspector		NY	New York
Inst.	Institute, Instituto			
Int.	International		OAS	Organization of American States
IRF	International Road Federation		Oax.	Oaxaca
irreg.	irregular		Oct.	October
Is	Islands		OECD	Organisation for Economic Co-operation and Development
ISIC	International Standard Industrial Classification		OECS	Organisation of Eastern Caribbean States
ITUC	International Trade Union Confederation		Of.	Oficina
IUU	illegal, unreported and unregulated		OH	Ohio
			OK	Oklahoma
Jal.	Jalisco		OPEC	Organization of the Petroleum Exporting Countries
Jan.	January		op. cit.	opere citato (in the work quoted)
Jr	Junior		opp.	opposite
Jt	Joint		OR	Oregon
			Org.	Organization
kg	kilogram(s)		ORIT	Organización Regional Interamericana de Trabajadores
kHz	Kilohertz		oz	troy ounces
km	kilometre(s)			
KS	Kansas		p.	page
kW	kilowatt(s)		PA	Pará, Pennsylvania
kWh	kilowatt hours		p.a.	per annum
KY	Kentucky		Parl.	Parliament(ary)
			PB	Paraíbo
LA	Louisiana		PC	Privy Counsellor
lb	pound(s)		PE	Pernambuco
LIBOR	London Inter-Bank Offered Rate		Perm. Rep.	Permanent Representative
Lic.	Licenciado		PI	Pianí
Licda	Licenciada		pl.	place
LNG	liquefied natural gas		PLC	Public Limited Company
LPG	liquefied petroleum gas		PMB	Private Mail Bag
Lt, Lieut	Lieutenant		POB	Post Office Box
Ltd, Ltda	Limited, Limitada		pp.	pages
			PR	Paraná

PRGF	Poverty Reduction and Growth Facility
Pres.	President
Prin.	Principal
Prof.	Professor
Propr	Proprietor
Prov.	Province; Provincial
Pte	Private
Pty	Proprietary
p.u.	paid up
publ.	publication; published
Publr(s)	Publisher(s)
Pue.	Puebla
Pvt.	Private
Q. Roo	Quintana Roo
QC	Queen's Counsel, Québec
q.v.	quod vide (to which refer)
Qro	Querétaro
Rd	Road
reg., regd	register; registered
reorg.	reorganized
Rep.	Republic; Republican; Representative
Repub.	Republic
res	reserve(s)
retd	retired
Rev.	Reverend
RI	Rhode Island
RJ	Rio de Janeiro
Rm	Room
RN	Rio Grande do Norte
RO	Rondônia
Rpto	Reparto
RR	Roraima
RS	Rio Grande do Sul
Rt	Right
S	South; Southern; San
SA	Société Anonyme, Sociedad Anónima (Limited Company)
SA de CV	Sociedad Anónima de Capital Variable (Variable Capital Company)
SACN	South American Community of Nations
SARL	Sociedade Anônima de Responsabilidade Limitada (Joint Stock Company of Limited Liability)
Sat.	Saturday
SC	Santa Catarina, South Carolina
SD	South Dakota
SDR(s)	Special Drawing Right(s)
Sec.	Secretary
Sen.	Senior; Senator
Sept.	September
Sgt	Sergeant
Sin.	Sinaloa
SITC	Standard International Trade Classification
SJ	Society of Jesus
SLP	San Luis Potosí
s/n	sin número (no number)
Soc.	Society
Son.	Sonora
SP	São Paulo
Sq.	Square
sq	square (in measurements)
Sr	Senior; Señor
Sra	Señora
St(s)	Saint(s); Street(s)

Sta	Santa
Ste	Sainte
subs.	subscriptions; subscribed
Suc.	Sucursal
Sun.	Sunday
Supt	Superintendent
Tab.	Tabasco
Tamps	Tamaulipas
Tce	Terrace
tech., techn.	technical
tel.	telephone
TEU	20-ft equivalent unit
Thurs.	Thursday
TJ	tetrajoule
Tlax.	Tlaxcala
TN	Tennessee
TO	Tocatins
Treas.	Treasurer
Tue.	Tuesday
TV	television
TX	Texas
u/a	unit of account
UEE	Unidade Ecónomica Estatal
UK	United Kingdom
UN	United Nations
UNCED	United Nations Conference on Environment and Development
UNCTAD	United Nations Conference on Trade and Development
UNDP	United Nations Development Programme
UNESCO	United Nations Educational, Scientific and Cultural Organization
UNHCHR	United Nations High Commissioner for Human Rights
UNHCR	United Nations High Commissioner for Refugees
Univ.	University
UNWTO	World Tourism Organization
USA (US)	United States of America (United States)
USAID	United States Agency for International Development
USSR	Union of Soviet Socialist Republics
Urb.	Urbanización (urban district)
UT	Utah
VA	Virginia
VAT	Value-Added Tax
v-CJD	new variant Creutzfeldt-Jakob disease
Ver.	Veracruz
VHF	Very High Frequency
VI	(US) Virgin Islands
viz.	videlicet (namely)
vol.(s)	volume(s)
W	West; Western
WA	Washington
Wed.	Wednesday
WFTU	World Federation of Trade Unions
WHO	World Health Organization
WI	Wisconsin
WTO	World Trade Organization
WV	West Virginia
WY	Wyoming
yr	year
Yuc.	Yucatán

INTERNATIONAL TELEPHONE CODES

To make international calls to telephone and fax numbers listed in *South America, Central America and the Caribbean*, dial the international code of the country from which you are calling, followed by the appropriate country code for the organization you wish to call (listed below), followed by the area code (if applicable) and telephone or fax number listed in the entry.

	Country code	+ GMT*
Anguilla	1264	–4
Antigua and Barbuda	1268	–4
Argentina	54	–3
Aruba	297	–4
Bahamas	1242	–5
Barbados	1246	–4
Belize	501	–6
Bermuda	1441	–4
Bolivia	591	–4
Bonaire	599	–4
Brazil	55	–3 to –4
British Virgin Islands	1284	–4
Cayman Islands	1345	–4
Chile	56	–4
Colombia	57	–4
Costa Rica	506	–6
Cuba	53	–4
Curaçao	599	–4
Dominica	1767	–4
Dominican Republic	1809	–4
Ecuador	593	–4
El Salvador	503	–6
Falkland Islands	500	–4
French Guiana	594	–3
Grenada	1473	–4
Guadeloupe	590	–4
Guatemala	502	–6
Guyana	592	–4
Haiti	509	–4
Honduras	504	–6
Jamaica	1876	–4
Martinique	596	–4

	Country code	+ GMT*
Mexico	52	–6 to –7
Montserrat	1664	–4
Nicaragua	505	–6
Panama	507	–4
Paraguay	595	–4
Peru	51	–4
Puerto Rico	1787	–4
Saba	599	–4
Saint-Barthélemy	590	–4
Saint Christopher and Nevis	1869	–4
Saint Lucia	1758	–4
Saint-Martin	590	–4
Saint Vincent and the Grenadines	1784	–4
Sint Eustatius	599	–4
Sint Maarten	1721	–4
Suriname	597	–3
Trinidad and Tobago	1868	–4
Turks and Caicos Islands	1649	–4
US Virgin Islands	1340	–4
Uruguay	598	–3
Venezuela	58	–4½

* Time difference in hours – Greenwhich Mean Time (GMT). The times listed compare the standard (winter) times. Some countries adopt Summer (Daylight Saving) Times—i.e. + 1 hour for part of the year.

Note: Telephone and fax numbers using the Inmarsat ocean region code 870 are listed in full. No country or area code is required, but it is necessary to precede the number with the international access code of the country from which the call is made.

EXPLANATORY NOTE ON THE DIRECTORY SECTION

The Directory section of each chapter covering a major country is arranged under the following, or similar, headings, where they apply:

THE CONSTITUTION

THE GOVERNMENT
   HEAD OF STATE
   CABINET/COUNCIL OF MINISTERS
   MINISTRIES

PRESIDENT AND LEGISLATURE

ELECTION COMMISSION

POLITICAL ORGANIZATIONS

DIPLOMATIC REPRESENTATION

JUDICIAL SYSTEM

RELIGION

THE PRESS

PUBLISHERS

BROADCASTING AND COMMUNICATIONS
   TELECOMMUNICATIONS
   RADIO
   TELEVISION

FINANCE
   CENTRAL BANK
   STATE BANKS
   DEVELOPMENT BANKS
   COMMERCIAL BANKS
   BANKING ASSOCIATIONS
   STOCK EXCHANGE
   INSURANCE

TRADE AND INDUSTRY
   GOVERNMENT AGENCIES
   DEVELOPMENT ORGANIZATIONS
   CHAMBERS OF COMMERCE
   INDUSTRIAL AND TRADE ASSOCIATIONS
   EMPLOYERS' ASSOCIATIONS
   MAJOR COMPANIES
   UTILITIES
   TRADE UNIONS

TRANSPORT
   RAILWAYS
   ROADS
   SHIPPING
   CIVIL AVIATION

TOURISM

DEFENCE

EDUCATION

South America

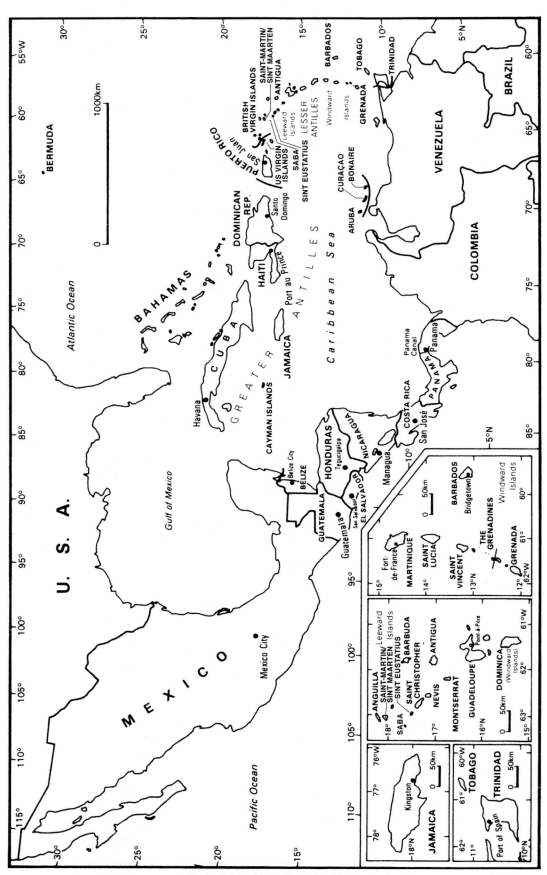

Central America and the Caribbean

PART ONE

General Survey

DEMOCRACY AND DIVERSITY IN LATIN AMERICA

Dr FRANCISCO PANIZZA

In the 21st century Latin America's turbulent political cycles of weak civilian governments and military coups have been replaced by the predictable regularity of electoral cycles that continue to frame the political landscape. The year 2013 marked the start of a new electoral cycle that will continue to 2016, during which 17 out of 18 countries in the region (with the exception of Mexico) will hold presidential elections. As it has become more democratic the region is also largely free of political violence. There are genuine prospects that the older and more violent armed conflict in the region, between the Colombian Government and the left-wing guerrillas of the Frente Nacional de Liberacion (FNL) is coming to an end. Yet, despite the significant political progress experienced by the region over the past 30 years, there are still significant challenges ahead.

While a majority of Latin Americans support democracy there is considerable dissatisfaction with how it works in practice. Regionwide support for democracy rose steadily from 48% of the population in 2001 to 61% in 2010, but dropped to 56% in 2013, while satisfaction with democracy, an indicator of how citizens perceive the performance of democratic institutions, fell from 44% to 39% over the same period, according to the polling organization Latinobarómetro. While military coups are largely of the past, democratic institutions remain fragile. Only 8% of adult Latin Americans consider there is full democracy in their country, while a majority believe either that there is no democracy (9%) or that it has important problems (46%), also according to Latinobarómetro. Questions have been raised about the abuse of incumbency in electoral campaigns, the influence of big business and drugs lords in campaign financing and corruption, and the colonization of the state by the political forces that control the Government. Political parties, trade unions, the legislature, the judiciary and the public administration are among the less trusted institutions in the region. Almost one-third of Latin Americans believe that democracy can work without political parties and 27% that it can work without Congress.

The rule of law is weak throughout the region. According to the World Bank, only Chile, Uruguay and Costa Rica figure among the top 50% of countries in the world for upholding the rule of law. While the rule of law is about more than personal security, criminal violence constitutes a real and present danger to social order. Latin America hosts 9% of the world population, but 27% of the world's murders take place in the region. With 82.1 homicides per 100,000 inhabitants, the murder rate in Honduras is the highest in the world and 10 of the 20 countries with the highest homicide rates in the world are in Latin America. Crime was regarded as their countries' main problem by 28% of Latin Americans in 2011, compared with 17% in 2007, and is identified as the main problem in 11 out of 18 countries polled by Latinobarómetro. High levels of socio-economic inequality, poorly trained, badly equipped and corrupt law enforcement agencies, and the illegal drugs trade are the main causes of criminal violence. Drugs-related violence is more prominent in Mexico. It is, however, in the smaller and poorer countries of Central America that criminal violence has a more devastating impact on the social fabric and political order. The murder rate in Honduras is almost four times higher than that of Mexico (21.5 per 100,000). El Salvador (66.1), Venezuela (49.0) and Colombia (33.4) are also among the countries with very high homicide rates, compared with the USA (4.6), Germany (0.8), and Japan (0.4), according to UN figures. Demands for a Mano Dura (Firm Hand) approach against crime contributed to the electoral victory of hardline former army general Otto Pérez Molina in Guatemala in November 2011.

Democratic stability and the dominance of electoral politics mean that there are low levels of political violence. Even in Colombia, the country with the largest and oldest guerrilla army in the region, there are signs that a negotiated solution to the conflict may be within reach. There has also been a decline in the riots and mass protests that led to the resignation of constitutionally elected Presidents in Argentina, Ecuador and Bolivia in the late 1990s and early 2000s and that contributed to the resignation of 20 constitutionally elected Presidents between 1980 and 2005. However in December 2013 at least seven people were killed in Argentina in a week of riots spurred by police strikes over pay in several provinces. Furthermore, since February 2014 Venezuela has been shaken by mass street protests against the Government of President Nicolás Maduro Moros, in which more than 40 people have died, according to the Venezuelan authorities.

In 2014 the people of Latin America are more prosperous than at any time in history. Most of the countries in the region are classified by the World Bank as high medium or medium developing economies. Eleven countries in the region are classified as having either a very high, or high, level of human development and only one (Haiti) is regarded as having a low level. In 2013 an estimated 27.9% of the population lived below the poverty line, compared with nearly 44% in 2002, according to figures from the UN's Economic Commission for Latin America and the Caribbean (ECLAC). Economic growth has contributed to the rise of a new middle class: according to figures from the World Bank, about 150m. Latin Americans have been incorporated into the middle classes over the past 10 years.

A large and prosperous middle class is regarded as a major social factor for democratic stability and political moderation. However, the emergence of a new lower middle class in a number of countries of the region presents distinct challenges to the region's political systems. In countries with radical populist governments, such as Venezuela (and to a lesser extent Ecuador and Bolivia), the middle classes are deeply divided politically, as the new lower middle classes support the incumbents while the traditional middle classes have strongly opposed the Governments of the late Hugo Chávez in Venezuela, Evo Morales in Bolivia and Rafael Correa in Ecuador for a variety of economic and political reasons. The split in the political allegiances of the middle classes has exacerbated political polarization. The losers so far have been the traditional middle classes, as the alliance between the popular sectors and the new lower middle classes have created a large social base of support for the left-of-centre and radical left administrations. However, as the new lower middle classes become more established, their demands for economic stability, personal security and better health and education services were likely to present new challenges to the governments of the region, irrespective of their political colours.

Progress notwithstanding, the region faces important social, economic and political challenges. Despite enjoying the best period of sustained economic growth for the past 30 years, in 2012 some 66m. Latin Americans were classified as 'indigent'. Moreover, despite some recent progress, Latin America is still the most unequal region in the world. High levels of economic inequality have political repercussions. Research by ECLAC has shown that both distrust of the state's political institutions and a perception of unfairness in the relations between the state and its citizens are high, and that both factors are associated with objectively measured inequality.

Economic growth remains too dependent on commodity prices and the region has made little progress in improving productivity and promoting a more sophisticated economic model based on high technology industries and services, technological innovation and the knowledge economy. According to certain rankings, no Latin American university figures among the top 150 world universities, and, while progress has been made in expanding primary education, educational levels in Latin America remain well below those of the Asian economies of similar levels of gross domestic product (GDP) per capita. If these problems are not addressed, some of the most prosperous countries of the region risk becoming caught in the middle-income trap: not cheap enough to compete with Asian countries exporting mass industrial goods and not productive enough to compete in the high value-added industrial market. Meanwhile, the region as a whole remains vulnerable to shifting prices in commodities and dependent on China's demand for its raw materials.

A slowdown in economic growth already visible in 2013–14 is likely to make it more difficult for governments to address their countries' still daunting problems of poverty and inequality. Less favourable international economic conditions have affected the countries of the region differently, with some, such as Colombia, Peru, Bolivia, Paraguay and Ecuador, still managing relatively high levels of growth and others, such as Argentina and Venezuela, likely to experience stagnation or negative growth in 2014. While the slowdown has not yet impacted political stability throughout the region, governments may struggle to match the citizens' expectations for better public services, as was reflected in mass protests in Brazil in the second half of 2013 and early 2014 against poor public services and excessive public spending in the organization of the World Cup football tournament.

Despite slower rates of economic growth since 2012 and persistent socio-economic problems a majority of the citizens of Latin America remain positive about their personal condition and optimistic about their countries' economic future. In 2013, in all countries, over one-half of inhabitants indicated they were satisfied with their lives. The percentage of Latin Americans who considered that their country's economic situation will improve in the long term increased from 31% in 2011 to 40% in 2013. Unlike satisfaction with life, however, the perception of progress showed wide variations across the region. In five countries around one-half of the population recognized progress in their country while in the other 13 countries, the perception of progress was limited. In eight countries, only one-third of the population had a perception of economic progress.

ELECTIONS AND ELECTORAL CYCLES

Latin America exhibits considerable political diversity. After being dominated by centre-right governments throughout the 1990s in the early 21st century a so-called 'pink tide' of left and left-of-centre candidates won office in some of the largest countries of the region. In early 2014, at the beginning of the current electoral wave, 10 out of 18 major Latin American countries have left-wing or left-of-centre Presidents and nearly two-thirds of Latin Americans lived under some form of left-leaning government. Leftist Presidents are in office in Argentina, Brazil, Bolivia, Chile, Costa Rica, Ecuador, El Salvador, Nicaragua, Uruguay and Venezuela. However, while electoral results can be aligned on a left–right continuum, government–opposition results are at least as important in assessing the region's political landscape. While relations between politics and economics are far from straightforward, votes for opposition parties often reflect citizens' discontent with economic conditions. In the case of Latin America, votes for the left and left-of-centre opposition candidates in the last years of the previous century, and the first few years of the current one, reflected a generalized disappointment with the free market reforms of the 1990s. It is surely not a coincidence that the rise of the left coincided with the 'lost half decade' of 1998–2002, in which per capita GDP contracted and the number of people living in poverty increased. When elections take place in the context of poor economic performance, incumbents tend to be punished regardless of their political orientation. As most incumbents were from the right and the centre-right, dissatisfaction with the status quo opened a window of opportunity for left-wing, as well as anti-establishment, candidates. In that sense, the victories of the left and left-of-centre political candidates had as much to do with popular demands for change as with the specific content of the changes on offer.

Economic conditions improved quite radically from around 2003, and the improvement was reflected in electoral performances. While the 'lost half-decade' of 1998–2002 acted as the background to the rise of the left, the economic upturn during 2003–12 provided the economic context of its political success in office. Unemployment, poverty and inequality took a downward trend, while real average wages and consumption rose. Higher tax revenue resulting from economic growth allowed left-of-centre governments to increase public spending, while simultaneously eliminating or narrowing the fiscal deficit and

repaying external debt obligations. Inflation remained low by the region's historical standards, although the commodities boom that boosted economic growth during the period also brought back inflationary pressures, particularly in Venezuela and Argentina. Paradoxically, the economic upturn was at least partly the result of the macroeconomic discipline preached by free market advocates, and high commodities prices resulted from the process of capitalist globalization denounced by the left.

The regional economic slowdown that started in 2012 has not yet had a significant impact in the standards of living of the majority of the population. The latest elections show that incumbents or their political successors are still favourites but opposition candidates have achieved some significant victories. Between January 2013 and June 2014 there were presidential elections in Honduras, Chile, Ecuador, Paraguay, Costa Rica, El Salvador, Panama and Colombia, while presidential polls will be held in Bolivia, Brazil and Uruguay late in 2014. Of the elections that have already taken place in 2013–14, opposition candidates won in Chile, Panama, Paraguay and Costa Rica. Presidents Rafael Correa and Juan Manuel Santos Calderón were re-elected in Ecuador and Colombia, respectively, and candidates from the ruling party won the presidency in El Salvador and Honduras. Later in 2014 President Evo Morales is a strong candidate for re-election in Bolivia and President Dilma Vana Rousseff is the frontrunner in Brazil, while in Uruguay, where re-election is not allowed, the candidate of the ruling Frente Amplio, former President Tabaré Vázquez, is also the favourite.

THE POLITICAL LANDSCAPE: A DIVERSE REGION

If generalizations about a leftward turn in Latin America must be qualified by the presence of right and right-of-centre governments in some of the largest countries in the region, such as Mexico and Colombia, differences between left-wing governments are as significant as those between left and right. The Governments of the late President Hugo Chávez and his successor Nicolás Maduro of Venezuela, Evo Morales of Bolivia and Rafael Correa of Ecuador have been regarded as representatives of radical populism in the region. Some observers also place the Government of President Cristina Fernández de Kirchner of Argentina in the same category. A contentious and highly charged concept, for which there is no agreed definition, populism by its very nature denotes an opposition to the status quo. As such, it appeals to the disenfranchised and the never enfranchised, who do not feel represented by existing institutions. Populism is the politics of anti-politics, with populist leaders presenting themselves as outsiders against vested economic interests and the political class. The anti-status quo element of populism makes it a common movement within societies deeply polarized on socio-economic, religious, ethnic and/or regional lines, in which important sections of the population regard themselves as oppressed or discriminated against by the dominant élite, and in which the state is unable to secure social cohesion. The concept of populism is not, however, without problems. To categorize together the Governments of Presidents Chávez, Maduro, Morales and Correa risks masking significant differences among the four leaders, as well as among their Governments. As candidates, Chávez, Morales and Correa campaigned as political outsiders. However, Chávez and Correa lacked the organized base of support that Morales enjoyed. Although strong, Morales' leadership does not fit the top-down style typical of populist leaders: his leadership, and indeed his administration, are embedded in the popular movements that first brought him to office in 2006 and have since limited the margins of autonomy of his administration.

An alternative, less normatively charged way of characterizing left-wing governments is to distinguish those who have sought to implement radical social and economic changes under the banner of so-called '21st century socialism' from the more moderate administrations that have been characterized as Latin American versions of social democracy. The Governments of Venezuela, Bolivia, Ecuador and Nicaragua have identified themselves with this new version of socialism. In common with classic socialism, 21st century socialism emphasizes the need for a strong presence of the state in the economy, state control of strategic industries and the importance of economic planning. There are, however, important differences in the extent of the four governments' rejection of market economics. Although they all denounce neo-liberalism, because the Venezuelan government draws much higher revenue from oil taxes than those of Morales and Correa, it is less constrained by international economic forces, and thus has been able to promote more radical economic change. While Argentina has a more developed and diversified economy than Venezuela, Bolivia and Ecuador and lacks the oil revenues of these countries, its increasingly protectionist and interventionist economic policies and the nationalization of the oil company Yacimientos Petrolíferos Fiscales (YPF) have been labelled as economic populism. In contrast with the 21st century socialist countries the left-of-centre Governments of Brazil, Chile (1990–2010 and 2014–18) and Uruguay have sought to combine business and market-friendly economic policies with social policies aimed at improving the standard of living of the poor and reducing inequalities. These administrations have welcomed foreign investment and remain financially integrated with the international money markets.

While the rise of the 'pink tide' in Latin America in the first decade of the 21st century was regarded as marking the rejection of the free market reformation that dominated the region in the 1990s, some of the strongest performing economies of the region in recent years have continued to follow free market economic policies. This applies to Mexico, Colombia and Chile, as well as to the nominally centre-left administration of President Ollanta Humala in Peru. The economies of the Pacific coast countries are becoming increasingly integrated with the Asia-Pacific economic area while simultaneously developing strong economic and political ties with the USA. Meanwhile, their Governments present a distinct alternative to the more interventionist and protectionist economies of the countries of the Mercado Común del Sur (MERCOSUR—Southern Common Market—Argentina, Brazil, Paraguay, Uruguay and Venezuela). Together with the differences among left-wing administrations analysed above, the rule of right-of-centre governments in some of the largest and most dynamic economies of the region reflects the increasing political pluralism of Latin America in the second decade of the 21st century.

Venezuela

The politics and policies of the late President Hugo Chávez deeply divided Venezuelan society. They also antagonized the US Administration and received a mixed reception elsewhere in Latin America. In the view of his supporters, Chávez deepened Venezuelan democracy, opened channels for popular participation and incorporated the excluded majority into the political system; supporters also argue that, while previous administrations favoured the middle classes, those of Chávez used oil revenue to benefit the poor. To his critics, however, Chávez was an authoritarian ruler who destroyed the country's liberal democracy, centralized power, harassed his critics and squandered oil revenue in order to consolidate his political base at home and pursue his ambitions of Latin American leadership abroad.

From his election to the presidency in 1998, Chávez used the economic windfall of high oil prices to finance social programmes and consolidate his political base. To this end, he implemented a series of special programmes, the so-called *misiones* (missions), to promote health care, housing, remedial education and food subsidies among the poor. These programmes were designed not only to bring the benefits of the welfare state to the poor, especially those in the informal sector, but also to alter the governance of the economy from one emphasizing atomistic participation in the market to one relying on co-operatives and state co-ordination. According to figures from ECLAC, the percentage of Venezuelans living below the poverty line fell from 49.9% in 1999 to 21.7% in 2012. Even Chávez's critics acknowledge that the *misiones* have helped sections of the population that previously had no access to social programmes. However, questions remain with regard to the sustainability of the Government's social policy, and, indeed, of its overall economic programme in light of stagnant oil output and mounting fiscal and economic problems.

President Chávez's illness dominated the country's political agenda until his death on 5 March 2013. A visibly unwell Chávez returned to Venezuela to campaign for the presidential election of 7 October 2012, which he won with the help of his charisma and a massive surge in public spending. However, shortly after the election Chávez returned to Cuba for further treatment and was unable to be sworn in for the new presidential term. Before leaving for Cuba, Chávez publicly endorsed his Vice-President, Nicolás Maduro, as his successor, in case he could not resume his public duties. During Chávez's illness Maduro effectively acted as President and was formally sworn as interim head of state on his death. New presidential elections were called for 14 April 2013, in accordance with the Constitution. Maduro campaigned as Chávez's heir, seeking to capitalize on the emotional bond between Chávez and the electorate. He even alleged that the spirit of Chávez had appeared to him in the form of a little bird. However, Maduro lacks Chávez's charisma and campaigning skills, and, with the economy in free fall since the October 2012 election, he only defeated the opposition candidate, the Governor of Miranda, Henrique Capriles Radonski, by a narrow 1.49% of the votes, according to official figures from the National Electoral Council. Capriles refused to acknowledge Maduro's victory, demanding a full recount of the electronic results, which was only partially granted by the electoral court. Maduro was sworn into office on 19 April 2013 for a six-year term.

Since February 2014 mass protests have alarmed the Maduro administration. The demonstrators, mainly students and middle-class citizens, took action in protest at lack of public security, high levels of inflation and shortages of basic consumer goods. Separate grievances rapidly coalesced into an anti-Government agenda with outright demands for the deposition of President Maduro. A heavy-handed police response and the arrest of opposition leader Leopoldo López Mendoza under the accusation of inciting violence brought further protests, which were harshly repressed by the Government. Some of the protests became violent. Hundreds of protesters were detained without trials and there were allegations of torture. The opposition alleged that armed militant groups loyal to the Government, known as *colectivos* had fired against the protesters. At least 40 persons, including demonstrators and members of the security forces, have been killed in protest-related violence, according to the Government's own figures. President Maduro has accused the opposition of promoting a coup and of plotting physically to eliminate him and has vowed to upheld the Constitution and the gains of the Bolivarian revolution. In April the foreign ministers of Ecuador, Colombia and Brazil, together with the Vatican representative in Venezuela, started a process of mediation between the Government and representatives of the opposition. However, at mid-2014 there has been no progress in the negotiations. President Maduro's position remains weak. The country is effectively divided into two halves and he does not have even the full support of the former supporters of Chávez. While the Government retains considerable support among the popular sectors, with the country's economy in recession and having the highest rate of inflation in the world, it is difficult to see how President Maduro can stabilize the tense political situation

Bolivia

President Evo Morales of Bolivia is another advocate of 21st century socialism. Morales won the 2005 presidential election with 53.7% of the valid votes cast, the highest share for any candidate since the country returned to democracy more than 20 years previously. He took office in early 2006 with a mandate for radical change and with high expectations among his popular base of support. The new President fulfilled one of his main electoral promises in striking fashion in May when he issued a decree nationalizing the country's oil and gas fields, and ordered the army to occupy the foreign companies' installations to secure them against sabotage. Foreign companies were to leave Bolivia unless they signed new contracts within six months recognizing state control. In October some 10 oil companies agreed new energy deals with the Government, which allowed the companies to continue operating in the country in partnership with the state-owned oil firm, Yacimientos Petrolíferos Fiscales Bolivianos (YPFB). The companies also agreed to pay the state higher royalties for their oil and gas sales. Telecommunications and mines were also nationalized and price controls were imposed on gas and foodstuffs, while the state distributed subsidized food to the poor. Morales' Government used the extra revenue accrued from higher gas royalties and prices to expand welfare provision, including the introduction of a non-contributory old age pension, and targeted cash handouts to poor households conditional upon their children's school attendance. Some estimates suggest that the payments reached one-quarter of Bolivia's 10m. citizens in 2009. In June 2006 the President launched a programme of agrarian reform by giving more than 77,000 sq km of land to indigenous peasant communities. The land handed over was state-owned, but Morales declared that his Government would also seize private holdings that were deemed not to be in productive use, in order to meet his target of redistributing around one-fifth of Bolivia's total land area over a five-year period.

President Morales further consolidated his hold on power by winning a second term in office in December 2009 with 64.2% of the popular vote and a wider margin of victory than in 2005. His share of the vote was significantly improved in the opposition strongholds of Santa Cruz, Tarija, Beni and Pando, which made the prospects of secession appear more remote. It was the first time since 1964 that an incumbent Bolivian President had secured re-election to a second term. The ruling party, Movimiento al Socialismo (MAS), also won a decisive two-thirds' majority in the Senate, previously controlled by the opposition. Morales' main priority in his second mandate was fully to implement the new Constitution and advance his programme of economic nationalism. In May 2010 the Government nationalized four electricity generation companies, and in May 2012 nationalized Transportadora de Electricidad, a Spanish-owned power-grid company that supplies 72% of the country's power, alleging that the company had underinvested. Critics of Morales' economic policy claim that nationalizations are discouraging much-needed foreign investment and depriving the country of technical and managerial expertise. They note that gas production has fallen since the outset of the programme of nationalization, owing to poor management by YPFB and declining private investment. After reports that natural gas reserves had fallen from 26,000m. cu ft in 2005 to 9,940m. cu ft in 2010 the Bolivian Government announced that new discoveries had increased proven reserves to 13,000m. cu. ft. Government sources claim that they are not against foreign investment, but 'want partners not patrons' and have promised fair compensation to expropriated firms.

While the impact of nationalizations on long-term investment and output is still unclear, the economy grew by a healthy 5.2% in 2011 and at about the same rate in 2012, prompted by the recovery in oil and gas prices. In May 2012 the international credit ratings agency Standard & Poor's raised the long-term sovereign rating on Bolivia to BB- from B+, with the outlook stable. According to Standard & Poor's statement, the upgrade reflected 'the improvement in the government's debt burden coupled with the country's strengthened external indicators—one of the strongest among its BB rated peers'. The statement noted that 'the general government debt burden fell to 31% of GDP in 2011 from 36% of GDP in 2010 owing in part to the government's low fiscal deficit and high nominal GDP growth'.

Social movements have challenged the Government on a number of issues. The Government's proposal to construct a road through the Isiboro Sécure Indigenous Territory and National Park (TIPNIS) raised strong opposition from local indigenous groups and environmentalists. Indigenous protesters marched on the capital, La Paz, and clashed with the police. The construction of the 300-km road, which was to be financed by Brazil's national development bank, is regarded by the Government as crucial for the physical integration of the country, but, in the face of the opposition to the project, the Government suspended the construction and promised a referendum to decide whether the area should be declared 'untouchable' or whether development projects should be permitted. In May 2013 the umbrella trade union organization, the Central Obrera Boliviana, staged a number of protests and strikes in support of demands for higher pensions and pay

rises. The protests reflect significant pockets of discontent with the Government of Morales among its natural supporters. None the less, in spite of his Government's fluctuating popularity, Morales remains the dominant figure in Bolivian politics, and his party, MAS, is the only nationwide organized political force. In a controversial decision, the country's constitutional court ruled in April 2013 that President Morales should be allowed to run for a third consecutive presidential term. He is a strong favourite in the election that was scheduled for October 2014.

Ecuador

Together with Chávez and Morales, President Correa of Ecuador completes the trio of radical left South American leaders. The context of Correa's electoral triumph in November 2006 bears strong similarities to the circumstances of Chávez's and Morales' victories. Over the previous decade Ecuador had been blighted by political instability and social tensions, during which time the country had had eight different Presidents, three of whom had been thrown out of office by street protests. It had a highly fragmented and weakly institutionalized party system which bred political volatility. Traditional parties were in decline, discredited because of allegations of corruption and economic mismanagement. Correa strongly denounced the Washington Consensus and what he perceived to be the evils of neo-liberalism. He advocated renegotiating oil contracts with multinational oil companies to increase royalties and use the revenue for the redistribution of wealth. One of the first measures that Correa implemented upon assuming office was to expel the World Bank's representative in the country. The Ecuadorean Minister of Finance stated that the Government would not submit its economic programme for the inspection of the IMF.

In the early days of his presidency, Correa embarked on a high-risk political strategy that entailed a series of rapid-fire plebiscites and elections giving him the electoral legitimacy to redraw the country's political institutions without too much consideration for the letter of the law. In his first months in office he doubled poverty assistance payments and credits available for housing loans, and reduced electricity rates for low-income consumers. He combined his redistributionist policies with high-profile confrontations with multinational companies, including a Brazilian construction company, and in 2008 defaulted on what his Government considered the 'illegitimate external debt'. Correa channelled the windfall from higher oil prices into targeted social programmes and higher public sector salaries; he also raised the minimum wage. However, Correa stressed that he did not intend to copy Chávez's political and economic models.

Correa was re-elected to a second term in April 2009, securing 52% of the vote and comfortably defeating his closest rival, Lucio Gutiérrez, who won only 28%. It was the first time in 30 years that the country had re-elected a President. Alianza País won the largest number of seats in the National Assembly, although it did not secure an absolute majority. In his inaugural speech, Correa promised to continue his so-called 'socialist revolution', the aim of which was to end poverty and strive for equality among all citizens. However, Correa's twin revolutions have encountered opposition from both the left and the right. In 2009 indigenous organizations mobilized against a water management bill that they claimed amounted to privatization and would negatively impact on farmers. At least one protester died in clashes between indigenous peasants and the police. In September 2010 Correa was held hostage for 11 hours in a military hospital by police officers disgruntled by the passage of a law which, among other things, cut their bonuses. The President was eventually rescued by police and army special forces. After his release, Correa rejected suggestions that he had been the victim of an attempted coup.

With the political opposition weak and divided, Correa's main confrontations have been with the media. In 2011 the President initiated a lawsuit against the *El Universo* newspaper, after a journalist, Emilio Palacio, published an article accusing him of having ordered an attack on a hospital during the police uprising of September 2010. In February 2012 the country's National Court of Justice ratified a lower court verdict that imposed a three-year prison sentence on the directors of *El Universo*, brothers Carlos, César and Nicolás Pérez, for criminal libel, together with a US $40m. fine for damages to the President. Correa's decision to present the lawsuit and the Court's verdict were strongly criticized by human rights organizations as an attack against press freedom. Following the verdict, the President dropped the charges while attacking the media, which he described as being run by 'the powers that be [fácticos]', which need to be 'confronted and defeated'.

In February 2013 Correa won a comfortable electoral victory to secure a third term in office. The President polled 57% of the votes against 23% for his nearest rival, Guillermo Lasso. Parties supporting the President also polled well, securing a strong majority in the National Assembly. Correa's victory reflected his strong popular support, particularly among the poor, the young and sectors of the middle class, as social programmes, subsidies, public spending and economic growth have benefited most sections of Ecuadorean society. The re-election of Correa highlighted the country's political stability in contrast with its turbulent past. Regional and local elections are scheduled for 2014 and national elections for 2017.

Argentina

The case of Argentina does not fall easily into a dichotomous classification between 21st century socialist and social democrat. While having some elements in common with the politics of Chávez, Morales and Correa, the administrations of the late Néstor Kirchner (2003–07) and his wife, Cristina Fernández de Kirchner (2007–11; 2011–2015), have never adopted the 21st century socialist banner. Néstor Kirchner was not a political outsider in the mould of Chávez or Morales and he operated in a more institutionalized political system. He came to office in 2003 in a country in which the previous year's economic crisis had produced a popular backlash against the political establishment, crystallized in the slogan 'Que se vayan todos' ('all politicians out'). Elected to the presidency with just 24.3% of the total votes, Néstor Kirchner sought to increase his popular support by denouncing neo-liberalism and appealing to the national popular tradition of his Peronist party, Partido Justicialista (PJ). He also sought to build an image as a defender of the Argentine people against powerful domestic and foreign interests. He clashed with the IMF, with the owners of privatized public utilities, with the country's external debt holders and even with the Roman Catholic Church. He forged a close political and economic alliance with Chávez, whose Government bought around US $5,000m. of Argentine debt between 2005 and early 2010. He concentrated power in the Executive, ruling by decree and broadening his political base of support by co-opting opposition state governors through the allocation of financial resources to the provinces on a discretionary basis and by forging alliances with social movements sympathetic to his policies, such as the *piquetero* movement.

The economic policy of the administration of Néstor Kirchner can be characterized as 'neo-developmentalist', after developmentalism, the interventionist economic doctrine that dominated economic policy-making in Latin America in the 1960s and the 1970s. In its current version, neo-developmentalism combines fiscal orthodoxy and heterodox state interventionism in a policy mix aimed at promoting exports and substituting imports. To this purpose, the Kirchner administration maintained high budgetary primary surpluses and supported a high US dollar export strategy. Export taxes, predominantly on highly priced primary exports such as beef, wheat and soya beans, were used to fund state spending and subsidize the public utilities, the tariffs of which have been frozen since the devaluation of the peso in 2002. Government funds were also used to support domestic industry. To offset the threat of rising inflation, Kirchner resorted to price controls, 'voluntary' agreements with producers and, allegedly, to the manipulation of the retail price index. Among the measures introduced to lower the price of foodstuffs by increasing domestic supply was the banning of exports of certain cuts of beef. Kirchner's economic policies resulted in high rates of economic growth that brought down unemployment into single figures and boosted his popularity, contributing to the electoral triumph of his wife, Cristina Fernández, in October 2007.

President Cristina Fernández de Kirchner has largely followed the politics and policies of her late husband. However, she hardly enjoyed a 'honeymoon' period. In the month following her inauguration in December 2007 she faced street protests in the capital, Buenos Aires, after power cuts left districts without energy for three days. More damagingly, in March 2008 a farmers' strike in protest at high export taxes for agricultural commodities precipitated a political crisis in which angry farmers erected roadblocks and disgruntled middle-class inhabitants staged political protests in major cities. Protests also reflected growing discontent among sectors of the population regarding crime, energy shortages and rising inflation. As a result of her perceived mismanagement of the confrontation with the farmers, President Fernández's popularity waned and, contending with an increasingly difficult economic situation, her Government has come to rely increasingly on the core support of the PJ in the industrial belt of Buenos Aires province. The Government's loss of support was reflected in the June 2009 mid-term elections, in which the ruling party, Frente para la Victoria (FPV), a faction of the PJ, lost control of both houses of the Congress. The party lost in the four main electoral districts, including the key province of Buenos Aires, home to more than 60% of the population. Increasing political polarization led to legislative gridlock and to tensions between the executive and the legislature. In an attempt to boost its popularity, the Government abandoned its initial fiscal prudence and increased spending on pensions, social security and infrastructure.

The unexpected death of former President Néstor Kirchner in October 2010 marked a turning point in the popularity of his wife. Political support for President Cristina Fernández soared after the death of her husband. The President's popular support was reflected in the presidential election of October 2011, in which Fernández's personal appeal, a strong economy and a weak and divided opposition delivered her an overwhelming victory. Since the election, however, the economic situation has deteriorated. Argentina remains unable to borrow money in the international financial markets, since it has not settled disputes with bondholders pending since the 2001 default, and relies on primary fiscal surpluses and a positive current account balance to finance its foreign currency needs. However, high public spending has turned the fiscal surpluses of Fernández's first mandate into a deficit. Facing capital flight, the Government has imposed strict capital controls. Tariff and non-tariff barriers were introduced on imports, in an attempt to preserve a positive balance of trade and the inflation index was manipulated by INDEC, the national statistics institute, to mask the rising cost of living. In April 2012 the President announced the nationalization of oil company YPF, a subsidiary of the Spanish oil company, Repsol, alleging that underinvestment from the company had turned Argentina from an oil exporter into a net oil and gas importer. The nationalization prompted strong protests from the Spanish Government, which threatened retaliatory measures against Argentina.

High inflation, import restrictions, exchange controls, slow economic growth and ongoing concerns regarding public security tilted public opinion against the ruling FPV's candidates in the October 2013 mid-term congressional elections. While the FPV still won the largest share of the votes nationwide, support for the party fell to around 33% from 54%, when Fernández was re-elected in 2011. A particularly heavy political blow for the Government was the defeat of the ruling party in the key electoral district of Buenos Aires province, where about one-third of the electorate lives. The victor, rising political star Sergio Massa, also from the PJ, was a former minister in Néstor Kirchner's Government and is regarded as a potential presidential candidate in 2015. While the FPV retained a majority in Congress, it is well below the two-thirds required to amend the Constitution that would have allowed Fernández de Kirchner to seek a second re-election in 2015.

With no natural candidate to succeed her and with a deteriorating economic situation, President Fernández de Kirchner could face a difficult end to her administration. Facing a run on foreign reserves, the Government devalued the peso in January 2014, while the Central Bank raised interest rates to restrain inflation and stem the demand for US dollars. The measures stabilized the economy at the cost of a fall in economic activity. The Government also took other steps towards economic orthodoxy. In February the board of Repsol accepted a compensation offer of at least US $5,000m. from the Government to settle the two-year dispute. In May the Government reached an agreement with the Paris Club of creditor nations on repaying overdue debts from the 2002 debt default. The agreement was considered to open the possibilities of accessing much needed international funds and foreign investment. However, Argentina's hope of accessing international financial markets suffered a setback in June 2014, when the US Supreme Court ruled that Argentina should pay in full around $1,300m. owed to bondholders who had refused to take part in the restructuring of the country's debt in 2005 and 2010. The bondholders also won the right to use the US courts to force Argentina to reveal where it owns assets around the world. The Government's failure to comply with the US court ruling resulted in a technical partial default in August 2014, a state of affairs that is likely to damage even further the already fragile confidence in the Argentinian economy.

Brazil

The administrations of Presidents Lula da Silva and Dilma Rousseff in Brazil are examples of the moderate left in Latin America, which in many aspects has been compared to the social democratic model. Often with their roots in traditional parties of the left, the social-democratic left has shifted from its radical roots towards the centre, as a result of the combination of political experience, electoral calculations and economic constraints. In power, the social-democratic left has adopted and adapted many of the market-friendly policies of the Washington Consensus, while attempting to redress its negative social impact by means of targeted social programmes and increasing investment in human capital. Social-democratic governments have sought to attract foreign investment to create the jobs that will both lift people out of poverty and provide tax revenue for investment in health and education. While seeking a more autonomous foreign policy with regard to the USA than their centre-right predecessors, centre-left governments have generally maintained good relations with the US Administration and with the multilateral financial agencies, such as the IMF and the World Bank.

In Brazil, three consecutive electoral defeats convinced Lula da Silva, the leader of the Partido dos Trabalhadores (PT), to broaden the party's electoral appeal prior to the 2002 election by promulgating an image of political moderation and economic responsibility. After winning the election, the new Government maintained a significant degree of continuity with the market-friendly economic policies of the previous administration of former President Fernando Henrique Cardoso, while expanding already existing social programmes and introducing new ones. After a difficult first year in office, economic growth picked up in the remaining three years of Lula da Silva's mandate. While the Government's moderate economic policies disappointed traditional PT supporters, the combination of low inflation, economic growth and targeted social programmes resulted in a reduction of economic inequality and in income gains for the poorest sectors of the population.

Satisfied with their welfare gains, in October 2006 voters rewarded Lula with a new four-year mandate. In his second term in office the administration of President Lula moved towards a more varied model of economic development which combined orthodox macroeconomic policies based on continuous fiscal discipline and inflation-targeting with increasing public and private investment in infrastructure and a more interventionist industrial policy. Brazil was not immune to the 2008–09 global recession, but, compared with the situation in other countries, the recession in Brazil was short and shallow (GDP contracted only modestly in 2009, by 0.2%). In an attempt to lessen the impact of the global downturn, the Government followed an activist policy of granting public investment and loans to ailing companies from the state-owned banks. Boosted by internal demand and by external demand from China and other emerging markets, the economy rebounded strongly in late 2009 and grew by over 6% in 2010.

As a result of Lula's extremely high levels of popularity, together with the robust condition of the economy, the candidate of the ruling PT, Dilma Rousseff, won the 2010 presiden-

tial election, defeating the centre-right opposition candidate, José Serra, in a run-off vote. Rousseff is a no-nonsense politician, with a past as a radical left activist who was imprisoned and tortured by the military dictatorship in the 1970s, and a reputation for efficiency. She has largely followed the successful economic policies of the previous Government, while seeking to invest in the country's infrastructure and promote structural reform in order to increase productivity. In spite of her popularity and large majority in parliament, Rousseff has struggled to pass legislation in Congress because of political unrest within her Government's broad congressional coalition. Differences among the coalition parties relate more to patronage and the allocation of ministerial posts than to ideological questions. The Rousseff administration has also been rocked by a series of corruption scandals, which have forced a number of ministers to resign.

While tens of millions of Brazilians have been lifted out of poverty in the past decade as a result of economic growth and the government's social policies, a wave of popular protests in the run up to the Football World Cup showed underlying discontent with the condition of society. The protests that started in June 2013 against a rise in public transport tickets in the city of São Paulo, soon spread throughout the country partly fuelled by the police's excessive use of force against the demonstrators. The protests were against alleged excessive public spending and corruption in the building of sporting facilities for the World Cup while the country badly needs to invest in public services such as health, transport and education. More broadly, the protests showed the disconnection between the citizens and the politicians, widely regarded as self-serving, corrupt and out of touch with ordinary people. President Rousseff acknowledged the legitimacy of the protesters' grievances and promised fresh investment in the public services, as well as political reform. The protests led to a fall in the approval rating of Rousseff. She is still the frontrunner for the October 2014 presidential election but her lead has been reduced in the first months of 2014, according to some opinion polls. Her main rival will be Aécio Neves of the centre-right Partido da Social Democracia Brasileira.

Brazil has been playing an increasingly assertive role in the international scene. Rousseff has continued the policy of her predecessor of prioritizing the configuration of a South American block of nations, in which Brazil exercises a clear but low profile leadership, and of boosting economic and political links with countries in Africa and Asia. However, she has kept a lower international profile than her predecessor, President Lula da Silva. Rousseff was to make an official visit to the USA in October 2013, the first by a Brazilian President since 1995, but the visit was abandoned when it emerged that the US Administration had tapped the President's telephone. Rousseff has also complained at the monetary policies of the USA and the countries of the European Union (EU) that have led to the over-appreciation of the country's currency, the real. China has become Brazil's main trading partner, reinforcing the country's increasing autonomy from the USA. Brazil's ultimate foreign policy objective is to gain a permanent seat in an enlarged UN Security Council.

Chile

The centre-left alliance Concertación por la Democracia (CPD), a coalition of Socialists, Christian Democrats and Radicals, founded in 1989 to oppose the dictatorship of General Augusto Pinochet, has been the first and most successful of the so-called social democratic left political forces in Latin America. During its 20 years in office (1990–2010), the CPD won four presidential elections and transformed Chile economically, socially and politically. Successive CPD administrations largely followed the free market economic model of the military Government headed by Gen. Pinochet, but implemented important measures to ensure that the benefits of economic growth reached those most in need. Since 1990, Chile has been the most successful economy in Latin America. The share of Chileans living below the poverty line fell from 38% in 1990 to less than 11.5% in 2009. There was also considerable investment in education, health and infrastructure. However, the slowdown in the country's high rates of economic growth in the second half of the 2000s, internal divisions within the CPD, and a general weariness with a political coalition that had been in office for almost two decades contributed to a mood of disillusionment with the Government. The mood was capitalized on by the centre-right candidate, Sebastián Piñera, who won the presidency in a run-off contest in January 2010. It was the first time in half a century that a right-wing candidate had won a presidential election in Chile. Piñera's victory, however, was more a reflection of a desire for political change than of a rightwards shift. The outgoing President, Michelle Bachelet, ended her mandate with high approval ratings and would have had a good chance of winning a second mandate had she not been constitutionally proscribed from seeking re-election. A multimillionaire businessman, Piñera campaigned as a social liberal and promised to maintain many of the CPD's social and economic policies while fighting crime and boosting economic growth and employment. Having stated that his main domestic priority was to combat poverty, he argued that if 1.5% of Chile's GDP were to be transferred directly to each poor family, it would end poverty in the country.

Piñera's honeymoon period in office was surprisingly brief. Underlying social tensions resulting from high levels of inequality and dissatisfaction with the élite-dominated political system erupted in a wave of street protests. These protests were led by students demanding reform of an educational system that allegedly fails to meet the needs of poor students and perpetuates social inequality. In spite of robust economic growth, President Piñera's mishandling of the protests and his failure to address the root causes of popular discontent led to the governing parties' heavy defeat in the presidential and parliamentary elections of November–December 2013. In the presidential election the candidate of Nueva Mayoría (NM—a coalition reconstituted from the CPD and including the Partido Comunista de Chile), former President Bachelet, defeated in a second round the candidate of the right-wing Alianza, former senator and Minister of Labour Evelyn Matthei Fornet, with 62.2% of the votes cast on a low turnout. In the parliamentary elections NM won control of both chambers.

President Bachelet campaigned on promises of change that, according to some analysts, place her to the left of previous CPD administrations. She pledged constitutional and educational reform to make the political system more representative of the electorate and the educational system fairer and more accessible for young people from low-income families. She promised free university education in six years' time and to create more public universities. To fund investment in education and other social policies, she also pledged to raise corporation tax from 20% to 25%, a measure that has been heavily criticized by defenders of Chile's free market model. She is also committed to legislate on abortion and same sex-marriage, initiatives that are expected to raise strong opposition from the powerful Catholic Church.

Uruguay

Together with Brazil, the Frente Amplio (FA) administrations of President Tabaré Vázquez (2005–10) and José Mujica (2010–14) are regarded as belonging to the moderate, social-democratic, left. The Government of President Vázquez, which took office in March 2005, broke the duopoly of power by the two traditional parties, the Blancos (whites or Conservatives) and the Colorados (reds or Liberals), that had ruled the country since independence. The new Government followed a market-friendly economic policy which had as its main goal the attraction of foreign investment. The Government's economic programme, which was inspired by the Chilean model, combined macroeconomic orthodoxy, fiscal prudence, corporatist agreements on wage demands between trade unions and businesses, and an emergency social programme similar to Brazil's family grant scheme. The Vázquez administration's management of the economy was remarkably successful. During its first four years in office, GDP grew by an average of 7% per year, while inflation was kept under control. Unemployment declined from a peak of almost 20% in 2002 to single figures in 2008, and there was a concomitant 13.7% reduction in the number of persons living below the poverty line. As part of a strategy of opening up new markets for exports, in January 2007, in a move that surprised its traditional left-wing supporters, the Government signed a Trade and Investment Framework Agreement (TIFA)

with the USA, which could lead to a future free trade agreement. Like other countries of the region, Uruguay suffered from the impact of the 2008–09 worldwide recession, but, while the economy slowed, it still registered positive growth of almost 3% in 2009.

In November 2009 the populace rewarded the ruling FA administration's social and economic policies by electing the party's candidate, José Mujica, as the new President (Vázquez having been constitutionally barred from seeking re-election). Mujica took office in March 2010. The Mujica Government showed considerable continuity with the policies of its predecessor, reaffirming the Vázquez administration's priorities of promoting domestic and international private investment, maintaining macroeconomic stability and investing in social policies. The economy rebounded strongly from the 2009 slowdown, with GDP growth of 8.5% in 2010 and 5.5% in 2011. Economic growth has continued in 2012–13, albeit at a lower rate, as result of the impact of protectionism in Argentina, low economic growth in Brazil and the general weakness of the world economy. The Mujica administration has been characterized by a number of liberal social initiatives, including the legalization of gay marriage, the decriminalization of abortion and the legalization of the cultivation and commercialization of marijuana. President Mujica announced in 2014 that Uruguay had agreed to the US Government's request to give asylum to a number of Guantánamo Bay prisoners. Presidential and parliamentary elections will take place in October 2014. The FA's candidate, former President Vázquez, is the leading candidate, although is not certain whether the FA will retain control of Parliament. His main rival will be Luis Lacalle Pou from the centre-right Partido Nacional (PN).

CENTRE-RIGHT GOVERNMENTS

Centre-right Governments are in office in Colombia, Guatemala, Honduras, Mexico, Panama, Paraguay and the Dominican Republic. These Governments have remained closer to the principles of the free market model that dominated the region throughout the 1990s. They have also maintained close economic and political links with the USA. Mexico is part of the North American Free Trade Agreement (NAFTA) and the other nations have signed free trade agreements with the USA. The USA provides financial assistance, logistical support and training to the Colombian military in their fight against drugs-traffickers and the Fuerzas Armadas Revolucionarias de Colombia (FARC) guerrilla group, and financial assistance to the Mexican Government in its war on drugs. However, differences between centre-right and centre-left governments on economic policy are a matter of grade rather than of substance, and there is more common ground between some centre-right and centre-left governments on economic policies than between different left-wing administrations. For instance, there has been very little variation in economic policy between the centre-left and centre-right governments in Chile. El Salvador and Nicaragua are part of the Dominican Republic-Central American Free Trade Agreement (CAFTA-DR) with the USA, and Peru has also signed a free trade agreement with the USA. Some observers of Latin America argue that, rather than a left–right division on economic policy, there is a Pacific–Atlantic coast division, whereby the countries of the Pacific rim—Mexico, Colombia, Peru and Chile—have established Latin America's newest free trade area, the Alianza Pacífico (see below), while the Atlantic-facing countries of MERCOSUR remain engaged in a more statist and protectionist development model.

Colombia

Under the presidency of Alvaro Uribe (2002–10) Colombia dodged Latin America's shift to the left. Uribe, a former Governor of the state of Antioquia, first contested the presidency as an independent Liberal Party candidate in 2002. He based his campaign on pledges of stepping up the military campaign against the FARC, the left-wing guerrilla group that controlled significant parts of the countryside. Once in office, Uribe was true to his promise. With financial assistance from the US Government under the so-called Plan Colombia, he strengthened the military and sent them into an offensive against the guerrilla forces with considerable success. He also negotiated the demobilization of the right-wing paramilitaries, the Autodefensas Unidas de Colombia. He ruled in a highly personalistic way, travelling the country and meeting local people in communitarian councils to listen to their demands. Uribe's success against the FARC brought him strong popularity, despite allegations against him of human rights violations by the security forces. He had a conflictive relationship with President Chávez of Venezuela, whom he accused of sheltering and financing the guerrilla forces, a claim that was rejected by Chávez, who in turn accused the Colombian Government of planning an invasion of Venezuela.

On the strength of his popularity, Uribe was re-elected in 2006 for a further four-year period. He continued his hardline policy against the guerrilla FARC, while promoting economic reforms and a free trade agreement with the USA. During his presidency, Colombia was the USA's main ally in South America. President Uribe maintained high levels of popularity throughout his second presidency but was constitutionally barred from seeking a third consecutive term. In the 2010 election he choose as his candidate the Minister of National Defence, Juan Manuel Santos, who defeated a strong challenge by the candidate of the Partido Verde, Antanas Mockus.

One of President Santos's first initiatives was to repair relations with Venezuela, which have improved considerably under his presidency. He has also sought to moderate the human rights abuses of the security forces and to promote social policies and housing programmes. In 2012 the Government confirmed that it had started peace negotiations with the FARC that could end the longest guerrilla war in Latin America. Among the main issues under negotiation were rural development, the FARC's participation in politics and a possible partial amnesty for crimes committed by the guerrillas. Santos's softer policy towards the armed group and his rapprochement with Venezuela have been strongly criticized by former President Uribe and have led to a breakdown in political relations between the two former allies. The 2014 presidential election became effectively a plebiscite on the peace process and a proxy contest between now bitter rivals Santos and Uribe. As he was unable to seek the presidency, Uribe supported the candidacy of former Minister of Finance Oscar Iván Zuluaga. Santos campaigned on the promise of driving forward the peace process, while Zuluaga claimed that Santos's peace process would grant impunity to FARC leaders and argued that rebel leaders should have to serve prison sentences after demobilizing. According to some estimates, more than 200,000 people, mostly civilians, have died as a result of the conflict and millions have been displaced. Since no candidate achieved an absolute majority in the first round, a run off took place on 15 June, in which Santos defeated Zuluaga by 51% to 45% of the votes cast. After his victory, Santos declared that he had been given a 'mandate for peace' by voters.

Mexico

Since the landmark election of 2000, which marked the end of the Partido Revolucionario Institucional (PRI)'s 70-year control of the Mexican state, until the inauguration of the PRI's candidate, Enrique Peña Nieto, in December 2013, Mexico was governed by Presidents from the centre-rightist Partido de Acción Nacional (PAN): Vicente Fox (2000–06) and Felipe Calderón (2006–12). However, neither of the two Presidents enjoyed a parliamentary majority, which was a major obstacle for passing legislation to reform areas such as the labour market, energy, tax and education. Since the NAFTA trade agreement with Canada and the USA came into force on 1 January 1994, the Mexican economy has been ever more closely integrated to that of the USA. The economic results have been mixed so far. The Mexican economy has been modernized and has attracted considerable foreign investment, but economic growth has been disappointing and its benefits have not been evenly distributed. In 2008–09 the Mexican economy suffered as a result of the economic downturn in the USA and Europe, with a 6.3% contraction in GDP in 2009. It has since recovered, growing by 5.6% in 2010, by some 4.0% in 2011 and by 3.9% in 2012. After winning a narrow victory in controversial circumstances against the left-wing candidate, Andrés Manuel López Obrador, in 2006, President Calderón made the war against drugs-traffickers the highest priority of his Government. To this end, he ordered the armed forces to join the police in combating the drug cartels. The result has been an unprecedented escalation in the levels of violence, which, according to some estimates, has led to 47,000 deaths since late 2006. While the Government argues that the high numbers of victims is a price worth paying for defeating the traffickers, considerable sectors of public opinion believe that its all-out war strategy is too costly in terms of human lives and unlikely ultimately to defeat the cartels. Mediocre economic growth, political stalemate and continuous high levels of violence negatively impacted the Government's popularity, as reflected in the defeat of the PAN candidate, Josefina Vásquez Mota, in the July 2012 presidential election.

The victory in 2012 of the PRI candidate, Enrique Peña Nieto, represented a return to the presidency of the party that ruled Mexico for 71 years. President Peña Nieto has been eager to use his honeymoon period to advance an ambitious reform agenda encapsulated in the so-called 'Pacto por Mexico' (Pact for Mexico), an agreement with the main opposition parties that aimed to pass up to 95 initiatives to modernize the Mexican economy. Among the measures already approved by Congress are an educational reform act and reform of judicial injunction procedures. The Government has also introduced a tax reform and opened up state monopoly Pemex to private investors.

Perhaps one of the most far-reaching of an already impressive list of reforms is that of the US $32,000m. telecommunications sector. On 10 June 2014 President Peña Nieto signed a constitutional amendment that transformed the government's role in telecommunications and expanded its power to curtail media monopolies. A new regulatory body, the Federal Telecommunications Institute (IFETEL), will be created to guarantee economic competition and content plurality, and to encourage universal coverage, convergence, quality and access. The telecommunications reform also mandates the federal Government to set up a non-profit, public service broadcast company to provide objective information and to broadcast independently produced content. However, the reforms are expected to raise strong opposition from a small group of powerful figures that control the telecommunications industry.

In spite of his reforming successes, President Peña Nieto's popularity has fallen sharply after his first year in office. During his first months in office the President faced some episodes of social unrest, particularly from a radical section of the teachers' union and from university students. While his Government has downgraded the political profile of the so-called 'war on drugs' that had been his predecessor's main priority, drug-related violence is still rife in many parts of the country. Furthermore, while the reforms are expected to improve Mexico's long-term economic prospects, GDP growth was just 1.3% in 2013, according to the World Bank, although a rise in growth is anticipated for 2014.

Peru

Peru is another example of the importance of considering variations between left-wing governments in the region as part of a continuum rather than as clear-cut classifications. Peru is one of the fastest growing economies in Latin America. However, the Government of President Alan García (2006–11) was highly unpopular, particularly among the poor people of the more undeveloped regions of the country that did not benefit from economic growth. The 2011 election ended in a run-off between the centre-right candidate, Keiko Fujimori, the daughter of imprisoned former President Alberto Fujimori, and the candidate of the left, Ollanta Humala, who won by 51% to 48%. The election of Humala illustrates the problems that arise when too much emphasis is placed on the personality of the leader without regard for political or economic context. In 2006 Humala campaigned as an outsider and an anti-status quo candidate on pledges to break away radically from Peru's political institutions and free market economic model. He was also particularly close to President Chávez and was widely seen as a representative of the radical populist left. In contrast, in the 2011 presidential campaign Humala became distinctly more moderate and consensus-seeking. While he promised to make the country 'more just and less unequal', he kept his distance from the Venezuelan leader and claimed that he was closer to the politics and policies of former Brazilian President Lula da Silva. At his inauguration Humala promised to respect investors' rights, the rule of law and the Constitution.

To the disappointment of those who expected radical change, Humala appointed a moderate Cabinet and his Government has followed orthodox economic policies. Since his inauguration, the economy has continued to perform strongly but the Government has faced protests by indigenous and local groups for alleged damages to water supplies, crops and the environment brought by mining, logging, and oil and gas concessions to foreign companies. Protests reflect the deep urban–rural divide in Peru and the weak presence of the state in some areas of the country. In spite of showing some of the highest rates of economic growth in Latin America, President Humala's popularity has declined sharply. His approval ratings fell to 25% by mid-2014, compared with 54% in 2013. The President is considered to lack strong leadership. His governing coalition has only 43 out of 130 seats in Congress and the President has effected five cabinet reshuffles in three years. Political parties are almost non-existent and the citizens consistently support political outsiders against incumbents. National elections are scheduled for April 2016. There is no natural successor for President Humala, who cannot seek re-election.

FOREIGN POLICY

Over the past decade Latin American countries have become more prosperous, more confident and more autonomous from the USA. The rise of China as one of the region's main trade partners has offered the countries of Latin America an outlet for their exports and a source of investment. During the first decade of the century Brazil's quest to become a sub-regional leader under the presidency of Lula da Silva was challenged by the petro-diplomacy of the late President Chávez of Venezuela. Chávez vigorously used his country's oil wealth to pursue a foreign policy aimed at promoting his 'Bolivarian' idea of Latin American integration and to consolidate his regional leadership. In 2004 Venezuela and Cuba sponsored the establishment of the so-called Alternativa Bolivariana para las Américas (the Bolivarian Alternative for the Americas— renamed the Bolivarian Alliance for the Peoples of our America/Alianza Bolivariana para los Pueblos de Nuestra América), which at mid-2014 included Antigua and Barbuda, Bolivia, Cuba, Dominica, Ecuador, Nicaragua, Saint Lucia, Saint Vincent and the Grenadines, and Venezuela, as an alternative project for political and economic integration under Venezuela's leadership. However, the lower international profile of President Lula's successor, Dilma Rousseff, and the death of Chávez, together with Venezuela's mounting economic problems, have lessened the two countries' competition for regional hegemony and opened space for wider processes of regional integration.

Political integration in Latin America has outpaced economic integration. In May 2008 12 South American countries signed a treaty to establish the Unión de Naciones Suramericanas (UNASUR—Union of South American Nations), which became a legal entity on 11 March 2011, when the constitutive treaty entered into force. The long-term goal of this new entity is to unite South America's two existing customs unions, MERCOSUR and the Andean Community. In its first years, however, UNASUR has been more a political than an economic entity. In December 2008 the member states approved the creation of a Consejo de Defensa Suramericano (South American Defence Council) and a Consejo de Salud Suramericano (South American Health Council). The political dimension of UNASUR came to prominence in September 2008, when its then acting head, Chilean President Michelle Bachelet, played an important mediating role in the conflict between the Bolivian President, Evo Morales, and the opposition, which brought the country to the verge of an armed confrontation. In 2009 UNASUR also sought to mediate in the conflict between Colombia and Venezuela following the announcement that the Colombian Government was to allow the USA to use military bases on its territory. And, more recently, a delegation from UNASUR countries have been attempting to mediate between the government and the opposition in Venezuela. A broader

regional body is the Comunidad de Estados Latinoamericanos y el Caribe (Community of Latin American and Caribbean States, CELAC). Established in Mexico in February 2010, CELAC brings together 33 Latin American and Caribbean nations, with a joint population of around 590m. people. CELAC is an inter-governmental forum aimed at driving forward the political, economic, social and cultural integration of the member countries and to promote independent and sustainable development based on democracy, equity and social justice.

In June 2012 Chile, Peru, Colombia and Mexico announced the formation of the Alianza Pacífico (Pacific Alliance—AP) which is the most recent of a number of criss-crossing regional and sub-regional trade and integration agreements. The AP is intended to expand trade between its member countries by lifting formal and informal barriers and integrating their economies more closely. It also aims to co-ordinate efforts to promote exports and attract foreign investment, and to take advantage of the countries' geographical location to expand trade with the Asia-Pacific region. The member countries' economies account for around 37% of the region's GDP and for 50% of its exports, and attracted 46% of regional foreign direct investment in 2013. All member states have free market economies, have signed free trade agreements with the US and have strong economic ties with the Asian Pacific countries. Over the past years the rate of economic growth of the countries of the AP was considerably higher than those of MERCOSUR. The new alliance has been perceived as a gathering of countries committed to trade liberalization and integration, in contrast to the increasingly protectionist MERCOSUR bloc dominated by Brazil and Argentina. However, President Bachelet of Chile, whose country is an associate member of MERCOSUR, has called for stronger economic ties between the two sub-regional blocs.

CONCLUSIONS

A quarter-century of almost uninterrupted democracy has brought political change as well as political diversity to Latin America. Traditional ruling élites and political forces have been displaced by new leaders and new parties which have successfully appealed to social and economic groups that felt excluded from the old political order. The electoral cycle that came to a close in 2012 showed that left and left-of-centre governments remained in office in a majority of countries of the region. It is still too soon to determine whether the new cycle that started in 2013 will change the regional balance of forces. In the elections that took place in 2013 and the first half of 2014 the left continued to perform well, winning presidential elections in Costa Rica, Chile, El Salvador and Ecuador. However, the region remains firmly plural, with centre and centre-right candidates winning in Colombia, Honduras, Panama and Paraguay. Perhaps it would be more productive to look at the political map of the region beyond left and right. In the vast majority of the countries of the region the main opposing political forces are centre left and centre right, rather than hard left and hard right, a situation not dissimilar to mature democracies in Europe and elsewhere. Moreover, elections are not necessarily fought along ideological lines, but the contest of incumbent against opposition candidate is always a deciding factor. As can be expected in a democratic election, citizens have chosen to reward incumbents who have performed well, or have voted for change when the incumbents have been less successful. Underpinning political stability is almost a decade of strong economic growth which has lifted an estimated 150m. people out of poverty and created a new middle class more interested in prosperity than in revolution. However, Latin America still faces considerable political and economic challenges in the years ahead. Elections have been mostly free and fair, but there is great variety in the shape and strength of political institutions, with some countries appearing as increasingly consolidated liberal democracies, while in others fragile political institutions remain strained by deep social and political divisions. Political violence is on the wane, but criminal violence, mostly related to drugs-trafficking, constitutes a real threat to social and political order, particularly in Mexico and some Central American countries.

Much remains to be done to transform commodity-led economic growth into sustainable development. With the commodity boom of 2003–08 easing off and the prospect of a rise in interest rates in the USA in the not too distant future, the extremely favourable international economic environment that was the main engine of growth in the first decade of the century is expected to become less benign. Furthermore, while the fall in poverty has been encouraging, the reduction in inequality has been much less impressive. An improvement in education standards will be crucial for further decline in the number of people living in poverty, and to decrease the still high levels of inequality.

Inequalities between countries are as important as inequalities within countries. While some countries in the region, such as Chile, Argentina, Uruguay, Brazil, Mexico and Panama, have GDP per capita that places them not too far from the statistical threshold of high-income economies, others such as Guatemala, Nicaragua and Honduras are classified as low middle-income economies and Haiti is a low-income economy. There are also significant differences in economic development. Brazil and Mexico have sophisticated industrial sectors but most of the economies of the region remain dependent on the export of basic commodities. Last but not least, there have been significant differences in the rates of economic growth over the past years, with countries such as Peru, Chile, Colombia and Panama growing well above the regional average. All these may suggest a 'two-speed' Latin America, with some countries characterized by consolidated democracies and prosperous economies, while others remain volatile politically and economically.

Internationally, Latin America continues to reassert its autonomy from the USA. The creation of new regional associations, such as UNASUR and the AP marks a new era for the integration of the countries of Latin America. However, political divisions and divergent economic integration strategies within the countries of the region, as exemplified by the AP, together with a reluctance to share sovereignty in supranational institutions, remain major obstacles to the achievement of deeper integration.

SELECTED REFERENCES

Corporación Latinobarómetro 2013 report. Available online at www.latinobarometro.org/latino/latinobarometro.jsp.

Economic Commission for Latin America and the Caribbean (ECLAC). *Preliminary Overview of Latin America and the Caribbean 2013*. Available online at www.eclac.org/default.asp?idioma=IN.

Panorama Social de América Latina 2013. Available online at www.cepal.org/cgi-bin/getProd.asp?xml=/publicaciones/xml/5/48455/P48455.xml&xsl=/tpl/p9f.xsl&base=/tpl/top-bottom.xsl.

Human Development Index 2013. Available online at hdr.undp.org/en/statistics/.

DRUGS POLICY REFORM IN LATIN AMERICA

THOMAS GRISAFFI

Latin America and the Caribbean together represent a critical zone for the production and trafficking of illicit drugs. The Andean region, including Bolivia, Colombia and Peru, is the world's foremost producer of cocaine. Mexico is the main producer of heroin in the Americas; Colombia, Mexico and Paraguay are all significant producers of cannabis; and synthetic drugs are increasingly manufactured in Central (and North) America. The main corridor for the transport of illegal drugs to the US market is through Central America, Mexico and the Caribbean (UNODC, 2013).

There is a voracious appetite for illicit drugs in the USA: it represents the single largest market for cocaine in the world, and consumers spend some US $100,000m. per year on illegal substances (Kilmer, Everingham et al, 2014). As a result of its excessive drugs consumption, the USA suffers from a heavy burden of crime and drugs-related health and social problems. Instead of tackling the structural inequalities that lead to drug addiction at home, politicians have described illicit drugs as a threat to national security and the battle has been taken to source regions. Over the past 30 years the USA has channelled thousands of millions of dollars to Latin American military and police forces to enable them to undertake counter-narcotics operations, with the aim of suppressing the production and trafficking of illegal drugs. The logic underlying the entire operation is that by reducing supply, the cost of illicit drugs will increase and this, in turn, will dissuade people in consumer countries from buying them (Caulkins, 2014).

Historically, the USA has dictated the terms of the 'war on drugs', and has used its political and economic might to crush any debate on alternatives. Of late, however, Latin American governments have pushed back against continuing with prohibitionist drugs policies. A regional debate has emerged, focused on the failure of present policies to achieve their desired objectives and on the high cost of implementing supply-reduction efforts (in terms of violence, corruption and institutional instability). Latin American leaders have argued for more effective and humane alternatives, including the creation of legal, regulated markets for narcotic substances and greater investment in harm-reduction practices. The past year marks an important period in the evolution of the global drug policy debate, including:

(i) The publication of a report commissioned by the Organization of American States (OAS) in April 2013 that expressed dissatisfaction with prohibitionist policies and the militarized supply-focused approach.

(ii) Uruguay's approval of the world's first national legal framework regulating the cultivation, trade and consumption of cannabis.

(iii) Colombia and Guatemala's stand at the 2013 UN General Assembly, where they claimed the drugs war had failed and that any long-term solution has to focus on the structural roots of drugs consumption, production and trafficking.

(iv) The Bolivian Government's successful efforts to legalize coca leaf consumption within its borders.

This essay begins by examining some of the objectives, methods and consequences of the US-designed and -funded 'war on drugs' in Latin America and the Caribbean. It then goes on to outline the emerging regional debate. The final section provides a brief overview of Bolivia's new approach to coca control, which, according to a recent report by the OAS, represents best practice. Overall, the essay illustrates that the alternative approaches championed by Latin American governments, which aim to reduce the harmful impacts generated by drugs and drugs-trafficking, may prove to be more effective in addressing the drugs problem in the long-term than the current militarized response.

THE 'WAR ON DRUGS'

For over a century the prohibitionist approach has shaped policies to deal with the production, trafficking, sale and consumption of psychoactive substances—including cannabis, cocaine and heroin. Significantly, these policies have been operationalized using hardline criminal policy tools. The US Administration's approach to domestic drugs control includes rigid legislation, enhanced law enforcement and high levels of incarceration (in 2012 the USA imprisoned 1.55m. people on drugs charges)[1]. Abroad, the US approach has been to curb the supply of illicit narcotics reaching the USA, through the eradication of illicit crops (mostly coca leaf—which is used to produce cocaine, but also opium poppy and marijuana)[2], law enforcement and the interdiction of drugs shipments (Youngers, 2006). The USA has ensured that its southern neighbours comply with its drugs policy goals, through what is termed 'certification'. This is an annual process undertaken by the USA to evaluate country performance against US-imposed anti-drugs targets. Countries that do not act in accordance with US strategy are punished by decertification; sanctions include the withholding of development aid, credit and trade benefits. In other words, any country that attempts to break with the US drugs war runs the risk of being politically and economically isolated.

Since the inauguration of the Andean Initiative[3] in 1989, the USA has devoted vast sums to its drugs war[4], building up what Youngers (2000) describes as an extensive 'narco-enforcement complex,' led by the US Department of Defense and including more than 50 federal agencies and bureaux. The USA has used its considerable resources to expand the role of both Latin American and US military forces in counter-drugs efforts, provide local security forces with logistical support and equipment, and to train civilian police forces in military tactics. Historically, US funding and weapons were restricted to anti-drugs operations; after 2001, however, they were also used to intervene against left-wing insurgencies in Peru and Colombia in the name of the 'war on terror' (Youngers, 2003). For example, in 2000 the US and Colombian Governments launched 'Plan Colombia'—a five-year, US $4,000m. 'aid' package (80% of which was earmarked for the Colombian police and military), with the stated aim of reducing narcotics production by one-half. However, the counter-narcotics security support, including state-of-the-art training, arms, aeroplanes and helicopters, was also used to strike at the guerrilla Fuerzas Armadas Revolucionarias de Colombia (FARC) (Hylton, 2006). The focus of the US approach, which prioritizes military and police assistance over aid for socioeconomic goals or institution-building, has produced what some policy analysts refer to as militarization—that is, the 'over-involvement of the armed forces in aspects of governance other than external defense' (Isacson, 2005: 17).

The objective of supply-side enforcement is to reduce the amount of drugs reaching the USA, but on this score the drugs war has clearly failed. The supply of drugs to the USA remains as robust as ever (Mejia, 2010)[5]. This is demonstrated by the fact that while the purity of cocaine has remained stable, the street price has consistently fallen since the 1980s. Similar patterns have also been observed for other drugs, including heroin and methamphetamine (Walsh, 2007). The disappointing results are a consequence of myopic policies that fail to address the underlying causes of drugs production and trafficking, such as poverty, social exclusion and weak institutions. Thus, victories in the war on drugs are generally only ever shortlived: when coca and poppy crops are eradicated, production moves to a different region (a phenomenon referred to as the 'balloon effect')[6]; drugs-traffickers are arrested but they are soon replaced; and when trafficking routes are disrupted they simply shift elsewhere.

The enormous cost of the drugs war, coupled with the fact that it is not actually achieving its stated goals, has prompted some observers to suggest that US foreign policy on drugs is not a stand-alone issue—rather, it is used as an instrument to push other less ostensible political and economic agendas. For instance, some academics have argued that the USA's motivation for escalating the drugs war at the end of the 1980s was to justify the build-up of a military presence in the region to protect US corporate interests in a post-cold war world (Grandin, 2006, Tokatlian, 2010).

THE LATIN AMERICAN DEBATE

Latin American leaders have grown weary of fighting what they perceive to be an unwinnable war. Their resolve to look for alternatives has been strengthened by the violence and corruption associated with the drugs trade. The scale of the problem is shocking; for example, the countries that lie on the main drugs-trafficking route from the Andes to the USA have among the highest murder rates in the world (UNODC, 2011). In spite of the violence, Latin American leaders do not view the drugs problem through the lens of 'national security', and they are actively seeking alternatives to the status quo. In August 2010 Mexico's President Felipe Calderón became the first incumbent head of state to call for a debate on whether to legalize drugs (*The Economist*, 2010); in an interview with *The Observer* newspaper in 2011, President Juan Manuel Santos of Colombia urged a major rethink of the 'war on drugs' (Mulholland, 2011); and at the 2013 World Economic Forum at Davos, Switzerland, Guatemala's President, Otto Pérez Molina, argued for the legal regulation of all drugs at a global level (Wearden, 2013).

There are strong arguments in support of the reformist agenda. One of the key points repeatedly made by Latin American leaders is that prohibition strengthens criminal organizations by handing them control of a lucrative and growing trade.[7] The massive profits derived from the drugs trade that flow untaxed, into criminal hands, have been used to equip private militias (often outgunning state enforcement) and to undermine state institutions through corruption. For example, in parts of Central America wealthy traffickers have even become de facto authorities, dispensing jobs and humanitarian assistance while simultaneously intimidating and corrupting local officials (Crisis Group, 2014). Some leaders, including Pérez Molina, have argued that the best way to crush trafficking organizations is to legalize drugs, which would deny cartels their main source of revenue. This position is supported by a recent study which argues that if marijuana were legalized in California and was then exported to other US states, Mexican drugs cartels would lose about one-fifth of their annual income (Kilmer, Caulkins, et al, 2010).

The drugs trade has undoubtedly had a harmful impact on the region, but so too have US-designed and -funded responses to it. Research illustrates that the drugs war has undermined human rights, civil liberties and democratic practices in Latin America (Youngers and Rosin, 2005). US-imposed anti-drugs legislation has led to a dramatic increase in sentences for drugs-related crimes—for instance, under Bolivia's notorious Law 1008 a small trafficker or dealer might end up with a sentence far longer than someone convicted for murder (Metaal and Youngers, 2011). As a result of such punitive laws, between 2006 and 2011 the number of female prisoners in Latin America almost doubled, from 40,000 to around 74,000—the vast majority of whom are in prison on non-violent drugs charges (Giacomello, 2013). Meanwhile, the US emphasis on using Latin American military forces to fight internal enemies has resulted in significant collateral damage. Mexico represents a prime example of the dangers posed by the militarized approach. In 2006 President Calderón deployed the army against the drugs gangs; this led to an escalation of violence, as cartels fought back against government forces but also fought each other for control over the trade. The total homicide rate in Mexico increased threefold within a period of just four years, from about eight homicides per 100,000 individuals in 2006 to more than 23 in 2010 (Mejia and Restrepo, 2014). Some estimates suggest that Mexico has suffered 70,000 murders as a result of drugs-related violence over the past seven years.

Colombia has also experienced pronounced cycles of violence as a result of the illegal drugs trade and the state's responses to it: Mejia and Restrepo (2014) suggest that it accounts for some 3,800 homicides every year. In coca growing regions, militarized crop eradication has pitted the security forces against local farmers, and this has provoked violent conflicts and opened up space for the violation of human rights, including extrajudicial

killings and wholesale massacres. Institutional damage has been further compounded by the impunity that US-funded forces frequently enjoy. Meanwhile the Government's aerial spraying of coca crops in Colombia[8] has made the lives of poor farmers even more precarious by causing environmental damage (including water contamination and land degradation) and serious health problems. Anthropologist, María Clemencia Ramírez (2011) records that residents in the spray zones suffer from a variety of ailments, including skin, respiratory and gastrointestinal problems. They also complain that spraying is indiscriminate and carried out without warning—as a result food and cash crops are also often affected by herbicides. The economic and humanitarian crisis provoked by aerial fumigation has forced people off their land—to join the ranks of Colombia's estimated 4.9m. to 5.5m. internally displaced people (Rincón-Ruiz and Kallis, 2013).

In 2009 the Latin American Commission on Drugs and Democracy, led by former Presidents Fernando Henrique Cardoso of Brazil, César Gaviria of Colombia and Ernesto Zedillo of Mexico, published a report calling for a public debate on alternatives to prohibitionist policies. Their proposals included treating drugs use as an issue of public health rather than as a matter of criminal law, decriminalizing marijuana and focusing repression on organized crime—as opposed to on the people who cultivate illicit crops. The report received a positive response, and the Commission subsequently gained the support of former UN Secretary-General Kofi Annan, George Schultz and Paul Volcker among dozens of other public figures. This advocacy opened up space for the subsequent rebellion spearheaded by Guatemala's President Pérez Molina in 2012.

Pérez Molina, a former head of military intelligence who was once responsible for executing the country's drugs war, became President of Guatemala in January 2012, having been elected on a platform of reducing crime. Soon after taking office, however, he stunned the US Administration of Barack Obama by announcing that the inability of the USA to reduce demand for illicit drugs left Guatemala with no option but to consider decriminalization. In March Pérez Molina convened a regional summit in Antigua, Guatemala, to discuss drugs policy options. The event was undermined by a disappointing turnout: the Presidents of Honduras, El Salvador and Nicaragua all withdrew, ostensibly as a result of US pressure. At the summit Pérez Molina presented a range of options, including the establishment of a dedicated regional court for drugs-trafficking offences with its own prison system; the depenalization of the transit of drugs along a North–South corridor; and the creation of a legal regulatory framework covering narcotic substances. The meeting did not end in political agreement, but it did ensure that drugs law reform was high on the agenda at the OAS Summit of the Americas held in Cartagena, Colombia, only a month later (Armenta, Metaal et al, 2012).

The April 2012 OAS summit marked a watershed in the Latin American drugs policy debate. For the first time, incumbent heads of state—including Pérez Molina, Colombia's Juan Manuel Santos, Costa Rica's Laura Chinchilla and Mexico's Felipe Calderón—questioned the efficacy of continuing with full-scale prohibition, and declared that all possibilities must be considered. Given the previous taboo on even discussing alternatives to the drugs war, the OAS summit marks a significant step towards change. Indeed, drugs policy analysts have characterized the event as releasing the 'genie from the bottle' (Youngers, 2012). The summit tasked the OAS with conducting a study to analyse the impact of present policy and to explore alternative approaches. The final report, published in April 2013, reflected Latin America's growing disenchantment with current drugs policy, and outlined serious alternatives to prohibition—including the decriminalization (meaning the removal of criminal penalties) or the legalization and regulation of certain drugs (starting with marijuana).

In September 2012 the Presidents of Colombia, Guatemala and Mexico took the regional debate to the UN General Assembly—where they issued a formal statement underscoring the need critically to review current drugs policies and called on the UN to analyse all available options, including regulatory market measures. Subsequently, it was announced that the UN General Assembly Special Session (UNGASS) on the 'world drug problem' would be brought forward to early 2016 (instead of 2019 as was previously planned). The momentum was maintained throughout the following year: in June 2013 the OAS adopted a declaration (known as the 'declaration of Antigua') that reiterated the futility of the current war on drugs and called for the OAS to hold a special session on drugs no later than 2014.[9] In September 2013 Colombia, Costa Rica, Guatemala and Mexico returned to the UN once more to call for a wide-ranging debate about the drugs issue in the lead up to the 2016 UNGASS. And finally, in March 2014, for the first time in its history, the Inter-American Commission on Human Rights (an autonomous organ of the OAS) granted a hearing to analyse the impacts of drugs policy on human rights in the Americas.

High-level debate has been accompanied by unilateral changes to drugs policy in some Latin American countries—chief among these is Uruguay, which, on 20 December 2013, became the first country in the world to legalize and regulate the production, marketing and consumption of cannabis. Coletta Youngers (2013), of the Washington Office on Latin America, argues that this development could encourage other reform-minded governments to explore similar initiatives. Mexico, Argentina and Brazil (all of which are experiencing rising domestic drug consumption) are investigating decriminalizing possession of small amounts of drugs for personal use, and increasing investment in harm-reduction programmes. Some Latin American countries are also addressing the issue of excessive sentences established in national drugs laws, which in most cases fail to distinguish between traffickers and consumers. In 2010 Brazil's Supreme Federal Tribunal ruled that the application of alternatives to incarceration should be allowed for low-level drugs offenders, noting that judges should have the right to discretion when sentencing. Meanwhile, in 2005 Ecuador took the unprecedented step of granting a pardon to low-level drugs couriers—an initiative that freed more than 2,000 people, the majority of whom did not reoffend (Armenta, Metaal et al, 2012).

Bolivia has led a battle for the decriminalization of coca leaf (a perennial shrub that has been consumed for millennia by people living in the Andean region). In early 2013 the UN agreed to amend the 1961 Single Convention on Narcotic Drugs[10]—the most important international legal framework for drugs control—to permit the traditional consumption of coca within Bolivian territory. Bolivia has, furthermore, advanced a radical method for controlling coca plantations, which allows voluntary crop eradication; this approach was commended in the OAS report and will be discussed in more detail below. Finally, it is not just Latin American countries where changes are taking place, the states of Washington and Colorado in the USA recently voted to legalize the possession of marijuana for personal use by adults over 21. Both states are in the process of creating systems for legal production and sale, subject to licensing, regulation and taxation.

The debate in the Americas has clearly moved far beyond the dogma of the 'war on drugs'. Nevertheless, progressive countries are still outnumbered by those committed to present policy. At the 2013 OAS summit Venezuela, Nicaragua, Panama, and El Salvador all spoke in favour of maintaining the status quo and neither Brazil nor Argentina articulated a reform agenda (Youngers, 2013). Furthermore, while the Obama Administration has been more diplomatic than its predecessors, and has even dropped the term 'war on drugs', the change in discourse has had little impact on the actual implementation of programmes or policies on the ground (Youngers, 2012). The UN's International Narcotics Control Board (INCB)[11] has also ignored the growing calls for policy reform. In the foreword to the INCB's 2013 annual report, the organization's President labelled reform initiatives as 'dangerous' and 'misguided'. Thus, it can be expected that reformist governments will face considerable opposition in the run up to the 2016 UNGASS.

BOLIVIA'S NEW APPROACH TO COCA CONTROL

According to UN estimates, Bolivia is the third largest producer of coca leaf, after Colombia and Peru (UNODC, 2012). One of Bolivia's two main coca growing regions is the Chapare, a tropical agricultural zone located in the centre of the country. The population comprises Quechua-speaking peasants and former miners and factory workers from the highlands—many of whom migrated to the region in the 1980s in search of alternative livelihoods in the coca-cocaine economy. Coca growers often point out that the only reason they took up coca cultivation in the first place was because it was one of the few options available to them in the wake of the economic reforms implemented under the Movimiento Nacionalista Revolucionario administration in the mid-1980s, which closed down state-owned mines and factories and put tens of thousands of people out of work (Grisaffi, 2010).

The 45,000 settler families established small, family-run farms. They cultivate a range of crops, including rice, bananas and citrus fruit, but it is the income generated by coca leaf that provides many with their only source of cash that is essential for survival. While the coca-cocaine industry represents a significant segment of the Bolivian economy (according to UN estimates, it is worth US $500m.–$700m. annually), the Chapare farmers are not the major beneficiaries. The UN has calculated that less than 1% of the value of European or US cocaine sales makes its way back to the Andean coca farmers. As a result, the basic quality of life in the Chapare has remained very low: beyond the main towns, people live in houses made from rough-cut planks and palm leaves, and they do not count on sanitation, running water or electricity.

In the early 1980s the US Administration launched a coca eradication programme in the Chapare, in an effort to tackle escalating coca production and cocaine-processing. The Bolivian military and police forces, working closely with the US Drug Enforcement Administration (DEA) and the Narcotics Affairs Section of the US embassy in La Paz, targeted the family-run farms and manually uprooted coca plantations. Forced eradication did dramatically reduce the amount of land under coca cultivation in the Chapare, but this came at a high price. Eradication outpaced the provision of alternative development assistance, and plunged the coca growers into severe economic crisis. More importantly, the security forces tasked with carrying out coca eradication missions killed and seriously wounded scores of peasant activists, raped women, torched homesteads and incarcerated and tortured hundreds of people[12] (Ledebur, 2005). Under the terms of the draconian Law 1008, which was pushed through the Bolivian congress under intense pressure from the US embassy in 1988, thousands of people were arrested for drugs-related offences on little or no evidence, and held indefinitely without charge.

In spite of (or some might say because of) military repression, the coca growers built a powerful agricultural union to contest the Bolivian Government's anti-coca policy. The coca union vowed to defend the right to grow coca leaf, which it classified as 'sacred' on the basis that it represented an important element of indigenous culture and religious practice (Grisaffi, 2010). In 2005 the coca union's political party, the Movimiento al Socialismo (MAS), secured an overwhelming victory in the presidential election, with the leader of the Chapare coca union, Evo Morales, becoming Bolivia's first indigenous head of state. Morales and the MAS subsequently won equally decisive majorities in the 2009 presidential and legislative elections.

On taking office at the beginning of 2006, President Morales made a radical break with the US-financed policies that focused on military/police suppression and the eradication of illicit crops. His new policy, popularly known as 'coca si, cocaina no' (coca yes, cocaine no), is a direct result of proposals put forward by Bolivia's coca grower unions. It envisions development with coca and treats the coca growers as partners in the fight against drugs-trafficking. There are four pillars to the new policy:

1. Limited coca cultivation: under the new regime, each member of the agricultural unions is permitted to grow a limited amount of coca, termed a *cato* (1,600 sq m). In addition, Morales has increased the extent of coca that can be grown nationally from 12,000 ha to 20,000 ha to supply the traditional legal market.

2. Decriminalization and industrialization of coca: the Bolivian Government makes a sharp distinction between coca leaf—the plant that Andeans have consumed for millennia—

and the illicit drug cocaine. It has proposed the industrialization of coca for legal uses, such as teas, shampoo, diet pills, wine and toothpaste. Moreover, Bolivia has urged the UN to decriminalize coca leaf, so that the country can export these coca-based products to other countries; this is not possible at present, as coca remains on the UN's list of controlled substances (Metaal et al., 2006). Unlike several other Latin American governments, however, the MAS administration is not in favour of decriminalizing cocaine.

3. Community-led control: responsibility for coca control has been transferred from the security forces to the country's agricultural federations. This policy is referred to as 'social control', and encourages the unions to exercise internal controls to restrict cultivation to one *cato* per member. Any coca produced beyond this limit is to be voluntarily uprooted. The policy works because coca growers identify strongly with the Morales administration, and take pride in self-governance. Furthermore, farmers consider that it is in their own best interest to respect the *cato* agreement—they understand that if coca cultivation is restricted, then coca prices will increase. The agricultural unions are also tasked with ensuring that coca is sold directly to official coca markets and is not diverted to drugs-traffickers.

4. 'Development First': the Government has promoted economic development in coca-growing regions, but—unlike the previous strategy—this has not been conditional on the eradication of coca. Furthermore, in contrast to the approach of the US Agency for International Development (USAID), development actors now work directly with the coca unions.

From the perspective of the Chapare coca growers, the new policy is a step in the right direction. The violence provoked by forced coca eradication is regarded as a thing of the past, and the coca growers have been able to re-establish themselves after years of impoverishment. The *cato* of coca generates an income of about US $200 dollars per month for each grower; this provides poor farmers with an economic safety net, and has allowed them to experiment with other legal crops without running the risk of destitution. Since 2006 the local economy has started to grow; this is clearly demonstrated by the proliferation of village fiestas, motorcycle ownership, thriving local businesses, home improvements and rising land prices in the region. In addition, the new policy respects the coca leaf, which the coca growers consider to be an important element of their culture. Notwithstanding these advances, however, there are challenges associated with implementing the new policy—not least the refusal by a minority of farmers to comply with the new regime (Grisaffi, 2013).

The Bolivian policy has been remarkably effective. A recent UN report suggests that the area under coca cultivation decreased by 19% in 2010–12, a far greater fall than in Peru where eradication was carried out. The UN attributes Bolivia's 'significant' decrease to 'effective control' through co-operative coca reduction and eradication (Ledebur and Youngers, 2013). The Bolivian Government has also made significant efforts to eradicate coca in areas that are not controlled by registered coca unions. In 2011 government forces eradicated a total of 10,500 ha of coca—28% more than in 2010. Moreover, despite having expelled the DEA in 2008, the Bolivian Government has achieved several important victories against drugs-traffickers. In 2010 the country's special anti-narcotics police force confiscated and destroyed more than 28 metric tons of cocaine paste and 5.5 tons of pure cocaine (UNODC, 2012); this represents a massive increase on the amount of cocaine interdicted 10 years previously. Anthropological research suggests that US-financed repression against growers was effective in convincing all Chapare residents that the police were enemies. However, today this is no longer the case and the coca growers are now willing to collaborate with the authorities in the fight against drugs-traffickers (Grisaffi, 2014). Prominent research organizations, including the Washington Office on Latin America and the Andean Information Network, have judged Morales' 'social control' approach in positive terms. They consider that the policy treats the coca growers as partners instead of as criminals, respects human rights, and offers poor farmers realistic economic alternatives. Furthermore, they contend that by tackling the root causes of the cultivation of illicit crops, the co-operative approach could be more effective in

reducing coca and cocaine production in the long term than was the previous strategy of forced eradication (Farthing and Kohl, 2012, Ledebur and Youngers, 2013).

Notwithstanding the persuasive figures, the USA has been very critical of this new approach. The White House Office of National Drug Control Policy argues that, despite the decrease in total coca acreage, potential annual cocaine production in Bolivia increased dramatically in 2011, to 265 metric tons (from 195 tons in 2010), as a result of better yields from existing plantations and innovative methods for processing cocaine. However, some drugs policy analysts have suggested that these figures are opaque and unrealistic (Ledebur and Youngers, 2013). Even so, in September 2013 the White House renewed the decertification of Bolivia for the fifth consecutive year, stating that the country had 'demonstrably failed to comply with its obligations to tackle drug traffic'. The USA did, none the less, sign a bilateral framework agreement with Bolivia in 2011, and it has continued to provide it with equipment and training for anti-drugs operations (although at a much reduced level). In January 2012 Bolivia, Brazil and the USA signed a trilateral coca monitoring agreement.

History has shown that eradicating illicit crops in source countries is counterproductive. It destroys local economies, provokes violent confrontations, and criminalizes some of the poorest and most vulnerable members of society. Furthermore, there is absolutely no evidence to suggest that eradicating coca crops in the Andes has an impact on the supply of drugs reaching US streets. Conversely, Bolivia's co-operative coca reduction policy is humane: it respects indigenous culture, and it creates a safe and secure environment in which alternative livelihood strategies can be tried out (Youngers and Walsh, 2010). Rather than remaining committed to a policy that has proved to be harmful, ineffective and unsustainable, US policy-makers would be well advised to learn lessons from the Bolivian experiment.

CONCLUSION

For decades, successive US administrations have pursued a supply-side drugs control strategy that has been harmful and that has failed to achieve its goals. Despite the thousands of millions of dollars spent and the lives lost, Latin America remains a major global exporter of illicit drugs, including cocaine, cannabis and heroin. Some Latin American leaders have tired of the violence, corruption and disappointing results associated with the drugs war. They have called into question the legal and ethical framework underlying the international drugs control system that transfers a large proportion of the costs to producer and transit countries. Latin American governments have proposed a range of initiatives including decriminalizing drugs for personal consumption; reducing penalties for drugs offences; creating corridors for the transit of illicit drugs, so that they can move unhindered to the market without destabilizing the entire region; increasing expenditure on harm-reduction programmes; and pursuing collaborative approaches to control illicit crops. Latin American leaders have also called on the USA to stem the flow of money and automatic weapons from that country. The present time marks a historic juncture in the debate regarding drugs policy, with Latin American leaders making ever-louder calls for 'regulation' as opposed to 'prohibition'. Whether they will be able to forge a new consensus in the run up to the 2016 UNGASS remains to be seen. However, it is worth remembering that drugs control policy has taken many different forms over the years, and so there is no reason to assume that the current prohibitionist policies will prevail (Paoli, Greenfield et al., 2012).

FOOTNOTES

[1] See www.drugpolicy.org/drug-war-statistics.

[2] The justification for the physical destruction of illicit crops is that it prevents them from being processed into drugs and subsequently traded on the international market.

[3] The Andean Initiative was a five-year, US $2,200m. plan targeting coca and cocaine production in the Andean region; the plan was 'front-loaded' with military and police assistance.

[4] Some estimates put US spending on counter-narcotics initiatives at US $20,000m.–$25,000m. per year.

[5] Mejia estimated that the amount of cocaine reaching US borders actually increased from 322 metric tons in 2000 to 402 tons in 2006.

[6] The trend of shifting production can be attributed to the fact that eradication forces up the price of coca, while simultaneously denying poor farmers their only source of income—thus leaving farmers with little choice but to replant illicit crops. Consequently, although the amount of coca in each country has fluctuated over the past 30 years, total coca acreage in the Andean region as a whole has remained remarkably stable, at around 200,000 ha. See Ramirez, S., and Youngers, C. *Drug Policy in the Andes: Seeking Humane and Effective Alternatives*. Stockhom, Lima and Atlanta, GA, The Carter Center and International IDEA, 2011.

[7] The UN Office on Drugs and Crime estimated that in 2003 the total retail value of the global illicit drug trade was US $320,000m., and the retail drug markets in the Americas were estimated to be worth $151,000m.

[8] Colombia is currently the only country in the Andean region that permits the aerial fumigation of coca plantations.

[9] The OAS special session on drugs will be held in Guatemala in September 2014.

[10] The justification for classifying coca as an illegal substance has its roots in a UN study published in 1950. This study has since been discredited as inaccurate and racist for its characterization of coca-chewing as a disgusting, backward and dangerous habit. Subsequent research undertaken by the World Health Organization and the UN Interregional Crime and Justice Research Institute comes out in favour of coca leaf, noting the positive therapeutic, nutritional and social functions associated with its use. However, as a result of diplomatic pressure from the USA, the report on the research was never published (Metaal, Jelsma, et al., 2006).

[11] The INCB is an independent organ for the implementation of the UN's drug conventions.

[12] Security forces killed 33 coca growers and injured 570, leading to retaliatory attacks that left 27 military and police dead in the Chapare between 1997 and 2001.

REFERENCES

Armenta, A., Metaal, P., and Jelsma, M. 'A breakthrough in the making? Shifts in the Latin American drug policy debate', in *Series on Legislative Reform of Drug Policies*, No. 21. Amsterdam, Transnational Institute, 2012.

Caulkins, J. *Effects of Prohibition, Enforcement and Interdiction on Drug Use. Ending the Drug Wars: Report of the LSE Expert Group on the Economics of Drug Policy*. J. Collins, London, London School of Economics IDEAS, 2014.

Crisis Group. *Corridor of Violence: the Guatemala- Honduras Border*. Latin America Report No 52. Brussels, Crisis Group, 2014.

The Economist. 'The Americas: Thinking the unthinkable; Mexico and drugs'. *The Economist*, pp. 28–29, 14 Aug. 2010.

Farthing, L., and Kohl, B. 'Supply-side harm reduction strategies: Bolivia's experiment with social control'. *International Journal of Drug Policy*, 23:6, pp. 488–494, 2012.

Giacomello, C. *Women, drug offenses and penitentiary systems in Latin America*. IDPC Briefing Paper. London, International Drug Policy Consortium, 2013.

Grandin, G. *Empire's Workshop: Latin America, the United States and the Rise of the New Imperialism*. New York, Metropolitan Books, 2006.

Grisaffi, T. '"We are Originarios... We just aren't from here": Coca leaf and Identity Politics in the Chapare, Bolivia', in *Bulletin of Latin American Research*, 29:4, pp. 425–439, 2010.

'"All of us are Presidents": Radical Democracy and Citizenship in the Chapare Province, Bolivia', in *Critique of Anthropology*, 33:1, pp. 47–65, 2013.

'Can you get rich from the Bolivian Cocaine Trade? Cocaine Paste Production in the Chapare', in *Andean Information Network Memo*. Retrieved 10 March 2014, from ain-bolivia. org/2014/03/can-you-get-rich-from-the-bolivian-cocaine-trade-cocaine-paste-production-in-the-chapare/.

Hristov, J. *Blood and Capital: The Paramilitarization of Colombia*. Athens, OH, Ohio University Press, 2009.

Hylton, F. *Evil Hour in Colombia*. London, Verso, 2006.

Isacson, A. 'The U.S. Military in the War on Drugs', in Youngers, C., and Rosin, E. (Eds). *Drugs and Democracy in Latin America: The Impact of U.S. Policy*. Washington Office on Latin America, Washington, DC, Lynne Rienner Publrs, Boulder, CO, and London, 2005.

Kilmer, B., et al. 'Reducing Drug Trafficking Revenues and Violence in Mexico: Would Legalizing Marijuana in California Help?'. RAND Corporation, 2010. www.rand.org/pubs/occasional_papers/op325.

What America's Users Spend on Illegal Drugs: 2000-2010. Washington DC, Office of National Drug Control Policy, 2014.

Ledebur, K. 'Bolivia: Clear Consequences', in Youngers, C., and Rosin, E. (Eds). *Drugs and Democracy in Latin America: The Impact of U.S. Policy*. Washington Office on Latin America, Washington, DC, Lynne Rienner Publrs, Boulder, CO, and London 2005.

Ledebur, K., and Youngers, C. 'From Conflict to Collaboration: An Innovative Approach to Reducing Coca Cultivation in Bolivia', in *Stability: International Journal of Security and Development*, 2:1, pp. 1–11, 2013.

Mejia, D. 'Evaluating Plan Colombia', in Keefer, P., and Loayza, N. (Eds). *Innocent Bystanders: Developing Countries and the War on Drugs*. New York, The World Bank and Palgrave Macmillan, 2010.

Mejia, D., and Restrepo, P. 'Why Is Strict Prohibition Collapsing? A Perspective from Producer and Transit Countries', in Collins, J. *Ending the Drug Wars: Report of the LSE Expert Group on the Economics of Drug Policy*. London, London School of Economics IDEAS, 2014.

Metaal, P., et al. 'Coca Yes, Cocaine, No? Legal Options for the Coca Leaf', in *TNI Briefing Series*. Amsterdam, Transnational Institute, 2006.

Metaal, P., and Youngers, C. 'Systems Overload: Drug Laws and Prisons in Latin America', in *Series on Legislative Reform of Drug Policies*. Amsterdam and Washington, DC, Transnational Institute and Washington Office on Latin America, 2011.

Mulholland, J. 'Juan Manuel Santos: It is time to think again about the war on drugs', in *The Observer*, 12 November 2011.

Paoli, L., Greenfield, V., and Reuter, P. 'Change Is Possible: The History of the International Drug Control Regime and Implications for Future Policymaking', in *Substance Use and Misuse*, 47:8–9, pp. 923–935, 2012.

Ramírez, M. C. *Between the Guerrillas and the State: The Cocalero Movement, Citizenship and Identity in the Colombian Amazon*. Durham, NC, and London, Duke University Press, 2011.

Ramirez, S., and Youngers, C. *Drug Policy in the Andes: Seeking Humane and Effective Alternatives*. Stockhom, Lima and Atlanta, GA, The Carter Center and International Institute for Democracy and Electoral Assistance (IDEA), 2011.

Rincón-Ruiz, A., and Kallis, G. 'Caught in the middle, Colombia's war on drugs and its effects on forest and people', in *Geoforum*, 46. Philadelphia, PA, Elsevier, 2013.

Tokatlian, J. G. 'La "guerra antidrogas" y el Comando Sur', in *Foreign Affairs Latinoamérica*, 10(1): pp. 43–50. New York, Council on Foreign Relations, 2010.

UN Office on Drugs and Crime (UNODC). *Global Study on Homicide: Trends, Context, Data*. Vienna, United Nations Publications, 2011.

Estado Plurinacional de Bolivia: Monitoreo de Cultivos de Coca. Oficina de las Naciones Unidas Contra la Droga y el Delito, La Paz, Bolivia, 2012.

World Drug Report 2013. Vienna, United Nations Publications, 2013.

Walsh, J. *Connecting the Dots: ONDCP's Reluctant Update on Cocaine Price and Purity*. Drug Policy Program Occasional Reports, Washington, DC, Washington Office on Latin America, 2007.

Wearden, G. 'George Soros backs Guatemalan President's call to end war on drugs', in *The Guardian*, 23 January 2013.

Youngers, C. 'Cocaine madness: Counternarcotics and militarization in the Andes', in *NACLA Report on the Americas*, Nov./Dec. 2000, pp. 16–23. New York, 2000.

'The U.S. and Latin America After 9-11 and Iraq', in *Foreign Policy in Focus*. Silver City, NM, and Washington, DC, 2003.

'Dangerous Consequences: The US 'War on Drugs' in Latin America', in Hershberg, E., and Rosen, F. (Eds). *Latin America After Neoliberalism: Turning the Tide in the 21st Century?* New York and London, The New Press and NACLA, 2006.

'Drug-Law Reform Genie Freed From Bottle at Summit of the Americas'. www.fpif.org/blog/drug-law_reform_genie_freed_from_bottle_at_summit_of_the_americas. 2012(a). Accessed 29th April 2013.

'U.S. Elections and the War on Drugs', in *NACLA Report on the Americas*, Winter, 2012. New York, 2012(b).

'The Drug Policy Reform Agenda in the Americas'. IDPC Briefing Paper. London, International Drug Policy Consortium, 2013.

Youngers, C., and Rosin, E. (Eds). *Drugs and Democracy in Latin America: The Impact of U.S. Policy*. Washington Office on Latin America, Washington, DC, Lynne Rienner Publrs, Boulder, CO, and London, 2005(a).

Youngers, C., and Walsh, J. *Development First: A More Humane and Promising Approach to Reducing Cultivation of Crops for Illicit Markets*. Washington Office on Latin America, Washington, DC, 2010.

CHINA'S GROWING INFLUENCE IN LATIN AMERICA

Dr HANS STEINMÜLLER

Chinese migrants and labourers have been in Latin America for several centuries, and both the People's Republic of China and Taiwan have had political and trade relations with the countries on the continent for decades. However, Chinese involvement in the continent has broadly increased during the last decade. Both Latin American countries and China recovered relatively quickly from the global financial crisis of 2008, and since then have deepened existing trade relations. Additionally, Chinese investment in the region has increased rapidly and is now funding numerous development projects. Chinese trade with Latin America is largely focused on agricultural and mineral products; Chinese investment also focuses on raw materials, often accompanied by infrastructure projects. This essay first presents some background of the current relations between China and Latin America. It then describes current economic and political developments, and focuses on the benefits and pitfalls of Chinese involvement on the continent, specifically the synergy and potential conflict of Chinese and Latin American interests in the exchange of natural materials for investment in infrastructure. The final section discusses mutual perceptions and provides a cautious prospect for further developments.

HISTORICAL BACKGROUND

The Chinese presence in Latin America dates back to the 16th century, when maritime commerce mainly between the ports of Manila and Acapulco brought Chinese products and people to the then viceroyalty of New Spain (Slack, 2010). Called 'Sangleys' by the Spaniards, Chinese Mestizos (i.e. of mixed indigenous and Spanish descent) from the Philippines came as sailors, slaves and servants to New Spain before Mexican independence. In the 19th century indentured Chinese labourers were forced to work in several Latin American countries, especially in the cotton and sugar plantations of Cuba and the mines and guano industry of Peru. The history of this 'coolie trade' (using the name given to the indentured labourers) is characterized by violent exploitation; but the coolies' marriage with local women led to the formation of the first Chinese Latin American communities (Lai and Tan, 2010). Small groups of refugees from the Nationalists (Kuomintang) arrived in Latin America after their defeat by the Chinese Communist Party on the mainland in 1949; since then there have been some Taiwanese communities, for instance in Ciudad del Este in Paraguay and in Buenos Aires in Argentina (Trejos and Chiang, 2012). Aside from Cuba, no Latin American nation recognized the People's Republic of China, which was established in 1949. China's break with the USSR in the 1960s, and the rapprochement of China and the USA, was followed by the formal establishment of diplomatic relations with a number of Latin American countries in the early 1970s, including Argentina, Chile, Mexico and Peru. However, the largest tide of Chinese involvement in the continent has occurred in the last 10 years. China has become the largest trade partner of Brazil, Chile and Peru, and a very important trade partner of most other Latin American nations. Ecuador and Peru are the main destinations of Chinese foreign direct investment (FDI) in mineral resources (Gonzalez-Vicente, 2012: 45); in these countries and elsewhere, Chinese mining projects are often coupled with large-scale infrastructure development undertaken by Chinese state-owned enterprises. Chinese businesses are investing in many different industries in Latin America, small-scale entrepreneurs are opening internet cafés and supermarkets all over the region, government enterprises are investing in oil extraction in the Amazon, and China is preparing to host annual meetings with the representatives of most Latin American nations and regional groups.

The rapid pace of Chinese investment in the region has sometimes led to the impression that there is an insurmountable gap between Chinese strategies and the established practices of Western governments and companies. It is important to bear in mind that Chinese involvement in Latin America has been part of the wider strategy of 'going out', which is accompanied by an internationalization of the Chinese state and companies; in this process, Chinese companies are adjusting their practices to those of international competitors (Gonzalez-Vicente, 2011). Hence, Chinese government agencies and corporations are also adjusting their strategies in certain ways to the situation in their respective host countries. Since the so-called era of 'reform and opening' began in the 1980s, Chinese investment, migration and political involvement has become widely felt almost everywhere in the world. China's rising global influence is clearly articulated with domestic developments: the relaxation of political control and the encouragement of local entrepreneurship since the 1980s, the opening of special economic zones, and the continuing state-ownership of strategic industries (especially in energy and infrastructure) are the background against which Chinese investment and migration abroad is taking place. Since the southern tour of Chinese leader Deng Xiaoping in 1992, the rapid privatization of state assets and state-led capitalist development in the People's Republic was accompanied by a surge of Chinese investments abroad. In 1999 the Government announced its 'going out' policy to support and increase Chinese investments abroad. Aside from balancing China's huge foreign exchange reserves, one important target of this strategy is to equip Chinese companies with the skills and experience to compete with global competitors, who are already operating in China. Following these changes, the developing world has become a major focus of China's foreign policy. Chinese involvement in Africa has been a focus of interest for Western journalists and academic observers (see, for instance, Alden, 2007; Rotberg, 2008; Raine, 2009). Similar developments have taken place elsewhere, and to some extent Chinese involvement in Latin America is comparable to China's relations with African countries (Alden, 2012). As in Africa, one particular interest of Chinese government and business in Latin America is to satisfy the country's increasing demand for oil, minerals, copper, iron and other metals. Partly in exchange for access to mineral resources and primary products, Chinese companies and government agencies have invested widely in infrastructure projects in Latin America. Chinese firms have received numerous contracts for road construction, and are involved in large hydro-electrical projects, oil production and mining extraction across the continent. The emerging literature on China in Latin America points to these core features of resource interest and Chinese investment (Cesarin and Moneta, 2005; Gallagher and Porzecanski, 2010; Armony and Strauss, 2012).

TRADE AND INVESTMENT

While China's trade volume with Latin America is still far lower than its trade with Asian countries, the People's Republic has already become the largest trading partner of Brazil, Chile and Peru. According to the Brazilian Ministry of Development, Industry and Foreign Trade, Brazil's bilateral trade with China grew by 10% in 2013 to reach US $83,300m. (Toh, 2014). A large part of Latin American exports to China are primary products, such as copper, iron ore, soy and oil. In 2009 agriculture and mining sector goods constituted 83% of Latin American exports to China (Gallagher and Porzecanski, 2010). Some observers predict that China will overtake the European Union (EU) as Latin America's second largest trade partner in 2016 (Toh, 2014), and some predict that it might eventually surpass the USA as Latin America's largest trading partner in about 15 years (Hakim and Myers, 2014).

By global region, Latin America was the second largest target of Chinese overseas foreign direct investment (OFDI) in 2011, receiving 13% of Chinese OFDI following Asia's 71.4%. However, 92% of Chinese OFDI to Latin America went to the British Virgin Islands and the Cayman Islands, and for a more balanced view of Chinese FDI to Latin America these two tax havens will henceforth be excluded from our analysis. Of the remaining FDI, large parts went to Brazil, Peru, Venezuela and Argentina, which are the main recipients of Chinese FDI in the region (Chen and Pérez Ludeña, 2013). Chinese companies play an important role in the oil and gas industry of several countries, and in the mining sector in others (specifically Brazil and Peru). The largest investments outside the natural resources sector have been to Brazil, where several Chinese manufacturers and at least one provider of electricity services operate. At the same time other countries, such as Chile and Mexico, have not yet received significant amounts of FDI from China. While Chinese FDI to the region has grown exponentially, China's overall share of FDI to Latin America is less than 7%, and thus far behind that of the USA and the EU, which, respectively, provide 25% and 40% of FDI to the region (Chen and Pérez Ludeña, 2013: 11).

In terms of trade and FDI, agriculture plays an important role for China in Latin America. Rapid urbanization and the effects of desertification and environmental pollution in China itself, together with concerns about volatility in food prices, have led Chinese government agencies and enterprises to search for investment opportunities in agricultural production and markets abroad. Aside from other staple crops, China has become a major importer of soy from Latin America. Agriculture-related involvement in Latin America is still mainly limited to trade; there has been much less investment in agriculture or so-called 'land-grabs' as has sometimes been suggested in the Western media (Myers, 2013).

Together with increased volumes of trade and FDI, China has also become a major provider of loans to Latin American countries. Chinese banks have issued more than US $100,000m. since Chinese lending to the region began in 2006. Recent estimates indicate a major increase in Chinese lending to Latin American countries in 2013, after a considerable slump in 2012 (Irwin and Gallagher, 2014). Chinese banks have emerged as an important alternative for Latin American countries, specifically for those that are considered high risk on global capital markets. These include the Governments of Venezuela and Argentina, which were the principal recipients of Chinese loans in 2013, with volumes of $50,600m. and $14,100m., respectively, since 2006.[1]

MUTUAL PERCEPTIONS AND INTERESTS

From a Chinese perspective, there are a number of core interests in Latin America: the region is a major provider of raw materials and an emerging market for China's manufactured products. Aside from these economic interests, the Chinese Government also has a number of geopolitical and strategic interests in the region, which include the search for allies that support China's position in international negotiations, including over its contentious relationship with Taiwan and possibly the limitation of US influence in Latin America (Ellis, 2009: 14-15; Leiteritz, 2012: 68).

Gallagher and Porzecanski (2010) discuss the tension between the first two interests and the potentially negative consequences for Latin American industrialization. If, in the short term, it seems that Chinese demand for primary products has only positive consequences for Latin America, ultimately, it might just extend the resource curse that has been haunting Latin American countries for decades, if not centuries. Add to this the fact that China is providing huge amounts of cheap manufactured products to the region, and it is clear that the prospects from this relationship are not necessarily optimal for Latin American industrialization and indigenous development.

Of specific interest is also the relationship between China and the long-standing interests of the USA in the region. A number of scholars have analysed these relationships as a 'triangle' of Latin American countries, the USA and China (see, for instance, Stallings, 2008, and the contributions to Dussel Peters et al, 2013). However, the notion of a 'triangle' should be cautioned for a number of reasons: specifically, it might suggest a unity of interests for Latin American countries which is actually absent, and it might neglect other important countries which play important roles in Latin America (Ellis, 2012).

There is actually much diversity in the positions of Latin American nations towards the USA and China. Chile and Peru, for instance, have negotiated bilateral free trade agreements (FTAs) with both the USA and China (Chile concluded its FTA with the USA in 2004 and with China in 2006; Peru signed FTAs with both countries in 2009). In both cases, the FTAs concluded with China focus on the 'old trade agenda' of extending the product lines of liberalized trade, tariff and market access; by contrast, the agreements of both countries with the USA cover the 'new trade agenda', including investment, services, trade-related intellectual property rights, competition and trade facilitation (Wise, 2012). In terms of foreign policy, China's approaches in Latin America can be broadly contrasted with those of the USA. Relations between the USA and Latin America have been traditionally characterized by the exercise of 'hard power', in the form of interventions, threats and the provision of financial and technical assistance with conditions attached for the recipient countries. The USA has, for instance, intervened more or less directly in left-leaning coups d'état in Guatemala (1954) and Chile (1973); in recent decades the exercise of 'hard power' can be seen in the employment of 'sticks and carrots' in trade relations (Dunkerley, 2008). The Chinese approach, in contrast, generally sticks to the principle of non-interference, in which trade agreements and development assistance have 'no strings attached'. Chinese 'soft power' is very attractive to some Latin American regimes, especially when compared with the more restrictive US foreign policy. While the USA limited its relations with the left-leaning regimes of President Evo Morales in Bolivia and the late President Hugo Chávez in Venezuela, China invited both leaders for official state visits to Beijing. It remains to be questioned, however, how far the attraction of Chinese 'soft power' will go for Latin American citizens and governments (Leiteritz, 2012).

One core issue in China's relationship with Latin America is the contentious status of Taiwan. Currently, 12 of the 22 countries that have diplomatic relations with Taiwan are from Latin America and the Caribbean. Aside from Paraguay, they are all located in Central America and the Caribbean (Belize, the Dominican Republic, El Salvador, Guatemala, Haiti, Honduras, Nicaragua, Panama, Paraguay, Saint Christopher and Nevis, St Lucia, and St Vincent and the Grenadines). While both China and Taiwan have used 'chequebook diplomacy' to gain support from Latin American nations, in the last decade China has successfully convinced both Dominica (in 2004) and Costa Rica (in 2007) to switch their allegiances; in both cases, the offer of significant aid packages, preferential trade agreements and infrastructure projects played a considerable role in the decision (Ellis, 2010).

The Taiwan issue is very important, but China is also looking for allies more broadly in the international arena. Building on its economic collaboration with Brazil, there have been some strategic partnerships in World Trade Organization negotiations between China and Brazil, for instance, sometimes including the other two so-called BRIC nations, Russia and India.

On the Latin American side, there are a number of different views of China, its recent development and its involvement in the region. While, on the one hand, China is a new actor on the international scene, which might not come with the 'baggage' of the historical relations with Europe and the USA, on the other hand, the particularity of the 'China Model' comes with a particular set of problems. If China offers a different paradigm of modernity without the memories of colonialism and imperialism, at the same time this 'modernity without enlightenment' might also further accentuate the unsettled problems of democracy and development in Latin American countries. In the rapidly increasing coverage of China in Latin American news outlets, one discovers not only predictable condemnation of human rights abuses and lack of democratic governance, but there is also some sense of confusion about the relative success of the 'China Model' and what it could mean for Latin America. In an analysis of China coverage in two major Colombian newspapers, Armony (2012) reveals precisely the Janus face of China's image in Latin America, which combines suspicion and admiration. At the same time, the discussions about China and Chinese investment in Latin America are becoming increasingly diverse and sophisticated, and the view that Chinese investment would favour illiberal and non-democratic settings is certainly too simplistic.

If we take Chinese investments in mining and energy as an example, there is a common view that Chinese companies prefer non-democratic policy contexts. For Chinese mining investment in Latin America, specifically in Ecuador and Peru, however, this is not the case. It has been shown that Chinese mining investments favour liberal investment regimes and relative political stability, and in these preferences Chinese mining companies are not very different from their Western counterparts. Additional factors which play important roles in Chinese investment decisions are the existing business relations and the presence of a Chinese community in the host country. Chinese FDI in mining is best understood in terms of individual mining companies in specific local settings, rather than a specific national strategy imposed by the Chinese Government. However, there are certain differences in the receptivity of Chinese companies to demands from civil society. Given that Chinese energy companies are to a large extent owned and controlled by government agencies, they do not rely on stock markets and shareholders, and their management is therefore less dependent on, and responsible to, outside demands (Gonzalez-Vicente, 2012). At the same time, several Chinese companies have made their first attempts at entering into a dialogue with civil society representatives, sometimes including representatives of indigenous peoples (for instance in Ecuador). The results need to be judged on a case-by-case basis, and in contexts where numerous multinational extractive industries operate (such as in Chile and Peru); it is far from certain that Chinese business practices are causing higher social and environmental costs when compared with other multinationals.

Anti-Chinese sentiment and protest is growing in some countries, and there are serious discussions about the benefits and pitfalls of China's relations with Latin America. Mexican manufacturers, for example, find it difficult to compete with cheaper Chinese imports, and these concerns have led in some cases to an antagonistic presentation of Chinese entrepreneurs in local media and sometimes also to acts of aggression against Chinese business (Hearn, 2012). The Government of Cuba, which still retains broad control over its national economy, has stepped up its efforts to centralize the commercial regulation of Chinese business, specifically the informal businesses in Havana's Chinatown (ibid).

Against the sometimes negative perceptions of cheap Chinese imports, irresponsible Chinese investors and an autocratic Government, China has intensified its 'soft power' efforts on the continent. Student exchanges, cultural diplomacy and the establishment of so-called Confucius Institutes play important roles here. Since 2004 hundreds of such institutes have been established all over the world in order to promote Chinese culture and language. The Confucius Institutes are under the supervision of the 'Han Ban', the Language Council affiliated to the Chinese Ministry of Education. Since 2004 at least 20 Confucius Institutes have been established in 11 Latin American countries, each of them affiliated to a local university, and in partnership with a Chinese university.

High-profile state visits are another major strategy. Soon after US President Barack Obama and Vice-President Joe Biden travelled to five Latin American countries (Costa Rica, Mexico, Brazil, Colombia, and Trinidad and Tobago) in May 2013, Chinese President Xi Jinping visited three of the same countries in June: Costa Rica, Mexico, and Trinidad and Tobago. Notwithstanding China's increased 'soft power' measures and influence in the region, the perception in most Latin American countries still ranks China and the Chinaese model as secondary for the continent, when compared with the USA. A poll of 40,000 participants in various Latin American countries found that a majority of 56.0% responded that they trusted the USA, while 50.8% of participants said that they trusted China. Similarly, when asked 'which country has the most influence in the region', 40.8% of the participants said the USA, against 20.3% which answered China (Azpuru and Zechmeister, 2014).

CONCLUSIONS

During the last decade China's influence in Latin America has grown exponentially. Measured in terms of trade volumes and FDI, China has established close ties with a number of Latin American nations. However, overall trade volumes are still small when compared to China's trade with Asia, Europe and North America. China's relationship with Latin America is characterized to a large extent by China's interest in raw materials and access to Latin American markets. As has been discussed, some countries have been able to benefit from this relationship; however, it also comes with certain risks, especially for Latin America's own manufacturing industries. Calls for the diversification of Chinese trade and investment have so far only led to limited changes; moreover, the possibilities for manufactured goods from Latin America to enter the Chinese market also remain limited.

While China has not yet overtaken the USA in terms of trade ties and political influence in the region, its growing links with the region, interest in raw materials and markets, and high degree of political engagement will demand continuous attention in the future. In terms of mutual perceptions, there have been also rapprochements between Latin America and China. Latin America, to some degree like Africa, presents a number of opportunities for China; yet there are also risks and potential misunderstandings. From the perspective of Latin Americans, China also ranks still behind the USA as a global power; it remains to be seen whether, and how, this will change in the future.

FOOTNOTE

[1] See China-Latin America Finance Database at www.the-dialogue.org/map_list.

REFERENCES

Alden, C. *China in Africa: Partner, Competitor or Hegemon?* London and New York, Zed Books, 2007.

'China and Africa: A Distant Mirror of Latin America', in *Colombia Internacional*, 75, pp. 19–47, 2012.

Armony, A. C. 'A View from Afar: How Colombia Sees China', in *The China Quarterly*, 209, pp. 178–97, 2012.

Armony, A. C., and Strauss, J. C. 'From Going Out (zouChuqu) to Arriving In (desembarco): Constructing a New Field of Inquiry in China–Latin America Interactions', in *The China Quarterly*, 209: 1–17, 2012.

Azpuru, D., and Zechmeister, E. J. 'Latin Americans' Perceptions of the United States and China', in *Americas Quarterly*. www.americasquarterly.org/latin-americans-perceptions-united-states-and-china. 2014. Accessed 3 July 2014.

Cesarin, S., and Moneta, C. (Eds). *China y America Latina. Nuevos enfoques sobre la cooperacion y desarrollo. Una segunda ruta de la seda?* Buenos Aires, BID-INTAL, 2005.

Chen, T., and Pérez Ludeña, M. 'Chinese Foreign Direct Investment in Latin America and the Caribbean', in *Working Paper for the Summit on the Global Agenda*, World Economic Forum. Available online at www.cepal.org/publicaciones/xml/1/51551/Chineseforeigndirectinvestment.pdf. 2013. Accessed 30 June 2014.

Delgado, G. *Making the Chinese Mexican: Global Migration, Localism, and Exclusion in the U.S.–Mexico Borderlands.* Stanford, CA, Stanford University Press, 2012.

Dunkerley, J. 2008. 'US Foreign Policy in Latin America', in Cox, M., and Stokes, D. (Eds). *US Foreign Policy*. pp. 292–312. Oxford and New York, Oxford University Press. 2008.

Dussel Peters, E., Hearn, A. H., and Shaiken, H. (Eds). *China and the New Triangular Relationships in the Americas: China and the Future of US-Mexico Relations*. University of Miami Center for Latin American Studies Publications, Miami, FL. Available online at scholarlyrepository.miami.edu/clas_publications/3. 2013. Accessed 30 June 2014.

Ellis, R. E. *China in Latin America: The Whats and Wherefores.* Boulder, CO, Lynne Rienner Publrs, 2009.

'Chinese Soft Power in Latin America: A Case Study', in *National Defense University*, 60:1, 2010. Available online at www.dtic.mil/cgi-bin/GetTRDoc?AD=ADA536568. Accessed 30 June 2014.

'The United States, Latin America and China: A "Triangular Relationship"?', in *Inter-American Dialogue Working Paper*. Available online at www10.iadb.org/intal/intalcdi/PE/2012/10211.pdf. Accessed 30 June 2014.

Gallagher, K. P., and Porzecanski, R. 'China and the Future of Latin American Industrialization', in *Issues in Brief*, No. 18, October 2010.

Gonzalez-Vicente, R. 'The Internationalization of the Chinese State', in *Political Geography*, Vol. 30, No. 7, pp. 402–11, 2011.

'Mapping Chinese Mining Investment in Latin America: Politics or Market?', in *The China Quarterly*, 209, pp. 35–58, 2012.

Hakim, P., and Myers, M. 'China and Latin America in 2013', in *China Policy Review*, 9 January 2014. Available online at www.thedialogue.org/page.cfm?pageID=32&pubid=3491. 2014. Accessed 30 June 2014.

Hearn, A. H. 'Harnessing the Dragon: Overseas Chinese Entrepreneurs in Mexico and Cuba', in *The China Quarterly*, 209, pp 111–33, 2012.

Irwin, A., and Gallagher, K. 'Chinese Finance to Latin America Tops $100 Billion Since 2005, Inter-American Dialogue'. China-Latin American Finance Database. Available online at thedialogue.org/page.cfm?pageID=32&pubid=3563. Accessed 30 June 2014.

Lai, W. L. 'Asian Diasporas and Tropical Migration in the Age of Empire: A Comparative Overview', in Lai, W. L., and Tan Chee-Beng (Eds). *The Chinese in Latin America and the Caribbean*. Leiden, Brill Academic Publrs, 2010.

Lai, W. L., and Tan Chee-Beng (Eds). *The Chinese in Latin America and the Caribbean*. Leiden, Brill Academic Publrs, 2010.

Leiteritz, R. 'China and Latin America: A Marriage Made in Heaven?', in *Colombia Internacional*, 75, pp. 49–81, June 2012.

Myers, M. 'China's Agricultural Engagement in Latin America', in *China and Latin America*. chinaandlatinamerica.com/2013/11/19/chinas-agricultural-engagement-in-latin-america-2/. Accessed 30 June 2014.

Raine, S. *China's African Challenges*. Abingdon, Routledge. 2009.

Rotberg, R. I. (Ed.). *China into Africa: Trade, Aid and Influence*. Baltimore, MD, Brookings Institution Press, 2008.

Slack, E. R. 'Sinifying New Spain: Cathay's Influence on Colonial Mexico via the Nao de China', in Lai, W. L., and Tan Chee-Beng (Eds). *The Chinese in Latin America and the Caribbean*, pp. 7–34. Leiden, Brill Academic Publrs, 2010.

Stallings, B. 'The US-China-Latin America Triangle: Implications for the Future', in Roett, R., and Paz, G. (Eds). *China's Expansion into the Western Hemisphere*. Washington, DC, Brookings Institution Press, 2008.

Toh, H. S. 'China's Trade with Latin America Set to Outpace EU within Two Years', in *South China Morning Post*. www.scmp.com/business/economy/article/1450313/chinas-trade-latin-america-set-outpace-eu-within-two-years. Accessed 30 June 2014.

Trejos, B., and Chiang, L.-H. N. 'Young Taiwanese Immigration to Argentina: The Challenges of Adaptations, Self-identity and Returning' in *International Journal of Asia Pacific Studies*, 8:2, pp. 113–143, 2012.

Wise, C. 'The China Conundrum: Economic Development Strategies Embraced by Small States in South America', in *Colombia Internacional*, 75, pp. 131–70, June 2012.

THE FUTURE OF CARIBBEAN ENERGY: THE RISE OF NEW ENERGY EXPORTERS

Dr KERON NILES

INTRODUCTION

Caribbean nations are heavily dependent on conventional (thermal) energy sources, particularly for transport and power generation. In fact, the archipelago of small island developing states (SIDS) nestled in the Caribbean Sea is almost entirely reliant on fossil fuels for commercial energy. These island economies are also particularly vulnerable to the impacts of climate change. This paper addresses the options available to Caribbean nations as they pertain to future energy development.

Specific attention will be paid to geopolitical considerations that are likely to influence energy policy decisions made within the foreseeable future. The term 'Caribbean', for the purposes of this paper, is used to refer to the archipelago of island states nestled in the Caribbean Sea as well as those nations of the surrounding coasts that are members of the Caribbean Community and Common Market (CARICOM)[1].

This paper will examine the unique arrangements in the Caribbean that have helped to shape the region's energy matrix up to the present day. Moreover, alternative ideas that could be utilized in the future to satisfy regional energy requirements will be explored. Yet, it should be noted that Caribbean energy futures will be considered within the context of the threat of climate change and persistently high oil prices. Hence, this discussion explains why a transition to alternative energy sources is required and provides a few examples of mechanisms that aim to enhance trade in natural gas and renewable electricity. In this regard, the emergence of new energy exporters is considered, not only in terms of their geopolitical significance but also their potential to aid a transition to sustainable energy.

A PORTRAIT OF FOSSIL FUEL DEPENDENCE: ENERGY CONSUMPTION IN THE CARIBBEAN

Energy consumption for commercial purposes in the Caribbean has been largely dominated by imported fossil fuels[2] since these nations were colonized and particularly from around the early 1900s (Niles and Lloyd, 2013). According to a *Benchmark Study of Caribbean Utilities* conducted in 2009, 98% of primary energy consumption in the region is thought to be fossil fuel based (KEMA, 2010).

The emphasis on liquid fuels has been partly due to the inability of SIDS to access the economies of scale enjoyed via the use of large coal steam generation plants for electricity production, which has resulted in a reliance on small-scale diesel electricity generation devices. Similarly, the inability of SIDS to pursue nuclear energy[3] also contributes to dependence upon liquid fuels for power generation (especially in cases

where a reasonable magnitude of hydroelectric resources are not present). Resultantly, with the exception of a few nations like Belize and Suriname, electricity production in the Caribbean can be described as 'petroleum intensive' (see Table 1).

Increased electricity demand in SIDS, unless satisfied via renewable or nuclear energy, will not only exacerbate their reliance on fossil fuels and add to the greenhouse gas emissions of these nations, but will also augment global demand for finite fossil fuels. Thus, should these economies continue to grow, the current proclivity towards conventional thermal electricity generation (using oil, gas or coal) is certain to make the power sector in these island nations more vulnerable to volatile fossil fuel prices and to possible greenhouse gas emission penalties in the future. This problem is also very serious in light of the finite nature of fossil fuels themselves. As the available supply of conventional fuels in the world begins to tighten, fuels may become accessible only to those with access to large secure stocks within their borders or those with sufficient financial resources to purchase them on the open market.

The small size of Caribbean markets also has the effect of making energy even more expensive. The limited demand for petroleum to service local energy requirements has meant that small territories are unable to benefit from economies of scale when purchasing oil on the international market. Additionally, many Caribbean nations do not straddle or rest on major international transportation routes. As a result, small island nations in the Caribbean are at times obliged to pay transportation premiums to have oil delivered to their shores. In this context, efforts to reduce fuel imports by promoting a transition to renewable energy can be viewed not only as a path to a greater degree of energy independence, but also as an economic imperative.

WHY A TRANSITION TO SUSTAINABLE ENERGY IS REQUIRED

Climate Change

The Intergovernmental Panel on Climate Change (IPCC) has now offered what is likely to be its most resolute determination to date. Its Fifth Assessment Report, published in 2013, asserts that 'warming of the climate system is unequivocal' and warns of rising sea levels and concentrations of greenhouse gases (Intergovernmental Panel on Climate Change, 2013). The susceptibility of SIDS is acknowledged in the Preamble to the UN Framework Convention on Climate Change, which recognizes that 'low-lying and other small island countries... are particularly vulnerable to the adverse effects of climate change' (UN Framework Convention on Climate Change, 1992).

Table 1: Net Electricity Generation by Type in CARICOM Member States in 2010

Country	Total Renewable Generation (%)	Total Fossil Fuel Generation (%)	Total Electricity Net Generation (MW)
Antigua and Barbuda	0.00	100	13.12
The Bahamas	0.00	100	220.17
Barbados	0.00	100	118.30
Belize	65.00	35	59.80
Dominica	30.85	69	11.46
Grenada	0.00	100	22.98
Guyana	0.00	100	79.86
Haiti	31.23	69	63.93
Jamaica	6.75	93	451.36
Montserrat	0.00	100	2.74
St Kitts and Nevis	0.00	100	15.40
St Lucia	0.00	100	40.84
St Vincent and the Grenadines	19.12	89	15.51
Suriname	55.10	45	179.10
Trinidad and Tobago	0.00	100	912.38

Source: US Energy Information Administration, 2013.

Moreover, in its Fourth Assessment Report, the IPCC noted that small islands, akin to those found in the Caribbean, have specific geographic 'characteristics which make them especially vulnerable to the effects of climate change' (Mimura et al., 2007). The report indicates that small islands are likely to suffer, *inter alia*, sea-level rise (which can cause flooding and coastal erosion) and more extreme and intense natural disasters, such as hurricanes, which can damage vital infrastructure. The small size of the island economies in the Caribbean also means that they possess fewer financial resources to respond to climate change impacts. In addition, climate change is likely to have significant adverse consequences upon key revenue-generating economic sectors in SIDS, like tourism.

However, it should be noted that largely due to their limited absolute energy demand, SIDS (arguably with the exception of Trinidad and Tobago[4]) are not large contributors to the problem of climate change, but are among the group of countries estimated to be impacted the most (Nurse et al., 2009). Anthropogenic climate change therefore constitutes a significant concern for Caribbean nations. Climate change not only threatens the very existence of some islands, but it also makes power sector investments more risky and costly as energy infrastructure will have to be built or retro-fitted to withstand more frequent and intense hurricanes.

Peak Oil

Peak oil refers to the transition from a period of easily attainable and affordable oil to a period characterized by a declining global annual supply of petroleum (Heinberg, 2006). It refers to that 'moment in time when the world will achieve its maximum rate of extraction; from then on... the amount of petroleum available to society on a daily or yearly basis will begin to dwindle' (Heinberg, 2007). This scenario reflects the reality that fossil fuels, like all other natural resources, are finite and will eventually become scarce. In the case of oil and gas, it is not merely the absence of fossil fuels in situ that brings about a shortage of supply, but rather, it is the depletion of easily attainable petroleum. In this regard, it is important to note that the global average for energy returned on energy invested (EROEI) for oil is declining. The EROEI is the ratio of the energy obtained from oil to the energy needed to afford its discovery, extraction and conversion to a useable liquid fuel.

The vulnerability of SIDS to the physical and economic risks brought about by climate change is therefore exacerbated when one considers anticipated 'peak oil' impacts, which will become an eminent concern when world demand for oil exceeds the available supply, causing the price of oil to increase for a prolonged period of time (Mobbs, 2005). Indeed, the International Energy Agency has already pronounced that 'the era of cheap oil is over' (International Energy Agency, 2008).

Stubbornly high oil prices are of particular concern since most Caribbean nations are largely, if not entirely, dependent upon fossil fuels for electricity generation (see Table 1). Moreover, electricity tariffs in most Caribbean countries are already among the highest in the world. Unless the power industries in these island nations find some means to 'wean themselves off' their addiction to petroleum[5] within the relatively near future, they will become even more vulnerable to global oil price increases, which, in turn, is likely to result in higher prices for electricity.

STAYING AFLOAT: SPECIAL ENERGY ARRANGEMENTS IN THE CARIBBEAN

Notwithstanding the above, the presence of energy exporters in the region has acted as a source of reprieve for Caribbean nations in the past. Trinidad and Tobago, Venezuela and Mexico have played a key role in terms of stabilizing the energy supply and offsetting oil price volatility. Being able to source petroleum from within the region has the practical benefit of helping to reduce overall transportation costs. Following the first 'oil shock' in 1973, the Governments of Mexico and Venezuela came together to make funds available with relatively generous and deferred payment conditions (i.e. 'soft financing') under the Ven/Mex Oil Facility. In 1980, moreover, as explained by Bryan (2011), Trinidad and Tobago 'offered its own CARICOM Oil Facility which provided for the incremental purchases of oil, fertiliser, and asphalt from [Trinidad and

Tobago] at 1979 prices'. Indeed, these forms of functional co-operation have continued to feature in the region.

In 2004 the Trinidad and Tobago Petroleum Fund was launched as a grant facility to be made available to CARICOM member states that were experiencing economic hardship because of persistently high oil prices, though the stated aims of the fund include economic development and poverty alleviation (Bryan, 2011; Caribbean Community Secretariat, 2006). In the following year Petrocaribe was established by the Government of Venezuela, allowing Caribbean nations to purchase oil at set prices under a deferred payment scheme. One significant difference between the earlier Ven/Mex Oil Facility and Petrocaribe is that the latter also includes direct assistance with the transportation and storage of petroleum products, thus helping to stabilize transportation costs by removing the need for private sector participation in this sub-sector. Though Bryan (2011) suspects that these initiatives are manifestations of geopolitical rivalry, measures of this nature can, and perhaps do, assist the island economies of the Caribbean to respond to supply shortages and oil price volatility (Williams, J., 2011; Broderick, 2011). The transition in leadership brought about by the death of the author of the Petrocaribe initiative, Venezuelan President Hugo Chávez, and the ensuing political instability in Venezuela raises important questions about the future of the mechanism. Indeed, it would be prudent for the 17 island nations that participate in the scheme (12 of which are members of CARICOM[6]) to make planning decisions that account for the potential loss of the benefits derived from Petrocaribe (Sanders, 2014).

THE GEOPOLITICS OF ENERGY FUTURES IN THE CARIBBEAN

The uncertainty surrounding future Venezuelan economic and foreign policy, and the potential impact upon Petrocaribe, provides sufficient incentive for participating island nations to explore alternative sources of supply. Moreover, the threat posed by climate change provides added impetus for Caribbean economies to transition to sustainable energy sources. Indeed, the challenges confronting the power sector in the Caribbean are compounded by diseconomies of scale and require innovative policy solutions that are environmentally benign and serve the socioeconomic and geopolitical interests of each island state. The section that follows explores two of the primary options currently being explored that could shape future energy supply policies in the region: building an inter-island pipeline to transport natural gas for electricity generation and an electrical interconnection of islands (particularly in the Eastern Caribbean)[7].

Trade in Natural Gas: the Eastern Caribbean Gas Pipeline

A number of power utilities and state energy agencies from across the region have already voiced a preference for natural gas-fuelled electricity generation, not only because of its lower price on the international market in recent times in comparison with oil, but also because it emits less carbon dioxide into the atmosphere than oil. The Eastern Caribbean Gas Pipeline represents a plan to construct a pipeline (of approximately 300 km) to transport this cheaper and cleaner fuel between Trinidad and Tobago[8] and Barbados to be used primarily for power generation. The proposed pipeline could also be extended to other Caribbean nations.

In tandem, it should be noted that a number of Caribbean nations are currently contemplating the acquisition of gas-fired electricity turbines in order to reduce vulnerability to high oil prices. Other Caribbean nations (not involved in the pipeline project) have already registered their support for the idea of a transition to gas as a more stable (in terms of price) and environmentally friendly fuel. In fact, the Jamaica Energy Action Plan (2009–12) listed natural gas as the 'country's diversification fuel of choice' (Government of Jamaica, 2010), and a mandate was issued that declared that any new conventional (thermal) power plants must be combined cycle natural gas facilities.

Notwithstanding the above, enthusiasm regarding a regional transition to natural gas is not universal. Instead, the idea is at times met with scepticism, largely due to the challenges associated with sourcing and transporting gas. Due to the small quantities used in the Caribbean, finding a long-term natural gas supplier may be challenging. Even though a growth in demand for natural gas could serve the region's geopolitical interests, it is uncertain whether Trinidad and Tobago would be willing to satisfy the energy requirements of other Caribbean nations. Even less clear is the mechanism that would be used to facilitate this and whether preferential prices would or should be offered to fellow CARICOM member states. It is worthwhile to note that a recent study by the Inter-American Development Bank asserted that the demand for liquefied natural gas in the Caribbean will probably be satisfied via Louisiana in the USA, due to the downward pressure that shale gas has placed on prices there (Bailey et al., 2013).

Overall, a transition to gas certainly seems desirable and viable in many Caribbean nations, regardless of whether the fuel is shipped or transported via pipeline. Future power plants in Barbados and Jamaica (at least in the short term) are highly likely to be gas-fired. In the case of Barbados, the Barbados Light and Power Company has already chosen to acquire dual-fired power plants that can utilize bunker fuel as well as natural gas as a part of the country's transition to the latter. Further decisions by Caribbean nations to use natural gas for power generation are likely to increase interest in intra-regional energy trade, particularly with respect to securing supplies of gas from the region's most southerly state.

Electricity Interconnection

Another regional alternative that needs to be considered (that is, apart from enhancing trade in natural gas) is the idea of an electrical connection between islands by subsea cable. In this case, rather than making use of fossil fuels, electricity would be generated using geothermal energy. The potential feasibility of this option lies in the existence of an inner arc of volcanic islands in the Eastern Caribbean[9]. In addition, many nations that comprise the archipelago are in relatively close proximity to one another (as compared with the Pacific region, for example, where island nations tend to be more scattered).

Indeed, the possibility of trading geothermal electricity is now being actively pursued and discussed, particularly in the case of prospective deals between Saint Christopher and Nevis and the US territory of Puerto Rico and between Dominica and the French Overseas Territories of Guadeloupe and Martinique (Brown, 2013). Even though the interconnection project between Saint Christopher and Nevis and Puerto Rico seems to have slowed due to cost concerns, pre-feasibility studies have already been conducted under the Energy and Climate Partnership of the Americas—a multilateral co-operation mechanism initiated by the US Administration of Barack Obama.

Having inter-island connections powered by geothermal electricity is considered to be particularly desirable due to the potential for such energy to be used as 'base-load'[10], which could serve to reduce dramatically dependence on fossil fuel imports. Moreover, the sale of electricity to other nations could serve as a valuable source of foreign exchange. This is likely to act as a welcome boost to the economies of Saint Christopher and Nevis and Dominica, which have traditionally relied on revenues earned via tourism.

Perhaps an even more fundamental consideration to be taken into account is the foreign relations element of a potential electrical interconnection between Caribbean nations. In fact, one could assert that the geopolitical dimension of this initiative is fundamental to how this project will be operationalized and how funds will be mobilized (Williams, J., 2011). This is partly owing to the fact that the USA and France possess the institutional and financial resources necessary to mobilize the funds required for such a venture. Additionally, in the short term, the large amount of technical assistance required to establish the infrastructure necessary to produce and export geothermal energy also provides the USA and France with new potential markets that their skilled service providers can use to gain valuable experience and leverage in the region[11]. Moreover, the interest of these two metropolitan nations in the completion of this initiative is firmly undergirded by their desire to reduce the dependency of their Caribbean territories on oil.

The official endorsement of the Nevis–Puerto Rico connection by the US Administration underscores the economic and geopolitical significance of the venture (Caribbean 360, 2011; Task Force on Puerto Rico's Status, 2011). In the case of France and the potential connections between Dominica and Guadeloupe and/or Martinique, it seems almost certain that the policy agenda insofar as it pertains to geothermal energy development is being driven primarily by the possibility of electricity exports to Guadeloupe and Martinique (Timothy, 2011).

Thus, one could perhaps postulate that current interest in geothermal electricity interconnection is being driven primarily by a desire to reduce dependence on oil, not only on the part of independent Caribbean states, but also on the part of developed (traditional donor) nations that wish to enhance the energy security of their island territories in the region. Moreover, energy trade may facilitate a deepening of political and economic ties between the metropolitan and Caribbean states involved in such agreements, which could serve to further mutual economic and geopolitical interests.

CARIBBEAN (RENEWABLE) ENERGY FUTURES?

Enhancing the development and deployment of renewable energy technologies (RETs), whether for export or domestic use, is essential to mitigating the socioeconomic impacts of climate change and peak oil. Renewable energy use has the potential to reduce simultaneously carbon dioxide emissions and dependence on fossil fuels. Furthermore, renewable energy options make use of indigenous energy sources, which can serve to reduce the (ever-fluctuating) cost of fuel imports and help to stabilize local balance of payments accounts and expenditure on foreign exchange. Perhaps even more importantly, RETs have the overall effect of enhancing what Weisser (2004) refers to as the 'three pillars of national energy policy: (i) economic efficiency, (ii) environmental performance and (iii) security and diversity of supply'. This is largely due to the fact (as mentioned earlier) that lower emissions and fuel costs make RETs economically and environmentally attractive in the medium-to-long term. The potential loss of benefits derived from Petrocaribe not only has the effect of incentivizing a transition from the use of oil for power generation, but it also creates space for other nations to enhance their geopolitical influence in the region, particularly by helping Caribbean nations to acquire and install RETs.

Moreover, opportunities to establish RETs with the capacity for export can create a scenario where the interests of independent Caribbean nations and those of traditional donor nations can be satisfied simultaneously. It is therefore unsurprising that the CARICOM Energy Policy, approved in March 2013, specifically encourages member states to pursue opportunities that entail cross border trade in electricity and natural gas. In this regard, it should be noted that preliminary discussions are currently underway exploring the potential export of hydroelectricity from Guyana. Regardless of the outcome of these deliberations, a proliferation of trade in electricity will create new energy exporters within the region, which could serve to enhance the geopolitical influence of exporting economies. Trade in electricity (as alluded to earlier) could emanate from geothermal reservoirs located in Dominica, Grenada, Guadeloupe, Martinique, Montserrat, Saint Christopher and Nevis, Saint Lucia, and Saint Vincent and the Grenadines, or from hydropower, most likely via Guyana. In terms of generation from geothermal sources, a number of scientific studies have already been undertaken in the aforementioned nations with geothermal potential. In fact, exploratory wells have already been drilled in Martinique, Saint Lucia and Nevis; production wells have been drilled in Montserrat and Dominica; and Guadeloupe has already taken large strides in this field by becoming the Caribbean's first geothermal energy producer in 1986 with a 4.2-MW plant that became fully operational in 1996 and was expanded to 15 MW in 2004 (Brophy and Poux, 2013). Increased energy trade in the region, via hydropower or geothermal electricity, would likely create new economic activities, contribute to job creation and reduce reliance on traditional energy-exporting nations like Trinidad and Tobago and Venezuela.

It should however be noted that the deployment of RETs is being actively pursued across the region. Measures promoting greater utilization of solar water heaters and solar photovoltaic technologies have already been implemented in different islands across the region, with particularly aggressive programmes in Barbados and Grenada. Wind farms already exist in Jamaica and Curaçao. Feasibility and other background studies to facilitate the construction of new wind farms are well underway in Barbados, Saint Lucia, Saint Vincent and the Grenadines, and Trinidad and Tobago. Yet, it should be noted that solar, wind, and less mature technologies such as tidal and wave energy are being considered within the context of a domestic energy supply. As a result, while a proliferation of solar and wind energy technologies should help to reduce expenditure on imported oil, the production of electricity from such devices is not being considered for export.

CONCLUSION

The possible emergence of new renewable energy exporters should be juxtaposed alongside existing arrangements and competing interests. Nations currently considering the development of indigenous resources for export will be competing with those nations already engaged in the export of hydrocarbons (such as Trinidad and Tobago, Venezuela and the USA) and those that are presently conducting exploration activities within their borders in search of commercially viable quantities of oil and gas to export (such as Barbados and Jamaica). In this regard, it should be noted that, even if the development of renewable energy for export is realized, a demand for petroleum will still exist as it is likely to be required to service the transportation sector for the foreseeable future. Thus, the Caribbean could witness the development of competitive intra-regional markets for trade in both conventional and renewable energy.

Attempts have been made to transition the region to renewable energy in the past. However, these efforts were only sustained when oil prices were high. When oil prices declined after the first and second global oil crises, interest in alternative energy waned. The overall result of this was an ongoing reliance on petroleum for transport and electric power that has persisted until the present day. If the dependence of SIDS on fossil fuels is to be arrested, greater deployment of RETs is required. One would therefore hope, particularly in light of the worsening threat of climate change, that a proliferation in trade of renewable electricity would help to propel the region towards a transition to sustainable energy. That said, while increased intra-regional trade in natural gas and/or electricity would almost certainly demand a greater degree of functional co-operation among Caribbean nations and would reduce greenhouse gas emissions, it would not necessarily curtail or reduce fossil fuel dependence (particularly if trade is utilized to service additional capacity requirements). Deliberate measures and policy instruments to discourage fossil fuel use may be required to boost efforts to transition to renewable energy. Indeed, reducing reliance on petroleum may prove to be even more urgent should the benefits derived from Petrocaribe cease to exist in the future.

FOOTNOTES

[1] According to Article 3 of the Revised Treaty of Chaguaramas, 2001 (establishing the Caribbean Community, including the CARICOM Single Market and Economy), CARICOM comprises Antigua and Barbuda, the Bahamas, Barbados, Belize, Dominica, Grenada, Guyana, Jamaica, Montserrat, Saint Christopher and Nevis, Saint Lucia, Saint Vincent and the Grenadines, Suriname, and Trinidad and Tobago. Haiti gained membership in 2002.

[2] Trinidad and Tobago, which is a longstanding producer and exporter of oil and gas, is an exception in this regard.

[3] Electricity generation using nuclear energy is not only capital intensive, but it requires a considerable degree of technical expertise to operate and maintain the power plants. As a dearth of financial and human resources is a major contributing factor to the current lack of indigenous investment in renewable energy technologies by SIDS, similar undertakings in nuclear energy are highly unlikely.

[4] In their 2008 article 'Trinidad and Tobago's CO2 Inventory and Techno-Economic Evaluation of Carbon Capture Options for Emis-

sions Mitigation', Boodlal, Furlonge and Williams highlighted that Trinidad and Tobago's carbon dioxide emissions per caput and per GDP ranked among the highest in the world at that time.

[5] Adapted from a quote by US President George W. Bush, featured in *The Oil Depletion Protocol* (Heinberg, 2006).

[6] The 12 signatory states to Petrocaribe that are members of CARICOM are: Antigua and Barbuda; the Bahamas; Belize; Dominica; Grenada; Guyana; Haiti; Jamaica; Saint Christopher and Nevis; Saint Lucia; Saint Vincent and the Grenadines; and Suriname.

[7] Proposed solutions like inter-island pipelines or subsea electrical interconnections may not be applicable among the SIDS of the Pacific region, where the islands are generally separated by greater distances and the energy consumption per caput is usually less.

[8] At the end of 2010 Trinidad and Tobago had 13,460,000m. cu ft of proven natural gas reserves. It should be noted, however, that the country's reserves stood at 14,420,000m. cu ft in 2009 and are believed to be in decline. For further details, see 'Ryder Scott: Trinidad and Tobago's proved gas reserves decline' (Williams, C., 2011).

[9] Volcanic islands in the Eastern Caribbean that have undergone feasibility studies for geothermal potential include Dominica, Grenada, Saint Christopher and Nevis, Saint Lucia, and Saint Vincent and the Grenadines.

[10] The term 'base-load' is usually used to refer to consistency of supply. As explained by Diesendorf, 'A conventional base-load power station is one that is in theory available 24 hours a day, seven days a week, and operates most of the time at full (rated) power.' None the less, he notes that 'In practice, base-load power stations break down from time to time and, as a result, can be out of action for weeks. Therefore, base-load power stations must have back-up.' For further details, see 'The Base Load Fallacy and other Fallacies disseminated by Renewable Energy Deniers' (Diesendorf, 2010).

[11] As an example, a subsea electrical interconnection is likely to require advanced engineering services, particularly due to the presence of very deep trenches in the Caribbean Sea. In this regard, preliminary studies of regional electricity interconnection were undertaken by a firm based in California, USA, in 2010.

REFERENCES

Bailey, J., Janson, N., and Espinasa, R. *Pre-Feasibility Study of the Potential Market for Natural Gas as a Fuel for Power Generation in the Caribbean.* Washington, DC, Inter-American Development Bank, 2013.

Broderick, L. Address of the Honourable Mr Laurence Broderick, Minister of State in the Ministry of Energy and Mining, Jamaica. Caribbean Renewable Energy Forum 2011. Bridgetown, Barbados, 2011.

Brophy, P., and Poux, B. *Status of Geothermal Development in the Islands of the Caribbean.* Geothermal Resources Council Annual Meeting 2013, International Session. Las Vegas, NV, 2013.

Brown, D. 'Nevis Embarks on Geothermal Energy Journey'. Inter Press Service. www.ipsnews.net/2013/12/nevis-embarks-geothermal-energy-journey, 2013.

Bryan, A. *Trinidad and Tobago's Strategic Culture.* Florida International University, Miami, FL, 2011.

Caribbean360. 'White House supports Nevis energy proposal'. www.caribbean360.com/index.php/business/329867.html#axzz23mywpLY5, 2011.

Caribbean Community Secretariat. *CDB, Petroleum Fund Assistance for Haiti's Recovery.* Turkeyen, Guyana, 2006.

Diesendorf, M. 'The Base Load Fallacy and other Fallacies Disseminated by Renewable Energy Deniers'. www.energy-science.org.au/BP16%20BaseLoad.pdf, 2010.

Government of Jamaica. *Action Plan 1: 2009–2012. Jamaica's Energy Policy 2009–2030.* Ministry of Energy and Mining, Kingston, 2010.

Heinberg, R. *The Oil Depletion Protocol: A Plan to Avert Oil Wars, Terrorism and Economic Collapse.* New Society Publrs, Gabriola Island, BC, 2006.

Peak Everything: Waking up to the Century of Decline in Earth's Resources. New Society Publrs, Gabriola Island, BC, 2007.

Intergovernmental Panel on Climate Change. Working Group I Contribution to the IPCC Fifth Assessment Report. Climate

Change 2013: The Physical Science Basis. *Summary for Policy Makers*. Geneva, 2013.

International Energy Agency. *World Energy Outlook*. Paris, 2013.

KEMA. *Benchmark Study of Caribbean Utilities. Sixth Update—Year 2009*. Caribbean Electric Utility Service Corpn, Arnhem, 2010.

Mimura, N., et al. *Small Islands. Climate Change 2007: Impacts, Adaptation and Vulnerability*. Contribution of Working Group II to the Fourth Assessment Report of the Intergovernmental Panel on Climate Change. Cambridge University Press, Cambridge, 2007.

Mobbs, P. *Energy Beyond Oil*. Troubador Publishing Ltd, Leicester, 2005.

Niles, K., and Lloyd, B. 'Small Island Developing States (SIDS) and energy aid: Impacts on the energy sector in the Caribbean and Pacific', in *Energy for Sustainable Development*, No. 17, pp. 521–530, Elsevier, 2013.

Nurse, K., Niles, K., and Dookie, D. 'Climate Change Policies and Tourism Competitiveness in Small Island Developing States'. *National Centres of Competence in Research Swiss Climate Research Conference on the International Dimensions of Climate Policies*. Bern, 2009.

Sanders, R. 'Petrocaribe—are we prepared for the worst?', in *Trinidad & Tobago Express*, 27 February 2014.

Task Force on Puerto Rico's Status. *Report by the President's Task Force on Puerto Rico's Status*. Washington, DC, 2011.

Timothy, J. 'Interview with Jason Timothy, Project Coordinator, Geothermal Project Management Unit'. Dominica, 13 October 2011.

UN Framework Convention on Climate Change. Secretariat for the UN Framework Convention on Climate Change, Bonn, 1992.

Weisser, D. 'Power sector reform in small island developing states: what role for renewable energy technologies?', in *Renewable and Sustainable Energy Reviews*, No. 8, pp. 101–127, 2004.

Williams, C. 'Ryder Scott: Trinidad and Tobago's proved gas reserves decline', in *Oil And Gas Journal*. www.ogj.com/articles/2011/08/ryder-scott-trinidad-and-tobagos-proved-gas-reserves-decline.html, 2011.

Williams, J. 'Interview with Joseph Williams, Programme Manager, Energy, the Caribbean Community'. 12 October 2011.

THE CARIBBEAN OVERSEAS TERRITORIES AND THE LIMITS OF AUTONOMY

Dr PETER CLEGG

INTRODUCTION

A number of countries in the Caribbean region have yet to gain independent status. They still have constitutional relationships, albeit under different systems, with their original metropolitan powers. At present, none of the islands wishes to stand on its own as a sovereign state. However, many governments and political parties of the islands are not satisfied with the status quo, and thus there has been considerable debate with regard to the extent to which greater autonomy might be provided to them. While the metropolitan powers have been generally willing to grant more autonomy, a situation is now developing whereby further change is highly unlikely, and in some cases there has in fact been a moderate repatriation of powers. This essay considers the nature of the political relationships in place, the important reforms that are being undertaken in an attempt to re-energize and reorganize links between the Caribbean overseas territories and their metropolitan centres, and the likelihood that an end point is being neared with regard to the awarding of further autonomy. This essay will also consider the increasingly important relationship that the European Union (EU) has with some of the territories, and how this link also influences the autonomy debate.

THE UNITED KINGDOM OVERSEAS TERRITORIES

The collapse of the Federation of the West Indies precipitated a period of decolonization in the English-speaking Caribbean from the early 1960s. Despite the trend towards self-rule a number of smaller territories were reluctant to follow suit. As a consequence, the British authorities had to establish a new governing framework for them, and the West Indies Act of 1962 was approved for this purpose. The Act remains today the foremost provision for the British Virgin Islands, the Cayman Islands, Montserrat, and the Turks and Caicos Islands. Anguilla was dealt with separately owing to its long association with Saint Christopher and Nevis, and the Anguilla Act 1980 became the principal source of authority. Bermuda, located in the West Atlantic but often grouped with the Caribbean territories, also retains its link with the United Kingdom under the Bermuda Constitution Act 1967.

Each Constitution allocates government responsibilities to the Crown (i.e. the British Government and the Governor) and the Overseas Territory, according to the nature of the responsibility. Those powers generally reserved for the Crown include defence and external affairs, as well as responsibility for internal security and the police, international and offshore financial relations, and the public service. The Crown also has responsibility for the maintenance of good governance. Meanwhile, individual territory governments have control over all aspects of policy that are not overseen by the Crown, including the economy, education, health, social security and immigration. However, ultimate control lies with the United Kingdom as the territories are constitutionally subordinate. Nevertheless, the arrangements were not intended to be permanent; rather, they were originally proposed as stepping stones on the route to independence, and so the balance of administrative responsibilities is in practice often ill-defined. Further, the British Government, via its Governors, is reluctant to use its full powers, even in areas where the Governor has responsibility—rather, consensus and persuasion are preferred. The United Kingdom is aware of the importance of maintaining relations with democratically elected governments, and this is particularly true of those Overseas Territories—the majority—that are no longer in receipt of British state funding. In order to manage most effectively this sometimes difficult relationship, the United Kingdom strives to achieve a balance between allowing territories the fullest autonomy that they desire and ensuring that it can discharge its responsibilities and minimize its exposure to potential liabilities. The United Kingdom can face moral, political and legal obligations to give support when a territory's resources are insufficient to meet its commitments, and thus the former feels it must retain certain levers of control.

Despite such constraints and occasional serious disagreements over policy, such as the United Kingdom's decision to impose legislation to decriminalize homosexual acts between consenting adults in private (2001), and the acceptance by Bermuda of four detainees of the US detention centre in Guantánamo Bay, Cuba, without the British Government's prior knowledge (2009), the territories' constitutional link with the United Kingdom has largely retained its popularity, in particular, because it helps to preserve their stability. Many of the citizens within the territories regard continuing dependence as a safeguard against weak or corrupt government. The political ties are also important for the economies of the territories, as they provide a measure of sovereign protection, which helps to reassure potential investors. The influence of English law and language and the United Kingdom's responsibility for defence and external affairs have been valuable. Furthermore, the quasi-independent status that exists for the territories provides room for manoeuvre in political and economic matters and creates an ambiguity that attracts international capital. British support has facilitated the transition into successful economies of many of the territories. For example, Bermuda had a gross domestic product (GDP) per head of US $85,762 in 2012 (according to UN estimates), and is one of the world's leading centres for international insurance companies, while the Cayman Islands had a GDP per head of US $58,942 in 2012 (according to UN estimates), and is the world's leading centre for 'hedge funds'. In short, these territories have recognized the advantages of retaining their present status, particularly if a comparison is made with the perilous economic position of many independent Commonwealth Caribbean countries.

Although the underlying nature of the relationship has not changed significantly in recent years, a number of important initiatives have been undertaken since the Conservative-led coalition Government took office in the United Kingdom in May 2010, and these are now considered. On 28 June 2012 a White Paper on the Overseas Territories, sub-titled *Security, Success and Sustainability*, was published by the Government. The White Paper set out the nature of the existing links between the United Kingdom and its Overseas Territories and the measures required to 'renew and strengthen' this relationship. The coalition Government felt—perhaps correctly—that towards the end of the previous Government's time in power relations with at least some of the territories were becoming increasingly fractious and that several political and economic problems in the territories required stronger corrective action, supported by a 'very strong positive vision'. Thus, the White Paper attempts a balance between promoting a more positive overall agenda while making clear the responsibilities and high standards of governance the territories must maintain.

From the outset, the White Paper refers to the 'valued partnership within the Realm' and the mutual benefits gained from the relationship. The White Paper also makes very clear that all United Kingdom government departments—not just the Foreign and Commonwealth Office (FCO) and the Department for International Development—are 'committed to engaging with supporting the Territories' to establish a mutually beneficial relationship. Stronger political links between the United Kingdom and the territories are also encouraged through a new Joint Ministerial Council, supported by a small secretariat, which replaced the more ad hoc and rather ineffective Overseas Territories Consultative Council. Further, the White Paper highlights the British Government's desire to promote broader engagement with the territories via local government, private companies and non-governmental organizations, as well as the sharing of best practice between the territories.

In relation to specific policy areas, the White Paper includes chapters on: defence, security and safety; economic development and resilience; the natural environment; good governance; education, health, culture and sport; and the territories' links with the wider world. Within these chapters two considerations stand out. First, territories must 'abide by the same basic standards of good government as in the UK', which means, *inter alia*, maintaining the highest standards in public life, strengthening the public service, and safeguarding fundamental rights and freedoms. Second, territories must follow 'prudent fiscal management and effective fiscal planning' to become as financially self-reliant as possible; if not, the British Government will intervene. However, the United Kingdom will strongly defend the territories' offshore financial sectors and provide financial support, including investments to promote growth, when called upon.

The publication of the White Paper was timely in reaffirming the importance of the relationship and setting out clearly the priorities of the British Government. However, the White Paper is, in many respects, very similar to the previous White Paper, *Partnership for Progress and Prosperity*, produced by the Labour administration in 1999. Because there is no desire on the part of the coalition to change the fundamental nature of the relationship and little pressure to force independence, managing relations in an effective manner is the most important challenge.

Beyond the White Paper, there have been several political and economic developments that are worth noting. In the Turks and Caicos Islands, a general election was held on 9 November 2012, just over three years after direct rule was imposed by the United Kingdom after serious allegations of corruption were revealed. The election was won very narrowly by the Progressive National Party (PNP), which had been in office when self-government was suspended in August 2009. Just prior to the election a new Constitution came into force, on 15 October 2012. Compared to the previous 2006 Constitution, the new version included stronger powers for the Governor and the British Government. The British authorities felt this was necessary to ensure that previous corruption and mismanagement in the territory could not reoccur.

With self-rule returned, but with greater British oversight, tensions were apparent between the Turks and Caicos Islands and the United Kingdom in 2013. In February Premier Rufus Ewing warned that there was a risk of 'chaos' in the country. He criticized the actions of the United Kingdom, and called for the 'full restoration' of democracy and the removal of 'colonial influences' from the Islands. In a strongly worded response, British Secretary of State for Foreign and Commonwealth Affairs William Hague accused the Premier of 'misrepresenting' the jurisdiction's situation, and he reminded him that the previous PNP Government had 'left behind a chaotic situation'. Hague continued, '[t]he UK government has invested much in helping put Turks and Caicos Islands back on the right path. I hope you will use this inheritance wisely'. The situation in the Turks and Caicos Islands remained difficult in 2014, and the forthcoming criminal trials of former premier Michael Misick and 11 others will be a key test of the territory's fresh start.

The Cayman Islands has also witnessed a period of political instability after Premier McKeeva Bush was arrested on suspicion of theft and allegedly importing explosive substances without valid permits in December 2012. (He was formally charged in March 2013 and his trial was scheduled for late 2014.) Subsequently, Bush lost a vote of no confidence in the House of Assembly after five of his colleagues supported the motion; those colleagues then formed a new Government. This move against Bush was precipitated in part by what had happened in the Turks and Caicos Islands: Cayman politicians felt it was necessary to act first, rather than risk a repeat of the Turks and Caicos experience. Indeed, the arrest of Bush was the culmination of a period of increasingly strained relations between the former Premier and the Governor and the FCO. During his premiership Bush had taken an aggressive stance towards the Governor and the British authorities: on many occasions he had referred to 'bureaucratic harassment' and 'meddling'. It is true that the Governor and the United Kingdom have taken a more pro-active role in the Cayman Islands, but there have been legitimate concerns about the path the territory has taken, in particular the overly dominant role Bush has played in Caymanian politics and the somewhat lax approach to budget management and government procurement.

Further, the United Kingdom's present engagement in the Cayman Islands (and in other territories) is framed by the previous unattended failings in the Turks and Caicos. The arrest of Bush was unconnected to the policy clashes that had taken place, but it is a sign that greater attention is now being paid to good governance, with a strong lead being taken by the Governor and the United Kingdom authorities. Former Premier Bush tried, but ultimately failed, to challenge the constitutional supremacy of the British Government, and as a consequence his own position was seriously undermined. Since Bush stepped down as head of government the mood music coming out of the Cayman Islands in relation to the United Kingdom has been more positive. There are indications that many in the Caymans believe that the politics of division and conflict have damaged the jurisdiction's reputation and undermined its economy. Efforts have been made to shape a more positive political climate. However, it is uncertain whether some other territories, including the Turks and Caicos Islands, will follow suit. The absence of mutual trust and confidence is a real barrier towards the awarding of further autonomy, and without improvements the British Government will be reluctant to move significantly on the issue.

Economically, there have also been a number of important developments. The territories suffered during the 2008–09 global recession from reduced activity in their financial services sector and declines in tourist arrivals and construction levels. International regulatory oversight was also tightened with new initiatives such as the Foreign Account Tax Compliance Act passed by the US Congress and the Organisation for Economic Co-operation and Development's Convention on Mutual Administrative Assistance in Tax Matters. As a result, economies stagnated and fiscal deficits increased. The growing budgetary pressures were particularly acute in Anguilla, the Cayman Islands and the Turks and Caicos Islands (the latter's situation being exacerbated by the previous Government's corruption and mismanagement). This has led the British Government to take a stronger hand in economic matters. For example, in both Anguilla and the Cayman Islands the United Kingdom forced revisions to local budgets to cut spending and raise revenue. Further, the United Kingdom and all the territories agreed Frameworks for Fiscal Responsibility—legislation that commits the territory governments to be prudent and transparent on fiscal and debt management, establishes borrowing limits, and lays down the stages that must be followed in the planning, development and execution of a project. However, there has been resistance in the territories to this stronger hand, particularly in Anguilla. Responding to the British Government's decision to withhold assent of the territory's budget, in 2011 Chief Minister Hubert Hughes called on Anguillans to 'throw off the yoke of oppression' and consider independence.

So it is clear that the level of economic oversight of the territories, both on the part of the United Kingdom and the international community, is increasing. The British coalition Government, with its austerity policies at home, feels it is necessary to encourage greater fiscal discipline in the territories. The United Kingdom wants the territories to be financially self-reliant. However, the increasing criticism of the territories' offshore financial centres might put that at risk. Notwithstanding, the United Kingdom remains a strong defender of the territories' right to maintain their role in the offshore sector. As the 2012 White Paper suggested, the United Kingdom 'will continue to represent the interests of those Territories which meet [international standards]' and 'will strongly support their right to compete freely in international markets'. One reason for this support is that 'the international financial centres in the territories can play a positive and complementary role to the UK-based financial services industry'. A second is that the United Kingdom wants the territories to be as economically independent as possible and the offshore sector helps them to be so.

How might the present economic trends impact on the territories and their attitudes towards greater political autonomy? Well, greater financial discipline may help them by consolidating their economic position and minimizing their vulnerability, despite some short-term resentment over the United Kingdom's greater involvement in economic matters. On the other hand, the more hostile international attitude to their financial services industries might make the territories less confident about asking for more autonomy. The territories may well prefer to maintain the link with the United Kingdom and the useful level of protection that it provides.

THE ISLANDS OF THE DUTCH CARIBBEAN

The Charter of the Kingdom of the Netherlands was agreed in 1954 and laid out the arrangements for a federal state, comprising three self-governing autonomous countries of supposedly equal standing: the Netherlands, Suriname and the Netherlands Antilles (Aruba, Bonaire, Curaçao, Saba, Sint Eustatius and Sint Maarten). Despite changes to the membership of the Kingdom (such as Bonaire, Saba and St Eustatius becoming special-status municipalities of the Netherlands), the original Charter remains in place, in part because any reform requires the consent of all parties. In principle, although not always in practice, the countries of the Kingdom are autonomous in relation to internal matters, such as government finance, social and economic development, cultural affairs, housing and education, while the Kingdom oversees defence, foreign affairs, Dutch nationality and extradition. Beyond the country-level autonomy, the Charter stipulates areas of communal responsibility, which by statute require the partners to co-operate. In the areas of human rights and freedoms, the rule of law and good governance, responsibility is shared between each country and the Kingdom, although ultimate responsibility for safeguarding standards in public life rests with the Kingdom. In the Charter, Articles 48 to 52 allow for higher supervision—in essence a tool of last resort—which allows the Dutch Crown to impose its authority. However, as with the United Kingdom, and for the same reasons, the Dutch authorities have been reluctant to use this power.

When the Charter was signed it was expected that the Caribbean countries would seek their independence at some time in the future, and as a consequence the Netherlands agreed to give them a significant measure of autonomy. Although Suriname gained its independence in 1975 and Aruba came close (before deciding on *status aparte*—separation from the Netherlands Antilles—in 1986), in the early 1990s a political consensus emerged on both sides of the Atlantic that the Netherlands Antilles and Aruba would be better off remaining part of the Kingdom, primarily owing to their relatively high standards of living, significant financial assistance, the duty of support when faced with natural disasters, and safeguards to maintain the rule of law and good governance. Therefore the temporary nature of the provisions of the Kingdom became permanent, and the Dutch Government in turn felt that a stronger role for the Kingdom was needed more effectively to oversee good governance in the territories. However, there was very strong opposition to this from the islands, and no reform was possible. Accordingly, the Dutch Government employed its financial assistance to the region to effect changes at the local level in areas such as the organization of the Antillean Government, prison conditions, police operations and criminal investigations. However, this rather piecemeal approach was not a substitute for proper reform.

As well as problems in Kingdom relations, the operation of the Netherlands Antilles was questioned. The government structure consisted of two tiers: the national level and the island level, with elections held every four years. However, as the island elections took place during the mid-point of the national government there was little time for stable government and effective policy-making. Further, after Aruba left the Netherlands Antilles the territory was out of balance and dominated by Curaçao, the largest island by far. Curaçao

felt that its interests were not being met because of the demands of the smaller islands, while those islands felt that Curaçao dominated the Antillean Government. As a result of these structural problems within the Kingdom and Antillean relationships, a number of serious difficulties manifested themselves in the Netherlands Antilles, including corruption, a substantial public debt, a high murder rate, significant levels of drugs-trafficking, inadequate environmental safeguards, and widespread social dislocation. There was also mounting public concern in the Netherlands about the situation; in part because of allied alarm over the poor level of integration of sizeable numbers of young Antillean migrants in the Netherlands. This led, in turn, to rising political opposition to the territories and their peoples.

In the face of such problems the Dutch Government made several attempts to negotiate with the islands to improve standards of governance, but initially all efforts failed. However, in 2004 attitudes changed owing to the worsening levels of violence and drugs-trafficking in the Netherlands Antilles which created a growing image of a failed state, and all parties agreed that the Antillean construct should be disbanded and a new set of relationships established. During 2004 and 2005 referendums were held in the islands and all but St Eustatius voted for the dissolution of the Netherlands Antilles; this was sufficient to bring the Antilles to an end. After a period of initial negotiations it was agreed in October 2006 that Bonaire, St Eustatius and Saba would become part of the Netherlands as special-status municipalities. This meant that the islands would be overseen by the Netherlands while retaining local government functions. Then, in November, the two larger territories, Curaçao and St Maarten, signed an agreement with the Dutch Government to become autonomous islands within the Kingdom, a similar status to that of Aruba. However, there was a pact that the Kingdom would (temporarily) oversee the public finances and the rule of law of the two islands. It was also agreed that the public debt of the Netherlands Antilles and of the island governments would be largely forgiven.

Despite expectations, the deadline of 15 December 2008 for the dissolution of the Netherlands Antilles was not met, following a series of disputes between the Kingdom partners. A new date of 10 October 2010 was then set for dissolution, and this was kept. However, the process continued to be difficult. For instance, there was strong opposition in those islands becoming Dutch municipalities to the introduction of gay marriage, abortion and euthanasia, but these changes were enacted in order to allow Bonaire, St Eustatius and Saba to accede to the Dutch Constitution. Further, on 15 May 2009 Curaçao voted in a non-binding referendum to support the island becoming an autonomous territory, but around 48% of voters rejected the plan. Opponents denounced the planned increase in administrative powers for the Dutch as 'neocolonialism'. Another dispute arose in October 2009 when Bonaire's new Government, led by the Aliansa Demokrátika Bonairiana (as the Partido Demokrátiko Boneriano was known from 2009 to September 2010), a progressive social democratic party, dismissed the idea of becoming a municipality of the Netherlands and instead argued for 'free association' status to provide the island with greater autonomy. Unsurprisingly, the Dutch were dismayed by the *volte-face*, arguing that everything had been agreed, and if public authority status was not acceptable the only other option would be independence. In the end, Bonaire agreed to adhere to the original agreement.

Since the dissolution of the Netherlands Antilles tensions remain, many stemming from the 2006 agreements. For example, both Curaçao and St Maarten have seen several draft budgets blocked by the Dutch financial supervision council. The council has felt the two local governments have not done enough to balance their budgets, although their financial positions were improving in 2014. Despite both St Maarten and Curaçao agitating for the termination of the Kingdom law on financial supervision, strong Dutch oversight remains. Further, the Dutch have concerns over the poor level of governance, particularly in St Maarten. In a parliamentary debate in April 2013, Minister of the Interior and Kingdom Relations Ronald Plasterk stated that there were too many rumours about corruption and violation of human rights in St

Maarten. Plasterk cautioned '[t]his causes much damage to the reputation of the Kingdom. The situation is very worrisome'. Since then new rules have been introduced to help clean up the political system. In Curaçao, meanwhile, the country is still dealing with the fall-out from the murder in May 2013 of Helmin Wiels, leader of the island's largest political party, the Pueblo Soberano (PS). Although the motive remains unclear, it has been suggested that organized crime was behind the killing owing to Wiels's work in combating corruption. In Bonaire, St Eustatius and Saba, significant funds are being disbursed by the Dutch Government to improve schools, prisons and hospitals. However, the populations are not happy with other aspects of the relationship, from retail price increases to what is seen as Dutch dominance in many areas of policy.

Up until now, for territories of the Dutch Caribbean, separation from each other—rather than independence from the Netherlands—has been the key concern. The subsequent process of reform has been very protracted and divisive, and the degree of autonomy awarded to each island after the dissolution of the Netherlands Antilles has been strictly limited, despite what many of them originally wanted. However, it is worth noting that, in the end, the Dutch metropolitan administration acceded to something it had resisted for many years—the islands enjoying separate relationships with the Netherlands.

However, there remains considerable dissatisfaction on all sides. In the Netherlands there are growing voices, including from within the Volkspartij voor Vrijheid en Democratie (People's Party for Freedom and Democracy), the largest party in government, that looser ties between the Kingdom partners (though some sort of Commonwealth) should be introduced, and that limitations be placed on the free travel from the islands to the Netherlands. Such views a decade ago would not have been contemplated. An underlying problem is that the metropolitan Government still does not have a clear and positive vision for the Kingdom. On the other hand, as highlighted above, there is unhappiness over the Netherlands' strong role in the islands. The percentage of Antilleans supporting independence has increased and the largest party in Curaçao's present coalition Government, the PS, is a pro-independence party and has called for a referendum on the issue. However, the party won only 23% of the vote in the 2012 general election, so it appears that there is some way to go before independence is a truly credible option. The PS has stated that independence could be achieved within 10 years if the economy is strengthened. A majority of the Dutch parliament would support Curaçao (and other territories) if it decided to go its own way.

THE FRENCH OVERSEAS DEPARTMENTS

Unlike the British, Dutch and US territories, the French Overseas Departments in the Caribbean are actually part of France. However, the political, economic and social challenges facing the Départements d'Outre-Mer (DOM) are similar to those in the other non-sovereign countries in the region. The law of assimilation of 19 March 1946 granted Martinique, Guadeloupe and French Guiana (together with Réunion in the Indian Ocean) the administrative status of Department so that all territorial institutions operate like their metropolitan equivalents in France. In addition, laws and regulations enacted in the metropolitan Government in Paris apply automatically to the DOM. A Prefect nominated by Paris represents the State and has responsibility for foreign relations, defence, law and order, and the provision of the national service. A Conseil Général (General Council) manages each Department. Directly elected by the inhabitants of the Department, the Council controls a local budget and oversees social issues, economic initiatives and day-to-day administration. Also, locally elected deputies and senators represent each DOM in the French parliament. In 1982 French President François Mitterand introduced greater decentralization into the system which established a new level of government—the Region—with a directly elected body, the Conseil Régional (Regional Council), whose main role was to promote social, economic, cultural and scientific development of the Region. In principle, each Region was to cover a few Departments. For geographical

and political reasons it was impossible to incorporate the four DOM within a single Region. Thus four overseas Regions were established; one for each DOM. Martinique, Guadeloupe, French Guiana and Réunion each then became a Department and a Region. The Region operates on the same geographical territory, same population and same electorate as the Department. This reform has caused significant problems for the DOM in terms of overlapping activities, increased administrative costs and local political rivalry.

Aware of the bureaucratic tensions in the DOM Prime Minister Lionel Jospin and his socialist government established a new programme for the territories in 2000, entitled Loi d'Orientation pour l'Outre-Mer, or LOOM. This gave members of the General Council and Regional Council in each DOM an opportunity to discuss and submit to the Prime Minister any proposal regarding an evolution of their status, including a move towards independence. However, the changes suggested were rather moderate, and focused on administrative reform. Notwithstanding, with the defeat of the Socialists in the 2002 French parliamentary elections, the LOOM process was halted and the Conservatives introduced a new decentralization reform. In response, the elected representatives of Martinique and Guadeloupe submitted a request for local referendums to take place on the evolution of their status. They asked for the reunification of the General Council and the Regional Council within a single elected assembly. In December 2003 the votes were held, but the results were unexpected as the proposed change was rejected in both territories. The outcomes highlighted the concern of voters that, if any alteration were made, the social and economic advantages emanating from the French state might be threatened, and that the gathering of local power in the hands of one person could lead to a decline in democratic standards and to a risk of autocracy. The voters appear to have thought that keeping two local bodies with two presidents would guarantee a certain degree of competition considered to be positive for the management of their Department.

Although the administrative structures of Guadeloupe and Martinique remained unchanged, Saint-Barthélemy and Saint-Martin, two islands administratively attached to Guadeloupe, used their right under the decentralization reform to revise their status. Both islands expressed a wish to escape Guadeloupe's management and become two distinct territories. During the local referendums that took place both electorates voted overwhelmingly in favour of this new status that would allow them legislative speciality, more local power and a more direct link with the metropolitan Government in Paris. On 7 February 2007 the French Parliament approved legislation granting Saint-Barthélemy and Saint-Martin their new status. They are now known as French Overseas Collectivities (Collectivités d'Outre-Mer or COM).

The political and legal assimilation of the DOM has taken place along with enormous injections of money from mainland France and increasingly from the EU, which has produced high levels of development. Financial transfers are spent on social security, health care, education, tax breaks and public employment. However, there are concerns about a model that does not allow the DOM to achieve self-sustained development despite good rates of growth. Indeed, growth is paradoxically derived from a considerable decline in the productive capacities of the territories. Thus, the significant monetary transfers provided have actually impeded economic development. In particular, the implementation of social legislation conceived for a developed country (i.e. mainland France) has distorted the economic performance of the small and formerly underdeveloped DOM. Therefore, they have been transformed from producer economies to heavily assisted welfare-based ones. The result is that 80% of required foods are imported, exports amount to only one-seventh of imports, high unemployment is endemic, and crime levels are increasing.

Some of these structural problems, exacerbated by the effects of the global financial crisis, were the cause of widespread protests in the DOM during the early part of 2009. Guadeloupe, in particular, was badly affected by a six-week general strike. Workers demanded action over low wages (in comparison with mainland France rather than with the rest of the Caribbean) and the high cost of living, which was, in part, caused by the high level of imports from France. Agreement was reached on a number of issues, but the protests also re-opened the debate about the DOM's relationship with France. In Martinique and French Guiana it was agreed that referendums should be held on whether the Departments should have greater autonomy and become autonomous territories governed by Article 74 (rather than Article 73) of the French Constitution. However, in January 2010 the voters in both Departments rejected the proposals by a convincing margin, but then subsequently agreed to the less significant reform of merging the Regional Council and General Council into a single body. This merger is scheduled to take place in 2015. The French Government accepted the results of the votes and suggested this now concluded the debate over Martinique's and French Guiana's constitutional relationship with France. In Guadeloupe, meanwhile, it was decided that a referendum was not appropriate. Rather, it was felt that a period of reflection and consensus-building was needed after the violent protests and civil unrest. This was reinforced in the elections for the Regional Council in March. Victorin Lurel's left-wing coalition retained power with an convincing share of the vote, while two parties led by key figures in the Liyannaj Kont Pwofitasyon, or 'Collective Against Exploitation', which organized the unrest, gained only 3% between them. Thus, the opportunity for further autonomy was not seized. Notwithstanding, there is discussion over whether the Regional and General Councils should be merged, and it was likely that a referendum would be held on the issue in the near future.

The European Union, the Overseas Countries and Territories and the Outermost Regions

Positioning itself within this complicated set of relations is the European Union (EU), which has separate links with the Overseas Countries and Territories (OCTs) and the outermost regions (ORs). The non-self-governing OCTs are not part of the EU and thus are not directly subject to EU law, but they do have associate status (under Part IV of the Treaty on the Functioning of the EU) and this provides an increasingly important level of economic and social support. In addition, there are the ORs which are integral but distant regions of EU member states, and include the French DOM and one COM (Saint-Martin). Unlike the OCTs, the ORs must adhere in full to the rights and obligations arising from the European Treaties.

Links with the OCTs were established in 1957 and for many years they were mainly 'light' versions of the agreements with the African, Caribbean and Pacific (ACP) group of countries. In addition, the administering powers, rather than the OCTs, led negotiations with the EU. However, more recently, the OCTs have gained a stronger voice within the EU. One consequence of this has been a new agreement—Council Decision 2013/755/EU on the Association of the Overseas Countries and Territories with the EU, adopted on 25 November 2013. The agreement aims to modernize the relationship between the EU and the OCTs, 'moving beyond development cooperation and focusing on a reciprocal relationship based on mutual interests'. The key provisions of the Decision include the establishment of closer economic relations between the EU and the OCTs, such as through an improvement in market access for OCT goods and services, and relaxation of the rules of origin. In addition, the agreement includes: enhancing OCTs' competitiveness; the strengthening of OCTs' resilience and reduction of their vulnerability; and the establishment of more reciprocal relations between the EU and OCTs based on mutual interests and shared values. There are also several financial instruments linked to the new Decision. Total EU funding for OCTs via the 11th European Development Fund (EDF, 2014–20) is €364.m., a sizeable increase on the previous allocation. Two-thirds of that amount will be allocated to individual OCTs. In addition to the EDF money, the OCTs will receive funding under programmes by way of the EU's general budget. The new Decision has been largely welcomed by the OCTs and will provide an important additional level of support above and beyond the metropolitan powers.

The ties between the ORs and the EU are obviously much closer. In the EU Treaty the ORs are covered by Article 349, which requires that EU policies must be adjusted to the regions' special circumstances. The EU believes that the regions face several difficulties in moving towards full development, such as remoteness, insularity, climate, economic dependence, and a narrow productive base. As a consequence, several programmes are in place to provide funding to support their development. Between 2007 and 2013 over €11,000m. was provided to the ORs; a figure very much higher than the amount going to the OCTs. In October 2008 a new Commission policy paper, 'The Outermost Regions—an asset for Europe' set two objectives: first, address new difficulties facing the ORs, such as globalization, climate change, demographic trends, and migratory flows; and second, exploit the regions' assets to boost economic development, with particular focus on sectors with high added-value, such as the agri-food industry, biodiversity, renewable energy, aerospace, and seismology, and to promote the regions' role as outposts of the EU in the world. For the ORs, this level of support is significant, and would be lost if they gained independence. One final point here is that, interestingly, Bonaire, St Eustatius and Saba could become ORs because of their special municipality status, but at present continue to be OCTs. They are hesitant to make the change because they feel the dominant image of the EU is one of excessive regulation, potentially increased intervention, and less autonomy. Thus, for the time being, more autonomy is preferable to greater levels of financial aid. Nevertheless, whether a territory is an OCT or an OR, the link with the EU is an important and additional benefit, which it otherwise would not have.

PUERTO RICO AND THE US VIRGIN ISLANDS

The other remaining metropolitan power in the Caribbean is the USA, with oversight of Puerto Rico and the US Virgin Islands. The current status of the Commonwealth of Puerto Rico was established in 1952, under Law 600. After the USA took control of Puerto Rico in 1898 and until 1952, the territory had little autonomy. Despite this, Puerto Ricans were granted US citizenship in 1917. Hence, they are US citizens by statute, and can move freely to the USA. When Law 600 was passed, it set out a new structure for relations that remains in place today, providing a degree of autonomy, although Puerto Rico's status means that it is neither state, nor federal territory nor colonial possession. Rather, it is an 'unincorporated' territory: the US Government has the authority to undertake unilateral action on a range of issues, including the right to revoke any law inconsistent with the Constitution of the USA, and to award or rescind regulatory privileges or advantages, such as US citizenship. The US Congress may even repeal Law 600 or annul Puerto Rico's Constitution. More specifically, the USA retains control over issues such as citizenship, defence, diplomacy, currency, immigration and foreign trade. Puerto Rico, meanwhile, has limited self-government in areas such as taxation, economic development, education and culture. The territory's current status provides also for local gubernatorial, legislative and mayoral elections, but not the right to vote in US federal elections. However, Puerto Ricans living in the USA are able to vote for the US President.

As the Cold War came to an end the question of Puerto Rico's status emerged as a key issue, and several attempts were made to resolve it in the early 1990s. In 1993 a referendum was held which offered three options: statehood (complete annexation to the US federal system as a state), independence, or remaining a commonwealth but with increased federal funding and autonomy. Neither statehood nor the commonwealth option enjoyed a clear majority, with the support of 46.2% and 48.4% of voters, respectively, while independence scored a mere 4%. A second referendum was held in 1998, but again the result was not decisive. This time there were five options on the ballot paper (statehood, independence, two definitions of commonwealth status, and 'none of the above'); 'none of the above' was the most popular, obtaining 50.2% of the vote, compared with 46.5% for statehood. This was a consequence of serious dissatisfaction regarding the design of the referendum by the administration of Pedro Rosselló without the agreement of the other political parties. In the decade that followed, the question of Puerto Rico's status declined in prominence as a political issue.

There were several reasons for the downgrading of the status issue. First, there was no consensus on the best way forward—either in Puerto Rico or the US Congress. Second, Puerto Rico accrues substantial economic benefits from its relationship with the USA and many in the territory were concerned that political change would undermine these benefits. For example, 30% of Puerto Rico's budget is accounted for by US federal grants, much of which is distributed as social welfare programmes to a large proportion of families. Third, national identity among the Spanish-speaking Puerto Ricans is strong, with a majority seeing themselves as a distinct nation and sharing a Puerto Rican, and not a US or Latino identity. However, Puerto Ricans do not wish to relinquish their US citizenship and the advantages that come with it, including significant circular migration between Puerto Rico and the continental USA. Puerto Rico has been called 'the nation on the move'. Thus, the paradoxical nature of national identity helped to muddy the political waters.

However, the status issue has now once again taken centre stage. One reason is that the territory is in the midst of its worst economic crisis in modern history. The Government of Puerto Rico is nearly bankrupt and the island's GDP has decreased by over 10% in the past decade. The result has been worsening social conditions with rising unemployment, significant poverty, drugs-trafficking and a high murder rate, prompting uneasy speculation in Puerto Rico that the lack of consensus on the status issue has caused a dangerous degree of stagnation to set in. A second and related reason is that funding caps have been placed on federal programmes, such as health care and housing schemes, owing to Puerto Rico's commonwealth status, which puts it at a disadvantage vis-à-vis other parts of the USA. Further, because the USA has signed a number of free trade agreements with other competitor jurisdictions in the region (such as Mexico and the Dominican Republic), Puerto Rico has lost its privileged trading position in the US market and its economic competitiveness has been negatively impacted. In addition, because the US Congress has ended the schemes that granted federal tax exemption to US corporations for earnings gained in Puerto Rico, the territory's status is now much less important to the USA.

There is also increasing political support to address the status issue. For example, prior to his election victory in 2008, US President Barack Obama pledged to resolve the territory's status question. While on a visit to the island in 2011, Obama stated '[w]hen the people of Puerto Rico make a clear decision, my administration will stand by you'. Furthermore, the US House of Representatives considered the issue in 2009 and 2010. This all led to a new vote on Puerto Rico's status in November 2012. The ballot included two questions. Voters were asked first whether they wanted the current territory status to continue: 54% said 'no' and 46% said 'yes, a clear rejection of the current status. Voters were then asked to give their preference among the three alternatives to the current status and the results were as follows: statehood, 44.4%; independence, 4.0%; and free association (or sovereign commonwealth status), 24.2%. Blank votes accounted for a significant 26.5%. So yet again the vote was inconclusive, and interestingly the share of the vote for statehood actually decreased by 2.1% from 1998.

In the absence of a clear result, President Obama and the US Congress did not comment on the 2012 vote. However, in April 2013 the US Administration announced the allocation of US $2.5m. 'for objective, nonpartisan voter education about, and a plebiscite on, options that resolve Puerto Rico's future political status'. Following that, Puerto Rico's Resident Com-

missioner to the House of Representatives presented Bill HR 2000, the Puerto Rico Status Resolution Act, proposing a simple statehood 'yes' or 'no' plebiscite. If another vote does take place and statehood is supported (by no mean a certainty), the US Congress would then have to introduce and approve the necessary legislation before it was signed off by the US President. However, this would not be a foregone conclusion as the issue is not a high priority for Congress and there is little consensus among its members on which status is preferable, with some of the opinion that the people of Puerto Rico are too 'foreign' to be incorporated into the USA.

In contrast to Puerto Rico, political status is not an issue in the US Virgin Islands, which includes St Thomas, St Croix and St John. The lack of a strong, distinct national identity, the use of English (but spoken with an 'African-derived' accent), its small size, the limited population (109,000—compared with 4m. for Puerto Rico) and its narrow productive base (mainly tourism) make it very difficult for the islands to move to either statehood or full independence. At present the islands are an organized non-incorporated territory, governed by a US Congressional Organic Act, and overseen by the US Office for Insular Affairs. This legal and administrative structure means that the US Virgin Islands has less political and economic autonomy than Puerto Rico.

CONCLUSION

In many respects the overseas territories in the Caribbean, regardless of the metropolitan power with which they are associated and the specific nature of that relationship, have a privileged position within the international system. The territories' citizens have a final guarantee against autocracy and economic collapse; many territories receive sizeable monetary assistance which has helped them in creating relatively high levels of development; and nationals possess the citizenship of their metropolitan powers, and in the case of the British, Dutch and French territories have freedom of movement across the EU. The EU also provides significant financial support and privileged access to its market. Consequently, there are no serious demands for independence in any of the territories. Furthermore, after a period of constitutional reflection and, in some cases, change, the likelihood of the territories gaining further autonomy is remote. In the British Overseas Territories and the Dutch Caribbean, further autonomy will now only be given with independence, and in select areas there has been a modest repatriation of powers to the respective central Governments in the United Kingdom and the Netherlands. In the French DOM there is no widespread desire for further autonomy, as clearly evidenced in a series of local referendums. Finally, while the situation in Puerto Rico is more difficult to predict, it is evident that independence is not a feasible option and many Puerto Ricans hope that statehood can be achieved, thereby locking the territory into the federal structure of the USA. For all territories, irrespective of their specific circumstances, there are clear and generally accepted limits to their autonomy. It is a case of 'this far and no further' with regard to the question of additional autonomy, and this will almost certainly remain the case for some time to come. Beyond these issues, it is perhaps most notable that some of the islands—particularly those formerly part of the Netherlands Antilles and Guadeloupe—have broken away from their neighbours and established direct links with the metropoles. Thus, inter-island antipathy and rivalry, and insular particularism, seem to be the primary motivators for a change in status.

VIOLENCE AND INSECURITY IN MEXICO

Dr GARETH A. JONES and Dr PETER WATT

When Enrique Peña Nieto took office as the 57th President of the United Mexican States on 1 December 2012, political commentators took stock of what had been a decade of rising violence and a widespread sense of insecurity. During the previous two administrations, the first of Vicente Fox Quesada (2000–06) and the second of Felipe Calderón Hinojosa (2006–12), Mexico had witnessed rising levels of crime, including murder and kidnap, many of which were associated with the prosecution of a 'war on drugs'. In many parts of the country, Mexicans expressed growing feelings of insecurity, just as they also became more accustomed to the sight of military units and military-style policing in daily life. The expectation in Mexico, and among observers abroad, not least in the security agencies of the USA, was that Peña Nieto's election might mark a change of policy, or at least emphasis. During his election campaign he had stressed the need to tackle public insecurity and violence, and signalled that there might be less attention paid to drugs-trafficking organizations (DTOs). Supporters commended a sensible adjustment of priorities, matching the demands of ordinary Mexicans, and reflecting a sense of failure in the 'war', while critics feared that it marked a return to a past when the political élite refused to acknowledge organized crime. For 71 years before 2000 the party of Peña Nieto, the Partido Revolucionario Institucional (PRI, Institutional Revolutionary Party), had held power through deals with business, trade unions, peasant groups, student organizations and, it was alleged, organized crime leaders, including incipient DTOs.

Little more than a year into his presidency, however, both former supporters and critics appeared to be deeply unhappy with the PRI's return to power. Polls conducted in early 2014 suggest that Peña Nieto is one of the most unpopular Mexican Presidents of the last 100 years, placing his approval rating at a meagre 37%. On the one hand, there exists a pervasive perception that changes in security policy are largely rhetorical and fail to address the grave structural socio-economic problems which contributed to the growth and influence of DTOs. On the other hand, Peña Nieto has spearheaded a wave of neoliberal structural reforms, privatizations and the process of selling off some of the country's key resources, particularly the partly state-run petroleum giant, Petróleos Mexicanos (PEMEX). These moves have exasperated the President's opponents, many of whom view current policy decisions as a dismantling of, and attack on, the progressive and democratic provisions guaranteed by the Mexican Constitution.

PUBLIC INSECURITY AND EVERYDAY VIOLENCE

The past decade has witnessed a rise in violent crime. The change has been dramatic and is increasingly spreading from remote parts of the country to have a pervasive presence in hitherto relatively unaffected areas. News of another act of violence has become an almost banal occurrence. Nevertheless, violence has become an important medium through which people understand daily events and take what they believe to be appropriate decisions. This is what some sociologists refer to as 'sociological imagination', the construct through which people make rational inferences from the information in the world around them (Castillo Berthier and Jones, 2009). In analysing news reports, Mexicans attribute periods of peace to political deals, and interpret shootings and arrests as either the legitimate actions of the state, a cynical propaganda campaign or further evidence of collusion between a politician with one DTO over another. In short, after a period from approximately the early 1940s when Mexicans' sense of identity could be distilled to a pride in the nation, in religion, tolerance, sociability and stability—notwithstanding considerable nostalgia inherent in these ideas, not least from the perspective of discrimination against indigenous groups—living with violence is now a key factor to understanding the Mexicans' sense of themselves, social morals, and their trust in the state and institutions.

This change in people's attitudes does have an empirical basis. Although Mexico is not the most violent country in Latin America—homicide rates in 2013 for Honduras (79.0 per 100,000), and in 2012 for Belize (44.3) and El Salvador (42.4) are significantly higher—the rate in Mexico is high, around 21.5 in 2012 and rising compared with the last decade. According to official figures, in 1995 the homicide rate was 16.9 per 100,000, which then fell to a low of 8.9 in 2004 before rising. By far the largest component of this increase is attributed to what is termed 'drug-related violence'; initially, a term popularized by national newspapers, especially *Reforma*, which was at the forefront of data collection and innovative presentation through its *Ejecutrómetro* (Execution-ometer), but became a term incorporated into government announcements and statistical profiles. In 2006 there were 2,200 drugs-related murders, increasing to 2,725 in 2007, more than 6,800 in 2008, 9,614 in 2009, 15,273 in 2010 and 16,466 in 2011. At this stage over one-half of all homicides in Mexico were attributed to the 'war on drugs', compared with about 10% of homicides in the early 2000s: the five-fold increase in drugs-related violence between 2007 and 2012 not only affected the national homicide rate but came to dominate it (Shirk, 2011).

An alarming corollary of the security crisis is the number of people reported as having been forcibly 'disappeared'. One internal government document leaked to the media catalogued over 26,000 disappearances during the presidency of Felipe Calderón, for example, and there are few signs that this trend is slowing. Discoveries of mass graves containing several or even dozens of bodies are becoming increasingly frequent. Although government rhetoric overwhelmingly blames such disappearances on DTOs, research by Human Rights Watch found that 149 out of 250 case studies of forced disappearances in Mexico 'were committed by members of every security force involved in public security operations, sometimes acting in conjunction with organized crime'.

In 2013, Peña Nieto's first full year in office, over 18,000 intentional homicides were recorded. In addition, about 2,600 kidnappings were reported, although the actual figure is probably significantly higher. A survey conducted by the Government's Instituto Nacional de Estadística y Geografía (INEGI, National Institute of Statistics and Geography) suggested that the number of kidnappings throughout the country was as high as 105,000 in 2012, but that in most instances these were never reported.

In the context of high homicide rates, it is important to understand two points. First, the prevalence of homicide is still geographically uneven across Mexico. According to data published by the UN Office on Drugs and Crime, homicides are concentrated in a few states: Chihuahua, Sinaloa, Guerrero and Baja California. These states accounted for about 11% of the national population but 41% of intentional homicides in 2010. Homicide within these states is also highly concentrated, with almost three-quarters of homicides in Baja California being recorded in Tijuana and two-thirds of homicides in the state of Chihuahua taking place in Ciudad Juárez (also known simply as Juárez). In 2008 about 1,600 people were killed in Juárez, a figure that rose to 2,575 in 2009 and to 2,738 in 2010, increasing the homicide rate for the city to 191 murders per 100,000 inhabitants. Residents of other cities such as Acapulco, Culiacán and Nuevo Laredo have also had to live with the reality of high levels of organized violent crime over the past decade (Shirk, 2011). What media attention to these high crime areas obscures is why some parts of Mexico, including Mexico City, have experienced low levels of violence—indeed homicide has fallen in Guanajuato, Tlaxcala and Zacatecas states without people giving this any attention—albeit there is an increased sense of everyday insecurity.

Second, the headline data rarely analyse who are the victims of violence and focus more enthusiastically on who are its perpetrators. If we look at the data on victims one can identify a clear gender divide. The ratio of homicide is about 10 to one for males and females. This ratio is broadly consistent from the mid-1990s onwards and regardless of whether the trend overall is rising or falling, high or low. If these figures are broken down by age, then, focusing on males, it is equally clear that the victims of homicide are likely to be males above the age of 15, and that the trend for male victimhood is consistent for all age groups except for 10–14-year-olds over the period from the mid-1990s. For all years the homicide rate is highest for men aged 30–35 years, followed closely by men aged 25–29 and 20–24. For men in their early 30s, the homicide rate in Mexico from 2007 was over 70 per 100,000, or, to put this another way, the rate for this gender and age group was nearing the level for Hondurans generally.

Such statistics, however, have little relation to the perceptions and debates on victimhood. In 2011 President Felipe Calderón was widely condemned for suggesting that the victims of crime were 'collateral' and implying that many of those killed since 2006 were probably not 'innocent' of involvement in the drug economy. In fact, despite the now vernacular usage of terms such as 'drug-related violence', official data offer only clumsy and incomplete analysis of how many of the people killed were involved in, or the direct victims of, DTOs or security forces. There is some suggestion that the data might under-report homicides related to the 'war on drugs' as DTOs have become proficient at disposing of bodies using acid baths and mass graves. It is also impossible from the data, based on homicide reports and death certificates, to ascertain what role people might have played in relation to the drug economy. Evidence from the early 1990s suggests that victims were often shippers (*transportistas*) who had lost consignments, or distributors unable to pay for advances—with a figure of 1,000 deaths per year suggested by one source. Since the early 2000s, however, the perception is that violence has involved more people with no connection with criminal activity. The killing of 52 people in a casino fire in Monterrey in 2011, which was reported as a revenge attack by a leading DTO, however, are also categorized as 'drug-related', even though none of the dead were identified as connected to rival DTOs or security forces; many of them were female office workers on a break. Suspicion abounds that it suits the Government to categorize as many deaths as possible as 'drugs-related' to bolster legitimacy for the 'war' or then to claim that it was winning.

The gulf between official rhetoric and the increasing popular disillusionment with the Government's drug war strategy, however, has seen the growth of new social movements which aim to change the parameters of mainstream debate. The student-led Yo Soy 132 (I am 132) and the ¡No Más Sangre! (No More Blood) movements have highlighted the Government's contradictory rhetoric relating to the security crisis and its efforts to use the mass media to manipulate and control its message. Popular movements like these—of which there are now many —have tapped into popular resentment and the recognition that corruption and co-operation with DTOs reaches all levels of government and big business. Furthermore, whereas the armed forces once retained a certain legitimacy among the population, they are now commonly viewed as contributing to the violence and breakdown in the rule of law as much as the cartels.

YOUTH GANGS AND THE *NARCO PANDILLA*

Far more attention has been focused on who has been conducting the homicides. One concern has been that youth gangs have become involved with organized crime and have shifted from being localized, low-skilled and poorly armed associations of young people without allegiance, to groups linked with the drug trade and possibly a DTO. Consequently, security agencies have become involved in attempts to measure gang presence. The Attorney-General's Special Investigative Office for Organized Crime (SIEDO) estimated in 2008, for example, that there might be as many as 1,500 gangs and 20,000 young people linked with drug-related violence. A 2010 submission by the Attorney-General to a Special Session of the Organization of American States estimated 214 gangs with links to DTOs. The evidence for youth gangs becoming actively, consistently and effectively involved with organized crime is ambiguous.

Youth gangs have a long history in Mexico and are a pervasive feature of many cities, mostly concentrated in lower income areas of the older *barrios* or *colonias*. For the most part these gangs—often termed *bandas* or *pandillas*—are 'social' groups with their own argots (*caló*), sometimes dress styles and tattoos, and motivated by fun, drug consumption and displays of masculine identity. They do undertake petty crime, but are poorly armed and restrict activities to their local neighbourhood or area of the city (Jones, 2013). Actual or potential gang members are under pressure to change their modus operandi. According to the World Bank, Mexico experienced low economic growth of about 1.2% between 1997 and 2001, followed by a decline in growth of 6.2% between 2002 and 2006, while the impressive 5.5% growth rate recorded between 2007 and 2011 was insufficient to prevent poverty worsening and moving an additional 3.2m. Mexicans beneath the poverty line. By contrast, the drugs economy has boomed. These gangs perceive the benefits of small-scale drug dealing, as well as consumption, involvement in protection rackets and better access to cast-off weaponry. For the most part, however, membership of these gangs diminishes with age, and 'turn over' of gangs in particular localities is high, with new groups replacing old in quick succession.

The exception to the rule of limited gang conversion to '*narco pandilla*' status suggests that shifts are dependent on particular gang conditions, relations with the drug trade and neighbourhood political affiliations. Recent reports for the *barrio* of Tepito in Mexico City—an important centre for both small-scale drug sales (*narcomenudeo*) and wholesale distribution—suggest that a leading gang, the Ojos Rojos ('Red Eyes'), that has been involved with protection, contraband and drug sales for many years has been challenged by La Mano de Osos gang ('The Bears') in order to take over drug distribution. Unlike previous 'turf wars' that would be resolved with fights or a targeted murder, La Mano de Osos has set about killing rival distributors and gang members. Although still relatively rare in Mexico City, Tepito has experienced a couple of mass killings, including use of 'drive-by' shooting. These *pandilla* to *narco pandilla* converts remain rare. Crucially, most lack the skills and tactics employed by DTOs or the transnational gangs. DTOs also seem wary of the reliability of gangs, and accounts from both Chihuahua and Michoacán indicate that gangs are often the victims of DTO incursion into an area rather than being incorporated into the organizations.

Nevertheless, gangs are caught up in a series of policing strategies that have adopted a 'toughened' stance towards them, whether they (self-)define as *bandas*, *pandillas* or '*narco*' varieties. In 1996 a new Law against Organized Delinquency brought both *bandas* and *pandillas* under the rubric of 'organized crime', initially justified through links with assault, robbery and vehicle theft. Reforms to the Penal Code in 2007 and 2009 associated gangs with kidnapping, drugs and terrorism. The difficulty at a street level is that security agencies and the media are conflating the *barrio* youth gang with groups that are associated with serious criminal organizations, sometimes on a transnational basis (Castillo Berthier and Jones, 2009). Two types of transnational gangs receive the majority of the attention. First, there are the Maras, the Mara Salvatrucha (MS-13) and Calle 18, which have their origins in El Salvador and the USA. The second type is 'Mexican' gangs that are either based in the cities along the US border or have networks with gangs in the USA, mostly in California and the south-west. It is worth identifying the characteristics of both types, their role in the drug economy and links with violence.

The Maras undertake a range of criminal activities from kidnapping to extortion, are accredited with a 'command' structure, and use violence to dominate social institutions and carve out space within which they may exert control over the local state. From the late 1990s and early 2000s Maras groups were identified in the areas of Tapachula, Suchiate and Huixtla in Chiapas, and parts of Oaxaca and Tabasco, with numbers reaching perhaps 3,000 in 2001. Although Chiapas actually recorded one of the lowest homicide rates of any state at the time, newspaper headlines in the early 2000s frequently referred to the Maras 'invading' Mexico. By 2008 the National Commission for Human Rights (CNDH) identified Maras in 23 states and the Federal District but suggested that total gang numbers were small. By contrast, the national intelligence agency (CISEN) and the US Agency for

International Development (USAID) Mexico Gang Report began to claim 5,000 to 20,000 Maras, with growing numbers along the border with the USA and in Mexico City. Public security agencies, including for Mexico City, announced the creation of anti-Maras units, as well as regional operations such as the 2005 International Plan for Combined anti-Gang Operations that involved security forces from Mexico, El Salvador, Guatemala, Honduras and the USA. Again, however, claims that thousands of Maras were present in Mexico were always doubtful. Indeed, a finding by the CNDH that more than 70% of 'Maras' apprehended in Mexico were actually Mexican rather than El Salvadoran or Guatemalan failed to receive much attention. There seemed little appetite for facts to impede a good story.

The more intriguing and possibly more credible case for 'gang' involvement with violence and especially 'drug related violence' over the past decade are the 'Mexican gangs of US origin'. There is good evidence that gangs of 'Mexican origin' but US citizenship are key actors in the present *narco* violence. A 2008 report informed by the head of the Anti-Gang Division of the Los Angeles Police Department claims that the DTOs are deliberately hiring 'Mexicans' with US citizenship residing in California to conduct killings in Tijuana, Mexicali and Rosarito. The best known gang of this type is La Eme (the 'Mexican Mafia'), which has a power base in the California prison system and has close ties with other Latino gangs in the USA, including possibly Calle 18. It is even claimed that La Eme may be involved directly in the drugs trade in Baja California, either in partnership with the Arellano Félix DTO, or, given its weaker position since the mid-2000s, as its replacement.

The upsurge of drug-related killings in Ciudad Juárez has also been linked with 'Mexican' gangs, although here the relation with the border is more complicated. The Juárez DTO has used the Aztecas (Barrio Azteca) gang to fight 'turf wars' with the Mexicles (Mexica) gang acting for the Sinaloa 'Pacific' DTO, as well as the smaller Artistas Asesinos (Doble A). All three gangs were established in Texas sometime in the mid-1980s and again have a powerful position within the prison system. As with La Eme, the core membership of these gangs remains quite small—the Aztecas and Los Mexicles claim a combined membership of about 3,000 people—and only some of these members have the necessary skills to operate as a quasi-paramilitary organization; in the case of the Aztecas this has involved setting up a separate group called La Linea from 'black' elements of the police. Rather, these gangs seem to operate in co-ordination with, or through the hire of indigenous *pandilla*, giving these gangs a more permanent presence in Juárez and the north than is the case with La Eme or Logan Heights in California.

At the same time, the capacity of these gang organizations should not be exaggerated. They do not represent a serious threat to the Mexican state and certainly lack the organization, training and size to take on police and military units. Moreover, the 'fear of gangs' should not distract observers from asking more relevant analytical questions, not the least of which is 'how did Mexico become embroiled in drug-related violence'?

THE RISE OF THE *NARCO*

Mexico has had a long history of involvement in the production and trade of drugs. Unlike in previous decades, however, this involvement was little discussed and combating DTOs did not form a central part of government discourse or policy. Rather, as outlined further below, organized crime, including DTOs, were 'integrated' into a political pact that emphasized stability. This pact was kept away from public view and with a controlled press, single-party dominance of the electoral system and a combination of clientelism and (threat of) violence against dissent, the 'bargain' was not subject to much scrutiny inside or outside the system. Before 2000 Mexico did not have a 'narrative' around which to discuss the nation's relationship with drugs and DTOs. The breakdown of authoritarian control, together with the rise of democracy, enabled a change of political logic and a 'war on drugs' that provided a narrative.

To understand the rise of the DTO, we must appreciate changes to the commodity chains for drugs and to the relative importance of Mexico. Although the focus of attention has been the trade in cocaine, the earliest significant DTOs, dating from the 1960s and 1970s, were involved in the production and/or shipment of marijuana and black tar heroin, with Mexican DTOs supplying about one-third of all heroin and marijuana entering the USA by 1991. The shift to cocaine, from the late 1970s, was an extension of these operations and was already significant by the 1980s. In 1991 about 350 metric tons of cocaine were already passing through Mexico. Since then, cocaine has grown in relative importance to DTO operations, with current shipments through Mexico estimated at over 1,000 tons and worth perhaps as much as US $38,000m. However, it is the impact of cocaine on DTO business practices and relations with the state that must be understood in order to appreciate the path to 'war'.

The precursor to these changes was the development of relations between Colombian traffickers and the early Mexican DTOs during the 1970s, when it is alleged that Juan Ramón Matta Ballesteros, a Honduran national, linked Alberto Sicilia Falcón, a Cuban émigré and head of drugs-smuggling through Tijuana, to the Cali-based DTO of Benjamín Herrera Zuleta. Sicilia Falcón's operation was soon challenged by the emerging DTO of Miguel Angel Félix Gallardo, Rafael Caro Quintero and Ernesto Fonseca Carrillo, which began to link the Mexican states of Sinaloa, Sonora, Durango and Jalisco, becoming known as the Guadalajara DTO, and by the Gulf DTO of Juan García Abrego, which became involved with the Cali DTO from around the mid-1980s. Before their involvement with cocaine, these DTOs shipped marijuana and black tar heroin in one direction and took advantage of high tariffs to 'import' a variety of consumer goods in the other. The DTO structures were based on strong family links and ties to regions, restricted by relations with farms and intermediary suppliers, and dependent on specific border crossing-points where bribery could be arranged. Cocaine, however, would transform these thin networks into complex structures with transnational reach, more diversified business interests and, most important of all, modified DTO links with the state.

In the early 1980s US President Ronald Reagan launched a crackdown on Colombian narcotraffickers who were using smuggling routes through the Caribbean basin in order to distribute narcotics in Miami. Seeking to avoid the risks now associated with smuggling into Florida, Colombian cartels furthered existing links with Mexican mafia organizations in order to use routes through Mexico. This proved advantageous to the Colombians because it allowed them to circumvent Reagan's South Florida Task Force, while leaving Mexican cartel foot soldiers to run the risk of lengthy prison sentences in US gaols instead. As a result of their well-developed distribution networks and contacts north of the border, however, Mexican DTOs were increasingly able to negotiate with the Colombian cartels and to set prices on their own terms.

The Mexican DTOs offered their Colombian counterparts a number of advantages over the service provided by *transportistas* operating air or maritime routes from Peru, or through Venezuela and the Caribbean. In addition to air and maritime routes, both via the west coast and the Gulf of Mexico, Mexican DTOs could provide access to tested mechanisms for crossing the land border. Critically, Mexican DTOs could switch transit routes and means quickly according to the anti-drugs operations of either the Mexican or US state, and reduce risks by having products in transit for shorter periods. Above all, however, Mexico offered opportunities for net bulk access to US markets. The high value to weight ratio of cocaine made it worthwhile to maximize the number of shipments, but Mexican DTOs began to use larger shipments; although a single interdiction might lose millions of dollars, the value of the larger loads would more than compensate. Stockpiling drugs ready for large shipments became a key component of the Mexican model. Offering reliability, frequency and bulk access, the main DTOs could charge higher fees—as much as one-half of a shipment's value—as well as operate as 'price makers', using their capacity either to flood or restrict the market in the short term and increase profit margins.

Another contributory factor which allowed DTOs to expand was the US Central Intelligence Agency (CIA)'s strategy of employing Mexican traffickers to ship money and arms to the counter-revolutionary forces, or 'Contras', in Nicaragua, whom the Reagan Administration was covertly supporting in an effort to overthrow the recently elected revolutionary Sandinista Government. Following a measure adopted by the US Congress, which limited funds available to support the Contras, elements within the US Government made a pact with Mexican drugs-traffickers which in essence gave a number of them relatively unrestricted access to operate in US cities. Combined with the increased traffic of narcotics coming north from Colombia, this represented remarkable international business opportunities for organizations such as the Guadalajara cartel.

The arrangements between Mexican and Colombian DTOs have not remained stable over time. Mexican DTOs have tended to operate with a variety of Colombian DTOs. The Juárez DTO of Amado Carrillo Fuentes, for example, had strong links with Rodríguez Orejuela of Cali, as well as with the Ochoa brothers in Medellín, while Osiel Cárdenas, who took over the Gulf DTO from García Abrego, also built connections with Cali traffickers, despite being in competition with the Juárez DTO. More recently, it was revealed that, although in conflict with each other, both the Sinaloa and Beltrán Leyva DTOs (an off-shoot of the Sinaloa DTO and named after the five brothers who founded it) had developed and maintained ties with the Norte del Valle DTO of Colombia. DTOs fighting a lethal conflict in Mexico might be dealing with the same Colombian DTO and agents in the supply chain, and even co-operating under 'pacts' to do so. The modus operandi of Mexican DTOs is extremely fluid and largely driven by pragmatism.

Despite the perceived shift of power away from Colombian DTOs to their Mexican counterparts, the latter do not appear to have become involved with the refinement and shipping of cocaine out of Colombia, Peru and Bolivia. They have, however, diversified their operations and geographical presence in other ways, notably increasing their presence in Central America since the late 1990s. This strategy is logical for a number of reasons. First, the shift to cocaine allowed Mexican DTOs to extend their geographical reach from a local area to the region in order to secure imports. Expanding into Guatemala and Honduras has provided more opportunities to diversify drugs routes, particularly given the relative power of Mexican DTOs compared with those in both countries. Second, it seems likely that the Mexican DTOs identified Guatemalan and Honduran political structures as being susceptible to infiltration and corruption, especially in areas such as Petén and San Marcos in Guatemala. The regional presence of Mexican DTOs has been vital to their survival in the past five years, as the Mexican state has prosecuted a 'war'. It is now estimated that one-third of the drugs consignments controlled by the Mexican DTOs arrive into Guatemala and Honduras from where 'lieutenants' can decide whether to route through or around Mexico to get shipments into the USA.

Economic policies introduced and advanced in the 1980s and 1990s also had a major effect on the development of organized crime in Mexico. Perhaps the most significant of these was the North American Free Trade Agreement (NAFTA) signed by President Carlos Salinas, which, while providing very favourable investment opportunities to wealthy Mexican and international investors and corporations, had the effect of pushing more people into poverty. This, in turn, led to increased internal migration from rural areas to urban centres and contributed to growing numbers of Mexicans who sought refuge from economic misery by crossing into the USA in search of work. NAFTA exacerbated already widespread poverty, allowing DTOs to recruit to their ranks ever more desperate unemployed people who were willing to take risks. Although US President Bill Clinton increased funds to militarize the US–Mexico border in order to curb the exodus of undocumented migrants, NAFTA saw the development of an improved transportation infrastructure which allowed for increased freight—and therefore opportunities to smuggle contraband—heading north, a business opening that was not lost on expanding DTOs.

The rise of the *narcos* in Mexico was also aided by the complicity of the international banking sector, particularly from the 1980s and 1990s onwards. All DTOs share the problem of how to make illicit profits enter the legal economy. According to Antonio Maria Costa, former director of the UN Office on Drugs and Crime, major international banks in need of liquid assets actively seek out the profits of drugs-trafficking and organized crime. For some critics, this aspect should be fundamental in addressing the security crisis in Mexico, for so long as the Mexican and international banking sector profits handsomely from the proceeds of criminal activity, it will be impossible to counter the wave of violence for which DTOs are responsible (Buscaglia, 2013). One way to combat the power and influence of organized crime in Mexico, goes this argument, would be to begin prosecuting bankers who launder money for the cartels, a tactic which has been met with tremendous resistance by both the Mexican and US Governments. In 2010, although the US federal authorities fined Wachovia of the Wells Fargo group US $110m. following an investigation into the bank's laundering of money on behalf of Mexican DTOs, none of its employees went to gaol. Then, in 2012, the US Department of Justice fined HSBC, Europe's largest bank, for its repeated violations under US law of the Banking Secrecy Act, the Trading with the Enemy Act and the USA Patriot Act, and for its lucrative business partnership with the Sinaloa cartel. The HSBC fine of $1,900m. was the largest in banking history. None the less, while drug war initiatives in both the USA and Mexico see users and small dealers going to gaol for years and even decades, critics point to the contradiction that not one of the HSBC or Wachovia bankers received a custodial sentence.

THE CONTROL OF THE *NARCO*

Perhaps the most significant impact of DTOs' involvement in cocaine was the change it made to their relationships with the Mexican state. Alberto Sicilia Falcón later claimed that his DTO was protected by the Dirección Federal de Seguridad (DFS), the agency tasked from 1947 with ensuring the internal security of Mexico, which, in practice, meant the suppression of left-wing movements. Sicilia identified as his principal contact Miguel Nazar Haro, allegedly the head of a secret group called the White Brigade during the 'dirty war', DFS deputy director from 1978–82 and subsequently director. Nazar Haro was an important player in a close group of politicians headed by two key figures, Fernando Gutiérrez Barrios and Manuel Bartlett. Gutiérrez Barrios joined the DFS in 1952, becoming its director during 1964–70, before serving in a variety of elected posts, including as Governor of Veracruz (1986–88). Bartlett rose through the ranks of the PRI, becoming Secretary of the Interior in 1982–88. Crucially, despite shifts in ideology and personality during the final decades of its 70-year rule, which lasted until 2000, this *camarilla* (cabal) has always remained near the centre of power. Under the so-called 'new broom' of President Carlos Salinas (1988–94), Gutiérrez Barrios was appointed Secretary of the Interior and Bartlett Secretary of Public Education, before the latter became Governor of the state of Puebla. Nor has the *camarilla* disappeared with the death of Gutiérrez Barrios in 2000 and the decline of Bartlett, a federal senator (2000–06 and 2012–present): rather, it has recreated itself around another generation, headed by Manlio Fabio Beltrones, who has served as Under-Secretary of the Interior (1988–91), as Governor of Sonora (1991–97), and as a federal senator and deputy.

The key point is that under the tutelage of Gutiérrez Barrios the DFS became a 'state within a state', negotiating with DTOs and protecting the political system. For the most part, the arrangement established with DTOs was the same as that applied to groups involved in other forms of organized crime or to leading trade union officials: keep certain activities away from public scrutiny, do not become involved in politics and provide funds or favours when requested. DTOs were encouraged to divide Mexico into *plazas* (territories), within which organizations would avoid each other or co-operate. In return, the state offered the 'guarantee' of protection and sometimes more. In the mid-1980s, for example, the US Drug Enforcement Administration (DEA) discovered interior ministry and army personnel working at a 220-acre ranch in Chihuahua used for growing marijuana and owned by Rafael Caro Quintero. Some DTO heads were even issued with DFS identification cards by José Antonio Zorrilla Pérez, Nazar Haro's successor, making them all but 'untouchable' within the criminal justice system. The line between the state and the DTOs was even more blurred by kinship arrangements. When Rodolfo Sánchez Duarte, the son of the Sinaloa Governor, Leopoldo Sánchez Celis, was killed in 1990, allegedly on the orders of DTO head Héctor 'El Güero' Palma Salazar in retaliation for the killing of his wife and children at the behest of Miguel Angel Félix Gallardo, it was noted that Félix Gallardo was godfather to Rodolfo Sánchez. With these connections in place, the DTOs were alike to standard cartels.

The period from 1985 to about 1990 marked a critical juncture in state-DTO relations. At the time when Mexican DTO involvement in the trafficking of cocaine was growing, the mechanism to negotiate protection with the state shifted to rely less on the mediation of the security apparatus. The link would remain, but it would be the DTOs that increasingly controlled the arrangement. According to the DEA, four of the five Attorney-Generals that served during the administration of Carlos Salinas had links with DTOs, and the Procuraduría de Justicia Federal (PFJ, Judicial Police) and the successor to the DFS, the CISEN, were widely regarded as compromised. However, DTOs now felt able to make deals direct with secretaries of state, including, according to the DEA, those responsible for key portfolios such as transport and agriculture. The quid pro quo in these arrangements would not be loyalty protection but funding enrichment. Cash-rich DTOs used 'shell' companies and financed the acquisition of equity in privatized enterprises, as well as the enormous number of state concessions and infrastructure programmes. Seminal to this argument is the allegation that the President's brother, Raúl Salinas, developed business relations with García Abrego of the Gulf DTO, as well as with individuals accused of money-laundering for the DTO, notably the fugitive President of the Banco Unión, Carlos Cabal Peniche. Despite only receiving a government salary, Raúl Salinas had bank accounts and real estate worth hundreds of millions of US dollars. The change in state-DTO relations may have extended to the PRI's presidential candidate for the 1994 election, Luis Donaldo Colosio, who was murdered during the electoral campaign. Some years after the assassination, a senior source in the PRI claimed that the Tijuana DTO might have found out about an agreement made by Colosio's team to favour the Sinaloa DTO once in office.

Carlos Salinas's successor as President, Ernesto Zedillo (1994–2000), distanced his administration from Gutiérrez Barrios and Bartlett. Lacking a personal power base, his strategy was to rely on a balance of technocrats, mostly former secretaries of state and directors of agencies in the Salinas administration, and politicians linked with the Atlacomulco group. Headed by patriarch Carlos Hank González, this group had been engrained in the political structure of Mexico since the 1960s. Hank had served as Governor of the state of Mexico, Regent of Mexico City (akin to Mayor), Secretary of Tourism and Secretary of Agriculture. His power, however, extended to business interests in real estate, petrol stations, construction, an airline, shipping, sport and gambling, and banking in Mexico and the USA. These interests have been the subject of investigations in the USA by the DEA, the Federal Bureau of Investigation, the National Drug Intelligence Center and the Federal Reserve Board, which have also examined the role of Hank's children, most notoriously his eldest son, who also served one term as Mayor of Tijuana. It is possible that Hank had links with more than one DTO. Members of the Atlacomulco group rose to prominence during Zedillo's presidency: notably, Emilio Chuayffet, a former Governor of the state of Mexico, was appointed Secretary of the Interior, while Arturo Montiel served as a senior official at the Secretariat of State for the Interior and later as Governor of the state of Mexico. Roberto Madrazo, former Governor of Tabasco and a future presidential candidate for the PRI, was also a member of the group and a close ally of Manlio Fabio Beltrones, a protégé of Gutiérrez Barrios. Many doubted whether President Zedillo, commanding a fragile legitimacy, was able to keep in check powerful interest groups.

LOSING CONTROL: DEMOCRACY AND DRUGS

The PRI's loss of the presidency in 2000 to the candidate of the Partido Acción Nacional (PAN, National Action Party), Vicente Fox, was widely celebrated, but the aftermath of his election had serious implications for the DTOs. In one version of events, popular in Washington, 'drugs-related' violence is an unintended consequence of 'democracy', although this idea lacks analytical traction. There are four dimensions to the way in which democratization has changed state-DTO relations and been partly responsible for violence. First, the loss of electoral power for the PRI, and with it access to business opportunities and corruption channels, put pressure on lower level party officials who now lacked the means to maintain the loyalty of *matones* (thugs), in some cases integrated into police forces, which therefore threatened the careful management of crime. In the second half of the 1990s, at the same time as the PRI began to recognize its loss of power, people began to notice an increase in street crime, car theft and abduction. Crime, moreover, became less predictable and possibly more violent. Small-scale criminals would see opportunities for working for shippers and dealers or undertaking theft, extortion and kidnap at the behest of incipient DTOs that used organized crime to raise capital for involvement in the drugs trade.

Second, democracy increased the number of actors with whom DTOs had to deal, and who were, in turn, freer of central control. Previously, a mayor or governor would be closely monitored from the centre, reports from *madrinas* (informants) going back to the Secretariat of State for the Interior, the PRI and, if required, the President. If deemed necessary, action could be taken to restrain a politician who was making deals likely to attract scandal. The decline of the PRI meant that the monitoring system collapsed, although it has been suggested that President Vicente Fox would still receive reports from the provinces but gave them little attention.

Third, democracy raised the price for political co-operation. Politicians were now in a position to make deals with one DTO rather than another, offering protection of *plazas* during their term of office. Accusations were made in this regard against former Governors such as Francisco Labastida (Sinaloa) and Manlio Fabio Beltrones, while in May 2010 Mario Villanueva, Governor of Quintana Roo in 1993–99, became the first former Governor to be extradited to the USA on charges of illicit gain from the drugs trade. Villanueva had been Mayor of Cancún, a city synonymous with money-laundering and where five of the last seven mayors have been arrested for connections with DTOs.

The case of Cancún's recent Mayor, Gregorio Sánchez, illustrates the fourth dimension, known as *narco-democracia* ('narco-democracy'). Sánchez was arrested in May 2010, shortly before elections to the governorship of Quintana Roo, for which he was the candidate of the Partido de la Revolución Democrática (PRD, Party of the Democratic Revolution) and ahead in the polls. The judge who issued the arrest warrant had been involved in the arrests in 2009 of 10 mayors in the state of Michoacán, all from the PRD and PRI, on the eve of elections. Charges were subsequently withdrawn, fuelling the suspicion that an association with drugs was being used as 'mud' to 'dirty' opposition candidates and justify the presence of the army during elections. One interesting response from the PRI has been a sustained effort to position itself as the party of 'stability', a thinly veiled code in the minds of many for a return to negotiated pacts with DTOs in return for less bloodshed. Hence, during the July 2009 mid-term congressional elections, the July 2010 gubernatorial polls and the 2012 presidential campaign PRI candidates spoke of continuing the fight against organized crime but with 'adjustments'.

Since President Peña Nieto took office, there has been little indication that government policy represents a departure from that of his predecessor. While there have been rhetorical shifts and a series of public relations campaigns aimed at winning back a disillusioned public, the army continues to occupy many areas and human rights violations and homicides continue unabated. Similarly, while Peña Nieto has achieved a number of public relations triumphs—not least the arrest in February 2014 of one of the world's most wanted men, Joaquín 'El Chapo' Guzmán Loera, leader of the Sinaloa cartel—picking off *capos* and kingpins does not address the structural problems that allowed for the growth of organized crime in Mexico.

Peña Nieto's electoral campaign emphasized strengthening the state and economy via further neo-liberal reforms. Nevertheless, the PRI Government is increasingly vulnerable to dissent, challenge and criticism. At the same time as Western media and élites were celebrating Peña Nieto as a modernizer unafraid to make unpopular but necessary reforms, groups of armed peasant vigilantes, or *autodefensas*, in rural areas (as in the state of Michoacán) began to form apparently independently in a direct challenge to the policies of federal government. These groups stated that they were taking the law into their own hands precisely because the authorities were either incapable of, or unwilling to, protect civilians from the Caballeros Templarios (Knights Templar) cartel. Almost immediately, in what was a tremendous embarrassment to Peña Nieto's Government, it appeared that groups of armed civilians were having more success in combating organized crime in a matter of weeks than the Government had achieved in its long-term 'war on drugs'.

One of the immediate reactions by the authorities in January 2014 was to send thousands more troops to Michoacán in order to disarm the vigilante *autodefensas*. This had the immediate effect of alienating even further a population already exhausted by, and mistrustful of, the Government's security policy. The newly arrived troops, who occupied the town of Nueva Italia, for example, failed to arrest any leaders of the Caballeros Templarios, instead shooting and killing four unarmed civilians, one of whom was an 11-year-old girl. The army also failed to prevent the cartel from intimidating local businesses, which, too afraid to challenge the Templarios, remained closed, despite the ostensible protection offered by federal government. In a blatant display of irreverence towards centralized political power and to remind everyone who was really in charge, the cartel firebombed a pharmacy within earshot of the military cordon.

STATE REFORM AND THE 'WAR ON DRUGS'

The DTOs emerged from a radical restructuring of politics and the state; they did not suddenly expand to take on a stable state. As the PAN replaced the PRI in government, accommodating the DTOs in a new political bargain was impossible. President Vicente Fox and his successor from December 2006, Felipe Calderón (also of the PAN), headed administrations that lacked the means and motivation to broker deals with the DTOs. However, Fox and Calderón had to control the DTOs without the guaranteed loyalty of agencies within the state, notably those involved with intelligence-gathering, policing and criminal prosecution. Both were thus confronted with the problem of having to conduct a profound reform of the state as part of the 'war on drugs', rather than in preparation for such a conflict.

A reform of the police was critical. Municipal and state police forces had long been criticized for their lack of professional training and co-ordination, as well as complicity with corruption. Reforming the municipal police in all 2,438 municipalities, many of which were controlled by mayors from opposition parties, was a daunting task. Instead, the National Programme for the Control of Drugs 2000–06 envisaged the use of federal police agents and the army in conventional policing roles. In 2005 Operation Secure Mexico began in the states of Tamaulipas, Sinaloa and Baja California, with army units and federal agents replacing municipal police. The move received a hostile reaction in Nuevo Laredo, Tamaulipas, when federal agents were shot at by municipal police before the 700-strong force was made to stand down. This approach continued under Calderón, who deployed federal police and the army to Tijuana, Baja California, removing around 2,300 local officers from duty. More subtly, Calderón also extended an approach adopted by President Zedillo by installing military officers in police roles, allocating senior posts to those with experience of anti-drugs operations. The appointment in 2008 of Gen. Javier del Real Magallanes, a former chief of the intelligence section of the armed forces and head of anti-drugs operations for northeast Mexico, as Under-Secretary of Police Strategy and Intelligence in the Secretariat for Public Security was regarded as particularly significant.

While relying on federal agencies, both Fox and Calderón had to cope with the knowledge that these same forces were compromised by links with DTOs. In a move that was more than a little suggestive of political expediency, six months after taking office President Calderón removed 284 federal police commanders, including the commanders of federal police agencies in all 31 states and the Federal District of Mexico, on the grounds of corruption. Unlike at the local level, nationally neither Fox nor Calderón had much option but to undertake reform. Fox created the Secretariat of State for Public Security to improve co-ordination between the security and justice systems, and a new federal agency for criminal investigation, the Agencia Federal de Investigación (AFI), to replace the much discredited PJF. Under Calderón, the powers of the federal agencies were expanded, with provision made for the use of wire-taps, searches without a warrant and the confiscation of property from people convicted of serious crime. Calderón also sought to co-ordinate efforts by placing the public security police (Policía Federal Preventiva, PFP) and the AFI under a single command. In 2005, however, a report by the office of the Attorney-General had indicated that 1,500 of 7,000 AFI agents were under investigation for criminal activity and that 457 were facing charges, including for the illegal detention and disappearance of DTO members. In 2009 Calderón was forced to replace the AFI with a 'new' federal police agency, the Policía Federal Ministerial, although it subsequently recruited former AFI personnel, and the PFP became the Policía Federal. New officers are trained at a special college in San Luis Potosí, with US advisers, screened for drugs use, and are subject to background financial checks and obliged to take polygraph tests at regular intervals.

In the circumstances, it is not surprising that President Calderón made extensive use of the military. What marked the Calderón approach as different from those of his predecessors, however, was the scale of deployment and the almost constant mobilization of units in parts of the country. Less than two weeks after taking office, Calderón launched Operation Michoacán, involving agents from the AFI, 5,300 troops and special forces. By 2009 48,750 army personnel were assigned to more than 20 anti-drugs operations. During the administration approximately one-third of the army was on drugs-related duty at any time, with a 2008 study by the Secretary of National Defence predicting that mobilization might need to be long-term. This is not a scenario that pleased all senior officers. Concerns have been expressed at the use of the military for internal security, at problems of desertion and at the rising number of human rights cases levelled at the army.

WINNING THE WAR?

In 2009 President Felipe Calderón declared that 'organized crime is in search of territorial control, there will be a war with no quarter given because there is no possibility of living with the drugs cartel (*el narco*). There is no turning back; it is them or us.' If the 'war on drugs' was about 'them or us', it is useful to ask which side has won? Most assessments are ambivalent. First, considering the number of people detained on drugs-related charges, this figure has amounted to about 12,000 per year between 2000 and 2006, but rose to 36,332 arrests in 2009. The Calderón Government argued that these arrests represented a significant proportion of DTO membership and disrupted operations. Critics suggested that most of those apprehended were small-scale dealers or shippers, rather than high-level bosses or those involved in money-laundering. Not for nothing are DTO leaders known colloquially as *cucarachas* (cockroaches), able to scuttle away from trouble. Such criticism has been challenged by the killing or arrest of leading DTO figures, including most prominent members of the Beltrán Leyva DTO, Nazario 'El Chayo' Moreno, founder of La Familia, Teodoro 'El Teo' García Simental of Tijuana DTO, Felipe Cabrera Sarabia of Sinaloa DTO, Marcos Jesus Hernandez Rodriguez ('El Chilango'), Iván Velázquez Caballero ('El Talibán'), Miguel Ángel Treviño Morales of the Zetas and Joaquín 'El Chapo' Guzmán, leader of the Sinaloa cartel. However, even the impact of high-profile arrests has probably been short-term. A DEA poster from a few years ago proclaimed successes against the Tijuana DTO, with 'arrested' stamped over photographs of seven of the nine leading members, including Javier and Eduardo Arellano Félix. Shortly afterwards a new poster was issued with photographs of a different 10 'most wanted' members of the organization.

One significant achievement concerns extradition. Until 2000 Mexico had only ever permitted the extradition of six citizens to the USA for crimes that might bring the death penalty, leaving DTO heads such as Miguel Angel Félix Gallardo, Rafael Caro Quintero and Osiel Cárdenas the opportunity to manage their organizations from Mexican prisons. In late 2005, however, the Mexican Supreme Court overturned a prohibition on extraditing fugitives who could face the death penalty. Extraditions quickly followed: 41 in 2005, reaching 107 in 2009. DTO leaders dislike prison life in the USA, as they are unable to see family, to communicate with lieutenants or to arrange the protection of fellow DTO inmates. Retribution has been dramatic. Although denied as being sabotage, an aeroplane crash in Mexico City in November 2008, in which the Secretary of the Interior, Juan Camilo Mouriño, and all others on board were killed, is claimed by an informed source to have been the work of DTOs. Also in the aircraft was José Luis Santiago Vasconcelos, formerly Assistant Attorney-General for International Affairs and Assistant Attorney-General at the federal agency charged with investigating organized crime, who was responsible for arranging the extradition of 15 major traffickers in January 2006.

A second gauge relates to the interdiction of drugs or their means of production in Mexico. The Calderón Government claimed that in the first years of the 'war' 33,019 farms for the cultivation of opium poppy were seized and 777 laboratories for processing cocaine and/or methamphetamine were destroyed. The numbers represent an increase on previous years, but critics have noted the definitional difficulties with the description 'farms' and the fact that laboratories can be reassembled at other locations within days. Between 2006 and 2010 the Mexican military claimed to have seized 22 metric tons of cocaine, which would represent about 3% of the total quantity being transported through Mexico to the USA, as well as 337 kg of opium paste and 233 kg of heroin. Although DEA and police reports in the USA have indicated an increase in street prices for cocaine, suggesting difficulties of supply, this may be due to production difficulties in Colombia. Indeed, the interdiction of cocaine has declined on the US side by almost one-half since 2006, whereas that of heroin has trebled since 2005. This might support the US Department of Justice's claim, in its report National Drug Threat Assessment 2010, that Mexican DTOs may be switching back to heroin as the export of choice. Whether this assessment is accurate, or justifies being considered a success, is difficult to judge. There is no evidence that DTO revenues have collapsed due to the 'war'.

A third indicator relates to claims that the increased level of 'drugs-related' violence is the result of DTO infighting (as arrests and interdiction mount) or inter-DTO conflicts during which the DTOs might fight each other to a standstill. Both theories have some merit. Although a process that began during the 1990s, when pacts with the state broke down, it seems as if the DTOs have become more violent both against the state and against other DTOs as a means to preserve territorial control and to extend into zones controlled by others. To these ends, the 'war' has accelerated and diversified the emergence of new violent actors. First, several paramilitary groups, either linked with one DTO or acting as mercenaries, have been established. The best known of these are the Zetas, formed by Arturo Guzmán Decena from a group of around 30 members of the air unit of the special forces, supported with recruitment from Guatemalan special forces (*Kaibiles*). Initially under the command of the Gulf DTO, the Zetas used their military training to mount sophisticated and ruthless attacks against opponents. In counterpart, the Negros and Pelones have operated on behalf of the Sinaloa DTO, most famously in the attempted takeover of Nuevo Laredo in 2005, although the Negros are alleged to have shifted allegiance to the Beltrán Leyva DTO until its relative demise, or become independent

under the direction of Edgar Valdez Villareal (known as La Barbie) before his arrest in August 2010.

The argument that increasing levels of violence indicate the break-up of the DTOs requires some caution. A brief history of DTOs reveals a propensity to fragment and realign. In the 1990s the Guadalajara DTO divided into the Tijuana and Sinaloa DTOs, after which the Sinaloa DTO headed by Joaquín 'El Chapo' Guzmán split, with the Beltrán Leyva brothers forming their own DTO. The Beltrán Leyva DTO subsequently associated with the Juárez and Tijuana DTOs, although these were in conflict, and grew rapidly in just two years until elder brother Arturo was killed in December 2009. The Juárez DTO survived the death of Amado Carrillo Fuentes in 1997, in part through maintaining a family line, as well as through Juan José Esparragoza Moreno's use of his Guadalajara DTO connections to broker a pact with the Sinaloa DTO and to draw upon support from the Caro Quintero Sonora DTO, which reformed around brothers Miguel and Jorge after lead figure Rafael was extradited to the USA. The arrangement between the Juárez, Sinaloa and Sonora DTOs is sometimes referred to as The Federation. The massive upsurge in murder in Ciudad Juárez from 2007, however, was largely attributed to the attempt by the Sinaloa DTO to take the city from the Juárez DTO. An equally fragile arrangement may have been negotiated by Esparragoza between the Juárez DTO and the Zetas, the latter having seemed to gain some control over the Gulf DTO, with reports suggesting that in 2008–09 the Zetas might have supplanted Osiel Cárdenas, and then splitting from the Gulf DTO and becoming its rival. Subsequent reports signalled the dissolution of the Zetas, as original members were killed or captured, only for indications in 2010 to suggest a split in the organization, with a new group, the New Zetas Organization, emerging, acting as both a paramilitary group and a DTO, and with links to a revived Beltrán Leyva DTO.

Finally, the Tijuana DTO declined after the arrests of Benjamín and Eduardo Arellano Félix and the 2002 death of Ramón Arellano Félix, but subsequently reappeared, despite having fewer links with other organizations. After a power battle between Eduardo, Javier, Francisco and Enedina Arellano Félix, Eduardo and Enedina emerged as the new heads of the DTO, and when Javier and Eduardo were arrested, Enedina took control, passing responsibilities to her son, Luis Fernando Sánchez Arellano. A 2008 split with former lieutenant Teodoro García Simenthal did not weaken the Tijuana DTO so much as necessitate the promotion of cell leaders. García Simenthal's arrest in January 2010 removed a rival who had formed links with another new and important DTO, Familia Michoacana, which has attempted to consolidate control of Michoacán and Guerrero, supported initially by the Gulf DTO and Zetas, although currently a rival of the latter, amid rumours of links to the Sinaloa DTO. The arrest of 'El Chapo' Guzmán, leader of the Sinaloa cartel, in February 2014 appeared to be a major victory in the war on the *narcos* for the Government of Peña Nieto. Nevertheless, although 'El Chapo' was Mexico's most powerful *capo*, his detention will probably not lead to any significant shifts in how DTOs operate. Although DTOs are intensely competitive organizations, they are not single, hierarchical structures, but controlled, complex organizations, bonded around family links and loose associations. Hence, claims about the actual number of DTOs vary wildly, from the figure of 30 provided by the DEA, to over 130 according to the Mexican Attorney-General's office. Breaking up one DTO will not signal a zero-sum demise but possibilities for parts to re-form, or groups to sell their services to others.

CONCLUSION

The 'war on drugs' declared by President Calderón in 2006 added a narrative thread to a conflict that had been under way for more than a decade, and which has its origins in the 1980s. Then, a shift by DTOs into cocaine necessitated changes to their organization and practice, which coincided with political changes that resulted in a more complicated state structure. As the PRI lost its apparently hegemonic grip on politics, as a group of politicians tied to the state security apparatus competed with politicians with business interests, as the state apparatus itself decentralized and the media became less controlled, so a space opened for DTOs to become more autonomous. More and larger DTOs emerged, although not to challenge the state, as interests remained largely coterminous. Beholden to groups in the PRI for stability, President Zedillo had limited scope to act decisively against the DTOs. By contrast, his successors had even less room for manoeuvre. On assuming the presidency in December 2006, Calderón inherited a country in which even in the arenas of 'public security' the Government lacked a nationwide reach, and confidence in the security institutions, especially the police, prosecutors' offices and intelligence agencies, was extremely limited. His successor, Enrique Peña Nieto, despite rhetorical differences, has done little of substance to change the overall nature of the Government's security strategy, relying on a heavy-handed military approach to the crisis.

In setting out to conduct a 'war' on the DTOs the Mexican Government took a high-risk decision. The price of failure would not be a spiral of drugs-related violence, which was an inevitable part of the process it has since been claimed with some justification. Rather, the threat was that a state that was not failing—the Mexican Government was reasonably effective at conduct of foreign affairs, economic policy (notwithstanding a drug economy equivalent to about 8% of GDP largely beyond its control), and ran extensive social programmes—might do so. In that scenario, alarmist predictions, such as those posited by Sullivan and Elkus (2008), claimed that 'A lawless Mexico will be a perfect staging ground for terrorists seeking to operate in North America. American policy-makers must act to protect our southern flank.' The view was shared by a range of private security consultancies and blogs, which endorsed the thesis that 'third-phase cartels', no longer limited to regional power bases, might associate with 'third-generation gangs' that have shifted from turf-based affiliations to transnational networks, with the potential to conduct 'fourth generation warfare'. The scenario predicted DTOs or transnational gangs in the employ of terrorist or anticapitalist groups looking to extend their cause.

For the US Government, Mexico has risen up the security agenda, and inter-agency co-operation between the USA and Mexico has increased substantially (Shirk, 2011). As recently as 2007, Mexico ranked 12th on the recipient list for funding through US foreign operations programmes. Mexico was deemed capable of financing its own anti-DTO initiatives and to require only occasional technical assistance and training in counter-insurgency measures. That view has changed. In 2010 it was rumoured that US Joint Special Operations Command had already approved a decision for Special Forces to operate covertly in Mexico to capture or eliminate DTO 'kingpins'. The former US Secretary of Homeland Security, Michael Chertoff, even seemed to reveal that the Government had taken precautionary steps in the event of the Mexican Government losing the 'war' when he revealed the existence of a 'contingency plan for border violence, so if we did get a significant spillover, we have a surge—if I may use that word—capability'.

For the average Mexican, the wider issues with DTOs and regional geopolitical crises seem far beyond daily concerns. A shoot-out in a shopping mall, the presence of army checkpoints on the highway and the almost daily body count on television are what matters. The electoral campaign of President Peña Nieto tapped into people's concerns with crime and violence as it affects them. The implicit promise of the campaign was that Peña Nieto—from Atlacomulco—would return Mexico to a period of 'stability'. The President has toned down the rhetoric of 'war', but there seems no evidence at present that he or factions within the PRI actually intend to return to pacts and bargains with the DTOs. In reality, circumstances have changed too much. Nevertheless, the challenge will be to deliver security on the street.

BIBLIOGRAPHIC REFERENCES

Buscaglia, E. *Vacíos de poder en México*. Mexico, DF, Debate, 2013.

Castillo Berthier, H., and Jones, G. A. 'Mean Streets: Gangs, Violence and Daily Life in Mexico', in Jones, G. A., and Rodgers, D. (Eds) *Youth Violence in Latin America: Gangs and Juvenile Justice in Perspective*. New York, PalgraveMacmillan, 2009: pp. 289–315.

Cockburn, A., and Clair, J. *Whiteout: The CIA, Drugs and the Press*. London, Verso, 1999.

Gootenburg, P. 'Cocaine's Long March North, 1900–2010', in *Latin American Politics and Society*. Miami, FL, University of Miami, 2012. Vol. 54, No. 1, pp. 159–180.

Human Rights Watch, *Mexico's Disappeared. The Enduring Cost of a Crisis Ignored*. New York, HRI, 2013.

Jones, G. A. 'Hecho en Mexico: gangs and public security over time, and now', in Rodgers, D., and Hazen, J. (Eds) *Global Gangs*. Minneapolis, MN, University of Minnesota Press, 2013.

Shirk, D. A. 'The Drug War in Mexico: Confronting a Shared Threat', *Special Report No 60*. New York, Council on Foreign Relations, March 2011.

Sullivan, J. P., and Elkus, A. 'State of Siege: Mexico's Criminal Insurgency'. smallwarsjournal.com (accessed 21 May 2010). Bethesda, MD, Small Wars Foundation, 2008.

Velasco, J. L. *Insurgency, Authoritarianism, and Drug Trafficking in Mexico's Democratization*. London, Routledge, 2012.

Watt, P., and Zepeda, R. *Drug War Mexico. Politics, Violence and Neoliberalism in the New Narcoeconomy*. London, Zed Books, 2012.

NATURAL HAZARDS IN THE CARIBBEAN

MARK WILSON

The small economies of the Caribbean islands, along with the mainland countries of Belize, Guyana and Suriname which share the islands' historical and cultural background, suffer from a number of economic and physical risks that are intensified by their lack of scale. These economies are of necessity skewed towards a small number of productive sectors, principally tourism, minerals and financial services, which are vulnerable to swings in international demand and commodity prices. At the same time, a single natural hazard event may affect the entire national territory. In larger mainland economies, by contrast, a single productive sector is less likely to play a dominant role, while natural hazard events generally affect a small percentage of the overall area, allowing the provision of support from unaffected regions, and leaving the macroeconomy broadly intact. However, when assessing smaller economies, donor organizations and risk assessment agencies remain likely in many cases to treat natural hazards as of secondary interest, maintaining their usual focus on macroeconomic risks; this can prove unwise, as a major earthquake, volcanic eruption or hurricane can cause damage equivalent to or larger than the entire annual gross domestic product (GDP) of a small economy, negating significant investments and social progress, and with consequences extending over years or even decades.

Within the Caribbean, the major risks are from geological hazards, principally earthquakes and volcanic eruptions, and from climatic hazards, of which the most dramatic are hurricanes, but with a risk also of significant disruption from tropical storms, floods and droughts. In both categories, minor events are relatively common, with major events less frequent but significantly more damaging, while the risk of climatic hazards is expected to increase over the present century as a result of climate change.

GEOLOGICAL RISKS

The Caribbean islands, along with northern Venezuela and Colombia as well as Central America, lie close to the boundaries of the Caribbean plate. This puts them at risk from volcanoes and earthquakes. There is an earthquake risk associated with all boundaries of the Caribbean plate. However, volcanic risk is more localized, and is associated with the Windward and Leeward Islands close to the eastern plate margin, where the Caribbean plate converges with the North American and South American plates, and with the western part of Central America, where the Caribbean plate converges with the Cocos plate underlying the adjacent portion of the Pacific Ocean. There is also some risk from tsunamis in most coastal areas.

EARTHQUAKE RISKS

A number of organizations maintain a network of seismic stations which monitor earthquake activity and share information. In the eastern Caribbean, for example, the Seismic Research Centre of the University of the West Indies, based in Trinidad, operates more than 50 seismic stations in the English-speaking islands, while other stations are maintained by national organizations in Venezuela, the French Caribbean, and the islands of the former Netherlands Antilles, as well as by the Montserrat Volcano Observatory. Islands such as Dominica and Martinique have as many as 14 operating stations.

Minor earthquakes are extremely frequent, and are not generally felt or noticed by humans, but release strain at plate boundaries with frequent small displacements. In islands such as Trinidad, somewhat larger events occur several times a year, and are noticeable; however, they do not generally cause structural damage or loss of life.

Two major earthquakes have caused devastating damage in the Caribbean islands since 1900; the Kingston earthquake in Jamaica in 1907, and the earthquake that devastated the Haitian capital, Port-au-Prince, in 2010. Both were associated with the Enriquillo-Plantain Garden fault, which lies approximately parallel to the northern boundary of the Caribbean plate. The total relative movement along this plate boundary averages close to 20 mm annually, of which 7 mm is accommodated by the Enriquillo-Plantain Garden fault. However, until 2010 there had been little movement along the Hispaniola section of the fault for more than 200 years, allowing stresses to build up that were released on 12 January of that year, with a sudden movement of close to 1.8 m. The Haitian 2010 earthquake was not particularly powerful: worldwide, there were 20 tremors of at least equal force in the following 12 months. However, it was particularly destructive for several reasons:

It was centred on a point just 25 km west of the city centre, rather than in a sparsely inhabited rural area.

It was relatively shallow, with a focus 13 km below the surface.

Port-au-Prince is built largely on unconsolidated rocks, which become unstable and shake violently during a major earthquake.

Haiti had no building code. Many structures in Port-au-Prince were badly built and unable to withstand an earthquake shock.

There was little public preparedness or contingency planning.

There is no accurate total of deaths or damage caused; estimates include figures of 220,000 dead and damage of US $8,000m., which would be close to 125% of annual GDP. Damage was severe in areas such as the suburb of Delmas, where migrant remittances and other resources had allowed the construction of concrete structures of several stories which collapsed during the earthquake, in many cases killing their occupants.

By comparison, an earthquake in Chile one month later, in February 2010, released approximately 500 times as much geological energy as the Haitian earthquake, but caused just 562 deaths, and, when measured in financial terms, slightly less damage, which in Chile's larger economy was equivalent to perhaps 4% of GDP.

The time, location and magnitude of earthquakes cannot be predicted. However, areas that are at risk can be mapped and differentiated. The US Geological Service has prepared probabilistic hazard maps for Puerto Rico and the US Virgin Islands, showing, for example, areas with a 10% probability of an earthquake exceeding a certain force within the next 50 years. Similar maps have been published by other organizations for areas within the Caribbean. In more general terms, it is possible to identify areas where stresses have accumulated for some years, and where there is therefore a strong chance of a powerful earthquake within the coming decades; the island of Trinidad has been mentioned in this context.

In order to reduce the risk of loss of life and financial damage, the most promising approaches appear to be ensuring that new structures are built to earthquake-resistant standards; avoiding construction, where possible, on recent marine deposits and other areas at risk from liquefaction; and maintaining a high level of public awareness and preparedness regarding appropriate safety procedures and precautions. However, the first two of these appear difficult to achieve, as the legal, administrative and enforcement framework for development control in most Caribbean countries is relatively weak.

Tsunami risks are comparatively low in the Caribbean, as the nature of the surrounding plate boundaries is, by comparison with the circum-Pacific region, less conducive to the type of shock that generates large waves. However, coastal regions are exposed to some degree of risk. There is also a perceptible risk that a very large landslide event outside the region, for example in the Canary Islands, could generate a 'mega-tsunami' large enough to affect the islands of the Caribbean and the coastline of the Guianas.

VOLCANIC RISKS

In the eastern Caribbean, there are 16 volcanic centres that have been active in the Holocene period (since the most recent ice age), distributed along a chain of islands running from Grenada in the south to Saba in the north, and including the submarine volcano of Kick 'Em Jenny to the north of Grenada. Larger islands have more than one centre; indeed, Dominica has five that have been active in the Holocene, as well as several earlier centres. In various islands, volcanic centres were given the name Soufrière in these areas by early French settlers, as there were surface deposits of sulphur. Most appear quiet to the casual observer, are covered with rainforest or other mature vegetation, and have not erupted during the five centuries since first European contact. However, appearances can be deceptive. There was, for example, no obvious indication before 1992 that Montserrat was more at risk than its neighbours. Other islands somewhat to the east, such as Barbados, are either not volcanic in origin or have not been active for an extended geological period, and are not therefore at risk.

There have been major eruptions in four eastern Caribbean islands since 1900. Mont Pelée on Martinique erupted in 1902 and 1929; on the first occasion, the town of St Pierre was destroyed, with approximately 30,000 killed. Soufrière on St Vincent erupted also in 1902, and again in 1979, on the first occasion with close to 1,600 deaths. The Guadeloupe Soufrière erupted in 1976, but with no loss of life. Most recently, the Soufrière Hills on the island of Montserrat erupted in 1995, and have remained active since; there have been around 20 deaths, and the southern two-thirds of the island was evacuated.

The case of Montserrat highlights the extreme nature of volcanic hazards and their destructive impact on a small island. In general, even the most powerful hurricanes and earthquakes leave a significant proportion of structures intact, with an immediate start to reconstruction and full recovery in most cases within months or years. In Montserrat, by contrast, the south of the island was evacuated twice in 1995 and has been continuously empty since 1996. Most structures have been buried by up to 12 m of volcanic ash, irrespective of structural and design standards, and continuing risks have ruled out any significant reconstruction while the volcano remains active. At its low point in 1998, the island retained less than one-quarter of its former population, with most moving to neighbouring islands such as Antigua, to the United Kingdom, the USA or elsewhere. Among the options considered by the British Government at that time was a full evacuation of the island. However, this was rejected, in part because of the cost of retaining an effective security presence, which would be needed for counter-narcotics and other security reasons. With volcanic risks in the north of island limited to light or moderate ashfalls, and a proportion of the island's inhabitants keen to stay, the decision was taken to establish infrastructure and support services to maintain a viable community there. A new airport, port, housing, government headquarters, electricity generating station, schools and other facilities were required, with the capital cost met mainly by UK grants and other donor sources. By 2012 the population had reached 42.5% of its former level, but public sector construction remained the dominant sector of the small economy, with other activities very weakly developed. Most agricultural land and all significant manufacturing had been in the south. There were efforts to stimulate tourism, with the volcano as an attraction for short stays, which met limited success. There is also a very small 'offshore' financial sector. From 2005, volcanic ash was quarried for export to neighbouring islands, where it was used in construction; from 2012, this material was exported from the port of Plymouth, the former capital.

In contrast to earthquakes, volcanic eruptions can to some extent be predicted, with the aid of the region's continuously recorded seismic network. Characteristic swarms of small earthquakes over a period of months or years may indicate the movement of magma (molten rock) towards the surface. Eighteen of these swarms were recorded in Montserrat from 1992 until the start of the eruption in June 1995. However, earthquake swarms are not necessarily followed by a volcanic eruption; this was the case with an intense swarm recorded in Dominica from 1998 to early 2000 and associated with the Plat Pays and Anglais volcanic centres. Earthquake swarms do, none the less, indicate an increased volcanic hazard, and a need for more intensive monitoring. If eruptive activity starts, residents under threat will be evacuated, greatly reducing the chance of casualties, although some of those within the danger zone will be reluctant to comply with advice or instructions. The University of the West Indies Seismic Research Centre has published a Volcanic Hazard Atlas, with maps showing areas in the eastern Caribbean islands that are at risk from ashfalls, pyroclastic flows and other threats. The areas shown form a significant proportion of the islands covered, and in some, such as Dominica, include the capital. It is not therefore possible to limit new residential, tourist or commercial development to areas outside the hazard zones. In some of the smaller islands, such as Nevis, the entire territory would be under severe threat in the case of an eruption on the scale of Montserrat's, with no potential safe zone. In the broadest terms, some observers have talked of a 25% probability of a further major eruption within the eastern Caribbean over a period of 25 years.

More positively, the existence of masses of hot rock relatively close to the surface in several eastern Caribbean islands raises the possibility of geothermal generation of electric power. The La Bouillante geothermal plant in Guadeloupe provides some 10% of the island's power needs. Test drilling in 2012 to investigate the possibilities for geothermal power in Dominica indicated that enough energy could be produced to supply much of the island's demand, with a surplus for export to Martinique and Guadeloupe. Investigations of geothermal potential were also in progress on Montserrat, Nevis and other islands.

HURRICANES AND TROPICAL STORMS

Hurricanes and tropical storms are far more frequent than significant earthquakes or volcanic eruptions, and may affect almost any part of the Caribbean and neighbouring tropical North Atlantic (although areas to the south of Trinidad are not at risk because they are too close to the equator for revolving storms to develop). Storm development is possible over warm seas, with a surface temperature of at least 27°C, and is most common during the 'hurricane season', which runs from June to November. However, storms are possible outside this period and have indeed started at least once in every month of the year. Based on the long-term average, there are 11 tropical storms (at least 63 km/h, with a name assigned alphabetically) each year in the Atlantic and Caribbean, of which six develop into hurricanes (of at least 119 km/h), and three into powerful hurricanes reaching Category Three (of five) on the Saffir-Simpson scale (at least 178 km/h). In general, the destructive power of the wind varies with the square of the wind speed. A large number of storms and hurricanes pass entirely over water bodies, but a significant number make landfall, either in the Caribbean or on the North American mainland.

Tropical storms and hurricanes, and weather systems that could become storms, are closely tracked by the US National Hurricane Centre in Miami and national meteorological services, and a number of computer models developed by international agencies are used to predict the expected track and strength. As a result, storm and hurricane watches and more definite warnings are issued for areas on or close to predicted tracks, while other data such as satellite images are readily available on the internet for public information. The level of public information on hurricane preparedness is relatively high, the nature of hazards is fairly well understood, and structures are in general more robust than in the early 20th century. For these reasons, the risk of loss of life from most hurricanes is now fairly low, in comparison with their historic counterparts, such as the 1780 hurricane which is believed to have caused at least 20,000 deaths in Martinique and elsewhere. However, a small number of hurricanes do cause significant loss of life, both from shipwrecks and from flooding and landslides in land areas. During Hurricane Mitch in 1998, for example, a 30-member crew was lost when an 88-m cruise ship, the *Fantome*, capsized off the coast of Central America (the passengers had been left on shore). Mitch also caused exceptional rainfall at some distance from the storm centre, over

Honduras and Nicaragua, where up to 9,000 were killed and up to 500,000 left homeless by landslides. The number of deaths does not necessarily bear a direct relation to the strength of the storm. Hurricane Ivan, an exceptionally strong Category Five storm, caused an estimated 96 deaths in the Caribbean and the US mainland in 2004. In the same year, Hurricane Jeanne passed north of Haiti as a tropical storm, but brought heavy rainfall (up to 325 mm) and severe flooding which left some 3,000 dead.

Even where loss of life is comparatively low, hurricanes may cause very significant economic damage, particularly in a small island where the entire national territory is affected. Hurricane Ivan was at Category Four strength when it hit Grenada; total damage was estimated at US $815m., an amount then equivalent to more than twice the island's annual GDP. A high proportion of houses—more than 80% according to some estimates—suffered some degree of damage, with many losing their roofs. Only 300 of the island's 1,700 hotel rooms remained usable. Of the nutmeg trees which supplied the main export crop, 90% were damaged or destroyed. Water supply, telecommunications, electricity supply and other public services were out of commission or severely disrupted for periods of varying length, while there was a short-term collapse of law and order, with a mass escape from the prison and an outbreak of looting. Many services were restored within weeks. The speed of recovery for different economic sectors depends to a great extent on their respective underlying health. In Grenada, cruise ships resumed their visits a month after Ivan; overall tourist spending was 23% below normal levels in 2005, but was back on track by 2006. Some nutmeg trees resumed growth after suffering severe wind damage, but where this was not the case, progress with replanting has been spectacularly slow. Few Grenadians are willing to undertake heavy agricultural work, while the construction sector offered attractive alternative employment opportunities after the storm. Nutmeg reaping and sales have since seen a partial recovery, but it is unlikely that the industry will return to its former level of output. Similar factors operate across the region. Hurricane Dean in 2007, followed by Tropical Storm Gustav in 2008, formed the final factor prompting the closure of Jamaica's banana export industry, the prospects of which had already been weakened by the loss of market protection in the European Union and rising production costs. In the tourism sector, hotels with other issues affecting investment or profitability have been slow to reopen; in 2013 the Royal Oasis on Grand Bahama remained closed and in a worsening state of repair after Hurricane Jeanne in 2004, with no immediate prospect of reconstruction, while Half Moon Bay on Antigua closed after Hurricane Luis in 1995, and remains the subject of a protracted dispute between the island's Government and the original owners.

FLOODS AND DROUGHTS

Floods and droughts are less spectacular than hurricanes or volcanic eruptions, and are less likely to receive international attention, but are also a severe hazard with a disproportionate impact on small economies. The wider Caribbean is affected by the El Niño/La Niña cycle of warm and cold currents off the western coast of South America, with the Guianas and eastern Caribbean in particular suffering from drought during El Niño events and heavy rainfall with an increased flood risk during the La Niña phase. Extreme droughts have led to crop failure for semi-subsistence farmers in southern Guyana, and bush fires and serious water shortages in the insular Caribbean. There was concern over drought conditions in mid-2014 for the insular Caribbean, with rainfall suppressed by the current phase of the Madden-Julian oscillation, a large-scale tropical pattern of atmospheric circulation, and an El Niño even forecast for the latter part of the year and early 2015. However, these conditions appeared to be producing an inactive hurricane season; by late July 2014 there had been only one named storm (Arthur), which formed well to the north of the Caribbean, off the east coast of the USA.

Flash flooding can damage roads or trigger landslides in mountainous areas within the Caribbean islands, while longer-term flooding is a frequent hazard in low-lying areas

such as the Caroni plains of Trinidad or the Guyanese coastlands, with crop damage, disruption of transport routes, and floodwater damage to houses and other buildings. Flooding in Guyana in January 2005 caused an estimated US $460m. in damage, then equivalent to one-third of annual GDP. Poor maintenance of drainage systems, soil erosion in the upper portion of river basins, deforestation, and dumping of household appliances and other objects in river channels may all contribute to flood hazards. In addition, flooding of low-lying coastal areas may be linked to storm surges which raise sea levels during major hurricanes. Severe flooding can occur outside the hurricane season. On Christmas Day in 2013 a strong upper-level trough over the Windward Islands produced exceptionally heavy rains. There was 300 mm of rainfall in some districts of Saint Vincent within 24 hours, with at least nine deaths and widespread infrastructural, housing and other damage valued at 17% of GDP. There were six deaths in Saint Lucia, and serious damage also on other islands.

MITIGATION, PLANNING AND RECONSTRUCTION

For any disaster with a sudden onset, the initial phase is one of severe disruption. Communications and public services are severely disrupted, and in extreme cases there may be a collapse of internal security, with problems such as looting. Immediate needs may include supplies of food and drinking water, medical assistance, emergency housing, restoration of law and order, and restoration of services such as telecommunications and electricity supply. In all of these areas, problems are exacerbated in small islands. Land-based evacuation ahead of a hurricane strike, as has been practised for coastal areas in the USA and for larger islands such as Cuba, is not an option. Relief supplies and personnel have to be imported through small ports and airports, which are likely themselves to have suffered disruption. Relatively small teams of managers and relief personnel are themselves dealing with the disruption of their own lives—or in extreme cases, such as Haiti's earthquake, are themselves among the missing. After overcoming these initial hurdles, there are phases of reconstruction, lasting months after a moderate hurricane or, at the extreme, for decades after a devastating event such as the Haiti earthquake or the Montserrat volcanic emergency. This process should in principle involve a substantial element of forward planning to reduce vulnerability to natural hazards in future years.

In principle, land use planning in the Caribbean should take account of spatial variations in disaster risk. In practice, this is rarely the case, in part because the most powerful earthquakes, hurricanes and volcanic events are rare, and perceived risks correspondingly low, and in part because areas at risk cover a high proportion of the land area of most Caribbean islands, while in the nearby mainland territories a high proportion of the population lives in low-lying coastal areas, and in the case of Guyana and Suriname often below sea level at high tide. Areas of recent marine deposits or reclaimed land, such as the upper-income residential area of Westmoorings in Trinidad, or the Point Lisas industrial estate on the same island, are subject to flood risks, and would be at risk from liquefaction during a powerful earthquake. At best, structures have been engineered with these considerations in mind. In a rare example of forward planning, the administrative capital of Belize (then British Honduras) was moved to the inland site of Belmopan in 1970, after the disastrous experience of Hurricane Hattie in 1961. However, the general pattern regionally has been of increased investment in coastal areas, with the growth of coastal cities and their suburbs, tourism, ports and industrial facilities, with corresponding risks of damage, tempered in some cases by restrictions on construction on the immediate foreshore. Building codes, and their enforcement, are at best uneven, and there is no agreed Caribbean standard. Indeed, the argument is sometimes advanced that a rigorous design requirement would reduce the provision of low-cost housing solutions to lower-income families. Where attempts have been made to relocate settlements even on a small scale, the results have been disappointing. In Jamaica, US $33m. was spent after Hurricane Ivan in 2004 to relocate 500 families from vulnerable south-coast villages; many residents, however, chose to remain in the original settlements, which were again damaged by Hurricane Dean in 2007.

Insurance against disaster risk remains problematic. There is sufficient historic data on hurricanes for reasonably accurate risk assessments, but earthquake and volcanic risk is harder to quantify. For individuals and small businesses, insurance is available, although some companies have been reluctant to write general insurance in some or all Caribbean countries, or have increased their premiums; in addition, most do not differentiate in assessing risks between high and low risk locations within the region.

For governments, disasters incur very large additional costs for both the current and capital budgets, while disrupting routine administrative capabilities and sharply reducing revenue collection. The Caribbean Catastrophe Risk Insurance Facility (CCRIF) was established after Hurricane Ivan, on the initiative of the Caribbean Community (CARICOM) and with assistance from the World Bank. It issues hurricane, earthquake and excess rainfall insurance policies, with payout based on parameters such as wind force or earthquake magnitude, rather than actual losses, as measured by the US National Hurricane Centre and the US Geological Survey; this allows payouts to be made within days of a disaster, rather than the months that would be needed with conventional insurance procedures, and provides immediate liquidity for government operations while longer-term assistance is mobilized over an extended period from donor agencies. Coverage of up to US $100m. is offered for a '15-year' hurricane or a '20-year' earthquake. Other products are under development with assistance from the CCRIF, including insurance for electricity distribution companies whose facilities are highly vulnerable to wind damage and need to be restored quickly so that other services and economic sectors can operate. The CCRIF operates as a non-profit 'mutual' entity, registered in the Cayman Islands.

CLIMATE CHANGE

Weather-related risks within the Caribbean, including hurricanes, floods and droughts, are expected to become more complex as the process of climate change unfolds over the current century. On most expectations, the frequency of extreme events will increase, leading to greater disaster risks, while sea-level rise will make low-lying coastal areas more vulnerable. Tourism will be exposed to hurricane and storm risk and rising sea levels, but also to other processes such as coral bleaching, reef damage and enhanced beach erosion. However, there is no simple linear relationship between climate change and disaster risk. Hurricane risk is likely to increase as a greater area of sea surface reaches a temperature above the threshold value of 27°C for a greater portion of the year; at the same time, hurricane formation is strongly influenced by upper-level wind patterns, which might at certain phases in some scenarios become less favourable for storm development; this is the case, for example, with El Niño events. The average annual number of tropical storms and hurricanes in the Caribbean and Atlantic increased from 11.6 in 1980–94 to 14.5 in 1995–2009. Overall, the risk of hurricane damage is likely to rise further, but this is not certain to be the case at all times and locations. Other projections based on a global temperature rise of 1.5°C–2.0°C include a 20% increase in the frequency of intense rains by 2050.

CONCLUSION

Worldwide, the IMF reported an increase in damage from natural disasters from an average annual of US $48,000m. in the 1950s to $575,000m. during the decade 1996–2005 (at constant 2005 prices), with the mean loss from each major event rising from $3,900m. in the 1980s to $10,000m. in the decade to 2005 (the latter figure being larger than the annual GDP of any country in the English-speaking Caribbean other than Jamaica or Trinidad and Tobago). A high and increasing disaster risk within the Caribbean is clearly foreseeable; however, the timing of each hazard is generally not predictable. While certain areas within each country are more exposed to risk, the exact locations that will in fact be affected cannot be foreseen. Increased planning to reduce vulnerability is desirable, but can in reality be expected only to a limited extent. For these reasons, international donor assistance is likely to remain a significant need within the region, as natural hazards threaten to wipe out the critical development gains of recent decades.

PART TWO

Country Surveys

ANGUILLA

Geography

PHYSICAL FEATURES

The United Kingdom Overseas Territory of Anguilla is in the north-eastern Caribbean and is the most northerly part of the Leeward Islands in the Lesser Antilles. The territory includes the islet of Sombrero, the pivot of the Lesser Antilles, between the main arc of the archipelago running south-eastwards and the Virgin Islands running westwards. The British Virgin Islands lie some 40 km (25 miles) to the west of the territory, but the nearest neighbour is only 8 km to the south—the French (northern) part of the island of Saint Martin (Sint Maarten), which is under the jurisdiction of France. Anguilla itself was previously part of the federation of Saint Christopher (Kitts)-Nevis-Anguilla, but seceded and reverted to British colonial status (Saint Kitts is over 110 km to the south-east). Anguilla comprises over 96 sq km (37 sq miles) of territory, the main island itself consisting of 91 sq km. This makes the colony the smallest territory in the Caribbean.

The main island, aligned roughly south-west to north-east, is long and narrow, which is why the French named it after an eel (Anguilla), echoing the Carib name, which meant a sea serpent (Malliouhana). It is a low, coral and limestone island, about 26 km in length and never wider than 5 km. The highest point on Anguilla is at Crocus Hill (65 m or 213 ft). Most of the more rugged terrain is at the north-eastern end of the island, where it faces into the Atlantic weather, sheltering some denser vegetation than the usual scrub of the arid interior behind 30-m cliffs. There are some areas of wetland along the 60 km or so of coastline, favoured by the island's varied bird life, but it tends to be the clear seas favoured by coral and the many wide, sandy beaches that draw more lucrative visitors.

Apart from the detached islets of Scrub Island, at the north-eastern tip of the main island, and the even smaller Anguillita, at the south-western tip, the territory also comprises a number of other islands and cays. To the north-west of the mainland is Dog Island and, just to the east of that, the Prickly Pear Cays and Seal Island. Further to the north-west, almost 50 km from Anguilla itself, is the sea-washed rock of Sombrero, uninhabited since its lighthouse was automated. The light, 51 m (166 ft) above the sea, serves shipping using the Anegada Passage from the Atlantic Ocean into the Caribbean Sea. The island, just over 1.5 km long, not even 0.5 km wide and around 10 m above sea level, is particularly rich in seabird life.

CLIMATE

The climate is a subtropical one, tempered by the north-eastern trade winds off the Atlantic. The lack of altitude means Anguilla often misses the rains, but also that it is prone to

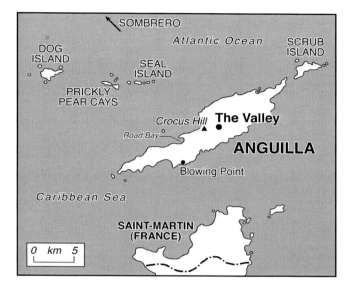

flooding, particularly during the June–September hurricane season. Annual rainfall is 36 ins (914 mm) per year and falls mainly between September and December. The mean temperature is 27°C (80°F), varying little over the course of the year.

POPULATION

There are some white and some mixed-race people native to Anguilla, but most of the population is black. Everyone speaks English, the official language, and most are adherents of one or other of numerous Christian denominations. Some 29% of the population was nominally Anglican, according to the latest available census figures, and 24% Methodist, with the Seventh-day Adventists, Baptists and Roman Catholics the next largest groups.

Preliminary census figures put the total population at 13,452 in 2011, with about 1,600 living in and around the capital, The Valley, which is located in the centre of the island, near the northern coast. Across the island, to the south-west, is the ferry terminal of Blowing Point, although the main anchorage is at Road Bay, directly north of that port.

History

MARK WILSON

Anguilla is a United Kingdom Overseas Territory. A Governor, who is the representative of the British monarch, has important reserve powers, including responsibility for national security and defence, the civil service, the judiciary and certain financial matters. A Chief Minister is responsible to the Legislative Council, similar in function to a parliament, which contains a majority of elected members. The Governor presides over an Executive Council, similar in function to a cabinet, which includes the Chief Minister and the other ministers. A Constitutional and Electoral Reform Commission was created in 2006 (see below), and proposals for a new constitution were to be discussed with the United Kingdom.

A few traces remain of the original Amerindian inhabitants. The first known European visitors were French, and named the island for its eel-like shape; however, the first European settlers were British, arriving in 1650. With a dry climate and thin soil, the island was not a major centre for plantation agriculture, and from 1825 it was tied increasingly closely in its administration to that of Saint Christopher and Nevis (St Kitts). From 1871 to 1956 Anguilla was a member of the Leeward Islands Federation, as part of the presidency of Saint Christopher. With the Leeward Islands Federation disbanded in 1957, Saint Christopher-Nevis-Anguilla joined the Federation of the West Indies in 1958 along with nine other British colonies. Following the departure of Jamaica and Trinidad and Tobago in 1962, the Federation collapsed, and an attempt to unite the remaining colonies as the 'little eight' was unsuccessful. Along with its neighbours, Saint Christopher-Nevis-Anguilla became a British Associated State in 1967, responsible for its own internal affairs, with the United Kingdom retaining control of external affairs and defence.

However, this arrangement was fiercely resisted by Anguilla, which feared domination by its larger neighbour, and in particular by Robert Llewellyn Bradshaw, leader of the St Kitts-Nevis-Anguilla Labour Party, which, in spite of its name, never had a substantial following outside the larger island.

Ronald Webster, leader of the People's Progressive Party (PPP), led a movement to break away from the three-island grouping. On 8 March 1967 Government House was burnt down, and on 30 May the island's small police detachment was expelled to the island of Saint Christopher. An armed attack on Saint Christopher on 10 June was unsuccessful, but a plebiscite on 11 July recorded 1,813 votes in favour of separation from the three-island grouping (there were five votes against). A further plebiscite in February 1969 resulted in 1,739 votes to four in favour of an independent republic. However, this move was rejected by the United Kingdom. William Whitlock, a British junior minister, was despatched to Anguilla as an envoy in early March, but was ejected from the island. On 19 March 300 British paratroops and marines invaded, followed by a detachment from the Metropolitan Police Force; thereafter the island was administered under a resident Commissioner. The British police left in 1972, when Anguilla established its own force.

From 1980, following Bradshaw's death and the inauguration of a new administration in Saint Christopher and Nevis, Anguilla formally became a British Dependent Territory under a Governor, and from 1998, a United Kingdom Overseas Territory. In local politics, office alternated between the PPP and the Anguilla National Alliance (ANA) of Emile (later Sir Emile) Gumbs, who held office in 1977–80 and from 1984 until his retirement in 1994. Thereafter, the two-party system became less clear. A general election in March 1994 gave two seats each to the ANA, the Anguilla United Party (AUP), and the Anguilla Democratic Party (ADP). A former ANA Minister of Finance, Osbourne Fleming, took the seventh legislative seat. Hubert Hughes, also a former ANA minister, but now leader of the AUP, formed a coalition with Victor Banks of the ADP, and became Chief Minister. In May controversy arose over the proposed appointment by the Governor of a nominated member to the Legislative Council, David Carty, who had failed to win a legislative seat in the March election. Hughes objected to Carty's nomination, and alleged that he had not been consulted over the appointment, a charge denied by the Governor. Despite a constitutional court ruling in Carty's favour, the Speaker refused to swear him in as a member of the House of Assembly in December 1995.

The announcement by the British Government in January 1997 that it was considering the extension of its powers in the Dependent Territories of the Caribbean attracted criticism from Hughes, as did the proposed reactivation of the Governor's reserve powers, whereby the Governor (with the consent of the British Government) can amend, veto or introduce legislation without the consent of the local legislature.

In a legislative election held on 4 March 1999, the AUP held its two seats, as did the ADP. Hughes therefore continued in office as leader of a coalition Government. The ANA, with Fleming now a member, also retained its three seats. However, in June the ADP leader, Victor Banks, left the governing coalition following a dispute about the ADP's role in government. Hughes therefore no longer enjoyed the support of a majority of the elected members; however, with several appointed members also sitting in the Legislative Council, the constitutional position was unclear. To force an eventual resolution, Banks and the three ANA members withdrew from the House of Assembly, thus denying it a quorum. This left the Government unable, in December, to introduce a budget for the following year or implement any policy. A fresh election was called for 3 March 2000.

The election of March 2000 left the ANA still with three parliamentary seats, the AUP still with two seats, while Banks (representing the ADP) and Edison Baird (an Independent) each held one. Fleming was appointed Chief Minister with support from four of the seven elected members. Banks became Minister of Finance, Economic Development, Investment and Commerce.

Following Anguilla's inclusion on an Organisation for Economic Co-operation and Development (OECD) blacklist of tax havens in 2000, the Government introduced a number of articles of legislation to combat money-laundering on the island, including the establishment of a 'Money Laundering Reporting Authority'. OECD removed Anguilla from the list in March 2002, declaring that the Government had made sufficient commitments to improve transparency and effective exchange of information on tax matters by the end of 2005. The establishment in 2004 of a new financial regulatory body, the Anguilla Financial Services Commission, represented a further commitment to transparency within the sector. However, in April 2009 Anguilla was included in OECD's so-called 'grey list' of territories that had committed to improving transparency in the financial sector but had not yet substantially implemented such change.

In June 2001 the Government officially approved the draft of its National Telecommunications Policy, which would liberalize the telecommunications sector. Cable & Wireless, the territory's sole telecommunications provider, in April 2003 signed an agreement with the Government to open the market for competition. In August the Government commenced the sale of 6m. shares at US $1 each in the Anguilla Electricity Company, a profit-making public utility, in order to raise funds for the EC $49.2m. expansion and reconstruction of Wallblake Airport (renamed Clayton J. Lloyd International Airport in 2010). The proceeds of the sale were to go primarily towards lengthening the airport's runway in order to accommodate larger aircraft. In May 2004 Edison Baird replaced Hubert Hughes as Leader of the Opposition after Albert Hughes resigned from the AUP and transferred his support to Baird.

At the general election held on 21 February 2005 there were some variations in party names or affiliations, but the same members were returned to government as in the previous ballot. The Anguilla United Front, an alliance comprising the ADP and the ANA, led by Osbourne Fleming, won four seats, while the Anguilla National Strategic Alliance secured two and the Anguilla United Movement (as the AUP had been renamed) one. However, it was anticipated that some of the existing representatives would retire from active politics prior to the holding of the next election. With the economy prospering, the Government was anxious to avoid the dangers of economic 'overheating' and social dislocation; to this effect, in October it announced that it would consider no additional investment proposals until May 2008; this moratorium was afterwards extended, although it was of less relevance in 2009 with most major projects at a halt from mid-2009. The Government expressed concern over the erosion of traditional values in Anguilla, and over short-term labour unrest on camps for migrant construction workers in 2007, stressing a desire to avoid the pattern of development that had evolved on neighbouring islands such as Saint Martin. In July 2006 Andrew George took office as Governor, in succession to Alan Huckle; Stanley Everton Reid, a lawyer and the country's first indigenous Deputy Governor, was sworn in later the same month. A report of the British parliamentary select committee on foreign affairs, completed in mid-2008, disclosed allegations that a single developer had been given permission for three large projects as a result of bribes paid to Anguillan government ministers, and recommended an independent inquiry; the Chief Minister denied the reports.

In January 2006 the Governor established a Constitutional and Electoral Reform Commission, to advance the work done by the previous electoral commission in 2001–04. A report detailing its recommendations was submitted to the Governor in August of that year. A series of public consultations commenced in March 2007. However, subsequent discussions with the United Kingdom were postponed, to allow the formation of a smaller committee comprising elected Assembly members from the Government and opposition parties assisted by local jurists; this body conducted public consultations throughout the island, and the resulting proposals were expected to be discussed with the United Kingdom in 2009, after which consultations between representatives of the Governments of Anguilla and the United Kingdom were to begin. The change of government in early 2010, however, meant discussions were delayed. Areas identified as in need of urgent amendment included the administration of justice, transparency in judicial proceedings, enforcement of constitutional rights, and the appointment of the island Governor and deputies. Furthermore, it recommended the expansion and restructuring of the Executive Council and House of Assembly to enable more efficient delivery of government functions, while increased responsibilities were to be conferred upon the Chief Minister and certain limitations imposed upon the Governor's powers, in order to improve the democratic process. Extensive electoral and judicial reform was also advocated. Broadly interpreted, the Commission's recommendations sought to advance Anguilla's ambitions towards greater responsibility for locally elected institutions, with the Governor's powers mainly limited to defence and security. The United Kingdom would, however, retain ultimate authority over constitutional questions and continue to possess significant reserve powers.

A general election was held on 15 February 2010. The AUM, led by former Chief Minister Hughes, won four of the seven elected seats in the House of Assembly. The AUF's parliamentary representation was reduced to two seats while the remaining seat was secured by Jerome Roberts of the APP, who subsequently joined the AUM administration. The AUF leader, Victor Banks, lost his seat in the Valley South constituency. Hughes' new administration included Edison Baird as Deputy Chief Minister and Minister of Social Development, and Walcott Richardson in the key post of Minister of Home Affairs, including Labour, Natural Resources, Lands, Physical Planning and Immigration. Lowering the unemployment rate was one of the stated priorities of the new Council. Hughes also took on the finance portfolio. In the following month the Chief Minister and the Governor announced the formation of a government task force further to improve financial transparency in Anguilla. The territory had recently been removed from OECD's 'grey list' of jurisdictions that failed to meet international tax standards (see above). One of the AUM's electoral pledges had been to strengthen the economically important financial sector.

There were reports from September 2010 of serious disagreements between the Governor and Chief Minister. The Governor announced in January 2011 that he would not agree the annual budget, presented in December 2010 by the Chief Minister in his capacity as Minister of Finance and agreed by the House of Assembly. The United Kingdom Government asked for cuts in expenditure and in public service employment, to achieve a balanced budget within three years. Two British-appointed financial consultants found in February 2011 that the budget would be workable if some additional revenue measures were implemented. However, this did not placate Chief Minister Hughes, who argued in favour of independence for Anguilla, stating that 'Britain has done nothing for black colonies, nothing but slavery'. In November he called the Governor a 'virtual dictator', while the United Kingdom in September again expressed concern over the widening fiscal deficit and called for corrective measures. Hughes has argued in favour of independence for Anguilla, and continues to use forceful language to describe his relations with the Governor and with London. He said in April 2013 that Anguilla and the United Kingdom were 'at war' over a proposed Framework for Fiscal Sustainability and Development, which he, none the less, signed a few days later, thus paving the way for the Governor to sign the annual budget. However, further differences emerged in mid-2013 over international sharing of tax information and related matters, with Anguilla, along with other British Overseas Territories resisting British pressure to sign a new treaty.

The Governor in February 2011 informed the Chief Minister of reports alleging abuse of office by Richardson, who had issued several hundred visa waivers to Caribbean nationals. In April the Governor used his reserve powers on security issues to override the Executive Council, instructing the minister to stop issuing waivers, arguing that there was no ministerial power to do so, and stating that some had been issued to known criminals. Richardson resigned in February 2013, more than two weeks after his arrest on two charges of sexual assault. The Caribbean Community and Common Market (CARICOM) agreed in March 2012 to make efforts to reduce tensions between the Governor and Chief Minister, while a United Kingdom White Paper published in June 2012 set out a strategy of greater British involvement in the governance of the remaining 14 British Overseas Territories, and stated that the present was not a suitable time to initiate further constitutional reform. Christina Scott was sworn in as Governor in July 2013.

The Anguilla United Movement in May 2014 launched its campaign for a general election which must be held by May 2015; the issue of independence was not raised.

Economy

MARK WILSON

Anguilla is a United Kingdom Overseas Territory in the eastern Caribbean, with an area of 96 sq km. Preliminary data from the May 2011 census indicated a population of 13,452, with a population density of 140 inhabitants. This represents an annual increase of 1.6% since the 2001 census, which recorded a population of 11,430. Anguilla is an associate member of the Caribbean Community and Common Market, or CARICOM, whose larger members formed a single market in 2006. It is also a member of the Organisation of Eastern Caribbean States (OECS), which links nine of the smaller Caribbean territories, while the Eastern Caribbean Central Bank (ECCB), based in Saint Christopher and Nevis, supervises its financial affairs.

The island has a prosperous middle-income economy, in spite of a sharp downturn in tourism and hotel construction at the end of the 2000s, with estimated per head gross domestic product (GDP), at market prices, at US $17,570 in 2011. In this small economy which is heavily dependent on tourism, recent economic performance has been volatile. Growth averaged 15.8% per year in 2005–07 as tourism and related investment boomed, and a labour shortage led to employment of workers from India, Mexico and elsewhere on hotel construction projects. However, the economy contracted by a cumulative 25% in 2008–13 as international tourism investment slowed significantly. Major tourism investment projects stalled and there was additional damage in 2010 from Hurricane Earl. The non-performing loan ratio at local banks increased to 36% by June 2011. Construction output decreased from EC $181m. in 2008 to an estimated EC $41m. in 2013, while foreign direct investment peaked at EC $387m. in 2006, equivalent to 24% of GDP, but fell to EC $31m. in 2010, recovering to EC $152m. in 2013. A study by the Caribbean Development Bank in 2008/09, at the end of the construction boom, estimated the poverty rate at 5.8%, by far the lowest figure in the OECS, with unemployment then at just 1.5%; since then, unemployment has increased.

The sharp downturn affected the fiscal balance. There was an overall budgetary deficit (before grants) peaking at EC $64.7m. in 2009, equivalent to some 9.7% of the sharply contracted GDP. However, the United Kingdom applied strict budgetary rules, which were a source of friction with locally elected politicians. Under pressure for restraint, the annual budget for 2011 provided for a 7% public sector pay cut and a 17% increase in revenue, with a temporary 'stabilization levy' or income tax. Public debt was EC $226m., equivalent to 30% of GDP, at the end of 2013, up from EC $191.5m. or 24% of GDP, three years earlier. The United Kingdom had pressed for more wide-ranging cuts to achieve fiscal balance within three years.

In the event, the overall balance moved to a surplus of EC $21.6m. in 2011, the result of a large stamp duty windfall stemming from the sale of a hotel property; it was then near balanced in 2012, with a deficit of EC $10.7m. recorded in 2013. The IMF in November 2012 called for urgent action to improve the health of the financial sector, stabilize public finances and increase long-term growth potential. The Fund advised the introduction of a value-added tax on goods and services, or a permanent income tax, and a reduction in current spending.

The 2012 budget, with the theme 'steadying the ship: moving cautiously ahead', accordingly proposed revenue measures and control of expenditure, with a goods and services tax to be introduced; however, there had been no move to bring this on stream by mid-2014. Anguilla was to receive €45m. in European Union grant funding in 2011–13, which would, to some extent, ease the difficult fiscal situation. The 2013 budget presented in November 2012 provided for a recurrent surplus of EC $5m. and capital spending of EC $32.6m. It was approved (with some changes) only after a sharp clash between Chief Minister Hughes and the United Kingdom authorities over a Framework for Fiscal Sustainability and Development. This was signed in April 2013 and was broadly similar to agreements on fiscal prudence reached with other British Caribbean territories; it provided for a significant reduction in debt ratios by 2017. Both revenue and expenditure in 2013 were below budget projections, with an overall budget deficit before grants of EC $10.7m., financed by European Development Fund grants. The 2014 budget took the theme 'cautiously optimistic—strengthening our resolve to rebuild our nation'. It provided for a balanced recurrent budget, with an EC $35.8m. capital budget, to be funded by British and European Union grants, a drawdown on reserves, and an EC $8.6m. loan.

Tourism is the mainstay of the economy, with hotels and restaurants accounting for an estimated 21.6% of GDP in 2013; the main attractions are the island's tranquillity, the clear surrounding waters, low rainfall, and white, sandy beaches. According to the Caribbean Tourism Organization, there were 69,068 stop-over visitors in 2013, an 11.1% decrease from the 2007 peak, with total spending of EC $329m. in 2013 (an improvement in current price terms on the previous peak of EC $310m. in 2007). The USA accounted for 56.5% of visitor arrivals in 2013. The ratio of tourists to local population is higher than on such islands as Antigua and Barbuda, Barbados or Jamaica. Most tourists stay in high-cost, luxury accommodation, and their high spending power per head is of considerable economic benefit. The island is not a port of call for cruise ships, which helps preserve its pleasant atmosphere. The main international carrier, American Airlines' American Eagle operation, ceased service to Clayton J. Lloyd International Airport in 2011; connections to neighbouring islands are provided by other smaller carriers.

During the recent boom, residential, commercial, public sector and tourism-related investment resulted in a high level of construction activity, which peaked at 22.2% of GDP in 2008 (falling back to 6.1% in 2013). A wave of luxury tourism proposals from 2000 gave rise to widespread concerns over economic overheating and rapid social change. Tourism-related investments proposed or in progress in 2005, and scheduled for completion by 2021, totalled US $1,800m., close to more than nine times the annual level of GDP. To guard against too fast a pace of growth, the Government announced a moratorium on new development proposals until May 2008. The moratorium was later extended, with a tourism master plan prepared in 2009, building on an economic and social impact analysis completed in 2008. However, the pace of tourism-related construction slowed sharply from the second half of 2008, with several hotel projects delayed or cancelled. The construction sector was estimated to have contracted by a cumulative 76% in 2009–12. There is no significant agricultural sector, but a few small-scale farmers keep livestock and grow food crops. There has also been some recent development of commercial fishing. There is no manufacturing industry. A small offshore medical school has operated since 2003, with student in residence for 16 months before completing their studies in the USA. A tourism master plan running to 2020 was adopted in 2013.

Banking, insurance and related activities made up 12.4% of GDP in 2013. There is a small offshore financial sector, which has been reasonably well regulated. Online company registration through an approved agent is quick and cost-effective, with revenue of EC $10m. in 2013: a total of 2,386 International Business Companies were added to the register in 2012. Following pressure from the Organisation for Economic Co-operation and Development (OECD), which, in 2000, included Anguilla on a list of tax havens, efforts were made to improve the transparency of the sector. As a result, in 2002 OECD removed Anguilla from its 'black list'. In 2009 Anguilla was included in OECD's so-called 'grey list' of jurisdictions that had committed to improving transparency in the financial sector, but had not yet substantially implemented such change; Anguilla was removed from the list in 2010. The administration of Hubert Hughes pledged to promote the financial services sector while ensuring that Anguilla remained on OECD's 'white list'; the OECD Global Forum on Transparency and Exchange of Information published a broadly positive peer review in 2011. In August 2013, however, the ECCB took control of two under-performing banks on the island, Caribbean Commercial Bank (Anguilla) and National Bank of Anguilla, and subsequently initiated a forensic audit of both institutions.

Statistical Survey

Source (unless otherwise stated): Government of Anguilla, The Secretariat, The Valley; tel. 497-2451; fax 497-3389; e-mail stats@gov.ai; internet gov.ai/statistics.

AREA AND POPULATION

Area (sq km): 96 (Anguilla 91, Sombrero 5).

Population: 11,430 at census of 9 May 2001; 13,452 (males 6,659, females 6,793) at census of 11 May 2011 (preliminary).

Density (at 2011 census): 140.1 per sq km.

Population by Age and Sex (at 2001 census): *0–14 years:* 3,202 (males 1,590, females 1,612); *15–64 years:* 7,356 (males 3,632, females 3,724); *65 years and over:* 872 (males 406, females 466); *Total* 11,430 (males 5,628, females 5,802).

Principal Towns (population at 2011 census, preliminary): North Side 1,980; South Hill 1,722; Stoney Ground 1,549; The Valley (capital) 1,067.

Births, Marriages and Deaths (2012): Registered live births 192 (birth rate 14.3 per 1,000); Registered marriages 56 (marriage rate 4.2 per 1,000); Registered deaths 37 (death rate 2.8 per 1,000). *2013:* Registered live births 101; Registered marriages 26; Registered deaths 40.

Life Expectancy (years at birth): 81.1 (males 78.5; females 83.7) in 2013. Source: Pan American Health Organization.

Economically Active Population (persons aged 15 years and over, census of 9 May 2001): Agriculture, fishing and mining 183; Manufacturing 135; Electricity, gas and water 81; Construction 830; Trade 556; Restaurants and hotels 1,587; Transport, storage and communications 379; Finance, insurance, real estate and business services 433; Public administration, social security 662; Education, health and social work 383; Other community, social and personal services 164; Private households with employed persons 164; *Sub-total* 4,773; Activities not stated 871; *Total employed* 5,644 (males 3,014, females 2,630); Unemployed 406 (males 208, females 198); *Total labour force* 6,050 (males 3,222, females 2,828). *July 2002:* Total employed 5,496 (males 3,009, females 2,487); Unemployed 465 (males 204, females 261); Total labour force 5,961 (Source: ILO).

HEALTH AND WELFARE

Total Fertility Rate (children per woman, 2013): 1.7.

Under-5 Mortality Rate (per 1,000 live births, 1997): 34.0.

Physicians (per 1,000 head, 2011): 0.9.

Hospital Beds (per 1,000 head, 2012): 2.1.

Health Expenditure (% of GDP, 2007): 3.0.

Access to Water (% of persons, 2012): 95.

Access to Sanitation (% of persons, 2012): 98.

Sources: Caribbean Development Bank, *Social and Economic Indicators 2004* and Pan American Health Organization.

For definitions, see explanatory note on p. vi.

AGRICULTURE, ETC.

Fishing (metric tons, live weight, 2012): Marine fishes 498; Caribbean spiny lobster 144; Stromboid conchs 480; Total catch 1,122. Source: FAO.

INDUSTRY

Electric Energy ('000 kWh): 91,335 in 2009; 98,532 in 2010; 88,679 in 2011. Source: Eastern Caribbean Central Bank.

FINANCE

Currency and Exchange Rates: 100 cents = 1 Eastern Caribbean dollar (EC $). *Sterling, US Dollar and Euro Equivalents* (30 May 2014): £1 sterling = EC $4.542; US $1 = EC $2.700; €1 = EC $3.675; EC $100 = £22.02 = US $37.04 = €27.21. *Exchange Rate:* Fixed at US $1 = EC $2.70 since July 1976.

Budget (EC $ million, 2013): *Revenue:* Tax revenue 147.5 (Taxes on domestic goods and services 52.5, Taxes on international trade and transactions 78.6, Taxes on property 3.6, Taxes on income and profits 12.8); Non-tax revenue 25.9; Total 173.4 *Expenditure:* Current expenditure 175.8 (Personal emoluments 80.3, Other goods and services 40.5, Transfers and subsidies 45.9, Interest payments 9.1); Capital expenditure 8.3; Total 184.1. Source: Eastern Caribbean Central Bank.

Cost of Living (Consumer Price Index; base: 2005 = 100): All items 129.6 in 2011; 134.7 in 2012; 139.1 in 2013. Source: IMF, *International Financial Statistics*.

Gross Domestic Product (EC $ million at constant 2006 prices): 702.27 in 2011; 655.48 in 2012; 649.34 in 2013 (estimate). Source: Eastern Caribbean Central Bank.

Expenditure on the Gross Domestic Product (EC $ million at current prices, 2013, estimates): Government final consumption expenditure 122.83; Private final consumption expenditure 623.48; Gross fixed capital formation 133.92; *Total domestic expenditure* 880.23; Exports of goods and services 384.31; *Less* Imports of goods and services 511.41; *GDP in purchasers' values* 753.13. Source: Eastern Caribbean Central Bank.

Gross Domestic Product by Economic Activity (EC $ million at current prices, 2013, estimates): Agriculture (including crops, livestock and fishing) 16.91; Mining and quarrying 2.39; Manufacturing 8.72; Electricity and water 26.59; Construction 41.07; Wholesale and retail trade 56.11; Hotels and restaurants 144.98; Transport and communications 61.52; Finance, insurance, real estate and business services 82.97; Real estate and housing 90.88; Public administration and defence 70.37; Education 24.69; Health 19.59; Other services 24.33; *Sub-total* 671.12; *Less* Financial intermediation services indirectly measured 33.51; *Gross value added in basic prices* 637.61; Taxes, *less* subsidies, on products 115.52; *GDP in purchasers' values* 753.13. Source: Eastern Caribbean Central Bank.

Balance of Payments (EC $ million, 2013): Goods (net) –332.96; Services (net) 222.28; *Balance on goods and services* –110.67; Income (net) –5.94; *Balance on goods, services and income* –116.61; Current transfers (net) –12.74; *Current balance* –129.35; Capital account (net) 31.97; Direct investment (net) 152.47; Portfolio investment

0.37; Other investments (net) –55.35; Net errors and omissions 2.68; *Overall balance* 2.78. Source: Eastern Caribbean Central Bank.

EXTERNAL TRADE

Principal Commodities (EC $ million, 2008): *Imports:* Food and live animals 56.4; Beverages and tobacco 39.7; Mineral fuels, lubricants, etc. 104.7; Chemicals and related products 53.2; Basic manufactures 215.1; Machinery and transport equipment 156.5; Miscellaneous manufactured articles 87.6; Total (incl. others) 733.7. *Exports* (incl. re-exports): Food and live animals 0.2; Beverages and tobacco 12.7; Basic manufactures 8.0; Machinery and transport equipment 8.1; Miscellaneous manufactured articles 0.2; Total (incl. others) 31.0. *2013* (estimates): Food and live animals 70.9; Beverages and tobacco 25.9; Mineral fuels, lubricants, etc. 62.4; Chemicals and related products 27.9; Basic manufactures 66.7; Machinery and transport equipment 72.6; Miscellaneous manufactured articles 54.4) Total (incl. others) 391.1; Total exports (incl. re-exports) 9.8 (Source: Eastern Caribbean Central Bank).

Principal Trading Partners (EC $ million, 2008): *Imports:* Barbados 4.7; Guyana 14.6; Puerto Rico 56.2; Trinidad and Tobago 106.2; United Kingdom 5.5; USA 375.9; US Virgin Islands 3.9; Total (incl. others) 733.7. *Exports* (incl. re-exports): British Virgin Islands 0.1; Guyana 11.9; United Kingdom 0.6; USA 4.6; Total (incl. others) 31.0. *2013* (estimates): Total imports 391.1; Total exports (incl. re-exports) 9.8 (Source: Eastern Caribbean Central Bank).

TRANSPORT

Road Traffic (motor vehicles in use at 31 December 2006): Passenger cars 4,155; Vans and lorries 92; Motorcycles and mopeds 22; Total 4,269 (Source: IRF, *World Road Statistics*).

Shipping: *Flag Registered Fleet* (at 31 December 2013): Number of vessels 5; Total displacement 1,127 grt. (Source: Lloyd's List Intelligence—www.lloydslistintelligence.com).

TOURISM

Visitor Arrivals: 123,558 (stop-overs 65,783, excursionists 57,775) in 2011; 129,391 (stop-overs 64,698, excursionists 64,693) in 2012; 151,303 (stop-overs 69,068, excursionists 82,235) in 2013.

Visitor Arrivals by Place of Residence (2013): Canada 9,931; Caribbean 8,560; United Kingdom 5,382; USA 85,415; Total (incl. others) 151,303.

Tourism Receipts (EC $ million): 301.7 in 2011; 304.5 in 2012; 328.7 in 2013. Source: Eastern Caribbean Central Bank.

COMMUNICATIONS MEDIA

Telephones (2013): 6,000 main lines in use.

Mobile Cellular Telephones (2013): 26,000 subscribers.

Internet Subscribers (2008): 3,700.

Broadband Subscribers (2013): 4,300.

Source: International Telecommunication Union.

EDUCATION

Pre-primary (2010/11 unless otherwise indicated): 11 schools (2003); 31 teachers; 434 pupils (males 226, females 208).

Primary (2010/11 unless otherwise indicated): 8 schools (2003); 111 teachers; 1,646 pupils (males 846, females 800).

Secondary (2010/11 unless otherwise indicated): 1 school (2002/03); 124 teachers; 1,059 pupils (males 523, females 536).

Tertiary (2007/08): 14 teachers; 54 students (9 males, 45 females).

Pupil-teacher Ratio (primary education, UNESCO estimate): 14.8 in 2010/11.

Adult Literacy Rate (UNESCO estimates): 95.4% (males 95.1%; females 95.7%) in 1995. Source: UNESCO, *Statistical Yearbook*.

Source (unless otherwise indicated): UNESCO Institute for Statistics.

Directory

The Constitution

The Constitution, established in 1976, accorded Anguilla the status of a British Dependent Territory. It formally became a separate dependency on 19 December 1980, and is administered under the Anguilla Constitution Orders of 1982 and 1990. British Dependent Territories were referred to as United Kingdom Overseas Territories from February 1998 and draft legislation confirming this change and granting citizens rights to full British citizenship and residence in the United Kingdom was published in March 1999. The British Overseas Territories Act entered into effect in May 2002. The British Government proposals also included the requirement that the Constitutions of Overseas Territories should be revised in order to conform to British and international standards. The process of revision of the Anguillan Constitution began in September 1999.

The British monarch is represented locally by a Governor, who presides over the Executive Council and the House of Assembly. The Governor is responsible for defence, external affairs (including international financial affairs), internal security (including the police), the public service, the judiciary and the audit. The Governor appoints a Deputy Governor. On matters relating to internal security, the public service and the appointment of an acting Governor or Deputy Governor, the Governor is required to consult the Chief Minister. The Executive Council consists of the Chief Minister and not more than three other ministers (appointed by the Governor from the elected members of the legislative House of Assembly) and two ex officio members (the Deputy Governor and the Attorney-General). The House of Assembly is elected for a maximum term of five years by universal adult suffrage and consists of seven elected members, two ex officio members (the Deputy Governor and the Attorney-General) and two nominated members who are appointed by the Governor, one upon the advice of the Chief Minister, and one after consultations with the Chief Minister and the Leader of the Opposition. The House elects a Speaker and a Deputy Speaker.

The Governor may order the dissolution of the House of Assembly if a resolution of no confidence is passed in the Government, and elections must be held within two months of the dissolution.

The Constitution provides for an Anguilla Belonger Commission, which determines cases of whether a person can be 'regarded as belonging to Anguilla' (i.e. having 'belonger' status). A belonger is someone of Anguillan birth or parentage, someone who has married a belonger, or someone who is a citizen of the United Kingdom Overseas Territories from Anguilla (by birth, parentage, adoption or naturalization). The Commission may grant belonger status to those who have been domiciled and ordinarily resident in Anguilla for not less than 15 years.

The Government

HEAD OF STATE

Queen: HM Queen ELIZABETH II.

Governor: CHRISTINA MARTHA ELENA SCOTT (took office 23 July 2013).

EXECUTIVE COUNCIL
(September 2014)

The Government is formed by the Anguilla United Movement (AUM) and the Anguilla Progressive Party (APP).

Chief Minister and Minister of Finance, Economic Development, Investments, Social Development and Tourism: HUBERT B. HUGHES (AUM).

Minister of Home Affairs, Natural Resources, Lands and Physical Planning: JEROME C. ROBERTS (APP).

Minister of Infrastructure, Communications, Utilities and Housing: EVAN GUMBS (AUM).

Parliamentary Secretary with responsibility for Tourism: HAYDN HUGHES.

Deputy Governor: STANLEY EVERTON REID.

Attorney-General: JAMES WOOD.

MINISTRIES

Office of the Governor: Government House, POB 60, The Valley; tel. 497-2622; fax 497-3314; e-mail governorsoffice@gov.ai.

Office of the Chief Minister: The Secretariat, POB 60, The Valley; tel. 497-3518; fax 497-3389; e-mail chief-minister@gov.ai.

All ministries are based in The Valley, mostly at the Secretariat (tel. 497-2451; internet www.gov.ai).

Legislature

HOUSE OF ASSEMBLY

Speaker: BARBARA WEBSTER-BOURNE.

Clerk to House of Assembly: ADELLA RICHARDSON.

Election, 15 February 2010

Party		% of votes	Seats
Anguilla United Movement (AUM)	.	32.67	4
Anguilla United Front (AUF)	. .	39.39	2
Anguilla Progressive Party (APP)	. .	14.71	1
Independent candidates	. . . .	13.24	—
Total	. . . .	100.00	7

There are also two ex officio members and two nominated members.

Political Organizations

Anguilla Progressive Party (APP): The Valley; Leader BRENT DAVIS.

Anguilla United Front (AUF): The Valley; tel. 497-4541; e-mail othlyn@unitedfront.ai; internet www.unitedfront.ai; f. 2000 by the alliance of the Anguilla Democratic Party and the Anguilla National Alliance; Leader VICTOR F. BANKS.

Anguilla United Movement (AUM): The Valley; tel. 497-0335; e-mail joanivy2002@yahoo.com; f. 1978; revived 1984; fmrly known as the Anguilla United Party—AUP; conservative; Leader HUBERT B. HUGHES.

Judicial System

Justice is administered by the High Court, Court of Appeal and Magistrates' Courts. Anguilla is under the jurisdiction of the Eastern Caribbean Supreme Court (ECSC). One of the ECSC's High Court Judges arbitrates in sittings of the territory's High Court.

High Court Judge: CHERYL MATHURIN.

Registrar: VERNETTE S. RICHARDSON.

Religion

CHRISTIANITY

The Anglican Communion

Anglicans in Anguilla are adherents of the Church in the Province of the West Indies, comprising eight dioceses. Anguilla forms part of the diocese of the North Eastern Caribbean and Aruba. The Bishop is resident in St John's, Antigua and Barbuda. According to the 2001 census, 29% of the population are Anglican.

The Roman Catholic Church

The diocese of St John's-Basseterre, suffragan to the archdiocese of Castries (Saint Lucia), includes Anguilla, Antigua and Barbuda, the British Virgin Islands, Montserrat and Saint Christopher and Nevis. The Bishop resides in St John's, Antigua and Barbuda. Some 6% of the population are Roman Catholic, according to census figures.

Roman Catholic Church: St Gerard's, POB 47, The Valley; tel. 497-2405; e-mail info@stgerards-anguilla.org; internet stgerards-anguilla.org; Pastor PAUL CZOCH.

Other Christian Churches

According to census figures, 24% of the population are Methodist.

Methodist Church: Epworth Manse, POB 5, 2640 The Valley; tel. 497-2612; fax 497-8460; e-mail methodism@anguillanet.com; internet www.lidmethodist.org; Supt Minister Rev. CLIFTON H. NILES.

The Seventh-day Adventist, Baptist, Church of God, Pentecostal, Jehovah's Witnesses, Evangelical, Brethren and Presbyterian churches are also represented.

The Press

Anguilla Life Magazine: POB 1622, The Valley; tel. 497-3080; fax 497-4196; f. 1998; 3 a year; Publr and Editor CLAIRE DEVENER; circ. 10,000.

Anguilla Official Gazette: House of Assembly, POB 60, The Valley AI-2640; tel. 497-5081; fax 498-2210; internet gazette.gov.ai; monthly; govt news-sheet.

The Anguillian Newspaper: POB 98, The Valley; tel. 497-3823; fax 497-8706; e-mail theanguillian@anguillanet.com; internet theanguillian.com; weekly; Editor A. NAT HODGE.

Design Anguilla Magazine: POB 5050, The Valley, AI 2640; tel. 584-8886; e-mail info@designanguilla.com; internet designanguilla .com; 4 a year; Publr ORRETT WYNTER.

The Light: Sandy Hill, POB 1373, The Valley; tel. 497-5058; fax 497-5641; e-mail thelight@anguillanet.com; f. 1993; owned by Hodgeco Publishing Inc; weekly newspaper; Editor GEORGE C. HODGE.

True ANGUILLA: The Valley; tel. 476-2883; e-mail info@ trueanguilla.com; internet trueanguilla.com; f. 2013; annual; tourist guide; Publr TRUDY NIXON.

What We Do in Anguilla: Sandy Hill, POB 1373, The Valley; tel. 497-5058; e-mail thelight@anguillanet.com; f. 1987; monthly newsletter, annual magazine; tourism; Editor GEORGE C. HODGE; circ. 20,000.

Broadcasting and Communications

TELECOMMUNICATIONS

LIME: POB 77, The Valley; tel. 804-2994; e-mail customerservice@ lime.com; internet www.lime.com; fmrly Cable & Wireless (Anguilla) Ltd; name changed as above 2008; contact centres in Jamaica and St Lucia; fixed-line, mobile and internet services; CEO (Caribbean) TONY RICE.

Wireless Ventures (Anguilla) Ltd: Babrow Bldg, The Valley; tel. 498-7500; fax 498-7510; e-mail customercareanguilla@digicelgroup .com; internet www.digicelanguilla.com; owned by Digicel Ltd (Bermuda); fmrly AT&T Wireless; CEO COLM DELVES; Country Man. JOHN GIDHARRY.

BROADCASTING

Radio

The Caribbean Beacon: Long Rd, POB 690, The Valley; Head Office: POB 7008, Columbus, GA 31908, USA; tel. 338-3030; fax 497-4311; f. 1981; religious and commercial; broadcasts 24 hours daily; Pres. MELLISA SCOTT; CEO B. MONSELL HAZELL.

Klass 92.9 FM: POB 339, The Valley; tel. 497-3791; e-mail info@ klass929.com; internet www.klass929.com; f. 2006; commercial; Owner ABNER BROOKS, Jr.

Kool FM: North Side, The Valley; tel. 497-0103; fax 497-0104; e-mail info@koolfm103.com; internet www.koolfm103.com; commercial; Man. ASHLEY BROOKS.

Radio Anguilla: Dept of Information and Broadcasting, Secretariat, POB 60, The Valley; tel. 497-2218; fax 497-5432; e-mail radioaxa@anguillanet.com; internet www.radioaxa.com; f. 1969; owned by the Govt of Anguilla; 250,000 listeners in the north-eastern Caribbean; broadcasts 17 hours daily; Dir FARRAH BANKS; Programme Man. KEITHSTONE GREAVES.

UP Beat Radio 97.7 FM: Cedar Ave, Rey Hill, POB 5045, The Valley, AI 2640; tel. 498-3354; fax 497-5995; e-mail info@hbr1075 .com; internet hbr1075.com; f. 2000; commercial; music and news; Dirs IWANDAI I. GUMBS, WHALDOMA (RAS B.) BROOKS.

ZJF FM: POB 333, The Valley; tel. 497-3919; fax 497-3909; f. 1989; commercial; Man. SELWYN BROOKS.

Television

Anguilla TV: tel. 476-7365; e-mail donna@islandeyetv.com; internet www.islandeyetv.com; operated by Eye TV; terrestrial channels 3 and 9; 24-hour local and international English language programming; Exec. Producer DONNA DAVIS.

Caribbean Cable Communications (Anguilla): Edwin Wallace Rey Dr., POB 336, The Valley; tel. 497-3600; fax 497-3602; e-mail customersupport@caribcable.com; internet www.caribcable.com; also broadcasts to Nevis; Pres. LEE BERTMAN.

Finance

(cap. = capital; res = reserves; dep. = deposits; m. = million; amounts in EC dollars)

BANKING

Central Bank

Eastern Caribbean Central Bank (ECCB): Fairplay Commercial Complex, POB 1385, The Valley; tel. 497-5050; fax 497-5150; e-mail eccbaxa@anguillanet.com; internet www.eccb-centralbank.org; HQ in Basseterre, St Christopher and Nevis; bank of issue and central monetary authority for Anguilla, Antigua and Barbuda, Dominica, Grenada, Montserrat, St Christopher and Nevis, St Lucia and St Vincent and the Grenadines; Gov. Sir K. DWIGHT VENNER; Man. Dir JENNIFER NERO.

Commercial Banks

Caribbean Commercial Bank (Anguilla) Ltd: 1 Mary's St, POB 23, The Valley; tel. 497-3917; fax 497-3570; e-mail service@ccb.ai; internet www.ccb.ai; f. 1976; put under control of Eastern Caribbean Central Bank in Aug. 2013; Chair. OSBOURNE B. FLEMING; Man. Dir STARRY WEBSTER-BENJAMIN.

CIBC FirstCaribbean International Bank Ltd: POB 140, The Valley; tel. 497-2301; fax 497-2980; e-mail care@cibcfcib.com; internet www.cibcfcib.com; f. 2002 as FirstCaribbean International Bank Ltd following merger of Caribbean operations of Barclays Bank PLC and CIBC, present name adopted in 2011; Exec. Chair. MICHAEL K. MANSOOR; CEO RIK PARKHILL.

National Bank of Anguilla Ltd (NBA): POB 44, The Valley; tel. 497-2101; fax 497-3310; e-mail nbabankl@anguillanet.com; internet www.nba.ai; f. 1985; 6% owned by Govt of Anguilla; cap. 30.6m., res 36.8m., dep. 784.5m. (March 2011); put under control of Eastern Caribbean Central Bank in Aug. 2013; Chair. CONRAD W. FLEMING; CEO E. VALENTINE BANKS.

Scotiabank Anguilla Ltd: Fairplay Commercial Centre, POB 250, The Valley; tel. 497-3333; fax 497-3344; e-mail bns.anguilla@ scotiabank.com; internet www.anguilla.scotiabank.com; f. 1989 as Bank of Nova Scotia Anguilla, present name adopted 1995; cap. 32,4m., res. 13,6m., dep. 225,5m. (Oct. 2010); Man. Dir PAMELA HERBERT-DANIEL.

Offshore Banks

Caribbean Commercial Investment Bank Ltd: 2 St Mary's St, POB 23, The Valley; tel. 497-2242; fax 497-7054; put under control of Eastern Caribbean Central Bank in Aug. 2013.

Foreign Commerce Bank Ltd: The Anguilla Professional Complex, POB 1648, The Valley; tel. 498-5576; fax 498-5578.

National Bank of Anguilla (Private Banking and Trust) Ltd: Conrad W. Fleming Corporate Bldg, St Mary's Rd, POB 44, The Valley; tel. 497-7096; fax 497-2296; put under control of Eastern Caribbean Central Bank in Aug. 2013.

Trust Companies

There were eight active trust companies registered with the Anguilla Financial Services Commission in 2014.

ATU General Trust (Anguilla) Inc: Mitchell House, POB 174, The Valley; tel. 498-8800; fax 498-8880; internet www.atu.li; f. 1995; subsidiary of ATU General Trust (BVI) Ltd.

Codan Trust Co (Anguilla) Ltd: Mitchell House, POB 147, The Valley; tel. 461-8800; fax 461-8880; e-mail anguilla@conyersdill.com; internet www.conyersdill.com; subsidiary of Conyers, Dill and Pearman, Bermuda; Man. GARETH THOMAS.

First Anguilla Trust Co Ltd: Mitchell House, POB 174, The Valley, AI 2640; tel. and fax 498-8800; fax 461-8880; e-mail information@firstanguilla.com; internet www.firstanguilla.com; f. 1995.

Geneva Trust Corpn: 201 Rogers Office Bldg, Edwin Wallace Rey Dr., POB 941, George Hill; tel. 518-1130; fax 553-5074; e-mail geneva@genevatrust.com; internet www.genevatrust.com; f. 2005 as the GenevaTrust Corpn; subsidiary of Geneva Assurance Ltd; CEO NADINE DE KOKER.

Lutea (Anguilla) Ltd: Heritage Suite, POB 1533, The Valley; tel. 498-0340; fax 498-0341; e-mail skalmera@lutea.com; internet www .lutea.com; owned by the Lutea Group of Cos, administered in Jersey (United Kingdom); Man. SOERIDA KALMERA.

Mossack Fonseca & Co (British Anguilla) Ltd: Mason Complex 25, POB 193, The Valley; tel. 498-7777; fax 497-3727; e-mail britishanguilla@mossfon.com; internet www.mossfon.com.

Noble Trust Co (Anguilla) Ltd: Mitchell House, POB 1321, The Valley; tel. 498-8005; fax 498-7402; e-mail info@noblegroup.ai; internet www.noblegroup.ch; HQ in Switzerland; Chair. and CEO SÉBASTIAN B. J. MOERMAN.

United Trust (Anguilla) Ltd: Brabow Bldg, POB 371, The Valley; tel. 497-4224; fax 497-4220; internet www.united-itrust.com/ anguilla; f. 2006; subsidiary of United International Holdings (Netherlands); CEO ROBERT STROEVE.

REGULATORY AUTHORITY

Anguilla Financial Services Commission: MAICO HQ Bldg, 2nd Floor, Cosley Dr., POB 1575, The Valley; tel. 497-5881; fax 497-5872; e-mail info@fsc.org.ai; internet www.fsc.org.ai; f. 2004; Chair. HELEN HATTON; Dir RICHARD HANDS.

STOCK EXCHANGE

Eastern Caribbean Securities Exchange: Bird Rock, Basseterre, Saint Christopher and Nevis; tel. (869) 466-7192; fax (869) 465-3798; e-mail info@ecseonline.com; internet www.ecseonline.com; f. 2001; regional securities market; 8 mem. territories—Anguilla, Antigua and Barbuda, Dominica, Grenada, Montserrat, St Christopher and Nevis, St Lucia, and St Vincent and the Grenadines; Chair. Sir K. DWIGHT VENNER; Gen. Man. TREVOR E. BLAKE.

INSURANCE

In 2014 there were 289 captive insurance companies registered in Anguilla.

Alliance Insurance Services Ltd: POB PW 5236, George Hill; tel. 498-7788; fax 498-7780; e-mail info@aisanguilla.com; internet www .aisanguilla.com; f. 2006; Man. Dir SANDRA LOVELL.

Captiva Global Ltd: POB 941, Edwin Wallace Rey Dr., George Hill; tel. 498-5858; fax 497-5504; e-mail info@captivagroup.net; Group Dir NOELLA M. THOMPSON; Group Man. Dir HARRY J. THOMPSON.

D-3 Enterprises Ltd: Caribbean Commercial Center, POB 1377, The Valley; tel. 497-3525; fax 497-3526; e-mail info@d3ent.com; internet www.d-3enterprises.com; represents the Atlantic Southern Insurance Co Ltd and the Caribbean Alliance Insurance Co Ltd; Gen. Man. CLEMENT RUAN.

Fidelity Insurance Co.: The Law Bldg POB 687, The Valley; tel. 497-0484; fax 497-5753; e-mail clientserv@fidinsco.com; internet www.fidinsco.com/about_anguilla.html; Dir KEITHLEY F. T. LAKE.

Gulf Insurance Ltd: POB 1254, South Hill; tel. 498-4853; fax 498-5852; e-mail chantalpiazzi@yahoo.com; internet www .gulfinsuranceltd.com; Dirs CHANTAL PIAZZI, MICHAEL PERMUY.

Malliouhana-Anico Insurance Co Ltd (MAICO): Herbert's Commercial Centre, Cosley Rd, POB 492, The Valley; tel. 497-3712; fax 497-3710; e-mail maico@anguillanet.com; internet www .maicoanguilla.com; f. 1988; wholly owned subsidiary of National Bank of Anguilla Ltd; Gen. Man. MONICA HODGE.

National Caribbean Insurance Co Ltd: Caribbean Commercial Complex, POB 323, The Valley; tel. 497-2865; fax 497-3783.

National General Insurance Co N.V. (NAGICO): Albert Lake Dr., The Valley; tel. 497-5940; fax 497-0510; e-mail info.anguilla@ nagico.com; internet www.nagico.com; f. 1982; CEO IMRAN MCSOOD-AMJAD; Man. CARLYN CARTY.

Trade and Industry

DEVELOPMENT ORGANIZATION

Anguilla Development Board: Cannon Ball Office Complex, Wallblake Rd, POB 285, The Valley; tel. 497-2595; fax 497-2959; e-mail adb@anguillanet.com; f. 1979; provides financial and technical assistance to fishing, agriculture, tourism and industry; Gen. Man. ALTHEA HODGE.

CHAMBER OF COMMERCE

Anguilla Chamber of Commerce and Industry: POB 321, The Valley; tel. 497-2839; fax 497-3880; e-mail acoci@caribcable.com; internet www.anguillachamber.com; Pres. KEITHLEY LAKE; Exec. Dir CARLTON PICKERING.

BUSINESS ASSOCIATION

Anguilla Commercial Registry: Ministry of Finance, POB 60, The Secretariat, The Valley; tel. 497-3881; fax 497-8053; e-mail support@ anguillafsd.com; internet www.commercialregistry.ai; enables online registration and incorporation of International Business Companies; Registrar LANSTON CONNOR.

UTILITIES

Electricity

Anguilla Electricity Co Ltd: POB 400, The Valley; tel. 497-5200; fax 497-5440; e-mail info@anglec.com; internet www.anglec.com; f. 1991; operates a power station and 12 generators; Chair. JAMES RICHARDSON; Gen. Man. THOMAS HODGE.

Water

Water Corpn of Anguilla: The Valley; CEO ROMMEL HUGHES.

TRADE UNIONS

Anguilla Civil Services Association (ACSA): POB 1320, The Valley; tel. 729-0120; e-mail anguillacsa@hotmail.com; Pres. GERARD GUMBS.

Anguilla Teachers' Union (ATU): POB 196, The Valley; tel. 235-1066; fax 929-2909; e-mail info@atu.ai; internet www.atu.ai; Pres. EMMA FERGUSON; Gen. Sec. GLEASON BROOKS; 188 mems.

Transport

ROADS

Anguilla has 175 km (108 miles) of roads, of which 46.9% are paved. There are 63 km of main roads and 112 km of secondary roads.

SHIPPING

There are three main seaports. The principal port of entry is Sandy Ground on Road Bay. The Corito Bay port is used by two oil companies for the import of petroleum products and propane. The Blowing Point port is the passenger terminal for ferries operating between Anguilla and Marigot (St-Martin). The other areas of entry are Cove, Forest, Island Harbour and Little Harbour. In December 2013 Anguilla's flag registered fleet comprised five vessels, with an aggregate displacement of some 1,127 grt.

Anguilla Air and Seaports Authority: c/o Permanent Secretary, MICUHAF, POB 60, The Valley; tel. 497-3476; fax 497-5258; e-mail larry.franklin@gov.ai; f. 2009; Chair. LANVIL HARRIGAN (acting); Supt (Ports) EDWIN HARRIS.

Link Ferries: Little Harbour; tel. 497-2231; fax 497-3290; e-mail fbconnor@anguillanet.com; internet www.link.ai; f. 1992; daily services to St Maarten and charter services to neighbouring islands and offshore quays; Capt. and Owner FRANKLYN CONNOR.

CIVIL AVIATION

Clayton J. Lloyd International Airport (known as Wallblake Airport until 2010), 3.2 km (2 miles) from The Valley, has an asphalt-surfaced runway with a length of 1,665 m (5,462 ft). Reconstruction and expansion of the airport in 2004 included an extension of the runway to accommodate mid-range aircraft. LIAT (see Civil Aviation, Antigua and Barbuda) and Winair regional airlines also operate from the airport.

Anguilla Air Services: POB 559, Clayton J. Lloyd International Airport; tel. 498-5922; fax 498-5921; e-mail info@anguillaairservices .com; internet www.anguillaairservices.com; f. Dec. 2006; operates passenger and cargo charter flights from Anguilla to neighbouring islands; official carrier for Winair (Winward Islands Airways) in Anguilla; Man. Dir CARL THOMAS.

Trans Anguilla Airways (2000) Ltd (TAA): POB 1329, Clayton J. Lloyd International Airport; tel. 497-8690; fax 497-8689; e-mail transang@anguillanet.com; internet www.transanguilla.com; f. 1996; air charter service in the Eastern Caribbean; Pres. VERNOL GUMBS; CEO LINCOLN GUMBS.

Tourism

Anguilla's sandy beaches and unspoilt natural beauty attract tourists and also day visitors from neighbouring St-Martin. Tourism receipts totalled an estimated EC $328.7m. in 2013 and visitor arrivals totalled 151,303 in the same year.

Anguilla Hotel and Tourism Association: Coronation Ave, POB 1020, The Valley; tel. 497-2944; fax 497-3091; e-mail ahtaadmin@ anguillanet.com; internet www.anguillahta.com; f. 1981; Pres. DELROY LAKE; Exec. Dir GILDA GUMBS-SAMUEL.

Anguilla Tourist Board: Coronation Ave, POB 1388, The Valley, AI 2640; tel. 497-2759; fax 497-2710; e-mail atbtour@ivisitanguilla .com; internet ivisitanguilla.com; Chair. BONNIE BLOOM; Dir CANDIS NILES.

Defence

The United Kingdom is responsible for the defence of Anguilla.

Education

Education is free and compulsory between the ages of five and 17 years. Primary education begins at five years of age and lasts for six years. Secondary education, beginning at 11 years of age, lasts for a further six years. There are six government primary schools and one government secondary school, on two campuses. According to UNESCO estimates, in 2008 enrolment at primary schools included 93% of children in the relevant age-group, while enrolment at secondary schools included 78% of pupils in the relevant age-group. Post-secondary education is undertaken abroad.

ANTIGUA AND BARBUDA

Geography

PHYSICAL FEATURES

Antigua and Barbuda is in the Leeward Islands, in the north-eastern Caribbean, the Atlantic Ocean spreading to the east. The country's nearest neighbour is the British dependency of Montserrat, 43 km (27 miles) to the south-west of Antigua island, but only 24 km south-east of Redonda, the uninhabited western outpost of Antigua and Barbuda. Guadeloupe, a part of France, lies to the south and Saint Christopher (Kitts) and Nevis to the west. The islands that continue the chain of the Lesser Antilles to the north-west are variously parts of the Dutch and French Antilles. Antigua and Barbuda has a total surface area of 442 sq km (171 sq miles), Antigua (280 sq km) being larger than Barbuda (161 sq km). Redonda covers only 1.6 sq km.

Most of the country consists of a flat, coral or limestone terrain, but there are higher areas anciently formed by volcanic activity (southern Antigua and Redonda). This contributes to an irregular shoreline of many beaches and harbours on the main island (in total, the country has 153 km of coastline). Antigua was the largest of the British Leeward Islands and, historically, the site of an important port (English Harbour) for the Royal Navy in the West Indies. The arid island is about 23 km long (east–west) and 18 km wide, and its complex coast is girdled by reefs and islets. In the south-west the largely treeless highlands culminate in Mount Obama (as Boggy Peak was renamed in 2009, 402 m—1,319 ft).

By contrast, Barbuda, 42 km north of Antigua, is an entirely low-lying island (the highest point above sea level, in the north-eastern, ambitiously named Highlands, reaches only 38 m), with smoother shores and only one harbour, the large Codrington Lagoon on the west. The Lagoon is formed by the south-westward jutting Palmetto Point on the central western coast and a long, narrow spit of land heading northwards from there and culminating in Cedar Tree Point, which runs in a north-easterly direction to form the narrow sea entrance. The other side of this northern entrance to the lagoon is formed by Goat Island (which is actually connected to the mainland by a narrow isthmus). South of the Lagoon is the Caribbean's largest colony of frigatebirds, and the island is home to many other birds, and to turtles.

The rocky, scrubby cone of Redonda, 55 km west-south-west of Antigua, lies in the western or inner of the two chains of islands that the Lesser Antilles split into here, between Montserrat and Nevis. It is just over 1.5 km long (north–south) and barely 0.5 km wide. Redonda has achieved some notoriety as a putative kingdom, established by the Irish Shiell family from Montserrat seven years before the United Kingdom formally annexed the island in 1872 (placing it under the jurisdiction of the Antiguan authorities). Those authorities never bothered to dispute the royal title, which became particularly noted in British literary circles after the Second World War, when the poet John Gawsworth ('King Juan') promoted its court with the creation of an 'intellectual aristocracy'. The title is now disputed, but sovereignty of Redonda is firmly vested in the Crown of Antigua and Barbuda, while actual possession by goats and birds is seldom challenged.

CLIMATE

Antigua and Barbuda is prone to hurricanes and droughts, the low altitudes drawing little of the moisture carried by the constant Atlantic trade winds. Antigua receives more rainfall

than Barbuda, at some 45 ins (1,143 mm) annually. Most rainfall is in September–November, at the end of the hurricane season. Average monthly temperatures range between 23°C and 29°C (73°F–85°F).

POPULATION

Most people are black, but there are some native whites (traditionally of British or Portuguese descent), as well as more recent communities from Syria and Lebanon. Moreover, as much as 10% of the population is reckoned to have emigrated from the Dominican Republic. Such groups often retain use of their own languages, but English is the official tongue. An English patois is also widely spoken. Most people are Christian, the main denomination (18% at the 2011 census) being the Anglican Communion, as represented by the Church in the Province of the West Indies, although there are also Seventh-day Adventists (12%), Pentecostalists (12%), Moravian (8%), Roman Catholic (8%), Methodists (6%) and Wesleyan (5%) communities.

There were 86,295 people in the country at the time of the May 2011 census (over 98% of them on Antigua). According to UN estimates, this had risen to 90,905 in mid-2014. There is a large immigrant population, notably from the Dominican Republic and Montserrat. Saint John's, in the north of Antigua, is the national capital, the largest city and the main port. It had a population of 22,193 people according to the 2011 census, while the chief town of Barbuda, Codrington, is home to most of the island's population of some 1,500. For administrative purposes, Barbuda is separate from Antigua (Redonda is also a separate unit), and the main island is divided into six parishes.

History

MARK WILSON

Antigua and Barbuda is a constitutional monarchy within the Commonwealth. Queen Elizabeth II is Head of State, and is represented in Antigua and Barbuda by a Governor-General. There is a bicameral legislature, Parliament, with an elected chamber.

Few traces remain of the islands' original Amerindian inhabitants. Christopher Columbus landed and named the main island Santa María de la Antigua in 1493, but the Spanish took very little interest in the islands, and the first permanent European settlement was by English colonists in 1632. The inlet of English Harbour provided shelter from hurricanes, and was a major British naval base in the 18th and 19th centuries. Antigua was captured by France only once, and very briefly, in 1666. Sugar was grown from 1674, and cultivation of this crop, and of cotton, was the dominant economic activity for most of the colonial period, with plantations worked until 1834 by slaves of African origin, and then by their descendants as free, but badly paid, labourers. Following emancipation, there was a high rate of emigration to other Caribbean countries, and later to Great Britain and North America. Antigua was a separate British colony until 1871, when it became the seat of government for the Leeward Islands Federation.

The Antigua Trades and Labour Union (ATLU) was founded in 1939, organizing the low-paid sugar workers and other manual employees. Vere C. Bird, Sr, became President of the ATLU in 1943 and, in 1946, founded the Antigua Labour Party (now known as the Antigua and Barbuda Labour Party, ABLP), which won a decisive election victory in the first elections under universal suffrage in 1951. During Bird's term of office Antigua and Barbuda, along with the other British possessions in the Caribbean, enjoyed steady improvements in living standards, education and social services. As a result, he won the fierce loyalty of most lower-income Antiguans.

Following the dissolution of the Leeward Islands Federation in 1957, Antigua and Barbuda joined the Federation of the West Indies in 1958, along with nine other British colonies. Following the departure of Jamaica and Trinidad and Tobago in 1962, the Federation collapsed and an attempt to unite the remaining colonies as the 'little eight' was unsuccessful. Along with its neighbours, Antigua and Barbuda became a British Associated State in 1967, responsible for its internal affairs, with the United Kingdom retaining control of external affairs and defence.

Vere Bird's ABLP remained in government until February 1971, when George Walter's Progressive Labour Movement (PLM) began a troubled period in office. Regaining power in 1976, the ABLP presided over the transition to independence on 1 November 1981.

After 1976 the ABLP won six successive election victories. The Bird family retained control of the party machinery, and continued to enjoy loyal popular support. Almost 29% of the labour force was employed directly by the state, and many public employees felt a close and personal bond with the ABLP's leadership. Several private sector businesses had close links with ABLP government ministers. Until November 2000 no radio or television station deemed to be critical of the Government was licensed to operate.

However, the Government's political credibility was damaged over an extended period by a series of scandals. Of these, the most widely documented concerned a Colombian diplomatic note delivered to the Antiguan permanent representative at the Organization of American States (OAS) in April 1990, stating that Israeli-manufactured weapons found on the property of a known Colombian drugs-trafficker had been traced to a delivery made to the Antigua Defence Force. The Prime Minister's eldest son, Vere Bird, Jr, was Minister of National Security at the time. The Governor-General appointed a British Queen's Counsel, Sir Louis Blom Cooper, to undertake a Commission of Inquiry. His conclusions included a recommendation that Bird, Jr, 'should not hold any public

office again'. Bird, Jr, was consequently dismissed from his post and banned for life from holding government office. The head of the Defence Force was also removed from office.

The Inquiry's conclusions helped to settle a succession struggle within the Bird family. Vere Bird, Sr, retired as leader of the ABLP in 1993 and was succeeded by another son, Lester Bryant Bird, who led the party into an election in March 1994. The campaign was hard fought. Three small opposition parties had merged in 1992 to form the United Progressive Party (UPP), led by Baldwin Spencer, a senior official of the Antigua Workers' Union. At the election, the UPP increased its parliamentary representation from one seat to five. The ABLP's share of the popular vote declined, but the party retained 11 seats, and Lester Bird became Prime Minister. In May 1996 Vere Bird, Jr, was controversially appointed to the post of Special Adviser to the Prime Minister.

At the next election, held in March 1999, the ABLP's share of the popular vote was further reduced, but the party gained an additional seat from the UPP. A Commonwealth observer team criticized the electoral process, while independent observers noted that large numbers of voters had been given generous gifts of food, or had been allowed to import vehicles duty-free in what the Prime Minister referred to as an exercise in 'poverty alleviation'. Vere Bird, Jr, was appointed Minister of Agriculture, Lands and Fisheries, on the basis that he had been elected to Parliament by voters who were aware of the findings of the Blom Cooper Commission of Inquiry.

In 2001 a further serious controversy developed over the management of the Government's Medical Benefits Scheme, which prompted the dismissal of the Attorney-General, Errol Cort, and the Leader of Government Business in the Senate, George 'Bacchanal' Walker. The Government reluctantly agreed to appoint a Commission of Inquiry into the management of the Scheme. The report of the Inquiry, published in 2002, detailed serious and systematic mismanagement, and recommended that the Director of Public Prosecutions should consider prosecuting 14 public officials, including two former health ministers. Some of these were subsequently charged.

In advance of the 2004 general election, a completely new electoral register was, with the assistance of the Electoral Office of Jamaica, prepared for the first time since 1975. Elimination of the names of the deceased and non-residents reduced the list by more than one-fifth, while voters were issued with identity cards including a photograph and fingerprint, decreasing the risk that illegitimate votes would be cast. At the election, held on 23 March 2004, the UPP increased its share of the vote to 55%, securing 12 of the 17 seats, with an additional seat for the UPP's ally, the Barbuda People's Movement. The ABLP took only 42% of the vote and four seats; both Lester Bird and Vere Bird, Jr, were defeated. Voter turnout, at 91%, was extremely high, and the election was widely seen as a watershed in national politics. Baldwin Spencer became Prime Minister, and committed his Government to a pragmatic reformist programme and the control of corruption and mismanagement. None the less, the ABLP retained a strong core of support, particularly in the civil service and police. Immediately before the election, a large number of files at the Prime Minister's office were destroyed, making it difficult for the incoming Government to establish the true state of public finances, debt or contracts with the private sector. Errol Cort, who had switched parties before the election, took Lester Bird's seat for the UPP and became finance minister in the new Cabinet.

The increasing prevalence of crime in the Caribbean region in recent years was also an important issue in Antigua, where the number of violent crimes had escalated rapidly: reported murders had risen from three, in both 2004 and 2005, to 19 in 2007. The number of reported murders declined slightly to 14 in 2008, but among those killed were a British honeymoon couple shot in their hotel cottage, whose deaths brought unwelcome international attention; two men were found guilty of this crime in 2011. There were 16 murders in 2009, but only seven in 2010, nine in 2011, 10 in 2012, and 12 in 2013. This last figure is equivalent to a per head murder rate of 14 per 100,000, which remains high by international standards and is more than three times that of the USA. The increase in violent crime was attributed in part to an escalation in drugs-related gang disputes, and to an increase in the number of criminal deportees repatriated from the USA. Drugs transshipment was a continuing problem, and is reported to have increased throughout the eastern Caribbean in 2013; the Government in 2009 estimated that 60% of the cocaine passing through the islands was destined for the United Kingdom, with 25% for the USA, 10% for the neighbouring island of Saint-Martin, and 5% consumed locally. The sole prison was overcrowded, insanitary, and ridden with gang violence and corruption, with 361 prisoners in 122 cells in 2014, and only 75 staff.

The IMF observed in the years following the 2004 election that the Government achieved progress in its attempt to restabilize the economy; however, the political atmosphere remained strongly polarized. Investigations into allegations against members of the former ABLP administration led to criminal charges against Lester Bird, several former cabinet ministers, and their financial associates, but procedural issues were raised to delay their progress through the judicial system. The office of the Special Task Force against Corruption and Organised Crime was damaged in an arson attack in January 2008. Divisions opened within the UPP from 2005, weakening its public image: one focus of contention was the Antigua Public Utilities Authority, which operates electricity, water and domestic telecommunications services, and the governing board of which was dismissed in November following indications of financial malpractice.

A further problem was continuing partisan support for the ABLP from former political appointees in the police force and public service. A report on the Royal Police Force of Antigua and Barbuda by Alphonse Breau, a retired Assistant Commissioner of the Royal Canadian Mounted Police concluded that the force was debilitated by political polarization, and suffered from weak operational standards, poor leadership, as well as problems with corruption, management, training and communications, and insufficient material resources. A former member of the Ottawa Police Service, Gary Nelson, became Commissioner of Police in Antigua in 2008, supported by three other Canadian officers on two-year contracts. Lester Bird stated that he viewed the appointments with 'utter abhorrence'. Nelson was replaced by Thomas Bennett, another Canadian, later in the year. When Bennett completed his contract in August 2010, he was replaced by Vere Browne, an Antiguan who had served for 30 years in the British Virgin Islands. A Canadian deputy commissioner, Neal Parker, remained in post until February 2012.

Allen Stanford, an investor of Texan origin (USA) who now has Antiguan citizenship, played an important role in the island's affairs from the early 1990s, when he moved his offshore banking activities from Montserrat, following their closure by the British authorities. He enjoyed a close relationship with the ABLP Government that was then in office, acquiring Antiguan citizenship and developing 'onshore' (Bank of Antigua) and offshore (Stanford International Bank) banks, property, construction and leisure companies, a daily newspaper (Antigua Sun), and a regional airline, Caribbean Star. The Stanford group was Antigua's second largest employer after the Government. However, Stanford distanced himself from the Bird regime ahead of the March 2004 election. Disagreements over a resort project developed by Stanford (see Economy) appear to have contributed to his rupture with the UPP Government in 2007, and Stanford's move to a new accommodation with the ABLP, on the nomination of which he had been conferred with a knighthood in 2006 (the title was revoked in 2009). Closure of his airline by early 2007 indicated growing financial difficulties, although Stanford was heavily involved in costly international and regional cricket sponsorship. The US authorities in February 2009 charged Stanford and several of his companies with organizing a fraudulent investment scheme. His lawyers argued in December 2010 that he was mentally unfit to stand trial; however, he was sentenced to 110 years in prison in June 2012. Indicating the weakness of local financial regulation, the

Antiguan Financial Services Regulatory Commission had in late 2008 given a clean bill of health to the Stanford International Bank. Its chief executive officer, Leroy King, was indicted by a grand jury in Houston, USA, in June 2009 for alleged corruption, and a court in Antigua ordered his extradition in April 2010; the High Court in February 2012 ruled against an appeal, as did the Eastern Caribbean Supreme Court in March, but he remained in Antigua on bail in mid-2014, with the Prime Minister supposedly to decide whether the extradition should proceed.

At a general election on 12 March 2009, the UPP Government lost ground to the ABLP opposition, still led by Lester Bird. The UPP's share of the popular vote declined to 51%, compared with 55% in 2004, and from 12 to nine seats, while the ABLP moved to 47% and seven seats. Lester Bird, now 71 years of age and still ABLP leader, regained his seat from Errol Cort. The Barbuda result was again narrow, with Trevor Walker of the Barbuda People's Movement defeating the ABLP candidate by a single vote. The voter turnout was 81%, a high figure, but down from 91% in 2004. The polling process did not run smoothly, with polling stations opening up to six hours late, and voters' lists, identity cards and ballot papers not ready for the scheduled start of the poll. However, election observers from the OAS, the Commonwealth, and the Caribbean Community and Common Market saw no evidence that either rival party was disproportionately affected.

Following the election, there was some remaining political uncertainty. Six defeated ABLP candidates initiated a legal challenge to the result, and an unsuccessful UPP candidate challenged the electoral list. There were widespread reports that Walker and several UPP members of Parliament, including Cort (now Minister of National Security), were offered substantial inducements to change sides. The Deputy Prime Minister, Wilmoth Daniel, resigned that post in early May 2009, but remained in the Cabinet with responsibility for health. Meanwhile, the High Court ruled in March that polling day irregularities were such that the election of three members of Parliament, including Spencer, was invalid, and that by-elections should be held for those seats; however, this ruling was, in October, overturned by the Eastern Caribbean Court of Appeal. Following an inquiry into alleged incompetence and misconduct, the Governor-General in January 2010 reconstituted the Electoral Commission, with some changes in membership and a new Chairman. Allegations of corruption under the ABLP Government remained under active consideration in mid-2013; a former minister, Hilroy Humphreys, was in April 2011 found guilty of fraudulent use of the Medical Benefits Scheme, and fined. At a contested ABLP convention in November 2012, Gaston Browne defeated Lester Bird in a leadership challenge; Browne is not, however, seen as representing a break with the past leadership. Meanwhile, the ABLP in March 2013 regained control of the Barbuda Island Council.

With the economy weak following the collapse of Allen Stanford's companies, and tourism suffering from the international recession, the UPP government continued to lose support in 2013–14. The party was decisively defeated at a general election on 12 June 2014, when it retained just three seats and 41.8% of the votes. The ABLP won 56.2% of votes cast and 14 seats. There was a high voter turnout of 90.3%. The new Cabinet appointed by incoming Prime Minister Gaston Browne included several stalwarts from the party's previous period in office, such as the former premier Lester Bird as Senior Minister, as well as Robin Yearwood, who had been appointed to his first cabinet post in 1980, and Molwyn Joseph, first appointed in 1984. Another cabinet member formerly in government was the new Attorney-General Steadroy 'Cutie' Benjamin, who also responsible for labour, immigration and the police. He had been charged by the police in 2008 with falsely certifying a photograph used in an application by a Jamaican migrant for a passport in the name of a recently deceased Antiguan. Benjamin stated that he believed the photograph to be correct and had no intention to deceive.

A dispute with the USA over restrictions on the use by US residents of internet gambling websites based in Antigua remained unresolved in mid-2014: a 2005 ruling by a World Trade Organization (WTO) appellate body stated that while the USA was entitled to regulate gambling, some existing legislation discriminated against offshore jurisdictions. However, Antigua maintained that the USA made no attempt to modify its legislation to ensure compliance with the ruling before the expiry of an April 2006 deadline. In October the US Congress approved legislation (the Unlawful Internet Gambling Enforcement Act) outlawing credit card payments to internet gambling websites, a move that the WTO in turn ruled illegal in March 2007. The USA announced in May that it would withdraw from any commitments relating to gambling under the General Agreement on Trade in Services, while Antigua attempted to gain wider international support for its position. As licensor and regulator for 32 internet gambling concerns within its jurisdiction, Antigua alleged that the prohibitive new legislation implemented by the USA had resulted in lost earnings, amounting to an estimated US $90m., and caused the loss of some 2,800 jobs, an estimate that most sources believed to be greatly exaggerated. Since the introduction of earlier US online gambling restrictions in 2000 it was claimed that revenue from the industry had declined from $1,000m. a year to $130m. in 2006. Licence fees and charges totalled almost $2.8m. The Government in June 2007 claimed the right to impose sanctions to the value of $3,400m. (three times the national gross domestic product) in compensation against the USA, through the withdrawal of intellectual property protection in Antigua for US trademarks, patents and industrial designs. Australia, Canada, India, Japan and the European Union also filed compensation claims. A WTO panel in December awarded Antigua the right to impose sanctions, but to the much lower value of $21m. a year; the USA offered $500,000. The World Intellectual Property Organization held that, notwithstanding the WTO ruling, Antigua remained bound by its obligations under the Berne Convention. The USA contended that the terms it had originally negotiated under the Agreement did not explicitly refer to internet gambling, thus rendering it exempt from the payment of the compensation. Nevertheless, the USA maintained its restrictions on internet gambling, and in November 2009 the founder of online gambling company BetOnSports was sentenced to 51 months in prison for violating racketeering and other laws. The USA in 2014 maintained its policy of prosecuting non-domestic internet gambling operations based in Antigua or elsewhere and believed to be in breach of US law. The internet gambling sector, along with drugs-trafficking and offshore finance, contributed to the US Department of State's classification of Antigua and Barbuda as a country of 'primary concern' in regard to money-laundering.

New 'passports for sale' legislation passed in March 2013 granted citizenship to those making a US $250,000 investment in Antigua's National Development Fund. The programme was officially inaugurated in October. There was widespread opposition to this move both inside and outside the island; two government senators were removed after voting against the measure. However, the ABLP supported the measure while in opposition, and stated on taking office in June 2014 that it would relax the 35-day residence and other requirements for citizenship, as these deterred potential business.

In 2006, at the annual meeting of the International Whaling Commission, Antigua voted, along with other members of the Organisation of Eastern Caribbean States (OECS), in favour of an end to a 20-year commercial whaling ban, despite lacking a recent whaling tradition and scientific expertise in the relevant issues. The Government's pro-whaling stance brought allegations that Japanese financial assistance had amounted to bribery (Japan led the campaign to end the ban), and that the vote had jeopardized relations with environmental groups and other foreign investors. Furthermore, at the Commission's annual meeting in 2007, Antigua was among several OECS countries to confirm their concurrence with a request, issued by Saint Vincent and the Grenadines, for an increase to those islands' commercial whaling quotas. An appeal for the protection of the indigenous and coastal population's rights to preserve their supposed traditional fishing practices—and for acknowledgement of earlier recommendations, by Saint Kitts and Nevis, that a policy of appropriate management of marine resources be adopted, as opposed to a complete ban—was presented to the Commission. Opposition to the proposed establishment of a marine mammal sanctuary in the French West Indies was also reiterated, particularly as marine territorial boundaries between the French dependencies and several Eastern Caribbean nations remained in dispute.

Antigua and Barbuda was the first of the OECS states to open diplomatic relations with the People's Republic of China, and in 2010 signed agreements providing US $50m. in financial assistance; in 2011 China agreed funding of 300m. yuan to finance a new airport terminal.

In July 2014 Prime Minister Browne announced his Government's intention to hold a referendum on replacing the Privy Council, based in the United Kingdom, with the Caribbean Court of Justice, in Trinidad and Tobago, as Antigua and Barbuda's final court of appeal.

Economy

MARK WILSON

Antigua and Barbuda is the third smallest country in the Western hemisphere, in terms of population, with some 86,295 inhabitants living on its 442 sq km at the 2011 census. However, the islands have developed a relatively prosperous middle-income economy, with a per head gross domestic product (GDP) at market prices peaking at US $12,766 in 2011.

The pace of economic growth picked up in the mid-2000s, increasing from a rise of 2.0% in 2001 to an average of 8.6% in 2003–07. However, the important tourism sector has been broadly stagnant since the mid-1990s, with a further downturn in 2008–10 as international demand declined sharply; remittances from overseas migrants and investment inflows also decreased, while the economy suffered intense pressure from the collapse of Allen Stanford's group of companies (see below). GDP grew by just 1.5% in 2008, and contracted by 10.7% in 2009, by 8.6% in 2010 and by a further 2.1% in 2011, before recovering weakly by 2.8% in 2012 and by an estimated 0.1% in 2013. Arrivals of stop-over tourists contracted by a cumulative 13.5% in 2009–10, as the international recession resulted in fewer tourist arrivals and reduced investment; arrivals in 2013 were still 10.6% below the 2008 peak. The construction sector grew by a cumulative 100.3% in 2004–07, stagnated in 2008,

then contracted by a cumulative 55% in 2009–11, as tourism-related and other private and public sector activity slowed sharply; cumulative growth of 15.5% in 2012–13 indicated only a partial recovery. Wholesale and retail trading activity contracted by a cumulative 37% in 2009–11, recovering by only 3.2% by 2013, while the balance of payments current deficit increased to EC $552m. or 16.6% of GDP, in 2013. Unemployment has increased, and was estimated at 10.2% by the 2011 census, but wages were high enough to attract immigrants from less prosperous Caribbean countries such as Dominica, the Dominican Republic and Guyana, with an estimated net annual inward migration rate of two per 1,000; the poverty rate was estimated at 18% in 2007 by the Caribbean Development Bank, one of the lowest in the Organisation of Eastern Caribbean States (OECS). However, migrant remittances into Antigua made up 4% of GDP in 2001–11.

There is concern about the extent of government debt: although debt had been reduced to an estimated 90% of GDP by December 2008 (from 128% of GDP in 2003), partly because of negotiated partial debt-forgiveness and -restructuring, the economic contraction of 2009 increased the debt-to-GDP ratio to 102% (according to IMF estimates), with arrears at 53% of

GDP. The 2005 budget introduced new taxes, including an income tax for the highest paid 25% of the population, while the efficiency of tax collections improved sharply and a value-added tax was introduced in 2007. The overall fiscal deficit moved from 12.4% of GDP in 2001 to 6.4% in 2007. Around 1,000 public service jobs (equivalent to 8% of total employment in the sector) were shed from 2006 through voluntary redundancy and early retirement programmes, contributing to a 11.3% reduction in central government salary costs, which were EC $277m. in 2013, down from EC $309m. in 2007. The economic difficulties of 2009 sharply decreased revenue and raised expenditure, with the fiscal deficit widening again to 18% of GDP (according to IMF data). The IMF in 2010 approved a US $128m. (SDR 81m.) stand-by loan, while the Government agreed to a three-year plan involving spending reductions, revenue-raising measures, public sector reform, a debt-management strategy and policy reforms to mitigate financial sector risks. The programme was completed with a 10th and final review in June 2013. Debt had been reduced to 88% of GDP at the end of 2012, still a high figure, while the overall fiscal deficit was back down to 1.2% of GDP by 2012, although public servants were again being paid late in 2013, an indication of serious cash flow difficulties. The IMF called for continued efforts to improve revenue administration, rationalize tax expenditures and move forward with civil service reform. State-owned enterprises remain a significant problem area, with employment and spending almost one-half that of the central government, as do large government-guaranteed debts and poor governance. The IMF in May 2014 noted a high degree of risk to the macroeconomic outlook stemming from an unsustainable fiscal deficit, which had risen again to 3.3% of GDP in 2013, with debt back to 92% of GDP, and a high ratio of non-performing loans in the banking system. The 2014 budget provided for a deficit of EC $63.8m., or 1.9% of GDP. The new Antigua and Barbuda Labour Party (ABLP) administration that took office in 2014 stated its intention not to seek further agreements with the IMF.

Antigua and Barbuda is a member of the Caribbean Community and Common Market (CARICOM), which formed the Caribbean Single Market in 2006. It is also a member of the OECS, which links nine of the smaller Caribbean territories (Antigua and Barbuda, Dominica, Grenada, Montserrat, Saint Christopher (St Kitts) and Nevis, Saint Lucia, and Saint Vincent and the Grenadines, with Anguilla and the British Virgin Islands as associate members), while the Eastern Caribbean Central Bank (ECCB), based in neighbouring Saint Christopher and Nevis, supervises its financial affairs. Antigua is of much greater economic significance than Barbuda, which is two-thirds the area of the main island, but which has a population of only some 1,500.

The main source of foreign exchange revenue is the service sector, principally tourism. The services sector contributed 81.9% of GDP in 2013. Gross tourism earnings totalled EC $831m. in that year, equivalent to 25.0% of GDP, which was 8.9% below the 2007 peak, even in current price terms, and not enough to cover the deficit on merchandise trade, estimated at EC $1,204m. in 2013, or 36.3% of GDP. The islands' main attractions are their white sandy beaches, of which there are reputed to be 365. There are also fine historic naval sites at English Harbour, Nelson's Dockyard and Shirley Heights in the south-east of Antigua. There were 237,765 stop-over tourist arrivals in 2013, of whom 36% came from the USA, 36% from Europe (mostly the United Kingdom) and 12% from Canada. Cruise ship passengers outnumber stop-over tourists, and totalled 533,280 in 2013, although, with much lower per head spending, they made a smaller contribution to the economy. Yachting and pleasure-boating is also an important and growing activity, centred on English Harbour, with 3,825 yachts bringing 29,053 visitors in 2013; Antigua's annual sailing week in April attracts several hundred yachts from across the Caribbean and worldwide. Barbuda has a small tourism industry, with three luxury hotels. In addition to tourism, an offshore medical school, Indian-owned since 2008 (Manipal Education), generated significant year-round spending by its 1,000 students, as well as staff.

The tourism industry has been somewhat stagnant in recent years. In 2012 hotels and restaurants accounted for an esti-mated 12.8% of GDP, down from a peak value of 17.3% in 2004. High labour costs have been a particular problem for the sector. Relations between the previous ABLP Government and established investors were not always good, and improved only to a limited extent under the subsequent United Progressive Party administration; an untractable dispute over the compulsory purchase of the former Half Moon Bay hotel, which was closed after Hurricane Luis in 1995, remained unsettled for some time, but appeared to have been resolved by a Privy Council ruling in February 2014. The incoming ABLP Government in June signed an outline agreement with Chinese investors for a tourism complex to include Guana Island on the north-east coast, to include five hotels, 1,300 holiday homes, and a golf course, marina and casino, to be built over 10 years at a cost of EC $2,000m. Inward foreign direct investment, much of it tourism-related, declined from EC $919m. in 2007 to EC $373m. in 2013.

Antigua serves as a hub for airline services to the smaller neighbouring islands, and is the headquarters of the major Eastern Caribbean airline, LIAT. The controlling shareholders of the airline are the Governments of Antigua, Barbados and Saint Vincent. However, the financial stability of the airline has been uneven, and has been affected by labour disputes since 2009.

There is an offshore financial services sector, which has been a source of international concern, and has contracted in size since 2000. The USA signed a Tax Information Exchange Treaty with Antigua and Barbuda in December 2001, although it is still listed by the US Department of State as a jurisdiction of 'primary concern' for money-laundering, with attention focusing on internet casinos, investment fraud and advance fee fraud as much as on funds derived from narcotics. Even though the country was never included on the Financial Action Task Force's list of 'non-co-operative' jurisdictions, Antigua and Barbuda was placed on a list of tax havens by the Organisation for Economic Co-operation and Development (OECD) in 2000; it was removed from this list in 2002 after the Government signed a commitment to move towards the exchange of information with civil and criminal tax investigators by 2005. However, Antigua and Barbuda withdrew from this agreement in 2004, citing the failure of some OECD members to make similar commitments, and in 2008 OECD included the islands in a 'grey list' of countries that did not yet have a significant number of Tax Information Exchange Agreements in place; sufficient agreements were signed to be removed from the list at the end of 2009. The territory was again placed on OECD's 'dark grey list' of territories that had failed sufficiently to comply with international financial standards in 2013, but removed once more from the list in Febuary 2014. In 2011 there were 14 licensed offshore banks; more than 30 other banks had been closed for regulatory reasons since 1999. There were also 3,497 International Business Corporations in 2010, down from 15,000 in 1997. In 2014 there were eight internet gambling companies, supervised in principle by the Directorate of Offshore Gaming, to which the owners of these sites paid annual licence fees totalling US $3.1m. in 2013; in 2010 gambling accounted for one-half of the 885 jobs in the offshore financial sector. In 2003 Antigua challenged US restrictions on internet gambling through the structures of the World Trade Organization (WTO), and in 2005 received a ruling that was interpreted as partly in its favour. However, by mid-2014 the USA had failed to modify its regulatory regime to achieve compliance (having outlawed credit card payments to internet gambling sites in 2006) and stated in 2007 that it would withdraw from any commitments on gambling made under the General Agreement on Trade in Services. The WTO in 2007 made a further ruling in favour of Antigua, which attempted vigorously to gather international support for its stance; in 2013 Antigua received final approval from the WTO to implement the 2007 ruling allowing suspension of US intellectual property rights to an annual value of US $21m. Nevertheless, US legal action against online gambling companies, including those registered in Antigua, continued in mid-2014. Indicating international recognition, Antigua in 2008 received 'white list' status from the United Kingdom, allowing internet casinos to advertise for British customers, subject to a licensing requirement. The Government in 2013 established an economic citizenship programme, claiming it would avoid the opportunities to international criminals afforded by programmes in St Kitts and Nevis, Dominica and elsewhere.

Allen Stanford, a US entrepreneur of Texan origin, moved to Antigua in the early 1990s, acquiring Antiguan citizenship and developing many businesses. The Stanford group became Antigua's second largest employer after the government, to which it provided loans totalling US $85m., then more than 10% of GDP. An agreement in 2004 provided for further funding, as well as an $18.5m. debt cancellation. Stanford also announced plans for a EC $3,000m. resort development, although a dispute over land ownership delayed progress on the scheme. Disagreements over this project contributed to Stanford's rupture with the Government in 2007, and his move to a new accommodation with the ABLP. In 2009 US authorities charged Stanford and several of his companies with organizing a fraudulent investment scheme and Stanford was sentenced to 110 years' imprisonment in June 2012 (see History).

Like its neighbours, Antigua and Barbuda suffered from the collapse in 2009 of a Trinidad-based insurance conglomerate, CL Financial, which posed risks to financial stability throughout the eastern Caribbean, with an important subsidiary, the British American Insurance Company (BAICO), declared insolvent. The IMF estimated the total eastern Caribbean exposure to the CL group at EC $2,100m., or 17% of the subregional GDP; Antigua and Barbuda's exposure to BAICO was estimated at EC $300m., or 9% of GDP. With troubles in both the offshore and domestic finance sectors, GDP attributable to the banking sector contracted by 14.2% in 2009 and a cumulative 7.6% in 2010–13. A local institution, the Antigua and Barbuda Investment Bank (ABIB), was unable to meet statutory reserve requirements in 2011 and was taken over by the ECCB, placing a further potential burden on public debt.

The Government has emphasized the importance of new technology, and telemarketing was seen as a promising area of activity. However, the islands have lagged behind their neighbours in liberalizing the telecommunications industry. There was competition in domestic cellular telephony, but landline services were provided only by the state-owned Antigua Public Utilities Authority (APUA). Southern Caribbean Fibre landed a cable in 2007, and the international voice call monopoly held by the local LIME (Cable & Wireless) expired in 2012, with new licences granted to APUA, Digicel, LIME and a local competitor. APUA's role of regulator was transferred in 2012 to the Telecommunications Division under the auspices of the Office of the Prime Minister. Overall, the state of utilities infrastructure is uneven. Electricity is distributed by APUA, and generated by both APUA and the private sector Antigua Power Company (APC); relations between the two companies and other matters relating to the sector have been the subject of complex legal disputes, in which a May 2013 court ruling in favour of APC appeared likely to prove costly for the Government; further legal action followed in 2014. Electricity supply has been inadequate, with frequent power cuts. Water supply is also inadequate, with APUA buying fresh water from private sector desalination plants. Its difficulties were compounded by consumer arrears, which totalled EC $172m., equivalent to 5.2% of GDP, in mid-2014; the incoming ABLP Government promised to write off all APUA debt from before the start of the year.

Since the closure of the sugar industry, most of the land has been uncultivated. Agriculture accounted for only 1.1% of GDP in 2013, with a further 1.0% from fishing. The state owns most rural land. This has given it close control over residential, commercial and tourism-orientated development projects. There was a very small manufacturing sector, which contributed an estimated 2.6% of GDP in 2013. It included a brewery and a paint company, which catered mainly for the domestic market.

Statistical Survey

Source (unless otherwise stated): Ministry of Finance, Economy and Public Administration, Coolidge Business Complex, Sir George Walter Highway, St John's; tel. 468-4600; e-mail minfinance@antigua.gov.ag; internet www.ab.gov.ag.

AREA AND POPULATION

Area: 441.6 sq km (170.5 sq miles).

Population: 76,886 at census of 28 May 2001; 86,295 (males 41,481, females 44,814) at census of 28 May 2011 (preliminary). *Mid-2014* (UN estimate): 90,905 (Source: UN, *World Population Prospects: The 2012 Revision*).

Density (at mid-2014): 205.9 per sq km.

Population by Age and Sex (UN estimates at mid-2014): *0–14 years:* 22,315 (males 11,191, females 11,124); *15–64 years:* 62,126 (males 29,519, females 32,607); *65 years and over:* 6,464 (males 2,731, females 3,733); *Total* 90,905 (males 43,441, females 47,464). Source: UN, *World Population Prospects: The 2012 Revision*.

Principal Town: St John's (capital), population 22,193 at 2011 census (preliminary).

Births, Marriages and Deaths (2007 unless otherwise indicated): Live births 1,240 (birth rate 14.44 per 1,000); Marriages 1,863; Deaths 504 (death rate 5.87 per 1,000). *2008:* Birth rate 16.8 per 1,000; Death rate 6.1 per 1,000. *2013:* Birth rate 16.1 per 1,000; Death rate 5.7 per 1,000 (Source: Pan American Health Organization).

Life Expectancy (years at birth): 75.7 (males 73.3; females 78.1) in 2012. Source: World Bank, World Development Indicators database.

Employment (persons aged 15 years and over, official estimates, 2008): Agriculture, hunting and forestry 789; Fishing 290; Mining and quarrying 121; Manufacturing 1,754; Electricity, gas and water supply 585; Construction 3,557; Wholesale and retail trade 5,516; Hotels and restaurants 5,783; Transport, storage and communications 3,203; Financial intermediation 1,195; Real estate, renting and business activities 1,665; Public administration and defence 4,986; Education 1,956; Health and social work 1,955; Other community, social and personal service activities 3,057; Households with employed persons 1,485; Extraterritorial organizations and bodies 572; Total employed 38,470 (males 19,321, females 19,149). Source: ILO.

HEALTH AND WELFARE

Key Indicators

Total Fertility Rate (children per woman, 2012): 2.1.

Under-5 Mortality Rate (per 1,000 live births, 2012): 10.

Physicians (per 1,000 head, 1999): 0.2.

Hospital Beds (per 1,000 head, 2010): 2.2.

Health Expenditure (2011): US $ per head (PPP): 1,061.

Health Expenditure (2011): % of GDP: 5.5.

Health Expenditure (2011): public (% of total): 73.7.

Access to Water (% of persons, 2012): 98.

Access to Sanitation (% of persons, 2011): 91.

Total Carbon Dioxide Emissions ('000 metric tons, 2010): 513.4.

Total Carbon Dioxide Emissions Per Head (metric tons, 2010): 5.9.

Human Development Index (2013): ranking: 61.

Human Development Index (2013): value: 0.774.

For sources and definitions, see explanatory note on p. vi.

AGRICULTURE, ETC.

Principal Crops ('000 metric tons, 2012, FAO estimates): Cantaloupes and other melons 1.0; Vegetables (incl. melons) 3.3; Guavas, mangoes and mangosteens 1.2; Fruits (excl. melons) 10.0.

Livestock ('000 head, 2012, FAO estimates): Asses 1.7; Cattle 15.0; Pigs 3.0; Sheep 23.0; Goats 37.0; Poultry 150.0.

Livestock Products ('000 metric tons, 2012, FAO estimates): Cattle meat 0.6; Cows' milk 6.0; Hen eggs 0.3.

Fishing (metric tons, live weight, 2012, estimates): Groupers and seabasses 120; Snappers and jobfishes 370; Grunts and sweetlips

110; Parrotfishes 120; Surgeonfishes 180; Triggerfishes and durgons 18; Caribbean spiny lobster 220; Stromboid conchs 1,350; Total catch (incl. others) 3,050.

Source: FAO.

INDUSTRY

Production (1988 estimates unless otherwise indicated): Rum 4,000 hectolitres; Wines and vodka 2,000 hectolitres; Electric energy (2009) 119m. kWh. Source: partly UN Industrial Commodity Statistics Database and Yearbook.

FINANCE

Currency and Exchange Rates: 100 cents = 1 Eastern Caribbean dollar (EC $). *Sterling, US Dollar and Euro Equivalents* (30 May 2014): £1 sterling = EC $4.542; US $1 = EC $2.700; €1 = EC $3.675; EC $100 = £22.02 = US $37.04 = €27.21. *Exchange rate:* Fixed at US $1 = EC $2.700 since July 1976.

Budget (EC $ million, 2013): *Revenue:* Tax revenue 555.2; Other current revenue 42.6; Capital revenue 1.3; Total 599.1 (excl. grants 0.0). *Expenditure:* Current expenditure 700.4 (Wages and salaries 276.9, Goods and services 147.7, Interest payments 66.0, Transfers and subsidies 209.9); Capital expenditure 43.1; Total 743.6. Source: Eastern Caribbean Central Bank.

International Reserves (US $ million at 31 December 2013): IMF special drawing rights 0.01; Reserve position in IMF 0.08; Foreign exchange 202.49; Total 202.58. Source: IMF, *International Financial Statistics*.

Money Supply (EC $ million at 31 December 2013): Currency outside depository corporations 136.59; Transferable deposits 868.92; Other deposits 2,178.72; *Broad money* 3,184.23. Source: IMF, *International Financial Statistics*.

Cost of Living (Consumer Price Index; base: January 2001 = 100): 128.9 in 2011; 131.3 in 2012; 132.7 in 2013. Source: Eastern Caribbean Central Bank.

Expenditure on the Gross Domestic Product (EC $ million at current prices, 2012): Government final consumption expenditure 566.87; Private final consumption expenditure 2,334.88; Gross capital formation 716.45; *Total domestic expenditure* 3,618.20; Exports of goods and services 1,462.18; *Less* Imports of goods and services 1,856.59; *GDP at market prices* 3,223.79. Source: Eastern Caribbean Central Bank.

Gross Domestic Product by Economic Activity (EC $ million at current prices, 2012): Agriculture, hunting, forestry and fishing 53.97; Mining and quarrying 21.62; Manufacturing 68.93; Electricity and water 107.84; Construction 260.27; Trade 411.24; Restaurants and hotels 362.27; Transport and communications 358.61; Finance, insurance, real estate and business services 655.44; Government services 246.01; Education 137.59; Health and social work 80.10; Other community, social and personal service activities 52.62; *Sub-total* 2,831.10; *Less* Financial intermediation services indirectly measured 84.93; *Gross value added in basic prices* 2,746.17; Taxes, less subsidies, on products 477.61; *GDP in market prices* 3,223.79. Source: Eastern Caribbean Central Bank.

Balance of Payments (EC $ million, 2013): Goods (net) –1,161.49; Services (net) 662.76; *Balance on goods and services* –498.73; Income (net) –135.36; *Balance on goods, services and income* –634.09; Current transfers (net) 82.21; *Current balance* –551.88; Capital account (net) 42.09; Direct investment (net) 362.58; Portfolio investment (net) 14.37; Other investments (net) 244.53; Net errors and omissions 2.89; *Overall balance* 114.57. Source: Eastern Caribbean Central Bank.

EXTERNAL TRADE

Total Trade (EC $ million): *Imports f.o.b.:* 1,271.96 in 2011; 1,437.43 in 2012; 1,372.87 in 2013. *Exports f.o.b.:* (incl. re-exports): 78.38 in 2011; 78.32 in 2012; 88.89 in 2013. Source: Eastern Caribbean Central Bank.

Principal Commodities (US $ million, 2013): *Imports:* Live animals and animal products 34.7 (Meat and edible meat offal 19.1; Dairy products, eggs, honey, edible animal products, etc. 10.4); Vegetables and vegetable products 21.5; Prepared foodstuffs; beverages, spirits, vinegar; tobacco and articles thereof 64.1 (Beverages, spirits and vinegar 23.1; Miscellaneous edible preparations 11.2); Chemicals and related products 29.1; Plastics, rubber, and articles thereof 13.3; Pulp of wood, paper and paperboard, and articles thereof 11.1; Textiles and textile articles 18.8; Iron and steel, other base metals and articles of base metal 23.7 (Articles of iron or steel 11.0); Machinery and mechanical appliances; electrical equipment; parts thereof 40.5 (Machinery, boilers, etc. 21.6; Electrical, electronic equipment 19.0); Vehicles, aircraft, vessels and associated transport equipment 26.0 (Vehicles other than railway, tramway 21.6); Miscel-

laneous manufactured articles 12.0; Total (incl. others) 344.6. *Exports:* Prepared foodstuffs; beverages, spirits, vinegar; tobacco and articles thereof 1.2 (Beverages, spirits and vinegar 1.1); Mineral products 4.2 (Mineral fuels, oils, distillation products, etc. 4.2); Textiles and textile articles 10.3 (Textile articles, sets, worn clothing, etc. 9.6); Iron and steel, other base metals and articles of base metal 3.8 (Iron and steel 1.8; Articles of iron or steel 1.5); Machinery and mechanical appliances; electrical equipment; parts thereof 4.3; (Machinery, boilers, etc. 1.8; Electrical, electronic equipment 2.5); Vehicles, aircraft, vessels and associated transport equipment 3.4 (Ships, boats and other floating structures 2.5); Miscellaneous manufactured articles 1.4 (Furniture, lighting, signs, prefabricated buildings 1.0); Total (incl. others) 33.1. Source: Trade Map-Trade Competitiveness Map, International Trade Centre, www.intracen.org/marketanalysis.

Principal Trading Partners (US $ million, 2013): *Imports:* Barbados 5.3; Brazil 6.5; Canada 5.7; China, People's Republic 19.7; Dominican Republic 4.4; France 5.2; Germany 3.6; Italy 4.1; Jamaica 5.4; Japan 10.3; Korea, Republic 4.7; Mexico 3.7; Netherlands 3.9; Saint Vincent and the Grenadines 5.8; Switzerland 3.9; Trinidad and Tobago 15.6; United Kingdom 14.2; USA 179.8; Total (incl. others) 344.6. *Exports:* Anguilla 0.4; Barbados 0.3; British Virgin Islands 1.0; Dominica 0.6; France (incl. Monaco) 0.9; French Polynesia 0.4; Hong Kong 0.7; Montserrat 1.0; New Zealand 1.8; Panama 0.5; Saint Christopher and Nevis 1.0; Saint Lucia 0.9; Saint Vincent and the Grenadines 0.7; Suriname 0.7; Taiwan 0.7; Trinidad and Tobago 0.6; United Kingdom 6.8; USA 8.8; Total (incl. others) 33.1. Source: Trade Map-Trade Competitiveness Map, International Trade Centre, www.intracen.org/marketanalysis.

TRANSPORT

Road Traffic (registered vehicles, 1998): Passenger motor cars and commercial vehicles 24,000. Source: UN, *Statistical Yearbook*.

Shipping: *Flag Registered Fleet* (at 31 December): 1,225 vessels (total displacement 10,120,815 grt) in 2013 (Source: Lloyd's List Intelligence—www.lloydslistintelligence.com).

Civil Aviation (traffic on scheduled services, 2009): Kilometres flown (million) 6; Passengers carried ('000) 748; Passenger-km (million) 123; Total ton-km (million) 11 (Source: UN, *Statistical Yearbook*). *2012* ('000): Passengers carried 1,310 (Source: World Bank, World Development Indicators database).

TOURISM

Visitor Arrivals: 870,240 (241,331 stop-over visitors, 24,403 yacht passengers, 604,506 cruise ship passengers) in 2011; 842,693 (246,926 stop-over visitors, 28,060 yacht passengers, 567,707 cruise ship passengers) in 2012; 792,332 (229,999 stop-over visitors, 29,053 yacht passengers, 533,280 cruise ship passengers) in 2013.

Tourism Receipts (EC $ million): 841.8 in 2011; 861.3 in 2012; 806.2 in 2013.

Source: Eastern Caribbean Central Bank.

COMMUNICATIONS MEDIA

Telephones (2013): 33,133 main lines in use.

Mobile Cellular Telephones (2013): 114,358 subscribers.

Internet Subscribers (2011): 14,600.

Broadband Subscribers (2013): 4,035.

Source: International Telecommunication Union.

EDUCATION

Pre-primary (2010/11 unless otherwise indicated): 31 schools; 165 teachers; 2,341 pupils.

Primary (2011/12 unless otherwise indicated): 55 schools (2000/01); 794 teachers (males 66, females 728, 2010/11); 10,453 students (males 5,413, females 5,040).

Secondary (2011/12 unless otherwise indicated): 14 schools (2000/01); 637 teachers (males 201, females 436, 2010/11); 7,907 students (males 3,920, females 3,987).

Special (2011/12 unless otherwise indicated): 2 schools (2000/01); 15 teachers (2000/01); 104 students (males 61, females 43).

Tertiary (2011/12 unless otherwise indicated): 2 colleges (1986); 173 teachers (males 66, females 107, 2009/10); 1,792 students (males 548, females 1,244). Source: UNESCO Institute for Statistics.

Pupil-teacher ratio (primary education, UNESCO estimate): 13.8 in 2011/12. Source: UNESCO Institute for Statistics.

Adult Literacy Rate: 99.0% (males 98.4, females 99.4) in 2011. Source: UNESCO Institute for Statistics.

Directory

The Constitution

The Constitution, which came into force at the independence of Antigua and Barbuda on 1 November 1981, states that Antigua and Barbuda is a 'unitary sovereign democratic state'. The main provisions of the Constitution are summarized below.

FUNDAMENTAL RIGHTS AND FREEDOMS

Regardless of race, place of origin, political opinion, colour, creed or sex, but subject to respect for the rights and freedoms of others and for the public interest, every person in Antigua and Barbuda is entitled to the rights of life, liberty, security of the person, the enjoyment of property and the protection of the law. Freedom of movement, of conscience, of expression (including freedom of the press), of peaceful assembly and of association is guaranteed, and the inviolability of family life, personal privacy, home and other property is maintained. Protection is afforded from discrimination on the grounds of race, sex, etc., and from slavery, forced labour, torture and inhuman treatment.

THE GOVERNOR-GENERAL

The British sovereign, as monarch of Antigua and Barbuda, is the Head of State and is represented by a Governor-General of local citizenship.

PARLIAMENT

Parliament consists of the Monarch, a 17-member Senate and the House of Representatives, which is composed of 17 elected members. Senators are appointed by the Governor-General: 11 on the advice of the Prime Minister (one of whom must be an inhabitant of Barbuda), four on the advice of the Leader of the Opposition, one at his or her own discretion and one on the advice of the Barbuda Council. The Barbuda Council is the principal organ of local government in that island, whose membership and functions are determined by Parliament. The life of Parliament is five years.

Each constituency returns one Representative to the House who is directly elected in accordance with the Constitution.

The Attorney-General, if not otherwise a member of the House, is an ex officio member but does not have the right to vote.

Every citizen over the age of 18 is eligible to vote.

Parliament may alter any of the provisions of the Constitution.

THE EXECUTIVE

Executive authority is vested in the Monarch and exercisable by the Governor-General. The Governor-General appoints as Prime Minister that member of the House who, in the Governor-General's view, is best able to command the support of the majority of the members of the House, and other ministers on the advice of the Prime Minister. The Governor-General may remove the Prime Minister from office if a resolution of no confidence is approved by the House and the Prime Minister does not either resign or advise the Governor-General to dissolve Parliament within seven days.

The Cabinet consists of the Prime Minister and other ministers and the Attorney-General.

The Leader of the Opposition is appointed by the Governor-General as that member of the House who, in the Governor-General's view, is best able to command the support of a majority of members of the House who do not support the Government.

CITIZENSHIP

All persons born in Antigua and Barbuda before independence who, immediately prior to independence, were citizens of the United Kingdom and Colonies automatically become citizens of Antigua and Barbuda. All persons born outside the country with a parent or grandparent possessing citizenship of Antigua and Barbuda automatically acquire citizenship, as do those born in the country after independence. Provision is made for the acquisition of citizenship by those to whom it would not automatically be granted.

The Government

HEAD OF STATE

Queen: HM Queen ELIZABETH II.

Governor-General: Dr RODNEY WILLIAMS (took office 14 August 2014).

CABINET

(September 2014)

The Government was formed by the Antigua and Barbuda Labour Party.

Prime Minister and Minister of Finance and Corporate Governance: GASTON A. BROWNE.

Attorney-General and Minister of Legal Affairs, Public Safety, Immigration and Labour: STEADROY C. O. BENJAMIN.

Minister of Agriculture, Lands, Fisheries and Barbuda Affairs: ARTHUR NIBBS.

Minister of Education, Science and Technology: MICHAEL BROWNE.

Minister of Foreign Affairs and International Trade: CHARLES HENRY FERNANDEZ.

Minister of Health and the Environment: MOLWYN JOSEPH.

Minister of Information, Broadcasting, Telecommunications and Information Technology: MELFORD NICHOLAS.

Minister of Public Utilities, Civil Aviation and Transportation: ROBIN YEARWOOD.

Minister of Works and Housing: EUSTACE (TECO) LAKE.

Minister of Social Transformation and Human Resource Development: SAMANTHA MARSHALL.

Minister of Tourism, Economic Development, Investment and Energy: ASOT MICHAEL.

Minister of Trade, Commerce, Industry, Sports, Culture and National Festivals: PAUL (CHET) GREENE.

Senior Minister: LESTER BIRD.

Minister of State in the Ministry of Finance and Corporate Governance: LENNOX O'REILLY WESTON.

MINISTRIES

Office of the Prime Minister: Queen Elizabeth Hwy, St John's; tel. 462-4610; fax 462-3225; internet www.antigua.gov.ag.

Ministry of Agriculture, Lands and Fisheries: Queen Elizabeth Hwy, St John's; tel. 462-1213; fax 462-6104; e-mail minagri@antigua.gov.ag.

Ministry of Education, Science and Technology: Govt Office Complex, Queen Elizabeth Hwy, St John's; tel. 462-4959; fax 462-4970; e-mail mineduc@ab.gov.ag; internet www.education.gov.ag.

Ministry of Finance and Corporate Governance: Govt Office Complex, Parliament Dr., St John's; tel. 462-2922; fax 462-4860; e-mail ps.finance2011@gmail.com.

Ministry of Foreign Affairs and International Trade: Queen Elizabeth Hwy, St John's; tel. 462-1052; fax 462-2482; e-mail foreignaffairs@ab.gov.ag; internet www.foreignaffairs.gov.ag.

Ministry of Health and the Environment: Popeshead St, St John's; tel. 562-6640.

Ministry of Information, Broadcasting, Telecommunications and Information Technology: St John's.

Ministry of Legal Affairs, Public Safety, Immigration and Labour: New Government Office Complex, Parliament Dr., St John's; tel. 462-0017; fax 462-2465; e-mail legalaffairs@antigua.gov.ag.

Ministry of Public Utilities, Civil Aviation and Transportation: St John's St, St John's; tel. 462-2953.

Ministry of Social Transformation and Human Resource Development: St John's.

Ministry of Tourism, Economic Development, Investment and Energy: Government Office Complex, Queen Elizabeth Hwy, St John's.

Ministry of Trade, Commerce, Industry, Sports, Culture and National Festivals: St John's.

Ministry of Works and Housing: St John's.

Legislature

PARLIAMENT

Senate

President: ALINCIA WILLIAMS-GRANT.

There are 17 nominated members.

House of Representatives

Speaker: Sir GERALD WATT.
General Election, 12 June 2014

Party	Votes cast	% of votes	Seats
Antigua and Barbuda Labour Party	24,212	56.21	14
United Progressive Party	17,994	41.77	3
Barbuda People's Movement	484	1.12	—
Others	202	0.47	—
Blank or invalid votes	185	0.43	
Total	**43,077**	**100.00**	**17**

The Attorney-General is also an ex-officio member of the House of Representatives.

Election Commission

Antigua and Barbuda Electoral Commission (ABEC): Queen Elizabeth Hwy, POB 664, St John's; tel. 562-4196; fax 562-4331; internet www.abec.gov.ag; f. 2001; Chief Elections Officer LORNA SIMON.

Political Organizations

Antigua and Barbuda Labour Party (ABLP): Nevis St, St John's; tel. 562-5401; internet www.ablp.ag; f. 1946; Leader GASTON BROWNE.

Barbuda People's Movement (BPM): Codrington; campaigns for separate status for Barbuda; allied to United Progressive Party; Leader THOMAS HILBOURNE FRANK.

Barbuda People's Movement for Change (BPMC): Codrington; f. 2004; effectively replaced Organisation for National Reconstruction, which was f. 1983 and re-f. 1988 as Barbuda Independence Movt; advocates self-govt for Barbuda; supports the Antigua Labour Party; Pres. ARTHUR SHABAZZ-NIBBS.

Barbudans for a Better Barbuda: Codrington; f. 2004 by fmr Gen. Sec. of Barbuda People's Movt for Change; Leader ORDRICK SAMUEL.

National Movement for Change (NMC): St John's; f. 2003; Leader ALISTAIR THOMAS.

Organisation for National Development: Upper St Mary's St, St John's; f. 2003 by breakaway faction of the United Progressive Party; Leader MELFORD NICHOLAS.

United Progressive Party (UPP): UPP Headquarters Bldg, Upper Nevis St, POB 2379, St John's; tel. 481-3888; fax 481-3877; e-mail info@uppantigua.com; internet www.uppantigua.com; f. 1992 by merger of the Antigua Caribbean Liberation Movt (f. 1979), the Progressive Labour Movt (f. 1970) and the United National Democratic Party (f. 1986); Leader BALDWIN SPENCER; Deputy Leader HAROLD E. E. LOVELL; Chair. LEON (CHAKU) SYMISTER.

Diplomatic Representation

EMBASSIES IN ANTIGUA AND BARBUDA

Brazil: Price Waterhouse Bldg, Old Parham Rd, St John's; tel. 562-7532; fax 562-7537; e-mail michael.neele@itamaraty.gov.br; Ambassador RAUL CAMPOS E CASTRO.

China, People's Republic: Cedar Valley, POB 1446, St John's; tel. 462-1125; fax 462-6425; e-mail chinaemb_ag@mfa.gov.cn; internet ag.chineseembassy.org/eng; Ambassador REN GONGPING.

Cuba: Coral Villas 6 Crosbies, St John's; tel. 562-5865; fax 562-5867; e-mail cubanembassy@candw.ag; internet www.cubadiplomatica.cu/antiguaybarbuda; Ambassador JOSÉ MANUEL INCLÁN EMBADE.

Venezuela: ALBA CARIBE Bldg, Old Parham Rd, POB 1201, St John's; tel. 462-1574; fax 462-1570; e-mail embaveneantigua@yahoo.es; Ambassador CARLOS AMADOR PÉREZ SILVA.

Judicial System

Justice is administered by the Eastern Caribbean Supreme Court (ECSC), based in Saint Lucia, which consists of a High Court of Justice and a Court of Appeal. Three of the Court's High Court Judges are resident in and responsible for Antigua and Barbuda, and preside over the Court of Summary Jurisdiction on the islands. One of two ECSC Masters, chiefly responsible for procedural and inter-locutory matters, is also resident in Antigua. Magistrates' Courts in the territory administer lesser cases.

High Court Judges: CLARE HENRY, BRIAN COTTLE, KEITH THOM.
Registrar: CECILE HILL.
Attorney-General: STEADROY C. O. BENJAMIN.

Religion

The majority of the inhabitants profess Christianity, and the largest denomination is the Church in the Province of the West Indies (Anglican Communion).

CHRISTIANITY

Antigua Christian Council: POB 863, St Mary's St, St John's; tel. 461-1135; fax 462-2383; f. 1964; five mem. churches; Pres. Bishop KENNETH RICHARDS; Treas. MARY-ROSE KNIGHT.

The Anglican Communion

Anglicans in Antigua and Barbuda are adherents of the Church in the Province of the West Indies. The diocese of the North Eastern Caribbean and Aruba comprises 12 islands: Antigua, St Kitts, Nevis, Anguilla, Barbuda, Montserrat, Dominica, Saba, St-Martin/St Maarten, Aruba, St-Barthélemy and St Eustatius. The Bishop is resident in St John's, Antigua and Barbuda. According to the 2011 census, some 18% of the population are Anglicans.

Bishop of the North Eastern Caribbean and Aruba: Rt Rev. LEROY ERROL BROOKS, Bishop's Lodge, POB 23, St John's; tel. 462-0151; fax 462-2090; e-mail dioceseofneca@hotmail.com; internet www.dioneca.org.

The Roman Catholic Church

The diocese of St John's-Basseterre, suffragan to the archdiocese of Castries (Saint Lucia), includes Anguilla, Antigua and Barbuda, the British Virgin Islands, Montserrat and Saint Christopher and Nevis. The Bishop participates in the Antilles Episcopal Conference (whose Secretariat is based in Trinidad and Tobago). Some 8% of the population are Roman Catholics, according to the 2011 census.

Bishop of St John's-Basseterre: Mgr KENNETH DAVID OSWIN RICHARDS, Chancery Offices, POB 836, St John's; tel. 461-1135; fax 462-2383; e-mail diocesesjb@gmail.com.

Other Christian Churches

According to the 2011 census, some 12% of the population are Seventh-day Adventists, 12% are Pentecostalists, 8% are Moravians, 6% are Methodists, 5% are Wesleyan, 4% are Church of God and 4% are Baptists.

East Caribbean Baptist Mission: POB 2678, St John's; tel. 462-2894; fax 462-6029; e-mail admin@baptistantigua.org; internet www.baptistantigua.org; f. 1991; mem. congregation of the Baptist Circuit of Churches in the East Caribbean Baptist Mission; Presiding Elder Dr HENSWORTH W. C. JONAS.

Methodist Church: Methodist Manse, Hodges Bay, POB 69, St John's; tel. 764-5998; fax 560-5922; e-mail novjosiah@hotmail.com; internet www.lidmethodist.org; Supt Rev. NOVELLE C. JOSIAH.

St John's Church of Christ: Golden Grove, Main Rd, St John's; tel. and fax 461-6732; e-mail stjcoclectureship2013@hotmail.com; internet www.stjohnscoc.com; Contact Evangelist CORNELIUS GEORGE.

St John's Evangelical Lutheran Church: Woods Centre, POB W77, St John's; tel. and fax 462-2896; e-mail sjluther@candw.ag; Principal ANDREW JOHNSTON; Pastors Rev. ANDREW JOHNSTON, Rev. JOSHUA STERNHAGEN, Rev. JASON RICHARDS, Rev. PAUL WORKENTINE.

The Press

Business Focus: Bryson's Office Complex, Suite 5A, Friar's Hill Rd, POB 180, St John's; tel. 481-7680; fax 481-7685; e-mail info@businessfocusantigua.com; internet www.businessfocusantigua.com; 6 a year; Man. Dir and Editor LOKESH SINGH.

Daily Observer: 15 Pavilion Dr., Coolidge, POB 1318, St John's; tel. 480-1750; fax 480-1757; e-mail editor@antiguaobserver.com; internet www.antiguaobserver.com; f. 1999; owned by the Observer Media Group; Gen. Man. CECILIA DERRICK; Editors CHERISSE CONSTANT, JULIET BENJAMIN; circ. 5,000.

Paradise Antigua and Barbuda: Bryson's Office Complex, Suite 5A, Friar's Hill Rd, POB 180, St John's; tel. 481-7680; fax 481-7685; e-mail info@paradiseantiguabarbuda.com; internet paradiseantiguabarbuda.com; annual tourism guide; Man. Dir and Editor LOKESH SINGH.

The Worker's Voice: Emancipation Hall, 46 North St, POB 3, St John's; tel. 462-0090; fax 462-4056; f. 1943; 2 a week; official organ of the Antigua Labour Party and the Antigua Trades and Labour Union; Editor Noel Thomas; circ. 6,000.

Publishers

Antigua Printing and Publishing Ltd: Factory Rd, POB 670, St John's; tel. 481-1500; fax 481-1515; e-mail antprint@candw.ag.

The Best of Books Ltd: Lower St Mary's St, St John's; tel. 562-3198; fax 562-3198; e-mail bestofbooks@yahoo.com; textbooks; authorized distributor of Macmillan Caribbean and Nelson Thornes books.

Caribbean Publishing Co Ltd: Ryan's Pl., Suite 1B, High St, POB 1451, St John's; tel. 462-2215; fax 462-0962; e-mail lan-sales@caribpub.com.

Regional Publications Ltd: Bryson's Office Complex, Suite 5A, Friar's Hill Rd, POB 180, St John's; tel. 481-7680; fax 481-7685; e-mail info@regionalpub.com; internet regionalpub.com; f. 2006; publishes the business periodical *Business Focus*, the local Yellow Pages and the annual tourist magazine *Paradise Antigua and Barbuda*; Man. Dir Lokesh Singh.

Treasure Island Publishing Ltd: Anchorage Dockyard Dr., POB W283, Woods Centre, St John's; tel. and fax 463-7414; e-mail colettif@candw.ag; internet www.thetreasureislands.com; Publr and Editor Francesca Coletti.

West Indies Publishing Ltd: Wood's Centre, POB W883, St John's; tel. 461-0565; fax 461-9750; e-mail wip@candw.ag; internet www.westindiespublishing.com; f. 1992; Publr Bertel Dejoie; Gen. Man. and Editor Alison Archer.

Broadcasting and Communications

TELECOMMUNICATIONS

Antigua Computer Technology Ltd (ACT): Old Parham Rd, St John's; tel. 480-5228; e-mail act@actol.net; internet www.act2000.net; f. 1989 as computer sales and repair service; internet provider since 2001.

Digicel Antigua and Barbuda: Antigua Wireless Ventures Ltd, POB W32, St John's; tel. 480-2050; fax 480-2060; e-mail customercareantiguaandbarbuda@digicelgroup.com; internet www.digicelantiguaandbarbuda.com; acquired Cingular Wireless' Caribbean operations and licences in 2005; owned by an Irish consortium; Chair. Denis O'Brien; Group CEO and Dir Colm Delves.

I-Mobile: Cassada Gardens, POB 416, St John's; tel. 480-7000; fax 480-7476; internet www.apua.ag; f. 2000 as PCS, relaunched in 2011 under present name; owned by Antigua Public Utilities Authority (see Trade and Industry—Utilities); digital mobile cellular telephone network; controls less than 20% of market; Chair. Clarvis Joseph; Man. (Telecommunications) Dalma Hill.

LIME: Cable & Wireless, Wireless Rd, Clare Hall, St John's; tel. 480-4000; e-mail customerservice@lime.com; internet www.lime.com/ag; fmrly Cable & Wireless (Antigua and Barbuda) Ltd; name changed as above in 2008; fixed-line, mobile telecommunications and internet services; monopoly ended in 2012; CEO (Caribbean) Tony Rice.

Regulatory Body

Telecommunications Division: part of the Office of the Prime Minister; see The Government—Ministries.

BROADCASTING

Radio

ABS Radio: POB 590, St John's; tel. 464-9376; fax 463-4525; e-mail davelpayne@hotmail.com; internet www.abstvradio.com; f. 1956; state-owned; Station Man. Dave Lester Payne.

Abundant Life Radio: Codrington Village, Barbuda; tel. 562-4821; e-mail afternoonpraise@gmail.com; internet www.abundantliferadioag.com; f. 2001; began broadcasting in Antigua in 2003; Christian station; daily, 24-hour broadcasts; Man. Dir Evangelist Clifton Francois.

Caribbean Radio Lighthouse: POB 1057, St John's; tel. 462-1454; fax 462-7420; e-mail info@radiolighthouse.org; internet www.radiolighthouse.org; f. 1975; religious broadcasts in Spanish and English; operated by Baptist Int. Mission Inc (USA); Station Man. Jerry Baker.

Crusader Radio: Redcliffe St, POB 2379, St John's; tel. 562-4610; e-mail crusaderradio@candw.ag; internet www.crusaderradio.com; f. 2003; Crusader Publishing & Broadcasting Ltd; official station of the UPP; Station Man. Conrad Pole.

Gem Radio Network: Tristan's Crescent Cedar Valley, POB W939, St John's; tel. 744-7768; fax 720-7017; e-mail gemfmstereo@gmail.com.

Observer Radio: POB 1318, St John's; tel. 460-0911; e-mail voice@antiguaobserver.com; internet www.antiguaobserver.com; f. 2001; owned by the Observer Media Group; Chair. (vacant).

ZDK Liberty Radio International (Radio ZDK): Grenville Radio Ltd, Bryant Pasture, Bird Rd, Ottos, POB 1100, St John's; tel. 462-1116; fax 462-1101; e-mail mail@radiozdk.com; internet www.radiozdk.com; f. 1970; commercial; also operates SUN Radio; Man. Dir Ivor Grenville Bird.

Television

ABS Television: POB 1280, St John's; tel. 462-0010; fax 462-1622; f. 1964; state-run.

CTV Entertainment Systems: POB 1536, St John's; tel. 462-4224; fax 462-4211; internet ctv.ag; cable television co; transmits 33 channels of US television 24 hours per day to subscribers; Programme Dir K. Bird.

Finance

(cap. = capital; res = reserves; dep. = deposits; m. = millions; br(s) = branch(es))

BANKING

The Eastern Caribbean Central Bank, based in Saint Christopher, is the central issuing and monetary authority for Antigua and Barbuda.

Antigua and Barbuda Development Bank: 27 St Mary's St, POB 1279, St John's; tel. 462-0838; fax 462-0839; f. 1974; Gen. Man. S. Alex Osborne.

Antigua Commercial Bank: St Mary's and Thames Sts, POB 95, Loans, St John's; tel. 481-4200; fax 481-4229; e-mail acb@acbonline.com; internet www.acbonline.com; f. 1955; auth. cap. EC $5m.; Chair. Davidson Charles; Man. Gladston S. Joseph; 2 brs.

Caribbean Union Bank Ltd: Friar's Hill Rd, POB W2010, St John's; tel. 481-8278; fax 481-8290; e-mail customerservice@cub.ag; internet www.caribbeanunionbank.com; f. 2005; total assets US $42.4m. (Sept. 2007); Chair. Clement Bird; Gen. Man. Gregory Gilpin-Payne; 2 brs.

CIBC FirstCaribbean International Bank: High and Market Sts, POB 225, St John's; tel. 480-5000; fax 462-4910; internet www.cibcfcib.com; f. 2002 as FirstCaribbean International Bank following merger of Caribbean operations of CIBC and Barclays Bank PLC; Barclays relinquished its stake in 2006; adopted current name in 2011; CEO Rik Parkhill; 2 brs.

Eastern Caribbean Amalgamated Bank (ECAB): 1000 Airport Blvd, Pavilion Dr., POB 315, Coolidge; tel. 480-5300; fax 480-5433; e-mail info@ecabank.com; internet www.ecabank.com; f. 1981 as Bank of Antigua; name changed in 2010 following purchase by Eastern Caribbean Amalgamated Financial Co Ltd in 2009; total assets EC $506m. (Sep. 2013); Chair. Craig J. Walter (acting); Gen. Man. Henry Hazel; 3 brs.

Global Bank of Commerce Ltd (GBC): Global Commerce Centre, Old Parham Rd, POB W1803, St John's; tel. 480-2240; fax 462-1831; e-mail customer.service@gbc.ag; internet www.globalbank.ag; f. 1983; int. financial services operator; Chair. and CEO Brian Stuart-Young; Gen. Man. Winston St Agathe; 1 br.

PKB Privatebank Ltd: 10 Redcliffe Quay, POB W791, St John's; tel. 481-1250; fax 481-1263; e-mail antiguabackoffice@pkb.ag; f. 1995 as Privat Kredit Bank, name changed 1998; owned by PKB PRIVATBANK, SA (Switzerland); CEO Umberto Trabaldo Togna.

RBC Royal Bank (Barbados) Ltd: 45 High St, POB 1324, St John's; tel. 462-4217; fax 462-5040; internet www.rbtt.com; CEO Suresh Sookoo; Man. Alan Hamel-Smith; 117 brs.

Scotiabank Antigua (Canada): High and Market Sts, POB 342, St John's; tel. 480-1500; fax 480-1554; e-mail bns.antigua@scotiabank.com; internet www.antigua.scotiabank.com; f. 1961 subsidiary of Bank of Nova Scotia, Canada; Country Man. Gordon Julien; Operations Man. Pascal Hughes; 2 brs.

Regulatory Body

Financial Services Regulatory Commission (FSRC): Royal Palm Pl., Friar's Hill Rd, POB 2674, St John's; tel. 481-3300; fax 463-0422; e-mail anuifsa@candw.ag; internet www.fsrc.gov.ag; fmrly known as International Financial Sector Regulatory Authority, adopted current name in 2002; Chair. Althea Crick; Administrator and CEO John Benjamin.

STOCK EXCHANGE

Eastern Caribbean Securities Exchange: tel. (869) 466-7192; fax (869) 465-3798; e-mail info@ecseonline.com; internet www .ecseonline.com; based in Basseterre, Saint Christopher and Nevis; f. 2001; regional securities market designed to facilitate the buying and selling of financial products for the 8 mem. territories—Anguilla, Antigua and Barbuda, Dominica, Grenada, Montserrat, St Kitts and Nevis, St Lucia and St Vincent and the Grenadines; Chair. Sir K. Dwight Venner; Gen. Man. Trevor E. Blake.

INSURANCE

Several foreign companies have offices in Antigua. Local insurance companies include the following:

ABI Insurance Co Ltd (ABII): ABI Financial Center, 156 Redcliffe St, POB 2386, St John's; tel. 480-2825; fax 480-2834; e-mail abii@abifinancial.com; internet www.abifinancial.com/abii; f. 1999; subsidiary of the ABI Financial Group; Chair. Bradley Lewis.

Antigua Insurance Co Ltd (ANICOL): Long St, POB 511, St John's; tel. 480-9000; fax 480-9035; e-mail anicol@candw.ag; internet www.anicolinsurance.com.

Brysons Insurance Agency: Friars Hill Rd, POB 162, St. John's; tel. 480-1220; fax 462-0320; e-mail office@brysonsinsurance.com; internet www.brysonsantigua.com; f. 1835; Gen. Man. Majorie Parchment.

Caribbean Alliance Insurance Co Ltd: Cnr Newgate and Cross Sts, POB 1609, St John's; tel. 484–2900; fax 481-2950; e-mail enquiries@caribbean alliance.com; internet www.caribbeanalliance .com; f. 1988; regional co covering Eastern Caribbean; Dir Asram Stram.

General Insurance Co Ltd: Upper Redcliffe St, POB 340, St John's; tel. 462-2346; fax 462-4482; e-mail info@gicantigua.com; internet www.gicantigua.com; Man. Dir Peter Blanchard.

Pan-American Life Insurance Co of the Eastern Caribbean: Selkridge Insurance Agency Ltd, 7 Woods Centre, Friar's Hill Rd, St John's; tel. 462-2042; fax 462–2466; internet www.palig.com; f. 2012; part of Pan-American Life Insurance Group (USA); CEO and Man. Dir (Caribbean) William R. Schulz, Jr; Gen. Agent Charlene Selkridge.

Sagicor Life Inc: Sagicor Financial Centre, 9 Factory Rd, St. John's; tel. 480-5500; fax 480-5520; e-mail info_antigua@sagicor.com; internet www.sagicorlife.com; f. 1863; Man. Dr Trevor Vigo.

Selkridge Insurance Agency Ltd: 7 Woods Centre, Friar's Hill Rd, POB W306, St John's; tel. 462-2042; fax 462-2466; e-mail selkins@candw.ag; internet www.selkridgeinsuranceantigua.com; f. 1961; agents for American Life Insurance Co (ALICO) and Island Heritage Insurance Co; Man. Charlene Selkridge.

State Insurance Co Ltd: Redcliffe St, POB 290, St John's; tel. 481-7804; fax 481-7860; e-mail stateins@candw.ag; f. 1977; fmrly State Insurance Corpn; privatized in March 2011; Chair. Dr Vincent Richards; Gen. Man. Lyndell Butler.

Trade and Industry

DEVELOPMENT ORGANIZATIONS

Antigua and Barbuda Investment Authority: Sagicor Financial Centre, POB 80, St John's; tel. 481-1000; fax 481-1020; e-mail abia@antigua.gov.ag; internet www.investantiguabarbuda.org; f. 2007; Exec. Dir Lestroy Samuel.

Citizenship by Investment Unit: 3rd Floor, ABI Financial Centre, Redcliffe St, POB W2074, St John's; tel. 562-8427; fax 562-8431; e-mail info@cip.gov.ag; internet cip.gov.ag; f. 2013; responsible for processing applications to the economic citizenship programme; Chair. Donald Myatt.

Development Control Authority: Cecil Charles Bldg, 1st Floor, Cross St, POB 895, St John's; tel. 462-2038; fax 462-6426; developing lands, regulating construction; Chair. Leon (Chaku) Symister.

St John's Development Corpn: Thames St, POB 1473, St John's; tel. 462-3925; fax 462-3931; e-mail info@stjohnsdevelopment.com; internet www.stjohnsdevelopment.com; f. 1986; manages the Heritage Quay Duty Free Shopping Complex, Vendors' Mall, Public Market and Cultural and Exhibition Complex; Chair. Sylvester Browne; Exec. Dir (vacant).

CHAMBER OF COMMERCE

Antigua and Barbuda Chamber of Commerce and Industry Ltd: Cnr of North and Popeshead Sts, POB 774, St John's; tel. 462-0743; fax 462-4575; e-mail chamcom@candw.ag; f. 1944 as Antigua Chamber of Commerce Ltd; name changed as above in 1991; Pres. Errol Samuel; Exec. Dir Holly Peters.

INDUSTRIAL AND TRADE ASSOCIATIONS

Antigua and Barbuda Manufacturers' Association (ABMA): POB 115, St John's; tel. 462-1536; fax 462-1912.

Antigua and Barbuda Marine Association (ABMA): English Harbour, St John's; tel. 562-5085; e-mail info@abma.ag; internet www.abma.ag; protection and improvement of marine industry; Pres. Franklyn Braithwaite.

EMPLOYERS' ORGANIZATIONS

Antigua and Barbuda Employers' Federation: Upper High St, POB 298, St John's; tel. 462-0247; fax 462-0449; e-mail aempfed@candw.ag; internet abef-anu.org; f. 1950; affiliated to the International Organization of Employers and the Caribbean Employers' Confederation; 135 mems; Pres. Acres Stowe.

Antigua and Barbuda Small Business Association Ltd (ABSBA): Cross and Tanner Sts, POB 1401, St John's; tel. and fax 461-5741; Pres. Lawrence King.

UTILITIES

Antigua Public Utilities Authority (APUA): Cnr Independence Ave and High St, POB 416, St John's; tel. 480-7000; fax 462-4131; e-mail support@apua.ag; internet www.apua.ag; f. 1973; state-owned; generation, transmission and distribution of electricity; telecommunications; colln, treatment, storage and distribution of water; Chair. Clarvis Joseph; Gen. Man. Esworth Martin.

Antigua Power Co Limited (APC): Old Parham Rd, POB 10, St John's; tel. 460-9461; fax 460-9462; e-mail cmills@candw.ag; electricity provider; Owner Francis Hadeed; Gen. Man. Calid Hassad.

Sembcorp (Antigua) Water: St John's; internet www.sembcorp .com; fmrly known as Eneserve; water supplier; Group Pres. and CEO Tang Kin Fei; Operations Man. Ricky Buckley.

TRADE UNIONS

Antigua and Barbuda Meteorological Officers' Association: c/o V. C. Bird Int. Airport, Gabatco, POB 1051, St John's; tel. and fax 462-4606; Pres. Cicely Charles.

Antigua and Barbuda Nurses Association (ABNA): Nurses HQ, Queen Elizabeth Hwy, St John's; tel. 462-0251; fax 462-5003; Pres. Henrietta James; Vice-Pres. Karen Josiah.

Antigua and Barbuda Public Service Association (ABPSA): Popeshead St, POB 1285, St John's; tel. 461-5821; fax 562-4571; e-mail abpsa_tradeunion@yahoo.com; Pres. Jannelle Wehner; Gen. Sec. Emile Floyd; 365 mems.

Antigua and Barbuda Trades Union Congress (ABTUC): c/o Antigua and Barbuda Workers' Union, Freedom Hall, Newgate St, POB 940, St John's; tel. 462-0442; fax 462-5220; e-mail awu@candw .ag; Pres. Kim Burdon; Gen. Sec. Natasha Mussington.

Antigua and Barbuda Union of Teachers: Factory Rd and Teachers' Lane, POB 853, St John's; tel. and fax 462-3750; e-mail gensec@abut.edu.ag; internet www.abut.edu.ag; f. 1926; Pres. Ashworth Azille; Gen. Sec. Annetta Alexander.

Antigua and Barbuda Workers' Union (ABWU): Freedom Hall, Newgate St, POB 940, St John's; tel. 462-2005; fax 462-5220; e-mail awu@candw.ag; f. 1967 following split with ATLU; not affiliated to any party; Pres. Esrome Roberts; Gen. Sec. Sen. David Massiah; 10,000 mems.

Antigua Trades and Labour Union (ATLU): 46 North St, POB 3, St John's; tel. 462-0090; fax 462-4056; e-mail atandlu@hotmail.com; f. 1939; affiliated to the Antigua Labour Party; Pres. Wigley George; Gen. Sec. Alrick Daniel; about 10,000 mems.

Leeward Islands Pilots Association (LIALPA): POB 2313, St John's; tel. 463-0439; fax 462-0929; Chair. Capt. Carl Burke.

Transport

ROADS

There are 384 km (239 miles) of main roads and 781 km (485 miles) of secondary dry-weather roads. Of the total 1,165 km (724 miles) of roads, only 33% are paved.

SHIPPING

The port of St John's has three operating harbours. The Deep Water Harbour handles cargo and is the main commercial pier. The other two harbours, Nevis Pier and Heritage Quay, are used by cruise ships and a number of foreign shipping lines. There are regular cargo and passenger services internationally and regionally. The other harbours in Antigua include Falmouth, English and Jolly on the south-eastern and southern parts of the island. In December 2013 Antigua and Barbuda's flag registered fleet comprised 1,225 vessels, with an aggregate displacement of some 10,120,815 grt.

Antigua and Barbuda Port Authority: Terminal Bldg, Deep Water Harbour, POB 1052, St John's; tel. 484-3400; fax 462-2510; e-mail abpa@port.gov.ag; internet www.port.gov.ag/hp.php; f. 1968; responsible to Ministry of Public Works and Transport; CEO DARWIN TELEMAQUE; Port Man. CURTIS DENNIE.

Barbuda Express: POB 958, St John's; tel. 560-7989; fax 460-0059; e-mail info@barbudaexpress.com; internet www.barbudaexpress.com; f. 2004; ferry services between the islands of Antigua and Barbuda; Owner GREG URLWIN; Man. FREDERIQUE BONFILS.

Brysons Shipping: Friar's Hill Rd, POB 162, St John's; tel. 480-1240; fax 462-0170; internet www.brysonsantigua.com; f. 1835; all shipping services; represents major cruise lines; local agent for CMA-CGM Group; Gen. Man. NATHAN DUNDAS.

Consolidated Maritime Services: CMS Enterprise Complex, Old Parham Rd, POB 2478, St John's; tel. 462-1224; fax 462-1227; e-mail caribms@candw.ag; shipping agents for Crowley Corpn and Navivan Corpn; liner and freight services; Gen. Man. TERRENCE D'ORNELLAS.

Geest Line: Francis Trading Agency Ltd, High St, POB 194, St John's; tel. 462-0854; fax 462-0849; e-mail quotes@geestline.com; internet www.geestline.com; operates between Europe and the Windward and Leeward islands; Man. Dir PETER DIXON.

Tropical Shipping: Antigua Maritime Agencies Ltd, Milburn House, Old Parham Rd, POB W1310, St John's; tel. 562-2934; fax 562-2935; internet www.tropical.com; f. 1992; operates between Canada, the USA and the Caribbean; Pres. MIKE PELLICCI.

Vernon Edwards Shipping Co: Thames St, POB 82, St John's; tel. 462-2034; fax 462-2035; e-mail vedwards@candw.ag; cargo service to and from San Juan, Puerto Rico; Man. Dir VERNON G. EDWARDS, Jr.

CIVIL AVIATION

Antigua's V. C. Bird (formerly Coolidge) International Airport, 9 km (5.6 miles) north-east of St John's, is modern and accommodates jet-engined aircraft. There is a small airstrip at Codrington on Barbuda. Antigua and Barbuda Airlines, a nominal company, controls international routes, but services to Europe and North America are operated by foreign airlines. Antigua and Barbuda is a shareholder in, and the headquarters of, the regional airline LIAT. Other regional services are operated by Caribbean Airlines (Trinidad and Tobago) and Air BVI (British Virgin Islands). In November 2011 construction of a new airport terminal at the V. C. Bird International Airport began, with Chinese financing. The new terminal was scheduled to open in September 2014.

LIAT Airlines: V. C. Bird Int. Airport, POB 819, St John's; tel. 480-5713; fax 480-5717; e-mail customerrelations@liatairline.com; internet www.liatairline.com; f. 1956 as Leeward Islands Air Transport Services; privatized in 1995; shares are held by the Govts of Antigua and Barbuda, Montserrat, Grenada, Barbados, Trinidad and Tobago, Jamaica, Guyana, Dominica, Saint Lucia, Saint Vincent and the Grenadines and Saint Christopher and Nevis (30.8%), Caribbean Airlines (29.2%), LIAT employees (13.3%) and private investors (26.7%); acquired Caribbean Star Airlines in 2007; scheduled passenger and cargo services to 19 destinations in the Caribbean; charter flights are also undertaken; Chair. Dr JEAN HOLDER; CEO DAVID EVANS.

Tourism

Tourism is the country's main industry. Antigua offers a reputed 365 beaches, an annual international sailing regatta and Carnival week, and the historic Nelson's Dockyard in English Harbour (a national park since 1985). Barbuda is less developed, but is noted for its beauty, wildlife and beaches of pink sand. In 2013 there were 229,999 stop-over visitors and 533,280 cruise ship passengers. Tourism receipts totalled EC $806.2m. in the same year.

Antigua & Barbuda Cruise Tourism Association (ABCTA): POB 2208, St John's; tel. 562-1746; fax 562-2858; e-mail abcta@candw.ag; internet www.abc-ta.com; f. 1995; Pres. NATHAN DUNDAS; 42 mems.

Antigua and Barbuda Department of Tourism: c/o Ministry of Tourism, Civil Aviation and Culture, Govt Complex, Queen Elizabeth Hwy, POB 363, St John's; tel. 462-0480; fax 462-2483; e-mail deptourism@antigua.gov.ag; internet www.antigua-barbuda.org; Dir-Gen. CORTHWRIGHT MARSHALL.

Antigua and Barbuda Tourism Authority (AHTA): ACB Financial Centre, High St, St John's; tel. 562-7600; fax 562-7602; e-mail info@aandbtourism.com; internet www.visitantiguabarbuda.com; CEO COLIN JAMES.

Antigua Hotels and Tourist Association (AHTA): Island House, Newgate St, POB 454, St John's; tel. 462-0374; fax 462-3702; e-mail ahta@candw.ag; internet www.antiguahotels.org; Exec. Dir NEIL FORRESTER.

Defence

There is a small defence force of 180 men (army 130, navy 50). There were also joint reserves numbering 80. The US Government leases two military bases on Antigua. Antigua and Barbuda participates in the US-sponsored Regional Security System. In 2014 Antigua and Barbuda signed a framework agreement on defence and security. The defence budget in 2013 was estimated at EC $70m.

Education

Education is compulsory for 11 years between five and 16 years of age. Primary education begins at the age of five and normally lasts for seven years. Secondary education, beginning at 12 years of age, lasts for five years, comprising a first cycle of three years and a second cycle of two years. In 2009/10 there were 63 primary and 20 secondary schools; the majority of schools are administered by the Government. According to UNESCO estimates, in 2012 enrolment at primary schools included 85% of the pupils in their relevant age-groups while that of secondary schools included 78% of pupils in their relevant age-groups. An estimated 72% of children in the appropriate age-group were enrolled in pre-primary education in 2012. Teacher training and technical training are available at the Antigua State College in St John's. An extra-mural department of the University of the West Indies offers several foundation courses leading to higher study at branches elsewhere. There are 11 other tertiary educational institutes. Government expenditure on the Ministry of Education, Sports and Youth Affairs in 2013 was projected at EC $84.4m. In late 2013 the Caribbean Development Bank provided a US $13.4m. loan to improve secondary education in the country.

Bibliography

For works on the Caribbean generally, see Select Bibliography (Books)

Antigua and the Antiguans: A Full Account of the Colony and its Inhabitants. Vols I & II, Cambridge, Cambridge University Press, 2011.

Antigua and Barbuda Foreign Policy and Government Guide, 5th edn. USA International Business Publications, 2004.

Dyde, B. *The Unsuspected Isle: A History of Antigua.* Oxford, Macmillan Caribbean, 2003.

Henry, P. *Shouldering Antigua and Barbuda: The Life of V. C. Bird.* London, Hansib Publishing (Caribbean) Ltd, 2010.

ARGENTINA

Geography

PHYSICAL FEATURES

The Argentine Republic is the second largest country in Latin America, after Brazil, and occupies the broad territories east of the Andes in the tapering southern half of South America. Along the Andes, from north to south, Argentina and Chile share the second longest land border in the Americas, at 5,150 km (3,198 miles), and it continues from north to south across the Isla Grande de Tierra del Fuego (the south-western city of Ushuaia is the most southerly city in the world). To the north is Bolivia (beyond an 832 km border) and to the north-east Paraguay (1,880 km). Also in the north-east, between south-eastern Paraguay and southern Brazil, Argentina extends an arm between the Paraná and Uruguay rivers; Brazil lies to the north, east and south-east of this region (the border is 1,224 km in length). The border with Uruguay (579 km) continues along the River Uruguay to the sea—Uruguay lies east across the river, but also to the north-east where the Argentinian capital, Buenos Aires, faces it across the great Río de la Plata (River Plate) estuary. In all, Argentina covers 2,780,403 sq km (1,073,519 sq miles), although it also claims a further 28,202 sq km of territory in the South Atlantic (the two British dependencies of the Falkland Islands, and of South Georgia and the South Sandwich Islands) and in Antarctica (where its claims partly overlap those of Chile and, again, of the United Kingdom).

Argentina lies between the converging lines drawn by the Continental Divide and the eastern coast of South America, but also includes the eastern part of the main island of Tierra del Fuego, the tip of the eastward-curling tail of the continent, which ends in a broken mass of islands (mainly held by Chile). Argentina includes the Islas de los Estados just to the east (further east, and a little north, are the Falklands, which Argentina claims as the Islas Malvinas). The country's coast-line, bulging in the north-east, then bitten by broad gulfs or bays southwards, is 4,989 km in length. Northern Argentina does not have a coast, but thrusts into the centre of the continent, extending the country's maximum length to some 3,330 km (it is 1,384 km at its widest), making north and south very different prospects, depending on latitude. Moreover, the terrain not only varies between the tropical rainforest of the north through fertile plains to the bleak landscape of Patagonia, but in the essential contrast between the plains and the high Andes. Indeed, Argentina contains both the highest and the lowest places in South America: Cerro Aconcagua (6,962 m or 22,841 ft), the highest mountain in the world outside the great ranges in the middle of Asia, is west of Mendoza; and the Laguna del Carbón (–105 m) is near Puerto San Julián in southern Patagonia. The country can be divided into the Andean highlands, the northern lowlands, the central plains of the Pampas (*pampa*) and the windswept Patagonian steppe.

The lower Patagonian Andes in the south (seldom exceeding 3,600 m) mount northwards into the main Andean cordillera, where some peaks rise above 6,400 m. Parallel ranges and spurs extend the mountainous terrain, which is generally inhospitable, except in some of the broader valleys, deep into north-western Argentina. Just south of here, in central Argentina, is the only other highland of significance, the Sierra de Córdoba (less than 3,000 m). The plains beneath these heights consist of the southern, Argentine, part of the Gran Chaco in the north, the Pampas stretching south for about 1,600 km, and Patagonia in the narrower south. From the far north to the Colorado many rivers disappear into sinks or empty into marshes, and the northern and central plains are dotted with lakes and swampy wetlands. In the north and north-east subtropical and tropical conditions vary the landscape with rainforest, notably the tannin-rich quebracho trees (which thrive on the peculiarly saline soil of the Chaco), but generally grasslands dominate the vast, sometimes gently undulating, but largely treeless, plains. Forests cover only

19% of Argentina, while pasturelands cover 52%. Vegetation also includes the pine forests of the Andes and of Tierra del Fuego, the hardy shrubs and brambles of Patagonia and the cacti and thorny bushes of the arid, mountainous north-west; however, grasslands dominate. The Pampas proper, the main region of fertile farmland and rich grazing for livestock, falls gently from about 600 m at the base of the Andean system in the west to sea level. Patagonia, semi-arid and with a more tortured terrain, has sharp contrasts between heights of over 1,500 m and depressions deeper than 30 m below sea level. Its desolate plains end in a lake district of waters fed by glaciers and icecaps (Argentina has 30,200 sq km of inland waters in total). The main rivers of the south, the Negro and the Colorado, are further north, while the most important rivers in the north are those that drain into the Plate—the Paraguay, the Paraná and the Uruguay. The fauna native to this varied land ranges from, for instance, the parrots, jaguars, tapirs and monkeys of the north, through the rheas (flightless, ostrich-like birds), armadillos, martens and deer of the Pampas, to the Andean condors, llamas, alpacas and guanacos.

CLIMATE

Apart from a small tropical area in the north-east and the subtropical Chaco (the Tropic of Capricorn passes through northernmost Argentina), most of the country has a temperate climate, although it is arid in the north-west, and the dry south gradually tends towards the subarctic. Most of the country is shadowed by the Andes and most rainfall is in the east. Altitude also affects the temperature. The lower Patagonian Andes leave the south exposed to the prevailing westerlies, which descend less humid from the mountains. The semi-arid Pampas ranges from cool to humid subtropical. The Pampas and the north-east can be subjected to violent windstorms, known as *pamperos*, while flooding and earthquakes can add to the natural hazards of the country. Average annual rainfall is at its height in the north (over 1,500 mm, or some 60 ins), becoming drier to the west and south—Buenos Aires, on the north-east coast, but at a central latitude, receives 950 mm (37 ins). The average minimum and maximum temperatures in

Buenos Aires range from winter's 8°C and 15°C (46°F–59°F) in July, to mid-summer's 20°C–30°C (67°F–86°F) in January. To the west, in the foothills of the Andes, the extremes can be more pronounced, while in the far north there have been summer temperatures of 45°C (113°F) recorded, and the average winter temperature in western (inland) Patagonia is 0°C (32°F).

POPULATION

Most Argentines are of European origin (85%), especially of Spanish and Italian extraction (but also British, French, German and Russian, for instance). Although most of the rest of the population are of mixed descent, these are relatively few compared to other Latin American countries and mainly originate from elsewhere in South America. According to the 2010 census, 2.4% of the population were indigenous, or of indigenous descent. Other ethnic groups are also well represented, such as the 1m. or so of Arab descent, and one of the largest Jewish communities in the world outside Israel. This rich racial diversity does not compromise the predominance of the Roman Catholic Church (some 76% of the population). According to a 2008 study by Consejo Nacional de Investigaciones Científicas y Técnicas, however, recent growth of evangelical Protestant communities owing to conversion has brought down

Roman Catholic numbers, which means that other Christian denominations (11%—increased from 2% in the last decade) and other faiths (1.2%—including Jews, Muslims or native traditions) are well represented. Furthermore, 11% of the population are estimated as agnostics and atheists. The official language is Spanish, although some minorities also retain use of their own native tongues for domestic purposes, and English, Italian, German and French are not uncommon. The three remaining Amerindian languages are Tehuelche, Guaraní and Quechua; most speakers of native tongues live in the north and west of the country.

According to mid-year estimates, in 2014 the total population of Argentina was 42.7m. About one-third of the population live in the greater metropolitan area of Buenos Aires, the capital. In all, some 86% of the population is classed as urban. After Buenos Aires (the city proper had an estimated population of 2.9m. at the 2010 census), the chief cities of Argentina are Córdoba (1.3m. at the 2010 census—north-west of Buenos Aires, its old rival, and midway to the Chilean border) and Rosario (1.2m.—upriver from Buenos Aires, on the Paraná). Argentina is a federal republic constituted of 23 provinces and one autonomous city (the Federal Capital, Buenos Aires).

History

Prof. COLIN M. LEWIS

INTRODUCTION

Col Juan Domingo Perón and his wife, Eva ('Evita') Duarte de Perón are iconic figures in contemporary Argentinian history, variously associated with social progress, political reform and modernization, and authoritarianism, corruption and chaos. Peronism has been the defining force in politics since the middle of the 20th century, becoming a 'brand' that Néstor Carlos Kirchner and his wife, Cristina Fernández de Kirchner (see below) have sought to capture and modernize over the last decade or so. How did this come about, and for how much longer can populist, highly personalized politics, such as that typified by Peronism/Kirchnerism continue to set the political agenda at a time when the country appears more polarized and unstable than ever? If Argentinian history may be depicted as a series of counterpoints—of democratic and authoritarian interludes, of institutional consolidation and destruction, of popular mobilization and repression, and of optimism and pessimism—is another moment of transition in prospect? As the country heads for presidential elections in October 2015, there are two certainties; that the Kirchner era will end and that the next regime will be Peronist.

Modern Argentina began to take shape after 1853, following the overthrow of the dictator Gen. Manuel de Rosas in the previous year. The liberal 1853 Constitution, which established a federal, republican system of government, was probably unique in that it accorded the vote to all native-born males without subjecting electors to property or literacy tests. The substance of federalism was secured in 1880 with the 'nationalization' of the city of Buenos Aires, which was separated from the province and became the national capital. Subsequent political developments of critical importance include: electoral reform in 1912, which made the ballot secret, established the principle of compulsory voting, and provided semi-proportional representation for runner-up parties; the 1930 military coup, which overturned a democratically elected Government, inaugurating a cycle of 'restricted politics', which included an electoral ban on the Radicals (Unión Cívica Radical—UCR); the 1946 electoral 'rupture' of Peronism; the approval of the short-lived 1949 Constitution (which extended the vote to women); the overthrow of Perón in 1955 and military efforts to proscribe Peronism; the 1976 military coup, which resulted in the installation of the so-called Proceso de Reorganización Nacional, a regime characterized by mass torture, murder and the 'disappearance' of thousands during

the 'dirty war'; the return of democracy in 1983; and the neo-liberal experiment of the 1990s, a period of rapid growth and political reorganization—a new Constitution was adopted in 1994, which culminated in the 2001–02 economic crisis that prompted street protests, and appeared to threaten social collapse and mass civil unrest.

Conventionally presented as a model for national consolidation, arrangements encapsulated in the 1853 Constitution and 1880 federalization of Buenos Aires could also be depicted as the project of a confederation of regional oligarchies designed to balance the interests of the interior and of the littoral provinces. Irrespective of the rights accorded by the 1853 Constitution, before the early 20th century access to political life remained restricted. This resulted in an explosion of demands for political participation by the middle classes around 1900, and by the working classes in the 1940s. Accordingly, in the 1910s, the UCR 'captured' the state and in the 1940s the Peronists did likewise. This widening of the political system occurred in a much shorter space of time than in many countries. However, the process of political inclusion was neither linear nor without problems. Yet, since 1983, notwithstanding several profound economic crises that in earlier periods would undoubtedly have triggered military intervention, democratic politics have prevailed.

STATE- AND NATION-BUILDING: OLIGARCHIC AND EARLY DEMOCRATIC POLITICS

By the 1880s mass immigration from Western Europe had made Argentina the third most populous country in Latin America after Brazil and Mexico. It was also the most urban: approximately one-half of the population lived in cities by 1914. Argentina was on course to becoming one of the wealthiest societies of the early 20th century. The result was the emergence of a civil society, enmeshed with the building of a state. The relationship between institutional consolidation and the emergence of political order was direct and causal. However, it was unclear to what extent nation-building occurred within a state open to all, or in a less permeable, more restricted structure. The 1880s saw the development of the Partido Autonomista Nacional (PAN), a coalition of regional oligarchies that came to monopolize national politics and eclipsed other organizations. Because the PAN did not have a well-defined internal organization, factional confrontations proliferated and came to replace open electoral contests. In effect, internal manoeuvring and intrigue within the PAN emerged as a substitute for competitive party politics. Real politics was conducted inside the PAN, rather than the institutions of the state, an arrangement that facilitated order rather than democratic consolidation, and survived virtually unchanged until 1916.

Mass immigration, population growth, and urbanization transformed society and politics. That the PAN became more centralized, and possibly isolated, was suggested by popular protest triggered by the commercial and financial panic of 1889–90 (the Baring Crisis), which provoked a series of events prefiguring those of 2001–02. These protests in 1889 ultimately resulted in 'reform from within'. Managed elections required a more patriotic and democratic patina. Electoral reform, sponsored by President Roque Sáenz Peña (1910–13) in 1912, led to the first free and fair elections in Argentine political history in 1916, the defeat of the PAN, and the ensuing Radical ascendancy of 1916–30. The rules of the political game had changed.

Mass and class politics did not necessarily imply ideology-based politics. Nevertheless, it was generally accepted that mass politics erupted into Argentine political life in the 1910s, and that the UCR was its initial beneficiary. The UCR successfully courted three distinct groups: dissident interior oligarchies; the growing urban, professional middle classes; and sections of the enfranchised working class (in 1914 around 70% of the Buenos Aires working class had been born abroad and was therefore effectively disenfranchised as rates of naturalization were very low). Two of these social classes were epitomized by UCR Presidents of the period: Hipólito Yrigoyen (1916–22 and 1928–30), a teacher and minor public official, and Marcelo T. de Alvear (1922–28), scion of an aristocratic family and prominent lawyer. These three groups remained the bases of party support during the years of proscription in the 1930s, and the time of unequal electoral contest with the Peronists in the 1940s and 1950s. The heterogeneous character of party membership probably accounted for the broadly conservative yet reformist stance of the UCR in the 1910s and 1920s. After the 1950s the party became more closely identified with the urban and rural middle class. Since around 2000 the UCR has maintained a significant, though declining, presence in municipal and provincial government, despite the virtual decimation of its representation at national level.

The 1929 worldwide economic depression brought an end to the democratic experiment and the return of 'oligarchic authoritarianism'. Institutional and conjunctural explanations are offered for the collapse of Argentine democracy in the 1930s. Arguably, fully functioning democratic organization had insufficient time to become firmly embedded before the shock struck. Rivals pointed to the authoritarian personality of Yrigoyen, and accused him of an abuse of power. Indeed, for some he was a proto-populist who fostered an exclusionary approach to politics and to government. If the PAN deployed electoral fraud, Yrigoyen did not hesitate to use UCR majorities in the Congreso (Congress) to overturn inconvenient results in provincial contests, nor to appoint federal administrators (*interventores*) to secure the desired electoral outcomes. Like the PAN, the UCR also emerged as a 'distributional coalition', channelling state resources to friends of the regime and denying them to its enemies. This exclusionary approach to politics, with parties that functioned as distributional electoral alliances, appeared to have become key features of Argentine political life, one that has since been perfected by the administrations of the Kirchners.

For some, the UCR was too progressive, provoking an inevitable conservative backlash; for others, it was insufficiently radical and failed to restructure Argentine society and polity so as to secure democracy. Opponents certainly accused UCR administrations of corruption and protested against the 'tyranny of democracy'—that is, its ability to manufacture electoral victories. The inertia of the administration in 1929–30, as the country slipped into economic disorder, fostered disillusion, providing an opportunity for opponents of the regime. Consequently, the 1930 military coup attracted a fair measure of support: there was general antipathy towards an elected administration seen as failing the Republic. During the 1930s economic internationalism and liberal democracy were under threat not only in Argentina; regimes abroad, especially Benito Mussolini's Italy and Francisco Franco's Spain (primary sources of immigration to Argentina in the early 20th century), served as an inspiration to anti-democratic elements in Argentina.

THE RISE, CONTAINMENT AND SURVIVAL OF PERONISM

Although originating in a military putsch, and dependent on the armed forces and police to contain opposition, the 'Concordancia' administrations of the 1930s presented a largely civilian façade. Politically, the Concordancia was a disparate grouping of liberals, conservatives and reformist socialists, precisely those groups that had been unable to loosen the UCR stranglehold on the presidency in the 1920s. Initially, the regime sought legitimacy in efficient macroeconomic management and, with the stabilization of the economy in the mid-1930s, in a measured return to democracy. Accident, in the form of the death of several consummate political operators, and the approach of the Second World War derailed the projected phased return to open politics. The regime lurched to the right, destroying the fragile party political balance that had delivered stability in the executive and legislature. Concurrently, elements within the military railed against the subordinate role assigned to the armed forces and the pro-Allied stance of the administration, notwithstanding its formal declaration of neutrality.

In 1943 a group of officers, of whom Col Juan Domingo Perón was one, acted. The technocrats and oligarchs were removed and a full military administration was installed. However, the armed forces were divided and ill-prepared for government. Elections were called in 1946. To the surprise of many, not least the US ambassador, who had campaigned actively in favour of the Alianza Democrática (the umbrella grouping established by existing political parties, some of whom had formed part of the Concordancia), Perón won fairly decisively. Between 1943 and 1945 Perón had assiduously cultivated the support of organized labour. As a result, he became the presidential candidate of the Partido Laborista, the hastily constructed political wing of the Confederación General de Trabajadores (CGT—General Confederation of Workers). Soon, independent labour leaders were sidelined and the Partido Laborista became the Partido Justicialista (PJ). In association with his charismatic wife, 'Evita', Perón established a regime that would become increasingly centralist, statist and anti-liberal. Its main sources of support were organized labour, developmentalist military officers, nationalists and, at least in the early years, elements of the Roman Catholic hierarchy attracted by the authoritarian, traditionalist, anti-secularist, moralistic stance of the administration.

Like the UCR in the 1910s and 1920s, the PJ of the 1940s defied easy definition. In electoral terms, the overwhelming strength of the party lay with the working class, largely the urban working class. State sector workers, too, were a major electoral bulwark. Nevertheless, the Peronists have not always enjoyed the unquestioning electoral support of labour, nor been exclusively dependent on it. As victories at elections in 1973, 1989, 1992 and 1995 indicated, the party often captured substantial support from the middle class; conversely, it failed to mobilize important elements of the working class in 1982 and 1999. More a movement than a party, the PJ has proven to be the least institutionalized political organization in Argentina. Peronism is a contending alliance of factions headed by regional leaders. These features derived from, and conferred power on, a highly personalistic leadership. This legacy of Carlos Saúl Menem (1989–99), reinforced under the administrations of the Néstor Carlos Kirchner (2003–07) and Cristina Fernández (2007–), means that the PJ continues as a constellation of competing sectional and regional interests, further exemplifying the categorization of Argentine political parties as 'distributional coalitions', and the PJ, in particular, as typifying clientelistic politics centred on the cult of the leader.

The 1946–55 Peronist administration, the *peronato*, can be divided into several distinct sub-periods. The first, which lasted until around 1949, was characterized by high levels of popular support, rapid social progress, economic nationalism verging on autarky and increasing centralization. This was the 'golden age' of Peronism, largely financed from windfall export earnings. The second phase ran from 1949 to about 1952 (when 'Evita' died). During this period high levels of mass support continued, but social tensions increased and the regime became much more authoritarian as the economy faltered. The final period witnessed the fracturing of the 'Peronist family': workers and nationalists were antagonized by a return to liberal orthodoxy reflected in wage cuts and the opening of the economy to foreign investment. The armed forces became alarmed at the threat of internal disorder. Intellectuals pointed to the isolation of the regime. The Roman Catholic Church was antagonized by proposed government interventions in education and family life, and by orchestrated demands for the canonization of 'Evita'.

Military governments of 1955 proposed to excise Peronism from Argentine politics and the Argentine psyche, to restore the market economy, and to prepare the country for an ordered return to civilian rule. The outcome was quite different. The nation was riven: for every committed Peronist, there was a vehement anti-Peronist. Equally, from the 1950s until the 1980s there would be only conditional support for democracy, and little consensus about the international position of the country.

Reconstructing society and polity, and re-establishing the international position of the country, exercised successive regimes in the 1950s and 1960s, but possibilities and outcomes remained confused. These were neatly illustrated by the coups of 1955. The first, headed by Gen. Eduardo Lonardi, persecuted Peronists and set about dismantling some of the agencies of economic intervention. However, the Lonardi regime appeared disinclined to eradicate other aspects of statism and nationalism, revoking contracts granted to foreign oil companies awarded during the last years of the *peronato*. The second coup of 1955 led to the installation of a more internationalist regime, headed by Gen. Pedro Aramburu (1955–58). Deregulation and export promotion were applied with vigour and Argentina submitted membership applications to the World Bank and the IMF. In 1958 Aramburu's regime gave way to the elected presidency of Radical Arturo Frondizi (1958–62), which encapsulated the inconsistencies in domestic politics and the difficulties of devising a sustainable external strategy. Although he had enjoyed a reputation as a radical nationalist, on assuming office Frondizi awarded risk concessions to foreign oil corporations. This was part of the so-called 'battle for oil'. The second campaign, the 'battle for healthy money', was based on an IMF adjustment package, a measure which also implied a pro-internationalist position.

Partly for electoral purposes, Frondizi sought to balance a liberal, internationalist stance in economic and trade policy with a radical diplomatic programme, courting communist Cuba and the Non-aligned Movement. Frondizi made the mistake of receiving communist guerrilla commander Ernesto 'Che' Guevara on a secret visit to Buenos Aires. This was too much for the military, although whether Frondizi's eventual removal from office was a result of liberal international economics, adventurous diplomacy, or an ambiguous relationship with the Peronists remained unclear. Successive civilian administrations of the 1960s, always closely scrutinized by the military, were no more successful in restabilizing domestic politics or redefining the international position of the country.

With the failure of the nominally developmentalist regime of Gen. Juan Carlos Onganía (1966–70), and its rise in mass protest characterized by urban uprisings, factory occupations, a spate of kidnappings directed against the heads of national and foreign corporations, and mounting guerrilla violence, the public and military looked to the exiled Perón for salvation. After Gen. Onganía's regime there followed the short-lived military presidencies of Gen. Roberto Levingston (1970–71) and Gen. Alejandro Agustín Lanusse (1971–73), under whose Government Perón was permitted to return from exile in Madrid, Spain, where he had been sheltered by Franco. Elected in March 1973, 'interim' President Héctor José Cámpora of the PJ was a fervent loyalist, who took office on 25 May and resigned in mid-July, triggering the need for new elections. Left-leaning, as well as a loyalist, Cámpora's name was taken

by the group of young activists who would later form the effective militia of the Néstor and Cristina Fernández Kirchner regimes. Returning in June, and elected in September, Perón arrived in a country that appeared to be falling apart. Standing for the presidency and vice-presidency, respectively, Perón and his new wife, María Estela ('Isabelita') Martínez de Perón, easily won the ballot. However, at 78 years of age, Perón was losing his touch, and was demonstrably unable to contain conflict within the movement, as shown by gun battles at party gatherings and on the streets. Most rapidly alienated were the Montoneros, a radical, anti-capitalist youth organization committed to armed struggle. Initially regarding Perón as a potential ally, they later declared war on the regime of 'Isabelita'. (Whether Néstor and Cristina Fernández Kirchner were members of the organization, or merely sympathizers, is strongly contested.) Assuming the presidency on the death of her husband, 'Isabelita' proved particularly ineffective. Shifting to the right, she soon became beholden to sections of the labour movement and national business, and shadowy criminal groups, including armed gangs controlled by her Minister for Social Welfare, José López Rega. The last days of her regime were marked by the open operation of official 'death squads', near anarchy and spiralling inflation. In this context, the military regime that took over in 1976 was almost welcomed.

Declaring a policy of alignment with the 'western, Christian, free world', the military regimes of the 1976–82 period subscribed to the doctrine of 'national security' initially popularized in US–Latin American policy-making circles. According to this doctrine, the principal threat to the nation was from internal subversion sponsored by an international Marxist conspiracy that took advantage of domestic social tensions. Following a dose of military discipline (more accurately, the use of state terror) and liberal economics, Argentine society would be purged of subversive elements. Hence, the regimes promised to deregulate and open the economy.

Estimates of the number who 'disappeared' during the 'dirty war' range between 10,000 and 30,000. For the regime, the defining moment occurred in 1982, when the domestic and international actions of the dictatorship descended into a tragicomedy of errors, culminating in the invasion of the Falkland Islands (Islas Malvinas) in April. These British-ruled islands in the South Atlantic had been claimed by Argentina since 1833. The events leading up to the invasion illustrated the arrogance and ignorance of the regime, which had completely misread both its influence abroad and the place of Argentina in the Americas and the wider world. Following the collapse of the liberal, debt-led economic programme, as the stock market went into meltdown with a series of spectacular bank failures, the currency collapsed and the country approached default. Fearful of a resurgence of street protest, the regime felt compelled to act. Deluded by his own rhetoric, misled by civilian foreign policy advisers and convinced of the capacity of the armed forces, Gen. Leopoldo Fortunato Galtieri announced from the balcony of the presidential palace (the Casa Rosada) to an enthusiastic crowd on 2 April that Argentine forces had taken Port Stanley in the Falklands. However, Argentina's ignominious defeat by the British followed on 14 June, the military lacking both the organizational capacity and the ability to resist the British task force dispatched to recover the islands.

THE RETURN OF DEMOCRACY

Political optimism and economic crisis were the inheritance of the incoming UCR Government of President Raúl Alfonsín in December 1983. A human rights lawyer who had consistently opposed the military and the war, Alfonsín was a committed democrat and constitutionalist. He represented the new face of Argentine politics. Perhaps this, as well as the association of some Peronists with the outgoing military regime, explained the electoral triumph of the UCR in the elections of 30 October. Alfonsín's victory was a watershed in Argentine political history: it was the first time that the PJ had been defeated in free, fully democratic elections.

The new administration was confronted by an expectant electorate demanding that those responsible for human rights abuses during the 'dirty war' be brought to justice. It also faced a cowed but dangerous armed forces, a recalcitrant and divided opposition, an empty treasury, and an international banking community determined that the democratic Government honour the foreign debt accumulated by the military. For Alfonsín, the restoration of democracy was a moral and practical imperative, as was principled internationalism. Indeed, the best means of securing civilian government at home would be to improve relations with neighbouring countries through the formation of the Southern Common Market (Mercado Común del Sur—MERCOSUR), the resolution of border disputes with Chile, the renunciation of the use of force in the settlement of international disputes, engagement in international forums and a commitment to the rule of international law.

Anticipating rewards for democratization from international institutions and foreign governments (and assuming that these would put pressure on the international banks), the administration initially prioritized social spending and negotiations with the military over debt resolution. This was all the more pressing, as the Government had to confront a number of barrack protests. Although these hardly threatened a coup (being concerned with affronts to 'military dignity' and spending cuts), they still represented a challenge to the Government and democratic consolidation. Drift, rather than strategy, typified the early economic stance of the Alfonsín presidency, though neither the debt nor the economy could be ignored indefinitely. A stand-by loan was obtained from the IMF in 1984, and when this failed to stabilize the economy, the heterodox 'Austral Plan' was launched in 1985. Initially popular, the Plan could have succeeded, but it was sabotaged by debt overhang, some technical flaws and, principally, by an electoral timetable that gave opponents ample opportunity to mobilize against it. The Plan ended in hyperinflation that proved detrimental to the UCR in the 1989 elections, and resulted in the transfer of power to incoming President Menem of the PJ, five months earlier than required by the Constitution.

To its detractors, the legacy of democracy in 1989 was fiscal indiscipline and social disorder, manifest in the looting of supermarkets. Nevertheless, for the first time in Argentine political history, an administration of one political hue, which had gained office as the result of free, unrestricted elections, handed over the government of the country to another freely elected administration of a different political party. Although the transfer of power occurred earlier than provided for by the Constitution, at a moment of profound crisis, there was no military intervention. Even if the Peronist victory in 1989 owed more to a protest against the UCR than a vote of confidence in Menem, the PJ victory was resounding. This, coupled with his skills as a coalition builder, gave Menem considerable freedom of manoeuvre. He employed these advantages to construct a broad alliance within and outside the traditional ranks of Peronism and, indeed, the party. Thus was formed the so-called popular-business alliance, which was to be responsible for the neo-liberal economic project designed to secure the new President's position in power, if not to institutionalize democracy.

Menem espoused 'realism' in politics and international economic relations. Following currency stabilization in 1991—the so-called 'Convertibility Plan'—foreign investment increased, as did the foreign debt. Internationalism also assumed a distinctly pro-US stance, reflected in positions taken in international forums and conflicts. The aspirations of the regime were signalled by the pledging of Argentine frigates to the international coalition involved in the Gulf War of 1991, the proposal to join the North Atlantic Treaty Organization (NATO), renewed commitment to MERCOSUR, which was gradually transformed from a free trade zone into something approaching a common market, and efforts to foster close collaboration between MERCOSUR and the European Union. In contrast to PJ administrations of the 21st century, Menem was determined to secure allies abroad, notably in the USA and Europe.

Ever the consummate populist politician, Menem reconfigured the PJ in his image and divided the opposition; he also secured constitutional reform in order to be able to stand for a second consecutive presidential term. Constitutional change was prepared by the Olivos Pact, an agreement between Menem and former President Alfonsín. The principal modifications introduced by the 1994 Constitution included an increase in provincial representation in the Senado (Senate) from two to three seats, the granting of province-style autonomy to the federal capital, a reduction in the length of the presidential term from six to four years, and a provision allowing a sitting President to seek immediate re-election (hitherto a consecutive presidential term had been proscribed, incumbents being required to stand down for at least one term). The 1994 settlement facilitated the re-election of Menem and secured the Convertibility Plan. The lessons of the PJ's midterm electoral victories during Menem's first term, and his second triumph in the 1995 presidential election, were that the electorate demanded economic stability and would not support political groupings deemed unlikely to deliver monetary order. Nevertheless, before and after 1995 Menem's political project represented a threat to democracy: he undermined accountability within the PJ, repeatedly changed the rules of the political game and institutionalized corruption. None the less, voters had few qualms about returning the PJ to office in 1995. Economic instability had driven traditional politics off the agenda. However, with an opposition alliance of the UCR and the Frente País Solidario (Frepaso) painstakingly constructed after 1997, and with both major political groupings committed to macroeconomic stability, the electorate was finally presented with a real choice in 1999.

The opposition victory in the 1999 presidential and congressional elections can be viewed as a demand for economic stability and political transparency. The elections were another benchmark in the consolidation of Argentine democracy. The third consecutive constitutionally prescribed change of government since 1983, the 1999 elections appeared to confirm institutional stability and offer a distinct opportunity for democratic consolidation. That the UCR's Fernando de la Rúa was elected President suggested the UCR had been forgiven by the electorate for the chaos of 1989. Carlos 'Chacho' Alvarez of Frepaso was elected Vice-President. Even if the economy was already moving into recession, there was confidence that corruption was on the wane and that democracy and stability could be saved. However, disappointment soon set in.

In retrospect, perhaps the Peronists were not as corrupt as popularly perceived, nor the Radicals as honest. In both parties there were those who struggled for greater internal democracy and accountability, while there were also those who were prepared to bend the rules. This became clear in 2000 when it was revealed that President de la Rúa had systematically bribed opposition senators in order to secure legislative majorities. Budget slippage (often a mask for illegal transfers of funds) and nepotism seemed to be as much a feature of the new administration as that of Menem and the PJ. Alvarez resigned in disgust. An apparent inability to resolve the spiralling political and economic crises, became almost as much a feature of the de la Rúa administration in 2001 as of the Yrigoyen Government in 1929–30. While other sectors bore the brunt of unemployment and falling wages, the political class continued to spend more on itself. Public anger was demonstrated in the October 2001 mid-term elections: the tallies of blank protest votes cast in such key areas as the gubernatorial contest in the province of Buenos Aires, and the senatorial contest in the city of Buenos Aires, were larger than the number of votes secured by the winning candidates. Less than two months later, with the imminent collapse of the Convertibility Plan, came street demonstrations and government paralysis. De la Rúa was forced to flee the Casa Rosada by helicopter, amid violent anti-Government protests around the palace.

DEMOCRACY WITHOUT DEMOCRATIC INSTITUTIONS?

In December 2001 Ramón Puerta, the President of the Senate, was sworn in as acting President of the Republic, in the absence of a Vice-President (the position had not been filled following the resignation of Alvarez). Within the space of two weeks, from 20 December 2001 to 1 January 2002, the presidency changed hands on five occasions as public protests continued. Ultimately, a joint session of both houses of the Congress elected Eduardo Duhalde as President. A former Governor of the province of Buenos Aires, Duhalde was the PJ candidate who had lost to de la Rúa in 1999.

Duhalde managed to hold both the administration and the country together, although he was less successful in keeping the PJ united. Although Duhalde had been nominated to serve out only the remainder of de la Rúa's term, it soon became clear that he aspired to stand for a further full four years—in effect, engineering his own election. He was prevented from doing so by an anti-Buenos Aires alliance of PJ Governors from interior provinces, fearful of the power amassed by the Buenos Aires faction of the party. Although there was no effective opposition, Peronist factions were unable to agree on a candidate for the 2003 election. Several Peronists indicated their willingness to stand, foremost among them being former President Menem and Néstor Kirchner, erstwhile Governor of the sparsely populated Patagonian province of Santa Cruz. Kirchner was favoured by Duhalde, who viewed his Santa Cruz colleague as malleable and able to defeat Menem, from whom Duhalde intended to wrest control of the PJ. In the event, Menem won the first round of the presidential election held in April 2003, obtaining 24.3% of the votes cast, ahead of Kirchner's 22.0%. A former UCR minister, Ricardo López Murphy, came third with 16.4% of the ballot.

In mid-May 2003, four days before the second-round run-off was scheduled, and with opinion polls showing that Kirchner was likely to win twice as many votes, Menem withdrew from the contest. He did so partly to be able to claim that he had never been defeated in an election and, it was asserted, to deny Kirchner the legitimacy of a landslide victory. In the event, Kirchner managed to marginalize both Menem and Duhalde. Following his inauguration, the new President immediately began to build a 'transverse alliance', based on groupings across the political spectrum. By favouring particular candidates in a succession of elections, such as the mayoral contest in Buenos Aires and interior governorships, and by supporting different factions in the October 2005 mid-term congressional elections, Kirchner created a loose confederation of individuals and interests in key provinces who were beholden to him. This was not the politics of consensus, however, as Kirchner was suspicious of potential enemies. Rather, it was personality-driven leadership sustained by the granting (or withholding) of favours. There was to be no institutionalizing of politics, and even less accountability. However, favours were not the only means used by Kirchner. Another mechanism was orchestrated street protest—the *piquetero* movement. 'Picketing', organized road blockades, to draw attention to specific issues originated in the 1990s as a form of spontaneous popular protest. By 2002–03, however, most factions of the PJ and parts of the labour movement were organizing their own *piquetero* groups, virtual mobs available for hire and answerable to political bosses. Increasingly, the most powerful of these was La Cámpora, nominally headed by Máximo, the playboy son of Néstor and Cristina Fernández.

The strategy was successful. Economic recovery, under way by 2003, and the renegotiation of most of the outstanding foreign debt in February 2005 generated massive federal fiscal surpluses. A judicious disposal of these funds secured for Kirchner the acquiescence of many provincial administrators and the isolation of troublesome groups, including antagonistic segments of the PJ and the labour movement. The allocation of federal funds was also deployed to divide a weak formal opposition: Kirchner bought the adhesion of some sections of the UCR and marginalized others. Although Kirchner and his then Minister of the Economy, Roberto Lavagna, were not responsible for the economic recovery, their delivery of exchange rate stability and relatively low levels of inflation, as well as new social assistance programmes, were notable achievements. Furthermore, their resolute stance in negotiations with the IMF and private foreign creditors generated confidence and domestic political capital: nationalist rhetoric and debt write-down yielded a considerable electoral dividend.

Nationalist posturing was not without cost, however. Bombastic language in international forums, and unilateral action against neighbouring countries, such as restricting imports from Brazil and suspending energy supplies to Chile, gained Argentina few allies. More worrying still, Argentina's continued uncompromising opposition to the establishment of a modern European-financed cellulose plant in Uruguay occasioned a sharp deterioration in diplomatic relations between the two countries, creating an impasse that the regime in Buenos Aires seemed unable, or unwilling, to resolve. As a result, the country's closest allies in Latin America appeared to be Venezuela and Bolivia, joined subsequently by Ecuador, Cuba and Iran, a 'left-wing' association that irked other members of MERCOSUR and made few friends for Argentina overseas. Despite membership of the Group of 20 (G20) organization, and participation in such forums as the left-of-centre Summit of Progressive Leaders, Argentina witnessed a decline in its international standing.

By 2005, with rising world commodity prices further fuelling economic growth and a dramatic increase in fiscal resources at the disposal of the federal Government, the rhetoric and action of the administration became even more populist and nationalist. Both at home and abroad the Government seemed consciously to be resurrecting the language and imagery of the first Peronist administration of the 1940s, a rhetoric that became even more pronounced after 2008. Images of Perón and 'Evita' were routinely included in Kirchner political propaganda. Néstor Kirchner showed himself to be unafraid to promote members of his family to high office. His wife, Cristina Fernández, obtained a seat in the Senate in October 2005, which proved to be the launch-pad for a successful presidential campaign two years later. Despite some setbacks in the final year of his presidency, notably the election of anti-Kirchner or opposition candidates to provincial governorships and the mayoralty of Buenos Aires, crude political arm-twisting and massive discretionary expenditure meant that Kirchner was able to deliver the presidency to his wife, as he stepped down as head of state to assume the leadership of the PJ.

In the elections of October 2007 the electorate was offered a choice of three Peronist factions and a plethora of opposition groupings. Although Fernández failed to take the three major cities (Buenos Aires, Córdoba and Rosario), she nevertheless obtained 44.9% of the vote. Her margin of victory over her nearest rival, Elisa Carrió of the centre-left Coalición Cívica, who obtained 23.0%, was well ahead of the 10 percentage points necessary to avoid a run-off election. The other principal candidate, Kirchner's former Minister of Economy and Production, Lavagna, of the centre-right Una Nación Avanzada, won 16.9% of votes cast. In effect, the three candidates who topped the presidential poll represented new electoral alliances, ephemeral groupings quite distinct from the former political parties, the PJ and the UCR. This pointed to a state of flux and a lack of institutionality in Argentine politics and political life, where traditional allegiances and national structures were breaking down. Although initially muted by continuing economic prosperity, these developments subsequently became more pronounced.

Within six months of the 2007 presidential elections, President Fernández's approval rating had fallen to around 20%, causing justifiable anxiety as the 2009 mid-term elections approached. Despite bringing forward the elections from 25 October 2009 to 28 June, on the pretext that early elections would enable legislators to focus their efforts on resolving the negative effects of global economic crisis, the results were a clear snub to the Government, which lost its majority in both legislative chambers. These losses were attributed to mismanagement of the economy, chaotic handling of farmer protests, a simmering dispute over taxation and gross manipulation of prices that had united diverse rural and urban groups and caused an irreparable rupture between President Fernández and her Vice-President, escalating anxiety about crime and security issues, and fears about inflation triggered by government manipulation of the official agency responsible for collating macroeconomic data. Furthermore, considerable unease had been prompted by the way in which the Kirchners had undermined democratic accountability and manipulated the media—most notably in mid-2009 when tax inspectors raided the offices of a well-regarded newspaper that had become critical of the Fernández administration.

The 2009 election results demonstrated various trends. The magnitude of the Government's loss of support was considerable. Néstor Kirchner was defeated by the candidate of the

Unión PRO centre-right opposition alliance in the contest for a congressional seat in the province of Buenos Aires, an electoral district in which the former President had previously been considered to be unassailable. Kirchner still secured a seat in the lower house as a result of the proportional representation voting system but his electoral loss provided a telling example of the fading fortunes of the Government. However, the opposition remained divided. Although Coalición Cívica Afirmación para una República Igualitaria (CCARI—a centre-left coalition nominally led by party President Elisa Carrió) came a close second to the official party list (gaining 29% of the popular vote compared with the latter's 31%), CCARI was extremely loose and rather different from the constellation that Carrió had headed in 2007. The most spectacular gains were registered by the fairly recently formed Unión PRO, headed by businessman Francisco de Naváez. These changes could be presented as democratic and generational renewal in the party political system. It was evident, however, that the 2009 mid-term results signalled growing discontent with existing institutions and political arrangements, and their fragility.

When Néstor Kirchner stepped down as President in 2007, conspiracy theorists argued that he had handed power to his wife in order to establish the Kirchner dynasty. Had he been elected in 2007, having served two consecutive terms he would have been constitutionally debarred from contesting the presidency again at any point in the future. By allowing Cristina Fernández to assume power in 2007, he ensured his eligibility to stand for re-election in 2011, which would in turn ensure her own in 2015—an interminable tango of the Kirchners. If there was substance to this story, the strategy was dealt a fatal blow in October 2010 with the death of Néstor, provoking fears of a weak administration in the run-up to presidential and congressional elections scheduled for October 2011. In the event, Cristina Fernández confounded critics, retaking the presidency with 54% of the vote, 10 percentage points more than she had achieved in 2007, and a remarkable recovery from the low opinion poll ratings in 2007 and 2008. Runner-up, Hermes Binner, former socialist Governor of the province of Santa Fé secured 17%. Arguably, it was a historic victory for Binner too. A well-respected regional political figure, he was the first socialist party candidate to gain such a significant share of the vote in federal elections.

Cynics attribute the re-election victory of President Fernández to the short memory of Argentine voters. More compelling explanations are to be found in the economic boom, and careful distribution of subsidies by the administration. Some 60% of Argentine voters were better off in 2011 than they had been in 2005, and those who were not were either unlikely to vote PJ or were hardened Peronists who had nowhere else to go. Inequality, having risen dramatically during the first decade of the 21st century, began to decline after 2010, gleaning further support for the Government. In addition, the political reference point for most voters remained the economic and political meltdown of 2001–02, since when the Kirchners had come to symbolize stability. Yet another explanation stems from a weak and divided opposition, which hardly offered a credible alternative to the incumbent administration. Furthermore, and despite views to the contrary expressed in 2010, Fernández was undoubtedly a consummate politician. Perhaps, too, she benefited from a sympathy vote following the death of Néstor. By promoting the cult of personality, she has sought to propel Néstor into the firmament of Peronist saviours of the country alongside 'Evita' and Perón himself, while emphasizing their shared credentials as radicals and nationalists, and as patrons of the poor. The language and stance of the regime has become increasingly populist. Most of the enterprises nationalized during the first Perón presidency, and privatized by Menem, have now been taken back by the state, or passed to allies of the regime. There has also been renewed sabre-rattling over the Falkland Islands. Some attribute shrill nationalism to confidence engendered by electoral victory in 2011, others to the increasingly fragile state of the economy—radical rhetoric serving to deflect attention from growing evidence of an impending crisis in state finances and productive sectors.

THE APOGEE AND DEMISE OF KIRCHNERISMO: WHAT NEXT?

Success in the 2011 general elections for the Frente para la Victoria (Victory Front) under Cristina Fernández was the high point of Kirchnerismo. Having obtained 54% then, the administration could only muster 33% of the national vote in the mid-term elections of October 2013, although it still came top of the poll. In the province of Buenos Aires, the largest electoral district in the country, Fernández only managed to secure 32% of the vote, with the dissident Frente Renovador (Renewal Front) branch of the PJ, headed by erstwhile ally, Sergio Massa, triumphing with 44%. The political model of 'direct democracy', involving popular mobilization and the use of state power to radicalize society in order to effect systemic change through the delivery of huge electoral majorities had broken. A series of *cacerolazos* (protests against corruption and scarcities) and large-scale anti-Kirchner street demonstrations between 2012 and 2014 indicated beyond doubt that the Government had no monopoly on mass popular mobilization.

Perhaps the 2013 election was one that the administration did not lose, or the opposition win, although the result put pay to any possibility of constitutional change that would have allowed Fernández to stand for a third presidential term. The elections were, however, financially as well as politically, costly for the regime. Initially, central bank reserves had been depleted to fund political sweeteners and, after the elections, to stabilize the economy and polity in the face of capital flight, accelerating inflation, exchange depreciation, and fears that a 'lame duck' president might not survive until the end of her term. These concerns were compounded by the state of Fernández's health, anxiety about her increasing isolation and the influence of radical ideologues from La Cámpora, an overtly Marxist clique. Having first promised that the Government would not change course, the President subsequently adopted a traditional Peronist stance when confronted by a crisis. She named Axel Kicillof, from La Cámpora, Minister of Economy (he had previously been number two at the ministry) and Jorge Capitanich, a successful businessman and politician from the interior on the right of the PJ, Cabinet Secretary. If this balancing act was designed to bring stability to the Government, it sent conflicting signals to the markets about who was in overall charge of strategy.

A renewed spate of intense popular protests at the beginning of 2014, which some commentators portrayed as echoing those of 2001–02 and which threatened the governability of the country, were contained. Possibly, because important sections of the political élite agreed that the interests of the country, and their own, were not best served by another institutional collapse. Such realism is likely to ensure that President Fernández will complete her term. Distinct groups within the Peronism spectrum are looking ahead to the elections of 2015 and recognize that the incoming government, irrespective of political hue, will have to pick up the pieces. This suggests that, while jockeying for position, factions will urge restraint. Moreover, Fernández needs to secure immunity from any possibility of a criminal prosecution after she steps down. However, substantial problems remain, including popular frustration at official corruption, anxiety about inflation and security, as well as concerns about governability.

Public disgust at corruption in official circles intensified with the high profile arraignment of Vice-President Amado Boudou in June 2014, on charges of bribery and conduct incompatible with public office. Boudou is a very close associate, long-protected by the President, and a drawn-out court case will further damage the reputation of Kirchner during her final year in office. Some have described such support for Boudou as misguided, others attribute it to the rumour that the Vice-President has declared that: '. . . if I go down, we all go down'. In the same month public anxiety about the management of the economy inevitably intensified with the US court decisions to uphold the claims of bondholders who did not settle in 2005 for debt repayment in full, despite the fact that current holders acquired the bonds at massive discounts. Failure to comply with legal decisions made by a New York court resulted in technical default in August 2014, and continuing uncertainty.

Non-partisan domestic actors are unconvinced by the Government's efforts to claim the moral high ground, while the public at large continues to be exercised by the condition of foreign exchange reserves and reputational damage.

In 2015 Capitanich may be a strong presidential contender from within the Government, provided that the economy shows signs of sustainable improvement—something that is by no means guaranteed. Another official contender, likely to gain if things go wrong for Capitanich, is Daniel Scioli, Governor of the province of Buenos Aires, and former Vice-President of Néstor Kirchner. Following his success in October 2013, Sergio Massa will only be able to build on that position if he manages to construct alliances within the PJ and beyond. How will Argentina look after Kirchnerismo? There will undoubtedly be less optimism in the country, although pessimism may be leavened by the prospect of change. There will be a realization that democratic institutions have been weakened, coupled with demands from significant sections of civil society for greater transparency. There may, too, be an acknowledgement of the positive impact of the middle years of the Kirchnerato, such as declining inequality, as well as regret at missed opportunities for societal and economic reconstruction during the long boom. Moreover, the country may aspire to more harmonious relationships with its neighbours and the wider international community.

Peronism outlived Perón and 'Evita' to become one of the dominant forces in the history and politics of the country from the mid-20th century. Its ideas and iconography were revived and exploited mercilessly by the Kirchners. However, Kirchnerismo is unlikely to survive its progenitors.

Economy

Prof. COLIN M. LEWIS

Default, albeit a technical one, at the beginning of August 2014 marked the inevitable culmination of chaotic mismanagement, compounded by posturing, of the Argentinian economy. This second default in a little over a dozen years had been preceded by a rapid depletion of foreign exchange reserves, the depreciation of the peso and rising inflation, all of which marked the fragility of the Argentinian economy, anxiety about which was reflected in the October 2013 mid-term election results. In the 2011 presidential elections, Cristina Fernández de Kirchner, who was standing for a second term, had won 54% of the popular vote; in the mid-terms, the administration secured just 33%. A government has to work extremely hard to engineer a 21 percentage point collapse in its share of the vote, or be extremely unlucky. In this instance, luck had nothing to do with the outcome of the poll, though luck had been instrumental in sustaining the Kirchner economic model, based on the dual strategy of surpluses and subsidies; namely maintaining positive balances in the fiscal and external accounts to fund subsidies to households and businesses. This strategy had delivered political stability in the aftermath of the 2001–02 economic crisis, and then recovery and growth after 2004. Today the economy is substantially larger than it was at the peak of the boom of the 1990s, which came to an end in 1997/98, though 2014/15 is likely to be problematic.

Many analysts have revised estimates of Argentina's gross domestic product (GDP) growth for 2013 upwards, with some predicting a final figure of around 5.0%, significantly higher than the 2% recorded by the World Bank for 2012. Yet most commentators continue to predict a marked slowdown in 2014. Between 2004 and 2011 the annual average rate of GDP growth was 7.6%. Indeed, as 9% was registered on several occasions during the period, this almost came to be regarded as the 'normal' annual rate of growth. Alas, this is no longer the case. Other indicators point to a similar trend, confirming underlying economic malaise and fragility, and confounding the expectations of profound and sustainable change encouraged during the early Kirchner years. The macroeconomic fundamentals are almost as precarious as in 2001–02 when the country confronted a profound crisis which precipitated the largest default in international debt history. *The 2013 Corruption Perceptions Index*, produced by Transparency International, ranks the country at 106 (out of a total of 177 states), down one place from 2010, and from a ranking of 57 (out of 91) in 2001. The World Economic Forum's *2013/14 Global Competitiveness Report* places the republic at 104 (out of 148), down from 85 (out of 133) in 2009/10; the 2013 World Bank Doing Business Index classes Argentina 124th, compared with 113th the previous year. For some, this slippage, in growth rates and international ranking, represents a telling comment on 'populist economics', as practised over the last decade or so.

The current pattern of growth confirms the Argentine paradox, of 'boom and bust' and of abrupt policy shifts. Around 1900 the country featured among the 10 wealthiest economies in the world, and ranked 12th as late as 1950. According to the *CIA World Factbook* for 2013, Argentina's GDP per head, measured in terms of purchasing power parity, placed the country 75th; Chile ranked 73rd and Brazil 105th. How could a country so favourably endowed with natural resources, and which was so well-placed in international economic rankings until the mid-20th century, have experienced such economic volatility over the last 60 years? This conundrum can only be understood by recognizing that the economic problems confronting the country are deep-seated. In addition, as the Kirchner era draws to a close, it is reasonable to ponder the legacy of 'Kirchneronomics': has the legacy compounded or confounded the conundrum?

RESOURCES AND EXPORT-LED GROWTH

The second largest country in South America, after Brazil, Argentina comprises a little over 2.78m. sq km. It is about one-third of the size of the continental USA, or similar in area to Western Europe. Almost the whole of the Republic is situated in the temperate zone of the Southern Hemisphere, though, owing to the sheer size of the country, there are considerable variations in climate and topography, a variety matched only by the range and wealth of natural resources. In recent decades the north-west and Patagonia have developed rapidly as centres of mining and energy production, with known deposits of petroleum and natural gas in the region being the third largest in Latin America. Along the Andes, in addition to traditional activities such as sheep-raising and wine production, new agricultural commodities were being developed and the region was beginning to realize fully its potential as a source of hydroelectric generation. The Pampas, the agricultural heartland of the country, although now increasingly planted with soya, has the potential to produce high yields of arable, pastoral and oleaginous commodities without the use of chemicals or artificial fertilizers, according Argentina a competitive advantage in the lucrative and expanding organic foods market, as well as an apparently limitless capacity to respond to surging global demand for more traditional temperate-region staples. Similarly dependent on the natural environment, new activities such as eco-tourism and extreme sports were emerging in the far north and south of the country. Critically, the ability to harness Argentina's abundant natural wealth and utilize its topographical and climatic diversity has depended on a number of interrelated factors, such as an efficient infrastructure, a stable political environment and an appropriate international trade regime.

Factor endowments, as during the current commodity price boom, underpinned the liberal growth model of the so-called *Belle Époque* (1870s–1910s), an arrangement that facilitated the production of a broadening mix of commodities for global markets. During this period the country became, successively, a major world supplier of wool, cereals (principally wheat and maize), and, with the development of refrigerated shipping, quality frozen and chilled meat, especially high-premium chilled beef. No other economy experienced such an exponential increase in the area under cultivation in such a short space of time, or exhibited such a dynamic primary commodity export profile.

As reflected in the first Baring Crisis of 1889–91, export-led growth was volatile. In a series of events that foreshadowed those of 2001–02, by the end of the 1880s overseas investors doubted the capacity or willingness of the state to extract sufficient income to honour its obligations. The supply of new credits dried up, gold flowed abroad, and the Government broke its bond with domestic and foreign creditors. There were riots and armed confrontations on the streets. Asset values declined and the recession deepened. However, prefiguring recovery in the early 21st century, buoyant world demand for commodities soon facilitated a surge in export production. At the time, and notwithstanding the instability of the arrangement, recovery and growth was viewed as validating the liberal model of economic openness and global engagement based on comparative natural advantage.

The First World War, however, weakened the model. During the 1920s world growth slowed and there was greater instability, not least in commodity prices. Hence, earlier economic stimulants such as trade expansion, foreign capital inflows and immigration, were less pronounced. The terms of trade were beginning to move against Argentine exports, and the scope for commodity diversification became increasingly limited as the frontier closed. Changes in the external commercial and financial context had an impact on the domestic political economy and prevailing economic ideology.

Broad changes in commodity production and export between the 1880s and 1920s would not have been possible without institutional flexibility, policy pragmatism and macroeconomic efficiency, notwithstanding the massive growth in the resource base. In the early 1930s there was a sharp contraction in the area of land under cultivation, which pointed to structural rigidity and a looming crisis of production. The transition from an extensive, to an intensive, growth model proved difficult. Between the 1930s and the 1980s an increase in the production of one commodity tended to be accompanied by a contraction in the supply of another. Moreover, after the 1940s the economy seemed incapable of increasing exports without constraining domestic consumption, or vice versa. Growth in one sector was often accompanied by retrenchment in another as factor inputs relocated: increased industrial production implied a contraction in resources available for agriculture, while generating inputs for agriculture meant curtailing resources available for manufacturing. Consequently, for much of the period encompassing the 1940s–80s there was only modest growth in productivity and aggregate production.

NATIONAL DEVELOPMENT AND INDUSTRIALIZATION: ILLUSION OR REALITY?

Pessimism about the robustness of world trade and finance in the post-Second World War period fostered in Argentina a policy shift towards state-sponsored national development, founded on positive assumptions about the capacity of domestic institutions. As in other countries, government intervened in the productive sectors and assumed a substantial role in the social sphere. The critical difference between Argentina and many other countries was that the issue of how to fund state growth was not addressed systematically. Initially, intervention was financed by wartime windfall gains in export prices and fiscal reforms introduced during the early depression years. Thereafter, inflation taxation became the easy expedient. From the early 1940s to the early 1950s, as the economy closed, Argentine rates of inflation were noticeably higher than those of comparable economies. There was a second, more pronounced phase of divergence from international rates of price change in the mid-1950s and late 1960s, and a third cycle of divergence, from the early 1970s to the late 1980s, when inflation rates were vastly higher than those of other countries, and which culminated in bouts of hyperinflation in 1989–90. At the beginning of the second decade of the 21st century, Argentine rates of inflation were again diverging substantially from regional and global norms.

It would be easy to blame these problems on populist strategies implemented by Peronist (PJ) administrations between 1946 and 1955. Arguably, it was not these strategies per se that provoked a break in the national growth trajectory and divergence from other economies. Rather, the cause lay in the way in which these strategies were implemented. Pro-industry ideas promulgated by the UN's Economic Commission for Latin America (as the Economic Commission for Latin America and the Caribbean—ECLAC—was then known) had broad appeal. Developmentalist (*desarrollista*) ideology was widely embraced during the presidency of Arturo Frondizi (1958–62). There was a concerted effort to address the problem of arbitrary policy change and to resolve structural deficiencies in a systematic fashion. Targeting such sectors as steel and energy was designed to correct the bias towards 'horizontal' industrial expansion, manifest during the rule of Col Juan Domingo Perón (1946–55) when policy distortions had favoured light industries, geared towards the manufacture of basic wage goods, and the proliferation of small firms. In its own terms, the Frondizi project was successful. Growth rates were high, if unpredictable. However, public sector deficits grew and, despite an improvement in the terms of trade, soaring imports and erratic export performance soon caused balance of payments deficits.

By the mid-1960s manufacturing accounted for around one-third of total economic activity, the composition of industrial output was more diverse than hitherto, and firms were larger. These two phenomena were related and largely driven by the 'transnationalization' of business. The participation of foreign firms became particularly pronounced in sectors such as petrochemicals, machinery and equipment, motor vehicles, chemicals, and non-ferrous metals. Increases in the scale of production were consistent with modest real reductions in the price of manufactures and efficiency gains. However, while foreign-owned corporations tended to invest in the upgrading of technology, national firms invested less and kept productions costs low by recruiting cheap, unskilled labour that was flooding into the cities from the countryside. The presence of the state (mainly military-owned firms) in manufacturing also grew. Across the manufacturing sector, a productivity gap was opening: all-round efficiency gains in sectors such as petrochemicals, chemicals and cellulose, and (some) metallurgical sectors were offset by slow productivity growth in other branches. This constrained expansion in overall productivity limited structural improvements in macroeconomic efficiency. Moreover, all businesses, however technically advanced, were dependent on the policy regime. As the productivity gap widened, distributional conflict (among economic sectors and between social groups) became a pronounced feature of the development model.

The 'bureaucratic-authoritarian' military regime installed in 1966, and presided over by Gen. Juan Carlos Onganía (1966–70), promised to resolve the efficiency gap and restore economic discipline. Onganía presented a 'business-friendly' face to the outside world. Foreign investment increased, precipitating another cycle of transnational corporate expansion, which, associated with structural developments sustained from the Frondizi presidency, facilitated a surge in the manufacture of consumer durables, notably motor vehicles and electrical goods. The pro-business policy stance of the regime did not bring much relief to the agricultural sector, which continued to suffer pressure to generate resources (notably foreign exchange) essential for industrial development. The international oil crisis of 1973 prompted another policy shift, associated with the return from exile of Perón, who believed rising world commodity prices would end sluggish growth and finance fundamental structural change that might yet facilitate national development focused on the domestic market. As in the late 1940s, windfall taxes on agricultural exports supported an expansion in public expenditure, which increased by more than 50% in real terms between 1972 and 1975. However, the boom could not last: after 1975 commodity prices and foreign reserves decreased sharply. Despite fiscal innovation, taxes failed to keep pace with expenditure. As the public sector deficit was monetized, inflation escalated and there was another crisis in the balance of payments. Conditions were thus aligned for the 1976 coup, and renewed efforts to restore the productivity deficit and stabilize the economy.

A REVOLUTION IN PRODUCTIVITY: RESTRUCTURING IN AUTHORITARIAN AND DEMOCRATIC CONTEXTS

Many sectors of society initially greeted with relief the so-called Proceso de Reorganización Nacional initiated by the armed forces in March 1976. The incoming military Government signalled a profound rupture with the pro-manufacturing consensus articulated by both civilian and military administrations since the 1940s. The collapse of the corporatist industrial alliance in the chaos of the last months of the administration of 'Isabelita' Martínez de Perón (1974–76), and the utter exhaustion of civil society, contributed to the new regime's autonomous power. The economy was opened and wages reduced: foreign capital flowed in and investment levels recovered; there was a near 40% contraction in real wages and exports grew, facilitated by the reduction in production costs and driven by the severe contraction in domestic demand. Inflation was brought under control, declining from an average monthly rate above 30% in the period immediately preceding the coup to almost zero by June 1976. Subsidies were reduced, and by 1977 the primary deficit had decreased to one-quarter of its 1975 level, remaining low for the remainder of the decade. With the 'depoliticization' of decision-making, the junta's economic team enjoyed considerable protection from sectoral lobbying. None the less, there were limits to 'reform'. Public expenditure was not brought fully under control and the military refused to relinquish businesses acquired since the 1940s, despite a supposed commitment to market economics. Furthermore, the armed forces exempted themselves from the discipline of the market and, in so doing, imposed greater fiscal pressure on other branches of public expenditure. As a share of the budget, military expenditure doubled in real terms during the second half of the decade.

Rooted in market logic, the economic model combined incentives and penalties. Unfortunately, not all economic agents behaved as expected. Rising government and household demand for credit meant that the financial sector was the main beneficiary of the boom: those with liquid assets found it more profitable to lend to the banks than to invest in production. Although companies raised funds to finance modernization, lending pressures limited the stock of resources available to business and drove up the real cost of domestic credit, even before the global spike in interest rates made further borrowing impracticable. Moreover, by 1980 public expenditure was higher than in 1976, and the budget deficit even larger. Domestic and external indebtedness was becoming uncontrollable, just as international interest rates were on the increase. Yet another boom was proving unsustainable: the era of 'easy money' (*plata dulce*) was about to end for companies, for consumers and for a Government that had based its legitimacy on growth, exchange rate stability and low inflation. All the signs of a structural crisis were in place: as in 1889, 1953–55, 1968, 1976, 1989, 1998, 2001 and 2013 there was evidence of financial sector distress, businesses dependent on state subsidies, capital flight, a precipitate decline in reserves and exchange rate slippage.

When the debt crisis and Falklands debacle (see History) resulted in the collapse of the Proceso regime in the 1982, the scene was set for a heterodox solution to the 'productivity crisis'. Launched in June 1985, the 'Austral Plan' was conceived as a 'war on inflation' by the democratically elected Government that had taken office in 1983. The project was a controversial blend of Keynesianism and monetarism. Acknowledging the need for macroeconomic stability, it broke the policy mould by seeking to stabilize through growth, rather than via a 'corrective' recession. Implemented in a democratic framework, unlike earlier 'corrections' of 1968 and 1976, the Austral Plan was another policy shock intended to change attitudes. A new currency, the austral, was phased in according to a sliding conversion table designed to prevent windfall gains and losses that often accompany sharp devaluations. A freeze on wages and prices was similarly adjusted for residual inflation, with fairly generous corrections being allowed for basic wages, and presented as a social pact involving the state, labour and business. Indexation was outlawed: the courts were banned from enforcing index clauses in contracts that linked prices to the rate of inflation. The Government committed itself to fiscal and monetary responsibility and privatization was on the agenda. Together, echoing the European social-democratic economic model, these measures and promises were intended to promote co-operation among all major interest groups—labour, business and the state—thereby ending the cycles of distributional conflict that had plagued the country since the 1940s.

Unfortunately, economic agents did not always co-operate, and the state appeared reluctant or unable to honour its side of the bargain. Although inflation remained under control and public confidence remained high, investment did not increase as hoped. Crucially, the freezing of wages and prices was extended beyond its intended time span, a step largely motivated by the imminence of elections. A wages and prices shock, such as that applied in July 1985, could work only once: the imposition of a second round of shock treatment reduced the credibility of the policy model and the administration, indicating that the strategy was unravelling. By February 1989 central bank reserves were exhausted, the currency was in free fall and hyperinflation had become inevitable. When presidential and congressional elections were held in May, the monthly rate of price increases touched 150%, representing an annual inflation rate of 5,000%. The scene was set for another dose of liberal correction.

In January 1991 President Carlos Saúl Menem (1989–95, 1995–99) appointed Domingo Cavallo as Minister of the Economy. Cavallo implemented the 'Convertibility Plan' based on a new monetary system and the reform of the state: privatization, the liberalization of capital markets and a renewed opening of the economy. Following a substantial devaluation, the domestic currency was to be completely underwritten by US dollars and foreign reserves held by the central bank, which was to be freed from political control and prohibited from printing money (that is, monetizing the fiscal deficit). The Convertibility Plan introduced a dual (or competitive) monetary system: pesos and US dollars circulated in parallel and were interchangeable. Private debts could be settled in pesos or dollars and the US dollar enjoyed the status of quasi-legal tender, with the exception that the Government would only accept payment of taxes in pesos. The central bank became, in effect, a currency board. Reform of the state meant removing the principal fiscal pressure points, specifically deficits generated by state-owned enterprises, provincial administrations and social security funds. The balance of the federal budget was to be restored by, on the revenue side, tax reform—entailing modernization of the fiscal structure and increasing the efficiency of tax collection—and, on the expenditure side, by the disposal of state enterprises, pension privatization and imposing discipline on the provinces.

Despite some technical flaws, the Convertibility Plan was successful, chiefly because there was a large measure of popular support and a reasonable (though not equitable) distribution of hardship. During the early years of the arrangement there was economic growth with low inflation. From 1991 to the end of 1994 output grew at an average annual rate of just under 8%, while the annual rate of inflation decreased sharply from 84% to less than 4%. Unemployment rose, but remained below 10% until 1994, despite the accelerating pace of privatization. Investment increased and general levels of productivity improved. However, despite the re-stabilization of the economy, and the beginning of profound structural reform, the success of the Convertibility Plan was undermined by corruption.

By the late 1990s the Menem administration had become a distributionist confederacy that preyed on the remnants of a failing state, conditions that contributed to opposition victories in the 1999 presidential and congressional elections. Institutionalized corruption exacted an economic and political price. Failure to close the fiscal gap resulted in renewed state borrowing. Unfortunately, interest rates remained stubbornly high, despite the removal of the risk to the exchange rate associated with the new currency regime. There were several reasons for this. First, the markets harboured doubts about the technicalities of sustaining the project, doubts that intensified after 1999, as debt-service and the fiscal gap necessitated additional borrowing. Second, as during the mid-1980s, rising government demand for credit kept rates high. Third, corruption drove the deficit. If Menem had little intention of curbing corruption, the Government of President Fernando de la Rúa that took office in December 1999 seemed equally unable, or unwilling, to curb expenditure. From 1991 to 2001 the fiscal deficit averaged 2% of GDP.

The immediate causes of the ensuing crisis dated from early 2001 and unfolded in two phases. The first phase occurred in early April when Cavallo made a decision to adjust the Convertibility Law and modify the Central Bank Charter. This followed the largest ever monthly withdrawal of deposits from the banking system: in March some US $5,500m. flowed out of the banks, compared with the previous record of $4,600m. at the height of the tequila crisis in 1994. Between April and mid-July 2001 a further $10,000m. was withdrawn from banks, precipitating a corresponding shrinkage of the domestic money supply and capital stock. This provoked a further credit slump—at a time when the economy was already more than three years into recession and bankruptcies were running at record levels—and precipitated the second phase: 'Plan Cero'. This was a monthly balancing of the budget that represented a desperate last attempt to reassure the public and the IMF, which was beginning to display a marked reluctance to advance further credit. This was followed in December by the freezing of bank accounts, public outrage and the collapse of the de la Rúa presidency. By this time more than $20,000m. had been removed from the domestic banking system. The country was without credit and virtually without money.

FROM KEYNESIANISM TO 'KIRCHNERONOMICS'

The intensity and extent of the 2001–02 crisis was reflected in a series of protests aimed at the political class and the banks, and the succession of five Presidents in two weeks. Symbolically, on 1 January 2002 the Congreso offered the presidency to Eduardo Duhalde, a Peronist and former Governor of the province of Buenos Aires, who had been defeated by de la Rúa in the 1999 presidential election. Remaining in office until May 2003, the Duhalde administration was forced to take difficult decisions in order to secure a positive legacy for its successor. The dual peso/US dollar monetary arrangement was abandoned, debt default was officially announced, the freeze on bank accounts was extended (with some minor exceptions), and an interim arrangement was sought with the IMF. Measures were taken to support the banking system and state finances, and a series of price agreements was negotiated with utility companies to prevent total social collapse. The principal anxieties were of a return of hyperinflation, precipitous devaluation of the peso, and violent public disorder. In the event, these fears were not realized, largely owing to the prudence of the regime (it had little alternative) and disciplined action by the new Minister of the Economy, Roberto Lavagna, appointed in April 2002. Lavagna was the sixth appointee to that post in 12 months, but he remained in office until November 2005, having been reappointed by Duhalde's successor, Néstor Carlos Kirchner (2003–07). President Kirchner was in turn succeeded by his wife, Cristina Fernández de Kirchner, in December 2007, who was re-elected in October 2011. This husband-to-wife succession ensured the strengthening and deepening of neo-populist economics that have characterized the post-2005 period.

An immediate benefit of debt default was the non-payment of interest and amortization charges. This reduced pressure on the budget—already contracting owing to the recession and near paralysis of the economy caused by the crisis—and allowed scarce fiscal resources to be devoted to emergency projects. A new revenue-sharing agreement was implemented in mid-2002 between the federal Government and the provinces, securing political support for the administration and preventing the failure of the state, while considerable sums were applied to social relief. Primary budget surpluses were soon being generated, and emergency taxes on exports gave the Government access to foreign exchange. This facilitated non-inflationary funding of government expenditure, initially the

innovative Heads of Households Programme (Programa Jefes y Jefas de Hogar), targeted at the poorest members of society (at the height of the 2001–02 crisis, over 55% households were categorized as living below the poverty line), and gave the central bank access to foreign exchange with which to manage the exchange rate. The Heads of Households Programme was subsequently diluted but complemented by a range of income support schemes introduced around 2011 that included child and education grants and unemployment benefit.

Measures like the Heads of Households and Social Inclusion Programmes were necessary and had important, progressive social consequences. Neo-Keynesian social expenditure certainly contributed to economic reactivation after 2003 and, in part, explains the current growth surge—child benefit allowances had a dramatic impact on domestic consumption from early 2010, when payments commenced. These social interventions—combined with the 'China effect' (the rise in commodity prices owing to increased Chinese demand) and the strong economic performance of Brazil (Argentina's principal trading partner)—partly explain why the country was relatively unscathed by the 2007–09 global financial crisis. The fact that Argentina had been largely absent (excluded) from international capital markets since the 2001–02 crash also contributed to the country's resilience. Yet, political manipulation of some of social programmes has provoked questions about their contribution to social cohesion, as well as their sustainability. Other structural constraints include productive and infrastructure capacity. As early as 2008 there was evidence that many branches of manufacturing were beginning to experience capacity constraints, suggesting that growth up to that point may have been due to the existence of idle installed plant. Addressing the capacity deficit proved politically expedient in the run-up to both the mid-term congressional elections in 2009 and the presidential election in 2011. In 2009 and 2011 there was a noticeable loosening of fiscal policy as the administration increased public expenditure on job-creating public works, ostensibly to lay the foundations for future growth. However, the investment deficit remains: the current system is incapable of sustaining high levels of expenditure on capital formation and subsidies. Primary surpluses are large, but since 2006 an increasing proportion of government expenditure has been absorbed by subsidies: compensation to oil companies to keep domestic fuel prices below international levels; subsidies to transport companies to cover rising costs and compensate for the failure to adjust charges; subsidies to favoured exporters to counteract the overvalued exchange rate; and diverse subsidies to producers and consumers in politically sensitive areas. The list is endless, driven by official efforts to check price increases and contain inflationary pressure. No economy can run on subsidies for ever. Although the arrangement seemed feasible when the fiscal and external accounts remained in substantial surplus, the short-sightedness of the Government's macroeconomic management is now becoming clear at precisely the moment when greater flexibility and efficiency is required to resolve domestic structural weaknesses. Post-presidential election increases in utility rates in 2011 showed that the administration recognizes that it had to decide between consumption subsidies and capital-creating subsidies. Yet, little of real significance has since been done.

The economic and political achievements of the new 'model' were reflected in public opinion polls and electoral gains for the Kirchners and, initially, the exchange rate—always a key indicator of macroeconomic performance and public assessment of policy competence. The rate of exchange remained remarkably stable from April 2003 until mid-2007, settling at around 3 pesos to the US dollar. After mid-2007, the peso began to decline, and although the slippage was initially slow, the rate of depreciation accelerated in late 2011 and by mid-2013 the peso stood at around 5.3 pesos to the US dollar, closing the year at about 6.0, despite increasingly tough measures aimed at closing down the unofficial 'blue' exchange market. The gap between the official and 'blue' rates of exchange peaked at about 70% in mid-2013 and again in early 2014, provoking street protests and a run on the banks. It was at this point in late January 2014 that the official rate was devalued from 6.0 to 8.0 pesos. Given that movements in the exchange rate can serve as indicators of public confidence and a proxy for the quality of economic management, the exchange rate correction early in 2014 can be taken as marking the end of 'Kirchneronomics'.

Until 2006 the economic team was generally well regarded, and the application of a neo-Keynesian strategy as necessary to facilitate economic recovery and growth, and prevent social disintegration. The principal features of the policy regime were, in addition to the accumulation of substantial fiscal surpluses and international reserves, price controls; targeted expenditure, initially focused mainly on emergency social projects and later the economic and social infrastructure; and, until very recently, exchange rate stability and low inflation. Most accounts acknowledged that the economic team had regained control of the economy by 2003, enabling the slow and arduous process of rebuilding the economic structures to begin, and for soon-to-be-disappointed optimists to create an opportunity for fundamental macroeconomic reform.

The extent to which the commodity boom underwrote recovery and growth was demonstrated by several indicators. Primary fiscal surpluses stabilized at around 3%. The rate of open unemployment, which reached more than 22% in early 2002 and was approximately 10% in mid-2006, returned to historic (pre-Convertibility Plan) levels of around 6% in 2008, with employment growing strongly thereafter. According to official data, the proportion of the population living below the poverty line in 2013 was 5.4%, down from 55% in 2002. Since 2010, inequality, which increased in the 1990s and soared during the crisis and early Kirchner presidencies, has fallen sharply, largely due to a growth in employment. With domestic manufacturing once again the focus of government attention, official data shows a strong recovery in industrial production after 2007, although with a sharp contraction in 2012 and poor performance in 2013 and 2014.

These achievements, however, should be considered in context. First, the level of external indebtedness remains high (higher in real terms than before the 2001 crisis) and debt service charges (expressed as a proportion of GDP) also remained above 2001 levels, despite the 2005 agreement with most foreign creditors. Second, investment remains at critically low levels. The partial recovery in direct foreign investment flows associated with the commodity boom and Chinese-style growth rates, has faltered and remains among the lowest in Latin America, at around 2% of GDP—by comparison, in 2012 capital inflow in Chile was equivalent to around 10% of GDP. This is connected to a third factor, business confidence—lack of investment signals a lack of confidence in the country and the Government. Since 2007, as the rhetoric and substance of economic policy became increasingly nationalistic, international enterprises have gradually, sometimes vociferously, withdrawn from Argentina, a process that intensified with the renationalization of Spanish oil company REPSOL's Argentine subsidiary YPF in 2012, and has continued since, with further companies leaving the country. Fourth, despite promises to address the problem, there is growing evidence of under-investment in public infrastructure, including transport, energy generation and supply, and key branches of manufacturing. Tragic railway accidents and the failure of energy supplies appear to illustrate this issue. Power blackouts have prompted memories of the energy shortages experienced between the 1950s and the 1970s, and have resulted in burgeoning energy imports that consume scarce foreign exchange in a country that was until recently an energy exporter. Fifth, the tax regime is unsustainable: government finances have become dependent on export taxes levied on a narrowing range of commodities. Initially justified as an emergency measure, when reapplied during the 2001–02 crisis, and subsequently presented as an 'equity' charge on an agro-export sector benefiting from the surge in commodity prices, these taxes have become counterproductive. Accompanied by export bans, successive increases in export tax rates have resulted in massive rural recapitalization (reversing a trend towards capital upgrading initiated in the 1990s), a switch to less heavily taxed commodities, and producer strikes. Farmer protests, accompanied by highway blockades and empty shelves in supermarkets, have become a recurrent feature, and have succeeded in uniting various farming groups and urban consumers against the Government. The fiscal system remains highly dependent on procyclical sales and commodities taxes: until the January 2014 correction there was little evidence that the regime had the willingness or the capacity to address fundamental flaws in the policy and business environments. Finally, there are the signals being sent by accelerating inflation and currency depreciation, that indicate a further deterioration over the next 12 months. For example, while official estimates of inflation hover around 10%, organized labour is demanding wage rises of 25%–30% to cover increases in the cost of living, and there is evidence that for some sectors and regions, the real rate of inflation is approximately 40%. These factors explain public unease and a lack of business confidence—except on the part of those firms closely connected with the regime. They also indicate that financing the state in a manner that is socially and economically progressive—and conducive to macroeconomic efficiency—remains unresolved.

THE ECONOMIC ENDGAME: HOW TO EXIT 'KIRCHNERONOMICS'

In some quarters, the radicalism observed in economic language and policies, particularly since the inauguration of the second Fernández de Kirchner administration, is attributed to a conscious project designed to restructure the fundamentals of the economy in order to reconfigure society and the state itself. Although much of the rhetoric may echo that of the first Perón administration, and a number of initiatives appear equally opportunistic, the current model is more ideologically driven and internally coherent. There is symmetry to its motivation and mechanisms. The agenda is anti-capitalist and anti-internationalist, or 'anti-globalization' given the current usage of the term. Associated with a faction of the youth wing of the PJ, La Cámpora, many key figures in the group formed their ideas about economics and politics in student movements of the 1990s, notably those protesting against the Menemist neoliberal 'Washington Consensus' programme (the policies adopted in conjunction with international financial institutions), and the cosy relationship between the state and domestic and foreign business. Yet others acknowledge the influence of notions of armed struggle forged during the chaos of the 1960s and 1970s, when Marxist activists on the fringe of the PJ, the Montoneros, fought to secure a more prominent position in the Peronist movement and government, elements with whom the Kirchners were engaged. Whether their world view was formed by assessments of events in the 1970s, or experiences of the 1990s, the current conjuncture is viewed by proponents of the project as a moment to be seized to forge a new future. Until his death in 2014, the intellectual guru of the administration was Ernesto Laclau, a distinguished Argentinian political sociologist, who had taught in Europe and the USA. The most influential figure in La Cámpora remains the youthful, charismatic Axel Kicillof, appointed as Deputy Minister of the Economy by President Fernández in 2011, and promoted to Minister of the Economy in November 2013.

Late 'Kirchneronomics' placed a renewed emphasis on autarchy and statism, purported to serve the interests of the country and the poor by generating jobs through the 'Argentinianization' of the productive structure and the reordering of society, and showed scant regard for conventional economics. As during the 2011 presidential election, when one senior official dismissed inflation as a problem for the middle classes, and business as corrupt (except for firms controlled by the state or interests close to the state), the language and substance of economic policy is confrontational and populist. Yet as shortages multiply, epitomized by the energy deficit—particularly acute in 2013/14, when the country relied on imports from neighbouring countries to cover the shortfall, and fill gaps on supermarket shelves—the level of activity remains dependent on resources generated by staple exports. It is this dependence that explains the careful monitoring of the foreign exchange market following correction and efforts to tighten the fiscal regime as commodity production fluctuates and the tax base shrank. With each escalation of the crisis, measures of last resort have become the norm, from the dismissal in 2007 of the team responsible for compiling inflation data at the Instituto Nacional de Estadística y Censos (INDEC—National Institute of Statistics and Censuses)—until then a highly respected agency—to the nationalization and looting of pension funds in 2008, to the successive re-statization of most businesses privatized during the Menem presidency, to the seizure of central bank reserves in 2010 (to pay off loans to international agencies), to the suppression of the exchange market in order to prevent capital flight, and a tightening of import controls—a cause of considerable tension with Brazil in April 2014. Such measures of last resort are now virtually exhausted.

The end of 'Kirchneronomics' has been marked by two events. First, the promotion of Kicillof from the number two to the number one position at the Ministry of the Economy, apparently consistent with the President's initial statement that there would be no change in the economic strategy, and the balancing designation of Jorge Capitanich, a pragmatic politician and successful businessman, as Cabinet Secretary (equivalent to the role of Prime Minister). Since the cabinet reshuffle, Capitanich has spearheaded key economic initiatives at home and overseas. Second, the long anticipated correction of January 2014: following political protest, capital flight and a surge in the gap between the official and blue rates of exchange, the peso was devalued and controls eased. As anticipated, a measure of calm returned to the foreign exchange markets, although fears about medium-term, macroeconomic stability remained.

Even before the correction, the administration had begun to reduce subsidies, as a means of curbing expenditure, accepting the inevitable impact on inflation, consumption and employment. There has also been a renewed focus on the debt. Strenuous efforts have been made to rein in provincial debt (and spending) and, as foreign currency reserves continue to dwindle, tentative moves have been made to re-establish credibility in overseas capital markets. Arranging a settlement with Paris Club institutional creditors and the so-called holdouts (small investors who refused to participate in the 2005 debt-write-down) will be crucial to any rapprochement with potential investors. This strategy is flawed. Although institutional creditors may be prepared to play a long game, private debt holders are not, their determination to press the Government being strengthened by string of US court decisions. While the administration has always maintained that it would never negotiate with so-called 'vulture' funds who hold most of the unsettled debt, by July 2014 it was being forced to the negotiating table, negotiations and appeals which continued in August, notwithstanding default. Failure to settle with the holdouts continued to destabilize Argentina, despite actual and promised settlements with the international financial institutions involved.

Looking ahead to 2015, the regime appears to be banking on export growth—although prices may be soft, there are forecasts of a bumper soya harvest—and capital inflows. Luck and credibility may be mutually reinforcing, serving to replenish fiscal and foreign currency reserves. If so, will the result be an addressing of the investment and productivity gaps, or renewed indiscipline and corruption?

CONCLUSION

Argentina is again at a critical juncture. There may be an opportunity to rebuild and reconstruct both infrastructure and confidence among consumers and investors. Bridges will also need to be rebuilt with regional and overseas partners, including Brazil, Uruguay and Chile, as well as with international institutions. Recent crises have been largely of domestic making. Tax policy continues to undermine the resilience and flexibility of the agrarian sector, leading to an overdependence on one commodity—soya. Business confidence has been severely damaged; many firms complain of chronic public underfunding of social overhead capital and of heavy-handed and inconsistent policy interventions. Although recovering as the harvest comes in, the trade surplus is narrow. Fiscal and foreign currency reserves, which declined catastrophically in the run-up to the October 2013 mid-term elections and haemorrhaged thereafter, will take time to rebuild. Once a major provider of food to the world and energy self-sufficient, in 2014 Argentina is again importing commodities it once exported. Government income remains dependent on the vagaries of the weather, on world demand for commodities, on the capacity (and willingness) of the rural sector to produce, and on the ability of local infrastructure to deliver goods to world markets at prices that cover costs, while generating sufficient returns to fund domestic profits and subsidies. Fiscal surpluses, initially deployed in an effective neo-Keynesian response to economic crises, have been squandered and squeezed by corruption. Having been discouraged by rhetoric and an official stance sometimes described as predatory, domestic savers and overseas investors will require considerable reassuring and a consistent approach to policy. The late Kirchner economic model failed; it is too early to predict what will follow.

Statistical Survey

Sources (unless otherwise stated): Instituto Nacional de Estadística y Censos, Avda Julio A. Roca 609, C1067AAB Buenos Aires; tel. (11) 4349-9200; fax (11) 4349-9601; e-mail ces@indec.mecon.gov.ar; internet www.indec.mecon.ar; Banco Central de la República Argentina, Reconquista 266, C1003ABF Buenos Aires; tel. (11) 4348-3500; fax (11) 4348-3955; e-mail sistema@bcra.gov.ar; internet www.bcra.gov.ar.

Area and Population

AREA, POPULATION AND DENSITY

Area (sq km)	2,780,403*
Population (census results)†	
17–18 November 2001	36,260,130
27 October 2010	
Males	19,523,766
Females	20,593,330
Total	40,117,096
Population (official estimates at 1 July)	
2012	41,733,271
2013	42,202,935
2014	42,669,500
Density (per sq km) at 1 July 2014	15.3

* 1,073,519 sq miles. The figure excludes the Falkland Islands (Islas Malvinas) and Antarctic territory claimed by Argentina.
† Figures exclude adjustment for underenumeration.

POPULATION BY AGE AND SEX
(official estimates at 1 July 2014)

	Males	Females	Total
0–14 years	5,542,809	5,254,737	10,797,546
15–64 years	13,493,877	13,852,524	27,346,401
65 years and over	1,859,517	2,666,036	4,525,553
Total	20,896,203	21,773,297	42,669,500

ADMINISTRATIVE DIVISIONS
(official estimates at 1 July 2014)

	Area (sq km)	Population	Density (per sq km)	Capital
Buenos Aires— City . . .	203	3,049,229	15,020.8	—
Buenos Aires— Province . .	307,571	16,476,149	53.6	La Plata
Catamarca . .	102,602	393,088	3.8	San Fernando del Valle de Catamarca
Chaco . . .	99,633	1,130,608	11.3	Resistencia
Chubut . .	224,686	556,319	2.5	Rawson
Córdoba . .	165,321	3,528,687	21.3	Córdoba
Corrientes . .	88,199	1,059,836	12.0	Corrientes
Entre Ríos . .	78,781	1,308,290	16.6	Paraná
Formosa . .	72,066	573,823	8.0	Formosa
Jujuy . . .	53,219	718,971	13.5	San Salvador de Jujuy
La Pampa . .	143,440	339,895	2.4	Santa Rosa
La Rioja . .	89,680	362,605	4.0	La Rioja
Mendoza . .	148,827	1,863,809	12.5	Mendoza
Misiones . .	29,801	1,174,542	39.4	Posadas
Neuquén . .	94,078	610,449	6.5	Neuquén
Río Negro . .	203,013	688,873	3.4	Viedma
Salta . . .	155,488	1,314,726	8.5	Salta
San Juan . .	89,651	730,408	8.1	San Juan
San Luis . .	76,748	469,889	6.1	San Luis
Santa Cruz . .	243,943	311,444	1.3	Río Gallegos
Santa Fe . .	133,007	3,369,365	25.3	Santa Fe
Santiago del Estero . .	136,351	918,147	6.7	Santiago del Estero
Tierra del Fuego .	21,571	148,143	6.9	Ushuaia
Tucumán . .	22,524	1,572,205	69.8	San Miguel de Tucumán
Total . . .	2,780,403	42,669,500	15.3	—

PRINCIPAL LOCALITIES
(population by provincial capital or departamento, 2010 census)

Buenos Aires (capital) . .	2,890,151*	San Fernando (Chaco) . .	390,874
Córdoba . . .	1,329,604	Confluencia (Neuquén) . .	362,673
Rosario (Santa Fe) .	1,193,605	Corrientes . .	358,223
(San Miguel de) Tucumán . .	548,866	Paraná (Entre Ríos)	339,930
Salta	536,113	General Roca (Río Negro) . .	320,921
Santa Fe . . .	525,093	Posadas (Misiones) .	324,756

* The population of the Greater Buenos Aires agglomeration, including the capital city, was 12,806,866. The population of the Province of Buenos Aires, excluding the capital city, was 15,525,084. Principal settlements within the Province of Buenos Aires included: La Matanza 1,775,816; La Plata 654,324; General Pueyrredón 618,989; Lomas de Zamora 616,279; Quilmes 582,943; Almirante Brown 552,902; Merlo 528,494; Lanús 459,263; Moreno 452,505; Florencio Varela 426,005; General San Martín 414,196; Tigre 376,381; Avellaneda 342,677; Tres de Febrero 340,071; Berazategui 324,244; Malvinas Argentinas 322,375; Morón 321,109; Bahía Blanca 301,572; Esteban Echeverría 300,959.

BIRTHS, MARRIAGES AND DEATHS

	Registered live births		Marriages		Registered deaths	
	Number	Rate (per 1,000)	Number	Rate (per 1,000)	Number	Rate (per 1,000)
2005 . .	712,220	18.5	132,720	3.4	293,529	7.6
2006 . .	696,451	17.9	134,496	3.5	292,313	7.5
2007 . .	700,792	17.8	136,437	3.5	315,852	8.0
2008 . .	746,460	18.8	133,060	3.3	302,133	7.6
2009 . .	745,336	18.6	126,081	3.1	304,525	7.6
2010 . .	756,176	18.7	123,208	3.0	318,602	7.9
2011 . .	758,042	18.5	128,797	3.1	319,059	7.8
2012 . .	738,318	17.9	131,922	3.2	319,539	7.7

Sources: Dirección de Estadísticas e Información en Salud (DEIS) and UN, *Demographic Yearbook* and *Population and Vital Statistics Report*.

Life expectancy (years at birth): 76.0 (males 72.4; females 79.8) in 2012 (Source: World Bank, World Development Indicators database).

ECONOMICALLY ACTIVE POPULATION
(labour force survey of 31 urban agglomerations, persons aged 10 years and over, 2006)

	Males	Females	Total
Agriculture, hunting and forestry.	59,242	13,640	72,882
Fishing	8,215	821	9,036
Mining and quarrying . . .	34,127	5,687	39,814
Manufacturing	988,343	422,321	1,410,664
Electricity, gas and water . .	38,066	5,991	44,057
Construction	854,764	29,917	884,681
Wholesale and retail trade; repair of motor vehicles, motorcycles and personal and household goods	1,263,477	755,160	2,018,637
Hotels and restaurants . .	213,854	166,975	380,829
Transport, storage and communications . . .	557,431	86,613	644,044
Financial intermediation . . .	95,938	93,497	189,435
Real estate, renting and business activities	528,349	281,460	809,809
Public administration and defence; compulsory social security . .	444,379	324,337	768,716
Education	185,900	620,900	806,800
Health and social work . .	163,470	426,735	590,205
Other community, social and personal services	317,127	229,607	546,734
Private households with employed persons	18,151	778,801	796,952
Extraterritorial organizations and bodies	2,031	164	2,195
Sub-total	5,772,864	4,242,626	10,015,490
Activities not adequately described	13,854	11,161	25,015
Total employed . . .	5,786,718	4,253,787	10,040,505
Unemployed	488,935	560,263	1,049,198
Total labour force . . .	6,275,653	4,814,050	11,089,703

2011 (labour force survey of 31 agglomerations at January–March, '000 persons aged 10 years and over): Total employed 10,605; Unemployed 846; Total labour force 11,451.

2012 (labour force survey of 31 agglomerations at January–March, '000 persons aged 10 years and over): Total employed 10,664; Unemployed 820; Total labour force 11,485.

2013 (labour force survey of 31 agglomerations at January–March, '000 persons aged 10 years and over): Total employed 10,748; Unemployed 925; Total labour force 11,673.

Health and Welfare

KEY INDICATORS

Total fertility rate (children per woman, 2012)	2.2
Under-5 mortality rate (per 1,000 live births, 2012) . . .	14
HIV (% of persons aged 15–49, 2012)	0.4
Physicians (per 1,000 head, 2004)	3.2
Hospital beds (per 1,000 head, 2010)	4.5
Health expenditure (2011): US $ per head (PPP)	1,393
Health expenditure (2011): % of GDP	7.9
Health expenditure (2011): public (% of total)	66.5
Access to water (% of persons, 2012)	99
Access to sanitation (% of persons, 2012)	97
Total carbon dioxide emissions ('000 metric tons, 2010) . .	180,511.7
Carbon dioxide emissions per head (metric tons, 2010) . .	4.5
Human Development Index (2013): ranking	49
Human Development Index (2013): value	0.808

For sources and definitions, see explanatory note on p. vi.

Agriculture

PRINCIPAL CROPS
('000 metric tons)

	2010	2011	2012
Wheat	15,876	14,501	8,198
Rice, paddy	1,243	1,748	1,568
Barley	2,964	4,086	5,158
Maize	22,677	23,800	21,196
Rye	44	43	40
Oats	660	415	496
Sorghum	3,629	4,458	4,252
Potatoes*	1,996	2,127	2,200
Sweet potatoes*	353	390	400
Cassava (Manioc)* . . .	182	185	187
Sugar cane*	25,960	26,960	25,000
Beans, dry	338	333	350*
Soybeans (Soya beans) . .	52,677	48,879	40,100
Groundnuts, with shell . .	611	702	686
Olives*	165	170	175
Sunflower seed	2,221	3,672	3,341
Artichokes*	85	101	106
Tomatoes*	721	699	715
Pumpkins, squash and gourds* .	327	338	345
Chillies and peppers, green* . .	145	133	138
Onions, dry*	723	718	726
Garlic*	129	120	135
Carrots and turnips* . . .	227	244	260
Watermelons*	122	124	127
Cantaloupes and other melons* .	77	77	80
Bananas*	171	172	175
Oranges	833	877*	900*
Tangerines, mandarins, clementines and satsumas	424	401*	415*
Lemons and limes	1,113	1,229*	1,300*
Grapefruit and pomelos . . .	189	189*	200*
Apples*	1,050	1,116	1,250
Pears*	704	691	700
Peaches and nectarines* . . .	318	285	290
Plums and sloes*	150	148	150
Grapes	2,617	2,890†	2,800*
Tea	89	97	100*
Mate	250	273*	290*
Tobacco, unmanufactured* . .	137	145	148

* FAO estimate(s).
† Unofficial figure.

Aggregate production ('000 metric tons, may include official, semi-official or estimated data): Total cereals 47,149 in 2010, 49,101 in 2011, 40,964 in 2012; Total roots and tubers 2,531 in 2010, 2,701 in 2011, 2,787 in 2012; Total vegetables (incl. melons) 3,351 in 2010, 3,464 in 2011, 3,557 in 2012; Total fruits (excl. melons) 7,645 in 2010, 8,070 in 2011, 8,260 in 2012.

Source: FAO.

LIVESTOCK
('000 head, year ending September)

	2010	2011	2012
Horses*	3,600	3,590	3,650
Asses*	98	98	98
Mules*	185	185	185
Cattle	48,950	46,000*	47,500
Pigs*	2,300	2,350	2,400
Sheep	15,025	14,731	16,300*
Goats*	4,250	4,280	4,350
Chickens*	98,000	100,000	105,000
Ducks*	2,500	2,550	2,600
Geese*	160	165	167
Turkeys	3,000	3,050	3,070

* FAO estimate(s).

Source: FAO.

LIVESTOCK PRODUCTS
('000 metric tons)

	2010	2011	2012
Cattle meat	2,630	2,497*	2,500†
Sheep meat†	44	47	49
Pig meat	281	301	305†
Horse meat	32	29	30†
Chicken meat†	1,597	1,648	1,664
Cows' milk	10,502	11,206	11,815*
Butter and ghee†	48	51	52
Cheese†	510	528	530
Hen eggs	554*	591*	600†
Honey	59	74†	75†
Wool, greasy	54	54†	55†

* Unofficial figure.
† FAO estimate(s).

Source: FAO.

Forestry

ROUNDWOOD REMOVALS
('000 cubic metres, excl. bark)

	2009	2010	2011
Sawlogs, veneer logs and logs for sleepers*	4,289	4,403	4,403
Pulpwood	5,250	5,874	5,874
Other industrial wood . . .	283	358	363
Fuel wood	4,267	4,375	4,547*
Total*	14,089	15,010	15,187

* FAO estimate(s).

2012: Production assumed to be unchanged from 2011 (FAO estimates).

Source: FAO.

SAWNWOOD PRODUCTION
('000 cubic metres, incl. railway sleepers)

	2008	2009	2010
Coniferous (softwood)	470	1,115	761
Broadleaved (hardwood) . . .	485	1,036	1,398
Total	955	2,151	2,159

2011–12: Production assumed to be unchanged from 2010 (FAO estimates).

Source: FAO.

Fishing

('000 metric tons, live weight)

	2010	2011	2012
Capture	811.7	793.3	738.1
Southern blue whiting . . .	11.6	3.5	8.4
Argentine hake	281.8	287.8	258.0
Patagonian grenadier . . .	82.7	70.9	59.6
Argentine red shrimp . . .	72.1	82.9	79.9
Patagonian scallop	50.9	47.8	36.8
Argentine shortfin squid . .	86.0	76.6	95.0
Aquaculture	2.7*	3.2*	3.0
Total catch	814.4*	796.5*	741.0

* FAO estimate.

Note: The data exclude aquatic animals, recorded by number rather than by weight. The number of dolphins and toothed whales caught was 121 in 2010; 180 in 2011; n.a. in 2012. The number of broad-nosed and spectacled caimans caught was 6,292 in 2010; 6,132 in 2011; 4,931 in 2012.

Source: FAO.

Mining

('000 metric tons unless otherwise indicated)

	2009	2010	2011
Crude petroleum ('000 barrels) .	230,885	224,077	214,142
Natural gas (million cu metres) .	36,708	35,625	34,060
Lead ore*	24.8	22.6	26.1
Zinc ore*	31.9	32.6	34.0
Aluminium (primary) . . .	410.2	412.8	432.0
Lithium:			
carbonate (metric tons) . .	8,574	11,178	10,000†
chloride (metric tons) . .	4,279	6,644	4,480†
Silver ore (kg)*	532,823	723,238	747,449
Copper ore*	143.1	140.0	116.7
Gold ore (kg)*	46,588	63,138	59,140
Fluorspar (metric tons) . . .	13,424	17,657	25,099
Boron (crude)	506.0	623.0	648.8
Gypsum (crude)	1,355.3	1,346.5	1,452.8
Clay (common)	6,941.7	7,313.4	8,323.9
Salt	1,477.5	1,532.1	1,884.9
Sand:			
for construction	27,183.5	31,345.8	33,455.2
Silica (glass) sand . . .	364.2	531.2	516.8
Limestone	15,746.7	17,309.8	19,782.4
Stone (various crushed) . . .	19,663.4	22,237.9	22,638.7
Rhodochrosite (kg) . . .	122,117	122,839	120,673
Quartzite (crushed)	946.7	1,164.4	1,292.5
Gemstones (kg)	119,650	45,054	45,000†

* Figures refer to the metal content of ores and concentrates.
† Estimate.

Source: US Geological Survey.

2012 (estimates): Crude petroleum 31.5m. metric tons; Natural gas 37,729m. cu metres (Source: BP, *Statistical review of World Energy*).

Industry

SELECTED PRODUCTS
('000 metric tons unless otherwise indicated)

	2011	2012	2013
Wheat flour	4,843	4,635	4,006
Beer (sales, '000 hectolitres)* .	21,433	20,408	21,082
Wine (sales, '000 hectolitres) . .	9,810	10,051	10,336
Cigarettes (sales, million packets)	2,188	2,173	2,116
Paper (excl. newspaper) . . .	1,623	1,607	1,597
Aluminium	416	413	440
Iron (primary)	4,471	3,683	4,115
Crude steel	5,611	4,996	5,186
Portland cement	11,592	10,716	11,892
Refined petroleum ('000 cu m)† .	36,087	37,668	37,890
Ethylene	655	680	695
Urea	1,159	1,179	1,123
Ammonia	759	757	734
Washing machines ('000 units) .	1,242	1,445	1,321
Home refrigerators ('000 units) .	822	897	840
Air conditioning units (domestic, '000)	1,801	1,549	1,653
Motor vehicles ('000)	577	497	507
Electric energy (million kWh) .	124,901	129,163*	n.a.

* Estimate(s).
† Provisional figures.

Finance

CURRENCY AND EXCHANGE RATES

Monetary Units
100 centavos = 1 nuevo peso argentino (new Argentine peso).

Sterling, Dollar and Euro Equivalents (30 May 2014)
£1 sterling = 13.508 new pesos;
US $1 = 8.030 new pesos;
€1 = 10.930 new pesos;
100 new pesos = £7.40 = $12.45 = €9.15.

Average Exchange Rate (new pesos per US $)
2011   4.110
2012   4.537
2013   5.459

Note: From April 1996 to December 2001 the official exchange rate was fixed at US $1 = 99.95 centavos. In January 2002 the Government abandoned this exchange rate and devalued the peso: initially there was a fixed official exchange rate of US $1 = 1.40 new pesos for trade and financial transactions, while a free market rate was applicable to other transactions. In February, however, a unified 'floating' exchange rate system, with the rate to be determined by market conditions, was introduced.

GENERAL GOVERNMENT BUDGET
(public sector accounts, million new pesos, forecasts)

Revenue	2013	2014	2015
Current revenue	732,572.9	930,876.4	1,102,095.1
Tax revenue	423,706.5	534,393.6	636,119.8
Social security contributions .	229,074.4	286,814.2	341,607.8
Sale of public goods and services	2,657.2	3,541.1	4,070.1
Property income	60,110.0	86,341.6	94,494.0
Current transfers . . .	782.4	550.3	4,589.5
Other current revenue . .	22.1	329.6	343.0
Capital revenue	863.9	287.9	356.5
Total	733,436.8	931,164.3	1,102,451.6

Expenditure	2013	2014	2015
Current expenditure . . .	684,593.0	820,881.3	950,060.8
Consumption expenditure . .	139,496.0	160,386.1	168,893.4
Property income	47,125.9	80,322.5	94,020.5
Social security benefits . . .	270,075.6	329,235.7	391,329.2
Current transfers	197,372.0	219,306.9	252,524.3
Capital expenditure . . .	95,529.8	106,703.9	146,139.6
Direct investment	42,765.7	53,630.0	70,144.4
Capital transfers	42,765.7	47,113.6	69,205.7
Financial investment . . .	5,249.4	5,960.3	6,789.5
Total	780,122.8	927,585.2	1,096,200.4

Note: Budget figures refer to the consolidated accounts of the central and local governments and state-owned companies and entities.

Source: Oficina Nacional de Presupuesto, Secretaría de Hacienda, Ministerio de Economía, Buenos Aires.

INTERNATIONAL RESERVES
(US $ million at 31 December)

	2011	2012	2013
Gold (national valuation) . . .	3,127	3,326	2,389
IMF special drawing rights . .	3,152	3,155	3,162
Foreign exchange	40,075	36,765	24,981
Total	46,354	43,246	30,532

Source: IMF, *International Financial Statistics*.

MONEY SUPPLY
(million new pesos at 31 December)

	2011	2012	2013
Currency outside banks . . .	151,282	209,979	257,805
Demand deposits at commercial banks	64,001	111,504	148,673
Total money	215,283	321,483	406,478

Source: IMF, *International Financial Statistics*.

COST OF LIVING
(Consumer Price Index for Buenos Aires metropolitan area; base: April 2008 = 100)

	2011	2012	2013
Food and beverages	127.9	141.0	151.7
Clothing	159.2	172.9	186.0
All items (incl. others) . . .	130.2	143.3	158.5

NATIONAL ACCOUNTS
(million new pesos at current prices, preliminary)

Expenditure on the Gross Domestic Product

	2011	2012	2013
Government final consumption expenditure	320,901	408,898	521,705
Private final consumption expenditure	1,483,448	1,812,550	2,234,633
Increase in stocks*	34,431	12,407	40,347
Gross fixed capital formation . .	426,493	463,358	568,855
Total domestic expenditure .	2,265,273	2,697,213	3,365,540
Exports of goods and services . .	409,633	433,651	478,041
Less Imports of goods and services	371,659	386,036	493,732
Gross domestic product (GDP) in market prices	2,303,246	2,744,829	3,349,848
GDP at constant 2004 prices .	836,889	844,807	869,739

* Including statistical discrepancy.

Gross Domestic Product by Economic Activity

	2011	2012	2013
Agriculture, forestry and hunting .	151,140	158,525	181,695
Fishing	3,490	3,930	8,405
Mining and quarrying	82,803	98,003	115,067
Manufacturing	351,897	391,847	439,244
Electricity, gas and water supply .	59,679	77,629	97,179
Construction	111,532	128,652	163,184
Wholesale and retail trade . .	253,164	292,343	346,380
Hotels and restaurants . . .	39,136	44,615	50,776
Transport, storage and communications	136,373	156,143	184,975
Financial intermediation . . .	60,754	81,684	101,539
Real estate, renting and business activities	258,037	299,957	366,292
Public administration and defence*	137,441	178,566	227,322
Education, health and social work	225,253	287,255	365,567
Other community, social and personal service activities† . .	114,481	152,055	199,101
Sub-total	1,985,180	2,351,205	2,846,725
Value-added tax	154,237	190,496	249,006
Import duties	14,678	16,643	23,551
Net taxes on products	149,152	186,485	230,567
GDP in market prices . . .	2,303,246	2,744,829	3,349,848

* Including extra-territorial organizations and bodies.
† Including private households with employed persons.

BALANCE OF PAYMENTS
(US $ million)

	2011	2012	2013
Exports of goods f.o.b.	84,051	80,927	83,026
Imports of goods f.o.b.	−71,126	−65,556	−70,871
Trade balance	12,925	15,372	12,155
Exports of services	15,610	15,107	14,415
Imports of services	−17,857	−18,473	−19,518
Balance on goods and services	10,678	12,006	7,052
Other income received (net) . .	−12,402	−11,503	−10,709
Balance on goods, services and income	−1,724	503	−3,657
Current transfers (net) . . .	547	−455	−673
Current balance	−2,271	48	−4,330
Capital account (net)	62	48	32
Net investment in banking sector .	6,900	−1,649	−1,154
Net investment in public sector .	−2,250	−3,648	183
Net investment in private sector .	−4,356	4,624	−4,928
Net errors and omissions . . .	−4,194	−2,727	−1,627
Overall balance	−6,108	−3,305	−11,824

External Trade

PRINCIPAL COMMODITIES
(US $ million)

Imports c.i.f.	2010	2011	2012*
Mineral fuels, lubricants and related products	4,479	9,402	8,878
Paper and cardboard . . .	1,010	1,152	1,044
Rubber and manufactures of rubber	1,183	1,494	1,284
Organic chemicals and related products	2,660	3,089	3,034
Pharmaceutical products . .	1,566	1,790	2,092
Plastic and manufactures of laminate	2,428	3,034	2,845
Metalliferous ore	1,423	1,547	1,385
Electrical machinery	6,980	8,316	7,707
Boilers, machines and mechanical appliances, etc.	8,540	11,050	9,897
Vehicles	10,125	12,880	12,054
Optical instruments and apparatus, etc.	1,227	1,637	1,615
Total (incl. others) . . .	56,793	74,319	68,508

* Provisional figures.

Exports f.o.b.	2010	2011	2012*
Meat and meat products . . .	1,694	1,905	1,802
Fish	1,307	1,438	1,306
Residues from the food industries and prepared animal feed . .	8,783	10,774	11,669
Fats and oils	5,192	7,034	5,929
Cereals	4,622	8,382	9,530
Oil seeds and oleaginous fruits .	5,338	5,995	3,796
Milk and milk products . . .	1,059	1,717	1,059
Skins and leathers	1,001	927	832
Mineral fuels, lubricants and related materials	5,388	4,956	4,962
Mineral by-products	1,820	1,889	2,116
Chemical products	1,925	2,856	2,542
Plastic and manufactures of laminate	1,346	1,536	1,388
Pearls, stones, metals and articles thereof	2,258	2,734	2,575
Metalliferous ore	1,201	1,494	1,391
Boilers and mechanical appliances, etc.	1,691	1,891	1,873
Vehicles	7,973	9,974	9,557
Total (incl. others) . . .	68,187	84,051	80,927

* Provisional figures.

2013 (preliminary): Total imports 73,655; Total exports 81,660.

PRINCIPAL TRADING PARTNERS
(US $ million)*

Imports c.i.f.	2010	2011	2012†
Bolivia	350	629	1,416
Brazil‡	17,950	22,181	17,907
Chile‡	885	1,093	1,011
China, People's Republic§ . .	7,678	10,573	9,952
France (incl. Monaco) . .	1,529	1,634	1,599
Germany	3,215	3,646	3,713
Italy	1,297	1,482	1,457
Japan	1,191	1,415	1,509
Korea, Republic	968	1,420	1,140
Mexico	1,817	2,533	2,251
Netherlands	394	435	1,130
Russia	397	792	1,125
Spain	1,024	1,396	1,320
Thailand	640	696	872
Trinidad and Tobago . . .	511	1,275	1,905
USA	6,125	7,700	8,388
Uruguay‡	587	606	520
Total (incl. others) . . .	56,793	74,319	68,508

Exports f.o.b.	2010	2011	2012†
Algeria	1,010	1,699	1,503
Brazil‡	14,425	17,347	16,495
Canada	1,402	4,845	2,194
Chile‡	4,490	4,845	5,065
China, People's Republic§ . .	6,117	6,232	5,021
Colombia	1,302	1,806	2,067
Germany	1,832	2,486	1,981
Egypt	979	1,746	1,013
India	1,321	1,087	1,183
Indonesia	852	1,542	1,634
Iran	1,453	1,092	984
Italy	1,586	2,018	1,172
Japan	855	843	1,223
Korea, Republic	780	981	1,379
Malaysia	813	706	870
Netherlands	2,367	2,627	2,236
Peru	1,121	1,808	1,924
South Africa	879	1,131	1,050
Spain	2,242	3,089	2,650
USA	3,656	4,248	4,089
Uruguay‡	1,554	1,996	1,983
Venezuela	1,424	1,867	2,225
Total (incl. others) . . .	68,187	84,051	80,927

* Imports by country of origin; exports by country of destination.
† Provisional figures.
‡ Including free trade zones.
§ Including Hong Kong and Macao.

Transport

RAILWAYS
(traffic)

	2010	2011	2012
Passengers carried ('000) . . .	421,392	346,225	284,353
Freight carried ('000 tons) . .	23,551	24,194	22,033
Passenger-km (million) . . .	8,588	7,083	5,845
Freight ton-km (million) . . .	12,112	12,198	10,583

ROAD TRAFFIC
('000 motor vehicles in use)

	2003	2004	2005
Passenger cars	4,668	4,926	5,230
Commercial vehicles	1,198	1,684	1,775

Source: UN, *Statistical Yearbook*.

2007 ('000 motor vehicles in use at 31 December): Total vehicles 12,399.9 (Source: IRF, *World Road Statistics*).

SHIPPING

Flag Registered Fleet
(at 31 December)

	2011	2012	2013
Number of vessels	395	398	409
Total displacement ('000 grt) . .	826.2	759.9	732.6

Source: Lloyd's List Intelligence (www.lloydslistintelligence.com).

International Seaborne Freight Traffic
('000 metric tons)

	2011	2012	2013
Goods unloaded	30,204	25,272	27,473

Source: UN, *Monthly Bulletin of Statistics*.

Total maritime freight handled ('000 metric tons): 163,764 in 2010; 175,539 in 2011; 169,453 in 2012 (Source: Dirección Nacional de Puertos).

CIVIL AVIATION

	2010	2011	2012
Passengers carried ('000) . . .	17,212	17,664	19,009
Total freight carried ('000 metric tons)	256	234	256

2009 (million): Kilometres flown 190; Passenger-km 21,286.

Tourism

TOURIST ARRIVALS BY REGION
('000 arrivals at Jorge Newbery and Ezeiza airports)

	2011	2012	2013
Europe	560.8	533.8	513.8
North America	289.9	277.2	257.9
South America	1,690.3	1,603.9	1,408.8
Brazil	886.8	817.2	667.3
Chile	220.0	220.6	219.0
Total (incl. others)	2,692.1	2,568.2	2,385.2

Spending by tourists (arrivals at Jorge Newbery and Ezeiza airports, US $ million): 3,514.0 in 2011; 3,095.7 in 2012; 2,631.5 in 2013.

Total tourist arrivals ('000 arrivals at frontiers, excl. excursionists): 5,705 in 2011; 5,585 in 2012; 5,571 in 2013 (provisional) (Source: World Tourism Organization).

Total tourism receipts (US $ million): 5,354 in 2011; 4,887 in 2012; 4,411 in 2013 (provisional) (Source: World Tourism Organization).

Communications Media

	2011	2012	2013
Telephones ('000 main lines in use)	9,722.5	9,455.6	9,662.1
Mobile cellular telephones ('000 handsets in use)	60,722.7	64,327.6	65,910.1
Broadband subscribers ('000) . .	4,558.8	5,147.6	5,742.5

Internet subscribers ('000): 3,995.3 in 2010.

Source: International Telecommunication Union.

Education

(2012 unless otherwise indicated)

	Institutions	Teachers	Students
Pre-primary	18,035	115,515	1,610,845
Primary	22,256	340,015	4,603,422
Secondary	21,281*	141,389*	3,813,545
Basic	14,155*	44,210*	2,330,757
Specialized	7,126*	97,179*	1,482,788
Higher			
University†	37	n.a.	1,273,156
Non-university	2,164	24,679	767,698

* 2007.
† 2004.

Source: partly Red Federal de Información Educativa, *Relevamiento*.

Pupil-teacher ratio (primary education, UNESCO estimate): 16.3 in 2007/08 (Source: UNESCO Institute for Statistics).

Adult literacy rate (UNESCO estimates): 97.9% (males 97.8%; females 97.9%) in 2011 (Source: UNESCO Institute for Statistics).

Directory

The Constitution

The return to civilian rule in 1983 represented a return to the principles of the 1853 Constitution, with some changes in electoral details. In August 1994 a new Constitution was approved, which contained 19 new articles, 40 amendments to existing articles and the addition of a chapter on New Rights and Guarantees. The Constitution is summarized below:

DECLARATIONS, RIGHTS AND GUARANTEES

Each province has the right to exercise its own administration of justice, municipal system and primary education. The Roman Catholic religion shall enjoy state protection; freedom of religious belief is guaranteed to all other denominations. The prior ethnical existence of indigenous peoples and their rights, as well as the common ownership of lands they traditionally occupy, are recognized. All inhabitants of the country have the right to work and exercise any legal trade; to petition the authorities; to leave or enter the Argentine territory; to use or dispose of their properties; to associate for a peaceable or useful purpose; to teach and acquire education; and to express freely their opinion in the press without censorship. The State does not admit any prerogative of blood, birth, privilege or titles of nobility. Equality is the basis of all duties and public offices. No citizens may be detained, except for reasons and in the manner prescribed by the law; or sentenced other than by virtue of a law existing prior to the offence and by decision of the competent tribunal after the hearing and defence of the person concerned. Private residence, property and correspondence are inviolable. No one may enter the home of a citizen or carry out any search in it without their consent, unless by a warrant from the competent authority; no one may suffer expropriation, except in case of public necessity and provided that the appropriate compensation has been paid in accordance with the provisions of the laws. In no case may the penalty of confiscation of property be imposed.

LEGISLATIVE POWER

Legislative power is vested in the bicameral Congreso (Congress), comprising the Cámara de Diputados (Chamber of Deputies) and the Senado (Senate). The composition of the Chamber of Deputies is determined according to the population of each province. Deputies are directly elected for a four-year term and are eligible for re-election; approximately one-half of the membership of the Chamber shall be renewed every two years. The Senate comprises 72 members (three from each province), directly elected for a six-year term, with one-third of the seats renewable every two years. The Vice-President of the nation sits as President of the Senate.

The powers of Congress include regulating foreign trade; fixing import and export duties; levying taxes for a specified time whenever the defence, common safety or general welfare of the State so requires; contracting loans on the nation's credit; regulating the internal and external debt and the currency system of the country; fixing the budget; and facilitating the prosperity and welfare of the nation. Congress must approve required and urgent decrees and delegated legislation. Congress also approves or rejects treaties, authorizes the Executive to declare war or make peace, and establishes the strength of the Armed Forces in peace and war.

EXECUTIVE POWER

Executive power is vested in the President, who is the supreme head of the nation and controls the general administration of the country. The President issues the instructions and rulings necessary for the execution of the laws of the country, and takes part in drawing up and promulgating those laws. The President appoints, with the approval of the Senate, the judges of the Supreme Court and all other competent tribunals, ambassadors, civil servants, members of the judiciary, senior officers of the Armed Forces and bishops. The President may also appoint and remove, without reference to another body, the cabinet ministers. The President is Commander-in-Chief of all the Armed Forces. The President and Vice-President are elected directly for a four-year term, renewable only once.

JUDICIAL POWER

Judicial power is exercised by the Supreme Court and all other competent tribunals. The Supreme Court is responsible for the internal administration of all tribunals.

PROVINCIAL GOVERNMENT

The 23 provinces retain all the power not delegated to the federal Government. They are governed by their own institutions and elect their own governors, legislators and officials. The City of Buenos Aires has its own autonomous Government.

The Government

HEAD OF STATE

President of the Nation: CRISTINA ELISABET FERNÁNDEZ DE KIRCHNER (took office 10 December 2007, re-elected 23 October 2011).
Vice-President: AMADO BOUDOU.

CABINET
(September 2014)

The Cabinet is composed of members of the Frente para la Victoria alliance.

Cabinet Chief: JORGE MILTON CAPITANICH.

Minister of the Interior and Transport: ANÍBAL FLORENCIO RANDAZZO.

Minister of Foreign Affairs, International Trade and Worship: HÉCTOR MARCOS TIMERMAN.

Minister of Defence: AGUSTÍN ROSSI.

Minister of Economy and Public Finance: AXEL KICILLOF.

Minister of Industry: DÉBORA ADRIANA GIORGI.

Minister of Tourism: CARLOS ENRIQUE MEYER.

Minister of Education: ALBERTO ESTANISLAO SILEONI.

Minister of Science, Technology and Productive Innovation: LINO BARAÑAO.

Minister of Labour, Employment and Social Security: CARLOS ALFONSO TOMADA.

Minister of Federal Planning, Public Investment and Services: JULIO MIGUEL DE VIDO.

Minister of Health: JUAN LUIS MANZUR.

Minister of Security: MARÍA CECILIA RODRÍGUEZ.

Minister of Justice and Human Rights: JULIO CÉSAR ALAK.

Minister of Social Development: ALICIA MARGARITA KIRCHNER.

Minister of Agriculture, Livestock and Fisheries: CARLOS HORACIO CASAMIQUELA.

Minister of Culture: TERESA ADELINA SELLARÉS.

MINISTRIES

General Secretariat to the Presidency: Balcarce 50, C1064AAB Buenos Aires; tel. and fax (11) 4344-3600; e-mail secretariageneral@presidencia.gov.ar; internet www.secretariageneral.gov.ar.

Office of the Cabinet Chief: Avda Julio Argentino Roca 782, C1067ABP Buenos Aires; tel. (11) 4331-1951; e-mail privada@jgm.gov.ar; internet www.jgm.gov.ar.

Ministry of Agriculture, Livestock and Fisheries: Avda Paseo Colón 982, C1063ACW Buenos Aires; tel. (11) 4349-2000; fax (11) 4349-2589; e-mail prensa1@minagri.gob.ar; internet www.minagri.gob.ar.

Ministry of Culture: Alvear 1690, C1014AAQ, Buenos Aires; tel. (11) 4129-2452; e-mail privada1@cultura.gob.ar; internet www.cultura.gob.ar.

Ministry of Defence: Azopardo 250, C1328ADB Buenos Aires; tel. (11) 4346-8800; e-mail mindef@mindef.gov.ar; internet www.mindef.gov.ar.

Ministry of Economy and Public Finance: Hipólito Yrigoyen 250, C1086AAB Buenos Aires; tel. (11) 4349-5000; e-mail ciudadano@mecon.gov.ar; internet www.mecon.gov.ar.

Ministry of Education: Pizzurno 935, C1020ACA Buenos Aires; tel. (11) 4129-1000; fax (11) 4129-1180; e-mail prensa@me.gov.ar; internet www.me.gov.ar.

Ministry of Federal Planning, Public Investment and Services: Hipólito Yrigoyen 250, 11°, Of. 1112, C1086AAB Buenos Aires; tel. (11) 4349-5000; internet www.minplan.gov.ar.

Ministry of Foreign Affairs, International Trade and Worship: Esmeralda 1212, C1007ABR Buenos Aires; tel. (11) 4819-7000; e-mail info@cancilleria.gob.ar; internet www.cancilleria.gov.ar.

Ministry of Health: 9 de Julio 1925, C1073ABA Buenos Aires; tel. (11) 4379-9000; fax (11) 4381-2182; e-mail prensa@msal.gov.ar; internet www.msal.gov.ar.

Ministry of Industry: Hipólito Yrigoyen 250, C1086AAB Buenos Aires; tel. (11) 4349-3000; e-mail prensa@industria.gob.ar; internet www.minprod.gob.ar.

Ministry of the Interior and Transport: 25 de Mayo 101/145, C1002ABC Buenos Aires; tel. (11) 4339-0800; fax (11) 4331-6376; e-mail info@mininterior.gov.ar; internet www.mininterior.gov.ar.

Ministry of Justice and Human Rights: Sarmiento 329, C1041AAG Buenos Aires; tel. (11) 5300-4000; e-mail prensa@jus.gov.ar; internet www.jus.gov.ar.

Ministry of Labour, Employment and Social Security: Avda Leandro N. Alem 650, C1001AAO Buenos Aires; tel. (11) 4311-2913; fax (11) 4312-7860; e-mail cfederal@trabajo.gov.ar; internet www.trabajo.gov.ar.

Ministry of Science, Technology and Productive Innovation: Avda Godoy Cruz 2320, C1425FQD Buenos Aires; tel. (11) 4899-5000; fax (11) 4312-8364; e-mail info@mincyt.gov.ar; internet www.mincyt.gov.ar.

Ministry of Security: Gelly y Obes 2289, C1425EMA Buenos Aires; internet www.minseg.gob.ar.

Ministry of Social Development: 9 de Julio 1925, 19°, C1073ABA Buenos Aires; tel. (11) 4379-3648; e-mail privadaministro@desarrollosocial.gov.ar; internet www.desarrollosocial.gov.ar.

Ministry of Tourism: Buenos Aires; e-mail info@turismo.gov.ar; internet www.turismo.gov.ar.

President and Legislature

PRESIDENT

Election, 23 October 2011

Candidates	Votes	% of valid votes cast
Cristina E. Fernández de Kirchner (Frente para la Victoria)	11,593,023	53.96
Hermes Juan Binner (Frente Amplio Progresista)	3,624,518	16.87
Ricardo Luis Alfonsín (Unión para el Desarrollo Social)	2,395,056	11.15
Alberto J. Rodríguez Saá (Alianza Compromiso Federal)	1,714,385	7.98
Eduardo Duhalde (Frente Popular)	1,264,609	5.89
Jorge Altamira (Frente de Izquierda y de los Trabajadores)	497,082	2.31
Elisa M. A. Carrió (Coalición Cívica Afirmación para una República Igualitaria)	396,171	1.84
Total valid votes*	21,484,844	100.00

* In addition, there were 678,724 blank and 206,030 spoiled ballots. There were also a further 23,921 contested votes.

CONGRESS

Chamber of Deputies

President: JULIÁN ANDRES DOMÍNGUEZ.

The Chamber of Deputies has 257 members, who hold office for a four-year term, with approximately one-half of the seats renewable every two years. The last election was held on 27 October 2013.

Distribution of Seats by Legislative Bloc, December 2013

	Seats
Frente para la Victoria	118
Unión Cívica Radical	41
Dissident Peronists*	33
Propuesta Republicana	20
Frente Amplio Progresista	15
Frente Cívico por Santiago	7
Nuevo Encuentro	4
Coalición Cívica ARI/UNEN	3
Frente de Izquierda y de los Trabajadores	3
Movimiento Popular Neuquino	3
Unidad Popular	3
Others	7
Total	257

* Including the Frente Renovador.

Senate

President: GERARDO ZAMORA (provisional).

The Senate has 72 directly elected members, three from each province. One-third of these seats are renewable every two years. The last election was held on 27 October 2013, in which, according to preliminary results, the FPV won 11 seats, the PRO, Frente Cívico por Santiago and the MPN two seats each, and the UNEN, Unión por Chaco, Alianza Unión por Entre Ríos, Frente Popular Salteño, Frente Popular, Alianza Frente Progresista and the Movimiento Popular Fueguino each won one seat.

Distribution of Seats by Legislative Bloc, December 2013

	Seats
Frente para la Victoria and allies	40
Unión Cívica Radical/Frente Amplio Progresista . .	19
Frente Renovador and allies	7
Propuesta Republicana and allies	3
Others	3
Total	72

Provincial Administrators

(September 2014)

Head of Government of the Autonomous City of Buenos Aires: MAURICIO MACRI (PRO).

Governor of the Province of Buenos Aires: DANIEL OSVALDO SCIOLI (FPV).

Governor of the Province of Catamarca: LUCÍA CORPACCI (FPV).

Governor of the Province of Chaco: JUAN CARLOS BACILEFF IVANOFF (acting).

Governor of the Province of Chubut: MARTÍN BUZZI (Modelo Chubut).

Governor of the Province of Córdoba: JOSÉ MANUEL DE LA SOTA (PJ).

Governor of the Province of Corrientes: RICARDO COLOMBI (UCR).

Governor of the Province of Entre Ríos: SERGIO DANIEL URRIBARRI (FPV).

Governor of the Province of Formosa: Dr GILDO INSFRÁN (PJ).

Governor of the Province of Jujuy: EDUARDO ALFREDO FELLNER (PJ).

Governor of the Province of La Pampa: OSCAR MARIO JORGE (PJ).

Governor of the Province of La Rioja: LUIS BEDER HERRERA (PJ).

Governor of the Province of Mendoza: FRANCISCO PÉREZ (FPV).

Governor of the Province of Misiones: MAURICE FABIÁN CLOSS (Frente Renovador de la Concordia).

Governor of the Province of Neuquén: JORGE AUGUSTO SAPAG (MPN).

Governor of the Province of Río Negro: ALBERTO WERETILNECK (FPV).

Governor of the Province of Salta: JUAN MANUEL URTUBEY (FPV).

Governor of the Province of San Juan: Dr JOSÉ LUIS GIOJA (FPV).

Governor of the Province of San Luis: CLAUDIO POGGI (Alianza Compromiso Federal).

Governor of the Province of Santa Cruz: DANIEL ROMAN PERALTA (FPV).

Governor of the Province of Santa Fe: ANTONIO BONFATTI (PS).

Governor of the Province of Santiago del Estero: CLAUDIA LEDESMA ABDALA DE ZAMORA (FPV/Frente Cívico por Santiago).

Governor of the Province of Tierra del Fuego, Antártida e Islas del Atlántico Sur: MARÍA FABIANA RÍOS (CCARI).

Governor of the Province of Tucumán: JOSÉ JORGE ALPEROVICH (PJ).

Election Commission

Dirección Nacional Electoral: 25 de Mayo 101, 3°, Of. 346, C1002ABC Buenos Aires; tel. (11) 4346-1683; fax (11) 4346-1634; e-mail elecciones@mininterior.gov.ar; internet www.elecciones.gov .ar; part of the Ministry of the Interior and Transport; Dir ALEJANDRO TULLIO.

Political Organizations

Bandera Vecinal: Rivadavia 8811, C1407DYK Buenos Aires; tel. (11) 5803-2555; e-mail banderavecinal@gmail.com; internet www .banderavecinal.org; f. 2012 following the merger of Gente en Acción (GEA) and Alternativa Social (AS); Pres. ALEJANDRO CARLOS BIONDINI; Sec.-Gen. GABRIEL KLOSTER.

Coalición Cívica ARI (Coalición Cívica Afirmación para una República Igualitaria—CCARI): Rivadavia 1475, C1022AAB Buenos Aires; tel. (11) 4384-1268; e-mail prensa@coalicioncivicaari.org.ar; internet coalicioncivicaari.org.ar; f. 2001 as Alternativa por una República de Iguales; progressive party; contested the 2013 legislative elections as mem. of the UNEN coalition, which forms a parliamentary bloc with the UCR; Sec.-Gen. PABLO JAVKIN; 48,000 mems.

Frente Amplio Progresista (FAP): f. 2011; centre-left; Leader HERMES JUAN BINNER; contested the 2011 presidential election with Partido Nuevo and the following parties:

> **Generación para un Encuentro Nacional (GEN):** Riobamba 67, 1°, C1025ABA Buenos Aires; tel. (11) 4951-9503; e-mail gen@ partidogen.com.ar; internet www.partidogen.com.ar; f. 2007; Leader MARGARITA ROSA STOLBIZER; Sec.-Gen. JUAN CARLOS JUÁREZ.

> **Movimiento Libres del Sur:** Humberto I 542, San Telmo, C1103ACL Buenos Aires; tel. (11) 4307-3724; e-mail contacto@ libresdelsur.org.ar; internet www.libresdelsur.org.ar; Leader HUMBERTO TUMINI.

> **Partido Socialista (PS):** Entre Ríos 488, 2°, Buenos Aires; tel. (11) 4383-2395; e-mail pscen@ar.inter.net; internet www .partidosocialista.org.ar; f. 2002 following merger of the Partido Socialista Democrático and the Partido Socialista Popular; Pres. HERMES JUAN BINNER; Sec.-Gen. ALFREDO LAZZERETTI; 115,000 mems.

> **Unidad Popular:** Rivadavia 2515, C1034ACE Buenos Aires; tel. (11) 2055-7778; e-mail info@corrienteup.org; internet corrienteup .org; comprises the Unidad Popular, Unión de los Neuquinos (UNE), Buenos Aires para Todos, Participación, Ética y Solidaridad (PARES) and Cruzada Renovadora de San Juan; Leader LILIANA PARADA.

Frente Cívico—Córdoba: Córdoba; regional party.

Frente Cívico por Santiago: Santiago del Estero; f. 2005; regional party; Leader GERARDO ZAMORA.

Frente de Izquierda y de los Trabajadores (FIT): La Rioja 853, C1221ACG Buenos Aires; tel. (11) 4932-9297; e-mail laverdadobrera@pts.org.ar; internet www.frentedeizquierda.org; f. 2011; left-wing; Pres. JORGE ALTAMIRA; comprises the following parties:

> **Partido Obrero:** Ayacucho 444/8, C1026AAB Buenos Aires; tel. (11) 4953-3824; fax (11) 4954-5829; e-mail secretariaprensapo@ gmail.com; internet www.po.org.ar; f. 1982; Trotskyist; Leader JORGE ALTAMIRA; 26,000 mems.

> **Partido de los Trabajadores Socialistas (PTS):** La Rioja 853, C1221ACG Buenos Aires; tel. (11) 4932-9297; e-mail pts@pts.org .ar; internet www.pts.org.ar; f. 1988 as a schism of Movimiento al Socialismo; Trotskyist; Pres. CHRISTIAN CASTILLO.

Movimiento de Integración y Desarrollo (MID): Ayacucho 49, C1025AAA Buenos Aires; tel. (11) 4954-0817; e-mail midcapital@ midnacional.com.ar; internet midnacional.com.ar; f. 1963; mem. of the Unidos por la Libertad y el Trabajo alliance formed to contest the 2013 elections; Leader EFRAÍN GUSTAVO PUYÓ PEÑA; 51,000 mems.

Movimiento Popular Neuquino (MPN): Neuquén; internet www .mpn.org.ar; f. 1961; provincial party; Pres. JORGE OMAR SOBISCH; 112,000 mems.

Movimiento Proyecto Sur: Sarandí 56, C1088AAI Buenos Aires; tel. (11) 4952-3103; e-mail sur@proyecto-sur.com.ar; internet www .proyecto-sur.com.ar; f. 2001 as an alliance comprising Partido Socialista Auténtico, Partido Proyecto Sur and Buenos Aires para Todos; contested the 2013 legislative elections as part of the UNEN coalition, which forms a parliamentary bloc with the UCR; Pres. FERNANDO 'PINO' SOLANAS.

Movimiento Socialista de los Trabajadores (MST): San Nicolás, Peru 439, Buenos Aires; tel. (11) 4342-7520; e-mail webmaster@mst .org.ar; internet www.mst.org.ar; f. 1944; Leader VILMA RIPOLL.

Nuevo Encuentro: Hipólito Yrigoyen 1189, 1°, Buenos Aires; tel. (11) 4381-0286; internet www.partidoencuentro.org.ar; f. 2009; centre-left; Leader MARTÍN SABBATELLA.

Partido del Campo Popular (PCP): Alicia Moreau de Justo 1150, Rosario; e-mail partidocampopopular@gmail.com; internet www.pcp .org.ar; f. 1991 as Movimiento por la Dignidad y la Independencia (Modin); present name adopted in 2008; nationalist; Pres. JOSÉ ALEJANDRO BONACCI; Sec. LUIS FERNANDO RETO; 15,000 mems.

Partido Comunista de Argentina: Entre Ríos 1039, C1080ABQ Buenos Aires; tel. and fax (11) 4304-0066; e-mail info@pca.org.ar; internet www.pca.org.ar; f. 1918; Leader PATRICIO ECHEGARAY.

Partido Demócrata Cristiano (PDC): Combate de los Pozos 1055, C1222AAK Buenos Aires; tel. (11) 4305-1229; fax (11) 4306-8242; e-mail pdcblog@fibertel.com.ar; internet www.democraciacristiana .org.ar; f. 1954; mem. of the Unidos por la Libertad y el Trabajo alliance formed to contest the 2013 elections; Pres. Dr JUAN BRUGGE; 51,000 mems.

Partido Demócrata Progresista (PDP): Entre Ríos 1443, Rosario; tel. (341) 440-0777; e-mail prensapdpsantafe@gmail.com; internet www.pdp.org.ar; f. 1914; Gen. Sec. CARLOS FAVARI; 36,000 mems.

Partido Federal: Avda de Mayo 962, 1°, Buenos Aires; tel. (11) 4338-3071; e-mail partido@federal.org.ar; internet www.federal.org .ar; f. 1983; mem. of the Unidos por la Libertad y el Trabajo alliance formed to contest the 2013 elections.

Partido Justicialista (PJ): Domingo Matheu 128/130, C1082ABD Buenos Aires; tel. (11) 4954-2450; fax (11) 4954-2421; e-mail contacto@pj.org.ar; internet www.pj.org.ar; f. 1945; broad grouping of Peronist parties; Pres. EDUARDO ALFREDO FELLNER; Vice-Pres. DANIEL OSVALDO SCIOLI; Sec.-Gen. JOSÉ LUIS GIOJA; 3.6m. mems; includes the following factions.

   Frente para la Victoria (FPV): e-mail webmaster@diarioelsol .com.ar; internet www.frenteparalavictoria.org; f. 2003; centre-left; ruling faction of the PJ; Leader CRISTINA FERNÁNDEZ DE KIRCHNER.

Partido Conservador Popular: Rivadavia 1645, (Entre EP°), C1033AAG Buenos Aires; tel. (11) 4372-3791; internet www .atalayaweb.com.ar/pcp; f. 1958; Pres. GUILLERMO DURAND CORNEJO.

Partido Frente Grande: Junín 156, entre Bartolomé Mitre y Perón, Buenos Aires; tel. (11) 3970-6480; e-mail info@frentegrande .org.ar; internet www.frentegrande.org.ar; f. 1993 as an electoral front; Pres. ADRIANA PUIGGRÓS; Sec.-Gen. HERMAN AVOSCÁN.

Partido Humanista: San Juan 1828, C1232AAN Buenos Aires; tel. (11) 6176-4132; e-mail phumanistaprensa@gmail.com; internet www.partidohumanista.org.ar; f. 1984; Gen. Sec. ESTHER SOSA.

Partido Intransigente: Riobamba 482, C1025ABJ Buenos Aires; tel. (11) 4954-2283; e-mail nacional@pi.org.ar; internet www.pi .org.ar; f. 1957; left-wing; Pres. Dr ENRIQUE GUSTAVO CARDESA; Sec. AMERICO PARODI; 57,000 mems.

   Frente Renovador (FR): Buenos Aires; internet www .frenterenovador.org.ar; dissident Peronist party; Leader SERGIO MASSA.

Partido Socialista Auténtico: Sarandí 56, C1081ACB Buenos Aires; tel. and fax (11) 4952-3103; e-mail consultas@psa.org.ar; internet www.psa.org.ar; Sec.-Gen. MARIO MAZZITELLI; 13,000 mems.

Política Abierta para la Integridad Social (PAIS): Corrientes 2141, Of. 10, C1043AAL Buenos Aires; tel. (11) 4383-6350; e-mail info@partidopais.com.ar; internet www.partidopais.com.ar; f. 1994 following split with the PJ; contested the 2011 elections as a mem. of the Alianza Compromiso Federal; Pres. FÉLIX MARIANO ACEVEDO.

Propuesta Republicana (PRO): Alsina 1325, C1088AAI Buenos Aires; e-mail info@pro.com.ar; internet www.pro.com.ar; f. 2005; centre-right; Leader MAURICIO MACRI.

Unión Celeste y Blanco: tel. (11) 4779-6418; e-mail union@ celesteyblanco.com; internet www.unioncelesteyblanco.com; mem. of the Unidos por la Libertad y el Trabajo alliance formed to contest the 2013 elections; Leader FRANCISCO DE NARVÁEZ.

Unión del Centro Democrático (UCeDé): Hipólito Yrigoyen 636, 6°B Buenos Aires; tel. (11) 4381-3763; internet ucedenacional .blogspot.com; f. 1980; contested the 2011 elections as a mem. of the Alianza Compromiso Federal; Pres. JORGE PEREYRA DE OLAZÁBAL; 77,000 mems.

Unión Cívica Radical (UCR): Alsina 1786, C1088AAR Buenos Aires; tel. and fax (11) 5199-0600; e-mail webmaster@ucr.org.ar; internet www.ucr.org.ar; f. 1890; moderate; contested the 2011 elections as mem. of the Unión para el Desarrollo Social coalition; Pres. LILIA PUIG DE STUBRIN; Gen. Sec. JUAN MANUEL CASELLA; 2.5m. mems.

Unión por Córdoba: Córdoba; Leader FRANCISCO J. FORTUNA.

Unión Popular: Maipú 3685, 1702, Buenos Aires; tel. (11) 4488-3279; e-mail pdounionpopular@yahoo.com.ar; internet www .partidounionpopular.org; mem. of the Unidos por la Libertad y el Trabajo alliance formed to contest the 2013 elections; Nat. Pres. Dr MARCELO D'ALESSANDRO; 16,000 mems.

OTHER ORGANIZATIONS

Asociación Madres de Plaza de Mayo: Hipólito Yrigoyen 1584, C1089AAD Buenos Aires; tel. (11) 4383-0377; fax (11) 4954-0381;

e-mail madres@madres.org; internet www.madres.org; f. 1979; formed by mothers of those who 'disappeared' during the years of military rule, it has since become a broad-based anti-poverty grouping with socialist aims; Founder and Leader HEBE MARÍA PASTOR DE BONAFINI.

Diplomatic Representation

EMBASSIES IN ARGENTINA

Albania: Juez Tedín 3036, 4°, C1425CWH Buenos Aires; tel. (11) 48093574; fax (11) 48078767; e-mail embassy.buenosaires@mfa.gov .al; Ambassador REZAR BREGU.

Algeria: Montevideo 1889, C1021AAE Buenos Aires; tel. (11) 4815-1271; fax (11) 4815-8837; e-mail embajadaargelia@fibertel.com.ar; Ambassador BENAOUDA HAMEL.

Angola: La Pampa 3452-56, C1430BXD Buenos Aires; tel. (11) 4554-8383; fax (11) 4554-8998; Ambassador HERMÍNIO JOAQUIM ESCÓRCIO.

Armenia: José Andrés Pacheco de Melo 1922, C1126AAD Buenos Aires; tel. (11) 4816-8710; fax (11) 4812-2803; e-mail armenia@ fibertel.com.ar; Ambassador VAHAGN MELIKYAN.

Australia: Villanueva 1400, C1426BMJ Buenos Aires; tel. (11) 4779-3500; fax (11) 4779-3581; e-mail info.ba.general@dfat.gov.au; internet www.argentina.embassy.gov.au; Ambassador PATRICIA ANN HOLMES.

Austria: French 3671, C1425AXC Buenos Aires; tel. (11) 4807-9185; fax (11) 4805-4016; e-mail buenos-aires-ob@bmeia.gv.at; internet www.bmeia.gv.at/botschaft/buenos-aires.html; Ambassador KARIN PROIDL.

Azerbaijan: Gorostiaga 2176, C1426BMC Buenos Aires; tel. (11) 4777-3655; fax (11) 4777-8928; e-mail buenosaires@azembassy.com .ar; internet www.azembassy.com.ar; Ambassador MAMMAD AHAMDZADA.

Belarus: Cazadores 2166, C1428AVH Buenos Aires; tel. (11) 4788-9394; fax (11) 4788-2322; e-mail argentina@mfa.gov.by; internet www.argentina.mfa.gov.by; Ambassador VICTOR KOZINTEV.

Belgium: Defensa 113, 8°, C1065AAA Buenos Aires; tel. (11) 4331-0066; fax (11) 4331-0814; e-mail BuenosAires@diplobel.fed.be; internet www.diplomatie.be/buenosaires; Ambassador PATRICK RENAULT.

Bolivia: Corrientes 545, 2°, C1043AAF Buenos Aires; tel. (11) 4394-1463; fax (11) 4394-0460; e-mail embolivia-baires@ree.gov.bo; internet www.embajadadebolivia.com.ar; Ambassador LIBORIO FLORES ENRIQUEZ.

Brazil: Cerrito 1350, C1010ABB Buenos Aires; tel. (11) 4515-2400; fax (11) 4515-2401; e-mail info@brasil.org.ar; internet www.brasil .org.ar; Ambassador EVERTON VIEIRA VARGAS.

Bulgaria: Mariscal A. J. de Sucre 1568, C1428DUT Buenos Aires; tel. (11) 4781-8644; fax (11) 4781-1214; e-mail embular@uolsinectis .com.ar; internet www.mfa.bg/embassies/argentina; Ambassador MAXIM GAYTANDJIEV.

Canada: Tagle 2828, C1425EEH Buenos Aires; tel. (11) 4808-1000; fax (11) 4808-1111; e-mail bairs-webmail@international.gc.ca; internet www.canadainternational.gc.ca/argentina-argentine; Ambassador GWYNETH A. KUTZ.

Chile: Tagle 2762, C1425EEF Buenos Aires; tel. (11) 4808-8600; fax (11) 4804-5927; e-mail echile.argentina@minrel.gov.cl; internet chileabroad.gov.cl/argentina; Ambassador MARCELO DÍAZ.

China, People's Republic: Crisólogo Larralde 5349, C1431APM Buenos Aires; tel. (11) 4547-8100; fax (11) 4545-1141; e-mail chinaemb_ar@mfa.gov.cn; internet ar.chineseembassy.org/esp; Ambassador YIN HENGMIN.

Colombia: Carlos Pellegrini 1363, 3°, C1011AAA Buenos Aires; tel. (11) 4325-0258; fax (11) 4322-9370; e-mail ebaires@cancilleria.gov .co; internet argentina.embajada.gov.co; Ambassador CARLOS ENRIQUE RODADO NORIEGA.

Congo, Democratic Republic: Arcos 2340, 2°, Depto G, C1428EON Buenos Aires; tel. (11) 4896-4963; e-mail rdcbuenos@ hotmail.com; Chargé d'affaires a.i. YEMBA LOHAKA.

Costa Rica: Pacheco de Melo 1833, 5°, C1126AAD Buenos Aires; tel. (11) 4802-5983; fax (11) 4801-3222; e-mail embarica@fibertel.com.ar; Ambassador LUIS ALBERTO CORDERO ARIAS.

Croatia: Gorostiaga 2104, C1426CTN Buenos Aires; tel. (11) 4777-6409; fax (11) 4777-9159; e-mail croemb.ar@mvpei.hr; Ambassador ŽELJKO BELAJ.

Cuba: Virrey del Pino 1810, Belgrano, C1426EGF Buenos Aires; tel. (11) 4782-9049; fax (11) 4786-7713; e-mail oficinaembajador@ar .embacuba.cu; internet www.cubadiplomatica.cu/argentina; Ambassador JORGE NÉSTOR LAMADRID MASCARÓ.

Czech Republic: Junín 1461, C1113AAM Buenos Aires; tel. (11) 4807-3107; fax (11) 4800-1088; e-mail buenosaires@embassy.mzv.cz; internet www.mzv.cz/buenosaires; Ambassador PETR KOPŘIVA.

Denmark: Avda Leandro N. Alem 1074, 9°, C1001AAS Buenos Aires; tel. (11) 4312-6901; fax (11) 4312-7857; e-mail bueamb@um.dk; internet www.argentina.um.dk; Ambassador GRETE SILLASEN.

Dominican Republic: Juncal 802, 6°, C1062ABF Buenos Aires; tel. (11) 4312-9378; fax (11) 4894-2078; e-mail embajadadombaires@fibertel.com.ar; Ambassador GUILLERMO EDUARDO PIÑA-CONTRERAS.

Ecuador: Quintana 585, 9°, C1129ABB Buenos Aires; tel. (11) 4804-0073; fax (11) 4804-0074; e-mail embecuador@embecuador.com.ar; Ambassador GLORIA PIEDAD VIDAL ILLINGWORTH.

Egypt: Virrey del Pino 3140, C1426EHF Buenos Aires; tel. (11) 4553-3311; fax (11) 4553-0067; e-mail embegypt@fibertel.com.ar; Ambassador REDA HABIB ZAKI.

El Salvador: Rodriguez Peña 1627 3°, C1011ACD Buenos Aires; tel. (11) 4813-2525; fax (11) 4812-9353; e-mail elsalvador@fibertel.com.ar; internet www.embajadaelsalvador.com.ar; Ambassador OSCAR ERNESTO MENJIBAR CHÁVEZ.

Finland: Santa Fe 846, 5°, C1059ABP Buenos Aires; tel. (11) 4312-0600; fax (11) 4312-0670; e-mail sanomat.bue@formin.fi; internet www.finlandia.org.ar; Ambassador JUKKA SIUKOSAARI.

France: Cerrito 1399, C1010ABA Buenos Aires; tel. (11) 4515-2930; fax (11) 4515-0120; e-mail ambafr@abaconet.com.ar; internet www.embafrancia-argentina.org; Ambassador JEAN-MICHEL CASA.

Georgia: 14 de Julio 1656, C1430END Buenos Aires; tel. (11) 4554-5176; e-mail buenosaires.emb@mfa.gov.ge; Ambassador GUELA SEKHNIACHVILI.

Germany: Villanueva 1055, C1426BMC Buenos Aires; tel. (11) 4778-2500; fax (11) 4778-2550; e-mail info@buenos-aires.diplo.de; internet www.buenos-aires.diplo.de; Ambassador BERNHARD GRAF VON WALDERSEE.

Greece: Mariscal Ramón Castilla 2952, C1425DZF Buenos Aires; tel. (11) 4805-1100; fax (11) 4806-4686; e-mail gremb.bay@mfa.gr; internet www.mfa.gr/buenosaires; Ambassador ELENI LEIVADITOU.

Guatemala: Juncal 802, 3° H, C1062ABF Buenos Aires; tel. (11) 4313-9180; fax (11) 4313-9181; e-mail embajadaguatemala@fibertel.com.ar; Ambassador CARLOS RAMIRO MARTÍNEZ ALVARADO.

Haiti: Avda Figueroa Alcorta 3297, C1425CKL Buenos Aires; tel. (11) 4802-0211; fax (11) 4802-3984; e-mail embajadahaiti@fibertel.com.ar; Chargé d'affaires a.i. JEANÇOIS JOSEPH.

Holy See: Marcelo T. de Alvear 1605, C1014AAD Buenos Aires; tel. (11) 4813-9697; fax (11) 4815-4097; e-mail nunciaturaapostolica@speedy.com.ar; Apostolic Nuncio Most Rev. EMIL PAUL TSCHERRIG (Titular Archbishop of Voli).

Honduras: Avda Callao 1564, 2°, C1024AAO Buenos Aires; tel. (11) 5199-7080; fax (11) 4804-1875; e-mail embajada@embajadadehonduras.com.ar; Chargé d'affaires a.i. DIMAS ALEXI ESCOBAR GUILLEN.

Hungary: Plaza 1726, C1430DGF Buenos Aires; tel. (11) 4553-4646; fax (11) 4555-6859; e-mail mission.bue@kum.hu; internet www.mfa.gov.hu/emb/buenosaires; Ambassador PÁL VARGA KORITÁR.

India: Torre Madero, 19°, Avda Eduardo Madero 942, C1106ACW Buenos Aires; tel. (11) 4393-4001; fax (11) 4393-4063; e-mail indemb@indembarg.org.ar; internet www.indembarg.org.ar; Ambassador Dr AMARENDRA KHATUA.

Indonesia: Mariscal Ramón Castilla 2901, C1425DZE Buenos Aires; tel. (11) 4807-2211; fax (11) 4802-4448; e-mail emindo@tournet.com.ar; internet www.indonesianembassy.org.ar; Ambassador NURMALA KARTINI PANDJAITAN SJAHRIR.

Iran: Avda Figueroa Alcorta 3229, C1425CKL Buenos Aires; tel. (11) 4802-1470; fax (11) 4805-4409; e-mail embajadairan@fibertel.com.ar; Chargé d'affaires HAHMAD REZA KHEIRMAND.

Ireland: Avda del Libertador 1068, Edif. Bluesky, 6°, Recoleta, C1112ABN Buenos Aires; tel. (11) 5787-0801; fax (11) 5787-0802; e-mail info@irlanda.org.ar; internet www.embassyofireland.org.ar; Ambassador JAMES MCINTYRE.

Israel: Avda de Mayo 701, 10°, C1084AAC Buenos Aires; tel. (11) 4338-2500; fax (11) 4338-2624; e-mail info@buenosaires.mfa.gov.il; internet buenosaires.mfa.gov.il; Ambassador DORIT SHAVIT.

Italy: Billinghurst 2577, C1425DTY Buenos Aires; tel. (11) 4011-2100; fax (11) 4011-2159; e-mail segreteria.buenosaires@esteri.it; internet www.ambbuenosaires.esteri.it; Ambassador TERESA CASTALDO.

Japan: Bouchard 547, 17°, C1106ABG Buenos Aires; tel. (11) 4318-8200; fax (11) 4318-8210; e-mail taishikan@japan.org.ar; internet www.ar.emb-japan.go.jp; Ambassador MASASHI MIZUKAMI.

Korea, Republic: Avda del Libertador 2395, C1425AAJ Buenos Aires; tel. (11) 4802-9665; fax (11) 4803-6993; e-mail argentina@mofa.go.kr; Ambassador BYUNG-KIL HAN.

Kuwait: Uruguay 739, C1015ABO Buenos Aires; tel. (11) 4374-7202; fax (11) 4374-0489; e-mail info@embajadadekuwait.com.ar; internet www.embajadadekuwait.com.ar; Ambassador SALAH MUBARAK AL-MUTAIRI.

Lebanon: Avda del Libertador 2354, C1425AAW Buenos Aires; tel. (11) 4802-0466; fax (11) 4802-0929; e-mail embajada@ellibano.com.ar; internet www.ellibano.com.ar; Ambassador ANTONIO NASER ANDARY.

Libya: Virrey del Pino 3432, C1426EHL Buenos Aires; tel. (11) 4553-4669; fax (11) 4551-6187; e-mail embajadadelibia@hotmail.com.ar; Chargé d'affaires a.i. MATOUG S. S. ABORAWI.

Malaysia: Villanueva 1040, C1426BMD Buenos Aires; tel. (11) 4776-2553; fax (11) 4776-0604; e-mail malbnaires@kln.gov.my; internet www.kln.gov.my/perwakilan/buenosaires; Ambassador Dato' MOHD ASHRI BIN MUDA (designate).

Mexico: Arcos 1650, C1426BGL Buenos Aires; tel. (11) 4118-8800; fax (11) 4118-8837; e-mail info@embamex.int.ar; internet embamex.sre.gob.mx/argentina; Ambassador FERNANDO JORGE TRENTI.

Morocco: Castex 3461, C1425CDG Buenos Aires; tel. (11) 4801-8154; fax (11) 4802-0136; e-mail sifamarruecos@fibertel.com.ar; Ambassador FOUAD YAZOURH.

Netherlands: Edif. Porteño II, Olga Cossettini 831, 3°, C1107CDC Buenos Aires; tel. (11) 4338-0050; fax (11) 4338-0060; e-mail bue@minbuza.nl; internet www.embajadaholanda.int.ar; Ambassador HEIN DE VRIES.

New Zealand: Carlos Pellegrini 1427, 5°, C1011AAC Buenos Aires; tel. (11) 5070-0700; fax (11) 5070-0720; e-mail kiwiarg@speedy.com.ar; internet www.nzembassy.com/argentina; Ambassador HAYDEN E. MONTGOMERY.

Nicaragua: Santa Fe 1845, 7°, Of. B, C1123AAA Buenos Aires; tel. (11) 4811-0973; fax (11) 4811-0973; e-mail zmasis@cancilleria.gob.ni; Ambassador NORMA MORENO SILVA.

Nigeria: Juez Estrada 2746, Palermo, C1425CPD Buenos Aires; tel. (11) 4328-8717; fax (11) 4807-1782; e-mail info@nigerianembassy.org; internet www.nigerianembassy.org.ar; Ambassador CHIVE KAAVE.

Norway: Carlos Pelegrini 1427, 2°, C1011AAC Buenos Aires; tel. (11) 3724-1200; fax (11) 4328-9048; e-mail emb.buenosaires@mfa.no; internet www.noruega.org.ar; Ambassador JANNE JULSRUD.

Pakistan: Gorostiaga 2176, C1426CTN Buenos Aires; tel. (11) 4775-1294; fax (11) 4776-1186; e-mail parepbaires@fibertel.com.ar; internet www.embassypakistan.com.ar; Ambassador IMTIAZ AHMAD.

Panama: Santa Fe 1461, 1°, C1060ABA Buenos Aires; tel. (11) 4811-1254; fax (11) 4814-0450; e-mail epar@fibertel.com.ar; internet www.embajadadepanama.com.ar; Ambassador MARIO ANTONIO BOYD GALINDO.

Paraguay: Las Heras 2545, C1425ASC Buenos Aires; tel. (11) 4802-3826; fax (11) 4807-7600; e-mail embaparba@fibertel.com.ar; Ambassador NICANOR DUARTE FRUTOS.

Peru: Avda del Libertador 1720, C1425AAQ Buenos Aires; tel. (11) 4802-2000; fax (11) 4802-5887; e-mail contacto@embajadadelperu.int.ar; internet www.embajadadelperu.int.ar; Ambassador JOSÉ LUIS NÉSTOR PÉREZ SÁNCHEZ-CERRO.

Philippines: Zapiola 1701, C1426AUI Buenos Aires; tel. (11) 4554-4015; fax (11) 4554-9194; e-mail pheba@fibertel.com.ar; internet www.buenosairespe.com.ar; Ambassador MARÍA AMELIA AQUINO.

Poland: Alejandro María de Aguado 2870, C1425CEB Buenos Aires; tel. (11) 4808-1700; fax (11) 4808-1701; e-mail secretaria.buenosaires@msz.gov.pl; internet www.buenosaires.polemb.net; Ambassador JACEK BAZAŃSKI.

Portugal: Maipú 942, 17°, C1006ACN Buenos Aires; tel. (11) 4312-3524; fax (11) 4311-2586; e-mail embpor@buenosaires.dgaccp.pt; internet www.embaixadaportugal.com.ar; Ambassador HENRIQUE SILVEIRA BORGES.

Qatar: Buenos Aires; tel. (11) 4318-9198; Ambassador FAHAD BIN IBRAHIM AL HAMAD AL MANA.

Romania: Arroyo 962–970, C1007AAD Buenos Aires; tel. (11) 4326-5888; fax (11) 4322-2630; e-mail embarombue@rumania.org.ar; internet www.rumania.org.ar; Chargé d'affaires a.i. SENA LATIF.

Russia: Rodríguez Peña 1741, C1021ABK Buenos Aires; tel. (11) 4813-1552; fax (11) 4815-6293; e-mail embrusia@gmail.com; internet www.argentina.mid.ru; Ambassador VICTOR KORONELLI.

Saudi Arabia: Alejandro María de Aguado 2881, C1425CEA Buenos Aires; tel. (11) 4802-0760; fax (11) 4806-1581; e-mail aremb@mofa.gov.sa; Ambassador TURKI M. A. AL-MADI.

Serbia: Marcelo T. de Alvear 1705, C1060AAG Buenos Aires; tel. (11) 4813-3446; fax (11) 4812-1070; e-mail serbembaires@ciudad.com.ar; internet www.buenosaires.mfa.gov.rs; Chargé d'affaires a.i. TAJANA CONIC.

Slovakia: Figueroa Alcorta 3240, C1425CKY Buenos Aires; tel. (11) 4801-3917; fax (11) 4801-4654; e-mail emb.buenosaires@mzv.sk; Ambassador PAVEL ŠÍPKA.

Slovenia: Santa Fe 846, 6°, C1059ABP Buenos Aires; tel. (11) 4894-0621; fax (11) 4312-8410; e-mail vba@gov.si; internet www .buenosaires.veleposlanistvo.si; Ambassador TOMAŽ MENCIN.

South Africa: Marcelo T. de Alvear 590, 8°, C1058AAF Buenos Aires; tel. (11) 4317-2900; fax (11) 4311-8993; e-mail embajador .argentina@foreign.gov.za; internet www.sudafrica.org.ar; Ambassador ZENANI MANDELA-DLAMINI.

Spain: Avda Figueroa Alcorta 3102, C1425CKX Buenos Aires; tel. (11) 4809-4900; fax (11) 4809-4919; e-mail emb.buenosaires@maec .es; internet www.maec.es/embajadas/buenosaires; Ambassador ESTANISLAO DE GRANDES PASCUAL.

Sweden: Tacuari 147, 6°, C1071AAC Buenos Aires; tel. (11) 4329-0800; fax (11) 4342-1697; e-mail ambassaden.buenos-aires@foreign .ministery.se; internet www.swedenabroad.com/buenosaires; Ambassador GUFRAN AL-NADAF.

Switzerland: Santa Fe 846, 12°, C1059ABP Buenos Aires; tel. (11) 4311-6491; fax (11) 4313-2998; e-mail bue.vertretung@eda.admin .ch; internet www.eda.admin.ch/buenosaires; Ambassador JOHANN STEPHAN MATYASSY.

Syria: Callao 956, C1023AAP Buenos Aires; tel. (11) 4813-2113; fax (11) 4814-3211; Chargé d'affaires a.i. HAMZEH DAWALIBI.

Thailand: Vuelta de Obligado 1947, 12°, C1428ADC Buenos Aires; tel. (11) 4780-0555; fax (11) 4782-1616; e-mail thaiembargen@ fibertel.com.ar; internet www.thaiembargen.org; Ambassador MEDHA PROMTHEP.

Tunisia: Ciudad de la Paz 3086, C1429ACD Buenos Aires; tel. (11) 4544-2618; fax (11) 4545-6369; e-mail atbuenosaires@infovia.com.ar; Ambassador HICHEM BAYOUDH.

Turkey: 11 de Septiembre 1382, C1426BKN Buenos Aires; tel. (11) 4788-3239; fax (11) 4784-9179; e-mail embajada.buenosaires@mfa .gov.tr; internet buenosaires.be.mfa.gov.tr; Ambassador TANER KARAKAS.

Ukraine: Conde 1763, C1426AZI Buenos Aires; tel. (11) 4552-0657; fax (11) 4552-6771; e-mail embucra@embucra.com.ar; internet www .mfa.gov.ua/argentina; Ambassador YURII DIUDIN.

United Arab Emirates: Olleros 2021, C1426BRK Buenos Aires; tel. (11) 4771-9716; fax (11) 4772-5169; Ambassador ABDULKHALEQ ALI SABED BIN DHAEER ALYAFEI.

United Kingdom: Dr Luis Agote 2412, C1425EOF Buenos Aires; tel. (11) 4808-2200; fax (11) 4808-2274; e-mail askinformation .baires@fco.gov.uk; internet ukinargentina.fco.gov.uk; Ambassador JOHN FREEMAN.

USA: Avda Colombia 4300, C1425GMN Buenos Aires; tel. (11) 5777-4533; fax (11) 5777-4240; internet argentina.usembassy.gov; Chargé d'affaires a.i. KEVIN K. SULLIVAN.

Uruguay: Las Heras 1907, C1127AAB Buenos Aires; tel. (11) 4807-3040; fax (11) 4807-3050; e-mail urubaires@embajadadeluruguay .com.ar; internet www.embajadadeluruguay.com.ar; Ambassador GUILLERMO JOSÉ POMI BARRIOLA.

Venezuela: Virrey Loreto 2035, C1426DXK Buenos Aires; tel. (11) 4788-4944; fax (11) 4784-4311; e-mail embaven@arnet.com.ar; Ambassador CARLOS EDUARDO MARTÍNEZ MENDOZA.

Viet Nam: 11 de Septiembre 1442, C1426BKP Buenos Aires; tel. (11) 4783-1802; fax (11) 4782-0078; e-mail sqvnartn@fibertel.com.ar; Ambassador THAO NGUYEN DINH.

Judicial System

SUPREME COURT

Corte Suprema: Talcahuano 550, 4°, C1013AAL Buenos Aires; tel. (11) 4370-4600; fax (11) 4340-2270; e-mail consultas@cjsn.gov.ar; internet www.csjn.gov.ar; mems of the Supreme Court are appointed by the President with the agreement of at least two-thirds of the Senate; mems can be dismissed by impeachment; Pres. RICARDO LUIS LORENZETTI; Vice-Pres. ELENA I. HIGHTON DE NOLASCO.

OTHER COURTS

Judges of the lower, national or further lower courts are appointed by the President, with the agreement of the Senate, and can be dismissed by impeachment. Judges retire on reaching 75 years of age.

The Federal Court of Appeal in Buenos Aires has three courts: civil and commercial, criminal, and administrative. There are six other courts of appeal in Buenos Aires: civil, commercial, criminal, peace, labour, and penal-economic. There are also federal appeal courts in La Plata, Bahía Blanca, Paraná, Rosario, Córdoba, Mendoza, Tucumán and Resistencia. In 1994 the Office of the Attorney-General was established and in 1997 a Council of Magistrates was created.

The provincial courts each have their own Supreme Court and a system of subsidiary courts. They deal with cases originating within and confined to the provinces.

Consejo de la Magistratura de la Nación: Avda Libertad 731, 2°, 1017 Buenos Aires; tel. (11) 4124-5394; fax (11) 4124-5394; e-mail propuestas@pjn.gov.ar; internet www.consejomagistratura.gov.ar; responsible for the selection of judges, of suspending or deposing them, and the administration of the judiciary; consists of 13 mems; six legislators, three national judges, two federal lawyers, one academic and a govt representative; Pres. Dr MARIO S. FERA; Sec.-Gen. Dr MARÍA SUSANA BERTERREIX.

Attorney-General: ALEJANDRA GILS CARBÓ.

Religion

CHRISTIANITY

The Roman Catholic Church

Some 76% of the population are Roman Catholics.

Argentina comprises 14 archdioceses, 51 dioceses (including one each for Uniate Catholics of the Ukrainian rite, of the Maronite rite and of the Armenian rite), four territorial prelatures and an apostolic exarchate for Catholics of the Melkite rite. The Bishop of San Gregorio de Narek en Buenos Aires is also the Apostolic Exarch of Latin America and Mexico for Catholics of the Armenian rite, and the Archbishop of Buenos Aires is also the Ordinary for Catholics of other Oriental rites.

Bishops' Conference (Conferencia Episcopal Argentina): Suipacha 1034, C1008AAV Buenos Aires; tel. (11) 4328-0993; fax (11) 4328-9570; e-mail seccea@cea.org.ar; internet www.episcopado.org; f. 1959; Pres. JOSÉ MARÍA ARANCEDO (Archbishop of Santa Fe de la Vera Cruz).

Armenian Rite

Bishop of San Gregorio de Narek en Buenos Aires: VARTÁN WALDIR BOGHOSSIAN, Charcas 3529, C1425BMU Buenos Aires; tel. (11) 4824-1613; fax (11) 4827-1975; e-mail exarmal@pcn.net; f. 1989.

Latin Rite

Archbishop of Bahía Blanca: GUILLERMO JOSÉ GARLATTI, Avda Colón 164, B8000FTO Bahía Blanca; tel. (291) 455-0707; fax (291) 452-2070; e-mail arzobis@arzobispadobahia.org.ar; internet www .arzobispadobahia.org.ar.

Archbishop of Buenos Aires: Cardinal MARIO AURELIO POLI, Rivadavia 415, C1002AAC Buenos Aires; tel. (11) 4343-0812; fax (11) 4334-8373; e-mail arzobispado@arzbaires.org.ar; internet www .arzbaires.org.ar.

Archbishop of Córdoba: CARLOS JOSÉ ÑÁÑEZ, Hipólito Irigoyen 98, X5000JHN Córdoba; tel. and fax (351) 422-1015; e-mail comunicacionpastoral@arzobispado.org.ar; internet www .arzobispadocba.org.ar.

Archbishop of Corrientes: ANDRÉS STANOVNIK, 9 de Julio 1543, W3400AZA Corrientes; tel. and fax (3783) 422436; e-mail arzobispadodecorrientes@gmail.com; internet www.arzcorrientes .com.ar.

Archbishop of La Plata: HÉCTOR RUBÉN AGUER, Calle 14 Centro 1009, B1900DVQ La Plata; tel. (221) 425-1656; e-mail arzobispadodelaplata@speedy.com.ar; internet www.arzolap.org.ar.

Archbishop of Mendoza: CARLOS MARÍA FRANZINI, Catamarca 98, M5500CKB Mendoza; tel. (261) 423-3862; fax (261) 429-5415; e-mail arzobispadomza@supernet.com.ar; internet www.arquimendoza .org.ar.

Archbishop of Mercedes-Luján: AGUSTÍN ROBERTO RADRIZZANI, Calle 22 745, B6600HDU Mercedes; tel. (2324) 432-412; fax (2324) 432-104; e-mail arzomerce.informacion@gmail.com; internet arquimercedes-lujan.com.ar.

Archbishop of Paraná: JUAN ALBERTO PUIGGARI, Monte Caseros 77, E3100ACA Paraná; tel. (343) 431-1440; fax (343) 423-0372; e-mail prensa@arzparan.org.ar; internet www.arzparan.org.ar.

Archbishop of Resistencia: FABRICIANO SIGAMPA, Bartolomé Mitre 363, Casilla 35, H3500BLG Resistencia; tel. and fax (3722) 441908; e-mail arzobrcia@arnet.com.ar.

Archbishop of Rosario: JOSÉ LUIS MOLLAGHAN, Córdoba 1677, S2000AWY Rosario; tel. (341) 425-1298; fax (341) 425-1207; e-mail arzobros@uolsinectis.com.ar; internet www.delrosario.org.ar.

Archbishop of Salta: MARIO ANTONIO CARGNELLO, España 596, A4400ANL Salta; tel. (387) 421-4306; fax (387) 421-3101; e-mail prensaarzobispado@ucasal.net; internet www.arquidiocesissalta .org.ar.

Archbishop of San Juan de Cuyo: ALFONSO ROGELIO DELGADO EVERS, Bartolomé Mitre 250 Oeste, J5402CXF San Juan; tel. (264)

422-2578; fax (264) 427-3530; e-mail arzobispadosanjuan@infovia
.com.ar; internet www.iglesiasanjuancuyo.org.ar.

Archbishop of Santa Fe de la Vera Cruz: JOSÉ MARÍA ARANCEDO,
Avda Brig.-Gen. E. López 2720, S3000DCJ Santa Fe; tel. (342) 459-
1780; fax (342) 459-4491; e-mail curia@arquisantafe.org.ar; internet
www.arquisantafe.org.ar.

Archbishop of Tucumán: ALFREDO ZECCA, Avda Sarmiento 895,
T4000GTI San Miguel de Tucumán; tel. (381) 431-0617; e-mail
arztuc@arnet.com.ar; internet www.arztucuman.org.ar.

Maronite Rite

Bishop of San Charbel en Buenos Aires: CHARBEL GEORGES
MERHI, Eparquía Maronita, Colegio San Marón, Paraguay 834,
C1057AAL Buenos Aires; tel. (11) 4311-7299; fax (11) 4312-8348;
e-mail   sanmaron@misionlibanesa.com;   internet   www
.misionlibanesa.com.ar.

Melkite Rite

Apostolic Exarch: ABDO ARBACH, Exarcado Apostólico Greco-
Melquita, Corrientes 276, X5000ANF Córdoba; tel. (351) 421-0625;
e-mail   catedralmelquitasanjorge@gmail.com;   internet   www
.exarcadoapostolicogreco-melkitacatolicoenargentina.com.

Ukrainian Rite

Bishop of Santa María del Patrocinio en Buenos Aires: Rt Rev.
DANIEL KOZELINSKI NETTO, Ramón L. Falcón 3950, Casilla 28,
C1407GSN Buenos Aires; tel. (11) 4671-4192; fax (11) 4671-7265;
e-mail pokrov@ciudad.com.ar.

The Anglican Communion

The Iglesia Anglicana del Cono Sur de América (Anglican Church of
the Southern Cone of America) comprises seven dioceses: Argentina,
Northern Argentina, Chile, Paraguay, Peru, Bolivia and Uruguay.

Bishop of Argentina: Rt Rev. GREGORY JAMES VENABLES, 25 de
Mayo 282, C1002ABF Buenos Aires; tel. (11) 4342-4618; fax (11)
4784-1277; e-mail diocesisanglibue@fibertel.com.ar; internet www
.anglicanaargentina.org.ar.

Bishop of Northern Argentina: Rt Rev. NICHOLAS JAMES QUESTED
DRAYSON, Iglesia Anglicana, Casilla 187, A4400ANL Salta; tel. (387)
431-1718; fax (371) 142-0100; e-mail nicobispo@gmail.com; jurisdiction extends to Jujuy, Salta, Tucumán, Catamarca, Santiago del
Estero, Formosa and Chaco.

Other Christian Churches

Church of Jesus Christ of Latter-Day Saints (Mormons):
Autopista Richieri y Puente 13, Ciudad Evita, B1778DUA Buenos
Aires; tel. (11) 4487-1848; internet www.lds.org; 412,095 mems.

Convención Evangélica Bautista Argentina (Baptist Evangelical Convention): Virrey Liniers 42, C1174ACB Buenos Aires; tel.
and fax (11) 4864-2711; e-mail administracion@confeba.org.ar;
internet www.confeba.org.ar; f. 1908; Pres. NÉSTOR GOLLUSCIO.

Federación Argentina de Iglesias Evangélicas (Argentine Federation of Evangelical Churches): Condarco 321, C1604AFE Buenos
Aires; tel. and fax (11) 4611-1437; e-mail presidencia@faie.org.ar;
internet www.faie.org.ar; f. 1938; 21 mem. churches; Pres. KARIN
KRUG; Sec. Dr ALBERTO ROLDÁN.

Iglesia Evangélica Luterana Argentina (Evangelical Lutheran
Church of Argentina): Ing. Silveyra 1639-41, B1607BQM Villa
Adelina, Buenos Aires; tel. (11) 4735-4155; fax (11) 4766-7948;
e-mail ielapresidente@arnet.com.ar; internet www.iela.org.ar;
f. 1905; 30,000 mems; Pres. CARLOS NAGEL.

Iglesia Evangélica Luterana Unida (United Evangelical
Lutheran Church): Marcos Sastre 2891, C1417FYE Buenos Aires;
tel. (11) 4501-3925; fax 4504-7358; e-mail contacto@ielu.org; internet
www.ielu.org; 11,000 mems; Pres. Rev. GUSTAVO GÓMEZ PASCUA.

Iglesia Evangélica Metodista Argentina (Methodist Church of
Argentina): Rivadavia 4044, 3°, C1205AAN Buenos Aires; tel. (11)
4981-4474; fax (11) 4981-0885; e-mail secretariaadministracion@
iglesiametodista.org.ar; internet www.iglesiametodista.org.ar;
f. 1836; Bishop FRANK DE NULLY BROWN.

Iglesia Evangélica del Río de la Plata (Evangelical Church of the
Plate River): Mariscal Sucre 2855, C1428DVY Buenos Aires; tel. (11)
4787-0436; fax (11) 4787-0335; e-mail presidente@ierp.org.ar;
internet www.iglesiaevangelica.org; f. 1899; 27,500 mems; Pres.
CARLOS ALFREDO DUARTE VOELKER; Gen. Sec. SONIA SKUPCH.

JUDAISM

There are about 230,000 Jews in Argentina, mostly in Buenos Aires.

Delegación de Asociaciones Israelitas Argentinas (DAIA)
(Delegation of Argentine Jewish Associations): Pasteur 633, 7°,
C1028AAM Buenos Aires; tel. and fax (11) 4378-3200; e-mail

daia@daia.org.ar; internet www.daia.org.ar; f. 1935; Pres. JULIO
SCHLOSSER; Exec. Dir VÍCTOR GARELIK.

The Press
PRINCIPAL DAILIES
Buenos Aires

Ambito Financiero: Paseo Colón 1196, C1063ACY Buenos Aires;
tel. (11) 4349-1500; fax (11) 4349-1505; e-mail editor@ambito.com.ar;
internet www.ambito.com.ar; f. 1976; morning (Mon.–Fri.); business;
Dir ORLANDO MARIO VIGNATTI; circ. 115,000.

Boletín Oficial de la República Argentina: Suipacha 767,
C1008AAO Buenos Aires; tel. and fax (11) 5218-8400; e-mail
dnro@boletinoficial.gov.ar;   internet   www.boletinoficial.gov.ar;
f. 1893; morning (Mon.–Fri.); official records publ; Dir Dr JORGE
EDUARDO FEIJOÓ; circ. 15,000.

Buenos Aires Herald: AvdaSan Juan 141, C1064AEB Buenos
Aires; tel. and fax (11) 4349-1524; e-mail info@buenosairesherald
.com; internet www.buenosairesherald.com; f. 1876; English; independent; morning; Editor-in-Chief SEBASTIÁN LACUNZA; circ. 20,000.

Clarín: Piedras 1743, C1140ABK Buenos Aires; tel. (11) 4309-7500;
fax (11) 4309-7559; e-mail cartas@claringlobal.com.ar; internet www
.clarin.com; f. 1945; morning; Dir ERNESTINA HERRERA DE NOBLE;
Editor RICARDO KIRSCHBAUM; circ. 342,749 (daily), 686,287 (Sun.).

Crónica: Avda Juan de Garay 130, C1063ABN Buenos Aires; tel.
(11) 5550-8608; fax (11) 4361-4237; e-mail info@cronica.com.ar;
internet www.cronica.com.ar; f. 1963; morning and evening; Dir
ALEJANDRO OLMOS; circ. 330,000 (morning), 190,000 (evening),
450,000 (Sun.).

El Cronista Comercial: Paseo Colón 740/6, 1°, C1063ACU Buenos
Aires; tel. (11) 4121-9300; fax (11) 4121-9301; e-mail publicidad@
cronista.com; internet www.cronista.com; f. 1908; morning; Dir
FERNANDO GONZÁLEZ; Editor WALTER BROWN; circ. 65,000.

La Nación: Bouchard 557, C1106ABG Buenos Aires; tel. (11) 4319-
1600; fax (11) 4319-1969; e-mail cescribano@lanacion.com.ar;
internet www.lanacion.com.ar; f. 1870; morning; independent;
Pres. JULIO SAGUIER; Editor-in-Chief JORGE LIOTTI; circ. 170,782
(2012).

Página 12: Solís 1525, C1134ADG Buenos Aires; tel. (11) 6772-4444;
fax (11) 6772-4428; e-mail publicidad@pagina12.com.ar; internet
www.pagina12.com.ar; f. 1987; morning; independent; Dir ERNESTO
TIFFENBERG; Pres. FERNANDO SOKOLOWICZ; circ. 280,000.

La Prensa: Azopardo 715, C1107ADK Buenos Aires; tel. (11) 4349-
1000; e-mail informaciongeneral@laprensa.com.ar; internet www
.laprensa.com.ar; f. 1869; morning; independent; Dir FLORENCIO
ALDREY IGLESIAS; circ. 100,000.

La Razón: Río Cuarto 1242, C1168AFF Buenos Aires; tel. and fax
(11) 4309-6000; e-mail lectores@larazon.com.ar; internet www
.larazon.com.ar; f. 1992; evening; Dir LUIS VINKER; circ. 62,000.

PRINCIPAL PROVINCIAL DAILIES
Catamarca

El Ancasti: Sarmiento 526, 1°, K4700EML Catamarca; tel. (3833)
431385; fax (3833) 453995; e-mail mzitelli@durhone.com.ar; internet
www.elancasti.com.ar; f. 1988; morning; Dir MARCELO SOSA; circ.
9,000.

Chaco

Norte: Carlos Pellegrini 744, H3500CDP Resistencia; tel. (362) 445-
1222; fax (362) 442-6047; e-mail webchaco@diarionorte.com;
internet www.diarionorte.com; f. 1968; Dir MIGUEL ANGEL FERNÁN-
DEZ; circ. 16,500.

Chubut

Crónica: Namuncurá 122, U9000BVD Comodoro Rivadavia; tel.
(297) 447-0117; fax (297) 447-1780; e-mail diariocronica@
diariocronica.com.ar; internet www.diariocronica.com.ar; f. 1962;
morning; Dir DANIEL CÉSAR ZAMIT; circ. 15,000.

Córdoba

Comercio y Justicia: Félix Paz 310, Alto Alberdi, X5002IGQ
Córdoba; tel. and fax (351) 488-0088; e-mail redaccion@
comerciojusticia.info; internet www.comerciojusticia.info; f. 1939;
morning; economic and legal news with periodic supplements on
architecture and administration; Dir JOSÉ MARÍA LAS HERAS; Editor-
in-Chief ADOLFO RUIZ; circ. 5,800.

La Voz del Interior: Monseñor P. Cabrera 6080, X5008HKJ
Córdoba; tel. (351) 475-7135; fax (351) 475-7282; e-mail
atencionalcliente@lavozdelinterior.com.ar;   internet   www

.lavozdelinterior.com.ar; f. 1904; morning; independent; Dir Dr CARLOS HUGO JORNET; circ. 50,340 (2012).

Corrientes

El Litoral: Hipólito Yrigoyen 990, W3400AST Corrientes; tel. and fax (379) 4410150; e-mail redaccion@ellitoral.com.ar; internet www.ellitoral.com.ar; f. 1960; morning; Dir CARLOS A. ROMERO FERIS; circ. 14,973 (2012).

Entre Ríos

El Diario: Buenos Aires y Urquiza, E2823XBC Paraná; tel. (343) 400-1000; fax (343) 431-9104; e-mail institucional@eldiario.com.ar; internet www.eldiario.com.ar; f. 1914; morning; Dir SEBASTIÁN ETCHEVEHERE; circ. 4,274.

El Heraldo: Quintana 42, E3200XAE Concordia; tel. (345) 421-5304; fax (345) 421-1397; e-mail redaccion@elheraldo.com.ar; internet www.elheraldo.com.ar; f. 1915; evening; Editor ROBERTO W. CAMINOS; circ. 10,000.

Mendoza

Los Andes: San Martín 1049, M5500AAK Mendoza; tel. (261) 449-1200; fax (261) 420-2011; e-mail aguardiola@losandes.com.ar; internet www.losandes.com.ar; f. 1982; morning; Dir ARTURO GUARDIOLA; circ. 30,400.

Misiones

El Territorio: Quaranta No 4307, N3301GAC Posadas; tel. and fax (3752) 451844; e-mail info@territoriodigital.com; internet www.territoriodigital.com.ar; f. 1925; Dir GONZALO PELTZER; Editor-in-Chief ROBERTO MAACK; circ. 4,707 (2012).

Provincia de Buenos Aires

El Atlántico: Bolívar 2975, B7600GDO Mar del Plata; e-mail cronicadelacosta@cronica.com.ar; internet www.cronicadelacosta.com; f. 1938; morning; Dir OSCAR ORTIZ; circ. 20,000.

La Capital: Avda Marcelino Champagnat 2551, B7604GXA Mar del Plata; tel. (223) 478-8490; e-mail contacto@lacapitalmdq.com.ar; internet www.lacapitalmdp.com; f. 1905; Editor-in-Chief OSCAR LARDIZÁBAL; circ. 32,000.

El Día: Avda A, Diagonal 80 815, B1900CCI La Plata; tel. (221) 425-0101; fax (221) 423-2996; e-mail lectores@eldia.com; internet www.eldia.com.ar; f. 1884; morning; independent; Dir RAÚL E. KRAISEL-BURD; circ. 35,292 (2012).

Ecos Diarios: Calle 62, No. 2486, B7630XAF Necochea; tel. and fax (2262) 430754; e-mail redaccion@ecosdiarios.com; internet www.ecosdiariosweb.com.ar; f. 1921; morning; independent; Dir MARÍA JOSEFINA IGNACIO; circ. 2,233 (2012).

La Nueva Provincia: Rodríguez 55, B8000HSA Bahía Blanca; tel. (291) 459-0000; fax (291) 459-0001; e-mail abel@lanueva.com; internet www.lanueva.com; f. 1898; morning; independent; Gen. Editor ABEL ESCUDERO ZADRAYEC; circ. 12,402 (2012).

El Nuevo Cronista: 5 Calle 619, B8000XAV Mercedes; tel. and fax (2324) 400111; e-mail redaccion@nuevocronista.com.ar; internet www.nuevocronista.com.ar; f. 1987; Dir CLAUDIO GUEVARA.

El Popular: Vicente López 2626, B7400CRH Olavarría; tel. and fax (22) 8442-0502; e-mail diario@elpopular.com.ar; internet elpopular.com.ar; f. 1899; morning; Dir JORGE GABRIEL BOTTA; circ. 5,086 (2012).

El Sol: Hipólito Yrigoyen 122, B1878FND Quilmes; tel. and fax (11) 4257-6325; e-mail elsol@elsolquilmes.com.ar; internet www.elsolquilmes.com.ar; f. 1927; Dir CARLOS E. BOTTASO; circ. 25,000.

La Voz del Pueblo: San Martín 991, B7500IKJ Tres Arroyos; tel. (2983) 430680; fax (2938) 430684; e-mail avisos@lavozdelpueblo.com.ar; internet www.lavozdelpueblo.com.ar; f. 1902; morning; independent; Dir MARIA RAMONA MACIEL; circ. 3,400.

Río Negro

Río Negro: 9 de Julio 733, R8332AAO General Roca; tel. (2941) 439300; fax (2941) 439638; e-mail publicidadonline@rionegro.com.ar; internet www.rionegro.com.ar; f. 1912; morning; Dir JULIO RAJNERI; Co-Dir NÉLIDA RAJNERI; circ. 30,000.

Salta

El Tribuno: Avda Ex Combatientes de Malvinas 3890, A4412BYA Salta; tel. (387) 424-6200; fax (387) 424-6240; e-mail gpublicidad@eltribuno.com.ar; internet www.eltribuno.info/salta; f. 1949; morning; Dir SERGIO ROMERO; circ. 20,000.

San Juan

Diario de Cuyo: Mendoza 380 Sur, J5402GUH San Juan; tel. (264) 429-0038; fax (264) 429-0063; e-mail comercialdc@diariodecuyo.com.ar; internet www.diariodecuyo.com.ar; f. 1947; morning; independent; Dir FRANCISCO B. MONTES; circ. 14,450.

San Luis

El Diario de La República: Lafinur 924, D5700ASO San Luis; tel. and fax (2623) 422037; e-mail redaccion@eldiariodelarepublica.com; internet www.eldiariodelarepublica.com; f. 1966; Dir ALBERTO RODRIGUEZ SAÁ; circ. 7,650.

Santa Fe

La Capital: Sarmiento 763, S2000CMK Rosario; tel. (341) 420-1100; fax (341) 420-1114; internet www.lacapital.com.ar; f. 1867; morning; independent; Dirs ORLANDO MARIO VIGNATTI, DANIEL EDUARDO VILA; circ. 40,000.

El Litoral: 25 de Mayo 3536, S3000DPJ Santa Fe; tel. (342) 450-2500; fax (342) 450-2530; e-mail publicidad@ellitoral.com; internet www.litoral.com.ar; f. 1918; morning; independent; Dir GUSTAVO VÍTTORI; circ. 14,973 (2012).

Santiago del Estero

El Liberal: Libertad 263, G4200CZC Santiago del Estero; tel. (385) 422-4400; fax (385) 422-4538; e-mail redaccion@elliberal.com.ar; internet www.elliberal.com.ar; f. 1898; morning; Dir GUSTAVO EDUARDO ICK; circ. 25,008 (2012).

Tucumán

La Gaceta: Mendoza 654, T4000DAN San Miguel de Tucumán; tel. (381) 484-2200; fax (381) 431-1597; e-mail redaccion@lagaceta.com.ar; internet www.lagaceta.com.ar; f. 1912; morning; independent; Dir DANIEL DESSEIN; circ. 53,219 (2012).

WEEKLY NEWSPAPER

Perfil: Chacabuco 271, 8°, C1069AAE Buenos Aires; tel. (11) 4341-9000; fax (11) 4341-8988; e-mail gangeli@perfil.com.ar; internet www.perfil.com; f. 2005; Saturday and Sunday; Gen. Editor GERMÁN ANGELI; circ. 38,600.

PERIODICALS

Aeroespacio (Revista Nacional Aeronáutica y Espacial): Avda Rafael Obligado 2580, C1425COA Buenos Aires; tel. and fax (11) 4514-1561; e-mail director@aeroespacio.com.ar; internet www.aeroespacio.com.ar; f. 1941; every 2 months; aeronautics; Dir ALEJANDRO BALLESPÍN; circ. 12,000.

Billiken: Azopardo 565, C1307ADG Buenos Aires; tel. (11) 4346-0107; fax (11) 4343-7040; e-mail billiken@atlantida.com.ar; internet www.billiken.com.ar; f. 1919; weekly; children's magazine; Dir JUAN CARLOS PORRAS; circ. 54,000.

Caras: Chacabuco 271, 8°, C1069AAE Buenos Aires; tel. (11) 4341-9000; fax (11) 4341-8988; e-mail correocaras@perfil.com.ar; internet www.caras.perfil.com; f. 1992; weekly; celebrities; Dir LILIANA CASTAÑO; circ. 41,000.

Chacra: The New Farm Company, SA, Paseo Colón 728, 7°B, C1063ACU Buenos Aires; tel. (11) 4342-4390; fax (11) 4343-0576; e-mail ventas@nfco.com.ar; internet www.revistachacra.com.ar; f. 1930; monthly; agriculture magazine; Dir RUBÉN BARTOLOMÉ; circ. 12,000.

El Economista: Paraguay 776, 8°, C1057AAJ Buenos Aires; tel. (11) 4312-3529; fax (11) 4314-7680; e-mail pperez@eleconomista.com.ar; internet www.eleconomista.com.ar; f. 1951; weekly; financial; Dir PATRICIA S. PÉREZ; circ. 37,800.

El Federal: Cap. General R. Freire 948, C1426AVT Buenos Aires; tel. (11) 4556-2900; fax (11) 4556-2990; e-mail eraies@infomedia.com.ar; internet revistaelfederal.com; weekly; farming and countryside; Editor ESTEBAN RAIES; circ. 18,900.

Gente: Azopardo 565, C1307ADG Buenos Aires; tel. (11) 4346-0240; e-mail genteonline@atlantida.com.ar; internet www.gente.com.ar; f. 1965; weekly; celebrities; Dir JORGE DE LUJÁN GUTIÉRREZ; circ. 45,000.

El Gráfico: Balcarce 510, 1064 Buenos Aires; tel. (11) 5235-5100; e-mail elgrafico@elgrafico.com.ar; internet www.elgrafico.com.ar; f. 1919; monthly; sport; Editor MARTIN MAZUR; circ. 40,000.

Mercado: Bartolomé Mitre 648, 8°, CP, Buenos Aires; tel. (11) 5254-9400; fax (11) 4343-7880; e-mail info@mercado.com.ar; internet www.mercado.com.ar; f. 1969; monthly; business; Dir MIGUEL ANGEL DIEZ; circ. 28,000.

Mundo Israelita, SA: Corrientes 4006, 4°, Of. 35, C1194ABS Buenos Aires; tel. (11) 4861-2224; fax (11) 4861-8434; e-mail mundoeditor@hotmail.com; internet www.mundoisraelita.com.ar;

f. 1923; owned by Mundo Editor, SA; fortnightly; Jewish interest; Editor-Dir Dr CORINA SCHVARTZAPEL; circ. 2,000.

Noticias de la Semana: Chacabuco 271, 8°, C1069AAE Buenos Aires; tel. (11) 4341-9000; fax (11) 4341-8988; e-mail correoticias@perfil.com; internet noticias.perfil.com; f. 1977; weekly; news and current affairs; Editor GUSTAVO GONZÁLEZ; circ. 63,000.

Para Ti: Azopardo 565, C1107ADG Buenos Aires; tel. (11) 4331-4591; fax (11) 4331-3272; e-mail parationline@atlantida.com.ar; internet www.parati.com.ar; f. 1922; weekly; women's interest; Dir JUAN CARLOS PORRAS; circ. 35,000.

La Prensa Médica Argentina: Junín 917, 2°D, C1113AAA Buenos Aires; tel. and fax (11) 4961-9213; e-mail presmedarg@hotmail.com; internet www.prensamedica.com.ar; f. 1914; monthly; medical; Editor Dr PABLO A. LÓPEZ; circ. 8,000.

Prensa Obrera: Ayacucho 444, C1026AAB Buenos Aires; tel. (11) 4953-3824; fax (11) 4953-7164; e-mail info@po.org.ar; internet www.po.org.ar; f. 1982; weekly; publ. of Partido Obrero; Editor J. CHRISTIAN RATH; circ. 16,000.

Saber Vivir: Magallanes 1315, C1288ABA Buenos Aires; tel. (11) 4303-2305; e-mail sabervivir@gentille.biz; internet www.sabervivir.com.ar; f. 1999; fortnightly; health; Dir RICARDO GENTILLE; circ. 81,000.

Veintitrés: Serrano 1650, C1414CHX Buenos Aires; tel. (11) 4775-0300; e-mail lectores@veintitres.com; internet www.veintitres.com; f. 1998; weekly; political and cultural; Dir JORGE CICUTTIN; circ. 35,000.

NEWS AGENCIES

Diarios y Noticias (DYN): Julio A. Roca 636, 8°, C1067ABO Buenos Aires; tel. (11) 4342-3040; fax (11) 4342-3043; e-mail editor@dyn.com.ar; internet www.dyn.com.ar; f. 1982; Chair. JOSÉ POCHAT; Dir HUGO E. GRIMALDI.

Noticias Argentinas, SA (NA): Moreno 769, 3°, C1091AAO Buenos Aires; tel. and fax (11) 4331-3850; e-mail infogral@noticiasargentinas.com; internet www.noticiasargentinas.com; f. 1973; Pres. FRANCISCO FASCETTO; Dir GABRIEL PROFITI.

Télam, SE: Bolívar 531, C1066AAK Buenos Aires; tel. (11) 4339-0330; fax (11) 4339-0353; e-mail telam@telam.com.ar; internet www.telam.com.ar; f. 1945; state-owned; Pres. SANTIAGO ALVAREZ; Gen. Man. Dr ESTEBAN ORESTES CARELLA.

PRESS ASSOCIATIONS

Asociación de Diarios del Interior de la República Argentina (ADIRA): Chacabuco 314, 4°, C1069AAH Buenos Aires; tel. (11) 4342-7003; e-mail adira@adira.org.ar; internet www.adira.org.ar; f. 1975; association for regional newspapers and periodicals; Pres. SEBASTIAN ZUELGARAY; Sec. NAHUEL CAPUTTO.

Asociación de Entidades Periodísticas Argentinas (ADEPA): Chacabuco 314, 3°, C1069AAH Buenos Aires; tel. and fax (11) 4331-1500; e-mail adepa@adepa.org.ar; internet www.adepa.org.ar; f. 1962; Pres. CARLOS JORNET; Sec.-Gen. CARLOS RAGO.

Publishers

Aguilar, Altea, Alfaguara, Taurus, SA de Ediciones: Leandro N. Alem 720, C1001AAP Buenos Aires; tel. (11) 4119-5000; fax (11) 4119-5021; e-mail info@alfaguara.com.ar; internet www.alfaguara.com.ar; f. 1946; part of Grupo Editorial Santillana Argentina; general, literature, children's books; Pres. EMILIANO MARTINEZ; Dir-Gen. ARMANDO COLLAZOS.

Aique Grupo Editor, SA: Francisco Acuña de Figueroa 352, C1180AAF Buenos Aires; tel. (11) 4867-7000; e-mail centrodocente@aique.com.ar; internet www.aique.com.ar; f. 1976; educational; Dir-Gen. MARÍA PÍA GAGLIARDI.

Amorrortu Editores, SA: Paraguay 1225, 7°, C1057AAS Buenos Aires; tel. (11) 4816-5812; fax (11) 4816-3321; e-mail info@amorrorteditores.com; internet www.amorrorteditores.com; f. 1967; academic, social sciences and humanities; Man. Dir HORACIO DE AMORRORTU.

A–Z Editora, SA: Paraguay 2351, C1121ABK Buenos Aires; tel. (11) 4961-4036; fax (11) 4961-0089; e-mail contacto@az.com.ar; internet www.az.com.ar; f. 1976; educational, children's, literature, social sciences, medicine, law; Pres. RAMIRO VILLALBA GARIBALDI.

Biblioteca Nacional de Maestros: c/o Ministerio de Educación, Pizzurno 935, planta baja, C1020ACA Buenos Aires; tel. (11) 4129-1272; fax (11) 4129-1268; e-mail bnminfo@me.gov.ar; internet www.bnm.me.gov.ar; f. 1884; Dir GRACIELA TERESA PERRONE.

Cosmopolita, SRL: Piedras 744, C1070AAP Buenos Aires; tel. (11) 4361-8925; fax (11) 4361-8049; e-mail cosmopolita09@yahoo.com.ar;

internet www.ed-cosmopolita.com.ar; f. 1940; science and technology; Man. Dir RUTH F. DE RAPP.

Crecer Creando Editorial: Viamonte 2052, C1056ABF Buenos Aires; tel. (11) 4372-4165; fax (11) 4371-9351; e-mail info@crecercreando.com.ar; internet www.crecercreando.com.ar; educational; Pres. CARLOS RIVERA.

De Los Cuatro Vientos Editorial: Venezuela 726, C1096ABD Buenos Aires; tel. and fax (11) 4331-4200; e-mail info@deloscuatrovientos.com.ar; internet www.deloscuatrovientos.com.ar; f. 2000; Dir PABLO GABRIEL ALBORNOZ; Editor MARIELA FERNANDA AQUILANO.

Edebé, SA: Don Bosco 4069, C1206ABM Buenos Aires; tel. (11) 4883-0111; fax (11) 4883-0115; tel. info@edebe.com.ar; internet www.edebe.com.ar; f. 1996; religious and educational literature for children; Gen. Man. NORA WAGNER.

Ediciones de la Flor SRL: Gorriti 3695, C1172ACE Buenos Aires; tel. (11) 4963-7950; fax (11) 4963-5616; e-mail edic-flor@datamarkets.com.ar; internet www.edicionesdelaflor.com.ar; f. 1966; fiction, poetry, theatre, juvenile, humour and scholarly; Co-Dirs ANA MARÍA MILER, DANIEL DIVINSKY.

Ediciones Gránica: Lavalle 1634, 3° G, C1048AAN Buenos Aires; tel. (11) 4374-1456; fax (11) 4373-0669; e-mail granica.ar@granicaeditor.com; internet www.granicaeditor.com; management, reference; Gen. Man. CLAUDIO IANNINI.

Ediciones Macchi, SA: Pacheco 3190, C1431FJN Buenos Aires; tel. and fax (11) 4542-7835; e-mail info@macchi.com; internet www.macchi.com; f. 1960; economic sciences; Pres. RAÚL LUIS MACCHI.

Ediciones Manantial, SRL: Avda de Mayo 1365, 6°, Of. 28, C1085ABD Buenos Aires; tel. (11) 4383-6059; fax (11) 4383-7350; e-mail info@emanantial.com.ar; internet www.emanantial.com.ar; f. 1984; social science, education and psychoanalysis; Gen. Man. CARLOS A. DE SANTOS.

Ediciones Nueva Visión, SAIC: Tucumán 3748, C1189AAV Buenos Aires; tel. (11) 4864-5050; fax (11) 4863-5980; e-mail ednuevavision@ciudad.com.ar; f. 1954; psychology, education, social sciences, linguistics; Man. Dir HAYDÉE P. DE GIACONE.

Ediciones del Signo: Julián Alvarez 2844, 1° A, C1425DHT Buenos Aires; tel. (11) 4804-4147; fax (11) 4782-1836; e-mail info@edicionesdelsigno.com.ar; internet www.edicionesdelsigno.com.ar; f. 1995; philosophy, psychoanalysis, politics and scholarly; Man. MICAELA GERCMAN.

Editorial Albatros, SACI: Torre Las Plazas, J. Salguero 2745, 5°, Of. 51, C1425DEL Buenos Aires; tel. (11) 4807-2030; fax (11) 4807-2010; e-mail info@albatros.com.ar; internet www.albatros.com.ar; f. 1945; technical, non-fiction, social sciences, sport, children's books, medicine and agriculture; Man. Dir ANDREA INÉS CANEVARO.

Editorial Argenta Sarlep, SA: Avda Corrientes 1250, 3°, Of. F, C1043AAZ Buenos Aires; tel. (11) 4382-9085; fax (11) 4381-6100; e-mail info@editorialargenta.com; internet www.editorialargenta.com; f. 1970; literature, poetry, theatre and reference; Man. ALEXANDER ERNST RENNES.

Editorial Bonum, SACI: Avda Corrientes 6687, C1427BPE Buenos Aires; tel. and fax (11) 4554-1414; e-mail marina@editorialbonum.com.ar; internet www.editorialbonum.com.ar; f. 1960; religious, educational and self-help; Pres. MARTÍN GREMMELSPACHER.

Editorial Catálogos, SRL: Avda Independencia 1860, C1225AAN Buenos Aires; tel. and fax (11) 4381-5708; e-mail catalogos@ciudad.com.ar; internet www.catalogossrl.com.ar; religion, literature, academic, general interest and self-help; Co-Dirs HORACIO GARCÍA, LEONARDO PÉREZ.

Editorial Claretiana: Lima 1360, C1138ACD Buenos Aires; tel. (11) 4305-9597; fax (11) 4305-6552; e-mail contacto@editorialclaretiana.com.ar; internet www.editorialclaretiana.com.ar; f. 1956; Catholicism; Man. Dir P. GUSTAVO M. LARRAZÁBAL.

Editorial Claridad, Heliasta, unaLuna, SA: Juncal 3451, C1425AYT Buenos Aires; tel. and fax (11) 4804-0472; e-mail editorial@editorialclaridad.com.ar; internet www.heliasta.com.ar; f. 1922; literature, biographies, social science, politics, reference, dictionaries; Co-Dirs Dra ANA MARÍA CABANELLAS DE LAS CUEVAS, GUILLERMO CABANELLAS DE LAS CUEVAS.

Editorial Errepar: Paraná 725, C1017AAO Buenos Aires; tel. (11) 4370-2002; fax (11) 4383-2202; e-mail clientes@errepar.com; internet www.errepar.com; f. 1976; encyclopaedias, technical and legal texts; Pres. RICARDO PARADA; Dir FRANCISCO CAÑADA.

Editorial Grupo Cero: Mansilla 2686, planta baja 1 y 2, C1425BPD Buenos Aires; tel. (11) 4966-1710; fax (11) 4966-1713; e-mail pedidos@editorialgrupocero.com; internet www.editorialgrupocero.com; fiction, poetry and psychoanalysis; Dir MARÍA NORMA MENASSA.

Editorial Guadalupe: Mansilla 3865, C1425BQA Buenos Aires; tel. and fax (11) 4826-8587; e-mail gerencia@editorialguadalupe.com.ar; internet www.editorialguadalupe.com.ar; f. 1895; social sciences, religion, anthropology, children's books and pedagogy; Man. Dir P. LUIS O. LIBERTI; Man. Editor LILIANA FERREIRÓS.

Editorial Hispano-Americana, SA (HASA): Rincón 686, C1227ACD Buenos Aires; tel. (11) 4943-7111; fax (11) 4943-7061; e-mail info@hasa.com.ar; internet www.hasa.com.ar; f. 1934; science and technology; Pres. Prof. HÉCTOR ALBERTO ALGARRA.

Editorial Inter-Médica, SAICI: Junín 917, 1°A, C1113AAC Buenos Aires; tel. (11) 4961-9234; fax (11) 4961-5572; e-mail info@inter-medica.com.ar; internet www.inter-medica.com.ar; f. 1959; medicine and veterinary; Pres. JORGE MODYEIEVSKY.

Editorial Juris: Moreno 1580, S2000DLF Rosario, Santa Fe; tel. (341) 426-7301; e-mail editorial@editorialjuris.com; internet www.editorialjuris.com; f. 1952; legal texts; Dir LUIS MAESANO.

Editorial Kier, SACIFI: Avda Santa Fe 1260, C1059ABT Buenos Aires; tel. (11) 4811-0507; fax (11) 4811-3395; e-mail info@kier.com.ar; internet www.kier.com.ar; f. 1907; Eastern doctrines and religions, astrology, parapsychology, tarot, I Ching, occultism, cabbala, freemasonry and natural medicine; Pres. HÉCTOR S. PIBERNUS; Dirs CRISTINA GRIGNA, OSVALDO PIBERNUS.

Editorial Losada, SA: Avda Corrientes 1551, C1042AAB Buenos Aires; tel. (11) 4375-5001; fax (11) 4373-4006; e-mail losada@editoriallosada.com; internet www.editoriallosada.com; f. 1938; general; Pres. JOSÉ JUAN FERNÁNDEZ REGUERA; Editor GONZALO LOSADA.

Editorial Médica Panamericana, SA: Marcelo T. de Alvear 2145, C1122AAG Buenos Aires; tel. (11) 4821-5520; fax (11) 4825-1214; e-mail info@medicapanamericana.com; internet www.medicapanamericana.com.ar; f. 1962; medicine and health sciences; Pres. HUGO BRIK.

Editorial Mercosur: Dean Funes 923, C1231ABI Buenos Aires; tel. (11) 4956-2297; e-mail info@editorialmercosur.com; internet www.editorialmercosur.com; self-help and general interest.

Editorial del Nuevo Extremo: Angel J. Carranza 1852, C1414COV Buenos Aires; tel. (11) 4773-3228; fax (11) 4773-8445; e-mail info@delnuevoextremo.com; internet www.delnuevoextremo.com; general interest; Pres. MIGUEL ANGEL LAMBRÉ; Dir TOMÁS LAMBRÉ.

Editorial Planeta Argentina, SAIC: Avda Independencia 1668, C1100ABQ Buenos Aires; tel. (11) 4124-9100; fax (11) 4124-9190; e-mail info@eplaneta.com.ar; internet www.editorialplaneta.com.ar; f. 1939; fiction, non-fiction, biographies, history, art, essays; subsidiary of Grupo Planeta, Spain; Editorial Dir ALBERTO DÍAZ.

Editorial Sigmar, SACI: Avda Belgrano 1580, 7°, C1093AAQ Buenos Aires; tel. (11) 4381-2510; fax (11) 4383-5633; e-mail editorial@sigmar.com.ar; internet www.sigmar.com.ar; f. 1941; children's books; Man. Dir ROBERTO CHWAT.

Editorial Stella: Viamonte 1984, C1056ABD Buenos Aires; tel. (11) 4374-0346; fax (11) 4374-8719; e-mail ventas@editorialstella.com.ar; internet www.editorialstella.com.ar; f. 1941; general non-fiction and textbooks; owned by Asociación Educacionista Argentina; Dir TELMO MEIRONE; Editor ADOLFO GARCÍA SÁEZ.

Editorial Troquel, SA: Olleros 1818, 4° I, C1426CRH Buenos Aires; tel. and fax (11) 4779-9444; e-mail info@troguel.com.ar; internet www.troquel.com.ar; f. 1954; general literature, religion, philosophy and education; Pres. GUSTAVO A. RESSIA.

Editorial Zeus, SRL: San Lorenzo 1329, S2000DNP Rosario, Santa Fe; tel. (341) 449-5585; fax (341) 425-4259; e-mail zeus@zeus.com.ar; internet www.editorial-zeus.com.ar; legal texts; Editor and Dir GUSTAVO L. CAVIGLIA.

EUDEBA (Editorial Universitaria de Buenos Aires): Avda Rivadavia 1573, C1033AAF Buenos Aires; tel. (11) 4383-8025; fax (11) 4383-2202; e-mail info@eudeba.com.ar; internet www.eudeba.com.ar; f. 1958; university textbooks and general interest publs; Pres. GONZALO ALVAREZ; Gen. Man. LUIS QUEVEDO.

Galerna: Lambaré 893, C1185ABA Buenos Aires; tel. (11) 4867-1661; fax (11) 4862-5031; e-mail contacto@galerna.net; internet www.galernalibros.com; fiction, theatre, poetry and scholarly; Pres. MATIAS SANABRIA; Dir HUGO LEVÍN.

Gram Editora: Cochabamba 1652, C1148ABF Buenos Aires; tel. (11) 4304-4833; fax (11) 4304-5692; e-mail grameditora@infovia.com.ar; internet www.grameditora.com.ar; f. 1990; education; Man. MANUEL HERRERO MONTES.

Grupo Editorial Lumen, SRL: Montevideo 604, 2°, C1019ABN, Buenos Aires; tel. (11) 4373-1414; fax (11) 4375-0453; e-mail contacto@lumen.com.ar; internet www.edlumen.net; f. 1958; imprints include Lumen (religion, spirituality, etc.), Magisterio (educational), Lumen-Hvmanitas (social sciences) and Lohlé-Lumen (politics, philosophy, literature); Man.Dir ALEJANDRO MARKER.

Grupo Santillana Argentina: Avda Leandro N. Alem 720, C1001AAP Buenos Aires; tel. (11) 4119-5000; e-mail info@santillana.com.ar; internet www.santillana.com.ar; f. 1963; part of Grupo Editorial Santillana (Spain); education; Dir-Gen. DAVID DELGADO DE ROBLES.

Kapelusz Editora, SA: San José 831, C1076AAQ Buenos Aires; tel. (11) 5236-5000; fax (11) 5236-5051; e-mail jvergara@kapelusz.com.ar; internet www.kapelusznorma.com.ar; f. 1905; textbooks, psychology, pedagogy, children's books; Vice-Pres. RAFAEL PASCUAL ROBLES.

LexisNexis Argentina: Carlos Pellegrini 887, 3°, C1013AAQ Buenos Aires; tel. (11) 5236-8800; fax (11) 5236-8811; e-mail info@lexisnexis.com.ar; internet www.lexisnexis.com.ar; f. 1999 upon acquisition of Depalma and Abeledo-Perrot; periodicals and books covering law, politics, sociology, philosophy, history and economics; Gen. Man. CAROLINA TRONGE.

Random House Mondadori: Humberto Primo 545, 1°, C1103ACK Buenos Aires; tel. (11) 5235-4400; fax (11) 4362-7364; e-mail info@rhm.com.ar; internet www.megustaleer.com.ar; f. 1939; general fiction and non-fiction; Man. Dir JUAN IGNACIO BOIDO.

Siglo Veintiuno Editores: Guatemala 4824, C1425BUP Buenos Aires; tel. and fax (11) 4770-9090; e-mail info@sigloxxieditores.com.ar; internet www.sigloxxieditores.com.ar; social science, history, economics, art; Editorial Dir CARLOS E. DIEZ.

PUBLISHERS' ASSOCIATIONS

Cámara Argentina del Libro: Avda Belgrano 1580, 4°, C1093AAQ Buenos Aires; tel. (11) 4381-8383; fax (11) 4381-9253; e-mail cal@editores.org.ar; internet www.editores.org.ar; f. 1938; Pres. ISAAC RUBINZAL; Exec. Dir DIANA SEGOVIA.

Cámara Argentina de Publicaciones: Lavalle 437, 5°, Of. A, C1047AAI Buenos Aires; tel. (11) 5218-9707; e-mail info@publicaciones.org.ar; internet www.publicaciones.org.ar; f. 1970; Pres. HÉCTOR DI MARCO; Sec. MARÍA PÍA GAGLIARDI.

Broadcasting and Communications

TELECOMMUNICATIONS

AT&T Argentina: Alicia Moreau de Justo 400, C1107AAH Buenos Aires; tel. (11) 4310-8700; fax (11) 4310-8706; e-mail info_Argentina@cla.att.com; internet www.att.com; Vice-Pres. (Canada, Caribbean and Latin America) MARY E. LIVINGSTON; Country Pres. ALEJANDRO ROSSI.

Claro Argentina, SA (AMX Argentina, SA): Edif. Corporativo, Avda de Mayo 878, C1084AAQ Buenos Aires; tel. (11) 4109-8888; e-mail nscocimarro@claro.com.ar; internet argentina.claro.com.ar; f. 1994 as CTI Móvil; wholly owned subsidiary of América Móvil, SA de CV (Mexico) since 2003; mobile cellular telephone services; CEO JULIO CARLOS PORRAS ZADIK.

Ericsson, SACI: Güemes 676, 1°, Vicente López PCIA, B1638CJF Buenos Aires; tel. (11) 4319-5500; fax (11) 4315-0629; e-mail infocom@cea.ericsson.se; internet www.ericsson.com; Head (Latin America) SERGIO QUIROGA DA CUNHA; Exec. Vice-Pres. (Argentina) DANIEL CARUSO.

Movistar: Avda Corrientes 655, 3°, C1043AAG Buenos Aires; tel. (11) 5321-0000; fax (11) 5321-1604; internet www.movistar.com.ar; 98% owned by Telefónicas Móviles, SA (Spain); operates mobile telephone network; Dir (Products and Services) LEANDRO MUSCIANO.

Nextel Communications Argentina, SRL: Olga Cossettini 363, Dique 4, C1107CCG Buenos Aires; tel. (11) 5359-0000; e-mail prensa@nextel.com.ar; internet www.nextel.com.ar; f. 1998; Pres. RUBEN BUTVILOFSKY.

Telcosur, SA: Don Bosco 3672, 5°, C1206ABF Buenos Aires; tel. (11) 4865-9060; e-mail telcosur@telcosur.com.ar; internet www.telcosur.com.ar; f. 1998; 99% owned by Transportador de Gas del Sur (TGS); Operations Man. EDUARDO VIGILANTE.

Telecom Argentina, SA: Alicia Moreau de Justo 50, 10°, C1107AAB Buenos Aires; tel. (11) 4968-4000; fax (11) 4968-1420; e-mail contactos@telecompersonal.com.ar; internet www.telecom.com.ar; provision of telecommunication services in the north of Argentina; provides wireless services under the brand Telecom Personal; Exec. Dir STEFANO DE ANGELIS; Gen. Sec. MARÍA D. CARRERA SALA.

Regulatory Body

Comisión Nacional de Comunicaciones (CNC): Perú 103, 1°, C1067AAC Buenos Aires; tel. (11) 4347-9501; fax (11) 4347-9897; internet www.cnc.gov.ar; f. 1996; Insp. CEFERINO NAMUNCURÁ.

BROADCASTING

Radio

Radio Nacional Argentina (RNA): Maipú 555, C1006ACE Buenos Aires; tel. (11) 4325-9100; fax (11) 4325-4313; e-mail direccionlra1@radionacional.gov.ar; internet www.radionacional.gov.ar; f. 1937; state-controlled, part of Radio y Televisión Argentina, SE; 6 national radio stations: AM 870; Nacional Folklórica; Nacional Clásica; Nacional Rock; Fútbol; and Radiodifusión Argentina al Exterior (f. 1947); 49 provincial stations; Exec. Dir MARÍA SEOANE.

Asociación de Radiodifusoras Privadas Argentinas (ARPA): Juan D. Perón 1561, 3°, C1037ACC Buenos Aires; tel. (11) 4371-5999; fax 4382-4483; e-mail arpaorg@arpa.org.ar; internet www.arpa.org .ar; f. 1958; asscn of privately owned commercial stations; Pres. Dr EDMUNDO O. RÉBORA; Exec. Dir HECTOR J. PARREIRA.

Television

América TV: Fitzroy 1650, C1414CHX Buenos Aires; tel. (11) 5032-2222; e-mail americanoticias@america2.com.ar; internet www .america2.com.ar; Pres. DANIEL VILA; CEO GUSTAVO CAPUA.

Canal 9 (Telearte, SA): Dorrego 1782, C1414CKZ Buenos Aires; tel. (11) 3220-9999; e-mail webmaster@canal9.com.ar; internet www .canal9.com.ar; f. 1960; private channel; Pres. CARLOS E. LOREFICE LYNCH; Dir-Gen. ENRIQUE TABOADA.

Canal 13: Lima 1261, C1138ACA Buenos Aires; tel. (11) 4305-0013; fax (11) 4331-8573; e-mail eltrecetv@artear.com; internet www .eltrecetv.com.ar; f. 1989; part of Arte Radiotelevisivo Argentino, SA; leased to a private concession in 1992; Gen. Man. DANIEL ZANARDI; Programme Man. PABLO CODEVILLA.

Telefé (Canal 11): Pavón 2444, C1248AAT Buenos Aires; tel. (11) 4941-9549; fax (11) 4942-6773; e-mail prensa@telefe.com.ar; internet www.telefe.com.ar; private channel; Pres. JUAN WAEHNER; Programme Man. CLAUDIO VILLARRUEL.

TV Pública Canal Siete: Avda Figueroa Alcorta 2977, C1425CKI Buenos Aires; tel. (11) 4808-2500; e-mail contacto@tvpublica.com.ar; internet www.tvpublica.com.ar; f. 1951; state-controlled, part of Radio y Televisión Argentina, SE; Pres. TRISTÁN BAUER; Exec. Dir MARTÍN BONAVETTI.

Asociación de Teleradiodifusoras Argentinas (ATA): Avda Córdoba 323, 6°, C1054AAC Buenos Aires; tel. (11) 4312-4208; fax (11) 4315-4681; e-mail info@ata.org.ar; internet www.ata.org.ar; f. 1959; asscn of 23 private television channels; Pres. RICARDO NOSIGLIA; Sec. PABLO CASEY.

Regulatory Bodies

Autoridad Federal de Servicios de Comunicación Audiovisual (AFSCA): Suipacha 765, 9°, C1008AAO Buenos Aires; tel. (11) 4320-4900; fax (11) 4394-6866; e-mail prensa@afsca.gob.ar; internet www.afsca.gov.ar; f. 1972 as Comisión Nacional de Radio y Televisión (CONART); name changed to Comité Federal de Radiodifusión (COMFER) in 1981; reorg. as a decentralized regulatory authority and adopted present name in 2009; controls various technical aspects of broadcasting and transmission of programmes; Pres. MARTÍN SABATELLA.

Secretaría de Comunicaciones: Sarmiento 151, 4°, C1041AAC Buenos Aires; tel. (11) 4318-9410; fax (11) 4318-9432; internet www .secom.gov.ar; co-ordinates 30 stations and the international service; Sec. CARLOS LISANDRO SALAS.

Finance

(cap. = capital; res = reserves; dep. = deposits; m. = million; br(s) = branch(es); amounts in nuevos pesos argentinos)

BANKING

Central Bank

Banco Central de la República Argentina: Reconquista 266, C1003ABF Buenos Aires; tel. (11) 4348-3500; fax (11) 4348-3955; e-mail sistema@bcra.gov.ar; internet www.bcra.gov.ar; f. 1935 as a central reserve bank; bank of issue; all capital is held by the state; cap. 14,604.7m., res 34,972.1m., dep. 108,855.3m. (Dec. 2009); Pres. JUAN CARLOS FÁBREGA.

Government-owned Commercial Banks

Banco del Chubut: Rivadavia 615, Rawson, U9103ANG Chubut; tel. (297) 448-2505; fax (297) 448-2513; e-mail contacto@chubutbank .com.ar; internet www.bancochubut.com.ar; f. 1959; cap. 198.6m., res 101.7m., dep. 2,971.6m. (June 2013); Chair. OSCAR ABEL ANTONENA; Gen. Man. HUGO GARNERO.

Banco de la Ciudad de Buenos Aires: Sarmiento 630, C1005AAH Buenos Aires; tel. (11) 4329-8600; fax (11) 4329-8729; e-mail Exterior@bancociudad.com.ar; internet www.bancociudad.com.ar; municipal bank; f. 1878; cap. 1,348.3m., res 991.2m., dep. 26,471.5m. (Dec. 2013); Chair. and Pres. FEDERICO ADOLFO STURZENEGGER; Gen. Man. GUILLERMO ANTONINO CASCIO; 65 brs.

Banco de Inversión y Comercio Exterior, SA (BICE): 25 de Mayo 526/532, C1002ABL Buenos Aires; tel. (11) 4313-9546; fax (11) 4311-5596; e-mail info@bice.com.ar; internet www.bice.com.ar;

f. 1991; cap. 489.2m., res 831.1m., dep. 651.1m. (Dec. 2011); Pres. MAURO ALEM; Gen. Man. JORGE GIACOMOTTI.

Banco de la Nación Argentina: Bartolomé Mitre 326, Capital Federal Of. 235, C1036AAF Buenos Aires; tel. (11) 4347-6000; fax (11) 4347-6316; e-mail prensabna@bna.com.ar; internet www.bna .com.ar; f. 1891; national bank; cap. 2,510.2m. (Dec. 2010), res 14,900.5m., dep. 180,020.3m. (Dec. 2012); Pres. JUAN IGNACIO FORLÓN; Gen. Man. RAÚL DUZEVIC; 645 brs.

Banco de la Pampa SEM: Carlos Pellegrini 255, L6300DRE Santa Rosa; tel. (295) 445-1000; e-mail cexterior@blp.com.ar; internet www .blp.com.ar; f. 1958; cap. 128.5m., res 131.1m., dep. 5,552.2m. (Dec. 2013); Chair. LAURA AZUCENA GALLUCCIO; Gen. Man. CARLOS DESINANO; 51 brs.

Banco de la Provincia de Buenos Aires: San Martín 137, 9°, C1004AAC, Buenos Aires; tel. (11) 4347-0000; fax (11) 4347-0299; e-mail gerenciageneral@bpba.com.ar; internet www.bapro.com.ar; f. 1822; provincial govt-owned bank; cap. 2,764.8m., (Dec. 2011), dep. 68,478.8m., res 3,431.2m. (Dec. 2013); Pres. GUSTAVO M. MARANGONI; Gen. Man. MARCELO H. GARCÍA; 343 brs.

Banco de la Provincia de Córdoba: San Jerónimo 166, esq. Buenos Aires, CP 5000, X5000AGD Córdoba; tel. (351) 420-7200; fax (11) 5811-8864; e-mail contgral@bancor.com.ar; internet www .bancor.com.ar; f. 1873; provincial bank; cap. 627.2m., res 95.1m., dep. 12,333.5m. (Dec. 2013); Pres. FABIÁN MAIDANA; Exec. Dir JOSÉ LUIS DOMINGUEZ; 143 brs.

Banco Provincia del Neuquén: Avda Argentina 41, 1°, Q8300AYA Neuquén; tel. (299) 449-6600; fax (299) 449-6900; e-mail institucional@bpn.com.ar; internet www.bpn.com.ar; f. 1960; cap. 210m., dep. 3,410m. (Dec. 2013); Pres. MARCOS GABRIEL KOOPMANN IRIZAR; Gen. Man. ADRIANA VELASCO; 22 brs.

Banco de Tierra del Fuego: Maipú 897, V9410BJQ Ushuaia; tel. (2901) 441600; fax (2901) 441671; e-mail info@bancotdf.com.ar; internet www.bancotdf.com.ar; national bank; cap. 200.7m., dep. 998.3m. (Dec. 2012); Pres. RICARDO IGLESIAS; Gen. Man. MIGUEL LANDERRECHE; 8 brs.

Nuevo Banco de Santa Fe, SA: San Martín 715, S2000CJI Rosario, Santa Fe; tel. (342) 429-4200; e-mail contactobc@bancobsf.com.ar; internet www.bancobsf.com.ar; f. 1847 as Banco Provincial de Santa Fe, adopted current name in 1998; provincial bank; cap. 91.1m., res 649.6m., dep. 15,726.1m. (Dec. 2013); Chair. ENRIQUE ESKINAZI; Exec. Dir MARCELO BUIL; 105 brs.

Private Commercial Banks

Banco BI Creditanstalt, SA: Bouchard 547, 24° y 25°, C1106ABG Buenos Aires; tel. (11) 4319-8400; fax (11) 4319-8230; e-mail info@ bicreditanstalt.com.ar; internet www.bicreditanstalt.com.ar; f. 1971 as Banco Interfinanzas; adopted current name 1997; cap. and res 444.8m., dep. 8.7m. (Dec. 2009); Pres. Dr DIEGO MIGUEL MARÍA ANGELINO; Gen. Man. RICARDO RIVERO HAEDO.

Banco CMF, SA: Macacha Güemes 150, Puerto Madero, C1106BKD Buenos Aires; tel. (11) 4318-6800; fax (11) 4318-6844; e-mail cmfb@ cmfb.com.ar; internet www.bancocmf.com.ar; f. 1978 as Corporación Metropolitana de Finanzas, SA; adopted current name in 1999; cap. 145.9m., res 97.7m., dep. 2,524.2m. (Dec. 2013); Pres. and Chair. JOSÉ ALBERTO BENEGAS LYNCH; Gen. Man. MARCOS PRIETO.

Banco COMAFI: Roque S. Peña 660, C1035AAO Buenos Aires; tel. (11) 4328-3020; fax (11) 4328-9068; e-mail contactenos@comafi.com .ar; internet www.comafi.com.ar; f. 1984; assumed control of 65% of Scotiabank Quilmes in 2002; cap. 36.7m., res 513m., dep. 5,299.9m. (June 2013); Pres. GUILLERMO CERVIÑO; CEO GUILLERMO LAJE; 56 brs.

Banco de Corrientes: 9 de Julio 1002, esq. San Juan, W3400AYQ Corrientes; tel. (3783) 479300; fax (3783) 479368; e-mail bcteservicios@bcoctes.com.ar; internet www.bancodecorrientes.com .ar; f. 1951 as Banco de la República de Corrientes; adopted current name in 1993 after transfer to private ownership; cap. 124.1m., dep. 1,780.1m. (Dec. 2011); Pres. Dr ALEJANDRO ABRAHAM; Gen. Man. CARLOS GUSTAVO MACORATTI; 33 brs.

Banco Finansur, SA: Sarmiento 700, esq. Maipú, C1041AAN Buenos Aires; tel. (11) 4324-3422; fax (11) 4322-4687; e-mail bafin@bancofinansur.com.ar; internet www.bancofinansur.com.ar; f. 1973; est. as Finansur Compañía Financiera, SA; adopted current name in 1993; cap. 32.7m., res 29.9m., dep. 791.8m. (Dec. 2012); Pres. JORGE SÁNCHEZ CÓRDOVA; 4 brs.

Banco Formosa SA: 25 de Mayo 102, 3600 Formosa; tel. (370) 429200; fax (370) 429844; internet www.bancodeformosa.com; cap. 19m., res 103.5m., dep. 1,580.5m. (Dec. 2012); Pres. MARTÍN JOSÉ CORTÉS; Gen. Man. RODRIGO HÉCTOR PENA.

Banco de Galicia y Buenos Aires, SA: Juan D. Perón 415, Casilla 86, C1038AAI Buenos Aires; tel. (11) 6329-0000; fax (11) 6329-6100; e-mail bancogalicia@bancogalicia.com.ar; internet www .bancogalicia.com.ar; f. 1905; cap. 562.3m., res 3,040.5m., dep. 39,991.1m. (Dec. 2012); Chair. SERGIO GRINENCO; CEO DANIEL LLAMBÍAS; 236 brs.

Banco Hipotecario, SA: Reconquista 101, C1003ABC Buenos Aires; tel. 4347-5000; fax 4342-2247; e-mail info@hipotecario.com .ar; internet www.hipotecario.com.ar; f. 1886; cap. 1,500m., res 1,926m., dep. 10,889.8m. (Dec. 2013); Chair. Dr GUSTAVO MATA.

Banco Industrial, SA (BIND): Sarmiento 530, C1041AAL, Buenos Aires; tel. (11) 5238-0200; fax (11) 4315-8113; e-mail info@ bancoindustrial.com.ar; internet www.bancoindustrial.com.ar; f. 1928 as Banco de Azul; operated as a co-operative until 1995; renamed Nuevo Banco Industrial de Azul in 1997, present name adopted 2010; cap. 177m., res 312.3m., dep. 4,737.9m. (Dec. 2013); Pres. CARLOTA EVELINA DURST; Gen. Man. LUIS LARA; 30 brs.

Banco Itaú Argentina, SA: Victoria Ocampo 360, C1107DAB Buenos Aires; tel. (11) 4378-8420; fax (11) 4372-0228; e-mail azorgno@itau.com.ar; internet www.itau.com.ar; fmrly Banco Itaú Argentina, SA; renamed as above following purchase of Banco del Buen Ayre, SA, in 1998; subsidiary of Banco Itaú, SA (Brazil); cap. 443.7m., res 266.5m., dep. 7,257.8m. (Dec. 2012); Pres. RICARDO VILLELA MARINO; Gen. Man. SERGIO SALOMON FELDMAN; 117 brs.

Banco Macro, SA: Sarmiento 447, 4°, C1041AAI Buenos Aires; tel. (11) 5222-6500; fax (11) 5222-6624; e-mail relacionesinstitucionales@macro.com.ar; internet www.macro.com .ar; f. 1988 as a commercial bank, merged with Banco Bansud in 2002 and renamed Macro Bansud; adopted current name 2006; cap. 594.5m., res 5,517.4m., dep. 43,427m. (Dec. 2013); Pres. JORGE HORACIO BRITO; 400 brs.

Banco Mariva, SA: Sarmiento 500, C1041AAJ Buenos Aires; tel. (11) 4321-2200; fax (11) 4321-2292; e-mail info@mariva.com.ar; internet www.mariva.com.ar; f. 1980; cap. 67.1m., res 56.6m., dep. 797.2m. (Dec. 2012); Pres. JOSÉ LUIS PARDO; Gen. Man. JOSÉ MARÍA FERNÁNDEZ.

Banco Patagonia, SA: Juan D. Perón 500, C1038AAJ Buenos Aires; tel. (11) 4132-6300; fax (11) 4132-6058; e-mail international@bancopatagonia.com.ar; internet www .bancopatagonia.com.ar; f. 1912; fmrly Banco Sudameris; adopted current name in 2004 following merger with Banco Patagonia; cap. 719.3m., res 2,673.5m., dep. 22,613.7m. (Dec. 2013); Pres. JOÃO CARLOS DE NÓBREGA PECEGO.

Banco Piano, SA: San Martín 345/347, C1004AAB Buenos Aires; tel. (11) 4325-6562; fax (11) 4325-4942; e-mail info@piano.com.ar; internet www.bancopiano.com.ar; f. 1992; cap. 45m., res 81.1m., dep. 1,416.5m. (June 2012); Pres. ALFREDO VICTORINO PIANO.

Banco de San Juan: Ignacio de la Roza 85, J5402DCA San Juan; tel. (264) 429-1000; fax (264) 421-4126; internet www.bancosanjuan .com; f. 1943; 20% owned by provincial govt of San Juan; 80% privately owned; cap. 20.7m., res 537.7m., dep. 19,836.9m. (Dec. 2012); Pres. ENRIQUE ESKENAZI; Gen. Man. MARIA SILVINA BELLANTIG TARDIO; 8 brs.

Banco Santander Río, SA: Bartolomé Mitre 480, 2°, C1036AAH Buenos Aires; tel. (11) 4341-1000; fax (11) 4341-1020; e-mail sgalvan@santanderrio.com.ar; internet www.santanderrio.com.ar; f. 1908 as Banco Río de la Plata; adopted current name 2007; owned by Banco Santander (Spain); cap. 6,693.4m., dep. 53,228.4m. (Dec. 2013); Pres. JOSÉ LUIS ENRIQUE CRISTOFANI; 370 brs.

Banco Santiago del Estero: Belgrano 529 Sur, G4200AAF Santiago del Estero; tel. (385) 450-2300; fax (385) 450-2319; e-mail bsegerencia@arnet.com.ar; internet www.bse.com.ar; Pres. NÉSTOR CARLOS ICK; Gen. Man. ALDO RENÉ MAZZOLENI.

Banco de Servicios y Transacciones, SA: Avda de Corrientes 1174, 3°, C1043AAY Buenos Aires; tel. (11) 5235-2300; fax (11) 5235-2305; e-mail info@bancost.com.ar; internet www.bancost.com.ar; cap. 139.8m., res 3.3m., dep. 1,165.9m. (Dec. 2012); Pres. PABLO BERNARDO PERALTA; Gen. Man. PABLO DAMIAN CONFORTI.

Banco Supervielle, SA: Bartolomé Mitre 434, C1036AAH Buenos Aires; tel. (11) 4324-8000; fax (11) 4324-8090; e-mail informes@ar .socgen.com; internet www.supervielle.com.ar; f. 1887; owned by Grupo Supervielle; took over Banco Regional de Cuyo in Oct. 2010; cap. 456.1m., res 730.8m., dep. 12,823.3m. (Dec. 2013); Pres. PATRICIO SUPERVIELLE; Gen. Man. JOSÉ LUÍS PANERO; 176 brs.

Banco Tucumán Grupo Macro, SA: San Miguel de Tucumán 4000, Tucumán; tel. (381) 4503300; fax (381) 4311957; e-mail bancodeltucuman@bancodeltucuman.com.ar; internet www .bancodeltucuman.com.ar; f. 1996, bought by Grupo Macro in 2005; cap. 43.9m., res 131.8m., dep. 3,775.7m. (Dec 2013); Pres. JORGE HORACIO BRITO.

Banco de Valores, SA: Sarmiento 310, C1041AAH Buenos Aires; tel. (11) 4323-6900; fax (11) 4334-1731; e-mail info@banval.sba.com .ar; internet www.bancodevalores.com; f. 1978; cap. 75m., res 169.4m., dep. 1,713.1m. (Dec. 2013); Pres. HÉCTOR JORGE BACQUÉ; Chair. EDUARDO ANTONIO SANTAMARINA; 1 br.

BBVA Banco Francés, SA: Reconquista 199, C1003ABC Buenos Aires; tel. (11) 4346-4000; fax (11) 4346-4320; e-mail mensajes@ bancofrances.com.ar; internet www.bancofrances.com; f. 1886 as Banco Francés del Río de la Plata, SA; changed name to Banco

Francés, SA, in 1998 following merger with Banco de Crédito Argentino; adopted current name in 2000; cap. 536.9m., res 4,595.1m., dep. 43,759.5m. (Dec. 2013); Pres. JORGE CARLOS BLEDEL; Gen. Man. ANTONIO MARTÍNEZ JORQUERA; 308 brs.

HSBC Bank Argentina, SA: Florida 201, 27°, C1005AAE Buenos Aires; tel. (11) 4320-2800; fax (11) 4132-2409; e-mail contactenos@ hsbc.com.ar; internet www.hsbc.com.ar; f. 1978 as Banco Roberts, SA; name changed to HSBC Banco Roberts, SA, in 1998; adopted current name in 1999; cap. 1,244.1m., res 688.4m., dep. 26,408.2m. (June 2013); Pres. and CEO GABRIEL MARTINO; 68 brs.

Industrial and Commercial Bank of China (Argentina), SA (ICBC): Cecilia Grierson 355, Dique 4, Puerto Madero, C1107CPG Buenos Aires; tel. (11) 4820-2000; fax (11) 4820-2184; internet www .icbc.com.ar; f. 2006; frmly known as Standard Bank Argentina, 80% bought by ICBC in 2012; cap. 1,344.6m., res 1,043.4m., dep. 19,283.1m. (Dec. 2013); Pres. WANG LILI; Gen. Man. ALEJANDRO LEDESMA; 98 brs.

Nuevo Banco de Entre Ríos, SA: Monte Caseros 128, E3100ACD Paraná; tel. (343) 420-1200; fax (343) 431-3869; e-mail info@ nuevobersa.com.ar; internet www.nuevobersa.com.ar; f. 1935 as Banco Entrerriano; provincial bank; transferred to private ownership in 1995; adopted present name in 2002; cap. 267m., res 139.2m., dep. 4,964.6m. (Dec. 2013); Pres. ENRIQUE ESKENAZI; Gen. Man. LUIS ROBERTO NÚÑEZ; 73 brs.

Nuevo Banco de la Rioja, SA: Rivadavia 702, F5300ACU La Rioja; tel. (3822) 430575; fax (3822) 430618; e-mail nblrsa@nblr.com.ar; internet www.nblr.com.ar; f. 1994; provincial bank; cap. 21m., res 40m., dep. 504.4m. (Dec. 2012); Pres. JORGE RODOLFO GONZÁLEZ; Gen. Man. JUAN JOSÉ MANUEL LOBATO; 13 brs.

Co-operative Bank

Banco Credicoop Cooperativo Ltdo: Reconquista 484, C1003ABJ Buenos Aires; tel. (11) 4320-5000; fax (11) 4320-5293; e-mail credicoop@bancocredicoop.coop; internet www .bancocredicoop.coop; f. 1979; cap. 1m., res 1,832.8m., dep. 26,074.4m. (June 2013); Chair., Pres. and CEO CARLOS HELLER; Gen. Man. GERARDO GALMÉS; 253 brs.

Bankers' Associations

Asociación de Bancos Argentinos (ADEBA): Juan D. Perón 564, 6°, C1038AAL Buenos Aires; tel. and fax (11) 5238-7790; e-mail info@ adebaargentina.com.ar; internet www.adeba.com.ar; f. 1972; Pres. JORGE HORACIO BRITO; Exec. Dir NORBERTO PERUZZOTTI; 28 mems.

Asociación de Bancos de la Argentina (ABA): San Martín 229, 12°, 1004 Buenos Aires; tel. (11) 4394-1836; fax (11) 4394-6340; e-mail webmaster@aba-argentina.com; internet www .aba-argentina.com; f. 1999 by merger of Asociación de Bancos de la República Argentina (f. 1919) and Asociación de Bancos Argentinos (f. 1972); Pres. CLAUDIO CESARIO; Sec. MARCELO BLANCO; 27 mems.

Asociación de Bancos Públicos y Privados de la República Argentina (ABAPPRA): Florida 470, 1°, C1005AAJ Buenos Aires; tel. and fax (11) 4322-5342; e-mail info@abappra.com.ar; internet www.abappra.com; f. 1959; Pres. JUAN IGNACIO FORLÓN; Exec. Dir DEMETRIO BRAVO AGUILAR; 31 mems.

STOCK EXCHANGES

Bolsa de Comercio de Buenos Aires (BCBA): Sarmiento 299, 1°, C1041AAE Buenos Aires; tel. (11) 4316-7000; fax (11) 4316-7011; e-mail info@bcba.sba.com.ar; internet www.bcba.sba.com.ar; f. 1854; Pres. ADELMO GABBI.

Mercado de Valores de Buenos Aires, SA: 25 de Mayo 367, 8°–10°, C1002ABG Buenos Aires; tel. and fax (11) 4316-6000; e-mail merval@merval.sba.com.ar; internet www.merval.sba.com.ar; f. 1929; Pres. CLAUDIO PÉRÉS MOORE.

There are also stock exchanges at Córdoba, Rosario, Mendoza and La Plata.

Supervisory Authority

Comisión Nacional de Valores (CNV): 25 de Mayo 175, C1002ABC Buenos Aires; tel. (11) 4329-4600; fax (11) 4331-0639; e-mail webadm@cnv.gov.ar; internet www.cnv.gob.ar; monitors capital markets; Pres. ALEJANDRO VANOLI; Gen. Man. RODOLFO CLAUDIO IRIBARREN.

INSURANCE

The following is a list of those offering all classes or a specialized service.

Supervisory Authority

Superintendencia de Seguros de la Nación: Julio A. Roca 721, 5°, C1067ABC Buenos Aires; tel. (11) 4338-4000; fax (11) 4331-9821;

e-mail consultasydenuncias@ssn.gov.ar; internet www.ssn.gov.ar; f. 1938; Supt JUAN A. BONTEMPO.

Major Companies

Allianz Argentina, Cía de Seguros, SA: Avda Corrientes 299, C1043AAC, Buenos Aires; tel. 4222-3443; fax 4320-7143; e-mail atencionalcliente@allianz.com.ar; internet www.allianz.com.ar; f. 1988; fmrly AGF Allianz Argentina; changed name as above 2007; CEO FABIANA CASTIÑEIRA.

Aseguradora de Créditos y Garantías, SA (ACG): Maipú 71, 4°, C1084ABA Buenos Aires; tel. (11) 4320-7200; fax (11) 4320-7277; e-mail infoacg@bristolgroup.com.ar; internet www.rsaacg.com.ar; f. 1965; part of the Bristol Group; Dir MARTÍN MOAR.

Aseguradores de Cauciones, SA: Paraguay 580, C1057AAF Buenos Aires; tel. (11) 5235-3734; fax (11) 5235-3784; e-mail consultas@caucion.com.ar; internet www.caucion.com.ar; f. 1968; all classes; Pres. JOSÉ DE VEDIA.

Berkley International Argentina, SA: Avda Carlos Pellegrini 1023, 1009, Buenos Aires; tel. (11) 4378-8100; e-mail comercial@berkley.com.ar; internet www.berkley.com.ar; f. 1908; part of Berkley International Latinoamérica; Pres. EDUARDO I. LLOBET.

Caja de Seguros, SA: Fitz Roy 957, C1414CHI Buenos Aires; tel. (11) 4857-8118; fax (11) 4857-8001; e-mail suc_villacrespo@lacaja.com.ar; internet www.lacaja.com.ar; f. 1992; Chair. GERARDO WERTHEIN.

CESCE Argentina—Seguro de Crédito y Garantías, SA: Corrientes 345, 7°, C1043AAD Buenos Aires; tel. (11) 4313-4303; fax (11) 4313-2919; e-mail info@casce.com.ar; internet www.casce.com.ar; f. 1967 as Cía Argentina de Seguros de Créditos a la Exportación; part of Grupo CESCE Internacional; covers credit and extraordinary and political risks for Argentine exports; Chair. EDUARDO ANGEL FORNS; Dir MANUEL ALVES.

Chiltington Internacional, SA: Reconquista 559, 8°, C1003ABK Buenos Aires; tel. (11) 4312-8600; fax (11) 4312-8884; e-mail msmith@chiltington.com.ar; internet chiltington.com; f. 1982; Regional Head MARTIN SMITH.

Chubb Argentina de Seguros, SA: Hipólito Bouchard 710, C1106ABL Buenos Aires; tel. (11) 4510-1500; fax (11) 4510-1545; e-mail argentinainfo@chubb.com; internet www.chubb.com/international/argentina; f. 2003; Pres. JOHN D. FINNEGAN.

Cía de Seguros La Mercantil Andina, SA: Avda Eduardo Madero 942, 17°, C1106ACW Buenos Aires; tel. 4310-5400; internet www.mercantilandina.com.ar; f. 1923; part of Grupo Pescarmona since 1978; Gen. Man. PEDRO MIRANTE.

El Comercio Seguros, SA: Maipú 71, baja, C1084ABA Buenos Aires; tel. (11) 4324-1300; fax (11) 4393-1311; e-mail gguerrero@bristolgroup.com.ar; internet www.bristolgroup.com.ar/ec; f. 1889; all classes; part of the Bristol Group; Exec. Dirs CLAUDIO LANDA, JORGE DURBANO; Man. GUIDO GUERRERO.

Generali Argentina, Cía de Seguros, SA: Reconquista 458, 3°, C1003ABJ, Buenos Aires; tel. 4857-7942; fax 4857-7946; e-mail infogenerali@generali.com.ar; internet www.generali.com.ar; f. 1948 as Assicurazioni Generali; changed name as above 1998; Gen. Man. HUGO BRIOSCHI.

HDI Seguros Argentina, SAC: Tte Gral D. Perón 650, 5°, C1038AAN Buenos Aires; tel. (11) 5300-3300; fax (11) 5811-0744; e-mail hdi@hdi.com.ar; internet www.hdi.com.ar; f. 1896 as L'Union IARD, known as L'UNION de Paris Compañía Argentina de Seguros in 2004–11; part of HDI Seguros group; general.

Liberty Seguros Argentina, SA: Avda Paseo Colón 357, C1063ACD Buenos Aires; tel. (11) 4104-0000; fax (11) 4346-0400; e-mail cap@integrityseguros.com.ar; internet www.libertyseguros.com.ar; f. 1995; acquired by Kranos Capital in March 2014; Pres. SUSANA AUGUSTÍN.

Mapfre Argentina: Juana Manso 205, C1107CBE Buenos Aires; tel. (11) 4320-9439; fax (11) 4320-9444; e-mail comunicacion@mapfre.com.ar; internet www.mapfre.com.ar; all classes; Pres. ALBERTO BERGES ROJO.

Prudential Seguros, SA: Avda Leandro N. Alem 855, 5°, C1001AAD Buenos Aires; tel. (11) 4891-5000; fax 4314-3435; e-mail atencionalcliente@prudential.com; internet www.prudentialseguros.com.ar; f. 2000; CEO MAURICIO ZANATTA.

RSA Argentina (United Kingdom): Lima 653, Buenos Aires; tel. (11) 4339-0000; fax (11) 4331-1453; e-mail atencion.cliente@rsagroup.com; internet www.rsagroup.com.ar fmrly known as Royal & Sun Alliance Seguroslife and general; Pres. FERRARO ROBERTO PASCUAL.

Victoria Seguros, SA: Florida 556, C1005AAL Buenos Aires; tel. (11) 4322-1100; fax (11) 4325-9016; e-mail seguros@victoria.com.ar; internet www.victoria.com.ar; f. 1921; Pres. SEBASTIÁN BAGÓ; Vice-Pres. and Exec. Dir DANIEL RICARDO SALAZAR.

Zurich Argentina Cía de Seguros, SA: Cerrito 1010, C1010AAV Buenos Aires; tel. (11) 4819-1010; e-mail servicioalcliente@zurich.com; internet www.zurich.com.ar; f. 1947; all classes; CEO ALCIDES RICARDES.

Insurance Association

Asociación Argentina de Cías de Seguros (AACS): 25 de Mayo 565, 2°, C1002ABK Buenos Aires; tel. (11) 4312-7790; fax (11) 4312-6300; e-mail info@aacs.org.ar; internet www.aacs.org.ar; f. 1894; 27 mems; Pres. FRANCISCO M. ASTELARRA.

Trade and Industry

GOVERNMENT AGENCIES

Agencia de Administración de Bienes del Estado (AABE): Avda José Ramos Mejía 1302, 3°, C1104AJN Buenos Aires; e-mail info@bienesdelestado.gob.ar; internet www.bienesdelestado.gob.ar; f. 2012 following dissolution of Organismo Nacional de Administración de Bienes del Estado; responsible for administration of state property; supervised by the Cabinet Chief; Pres. Dr ANTONIO ALBERTO VULCANO.

Consejo Federal de Inversiones: San Martín 871, C1004AAQ Buenos Aires; tel. (11) 4317-0700; fax (11) 4315-1238; e-mail administrator@cfired.org.ar; internet www.cfired.org.ar; f. 1959; federal board to co-ordinate domestic and foreign investment and provide technological aid for the provinces; Sec.-Gen. JUAN JOSÉ CIÁCERA.

Dirección de Forestación (DF): Paseo Colón 982, Anexo Jardín, C1063ACW Buenos Aires; tel. (11) 4349-2103; fax (11) 4349-2833; e-mail forest@minagri.gob.ar; internet www.forestacion.gov.ar; assumed the responsibilities of the national forestry commission (Instituto Forestal Nacional—IFONA) in 1991, following its dissolution; supervised by the Secretaría de Agricultura, Ganadería, Pesca y Alimentos; maintains the Centro de Documentación e Información Forestal; Dir MIRTA ROSA LARRIEU.

Instituto de Desarrollo Económico y Social (IDES): Aráoz 2838, C1425DGT Buenos Aires; tel. (11) 4804-4949; fax (11) 4804-5856; e-mail ides@ides.org.ar; internet www.ides.org.ar; f. 1960; investigation into social sciences and promotion of social and economic devt; 1,100 mems; Pres. ALEJANDRO DUJOVNE.

Instituto Nacional de Tecnología Agropecuaria (INTA): Rivadavia 1439, C1033AAE Buenos Aires; tel. (11) 4338-4600; internet inta.gob.ar; f. 1956; research and support for technological advances in agriculture; Pres. FRANCISCO JUAN OSCAR ANGLESIO.

Subsecretaría de Desarrollo de Inversiones y Promoción Comercial: Esmeralda 1212, 6°, C1005AAG Buenos Aires; tel. (11) 4819-7488; fax (11) 4819-7269; e-mail info@inversiones.gob.ar; internet www.inversiones.gob.ar; fmrly Agencia Nacional de Desarrollo de Inversiones (ProsperAr); promotion of investment in Argentina; Dir CARLOS BIANCO.

Unidad de Coordinación y Evaluación de Subsidios al Consumo Interno (UCESCI): Hipólito Yrigoyen 250, Buenos Aires; tel. (11) 4349-5000; e-mail ucesci@ucesci.gob.ar; internet www.ucesci.gob.ar; f. 2011 following dissolution of Oficina Nacional de Control Comercial Agropecuario; promotion and development of the agricultural sector; supervised jtly by the Ministries of Economy and Public Finance, Agriculture, Livestock and Fisheries, and Industry; Exec. Sec. LISANDRO TANZI.

DEVELOPMENT ORGANIZATIONS

Instituto Argentino del Petróleo y Gas: Maipú 639, C1006ACG Buenos Aires; tel. (11) 5277-4274; fax (11) 5277-4263; e-mail informa@iapg.org.ar; internet www.iapg.org.ar; f. 1957; promotes the devt of petroleum exploration and research; Pres. ERNESTO LÓPEZ ANADÓN.

Instituto para el Desarrollo Social Argentino (IDESA): Montevideo 451, 11°, Of. 33, C1019ABI Buenos Aires; tel. (11) 4374-7660; e-mail atorres@idesa.org; internet www.idesa.org; centre for research in public policies related to social devt; Pres. OSVALDO GIORDANO; Exec. Dir ALEJANDRA TORRES.

Sociedad Rural Argentina: Florida 460, C1005AAJ Buenos Aires; tel. (11) 4324-4700; e-mail acciongremial@sra.org.ar; internet www.sra.org.ar; f. 1866; private org. to promote the devt of agriculture; Pres. Dr LUIS MIGUEL ETCHEVEHERE; 9,400 mems.

CHAMBERS OF COMMERCE

Cámara Argentina de Comercio: Leandro N. Alem 36, C1003AAN Buenos Aires; tel. (11) 5300-9000; fax (11) 5300-9058; e-mail difusion2@cac.com.ar; internet www.cac.com.ar; f. 1927; Pres. CARLOS RAÚL DE LA VEGA; Sec. ALBERTO O. DRAGOTTO.

Cámara de Comercio Argentino Brasileña: Montevideo 770, 12°, C1019ABP Buenos Aires; tel. (11) 4811-4503; e-mail institucionales@cambras.org.ar; internet www.cambras.org.ar; Pres. JORGE RODRÍGUEZ APARICIO.

Cámara de Comercio de los Estados Unidos en la República Argentina (AMCHAM): Viamonte 1133, 8°, C1053ABW Buenos Aires; tel. (11) 4371-4500; fax (11) 4371-8400; e-mail amcham@ amchamar.com.ar; internet www.amchamar.com.ar; f. 1918; US Chamber of Commerce; Pres. JUAN MANUEL VAQUER; CEO ALEJANDRO DÍAZ.

Cámara de Comercio Exterior de Rosario: Córdoba 1868, 1°, Of. 114 y 115, Rosario, S2000AXD Santa Fe; tel. and fax (341) 425-7147; e-mail ccer@commerce.com.ar; internet www.commerce.com.ar; f. 1958; deals with imports and exports; Pres. JUAN CARLOS RETAMERO; Vice-Pres. GUILLERMO BECCANI; 150 mems.

Cámara de Comercio, Industria y Producción de la República Argentina: Florida 1/15, 4°, C1005AAA Buenos Aires; tel. (11) 4342-8252; fax (11) 4331-9116; e-mail correo@cacipra.org.ar; internet www.cacipra.org.ar; f. 1913; Pres. Dr CARLOS A. CANTA YOY; 1,500 mems.

Cámara de Comercio Italiana de Rosario: Córdoba 1868, 1°, S2000AXD, Rosario; tel. and fax (341) 426-6789; e-mail info@ italrosario.com; internet www.ccir.com.ar; f. 1985; promotes Argentine–Italian trade; Pres. EDUARDO ROMAGNOLI; Sec.-Gen. GUSTAVO MICATROTTA; 104 mems.

Cámara de Exportadores de la República Argentina: Roque Sáenz Peña 740, 1°, C1035AAP Buenos Aires; tel. and fax (11) 4394-4482; e-mail contacto@cera.org.ar; internet www.cera.org.ar; f. 1943; export promotion; 700 mems; Pres. Dr ENRIQUE S. MANTILLA; Gen. Man. RUBÉN E. GIORDANO.

Similar chambers are located in most of the larger centres, and there are many other foreign chambers of commerce.

INDUSTRIAL AND TRADE ASSOCIATIONS

Asociación Argentina de Productores Porcinos: Florida 520, 2°, Of. 205, C1005AAL Buenos Aires; internet www.porcinos.org.ar; f. 1922; promotion of pork products; Pres. JUAN LUIS UCCELLI.

Asociación de Importadores y Exportadores de la República Argentina: Manuel Belgrano 124, 1°, C1092AAO Buenos Aires; tel. (11) 4342-0010; fax (11) 4342-1312; e-mail aiera@aiera.org.ar; internet www.aiera.org; f. 1966; Pres. JUAN CARLOS PEREYRA; Man. ADRIANO A. DE FINA.

Asociación Empresaria Argentina (AEA): Madero 1020, 22°, C1408BRT Buenos Aires; internet www.aeanet.net; f. 2002; represents private sector cos; Pres. JAIME CAMPOS.

Bodegas de Argentina: Thames 2334, 16A, C1425FIH Buenos Aires; tel. (11) 5786-1220; fax (11) 5786-1266; e-mail info@ bodegasdeargentinaac.com; internet www.bodegasdeargentina.com; f. 2001 following merger between Centro de Bodegueros de Mendoza and Asociación Vitivinícola Argentina; wine industry; Pres. JUAN JOSÉ CANAY.

Cámara de la Industria Aceitera de la República Argentina—Centro de Exportadores de Cereales: Bouchard 454, 7°, C1106ABS Buenos Aires; tel. (11) 4311-4477; fax (11) 4311-3899; internet www.ciaracec.com.ar; f. 1980; vegetable oil producers and grain exporters; 49 mems; Pres. ALBERTO RODRIGUEZ.

Cámara de la Industria Química y Petroquímica (CIQyP): Avda Córdoba 629, 4°, C1054AAF Buenos Aires; tel. (11) 4313-1000; fax (11) 4313-1059; e-mail informacion@ciqyp.org.ar; internet www.ciqyp.org.ar; Pres. ALBERTO CANCIO; Exec. Dir JOSÉ MARÍA FUMAGALLI.

Cámara de Informática y Comunicaciones de la República Argentina (CICOMRA): Avda Córdoba 744, 2° D, C1054AAT Buenos Aires; tel. (11) 4325-8839; fax (11) 4325-9604; e-mail gerente@cicomra.org.ar; internet www.cicomra.org.ar; f. 1985; represents enterprises in the communications sector; Pres. NORBERTO CAPELLÁN; Exec. Dir ALFREDO BALLARINO.

Confederación Argentina de la Mediana Empresa (CAME): Florida 15, 3°, C1005AAA Buenos Aires; tel. (11) 5556-5556; fax (11) 5556-5502; e-mail info@came.org.ar; internet redcame.org.ar; f. 1956; fmrly Coordinadora de Actividades Mercantiles Empresarias; adopted current name 2006; small and medium enterprises; Pres. OSVALDO CORNIDE.

Confederación Intercooperativa Agropecuaria Ltda (CONINAGRO): Lavalle 348, 4°, C1047AAH Buenos Aires; tel. (11) 4311-4664; fax (11) 4311-0623; internet www.coninagro.org.ar; f. 1958; farming co-operative; Pres. CARLOS ALBERTO GARETTO; Gen. Man. DANIEL EDUARDO ASSEFF.

Confederaciones Rurales Argentinas (CRA): México 628, 2°, C1097AAN Buenos Aires; tel. (11) 4300-4451; fax (11) 4300-4471; internet www.cra.org.ar; f. 1943; promotion and devt of agricultural activities; 14 feds comprising over 300 mem. orgs, representing 109,000 farmers; Pres. Dr RUBÉN FERRERO.

Consorcio de Exportadores de Carnes Argentinas (ABC): San Martín 575, 5°B, C1004AAK Buenos Aires; tel. (11) 4394-9734; fax (11) 4394-9658; e-mail gerencia@abc-consorcio.com.ar; internet www.abc-consorcio.com.ar; f. 2002 following the merger between the Asociación de Industrias Argentinas de Carnes and several meat exporters; meat industry; refrigerated and canned beef and mutton; Pres. MARIO DARÍO RAVETTINO.

Federación Agraria Argentina (FAA): Alfonsina Storni 745, S2000DYA Rosario, Santa Fe; tel. (341) 512-2000; fax (341) 512-2001; e-mail comunicacion@faa.com.ar; internet www.faa.com.ar; f. 1912; oversees the interests of small and medium-sized grain producers; Pres. EDUARDO BUZZI.

Federación Lanera Argentina: 25 de Mayo 516, 4°, C1002ABL Buenos Aires; tel. (11) 5199-5617; e-mail info@flasite.com; internet www.flasite.com; f. 1929; wool industry; Pres. RAÚL ERNESTO ZAMBONI; Sec. JUAN PABLO LEFEBVRE; 40 mems.

Unión Industrial Argentina (UIA): Avda de Mayo 1147/57, C1085ABB Buenos Aires; tel. (11) 4124-2300; fax (11) 4124-2301; e-mail uia@uia.org.ar; internet www.uia.org.ar; f. 1887; re-established in 1974 with the fusion of the Confederación Industrial Argentina (CINA) and the Confederación General de la Industria; following the dissolution of the CINA in 1977, the UIA was formed in 1979; asscn of mfrs, representing industrial corpns; Pres. Dr HÉCTOR MENDEZ; Sec. JOSÉ IGNACIO DE MENDIGUREN.

STATE HYDROCARBON COMPANY

YPF, SA: Macacha Güemes 515, CP 1364, C1106BKK Buenos Aires; tel. (11) 4329-2000; fax (11) 4329-5717; e-mail federico.etiennot@ypf.com; internet www.ypf.com; f. 1922 as Yacimientos Petrolíferos Fiscales, a state-owned company; bought by Repsol (Spain) and changed name as Repsol YPF, SA in 1992; in 2012 the Govt announced it was expropriating 51% of Repsol's shares in YPF; final Repsol shares sold in May 2013; petroleum and gas exploration and production; CEO MIGUEL MATÍAS GALUCCIO; 9,750 employees.

YPF Tecnología, SA: La Plata; f. 2012; 51% owned by YPF and 49% owned by Consejo Nacional de Investigaciones Científicas y Técnicas; devt of oil and gas exploration and exploitation techniques.

MAJOR COMPANIES

AcerBrag, SA (Aceros Bragado): Panamericana Km 49.5, Edif. Boreau Pilar, 3°, 1629 Pilar, CD1629 Buenos Aires; tel. (11) 4006-7100; fax (11) 4006-7101; internet www.acerbrag.com; f. 1964; foundry, mill rolls, bearing trucks, laminating; 53% owned by Votorantim Metais, Brazil; Gen. Man. GUSTAVO GONZAGA DE OLIVEIRA; 495 employees.

Acindar, SA: Dr Ignacio Arieta 4936, B1766DQP Tablada, Buenos Aires; tel. (11) 5077-5000; fax (11) 4719-8501; e-mail sac@acindar.com.ar; internet www.acindar.com.ar; f. 1942; production of iron and steel; part of ArcelorMittal group (Luxembourg); CEO JOSÉ GIRAUDO; Exec. Dir GABRIEL DATTILO; 3,922 employees.

ADM Argentina, SA: Maipu 942, 7°, C1006ACN, Buenos Aires; tel. (11) 4114-5100; internet www.adm.com; f. 1999; food grain exporter; subsidiary of Archer Daniels Midland Co, USA; Pres. (South America) VALMOR SCHAFFER.

Agrometal, SA: Misiones 1974, X2659BIN Monte Maíz, Córdoba; tel. (34) 6847-1311; fax (34) 6847-1804; internet www.agrometal.com; manufacture of agricultural machinery; Pres. ROSANA MARÍA NEGRINI.

Alpargatas, SAIC: Azara 841, C1267ABQ Buenos Aires; tel. (11) 4124-2400; fax (11) 4303-2401; e-mail asuntoslegales@alpargatas.com.ar; internet www.alpargatas.com.ar; f. 1885; textile and footwear mfrs; Pres. MÁRCIO LUIZ SIMOES UTSCH; 4,000 employees.

ALUAR (Aluminio Argentino, SAIC): Pasteur 4600, B1644AMV Victoria, Buenos Aires; tel. (11) 4725-8000; fax (11) 4725-8091; internet www.aluar.com.ar; f. 1974; aluminium production; Pres. JAVIER SANTIAGO MADANES QUINTANILLA; 2,216 employees.

Atanor, SCA: Albarellos 4914, B1605AFR Munro, Buenos Aires; tel. (11) 4721-3400; internet www.atanor.com.ar; f. 1943; producers of chemicals, petrochemicals, agrochemicals and sugar; Pres. MIGUEL ANGEL GONZÁLEZ; 768 employees.

Axion Energy Argentina, SRL: Torre Boston, 19°, Carlos María Della Paolera 265, C1001ADA Buenos Aires; tel. (11) 4705-7000; fax (11) 4319-1163; e-mail csslubes-arg@axionenergy.com; internet www.axionenergy.com; f. 1911; active in all spheres of the petroleum industry; acquired by Bridas Corpn in 2012; Pres. ANTONIO ESTRANYY GENDRE; Gen. Man. CLAUDIO GRAJEWER; 2,200 employees.

Bayer Argentina, SA: Ricardo Gutiérrez 3652, B1605EHD Munro, Buenos Aires; tel. (11) 4762-7000; fax (11) 4762-7100; internet www.bayer.com.ar; f. 1911; production of chemicals, agrochemicals and pharmaceuticals; subsidiary of Bayer AG, Germany; Pres. and CEO KURT SOLAND.

BGH, SA: Brasil 731, C1154AAK Buenos Aires; tel. (11) 4309-2000; fax (11) 6310-4033; e-mail info@bgh.com.ar; internet www.bgh.com.ar; electronic appliances mfrs; f. 1913 as Boris Garfunkel e Hijos; Pres. ALBERTO HOJMAN; Gen. Man. GUSTAVO CASTELLI.

Boldt, SA: Aristóbulo del Valle 1257, C1295ADA Buenos Aires; tel. (11) 4309-5400; fax (11) 4361-3435; e-mail contact@boldt.com.ar; internet www.boldt.com.ar; information technology, telecommunications, land and leisure management; Chair. ANTONIO ANGEL TABANELLI; 932 employees.

Borax Argentina, SA: Huaytiquina 227, Campo Quijano, A4407AVE Salta; tel. (38) 7490-4030; fax (38) 4920-4031; e-mail boraxargentina@borax.com; internet www.borax.com; owned by Rio Tinto (UK and Australia); mining of borates; Pres. ALBERTO CARLOS TRUNZO.

Bunge Argentina: Avda 25 de Mayo 501, 1002, Buenos Aires; tel. (11) 5169-3200; fax (11) 4382-5605; e-mail BAR.comm@bunge.com; internet www.bungeargentina.com; f. 1884; agri-business; subsidiary of Bunge Ltd, USA; CEO ENRIQUE HUMANES.

Cargill, SA: Leandro N. Alem 928, C1001AAR, Buenos Aires; tel. (11) 4317-7000; fax (11) 4317-7077; e-mail Atencion_Clientes@cargill.com; internet www.cargill.com.ar; f. 1947; agri-business; Pres. HUGO KRAJNC; 4,000 employees.

Celulosa Argentina, SA: Avda H. Pomilio, S2154FVS Capitán Bermúdez, Santa Fe; tel. (341) 491-1402; fax (341) 491-1401; e-mail contacto.comercial@celulosaargentina.com.ar; internet www.celulosaargentina.com.ar; f. 1929; mfrs of paper and paper products; Pres. DOUGLAS ALBRECHT; 1,900 employees.

Cencosud, SA: Larrea 847, 1°, 1117 Buenos Aires; tel. (11) 4964-8000; fax (11) 4964-8039; e-mail laempresa@disco.com.ar; internet www.cencosud.com.ar; f. 1961; owned by Cencosud, SA (Chile); supermarket chain; outlet brands include Easy, Jumbo, Disco and Vea; Pres. HORST PAULMANN.

Cervecería y Maltería Quilmes, SAICA: 12 de Octubre y Gran Canaria s/n, B1878AAB Quilmes, Buenos Aires; tel. (11) 4394-1700; fax (11) 4326-0026; e-mail contacto@cerveceriaymalteriaquilmes.com; internet www.cerveceriaymalteriaquilmes.com; f. 1888; beer and malt producers; part of Anheuser-Busch InBev, Belgium; Exec. Dir FRANCISCÓ SÁ; 4,700 employees.

Chevron Argentina, SRL: Peron 925, 4°, C1038AAS Buenos Aires; tel. (11) 4320-7400; internet www.chevron.com/countries/argentina; wholly owned subsidiary of Chevron Corpn, USA; Pres. MICHAEL KOCH.

Coca-Cola Andina Argentina, SA: Ruta 19, Km 3.7, CP X5001CD2, Córdoba; tel. (351) 496-8800; fax (351) 496-8826; internet www.koandina.com; f. 1995 in Argentina following Grupo Andina's purchase of Mendoza Refrescos and Rosario Refrescos; owned by Embotelladora Andina, SA; bottling co for Coca-Cola; Chair. JUAN CLARO GONZÁLEZ.

Dow Química Argentina, SA: Blvd Cecilia Grierson 355, Dique IV, 25°, Puerto Madero, C1107CPG Buenos Aires; tel. (11) 4319-0100; fax (11) 4319-0381; e-mail fbepoli@dow.com; internet www.dow.com/argentina; fmrly PBBPolisur, SA; wholly owned by Dow Chemical since 2005; petrochemicals; Pres. GASTÓN REMY.

DuPont Argentina: Ingeniero Butty 240, 10°, C1001AFB Buenos Aires; tel. (11)4021-4700; fax (11) 4021-4737; e-mail Gabriela.capacete@arg.dupont.com; internet www.dupont.com.ar; f. 1937; polymer production; Pres. JUAN VAQUER; 600 employees.

Dycasa, SA: Leandro N. Alem 986, 4°, C1001AAR Buenos Aires; tel. (11) 4318-0200; fax (11) 4318-0230; e-mail comercial@dycasa.com.ar; internet www.dycasa.com; f. 1968; part of Grupo ACS, Spain; construction; Pres. PABLO RUIZ PARRILLA.

Eco de los Andes, SA: 12 de Octubre y Gran Canaria, C1878AAB Quilmes; e-mail ecocontacto@quilmes.com.ar; internet www.ecodelosandes.com.ar; f. 1994; 51% owned by Nestlé Waters (Switzerland) and 49% owned by Quilmes Industrial, Luxembourg; bottled water producer.

Ferrum, SA de Cerámica y Metalurgia: España 496, B1870BWJ Avellaneda, Buenos Aires; tel. (11) 4222-1500; fax (11) 4229-6244; e-mail info@ferrum.com; internet www.ferrum.com; f. 1911; mfrs of sanitary products and building materials; Pres. GUILLERMO VIEGENER; Man. Dir DANIEL H. CALABRÓ.

Ford Argentina, SA: Henry Ford/Ruta Panamericana s/n, Ricardo Rojas, 1617 Buenos Aires; tel. (11) 4756-9000; fax (11) 4756-9001; e-mail cacford@ford.com; internet www.ford.com.ar; f. 1913; manufacture of motor vehicles; owned by Ford Motor Co, USA; Pres. ENRIQUE ALEMAÑY; 5,200 employees.

General Electric Technical Services Co, Inc: Leandro N. Alem 619, 9°, 1001 Buenos Aires; tel. (11) 4489-8989; fax (11) 4489-8989; internet www.ge.com/ar; f. 1920; sales of industrial equipment; engineering services; subsidiary of International General Electric Co, USA; Pres. REINALDO GARCÍA; 900 employees.

Grimoldi, SA: Zapiola 1863, B1712ISQ Castelar, Buenos Aires; e-mail nretamar@mail.grimoldi.com.ar; internet www.grimoldi.com.ar; footwear retailers; Pres. ALBERTO LUIS GRIMOLDI.

Grupo Arcor: Maipú 1210, 2°, 3° y 6°, C1006ACT Buenos Aires; tel. (11) 4310-9500; internet www.arcor.com.ar; f. 1951; chocolate and candy products; Pres. LUIS ALEJANDRO PAGANI; Exec. Dir JUAN RODRÍGUEZ NOUCHE.

Holcim (Argentina), SA: A. Moreau de Justo 140, 1°, C1107AAD Buenos Aires; tel. (11) 4510-4800; fax (11) 4510-4859; e-mail conexion.argentina@holcim.com; internet www.holcim.com.ar; f. 1930 as Cementos Minetti; name changed as above in 2011; mfrs of hydraulic cement; Pres. Dr UBALDO JOSÉ AGUIRRE; CEO JUAN JAVIER NEGRI; 830 employees.

IBM Argentina, SA: Hipólito Yrigoyen 2149, Martínez, C1089AAO Buenos Aires; tel. (11) 4898-4898; fax (11) 4313-2360; e-mail ibm_directo@ar.ibm.com; internet www.ibm.com.ar; f. 1923; computer hardware and software; owned by IBM Corpn, USA; Gen. Man. ROBERTO ALEXANDER; 7,200 employees.

Inversiones y Representaciones, SA (IRSA): Edif. Intercontinental Plaza, 22°, Moreno 877, C1091AAQ Buenos Aires; tel. (11) 4323-7400; fax (11) 4323-7480; e-mail finanzas@irsa.com.ar; internet www.irsa.com.ar; f. 1943; land and property development; Chair. EDUARDO SERGIO ELSZTAIN.

Laboratorios Bagó, SA: Bernardo de Yrigoyen 248, C1072AAF Buenos Aires; tel. (11) 4344-2000; fax (11) 4334-5813; e-mail hdacunha@bago.co.ar; internet www.bago.com/BagoArg; f. 1934; pharmaceuticals; Dir-Gen. Dr JUAN PABLO BAGÓ; 936 employees.

Ledesma, SAAIC: Corrientes 415, 8°, C1043AAE Buenos Aires; tel. (11) 4378-1555; fax (11) 4325-7666; e-mail adiciancio@ledesma.com.ar; internet www.ledesma.com.ar; f. 1908; sugar, paper and fruit producers; Pres. Dr CARLOS HERMINIO BLAQUIER; 3,970 employees.

Louis Dreyfus Commodities Argentina, SA: Olga Cossettini 240, 2°, C1107CCF, Buenos Aires; tel. (11) 4324-6900; fax (11) 4318-6943; internet www.ldc.com.ar; f. 1925; agri-business; Head, South and West Latin America GONZALO RAMIREZ MARTIARENA; Exec. Chair. SERGE SCHOEN.

Loma Negra, CIASA: Reconquista 1088, 7°, 1003 Buenos Aires; tel. (11) 4319-3000; fax (11) 4319-3003; e-mail info@lomanegra.com.ar; internet www.lomanegra.com.ar; f. 1926; subsidiary of Camargo Corrêa, SA (Brazil); cement and building materials manufacturing; Dir-Gen. OSVALDO SCHÜTZ.

Massalin Particulares, SA: Leandro N. Alem 466, 9°, C1003AAR Buenos Aires; tel. and fax (11) 4705-2200; f. 1980; owned by Philip Morris Int; cigarette and tobacco producers; Pres., Latin America and Canada MARTIN KING; 2,600 employees.

Mondelez International Argentina: Henry Ford 3200, B1610BKW Ricardo Rojas, Tigre, Buenos Aires; tel. (33) 2741-2600; fax (33) 2745-6000; e-mail consultas.ar@kraftla.com; internet www.mondelezinternational.com; f. 1933; fmrly Kraft Foods; changed name as above in 2012; chocolate, sweets and frozen confectionery; Pres. GUSTAVO ABELENDA.

Mercedes-Benz Argentina, SA: Blvd Azucena Villaflor 435, Puerto Madero, C1107CII Buenos Aires; tel. (11) 4808-8700; fax (11) 4808-8701; e-mail soledad.carranza@daimler.com; internet www.mercedes-benz.com.ar; f. 1951; mfrs of trucks, buses and engines; subsidiary of Daimler AG, Germany; Pres. ROLAND ZEY; 2,000 employees.

Molinos Río de la Plata, SA: Uruguay 4075, B1644HKG Victoria, Buenos Aires; tel. (11) 4340-1100; fax (11) 4340-1200; e-mail info@molinos.com.ar; internet www.molinos.com.ar; f. 1902; mfrs of flour and grain products; part of the Pérez Companc group; Pres. LUIS PEREZ COMPANC; 5,000 employees.

Morixe Hermanos, SA: Santa Fe 846, 8°, C1059ABP Buenos Aires; tel. (11) 4312-8500; fax (11) 4431-4079; e-mail info@morixehnos.com.ar; internet www.morixe.com.ar; f. 1923; flour and grain processing; Pres. FERNANDO ANDRÉS SANSUSTE.

Nestlé Argentina: Libertador 1855, Vicente López, C1425AAE Buenos Aires; tel. (11) 4329-8100; fax (11) 4329-8200; e-mail comunicaciones.corporativas@ar.nestle.com; internet www.nestle.com.ar; mfrs of condensed milk, instant coffee, milk powder and confectionery; subsidiary of Nestlé, SA (Switzerland); f. 1930; Pres. and CEO FÉLIX ALLEMANN; 3,400 employees.

Nobleza-Piccardo, SAICF: San Martín 645, CP 899, B1650HVE Buenos Aires; tel. (11) 4724-8444; fax (11) 4313-2499; e-mail pablo_cattoni@bat.com; internet www.noblezapiccardo.com; f. 1898; cigarette and tobacco mfrs; owned by British American Tobacco (UK); Gen. Man. JORGE DAVYT; 1,200 employees.

Peugeot Citroën Argentina, SA: Juan Domingo Perón 1001, Villa Bosch, 1684 Provincia de Buenos Aires; tel. (11) 4734-3005; fax (11) 4734-3007; e-mail info@psa-peugeot-citroen.com.ar; internet www.psa-peugeot-citroen.com.ar; f. 1965 as Sevel Argentina, SA; subsidiary of PSA Peugeot Citroën, France; automobile mfrs; Pres. and Dir-Gen. CARLOS GOMES; 3,600 employees.

Philips Argentina, SA: Vedía 3892, C1430DAL Buenos Aires; tel. (11) 4546-7777; fax (11) 4546-7600; internet www.philips.com.ar; f. 1935; mfrs of electrical equipment; subsidiary of Koninklijke Philips Electronics NV, Netherlands; CEO GUSTAVO VERNA.

Pirelli Neumaticos, SAIC: Cervantes 1901, Merlo, 1722 Buenos Aires; tel. (11) 4489-6000; fax (11) 4489-6603; internet www.pirelli .com.ar; tyre mfr; Pres. FRANCO LIVINI; f. 1948; 1,900 employees.

Pluspetrol Exploración y Producción, SA: Edif. Pluspetrol, Lima 339, C1073AAG Buenos Aires; tel. (11) 4340-2222; fax (11) 4340-2215; e-mail rrhh-cv@pluspetrol.net; internet www.pluspetrol .net; f. 1977; oil and gas exploration and production; Country Man. ELISEO BOUZA; 497 employees.

Renault Argentina, SA: Fray Justo María de Oro 1744, 1414 Buenos Aires; tel. (11) 4778-2000; fax (11) 4778-2023; e-mail src-renault.argentina@renault.com; internet www.renault.com.ar; f. 1955 as Ciadea, SA; subsidiary of Renault, SA, France; motor vehicle mfrs; Pres. THIERRY KOSKAS; 2,211 employees.

Rigolleau, SA: Lisandro de la Torre 1651, Berazategui, B1884MFK Buenos Aires; tel. (11) 4256-2010; fax (11) 4256-2544; e-mail info@ rigolleau.com.ar; internet www.rigolleau.com.ar; f. 1882; makers of glass and glass products; Pres. ENRIQUE FRANCISCO CATTORINI; 1,485 employees.

Roggio, SA: La Voz del Interior 8500, X5000FMR Córdoba; tel. (351) 638-0000; fax (351) 638-0001; e-mail contacto@roggio.com.ar; internet www.roggio.com.ar; f. 1908; group of construction companies; Pres. VITO REMO ROGGIO; 2,156 employees.

Shell Compañía Argentina de Petróleo, SA: Roque Saenz Peña 788, C1035AAP Buenos Aires; tel. (11) 4130-2000; e-mail consultas@ shelldirecto.com.ar; internet www.shell.com.ar; f. 1922; active in all spheres of the petroleum industry; owned by Royal Dutch Shell; Pres. (Argentina) JUAN JOSÉ ARANGUREN.

Tabacal Agroindustria: Leandro N. Alem 986, 9°, C1001AAR Buenos Aires; tel. (11) 5167-2100; fax (11) 4576-7720; e-mail ingenio@tabacal.com.ar; internet www.tabacal.com.ar; f. 1920; sugar and alcohol production; owned by Seaboard Corpn of the USA; Pres. HUGO ROSSI.

Techint Compañía Técnica Internacional, SACI: Torre Bouchard Plaza, Hipólito Bouchard 557, C1106ABG Buenos Aires; tel. (11) 4018-4100; fax (11) 4018-1000; e-mail info@techint.com; internet engineering.techint.com; f. 1946; steel and petroleum extraction and refining; part of the Techint Group; Exec. Pres. and CEO CARLOS BACHER.

Ternium Siderar, SA: Edif. Carlos Pellegrini, 20°, Leandro N. Alem 1067, C1001AAF Buenos Aires; tel. (11) 4018-2100; fax (11) 4018-1000; e-mail aparej@siderar.com; internet www.ternium.com.ar; f. 1962; part of the Techint Group; mfrs of steel; also operates in Mexico and Venezuela; CEO DANIEL AGUSTÍN NOVEGIL; 5,695 employees.

UTILITIES

Regulatory Authorities

Compañía Administradora del Mercado Mayorista Eléctrico, SA (CAMMESA): Avda Madero 942, 1°, C1106ACW Buenos Aires; tel. (11) 4319-3700; e-mail agentes@cammesa.com.ar; internet portalweb.cammesa.com; f. 1992; responsible for administering the wholesale electricity market; 20% state-owned, 80% by electricity companies; Pres. JULIO MIGUEL DE VIDO (Minister of Federal Planning, Public Investment and Services); Gen. Man. JUAN MANUEL ABUD.

Ente Nacional Regulador de la Electricidad (ENRE): Avda Eduardo Madero 1020, 10°, C1106ACX Buenos Aires; tel. (11) 4510-4600; fax (11) 4510-4210; internet www.enre.gov.ar; f. 1993; agency for regulation and control of electricity generation, transmission and distribution; Pres. RICARDO MARTÍNEZ LEONE.

Ente Nacional Regulador del Gas (ENARGAS): Suipacha 636, 10°, C1008AAN Buenos Aires; tel. (11) 4325-2500; fax (11) 4348-0550; internet www.enargas.gov.ar; regulates and monitors gas utilities; brought under govt control in 2007; Insp. ANTONIO LUIS PRONSATO.

Electricity

AES Argentina: Román Subiza 1960, San Nicolás de los Arroyos, CP 2900, Buenos Aires; tel. (336) 448-7100; fax (336) 448-7103; e-mail rrii@aes.com; internet www.aesargentina.com.ar; f. 1993; subsidiary of AES Corpn, USA; owns and operates 6 hydroelectric plants: Alicura, Cabra Corral, Caracoles, El Tunal, Quebrada de Ullum and Ullum; and three thermoelectric plants: AES Paraná, Central Sarmiento and Central Térmica San Nicolás; Pres. PATRICIO TESTORELLI.

Central Hidroeléctrica El Chocón, SA: Avda España 3301, C1107ANA Buenos Aires; tel. (11) 4300-5002; e-mail clujambio@ elchoconsa.com.ar; internet www.hidroelectricaelchocon.com; Gen. Man. FERNANDO CLAUDIO ANTOGNAZZA.

Central Puerto, SA (CEPU): Tomás Edison 2701, Dársena E, Puerto de Buenos Aires, C1104BAB Buenos Aires; tel. (11) 4317-5000; fax (11) 4317-5099; e-mail info@centralpuerto.com; internet www.centralpuerto.com; electricity generating co; Pres. JOSÉ MARÍA VÁZQUEZ.

Comisión Nacional de Energía Atómica (CNEA): Avda del Libertador 8250, C1429BNP Buenos Aires; tel. (11) 4704-1000; fax (11) 4704-1154; e-mail comunicacion@cnea.gov.ar; internet www .cnea.gov.ar; f. 1950; nuclear energy science and technology; operates 3 nuclear power stations for research purposes; Pres. NORMA LUISA BOERO.

Comisión Técnica Mixta de Salto Grande (CTMSG): Leandro N. Alem 449, C1003AAE Buenos Aires; tel. (11) 5554-3400; fax (11) 5554-3402; e-mail secgral@saltogrande.org; internet www .saltogrande.org; operates Salto Grande hydroelectric station, which has an installed capacity of 650 MW; jt Argentine-Uruguayan project; Pres., Argentine delegation JUAN CARLOS CRESTO; Gen. Mans JUAN CARLOS CRESTO (Argentina), GABRIEL RODRÍGUEZ (Uruguay).

Dirección Provincial de Energía: Calle 55, 629, entre 7 y 8, La Plata, B1900BGY Buenos Aires; tel. and fax (221) 427-1185; e-mail dpe@dpe.mosp.gba.gov.ar; internet www.dpe.mosp.gba.gov.ar; f. 1957 as Dirección de Energía de la Provincia de Buenos Aires; name changed as above in 2000; electricity co for province of Buenos Aires; Dir NÉSTOR CALLEGARI.

Empresa Distribuidora y Comercializadora Norte, SA (EDENOR): Avda del Libertador 6363, C1428ARG Buenos Aires; tel. (11) 4346-8400; fax (11) 4346-5441; e-mail ofitel@edenor.com.ar; internet www.edenor.com.ar; f. 1992; distribution of electricity; Pres. RICARDO ALEJANDRO TORRES; Dir-Gen. EDGARDO ALBERTO VOLOSIN.

Empresa Distribuidora Sur, SA (EDESUR): San José 140, C1076AAD Buenos Aires; tel. (11) 4381-8981; fax (11) 4383-3699; e-mail emailservicio@edesur.com.ar; internet www.edesur.com.ar; f. 1992; distribution of electricity; Gen. Man. ANTONIO JEREZ AGUDO.

Endesa Costanera, SA (CECCO): España 3301, C1107ANA Buenos Aires; tel. (11) 4307-3040; fax (11) 4300-4168; e-mail comercialweb@ccostanera.com.ar; internet www.endesacostanera .com; subsidiary of Endesa (Spain); generation, transmission, distribution and sale of thermal electric energy; Pres. JOAQUÍN GALINDO VÉLEZ; Gen. Man. JOSÉ MIGUEL GRANGED BRUÑEN.

Energía Argentina, SA (ENARSA): Avda Libertador 1068, 2°, C1112ABN Buenos Aires; tel. and fax (11) 4801-9325; e-mail contacto@enarsa.com.ar; internet www.enarsa.com.ar; f. 2004; state-owned; generation and distribution of electricity, especially from renewable sources; exploration, extraction and distribution of natural gas and petroleum; Pres. WALTER FAGYAS; Gen. Man. JUAN JOSÉ CARABAJALES.

Entidad Binacional Yacyretá: Eduardo Madero 942, 21°, C1106ACW Buenos Aires; tel. (11) 4510-7500; e-mail rrpp@eby.org .ar; internet www.eby.org.ar; operates the hydroelectric dam at Yacyretá on the Paraná river; owned jtly by Argentina and Paraguay; completed in 1998, it is one of the world's largest hydroelectric complexes, consisting of 20 generators with a total generating capacity of 3,200 MW; 14,673 GWh of electricity produced in 2007; Exec. Dir OSCAR ALFREDO THOMAS.

Hidroeléctrica Piedra del Aguila, SA: Ruta Nacional 237 km, 1450.5, Piedra del Aguila 16, CP 8315, Neuquén; tel. (2942) 493-152; fax (2942) 493-166; e-mail info@hpda.com.ar; internet www .gruposadesa.com.ar; f. 1993; owned by Grupo SADESA; electricity generation and distribution in the provinces of Neuquén and Río Negro; Pres. JOSÉ MARÍA VÁZQUEZ; Gen. Man. HORACIO TURRI.

Hidronor Ingeniería y Servicios, SA (HISSA): Hipólito Yrigoyen 1530, 6°B, C1089AAD Buenos Aires; tel. (11) 4382-6316; fax (11) 4382-5111; e-mail hidronor@ciudad.com.ar; internet www.hissa.com .ar; f. 1967; fmrly HIDRONOR, SA, the largest producer of electricity in Argentina; privatized in 1994; responsible for developing the hydroelectric potential of the Limay and neighbouring rivers; Pres. CARLOS ALBERTO ROCCA.

Petrobrás Energía, SA: Maipú 1, 22°, C1084ABA Buenos Aires; tel. (11) 4344-6000; fax (11) 4344-6315; e-mail ricardo.monge@ petrobras.com; internet www.petrobras.com.ar; f. 1946 as Pérez Companc, SA; petroleum interests acquired by Petrobrás of Brazil in 2003; operates the hydroelectric dam at Pichi Picún Leufu; Exec. Dir RONALDO BATISTA ASUNÇAO.

Transener, SA: Paseo Colón 728, 6°, C1063ACU Buenos Aires; tel. (11) 4342-6925; fax (11) 4342-7147; e-mail info-trans@transx.com.ar; internet www.transener.com.ar; energy transmission co; Gen. Man. ANDRÉS G. COLOMBO.

Gas

Asociación de Distribuidores de Gas (ADIGAS): Suipacha 1067, 5°, C1008AAU Buenos Aires; tel. (15) 4980-0005; e-mail consultas@ adigas.com.ar; internet www.adigas.com.ar; f. 1993 to represent newly privatized gas companies; Pres. ENRIQUE FLAIBAN.

Distribuidora de Gas del Centro, SA: Ituzaingó 774, Córdoba; tel. (351) 468-8108; fax (351) 468-1568; e-mail clientescentro@ecogas .com.ar; internet www.ecogas.com.ar/appweb/leo/centro/centro.php; state-owned co; distributes natural gas in Córdoba, Catamarca and La Rioja; Gen. Man. DONALDO SLOOG.

Distribuidora de Gas Cuyana, SA: Ituzaingó 774, Córdoba; tel. (351) 468-8108; fax (351) 468-1568; e-mail clientescuyo@ecogas.com .ar; internet www.ecogas.com.ar/appweb/leo/cuyo/cuyo.php; state-owned co; distributes natural gas in Mendoza, San Juan, San Luis; Pres. EDUARDO A. HURTADO.

Energía Argentina, SA (ENARSA): see Electricity.

Gas Natural Fenosa, SA: Isabel la Católica 939, C1268ACS Buenos Aires; tel. (11) 4754-1137; e-mail comercial@gasnaturalban.com.ar; internet www.gasnaturalban.com.ar; f. 1992 as Gas Natural BAN; changed name as above 2011; distribution of natural gas; Pres. HORACIO CRISTIANI.

Metrogás, SA: Gregorio Aráoz de Lamadrid 1360, C1267AAB Buenos Aires; tel. (11) 4309-1000; fax (11) 4309-1025; e-mail atencionclientes@metrogas.com.ar; internet www.metrogas.com.ar; f. 1992; 70% state-owned; gas distribution, mainly in Buenos Aires region; Dir-Gen. MARCELO ADRIÁN NÚÑEZ.

Transportadora de Gas del Norte, SA: Don Bosco 3672, 3°, C1206ABF Buenos Aires; tel. (11) 4008-2000; fax (11) 4008-2242; internet www.tgn.com.ar; f. 1992; distributes natural gas; Pres. SANTIAGO MARFORT.

Transportadora de Gas del Sur, SA (TGS): Don Bosco 3672, 6°, C1206ABF Buenos Aires; tel. (11) 4865-9050; fax (11) 4865-9059; e-mail totgs@tgs.com.ar; internet www.tgs.com.ar; f. 1992; processing and transport of natural gas; Pres. RICARDO ISIDRO MONGE; Dir-Gen. JAMES GREMES CORDERO.

Water

Agua y Saneamientos Argentinos, SA (AySA): Tucumán 752, C1049APP Buenos Aires; tel. (11) 6319-0000; fax (11) 6139-2460; e-mail prensa@aysa.com.ar; internet www.aysa.com.ar; f. 2006; 90% state-owned; distribution of water in the Buenos Aires metropolitan area; Dir-Gen. Dr CARLOS HUMBERTO BEN.

TRADE UNIONS

Central de Trabajadores de la Argentinos (CTA): Piedras 1065, C1070AAU Buenos Aires; tel. (11) 4307-3829; fax (11) 4300-1015; e-mail prensacentral@cta.org.ar; internet www.cta.org.ar; f. 1992; dissident trade union confederation; Gen. Sec. HUGO YASKY.

CGT Azul y Blanca: Avda Belgrano 1280, C1093AAN Buenos Aires; f. 2008 by dissident faction of CGT comprising c. 60 unions; Sec.-Gen. LUIS BARRIONUEVO.

Confederación General del Trabajo (CGT) (General Confederation of Labour): Azopardo 802, C1107ADN Buenos Aires; tel. (11) 4334-0596; fax (11) 4334-0599; e-mail secgral@cgtra.org.ar; internet www.cgtra.org.ar; f. 1930; Peronist; represents approx. 90% of Argentina's 1,100 trade unions; Sec.-Gen. ANTONIO CALÓ.

Federación Argentina de Trabajadores de Luz y Fuerza (FATLYF): Lima 163, C1073AAC, Buenos Aires, DF; tel. (11) 4383-4541; e-mail secretariageneral@fatlyf.org; internet www .fatlyf.org; f. 1948; affiliated to the CGT; Sec.-Gen. JULIO CÉSAR IERACI.

Unión Argentina de Trabajadores Rurales y Estibadores (UATRE) (Argentine Union of Rural Workers and Stevedores): Reconquista 630, 4° y 5°, C1003ABN, Buenos Aires; tel. (11) 4312-2500; e-mail igualdadygenero@uatre.org.ar; internet www.uatre.org .ar; Gen. Sec. GERÓNIMO (MOMO) VENEGAS.

Unión Ferroviaria (UF): Avda Independencia 2880, C1225AAX Buenos Aires; tel. (11) 4957-4921; fax 4957-4928; e-mail info@ unionferroviaria.org.ar; internet www.unionferroviaria.org.ar; f. 1922; train workers' union; part of the CGT; Sec.-Gen. SERGIO ADRIAN SASIA.

Transport

Comisión Nacional de Regulación del Transporte (CNRT): Maipú 88, Apdo 129, C1000WAB Buenos Aires; tel. (11) 4819-3000; e-mail cnrt@miv.gov.ar; internet www.cnrt.gov.ar; f. 1996; regulates domestic and international transport services; Insp. Dr FERNANDO RODRIGO MANZANARES.

Secretaría de Transporte de la Nación: Hipólito Yrigoyen 250, 12°, C1086AAB Buenos Aires; tel. (11) 4349-7254; fax (11) 4349-7201; e-mail transporte@minplan.gov.ar; internet www.transporte.gov.ar; Sec. ALEJANDRO RAMOS.

RAILWAYS

There are direct rail links with the Bolivian Railways network to Santa Cruz de la Sierra and La Paz; with Chile, through the Las Cuevas–Caracoles tunnel (across the Andes) and between Salta and Antofagasta; with Brazil, across the Paso de los Libres and Uruguayana bridge; with Paraguay (between Posadas and Encarnación by ferry-boat); and with Uruguay (between Concordia and Salto). In 2012 there were 25,023 km of tracks.

Following privatization in the early 1990s the state-run Ferrocarriles Argentinos was replaced by Ente Nacional de Administración de Bienes Ferroviarios (which was subsumed by the Organismo Nacional de Administración de Bienes in 2000), which assumed responsibility for railway infrastructure and the rolling stock not already sold off. The Buenos Aires commuter system was divided into eight concerns (one of which incorporates the underground railway system) and sold to private operators as 10- or 20-year (subsidized) concessions. In 2013 the Government of Buenos Aires took control of the metro network from the federal Government. The railway network is regulated by the Comisión Nacional de Regulación del Transporte (CNRT—see above). Construction of a 710-km high-speed railway linking Buenos Aires, Rosario and Córdoba was planned, although by 2014 the project remained stalled.

ALL Central: Santa Fe 4636, 3°, C1425BHV Buenos Aires; tel. (11) 4778-2425; fax (11) 4778-2493; internet en.all-logistica.com; f. 1993 as Ferrocarril Buenos Aires al Pacífico San Martín; bought by Brazil's América Latina Logística (ALL), SA, in 1999; nationalized in 2013; operates freight services on the San Martín line.

ALL Mesopotámica: Santa Fe 4636, 3°, C1425BHV Buenos Aires; tel. (11) 4778-2425; fax (11) 4778-2493; internet en.all-logistica.com; f. 1993 as Ferrocarril Mesopotámico; bought by Brazil's América Latina Logística (ALL), SA, in 1999; nationalized in 2013; operates freight services on the Urquiza lines; 2,704 km of track.

Cámara de Industriales Ferroviarios: Alsina 1609, 1°, C1088AAO Buenos Aires; tel. (11) 4382-0598; e-mail cifra@ argentina.com; private org. to promote the devt of Argentine railway industries; Pres. ANA MARÍA GHIBAUDI.

Ferrobaires: Gen. Hornos 11, 4°, C1154ACA Buenos Aires; tel. (11) 4304-0028; fax (11) 4305-5933; e-mail info@ferrobaires.gba.gov.ar; internet www.ferrobaires.gba.gov.ar; f. 1993; owned by the govt of the Province of Buenos Aires; local services; Admin. ANTONIO MALTANA; Gen. Man. Dr JOSÉ PUCCIARELLI.

Ferroexpreso Pampeano, SA (FEPSA): Consea 1073, C1426AQU Buenos Aires; tel. (11) 4510-4900; e-mail feppau@fepsa.com.ar; operates services on the Rosario–Bahía Blanca grain lines; 5,094 km of track; Gen. Man. JUAN CARLOS ROSSI.

Ferrosur Roca (FR): Reconquista 1088, 7°, C1003ABV Buenos Aires; tel. (11) 4319-3000; fax (11) 4319-3901; e-mail ferrosur@elsitio .net; internet www.ferrosur.com.ar; f. 1993; operator of freight services on the Roca lines; Gen. Man. PABLO TERRADAS; 3,000 km of track.

Ferrovías: Avda Dr Ramos Mejía 1430, Estación Retiro, C1104AJO Buenos Aires; tel. (11) 4314-1444; fax (11) 3311-1181; e-mail atencionalpasajero@ferrovias.com.ar; internet www.ferrovias.com .ar; f. 1994; operates northern commuter line (Belgrano Norte) in Buenos Aires; Pres. GABRIEL ROMERO.

Metrovías (MV): Bartolomé Mitre 3342, C1201AAL Buenos Aires; tel. (11) 4959-6800; fax (11) 4553-9270; e-mail info@metrovias.com .ar; internet www.metrovias.com.ar; f. 1994; operates Subterráneos de Buenos Aires (Subte, although govt of Buenos Aires responsible for network), a light rail line (Premetro) and Urquiza commuter line; Pres. ALBERTO ESTEBÁN VERRA.

Nuevo Central Argentino, SA (NCA): Avda Alberdi 50, Rosario; tel. (3411) 437-6561; e-mail seleccion@nca.com.ar; internet www.nca .com.ar; f. 1993; operates freight services on the Bartolomé Mitre lines; Pres. MIGUEL ALBERTO ACEVEDO; Gen. Man. HORACIO DÍAZ HERMELO; 5,011 km of track.

Subterráneos de Buenos Aires (Subte): Agüero 48, C1201AAL Buenos Aires; tel. (11) 5166-5800; e-mail info@sbase.com.ar; internet www.buenosaires.gob.ar/subte; f. 1913; completely state-owned in 1951–93, responsibility for operations was transferred in 1993 to a private consortium, Metrovías, with control returned to the Municipalidad de la Ciudad de Buenos Aires (from the federal authorities) from 2012; 6 underground lines totalling 53.7 km, 74 stations, and a 7.4 km light rail line (Premetro) with 17 stations; 3 additional lines planned; Pres. JUAN PABLO PICCARDO.

ROADS

In 2010 the intercity road network comprised 231,374 km of roads, of which 30% were paved. Of the total, 38,313 km were under the national road network and 191,812 km formed the provincial road network. In the national network, 87% of roads are paved, whereas only 20% of provincial roads are paved. Four branches of the Pan-American highway run from Buenos Aires to the borders of Chile, Bolivia, Paraguay and Brazil. In 2006 the Inter-American Development Bank financed road development in the Norte Grande region with US $1,200m. A further $300m. for the second phase of the project was approved in 2012.

Asociación Argentina de Empresarios Transporte Automotor (AAETA): Bernardo de Irigoyen 330, 6°, C1072AAH Buenos Aires; tel. (11) 4334-3254; fax (11) 4334-6513; e-mail info@aaeta.org.ar; internet www.aaeta.org.ar; f. 1941; Pres. EDUARDO ZBIKOSKI; Gen. Man. MARCELO GONZALVEZ.

Autobuses Sudamericanos, SA: Tres Arroyos 287, C1414EAC Buenos Aires; tel. (11) 4857-3065; fax (11) 4307-1956; f. 1928; international bus services; car and bus rentals; charter bus services; Pres. ARMANDO SCHLECKER HIRSCH; Gen. Man. MIGUEL ANGEL RUGGIERO.

Dirección Nacional de Vialidad: Julio A. Roca 783, C1067ABC Buenos Aires; tel. (11) 4343-8520; internet www.vialidad.gov.ar; controlled by the Ministry of the Interior and Transport; Gen. Man. NELSON GUILLERMO PERIOTTI.

Federación Argentina de Entidades Empresarias de Autotransporte de Cargas (FADEEAC): Sánchez de Bustamante 54, C1173AAB Buenos Aires; tel. (11) 4860-7700; fax (11) 4383-7870; e-mail fadeeac@fadeeac.org.ar; internet www.fadeeac.org.ar; Pres. DANIEL INDART.

INLAND WATERWAYS

There is considerable traffic in coastal and river shipping, mainly carrying petroleum and its derivatives.

Dirección Nacional de Vías Navegables: Avda España 221, 4°, Buenos Aires; tel. (11) 4361-5964; e-mail amparadela@yahoo.com.ar; internet www.sspyvn.gov.ar; part of the Transport Secretariat of the Ministry of Federal Planning, Public Investment and Services; responsible for the maintenance and improvement of waterways, and dredging operations; Dir Dr JOSÉ BENI.

SHIPPING

There are more than 100 ports, of which the most important are Buenos Aires, Quequén and Bahía Blanca. There are specialized terminals at Ensenada, Comodoro Rivadavia, San Lorenzo and Campana (petroleum); Bahía Blanca, Rosario, Santa Fe, Villa Concepción, Mar del Plata and Quequén (cereals); and San Nicolás and San Fernando (raw and construction materials). In 2013 Argentina's flag registered fleet totalled 409 vessels, totalling 732,587 grt.

Administración General de Puertos: Avda Ing. Huergo 431, 1°, C1107AOE Buenos Aires; tel. (11) 4342-1727; fax (11) 4342-6836; e-mail institucionales@puertobuenosaires.gov.ar; internet www.puertobuenosaires.gov.ar; f. 1956 as a state enterprise for administration of all national sea- and river-ports; following privatization of much of its activity in the mid-1990s, operates the port of Buenos Aires; Gen. Man. Dr JORGE FRANCISCO CHOLVIS.

Consorcio de Gestión del Puerto de Bahía Blanca: Dr Mario M. Guido s/n, 8103 Provincia de Buenos Aires; internet www.puertobahiablanca.com; Pres. HUGO ANTONIO BORELLI; Gen. Man. VALENTÍN D. MORAN.

Terminales Río de la Plata: Avda Ramón Castillo y Avda Cdre Py, Puerto Nuevo, Buenos Aires; tel. (11) 4319-9500; e-mail atencionalcliente@trp.com.ar; internet www.trp.com.ar; operates 1 of 5 cargo and container terminals in the port of Buenos Aires; Gen. Man. GUSTAVO FIGUEROLA.

CIVIL AVIATION

Argentina has 10 international airports (Aeroparque Jorge Newbery, Córdoba, Corrientes, El Plumerillo, Ezeiza, Jujuy, Resistencia, Río Gallegos, Salta and San Carlos de Bariloche). Ezeiza, 22 km from Buenos Aires, is one of the most important air terminals in Latin America.

Aerolíneas Argentinas: Bouchard 547, 9°, C1106ABG Buenos Aires; tel. (11) 4317-3000; fax (11) 4320-2116; internet www.aerolineas.com.ar; f. 1950; bought by Grupo Marsans (Spain) in 2001; renationalized in 2008; services to North and Central America, Europe, the Far East, New Zealand, South Africa and destinations throughout South America; the internal network covers the whole country; passengers, mail and freight are carried; Pres. Dr MARIANO RECALDE.

Austral Líneas Aéreas: Corrientes 485, 9°, C1043AAE Buenos Aires; tel. (11) 4317-3600; fax (11) 4317-3777; internet www.austral.com.ar; f. 1971; domestic flights.

Líneas Aéreas del Estado (LADE): Perú 710, San Telmo, C1068AAF Buenos Aires; tel. (11) 5353-2387; fax (11) 4362-4899; e-mail informes@lade.com.ar; internet www.lade.com.ar; f. 1940; domestic flights.

Sol Líneas Aéreas: Aeropuerto Internacional Rosario, Entre Ríos 986, S2000CRR Rosario; tel. (11) 6091-0032; e-mail contacto@sol.com.ar; internet www.sol.com.ar; f. 2005; services between Argentina and Uruguay; Pres. HORACIO ANGELI.

Tourism

Argentina's superb tourist attractions include the Andes mountains, the lake district centred on Bariloche (where there is a National Park), Patagonia, the Atlantic beaches and Mar del Plata, the Iguazú falls, the Pampas and Tierra del Fuego. Tourism receipts totalled a provisional US $4,411m. in 2013, when visitor arrivals totalled an estimated 5.6m.

Asociación Argentina de Agencias de Viajes y Turismo (AAAVYT): Viamonte 640, 10°, B6015XAA Buenos Aires; tel. (11) 4325-4691; fax (11) 4322-9641; e-mail secretaria@aaavyt.org.ar; internet www.aaavyt.org.ar; f. 1951; Pres. FABRICIO DI GIAMBATTISTA; Exec. Dir GERARDO BELIO.

Instituto Nacional de Promoción Turística (INPROTUR): Paraguay 866, 8°, C1057AAL Buenos Aires; tel. (11) 4850-1400; fax (11) 4313-6834; e-mail inprotur@turismo.gov.ar; internet www.argentina.travel; f. 2005; Pres. ENRIQUE MEYER; Exec. Sec. ROBERTO PALAIS.

Defence

As assessed at November 2013, Argentina's Armed Forces numbered an estimated 73,100: Army 38,500, Navy 20,000 (including Naval Air Force), Air Force 14,600. There were also paramilitary forces numbering 31,250. Conscription was ended in 1995 and a professional (voluntary) military service was created in its place.

Defence Budget: An estimated 26,300m. new pesos in 2013.

Chair. of the Joint Chiefs of Staff: Gen. LUIS MARÍA CARENA.

Chief of Staff (Army): Gen. CÉSAR SANTOS GERARDO DEL CORAZÓN DE JESÚS MILANI.

Chief of Staff (Navy): Rear-Adm. GASTÓN FERNANDO ERICE.

Chief of Staff (Air Force): Brig. MARIO MIGUEL CALLEJO.

Education

Education from pre-school to university level is available free of charge. Education is officially compulsory for all children at primary level, between the ages of six and 14 years. Secondary education lasts for between five and six years, depending on the type of course: the normal certificate of education (bachillerato) takes five years, a course leading to a commercial bachillerato lasts five years, and one leading to a technical or agricultural bachillerato takes six years. Technical education is supervised by the Consejo Nacional de Educación Técnica. Non-university higher education, usually leading to a teaching qualification, is for three or four years, while university courses last for four years or more. There were three main categories of universities: national, which are supported by the federal budget; provincial (or state), supported by the provincial governments; and private, supported entirely by private initiative, but authorized to function by the Ministry of Education. Enrolment at primary schools in 2005 included 99% of the relevant age-group, while enrolment at secondary schools in 2011 included 85% of pupils in the relevant age-group. Government expenditure on education in 2013 was 34,462.3m. new pesos, equivalent to 5.5% of government expenditure.

Bibliography

For works on South America generally, see Select Bibliography (Books)

Alexander, R. *A History of Organized Labor in Argentina*. Westport, CT, Praeger Publrs, 2003.

Alonso, P. *Between Revolution and the Ballot Box: The Origins of the Argentine Radical Party*. Cambridge, Cambridge University Press, 2000.

Arceneaux, C. L. *Bounded Missions: Military Regimes and Democratization in the Southern Cone and Brazil*. University Park, PA, Penn State University Press, 2001.

Auyero, J. *Poor People's Politics: Peronist Survival Networks and the Legacy of Evita*. Durham, NC, Duke University Press, 2001.

Barton, R., and Tedesco, L. *The State of Democracy in Latin America: Post-Transitional Conflicts in Argentina and Chile*. London, Routledge, 2004.

Blustein P. *And the Money Kept Rolling In (and Out): Wall Street, the IMF, and the Bankrupting of Argentina*. London, Public Affairs, 2005.

Brennan, J. P., and Rougier, M. *The Politics of National Capitalism: Peronism and the Argentine Bourgeoisie, 1946–1976*. University Park, PA, Penn State University Press, 2009.

Chudnovsky, D., and López, A. *The Elusive Quest for Growth in Argentina*. Basingstoke, Palgrave Macmillan, 2007.

Corrales, J. *Presidents Without Parties: The Politics of Economic Reform in Argentina and Venezuela in the 1990s*. University Park, PA, Penn State University Press, 2002.

Dominguez, J. I., and Shifter, M. (Eds). *Constructing Democratic Governance in Latin America (An Inter-American Dialogue Book)*. Baltimore, MD, Johns Hopkins University Press, 2003.

Epstein, E. (Ed.). *Broken Promises? The Argentine Crisis and Argentine Democracy*. Lanham, MD, Lexington Books, 2006.

Fuentes, C. *Contesting the Iron Fist: Advocacy Networks and Police Violence in Democratic Argentina and Chile*. London, Routledge, 2007.

Goñi, U. *The Real Odessa: How Perón Brought the Nazi War Criminals to Argentina*. London, Granta, 2003.

González, Martín Abel *The Genesis of the Falklands (Malvinas) Conflict: Argentina, Britain and the Failed Negotiations of the 1960s (Security, Conflict and Cooperation in the Contemporary World)*. USA, Palgrave Macmillan, 2013.

Grimson, A., and Kessler, G. *On Argentina and the Southern Cone: Neoliberalism and National Imaginations*. London, Routledge, 2005.

Guy, D. J. *Women Build the Welfare State: Performing Charity and Creating Rights in Argentina, 1880–1955*. Durham, NC, Duke University Press, 2009.

Helmke, G. *Courts Under Constraints: Judges, Generals, and Presidents in Argentina (Cambridge Studies in Comparative Politics)*. Cambridge, Cambridge University Press, 2005.

Hornbeck, J. F. *Argentina's Post-Crisis Economic Reform: Challenges for US Policy*. Washington, DC, Congressional Research Service, 2013.

Karush, M. B., and Chamosa, O. (Eds). *The New Cultural History of Peronism: Power and Identity in Mid-Twentieth-Century Argentina*. Durham, NC, Duke University Press, 2010.

Lessa, F. and Druliolle, V. (Eds). *The Memory of State Terrorism in the Southern Cone. Argentina, Chile and Uruguay*. USA, Palgrave Macmillan, 2011

Levine, L. W. W., Levine, L. W., and Ortiz, F. *Inside Argentina from Peron to Menem: 1950–2000 from an American Point of View*. Ojai, CA, Edwin House Publishing, 2001.

Levitsky, S. *Transforming Labour-Based Parties in Latin America: Argentine Peronism in Comparative Perspective*. Cambridge, Cambridge University Press, 2003.

(Ed.). *Argentine Democracy: The Politics of Institutional Weakness*. Philadelphia, PA, University of Pennsylvania Press, 2006.

Lewis, D. K. *The History of Argentina (Greenwood Histories of the Modern Nations)*. New York, Palgrave Macmillan, 2003.

Lewis, P. H. *Guerrillas and Generals: The 'Dirty War' in Argentina*. Westport, CT, Greenwood Publishing Group, 2001.

Llanos, M. *Privatization and Democracy in Argentina: An Analysis of President-Congress Relations*. New York, Palgrave, 2002.

Marchak, P. *God's Assassins: State Terrorism in Argentina in the 1970s*. Montréal, QC, McGill-Queens University Press, 2002.

Middlebrook, M. *The Argentine Fight for the Falklands*. London, Pen & Sword Books, 2003.

Mussa, M. *Argentina and the Fund: From Triumph to Tragedy*. Washington, DC, Institute for International Economics, 2002.

Norden, D., and Russell, R. *The United States and Argentina: Changing Relations in a Changing World*. London, Routledge, 2002.

Osiel, M. J. *Mass Atrocity, Ordinary Evil and Hannah Arendt: Criminal Consciousness in Argentina's Dirty War*. New Haven, CT, Yale University Press, 2002.

Podalsky, L. *Specular City: The Transformation of Culture, Consumption and Space after Peron*. Philadelphia, PA, Temple University Press, 2004.

Powers, N. *Grassroots Expectations of Democracy and Economy: Argentina in Comparative Perspective*. Pittsburgh, PA, University of Pittsburgh Press, 2001.

Robben, A. C. G. M. *Political Violence and Trauma in Argentina*. Philadelphia, PA, University of Pennsylvania Press, 2005.

Rock, D. *State Building and Political Movements in Argentina, 1860–1916*. Palo Alto, CA, Stanford University Press, 2002.

Politics in Argentina, 1890–1930: The Rise and Fall of Radicalism. Cambridge, Cambridge University Press, 2009.

Romero, J. L. *Las Ideas Políticas en Argentina*. Buenos Aires, Fondo de Cultura Económica Argentina, 2002.

Romero, L. A. *A History of Argentina in the Twentieth Century*. University Park, PA, Penn State University Press, 2002.

Sabato, H. *The Many and the Few: Political Participation in Republican Buenos Aires*. Palo Alto, CA, Stanford University Press, 2001.

Sheinin, D. M. K. *Argentina and the United States: An Alliance Contained*. Athens, GA, University of Georgia Press, 2006.

Spektorowski, A. *The Origins of Argentina's Revolution of the Right*. Notre Dame, IN, University of Notre Dame Press, 2003.

Teichman, J. A. *The Politics of Freeing Markets in Latin America: Chile, Argentina, and Mexico*. Chapel Hill, NC, University of North Carolina Press, 2001.

Wright, T. C. *State Terrorism in Latin America: Chile, Argentina, and International Human Rights*. Lanham, MD, Rowman & Littlefield Publrs, 2007.

ARUBA

Geography

PHYSICAL FEATURES

Aruba is a constituent of the quadripartite Kingdom of the Netherlands, together with the metropolitan country in Europe and Curaçao and Sint Maarten (these last two gained *status aparte* in 2010, as Aruba had done in 1986). The island of Aruba is one of the Lesser Antilles, lying in the southern Caribbean, the most westerly of that part of the chain paralleling the South American coast. Indeed, the island lies just 25 km (16 miles) north of mainland Venezuela (the Paraguná peninsula). It is 68 km west of Curaçao. With Curaçao and Bonaire, Aruba constitutes what the Dutch confusingly call the 'Leeward Islands' (Benedenwindse Eilands). They are more familiarly called the 'ABC islands'. Aruba covers an area of 180 sq km (69.5 sq miles).

Aruba is the smallest of the three Dutch islands in the southern Caribbean. It is about 32 km at its longest (running from the south-east to the north-west) and almost 10 km at its widest. The island tapers fairly evenly towards the south-east, but the northerly facing weather coast extends further than the other, gentler shore, as, to the north-west of the capital, Oranjestad, the coast turns abruptly towards the north-east, curving into a western coastline that arcs up to the pointing north-western tip of Aruba. Most of the main towns and tourist resorts are on the leeward, reef-fringed western and southern shores. There are over 68 km of seashore. The interior (*cunucu*) of the dry island is naturally covered by scrub, cacti and wind-bent divi divi (*watapana*) trees, and little land is farmed. The lack of trees results from human exploitation of the scarce wood resources, although the more endangered native species are now protected, and there are replanting programmes and initiatives designed to keep goats out of vulnerable areas. Bird life is rich, particularly during November–January, when migratory species swell the local avian population. The terrain is generally flat, although there are some hills, the highest being Jamanota (189 m or 620 ft). There are no rivers.

CLIMATE

Aruba has an even, tropical marine climate, with minimal seasonal temperature variation—the average is fairly constant at 27°C (81°F), seldom registering below 26°C or above 32°C. August, September and October are the hottest months, while December–February is slightly cooler than the rest of the year. The island is outside the Caribbean hurricane belt (although it is constantly cooled by the trade winds) and is very dry. There are only an average of 510 mm (20 ins) of rainfall per year, mostly falling in October–December.

POPULATION

The main ethnic group (80%) is of mixed white and Amerindian (Arawak) race (there have been no full-blooded Amerindians since the late 19th century), but, as a long-established and

cosmopolitan trading centre, Aruba has attracted a rich diversity of communities and racial groups. As in the other southern Dutch Antilles, this varied background has given rise to a widely spoken Creole language, Papiamento, of mixed Portuguese, Spanish, Dutch and English descent. The official language is Dutch, although English and Spanish are also widely spoken. The historic influence of Latin America on this part of the Dutch Caribbean is revealed by estimates of religious affiliation—the principal faith of Aruba is the Roman Catholic denomination of Christianity, to which 76% of the population adhere. A further 3% are Protestant, while other groups represented include Jehovah's Witnesses, Methodists, Seventh-day Adventists and Anglicans.

The total population in mid-2014 was an estimated 103,433, although during the course of a typical year almost 1m. visit as stop-over tourists and well over 500,000 more visit as passing cruise ship passengers. Oranjestad (with a population of 28,294 at the 2010 census) is at the more northerly end of the south-western coast, with the 'oil town' of Sint Nicolaas at the southern end. Inland, near the western shore, is Noord, and in the centre of the island lies Santa Cruz.

History

CHARLES ARTHUR

Revised for this edition by the editorial staff

Aruba's history has been closely linked to those of five other Caribbean islands that were colonized by the Dutch in the 17th century and administered as one entity by the Netherlands from 1845 until 1986. In that year Aruba left the federation of the Netherlands Antilles, having been granted *status aparte* by the Dutch Government, to become a self-governing part of the Kingdom of the Netherlands.

Aruba, which had been inhabited for some centuries by Arawak people, was discovered by the Spanish in 1499. The Spanish colony was limited in scope, and in contrast to most other Caribbean islands, Aruba did not develop a plantation society. Instead, the Spanish sent many of the indigenous people to Hispaniola (today the island shared by Haiti and the Dominican Republic), where they were enslaved in the mines. In the 1630s the Dutch West India Company developed an increasingly strong presence on Aruba, and in 1648 the Dutch took formal possession of the island. Apart from a brief spell under British control in 1805–16, Aruba remained a Dutch colony until after the Second World War. Periods of economic prosperity occurred during the 18th century when the island thrived first as a source of sea salt and then as a trading centre, and were further evidenced during the 19th century when gold was discovered and vigorously mined until the early years of the 20th century, when the supply dwindled and mining ceased to be prosperous. The basis of the island's modern day economy was established in 1929 when, following the discovery of extensive petroleum reserves in the neighbouring territory of Venezuela, the Lago Oil and Transport Company (a subsidiary of the Standard Oil Company of the USA, now the ExxonMobil Corporation) established an oil refinery at the eastern end of the island, at Sint (St) Nicolaas. At around the same time, Royal Dutch Shell built another refinery on the opposite end of the island. The refining of petroleum transformed the island's economy and ensured another period of economic prosperity.

In the years following the end of the Second World War, Aruba's economy received a further boost when the capital city of Oranjestad became a regular port of call for Caribbean cruise ships. A tourism industry soon developed, at first limited to cruise ship visits, and in 1959 the first luxury hotel opened in Aruba. The increasing wealth and prosperity encouraged islanders to agitate for a separation from the other Dutch colonies in the Caribbean. Although its status as a Dutch colony came to an end in 1951, when it formed its own government within the political structure of the Netherlands Antilles, in 1954 it was made part of the federation of the Netherlands Antilles along with Bonaire and Curaçao, and the three islands further to the north, St Eustatius, St Maarten and Saba.

Aruba's citizens increasingly came to resent the unequal relationship within the Netherlands Antilles because the seat of the federal government was in Curaçao, but also because it was felt that Curaçao had too much influence over domestic issues while Aruba's interests were not sufficiently protected. The island's main political party, the Movimiento Electoral di Pueblo (MEP—People's Electoral Movement), campaigned for independence for Aruba, and in a referendum in March 1977 some 82% of those taking part voted in favour of withdrawal from the Antillean federation. Following drawn-out negotiations with the Dutch, in 1983 agreement was reached providing for Aruba's secession from the federation in 1986 and full independence 10 years later. In the interim it was agreed that Aruba would maintain a co-operative union in monetary and economic affairs with the other five members of the federation, and that the Netherlands would maintain its authority over matters of foreign affairs and defence.

Aruba achieved its new *status aparte* on 1 January 1986. Its first Prime Minister was Henny Eman, who headed a coalition consisting of the Arubaanse Volkspartij (AVP) and three smaller parties, as well as the Partido Democrático Arubano (PDA), the Partido Patriotico di Aruba (PPA) and the Acción Democrático Nacional (ADN). In the same year the Lago refinery in Sint Nicolaas closed. Unemployment rose to 20% and GDP dropped by 18% during the first year of the *status aparte*. With the support of the Netherlands and the IMF, an adjustment programme was drafted, which focused on the expansion of the tourism and construction sectors. In 1989 production at the refinery resumed under a new owner, Coastal Oil Company.

Aruba's electoral system is based on proportional representation, and, as no one party is usually able to win a majority of seats in the 21-seat Staten (parliament), the result of the elections held once every four years has traditionally been the creation of unstable coalition governments. The 1989 election brought a change in government: the MEP formed an administration with two small parties, the PPA and the ADN. This coalition remained in office for two terms. The AVP formed a coalition Government from 1995 to 2001. However, in elections in 2001 the MEP won an absolute majority, and formed Aruba's first ever one-party government. In the general election held in September 2005 the MEP won another outright victory.

Popular disillusion with the deteriorating economic conditions was a key determinant in the legislative election held on 25 September 2009, from which the opposition AVP emerged victorious, with 12 of the 21 seats in the Staten. The MEP secured only eight seats. MEP leader and outgoing Prime Minister, Nelson Oduber, who had presided over a fractious and deteriorating relationship with the Netherlands, blamed the party's poor performance on interference by the Dutch authorities—an investigation into corruption on the island had been launched by the Netherlands shortly prior to the election.

The AVP Government's early initiatives focused on the economy. In addition to economic problems brought about by the international recession, government budgets came under pressure from 2009 owing to a variety of factors. There was an expansion of the public sector by around 1,500 posts, and the administration was also liable for the claims received as a result of failed hotel projects (arising from an earlier government guarantee on non-performing loans). The introduction of a new national health system (Algemene Ziektekostenverzekering—AZV) also increased the burden on state revenues. The AVP administration focused on longer-term initiatives to boost the economy, including reviving the flagging tourism industry, promoting the use of renewable energy, and improving relations with the Netherlands. The Prime Minister, Mike Eman, also initiated moves to improve relations with the other islands of the former Netherlands Antilles, and with Venezuela. A major challenge for the Government was the reopening of the refinery at St Nicolaas, which had been shut down by Coastal. The refinery finally resumed operations in January 2011, but in March 2012 its owner (Valero Energy Corporation of the USA) closed the refinery again. Valero held talks with other oil companies to discuss a potential takeover of the refinery, but no firm offers were received. Thus, in September Valero announced its intention to convert the plant into an oil depot, resulting in many refinery workers losing their jobs.

A general election was held on 27 September 2013. The AVP secured a second term in office, increasing its parliamentary representation to 13 seats. The MEP secured seven seats, while the Partido Democracia Real won one seat. Turnout was 84%. Eman pledged to continue his efforts to rekindle the island's ailing economy. Elections to the European Parliament took place in Aruba on 22 May 2014. The Christen Democratisch

Appèl (Christian Democratic Appeal) won the majority of the local ballot, although the rate of participation by the electorate was very low.

In July 2014 Eman declared that he was staging a hunger strike in protest against the recent actions of the Dutch Government, which, owing to concerns about Aruba's precarious fiscal position, had withheld approval of the Eman adminis-tration's proposed 2014 budget and had ordered the Governor to conduct an investigation into the island's finances. Although the Dutch authorities insisted that they had acted lawfully, Eman claimed that these measures constituted a violation of Aruba's autonomy, and the Prime Minister affirmed his intention to maintain his hunger strike until the Governor authorized the 2014 budget.

Economy

Based on an earlier article by CHARLES ARTHUR and subsequently revised by ROLAND VAN DEN BERGH and the editorial staff

For much of the 20th century Aruba's economy revolved around oil-processing, but in the mid-1980s, following the closure of the Lago refinery, there was an enforced move to concentrate instead on the development of the tourism sector. Tourism showed especially strong growth in the 1990s and, as a consequence, tourism-related industries—particularly construction—boomed, contributing to strong economic growth and to a low unemployment rate. Today Aruba's main industries are tourism, until recently oil-refining, offshore financial services, transport (mainly shipping), and free zone activities. The island possesses few natural resources, and is heavily dependent on imports of all kind of merchandise, including food and manufactures.

Throughout the 1990s growth remained steady, largely owing to a vibrant tourism industry and investment in oil-refining, and averaged 5.1% per year in 1991–2000. After such a prolonged period of economic success, the trend abated. In the first decade of the 21st century the growth rate fluctuated. The terrorist attacks in the USA in September 2001 badly affected the tourism and construction sectors. A sharp increase in investment in 2003 prompted a recovery, and in 2004 the renewed growth in stay-over tourism of 13% and related expansion in construction contributed to strong real gross domestic product (GDP) growth of 7.9%. However, as the performance of the tourism sector weakened again, economic growth slowed during 2005–08. In 2009 the economy fell into a deep recession, contracting by 11.3%. The main causes were the closure of the Valero oil refinery and, to a lesser extent, the world economic recession, which caused a slight decrease in tourist arrivals but a severe decline in investments, in particular in tourism and tourism-related activities.

Despite a more favourable economic environment in 2010, the economy suffered from a slow recovery in tourism and delays in reopening the Valero oil refinery, and real GDP contracted by 3.3%. The reopening of the refinery in January 2011 and favourable developments in tourism resulted in economic growth of 3.5% in 2011. However, refining activities were halted again in March 2012, leading to a decline in exports and an increase in unemployment. The negative economic repercussions of the closure were partially offset by the strong performance of the tourism industry during 2012, but a 1.3% contraction in real GDP was registered in that year, none the less. A further rise in tourist numbers, combined with an increase in domestic consumption (a consequence of lower utility prices), precipitated a robust economic recovery in 2013, with real GDP expanding by 3.9%. The central bank forecast further economic growth of 2.7% in 2014, predicated on expected increases in investment and tourist arrivals.

For the last two decades Aruba has been one of the most prosperous economies in the region, its real GDP per caput, at 31,100 Aruban florins in 2013, was among the highest in the Caribbean. Aruba enjoyed relatively low unemployment rates, particularly during the 1990s. Its tourism and oil-refining industries have attracted migrant labour to cover the short-falls in its labour market, resulting in an increase in the population from 67,382 in 1991 to 107,159 in early 2014. This has made Aruba one of the most densely populated islands in the Caribbean. Unemployment increased to 11.4% in 2003, before declining gradually to 6.9% in 2008. The unemployment rate rose again in 2009 to 10.3%, owing to the deterioration in the wider economy and exacerbated in particular by the closure in September of the Valero oil refinery (see below). By 2013 the unemployment rate had decreased to 7.6%.

Tourism remained the mainstay of the Aruban economy. According to the World Travel and Tourism Council (WTTC), in 2013 the sector, directly or indirectly, accounted for 84.1% of total output and 86.2% of total employment on the island. The sandy white beaches, particularly along the southern coast, are a major attraction, along with reefs offering good diving and liberal casino laws. The construction of new hotels and time share apartments, combined with an aggressive marketing campaign, succeeded in effecting and maintaining a continuous boom in the sector during the early years of the 21st century. However, dependence on tourism left the economy vulnerable to outside shocks. This was highlighted in 2005 when a US teenager went missing on the island, generating large amounts of negative publicity in the USA, by far the most important source of visitors. As a result, the number of stay-over tourists visiting Aruba declined in 2006 to 694,400 (from 732,500 in 2005). By 2008, however, the number of stay-over tourists had recovered to 826,200. As a result of the world economic recession in general, and in particular in the USA, tourism performed moderately in 2009, with stop-over arrivals decreasing to 810,100. Although economic problems in the USA and Europe continued to have a negative impact on the growth in tourist arrivals and tourism investments, the number of stay-over tourists rose steadily from 2010, reaching 979,256 in 2013.

The main markets for tourism are the USA, Venezuela, Canada and the Netherlands, with the USA accounting for 56.8% of all tourist arrivals in 2013. The number of cruise ship passengers fell in 2010–12, to 582,309 in the latter year, before recording a sharp increase in 2013, reaching 688,568. The WTTC expected that tourism in Aruba would continue to grow at a moderate level of around 3% per year in the foreseeable future.

Oil-refining was, until 2012, the other dominant industry in Aruba. In 1929 the Lago Oil and Transport Company, a subsidiary of US energy company ExxonMobil, built a refinery at the eastern end of the island. At the time it was the largest refinery in the world, employing more than 8,000 people, and for most of the 20th century it was the main driver of Aruba's economy. In 1985 Exxon closed the refinery owing to a reduced worldwide demand for oil, causing a profound shock to the Aruban economy. In 1989 the Coastal Oil Company, attracted by fiscal concessions, bought the Lago oil refinery facility and reopened it on a smaller scale. Coastal increased its production capacity from 150,000 barrels per day (b/d) in 1989 to 280,000 b/d in 2000. Another US-based company, El Paso, took over Coastal in 2001. However, the quantity of oil refined declined, and in 2004 Coastal sold the refinery. The new owner, the Valero Energy Corporation, renamed the facility the Valero Aruba Refinery, and in 2006 it had a total throughput capacity of 315,000 b/d. However, by 2007 this had declined to 275,000 b/d. In 2008 Valero announced plans to sell the refinery because high oil prices had narrowed processing margins, and the global economic downturn had made financing more difficult. Valero subsequently closed the refinery in 2009, resulting in the loss of over 700 jobs. The refinery was Aruba's largest single employer, and its importance to the economy was reflected by the substantial contribution to GDP of the industrial sector, which was an estimated 10.2% in 2006. In 2010 negotiations between the Government and Valero resulted in the resolution of a long-running dispute regarding unpaid taxes, reviving hopes for an eventual sale of the refinery, although it did not resume operations until January 2011. However, the reopening was only for a short period of time, and the refinery shut down once again in March 2012. Valero subsequently held talks with interested investors and operators to discuss the continuation of refinery activities in Aruba. However, in September, in the absence of any firm offers, Valero declared that it would convert the facility into an oil depot, precipitating further job losses.

A financial services sector grew strongly in the 1990s, helped by the deregulation of the financial services industry and better legislation. The offshore financial sector is important to Aruba, although it is small compared with other Caribbean offshore centres. In 2008 Aruba was removed from a 'black list' and put on the 'white list' of international tax havens published by the Organisation for Economic Co-operation and Development after the Government signed tax information exchange agreements and agreements for the avoidance of double taxation. The Financial Action Task Force, however, has put Aruba under enhanced surveillance. A committee was installed, chaired by the Minister-President, to improve the regulations and monitoring related to money-laundering and the financing of terrorism.

Owing to the scarcity of arable land, the poor quality of the soil and the shortage of water for irrigation, Aruba's agricultural sector is small. The main commercial crop is aloe, which is used in the manufacture of cosmetics and pharmaceuticals. Only a few other agricultural products are grown domestically, and Aruba depends heavily on imports of food. There is a small informal fishing industry.

The tourism boom and a housing shortage have boosted construction activity since the 1990s, and made this sector one of the main drivers of economic growth in Aruba. The construction sector experienced steady growth during the mid-2000s, in particular in relation to the building of condominiums, the expansion of the number of hotel rooms, and other real estate developments. Condominium construction had been expected to boom in 2007–12, with more than 2,000 new units planned for resort areas and other parts of the island, such as Weststraat (Oranjestad), Palm Beach, Malmok and Tierra del Sol. However, the global economic crisis led to the suspension of many of these projects as buyers, mostly from the USA, exercised caution. Future investments would depend very much on whether a new owner for the refinery could be found and on public investment in, for instance, Aruba's hospital and *linearpark*, a 10 mile strip reaching from the airport to Arashi Beach by the light house.

The Queen Beatrix International Airport outside Oranjestad is served by numerous airlines linking the island with the Caribbean, North America, Latin America and Europe. After substantial renovation and expansion, the airport was able to handle 2.6m. passengers per year. The island has some small privately operated national airlines. Aruba does not have a railway system, but a tourist tram network in the centre of the capital opened in early 2013. The road network is in good condition. The main seaport is at Oranjestad, where the harbour can accommodate large ocean-going vessels.

In 2002 the Staten adopted a law allowing the liberalization of the telecommunications market. The state telecommunications company Servicio di Telecomunicacion di Aruba NV (SETAR) was privatized in 2003. The explosion in mobile telephone use was reflected in the relative percentages of the population with subscriptions to fixed line (34%) and mobile telephone services (135%) in 2013. Internet access has grown steadily, from 15% in 2000 to 79% in 2013.

Exports through the island's free zone peaked at US $295m. in 1997, but have since fallen as demand has dropped away. Recent figures show a revival of the free zone trade, with export rising from $67m. in 2007 to $148m. in 2011. Refined oil was Aruba's most important merchandise export until the closure of the Valero refinery in 2012. In the absence of any significant local manufacturing, most consumer items, foodstuffs and machinery items are imported. There is a significant merchandise trade deficit. In 2013 imports totalled 2,084m. Aruban florins, not including oil products, while exports stood at just 75m. Aruban florins. Aruba's main trading partners are the USA, the Netherlands, the other islands of the former Netherlands Antilles, Colombia and Venezuela.

With the exception of 2000, 2003 and 2008 the Government has run a fiscal deficit in every year since achieving *status aparte* in 1986. Successive Governments have attempted to reduce the deficit, apart from in 2001–02, when a counter-cyclical spending policy was adopted. After a good economic and fiscal performance in 2003, when the fiscal accounts moved into surplus, the Government loosened policy in 2004, resulting in a deficit of 8.9% of GDP. Continued deficits have led to an accumulation of public debt. During 2009–10 Aruba's public sector finances deteriorated sharply, in line with falling GDP during those years. In 2011 the fiscal deficit worsened as a result of a substantial decrease in tax income whereas government expenditures decreased only moderately, increasing the fiscal deficit to 7.1% of GDP. The deficit widened to 9.8% of GDP in 2012 but narrowed to 7.2% of GDP in 2013. The total debt owed by the Government increased to 73.6% of GDP in 2013 (of which 52% was domestic and 48% foreign debt).

The Aruban florin was introduced after the island gained *status aparte* within the Kingdom of the Netherlands, at the rate of 1 florin = US $0.55, a rate that had increased slightly to 1 florin = $0.56 by mid-2014. The exchange rate has been stable because no balance of payment problems exist. Aruba had net foreign assets equivalent to 4.1 months of current account payments (excluding the oil sector) in 2013. The large trade deficit is, to a large extent, compensated for by the services balance. In 2011–13 annual average inflation was 4.4%, 0.6% and –2.4%, respectively.

Statistical Survey

Sources (unless otherwise stated): Central Bureau of Statistics, Ministry of Finance and Government Organization, Sun Plaza Bldg, 3rd Floor, L. G. Smith Blvd 160, Oranjestad; tel. 5837433; fax 5838057; internet www.cbs.aw; Centrale Bank van Aruba, J. E. Irausquin Blvd 8, POB 18, Oranjestad; tel. 5252100; fax 5252101; e-mail cbaua@setarnet.aw; internet www.cbaruba.org.

AREA AND POPULATION

Area: 180 sq km (69.5 sq miles).

Population: 90,506 at census of 14 October 2000; 101,484 (males 48,241, females 53,243) at census of 29 September 2010. *Mid-2014* (UN estimate): 103,433 Source: UN, *World Population Prospects: The 2012 Revision.*

Density (at mid-2014): 574.6 per sq km.

Population by Age and Sex (UN estimates at mid-2014): *0–14 years:* 19,495 (males 9,935, females 9,560); *15–64 years:* 71,757 (males 34,052, females 37,705); *65 years and over:* 12,181 (males 5,210, females 6,971); *Total* 103,433 (males 49,197, females 54,236). Source: UN, *World Population Prospects: The 2012 Revision.*

Principal Town (population at 2010 census): Oranjestad (capital) 28,294. *Mid-2014* (UN estimate, incl. suburbs): Oranjestad (capital) 29,041 (Source: UN, *World Urbanization Prospects: The 2014 Revision*).

Births, Marriages and Deaths (2012 unless otherwise indicated): Live births 1,154 (birth rate 10.8 per 1,000); Marriages 768 (marriage rate 7.5 per 1,000, 2011); Deaths 560 (death rate 5.7 per 1,000).

Life Expectancy (years at birth): 75.2 (males 72.8; females 77.7) in 2012. Source: World Bank, *World Development Indicators* database.

Immigration and Emigration (2013): Immigration 3,335; Emigration 2,291.

Economically Active Population (persons aged 14 years and over, 2010 census): Agriculture, hunting and forestry 297; Mining and quarrying 24; Manufacturing 2,334; Electricity, gas and water 529; Construction 3,851; Wholesale and retail trade, repairs 7,523; Hotels and restaurants 9,526; Transport, storage and communications 2,475; Financial intermediation 1,593; Real estate, renting and business activities 4,224; Public administration, defence and social security 4,570; Education 2,078; Health and social work 2,526; Other community, social and personal services 3,492; Private households with employed persons 1,242; Extraterritorial organizations and bodies 14; *Sub-total* 46,299; Activities not adequately defined 227; *Total employed* 46,526; Unemployed 5,519; *Total labour force* 52,045 (males 26,184, females 25,861).

HEALTH AND WELFARE

Total Fertility Rate (children per woman, 2011): 1.8.

Under-5 Mortality Rate (per 1,000 live births, 2010): 16.8.

Physicians (per 1,000 head, 2012): 1.92.

Hospital Beds (per 1,000 head, 2009): 2.8.

Health Expenditure (% of GDP, 2010): 10.0.

Total Carbon Dioxide Emissions ('000 metric tons, 2010): 2,321.2.

Carbon Dioxide Emissions Per Head (metric tons, 2010): 22.8.

Source: partly Pan American Health Organization.

For definitions, see explanatory note on p. vi.

FISHING

Total catch (all capture, metric tons, live weight, 2012): Groupers 10; Snappers and jobfishes 38; Wahoo 45; Other marine fishes 45; Total 138. Source: FAO.

INDUSTRY

Electric Energy (million kWh, 2013): 779.7.

FINANCE

Currency and Exchange Rates: 100 cents = 1 Aruban gulden (guilder) or florin (AFl.). *Sterling, Dollar and Euro Equivalents* (30 May 2014): £1 sterling = AFl. 3.011; US $1 = AFl. 1.790; €1 = AFl. 2.436; AFl. 100 = £33.21 = $55.87 = €41.04. Note: the Aruban florin was introduced in January 1986, replacing (at par) the Netherlands Antilles guilder or florin (NA Fl.). Since its introduction, the currency has had a fixed exchange rate of US $1 = AFl. 1.79.

Budget (AFl. million, 2013, provisional): *Revenue:* Tax revenue 942.0; Non-tax revenue 195.0; Total 1,137.0. *Expenditure:* Wages 387.6; Wage subsidies 168.2; Goods and services 256.5; Interest payments 164.5; Investments 39.9; Transfer to the General Health Insurance (AZV) 101.5; Total (incl. others) 1,432.3.

International Reserves (US $ million at 31 December 2013): Gold 133.7; Foreign exchange 532.7; *Total* 666.4. Source: IMF, *International Financial Statistics*.

Money Supply (AFl. million at 31 December 2013): Currency outside banks 213.6; Demand deposits at commercial banks 1,501.0; *Total money* 1,714.6. Source: IMF, *International Financial Statistics*.

Cost of Living (Consumer Price Index; base: December 2006 = 100): All items 119.4 in 2011; 120.1 in 2012; 117.3 in 2013.

Gross Domestic Product (AFl. million at constant 2000 prices): 3,095 in 2010; 3,211 in 2011; 3,171 in 2012; 3,293 in 2013.

Expenditure on the Gross Domestic Product (AFl. million at current prices, 2013): Final consumption expenditure 4,244; Gross capital formation 1,062; *Total domestic expenditure* 5,306; Exports of goods and services 3,157; *Less* Imports of goods and services 3,828; *GDP in purchasers' values* 4,634.

Gross Domestic Product by Economic Activity (AFl. million at current prices, 2012): Agriculture, hunting, forestry and fishing 21; Mining and utilities 255; Manufacturing 191; Construction 236; Wholesale, retail trade, restaurants and hotels 847; Transport, storage and communications 410; Other activities 2,464; *Total gross value added* 4,425; Net taxes on products 130 (figure obtained as a residual); *GDP in purchasers' values* 4,555. Source: UN National Accounts Main Aggregates Database.

Balance of Payments (US $ million, 2012): Exports of goods f.o.b. 1,388.6; Imports of goods f.o.b. −2,039.0; *Balance on goods* −650.4; Exports of services 1,758.3; Imports of services −817.4; *Balance on goods and services* 290.6; Primary income received 37.0; Primary income paid −129.0; *Balance on goods, services and primary income* −198.6; Secondary income received 77.4; Secondary income paid −152.1; *Current balance* 123.9; Capital account (net) 1.2; Direct investment assets −2.8; Direct investment from liabilities −140.0; Portfolio investment assets −18.3; Portfolio investment liabilities 164.9; Financial derivatives and employee stock options (net) 1.6; Other investment assets 35.2; Other investment liabilities −94.2; Net errors and omissions −5.2; *Reserves and related items* 66.3. Source: IMF, *International Financial Statistics*.

EXTERNAL TRADE

Principal Commodities (AFl. million, 2013): *Imports c.i.f.:* Live animals and animal products 156.2; Food products 243.2; Chemical products 180.2; Base metals and articles thereof 92.8; Machinery and electrical equipment 298.9; Transport equipment 141.0; Total (incl. others) 2,083.5. *Exports f.o.b.:* Live animals and animal products 0.4; Machinery and electrical equipment 11.0; Transport equipment 4.8; Art objects and collectors' items 7.9; Total (incl. others) 74.7. Note: Figures exclude transactions involving mineral fuels and those of the Free Trade Zone of Aruba.

Principal Trading Partners (AFl. million, 2013): *Imports c.i.f.:* Brazil 27.7; Colombia 36.8; Japan 18.5; Netherlands 251.4; former Netherlands Antilles 44.3; Panama 65.2; USA 1,154.2; Venezuela 25.2; Total (incl. others) 2,083.5. *Exports f.o.b.:* Colombia 2.1; Netherlands 12.0; former Netherlands Antilles 6.7; USA 37.0; Venezuela 1.4; Total (incl. others) 74.7. Note: Figures exclude transactions of the petroleum sector and those of the Free Trade Zone of Aruba.

TRANSPORT

Road Traffic (motor vehicles registered, December 2012): Passenger cars 55,874; Lorries 1,054; Buses 131; Taxis 380; Rental cars 3,439; Government cars 537; Motorcycles 1,988; Total (incl. others) 63,808.

Shipping: *Arrivals* (2011): 2,098 vessels. *Flag Registered Fleet* (31 December 2013): Number of vessels 1; Total displacement 221 grt (Source: Lloyd's List Intelligence—www.lloydslistintelligence.com).

Civil Aviation: *Aircraft Landings:* 19,097 in 2010; 19,225 in 2011; 20,542 in 2012. *Passenger Arrivals:* 919,281 in 2010; 980,544 in 2011; 1,020,731 in 2012.

TOURISM

Tourist Arrivals: 1,468,866 (868,973 stop-over visitors, 599,893 cruise ship passengers) in 2011; 1,486,243 (903,934 stop-over visitors, 582,309 cruise ship passengers) in 2012; 1,667,824 (979,256 stop-over visitors, 688,568 cruise ship passengers) in 2013.

Stop-over Visitors by Country of Origin (2013): Netherlands 37,788; USA 556,296; Venezuela 188,020; Total (incl. others) 979,256.

Tourism Receipts (AFl. million): 2,414.6 in 2011; 2,505.0 in 2012; 2,679.7 in 2013.

COMMUNICATIONS MEDIA

Telephones (2013): 35,000 main lines in use.

Mobile Cellular Telephones (2013): 138,800 subscribers.

Internet Subscribers (2008): 18,400.

Broadband Subscribers (2013): 19,200.

Source: International Telecommunication Union.

EDUCATION

Pre-primary (September 2011): 28 schools (provisional); 2,874 pupils; 140 teachers.

Primary (September 2011): 38 schools (provisional); 9,130 pupils; 498 teachers.

General Secondary (September 2011 unless otherwise indicated): 9 schools (provisional); 7,592 pupils (2009/10); 544 teachers (2009/10).

Technical-Vocational (September 2011, provisional): 1 school; 1,881 pupils; 175 teachers.

Community College (1999/2000): 1 school; 1,187 pupils; 106 teachers.

University (September 2011, provisional): 1 university; 163 students; 29 tutors.

Teacher Training (September 2011, provisional, unless otherwise indicated): 1 institution; 132 students; 59 teachers (2008).

Special Education (September 2010): 5 schools; 549 pupils; 78 teachers.

Private, Non-aided (September 2008): 7 schools; 530 pupils; 47 teachers.

International School (2000/01): 1 school; 154 pupils; 25 teachers.

Pupil-teacher Ratio (primary education, UNESCO estimate): 14.8 in 2011/12 (Source: UNESCO Institute for Statistics).

Adult Literacy Rate (UNESCO estimates, 2010): 96.7% (males 96.9%; females 96.8%) (Source: UNESCO Institute for Statistics).

Directory

The Constitution

On 1 January 1986 Aruba acquired separate status (*status aparte*) within the Kingdom of the Netherlands. The form of government is embodied in the Charter of the Kingdom of the Netherlands (operational from 20 December 1954). The Netherlands, Aruba, Curaçao and Sint (St) Maarten each enjoy full autonomy in domestic and internal affairs, and are united on a basis of equality for the protection of their common interests and the granting of mutual assistance. In economic and monetary affairs there is a co-operative union between Aruba and Curaçao and St Maarten.

The Governor, who is appointed by the Dutch Crown for a term of six years, represents the monarch of the Netherlands in Aruba. The Government of Aruba appoints a minister plenipotentiary to represent it in the Government of the Kingdom. Whenever the Netherlands Council of Ministers is dealing with matters coming under the heading of joint affairs of the realm (in practice mainly foreign affairs and defence), the Council assumes the status of Council of Ministers of the Kingdom. In that event, Aruba's Minister Plenipotentiary takes part, with full voting powers, in the deliberations.

A legislative proposal regarding affairs of the realm and applying to Aruba as well as to the metropolitan Netherlands is sent, simultaneously with its submission, to the Staten Generaal (the Netherlands parliament) and to the Staten (States) of Aruba. The latter body can report in writing to the States on the draft Kingdom Statute and designate one or more special delegates to attend the debates and furnish information in the meetings of the Chambers of the States. Before the final vote on a draft the Minister Plenipotentiary has the right to express an opinion on it. If he disapproves of the draft, and if in the Second Chamber a three-fifths' majority of the votes cast is not obtained, the discussions on the draft are suspended and further deliberations take place in the Council of Ministers of the Kingdom. When special delegates attend the meetings of the Chambers, this right devolves upon the delegates of the parliamentary body designated for this purpose.

The Governor has executive power in external affairs, which he exercises in co-operation with the Council of Ministers. He is assisted by an advisory council, which consists of at least five members appointed by him.

Executive power in internal affairs is vested in a nominated Council of Ministers, responsible to the States. The legislature consists of 21 members, who are elected by universal adult suffrage for four years (subject to dissolution), on the basis of proportional representation. Inhabitants have the right to vote if they have Dutch nationality and have reached 18 years of age.

The Government

HEAD OF STATE

King of the Netherlands: HM King WILLEM-ALEXANDER.

Governor: FREDIS J. REFUNJOL (took office 7 May 2004).

COUNCIL OF MINISTERS
(September 2014)

The Government is formed by the Arubaanse Volkspartij.

Prime Minister and Minister of General Affairs, Science, Innovation and Sustainable Development: MICHIEL GODFRIED EMAN.

Minister of Territorial Development, Infrastructure and Integration: OSLIN BENITO SEVINGER.

Minister of Economic Affairs, Communications, Energy and the Environment: MIKE ERIC DE MEZA.

Minister of Tourism, Transport, Primary Industries and Culture: OTMAR ENRIQUE ODUBER.

Minister of Finance and Government Organization: ANGEL ROALD BERMUDEZ.

Minister of Justice: ARTHUR LAWRENCE DOWERS.

Minister of Education and Family: MICHELLE JANICE HOOYBOER-WINKLAAR.

Minister of Public Health, the Elderly Population and Sports: CARLOS ALEX SCHWENGLE.

Minister of Social Affairs, Youth and Labour: PAULDRICK FRANÇOIS TEODORIC CROES.

Minister Plenipotentiary and Member of the Council of Ministers of the Realm for Aruba in the Netherlands: ALFONSO BOEKHOUDT.

Minister Plenipotentiary of the Realm for Aruba in Washington, DC (USA): JOCELYNE CROES.

Secretary to the Council of Ministers: NICOLE HOEVERTSZ.

MINISTRIES

Office of the Governor: Plaza Henny Eman 3, POB 53, Oranjestad; tel. 5834445; fax 5820730; e-mail info@kabga.aw; internet www.kabga.aw.

Office of the Prime Minister: Government Offices, L. G. Smith Blvd 76, Oranjestad; tel. 5880300; fax 5880024.

Ministry of Economic Affairs, Communications, Energy and the Environment: L. G. Smith Blvd 76, Oranjestad; tel. 5885455; fax 5827526.

Ministry of Education and Family: L. G. Smith Blvd 76, Oranjestad; tel. 5284971; fax 5827531.

Ministry of Finance and Government Organization: Sun Plaza Bldg, 3rd Floor, L. G. Smith Blvd 76, Oranjestad; tel. 5833457; fax 5827538.

Ministry of General Affairs, Science, Innovation and Sustainable Development: L. G. Smith Blvd 76, Oranjestad; tel. 5830001; fax 5827513; e-mail rekenkamer@aruba.gov.aw.

Ministry of Justice: L. G. Smith Blvd 76, Oranjestad; tel. 5830004; fax 5827518.

Ministry of Public Health, the Elderly Population and Sports: L. G. Smith Blvd 76, Oranjestad; tel. 5825751; fax 5827569.

Ministry of Social Affairs, Youth and Labour: L. G. Smith Blvd 76, Oranjestad; tel. 5288998; fax 5285045.

Ministry of Territorial Development, Infrastructure and Integration: L. G. Smith Blvd 76, Oranjestad; tel. 5284945; fax 5827538.

Ministry of Tourism, Transport, Primary Industries and Culture: L. G. Smith Blvd 76, Oranjestad; tel. 5827718; fax 5827556.

Office of the Minister Plenipotentiary for Aruba in the Netherlands: R. J. Schimmelpennincklaan 1, 2517 JN The Hague, Netherlands; tel. (70) 3566200; fax (70) 3451446; e-mail info@arubahuis.nl; internet www.arubahuis.nl.

Office of the Minister Plenipotentiary for Aruba in Washington, DC (USA): 4200 Linnean Ave, NW, Washington, DC 20008, USA; tel. (202) 274-2601; fax (202) 237-8303; e-mail was-plvcdp@minbuza.nl.

Legislature

STATES
(Staten)

President: MARISOL LOPEZ-TROMP.

General Election, 27 September 2013

Party	Seats
Arubaanse Volkspartij (AVP)	13
Movimiento Electoral di Pueblo (MEP)	7
Partido Democracia Real (PDR)	1
Total	**21**

Political Organizations

Arubaanse Volkspartij (AVP) (Aruba People's Party): Avda Alo Tromp 56, Oranjestad; tel. 5830911; fax 5837963; internet www.avp .net; f. 1942; advocates Aruba's separate status; Leader MICHIEL GODFRIED EMAN.

Movimiento Electoral di Pueblo (MEP) (People's Electoral Movement): Santa Cruz 74D, Santa Cruz; tel. 5856917; fax 5850768; e-mail info@mep.aw; internet www.mep.aw; f. 1971; socialist; 1,200 mems; Pres. and Leader EVELYN WEVER-CROES.

Partido Democracia Real (PDR) (Real Democracy Party): Oranjestad; tel. 5941900; e-mail andin.bikker@gmail.com; internet www .votapdr.com; f. 2004; Leader ANDIN C. G. BIKKER.

Partido Patriotico di Aruba (PPA) (Patriotic Party of Aruba): Clavelstraat 5, Sint Nicolaas; tel. 5844609; e-mail nisbet@ppa-aruba .org; internet www.ppa-aruba.org; f. 1949; social democratic; opposed to complete independence for Aruba; Leader BENEDICT (BENNY) JOCELYN MONTGOMERY NISBET.

RED Democratico (RED Democratic Network): Belgiestraat 14, Oranjestad; tel. 5820213; e-mail info@red.aw; f. 2003; Leader DIONISIA THERESITA DE CUBA.

Union Patriotico Progresista (UPP): Oranjestad; Leader CANDELARIO A. S. D. WEVER.

Judicial System

Legal authority is exercised by the Joint Court of Justice of Aruba, Curaçao and St Maarten and of Bonaire, St Eustatius and Saba. Its headquarters are in Curaçao. The Joint Court hears civil, criminal and administrative cases in the first instance and on appeal. The Supreme Court of the Netherlands (based in The Hague) is the court of Final Instance for any appeal.

Joint Court of Justice: Wayaca 33E, Oranjestad; tel. 5822294; fax 5821241; internet www.gemhofvanjustitie.org/vestigingen/aruba; hears cases in the first instance.

Attorney-General: ROBERT F. PIETERSZ.

Religion

CHRISTIANITY

The Roman Catholic Church

Roman Catholics form the largest religious community, numbering 76% of the population, according to the 2010 census. Aruba forms part of the diocese of Willemstad (Curaçao), comprising Aruba, Bonaire, Curaçao, St Maarten, St Eustatius and Saba. Willemstad is part of the archdiocese of Port of Spain (Trinidad and Tobago).

Roman Catholic Church (St Fransiscus Church): J. Yrausquin Plein 3, POB 445, Oranjestad; tel. 5821434; fax 5821276; e-mail parokiasanfrancisco@yahoo.com.

The Anglican Communion

Within the Church in the Province of the West Indies, Aruba forms part of the diocese of the North Eastern Caribbean and Aruba. The Bishop is resident in St John's, Antigua and Barbuda. About 0.5% of the population were Anglican, according to the 2010 census.

Anglican Church: Holy Cross, Weg Seroe Pretoe 31, Sint Nicolaas; tel. 5845142; fax 5843394; e-mail holycross@setarnet.aw.

Other Christian Churches

According to the 2010 census, 3% of the population were Protestant, 2% Jehovah's Witnesses, 1% Methodist, and 1% Seventh-day Adventist.

Baptist Church: Aruba Baptist Mission, SBC, Paradera 98-C; tel. 5883893.

Church of Christ: Pastoor Hendrikstraat 107, POB 2206, Sint Nicolaas; tel. 5848172; e-mail lwaymire@setarnet.aw; Minister LARRY WAYMIRE.

Church of Jesus Christ of Latter-Day Saints: Dadelstraat 16, Oranjestad; tel. 5823507.

Dutch Protestant Church: Wilhelminastraat 1, Oranjestad; tel. 5821435; e-mail protestantsegemeente@setarnet.aw.

Evangelical Church of San Nicolas: Jasmijnstraat 7, Sint Nicolaas; tel. 5848973; e-mail norbeth@setarnet.aw; internet www .goodnewsaruba.org; f. 1970; Pastor NORMAN BROWNE.

Faith Revival Center: Rooi Afo 10, Paradera; tel. 5831010; fax 5833070; e-mail frc_aruba@yahoo.com; internet faithrevival .googlepages.com.

Iglesia Evangelica Pentecostal: Asamblea di Dios, Reamurstraat 2, Oranjestad; tel. 5831940.

Jehovah's Witnesses: Guyabastraat 3, Oranjestad; tel. 5828963.

Methodist Church: Bernhardstraat 245, Sint Nicolaas; tel. 5845243; fax 5934810; e-mail relismartinriley@yahoo.com; Supt Rev. RELIS F. MARTIN-RILEY.

New Apostolic Church: Goletstraat 5, Oranjestad; tel. 5833762; Pastor A. DEN HAMER.

Seventh-day Adventist: Pos Chiquito 47A, POB 66, Oranjestad; tel. 5840777; e-mail misionaruba@gmail.com; internet misionaruba .interamerica.org; Pres. MARTIN FORBES.

JUDAISM

According to 2010 census figures, 0.4% of the population was Jewish.

Beth Israel Aruba Synagogue: Adriaan Laclé Blvd 2, POB 655, Oranjestad; tel. 5823272; e-mail rabbi@bethisraelaruba.com; internet www.bethisraelaruba.com; Rabbi DANIEL KRIPPER.

BAHÁ'Í FAITH

Spiritual Assembly: Bucutiweg 19, Oranjestad; tel. 5823104; Contact M. CHRISTIAN.

The Press

DAILIES

Amigoe di Aruba: Bilderdijkstraat 16-2, POB 323, Oranjestad; tel. 5824333; fax 5822368; e-mail arubaredactie@amigoe.com; internet www.amigoe.com; f. 1884; Dutch; Dir SIGRID HAMMELBURG; Editor JEAN MENTENS; circ. 12,000.

Aruba Daily: Engelandstraat 29, POB 577, Oranjestad; tel. 7346150; e-mail news@aruba-daily.com; internet aruba-daily.com; English; Mon.–Sat. morning; Publr RENE VAN NOREL.

Aruba Today: Weststraat 22, Oranjestad; tel. 5827800; fax 5827093; e-mail info@arubatoday.com; internet www.arubatoday .com; English; Editor-in-Chief JULIA C. RENFRO.

Bon Dia Aruba: Weststraat 22, Oranjestad; tel. 5827800; fax 5827044; e-mail noticia@bondia.com; internet www.bondia.com; Papiamento; Dir JOHN CHEMALY, Jr.

Diario: Engelandstraat 29, POB 577, Oranjestad; tel. 5826747; fax 5828551; e-mail noticia@diario.aw; internet www.diarioaruba.aw; f. 1980; Papiamento; morning; Editor and Man. JOSSY M. MANSUR; circ. 15,000.

The Morning News: Caya G. F. (Betico) Croes 111, Oranjestad; tel. 5889517; fax 5889518; e-mail themorningnewsaruba@gmail.com; internet www.themorningnewsaruba.com; f. 2010 by staff of defunct *The News* daily; English; daily.

Publishers

Aruba Experience Publications NV: Miramar Bldg, 3rd Floor, Of. 306, L. G. Smith Blvd 62, Oranjestad; tel. 5887878; fax 5384520; e-mail info@arubaexperience.com; internet www.arubaexperience .com; f. 1985; Gen. Man. SUSAN RUITER.

Caribbean Publishing Co Ltd (CPC): L. G. Smith Blvd 116, Oranjestad; tel. 5820485; fax 5820484; e-mail infoarubayp@ globaldirectories.com; internet arubayp.com; subsidiary of Global Directories Ltd, Bermuda.

De Wit and Van Dorp Aruba: Tanki Leendert 103B, Oranjestad; tel. 5823076; fax 5821575; e-mail info@dewitvandorp.com; f. 1948; Gen. Man. LYANNE BEAUJON.

Editorial Charuba: Beatrixstraat 23, Oranjestad; tel. 5943773; fax 5827526; e-mail alivaro@hotmail.com; f. 1982; Pres. ALICE VAN ROMONDT.

ProGraphics Inc: Italiestraat 5, POB 201, Oranjestad; tel. 5824550; fax 5833072; e-mail info@prographicsaruba.com; internet www.prographicsaruba.com; f. 2001; fmrly VAD Printers Inc; Gen. Man. HEIN VAN DER PUTTEN.

Broadcasting and Communications

TELECOMMUNICATIONS

Digicel Aruba: Marisol Bldg, L. G. Smith Blvd 60, POB 662, Oranjestad; tel. 5222222; fax 5222223; e-mail customercarearuba@ digicelgroup.com; internet www.digicelaruba.com; f. 2003; owned by an Irish consortium; established a mobile cellular telephone network connecting Aruba with Bonaire and Curaçao in 2006; Chair. DENIS

O'Brien; CEO (Dutch Caribbean) Sander Gielen; Gen. Man. (Aruba) Remko van der Veldt.

SETAR (Servicio di Telecomunicacion di Aruba NV): Seroe Blanco z/n, POB 13, Oranjestad; tel. 5251000; fax 5251515; e-mail sysop@setarnet.aw; internet www.setar.aw; f. 1986; Man. Dir Roland Croes.

BROADCASTING

Radio

Canal 90 FM Stereo: Van Leeuwenhoekstraat 26, Oranjestad; tel. 5821601; fax 837340; e-mail canal90fm@gmail.com; internet www.canal90fm.aw/index2.htm; Producer M. Gravenhorst.

Cool FM 98.9: Caya Betico Croes 23, Oranjestad; tel. 5833100; fax 5833101; e-mail publica@coolaruba.com; internet www.coolaruba.com; part of A & K Broadcasting Corpn NV; Dir Alexander Ponson.

Hit 94 FM: Caya Ernesto Petronia 68, Oranjestad; tel. 5820694; fax 5820494; e-mail hit94@setarnet.aw; internet www.hit94fm.com; f. 1993; Dir Johnny Habibe.

Magic 96.5 FM: Caya G. F. (Betico) Croes 164, Oranjestad; tel. 5865353; fax 5835354; internet www.magic965.com; Owner and Dir Erin J. Croes.

Power FM 101.7: Piedra Plat 44 C-D, Lok 12, Paradera; tel. 5851017; e-mail info@blizz.aw; internet blizz.aw; fmrly Blizz FM; name changed as above in 2012; Man. Ruben (Scorpio) Garcia.

Radio Carina FM 97.9: Datustraat 10A, Oranjestad; tel. 5821450; fax 5831955; commercial station; programmes in Dutch, English, Spanish and Papiamento; Dir-Gen. Albert R. Dieffenthaler.

Radio Caruso Booy FM: G. M. de Bruynewijk 49, Savaneta; tel. 5847752; fax 5843351; e-mail radiocarusobooy@hotmail.com; commercial station; broadcasts for 24 hrs a day; programmes in Dutch, English, Spanish and Papiamento; Gen. Man. Sira Booy.

Radio Victoria: Washington 23A, POB 5291, Oranjestad; tel. and fax 5873444; e-mail radiovictoria@setarnet.aw; internet www.srv931fm.org; f. 1958; religious and cultural FM radio station owned by the Radio Victoria Foundation; programmes in Dutch, English, Spanish, Papiamento, Dutch, Tagalog, Creole and Mandarin; Pres. N. J. F. Arts.

Voz di Aruba (Voice of Aruba): Van Leeuwenhoekstraat 26, POB 219, Oranjestad; tel. 5823355; fax 5837340; commercial radio station; programmes in Dutch, English, Spanish and Papiamento; also operates Canal 90 on FM; Dir A. M. Arends, Jr.

Television

ABC Aruba Broadcasting Co NV (ATV): Royal Plaza Suite 223, POB 5040, Oranjestad; tel. 5838150; fax 5838434; e-mail emily@15atv.com; internet www.15atv.com; Rep. Emily Hudson.

Telearuba NV: Pos Chiquito 1A, POB 392, Oranjestad; tel. 5851000; fax 5851111; e-mail info@telearuba.aw; internet www.telearuba.aw; f. 1963; fmrly operated by Netherlands Antilles Television Co; commercial; acquired by SETAR in March 2005; Gen. Man. M. Marchena.

Finance

(cap. = capital; res = reserves; dep. = deposits; m. = million; br(s) = branch(es); amounts in Aruban florins, unless otherwise stated)

BANKING

Central Bank

Centrale Bank van Aruba: J. E. Irausquin Blvd 8, POB 18, Oranjestad; tel. 5252100; fax 5252101; e-mail cbaua@setarnet.aw; internet www.cbaruba.org; f. 1986; cap. 10.0m., res 174.8m., dep. 884.7m. (Dec. 2009); Chair. C. G. Maduro; Pres. Jeanette R. Figaroa-Semeleer.

Commercial Banks

Aruba Bank NV: Camacuri 12, POB 192, Oranjestad; tel. 5277777; fax 5277715; e-mail info@arubabank.com; internet www.arubabank.com; f. 1925; acquired Interbank Aruba NV in 2003; total assets US $1,690m. (Dec. 2012); Chair. B. W. H. Guis; 5 brs.

Banco di Caribe NV: Vondellaan 31, POB 493, Oranjestad; tel. 5232000; fax 5832422; e-mail management@bancodicaribe.com; internet www.bancodicaribe.com; f. 1987; Gen. Man. and CEO Idefons D. Simon; 1 br.

Caribbean Mercantile Bank NV: Caya G. F. (Betico) Croes 53, POB 28, Oranjestad; tel. 5823118; fax 5824373; e-mail executive_office@cmbnv.com; internet www.cmbnv.com; f. 1963; cap. 4.0m., dep. 1,228.6m. (Dec. 2012); Chair. Lionel Capriles, II; Gen. Man. J. E. Wolter; 6 brs.

RBC Royal Bank (Aruba) NV: Italiestraat 36, Sasakiweg, Oranjestad; tel. 5233100; fax 58821576; e-mail tt-info@rbc.com; internet www.rbtt.com; f. 2001; fmrly First National Bank of Aruba NV (f. 1985 and acquired by Royal Bank of Trinidad and Tobago Ltd in 1998); name changed as above Mar. 2012; cap. 43.8m., res 17.6m., dep. 997.4m. (Dec. 2012); Chair. Peter J. July; 4 brs.

Investment Bank

AIB Bank NV: Wilhelminastraat 34–36, POB 1011, Oranjestad; tel. 5827327; fax 5827461; e-mail info@aib-bank.com; internet www.aib-bank.com; f. 1987 as Aruban Investment Bank; name changed as above in April 2004; total assets 149.0m. (Dec. 2005); Man. Dir Frendsel W. Giel.

Mortgage Bank

Fundacion Cas pa Comunidad Arubano (FCCA): Sabana Blanco 66, Oranjestad; tel. 5223222; fax 5836272; e-mail info@fcca.com; internet www.fcca.com; f. 1979; Man. Dir Peter van Poppel.

INSURANCE

There were seven life insurance companies and 13 non-life insurance companies active in Aruba in 2011.

Pan-American Life Insurance Company of Aruba, NV: Sun Plaza Suite 100, L. G. Smith Blvd 160, Oranjestad; tel. 5821184; fax 5823880; internet www.palig.com; f. 2012; part of Pan-American Life Insurance Group (USA); CEO and Man. Dir (Caribbean) William R. Schulz, Jr; Gen. Man. Valery Sinot.

Association

Insurance Association of Aruba (IAA): Sun Plaza 202, Oranjestad; tel. 5825500; fax 5822126; e-mail prakash.gupta@aig.com; Pres. Prakash Gupta; 17 mems.

Trade and Industry

DEVELOPMENT ORGANIZATIONS

Department of Agriculture, Husbandry and Fisheries (DLVV): Piedra Plat 114A, Paradera, Oranjestad; tel. 5858102; fax 5855639; e-mail dlvv@aruba.gov.aw; internet www.overheid.aw; f. 1976; Dir T. G. Damian.

Department of Economic Affairs, Commerce and Industry (Directie Economische Zaken, Handel en Industrie): Sun Plaza Bldg, L. G. Smith Blvd 160, Oranjestad; tel. 5821181; fax 5834494; e-mail deaci@setarnet.aw; internet www.arubaeconomicaffairs.aw; f. 1986; Dir Maria Dijkhoff-Pita.

CHAMBERS OF COMMERCE AND INDUSTRY

Aruba Chamber of Commerce and Industry: J. E. Irausquin Blvd 10, POB 140, Oranjestad; tel. 5821566; fax 5883962; e-mail info@arubachamber.com; internet www.arubachamber.com; f. 1930; Pres. Omar F. Tromp; Exec. Dir Leonicio J. Maduro.

Association of Dutch Caribbean Chambers of Commerce & Industry: J. E. Irausquin Blvd 10, POB 140, Oranjestad; tel. 5821566; fax 5883962; e-mail secretariat@arubachamber.com; f. 2011; asscn of chambers of commerce in Aruba, Bonaire, Curaçao, Saba, Sint Eustatius and Sint Maarten.

TRADE ASSOCIATION

Aruba Trade and Industry Association (ATIA): ATIA Bldg, Pedro Gallegostraat 6, Dakota, POB 562, Oranjestad; tel. 5827593; fax 5833068; e-mail atiaruba@setarnet.aw; internet www.atiaruba.org; f. 1945; Chair. Michel Henriquez; Dir Igmar Reyes; 250 mems.

MAJOR COMPANIES

Albo Aruba NV: Barcadera 122, Oranjestad; tel. 5285808; fax 5853766; e-mail info@alboaruba.com; internet www.alboaruba.com; f. 1980, combining Albo Bonaire NV and Bonbocemi NV; civil construction; subsidiary of Albo Holding Co NV; Man. Dir Folkert G. van der Woude.

Arena Contractors: Arendstraat 120-F, Oranjestad; tel. 5881310; fax 5838514; internet www.arenacontractorsnv.com; f. 2006; manpower services and clay products; Man. Dir Edith Maria Perez.

Aruba Aloe Balm NV: Pitastraat 115, Hato, Oranjestad; tel. 5883222; fax 5826081; e-mail customerservice@arubaaloe.com; internet www.arubaaloe.com; f. 1890; aloe-based skin care products; Man. Dir Louis Posner.

Arubaanse Verffabriek NV (Arvefa): L. G. Smith Blvd 144, POB 297, Oranjestad; tel. 5822519; fax 5827225; e-mail farts@arvefa.com; internet www.arvefa.com; f. 1969; manufactures paints and fillers; Man. Fred Arts.

Arubaanse Wegenbouw Maatschappij NV (Aruba Road Construction Co): Barcadera 122, Oranjestad; tel. 5853007; fax 5853766; e-mail info@awmaruba.com; internet www.awmaruba.com; f. 1960; wholly owned subsidiary of Albo Holding Co NV; Man. Dir MICHIEL J. L. DAEMS; 100 employees.

Aruba Marriott Resort and Stellaris Casino: L. G. Smith Blvd 101, Palm Beach, Oranjestad; tel. 5869000; fax 5206227; e-mail marriott@setarnet.aw; internet www.marriottaruba.com; Vice-Pres. and Gen. Man. TOM CALAME; 670 employees.

Aruba Trading Company (Aruba Handel Maatschappij NV): Weststraat 15–17, POB 156, Oranjestad; tel. 5823950; fax 5832165; e-mail info@arubatrading.com; internet www.arubatrading.com; f. 1933; distribution of general goods, incl. food and drink, clothing and household items; Chair. RAOUL C. HENRIQUEZ; CEO ISAAC WAINCIER; 80 employees.

Aruhiba Cigars: L. G. Smith Blvd 330, Palm Beach, Oranjestad; tel. 5867833; e-mail aruhibacigars@gmail.com; internet www.aruhibacigars.com; tobacco; CEO BENJAMIN PETROCCHI.

Arupro Chemical & Agencies: Van Gallenstraat 4, Industrial Zone, San Nicolas; tel. 5844658; fax 5842641; internet www.arupro-agencies.com; f. 1999; chemicals, detergents; Gen. Man. ANDRES HERNANDEZ.

ATCO (Associated Transport Company): Sabana Blanco 2, POB 189, Oranjestad; tel. 5821523; fax 5886761; e-mail info@atco.aw; internet www.atcoaruba.com; f. 1949; part of MetaCorp conglomerate; provides heavy lifting and transport equipment services to construction and petrochemical industries; mfr of concrete and paving materials; operates waste management and recycling services.

Brouwerij Nacional Balashi NV: POB 5317, Balashi; tel. 5922544; fax 5236544; internet www.balashi.com; f. 1998; brewery; owned by MetaCorp NV conglomerate; Man. Dir EDUARD L. J. DE VEER.

Caribbean Paint Factory Aruba NV: Sabana Blanco 16A, POB 273, Oranjestad; tel. 5825339; fax 5837063; e-mail akamermans@setarnet.aw; internet www.cpfaruba.com; f. 1986; paint mfr; Dir ANTONY KAMERMANS.

Deli Caribbean (Aruba): Schotlandstraat 51, Suite 8- E, Oranjestad; tel. 583 2373; e-mail info@delicaribbean.com; internet www.delicaribbean.com; importers and suppliers of food products; Gen. Man. RICK WOUTERS.

Ecolab Aruba NV: Schotlandstraat 73, Oranjestad; tel. 5820765; fax 5820799; e-mail ronald.ligeon@ecolab.com; internet www.ecolab.com; Man. RONALD LIGEON.

Hyatt Regency Aruba Resort & Casino: J. A. Irausquin Blvd 85, Palm Beach, Oranjestad; tel. 5861234; fax 5861682; e-mail adventure.concierge@hyatt.com; internet www.aruba.hyatt.com; f. 1990; Hyatt Hotels Corpn; Gen. Man. FRED HOFFMAN; 670 employees.

Ling & Sons: Schotlandstraat 41, Oranjestad; tel. 5832370; fax 5887718; e-mail info@lingandsons.com; internet www.lingandsons.com; f. 1965; groceries retailer and wholesaler; mem. of the Independent Grocers Asscn; Gen. Man. CLIFTON LING.

Nos Cunucu—The Land Farm: Shete 7-Z; tel. 5855231; e-mail thelandfarm@gmail.com; internet www.noscunucuaruba.com; groceries; Man. Dir ARI LICHTENSTEIN.

Palmera Quality Products NV: L. G. Smith Blvd 140, POB 95, Oranjestad; tel. 5822122; fax 5821048; e-mail palmeraquality@setarnet.aw; internet www.rumpalmera.com; f. 1965; alcoholic beverages; Man. Dirs ALBERT C. EMAN, ETHAN WONG; 30 employees.

Thiel Corpn, NV: J. G. Emanstraat 118A, POB 614, Oranjestad; tel. 5837286; fax 5831545; e-mail info@thielcorp.aw; internet thielcorp.com; building equipment suppliers and cement producers; owns *Barcadera Cement Aruba*; Dir ANTHONY THIEL.

Valero Energy Corporation: 5 Lago Weg, Sint Nicolaas; internet www.valero.com; owns island's oil refinery, Valero Aruba Refining Co NV; refinery closed in 2012; currently operating as fuel storage facility; CEO WILLIAM R. KLESSE.

Visser Holding Aruba, NV: Italiestraat 24, Oranjestad; tel. 5835212; fax 5838290; internet www.visserholding.com; f. 1967; pharmaceutical supplier; CEO RICHARD VISSER; Gen. Man. HANS MONDRIA.

UTILITIES

Electricity and Water

Utilities Aruba NV: Schelpstraat 12, Oranjestad; tel. 5828277; fax 5828682; e-mail info@utilitiesarubanv.com; internet www.utilitiesarubanv.com; govt-owned holding co; Man. Dir Dr FRANKLIN HOEVERTSZ.

Electriciteit-Maatschappij Aruba (ELMAR) NV: Wilhelminastraat 110, POB 202, Oranjestad; tel. 5237100; fax 5828991; e-mail info@elmar.aw; internet www.elmar.aw; independently managed co, residing under Utilities Aruba NV; electricity distribution; Man. Dir ROBERT HENRIQUEZ; 160 employees.

Water en Energiebedrijf Aruba (WEB) NV: Balashi 76, POB 575, Oranjestad; tel. 5254600; fax 5857681; e-mail info@webaruba.com; internet www.webaruba.com; f. 1991; independently managed co, residing under Utilities Aruba NV; production and distribution of industrial and potable water, and electricity generation; Man. Dir OSLIN J. BOEKHOUDT.

Gas

Aruba Gas Supply Company Ltd (ARUGAS): Barcadera z/n, POB 190, Oranjestad; tel. 5851198; fax 5852187; e-mail sales@arugas.com; internet www.arugas.com; f. 1940; Man. R. P. GEERMAN.

BOC Gases Aruba NV: Balashi z/n, POB 387, Oranjestad; tel. 5852624; fax 5852823; e-mail bocaruba@setarnet.aw; internet www.linde-worldwide.com; acquired by the Linde Group global industrial gases and engineering org. in 2006; Man. Dir J. KENT MASTERS (responsible for Americas, South Pacific and Africa).

TRADE UNION

Federacion di Trahadornan di Aruba (FTA) (Aruban Workers' Federation): Bernhardstraat 23, Sint Nicolaas; tel. 5845448; fax 5845504; e-mail info@fta.aw; internet www.fta.aw; f. 1964; independent; affiliated with the International Trade Union Confed; Pres. JOSÉ RUDOLF (RUDY) GEERMAN; Vice-Pres. HUBERT MARIANO DIRKSZ.

Transport

There are no railways, but Aruba has a network of all-weather roads.

Arubus NV: Sabana Blanco 67, Oranjestad; tel. 5202300; fax 5828633; e-mail marketing@arubus.com; internet www.arubus.com; f. 1979; state-owned company providing public transport services; runs a fleet of 48 buses; Man. Dir TEO CROES.

SHIPPING

The island's principal seaport is Oranjestad, whose harbour can accommodate ocean-going vessels. There are also ports at Barcadera and Sint Nicolaas.

Aruba Ports Authority NV: Port Administration Bldg, L. G. Smith Blvd 23, Oranjestad; tel. 5234300; fax 5234343; e-mail info@arubaports.com; internet www.arubaports.com; f. 1981; responsible for the administration of the ports of Oranjestad and Barcadera; Man. Dir JOSSY FIGUAROA.

Principal Shipping Companies

Aruba Stevedoring Co (ASTEC), NV: Port Administration Bldg, L. G. Smith Blvd 23, Oranjestad; tel. 5822558; fax 5834570; e-mail astec_admin@setarnet.aw; f. 1983; Man. Dir ERNAND MIKE DE L'ISLE.

Global Marine Services NV: De la Sallestraat 71-D, Oranjestad; tel. 5887212; fax 5887210; e-mail info@globalmarineservicesnv.co; internet www.globalmarineservicesnv.com; f. 2004; ship agent, liner shipping services, STS operations and freight services; Man. MARIA WINKEL.

Rocargo Services Aruba, NV: Lago Heightstraat 28, Lago Heights, POB 2527, San Nicolas; tel. 5844900; fax 5844880; e-mail rocargoaruba@rocargo.com; internet www.rocargo.com; f. 1994; shipping and port agents, cargo handling and transportation; Man. JOOP KRAAIJEVELD.

SEL Maduro & Sons (Aruba) Inc: Rockefellerstraat 1, Oranjestad; tel. 55826039; fax 5826136; e-mail vessel_coll@selmaduro.com; internet www.selmaduro.com; ship husbandry and port agent; also provides container services, cargo services, moving services, real estate and travel services; Man. Dir HANS BEAUJON (acting); Man. GRACEO DUNLOCK (Shipping and Container Services).

VR Shipping NV: Executive Bldg, Frankrijkstraat 1, POB 633, Oranjestad; tel. 5821953; fax 5825988; e-mail bronswinkelh@vrshipping.com; internet www.vrshipping.com; f. 1975 as Anthony Veder & Co; name changed as above 2000; Man. HANLEY BRONSWINKEL.

CIVIL AVIATION

The Queen Beatrix International Airport (Aeropuerto Internacional Reina Beatrix), about 2.5 km from Oranjestad, is served by numerous airlines (including Dutch Antilles Express, based in Curaçao), linking the island with destinations in the Caribbean, Europe, the USA, and Central and South America. The airport in 2014 was undergoing a three-stage expansion project, estimated to cost between US $18m.–$29m.

Aruba Airport Authority NV: Queen Beatrix International Airport, Wayaca z/n, Oranjestad; tel. 5242424; fax 5834229; e-mail p.steinmetz@airportaruba.com; internet www.airportaruba.com; Man. Dir PETER STEINMETZ.

Tiara Air: Sabana Blanco 70E, Suite 11, Oranjestad; tel. 5884272; fax 5885002; e-mail sales@tiara-air.com; internet www.tiara-air.com; daily flights to Colombia and Venezuela, scheduled flights to Bonaire, Curaçao; Pres. ALEJANDRO MUYALE.

Tourism

Aruba's white sandy beaches, particularly along the southern coast, are an attraction for foreign visitors, and tourism is a major industry. The number of hotel rooms totalled 7,441 in 2009. In 2013 some 1,667,824 tourists visited Aruba, of whom 979,256 were stop-over visitors and 688,568 were cruise ship passengers. Most stop-over visitors came from the USA (57% in 2013), Venezuela (19%) and the Netherlands (4%). Receipts from tourism totalled A Fl. 2,679.7m. in 2013.

Aruba Cruise Tourism: Royal Plaza Mall, Suite 230, L. G. Smith Blvd 94, POB 5254, Oranjestad; tel. 5833648; fax 5835088; e-mail cruiseinfo@aruba.com; internet cruise.aruba.com; f. 1995 as the Cruise Tourism Authority—Aruba; name changed as above in 2005; non-profit government organization; Gen. Man. GLORIA VEGA.

Aruba Hotel and Tourism Association (AHATA): L. G. Smith Blvd 174, POB 542, Oranjestad; tel. 5822607; fax 5824202; e-mail info@ahata.com; internet www.ahata.com; f. 1965; 101 mems; Chair. EWALD BIEMANS; Pres. and CEO JAMES HEPPLE.

Aruba Tourism Authority (ATA): L. G. Smith Blvd 172, Eagle, Oranjestad; tel. 5823777; fax 5834702; e-mail support@aruba.com; internet www.aruba.com; f. 1953; CEO RONELLA TJIN ASJOE-CROES.

Defence

The Netherlands is responsible for Aruba's defence, and military service is compulsory. The Dutch-appointed Governor is Commander-in-Chief of the armed forces on the island. A Dutch naval contingent is stationed in Curaçao and Aruba.

Education

A Compulsory Education Act was introduced in 1999 for those aged between four and 16 years. Kindergarten begins at four years of age. Primary education begins at six years of age and lasts for six years. Secondary education, beginning at the age of 12, lasts for up to six years. In 2010 enrolment at primary schools included 99% of pupils in the relevant age-group, while enrolment at secondary schools in 2011 was 77%. The main language of instruction is Dutch, but Papiamento (using a different spelling system from that of Bonaire and Curaçao) is used in kindergarten and primary education, and is also being introduced into the curriculum in all schools. There is one public university in Aruba, the Universiteit van Aruba. There is also a teacher training college and a number of private institutions, including two medical schools. In addition, there is a community college. However, the majority of students continue their studies abroad, generally in the Netherlands. General government spending on education in 2010 was equivalent to 18.3% of total expenditure.

Bibliography

Croes, R. R. *Anatomy of Demand in International Tourism: The Case of Aruba.* Saarbrücken, LAP LAMBERT Academic Publishing, 2010.

Haanappel, P., *et al* (Eds). *The Civil Code of the Netherlands Antilles and Aruba.* Alphen aan den Rijn, Kluwer Law International, 2002.

International Monetary Fund. *The Kingdom of the Netherlands—Aruba: 2007 Article IV Consultation—Staff Report; Public Informa-tion Notice on the Executive Board Discussion; and Statement by the Executive Director for the Kingdom of the Netherlands—Aruba.* Washington, DC, IMF Staff Country Report, 2008.

Oostindie, G. *Paradise Overseas: The Dutch Caribbean: Colonialism and its Transatlantic Legacies.* Oxford, Macmillan Caribbean, 2005.

THE BAHAMAS

Geography

PHYSICAL FEATURES

The Commonwealth of the Bahamas forms part of the West Indies; however, as it is located to the north of the Greater Antilles and east of Florida (USA), the archipelago lies in the Atlantic Ocean, not the Caribbean Sea. The island chain begins some 80 km (50 miles) off the coast of south-eastern Florida, arcing south and east to tail off in the Turks and Caicos Islands, a British dependency that lies just over 60 km south-east of Mayaguana and to the west of Great Inagua, the southernmost of the Bahamas. The country ends here, just to the north of the Windward Passage between the Antillean islands of Cuba and Hispaniola, giving the Bahamas two more international neighbours less than 100 km from its shores—Haiti to the south-east and Cuba to the south. The Tropic of Cancer bisects the country, crossing Long Island. The myriad islands of the Bahamas cover 13,939 sq km (5,382 sq miles), of which 3,870 sq km are enclosed or inland waters.

There are almost 700 islands and some 2,000 cays (keys) and rocky islets in the Bahamas, giving the country coastlines that total 3,542 km in length. Most of the islands are coralline, usually flat, many of the larger ones being long and thin. Low hills relieve the landscape in places, the highest point in the country being Mt Alvernia (63 m or 207 ft) on Cat Island (once believed to be the San Salvador where the Italian navigator Christopher Columbus first set foot in the Americas). This terrain, as well as the dry climate, does not support much arable land. In the north of the archipelago is Grand Bahama, the main island nearest to Florida, while to its east, marking the other edge of the Little Bahama Bank, are Little Abaco and Great Abaco. To the south of Grand Bahama is the Great Bahama Bank, marked above sea level by the landmass of Andros, the largest island in the country, as well as Bimini and Berry and Williams Islands. East of Andros, beyond the continuation of the Northeast Providence Channel known as the Tongue of the Ocean (which plunges some 6,000 m beneath the surface), rises the relatively small, but densely populated, island of New Providence, the location of Nassau, the national capital. East of New Providence, Eleuthera continues the chain of long, thin islands heading south from Great Abaco, with Cat Island and Long Island following. East of Cat Island and Long Island is, among others, the island now called San Salvador (formerly Watling Island), while to the west is Great Exuma, another long, thin stretch of territory. By now heading more east than south, the remaining large islands of the Bahamas include Crooked and Acklins Islands and, beyond the Mayaguana Passage, Mayaguana itself and, to its south, Little Inagua (where Bahamian territory comes closest to the Turks and Caicos Islands—West Caicos) and Great Inagua, the latter dominated by Lake Rosa at its heart. Particularly to the west of the main chain of islands and islets, numerous reefs and cays dot the ocean, extending the country's territorial waters to cover well over 0.25m. sq km. The Andros Barrier Reef is the third largest such reef in the world and the largest, after that of Belize, in the Americas.

CLIMATE

The climate is tropical marine, moderated by the Gulf Stream and the Atlantic trade winds. The islands are prone to hurri-

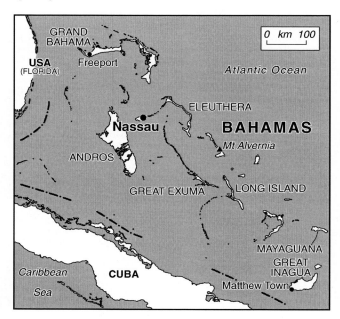

canes, which can be particularly devastating given the low-lying terrain. Precipitation is not profuse, and the annual average is 1,360 mm (53 ins), falling mostly in June and then the four months thereafter. Seasonal variations in temperature are slight, with the weather always being warm—the month with the highest average daily maximum temperature is August (89.3°F or 31.8°C), while the lowest daily minimum is in January (62.1°F or 16.7°C).

POPULATION

The population is predominantly black (93%, according to the 2010 census). The white population comprised about 5% of the population in 2010. The people of the Bahamas are generally Christian, the largest denomination being the Baptists (35% in 2010), but there are also numerous other Protestant denominations, as well as sizeable Anglican (14%) and Roman Catholic (12%) communities. The main language in use, as well as the official one, is English.

In mid-2014 the total population of the Bahamas was officially estimated at 364,000. Just over two-thirds of the population lived in the capital, Nassau, on New Providence. In mid-2012 the city and its suburbs housed an estimated 248,948 people. The other islands, of which about 29 are inhabited, are known as the Out Islands or Family Islands. The more populous ones are Grand Bahama, where the second largest city, Freeport, is located, Eleuthera, the original site of settlement by the British, and Andros. The country is divided into 32 administrative districts.

History

MARK WILSON

INTRODUCTION

The nearly 700 islands and 2,000 uninhabited cays that make up the Bahamian archipelago stretch in a 1,220 km arc towards the northern edge of the Caribbean from a point some 80 km off the coast of Florida (USA). One of the islands, San Salvador or Watling Island, is widely believed to have been the navigator Christopher Columbus's first landfall in the New World, in October 1492. The Spanish are thought to have deported and enslaved the original Lucayan inhabitants, but otherwise took little interest in the dry and somewhat barren islands. The British also found little to attract them to the islands, although a royal charter permitting their exploitation was granted to Sir Robert Heath in 1629. The first British settlers were Puritans from Bermuda, who arrived on Eleuthera in 1647. Other migrants from Bermuda also came, to seek salt. New Providence became the site of the capital, Nassau, from 1666. The other islands became collectively known as the Out Islands and, more recently, as the Family Islands. The soil and climate were not suitable for commercial agriculture, and piracy became the basis of the economy, until its eradication in 1719 by the British Governor, Capt. Woodes Rogers.

Population growth was slow. As recently as 1782 there were only 4,000 inhabitants, of whom some 43% were white. However, with the ending of the American War of Independence at this time, loyalist settlers who had been expelled from the former British colonies on the mainland arrived. New Englanders settled some of the smaller islands as fishermen, while southerners brought slaves and established cotton plantations on some of the larger islands. Within four years, the population had grown to 8,950, of whom 67% were black. However, the cotton plantations were soon abandoned, owing to insect pests and soil exhaustion. In total, fewer than 10,000 slaves were landed in the colony, and many were freed from bondage long before emancipation in 1834, when the population was an estimated 21,000. Then, as now, whites formed a significant minority. A further minority group originated directly from Africa, without any experience of New World slavery: several Bahamian villages were built on land granted to Africans freed by the British navy from captured Spanish vessels, intercepted *en route* to Cuba, following the abolition of the slave trade. Poor soil and a dry climate continued to prevent the development of plantation agriculture. The economy was based successively on plundering wrecks, gun-running during the American Civil War (1861–65), the cultivation of citrus and pineapples, sponge-fishing and the smuggling of rum and whisky during the US 'Prohibition' of alcoholic liquors in 1919–33.

Although there was some miscegenation, a rigid colour bar prevented black advancement. Accordingly, when a representative House of Assembly was established in 1729, it was an exclusive preserve of the white settlers and merchants. Despite being briefly suspended in 1776, when the colony was captured by the rebel American colonists, and again in 1782 when it surrendered to the Spanish, the House of Assembly remained a permanent feature of Bahamian politics.

Although free black property owners were able to vote from 1807, and the Assembly had four non-white members by as early as 1834, political and economic life was controlled, to all intents and purposes, by a white merchant élite, the so-called 'Bay Street Boys' (named after Nassau's main commercial street). This oligarchy practised blatant electoral bribery in small Out Island constituencies, where the secret ballot was not introduced until 1949. The élite's electoral power was challenged by just a small number of black and mixed-race members and by Sir Etienne Dupuch's *Nassau Tribune*.

POLITICAL AWAKENING

Black political awakening can be traced to the so-called Burma Road riots in 1942. By this time, after centuries of extreme variations in the island's fortunes, the economy was beginning to expand, with tourism growing steadily from the 1920s and the construction of US military bases required by the Second World War. The riots erupted over the issue of differential wages paid during the construction of a US Air Force base, to foreign and white workers on the one hand and to black Bahamians on the other. Two people were killed and 25 injured in the riots, which were followed by significant pay increases for black workers. The colony's first political party, the Progressive Liberal Party (PLP), was founded by a group of mixed-race professionals in 1953. In 1956 Sir Etienne Dupuch successfully advocated legislation to outlaw racial discrimination in public places. The 'Bay Street Boys' responded to the formation of the PLP by creating the United Bahamian Party (UBP). Lynden (later Sir Lynden) Pindling, a newly qualified black lawyer, later took over the leadership of the PLP, breaking with an older generation of mainly mixed-race PLP politicians. A tourism industry strike in 1958 was followed by universal male suffrage and the creation of four seats in New Providence, to reduce under-representation of the most densely populated island. The UBP benefited from the continuing over-representation of the less populous islands and won a majority of seats in the 1962 election, with only 36% of the popular vote, less than the 45% polled by the PLP. However, reports of the privately owned Grand Bahama Port Authority, which had recently been granted a casino licence, paying large consultancy fees to cabinet ministers severely damaged the reputation of the oligarchy.

INDEPENDENCE

In the historic January 1967 general election vigorous PLP campaigning resulted in each party winning 18 seats in the 38-seat House of Assembly. The sole representative of the Labour Party held the balance of power, and pledged his support for the PLP, which was therefore able to form a Government; Pindling, hailed as the 'Black Moses', became premier. Because of the insistence by the PLP on black advancement, local control over immigration was regarded as especially important, and the import of mainly white, expatriate labour became progressively restricted.

The PLP won the 1968 election; after further endorsement at a general election in 1972, the party led the country to independence in 1973. There was, however, growing middle-class resentment at Pindling's dictatorial style of leadership, while allegations of corruption became widespread. Dissident members resigned from the PLP, and in 1972 merged with the remnants of the UBP to form a new opposition party, the Free National Movement (FNM).

By the mid-1970s drugs-trafficking and money-laundering had become significant activities in the Bahamas. Worse still was a virtual epidemic in the local use of drugs and a dramatic increase in violent crime. Initially, Pindling resisted pressure from the USA; however, in 1983 he was publicly accused by a US television network of personal involvement and was forced to establish a Royal Commission to investigate the issue.

The Commission reported in December 1984. Although no evidence was published implicating Pindling, the same could not be said of several other ministers. Nevertheless, a minority report noted a prominent Bahamian businessman, Everette Bannister, had made substantial payments to Pindling, enabling the Prime Minister to spend more than eight times his official salary. Few dismissals followed and Pindling was re-endorsed as party leader at the 1985 PLP convention. Two cabinet ministers, Hubert Ingraham and Perry Christie, who shared a legal practice, resigned in protest.

The damage caused to Bahamian-US relations was serious. The US Administration's concern went beyond trafficking: the strict banking secrecy laws, under which US and other offshore banks in the islands operated, were also criticized because of their misuse by criminals. Moreover, US companies and individuals who used Bahamian banks deprived the US Internal Revenue Service of tax income. Consequently, the Bahamas was excluded from the US Caribbean Basin Initiative, and tax concessions were not granted to US insurance companies wishing to exploit Bahamian offshore facilities, nor to US corporations holding conventions in the islands. The Bahamas Government denounced US demands to be allowed access to bank records and be permitted to search for drugs as an 'imperialist' infringement of sovereignty.

Aware of increasing public concern and international pressure, Pindling realized that co-operation with the USA was essential. A compromise was reached: drugs searches in the Bahamas could be made by the US Coastguard and the Drug Enforcement Agency (DEA), but only with the involvement of the Bahamian police. Expenditure on coastguard and defence forces was increased, and several notable Colombian smugglers were arrested. Other measures followed: free passage and diplomatic immunity were granted to DEA agents; a joint drugs-interdiction force was formed; and in 1989 both countries signed a Mutual Legal Assistance Treaty, providing for collaboration in the investigation of criminal allegations within the offshore financial industry. A similar agreement was also signed with Canada. However, drugs-trafficking continued to pose a problem, despite the limited success of anti-smuggling measures.

DOMESTIC POLITICS AND THE RISE OF THE FNM

The PLP remained the dominant political force in the 1980s, accusing the FNM of subservience to the USA and to local white Bahamian interests. However, the party lost some ground in the 1987 election. Christie and Ingraham were elected as independents, but in 1990 Ingraham joined the FMN, becoming party leader one month later after the death of Cecil Wallace-Whitfield. Perry Christie rejoined the PLP shortly afterwards.

Prospects for the FNM improved as the economy worsened. Measures taken under US pressure against cocaine-smuggling and money-laundering reduced the free flow of funds into the economy from the mid-1980s. A consequent fall in consumer demand induced a recession in the formal sector of the economy, followed by a decline in tourist arrivals. As a result, Pindling was forced to introduce three successive austerity budgets and restraints on credit. In addition, the Government was damaged by new scandals, this time over widespread corruption in state-owned businesses. A vigorous campaign by the FNM resulted in the defeat of the PLP in the general election of August 1992. Ingraham became Prime Minister, and the extent of economic mismanagement and of corrupt practices in several public corporations under the PLP regime only then began to become apparent.

The FNM's confident campaign prior to the March 1997 general election culminated in a clear victory. Sir Lynden resigned as PLP leader in April, and later announced his retirement from Parliament, after 41 years. Perry Christie succeeded him as party leader.

In spite of the FNM's 10-year record of economic success, and a dramatic improvement in the standard of government, the party was increasingly perceived as élitist, autocratic and subservient to the interests of foreign investors. From the late 1990s expansion of large hotels such as Sun International's Atlantis resort on Paradise Island just north of Nassau led to concerns over beach access. There was vigorous trade union opposition in 2000 to the proposed privatization of the Bahamas Telecommunications Corporation (BaTelCo). From late 2000 sections of the financial community and the legal profession were disturbed by the Government's willingness to co-operate with international moves by the Financial Action Task Force on Money Laundering (FATF, based in Paris, France), and by the Organisation for Economic Co-operation and Development's (OECD) initiative against tax evasion (see below).

These considerations laid the ground for a sharp turnaround in the fortunes of the two main parties, which gathered force from mid-2001. In line with Ingraham's long-standing commitment to step down as premier after two terms in office, the FNM elected Orville Alton Thompson (Tommy) Turnquest to succeed him in August. Turnquest was widely accused of having used improper methods to influence delegates, and was seen as a significantly less substantial figure than Ingraham. His father, Sir Orville Alton Thompson Turnquest, was Governor-General, but, in order to prevent a possible conflict of

interest, he was replaced in this office by Dame Ivy Dumont, a respected former Minister of Education.

An FNM proposal to amend the Constitution, originally put forward before the 1997 election, suddenly gathered pace at the beginning of 2002. Five proposed amendments were put to a referendum on 27 February. These included: the appointment of an independent Director of Public Prosecutions; the establishment of an independent body to oversee teachers' employment; the appointment of an independent Parliamentary Electoral Commissioner; and the creation of a Boundaries Commission. The PLP voted for the amendments in Parliament, but campaigned for a 'no' vote in the referendum, on the grounds that the reforms had been rushed and ill-prepared. To the consternation of the Government, the population rejected all five proposals by large margins.

THE 2002 ELECTIONS

A general election was held on 2 May 2002. The PLP took 29 of the 40 seats in the House of Assembly, while the FNM's legislative representation was reduced to seven seats, with the four remaining seats taken by independent candidates. Only one FNM cabinet minister was re-elected to Parliament; Turnquest lost his seat, but was nominated by his party to the Senate and remained party leader. Perry Christie was appointed Prime Minister.

The new Government pledged to establish a national health insurance system, as well as constitutional reform; commissions were subsequently established to develop detailed proposals with regard to these commitments. The commission on health insurance reported in May 2004, with annual costs later estimated at US $235m., but implementation was not expected until after the 2007 general election. A constitutional reform commission reported in March 2006: it recommended the replacement of Queen Elizabeth II as head of state with a President, who would have some limited real powers, including the appointment of independent senators, of the Chief Justice, and of other judges. Other proposals included the creation of an independent electoral and boundaries commission. None of these proposals was fulfilled during the Christie Government's single term in office.

The Bahamas' judicial system underwent significant disruption in November 2006 when the Cabinet's failure to appoint a commission to review judicial salaries was declared illegal by a supreme court ruling, and therefore to have compromised the independence of the judiciary. Closure of the country's magistrates' courts was anticipated pending the outcome of an appeal. Despite the judicial pay controversy, in December a contingent of Law Lords from the Privy Council sat in the Court of Appeal in Nassau, the first instance of the country's final appellate court operating outside London, United Kingdom. The Bahamas retained the Privy Council as its final appellate court, in contrast to several other Caribbean countries that had instituted the Caribbean Court of Justice following its inauguration in April 2005.

THE FNM IN OFFICE

A general election was held on 2 May 2007, exactly five years after the previous poll. After a closely fought campaign, the FNM took 23 of the 41 seats in the enlarged House of Assembly, with the remaining 18 going to PLP members and allied independents. The FNM took 49.8% of the popular vote, with 47.0% going to the PLP and its allies, and the remainder to non-aligned independents and a minor party. Voter turnout was high, at 91.3%. The PLP's parliamentary strength was weakened in January 2008, when a member of parliament, Kenyatta Gibson, left the party to sit as an independent; he formally joined the FNM a year later.

Hubert Ingraham returned as Prime Minister after the poll, also assuming the portfolio for finance; Turnquest, once more in the House of Assembly, became Minister of National Security, while Zhivargo Laing emerged as another influential figure, being appointed Minister of State in the Ministry of Finance. The PLP remained weak and divided after the election, with a question over Christie's long-term future as party leader; however, he was re-elected by a party conference in October 2009, with 1,158 votes to 204 for his nearest rival,

Bernard Nottage. To the embarrassment of the party, a PLP senator and former member of parliament, Pleasant Bridgewater, was charged with conspiracy in January 2009 after an alleged attempt to extort US $25m. from the US actor John Travolta after the sudden death of his son on Grand Bahama. A court process ended in October with a mistrial, when an FNM member of parliament, Picewell Forbes, mistakenly told a party convention that Bridgewater had been found innocent; the jury was still deliberating at the time, and the judge aborted the process fearing jury contamination. The FNM's parliamentary strength was reduced slightly in March 2011 after a former junior minister of tourism, Branville McCartney, left the party to form the Democratic National Alliance, which won support from voters disillusioned with the two main parties.

RETURN OF THE PLP

At the general election held on 7 May 2012, the PLP once more gained office, with 48.6% of the popular vote, a marginal increase from 2007, but with 29 of 38 seats in a smaller parliament. With the economy remaining weak and some electors ready for a change, the FNM vote declined to 42.1%, with the party retaining nine seats. The DNA performed respectably, with 8.5% of the poll, but took no seats. McCartney failed to retain his place in parliament. With his 65th birthday approaching in August, Ingraham resigned (for a second time) as FNM leader and Leader of the Opposition immediately after the election, and was succeeded by Hubert Minnis. His former seat fell to the PLP in a by-election held in October after 35 years as an FNM stronghold.

The Government in 2013 called a referendum on a proposal to legalize internet gambling in 'webshops', which operate openly but outside the law, and on whether to institute a national lottery. In the vote, held on 28 January, both propositions were defeated, by 61% and 59%, respectively, with a turnout of 45%. However, by mid-2014 the 'webshops' remained in operation; the Government held that the referendum had been advisory and non-binding, and proposed in the May 2014 budget to license and tax their operation. A referendum on offshore oil extraction was proposed in principle for the second half of 2015; however, exploratory drilling was to be permitted in advance of the poll. A Constitutional Commission reported in July 2013, but recommended only minor changes.

REGIONAL ISSUES

In the late 1990s there was a resurgence in drugs-trafficking in the Bahamas, as the Mexican route for Colombian cocaine became more difficult and Haiti, just south of the Bahamas, increased its importance as a transshipment point, as did Jamaica. A lull followed after 2000, but a further resurgence was reported in 2013. A report published in 2005 by the US Department of State suggested some 20 metric tons of cocaine were transshipped each year through the Jamaica–Cuba–Bahamas corridor. Moreover, an earlier analysis of balance-of-payments statistics by the US embassy in Nassau suggested that cocaine- and marijuana-smuggling resulted in foreign exchange inflows of US $200m.–$300m. annually, a sum equivalent to 11%–17% of formal-sector merchandise imports, or 4%–7% of gross domestic product. On this basis, the report suggested drugs transshipment might rival, or even surpass, the Bahamian banking industry in economic impact. In 2008 some 25 suspicious speedboats were detected in or over Bahamian waters but could not be intercepted. The USA was also concerned about the transshipment of drugs and other contraband in commercial cargo, for example in Freeport's container port, where approximately 3 tons of cocaine were seized in 2007–11. There are an estimated 12–15 major drugs-trafficking organizations operating in the country.

The USA in 2014 once more included the Bahamas on a list of 22 major drugs transshipment countries and on a list of 65 major money-laundering countries or territories 'of primary concern'. Co-operation between the US and Bahamian authorities is generally fairly close. A Canadian consultancy, Emergo International, completed a full review of the defence force in January 2006. Preliminary findings indicated a 'desperate'

need for reorganization; the final report, however, was not made public. The then serving Commissioner of Police, Reginald Ferguson, said in March 2009 that police corruption was a major concern. The USA has donated six fast interceptor boats to the coastguard and three to the police force, and has built a hanger on the southern island of Inagua, allowing it to station helicopters there for work in the southern Bahamas and Turks and Caicos. The coastguard also had two 60-metre offshore patrol vessels and three patrol vessels, as well as smaller craft, based in Nassau, Inagua and Grand Bahama. In addition, there are three fixed-wing surveillance aircraft; the police also have eight smaller craft. The defence force in May 2014 acquired the first of nine new vessels from the Damen Shipyards Group. The USA also maintains an Atlantic Undersea Test Evaluation Centre on the island of Andros to test and evaluate naval operations, equipment and procedures.

Drugs-trafficking and violent crime continues to be a problem. The prison, which is designed for 750, held 1,433 inmates in 2013. The murder rate rose from 14 per 100,000 in 2004 to 36 per 100,000 in 2011, falling back slightly to 33 per 100,000 in 2013. A high proportion of murders appeared to be drugs- or gang-related. The US Embassy in 2014 referred to the level of violent crime in Nassau as 'critical', and expressed concern over the increasing number of sexual assaults and armed robberies, of which the police recorded 1,022 in 2013, and with many of them directed at tourists. Two US citizens were killed in 2013, and a consular officer attacked in June of that year. Although a suspect was identified for a fairly high proportion of murders (80% of murders committed in 2012, for example) successful prosecutions were rare. For the five years to 2009 there were 349 murders, but only 10 people convicted, with a further eight found guilty of manslaughter. The Attorney-General, Allyson Maynard-Gibson, said in June 2012 that more than 400 people who had been charged with murder were free on bail at that time. A high proportion of cases which do find their way to court stem from domestic, rather than gang, violence. The reach of the drugs trade was illustrated in the 2006 trial of two men accused of murdering the son of the Minister of Trade in 2002; both defence and prosecution alleged that the killing stemmed from the theft of a commercial consignment of cocaine. Extradition from the Bahamas to the USA was also difficult. One high-profile alleged trafficker, Samuel 'Ninety' Knowles, resisted extradition from 2001 until 2006, when he was sent for trial in Florida; he was found guilty in 2008 of trafficking several tons of cocaine and sentenced to 35 years in prison. Two other alleged traffickers, Dwight and Keva Major, were extradited in 2008 after a five-year legal battle.

In 2007 the PLP Government was accused by the FNM, then in opposition, of colluding with US authorities to induce five Bahamian employees of the Lynden Pindling International Airport to travel to the USA for the purposes of arrest and trial on charges of drugs-trafficking, by scheduling training sessions in Florida; all five were found guilty. Cocaine seizures totalled 1.01 metric tons in 2013, exceeding the combined total of the three previous years (when approximately 28 tons of marijuana, with 20,461 marijuana plants, were eradicated).

In 2000 the Bahamas was included by the FATF on a 'black list' of jurisdictions considered to be failing in attempts to combat money-laundering. As a result, the Government devoted considerable political attention to reform of the offshore financial sector. New legislation established a Financial Intelligence Unit in October, improved the mechanism for international co-operation in criminal proceedings, and required international business companies to keep records showing their beneficial ownership. A further law was passed increasing the regulatory capacity of the Central Bank. As a result of the measures, in 2001 the FATF removed the Bahamas from its list of non-co-operative countries. An agreement to exchange information on tax with the USA came into effect in 2003. Ongoing US concerns included continued money-laundering through the purchase of real estate, large vehicles, boats and jewellery, and through a web of legitimate businesses and international business companies registered in the offshore financial sector, as well as the apparent lack of sufficient resources for the enforcement of existing legislation, and the need for a public registry showing the beneficial owners of offshore entities.

Illustrating the continuing use of the Bahamas by controversial figures, Viktor Kožen, a Czech-born financier with Grenadian, Venezuelan and Irish nationality, in 2012 appeared to have successfully resisted extradition to both the USA and the Czech Republic on corruption charges linked, *inter alia*, to privatizations in Azerbaijan. His attorney, Philip Davis, has been a deputy leader of the PLP since October 2009 and was sworn in as Deputy Prime Minister after the 2012 election. He is a former legal partner of Perry Christie (as is Hubert Ingraham), and acted formerly for Samuel 'Ninety' Knowles in resisting extradition to the USA. Arrested in 2005, Kožen was released on bail in 2007. The high court initially ruled in his favour in 2007 on the basis that corruption of foreign officials was not an offence in the Bahamas; the state lost a local appeal in 2010, as well as a further appeal to the Privy Council, which ruled in March 2012.

Another ongoing security concern is illegal migration from Haiti. The census of 2010 reported that mainly legal migrants from Haiti made up 11% of the resident population, up from 7% in 2000, with illegal migrants comprising a further 10%, according to some estimates; however, in 2000–08 approximately 51,000 Haitian illegal migrants and refugees were deported from the Bahamas, while a further 15,500 were intercepted at sea; repatriations have continued at a similar rate, in spite of an appeal by the UN High Commissioner for Refugees for a more lenient approach following the 2010 Haiti earthquake; 2,525 Haitians were deported in 2012. There are frequent reports of poor conditions at the detention centre used to hold illegal migrants. About 11% of all births nationally were to Haitian mothers, rising to more than 50% in major public clinics on the island of Abaco; children born in the Bahamas to foreign parents have no automatic right to citizenship, and may apply for naturalization only during the 12 months after their 18th birthday. There was also a substantial volume of illegal migration from Jamaica and Cuba, while illegal migrants from the People's Republic of China also used the Bahamas as a transit point for entry to the USA, a flow which was expected to increase with the employment of up to 5,000 Chinese workers on the Baha Mar tourism construction project from 2011. Meanwhile, a 'Bahamians first' policy announced in March 2013 led to a reduction in overseas professional staff as well as unskilled migrants. In addition to the financing and construction of the Baha Mar scheme, Chinese companies were involved in other infrastructural projects, while Hutchison Whampoa, based in Hong Kong, had extensive port, infrastructural and tourism interests on Grand Bahama. A maritime border with Cuba was finalized in 2011 after 20 years of negotiations; this would allow both countries to move forward more easily with marine oil and gas exploration. Negotiations to establish a maritime boundary with the USA were initiated in 2012 and were ongoing in 2014.

Economy

MARK WILSON

The economy of the Bahamas is one of the most prosperous of the Caribbean and Latin American nations, with a per head gross domestic product (GDP) of some US $21,908 in 2012, a higher figure than any independent country in Latin America and the Caribbean (the Bahamian dollar is at par with the US dollar). However, the economy experienced difficulties in 2008–14 as a result of the international recession, with its Standard & Poor's credit rating reduced from A– to BBB/A–2 and a negative outlook assigned in September 2012; Moody's downgraded the Bahamas from A3 to Baa1 with a negative outlook in December 2012. The country was rated 51st of 187 countries in the UN Development Programme's Human Development Index in 2014—fifth in the Latin America and Caribbean region; in the Caribbean, only Cuba, which was placed 44th, was rated higher. The population was 353,658 at the 2010 census, and projected to be 368,100 in mid-2015, of whom 70% (according to the 2010 census) were in Nassau (New Providence), 15% on Grand Bahama and 15% on the other Family Islands. The average annual rate of increase between 2003 and 2012 was 1.8%.

During 2001–04 the economy was virtually stagnant, with tourism performing weakly. Economic expansion recovered slightly to 3.4% in 2005, but growth slipped back to 1.4% in 2007. As the international recession hit US consumer demand in 2008–09, financial services, tourist arrivals and hotel construction slowed, and GDP contracted, by 2.3% in 2008 and then more steeply, by 4.2%, in 2009; this was followed by a weak and partial recovery, with growth of 1.5% in 2010, 1.1% in 2011, 1.0% in 2012 and a mere 0.7%, according to preliminary figures, in 2013. Foreign direct investment has been very high since the late 1990s and stood at 12.5% in 2008. Although some major hotel projects were on hold from then, overall inward investment remained high in spite of the recession, at 9.6% of GDP in 2009, 12.2% in 2010 and 12.3% in 2011 as the very large Baha Mar project came under way, before slipping to 7.1% of GDP in 2012. Unemployment rose sharply from 8.7% in 2008, peaking at 15.9% in 2011 as the recession hit, and still high in 2013, at 15.4%.

There is no personal or corporate income tax in the Bahamas. Duties on imports and other trade taxes accounted for 45.1% of Government revenue in 2012/13. With high taxes on consumption of goods, retail prices were high, although the inflation rate was relatively low. Retail prices increased at an average annual rate of 2.6% in 2005–12, spiking briefly at 4.7% in 2008, as international energy and food commodity costs rose sharply, but falling back to 1.2% in 2012 and to 0.5% in 2013. Taxes directly related to tourism (hotel occupancy tax, departure tax and gaming tax) made up a further 14.4% of government revenue in 2012/13. However, the small tax base posed problems. In spite of successive tax increases, government recurrent revenue was equivalent to only an estimated 16.6% of GDP in 2012/13, much lower than in other Caribbean islands. The Bahamas is the only Western hemisphere country not to be a member of the World Trade Organization (WTO), but was given observer status in 2000 and applied for membership in 2001, with accession negotiations under way in 2014, but proceeding slowly. WTO membership would require a restructuring of the revenue system; accordingly, from 2008 the Government moved away from import duties and towards excise duties, and intends to introduce a value added tax (VAT) to protect the tax base while avoiding the need for an income tax. This proposal met with strong private sector and other opposition, however, forcing the Government to postpone its introduction to January 2015 and to halve the initial rate, to 7.5%. Membership of the Caribbean Community and Common Market (CARICOM) single market and economy was not likely as public opinion remained strongly opposed to free trade and wary of Jamaica and the 'neighbours to the south'. The Government signed an Economic Partnership Agreement (EPA) with the European Union (EU) in 2008: this involved a commitment to free trade for most imports from the EU after a 25-year transition period from 2011. However, the Bahamas did not commit to the EPA's stipulations on trade in services, and in 2010 reached a separate agreement on this area, which was more restrictive than those adopted by other Caribbean countries, reserving activities such as retailing, real estate, advertising and restaurants for Bahamian businesses.

Both recurrent and overall fiscal accounts moved sharply into deficit from the last quarter of 2001, with revenue adversely affected by the downturn in tourism and in domestic consumer demand. The deficit averaged 2.3% of GDP from 2001/02 to 2006/07, dipping to 1.6% in 2007/08, but rising sharply to 4.5% in 2008/09 and to 5.1% in 2009/10 as the international recession affected revenues and led to additional spending commitments, setting back the Government's earlier proposals for achieving a balanced budget by 2012/13. The deficit was reduced to 2.1% in 2010/11, with substantial stamp duty revenue, equivalent to 1.5% of GDP, from the sign-off of the Baha Mar tourism project and the sale of the Bahamas Oil Refining Company (BORCO). However, the fiscal deficit increased to a worrying 5.5% in 2011/12, a pre-election year, with tax holidays extended and some relaxation of public sector salary policy. There was an even higher deficit of 6.3% for 2012/13, with an estimated deficit equivalent to 5.4% of GDP for 2013/14; the Government intended to bring this down to 3.2% in 2014/15. Total public and government-guaranteed debt grew from 30% of GDP in 2000 to 66% by the end of 2013. Until recently, historic debt levels were considered to be fairly manageable by Caribbean standards, but the rate of increase in the ratio over the past few years has become a source of serious concern. Central government debt was equivalent to 59% of GDP at the end of 2013, significantly above the Government's target range of 30%–35%. Interest payments on debt were US $197.7m. in 2012/13, up from $116.9m. in 2005/06, and equivalent to 14.6% of the revenue of $1,354.6m. With substantial domestic borrowing, the foreign debt-service ratio net of refinancing was fairly modest, at an estimated 5.1% of the value of exports of goods and services in 2013 (net of refinancing obligations for public corporations' debt). Salaries and related expenses accounted for 38.4% of total recurrent expenditure in 2012/13, down from 51.4% in 1993/94, marking a decrease in public sector employment and an increase in public salary restraint, as well as a rise in interest payments.

Plans first mooted in 1997 to privatize the Bahamas Telecommunications Corporation (BaTelCo, later restructured as BTC) were slow to bear fruit. However the Government completed the sale of a 51% stake to Cable and Wireless for US $210m. in 2011, reducing the borrowing requirement; however, prior to the general election in May 2012, the Progressive Liberal Party (PLP) opposed this sale. In June 2013 PLP Prime Minister Perry Christie proposed increasing the government stake in BTC from 49% to 51% in return for an extension of the company's monopoly rights to mobile cellular services beyond the scheduled liberalization date of March 2014. Instead, an agreement in January 2014 provided for 2% of shares to be held by a BTC Foundation 'in trust for the Bahamian people', an arrangement which, if completed, would leave Cable and Wireless with management control. No progress had been made by mid-2014 on long-standing suggestions for the privatization of the Bahamas Electricity Corporation (BEC) or the national airline, Bahamasair Holdings Ltd, which had a history of heavy financial losses, although a more detailed privatization plan for BEC was issued in January. However, an agreement was finalized with a Canadian company in 2006 for the management of Lynden Pindling International Airport in Nassau under a 30-year contract, with a $410m. redevelopment plan completed in 2013.

In 1955 an area of 603 sq km (233 sq miles), approximately one-third of the island of Grand Bahama, was granted to the privately owned Grand Bahama Port Authority (GBPA), with important tax concessions under the Hawksbill Creek Agreement. Freeport, which owed its existence entirely to that Agreement, developed considerably. The GBPA aimed originally to construct a manufacturing centre. The focus then shifted to tourism and residential development. Within Freeport, the operation of the port and airport, land development and the management of the water and electricity supply were private sector activities. Under successive PLP governments, Grand Bahama was regarded as an opposition stronghold, and was consequently neglected by the central administration. The petroleum refinery and cement plant were closed, and tourism stagnated. In 1993, with the Free National Movement in office, the Hawksbill Creek Agreement was extended to 2054, with tax exemptions running to 2015. This contributed to renewed economic development, with a Hong Kong-owned company, Hutchison Whampoa, the principal investor. A legal dispute developed from 2004 between the British shareholders in the GBPA, Sir Jack Hayward and the heirs of his associate, Edward St George; the main dispute appeared to have been resolved by 2010, but legal wrangling continued. With unemployment on Grand Bahama at 18.0% of the labour force in 2012, the incoming PLP Government proposed to extend tax concessions to the eastern and western parts of the island, outside the original Freeport area, and to extend substantial tax concessions to Grand Bahama hotels; however, by mid-2014 the major change had been the imposition of additional government charges and levies, which were the subject of legal dispute under the Hawksbill Creek Agreement.

On the more populated island of New Providence, a public-private sector partnership in 2012 completed a US $60m. container port development on Arawak Cay, relieving pressure on the city centre waterfront. The Out Islands, or Family Islands, vary enormously in the degree of economic development achieved. In the northern Bahamas, activities such as tourism and fishing have brought prosperity to a number of islands, including Abaco, Spanish Wells, Eleuthera and Bimini. In contrast, some islands in the southern Bahamas, such as Mayaguana, Acklins and Crooked Island, have small populations and a very limited range of economic activity. Stimulating growth on these islands with airport development and an 'anchor' tourism project formed a central element of the Government's economic agenda in the 2000s, but progress on this agenda slowed from 2007 as a difficult borrowing environment halted most resort construction.

TOURISM

Tourism forms the basis of prosperity in the Bahamas, and remains by far the most important sector of the economy. The islands are closer to the USA than most other destinations in the Caribbean. Thus, commercial tourism developed comparatively early, with the construction of the Royal Victoria Hotel in Nassau commencing just before the American Civil War of the 1860s. Luxury winter tourism developed further between 1920 and 1940, and from the 1950s jet travel opened the islands as a mass-market destination. Expansion of the tourism sector led to rapid growth in commercial activity and a significant improvement in living standards.

The increase in tourism investment involved the reconstruction of most of the existing hotels in Nassau, followed, in 1999–2001, by the major properties on Grand Bahama. This activity involved the development, at a cost of US $450m., of the Atlantis resort on Paradise Island. After completion of its Phase II, the project included 2,395 rooms and employed 5,600 staff, equivalent to about 4% of national employment. Following the Government's decision to invest substantially in airport, road, water and electricity improvements, and its commitment to a further 11 years of tax concessions and up to $4m. per year in marketing assistance over five years, in 2003 the owners of the Atlantis resort, Kerzner International, announced a further $600m. Phase III expansion, increased in scope to $1,000m. one year later. This included 1,500 additional hotel rooms, and an increase in staff numbers to 9,000. In 2004 Kerzner purchased the neighbouring Club Méditerranée property on Paradise Island for $40m., and in 2005 the company bought the island's Hurricane Hole marina. However, in 2012, with Kerzner International struggling with debt, the Atlantis resort and associated properties were sold to Brookfield Asset Management, a Canadian-registered company with $180,000m. in assets. Brookfield announced in July 2014 that US $1,900m. in debt had been refinanced, opening the way for a further expansion programme. Kerzner was also, from September, to be replaced as operator by Brookfield Hospitality, using the Marriott brand.

The Baha Mar Development Company, owned by a locally resident investor, in 2005 agreed to buy the Wyndham Nassau Resort, Crystal Palace Casino and Nassau Beach Hotel, and also purchased the Radisson Cable Beach Resort, the last remaining major property of the state-owned Hotel Corporation, along with a substantial area of government-owned land. The US $2,600m. project aimed to develop hotels with 3,450 rooms, a 0.7-ha casino, a golf course, 1 ha of convention space, residential units and a marina, and to employ a staff of 6,500 on completion. In 2010 a joint venture was agreed with the Export-Import Bank of China and China State Construction Engineering Corporation. However, there was some local disquiet over the proposed employment of several thousand Chinese workers in the construction phase. With construction due for completion in December 2014 (and the resort scheduled to open in March 2015), management agreements had been signed with the Hyatt Hotels Corporation, SLS Hotels, Rosewood Hotels and Resorts and Global Gaming Asset Management.

Most of Nassau's hotel properties are large, and many belong to international chains, a great asset for US marketing, which relies heavily on branding. In 1997 the largest properties owned by the Hotel Corporation were sold to Hutchison Whampoa, which undertook a US $400m. redevelopment and reopened the Our Lucaya complex in 2000. The Princess Resort and Casino reopened in 2000 after a $42m. renovation as the 965-room Resort at Bahamia; renamed the Royal Oasis, it was closed after Hurricane Frances in 2004, with substantial debts owed to the Government, staff and local businesses, and remained closed and deteriorating in mid-2014. In spite of their excellent beaches and wildlife resources, most of the Family Islands remained relatively undeveloped until the 2000s. There are few direct air links to the north-eastern USA, and travel via Nassau can be inconvenient. Airport improvements in Nassau and the Family Islands have formed an important component of the Government's economic strategy, and large-scale developments were built or planned on several islands, including Eleuthera, Abaco and San Salvador. In 2006 proposals were published for large-scale resorts (with airports to serve them) on smaller and more remote islands, such as Rum Cay, which had only 70 inhabitants, or Mayaguana, with 262; the Government's aim was for each island to have at least one 'anchor' property to underpin its development. However, weakness in the US tourism, real estate and financial markets delayed projects still in the planning stage. A $140m. resort on Exuma was purchased and renovated by the Sandals group in 2010.

Agriculture and manufacturing are poorly developed, and tourism operators purchase little locally. Food, furnishings and even souvenirs are generally shipped in from Miami, USA; some construction projects have imported pre-assembled and pre-fitted hotel rooms, thus minimizing the need for local labour. For this reason, retained earnings are poor. In addition, many major hotel projects are given important tax concessions, reportedly equivalent in value to 20% of the development cost for the Atlantis Phase III projects.

Stop-over arrivals reached an all-time high of 1.61m. in 2005; however, numbers slipped to 1.33m. in 2009 following the 2007 introduction of a passport requirement by the USA for returning residents, as well as the sharp downturn in consumer demand stemming from the international recession. Stop-over arrivals totalled 1.36m. in 2013. Cruise ship passenger numbers in 2013 totalled 4.71m., a 166% increase since 1998. The opening of 'private island' facilities by cruise lines and a refurbished cruise port facility in Nassau contributed to an increase in cruise ship passenger arrivals, which totalled 4.71m. in 2013. This represented a 6.2% increase over 2012, with short cruises from Florida, USA, to the Bahamas providing a low-cost form of Caribbean travel. The Bahamas received more than twice as many cruise ship passengers as any other English-speaking Caribbean destination, although with much lower per head spending ($93 in 2012) than stop-over tourists ($1,334). Hotel room occupancy in Nassau fell to 58.0% in 2010, owing to lower tourism demand, dipping to just 36.0% on Grand Bahama and the Family Islands. Compounding the difficulties, average Nassau room rates fell by 9.3% in 2009 and by a further 2.7% in 2010, with declines also on other islands.

Meanwhile, tourism receipts rose to a peak of $2,501m. in 2008, falling back to $2,014m. in 2009 under the impact of the international recession, but with a partial recovery, to $2,162m., in 2013. Travel receipts in 2013 comprised 62.9% of earnings from goods and services, and covered 69.6% of the value of all goods imported to the Bahamas. In 2013 the hotel and restaurant sector directly contributed 10.8% of GDP. Owing to the proximity of the USA, the European market is less important to the Bahamian tourism industry than it is to that of the rest of the Caribbean. In 2012 some 78.1% of stop-over arrivals had travelled from the USA. In the same year 9.1% of visitors came from Canada and 5.9% came from Europe.

OFFSHORE FINANCE AND REGISTRATION

Nassau is a major international financial centre, the largest offshore centre in the Caribbean, with domestic and international banking and insurance (and real estate) accounting for 32.6% of GDP in 2013. Offshore banks account for 98% of the financial sector. In 2012 international banks in the Bahamas held US $583,000m. in assets. Despite this, from being one of the world's best known offshore centres, dating from the 1920s, the financial services industry in the Bahamas lost market share almost every year from the early 1980s. Nassau lost market share partly because there was no longer a tax advantage in booking large international loans offshore, which had in any event accounted for relatively little value added. Furthermore, in the more economically significant business of private banking and trust management, the reputation of the Bahamas was severely damaged by extensive money-laundering activity. Many financial institutions had to defend themselves against the persistent enquiries of overseas law-enforcement and tax authorities (mainly from the USA), and a number reduced their operations or chose alternative centres, notably the Cayman Islands. In addition, aggressive marketing of company registration and other services by newer financial centres, such as the British Virgin Islands, allowed them to capture a share of the market that they did not thereafter relinquish, while there has been strong growth in Asian financial centres at the expense of the Caribbean market share.

Resolute action was taken to cleanse the industry of illegal funds and to remove the minority damaging the industry's reputation. The reforms began in 1989, accelerating from 1992. However, in 2000 the intergovernmental body charged with combating money-laundering, the Financial Action Task Force on Money Laundering (FATF, based in Paris, France) included the Bahamas in a list of 'non-co-operative' jurisdictions. The Bahamas was the subject of an advisory statement from the US Treasury, which asked US financial institutions to apply 'enhanced scrutiny' to transactions with the country. In response, the Bahamian authorities accelerated their efforts to bring the jurisdiction into line with international requirements and the Bahamas was removed from the FATF 'black list' in 2001. In 2002 the Bahamas concluded a tax information-exchange agreement with the USA. In 2004 the FATF expressed concern that the Government was lax in responding to regulatory requests, and in 2009 placed the Bahamas on a 'grey list' of countries that had not yet taken sufficient steps to negotiate tax information exchange agreements with international partners; the Bahamas was taken off the list in 2010 after 21 agreements had been concluded. However, in 2014 the US Department of State continued to classify it as a jurisdiction of 'primary concern' for money-laundering, largely because of the size of the offshore sector; it also appealed for reforms such as a public registry of beneficial owners of offshore entities, and the provision of adequate resources to investigate and prosecute apparent breaches of regulations and to comply with international information requests.

The Bahamas International Securities Exchange (BISX) opened in 2000, and, although trading volumes and commission income remained low, the Exchange recorded its first year of profit in 2010. In 2011 BISX was registered by the US Securities and Exchange Commission as a Designated Offshore Securities Market. At the end of 2013 the Exchange was trading the shares of 22 local companies with total market capitalization of over US $3,000m.

Financial services suffered as a result of the international recession from 2008. Local expenditure by offshore companies was US $170.1m. in 2013, down from $233.8m. in 2008, and equivalent to only 3.5% of imports of goods and services. Total employment in banking was 4,773 in 2012, close to 3% of the employed labour force, with 1,125 employed in offshore banks, and on average earnings more than twice as high as in domestic institutions. Bahamas law required that offshore banks must maintain a physical presence in the Bahamas. With other licences lapsing later, 113 offshore banks and trust companies with public licences remained in operation at the end of 2012, with a further 147 on restricted licences. The requirement to maintain an office and employ staff meant that the remaining banks each had a more significant economic impact.

Company registration witnessed spectacular growth following the International Business Company Act of 1990. Financial sector professionals in the Bahamas have always insisted that most offshore business is legitimate. As a result of new requirements that beneficial owners should be identifiable, the number of new International Business Companies (IBCs) registered in 2003 was less than one-fifth of the new registrations recorded in 2000, while many existing IBCs failed to renew their registration. In 2012 there were 166,344 registered IBCs, of which approximately one-quarter were active; there were 2,843 new registrations during that year.

The other area of offshore activity that continues to perform well is that of ship registration. The Bahamas ship registry, relaunched after the adoption of the Bahamas Maritime Authority Act in 1995, is the world's third largest in terms of gross registered tonnage, behind Panama and Liberia. It is managed by the Bahamas Maritime Authority, which has offices in Nassau, London, New York (USA), Hong Kong (China) and Piraeus (Greece); by December 2013 the Authority had registered 1,493 vessels, with total displacement of 57m. grt. The international container-transshipment terminal at Freeport, Grand Bahama, acts as an intercontinental hub port serving North America, the Caribbean and South America. Throughput at the terminal was 1.2m. units in 2012. A 320-ha industrial park has also been developed, and a fifth-phase expansion programme was to start in 2014.

INDUSTRY

Industrial development was a relatively late arrival in the Bahamas, dating from the formation of the Grand Bahama Development Company in 1960, based in the free trade zone in Freeport, itself only established by the 1955 Hawksbill Creek Agreement. Freeport was at first dominated by ship-bunkering and petroleum-refining. However, proposals to develop Grand Bahama as a major industrial centre did not come to fruition; high labour and utilities costs, and the small size of the local market, combined to limit severely the development of industrial activity, although a number of manufacturers produced for the local market. Until 2009 Bacardi operated a rum distillery in Nassau, which made use of imported molasses and bulk rum to produce blended rums for export to Europe under the Cotonou Agreement. Rum exports contributed 5.5% of domestic exports in 2007. A reduction in duties on all rum entering the European market greatly reduced the comparative advantage of Bahamian production and production was switched to a larger plant in Puerto Rico.

Of greater significance are a number of enclave industries located on Grand Bahama that benefit from the island's tax concessions and port facilities. A Freeport company has facilities for the repair of containers, fabrication of steel structures and instrumentation system maintenance. There is also a plant producing expandable polystyrene. A 320-m dry dock, the largest in the Americas, was in operation from 2002, and by 2009 there were two additional dry docks on the site. Engineering skills shortages kept down the number of local staff, although a training centre was attempting to increase the number of Bahamian staff. A separate operation included the world's largest covered yacht repair facility. Also on Grand Bahama, Gold Rock Creek studios opened in 2005 as an international centre for filming, with two very large water tanks for marine scenes; however, there has been very little use of this facility, and its future was uncertain at mid-2014. The former oil refinery on Grand Bahama was operated as an oil storage facility, and in 2014 was owned by Buckeye Partners, a US pipeline and oil terminal company, which operated with a storage capacity of 21.5m. barrels. On the remote island of Inagua in the southern Bahamas, the main employer is the Morton Salt Company, which produces salt through the evaporation of sea water. Production is reduced in periods of high rainfall. Exports of salt in 2007 were worth $6.6m. or 1.7% of domestic exports.

Industry (including construction and utilities) employed 12.5% of the working population in 2012 (construction accounted for 6.3%). Manufacturing contributed a preliminary 4.0% of GDP in 2013, with construction contributing a further 10.0%, electricity and water 2.1%, and mining and quarrying 0.8%. However, high wages and costs continued to be serious disadvantages. Installed electricity capacity in Nassau and the Family Islands (excluding Grand Bahama) in 2012 was 438 MW.

There has been some interest in petroleum and natural gas exploration. Negotiations were completed in October 2011 for an agreed maritime boundary with Cuba, which will allow exploration of promising areas to the south of the small island of Cay Sal; maritime boundary talks were ongoing with the USA 2014, and talks have also been held with the United Kingdom in relation to the Turks and Caicos Islands. Bahamas Petroleum Company, incorporated in the Isle of Man (in the United Kingdom), has since 2006 held oil concessions in Bahamian waters, some in partnership with Statoil of Norway. Initial two-dimensional seismic surveys revealed large geological structures which, in the view of Bahamas Petroleum Company, have a 25%–30% probability of containing significant quantities of oil or gas. The company completed three-dimensional seismic surveys in 2011, to be followed by exploratory drilling by April 2015 in order to meet its licence obligations. The PLP Government announced in April 2013 that exploratory drilling would be allowed ahead of a referendum in late 2014 or 2015, in which voters would decide on the principle of commercial extraction. Past oil exploration initiatives have not met with success; Kerr McGee and Talisman of Canada abandoned a licence for an area north of Grand Bahama in 2006 after completing a seismic survey in 2004.

AGRICULTURE AND FISHING

Agriculture (excluding fishing) has never played a leading role in the Bahamian economy, and in 2013 the sector was estimated to account for only 1.8% of GDP. More than 80% of food is imported. Agricultural resources are severely limited since rainfall is low, few areas have groundwater for irrigation and much of the land consists of bare limestone rock with only scattered patches of soil.

Agricultural production accounts for only 1% of total land area. There are small-scale farmers on many of the Family Islands, who produce livestock, fruit and vegetables in limited quantities for local markets. Larger commercial farms on New Providence, the most populous island, produce eggs and poultry. Feed and other supplies are imported. Ornamental plants and flowers account for about 10%–15% of agricultural production. Following government efforts to make land available to local and foreign investors for fruit and vegetable farming, by 1995 over 8,000 ha were devoted to citrus fruit cultivation. However, commercial citrus production experienced a serious setback in 2004–05, when all trees on two major farms, covering a total of 2,500 ha, were uprooted after an outbreak of citrus canker disease. The outcome of this was that fruit and vegetable exports fell to US $1.2m. in 2007, one-10th of the total a decade earlier. To protect local producers, imports of some crops, such as bananas, are restricted. A number of sizeable agro-businesses in the larger islands of the northern Bahamas operate as enclave industries, growing crops for export. Some farms use crushed limestone rock as a growing medium, and nutrients are sometimes added to groundwater used for irrigation.

Commercial fishing remains an important economic activity on some of the smaller islands, such as Spanish Wells, contributing about 0.9% of national GDP. Exports of crawfish (spiny lobster) amounted to US $81.4m. in 2007, with an additional $1.9m. from other fisheries exports; fears of overfishing led to tighter limits on the catch per vessel from mid-2006. Such primary economic activities, however, remain peripheral in their contribution to the national wealth of the Bahamas.

Statistical Survey

Source (unless otherwise stated): Department of Statistics, Clarence A. Bain Bldg, Thompson Blvd, POB N-3904, Nassau; tel. 302-2400; fax 325-5149; e-mail dpsdp@bahamas.gov.bs; internet statistics.bahamas.gov.bs/index.php; The Central Bank of the Bahamas, Frederick St, POB N-4868, Nassau; tel. 322-2193; fax 322-4321; e-mail cbob@centralbankbahamas.com; internet www.centralbankbahamas.com.

AREA AND POPULATION

Area: 13,939 sq km (5,382 sq miles).

Population: 303,611 at census of 1 May 2000; 351,461 (males 170,257, females 181,204) at census of 3 May 2010; 364,000 at mid-2014 (official estimate). *By Island* (census of 2010): New Providence 246,329; Grand Bahama 51,368; Eleuthera 8,202; Andros 7,490; Others 38,072.

Density (at mid-2014): 26.1 per sq km.

Population by Age and Sex ('000, official estimates at mid-2014): *0–14 years:* 87.0 (males 44.8, females 42.2); *15–64 years:* 252.6 (males 122.8, females 129.8); *65 years and over:* 24.4 (males 10.2, females 14.2); *Total* 364.0 (males 177.8, females 186.2).

Principal Town (incl. suburbs, UN estimate): Nassau (capital) 266,765 in mid-2014. Source: UN, *World Urbanization Prospects: The 2014 Revision*.

Births, Marriages and Deaths (2013, provisional): Registered live births 3,935 (birth rate 10.7 per 1,000); Registered deaths 2,062 (death rate 5.6 per 1,000); Registered marriages 3,617 (marriage rate 9.8 per 1,000).

Life Expectancy (years at birth): 74.9 (males 72.0; females 78.0) in 2012. Source: World Bank, World Development Indicators database.

Economically Active Population (persons aged 15 years and over, excl. armed forces, 2012): Agriculture, hunting, forestry and fishing 4,955; Mining, quarrying, electricity, gas and water 3,095; Manufacturing 7,150; Construction 10,400; Wholesale and retail trade 26,975; Hotels and restaurants 24,480; Transport, storage and communications 13,945; Finance, insurance, real estate and other business services 25,370; Community, social and personal services 48,885; *Total employed* 165,255 (males 82,065, females 83,190); Unemployed 26,950 (males 13,440, females 13,510); *Total labour force* 192,205 (males 95,505, females 96,700). *2013:* Total employed 166,595 (males 82,170, females 84,425); Unemployed 30,285 (males 15,375, females 14,910); Total labour force 196,880 (males 99,335, females 97,545).

HEALTH AND WELFARE

Key Indicators

Total Fertility Rate (children per woman, 2012): 1.9.

Under-5 Mortality Rate (per 1,000 live births, 2012): 17.

HIV/AIDS (estimated % of persons aged 15–49, 2011): 2.8.

Physicians (per 1,000 head, 2008): 2.8.

Hospital Beds (per 1,000 head, 2009): 3.1.

Health Expenditure (2011): US $ per head (PPP): 2,325.

Health Expenditure (2011): % of GDP: 7.5.

Health Expenditure (2011): public (% of total): 45.6.

Access to Water (% of persons, 2012): 98.

Access to Sanitation (% of persons, 2012): 92.

Total Carbon Dioxide Emissions ('000 metric tons, 2010): 2,464.2.

Total Carbon Dioxide Emissions Per Head (metric tons, 2010): 6.8.

Human Development Index (2013): ranking: 51.

Human Development Index (2013): value: 0.789.

For sources and definitions, see explanatory note on p. vi.

AGRICULTURE, ETC.

Principal Crops ('000 metric tons, 2012 unless otherwise indicated): Sweet potatoes 0.8 (FAO estimate); Sugar cane 57.5 (FAO estimate); Bananas 9.5; Lemons and limes 3.1; Grapefruit and pomelos 20.4; Vegetables (incl. melons) 29.4; Fruits (excl. melons) 48.3.

Livestock ('000 head, year ending September 2012, FAO estimates): Cattle 0.8; Pigs 5.0; Sheep 6.6; Goats 15.0; Poultry 3,000.

Livestock Products ('000 metric tons, 2012, FAO estimates): Chicken meat 6.6; Cows' milk 0.8; Goat's milk 2.0; Hen eggs 1.3.

Forestry ('000 cubic metres, 2012, FAO estimates): *Roundwood Removals (excl. bark):* Sawlogs and veneer logs 17 (output assumed to be unchanged since 1992); *Sawnwood Production (incl. railway sleepers):* Coniferous (softwood) 1.4 (output assumed to be unchanged since 1970).

Fishing (all capture, metric tons, live weight, 2012): Nassau grouper 103; Snappers 552; Caribbean spiny lobster 12,051; Stromboid conchs 6,413; Total catch (incl. others) 19,462.

Source: FAO.

MINING

Production ('000 metric tons, 2011, preliminary figures): Unrefined salt 1,000.0; Aragonite 1.5. Source: US Geological Survey.

INDUSTRY

Production (million kWh, 2013): Electric energy 1,936.8.

FINANCE

Currency and Exchange Rates: 100 cents = 1 Bahamian dollar (B $). *Sterling, US Dollar and Euro Equivalents* (30 May 2014): £1 sterling = B $1.682; US $1 = B $1.000; €1 = B $1.361; B $100 = £59.45 = US $100.00 = €73.47. *Exchange Rate:* Since February 1970 the official exchange rate, applicable to most transactions, has been US $1 = B $1, i.e. the Bahamian dollar has been at par with the US dollar. There is also an investment currency rate, applicable to certain capital transactions between residents and non-residents and to direct investments outside the Bahamas. Since 1987 this exchange rate has been fixed at US $1 = B $1.225.

General Budget (B $ million, 2013/14, budget, preliminary): *Revenue:* Taxation 1,325.8 (Taxes on international trade and transactions 660.2; Taxes on property 110.6; Taxes on companies 180.0); Other current revenue 159.4; Capital revenue 0.0; Grants 8.0; Total 1,493.2. *Expenditure:* Current expenditure 1,635.2 (Wages and salaries 649.6; Goods and services 314.5; Interest payments 229.4; Subsidies and transfers 441.7); Capital expenditure and net lending 235.3; Total 1,870.5.

International Reserves (B $ million at 31 December 2012): IMF special drawing rights 28.4; Reserve position in IMF 9.6; Foreign exchange 808.9; Total 846.9. *2013:* IMF special drawing rights 58.7; Reserve position in IMF 9.7. Source: IMF, *International Financial Statistics*.

Money Supply (B $ million at 31 December 2013): Currency outside banks 215; Demand deposits at deposit money banks 1,385; Total money (incl. others) 1,611. Source: IMF, *International Financial Statistics*.

Cost of Living (Consumer Price Index; base: 2005 = 100): All items 118.0 in 2011; 119.4 in 2012; 120.0 in 2013. Source: IMF, *International Financial Statistics*.

Gross Domestic Product (B $ million at constant 2006 prices): 7,761.6 in 2011; 7,841.8 in 2012 (provisional); 7,894.2 in 2013 (preliminary).

Expenditure on the Gross Domestic Product (B $ million at current prices, 2013, preliminary): Government final consumption expenditure 1,352.0; Private final consumption expenditure 5,917.3; Change in stocks 103.3; Gross fixed capital formation 2,212.2; *Total domestic expenditure* 9,584.8; Exports of goods and services 3,532.2; *Less* Imports of goods and services 4,696.7; *GDP in purchasers' values* 8,420.4.

Gross Domestic Product by Economic Activity (B $ million at current prices, 2013, preliminary): Agriculture, hunting, forestry and fishing 151.5; Mining and quarrying 66.0; Electricity and water 174.4; Construction 828.4; Wholesale and retail trade 822.4; Restaurants and hotels 894.1; Transport, storage and communications 673.1; Finance, insurance, real estate and business services 2,696.9; Government services 512.7; Education 339.3; Health 309.3; Other community, social and personal services 475.1; *Sub-total* 8,273.8; *Less* Financial intermediation services indirectly measured –617.8; *Gross value added in basic prices* 7,656.0; Net indirect taxes 764.4; *GDP in purchasers' values* 8,420.4.

Balance of Payments (B $ million, 2013, preliminary): Exports of goods f.o.b. 909.3; Imports of goods f.o.b. –3,126.4; *Trade balance* –2,217.3; Services (net) 902.4; *Balance on goods and services* –1,314.7; Other income (net) –329.1; *Balance on goods, services and income* –1,643.8; Current transfers (net) 7.1; *Current balance* –1,636.8; Capital account (net) –9.6; Financial account (net) 999.6; Net errors and omissions 578.2; *Overall balance* –68.6.

EXTERNAL TRADE

Principal Commodities (B $ million, 2012, distribution according to HS): *Imports c.i.f.:* Food and live animals 483.7; Beverages and tobacco 83.6; Crude materials, inedible, excl. fuels 68.0; Mineral products 874.8; Products of chemical or allied industries 398.3; Manufactured goods classified chiefly by material 524.3; Machinery and transport equipment 688.0; Miscellaneous manufactured articles 382.2; Total (incl. others) 3,647.0. *Exports (incl. re-exports) f.o.b.:* Food and live animals 81.7; Mineral products 319.7; Products of chemical or allied industries 281.6; Machinery and transport equipment 63.8; Total (incl. others) 827.7.

Principal Trading Partners (non-petroleum transactions, B $ million, 2012): *Imports c.i.f.:* Canada 19.9; United Kingdom 17.5; USA 2,414.3; Total (incl. others) 2,772.2. *Exports f.o.b.:* Canada 25.9; United Kingdom 12.4; USA 357.1; Total (incl. others) 559.9.

TRANSPORT

Road Traffic (vehicles in use at 31 December 2007): Total 27,058. Source: IRF, *World Road Statistics*.

Shipping: *Flag Registered Fleet* (at 31 December 2013): Number 1,493; Displacement ('000 grt) 56,663. Source: Lloyd's List Intelligence (www.lloydslistintelligence.com).

Civil Aviation (2009): Kilometres flown (million) 8; Passengers carried ('000) 979; Passenger-km (million) 276; Total ton-km of freight (million) 25 (Source: UN, *Statistical Yearbook*). Passengers carried ('000): 968 in 2010; 1,056 in 2011; 1,048 in 2012 (Source: World Bank, World Development Indicators database).

TOURISM

Visitor Arrivals ('000): 5,588 (1,268 by air, 4,320 by sea) in 2011; 5,940 (1,357 by air, 4,583 by sea) in 2012; 6,151 (1,281 by air, 4,870 by sea) in 2013.

Tourism Receipts (B $ million, excl. passenger transport): 2,163 in 2010; 2,142 in 2011; 2,311 in 2012 (provisional) (Source: partly World Tourism Organization).

COMMUNICATIONS MEDIA

Telephones: 136,000 main lines in use in 2013.

Mobile Cellular Telephones: 287,000 subscribers in 2013.

Internet Subscribers: 24,700 in 2010.

Broadband Subscribers: 15,500 in 2013.

Source: International Telecommunication Union.

EDUCATION

Pre-primary (2002/03, unless otherwise indicated): 20 schools (1996/97); 338 teachers (all females); 3,771 pupils (males 1,931, females 1,840).

Primary (2009/10 unless otherwise indicated): 113 schools (1996/97); 2,402 teachers (males 192, females 2,210); 33,977 pupils (males 17,139 females 16,838).

Secondary (2009/10 unless otherwise indicated): 37 junior/senior high schools (1990); 2,837 teachers (males 669, females 2,168); 34,406 students (males 16,917, females 17,489).

Tertiary (1987): 249 teachers; 5,305 students. In 2002 there were 3,463 students registered at the College of the Bahamas.

Pupil-teacher Ratio (primary education, UNESCO estimate): 14.1 in 2009/10.

Sources: UNESCO, *Statistical Yearbook*; UN, Economic Commission for Latin America and the Caribbean, *Statistical Yearbook*; Caribbean Development Bank, *Social and Economic Indicators 2001*.

Adult Literacy Rate (UNESCO estimates): 95.0% (males 95.0%; females 95.0%) in 2003. Source: UN Development Programme, *Human Development Report*.

Directory

The Constitution

A representative House of Assembly was first established in 1729, although universal adult suffrage was not introduced until 1962. A new Constitution for the Commonwealth of the Bahamas came into force at independence, on 10 July 1973. The main provisions of the Constitution are summarized below.

Parliament consists of a Governor-General (representing the British monarch, who is Head of State), a nominated Senate and an elected House of Assembly. The Governor-General appoints the Prime Minister and, on the latter's recommendation, the remainder of the Cabinet. Apart from the Prime Minister, the Cabinet has no fewer than eight other ministers, of whom one is the Attorney-General. The Governor-General also appoints a Leader of the Opposition.

The Senate (upper house) consists of 16 members, of whom nine are appointed by the Governor-General on the advice of the Prime Minister, four on the advice of the Leader of the Opposition and three on the Prime Minister's advice after consultation with the Leader of the Opposition. The House of Assembly (lower house) has 41 members. A Constituencies Commission reviews numbers and boundaries at intervals of not more than five years and can recommend alterations for the approval of the House. The life of Parliament is limited to a maximum of five years.

The Constitution provides for a Supreme Court and a Court of Appeal.

The Government

HEAD OF STATE

Queen: HM Queen ELIZABETH II.

Governor-General: Dame MARGUERITE PINDLING (took office 8 July 2014).

THE CABINET
(September 2014)

The Cabinet is formed by the Progressive Liberal Party.

Prime Minister and Minister of Finance: PERRY GLADSTONE CHRISTIE.

Deputy Prime Minister and Minister of Works and Urban Development: PHILIP EDWARD BRAVE DAVIS.

Minister of Foreign Affairs and Immigration: FREDERICK MITCHELL.

Minister of National Security: Dr BERNARD J. NOTTAGE.

Minister of Tourism: OBEDIAH WILCHCOMBE.

Minister of Agriculture, Marine Resources and Local Government: ALFRED GRAY.

Minister of Education, Science and Technology: JEROME FITZGERALD.

Minister of Financial Services: RYAN PINDER.

Minister of Health: Dr PERRY GOMEZ.

Minister of Transport and Aviation: GLENYS HANNA MARTIN.

Minister of Environment and Housing: KENDRED DORSETT.

Attorney-General and Minister of Legal Affairs: ALLYSON MAYNARD GIBSON.

Minister of Labour and National Insurance: SHANE GIBSON.

Minister of Youth, Sports and Culture: DANIEL JOHNSON.

Minister of Social Services and Community Development: MELANIE GRIFFIN.

Minister for Grand Bahama: Dr MICHAEL DARVILLE.

Minister of State in the Ministry of Finance: MICHAEL HALKITIS.

Minister of State in the Ministry of National Security: KEITH BELL.

Minister of State in the Ministry of Legal Affairs: DAMIEN GOMEZ.

Minister of State in the Ministry of Transport and Aviation: HOPE STRACHAN.

Minister in the Office of the Prime Minister with responsibility for Investments: KHAALIS ROLLE.

MINISTRIES

Attorney-General's Office and Ministry of Legal Affairs: Post Office Bldg, 7th Floor, East Hill St, POB N-3007, Nassau; tel. 322-1141; fax 322-2255; e-mail attorneygeneral@bahamas.gov.bs.

Office of the Prime Minister: Sir Cecil Wallace-Whitfield Centre, West Bay St, POB CB-10980, Nassau; tel. 327-5826; fax 327-5806; e-mail primeminister@bahamas.gov.bs.

Office of the Deputy Prime Minister: John F. Kennedy Dr., POB N-8156, Nassau; tel. 322-4830; fax 326-7344.

Ministry of Agriculture, Marine Resources and Local Government: Traders Bldg, East Bay St, POB N-3028, Nassau; tel. 397-7400; fax 322-8632; e-mail minagriculturemarine@bahamas.gov.bs.

Ministry of Education, Science and Technology: Thompson Blvd, POB N-3913, Nassau; tel. 502-2700; fax 322-8491; e-mail info@bahamaseducation.com; internet www.bahamaseducation.com.

Ministry of Environment and Housing: Charlotte House, Charlotte St, POB N-275, Nassau; tel. 322-6005; fax 326-2650.

Ministry of Finance: Sir Cecil Wallace-Whitfield Centre, West Bay St, POB N-3017, Nassau; tel. 327-1530; fax 327-1618; e-mail mofgeneral@bahamas.gov.bs; internet www.bahamas.gov.bs/finance.

Ministry of Financial Services and Investments: 3rd Floor, Manx Corporate Centre, West Bay St, POB N-4843, Nassau; tel. 328-5071; fax 328-8090.

Ministry of Foreign Affairs and Immigration: Goodman's Bay Corporate Centre, West Bay St, POB N-3746, Nassau; tel. 322-7624; fax 356-3967; e-mail mofa@bahamas.gov.bs.

Ministry for Grand Bahama: 4th Floor, Harold de'Gregory Complex, Freeport; tel. 352-8525; fax 352-8520; e-mail grbgeneral@bahamas.gov.bs.

Ministry of Health: Poinciana Bldg, Meeting and Augusta Sts, POB N-3730, Nassau; tel. 502-4700; fax 502-4711; internet www.bahamas.gov.bs/health.

Ministry of Labour and National Insurance: British Colonial Hilton, 1 Bay St, Nassau; tel. 322-3105.

Ministry of National Security: Churchill Bldg, 3rd Floor, Rawson Sq., POB N-3217, Nassau; tel. 356-6792; fax 356-6087; e-mail nationalsecurity@bahamas.gov.bs.

Ministry of Social Services and Community Development: Post Office, East Hill St, Nassau; tel. 325-2261; fax 356-6228.

Ministry of Tourism: Bolam House, George St, POB N-3701, Nassau; tel. 302-2000; fax 302-2098; e-mail tourism@bahamas.com; internet www.bahamas.com.

Ministry of Transport and Aviation: Manx Bldg, West Bay St, Nassau; tel. 328-2701; fax 328-1324; e-mail admin@mowt.bs.

Ministry of Works and Urban Development: John F. Kennedy Dr., POB N-8156, Nassau; tel. 322-4830; fax 326-7344; e-mail publicworks@bahamas.gov.bs.

Ministry of Youth, Sports and Culture: Thompson Blvd, POB N-4891, Nassau; tel. 502-0600; fax 326-0085; internet youthmysc@bahamas.gov.bs.

Legislature

PARLIAMENT

Senate

President: SHARON WILSON.

There are 16 nominated members.

House of Assembly

Speaker: KENDAL MAJOR.
General Election, 7 May 2012

Party	% of votes	Seats
Progressive Liberal Party (PLP) . . .	48.62	29
Free National Movement (FNM) . . .	42.09	9
Democratic National Alliance (DNA) . .	8.48	—
Independent	0.75	—
Total valid votes	100.00	38

Election Commission

Office of the Parliamentary Commissioner: c/o Ministry of National Security, Farrington Rd, POB N-1653, Nassau; tel. 397-2000; fax 322-1637; e-mail errolbethel@hotmail.com; internet www.bahamas.gov.bs/parliamentary; Commr ERROL W. BETHEL.

Political Organizations

Bahamas Constitution Party (BCP): Nassau; internet hope4bahamalandbcp.blogspot.in; conservative, Christian; Leader S. ALI MCINTOSH.

Democratic National Alliance (DNA): Prince Charles Dr. Shopping Center (Above KFC), Prince Charles Dr., POB AP59217, Nassau; tel. 326-9362; e-mail info@mydnaparty.org; internet www.mydnaparty.org; f. 2011; Leader BRANVILLE MCCARTNEY.

Free National Movement (FNM): 144 Mackey St, POB N-10713, Nassau; tel. 393-7853; fax 393-7914; e-mail info@fnm2012.org; internet www.fnm2012.org; f. 1972; incorporated Bahamas Democratic Movt (f. 2000) in 2011; Leader Dr HUBERT MINNIS.

Progressive Liberal Party (PLP): Sir Lynden Pindling Centre, PLP House, Farrington Rd, POB N-547, Nassau; tel. 326-9688; fax 328-0808; internet myplp.org; f. 1953; centrist party; Chair. BRADLEY ROBERTS; Leader PERRY G. CHRISTIE.

Diplomatic Representation

EMBASSIES IN THE BAHAMAS

Brazil: Sandringham House, 83 Shirley St, POB SS-6265, Nassau; tel. 356-7613; fax 356-7617; e-mail brasembnassau@yahoo.com.br; Charge d'affaires a.i. ALEXANDRE DE AZEVEDO SILVEIRA.

China, People's Republic: East Shirley St, POB SS-6389, Nassau; tel. 393-1415; fax 393-0733; e-mail chinaemb_bs@mfa.gov.cn; internet bs.china-embassy.org; Ambassador YUAN GUISEN.

Cuba: Miller House, 61 Collins Ave, POB EE-15679, Nassau; tel. 356-3473; fax 356-3472; e-mail cubanembassy@coralwave.com; internet www.cubadiplomatica.cu/bahamas; Ambassador ENERSTO SOBERÓN GUZMÁN.

Haiti: Sears House, Shirley St and Sears Rd, POB N-3036, Nassau; tel. 326-0325; fax 322-7712; Ambassador ANTONIO RODRIGUE.

San Marino: 291, The Office of the Old Fort Bay, Bldg 2, Western Rd, POB N-7776, Nassau; tel. 362-4382; fax 362-4669; e-mail smembassy@coralwave.com; Ambassador GIULIA GHIRARDI BORGHESE.

USA: Mosmar Bldg, Queen St, POB N-8197, Nassau; tel. 322-1181; fax 328-7838; e-mail embassynassau@state.gov; internet nassau.usembassy.gov; Chargé d'affaires a.i. JOHN DINKELMAN.

Judicial System

The Judicial Committee of the Privy Council (based in the United Kingdom), the Bahamas Court of Appeal, the Supreme Court and the Magistrates' Courts are the main courts of the Bahamian judicial system.

All courts have both a criminal and civil jurisdiction. The Magistrates' Courts are presided over by professionally qualified Stipendiary and Circuit Magistrates in New Providence and Grand Bahama, and by Island Administrators sitting as Magistrates in the Family Islands.

Whereas all magistrates are empowered to try offences that may be tried summarily, a Stipendiary and Circuit Magistrate may, with the consent of the accused, also try certain less serious indictable offences. Magistrates also hear inquests, although their jurisdiction is limited by law.

The Supreme Court consists of the Chief Justice, two Senior Justices and six Justices. The Supreme Court also sits in Freeport, with two Justices.

Appeals in almost all matters lie from the Supreme Court to the Court of Appeal, with further appeal in certain instances to the Judicial Committee of the Privy Council.

Supreme Court of the Bahamas: Bank Lane, POB N-167, Nassau; tel. 322-3315; fax 323-6463; e-mail registrar@courts.gov.bs; internet www.courts.gov.bs; Chief Justice Sir MICHAEL L. BARNETT.

Court of Appeal: Claughton House, 3rd Floor, POB N-3209, Nassau; tel. 328-5400; fax 323-4659; e-mail info@courtofappeal.org.bs; internet www.courtofappeal.org.bs; Pres. ANITA ALLEN.

Office of the Registrar-General: Shirley House, 50 Shirley St, POB N-532, Nassau; tel. 397-8954; e-mail registrargeneral@bahamas.gov.bs; internet www.bahamas.gov.bs/rgd; Registrar-Gen. JACINDA P. BUTLER.

Religion

Most of the population profess Christianity, but there are also small communities of Jews, Hindus, Muslims and Rastafarians.

CHRISTIANITY

Bahamas Christian Council: POB N-3103, Nassau; tel. 326-7114; f. 1948; 27 mem. churches; Pres. Rev. RANFORD PATTERSON.

The Baptist Church

According to the 2010 census, some 35% of the population are Baptists.

Bahamas National Baptist Missionary and Educational Convention: Blue Hill Rd, POB N-4435, Nassau; tel. 325-0729; fax 326-5473; internet bahamasbaptist.com; mem. of the Baptist World Alliance; 270 churches and c. 75,000 mems; Pres. Dr ANTHONY CARROLL.

The Roman Catholic Church

The Bahamas comprises the single archdiocese of Nassau. According to the 2010 census, some 12% of the population are Roman Catholics. The Archbishop participates in the Antilles Episcopal Conference (whose Secretariat is based in Port of Spain, Trinidad). The Turks and Caicos Islands are also under the jurisdiction of the Archbishop of Nassau.

Archbishop of Nassau: Most Rev. PATRICK PINDER, Archdiocesan Pastoral Centre, West St North, POB N-8187, Nassau; tel. 322-8919; fax 322-2599; e-mail rcchancery@batelnet.bs; internet www .archdioceseofnassau.org.

The Anglican Communion

Anglicans in the Bahamas, who account for some 14% of the population, according to the 2010 census, are adherents of the Church in the Province of the West Indies, comprising eight dioceses. The Archbishop of the Province currently is the Bishop of Barbados. The diocese of the Bahamas also includes the Turks and Caicos Islands.

Bishop of the Bahamas and the Turks and Caicos Islands: Rt Rev. LAISH Z. BOYD, Bishop's Lodge, Sands Rd, POB N-656, Nassau; tel. 322-3015; fax 322-7943; e-mail media@bahamasanglicans.org; internet www.bahamasanglicans.org.

Other Christian Churches

According to the 2010 census, 9% of the population are Pentecostalists, 4% are Seventh-day Adventists, 4% are Methodists and 2% belong to the Church of God.

Bahamas Conference of the Methodist Church: Baltic Ave, Off Mackey St, POB SS-5103, Nassau; tel. 393-3726; fax 393-8135; e-mail bcmc@bahamasmethodist.org; internet bahamasmethodist .org; 34 mem. churches; Pres. CHRISTOPHER NEELY.

Bahamas Conference of Seventh-day Adventists: Tonique Williams-Darling Hwy, POB N-356, Nassau; tel. 341-4021; fax 341-4088; e-mail southbahamasconference@gmail.com; internet www.southbahamasconference.org; Pres. PAUL A. SCAVELLA.

Greek Orthodox Church: Church of the Annunciation, West St, POB N-823, Nassau; tel. 326-0850; fax 326-0851; e-mail officemanager.agoc@gmail.com; internet www.orthodoxbahamas .com; f. 1928; part of the Archdiocese of North and South America, based in New York (USA); Priest Rev. THEODORE ROUPAS.

Other denominations include Brethren, Jehovah's Witnesses, Assemblies of God, Presbyterian, Greek Orthodox, Lutheran and Church of the Latter Day Saints (Mormons).

OTHER RELIGIONS

Bahá'í Faith

Adherents to the Bahá'í Faith numbered 65 at the 2010 census.

Bahá'í National Spiritual Assembly: POB N-7105, Nassau; tel. 326-0607; e-mail nsabaha@mail.com; internet www.bahai.org; Sec. AYANNA MAYCOCK.

Islam

There is a small community of Muslims, numbering 306 at the 2010 census.

Islamic Centre: Carmichael Rd, POB N-10711, Nassau; tel. 341-6612; fax 364-6233; e-mail questions@jamaa-ahlussunnah-bahamas .com; internet www.jamaa-ahlussunnah-bahamas.com; fmrly Jamaat ul-Islam of the Commonwealth of the Bahamas.

Judaism

Most of the Bahamian Jewish community, numbering 191 at the 2010 census, are based on Grand Bahama.

Nassau Jewish Congregation: POB N-95, Nassau; tel. 325-8416; e-mail gangieval@gmail.com; f. 1996; Sec. JANEEN VALENTINE ISAACS.

The Press

NEWSPAPERS

The Abaconian: Marsh Harbour, POB AB-20551, Abaco; tel. 367-3200; fax 367-3677; e-mail abaconiannews@gmail.com; internet abaconian.com; f. 1993; privately owned; local news; Editor BRADLEY ALBURY.

The Bahama Journal: Media House, East St North, POB N-8610, Nassau; tel. 325-3082; fax 325-3996; internet www.jonesbahamas .com; f. 1987; daily; Publr WENDALL JONES; circ. 5,000.

Bahamas Press: Nassau; e-mail media@bahamaspress.com; internet www.bahamaspress.com; online newspaper; f. 2007; Editor ALEXANDER JAMES.

The Eleutheran: Cupid's Cay, POB EL-25046, Governor's Harbour, Eleuthera; tel. 422-9350; fax 332-2993; e-mail editor@theeleutheran .com; internet www.eleutheranews.com; Man. Editor ELIZABETH BRYAN.

The Freeport News: Cedar St, POB F-40007, Freeport; tel. 352-8321; fax 351-3449; e-mail tfneditor@nasguard.com; internet freeport.nassauguardian.net; f. 1961; owned by *The Nassau Guardian*; daily; Publr ANTHONY FERGUSON; Man. Editor JOHN FLEET; circ. 5,000.

The Nassau Guardian: 4 Carter St, Oakes Field, POB N-3011, Nassau; tel. 302-2300; fax 328-8943; e-mail editor@nasguard.com; internet www.thenassauguardian.com; f. 1844; daily; Pres. ANTHONY FERGUSON; Man. Editor ERICA WELLS; circ. 15,000.

The Tribune: Shirley St, POB N-3207, Nassau; tel. 322-1986; fax 328-2398; e-mail tips@tribunemedia.net; internet www.tribune242 .com; f. 1903; daily; Publr and Editor EILEEN CARRON; circ. 15,000.

PERIODICALS

The Bahamas Financial Digest and Business Today: Miramar House, 2nd Floor, Bay and Christie Sts, POB N-4271, Nassau; tel. 356-2981; fax 326-2849; e-mail info@smgbahamas.com; f. 1973; 4 a year; business and investment; Publr and Editor MICHAEL A. SYMONETTE; circ. 15,890.

Ca Mari: POB N-3672, Nassau; tel. 565-9069; e-mail camari@ camariinc.com; internet www.camariinc.com; lifestyle magazine for women; Editor-in-Chief CAMILLE KENNY.

Insitu Arch: West Bay St, SP-60785, Nassau; tel. 376-4600; fax 327-8931; e-mail info@insitumag.com; internet www.insitumag.com; architecture; quarterly; CEO MARCUS LAING.

Nu Woman: Freddie Munnings Manor, Harbour Bay, CB-13236, Nassau; tel. 676-7908; fax 479-2318; e-mail info@nuwomanmagazine .com; internet www.nuwomanmagazine.com; f. 2007; lifestyle magazine for women; quarterly; Publr and Editor-in-Chief ERICA MEUS-SAUNDERS.

What's On Bahamas: Woodes Rogers Wharf, POB CB-11713, Nassau; tel. 323-2323; fax 322-3428; e-mail info@whatsonbahamas .com; internet www.whatsonbahamas.com; monthly; Publr NEIL ABERLE.

Publishers

Aberland Publications Ltd: Woodes Rodger's Wharf, CB-11713, Nassau; tel. 323-2323; fax 322-3428; e-mail submissions@ whatsonbahamas.com; internet www.whatsonbahamas.com; Publr ANDREW BERLANDA.

Dupuch Publications Ltd: 51 Hawthorne Rd, Oakes Field, POB N-7513, Nassau; tel. 323-5665; fax 323-5728; e-mail info@dupuch.com; internet www.dupuch.com; f. 1959; publishes *Bahamas Handbook*, *The Bahamas Investor*, *Trailblazer* maps, *What To Do* magazines, *Welcome Bahamas* and *Dining and Entertainment Guide*; Publr ETIENNE DUPUCH, Jr.

Guanima Press Ltd: East Bay St, POB CB-13151, Nassau; tel. and fax 393-3221; e-mail bookstore@guanimapress.com; internet www .guanima.com; f. 1992; Owner P. MEICHOLAS.

Media Enterprises Ltd: 31 Shirley Park Ave, POB N-9240, Nassau; tel. 325-8210; fax 325-8065; e-mail info@bahamasmedia .com; internet www.bahamasmedia.com; f. 1984; educational and other non-fiction books; authorized representative for Macmillan Caribbean, Oxford University Press and Nelson Thornes; Pres. and Gen. Man. LARRY A. SMITH; Publishing Dir NEIL E. SEALEY.

Broadcasting and Communications

REGULATORY AUTHORITY

Utilities Regulation and Competition Authority (URCA): UBS Annex Bldg, East Bay St, POB N-4860, Nassau; tel. 393-0234; fax 393-0153; e-mail info@urcabahamas.bs; internet www.urcabahamas .bs; f. 2009; replaced both the Public Utilities Commission and the Television Regulatory Authority; regulatory authority for electronic communications and broadcasting (including cable television); Chair. RANDOL DORSETT; CEO KATHLEEN RIVIERE-SMITH.

TELECOMMUNICATIONS

Bahamas Telecommunications Co (BTC): John F. Kennedy Dr., POB N-3048, Nassau; tel. 302-7008; fax 326-8423; e-mail help@ batelnet.bs; internet www.btcbahamas.com; f. 1966, fmrly known as BaTelCo; 51% stake acquired by Cable and Wireless (United Kingdom) in 2011; Chair. MARTIN JOOS (acting); CEO GEOFF HOUSTON.

Cable Bahamas Ltd: Robinson Rd at Marathon, POB CB-13050, Nassau; tel. 356-8940; fax 356-8997; e-mail info@cablebahamas.com; internet www.cablebahamas.com; f. 1995; provides cable television and internet services; Chair. PHILIP KEEPING; Pres. and CEO ANTHONY BUTLER.

BROADCASTING

Radio

Broadcasting Corporation of the Bahamas: Harcourt 'Rusty' Bethel Dr., 3rd Terrace, Centreville, POB N-1347, Nassau; tel. 502-3800; fax 322-6598; e-mail info@znsbahamas.com; internet www .znsbahamas.com; f. 1936; govt-owned; operates the ZNS radio and television network; Chair. Rev. Dr WILLIAM L. THOMPSON; Gen. Man. EDWIN LIGHTBOURNE.

Radio ZNS Bahamas: internet www.znsbahamas.com; f. 1936; broadcasts 24 hours per day on 4 stations: the main Radio Bahamas ZNS1, Radio New Providence ZNS2, which are both based in Nassau, Radio Power 104.5 FM, and the Northern Service (ZNS3—Freeport); Station Man. ANTHONY FORSTER.

Cool 96 FM: Yellow Pine St, POB F-40773, Freeport, Grand Bahama; tel. 351-2665; fax 352-8709; e-mail cool96@coralwave .com; internet cool96fm.com; f. 1995; opened office in Nassau in Jan. 2005; Pres. and Gen. Man. ANDREA GOTTLIEB.

Gems Radio: 51 Sears Hill, POB SS-6094, Nassau; tel. 326-4381; fax 326-4371; e-mail shenac@gemsbahamas.com; internet gemsbahamas.com; f. 2006; subsidiary of Bartlett-McWeeney Communications Ltd; Programming Dir SHENA CARROL.

Island FM: EdMark House, Dowdeswell St, POB N-1807, Nassau; tel. 322-8826; fax 356-4515; internet www.islandfmonline.com; Owner EDDIE CARTER.

Love 97 FM: Bahamas Media House, East St North, POB N-3909, Nassau; tel. 356-4960; fax 356-7256; e-mail twilliams@ jonescommunications.com; internet www.jonesbahamas.com; operated by Jones Communications Ltd.

More 94 FM: Carmichael Rd, POB CR-54245, Nassau; tel. 361-2447; fax 361-2448; e-mail media@more94fm.com; internet www .more94fm.com.

One Hundred JAMZ: Shirley and Deveaux St, POB N-3207, Nassau; tel. 677-0950; fax 356-5343; e-mail michelle@100jamz .com; internet www.100jamz.com; operated by *The Tribune* newspaper; Gen. Man. STEPHEN HAUGHEY; Programme Dir ERIC WARD.

Television

Broadcasting Corporation of the Bahamas: see Radio.

JCN Channel 14: East St North 99999, New Providence, Nassau; tel. 356-9071; fax 356-9073; internet www.jonesbahamas.com; subsidiary of the Jones Communications Network; CEO WENDALL JONES.

US television programmes and some satellite programmes can be received. Most islands have a cable television service.

Finance

The Bahamas has developed into one of the world's foremost financial centres (there are no corporation, income, capital gains or withholding taxes or estate duties), and finance has become a significant feature of the economy. There were 260 offshore banks and trust companies in operation in the islands at the end of 2012.

BANKING

(cap. = capital; res = reserves; dep. = deposits; m. = million; br(s) = branch(es))

Central Bank

The Central Bank of the Bahamas: Frederick St, POB N-4868, Nassau; tel. 302-2600; fax 322-4321; e-mail cbob@ centralbankbahamas.com; internet www.centralbankbahamas .com; f. 1974; bank of issue; cap. B \$3.0m., res B \$127.1m., dep. B \$411.4m. (Dec. 2009); Gov. and Chair. WENDY M. CRAIGG.

Development Bank

The Bahamas Development Bank: Cable Beach, West Bay St, POB N-3034, Nassau; tel. 702-5700; fax 327-5047; e-mail cserv@ bahamasdevelopmentbank.com; internet bahamasdevelopmentbank.com; f. 1978 to fund approved projects and channel funds into appropriate investments; total assets B \$58.3m. (Dec. 2004); Chair. CALVIN KNOWLES; Man. Dir ARINTHIA S. KOMOLAFE; 1 br.

Principal Banks

Bank of the Bahamas Ltd (Bank of the Bahamas International): Claughton House, Shirley and Charlotte Sts, POB N-7118, Nassau; tel. 397-3000; fax 325-2762; e-mail bob.info@ BankBahamas.com; internet www.bankbahamas.com; f. 1970; est. as Bank of Montreal (Bahamas and Caribbean); name changed as above in 2002; 50% owned by Govt, 50% owned by c. 4,000 Bahamian shareholders; cap. B \$50.0m., res B \$32.6m., dep. B \$649.3m. (Jan. 2013); Chair. MACGREGOR ROBERTSON; Man. Dir PAUL JOSEPH MCWEENEY; 13 brs.

BSI Overseas (Bahamas) Ltd (Italy): Goodman's Bay Corporate Centre, West Bay St, Sea View Dr., POB N-7130, Nassau; tel. 502-2200; fax 502-2230; e-mail info@bsibank.com; internet www.bs .bsibank.com; f. 1969 as Banca della Svizzera Italiana (Overseas) Ltd; name changed as above 1991; wholly owned subsidiary of BSI SA Lugano; cap. US \$10.0m., res US \$18.2m., dep. US \$3,857.8m. (Jan. 2013); Chair. VINCENZO PIANTEDOSI; CEO STEFANO CODURI.

CIBC FirstCaribbean International Bank: FirstCaribbean Financial Centre, Shirley St, POB N-8350, Nassau; tel. 322-8455; fax 326-6552; internet www.cibcfcib.com; f. 2002 following merger of Caribbean operations of Barclays Bank PLC and CIBC, present name adopted 2011; Barclays Bank relinquished its stake to CIBC in 2006; cap. B \$477.2m., res B \$−14.8m., dep. B \$2,499.3m. (Oct. 2013); CEO RIK PARKHILL; Man. Dir (Bahamas, Turks and Caicos) MARIE RODLAND-ALLEN; 15 brs.

Citibank NA (USA): Citibank Bldg, 4th Floor, Thompson Blvd, Oakes Field, POB N-8158, Nassau; tel. 302-8500; fax 323-3088; internet www.citibank.com; CEO MICHAEL CORBAT; 2 brs.

Commonwealth Bank Ltd: The Plaza, Mackey St, POB SS 5541, Nassau; tel. 502-6200; fax 394-5807; e-mail cbinquiry@combankltd .com; internet www.combankltd.com; f. 1960; cap. B \$86.9m., res B \$37.1m., dep. B \$1,203.0m. (Jan. 2013); Chair. WILLIAM BATEMAN SANDS, Jr; Pres. IAN ANDREW JENNINGS; 11 brs.

Crédit Agricole Suisse Bank & Trust (Bahamas) Ltd: Goodman's Bay Corporate Centre, Ground Floor, West Bay St, POB N-3015, Nassau; tel. 502-8100; fax 502-8166; internet www.ca-suisse .bs; f. 1978; 100% owned by Crédit Agricole (Suisse) SA, Geneva (Switzerland); fmrly National Bank of Canada (International) Ltd; name changed as above 2008; Chair. JEAN BOUYSSET.

Crédit Suisse (Bahamas) Ltd (Switzerland): Bahamas Financial Centre, 4th Floor, Shirley and Charlotte Sts, POB N-4928, Nassau; tel. 356-8100; fax 326-6589; internet www.credit-suisse.com/bs; f. 1968; subsidiary of Crédit Suisse Zurich; portfolio and asset management, offshore co management, trustee services, foreign exchange; Man. Dir ANTOINETTE RUSSELL.

Edmond de Rothschild (Bahamas) Ltd (Switzerland): Lyford Financial Centre, Lyford Cay 2, West Bay St, POB SP-63948, Nassau; tel. 702-8000; fax 702-8008; e-mail dswaby@bper.ch; internet www.edmond-de-rothschild.bs; f. 1997; owned by Banque Privée Edmond de Rothschild SA (Switzerland); cap. 15.0m. Swiss francs, res 23.9m. Swiss francs, dep. 442.9m. Swiss francs (Jan. 2013); Chair. MANUEL LEUTHOLD; CEO GIAN FADRI PINOESCH.

Guaranty Trust Bank Ltd: Lyford Manor Ltd, Lyford Cay, POB N-4918, Nassau; tel. 362-7200; fax 362-7210; e-mail info@ guarantybahamas.com; internet www.guarantybahamas.com; f. 1962; cap. US \$21.0m., res US \$0.3m., dep. US \$72.4m. (Dec. 2011); Chair. Sir WILLIAM C. ALLEN; Man. Dir JAMES P. COYLE.

Pictet Bank and Trust Ltd (Switzerland): Bldg No. 1, Bayside Executive Park, West Bay St and Blake Rd, POB N-4837, Nassau; tel. 302-2222; fax 327-6610; e-mail pbtbah@bahamas.net.bs; internet www.pictet.com; f. 1978; cap. US \$1.0m., res US \$10.0m., dep. US \$126.2m. (Dec. 1995); Pres., Dir and Gen. Man. YVES LOURDIN.

Private Investment Bank Ltd: Devonshire House, Queen St, POB N-3918, Nassau; tel. 302-5950; fax 302-5970; e-mail valerio.zanchi@pib.bs; internet www.bfsb-bahamas.com; f. 1984 as Bank Worms and Co International Ltd; est. renamed in 1990, 1996 and 1998; in 2000 merged with Geneva Private Bank and Trust (Bahamas) Ltd; wholly owned by Banque de Patrimoines Privés Genève BPG SA (Switzerland); cap. US $3.0m., res US $12.0m., dep. US $163.6m. (Dec. 2009); Gen. Man VALERIO ZANCHI.

Royal Bank of Canada Ltd (Canada): 323 Bay St, POB N-7549, Nassau; tel. 322-8700; fax 328-7145; e-mail banks@rbc.com; internet www.rbc.com; f. 1869; Pres. and CEO GORDON M. NIXON; 25 brs.

Scotiabank (Bahamas) Ltd (Canada): Scotiabank Bldg, Rawson Sq., POB N-7518, Nassau; tel. 356-1400; fax 326-0991; e-mail scotiabank.bs@scotiabank.com; internet www.bahamas.scotiabank.com; f. 1956; cap. B $25m., res B $40m., dep. B $1,843.9m. (Dec. 2013); Chair. ANTHONY C. ALLEN; Man. Dir SEAN ALBERT; 20 brs.

Société Générale Private Banking (Bahamas) Ltd (United Kingdom): Lyford Cay House, West Bay St, POB N-7785, Nassau; tel. 302-5000; fax 326-6709; e-mail renaud.vielfaure@socgen.com; internet www.privatebanking.societegenerale.com; f. 1936; became SG Hambros Bank and Trust (Bahamas) Ltd in 1998; cap. B $2.0m., res –B $3.2m., dep. B $435.2m. (Dec. 2008); Chair. JEAN-PIERRE FLAIS.

UBS (Bahamas) Ltd (Switzerland): UBS House, East Bay St, POB N-7757, Nassau; tel. 394-9300; fax 394-9333; internet www.ubs.com/bahamas; f. 1968 as Swiss Bank Corpn (Overseas) Ltd name changed as above 1998; wholly owned by UBS AG (Switzerland); Pres. (Latin America) GABRIEL CASTELLO; Group CEO SERGIO P. ERMOTTI.

Principal Bahamian Trust Companies

Ansbacher (Bahamas) Ltd: 308 East Bay St, POB N-7768, Nassau; tel. 322-1161; fax 326-5020; e-mail info@ansbacher.bs; internet www.ansbacher.bs; f. 1957; offers bank and trust services; total assets US $128m. (2012); Man. Dir CARLTON MORTIER.

Bank of Nova Scotia Trust Co (Bahamas) Ltd: Scotia House, 404 East Bay St, POB N-3016, Nassau; tel. 502-5700; fax 326-0991; e-mail info.bahamas@scotiatrust.com; internet www.bahamas.scotiabank.com; wholly owned by the Bank of Nova Scotia; Chair. CATHY WELLING.

CIBC Trust Company (Bahamas) Ltd: Goodman's Bay Corporate Centre, West Bay St, POB N3933, Nassau; tel. 356-1800; fax 322-3692; internet www.cibc.com; f. 1957.

Winterbotham Trust Co Ltd: Winterbotham Pl., Marlborough and Queen Sts, POB N-3026, Nassau; tel. 356-5454; fax 356-9432; e-mail ihooper@winterbotham.com; internet www.winterbotham.com; total assets US $23.1m. (June 2013); Chair. ANDREW LAW; 2 brs.

Bankers' Organizations

Association of International Banks and Trust Companies in the Bahamas: Montague Sterling Centre, 2nd Floor, East Bay St, POB N-7880, Nassau; tel. 393-5500; fax 393-5501; e-mail info@aibt-bahamas.com; internet www.aibt-bahamas.com; f. 1976; Chair. ANTOINETTE RUSSELL.

Bahamas Financial Services Board (BFSB): Montague Sterling Centre, East Bay St, POB N-1764, Nassau; tel. 393-7001; fax 393-7712; e-mail info@bfsb-bahamas.com; internet www.bfsb-bahamas.com; f. 1998; jt govt/private initiative responsible for industry promotion and overseas marketing of financial services; CEO and Exec. Dir ALIYA ALLEN; Chair. PRINCE RAHMING.

Bahamas Institute of Financial Services (BIFS): Verandah House, Market St and Trinity Pl., POB N-3202, Nassau; tel. 325-4921; fax 325-5674; e-mail info@bifs-bahamas.com; internet www.bifs-bahamas.com; f. 1974 as Bahamas Institute of Bankers, name changed as above 2003; Pres. TANYA MCCARTNEY.

STOCK EXCHANGE

Bahamas International Securities Exchange (BISX): Fort Nassau Centre, 2nd Floor, British Colonial Hilton, Bay St, POB EE-15672, Nassau; tel. 323-2330; fax 323-2320; e-mail info@bisxbahamas.com; internet www.bisxbahamas.com; f. 1999; 28 primary listings and 24 mutual funds in Feb. 2014; Chair. IAN FAIR; CEO KEITH DAVIES.

INSURANCE

BAF Financial: Independence Dr., POB N-4815, Nassau; tel. 461-1000; fax 361-2524; e-mail info@mybafsolutions.com; internet bahamas.mybafsolutions.com; f. 1920; est. as British American Insurance Co; name changed to British American Financial in 2007; rebranded as above in 2010; owned by local consortium, BAB Holdings Ltd, since 2007; Chair. BASIL L. SANDS; Pres. and CEO CHESTER COOPER.

Bahamas First General Insurance Co Ltd: Bahamas First Centre, 32 Collins Ave, POB SS-6238, Nassau; tel. 302-3900; fax 302-3901; e-mail info@bahamasfirst.com; internet www.bahamasfirst.com; f. 1983; Chair. IAN D. FAIR; Pres. and CEO PATRICK G. W. WARD.

Carib Insurance Agency Ltd: POB N-4200, Nassau; tel. 322-8210; fax 322-5277; e-mail info@carib.com.bs; Contact RICHARD URIASZ.

Colina General Insurance Ltd: 308 Bay St, POB N-4728, Nassau; tel. 396-2100; fax 393-1710; internet www.colinageneral.com; fmrly known as Colina Imperial Insurance Ltd; Colina Insurance Co merged with Global Life Assurance Bahamas in 2002; operates under above name; fully owned subsidiary of Colina Holdings Bahamas Ltd; Chair. TERENCE HILTS; Exec. Vice-Chair. and CEO EMANUEL M. ALEXIOU.

Family Guardian Insurance Co Ltd (FamGuard): East Bay & Shirley St, POB SS-6232, Nassau; tel. 396-4000; fax 393-1100; e-mail info@familyguardian.com; internet www.familyguardian.com; f. 1965; life and health; fully owned subsidiary of FamGuard Corpn Ltd; Pres. and CEO PATRICIA A. HERMANNS.

Insurance Company of the Bahamas (ICB): 33 Collins Ave, POB N-8320, Nassau; tel. 326–3100; fax 326-3132; e-mail tomduff@icbbahamas.com; internet www.icbbahamas.com; f. 1996; all non-life insurance; 40% owned by J. S. Johnson & Co Ltd; Gen. Man. TOM DUFF.

J. S. Johnson & Co Ltd: 33 Collins Ave, POB N-8337, Nassau; tel. 397-2100; fax 323-3720; internet jsjohnson.com; f. 1919; general insurance; Man. Dir ALISTER I. MCKELLAR.

Moseley Burnside Insurance Agency Ltd: POB N-3208, Nassau; tel. 394-8305; fax 394-8309; e-mail info@mbiabahamas.com; part of Bahamas First Holdings Ltd; Contact FRANCES OLIVER MCKENZIE.

NUA Insurance Agents and Brokers: The R. H. Bobby Symonette Bldg, Third Terrace and Collins Ave, POB N-4870, Nassau; tel. 302-9100; fax 328–5974; e-mail info@nuacainsurance.com; internet www.nuacainsurance.com; f. 1966; Man. Dir WARREN T. ROLLE.

RoyalStar Assurance: John F. Kennedy Dr., POB N-4391, Nassau; tel. 328-7888; fax 325-3151; internet rsabahamas.com; Man. Dir ANTON A. SAUNDERS.

Security and General Insurance Co Ltd: Atlantic House, Second Terrace and Collins Ave, POB N-3540, Nassau; tel. 326-7100; fax 325-0948; internet bahamas.cgigroup.com; owned by Colonial Group International (Bermuda).

Star General Insurance Agency Ltd: Second Terrace West, Centreville, POB N-1108, Nassau; tel. 322-2058; fax 326-1591; e-mail stargen@stargeneralnp.com; internet www.stargeneralbahamas.com; f. 1987.

Summit Insurance Co Ltd: 42 Montrose Ave, Sears Hill, POB SS-19028, Nassau; tel. 677-7878; fax 677-7873; e-mail info@summitbah.com; internet www.summitbahamas.com; f. 1994; Chair. CEDRIC A. SAUNDERS; Gen. Man. and Dir TIMOTHY N. INGRAHAM.

Sunshine Insurance Agents and Brokers Ltd: Sunshine House, East Shirley St, POB N-3180, Nassau; tel. 502-6500; fax 394-3101; e-mail info@sunshine-insurance.com; internet www.sunshine-insurance.com; f. 1972.

Association

Bahamas Insurance Association (BIA): Royal Palm Mall, Unit 8, Mackey St, POB N-860, Nassau; tel. 394-6625; fax 394-6626; e-mail bgia@coralwave.com; internet www.bahamasinsurance.org; Chair. HOWARD KNOWLES; Co-ordinator Dr RHONDA CHIPMAN-JOHNSON; 29 mems.

Trade and Industry

DEVELOPMENT ORGANIZATIONS

Bahamas Agricultural and Industrial Corpn (BAIC): BAIC Bldg, East Bay St, POB N-4940, Nassau; tel. 322-3740; fax 322-2123; e-mail baic@bahamas.gov.bs; internet www.bahamas.gov.bs/baic; f. 1981; an amalgamation of Bahamas Development Corpn and Bahamas Agricultural Corpn for the promotion of greater co-operation between tourism and other sectors of the economy through the development of small and medium-sized enterprises; Chair. ARNOLD FORBES; Gen. Man. BENJAMIN RAHMING.

Bahamas Investment Authority: Sir Cecil Wallace-Whitfield Centre, West Bay St, POB CB-10990, Nassau; tel. 327-5826; fax 327-5806; e-mail bia@bahamas.gov.bs; govt-owned; operates from the Office of the Prime Minister; Dir of Investments JOY JIBRILU.

Nassau Paradise Island Promotion Board: Hotel Center, S. G. Hambros Bldg, West Bay St, Nassau; tel. 322-8381; fax 326-5346; e-mail michael@npipb.com; internet www.nassauparadiseisland

.com; f. 1973; Chair. GEORGE R. MYERS; Vice-Chair. GEORGE MARKANTONIS; 17 mems.

CHAMBERS OF COMMERCE

Bahamas Chamber of Commerce and Employers Confederation (BCCEC): Shirley St and Collins Ave, POB N-665, Nassau; tel. 322-2145; fax 322-4649; e-mail info@thebahamaschamber.com; internet www.thebahamaschamber.com; f. 1935 as Bahamas Chamber of Commerce; changed name as above after merger with Bahamas Employers Conf; Pres. CHESTER COOPER; Exec. Dir KESHELLE KERR; over 500 mems.

Grand Bahama Chamber of Commerce: 5 Mall Dr., POB F-40808, Freeport, Grand Bahama; tel. 352-8329; fax 352-3280; e-mail gbchamberofcommerceassistant@hotmail.com; internet www.gbchamber.org; Pres. BARRY MALCOLM; Exec. Dir MERCYNTH FERGUSON; 264 mems.

EMPLOYERS' ASSOCIATIONS

Bahamian Contractors' Association: POB N-9286, Nassau; tel. 322-2145; fax 322-4649; e-mail info@bahamiancontractors.org; internet www.bahamascontractors.org; f. 1959; Pres. GODFREY FORBES; Sec. ROBYN OGILVIE.

Bahamas Hotel Employers' Association: SG Hambros Bldg, West Bay, POB N-7799, Nassau; tel. 322-2262; fax 502-4221; e-mail bhea4mcr@hotmail.com; f. 1958; Pres. J. BARRIE FARRINGTON; Exec. Vice-Pres. MICHAEL C. RECKLEY; 16 mems.

Bahamas Institute of Chartered Accountants: Maritima House, 2nd Floor, Frederick St, POB N-7037, Nassau; tel. 326-6619; fax 326-6618; e-mail secbica@batelnet.bs; internet www.bica.bs; f. 1971; Pres. JASMINE DAVIS.

Bahamas Motor Dealers' Association (BMDA): POB SS-6213, Nassau; tel. 302-1030; internet www.bmda.bs; 16 mem. cos.

Bahamas Real Estate Association: Dowdeswell St, POB N-8860, Nassau; tel. 356-4578; fax 356-4501; e-mail info@bahamasrealestateassociation.com; internet www.bahamasrealestateassociation.com; f. 1959; Pres. FRANON WILSON; Sec. DONNA JONES; 400 mems.

Professional Engineers Board (PEB): 3 21st Century Rd, POB N-3817, Nassau; tel. 328-3574; e-mail info@pebahamas.org; internet www.pebahamas.org; f. 2004; Chair. ROBERT DEAL.

MAJOR COMPANIES

AML Foods Ltd: Town Center Mall, 2nd Level, Blue Hill Rd, POB SS-6322, Nassau; tel. 677-7200; fax 356-7822; e-mail info@amlfoods.com; internet www.amlfoods.com; retail stores chain; Chair. DIONISIO D'AGUILAR; Pres. and CEO GAVIN WATCHORN.

Baha Mar Development Co Ltd: Baha Mar Resorts Ltd, West Bay St, POB CB-10977, Nassau; tel. 677-9000; fax 677-9100; e-mail info@bahamar.com; internet www.bahamar.com; subsidiary of Baha Mar Resorts Ltd; developer of a 1,000 acre resort at Nassau; jt venture with Export-Import Bank of China and China State Construction Engineering Corpn; Chair. and CEO SARKIS IZMIRLIAN; Pres. TOM DUNLAP.

Bahamas Food Services Ltd (BFS): Gladstone Rd, POB N-4401, Nassau; tel. 361-2000; fax 461-6100; e-mail foodsales@bahamafood.com; internet www.bahamafood.com; f. 1971; fmrly Island Sea Food (ISF); distributors of agricultural and seafood products; Man. MELANIE FARRANT; 300 employees.

Bahamas Marine Construction Co Ltd: Lyford Cay House, Western Rd, POB N-641, Nassau; tel. 362-4018; fax 362-4081; e-mail crogers@mosko.com; internet www.mosko.com/building/marine.html; f. 1980; owned by the Mosko Group of Cos, Bahamas; construction of ports, docks and marinas; Chair. JAMES GEORGE MOSKO; 111 employees.

Bahamas Oil Refining Co International Ltd (BORCO): West Sunrise Highway, POB F-42435, Freeport; tel. 350-2106; fax 359-5206; e-mail jhollingsworth@buckeye.com; internet www.buckeyeglobalmarine.com; f. 1964; petroleum distribution; storage terminal facility; fmrly Vopak Terminal Bahamas; subsidiary of Buckeye Partners (USA); Man. JEFF HOLLINGSWORTH; 108 employees.

Bahamas Petroleum Co PLC: Nassau Office, Bldg 3, Western Rd, Mount Pleasant Village, POB SP-64135, Nassau; tel. 362-5120; fax 362-5125; e-mail info.nassau@bpcplc.com; internet www.bpcplc.com; oil and gas exploration; incorporated in Isle of Man (United Kingdom) but owns BPC Ltd (incorporated in the Bahamas); CEO SIMON CRAIG POTTER.

Bahamas Realty Ltd: POB N-1132, Nassau; tel. 396-0000; fax 396-0010; e-mail info@bahamasrealty.bs; internet www.bahamasrealty.bs; f. 1978 as Caribbean Management and Sales Ltd; real estate; Pres. ROBIN B. BROWNRIGG; CEO LARRY ROBERTS.

Bahamian Brewery & Beverage Co: POB F-42409, Freeport; tel. 352-4070; fax 352-4076; internet www.bahamianbrewery.com; f. 2008; Owner JAMES SANDS.

FOCOL Holdings Co Ltd (FCL): Queens Hwy, POB F-42458, Freeport; tel. 352-8131; fax 352-2986; e-mail sales.focol@batelnet.bs; f. 1981; fmrly Freeport Oil Holdings Co; Chair. ALBERT MILLER; Man. Dir ANTHONY ROBINSON.

Grand Bahama Development Co Ltd: G. B. Port Authority Bldg, Pioneers Way and East Mall, POB F-42666, Freeport; tel. 350-9311; fax 350-9323; e-mail infosupport@gbdevco.com; internet www.gbdevco.com; f. 1961; holding co; Pres. and CEO GRAHAM TORODE; 300 employees.

Grand Bahama Snack Food Wholesale: Queen's Hwy, POB F-40797, Freeport; tel. 352-8868; fax 352-4173; f. 1960; snack food and drinks wholesalers and retailers; Pres. GWENDOLYN NEWBOLD.

H. G. Christie Ltd: Millar's Court, POB N-8164, Nassau; tel. 322-1041; fax 326-5642; e-mail sales@hgchristie.com; internet www.hgchristie.com; f. 1922; real estate service; Pres. PETER CHRISTIE; Vice-Pres. JOHN CHRISTIE.

Hutchison Port Holdings (HPH): Headquarters Bldg, Container Port Rd, Queen's Hwy, POB F-42465, Freeport; tel. 350-8000; fax 350-8044; internet www.freeportcontainerport.com; port holding co; owned by Hutchison Whampoa of Hong Kong; subsidiaries include Grand Bahama Airport Co, Freeport Container Port and Freeport Harbour Co; Group Man. Dir JOHN E. MEREDITH; CEO GARY GILBERT.

J. S. R. Real Estate Ltd: Pioneers Professional Plaza, POB F-40093, Freeport; tel. 352-7201; fax 352-7203; e-mail jsrreal@batelnet.bs; internet jsrbahamasrealestate.com; f. 1957; real estate, developments, condominiums, residency and investing; Pres. LEE VAN LEW.

Kerzner International (Bahamas) Ltd: c/o Holiday Inn, POB N-4777, Paradise Island; tel. 363-2000; fax 363-3703; e-mail meagan.mccutcheon@kerzner.com; internet www.kerzner.com; South African co; hotel owners; CEO ALAN LEIBMAN; Pres. and Man. Dir (Bahamas) GEORGE MARKANTONIS.

Morton Salt Co (Bahamas): Gregory St, Matthew Town, Inagua; tel. 339-1300; internet www.mortonsalt.com; f. 1954 when West Chemical Co was amalgamated into Morton Salt Co; bought by K+S Aktiengesellschaft (Germany) in 2008; Group CEO CHRISTIAN HERRMANN.

Mosko's United Construction Ltd: House of Mosko, Bay St and Victoria Ave, POB N-641, Nassau; tel. 362-4018; fax 362-4081; e-mail tmcdermott@mosko.com; internet www.mosko.com/building/united; f. 1958; owned by the Mosko Group of Cos, Bahamas; Pres. GEORGE MOSKO; 567 employees.

PharmaChem Technologies Grand Bahama Ltd (Novasep—Freeport): West Sunrise Hwy, POB F-42430, Freeport; tel. 352-8171; fax 352-7078; e-mail rthompson@pharmachemtech.com; f. 1967 by Syntex; pharmaceutical products mfr; acquired by Novasep (France) in 2007; Pres. PIETRO STEFANUTTI; CEO ANGELO CARMINATI.

Taylor Industries Ltd: 111 Shirley St, POB N-4806, Nassau; tel. 322-8941; fax 328-0453; e-mail generalinfo@taylor-industries.com; internet www.taylor-industries.com; f. 1945; electrical appliances and supplies; Pres. and Gen. Man. DEREK TAYLOR; 87 employees.

Templeton Global Advisors Ltd: Lyford Cay, POB N-7759, Nassau; tel. 362-4600; fax 362-4308; e-mail csweeti@templeton.com; f. 1986; investment consultants and security brokers; Pres. CINDY SWEETING; 400 employees.

UTILITIES

Electricity

Bahamas Electricity Corpn (BEC): Big Pond and Tucker Rds, POB N-7509, Nassau; tel. 302-1000; fax 323-6852; e-mail customercare@bahamaselectricity.com; internet www.bahamaselectricity.com; f. 1956; state-owned, scheduled for privatization; provides electricity to approx. 100,000 customers; Exec. Chair. LESLIE MILLER; Gen. Man. KEVIN A. BASDEN.

Grand Bahama Power Co (GBPC): Pioneers Way & East Mall Dr., POB F-40888, Freeport; tel. 350-9000; fax 351-5008; e-mail customerservice@gb-power.com; internet www.gb-power.com; f. 1962 as Freeport Power Co Ltd; 80% owned by Emera (Canada); Pres. and CEO SARAH MacDONALD.

Gas

Tropigas: Gladstone Rd, POB SS-5833, Nassau; tel. 361-2695; fax 341-4875.

Water

Bahamas Water and Sewerage Corpn (WSC): 87 Thompson Blvd, POB N-3905, Nassau; tel. 322-5500; fax 328-3896; e-mail wccomplaints@wsc.com.bs; internet www.wsc.com.bs; f. 1976; state-run; Chair. BRADLEY B. ROBERTS; Gen. Man. GLEN LAVILLE.

TRADE UNIONS
Confederations

Commonwealth of the Bahamas Trade Union Congress: 3 Warwick St, POB N-3399, Nassau; tel. 394-6301; fax 394-7401; e-mail tuc@bahamas.net.bs; Pres. OBIE FERGUSON, Jr; Gen. Sec. TIMOTHY MOORE; 12,500 mems.

National Congress of Trade Unions (NCTUB): Horseshoe Dr., POB GT-2887, Nassau; tel. 356-7459; fax 356-7457; e-mail ncongress@hotmail.com; internet nctu-bahamas.org; f. 1995; Pres. JENNIFER ISAACS-DOTSON; Gen. Sec. ROBERT FARQUHARSON; 20,000 mems.

Principal Trade Unions

Airport, Airline and Allied Workers' Union: Workers' House, Harold Rd, POB N-3364, Nassau; tel. 323-5030; fax 326-8763; e-mail aaawu@batelnet.bs; f. 1958; Acting Pres. and Gen. Sec. ANTHONY BAIN.

Bahamas Communications and Public Officers' Union: Farrington Rd, POB N-3190, Nassau; tel. 322-1537; fax 323-8719; e-mail union@bcpou.com; internet bcpou.org; f. 1973; Pres. BERNARD EVANS; Gen. Sec. DENISE WILSON; 2,100 mems.

Bahamas Doctors' Union: School Lane, Nassau; tel. 326-4166; Pres. PHILIP SEALY; Gen. Sec. GEORGE SHERMAN.

Bahamas Electrical Workers' Union (BEWU): 52 Poinciana Dr., POB GT-2535, Nassau; tel. 322-4289; fax 322-4711; e-mail bewupresident2002@hotmail.com; Pres. and Gen. Sec. STEPHANO GREENE.

Bahamas Gaming and Allied Workers' Union: Taxi Union Bldg, Old Airport Rd, POB F-43070, Freeport; tel. 375-9804; fax 352-8837; e-mail bgawu@hotmail.com; internet bgaworkersunion.tripod.com; Pres. DENNIS BRITTON; Vice-Pres. WILLIAM MARTINBOROUGH.

Bahamas Hotel, Catering and Allied Workers' Union: Harold Rd, POB GT-2514, Nassau; tel. 325-0807; fax 325-6546; e-mail bhcawu@batelnet.bs; f. 1958; Pres. NICOLE MARTIN; Vice-Pres. DARRIN WOODS; 6,500 mems.

Bahamas Musicians' and Entertainers' Union: Horseshoe Dr., POB N-880, Nassau; tel. 322-3734; fax 323-3537; f. 1958; Pres. PERCIVAL SWEETING; Gen. Sec. PORTIA NOTTAGE; 410 mems.

Bahamas Nurses' Union: Centreville, Eighth Terrace, POB N-11530, Nassau; tel. and fax 325-3008; e-mail bnu_17199@hotmail.com; Pres. CLEOLA HAMILTON; Gen. Sec. ANEKA JOHNSON.

Bahamas Public Services Union: Wulff Rd, POB N-4692, Nassau; tel. 325-0038; fax 323-5287; e-mail bpsu@batelnet.bs; internet www.bpsubahamas.com; f. 1959; Pres. JOHN PINDER; Sec.-Gen. STEVEN J. MILLER; 4,247 mems.

Bahamas Taxi-Cab Union: Nassau St, POB N-1077, Nassau; tel. 323-5818; fax 323-6919; e-mail btcunion@coralwave.com; internet www.bahamastaxicabunion.com; Pres. LEON GRIFFIN; Gen. Sec. ROSCOE WEECH.

Bahamas Union of Teachers (BUT): Teachers' National Secretariat, 104 Bethel Ave, Stapledon Gardens, POB N-3482, Nassau; tel. 323-4491; fax 323-7086; e-mail idatp@hotmail.com; internet teachersvoicebahamas.com; f. 1945; Pres. BELINDA WILSON; Sec.-Gen. STEPHEN McPHEE; 4,000 mems.

Eastside Stevedores' Union: Wulff Rd, POB GT-2813, Nassau; tel. 322-4069; fax 323-7566; f. 1972; Pres. DAVID BETHEL; Gen. Sec. HAROLDINE STUBBS, Jr.

Transport

ROADS

There are about 1,600 km (994 miles) of roads in New Providence and 1,368 km (850 miles) in the Family Islands, mainly on Grand Bahama, Cat Island, Eleuthera, Exuma and Long Island. In 2001 57.4% of roads were paved.

SHIPPING

The principal seaport is at Nassau (New Providence), which can accommodate the very largest cruise ships. Passenger arrivals exceed 2m. annually. The other main ports are at Freeport (Grand Bahama), where a container terminal opened in 1997, and Matthew Town (Inagua). There are also modern berthing facilities for cruise ships at Potters Cay (New Providence), Governor's Harbour (Eleuthera), Morgan's Bluff (North Andros) and George Town (Exuma). In 2012 plans were approved for construction of a new port in northern Abaco, financed by the Export-Import Bank of China at the cost of US $39m. Construction of the 35-acre project was expected to begin in 2014 and take two years.

The Bahamas converted to free flag status in 1976. In December 2013 the fleet comprised 1,493 vessels, totalling 56,663,130 grt (the third largest national fleet in the world).

There is a weekly cargo and passenger service to all the Family Islands.

Bahamas Maritime Authority: Shirlaw House, 87 Shirley St, POB N-4679, Nassau; tel. 356-5772; fax 356-5889; e-mail nassau@bahamasmaritime.com; internet www.bahamasmaritime.com; f. 1995; promotes ship registration and co-ordinates maritime administration; state-owned; CEO and Man. Dir Cdre DAVY F. ROLLE.

Freeport Harbour Co Ltd: POB F-42465, Freeport; tel. 350-8000; fax 350-8044; internet www.freeportcontainerport.com; owned by Hutchison Port Holdings (HPH), Hong Kong; CEO GARY GILBERT; Dir ORLANDO FORBES.

Grand Bahama Port Authority (GBPA): Pioneer's Way and East Mall Dr., POB F-42666, Freeport; tel. 350-9002; fax 352-6184; e-mail fstubbs@gbpa.com; internet www.gbpa.com; f. 1955; Chair. HANNES BABAK; Pres. IAN ROLLE.

Principal Shipping Companies

Bahamas Ferries: Potters Cay West, Nassau; tel. 323-2166; fax 393-7451; e-mail customerservice@bahamasferries.com; internet www.bahamasferries.com; f. 1999; services Spanish Wells, Harbour Island, Current Island and Governors Harbour in Eleuthera, Morgan's Bluff and Fresh Creek in Andros, Sandy Point in Abaco and George Town in Exuma; Gen. Man. ALAN BAX.

Campbell Shipping Co Ltd (CSCL): Dockendale House, 3rd Floor, West Bay St, POB N-3033, Nassau; tel. 325-0448; fax 328-1542; internet csship.com; f. 1973 as Dockendale Shipping Co; bought by CSCL in 2006; ship management; Man. Dir CHANDLER B. T. SANDS.

Dean's Shipping Co: 11 Parkgate, POB EE17318, Nassau; tel. 394-0245; fax 394-0253; e-mail deansshippingco@gmail.com; internet www.deanshipping.com; Man. TWEED DEAN.

Freeport Ship Services: 8 Logwood Rd, POB F-40423, Freeport; tel. 351-4343; fax 351-4332; e-mail info@freeportshipservices.com; internet www.freeportshipservices.com; f. 2003; privately owned co; affiliated to United Shipping Co Ltd; agents, customs brokers, logistics providers, chandlers; Pres. JEREMY CAFFERATA; Gen. Man. JOHN LANE.

Tropical Shipping Co Ltd: Container Terminals Ltd, John Alfred Dock, Bay St, POB N-8183, Nassau; tel. 322-1012; fax 323-7566; internet www.tropical.com; Pres. MIKE PELLICCI.

United Abaco Shipping Co Ltd: Marsh Harbour, POB AB-20737, Abaco; tel. 367-2091; fax 367-2235; e-mail unitedabacoshippingco@coralwave.com; internet www.unitedabacoshipping.com; Man. SIDNEY ALBURY.

United Shipping Co (Nassau) Ltd: Centreville House, 5th Floor, Terrace 2, West Centreville, POB N-4005, Nassau; tel. 322-1341; fax 323-8779; e-mail operations@unitedshippingnassau.com; internet www.uscbahamas.com; sister co of Freeport Ship Services; Gen. Man. RICH RYAN.

CIVIL AVIATION

Lynden Pindling International Airport (formerly Nassau International Airport) (15 km—9 miles—outside the capital), Freeport International Airport (5 km—3 miles—outside the city, on Grand Bahama) and Marsh Harbour International Airport (on Abaco Island) are the main terminals for international and internal services. There are also important airports at West End (Grand Bahama) and Rock Sound (Eleuthera) and some 50 smaller airports and landing strips throughout the islands. An estimated US $200m. development of Lynden Pindling International Airport was completed in late 2013, and in May 2014 a new terminal at Marsh Harbour International Airport was opened.

Bahamasair Holdings Ltd: Windsor Field, POB N-4881, Nassau; tel. 702-4100; fax 702-4180; e-mail astuart@bahamasair.com; internet bahamasair.com; f. 1973; state-owned, proposed privatization plans shelved indefinitely by 2009; scheduled services between Nassau, Freeport, Cuba, Jamaica, Dominican Republic, Turks and Caicos Islands, destinations within the USA and 20 locations within the Family Islands; Chair. VALENTINE GRIMES; Man. Dir HENRY WOODS.

Western Air Limited: San Andros International Airport, POB AP 532900, North Andros, Nassau; tel. 329-4000; fax 329-4013; e-mail westernairltd@gmail.com; internet www.westernairbahamas.com; f. 2001; private, wholly Bahamian-owned company; scheduled services between Nassau, Freeport, San Andros and Bimini, and to Cuba, and on-demand charter flights throughout the Bahamas, the Caribbean and Central and South America; Pres. and CEO REX ROLLE.

Tourism

The mild climate and beautiful beaches attract many tourists. In 2013 tourist arrivals totalled some 6,151,000, including 4,870,000 visitors by sea. The majority of stop-over arrivals were from the USA. Receipts from the tourism industry stood at a provisional B $2,311m. in 2012.

Ministry of Tourism: Bolam House, George St, POB N-3701, Nassau; tel. 302-2000; fax 302-2098; e-mail tourism@bahamas.com; internet www.bahamas.com; Dir-Gen. JOY JIBRILU.

Bahamas Hotel Association: Serenity House, East Bay St, POB N-7799, Nassau; tel. 322-8381; fax 502-4246; e-mail bha@bahamashotels.org; internet www.bhahotels.com; Pres. STUART BOWE; Exec. Vice-Pres. FRANK COMITO.

Hotel Corporation of the Bahamas: Bolam Bldg, George St, POB N-3701, Nassau; tel. 302-2000; fax 356-4846; operates from Office of the Prime Minister; to become the Tourism Devt Corpn; Chair. MICHAEL SCOTT; CEO DAVID JOHNSON.

Nassau Tourism Development Board: POB N-4740, Nassau; tel. 326-0992; fax 323-2998; e-mail linkages@batelnet.bs; f. 1995; Chair. CHARLES KLONARIS.

Defence

The Royal Bahamian Defence Force, a paramilitary coastguard, is the only security force in the Bahamas, and numbered 850, as assessed at November 2013. Increasing concerns over rising crime levels in the Caribbean region prompted the recruitment of an additional 100 personnel to the Royal Bahamas Defence Force and 200 officers to the Royal Bahamas Police Force in 2007.

Defence Budget: an estimated B $87m. in 2014.

Commodore: RODERICK BOWE.

Education

Education is compulsory between the ages of five and 16 years, and is provided free of charge in government schools. There are several private and denominational schools. Primary education begins at five years of age and lasts for six years. Secondary education, beginning at the age of 11, also lasts for six years and is divided into two equal cycles. In 2010 some 98% of children in the relevant age-group were enrolled at primary level, while 86% of children in the relevant age-group were enrolled at secondary level. The University of the West Indies has an extra-mural department in Nassau, offering degree courses in hotel management and tourism. Ross University School of Medicine, which has a 126-acre campus on Grand Bahama for overseas medical students, began teaching activities in 2009. Technical, teacher-training and professional qualifications can be obtained at the three campuses of the College of the Bahamas.

In 2013/14 the estimated recurrent expenditure allocated to the Ministry of Education, Science and Technology was B $199.6m., equivalent to 11.4% of total recurrent expenditure.

Bibliography

For works on the Caribbean generally, see Select Bibliography (Books)

Craton, M., and Saunders, G. *Islanders in the Stream: A History of the Bahamian People: From the Ending of Slavery to the Twenty-First Century*, Vol. I. Athens, GA, University of Georgia Press, 1998.

   Islanders in the Stream: A History of the Bahamian People: From the Ending of Slavery to the Twenty-First Century, Vol II. Athens, GA, University of Georgia Press, 2000.

Culmer Jenkins, O. *Bahamian Memories*. Gainesville, FL, University Press of Florida, 2008.

Eneas, G. *Agriculture in the Bahamas: Historical Development 1492–1992*. Nassau, Media Publishing Ltd, 1998.

Howard, R. *Black Seminoles in the Bahamas*. Gainesville, FL, University Press of Florida, 2002.

Johnson, H. *Bahamas—Slavery to Servitude, 1783–1933*. Gainesville, FL, University Press of Florida, 1997.

Johnson, W. B. *Race Relations in the Bahamas 1784–1834: The Nonviolent Transformation from a Slave to a Free Society*. Fayetteville, AK, University of Arkansas Press, 2000.

McCartney, D. M. *Bahamian Culture and Factors Which Impact Upon It*. Pittsburgh, PA, Dorrance Publishing Co Inc, 2004.

Storr, V. H. *Enterprising Slaves and Master Pirates: Understanding Economic Life in the Bahamas*. Bern, Peter Lang Publishing, 2004.

Strachan, I. *Paradise and Plantation: Tourism and Culture in the Anglophone Caribbean*. Charlottesville, VA, University of Virginia Press, 2003.

Toogood, M. and Smith, L. *The Bahamas: Portrait of an Archipelago*. Oxford, Macmillan Caribbean, 2004.

BARBADOS

Geography

PHYSICAL FEATURES

Barbados lies in the Lesser Antilles, between the Atlantic Ocean and the Caribbean Sea. It is the most easterly of the West Indian islands, and its nearest neighbour is Saint Vincent and the Grenadines, about 160 km (100 miles) to the west. The island nation has an area of 430 sq km (166 sq miles).

The wider southern part of the island of Barbados continues in the north-west, tapering northwards. The terrain is generally flat limestone scored by deep, vegetation-filled gullies, gently rising into a central highland area, especially in the north-east, where Mt Hillaby reaches 336 m (1,103 ft). The 97 km (156 miles) of coast are more rugged in the east and north, protecting the island from the worst of the oceanic weather and sheltering the gentler waters and beaches of the west. Reefs surround much of Barbados. There are rivers in the north-eastern Scotland District, where the ancient limestone cap has been eroded to expose even older rocks. The well-watered island is fertile, and two types of flora warrant particular mention: the typical local fig trees, with their aerial roots, which are believed to be the origin of the island's name (Los Barbados, 'the bearded ones', of Pedro a Campos of Portugal in 1536); and the grapefruit, which originates on Barbados. Wildlife includes the Barbados green monkey (vervet monkeys originally transported from West Africa), the red-footed tortoise, and *Leptotyphlops carlae*, the world's smallest snake.

CLIMATE

The climate is tropical, but exposure to the Atlantic alleviates the extremes. Indeed, when the wind is strong off the ocean, certainly in the highlands it can become chilly. Generally, the average temperature is 27°C (81°F). The rainy season is between June and October, when there are likely to be hurricanes, although Barbados is on the edge of the region prone to them.

POPULATION

The people of the island, Barbadians (Bajans), are predominantly black (92% at the 2010 census), but there is still a white

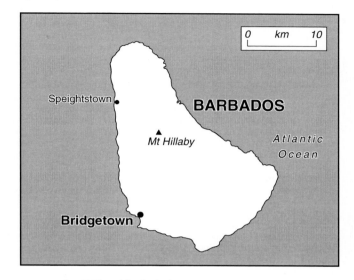

community (3%), with the balance comprising mixed-race and Asian groups. Most of the people are Christians, the largest denomination being the Anglican Church, claiming the adherence of 24% of the population in 2010, followed by Pentecostalists with 20%, Adventists 6% and Methodists 4%. Roman Catholics account for 4% of the islanders. More than 100 religions and sects are represented on the island. There are small Muslim, Hindu and Jewish communities—the synagogue is built on the site of one of the first two built in the Americas. English is the universal and official language.

The total population was 286,063 in mid-2014, making Barbados one of the most densely populated countries in the Caribbean. The capital and main port, Bridgetown, is on the south-western coast. In 2011 Bridgetown was designated a UNESCO World Heritage Site. On the coast in the north-west, Speightstown is the chief commercial centre for the north of the island. There are 11 parishes.

History

MARK WILSON

The Amerindians who settled Barbados from around AD 350 left the island during the 16th century, so that the first British settlers, who arrived in 1627, found no indigenous inhabitants. Barbados remained under British sovereignty until political independence in 1966, thereby earning itself the sobriquet 'Little England', and Barbadians played an important role in the settlement and administration of Britain's other Caribbean possessions. The first British settlers were smallholders growing tobacco and other crops, using the labour of indentured servants. However, fundamental change came with the introduction in the 1640s of sugar cane, by Dutch merchants, who brought plants from the Dutch settlements in Brazil. Sugar production required considerable labour and capital for the manufacturing process, a large workforce and extensive acreage, so estate owners supplanted the smallholders and, increasingly, slaves (of African origin) replaced the European servants. Although the first slaves arrived in 1627, they were few in number until the 1640s. By 1655 slaves formed 47% of a population of 43,000 and by 1712 they formed 77% of a total

population of some 54,500. Many whites moved on to other British settlements in the Caribbean, or on to the American mainland. Those who stayed, unless they were landowners, became craftsmen, overseers or merchants, or in some cases led a marginal and socially isolated existence as 'poor whites'. The black slave population was harshly treated and there were attempted slave revolts in 1675, 1692, 1702 and 1816. Slavery was eventually abolished in 1834, but its legacy was a highly stratified class-based society, still based, to some extent, on gradations of colour.

The British settlers established a House of Assembly in 1639 to represent their interests. Based on the 'representational system', the franchise was strictly limited by a property qualification. De facto power was exercised by the House of Assembly through its control of the public purse; hence it was able to hinder any attempt at reform by successive Governors. In 1876 the British Governor, John Pope Hennessy, proposed the establishment of a confederation to link Barbados and the Windward Islands. This suggestion was resisted by the Assembly, but was seen by many blacks as a partial solution to their difficulties. Eight people were killed in the ensuing Confederation Riots. The first mixed-race member of the Assembly, Samuel Jackman Prescod, was elected in 1843, and the franchise was significantly widened in 1884. However, even the reformed property qualification continued to exclude the majority of blacks from the franchise. In 1856 the Assembly introduced district medical officers, and a Board of Education was formed in 1878, under the influence of the Anglican bishop, John Mitchinson. A non-white professional middle class emerged during the 19th century; Sir Conrad Reeves, a mixed-race politician and lawyer, was Chief Justice from 1886 to 1902. However, further political and social advance was to wait until the rise of the labour movement in the 1930s.

Charles Duncan O'Neal founded the Democratic League, influenced by Fabian principles, in 1924. Its first member, Chrissie Brathwaite, was elected to the Assembly in the same year, and the Working Men's Association was founded in 1926. The poor economic climate and the impoverished condition of most Barbadians led, as was also the case in most of the other British West Indian territories, to labour disturbances. In July 1937 14 people were killed and 47 injured in island-wide riots. A later commission of inquiry expressed no surprise at the disturbances, once the inequalities in Barbadian society at the time were revealed. The Barbados Progressive League was founded in 1938, its leaders including Grantley (later Sir Grantley) Adams. It secured five seats in the House of Assembly in 1940 and was strengthened considerably by an alliance with the Barbados Workers' Union (BWU), founded by Adams and Hugh Springer. In 1943 the League successfully campaigned for an extension of the franchise. In the 1944 general election the League won seven seats, while eight were attained by Wynter Crawford's more radical West Indian National Congress Party and eight by the traditionalist Electors' Association, established by the landowning and merchant élite. Adams and other elected members subsequently joined the Executive Committee, the principal policy-making instrument. The League was renamed the Barbados Labour Party (BLP) in 1946, and achieved growth at the expense of both other parties in the elections held in 1946 and 1948.

Universal adult suffrage was introduced in 1950 and in the general election held in 1951 the BLP won 16 of the 24 seats. Ministerial government was introduced in 1954 and Adams was appointed Premier. He subsequently became Prime Minister of the West Indies Federation, from January 1958 until its dissolution in 1962, and was succeeded as Premier of Barbados by Dr Hugh Cummins.

Following the 1951 election victory, those who favoured a more socialist approach, such as Errol Barrow, became disenchanted with those, like Adams, who favoured gradualist policies. In 1955 a small group, later named the Democratic Labour Party (DLP), led by Barrow, split from the BLP and joined forces with former members of the Congress Party. The BLP won 15 seats in the subsequent 1956 election, with the DLP and the Progressive Conservative Party each obtaining four. In October 1961 full internal self-government was granted and, in the ensuing general election, the DLP won 16 seats to the BLP's five, with one Independent seat and four for the traditionalist Barbados National Party. Britain tried to promote an association of Barbados with the neighbouring Leeward and Windward Islands, following the collapse of the West Indies Federation in 1962. However, this attempt was unsuccessful, and Barrow led Barbados to separate independence in November 1966 and became its first Prime Minister. Thereafter, a two-party system, based on the two Labour parties, prevailed.

The DLP was ousted from power in 1976 and the BLP leader, J. M. G. M. (Tom) Adams, son of Sir Grantley Adams, became Prime Minister. The BLP also won the 1981 election, securing 17 of the 27 seats in the newly enlarged House of Assembly. Adams played a leading role in support of the US military intervention in Grenada in 1983. He died suddenly in 1985 and was succeeded by Bernard St John, under whose leadership the BLP was heavily defeated by the DLP in the May 1986 election, when the BLP won only three seats. St John lost his seat and a former Minister of Foreign Affairs, Henry (later Sir Henry) Forde, assumed the BLP leadership. Errol Barrow once again

became Prime Minister. The underlying reason for the Government's defeat lay in the country's past history. The issue of racism and 'white power' was never far from the surface; the BLP had become too closely identified, in many people's view, with the light-coloured business élite, from which it received substantial funds. Barrow, on the other hand, appealed to the black population and promised tax reforms to aid the black middle class. There was also dissatisfaction with the BLP's strong identification with US policy in the region, which offended nationalist sensibilities. Barrow's stand on this and other regional issues made him an imposing political force. His sudden death in June 1987 was, however, not entirely unexpected, given his refusal of medical advice pertaining to his strenuous work schedule. He was succeeded by his one-time deputy, Erskine Sandiford.

Sandiford's first political test was the resignation, in September 1987, of the Minister of Finance, Dr Richard (Richie) Haynes, who regarded himself as a possible future Prime Minister. At the same time, the economic situation began to deteriorate, partly as a result of Haynes' tax measures and partly owing to the closure in 1986 of the island's main manufacturing operation, a semi-conductor plant. In 1989 Haynes formed the National Democratic Party (NDP), with three other DLP parliamentarians, thus displacing Forde as the official Leader of the Opposition. In the general election of January 1991 the BLP won 10 seats to the DLP's 18. The fortunes of the BLP were restored with those of the two-party system; all four NDP members lost their seats. Support for the Sandiford regime declined rapidly thereafter, as austerity measures were introduced as a condition of IMF assistance to the economy, made necessary by a serious economic crisis. This situation was exploited to great effect by a rejuvenated BLP, led by a dynamic new leader, Owen Arthur. The BLP won a majority of seats at the general election of September 1994. Arthur became Prime Minister.

Arthur, a former professional economist, promoted economic recovery and international competitiveness in order to reduce the high levels of unemployment in the country. He proved himself capable of populist gestures, passing a constitutional amendment forbidding future reductions in pay for public employees. He also significantly broadened the BLP's support base, retaining its links with the business community while at the same time attracting a considerable number of nationalist intellectuals and trade unionists. In 1997 a public holiday to mark Emancipation Day was declared, and a National Heroes' Day was introduced on the anniversary of the birth of Sir Grantley Adams. The anniversary of the 1937 riots was declared a 'day of national significance', and a pilot project was commenced towards the teaching of black studies in primary and secondary schools.

Support from across the political spectrum and a rapidly growing economy helped the BLP to achieve an unprecedented victory in the general election of 20 January 1999, winning 26 of the 28 seats in the House of Assembly. The opposition DLP emerged from the election severely weakened, gaining only two seats; a dispute from September 2001 between its two members of parliament over the party leadership further undermined its strength.

In August 2000 Arthur announced that a referendum would be held on the replacement of the monarchy with a republic, a proposal that had the support of all political parties. However, a series of fierce political controversies in Trinidad and Tobago over the constitutional powers of the President in 2000–02 led to an enhanced appreciation of the need for careful consideration of the relationship between an elected government and a ceremonial President. In 2002 the Deputy Prime Minister and Minister of Foreign Affairs and Foreign Trade, Billie Miller, announced that new constitutional legislation would be drafted by the end of the year; however, the only change made was an amendment approved in September to override human rights judgments by the Privy Council, making it easier to make use of the death penalty.

A general election was held in May 2003, one year ahead of the constitutional deadline. With a strong economic record, in spite of a recent downturn in tourism, Owen Arthur led the BLP to a third successive electoral victory. However, the DLP increased its share of the popular vote to 44% and its parliamentary strength to seven seats; moreover, the Government held a further four seats by only narrow margins. Some voters were concerned over allegations of serious mismanagement in tourism, waste disposal and other public sector projects, and were at the same time concerned to temper the perceived arrogance of the BLP Government, while expecting it to remain in office. Clyde Mascoll was appointed opposition leader, quieting the DLP's leadership dispute. However, David Thompson was elected in November 2005 to the newly created post of party leader, and in January 2006 was chosen by a majority of elected opposition parliamentarians as constitutional Leader of the Opposition. Mascoll then defected from the DLP to the BLP, bringing the parliamentary strength of the ruling party to 24.

In February 2005 Arthur resurrected the proposal for Barbados' transformation to a republic with the announcement that a referendum to decide the issue—first disclosed as an objective of the BLP's third term in office by the Governor-General in June 2003—would be held by the end of the year. However, it was later announced that the referendum would be further postponed. It had been hoped that the 40th anniversary of Barbados' independence from British colonial rule, celebrated in November 2006, would induce the promised referendum. However, such a consultation remained unrealized in mid-2011 after Deputy Prime Minister Mia Mottley revoked a statement made in 2007 in which she had announced that the referendum would be held concurrently with the next legislative elections. The DLP Government that replaced her party in power from 2008 made no further move for transition to a republic.

A general election was held on 15 January 2008, with the BLP again suffering from allegations of arrogance and midscale corruption, as well as from concerns over rising food and energy prices and the management of public sector infrastructure projects. The DLP returned to office after winning 20 of the 30 legislative seats and 53% of the popular vote, forming a new Government led by David Thompson. Arthur resigned as BLP leader immediately after the election, and was succeeded by Mottley; however, the new leader was removed by her parliamentary team in October 2010, and Arthur was again made opposition leader. More significantly, the Prime Minister announced in June that he would take a two month leave of absence; it was subsequently announced that he was suffering from prostate cancer, and he died in October. His successor was the former Deputy Prime Minister, Minister of Home Affairs and Attorney-General, Freundel Stuart, who had been appointed Acting Prime Minister from July. During Thompson's illness, Adriel Brathwaite was appointed Attorney General and Minister of Home Affairs, and Christopher Sinckler became Minister of Finance. Thompson's widow, Mara, won his parliamentary seat in a January 2011 by-election, with 89% of votes cast.

Stuart made little personal impact on the Barbadian public and support for the Government was undermined by the lacklustre performance of the economy, job losses in tourism and elsewhere, and tax increases introduced to narrow the fiscal deficit. Nevertheless, the DLP narrowly retained office in a general election held on 21 February 2013, taking 16 of the 30 seats and 51.3% of the popular vote. Four days after its defeat in the polls the BLP again replaced Arthur with Mottley as party leader; remaining dissatisfied with his successor's leadership, Arthur in July 2014 resigned from the DLP, sitting from them in parliament as an independent. Under pressure from a deteriorating economy and forced to take austerity measures, the DLP appeared to have lost significant popular support by mid-2014, but its parliamentary position remained secure.

Legislation enacted in 2005 made Barbados one of only two countries (from 2010, three) to make the new Caribbean Court of Justice (CCJ) its final court of appeal, replacing the Privy Council in London, United Kingdom. The CCJ issued its first significant ruling in November 2006, endorsing a decision of the Court of Appeal of Barbados to commute to life imprisonment the death penalties given to two convicted murderers, and so demonstrating the CCJ's ambivalence on the reinstatement of capital punishment (the last execution in Barbados occurred in 1984). Barbados has, in general, been an enthusi-

astic supporter of Caribbean integration, but alleged maltreatment of visitors from other islands by immigration officials has aroused resentment elsewhere in the region, particularly in Guyana and Jamaica. A total of 274 Jamaicans were turned back from Barbados in 2010, while only five Barbadians were refused entry to Jamaica over the three-year period from 2008. The CCJ in October 2013 ruled that Caribbean Community and Common Market (CARICOM) nationals have a right of entry except where there is 'a genuine, present and sufficiently serious threat affecting one of the fundamental interests of society'; the Court ordered compensation of US $38,600 for a Jamaican woman who had been refused entry.

Barbados played a leading role in the 2000s in moves by offshore financial centres to block initiatives by the Organisation for Economic Co-operation and Development (OECD, based in Paris, France) against tax havens, and by the intergovernmental Financial Action Task Force on Money Laundering (FATF, also based in Paris—see Economy). However, the country has an active anti-money-laundering policy although it remains vulnerable to laundering of both locally derived drugs proceeds and of overseas funds derived mainly from fraud operations. The offshore financial sector is relatively clean, with a strong international reputation, and benefits from a network of 25 double taxation treaties—a single CARICOM treaty with 14 regional partners brings the number of countries covered to 38.

A dispute with Trinidad and Tobago over the delimitation of the Exclusive Economic Zone and fishing rights for Barbadian vessels within Tobago waters escalated in 2004. Although fisheries issues attracted most attention, considerable importance was also attached to geological structures close to the median line between the countries that may contain significant quantities of petroleum and natural gas. Barbados imposed a temporary licensing requirement on some Trinidad and Tobago exports, and referred the maritime dispute for arbitration under the UN Convention on the Law of the Sea. A tribunal ruled in 2006, establishing a boundary following the line of equidistance between the two states for most of its length and reaching to the limits of the 200 nautical mile Exclusive Economic Zone. This gave Barbados a large area to the south-east, which had been claimed by Trinidad and Tobago, and was thought to have potential for deep-water petroleum and gas exploration. The tribunal rejected the Barbadian claim to a large area to the north of Tobago, but instructed the two countries to negotiate a fishing agreement for this area 'in good faith'; however, no significant progress on this front had been made by mid-2013. The Permanent Court of Arbitration's ruling conferred security on these new demarcations of jurisdiction, enabling Barbados in 2007 to open the auctioning of oil exploration rights for offshore blocks to leading hydrocarbon companies. A bid round for 24 offshore blocks was opened in 2008. With oil prices low and capital markets weak at that point, results were disappointing. BHP Billiton was awarded two blocks, with a three-year seismic survey and data analysis programme. Barbados was in 2008 the first small island state to claim a further 150 nautical miles of Extended Continental Shelf beyond the Exclusive Economic Zone under Article 76 of the UN Convention on the Law of the Sea, acting a full year ahead of the deadline for such submissions; a revised claim was submitted in July 2011, with overlapping claims by Trinidad and Tobago and Venezuela expected to give rise to disagreements. Maritime boundaries have also been agreed with Guyana, and in October 2009 with France (covering the French Overseas Department of Martinique).

Although Barbados is better ordered than most Caribbean islands, violent crime and drugs-trafficking are of serious concern. The US Department of State reported an increase in cocaine transshipment through Barbados since 2004, while marijuana is imported from Saint Vincent and Jamaica. Barbados police estimated around 5% of total drug consignment volumes remained on the island for local consumption in 2009, with 60% moving on to the United Kingdom, 15% to Canada, 10% to the USA and 10% to other Caribbean markets. Marijuana is perhaps imported by between eight and 12 local traffickers, and cocaine mainly by Trinidadians, Guyanese, Venezuelans and Colombians, who use pleasure boats, 'mules', and air cargo; these were reported in 2011 to be developing increasingly close operational links with their Venezuelan counterparts. The US Department of State noted concerns over corruption within the coastguard, as go-fast boats appear able to penetrate local defences; in 2011 89% of cannabis seizures and 10% of cocaine seizures were made at sea. The murder rate was nine per 100,000 in 2013 (with a recent high of 13 in 2006); this remained low by regional standards but was approximately twice that of the USA. Some violent crimes against visitors, such as the murder of a British man in June 2014, received significant coverage overseas, damaging the image of Barbados as a relaxed and peaceful destination for tourism. The recent economic downturn appeared to have led to an increase in property crime; police in 2011 reported a sharp increase in theft from the person, and sales of gold for cash were banned in 2013 for security reasons. Confidence in the police was reasonably high; however, the former police commissioner Darwin Dottin was sent on pre-retirement leave in 2013 after concerns were raised over 'tapping' of the telephones of public officials and politicians. He was replaced by Tyrone Griffith. In an effort to improve marine security, Barbados extended the capabilities of its coastguard from 2006, the completion in the previous year of a new coastguard headquarters and base paving the way for the delivery in 2007–09 of three 42-m offshore patrol vessels. Barbados in 2010 agreed to borrow US $65m. from ING Bank to finance the purchase of eight smaller boats, an improved coastal radar system (with the aim of achieving 360° coastal coverage), and two helicopters.

Economy

MARK WILSON

Barbados is more economically and socially developed than most of the English-speaking Caribbean, with a per-head gross domestic product (GDP) at market prices of US $16,150 in 2013, among the highest in the region. The island functions as an air transport hub for the eastern Caribbean and is the site of the headquarters of several regional organizations. With high standards of education, infrastructure and health care, in 2014 the island was ranked third in the Caribbean by the Human Development Index, produced by the UN Development Programme, although, at 59th worldwide, it remained behind most members of the Organisation for Economic Co-operation and Development (OECD). The relative success was all the more remarkable because the country had one of the highest population densities in the world (some 646.1 per sq km at the 2010 census, with a population of 277,821 living on an area of 430 sq km).

However, Barbados has in recent years suffered from increasing economic difficulties. After an extended period of steady growth from the early 1990s, the economy of Barbados has suffered since 2008 from the effects of the global economic recession and a decline in tourism demand. The economy contracted by 4.1% in 2009, then grew by just 0.3% in 2010 and 0.8% in 2011; this was followed by zero growth in 2012 and a contraction of 0.2% in 2013. Unemployment rose to an average of 11.6% in 2013, from 7.4% in 2007, and rose further in the first half of 2014 as the Government laid off up to 2,800 low-paid workers, equivalent in number to 2% of the labour force.

Although some consumer prices are high by international standards, the underlying rate of inflation has historically been modest. However, increased international oil prices raised the inflation rate in recent years, as did an increased rate of value-added tax (VAT) from 2010; retail prices increased by 9.4% in 2011. According to official figures, inflation then slowed to 4.5% in 2012 and to 1.8% in 2013.

Recent economic difficulties have had a strongly adverse effect on the fiscal balance. Historically, governments took a reasonably cautious approach to budgeting and overall fiscal deficits remained under control, with the current account largely in surplus. The introduction of VAT in 1997 contributed to the deficit reaching a low point of 0.1% of GDP in 1999. The fiscal deficit averaged a manageable 2.7% in 2003–07, albeit with some substantial extra-budgetary spending, for example on improvements to the airport. However, the deficit increased again significantly as a result of the economic downturn, reaching 8.8% in 2010 as revenue from corporate income tax and other sources fell sharply, while spending on capital programmes, goods, services and salaries was reduced, and interest payments, pension payments and the subsidy to the University of the West Indies, which offered free tuition, continued to increase. The deficit was initially financed mainly by long-term borrowing from local institutions, particularly the National Insurance Board, and in 2009 also by a bond issue led by the Bank of Nova Scotia in Trinidad and Tobago. In November 2010 the Government introduced a Medium Term Financial Strategy, intended to bring the fiscal accounts into balance by 2014/15. This increased the rate of VAT from 15% to 17.5% and increased fuel tax, which, along with other measures, was intended to increase the annual tax take by 2.4% of GDP. These measures reduced the deficit to 4.4% in 2011, but it then increased rapidly to 8.0% in 2012 and to 11.3% in 2013, financed mainly by short-term borrowing from domestic financial institutions and the Central Bank; the ceiling on local borrowing increased from US $750m. at the start of 2013 to US $2,500m. in June 2014. There was also significant long-term borrowing from the National Insurance Scheme, two-thirds of the portfolio of which was government debt in 2014, a ratio significantly above actuarial recommendations. The IMF in 2011 proposed a freeze on public sector salaries, higher charges by public enterprises, further privatization, reduced transfers to bodies such as the University of the West Indies, and reduced tax exemptions. However, the Government was unwilling to launch any dramatic fiscal initiatives in advance of the February 2013 general election, while it was afterwards constrained by its narrow parliamentary majority.

The debt-to-GDP ratio climbed from less than 60% in 2009 to 94% in September 2013; including government securities held by the National Insurance Scheme, it rose from about 80% of GDP in 2009 to 128% in 2013. External debt interest was estimated at 7% of foreign exchange earnings for 2013, and total interest at 24% of government revenue, rising to 29% in the first quarter of 2014. With debt ratios rising, Moody's Investor Service in 2011 downgraded its domestic currency rating for Barbados from investment grade in December 2012; by June 2014 its rating had reached B3, indicating speculative debt with a high credit risk. Standard & Poor's in July 2012 also moved its Barbados rating to BB+/B from BBB–/A-3, and in November 2013 to BB–.

After several years in surplus, the current account went into deficit in the late 1990s. The deficit rose to more than 12% of GDP in 2005, a level admitted by the Government to be unsustainable. The deficit fell back to 5.5% of GDP in 2007, but rose sharply to 11.2% of GDP in 2008, as goods imports reached an all-time high of US $1,811m., partly because of high oil prices, and tourism earnings stagnated. However, a decline in imports compensated in the following period for weaker tourism earnings, so that the current account deficit fell back to 5.8% of GDP in 2010. However, it increased sharply again, to 11.4% of GDP in 2011, 10.1% in 2012 and an estimated 11.4% in 2013. Partly balancing the current account payments deficit, there have been strong capital inflows, averaging US $306m. in 2004–12, and standing at US $229m. in 2013. The nature of these flows varied, with long-term private sector investments peaking at US $626m. in 2006, falling to US $198m. in 2010 as tourism investments slowed, and increasing again in 2012 to US $309m. In 2011 a major item was proceeds of US $94m. from sales of minority holdings in the Barbados Light and Power Co to Emera Inc of Canada.

In spite of recent economic difficulties, overseas borrowing has maintained the reserves position, at the cost of further increases in debt. Reserves generally follow a strong seasonal pattern, with tourism inflows during the early part of the year, a peak in the second quarter and net outflows thereafter. In addition, there are periodic capital inflows from tourism-related investments and other sources. In recent years tourism and investment inflows have been weaker than normal; in 2013 reserves were reduced by US $150.5m. in spite of US $150m. in high-interest borrowing from Credit Suisse, and ended the year at equivalent to 15 weeks' import cover, down from 19.5 weeks' a year earlier. A further US $75m was borrowed from Credit Suisse in the first quarter of 2014.

The IMF in January 2014 highlighted the difficulties facing Barbados, and proposed a front-loaded fiscal adjustment plan, with improved public sector management, increased taxation and charges for public services, spending cuts, an end to deficit financing from the Central Bank, higher interest rates, better targeting of social benefits, and reductions in real labour costs. The IMF warned that existing policies would create difficulties in maintenance of the currency peg of two Barbados dollars to one US dollar, which was seen as a central policy priority by the Government, opposition, trade unions and private sector alike.

TOURISM

Barbados has a well-established tourism industry, directly employing 11.1% of the working population in 2013 (according to the World Travel and Tourism Council). The industry grew strongly in the 1990s; stop-over tourist arrivals increased by 34.3% between 1992 and 2000. As a result of uncertain market conditions in the USA and a decrease in the local purchasing power of sterling for tourists from the United Kingdom, the number of stop-over arrivals decreased in the early 2000s, but, by 2007, had recovered to a high of 573,900. However, stop-over arrivals were slightly down from 2008, and in 2013 totalled 509,765. With shorter average stays and lower per-head spending, revenue in 2013 was 23% lower than in 2008, in cash terms and without allowing for inflation. Trinidad-owned Almond group was in severe difficulties from mid-2012, partly because of deep discounting to attract high-volume business. Its largest property, Almond Beach Village, was closed with the loss of 500 jobs; it was sold to the Government, which planned to demolish, redevelop and sell it to the Jamaica-based Sandals group in August 2014. In December 2013 another Almond property, the Casuarina resort, was sold directly to Sandals, which received substantial tax and duty concessions, raising concerns among other operators.

Tourism accounted for an estimated 11% of GDP and contributed 48% of foreign exchange earnings from goods and non-factor services in 2013. Barbados is a home port for some cruises in the eastern Caribbean, and consequently cruise traffic brings more benefits to the local economy than to some other islands. The number of cruise ship passengers fluctuated as cruise lines switched routes, and totalled 570,263 in 2013.

Labour costs in Barbados were much higher than in some competing destinations and the landscape less immediately striking. However, the island enjoyed a high percentage of repeat visitors. All-inclusive holiday packages accounted for a relatively small market share until the advent of Sandals, thus encouraging spending outside hotel premises. There were 155 registered properties in 2011, with a total of 6,659 rooms. New construction slowed under the impact of the economic recession in 2009–12, while several properties had been converted to self-catering condominiums and apartments. Industry concerns included high operating costs and a low room-occupancy rate, which was 56% in 2010. Barbados' tourism has been particularly successful in the United Kingdom, which in 2013 accounted for some 33.2% of tourist arrivals. The lack of large brand name hotels was partly responsible for Barbados' poor performance in North America, which also impeded the development of conference and incentive tourism. However, there was some reversal in this trend from 2005 following the opening of the Hilton hotel, as well as special marketing promotions in the US market. As a result, US tourists comprised 23.7% of the total in 2013 (compared with 20.6% in 2000). Sandals was expected to attract further US business.

Tourist accommodation was concentrated on the sheltered south and west coasts, which were highly urbanized. Since 1980 the number of hotel rooms in Barbados has decreased by 20%; over the same period, hotel accommodation has expanded almost four-fold in Saint Lucia and three-fold in Jamaica. Several large properties had been closed from 2010 to mid-2014, and a recovery in room stock depended on redevelopment of sites that were already used for tourism or other urban purposes—such as the planned eventual redevelopment of the former Mobil petroleum refinery site for tourism. The Government in 2014 had not followed through on moves initiated three years earlier to acquire the historic, but derelict, Sam Lord's property on the south-east coast from CL Financial, a Trinidadian insurance conglomerate which collapsed in 2009 (see below); the buildings had been further damaged by vandalism and fire. Construction of a Four Seasons resort on the former west coast Cunard Paradise Beach property was halted in 2009 with the developers also in financial difficulties, and efforts by the Government to assist the resumption of work by taking a 20% equity stake in return for a US $60m. loan guarantee, along with a proposed US $55m. investment by the Inter-American Development Bank and ANSA Merchant Bank of Trinidad and Tobago, had not, by mid-2014, led to a resumption in construction activity; by this time, this valuable beachfront site had been unused for more than 20 years, representing a major lost opportunity.

FINANCIAL AND INFORMATION SERVICES

Barbados has a well-developed local banking and insurance industry. The largest regional commercial bank, CIBC First-Caribbean, is headquartered in Barbados. With assets of US $11,400m. in 2013, it was formed in 2002 through a merger of the Caribbean interests of the Canadian Imperial Bank of Commerce (CIBC) and Barclays Bank (which sold its interest to CIBC in 2006). Sagicor, a major insurance company with interests throughout the region and assets in 2012 of US $5,300m., was also formed in 2002 through the merger of the two largest Barbados-based insurers; in 2005 it expanded into North America, buying an unlisted US company, American Founders' Life, and it is listed on the London Stock Exchange as well as on Caribbean exchanges. The International Finance Corporation, a World Bank subsidiary, in 2011 took a 4% stake, with an investment of US $100m. There was a small local stock exchange, on which 15 locally based companies had a market capitalization of Bds $5,424m. in June 2014. In addition, four Trinidadian and Jamaican companies had cross-listings on the Barbados exchange, bringing total capitalization in June 2014 to Bds $8,222m. Several major Barbados-based companies passed into Trinidadian control after 2000. The majority of Sagicor's shares are now held by Trinidad residents, while in 2008 Trinidadian group Neal & Massy (known as Massy from 2014) completed the purchase of the major local conglomerate, Barbados Shipping and Trading. A Canadian investor, Emera Inc, in 2011 acquired an 80% stake in the only electricity provider, Barbados Light and Power Co. Stock exchange trading fell off sharply from 2007 with the economic downturn, moving from 7% of GDP to less than 0.5%.

The financial sector suffered from the collapse of the Trinidad-based insurance conglomerate CL Financial in 2009, which left the life portfolio of its Barbados subsidiaries with excess liabilities equivalent to 4.4% of GDP; these companies were taken into judicial management, while the IMF commented adversely on the quality of local financial supervision. A police investigation into the local affairs of the company was referred to the Director of Public Prosecutions in 2011; the company had continued to write new business into 2010, in violation of an 2009 order by the Central Bank, while a settlement had not yet been finalized with all policyholders by mid-2014.

The offshore financial sector, mainly specializing in insurance, was encouraged by the negotiation of 25 double taxation agreements with a total of 38 other countries by mid-2014, the full network creating niche opportunities not open to larger offshore sectors such as those of the Bahamas, Bermuda or the Cayman Islands; however, OECD noted in 2011 that some elements of an effective tax information exchange regime were not in place. The offshore sector was a significant employer and foreign exchange earner; under Barbados regulations a high proportion of offshore entities maintained an office and employed local staff, rather than existing simply on paper. However, there were concerns that changes in the Canadian tax regime have made Barbados less attractive as an offshore regime, to the great disadvantage of the financial sector. Barbados has a fairly high standard of financial regulation. Since Barbados is a 'low tax' rather than 'no tax' regime, offshore companies contributed more than 50% of corporate income tax revenue in 2009 and more than 10% of total government revenue; however, its contribution has since fallen, and the offshore sector is not in the same league as that of the Cayman Islands or British Virgin Islands. According to Invest Barbados, the international business sector's contribution to tax revenue was still less than Bds $200m. in 2012, compared with about Bds $350m. in 2007. The number of new offshore entities registered grew steadily up to 2007, but declined by 40% thereafter to 2012. There is an active anti-money-laundering regime. Active regulation discouraged more dubious clients, but attracted businesses such as captive insurance companies.

International developments in the first decade of the 21st century placed all offshore financial services sectors under increasing pressure. Following a World Trade Organization ruling, US foreign sales corporations, a niche market for Barbados, were phased out from 2000. The island's inclusion on the OECD list of 'unco-operative tax havens' in that year received a hostile reaction from the Barbadian Government, which played a leading role in international lobbying by offshore centres against OECD's initiative and that of the Financial Action Task Force on Money Laundering (based in Paris, France). Barbados was removed from the OECD list in 2002, after the organization modified its criteria for the definition of a tax haven. Although, unlike many other jurisdictions included on OECD's 'black list', Barbados did not pledge to reform its financial sector, the Government did introduce legislative changes intended to improve financial transparency, as well as demonstrating a willingness to enter into tax information exchange agreements with other countries. For this reason Barbados was the only Caribbean country to be placed on a 'white list' of financial jurisdictions by OECD in 2009.

With cellular service providers in operation, and competitive fixed-wireless, broadband, international fibre-optic cable and local landline services already licensed, liberalization of the telecommunications sector was well advanced in 2014.

MANUFACTURING

The principal manufacturing industries employed 9,000 people, representing about 7.1% of the total active workforce, in 2013; manufacturing accounted for 4.1% of GDP in 2013. However, Barbados still had a range of manufacturing industries, producing consumer products and cement for the local and regional market, as well as export products, although labour costs were higher than in most Caribbean islands and power costs much higher than in Trinidad and Tobago. A strong point has been the rum industry, with brands such as Malibu produced locally for export, as well as traditional Barbadian brands. Rum exports stood at Bds $86.1m. in 2013, more than five times the value of sugar exports.

Following the removal of most trade barriers in the 1990s, the clothing and wooden furniture industries virtually disappeared. However, the more efficient producers in other branches of manufacturing managed to survive and, in some cases, to expand their export sales. The remaining heavy industrial plant was the Arawak cement plant in the north of the island, owned by a Trinidadian company, which used local limestone. Capacity was 360,000 metric tons; however, with the economy in recession in 2013, sales were only 237,500 tons, 25% lower than in 2007, with 65% of the plant's output being exported. The construction industry contracted by a cumulative 37% in 2007–13 as the economy suffered from continuing stagnation, but still contributed 5.8% of GDP in

2013, and employed 9.6% of the working population (17.1% of male workers).

Petroleum production was another industrial activity. However, continued drilling programmes have had disappointing results, and output was an estimated 259,500 barrels in 2013. Proposals were announced in 2014 to privatize the only producer, the Barbados National Oil Company. Crude petroleum was exported to Trinidad and Tobago for refining; partly to protect this arrangement, Barbados remained outside Venezuela's Petrocaribe preferential oil supply agreement. Natural gas production was 20.0m. cu m in 2012. With local gas resources limited in extent, there were proposals to import gas from Trinidad and Tobago by pipeline for electricity generation and other uses. Initial seismic surveys for offshore petroleum and gas showed promising deep-water geological prospects. The southern boundaries of the Exclusive Economic Zone were fixed by arbitration under the UN Convention on the Law of the Sea in 2006, and a bidding round for exploration and production contracts was completed in 2008. However, the response was disappointing, with the financial environment inauspicious for high-risk deep water exploration.

SUGAR AND AGRICULTURE

Sugar was the mainstay of the economy until the rise of the tourism industry in the mid-20th century. In 1946 the sugar industry accounted for 37.8% of GDP and 55% of foreign exchange earnings, employing some 25,100 people. By 2013, however, the industry accounted for only 0.7% of GDP, 0.4% of foreign exchange earnings from goods and services, and less than 1.0% of total employment.

In spite of a guaranteed price for exports to Europe, the sugar industry suffered from severe economic problems from the 1980s. These related in part to high production costs and inefficiencies associated with the traditional management system. Farmers also left many sugar farms uncultivated, in order to capitalize upon the high prices that could sometimes be obtained for land set aside for urban development. In 1992 Barbados Sugar Industries Ltd, which owned and operated the factories, was forced into receivership. The factories and the most heavily indebted estates were placed under the management of the Barbados Agricultural Management Company.

As a result of declining production, in 2003 Barbados surrendered part of its valuable European Union (EU) quota of 54,000 metric tons of sugar (worth some US $24m. in foreign exchange); production of raw cane sugar in 2012 was approximately 20,000 tons, falling to 17,000 tons in 2013. The remainder of the EU sugar quota was to be abolished from 2017, a move that would cause a fall in prices, according to Caribbean farmers. The rum industry was forced to import most of its rising annual requirement of molasses. Production costs for Barbados sugar have for many years been significantly greater than export prices, and were estimated at close to Bds $2,000 per ton in the years after 2000. Even before reform of the EU's sugar regime, additional, locally funded subsidies were already required to keep the industry afloat; with the abolition of the guaranteed price from 2009, maintaining the industry in its current form will be increasingly costly, while closure would carry a heavy political and environmental price. The Government in 2013 announced a US $270m. proposal for a new factory to produce high-value packaged sugars, with use of cane waste and other biomass for electricity generation; however, no realistic financial proposals were in place by mid-2014. The soil holds nutrients well, but is thin. Rainfall is generally adequate, but there are occasional severe droughts. Groundwater supplies are not sufficient for large-scale irrigation. These problems impede the development of other agricultural activities. There is some commercial production of vegetables and root crops. The island is virtually self-sufficient in poultry products and in fresh milk, activities that depend to a significant extent on imported inputs. There is some pig farming and lamb is produced from the local Black Belly short-haired sheep. However, despite some self-sufficiency, in 2013 agricultural production (including fishing, but excluding sugar) contributed only an estimated 4.1% of GDP and (including sugar and fishing) employed 2.7% of the working population.

Statistical Survey

Sources (unless otherwise stated): Barbados Statistical Service, National Insurance Bldg, 3rd Floor, Fairchild St, Bridgetown; tel. 427-7841; fax 435-2198; e-mail barstats@caribsurf.com; internet www.barstats.gov.bb; Central Bank of Barbados, Tom Adams Financial Centre, Spry St, POB 1016, Bridgetown; tel. 436-6870; fax 427-9559; e-mail cbb.libr@caribsurf.com; internet www.centralbank.org.bb.

AREA AND POPULATION

Area: 430 sq km (166 sq miles).

Population: 268,792 at census of 1 May 2000; 277,821 (males 133,018, females 144,803) at census of 2 May 2010. *Mid-2014* (UN estimate): 286,063 (Source: UN, *World Population Prospects: The 2012 Revision*).

Density (at mid-2014): 665.3 per sq km.

Population by Age and Sex (UN estimates at mid-2014): *0–14 years:* 53,688 (males 27,317, females 26,371); *15–64 years:* 200,733 (males 102,043, females 98,690); *65 years and over:* 31,642 (males 13,371, females 18,271); *Total* 286,063 (males 142,731, females 143,332) (Source: UN, *World Population Prospects: The 2012 Revision*).

Population by Ethnic Group (self–declaration at 2010 census): Black 209,109; White 6,135; Mixed race 7,034; Total (incl. others) 226,193. Note: Classification of ethnic groups reflects national methodology. Data exclude institutional population (2,513) and adjustment for underenumeration (49,115).

Parishes (population at 2010 census): Christ Church 54,336; St Andrew 5,139; St George 19,767; St James 28,498; St John 8,963; St Joseph 6,620; St Lucy 9,758; St Michael 88,529; St Peter 11,300; St Philip 30,662; St Thomas 14,249; *Total* 277,821.

Principal Towns (population at 2000 census, preliminary): Bridgetown (capital) 5,996; Speightstown 2,604; Holetown 1,087; Oistins 1,203. *Mid-2014* (population in '000, incl. suburbs): Bridgetown 90 (Source: UN, *World Urbanization Prospects: The 2014 Revision*).

Births, Marriages and Deaths (2007, unless otherwise indicated): Live births 3,537 (birth rate 12.9 per 1,000); Marriages (2000) 3,518 (marriage rate 13.1 per 1,000); Deaths 2,213 (death rate 8.1 per 1,000). Source: partly UN, *Population and Vital Statistics Report*. *2013:* Crude birth rate 12.1 per 1,000; Crude death rate 8.4 per 1,000 (Source: Pan American Health Organization).

Life Expectancy (years at birth): 75.1 (males 72.8; females 77.6) in 2012 (Source: World Bank, World Development Indicators database).

Economically Active Population (labour force sample surveys, '000 persons aged 15 years and over, excl. armed forces, 2013): Agriculture, forestry and fishing 3.4; Manufacturing 9.0; Electricity, gas and water 2.8; Construction and quarrying 12.1; Wholesale and retail trade 20.5; Tourism 13.3; Transport, storage and communications 6.6; Finance and insurance 5.8; Professional, scientific and technical services 4.2; Administrative and support services 6.3; Public administration and defence 11.6; Education 7.5; Health and social welfare 6.3; Household employees 5.2; Other services 11.6; *Total employed* 126.2 (males 64.3, females 61.9); Unemployed 16.6 (males 8.5, females 8.1); *Total labour force* 142.9 (males 72.9, females 70.0).

HEALTH AND WELFARE
Key Indicators

Total Fertility Rate (children per woman, 2012): 1.8.

Under-5 Mortality Rate (per 1,000 live births, 2012): 18.

HIV/AIDS (% of persons aged 15–49, 2011, estimate): 0.9.

Physicians (per 1,000 head, 2005): 1.8.

Hospital Beds (per 1,000 head, 2009): 6.8.

Health Expenditure (2011): US $ per head (PPP): 1,450.

Health Expenditure (2011): % of GDP: 7.2.

Health Expenditure (2011): public (% of total): 66.0.

Total Carbon Dioxide Emissions ('000 metric tons, 2010): 1,503.5.

Total Carbon Dioxide Emissions Per Head (metric tons, 2010): 5.4.

Human Development Index (2013): ranking: 59.

Human Development Index (2013): value: 0.776.

For sources and definitions, see explanatory note on p. vi.

AGRICULTURE, ETC.

Principal Crops ('000 metric tons, 2012, FAO estimates): Sweet potatoes 0.6; Yams 0.2; Avocados 0.7; Pulses 1.9; Coconuts 2.0; Tomatoes 0.9; Cucumbers 1.2; Chillies and peppers, green 0.4; Onions, dry 0.4; String beans 0.9; Carrots and turnips 0.2; Okra 0.3; Maize 0.3; Bananas 1.0.

Livestock ('000 head, year ending September 2012, FAO estimates): Horses 1.3; Asses 2.3; Mules 2.0; Cattle 11.0; Pigs 22.5; Sheep 13.0; Goats 5.3; Poultry 3,660.

Livestock Products ('000 metric tons, 2012, FAO estimates): Cattle meat 0.2; Pig meat 3.0; Chicken meat 14.7; Cows' milk 6.0; Hen eggs 2.1.

Forestry ('000 cubic metres, 2012, FAO estimates): Roundwood removals 10.9.

Fishing (metric tons, live weight, 2012, FAO estimates): Total catch 1,374 (Yellowfin tuna 195; Flying fishes 354; Common dolphinfish 354).

Source: FAO.

MINING

Production (2011, provisional): Natural gas 16.0m. cu m; Crude petroleum 300,000 barrels; Cement 300,000 metric tons. Source: US Geological Survey.

INDUSTRY

Selected Products (2010 unless otherwise indicated): Raw sugar 24,560 metric tons; Rum 11,000,000 litres (2003); Beer 7,100,000 litres (2009); Cigarettes 65m. (1995); Batteries 17,165 (official estimate, 1998); Electric energy 1,027.7m. kWh. Sources: partly UN Industrial Commodity Statistics Database, and IMF, *Barbados: Statistical Appendix* (May 2004).

FINANCE

Currency and Exchange Rates: 100 cents = 1 Barbados dollar (Bds $). *Sterling, US Dollar and Euro Equivalents* (30 May 2014): £1 sterling = Bds $3.364; US $1 = Bds $2.000; €1 = Bds $2.722; Bds $100 = £29.72 = US $50.00 = €36.73. *Exchange Rate:* Fixed at US $1 = Bds $2.000 since 1986.

Budget (Bds $ million, year ending 31 March 2014, estimates): *Revenue:* Tax revenue 1,995.0 (Direct taxes 739.5, Indirect taxes 1,255.4); Non-tax revenue and grants 103.5; Total 2,098.4. *Expenditure:* Current 2,908.6 (Wages and salaries 872.0, Other goods and services 375.1, Interest payments 606.9, Transfers and subsidies 1,054.6); Capital (incl. net lending) 145.0; Total 3,053.6.

International Reserves (US $ million at 31 December 2013): IMF special drawing rights 87.00; Reserve position in IMF 8.94; Foreign exchange 598.83; *Total* 694.77. Source: IMF, *International Financial Statistics*.

Money Supply (Bds $ million at 31 December 2009): Currency outside depository corporations 494.0; Transferable deposits 3,098.2; Other deposits 7,355.6; *Broad money* 10,947.8. Source: IMF, *International Financial Statistics*.

Cost of Living (Consumer Price Index; base: 2005 = 100): All items 149.3 in 2011; 153.1 in 2012; 155.5 in 2013. Source: IMF, *International Financial Statistics*.

Gross Domestic Product (Bds $ million at constant 1974 prices): 1,076.0 in 2011; 1,076.1 in 2012; 1,074.5 in 2013.

Expenditure on the Gross Domestic Product (Bds $ million at current prices, 2012): Government final consumption expenditure 1,364.4; Private final consumption expenditure 6,780.0; Gross capital formation 1,204.2; *Total domestic expenditure* 9,348.6; Exports of goods and services 3,589.6; *Less* Imports of goods and services 4,590.8; Statistical discrepancy 102.5; *GDP in purchasers' values* 8,449.7. *2013* (provisional): GDP in purchasers' values 8,431.7.

Gross Domestic Product by Economic Activity (estimates, Bds $ million at current prices, 2012): Agriculture, hunting, forestry and fishing 103.7; Mining and quarrying 20.8; Manufacturing 489.9; Electricity, gas and water 224.2; Construction 370.9; Wholesale and retail trade 741.9; Hotels and restaurants 965.9; Transport, storage and communications 846.0; Finance, insurance, real estate and business services 2,233.1; Government services 951.7; Other community, social and personal services 379.0; *Sub-total* 7,327.1; *Less* Financial intermediation services indirectly measured (FISIM) 166.2; *GDP at factor cost* 7,160.9; Indirect taxes, less subsidies 1,391.3; Statistical discrepancy –102.5; *GDP in purchasers' values* 8,449.7. *2013* (provisional): GDP in purchasers' values 8,431.7.

Balance of Payments (Bds $ million, 2010): Exports of goods f.o.b. 861.4; Imports of goods f.o.b. –3,014.7; *Trade balance* –2,153.3; Exports of services 3,247.4; Imports of services –1,465.3; *Balance on goods and services* –371.2; Other income received 472.4; Other income paid –696.2; *Balance on goods, services and income* –595.0; Current transfers received 222.3; Current transfers paid –144.5; *Current balance* –517.2; Capital and financial accounts (net) 512.1; Net errors and omissions 66.1; *Overall balance* 61.0.

EXTERNAL TRADE

Principal Commodities (distribution by HS, US $ '000, 2013): *Imports c.i.f.:* Live animals and animal products 70.4; Vegetables and vegetable products 78.5; Prepared foodstuffs; beverages, spirits, vinegar; tobacco and articles thereof 190.1; Mineral products 488.1 (Mineral fuels, oils, distillation products, etc. 482.8); Chemicals and related products 159.5 (Pharmaceuticals 64.7); Plastics, rubber, and articles thereof 72.6 (Plastic goods 57.8); Iron and steel, other base metals and articles of base metal 69.4; Machinery and mechanical appliances, electrical equipment and parts thereof 247.3 (Machinery, boilers, etc. 126.4; Electrical, electronic equipment 120.9); Vehicles, aircraft, vessels and associated transport equipment 79.8 (Road vehicles 69.4); Total (incl. others) 1,768.7. *Exports f.o.b.:* Prepared foodstuffs; beverages, spirits, vinegar; tobacco and articles thereof 79.1 (Beverages, spirits and vinegar 52.7); Mineral products 173.6 (Mineral fuels, oils, distillation products, etc. 152.5); Chemicals and related products 72.2 (Pharmaceutical 46.9); Pulp of wood, paper and paperboard, and articles thereof 16.5 (Paper and paperboard, articles of pulp, paper and board 14.5); Iron and steel, other base metals and articles of base metal 14.2; Machinery and mechanical appliances, electrical equipment and parts thereof 18.7; Optical, medical apparatus, clocks and watches, musical instruments and parts thereof 32.3 (Optical, photo, technical, medical, etc apparatus 23.1); Total (incl. others) 467.4 (Source: Trade Map-Trade Competitiveness Map, International Trade Centre, www.intracen.org/marketanalysis).

Principal Trading Partners (distribution by HS, US $ '000, 2013): *Imports c.i.f.:* Brazil 21.2; Canada 49.6; China, People's Republic 78.3; France 34.6; Germany 22.9; Japan 34.6; Mexico 34.9; New Zealand 23.8; Suriname 87.1; Switzerland 18.1; Trinidad and Tobago 463.9; United Kingdom 71.6; USA 584.2; Total (incl. others) 1,768.7. *Exports f.o.b.:* Antigua and Barbuda 9.1; Canada 11.9; China, People's Republic 10.3; Guyana 21.4; Jamaica 20.7; Saint Lucia 20.1; Saint Vincent and the Grenadines 11.7; Trinidad and Tobago 53.9; United Kingdom 8.5; USA 85.0; Total (incl. others) 467.4 (Source: Trade Map-Trade Competitiveness Map, International Trade Centre, www.intracen.org/marketanalysis).

TRANSPORT

Road Traffic (motor vehicles in use, 2007): Passenger cars 103,535; Buses and coaches 631; Lorries and vans 15,151; Motorcycles and mopeds 2,525. Source: IRF, *World Road Statistics*.

Shipping: *Total Goods Handled* ('000 metric tons, 2010): 1,082 (Source: Barbados Port Authority). *Flag Registered Fleet* (at 31 December 2013): Number of vessels 138; Total displacement 882,619 grt (Source: Lloyd's List Intelligence—www.lloydslistintelligence.com).

Civil Aviation (1994): Aircraft movements 36,100; Freight loaded 5,052.3 metric tons; Freight unloaded 8,548.3 metric tons.

TOURISM

Tourist Arrivals ('000 persons): *Stop-overs:* 567.7 in 2011; 536.3 in 2012; 508.5 in 2013 (provisional). *Cruise-ship passengers:* 609.8 in 2011; 517.4 in 2012; 570.3 in 2013 (provisional).

Tourist Arrivals by Country ('000 visitor stop-overs, 2013, provisional): Canada 67.3; Germany 10.3; Trinidad and Tobago 31.6; Other CARICOM 55.7; United Kingdom 168.7; USA 120.6; Total (incl. others) 508.5.

Tourism Receipts (US $ million, excl. passenger transport): 963 in 2011; 907 in 2012; 912 in 2013 (provisional) (Source: World Tourism Organization).

COMMUNICATIONS MEDIA

Telephones (2013): 148,735 main lines in use.

Mobile Cellular Telephones (2013): 307,708 subscribers.

Internet Subscribers (2009): 61,000.

Broadband Subscribers (2013): 67,798.

Source: International Telecommunication Union.

EDUCATION

Pre-primary (2010/11 unless otherwise indicated): 84 schools (1995/96); 348 teachers (males 14, females 334); 5,620 pupils (males 2,836, females 2,784).

Primary (2010/11 unless otherwise indicated): 109 schools (2005/06); 1,720 teachers (males 382, females 1,338); 22,509 pupils (males 11,559, females 10,950).

Secondary (2005/06 unless otherwise indicated): 32 schools; 1,430 teachers (males 589, females 841); 19,696 pupils (males 9,809, females 9,887) (2010/11).

Tertiary (2010/11 unless otherwise indicated): 4 schools (2002); 786 teachers (males 403, females 383) (2006/07); 12,421 students (males 3,833, females 8,588).

Sources: Ministry of Education, Science, Technology and Innovation and UNESCO Institute for Statistics.

Pupil-teacher Ratio (primary education, UNESCO estimate): 13.1 in 2010/11 (Source: UNESCO Institute for Statistics).

Adult Literacy Rate (UN estimates): 99.7% (males 99.7%; females 99.7%) in 2003. Source: UN Development Programme, *Human Development Report*.

Directory

The Constitution

The parliamentary system has been established since the 17th century, when the first Assembly sat, in 1639, and the Charter of Barbados was granted, in 1652. A new Constitution came into force on 30 November 1966, when Barbados became independent. Under its terms, protection is afforded to individuals from slavery and forced labour, inhuman treatment, deprivation of property, arbitrary search and entry, and racial discrimination; freedom of conscience, expression, assembly, and movement are guaranteed.

Executive power is nominally vested in the British monarch, as Head of State, represented in Barbados by a Governor-General, who appoints the Prime Minister and, on the advice of the Prime Minister, appoints other ministers and some senators.

The Cabinet consists of the Prime Minister, appointed by the Governor-General as being the person best able to command a majority in the House of Assembly, and not fewer than five other ministers. Provision is also made for a Privy Council, presided over by the Governor-General.

Parliament consists of the Governor-General and a bicameral legislature, comprising the Senate and the House of Assembly. The Senate has 21 members: 12 appointed by the Governor-General on the advice of the Prime Minister, two on the advice of the Leader of the Opposition and seven as representatives of such interests as the Governor-General considers appropriate. The House of Assembly has (since 2003) 30 members, elected by universal adult suffrage for a term of five years (subject to dissolution). The minimum voting age is 18 years.

The Constitution also provides for the establishment of Service Commissions for the Judicial and Legal Service, the Public Service, the Police Service and the Statutory Boards Service. These Commissions are exempt from legal investigation; they have executive powers relating to appointments, dismissals and disciplinary control of the services for which they are responsible.

The Government

HEAD OF STATE

Queen: HM Queen ELIZABETH II.

Governor-General: Sir ELLIOT FITZROY BELGRAVE (took office 1 June 2012).

THE CABINET
(September 2014)

The Cabinet is formed by the Democratic Labour Party.

Prime Minister and Minister of National Security, the Public Services and Urban Development: FREUNDEL JEROME STUART.

Attorney-General and Minister of Home Affairs: ADRIEL BRATHWAITE.

Minister of Finance and Economic Affairs: CHRISTOPHER SINCKLER.

Minister of Education, Science, Technology and Innovation: RONALD JONES.

Minister of Housing, Lands and Rural Development: DENIS KELLMAN.

Minister of Tourism and International Transport: RICHARD SEALY.

Minister of Social Care, Constituency Empowerment and Community Development: STEVEN BLACKETT.

Minister of Transport and Works: MICHAEL LASHLEY.

Minister of Culture, Sports and Youth: STEPHEN LASHLEY.

Minister of Drainage and the Environment: DENIS LOWE.

Minister of Agriculture, Food, Fisheries and Water Resource Management: DAVID ESTWICK.

Minister of Health: JOHN BOYCE.

Minister of Foreign Affairs and Foreign Trade: MAXINE MCCLEAN.

Minister of Industry, International Business, Commerce and Small Business Development: DONVILLE INNISS.

Minister of Labour, Social Security and Human Resource Development: Dr ESTHER BYER SUCKOO.

Minister of State in the Prime Minister's Office: PATRICK TODD.

MINISTRIES

Office of the Prime Minister: Government HQ, Bay St, St Michael; tel. 436-6435; fax 436-9280; e-mail info@primeminister.gov.bb; internet www.primeminister.gov.bb.

Ministry of Agriculture, Food, Fisheries and Water Resource Management: Graeme Hall, POB 505, Christ Church; tel. 434-5000; fax 420-8444; e-mail info@agriculture.gov.bb; internet www.agriculture.gov.bb.

Ministry of Culture, Sports and Youth: Constitution Rd, St Michael; tel. 430-2704; fax 436-8909.

Ministry of Drainage and the Environment: S. P. Musson Bldg, Hinks St, St Michael; tel. 467-5700; fax 437-8859; e-mail ps_environment@gob.bb.

Ministry of Education, Science, Technology and Innovation: Elsie Payne Complex, Constitution Rd, St Michael; tel. 430-2709; fax 436-2411; e-mail ps@mes.gov.bb; internet www.mes.gov.bb.

Ministry of Finance and Economic Affairs: East Wing, Warrens Office Complex, St Michael; tel. 426-3179; fax 436-9280; e-mail pspowlett@gob.bb.

Ministry of Foreign Affairs and Foreign Trade: 1 Culloden Rd, St Michael; tel. 429-7108; fax 429-6652; e-mail barbados@foreign.gov.bb; internet www.foreign.gov.bb.

Ministry of Health: Jemmott's Lane, St Michael; tel. 426-5570; fax 426-4669.

Ministry of Home Affairs: General Post Office Bldg, Level 5, Cheapside, St Michael; tel. 228-8950; fax 437-3794; e-mail mha@caribsurf.com; internet ps@mha.gov.bb.

Ministry of Housing, Lands and Rural Development: National Housing Corpn Bldg, 'The Garden', Country Rd, St Michael; tel. 426-5041; fax 435-0174; e-mail info@bhta.org.

Ministry of Industry, International Business, Commerce and Small Business Development: British American Insurance Bldg, 2nd Floor, Magazine Lane, Bridgetown, St Michael; tel. 439-7483; fax 271-6155.

Ministry of Labour, Social Security and Human Resource Development: The Warrens Office Complex, 3rd Floor West, Warrens, St Michael; tel. 310-1400; fax 425-0266; e-mail vburnett@labour.gov.bb; internet labour.caribyte.com/index.

Ministry of National Security, the Public Services and Urban Development: E. Humphrey Walcott Bldg, Culloden Rd, St Michael; tel. 426-4617.

Ministry of Social Care, Constituency Empowerment and Community Development: The Warrens Office Complex, 4th Floor, Warrens, St Michael; tel. 310-1604; fax 424-2908; e-mail info@socialtransformation.gov.bb; internet www.socialcare.gov.bb.

Ministry of Tourism and International Transport: Lloyd Erskine Sandiford Centre, Two Mile Hill, St Michael; tel. 430-7500; fax 436-4828; e-mail info@tourism.gov.bb; internet www.tourism.gov.bb.

Ministry of Transport and Works: Pine East West Blvd, St Michael; tel. 429-2191; fax 437-8133; e-mail mpttech@caribsurf.com; internet www.mtw.gov.bb.

Office of the Attorney-General: Cedar Court, Wildey Business Park, Wildey Rd, St Michael; tel. 431-7700; fax 228-5433; e-mail ps@oag.gov.bb.

Legislature

PARLIAMENT

Senate

President: KERRYANN F. IFILL.
There are 21 members.

House of Assembly

Speaker: MICHAEL A. CARRINGTON.
General Election, 21 February 2013

Party							Seats
Democratic Labour Party (DLP)	.	.	.	.	.	.	16
Barbados Labour Party (BLP)	.	.	.	.	.	.	14
Total	.	.	.	.	.	.	**30**

Election Commission

Electoral and Boundaries Commission: National Insurance Bldg, Ground Floor, Fairchild St, Bridgetown BB11122; tel. 227-5817; fax 437-8229; e-mail electoral@barbados.gov.bb; internet www.electoral.barbados.gov.bb; Chief Electoral Officer ANGELA TAYLOR.

Political Organizations

Barbados Labour Party (BLP): Grantley Adams House, 111 Roebuck St, Bridgetown; tel. 429-1990; fax 427-8792; e-mail will99@caribsurf.com; internet www.blp.org.bb; f. 1938 as Barbados Progressive League, name changed as above 1946; moderate social democrat; Leader MIA MOTTLEY.

Clement Payne Movement (CPM): Crumpton St, Bridgetown; tel. 435-2334; fax 437-8216; e-mail cpmbarbados2@yahoo.com; f. 1988 in honour of national hero; non-electoral founding assoc. of the PEP; links to the Pan-Caribbean Congress and promotes international Pan-Africanism; Pres. DAVID A. COMISSIONG; Gen. Sec. BOBBY CLARKE.

People's Empowerment Party (PEP): Clement Payne Cultural Centre, Crumpton St, Bridgetown; tel. 423-6089; fax 437-8216; e-mail pepbarbados@gmx.com; internet pepbarbados.blogspot.com; f. 2006 by the Clement Payne Movt; left-of-centre; Leader DAVID COMISSIONG.

Democratic Labour Party (DLP): 'Kennington', George St, Belleville, St Michael; tel. 429-3104; fax 427-0548; internet www.dlpbarbados.org; f. 1955; Pres. and Leader FREUNDEL STUART; Gen. Sec. DONVILLE INNISS.

Diplomatic Representation

EMBASSIES AND HIGH COMMISSIONS IN BARBADOS

Brazil: The Courtyard, Hastings, POB BB15156, Christ Church; tel. 427-1735; fax 427-1744; e-mail brasemb.bridgetown@itamaraty.gov.br; internet bridgetown.itamaraty.gov.br; Ambassador APPIO CLAUDIO MUNIZ ACQUARONE.

Canada: Bishops Court Hill, Pine Rd, POB 404, Bridgetown; tel. 429-3550; fax 429-3780; e-mail bdgtn@international.gc.ca; internet www.canadainternational.gc.ca/barbados-barbade; High Commissioner RICHARD HANLEY.

China, People's Republic: 17 Golf View Terrace, Golf Club Rd, POB 428, Rockley, Christ Church; tel. 435-6890; fax 435-8300; e-mail chinaemb_bb@mfa.gov.cn; internet bb.chineseembassy.org; Ambassador WANG KE.

Cuba: No. 13, Edgehill Heights, Phase 2, St Thomas; tel. 271-9209; fax 271-9325; e-mail consulcuba@caribsurf.com; internet www.cubadiplomatica.cu/barbados; Ambassador LISSETTE BÁRBARA PÉREZ PÉREZ.

New Zealand: Lower Collymore Rock, Bridgetown; High Commissioner JAN HENDERSON.

United Kingdom: Lower Collymore Rock, POB 676, Bridgetown; tel. 430-7800; fax 430-7860; e-mail ukinbarbados@fco.gov.uk; internet www.gov.uk/world/barbados; High Commissioner VICTORIA GLYNIS DEAN.

USA: Wildey Business Park, Wildey, POB 302, Bridgetown BB14006; tel. 227-4000; fax 227-4088; e-mail BridgetownPublicAffairs@state.gov; internet bridgetown .usembassy.gov; Ambassador LARRY LEON PALMER.

Venezuela: Hastings, Main Rd, Christ Church; tel. 435-7619; fax 435-7830; e-mail embavenbdos@gmail.com; Ambassador JOSÉ GÓMEZ FEBRES.

Judicial System

Justice is administered by the Supreme Court of Judicature, which consists of a High Court and a Court of Appeal. Final appeal lies with the Caribbean Court of Justice, which was inaugurated in Port of Spain, Trinidad and Tobago, in April 2005; previously, final appeals were administered by the Judicial Committee of the Privy Council in the United Kingdom. There are Magistrates' Courts for lesser offences, with appeal to the Court of Appeal.

Supreme Court: Supreme Court Complex, Whitepark Rd, Bridgetown; tel. 434-9970; fax 426-2405; e-mail registrar@lawcourts.gov .bb; internet www.lawcourts.gov.bb; Chief Justice MARSTON GIBSON; Registrar LAURIE-ANN SMITH-BOVELL.

Office of the Attorney-General: Jones Bldg, Wildey Business Park, Wildey, St Michael; tel. 621-0110; fax 228-5433; e-mail attygen@caribsurf.com; Attorney-Gen. ADRIEL BRATHWAITE.

Religion

More than 100 religious denominations and sects are represented in Barbados, but the vast majority of the population profess Christianity.

CHRISTIANITY

Barbados Christian Council: Caribbean Conference of Churches Bldg, George St and Collymore Rock, St Michael; tel. 426-6014; Chair. Mgr VINCENT BLACKETT.

The Anglican Communion

According to the latest available census figures (2010), some 24% of the population are Anglicans. Anglicans in Barbados are adherents of the Church in the Province of the West Indies, comprising eight dioceses. The Archbishop of the Province currently is the Bishop of Barbados.

Bishop of Barbados: Rt Rev. JOHN WALDER DUNLOP HOLDER, Diocese of Barbados, Mandeville House, Henry's Lane, Collymore Rock, St Michael; tel. 426-2761; fax 426-0871; e-mail mandeville@ sunbeach.com; internet www.anglican.bb.

The Roman Catholic Church

According to the 2010 census, some 4% of the population are Roman Catholics. Barbados comprises a single diocese, which is suffragan to the archdiocese of Port of Spain (Trinidad and Tobago). The Bishop participates in the Antilles Episcopal Conference (currently based in Port of Spain, Trinidad and Tobago).

Bishop of Bridgetown: CHARLES JASON GORDON, Bishop's House, Ladymeade Gardens, St Michael, POB 1223, Bridgetown; tel. 426-3510; fax 429-6198; e-mail rcbishopbgl@caribsurf.com.

Other Churches

According to the 2010 census, other significant denominations in terms of number of adherents include Pentecostal (20% of the population), Adventist (6%), Methodist (4%), Nazarene (3%), Wesleyan (3%), Church of God (2%), Jehovah's Witnesses (2%) and Baptist (2%).

Church of God: Chapman St, POB 1, St Michael; tel. 426-5327; fax 228-2184; e-mail generalassemblychog@caribsurf.com; internet chogbarbados.org; Chair., Gen. Assembly Rev. M. GOODRIDGE; Pres. Rev. LIONEL L. GIBSON.

Church of Jesus Christ of Latter-Day Saints (Mormons): Black Rock Main Rd, Black Rock, St Michael; tel. 228-0210.

Church of the Nazarene (Barbados District): District Office, POB 3003E, Eagle Hall, St Michael; tel. 435-4444; fax 435-6486; internet nazarenebb.org; f. 1926; Supt Rev. Dr. ORLANDO D. SEALE.

Jerusalem Apostolic Spiritual Baptist Church: Ealing Grove, Christ Church; f. 1957; 10,000 mems; Archbishop GRANVILLE WILLIAMS.

Methodist Church: Bethel Church Office, Bay St, Bridgetown; tel. and fax 426-2223; e-mail methodist@caribsurf.com.

Seventh-day Adventists (East Caribbean Conference): Brydens Ave, Brittons Hill, POB 223, St Michael; tel. 429-7234; fax 429-8055; e-mail thepresidenteccsda@gmail.com; internet www .eastcarib.org; f. 1926; Pres. ROBINSON FRANCIS.

Spiritual Baptist Social and Community Development Ministries: Bridgetown; f. 2010; Chair. Rev. ODAIN BLACKMAN.

Wesleyan Holiness Church: Barbados District, POB 59, Bridgetown; tel. 429-3692; e-mail w.h.bdist@caribsurf.com; f. 1912 in Barbados; 38 churches; Gen. Supt Rev. ANTHONY WORRELL.

Other denominations include the Apostolic Church, the Bethel Evangelical Church, the Brethren Church, the Moravian Church, the Salvation Army, Presbyterian congregations, the African Methodist Episcopal Church and the United Holy Church of America.

OTHER RELIGIONS

In addition to the faiths listed below, there are also small communities of Rastafarians (1% of the population in 2010) and those of the Baha'í Faith.

Islam

According to the 2010 census, around 1% of the population are Muslims.

Islamic Teaching Centre: Harts Gap, Hastings, Bridgetown; tel. 427-0120.

Judaism

According to the 2010 census, there were 103 Jews on the island (less than 1% of the population).

Jewish Community: Shaare Tzedek Synagogue, Rockley New Rd, Christ Church; Nidhe Israel Synagogue, Synagogue Lane, POB 651, Bridgetown; tel. 437-0970; fax 437-0829; Pres. JACOB HASSID; Sec. SHARON ORAN.

Hinduism

According to the census of 2010, there are 840 Hindus on the island (less than 1% of the population).

Hindu Community: Hindu Temple, Synagogue Lane, Bridgetown; tel. 434-4638.

The Press

Barbados Advocate: POB 230, St Michael; tel. 467-2000; fax 434-2020; e-mail news@barbadosadvocate.com; internet www .barbadosadvocate.com; f. 1895; daily; Publr ANTHONY T. BRYAN; Man. Editor YAJAIRA ARCHIBALD; circ. 11,413.

The Broad Street Journal: Boarded Hall House, Boarded Hall, St. George; tel. 437-4592; e-mail bsjbarbados@gmail.com; internet www .broadstreetjournalbarbados.com; f. 1993; online; business; Publr and Editor PATRICK R. HOYOS.

The Nation: Nation House, Fontabelle, POB 1203, St Michael BB11000; tel. 430-5400; fax 427-6968; e-mail webmaster@ nationnews.com; internet www.nationnews.com; f. 1973; daily; also publishes *The Midweek Nation, The Weekend Nation, The Sun on Saturday, The Sunday Sun* (q.v.) and *The Visitor* (a free publ. for tourists); owned by One Caribbean Media Ltd; Publr VIVIAN-ANNE GITTENS; Editor-in-Chief ROY MORRIS; circ. 31,533 (Daily), 51,440 (Sun.).

Sunday Advocate: POB 230, St Michael; tel. 467-2000; fax 434-1000; e-mail news@sunbeach.net; internet www.barbadosadvocate .com; f. 1895; Exec. Editor GILLIAN MARSHALL; circ. 17,490.

The Sunday Sun: Nation House, Fontabelle, POB 1203, St Michael BB11000; tel. 430-5400; fax 427-6968; e-mail webmaster@ nationnews.com; internet www.nationnews.com; f. 1977; owned by One Caribbean Media Ltd; Publr VIVIAN-ANNE GITTENS; Editor-in-Chief KAYMAR JORDAN; circ. 48,824.

NEWS AGENCY

Caribbean Media Corporation (CMC): Harbour Industrial Estate, Unit 1B, Bldg 6A, St Michael BB11145; tel. 467-1000; fax 429-4355; e-mail admin@cmccaribbean.com; internet www .cananews.net; f. 2000; formed by merger of Caribbean News Agency (CANA) and Caribbean Broadcasting Union; Dir PATRICK COZIER.

Publishers

Advocate Publishers (2000) Inc: POB 230, Fontabelle, St Michael; tel. 467-2000; fax 434-2020; e-mail news@barbadosadvocate.com; internet www.barbadosadvocate.com; Dir HENRY MOULTON.

Miller Publishing Co: Edgehill, St Thomas; tel. 421-6700; fax 421-6707; e-mail keith@millerpublishing.net; internet millerpublishing.net; f. 1983; publishes general interest books, tourism and business guides; Jt Man. Dirs KEITH MILLER, SALLY MILLER.

Nation Publishing Co Ltd: Nation House, Fontabelle, POB 1203, Fontabelle, St Michael BB11000; tel. 430-5400; fax 427-6968; internet www.nationpublishing.com; f. 1973; owned by One Caribbean Media Ltd; publishes daily edns of *The Nation* newspaper, as well as *The Midweek Nation, The Weekend Nation, The Sun on Saturday, The Sunday Sun* (q.v.), *The Visitor* (a free publ. for tourists), *Friends, Ignition Plus, Barbados Business Authority, Better Health* and *Nation Work Book*; Chair. HAROLD HOYTE; Publr and CEO VIVIAN-ANNE GITTENS.

Broadcasting and Communications

TELECOMMUNICATIONS

Columbus International Inc: Suite 205-207, Dowell House, cnr Roebuck and Palmetto St, Bridgetown; tel. 602-4668; internet www.columbus.co; f. 2004; internet and private telecommunications network provider; CEO BRENDAN PADDICK.

Digicel Barbados Ltd: The Courtyard, Hastings, Christ Church; tel. 434-3444; fax 426-3444; e-mail BDS_CustomerCare_External@digicelgroup.com; internet www.digicelbarbados.com; f. 2001; awarded licence to operate cellular telephone services in 2003; approval granted in 2006 for the acquisition of Cingular Wireless' operation in Barbados; owned by an Irish consortium; CEO BARRY O'BRIEN.

LIME: Carlisle House, Hincks St, Bridgetown, St Michael; tel. 292-5050; e-mail CallCenterSupport@lime.com; internet www.lime.com; f. 1984; fmrly Cable & Wireless (Barbados) Ltd; Barbados External Telecommunications Ltd became Cable & Wireless BET Ltd; name changed as above in 2008; owned by Cable & Wireless PLC (United Kingdom); provides international telecommunications and internet services; contact centres in Jamaica and Saint Lucia; CEO (Caribbean) MARTIN JOOS (acting); Man. Dir ALEX MCDONALD.

Sunbeach Communications: 'San Remo', Belmont Rd, St Michael; tel. 233-6092; fax 228-6330; e-mail customerservice@sunbeach.net; internet www.sunbeach.net; f. 1995 as an internet service provider; licence to operate cellular telephone services obtained in 2003; launch of cellular operations postponed indefinitely in 2007; Vtel (Saint Lucia) acquired controlling 52.9% share in Dec. 2006; CEO JUDY TROTTER.

BROADCASTING

Radio

Barbados Broadcasting Service Ltd: Astoria, St George, Bridgetown; tel. 437-9550; fax 437-9203; e-mail action@sunbeach.net; f. 1981; operates BBS FM and Faith 102.1 FM (religious broadcasting); Man. Dir GAIL S. PADMORE.

Caribbean Broadcasting Corporation (CBC): The Pine, POB 900, Wildey, St Michael; tel. 467-5400; fax 429-4795; e-mail customerservices@cbc.bb; internet www.cbc.bb; f. 1963; state-owned; operates 3 radio stations; Gen. Man. LARS SÖDERSTRÖM.

  CBC Radio 900 AM: Caribbean Broadcasting Corpn, The Pine, St Michael; tel. 434-1900; fax 429-4795; e-mail pbowen@cbc.bb; internet www.947fm.bb; f. 1963; spoken word and news.

  Quality 100.7 FM: Caribbean Broadcasting Corpn, The Pine, St Michael; tel. 434-1007; fax 429-4795; e-mail dsthill@cbc.bb; internet www.qfm.bb; international and regional music, incl. folk, classical, etc.

  The One 98.1 FM: Caribbean Broadcasting Corpn, The Pine, St Michael; tel. 434-1981; fax 429-4795; e-mail webmaster@theone.bb; internet www.theone.bb; f. 1984; popular music.

One Caribbean Media Ltd (OCM): River Rd, POB 1267, Bridgetown; tel. 430-7300; fax 426-5377; e-mail ocmnetwork@ocmnetwork.net; internet ocmnetwork.net; f. 2007 after Starcom Network Inc (SNI) with CCCL and GBN became the OCM Network; operates 4 radio stations: Gospel 790 AM, Hott 95.3 FM, LOVE FM 104, VOB 92.9 FM; Group CEO DAWN THOMAS.

Television

CBC-TV 8: The Pine, POB 900, Wildey, St Michael; tel. 467-5400; fax 429-4795; e-mail news@cbc.bb; internet www.cbc.bb; f. 1964; part of the Caribbean Broadcasting Corpn (q.v.); Channel Eight is the main

national service, broadcasting 24 hours daily; a maximum of 115 digital subscription channels will be available through Multi-Choice Television; Dir of Television CECILY CLARKE-RICHMOND.

DIRECTV: Nation House, Roebuck St, Bridgetown, St Michael; tel. 435-7362; fax 228-5553; e-mail info@directvtt.com; internet www.directvcaribbean.com/bb; digital satellite television service; owned by the OCM Network; Administrator M. OWANA SKEETE.

Finance

In 2013 there were 46 offshore banks registered in Barbados.

REGULATORY AUTHORITY

Financial Services Commission: 34 Warrens Industrial Park, St Michael; tel. 421-2142; fax 421-2146; e-mail seccom@caribsurf.com; internet www.fsc.gov.bb; f. 2011 to regulate and supervise the operations of the non-banking financial sector.

BANKING

(cap. = capital; res = reserves; dep. = deposits; brs = branches; m. = million; amounts in Barbados dollars unless otherwise indicated)

Central Bank

Central Bank of Barbados: Tom Adams Financial Centre, Spry St, POB 1016, Bridgetown BB11126; tel. 436-6870; fax 427-9559; e-mail info@centralbank.org.bb; internet www.centralbank.org.bb; f. 1972; bank of issue; cap. 2.0m., res 6.5m., dep. 712.3m. (Dec. 2009); Gov. R. DELISLE WORRELL.

Commercial Banks

CIBC FirstCaribbean International Bank: Warrens, POB 503, St Michael; tel. 367-2300; fax 424-8977; e-mail care@cibcfcib.com; internet www.cibcfcib.com; f. 2002 as FirstCaribbean International Bank following merger of Barclays and Canadian Imperial Bank of Commerce (CIBC)'s Caribbean operations; Barclays relinquished its stake to CIBC in 2006, present name adopted in 2011; cap. US $1,193.1m., res US $–229.6m., dep. US $9,608.3m. (Oct. 2013); CEO RIK PARKHILL; Man. Dir (Barbados) DONNA WELLINGTON; 69 brs in region.

First Citizens Bank (Barbados) Ltd: The Mutual Bldg, 1 Beckwith Pl., Lower Broad St, Bridgetown; tel. 431-4500; fax 430-0222; e-mail contact@firstcitizensbb.com; internet www.firstcitizensbb.com/barbados; f. 2003 as Mutual Bank of the Caribbean, name later changed to Butterfield Bank (Barbados); acquired by First Citizens Bank (Trinidad and Tobago) in 2012; cap. 36.9m., res 12.5m., dep. 531.3m. (Dec. 2013); CEO GLYNE HARRISON.

RBC Royal Bank Barbados: Broad St, POB 68, Bridgetown BB11000; tel. 467-4000; fax 426-4139; internet www.rbcroyalbank.com/caribbean/barbados/; f. 1911; subsidiary of RBC Financial Group, Canada; CEO (Caribbean) SURESH SOOKOO.

Republic Bank (Barbados) Ltd: Independence Sq., POB 1002, Bridgetown, St Michael; tel. 431-5700; fax 429-2606; e-mail info@republicbarbados.com; internet www.republicbarbados.com; f. 1978; fmrly Barbados National Bank Inc; present name adopted 2012; cap. 48.0m., res 137.3m., dep. 1,695.4m. (Sept. 2012); Chair. RONALD F. D. HARFORD; Man. Dir DAVID DULAL-WHITEWAY; 9 brs.

Scotiabank (Canada): CGI Tower, 1st Floor, Warrens, St Michael; tel. 426-7000; fax 425-2394; internet www.scotiabank.com/bb; f. 1956; Man. Dir (Caribbean East) DAVID NOEL; 8 brs.

Regional Development Bank

Caribbean Development Bank: POB 408, Wildey, St Michael BB11000; tel. 431-1600; fax 426-7269; e-mail info@caribank.org; internet www.caribank.org; f. 1970; cap. US $256.3m., res US $9.2m., (Dec. 2013), dep. US $20.0m. (Dec. 2012); Pres. Dr WILLIAM WARREN SMITH.

Trust Companies

Alexandria Trust Corpn: Deighton House, Cnr of Deighton and Dayrell's Rds, St Michael BB14030; tel. 228-8402; fax 228-3847; e-mail barbara.ogorman@atcbarbados.com; internet www.alexandriabancorp.com; wholly owned by Guardian Capital Group Ltd (Canada); Man. Dir ROBERT F. MADDEN; Gen. Man. BARBARA O'GORMAN.

The Blue Financial Group: Braemar Court, Deighton Rd, St Michael BB14017; tel. 467-6677; fax 467-6678; e-mail info@stmichael.bb; internet www.thebluefinancialgroup.com; f. 1987; fmrly St Michael Trust Corpn; Pres. IAN HUTCHISON.

Capita Financial Services Inc: Walrond St, Bridgetown BB11127; tel. 431-4716; fax 426-6168; e-mail info@capitacaribbean.com; internet www.capitacaribbean.com; f. 1984; incorporated as

Clico Mortgage & Finance Corpn; name changed as above in 2010; subsidiary of Barbados Public Workers' Cooperative Credit Union Ltd; Chair. CARLOS HOLDER; Pres. and CEO ANDREW ST. JOHN.

CCG Trust Corpn: 1 Chelston Park, Collymore Rock, St Michael; tel. 427-8174; fax 429-7995; e-mail john.walker@cit.com; owned by CIT Group, Inc.

CIBC FirstCaribbean International Trust and Merchant Bank (Barbados) Ltd: CIBC Centre, Warrens, POB 503, St Michael; tel. 367-2300; fax 424-8977; internet www.cibcfcib.com; known as CIBC Trust and Merchant Bank until 2002; Exec. Chair. MICHAEL MANSOOR; Exec. Dir RIK PARKHILL.

Concorde Bank Ltd: The Corporate Centre, Bush Hill, Bay St, POB 1161, Bridgetown BB11000; tel. 430-5320; fax 429-7996; e-mail concorde@concordebb.com; f. 1987; cap. 2.8m., res 2m., dep. 41.9m. (June 2013); Pres. and Chair. GERARD LUSSAN; Gen. Man. A. MARINA CORBIN.

DGM Bank & Trust Inc: Hastings Financial Centre, 2°, Hastings, Christ Church B15154; tel. 434-4850; fax 431-3439; e-mail info@dgmgroup.com; internet www.dgmbank.com; f. 1996, fmrly Altamira International Bank; Chair. GEOFFREY CAVE.

Globe Finance Inc: Rendezvous Court, Suite 6, Rendezvous Main Rd, Christ Church BB15112; tel. 426-4755; fax 426-4772; e-mail info@globefinanceinc.com; internet www.globefinanceinc.com; f. 1998; Man. Dir RONALD DAVIS.

J&T Bank and Trust: Lauriston House, Lower Collymore Rock, POB 1132, Bridgetown, St Michael BB11000; tel. 430-8650; fax 430-5335; e-mail info@jtbanktrust.com; internet www.jtbanktrust.com; fmrly known as Bayshore Bank and Trust; Man. Dir L. PENNY ETTINGER.

Republic Finance and Trust Corpn: BNB Bldg, 2nd Floor, Independence Sq., Bridgetown; tel. 431-5700; fax 429-8389; internet www.republicbarbados.com; f. as BNB Finance and Trust Corpn; subsidiary of Republic Bank (Barbados) Ltd; Man. ERIC SCOTT.

Royal Bank of Canada Financial Corporation: Bldg 2, 2nd Floor, Chelston Park, Collymore Rock, POB 986, St Michael; tel. 429-4923; fax 429-3800; internet www.rbcroyalbank.com; Pres. and CEO GORDON M. NIXON.

Royal Fidelity Merchant Bank and Trust (Barbados) Ltd: Royal Fidelity House, 27 Pine Rd, POB 1338, St Michael BB11113; tel. 435-1955; fax 435-1964; e-mail info@royalfidelity.com; internet www.royalfidelity.com/barbados; Pres. MICHAEL A. ANDERSON.

Signia Financial Group Inc: Carlisle House, Hinks St, Bridgetown; tel. 434-2360; fax 434-0057; e-mail info@signiafinancial.com; internet www.signiafinancial.com; f. 2003, fmrly General Finance; Chair. GEOFFREY CAVE; CEO PAUL ASHBY.

STOCK EXCHANGE

Barbados Stock Exchange Inc (BSE): Eighth Ave, Belleville, St Michael BB11114; tel. 436-9871; fax 429-8942; e-mail marlon.yarde@bse.com.bb; internet www.bse.com.bb; f. 1987 as the Securities Exchange of Barbados; in 1989 the Govts of Barbados, Trinidad and Tobago and Jamaica agreed to link exchanges; cross-trading began in 1991; reincorporated in 2001; CEO and Gen. Man. MARLON YARDE.

INSURANCE

The leading British and a number of US and Canadian companies have agents in Barbados. In 2014 there were 238 exempt and qualified exempt insurance companies registered in the country. Domestic insurance companies include the following:

Insurance Corporation of Barbados Ltd (ICBL): Roebuck St, POB 11000, Bridgetown; tel. 434-6000; fax 426-3393; e-mail icb@icb.com.bb; internet www.icb.com.bb; f. 1978; 51% owned by BF&M Ltd of Bermuda; cap. Bds $39m.; Chair. R. JOHN WIGHT; Man. Dir and CEO INGRID INNES.

McLarens: Warrens Complex, 106 Warrens Terrace East, Suite 3, POB 5004, St Michael BB28000; tel. 438-9231; e-mail david.hobson@mclarens.com; internet www.mclarens.com; fmrly McLarens Young International; renamed as above in 2012; Regional Dir, Caribbean KEVIN INNES.

Pan-American International Insurance Corpn: POB 197, Cheapside, Bridgetown; tel. 427-5320; fax 427-6596; internet www.palig.com; f. 2012; part of Pan-American Life Insurance Group (USA); Pres. and CEO BRUCE PARKER; Gen. Man. KEITH KING.

Sagicor: Sagicor Financial Centre, Lower Collymore Rock, Wildey, St Michael; tel. 467-7500; fax 436-8829; e-mail info@sagicor.com; internet www.sagicor.com; f. 1840 as Barbados Mutual Life Assurance Society (BMLAS); changed name as above in 2002 after acquiring majority ownership of Life of Barbados (LOB) Ltd; Chair. STEPHEN MCNAMARA; Pres. and CEO DODRIDGE D. MILLER.

United Insurance Co Ltd: United Insurance Centre, Lower Broad St, POB 1215, Bridgetown; tel. 430-1900; fax 436-7573; e-mail mail@unitedinsure.com; internet unitedinsure.com; f. 1976; CEO HOWARD HALL; Regional Man. CECILE COX.

USA Risk Group (Barbados) Ltd: Golden Anchorage Complex, Sunset Crest, St James; tel. 432-6467; fax 483-1850; e-mail mhole@usarisk.bb; internet www.usarisk.com/; Man. MARTIN HOLE.

Association

Insurance Association of the Caribbean Inc (IAC): The Thomas Pierce Bldg, Lower Collymore Rock, St Michael BB11115; tel. 427-5608; fax 427-7277; e-mail info@iac-caribbean.com; internet www.iac-caribbean.com; regional asscn; Pres. DAVID ALLEYNE; Man. JANELLE THOMPSON.

Trade and Industry

GOVERNMENT AGENCY

Barbados Agricultural Management Co Ltd (BAMC): Warrens, POB 719C, St Michael; tel. 425-0010; fax 421-7879; e-mail lparris@bamc.net.bb; f. 1993; Gen. Man. LESLIE PARRIS.

DEVELOPMENT ORGANIZATIONS

Barbados Agriculture Development and Marketing Corpn (BADMC): Fairy Valley Plantation House, Fairy Valley, Christ Church; tel. 428-0250; fax 428-0152; e-mail badmc@agriculture.gov.bb; internet www.agriculture.gov.bb; f. 1993 by merger; programme of diversification and land reforms; CEO FAY BEST.

Barbados Investment and Development Corpn (BIDC): Pelican House, Princess Alice Hwy, POB 1250, Bridgetown BB11000; tel. 427-5350; fax 426-7802; e-mail bidc@bidc.org; internet www.bidc.com; f. 1992 by merger; facilitates the devt of the industrial sector, especially in the areas of manufacturing, information technology and financial services; offers free consultancy to investors; provides factory space for lease or rent; administers the Fiscal Incentives Legislation; Chair. BENSON STRAKER; CEO LEROY MCCLEAN.

Barbados Small Business Association: 1 Pelican Industrial Park, Bridgetown; tel. 228-0162; fax 228-0163; e-mail theoffice@sba.org.bb; internet www.sba.org.bb; f. 1982; non-profit org. representing interests of small businesses; Pres. CELESTE FOSTER.

CHAMBER OF COMMERCE

Barbados Chamber of Commerce and Industry: Braemar Court, Deighton Rd, St Michael; tel. 434-4750; fax 228-2907; e-mail bcci@bdscham.com; internet www.barbadoschamberofcommerce.com; f. 1825; 220 mem. firms; some 345 reps; Exec. Dir LISA GALE.

INDUSTRIAL AND TRADE ASSOCIATIONS

Barbados Agricultural Society: The Grotto, Beckles Rd, St Michael; tel. 436-6683; fax 435-0651; e-mail agrofest@basonevoice.org; internet www.basonevoice.org; CEO JAMES PAUL.

Barbados Association of Professional Engineers: Christie Bldg, Garrison Hill, St Michael BB14038; tel. 429-6105; fax 434-6673; e-mail info@bape.org; internet www.bape.org; f. 1964; Pres. GREG PARRIS; Hon. Sec. JASON MARSHALL; 213 mems.

Barbados International Business Association (BIBA): 19 Pine Rd, Belleville, St Michael; tel. 436-2422; fax 434-2423; e-mail biba@biba.bb; internet www.biba.bb; f. 1993 as Barbados Asscn of International Business Cos and Offshore Banks (BAIBCOB); changed name as above in 1997; org. comprising cos engaged in int. business; Pres. CONNIE SMITH; Exec. Dir HENDERSON HOLMES; 187 mem. cos.

Barbados Manufacturers' Association: Suite 201, Bldg 8, Harbour Industrial Park, St Michael; tel. 426-4474; fax 436-5182; e-mail info@bma.bb; internet www.bma.bb; f. 1964; Pres. KARLENE NICHOLLS; Exec. Dir BOBBI MCKAY; 110 mem. firms.

Barbados Sugar Industry Ltd (BSIL): Bridgetown; f. 1973; operates sugar factories and supervises transport and storage of sugar products; Chair. Dr ATLEE BRATHWAITE.

EMPLOYERS' ORGANIZATION

Barbados Employers' Confederation (BEC): Braemar Court, Deighton Rd, POB 33B, Brittons Hill, St Michael; tel. 435-4753; fax 435-2907; e-mail becon@barbadosemployers.com; internet barbadosemployers.com; f. 1956; Pres. IAN GOODING-EDGHILL; Exec. Dir TONY WALCOTT; 235 mems (incl. assoc. mems).

MAJOR COMPANIES

ADM Barbados Mills Ltd: Flour Mill Complex, Spring Garden Hwy, POB 260, Bridgetown, St Michael; tel. 427-8880; fax 427-8886; e-mail bfm@admbml.com; internet www.admworld.com; f. 1977; manufacturer of flour and other grain-derived products; Chair., Pres. and CEO PATRICIA A. WOERTZ; more than 40 employees.

Arawak Cement Co Ltd: Checker Hall, St Lucy; tel. 439-9880; fax 439-7976; e-mail arawak@arawakcement.com.bb; internet www.arawakcement.com.bb; f. 1981; manufacture and marketing of cement and lime (quicklime and hydrated lime); 100% owned by Trinidad Cement Ltd; sales US $30m. (2003); Chair. CARLOS HEE HOUNG; Gen. Man. DERRICK ISAAC; more than 250 employees.

Banks Holdings Ltd (BHL): Pine Hill Dairy Complex, The Pine, St Michael BB11000; tel. 227-6700; fax 427-0772; e-mail bhl@banksholdings.com.bb; internet www.thebhlgroup.com; f. 1991, after Banks (Barbados) Breweries acquired Barbados Bottling Co Ltd; beverage conglomerate; Chair. ANTHONY KING; CEO and Man. Dir RICHARD COZIER.

> **B & B Distribution Ltd:** Newton, Christ Church; tel. 418-2900; fax 418-2970; e-mail bandb@banksholdings.com.bb; internet www.thebhlgroup.com; f. 1994; distribution of finished BHL products; Gen. Man. JEREMY WHITELAW.

> **Banks (Barbados) Breweries Ltd:** Pine Hill Dairy Complex, The Pine, St. Michael, BB14000; tel. 227-6750; fax 227-6790; e-mail info@banksbeer.com; internet www.banksbeer.com; f. 1961; brewing and bottling of alcoholic and non-alcoholic beverages; Gen. Man. AKASH RAGBIR.

> **Barbados Bottling Co Ltd:** Newton, Christ Church; tel. 418-3300; fax 418-3350; e-mail bbc@thebhlgroup.com; manufacturer of soft drinks; f. 1944; acquired by BHL in 1992; Gen. Man. WILLIAM HASLETT.

> **Barbados Dairy Industries Ltd:** The Pine, St Michael; tel. 430-4100; fax 227-6660; e-mail phd@thebhlgroup.com; f. 1966; acquired by BHL in 1997; manufacturer of dairy and related products; Sec. C. S. A. JONES.

> **Plastic Containers Ltd:** Thornbury Hill, Christ Church; tel. 428-7780; fax 428-7112; e-mail pcl@banksholdings.com.bb; acquired by BHL in 1991; manufacturers of plastic bottles.

BICO Ltd: Harbour Industrial Estate, Bridgetown BB11145; tel. 430-2100; fax 426-2198; e-mail admin@bicoicecream.com; internet www.bicoicecream.com; f. 1901; manufacturer and distributor of ice cream; distributor of frozen dough and pastries; operators of public cold-storage facilities; CEO F. EDWIN THIRLWELL; 120 employees.

BRC West Indies Ltd: Cane Garden, St Thomas; tel. 425-0371; fax 425-2941; e-mail brc@caribsurf.com; internet www.brcwestindies.com; f. 1979; manufacturer of wire mesh and steel products; Gen. Man. PETER COLLETT; 42 employees.

Bryden's Distribution (Barbados) Ltd: Barbarees Hill, POB 403, Bridgetown, St Michael; tel. 431-2600; fax 426-0755; e-mail barbados@brydens.com; internet www.brydens.com/barbados; f. 1898; wholly owned subsidiary of ANSA McAL (Barbados); mem. of the Trinidad-based ANSA McAL Group; manufacturers' representative and distributor for food and beverages, pharmaceuticals, photographic supplies, personal care and household cleaners; CEO ANDREW LEWIS; 1,200 employees.

DaCosta Mannings Retail Ltd: POB 1227C, Bridgetown BB11000; tel. 431-8700; fax 429-5905; e-mail info@dmi.com; internet www.dacostamannings.com; f. 1995 after merger of DaCosta Ltd and Mannings, Wilkinson & Challenor; trade in building materials, furniture and hardware products; subsidiary of Barbados Shipping and Trading Company (see under Shipping); CEO TERRANCE MAHON; 276 employees.

Edghill Associates Ltd: Websters Industrial Park, Wildey, St Michael; tel. 427-2941; fax 426-5958; e-mail edghill@caribsurf.com; heavy construction; Dir RICHARD EDGHILL; 300 employees.

Goddard Enterprises Ltd (GEL): POB 502, Bridgetown; tel. 430-5700; fax 436-8934; e-mail gelinfo@thegelgroup.com; internet www.goddardenterprisesltd.com; f. 1921; rum production, meat processing, bakery production, in-flight and airport-terminal catering, duty-free sales, lumber and building supplies, air conditioning and electrical contracting, insurance and financial services, shipping agent, automotive agency; sales Bds $889m. (2008/09); Chair. CHARLES HERBERT; Man. Dir ANTHONY ALI; 4,412 employees in the Caribbean, Central and Latin America (2008/09).

Hanschell Inniss Ltd: Goddard's Complex, Kensington, Fontabelle, St Michael; tel. 426-3544; fax 427-6938; e-mail camilla_greaves@goddent.com; internet www.hanschellinnissltd.com; manufacture and distribution of food and soft drinks; f. 1884; owned by Goddard Enterprises Ltd since 1973; 190 employees.

Mico Garment Factory Ltd: Harbour Industrial Park, Harbour Rd, POB 621, Bridgetown; tel. 426-1883; fax 429-7267; e-mail misons@trinidad.net; f. 1964; clothing mfrs, licensed mfr for Philips Van Heusen in Caribbean; Chair. MOHAMMED IBRAHIM JUMAN; Man. Dir ANSAR JUMAN; 143 employees.

Mount Gay Distilleries Ltd: Exmouth Gap, Brandons, Spring Garden Highway, St Michael; tel. 227-8800; fax 425-8770; e-mail cjordan@caribsurf.com; internet www.mountgay.com; f. 1955; bought by Rémy-Cointreau, part of the Maxxium alliance, in 1989; rum distilling; Man. Dir RAPHAEL GRISONI; 55 employees.

Roberts Manufacturing Co Ltd: POB 1275, Lower Estate, Bridgetown, St Michael; tel. 429-2131; fax 426-5604; e-mail roberts@rmco.com; internet www.rmco.com; f. 1944; subsidiary of Barbados Shipping and Trading Co Ltd (see under Shipping); manufacturers of shortening, margarine, edible oils and animal feeds; Man. Dir D. G. FOSTER; 160 employees.

R. L. Seale and Co Ltd: Clarence House, Tudor Bridge, POB 864, St Michael; tel. 426-0334; fax 436-6003; e-mail rseale@caribsurf.com; f. 1926; manufacture and distribution of rum, sale of food; Chair. and Man. Dir Sir DAVID SEALE; 275 employees.

The West Indies Rum Distillery Ltd: Brighton, Black Rock, St Michael; tel. 425-9301; fax 425-7236; e-mail info@westindiesrum.com; internet www.westindiesrum.com; f. 1893; 88% shares owned by Goddard Enterprises Ltd; main brands are Cockspur, Malibu, Gilbeys and Popov; Man. Dir ANDREW HASSELL; 62 employees.

C. O. Williams Construction Ltd: POB 871E, Lears, St Michael; tel. 436-3910; fax 427-5336; e-mail info@cow.bb; internet www.cow.bb; f. 1960; Chair. Sir CHARLES OTHNEIL WILLIAMS.

UTILITIES

Electricity

Barbados Light and Power Co (BL & P): POB 142, Garrison Hill, St Michael; tel. 626-4300; fax 228-1396; internet www.blpc.com.bb; f. 1911; 80% owned by Emera (Canada); electricity generator and distributor; operates 3 stations with a combined capacity of 209,500 kW; Chair. ANDREW GITTENS; Man. Dir MARK KING.

Gas

Barbados National Oil Co Ltd (BNOCL): POB 175, Woodbourne, St Philip; tel. 420-1800; fax 420-1818; e-mail gibbsw@bnocl.com; internet www.bnocl.com; f. 1982; state-owned, although plans for privatization announced in 2014; exploration and extraction of petroleum and natural gas; Chair. Dr LEONARD NURSE; Gen. Man. WINTON GIBBS; 88 employees.

National Petroleum Corporation (NPC): Wildey, POB 175, St Michael; tel. 430-4020; fax 426-4326; e-mail customerserv@npc.com.bb; internet npc.com.bb; gas production and distribution; Chair. HARCOURT LEWIS; Gen. Man. JAMES BROWNE.

Water

Barbados Water Authority: Pine East-West Blvd, The Pine, St Michael; tel. 424-1650; fax 424-2362; e-mail bwa@caribsurf.com; internet www.bwa.bb; f. 1980; Exec. Chair. ARNI WALTERS; Gen. Man. CHARLES MARVILLE (acting).

TRADE UNIONS

Barbados Police Association: Speightstown, St Peter; tel. 432-0447; e-mail rpba@caribsurf.com; Pres. Sgt MICHAEL SOBERS; Gen. Sec. SAMUEL HINDS.

Barbados Registered Nurses Association: Gibson House, Lower Collymore Rock, St. Michael, POB 120C, Bridgetown; tel. 427-5627; fax 436-6279; e-mail brna@sunbeach.net; Pres. BLONDELLE MULLIN.

Barbados Secondary Teachers' Union: The Patrick Frost Centre, Eighth Ave, Belleville, St Michael; tel. and fax 429-7676; e-mail bstu_org@yahoo.com; internet www.bstu.org; f. 1946 as Asscn of Asst Teachers in Secondary Schools; present name adopted 1970; Pres. MARY-ANN REDMAN; Gen. Sec. MONA ROBINSON; 440 mems.

Barbados Union of Teachers: Merry Hill, Welches, POB 58, St Michael; tel. 436-6139; fax 426-9890; e-mail but@hotmail.com; internet butbarbados.org; f. 1974; Pres. KAREN BEST; Gen. Sec. HERBERT GITTENS; 1,800 mems.

Barbados Workers' Union (BWU): 'Solidarity' House, Harmony Hall, POB 172, St Michael; tel. 426-3492; fax 436-6496; e-mail bwu@caribsurf.com; internet www.bwu-bb.org; f. 1941; Pres.-Gen. LINDA BROOKS; Gen. Sec. Sir ROY TROTMAN; 25,000 mems.

Caribbean Congress of Labour (CCL): St Michael, Barbados; f. 1960; regional trade union fed; Pres. DAVID MESSIAH; Gen. Sec. LINCOLN LEWIS.

National Union of Public Workers: Dalkeith Rd, POB 174, St Michael; tel. 426-1764; fax 436-1795; e-mail nupwbarbados@sunbeach.net; internet www.nupwbarbados.org; f. 1944 as the Barbados Civil Service Asscn, present name adopted in 1971; Pres. WALTER MALONEY; Gen. Sec. DENNIS L. CLARKE; c. 8,000 mems.

Transport

ROADS

In 2012 there was a network of 1,600 km (994 miles) of paved roads.

Barbados Transport Board: Weymouth, Roebuck St, St Michael BB11083; tel. 310-3500; fax 310-3573; e-mail customerservice@transportboard.com; internet www.transportboard.com; f. 1955; part of the Ministry of Transport and Works; Gen. Man. SANDRA FORDE.

SHIPPING

Bridgetown harbour has berths for eight ships and simultaneous bunkering facilities for five. A new cruise ship pier was built in the mid-2000s. In December 2013 the flag registered fleet comprised 138 vessels, totalling 882,619 grt, of which 21 were bulk carriers and 58 were general cargo ships.

Barbados Port Inc: University Row, Princess Alice Hwy, Bridgetown; tel. 430-6100; fax 429-5348; e-mail administrator@barbadosport.com; internet www.barbadosport.com; f. 1979 as the Barbados Port Authority and incorporated in 2003; Chair. DAVID HARDING; Man. Dir and CEO DAVID JEAN MARIE.

The Shipping Association of Barbados: Trident House, 2nd Floor, Broad St, Bridgetown; tel. 427-9860; fax 426-8392; e-mail info@shippingbarbados.com; internet www.shippingbarbados.com; f. 1981; Pres. ROVEL MORRIS; Exec. Vice-Pres. EMERSON ALLEYNE.

Principal Shipping Companies

Booth Steamship Co (Barbados) Ltd: Prescod Blvd, St Michael BB11124; tel. 436-6094; fax 426-0484; e-mail info@boothsteamship.com; internet www.boothsteamship.com; f. 1961; represents Crowley Liner Services, Mediterranean Shipping Co (MSC), Inchcape Shipping Services; Chair. RANDALL I. BANFIELD; Gen. Man. NOEL M. NURSE.

DaCosta Mannings Inc (DMI): Brandons, POB 103, St Michael; tel. 430-4800; fax 431-0051; e-mail sales@dmishipping.com; internet www.dmishipping.com; f. 1995 following merger of DaCosta Ltd and Manning, Wilkinson & Challenor Ltd; agent for P & O Nedlloyd, Princess Cruises, Bernuth Agencies, Columbus/Hamburg Sud and K Line; Exec. Dir MARK SEALY; Gen. Man. GLYNE ST HILL.

Eric Hassell and Son Ltd: Carlisle House, Hincks St, Bridgetown; tel. 436-6102; fax 429-3416; e-mail info@erichassellandson.com; internet www.erichassellandson.com; f. 1969; represents Seaboard Marine; Man. Dir ERICA LUKE; Operations Man. MITCHELL FORDE.

Sea Freight Agencies and Stevedoring Ltd: Atlantis Bldg, Shallow Draught, Bridgetown Port, Bridgetown; tel. 429-9688; fax 429-5107; e-mail operations@seafrt.com; internet www.seafrt.com; f. 2011; ship agent and stevedoring contractor; represents the Geest Line and Clipper Inter-American Line; Man. Dir ROVEL MORRIS; Man. (Operations) GLADSTONE WHARTON.

Seaboard International Shipping Company Ltd, Barbados: St James House, Second St, St James; tel. 432-4000; fax 432-4004; e-mail melb@seaboardintl.com; internet www.seaboardintl.com; f. 1936; parent co in Vancouver (Canada); Rep. MEL BJORNDAL.

Tropical Shipping: Goddards Shipping & Tours Ltd, Goddards Complex, Fontabelle Rd, POB 1283, St Michael; tel. 426-9918; fax 426-7322; e-mail gst_shipagent@goddent.com; internet www.tropical.com; Pres. MIKE PELLICCI; Gen. Man. ROVEL MORRIS.

CIVIL AVIATION

The principal airport is Grantley Adams International Airport, at Seawell, 18 km (11 miles) from Bridgetown and with a runway over 11,000 feet long. Barbados is served by a number of regional and international airlines, including Air Jamaica, LIAT Airlines (see Antigua and Barbuda), Air Canada and British Airways.

Barbados Civil Aviation Department: Grantley Adams Industrial Park, Bldg 4, Christ Church BB17089; tel. 428-0930; fax 428-2539; e-mail civilav@sunbeach.net; internet www.bcad.gov.bb; Dir MITCHINSON H. BECKLES.

Tourism

The natural attractions of the island consist chiefly of the warm climate and varied scenery. In addition, there are many facilities for outdoor sports of all kinds. In 2013 the number of stop-over tourist arrivals was an estimated 508,500, while the number of visiting cruise ship passengers was an estimated 570,300. Tourism receipts (excluding passenger transport) totalled a provisional US $912m. in 2013. In 2012 the Inter-American Development Bank confirmed a US $55m. loan for the construction of an eco-friendly Four Seasons hotel.

Barbados Hotel and Tourism Association (BHTA): Fourth Ave, Belleville, St Michael; tel. 426-5041; fax 429-2845; e-mail info@bhta.org; internet www.bhta.org; f. 1952 as the Barbados Hotel Asscn; adopted present name in 1994; non-profit trade asscn; Pres. SUNIL CHATRANI.

Barbados Tourism Marketing Inc: Harbour Rd, POB 242, Bridgetown; tel. 427-2623; fax 426-4080; e-mail btainfo@visitbarbados.org; internet www.visitbarbados.org; f. 1993 as Barbados Tourism Authority to replace Barbados Board of Tourism; restructured in 2014 under present name and the Barbados Tourism Product Authority; CEO WILLIAM GRIFFITH.

Defence

The Barbados Defence Force is divided into regular defence units and a coastguard service with armed patrol boats. The total strength of the armed forces, as assessed at November 2013, was an estimated 610, comprising an army of 500 members and a navy (coastguard) of 110. There was also a reserve force of 430 members.

Defence Budget: an estimated Bds $66m. in 2013.

Chief of Staff: Col ALVIN QUINTYNE.

Education

Education is compulsory for 12 years, between five and 16 years of age. Primary education begins at the age of five and lasts for seven years. Secondary education, beginning at 12 years of age, lasts for six years. In 2010/11 22,509 pupils were enrolled at primary schools, while there were 19,696 pupils at secondary schools. Tuition at all government schools is free. There were 12,421 students in higher education in 2010/11. Degree courses are offered at the Cave Hill campus of the University of the West Indies. A two-year clinical-training programme for medical students is conducted by the School of Clinic Medicine and Research of the University, while an in-service training programme for teachers is provided by the School of Education. Approved government expenditure on education for 2012/13 was Bds $509.0m.

Bibliography

For works on the Caribbean generally, see Select Bibliography (Books)

Beckles, H. *A History of Barbados: From Amerindian Settlement to Caribbean Single Market*, 2nd edn. Cambridge, Cambridge University Press, 2007.

Broberg, M. *Barbados*. New York, Chelsea House Publications, 1998.

Carmichael, T. A. *Barbados: Thirty Years of Independence*. Kingston, Ian Randle Publrs, 1996.

Drummond, I., and Marsden, T. *The Condition of Sustainability*. London, Routledge, 1999.

Girvan, N. (Ed.). *Poverty, Empowerment and Social Development in the Caribbean*. Bridgetown, Canoe Press, 1997.

Gragg, L. *Englishmen Transplanted: The English Colonization of Barbados 1627-1660*. Oxford, Oxford University Press, 2003.

Henderson, C. *Business in Bim: A Business History of Barbados 1900-2000*. Kingston, Ian Randle Publrs, 2008.

Jones, C. *Engendering Whiteness: White Women and Colonialism in Barbados and North Carolina, 1627-1865*. Manchester, Manchester University Press, 2007.

Ligon, R. *A True and Exact History of the Island of Barbados*. London, Frank Cass Publrs, 2013.

Menard, R. R. *Sweet Negotiations: Sugar, Slavery, and Plantation Agriculture in Early Barbados*. Charlottesville, VA, University of Virginia Press, 2006.

Schomburg, R. *History of Barbados*. London, Frank Cass Publrs, 1998.

BELIZE

Geography

PHYSICAL FEATURES

Belize is situated on the north-eastern shores of Central America. Mexico lies to the north, beyond a 250-km (155-mile) border, and Guatemala to the west and south, beyond a 266-km border, with Honduras in the south-east, across the Gulf of Honduras. Belize is a Central American, Commonwealth country, which was known as British Honduras until 1973, when it was a dependent territory of the United Kingdom. It became independent only in 1981, the last country on the American mainland to do so, but its history and culture have made it more usually associated with the anglophone West Indian states than with its Spanish-speaking neighbours (it is the only Central American country not to have a Pacific coast). These neighbours also have territorial claims on Belize, with Guatemala going so far as only to recognize the country's independence in September 1991. The Organization of American States (OAS) is currently mediating the disputes over Guatemala's territorial claims and its rights of maritime access to the Caribbean. There are also problems associated with the 2000 agreement on managing disagreements within the 'Lines of Adjacency' (1 km either side of the Belize–Guatemala border), which attempt to limit illegal immigration (by 'squatters') coming into Belize. Honduras claims the Sapodilla Cays. The current total area of Belize covers 22,965 sq km (8,867 sq miles), making it about the size of Wales (United Kingdom) but with a population less than that of Cardiff, the Welsh capital.

The territory of Belize, which includes 160 sq km of inland waters and a maritime littoral of 386 km, is a flat, swampy coastal plain, with low mountains in the south. A new survey of the Maya Mountains recently superseded Victoria Peak, in the south-east, with the nearby peak of Doyle's Delight (1,174 m or 3,853 ft) as the highest point in the country. The low-lying north of the country was once the bed of the sea, and supports scrubby vegetation or dense tropical hardwood forest. Particularly in this area, the landscape is typified by jungles laced with a seasonally navigable river network. Central Belize has sandy soil, supporting savannah grasslands, while to the south the land rises into the lofty Mountain Pine Ridge area and, thence, the Maya Mountains, which continue west into Guatemala. Here rainfall fuels the many streams, such as the Macal (which, with the Mopan, becomes the River Belize). South of the watershed is a more precipitous landscape, with short, fast streams carrying fertile soils and detritus to the coast, which permits not only a flourishing agriculture but also the longer-established tropical rainforest. Belize's shores are guarded by a coral barrier-reef system that is second in size only to the Great Barrier Reef of Australia. This extends the territory of the country to include a number of islands and cays (mangrove cays and island cays) offshore, in the Caribbean Sea. At almost 300 km in length, it is certainly the longest reef in the Americas. Two-fifths of the country, including the marine environment, is protected by parks and reserves.

CLIMATE

The climate is tropical and very hot and humid, despite the prevailing winds off the Caribbean. The country has an annual mean temperature of 79°F (26°C), with maximums seldom above 96°F (36°C) or below 60°F (16°C), even at night. The rainy season is in May–November, with hurricanes likely from June. The coast is prone to flooding, particularly in the south. The dry season is in February–May. Average annual rainfall ranges from 50 ins (1,270 mm) in the north to 170 ins (4,320 mm) in the south. Complications in this pattern have been observed in recent years, noticeably owing to the El Niño phenomenon and the effects of climate change.

POPULATION

The racial balance in Belize has changed since independence, mainly owing to immigration. The growing mixed Maya-Spanish population accounted for 50% of the total in 2010, while the previously dominant, black Creole population accounted for 21%. The autochthonous Amerindians consisted mainly of the Maya (10%), although there were also immigrant, mixed-race Garifuna (5%) peoples. Those of mixed ethnicity totalled 6%, and there were also those of European descent (including German Mennonites), East Indians and Asians. This changing balance of population has not had a discernible effect on the pattern of religious adherence, with Roman Catholics accounting for 40% of the population. Other Christian denominations command the faith of the majority of the remainder of the population (mainly Pentecostalists, Seventh-day Adventists, Anglicans, Mennonites, Baptists and Methodists). English is the official language, but immigration (often originally illegal) from the neighbouring Hispanic countries means that Spanish is now widely spoken. There is also a Creole dialect in use and native speakers of Amerindian tongues such as Maya, Garifuna and Ketchi.

The total population was 339,758 in mid-2014, according to UN estimates, making Belize the smallest country of Central America in terms of population (El Salvador is slightly smaller in extent). The capital since 1972 has been Belmopan, in the centre of the country, although, according to UN estimates, it still had a population of only 14,472 in mid-2011. The old capital on the coast, Belize City, remains the largest urban centre (65,042 at the 2010 census), and San Ignacio near the central western border also has a larger population than the capital. The chief town of the south is Punta Gorda. The country is the least urbanized in Central America, with only about 10% of the population living in urban areas. Belize is divided into six districts.

History

MARK WILSON

Based on an earlier article by CHARLES ARTHUR

INTRODUCTION

The lands on the eastern side of the Central American isthmus that are today known as Belize were once part of the Mayan system of city states, but when the Spanish arrived in the 16th century these had long since collapsed. Spain never achieved uncontested control over the territory or the indigenous Maya, and the first Europeans to establish a permanent presence were British buccaneers and woodcutters who settled in coastal areas near present-day Belize City. The first recorded British settlement was established in 1638. Disease and destructive Spanish colonial policies had decimated the Mayan population, and those who survived lived inland, away from the coast. The country has remained sparsely populated ever since. In 1763 the Treaty of Paris granted British subjects the privilege of wood-cutting along the coast of the Gulf of Honduras, but retained Spanish sovereignty over the territory, and Spanish forces throughout the 18th century attempted to expel the British settlers. Defeat in a series of battles in 1798 fought around the islands and reefs off the coast, known as the battle at St George's Caye, was Spain's last attempt to gain control; in 1802 Spain recognized British sovereignty under the Treaty of Amiens. In 1859 the neighbouring country to the west, Guatemala, signed a treaty recognizing its border with British Honduras on the understanding that a road would be constructed linking Guatemala with the Caribbean coast (the road was not built and, as a result, Guatemala later declared the treaty invalid). 'Bayman' settlers had elected their own magistrates as early as 1738, although these were recognized neither by Spain nor the United Kingdom. A formal Constitution with a legislative assembly was introduced in 1854 to replace the earlier public meeting of settlers, and in 1862 Belize became the colony of British Honduras, although it remained a dependency of Jamaica until 1884.

During the 18th century several thousand African slaves were brought into the territory, many of them via islands in the Caribbean but some direct from Africa, and were put to work felling logwood and later mahogany. By the time slavery was abolished in British colonies in 1833 the population comprised Africans, Mestizos (of mixed Mayan and European descent), indigenous Mayas, and a number of Garifuna (mixed African and Amerindian people originally deported from St Vincent to the Honduran island of Roatán in 1797), as well as a mainly British colonial élite. In the mid-19th century the still-small population was significantly augmented when thousands of Mayan and Mestizo refugees from the Caste War of Yucatán (1847–1901) fled south into British Honduras. Many of them settled in the north of the colony where they established small farms. The appointed Legislative Council, which replaced the Assembly from 1871, included some Creole members from 1892.

Well into the 20th century the social and economic life of the colony revolved around the felling and export of timber, although the industry was depressed for extended periods from the mid-19th century. Extraction of chicle, a naturally occurring by-product of the sapodilla tree, for use in chewing gum was an important activity from the 1880s. Unlike the other Central American countries, a plantation economy was not developed, and with logging requiring relatively few workers, the population remained small. The timber industry came to be dominated by a handful of companies, one of which, the British Honduras Company (renamed the Belize Estate and Produce Company—BEC—in 1875), eventually owned one-half of all the private land in the colony.

The Great Depression of the early 1930s had serious repercussions in British Honduras. Export prices were reduced, imports dropped sharply, and unemployment increased. In 1931 a major hurricane destroyed most of the capital, Belize City, adding to the mounting social and economic problems. During the 1930s workers began to organize to demand better pay, as well as an end to exploitative conditions of employment, and the unemployed to demand jobs. After a wave of strikes and demonstrations in 1934, reforms introduced in 1936 included elections for six of the 13 seats on the Legislative Council, albeit with a very restrictive property limit on the franchise. Further reforms in 1941 and 1943 permitted trade unions, and reduced some of the restrictions on workers' rights. The Second World War revived the timber industry and stimulated work opportunities abroad, but from 1945 widespread unemployment and poverty among the working class, especially in Belize City, galvanized a movement that questioned both the colonial set-up and the dominance of the small number of wealthy land-owners and merchants. The devaluation of the currency on the last day of 1949 (in line with Sterling devaluation three months earlier) resulted in price increases and the immediate worsening of the workers' situation. Protests against devaluation evolved into a campaign against the entire colonial system, and in September 1950 the People's United Party (PUP) formed with the objective of gaining political and economic independence for the people of the colony. The PUP was closely aligned with the General Workers' Union (GWU), and in October 1952 the two called a national strike to protest against worsening economic conditions. After 10 days the Government and the main companies, but not including the BEC, agreed to negotiate with the union for better wages and working conditions. The BEC held out and succeeded in breaking the strike without making any concessions, but the strike was considered a victory and the prestige of the PUP and the GWU were considerably enhanced. The PUP then focused on a campaign to win universal suffrage. Several years of campaigning, during which a number of leading figures were jailed for sedition, culminated in 1954 with a new Constitution allowing all literate citizens over the age of 21 to vote, and in a general election held in the same year the PUP, under the leadership of George Price, won eight of the nine seats in the new Legislative Assembly with 66% of the popular vote.

THE RISE OF THE PUP

There followed a long period of PUP domination of the political scene. In 1961, after a constitutional reform introducing the ministerial system, the party won all 18 seats in an enlarged legislature, and Price was appointed First Minister by the British Governor. Further reforms led to a new Constitution in 1964 that significantly reduced the powers of the British Governor, and set up a Cabinet of Ministers headed by a Premier who would be the leader of the majority party in a bicameral National Assembly, composed of a House of Representatives and a Senate. The reforms effectively granted the colony internal self-government, and in an election in 1965 another PUP landslide victory over the opposition National Independence Party saw Price become Premier. Under Price the decision was taken to move the capital away from Belize City, which was prone to hurricane damage, and over several years a new capital, Belmopan, was built at the exact geographical centre of the country. In January 1972 Belmopan was declared the new capital, although Belize City remains the nation's largest city and port. In June 1973 the colony was officially renamed Belize. In September the three main opposition parties—liberals and social democrats concerned about the PUP's apparent progression to one-party rule—merged to form the United Democratic Party (UDP). In the general election of 1974 the UDP won six of the 18 seats in the House of Representatives, and in the following year confirmed its arrival as a major political force by winning control of six of the nine seats on the Belize City Council.

During the 1960s and 1970s the PUP followed a centre-left orientation with a focus on leading the colony to full independence. For over two decades this aim was thwarted because of concerns over the territorial claims of neighbouring Guatemala. In 1945 Guatemala had cited the failure of the British to build a road through the colony to the Caribbean coast as reason to renege on the 1859 treaty, and a new Guatemalan Constitution declared British Honduras to be part of Guatemala. After the colony was granted self-government in 1964 Guatemala renewed its land claim, and threatened to use force if the colony became independent without first settling the claim. Protracted negotiations continued throughout the 1960s but collapsed in 1972, at which point the United Kingdom established a permanent military garrison in the colony to deter any prospect of a Guatemalan invasion. In 1975 Guatemala demanded that Belize give up all the land south of the Monkey River—approximately one-quarter of the colony's territory—as a way of settling the dispute. Faced with this escalation the PUP Government embarked on a new strategy designed to win international support for its independence and for its territorial integrity. A concerted campaign succeeded in winning the advocacy of the Caribbean Community and Common Market (CARICOM) and the Non-aligned Movement. The Central American republics were also gradually won over, and the fall of the Somoza dictatorship in Nicaragua in 1979 deprived Guatemala of its most committed supporter in the region. In 1980 the USA changed its policy of neutrality and voted in favour of a UN resolution calling for the independence of Belize, with all its territory, before the next UN session in 1981.

INDEPENDENCE

In the general election of November 1979 the PUP ran on a platform endorsing independence. The UDP, by contrast, favoured delaying independence until the territorial dispute with Guatemala had been resolved, and pinned its hopes on winning the youth vote, as the suffrage had been extended to those of 18 years of age and over. The election became a referendum on independence, and although the PUP won only 52% of the vote, it carried 13 of the 18 seats in the House of Representatives and thus received a mandate for the preparation of an independence constitution. Following the UN resolution in favour of Belize's independence, the Price administration made a last attempt to reach an agreement with Guatemala. In March 1981 the United Kingdom, Guatemala and Belize signed the Heads of Agreement document outlining proposals for Guatemala to recognize an independent Belize within its existing borders. This depended upon reaching agreement on allowing Guatemala to use certain coastal cays, enjoy free port facilities and the freedom of transit on two roads, as well as a number of other border and national security issues. The proposals were interpreted by some sections of the Belizean population as unacceptable concessions, and trade unionists and students led a strike and a number of violent protests against the agreement, prompting the Government to declare a state of emergency. When Guatemala again withdrew from the negotiations under domestic right-wing pressure, the United Kingdom confirmed it would protect an independent Belize. Independence was declared on 21 September 1981 without any agreement with Guatemala, and with the UDP boycotting the independence ceremony.

In the general election of 1984 the UDP, capitalizing on the popularity of its leader, Manuel Esquivel, won 21 of the 28 seats in the newly enlarged House of Representatives, ending 30 years of PUP domination. The UDP confirmed its strength when it prevailed in the municipal elections in March 1985, winning control of five of the eight municipal councils. The new Government carried out an economic adjustment programme in conjunction with the IMF, including cuts in public expenditure and the provision of incentives to diversify the economy. The reforms, together with favourable changes in the international economy, contributed to a profound economic recovery during the late 1980s. Buoyed by the country's strong economic growth, in late 1989 Esquivel called an election several months sooner than necessary. However, the PUP campaigned strongly on a nationalist platform, criticizing the UDP Government's policy of selling Belizean citizenship (although similar 'economic citizenship' programmes were operated by PUP governments in 1979–84 and after 1998) and accusing it of excessive reliance on foreign investment to the detriment of

Belizeans. The combination of the PUP's effective 'Belizeans First' campaign and the existence of internal divisions within the UDP contributed to a narrow victory for Price's PUP.

Party politics in Belize has continued to be dominated by the PUP and the UDP, with third parties failing to make any lasting impact. There are few ideological differences between the two parties, and neither holds any exclusive appeal for either of Belize's two main ethnic groups—the English-speaking Creoles of black African descent and the Spanish-speaking Mestizos. The electorate has often been more or less evenly divided in its support for the two, and in several elections the difference in the numbers voting for each party has been a matter of just one or two per cent. The close-fought nature of Belize's electoral contests was highlighted in 1993 when the UDP polled 49% of the vote against the PUP's 51%, but returned to power as it had won 16 seats against the PUP's 13 in the 29-seat House of Representatives.

THE DOMESTIC RAMIFICATIONS OF INTERNATIONAL POLITICS

The UDP's second term in office was notable for the continuing repercussions of Guatemala's territorial claim. In 1991 Guatemala had recognized Belize's right to exist, and, as a result, in 1993 the United Kingdom decided there was no longer any need to maintain a permanent military presence in Belize. The progressive reduction in the size of the British military force (from a high of 1,350) had pronounced negative effects on the Belizean economy, and added to economic woes that turned the electorate against the UDP Government. The public was also disenchanted by the renewal of the Guatemalan threat following the UDP's suspension of a non-aggression pact agreed between the two countries under the previous PUP administration. In March 1994 Guatemala renewed its territorial claim.

By 1998 the incumbent UDP was widely perceived as incompetent, especially in terms of managing the economy. In 1996 a government survey had revealed that one-third of the population lived below the poverty line. Accusations of ministerial corruption exacerbated the discontent. Meanwhile, in opposition, the PUP had regrouped under a new leader, Said Musa, who had replaced the veteran George Price in 1996. In the August 1998 election the PUP won a substantial 60% of the vote, taking 26 of the 29 seats. Esquivel lost his seat and immediately resigned as UDP leader, being replaced by Dean Barrow.

The new PUP Government inherited an economy in a precarious state, with unemployment at 14% and a constrictive dependence on exports of sugar, citrus fruits and bananas. Earlier attempts to diversify had seen the development of a financial services sector and a shipping registry system, and the PUP relied on these to attract foreign investment. However, from 1999 the USA and the United Kingdom began to raise serious concerns about the country's offshore banking system.

A particular focus was put on the financial empire established in Belize by the billionaire businessman Michael (from 2000 Lord) Ashcroft in the early 1990s. Ashcroft—who spent much of his childhood in Belize, holds dual Belizean-British nationality, was treasurer of the British Conservative Party in 1998–2001, and has since 2005 been its deputy chairman—was alleged to have made large donations to the PUP when it was in opposition. He benefited also from several pieces of legislation introduced by the new PUP Government; these included a law giving tax-exempt status to companies including Ashcroft's 'offshore' holding company Belize Holdings, and the granting of the exclusive right to the Ashcroft-controlled Belize Bank to set up 'offshore' companies in Belize for US and British citizens.

THE 2003 GENERAL ELECTION

In March 2003 the PUP called an election, and focused its campaign on several years of steady economic growth and its record of increased spending on health, education and housing. The UDP strongly criticized the Government for alleged corruption, but although it succeeded in increasing its share of the vote, it was not enough to stop the PUP from emerging victorious. The PUP won 53% of the vote to the UDP's 46%, giving the PUP 22 seats and the UDP seven. The election result was notable for being the first time that either party had won two consecutive elections since independence.

In terms of domestic politics, the PUP's second term proved disastrous, and there were frequent charges of corruption and poor macroeconomic management from the opposition UDP, business organizations and international observers, as the expansionary fiscal policies, rapidly rising debt and widespread mismanagement of the PUP's first term had destroyed public trust while necessitating unpopular austerity measures. In January 2005 civil unrest broke out in Belmopan, provoked by the release of a new national budget that instituted significant tax increases. On 21 January a large demonstration at the National Assembly called by the National Trade Union Congress of Belize (NTUCB) and the Belize Chamber of Commerce ended in violent clashes between protesters and riot police. The following day the Belize National Teachers' Union added to the pressure on the Government by launching a strike that left the majority of schools closed. A planned general strike was averted when the Government negotiated a deal with the NTUCB that included salary increases for its members and a suspension of the budget's tax increases pending a review. The Government then reneged on the deal, and in mid-March, as government machinations regarding the ownership of the privatized telecommunications monopoly Belize Telecommunications Ltd continued, the Belize Communication Workers' Union began protests to demand renationalization, including a work stoppage that cut off telephone lines across the country and international connections. Anti-Government protests culminated in a riot in Belize City on 20 April, in which one person was killed and many injured. After the Government turned to the IMF to negotiate adjustments in debt payments, and agreed to renationalize the water service, the protests subsided. In local elections in March 2006 the full strength of the opposition was demonstrated when the UDP swept to power in all nine city and municipal councils, taking 64 of the 67 seats and 60% of the popular vote. The Government continued to be dogged by financial problems, and it was forced to default on debt payments in December, and to renegotiate the country's external debt in early 2007 with international creditors.

The opposition repeatedly aired accusations of corruption, and in 2006 Musa was forced to appoint commissions to investigate the Social Security Board (SSB) and the Development Finance Corporation (DFC). The SSB investigation resulted in resignations and dismissals of key personnel, while the report into the DFC found that it had authorized the use of millions of dollars in public, domestic, and international loan funds inappropriately to assist the business interests of certain citizens. Further problems arose over the Government's handling of the health sector, and in particular the decision to guarantee the debts of a private health company, Universal Health Services. In May 2007 the issue of the loan guarantee split the Government, and Prime Minister Musa dismissed three ministers who opposed it, in a further twist to the factional fights that had led to 10 cabinet reorganizations since October 2001. Further anti-Government protests only subsided once Musa announced that the company's debt of US $16m. could be serviced without the need for 'tax-payer involvement'. (The issue was to return to haunt the PUP when, following the February 2008 election, it was revealed that some $10m. donated to the Government by Venezuela for public housing had been used to pay the debt guarantee and ended up with Ashcroft's Belize Bank.)

THE UDP IN POWER

The 2008 election produced a clear victory for the UDP. The party had repeatedly accused the Musa administration of corruption and mismanagement, and it made these charges the focus of its campaign, while the PUP used US $10m. in Venezuelan funds to make cash payments to voters. Discontent with the PUP's role in a series of financial scandals contributed to a 7 February election result in which the UDP won 57% of the vote to the PUP's 41%, giving the UDP 25 seats and the PUP six. UDP leader Dean Barrow became the first black Prime Minister of Belize. Musa stood down as PUP leader following

the defeat, and Johnny Briceño, from the reformist wing of the party, was named as his successor; however, deep splits within the party persisted, with a team of five deputy leaders needed to preserve a balance between the rival factions. Barrow vowed to investigate missing public funds and other aspects of alleged government corruption. One of his first actions was to appoint a team to investigate what had happened to the $10m. that the country had received from Venezuela for public housing under the previous administration.

Hampered by severe financial difficulties, the new Government was also enmeshed in a series of complex court cases with locally prominent companies, some of them linked to Lord Ashcroft, described by the premier in his 2009 budget presentation as 'close to acquiring the status of an enemy of the people'. Belize Bank was in 2008 forced to pay the disputed Venezuelan US $10m. donation to the Government, although the rights of the case remained subject to legal dispute. Belize Bank won a favourable ruling in a related dispute over tax exemptions in the London Court of Arbitration; however, the Caribbean Court of Justice ruled in July 2013 that this should not be enforced, as the exemptions were 'repugnant to the established legal order of Belize'. An attempt to charge Musa and former Minister of Housing and Urban Development Ralph Fonseca with theft was defeated after initial court hearings. There was also a complex dispute with the telecommunications company, restructured as Belize Telemedia Ltd (BTL). With the dispute still unresolved, BTL was nationalized by act of parliament in August 2009. In June 2011, however, the Court of Appeal ruled that the state takeover had been unconstitutional. After a confused week in which both the government-appointed Board and the former majority shareholders claimed control, the National Assembly again nationalized the company on 4 July, with legislation that attempted to address the constitutional issues raised by the previous court ruling. There had also been repeated disputes over allowable rates and charges between Canadian-owned Belize Electricity Ltd (BEL) and the Public Utilities Commission (PUC); these too reached a crisis in mid-2011. With the company's revenue adversely affected by a 2008 ruling of the PUC, BEL found itself unable to pay either domestic generators of electricity or Mexico's state utility Comisión Federal de Electricidad, which supplied power through cross-border cables. Asked to provide emergency finance, the Government renationalized the company. To secure the nationalization of Telemedia and BEL against further challenges, in July 2011 the National Assembly approved a constitutional amendment that required public ownership of listed utility providers; the measure came into force in October. In a judgment that was viewed by some observers as rather opaque, the local courts ruled in June 2012 that the reacquisition of BTL in 2011 had not met legal requirements, but that no consequential relief was to be granted to the former shareholders. This judgment was reversed by the Belize Court of Appeal in May 2014, with a final appeal by the former shareholders to be heard by the Caribbean Court of Justice. The Government was largely unsuccessful in its attempts to divest shares to private sector investors, while the payment of BTL dividends to public sector shareholders was blocked in December 2012 by a court order. Legal cases relating to both nationalizations remained before the courts in mid-2014, and the amount of compensation due to the former owners had yet to be settled. A further dispute developed in June 2013, when the Government assumed direct control of the offshore companies registry and the shipping registry, on the basis that a management contract extension issued by the Musa administration in 2005 to Belize International Service Ltd, a company linked to Lord Ashcroft, was invalid. Meanwhile, an affiliate of Lufthansa Consulting, Newco, won a $4.3m. arbitration settlement in 2008, in compensation for the Musa Government's cancellation of an airport management contract; however, Newco was unable to secure enforcement of this ruling through the local courts.

The Government in April 2008 proposed constitutional reforms under which Prime Ministers would be limited to three parliamentary terms in office; public contracts would be open to scrutiny; the state's right to mineral deposits would be strengthened; there would be no requirement to hold a referendum on legislation affecting human rights; and an additional independent senator representing non-governmental organizations (NGOs) would deprive the Government of its upper-house majority. While most of these proposals were approved by the National Assembly in August, they were subject to legal challenges and appeared by mid-2014 to have been abandoned by the Government.

Meanwhile, the Government's continuing electoral strength was apparent in local elections in March 2009, when it again won 64 of the 67 seats; the PUP took only three in the Orange Walk district, Briceño's home base. The UDP's parliamentary strength was reduced to 24 deputies in March 2011, when a parliamentary representative, Marcel Cardona, was held to have resigned from the party with a strenuous attack on government policy during the budget debate.

Johnny Briceño resigned as PUP leader in October 2011. He cited health reasons, but it was thought that his position had become untenable owing to the refusal of the party's wealthiest supporters to contribute funds; the organization was heavily in debt, and reportedly unable to meet regular social security payments. Former Attorney-General Francis Fonseca, an ally of Musa's 'old guard' faction, was designated as the new party leader in November.

Further difficulties for the Government arose from an attempt by the Belize Coalition to Save our Natural Heritage, an environmental group, to call a referendum on its proposal to ban offshore oil drilling. The coalition claimed in December 2011 to have collected 20,160 signatures, exceeding the required 10% of the electorate. Some 8,042 of these were subsequently declared to be invalid, although supporters of the referendum in June 2012 won the right to a judicial review of that declaration. Meanwhile, the group called an unofficial poll in February which attracted 29,235 participants, of whom 96% voted against offshore drilling. In response, Barrow stated that he was now in favour of an official referendum, after an interval of approximately two years.

With the economy suffering from the effects of the protracted international downturn but the PUP still in some disarray, the Government called an election for 7 March 2012, one year before the constitutional deadline. The UDP secured 49.3% of the popular vote, retaining 17 of the 31 seats, but losing eight to the PUP, which increased its representation in the lower house to 14. The Government, therefore, lost its two-thirds' majority, which had allowed it to adopt constitutional amendments without opposition support. In concurrent local elections, the UDP held six of the nine municipalities, including Belize City.

The standing of the Government since 2012 has been further weakened by a number of corruption scandals, many of them relating to passports, citizenship and migration issues. The most serious of these led to the resignation in September 2013 of the junior immigration minister Elvin Penner, over a fraudulent Belizean passport issued with his assistance to a South Korean held in a Taiwanese prison. Procedures were subsequently tightened, but the opposition argued that further legal action should have been taken. An attempt by the PUP to initiate a recall process to force a by-election in Penner's parliamentary seat was unsuccessful.

In June 2009 the Barrow Government announced its intentions to replace the Privy Council (based in the United Kingdom) with the Caribbean Court of Justice as Belize's final court of appeals. Following an amendment to the Constitution, this change came into effect at the beginning of June 2010. In an unusual judgment in June 2011, the Caribbean Court ruled (in a split three-to-two majority verdict by a panel of judges) that the Attorney-General was able to initiate an action in tort against two former PUP government ministers for alleged corruption; this represented a departure from standard common-law jurisprudence, which allowed for the use of criminal prosecution, rather than civil tort procedure.

Successive Belizean administrations have grappled with the seemingly intractable dispute with Guatemala, but without much success. In 1998 a joint commission to address immigration and cross-border traffic was established, and in May 2000 bilateral talks under the aegis of the Organization of American States (OAS) began in Washington, DC, USA. However, continuing tensions on the border undermined the talks. Proposals presented in September 2002 provided for a US $200m. international assistance package; an international border eco-

logical park shared with Honduras; and concessions by Belize and Honduras to allow Guatemala a corridor of territorial sea and a narrow Exclusive Economic Zone in the Caribbean. However, Guatemala rejected the proposals in August 2003 for domestic political reasons.

Although intermittent border incidents have continued, an international 'Group of Friends' continued to press for a resolution, and a bilateral co-operation agreement signed in February 2003 provided for a transition process and confidence-building measures. An Agreement on a Framework for Negotiations was signed, again with guidance from the OAS, in September 2005, providing for a joint Belizean-Guatemalan commission to encourage initiatives in bilateral trade, tourism and resource conservation. This was followed by a partial scope trade agreement, which was concluded, in principle, in June 2006, but remained unratified by Guatemala's legislature until October 2009; as a result, the agreement was not implemented until April 2010. Meanwhile, with no agreed settlement to the bilateral border dispute in sight, the OAS in November 2007 proposed referral to the International Court of Justice for binding arbitration. Both sides agreed to the proposal in December 2008, subject to simultaneous referendums in each country and in April 2012 it was agreed that referendums would be held on 6 October 2013. However, Guatemala announced in March 2013 that it would not hold a referendum on that date, citing concerns over a Belizean law that required a 60% voter participation rate; there had been no further progress on this initiative by mid-2014. Sporadic minor border skirmishes continued to be reported, as did illegal activity by Guatemalan loggers, hunters and farmers in the Chiquibul forest on the Belizean side of the border.

Relations with Mexico and other Central American neighbours remain good, and Belize is the only country to be a member of both the CARICOM group and the Central American Integration System. Although English remains the sole official language, Belize is in practice bilingual and multicultural, with Mestizos comprising 50% of the population, according to the 2010 census, followed by Creoles (21%), Maya Amerindians (10%), Garifuna (5%) and Mennonites from North America (4%). The foreign-born population constituted 15% of the total; of whom more than three-quarters were from Central America or Mexico. The proportion of Roman Catholics was 40%, compared with 50% in 2000, with an increase in Pentecostals (to 9%) and those with no religious affiliation (to 16%).

Another international relations issue has been the use of Belizean territory for the transshipment of illicit drugs. Although Belize had been removed from the USA's list of major drug transit countries in 1999, during the early years of the 21st century there was strong evidence that the country—and its territorial waters and airspace—was being used for the transshipment of cocaine from Colombia to Mexico, and ultimately to the USA, and Belize was again placed on the list in 2011. There is no coastal radar system to track suspicious vessels. The US authorities reported that underdeveloped infrastructure, a lack of resources, and a small population limited local efforts to suppress the cocaine-trafficking, with problems compounded by corruption, failures of political will, poor intelligence-gathering and analysis, problems with the judiciary, and a weak public prosecution staff. Although the extradition process was slow, the USA noted Belize's positive response to requests outside of the extradition framework for the repatriation of criminal fugitives, six of whom were returned to the USA in 2013. Large shipments of other precursor drugs, phenyl acetic acid and ethyl phenyl acetate, were intercepted in 2010 and 2011; with a shipment of six containers of methylamine hydrocholoride—enough to produce 400 tons of meta-amphetamine—declared as 'fertilizer' and intercepted in March 2012. In the first 10 months of 2013 drugs seizures included just 3 kg of cocaine and 4 kg of crystal methamphetamine, but 115 metric tons of marijuana. However, there were no successful major drug prosecutions. Decriminalization of the possession of small quantities of marijuana was under consideration in 2014.

In Belize the drugs problem was regarded as serious, not only due to local consumption, but also because of the involvement of drugs-traffickers in money-laundering, and with the increasingly murderous criminal street gangs, particularly in Belize City; there were 145 murders in 2012, a rate of 46 per 100,000, almost 10 times that of the USA, and, according to UN Office on Drugs and Crime figures, the fourth highest in the world after Honduras, El Salvador and Côte d'Ivoire. The number of murders was brought down to 99 in 2013, in part because of labour-intensive construction projects in Belize City, and the introduction of precinct-based policing. Convictions are rare, as eye witnesses are frequently either killed before a court hearing, or are unwilling to testify. There was some concern locally over the downsizing of the British BATSUB (British Army Training Support Unit Belize) force from a strength of 70 to eight or fewer, announced in December 2010, and the withdrawal of its valued helicopter support. The police anti-drugs unit cannot respond promptly to reports of unauthorized air traffic in remote areas. The USA also lists Belize as a country 'of primary concern' whose offshore financial sector and online casinos, as well as the Corozal Free Zone on the Mexican border, are vulnerable to money-laundering. The financial intelligence unit has a small staff with limited training or experience, and appears subject to political pressure. The USA has appealed for tighter rules on wire transfers, beneficial ownership and customer due diligence. The Caribbean Financial Action Task Force (CFATF) in May 2013 warned Belize that it would face counter-measures, such as enhanced overseas scrutiny of its financial transactions, if it did not strengthen its money-laundering controls by November. Last minute legislation approved by the National Assembly in October was seen as inadequate: evidence of implementation and enforcement was also required, and the CFATF called on its members to consider counter-measures to protect their financial systems from Belizean risks.

Strong US support for anti-trafficking efforts focused on assistance to police counter-narcotics units, the Defence Force, the Belize National Coast Guard, investigative, forensic and prosecutor units, the Financial Intelligence Unit, and the Mobile Interdiction Team for border security. Belize was the only English-speaking Caribbean country to have ratified a Caribbean Regional Agreement on Maritime Counter Narcotics with the USA. Concerns existed regarding the effectiveness of the police force, not least because a significant number of officers had been charged with corruption, murder and other serious offences. Training of new and serving police officers was upgraded in 2011, while a controversial Gang Suppression Unit was formed to take draconian action against alleged violent criminal groups. New legislation, adopted in 2010 and 2011, provided for the interception of communications, increased penalties for crimes of violence, the introduction of written witness statements in place of court appearances, and the use of trials by judge without jury for cases involving murder and related offences. In November 2012 the police were granted the power to search without a warrant and to control movement in designated 'crime-ridden areas'.

Economy

MARK WILSON

Based on an earlier article by CHARLES ARTHUR

INTRODUCTION

During the colonial period the economy was based on the export of a series of commodities: logwood in the 17th and 18th centuries, mahogany in the 19th century, and then sugar from the middle of the 20th century. In the second half of the 20th century there was some diversification of the economy. Non-traditional exports—principally citrus products, bananas and papaya—flourished, a single export garment factory was established, and tourism began to develop. In the 1990s the country's offshore financial services and fishing sectors were also successful. At the end of the 20th century the economy was expanding rapidly, although it remained vulnerable to the impact of hurricanes and changes in the terms of trade for its main exports, and to macroeconomic difficulties resulting from a rapid increase in government debt and serious mismanagement of state institutions. Expansionary fiscal policies produced a spurt in gross domestic product (GDP), peaking at 13.0% in 2000, with growth averaging 3.0% in 2003–12. After expanding by 3.8% in 2008, the economy registered just 0.3% in 2009, but demonstrated a recovery from 2010, with growth of 3.1% in that year and 2.1% in 2011, rising to 4.0% in 2012 as the effects of poor weather on commodity and hydroelectricity production in the previous year receded. However, growth slowed to a barely perceptible 0.1% in 2013, with the small oil field approaching depletion and adverse weather affecting agriculture.

According to the 2010 census, the population of Belize totalled 312,698, with an average annual increase of 2.7% since the previous census in 2000; the population in 2013 was estimated at 347,800. The labour force grew in the course of the late 20th century as migrant workers from Central America (some of them fleeing political violence) eased periodic labour shortages. In addition, the influx of a great many immigrants each year, many of whom stay and settle in Belize, has changed the ethnic composition of the population and created a potential source of social tension, with 15% of the total population born outside the country, and Belizeans of Hispanic Mestizo origin now by far the largest ethnic group, comprising 50% of the total. There were approximately 30,000 economically active individuals in 1970, with the number rising to 89,572 in 2000 and to 149,355 in 2013, when the employed labour force totalled 128,134. Nevertheless, the labour force in Belize remains small in relation to those of the neighbouring Central American republics. Unemployment increased to an estimated 14.2% in September 2013. In 2013 remittances from approximately 59,000 emigrants—most living in the USA—totalled US \$72.2m., or 4.5% of GDP. The alleviation of poverty continued to be a major challenge. An official survey conducted in 2009 classed some 43% of the population as poor, up from 33% at the time of the previous survey in 2002.

AGRICULTURE AND FISHING

Agriculture is a mainstay of the economy, accounting for 9.7% of GDP in 2013, with a further 5.7% from fishing. Agriculture and fishing provided 20.7% of employment in 2006 and 49% of exports in 2013, with a further 13% of exports by value from fishing.

Sugar cane is grown mainly by small-scale farmers in northern Belize, with a single sugar factory at Tower Hill operated by Belize Sugar Industries Ltd (BSI), which produced 120,238 metric tons in 2012/13. In 2012/13 production of sugar cane increased by just 0.7%, while in 2013 exports rose by 7.4%, to 105,948 tons, but export earnings from the crop remained virtually unchanged from the previous year, with lower international prices and a depreciation of the euro against the US dollar, to which the local currency is linked. Sugar and molasses accounted for 17.1% of domestic exports in 2013. With the benefits of the European Union (EU)'s import quotas to be removed from 2017, which would result in lower EU import prices for Caribbean sugar, the outlook for the industry was uncertain in view of high costs. The Belize Sugar Cane Farmers' Association (BSCFA) obtained Fairtrade certification in 2008, resulting in additional revenue of US \$60 per metric ton, which was to be spent on development of the industry and social development in the sugar cane belt. The industry has been damaged by industrial disputes; in 2009 violent protests by sugar farmers prevented the use of a 'core sampler' to gauge the quality of cane deliveries and resulted in 12 people being injured and one killed in a confrontation with police. There was also an ongoing dispute between the BSCFA and a breakaway group, the United Cane Farmers' Association, which received official recognition in 2009. The Belcogen co-generation plant, construction of which was completed in 2009, was intended to generate 13.5 MW of electricity from sugar cane waste, of which 9 MW was to be sold to Belize Electricity Ltd (BEL—see Energy and Infrastructure, below); however, the plant severely underperformed in its first season of operation, producing only 1 MW of power, while a dispute over payments for the waste product (bagasse) used to generate electricity (along with heavy rains) caused a damaging two-month delay to the start of the 2013/14 sugar crop. The sugar industry's revolving credit facility with ING Bank was not renewed in September 2010; a bridge loan from the Government and pre-shipment finance from Tate & Lyle provided short-term working capital, and with improved industry performance the ING facility was restored for 2011/12. American Sugar Refining (ASR), the parent company of Tate & Lyle, bought an 81% majority shareholding from the Belize Employees' Holdings Trust for US $62m. in September 2012, investing $100m. to clear the company's debts and modernize the factory. ASR intended to increase cane yields by up to two-thirds, and to improve and expand the sugar factory.

Citrus fruit production—mainly oranges and grapefruit—expanded in the 1980s when foreign demand for citrus concentrate for use in the production of fruit juices soared, and in the 1990s the sector was developed further when new areas were planted with citrus trees. Citrus concentrates accounted for 17.0% of total exports in 2013; nearly all the citrus fruit grown is processed for export. In the late 2000s the Belize Citrus Growers' Association (BCGA) had 1,000 members, mostly in the Stann Creek valley and in central and southern Belize, of whom the 65 largest with more than 40 ha accounted for three-quarters of total production. A Barbados beverage company, Banks Holdings Ltd, acquired a 47% stake in the processing company Citrus Products of Belize Ltd in 2007, following which a major investment programme upgraded processing, packaging and by-product technology. New borrowing resulted in a financial loss for the year to September 2009, with no dividend paid to the BCGA, which led to a bitter dispute between the BCGA and Citrus Products of Belize over board membership and company policy. This dispute appeared to have been resolved in 2014, with the Social Security Board acquiring a 10% shareholding through a debt-equity swap and additional directors working to achieve a boardroom consensus. Production fell by 29% in volume terms in 2013 because of outbreaks of plant disease and adverse weather conditions; these problems were compounded by a decline in international prices.

Bananas are grown mainly by small and medium farms of 40 ha–200 ha in southern Belize, with sales and marketing co-ordinated by the Banana Growers' Association. Bananas accounted for 14.1% of exports in 2013, with most sold to the EU under preferential marketing arrangements under a marketing agreement with Fyffes PLC (Ireland), which was renewed for five years from 2013 with a 10% price increase. However, the degree of protection has been substantially reduced since the 1990s and the remaining tariff advantage was to be reduced further by 2016. Costs were higher than those of Latin American producers, but lower than those of the Caribbean islands, and the future of the industry was uncertain. Production and export volume declined in 2013 because of adverse weather conditions, with overseas sales at 98,820 metric tons.

The other significant export crop is papaya, which is grown mainly by large farms in northern Belize for the US market, and accounted for 3.3% of exports in 2013. Production increased in 2013 with new acreage brought into production. Traditionally, the crops grown for the local market include corn, sorghum, rice and beans.

The fishing sector expanded rapidly in the 1990s when shrimp-farming began in earnest, supplementing more traditional activities such as offshore fishing for lobster and conch, and represented 5.7% of GDP in 2013. The industry recovered from a downturn over the previous few years, when low prices, disease outbreaks and the high cost of intensifying production techniques contributed to a decline in farmed shrimp, while the capture of wild marine shrimp also declined, reflecting the over-exploitation of shrimp fishing grounds in southern Belize and repeated hurricane damage to marine habitats. Fishing and fish-processing employed just over 2,000 people in 2006 (2% of the labour force), with most marine commercial fishers organized in marketing and processing co-operatives. Marine products accounted for 13% of total exports in 2013.

MANUFACTURING AND CONSTRUCTION

The manufacturing sector is small, and accounted for an estimated 10.7% of GDP in 2013 (of which the major component was petroleum extraction, which is grouped statistically with manufacturing). The major activities are the processing of primary products, principally sugar, citrus fruit and shrimp, and food-processing for the domestic market, as well as production of consumer products such as beer (Belikin) and soft drinks. There was until 2008 a single US-owned company, Williamson Industries, producing work-wear for export. This benefited from trade concessions under the Caribbean Basin Initiative, but could not survive increased competition from the People's Republic of China with the end of the Multi-Fibre Arrangement in 2005.

Construction accounted for 3.1% of GDP in 2013. Both private and public sector construction have suffered in recent years from depressed demand, although some aid-financed public sector construction and infrastructure projects have moved forward.

PETROLEUM EXTRACTION

A small firm, Belize Natural Energy Ltd (BNE), struck petroleum in the Spanish Lookout field, some 55 km north-west of the capital, Belmopan, in 2005. This followed 50 years of intermittent exploration by small local and overseas companies. In 2006—the first year of production—the volume of petroleum extracted reached 811,000 barrels, and the boost from oil production added almost 4% to GDP in 2006–07, accounting for most of the overall cumulative GDP growth of 5.9% over the two years. BNE discovered a smaller field at Never Delay in the Cayo District, and this was declared commercial in 2009. Exports rose by 13% to 1.43m. barrels in 2010, but output from the fields fell to 792,339m. barrels in 2013, and was expected to decline to 284,000 barrels in 2019, as reserves of 23m. barrels were depleted. At mid-2013 a number of small oil companies had been granted further exploration and production licences, onshore and offshore, and enjoyed some promising prospects. However, there was opposition to offshore and onshore drilling from influential non-governmental organizations, and from the People's United Party, which had issued most of the offshore licences prior to losing office in 2008. Environmental groups appealed for a national referendum on the issue, and in April 2013 won a court case that resulted in the invalidation of six offshore exploration contracts on the grounds that they did not comply with environmental legislation; legal disputes were still before the courts in 2014. All of Belize's oil is exported, as there is no local refinery. Oil accounted for 22.3% of exports in 2013, with revenues 52% lower than in 2011 as a result of reduced production. The petroleum industry has been an important source of revenue for a cash-poor administration since 2006, but tax mechanisms have been a continuing source of dispute with BNE, which in 2011 lost its licence for further exploration within its existing concession. A windfall tax on oil profits was enacted in 2009, which comes into effect with prices over US $90 per barrel, but proposals for an oil revenue investment fund have not been followed through. Oil export revenue contributed an estimated 4.7% of GDP in 2013.

ENERGY AND INFRASTRUCTURE

Despite the recent petroleum discovery, the lack of any refining capacity means that all fossil fuels are imported; fuels (including cross-border electricity) accounted for 22% of domestic imports in 2013. Belize signed up in 2006 to Venezuela's

Petrocaribe initiative, a deal under which Venezuela supplies oil to Belize (and other Caribbean countries) on preferential terms, with a proportion of purchases financed by low-interest loans, leading not to lower oil prices, but to the possibility of low interest loans for public sector social programmes. Debt to Venezuela amounted to US $36m. at the end of 2012.

Belize Electricity Limited (BEL), the sole electricity distributor, has been state-owned since 2010, but was from 1993 until then 70% owned by a Canadian company, Fortis. Fortis had frequent disputes with the statutory regulator, the Public Utilities Commission (PUC) over rates and charges, which were (and are) the second lowest among the members of the Caribbean Community and Common Market (CARICOM), after those of Trinidad and Tobago. As a result, the company found itself unable to pay its suppliers, and appealed to the Government for assistance. In response, the Government nationalized BEL, a move that it subsequently sought to secure through a constitutional amendment (see below). An associated Fortis company, Belize Electric Company Limited (BECOL), owns three hydroelectric plants on the Macal river, with a total capacity of 51 MW (depending in part on water levels), of which the newest, at Vaca Falls, was commissioned in 2010. Other domestic suppliers include the Belcogen plant, which produces 9 MW in peak season using sugar cane waste, and independent producers Hydro Maya and Belize Aquaculture, with a combined capacity of 13 MW. However, with peak demand at 74 MW in 2009 and rising, BEL buys much of its supply from Mexico's national power company, the Comisión Federal de Electricidad, the proportion of which rises in extended periods of dry weather; electricity purchases accounted for 4.9% of Belize's domestic imports in 2013. In that year electricity and water supply accounted for 5.6% of GDP.

Belize has four major roads, connecting the former capital, Belize City, with the two official crossings on the Belize–Mexico border, and the two with Guatemala, in western and southern Belize. Regular bus services operate to and from all main towns. The main airport, the Philip S. W. Goldson International Airport, is situated 16 km from Belize City. Domestic air services provide connections to all the main towns and to four of the offshore islands. A modern weather radar system, part of the World Meteorological Network, gives early warning of approaching hurricanes. The main port, which is capable of handling containerized shipping, is in Belize City, and is operated by Port of Belize Ltd, which was privatized in 2002, and has difficult relations with the Government. Port of Belize in 2002 acquired the port facility at Commerce Bight in southern Belize, which is not fully in use; following a complex legal dispute, the Government resumed control in August 2013. The port of Big Creek, also in southern Belize, is owned by citrus and banana interests, and is used for fruit, shrimp and oil exports, as well as general cargo.

The monopoly held by Belize Telecommunications Ltd (BTL) ended formally in 2002. The current successor company, Belize Telemedia Ltd, had competition from a mobile start-up company, SpeedNet Ltd, which began operations in 2004, but the two companies now appear to have been in allied ownership, with both reportedly possessing indirect links to the billionaire businessman Lord Ashcroft. BTL's ownership history since privatization has been complex, and subject to a convoluted series of legal disputes, involving at times the PUC, Lord Ashcroft, the Government, and Robert Prosser, an entrepreneur based in the US Virgin Islands. Matters were complicated by large government-guaranteed debts incurred by a failed internet start-up company, Intelco. In 2008–09 BTL was in dispute with the Government over a 2005 'accommodation agreement' negotiated in secret by the former Musa administration, under which BTL claims tax privileges and a 14% guaranteed return on investment; the Government, meanwhile, increased the rate of business taxation on telephone companies from 19% to 24.5% of gross sales revenue in December 2008. With legal proceedings over these and other issues in progress, BTL was nationalized in 2009, leading to further complex disputes including the matter of compensation. The appeal court ruled in June 2011 that the 2009 nationalization had been unconstitutional. After some confusion the National Assembly again nationalized the company in July 2011, with

legislation that addressed the constitutional issues raised by the previous court ruling. In order to secure the nationalization of Telemedia and BEL against further challenges, later in July the National Assembly, with some opposition support, approved a constitutional amendment requiring public ownership of listed utility providers; this measure was finalized after the required 90-day period of consultation. However, an initial 2012 court ruling cast some doubt over the legality of the 2011 nationalization, and a further court order blocked the payment of dividends to the public sector shareholders of BTL. Meanwhile, Telemedia had in 2008 extended its interests to television, acquiring a controlling stake in one of the two national networks, Channel 5 Belize, which was excluded from the 2009 nationalization and therefore remained in the control of companies linked to Lord Ashcroft. According to World Bank statistics, fixed-line penetration was 7.8 per 100 population in 2012, and 53 per 100 for mobile telephones. According to the 2010 census, one-quarter of the population over five years old had used the internet during the previous three months, a figure that rose to 45% for the 15–24 age-group.

TOURISM AND ENVIRONMENT

The tourism industry began to expand substantially in the 1980s, and it has since overtaken agricultural production as the most important source of foreign exchange for the Belizean economy. In 2013 tourism earnings of BZ $650.3m. were equivalent in value to 41% of domestic goods imports, and to 20% of GDP. The number of hotel rooms increased from 3,708 in 1995 to 6,536 in 2008. This success is based on the appeal of a combination of factors: the climate, the second longest barrier reef in the world, numerous islands, excellent fishing and safe waters, extensive undeveloped rainforest areas, and important Mayan ruins. The authorities have encouraged controlled development, aware of the danger of damaging the country's ecological balance, and Belize has developed a reputation for eco-tourism. The number of stop-over visitors rose steadily to 251,422 in 2007, but declined thereafter, falling back to 232,373 in 2009, owing to weak international demand, before recovering to 294,176 in 2013; of total tourist arrivals in 2013, some 62% were from the USA, 9% from Canada, and 11% from Europe. With the opening of a cruise ship facility in Belize City, cruise passenger numbers increased from 48,116 in 2001 to a peak of 851,436 in 2004. However, cruise traffic has since fluctuated as cruise lines again shifted their itineraries, and stood at 677,350 visitors in 2013. As there is no cruise ship berth, passengers must disembark by tender, making the destination less attractive. Plans for new cruise port facilities have been under consideration since 2004. A non-binding outline agreement was reached in July 2013 with Norwegian Cruise Lines to develop Harvest Cay, located offshore from southern Belize; however, this and other proposals remained controversial. In 2013 hotels and restaurants accounted for 4.5% of GDP, and in 2006 they provided just under 14,000 jobs, meaning that tourism retained its position as the country's fourth largest employer.

Belize is one of the world's most biologically diverse nations, with the integrity of its natural resources still very much intact. With only 347,800 people in 2013 inhabiting 22,965 sq km (8,867 sq miles), the population density, at 15.1 per sq km, was the lowest in Central America and one of the lowest in the world. In recent decades, as tourism has emerged as one of the main motors of the economy, the authorities have led efforts to balance development with conservation of the country's natural resources: 46% of the land is under some form of legally protected status, and there is an extensive network of marine conservation areas. The Protected Areas Conservation Trust Act was adopted in 1996, introducing a small conservation fee to be paid by each tourist on departure from the country, and a 20% commission from cruise ship passenger fees. The Trust issues grants for the conservation, preservation, enhancement and management of Belize's natural resources and protected areas. Protecting the country's natural and historical environment will be critical to the sustainability of Belize's tourism industry, and there is concern about both the number of tourists and the recent discovery of petroleum in the Cayo District, which has triggered interest in Belize on the part of other petroleum companies engaged in exploration activities within protected marine and forest areas. There are also concerns that the low-lying coastal zone, offshore islands and barrier reef are vulnerable to rising sea levels and any increase in hurricane activity.

TRADE AND BALANCE OF PAYMENTS

While tourism and other services, as well as remittances, are increasingly important, the economy continues to be characterized by a small productive base, and like any other small country relies heavily on foreign trade. In recent years the cost of imports—particularly fuel—has risen, while there have been continuing imports of capital goods for electricity generation, telecommunications and the oil industry, and traditional domestic exports have faced difficulties, while petroleum exports have declined steeply since 2010. In 2013 the merchandise trade deficit was 16.5% of GDP. Major domestic exports were agricultural products (sugar, bananas, citrus and papayas), fisheries products and oil. Sales of imported goods from free zones, principally at Corozal on the Mexican border, in 2011 brought earnings equivalent to 24% of domestic exports. The merchandise trade deficit was covered in part by net earnings from tourism and other services, and by remittances from overseas Belizeans, with a current account deficit equivalent to 1.8% of GDP in 2013. This was broadly covered by a capital account surplus, with foreign direct investment in oil, real estate, tourism and other sectors, as well as official assistance inflows.

In 2013, according to the Central Bank, the USA was the market for 23% of exports, principally shrimp and marine products, citrus, papaya and oil. The United Kingdom purchased 16% of exports, mainly sugar and bananas, with a further 8% to other European countries. Exports to CARICOM members, including citrus products, accounted for 8%. Exports to Mexico, mainly from the Corozal Free Zone, made up 43%. The USA was also the main source of imports, at 32%, with 14% from Central America and a further 11% from Mexico; China accounted for 11% of direct imports. Only 1% of imports were sourced from the United Kingdom, and 3.5% from mainland Europe.

PUBLIC FINANCES

Belize had extremely high levels of external debt, low reserves, and a high current account deficit, making it vulnerable to external shocks. This resulted from budget deficits running as high as 11.3% of GDP in 2001, and averaging 7.5% in 2002–06, with a high level of public borrowing, some of it on onerous commercial terms, and major unannounced tax concessions and loan guarantees granted to favoured private sector companies. The impact of years of expansionary policies, driven by increased government spending and borrowing, was confirmed when in 2006 the Government announced it would not be able to meet its repayment obligations to external creditors. Efforts to restructure the country's external debt of almost US $1,000m. were completed in 2007. Holders of eligible debt exchanged their claims for a new 22-year 'superbond', with interest initially reduced to 4.25%. However, this would increase to 6.0% from 2010, and to 8.5% from 2012, with twice-yearly principal repayments running for 10 years from 2019 to 2029. Arguing that current debt levels were unsustainable with a projected financing gap of 85% of GDP for 2014, the Government proposed to renegotiate the agreement and in August 2012 suspended interest payments. An agreement, concluded in February 2013, reduced the interest rate to 5% from March, rising to 6.8% from August 2017, with the maturity extended by nine years to 2038 and principal repayments to start from 2019. The Government estimated that it would save $247m. by 2017.

Despite the successful debt-restructuring, the debt burden remained high and was equivalent to 67% of GDP at the end of 2013, according to the Central Bank. External reserves remain modest, but were equivalent to 6.0 months of import cover in 2013, from only 0.8 months in 2005.

From 2007 revenues were enhanced by income from the newly discovered Spanish Lookout oilfield, and under international and domestic pressure the fiscal deficit was reined back to 1.2% of GDP in 2007. Following the election of the United Democratic Party (UDP) Government in 2008, the overall fiscal balance moved to a surplus of 1.5% of GDP, the first positive fiscal balance for 20 years, in spite of an increase in capital spending on externally funded projects. This resulted in part from strong oil revenues. In both 2007 and 2008 the fiscal balance benefited from substantial grants from Venezuela, Taiwan and other sources, which in 2008 were equivalent to 2.0% of GDP, while external interest payments declined as a result of the 2007 debt restructuring. The fiscal balance also benefited in 2008 from the strong stance taken by the Government in relation to disputed tax payments by major private sector companies, which was upheld at this time by the courts but would be subject to reverse in the event of an adverse ruling at final appeal. Despite the improved fiscal balance, the economy suffered in 2008 from a sharp downturn in international tourism, high international commodity prices, severe flood damage, and weak performance by most major export sectors, while grant inflows fell from 3.3% of GDP in 2007 to 1.4% of GDP in 2012. As a result, the fiscal balance deteriorated sharply to a 2.9% deficit in 2009, and the budget for 2010/11 increased value-added tax from 10.0% to 12.5%, and also raised the tax rates on oil and electricity production. The deficit declined to 1.7% of GDP in 2010, 0.8% in both 2011 and 2012, and to 1.1% in 2013, but remained a source of potential concern. In spite of this slight positive trend, the IMF in 2013 argued for further fiscal consolidation, while the Government maintained a firm position against public sector salary increases. The IMF also expressed concern regarding a rise in non-performing loans within the banking system, which in 2011 made up 20% of the total loan portfolio of domestic banks, and 26% for offshore institutions; however, the ratio declined to 11% in 2012. Meanwhile, the Caribbean Financial Action Task Force in November 2013 called for counter-measures, such as enhanced overseas scrutiny of its financial transactions, as the country had not sufficiently strengthened its money-laundering controls, in spite of legislation passed in October.

OUTLOOK

Belize had potential for further development in commercial agriculture and tourism, while petroleum exploration was in progress and had fair prospects of success. Inflation was low, standing at 0.5% in 2013. The continuing move towards transparency and improved public finances was expected to bring positive results, while hydroelectric and co-generation plants would reduce dependence on fossil fuels. However, there were concerns over the erosion and removal of EU trade preferences for sugar and bananas, while more broadly the economy remained vulnerable to fluctuations in the price of its major export commodities, to weakness in international demand for tourism, and to hurricanes. The Government remained in conflict with major local and foreign-owned companies over taxation, compensation for nationalization and other matters, and an adverse court ruling on final appeal would seriously affect public finances; the IMF estimated these contingent liabilities at 17% of GDP, and argued that they should be added to the debt figures. The IMF in 2013 urged the Government to use the reprieve provided by the debt-restructuring to address existing vulnerabilities and emerging risks through robust fiscal consolidation, active debt management, financial sector reform and measures to buttress external sector resilience, complemented by structural reforms to enhance competitiveness and growth.

Statistical Survey

Sources (unless otherwise stated): Statistical Institute of Belize, 1902 Constitution Drive, Belmopan; tel. 822-2207; internet www.statisticsbelize .org.bz; Central Bank of Belize, Gabourel Lane, POB 852, Belize City; tel. 223-6194; fax 223-6226; e-mail cenbank@btl.net; internet www .centralbank.org.bz.

AREA AND POPULATION

Area: 22,965 sq km (8,867 sq miles).

Population: 240,204 at census of 12 May 2000; 312,698 (males 157,935, females 154,763) at census of 12 May 2010. *Mid-2014:* (UN estimate): 339,758 (Source: UN, *World Population Prospects: The 2012 Revision*).

Density (at mid-2014): 14.8 per sq km.

Population by Age and Sex (UN estimates at mid-2014): *0–14 years:* 113,316 (males 57,345, females 55,971); *15–64 years:* 212,789 (males 106,075, females 106,714); *65 years and over:* 13,653 (males 6,250, females 7,403); *Total* 339,758 (males 169,670, females 170,088). Source: UN, *World Population Prospects: The 2012 Revision*.

Districts (population at 2010 census): Belize 89,247; Cayo 72,899; Orange Walk 45,419; Corozal 40,354; Stann Creek 32,166; Toledo 30,538. Note: Figures exclude homeless (118) and institutionalized population (1,957).

Principal Towns (population at 2010 census): Belize City (former capital) 65,042; San Ignacio/Santa Elena 16,977; Orange Walk 13,400; Belmopan (capital) 13,351; San Pedro 11,510; Corozal 9,901; Dangriga (fmrly Stann Creek) 9,096; Benque Viejo 5,824; Punta Gorda 5,205. *Mid-2014* (UN estimate, incl. suburbs): Belmopan 16,921 (Source: UN, *World Urbanization Prospects: The 2014 Revision*).

Births, Marriages and Deaths (2009 unless otherwise indicated): Registered live births 7,126 (birth rate 22.1 per 1,000, 2008); Registered marriages 1,895 (marriage rate 5.7 per 1,000); Registered deaths 1,453 (death rate 4.4 per 1,000).

Life Expectancy (years at birth): 73.7 (males 70.7; females 76.8) in 2012. Source: World Bank, World Development Indicators database.

Economically Active Population (April 2006): Agriculture 18,406; Forestry 733; Fishing 2,070; Mining and quarrying 434; Manufacturing 7,363; Electricity, gas and water 879; Construction 7,390; Wholesale and retail trade and repairs 16,722; Tourism (incl. restaurants and hotels) 13,981; Transport, storage and communications 4,352; Financial intermediation 1,800; Real estate, renting and business activities 2,431; General government services 9,345; Community, social and personal services 16,041; Other 285; *Total employed* 102,233. *Total labour force* (persons aged 14 years and over, September 2009): 144,364 (employed 126,188, unemployed 18,176). *2010 Census:* Total employed 100,537; Unemployed 30,180; Total labour force 130,717 (males 79,760, females 50,957). *September 2013:* Total employed 128,134; Unemployed 21,221; Total labour force 149,355.

HEALTH AND WELFARE

Key Indicators

Total Fertility Rate (children per woman, 2012): 2.7.

Under-5 Mortality Rate (per 1,000 live births, 2012): 18.

HIV/AIDS (% of persons aged 15–49, 2012): 1.4.

Physicians (per 1,000 head, 2009): 0.8.

Hospital Beds (per 1,000 head, 2010): 1.2.

Health Expenditure (2011): US $ per head (PPP): 434.

Health Expenditure (2011): % of GDP: 5.8.

Health Expenditure (2011): public (% of total): 66.5.

Access to Water (% of persons, 2012): 99.

Access to Sanitation (% of persons, 2012): 91.

Total Carbon Dioxide Emissions ('000 metric tons, 2010): 21.7.

Carbon Dioxide Emissions Per Head (metric tons, 2010): 1.4.

Human Development Index (2013): ranking: 84.

Human Development Index (2013): value: 0.732.

For sources and definitions, see explanatory note on p. vi.

AGRICULTURE, ETC.

Principal Crops ('000 metric tons, 2012): Rice, paddy 22.0; Maize 65.0; Sorghum 12.0; Sugar cane 1,070.0; Beans, dry 4.0; Fresh vegetables 4.5; Bananas 76.0; Plantains 12.0; Oranges 190.0; Grapefruit and pomelos 56.0; Papayas 24.0. *Aggregate Production* ('000 metric tons, may include official, semi-official or estimated data): Vegetables (incl. melons) 11.8; Fruits (excl. melons) 362.9.

Livestock ('000 head, year ending September 2012, FAO estimates): Horses 6; Cattle 92; Pigs 17; Sheep 13; Chickens 1,550.

Livestock Products ('000 metric tons, 2012, FAO estimates): Cattle meat 1.6; Chicken meat 14.4; Pig meat 1.4; Cows' milk 5.4; Hen eggs 2.0.

Forestry (2012): *Roundwood Removals* ('000 cubic metres, excl. bark, FAO estimates): Sawlogs, veneer logs and logs for sleepers 41; Fuel wood 126; Total 167. *Sawnwood Production* ('000 cubic metres, incl. railway sleepers, FAO estimates): Coniferous (softwood) 5; Broadleaved (hardwood) 30; Total 35.

Fishing ('000 metric tons, live weight, 2012): Capture 149.8 (Albacore 0.4; Caribbean spiny lobster 0.6; Stromboid conchs 3.6; Yellowfin tuna 6.0); Aquaculture 5.9 (White leg shrimp 5.8); *Total catch* 155.7.

Source: FAO.

INDUSTRY

Production (2005, unless otherwise indicated): Raw sugar 118,339 long tons (2012/13); Molasses 34,508 long tons (2012/13); Cigarettes 78 million; Beer 1,891,000 gallons; Batteries 6,000; Flour 26,959,000 lb; Fertilizers 26,874,000 short tons; Garments 611,900 items; Soft drinks 4,929,000 gallons; Citrus concentrates 2,973,000 gallons (2004); Single strength juices 2,102,000 gallons (2004). Source: mainly IMF, *Belize: Selected Issues and Statistical Appendix* (October 2006).

FINANCE

Currency and Exchange Rates: 100 cents = 1 Belizean dollar (BZ $). *Sterling, US Dollar and Euro Equivalents* (30 May 2014): £1 sterling = BZ $3.364; US $1 = BZ $2.000; €1 = BZ $2.722; BZ $100 = £29.72 = US $50.00 = €36.73. *Exchange rate:* Fixed at US $1 = BZ $2.000 since May 1976.

Budget (BZ $ million, year ending 31 March 2014, provisional): *Revenue:* Taxation 727.0 (Taxes on income and profits 233.8, Taxes on property 7.2, Taxes on goods and services 282.6, International trade and transactions 203.5); Other current revenue 99.3; Capital revenue 5.1; Total 831.4, excl. grants (41.1). *Expenditure:* Current expenditure 777.9 (Personal emoluments 313.2, Pensions 55.2, Goods and services 181.5, Debt service 95.9, Subsidies and current transfers 132.0); Capital expenditure 156.2; Total 934.1.

International Reserves (US $ million at 31 December 2013): IMF special drawing rights 30.83; Reserve position in the IMF 6.53; Foreign exchange 365.40; *Total* 402.75. Source: IMF, *International Financial Statistics.*

Money Supply (BZ $ million at 31 December 2013): Currency outside depository corporations 211.72; Transferable deposits 910.21; Other deposits 1,354.65; *Broad money* 2,476.57. Source: IMF, *International Financial Statistics.*

Cost of Living (Consumer Price Index; base: 2005 = 100): 111.1 in 2011; 115.8 in 2012; 117.2 in 2013. Source: IMF, *International Financial Statistics.*

Expenditure on the Gross Domestic Product (BZ $ million at current prices, 2012, preliminary): Government final consumption expenditure 471.6; Private final consumption expenditure 2,212.8; Gross fixed capital formation 505.7; Change in inventories –1.9; *Gross domestic expenditure* 3,188.1; Exports of goods and services 1,913.5; *Less* Imports of goods and services 1,980.6; Statistical discrepancy 24.2; *GDP at market prices* 3,145.2.

Gross Domestic Product by Economic Activity (BZ $ million at current prices, 2012, preliminary): Agriculture, hunting, forestry and fishing 398.7; Mining and quarrying 15.1; Electricity, gas and water 72.7; Manufacturing 374.9; Construction 87.8; Wholesale and retail trade, repairs 466.0; Hotels and restaurants 137.7; Transport, storage and communications 345.5; Financial intermediation 236.9; Real estate, renting and business activities 195.4; Government services 320.6; Other activities 208.1; *Sub-total* 2,859.5; *Less* Financial intermediation services indirectly measured (FISIM) 121.8; *GDP at factor cost* 2,737.7; Taxes on products, less subsidies 407.5; *GDP at market prices* 3,145.2.

Balance of Payments (US $ million, 2013): Exports of goods 608.6; Imports of goods –875.9; *Balance on goods* –267.3; Exports of services 448.1; Imports of services –207.8; *Balance on goods and ser-*

vices –27.1; Primary income received 6.1; Primary income paid –124.0; *Balance on goods, services and primary income* –145.1; Secondary income (net) 72.9; *Current balance* –72.1; Capital account (net) 37.7; Financial account (net) 134.4; Net errors and omissions 17.3; *Reserves and related items* 117.3 (Source: IMF, *International Financial Statistics*).

EXTERNAL TRADE

Principal Commodities (BZ $ million, 2013): *Imports c.i.f.:* Food and live animals 202.9; Mineral fuels and lubricants 275.8; Chemicals and related products 167.6; Manufactured goods 228.7; Miscellaneous manufactured articles 135.5; Machinery and transport equipment 345.1; Commercial free zone 332.8; Export processing zone 80.6; Total (incl. others) 1,855.6. *Exports f.o.b.:* Citrus concentrate 106.6; Marine products 79.8; Sugar 107.4; Bananas 88.5; Papaya 20.7; Crude petroleum 140.2; Total (incl. others) 627.6.

Principal Trading Partners (BZ $ million, 2013): *Imports c.i.f.:* China, People's Republic 211.4; Costa Rica 27.4; Jamaica 19.1; Mexico 211.9; Panama 51.7; Trinidad and Tobago 30.4; United Kingdom 21.2; USA 597.3; Total (incl. others) 1,855.6. *Exports f.o.b.:* Guyana 13.4; Ireland 26.4; Jamaica 33.7; Japan 7.5; Mexico 15.4; Netherlands 45.8; Puerto Rico 6.8; Spain 6.3; Trinidad and Tobago 32.1; United Kingdom 169.7; USA 245.3; Total (incl. others) 627.6.

TRANSPORT

Road Traffic (vehicles in use, 2007): Public vehicles 3,612 (Buses 769, Taxis 2,843); Passenger cars 14,156; Motorcycles 2,389; Pick-up vehicles 15,181; Goods vehicles 4,757; Total vehicles (incl. others) 56,094.

Shipping: *Flag Registered Fleet* (at 31 December 2013): Number of vessels 1,038; Total displacement 2,372,268 grt. Source: Lloyd's List Intelligence (www.lloydslistintelligence.com).

Civil Aviation (traffic at Philip Goldson International Airport, 2011): Aircraft movement 27,135; Passengers carried 464,732 (Passenger arrivals 244,006, Passenger departures 220,726) Freight carried 1,006 metric tons.

TOURISM

Tourist Arrivals: 914,797 (cruise ship passengers 688,165, stopover visitors 226,632) in 2010; 888,047 (cruise ship passengers 654,790, stop-over visitors 233,257) in 2011; 833,952 (cruise ship passengers 576,661, stop-over visitors 257,291) in 2012.

Stop-over Visitors by Country of Origin (2012): Guatemala 958; Mexico 5,048; USA 175,957; Total (incl. others) 257,291.

Tourism Receipts (US $ million, excl. passenger transport): 247 in 2011; 298 in 2012; 351 in 2013 (provisional). Source: World Tourism Organization.

COMMUNICATIONS MEDIA

Telephones (2013): 24,000 main lines in use.

Mobile Cellular Telephones (2013): 175,700 subscribers.

Internet Subscribers (2010): 9,400.

Broadband Subscribers (2013): 10,400.

Source: International Telecommunication Union.

EDUCATION

Pre-primary (2012/13): 213 schools, 435 teachers, 7,400 students (males 3,764, females 3,636).

Primary (2012/13): 294 schools, 3,299 teachers, 68,812 students (males 35,287, females 33,525).

Secondary (2012/13): 52 schools, 1,420 teachers, 20,539 students (males 9,897, females 10,642).

Higher (2012/13 unless otherwise indicated): 12 institutions (1997/98), 242 teachers, 4,652 students (all females).

Vocational/Technical (2012/13): 77 teachers, 719 students (males 542, females 177).

Pupil-teacher Ratio (primary education, UNESCO estimate): 21.6 in 2011/12.

Source: Ministry of Education, Youth and Sports; UNESCO Institute for Statistics.

Adult Literacy Rate (UNESCO estimates): 76.9% (males 77.1%; females 76.7%) in 2003. Source: UN Development Programme, *Human Development Report*.

Directory

The Constitution

The Constitution came into effect at the independence of Belize on 21 September 1981. Its main provisions are summarized below:

FUNDAMENTAL RIGHTS AND FREEDOMS

Regardless of race, place of origin, political opinions, colour, creed or sex, but subject to respect for the rights and freedoms of others and for the public interest, every person in Belize is entitled to the rights of life, liberty, security of the person, and the protection of the law. Freedom of movement, of conscience, of expression, of assembly and of association, and the right to work are guaranteed, and the inviolability of family life, personal privacy, home and other property, and human dignity is upheld. Protection is afforded from discrimination on the grounds of race, sex, etc., and from slavery, forced labour and inhuman treatment.

CITIZENSHIP

All persons born in Belize before independence who, immediately prior to independence, were citizens of the United Kingdom and Colonies automatically become citizens of Belize. All persons born outside the country having a husband, parent or grandparent in possession of Belizean citizenship automatically acquire citizenship, as do those born in the country after independence. Provision is made such that persons who do not automatically become citizens of Belize may be registered as such.

THE GOVERNOR-GENERAL

The British monarch, as Head of State, is represented in Belize by a Governor-General, a Belizean national.

Belize Advisory Council

The Council consists of not less than six people 'of integrity and high national standing', appointed by the Governor-General for up to 10 years upon the advice of the Prime Minister. The Leader of the Opposition must concur with the appointment of two members and be consulted about the remainder. The Council exists to advise the Governor-General, particularly in the exercise of the prerogative of mercy, and to convene as a tribunal to consider the removal from office of certain senior public servants and judges.

THE EXECUTIVE

Executive authority is vested in the British monarch and exercised by the Governor-General. The Governor-General appoints as Prime Minister that member of the House of Representatives who, in the Governor-General's view, is best able to command the support of the majority of the members of the House, and appoints a Deputy Prime Minister and other Ministers on the advice of the Prime Minister. The Governor-General may remove the Prime Minister from office if a resolution of no confidence is approved by the House and the Prime Minister does not, within seven days, either resign or advise the Governor-General to dissolve the National Assembly. The Cabinet consists of the Prime Minister and other Ministers.

The Leader of the Opposition is appointed by the Governor-General as that member of the House who, in the Governor-General's view, is best able to command the support of a majority of the members of the House who do not support the Government.

THE LEGISLATURE

The Legislature consists of a National Assembly comprising two chambers: the Senate, with 12 nominated members; and the House of Representatives, with 31 elected members. The Assembly's normal term is five years. Senators are appointed by the Governor-General: six on the advice of the Prime Minister; three on the advice of the Leader of the Opposition or on the advice of persons selected by the Governor-General; and one each on the advice of the Belize Council of Churches together with the Evangelical Association of Churches, the Belize Chamber of Commerce and Industry and the Belize Better Business Bureau, and the National Trade Union Congress in agreement with the Civil Society Steering Committee. If any person who is not a Senator is elected to be President of the Senate, he or she shall be an ex-officio Senator in addition to the 12 nominees.

Each constituency returns one Representative to the House, who is directly elected in accordance with the Constitution.

If a person who is not a member of the House is elected to be Speaker of the House, he or she shall be an ex-officio member in addition to the 31 members directly elected. Every citizen older than 18 years is eligible to vote. The National Assembly may alter any of the provisions of the Constitution.

The Government

HEAD OF STATE

Queen: HM Queen ELIZABETH II.

Governor-General: Sir COLVILLE YOUNG (appointed 17 November 1993).

THE CABINET
(September 2014)

The Government is formed by the United Democratic Party.

Prime Minister and Minister of Finance and Economic Development: DEAN O. BARROW.

Deputy Prime Minister and Minister of Natural Resources and of Agriculture: GASPAR VEGA.

Attorney-General and Minister of Foreign Affairs: WILFRED ELRINGTON.

Minister of Trade, Investment Promotion, Private Sector Development and Consumer Protection: ERWIN CONTRERAS.

Minister of Education, Youth and Sports: PATRICK FABER.

Minister of National Security: JOHN SALDIVAR.

Minister of Housing and Urban Development: MICHAEL FINNEGAN.

Minister of Works and Transport: RENE MONTERO.

Minister of Tourism and Culture: MANUEL HEREDIA, Jr.

Minister of Health: PABLO MARIN.

Minister of Labour, Local Government, Rural Development and National Emergency Management: GODWIN HULSE.

Minister of the Public Service and Elections and Boundaries: CHARLES GIBSON.

Minister of Forestry, Fisheries and Sustainable Development: LISELLE ALAMILLA.

Minister of Human Development, Social Transformation and Poverty Alleviation: ANTHONY MARTINEZ.

Minister of Energy, Science and Technology and Public Utilities: JOY GRANT.

There are, in addition, six Ministers of State.

MINISTRIES

Office of the Prime Minister: Sir Edney Cain Bldg, 3rd Floor, Left Wing, Belmopan; tel. 822-2346; fax 822-0898; e-mail secretarypm@opm.gov.bz; internet www.opm.gov.bz.

Ministry of Agriculture: West Block Bldg, 2nd Floor, Belmopan; tel. 822-2241; fax 822-2409; e-mail info@agriculture.gov.bz; internet www.agriculture.gov.bz.

Ministry of Education, Youth and Sports: West Block Bldg, 3rd Floor, Belmopan; tel. 822-2380; fax 822-3389; e-mail moeducation.moes@gmail.com; internet www.moes.gov.bz.

Ministry of Energy, Science and Technology and Public Utilities: Market Sq., Cayo District, Belmopan; tel. 822-0160; fax 822-0433; e-mail minister.sec@mysc.gov.bz; internet estpu.gov.bz.

Ministry of Finance and Economic Development: New Administration Bldg, Belmopan; tel. 822-2362; fax 822-2886; e-mail econdev@btl.net; internet www.mof.gov.bz.

Ministry of Foreign Affairs: NEMO Bldg, 2nd Floor, POB 174, Belmopan; tel. 822-2167; fax 822-2854; e-mail belizemfa@btl.net; internet www.mfa.gov.bz.

Ministry of Forestry, Fisheries and Sustainable Development: Sir Edney Cain Bldg, Ground Floor, Left Wing, Belmopan; tel. 822-2526; fax 822-3673; internet www.forestdepartment.gov.bz (Forestry), www.agriculture.gov.bz/Fisheries_Dept.html (Fisheries), www.doe.gov.bz (Environment).

Ministry of Health: East Block Bldg, Independence Plaza, Belmopan; tel. 822-2068; fax 822-2942; e-mail seniorsecretary@health.gov.bz; internet health.gov.bz/moh.

Ministry of Housing and Urban Development: Sir Edney Cain Bldg, 2nd Floor, Left Wing, Belmopan; tel. 822-1039; fax 822-3337; e-mail ministry@housing.gov.bz.

Ministry of Human Development, Social Transformation and Poverty Alleviation: West Block Bldg, Independence Plaza, Belmopan; tel. 822-2161; fax 822-3175; e-mail secretary@humandev.gov.bz.

Ministry of Labour, Local Government, Rural Development and National Emergency Management: 6/8 Trinity Blvd, Belmopan; tel. 822-2297; fax 822-0156; e-mail labour.comm@labour.gov.bz.

Ministry of National Security: Curl Thompson Bldg, Belmopan; tel. 822-2817; fax 822-2195; e-mail minofnatsec@mns.gov.bz.

Ministry of Natural Resources: Market Sq., Belmopan; tel. 822-3286; fax 822-2333; e-mail minister@mnrei.gov.bz; internet www.mnrei.gov.bz.

Ministry of the Public Service and Elections and Boundaries: Sir Edney Cain Bldg, Ground Floor, Left Wing, Belmopan; tel. 822-0929; fax 822-2206; e-mail ceo@mps.gov.bz; internet www.gob.gov.bz.

Ministry of Tourism and Culture: 106 South St, Belize City; tel. 227-2801; fax 227-2810; e-mail dcabelize@btl.net; internet www.belizetourism.org (Tourism); www.nichbelize.org (Culture).

Ministry of Trade, Investment Promotion, Private Sector Development and Consumer Protection: Sir Edney Cain Bldg, Ground Floor, Left Wing, Belmopan; tel. 822-2526; fax 822-3673; e-mail foreigntrade@btl.net.

Ministry of Works and Transport: New 2 Power Lane, Belmopan; tel. 822-2136; fax 822-3282; e-mail works@btl.net, departmentoftransport@yahoo.com.

Office of the Attorney-General: General Office, Belmopan; tel. 822-2504; fax 822-3390; e-mail agministrybze@yahoo.com.

Legislature

NATIONAL ASSEMBLY

The Senate

President: MARCO PECH.

There are 12 nominated members in addition to the current ex officio President.

House of Representatives

Speaker: MICHAEL PEYREFITTE.

Clerk: EDDIE WEBSTER.

General Election, 7 March 2012

	Valid votes cast	% of total	Seats
United Democratic Party (UDP)	61,903	49.33	17
People's United Party (PUP) .	61,556	49.05	14
Others	2,032	1.62	—
Total valid votes* . . .	125,491	100.00	31

* In addition, there were 4,767 blank, invalid or spoiled votes cast.

Election Commissions

Elections and Boundaries Commission: Belize City; internet www.elections.gov.bz; f. 1978; appointed by Governor-Gen; comprises Chair. and 4 mems; separate entity to the Elections and Boundaries Dept; Chair. BERNARD PITTS.

Elections and Boundaries Department: Charles Bartlett Hyde Bldg, Mahogany St Extension, POB 913, Belize City; tel. 222-4042; fax 222-4991; e-mail electbound@btl.net; internet www.elections.gov.bz; f. 1989; dept under the Ministry of the Public Service and Elections and Boundaries; Chief Elections Officer JOSEPHINE TAMAI.

Political Organizations

People's National Party (PNP): 57 Main St, Punta Gorda Town, Toledo Dist; tel. 610-0978; fax 225-2571; e-mail info@pnpbelize.org; internet www.pnpbelize.org; f. 2007; Leader WIL MAHEIA.

People's United Party (PUP): 3 Queen St, Belize City; tel. 677-9169; fax 223-3476; internet www.pup.org.bz; f. 1950; based on organized labour; publs *The Belize Times*; Leader FRANCIS WILLIAM FONSECA; Chair. HENRY USHER; Sec.-Gen. MYRTLE PALACIO.

United Democratic Party (UDP): South End Bel-China Bridge, POB 1898, Belize City; tel. 227-2576; fax 227-6441; e-mail unitedd@ btl.net; internet www.udp.org.bz; f. 1974 by merger of People's Development Movement, Liberal Party and National Independence Party; conservative; Leader DEAN BARROW; Chair. ALBERTO AUGUST.

Vision Inspired by the People (VIP): VIP Secretariat, Unit 2, Garden City Hotel, Belmopan, Belize City; e-mail vipbelize@gmail .com; f. 2005; Chair. ROBERT (BOBBY) LOPEZ.

Diplomatic Representation

EMBASSIES AND HIGH COMMISSION IN BELIZE

Brazil: 12 Floral Park Ave, POB 548, Belmopan; tel. 822-0460; fax 822-0461; e-mail brasemb.belmopan@itamaraty.gov.br; internet belmopan.itamaraty.gov.br; Ambassador LUCIO PIRES DE AMORIM.

Costa Rica: 1 Marigold St, Orchid Garden Extension, POB 288, Belmopan; tel. 822-1582; fax 822-1583; e-mail embaticabz@gmail .com; Ambassador INGRID HERMANN ESCRIBANO.

Cuba: 6087 Manatee Dr., Buttonwood Bay, POB 1775, Belize City; tel. 223-5345; fax 223-1105; e-mail embacuba@btl.net; internet www .cubadiplomatica.cu/belice; Ambassador JOSÉ PRIETO CINTADO.

El Salvador: 13 Citron St, Cohune Walk, POB 215, Belmopan; tel. 823-3404; fax 823-3569; e-mail embasalva@btl.net; Ambassador ROLANDO ROBERTO BRIZUELA RAMOS.

Guatemala: 8 A St, King's Park, POB 1771, Belize City; tel. 223-3150; fax 223-5140; e-mail embbelice@minex.gob.gt; Ambassador MANUEL ARTURO TÉLLEZ MIRALDA.

Honduras: 2½ Miles, Northern Hwy, POB 285, Belize City; tel. 224-5889; fax 223-0562; e-mail embahonbe@yahoo.com; Ambassador SANDRA ROSALES ABELLA.

Mexico: 3 North Ring Rd, Embassy Sq., Belmopan; tel. 822-2480; fax 822-2487; e-mail embamexbze@btl.net; internet www.sre.gob.mx/ belice; Ambassador MARIO VELÁZQUEZ SUAREZ.

Nicaragua: 1 South St, Belize City; tel. and fax 227-0335; e-mail belkysgrl@yahoo.com; Ambassador GILDA MARIA BOLT GONZÁLEZ (resident in El Salvador).

Taiwan (Republic of China): 20 North Park St, POB 1020, Belize City; tel. 227-8744; fax 223-3082; e-mail embroc@btl.net; internet www.taiwanembassy.org/bz; Ambassador BENJAMIN HO.

United Kingdom: Embassy Sq., POB 91, Belmopan; tel. 822-2146; fax 822-2761; e-mail brithicom@btl.net; internet ukinbelize.fco.gov .uk; High Commissioner PETER HUGHES.

USA: Floral Park Rd, POB 286, Belmopan; tel. 822-4011; fax 822-4012; e-mail embbelize@state.gov; internet belize.usembassy.gov; Ambassador CARLOS ROBERTO MORENO.

Venezuela: 17 Orchid Garden St, POB 49, Belmopan; tel. 822-2384; fax 822-2022; e-mail embaven@btl.net; Ambassador YOEL DEL VALLE PÉREZ MARCANO.

Judicial System

Summary Jurisdiction Courts (criminal jurisdiction) and District Courts (civil jurisdiction), presided over by magistrates, are established in each of the six judicial districts. Summary Jurisdiction Courts have a wide jurisdiction in summary offences and a limited jurisdiction in indictable matters. Appeals lie to the Supreme Court, which has jurisdiction corresponding to the English High Court of Justice. From the Supreme Court further appeals lie to a Court of Appeal. Since June 2010 final appeals are made to the Caribbean Court of Justice, based in Trinidad and Tobago, rather than to the Privy Council in the United Kingdom.

Court of Appeal: Belize City; tel. 227-3490; internet www .belizejudiciary.org/web/court-of-appeal-2/; f. 1967; Pres. MANUEL SOSA.

Supreme Court: Supreme Court Bldg, Belize City; tel. 227-7377; fax 227-0181; e-mail info@belizejudiciary.org; internet www .belizejudiciary.org; Chief Justice KENNETH BENJAMIN; Registrar VELDA FLOWERS.

Magistrates' Court: Paslow Bldg, Belize City; tel. 227-7164; fax 227-6268; e-mail magistratecourtbz@gmail.com; internet www .belizejudiciary.org/web/magistracy; Chief Magistrate ANN MARIE SMITH.

Attorney-General: WILFRED ELRINGTON.

Religion

CHRISTIANITY

Most of the population are Christian, the largest denomination being the Roman Catholic Church.

Belize Council of Churches: 149 Allenby St, POB 508, Belize City; tel. 227-7077; f. 1957 as Church World Service Cttee; present name adopted 1984; 9 mem. churches, 4 assoc. bodies; Pres. Rev. ROOSE-VELT PAPOULOUTE; Sec. KAREN TAYLOR.

The Roman Catholic Church

According to the 2010 census, 40.4% of the population are Roman Catholics. Belize comprises the single diocese of Belize City-Belmopan, suffragan to the archdiocese of Kingston in Jamaica. The Bishop participates in the Antilles Episcopal Conference (whose secretariat is based in Port of Spain, Trinidad and Tobago).

Bishop of Belize City-Belmopan: DORICK MCGOWAN WRIGHT, Bishop's House, 144 North Front St, POB 616, Belize City; tel. 223-6919; fax 223-1922; e-mail info@catholic.bz; internet catholic.bz.

The Anglican Communion

Anglicans in Belize, accounting for some 4.6% of the population at the 2010 census, belong to the Church in the Province of the West Indies, comprising eight dioceses. The Archbishop of the Province currently is the Bishop of Barbados.

Bishop of Belize: Rt Rev. PHILIP S. WRIGHT, Rectory Lane, POB 535, Belize City; tel. 227-3029; fax 227-6898; e-mail diocese@ belizeanglican.org; internet www.belize.anglican.org.

Protestant Churches

According to the 2010 census, some 8.5% of the population are Pentecostalists, 5.5% Seventh-day Adventists, 3.8% Mennonites, 3.6% Baptists and 2.9% Methodists.

Mennonite Congregations in Belize: POB 427, Belize City; tel. 823-0137; fax 823-0101; f. 1958; in 2010 there were an estimated 11,658 mems living in Mennonite settlements, the largest of which was Altkolonier Mennonitengemeinde, followed by Beachy Amish Mennonite Fellowship, Caribbean Light and Truth, Church of God in Christ, Evangelical Mennonite Mission Conference, Iglesia Evangélica Menonita de Belice, among others; Bishop AARON HARDER.

Methodist Church in the Caribbean and the Americas (Belize/Honduras District) (MCCA): 75 Albert St, POB 212, Belize City; tel. 227-7173; fax 227-5870; e-mail roodypap@btl.net; internet www.mccalive.org; f. 1824; c. 1,827 mems; District Pres. Rev. ROOSVELT PAPOULOUTE.

Other denominations active in the country include the Nazarene Church, Jehovah's Witnesses, Mormons and the Salvation Army.

OTHER RELIGIONS

There are also small communities of Hindus (612, according to the census of 2010), Muslims (577 in 2010) and Bahá'ís (202 in 2010), together accounting for less than 1% of the population.

The Press

Amandala: Amandala Press, 3304 Partridge St, POB 15, Belize City; tel. 202-4476; fax 222-4702; e-mail info@amandala.com.bz; internet www.amandala.com.bz; f. 1969; 2 a week; independent; Publr EVAN X. HYDE; Editor RUSSELL VELLOS; circ. 45,000.

Ambergris Today: Pescador Dr., POB 23, San Pedro Town, Ambergris Caye; tel. 226-3462; fax 226-3483; e-mail ambergristoday@yahoo .com; internet www.ambergristoday.com; weekly; independent; Editor DORIAN NUÑEZ.

The Belize Ag Report: POB 150, San Ignacio, Cayo District; tel. 663-6777; e-mail belizeagreport@gmail.com; internet belizeagreport .com; agriculture newsletter; fortnightly; Editor BETH GOULD ROBERSON.

The Belize Times: 3 Queen St, POB 506, Belize City; tel. 671-8385; fax 223-1940; e-mail editortimes@yahoo.com; internet www .belizetimes.bz; f. 1956; weekly; party political paper of PUP; Editor-in-Chief ALBERTO VELLOS; circ. 6,000.

Government Gazette: Print Belize Ltd, 1 Power Lane, Belmopan; tel. 822-0194; fax 822-3367; e-mail admin@printbze.com; f. 1871; official; weekly; CEO LAWRENCE J. NICHOLAS.

The Guardian: Ebony St and Bel-China Bridge, POB 1898, Belize City; tel. 207-5346; fax 227-5343; e-mail guardian@btl.net; internet www.guardian.bz; weekly; party political paper of UDP; Editor ALFONSO NOBLE; circ. 5,000.

The National Perspective: 25 Nanche St, Belmopan; tel. 635-3506; e-mail nationalperspectiveeditor@gmail.com; internet nationalperspectivebz.com; f. 2008; weekly; PUP oriented; Publr and Editor OMAR SILVA.

The Reporter: 147 West St, POB 707, Belize City; tel. 227-2503; fax 227-8278; e-mail editor@belizereporter.bz; internet www.reporter .bz; f. 1967; weekly; Editor DYON ELLIOT; circ. 6,500.

The San Pedro Sun: 63 Barrier Reef Dr., POB 35, San Pedro Town, Ambergris Caye; tel. 226-2070; fax 226-2905; e-mail spsun@ sanpedrosun.com; internet www.sanpedrosun.com; f. 1993; weekly; Publr RON SNIFFIN; Editor TAMARA SNIFFIN.

Publishers

Angelus Press Ltd: 10 Queen St, POB 1757, Belize City; tel. 223-5777; fax 227-8825; e-mail angel@btl.net; f. 1885; owned by the Santiago Castillo Group since 1997; Gen. Man. AMPARO MASSON NOBLE.

Cubola Productions: Montserrat Casademunt, 35 Elizabeth St, Benque Viejo del Carmen; tel. 823-2083; fax 823-2240; e-mail cubolabz@btl.net; internet www.cubola.com; Dir MONTSERRAT CASADEMUNT.

Print Belize Ltd: 1 Power Lane, Belmopan; tel. 822-2293; fax 822-0194; e-mail admin@printbelize.com; internet www.printbelize.com; f. 1871; responsible for printing, binding and engraving requirements of all govt depts and ministries; publications include annual govt estimates, govt magazines and the official *Government Gazette*; CEO LAWRENCE J. NICHOLAS.

Broadcasting and Communications

TELECOMMUNICATIONS

Belize Telemedia Ltd: Esquivel Telecom Centre, St Thomas St, POB 603, Belize City; tel. 223-2868; fax 223-1800; e-mail prdept@btl .net; internet www.belizetelemedia.net; f. May 2007; fmrly Belize Telecommunications Ltd (subsidiary of Innovative Communication Corpn (ICC) until taken over by the Govt in 2005); nationalized Aug. 2009; partially privatized in 2010; Exec. Chair. NESTOR VASQUEZ.

SpeedNet Communications Ltd: 2½ miles Northern Hwy, Belize City; tel. 280-1000; fax 223-1919; e-mail sduncan@speednet-wireless .com; internet www.smart-bz.com; f. 2003; commenced services in 2005; mobile cellular telecommunications provider under the brand name Smart; Man. (IT) SEAN DUNCAN.

Regulatory Authority

Public Utilities Commission (PUC): see Utilities—Regulatory Body.

BROADCASTING

Radio

KREM Radio Ltd: 3304 Partridge St, POB 15, Belize City; tel. 202-4409; fax 222-4220; e-mail contact@krembz.com; internet www .krembz.com; f. 1989; commercial; private radio station; Station Man. MICHAEL HYDE.

Love FM: 7145 Slaughterhouse Rd, POB 1865, Belize City; tel. 203-0528; fax 203-0529; e-mail lovefmbelize@yahoo.com; internet www .lovefm.com; f. 1992; purchased Friends FM in 1998; CEO RENE VILLANUEVA, Sr.

Other private radio stations broadcasting in Belize include: Estereo Amor, More FM, My Refuge Christian Radio, Radio 2000 and Voice of America.

Television

Centaur Cable Network (CTV): 31 Clarke St, Orange Walk; tel. 670-2216; fax 322-2216; e-mail jeb@centaurcablenetwork.com; internet www.ctv3belizenews.com; f. 1989; commercial; Man. Dir JAIME BRICEÑO.

Channel 5 Belize: Great Belize Productions Ltd, 2882 Coney Dr., POB 1314, Belize City; tel. 223-7781; fax 223-4936; e-mail gbtv@btl .com; internet www.channel5belize.com; f. 1991; CEO AMALIA MAI.

Tropical Vision (Channel 7): 73 Albert St, Belize City; tel. 223-5589; fax 227-5602; e-mail tvseven@btl.net; internet 7newsbelize .com; commercial; Man. Dir NESTOR VASQUEZ.

Regulatory Authority

Belize Broadcasting Authority (BBA): 7 Gabourel Lane, Belize City; tel. and fax 223-3953; e-mail broadcasting_bze@hotmail.com; regulatory authority; Chair. LOUIS LESLIE.

Finance

(cap. = capital; res = reserves; dep. = deposits; brs = branches; amounts in BZ $, unless otherwise indicated)

BANKING

Central Bank

Central Bank of Belize: Gabourel Lane, POB 852, Belize City; tel. 223-6194; fax 223-6226; e-mail cenbank@btl.net; internet www .centralbank.org.bz; f. 1982; cap. 10m., res 23.9m., dep. 337.9m. (2009); Gov. GLENFORD YSAGUIRRE; Chair. Sir MANUEL ESQUIVEL.

Development Bank

Development Finance Corporation: Bliss Parade, Belmopan; tel. 822-2360; fax 822-3096; e-mail info@dfcbelize.org; internet www .dfcbelize.org; f. 1972; issued cap. 10m.; 5 brs; Chair. DENNIS JONES.

Other Banks

Atlantic Bank Ltd: Cnr Freetown Rd and Cleghorn St, POB 481, Belize City; tel. 223-4123; fax 223-3907; e-mail atlantic@atlabank .com; internet www.atlabank.com; f. 1970; 55% owned by Honduran co Sociedad Nacional de Inversiones, SA (SONISA); cap. $18m., res $31.1m., dep. US $495m. (Dec. 2012); Gen. Man. SANDRA BEDRAN; 8 brs.

Atlantic International Bank Ltd: Cnr Withfield Tower, 2nd Floor, 4792 Coney Dr., POB 1811, Belize City; tel. 223-3152; fax 223-3528; e-mail info@atlanticibl.com; internet www.atlanticibl .com; f. 2000; affiliated to Atlantic Bank Ltd; CEO RICARDO PELAYO.

Belize Bank International: Matalon Business Center, 2nd Floor, POB 364, Belize City; tel. 227-0697; fax 227-0986; e-mail services@ bcbankinternational.com; internet bcbankinternational.com; fmrly British Caribbean Bank International; name changed as above in 2012.

Belize Bank Ltd: 60 Market Sq., POB 364, Belize City; tel. 227-7132; fax 227-2712; e-mail bblbz@belizebank.com; internet www .belizebank.com; subsidiary of BCB Holdings; cap. US $2.2m., res US $2.1m., dep. US $489m. (March 2010); Chair. LYNDON GUISEPPI; 12 brs.

Caye International Bank Ltd (CIBL): Coconut Dr., San Pedro, POB 11, Ambergris Caye; tel. 226-2388; fax 226-2892; e-mail cibl@btl .net; internet www.cayebank.bz; Chair. JOEL NAGEL.

Choice Bank Ltd: Power Point Bldg, Ground Floor, Cnr Hudson St and Marine Parade Blvd, POB 2494, Belize City; tel. 223-6850; e-mail info@choicebankltd.com; internet www.choicebankltd.com.

CIBC FirstCaribbean International Bank: 21 Albert St, POB 363, Belize City; tel. 227-7211; fax 227-8572; e-mail care@cibcfcib .com; internet www.cibcfcib.com; f. 2002 by merger of CIBC West Indies Holdings and Barclays Bank PLC Caribbean operations; Barclays relinquished its stake to CIBC in 2006, present name adopted in 2011; Exec. Dir RIK PARKHILL; 5 brs.

Heritage Bank Ltd: 106 Princess Margaret Dr., POB 1988, Belize City; tel. 223-6783; fax 223-6785; e-mail services@banking.bz; internet www.heritageibt.com/domestic; f. 2001 as Alliance Bank of Belize Ltd; name changed as above in 2010; Pres. and CEO JAMES M. FLOYD; 3 brs.

Heritage International Bank and Trust Ltd: 35 Barrack Rd, POB 1867, Belize City; tel. 223-5698; fax 223-0368; e-mail services@ banking.bz; internet www.heritageibt.com/international; f. 1998 as Provident Bank and Trust of Belize; name changed as above in 2010; cap. US $7.5m., res US $2.4m., dep. US $186.7m. (Dec. 2012)); Man. Dir STEPHEN DUNCAN.

National Bank of Belize: Cnr Forest Dr. and Hummingbird Hwy, Belmopan; tel. 822-0957; e-mail services@nbbltd.com; f. 2012, began operations Sept. 2013; state-owned; Chair. JOY GRANT; Man. Dir JOSÉ KARIM MARIN.

Scotiabank Belize Ltd: Albert St, POB 708, Belize City; tel. 227-7027; fax 227-7416; e-mail belize.scotia@scotiabank.com; internet www.scotiabank.com/bz; f. 1968; Pres. and CEO RICHARD E. WAUGH; Man. Dir PAT ANDREWS; 11 brs.

There are also a number of credit unions active in Belize.

INSURANCE

The insurance sector is regulated by the Office of the Supervisor of Insurance, part of the Ministry of Finance and Economic Development.

Atlantic Insurance Company Ltd: Atlantic Bank Bldg, 3rd Floor, Cnr Cleghorn St and Freetown Rd, POB 1447, Belize City; tel. 223-2657; fax 223-2658; e-mail info@atlanticinsurancebz.com; internet www.atlanticinsurancebz.com; f. 1991; part of the Atlantic Group of Cos; holding co, Sociedad Nacional de Inversiones, SA, (SONISA); Gen. Man. MARTHA GUERRA.

Belize Insurance Centre Ltd: 212 North Front St, Belize City; tel. 227-7310; fax 227-4803; e-mail info@belizeinsurance.com; internet www.belizeinsurance.com; f. 1972; insurance broker; subsidiary of Fraser Fontaine & Kong Ltd (Jamaica); acts as an agent for Guardian Life Ltd and United Insurance Co Ltd; Chair. G. RICHARD FONTAINE; Gen. Man. CYNTHIA AWE.

Insurance Corporation of Belize Ltd: 16 Daly St, Belize City; tel. 224-5328; fax 223-1317; e-mail icb@icbinsurance.com; internet www.icbinsurance.com; f. 1982; general insurance; Exec. Dir ERDULFO NUÑEZ.

RF & G Insurance Co Ltd: Gordon House, 1 Coney Dr., POB 661, Belize City; tel. 223-5734; fax 223-6734; e-mail info@rfginsurancebelize.com; internet www.rfginsurancebelize.com; f. 2005 by merger of F&G Insurance and Regent Insurance; underwriters of all major classes of insurance; mem. of the Roe Group of Cos; Chair. CHRISTOPHER ROE.

RF & G Life Insurance Company Ltd: Gordon House, 4th Floor, 1 Coney Dr., POB 661, Belize City; tel. 223-5734; fax 223-6734; e-mail info@rfglife.com; internet www.rfglife.com; f. 2005 through merger of the Life and Medical portfolios of F&G Insurance Co into Regent Life; mem. of the Roe Group of Cos; Chair. BRIAN D. ROE; Gen. Man. RHONDA LECKY.

Trade and Industry

STATUTORY BODIES

Belize Agricultural Health Authority: Cnr Forest Dr. and Hummingbird Hwy, POB 169, Belmopan; tel. 822-0818; fax 822-0271; e-mail baha@btl.net; internet www.baha.bz; Man. Dir EMIR CRUZ.

Belize Marketing and Development Corporation (BMDC): 117 North Front St, POB 633, Belize City; tel. 227-3409; fax 227-7656; f. 1948 as Belize Marketing Board to encourage the growing of staple food crops; renamed as above in 2003; promotes domestic produce; Man. Dir ROQUE MAI.

Belize Social Investment Fund: 1902 Constitution Dr., Belmopan; tel. 822 0239; fax 822 0508; e-mail daniel.cano@sifbelize.org; internet sifbelize.org; f. 1996; Exec. Dir NELLIE TRENCH (acting).

Coastal Zone Management Authority and Institute (CZMAI): POB 1884, Belize City; tel. 223-0719; fax 223-5738; e-mail czmbze@btl.net; internet www.coastalzonebelize.org; Man. Dir VINCENT GILLETT.

Pesticides Control Board (PCB): Central Farm, Cayo District; tel. 824-2640; fax 824-3486; e-mail pcbinfo@btl.net; internet www.pcbbelize.com; Chair. ANIL SINHA (acting).

DEVELOPMENT ORGANIZATION

Belize Trade and Investment Development Service (BELTRAIDE): 14 Orchid Garden St, Belmopan; tel. 822-3737; fax 822-0595; e-mail beltraide@belizeinvest.org.bz; internet www.belizeinvest.org.bz; f. 1986 as a joint govt and private sector institution to encourage export and investment; Exec. Chair. MICHAEL SINGH; Exec. Dir NICOLAS RUIZ.

CHAMBERS OF COMMERCE

American Chamber of Commerce of Belize: 1 Mapp St, POB 75, Belize City; tel. 224-5352; fax 222-4265; e-mail info@amchambelize.org; internet www.amchambelize.org; Pres. LYNETTE SINGH-ROSS; Sec. CON MURPHY.

Belize Chamber of Commerce and Industry (BCCI): 4792 Coney Dr., Withfield Tower, 1st Floor, POB 291, Belize City; tel. 223-5330; fax 223-5333; e-mail bcci@belize.org; internet www.belize.org; f. 1920; Pres. ARTURO VASQUEZ; CEO KIM AIKMAN; 300 mems.

EMPLOYERS' ASSOCIATIONS

Banana Growers' Association: Big Creek, Independence Village, Stann Creek District; tel. 523-2000; fax 523-2112; e-mail banana@btl.net; Chair. ANTONIO (TONY) ZABANEH.

Belize Citrus Growers Association (BCGA): Mile 9, Stann Creek Valley Rd, POB 7, Dangriga, Stann Creek District; tel. 522-3585; fax 522-2686; e-mail cga@belizecitrus.org; internet www.belizecitrus.org; f. 1967; Chair. ECCLESTON IRVING; CEO HENRY N. ANDERSON.

Belize Livestock Producers' Association (BLPA): 47½ miles Western Hwy, POB 183, Belmopan; tel. 822-3883; e-mail blpa@btl.net; internet www.blpabz.org; f. 1972; Chair. JOHN CARR.

Belize Sugar Cane Farmers' Association (BSCFA): 34 San Antonio Rd, Orange Walk; tel. 322-2005; fax 322-3171; f. 1959 to assist cane farmers and negotiate with the Sugar Cane Board and manufacturers on their behalf; Chair. ALFREDO ORTEGA; 16 district brs.

MAJOR COMPANIES

BCB Holdings Ltd: 60 Market Sq., POB 1764, Belize City; tel. 227-7132; fax 227-5854; e-mail info@bbholdingslimited.com; internet www.bcbholdings.com; fmrly Carlisle Holdings Ltd, changed name to BB Holdings in 2005; current name adopted 2009; holding co with banking and financial services operations in Belize; investments in infrastructure development and agro-processing and distribution in Central America and the Caribbean region; CEO LYNDON GUISEPPI; 437 employees.

Belize Brewing Co Ltd: 1 King St, POB 1068, Belize City; tel. 227-7031; fax 227-7062; e-mail belikin@bowenbz.com; internet www.belikin.com; f. 1969; subsidiary of Bowen & Bowen Ltd; producers of malt liquors; Pres. KEVIN M. BOWEN; Gen. Man HILBERTO (HILLY) MARTINEZ; 120 employees.

Belize Estate Co Ltd: Slaughterhouse Rd, POB 151, Belize City; tel. 223-1783; fax 223-1367; e-mail bec@btl.net; internet www.belizeestateshipping.com; f. 1875; acquired by Bowen & Bowen Ltd in 1983; importers, shipping agents, main agents for Kia and Ford, Maersk Lines and Lloyd's agent for Belize, operation of tourist enterprises; Man. Dir WILLIAM F. BOWMAN; 94 employees.

Belize Natural Energy Ltd (BNE): Spanish Lookout Rd, Mile 3, POB 279, Iguana Creek, Cayo, Belmopan; tel. 823-0354; fax 823-0415; e-mail info@belizeenergy.bz; internet www.belizenaturalenergy.bz; f. 2002; owned by US and Irish interests; oil and gas exploration and production; Pres. and CEO Dr GILBERT CANTON.

Belize Sugar Industries Ltd: Tower Hill, POB 29, Orange Walk; tel. 322-2150; fax 322-3241; e-mail ceobelizesugar@btl.net; f. 1935; public co; raw sugar manufacturers; CEO JOSÉ MONTALVO; 650 employees.

Castillo Sanchez & Burrell, LLP (CSB): 40A Central American Blvd, POB 1235, Belize City; tel. 227-3020; fax 227-5792; e-mail info@csb-llp.com; internet www.csb-llp.com; accountancy, management consultancy, offshore services; Sr Partner GIACOMO SANCHEZ.

Citrus Products of Belize Ltd: 12 Miles, Stann Creek Valley Rd, Pomona Village, Stann Creek District; tel. 522-2055; fax 522-2810; e-mail info@citrusproductsbelize.com; internet www.citrusproductsbelize.com; f. 1948 as Citrus Co of Belize Ltd; present name adopted in 2002; citrus fruit growers and processors; 46.58% owned by Bank Holdings Ltd of Barbados; Chair. DOUGLAS SINGH; Interim CEO JAIME ALPUCHE.

Femagra Industries Ltd: ½ Mile, Hummingbird Hwy, POB 65, Belmopan City; tel. 822-3909; fax 882-3910; e-mail fernando@femagra.com; internet www.femagra.com; f. 1984; chemical- and food-processing, water-purifying; Gen. Man. FERNANDO MOLINA.

Hofius Ltd: 19 Albert St, POB 226, Belize City; tel. 227-7231; fax 227-4751; e-mail info@hofiusbelize.com; internet www.hofiusbelize.com; f. 1892; hardware and home products, real estate sales, boats and marine fittings, food distribution; Gen. Man. JACQUELINE ROE; 50 employees.

Marine Farms Belize: Mile 5½ Western Highway, POB 1778, Belize City; tel. 222-5038; fax 222-4102; e-mail info@marinefarmsbelize.com; internet www.marinefarmsbelize.com; f. 2006; owned by Marine Farms ASA (Norway); fish farming and processing; CEO BJØRN MYRSETH; 30 employees (2007).

Netkom Internet Solutions: 18 Leslie St, Kings Park, POB 855, Belize City; tel. 223-3274; e-mail support@netkombelize.com; internet www.mybelizeadventure.com/netkombelize; internet consultancy and provider of digital media production services.

Northern Fishermen Cooperative Society: 49 North Front St, POB 647, Belize City; tel. 224-4488; fax 223-0978; e-mail norficoop@btl.net; producers, processors and exporters of seafood products; Gen. Man. ROBERT USHER.

Prosser Fertilizer and Agrotec Co: Mile 8 Western Hwy, POB 566, Belize City; tel. 223-5410; fax 222-5548; e-mail prosserfertilizer@gmail.com; manufacture of industrial chemicals and fertilizers; Chair. and CEO SALVADOR ESPAT.

Puma Energy Belize: Caesar Ridge Rd, POB 328, Belize City; tel. 227-7323; fax 227-7726; e-mail freddy.flores@puma-energy.com; internet www.pumaenergy.com/en/regions/americas/belize; subsidiary of Puma Energy Ltd, Switzerland; petroleum exploration and distribution; Man. FREDDY FLORES.

The Roe Group: Gordon House, 1 Coney Dr., Belize City; tel. 223-6124; fax 227-1357; e-mail info@roegroupbelize.com; internet www.roegroupbelize.com; f. 1961; 16 cos; agriculture, distribution and sales, financial services, manufacturing, real estate and tourism; Chair. BRIAN D. ROE; CEO CHRISTOPHER ROE.

Madisco: 42 Cleghorn St, POB 34, Belize City; tel. 223-1821; fax 223-1797; e-mail gm@madisco.bz; internet www.madisco.bz; mem. of the Roe Group (q.v.); marketing and distribution; Contact PARVEEN WILLIAMS HAMILTON.

Santiago Castillo Ltd: San Cas Plaza-Belcan Bridge, POB 69, Belize City; tel. 223-0610; internet www.santiagocastillo.com; f. 1926; part of the Santiago Castillo Group; food distribution; runs the Save-U supermarket and the TASTEE brand; Pres. LORENA CASTILLO; CEO SANTIAGO SANTINO CASTILLO.

Sol Belize Ltd: 2.5 miles Northern Hwy, POB 608, Belize City; tel. 223-0406; fax 223-0704; e-mail info.belize@solpetroleum.com; internet solpetroleum.com/belize; f. 1938; subsidiary of Interamericana Trading Ltd (Barbados); marketing and distribution of petroleum, petroleum products and chemical products; Gen. Man. RUFINO LIN; 14 employees.

UTILITIES

Regulatory Body

Public Utilities Commission (PUC): 41 Gabourel Lane, POB 300, Belize City; tel. 223-4938; fax 223-6818; e-mail info@puc.bz; internet www.puc.bz; f. 1999; regulatory body, headed by commissioners; replaced the Offices of Electricity Supply and of Telecommunications following enaction of the Public Utilities Commission Act in 1999; Chair. JOHN AVERY.

Electricity

Belize Electric Co Ltd (BECOL): Hydro Benque Rd, POB 87, San Ignacio, Cayo; tel. 824-3016; fax 824-4512; e-mail stephen@becol.com.bz; internet www.fortisinc.com; wholly owned subsidiary of Fortis Inc (Canada); operates Mollejón 25.2-MW hydroelectric plant, Chalillo 7.3-MW hydroelectric facility and Vaca hydroelectric plant which supply electricity to Belize Electricity Ltd (BEL—see below); Pres. and CEO H. STANLEY MARSHALL.

Belize Electricity Ltd (BEL): 2½ miles Northern Hwy, POB 327, Belize City; tel. 227-0954; fax 223-0891; e-mail pr@bel.com.bz; internet www.bel.com.bz; fmrly Belize Electricity Board, changed name upon privatization in 1992; nationalized in 2011; 70.2% owned by the Govt of Belize and 26.9% owned by Social Security Board; Pres. and CEO JEFFREY LOCKE; Chair. RODWELL WILLIAMS; 296 employees.

> **Belize Co-Generation Energy Ltd (BELCOGEN):** Tower Hill, Orange Walk Town; operations began 2009; jtly owned by BEL and Belize Sugar Industries Ltd; 31.5 MW biomass plant fuelled by bagasse (sugar cane fibre); Man. Dir JOEY MONTALVO.

Water

Belize Water Services Ltd: 7 Central American Blvd, POB 150, Belize City; tel. 222-4757; fax 222-4759; e-mail bws_ceosec@btl.net; internet www.bws.bz; f. 1971 as Water and Sewerage Authority (WASA); changed name upon privatization in 2001; renationalized in Oct. 2005 prior to partial reprivatization in early 2006; Chair. ALBERTO AUGUST; CEO ALVAN HAYNES.

TRADE UNIONS

National Trade Union Congress of Belize (NTUCB): POB 2359, Belize City; tel. 227-2678; fax 227-2864; e-mail ntucb@btl.net; f. 1966; Pres. DYLAN RENEAU; Gen. Sec. REBECCA SUAZO.

Principal Unions

Belize Communications Workers' Union (BCWU): POB 1291, Belize City; tel. 223-4809; fax 224-4300; e-mail bcwu@btl.net; f. 1989; Pres. LEANN BARDALEZ; Gen. Sec. EMILY TURNER.

Belize Energy Workers' Union: c/o Belize Electricity Ltd, 2½ miles Northern Hwy, POB 1066, Belize City; tel. 227-0954; e-mail bewunion@gmail.com; Pres. SEAN NICHOLAS; Gen. Sec. DORLA STAINE.

Belize National Teachers' Union: NGO Crescent, POB 382, Belize City; tel. 223-4811; fax 223-5233; e-mail admin@bntubelize.org; internet www.bntubelize.org; f. 1970 following merger between the British Honduras Union of Teachers (BHUT) and the Catholic Education Asscn (CEA); adopted present name in 1976; Pres. LUKE PALACIO; Exec. Sec. KEESHA YOUNG; 1,000 mems.

Belize Water Services Workers' Union: Belize City; tel. 223-4809; e-mail bwswu@yahoo.com; Pres. LORELEI WESTBY.

Belize Workers' Union: Tate St, Orange Walk; tel. 822-2327; e-mail bwu@btl.net; Pres. RAMIRO RAMON; Sec. BALDEMAR MAGANA.

Christian Workers' Union: 107B Cemetery Rd, POB 533, Belize City; tel. 227-2150; fax 227-8470; e-mail cwu@btl.net; f. 1962; general; Pres. AUDREY MATURA-SHEPHERD; 1,000 mems.

Public Service Union of Belize: Hilltop Complex, POB 458, Belmopan; tel. 802-3885; fax 822-0283; e-mail belizepsu@btl.net; internet psubelize.com; f. 1922; public workers; Pres. MARVIN BLADES; Gen. Sec. MARIO CALIZ; 1,600 mems.

Transport

Department of Transport: NEMO Bldg, Belmopan; tel. 822-2135; fax 822-3317; e-mail departmentoftransport@yahoo.com; Commr GARETH MURILLO.

RAILWAYS

There are no railways in Belize.

ROADS

There are 2,872 km of roads, of which some 2,210 km (1,600 km of gravel roads, 300 km of improved earth roads and 310 km of unimproved earth roads) are unpaved. A double-lane bridge was built over the Sibun River in 2004, and over Silver Creek in 2006. The Middlesex Bridge over Stann Creek was reconstructed in 2010. There are four major highways that connect all the major cities and towns and lead to the Mexican and Guatemalan borders. Work began on the BZ $48m. Southern Highway in 2011, connecting the south of the country to the Guatemala border. The project was financed by the Kuwaiti Fund for Economic Development and the Development Fund of the Organization of Petroleum Exporting Countries.

SHIPPING

There is a deep-water port at Belize City and a second port at Commerce Bight, near Dangriga (formerly Stann Creek), to the south of Belize City. There is a port for the export of bananas at Big Creek and additional ports at Corozal and Punta Gorda. At 31 December 2013 the flag registered fleet comprised 1,038 vessels, totalling 2,372,268 grt, of which nine were gas tankers, 25 were bulk carriers and 386 were general cargo ships.

Belize Ports Authority: 120 North Front St, POB 633, Belize City; tel. 223-0752; fax 223-0710; e-mail bzportauth@btl.net; internet www.portauthority.bz; f. 1980; Commr of Ports MERLENE MARTINEZ.

Marine & Services Ltd: Blake Bldg, Suite 203, Cnr Hudson and Eyre St, POB 611, Belize City; tel. 227-2113; fax 227-5404; e-mail info@marineservices.bz; internet www.marineservices.bz; f. 1975; shipping and cargo services, cruise line agent; Man. JOSE GALLEGO.

Port of Belize Ltd: Caesar Ridge Rd, POB 2674, Belize City; tel. and fax 223-2439; fax 223-3571; e-mail info@portofbelize.com; internet www.portofbelize.com; operates the main port facility; CEO ARTURO VASQUEZ; Deputy CEO FRANZINE WAIGHT.

CIVIL AVIATION

Philip S. W. Goldson International Airport, 16 km (10 miles) from Belize City, can accommodate medium-sized jet-engined aircraft. There are 37 airstrips for light aircraft on internal flights near the major towns and offshore islands.

Belize Airports Authority (BAA): POB 1564, Belize City; tel. 225-2045; fax 225-2439; e-mail bzeaa@btl.net; Chair. JOHN WAIGHT; Gen. Man. (vacant).

Department of Civil Aviation: POB 367, Belize City; tel. 225-2052; fax 225-2533; e-mail dcabelize@btl.net; internet www.civilaviation.gov.bz; f. 1931; Dir LINDSAY GARBUTT.

Maya Island Air: Municipal Airstrip, Bldg 1, 2nd Floor, POB 458, Belize City; tel. 223-1140; fax 223-1722; e-mail regional@mayaislandair.com; internet www.mayaislandair.com; f. 1961 as merger between Maya Airways Ltd and Island Air; operated by Belize Air Group; internal services, centred on Belize City, and charter flights to neighbouring countries; CEO LOUIS ZABANEH; Gen. Man. CARLOS VARGAS.

Tropic Air: San Pedro, POB 20, Ambergris Caye; tel. 226-2012; fax 226-2338; e-mail reservations@tropicair.com; internet www.tropicair.com; f. 1979; operates internal services and services to Guatemala; Pres. JOHN GREIF, III; CEO STEVEN SCHULTE.

Tourism

The main tourist attractions are the beaches and the barrier reef, diving, fishing and the Mayan archaeological sites. There are nine major wildlife reserves, and government policy is to develop eco-tourism, based on the attractions of an unspoiled environment and Belize's natural history. The country's wildlife includes howler monkeys and 500 species of birds, and its barrier reef is the second largest in the world. In 2012 there were 833,952 tourist arrivals, of which some 576,661 were cruise ship passengers and 257,291 were stop-over visitors. Tourism receipts totalled a provisional US $351m. in 2013.

Belize Tourism Board: 64 Regent St, POB 325, Belize City; tel. 227-2420; fax 227-2423; e-mail btb@travelbelize.org; internet btb.travelbelize.org/btb; f. 1964; fmrly Belize Tourist Bureau; 8 mems; CEO TRACY PANTON; Chair. CARLA BARNETT.

Belize Tourism Industry Association (BTIA): 10 North Park St, POB 62, Belize City; tel. 227-1144; fax 227-8710; e-mail info@btia .org; internet www.btia.org; f. 1985; promotes sustainable tourism; Pres. HERBERT HAYLOCK; Exec. Dir EFREN PEREZ; 500 mems.

Defence Budget: an estimated BZ $36m. in 2013.

Belize Defence Force Commandant: Col DAVID NEJEMIAH JONES.

Defence

The Belize Defence Force was formed in 1978 and was based on a combination of the existing Police Special Force and the Belize Volunteer Guard. Military service is voluntary, but provision has been made for the establishment of National Service, if necessary, to supplement normal recruitment. As assessed at November 2013, the regular armed forces totalled approximately 1,050 and there were some 700 militia reserves. The British Army Training Support Unit Belize was withdrawn at the end of 2010. In 2005 the Belize National Coast Guard Service was inaugurated to combat drugs-trafficking, illegal immigration and illegal fishing in Belize's territorial waters. The Coast Guard comprised 58 volunteer officers from the Belize Defence Force, the Belize Police Department, the Customs and Excise Department, the National Fire Service, the Department of Immigration and Nationality Services, the Ports Authority, and the Fisheries Department.

Education

Education is compulsory for all children for a period of 10 years between the ages of five and 14 years. Primary education, beginning at five years of age and lasting for eight years, is provided free of charge, principally through subsidized denominational schools under government control. In 2012/13 there were 68,812 pupils enrolled in primary institutions. Secondary education, beginning at the age of 13, lasts for four years. Some 20,539 students were enrolled in secondary education in 2012/13.

In 2012/13 there were 4,652 students enrolled in higher, technical or vocational colleges. The main institution of higher education is the University of Belize, which was formed in 2000 through the amalgamation of five higher education institutions. The private Galen University also offers degree courses. There is an extra-mural branch of the University of the West Indies in Belize. Government expenditure on education in the financial year 2013/14 was projected at BZ $207.2m.

Bibliography

For works on the Caribbean generally, see Select Bibliography (Books)

Bolland, O. N. *Colonialism and Resistance in Belize, Essays in Historical Sociology.* revised edn, Belize, Cubola Productions, 2003.

Bulmer-Thomas, B., and Bulmer-Thomas, V. *The Economic History of Belize.* Belize, Cubola Productions, 2012.

Grant, C. H. *The Making of Modern Belize: Politics, Society and British Colonialism in Central America.* Cambridge, Cambridge University Press, 2008.

Guderjan, Thomas H. *The Nature of an Ancient Maya City: Resources, Interaction, and Power at Blue Creek, Belize.* Tuscaloosa, AL, University of Alabama Press, 2007.

Kroshus Medina, L. *Negotiating Economic Development: Identity Formation and Collective Action in Belize.* Tucson, AZ, University of Arizona Press, 2004.

MacPherson, A. S. *From Colony to Nation: Women Activists and the Gendering of Politics in Belize, 1912–1982.* Lincoln, NE, University of Nebraska Press, 2007.

Musa, S., and Smith, G. P. (Eds). *Belize: A Caribbean Nation in Central America—Selected Speeches of Said Musa.* Kingston, Ian Randle Publrs, 2006.

Roessingh, C. *The Belizean Garifuna: Organization of Identity in an Ethnic Community in Central America.* Amsterdam, Rozenberg, 2002.

Shoman, A. *Belize's Independence and Decolonization in Latin America: Guatemala, Britain, and the UN.* New York, Palgrave Macmillan, 2010.

Simmons, D. C. *Confederate Settlements in British Honduras.* Jefferson, NC, McFarland & Co, 2001.

Sutherland, A. *The Making of Belize.* Westport, CT, Bergin & Garvey, 1998.

Thomson, P. *Belize: A Concise History.* Oxford, Macmillan Caribbean, 2005.

Turner, B. L., and Harrison, P. D. (Eds). *Pulltrouser Swamp: Ancient Maya Habitat, Agriculture and Settlement in Northern Belize.* Salt Lake City, UT, University of Utah Press, 2000.

Twigg, A. *Understanding Belize: A Historical Guide.* Madeira Park, BC, Harbour Publishing, 2006.

BERMUDA

Geography

PHYSICAL FEATURES

Bermuda lies in the North Atlantic, about 900 km (560 miles) east of Cape Hatteras in North Carolina (USA), and is an Overseas Territory of the United Kingdom (indeed, it is the oldest British colony). Although geographically part of North America, Bermuda shares many of the features of the West Indian islands, and is generally included in that region—it is north-west of the Bahamian archipelago and north of the Virgin Islands. Bermuda, located on what were called the Somers Islands, has an area of only 53.3 sq km, making it the smallest territory in the Western hemisphere.

Bermuda is built of coral perching on the southern rim of the summit of an underwater volcanic mountain. The 103 km (64 miles) of coastline define some 138 islands and islets, which are strung out across 35 km, running south-westwards from St George's Island to hook around the Great Sound in the south and taper off in a more northerly direction. There are many surrounding reefs, banks and islets. About 20 of the islands are inhabited and seven are linked by bridges and causeways. South of St George's is St David's Island, then Great Bermuda or Main Island (23 km in length). The landscape is richly vegetated, although there is now little land used for farming (over two-fifths of the territory is kept rural and undeveloped), with low hills separated by fertile depressions. The highest point is in the far south, at Gibbs Hill (78 m or 256 ft), itself surmounted by a 36-m, cast-iron lighthouse.

CLIMATE

The subtropical climate is influenced by the Gulf Stream, which enables Bermuda to consist of the most northerly coral islands in the world. The weather is mild, but humid, with strong winds common in winter. Hurricanes can occur between June and November. The good, year-round rainfall (averaging some 1,500 mm—59 ins—annually) makes up for the scarcity of natural freshwater resources. The annual average temperature is 76°F (24°C), ranging between an average minimum of 59°F (15°C) in February and a maximum of 85°F (29°C) in August.

POPULATION

Bermuda, named for the Spanish sailor who visited it in the early years of the 16th century, was only inhabited in the 17th

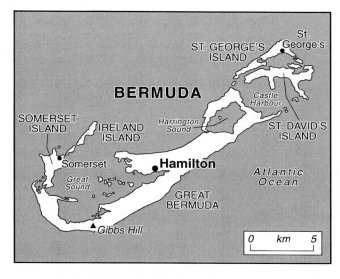

century, by the British. The black population forms the majority (60% of the total in 2010). Most people are Christian, with the main (of many) denominations being the Anglican Church (16% in 2010), the Roman Catholic Church and the African Methodist Episcopalian Church. English is the official language. There is a reasonably significant Portuguese-speaking community.

The total population according to mid-year projections was 61,777 in mid-2014, giving a population density of some 1,159.0 per sq km. Bermuda is the most densely populated territory of the Americas. The capital is at Hamilton, near the centre of Main Island and on the north-eastern shores of the Great Sound, which had an estimated population of 11,065 in 2011. It is one of two municipalities in the territory, the other being that of St George's, the original settlement and old capital in the north. There are also three villages on the islands, while for administrative purposes there are nine parishes.

History

Bermuda is a Crown Colony of the United Kingdom. The British monarch is represented in the islands by a Governor.

The 1968 Constitution gave Bermuda (the oldest British colony, established in 1684) internal self-government. The 1968 elections were won by the moderate, multiracial United Bermuda Party (UBP). However, Bermudian society was riven by racial tensions and in the early 1970s there was a considerable level of violence. Shooting incidents in 1973 notably resulted in the assassination of the Governor of the Colony. At the 1976 election the UBP remained in power, although it lost seats to the mainly black, pro-independence, left-wing Progressive Labour Party (PLP). In 1980 the UBP only narrowly retained power, but regained the seats it had lost in the following election, in 1983. Meanwhile, in 1982, John (later Sir John) W. Swan became party leader and Premier. The UBP won a decisive victory in the 1985 elections, and a less decisive one in the 1989 elections. However, it remained in government after the 1993 general election.

In August 1995 a referendum was held on independence from the United Kingdom, at which some 74% of participants registered their opposition to independence. The debate polarized opinion within the ruling party, and Swan subsequently resigned as Premier and as leader of the UBP. The erstwhile finance minister, Dr David Saul, succeeded him in both posts. Saul remained neutral on the independence issue, and the divisions within the UBP deepened under his leadership. Having failed to restore party unity, Saul resigned as Premier and UBP leader in March 1997. Pamela Gordon replaced him.

The PLP won its first ever majority in the House of Assembly at elections in November 1998. On becoming Premier, PLP leader Jennifer Smith declared that no immediate moves towards independence were planned, although it remained a stated aim of the party. In February 1999 Smith reassured members of the Organisation for Economic Co-operation and Development (OECD) that Bermuda would strive to improve regulation of the offshore financial services sector. Following OECD's investigation into tax havens, in 2000 Bermuda pledged to conform to international standards on financial transparency before the end of 2005.

In 2001 the Government and the opposition UBP fundamentally disagreed about proposed changes to the voting system and electoral boundaries. Racial issues were at the heart of the conflict, with the PLP claiming the present system favoured the traditionally 'white' UBP. In January the UBP submitted an 8,500-signature petition to the British Government, demanding a constitutional conference or referendum on proposed changes to the island's constituency boundaries. The British Foreign and Commonwealth Office (FCO), however, stated that a constitutional conference was unnecessary, and in April it began consultations over the proposed changes. The commission recommended reducing the number of seats in the House of Assembly by four, to 36. In addition, whereas deputies had previously been elected from 20 two-member constituencies, under the proposed scheme each member of parliament would be elected by a separate constituency. The FCO approved the changes before the 2003 general election.

In May 2002 the British Overseas Territories Act, having received royal assent in the United Kingdom in February, came into force and granted British citizenship to the people of its Overseas Territories, including Bermuda. Under the new law Bermudians would be able to hold British passports and work in the United Kingdom and anywhere else in the European Union.

Elections to the smaller 36-seat House of Assembly were held in July 2003 and were dominated by resentment towards wealthy foreign workers and criticism of the personal style of Smith, regarded by many as uncommunicative and aloof. The PLP retained its majority in parliament, securing 22 seats, but its share of the popular vote was reduced to 52% (compared with 48% for the UBP). Smith resigned as Premier and was replaced by the erstwhile Minister of Works and Engineering, W. Alexander Scott. In February 2004 Scott announced that his Government would initiate a 'relaxed public discussion' on the subject of achieving independence from the United Kingdom.

Scott's premiership ended in late October 2006 after he was defeated in a PLP leadership contest; party delegates voted in former Deputy Premier Ewart Brown as his successor. The new Government's stated intention to address disruptive racial tensions among the island's communities was a matter of particular pertinence to the opposition UBP, embroiled as it was in an internal racial discrimination controversy which, in January 2007, precipitated the resignations of House of Assembly member Jamahl Simmons and party Chair Gwyneth Rawlins. Both alleged serious charges of racial discrimination against factions within the party. Demands for the resignation of leader Wayne Furbert ensued, with senior members asserting that intra-party schisms and dissension arising from the racism dispute threatened to undermine the UBP's political power. Such public wrangling further provoked speculation of an early general election—ahead of the 2008 constitutional deadline—whereby Premier Brown might take advantage of an opposition in disarray. Following a vote of no confidence by a majority within the UBP, Furbert resigned on 29 March; deputy leader Michael Dunkley was elected unopposed as his successor.

In January 2005 the Bermuda Independence Commission was established, in co-operation with the UN Committee on Decolonization, in order to investigate and report on the implications of transition to self-rule. In November the Commission submitted its report; however, its findings were criticized for being biased, as they failed to include contributions from the UBP, using only the ruling PLP's submission. In an attempt to quell the criticism, Scott declared that discussions would take place in 2006 on the future status of Bermuda. However, public opinion remained strongly in favour of maintaining links with the United Kingdom: according to opinion polls in June 2005, only 20% of the public supported independence, while an overwhelming 65% opposed complete secession from the United Kingdom. In March both the UN and the British Government indicated their support for a referendum on the issue; however, Scott maintained that the question of independence should be decided at the next general election. The issue of independence created political tension between the population's black majority, from which the PLP drew much of its support, and the white minority.

The issue of future independence for Bermuda arose again in March 2007 when Premier Brown declared such an eventuality 'inevitable', but unlikely to feature prominently in preparations for the impending election. Pursuing such a contentious objective was deemed likely to jeopardize the PLP's chances of success. Brown indicated that constitutional revisions must be effected and the entrenchment of economic dependence upon the United Kingdom in the national ideology be reversed before advances towards such an historical development could be achieved. However, relations with the United Kingdom had become increasingly strained following the unauthorized disclosure, by a source within the Bermudian police force, of documents relating to a scandal in which the Premier, among other high-profile government officials, was implicated. Brown maintained that the previous inquiry into the alleged corrupt arrangement between government personnel (including himself) and the state-owned Bermuda Housing Corporation (BHC)—whereby substantial sums of public money were appropriated for private benefit—had exonerated him of any wrongdoing. Moreover, he blamed Governor Sir John Vereker for failing to ensure the documents' security, thereby allowing the information into the public realm.

Despite speculation that the events had gravely damaged Premier Brown's reputation and the PLP's popularity, in a general election held on 18 December 2007 the PLP secured a third consecutive term in office with 53% of the votes cast, while the UBP won 47% of the ballot. The parties' representation in the legislature remained as at the 2003 election: 22 seats for the PLP and 14 seats for the UBP. Brown was duly sworn in as Premier two days later. Allegations of corruption and issues of race featured prominently in the election campaign, with PLP candidates employing inflammatory rhetoric to suggest that the UBP, if elected, would install a regime oppressive to the black population. After failing to win the constituency seat he contested, Michael Dunkley was replaced as leader of the UBP by Kim Swan, hitherto the party's leader in the Senate.

The allegations of corruption at the BHC featured in a report issued by the FCO regarding the British Overseas Territories in July 2008, which recommended that the Government make clear the measures it had taken to investigate the allegations and also advised it to improve transparency on a wider scale, to include the establishment of an independent electoral commission. The document further recommended the extension of voting rights to 'non-Belongers' and an end to the practice of conscription.

A political dispute developed in June 2009 after it was revealed that the PLP Government had agreed with US authorities to allow four Chinese Uygur (Uighur) Muslim separatists to settle in Bermuda following their release from the US detention centre at Guantánamo Bay, Cuba. The UBP claimed that Brown had acted 'autocratically' by accepting the former detainees without consultation with either the Cabinet, the Governor or the British Government. On 20 June the opposition brought a motion of no confidence in the House of Assembly, which the Government survived by 22 to 11 votes. Following the vote, the Minister of Culture and Social Rehabilitation, Dale Butler, resigned in protest against the Premier's handling of the affair. The FCO also remonstrated with the Government for its lack of consultation, claiming that the matter fell outside the Bermudian authorities' remit. Nonetheless, following a security assessment of the Uygurs, the FCO concluded that they did not pose a 'significant risk'. By mid-2014 the Uygurs had yet to gain Bermudan citizenship.

Continued divisions within the UBP prompted the defection from the party of five members of the House of Assembly in 2009, reducing its representation in the chamber to nine seats. While two, including former UBP leader Wayne Furbert, subsequently chose to sit as independents in the House of Assembly, three joined other erstwhile members of the UBP in forming a new political organization, the Bermuda Democratic Alliance (BDA), in November. Craig Cannonier, a businessman, and Michael Fahy, a former UBP senator, were elected as leader and Chairman of the BDA, respectively, at the party's inaugural conference in February 2010.

Brown resigned as Premier, and PLP leader, on 28 October 2010 in accordance with an earlier pledge to serve only one four-year term. Deputy Premier and Minister of Finance Paula Cox won the PLP leadership election, and was inaugurated as the new Premier on 29 October.

The planned merger of the UBP and its breakaway faction, the BDA, was suspended in May 2011 after Swan objected to the union, which involved the replacement of the UBP and the BDA with a new party, the One Bermuda Alliance (OBA). Although Swan launched a successful legal challenge to prevent the dissolution of the UBP, the OBA was founded later that month by seven of the nine UBP deputies and all three BDA representatives, with the new grouping becoming the largest opposition bloc in the House of Assembly. Craig Cannonier was elected as OBA leader in September and was inaugurated as leader of the opposition in November following his victory in a parliamentary by-election earlier that month.

Elections to the House of Assembly took place on 17 December 2012. The OBA emerged victorious, winning 51.7% of the ballot and 19 seats in the legislature, compared with 46.1% and 17 seats, respectively, for the PLP. Turnout was recorded at 70.7%. Cannonier assumed the premiership on the following day. His Cabinet, which was installed on 20 December, included Michael Dunkley as Deputy Premier and Minister of Public Safety, Everard (Bob) Richards as Minister of Finance, Michael Fahy as Minister of Home Affairs, and Mark Pettingill as Attorney-General and Minister of Justice. Promoting economic recovery was declared to be the main aim of the new Government. Cox failed to retain her seat in the election and consequently resigned as PLP leader; Marc Bean was elected as her replacement. The UBP did not contest the election (Swan unsuccessfully stood as an independent), effectively marking the dissolution of the party.

In December 2013, in accordance with a recommendation by the Spending and Government Efficiency Commission, Cannonier dismissed three ministers and merged their previous responsibilities into existing portfolios. The Premier provoked controversy later that month after reneging on an earlier pledge to hold a referendum on the legalization of casinos. Cannonier, who supported the introduction of casino gambling, declared that a vote in the OBA-controlled House of Assembly would be conducted instead.

However, Cannonier resigned as Premier on 19 May 2014 following persistent PLP insinuations that he and his party had received inducements from a wealthy US property developer, Nathan Landow, in exchange for preferential treatment from the Government. It was reported that an OBA-affiliated organization had accepted a large campaign donation from Landow and his associates prior to the 2012 elections, and Cannonier admitted that he and other ministers had made use of Landow's private jet for official business in early 2013. While repeatedly denying that he had acted unlawfully, Cannonier conceded that there had been a lack of transparency surrounding his dealings with Landow and that this had undermined his

leadership. Dunkley was inaugurated as Premier on 20 May 2014. Pettingill, who had also travelled in Landow's aircraft in 2013, tendered his resignation two days later; he was succeeded by Trevor Moniz. In June Richards was appointed as Deputy Premier in addition to his existing responsibilities.

The PLP commenced a legislative boycott in July 2014 in protest against Governor George Fergusson's refusal, on the grounds of cost and insufficient evidence, to establish a commission of inquiry into a number of irregular land purchases dating from the 1920s–70s. The PLP, which had sponsored a successful parliamentary motion in support of the formation of such a commission, claimed that Fergusson had 'disrespected the will of the people' and demanded his recall and the dissolution of the House of Assembly. The British Government, however, rejected these demands.

Scrutiny of Bermuda's burgeoning financial services industry intensified in 2006, with an increased incidence of money-laundering and embezzlement. The arrest in Bermuda of Dutch businessman and oil magnate John Deuss in October attracted considerable media interest; Deuss was compelled to resign as Chairman and CEO of Bermuda Commercial Bank following allegations of money-laundering, and extradited to the Netherlands. Nevertheless, the House of Assembly ratified the Investment Funds Act 2006 in December; the legislation was designed to facilitate the registration and licensing of investment funds in the territory, by eliminating 'unnecessary' administrative protocols, and to encourage further expansion in a sector already attractive to international fund operators. Scrutiny of the financial sector was compounded in 2008 when the FCO report (see above) recommended that the country make further progress in improving financial regulation, particularly with regards to combating money-laundering. In April 2009 Bermuda was included in OECD's so-called 'grey list' of territories that had committed to but not yet implemented an internationally agreed standard of transparency measures. However, Bermuda was the first jurisdiction to be removed from the list two months later after it signed its 12th tax information-sharing agreement. (By early 2014 the Government had signed a further 26 such agreements.) After discussions with the British authorities, in November 2013 an accord was formalized in which Bermuda agreed to share information with the United Kingdom about bank accounts held in the territory. (A similar accord was also concluded with the US Administration in the following month.) In June, meanwhile, British Prime Minister David Cameron met with government officials from Bermuda and other United Kingdom Overseas Territories to discuss the further restructuring of their offshore financial sectors. Following the meeting, Cameron announced that the territories had pledged to maintain company ownership registers and to adopt OECD's Multilateral Convention on Mutual Administrative Assistance in Tax Matters. Bermuda acceded to the OECD Convention in November, and the instrument entered into force in March 2014.

Economy

Service industries, particularly the business, financial and tourism sectors, contributed 93.7% of gross domestic product (GDP) in 2012 and engaged 88.1% of the employed labour force in 2013. In 2013 13.2% of the employed labour force worked in restaurants and hotels. The majority of tourists come from the USA (72.4% of total arrivals by air in 2013), Canada and the United Kingdom. During the 2000s there was a continuing attempt to expand the tourism sector and reduce reliance on the insurance sector. To halt a decline in receipts, the industry rebranded Bermuda as a luxury destination in an attempt to attract higher spending visitors. By 2007 the number of visitor arrivals had risen to 659,572. However, the onset of the international financial crisis resulted in the number of tourist arrivals declining by 16.6% in 2008, to 550,021. Overall visitor arrivals improved in both 2009 and 2010, by 0.8% and 4.7%, respectively; however, the increases were owing to rises in

cruise ship visitors rather than the higher spending arrivals by air. The opening of a mega-cruise port in 2009 also boosted tourism. Total arrivals increased to 651,749 in 2011; cruise ship visitors rose by 19.5% in that year, although the number of tourists arriving by air only grew by 1.6%. However, total arrivals declined to 610,325 in 2012 and, despite a 1.8% rise in air arrivals, to 576,373 in 2013. Tourism receipts totalled US $385.5m. in 2010, rising to $434.8m. in 2011 before decreasing to $392.1m. in 2012 and $391.0m. in 2013. After contracting by 15.5% in 2009, the GDP of the hotel and restaurant sector expanded by 12.5% in 2010 and by a further 4.1% in 2011, before declining once again in 2012, by 1.2%.

An estimated 28.5% of the employed workforce were engaged directly in the financial, real estate and business sectors in 2013. Offshore commercial and financial services were a significant foreign exchange earner. International business accounted for 23.9% of GDP in 2012, while new companies registered in Bermuda in 2013 numbered 1,020, a 14.9% increase on the previous year's figure. Total active international companies reached 15,387 in 2013.

Bermuda is almost entirely dependent on imports, mainly from the USA, and has few export commodities. Therefore, it consistently records a large visible trade deficit (an estimated B $1,007m. in 2013). Receipts from the service industries normally ensure a surplus on the current account of the balance of payments (an estimated $754m. in 2013). The USA is the principal source of imports (providing 69.7% of total imports in 2012) and the principal market for exports. Other important trading partners include Canada, the United Kingdom and Venezuela. The main exports are rum, flowers, medicinal and pharmaceutical products, and re-exported petroleum products. Machinery and transport equipment, petroleum, and food, beverages and tobacco are the primary imports.

Industry (including manufacturing, construction, quarrying and public utilities) contributed 5.6% of GDP in 2012; the manufacturing, construction and utilities sectors engaged 10.3% of the employed workforce in 2013. The principal industrial sector is construction, which (including quarrying) contributed 3.1% of GDP in 2012 and (excluding quarrying) engaged 7.2% of the employed labour force in 2013. Construction registered a fourth successive year of decline in 2012, when the sector contracted by 11.8%. Smaller industries include ship repair, small boat building and manufacture of paint, perfume, pharmaceuticals, mineral-water extracts and handicrafts. Energy requirements are met primarily by the import of mineral fuels (accounting for 10.6% of total imports in 2012).

The average annual rate of inflation was 3.0% in 2002–12. The rate averaged 1.8% in 2013. In 2013 the official unemployment rate was recorded at 7.0%.

Bermuda's overall GDP increased, in real terms, at an average annual rate of 0.5% in 2001–11. The impact of the global recession on the tourism and international business sectors meant that real GDP contracted by 5.3% in 2009, 2.1% in 2010, 3.3% in 2011, 4.9% in 2012 and an estimated 2.0%– 2.5% in 2013, although a return to growth was expected in late 2014. Owing to the islands' heavy dependence on the tourism and offshore finance sectors, this was conditional on the continued recovery of the US economy.

Statistical Survey

Source: Dept of Statistics, Cabinet Office, POB HM 3015, Hamilton HM MX; tel. 297-7761; fax 295-8390; e-mail statistics@gov.bm; internet www .statistics.gov.bm.

AREA AND POPULATION

Area: 53.3 sq km (20.59 sq miles).

Population (civilian, non-institutional): 62,059 at census of 20 May 2000; 64,237 (males 30,858, females 33,379) at census of 20 May 2010. *Mid-2014* (official projection): 61,777.

Density (mid-2014): 1,159.0 per sq km.

Population by Age and Sex (official projections at mid-2014): *0–14 years:* 9,571 (males 4,845, females 4,726); *15–64 years:* 42,252 (males 20,419, females 21,833); *65 years and over:* 9,954 (males 4,235, females 5,719); *Total* 61,777 (males 29,499, females 32,278).

Principal Town (UN estimate at mid-2014): Hamilton (capital) 10,334. Source: UN, *World Urbanization Prospects: The 2014 Revision.*

Births, Marriages and Deaths (2012): Live births 648 (birth rate 10.4 per 1,000); Marriages 601 (marriage rate 9.6 per 1,000); Deaths 422 (death rate 6.8 per 1,000).

Life Expectancy (years at birth, 2012): 79.3 (males 76.6; females 82.1). Source: World Bank, World Development Indicators database.

Employment (persons aged 16 years and over, labour force survey, 2013): Agriculture, forestry, fishing, mining and quarrying 585; Manufacturing 618; Electricity, gas and water 486; Construction 2,603; Wholesale and retail trade 4,465; Hotels and restaurants 4,741; Transport and communications 2,157; Financial intermediation 2,414; Real estate 333; Business activities 3,511; Public administration 4,479; Education, health and social services 3,383; Other community, social and personal services 2,069; International business activity 3,992; *Sub-total* 35,836; Not classifiable by economic activity 153; *Total employed* 35,989 (males 18,193, females 17,796); Unemployed 2,569; *Total labour force* 38,558.

HEALTH AND WELFARE

Total Fertility Rate (children per woman, 2013): 2.0.

Physicians (per 1,000 head, 2005): 2.1.

Hospital Beds (per 1,000 head, 2012): 5.2.

Health Expenditure (% of GDP, 2004): 4.3.

Health Expenditure (public, % of total, 1995): 53.2.

Total Carbon Dioxide Emissions ('000 metric tons, 2010): 476.7.

Carbon Dioxide Emissions Per Head (metric tons, 2010): 7.3.

Source: partly Pan American Health Organization.

For other sources and definitions, see explanatory note on p. vi.

AGRICULTURE, ETC.

Principal Crops (metric tons, 2012, FAO estimates): Potatoes 1,100; Carrots and turnips 400; Vegetables and melons 3,836; Bananas 325.

Livestock (2012, FAO estimates): Cattle 660; Horses 1,000; Pigs 800.

Livestock Products (metric tons, 2012, FAO estimates): Cows' milk 1,465; Hen eggs 360.

Fishing (metric tons, live weight, 2012): Groupers 49; Snappers and jobfishes 40; Wahoo 88; Yellowfin tuna 66; Carangids 78; Caribbean spiny lobster 47; Total catch (incl. others) 516.

Source: FAO.

INDUSTRY

Electric Energy (production, million kWh): 645 in 2008; 733 in 2009; 730 in 2010. Source: UN Industrial Commodity Statistics Database.

FINANCE

Currency and Exchange Rates: 100 cents = 1 Bermuda dollar (B $). *Sterling, US Dollar and Euro Equivalents* (30 May 2014): £1 sterling = B $1.682; US $1 = B $1.000; €1 = B $1.361; B $100 = £59.45 = US $100.00 = €73.47. *Exchange Rate:* The Bermuda dollar is at par with the US dollar. Note: US and Canadian currencies are also accepted.

Budget (B $ million, 2013/14, estimates): Total current account revenue 892.6; Total current account expenditure 1,016.1; Total capital expenditure 62.5.

Cost of Living (Consumer Price Index; base: 2000 = 100): All items 139.2 in 2011; 142.6 in 2012; 145.1 in 2013. Source: ILO.

Gross Domestic Product (B $ million at constant 2006 prices): 5,242.6 in 2010; 5,067.5 in 2011; 4,820.8 in 2012.

Expenditure on the Gross Domestic Product (B $ million at current prices, 2012, UN estimates): Government final consumption expenditure 1,111.2; Private final consumption expenditure 4,143.8; Gross fixed capital formation 1,048.6; Change in inventories 58.5; *Total domestic expenditure* 6,362.1; Exports of goods and services 2,312.7; *Less* Imports of goods and services 3,081.8; *GDP in purchasers' values* 5,593.1. Source: UN Statistics Division, National Accounts Main Aggregates Database.

Gross Domestic Product by Economic Activity (B $ million at current prices, 2012): Agriculture, forestry and fishing 41.2; Manufacturing 52.1; Electricity, gas and water 86.6; Construction and quarrying 179.8; Wholesale and retail trade and repair services 372.4; Restaurants and hotels 246.9; Transport and communications 268.7; Financial intermediation 694.2; Real estate and renting activities 949.6; Business activities 511.5; Public administration 353.0; Education, health and social work 478.2; Other community, social and personal services 120.8; International business activity 1,371.6; *Sub-total* 5,726.7; *Less* Imputed bank service charges 424.0; Taxes and duties on imports 170.8; *GDP in purchasers' values* 5,473.5.

Balance of Payments (B $ million, 2013): Exports of goods f.o.b. 13; Imports of goods f.o.b. −1,020; *Trade balance* −1,007; Receipts from services and income 3,810; Payments on services and income −2,049; *Current balance* 754; Direct investment (net) 4; Portfolio investment (net) −1,372; Financial derivatives (net) −112; Other investments (net) 793; Reserve assets (net) −11; *Overall balance* 56.

EXTERNAL TRADE

Principal Commodities (US $ million, 2012): *Imports:* Food, beverages and tobacco 181.7; Mineral fuels and lubricants 93.6; Chemicals and related products 80.4; Basic manufactures 55.8; Machinery and transport equipment 157.5; Total (incl. others) 884.4. *Exports:* Total 16.9.

Principal Trading Partners (US $ million): *Imports* (2012): Canada 96.2; Caribbean countries 23.7; United Kingdom 33.1; USA 616.7; Total (incl. others) 884.4. *Exports* (1995): France 7.5; United Kingdom 3.9; USA 31.3; Total (incl. others) 62.9. *2012:* Total exports 16.9.

TRANSPORT

Road Traffic (vehicles in use, 2012): Private cars 21,707; Motorcycles 19,641; Buses, taxis and limousines 769; Trucks and tank wagons 3,746; Other 1,596; Total 47,459.

Shipping: *Ship Arrivals* (2004): Cruise ships 161; Cargo ships 186; Oil and gas tankers 21. *Flag Registered Fleet* (at 31 December 2013): Vessels 194; Total displacement 11,316,128 grt (Source: Lloyd's List Intelligence—www.lloydslistintelligence.com).

Civil Aviation (2012): Aircraft arrivals 12,827; Passengers 389,846; Air cargo 3,046,940 kg; Air mail 403,686 kg.

TOURISM

Visitor Arrivals: 651,749 (arrivals by air 236,038, cruise ship passengers 415,711) in 2011; 610,325 (arrivals by air 232,063, cruise ship passengers 378,262) in 2012; 576,373 (arrivals by air 236,343, cruise ship passengers 340,030) in 2013.

Visitors by Country of Origin (arrivals by air, 2013): Canada 27,613; United Kingdom 23,610; USA 171,215; Total (incl. others) 236,343.

Tourism Receipts (US $ million, incl. passenger transport): 434.8 in 2011; 392.1 in 2012; 391.0 in 2013.

COMMUNICATIONS MEDIA

Telephones (2013): 72,000 main lines in use.

Mobile Cellular Telephones (2013): 94,300 subscribers.

Internet Users (2009): 54,000.

Broadband Subscribers (2013): 40,100.

Source: International Telecommunication Union.

EDUCATION

Pre-primary (2012/13, unless otherwise indicated): 12 schools (2006); 55 teachers (2010/11); 389 pupils.

Primary: 17 (and 5 middle) schools (2006); 486 teachers (2010/11); 4,122 pupils (2012/13).

Senior: 18 schools (1999); 670 teachers (2010/11); 4,175 pupils (2012/13)*.

Higher: 1 institution (2002); 71 teachers (2010/11); 1,207 students (2012/13).

* Including 7 private schools.

2004: Local student enrolment 10,594 (government schools including pre-school 6,370, private schools excluding pre-school 3,512, Bermuda College 712); Teachers 1,310.

Pupil-teacher Ratio (primary education, UNESCO estimate): 8.9 in 2010/11. Source: UNESCO Institute for Statistics.

Adult Literacy Rate (UNESCO estimates): 99% (males 98%; females 99%) in 1998 (Source: UNESCO, *Statistical Yearbook*).

Directory

The Constitution

The Constitution, introduced on 8 June 1968 and amended in 1973 and 1979, contains provisions relating to the protection of fundamental rights and freedoms of the individual; the powers and duties of the Governor; the composition, powers and procedure of the Legislature; the Cabinet; the judiciary; the public service and finance.

The British monarch is represented by an appointed Governor, who retains responsibility for external affairs, defence, internal security and the police.

The Legislature consists of the monarch, the Senate and the House of Assembly. Three members of the Senate are appointed at the Governor's discretion, five on the advice of the Government leader and three on the advice of the Opposition leader. The Senate elects a President and Vice-President. The House of Assembly, consisting of 36 members elected under universal adult franchise, elects a Speaker and a Deputy Speaker, and sits for a five-year term.

The Cabinet consists of the Premier and at least six other members of the Legislature. The Governor appoints the majority leader in the House of Assembly as Premier, who in turn nominates the other members of the Cabinet. They are assigned responsibilities for government departments and other business and, in some cases, are assisted by Permanent Cabinet Secretaries.

The Cabinet is presided over by the Premier. The Governor's Council enables the Governor to consult with the Premier and two other members of the Cabinet nominated by the Premier on matters for which the Governor has responsibility. The Secretary to the Cabinet, who heads the public service, acts as secretary to the Governor's Council.

Voters must be British subjects aged 18 years or over (lowered from 21 years in 1990), and, if not possessing Bermudian status, must have been registered as electors on 1 May 1976. Candidates for election must qualify as electors, and must possess Bermudian status.

Under the British Overseas Territories Act, which entered into effect in May 2002, Bermudian citizens have the right to United Kingdom citizenship and the right of abode in the United Kingdom. British citizens do not enjoy reciprocal rights.

The Government

HEAD OF STATE

Queen: HM Queen ELIZABETH II.

Governor and Commander-in-Chief: GEORGE DUNCAN FERGUSSON (took office 23 May 2012).

Deputy Governor: GINNY FERSON.

CABINET
(September 2014)

The Government is formed by the One Bermuda Alliance.

Premier and Minister of National Security: MICHAEL HENRY DUNKLEY.

Deputy Premier and Minister of Finance: EVERARD TRENTON (BOB) RICHARDS.

Minister of Health, Seniors and the Environment: JEANNE ATHERDEN.

Minister of Education and Economic Development: Dr GRANT GIBBONS.

Minister of Tourism Development and Transport: SHAWN GRANVILLE CROCKWELL.

Minister of Public Works: PATRICIA JASMINE GORDON PAMPLIN.

Minister of Community, Culture and Sports: REGINALD WAYNE EUGENE SCOTT.

Minister of Home Affairs: Sen. MICHAEL FAHY.

Attorney-General and Minister of Legal Affairs: TREVOR MONIZ.

MINISTRIES

Office of the Governor: Government House, 11 Langton Hill, Pembroke HM 13; tel. 292-3600; fax 292-6831; e-mail executiveofficer@gov.bm; internet www.gov.bm.

Office of the Premier: Cabinet Office, Cabinet Bldg, 105 Front St, Hamilton HM 12; tel. 292-5501; fax 292-8397; e-mail premier@gov.bm; internet www.gov.bm.

Ministry of Community, Culture and Sports: Hamilton HM 12; tel. 292-0187.

Ministry of Education and Economic Development: 14 Waller's Point Rd, St David's DD 03; tel. 278-3300; fax 278-3348; e-mail reve@gov.bm; internet www.moed.bm.

Ministry of Finance: Govt Admin. Bldg, 2nd Floor, 30 Parliament St, Hamilton HM 12; tel. 295-5151; fax 295-5727.

Ministry of Health, Seniors and the Environment: Continental Bldg, 25 Church St, POB 380, Hamilton HM 12; tel. 278-4900; fax 292-2622.

Ministry of Home Affairs: Govt Admin. Bldg, 30 Parliament St, Hamilton HM12.

Ministry of Legal Affairs and Attorney-General's Chambers: Penthouse Floor, Global House, 43 Church St, Hamilton HM 12; tel. 292-2463; fax 292-3608; e-mail agc@gov.bm; internet www.bermudalaws.bm.

Ministry of National Security: Govt Admin. Bldg, 1st Floor, 30 Parliament St, POB HM 1364, Hamilton HM 12; tel. 297-7819; fax 295-4780.

Ministry of Public Works: 3rd Floor, General Post Office Bldg, 56 Church St, Hamilton HM 12; tel. 295-5151; fax 295-0170; e-mail nfox@bdagov.bm.

Ministry of Tourism Development and Transport: TCD Bldg, 11 North St, Hamilton HM11; tel. 295-3130; fax 295-1013.

Legislature

SENATE

President: CAROLANNE M. BASSETT.

Clerk: CLARK SOMNER.
There are 11 nominated members.

HOUSE OF ASSEMBLY

Speaker: K. H. (RANDOLPH) HORTON.

Clerk: SHERNETTE WOLFE; tel. 292-7408; fax 292-2006; e-mail swolffe@parliament.bm.

General Election, 17 December 2012

Party	% of votes	Seats
One Bermuda Alliance (OBA)	51.68	19
Progressive Labour Party (PLP)	46.07	17
Independent	2.25	—
Total valid votes	100.00	36

Political Organizations

One Bermuda Alliance (OBA): 58 Reid St, POB 1940, Hamilton HM HX; tel. 294-3264; e-mail info@oba.bm; internet www.oba.bm; f. 2011 by fmr mems of the United Bermuda Party and the Bermuda Democratic Alliance; Leader CRAIG CANNONIER; Chair. SUSAN JACKSON (acting); Leader MICHAEL DUNKLEY.

Progressive Labour Party (PLP): Alaska Hall, 16 Court St, POB 1367, Hamilton HM 17; tel. 292-2264; fax 295-7890; e-mail info@plp.bm; internet www.plp.bm; f. 1963; advocates the 'Bermudianization' of the economy, more equitable taxation, a more developed system of welfare and preparation for independence; Leader MARC A. R. BEAN; Chair. MAYNARD DILL; Sec.-Gen. TULANI O. BULFORD.

Judicial System

Supreme Court: 113 Front St, Hamilton HM 12; tel. 292-1350; fax 292-2268; unlimited civil jurisdiction and jurisdiction over all serious criminal matters; also hears civil and criminal appeals from the Magistrates' Courts; Chief Justice IAN R. C. KAWALEY; Registrar CHARLENE A. SCOTT.

Court of Appeal: Hamilton HM 12; f. 1964; Pres. EDWARD ZACCA.

Director of Public Prosecutions: RORY FIELD.

There are also three Magistrates' Courts with a limited civil jurisdiction and jurisdiction over all petty offences.

Religion

CHRISTIANITY

The Anglican Communion

According to 2010 census figures, some 16% of the population are Anglicans. The Anglican Church of Bermuda consists of a single, extra-provincial diocese, directly under the metropolitan jurisdiction of the Archbishop of Canterbury, the Primate of All England.

Bishop of Bermuda: Rt Rev. NICHOLAS DILL, Bishop's Lodge, 18 Ferrar's Lane, Pembroke HM 08; POB HM 769, Hamilton HM CX; tel. 292-6987; fax 292-5421; internet www.anglican.bm.

The Roman Catholic Church

According to 2010 census figures, some 15% of the population are Roman Catholics. Bermuda forms a single diocese, suffragan to the archdiocese of Kingston in Jamaica. The Bishop participates in the Antilles Episcopal Conference (currently based in Port of Spain, Trinidad and Tobago).

Bishop of Hamilton in Bermuda: ROBERT JOSEPH KURTZ, 2 Astwood Rd, POB HM 1191, Hamilton HM EX; tel. 232-4414; fax 232-4447; e-mail rjkurtz@northrock.bm.

Other Christian Churches

According to the 2010 census, 9% of the population are African Methodist Episcopalians, 7% are Seventh-day Adventists, 4% are Pentecostalists and 3% are Methodists. The Presbyterian Church, the Church of God, Jehovah's Witnesses, Baptist Church, the Salvation Army, the Brethren Church, the Church of Christ, the New Testament Churches of God, the Ethiopian Orthodox Church and the Lutherans are also active in Bermuda.

Baptist Church: Emmanuel Baptist Church, 35 Dundonald St, Hamilton HM 10; tel. 295-6555; fax 296-4491; Pastor RONALD K. SMITH.

Wesley Methodist Church: 41 Church St, Hamilton HM 12; tel. 292-0418; fax 295-9460; e-mail info@wesley.bm; internet www.wesley.bm; Rev. CALVIN STONE.

The Press

The Bermuda Sun: 19 Elliott St, POB HM 1241, Hamilton HM FX; tel. 295-3902; fax 292-5597; e-mail feedback@bermudasun.bm; internet www.bermudasun.bm; f. 1964; 2 a week; official govt gazette; Co-Publr and Editor-in-Chief TONY MCWILLIAM; circ. 12,500.

The Bermudian: POB HM 283, Hamilton HM AX; tel. 232-7041; fax 232-7042; e-mail info@thebermudian.com; internet www.thebermudian.com; f. 1930; monthly; pictorial and lifestyle magazine; Editor TINA STEVENSON; circ. 7,500.

Bermudian Business: POB HM 283, Hamilton HM AX; tel. 232-7041; fax 232-7042; e-mail info@thebermudian.com; internet www.bermudianbusiness.com; f. 1996; publ. by The Bermudian Publishing Co Ltd; Publr TINA STEVENSON; circ. 2,500.

The Royal Gazette: 2 Par-la-Ville Rd, POB HM 1025, Hamilton HM DX; tel. 295-5881; fax 292-2498; e-mail letters@royalgazette.bm; internet www.theroyalgazette.com; f. 1828; morning daily; incorporates *The Colonist* and *Daily News* (f. 1866); Editor (vacant); circ. 17,500.

The Worker's Voice: 49 Union Sq., Hamilton HM 12; tel. 292-0044; fax 295-7992; e-mail csmith@biu.bm; internet www.biu.bm/#!workers-voice/c1wi0; fortnightly; organ of the Bermuda Industrial Union; Editor-in-Chief CALVIN SMITH.

This Week in Bermuda: 13 Addendum Lane, Pembroke, POB 937, HM 07; tel. 295-1189; fax 295-3445; e-mail info@twib.bm; internet www.thisweek.bm; Editor CANDICE E. DICKINSON; Gen. Man. HORST AUGUSTIMOVIC.

Publishers

Bermuda Maritime Museum Press: POB MA 133, Sandys MA BX; tel. 234-1333; fax 234-1735; e-mail info@bmm.bm; internet www.bmm.bm; publishes books, *MARITimes* magazine, *Bermuda Journal of Archaeology and Maritime History*; Chair. ROBERT STEINHOFF.

Bermudian Publishing Co Ltd: POB HM 283, Hamilton HM AX; tel. 232-7041; fax 232-7042; e-mail info@thebermudian.com; internet www.thebermudian.com; social sciences, sociology, sports; Editor TINA STEVENSON.

MediaHouse Ltd: 19 Elliot St, Hamilton HM 10; tel. 295-1944; e-mail rfrench@mediahouse.com; internet www.mediahouse.com; f. 1959 as Island Press; rebranded as above in 2005; newspapers, magazines, directories; CEO RANDY FRENCH.

Broadcasting and Communications

TELECOMMUNICATIONS

Bermuda Digital Communications/CellularOne: 22 Reid St, Hamilton HM 3262; tel. 296-4010; fax 296-4020; e-mail info@cellularone.bm; internet www.cellularone.bm; f. 1998; mobile cellular telephone operator; CEO KURT EVE.

Bermuda Telephone Co (BTC): 30 Victoria St, POB 1021, Hamilton HM DX; tel. 295-1001; fax 295-1192; e-mail customersupport@btc.bm; internet www.btc.bm; f. 1987; owned by KeyTech Ltd, plans to sell to Barrie OpCo Ltd announced in July 2014; Pres. and CEO LLOYD FRAY.

Digicel Bermuda: Washington Mall, 22 Church St, Phase II, POB 896, Hamilton HM 11; tel. 500-5000; fax 295-3235; e-mail info.bermuda@digicelgroup.com; internet www.digicelbermuda.com; f. 2005; mobile telecommunications and internet services provider; CEO (Bermuda) WAYNE MICHAEL CAINES.

LinkBermuda Ltd: 1 Middle Rd, Smith's FL 03, POB HM 151, Hamilton HM AX; tel. 497-7000; fax 296-4490; e-mail helpdesk@LinkBermuda.com; internet www.LinkBermuda.com; new fibre optic submarine cable, Gemini Bermuda, installed in 2007; acquired by the Bragg Group, Canada, in 2011; CEO ANN PETLEY-JONES.

Logic Communications Ltd: 22 Church St, Hamilton, HM 11; tel. 296-9600; fax 295-1149; e-mail support@logic.bm; internet www.logic.bm; f. 1997; TV, telephone and internet service orovider; CEO VICKI COELHO.

TeleBermuda International Ltd (TBI): Victoria Pl., 1st Floor, 31 Victoria St, POB HM 3043, Hamilton HM 10; tel. 296-9000; fax 296-9010; e-mail business@telebermuda.com; internet www.telebermuda.com; f. 1997; a division of GlobeNet Communications, provides an international voice and data service; owns a fibre optic network connecting Bermuda, Cayman Islands and the USA; Pres. and COO GREGORY SWAN.

BROADCASTING

Radio

Bermuda Broadcasting Co: POB HM 452, Hamilton HM BX; tel. 295-2828; fax 295-4282; e-mail zbmzfb@bermudabroadcasting.com; f. 1982 as merger of ZBM (f. 1943) and ZFB (f. 1962); operates 4 radio stations; CEO ULRIC P. (RICK) RICHARDSON; Comptroller MALCOLM R. FLETCHER.

DeFontes Broadcasting Co Ltd (VSB): 94 Reid St, POB HM 1450, Hamilton HM FX; tel. 292-0050; fax 295-1658; e-mail news@vsbbermuda.com; internet www.vsbbermuda.com; f. 1981 as St George's Broadcasting Co; commercial; 4 radio stations; Pres. KENNETH DEFONTES; Station Man. MIKE BISHOP.

Television

Bermuda Broadcasting Co: see Radio; operates 2 TV stations (Channels 7 and 9).

Bermuda Cablevision Ltd: 19 Laffan St, POB 1642, Hamilton HM GX; tel. 292-5544; fax 295-3023; e-mail info@cablevision.bm; internet www.cablevision.bm; f. 1988; 180 channels; Gen. Man. TERRY ROBERSON.

DeFontes Broadcasting Co Ltd (VSB): see Radio; operates 1 TV station.

Finance

(cap. = capital; res = reserves; dep. = deposits; m. = million; brs = branches; amounts in Bermuda dollars, unless otherwise stated)

BANKING

Central Bank

Bermuda Monetary Authority: BMA House, 43 Victoria St, Hamilton HM 12; tel. 295-5278; fax 292-7471; e-mail info@bma.bm; internet www.bma.bm; f. 1969; central issuing and monetary authority; cap. 20.0m., res 24.7m., total assets 187.4m. (Dec. 2009); Chair. GERALD SIMONS; CEO JEREMY COX.

Commercial Banks

Bank of N. T. Butterfield & Son Ltd: 65 Front St, POB HM 195, Hamilton HM 12; tel. 295-1111; fax 292-4365; e-mail contact@bntb.bm; internet www.bm.butterfieldgroup.com; f. 1858; inc. 1904; cap. 5.5m., res 1,313.2m., dep. 8,228m. (Dec. 2010); Chair. BRENDAN MCDONAUGH; Pres. and CEO BRADFORD KOPP; 4 brs.

Bermuda Commercial Bank Ltd: Bermuda Commercial Bank Bldg, 19 Par-la-Ville Rd, POB 1748, Hamilton HM GX; tel. 295-5678; fax 295-8091; e-mail elambert@bcb.bm; internet www.bermuda-bcb.com; f. 1969; cap. US $16.8m., res US $8.3m., dep. US $457.5m. (Sept. 2012); CEO PETER HORTON; Chief Financial Officer LASANTHA THENNAKOON.

HSBC Bank Bermuda Ltd: 6 Front St, POB HM 1020, Hamilton HM 11; tel. 295-4000; fax 295-7093; e-mail customer.care@hsbc.bm; internet www.hsbc.bm; f. 1889; fmrly Bank of Bermuda Ltd; 100% acquired by HSBC Asia Holdings BV (Netherlands) in Feb. 2004; name changed as above in May 2010; cap. US $30.0m., res US $432.6m., dep. US $9,752.1m. (Dec. 2010); Chair. PHILLIP BUTTERFIELD; CEO RICHARD MOSELEY; 7 brs.

STOCK EXCHANGE

Bermuda Stock Exchange: 30 Victoria St, 3rd Floor, POB 1369, Hamilton HM FX; tel. 292-7212; fax 292-7619; e-mail info@bsx.com; internet www.bsx.com; f. 1971; more than 600 listed equities, funds, debt issues and depositary programmes; Chair. DAVID BROWN; Pres. and CEO GREG WOJCIECHOWSKI.

INSURANCE

The majority of insurance companies in Bermuda are subsidiaries of foreign insurance companies, or owned by foreign industrial or financial concerns.

Major Companies

ACE Bermuda: ACE Bldg, 17 Woodbourne Ave, POB HM 1015, Hamilton HM DX; tel. 295-5200; fax 298-9620; e-mail info@acebermuda.com; internet www.acebermuda.com; f. 1985; total revenue $14,154m. (Dec. 2007); Pres. G. REES FLETCHER; Regional Exec. and COO ALLISON TOWLSON.

American Safety Reinsurance Ltd (ASRE): The Boyle Bldg, 2nd Floor, 31 Queen St, Hamilton HM 11; tel. 296-8560; fax 296-8561; e-mail npascall@amsafety.bm; internet www.amsafety.bm; subsidiary of American Safety Insurance Holdings, Ltd; Chief Officer NICHOLAS PASCALL.

Argus Insurance Co Ltd: Argus Insurance Bldg, 14 Wesley St, POB HM 1064, Hamilton HM EX; tel. 295-2021; fax 295-6591; e-mail insurance@argus.bm; internet www.argus.bm; Chair. SHEILA E. NICOLL; CEO ALISON HILL.

BF&M Ltd: BF&M Insurance Bldg, 112 Pitts Bay Rd, Pembroke HM 08; tel. 295-5566; fax 292-8604; e-mail jwight@bfm.bm; internet www.bfm.bm; holding co for insurance and insurance-related cos; CEO JOHN WIGHT.

Colonial Insurance Co Ltd: Jardine House, 33–35 Reid St, POB 1559, Hamilton HM 12; tel. 296-3700; fax 295-1367; internet bermuda.cgigroup.com; part of Colonial Group International, also owns Colonial Medical Insurance and Colonial Life Assurance.

Flagstone Reinsurance: Wellesley House, 2nd Floor, 90 Pitts Bay Rd, Pembroke HM 08; tel. 278-4300; fax 296-9879; e-mail info@flagstonere.com; internet www.flagstonere.bm; CEO DAVID BROWN.

Hiscox Insurance Co (Bermuda) Ltd (Hiscox Bermuda): Wessex House, 4th Floor, 45 Reid St, Hamilton, HM12; tel. 278-8300; fax 278-8301; e-mail jeremy.pinchin@hiscox.bm; internet www.hiscox.bm; CEO JEREMY PINCHIN.

Validus Reinsurance Ltd: 48 Par-la-Ville Rd, Suite 1790, Hamilton HM 11; tel. 278-9000; fax 278-9090; e-mail conan.ward@validusre.bm; internet www.validusre.bm; f. 2005; general reinsurance coverage; CEO CONAN M. WARD.

XL Insurance Co Ltd: Brian O'Hara House, 1 Bermudiana Rd, Hamilton HM 08; tel. 292-8515; fax 292-5280; e-mail contact.xli@xlgroup.com; internet www.xlinsurance.com; CEO DAVID B. DUCLOS.

ASSOCIATIONS

Association of Bermuda Insurers and Reinsurers (ABIR): XL House, 1 Bermudiana Rd, Hamilton HM 11; tel. 294-7221; fax 296-4207; e-mail leila.madeiros@abir.bm; internet www.abir.bm; represents international insurers and reinsurers; Pres. and Exec. Dir BRADLEY L. KADING.

Bermuda Insurance Management Association (BIMA): POB HM 824, Hamilton HM DX; tel. 295-6015; fax 295-1702; e-mail grichmond@dyna.bm; internet www.bima.bm; f. 1978; manages over 1,200 insurance and reinsurance cos; liaises with govt and other financial orgs; Pres. ROBERT PATON.

Trade and Industry

GOVERNMENT AGENCY

Bermuda Registrar of Companies: Government Administration Bldg, 30 Parliament St, Hamilton HM 12; tel. 297-7530; fax 292-6640; e-mail jfsmith@gov.bm; internet www.roc.gov.bm; Registrar of Companies STEPHEN LOWE.

DEVELOPMENT ORGANIZATIONS

Bermuda Business Development Agency (BDA): Maxwell Roberts Bldg, 1 Church St, Hamilton HM 11; tel. 292-0632; fax 292-1797; e-mail info@bermudabda.com; internet www.bermudabda.com; f. 2013 following merger of BBDC with Business Bermuda and the Insurance Devt Council; CEO Ross D. Webber.

Bermuda Economic Development Corpn (BSBDC): Sofia House, 48 Church St, POB HM 637, Hamilton HM CX; tel. 292-5570; fax 295-1600; e-mail info@bsbdc.bm; internet www.bedc.bm; f. 1980; funded jtly by the Govt and private banks; guarantees loans to small businesses; responsible for establishing economic empowerment zones; Gen. Man. Lucretia Ming.

CHAMBER OF COMMERCE

Bermuda Chamber of Commerce: 1 Point Pleasant Rd, POB HM 655, Hamilton HM CX; tel. 295-4201; fax 292-5779; e-mail info@bermudacommerce.com; internet www.bermudacommerce.com; f. 1907; Pres. Kristi Grayston; Exec. Dir Joanne MacPhee; 750 mems.

EMPLOYERS' ASSOCIATIONS

Bermuda Employers' Council: 4 Park Rd, Hamilton HM 11; tel. 295-5070; fax 295-1966; e-mail kjensen@bec.bm; internet www.bec.bm; f. 1960; advisory body on employment and labour relations; Pres. Keith Jensen; 420 mems.

Construction Association of Bermuda: POB HM 238, Hamilton HM AX; tel. 292-0633; fax 292-0564; e-mail caob@logic.bm; internet www.constructionbermuda.com; f. 1968; Pres. Charles Dunstan; 90 mems.

Hotel Employers of Bermuda: c/o Bermuda Hotel Asscn, Carmel, 61 King St, Hamilton HM 19; tel. 295-2127; fax 292-6671; f. 1968; CEO Stephen Todd; 8 mems.

UTILITIES

Electricity

Bermuda Electric Light Co Ltd (BELCO): 27 Serpentine Rd, POB HM 1026, Hamilton HM DX; tel. 295-5111; fax 292-8975; e-mail info@belco.bm; internet www.belco.bm; f. 1904 as the Bermuda Electric Light, Power & Traction Co (BELPT); owned by Ascendant Group Ltd; Chair. Reginald S. Minors; Pres. Walter M. Higgins.

Gas

Bermuda Gas & Utility Co Ltd: 25 Serpentine Rd, Pembroke, POB 373, HM BX; tel. 295-3111; fax 295-8311; e-mail info@bermudagas.bm; internet www.bermudagas.bm; f. 1936; owned by Ascendant Group Ltd; Gen. Man. Judith Uddin.

TRADE UNIONS

In 2007 trade union membership was estimated at approximately 9,140. There are nine registered trade unions, eight of which profess membership of the Bermuda Trades Union Congress.

Bermuda Industrial Union: 49 Union Sq., Hamilton HM 12; tel. 292-0044; fax 295-7992; e-mail biu@biu.bm; internet www.biu.bm; f. 1946; Pres. Chris Furbert; Gen. Sec. Helena (Molly) Burgess; 5,202 mems.

Bermuda Trades Union Congress (BTUC): POB 2080, Hamilton HM HX; tel. 292-6515; fax 292-0697; e-mail mcharles@ibl.bm; Pres. Wendell (Shine) Hayward; Gen. Sec. Michael Charles.

Bermuda Federation of Musicians and Variety Artists: 49 Par-la-Ville Rd, Suite 798, Hamilton HM 11; tel. 291-0138; Sec.-Gen. Lloyd Simmons; 318 mems.

Bermuda Public Services Union: POB HM 763, Hamilton HM CX; tel. 292-6985; fax 292-1149; e-mail osimmons@bpsu.bm; internet www.bpsu.bm; re-formed 1961; Pres. Kevin Grant; Gen. Sec. Edward G. Ball, Jr; c. 3,500 mems. **Bermuda Union of Teachers:** 72 Church St, POB HM 726, Hamilton HM CX; tel. 292-6515; fax 292-0697; e-mail butunion@ibl.bm; internet www.but.bm; f. 1919; Pres. Keisha Douglas; Gen. Sec. Michael A. Charles; 700 mems.

Transport

ROADS

There are some 225 km (140 miles) of public highways and 222 km of private roads, with almost 6 km reserved for cyclists and pedestrians. All the roads are paved. Each household is permitted only one passenger vehicle, and visitors may only hire mopeds, to limit traffic congestion.

SHIPPING

The chief port of Bermuda is Hamilton, followed by St George's and King's Wharf. All three are used by freight and cruise ships. There is also a 'free' port, Freeport, on Ireland Island. Proposals in 2000 to enlarge Hamilton docks in order to accommodate larger cruise ships prompted fears that such an enlargement would place excessive strain on the island's environment and infrastructure. Bermuda is a 'free flag' nation, and at December 2013 the shipping register comprised 194 vessels, totalling 11,316,128 grt, of which 15 were bulk carriers, 43 gas tankers and 31 were general cargo ships.

Department of Marine and Ports Services: 4 Crow Lane, East Broadway, POB HM 180, Hamilton HM AX; tel. 295-6575; fax 295-5523; e-mail marineports@bolagov.bm; internet www.marineandports.bm; Dir Francis Richardson; Harbour Master David Simmons.

Department of Maritime Administration: Magnolia Pl., 2nd Floor, 45 Victoria St, POB HM 1628, Hamilton HM GX; tel. 295-7251; fax 295-3718; e-mail enquiries.bermudashipping@gov.bm; internet www.bermudashipping.bm; f. 1789; Chief Surveyor Simon Hill; Registrar of Shipping Edward Robinson.

Principal Shipping Companies

B & H Ocean Carriers Ltd: Par-la-Ville Pl., 3rd Floor, 14 Par-la-Ville Rd, POB HM 2257, Hamilton HM JX; tel. 295-6875; fax 295-6796; e-mail info@bhcousa.com; internet www.bhocean.com; f. 1988; Chair. Michael S. Hudner.

Bermuda Forwarders Ltd: 2 Mill Creek Park, POB HM 511, Hamilton HM CX; tel. 292-4600; fax 292-1859; e-mail info@bermudaforwarders.com; internet www.bermudaforwarders.com; f. 1955; international import and export handlers; Pres. Toby Kempe.

Bermuda Worldwide Shipping Ltd: 4 Mill Reach Lane, Pembroke, POB FL404, Flatts FLBX; tel. 292-9649; fax 292-4563; e-mail info@bdashipping.bm; internet www.bdashipping.bm; Pres. Roger Moniz.

Bernhard Schulte Shipmanagement (Bermuda) Ltd Partnership: Richmond House, 12 Par-la-Ville Rd, POB HM 2089, Hamilton HM HX; tel. 295-0614; fax 292-1549; e-mail management@amlp.bm; internet www.bs-shipmanagement.com; f. 2008 by the merger of Hanseatic Shipping, Dorchester Atlantic Marine, Eurasia Group and Vorsetzen Bereederungs- und Schiffahrtskontor; owned by the Schulte Group; CEO Rajesh Bajpaee.

BEST Shipping: 3 Addendum Lane North, Pembroke, Hamilton HM 07; tel. 292-8080; fax 295-1713; e-mail info@best.bm; internet www.best.bm; f. 1987 as Bermuda Export Sea Transfer Ltd; sea and air freight services; Pres. and Man. Dir David Sousa.

Container Ship Management Ltd: 14 Par-la-Ville Rd, POB HM 2266, Hamilton HM JX; tel. 295-1624; fax 295-3781; e-mail bcl@csm.bm; internet www.bcl.bm; f. 1980; privately owned; Chair. John H. K. White; Pres. and CEO Geoffrey Frith.

Gearbulk Holding Ltd: Par-la-Ville Pl., 14 Par-la-Ville Rd, POB HM 2257, Hamilton HM JX; tel. 295-2184; fax 295-2234; internet www.gearbulk.com; f. 1968; Pres. Arthur E. M. Jones.

Golden Ocean Group Ltd: Par-la-Ville Pl., 14 Par-la-Ville Rd, POB HM 1593, Hamilton HM 08; tel. 295-6935; fax 295-3494; e-mail tor@frontmgt.no; internet www.goldenocean.no; Chair., Pres. and CEO John Fredrikson; Exec. Dir Herman Billung.

Meyer Shipping: Waverley Bldg, 35 Church St, Hamilton HM 12; tel. 296-9798; fax 295-4556; e-mail shipping@meyer.bm; internet www.meyer.bm; f. 1867; subsidiary of the Meyer Group of Cos; Exec. Vice-Pres. Joe Simas.

CIVIL AVIATION

The L. F. Wade International Airport is served by several international airlines.

Department of Civil Aviation: Channel House, Suite 2, 12 Longfield Rd, Southside, POB GE 218, St George's GE BX; tel. 293-1640; fax 293-2417; e-mail info@dca.gov.bm; internet www.dca.gov.bm; Dir Thomas Dunstan.

L. F. Wade International Airport: 3 Cahow Way, St George's GE CX; tel. 293-2470; e-mail dao@gov.bm; internet www.bermudaairport.aero; fmrly Bermuda International Airport, adopted present name 2007; Gen. Man. Aaron Adderley.

Tourism

Tourism is the principal industry of Bermuda and is government-sponsored. The great attractions of the islands are the climate, scenery and facilities for outdoor entertainment of all types. In 2010 there were 44 licensed hotels and 2,659 rooms. In 2013 a total of 576,373 tourists (including 340,030 cruise ship passengers) visited

Bermuda. The industry earned an estimated US $391m. in the same year.

Bermuda Hotel Association: Carmel, 61 King St, Hamilton HM 19; tel. 295-2127; fax 292-6671; internet www.experiencebermuda .com; Pres. J. P. MARTENS; CEO STEPHEN TODD; 37 mem. hotels.

Bermuda Tourism Authority: Global House, 43 Church St, Hamilton; tel. 296-9200; fax 292-7537; e-mail contact@ bermudatourism.com; internet www.bermudatourism.com; fmrly Bermuda Dept of Tourism; denationalized and adopted present name in 2013; Chair. DAVID DODWELL; CEO BILL HANBURY.

Defence

The local defence force is the Bermuda Regiment, which employs selective conscription. According to the 2013/14 budget statement, some B $156.1m. was allocated to national security, representing 15.3% of total current expenditure.

Education

There is free compulsory education in government schools between the ages of five and 16 years, and a number of scholarships are awarded for higher education and teacher training. There are also seven private secondary schools, which charge fees. In 2011 enrolment at primary level institutions was equivalent to an estimated 90% of children in the relevant age-group, while at the secondary level it was equivalent to an estimated 77% of pupils in the relevant age-group. The Bermuda College is the only post-secondary educational institution. Extramural degree courses are available through Queen's University, Canada, and Indiana and Maryland Universities, USA. A Career Pathways programme to prepare students for business and industry was introduced in 2012/13. The 2013/14 budget allocated an estimated B $153.9m. to the Ministry of Education and Economic Development, representing 15.1% of total current expenditure.

BOLIVIA

Geography

PHYSICAL FEATURES

The Republic of Bolivia lies at the heart of the South American continent, in the centre-west, set on the high Andes, but reaching down into the Amazon basin. The country is land-locked, and has been since 1884, when it lost the Atacama Desert region to Chile (with which it still maintains demands for a sovereign corridor to the Pacific). The border with Chile, 861 km (535 miles) in extent, is in the south-west, while the rest of the western border, further north, is with Peru (900 km in extent). Brazil (with which Bolivia has a long, 3,400-km border) is to the north and north-east; the other landlocked country of the continent, Paraguay (750 km), to the south-east; and Argentina (832 km) to the south. The country is the fifth largest in South America, the size of France and Spain together, and covers 1,098,581 sq km (424,164 sq miles).

Bolivia's maximum length, from north to south, is about 1,530 km and its maximum breadth 1,450 km. Known as a 'rooftop of the world' from the setting of its lofty plateau amid the high Andes (which account for about one-third of the territory), the country also reaches down the eastern slopes of the mountains into vast grassy plains threaded by rivers with densely forested banks (Oriente). The high plateau is known as the *altiplano* and the lower slopes and valleys as the Yungas, while in the south-east the plains of the Amazonian–Chaco lowlands are known as the Llanos. The Andes form two main ranges in western Bolivia, the lower Cordillera Occidental along the border with Chile and, further inland, the great peaks of the broader Cordillera Oriental (Cordillera Real), also crossing from north to south, but in the centre-west of the country. Between the ranges is the main plateau, about 800 km long and 130 km wide, arid in the south, but in the north the country shares Lake Titicaca, the highest navigable lake in the world (at 3,805 m or 12,488 ft), with Peru. The region consists of snowy peaks and broad, windy plateaux over 4,000 m above sea level, often barren but for ichu (a coarse grass). The highest peak is Illimani (6,462 m). The Yungas consists of the lower, eastern slopes of the Cordillera Oriental, the fertile, forested and well-watered, but steep, valleys, separating the plateau region and the plains. Then, east and north-east of the mountains are the great Amazonian plains. South of them, beyond the low Chiquitos hills, is the Bolivian portion of the dry plains of the fought-over Chaco, the Llanos. Vast swathes of the plains become swampland during the rainy season, but the drier parts provide rich grazing for livestock. The plains are covered by great grasslands, although along the rivers, particularly in the north-east, there are stretches of dense tropical rainforest (forests cover about one-half of the country). Rivers drain either into the Amazon basin or into the system of the Río de la Plata (River Plate)—the lowest point in Bolivia, at 90 m above sea level, is the Paraguay river, part of the latter system, as it leaves the country. This vast, sparsely populated and rough countryside has also enabled Bolivia to become the world's third largest cultivator of coca (after Colombia and Peru).

CLIMATE

The country is situated entirely in the tropics, but its varied elevation gives it a wide range of climates. It is cold and dry in the mountainous south-west, but it is much warmer and wetter at lower altitudes. Being south of the Equator, winter is in the middle of the calendar year. The mean annual temperature in the *altiplano*, where most people live, is 8°C (46°F) and in the Llanos 26°C (79°F). The Yungas is more subtropical than the higher slopes. The main rain-bearing winds are those that cross the Amazon basin, and the north-east, particularly, is prone to flooding during the wet season (December–January),

although droughts here are equally possible. The Llanos gets drier towards the south.

POPULATION

Just under one-half of the population is Amerindian, native American, and has only been involved in the activities of the state and the benefits of its economy since the 1950s, when greater social mobility was encouraged, to the detriment of the white ruling élite. About 41% of the population aged 15 or over are Amerindian, or predominantly Amerindian, according to the 2012 census, mainly Quechua or Aymará. Bolivia was, anciently, home to a flourishing Aymará civilization based around Titicaca, but was later conquered by the Quechua-speaking Incas from the north. Given that only 36% of Bolivians use Spanish as their principal language, it is no surprise to find that Quechua and Aymará have joined it as official languages. Guaraní is the main one of the other indigenous languages in use. Although other aspects of native tradition are powerful in Bolivian culture, some homogeneity was provided by the prevalence of at least nominal, if adapted, Roman Catholic Christianity (still over 80% of the population). There are also increasing numbers of Protestant denominations, particularly the more evangelical ones, while the Bahá'ís claim almost 3%.

The total population according to the November 2012 census was 10,027,254, with most people living in the mountains (although the eastern lowlands have become more populated since the second half of the 20th century, owing to the exploitation of the hydrocarbons resources there), but less than two-fifths in rural areas. Bolivia is one of the least densely populated Latin American countries. The administrative capital and largest city (with its suburbs) is La Paz, in the west, at the northern end of the *altiplano*, and, at 3,640 m, the highest capital in the world. The judicial and constitutional capital is Sucre, in the centre-south. Between them, also in the highlands, are Cochabamba, at the centre of a fertile farming area, and the mining town of Oruro, more to the west. To the east, on the edge of the plains, is Santa Cruz de la Sierra, which is the only metropolis in Bolivia to have over 1m. people in the city proper. The country is divided into nine departments for administrative purposes.

History

Dr JOHN CRABTREE

INTRODUCTION

Indigenous civilizations flourished in what is now Bolivia long before the Spanish Conquest of the 16th century. In the mid-15th century the Inca empire extended its control over highland Bolivia, integrating the region around Lake Titicaca, and by the late 15th century Inca rule stretched from southern Colombia to northern Argentina. The Spanish invasion in 1533 quickly led to the creation of a new empire, with the establishment of the cities of Chuquisaca (today's Sucre) and La Paz during the 1540s. The discovery of enormous silver deposits at the Cerro Rico in Potosí in 1545 conferred on these territories huge economic importance, and by the end of the 16th century Potosí had become the largest city in the Americas. The development of mining in Potosí and elsewhere provided the stimulus for agricultural development in the inter-Andean valleys which became the territory's main 'bread basket'.

COLONIAL AND REPUBLICAN BOLIVIA

Spanish rule was exercised from Lima in Peru and lasted until the independent republic of Bolivia was established in 1825. As elsewhere in the Spanish colonies, the indigenous population was reduced to subservient status. However, indigenous culture proved more durable in the central Andes, and there were many rebellions against Spanish rule. The most important were the rebellions of Tupac Amaru and Tupaj Katari in southern Peru and western Bolivia, respectively. Both were put down with great violence. The decline in the power of Lima in the late 18th century encouraged the atomization of empire and the development of local power centres. In Bolivia, the most important was Chuquisaca, where independence was proclaimed following Simón Bolívar's victories over the Spanish armies in Peru. Bolivia's first President was José Antonio de Sucre.

At the outset, Bolivia was composed of a number of quasi-independent 'departments' that loosely reflected the system of *intendencias* (mayoralties) established by the colonial administration. However, Bolívar, after whom the new country was named, rejected federalism as a system of government. The struggle for hegemony between power centres, particularly between Sucre and La Paz, was one of the main factors behind Bolivia's chronic instability during much of the 19th century. The supremacy of La Paz was finally clinched after a civil war in 1899. Meanwhile, the country was dealt a rude shock during the War of the Pacific (1879–83), when it lost its Pacific department, based on Antofagasta, to Chile. Bolivia has repeatedly sought to regain its access to the sea, but so far without success.

The Chaco War and its Legacy

Bolivia's territorial integrity continued to suffer at the hands of its neighbours. In 1903 it lost Acre to Brazil, and then in 1935—following the Chaco War (1932–35)—it lost a large swathe of this semi-desert region to Paraguay. The experience of this bloody war, involving the mobilization of indigenous peasants, became one of the main catalysts of the development of Bolivian nationalism and causes of the 1952 'national' revolution. Domestic politics had stabilized in the 1880s with the emergence of an élite-run two-party system, a system that was already showing signs of weakness and which was dealt a body blow by the disastrous defeat in the Chaco.

The emergence of new forces in Bolivian politics, particularly on the left, became evident in the 1930s. Nationalist military governments, opposed to the élite (known in Bolivia as the *rosca*), sought to engineer important reforms. In 1937 the Government of David Toro Ruilova took the Bolivian assets of Standard Oil into state control, establishing Yacimientos Petrolíferos Fiscales Bolivianos (YPFB). In 1938 the Government of Germán Busch created a Ministry of Labour. That year also saw a constitutional reform that, among other things, rejected economic liberalism in favour of greater state intervention. In 1941 the Movimiento Nacionalista Revolucionario

(MNR) was established; the new party eschewed class-based politics and followed a nationalist ideology, influenced by the development of populist movements elsewhere in Latin America. Reflecting the increased salience of organized labour, the mineworkers in 1944 set up the Federación Sindical de Trabajadores Mineros de Bolivia (FSTMB). A coup the previous year brought to power Gualberto Villaroel, backed by the increasingly influential MNR. However, Villaroel and the MNR were overturned by an élite-backed coup in 1946.

THE 1952 REVOLUTION AND ITS LEGACY

The revolution of 1952 represented an important watershed, finally breaking the power of the mining élites—the so-called 'tin barons' (the Patiño, Aramayo and Hochschild families)—and ushering in a period of state-led development. The 1952 revolution occurred in the wake of the MNR's election victory in the previous year. This had been met with a military coup that prevented the MNR's presidential candidate, Víctor Paz Estenssoro, from taking power. The revolution involved three days of fighting in which armed workers and deserting conscripts overwhelmed the army. Paz Estenssoro became the new President, with the other main MNR leader, Hernán Siles Zuazo, his Vice-President.

Reformist Impulse

The new Government introduced some far-reaching changes. The first of these was universal suffrage, giving the vote to the country's previously marginalized indigenous peasant population. It then announced the nationalization of the country's largest mines, belonging to Patiño, Aramayo and Hochschild, which, in turn, led to the formation of the Corporación Minera de Bolivia (COMIBOL). Finally, in 1953, the Government announced its agrarian reform programme. This involved the formal ending of peonage and the division of large, landed estates among the *campesinos* (peasantry), as they became known after 1952. In fact, the reform programme was more a ratification of the land seizures that had taken place the year before. In terms of territory, the land reform had most impact in the *altiplano* and the inter-Andean valleys; it did not affect the eastern half of the country, where there was little pressure on available land and no organized *campesino* presence.

The revolution greatly added to the power of organized labour in Bolivia. Led by the FSTMB, which had played an important role in the insurrection, the new Government swiftly organized existing unions into a powerful confederation, the Central Obrera Boliviana (COB). The COB was effectively dominated by the mineworkers. The key figure linking the Government and the new union structure was Juan Lechín Oquendo. At the same time as pushing through the agrarian reform, the MNR Government sought to organize its peasant base into peasant unions.

Conservative Shift

Concerned by this leftwards lurch in Bolivian politics, coming as it did at the height of the Cold War, the US Administration sought to coax the new Government into a more moderate position. In particular, the USA sought to wean Paz Estenssoro away from Lechín and the COB. The economic crisis of 1956–57, which ended in rampant inflation, provided the opportunity to win over key sectors of the MNR leadership. The USA was able to provide much-needed finance in return for a stabilization plan that ran counter to the MNR's more left-wing policies. This was institutionalized in 1961 by the Plan Triangular, which sought to rehabilitate the country's mines on the condition that COMIBOL was reorganized and its number of employees reduced.

The post-revolutionary Governments—of Paz Estenssoro (1952–56 and 1960–64) and Siles Zuazo (1956–60)—also strove to develop the eastern part of the country, promoting agriculture so as to reduce Bolivia's dependence on mining exports. This diversification strategy had been suggested in the 1940s by the US Bohan Commission. Economic integration was facilitated by the completion in 1954 of a highway linking Santa Cruz with Cochabamba and La Paz. In the 1950s and early 1960s large-scale funding was made available to develop cash crop agriculture, and the MNR Governments devised official programmes to encourage migration of labour from the west of the country to the eastern lowlands. Spurred on economically by the development of petroleum resources in Santa Cruz department, growth rates far outpaced those of other parts of Bolivia. This encouraged, in turn, the emergence of a powerful, conservative élite, concerned to promote its department's interests irrespective of the rest of the country. Its mouthpiece was the Comité pro Santa Cruz.

Military Predominance, 1964–78

The period of MNR rule was brought to an abrupt end in November 1964, when the armed forces took power. Paz Estenssoro was overthrown by his Vice-President, Gen. René Barrientos Ortuño. In 1966 Barrientos, who enjoyed a good deal of popularity, won a presidential election. However, he died in a plane crash in 1969. He was succeeded by his Vice-President, Luis Adolfo Siles Salinas, who in turn was overthrown in a coup in the same year by Gen. Alfredo Ovando Candía. In October 1970 Ovando was himself thrown out of office by a leftist army general, Juan José Torres González. Pursuing an agenda of radical reforms, Torres was ejected in 1971 in a coup organized by Col (later Gen.) Hugo Bánzer Suárez and the right wing of the army. Bánzer went on to rule Bolivia for a comparatively long period, until 1978.

The new Bánzer administration enjoyed the decided support of the USA and the new élite of Santa Cruz. Effectively destroyed in 1952, the army had emerged as a key factor of political power in the years that followed. The USA provided important support in terms of money and training. However, as the ideological gyrations that took place after the death of Barrientos suggested, the army was not a cohesive force in political terms. Under Bánzer, however, the army adopted a more right-wing posture. It sought further to secure Santa Cruz's privileged position and to curb the power of the COB and the FSTMB.

Contested Interlude, 1978–82

The fall of Bánzer in 1978 led to a period of short-lived Governments, both military and civilian. Under US pressure to return the country to democracy, three presidential elections in so many years (1978, 1979 and 1980) failed to resolve the log-jam in Bolivian politics. Then, in 1980, in a coup designed to put an end to this short-lived 'democratic opening', a group of military officers closely connected to Bolivia's drugs production interests seized power. Three military Presidents ensued: Gen. Luis García Meza (1980–81), Gen. Celso Torrelio Villa (1981–82) and Gen. Guido Vildoso Calderón (1982). None of these Governments managed to generate domestic legitimacy and, externally, they faced US hostility because of two new departures in that country's foreign policy: the salience of illegal narcotics production and the support for democratization in Latin America. Economic crisis led to the military finally handing over power in 1982 to Siles Zuazo, the victor of the presidential election in 1980.

RETURN TO CONSTITUTIONAL RULE

The presidency of Siles Zuazo marked the beginning of the democratic period in Bolivian politics, which has lasted to the present. However, the Siles Government found itself wracked by internal dissension between the parties of which it was composed: Siles' Movimiento Nacionalista Revolucionario de Izquierda (MNRI—Siles had left the MNR proper and formed his own party in 1971), the Movimiento de la Izquierda Revolucionaria (MIR) and the Partido Comunista de Bolivia (PCB). It also had to contend with the effects of the debt crisis and simultaneously confront serious labour unrest. The Government was unable to control prices in a process of escalating hyperinflation. Responding finally to a general strike called by the COB, Siles was obliged to hold a presidential election one year early. This was duly held in July 1985, and was won by Siles' old partner in the 1952 revolution, Víctor Paz Estenssoro.

The Return of Paz Estenssoro, 1985–89

The return of Paz Estenssoro to the presidency, after 21 years, opened a new chapter in the life of this wily and experienced politician. The man who had led Bolivia as it entered its most interventionist period was the same man who presided over a period of economic liberalization. The so-called New Economic Policy, warmly supported by the international financial community, was a determined effort to achieve stabilization via trade and currency liberalization and fiscal and monetary orthodoxy. However, it had major social costs, which the Government did little to mitigate. In particular, the New Economic Policy involved a massive reorganization of the public sector, especially the state mining industry. Responding also to a sharp collapse in tin prices on international metals markets, the Government effectively closed down this sector, with the loss of some 25,000 jobs.

Although elected with the support of the MIR, Paz Estenssoro quickly moved into a working relationship with Bánzer's right-wing Acción Democrática Nacionalista (ADN). His policies were premised on close collaboration with the business sector, and all ties with the unions were severed. One of the main architects of stabilization was one of Bolivia's wealthiest private sector mine owners, Gonzalo Sánchez de Lozada. The Government also won the enthusiastic support of the World Bank, which provided Bolivia with a much-needed financial infusion. The positive effects of stabilization on domestic prices were quickly felt, helping to provide political support for the Paz Estenssoro administration. The President also found himself the beneficiary of the declining political clout of both the trade union movement and the army. The former mounted several attempts to protest against the Government's policies, but these had little effect. The reputation of the latter had been badly damaged by its former involvement in drugs-trafficking.

Jaime Paz Zamora, 1989–93

The 1989 elections brought to office Jaime Paz Zamora, leader of the MIR and Paz Estenssoro's nephew. Although Paz Zamora was actually third-placed in the elections, he managed to engineer a pact with Bánzer (who came second) to deprive the front-running MNR candidate, Sánchez de Lozada, of the presidency. Although Bánzer failed this time in his ambition to return to the presidency by constitutional means, the ADN was given a great deal of influence in the new Government, which continued the broad pro-business thrust of the previous administration. A timid privatization programme was launched. However, in spite of this conversion, Paz Zamora never enjoyed the trust of the USA owing to his alleged connections with drug interests.

The late 1980s and early 1990s saw the emergence of parties that drew their support primarily from popular sectors and which had a populist message. These were Conciencia de Patria (Condepa), set up in 1988, and Unidad Cívica Solidaridad (UCS), established in 1989. These parties represented an important departure from the more traditional parties, and offered a conduit for dissent. They tended to prosper at the expense of the older parties of the left. Another growing force was the emergence of indigenist politics, particularly among Aymará-speaking peoples of the *altiplano*. This was associated with the so-called Kataristas, who sought to create an independent force among the peasantry. Katarismo involved various strands that veered from class-based politics through to a more overt form of race politics.

Sánchez de Lozada, 1993–97

Deprived of the presidency in 1989, Sánchez de Lozada narrowly managed to achieve his ambition in 1993 with the help of UCS, the Movimiento Bolivia Libre, a splinter group from the MIR, and a small faction of the Kataristas. Sánchez de Lozada was primarily concerned to pursue the liberalizing agenda he had begun as Paz Estenssoro's Minister of Planning, as well as to consolidate the model politically by spreading the benefits of reform more widely. He argued that privatization was the key to sustainable growth and thus higher living standards. He called his model 'capitalization', since it was a hybrid scheme of privatization that involved foreign partners 'capitalizing' state companies by investing the estimated value of the company and taking management control. The existing stock value of the company would then be invested and provide income for a pension benefit called the Bonosol. By far the most important public company to be capitalized was YPFB.

Another key reform designed to build political support was Popular Participation, which involved the expansion of municipal government. Not only did it create a large number of municipalities in rural areas where the state had hardly existed previously, it also greatly increased the amount of spending channelled through them. It provided a mechanism through which to tackle extreme poverty, harnessing local civil society in exercising oversight into the way government money was applied. However, its critics charged that it sought to strengthen the hand of the President at the local level and to sap the strength of departmental-level institutions. Other innovative reforms pursued by the Sánchez de Lozada administration included plurilingual educational reforms and an attempt to revamp agrarian reform and apply it to eastern Bolivia.

Consensus Breakdown, 1997–2002

The hope that such reforms would help keep the MNR in power, however, proved misplaced, and in the 1997 elections Bánzer emerged victorious at the head of what he called his 'megacoalition'—an amalgam of the ADN, the MIR, UCS and Condepa. This proved an unwieldy mixture of elements, and the Government soon gained an unfortunate reputation for crony politics, corruption and graft. Though Bánzer was elected for a five-year term, his ailing health meant that he had to resign a year early, in 2001, and confer power on his Vice-President, Jorge Quiroga Ramírez.

Virulent opposition emerged to Bánzer and his policies in a number of areas. First, and most significant, was the reaction of the country's coca farmers, led by Juan Evo Morales Aima, to Bánzer's 'zero tolerance' policy on drugs cultivation. Use of the army to eradicate coca in the Chapare district of Cochabamba brought an energetic response from the *cocaleros*, many of them displaced mineworkers who had lost their jobs in 1985. Second, there were growing signs of unrest on the *altiplano*, where indigenist leader Felipe Quispe emerged as the *mallku*, or the self-styled leader of the 'Aymará nation'. Quispe became adept at the use of roadblocks and other forms of direct action to make demands on the Government. Finally, the attempt to privatize water supplies in Cochabamba precipitated the so-called 'water war', a massive local protest in 1999 and 2000, which ended with the Government ignominiously backing down.

Breakdown in the System of Pacts

The return of Sánchez de Lozada to office in 2002 compounded this sense of growing tension. Sánchez de Lozada failed to bring 'new ideas' to the fore in the way he had in his first administration. However, it was his handling of plans to sell Bolivian gas to the USA via a pipeline passing through northern Chile that proved the catalyst for the premature collapse of his Government. Riots in El Alto, dubbed the 'gas war', resulted in a violent stand-off, in which many were killed. Deserted by his allies and with doubts as to the loyalty of the army, Sánchez de Lozada agreed to step down from office in October 2003. He was replaced by his Vice-President, Carlos Mesa Gisbert, who agreed to meet a list of opposition demands known as the 'October agenda'.

President Mesa moved ahead with demands to put a series of questions about gas exploitation to a referendum. This authorized the Government to push ahead with a new hydrocarbons law that was much more nationalist in flavour than the scheme devised in 1996 by Sánchez de Lozada to attract foreign investors. However, ultimately, Mesa was reluctant to put his name to new legislation approved by the Congreso (Congress). With the tide of public unrest rapidly rising once again, he resigned in June 2005, giving way to a short interim administration headed by the President of the Supreme Court, Eduardo Rodríguez Veltzé, whose main achievement was to hold fresh presidential and legislative elections in December. Elections were also held for departmental prefects for the first time.

EVO MORALES, 2006–

The landslide victory of Evo Morales in the presidential election of 18 December 2005, with a massive 53.7% of the votes cast (avoiding the need for a vote in the Congress), represented a landmark in recent Bolivian history. His party, the Movimiento al Socialismo (MAS), also won a majority of seats, 72, in the 130-seat Cámara de Diputados (Chamber of Deputies), and only narrowly missed winning a majority in the Senate, securing 12 of the 27 upper house seats. The election therefore brought to an end the discredited system of party pacts. Morales was the first 'indigenous' head of state in a country where a mestizo minority had traditionally predominated. His rise to power from the humblest of backgrounds added to this symbolism, augmenting his legitimacy.

New Policy Direction

Morales abandoned the neo-liberal policies that had prevailed since 1985. The first major sign of this was his 'renationalizing' of Bolivia's oil and gas industry in May 2006, forcing foreign investors to sign new contracts that enhanced the role of YPFB and greatly increased the taxes payable to the state. Morales' Government also sought to extend power to those who had traditionally been excluded from Bolivian politics, especially the country's indigenous majority. Morales' first Cabinet included many from the social movements that had opposed successive previous Governments. Indeed, the MAS was less a political party as such, more a coalition of disparate social movements, united mainly by their support for Morales.

In foreign affairs, the new President immediately forged close ties with the left-wing administrations of Venezuela and Cuba, but at the same time developed a close rapport with Presidents Luiz Inácio Lula da Silva in Brazil and Néstor Carlos Kirchner in Argentina. The US Administration of George W. Bush avoided outright confrontation with Bolivia, in spite of marked differences between the two countries over coca cultivation.

Opposition to Morales

However, domestic opposition to Morales quickly made itself felt over his plans to rewrite the country's Constitution. Elected in July 2006, a Constituent Assembly was given one year to produce a draft constitution, which would then be submitted to a referendum. The conservative minority in the Constituent Assembly, backed by strong support from Santa Cruz and other anti-Morales strongholds, adroitly used its influence to stymie the MAS's agenda. The opposition was particularly insistent that the Government honour commitments towards greater regional and departmental autonomy. Due to the extent of opposition, the deadline for completing the constitution was extended to December 2007. In the end, with that deadline fast approaching and the opposition blocking final agreement, the MAS majority and its allies approved their own constitutional text, with the main opposition party, Poder Democrático y Social (PODEMOS), boycotting the final sessions.

Negotiating the New Constitution

In defiance of the new constitutional text, the opposition—led by the civic authorities in Santa Cruz—published a 'statute of autonomy' for the department at the end of 2007, a document proclaiming a wide measure of independence from central government. Similar pronouncements were made subsequently in Tarija, Beni and Pando. Negotiations between the Government and opposition prefects proved fruitless. Refusing any compromise, the authorities in Santa Cruz held a referendum on the autonomy proposal. Overwhelming local support for the autonomy statute in Santa Cruz led to similar outcomes in Beni, Pando and Tarija.

However, in the second half of 2008 the Morales Government managed to regain the initiative. In a recall referendum held in August, Morales was ratified as President by two-thirds of the electorate. Although the prefects of the four eastern departments were also ratified, two opposition prefects—those of La Paz and Cochabamba—were voted out of office. A bout of political violence in September in the eastern *media luna* ended in international mediation and the signing of an agreement that paved the way to a referendum on a somewhat amended version of the new constitution in January 2009. The

Constitution, duly ratified, was promulgated by Morales at the beginning of February. The July 2010 autonomies law set out more detailed proposals for decentralization.

Morales' Second Term

Fresh presidential and legislative elections under the terms of the new Constitution were held on 6 December 2009. In the presidential election, Morales and his Vice-President, Alvaro Marcelo García Linera, were re-elected for a further five-year term, with Morales securing a massive 64.2% of the vote compared with only 26.5% for Manfred Reyes Villa, candidate of the recently formed right-wing Plan Progreso para Bolivia—Convergencia Nacional. In the legislative poll, the MAS won 88 seats in the Chamber of Deputies and 26 seats in the newly enlarged 36-seat Senado Nacional (Senate). Altogether, the MAS won more than two-thirds of the seats in the renamed Asamblea Legislativa Plurinacional (Plurinational Legislative Assembly), sufficient (should it wish to do so) to amend the Constitution. Further polls were held in April 2010 to elect departmental governors (as prefects became known), departmental assemblies, local mayors and local councils. These, too, produced positive results for the MAS, though not on the same scale as the presidential election. At the departmental level, the party won six out of nine governorships, with opposition incumbents winning in Santa Cruz, Beni and Tarija, but not in Pando. At the municipal level, the MAS won in only three out of 10 major cities (the nine departmental capitals plus El Alto), although it won the great majority of mayoral contests in rural areas.

Having been re-elected in 2009, President Morales seemed to be in a strong position to push ahead with his Government's agenda of implementing the terms of the new Constitution. He enjoyed electoral legitimacy, a strong popular following, and was in charge of a Government with the fiscal resources to implement its plans. The opposition appeared demoralized and leaderless at the national level. However, Morales' second administration proved more problematic than many thought at the outset. In the last days of 2010 he incurred widespread popular antipathy as a result of the decision to raise fuel prices by between 70% and 90%, a move that he was subsequently forced to abandon. His relations with the unions and some of the country's social movements deteriorated during 2011 and 2012. Marches by indigenous peoples from the lowlands against plans to build a road through a protected area, the Territorio Indígena y Parque Nacional Isiboro Sécure (TIPNIS), provided a catalyst for renewed opposition. The first half of 2012 saw a series of strikes and protests against the Government and its policies, including a renewed march by indigenous peoples against government plans for the TIPNIS. As a result of this pressure, and with elections due in 2014, the Morales administration suspended the TIPNIS project following a controversial consultation with the communities affected.

From mid-2012 Morales managed to regain some of the support that he had lost since 2011. The number of protests against the Government declined, revealing the weakness of the opposition as a whole. In June 2012, moreover, the Confederación de Pueblos Indígenas de Bolivia split, dividing the indigenous movements opposed to the TIPNIS road. Nevertheless, the Government subsequently came under pressure from other social movements, particularly those associated with the mining industry. In March 2014 workers from mining co-operatives mobilized in an unsuccessful attempt to prevent changes to the mining law, which they regarded as a threat to their interests. The miners demanded an amendment to the law that would enable them to enter into contracts with third parties in the private sector, but this was deemed to be unconstitutional and was thus rejected. The dispute, however, led to the dismissal of Mario Virreira as Minister of Mines and Metallurgy. The Government also came under regular pressure from trade unions over wage settlements. While the Morales administration sought to resist union demands for fear of inflationary consequences, it significantly raised the minimum wage. Meanwhile, in April 2014 disgruntled junior officers in the armed forces staged a protest against alleged institutional racism within the military hierarchy. They made it clear, however, that this did not constitute an attempted coup against the Government. The authorities successfully isolated the purported ringleaders of the movement.

PROSPECTS

Campaigning for the October presidential and legislative elections began in early 2014, with Morales and García Linera standing once again as the candidates of the MAS. Their main opponents were Juan del Granado Cosío of the Movimiento sin Miedo, a former ally of the MAS; Samuel Doria Medina from the centre-right Frente de Unidad Nacional; and Rubén Costas Aguilera, the Governor of Santa Cruz, who was the candidate of the Movimiento Demócrata Social, allied with the Unidad Nacional. By mid-2014 attempts were under way to overcome ideological differences and present a single opposition candidate. None the less, after eight years in office, Morales remained the dominant figure in Bolivian politics, unchallenged within the ruling MAS and far more popular than any of the most prominent opposition leaders. Not only was he widely credited for having presided over a period of significant reform, but he retained a 'common touch' with the electorate because of his own humble background. He also benefited from the divisions between his opponents, while exploiting the significant advantages of incumbency to promote his presidential image. A third term in office for Morales, ending in 2020, therefore seemed probable. Municipal and gubernatorial elections were scheduled to be held in the first half of 2015.

Economy

Dr JOHN CRABTREE

MACROECONOMY

Overall Policy Direction

Since taking power in 2006, the administration of Evo Morales has sought to reverse many of the liberalizing economic policies adopted in recent years. It has taken a more interventionist approach to economic management, increasing the powers and responsibilities of state companies. This has been particularly noticeable in the hydrocarbons industry, which provides Bolivia with its main source of export revenues. Contracts with foreign investors in the gas sector have been forcibly revised, and the corporate tax burden has been raised substantially. In other respects, however, the Ministry of Economy and Public Finance and the central bank have pursued relatively orthodox monetary, fiscal and exchange rate policies. Largely as a result of buoyant commodity prices in recent years, the economy has

grown quickly (at least by historical standards), and poverty rates have declined. Moreover, levels of indebtedness have decreased, international reserves have risen and the country's international credit rating has improved as a consequence.

The strategic objectives of the new Morales administration were set out in its five-year development plan in 2006. This set out a blueprint for policy until 2011, and sought to make Bolivia a fairer and more democratic society, less dependent on the international economy as the source of growth. The plan was broadly renewed in 2011. It is based on the assumption that investment will continue to increase, therefore helping to expand productive capacity and to generate additional revenues, which can be spent on (among other things) reducing poverty. In the past, the majority of investment had been absorbed by the hydrocarbons industry. However, the linkages between this and the rest of the economy have been notoriously weak, and there were concerns that the Morales Government's hydrocarbons 'nationalization' policy (see below) would act as a disincentive to foreign investment. Given the growth of gas and mining revenues, the economy became more dependent on primary exports than ever.

Economic Growth

In 2013 the economy grew by 6.8%, the fastest rate in decades and among the fastest in Latin America, continuing a growth trend that had begun in 2003. Bolivia emerged relatively unscathed from the global downturn, again achieving one of the highest growth rates (3.4%) in Latin America in 2009. The economy expanded by a further 6.1% in 2010, and 6.2% in 2011 and 2012. The recent dynamic in the economy has responded more to domestic than external demand, although since 2006 the economy has benefited from both buoyant international prices for and increased output of the country's main commodity exports, notably minerals and natural gas. Bolivia has also benefited from the relative dynamism of Argentina and Brazil, its most important markets. The increased rhythm of growth pushed nominal gross domestic product (GDP) per head up to US $2,470 in 2013, according to Ministry of Economy and Public Finance figures, up from $1,182 in 2006.

Following many years of stagnation, Bolivia's rate of growth recovered in the mid-1990s, in part because of the investment stimulated by the privatization programme of President Gonzalo Sánchez de Lozada (1993–97), especially in hydrocarbons. The building of new infrastructure—particularly the gas pipeline to Brazil—provided a fillip to the economy. However, Bolivia found itself highly exposed to economic crises within its larger neighbours—first Brazil in the late 1990s and then Argentina in the early 2000s. The slowing of growth rates from 1998 coincided with the collapse in the popularity of successive governments and the onset of a wave of protests that was to lead to the assumption of office by the new Morales administration. The Morales Government has taken advantage of higher growth to increase social spending.

Inflation

Inflation, which reached a peak of nearly 14% on an annualized basis at the beginning of 2008, declined in 2009 and early 2010 before accelerating once again in the second half of that year and the first quarter of 2011 (when it reached 11%), partly as a result of the increase in food and fuel import prices but also because of the impact of adverse climatic conditions on the local supply of foodstuffs. By the end of 2013 inflation had decreased to 6.5%—higher than the rate forecast by the central bank, but within its target range. Government policy has been to use cautious monetary and exchange rate measures to prevent the emergence of inflationary pressures. In the early 1980s Bolivia was considered a byword for reckless monetary and fiscal policies that resulted in hyperinflation. Stabilization was one of the main achievements of the Víctor Paz Estenssoro Government (1985–89) and its successors. Although Bolivia ran large fiscal deficits through the 1990s, it was able to finance these by drawing down generous credits from the international financial and aid communities. Between 2006 and 2013 Bolivia maintained a fiscal surplus, with higher revenues derived mainly from the hike in hydrocarbon production tax rates. In 2013 there was a small surplus equivalent to 0.1% of GDP, compared with a surplus of 1.8% of GDP in 2012.

Foreign Trade

In 2013 Bolivia saw its trade surplus decline to US $2,768m., down from $3,521m. in 2012. This was largely owing to a 12% increase in imports and a reduction in the value of mineral shipments. Exports in 2013 reached a record $12,208m., up from $9,146m. in 2011, of which just over one-half came from the hydrocarbons sector. Increased sales of natural gas to Argentina bolstered gas export revenues, more than offsetting the decline in mineral exports. Total imports for 2013 were also a record at $9,353m., an increase of 12.9% compared with the previous year; most of these imports comprised intermediate and capital goods. Until 2011 Bolivia had benefited from the boom in world mineral prices in what had previously been a depressed sector. Bolivia's export performance also profited from the San Cristóbal zinc and silver mine coming on stream in 2007. However, in 2013 prices generally declined in this sector for key export commodities such as zinc, silver and tin. Silver is now the country's single most important mineral export, followed by zinc and gold. Buoyant world prices in recent years have encouraged higher production from mines that were previously abandoned in the 1980s, although production levels dipped in 2012 and 2013.

Export performance since 2009 has also been affected by the withdrawal of US trade preferences with the curtailment of the Andean Trade Preferences and Drug Eradication Act (ATP-DEA). Worst affected have been exporters of manufactured items, particularly textiles and clothing. Bolivia is a founder member of the Comunidad Andina de Naciones (CAN—Andean Community of Nations) and an associate member of the Southern Common Market (Mercado Común del Sur—Mercosur), established by Brazil, Argentina, Paraguay and Uruguay. It is also a member of the Bolivarian Alliance for the Peoples of our America (Alianza Bolivariana para los Pueblos de Nuestra América—ALBA), alongside Venezuela, Ecuador and Cuba, among others. Moreover, Bolivia enjoys access to the European Union (EU)'s Generalized System of Preferences.

Balance of Payments

Improved terms of trade have helped to ameliorate the balance of payments situation in recent years. In 2013 Bolivia achieved a balance of payments surplus of US $1,021m., lower than in 2012 ($1,712m.) and in 2011 ($2,161m.). This was largely the result of a $1,012m. surplus on the current account, the equivalent of 5.2% of GDP, down from $2,258m. in the previous year. The main reason for this decrease was the lower trade surplus. Remittances amounted to just over $287m. in the first quarter of 2014, of which 47% came from Bolivians resident in Spain. At the end of 2013 net foreign reserves stood at just over $14,400m., equivalent to around 47% of GDP. The balance of payments in 2013 also benefited from a positive net inflow of foreign investment of $1,749m. (compared with $1,060m. in 2012), with 80% of this going to the hydrocarbons sector. Furthermore, Bolivia has benefited from debt relief from multilateral lenders, principally the World Bank. In 2012 Bolivia, for the first time in nearly a century, tapped international bond markets, taking advantage of its improved international credit rating.

Fiscal Situation

Preliminary finance ministry figures suggested that there was a public sector fiscal surplus equivalent to 0.8% of GDP in 2013, down from 1.8% in the previous year. Increased gas sales boosted treasury income in 2013, but spending, especially public sector investment, rose more than proportionately. The robust fiscal performance of recent years reflected the hike in taxes on gas output since the nationalization of gas in 2006, with income augmented by the increase in sales to Argentina since 2011. As recently as 2003 Bolivia's fiscal deficit stood at 9.0% of GDP. Part of the reason for this shortfall was the privatization of pensions, which reduced levels of revenue from pension contributions while existing spending commitments continued.

ECONOMIC SECTORS

Hydrocarbons

Petroleum was first discovered in Bolivia in 1927. Until the sector was nationalized in 1937, the main company involved was Standard Oil of New Jersey, USA. Under the state company that emerged, Yacimientos Petrolíferos Fiscales Bolivianos (YPFB), no major new discoveries were made, and it was only in 1953 that Bolivia became self-sufficient in oil. In 1954 state policy changed, and private investment was sought, the main company being Bolivian Gulf Oil. New discoveries of petroleum and gas were made by Bolivian Gulf Oil, and pipelines were constructed linking Bolivia to the Pacific and to Argentina. In 1969 the assets of Bolivian Gulf Oil were taken over by YPFB. A stable system was created in which the private and public sectors coexisted, with YPFB awarding operating contracts to private sector companies. Then, in 1996, the Sánchez de Lozada Government 'capitalized' YPFB and turned over production to the private sector through shared risk contracts. Attracted by the generous terms on offer, several major international oil and gas companies invested in Bolivia, principal among them Petrobras of Brazil, Repsol of Spain, Total of France and British Gas (known as BG from 1997) of the United Kingdom. The new regime quickly led to important discoveries in the gas sector, mainly in the department of Tarija. Official 'proven' reserves of gas increased from 4,200,000m. cu ft in 1998 to 28,700,000m. cu ft in 2003. Proven plus probable reserves increased from 6,600,000m. cu ft to 54,900,000m. cu ft over the same period. However, a more recent assessment, conducted by the US firm Ryder Scott in 2009, suggested that the level of proven reserves was only around 10,000,000m. cu ft. To exploit Bolivia's gas potential, a pipeline was constructed, at a cost of US $450m., linking Río Grande in Bolivia with São Paulo in Brazil. Gas output averaged 54.4m. cu m per day in 2013, compared with 19.6m. cu m per day in 2001. A new assessment of Bolivia's gas reserves was under way in mid-2014.

At the beginning of the 21st century attention was devoted to developing new markets for Bolivian gas, and a project was designed to export gas to Mexico and the USA by piping it across the Andes, liquefying it and then shipping it northwards. The project sparked a furious polemic within Bolivia. This partly focused on the transhipment of gas through Chile, Bolivia's traditional enemy, but it also raised wider questions about the terms on which foreign companies were operating in Bolivia and the modest returns to the Bolivian economy. The resultant 'gas war' of 2003 led to the ousting of Sánchez de Lozada. A referendum in 2004 on the country's approach to the gas question, and, in particular, on the proposal to build a Chilean pipeline compelled the Government to reformulate its hydrocarbons legislation, and a new law was approved in 2005. This raised the taxes payable by foreign investors and changed the contractual relationship between them and YPFB.

Following the electoral victory of Evo Morales in 2005, the new administration announced its intention to 'nationalize' (for the third time) the hydrocarbons industry. Foreign companies were given 180 days in which to switch to new contracts or else leave the country. In the event, all the companies accepted the new terms offered to them within the deadline prescribed. As well as switching the contracts to service contracts, the new regulations established substantially higher new tax rates payable to the state: the highest rate established was 81% of the value of production. The new legislation afforded a greatly enhanced role to YPFB in the production process. In May 2008 the Government extended its ownership of the industry by acquiring a majority shareholding in several pipeline companies.

The second main strand in the Morales administration's gas policy was to renegotiate the terms whereby Argentina and Brazil bought gas from Bolivia. In the case of Argentina, in 2006 the Government of Néstor Carlos Kirchner agreed to increase both the volume purchased and price paid for Bolivian gas. Plans were also announced to build a new pipeline to Santa Fe in north-eastern Argentina. In May 2014 the Bolivian Government announced that it had agreed to supply up to 19m. cu m per day to Argentina, mainly from the Margarita field in Tarija. To supply more would involve expanding pipelines on the Argentine side of the frontier. Brazil, meanwhile, was buying 30.5m. cu m per day from Bolivia, just below the latter's maximum supply capacity. Domestic demand in Bolivia accounted for 10m. cu m per day, of which 55% was used for generating electricity. There is a reasonable probability that Bolivia's declining gas reserves will increase again once more systematic prospecting gets under way, but investment depends on opening up new markets. In 2011 Total announced an important discovery in Santa Cruz that will raise proven reserves considerably. However, foreign oil and gas companies (most of which have recovered their initial investment in Bolivia) have shown themselves reluctant to devote substantial resources to exploration while the contractual conditions are relatively unfavourable. Brazil's commitment to becoming self-sufficient in gas in the longer term has also deterred investment.

Mining

From the earliest colonial times, what was to become Bolivia found itself integrated into the world economy as a supplier of minerals. The discovery of the enormous silver reserves of the

Cerro Rico in Potosí gave the country huge economic significance. The importance of silver-mining declined by the 19th century, and in the 20th century tin-mining became the economic mainstay. Tin-mining was dominated in the first half of the 20th century by the Patiño, Hochschild and Aramayo families, but by the time the mines were nationalized in 1952, ore grades were decreasing rapidly. With its underground mines, Bolivia found it increasingly difficult to compete with open-cast tin-mining in Indonesia, Malaysia and Brazil. In 1985 the world tin market collapsed, and Bolivia was obliged to close its main mining centres. The only major mining centre to continue in production was at Huanuni, which was sold to the private sector in the 1990s. However, other private sector mining companies were better placed than the former state mining company, Corporación Minera de Bolivia (COMIBOL), to stay in business.

The recovery of prices in the early 2000s led to a revival of interest in the mining sector. A steady rise in mineral prices, stimulated mainly by demand from the People's Republic of China and India for raw materials, pushed up the value of exports. In the main this was because of higher prices, but these in turn prompted miners to expand production to meet the demand. The official value of exports of (non-hydrocarbons) minerals stood at US $369m. in 2003; by 2013 this had reached $3,055m. The decline in world mineral prices towards the end of 2008 did affect Bolivia, but export values decreased only by a fairly modest 4.8% in 2009. The composition of exports has changed greatly, meanwhile. Tin is no longer the main source of foreign exchange in the mining industry, having been overtaken by silver, zinc and gold. Silver accounted for just under 33% of export revenue from minerals in 2013, according to provisional figures ($1,001m.), followed by zinc ($750m.) and then gold ($562m.).

After the virtual closure of COMIBOL in 1985, the structure of the industry changed radically. The so-called 'minería mediana' (privately owned mines) took over from the public sector. The most important company here until recently was Sinchi Wayra, the firm owned by former President Sánchez de Lozada. In 2005 Sánchez de Lozada sold Sinchi Wayra, which owned several of Bolivia's most profitable mines, as well as the smelter at Vinto (near Oruro), to the Swiss-based company Glencore International AG. In 2007, however, the Morales Government announced that it was taking Vinto, built and formerly owned by the state, back into public ownership. It considered that Vinto had been improperly acquired by the private sector at a reduced price. The Government has taken steps to invest in Vinto, as well as in a silver- and lead-processing plant at Karachipampa, near Potosí. It has also sought to relaunch COMIBOL and to give it a much more prominent role in the industry.

Many of the former state-owned mines continued to be operated by self-employed workers who sold the ores they extracted to private intermediaries. The rise in mineral prices in the years after 2003 attracted workers back into the industry. At Siglo XX, for instance, formerly Bolivia's most important tin mine, there were more workers in 2012 than in 1985, mostly operating in extremely dangerous conditions. Such workers accounted for 80% of the mining labour force.

As well as seeking to revive COMIBOL, the Morales Government took steps to increase the taxes payable by the sector to the state. Mining contributed only US $58m. to the state in 2006 on exports earnings of over $1,000m. The Government sought to make the new Complementary Mining Tax (Complementario a la Minería) incremental, so that its yield reflected the upward shift in international prices. However, the implementation of such reforms encountered significant resistance from miners and mining companies, not least from the self-employed sector of 'cooperativistas'. A new, long-delayed, mining law, incorporating further tax changes, had been expected to be adopted in 2014. However, its introduction was postponed again in March on account of inconsistencies in its text with constitutional provisions that prevent cooperatives from entering into agreements with private companies without prior consent from the state.

As in the case of hydrocarbons, a major problem is the lack of investment. Mining investment has been at a very low level for more than 50 years, and relatively little of the country has been properly prospected. Investors have been deterred by political instability and by the existence of more attractive operating conditions in neighbouring countries, notably in Chile and Peru. None the less, the San Cristóbal mine and the San Bartolomé scheme, both in Potosí, have substantially increased Bolivia's productive capacity in silver and zinc. San Cristóbal, which is Bolivia's largest silver mine, entered into production in 2007. San Bartolomé is a project to apply new technology to reworking the tailings of the historic Cerro Rico mine, just outside the city of Potosí.

In 2007 the Government signed a contract with Jindal Steel and Power Ltd of India, together with its local subsidiary, Jindal Steel Bolivia, to develop the giant El Mutún iron ore deposit in eastern Santa Cruz, close to the Brazilian frontier. However, the contract was hindered by disagreements between Jindal and the Government, and investments lagged well behind the agreed timetable. In 2012 Jindal withdrew from Bolivia, leaving a subsidiary of COMIBOL to develop iron and steel production at El Mutún. Another scheme is to develop lithium from the Salar de Uyuni in Potosí. Bolivia has the world's largest reserves of this commodity, a key element in the development of batteries for use in electric cars. The Morales administration is seeking foreign investment to develop lithium, but on the basis of industrializing its use. To this end, in 2012 the Government signed a preliminary agreement with POSCO, a South Korean consortium.

Agriculture

Although Bolivia's main contribution to international commerce is through the extraction of gas and minerals (mining and hydrocarbons accounted for 14% of GDP in 2013), agriculture contributed 10% of GDP in that year and is an important source of employment. While rapid urbanization has reduced the proportion of people living on the land, Bolivia remains a much more rural country than most in Latin America. Agriculture is highly segmented, reflecting the geographical diversity of the country. There are three main types of agriculture: small-scale peasant agriculture in the highlands, where the quality of the soil is mainly poor, and where there is a mixture of livestock-rearing (mainly alpacas and llamas) and basic crops such as potatoes and some grains; small-scale agriculture (mainly crops) in the inter-Andean valleys (principally around Cochabamba, Sucre and Tarija), where the quality of the land is considerably better and the climate less extreme; and extensive export-orientated agriculture and cattle-rearing in the eastern lowland departments of Santa Cruz and Beni.

From a commercial point of view, the most dynamic sector in recent years has been soya. Produced mainly in Santa Cruz, soya took over in the 1980s from more traditional crops (such as sugar and cotton) as Bolivia's prime agricultural export commodity. Soya products (including oil) accounted for exports of US $1,175m. in 2013, up from $824m. in 2012. The scale of soya production depends both on climatic and market conditions. Bolivia has enjoyed a niche within the CAN as a privileged supplier of soya to Peru and Colombia. It also supplies Venezuela. However, its comparative advantages over much larger and lower-cost producers threatened to be eroded if the CAN and Mercosur eventually were to merge. Moreover, the growth in soya cultivation has taken place with scant regard for ecological considerations, and there are growing problems of desertification emerging in parts of the Bolivian lowlands.

Other forms of export agriculture also come predominantly from the lowlands. In 2013 these included quinoa (US $153m.), Brazil nuts ($122m.), sugar ($72m.) and timber ($49m.). In all probability, timber exports are worth far more than the official figure suggests, since the scale of illegal logging in Bolivia is large. Brazil nuts, mainly destined for the EU market, provide an important livelihood for small-scale producers in the northern departments of Beni and Pando, with prices reaching record levels in 2011. Other agricultural exports include coffee and cotton.

Coca

One of Bolivia's most lucrative forms of agriculture is coca, the raw material for cocaine. Coca has been grown in Bolivia since earliest times, and it is still widely used as a palliative to stave off hunger, fatigue and altitude sickness. It also has religious uses. However, its economic importance in recent decades lies in its illegal use for the manufacture of cocaine. Since the 1980s successive governments have come under strong pressure from the USA to eradicate coca. These attempts have led to strenuous resistance from those whose livelihoods depend on coca production. The *cocaleros* have emerged in recent years as one of Bolivia's best organized and most militant social movements, and the political rise of President Evo Morales, former leader of the Chapare *cocaleros*, owes much to attempts to eradicate coca.

Coca eradication reached its peak under the Government of Hugo Bánzer Suárez (1997–2001), whose strict stance on coca cultivation was strongly supported by the US Administration. The decline in coca acreages at that time has since been reversed, reflecting the increased political power at the national level of the *cocaleros*. At its maximum, coca production in Bolivia involved cultivation of 48,000 ha in 1996, according to figures published by the UN Office on Drugs and Crime. Between 2006 and 2010 the area under cultivation increased fairly marginally from 27,500 ha to 31,000 ha, and in 2011 and 2012 there were substantial decreases. The main production areas are in the Yungas valleys of La Paz department and the lowland Chapare district of Cochabamba: the area cultivated fell in both areas in 2013 by 7% and 12%, respectively. The policy of the Morales Government has been more permissive towards coca production than some of its predecessors. However, the Government asserted that it was doing more to stem illegal shipments of cocaine and cocaine paste. In 2013 there was a 3% increase in the area eradicated over the previous year, although seizures of cocaine paste and pure cocaine fell, compared with 2012. However, the Morales Government has been strongly criticized by the USA for not doing enough to counter drugs-trafficking, particularly since Morales expelled officials from the US Drug Enforcement Administration at the end of 2008.

Manufacturing

Manufacturing accounted for 10% of GDP in 2013, with the sector registering growth of 6.0%. However, Bolivia is one of South America's least industrialized countries. Much of what is classed as manufacturing is simply light processing of agricultural or mineral production. None the less, rapid urbanization has led to a growing demand for manufactured goods, and a proportion of these are produced locally. Bolivia has also increased its exports of manufactured goods in recent years, especially in areas such as clothing, textiles and jewellery. Major Bolivian cities, including La Paz, Cochabamba and Santa Cruz, all have industrial areas, and manufacturing is of ever greater importance in providing urban employment.

The most important market for manufactured goods is the USA, where ATPDEA acted as a spur to export activity in this area. However, since Bolivia's access to ATPDEA benefits was ended in 2009, Bolivian exporters—mainly in El Alto—have suffered some market loss.

The Morales Government is pursuing a policy of industrializing key export commodities in order to increase the added value remaining in the country. However, such initiatives are in the early stages of development. Projects include a scheme to manufacture steel from the iron ore resources at El Mutún, various operations to process other minerals (including lithium), and a plan to produce petrochemicals from the country's gas resources. There are also moves under way to process agricultural production, such as the building of citrus- and dairy-processing units.

Transport

Given its geographic location at the centre of South America, Bolivia has major potential as a transport hub for the region. In particular, it offers a route by which output from Brazil can reach the Pacific for transhipment to Asia. However, the country's rugged terrain and the poor quality of its infrastructure have hindered the development of this potential. Its railway network is in a poor state of repair, especially the eastern section in Santa Cruz, and the eastern and western networks do not interconnect. Major efforts have been made to upgrade road connections to facilitate international transport. However, the maintenance of road networks is poor, and climatic conditions are such that land transport links are frequently interrupted.

Tourism

Bolivia has experienced a large increase in international tourist arrivals over the last 20 years. Its dramatic geography and its cultural wealth mean that it has a great appeal to tourists. However, beyond the main cities, tourism infrastructure—such as hotels and restaurants—is often not of a high standard. Poor transport is also a deterrent, particularly the paucity and relative expense of international air links. Moreover, as elsewhere in Latin America, increasing crime rates can present a disincentive to visitors.

CONCLUSIONS AND PROSPECTS

Bolivia is likely to remain as one of Latin America's fastest growing economies in 2014, with real GDP expected to increase by over 5%. Bolivia's high level of international reserves means that it enjoys an important balance of payments cushion, and this has led to increases in its international credit ratings. The Morales administration has made clear its determination to avoid the inflationary policies characteristic of macroeconomic management in the past. However, in the longer term the economy remains perilously dependent on a handful of commodities for which prices have been buoyant in recent years, but which could easily decline in value. Also, the Government's failure to attract the scale of investment that has characterized other countries in the region (notably Chile and Peru) raises questions about the economy's ability to sustain its growth trajectory. Large-scale investment is particularly urgent in the gas sector to prevent a decline in production after 2016. Investors are concerned that demand for Bolivian gas in Brazil and Argentina may decrease if these two countries are able to develop their own copious gas resources. In spite of policies designed to foster an industrial capacity in some sectors, Bolivia will remain primarily an exporter of unprocessed raw materials. Since its export industries are largely capital intensive, this pattern of growth will do little to absorb a rapidly growing domestic supply of labour, much of which is currently employed in the informal sector.

Statistical Survey

Sources (unless otherwise indicated): Instituto Nacional de Estadística, José Carrasco 1391, Casilla 6129, La Paz; tel. (2) 222-2333; internet www.ine.gob.bo; Banco Central de Bolivia, Avda Ayacucho, esq. Mercado, Casilla 3118, La Paz; tel. (2) 240-9090; fax (2) 240-6614; e-mail bancocentraldebolivia@bcb.gob.bo; internet www.bcb.gob.bo.

Area and Population

AREA, POPULATION AND DENSITY

Area (sq km)	
Land	1,084,391
Inland water	14,190
Total	1,098,581*
Population (census results)†	
5 September 2001	8,274,325
21 November 2012	
Males	5,005,365
Females	5,021,889
Total	10,027,254
Population (UN estimates at mid-year)‡	
2013	10,671,201
2014	10,847,660
Density (per sq km) at mid-2014	9.9

* 424,164 sq miles.

† Figures exclude adjustment for underenumeration.

‡ Source: UN, *World Population Prospects: The 2012 Revision*; estimates not adjusted to take account of the results of the 2012 census.

POPULATION BY AGE AND SEX
(population at 2012 census)

	Males	Females	Total
0–14 years	1,597,872	1,512,650	3,110,522
15–64 years	3,119,500	3,184,003	6,303,503
65 years and over	287,993	325,236	613,229
Total	**5,005,365**	**5,021,889**	**10,027,254**

DEPARTMENTS
(population at census of November 2012)

	Area (sq km)*	Population	Density (per sq km)	Capital (population)†
Beni . . .	213,564	421,196	2.0	Trinidad (99,443)
Chuquisaca .	51,524	576,153	11.2	Sucre (312,024)
Cochabamba .	55,631	1,758,143	31.6	Cochabamba (631,304)
La Paz . .	133,985	2,706,351	20.2	La Paz (852,438)
Oruro . . .	53,588	494,178	9.2	Oruro (218,882)
Pando . . .	63,827	110,436	1.7	Cobija (44,867)
Potosí . . .	118,218	823,517	7.0	Potosí (168,831)
Santa Cruz .	370,621	2,655,084	7.2	Santa Cruz de la Sierra (1,697,630)
Tarija . . .	37,623	482,196	12.8	Tarija (216,138)
Total . . .	**1,098,581**	**10,027,254**	**9.1**	

* As at 2001 census.

† Official population projections, 2011.

PRINCIPAL TOWNS
(official projections, 2011)

Santa Cruz de la Sierra . . .	1,697,630	Sacaba	183,386
El Alto	974,754	Potosí	168,831
La Paz (administrative capital) . .	852,438	Quillacollo . . .	145,594
Cochabamba . .	631,304	Yacuiba	141,595
Sucre (legal capital)	312,024	Riberalta . . .	102,993
Oruro	218,882	Montero . . .	101,224
Tarija	216,138	Trinidad . . .	99,443

BIRTHS AND DEATHS
(annual averages, UN estimates)

	1995–2000	2000–05	2005–10
Birth rate (per 1,000)	32.7	30.3	27.3
Death rate (per 1,000)	8.9	8.1	7.5

Source: UN, *World Population Prospects: The 2012 Revision*.

Life expectancy (years at birth): 66.9 (males 64.8; females 69.2) in 2012 (Source: World Bank, World Development Indicators database).

ECONOMICALLY ACTIVE POPULATION
(labour force survey, '000 persons aged 10 years and over)

	2005	2006	2007
Agriculture, hunting, forestry and fishing	1,643.6	1,797.4	1,686.7
Mining and quarrying	71.0	55.5	72.4
Manufacturing	465.5	477.8	514.9
Electricity, gas and water supply	13.9	13.0	15.4
Construction	275.3	248.1	316.3
Wholesale and retail trade; repair of motor vehicles, motorcycles and personal and household goods	629.3	647.3	673.8
Hotels and restaurants	171.4	186.7	159.3
Transport, storage and communications	256.3	251.5	272.4
Financial intermediation	13.1	23.3	28.0
Real estate, renting and business activities	104.6	152.0	136.9
Public administration and defence; compulsory social security	91.1	115.2	152.3
Education	192.7	217.9	222.9
Health and social work	64.0	96.9	109.3
Other community, social and personal service activities	153.0	147.5	149.0
Private households with employed persons	108.3	119.6	160.7
Extraterritorial organizations and bodies	4.0	0.6	1.9
Total employed	4,257.2	4,550.3	4,672.4
Unemployed	245.2	243.5	255.0
Total labour force	4,502.4	4,793.8	4,927.4
Males	2,468.2	2,624.6	2,699.4
Females	2,034.2	2,169.2	2,228.0

Source: ILO.

2011 (household survey in November—December, persons aged 10 years and over): Total employed 5,361,425; Unemployed 146,766; Total labour force 5,508,191.

Health and Welfare

KEY INDICATORS

Total fertility rate (children per woman, 2012)	3.3
Under-5 mortality rate (per 1,000 live births, 2012)	41
HIV/AIDS (% of persons aged 15–49, 2012)	0.3
Physicians (per 1,000 head, 2011)	0.5
Hospital beds (per 1,000 head, 2009)	1.1
Health expenditure (2011): US $ per head (PPP)	248
Health expenditure (2011): % of GDP	5.0
Health expenditure (2011): public (% of total)	70.8
Access to water (% of persons, 2012)	88
Access to sanitation (% of persons, 2012)	46
Total carbon dioxide emissions ('000 metric tons, 2010)	15,456.4
Carbon dioxide emissions per head (metric tons, 2010)	1.5
Human Development Index (2013): ranking	113
Human Development Index (2013): value	0.667

For sources and definitions, see explanatory note on p. vi.

Agriculture

PRINCIPAL CROPS
('000 metric tons)

	2010	2011	2012
Wheat	255.4	249.7	200.0*
Rice, paddy	449.5	471.5	440.0*
Barley	47.6	51.1	49.0†
Maize	718.0	1,020.2	1,006.0†
Sorghum	335.5	389.5	478.0†
Potatoes	975.4	966.4	900.0*
Cassava (Manioc)	255.3	242.6	250.0*
Sugar cane	5,826.2	5,869.6	6,500.0*
Brazil nuts*	45.0	45.0	45.0
Chestnuts*	54.0	56.0	57.0
Soybeans (Soya beans)	1,917.2	2,299.9	2,400.0†
Sunflower seeds	310.8	152.7	250.0†
Tomatoes	53.1	49.5	50.0*
Pumpkins, squash and gourds*	20.1	20.2	22.0
Onions, dry	81.0	88.5	92.0*
Peas, green*	25.8	25.9	26.0
Carrots and turnips	26.9	27.0	30.0*
Maize, green	22.2	21.3	23.0*
Watermelons	15.6	15.4	16.5*
Bananas	158.2	203.4	210.0*
Plantains	338.9	336.3	350.0
Oranges	170.8	172.6	175.0
Tangerines, mandarins, clementines and satsumas	130.1	135.2	137.0
Lemons and limes	17.8	17.9	19.0
Grapes	25.0	26.9	28.0*
Papayas	7.6	7.4	7.2*
Coffee, green	28.8*	28.5	35.0*

* FAO estimate(s).
† Unofficial figure.

Aggregate production ('000 metric tons, may include official, semi-official or estimated data): Total cereals 1,849 in 2010, 2,227 in 2011, 2,218 in 2012; Total roots and tubers 1,290 in 2010, 1,267 in 2011, 1,210 in 2012; Total vegetables (incl. melons) 358 in 2010, 359 in 2011, 379 in 2012; Total fruits (excl. melons) 973 in 2010, 1,016 in 2011, 1,046 in 2012.

Source: FAO.

LIVESTOCK
('000 head, year ending September)

	2010	2011	2012
Horses*	478	483	487
Asses*	635	635	635
Mules*	82	82	82
Cattle	8,190	8,400	8,611
Pigs	2,641	2,713	2,800*
Sheep	8,701	8,878	8,900*
Goats	2,199	2,255	2,300*
Chickens	198,380	195,001	195,000*
Ducks*	300	305	307
Turkeys*	155	155	155

* FAO estimate(s).
Source: FAO.

LIVESTOCK PRODUCTS
('000 metric tons)

	2010	2011	2012
Cattle meat	202.3	205.2	215.3
Sheep meat	12.5	13.0	14.0*
Goat meat	5.3	5.3	5.5*
Pig meat	83.9	86.3	88.0*
Chicken meat	383.1	376.1	373.9
Cows' milk	371.7	381.5	392.0*
Sheep's milk*	33.5	33.5	34.0
Goats' milk	26.9	28.3	30.0*
Hen eggs†	69.8	73.1	74.8
Wool, greasy*	6.6	6.6	6.6

* FAO estimate(s).
† Unofficial figures.
Source: FAO.

Forestry

ROUNDWOOD REMOVALS
('000 cubic metres, excl. bark)

	2010	2011	2012
Sawlogs, veneer logs and logs for sleepers	913*	913*	913†
Fuel wood†	2,350	2,368	2,386
Total†	3,263	3,281	3,299

* Unofficial figure.
† FAO estimate(s).
Source: FAO.

SAWNWOOD PRODUCTION
('000 cubic metres, incl. railway sleepers, unofficial figures)

	2008	2009	2010
Coniferous (softwood)	2	3	7
Broadleaved (hardwood) . . .	459	459	459
Total	461	462	466

2011–12: Production assumed to be unchanged from 2010 (FAO estimates).
Source: FAO.

Fishing

(metric tons, live weight)

	2010	2011	2012
Capture	6,946	6,677	6,820
Freshwater fishes . . .	6,196	6,510	6,670
Silversides (sand smelts) . .	750	167	150
Aquaculture	856	966	1,060
Rainbow trout	360	414	455
Total catch	7,802	7,643	7,880

Note: Figures exclude crocodiles and alligators, recorded by number rather than by weight. The number of spectacled caimans caught was: 24,192 in 2010; 48,612 in 2011; 55,914 in 2012.
Source: FAO.

Mining

(metric tons unless otherwise indicated; figures for metallic minerals refer to the metal content of ores)

	2009	2010	2011
Crude petroleum ('000 barrels) .	12,329	12,607	12,600*
Natural gas (million cu m) . .	13,411	15,227	15,714
Copper	882	2,063	4,176
Tin	19,575	20,190	20,373
Lead	84,538	72,803	100,051
Zinc	430,879	411,409	427,129
Tungsten (Wolfram)	1,023	1,204	1,124
Antimony	2,990	4,980	3,947
Silver (kg)	1,325,729	1,259,388	1,213,586
Gold (kg)	7,217	6,394	6,513

* Estimate.
Source: US Geological Survey.

Industry

SELECTED PRODUCTS
('000 42-gallon barrels unless otherwise indicated)

	2009	2010	2011
Cement ('000 metric tons) . .	2,292	2,414	2,658
Liquefied petroleum gas . . .	645*	945	950*
Distillate fuel oil	4,100*	4,043	4,000
Kerosene	100*	127	125
Motor spirit (petrol) . . .	5,530*	5,492	5,500

* Estimate.

Electric energy (million kWh): 4,778 in 2005.

Source: partly US Geological Survey.

Finance

CURRENCY AND EXCHANGE RATES

Monetary Units
100 centavos = 1 boliviano (B).

Sterling, Dollar and Euro Equivalents (30 May 2014)
£1 sterling = 11.624 bolivianos;
US $1 = 6.910 bolivianos;
€1 = 9.405 bolivianos;
100 bolivianos = £8.60 = $14.47 = €10.63.

Average Exchange Rate (bolivianos per US $)
2011   6.94
2012   6.91
2013   6.91

GOVERNMENT FINANCE
(consolidated public sector accounts, million bolivianos)

Revenue	2011	2012*	2013*
Tax revenue	29,433.5	34,198.1	39,974.0
Internal	26,144.2	30,914.1	36,221.3
Customs	2,095.9	2,317.0	2,710.2
Mining royalties	1,193.4	967.0	1,042.6
Duties on hydrocarbons . . .	2,432.2	2,447.9	2,891.3
Sale of hydrocarbons . . .	30,830.1	39,560.6	47,035.8
Other public sector sales . .	5,248.6	5,393.3	6,397.6
Other current revenue . . .	4,780.8	3,366.3	4,553.3
Current transfers	1,514.9	1,770.6	2,174.5
Capital revenue	1,374.5	1,253.2	712.3
Total	75,614.6	87,990.0	103,738.8

Expenditure	2011	2012*	2013*
Current expenditure	52,119.2	59,446.2	68,032.7
Personal services	16,726.4	18,082.6	20,775.8
Goods and services . . .	22,764.1	25,785.4	29,529.3
Interest on debt	1,991.4	1,887.4	1,473.5
External	734.2	573.9	774.4
Internal	1,257.2	1,313.5	699.1
Current transfers	9,519.4	11,497.6	12,704.7
Other current expenditure . .	1,117.9	2,193.2	3,549.4
Capital expenditure	22,113.3	25,255.9	34,330.0
Total	74,232.5	84,702.0	102,362.7

* Preliminary figures.

INTERNATIONAL RESERVES
(US $ million at 31 December)

	2011	2012	2013
Gold (national valuation) . . .	2,109.1	2,267.3	1,647.4
IMF special drawing rights . .	253.2	254.2	256.7
Reserve position in IMF . . .	13.6	13.6	13.7
Foreign exchange	9,643.9	11,391.4	12,512.4
Total	12,019.8	13,926.5	14,430.1

Source: IMF, *International Financial Statistics*.

MONEY SUPPLY
(million bolivianos at 31 December)

	2011	2012	2013
Currency outside depository corporations	25,814	29,305	32,716
Transferable deposits	30,956	39,073	47,365
Other deposits	56,638	68,322	80,152
Securities other than shares	758	1,211	1,867
Broad money	114,165	137,911	162,101

Source: IMF, *International Financial Statistics*.

COST OF LIVING
(Consumer Price Index for urban areas; base: 2007 = 100)

	2011	2012	2013
All items	130.2	136.1	143.9

NATIONAL ACCOUNTS
(million bolivianos at current prices, preliminary)

Expenditure on the Gross Domestic Product

	2011	2012	2013
Government final consumption expenditure	22,901.9	25,152.8	29,324.1
Private final consumption expenditure	101,250.6	111,327.7	127,191.3
Increase in stocks	967.3	−1,080.9	−182.9
Gross fixed capital formation	31,531.1	34,074.0	40,388.7
Total domestic expenditure	156,650.9	169,473.6	196,721.2
Exports of goods and services	73,294.3	88,273.4	93,412.6
Less Imports of goods and services	63,814.1	70,711.5	78,680.0
GDP at market prices	166,131.0	187,035.4	211,453.7
GDP at constant 1990 prices	34,271.6	36,045.7	38,487.8

Gross Domestic Product by Economic Activity

	2011	2012	2013
Agriculture, hunting, forestry and fishing	16,246.6	18,371.2	21,124.1
Mining and quarrying	25,767.1	27,375.0	29,908.0
Manufacturing	17,192.7	19,123.9	21,041.1
Electricity, gas and water	3,301.1	3,551.1	3,915.5
Construction	4,242.3	4,872.0	5,577.1
Trade	11,832.4	12,505.8	13,608.5
Transport, storage and communications	13,959.6	14,942.5	16,664.9
Finance, insurance, real estate and business services	13,378.5	16,311.3	18,541.1
Government services	19,340.7	21,373.3	24,814.8
Other services	9,949.8	10,871.6	11,930.3
Sub-total	135,210.8	149,297.7	167,125.4
Value-added tax	} 36,459.9	44,974.2	52,894.2
Import duties			
Less Imputed bank charge	5,539.7	7,236.5	8,565.8
GDP in purchasers' values	166,131.0	187,035.4	211,453.7

BALANCE OF PAYMENTS
(US $ million)

	2010	2011	2012
Exports of goods	6,129.3	8,174.8	11,109.8
Imports of goods	−5,006.8	−7,126.4	−7,694.0
Balance on goods	1,122.5	1,048.5	3,415.8
Exports of services	707.7	948.0	1,080.7
Imports of services	−1,148.8	−1,650.7	−1,994.8
Balance on goods and services	681.4	345.8	2,501.6
Primary income received	81.7	136.8	141.4
Primary income paid	−970.6	−1,122.5	−1,770.7
Balance on goods, services and primary income	−207.5	−640.0	872.4
Secondary income received	1,187.6	1,299.3	1,416.8
Secondary income paid	−106.3	−122.2	−151.0

—*continued*	2010	2011	2012
Current balance	873.7	537.2	2,138.1
Capital account (net)	−7.2	5.9	5.7
Direct investment assets	28.8	−0.3	—
Direct investment liabilities	622.0	858.9	1,060.0
Portfolio investment assets	90.1	156.0	−360.3
Other investment assets	−32.3	−127.8	−2,342.1
Other investment liabilities	151.4	636.0	2,171.1
Net errors and omissions	−802.3	94.8	−960.8
Reserves and related items	924.3	2,160.8	1,711.7

Source: IMF, *International Financial Statistics*.

External Trade

PRINCIPAL COMMODITIES
(distribution by SITC, US $ million)

Imports c.i.f.	2011	2012*	2013*
Food and live animals	564.0	523.8	591.0
Crude materials (inedible) except fuels	81.8	82.3	84.5
Mineral fuels, lubricants, etc.	1,111.2	1,286.5	1,291.6
Chemicals and related products	1,117.5	1,255.3	1,372.2
Basic manufactures	1,418.8	1,560.1	1,611.8
Machinery and transport equipment	2,981.7	3,054.3	3,627.5
Miscellaneous manufactured articles	575.2	682.6	634.0
Total (incl. others)	7,935.7	8,590.1	9,353.0

Exports f.o.b.	2011	2012*	2013*
Food and live animals	746.8	973.8	1,218.8
Crude materials (inedible) except fuels	2,589.9	2,387.5	2,424.3
Mineral fuels, lubricants, etc.	4,148.7	5,909.9	6,681.0
Animal and vegetable oils, fats and waxes	326.8	373.5	359.4
Basic manufactures	799.1	640.2	622.0
Machinery and transport equipment	8.5	23.4	8.4
Miscellaneous manufactured articles	116.4	126.0	170.9
Total (incl. others)	9,145.8	11,814.6	12,207.6

* Preliminary figures.

PRINCIPAL TRADING PARTNERS
(US $ million)

Imports c.i.f.	2011	2012*	2013*
Argentina	966.4	1,066.6	1,019.9
Brazil	1,395.5	1,524.5	1,599.7
Chile	308.5	383.6	573.8
China, People's Republic	1,112.7	1,293.7	1,253.8
Colombia	195.0	162.3	183.4
Germany	142.9	164.9	236.4
India	76.3	86.2	108.1
Italy	93.8	173.8	119.6
Japan	598.9	387.6	469.3
Korea, Republic	67.9	74.5	101.5
Mexico	188.9	236.4	279.8
Netherlands	19.1	59.7	147.8
Peru	472.3	558.8	601.0
Singapore	4.9	71.0	95.8
Spain	101.9	100.9	184.4
Sweden	169.3	93.7	204.9
Switzerland	21.1	48.8	139.0
USA	889.6	940.1	1,170.4
Venezuela	526.2	444.4	15.6
Total (incl. others)	7,935.7	8,590.1	9,353.0

Exports	2011	2012*	2013*
Argentina	1,059.1	2,110.5	2,508.9
Australia	125.1	113.2	163.4
Belgium-Luxembourg	377.7	334.6	242.7
Brazil	3,030.1	3,665.3	4,030.6
Canada	194.2	152.3	164.4
Chile	149.8	226.0	153.9
China, People's Republic . . .	336.6	316.5	320.1
Colombia	259.3	413.3	675.2
Ecuador	89.6	221.2	145.1
Japan	540.0	441.8	417.7
Korea, Republic	419.1	358.0	404.6
Netherlands	54.4	34.0	190.4
Peru	461.0	627.6	627.9
Spain	93.6	63.8	110.2
Switzerland (incl. Liechtenstein) .	306.0	272.5	165.6
United Kingdom	155.7	106.7	105.5
USA	876.5	1,746.4	1,212.4
Venezuela	286.4	309.0	142.9
Total (incl. others)	**9,145.8**	**11,814.6**	**12,207.6**

*Preliminary.

Transport

RAILWAYS
(traffic)

	2002	2003	2004
Passenger-km (million) . . .	280	283	286
Net ton-km (million)	873	901	1,058

Source: UN, *Statistical Yearbook*.

ROAD TRAFFIC
(motor vehicles in use at 31 December)

	2002	2003	2004
Passenger cars	26,229	127,222	138,729
Buses	27,226	43,588	49,133
Lorries and vans	30,539	225,028	251,801
Motorcycles	1,125	15,467	19,426

2007: Passenger cars 174,912; Buses 6,996; Lorries and vans 468,763; Motorcycles 34,982.

Source: IRF, *World Road Statistics*.

SHIPPING
Flag Registered Fleet
(at 31 December)

	2011	2012	2013
Number of vessels	117	131	118
Total displacement ('000 grt) . .	170.1	210.2	132.4

Source: Lloyd's List Intelligence (www.lloydslistintelligence.com).

CIVIL AVIATION
(traffic on scheduled services, millions)

	2010	2011
Kilometres flown	22	26
Passengers carried	1.8	2.1
Passenger-km	1,603	2,097
Total ton-km	161	226

Source: UN, *Statistical Yearbook*.

Passengers carried (million): 1.8 in 2012 (Source: World Bank, World Development Indicators database).

Tourism

TOURIST ARRIVALS
(non-resident tourists arriving at hotels and similar establishments)

Country of origin	2010	2011	2012
Argentina	58,347	62,816	62,816
Brazil	37,707	40,908	41,139
Canada	11,217	12,951	13,024
Chile	27,052	30,947	31,122
Colombia	11,235	12,813	12,885
France	28,491	30,697	30,870
Germany	25,154	26,406	26,555
Israel	13,066	12,847	12,919
Peru	90,332	96,582	97,127
Spain	18,834	19,001	19,108
Switzerland	10,705	10,623	10,683
United Kingdom	23,278	24,425	24,563
USA	44,561	50,162	50,445
Total (incl. others)	**527,200**	**560,325**	**563,486**

Tourism receipts (US $ million, excl. passenger transport): 379 in 2010; 481 in 2011; 532 in 2012.

Source: World Tourism Organization.

Communications Media

	2011	2012	2013
Telephones ('000 main lines in use)	878.5	879.3	874.4
Mobile cellular telephones ('000 subscribers)	8,353.3	9,493.2	10,425.7
Internet subscribers ('000) . .	116.8	n.a.	n.a.
Broadband subscribers ('000) . .	65.9	110.6	141.8

Source: International Telecommunication Union.

Education

(2010/11 unless otherwise indicated, estimates)

	Institutions	Teachers	Students ('000)		
			Males	Females	Total
Pre-primary .	2,294*	6,126†	131.9	126.2	258.1
Primary . . .	12,639‡	62,430†	713.9	675.8	1,389.7
Secondary:					
general . .	n.a.	57,912†	540.2§	518.1§	1,058.3§
technical/ vocational .	n.a.	2,148‖	17.3¶	32.3¶	49.6¶
Tertiary† . .	n.a.	15,685	193.8	158.8	352.6

* 1988.
† 2006/07.
‡ 1987.
§ 2009/10.
‖ 2003/04.
¶ 2002/03.

Pupil-teacher ratio (primary education, UNESCO estimate): 24.2 in 2006/07.

Adult literacy rate (UNESCO estimates): 94.5% (males 97.1%; females 91.9%) in 2012.

Source: UNESCO Institute for Statistics.

Directory

The Constitution

Bolivia became an independent republic in 1825 and received its first Constitution in November 1826. Since that date a number of new Constitutions have been promulgated. Following the *coup d'état* of November 1964, the Constitution of 1947 was revived. Executive power is vested in the President, who chairs the Cabinet. A revised Constitution was signed into law in February 2009, according to which the President, who is elected by direct suffrage for a five-year term, can seek re-election for a second consecutive term. In the event of the President's death or failure to assume office, the Vice-President or, failing the Vice-President, the President of the Senate (Senado Nacional), of the Chamber of Deputies (Cámara de Diputados) or of the Supreme Tribunal of Justice, in that order, becomes interim Head of State.

The President has power to appoint members of the Cabinet and diplomatic representatives from a panel proposed by the Senate. The President is responsible for the conduct of foreign affairs and is also empowered to issue decrees and to initiate legislation by special messages to the Plurinational Legislative Assembly (Asamblea Legislativa Plurinacional).

The Plurinational Legislative Assembly consists of a 36-member Senate and a 130-member Chamber of Deputies. The Assembly meets annually and its ordinary sessions last only 90 working days, which may be extended to 120. Each of the nine departments (La Paz, Chuquisaca, Oruro, Beni, Santa Cruz, Potosí, Tarija, Cochabamba and Pando), into which the country is divided for administrative purposes, elects four senators. Members of both houses are elected for five years.

The supreme administrative, political and military authority in each department is vested in a Governor (known as a Prefect until 2010). Until 2005, Prefects were appointed by the President; however, the first direct elections for departmental Prefects were held in that year. The sub-divisions of each department are known as provinces. The provinces are further divided into cantons. There are 94 provinces and some 1,000 cantons. The capital of each department has its autonomous municipal council and controls its own revenue and expenditure.

Public order, education and roads are under national control.

A decree issued in July 1952 conferred the franchise on all persons who had reached the age of 21 years, whether literate or illiterate. Previously the franchise had been restricted to literate persons. (The voting age for married persons was lowered to 18 years at the 1989 elections.)

A revised Constitution was approved by some 61% of voters in a referendum in January 2009 and came into effect in the following month. The new Constitution provided for greater autonomy for indigenous communities, enshrined state control over key economic sectors (most notably natural resources), imposed restrictions on the size of land holdings, removed Roman Catholicism as the state religion and aimed to make the judiciary more transparent and accountable by introducing elections to federal courts. The first such ballots were held in October 2011.

The Government

HEAD OF STATE

President: Juan Evo Morales Aima (took office 22 January 2006, re-elected 6 December 2009).

Vice-President: Alvaro Marcelo García Linera.

THE CABINET
(September 2014)

The Cabinet is composed of members of the Movimiento al Socialismo.

Minister of Foreign Affairs and Worship: David Choquehuanca Céspedes.

Minister of the Interior: Jorge Pérez Valenzuela.

Minister of National Defence: Rubén Saavedra Soto.

Minister of Justice: Elizabeth Zaida Gutiérrez Salazar.

Minister of Economy and Public Finance: Luis Alberto Arce Catacora.

Minister of Development Planning: Elba Viviana Caro Hinojosa.

Minister of the Presidency: Juan Ramón Quintana.

Minister of Autonomy: Claudia Peña Claros.

Minister of Institutional Transparency and the Fight against Corruption: Nardi Suxo Iturry.

Minister of Health and Sports: Juan Carlos Calvimontes Camargo.

Minister of Labour, Employment and Social Security: Daniel Santalla Tórrez.

Minister of Education: Roberto Aguilar Gómez.

Minister of Rural Development and Lands: Nemesia Achacollo Tola.

Minister of Hydrocarbons and Energy: Juan José Sosa Soruco.

Minister of Mines and Metallurgy: César Navarro.

Minister of Public Works, Services and Housing: Vladimir Sánchez Escobar.

Minister of Water and the Environment: José Zamora Gutiérrez.

Minister of Culture and Tourism: Pablo César Groux Canedo.

Minister of Productive Development and Plural Economy: Ana Teresa Morales Olivera.

Minister of Communications: Amanda Dávila Torres.

MINISTRIES

Office of the Vice-President: Edif. de la Vicepresidencia del Estado, Calle Ayacucho, esq. Mercado 308, Casilla 7056, La Paz; tel. (2) 214-2000; fax (2) 220-1211; internet www.vicepresidencia.gob.bo.

Ministry of Autonomy: Edif. Ex CONAVI, Avda 20 de Octubre, esq. Fernando Guachalla 2230, Casilla 1397, La Paz; tel. (2) 211-0930; fax (2) 211-3613; e-mail contacto@autonomia.gob.bo; internet www.autonomia.gob.bo.

Ministry of Communications: Edif. La Urbana, 4°, Avda Camacho 1485, La Paz; tel. (2) 220-0402; fax (2) 220-0509; e-mail comunicacion@comunicacion.gob.bo; internet www.comunicacion.gob.bo.

Ministry of Culture and Tourism: Palacio Chico, Calle Ayacucho, esq. Potosí, Casilla 7846, La Paz; tel. (2) 220-0910; fax (2) 220-2628; e-mail despacho@minculturas.gob.bo; internet www.minculturas.gob.bo.

Ministry of Development Planning: Avda Mariscal Santa Cruz, esq. Oruro 1092, Casilla 12814, La Paz; tel. (2) 211-6000; fax (2) 231-7320; e-mail comunicacion@planificacion.gob.bo; internet www.planificacion.gob.bo.

Ministry of Economy and Public Finance: Edif. Palacio de Comunicaciones, 19°, CP 3744, La Paz; tel. (2) 220-3434; fax (2) 235-9955; e-mail ministro_web@economiayfinanzas.gob.bo; internet www.economiayfinanzas.gob.bo.

Ministry of Education: Avda Arce 2147, Casilla 3116, La Paz; tel. and fax (2) 244-2414; e-mail webmaster@minedu.gob.bo; internet www.minedu.gob.bo.

Ministry of Foreign Affairs and Worship: Plaza Murillo, Calle Ingavi, esq. Calle Junín, La Paz; tel. (2) 240-8900; fax (2) 240-8905; e-mail mreuno@rree.gob.bo; internet www.rree.gob.bo.

Ministry of Health and Sports: Plaza del Estudiante, esq. Cañada Strongest s/n, La Paz; tel. (2) 249-0554; fax (2) 248-6654; e-mail info@sns.gob.bo; internet www.sns.gob.bo.

Ministry of Hydrocarbons and Energy: Edif. Centro de Comunicaciones, 12°, Avda Mariscal Santa Cruz, esq. Calle Oruro, La Paz; tel. (2) 237-4050; fax (2) 214-1307; e-mail minehidro@hidrocarburos.gob.bo; internet www.hidrocarburos.gob.bo.

Ministry of Institutional Transparency and the Fight against Corruption: Edif. Capitán Ravelo, 3°–9°, Calle Capitán Ravelo 2101, esq. Montevideo, La Paz; tel. 211-5773; fax 215-3084; internet www.transparencia.gob.bo.

Ministry of the Interior: Avda Arce 2409, esq. Belisario Salinas 2409, Casilla 7110, La Paz; tel. (2) 244-0466; fax (2) 244-0466; e-mail mail@mingobierno.gob.bo; internet www.mingobierno.gob.bo.

Ministry of Justice: Avda 16 de Julio (El Prado) 1769, La Paz; tel. (2) 212-4725; fax (2) 231-5468; e-mail ministerio@justicia.go.bo; internet www.justicia.gob.bo.

Ministry of Labour, Employment and Social Security: Calle Yanacocha, esq. Mercado, Zona Central, La Paz; tel. (2) 240-8606; fax (2) 237-1387; e-mail info@mintrabajo.gob.bo; internet www.mintrabajo.gob.bo.

Ministry of Mines and Metallurgy: Edif. Palacio de Comunicaciones, 14°, Avda Mariscal Santa Cruz, Casilla 8686, La Paz; tel. (2) 237-1165; fax (2) 239-1241; e-mail mineria@mineria.gob.bo; internet www.mineria.gob.bo.

Ministry of National Defence: Calle 20 de Octubre 2502, esq. Pedro Salazar, La Paz; tel. (2) 243-2525; fax (2) 243-3153; e-mail utransparencia@mindef.gob.bo; internet www.mindef.gob.bo.

Ministry of the Presidency: Palacio de Gobierno, Calle Ayacucho, esq. Comercio s/n, Casilla 3278, La Paz; tel. (2) 220-2321; fax (2) 237-1388; e-mail correo@presidencia.gob.bo; internet www.presidencia.gob.bo.

Ministry of Productive Development and Plural Economy: Edif. Centro de Comunicaciones, 20°, Avda Mariscal Santa Cruz, esq. Calle Oruro, La Paz; tel. (2) 212-4235; fax (2) 212-4240; e-mail escribanos@produccion.gob.bo; internet www.produccion.gob.bo.

Ministry of Public Works, Services and Housing: Edif. Centro de Comunicaciones, 5°, Avda Mariscal Santa Cruz, esq. Calle Oruro, La Paz; tel. (2) 211-9999; e-mail obraspublicas@oopp.gob.bo; internet www.oopp.gob.bo.

Ministry of Rural Development and Lands: Avda Camacho 1471, entre Calle Bueno y Loayza, La Paz; tel. (2) 211-1103; fax (2) 211-1067; e-mail contacto@agrobolivia.gob.bo; internet www.agrobolivia.gob.bo.

Ministry of Water and the Environment: Capitán Castrillo 434, entre Calles 20 de Octubre y Héroes del Acre, Zona San Pedro, La Paz; tel. (2) 211-5571; fax (2) 211-8582; e-mail gary.suarez@minagua.gov.bo; internet www.mmaya.gob.bo.

President and Legislature

PRESIDENT

Election, 6 December 2009

Candidate	Valid votes	% of valid votes cast
Juan Evo Morales Aima (MAS) .	2,943,209	64.22
Manfred Reyes Villa (PPB—CN)	1,212,795	26.46
Samuel Doria Medina (UN) .	258,971	5.65
René Joaquino Suárez González (AS)	106,027	2.31
Others	61,784	1.35
Total (incl. others)*	4,582,786	100.00

* In addition, there were 156,290 blank votes and 120,364 spoiled votes.

PLURINATIONAL LEGISLATIVE ASSEMBLY
(Asamblea Legislativa Plurinacional)

President of the Senate: EUGENIO ROJAS APAZA (MAS).

President of the Chamber of Deputies: MARCELO WILLIAM ELIO CHÁVEZ (MAS).

General Election, 6 December 2009

	Seats	
Party	Chamber of Deputies	Senate
Movimiento al Socialismo (MAS) . .	88	26
Plan Progreso para Bolivia—Convergencia National (PPB—CN) .	37	10
Frente de Unidad Nacional (UN) .	3	—
Alianza Social (AS)	2	—
Total	130	36

Governors

DEPARTMENTS
(September 2014)

Beni: CARMELO LENZ FREDERIKSEN.

Chuquisaca: ESTEBAN URQUIZU CUÉLLAR.

Cochabamba: EDMUNDO NOVILLO AGUILAR.

La Paz: CÉSAR HUGO COCARICO YANA.

Oruro: SANTOS JAVIER TITO VÉLIZ.

Pando: LUIS ADOLFO FLORES ROBERTS.

Potosí: FÉLIX GONZÁLEZ BERNAL.

Santa Cruz: RUBÉN DARÍO COSTAS AGUILERA.

Tarija: LINO CONDORI ARAMAYO.

Election Commission

Organo Electoral Plurinacional (OEP): Plaza Abaroa, Avda Sánchez Lima 2440, esq. Pedro Salazar, Sopocachi, CP 8748, La Paz; tel. (2) 242-4221; fax (2) 242-3175; internet www.oep.org.bo; f. 1956 as Corte Nacional Electoral; replaced by OEP in 2010; consists of the Supreme Electoral Tribunal (Tribunal Supremo Electoral—TSE) and nine Departmental Electoral Tribunals, as well as Electoral Judges, the Juries at Election Tables, and Electoral Notaries; the TSE has the highest national jurisdiction; Pres. Dr WILMA VELASCO AGUILAR.

Political Organizations

Comité pro Santa Cruz (CpSC): Avda Cañada Strongest 70, CP 2630, Santa Cruz; tel. (3) 359-7338; e-mail info@comiteprosantacruz.org.bo; internet www.comiteprosantacruz.org.bo; f. 1950; regional autonomist grouping; Leader FERNANDO CASTEDO CADARIO.

Frente Revolucionario de Izquierda (FRI): Avda Busch 1191 y Pasaje Jamaica, Miraflores, La Paz; tel. (2) 222-5488; e-mail ssiemprefri@gmail.com; left-wing; f. 1978; Leader OSCAR ZAMORA MOTETE.

Frente para la Victoria (FPV): Edif. Ugarte de Ingeniería, Penthouse 1, Calle Loayza 255 entre Avda Camacho y Calle Mercado, La Paz; e-mail fpvbolivia@hotmail.com; f. 2006; centre-right; Leader ELISEO RODRÍGUEZ PARI.

Movimiento Demócrata Social (MDS): f. 2013; right-wing; contesting the 2014 elections as part of the Concertación de la Unidad Demócrata alliance with the Unidad Democrática; Leader RUBÉN DARÍO COSTAS AGUILERA.

Movimiento sin Miedo (MSM): Avda 20 de Octubre y Conchitas 1743, frente al Colegio Bolívar, La Paz; tel. (2) 248-9935; e-mail somossimiedo@msm.bo; internet www.msm.bo; f. 1999; left-wing; Leader JUAN DEL GRANADO COSÍO.

Movimiento Nacionalista Revolucionario (MNR): Avda Hernando Siles 21, Curva Sur del Estado Hernando Siles, La Paz; tel. (2) 212-8475; fax (2) 212-8479; e-mail mnr@bolivian.com; internet www.bolivian.com/mnr; f. 1942; centre-right; Nat. Dir JHONNY TORRES.

Movimiento al Socialismo (MAS): Calle Benedicto Vincenti 960, Sopocachi, La Paz; tel. 72970205 (mobile); f. 1987; also known as the Movimiento al Socialismo—Instrumento Político por la Soberanía de los Pueblos (MAS—IPSP); left-wing; promotes equality for indigenous people, peasants and workers; Leader JUAN EVO MORALES AIMA.

Partido Demócrata Cristiano (PDC): Calle Colón 812, 2°, esq. Sucre, Casilla 4345, La Paz; tel. 70655693 (mobile); e-mail josuva2002@hotmail.com; f. 1954; Pres. JORGE SUÁREZ VARGAS.

Partido Obrero Revolucionario (POR): Correo Central, La Paz; f. 1935; Trotskyist; not officially recognized by the Supreme Electoral Tribunal; Leader GUILLERMO LORA.

Partido Verde de Bolivia—Instrumento de la Ecologia Politica (PVB): internet www.partidoverdebolivia.org; f. 2007; Sec. MARGOT SORIA SARAVIA; Presidential candidate FERNANDO VARGAS.

Plan Progreso para Bolivia—Convergencia Nacional (PPB—CN): Of. Radio Ciudad, Plaza del Estudiante 1907, Zona Central, La Paz; f. 2007; not contesting the 2014 elections.

Unidad Cívica Solidaridad (UCS): Edif. La Primera Bloque B, 17°, Of. 7 y 8, Avda Mariscal Santa Cruz 1364, La Paz; tel. (2) 236-0297; fax (2) 237-2200; e-mail unidadcivicasolidaridad@hotmail.com; f. 1989; populist; Leader JHONNY FERNÁNDEZ SAUCEDO.

Unidad Democrática (UD): Calle Fernando Guachalla, esq. Jacinto Benavente 2190, La Paz; tel. and fax (2) 211-5110; f. 2003 as Unidad Nacional; contesting the 2014 elections as part of the Concertación de la Unidad Demócrata alliance with the Movimiento Demócrata Social; Leader SAMUEL DORIA MEDINA.

OTHER ORGANIZATION

Confederación de Pueblos Indígenas de Bolivia (CIDOB): Blvd San Juan, Calle 2, Santa Cruz; tel. (3) 344-6858; fax (3) 341-5929; e-mail cidob@cidob-bo.org; internet www.cidob-bo.org; f. 1982; represents indigenous peoples and communities; Pres. ADOLFO CHÁVEZ BEYUMA.

Diplomatic Representation

EMBASSIES IN BOLIVIA

Argentina: Calle Aspiazú 497, esq. Sánchez Lima, Casilla 64, La Paz; tel. (2) 241-7737; fax (2) 242-2727; e-mail ebolv@mrecic.gov.ar; internet www.ebolv.mrecic.gov.ar; Ambassador SERGIO ARIEL BASTEIRO.

Brazil: Edif. Multicentro, Torre B, Avda Arce s/n, esq. Rosendo Gutiérrez, Sopocachi, Casilla 429, La Paz; tel. (2) 216-6400; fax (2) 244-0043; e-mail embajadabrasil@brasil.org.bo; internet www.brasil .org.bo; Ambassador RAYMUNDO SANTOS ROCHA MAGNO.

China, People's Republic: Calle 1 8532, Los Pinos, Calacoto, Casilla 10005, La Paz; tel. (2) 279-3851; fax (2) 279-7121; e-mail chinaemb_bo@mfa.gov.cn; internet bo.china-embassy.org/esp; Ambassador LI DONG.

Colombia: Calle Roberto Prudencio 797, entre Calle 15 y 16 de Calacoto, Casilla 1418, Calacoto, La Paz; tel. (2) 279-0386; fax (2) 277-5670; e-mail bolivia@cancilleria.gov.co; internet bolivia.embajada .gov.co; Ambassador MARTHA CECILIA PINILLA PERDOMO.

Cuba: Calle Gobles 6246, entre calles 11 y 12, Bajo Irpavi, Zona Sur, La Paz; tel. (2) 272-1646; fax (2) 272-3419; e-mail embajador@ embacubabol.com; internet www.cubadiplomatica.cu/bolivia; Ambassador ROLANDO ANTONIO GÓMEZ GONZÁLEZ.

Denmark: Edif. Fortaleza, 9°, Avda Arce 2799, esq. Cordero, Casilla 9860, La Paz; tel. (2) 243-2070; fax (2) 243-3150; e-mail lpbamb@um .dk; internet www.amblapaz.um.dk; Ambassador OLE THONKE.

Ecuador: Calle 14, No 8136, Calacoto, Casilla 406, La Paz; tel. (2) 211-5869; fax (2) 279-5079; e-mail eecuabolivia@mmrree.gov.ec; Ambassador RICARDO ULCUANGO.

Egypt: Avda Ballivián 599, esq. Calle 12, Casilla 2956, La Paz; tel. (2) 278-6511; fax (2) 278-4325; e-mail embassy.lapaz@mfa.gov.eg; internet www.mfa.gov.eg/Lapaz_Emb; Ambassador HANI MUHAM-MAD BASSIYONI MAHMOUD.

France: Avda Hernando Siles 5390, esq. Calle 8 de Obrajes, Casilla 717, La Paz; tel. (2) 214-9900; fax (2) 214-9901; e-mail information@ ambafrance-bo.org; internet www.ambafrance-bo.org; Ambassador MICHEL PINARD.

Germany: Avda Arce 2395, esq. Belisario Salinas, Casilla 5265, La Paz; tel. (2) 244-0066; fax (2) 244-1441; e-mail info@la-paz.diplo.de; internet www.la-paz.diplo.de; Ambassador PETER LINDER.

Holy See: Avda Arce 2990, San Jorge, Casilla 136, La Paz; tel. (2) 243-1007; fax (2) 243-2120; e-mail nunciaturabolivia@gmail.com; Apostolic Nuncio Most Rev. GIAMBATTISTA DIQUATTRO (Titular Archbishop of Giru Mons).

Iran: Calle 11, No 7805, esq. Avda Infouentes Calacoto, La Paz; tel. (2) 277-5749; fax (2) 277-5747; e-mail iranbolivi@yahoo.com; Ambassador ALIREZA GHEZILI.

Italy: Calle 5 (Jordán Cuellar) 458, Obrajes, Casilla 626, La Paz; tel. (2) 278-8506; fax (2) 278-8178; e-mail segreteria.lapaz@esteri.it; internet www.amblapaz.esteri.it; Ambassador LUIGI DE CHIARA.

Japan: Calle Rosendo Gutiérrez 497, esq. Sánchez Lima, Casilla 2725, La Paz; tel. (2) 241-9110; fax (2) 241-1919; e-mail coopjapon@ acelerate.com; internet www.bo.emb-japan.go.jp; Ambassador HIDE-HIRO TSUBAKI.

Korea, Republic: Edif. Torre Lucía, 6°, Calle 13, Calacoto, La Paz; tel. (2) 211-0361; fax (2) 211-0365; e-mail coreabolivia@gmail.com; internet bol.mofat.go.kr; Ambassador CHUN YOUNG-WOOK.

Mexico: Avda Ballivián 1174, entre Calles 17 y 18, Calacoto, Casilla 430, La Paz; tel. (2) 277-1871; fax (2) 277-1855; e-mail embamex@ embamexbolivia.org; internet www.sre.gob.mx/bolivia; Ambassador ARMANDO ARRIAZOLA PETO-RUEDA.

Nicaragua: Calle 6 de Obrajes, entre Avda 14 de Setiembre y Avda Hernando Siles 481, La Paz; tel. (2) 211-5563; e-mail echevez@ cancilleria.gob.ni; Ambassador ELÍAS CHÉVEZ OBANDO.

Panama: Calle 10, No 7853, Calacoto, Casilla 678, La Paz; tel. (2) 278-7334; fax (2) 279-7290; e-mail empanbol@ceibo.entelnet.bo; internet www.empanbol.org; Ambassador AFRANIO HERRERA GARCÍA.

Paraguay: Edif. Illimani II, 1°, Of. 101, Avda 6 de Agosto, esq. Pedro Salazar, Sopocachi, Casilla 882, La Paz; tel. (2) 243-3176; fax (2) 243-2201; e-mail embaparbolivia@mre.gov.py; Chargé d'affaires a.i. OSVALDO BITTAR VICIOSO.

Peru: Calle Fernando Guachalla 300, Sopocachi, Casilla 668, La Paz; tel. (2) 244-1250; fax (2) 244-1240; e-mail embbol@caoba.entelnet.bo; internet www.embaperubolivia.com; Ambassador SILVIA ELENA ALFARO ESPINOSA.

Russia: Avda Walter Guevara Arce 8129, Calacoto, Casilla 5494, La Paz; tel. (2) 278-6419; fax (2) 278-6531; e-mail embrusia@acelerate .com; Ambassador ALEXÉI SAZONOV.

Spain: Avda 6 de Agosto 2827, Casilla 282, La Paz; tel. (2) 243-3518; fax (2) 243-2752; e-mail emb.lapaz@maec.es; internet www.maec.es/ embajadas/lapaz; Ambassador ÁNGEL MARÍA VÁZQUEZ DÍAZ DE TUESTA.

Sweden: Edif. Multicine, 11°, Avda Arce 2631, La Paz; tel. (2) 297-9630; fax (2) 297-9631; e-mail ambassaden.la-paz @foreign.ministry .se; internet www.swedenabroad.com; Ambassador MARIE ANDERS-SON DE FRUTOS.

Switzerland: Calle 13, esq. Avda 14 de Setiembre, Obrajes, Casilla 9356, La Paz; tel. (2) 275-1225; fax (2) 214-0885; e-mail paz

.vertretung@eda.admin.ch; internet www.eda.admin.ch/lapaz; Ambassador PETER BISCHOF.

United Kingdom: Avda Arce 2732, Casilla 694, La Paz; tel. (2) 243-3424; fax (2) 243-1073; e-mail ukinbolivia@gmail.com; internet www .ukinbolivia.fco.gov.uk; Ambassador ROSS PATRICK DENNY.

USA: Avda Arce 2780, Casilla 425, La Paz; tel. (2) 216-8000; fax (2) 216-8111; e-mail consularlapaz@state.com; internet bolivia .usembassy.gov; Chargé d'affaires a.i. LARRY L. MEMMOTT.

Uruguay: Calle 16, No 8247, entre Calle B y Roberto Prudencio, Calacoto, La Paz; tel. (2) 279-1482; fax (2) 279-3976; e-mail urulivia@ acelerate.com; internet www.embauruguaybol.com; Ambassador CARLOS MARIO FLANAGAN BENTOS.

Venezuela: Calle 12, esq. Costanerita 1000, Obrajes, Casilla 441, La Paz; tel. (2) 278-8501; fax (2) 278-8711; e-mail embve.bopaz@mppre .gob.ve; internet bolivia.embajada.gob.ve; Ambassador CRISBEYLEE GONZÁLES HERNÁNDEZ.

Judicial System

In October 2011, following a constitutional amendment, direct elections were held to elect judges to the Constitutional Court, Supreme Court, Council of Magistrates and a newly established Agro-Environmental Court.

CONSTITUTIONAL COURT

Tribunal Constitucional Plurinacional: Avda del Maestro 300, Sucre; tel. (4) 644-0455; fax (4) 642-1871; e-mail tcp@tcpbolivia.bo; internet www.tcpbolivia.bo; f. 1994; seven mems; Pres. (vacant).

SUPREME COURT

Judicial power is vested in the Supreme Tribunal of Justice. There are nine judges and a further nine alternates, directly elected for a term of six years. The court is divided into five chambers. One chamber deals with civil cases, two chambers deal with criminal cases, a further two deal with administrative and social cases. The President of the Supreme Tribunal of Justice presides over joint sessions of the courts and attends the joint sessions for cassation cases.

Tribunal Suprema de Justicia: Parque Bolívar, Casilla 211 y 321, Sucre; tel. (4) 645-3200; fax (4) 646-2696; e-mail cortesuprema@ poderjudicial.gob.bo; internet suprema.poderjudicial.gob.bo; Pres. JORGE VON BORRIES.

COUNCIL OF MAGISTRATES

Consejo de la Magistratura: Calle Luis Paz (Ex Pilinco) 290, Sucre; tel. (4) 646-1600; internet www.organojudicial.gob.bo/consejo; f. 2011; five judges, with five alternates; Pres. CRISTINA MAMANI AGUILAR.

AGRO-ENVIRONMENTAL COURT

The Agro-Environmental Court was founded in 2011. It comprises seven judges, elected by popular vote for a six-year term.

President: LUCIO FUENTES.

DISTRICT COURTS

There is a District Court sitting in each Department, and additional provincial and local courts to try minor cases.

ATTORNEY-GENERAL

In addition to the Attorney-General at Sucre (appointed by the President on the proposal of the Senate), there is a District Attorney in each Department as well as circuit judges.

Attorney-General: HUGO RAÚL MONTERO LARA.

Religion

CHRISTIANITY

The Roman Catholic Church

Some 83% of the population are Roman Catholics. Bolivia comprises four archdioceses, six dioceses, two Territorial Prelatures and five Apostolic Vicariates.

Bishops' Conference: Conferencia Episcopal Boliviana, Calle Potosí 814, Casilla 2309, La Paz; tel. (2) 240-6855; fax (2) 240-6941; e-mail asc@scbbs-bo.com; internet www.iglesia.org.bo; f. 1972; Pres. Cardinal OSCAR APARICIO (Bishop of Castrense).

Archbishop of Cochabamba: Most Rev. TITO SOLARI CAPELLARI, Avda Heroínas 152, esq. Zenteno Anaya, Casilla 129, Cochabamba;

tel. (4) 425-6562; fax (4) 425-0522; e-mail arzobispado@iglesiacbba .org; internet www.iglesiacbba.org.

Archbishop of La Paz: Most Rev. EDMUNDO LUIS FLAVIO ABASTO-FLOR MONTERO, Calle Ballivián 1277, Casilla 259, La Paz; tel. (2) 220-3690; fax (2) 220-3672; e-mail arzobispadodelapaz@yahoo.es; internet www.arzobispadolapaz.org.

Archbishop of Santa Cruz de la Sierra: Cardinal SERGIO ALFREDO GUALBERTI CALANDRINA, Calle Ingavi 49, Manzana Uno, Casilla 25, Santa Cruz; tel. (3) 332-4416; fax (3) 333-0181; e-mail cancilleria@cotas.com.bo; internet www.iglesiasantacruz.org.

Archbishop of Sucre: Most Rev. JESÚS JUÁREZ PÁRRAGA, Calle Guillermo Loayza 100B, Casilla 205, Sucre; tel. (4) 645-1587; fax (4) 646-0336; e-mail pascar@arquidiocesisdesucre.org.bo; internet www .arquidiocesisdesucre.org.bo.

The Anglican Communion

The diocese of Bolivia falls within the province of Iglesia Anglicana del Cono Sur de América (Anglican Church of the Southern Cone of America).

Inglesia Anglicana Episcopal de Bolivia: Avda Simón López, esq. Melchor Perez, Casilla 848, Cochabamba; tel. (4) 440-1168; e-mail BpFrank@sams-usa.org; internet iglesiaanglicanadebolivia .org; Bishop Rev. FRANK RAYMOND LYONS.

Other Christian Churches

Church of Jesus Christ of Latter-Day Saints (Mormons): Avda Melchor Urquidi 1500, Alto Queru, Cochabamba; tel. (4) 429-3161; internet www.lds.org; 182,964 mems.

Convención Bautista Boliviana (Baptist Convention of Bolivia): Avda Cesar Cronembold 109, Casilla 3147, Santa Cruz; tel. (3) 343-0717; e-mail convencion@cotas.com.bo; internet conbabol.org; f. 1947; Pres. RUTH NOEMÍ COULTHARD DE MANSILLA.

Iglesia Evangélica Luterana Boliviana: Calle Rio Pirai 958, Casilla 8471, La Paz; tel. (2) 238-3442; fax (2) 238-0073; e-mail eaf2000@hotmail.es; f. 1972; Pres. Rev. EMILIO ASLLA.

Iglesia Evangélica Metodista en Bolivia (Evangelical Methodist Church in Bolivia): Avda 16 de Julio 1636, Casillas 356 y 8347, La Paz; tel. (2) 290-0710; fax (2) 290-0726; internet www.iemb.cc; autonomous since 1969; 10,000 mems; Bishop Rev. JAVIER ROJAS TERÁN.

Unión Bautista Boliviana (Baptist Union of Bolivia): Calle Jordan 0-0369, Casilla 2199, La Paz; tel. (2) 458-3538; fax (2) 425-0212; e-mail info@ubb.org.bo; internet ubb.org.bo; Pres. Rev. REYES BALTAZAR QUISPE YAPITA; Exec. Dir YOLANDA OROPEZA DE FLORES.

BAHÁ'Í FAITH

National Spiritual Assembly of the Bahá'ís of Bolivia: Avda Libertador 1, Obrajes, Casilla 1613, La Paz; tel. (2) 278-5058; e-mail secretariat@bahai.org.bo; internet bahai.org.bo; f. 1961; mems resident in 5,161 localities; Sec. JOAN HERNANDEZ.

The Press

DAILY NEWSPAPERS

Cochabamba

Opinión: Calle General Achá 252, Casilla 287, Cochabamba; tel. (4) 425-4400; fax (4) 441-5121; e-mail opinion@opinion.com.bo; internet www.opinion.com.bo; f. 1985; Dir FEDERICO SABAT LARA; Chief Editor MARÍA LUISA MERCADO.

Los Tiempos: Edif. Los Tiempos, Plaza Quintanilla, Casilla 525, Cochabamba; tel. (4) 425-4562; fax (4) 425-7773; e-mail lostiempos@lostiempos-bolivia.com; internet www.lostiempos.com; f. 1943; morning; independent; Pres. EDUARDO CANELAS TÁRDIO; Man. Editor ELIZABETH ARRÁZOLA SANDOVAL; circ. 19,000.

La Paz

El Diario: Calle Loayza 118, Casilla 5, La Paz; tel. (2) 215-0900; fax (2) 215-0902; e-mail redinfo@diario.net; internet www.eldiario.net; f. 1904; morning; conservative; Gen. Man. JORGE CARRASCO GUZMÁN; Man. Editor FERNANDO VALDIVIA DELGADO; circ. 55,000.

Jornada: Edif. Almirante Grau 672, Zona San Pedro, Casilla 1628, La Paz; tel. (2) 248-8163; fax (2) 248-7487; e-mail cartas@jornadanet .com; internet www.jornadanet.com; f. 1964; evening; independent; Dir DAVID RÍOS ARANDA; circ. 11,500.

Página Siete: Calle Rosendo Reyes 16, esq. 27, Cota Cota, La Paz; tel. (2) 261-1700; e-mail paginasiete@paginasiete.bo; internet www .paginasiete.bo; Dir RAÚL PEÑARANDA UNDURRAGA; Editor MARTÍN ZELAYA SÁNCHEZ.

La Prensa: Mayor Lopera 230, Villa Fátima, Casilla 5614, La Paz; tel. (2) 221-8821; fax (2) 220-2509; e-mail laprensa@laprensa.com.bo; internet www.laprensa.com.bo; Dir-Gen. DIEGO CANELAS MONTAÑO; Chief Editor FABIANA CARRAZANA PAZ.

La Razón: Colinas de Santa Rita, Alto Auquisamaña (Zona Sur), Casilla 13100, La Paz; tel. (2) 277-1415; fax (2) 277-0908; e-mail larazon@la-razon.com; internet www.la-razon.com; f. 1990; Dir CLAUDIA BENAVENTE P.; Man. Editor CARLOS ORÍAS B.; circ. 35,000.

Oruro

La Patria: Avda Camacho 1892, entre Murguía y Aldana, Casilla 48, Oruro; tel. (2) 525-0780; fax (2) 525-0782; e-mail info@lapatria.com .bo; internet www.lapatriaenlinea.com; f. 1919; morning; independent; Dir ENRIQUE MIRALLES BONNECARRERE; Chief Editor JORGE LAZZO QUINTEROS; circ. 6,000.

Potosí

El Potosí: Calle Cochabamba 35 (Junto a Unidad Sanitaria), Potosí; tel. (2) 622-2601; fax (2) 622-7835; e-mail elpotosi@entelnet.bo; internet www.elpotosi.net; f. 2001; Dir JUAN JOSÉ TORO MONTOYA; Man. Editor GUILLERMO BULLAÍN IÑIGUEZ.

Santa Cruz

El Deber: Avda El Trompillo 1144, 2º, Casilla 1144, Santa Cruz; tel. (3) 353-8000; fax (3) 353-9053; e-mail web@eldeber.com.bo; internet www.eldeber.com.bo; f. 1953; morning; independent; Exec. Dir Dr PEDRO RIVERO MERCADO; Man. Editor TUFFÍ ARÉ VÁZQUEZ; circ. 35,000.

El Día: Avda Cristo Redentor 3355, Casilla 5344, Santa Cruz; tel. (3) 343-4040; fax (3) 342-4041; e-mail eldia@edadsa.com.bo; internet www.eldia.com.bo; f. 1987; Dir ALDO AGUIERA; Man. Editor RÓGER CUÉLLAR.

La Estrella del Oriente: Calle Republiquetas 353, Santa Cruz; tel. (3) 332-9011; fax (3) 332-9012; e-mail laestrelladeloriente@laestrella .bo; internet www.laestrelladeloriente.com; f. 1864; Dir CARLOS SUBIRANA SUÁREZ; Chief Editor MAURICIO MELGAR.

El Mundo: Parque Industrial, Manzana-7, Casilla 1984, Santa Cruz; tel. (3) 346-4646; fax (3) 346-3322; e-mail redaccion@mail .elmundo.com.bo; internet www.elmundo.com.bo; f. 1979; morning; owned by Santa Cruz Industrialists' Asscn; Pres. JOSÉ LUIS DURÁN SAUCEDO; Chief Editor CARLOS CALIZAYA AYAVIRI; circ. 15,000.

Sucre

Correo del Sur: Calle Kilómetro 7, No 202, Casilla 242, Sucre; tel. (4) 646-3202; fax (4) 646-0152; e-mail correo7@entelnet.bo; internet www.correodelsur.com; f. 1987; Dir MARCO ANTONIO DIPP MUKLED; Man. Editor RAYKHA FLORES COSSIO.

PERIODICALS

Actualidad Boliviana Confidencial (ABC): Edif. Villazón, 10º, Of. 10A, Avda Villazón, La Paz; tel. (2) 231-3781; internet www .abceconomia.com; f. 1966; weekly; Dir HUGO GONZÁLEZ RIOJA; circ. 6,000.

Agricultura Ecológica: Pasaje F, No 2958, Urb. El Profesional, Casilla 1999, Cochabamba; tel. (4) 442-3838; fax (4) 442-3636; e-mail info@agrecolandes.org; internet www.agrecolandes.org; f. 2005; publ. by the Centro de Información e Intercambio para la Agricultura Ecológica (AGRECOL); yearly; Exec. Dir and Editor RUBÉN MALDONADO.

ANF-Notas: Edif. Mariscal de Ayacucho, 5º, Of. 501, Calle Loayza 233, Casilla 5782, La Paz; tel. (2) 233-5577; fax (2) 233-7607; e-mail anf@noticiasfides.com; internet www.noticiasfides.com; f. 1963; publ. by ANF; weekly; political analysis; Dir P. SERGIO MONTES.

Cosas: Calle Inofuentes 1348, entre calles 19 y 20 de Calacoto, La Paz; tel. (2) 215-0191; e-mail cosasbolivia@cosas.com; internet www .cosasbolivia.com; monthly; lifestyle; Dir CARLA TEJERINA DE CABE-ZAS; Editor MARTHA OIAZO.

Datos: Edif. Quipus, 5º, Pasaje Jauregui No 2248, Sopocachi, Casilla 14390, La Paz; tel. (2) 244-0621; e-mail datos@datos-bo.com; internet www.datos-bo.com; monthly; politics and current affairs; Dir CARLOS RODRÍGUEZ.

Ecos: Calle Kilómetro 7 No 202, Sucre; tel. (4) 646-1531; e-mail contacto@ecos.com.bo; internet www.ecos.com.bo; weekly; entertainment and fashion; Editor OSCAR DÍAZ ARNAU.

Miradas: Edif. Torre Azul, 18º, Avda 20 de Octubre 2665, La Paz; tel. (2) 261-1700; e-mail paginasiete@paginasiete.bo; internet www .paginasiete.bo; weekly; arts; Editor MARCO ZELAYA.

Nueva Economía: Pedro Salazar 2477, La Paz; tel. (2) 291-1600; e-mail dgutierrez@nuevaeconomia.com.bo; internet nuevaeconomia .com.bo; financial; weekly; Gen. Man. JORGE VACA HEREDIA; Editor DANIEL GUTIÉRREZ CARRIÓN.

Oxígeno: Calle Harrison 1957-A, entre Diaz Romero y Villalobos, Miraflores, La Paz; tel. (2) 224-8040; e-mail oxigeno@oxigenobolivia .com; internet www.oxigenobolivia.com; monthly; society, general affairs; Dir Grover Yapura Aruquipa; Editor Liliana Carrillo Valenzuela.

PRESS ASSOCIATIONS

Asociación Nacional de la Prensa (ANP): Claudio Aliaga 1290, 2°, San Miguel, La Paz; tel. (2) 279-4208; internet www.anpbolivia .com; f. 1976; private; Pres. Ana María Tineo; Exec. Dir Juan León Cornejo.

Asociación de Periodistas de La Paz (APLP): Edif. Las Dos Torres, Avda 6 de Agosto 2170, Casilla 477, La Paz; tel. (2) 243-0345; fax (2) 243-6006; internet www.aplp.org.bo; f. 1929; Pres. Antonio Vargas Ríos; Sec.-Gen. Ghilka Sulma Sanabria Pradel.

NEWS AGENCIES

Agencia Boliviana de Información: Calle Colón, casi esq. Ballivian, Casilla 6500, La Paz; tel. (2) 211-3782; fax (2) 220-4370; e-mail abi@abi.bo; internet www.abi.bo; govt-owned; Dir Jorge Rey Cuba Akiyama; Man. Editor Rubén David Sandi Lora.

Agencia de Noticias Fides (ANF): Edif. Mariscal de Ayacucho, 5°, Of. 501, Calle Loayza, Casilla 5782, La Paz; tel. (2) 236-5152; fax (2) 236-5153; e-mail anf@noticiasfides.com; internet www.noticiasfides .bo; f. 1963; owned by the Roman Catholic Church; Dir Sergio Ricardo Montes Rondón; Editor Jaime Loayza Zegarra.

Publishers

Editorial los Amigos del Libro: Edif. Alba I, 3°, Of. 312, Calle España O-153, Cochabamba; tel. (4) 425-6005; fax (4) 450-4151; e-mail gutten@librosbolivia.com; internet www.librosbolivia.com; f. 1945; general; Gen. Man. Ingrid Guttentag.

Editorial Bruño: Loayza 167, Casilla 4809, La Paz; tel. (2) 233-1254; fax (2) 233-5043; f. 1964; Dir Ignacio Loma Gutiérrez.

Editorial Comunicarte: Avda Cañoto 360, Santa Cruz; tel. (3) 332-3111; fax (3) 336-9332; e-mail comunicarte@comunicarte.com.bo; internet www.comunicarte.com.bo; Gen. Man. Ana María Artigas.

Editorial Don Bosco: Villa Tejada Rectangular, Avda La Paz, esq. Avda Cívica, Casilla 4458, La Paz; tel. (2) 281-7325; fax (2) 281-7294; e-mail editorialdonbosco@gmail.com; internet www .editorial-donbosco.com; f. 1896; social sciences and literature.

Editorial Gente Comun: Villa Fátima, Avda de las Américas 764, La Paz; tel. (2) 221-4493; e-mail marcel@editorialgentecomun.com; internet editorialgentecomun.com; Dir Ariel Mustafá.

Editorial Icthus: Calle Miguel Angel Valda 121, Sucre; tel. (4) 642-7345; e-mail icthus@entelnet.bo; internet www.innset.com.bo; f. 1967; general and textbooks; Man. Dir Fabiola Gorena.

Editorial Verbo Divino: Avda Juan de la Rosa O-2216, Casilla 191, Cochabamba; tel. (4) 428-6297; fax (4) 442-0733; e-mail info@ verbodivino-bo.com; internet www.verbodivino-bo.com; f. 1997; Christian literature; part of Grupo Editorial Verbo Divino; Gen. Man. Pedro Pitura.

Gisbert y Cía, SA: Calle Comercio 1270, Casilla 195, La Paz; tel. (2) 220-2626; fax (2) 220-2911; e-mail info@libreriagisbert.com; internet www.libreriagisbert.com; f. 1907; textbooks, history, law and general; Pres. Antonio Schulczewski Gisbert; Promotions Man. María del Carmen Schulczewski; Admin. Man. Sergio García.

Grupo Editorial La Hoguera: Edif. Gabriela, 2°, Calle Beni 678, Santa Cruz; tel. (3) 335-4426; fax (3) 311-7821; e-mail lahoguera@ lahoguera.com; internet www.lahoguera.com; f. 1990; Pres. Alfonso Cortez; Dir-Gen. Mauricio Méndez.

Idearia: Calle 8, Este 19, Barrio Hamacas, Santa Cruz; tel. (3) 339-8381; e-mail idearia@idearia.net; internet www.idearia.net; children's literature and magazines; Gen. Man. Gabriela Ichaso.

Librería Editorial Juventud: Plaza Murillo 519, Casilla 1489, La Paz; tel. (2) 240-6248; f. 1946; textbooks and general; Dir Gustavo Urquizo Mendoza.

Martínez Acchini, SRL Libros: Edif. Illampu, Avda Arce 2132, La Paz; tel. (2) 244-1112; internet martinezacchini.com; f. 1975; Man. Dir Ernesto Martínez.

Master Bolivia: Calle Velasco 268, Santa Cruz; tel. (3) 333-2413; fax (3) 311-2260; e-mail info@masterbolivia.com; internet masterbolivia .com.

El Pauro Ediciones: Calle Vallegrande 424, Santa Cruz; tel. (3) 339-4916; e-mail elpauroed@cotas.com.bo; internet elpauroediciones .com; Gen. Man. Magdalena Márquez.

Plural Editores: Calle Rosendo Gutiérrez 595, esq. Avda Ecuador, La Paz; tel. (2) 241-1018; e-mail plural@plural.bo; internet www .plural.bo; f. 1999; Exec. Dir José Antonio Quiroga.

Rodel Ediciones: Calle Mandioré 46, Santa Cruz; tel. (3) 337-8689; fax (3) 337-0246; e-mail info@rodelediciones.com; internet rodelediciones.com; Pres. Jorge Luis Rodríguez.

Santillana de Ediciones, SA: Calle 13, No 8078, Calacoto, La Paz; tel. (2) 277-4242; fax (2) 277-1056; e-mail info@santillanabo.com; internet www.santillanabo.com; f. 1994; Gen. Man. Carola Ossio.

PUBLISHERS' ASSOCIATION

Cámara Boliviana del Libro: Calle Capitán Ravelo 2116, Casilla 682, La Paz; tel. and fax (2) 211-3264; e-mail cabolib@entelnet.bo; internet www.camaralibrolapaz.org.bo; f. 1947; Pres. Ernesto Martínez Acchini; Vice-Pres. Carla María Berdegué; Gen. Man. Ana Patricia Navarro.

Broadcasting and Communications

TELECOMMUNICATIONS

Bolitel, SRL (Bolivia Telecomunicación, SRL): Calle Mercado, esq. Independencia, Santa Cruz; tel. (3) 364-2424; fax (3) 364-3973; e-mail info@libre.com.bo; internet www.libre.com.bo; f. 2008; part of the UNAGRO corpn; Man. Mauricio Pinto.

Empresa Nacional de Telecomunicaciones, SA (ENTEL): Calle Federico Suazo 1771, Casilla 4450, La Paz; tel. (2) 214-1010; fax (2) 239-1789; e-mail contacto@entelsa.entelnet.bo; internet www.entel .bo; f. 1965; privatized under the Govt's capitalization programme in 1995; reverted to state ownership in 2008; Pres. Carlos Reyes Montaño; Gen. Man. Roy Roque Méndez.

Tigo (Telefónica Celular de Bolivia): Avda Viedma 648, Santa Cruz; tel. (3) 333-5227; fax (3) 335-8790; e-mail atencionalcliente@tigo.com .bo; internet www.tigo.com.bo; f. 2005; part of Millicom International Cellular, SA (MIC); Chief Officer, Latin America Mario Zanotti; Gen. Man. Pablo Guardia.

Viva GSM (NuevaTel PCS de Bolivia, SA): Edif. Multicentro, Calle Capitán Ravelo, esq. R. Gutiérrez 2289, Casilla 11875, Sopocachi, La Paz; tel. (2) 244-2420; fax (2) 244-2353; e-mail infoa@nuevatel.com; internet www.nuevatel.com; f. 1999; Regional Man. Virginia Retamoso.

Regulatory Authorities

Autoridad de Fiscalización y Control Social de Transportes y Telecomunicaciones (ATT): Calle 13, Nos 8260 y 8280, entre Sauces y Costanera, Calacoto, Casilla 6692, La Paz; tel. (2) 277-2266; fax (2) 277-2299; e-mail informaciones@att.gob.bo; internet www.att .gob.bo; supervises and regulates the activities and services provided by telecommunications operators; Exec. Dir Pedro Clifford Paravicini Hurtado.

Superintendencia de Telecomunicaciones: Calle 13, No 8260, Calacoto, La Paz; tel. (2) 277-2266; fax (2) 277-2299; e-mail supertel@ ceibo.entelnet.bo; internet www.sittel.gov.bo; f. 1995; govt-controlled broadcasting authority; Supt Jorge Nava Amador.

BROADCASTING

Radio

Educación Radiofónica de Bolivia (ERBOL): Edif. Smith, Calle Ballivián 1323, 4°, Casilla 5946, La Paz; tel. (2) 204-0111; fax (2) 220-3888; e-mail erbol@erbol.com.bo; internet www.erbol.com.bo; f. 1967; asscn of 28 educational radio stations in Bolivia; Dir Windsor José Salas Guisbert.

Radio Fides: La Paz; e-mail sistemas@radiofides.com; internet www.radiofides.com; f. 1939; network of 28 radio stations; Roman Catholic; Dir Eduardo Pérez Iribarne.

Red Patria Nueva: Avda Camacho 1485, 6°, La Paz; tel. (2) 220-0473; fax (2) 200-390; e-mail illimani@comunica.gov.bo; internet www.patrianueva.bo; f. 1932 as Compañía Radio Boliviana; govt-owned network; broadcasts across the country, often as Radio Illimani; Dir Iván Maldonado Cortéz.

Television

ATB Red Nacional (Canal 9): Avda Argentina 2057, Casilla 9285, La Paz; tel. and fax (2) 222-9922; e-mail noticias@atb.com.bo; internet www.atb.com.bo; f. 1984; privately owned television network; part of Grupo Prisa, SA; Man. Roxana Alcoba.

Bolivisión (Canal 4): Parque Demetrio Canelas 1543, Casilla 6067, Cochabamba; tel. (4) 428-4318; fax (4) 428-4319; e-mail jimmystrauch@redbolivision.tv; internet www.redbolivision.tv.bo; f. 1997; privately owned television network; Exec. Pres. Ernesto Asbún Gazaui; Gen. Man. Javier Carmona del Solar.

Red Uno: Calle Romecín Campos 592, Sopocachi, La Paz; tel. (2) 242-1111; fax (2) 241-0939; e-mail notivision@reduno.com.bo; internet www.reduno.com.bo; f. 1985; commercial television station; offices in

La Paz, Santa Cruz and Cochabamba; Dir MARIO ROJAS; Gen. Man. JULIO ROMERO.

Televisión Boliviana (TVB—Canal 7): Edif. La Urbana, 6°, Avda Camacho 1485, Casilla 900, La Paz; tel. (2) 220-3404; fax (2) 220-3973; e-mail info@boliviatv.bo; internet www.boliviatv.bo; f. 1969; govt network operating stations in La Paz, Oruro, Cochabamba, Potosí, Chuquisaca, Pando, Beni, Tarija and Santa Cruz; Gen. Man. MARCO ANTONIO SANTIVAÑEZ SORIA.

Televisión Universitaria (Canal 13): Edif. Hoy, 12°–13°, Avda 6 de Agosto 2170, Casilla 13383, La Paz; tel. and fax (2) 244-1313; e-mail canal13@umsa.bo; internet tvu.umsa.bo; f. 1980; educational programmes; stations in Oruro, Cochabamba, Potosí, Sucre, Tarija, Beni and Santa Cruz; Dir OMAR GÓMEZ LIZARRO.

Unitel (Canal 9): Km 5, Carretera antigua a Cochabamba, Santa Cruz; tel. (3) 352-7686; fax (3) 352-7688; e-mail canal9@unitel.com.bo; internet www.unitel.tv; f. 1997; privately owned television network; Vice-Pres. HUGO PÁRRAGA.

Regulatory Authority

Asociación Boliviana de Radiodifusoras (ASBORA): Edif. Jazmín, 10°, Avda 20 de Octubre 2019, Casilla 5324, La Paz; tel. (2) 236-5154; fax (2) 236-3069; broadcasting authority; Pres. RAÚL NOVILLO ALARCÓN.

Finance

(cap. = capital; res = reserves; dep. = deposits; m. = million; br(s) = branch(es); amounts are in bolivianos, unless otherwise stated)

BANKING

Supervisory Authority

Autoridad de Supervisión del Sistema Financiero: Plaza Isabel la Católica 2507, Casilla 447, La Paz; tel. (2) 243-1919; fax (2) 243-0028; e-mail asfi@asfi.gov.bo; internet www.asfi.gov.bo; f. 1928; fmrly Superintendencia de Bancos y Entidados Financieras; name changed as above in 2009; Exec. Dir ERNESTO RIVERO VILLARROEL.

Central Bank

Banco Central de Bolivia: Avda Ayacucho, esq. Mercado, Casilla 3118, La Paz; tel. (2) 240-9090; fax (2) 240-6614; e-mail bancocentraldebolivia@bcb.gob.bo; internet www.bcb.gob.bo; f. 1911 as Banco de la Nación Boliviana; name changed as above in 1928; bank of issue; cap. 515.7m., res 7,807.9m., dep. 47,441.2m. (Dec. 2009); Pres. MARCELO ZABALAGA ESTRADA; Gen. Man. WILMA PÉREZ PAPUTSACHIS (acting).

Commercial Banks

Banco Bisa, SA: Avda 16 de Julio 1628, Casilla 1290, La Paz; tel. (2) 231-7272; fax (2) 239-0033; e-mail bancobisa@grupobisa.com; internet www.bisa.com; f. 1963; cap. 927.4m., res 128.6m., dep. 10,739.2m. (Dec. 2012); Pres., CEO and Chair. Ing. JULIO LEÓN PRADO.

Banco de Crédito de Bolivia, SA: Calle Colón, esq. Mercado 1308, Casilla 907, La Paz; tel. (2) 217-5000; fax (2) 217-5115; e-mail cnavarro@bancred.com.bo; internet www.bcp.com.bo; f. 1993 as Banco Popular del Perú, SA; name changed as above 1994; owned by Banco de Crédito del Perú; cap. 315.5m., res 432.8m., dep. 8,267.6m. (Dec. 2012); Chair. DIONISIO ROMERO; CEO JORGE ALBERTO MUJICA GIANOLI; 8 brs.

Banco Económico, SA-SCZ: Calle Ayacucho 166, Casilla 5603, Santa Cruz; tel. (3) 315-5500; fax (3) 336-1184; e-mail baneco@baneco.com.bo; internet www.baneco.com.bo; f. 1990; dep. US $244.9m., cap. US $24.4m., total assets US $269.3m. (Dec. 2006); Pres. IVO MATEO KULJIS FÜCHTNER; 25 brs.

Banco Ganadero, SA-Santa Cruz: Calle Bolivar 99, esq. Beni, Santa Cruz; tel. (3) 336-1616; fax (3) 336-1617; internet www.bg.com.bo; f. 1994; cap. 251.5m., res 43.1m., dep. 2,670m. (Dec. 2012); Pres. FERNANDO MONASTERIO NIEME; Gen. Man. RONALD GUTIÉRREZ LÓPEZ.

Banco Mercantil Santa Cruz, SA: Calle Ayacucho, esq. Mercado 295, Casilla 423, La Paz; tel. (2) 240-9040; fax (2) 240-9158; e-mail asalinas@bancomercantil.com.bo; internet www.bmsc.com.bo; f. 1905 as Banco Mercantil, SA; acquired Banco Santa Cruz in 2006 and changed name as above; cap. 649.4m., res 408.7m., dep. 13,928.7m. (Dec. 2012); Chair. DARKO ZUAZO BATCHELDER; 37 brs.

Banco Nacional de Bolivia: Avda Camacho, esq. Colón 1296, Casilla 360, La Paz; tel. (2) 233-2323; fax (2) 233-1851; e-mail info@bnb.com.bo; internet www.bnb.com.bo; f. 1871; 67.27% owned by Grupo Bedoya; cap. 618.9m., res 256.8m., dep. 11,339.6m. (Dec. 2012); Pres. IGNACIO BEDOYA SÁENZ; Gen. Man. PABLO BEDOYA SÁENZ; 9 brs.

Banco Solidario, SA (BancoSol): Calle Nicolás Acosta 289, Casilla 13176, La Paz; tel. (2) 248-4242; fax (2) 248-6533; e-mail info@bancosol.com.bo; internet www.bancosol.com.bo; f. 1992; cap. 270.4m., res 97.1m., dep. 5,041m. (Dec. 2012); Gen. Man. KURT KÖNIGSFEST SANABRIA.

Banco Unión, SA: Calle Libertad 156, POB 4057, Santa Cruz; e-mail info@bancounion.com.bo; internet www.bancounion.com.bo; f. 1982; cap. 400.6m., res 379.3m., dep. 10,225.6m. (Dec. 2012); Pres. DIEGO ALEJANDRO PÉREZ CUETO; Gen. Man. MARCIA VILLARROEL GONZÁLES; 9 brs.

Credit Institution

PRODEM: Avda Camacho 1277, esq. Colón, La Paz; tel. (2) 211-3227; fax (2) 214-7632; e-mail info@prodemffp.com.bo; internet www.prodemffp.com.bo; f. 2000; microcredit institution; Gen. Man. JOSÉ NOEL ZAMORA; 250 brs.

Banking Association

Asociación de Bancos Privados de Bolivia (ASOBAN): Edif. Cámara Nacional de Comercio, 15°, Avda Mariscal Santa Cruz, esq. Colombia 1392, Casilla 5822, La Paz; tel. (2) 237-6164; fax (2) 239-1093; e-mail info@asoban.bo; internet www.asoban.bo; f. 1957; Pres. JUAN CARLOS SALAUES; Vice-Pres KURT KOENIGFEST SANABRIA, RONALD GUTIERREZ LOPEZ; 18 mems.

STOCK EXCHANGE

Bolsa Boliviana de Valores, SA: Calle Montevideo 142, Casilla 12521, La Paz; tel. (2) 244-3232; fax (2) 244-2308; e-mail info@bolsa-valores-bolivia.com; internet www.bbv.com.bo; f. 1989; Pres. JOSÉ TRIGO VALDIVIA; Gen. Man. JAVIER ANEIVA.

INSURANCE

Supervisory Authority

Autoridad de Fiscalización y Control de Pensiones y Seguros (APS): Edif. Torres Gundlach Este, 6°, Calle Reyes Ortiz, esq. Federico Zuazo, Casilla 10794, La Paz; tel. (2) 233-1212; fax (2) 231-2223; e-mail contactenos@aps.gob.bo; internet www.aps.gob.bo; Exec. Dir IVÁN ROJAS YANGUAS.

Major Companies

Alianza, Cía de Seguros y Reaseguros, SA: Avda 20 de Octubre 2680, esq. Campos, Zona San Jorge, Casilla 1043, La Paz; tel. (2) 243-2121; fax (2) 243-2713; e-mail info@alianzaseguros.com; internet www.alianza.com.bo; f. 1991; Exec. Dir ALEJANDRO YBARRA CARRASCO.

Alianza Vida Seguros y Reaseguros, SA: Avda Roca y Corornado, Calle Mario Gutiérrez 3325 esq., Santa Cruz; tel. (3) 363-2727; fax (3) 363-2700; e-mail vida@alianzaseguros.com; internet www.alianza.com.bo; f. 1999; Gen. Man. ALEJANDRO YBARRA CARRASCO.

Bisa Seguros y Reaseguros, SA: Edif. Multicine, 14°, Avda Arce 2631, La Paz; tel. (2) 217-7000; fax (2) 214-8724; e-mail bisaseguros@grupobisa.com; internet www.bisaseguros.com; f. 1991; part of Grupo Bisa; Pres. JULIO LEÓN PRADO; Exec. Vice-Pres. JULIO JAIME GUMUCIO.

La Boliviana Ciacruz de Seguros y Reaseguros, SA: Edif. La Boliviana Ciacruz, Calle Colón 288, Casilla 628, La Paz; tel. (2) 220-3131; fax (2) 220-3902; e-mail info@lbc.bo; internet www.lbc.bo; f. 1964; owned by Zurich Bolivia group; all classes; Pres. GONZALO BEDOYA HERRERA.

Bupa Insurance (Bolivia), SA: Calle 9 este, No 9, esq. Pasillo A, Zona Equipetrol, Santa Cruz; tel. (3) 341-2841; fax (3) 341-2832; e-mail bolivia@bupa.com.bo; internet www.bupasalud.com.bo; health insurance; Pres. ANTHONY CABRELLI.

Cía de Seguros y Reaseguros Fortaleza, SA: Avda Virgen de Cotoca 2080, La Paz; tel. (3) 348-7273; fax (3) 349-7675; e-mail oficinanacional@fortalezaseguros.com.bo; internet www.grupofortaleza.com.bo; Pres. GUIDO EDWIN HINOJOSA CARDOSO; Gen. Man. PATRICIO HINOJOSA J.

Credinform International, SA de Seguros: Edif. Credinform, Calle Julio Patiño NRO, La Paz; tel. (2) 231-5566; fax (2) 220-3917; e-mail credinform@credinformsa.com; internet www.credinformsa.com; f. 1954; all classes; Pres. Dr ROBÍN BARRAGÁN PELÁEZ; Gen. Man. MIGUEL ANGEL BARRAGÁN IBARGÜEN.

Latina Seguros Patrimoniales, SA: Avda Monseñor Rivero 223, esq. Asunción, Casilla 3087, Santa Cruz; tel. (3) 371-6565; fax (3) 371-6905; e-mail latinaseguros@latinaseguros.com.bo; internet www.latina-seguros.com.bo; f. 2007; part of Grupo Nacional Vida; Exec. Vice-Pres. JOSÉ LUÍS CAMACHO MISERENDINO; Gen. Man. RAMIRO JESÚS QUIROGA SAN MARTÍN.

Nacional Vida Seguros de Personas, SA: Avda Monseñor Rivero 223, esq. Asunción, Santa Cruz; tel. (3) 371-6262; fax (3) 333-7969;

e-mail nacionalvida@nacionalvida.com.bo; internet www
.nacionalvida.com.bo; f. 1999; Pres. MARIO AVELINO MORENO VIRUEZ;
Gen. Man. LUIS ALVARO TOLEDO PEÑARANDA.

Seguros Illimani, SA: Edif. Mariscal de Ayacucho, 10°, Calle
Loayza 233, Casilla 133, La Paz; tel. (2) 220-3040; fax (2) 239-
1149; e-mail info@segurosillimani.com.bo; internet www
.segurosillimani.com.bo; f. 1979; all classes; Exec. Pres. FERNANDO
ARCE G.

La Vitalicia Seguros y Reaseguros de Vida, SA: Edif. Hoy, Avda
6 de Agosto 2860, Casilla 8424, La Paz; tel. (2) 215-7800; fax (2) 211-
3480; e-mail aibanez@grupobisa.com; internet www
.lavitaliciaseguros.com; f. 1998; part of Grupo Bisa; Pres. JULIO LEÓN
PRADO; Exec. Vice-Pres. LUIS ALFONSO IBAÑEZ MONTES.

Insurance Association

Asociación Boliviana de Aseguradores: Edif. Castilla, 5°, Of.
510, Calle Loayza, esq. Mercado 250, Casilla 4804, La Paz; tel. (2)
231-0056; fax (2) 220-1088; e-mail info@ababolivia.org; internet
www.ababolivia.org; f. 1950; Pres. NELSON JIMÉNEZ; Gen. Man. Dr
JUSTINO AVENDAÑO RENEDO.

Trade and Industry

DEVELOPMENT ORGANIZATIONS

**Centro de Estudios para el Desarrollo Laboral y Agrario
(CEDLA):** Avda Jaimes Freyre 2940, esq. Muñoz Cornejo, Casilla
8630, La Paz; tel. (2) 241-2429; fax (2) 241-4625; e-mail jgomez@cedla
.org; internet www.cedla.org; f. 1985; agrarian and labour development; Exec. Dir JAVIER GÓMEZ AGUILAR.

Fondo Nacional de Desarrollo Regional (FNDR): Calle Pedro
Salazar, esq. Andrés Muñoz 631, Sopocachi, Casilla 12613, La Paz;
tel. (2) 241-7575; fax (2) 242-2267; e-mail transparencia@fndr.gob.bo;
internet www.fndr.gob.bo; f. 1987; promotes local and regional devt,
offering financing and support; assumed temporary responsibility
for water supply in La Paz in 2007 following annulment of contracts
with private water cos; Exec. Dir MARÍA ELENA ANGELERI BERNAL.

CHAMBERS OF COMMERCE

Cámara de Comercio de Oruro: Edif. Cámara de Comercio,
Pasaje Guachalla, La Plata, Casilla 148, Oruro; tel. (2) 525-0606;
fax (2) 525-2615; e-mail contacto@camaradecomerciodeoruro.com;
internet www.camaradecomerciodeoruro.com; f. 1895; Pres. FRAN-
CISCO MENA GONZALES; Gen. Man. VÍCTOR HUGO RODRÍGUEZ GARCÍA;
165 mems.

Cámara de Comercio y Servicios de Cochabamba: Calle Sucre
E-0336, Casilla 493, Cochabamba; tel. (4) 425-7715; fax (4) 425-7717;
e-mail gerencia@cadeco.org; internet www.cadeco.org; f. 1922; Pres.
ALDO GASTÓN VACAFLORES CHIARELLA; Gen. Man. FERNANDO
ALDAZOSA S.

**Cámara Departamental de Industria, Comercio y Servicios
de Tarija:** Calle Bolívar, entre Mendez y Suipacha, Zona Central,
Casilla 74, Tarija; tel. (4) 664-2737; fax (4) 611-3636; e-mail
caincotar@entelnet.bo; f. 2005; Pres. VÍCTOR FERNÁNDEZ.

Cámara de Exportadores de La Paz (CAMEX): Avda Arce 2021
esq. Goitia, Sopocachi, Casilla 789, La Paz; tel. (2) 244-4310; fax (2)
244-2842; e-mail info@camexbolivia.com; internet www
.camexbolivia.com; f. 1993; Pres. LARRY SERRATE; Gen. Man. BEATRIZ
ESPINOZA CALDERÓN.

Cámara de Exportadores de Santa Cruz (CADEX): Avda
Velarde 131, Santa Cruz; tel. (3) 336-2030; fax (3) 332-1509; e-mail
cadex@cadex.org; internet www.cadex.org; f. 1986; Pres. WILFREDO
ROJO PARADA; Gen. Man. OSWALDO BARRIGA KARLBAUM.

Cámara de Industria y Comercio de Chuquisaca: Calle España
64, 2°, Casilla 33, Sucre; tel. (4) 645-1194; fax (4) 645-1850; e-mail
empresario@caincochuquisaca.net; internet www.caincochuquisaca
.net; f. 1893; Pres. LUIS MARÍA PORCEL IBAÑEZ; Gen. Man. LORENZO
CATALÁ SUBIETA.

**Cámara de Industria, Comercio, Servicios y Turismo de
Santa Cruz (CAINCO):** Torre Cainco, Avda Las Américas, 7°,
Casilla 180, Santa Cruz; tel. (3) 333-4555; fax (3) 334-2353; e-mail
cainco@cainco.org.bo; internet www.cainco.org.bo; f. 1915; Pres. LUIS
FERNANDO BARBERY.

Cámara Nacional de Comercio: Edif. Cámara Nacional de
Comercio, Avda Mariscal Santa Cruz 1392, 1° y 2°, Casilla 7, La
Paz; tel. (2) 237-8606; fax (2) 239-1004; e-mail cnc@boliviacomercio
.org.bo; internet www.boliviacomercio.org.bo; f. 1929; 30 brs and
special brs; Pres. FERNANDO CÁCERES PACHECO; Gen. Man. JAVIER
HINOJOSA.

Cámara Nacional de Comercio Boliviano Brasileña: Edif. San
Pablo, 11°, Of. 1105, Avda 16 de Julio 1472, La Paz; tel. (2) 231-4249;
fax (2) 231-4247; e-mail cambobra@entelnet.bo; internet www
.cambobra.com; f. 1984; Pres. JOÃO GERALDO RAYMUNDO; Gen. Man.
CARLOS A. LARRAZÁBAL ANTEZANA.

Cámara Nacional de Exportadores de Bolivia (CANEB): Avda
Arce 2017, esq. c. Goitia, Casilla 12145, La Paz; tel. (2) 244-3529; fax
(2) 244-1491; e-mail secretaria@caneb.org.bo; internet www.caneb
.org.bo; f. 1969; fmrly Asociación Nacional de Exportadores de
Bolivia; adopted current name in 1993; Pres. GUILLERMO POU MUNT.

Cámara Nacional de Industrias de Bolivia: Edif. Cámara
Nacional de Comercio, 14°, Avda Mariscal Santa Cruz 1392, Casilla
611, La Paz; tel. (2) 237-4477; fax (2) 236-2766; e-mail cni@cnibolivia
.com; internet www.cnibolivia.com; f. 1937; 8 depts throughout
Bolivia; Pres. ARMANDO GUMUCIO KARSTULOVIC; Gen. Man. FERNANDO
HINOJOSA.

INDUSTRIAL AND TRADE ASSOCIATIONS

Cámara Agropecuaria del Oriente: Avda Roca y Coronado s/n,
(Predios de Fexpocruz), Casilla 116, Santa Cruz; tel. (3) 352-2200; fax
(3) 352-2621; e-mail comunicacion@cao.org.bo; internet www.cao.org
.bo; f. 1964; agriculture and livestock asscn for eastern Bolivia; Gen.
Man. EDILBERTO OSINAGA ROSADO.

Cámara Boliviana de Hidrocarburos: Radial 17 1/2 y Sexto
Anillo, Casilla 3920, Santa Cruz; tel. (3) 353-8799; fax (3) 357-
7868; e-mail cbhe@cbhe.org.bo; internet www.cbhe.org.bo; f. 1986;
Pres. CLAUDIA CRONENBOLD; Exec. Dir RAÚL KIEFFER GUZMAN.

Cámara Forestal de Bolivia: Prolongación Manuel Ignacio Salvatierra 1055, Casilla 346, Santa Cruz; tel. (3) 333-2699; fax (3) 333-
1456; e-mail camaraforestal@cfb.org.bo; internet www.cfb.org.bo;
f. 1969; represents the interests of the Bolivian timber industry; Pres.
PEDRO COLANZI SERRATE.

**Federación de Caficultores Exportadores de Bolivia (FECA-
FEB):** Avda Juan Pablo II 2926, frente a la FAB, El Alto, La Paz; tel.
and fax (2) 284-6310; e-mail directorio@fecafeb.com; internet www
.fecafeb.com; f. 1991; independent nat. fed. of the small coffee
producers' orgs; 30 mem. orgs; Pres. EUGENIO VILLCA QUISPE.

Instituto Boliviano de Comercio Exterior (IBCE): Of. 1010, 10°,
Edif. 16 de Julio, Paseo El Prado, Casilla 4738, La Paz; tel. (2) 290-
0424; fax (2) 290-0425; internet www.ibce.org.bo; f. 1986; trade
promotion institute; Pres. JOSÉ LUIS LANDIVAR BOWLES; Gen. Man.
GARY A. RODRÍGUEZ A.

EMPLOYERS' ASSOCIATIONS

Asociación Nacional de Mineros Medianos: Calle Pedro Salazar
600, esq. Presbítero Medina, Casilla 6190, La Paz; tel. (2) 241-7522;
fax (2) 241-4123; e-mail anmm@caoba.entelnet.bo; f. 1939; asscn of 14
private medium-sized mining cos; Pres. HUMBERTO RADA; Sec.-Gen.
Dr EDUARDO CAPRILLES.

Confederación de Empresarios Privados de Bolivia (CEPB):
Calle Méndez Arcos 117, Plaza España, Zona Sopocachi, Casilla
4239, La Paz; tel. (2) 242-0999; fax (2) 242-1272; e-mail cepb@cepb
.org.bo; internet www.cepb.org.bo; largest national employers' org.;
Pres. DANIEL SÁNCHEZ SOLIZ; Exec. Sec. RODRIGO AGREDA GÓMEZ.

**Confederación Nacional de la Micro y Pequeña Empresa de
Bolivia (Conamype):** Edif. de Col, 11°, Of. 1102, Avda Montes 768,
La Paz; e-mail conamype_bolivia_2011_2013@hotmail.com; internet
conamype.galeon.com; f. 2003; small businesses' org.; Pres. MANUEL
RODRÍGUEZ.

STATE HYDROCARBONS COMPANIES

Corporación Minera de Bolivia (COMIBOL): Avda Camacho
1396, esq. Loayza, La Paz; tel. (2) 268-2100; fax (2) 235-7979; e-mail
info@comibol.gob.bo; internet www.comibol.gob.bo; f. 1952; state
mining corpn; owns both mines and processing plants; Pres. EDGAR
ESTEBAN HURTADO MOLLINEDO; 26,000 employees.

Empresa Metalúrgica Karachipampa (EMK): Potosí; f. 1985,
but not operational until 2013; part of COMIBOL; lead, zinc, silver
and gold smelting.

Empresa Metalúrgica Vinto (EMV): Carretera Potosí Km 7.5,
Casilla 612, Oruro; tel. (2) 527-8094; fax (2) 527-8024; e-mail info@
vinto.gob.bo; internet www.vinto.gob.bo; f. 1966; smelting of non-
ferrous minerals and special alloys; majority of shares previously
owned by Glencore (Switzerland); renationalized in 2007; took
control of Glencore-owned Vinto-Antimony plant in 2010 following
renationalization; Gen. Man. RAMIRO VILLAVICENCIO NIÑO DE
GUZMÁN; 950 employees.

Empresa Minera Corocoro (EMC): Corocoro, La Paz; tel. (2)
213-9374; fax (2) 213-4365; e-mail info@mineracorocoro.com;
internet www.mineracorocoro.com; f. 2009; copper production;
Gen. Man. GUSTAVO CHOQUE VELÁSQUEZ.

Yacimientos Petrolíferos Fiscales Bolivianos (YPFB): Calle
Bueno 185, 6°, Casilla 401, La Paz; tel. (2) 217-6300; fax (2) 237-3375;
e-mail webmaster@ypfb.gob.bo; internet www.ypfb.gob.bo; f. 1936;
exploration, drilling, production, refining, transportation and dis-

tribution of petroleum; re-nationalized in 2006; Pres. CARLOS VILLEGAS QUIROGA; 4,900 employees.

YPFB Andina, SA: Avda José Estenssoro 100, Santa Cruz; tel. (3) 371-3529; fax (3) 371-3540; e-mail Jorge.roca@ypfb-andina.com .bo; internet www.ypfb-andina.com.bo; f. 2008; fmrly Repsol YPF Bolivia; exploration and production in the San Antonio and San Alberto regions; produces 60% of the country's natural gas; Pres. JORGE ORTÍZ PAUCARA.

YPFB Chaco, SA: Edif. Centro Empresarial Equipetrol, 6°, Avda San Martín 1700, Equipetrol Norte, Casilla 6428, Santa Cruz; tel. (3) 345-3700; fax (3) 345-3710; e-mail transparencia@ypfbchaco .com.bo; internet www.ypfbchaco.com.bo; f. 1999; wholly owned subsidiary of BP (United Kingdom); oil and gas exploration and production; Exec. Pres. RAFAEL MARTÍNEZ VACA; Gen. Man. CARLOS EDUARDO SÁNCHEZ CHAVARRÍA.

YPFB Petroandina, SAM: Edif. Londres, 4°, Avda Busch 1689, La Paz; tel. (2) 237-0209; internet www.ypfbpetroandina.com.bo; f. 2007; 60% shares owned by YPFB and 40% shares owned by PDVSA, Venezuela; Gen. Man. FERNANDO SALAZAR.

YPFB Refinación, SA: Edif. Nago, Calle Celso Castedo 39, Casilla 804, Santa Cruz; tel. (3) 363-2000; fax 363-2023; internet www.ypfbrefinacion.com.bo; fmrly Petrobras Bolivia Refinación; name changed as above in 2010; Pres. MAURICIO TRIBEÑO CONTRERAS; Gen. Man. GUILLERMO LUIS ACHÁ MORALES.

MAJOR COMPANIES

ADM-SAO, SA: Parque Industrial Pl-M9, Casilla 1295, Santa Cruz; tel. (3) 346-0888; fax (3) 346-3941; e-mail admsao@admworld.com; internet www.admsao.com; f. 1902; edible vegetable oils and soya-bean products; Pres. JUAN R. LUCIANO; Gen. Man. HERNÁN BARRÓN; 560 employees.

América Textil, SA (Ametex): Calle Yanacachi 1489, Villa Fatima, Casilla 2137, La Paz; tel. (2) 221-9595; fax (2) 221-9707; e-mail contacto@americatextil.com; internet www.americatextil.com; textile exporter to the USA; Exec. Pres. MARCOS IBERKLEID; Gen. Man. MARCO DE LA ROCHA; 3,500 employees.

Cartonbol (Cartones de Bolivia): Avda 24 de Junio Km 3, 1/5 Carretera a Vinto, Oruro; tel. (2) 5117-7012; e-mail cartonbol@ sedem.gob.bo; internet www.cartonbol.com.bo; f. 2007; state-owned; cardboard box mfr; Gen. Man. PATRICIA BALLIVIÁN.

Cervecería Boliviana Nacional, SA (CBN): Avda Montes 400, Casilla 421, La Paz; tel. (2) 245-5455; fax (2) 245-5344; e-mail cbn@ pacena.com; internet cbn.bo; f. 1920; brewing; Gen. Man. IBO BLAZICEVIC; 802 employees.

Compañía Industrial Azucarera San Aurelio, SA (CIASA): Avda San Aurelio, esq. 4 Anillo, Zona Sud, Casilla 94, Santa Cruz; tel. (3) 353-4343; fax (3) 352-1182; e-mail ciasacomercial@ciasa.com.bo; internet www.sanaurelio.com; sugar-refining and alcohol distillery; f. 1951; Pres. RAMÓN AURELIO GUTIÉRREZ SOSA; Gen. Man. JORGE GUTIÉRREZ G.; 800 employees.

Compañía Industrial Maderera Ltda (CIMAL): Parque Industrial Manzana 10, Casilla 700, Santa Cruz de la Sierra; tel. (3) 346-0404; fax (3) 346-1502; e-mail cimal@gruporoda.com; internet www .cimal.com.bo; f. 1974; sawmill operations; Pres. CRISTÓBAL RODA DAZA; Gen. Man. LARRY GRANT HANSLER; 265 employees.

Compañía Industrial de Tabacos, SA: Avda Chacaltaya 2141, Zona Achachicala, Casilla 210, La Paz; tel. (2) 230-5353; fax (2) 230-7272; e-mail citsa@citbolivia.com; internet www.citbolivia.com; f. 1934; cigarette mfrs; Pres. RAÚL ADLER KAVLIN; Gen. Man. JORGE H. PAREJA; 200 employees.

Cooperativa Boliviana de Cemento Industrias y Servicios (COBOCE): Avda San Martín 558, Cochabamba; tel. (2) 426-2547; fax (2) 422-2485; e-mail cem@coboce.com; internet www.coboce.com; f. 1966; manufacture and distribution of cement; Chair. LUIS SAINZ HINOJOSA; Gen. Man. Dr FERNANDO QUIROGA; 455 employees.

Droguería Inti, SA: Calle Lucas Jaimes 1959, Casilla 1421, La Paz; tel. (2) 217-6600; fax (2) 222-1981; e-mail drogueria@inti.com.bo; internet www.inti.com.bo; f. 1947; manufacture and distribution of pharmaceuticals; Pres. FRIEDRICH OHNES TANZER; Gen. Man. CHRISTIAN SCHILLING DALGAS; 365 employees.

Empresa Minera Inti Raymi, SA (Kori Kollo): Avda Fuerza Naval 55, entre Calle 22 y 23 de Calacoto, La Paz; tel. (2) 279-7676; fax (2) 279-7273; internet emirsa.com; f. 1982; owned by Procesadora de Minerales, Guatemala; gold-mining; owns the Kori Kollo and Kori Chaca mines; Pres. JOSÉ MERCADO ROCABADO; Gen. Man. LUIS TEJADA PONCE; 600 employees.

Empresa Pública Nacional Estratégica de Textiles (Enatex): Villa Fatima, Calle Yanacachi 1489, Casilla 591, La Paz; tel. (2) 221-9595; fax (2) 229-1707; e-mail enatex@enatex.com.bo; internet www .enatex.com.bo; f. 2012; textile; Gen. Man. BETTY SILVA.

Fábrica Nacional de Cemento, SA (FANCESA): Pasaje Armando Alba 80, Sucre; tel. (4) 645-3882; fax (4) 644-1221; e-mail

info@fancesa.com; internet www.fancesa.com; f. 1959; mfrs of cement; Pres. EDUARDO RIVERO ZURITA; Gen. Man. MIRKO IVO GARDILCIC CALVO; 300 employees.

Gravetal Bolivia, SA: Edif. Banco Nacional de Bolivia, 6° y 7°, René Moreno 258, Casilla 5503, Santa Cruz; tel. (3) 336-3601; fax (3) 332-4723; e-mail gerencia@gravetal.com.bo; internet www.gravetal.com .bo; f. 1992; production of soyabean oil and soyabean meal; Pres. JUAN VALDIVIA ALMANZA; Gen. Man. OLDEMAR CESAR WOHLKE (acting).

Industrias de Aceite, SA (FINO): Carretera al Norte Km 6.5; Casilla 1759, Santa Cruz; tel. (3) 344-3000; fax (3) 344-3070; e-mail fino@fino.com.bo; internet www.fino.com.bo; f. 1944; owned by Grupo Romero of Peru; manufacture of edible vegetable oils; Pres. and Gen. Man. RENZO VALAREZO CINO; 1,080 employees.

Ingenio Azucarero Guabirá, SA: Carretera al Norte Km 56, Casilla 2069, Guabirá, Montero, Santa Cruz; tel. (3) 922-0225; fax (3) 922-0730; e-mail lfvasquez@guabira.com; internet guabira.com; f. 1956; processing and refining of sugar cane and alcohol distillation; Pres. CARLOS E. ROJAS AMELUNGE; Gen. Man. RUDIGER TREPP DEL C.

Jindal Steel Bolivia, SA (JSB): Edif. Tacuaral, 4°, Of. 402–403, Avda San Martín 1800, Equipetrol Norte, Santa Cruz; tel. (3) 341-6000; fax (3) 341-6775; e-mail info@jindalbolivia.com; internet www .jindalbolivia.com; subsidiary of Jindal Steel & Power Ltd, India; operates in a joint venture with Empresa Siderúrgica del Mutún (ESM); mining and steel manufacture; Pres. and CEO CARLOS H. MAZZI FERNÁNDEZ.

Minera San Cristóbal, SA (MSC): Torre KETAL, 5°, Calle 15, Calacoto, Casilla 13790, La Paz; tel. (2) 262-3400; fax (2) 211-7950; e-mail informaciones@minerasancristobal.com; internet www .minerasancristobal.com; f. 2000; subsidiary of Sumitomo Corpn, Japan; Pres. HARUO MATSUZAKI; Gen. Man. DONALD PRAHL.

La Papelera, SA: Avda Clemente Inofuentes 836, entre 14 y 15, Calacoto, La Paz; tel. (2) 279-4022; fax (2) 279-3952; e-mail lapapelera@papelera.com; internet www.lapapelera.com; f. 1941; paper and plastics mfrs; Pres. EMILIO VON BERGEN; Gen. Man. JUAN CARLOS ARNEZ; 150 employees.

Petrobras Bolivia, SA: Avda Leigue Castedo 1700, Equipetrol Norte, Santa Cruz; tel. (3) 366-7000; fax (3) 358-6031; e-mail com .institucional@petrobras.com; internet www.petrobras.com/bolivia; f. 1995; subsidiary of Petrobras (Brazil); oil and gas exploration and production; Gen. Man. CLAUDIO CASTEJÓN; 1,500 employees.

Petroquim, SRL: 4to Anillo s/n, P.I. Mz. 25, CP 3445, Santa Cruz; tel. (3) 348-8000; fax (3) 348-8200; e-mail info@petroquim.net; internet www.petroquim.net; petrochemicals; Gen. Man. ANDRÉS RODRÍGUEZ.

Pluspetrol Bolivia Corporation, SA: Avda Grigota, esq. Calle Las Palmas, Santa Cruz; tel. (3) 359-4000; fax (3) 354-8080; e-mail ocosta@pluspetrol.net; internet www.pluspetrolbolivia.com.bo; f. 1990; oil and gas exploration and production; Chair. and Pres. LUIS ALBERTO REY.

Saite, SRL (Sociedad Agropecuaria Industrial y Técnica): Calle Esquillana 4014, Urb. Cosmos 79, Zona Collpani, El Alto, La Paz; tel. (2) 283-1779; fax (2) 283-2262; e-mail info@quinuasaite.com.bo; internet www.quinuasaite.com.bo; f. 1987; organic food products; Pres. DIONICIO HUAYLLANI.

Sinchi Wayra, SA: Edif. Multicentro, Torre B, 1° y 2°, Avda Arce, esq. Rosendo Gutiérrez 2299, Casilla 4326, La Paz; tel. (2) 244-4849; fax (2) 244-4126; e-mail fhartmann@sinchiwayra.com.bo; f. 1965; mining and processing of lead and zinc ores and precious metals; wholly owned by a subsidiary of Glencore (Switzerland); operated the Colquiri tin/zinc mine until it was nationalized in June 2012; Pres. EDUARDO CAPRILES; 2,200 employees.

Sociedad Boliviana de Cemento, SA (SOBOCE): Calle Mercado 1075, 1°, Casilla 557, La Paz; tel. (2) 240-6040; fax (2) 240-7557; e-mail info@soboce.com; internet www.soboce.com; f. 1925; mfrs of cement; Pres. HORST GREBE LÓPEZ; Gen. Man. ARMANDO GUMUCIO; 710 employees.

Sociedad Comercial e Industrial Hansa Ltda (HANSA): Edif. Hansa, Calle Yanacocha, esq. Mercado 1004, Casilla 10800, La Paz; tel. (2) 214-9800; fax (2) 240-7788; e-mail gpetit@hansa.com.bo; internet www.hansa.com.bo; f. 1954; import and trading of telecommunications equipment, hardware, industrial machinery, motor vehicles and mining equipment; Pres. GEORGES PETIT; 370 employees.

UTILITIES

Electricity

Autoridad de Fiscalización y Control Social de Electricidad (AE): Avda 16 de Julio 1571, Zona Central, La Paz; tel. (2) 231-2401; fax (2) 231-2393; e-mail autoridaddeelectricidad@ae.gob.bo; internet www.ae.gob.bo; f. 1994; fmrly Superintendencia de Electricidad; regulates the electricity sector; Exec. Dir RICHARD ALCOCER GARNICA.

Alternative Energy Systems Ltd (Talleres AES): Calle Agustín Virreyra 962, Dpto 8A, Cochabamba; tel. and fax (4) 440-0064; e-mail aesbol@freeyellow.com; internet rampump@hotmail.com; f. 1986; specialist mfrs of alternative energy products including small water turbines, equipment for small hydro plants and pumping stations; Gen. Man. MIGUEL ALANDIA.

Compañía Boliviana de Energía Eléctrica, SA (COBEE): Avda Hernando Siles 5635, Casilla 353, La Paz; tel. (2) 278-2474; fax (2) 278-5920; e-mail cobee@cobee.com; internet www.cobee.com; f. 1925; largest private power producer and distributor, serving the areas of La Paz and Oruro; mainly hydroelectric; Pres. and Gen. Man. RENÉ SERGIO PEREIRA.

Compañía Eléctrica Central Bulo Bulo, SA (CECBB): Calle José de los Ríos 1772, 2°, entre Avda América Este y Parque Facundo Quiroga, Cochabamba; tel. (4) 414-1123; e-mail termoelectrica@centralbulobulo.com; internet www.centralbulobulo.com; f. 1999; owned by Empresa Petrolera Chaco, SA; generator co; Gen. Man. RAMIRO BECERRA FLORES.

Compañía Eléctrica Sucre, SA (CESSA): Calle Ayacucho 254, Sucre; tel. (4) 645-3126; fax (4) 646-0292; e-mail cessa@mara.scr.entelnet.bo; internet www.cessasucre.com; f. 1924; electricity distributor; Pres. MILTON BARÓN; Gen. Man. ALFREDO DEHESA.

Cooperativa Rural de Electrificación Ltda (CRE): Avda Busch, esq. Honduras, Santa Cruz; tel. (3) 336-6666; fax (3) 332-4936; e-mail webmaster@cre.com.bo; internet www.cre.com.bo; f. 1965; electricity distributor; Pres. MIGUEL CASTEDO SUÁREZ; Gen. Man. CARMELO PAZ DURÁN.

Delapaz (Distribuidora de Electricidad de La Paz): Avda Illimani 1973, Miraflores, Casilla 10511, La Paz; tel. (2) 222-2200; fax (2) 222-3756; e-mail cpacheco@electropaz.com.bo; internet www.electropaz.com.bo; f. 1995 as Electropaz; adopted present name 2013; distributor serving La Paz area; owned by Iberdrola (Spain), renationalized in Jan. 2013; Gen. Man. RENÉ USTARIZ.

Empresa Luz y Fuerza Eléctrica de Oruro, SA (ELFEOSA): Calle Catacora y 12 de Octubre, Zona Cementerio, Casilla 53, Oruro; tel. (2) 525-2233; fax (2) 525-2233; e-mail info@elfeosa.info; internet www.elfeosa.info; f. 1921; distributor serving Oruro; owned by Iberdrola (Spain), renationalized in Jan. 2013; Gen. Man. HUMBERTO VILLEGAS GUZMÁN.

Empresa Nacional de Electricidad, SA (ENDE): Avda Balliván 503, Edif. Colón, 8°, Casilla 565, Cochabamba; tel. (4) 452-0317; fax (4) 452-0318; e-mail ende@ende.bo; internet www.ende.bo; f. 1962, privatized 1995, renationalized 2007; divided into three arms concerned with generation, transmission and distribution; also operates ENDE ANDINA (f. 2007), a jt venture with Venezuela; Exec. Pres. ARTURO IPORRE (acting); the following companies were renationalized in 2010 and placed under the control of ENDE:

> **Empresa Eléctrica Corani, SA:** Edif. Las Torres Sófer I, 9°, Avda Oquendo 654, Casilla 5165, Cochabamba; tel. (4) 423-5700; fax (4) 411-5192; e-mail corani@corani.bo; internet corani.bo; f. 1995; generator co; 802.60 GWh generation in 2006 in conjunction with Santa Isabel; Gen. Man. LUIS CARLOS ROCABADO ZANNIER.
>
> **Empresa Eléctrica Guaracachi, SA (EGSA):** Avda Brasil y Tercer Anillo Interno, Casilla 336, Santa Cruz; tel. (3) 346-4632; fax (3) 346-5888; e-mail central@egsa.com.bo; internet www.guaracachi.com.bo; f. 1995; generator co; 445 MW capacity in 2008; Gen. Man. EDUARDO PAZ CASTRO.
>
> **Empresa Eléctrica Valle Hermoso, SA (EVH):** Calle Tarija 1425, esq. Adela Zamudio, Cala Cala, Cochabamba; tel. (4) 424-0544; fax (4) 411-5195; e-mail info@evh.bo; internet www.evh.bo; f. 1995; generator co; operates subsidiary Río Eléctrico, SA; Gen. Man. RENÉ FRANCISCO CABERO CALATAYUD.
>
> **Empresa de Luz y Fuerza Eléctrica Cochabamba, SA (ELFEC):** Avda Heroínas 0-686, Casilla 89, Cochabamba; tel. (4) 420-0125; fax (4) 425-9427; e-mail vustariz@elfec.com; internet www.elfec.com; f. 1908; electricity distributor; Gen. Man. RONALD ZAMBRANA MURILLO.

Hidroeléctrica Boliviana, SA: Avda Fuerza Naval 22, Zona Calcoto, La Paz; tel. (2) 277-0765; fax (2) 277-0933; e-mail hb@hidrobol.com; internet www.hidrobol.com; 317 GWh generation in 2008; Gen. Man. Ing. ANGEL HUMBERTO ZANNIER CLAROS.

Transportadora de Electricidad, SA (TDE): Calle Colombia 0-0655, Casilla 640, Cochabamba; tel. (4) 425-9500; fax (4) 425-9516; e-mail tde@tde.com.bo; internet www.tde.com.bo; f. 1997; fmrly subsidiary of Red Eléctrica Española (REE), Spain; nationalized in May 2012; Gen. Man. ROBERTO PEREDO ECHAZÚ.

Gas

Numerous distributors of natural gas exist throughout the country, many of which are owned by the petroleum distributor, Yacimientos Petrolíferos Fiscales Bolivianos (YPFB)—see State Hydrocarbons Companies.

Gas TransBoliviano, SA (GTB): Km. 7.5 Carretera a Cochabamba, Casilla 3137, Santa Cruz; tel. (3) 371-4900; fax (3) 371-4009; e-mail rquintana@gtb.com.bo; internet www.gastransboliviano.com; Pres. SANTIAGO SOLOGUREN PAZ; Gen. Man. KATYA DIEDERICH.

Water

Autoridad de Fiscalización y Control Social de Agua Potable y Saneamiento Básico (AAPS): Edif. Cámara de Comercio, Avda Mariscal Santa Cruz 1392, 4° y 16°, Casilla 4245, La Paz; tel. (2) 231-0801; fax (2) 231-0554; e-mail contactos@aaps.gob.bo; internet www.aaps.gob.bo; f. 1999; fmrly Superintendencia de Saneamiento Básico (SISAB); decentralized regulatory authority for urban water supplies and grants service concessions and licences; Exec. Dir EDSON SOLARES.

Empresa Pública Social de Agua y Saneamiento (EPSAS): Avda de las Américas 705, Villa Fátima, Casilla 9359, La Paz; tel. (2) 221-0295; fax (2) 221-2454; e-mail info@epsas.com.bo; internet www.epsas.com.bo; f. 2007; state-owned water and sewerage provider in La Paz and El Alto; Gen. Man. WILLIAM MARCA.

TRADE UNIONS

Central Obrera Boliviana (COB): Edif. COB, Calle Pisagua 618, Casilla 6552, La Paz; tel. (2) 352-426; fax (2) 281-201; e-mail postmast@cob-bolivia.org; f. 1952; main union confederation; 800,000 mems; Exec. Sec. JUAN CARLOS TRUJILLO.

Central Obrera Departamental de La Paz: Plaza Zalles 284, Estación Central, La Paz; tel. (2) 245-8741; e-mail codlp@hotmail.com; affiliated to the COB; Exec. Sec. MARTÍN AGUILAR.

Confederación General de Trabajadores Fabriles de Bolivia (CGTFB): Avda Armentia 452, Casilla 21590, La Paz; tel. (2) 228-1524; fax (2) 228-5783; e-mail cgtfb@hotmail.com; f. 1951; manufacturing workers' union; Exec. Sec. VICTOR PEDRO QUISPE TICONA.

Confederación Sindical Unica de los Trabajadores Campesinos de Bolivia (CSUTCB): Avda Saavedra 2045, Miraflores, Casilla 11589, La Paz; tel. (2) 224-6232; fax (2) 224-6300; e-mail csutcbbolivia@gmail.com; internet www.csutcb.org; f. 1979; peasant farmers' union; affiliated to the COB; Exec. Sec. DAMIÁN CONDORI.

Federación Nacional de Cooperativas Mineras de Bolivia (FENCOMIN): Edif. Hansa, 16°, Avda Mariscal Santa Cruz, entre Yanacocha y Socabaya, La Paz; tel. (2) 212-0552; internet www.fencomin.com; Pres. ALEJANDRO SANTOS.

Federación Sindical de Trabajadores Mineros de Bolivia (FSTMB): Plaza Venezuela 147, Casilla 14565, La Paz; tel. (2) 235-9656; fax (2) 231-7764; e-mail fstmb1944@hotmail.com; internet sites.google.com/site/fstmb2003/; f. 1944; mineworkers' union; affiliated to the COB; Exec. Sec. MIGUEL PÉREZ; 27,000 mems.

Transport

RAILWAYS

In 2009 there were 2,866 km of railway lines in the country. There are direct rail links with Argentina, Brazil and Chile. A ferry connects the railhead at Guaqui, Bolivia to the railhead at Puno in Peru across Lake Titicaca.

Empresa Nacional de Ferrocarriles (ENFE): Estación Central de Ferrocarriles, Plaza Zalles, Casilla 428, La Paz; tel. (2) 232-7401; fax (2) 239-2677; f. 1964; privatized in 1995; renationalized in 2010; total networks: 3,698 km (2008); Andina network: 2,274 km; Oriental (Eastern) network: 1,424 km; Pres. JOSÉ MANUEL PINTO CLAURE.

> **Empresa Ferroviaria Andino, SA** (Red Occidental): Calle Quintin Barrios 791, entre Avda Ecuador y Calle Cervantes, Plaza España, Casilla 4350, La Paz; tel. and fax (2) 241-4400; e-mail efasa@fca.com.bo; internet www.fca.com.bo; f. 1996; has two lines: *Expreso del Sur* connects Oruro to Uyuni, towards the border of Argentina and *Wara Wara del Sur* connects Uyuni Salt Flats to Chile; other sections of the line connect La Paz with Cochabamba, Sucre and Potosí; Pres. MIGUEL SEPÚLVEDA CAMPOS; Gen. Man. EDUARDO MACLEAN ABAROA.**Empresa Ferroviaria Oriental, SA (FCOSA):** Avda Montes Final s/n, Casilla 3569, Santa Cruz; tel. (3) 338-7000; fax (3) 338-7105; e-mail ferroviaria@fo.com.bo; internet www.fo.com.bo; f. 1996; connects Santa Cruz with São Paulo, Brazil and Yacuiba on the Argentine border; Chair. RAFAEL ENRIQUE ABREU ANSELMI; Gen. Man. RICARDO FERNANDEZ DURÁN.

ROADS

In 2010 Bolivia had some 80,488 km of roads, of which an estimated 8.5% were paved. Of the total 16,515 km were under the national road network and 23,716 km formed the regional road network. Almost the entire road network is concentrated in the *altiplano* region and the Andes valleys. The Pan-American Highway, linking Argentina and Peru, crosses Bolivia from south to north-west. In 2010 the Administradora Boliviana de Carreteras commenced work on consolidating the Corredor al Norte, which would integrate the departments of La Paz, Beni and Pando. Also known as the Corredor Amazónico, the 1,357-km stretch would also improve Bolivia's connections with neighbouring countries.

Administradora Boliviana de Carreteras (ABC): Edif. Centro de Comunicaciones, 8°, Avda Mariscal Santa Cruz, La Paz; tel. (2) 235-7220; fax (2) 239-1764; e-mail abc@abc.gob.bo; internet www.abc .gob.bo; f. 2006; planning and devt of national highways; Pres. ANTONIO MULLISACA.

INLAND WATERWAYS AND SHIPPING

By agreement with Paraguay in 1938, Bolivia has an outlet on the River Paraguay. This arrangement, together with navigation rights on the Paraná, gives Bolivia access to the River Plate and the sea. The River Paraguay is navigable for vessels of 12-ft draught for 288 km beyond Asunción, in Paraguay, and for smaller boats another 960 km to Corumbá in Brazil.

Bolivia has duty-free access to the Brazilian coastal ports of Belém and Santos and the inland ports of Corumbá and Port Velho, as well as to free port facilities at Rosario, Argentina, on the River Paraná, and to the Peruvian port of Ilo. Most of Bolivia's foreign trade is handled through the ports of Matarani (Peru), Antofagasta and Arica (Chile), Rosario and Buenos Aires (Argentina) and Santos (Brazil). An agreement between Bolivia and Chile to reform Bolivia's access arrangements to the port of Arica came into effect in 1996. At 31 December 2013 the flag registered fleet comprised 118 vessels, totalling 132,356 grt.

CIVIL AVIATION

Bolivia has 30 airports, including the three international airports at La Paz (El Alto), Santa Cruz (Viru-Viru) and Cochabamba. In 2013 the Government of Evo Morales announced the nationalization of these three airports, hitherto operated by a Spanish company. Later that year plans to open two more international airports, in Cochabamba and Chuquisaca, in 2014, were announced.

Dirección General de Aeronáutica Civil: Edif. Multicine, 9°, Avda Arce 2631, Casilla 9360, La Paz; tel. (2) 244-4450; fax (2) 211-9323; internet www.dgac.gob.bo; f. 1947; Exec. Dir Gen. LUIS COÍMBRA BUSCH.

Boliviana de Aviación: Calle Jordán 202, esq. Nataniel Aguirre, Cochabamba; tel. (4) 411-4643; fax (4) 411-6477; e-mail ventasweb@ boa.bo; internet boa.bo; f. 2007; state-owned; Gen. Man. RONALD SALVADOR CASSO CASSO.

Transportes Aéreos Bolivianos (TAB): El Alto, Internacional Aeropuerto, Casilla 12237, La Paz; tel. (2) 284-0556; e-mail tabair@ tabairlines.com; internet www.tabairlines.com; f. 1977; Gen. Man. Col FRANZ TAMAYO.

Transportes Aéreos Militares: Avda Montes 738, esq. Jose Maria Serrano, La Paz; tel. (2) 268-1101; fax (2) 268-1102; internet www

.tam.bo; internal passenger and cargo services; Dir-Gen. Col JULIO CESAR VILLARROEL CAMACHO.

Tourism

Bolivia's tourist attractions include Lake Titicaca, at 3,805 m (12,488 ft) above sea level, pre-Incan ruins at Tiwanaku, Chacaltaya, in the Andes mountains, which has the highest ski-run in the world, and the UNESCO World Cultural Heritage Sites of Potosí and Sucre. In 2012 receipts from tourism totalled US $532m. Visitor arrivals totalled 563,486 in the same year.

Asociación Boliviana de Agencias de Viajes y Turismo (ABA-VYT): Calle Boliviar 27, 2°, Zonca Central, Santa Cruz; tel. (3) 332-7110; fax (3) 332-1634; e-mail abavyt@acelerate.com; f. 1984; Pres. LOURDES OMOYA BENITEZ.

Dirección General de Turismo: Edif. Cámara Nacional de Comercial, Avda Mariscal Santa Cruz, 11°, Casilla 1868, La Paz; tel. (2) 236-3326; fax (2) 220-2628; Vice-Minister of Tourism MARKO MARCELO MACHICAO BANKOVIC.

Defence

As assessed at November 2013, Bolivia's armed forces numbered 46,100: army 34,800 (including 25,000 conscripts), navy 4,800, air force 6,500. There was also a paramilitary force numbering 37,100. Military service, lasting one year, is selective.

Defence Expenditure: budgeted at 2,560m. bolivianos in 2013.

Commander-in-Chief of the Armed Forces: Adm. VÍCTOR BALDIVIESO HACHÉ.

General Commander of the Army: Maj.-Gen. FERNANDO ZEBALLOS CORTEZ.

General Commander of the Air Force: Brig.-Gen. VÍCTOR HUGO MENESES GÓMEZ.

General Commander of the Naval Forces: Vice-Adm. GONZALO ALCÓN ALIAGA.

Education

Primary education, beginning at six years of age and lasting for eight years, is officially compulsory and is available free of charge. Secondary education, which is not compulsory, begins at 14 years of age and lasts for up to four years. In 2011 enrolment at primary schools included 83% of pupils in the relevant age-group. In 2011 enrolment at secondary schools included 68% of students in the relevant age-group. There are 17 state universities and 68 private universities. The provision for education in the 2012 central government budget was 11,000m. bolivianos.

Bibliography

For works on South America generally, see Select Bibliography (Books)

Crabtree, J. *Patterns of Protest: Politics and Social Movements in Bolivia.* London, Latin America Bureau, 2005.

Crabtree, J., and Chaplin, A. *Bolivia: Processes of Change.* London, Zed Books, 2013.

Crabtree, J., and Whitehead, L. (Eds). *Unresolved Tensions: Bolivia Past and Present.* Pittsburgh, PA, University of Pittsburgh Press, 2008.

Dunkerley, J. *Bolivia: Revolution and the Power of History in the Present. Essays.* London, Institute for the Study of the Americas, 2007.

Fifer, J. V. *Bolivia: Land, Location and Politics Since 1825.* Cambridge, Cambridge University Press, 2008.

Gamarra, E. A. *Bolivia on the Brink.* New York, Council on Foreign Relations, 2007.

Gotkowitz, L. *A Revolution for Our Rights: Indigenous Struggles for Land and Justice in Bolivia.* Durham, NC, Duke University Press, 2008.

Grindle, M., and Domingo, P. (Eds). *Proclaiming Revolution: Bolivia in Comparative Perspective.* London, Harvard University David Rockefeller Center for Latin American Studies and the Institute for Latin American Studies, 2003.

Gustafson, B. D. *New Languages of the State: Indigenous Resurgence and the Politics of Knowledge in Bolivia.* Durham, NC, Duke University Press, 2009.

Healy, K. *Llamas, Weavings and Organic Chocolate: Multilateral Grassroots Development in the Andes and Amazon of Bolivia.* Notre Dame, IN, University of Notre Dame Press, 2000.

Hylton, F., and Thomson, S. *Revolutionary Horizons: Popular Struggle in Bolivia.* London and New York, Verso, 2007.

James, D. (Ed.). *The Complete Bolivian Diaries of Che Guevara.* New York, Cooper Square Press, 2000.

Jemio, L. C. *Debt, Crisis and Reform in Bolivia: Biting the Bullet.* The Hague, Institute of Social Studies, 2001.

Klein, H. S. *Bolivia: The Evolution of a Multi-Ethnic Society.* 2nd edn, New York, Oxford University Press, 1992.

  A Concise History of Bolivia. Cambridge, Cambridge University Press, 2003.

Kohl, B., and Farthing, L. *Impasse in Bolivia: Neoliberal Hegemony and Popular Resistance.* London, Zed Books, 2006.

Lehman, K. D. *Bolivia and the United States: A Limited Partnership.* Athens, GA, University of Georgia Press, 1999.

Muñoz-Pogossian, B. *Electoral Rules and the Transformation of Bolivian Politics: The Rise of Evo Morales*. Basingstoke, Palgrave Macmillan, 2010.

Olivera, O. *¡Cochabamba! Water War in Bolivia*. Cambridge, MA, Southend Books, 2004.

Pearce, A. (Ed.). *Evo Morales and the Movimiento Al Socialismo in Bolivia: The first term in context, 2006–2010*. London, Institute for the Study of the Americas, 2011.

Powers, W. *Whispering in the Giant's Ear: A Frontline Chronicle from Bolivia's War on Globalization*. New York, Bloomsbury USA, 2006.

Saldana, R. *Fertile Ground: Che Guevara and Bolivia*. New York, Pathfinder Press, 2001.

Sándor John, S. *Bolivia's Radical Tradition: Permanent Revolution in the Andes*. Tucson, AZ, University of Arizona Press, 2009.

Smale, R. L. *I Sweat the Flavor of Tin: Labor Activism in Early Twentieth-Century Bolivia*. Pittsburgh, PA, University of Pittsburgh Press, 2010.

Webber, J. R. *From Rebellion to Reform in Bolivia: Class Struggle, Indigenous Liberation, and the Politics of Evo Morales*. Chicago, IL, Haymarket Books, 2011.

BONAIRE

Bonaire lies about 80 km (50 miles) off the coast of Venezuela. The territory consists of Bonaire and, nestled in its western crescent, the uninhabited islet of Klein Bonaire. Together with Aruba and Curaçao, Bonaire forms the Benedenwindse Eilands or Leeward Islands. The climate is tropical, moderated by the sea, with an average annual temperature of 27.5°C (81°F) and little rainfall. The official languages are Dutch and Papiamento (a mixture of Dutch, Spanish, Portuguese, English, Arawak Indian and several West African dialects), which is the dominant language of the Leeward Islands. Almost all of the inhabitants, which numbered 18,413 at 1 January 2014, profess Christianity, predominantly Roman Catholicism. The population density of the territory was 63.9 persons per sq km in January 2014. The state flag (proportions 2 by 3) has a large blue triangle in the lower right corner and a smaller yellow triangle in the upper left corner. The triangles are separated by a white strip, inside of which is a black compass and a red six-pointed star (each point represents one of the original six villages of Bonaire). The capital is Kralendijk, on the western coast of the island; Rincon, situated in the north-west of Bonaire, is the territory's only other town.

The Leeward Islands, already settled by communities of Arawak Indians, were discovered by the Spanish in 1499 and named after the Arawak word 'Bo-nah', or 'low land.' The islands were seized by the Dutch in the 1630s. After frequent changes in possession, the islands were finally confirmed as Dutch territory in 1816. The Dutch established a government plantation system based on commercial crops and on the island's main resource, salt. Slavery was abolished in 1863. Together with the Windward Islands (comprising Sint (St) Eustatius, Saba and Sint (St) Maarten), Bonaire was administered as Curaçao and Dependencies between 1845 and 1948. During the Second World War Queen Wilhelmina of the Netherlands promised independence, and in 1954 a Charter gave the federation of six islands full autonomy in domestic affairs, and declared it to be an integral part of the Kingdom of the Netherlands.

The tourism industry developed from the 1950s. Bonaire was also allocated resources from the Netherlands. With the advent of the Bonaire Petroleum Corporation (BOPEC) in 1975, the island acquired a terminal to receive oil for transfer from large to small tankers.

From 1954 until 2010 Bonaire was a constituent part of the Netherlands Antilles (a six-member federation until 1986 when Aruba gained separate status). Political allegiances were generally divided along island, rather than policy, lines. This led to a series of unstable coalitions governing the federation. By the early 1990s it had become clear that although the metropolitan Dutch Government was unwilling to allow the complete disintegration of the federation, it would consider a less centralized system, or the creation of two federations in the separate island groups.

A referendum on status was conducted on Bonaire in October 1994 (simultaneous plebiscites were also held on St Maarten, St Eustatius and Saba). Some 88% of voters favoured continued federation with the Netherlands.

On 8 October 2004 the Jesurun Commission, established by the Dutch and Antillean Governments and headed by Edsel Jesurun (a former Governor of the Netherlands Antilles), recommended the dissolution of the Netherlands Antilles. The Commission proposed that Bonaire, along with Saba and St Eustatius, should be directly administered by the Dutch Government. In September, in an official referendum, a majority of voters (59%) on Bonaire strongly favoured becoming part of the Netherlands. On 3 December 2005 a preliminary agreement with the Dutch Government that the extant federation be dissolved by 1 July 2007 was duly signed in Curaçao. Under the new structure, Bonaire was to become a koninkrijseilande, or kingdom island, with direct ties to the Netherlands, a status equivalent to that of a Dutch province. The future status of Bonaire was subsequently refined to that of a bijzondere gemeete, or special municipality, similar in most ways to other metropolitan Dutch municipalities, although with separate social security and currency arrangements.

An agreement confirming Bonaire's impending accession to special municipality status was signed in The Hague, Netherlands, on 12 October 2006, and included provisions for citizens of the island to participate in Dutch national and local elections and in the election of candidates to the European Parliament. A further transition accord was signed by the Netherlands Antilles central Government, the Island Council of Bonaire, and the Netherlands on 12 February 2007, envisaging the Bonaire's complete secession from the federation. Under the terms of this covenant, the Netherlands was to pledge over NA Fl. 1,000m. to facilitate the process of disintegration, with each participating island receiving individual allocations. The metropolitan administration also agreed to write off almost three-quarters of the Antilles' debt.

A meeting was held in Curaçao on 15 December 2008 at which the Dutch Prime Minister, Jan Peter Balkenende, and the Antillean premier, Emily de Jongh-Elhage, signed an agreement confirming the new status of the island. In September 2009, at a meeting of the Dutch State Secretary for the Interior and Kingdom Relations, Ank Bijleveld-Schouten, and representatives of the Netherlands Antilles, it was agreed that the target date for dissolution of the federation would be 10 October 2010.

The Dutch Government postponed the payment of Bonaire's debt in October 2009, after the island's recently formed Executive Council, led by the Partido Demokrátiko Boneriano (PDB), proposed a free association status with the Netherlands, involving greater independence, rather than the planned integration as a municipality. The Dutch Government asserted the island could adopt municipality status or assume full self-governance. None the less, the Executive Council proceeded to schedule a referendum on its proposal. In February 2010 Frits Goedgedrag, the Governor of the Netherlands Antilles, cancelled the plebiscite on the grounds that it contravened international law. Nevertheless, the referendum was held in December, although low turnout meant the result was declared invalid. The Unión Patriótico Boneriano (UPB), which had taken office in September, had urged the electorate to boycott the plebiscite.

On 10 October 2010, following the formal dissolution of the Netherlands Antilles, Bonaire officially became a special municipality of the Netherlands. The US dollar was formally adopted as the island's currency from 1 January 2011, replacing the Netherlands Antilles guilder; the Island Council had opposed the introduction of the euro, the currency of the Netherlands.

At elections to the Island Council on 2 March 2011 the UPB secured four of the nine seats available. The PDB won three seats and the recently formed Movementu Boneiru Liber and Partido Pro Hustisia & Union each won one seat. A coalition Government was subsequently formed. Lydia Emerencia was sworn in as the island's new Lieutenant-Governor in March 2012.

Owing to Bonaire's change in administrative status, the island's residents were henceforth entitled to vote in Dutch polls. The islanders first opportunity to exercise this right came on 12 September 2012, when elections to the Tweede Kamer (Second Chamber—the lower house of the Dutch parliament) were conducted. The Partij van de Arbeid received 23.9% of the valid votes cast in Bonaire, while the Volkspartij voor Vrijheid en Democratie (VVD) garnered 20.9%, the Christen Democratisch Appèl 19.3% and Democraten 66 (D66) 11.5%. The rate of participation by the electorate was just 24.8% (compared with 74.6% nationwide). Commentators attributed this very low turnout to a lack of campaigning on the island.

In September 2013 Pablo (James) Kroon became the new leader of the UPB, replacing Ramonsito Booi. On 26 November the Island Council endorsed a motion of no confidence in Emerencia, and she announced her resignation as Lieutenant-Governor three days later. Legislators accused Emerencia of, *inter alia*, adopting a unilateral decision-making style and travelling abroad on official business too frequently. However, some observers suspected that the UPB had approved the no confidence motion in retaliation for the active support that the Lieutenant-Governor had given to various corruption investigations on the island, which had led to legal action being pursued against Booi and another senior UPB politician—former Executive Council member Burney El Hage. (The Dutch Kingdom Representative in Bonaire, Saba and St Eustatius, Wilbert Stolte, resigned in May 2014 following allegations that he had misappropriated public funds and that he had intervened in the Bonaire corruption inquiries in an effort to protect his allies in the UPB.) Emerencia officially relinquished her duties on 1 March 2014; she was succeeded as Lieutenant-Governor by Edison Rijna. Later that month the Island Council unanimously endorsed a proposal to conduct another referendum on Bonaire's constitutional status. The Dutch Government declared that it had no objections to such a poll being organized. The timing and structure of the planned plebiscite were under discussion in mid-2014.

Elections to the European Parliament took place in Bonaire on 22 May 2014. The 'ikkiesvooreerlijk.eu' list secured 26.9% of the local ballot, compared with 22.0% for D66 and 15.7% for the VVD. Turnout, however, was just 12.0%.

Tourism is the economic mainstay of Bonaire. The island is a well-known destination for diving and as a place of environmental diversity. Tourism numbers increased substantially between 2003 and 2007. According to the Caribbean Tourism Organization, in 2007 74,300 stay-over tourists were registered. This figure remained unchanged in 2008, but declined to 67,000 in 2009, before rising in 2010 to 70,500. Approximately 82,000 air passenger arrivals were recorded in 2012, with the majority travelling from the Netherlands and the USA. There was a 5.8% increase in tourist numbers during the first half of 2013, following a significant rise in visitors from Latin

America. To some extent, the growth in tourism was related to second-home ownership. When it became known in 2006 that Bonaire would become part of the Netherlands, interest in real estate investment increased, reinforced by a favourable (euro) exchange rate. However, the financial crisis from 2008, as well as a more expensive dollar and the introduction of a tax on second homes, ended the boom. Cruise tourism developed from around 40,000 cruise visitors in 2000, to 226,000 in 2010.

The BOPEC oil terminal, operated and owned by the Venezuelan state-run oil company PDVSA, receives about 20–25 tankers per month. The 23-tank, 12m.-barrel facility is used for unloading Venezuelan oil, most of which is shipped to the People's Republic of China. Other larger businesses are partly government-owned, such as the telephone companies and the utility company (electricity production stood at 91m. kWh in 2012). The largest employer on the island is the trade, transport, hotels and catering sector, providing 31% of all employment in 2012. Bonaire had a labour force of 9,383 in that year, of which 546 were unemployed (5.8%). In 2009 the island imported goods worth NA Fl. 209m. and exported goods worth NA Fl. 16m. In 2012 the inflation rate was 2.9%, although this declined to 1.7% in 2013. Gross domestic product (GDP) was estimated at US $364.2m. in 2012, with GDP per caput totalling $21,000.

Bonaire's economic prospects are generally positive. The Dutch Government is investing in social and economic infrastructure. Substantial expenditure has been made in environment protection, education, airport facilities and health care. This investment, it is hoped, will trigger private sector activity and, thus, generate economic growth.

Directory

The Government

HEAD OF STATE

King of the Netherlands: HM King WILLEM-ALEXANDER.

Lieutenant-Governor: EDISON E. RIJNA (acting), Bestuurskantoor, Wilhelminaplein 1, Kralendijk; tel. 717-5330; fax 717-2824; e-mail gezag@bonairelive.com; internet www.bonairegov.an.

ISLAND COUNCIL
(September 2014)

The Government is formed by a coalition of the Unión Patriótiko Boneriano (UPB), the Partido Demokrátiko Boneriano (PDB), the Movementu Boneiru Liber (MBL) and the Frakshon Santana.

Island Council: JEFFERY LEVENSTONE (UPB), MELENA WINKLAAR (UPB), MARITZA SILBERIE (UPB), REYNOLD WILSOE (UPB), BENITO DIRKSZ (MBL), ROBERT BEUKENBOOM (PDB), MARUGIA JANGA (PDB), CLARK ABRAHAM (PDB), RAFAEL SANTANA (Frakshon Santana).

Election, 2 March 2011

Party	Seats
Unión Patriótico Boneriano (UPB)	4
Partido Demokrátiko Boneriano (PDB) . . .	3
Movementu Boneiru Liber (MBL) . . .	1
Partido Pro Hustisia & Union (PHU) . . .	1
Total	9

Island Secretary: WILLEM CECILIA (acting).

Executive Council: EDISON E. RIJNA (Lt-Governor), C. J. ELS, PABLO JAMES KROON, EDSEL S. WINKLAAR.

MINISTRY

National Office for the Caribbean Netherlands Bonaire (Rijksdienst Caribisch Nederland Bonaire): Kaya International z/n, POB 357, Kralendijk; tel. 715-8303; fax 715-8330; e-mail info@rijksvertegenwoordiger.nl; internet www.rijksdienstcn.com; Kingdom Rep. GILBERT ISABELLA.

Political Organizations

Frakshon Santana: Kralendijk; Leader RAFAEL SANTANA.

Movementu Boneiru Liber (MBL) (Free Bonaire Movement): Passangrahan, Plasa Reina Wilhelmina, Kralendijk; tel. 717-4008; fax 717-6125; e-mail movementu@gmail.com; internet www.vota-mbl.com; f. 2010; Leader BENITO DIRKSZ; Sec. JOSÉ A. E. CAPELLA.

Partido Demokrátiko Boneriano (PDB) (Bonaire Democratic Party): Kaya America 13A, POB 294, Kralendijk; tel. 717-8903; fax 717-5923; e-mail info@partido-demokrat.org; internet partido-demokrat.org; f. 1954; also known as Democratische Partij—Bonaire (DPB); liberal, promotes self-governance for Bonaire; known as the Aliansa Demokrátika Bonairiana in 2009–10; Leader ROBBY BEUKENBOOM.

Partido Pro Hustisia & Union (PHU): Kralendijk; tel. 796-2650; e-mail m.bijkerk@telbonet.an; internet www.phubonaire.com; f. 2010; Pres. RAFAEL A. SANTANA.

Unión Patriótiko Boneriano (UPB) (Patriotic Union of Bonaire): Kaya Sabana 22, Kralendijk; tel. 717-8906; fax 717-5552; e-mail info@votaupb.com; internet votaupb.com; f. 1969; 2,134 mems; Christian democratic; Leader PABLO (JAMES) KROON; Sec.-Gen. C. V. WINKLAAR.

Judicial System

Legal authority is exercised by the Joint Court of Justice of Aruba, Curaçao and St Maarten and of Bonaire, St Eustatius and Saba. Its headquarters are in Curaçao. The Joint Court hears civil, criminal and administrative cases in the first instance and on appeal.

Joint Court of Justice: Plasa Reina Wilhelmina (Fort Oranje), Kralendijk; tel. 717-8172; fax 717-5779; e-mail griffiebonaire@caribjustitia.org; internet www.gemhofvanjustitie.org/vestigingen/bonaire; hears cases in the first instance; Pres. EVERT JAN VAN DER POEL.

Attorney-General: GUUS SCHRAM.

Religion

Almost all of the inhabitants profess Christianity, predominantly Roman Catholicism.

The Press

Arco Bonaire: Kaya Isabel 1, Kralendijk; tel. 717-2427; e-mail info@arcocarib.com; internet www.arcocarib.com; magazine; Editor M. BIJKERK.

Bonaire Reporter: Kaya Gobernador Nicolaas Debrot 200-6, POB 407, Kralendijk; tel. and fax 786-6125; fax 786-6518; e-mail info@bonairenews.com; internet www.bonairereporter.com; English; weekly; Publ. GEORGE DeSALVO; Editor-in-Chief LAURA DeSALVO.

Broadcasting and Communications

TELECOMMUNICATIONS

Chippie Bonaire: Kaya Caracas 2, Kralendijk; tel. 717-0117; fax 717-0119; e-mail info@uts.an; internet www.chippie.an; mobile telecommunication provider; subsidiary of UTS Group, Curaçao.

Digicel Bonaire: Kaya Grandi 26, Kralendijk; tel. 717-4400; fax 717-4466; e-mail customercare@digicelcuracao.com; internet www.digicelbonaire.com; f. 1999; bought majority shareholding of Antilliano Por NV in April 2006; Digicel acquired mobile business of TELBO (Bonaire) in Dec. 2006; Chair. DENIS O'BRIEN; CEO (Dutch Caribbean) SANDER GIELEN.

Telbo NV (Telefonia Bonairiano NV): Kaya Libertador Simon Bolivar 8, Kralendijk; tel. 715-7000; fax 717-5007; e-mail info@telbo.an; internet www.telbo.an; f. 1983; owned by Bonaire Holding Maatschappij (govt-controlled holding co); fixed-line telecommunications and internet service provider; Gen. Man. GILBERT DE BREE.

BROADCASTING
Radio

Radiodifusión Boneriana NV: Kaya Gobernador Nicolaas Debrot 2, Kralendijk; tel. 717-5947; fax 717-8220; e-mail vozdibonaire@gmail.com; internet www.vozdibonaire.com; f. 1962; Owner FELICIANO DA SILVA PILOTO.

Alpha FM: broadcasts in Spanish.

Mega FM: internet www.megahitfm.com; broadcasts in Dutch.

Voz di Bonaire (PJB2) (Voice of Bonaire): broadcasts in Papiamento.

Trans World Radio (TWR): Kaya Gobernador Nicolaas Debrot 64, Kralendijk; tel. 717-8800; fax 717-8808; e-mail 800am@twr.org; internet www.twr.org; f. 1964; religious, educational and cultural station; programmes to South, Central and North America, and Caribbean, in 5 languages; Pres. LAUREN LIBBY; Station Dir JOSEPH BARKER.

Television

Relay stations provide Bonaire with television programmes from Curaçao.

Finance

BANKING

Regulatory Authority

College Financieel Toezicht (CFT): De Rouvilleweg 39, Willemstad, Curaçao; tel. (9) 461-9081; e-mail info@cft.an; internet www.cft.an; f. 2007; bd of financial supervision; oversees financial administration in Bonaire, Sint Eustatius and Saba; Chair. AGE BAKKER; Rep. of Bonaire, Saba and St Eustatius THEODORE M. PANDT.

Commercial Banks

Girobank, NV: 12 Kaya L.D. Gerharts, Kralendijk; tel. 717-8115; e-mail info@gironet.com; internet www.girobank.net; f. 1965; Pres. and CEO ERIC GARCIA; Man. JOAN SILIE.

Maduro & Curiel's Bank (Bonaire), NV: 1 Kaya L. D. Gerharts, Kralendijk; tel. 715-5520; e-mail info@mcbbonaire.com; internet www.mcbbonaire.com; Man. Dir LEONARD DOMACASSÉ.

Banking Associations

Bonaire Bankers' Association: Maduro & Curiel's Bank (Bonaire) NV, Kaya L. D. Gerharts 1, POB 366, Kralendijk; tel. 717-5520; fax 717-5884; Man. Dir RUDY GOMEZ.

INSURANCE

ENNIA Bonaire: Centrumgebied z/n, POB 349, Kralendijk; tel. 717-8546; fax 717-7546; e-mail mail@ennia.com; internet www.ennia-bonaire.com; f. 1948; part of ENNIA Caribe Holding, NV; Pres. RALPH PALM.

NAGICO Bonaire (National General Insurance Corpn): Kaya Gilberto F. Betico Croes 2, Kralendijk; tel. 717-3022; fax 717-3029; e-mail info.bonaire@nagico.com; internet www.nagico.com; Exec. Dir DETLEF HOOYBOER.

RSA Bonaire: Bonaire District Plaza, Unit 4, Kaya Gobernador Nicolaas Debrot, Kralendijk; tel. 717-8811; fax 717-2112; e-mail info@dc.myguardiangroup.com; internet myguardiangroup.cw; f. 1889; Group Pres. STEVEN MARTINA.

Trade and Industry

CHAMBER OF COMMERCE

Bonaire Chamber of Commerce and Industry: Kaya Grandi 67, POB 52, Kralendijk; tel. 717-5595; fax 717-8995; e-mail office@kvkbonaire.com; internet www.bonairechamber.com; Chair. MARICELLA CROES-ODUBER.

MAJOR COMPANIES

BOPEC (Bonaire Petroleum Corporation NV): Plantage Brasil, POB 117, Kralendijk; tel. 717-8177; fax 717-8266; e-mail bopec@bonairelive.com; oil terminal with storage capacity of 10.1m. barrels; bought by PDVSA (Venezuela) in 1989; Gen. Man. HUMBERTO NIEVES.

Cargill Salt Bonaire NV: Kralendijk; internet www.cargillsalt.com; salt production and export; has operated the Solar Salt Works since 1997 when Cargill Salt acquired the North American assets of Akzo Nobel Salt Inc; Man. JOHANNES MARINUS HENDRIKUS GIELEN.

Firgos Bonaire, NV: Kaya Tintorero 2, Kralendijk; tel. 717-4249; fax 717-7757; e-mail info@firgosbonaire.nl; internet www.firgosbonaire.nl; f. 2007; packaging material; Man. Dir ANDRE HENDRIKS GEERT.

Hidrofor Bonaire, NV: Kaya Amsterdam 27, POB 457, Kralendijk; tel. 717-2949; fax 717-5448; e-mail pools@bonairepools.com; internet www.bonairepools.com; f. 1997; pool construction; Man. Dir NICOLAAS WILHELMUS MOSTERT.

UTILITIES

Contour Global Bonaire: Kaminda Turistiko 1000, Postbus 281, Kralendijk; tel. 699-2802; e-mail caribbean.inquiry@contourglobal.com; internet www.ecopowerbonaire-bv.com; f. 2007 as EcoPower Bonaire BV; sustainable energy producer; acquired by ContourGlobal, LLC (USA) and changed name as above in May 2013; 24-MW integrated wind and diesel power plant; Plant Man. VINCENT KOOIJ.

Water & Energiebedrijf Bonaire (WEB) NV: Kaya Carlos A. Nicolaas 3, POB 381, Kralendijk; tel. 715-8244; fax 717-8756; e-mail web@webbonaire.com; internet webbonaire.com; f. 1978; Dir ALFREDO KOOLMAN.

TRADE UNIONS

Algemene Federatie van Bonaireaanse Werknemers (AFBW): Kaya Korona 13, Kralendijk; tel. 717-5437; Pres. NILCO ROLLAN.

Federashon Bonaireana di Trabou (FEDEBON): Kaya Krabè 6, POB 324, Nikiboko; tel. and fax 717-8845; e-mail geroldbernabela@bonairelive.com; Pres. GEROLD BERNABELA.

Transport

There are no railways, but Bonaire has a network of all-weather roads. There is public transportation on the island in the form of buses, mini-vans and taxis.

SHIPPING

There are no ferry services between Bonaire and neighbouring islands; however, there are chartered boats. The port of Kralendijk has piers for dry cargo transfer and cruise vessels. At 31 December 2013 the flag registered fleet comprised one vessel.

Bonaire Port Authority, NV: Fort Oranje, Harbour Office, Kralendijk; tel. 717-8151; fax 717-8797.

Rocargo Services Bonaire, NV: Kaya Industria No. 12, POB 20, Kralendijk; tel. 717-8922; fax 717-8524; e-mail rocargobonaire@rocargo.com; internet www.rocargo.com; f. 1982; ship and liner agency, cargo and freight handlers; Man. MARIELA GOELOE DORTALINA.

CIVIL AVIATION

Bonaire International Airport, NV (Flamingo Airport) at Kralendijk has a runway of 2,880 m (9,449 ft). Bonaire is served by numerous airlines (including Delta, KLM, Air Berlin and United Airlines), linking the island with destinations in the Caribbean, Europe, the USA and South America.

Bonaire International Airport, NV (Flamingo Airport): Plasa Medardo SV Thielman 1, Kralendijk; tel. 717-5600; fax 717-5607; e-mail info@flamingoairport.com; internet www.flamingoairport.com; f. 1945; Man. Dir GEORGE SOLIANA.

Tourism

Bonaire's attractions include scuba-diving and snorkelling facilities, flamingo and donkey sanctuaries, Bonaire National Marine Park, the historic rock paintings of Caquieto Indians and the white, sandy beaches. In 2012 visitor arrivals to the island by air totalled 82,000. In 2010 tourism receipts totalled an estimated US $121m.

Bonaire Hotel and Tourism Association (BONHATA): Kaya Soeur Bartola 15A, POB 358, Kralendijk; tel. 717-5134; fax 717-8534; e-mail info@bonhata.org; internet www.ilovebonaire.com; f. 1980; CEO IRENE DINGJAN.

Tourism Corporation Bonaire (TCB): Kaya Grandi 2, Kralendijk; tel. 717-8322; fax 717-8408; e-mail info@tourismbonaire.com; internet www.tourismbonaire.com; Dir ETHSEL PIETERNELLA.

Defence

The Netherlands is responsible for the defence of Bonaire.

Education

The education system is the same as that of the Netherlands. Dutch is the principal language of instruction, although instruction in Papiamento is also used in primary schools.

BRAZIL

Geography

PHYSICAL FEATURES

The Federative Republic of Brazil is the largest country in Latin America, occupying much of the east of South America. Nearly one-half of the continent is in Brazil. Its longest border is with Bolivia (3,400 km or 2,111 miles), which lies to the south-west, next to Paraguay (1,290 km of border). Brazil then thrusts southwards, between the Atlantic coast and an extension of Argentina (1,224 km) to the west, ending in a 985-km border with Uruguay to the south. In the north is the Guianan coast (from east to west, French Guiana—673 km, Suriname—597 km and Guyana—1,119 km) and then Venezuela (2,200 km). Colombia pushes south to form the northern part of the western border (1,643 km), in north-west Brazil, with Peru also lying to the west, beyond a 1,560-km frontier. Of all the South American territories, only Ecuador and Chile do not have borders with Brazil. Brazil has an uncontested territorial dispute with Uruguay over small river islands in the Quarai (Cuareim) and the Arroio Invernada (Arroyo de la Invernada). Somewhat smaller than the USA, Brazil covers an area of 8,514,877 sq km (3,287,611 sq miles), making it the fifth largest country in the world.

Brazil, which also includes a number of offshore islands and islets, has 7,491 km of coastline, formed where South America bulges eastwards and then begins to taper south. The Amazon enters the Atlantic on the north-eastern coast of South America, and the mouth of the river is complicated by many channels and islands (the largest is Marajó), as well as swamps, mangroves and flooding, features common until higher land begins in eastern Brazil. Here the north-eastern highlands make the coast more defined, smoother and drier, with stretches of dunes, although there are still occasional mangroves and lagoons beyond São Roque cape, where the eastern bulge of the continent turns south. To the south-west, beneath the south-eastern highlands, the shore is varied by sandy spits and beaches, as well as lagoons and marshes, but for 1,000 km beyond Rio de Janeiro, the coastal plains are reduced to occasional patches, as the highlands often come sheer to the sea. Most of the country's territory, however, is defined by political rather than natural borders, although in the north the Guianan highlands help establish the line. These forested heights cover only 2% of the country and are generally considered to be part of the Amazon basin, but they also include Brazil's highest mountain, Pico da Neblina (3,014 m or 9,892 ft), which lies in the north-west, on the border with southern Venezuela. The Amazon basin itself, which accounts for about one-third of the country, spreads across the north of Brazil, pushing it west, deeply into the heart of the continent. Brazil also shares the basin of the much smaller River Plate (Río de la Plata) system, in the south, while coastal plains constitute the only other area of lowland in the country. In the midst of these other features, and in marked contrast to the dense jungles of the Amazonian lowlands, are the open Brazilian highlands, an eroded plateau of jumbled mountain ranges and river valleys, running from the easternmost end of the country towards the south-west, generally just inland from the coast. However, once human and economic geography is taken into account, Brazil is usually described as consisting of five regions: the north (most of the Amazon basin and the Guianan highlands—45% of the territory, but only 8% of the population); the north-east (essentially the eastern bulge, the north-eastern end of the Brazilian highlands—the area first settled by Europeans and their African slaves—28% of the population); the south-east (the other, higher end of the highlands—11% of the territory, but 42% of the population); the south (the smallest region, temperate in climate, 14% of the population); and, finally, the landlocked centre-west, sparsely populated (7% of the population), but including the capital city, Brasília (this region is a transitional region, including the edges of the Amazonian plains to the north, the Brazilian highlands to the south and

east, and the upper lowlands of the River Plate basin in the west). All these vast territories include surprisingly little fertile land and, although the range of crops produced is wide, relatively small amounts of land are cultivated. Grasslands are used extensively for pasture.

The main lowland area of Brazil is the Amazon basin, which is flat, or gently rolling, seldom exceeding 150 m above sea level and covered in the largest rainforest in the world. The Amazon and its tributaries are prone to seasonal flooding, inundating the level, swampy areas known as *varzeas*. Similarly, the headwaters of the Paraná and Paraguay can flood the important wetlands of the Pantanal, where the hills of the Brazilian highlands yield to the plains of the River Plate basin (the Chaco spreads through Paraguay to the south). The Pantanal forms the western end of the centre-west region, dividing the Amazonian north from the south-eastern highlands. Finally, there are the coastal plains, extending for thousands of kilometres from the north-east to the border with Uruguay. Up to 60 km in width in the north-east, the coastal plains are negligible south of Rio de Janeiro, where the Serra do Mar form a sharp edge along the shore. The plains only broaden again in the far south, as they widen towards the Pampas and, inland, the Chaco.

The Brazilian highlands are a huge block of geologically ancient rocks, falling away to the north-east and north. In the south-eastern region of the country the highlands consist of a complex mass of ridges and ranges, some dropping steeply into the sea, and generally with elevations of around 1,200 m, although the highest summits reach about 2,800 m. The main ranges include the Serra do Mar and the Serra da Mantiqueira. Inland from the coastal ranges is a broad plateau, hills lowering themselves into the centre-west and towards the Amazonian lowlands. Likewise, the highlands fall away to the north-east, as they parallel the coast and form the solid core of the eastern bulge of South America. Here are low, rolling hills, with the semi-arid interior known as the Sertão. As mentioned above, the north side of the Amazon basin is defined by the highlands separating Brazil from the Guiana coast and from the drainage area of the Orinoco. Out of these highlands, but mainly from the Andes to the west, flow the main rivers of Brazil, which can be grouped in eight systems, together carrying about one-fifth of the world's running water. The Amazon itself is the second longest river in the world, after the Nile in Africa, at 6,516 km (most of it flowing through Brazil, but still navigable into Peru). However, some of its tributaries are mighty rivers in themselves, notably the Tocantins, which joins the Amazon from the south, near its mouth. The second river system is that of the south-draining Paraná, which empties into the Plate (between Uruguay and Argentina), draining much of the south, south-east and centre-west of Brazil. The principal river of the eastern plateau region is the São Francisco, which flows north through the highlands until it turns east into the Atlantic.

The vegetation of this varied landscape is diverse, ranging from tropical and temperate woodland, through savannah and often swampy grasslands, to semi-arid scrub. Many of the species sheltering in these environments are still unknown, although already threatened, particularly by deforestation, and also by mining and industrial pollution. Wooded areas account for 58% of Brazil's total, but it is the great jungle of the Amazon, the largest rainforest (despite massive and continuing encroachments) in the world, covering two-fifths of Brazil's territory, which dominates. The luxuriant vegetation hosts a massively varied array of ecosystems and a good proportion of the many species found in Brazil. There are almost 400 species of mammal found in Brazil—such as endangered jaguars, rare bush dogs, anteaters, deer (for instance, the endangered Pantanal deer), monkeys, and tapirs—but, more impressively perhaps, the country has among the most diverse populations of birds (more than 1,600 species) and amphibians (more than 500 species), as well as about 1,500 species of freshwater fish, of which more than two-thirds are found in the Amazon basin. There are over 100,000 invertebrate species, of which 70,000 are insects, although it should be noted that, given the scale, all these figures are estimates. Much of this wealth is threatened, the Amazon increasingly affected by deforestation since the 1970s (much of the eastern and southern uplands have already been denuded of their widest variety since 1500), although some 3.3m. sq km of rainforest remain. One tree species should be mentioned, as it gave the country its name—the pau brasil or brazilwood tree provided dyewood, the first commodity to be exported by Europeans from Brazil. Grasslands have also been economically exploited (pasture covers 22% of the country), with both savannah and rich wetlands used for ranching—in areas such as the Pantanal, the Sertão, the Cerrado (in the centre-west, where the rainforest yields to a more open and varied landscape of trees and bushes, as well as grassland) and the Campos of the far south.

CLIMATE

Over such a large area, the climate is obviously extremely varied. All but the extreme north (the Equator passes across the mouth of the Amazon) and the far south lies within the Tropic of Capricorn (which passes through São Paulo). Most of the country has annual average temperatures of over 22°C (72°F), but in the far south and in the high country it occasionally falls lower than this, with seasonal variations also more pronounced. Northern Brazil largely has a tropical wet climate, with much rainfall and virtually no dry season. Temperatures average 25°C (77°F), varying more between night and day than by time of year, and average rainfall is about 2,200 mm per year. It is oppressively humid in the Amazon. In central Brazil rainfall (1,600 mm annually) is more seasonal, typical for a savannah area (80% falls in summer, October–March). The interior north-east, or Sertão, is even more pronouncedly seasonal in its little rainfall (only 800 mm per year—almost all falling within only two or three months), although precipitation is very liable to fail completely, causing drought (temperatures are extremely hot, able to exceed 40°C–104°F). In the south-east the tropical climate is moderated by altitude, with winter temperatures averaging below 18°C (64°F) and annual rainfall at 1,400 mm (falling mainly in the summer). The south has a subtropical climate, verging on the temperate, with cool winters that can produce a few frosts and even some snow at higher elevations. Annual rainfall is 1,500 mm, fairly evenly spread throughout the year.

POPULATION

Brazil is the only lusophone country in the Western hemisphere, owing to the 1494 Treaty of Tordesillas, which modified a papal arbitration between Portugal and Spain of the previous year. Most of the 'New World' was accorded to Spain, but moving the original Line of Demarcation further west ensured that Portugal gained territory here too. By the 1777 Treaty of Ildefonso (confirming principles established in 1750), Portugal also gained vast territories west again of the 1494 Line. As a result, modern Brazil is a unique blending of Portuguese settlers and their forcibly imported African labour with native Amerindians and later waves of immigration (usually from Europe). There is also a noticeably more relaxed attitude to race in Brazil than in many countries, with the Portuguese joined by many other European settlers and the African slaves taken not only from West Africa (as in much of the Caribbean), but also from Congo, Angola and Mozambique. About 48% of the population are classed as white, according to the 2010 census, a further 43% identified as mixed race, and 8% as black. Less than 1% of the population were classed as indigenous. Portuguese, with some regional variation, is the most widely used as well as the official language, although German and Italian, for instance, are still used in parts of the south (English and French tend to be the main second languages of the educated). Local dialects have incorporated Amerindian and African words. There are still over 100 indigenous Amerindian languages, of which the main ones belong to the Tupí, Gê, Arawak, Carib (Garib) and Nambicuara groups. Caribs and Arawaks are the main peoples of the north, the Tupí-Guaraní of the east coast and the Amazon river valley, the Gê of eastern and southern Brazil, and the Pano in the west. Most Amerindians survive in the north and west. Virtually all groups, excluding the more remote tribes of the Amazon and more recent immigrants from non-Christian backgrounds, tend to be at least nominally Roman Catholic (65%), making Brazil the largest Roman Catholic country in the world. Christian adherence is sometimes supplemented by parallel belief systems. Some 22% of the population are classified as Evangelical Christian. A growing number of the urban middle class are also followers of Spiritism, while Afro-Brazilian blendings have produced religions such as Candomblé and Umbanda, relatively widespread in areas such as the north-east.

According to official estimates, the population was 201.0m. in mid-2013, making Brazil the second most populous country in the Americas after the USA. The social legacy of a plantation society means there is still much inequality and poverty, especially in the countryside, although after massive urban migration the rural population accounts for only about one-fifth of the total. One-fifth of Brazilians live in cities of over 1m., the largest being São Paulo, the biggest city in South America and the country's main industrial centre (an estimated 11.8m. according to official estimates in mid-2013. The second most populous city is the old capital (1763–1960), Rio de Janeiro, which remains an important port and the commercial centre of the country (6.4m. in 2013). Both cities were founded on the scant coastal plains of the south-east region, Rio de Janeiro further east up the coast. The cities, followed by Salvador (2.9m.) in the north-east and Brasília (2.8m.), are the most densely populated parts of the country. Brasília, the federal capital since 1960, was purposely located away from the coast (four-fifths of Brazilians live within 350 km of the sea) and from the crowded south-east, nearer the centre of the country. Fortaleza (formerly Ceará—2.6m.), also in the north-east, and Belo Horizonte (2.5m.), in Minas Gerais, to the north of Rio de Janeiro, all have populations of a similar size to that of the capital. Curitiba and Porto Alegre in the south, Recife (formerly Pernambuco) on the north-east coast, the great inland Amazonian city of Manaus, Belém, at the mouth of the river, Goiânia, to the south-west of Brasília, Campinhas, to the north-west of São Paulo, and São Gonçalo, all had populations over 1m. (Guarulhos, a suburb of São Paulo, is also classed as a separate city, and had 1.3m. people in mid-2013). Brazil is a federal country, consisting of 26 states and one Federal District (Distrito Federal).

History

DR FRANCISCO PANIZZA

Based on an earlier article by PROF. DAVID FLEISCHER

Brazil was Portugal's only American colony, and survived as a single unit after independence to become Latin America's only Portuguese-speaking nation. During the period of Portuguese colonial rule, millions of Africans were forcibly transported to Brazil to work as slaves. As a result of the flight of the Portuguese royal family to the colony in 1808, Brazil attained independence in 1822 under Prince Pedro, who became Emperor Pedro I of Brazil. The country remained a monarchy until 1889, when a republic was declared, one year after the abolition of slavery. A federalist Constitution was adopted in 1891. This First Republic became a decentralized, federal regime and endured until it was overthrown in 1930, in a revolution that brought Dr Getúlio Vargas to power. Vargas oversaw the introduction of a new and more centralized Constitution in 1934, but established a military-backed dictatorship in 1937 rather than retire from the presidency following elections due to be held in 1938. During his 15-year tenure of power, Vargas recentralized the political system, initiated state reforms, encouraged import substitution and developed the steel industry. Vargas's regime (the 'Estado Novo') lasted until 1945, when the military withdrew its support and forced Vargas from power.

THE RESTORATION OF DEMOCRACY

The restoration of democracy with the new Constitution of 1946 gave most Brazilians their first experience of political involvement and inaugurated nearly two decades of continuous but unstable party competition. The period was dominated by Vargas, now presenting himself, with some success, as a champion of the masses, and his heirs. They were grouped in the broadly conservative, rural-based Partido Social Democrático and the leftist and increasingly influential, urban-based Partido Trabalhista Brasileiro (PTB), and were opposed by the liberal União Democrática Nacional (UDN) and at times by the Partido Social Progressista. Vargas was elected to the presidency in 1950, but committed suicide in 1954, when the military demanded his resignation.

Over the next 10 years Brazil gradually declined into a state of acute political crisis. Industrialization proceeded rapidly under the presidency of Juscelino Kubitschek (1956–61), but the economic strains that were created, and the political tensions arising out of urbanization and swift social change proved too great for the fragile political system. As pressure mounted for social and structural reform, the UDN secured the presidency for the first time, through an independent, Jânio Quadros, at elections in October 1960. However, in January 1961 Quadros resigned, alleging lack of support from the bicameral legislature, the Congresso Nacional (National Congress), and the country was plunged into crisis. He was succeeded by the Vice-President, PTB leader João Goulart, after the military had forced the Congresso to change from a presidential to a parliamentary system, with Tancredo de Almeida Neves as Prime Minister.

Under pressure from the left to adopt a radical programme, Goulart at first hesitated but, after regaining presidential powers in a referendum held in January 1963, and lacking a majority in the Congresso Nacional, he moved to respond to such demands by decree. Before the ensuing radicalization was far advanced, the military intervened, seizing power on 1 April 1964. The military coup brought an end to two decades of fragile democracy, marked by a refusal on the part of the privileged élites to countenance any degree of social reform, and a general failure on the part of political parties to establish themselves as independent actors, rather than as clientelistic groupings reliant upon the patronage powers of the State.

MILITARY RULE AFTER 1964

The 21-year military regime was a curious hybrid, quite distinct from the military governments in Argentina, Chile, Peru and Uruguay. The armed forces concentrated power in their own hands, but kept the Congresso Nacional in session (except for an extended period in 1968–69 and briefly in 1977) while denying it autonomy, and held regular elections for the Congresso, state legislatures, and local mayors and city councils. Successive purges removed all but the most moderate opponents of the regime. The five military Presidents were vested with power to govern by decree, and the parties existing in 1964 were replaced by a two-party system in 1966, with pro-Government forces congregating in the majority Aliança Renovadora Nacional (ARENA) and the remaining opposition members grouped in the Movimento Democrático Brasileiro (MDB).

The dictatorship was at its most harsh between 1968 and 1974, particularly under Gen. Emílio Garrastazu Médici. The already highly authoritarian Constitution approved in 1967 was heavily amended in 1969 to strengthen further the power of the military executive, and the elections of 1970, held in conditions that made meaningful competition impossible, gave emphatic majorities to the government party. Throughout this period, the retention of a system of political parties, combined with a concentration of powers of decision in the military executive, pushed to extremes the tendency for the governing party to act as a clientelistic machine. In 1974 Gen. Ernesto Geisel (who held the presidency in 1974–79), relying on the appeal of limited liberalization and Brazil's burst of economic growth after a period of recession had ended in 1967, allowed more open elections. The electoral system protected the government majority, but the unexpected gains made by the MDB, particularly in the elections for one-third of the upper house of the Congresso Nacional, the Senado Federal (Federal Senate), may be seen in retrospect as marking the beginning of the long retreat of the military from power. Following the 1973 petroleum crisis, Brazil's economy stagnated, but the less restricted elections in November 1974 provided political legitimacy to, and bolstered support for, Geisel's regime.

From 1974 onwards the military lacked a natural majority in the country, but persisted in holding elections on schedule, seeking to maintain its hold on power by a series of expedient measures such as the indirect election (to all intents and purposes, the appointment) of one-third of the Senado Federal in 1978. This failed, however, to conceal either the military's unpopularity or its waning self-confidence. Geisel's successor, Gen. João Baptista de Figueiredo (1979–85), was the beneficiary of a decision to prolong the presidential mandate by one year, but it fell to him to oversee the departure of the military from power.

An attempt to regain the initiative by dissolving the two-party system in 1979 in a bid to divide the opposition and to halt the advance of the reorganized and increasingly effective MDB, failed in its objective. ARENA was shorn of some of its moderate elements and reconstituted as the Partido Democrático Social (PDS), while a number of new opposition parties appeared, led by the renamed Partido do Movimento Democrático Brasileiro (PMDB), which was reduced to half the strength of its predecessor, the MDB. Most prominent among the new parties were the Partido dos Trabalhadores (PT), led by Luiz Inácio Lula da Silva, a labour union organizer, and the Partido Democrático Trabalhista (PDT), led by Goulart's brother-in-law, Leonel de Moura Brizola.

THE WANING OF MILITARY AUTHORITY

By 1982, five years of social mobilization and protest, focused primarily on the factories and working-class communities of São Paulo, and co-ordinated as much by the Roman Catholic

Church as by the political parties and labour unions, had put the military on the defensive. The 1982 elections gave the governorships of the 10 leading states to the opposition (with direct gubernatorial elections for the first time since 1965) and would have given the combined opposition forces a majority in the lower house of the Congreso, the Câmara dos Deputados (Chamber of Deputies), had the PTB not formed a coalition with the PDS. In April 1984 a substantial vote by the Câmara in favour of introducing direct elections failed to gain the required two-thirds' majority. However, the military executive lost control of its own party, and the official nomination for its presidential candidate went to the civilian industrialist and financier Paulo Salim Maluf, former Governor of São Paulo. His aggressive style provoked a division of the government party and led, eventually, to the formation of the Partido da Frente Liberal (PFL). This grouping gave its support to the PMDB candidate, Tancredo Neves, and secured the vice-presidential candidacy for José Sarney, the erstwhile leader of the pro-Government PDS who had played an instrumental role in the creation of the PFL. As a result, the electoral college that was to elect the President became opposition-controlled. Lacking other options, the military accepted Neves' victory, achieved by a massive 300-vote majority in the 686-member college when voting took place on 15 January 1985. The transfer of power took place as scheduled on 15 March, but Neves, then 74 years old, required surgical treatment on the eve of his accession. As a result, José Sarney was sworn in as acting President. He assumed full presidential powers after Neves' death in April.

THE RETURN TO DEMOCRACY, 1985

Brazil returned to competitive liberal democracy in challenging circumstances. Economic growth was faltering as inflation spiralled far beyond the levels it had reached when the military intervened in 1964. Socially, the strains of rapid industrialization and urbanization over previous decades had been exacerbated by the sharp worsening of income distribution over the period of military rule, leading to growing malnutrition and absolute poverty in urban and rural areas alike. Amid a general recognition of the need for political and social reform and substantial economic redistribution, civilian politicians were under pressure to address a range of issues that had been neglected during the military period. Initial suspicion arising from Sarney's recent links with the armed forces limited his popular appeal, and his relations with the dominant PMDB proved to be difficult. However, he pledged to implement the programme that Neves had proposed, including the convocation of a National Constituent Assembly and the introduction of direct elections to the presidency, and he reached a peak of popularity in 1986, as a consequence of the temporary success of the Cruzado Plan, an anti-inflation, price and wage freeze programme announced in February. The election, in November, of the Congreso Nacional marked the first stage in the transition to the adoption of a new constitution and a full return to democracy; the election was also a zenith for the PMDB, which won 22 of the 23 state governorships and absolute majorities in both houses of the Congreso.

However, the apparent economic and political success of the transition to democracy proved short-lived. The key measures of the Cruzado Plan were abandoned immediately after the November 1986 elections, and it collapsed altogether in early 1987. Debates over the new constitution were dominated by rivalry between the President and the unicameral National Constituent Assembly, and conflict over the extent to which commitments to social reform should be written into the document. Part of the problem lay in the changed character of the once reformist PMDB. Since its establishment as the leading opposition force in the 1970s, it had attracted the support of conservatives who abandoned the PDS as the latter's prospects faded. Thus, by 1986 the PMDB was no longer a party committed to genuine reform. A new Constitution was finally promulgated in October 1988. It provided for a five-year presidential term and adopted a conservative stance, particularly with regard to land reform. The PMDB had split in June of that year, with many of its founders, including the political exile and São Paulo senator Fernando Henrique

Cardoso, joining a new social democratic party, the Partido da Social Democracia Brasileira (PSDB). Signs of a serious challenge from the left emerged in the municipal elections of November, at which da Silva's hitherto small PT gained control of the city of São Paulo, as well as 37 other major towns and cities across the country.

THE RISE AND FALL OF COLLOR DE MELLO

The first direct presidential election since 1960 was held on 15 November 1989. In the first round of voting Fernando Collor de Mello, leader of the tiny Partido de Reconstrução Nacional (PRN), took 30.5% of the valid votes cast, compared with da Silva's 17.2%. As the Constitution required an absolute majority, a second round of voting was held, just over one month later, at which Collor de Mello defeated da Silva, obtaining 53% of the votes.

President Collor de Mello introduced a radical reform programme aimed at reducing public sector employment, lowering government expenditure and liberalizing the economy. At the same time, in 1991, Brazil, in conjunction with Argentina, Paraguay and Uruguay, began to establish the free trade zone known as MERCOSUL (Mercado Comum do Sul, or, in Spanish, Mercado Común del Sur—MERCOSUR). However, the initial results of these reforms were disappointing, with a sharp recession in 1990 followed by a resumption of inflation in 1991. Collor de Mello found his popularity and congressional support dwindling, even after the poor performance of the left at legislative elections held in October 1990, where the PRN also achieved disappointing results.

President Collor de Mello's position deteriorated further in 1991 when he failed to persuade the PSDB and other congressional parties to support a new reform programme, and he resorted to governing by decree. The Câmara dos Deputados subsequently voted to bring forward a referendum on changing to a parliamentary system of government. However, Collor de Mello intervened and in December the Senado defeated the measure. After a series of corruption scandals emerged in early 1992, leading to a number of ministerial resignations, in May Collor de Mello's brother, Pedro, launched a national campaign against the President's campaign manager, Paulo César Farias. The ensuing succession of corruption scandals soon involved Collor de Mello himself and ultimately led to his downfall. The Câmara voted to commence impeachment proceedings against the President, who was suspended from office on 28 September. The Senado subsequently convicted Collor de Mello of 'political crimes' and he was impeached on 30 December. Vice-President Itamar Franco, who had been appointed acting President in September, was confirmed as President on the same day.

TRANSITION TO DEMOCRACY IN CRISIS, 1993–94

With the coming to power of Franco, the crisis surrounding the attempted transition to democracy deepened further. A number of serious problems, some with deep historical roots, made decisive action imperative, but Franco lacked both the necessary political experience and the organized political support that would have made effective government possible. Inflation continued to worsen and threatened to spiral entirely out of control. Economic growth also continued to falter, while levels of foreign investment dwindled as international confidence in the Brazilian economy declined further. On the political side, pressure was already mounting for reform of the 1988 Constitution, while public discontent with politicians in general brought the future of the transition into question. Most seriously, Brazil's political party system, chronically weak and prone to fragmentation throughout the republican period, appeared once again to be in terminal decline. No party was able to elect a President, to provide majority support in the Congreso Nacional for the resulting administration, nor to exert sufficient authority over powerful élites to achieve either economic stability or social reform.

Economic affairs were dominated by the effort to introduce a credible programme of economic adjustment backed by fiscal reforms. There was an urgent need to reduce inflation dramatically, restore growth, balance the budget and address the pressing problem of the steadily worsening distribution of income. The new Minister of Finance, Fernando Henrique Cardoso, therefore sought repeatedly, but largely unsuccessfully, to introduce a series of wide-ranging structural reforms to the fiscal system. By early 1994 he had succeeded in introducing a limited fiscal reform package, incorporating selected expenditure reductions and the establishment of a Social Emergency Fund.

THE PRESIDENTIAL ELECTION AND THE REAL PLAN, 1994

With the Government weak and the Congresso Nacional discredited, the immediate beneficiaries were the PT and da Silva, who emerged as the left wing's leading contender in the presidential election that was scheduled for October 1994. A consensus eventually emerged in the Government, with business and army circles favouring the candidacy of centrist Minister of Finance Cardoso. The final stages of the Franco presidency were dominated by the long-awaited programme of economic reform, the centrepiece of which was the introduction, on 1 July, of a new currency, the real, pegged to the US dollar. The initial impact of the measures, known as the Real Plan, appeared broadly positive as inflation was dramatically reduced and the real incomes of poorer groups increased. This proved a very powerful election instrument, and at the election, on 3 October, Cardoso secured the presidency without the need to proceed to a second ballot. PSDB governors were also elected in the important central states of São Paulo, Minas Gerais and Rio de Janeiro. The election of Cardoso and his allies appeared to demonstrate that Brazilian voters had opted for a path of continuity with moderate reform rather than radical change or conservative reaction.

CARDOSO'S FIRST TERM, 1995–98

When President Cardoso assumed office on 1 January 1995, he committed himself to a series of key constitutional reforms, aimed at accelerating the modernization of the economic and social fabric and overcoming the federal Government's fiscal crisis. The principal reforms envisaged were: a liberalization of the petroleum, electricity and telecommunications sectors; the permitting of foreign investment in mining and hydroelectric projects; reform of the civil service; a major overhaul of the social security system; fundamental alterations to the federal Government's taxation and budgetary regimes; and the achievement of a more even pattern of landholding in rural areas. Cardoso enjoyed some initial success with the approval, in early 1995, of constitutional changes terminating state monopolies and permitting foreign investment in the above-named sectors. In addition, the programme of economic liberalization was given impetus by the full implementation of the MERCOSUL free trade area on 1 January. Furthermore, in December Brazil signed an agreement to establish a Free Trade Area of the Americas (FTAA). However, the reform programme encountered a number of obstacles during 1996 and 1997. In particular, the Government struggled to exercise control over the budget deficit. The constitutionally mandated transfers of funds between the federal Government and the state and municipal governments led to a weakening of the former's fiscal position as expenditures expanded. Slow progress in the reform of the civil service and the social security system meant that other major items of expenditure could not be reduced in compensation. The lack of progress in the reform of the landholding system resulted in a growing number of confrontations between landless peasants, represented by the Movimento dos Trabalhadores Rurais Sem Terra (MST), and landowners. The impasse in the reform programme was exacerbated by divisions between the two main parties of the coalition: President Cardoso's social democratic PSDB and the conservative PFL.

Although fiscal, social security and administrative reforms remained delayed, considerably more progress was made with the privatization and economic liberalization programmes. In 1996 steps were taken towards the sale of the Brazilian electricity network, Centrais Elétricas Brasileiras, SA (Eletrobras). The transfers to private ownership of the federal rail network, Rede Ferroviária Federal, SA, and the huge mining group Companhia Vale do Rio Doce, SA were completed in the following year. From 1997 onwards a series of other major privatizations occurred, many in the energy sector. By far the most significant privatization to date, however, was implemented in the telecommunications sector with the sale of the subsidiaries of Telecomunicações Brasileiras, SA in July 1998. The Government also accelerated its attempts to privatize the state banking sector in the late 1990s. In August 1997 legislation was implemented enabling the liberalization of the petroleum sector. In a radical departure, the new regulatory framework for the sector allowed the participation of foreign enterprises in the exploration for petroleum within Brazil, thus ending the monopoly status that the state-owned Petróleo Brasileiro, SA (Petrobras) had enjoyed since its foundation in 1953.

Despite these achievements in economic policy, lack of progress on constitutional reform left unaddressed a series of lingering macroeconomic problems. In particular, the Brazilian economy remained unable to escape from its tendency to accumulate heavy internal and external deficits. The persistence of these deficits became an increasing source of concern to international investors in 1997, and serious doubts were expressed in international financial markets as to the ability of the Brazilian Government to avoid a rapid, unplanned devaluation of the real. In order to maintain the valuation of the currency and avoid a resurgence of inflation, President Cardoso introduced a series of emergency measures intended to lower the budget deficit in November. In underlining the need for further progress on structural reform, the crisis induced notable advances in the passage of important legislation through the Câmara dos Deputados. In January 1998 crucial social security reforms were successfully enacted, while the Government's civil service reforms were finally approved in March. However, the international financial climate deteriorated in mid-1998, and investors began to withdraw resources from Brazil in ever-increasing quantities, causing a sharp decline in international reserves and testing the Government's ability to defend the value of the real.

By September 1998 Brazil was experiencing a period of economic crisis in which the sustainability of the Real Plan seemed increasingly in doubt. Nevertheless, at the presidential election held in October Cardoso became the first President to be re-elected for a consecutive term in office, securing 53% of the valid votes cast, compared with 32% for his closest rival, da Silva. The results of the legislative and gubernatorial elections, however, were not as favourable for Cardoso's PSDB. Although the governing coalition in the Câmara dos Deputados secured 377 of the 513 seats, the PSDB's 99 seats did not constitute a significant increase in the party's overall legislative representation. The election of populist, anti-Cardoso state governors in Minas Gerais, Rio de Janeiro and Rio Grande do Sul provided focal points for increasingly vocal regional opposition to the federal Government.

CARDOSO'S SECOND TERM, 1998–2002

Despite the generally favourable domestic and international reaction to Cardoso's re-election, Brazil's economic situation continued to deteriorate in late 1998. In November a US $41,000m. agreement was concluded with the IMF, imposing stronger fiscal austerity on Brazil. In December the Câmara dos Deputados voted to reject a significant government fiscal reform measure affecting public-employee pension contributions. The failure of this legislation increased concerns over the Government's ability to meet IMF targets and led to further outflows of foreign capital. By January 1999 it became apparent that the fixed exchange-rate policy pursued by the Government was becoming untenable. Faced with the imminent prospect of a complete depletion of foreign exchange reserves, on 13 January the Central Bank announced that the real was to float freely against the US dollar. Following the flotation, the real swiftly depreciated.

While the devaluation of the real did not affect the economy as severely as had been predicted, it did have the effect of galvanizing congressional opinion in favour of accelerating the fiscal and structural reform programme. In an important measure designed to reduce the recurrent deficits of the social security system, the Congresso Nacional finally approved the Fator Previdenciário in November 1999, which created a greater correspondence between social security contributions and pension payments in the private sector. Furthermore, in April 2000 legislation on fiscal responsibility was approved by the Senado, establishing stricter regulations for the setting of state and municipal budgets. However, the Cardoso Government remained frustrated in its attempts to introduce comprehensive taxation reform.

Left-wing opposition parties performed well in the municipal elections of October 2000, in advance of the presidential election of 2002. Furthermore, throughout 2000 and 2001 the Government and Congresso Nacional were embroiled in an extensive scandal involving allegations of embezzlement and corruption at senior levels. In November 2000 a congressional investigating committee published a report on organized drugs-trafficking and crime in Brazil, implicating a number of state deputies and mayors, as well as members of the Congresso Nacional, prosecutors, police, the judiciary and the armed forces. The ongoing corruption controversy and the departure in May 2001 of the President of the Senado, Antônio Carlos Magalhães, amid allegations of impropriety both acted to stall the Government's ambitious legislative programme and to taint the Government's hard-won reputation for competent economic management.

In the months preceding the October 2002 presidential election President Cardoso's coalition found itself in severe difficulties. Its most cohesive party, the PFL, had withdrawn from the governing coalition in March, the support of the PMDB was doubtful, and the PTB had declared its support for the candidacy of Ciro Gomes of the Partido Progressista Socialista (PPS). Nevertheless, Cardoso attempted to mobilize support for the PSDB candidate, José Serra, and succeeded in persuading the PMDB to enter into a formal alliance with the PSDB. By April Serra had emerged as second favourite in the presidential contest, behind the PT's da Silva. However, following press revelations in May regarding a number of scandals dating back to the mid- and late 1990s, the PSDB candidate's popularity decreased significantly. In the same month it also became apparent to international financial markets that Brazil's macroeconomic situation was deteriorating, and analysts questioned Brazil's capacity to honour its large debt. Amid insinuations that Brazil was in danger of suffering the economic crisis recently experienced by Argentina were an 'incompetent' President and economic team to be elected, da Silva's popularity rating also fell. The concerns by the international financial community regarding an imminent da Silva victory had a considerable negative impact on Brazil in mid-2002. Banks sharply reduced short-term trade credits, Brazil's risk evaluation soared, the real devalued strongly against the US dollar, and international reserves dwindled. As in 1998, the Cardoso Government again sought IMF assistance and quickly concluded a new 15-month agreement, worth US \$30,000m., in August 2002. In an attempt to allay fears, the PT's campaign platform took a sharp turn to the centre and attracted the support of several prominent business leaders.

The elections of October 2002 produced a decisive victory for the left. In the presidential contest da Silva nearly achieved an absolute majority (46.4%) in the first round, held on 6 October. Gomes, and Antônio Garotinho of the Partido Socialista Brasileiro (PSB), supported da Silva in the 27 October run-off, in which the PT candidate defeated Serra by an unprecedented margin, attracting 61.3% of the valid votes cast. In elections to the Congresso Nacional, the pro-da Silva parties elected 218 deputies and 31 senators, a considerable increase over 1998, but still fewer than the respective 257- and 41-member absolute majorities. The PT returned the largest delegation in the Câmara dos Deputados, with 91 federal deputies.

THE PT IN POWER

Lula da Silva was sworn in as President on 2 January 2003, and the new Congresso Nacional took office on 1 February. Da Silva's Cabinet was recruited from his electoral coalition, with a heavy concentration of PT militants, along with representatives from other allied parties. However, two prominent business leaders were also appointed. Many had feared that the

policy initiatives of the new da Silva Government would be impeded in the Congresso by a lack of majorities. However, the new President's team (led by Cabinet Chief José Dirceu) adroitly used the same power mechanisms (federal appointments and disbursements) as Cardoso to consolidate absolute majorities.

The new Minister of Finance, Antônio Palocci, and his economic team unequivocally pursued a fiscal austerity programme even more rigorous than that of the previous Government. This approach won enthusiastic approval from the IMF, and in the first five months of 2003 the trade surplus, tax collections and foreign direct investment all increased significantly, while the current account deficit decreased. Brazil's risk evaluation improved significantly.

On assuming office, the PT Government faced the problem of high deficits in a stagnating economy with low inflation. Thus, the da Silva Government's two key priorities were social security and tax reforms. However, da Silva's proposals to reform the deficit-ridden social security system were deemed 'heresy' by PT radicals. A first round vote on social security reform in August 2003 was only narrowly approved by the lower house, while a separate vote on the introduction of an 11% levy on public servants' pensions was adopted only with votes from opposition deputies. None the less, in September a more cohesive government coalition was able to approve the tax reform in the lower house without help from the opposition. In December the Senado finally ratified the two reforms.

In January 2004 da Silva effected a cabinet reorganization, in which representatives of the PMDB were appointed to the Government in an attempt to boost support for his administration. However, in February a videotape exposed allegedly corrupt campaign finance dealings in May 2002 by his congressional relations chief, Waldomiro Diniz. In April 2004 the Partido Liberal's (PL) three senators withdrew their support for the ruling coalition, thus reducing the Government's majority in the Senado to just three seats.

A four-month recess of the Congresso Nacional due to municipal elections delayed the Government's reform agenda in the second half of 2004. However, in early 2005 the Congresso approved protracted judicial reforms that established external control councils for the judiciary and public prosecutors. The Government was weakened in February after the PT lost the presidency of the Câmara dos Deputados. Severino Cavalcanti of the Partido Progressista (PP) was elected to head the lower house. Although the PP was part of the pro-Government bloc in the Câmara, Cavalcanti pursued an independent strategy as President of the chamber and, as a result, the Government's legislative agenda encountered obstacles.

In May 2005 several cases of government corruption were revealed by federal police investigations, and a major scandal erupted in early June. A videotape emerged that allegedly proved that a bribes-for-contracts scheme was in operation at the state postal service, the Empresa Brasileira de Correios e Telégrafos. A senior postal service employee claimed on the tape that the scheme was operated by PTB appointees, organized by Roberto Jefferson Monteiro, the party's national president. A similar scheme was subsequently revealed to be in operation at the state-owned reinsurance institution, the IRB-Brasil Resseguros. Jefferson denied the allegations and, in turn, publicly accused the PT of operating a bribery scheme in 2003–04, whereby PL and PP deputies received a monthly allowance (*mensalão*) for voting in support of government-sponsored legislation. Testifying before the Câmara dos Deputados's ethics council (Conselho de Ética e Decoro Parlamentar), Jefferson repeated his earlier accusation that President da Silva's Cabinet Chief, José Dirceu, had organized the bribery scheme. As a result, Dirceu resigned from the Government and was replaced by Dilma Vana Rousseff, hitherto Minister of Mines and Energy. The PT's Secretary-General, President and Treasurer also resigned their posts in July after being implicated in the scandal. Meanwhile, in late May the Congresso Nacional instituted a committee to investigate the accusations relating to the postal service and, following Jefferson's testimony, into the *mensalão* allegations. In June Jefferson took a leave of absence from the PTB presidency while the investigations continued.

In September 2005 the three congressional investigating committees (CPIs—Comissões Parlamentares de Inquéritos) dealing with the *mensalão* scandal proposed that 19 deputies be expelled from the Congresso Nacional. Following the further discovery that PT officials had signed dubious loan contracts with two banks to disguise the *mensalão* operations, they too were forced to resign. The PT's refusal to reform its institutions inflicted considerable damage on the party's image.

THE 2006 ELECTIONS

Not surprisingly, the CPIs had a negative impact on President da Silva's poll ratings in late 2005. However, by early 2006 da Silva's approval ratings had improved considerably through a combination of circumstance and a series of popular measures: rates of inflation, unemployment and interest had all decreased, and special consigned credit loans had been introduced, as well as a substantial increase in the minimum wage. Furthermore, the Bolsa Família (Family Allowance) programme met with considerable success, benefiting some 11m. poor families. In September, however, the Government was again implicated in a scandal after the federal police arrested a group of PT militants at a São Paulo hotel. The party members had suitcases filled with R $1.7m. in cash and were allegedly negotiating the purchase of a damaging dossier from the perpetrators of a scandal in which federal health officials in 2003 had accepted bribes in return for buying ambulances and other emergency equipment at inflated prices. Eight PT militants were involved, some with close ties to the President and others holding federal government posts.

At the first round presidential ballot, held on 1 October 2006, President da Silva received 48.6% of the valid votes cast, just short of an absolute majority. Da Silva's failure to secure a second term without need for a second ballot was attributed to the so-called 'dossier scandal' in the previous month. Da Silva's closest rival, the PSDB's candidate, São Paulo Governor Geraldo Alckmin, received 41.6% of the ballot. At the run-off poll, held on 29 October, Alckmin was unable to close the gap, garnering 39.2% of the valid votes, compared with the 60.8% attracted by the incumbent President. In concurrent elections to the Senado, in which 27 seats (one per state) were contested, the PFL elected six senators, the PSDB five, the PMDB four and the PT only two. As a result, the PFL counted 18 senators in total and was thus expected to select the new Senado President. The PMDB had 15 senators but, through several senators switching party allegiance, its representation had increased to 20 senators by February 2007, when the Câmara and Senado were scheduled to elect their new presiding officers. As a result, the PMDB re-elected Senator Renan Calheiros (a staunch ally of the President) to lead the upper house.

In the concurrent lower house elections, the PT returned 83 deputies and became the second largest party, behind the PMDB with 89 deputies. By tradition, the largest party in the legislature selected the new Câmara President; however, the PMDB agreed to support the PT candidate, Arlindo Chinaglia, in return for the PT's support of the PMDB candidate in the Senado. It was also agreed that in 2009 the reverse would occur: the PT would elect the Senado President and the PMDB the Câmara President. Following considerable political manoeuvring, the pro-da Silva coalition in the Câmara constructed an 11-party alliance that was equivalent to 70% of the chamber.

DA SILVA'S SECOND TERM

President da Silva's new Government was not fully constituted until late March 2007, as the President had to take into consideration the demands of the 11 coalition parties in the allocation of posts. The cabinet quota of the PT was reduced to accommodate the PMDB and other coalition partners, much to the displeasure of party members. Early in his second term, President da Silva changed the armed forces commandants. The new Chief of Staff of the Air Force, Brig.-Gen. Juniti Saito, faced an almost immediate institutional crisis: a national air travel 'blackout' provoked by flight controllers who were dissatisfied with their working conditions and who demanded 'demilitarization' of their sector (80% of air traffic controllers

were non-commissioned officers in the air force). In May the Senado and Câmara installed CPIs to investigate the issues surrounding the crash of an aeroplane in northern Mato Grosso, in September 2006, which killed all 154 people on board. Flight controllers were accused of causing the disaster. A further aeroplane crash, at São Paulo's Congonhas airport in July 2007, killed almost 200 people and increased pressure on the Government to reform the aviation sector. Following the second disaster Minister of Defence Waldir Pires was dismissed from his post and was succeeded by Nelson Jobim, a former Minister of Justice, who moved quickly to force the replacement of the directorate of the Agência Nacional de Aviação Civil (National Civil Aviation Agency).

Meanwhile, in February 2007 the Higher Electoral Court (Tribunal Superior Eleitoral—TSE) rendered an important interpretation of election and party legislation: that the mandate of those elected under proportional representation belonged to the party and not to the individual deputy. Thus, when a deputy changed parties, he or she would lose the seat and be replaced by the next alternate on that party's list. By late March 37 deputies had changed parties since their election in October 2006. Three opposition parties (the PFL, PSDB and PPS) had lost 22 deputies to the pro-Government coalition parties and immediately sought redress in the Supremo Tribunal Federal (Supreme Federal Court) to restore their lost seats. In October the Supreme Court confirmed the TSE resolution, and the TSE began receiving cases from the state election courts requesting the replacement of elected officials who had changed parties after the February adjudication.

In April 2007 the federal police began a sequence of operations against alleged corruption within the judiciary and executive. In May a major operation led to the arrests of 46 people suspected of involvement in a scandal whereby a construction firm, Guatama Construtora, was alleged to have bribed federal and state government officials in order to secure procurement contracts. Several governors and former governors were implicated, and in late May the Minister of Mines and Energy, Silas Rondeau, was forced to resign. In June the federal police launched an operation against illegal organized gambling operations in nine states. As in the *mensalão* affair in 2005 and the 'dossier scandal' in September 2006, several people from the PT and close to the President were implicated. However, the scandals were not confined to the PT: in May 2007 the powerful PMDB Senado President, Renan Calheiros, was accused of allowing a lobbyist for a construction company to make child-support payments for his illegitimate child. Although Calheiros protested his innocence, the case threatened to weaken the PT-PMDB alliance. Federal police and auditors subsequently identified a scheme of false sales receipts and other discrepancies relating to Calheiros's attempts to justify the lobbyist's expenditure. The Senado's ethics council investigated Calheiros on five counts and recommended his expulsion from the Senado. However, he refused to take a leave of absence from the Senado presidency and used his office to favour his defence. In September the Senado voted not to expel Calheiros, although in the following month he took a 45-day leave of absence. Finally, in December Calheiros resigned the presidency of the Senado, and later on the same day the upper house again voted not to expel him. This long-running episode prevented the Congresso Nacional from approving any major legislation during the latter half of 2007. Meanwhile, in August the Supreme Court indicted 40 people, including a number of deputies, implicated in the *mensalão* scandal of 2005.

During da Silva's first term many development projects, especially new hydroelectric installations, were delayed or thwarted owing to the refusal of the Brazilian Institute of Environment and Renewable Natural Resources (Instituto Brasileiro do Meio Ambiente e dos Recursos Naturais Renováveis—IBAMA) to grant the projects environmental impact licences. The President became frustrated by these impediments to economic growth, and in April 2007 dismissed most of the leadership in the Ministry of the Environment and transferred the conservation responsibilities of IBAMA to a new body. Da Silva subsequently recruited expert technicians from the World Bank and the Inter-American Development Bank to elaborate the impact licences for two new hydroelectric plants on the Madeira River. The concessions to construct the plants were subsequently awarded in December 2007 and May 2008, respectively. Also in May 2008 the Minister of the Environment, Marina Silva, resigned and returned to her seat in the Senado. Silva had opposed a number of President da Silva's policies, including the hydroelectric schemes and other plans for development of the Amazon region, on environmental grounds.

Meanwhile, in December 2007 the opposition in the Senado was able to defeat a constitutional amendment to renew the Contribuição Provisória Sobre Movimentação Financeira (CPMF), a tax of 0.38% on financial transactions that had been introduced in 1993 under President Franco and that raised some R $40,000m. a year in federal revenues. In June 2008, however, the Câmara dos Deputados approved the creation of the Contribuição Social para a Saude, a 0.1% tax on financial transactions for the sole purpose of funding health care. In spite of the loss of the CPMF, federal revenues increased in 2008.

Municipal elections held in October 2008 resulted in gains for both the PMDB (which won the greatest number of votes and of mayoralties) and the PT, and a decline in the share of the vote for the PSDB and the Democratas (DEM—as the PFL had been renamed in 2007). However, the PT suffered a defeat in the high-profile contest for Mayor of São Paulo, where its candidate failed to unseat the incumbent Gilberto Kassab of the DEM.

In 2009 some of President da Silva's supporters began a movement to amend the Constitution in order to allow the President to serve for a third consecutive term. Da Silva rejected the move and started instead to promote his Cabinet Chief, Dilma Rousseff, as his chosen successor. Although constitutionally barred from engaging in electoral politics, President da Silva toured the country with Rousseff, inaugurating public works financed by the Government's successful Growth Acceleration Programme (Programa de Aceleração do Crecimento—PAC). During these events, the President introduced Rousseff as 'the mother of the PAC'. In June 2010 Rousseff was confirmed as the PT's nominee for head of state.

THE 2010 ELECTIONS

Presidential, congressional and state elections took place on 3 October 2010. As no presidential candidate received more than one-half of the vote in the first round, a run-off ballot was held on 31 October in which the PT's candidate, Dilma Rousseff, defeated the candidate for the centre-right PSDB, José Serra, by 56% to 44% of the valid votes cast. The result constituted the third consecutive electoral victory for the PT, thus confirming the party's dominant position in Brazilian politics. Rousseff, a relative unknown in Brazilian politics at the start of the electoral campaign, owed her victory to da Silva's extraordinary popularity (he left office with an approval rating of over 80%) and to a buoyant economy that had lifted millions of Brazilians out of poverty and expanded the middle classes. Rousseff had campaigned on the record of da Silva's administrations and had also warned that a victory for Serra would put the Government's popular social programmes, such as the Bolsa Família, under threat. During the electoral campaign there was, however, relatively very little that had separated the two leading candidates in terms of economic policy. They were both committed to maintaining macroeconomic stability and a broadly orthodox, market-friendly, economic model combined with redistributive social policies, although Rousseff favoured a more activist state and a bigger role for state enterprises, particularly in sectors such as banking and petroleum and gas production.

The congressional elections saw the PT becoming the party with the largest representation in the 513-member Câmara dos Deputados, with 88 seats. However, despite increasing its share of the vote, the party fell far short of securing a majority of its own in the lower house, which is extremely hard to achieve given Brazil's proportional representation electoral system and its highly fragmented party system. None the less, the 10 parties that together formed the broad centre-left governing coalition controlled 373 of the Câmara seats, thus

giving Rousseff a large working majority. The PSDB-headed opposition secured just 96 of the seats in the lower house, its lowest share in 16 years. The PT also increased its representation in the Senado (where 54 of the 81 seats were contested), to 15 seats, while the PMDB retained the most upper house seats, with 20; following the elections, other allied parties held an additional 19 seats, including the Partido da República, the PP and the PDT, with four each, and the PSB, with three. The PSDB was represented by 11 senators, and the DEM and the PTB by six each. However, the opposition parties performed better in the state elections; the PSDB won eight governorships and its ally in opposition, the DEM, a further two, including the governorships in the key states of São Paulo and Minas Gerais.

THE ROUSSEFF ADMINISTRATION

Rousseff came to office with a reputation as a highly competent state manager and this was soon put to the test. In January 2011, just days after Rousseff's inauguration, Brazil suffered catastrophic floods in the states of São Paulo and Rio de Janeiro that left more than 1,000 people dead and around 25,000 homeless. President Rousseff's decisive reactions to the natural disaster, including the approval of R $780m. (US $466m.) in emergency funds, the engagement of the armed forces in the relief effort, and her commitment to address the country's estimated housing deficit of around 5.8m. units, gained her strong praise from across the political spectrum.

Nevertheless, Rousseff's popularity did not easily translate into congressional support. Although her 16-party coalition held a nominal 80% of the seats in the Congresso, ideological differences and the unwieldy nature of the country's political parties made it difficult to rely on party discipline to get legislation approved by the legislature. Instead, governments traditionally relied on the distribution among coalition parties of ministerial posts and other public sector positions to secure their support. However, the various parties in the governing coalition complained that Rousseff had not given them enough positions in the administration and that communications between the Government and its parliamentary support base were poor. Discontent within the coalition made it difficult for the Rousseff administration to gain sufficient support for legislation regarded as controversial or impinging upon powerful vested interests. The Government had some limited successes, most notably the approval of a public sector pensions reform bill, which reduced the state's future pension liabilities, and the adoption of legislation establishing the legal framework for hosting the 2014 Fédération Internationale de Football Association (FIFA) World Cup tournament. However, Rousseff was forced to veto several dispositions of a controversial new forestry code that significantly weakened environmental protection in the Amazon rainforest. More broadly, the Government was reluctant to risk defeat by sending to the Congresso much-needed labour, taxation and political reforms.

After increasing at an average annual rate of 4.5% between 2004 and 2010, economic growth decelerated during Rousseff's administration: the economy expanded by 2.7% in 2011 and by just 0.9% in 2012. Growth increased to 2.3% in 2013, but this figure was well below expectations and was lower than that of the most dynamic Latin American economies and of other regions' emerging economies. The Central Bank projected growth of just 1.6% in 2014. Only Argentina and Venezuela were expected to expand less than Brazil in that year. Low economic growth was a reflection of the long-term bottlenecks in the Brazilian economy associated with relatively low levels of investment, inflated and inefficient public spending, high labour and social security costs, wage and social security indexation, low labour productivity, and poor infrastructure. Further issues undermining the economy included a softening of Chinese demand for Brazilian commodities, weaker labour market conditions, a tightening of monetary policy and relatively high inflation, which was affecting household consumption. In order to secure sustainable development beyond the current commodity boom, the Government will need to proceed with structural reforms, particularly those regarding tax, labour and the state that had stalled during da Silva's second term in office and Rousseff's first term.

Confronted by a deteriorating economic situation, the Government implemented a series of fiscal and credit measures during 2012, including the reduction or elimination of various taxes and measures to boost industrial output, enhance competitiveness and reduce production costs. In a further step towards economic protectionism, the authorities announced that they would prioritize government purchases of nationally produced medicines and construction equipment to stimulate domestic production. However, these measures largely failed to produce the desired outcome. In a further attempt to boost economic growth, the Government announced in June 2014 that it was extending tax breaks for the automobile and furniture industries until the end of the year. The six-month extension marked a change in policy for the Government, which had previously declared that it would end the tax breaks in order to increase fiscal revenue. It was estimated that the extension would cost the state almost R $1,000m. in lost revenue.

While failing to stimulate the economy, higher public spending and lower interest rates, together with above-inflation rises in the minimum wage and other social security payments, had the effect of increasing the fiscal deficit. Public finances deteriorated under the Rousseff administration, leading the credit ratings agency Standard & Poor's to downgrade the country's sovereign debt rating in March 2014 to the bottom rung of the investment grade. At the equivalent of 1.9% of gross domestic product (GDP), the public sector primary surplus (the balance before debt interest payments) in 2013 was well below the target of 2.3% of GDP. The Government announced a reduction of R $44,000m. (US $18,700m.) in expenditure in the 2014 budget in an attempt to meet a planned surplus target of 1.9% of GDP. However, high spending during this election year was making the target difficult to meet, and the Government was unlikely to undertake any significant economic adjustment before the presidential poll in October. With more than 80% of government spending allocated by law, reducing public expenditure was a significant challenge. Moreover, the urgency and importance of a fiscal adjustment to constrain inflation needed to be balanced against the requirement for investment in infrastructure, public security, health and education, all of which required substantial improvement. Inflation was recorded at 6.4% in May 2014, well above the Central Bank's target of 4.5%. In an effort to curb rising prices, in 2013 the Central Bank reversed the interest rate reductions of 2011 and 2012 and raised the SELIC (Sistema Especial de Liquidação e Custódia) benchmark interest rate to 11%. While inflation was forecast to ease in the second half of 2014, high indexation, a tight labour market and elevated food prices were expected to contribute to an inflation rate above the 4.5% target in 2014–15. The current account deficit, meanwhile, increased substantially in 2013, to 3.6% of GDP, and was expected to remain at about the same level in 2014. The widening of the deficit was due to a decline in the trade balance surplus, high spending by Brazilians travelling abroad and the repatriation of profits by multinational corporations. The deficit in the current account was expected to be covered by foreign direct investment, which was projected to reach US $63,000m. in 2014.

One of President Rousseff's stated priorities on assuming office was the elimination of absolute poverty. In June 2011 she announced an expansion of the Government's highly popular social programmes, including the flagship Bolsa Família conditional cash transfer programme. Rousseff's social programme, Brasil Sem Miséria (Brazil Without Misery), aimed to focus on the 16.2m. Brazilians who continued to live in extreme poverty and was forecast to cost an annual R $20,000m. (US $13,000m.) over a four-year period. In May 2012 Rousseff announced that low-income families with at least one child under the age of six, already recipients of the Bolsa Família, would receive an additional monthly payment of R $70 (US $35). The President proclaimed that the new scheme would benefit 18m. people, mostly in the impoverished north-east of the country. In April 2014 Rousseff signed a decree increasing the income tax threshold by 4.55% and raising the Bolsa Família stipend by 10%. Rousseff also pledged to continue to implement above-inflation increases in the minimum wage, arguing that this policy had assisted millions of workers and had bolstered domestic demand. Increases in social security payments and the minimum wage had indeed benefited the poor and contributed to a reduction in income inequality in one of the world's most unequal societies. However, if economic growth continued to falter and inflation to rise, it would be difficult to maintain the upward trend in salaries, social security payments and household incomes that had boosted domestic consumption and the President's popularity.

Meanwhile, during 2012 a total of 25 senior PT officials and former government ministers were found guilty of involvement with the *mensalão* vote-buying scheme, tied to the administration of former President Lula da Silva. Among those convicted was José Dirceu, da Silva's Chief of Staff from 2003 to 2005. The trial, however, appeared not to have a significant effect on support for the ruling coalition in the municipal elections of October 2012 in which the PT and its ally, the PMDB, won the third largest and the largest number of cities, respectively, including the mayorship of São Paulo.

The Government was taken off guard by a wave of mass social protests in June 2013. The demonstrations began as small-scale protests over relatively modest rises in public transport fares in São Paulo and other Brazilian cities but soon morphed into mass anti-establishment demonstrations in cities across the country. The protests were about a wide range of issues. Prominent among these were political corruption, the costs of hosting the FIFA World Cup in 2014 and a lack of investment in health and education. Most of the protests were peaceful, but there were some sporadic episodes of looting and violence, and the disproportionately harsh response of the police was criticized. Reacting to the protests, President Rousseff asserted that she was listening to the voices from the street and that Brazil was ready to move forward. In a televised address to state governors and mayors on 24 June 2013, she proposed 'five pacts with the people'. These included tougher penalties for corruption, a referendum to convene a constituent assembly to consider political reform, and investment of R $50,000m. (US $25,000m.) in public transport. She also reaffirmed a previous commitment to invest oil royalties in education and recruit foreign doctors to improve the public health system. However, the President's pledges only partially defused popular discontent, as street protests continued, albeit at a lower level of intensity, in the first half of 2014. Embarrassingly, Rousseff was heckled by spectators during the opening ceremony for the FIFA World Cup in São Paulo in June.

In June 2014 the PT officially nominated Rousseff as the party's candidate for the October presidential election. Despite a decline in her popularity resulting from the social unrest and the deteriorating economy, Rousseff remained a strong favourite to win a second term. By July opinion polls placed her comfortably ahead of her main rivals. It was not clear, however, whether she would have enough votes to win in the first round. While questions could be raised about the long-term sustainability of Brazil's economic model—based on high public spending, rising wages and social security payments, and the availability of cheap credit to stimulate internal demand—the Government's policies had lifted millions of Brazilians out of poverty and created a new lower middle class. During the electoral campaign Rousseff accused her presidential rivals of seeking to reverse the social gains that had been achieved after 12 years of PT rule. Rousseff's candidacy was backed by a broad coalition of parties that extended across the left–right ideological divide and ensured the President the support of a majority of the candidates for state governors. Moreover, Rousseff enjoyed a considerable advantage over her presidential opponents since television campaign time was allocated in proportion to the number of seats controlled by each party in the Congresso. Rousseff's main rivals were senator Aécio Neves of the centrist PSDB and Eduardo Campos of the centre-left PSB. However, Campos was killed in a aeroplane crash in August; he was replaced as the PSB candidate by his vice-presidential candidate, Marina Silva.

FOREIGN POLICY UNDER THE PT

Under President da Silva, Brazil continued to pursue its ambition of securing one of the proposed additional permanent seats on the UN Security Council, a goal opposed by Argentina and Mexico. To this end, in 2005 the Group of Four (G4), comprising Brazil, India, Japan and Germany, was organized for the purpose of supporting one another's bid for a permanent seat. Brazil led demands from a group of emerging nations towards the Group of Eight industrialized countries (G8) for a reduction of subsidies and protectionist policies, particularly subsidies on agricultural products. In June 2004 a complaint against US cotton subsidies brought by Brazil was upheld by the World Trade Organization (WTO), and in August a similar complaint against European Union (EU) sugar subsidies was sustained.

In December 2004 Brazil was one of 12 countries that were signatories to the agreement, signed in Cusco, Peru, creating the South American Community of Nations (Comunidade Sul-Americana de Nações), intended to promote greater regional economic integration. The organization was renamed the Union of South American Nations (União das Nações Sul-Americanas—UNASUL/Unión de Naciones Suramericanas—UNASUR) at the South American Energy Summit held in Venezuela in April 2007. UNASUL was formally constituted in May 2008. Following Colombia's military incursion into Ecuador in March and the resulting diplomatic confrontation, President da Silva was active in promoting the establishment of a South American Defence Council, under the auspices of UNASUL, to guarantee peace and security in the region. The Council was duly inaugurated in March 2009.

In 2010 da Silva continued with his high-profile campaign to project Brazil as a global player with the ultimate goal of securing a permanent seat in a reformed UN Security Council. As part of this strategy, he continued to develop political and economic links with the developing world (south–south relations) and with other emerging powers, particularly with the other so-called BRIC countries: Russia, India and the People's Republic of China. President da Silva was a strong voice in the G20 group of nations, joining the other BRIC countries in demanding reform of international financial and political institutions better to reflect a changing world order. In this context, Brazil has sought to assert a growing autonomy from the USA while projecting the country as a consensus builder and an honest broker in international affairs. While relations with the USA are generally good and the current Administration of Barack Obama sees Brazil as a regional leader and a stabilizing force in Latin America, there has been friction between the two countries, particularly concerning da Silva's claim to have brokered a deal with Iran in May 2010 regarding the processing of nuclear fuel, which the USA considered merely a delaying tactic by Iran to prevent the imposition of sanctions. The US Government was also uneasy over President da Silva's reluctance to voice concerns about the erosion of democracy in Venezuela and his failure to condemn human rights abuses in Cuba.

During her first term in office President Rousseff generally maintained da Silva's foreign policy priorities while introducing some nuances in dealing with specific issues. Her Government's key priority was to maintain the impetus to transform Brazil into a major international actor. In 2011–12 Rousseff met some of the most important world leaders, including President Obama, German Chancellor Angela Merkel, and the leaders of Russia, India, China and South Africa. Brazilian Minister of Foreign Affairs Antônio de Aguiar Patriota stated in a Senate hearing in May 2012 that Brazil 'is emerging for the first time as a world power among already established powers'. He attributed Brazil's growing international prominence to the size of its economy (the sixth largest in the world), its progress in reducing poverty, its energy self-sufficiency, its active membership of the G20 group and its development of south–south relations, particularly with the other BRIC countries. The appointment in May of Roberto Azevedo, a Brazilian diplomat, as Director-General of the World Trade Organization (WTO) was seen as further evidence of the country's status on the international stage. Relations with China, Brazil's main trading partner and one of the major sources of foreign direct investment in Brazil, were expected to continue to grow in importance, both politically and economically.

President Rousseff departed from da Silva's position of invoking the principle of non-intervention in other countries' internal affairs by condemning human rights violations in Iran. She also took steps to repair the country's strategic relations with the USA, which were placed under strain during the latter years of da Silva's administration. Reflecting the amelioration in relations between the two countries, President Obama visited Brazil in March 2011 during his first official visit to South America. Although Rousseff had been expected to reciprocate with a state visit to the USA in October 2013, the first by a Brazilian President since 1995, this was cancelled following reports that the USA had spied on her personal communications and those of other Brazilians. Bilateral tension had also been generated by the failure of the US President to endorse Brazil's primary foreign policy goal of attaining a permanent seat in the UN Security Council. Furthermore, in June 2012 Mike Hammer, the US Assistant Secretary of State for Public Affairs, appealed for 'more action' from Brazil to increase pressure against Syrian President Lt-Gen. Bashar al-Assad, whose regime was orchestrating a brutal crackdown against anti-Government elements. For her part, Rousseff repeatedly blamed US and EU monetary policies for precipitating a 'currency war', causing the currencies of developing countries to appreciate in detriment to their competitiveness in global markets.

The death of President Hugo Chávez and Venezuela's economic problems have weakened Venezuela's position as Brazil's main competitor for influence in Latin America. However, the emergence of the Alianza Pacífico bloc of free trading nations (Chile, Colombia, Mexico and Peru) was perceived as a challenge to Brazil's regional leadership and as presenting an alternative to the Mercado Comum do Sul's (MERCOSUL/MERCOSUR) increasingly protectionist trade policies. In an effort to stabilize Venezuela's fragile Government, Brazil endorsed President Nicolás Maduro's electoral victory, despite accusations of fraud by the opposition.

Argentina remains Brazil's main strategic ally in South America. However, Brazilian exporters have complained about Argentina's economic protectionism, which results in Brazilian exports to Argentina being blocked, contrary to the rules of MERCOSUL. Further disagreements among the two countries arose in relation to negotiations over a co-operation and trade agreement between MERCOSUL and the EU. Brazil maintained that Argentina's protectionist policies were hindering progress on this front, and Brazilian sources suggested that if no agreement was reached with Argentina over a common proposal Brazil could support a two-speed process under which Brazil, Paraguay and Uruguay would present a more ambitious tariff reduction framework that would exclude Argentina. Brazil's decision to prioritize the WTO's multilateral trade liberalization negotiations and the protectionist policies of MERCOSUL prevented the country from pursuing bilateral trade agreements with other countries. However, the loss of trade preferences with the EU and the poor prospects for multilateral trade liberalization revived Brazil's interest in concluding an agreement with the EU.

Economy

Dr AME BERGÉS

INTRODUCTION

Brazil is the sixth largest economy in the world and the second largest emerging market, with an estimated gross domestic product (GDP), on an international purchasing-power parity (PPP) basis, of US $2,243,000m. and a population of around 201m. in 2013.

Although agricultural production and the export of raw materials have always played an important economic role, Brazil was one of earliest industrial powers in Latin America. Whereas dependency on sugar and other large-scale, labour- and land-intensive agricultural commodities underpinned later development in much of Latin America and the Caribbean, the particularities of coffee production in the 19th century lent themselves to a concentration of income in the hands of the São Paulo landed classes, who, in turn, diverted coffee profits into transportation networks, and other industrial and commercial enterprises. These nascent industries received a further boost from the interruption of trade during the First and Second World Wars, which effectively protected domestic industrial production from foreign imports. As early as 1947, the manufacturing sector had displaced agriculture as the country's principal productive sector. However, manufactures did not comprise a significant proportion of Brazilian exports until the last quarter of the 20th century. Manufacturing exports were predominantly resource-based products, such as processed foods and beverages. Over the past two decades, however, the composition of Brazilian exports has begun to reflect the technological upgrading of national industries, particularly high-technology and sophisticated heavy manufactures, including telecommunications equipment, automobiles and aircraft. In addition to high-technology, information technology, software, and services sectors have also performed well.

Until the last decade, consistent economic growth and macroeconomic stability had eluded Brazil. Economic growth rates rocketed thanks to record prices of primary commodity goods in world markets, and world demand for hydrocarbons and biofuels. From 2004 until the financial crisis of 2008, Brazil's economy grew at a record pace of 4.5% per year.

Crucially, economic growth has been accompanied by equally remarkable improvements in living standards and significant achievements in the eradication of poverty. As of 2012 life expectancy at birth had reached 73.6 years, literacy rates exceeded 90%, and, among young people aged 15–24, reached 98%. Fewer than 10% of Brazilians live on less than US $5 (at PPP) per day, and just 6.1% of the population lived on less than $1.25 (at PPP) per day. These advancements in the field of human welfare are testament to the foundation in basic health and education that was constructed during the period of inward-looking growth in the middle decades of the 20th century, particularly the plan of President Getúlio Dornelles Vargas (1930–45) for industrialization, and point to the intensive social welfare programmes—including the much-lauded and -emulated Bolsa Família (Family Fund) initiative—which were intended to insulate and protect the poor and marginalized from economic volatility during the 1990s and early 2000s.

The shift in the Brazilian economic model away from inward-looking, state-led growth characteristic throughout the Latin American region in the middle decades of the 20th century, was prompted in great measure by the hyperinflationary episodes of the 1980s. Brazil's experience of hyperinflation proved instrumental in generating the political capital needed to push through the market-orientated economic reforms initiated under President Fernando Collor de Mello (1990–92) and strengthened under President Fernando Henrique Cardoso (1995–2002). However, as dissatisfaction with fiscal austerity and worsening income and social inequality grew, so did popular support for the Partido dos Trabalhadores (PT), culminating in the victory of the PT presidential candidate, Luiz Inácio Lula da Silva, in the 2002 election and Lula's successor,

Dilma Vana Rousseff, in the 2010 election. Concerns that the left-leaning PT administrations would reverse market-friendly policies proved to be unfounded. Indeed, policy pragmatism has increasingly characterized the Brazilian economy under the governance of the PT, whatever its underlying ideology. Brazil's economy in the 21st century could be described as a hybridization of interventionist and free market approaches that has been made possible by Brazil's market size, both international as well as domestic. The policy framework has elements that are both export-orientated and foreign investment friendly, but also inward-looking and protective. Fiscal policy is counter-cyclical, but focused on inflation and on the exchange rate. Economic growth is regarded not as the end, but as the means to social ends: in particular, broader access to better health and education, environmental protection, and a reduction in poverty, destitution, and infant/maternal mortality.

PRODUCTION

The country of Brazil comprises five main regions with varied specialization in economic commodities: the north (mainly rubber, brazil nuts, and iron ore and manganese extraction); the north-east (sugar cane, cotton, soy and cocoa); the centre-west (livestock and cotton); the south-east (coffee, cotton, livestock and sugar cane); and the south (livestock, wheat, lumber and soy). Industrial production is centred in the south and the south-east.

The largest component of the Brazilian economy is the services sector, accounting for 69.3% of GDP in 2013, followed by the industrial sector with a share of 25.0% and agriculture with 5.7%. The services sector also accounts for two-thirds of employment, and has experienced robust growth totalling 35% since 2004, and 4.4% since 2010. Since the commodity price boom of 2004, agricultural value added has grown by 23% in real terms, while that of industry has risen by 20%. In recent years, however, both agricultural and industrial value added have contracted, to just 1.5% and 0.7%, respectively.

Agriculture

The agri-business sector plays a sizeable role in the Brazilian economy. The sector employs 13% of the labour force, accounts for 36% of exports, and 33% of Brazil's total surface area is dedicated to agriculture. Brazil's main agricultural products are beef (accounting for 28% of the value of agricultural production in 2011), followed by chicken (22%), soybeans (10%), sugar cane (7%), maize (5%) and milk (5%). The use of genetically modified crops has been on the rise, particularly in soy, maize, and cotton, making Brazil the second largest cultivator of genetically modified crops, after the USA.

Brazil is among the top world producers of cotton, beef, poultry, sugar, coffee, orange juice, tropical fruits, and soybeans for export. Record prices since 2004 spurred investment in agriculture, which, combined with favourable climatic conditions, resulted in sugar cane, soybean and maize achieving record harvests in 2008, 2010, 2012 and 2013. Agricultural output is projected to grow by more than 40% over the next few decades—significantly more than projections for the world's two other main agricultural producers, India (21%) and the People's Republic of China (26%).

The improvements in productivity seen today are partly due to better farm management practices, investments in modern equipment, and soil improvements. Brazilian efforts to tackle rural poverty through land-based poverty alleviation programmes such as the Crédito Fundiário—Combate à Pobreza Rural, have also contributed to a rise in productivity gains. Based on the earlier community-centred pilot land reform programme, Cédula da Terra, these efforts saw land distributed to some 372,500 families between 1995 and 2008.

Rural poverty and concerns about rising domestic food prices have informed a number of programmes in recent years charged with the multiple aims of productivity improvements, environmental conservation, and tackling rural poverty and unemployment. These include grants for the recovery of deforested lands and the implementation of more environmentally friendly agricultural practices, technical assistance, and training to producers (e.g. Programa de Integração Lavoura-Pecuária—ProLaPec and Programa de Estímulo a Prodacão Agropecuária Sustentável—ProdUsa). Other programmes target family farmers, facilitating subsidized credit for equipment purchases, land recovery, and development, and target specific sectors such as agro-industry, sustainable food production, and ecological and organic farming (e.g. Programa Nacional de Fortalecimento da Agricultura Familia—ProNAF).

Industry

The industrial sector in Brazil employs about 22% of the labour force, and manufactures accounting for 35% of exports. In recent years, however, industrial growth performance has been inconsistent, buoyed at times by robust consumer spending and by building works and construction in the run-up to the 2014 Fédération Internationale de Football Association (FIFA) World Cup tournament and the 2016 Olympic Games, but stymied at times by rising energy and labour costs, and lack of access to cheap credit for investment. Brazil, nevertheless, has one of the most sophisticated and diverse industrial sectors among emerging markets. Production spans a wide breadth: from natural resource-based commodities such as iron ore, steel, and petrochemicals, to light consumer goods like footwear, toys, and electronics, to high value-added and research and development manufactures such as automobiles, rail cars and locomotives, aircraft and satellites, and pharmaceuticals.

Brazil's industrial powerhouses are petroleum and ethanol. With 13,220m. barrels of proven petroleum reserves at January 2014, Brazil has the second largest reserves in South America, after Venezuela, and the 16th largest in the world. Brazil currently ranks 11th in world production, with 2.7m. barrels per day (b/d). With control over 95% of crude petroleum production, the state-owned petroleum company, Petróleo Brasileiro, SA (Petrobras), is the single most important player in the petroleum industry.

Petrobras is also the largest producer and wholesale supplier of natural gas in Brazil, with control of 90% of the country's natural gas reserves. Despite proven natural gas reserves of 389,920m. cu m (in 2014), Brazil produced just 16,940m. cu m, meeting only approximately 55% of its natural gas consumption requirements, importing the rest mostly from Bolivia. Challenges include balancing the country's vast and growing energy requirements—Brazil ranked eighth in world primary energy consumption in 2011—with efforts to fight climate change and deforestation. Brazil is spearheading the global search for alternative energy sources through investment in ethanol and biodiesel production, research into cellulosic ethanol (derived mainly from sugar cane, but also from sorghum, corn, and castor beans) and aviation biofuels, and setting minimum blend requirements for the use of bioethanol in gasoline and biodiesel (derived from soybean oil and animal fats) in diesel.

Brazil is spearheading research into renewable energy, accounting for nearly all of Latin America's investment in this sector, and in 2011 positioned itself as a global leader in combating climate change with the creation of the Fundo Nacional sobre Mudança do Clima (National Fund on Climate Change). The Fund, which focuses on reducing greenhouse gas emissions (particularly in the agricultural, energy and steel sectors), deforestation and forest degradation, aims to allocate R $1,000m. per year to qualified projects by 2015.

By volume, Brazil's automobile manufacturing industry is ranked the 10th largest in the world. Domestic ethanol production (totalling 392,000 b/d in 2011), combined with higher domestic prices for petrol and government regulations supporting the use of biofuels, has seen a massive increase in the use of flexible-fuel vehicles. Since their launch in 2003, the production of such vehicles has surged from 1.69m. to 27.7m. by 2012. Most production is destined for domestic consumption (just over 79% of flex-fuel vehicles in Brazil are manufactured locally), while roughly 13% is for export.

Brazil also has some of the largest domestic consumer markets in the world, with the third largest soft drinks market, the fourth largest car market, and the fifth largest beer market and

telecommunications market. Brazil's confectionery and food and beverages markets also rank among the world's largest. The sheer size and growth potential of Brazil's consumer markets have made it an attractive destination for foreign investment, and indeed both domestic consumption and foreign direct investment are credited with Brazil's rapid economic recovery from the 2008 global financial crisis.

Brazil's electricity market is the largest in Latin America. Although Brazil currently has two nuclear power plants, with a third under construction, these accounted for just 2.9% of total electricity supply in 2011. Similarly, electricity derived from natural gas, petroleum and coal comprises only a small share (9.8%). Most of the country's energy requirements are met by hydroelectric power (80.5% of Brazil's total electricity supply), although the pace of growth of other renewable energy sources is expected to continue to accelerate. The contribution of non-hydroelectric renewable energy towards Brazil's energy requirements is around 6.6%.

Productive investment, however, is lagging. The Government has introduced a wide range of stimulus measures to redress this, including the 2007 and 2010 Growth Acceleration Plan (Plano de Aceleração do Crescimento—PAC), and the 2011 Brasil Maior plan. These have sought to encourage domestic investment in key industries such as petroleum and gas exploration, electric power generation, agribusiness, nano- and bio-technology, transportation and infrastructure, biofuels, sanitation and housing, through soft loans, reductions in electricity rates, payroll reductions, and other tax incentives. Combined PAC investments were forecast to reach US $526,000m. during 2011–14. As of December 2013, 82.3% of projects planned have been completed, and roughly 76% of the budget allocated.

Efforts to boost industrial production have also targeted support for small and medium enterprises through public-private partnerships such as the Grupo de Trabalho Permanente para Arranjos Produtivos Locais (Permanent Working Group for Local Production Clusters), the Fundo de Aval da Micro e Pequena Empresa (Guarantee Fund for Micro and Small Enterprises), the Serviço Brasileiro de Apoio às Micro e Pequenas Empresas (SEBRAE—Brazilian Micro and Small Enterprise Support Service), the Financiadora de Estudios y Proyectos (FINEP—Funding for Studies and Projects), as well as through the provision of soft loans from the Banco Nacional do Desenvolvimento Econômico e Social (BNDES—Brazilian Development Bank).

In addition to targeting small and medium enterprises, other recent initiatives aimed at stimulating investment include simplification of the tax system, the introduction of tax-advantaged bonds for infrastructure and research and development investment, as well as labour skilling/upgrading through the Programa Nacional de Acesso ao Ensino Técnico e Emprego (PRONATEC—National Programme of Access to Technical Education and Employment) and scholarship programmes such as Ciência Sem Fronteiras (Science Without Borders).

However, productive investment has been slow to respond to stimulus measures. The 2012 GDP share of fixed capital formation has remained at its 2010 level of 18.4%, which is not even one-half of that for China (47%), and well below productive investment in Chile (24%), Peru (28%), Mexico (23%), and Nicaragua (25%).

Services

The Brazilian services sector is varied and sophisticated, encompassing health care, education, commerce and transportation logistics, financial services, telecommunications, and media. Brazil ranks among the top six countries in the world in terms of number of internet users, and has the largest banking system in Latin America. The banking system is highly concentrated: the percentage of banking sector assets held by Brazil's 10 largest banks rose from 80% of the total in 2005 to 85% in September 2011. Although some of the largest banks are foreign owned, foreign participation in the banking system has been relatively limited in comparison to the rest of Latin America. The top four banks, in terms of assets, are all Brazilian. The largest, Banco do Brasil, SA, which is owned by the federal Government, held 17.98% of the banking sector's total assets in 2011, followed by Itaú Unibanco, SA, which is the largest private banking institution in Latin America, with 16.05%. Other key players are Banco Bradesco, SA, the second largest private bank in the region, with 12.61%, the BNDES (11.25%) and the state-owned Caixa Econômica Federal (10.05%). The fifth largest commercial bank in Brazil is foreign-owned: Banco Santander Brasil, SA, a subsidiary of Banco Santander, with 8.37% of the country's total banking assets. State-controlled banks, including the Caixa Econômica Federal and the BNDES, accounted for some 40% of banking sector assets in 2011, and are responsible for the bulk of rural financing operations.

TRADE

Despite strong export performance over the past decade or so, the balance of trade, while still positive, has worsened in recent years. Although Brazilian exports rebounded from the international economic crisis and protracted global recovery, rising from US $159,000m. in 2009 to $242,000m. in 2013, growth in import demand resulted in a narrower trade surplus of just $2,560m. in 2013.

China is Brazil's main export and import partner, following a shift in trade beginning in 2008 towards the other so-called BRICS countries (Russia, India, China and South Africa—the latter since 2010), as well as the member nations of the North American Free Trade Agreement (Canada, Mexico and the USA) and Latin America. In 2013 Asia accounted for 32% of Brazil's exports and China 19% alone, followed by Latin America with 22%, the European Union with 20%, and the USA with 10%.

A marked trend has been the expansion of exports to developing economies (especially non-traditional markets), notably East Asia, and Africa, the Arab Peninsula and the Middle East (20.0% and 3.7% in 2012, respectively). Brazil's other main import partners, besides China, are the USA, Argentina, and Germany. Manufactures, primarily machinery, electrical and transport equipment, chemical products, petroleum, automotive parts and electronics, account for the greatest share of imports (approximately 73% since 2000).

Traditionally dominated by primary commodities, export composition has seen a radical shift since the 1960s. From just 3% of total exports in the 1960s, manufactures rose to average between 50% and 60% of exports during 1996–2006. Although their contribution to total exports has been trending downwards to 35% in 2012, due to the commodity boom, manufactures grew by 21% in nominal terms in the past five years to reach US $85,000m. in 2012. Nonetheless, Brazil's most important exports today are all primary commodities: iron ore, crude petroleum and fuels, soybeans and soy meal, sugar, poultry and coffee. Prominent among Brazilian manufactured and semi-manufactured exports in 2012 were foods, beverages and tobacco (accounting for 30.3% of the total), followed by metallic products (14.6%), automobiles (9.8%), machinery and equipment (7.6%) and chemical products (7.1%). As Brazil's manufacturing industry has become increasingly sophisticated, so too has export market penetration of high- and medium-technology products, notably aircraft, transport equipment parts, telecommunications equipment and automobiles. However, the share of high- and medium-technology manufactures in industrial exports declined from an all-time high of 35.6% in 2000 to a low of 22.6% in 2010, before recovering to 33.9% in 2012.

FOREIGN DIRECT INVESTMENT

Brazil's record growth rates and stable macroeconomic environment, combined with the growth potential implied by an increasingly affluent middle class and expanding domestic consumer base, boosted foreign direct investment (FDI) to a peak of US $66,700m. in 2011, although it has since declined slightly to $64,000m. in 2013.

The main sources of FDI are the USA, the United Kingdom, Spain, China, Germany, Japan, and France, with investment mainly orientated towards financial services, basic metallurgy and steel, and vehicles. Many of the multinational companies currently operating in Brazil originally acquired local operations through debt-equity swaps under President Collor de Mello's National Privatization Programme (Programa Nacio-

nal de Desestatização—PND). The PND saw 33 state-owned enterprises sold between 1990 and 1994, including Empresa Brasileira de Aeronáutica, SA (Embraer), an aircraft and aerospace services company. The big push towards privatization at both federal and state level came under President Cardoso: between 1995 and 1998 some 80 state-owned enterprises were privatized, including the Companhia Vale do Rio Doce mining company (now Vale), as well as railways, telecommunications, ports, electricity distribution and generation, and water and sanitation services.

Despite the opening up of the petroleum sector in 1997, foreign operations in the sector are few and far between. The first foreign crude petroleum production operation in Brazil was Royal Dutch Shell's Bijupira-Salema project in the Campos Basin. Other important foreign companies in the Brazilian petroleum sector are Chevron and Norsk Hydro. The first and only upstream petroleum project without any participation from Petrobras was Devon Energy Corporation's Polvo field, which began production in August 2007. Since 2010, new legislation has extended government control over the sector, making Petrobras the sole operator of new fields and granting it a minimum 30% stake in all future joint ventures.

Brazilian direct investment abroad was negligible until the latter half of the 2000s, when it grew to average US $26,500m. over the last eight years, allowing Brazil to become a net creditor for the first time ever in 2009. Although a net creditor again for the last three years, the margin has fallen dramatically from $10,000m. in 2009 to $3,500m. in 2013. The main destination of Brazilian investment is in industry, accounting for 56% of outward investment in 2010–13 (mainly foodstuff and basic metallurgy), followed by financial services (22.6%).

Spearheading outward FDI is Vale, which has mining operations and investments in Finland, Canada, Australia, Mongolia, China, India, Angola, South Africa, Chile and Peru, followed by Petrobras and Metalúrgica Gerdau, SA. Other major Brazilian multinationals include heavy construction companies and high-technology groups, such as Votorantim Cimentos (one of the 10 largest cement companies in the world), Camargo Corrêa, Embraer, Itautec, and Odebrecht. The rapid increase in outward investment is also, in good measure, the result of the rapid internationalization of a small number of established enterprises in the food and beverages sector (including Sadia, Perdigão Agroindustrial, and AmBev) and the personal care and cosmetics products sector.

MACROECONOMIC POLICY

Monetary Policy

As in many Latin American countries, managing inflation and exchange rate appreciation remains a priority for the Brazilian monetary authorities. It was only a few decades ago that inflation rates were brought down from a peak of 2,500% in 1993, to 1.6% in 1997. Brazil has followed a flexible exchange rate regime with an inflation target since 1997. As the real lost 68.5% of its value between 2000 and 2005, inflation declined from 8.9% in 1999 (and a peak of 12.5% in 2002 at the height of Argentina's economic crisis) to an average of around 3.8% in 2006-08. This controlled inflation led the Monetary Policy Committee (Comité de Política Monetária—COPOM) gradually to reduce the benchmark interest rate, known as the SELIC, from 19.75% in September 2005 to 13.25% in December 2006 and 11.25% in September 2007. Rising food and energy prices led to the implementation of more stringent monetary policy in the form of minimum reserve requirements on interbank deposits and an increase in the benchmark rate to 11.75% in 2008, although the SELIC was subsequently reduced to 10.25% in May 2009 and 8.75% in October 2009 as part of the economic stimulus package. The SELIC rose to 12.5% in 2011 in response to appreciation of the real and inflation overshooting the target ceiling. Although the SELIC was reduced to 7.25% by the third quarter of 2012, and stood at 8% in early 2013, the benchmark interest rate was raised gradually to 11% by April 2014, in response to consumer price pressures.

Fiscal Policy

Policy pragmatism under the current administration has seen a combination of fiscal discipline as enshrined in legislation on fiscal responsibility enacted in 2000, and counter-cyclical fiscal policy in response to the economic downturn. Efforts to maintain fiscal discipline have seen Brazil achieve one of the highest rates of tax collection in Latin America, averaging 22.3% of GDP in the last decade compared to 18.5% in 1997–99. This level of tax revenue, combined with a commitment to fiscal discipline (enshrined in legislation on fiscal responsibility enacted in 2000), has been instrumental in lowering the public internal debt from 50.6% in 2007 to 35.3% in 2011.

External debt has also been managed judiciously. Brazil repaid its debt to the IMF in 2005, and reduced foreign debt to US $193,200m. by 2007, from $236,600m. in 2003, leading the Standard & Poor's and Fitch Ratings credit rating agencies to raise Brazil's sovereign credit rating to 'investment' grade in 2008.

The immediate impact of the 2008 global financial crisis, and the loosening of fiscal policy, was an increase in foreign debt to US $211,300m. in September. Nonetheless, public debt in 2012 was still well below 2008 levels (at $116,600m.), with the debt ratio to gross national income (GNI) averaging 17.7% in 2009–13.

Export growth and foreign investment to the country helped Brazil to strengthen its international reserve position from US $49,000m. in 2003 to $373,161m. in 2012. However, the subsequent deterioration in the balance of trade in 2013, coupled with the slowdown in foreign investment, resulted in a balance of payments deficit of $5,900m. for the first time in a decade. Concerns about the state's ability to maintain macroeconomic stability against a backdrop of narrowing trade surplus and slowdown in inward FDI have prompted the credit rating agencies to reduce expectations of Brazil's outlook. Public sector outlays relating to the FIFA World Cup and the 2016 Olympic Games are growing, and forthcoming elections in 2014 will no doubt put pressure on the state to postpone adjustments until afterwards. Public employee salaries have been increasing and Brazil's social security deficit is widening. Volatile economic growth affects the corporate profit tax intake, as do stimulus measures for domestic industries. At the same time, the state is coping with widespread public protests against the cost of transport, against the designation of public funds for investments of dubious economic benefit to the wider public, and against slow progress in the areas of social and income equality.

LABOUR MARKETS AND SOCIAL POLICY

The services sector provided employment for some 62.5% of the employed labour force in 2011, while agriculture contributed 15.7%, and industry (including mining, manufacturing, construction and power) 21.8%. Labour market indicators have improved significantly since the 1980s and 1990s. The Brazilian labour force expanded from 62.4m. in 1990 to 83.4m. in 2000 and to an estimated 104.7m. in 2012. Unemployment declined from 7.9% in 2008 to 6.0% in 2011, and to a historic low of 5.4% in for 2013, thus making Brazil the country with the world's fastest rate in reduction of unemployment over the last five years. Job creation in the formal sector has remained steady even as economic growth has slowed. From 12.3% in 2003, unemployment in the six largest metropolitan areas (Belo Horizonte, Porto Alegre, Recife, Rio de Janeiro, Salvador and São Paulo) fell to 9.3% by 2007, 5.5% in 2012, and 4.6% in 2013. At the same time, minimum wage increases have so far exceeded the pace of inflation. In fact, over the past decade, average income has risen by 16% in real terms, and for women and informal workers the increase has been even greater (at 22.3% and 21.2%, respectively). For the poorest 10% of the Brazilian population, per head income rose by some 91% over the past decade. Surprisingly, although the 1990s witnessed an increase in informal employment, from 37.0% in 1990 to 45.3% in 2000, employment in the formal sector rose over the past decade from 45.3% in 2000 to 56.0% by 2011.

Brazil has also seen dramatic improvements in health and education indicators. Infant mortality decreased from 45.2 deaths per thousand births in 1992 to 27.8 in 2002 and 20.5 in 2011. The prevalence of under-nourishment in the total population has more than halved since the early 1990s, falling from 14.9% in 1990–92 to 11.1% in 2000–02 and to 6.9% in 2010–12. Literacy rates improved from 86.9% in 2000 to 88.6% in 2005, rising to 90.3% by 2010. The number of children in the relevant age-group attending school increased from 85.0% in 1990 to 98.2% in 2010. Consequently, literacy rates among young men and women aged between 15 and 24 years are currently even higher than the average, at 97% and 99%, respectively.

Schooling rates at both secondary and tertiary level have also improved over the last decade or so, increasing from 81.0% in 2000 to 83.7% in 2011 and from 27.0% in 2000 to 51.3% in 2011, respectively. Although discrepancies along racial and income lines remained—rates of university attendance among Afro-Brazilian and mixed-race teenagers in 2011 were still well below those of whites (35.8% compared to 65.7%)—there have been dramatic improvements: high school attendance rates for students aged between 15 and 17 years from low-income households rose from 13.0% in 2000 to 36.8% in 2011, and rates for Afro-Brazilian and mixed-race teenagers increased from 24.4% to 45.3% over the same period. Efforts to redress the remaining imbalance have included the passage of a new affirmative action law in August 2011 requiring public universities to allocate one-half of their places to underprivileged students from public schools.

Targeted income support and land-based poverty alleviation programmes helped to mitigate the impact of the global financial crisis, and have been instrumental in reducing extreme poverty in both rural and urban areas. In fact, Brazil's success story could arguably be the 30m. people who have been moved out of poverty and into the middle class over the last decade. The expansion of the middle class is reflected in the decline in the Gini coefficient (a measure of the concentration of income) from 0.640 in 1999 to 0.508 in 2011. Rural income inequality has also declined. Under the land-based Crédito Fundiário programme, for instance, beneficiaries' incomes increased by an average of 181% in 1998–2003 and by 145% in 2003–05. In addition, the Gini coefficient in rural areas decreased from 0.577 in 1999 to 0.538 in 2006. Brazil's much lauded poverty alleviation programme, Bolsa Família, which ties cash transfers to children's school attendance and participation in various government-sponsored vaccination and nutrition programmes, expanded its coverage from 8.5m. families at the end of 2005 to 12.9m. households in 2010. In 2011 the Rousseff administration inaugurated Brasil Sem Miséria (Brazil Without Misery), a multi-faceted approach aimed at targeting the 16.2m. people still living in extreme poverty, particularly in the north-east of Brazil, where 59% of the extremely poor are concentrated. About 60% of the new homes constructed under the My Home, My Life (Minha Casa, Minha Vida—MCMV) programme, a subsidized loan programme funded by the second phase of the PAC, have been allocated to poor families with a monthly income of less than R $1,395 (US $705). Other new initiatives include the expansion and improvement of the Unified Health System (Sistema Único de Saúde) through the Better at Home (Melhor em Casa) programme, tasked with providing access to home care, and SOS Emergências, which focuses on emergency care.

OUTLOOK

The Brazilian economy continues to show signs of resilience and macroeconomic stability. The Rousseff administration has thus far maintained its commitment to the promotion of innovation and investment in research and development, the eradication of poverty, and the enhancement of the quality of the Brazilian labour force. Brazil is on the cusp of becoming a world power, but still confronts a number of short- and long-term economic challenges. Brazil's rapid economic recovery, from a 0.8% contraction in GDP in 2008 to growth of 2.3% in 2013, was made possible by its strong international reserves position and by robust domestic demand. Its future growth outlook will depend on how the monetary and fiscal authorities manage macroeconomic stability, namely inflation and exchange rate appreciation, on whether domestic industries respond to incentives to boost productive investment, and on the extent to which private consumption, so far made possible by a growing middle class with access to easy consumer credit, is able to continue to finance economic growth at a time of weak foreign investment inflows and a shallow balance of trade surplus.

Statistical Survey

Sources (unless otherwise stated): Economic Research Department, Banco Central do Brasil, SBS, Quadra 03, Bloco B, 70074-900 Brasília, DF; tel. (61) 3414-1074; fax (61) 3414-2036; e-mail coace.depec.@bcb.gov.br; internet www.bcb.gov.br; Instituto Brasileiro de Geografia e Estatística (IBGE), Centro de Documentação e Disseminação de Informações (CDDI), Rua Gen. Canabarro 706, 2° andar, Maracanã, 20271-201 Rio de Janeiro, RJ; tel. (21) 2142-4781; fax (21) 2142-4933; e-mail ibge@ibge.bov.br; internet www.ibge.gov.br.

Area and Population

AREA, POPULATION AND DENSITY

Area (sq km)	8,514,877*
Population (census results)†	
1 August 2000	169,590,693
1 August 2010	
Males	93,406,990
Females	97,348,809
Total	190,755,799
Population (official estimates at mid-year)	
2011	192,379,287
2012	193,946,886
2013	201,032,714
Density (per sq km) at mid-2013	23.6

* 3,287,611 sq miles.

† Excluding Indian jungle population (numbering 45,429 in 1950).

POPULATION BY AGE AND SEX
(official estimates at mid-2013)

	Males	Females	Total
0–14 years	24,776,943	23,754,709	48,531,652
15–64 years	68,179,905	69,451,071	137,630,976
65 years and over	6,380,010	8,490,076	14,870,086
Total	99,336,858	101,695,856	201,032,714

ADMINISTRATIVE DIVISIONS
(official population estimates at mid-2013)

State	Area (sq km)	Population	Density (per sq km)	Capital
Acre (AC) . .	152,581	776,463	5.1	Rio Branco
Alagoas (AL) . .	27,768	3,300,935	118.9	Maceió
Amapá (AP) . .	142,815	734,996	5.1	Macapá
Amazonas (AM) . .	1,570,746	3,807,921	2.4	Manaus
Bahia (BA) . .	564,693	15,044,137	26.6	Salvador
Ceará (CE) . .	148,826	8,778,576	59.0	Fortaleza
Distrito Federal (DF) . . .	5,802	2,789,761	480.8	Brasília
Espírito Santo (ES)	46,078	3,839,366	83.3	Vitória
Goiás (GO) . .	340,087	6,434,048	18.9	Goiânia
Maranhão (MA) .	331,983	6,794,301	20.5	São Luís
Mato Grosso (MT) .	903,358	3,182,113	3.5	Cuiabá
Mato Grosso do Sul (MS)	357,125	2,587,269	7.2	Campo Grande
Minas Gerais (MG)	586,528	20,593,356	35.1	Belo Horizonte
Pará (PA) . . .	1,247,690	7,969,654	6.4	Belém
Paraíba (PB) . .	56,440	3,914,421	69.4	João Pessoa
Paraná (PR) . .	199,315	10,997,465	55.2	Curitiba
Pernambuco (PE) .	98,312	9,208,550	93.7	Recife
Piauí (PI) . .	251,529	3,184,166	12.7	Teresina
Rio de Janeiro (RJ)	43,696	16,369,179	374.6	Rio de Janeiro
Rio Grande do Norte (RN) . .	52,797	3,373,959	63.9	Natal
Rio Grande do Sul (RS) . . .	281,749	11,164,043	39.6	Porto Alegre
Rondônia (RO) .	237,576	1,728,214	7.3	Porto Velho
Roraima (RR) .	224,299	488,072	2.2	Boa Vista
Santa Catarina (SC)	95,346	6,634,254	69.6	Florianópolis
São Paulo (SP) .	248,209	43,663,669	175.9	São Paulo
Sergipe (SE) .	21,910	2,195,662	100.2	Aracaju
Tocantins (TO) .	277,621	1,478,164	5.3	Palmas
Total	8,514,877	201,032,714	23.6	—

PRINCIPAL TOWNS
(official estimates at mid-2013)*

São Paulo . .	11,821,873		Uberlândia . . .	646,673
Rio de Janeiro .	6,429,923		Contagem . . .	637,961
Salvador . .	2,883,682		Sorocaba . . .	629,231
Brasília (capital) .	2,789,761		Aracaju	614,577
Fortaleza . .	2,551,806		Feira de Santana .	606,139
Belo Horizonte .	2,479,165		Cuiabá . . .	569,830
Manaus . .	1,982,177		Joinville . . .	546,981
Curitiba . .	1,848,946		Juíz de Fora . .	545,942
Recife . . .	1,599,513		Londrina . . .	537,566
Porto Alegre .	1,467,816		Aparecida de Goiânia . .	500,619
Belém . .	1,425,922		Niterói . . .	494,200
Goiânia . .	1,393,575		Ananindeua . .	493,976
Guarulhos . .	1,299,249		Porto Velho . .	484,992
Campinas . .	1,144,862		Belford Roxo . .	477,583
São Luís . .	1,053,922		Campos dos Goytacazes . .	477,208
São Gonçalo .	1,025,507		Serra . . .	467,318
Maceió . . .	996,733		Caxias do Sul . .	465,304
Duque de Caxias .	873,921		São João de Meriti .	460,799
Natal . . .	853,928		Vila Velha . .	458,489
Teresina . .	836,475		Florianópolis . .	453,285
Campo Grande .	832,352		Mauá	444,136
São Bernardo do Campo . .	805,895		Macapá . . .	437,256
Nova Iguaçu . .	804,815		São José do Rio Preto	434,039
João Pessoa . .	769,607		Santos . . .	433,153
Santo André . .	704,942		Mogi das Cruzes .	414,907
Osasco . . .	691,652		Diadema . . .	406,718
Jaboatão dos Guararapes . .	675,599		Betim . . .	406,474
São José dos Campos	673,255		Campina Grande .	400,002
Ribeirão Preto . .	649,556			

* Figures refer to *municípios*, which may contain rural districts.

BIRTHS, MARRIAGES AND DEATHS
(official estimates based on annual registrations)

	Live births		Marriages	Deaths	
	Number*	Rate (per 1,000)	Number	Number	Rate (per 1,000)
2005 . .	3,329,431	18.2	835,846	996,931	5.4
2006 . .	3,172,000	17.1	889,828	1,023,814	5.5
2007 . .	3,080,266	16.4	916,006	1,036,405	5.5
2008 . .	3,107,927	16.4	959,901	1,060,365	5.6
2009 . .	3,045,696	15.9	935,116	1,083,399	5.7
2010 . .	2,985,406	15.7	977,620	1,132,701	5.1
2011 . .	3,044,594	15.8	1,026,736	1,163,740	6.0
2012 . .	2,998,281	15.5	1,041,440	1,165,751	6.0

* Including births registered but not occurring during that year: 448,243 in 2005; 368,062 in 2006; 324,895 in 2007; 309,885 in 2008; 281,054 in 2009; 224,445 in 2010; 219,818 in 2011; 185,764 in 2012.

Life expectancy (years at birth): 73.6 (males 70.1; females 77.3) in 2012 (Source: World Bank, World Development Indicators database).

ECONOMICALLY ACTIVE POPULATION

('000 persons aged 10 years and over, labour force sample survey at September)*

	2009	2011†	2012
Agriculture, hunting, forestry and fishing	15,715	14,682	13,368
Industry (excl. construction)	13,598	12,509	13,161
Manufacturing industries	12,815	11,787	12,441
Construction	6,895	7,814	8,218
Commerce and repair of motor vehicles and household goods	16,484	16,660	16,688
Hotels and restaurants	3,623	4,570	4,471
Transport, storage and communication	4,436	5,109	5,252
Public administration	4,754	5,081	5,178
Education, health and social services	8,681	8,627	9,100
Domestic services	7,223	6,653	6,355
Other community, social and personal services	3,928	3,538	3,748
Other activities	7,150	8,120	8,307
Sub-total	92,487	93,363	93,846
Activities not adequately defined	202	130	69
Total employed	92,689	93,493	93,915
Unemployed	8,421	6,730	6,149
Total labour force	101,110	100,223	100,064

* Data coverage excludes rural areas of Acre, Amapá, Amazonas, Pará, Rondônia and Roraima.

† No survey was conducted in 2010, owing to the population census in that year.

Health and Welfare

KEY INDICATORS

Total fertility rate (children per woman, 2012)	1.8
Under-5 mortality rate (per 1,000 live births, 2012)	14
HIV/AIDS (% of persons aged 15–49, 2011)	0.3
Physicians (per 1,000 head, 2009)	1.8
Hospital beds (per 1,000 head, 2010)	2.4
Health expenditure (2011): US $ per head (PPP)	1,035
Health expenditure (2011): % of GDP	8.9
Health expenditure (2011): public (% of total)	45.7
Access to water (% of persons, 2012)	98
Access to sanitation (% of persons, 2012)	81
Total carbon dioxide emissions ('000 metric tons, 2010)	419,754.2
Carbon dioxide emissions per head (metric tons, 2010)	2.2
Human Development Index (2013): ranking	79
Human Development Index (2013): value	0.744

For sources and definitions, see explanatory note on p. vi.

Agriculture

PRINCIPAL CROPS

('000 metric tons)

	2010	2011	2012
Wheat	6,171	5,690	4,418
Rice, paddy	11,236	13,477	11,550
Barley	279	304	265
Maize	55,364	55,660	71,073
Oats	395	373	431
Sorghum	1,532	1,931	2,017
Buckwheat*	57	57	60
Potatoes	3,548	3,917	3,732
Sweet potatoes	495	545	479
Cassava (Manioc)	24,967	25,349	23,045
Yams*	233	244	246
Sugar cane	717,464	734,006	721,077
Beans, dry	3,159	3,435	2,795
Brazil nuts, with shell	40	42	44*
Cashew nuts, with shell	104	231	81
Soybeans (Soya beans)	68,756	74,815	65,849
Groundnuts, with shell	261	311	334
Coconuts	2,843	2,944	2,888

—continued	2010	2011	2012
Oil palm fruit	1,293	1,301	1,241
Castor oil seed	95	120	26
Sunflower seed	87	78	124
Tomatoes	4,107	4,417	3,874
Onions, dry	1,753	1,523	1,519
Garlic	104	143	107
Watermelons	2,053	2,199	2,080
Cantaloupes and other melons	478	499	575
Bananas	6,969	7,329	6,902
Oranges	18,503	19,811	18,013
Tangerines, mandarins, clementines and satsumas	1,122	1,005	960
Lemons and limes	1,021	1,127	1,208
Grapefruit and pomelos*	71	75	78
Apples	1,279	1,339	1,335
Peaches and nectarines	222	222	233
Grapes	1,355	1,542	1,515
Guavas, mangoes, mangosteens	1,190	1,250	1,176
Avocados	153	160	160
Pineapples	2,206	2,365	2,478
Persimmons	167	155	158
Cashew-apple*	1,694	1,788	1,805
Papayas	1,872	1,854	1,518
Coffee, green	2,907	2,700	3,038
Cocoa beans	235	249	253
Mate	430	444	513
Sisal	247	284	89
Tobacco, unmanufactured	788	952	811
Natural rubber	134	164	177

* FAO estimate(s).

Aggregate production ('000 metric tons, may include official, semi-official or estimated data): Total cereals 75,161 in 2010, 77,586 in 2011, 89,908 in 2012; Total roots and tubers 29,243 in 2010, 30,055 in 2011, 27,502 in 2012; Total vegetables (incl. melons) 11,233 in 2010, 11,611 in 2011, 11,055 in 2012; Total fruits (excl. melons) 38,793 in 2010, 40,997 in 2011, 38,369 in 2012.

Source: FAO.

LIVESTOCK

('000 head, year ending September)

	2010	2011	2012
Cattle	209,541	212,815	211,279
Buffaloes	1,185	1,278	1,262
Horses	5,514	5,511	5,363
Asses	1,002	975	903
Mules	1,277	1,269	1,222
Pigs	38,957	39,307	38,796
Sheep	17,381	17,668	16,789
Goats	9,313	9,386	8,646
Chickens	1,238,912	1,268,209	1,245,269
Ducks*	3,700	3,750	3,800
Turkeys*	26,900	27,100	28,300

* FAO estimates.

Source: FAO.

LIVESTOCK PRODUCTS

('000 metric tons)

	2010	2011	2012
Cattle meat*	9,115	9,030	9,307
Sheep meat†	82	84	85
Goat meat†	29	29	30
Pig meat	3,195*	3,370	3,465
Horse meat†	22	22	23
Chicken meat	10,693	11,422	11,533
Cows' milk	30,715	32,096	32,304
Goats' milk†	148	149	150
Hen eggs*	1,948	2,037	2,084
Other poultry eggs	139	156	160†
Natural honey	38	42	34
Wool, greasy	12	12	12

* Unofficial figures.

† FAO estimate(s).

Source: FAO.

Forestry

ROUNDWOOD REMOVALS
('000 cubic metres, excl. bark, FAO estimates)

	2010	2011	2012
Sawlogs, veneer logs and logs for sleepers	50,574	55,289	62,950
Pulpwood	69,779	75,882	73,837
Other industrial wood . . .	8,047	8,798	10,017
Fuel wood	143,101	144,050	145,016
Total	271,501	284,019	291,820

Source: FAO.

SAWNWOOD PRODUCTION
('000 cubic metres, incl. railway sleepers)

	2010	2011	2012
Coniferous (softwood)* . . .	8,970	9,100	9,200
Broadleaved (hardwood) . . .	16,110†	16,110*	16,110†
Total	25,080	25,210	25,310

* Unofficial figure(s).
† FAO estimate.

Source: FAO.

Fishing

('000 metric tons, live weight)

	2010	2011	2012
Capture	785.4	803.3	843.0
Characins	90.4	91.6	98.0
Freshwater siluroids . .	30.0	30.3	32.4
Weakfishes	48.6	45.4	48.5
Whitemouth croaker . .	43.2	43.2	46.2
Brazilian sardinella . .	62.1	76.0	92.7
Aquaculture	479.6*	629.6*	707.5
Common carp	94.6	14.0	15.8
Tilapias	155.5	253.8	286.5
Whiteleg shrimp . . .	69.4	65.7	74.1
Total catch	1,265.0*	1,432.9*	1,550.5

* FAO estimate.

Note: Figures exclude aquatic mammals, recorded by number rather than by weight. The number of whales and dolphins caught was: 70 in 2010; 45 in 2011; 26 in 2012. Also excluded are crocodiles: the number of broad-nosed, black and spectacled caimans caught was: 1,101 in 2010; 9,036 in 2011; 6,320 in 2012.

Source: FAO.

Mining

('000 metric tons unless otherwise indicated)

	2009	2010	2011[1]
Hard coal[2]	5,818	6,310	6,330
Crude petroleum ('000 barrels) .	714,041	752,253	770,179
Natural gas (million cu m) .	21,142	22,922	24,090
Iron ore:[3]			
gross weight	298,528	372,120	391,098
metal content	198,771	247,772	260,408
Copper (metric tons) . . .	231,399	224,292	232,900
Nickel ore (metric tons)[4] . .	41,059	108,983	110,960
Bauxite	26,074	32,028	34,494
Lead concentrates (metric tons)[4] .	15,890	19,650	19,700
Zinc (metric tons)	242,136	288,107	281,190
Tin concentrates (metric tons)[4] .	9,500	10,400	9,550
Chromium ore (metric tons)[5] . .	246,900	258,308	258,300
Tungsten concentrates (metric tons)[4]	192	166	170
Ilmenite (metric tons) . . .	52,800	166,000	166,000
Rutile (metric tons) . . .	2,737	2,519	2,520
Zirconium concentrates (metric tons)[6]	34,248	23,235	23,200
Silver (kg)[7]	35,500	37,000	36,500

—continued	2009	2010	2011[1]
Gold (kg)	60,330	62,047	60,250
Bentonite (beneficiated) . . .	264	532	532
Kaolin (beneficiated) . . .	1,987	2,200	1,712
Magnesite (beneficiated) . . .	410	484	484
Phosphate rock[8]	6,084	6,192	6,200
Potash salts[9]	452	418	418
Fluorspar (Fluorite) (metric tons)[10]	43,964	25,814	25,850
Barite (Barytes) (beneficiated) (metric tons)	49,847	41,385	41,400
Quartz (natural crystals) (metric tons)	11,588	13,024	13,000
Salt (unrefined):			
marine	4,462	5,615	5,600
rock	1,443	1,415	1,400
Gypsum and anhydrite (crude) .	2,348	2,750	2,750
Graphite (natural) (metric tons)[2] .	59,425	72,623	76,330
Asbestos (fibre) (metric tons) . .	288,452	302,257	302,300
Mica (metric tons)[11] . . .	4,000	4,000	4,000
Vermiculite concentrates (metric tons)	50,438	49,976	55,000
Talc and pyrophyllite (crude) .	578	655	655
Diamonds, gem and industrial ('000 carats)[11,12]	21	25	25

[1] Preliminary figures.
[2] Figures refer to marketable products.
[3] Includes sponge iron (metric tons) 270,000 in 2009–11 (estimates).
[4] Figures refer to the metal content of ores and concentrates.
[5] Figures refer to the chromic oxide (Cr_2O_3) content.
[6] Including production of baddeleyite-caldasite.
[7] Figures refer to primary production only. The production of secondary silver (in kg, estimates): was: 31,000 in 2009; 32,000 in 2010; 32,000 in 2011 (preliminary figure).
[8] Figures refer to the gross weight of concentrates. The phosphoric acid (P_2O_5) content (in '000 metric tons) was: 2,163 in 2009; 2,179 in 2010; 2,200 in 2011 (preliminary figure).
[9] Figures refer to the potassium oxide (K_2O) content.
[10] Acid-grade and metallurgical-grade concentrates.
[11] Estimated production.
[12] Figures refer to officially reported diamond output plus official Brazilian estimates of diamond output by independent miners (*garimpeiros*).

Source: US Geological Survey.

Industry

SELECTED PRODUCTS
('000 metric tons unless otherwise indicated)

	2009	2010	2011
Beef—fresh or chilled . . .	3,476	3,492	4,675
Frozen poultry meats and giblets .	5,687	6,842	7,869
Sugar (granulated)	17,583	19,794	17,536
Beer ('000 hl)	n.a.	130,432	137,435
Soft drinks ('000 hl) . . .	142,041	166,323	167,252
Gas-diesel oil (distillate fuel oil, '000 cu m)	45,949	44,173	50,725
Residual fuel oils ('000 cu m) .	30,720	29,948	26,974
Naphthas for petrochemicals ('000 cu m)	9,187	9,022	8,233
Liquefied petroleum gas . . .	12,159	13,379	13,274
Ethylene—unsaturated . . .	2,772	n.a.	1,035
Fertilizers with nitrogen, phosphorus and potassium . .	15,057	17,207	18,944
Chemical wood pulp, cellulose .	9,856	10,467	10,467
Iron	5,028	6,670	7,009
Iron ore*	315,744	299,304	316,878
Hot rolled coils of carbon steel— uncoated	4,961	2,917	2,504
Trucks (units)†	100,832	144,412	164,243
Motorcycles (units)	1,391,865	1,590,697	1,928,754
Mobile cellular telephones ('000 units)	55,854	57,618	60,842

* Prepared forms, including concentrates, ball bearings, etc.
† Vehicles with diesel engines and maximum load capacity in excess of five metric tons.

Motor vehicles (excl. trucks): 2,473,586 in 2007.

Electric energy (million kWh): 463,120 in 2008; 466,158 in 2009; 515,798 in 2010 (Source: UN Industrial Commodity Statistics Database).

Finance

CURRENCY AND EXCHANGE RATES

Monetary Units
100 centavos = 1 real (plural: reais).

Sterling, Dollar and Euro Equivalents (30 May 2014)
£1 sterling = 3.765 reais;
US $1 = 2.238 reais;
€1 = 3.047 reais;
100 reais = £26.56 = $44.67 = €32.82.

Average Exchange Rates (reais per US $)
2011   1.6728
2012   1.9531
2013   2.1569

Note: In March 1986 the cruzeiro (CR $) was replaced by a new currency unit, the cruzado (CZ $), equivalent to 1,000 cruzeiros. In January 1989 the cruzado was, in turn, replaced by the new cruzado (NCZ $), equivalent to CZ $1,000 and initially at par with the US dollar (US $). In March 1990 the new cruzado was replaced by the cruzeiro (CR $), at an exchange rate of one new cruzado for one cruzeiro. In August 1993 the cruzeiro was replaced by the cruzeiro real, equivalent to CR $1,000. On 1 March 1994, in preparation for the introduction of a new currency, a transitional accounting unit, the Unidade Real de Valor (at par with the US $), came into operation, alongside the cruzeiro real. On 1 July 1994 the cruzeiro real was replaced by the real (R $), also at par with the US $ and thus equivalent to 2,750 cruzeiros reais.

BUDGET
(R $ million)

Revenue	2011	2012	2013
National treasury revenues . .	741,297	783,439	871,158
Gross revenues*	757,429	802,831	894,678
Restitutions	−15,858	−19,249	−23,468
Fiscal incentives	−274	−142	−52
Social security revenues . . .	245,892	275,765	307,147
Urban	240,536	270,002	300,991
Rural	5,356	5,763	6,156
Central bank revenues . . .	3,217	3,002	2,795
Total	990,406	1,062,206	1,181,100

Expenditure	2011	2012	2013
Transfers to state and local governments	172,483	181,377	189,987
Treasury expenditures	439,191	484,623	552,925
Payroll*	179,277	186,097	202,744
Worker support fund (FAT) .	34,660	39,330	44,688
Economic subsidies and grants† .	10,517	11,272	44,688
Assistance benefits (LOAS/RMV)	24,905	29,207	33,523
Other current and capital expenditures	187,696	216,399	251,853
Transfer to central bank . .	2,136	2,317	2,112
Social security benefits . . .	281,438	316,590	357,003
Central bank expenditures . .	3,769	3,755	4,113
Total	896,881	986,344	1,104,028

* Excludes the employer share of federal civil service payments from revenues originating in contributions to the Social Security Plan (CPSS) and personnel outlays.
† Includes judicially determined repayments related to the Rural Unified and Industrial Unified initiatives.

Source: Ministério da Fazenda, Brasília, DF.

INTERNATIONAL RESERVES
(US $ million at 31 December)

	2011	2012	2013
Gold (national valuation) . .	1,654	3,581	2,592
IMF special drawing rights . .	3,979	3,986	3,996
Reserve position in the IMF . .	2,993	3,483	3,190
Foreign exchange	343,384	362,097	349,028
Total	352,010	373,147	358,806

Source: IMF, *International Financial Statistics*.

MONEY SUPPLY
(R $ million at 31 December)

	2011	2012	2013
Currency outside depository corporations	131,727	149,627	163,864
Transferable deposits	152,579	182,279	189,798
Other deposits	2,603,033	2,413,439	2,628,278
Securities other than shares . .	193,472	810,387	890,817
Broad money	3,080,811	3,555,732	3,872,757

Source: IMF, *International Financial Statistics*.

COST OF LIVING
(Consumer Price Index; base: 2000 = 100)

	2010	2011	2012
Food	204.6	222.7	240.8
All items (incl. others) . . .	190.4	203.0	214.0

2013: All items 227.2.

Source: ILO.

NATIONAL ACCOUNTS
(R $ million at current prices)

National Income and Product

	2011	2012	2013
Gross domestic product (GDP) in market prices	4,143,013	4,392,094	4,844,815
Wages and salaries	948	1,001	1,106
Primary incomes received from abroad (net)	−79,076	−69,818	−85,831
Gross national income (GNI) .	4,064,885	4,323,277	4,760,090
Current transfers received from abroad (net)	4,998	5,581	7,260
Net national disposable income	4,069,883	4,328,858	4,767,351

Expenditure on the Gross Domestic Product

	2011	2012	2013
Final consumption expenditure .	3,356,136	3,686,020	4,098,222
Households	2,499,489	2,750,191	3,033,694
General government	856,647	935,829	1,064,528
Gross capital formation . . .	817,260	769,606	866,911
Gross fixed capital formation .	798,720	798,142	880,935
Changes in inventories . . .	18,540	−28,537	−14,024
Total domestic expenditure .	4,173,396	4,455,626	4,965,133
Exports of goods and services . .	492,570	552,843	608,209
Less Imports of goods and services	522,953	616,374	728,529
GDP in market prices	4,143,013	4,392,094	4,844,815

Gross Domestic Product by Economic Activity

	2011	2012	2013
Agriculture, hunting, forestry and fishing	192,653	198,137	234,594
Mining and quarrying	143,924	159,002	168,883
Manufacturing	515,441	482,494	539,673
Electricity, gas and water . . .	108,724	114,637	96,305
Construction	204,067	213,100	221,763
Trade, restaurants and hotels .	446,606	474,743	522,789
Transport, storage and communications	180,997	201,226	218,117
Information services	107,589	107,519	108,175
Financial intermediation, insurance, and related services .	262,482	266,793	285,462
Real estate and renting . . .	278,402	305,726	340,449
Government, health and education services	576,541	618,464	727,992
Other services	513,445	583,228	646,176
Gross value added in basic prices	3,530,871	3,725,069	4,110,377
Taxes, less subsidies, on products .	612,142	667,025	734,438
GDP in market prices . . .	4,143,013	4,392,094	4,844,815

BALANCE OF PAYMENTS
(US $ million)

	2011	2012	2013
Exports of goods	256,040	242,580	242,179
Imports of goods	−226,233	−223,149	−239,621
Balance on goods	29,807	19,431	2,558
Exports of services	38,209	39,864	39,118
Imports of services	−76,161	−80,939	−86,641
Balance on goods and services	−8,145	−21,645	−44,965
Primary income received . . .	10,753	10,888	10,071
Primary income paid	−58,072	−46,335	−49,843
Balance on goods, services and primary income	−55,464	−57,092	−84,738
Secondary income received . .	4,915	4,626	5,476
Secondary income paid . . .	−1,931	−1,780	−2,112
Current balance	−52,480	−54,246	−81,374
Capital account (net) . . .	1,573	−1,877	1,194
Direct investment assets . . .	−3,850	−8,017	−13,351
Direct investment liabilities . .	71,539	76,111	80,892
Portfolio investment assets . .	16,858	−8,260	−8,974
Portfolio investment liabilities .	18,453	16,534	34,664
Financial derivatives assets . .	252	150	382
Financial derivatives liabilities .	−249	−125	−271
Other investment assets . . .	−38,984	−24,278	−39,558
Other investment liabilities . .	46,796	22,525	19,636
Net errors and omissions . . .	−1,274	384	835
Reserves and related items .	58,635	18,899	−5,924

Source: IMF, *International Financial Statistics.*

External Trade

PRINCIPAL COMMODITIES
(distribution by HS, US $ million)

Imports f.o.b.	2011	2012	2013
Mineral products . . .	44,559.2	42,218.5	48,027.4
Mineral fuels, oils, distillation products, etc.	41,968.2	40,187.2	45,693.8
Crude petroleum oils . . .	14,080.6	13,405.8	16,320.0
Petroleum oils, not crude . .	16,905.1	16,365.1	17,757.0
Petroleum gases	4,592.4	5,959.6	7,997.9
Chemicals and related products	34,600.7	35,628.4	38,233.1
Organic chemicals	9,396.6	9,914.7	10,735.8
Pharmaceutical products . .	6,499.2	6,840.9	7,420.1
Fertilizers	9,138.4	8,583.8	8,885.5
Plastics, rubber and articles of plastics and rubber . . .	13,206.9	12,507.4	13,599.4
Plastics and articles thereof . .	8,104.3	7,967.7	8,848.6
Base metals and articles thereof	14,246.8	13,788.4	13,704.7
Machinery and mechanical appliances, electrical equipment	60,098.2	60,163.1	64,032.0
Machinery, boilers, etc. . . .	33,703.1	34,674.0	35,757.5
Electrical and electronic equipment	26,395.1	25,489.1	28,274.4
Vehicles, aircraft, vessels and transport equipment . . .	26,374.3	25,208.0	26,497.8
Vehicles other than railway, tramway	22,620.9	21,309.4	22,418.6
Cars (incl. station wagons) . .	11,891.4	9,566.7	9,081.2
Parts and accessories of motor vehicles	6,317.6	6,771.5	8,296.7
Optical, medical apparatus, etc.; clocks and watches; musical instruments; parts thereof	6,762.4	6,913.2	7,533.2
Total (incl. others) . . .	226,243.4	223,149.1	239,620.9

Exports f.o.b.	2011	2012	2013
Live animals and animal products	15,214.5	15,364.6	16,630.8
Meat and edible meat offal . .	13,722.9	13,703.0	14,786.2
Vegetable products	30,040.9	31,357.0	36,112.9
Coffee, tea, maté and spices . .	8,324.9	6,022.8	4,954.3
Coffee	8,026.4	5,740.3	4,598.1
Oil seed, oleagic fruits, grain, seed, fruit, etc.	16,531.3	17,682.0	23,027.2
Soya beans	16,327.3	17,248.3	22,812.3
Prepared foodstuffs, beverages, spirits, tobacco, etc.	31,786.7	31,419.9	30,277.3
Sugars and sugar confectionery .	15,154.1	13,030.3	12,013.9
Cane or beet sugar and chemically pure sucrose in solid form	14,941.7	12,650.8	11,842.5
Mineral products	76,613.6	65,433.8	53,705.6
Ores, slag and ash	44,216.6	33,244.4	35,082.7
Iron ores and concentrates (incl. roasted iron pyrites) . . .	41,817.3	30,989.3	32,491.5
Mineral fuels, oils, distillation products, etc.	31,619.4	31,420.0	17,822.2
Crude petroleum oils . . .	21,603.3	20,305.9	12,956.6
Chemicals and related products	12,258.4	11,570.0	11,156.6
Base metals and articles thereof	18,940.9	17,240.1	14,805.3
Iron and steel	12,013.9	10,711.0	8,372.3
Machinery and mechanical appliances, electrical equipment	19,225.4	18,805.5	17,638.1
Machinery, boilers, etc. . . .	14,084.4	13,880.6	12,890.2
Vehicles, aircraft, vessels and transport equipment . . .	19,575.4	19,436.7	26,573.9
Vehicles other than railway, tramway	13,760.9	12,569.5	14,089.3
Ships, boats and other floating structures	1,152.8	1,548.8	7,933.7
Light vessels, dredgers; floating docks; floating/submersible drill platforms	1,042.9	1,457.8	7,735.5
Total (incl. others)	256,038.7	242,579.8	242,178.6

Source: Trade Map-Trade Competitiveness Map, International Trade Centre, www.intracen.org/marketanalysis.

PRINCIPAL TRADING PARTNERS
(US $ million)

Imports f.o.b.	2011	2012	2013
Algeria	3,136.8	3,197.9	3,074.8
Argentina	16,906.1	16,444.1	16,462.9
Bolivia	2,863.4	3,431.0	3,937.7
Canada	3,553.3	3,072.1	3,001.5
Chile	4,569.5	4,164.6	4,328.3
China, People's Republic . . .	32,788.4	34,248.5	37,302.2
France (incl. Monaco)	5,471.3	5,918.6	6,509.4
Germany	15,212.9	14,208.9	15,182.0
India	6,081.0	5,042.8	6,357.3
Italy	6,228.3	6,206.9	6,724.1
Japan	7,871.8	7,734.7	7,081.7
Korea, Republic	10,097.0	9,097.7	9,491.3
Malaysia	2,287.4	2,083.6	2,211.7
Mexico	5,130.2	6,075.1	5,794.8
Netherlands	2,265.4	3,106.4	2,344.6
Nigeria	8,386.4	8,012.2	9,647.5
Russia	2,944.2	2,790.7	2,676.1
Saudi Arabia	3,093.0	3,192.9	3,194.2
Spain	3,298.2	3,540.1	4,486.4
Switzerland (incl. Liechtenstein) .	2,845.9	2,782.8	2,951.9
Taiwan	3,509.4	3,168.8	2,937.8
Thailand	2,399.3	2,503.9	2,383.9
United Kingdom	3,375.6	3,505.2	3,614.2
USA	34,233.5	32,607.9	36,279.6
Total (incl. others)	226,243.4	223,149.1	239,620.9

Exports f.o.b.	2011	2012	2013
Argentina	22,709.3	17,997.7	19,615.4
Belgium-Luxembourg	3,959.7	3,741.6	3,593.8
Canada	3,129.5	3,079.9	2,701.7
Chile	5,418.1	4,602.2	4,483.8
China, People's Republic	44,314.6	41,227.5	46,026.2
Colombia	2,577.4	2,834.5	2,703.1
Egypt	2,624.0	2,711.9	2,201.6
France (incl. Monaco)	4,359.3	4,139.4	3,423.4
Germany	9,039.1	7,277.1	6,551.7
Hong Kong	2,176.3	2,458.1	3,339.2
India	3,200.7	5,576.9	3,130.1
Italy	5,440.9	4,580.7	4,098.1
Japan	9,473.1	7,955.7	7,964.0
Korea, Republic	4,693.9	4,501.1	4,720.0
Mexico	3,959.7	4,003.0	4,230.3
Netherlands	13,639.7	15,040.7	17,325.9
Panama	418.7	397.4	4,423.1
Paraguay	2,968.6	2,617.5	2,996.6
Peru	2,262.9	2,415.2	2,147.2
Russia	4,216.3	3,140.8	2,974.1
Saint Lucia	2,943.3	1,253.5	100.7
Saudi Arabia	3,476.4	3,000.1	2,838.8
Singapore	2,786.5	2,942.6	1,905.4
Spain	4,705.5	3,688.7	3,576.0
United Arab Emirates	2,169.2	2,456.8	2,588.8
United Kingdom	5,229.8	4,519.4	4,101.9
USA	25,943.0	26,849.9	24,861.8
Venezuela	4,591.8	5,056.0	4,849.8
Total (incl. others)	256,038.7	242,579.8	242,178.6

Source: Trade Map-Trade Competitiveness Map, International Trade Centre, www.intracen.org/marketanalysis.

Transport

RAILWAYS
(figures are rounded)

	2005	2006	2007
Passengers ('000):			
Long distance	1,451	1,481	1,414
Metropolitan	144,300	n.a.	n.a.
Passenger-km ('000, long distance only)	451,943	463,517	444,094
Freight ('000 metric tons)	388,592	389,109	414,926
Freight ton-km (million)	221,633	238,054	257,118

2008: Freight ('000 metric tons) 426,514; Freight ton-km (million) 266,967.

Source: Agência Nacional de Transportes Terrestres (ANTT), Ministério dos Transportes, Brasília.

ROAD TRAFFIC
(motor vehicles in use at 31 December)

	2007	2008	2009
Passenger cars	30,282,855	32,054,684	34,536,667
Vans and lorries	5,709,063	7,528,326	n.a.
Buses and coaches	1,985,761	633,122	673,084
Motorcycles and mopeds	10,921,686	13,088,074	14,688,678
Total (incl. others)	48,899,365	53,304,206	n.a.

Source: IRF, *World Road Statistics*.

SHIPPING
Flag Registered Fleet
(at 31 December)

	2011	2012	2013
Number of vessels	744	781	823
Total displacement ('000 grt)	2,914.8	2,920.4	3,156.5

Source: Lloyd's List Intelligence (www.lloydslistintelligence.com).

CIVIL AVIATION
(traffic)

	2010	2011
Kilometres flown (million)	791	921
Passengers carried ('000)	74,598	87,891
Passenger-km (million)	90,619	105,728
Total ton-km (million)	9,070	10,888

Source: UN, *Statistical Yearbook*.

Passengers carried ('000): 94,618 in 2012 (Source: World Bank, World Development Indicators database).

Tourism

FOREIGN TOURIST ARRIVALS

Country of origin	2010	2011	2012
Argentina	1,399,592	1,593,775	1,671,604
Bolivia	99,359	85,429	112,639
Chile	200,724	217,200	250,586
Colombia	85,567	91,345	100,324
France	199,719	207,890	218,626
Germany	226,630	241,739	258,437
Italy	245,491	229,484	230,114
Paraguay	194,340	192,730	246,401
Portugal	189,065	183,728	168,649
Spain	179,340	190,392	180,406
United Kingdom	167,355	149,564	155,548
USA	641,377	594,947	586,463
Uruguay	228,545	261,204	253,864
Total (incl. others)	5,161,379	5,433,354	5,676,843

Source: Instituto Brasileiro de Turismo—EMBRATUR, Brasília.

Receipts from tourism (US $ million, excl. passenger transport): 6,555 in 2011; 6,645 in 2012; 6,711 in 2013 (provisional) (Source: World Tourism Organization).

Communications Media

	2011	2012	2013
Telephones in use ('000 main lines)	43,025.8	44,305.3	44,631.4
Mobile cellular telephones ('000 subscribers)	234,357.5	248,323.7	271,099.8
Internet subscribers ('000)	22,898.3	n.a.	n.a.
Broadband subscribers ('000)	16,855.1	18,186.5	20,190.9

Source: International Telecommunication Union.

Education

(2013 unless otherwise indicated)

	Institutions	Teachers	Students
Pre-primary	107,320	474,591	7,590,600
Literacy classes (Classe de Alfabetização)*	27,670	37,508	598,589
Primary	141,260	1,409,991	29,069,281
Secondary	27,450	509,403	8,312,815
Special	4,071	29,827	194,421
Technical and vocational	4,579	73,904	1,102,661
Higher	3,059	379,240	4,421,591

* 2003 figures.

Source: Ministério da Educação, Brasília.

Pupil-teacher ratio (primary education, UN estimate): 21.3 in 2010/11 (Source: UNESCO Institute for Statistics).

Adult literacy rate (UNESCO estimates): 91.3% (males 91.0%; females 91.6%) in 2012 (Source: UNESCO Institute for Statistics).

Directory

The Constitution

A new Constitution was promulgated on 5 October 1988. The following is a summary of the main provisions:

The Federative Republic of Brazil, formed by the indissoluble union of the States, the Municipalities and the Federal District, is constituted as a democratic state. All power emanates from the people. The Federative Republic of Brazil seeks the economic, political, social and cultural integration of the peoples of Latin America.

All are equal before the law. The inviolability of the right to life, freedom, equality, security and property is guaranteed. No one shall be subjected to torture. Freedom of thought, conscience, religious belief and expression are guaranteed, as is privacy. The principles of habeas corpus and 'habeas data' (the latter giving citizens access to personal information held in government data banks) are granted. There is freedom of association, and the right to strike is guaranteed.

There is universal suffrage by direct secret ballot. Voting is compulsory for literate persons between 18 and 69 years of age, and optional for those who are illiterate, those over 70 years of age and those aged 16 and 17.

Brasília is the federal capital. The Union's competence includes maintaining relations with foreign states, and taking part in international organizations; declaring war and making peace; guaranteeing national defence; decreeing a state of siege; issuing currency; supervising credits, etc.; formulating and implementing plans for economic and social development; maintaining national services, including communications, energy, the judiciary and the police; legislating on civil, commercial, penal, procedural, electoral, agrarian, maritime, aeronautical, spatial and labour law, etc. The Union, States, Federal District and Municipalities must protect the Constitution, laws and democratic institutions, and preserve national heritage.

The States are responsible for electing their Governors by universal suffrage and direct secret ballot for a four-year term. The organization of the Municipalities, the Federal District and the Territories is regulated by law.

The Union may intervene in the States and in the Federal District only in certain circumstances, such as a threat to national security or public order, and then only after reference to the Congresso Nacional (National Congress).

LEGISLATIVE POWER

Legislative power is exercised by the National Congress (Congresso Nacional), which is composed of the Chamber of Deputies (Câmara dos Deputados) and the Federal Senate (Senado Federal). Elections for deputies and senators take place simultaneously throughout the country; candidates for the Congress must be Brazilian by birth and have full exercise of their political rights. They must be at least 21 years of age in the case of deputies and at least 35 years of age in the case of senators. The Congress meets twice a year in ordinary sessions, and extraordinary sessions may be convened by the President of the Republic, the Presidents of both houses, or at the request of the majority of the members of either house.

The Chamber of Deputies is made up of representatives of the people, elected by a system of proportional representation in each State, Territory and the Federal District for a period of four years. The total number of deputies representing the States and the Federal District will be established in proportion to the population; each Territory will elect four deputies.

The Senate is composed of representatives of the States and the Federal District, elected according to the principle of majority. Each State and the Federal District will elect three senators with a mandate of eight years, with elections after four years for one-third of the members and after another four years for the remaining two-thirds. Each Senator is elected with two substitutes. The Senate approves, by secret ballot, the choice of Magistrates (when required by the Constitution), of the Attorney-General of the Republic, of the Ministers of the Accounts Tribunal, of the Territorial Governors, of the president and directors of the Central Bank and of the permanent heads of diplomatic missions.

The Congress is responsible for deciding on all matters within the competence of the Union, especially fiscal and budgetary arrangements, national, regional and local plans and programmes, the strength of the armed forces, and territorial limits. It is also responsible for making definitive resolutions on international treaties, and for authorizing the President to declare war.

The powers of the Chamber of Deputies include authorizing the instigation of legal proceedings against the President and Vice-President of the Republic and Ministers of State. The Senate may indict and impose sentence on the President and Vice-President of the Republic and Ministers of State.

Constitutional amendments may be proposed by at least one-third of the members of either house, by the President or by more than one-half of the legislative assemblies of the units of the Federation. Amendments must be ratified by three-fifths of the members of each house. The Constitution may not be amended during times of national emergency, such as a state of siege.

EXECUTIVE POWER

Executive power is exercised by the President of the Republic, aided by the Ministers of State. Candidates for the Presidency and Vice-Presidency must be Brazilian-born, be in full exercise of their political rights and be over 35 years of age. The candidate who obtains an absolute majority of votes will be elected President. If no candidate attains an absolute majority, the two candidates who have received the most votes proceed to a second round of voting, at which the candidate obtaining the majority of valid votes will be elected President. The President holds office for a term of four years and (under an amendment adopted in 1997) is eligible for re-election.

The Ministers of State are chosen by the President, and their duties include countersigning acts and decrees signed by the President, expediting instructions for the enactment of laws, decrees and regulations, and presentation to the President of an annual report of their activities.

The Council of the Republic is the higher consultative organ of the President of the Republic. It comprises the Vice-President of the Republic, the Presidents of the legislative houses, the leaders of the majority and of the minority in each house, the Minister of Justice, two members appointed by the President of the Republic, two elected by the Senate and two elected by the Chamber, the latter six having a mandate of three years.

The National Defence Council advises the President on matters relating to national sovereignty and defence. It comprises the Vice-President of the Republic, the Presidents of both legislative houses, the Minister of Justice, military Ministers and the Ministers of Foreign Affairs and of Planning.

JUDICIAL POWER

Judicial power in the Union is exercised by the Supreme Federal Court; the Higher Court of Justice; the Regional Federal Courts and federal judges; Labour Courts and judges; Electoral Courts and judges; Military Courts and judges; and the States' Courts and judges. Judges are appointed for life; they may not undertake any other employment. The Courts elect their own controlling organs and organize their own internal structure.

The Supreme Federal Court, situated in the Union capital, has jurisdiction over the whole national territory and is composed of 11 ministers. The ministers are nominated by the President after approval by the Senate, from Brazilian-born citizens, between the ages of 35 and 65 years, of proved judicial knowledge and experience.

The Government

HEAD OF STATE

President: Dilma Vana Rousseff (PT) (took office 1 January 2011).
Vice-President: Michel Miguel Elias Temer Lulia (PMDB).

THE CABINET
(September 2014)

The Cabinet is composed of members of the Partido dos Trabalhadores (PT), the Partido do Movimento Democrático Brasileiro (PMDB), the Partido da República (PR), the Partido Republicano Brasiliero (PRB), the Partido Comunista do Brasil (PC do B), the Partido Democrático Trabalhista (PDT), the Partido Republicano da Ordem Social (PROS), and Independents (Ind.).

Cabinet Chief: Aloízio Mercadante (PT).

Minister of Foreign Affairs: Luiz Alberto Figueiredo Machado (Ind.).

Minister of Justice: José Eduardo Cardozo (PT).

Minister of Finance: Guido Mantega (PT).

Minister of Defence: Celso Amorim (PT).

Minister of Agriculture, Livestock and Food Supply: Neri Geller (PMDB).

Minister of Agrarian Development: Miguel Rossetto (PT).

Minister of Labour and Employment: Manoel Dias (PDT).

Minister of Transport: Paulo Sérgio Passos (PR).

Minister of Cities: Gilberto Magalhães Occhi (Ind.).

Minister of Planning, Budget and Administration: Miriam Belchior (PT).

Minister of Mines and Energy: Edison Lobão (PMDB).

Minister of Culture: MARTA SUPLICY (PT).

Minister of the Environment: IZABELLA MÔNICA VIEIRA TEIXEIRA (Ind.).

Minister of Development, Industry and Foreign Trade: MAURO BORGES LEMOS.

Minister of Education: JOSÉ HENRIQUE PAIM FERNANDES (PT).

Minister of Health: ARTHUR CHIORO (PT).

Minister of National Integration: FRANCISCO JOSÉ COELHO TEIXEIRA (PROS).

Minister of Social Security: GARIBALDI ALVES FILHO (PMDB).

Minister of Social Development and the Fight against Hunger: TEREZA CAMPELO (PT).

Minister of Communications: PAULO BERNARDO SILVA (PT).

Minister of Science, Technology and Innovation: CLÉLIO CAMPOLINA DINIZ (PMDB).

Minister of Sport: JOSÉ ALDO REBELO FIGUEIREDO (PC do B).

Minister of Tourism: VINICIUS NOBRE LAGES (PMDB).

Minister of Fisheries and Aquaculture: EDUARDO LOPES (PRB).

Prosecutor-General: RODRIGO JANOT.

Attorney-General: LUÍS INÁCIO LUCENA ADAMS.

Comptroller-General: JORGE HAGE SOBRINHO.

Chief Minister of the Office of Institutional Security: Gen. JOSÉ ELITO CARVALHO SIQUEIRA.

SECRETARIES

Secretary of Strategic Affairs: MARCELO CÔRTES NERI.

Secretary of Civil Aviation: MOREIRA FRANCO.

Secretary of Social Communication: THOMAS TRAUMANN.

Secretary of Human Rights: MARIA DO ROSÁRIO.

Secretary of Policies for the Promotion of Racial Equality: LUIZA HELENA DE BAIRROS.

Secretary of Women's Policies: ELEONORA MENICUCCI DE OLIVEIRA.

Secretary of Ports: CÉSAR BORGES.

Secretary of Institutional Relations: IDELI SALVATTI.

Secretary for Small- and Micro-Businesses: GUILHERME AFIF DOMINGOS.

Secretary-General: GILBERTO CARVALHO.

MINISTRIES AND SECRETARIATS

Office of the President: Palácio do Planalto, 3° andar, Praça dos Três Poderes, 70150-900 Brasília, DF; tel. (61) 3411-1221; fax 3411-2222; e-mail protocolo@planalto.gov.br; internet www2.planalto.gov.br.

Office of the Civilian Cabinet: Palácio do Planalto, 4° andar, Praça dos Três Poderes, 70150-900 Brasília, DF; tel. (61) 3411-1221; fax (61) 3411-2222; e-mail sicplanalto@planalto.gov.br; internet www.casacivil.planalto.gov.br.

Ministry of Agrarian Development: Esplanada dos Ministérios, Bloco A, 8° andar, Ala Norte, 70050-902 Brasília, DF; tel. (61) 2020-0002; fax (61) 2020-0061; e-mail miguel.rossetto@mda.gov.br; internet www.mda.gov.br.

Ministry of Agriculture, Livestock and Food Supply: Esplanada dos Ministérios, Bloco D, Anexo B, 70043-900 Brasília, DF; tel. (61) 3218-2828; fax (61) 3218-2401; e-mail gm@agricultura.gov.br; internet www.agricultura.gov.br.

Ministry of Cities: Edif. Telemundi II, 14° andar, Setor de Autarquias Sul, Quadra 01, Lote 01/06, Bloco H, 700700-10 Brasília, DF; tel. (61) 2108-1000; fax (61) 2108-1415; e-mail cidades@cidades.gov.br; internet www.cidades.gov.br.

Ministry of Communications: Esplanada dos Ministérios, Bloco R, 8° andar, 70044-900 Brasília, DF; tel. (61) 2027-6200; fax (61) 3311-6731; e-mail falecomoministerio@comunicacoes.gov.br; internet www.mc.gov.br.

Ministry of Culture: Esplanada dos Ministérios, Bloco B, 4° andar, 70068-900 Brasília, DF; tel. (61) 2024-2000; fax (61) 3225-9162; e-mail gm@cultura.gov.br; internet www.cultura.gov.br.

Ministry of Defence: Esplanada dos Ministérios, Bloco Q, 70049-900 Brasília, DF; tel. (61) 3312-4000; fax (61) 3225-4151; e-mail faleconosco@defesa.gov.br; internet www.defesa.gov.br.

Ministry of Development, Industry and Foreign Trade: Esplanada dos Ministérios, Bloco J, 70053-900 Brasília, DF; tel. (61) 2027-7000; fax (61) 2027-7230; e-mail asint@desenvolvimento.gov.br; internet www.desenvolvimento.gov.br.

Ministry of Education: Esplanada dos Ministérios, Bloco L, 8° andar, Sala 805, 70047-900 Brasília, DF; tel. (61) 2022-7828; fax (61) 2022-7858; e-mail gabinetedoministro@mec.gov.br; internet www.mec.gov.br.

Ministry of the Environment: Esplanada dos Ministérios, Bloco B, 5°–9° andares, 70068-900 Brasília, DF; tel. (61) 2028-1057; fax (61) 2028-1756; e-mail webmaster@mma.gov.br; internet www.mma.gov.br.

Ministry of Finance: Esplanada dos Ministérios, Bloco P, 5° andar, 70048-900 Brasília, DF; tel. (61) 3412-2000; fax (61) 3412-1721; e-mail gabinete.df.gmf@fazenda.gov.br; internet www.fazenda.gov.br.

Ministry of Fisheries and Aquaculture: Edif. Carlton Tower, SBS Quadra 2, Lote 10, Bloco J, 70043-900 Brasília DF; tel. (61) 2023-3000; fax (61) 2023-3916; e-mail comunicacao@mpa.gov.br; internet www.mpa.gov.br.

Ministry of Foreign Affairs: Palácio do Itamaraty, Térreo, Esplanada dos Ministérios, Bloco H, 70170-900 Brasília, DF; tel. (61) 3411-8006; fax (61) 3225-8002; e-mail imprensa@itamaraty.gov.br; internet www.itamaraty.gov.br.

Ministry of Health: Esplanada dos Ministérios, Bloco G, 70058-900 Brasília, DF; tel. (61) 3315-3283; e-mail leandro.viegas@saude.gov.br; internet www.saude.gov.br.

Ministry of Justice: Esplanada dos Ministérios, Bloco T, 70064-900 Brasília, DF; tel. (61) 3429-3000; fax (61) 3224-0954; e-mail acs@mj.gov.br; internet www.mj.gov.br.

Ministry of Labour and Employment: Esplanada dos Ministérios, Bloco F, 5° andar, 70059-900 Brasília, DF; tel. (61) 3317-6000; fax (61) 3317-8245; e-mail ouvidoria@mte.gov.br; internet www.mte.gov.br.

Ministry of Mines and Energy: Esplanada dos Ministérios, Bloco U, 70065-900 Brasília, DF; tel. (61) 3319-5555; fax (61) 3319-5074; e-mail gabinete@mme.gov.br; internet www.mme.gov.br.

Ministry of National Integration: Esplanada dos Ministérios, Bloco E, 8° andar, 70067-901 Brasília, DF; tel. (61) 3414-5814; fax (61) 3321-5914; e-mail impresa@integracao.gov.br; internet www.integracao.gov.br.

Ministry of Planning, Budget and Administration: Esplanada dos Ministérios, Bloco K, 7° andar, 70040-906 Brasília, DF; tel. (61) 2020-4102; fax (61) 2020-5009; e-mail ministro@planejamento.gov.br; internet www.planejamento.gov.br.

Ministry of Science, Technology and Innovation: Esplanada dos Ministérios, Bloco E, 4° andar, 70067-900 Brasília, DF; tel. (61) 3317-7500; fax (61) 3317-7764; e-mail webgab@mct.gov.br; internet www.mct.gov.br.

Ministry of Social Development and the Fight against Hunger: Esplanada dos Ministérios, Bloco C, 5° andar, 70046-900 Brasília, DF; tel. (61) 3433-1029; e-mail ministro.mds@mds.gov.br; internet www.mds.gov.br.

Ministry of Social Security: Esplanada dos Ministérios, Bloco F, 8° andar, 70059-900 Brasília, DF; tel. (61) 2021-5000; fax (61) 2021-5407; e-mail gm.mps@previdencia.gov.br; internet www.mps.gov.br.

Ministry of Sport: Esplanada dos Ministérios, Bloco A, 70054-906 Brasília, DF; tel. (61) 3217-1800; fax (61) 3217-1707; e-mail gabmin@esporte.gov.br; internet www.esporte.gov.br.

Ministry of Tourism: Esplanada dos Ministérios, Bloco U, 2° e 3° andar, 70065-900 Brasília, DF; tel. (61) 2023-7024; fax (61) 2023-7096; e-mail ouvidoria@turismo.gov.br; internet www.turismo.gov.br.

Ministry of Transport: Esplanada dos Ministérios, Bloco R, 6° andar, 70044-900 Brasília, DF; tel. (61) 2029-7000; fax (61) 2029-7876; e-mail paulo.passos@transportes.gov.br; internet www.transportes.gov.br.

Office of Institutional Security: Brasília, DF.

Secretariat-General of the Presidency: Praça dos Três Poderes, Palácio do Planalto, 4° andar, 70150-900 Brasília, DF; tel. (61) 3411-1225; e-mail sg@planalto.gov.br; internet www.secretariageral.gov.br.

Secretariat of Civil Aviation: Brasília, DF.

Secretariat of Human Rights: Edif. Parque Cidade Corporate, Torre A, 10° andar, Setor Comercial Sul B, Quadra 9, Lote C, 70308-200 Brasília, DF; tel. (61) 2025-3536; fax (61) 2025-3106; e-mail direitoshumanos@sedh.gov.br; internet www.direitoshumanos.gov.br.

Secretariat of Institutional Relations: Palácio do Planalto, 4° andar, Sala 404, Praça dos Três Poderes, 70150-900 Brasília, DF; tel. (61) 3411-1585; fax (61) 3411-1503; e-mail sri.gabinete@planalto.gov.br; internet www.relacoesinstitucionais.gov.br.

Secretariat of Policies for the Promotion of Racial Equality: Esplanada dos Ministérios, Bloco A, 9° andar, 70054-906 Brasília, DF; tel. (61) 2025-7043; fax (61) 3226-5625; e-mail seppir.imprensa@planalto.gov.br; internet www.seppir.gov.br.

Secretariat of Ports: Centro Empresarial Varig, Pétala C Mezanino, Sala 1403, SCN Quadra 04, Bloco B, 70714-900 Brasília, DF; tel. (61) 3411-3704; fax (61) 3326-3025; e-mail faleconosco@portosdobrasil.gov.br; internet www.portosdobrasil.gov.br.

Secretariat of Small- and Micro-Businesses: Brasília, DF.

Secretariat of Social Communication: Esplanada dos Ministérios, Bloco A, 70054-900 Brasília, DF; tel. (61) 3411-1279; fax (61) 3226-8316; internet www.secom.gov.br.

Secretariat of Strategic Affairs: Esplanada dos Ministérios, Bloco O, 7° andar, 8° e 9° andares, 70052-900 Brasília, DF; tel. (61) 3411-4674; e-mail falecomministro.sae@presidencia.gov.br; internet www.sae.gov.br.

Secretariat of Women's Policies: Via N1 Leste, Pavilhão das Metas, Praça dos Três Poderes, Zona Cívico-Administrativa, 70150-908 Brasília, DF; tel. (61) 3411-4246; fax (61) 3327-7464; e-mail spmulheres@spmulheres.gov.br; internet www.sepm.gov.br.

President and Legislature

PRESIDENT

Election, First Round, 3 October 2010

Candidate	Votes	% of valid votes
Dilma Vana Rousseff (PT) . . .	47,651,434	46.91
José Serra (PSDB)	33,132,283	32.61
Marina Silva (PV)	19,636,359	19.33
Plínio de Arruda Sampaio (PSOL) .	886,816	0.87
José Maria Eymael (PSDC) . .	89,350	0.09
José Maria de Almeida (PSTU) . .	84,609	0.08
Levy Fidelix (PRTB)	57,960	0.06
Ivan Pinheiro (PCB)	39,136	0.04
Rui Costa Pimenta (PCO) . . .	12,206	0.01
Total*	101,590,153	100.00

* In addition, there were 3,479,340 blank and 6,124,254 spoiled votes.

Election, Second Round, 31 October 2010

Candidate	Votes	% of valid votes
Dilma Vana Rousseff (PT) . . .	55,725,529	56.04
José Serra (PSDB)	43,711,388	43.96
Total*	99,436,917	100.00

* In addition, there were 2,452,597 blank ballots and 4,689,428 spoiled ballots.

NATIONAL CONGRESS

Chamber of Deputies
(Câmara dos Deputados)

Chamber of Deputies: Palácio do Congresso Nacional, Edif. Principal, Praça dos Três Poderes, 70160-900 Brasília, DF; tel. (61) 3216-0000; e-mail presidencia@camara.gov.br; internet www.camara.gov.br.

President: HENRIQUE EDUARDO ALVES (PMDB).

The Chamber has 513 members who hold office for a four-year term.

General Election, 3 October 2010

Party	Votes	% of valid votes	Seats
Partido dos Trabalhadores (PT) .	16,289,199	16.9	88
Partido do Movimento Democrático Brasileiro (PMDB)	12,537,252	13.0	79
Partido da Social Democracia Brasileira (PSDB)	11,477,380	11.9	53
Democratas (DEM)	7,301,171	7.6	43
Partido da República (PR) . .	7,311,655	7.6	41
Partido Progressista (PP) . . .	6,330,062	6.6	41
Partido Socialista Brasileiro (PSB) .	6,851,053	7.1	34
Partido Democrático Trabalhista (PDT)	4,854,602	5.0	28
Partido Trabalhista Brasileiro (PTB)	4,038,239	4.2	21
Partido Social Cristão (PSC) . .	3,072,546	3.2	17
Partido Verde (PV)	3,710,366	3.8	15
Partido Comunista do Brasil (PC do B)	2,748,290	2.8	15
Partido Popular Socialista (PPS) .	2,536,809	2.6	12

Party—*continued*	Votes	% of valid votes	Seats
Partido Republicano Brasileiro (PRB)	1,633,500	1.7	8
Partido da Mobilização Nacional (PMN)	1,086,705	1.1	4
Partido Socialismo e Liberdade (PSOL)	1,142,737	1.2	3
Partido Trabalhista do Brasil (PT do B)	642,422	0.7	3
Partido Humanista da Solidariedade (PHS)	764,412	0.8	2
Partido Renovador Trabalhista Brasileira (PRTB)	307,925	0.3	2
Partido Republicano Progressista (PRP)	307,188	0.3	2
Partido Trabalhista Cristão (PTC) .	595,431	0.6	1
Partido Social Liberal (PSL) . .	499,963	0.5	1
Total (incl. others)	96,580,011	100.0	513

Federal Senate
(Senado Federal)

Federal Senate: Palácio do Congresso Nacional, Praça dos Três Poderes, 70165-900 Brasília, DF; tel. (61) 3311-4141; fax (61) 3311-3190; e-mail asimpre@senado.gov.br; internet www.senado.gov.br.

President: RENAN CALHEIROS (PMDB).

The 81 members of the Senate are elected by the 26 states and the Federal District (three senators for each) according to the principle of majority. The Senate's term of office is eight years, with elections after four years for one-third of the members and after another four years for the remaining two-thirds.

In the elections of 3 October 2010 54 seats were contested. In that month the PMDB was represented by 20 senators, the PT by 15, the PSDB by 11, the PTB and the DEM by six each, the PR, the PP and the PDT by four each, the PSB by three, the PSOL and the PC do B by two each and the PRB, the PPS, the PSC and the PMN by one each.

Governors

STATES
(September 2014)

Acre: SEBASTIÃO AFONSO VIANA MACEDO NEVES (PT).

Alagoas: TEOTÔNIO BRANDÃO VILELA FILHO (PSDB).

Amapá: CARLOS CAMILO GÓES CAPIBERIBE (PSB).

Amazonas: JOSÉ MELO DE OLIVEIRA (PROS).

Bahia: JACQUES WAGNER (PT).

Ceará: CID GOMES (PSB).

Espírito Santo: RENATO CASAGRANDE (PSB).

Goiás: MARCONI FERREIRA PERILLO JÚNIOR (PSDB).

Maranhão: ROSEANA SARNEY (PMDB).

Mato Grosso: SILVAL CUNHA BARBOSA (PMDB).

Mato Grosso do Sul: ANDRÉ PUCCINELLI (PMDB).

Minas Gerais: ALBERTO PINTO COELHO JÚNIOR (PP).

Pará: SIMÃO ROBSON OLIVEIRA JATENE (PSDB).

Paraíba: RICARDO VIEIRA COUTINHO (PSB).

Paraná: CARLOS ALBERTO RICHA (PSDB).

Pernambuco: JOÃO SOARES LYRA NETO (PMDB).

Piauí: ANTÔNIO JOSÉ DE MORAES SOUZA FILHO (PMDB).

Rio de Janeiro: LUIZ FERNANDO PEZÃO (PMDB, acting).

Rio Grande do Norte: ROSALBA CIARLINI ROSADO (DEM).

Rio Grande do Sul: TARSO FERNANDO HERZ GENRO (PT).

Rondônia: CONFÚCIO AIRES DE MOURA (PMDB).

Roraima: FRANCISCO (CHICO) DE ASSIS RODRIGUES (PSB).

Santa Catarina: JOÃO RAIMUNDO COLOMBO (DEM).

São Paulo: GERALDO ALCKMIN FILHO (PSDB).

Sergipe: JACKSON BARRETO DE LIMA (acting, PT).

Tocantins: SANDOVAL LOBO CARDOSO (PMDB).

FEDERAL DISTRICT

Brasília: AGNELO SANTOS QUEIROZ FILHO (PT).

Election Commission

Tribunal Superior Eleitoral (TSE): Setor de Administração Federal Sul (SAFS), Quadra 7, Lotes 1/2, 70070-600 Brasília, DF; tel. (61) 3030-7000; fax (61) 3030-9850; e-mail webmaster@tse.gov.br; internet www.tse.gov.br; f. 1945; Pres. CÁRMEN LÚCIA ANTUNES ROCHA; Inspector-Gen., Elections LAURITA HILÁRIO VAZ.

Political Organizations

Democratas (DEM): Senado Federal, Anexo 1, 26° andar, 70165-900 Brasília, DF; tel. (61) 3311-4305; fax (61) 3224-1912; e-mail democratas25@democratas.org.br; internet www.dem.org.br; f. 1985 as the Partido da Frente Liberal; refounded in 2007 under present name; Pres. JOSÉ AGRIPINO MAIA; Sec.-Gen. ONYX LORENZONI.

Partido da Causa Operaria (PCO): SCS, Quadra 2, Edif. São Paulo, Sala 310, 70314-900 Brasília, DF; tel. (11) 5584-9322; fax (11) 5584-9322; e-mail pco@pco.org.br; internet www.pco.org.br; f. 1997; Pres. RUI COSTA PIMENTA.

Partido Comunista do Brasil (PC do B): Rua Rego Freitas 192, 01220-907 São Paulo, SP; tel. and fax (11) 3054-1800; e-mail comitecentral@pcdob.org.br; internet www.pcdob.org.br; f. 1922; Pres. JOSÉ RENATO RABELO; Sec.-Gen. WALTER SORRENTINO; 185,000 mems.

Partido Democrático Trabalhista (PDT): Rua do Teatro 39, Praça Tiradentes, 20010-190 Rio de Janeiro, RJ; tel. (21) 2232-1016; fax (21) 2232-0121; e-mail fio@pdt.org.br; internet www.pdt .org.br; f. 1980; fmrly the Partido Trabalhista Brasileiro, renamed 1980 when that name was awarded to a dissident group following controversial judicial proceedings; mem. of Socialist International; Pres. CARLOS LUPI; Sec.-Gen. MANOEL DIAS.

Partido Ecológico Nacional (PEN): SHN, Quadra 2, Bloco F, Conj. 1510, Sala B, Asa Norte, 70702-000 Brasília, DF; tel. and fax (61) 3326-4555; e-mail pen@pen51.org.br; internet www.pen51.org .br; f. 2012; Pres. ADILSON BARROSO OLIVEIRA.

Partido Humanista da Solidariedade (PHS): SHI/SUL, QL 2, Conj. 3, Casa 13, Lago Sul, 71610-035 Brasília, DF; tel. (61) 3321-3131; fax (61) 3224-0726; e-mail contato@phs.org.br; internet www .phs.org.br; f. 2013; Pres. EDUARDO MACHADO E SILVA RODRIGUES.

Partido da Mobilização Nacional (PMN): Rua Martins Fontes 197, 3° andar, Conj. 32, 01050-906 São Paulo, SP; tel. (11) 3214-4261; fax (11) 3120-2669; e-mail pmn33@pmn.org.br; internet www.pmn .org.br; f. 1984; Pres. OSCAR NORONHA FILHO; Sec.-Gen. TELMA RIBEIRO DOS SANTOS.

Partido do Movimento Democrático Brasileiro (PMDB): Câmara dos Deputados, Edif. Principal, Ala B, Sala 6, Praça dos Três Poderes, 70160-900 Brasília, DF; tel. (61) 3215-9206; fax (61) 3215-9220; e-mail pmdb@pmdb.org.br; internet www.pmdb.org.br; f. 1980 by moderate elements of fmr Movimento Democrático Brasileiro; merged with Partido Popular in 1982; Pres. MICHEL TEMER; Sec.-Gen. MAURO LOPES; factions include the Históricos and the Movimento da Unidade Progressiva (MUP).

Partido Pátria Livre (PPL): SCS, Quadra 1, Bloco L, 17°, Sala 1114, 70301-000 Brasília, DF; tel. (61) 3225-1396; fax (61) 3225-1396; e-mail df.patrialivre@hotmail.com; f. 2011; Pres. SÉRGIO RUBENS DE ARAÚJO TORRES.

Partido Popular Socialista (PPS): SCS, Quadra 7, Bloco A, Edif. Executive Tower, Sala 826/828, Pátio Brasil Shopping, Setor Comercial Sul, 70307-901 Brasília, DF; tel. (61) 3218-4123; fax (61) 3218-4112; e-mail pps23@pps.org.br; internet www.pps.org.br; f. 1922; Pres. ROBERTO JOÃO PEREIRA FREIRE; Sec.-Gen. RUBENS BUENO.

Partido Progressista (PP): Senado Federal, Anexo 1, 17° andar, Sala 1704, 70165-900 Brasília, DF; tel. (61) 3311-3041; fax (61) 3322-6938; e-mail pp@pp.org.br; internet www.pp.org.br; f. 1995 as Partido Progressista Brasileiro by merger of Partido Progressista Reformador, Partido Progressista and Partido Republicano Progressista; adopted present name 2003; right-wing; Pres. CIRO NOGUEIRA; Sec.-Gen. ALDO DA ROSA.

Partido Renovador Trabalhista Brasileiro (PRTB): SHN, Quadra 2, Bloco F, Edif. Executive Tower, 70702-906 Brasília, DF; tel. (61) 3328-6128; fax (11) 5097-9993; e-mail prtb@prtb.org.br; internet www.prtb.org.br; f. 2004; Pres. JOSÉ LEVY FIDELIX DA CRUZ.

Partido da República (PR): SCN, Edif. Liberty Mall, Quadra 02, Bloco D, Torre A, Salas 601/606, Asa Norte, 70712-903 Brasília, DF; tel. and fax (61) 3202-9922; e-mail pr22@partidodarepublica.org.br; internet www.partidodarepublica.org.br; f. 2006 by merger of Partido Liberal and Partido de Reedificação da Ordem Nacional; Pres. ALFREDO PEREIRA DO NASCIMENTO.

Partido Republicano Brasileiro (PRB): SDS, Bloco L 30, Edif. Miguel Badya, 3° andar, Sala 320, 70394-901 Brasília, DF; tel. and fax (61) 3223-9069; e-mail faleconosco@prb10.org.br; internet www

.prb10.org.br; f. 2005 as Partido Municipalista Renovador; name changed as above in 2006; political wing of Igreja Universal do Reino de Deus; Pres. MARCOS ANTÔNIO PEREIRA; Sec.-Gen. EVANDRO GARLA.

Partido Republicano da Ordem Social (PROS): SAS, Quadra 05, Bloco K, Salas 1007–08, Asa Sul, 70070-937 Brasília, DF; tel. (61) 3322-4030; fax (61) 3223-8053; e-mail contato@pros.org.br; internet www.pros.org.br; f. 2013; Pres. EURÍPEDES GOMES DE MACEDO JÚNIOR.

Partido Republicano Progressista (PRP): SRTVS, Quadra 701, Bloco E, Edif. Palácio do Rádio II, 70340-902 Brasília, DF; tel. (61) 3037-4044; fax (61) 3039-4044; e-mail prpnacionalsrp@terra.com.br; internet www.prp.org.br; f. 2013; Pres OVASCO ROMA ALTIMARI RESENDE.

Partido Social Cristão (PSC): Rua Pouso Alegre 1388, Santa Teresa, 31015-030 Belo Horizonte, MG; tel. (31) 3467-1390; fax (31) 3467-6522; e-mail psc@psc.org.br; internet www.psc.org.br; f. 1970 as Partido Democrático Republicano; Pres. VITOR JORGE ADBALA NÓSSEIS; Sec.-Gen. ANTONIO OLIBONI.

Partido da Social Democracia Brasileira (PSDB): SGAS, Quadra 607, Edif. Metrópolis, Asa Sul, Cobertura 2, 70200-670 Brasília, DF; tel. (61) 3424-0500; fax (61) 3424-0515; e-mail tucano@psdb.org.br; internet www.psdb.org.br; f. 1988; centre; formed by dissident mems of parties incl. the PMDB, PFL, PDT, PSB and PTB; Pres. AÉCIO NEVES; Sec.-Gen. ANTÔNIO CARLOS MENDES THAME.

Partido Social Democrata Cristão (PSDC): SCS, Quadra 1, Bloco I, Edif. Central, Sala 402, 70304-900 Brasília, DF; tel. (61) 3225-1427; fax (61) 3225-1427; e-mail secretaria@psdc.org.br; internet www.psdc.org.br; f. 2011; Pres. JOSÉ MARIA EYMAEL.

Partido Social Democrático (PSD): e-mail contato@psd.org.br; internet www.psd.org.br; f. 2011; Pres. GILBERTO KASSAB; Sec.-Gen. SAULO QUEIROZ.

Partido Social Liberal (PSL): SCS, Quadra 01, Bloco E, Edif. Ceará, Sala 1004, 70303-900 Brasília, DF; tel. (61) 3322-1721; fax (61) 3032-6832; e-mail contato@pslnacional.org.br; internet www .pslnacional.org.br; f. 1994; Pres. LUCIANO CALDAS BIVAR; Sec.-Gen. ROBERTO SIQUEIRA GOMES.

Partido Socialismo e Liberdade (PSOL): SCS, Quadra 01, Bloco E, Edif. Ceará, Salas 1203–04, 70303-900 Brasília, DF; tel. (61) 3963-1750; fax (61) 3039-6356; e-mail secretariageral@psol50.org.br; internet psol50.org.br; f. 2004 by fmr PT mems; Pres. IVAN VALENTE; Secs-Gen. EDILSON FRANCISCO DA SILVA, MARIO AGRA JUNIOR.

Partido Socialista Brasileiro (PSB): SCLN 304, Bloco A, Sobreloja 1, Entrada 63, 70736-510 Brasília, DF; tel. and fax (61) 3327-6405; e-mail psb@psbnacional.org.br; internet www.psbnacional.org .br; f. 1945 as the Esquerda Democrática, renamed 1947; Pres. ROBERTO AMARAL; Sec.-Gen. JOSÉ RENATO CASAGRANDE.

Partido Socialista dos Trabalhadores Unificado (PSTU): SCS, SL 215, Quadra 6, Bloco A, Edif. Carioca 240, Asa Sul, 70306-000 Brasília, DF; tel. (61) 3226-1016; fax (61) 3226-1016; e-mail pstu@ pstu.org.br; internet www.pstu.org.br; f. 2010; Pres. JOSÉ MARIA ALMEIDA.

Partido Social Liberal (PSL): SCS, SL 1203, Quadra 1, Bloco E, Edif. Ceará, Setor Comercial Sul, 70303-900 Brasília, DF; tel. (61) 3322-1721; fax (61) 3225-1805; e-mail contato@pslnacional.org.br; internet www.psl.org.br; f. 1998; Pres. LUCIANO CALDAS BIVAR.

Partido dos Trabalhadores (PT): SCS, Quadra 2, Bloco C, Edif. Toufic, Sala 256, 70302-000 São Paulo, SP; tel. (11) 3213-1313; fax (11) 3213-1360; e-mail presidencia@pt.org.br; internet www.pt.org .br; f. 1980; first independent labour party; associated with the *autêntico* br. of the trade union movt; 500,000 mems; Pres. RUI FALCÃO; Sec.-Gen. PAULO TEIXEIRA.

Partido Trabalhista Nacional (PTN): SRTVS 701, Torre 1, SL 422, Edif. Assis Chateaubriand, Asa Sul, 70340-000 Brasília, DF; tel. (61) 3368-1323; fax (61) 3368-1323; e-mail ptnbrasil@ptn.org.br; internet www.ptn.org.br; f. 1997; Pres. JOSÉ MASCI DE ABREU.

Partido Trabalhista Brasileiro (PTB): SEPN, Quadra 504, Bloco A, Edif. Ana Carolina, Sala 100, Cobertura, 70730-521 Brasília DF; tel. (61) 2101-1414; fax (61) 2101-1400; e-mail ptb@ptb.org.br; internet www.ptb.org.br; f. 1980; Pres. ROBERTO JEFFERSON MONTEIRO FRANCISCO; Sec.-Gen. ANTÔNIO CARLOS DE CAMPOS MACHADO.

Partido Trabalhista do Brasil (PT do B): SHIS, QI 5, BlocoF, 130°, Centro Comercial Gilberto Salomão, Sobreloja 224, Lago Sul, 71615-907 Brasília, DF; tel. (61) 3248-1929; fax (61) 3248-5909; e-mail ptdobnac@yahoo.com.br; internet www.ptdob.org.br; f. 1994; Pres. LUIS HENRIQUE DE OLIVEIRA RESENDE.

Partido Trabalhista Cristão (PTC): Edif. Rodolpho De Paoli, Sala 506, Av. Nilo Peçanha 50, Centro, 20020-906 Rio de Janeiro, RJ; tel. (21) 2220-1832; e-mail ptcnacional@uol.com.br; internet www .ptc36nacional.com.br; f. 1989 as the Partido da Reconstrução Nacional, renamed 1997; Christian party; Pres. DANIEL S. TOURINHO.

Partido Verde (PV): Edif. Miguel Badya, Bloco L, Sala 218, Asa Sul, 70394-901 Brasília, DF; tel. (61) 3366-1569; e-mail nacional@pv.org

.br; internet www.pv.org.br; f. 1990; Pres. José Luis de França Penna; Organizing Sec. Carla Piranda.

Solidariedade: Rua Colônia da Glória 390, Salas 3 e 6, Vila Mariana, 04113-000 São Paulo, SP; tel. (11) 3053-4700; e-mail falecom@solidariedade.org.br; internet www.solidariedade.org.br; f. 2012; Pres. Paulo Pereira da Silva.

OTHER ORGANIZATIONS

Movimento dos Trabalhadores Rurais Sem Terra (MST): Alameda Barão de Limeira, 1232 Campos Elíseos, 01202-002 São Paulo, SP; tel. (11) 3361-3866; e-mail semterra@mst.org.br; internet www.mst.org.br; f. 1984; landless peasant movt; Pres. João Pedro Stédile; Nat. Co-ordinator Marina dos Santos.

Other rural movements include the Organização da Luto no Campo (OLC) and the Movimento de Liberação dos Sem Terra (MLST), a dissident faction of the MST.

Diplomatic Representation

EMBASSIES IN BRAZIL

Albania: SMDB, Conj. 4, Lote 3, Casa D, Lago Sul, 71680-040 Brasília, DF; tel. (61) 3364-0519; fax (61) 3364-0619; e-mail embassy.brasilia@mfa.gov.al; Ambassador Tatiana Gjonaj.

Algeria: SHIS, QI 09, Conj. 13, Casa 01, Lago Sul, 70472-900 Brasília, DF; tel. (61) 3248-4039; fax (61) 3248-4691; e-mail sanag277@terra.com.br; internet www.embaixadadaargelia.com.br; Ambassador Djamel-Eddine Omar Bennaoum.

Angola: SHIS, QL 06, Conj. 5, Casa 01, 71620-055 Brasília, DF; tel. (61) 3248-0761; fax (61) 3248-1567; e-mail embangola@embaixadadeangola.com.br; internet www.embaixadadeangola.com.br; Ambassador Nelson Manuel Cosme.

Argentina: SES Quadra 803, Lote 12, 70200-030 Brasília, DF; tel. (61) 3212-7600; fax (61) 3364-7666; e-mail ebras@mrecic.gov.br; internet www.brasil.embajada-argentina.gov.ar; Ambassador Luis María Kreckler.

Armenia: SHIS, QL 28, Conj. 3, Casa 04, South Lake, 71665-235 Brasília, DF; e-mail armgenconsulatesan-paulo@mfa.am; Ambassador Ashot Galoyan.

Australia: SES, Av. das Nações, Quadra 801, Conj. K, Lote 7, 70200-010 Brasília, DF; tel. (61) 3226-3111; fax (61) 3226-1112; e-mail embaustr@dfat.gov.au; internet www.brazil.embassy.gov.au; Ambassador Patrick Lawless.

Austria: SES, Av. das Nações, Quadra 811, Lote 40, 70426-900 Brasília, DF; tel. (61) 3443-3111; fax (61) 3443-5233; e-mail brasilia-ob@bmeia.gv.at; internet www.embaixadadaaustria.com.br; Ambassador Marianne Feldmann.

Azerbaijan: SHIS, QI 9, Conj. 15, Casa 15, Lago Sul, 71625-150 Brasília, DF; tel. (61) 3253-9803; fax (61) 3253-9812; e-mail embaixada@azembassy.org.br; internet www.azembassy.org.br; Ambassador Elnur Sultanov.

Bangladesh: SHIS, QL 24, Conj. 8, Casa 3, Lago Sul, 71665-085 Brasília, DF; tel. (61) 3367-3699; fax (61) 3522-8634; e-mail bdoot.brasilia@gmail.com; Ambassador Mohamed Mijarul Quayes.

Barbados: SHIS, QI 13, Conj. 10, Casa 03, Lago Sul, 71635-100 Brasília, DF; tel. (61) 3526-8310; fax (61) 3546-8310; e-mail brasilia@foreign.gov.bb; Ambassador Yvette Goddard.

Belarus: SHIS, Lago Sul, Quadra 12, Conj. 06, Casa 09, 71630-265 Brasília, DF; tel. (61) 3543-0481; fax (61) 3543-0469; e-mail belarus.emb@terra.com.br; internet brazil.mfa.gov.by; Ambassador Leonid Krupets.

Belgium: SES, Av. das Nações, Quadra 809, Lote 32, 70422-900 Brasília, DF; tel. (61) 3443-1133; fax (61) 3443-1219; e-mail brasilia@diplobel.org; internet www.diplomatie.be/brasilia; Ambassador Jozef Smets.

Benin: SHIS, QI 9, Conj. 11, Casa 24, Lago Sul, 71625-110 Brasília, DF; tel. (61) 3248-2192; fax (61) 3263-0739; e-mail ambabeninbrasilia@yahoo.fr; Ambassador Isidore Benjamin Amédée Monsi.

Bolivia: SHIS, QI 19, Conj. 13, Casa 19, Lago Sul, 71655-130 Brasília, DF; tel. (61) 3366-3432; fax (61) 3366-3136; e-mail embolivia@embolivia.org.br; internet www.embolivia.org.br; Ambassador Jerjes Justiniano Talavera.

Botswana: SHIS, QI 09, Conj. 16, Casa 03, Lago Sul, 71625-160 Brasília, DF; tel. (61) 3120-1250; fax (61) 3120-1271; e-mail info@botbraz.org.br; Ambassador Bernadette Sebage Rathedi.

Bulgaria: Asa Norte, SEN 8, 70800-911 Brasília, DF; tel. (61) 3223-6193; fax (61) 3323-3285; e-mail Embassy.Brasilia@mfa.bg; internet www.mfa.bg/embassies/brazil; Ambassador Valeriy Ivanov Yotov.

Burkina Faso: SHIS QI 09, Conj. 13, Casa 12, Lago Sul, 71605-001 Brasília, DF; tel. (61) 3366-4636; fax (61) 3366-3210; e-mail amburkinabras@gmail.com; internet www.burkina.org.br; Ambassador Alain Francis Gustave Ilboudo.

Burundi: SHIS, QI 21, Conj. 1, Casa 10, Lago Sul, 71655-210, Brasília, DF; tel. (61) 3248-1814; fax (61) 3248-1569; e-mail ambaburundibrasilia@gmail.com; Ambassador Gaudence Sindayigaya.

Cabo Verde: SHIS, QL 14, Conj. 03, Casa 08, Lago Sul, 71640-035 Brasília, DF; tel. (61) 3248-0543; fax (61) 3364-4059; e-mail embcvbrasil@embcv.org.br; internet www.embcv.org.br; Ambassador Domingos Dias Pereira Mascarenhas.

Cameroon: SHIS, QI 15, Conj. 14, Casa 17, 71635-340 Brasília, DF; tel. (61) 3248-5403; fax (61) 3248-0443; e-mail embcameroun@embcameroun.org.br; internet www.embcameroun.org.br; Ambassador Martin Agbor Mbeng.

Canada: SES, Av. das Nações, Quadra 803, Lote 16, 70410-900 Brasília, DF; tel. (61) 3424-5400; fax (61) 3424-5490; e-mail brsla@international.gc.ca; internet www.canadainternational.gc.ca/brazil; Ambassador Jamal Khokhar.

Chile: SES, Av. das Nações, Quadra 803, Lote 11, Asa Sul, 70407-900 Brasília, DF; tel. (61) 2103-5151; fax (61) 3322-2966; e-mail embchile@embchile.org.br; internet chileabroad.gov.cl/brasil; Ambassador Jaime Gazmuri Mujica.

China, People's Republic: SES, Av. das Nações, Quadra 813, Lote 51, Asa Sul, 70443-900 Brasília, DF; tel. (61) 2198-8200; fax (61) 3346-3299; e-mail chinaemb_br@mfa.gov.cn; internet br.china-embassy.org/por; Ambassador Li Jinzhang.

Colombia: SES, Av. das Nações, Quadra 803, Lote 10, 70444-900 Brasília, DF; tel. (61) 3214-8900; fax (61) 3224-4732; e-mail ebrasili@cancilleria.gov.co; internet www.embajadaenbrasil.gov.co; Ambassador Patricia Eugenia Cárdenas Santamaría.

Congo, Democratic Republic: SHIS, QL 13, Conj. 08, Casa 21, Lago Sul, 71635-080 Brasília, DF; tel. (61) 3214-8900; fax (61) 3536-1285; e-mail ambaredeco@ig.com.br; Chargé d'affaires a.i. Nadine Osório Tchamlesso.

Congo, Republic: SHIS, QL 8, Conj. 05, Casa 06, Lago Sul, 71620-255 Brasília, DF; tel. and fax (61) 3532-0440; e-mail ambacobrazza@gmail.com; Ambassador Louis-Sylvain Goma.

Costa Rica: SRTV/N 701, Conj. C, Ala A, Salas 308/310, Edif. Centro Empresarial Norte, 70719-903 Brasília, DF; tel. (61) 3032-8450; fax (61) 3032-8452; e-mail embcr.brasil@gmail.com; Ambassador Víctor Monge Chacón.

Côte d'Ivoire: SEN, Av. das Nações, Lote 09, 70473-900 Brasília, DF; tel. (61) 3321-7320; fax (61) 3321-1306; e-mail cotedivoire@cotedivoire.org.br; internet www.cotedivoire.org.br; Ambassador Sylvestre Aka Amon Kassi.

Croatia: SHIS, QI 09, Conj. 11, Casa 03, 71625-110 Brasília, DF; tel. (61) 3248-0610; fax (61) 3248-1708; e-mail croemb.brasilia@mvpei.hr; Ambassador Drago Stambuk.

Cuba: SHIS, QI 05, Conj. 18, Casa 01, Lago Sul, 71615-180 Brasília, DF; tel. (61) 3248-4710; fax (61) 3248-6778; e-mail embacuba@uol.com.br; internet embacu.cubaminrex.cu/brasil; Ambassador María Elena Ruíz Capote.

Cyprus: SHIS, QI 09, Conj. 20, Casa 2, Lago Sul, 71625-200 Brasília, DF; tel. (61) 3541-6892; e-mail mmavrommatis@mfa.gov.cy; Ambassador Martha A. Mavrommatis.

Czech Republic: SES 805, Lote 21A, Via L3 Sul, Asa Sul, 70200-901 Brasília, DF; tel. (61) 3242-7785; fax (61) 3242-7833; e-mail brasilia@embassy.mzv.cz; internet www.mzv.cz/brasilia; Ambassador Jirí Havlík.

Denmark: SES, Av. das Nações, Quadra 807, Lote 26, 70200-900 Brasília, DF; tel. (61) 3878-4500; fax (61) 3878-4509; e-mail bsbamb@um.dk; internet www.ambbrasilia.um.dk; Ambassador Svend Roed Nielsen.

Dominican Republic: SHIS, QL 06, Conj. 07, Casa 02, 71626-075 Brasília, DF; tel. (61) 3248-1405; fax (61) 3364-3214; e-mail embaixada@republicadominicana.org.br; internet www.republicadominicana.org.br; Ambassador Héctor Dionisio Pérez Fernández.

Ecuador: SHIS, QL 10, Conj. 08, Casa 01, 71630-085 Brasília, DF; tel. (61) 3248-5560; fax (61) 3248-1290; e-mail embeq@solar.com.br; internet www.embequador.org.br; Ambassador Horacio Sevilla Borja.

Egypt: SEN, Av. das Nações, Lote 12, 70435-900 Brasília, DF; tel. (61) 3323-8800; fax (61) 3323-1039; e-mail embegito@opendf.com.br; internet www.opengate.com.br/embegito; Ambassador Hossam Eldin Mohamed Ibrahim Zaki.

El Salvador: SHIS, QL 22, Conj. 7, Casa 8, Lago Sul, 71650-275 Brasília, DF; tel. (61) 3364-4141; fax (61) 3541-4101; e-mail elsalvador@embelsalvador.brte.com.br; Ambassador Rina del Socorro Angulo.

Equatorial Guinea: SHIS, QL 10, Conj. 09, Casa 01, Lago Sul, 70630-095 Brasília, DF; tel. (61) 3364-4185; fax (61) 3364-1641; e-mail embaixada@embrge.brtdata.com.br; Ambassador BENIGNO PEDRO MATUTE TANG.

Ethiopia: SHIS QI 7, Conj. 4, Casa 9, Lago Sul, Brasília, DF; tel. (61) 3248-0361; fax (61) 3248-0367; e-mail ethiobrazil@ethiopianembassy .org.br; internet www.ethiopianembassy.org.br; Ambassador SIN-KNESH EJIGU.

Fiji: QI 22, Conj. 10, Casa 13, Lago Sul, 71650-035 Brasília, DF; tel. (61) 3548-8100; Ambassador CAMA TUIQILAQILA TUILOMA.

Finland: SES, Av. das Nações, Quadra 807, Lote 27, 70417-900 Brasília, DF; tel. (61) 3443-7151; fax (61) 3443-3315; e-mail sanomat .bra@formin.fi; internet www.finlandia.org.br; Ambassador JARÍ LUOTO.

France: SES, Av. das Nações, Quadra 801, Lote 04, 70404-900 Brasília, DF; tel. (61) 3222-3999; fax (61) 3222-3917; e-mail france@ambafrance.org.br; internet ambafrance-br.org; Ambassador DENIS PIETTON.

Gabon: SHIS, QL 09, Conj. 09, Casa 19, Lago Sul, 71625-160 Brasília, DF; tel. (61) 3248-3536; fax (61) 3248-2241; e-mail embgabao@yahoo.com.br; Ambassador JÉRÔME ANGOUO.

Georgia: SHIS, QI 7, Conj. 11, Casa 01, Lago Sul, 71615-310 Brasília, DF; tel. (61) 3366-1101; fax (61) 3366-1161; e-mail brazil .emb@mfa.gov.ge; Ambassador OTAR BERDZENISHVILI.

Germany: SES, Av. das Nações, Quadra 807, Lote 25, 70415-900 Brasília, DF; tel. (61) 3442-7000; fax (61) 3443-7508; e-mail info@ alemanja.org; internet www.brasilia.diplo.de; Ambassador WILFRIED GROLIG.

Ghana: SHIS, QL 10, Conj. 08, Casa 02, 71630-085 Brasília, DF; tel. (61) 3248-6047; fax (61) 3248-7913; e-mail ghaembra@zaz.com.br; Ambassador Brig.-Gen. WALLACE GBEDEMAH.

Greece: SES, Av. das Nações, Quadra 805, Lote 22, 70480-900 Brasília, DF; tel. (61) 3443-6573; fax (61) 3443-6902; e-mail gremb .bra@mfa.gr; internet www.emb-grecia.org.br; Ambassador DIMITRI ALEXANDRAKIS.

Guatemala: SHIS, QI 03, Conj. 09, Casa 07, Lago Sul, 71615-330 Brasília, DF; tel. (61) 3248-4175; fax (61) 3248-6678; e-mail embaguate.brasil@gmail.com; internet www.brasil.minex.gob.gt; Ambassador JULIO ARMANDO MARTINI-HERRERA.

Guinea: SHIS, QL 02, Conj. 07, Casa 09, Lago Sul, 71610-075 Brasília, DF; tel. (61) 3365-1301; fax (61) 3365-4921; e-mail ambaguibrasil@terra.com.br; Ambassador MOHAMED YOULA.

Guinea-Bissau: SHIS, QL 02, Conj. 3, Casa 18, Lago Sul, 71610-035 Brasília, DF; tel. (61) 3366-1098; fax (61) 3366-1554; Ambassador EUGÉNIA PEREIRA SALDANHA ARAÚJO.

Guyana: SHIS, QI 05, Conj. 19, Casa 24, 71615-190 Brasília, DF; tel. (61) 3248-0874; fax (61) 3248-0886; e-mail embguyana@embguyana .org.br; internet www.embguyana.org.br; Ambassador MERLIN UDHO.

Haiti: SHIS, QI 13, Conj. 08, Casa 18, Lago Sul, 71635-080 Brasília, DF; tel. (61) 3248-6860; fax (61) 3248-7472; e-mail embhaiti@terra .com.br; Ambassador MADSEN CHÉRUBIN.

Holy See: SES, Av. das Nações, Quadra 801, Lote 01, 70401-900 Brasília, DF; tel. (61) 3223-0794; fax (61) 3224-9365; e-mail nunapost@solar.com.br; Apostolic Nuncio Most Rev. GIOVANNI D'ANIELLO (Titular Archbishop of Pesto).

Honduras: SHIS, QI 19, Conj. 07, Casa 34, Lago Sul, 71655-070 Brasília, DF; tel. (61) 3366-4082; fax (61) 3366-4618; e-mail embajada@embajadahondurasbrasil.com; internet www .embajadahondurasbrasil.com; Ambassador JAIME GÜELL BOGRÁN.

Hungary: SES, Av. das Nações, Quadra 805, Lote 19, 70413-900 Brasília, DF; tel. (61) 3443-0836; fax (61) 3443-3434; e-mail mission .brz@kum.hu; internet www.mfa.gov.hu/emb/brasilia; Ambassador Dr CSABA SZIJJARTO.

India: SES 805, Lote 24, 70452-901 Brasília, DF; tel. (61) 3248-4006; fax (61) 3248-7849; e-mail indemb@indianembassy.org.br; internet www.indianembassy.org.br; Ambassador ASHOK TOMAR.

Indonesia: SES, Av. das Nações, Quadra 805, Lote 20, 70479-900 Brasília, DF; tel. (61) 3443-8800; fax (61) 3443-6732; e-mail contato@ embaixadadaindonesia.org; internet www.embaixadadaindonesia .org; Ambassador SUDARYOMO HARTOSUDARMO.

Iran: SES, Av. das Nações, Quadra 809, Lote 31, 70421-900 Brasília, DF; tel. (61) 3242-5733; fax (61) 3224-9640; e-mail secretaria@ irembassy.com; internet brasilia.mfa.gov.ir; Ambassador MOHAMMAD ALI GHANEZADEH EZABADI.

Iraq: SES, Av. das Nações, Quadra 815, Lote 64, 70430-900 Brasília, DF; tel. (61) 3346-2822; fax (61) 3346-7442; e-mail brzemb@mofaml .gov.iq; Ambassador ADEL MUSTAFA KAMIL AL-KURDI.

Ireland: SHIS, QL 12, Conj. 05, Casa 09, Lago Sul, 71630-255 Brasília, DF; tel. (61) 3248-8800; fax (61) 3248-8816; e-mail brasiliaembassy@dfa.ie; internet www.embaixada-irlanda.org.br; Ambassador FRANK SHERIDAN.

Israel: SES, Av. das Nações, Quadra 809, Lote 38, 70424-900 Brasília, DF; tel. (61) 2105-0500; fax (61) 3443-8107; e-mail info@ brasilia.mfa.gov.il; internet brasilia.mfa.gov.il; Ambassador RAFAEL ELDAD.

Italy: SES, Av. das Nações, Quadra 807, Lote 30, 70420-900 Brasília, DF; tel. (61) 3442-9900; fax (61) 3443-1231; e-mail ambasciata .brasilia@esteri.it; internet www.ambbrasilia.esteri.it; Ambassador RAFFAELE TROMBETTA.

Jamaica: SHIS, QL 02, Conj. 04, Casa 02, Lago Sul, 71610-045 Brasília, DF; tel. (61) 2192-9774; fax (61) 2192-9772; e-mail jamaicanembassy.brazil@gmail.com; Ambassador ALISON STONE ROOFE.

Japan: SES, Av. das Nações, Quadra 811, Lote 39, 70425-900 Brasília, DF; tel. (61) 3442-4200; fax (61) 3442-2499; e-mail consularjapao@yawl.com.br; internet www.br.emb-japan.go.jp; Ambassador KUNIO UMEDA.

Jordan: SHIS, QI 09, Conj. 18, Casa 14, Lago Sul, 71625-180 Brasília, DF; tel. (61) 3248-5414; fax (61) 3248-1698; e-mail emb .jordania@apis.com.br; Ambassador MALEK EID OTALLA TWAL.

Kazakhstan: SHIS, QI 9, Conj. 03, Casa 8, Lago Sul, 71625-030 Brasília, DF; tel. (61) 3879-4602; fax (61) 3879-4604; e-mail embassykz@gmail.com; Ambassador BAKYTZHAN ORDABAYEV.

Kenya: SHIS, QL 10, Conj. 08, Casa 08, Lago Sul, 71630-085 Brasília, DF; tel. (61) 3364-0691; fax (61) 3364-0978; e-mail info@ kenyaembassybrazil.com.br; internet www.kenyaembassy.com.br; Ambassador PETER KIRIMI KABERIA.

Korea, Democratic People's Republic: SHIS, QI 25, Conj. 10, Casa 11, Lago Sul, 71660-300 Brasília, DF; tel. (61) 3367-1940; fax (61) 3367-3177; e-mail embrpdcoreia@hotmail.com; Ambassador KIM THAE JONG.

Korea, Republic: SEN, Av. das Nações, Lote 14, 70800-915 Brasília, DF; tel. (61) 3321-2500; fax (61) 3321-2508; e-mail emb-br@ mofa.go.kr; internet bra-brasilia.mofa.go.kr; Ambassador BON-WOO KOO.

Kuwait: SHIS, QI 05, Chácara 30, Lago Sul, 71600-550 Brasília, DF; tel. (61) 3213-2333; fax (61) 3248-0969; e-mail kuwait@opendf.com .br; Ambassador AYADA MEBRED AL-SAIDI.

Lebanon: SES, Av. das Nações, Quadra 805, Lote 17, 70411-900 Brasília, DF; tel. (61) 3443-5552; fax (61) 3443-8574; e-mail embaixada@libano.org.br; internet www.libano.org.br; Ambassador JOSEPH SAYAH.

Libya: SHIS, QI 15, Chácara 26, Lago Sul, 71600-750 Brasília, DF; tel. (61) 3248-6710; fax (61) 3248-0598; e-mail emblibia@terra.com .br; Ambassador KHALED ZAYED RAMADAN DAHAN.

Malawi: SHIS, QI 15, Conj. 01, Casa 03, Lago Sul, 71635-230 Brasília, DF; tel. (61) 3366-1337; fax (61) 3365-2149; e-mail malawiembassybrasil@bol.com.br; Ambassador FRANCIS MOTO.

Malaysia: SHIS, QI 05, Chácara 62, Lago Sul, 70477-900 Brasília, DF; tel. (61) 3248-5008; fax (61) 3248-6307; e-mail mwbrasilia@terra .com.br; internet www.kln.gov.my/perwakilan/brasilia; Ambassador SUDHA DEVI.

Mauritania: SHIS, QI 9, Conj. 3, Casa 09, Lago Sul, 71625-030 Brasília, DF; tel. (61) 3797-3995; fax (61) 3365-3079; e-mail ambarimbrasilia@mauritania.org.br; internet www.mauritania.org .br; Ambassador BAH NAGI KEBD ABDALLAHI.

Mexico: SES, Av. das Nações, Quadra 805, Lote 18, 70412-900 Brasília, DF; tel. (61) 3204-5200; fax (61) 3204-5201; e-mail embamexbra@cabonet.com.br; internet portal.sre.gob.mx/brasil; Ambassador BEATRIZ ELENA PAREDES RANGEL.

Mongolia: Brasilia, DF; Ambassador CHULUUNBAATARYN SOSORMAA.

Morocco: SEN, Av. das Nações, Quadra 801, Lote 02, Asa Norte, 70432-900 Brasília, DF; tel. (61) 3321-3994; fax (61) 3321-0745; e-mail sifamabr@onix.com.br; Ambassador LARBI MOUKHARIQ.

Mozambique: SHIS, QL 12, Conj. 07, Casa 09, Lago Sul, 71630-275 Brasília, DF; tel. (61) 3248-4222; fax (61) 3248-3917; e-mail embamoc-bsb@uol.com; internet www.mozambique.org.br; Ambassador MANUEL TOMÁS LUBISSE.

Myanmar: SHIS, QI 25, Conj. 05, Casa 14, Lago Sul, 71660-250 Brasília, DF; tel. (61) 3248-3747; fax (61) 3364-2747; e-mail mebrsl@ brnet.com.br; internet www.myanmarbsb.org; Ambassador THIRI PIYANCHI U TUN NAY LINN.

Namibia: SHIS, QI 09, Conj. 08, Casa 11, Lago Sul, 71625-080 Brasília, DF; tel. (61) 3248-6274; fax (61) 3248-7135; e-mail info@ embassyofnamibia.org.br; internet www.embassyofnamibia.org.br; Ambassador LINEEKELA JOSEPHAT MBOTI.

Nepal: SHIS, QI 11, Conj.03, Casa 20, Lago Sul, 71625-230 Brasília, DF; tel. (61) 3541-1232; fax (61) 3541-1229; e-mail embaixadanepal@ gmail.com; Ambassador PRADHUMNA BIKRAM SHAH.

Netherlands: SES, Av. das Nações, Quadra 801, Lote 05, 70405-900 Brasília, DF; tel. (61) 3961-3200; fax (61) 3961-3234; e-mail bra@minbuza.nl; internet www.mfa.nl/brasil; Ambassador KEES PIETER RADE.

New Zealand: SHIS, QI 09, Conj. 16, Casa 01, 71625-160 Brasília, DF; tel. (61) 3248-9900; fax (61) 3248-9916; e-mail zelandia@nwi.com.br; internet www.nzembassy.com/brazil; Ambassador JEFFREY MCALISTER.

Nicaragua: SHIS, QL 21, Conj. 10, Casa 14, Lago Sul, 71655-340 Brasília, DF; tel. (61) 3366-3297; e-mail embanicbrasil@cancilleria.gob.ni; Ambassador LORENA DEL CARMEN MARTÍNEZ.

Nigeria: SEN, Av. das Nações, Lote 05, 70800-400 Brasília, DF; tel. (61) 3208-1700; fax (61) 3226-5192; e-mail admin@nigerianembassy-brazil.org; internet www.nigerianembassy-brazil.org; Ambassador VINCENT ADAMU EMOZOZO.

Norway: SES, Av. das Nações, Quadra 807, Lote 28, 70418-900 Brasília, DF; tel. (61) 3443-8720; fax (61) 3443-2942; e-mail emb.brasilia@mfa.no; internet www.noruega.org.br; Ambassador AUD MARIT WIIG.

Pakistan: SHIS, QL 12, Conj. 02, Casa 19, Lago Sul, 71630-225 Brasília, DF; tel. (61) 3364-1632; fax (61) 3248-0246; e-mail parepbrasilia@yahoo.com; internet www.pakistan.org.br; Ambassador NASRULLAH KHAN.

Panama: SES, Av. das Nações, Quadra 803, Lote 09, 70200-030 Brasília, DF; tel. (61) 3323-6177; fax (61) 3323-2885; e-mail contacto@panaembabrasil.com.br; Ambassador GABRIELA GARCÍA CARRANZA.

Paraguay: SES, Av. das Nações, Quadra 811, Lote 42, 70427-900 Brasília, DF; tel. (61) 3242-3732; fax (61) 3242-4605; e-mail secretaria@embaparaguai.org.br; internet www.embaparaguai.org.br; Ambassador MANUEL MARÍA CÁCERES CARDOZO.

Peru: SES, Av. das Nações, Quadra 811, Lote 43, 70428-900 Brasília, DF; tel. (61) 3242-9933; fax (61) 3225-9136; e-mail embperu@embperu.org.br; internet www.embperu.org.br; Ambassador JORGE PORFIRIO BAYONA MEDINA.

Philippines: SEN, Av. das Nações, Lote 01, 70431-900 Brasília, DF; tel. (61) 3223-5143; fax (61) 3226-7411; e-mail brasiliape@turbo.com.br; Ambassador EVA G. BETITA.

Poland: SES, Av. das Nações, Quadra 809, Lote 33, 70423-900 Brasília, DF; tel. (61) 3212-8000; fax (61) 3242-8543; e-mail brasilia.embaixada@msz.gov.pl; internet www.brasilia.msz.gov.pl; Ambassador ANDRZEJ MARIA BRAITER.

Portugal: SES Sul, Av. das Nações, Quadra 801, Lote 02, 70402-900 Brasília, DF; tel. (61) 3032-9600; fax (61) 3032-9642; e-mail embaixadadeportugal@embaixadadeportugal.org.br; internet www.embaixadadeportugal.org.br; Ambassador FRANCISCO MARIA DE SOUSA RIBEIRO TELLES.

Qatar: SHIS, QL 20, Conj. 01, Casa 19, Lago Sul, 71650-115 Brasília, DF; tel. (61) 3366-1005; fax (61) 3366-1115; e-mail qatarbsb@embcatar.org.br; Ambassador MOHAMED AHMAD AL-HAYKI.

Romania: SEN, Av. das Nações, Lote 06, 70456-900 Brasília, DF; tel. (61) 3226-0746; fax (61) 3226-6629; e-mail romenia@solar.com.br; Ambassador DIANA ANCA RADU.

Russia: SES, Av. das Nações, Quadra 801, Lote A, 70476-900 Brasília, DF; tel. (61) 3223-3094; fax (61) 3226-7319; e-mail emb@embrus.brte.com.br; internet www.brazil.mid.ru; Ambassador SERGUEY POGÓSSOVITCH AKOPOV.

Saudi Arabia: SHIS, QL 9, Conj. 09, Casa 18, 71625-090 Brasília, DF; tel. (61) 3248-3523; fax (61) 3284-1142; e-mail bremb@mofa.gov.sa; internet www.saudiembassy.org.br; Ambassador HISHAM SULTAN BIN ZAFIR ALQAHTANI.

Senegal: SEN, Av. das Nações, Lote 18, 70800-400 Brasília, DF; tel. (61) 3223-6110; fax (61) 3322-7822; e-mail senebrasilia@senebrasilia.com.br; internet www.senebrasilia.org.br; Ambassador El Hadj AMADOU NIANG.

Serbia: SES, Av. das Nações, Quadra 803, Lote 15, 70409-900 Brasília, DF; tel. (61) 3223-7272; fax (61) 3223-8462; e-mail embaixadaservia@terra.com.br; Ambassador LJUBOMIR MILIC.

Singapore: SHIS QL 24, Conj. 3, Casa 11, Lago Sul, 71665-035 Brasília, DF; tel. (61) 2191-6565; fax (61) 2191-6580; e-mail singemb_bsb@sgmfa.gov.sg; internet www.mfa.gov.sg/brasilia; Ambassador CHIAU BENG CHOO.

Slovakia: SES, Av. das Nações, Quadra 805, Lote 21B, 70200-902 Brasília, DF; tel. (61) 3443-1263; fax (61) 3443-1267; e-mail emb.brasilia@mzv.sk; internet www.mzv.sk/brazilia; Ambassador MILAN CIGÁŇ.

Slovenia: SHIS, QL 08, Conj. 08, Casa 07, Lago Sul, 71620-285 Brasília, DF; tel. (61) 3365-1445; fax (61) 3365-1440; e-mail vbi@gov.si; internet www.brasilia.embassy.si; Ambassador MILENA ŠMIT.

South Africa: SES, Av. das Nações, Quadra 801, Lote 06, 70406-900 Brasília, DF; tel. (61) 3312-9500; fax (61) 3322-8491; e-mail brasilia.general@foreign.gov.za; internet www.africadosul.org.br; Ambassador MOHAKAMA NYANGWENI MBETE.

Spain: SES, Av. das Nações, Quadra 811, Lote 44, 70429-900 Brasília, DF; tel. (61) 3701-1600; fax (61) 3242-1781; e-mail emb.brasilia@maec.es; Ambassador MANUEL DE LA CÁMARA HERMOSO.

Sri Lanka: SHIS, QI 13, Conj. 13, Casa 01, Lago Sul, 71635-130 Brasília, DF; tel. (61) 3248-2701; fax (61) 3364-5430; e-mail lankaemb@yawl.com.br; Ambassador RAJA A. EDIRISURIYA.

Sudan: SHIS, QI 11, Conj. 05, Casa 13, Lago Sul, 71625-250 Brasília, DF; tel. (61) 3248-4835; fax (61) 3248-4833; e-mail sudanbrasilia@yahoo.com; Ambassador ABD ELGHANI ELNAIM AWAD ELKARIM.

Suriname: SHIS, QI 09, Conj. 08, Casa 24, 71625-080 Brasília, DF; tel. (61) 3248-6706; fax (61) 3248-3791; e-mail surinameemb@terra.com.br; Ambassador MARLON FAISAL MOHAMED HOESEIN.

Sweden: SES, Av. das Nações, Quadra 807, Lote 29, 70419-900 Brasília, DF; tel. (61) 3442-5200; fax (61) 3443-1187; e-mail ambassaden.brasilia@gov.se; internet www.suecia.org.br; Ambassador MAGNUS ROBACH.

Switzerland: SES, Av. das Nações, Quadra 811, Lote 41, 70448-900 Brasília, DF; tel. (61) 3443-5500; fax (61) 3443-5711; e-mail bra.vertretung@eda.admin.ch; internet www.dfae.admin.ch/brasilia; Ambassador ANDRÉ REGLI.

Syria: SEN, Av. das Nações, Lote 11, 70434-900 Brasília, DF; tel. (61) 3226-0970; fax (61) 3223-2595; e-mail embsiria@uol.com.br; Chargé d'affaires a.i. GHASSAN NSEIR.

Tanzania: SHIS, QI 09, Conj. 16, Casa 20, Lago Sul, 71615-190 Brasília, DF; tel. (61) 3364-2629; fax (61) 3248-3361; e-mail tanrepbrasilia@yahoo.com.br; Ambassador FRANCIS AMBAKISYE MALAMBUGI.

Thailand: SEN, Av. das Nações, Lote 10, 70800-912 Brasília, DF; tel. (61) 3224-6943; fax (61) 3223-7502; e-mail thaiembbrazil@gmail.com; internet www.thaiembassybrazil.com; Ambassador PITCHAYAPHANT CHARNBHUMIDOL.

Timor-Leste: SHIS, QI 11, Conj. 10, Casa 19, Lago Sul, 71625-300 Brasília, DF; tel. and fax (61) 3366-2755; e-mail embaixada@embaixadatimorleste.com.br; Ambassador GREGÓRIO JOSÉ DA CONCEIÇÃO FERREIRA DE SOUSA.

Trinidad and Tobago: SHIS, QL 02, Conj. 02, Casa 01, 71665-028 Brasília, DF; tel. (61) 3365-1132; fax (61) 3365-1733; e-mail trinbagoemb@gmail.com; Ambassador Dr HAMZA RAFEEQ.

Tunisia: SHIS, QI 11, Conj. 06, Casa 06, Lago Sul, 71625-260 Brasília, DF; tel. (61) 3248-7366; fax (61) 3248-7355; e-mail at.brasilia@terra.com.br; Ambassador SABRI BACHTOBJI.

Turkey: SES, Av. das Nações, Quadra 805, Lote 23, 70452-900 Brasília, DF; tel. (61) 3242-1850; fax (61) 3242-1448; e-mail embassy.brasil@mfa.gov.tr; internet brasilia.emb.mfa.gov.tr; Ambassador HÜSEYIN LAZIP DIRIÖZ.

Ukraine: SHIS, QI 05, Conj. 04, Casa 02, Lago Sul, 71615-040 Brasília, DF; tel. (61) 3365-1457; fax (61) 3365-2127; e-mail emb_br@mfa.gov.ua; internet www.mfa.gov.ua/brazil; Ambassador ROSTYSLAV TRONENKO.

United Arab Emirates: SHIS, QI 05, Chácara 54, 70800-400 Brasília, DF; tel. (61) 3248-0717; fax (61) 3248-7543; e-mail uae@uae.org.br; internet www.uae.org.br; Ambassador SULTAN RASHED AL-KAITOOB.

United Kingdom: SES, Av. das Nações, Quadra 801, Conj. K, Lote 08, 70408-900 Brasília, DF; tel. (61) 3329-2300; fax (61) 3329-2369; e-mail press.brasilia@fco.gov.uk; internet ukinbrazil.fco.gov.uk; Ambassador ALEXANDER WYKEHAM ELLIS.

USA: SES, Av. das Nações, Quadra 801, Lote 03, 70403-900 Brasília, DF; tel. (61) 3312-7000; fax (61) 3225-9136; e-mail ircbsb@state.gov; internet brasilia.usembassy.gov; Ambassador LILIANA AYALDE.

Uruguay: SES, Av. das Nações, Quadra 803, Lote 14, 70450-900 Brasília, DF; tel. (61) 3322-1200; fax (61) 3322-6534; e-mail urubras@emburuguai.org.br; internet www.emburuguai.org.br; Ambassador CARLOS DANIEL AMORÍN TENCONI.

Venezuela: SES, Av. das Nações, Quadra 803, Lote 13, 70451-900 Brasília, DF; tel. (61) 2101-1011; fax (61) 3321-0871; e-mail emb@embvenezuela.org.br; internet www.embvenezuela.org.br; Ambassador DIEGO ALFREDO MOLERO BELLAVIA.

Viet Nam: SHIS, QI 09, Conj. 10, Casa 01, Lago Sul, 71625-100 Brasília, DF; tel. (61) 3364-5876; fax (61) 3364-5836; e-mail embavina@yahoo.com; internet www.vietnamembassy-brazil.org/vi; Ambassador NGUYÊN VAN KIEN.

Zambia: SHIS, QL 10, Conj. 10, Casa 17, Lago Sul, 71630-065 Brasília, DF; tel. and fax (61) 3248-3277; fax (61) 3248-3494; e-mail zambiansbrasil@embaixadazambia.org.br; Ambassador CYNTHIA JANGULO.

Zimbabwe: SHIS, QI 03, Conj. 10, Casa 13, Lago Sul, 71605-300 Brasília, DF; tel. (61) 3365-4801; fax (61) 3365-4803; e-mail zimbrasilia@uol.com.br; Ambassador THOMAS SUKUTAI BVUMA.

Judicial System

The judicial powers of the State are held by the following: the Supreme Federal Court (Supremo Tribunal Federal), the Higher Court of Justice, the five Regional Federal Courts and Federal Judges, the Higher Labour Court, the 24 Regional Labour Courts, the Conciliation and Judgment Councils and Labour Judges, the Higher Electoral Court, the 27 Regional Electoral Courts, the Electoral Judges and Electoral Councils, the Higher Military Court, the Military Courts and Military Judges, the Courts of the States and Judges of the States, the Court of the Federal District and of the Territories and Judges of the Federal District and of the Territories.

The Supreme Federal Court comprises 11 ministers, nominated by the President and approved by the Senado. Its most important role is to rule on the final interpretation of the Constitution. The Supreme Federal Court has the power to declare an act of Congress void if it is unconstitutional. It judges offences committed by persons such as the President, the Vice-President, members of the Congresso Nacional, Ministers of State, its own members, the Attorney-General, judges of other higher courts, and heads of permanent diplomatic missions. It also judges cases of litigation between the Union and the States, between the States, or between foreign nations and the Union or the States, disputes as to jurisdiction between higher Courts, or between the latter and any other court, in cases involving the extradition of criminals, and others related to the writs of habeas corpus and habeas data, and in other cases.

The Higher Court of Justice comprises 33 members, appointed by the President and approved by the Senado. Its jurisdiction includes the judgment of offences committed by State Governors. The Regional Federal Courts comprise at least seven judges, recruited when possible in the respective region and appointed by the President of the Republic. The Higher Labour Court comprises 17 members, appointed by the President and approved by the Senado. The judges of the Regional Labour Courts are also appointed by the President. The Regional Electoral Courts are composed of seven members. The Higher Military Court comprises 15 life members, appointed by the President and approved by the Senado: three from the navy, four from the army, three from the air force and five civilian members. The States are responsible for the administration of their own justice, according to the principles established by the Constitution.

Supremo Tribunal Federal: Praça dos Três Poderes, 70175-900 Brasília, DF; tel. (61) 3217-3000; fax (61) 3217-4412; internet www.stf.jus.br; Pres. RICARDO LEWANDOWSKI.

Attorney-General: LUÍS INÁCIO LUCENA ADAMS.

Prosecutor-General: RODRIGO JANOT.

Religion

CHRISTIANITY

Conselho Nacional de Igrejas Cristãs do Brasil (CONIC) (National Council of Christian Churches in Brazil): Edif. Ceará, Sala 713, SCS, Quadra 01, Bloco E, 70303-900 Brasília, DF; tel. and fax (61) 3321-4034; e-mail conic@conic.org.br; internet www.conic.org.br; f. 1982; eight mem. churches; Pres. Bishop MANOEL JOÃO FRANCISCO; Exec. Sec. Pastor ROMI MÁRCIA BENCKE.

The Roman Catholic Church

Brazil comprises 45 archdioceses (including one for Catholics of the Ukrainian Rite), 213 dioceses (including one each for Catholics of the Maronite, Melkite and Ukrainian Rites), 11 territorial prelatures and one personal apostolic administration. The Archbishop of São Sebastião do Rio de Janeiro is also the Ordinary for Catholics of other Oriental Rites in Brazil. According to the 2010 census, some 65% of the population were Roman Catholics.

Bishops' Conference: Conferência Nacional dos Bispos do Brasil, SES, Quadra 801, Conj. B, 70401-900 Brasília, DF; tel. (61) 2103-8300; fax (61) 2103-8303; e-mail cnbb@cnbb.org.br; internet www.cnbb.org.br; f. 1952; statutes approved 2002; Pres. RAYMUNDO DAMASCENO ASSIS (Archbishop of Aparecida, SP); Sec.-Gen. ANTÔNIO SILVA DA PAIXÃO.

Latin Rite

Archbishop of São Salvador da Bahia, BA, and Primate of Brazil: MURILO SEBASTIÃO RAMOS KRIEGER, Cúria Metropolitana, Av. Leovigildo Filgueiras, García 270, 40100-000 Salvador, BA; tel. (71) 4009-6666; e-mail contato@arquidiocesesalvador.org.br; internet www.arquidiocesesalvador.org.br.

Archbishop of Aparecida, SP: Cardinal RAYMUNDO DAMASCENO ASSIS.

Archbishop of Aracaju, SE: JOSÉ PALMEIRA LESSA.

Archbishop of Belém do Pará, PA: ALBERTO TAVEIRO CORRÊA.

Archbishop of Belo Horizonte, MG: WALMOR OLIVEIRA DE AZEVEDO.

Archbishop of Botucatu, SP: MAURÍCIO GROTTO DE CAMARGO.

Archbishop of Brasília, DF: SÉRGIO DA ROCHA.

Archbishop of Campinas, SP: AIRTON JOSÉ DOS SANTOS.

Archbishop of Campo Grande, MS: DIMAS LARA BARBOSA.

Archbishop of Cascavel, PR: MAURO APARECIDO DOS SANTOS.

Archbishop of Cuiabá, MT: MILTON ANTÔNIO DOS SANTOS.

Archbishop of Curitiba, PR: (vacant).

Archbishop of Diamantina, MG: JOÃO BOSCO OLIVER DE FARIA.

Archbishop of Feira de Santana, BA: ITAMAR NAVILDO VIAN.

Archbishop of Florianópolis, SC: WILSON TADEU JÖNCK.

Archbishop of Fortaleza, CE: JOSÉ ANTÔNIO APARECIDO TOSI MARQUES.

Archbishop of Goiânia, GO: WASHINGTON CRUZ.

Archbishop of Juíz de Fora, MG: GIL ANTÔNIO MOREIRA.

Archbishop of Londrina, PR: ORLANDO BRANDES.

Archbishop of Maceió, AL: ANTÔNIO MUNIZ FERNANDES.

Archbishop of Manaus, AM: SÉRGIO EDUARDO CASTRANI.

Archbishop of Mariana, MG: GERALDO LYRIO ROCHA.

Archbishop of Maringá, PR: ANUAR BATTISTI.

Archbishop of Montes Claros, MG: JOSÉ ALBERTO MOURA.

Archbishop of Natal, RN: JAIME VIEIRA ROCHA.

Archbishop of Niterói, RJ: JOSÉ FRANCISCO REZENDE DIAS.

Archbishop of Olinda e Recife, PE: ANTONIO FERNANDO SABURIDO.

Archbishop of Palmas, PR: PEDRO BRITO GUIMARÃES.

Archbishop of Paraíba, PB: ALDO DE CILLO PAGOTTO.

Archbishop of Passo Fundo, RS: ANTÔNIO CARLOS ALTIERI.

Archbishop of Pelotas, RS: JACINTO BERGMANN.

Archbishop of Porto Alegre, RS: JAIME SPENGLER.

Archbishop of Porto Velho, RO: ESMERALDO BARRETO DE FARIAS.

Archbishop of Pouso Alegre, MG: JOSÉ LUIZ MAJELLA DELGADO.

Archbishop of Ribeirão Preto, SP: MOACIR SILVA.

Archbishop of Santa Maria, RS: HÉLIO ADELAR RUBERT.

Archbishop of São Luís do Maranhão, MA: JOSÉ BELISÁRIO DA SILVA.

Archbishop of São Paulo, SP: Cardinal ODILO PEDRO SCHERER.

Archbishop of São Sebastião do Rio de Janeiro, RJ: Cardinal ORANI JOÃO TEMPESTA.

Archbishop of Sorocaba, SP: EDUARDO BENES DE SALES RODRIGUES.

Archbishop of Teresina, PI: JACINTO FURTADO DE BRITO SOBRINHO.

Archbishop of Uberaba, MG: PAULO MENDES PEIXOTO.

Archbishop of Vitória, ES: LUIZ MANCILHA VILELA.

Archbishop of Vitória da Conquista, BA: LUIS GONZAGA SILVA PEPEU.

Ukrainian Rite

Archbishop of São João Batista em Curitiba, PR: VALDOMIRO KOUBETCH.

Bishop of Imaculada Conceição in Prudentópolis, PR: MERON MAZUR.

Maronite Rite

Bishop of Nossa Senhora do Líbano em São Paulo, SP: EDGAR MADI.

Melkite Rite

Bishop of Nossa Senhora do Paraíso em São Paulo, SP: FARES MAAKAROUN.

The Anglican Communion

Anglicans form the Episcopal Anglican Church of Brazil (Igreja Episcopal Anglicana do Brasil), comprising eight dioceses.

Igreja Episcopal Anglicana do Brasil: Praça Olavo Bilac 63, Campos Elíseos, 01201-050 São Paulo, SP; tel. and fax (11) 3667-8161; e-mail sec.geral@ieab.org.br; internet www.ieab.org.br; f. 1890; 103,021 mems (1997); Primate Rt Rev. MAURÍCIO JOSÉ ARAÚJO DE ANDRADE; Sec.-Gen. Rev. ARTHUR CAVALCANTE.

Other Christian Churches

According to the 2010 census, 22% of the population are Evangelical Christians.

Church of Jesus Christ of Latter-Day Saints (Mormons): Av. Prof. Francisco Morato 2390, Caxingui 05512-900 São Paulo, SP; tel. (11) 3723-7600; internet www.lds.org; 1.2m. mems.

Igreja Cristã Reformada do Campo Belo (Christian Reformed Church of Campo Belo): Rua Gabrielle D'annuzio 952, Campo Belo, Zona Sul, São Paulo, SP; tel. (11) 5561-6399; internet www .icrcampobelo.com.br; f. 1958; Pastor Rev. VALDECI SANTOS.

Igreja Evangélica de Confissão Luterana no Brasil (IECLB): Rua Senhor dos Passos 202, 4° andar, 90020-180 Porto Alegre, RS; tel. (51) 3284-5400; fax (51) 3284-5419; e-mail presidencia@ieclb.org .br; internet www.luteranos.org.br; f. 1949; 717,000 mems; Pres. Pastor Dr NESTOR PAULO FRIEDRICH; Sec.-Gen. INGRIT VOGT.

Igreja Evangélica Congregacional do Brasil: Rua Mauá 33, Centro, 98900-000 Santa Rosa, RS; tel. (55) 3512-6449; e-mail pastorivo@iecb.org.br; internet www.iecb.org.br; f. 1942; 148,836 mems (2000); Pres. Rev. IVO KÖHN.

Igreja Evangélica Luterana do Brasil: Av. Cel. Lucas de Oliveira 894, Bairro Mont'Serrat, 90440-010 Porto Alegre, RS; tel. (51) 3332-2111; fax (51) 3332-8145; e-mail ielb@ielb.org.br; internet www.ielb .org.br; f. 1904; 233,416 mems; Pres. Rev. EGON KOPERECK; Sec. Rev. Dr REUBENS JOSÉ OGG.

Igreja Maná do Brasil: Rua Arthur Guilardi 153, Jardin Recreio, 12910-150 Bragança Paulista, SP; tel. (11) 4032-8104; e-mail faleconosco@igrejamana.com.br; internet www.igrejamana.com.br; Pastor JORGE TADEU.

Igreja Metodista do Brasil: Av. Piassanguaba 3031, Planalto Paulista, 04060-004 São Paulo, SP; tel. (11) 2813-8600; fax (11) 2813-8632; e-mail sede.nacional@metodista.org.br; internet www .metodista.org.br; 240,000 mems (2010); Exec. Sec. Bishop ADONIAS PEREIRA LAGO.

Igreja Presbiteriana Unida do Brasil (IPU): Edif. Vitória Center, Av. Princesa Isabel 629, 29010-360 Vitória, ES; tel. and fax (27) 3222-8024; e-mail ipu@ipu.org.br; internet www.ipu.org.br; f. 1978; Moderator Rev. ANITA SUE WRIGHT TORRES.

Jehovah's Witnesses: Associação Torre de Vigia de Bíblias e Tratados, CP 92, Tatuí, 18270-970 São Paulo, SP; tel. (11) 3322-9000; 1.4m. adherents (2010).

BAHÁ'Í FAITH

Assembleia Espiritual Nacional dos Bahá'ís do Brasil (National Spiritual Assembly of Bahá'ís of Brazil): SHIS, QL 08, Conj. 02, CP 7035, 71620-970 Brasília, DF; tel. (61) 3255-2200; fax (61) 3364-3470; e-mail info@bahai.org.br; internet www.bahai.org .br; f. 1965; Nat.-Sec. CARLOS ALBERTO SILVA.

BUDDHISM

Sociedade Budista do Brasil (Buddhist Society—Rio Buddhist Vihara): Dom Joaquim Mamede 45, Lagoinha, Santa Tereza, 20241-390 Rio de Janeiro, RJ; tel. (21) 2245-4331; e-mail sbb@ sociedadebudistadobrasil.org; internet www .sociedadebudistadobrasil.org; f. 1972; Pres. JOÃO NERY RAFAEL.

OTHER RELIGIONS

Federação Espírita Brasileira (Brazilian Spiritist Federation): SGAN 603, Conj. F, Av. L2 Norte, 70830-106, Brasília, DF; tel. (61) 2101-6161; internet www.febnet.org.br; Pres. ANTONIO CESAR PERRI DE CARVALHO; 3.8m. followers (2010).

Sociedade Taoísta do Brasil (Taoist Society): Rua Cosme Velho 355, Cosme Velho, 22241-090 Rio de Janeiro, RJ; tel. (21) 2285-1937; e-mail secretaria@taoismo.org.br; internet www.taoismo.org.br; f. 1991; Pres. WU JYH CHERNG.

The Press

The most striking feature of the Brazilian press is the relatively small circulation of newspapers in comparison with the size of the population. This is mainly owing to high costs resulting from distribution difficulties. In consequence, there are no national newspapers.

DAILY NEWSPAPERS

Belém, PA

O Liberal: Av. 25 de Setembro 2473, Marco, 66093-000 Belém, PA; tel. (91) 3216-1138; e-mail redacao@orm.com.br; internet www.orm .com.br/oliberal; f. 1946; Gen. Man. MICHEL PSAROS; Editor ELISÂNGELA SOARES; circ. 43,000.

Belo Horizonte, MG

Diário do Comércio: Av. Américo Vespúcio 1660, Nova Esperança, 31230-250 Belo Horizonte, MG; tel. (31) 3469-2000; fax (31) 3469-2043; e-mail redacaodc@diariodocomercio.com.br; internet www

.diariodocomercio.com.br; f. 1932; Editor-in-Chief AMAURY PIMENTA DE PINHO; Exec. Dir YVAN MULLS.

Estado de Minas: Av. Getúlio Vargas 291, 8° andar, 30112-020 Belo Horizonte, MG; tel. (31) 3263-5800; fax (31) 3263-5424; e-mail fale .conosco@em.com.br; internet www.em.com.br; f. 1928; morning; independent; Chief Editor CARLOS MARCELO CARVALHO; circ. 80,136.

Hoje em Dia: Rua Padre Rolim 652, Santa Efigênia, 30130-916 Belo Horizonte, MG; tel. (31) 3236-8000; fax (31) 3236-8010; e-mail jornalismo@hojeemdia.com.br; internet www.hojeemdia.com.br; Pres. FLÁVIO JACQUES CARNEIRO; Editor-in-Chief CHICO MENDONÇA; circ. 48,800.

Blumenau, SC

Jornal de Santa Catarina: Rua Bahia 2291, 89031-002 Blumenau, SC; tel. (47) 3221-1400; fax (48) 3221-1405; e-mail redacao@santa .com.br; internet jornaldesantacatarina.clicrbs.com.br/sc; f. 1971; Chief Editor EVANDRO ASSIS; circ. 19,402.

Brasília, DF

Correio Braziliense: Edif. Edilson Varela, SIG, Quadra 02, Lote 340, 70610-901 Brasília, DF; tel. (61) 3342-1000; fax (61) 3342-1306; e-mail anadubeux.df@dabr.com.br; internet www.correiobraziliense .com.br; f. 1960; Pres. and Dir ALVARO TEIXEIRA DA COSTA; Editor-in-Chief ANA DUBEUX; circ. 56,321.

Jornal de Brasília: SIG, Trecho 1, Lote 765, 70610-410 Brasília, DF; tel. (61) 3343-8000; fax (61) 3226-6735; e-mail redacao@ jornaldebrasilia.com.br; internet www.jornaldebrasilia.com.br; f. 1972; Editor-in-Chief PAULO GUSMÃO; circ. 25,000.

Campinas, SP

Correio Popular: Rua 7 de Setembro 189, Vila Industrial, 13035-350 Campinas, SP; tel. (19) 3736-3050; fax (19) 3234-8984; e-mail correiopontocom@rac.com.br; internet www.cpopular.com.br; f. 1927; Editorial Dir NELSON HOMEM DE MELLO; circ. 32,044.

Contagem, MG

Super Notícia: Av. Babita Camargos 1645, 32210-180 Contagem, MG; tel. (31) 2101-3901; e-mail luciacastro@otempo.com.br; internet www.supernoticia.com.br; f. 2002; Editor LÚCIA CASTRO; circ. 293,572.

Curitiba, PR

O Estado do Paraná: Rua José Loureiro 282, Centro, 80010-020 Curitiba, PR; tel. (41) 3321-5000; fax (41) 3331-5167; e-mail fale@ pron.com.br; internet www.parana-online.com.br; f. 1951; Pres. ANA AMÉLIA CUNHA PEREIRA FILIZOLA; Editorial Dir RAFAEL TAVARES DE MELLO; circ. 15,000.

Gazeta do Povo: Rua Pedro Ivo 459, Centro, 80010-020 Curitiba, PR; tel. (41) 3321-5470; fax (41) 3321-5300; e-mail guia@ gazetadopovo.com.br; internet www.gazetadopovo.com.br; f. 1919; Editorial Dir MARIA SANDRA GONÇALVES; circ. 43,513.

Jornal Bem Paraná: Rua Dr Roberto Barrozo 22, Centro Cívico, 80530-120 Curitiba, PR; tel. (41) 3350-6600; fax (41) 3350-6650; e-mail contato@bemparana.com.br; internet www.bemparana.com .br; f. 1983 as Jornal do Estado; adopted present name in 2013; Editor-in-Chief JOSIANNE RITZ.

Fortaleza, CE

Diário do Nordeste: Editora Verdes Mares Ltda, Praça da Impresa, C.G.C. 07209-299 Fortaleza, CE; tel. (85) 3266-9773; fax (85) 3266-9797; e-mail aloredacao@diariodonordeste.com.br; internet diariodonordeste.globo.com; Editorial Dir ILDEFONSO RODRIGUES; circ. 33,114.

Jornal O Povo: Av. Aguanambi 282, 60055 Fortaleza, CE; tel. (85) 3255-6250; fax (85) 3231-5792; e-mail centraldeatendimento@opovo .com.br; internet www.opovo.com.br; f. 1928; evening; Exec. Editor FÁTIMA SUDÁRIO; circ. 23,216.

Goiânia, GO

Diário da Manhã: Av. Anhanguera 2833, Setor Leste Universitário, 74610-010 Goiânia, GO; tel. (62) 3267-1000; e-mail opiniao@dm.com .br; internet www.dm.com.br; f. 1980; Editor BATISTA CUSTÓDIO; circ. 16,000.

O Popular: Rua Thómas Edson, Quadra 07, No 400, Setor Serrinha, 74835-130 Goiânia, GO; tel. (62) 3250-1028; fax (62) 3250-1260; e-mail dca@opopular.com.br; internet www.opopular.com.br; f. 1938; Editor-in-Chief CILEIDE ALVES; circ. 31,971.

João Pessoa, PB

Correio da Paraíba: Av. Pedro II, Centro, João Pessoa, PB; tel. (83) 3216-5000; fax (83) 3216-5009; e-mail assinante@portalcorreio.com

.br; internet www.correiodaparaiba.com.br; Exec. Dir BEATRIZ RIBEIRO; Editor-in-Chief WALTER GALVÃO.

Londrina, PR

Folha de Londrina: Rua Piauí 241, 86010-420 Londrina, PR; tel. (43) 3374-2020; fax (43) 3339-1412; e-mail contato@folhadelondrina .com.br; internet www.folhaweb.com.br; f. 1948; Editor-in-Chief FERNANDA MAZZINI; circ. 33,113.

Manaus, AM

A Crítica: Av. André Araújo 1924A, Aleixo-Cidade das Comunicações, 69060-001 Manaus, AM; tel. (92) 3643-1200; fax (92) 3643-1234; e-mail aruana@acritica.com.br; internet www.acritica.com.br; f. 1949; Chair. RITTA ARAÚJO CALDERARO; Editorial Dir ARUANA BRIANEZI; circ. 19,000.

Natal, RN

Diario de Natal: Av. Deodoro da Fonseca 245, Petrópolis, 59012-600 Natal, RN; tel. (84) 4009-0166; e-mail redacao.rn@diariosassociados .com.br; internet www.diariodenatal.com.br; Exec. Editor JULISKA AZEVEDO.

Niterói, RJ

O Fluminense: Rua Visconde de Itaboraí 184, Centro, 24035-900 Niterói, RJ; tel. (21) 2125-3000; fax (21) 2620-8636; e-mail reportagem@ofluminense.com.br; internet www.ofluminense.com .br; f. 1878; Man. Editor SANDRA DUARTE; circ. 80,000.

A Tribuna: Rua Barão do Amazonas 31, Ponta D'areia, 2403-0111 Niterói, RJ; tel. (21) 2719-1886; e-mail icarai@urbi.com.br; internet www.atribunarj.com.br; f. 1936; daily; Dir-Supt GUSTAVO SANTANO AMÓRO; circ. 10,000.

Palmas, TO

O Girassol: Edif. Office Center, Salas 408–410, Av. Teotônio Segurado, 101 Sul, Conj. 01, Lote 06, 77015-002 Palmas, TO; tel. and fax (63) 3225-5456; e-mail ogirassol@uol.com.br; internet www.ogirassol .com.br; f. 2000; Editor-in-Chief WILBERGSON ESTRELA GOMES; Exec. Editor SONIELSON LUCIANO DE SOUSA.

Porto Alegre, RS

Zero Hora: Av. Ipiranga 1075, Azenha, 90169-900 Porto Alegre, RS; tel. (51) 3218-4300; fax (51) 3218-4700; e-mail leitor@zerohora.com .br; internet zerohora.clicrbs.com.br/rs; f. 1964; Editor-in-Chief NILSON VARGAS; circ. 188,561.

Recife, PE

Diário de Pernambuco: Rua do Veiga 600, Santo Amaro, 50040-110 Recife, PE; tel. (81) 2122-7555; fax (81) 2122-7544; e-mail faleconosco@diariodepernambuco.com.br; internet www .diariodepernambuco.com.br; f. 1825; morning; independent; Editorial Dir VERA OGANDO; circ. 24,762.

Ribeirão Preto, SP

Jornal Tribuna da Ribeirão Preto: Rua São Sebastião 1380, Centro, 14015-040 Ribeirão Preto, SP; tel. and fax (16) 3632-2200; e-mail tribuna@tribunaribeirao.com.br; internet www .tribunaribeirao.com.br; Editor HILTON HARTMANN; circ. 16,000.

Rio de Janeiro, RJ

O Dia: Rua Riachuelo 359, Centro, 20235-900 Rio de Janeiro, RJ; fax (21) 2507-1228; e-mail aziz.filho@odia.com.br; internet odia.ig.com .br; f. 1951; morning; centrist labour; Publr RAMIRO ALVES; Editor-in-Chief AZIZ FILHO; circ. 50,288.

O Globo: Rua Irineu Marinho 35, CP 1090, 20233-900 Rio de Janeiro, RJ; tel. (21) 2534-5000; fax (21) 2534-5510; internet oglobo.globo.com; f. 1925; morning; Editor-in-Chief ASCÂNIO SELEME; circ. 256,259.

Jornal do Brasil: Av. Paulo de Frontin 568, Fundos, Rio Comprido, 20261-243 Rio de Janeiro, RJ; tel. (21) 2323-1000; e-mail cartas@jb .com.br; internet www.jb.com.br; f. 1891; print edn suspended July 2010, online only; Catholic, liberal; Editor TALES FARIA.

Lance: Rua Santa Maria 47, Cidade Nova, 20211-210 Rio de Janeiro, RJ; tel. (21) 4063-6350; internet www.lancenet.com.br; sports, daily; Editor LUIZ FERNANDO GOMES; circ.84,983.

Salvador, BA

Correio da Bahia: Rua Aristides Novis 123, Federação, 40310-630 Salvador, BA; tel. (71) 3533-3030; fax (71) 3203-1045; e-mail redacao@correio24horas.com.br; internet www.correio24horas.com .br; f. 1978; Editor-in-Chief SERGIO COSTA; circ. 34,681.

A Tarde: Rua Prof. Milton Cayres de Brito 204, Caminho das Árvores, 41820-570 Salvador, BA; tel. (71) 3340-8500; fax (71) 3231-8800; e-mail suporte@atarde.com.br; internet www.atarde .com.br; f. 1912; evening; Editor-in-Chief VAGUINALDO MARINHEIRO; circ. 45,377.

Santarém, PA

O Impacto—O Jornal da Amazônia: Av. Presidente Vargas 3721, Caranazal, 68040-060 Santarém, PA; tel. (93) 3523-3330; fax (93) 3523-9131; e-mail oimpacto@oimpacto.com.br; internet www .oimpacto.com.br; Editor-in-Chief JERFFESON ROCHA.

Santo André, SP

Diário do Grande ABC: Rua Catequese 562, Bairro Jardim, 09090-900 Santo André, SP; tel. (11) 4435-8100; fax (11) 4434-8250; e-mail online@dgabc.com.br; internet www.dgabc.com.br; f. 1958; Editor-in-Chief EVALDO NOVELINI; circ. 78,500.

Santos, SP

A Tribuna: Rua João Pessoa 129, 2º e 3º andares, Centro, 11013-900 Santos, SP; tel. (13) 2102-7000; fax (13) 3219-7329; e-mail redacao@ atribuna.com.br; internet www.atribuna.com.br; f. 1984; Exec. Editor ARMINDA AUGUSTO; Editor-in-Chief CARLOS CONDE; circ. 20,751.

São Luís, MA

O Imparcial: Empresa Pacotilha Ltda, Rua Assis Chateaubriand s/ n, Renascença 2, 65075-670 São Luís, MA; tel. (98) 3212-2000; e-mail redacao@oimparcial.com.br; internet www.oimparcial.com.br; f. 1926; Editor-in-Chief PEDRO HENRIQUE FREIRE; circ. 8,000.

São Paulo, SP

DCI (Diário Comércio, Indústria e Serviços): Rua Major Quedinho 90, 7º andar, centro, 01050-030 São Paulo, SP; tel. (11) 5095-5200; fax (11) 5095-5308; e-mail redacao@dci.com.br; internet www.dci.com .br; f. 1933; morning; Editor-in-Chief LILIANA LAVORATTI; circ. 50,000.

Diário do Comércio: Associação Comercial de São Paulo, Rua Boa Vista 51, 6º andar, Centro, 01014-911 São Paulo, SP; tel. (11) 3244-3322; fax (11) 3244-3046; e-mail faleconosco@dcomercio.com.br; internet www.dcomercio.com.br; Editorial Dir MOISÉS RABINOVICI.

Diário de São Paulo: Rua Américo Vespúcio 1001, Menck, 06273-070 Osasco, SP; tel. (11) 3235-7800; e-mail contato@diariosp.com.br; internet www.diariosp.com.br; f. 1884; fmrly *Diário Popular*; evening; owned by O Globo; Editor-in-Chief CARLOS FREY DE ALENCAR; circ. 38,840.

O Estado de São Paulo: Av. Engenheiro Caetano Alvares 55, Bairro do Limão, 02598-900 São Paulo, SP; tel. (11) 3856-5400; fax (11) 3856-2940; e-mail falecom.estado@grupoestado.com.br; internet www.estado.com.br; f. 1875; morning; independent; Editor-in-Chief ROBERTO GAZZI; circ. 263,046.

Folha de São Paulo: Alameda Barão de Limeira 425, 6º andar, Campos Elíseos, 01202-900 São Paulo, SP; tel. (11) 3224-4759; fax (11) 3224-7550; e-mail falecomagente@folha.com.br; internet www .folha.uol.com.br; f. 1921; morning; Editorial Dir OTAVIO FRIAS FILHO; circ. 286,398.

Vitória, ES

A Gazeta: Rua Charic Murad 902, 29050 Vitória, ES; tel. (27) 3321-8333; fax (27) 3321-8720; e-mail ahees@redegazeta.com.br; internet gazetaonline.globo.com; f. 1928; Exec. Editor ANDRÉ HEES; circ. 26,785.

PERIODICALS

Rio de Janeiro, RJ

Antenna-Eletrônica Popular: Av. Marechal Floriano 151, Centro, 20080-005 Rio de Janeiro, RJ; tel. (21) 2223-2442; fax (21) 2263-8840; e-mail antenna@anep.com.br; internet www.anep.com.br; f. 1926; monthly; telecommunications and electronics, radio, TV, hi-fi, amateur and CB radio; Dir MARIA BEATRIZ AFFONSO PENNA; circ. 15,000.

Conjuntura Econômica: Rua Barão de Itambi 60, 7º andar, Botafogo, 22231-000 Rio de Janeiro, RJ; tel. (21) 2559-6040; fax (21) 2559-6039; e-mail eleonora@conjunturainstitucional.com.br; internet www.fgv.br/ibre/cecon; f. 1947; monthly; economics and finance; published by Fundação Getúlio Vargas; Editor-in-Chief CLAUDIO CONCEIÇÃO; circ. 15,000.

ECO21: Av. Copacabana 2, Gr. 301, 22010-122 Rio de Janeiro, RJ; tel. (21) 2275-1490; e-mail eco21@eco21.com.br; internet www.eco21 .com.br; f. 1990; monthly; ecological issues; Editor RENÉ CAPRILES.

São Paulo, SP

Ana Maria: Editora Abril, Av. das Nações Unidas 7221, 05425-902 São Paulo, SP; tel. (11) 3037-2000; fax (11) 3037-4734; e-mail anamaria.abril@atleitor.com.br; internet mdemulher.abril.com.br/revistas/anamaria; weekly; women's interest; Dir HELENA BAGNOLI; Editor-in-Chief LIDICE BÁ; circ. 222,171.

Caras: Av. Juscelino Kubitschek 1400, 13º andar, 04543-000 São Paulo, SP; tel. (11) 2197-2000; fax (11) 3086-4738; e-mail atendimento@caras.com.br; internet novoportal.caras.uol.com.br; f. 1993; weekly; celebrities; Editor VALENÇA SOTERO; circ. 308,465.

Caros Amigos: Rua Paris 856, Sumaré, 01257-040 São Paulo, SP; tel. (11) 3123-6600; fax (11) 3123-6609; e-mail atendimento@carosamigos.com.br; internet www.carosamigos.com.br; f. 1997; monthly; political; Editor ARAY NABUCO (acting); circ. 37,000.

CartaCapital: Alameda Santos 1800, 7º andar, Cerqueira César, 01418-200 São Paulo, SP; tel. (11) 3474-0161; e-mail redacao@cartacapital.com.br; internet www.cartacapital.com.br; f. 1994; weekly; politics and economics; Editor-in-Chief SERGIO LIRIO; circ. 32,570.

Casa e Jardim: Av. Jaguaré 1485, 05346-902 São Paulo, SP; tel. (11) 3767-7000; fax (11) 3767-7936; e-mail casaejardim@edglobo.com.br; internet revistacasaejardim.globo.com; f. 1953; monthly; homes and gardens, illustrated; Editor-in-Chief THAÍS LAUTON; circ. 100,811.

Claudia: Editora Abril, Av. das Nações Unidas 7221, Pinheiros, 05425-902 São Paulo, SP; tel. (11) 3037-2000; fax (11) 5087-2100; e-mail claudia.abril@atleitor.com.br; internet claudia.abril.com.br; f. 1962; monthly; women's interest; Dir PAULA MAGESTE; Editor-in-Chief DAGMAR SERPA; circ. 402,940.

Contigo!: Editora Abril, Av. das Nações Unidas 7221, 5º andar, 05425-902 São Paulo, SP; tel. (11) 3037-2000; fax (11) 3037-4734; e-mail contigo.abril@atleitor.com.br; internet contigo.abril.com.br; f. 1963; weekly; entertainment and celebrity news; Editor-in-Chief DENISE GIANOGLIO; circ. 148,569.

Cult: Praça Santo Agostinho 70, 10º andar, Paraíso, 01533-070 São Paulo, SP; tel. (11) 3385-3385; fax (11) 3385-3386; e-mail redacao@revistacult.com.br; internet revistacult.uol.com.br; f. 1997; monthly; art and culture; Editorial Dir DAYSI BREGANTINI.

Digesto Econômico: Associação Comercial de São Paulo, Rua Boa Vista 51, 6º andar, Centro, 01014-911 São Paulo, SP; tel. (11) 3244-3055; fax (11) 3244-3046; e-mail admdiario@acsp.com.br; internet www.dcomercio.com.br; fortnightly; Chief Editor JOSÉ GUILHERME RODRIGUEZ FERREIRA.

Elle: Editora Abril, Av. das Nações Unidas 7221, 16º andar, Pinheiros, 05425-902 São Paulo, SP; tel. (11) 3037-3545; fax (11) 3037-5451; e-mail elle.abril@atleitor.com.br; internet elle.abril.com.br; f. 1988; monthly; women's interest; Editor-in-Chief RENATA PIZA; circ. 100,000.

Época: Av. Jaguaré 1485, 05346-902 São Paulo, SP; tel. (11) 3767-7000; e-mail epoca@edglobo.com.br; internet revistaepoca.globo.com; f. 1998; news weekly; Editor-in-Chief JOÃO GABRIEL DE LIMA; circ. 416,744.

Exame: Editora Abril, Av. das Nações Unidas 7221, Pinheiros, 05425-902 São Paulo, SP; tel. (11) 3037-2000; fax (11) 3037-2027; e-mail redacao.exame@abril.com.br; internet www.exame.com.br; f. 1967; 2 a week; business; Editor-in-Chief TIAGO LETHBRIDGE; circ. 168,300.

Glamour: Rua de Rocio 350, 04552-000 São Paulo, SP; tel. (11) 2322-4617; fax (11) 2322-4699; e-mail glamour@edglobo.com.br; internet revistaglamour.globo.com; f. 2012; monthly; women's interest; Editor-in-Chief MÔNICA SALGADO.

ISTOÉ: Rua William Speers 1088, 05067-900 São Paulo, SP; tel. (11) 3618-4200; fax (11) 3618-4324; e-mail leitor@istoe.com.br; internet www.istoe.com.br; politics and current affairs; Editorial Dir CARLOS JOSÉ MARQUES; circ. 340,764.

Máquinas e Metais: Alameda Olga 315, 01155-900 São Paulo, SP; tel. (11) 3824-5300; fax (11) 3666-9585; e-mail infomm@arandanet.com.br; internet www.arandanet.com.br; f. 1964; monthly; machine and metal industries; Editorial Dir JOSÉ ROBERTO GONÇALVES; circ. 15,000.

Marie Claire: Av. Jaguaré 1485, 05346-902 São Paulo, SP; tel. (11) 3767-7000; fax (11) 3767-7833; e-mail mclaire@edglobo.com.br; internet revistamarieclaire.globo.com; monthly; women's interest; Editorial Dir MÔNICA DE ALBUQUERQUE LINS SERINO; circ. 199,831.

Micromundo-Computerworld do Brasil: Rua Caçapava 79, 01408 São Paulo, SP; tel. (11) 3289-1767; e-mail cw@nowdigital.com.br; internet www.computerworld.com.br; f. 1976; bimonthly; computers; Exec. Editor EDILEUZA SOARES; circ. 38,000.

Nova Escola: Editora Abril, Av. das Nações Unidas 7221, 6º andar, 05425-902 São Paulo, SP; tel. (11) 3037-2000; fax (11) 3037-4322; e-mail novaescola@atleitor.com.br; internet revistaescola.abril.com.br; f. 1986; monthly; education; Editor-in-Chief DENISE PELLEGRINI; circ. 451,125.

Pais & Filhos: Av. Rebouças 3181, Pinheiros, 05401-400 São Paulo, SP; tel. (11) 3511-2200; fax (11) 3512-9458; e-mail revista@revistapaisefilhos.com.br; internet www.revistapaisefilhos.com.br; monthly; child health; Editor MARIANA SETUBAL.

Placar: Editora Abril, Av. das Nações Unidas 7221, 14º andar, Pinheiros, 05425-902 São Paulo, SP; tel. (11) 3037-2000; fax (11) 5087-2100; e-mail placar.abril@atleitor.com.br; internet placar.abril.com.br; f. 1970; monthly; soccer; Editor-in-Chief MARCOS SERGIO SILVA; circ. 127,000.

Quatro Rodas: Editora Abril, Av. das Nações Unidas 7221, 14º andar, 05425-902 São Paulo, SP; fax (11) 3037-5039; internet quatrorodas.abril.com.br; f. 1960; monthly; motoring; Editor-in-Chief ZECA CHAVES; circ. 190,139.

Revista O Carreteiro: Rua Palacete das Aguias 395, Vila Alexandria, 04635-021 São Paulo, SP; tel. (11) 5035-0000; fax (11) 5031-8647; e-mail revista@ocarreteiro.com.br; internet www.revistaocarreteiro.com.br; f. 1970; monthly; transport; Editor JOÃO GERALDO; circ. 100,000.

Saúde: Editora Abril, Av. das Nações Unidas 7221, 16º andar, Pinheiros, 05425-902 São Paulo, SP; tel. (11) 3037-4885; fax (11) 3037-4867; e-mail saude.abril@atleitor.com.br; internet saude.abril.com.br; monthly; health; Editor-in-Chief FÁBIO DE OLIVEIRA; circ. 183,250.

Superinteressante: Editora Abril, Av. das Nações Unidas 7221, 8º andar, 05425-902 São Paulo, SP; tel. (11) 3037-2000; fax (11) 3037-5891; e-mail superleitor.abril@atleitor.com.br; internet super.abril.com.br; f. 1987; monthly; popular science; Editor-in-Chief RAFAEL KENSKI; circ. 354,947.

Veja: Editora Abril, Av. das Nações Unidas 7221, Pinheiros, 05425-902 São Paulo, SP; tel. (11) 3347-2121; fax (11) 3037-5638; e-mail veja@abril.com.br; internet veja.abril.com.br; f. 1968; weekly; Editor-in-Chief FÁBIO ALTMAN; circ. 1,099,078.

NEWS AGENCIES

Agência o Estado de São Paulo: Av. Eng. Caetano Alvares 55, Bairro do Limão, 02588-900 São Paulo, SP; tel. (11) 3856-3500; fax (11) 3856-2940; e-mail falecom.estado@grupoestado.com.br; internet www.estadao.com.br; Rep. SAMUEL DIRCEU F. BUENO.

Agência O Globo: Rua Irineu Marinho 70, 4º andar, Cidade Nova, 20230-901 Rio de Janeiro, RJ; tel. (21) 2534-5656; e-mail agenciaoglobo@oglobo.com.br; internet www.agenciaoglobo.com.br; f. 1974; Man. RICARDO MELLO.

PRESS ASSOCIATIONS

Associação Brasileira de Imprensa (ABI): Rua Araújo Porto Alegre 71, Centro, 20030-012 Rio de Janeiro, RJ; tel. (21) 2282-1292; e-mail abi@abi.org.br; internet www.abi.org.br; f. 1908; asscn for journalistic rights and assistance; 4,000 mems; Pres. MAURÍCIO AZÊDO.

Associação Nacional de Editores de Revistas (ANER): Rua Deputado Lacerda Franco 300, 15º, Conj. 155, 05418-000 São Paulo, SP; tel. (11) 3030-9390; fax (11) 3030-9393; e-mail info@aner.org.br; internet www.aner.org.br; f. 1986; Pres. FREDERIC KACHAR; Exec. Dir MARIA CÉLIA FURTADO.

Federação Nacional dos Jornalistas (FENAJ): SCLRN 704, Bloco F, Loja 20, 70730-536 Brasília, DF; tel. (61) 3244-0650; fax (61) 3242-6616; e-mail fenaj@fenaj.org.br; internet www.fenaj.org.br; f. 1946; represents 31 regional unions; Pres. CELSO SCHRÖDER; Sec.-Gen. GUTO CAMARGO.

Publishers

Abril Educação, SA: Av. das Nações Unidas 7221, Pinheiros, 05425-902 São Paulo, SP; internet www.abrileducacao.com.br; f. 1960; owned by Grupo Abril; educational resources; imprints include Editora Atica (f. 1965) and Editora Scipione (f. 1983); Pres. GIANCARLO CIVITA.

Aymará Edições e Tecnologia, Ltda: Rua Lamenha Lins 1709, Rebouças, 80220-080 Curitiba, PR; tel. (41) 3213-3500; fax (41) 3213-3501; e-mail debora.nunes@aymara.com.br; internet www.aymara.com.br; academic; Pres. ANDRÉ CALDEIRA.

Barsa Planeta Internacional: Edif. New York, 4º andar, Centro Empresarial Agua Branca, Av. Francisco Matarazzo 1500, 05001-100 São Paulo, SP; tel. (11) 3225-1990; fax (11) 3225-1960; e-mail atendimento@barsaplaneta.com.br; internet brasil.planetasaber.com; f. 1949; reference books.

Cengage Learning: Prédio 11, Torre A, Conj. 12, Condomínio E-Business Park, Rua Werner Siemens 111, Lapa de Baixo, 05069-900 São Paulo, SP; tel. (11) 3665-9900; fax (11) 3665-9901; e-mail milagros.valderrama@cengage.com; internet www.cengage.com.br; f. 1960 as Editora Pioneira; architecture, computers, political and social sciences, business studies, languages, children's books; Dir MILAGROS VALDERRAMA.

Cortez Editora: Rua Monte Alegre 1074, 05014-001 São Paulo, SP; tel. (11) 3611-9696; fax (11) 3864-0111; e-mail erivan@cortezeditora .com.br; internet www.cortezeditora.com.br; f. 1980; children's literature, linguistics and social sciences; Dir ERIVAN GOMES.

Ediouro Publicações, SA: Rua Nova Jerusalém 345, CP 1880, Bonsucesso, 21042-235 Rio de Janeiro, RJ; tel. (21) 3882-8416; fax (21) 3882-8200; e-mail livros@ediouro.com.br; internet www.ediouro .com.br; f. 1939; part of Empresas Ediouro; general interest, leisure magazines, textbooks; Pres. JORGE CARNEIRO.

Editora Abril, SA: Av. das Nações Unidas 7221, Pinheiros, 05425-902 São Paulo, SP; tel. (11) 3037-2000; fax (11) 5087-2100; e-mail abril@abril.com.br; internet www.abril.com.br; f. 1950; owned by Grupo Abril; magazines; Pres. FÁBIO COLLETTI BARBOSA.

Editora Atlas, SA: Rua Conselheiro Nébias 1384, 01203-904 São Paulo, SP; tel. (11) 3357-9144; fax (11) 3331-7830; e-mail atendimento@editora-atlas.com.br; internet www.editoraatlas.com .br; f. 1944; business administration, economics, accounting, law, education, social sciences; Pres. LUIZ HERRMANN, Jr.

Editora Blucher: Rua Pedroso Alvarenga 1245, 4° andar, 04531-012 São Paulo, SP; tel. (11) 3078-5366; fax (11) 3079-2707; e-mail eduardo@blucher.com.br; internet www.blucher.com.br; f. 1957; science and engineering; Dir EDUARDO BLÜCHER.

Editora do Brasil, SA: Rua Conselheiro Nébias 887, Campos Elíseos, CP 4986, 01203-001 São Paulo, SP; tel. (11) 3226-0211; fax (11) 3222-5583; e-mail editora@editoradobrasil.com.br; internet www.editoradobrasil.com.br; f. 1943; education; Pres. MARIA APPARECIDA CAVALCANTE COSTA.

Editora Brasiliense, SA: Rua Mourato Coelho 111, Pinheiros, 05417-010 São Paulo, SP; tel. and fax (11) 3087-0000; e-mail brasilienseedit@uol.com.br; internet www.editorabrasiliense.com .br; f. 1943; education, racism, gender studies, human rights, ecology, history, literature, social sciences; Pres. YOLANDA C. DA SILVA PRADO.

Editora Campus-Elsevier: Rua Sete de Setembro 111, 16° andar, 20050-002 Rio de Janeiro, RJ; tel. (21) 3970-9300; fax (21) 2507-1991; e-mail info@elsevier.com.br; internet www.campus.com.br; f. 1976; business, computing, non-fiction; imprint of Elsevier since 2002; Pres. CLAUDIO ROTHMULLER; Dir IGDAL PARNES.

Editora Canção Nova: Rua São Bento 43, Centro, 01011-000 São Paulo, SP; tel. (11) 3106-9080; e-mail editora@cancaonova.com; internet editora.cancaonova.com; f. 1996; spiritual literature and children's books; Dir CRISTIANA MARIA NEGRÃO.

Editora Delta, SA (Mundo da Criança): Av. Nilo Peçanha 50, Centro 2817, 20020-100 Rio de Janeiro, RJ; tel. (21) (21) 2533-6673; e-mail falcconosco@mundodacrianca.com; internet www.mundodacrianca .com; f. 1930; reference books; Pres. ANDRÉ KOOGAN BREITMAN.

Editora FTD, SA: Rua Rui Barbosa 156, Bairro Bela Vista, 01326-010 São Paulo, SP; tel. (11) 3253-5011; fax (11) 3288-0132; e-mail ftd@ ftd.com.br; internet www.ftd.com.br; f. 1902; textbooks; Pres. DÉLCIO AFONSO BALESTRIN; Dir CECILIANY ALVES.

Editora Globo, SA: Av. Jaguaré 1485, 3° andar, 05346-902 São Paulo, SP; tel. (11) 3767-7400; fax (11) 3767-7870; e-mail globolivros@edglobo.com.br; internet globolivros.globo.com; f. 1957; fiction, engineering, agriculture, cookery, environmental studies; Dir-Gen. FREDERIC ZOGHAIB KACHAR.

Editora Lê, SA: Rua Januária 437, Floresta, 31110-060 Belo Horizonte, MG; tel. (31) 3423-3200; fax (31) 2517-3003; e-mail editora@le.com.br; internet www.le.com.br; f. 1967; textbooks; Dir JOSÉ ALENCAR MAYRINK.

Editora Manole: Av. Ceci 672, Tamboré, 06460-120 Barueri, SP; tel. (11) 4196-6000; e-mail info@manole.com.br; internet www .manole.com.br; includes the imprints Minha Editora and Amarylis Editora; Dir AMARYLIS MANOLE.

Editora Melhoramentos, Ltda: Rua Tito 479, Vila Romana, 05051-000 São Paulo, SP; tel. (11) 3874-0800; fax (11) 3874-0855; e-mail sac@melhoramentos.com.br; internet www .livrariamelhoramentos.com.br; f. 1890; general non-fiction, children's books, dictionaries; Dir BRENO LERNER.

Editora Moderna, Ltda: Rua Padre Adelino 758, Belenzinho, 03303-904 São Paulo, SP; tel. (11) 2790-1300; fax (11) 2602-5510; e-mail falcconosco@moderna.com.br; internet www.moderna.com .br; f. 1968; Pres. RICARDO ARISSA FELTRE.

Editora Nova Fronteira, SA: Rua Nova Jerusalém 345, Bonsucesso, 21042-230 Rio de Janeiro, RJ; tel. (21) 2131-1111; fax (21) 2537-2009; e-mail sac@novafronteira.com.br; internet www .novafronteira.com.br; f. 1965; acquired by Empresas Ediouro in 2006; fiction, psychology, history, politics, science fiction, poetry, leisure, reference; Exec. Dir MAURO PALERMO.

Editora Positivo: Rua Major Heitor Guimarães 174, Seminário, 80400-120 Curitiba, PR; tel. (41) 3212-3500; fax (41) 3336-5135;

e-mail vendas@editorapositivo.com.br; internet www .editorapositivo.com.br; f. 1980; Dir-Gen. EMERSON SANTOS.

Editora Record, SA: Rua Argentina 171, São Cristóvão, CP 884, 20921-380 Rio de Janeiro, RJ; tel. (21) 2585-2000; fax (21) 2585-2085; e-mail record@record.com.br; internet www.record.com.br; f. 1942; part of Grupo Editorial Record; general fiction and non-fiction, education, textbooks, fine arts; Pres. SÉRGIO MACHADO.

Editora Revista dos Tribunais, Ltda: Rua do Bosque 820, 01136-000 São Paulo, SP; tel. (11) 3613-8400; fax (11) 3613-8450; e-mail sac@rt.com.br; internet www.rt.com.br; f. 1912; acquired by Thomson Reuters in 2010; law and jurisprudence books and periodicals; Pres. GONZALO LISSARRAGUE; CEO BELINELO ANTONIO.

Editora Rideel, Ltda: Av. Casa Verde 455, Casa Verde, 02519-000 São Paulo, SP; tel. and fax (11) 2238-5100; e-mail sac@rideel.com.br; internet www.rideel.com.br; f. 1971; general; Dir ITALO AMADIO.

Editora Saraiva: Rua Henrique Schaumann 270, Cerqueira César, 05413-909 São Paulo, SP; tel. (11) 3613-3000; fax (11) 3611-3308; e-mail saceditorasaraiva@editorasaraiva.com.br; internet www .editorasaraiva.com.br; f. 1914; education, textbooks, law, economics, general fiction and non-fiction; Pres. JORGE EDUARDO SARAIVA.

Editora Vozes, Ltda: Rua Frei Luís 100, CP 90023, Centro, 25689-900 Petrópolis, RJ; tel. (24) 2233-9000; fax (24) 2231-4676; e-mail editorial@vozes.com.br; internet www.universovozes.com.br; f. 1901; Catholic publrs; theology, philosophy, history, linguistics, science, psychology, fiction, education, etc.; Dir ANTÔNIO MOSER.

Global Editora: Rua Pirapitingüi 111, Liberdade, 01508-020 São Paolo, SP; tel. (11) 3277-7999; fax (11) 3277-8141; e-mail global@ globaleditora.com.br; internet www.globaleditora.com.br; f. 1973; Dir LUIZ ALVES JÚNIOR.

Instituto Brasileiro de Edições Pedagógicas, Ltda (Editora IBEP): Av. Alexandre Mackenzie 619, Jaguaré, 05322-000 São Paulo, SP; tel. (11) 2799-7799; fax (11) 6694-5338; e-mail editoras@ ibep-nacional.com.br; internet www.editoraibep.com.br; f. 1965; part of Grupo IBEP; textbooks; Dirs JORGE YUNES, PAULO CORNADO MARTI.

Lex Editora, SA: Rua da Consolação 77, Centro, 01301-000 São Paulo, SP; tel. (11) 2126-6000; fax (11) 2126-6020; e-mail editorial@ lex.com.br; internet www.lex.com.br; f. 1937; legislation and jurisprudence; Pres. CARLOS SERGIO SERRA; Exec. Dir FÁBIO PAIXÃO.

Pallas Editora: Rua Frederico de Albuquerque 56, Higienópolis, 21050-840 Rio de Janeiro, RJ; tel. and fax (21) 2270-0186; e-mail pallas@pallaseditora.com.br; internet www.pallaseditora.com.br; f. 1980; Afro-Brazilian culture; Pres. CRISTINA FERNANDES WARTH.

Yendis Editora: Estrada das Lágrimas, 111, 09581-300 São Caetano do Sul, SP; tel. (11) 4224-9400; fax (11) 4224-9403; e-mail dirce@ yendis.com.br; internet www.yendis.com.br; Dir MAXWELL MEDEIROS FERNANDES.

PUBLISHERS' ASSOCIATIONS

Associação Brasileira de Difusão do Livro (ABDL) (Brazilian Association of Door-to-Door Booksellers): Rua Marquês de Itu 408-71, CP 01223-000, São Paulo, SP; internet www.abdl.com.br; f. 1987; non-profit org.; Pres. LUÍS ANTONIO TORELLI.

Associação Brasileira de Editores de Livros Escolares (Abrelivros): Rua Funchal 263, Conj. 61/62, Vila Olímpia, 04551-060 São Paulo, SP; tel. and fax (11) 3826-9071; e-mail contato@abrelivros.org .br; internet www.abrelivros.org.br; f. 1991; 28 mems; Pres. JORGE YUNES; Gen. Man. BEATRIZ GRELLET.

Associação Brasileira do Livro (ABL): Av. 13 de Maio 23, 16° andar, Sala 1619/1620, 20031-000 Rio de Janeiro, RJ; tel. and fax (21) 2240-9115; e-mail abralivro@uol.com.br; internet www.abralivro .com.br; f. 1955; Pres. ADENILSON JARBAS CABRAL.

Câmara Brasileira do Livro: Rua Cristiano Viana 91, Pinheiros, 05411-000 São Paulo, SP; tel. and fax (11) 3069-1300; e-mail cbl@cbl .org.br; internet www.cbl.org.br; f. 1946; Pres. ROSELY BOSCHINI.

Sindicato Nacional dos Editores de Livros (SNEL): Rua da Ajuda 35, 18° andar, Centro, 20040-000 Rio de Janeiro, RJ; tel. (21) 2533-0399; fax (21) 2533-0422; e-mail snel@snel.org.br; internet www.snel.org.br; 200 mems; Pres. SONIA MACHADO JARDIM.

Broadcasting and Communications

TELECOMMUNICATIONS

AT&T Brazil: Torre Sul, 7°, Rua James Joule 65, São Paulo, SP; tel. (11) 3885-0080; internet www.att.com.br; Vice-Pres. (Caribbean and Latin America) MARY LIVINGSTON.

Claro: Rua Florida 1970, Bairro Cidade Monções, 40432-544 São Paulo, SP; internet www.claro.com.br; f. 2003 by mergers; owned by América Móvil, SA de CV (Mexico); mobile cellular provider; 67m. subscribers (2013); CEO CARLOS ZENTENO DE LOS SANTOS.

CTBC (Companhia de Telecomunicações do Brasil Central): Rua Machado de Assis 333, Centro, 38400-112 Uberlândia, MG; tel. (34) 3256-2033; fax (34) 3236-7723; e-mail tatianes@ctbc.com.br; internet www.ctbc.com.br; f. 1954; owned by Grupo Algar; mobile and fixed line provider in central Brazil; Pres. DIVINO SEBASTIÃO DE SOUZA.

Empresa Brasileira de Telecomunicações, SA (Embratel): Av. Presidente Vargas 1012, CP 2586, 20179-900 Rio de Janeiro, RJ; tel. (21) 2519-8182; e-mail cmsocial@embratel.net.br; internet www .embratel.com.br; f. 1965; operates national and international telecommunications system; owned by Telmex (Teléfonos de Mexico, SA); Pres. JOSÉ FORMOSO MARTÍNEZ.

GVT (Global Village Telecom): Av. Dario Lopes dos Santos 2197, 8° andar, Centro Cívico, CEP 80210-010, Curitiba, PR; tel. (41) 3025-9900; fax (41) 3025-9922; e-mail comunicacacocorporativo@gvt.com .br; internet www.gvt.com.br; f. 2000; owned by Vivendi (France); broadband internet, fixed telephone and pay TV services.

Nextel Telecomunicações Ltda: Av. das Nações Unidas 14171, Morumbi, 04795-100 São Paulo, SP; tel. (11) 4004-6611; e-mail assessoria.imprensa@nextel.com.br; internet www.nextel.com.br; f. 1997; part of NII Holdings, Inc. (USA); digital radio, mobile cellular and wireless services provider; Pres. SERGIO CHAIA.

Oi (Tele Norte Leste Participações, SA): Rua Lauro Müller 116, 22° andar, Botafogo, Rio de Janeiro, RJ; tel. (21) 2815-2921; fax (21) 2571-3050; internet www.novaoi.com.br; f. 1998 as Telemar; 22% owned by Portugal Telecom, full merger planned in early 2014; fixed line and mobile operator; 50m. subscribers (2013); CEO ZEINAL BAVA.

Sercomtel Celular, SA: Rua João Cândido 555, 86010-000 Londrina, PR; e-mail casc@sercomtel.com.br; internet www .sercomtelcelular.com.br; f. 1998; mobile cellular network provider; Pres. OSWALDO PITOL.

Telefônica SP: Rua Martiniano de Carvalho 851, Bela Vista, 01321-000 São Paulo, SP; tel. (11) 3549-7200; fax (11) 3549-7202; e-mail telefonicabr@telefonica.com.br; internet www.telefonica.com.br; fmrly Telecomunicações de São Paulo (Telesp), privatized in 1998; subsidiary of Telefónica, SA (Spain); 41m. customers; Pres. ANTONIO CARLOS VALENTE DA SILVA.

> **Telemig Celular:** internet www.telemigcelular.com.br; mobile cellular provider in Minas Gerais; 2.6m. customers.

> **Vivo:** Av. Chucri Zaidan 2460, 5°, 04583-110 São Paulo, SP; tel. (11) 5105-1001; internet www.vivo.com.br; owned by Telefónica Móviles, SA of Spain; Telefónica bought Portugal Telecom's share in 2010; 77m. customers (2013); CEO PAULO CESAR TEIXEIRA.

TIM (Telecom Italia Mobile): Av. das Américas 3434, 5° andar, Barra da Tijuca, 22640-102 Rio de Janeiro, RJ; internet www.tim.com.br; f. 1998 in Brazil; subsidiary of Telecom Italia (Italy); mobile cellular provider; 73m. customers (2013); Pres. MANOEL HORÁCIO FRANCISCO DA SILVA; Dir ANDREA MANGONI.

Regulatory Authority

Agência Nacional de Telecomunicações (ANATEL): SAUS Quadra 06, Blocos C, E, F e H, 70070-940 Brasília, DF; tel. (61) 2312-2000; fax (61) 2312-2264; e-mail biblioteca@anatel.gov.br; internet www.anatel.gov.br; f. 1998; regional office in each state; Pres. JOÃO BATISTA DE REZENDE; Exec. Supt MARILDA MOREIRA.

BROADCASTING

Empresa Brasil de Comunicação (EBC): Edif. Venâncio 2000, 1° andar Inferior, SCS, Quadra 08, Bloco B–60, Asa Sul, 70333-900 Brasília, DF; tel. (61) 3799-5700; e-mail comunicacao@ebc.com.br; internet www.ebc.com.br; f. 1975, as Empresa Brasileira de Radiodifusão (RADIOBRÁS); re-established as above in 2007; state-run radio and television network; manages public broadcasters; Pres. NELSON BREVE; Dir-Gen. EDUARDO CASTRO.

Radio

The main broadcasting stations in Rio de Janeiro are: Rádio Nacional, Rádio Globo, Rádio Eldorado, Rádio Jornal do Brasil, Rádio Tupi and Rádio Mundial. In São Paulo the main stations are Rádio Bandeirantes, Rádio Mulher, Rádio Eldorado, Rádio Gazeta and Rádio Excelsior; and in Brasília: Rádio Nacional, Rádio Alvorada, Rádio Planalto and Rádio Capital.

The state-run corporation Empresa Brasil de Comunicação (q.v.) owns the following radio stations:

Rádio MEC AM/FM do Rio de Janeiro: Praça da República 141-A, Centro, 20211-350 Rio de Janeiro, RJ; tel. (21) 2117-7853; e-mail ouvinte@radiomec.com.br; internet radiomec.com.br; f. 2004; Supt ORLANDO GUILHON.

Rádio Nacional AM de Brasília: CP 259, 70710-750 Brasília, DF; tel. (61) 3799-5167; fax (61) 3799-5169; e-mail centraldoouvinte@ebc .com.br; f. 1958; Man. CRISTINA GUIMARÃES.

Rádio Nacional da Amazônia-OC: CP 258, 70359-970 Brasília, DF; f. 1977; Regional Man. SOFÍA HAMMOE; Co-ordinator LUCIANA COUTO.

Rádio Nacional FM de Brasília: CP 070747, 70720-502 Brasília, DF; e-mail ouvinte@radiomec.com.br; f. 1976; broadcasts to the Federal District and surrounding areas; Man. CARLOS SENNA.

Television

The main television networks are:

RBS TV: Rua do Acampamento 2550, Passo do Príncipe, 96425-250 Bagé, RS; tel. (53) 3240-5300; fax (53) 3240-5305; internet www.rbs .com.br; f. 1957; major regional network; operates Canal Rural and TVCOM; Group Pres. NELSON PACHECO SIROTSKY; Exec. Dir EDUARDO SIROTSKY MELZER.

TV Bandeirantes: Rádio e Televisão Bandeirantes Ltda, Rua Radiantes 13, Morumbi, 05699-900 São Paulo, SP; tel. (11) 3742-3011; fax (11) 3745-7622; e-mail cat@band.com.br; internet www .band.com.br; 65 TV stations and repeaters throughout Brazil; Pres. JOÃO CARLOS SAAD.

TV Brasil Internacional (TVBI): CP 8640, 70312-970 Brasília, DF; tel. (61) 3799-5889; fax (61) 3799-5888; e-mail tvbrasilinternacional@ebc.com.br; internet www.tvbrasil.ebc.com .br/internacional; f. 2010; owned by Empresa Brasil de Comunicação (EBC); broadcasts internationally via satellite in Portuguese; Programme Dir RICARDO SOARES; Programme Man. MAX GONÇALVES.

TV Nacional/TV Brasil (Canal 2): Rua da Relação 18, Lapa, 20231-110 Rio de Janeiro, RJ; tel. (21) 2117-6208; e-mail sap@tvbrasil.org .br; internet www.tvbrasil.org.br; public tv station; broadcasts to the Federal District and surrounding areas; operated by Empresa Brasil de Comunicação (EBC); Dir-Gen. NELSON BREVE.

TV Record—Rádio e Televisão Record, SA: Rua de Bosque 1393, Barra Funda, 01136-001 São Paulo, SP; tel. (11) 3660-4761; fax (11) 3660-4756; e-mail tvrecord@rederecord.com.br; internet rederecord .r7.com; f. 1953; Dir ALEXANDRE RAPOSO.

TV Rede Globo: Rua Lopes Quintas 303, Jardim Botânico, 22460-010 Rio de Janeiro, RJ; tel. (21) 2444-4725; fax (21) 2294-2092; e-mail cgcom-br@tvglobo.com.br; internet redeglobo.globo.com; f. 1965; 8 stations; national network; Exec. Pres. ROBERTO IRINEU MARINHO.

TV SBT—Sistema Brasileira de Televisão—Canal 4 de São Paulo, SA: Av. das Comunicações 4, Vila Jaraguá, Osasco, 06278-905 São Paulo, SP; tel. (11) 7087-3000; fax (11) 7087-3509; internet www.sbt.com.br; 107 local TV channels; Dir-Gen. DANIEL SLAVIERO.

Broadcasting Associations

Associação Brasileira de Emissoras de Rádio e Televisão (ABERT): Edif.Via Esplanada, SAF/SUL Quadra 02, Lote 04, Bloco D, Sala 101, 70770-600 Brasília, DF; tel. (61) 2104-4600; fax (61) 2104-4611; e-mail abert@abert.org.br; internet www.abert.org.br; f. 1962; Pres. DANIEL PIMENTEL SLAVIERO; Exec. Dir VICENTE JORGE RODRIGUES.

There are regional associations for Bahia, Ceará, Goiás, Minas Gerais, Rio Grande do Sul, Santa Catarina, São Paulo, Amazonas, Distrito Federal, Mato Grosso and Mato Grosso do Sul (combined), and Sergipe.

Finance

(cap. = capital; res = reserves; dep. = deposits; m. = million; br(s) = branch(es); amounts in reais, unless otherwise stated)

BANKING

Conselho Monetário Nacional (CMN): Setor Bancário Sul, Quadra 03, Bloco B, Edif. Sede do Banco do Brasil, 21° andar, 70074-900 Brasília, DF; tel. (61) 3414-1945; fax (61) 3414-2528; e-mail cmn@bcb.gov.br; internet www.bcb.gov.br/?CMN; f. 1964 to formulate monetary policy and to supervise the banking system; Pres. GUIDO MANTEGA (Minister of Finance).

Central Bank

Banco Central do Brasil: SBS, Quadra 03, Mezanino 01, Bloco B, 70074-900 Brasília, DF; tel. (61) 3414-1414; fax (61) 3414-2553; e-mail cap.secresecre.surel@bcb.gov.br; internet www.bcb.gov.br; f. 1965; est. to execute the decisions of the Conselho Monetário Nacional; bank of issue; total assets 1,157,596.2m. (Dec. 2009); Gov. ALEXANDRE ANTONIO TOMBINI; 10 brs.

State Commercial Banks

Banco da Amazônia, SA: Av. Presidente Vargas 800, 3° andar, 66017-000 Belém, PA; tel. (91) 4008-3287; fax (91) 4008-3663; e-mail cambio@bancoamazonia.com.br; internet www.bancoamazonia

.com.br; f. 1942; state-owned; cap. 1,219.7m., res –494.5m., dep. 3,243.9m. (Dec. 2013); Pres. VALMIR PEDRO ROSSI; 123 brs.

Banco do Brasil, SA: SBS, Quadra 01, Bloco C, Lote 32, Edif. Sede III, 70073-901 Brasília, DF; tel. (61) 3310-4500; fax (61) 3310-2444; e-mail ri@bb.com.br; internet www.bb.com.br; f. 1808; cap. 54,000m., res 21,043.2m., dep. 487,386.8m. (Dec. 2013); CEO ALDEMIR BENDINE.

Banco do Estado do Pará: Edif. Banpará, 4° andar, Av. Presidente Vargas 251, Campina, 66010-000 Belém, PA; tel. (91) 3348-3295; fax (91) 3224-4707; internet www.banparanet.com.br; f. 1961; cap. 400.4m., res 105.6m., dep. 3,662.3m. (Dec. 2013); Pres. AUGUSTO SÉRGIO AMORIM COSTA; 24 brs.

Banco do Estado do Rio Grande do Sul, SA (Banrisul): Rua Capitão Montanha 177, Centro, 90010-040 Porto Alegre, RS; tel. (51) 3215-2501; fax (51) 3215-1715; e-mail cambio_dg@banrisul.com.br; internet www.banrisul.com.br; f. 1928; cap. 3,750m., res –181.2.5m., dep. 35,105.2m. (Dec. 2013); Pres. TÚLIO LUIZ ZAMIN; 473 brs.

Banco do Nordeste do Brasil, SA: Av. Pedro Ramalho 5700, Passaré, CP 628, 60743-902 Fortaleza, CE; tel. (85) 3299-3000; fax (85) 3299-3674; e-mail ri@bnb.gov.br; internet www.bnb.gov.br; f. 1952; cap. 2,437m., res 602.8m., dep. 16,147.6m. (Dec. 2013); Pres. ARY JOEL DE ABREU LANZARIN; 187 brs.

BANESTES, SA—Banco do Estado do Espírito Santo: Edif. Palas Center, Bloco B, 9° andar, Av. Princesa Isabel 574, Centro, 29010-931 Espírito Santo, ES; tel. (27) 3383-1465; fax (27) 9831-6034; e-mail ri@banestes.com.br; internet www.banestes.com.br; f. 1937; cap. 725.7m., res 238.2m., dep. 7,800.5m. (Dec. 2013); CEO GUILHERME GOMES DIAS.

Private Banks

Banco ABC Brasil, SA: Av. Juscelino Kubitschek 1400, 4° andar, Itaim Bibi, 04543-000 São Paulo, SP; tel. (11) 3170-2000; fax (11) 3170-2001; e-mail abcbrasil@abcbrasil.com.br; internet www .abcbrasil.com.br; f. 1983 as Banco Roma de Investimentos; 59% owned by Arab Banking Corpn BSC (Bahrain); cap. 1,041.9m., res 410.9m., dep. 4,897.1m. (Dec. 2012); Pres. and Gen. Man. ANIS CHACUR NETO; 4 brs.

Banco Alfa de Investimento, SA: Alameda Santos 466, Cerqueira César, 01418-000 Paraíso, SP; tel. (11) 4004-3344; fax (11) 3171-2438; e-mail alfanet@alfanet.com.br; internet www.alfanet.com.br; f. 1998; cap. 500m., res 650m., dep. 5,790.5m. (Dec. 2012); Chair. PAULO GUILHERME MONTEIRO LOBATO RIBEIRO; Pres. FABIO ALBERTO AMOROSINO; 12 brs.

Banco BBM, SA: Rua Miguel Calmon 398, 2° andar, Parte Comércio, 40015-010 Salvador, BA; tel. (71) 3326-4721; fax (71) 3254-2703; e-mail bancobbm@bancobbm.com.br; internet www.bancobbm.com .br; f. 1858; est. as Banco de Bahia; present name adopted 1998; cap. 413.1m., res 149.4m., dep. 679.1m. (Dec. 2013); Pres. PEDRO HENRIQUE MARIANI BITTENCOURT; 3 brs.

Banco BMG, SA: Av. Alvares Cabral 1707, Santo Agostinho, 30170-001 Belo Horizonte, MG; tel. (31) 3290-3700; fax (31) 3290-3168; e-mail ri@bancobmg.com.br; internet www.bancobmg.com.br; f. 1930; cap. 2,805.1m., res 593.5m., dep. 7,991.4m. (Dec. 2013); Pres. RICARDO ANNES GUIMARÃES; 14 brs.

Banco Bradesco, SA: Cidade de Deus, Vila Yara, 06029-900 Osasco, SP; tel. (11) 3684-2126; fax (11) 3684-4630; internet www .bradesco.com.br; f. 1943; est. as Banco Brasileiro de Descontos; present name adopted 1989; cap. 30,100m., res 40,495.2m., dep. 387,411.4m. (Dec. 2012); Chair. LÁZARO DE MELLO BRANDÃO; Pres. and CEO LUIZ CARLOS TRABUCO CAPPI; 3,358 brs.

Banco BTG Pactual, SA: Torre Corcovado, 6°, Praia de Botafago 501, 22250-040 Rio de Janeiro, RJ; tel. (21) 3262-9600; fax (21) 2514-8600; internet www.btgpactual.com; f. 1983; fmrly Banco UBS Pactual; present name adopted 2008 following acquisition by BTG Pactual; cap. 6,355.3m., res 3,649.4m., dep. 37,552.8m. (Dec. 2013); Pres. ANDRÉ ESTEVES; 5 brs.

Banco Fibra: Av. Presidente Juscelino Kubitschek 360, 4°–9° andares, 04543-000 São Paulo, SP; tel. (11) 3847-6700; fax (11) 3847-6962; e-mail ri@bancofibra.com.br; internet www.bancofibra .com.br; f. 1989; cap. 1,564.8m., res 314.5m., dep. 5,847.6m. (Dec. 2013); CEO FELIX CARDAMONE.

Banco Industrial do Brasil: Av. Juscelino Kubitschek 1703, 1°–4° andares, Itaim Bibi, 04543-000 São Paulo, SP; tel. (11) 3049-9700; fax (11) 3049-9810; internet www.bancoindustrial.com.br; f. 1994; cap. 367.2m., res 77.4m., dep. 1,266.1m. (Dec. 2013); Pres. CARLOS ALBERTO MANSUR.

Banco Industrial e Comercial, SA (Bicbanco): Av. Brigadeiro Faria Lima 4440, 5° andar, 04538-132 São Paulo, SP; tel. (11) 2173-9000; fax (11) 2173-9101; internet www.bicbanco.com.br; f. 1938; 72% bought by China Construction Bank in Oct. 2013; cap. 1,434.2m., res 474.9m., dep. 7,940.6m. (Dec. 2013); Pres. JOSÉ BEZERRA DE MENEZES; 37 brs.

Banco Indusval & Partners, SA (Banco Indusval Multistock): Rua Iguatemi 151, 6° andar, Centro, 01451-011 São Paulo, SP; tel. (11) 3315-6777; fax (11) 3315-0130; e-mail banco@indusval.com.br; internet www.bip.b.br; f. 1980; fmrly Banco Indusval; adopted present name in 2011; cap. 572.4m., res 18.3m., dep. 2,516.5m. (Dec. 2012); Chair. MANOEL FELIX CINTRA NETO; Pres. JAIR RIBEIRO DA SILVA NETO.

Banco Itaú BBA, SA: Av. Brig. Faria Lima 3400, 3° ao 8° andar, 04538-132 São Paulo, SP; tel. (11) 3708-8000; fax (11) 3708-8172; e-mail bancoitaubba@itaubba.com.br; internet www.itaubba.com .br; f. as Banco do Estado de Minas Gerais, SA in 1945; acquired by Banco Itaú in 2002, present name adopted 2004; part of Itaú Unibanco Holdings, SA from 2008; cap. 4,224.1m., res 2,059.1m., dep. 181,311.3m. (Dec. 2012); Pres. and CEO CANDIDO BOTELHO BRACHER; 11 brs.

Banco Mercantil do Brasil, SA: Rua Rio de Janeiro 654, Centro, 30160-912 Belo Horizonte, MG; tel. (31) 3057-6314; fax (31) 3057-6475; e-mail sac@mercantil.com.br; internet www.mercantil.com.br; f. 1943; est. as Banco Mercantil de Minas Gerais, SA; cap. 399.5m., res 426.1m., dep. 7,972.2m. (Dec. 2012); Pres. MILTON DE ARAÚJO; 171 brs.

Banco Paulista, SA: Av. Brigadeiro Faria Lima, 1355 Jardim Paulistano, 2° andar, 01452-002 São Paulo, SP; tel. (11) 3299-2000; fax (11) 3299-2363; e-mail cambiobp@bancopaulista.com.br; internet www.bancopaulista.com.br; f. 1989; cap. 127m., res 2.4m., dep. 568.2m. (Dec. 2013); CEO ALVARO AUGUSTO VIDIGAL.

Banco Pine, SA: Eldorado Business Tower, Av. das Nações Unidas 8501, 30° andar, 05425-070 São Paulo, SP; tel. (11) 3372-5200; fax (11) 3372-5404; e-mail bancopine@uol.com.br; internet www .bancopine.com.br; f. 1997; cap. 1,112.2m., res 165.7m., dep. 5,004.4m. (Dec. 2013); Chair. NORBERTO NOGUEIRA PINHEIRO.

Banco Safra, SA: Av. Paulista 2100, 9° andar, Cerqueira Cesar, 01310-930 São Paulo, SP; tel. (11) 3175-7575; fax (11) 3175-8466; internet www.safra.com.br; f. 1940; cap. 4,362.4m., res 4,530.1m., dep. 10,624.4m. (Dec. 2013); Pres. ROSSANO MARANHÃO PINTO; 104 brs.

Banco Santander Brasil, SA: Av. Presidente Juscelino Kubitschek 2041, E 2235, Bloco A, Vila Olimpia, 04543-011 São Paulo, SP; tel. (11) 3553-5533; fax (11) 3553-5534; internet www .santander.com.br; f. 2006; est. as Banco Santander Banespa, SA by merger; present name adopted 2007; owned by Banco Santander, SA (Spain); cap. 62,634.5m., res 13,008.1m., dep. 189,508.2m. (Dec. 2013); Chair. CELSO CLEMENTE GIACOMETTI; 2,636 brs.

Banco Société Générale Brasil, SA: Av. Paulista 2300, 9° andar, Cerqueira Cesar, 01310-300 São Paulo, SP; tel. (11) 3217-8000; fax (11) 3217-8110; e-mail faleconosco@sgcib.com; internet www .sgbrasil.com.br; f. 1981; est. as Banco Sogeral; present name adopted 2001; cap. 2,374.9m., res 10.1m., dep. 711.9m. (Dec. 2013); Pres. FRANCIS HENRI MAX REPKA.

Banco Votorantim, SA: Av. das Nações Unidas 14171, Torre A, 18° andar, Vila Gertrudes, 04794-000 São Paulo, SP; tel. (11) 5185-1700; fax (11) 5185-1900; e-mail webmaster@bancovotorantim.com.br; internet www.bancovotorantim.com.br; f. 1991; cap. 7,125.7m., res –9.6m., dep. 8,252.9m. (Dec. 2013); Pres. ALDEMIR BENDINE.

Banif—Banco Internacional do Funchal (Brasil), SA: Rua Minas de Prata 30, 16°–17° andares, Vila Olímpia, 04552-080 São Paulo, SP; tel. (11) 3165-2124; fax (11) 3167-3960; e-mail bc_matriz@ bancobanif.com.br; internet www.bancobanif.com.br; f. 1999 as Banco Banif Primus, SA; present name adopted 2005; owned by Banif Comercial SGPS, SA (Portugal); cap. 707.8m., res 15.3m., dep. 679.8m. (Dec. 2013); Chair. GLADSTONE MEDEIROS DE SIQUEIRA; 13 brs.

Itaú Unibanco Holding, SA: Praça Alfredo Egydio de Souza Aranha 100, Torre Olavo Setubal, Parque Jabaquara, 04344-902 São Paulo, SP; tel. (11) 50190-9980; fax (11) 5019-9986; e-mail investor.relations@itau-unibanco.com.br; internet www .itau-unibanco.com.br; f. 1924 as Unibanco; Banco Itaú est. in 1944 as Banco Central de Crédito; renamed Banco Itaú, SA in 1973; Unibanco and Itaú merged in 2008 and named changed as above; cap. 39,676.3m., res 450.2m., dep. 404,881.3m. (Dec. 2011); Pres. and CEO ROBERTO SETUBAL; Chair. PEDRO MOREIRA SALLES; 3,893 brs.

Development Banks

Banco de Desenvolvimento de Minas Gerais, SA (BDMG): Rua da Bahia 1600, Lourdes, 30160-907 Belo Horizonte, MG; tel. (31) 3219-8000; fax (31) 3226-3292; internet www.bdmg.mg.gov.br; f. 1962; owned by the state of Minas Gerais; long-term credit operations; cap. 1,659.7m., res 53.8m., dep. 51.9m. (Dec. 2013); Pres. PAULO DE TARSO ALMEIDA PAIVA.

Banco Nacional do Desenvolvimento Econômico e Social (BNDES): Av. República do Chile 100, Centro, 20031-917 Rio de Janeiro, RJ; tel. (21) 2172-7447; fax (21) 2533-1538; e-mail gerai@ bndes.gov.br; internet www.bndes.gov.br; f. 1952 to act as main instrument for financing of govt devt schemes and to support programmes for the devt of the national economy; socioenvironmental devt and the modernization of public administration; cap. 36,340.5m., res 26,974.5m., dep. 22,540.5m. (Dec. 2013); Pres. LUCIANO COUTINHO.

Investment Banks

BES Investimento do Brasil, SA- Banco de Investimento: Av. Brigadeiro Faria Lima 3729, 6° andar, 04538-905 São Paulo, SP; tel. (11) 3074–7444; fax (11) 3074-7469; e-mail besinvestimento@ besinvestimento.com.br; internet www.besinvestimento.com.br; f. 2000; part of Banco Espírito Santo de Investimento, SA (Portugal); cap. 420m., res 245.7m., dep. 2,964.1m. (Dec. 2013); CEO RICARDO ESPÍRITO SANTO.

BRKB Distribuidora de Títulos e Valores Mobiliários, SA: Av. Almirante Barroso 52, 30° andar, Centro, 20031-000 Rio de Janeiro, RJ; tel. (21) 3231-3000; fax (21) 3231-3231; internet www.brkbdtvm .com.br; f. 1989; frmly known as Banco Brascan, SA; cap. 155.6m., res 6.4m., dep. 224.1m. (Dec. 2011); Pres. VALDECYR MACIEL GOMES.

State-owned Savings Bank

Caixa Econômica Federal: SBS, Quadra 04, Lotes 3–4, 16° andar, 70092-900 Brasília, DF; tel. (61) 3206-9840; fax (61) 3206-0267; e-mail genit04@caixa.gov.br; internet www.caixa.gov.br; f. 1861; cap. 22,054.8m., res 2,580.5m., dep. 333,165.5m. (Dec. 2012); Pres. JORGE FONTES HEREDA; 4,000 brs.

Foreign Banks

Banco Sumitomo Mitsui Brasileiro, SA: Av. Paulista 37, 11° andar, Conj. 12, Bela Vista, 01311-902 São Paulo, SP; tel. (11) 3178-8000; fax (11) 3178-8189; internet www.smbcgroup.com.br; f. 1958; present name adopted 2001; cap. 667.8m., res 10.6m., dep. 1,310.1m. (Dec. 2013); Pres. TAKAAKI OTANI; 1 br.

Banco de Tokyo-Mitsubishi UFJ Brasil, SA: Av. Paulista 1274, Bela Vista, 01310-925 São Paulo, SP; tel. (11) 3268-0211; fax (11) 3268-0263; internet www.br.bk.mufg.jp; f. 1919 as Yokohama Specie Bank of Japan; cap. 853m., res 256.7m., dep. 2,039.7m. (Dec. 2013); Pres. TOSHIFUMI MURATA; 1 br.

Deutsche Bank, SA—Banco Alemão: Av. Brigadeiro Faria Lima 3900, 13–15° andares, Itaim Bibi, 04598-132 São Paulo, SP; tel. (11) 2113-5000; fax (11) 2113-5100; internet www.db.com/brasil; f. 1911; cap. 996.5m., res 33m., dep. 2,472.7m. (Dec. 2013); Pres. BERNARDO PARNES; 2 brs.

HSBC Bank Brasil, SA—Banco Multiplo: Edif. Palácio Avenida, 4° andar, Travessa Oliveira Belo 34, Centro, 80020-030 Curitiba, PR; tel. (41) 3321-6161; fax (41) 3646-3581; internet www.hsbc.com.br; f. 1997; cap. 5,993.9m., res 232.3m., dep. 868,906.9m. (Dec. 2012); Pres. and CEO ANDRE BRANDÃO; 866 brs.

Scotiabank Brasil, SA Banco Múltiplo (Canada): Av. Brig. Faria Lima 2277, 7° andar, 01452-000 São Paulo, SP; tel. (11) 2202-8100; fax (11) 2202-8200; e-mail scotiabank.saopaulo@br.scotiabank.com; internet www.br.scotiabank.com; f. 2008 in Brazil took over Dresdner Bank Brasil in 2011; Chair. WINSTON FRITSCH.

Banking Associations

Associação Brasileira das Entidades dos Mercados Financeiro e de Capitais (ANBIMA): Edif. Eldorado Business Tower, Av. das Nações Unidas 8501, 21° andar, Conj. A, Pinheiros, 05425-070 São Paulo, SP; tel. (11) 3471-4200; fax (11) 3471-4230; e-mail anbid@anbid.com.br; internet www.anbima.com.br; fmrly Associação Nacional dos Bancos de Investimentos; changed name as above in 2009 following re-integration; investment banks; Pres. DENISE PAULI PAVARINA; Supt JOSÉ CARLOS DOHERTY.

Federação Brasileira dos Bancos: Av. Brigadeiro Faria Lima 1485, 14° andar, Torre Norte, Pinheiros, 01452-921 São Paulo, SP; tel. (11) 3244-9800; fax (11) 3031-4106; e-mail imprensa@febraban .org.br; internet www.febraban.org.br; f. 1967; Pres. FABIO COLLETTI BARBOSA; 120 mems.

Federação dos Empregados em Estabelecimentos Bancários de São Paulo e Mato Grosso do Sul (Feeb-SP/MS): Rua Boa Vista 76, 10° andar, Centro, 01014-000 São Paulo, SP; tel. (11) 3116-7070; fax (11) 3104-2422; internet www.feeb-spms.org.br; f. 1956; Pres. DAVID ZAIA.

Sindicato dos Bancos dos Estados do Rio de Janeiro e Espírito Santo: Rua do Ouvidor 50, 12° andar, 20040-004 Rio de Janeiro, RJ; tel. (21) 2253-1538; fax (21) 2253-6032; e-mail aberj@ aberj.com.br; internet www.aberj.com.br; f. 1935; Pres. CARLOS ALBERTO VIEIRA.

There are other banking associations in Maceió, Salvador, Fortaleza, Belo Horizonte, João Pessoa, Recife and Porto Alegre.

STOCK EXCHANGES

Comissão de Valores Mobiliários (CVM): Rua 7 de Setembro 111, Centro, 20050-901 Rio de Janeiro, RJ; tel. (21) 3554-8531; fax (21) 3554-8211; e-mail ouvidor@cvm.gov.br; internet www.cvm.gov.br; f. 1977 to supervise the operations of the stock exchanges and develop the Brazilian securities market; regional offices in Brasília and São Paulo; Chair. LEONARDO GOMES PEREIRA.

BM&F BOVESPA, SA (Bolsa de Valores, Mercadorias e Futuros): Praça Antônio Prado 48 Centro, 01010-901 São Paulo, SP; tel. (11) 2565-4000; fax (11) 2565-5314; e-mail ri@bmfbovespa.com.br; internet www.bmfbovespa.com.br; f. 2008 by merger of Bolsa de Mercadorias e Futuros (BM&F—Mercantile and Futures Exchange) and Bolsa de Valores de São Paulo (BOVESPA—São Paulo Stock Exchange); offices in São Paulo, Rio de Janeiro, New York (USA), Shanghai (People's Republic of China) and London (UK); Pres. PEDRO PARENTE; CEO EDEMIR PINTO.

There are commodity exchanges at Paraná, Porto Alegre, Vitória, Recife, Santos and São Paulo.

INSURANCE

Supervisory Authorities

Conselho de Recursos do Sistema Nacional de Seguros Privados, de Previdência Aberta e de Capitalização (CRSNSP): Av. Presidente Vargas 730, 20071-900 Rio de Janeiro, RJ; tel. (21) 3233-4115; internet www.fazenda.gov.br/portugues/orgaos/crsnsp/ crsnsp.html; f. 1966 as Conselho Nacional de Seguros Privados (CNSP); changed name in 1998; part of the Ministry of Finance; Pres. ANA MARIA MELO NETTO; Sec. THERESA CHRISTINA CUNHA MARTINS.

Superintendência de Seguros Privados (SUSEP): Av. Presidente Vargas, 730 Centro, 20071-900 Rio de Janeiro, RJ; tel. (21) 3233-4000; e-mail gabinete.rj@susep.gov.br; internet www.susep .gov.br; f. 1966; part of the Ministry of Finance; offices in Brasília, São Paulo and Porto Alegre; Supt ROBERT WESTENBERGER.

Principal Companies

The following is a list of the principal national insurance companies, selected on the basis of assets.

Bradesco Seguros e Previdência, SA: Av. Paulista 1415, Bela Vista, São Paulo, 01310-100; tel. (21) 2503-1101; fax (21) 2293-9489; internet www.bradescoseguros.com.br; f. 1934; general; Pres. MARCO ANTONIO ROSSI.

Bradesco Vida e Previdência, SA: Cidade de Deus s/n, Vila Yara, São Paulo, SP; tel. (11) 3684-2122; fax (11) 3684-5068; internet www .bradescoprevidencia.com.br; f. 2001; life insurance; Pres. LÚCIO FLÁVIO DE OLIVEIRA.

Brasilprev Seguros e Prevedência, SA: Rua Alexandre Dumas 1671, 04717-004 São Paulo, SP; tel. (11) 5185-4240; e-mail atendimento@brasilprev.com.br; internet www.brasilprev.com.br; f. 1993; all classes; 50% owned by Banco do Brasil; Dir ALEXANDRE CORRÊA ABREU.

Caixa Seguros: Edif. No 1, 15° andar, SCN Quadra 01, Bloco A, Asa Norte, 70711-900 Brasília, DF; tel. (61) 2192-2400; fax (61) 3328-0600; internet www.caixaseguros.com.br; f. 1967; fmrly Sasse, Cia Nacional de Seguros; adopted current name 2000; general; Pres. THIERRY MARC CLAUDE CLAUDON.

Caixa Vida e Previdência, SA: Edif. No 1, 13° andar, SCN Quadra 1, Bloco A, 70711-900 Brasília, DF; tel. (61) 2192-2400; fax (61) 3328-0600; internet www.caixavidaeprevidencia.com.br; part of Caixa Seguros group; Dir JUVÊNCIO CAVALCANTE BRAGA.

Cia de Seguros Aliança do Brasil, SA (BB Seguros): Rua Manuel da Nóbrega 1280, 9° andar, 04001-004 São Paulo, SP; tel. (11) 3885-0807; e-mail imprensa@aliancadobrasil.com.br; internet www .bbseguros.com.br; f. 1996; CEO ROBERTO BARROSO; Pres. ALLAN SIMOES TOLEDO.

Crédito y Caución Seguradora de Crédito à Exportação, SA: Av. Angélica 2530, 10° andar, Consolaçao, 01228-200 São Paulo, SP; tel. (11) 3100-1100; fax (11) 3100-1109; e-mail saopaulo@ creditoycaucion.com.br; internet www.creditoycaucion.com.br; f. 1997 (in Brazil); Dir-Gen. DANIEL NOBRE.

HSBC Vida e Previdência (Brasil), SA: Rua Teniente Francisco Ferreira de Souza 805, Bloco 1, Ala 4, Vila Hauer, 81630-010 Curitaba, PR; tel. (41) 4004-4722; fax (41) 3523-2320; e-mail spariz@hsbc.com.vr; internet www.hsbc.com.br; f. 1938; all classes; Man. Dir FERNANDO ALVES MOREIRA.

Icatu Hartford Seguros, SA: Praça 22 de Abril 36, 20021-370 Rio de Janeiro, RJ; tel. (21) 3824-3900; fax 3824-6678; e-mail atendimento_internet@icatuseguros.com.br; internet www .icatuseguros.com.br; f. 1991; Pres. LUCIANO SNEL.

IRB-Brasil Resseguros: Av. Marechal Câmara 171, Castelo, 20020-901 Rio de Janeiro, RJ; tel. (21) 2272-0200; fax (21) 2272-2800; e-mail info@irb-brasilre.com.br; internet www.irb-brasilre .com.br; f. 1939; state-owned reinsurance co; fmrly Instituto de Resseguros do Brasil; CEO LEONARDO ANDRÉ PAIXÃO; Exec. Pres. MARIO DI CROCE.

Itaú Seguros, SA: Praça Alfredo Egydio de Souza Aranha 100, Bloco A, 04344-920 São Paulo, SP; tel. (11) 5019-3322; fax (11) 5019-3530; e-mail itauseguros@itauseguros.com.br; internet www.itauseguros .com.br; f. 1921; all classes; Pres. ROBERTO EGYDIO SETUBAL.

Liberty Seguros, SA: Rua Dr Geraldo Campos Moreira 110, 04571-020 São Paulo, SP; tel. (11) 5503-4000; fax (11) 5505-2122; internet www.libertyseguros.com.br; f. 1906; general; Pres. LUIZ FRANCISCO CAMPOS.

Marítima Seguros, SA: Rua Col Xavier de Toledo 114 e 140, 10° andar, São Paulo, SP; tel. (11) 3156-1000; fax (11) 3156-1712; internet www.maritima.com.br; f. 1943; Pres. FRANCISCO CAIUBY VIDIGAL; Exec. Dir MARIO JORGE PEREIRA.

Porto Seguro Cia de Seguros Gerais: Av. Rio Branco 1489, Campos Elíseos, 01204-001 São Paulo, SP; tel. (11) 3366-2050; fax (11) 3366-5175; internet www.portoseguro.com.br; f. 1945; life, automotive and risk; Chair. JAYME BRASIL GARFINKEL.

Sul América Cia Nacional de Seguros, SA: Rua da Beatriz Larragoiti Lucas 121, Cidade Nova, 20211-903 Rio de Janeiro, RJ; tel. (21) 2506-8585; fax (21) 2506-8807; internet www.sulamerica .com.br; f. 1895; life and risk; Chair. PATRICK ANTONIO DE LARRAGOITI LUCAS; CEO GABRIEL FAGUNDES FILHO.

Tokio Marine Seguradora, SA: Rua Samapiao Viana 44, 04004-902 Paraíso, SP; tel. (11) 2138-8904; fax (11) 3265-7505; e-mail tokiomarine@planin.com; internet www.tokiomarine.com.br; f. 1969 as Real Seguros, SA; adopted current name 2008; owned by Tokio Marine Holdings (Japan); general; Pres. AKIRA HARASHIMA.

Insurance Associations

Confederação Nacional das Empresas de Seguros Gerais, Previdência Privada e Vida, Saúde Suplementar e Capitalização (CNseg): Rua Senador Dantas 74, 12° andar, Centro, 20031-205 Rio de Janeiro, RJ; tel. (21) 2510-7777; e-mail suporte@cnseg.org .br; internet www.cnseg.org.br; f. 1951 as Federação Nacional das Empresas de Seguros Privados e de Capitalização; reformulated as above 2008; 4 subordinate feds; Pres. JORGE HILÁRIO GOUVÊA VIEIRA.

> **Federação Nacional de Capitalização (FenaCap):** Rua Senador Dantas 74, 8° andar, Centro, 20031-205 Rio de Janeiro, RJ; tel. (21) 2510-7777; internet www.cnseg.org.br/fenacap; f. 2007; Pres. MARCO ANTONIO DA SILVA BARROS.

> **Federação Nacional de Previdência Privada e Vida (FenaPrevi):** Rua Senador Dantas 74, 11° andar, Centro, 20031-205 Rio de Janeiro, RJ; tel. (21) 2510-7777; internet www.cnseg.org.br/ fenaprevi; Pres. MARCO ANTONIO ROSSI.

> **Federação Nacional de Saúde Suplementar (FenaSaúde):** Rua Senador Dantas 74, 8° andar, Centro, 20031-205 Rio de Janeiro, RJ; tel. (21) 2510-7777; e-mail fenasaude@approach .com.br; internet www.cnseg.org.br/fensaude; Pres. MARCIO SERÔA DE ARAUJO CORIOLANO; Exec. Dir JOSÉ CECHIN.

> **Federação Nacional de Seguros Gerais (FenSeg):** Rua Senador Dantas 74, 8° andar, Centro, 20031-205 Rio de Janeiro, RJ; tel. (21) 2510-7777; internet www.cnseg.org.br/fenseg; f. 2007; Pres. PAULO MIGUEL MARRACCINI.

Federação Nacional dos Corretores de Seguros Privados e de Resseguros, de Capitalização, de Previdência Privada e das Empresas Corretoras de Seguros e de Resseguros (FENACOR): Rua Senador Dantas 74, 10° andar, 20031-205 Rio de Janeiro, RJ; tel. (21) 3077-4777; fax (21) 3077-4799; e-mail presidencia@ fenacor.com.br; internet www.fenacor.com.br; f. 1975; Pres. ROBERT BITTAR (acting).

Trade and Industry

GOVERNMENT AGENCIES

Agência Nacional de Petróleo, Gás Natural e Biocombustíveis (ANP): Av. Rio Branco 65, 12°–22° andar, 20090-004 Rio de Janeiro, RJ; tel. (21) 2112-8100; fax (21) 2112-8129; e-mail imprensa@anp.gov.br; internet www.anp.gov.br; f. 1998; regulatory body of the petroleum, natural gas and biofuels industries; Dir-Gen. MAGDA MARIA DE REGINA CHAMBRIARD.

Agência de Promoção de Exportações do Brasil (APEX Brasil): Edif. Apex-Brasil, SBN, Quadra 02, Lote 11, 70040-020 Brasília, DF; tel. (61) 3426-0202; fax (61) 3426-0263; e-mail apex@apexbrasil .com.br; internet www.apexbrasil.com.br; f. 2003; promotes Brazilian exports; CEO MAURICIO BORGES.

Câmara de Comércio Exterior (CAMEX): Ministério do Desenvolvimento, Indústria e Comércio Exterior, Esplanada dos Ministérios, Bloco J, Sala 700, 70053-900 Brasília, DF; tel. (61) 2027-7050; e-mail camex@mdic.gov.br; internet www.camex.gov.br; f. 2003; part of Ministry of Development, Industry and Foreign Trade; formulates and co-ordinates export policies; Exec. Sec. ANDRÉ ALVIM DE PAULA RIZZO.

Companhia de Pesquisa de Recursos Minerais (CPRM): Av. SGAN, Quadra 603, Conj. J, Parte A, 1° andar, 70830-030 Brasília, DF; tel. (61) 2192-8252; fax (61) 3224-1616; e-mail cprmsede@df .cprm.gov.br; internet www.cprm.gov.br; mining research, attached to the Ministry of Mines and Energy; 8 regional offices; Exec. Dir MANOEL BARRETTO DA ROCHA NETO.

Confederação Nacional da Agricultura e Pecuária do Brasil (CNA): SGAN, Quadra 601, Módulo K, 70830-903 Brasília, DF; tel. (61) 2109-1400; fax (61) 2109-1490; internet www.canaldoprodutor .com.br; represents and defends the interests of farmers; 27 agricultural fed. mems; Pres. KÁTIA ABREU.

Conselho Nacional de Desenvolvimento Científico e Tecnológico (CNPq): Edif. Santos Dumont, SHIS, Quadra 01, Conj. B, Blocos A, B, C e D, Lago Sul, 71605-001 Brasília, DF; tel. (61) 2108-9000; fax (61) 2108-9394; e-mail presidencia@cnpq.br; internet www .cnpq.br; f. 1951; scientific and technological development council; Pres. GLAUCIUS OLIVA.

Conselho Nacional de Desenvolvimento Rural Sustentável (CONDRAF): Edif. Sarkis, SBN, Quadra 01, Bloco D, 70057-900 Brasília, DF; tel. (61) 2020-0285; e-mail condraf@mda.gov.br; internet sistemas.mda.gov.br/condraf; f. 2000 to promote sustainable rural development; Exec. Sec. ROBERTO NASCIMENTO.

Empresa Brasileira de Pesquisa Agropecuária (EMBRAPA): Edif. Sede, Parque Estação Biológica (PqEB) s/n, Av. W3 Norte (final), CP 40315, 70770-901 Brasília, DF; tel. (61) 3448-4433; fax (61) 3448-4890; e-mail presid@sede.embrapa.br; internet www .embrapa.br; f. 1973; attached to the Ministry of Agriculture, Livestock and Food Supply; agricultural research; Pres. MAURÍCIO ANTÔNIO LOPES.

Instituto Brasileiro do Meio Ambiente e Recursos Naturais Renováveis (IBAMA): Edif. Sede IBAMA, SCEN Trecho 2, 70818-900 Brasília, DF; tel. (61) 3316-1001; fax (61) 3226-1025; e-mail presid.sede@ibama.gov.br; internet www.ibama.gov.br; f. 1989; authorizes environmentally sensitive devt projects; Pres. Dr VOLNEY ZANARDI.

Instituto Nacional de Colonização e Reforma Agraria (INCRA): Edif. Palácio do Desenvolvimento, SBN, Quadra 01, Bloco D, 70057-900 Brasília, DF; tel. (61) 3411-7474; fax (61) 3411-7404; e-mail publico@incra.gov.br; internet www.incra.gov.br; f. 1970; land reform agency; Pres. CARLOS MÁRIO GUEDES DE GUEDES.

Instituto Nacional da Propriedade Industrial (INPI): Praça Mauá 7, 18° andar, Centro, 20081-240 Rio de Janeiro, RJ; tel. (21) 2139-3000; fax (21) 2263-2539; e-mail sic@inpi.gov.br; internet www .inpi.gov.br; f. 1970; part of Ministry of Development, Industry and Foreign Trade; intellectual property, etc.; Pres. OTÁVIO BRANDELLI.

Instituto de Pesquisa Econômica Aplicada (IPEA): Av. Presidente António Carlos 51, 15° andar, 20020-010 Rio de Janeiro, RJ; tel. (21) 3804-8000; fax (21) 2240-1920; e-mail faleconosco@ipea.gov .br; internet www.ipea.gov.br; f. 1970; economics and planning institute; Pres. SERGEI SUAREZ DILLON SOARES.

REGIONAL DEVELOPMENT ORGANIZATIONS

Companhia de Desenvolvimento dos Vales do São Francisco e do Parnaíba (CODEVASF): Edif. Manoel Novaes, SGAN, Quadra 601, Conj. 1, 70830-901 Brasília, DF; tel. (61) 3312-4611; fax (61) 3312-4680; e-mail tenio.pereira@codevasf.gov.br; internet www .codevasf.gov.br; f. 1974; promotes integrated development of resources of São Francisco and Parnaíba Valley; part of Ministry of National Integration; Pres. ELMO VAZ BASTOS DE MATOS.

Superintendência do Desenvolvimento da Amazônia (SUDAM): Av. Almirante Barroso 426, Marco, 66090-900 Belém, PA; tel. (91) 4008-5443; fax (91) 4008-5456; e-mail ouvidoria@sudam .gov.br; internet www.sudam.gov.br; f. 2001 to co-ordinate the devt of resources in Amazon region; Supt DJALMA BEZERRA MELLO.

Superintendência de Desenvolvimento do Nordeste (SUDENE): Praça Ministro João Gonçalves de Souza s/n, Engenho do Meio, 50670-900 Recife, PE; tel. (81) 2102-2114; fax (81) 2102-2575; e-mail gabinete@sudene.gov.br; internet www.sudene.gov.br; f. 2007 to replace Agência de Desenvolvimento do Nordeste (f. 2001); Supt LUIZ GONZAGA PAES LANDIM.

Superintendência da Zona Franca de Manaus (SUFRAMA): Av. Ministro João Gonçalves de Souza 1424, Distrito Industrial, 69075-830 Manaus, AM; tel. (92) 3321-7000; fax (92) 3237-6549; e-mail super@suframa.gov.br; internet www.suframa.gov.br; assists in the devt of the Manaus Free Zone; Supt THOMAZ AFONSO QUEIROZ NOGUEIRA.

AGRICULTURAL, INDUSTRIAL AND TRADE ORGANIZATIONS

Associação Brasileira do Alumínio (ABAL): Rua Humberto I 220, 4° andar, Vila Mariana, 04018-030 São Paulo, SP; tel. (11) 5904-6450; fax (11) 5904-6459; e-mail aluminio@abal.org.br; internet www

.abal.org.br; f. 1970; represents aluminium producing and processing cos; 66 mem. cos; Pres. ADJARMA AZEVEDO.

Associação Brasileira de Celulose e Papel—Bracelpa: Rua Olimpíadas, 66, 9° and Bairro Vl. Olímpia São Paulo, São Paulo, SP; tel. (11) 3018-7800; fax (11) 3018-7813; e-mail faleconosco@bracelpa.org.br; internet www.bracelpa.org.br; f. 1932; pulp and paper asscn; Exec. Dir ELIZABETH CARVALHAES.

Associação Brasileira das Empresas Importadoras de Veículos Automotores (ABEIVA): Rua Dr Renato Paes de Barros 717, Conjunto 113, 11° andar, Itaim Bibi, 04530–001 São Paulo, SP; tel. (11) 3078-3989; e-mail abeiva@abeiva.com.br; internet www .abeiva.com.br; f. 1991; car importers' asscn'; Pres. MORCEL VISCONDE; Exec. Man. JOSÉ NELSON CORREA.

Associação Brasileira das Indústrias de Óleos Vegetais (Abiove) (Brazilian Association of Vegetable Oil Industries): Av. Vereador José Diniz 3707, 7° andar, Conj. 73, 04603-004 São Paulo, SP; tel. (11) 5536-0733; fax (11) 5536-9816; e-mail abiove@abiove .com.br; internet www.abiove.com.br; f. 1981; 11 mem. cos; Pres. CARLO LOVATELLI.

Associação Brasileira da Infraestrutura e Indústrias de Base (ABDIB): Praça Monteiro Lobato, 36 Butantã, 05506-030 São Paulo, SP; tel. (11) 3094-1950; fax (11) 3094-1949; e-mail abdib@abdib.org .br; internet www.abdib.org.br; f. 1955; Pres. WILSON FERREIRA JUNIOR; 144 mems.

Associação Brasileira dos Produtores de Algodão (ABRAPA): Edif. Barão do Rio Branco, Terraço 02, 4° andar, SIG, Quadra 01, Lotes 495, 505 e 515, 70610-410 Brasília, DF; tel. (61) 3028-9700; fax (61) 3028-9707; e-mail faleconosco@abrapa.com.br; internet www .abrapa.com.br; f. 1999; cotton producers' asscn; Pres. GILSON FERRÚCIO PINESSO; Exec. Dir MARCIO PORTOCARRERO.

Associação Comercial do Rio de Janeiro (ACRJ): Rua da Calendária 9, 11°–12° andares, Centro, 20091-020 Rio de Janeiro, RJ; tel. and fax (21) 2514-1229; e-mail acrj@acrj.org.br; internet www .acrj.org.br; f. 1820; Pres. ANTONIO BARROS LEAL.

Associação Comercial de São Paulo (ACSP): Rua Boa Vista 51, Centro, 01014-911 São Paulo, SP; tel. (11) 3244-3322; fax (11) 3244-3355; e-mail infocem@acsp.com.br; internet www.acsp.com.br; f. 1894; Pres. ROGÉRIO PINTO COELHO AMATO.

Associação de Comércio Exterior do Brasil (AEB) (Brazilian Foreign Trade Association): Av. General Justo 335, 4° andar, 20021-130 Rio de Janeiro, RJ; tel. (21) 2544-0048; fax (21) 2544-0577; e-mail aebbras@aeb.org.br; internet www.aeb.org.br; exporters' asscn; Pres. JOSÉ AUGUSTO DE CASTRO; Exec. Vice-Pres. FÁBIO MARTINS FARIA.

Associação Nacional dos Exportadores de Cereais (ANEC): Av. Brigadeiro Faria Lima 1656, 8° andar, Conj. 81, Jardim Paulistano, 01451-001 São Paulo, SP; tel. (11) 3039-5599; fax (11) 3039-5598; e-mail anec@anec.com.br; internet www.anec.com.br; f. 1965; grain exporters' asscn; Pres. FELÍCIO PASCHOAL DA C. AGUIAR; Dir-Gen. SÉRGIO CASTANHO TEIXEIRA MENDES.

Associação Nacional dos Fabricantes de Veículos Automotores (ANFAVEA): Av. Indianópolis 496, 04062-900 São Paulo, SP; tel. (11) 2193-7800; fax (11) 2193-7825; internet www.anfavea.com .br; f. 1956; motor vehicle manufacturers' asscn; 27 mems; Pres. LUIZ MOAN YABIKU JUNIOR; Exec. Dir AURÉLIO SANTANA.

Centro das Indústrias do Estado de São Paulo (CIESP): Av. Paulista 1313, 01311-923 São Paulo, SP; tel. (11) 3549-3232; e-mail atendimento@ciesp.com.br; internet www.ciesp.com.br; f. 1928; asscn of small and medium-sized businesses; Pres. PAULO ANTONIO SKEF.

Confederação da Agricultura e Pecuária do Brasil (CNA): SGAN, Quadra 601, Modulo K, 70830-903 Brasília, DF; tel. (61) 2109-1400; fax (61) 2109-1490; e-mail cna@cna.org.br; internet www .canaldoprodutor.com.br; f. 1964; national agricultural confederation; Pres. JOÃO MARTINS DA SILVA JUNIOR; Exec. Vice-Pres. FÁBIO DE SALLES MEIRELLES FILHO.

Confederação Nacional do Comércio (CNC): Av. General Justo 307, 20021-130 Rio de Janeiro, RJ; tel. (21) 3804-9200; e-mail cncrj@cnc.com.br; internet www.portaldocomercio.org.br; 35 affiliated feds of commerce; Pres. ANTÔNIO JOSÉ DOMINGUES DE OLIVEIRA SANTOS.

Confederação Nacional da Indústria (CNI) (National Confederation of Industry): Edif. Roberto Simonsen, SBN, Quadra 01, Bloco C, 70040-903 Brasília, DF; tel. (61) 3317-9993; fax (61) 3317-9994; e-mail sac@cni.org.br; internet www.cni.org.br; f. 1938; comprises 27 state industrial feds; Pres. ROBSON BRAGA DE ANDRADE.

Conselho dos Exportadores de Café Verde do Brasil (CECAFE): Av. Nove de Julho 4865, Torre A, Conj. 61, Chácara Itaim, 01407-200 São Paulo, SP; tel. (11) 3079-3755; fax (11) 3167-4060; e-mail cecafe@cecafe.com.br; internet www.cecafe.com.br; f. 1999 through merger of Federação Brasileira dos Exportadores de Café and Associação Brasileira dos Exportadores de Café; council of green coffee exporters; Pres. JOÃO ANTÔNIO LIAN; Dir-Gen. GUILHERME BRAGA ABREU PIRES FILHO.

Federação das Indústrias do Estado do Rio de Janeiro (FIRJAN): Centro Empresarial FIRJAN, Av. Graça Aranha 1, Rio de Janeiro, RJ; tel. (21) 2563-4389; e-mail centrodeatendimento@firjan .org.br; internet www.firjan.org.br; Pres. EDUARDO EUGENIO GOUVÊA VIEIRA; regional manufacturers' asscn; 103 affiliated syndicates representing almost 16,000 cos.

Federação das Indústrias do Estado de São Paulo (FIESP): Av. Paulista 1313, 01311-923 São Paulo, SP; tel. (11) 3549-4499; e-mail relacionamento@fiesp.org.br; internet www.fiesp.org.br; regional manufacturers' asscn; Pres. PAULO ANTONIO SKAF.

Instituto Aço Brasil: Av. Rio Branco 181, 28° andar, 20040-007 Rio de Janeiro, RJ; tel. (21) 3445-6300; fax (21) 2262-2234; e-mail acobrasil@acobrasil.org.br; internet www.acobrasil.org.br; f. 1963; fmrly Instituto Brasileiro de Siderurgia (IBS); steel cos' org.; Pres. BENJAMIN BAPTISTA FILHO; Exec. Chair MARCO POLO DE MELLO LOPES.

Instituto Brasileiro do Mineração (IBRAM) (Brazilian Mining Association): SHIS, Quadra 12, Conj. 0, Casa 4, 71630-205 Brasília, DF; tel. (61) 3364-7200; fax (61) 3364-7272; e-mail ibram@ibram.org .br; internet www.ibram.org.br; f. 1976 to foster the devt of the mining industry; Pres. and Dir JOSÉ FERNANDO COURA.

Instituto Nacional de Tecnologia (INT): Av. Venezuela 82, 8° andar, 20081-312 Rio de Janeiro, RJ; tel. (21) 2123-1100; fax (21) 2123-1284; e-mail dcom@int.gov.br; internet www.int.gov.br; f. 1921; co-operates in national industrial devt; Dir DOMINGOS MANFREDI NAVEIRO.

Serviço de Apoio às Micro e Pequenas Empresas (Sebrae): SEPN, Quadra 515, Lote 03, Bloco C, Asa Norte, 70770-530 Brasília, DF; tel. (61) 3348-7100; fax (61) 3347-3581; internet www.sebrae .com.br; f. 1972; supports small and medium-sized enterprises; Exec. Dir LUIZ EDUARDO PEREIRA BARRETTO FILHO.

União Democrática Ruralista (UDR): Av. Col Marcondes 983, 6° andar, Sala 62, Centro, 19010-080 Presidente Prudente, SP; tel. (11) 3221-1082; fax (11) 3232-4622; e-mail udr.org@uol.com.br; internet www.udr.org.br; landowners' org.; Pres. LUIZ ANTÔNIO NABHAN GARCIA.

União da Industria de Cana-de-Açúcar (UNICA): Av. Brigadeiro Faria Lima 2179, 9° andar, Jardim Paulistano, 01452-000 São Paulo, SP; tel. (11) 3093-4949; fax (11) 3812-1416; e-mail unica@unica.com.br; internet www.unica.com.br; f. 1997; sugar and bioethanol asscn; offices in USA and Belgium; Pres. ELIZABETH FARINA; Exec. Dir EDUARDO LEÃO DE SOUSA.

STATE HYDROCARBONS COMPANIES

Petróleo Brasileiro, SA (Petrobras): Av. República do Chile 65, Centro, 20031-912 Rio de Janeiro, RJ; tel. (21) 3224-1510; fax (21) 3224-6055; e-mail sac@petrobras.com.br; internet www.petrobras .com.br; f. 1953; production of petroleum and petroleum products; owns 16 oil refineries; CEO MARIA DAS GRAÇAS SILVA FOSTER; Sec.-Gen. HÉLIO SHIGUENOBU FUJIKAWA; 53,933 employees; subsidiary cos are Petrobras Transporte, SA (Transpetro), Petrobras Comercializadora de Energia, Ltda, Petrobras Negócios Eletrônicos, SA, Petrobras International Finance Co (PIFCO) and Downstream Participações, SA, and cos listed below:

Petrobras Biocombustível, SA (Petrobras Biofuel): Av. República do Chile 500, 27°, Centro, 20031-912 Rio de Janeiro, RJ; tel. (21) 3224-6283; fax (21) 3224-6055; e-mail biocombustivel@petrobras.com.br; internet www.petrobrasbiocombustivel.com.br; f. 2008; 5 biodiesel plants; 10 ethanol plants, 9 in Brazil and 1 in Mozambique; Pres. MIGUEL SOLDATELLI ROSSETTO.

Petrobras Distribuidora, SA: Rua General Canabarro 500, Maracanã, 20271-900 Rio de Janeiro, RJ; tel. (21) 3876-4477; fax (21) 3876-4977; internet www.br.com.br; f. 1971; distribution of all petroleum by-products; Pres. JOSÉ LIMA DE ANDRADE NETO; 3,758 employees.

Petrobras Gás, SA (Gaspetro): Av. República do Chile 65, Centro, 20031-912 Rio de Janeiro, RJ; tel. (21) 3534-0439; fax (21) 3534-1080; e-mail sac@petrobras.com.br; internet www .gaspetro.com.br; f. 1998; Pres. JOSÉ MARIA CARVALHO RESENDE.

Petrobras Química, SA (Petroquisa): Av. República do Chile 65, 9° andar, Centro, 20031-912 Rio de Janeiro, RJ; tel. (21) 3224-1455; fax (21) 2262-1521; e-mail contato.petroquisa@petrobras .com.br; internet www.petroquisa.com.br; f. 1968; petrochemicals industry; controls 27 affiliated cos and 4 subsidiaries; Dir PATRICK FAIRON.

Pré-Sal Petróleo, SA (PPSA): f. 2010; state-owned; manages exploration of petroleum and natural gas beneath the salt layer along the Brazilian coast; Pres. OSWALDO ATUNES PEDROSA JÚNIOR.

Refinaria de Petróleos de Manguinhos: Av. Brasil 3141, Manguinhos, 20930-041 Rio de Janeiro, RJ; tel. (21) 3891-2000; e-mail webmaster@rpdm.com.br; internet www.manguinhosrefinaria.com .br; f. 1954; acquired by Grupo Andrade Magro in 2008; nationalization announced in Nov. 2012; Chair. CARLOS FILIPE RIZZO; Pres. and CEO PAULO HENRIQUE OLIVEIRA DE MENEZES.

MAJOR COMPANIES

Chemicals, Petrochemicals and Petroleum

Braskem, SA: Edif. Odebrecht, 120, Rua Lemos Monteiro, 05501-050 São Paulo, SP; tel. (11) 3643-2744; fax (11) 3443-9017; internet www.braskem.com.br; f. 2002; part of Odebrecht group; 18 chemical plants; Pres. CARLOS FADIGAS DE SOUZA; 4,800 employees.

Empresas Petróleo Ipiranga, SA (IPQ): Rua Francisco Eugênio 329, 20948-900 Rio de Janeiro, RJ; tel. (21) 2574-5858; fax (21) 2569-8796; internet www.ipiranga.com.br; f. 1959; petroleum, petroleum products and natural gas; Pres. JOÃO PEDRO GOUVÊA VIEIRA; Vice-Pres. SÉRGIO SILVEIRA SARAIVA; 3,653 employees.

Distribuidora de Productos de Petróleo Ipiranga, SA: Av. Dolores Alcaraz Caldas 90, Praia das Belas, 90110-180 Porto Alegre, RS; tel. (51) 3216-4411; fax (51) 3224-0501; internet www.ipiranga.com.br; f. 1957; distribution of petroleum derivatives; cap. US $1,482.4m., sales $9,772.5m. (2005); Pres. SÉRGIO SILVEIRA SARAIVA; 1,500 employees.

Metals and Mining

Aços Villares, SA: Av. das Nações Unidas 8501, Bloco A, 5° andar, Pinheiros, 05425-070 São Paulo, SP; tel. (11) 3094-6600; fax (11) 3094-6524; internet www.acosvillares.com.br; f. 1944; part of Sidenor group; steel producers; Pres. PAULO FERNANDO BINS DE VASCONCELLOS; CEO ANDRÉ BIER GERDAU JOHANNPETER; 4,307 employees.

Alcoa Alumínio, SA: Av. das Nações Unidas 12901, Torre Oeste 16° andar, Brooklin Novo, 04578-000 São Paulo, SP; tel. (11) 3296-3300; fax (11) 3741-8300; internet www.alcoa.com.br; f. 1965; subsidiary of Alcoa Inc (USA); extraction and processing of bauxite; Pres. (Latin America and Caribbean) AQUILINO PAOLUCCI; 4,447 employees.

ArcelorMittal Brasil: Av. Carandaí 1115, 30130-915 Belo Horizonte, MG; tel. (31) 3219-1122; fax (31) 3235-4294; internet www.arcelor.com.br; f. 1921; formed by merger of Companhia Siderúrgica Belgo-Mineira, Companhia Siderúrgica de Tubarão, and Vega do Sul; owned by ArcelorMittal, Luxembourg; steel mill; bought ACESITA in 2010; Pres. JOSÉ ARMANDO DE FIGUEIREDO CAMPOS; CEO BENJAMIN MÁRIO BAPTISTA FILHO; 15,000 employees.

Companhia Brasileira de Metalurgia e Mineração (CBMM): Córrego da Mata s/n, CP 8, 38183-970 Araxá, MG; tel. (34) 3669-3000; fax (34) 3669-3100; e-mail cbmm@cbmm.com.br; internet www.cbmm.com.br; f. 1955; extraction and processing of niobium, manufacturing of niobium products; CEO TADEU CARNEIRO.

Companhia Siderúrgica Nacional (CSN): Av. Brigadeiro Faria Lima 3400, 20° andar, Itaim Bibi, 04538-132 São Paulo, SP; tel. (11) 3049-7100; fax (11) 3049-7102; e-mail imprensa@csn.com.br; internet www.csn.com.br; f. 1941; privatized 1993; steel; Chair. and CEO BENJAMIN STEINBRUCH; 8,000 employees.

Fusion Metais do Brasil Ltda: Rua Maria Bellini Fachinni, 44 Jardim Presidente Tancredo Neves, 13607-095 Araras, SP; tel. (19) 3544-4738; fax (19) 3542-0054; e-mail contato@fusionmetais.com.br; internet www.fusionmetais.com.br; brass, bronze and cast iron products; Gen. Man. TIAGO AMARAL.

Grupo Gerdau: Av. Farrapos 1811, 90220-005 Porto Alegre, RS; tel. (51) 3323-2000; fax (51) 3323-2222; internet www.gerdau.com.br; f. 1901; long steel group; Pres. JORGE GERDAU JOHANNPETER; CEO ANDRÉ BIER GERDAU JOHANNPETER; cos in the group include Gerdau Ameristeel Corpn and Metalúrgica Gerdau, SA.

Paranapanema, SA: Via do Cobre, 3700 Área Industrial Oeste, COPEC, 42850-000 Dias Dávila, BA; tel. (71) 2203-1210; fax (71) 2203-1484; e-mail dri@paranapanema.com.br; internet www.paranapanema.com.br; f. 1961; copper and fertilizer production; Chair. ALBANO CHAGAS VIEIRA.

SMS Siemag Equipamentos e Serviços, Ltda: Av. 2, 230 Distrito Industrial Parque Norte, 33200-000 Vespasiano, MG; tel. (31) 2125-1160; fax (31) 2125-1408; e-mail consulta@sms-siemag.com.br; internet www.sms-siemag.com.br; f. 1977; subsidiary of SMS Siemag, Germany; steel mills and hot metal production; Group Pres. and CEO BURKHARD DAHMEN.

Usinas Siderúrgicas de Minas Gerais, SA (USIMINAS): Rua Prof. José Vieira de Mendonça 3011, Engenho Nogueira, CP 806, 31310-260 Belo Horizonte, MG; tel. (31) 3499-8000; fax (31) 3499-8899; e-mail imprensa@usiminas.com.br; internet www.usiminas.com.br; f. 1956; consists of 13 cos with activities in mining, steel and iron; privatized in 1991; Pres. PAULO PENIDO PINTO MARQUES; CEO JULIÁN ALBERTO EGUREN; 30,000 employees.

Vale, SA (Companhia Vale do Rio Doce, SA): Av. Graça Aranha 26, 12° andar, Bairro Castelo, 20030-900 Rio de Janeiro, RJ; tel. (21) 3814-4540; fax (21) 3814-9935; internet www.vale.com.br; f. 1942; fmr state-owned mining co, privatized in 1997; owns and operates two systems: in the north, the Carajás iron ore mine and railway, and port of Ponta da Madeira; in the south, the Itabira iron ore mine, the Vitória–Minas railway and the port of Tubarão; iron ore, gold producer; also involved in forestry and pulp production, aluminium and other minerals; Pres. and CEO MURILO PINTO DE OLIVEIRA FERREIRA; 15,500 employees.

Votorantim Metais: Praça Ramos de Azevedo 254, 5° e 6° andares, 01037-912 São Paulo, SP; tel. (11) 2159-3100; fax (11) 3222-9975; internet www.votorantim.com.br; part of Votorantim Group; aluminium and zinc extraction and processing, long steel; subsidiary cos include Companhia Mineira do Metais, Companhia Niquel Tocatins and Companhia Paraibuna de Metais; Pres. and CEO TITO BOTELHO MARTINS JUNIOR; 3,500 employees.

White Martins Gases Industriais, Ltda: Rua Mayrink Veiga 9, Centro, 20090-050 Rio de Janeiro, RJ; tel. (21) 2588-6622; fax (21) 2588-6683; e-mail atendimento@sac.whitemartins.com.br; internet www.whitemartins.com.br; f. 1912; almost 100% owned by Praxair; mfrs and distributors of industrial gases, welding equipment and seamless cylinders; CEO DOMINGOS BULUS; 10,000 employees.

Motor Vehicles and Aircraft

Embraer, SA: Av. Brig. Faria Lima 2170, Putim, 12227-901 São José dos Campos, SP; tel. (12) 3927-4404; fax (12) 3922-6070; e-mail investor.relations@embraer.com.br; internet www.embraer.com.br; f. 1969 as state-owned Empresa Brasileira de Aeronautica, SA; privatized in 1994; present name adopted Nov. 2010; aeronautics industry; Chair. ALEXANDRE GONÇALVES SILVA; Pres. and CEO FREDERICO FLEURY CURADO; 17,375 employees.

Fiat do Brasil, SA: Rua Senador Milton Campos 175, Vila da Serra, 34000-000 Nova Lima, MG; tel. (31) 3589-4000; fax (31) 3589-4040; e-mail bogutchi@fiat.com; internet www.fiat.com.br; f. 1989; subsidiary of Fiat of Italy; produces 730,000 vehicles per year; Pres. and Dir CLEDORVINO BELINI; 9,400 employees.

Ford Brasil, Ltda: Av. Taboão 899, Prédio 6, CP 9308, 09655-900 São Bernardo do Campo, SP; tel. (11) 4174-8235; fax (11) 848-9057; internet www.ford.com.br; f. 1987; subsidiary of Ford Motor Co (USA); motor vehicles; Pres. STEVEN ARMSTRONG; 6,500 employees.

General Motors do Brasil: Av. Goiás 1805, São Caetano do Sul, 09521-000 São Paulo; tel. (51) 4234-3043; internet chevrolet.com.br; f. 1925; subsidiary of General Motors Co of the USA; Pres. and Man. Dir JAIME ARDILA; 21,180 employees.

Iochpe-Maxion, SA: Rua Luigi Galvani 146, 13° andar, 04575-020 São Paulo, SP; tel. (11) 5508-3800; fax (11) 5506-7353; e-mail ri@iochpe.com.br; internet iochpe-maxion.com.br; f. 1918; motor vehicle mfrs; Chair. IVONCY BROCHMANN IOSCHPE; Pres. and CEO DANIEL IOSCHPE; 6,500 employees.

Magneti Marelli Cofap Autopeças: Av. Manoel da Nóbrega 350, Capuava, 09310-120 Mauá, SP; tel. (11) 4474-1357; fax (11) 4474-1357; e-mail erv.saopaulo@marellicofap.com.br; internet www.mmcofap.com.br; f. 1951; mfrs of motor vehicle components; Pres. ELIANA GIANNOCCARO; 7,100 employees.

Mercedes-Benz do Brasil, SA: Av. Mercedes Benz 679, Distrito Industrial, 13054-750 Campinas, SP; tel. (19) 3725-3333; fax (19) 3725-3635; internet www.mercedes-benz.com.br; f. 1953 as Mercedes Benz do Brasil, SA; subsidiary of DaimlerChrysler AG of Germany; motor-car, truck and bus-chassis production; CEO PHILIPP SCHIEMER; 13,209 employees.

Volkswagen do Brasil, SA: Via Anchieta km 23, 5, CP 1048, 09823-990 São Bernardo do Campo, SP; tel. (11) 4347-2355; fax (11) 578-0947; e-mail info@vm.com.br; internet www.vm.com.br; f. 1953; subsidiary of Volkswagen AG of Germany; manufacture of trucks and passenger commercial vehicles; Pres. THOMAS SCHMALL; 22,000 employees.

Rubber, Textiles and Paper

Celulose Nipo-Brasileira (CENIBRA): Rua Bernardo Guimarães 245, 8° andar, Bairro Funcionários, 30140-080 Belo Horizonte, MG; tel. (31) 3235-4041; fax (31) 3235-4002; e-mail comercial@cenibra.com.br; internet www.cenibra.com.br; f. 1973; owned by Japan Brazil Paper and Pulp Resources Development Co Ltd (JBP); eucalyptus pulp paper; Pres. PAULO EDUARDO DE ROCHA BRANT; 1,600 employees.

Eldorado Celulose e Papel, SA: Rua General Furtado do Nascimento, 66 Alto de Pinheiros, 05465-070 São Paulo, SP; tel. (11) 2505-0200; internet www.eldoradobrasil.com.br; f. 2012; subsidiary of JBS, SA; CEO JOSÉ CARLOS GRUBISICH.

Fibria Celulose, SA: Alameda Santos 1357, 6° andar, 01419-908 São Paulo, SP; tel. (11) 2138-4000; e-mail ir@fibria.com.br; internet www.fibria.com.br; f. 2009; following merger between Aracruz Celulose and Votorantim Celulose e Papel (VCP); Chair. JOSÉ LUCIANO PENIDO; CEO MARCELO STRUFALDI CASTELLI; 15,000 employees.

Indústrias Klabin de Papel e Celulose, SA (Klabin): Av. Brig. Faria Lima 3600, Itaim Bibi, 04538-132 São Paulo, SP; tel. (11) 3046-5800; fax (11) 3225-4067; e-mail invest@klabin.com.br; internet www

.klabin.com.br; f. 1934; paper and paper products; Chair. DANIEL MIGUEL KLABIN; Gen. Man. FABIO SCHVARTSMAN; 13,432 employees.

LANXESS Elastomers of Brazil, SA: Av. Maria Coelho Aguiar 215, Bloco B, 2° andar, 05804-902 Jardim São Luis, São Paulo, SP; tel. (21) 3741-2500; fax (21) 2776-1510; internet www.lanxess.com.br; f. 1977 as a subsidiary of Petroquisa; 70% shares bought by LANXESS Holdings in 2008; synthetic rubber; CEO MARCELO LACERDA; 900 employees.

Pirelli Pneus, SA: Av. Capuava 603, Vila Homero Thon, 09111-310 Santo André, SP; fax (11) 4998-5512; e-mail webpneus@pirelli.com.br; internet www.pirelli.com.br; f. 1988; owned by Pirelli of Italy; makers of rubber inner tubes and tyres; CEO PAUL HEMBREY; 6,798 employees.

Stora Enso Arapoti, Ltda: Alameda Itú 852, 6° e 8° andares, Cerqueira César, 01421-001 São Paulo, SP; tel. (11) 3065-5200; fax (11) 3065-5214; internet www.storaenso.com; f. 1998; fmrly Vinson Indústria de Papel Arapoti Ltda and Vinson Empreendimentos Agricolas Ltda; bought by Stora Enso (Finland) in 2006; paper mfrs; Group CEO JOUKO KARVINEN; 370 employees.

Suzano Papel e Celulose, SA: Av. Tancredo Neves 274, Bloco B, Sala 121, 122 e 123 Caminho das Arvores, 41820-020 Salvador, BA; tel. (71) 3797-7900; fax (71) 3797-7906; e-mail suzano@suzano.com.br; internet www.suzano.com.br; f. 1923; makes and distributes eucalyptus pulp and paper products; CEO WALTER SCHALKA; 3,425 employees.

Tecelagem Kuehnrich, SA (TEKA): Rua Paulo Kuehnrich 68, Bairro Itoupava Norte, 89052-900 Blumenau, SC; tel. (47) 3321-5000; fax (47) 3321-5050; e-mail sac@teka.com.br; internet www.teka.com.br; f. 1935; textile mfrs; Pres. FREDERICO KUEHNRICH NETO; CEO MARCELLO STEWERS; 4,500 employees.

Construction

Camargo Corrêa, SA: Rua Funchal 160, Vila Olímpia, 04551-903 São Paulo, SP; tel. (11) 3841-5511; fax (11) 3841-5849; e-mail faleconosco@camargocorrea.com.br; internet www.camargocorrea.com.br; f. 1939; heavy construction, engineering, cement; part of the Camargo Corrêa Group; 25 subsidiary cos; Chair. VITOR HALLACK; Man. Dir JOSÉ ALBERTO DINIZ; 56,800 employees.

Construtora Andrade Gutierrez, SA: Av. do Contorno 8123, Cidade Jardim, 30110-910 Belo Horizonte, MG; tel. (31) 3290-6699; internet www.agsa.com.br; f. 1948; subsidiary of Andrade Gutierrez, SA; heavy construction and civil engineering; Pres. SÉRGIO LINS ANDRADE; 34,161 employees.

Construtora Norberto Odebrecht, SA: Praia de Botafogo 300, 10° andar, Botafogo, 22250-040 Rio de Janeiro, RJ; tel. (21) 2559-3000; fax (21) 2552-4448; e-mail info@odebrecht.com.br; internet www.odebrecht-ec.com; f. 1944; part of Odebrecht group; subsidiaries include CBPO Engenharia Ltda, Odebrecht Empreendimentos Imobiliários Ltda, Lumina Engenharia Ambiental Ltda; CEO PAULO OLIVEIRA LACERDA DE MELO; 27,159 employees.

Construtora Queiroz Galvão, SA: Av. Rio Branco 156, 30° andar, Centro, 20040-901 Rio de Janeiro, RJ; tel. (21) 2131-7100; fax (21) 2131-9367; internet www.queirozgalvao.com; f. 1953; civil engineering and construction projects; Pres. ANTÔNIO DE QUEIROZ GALVÃO; Man. Dir JOÃO ANTÔNIO DE QUEIROZ GALVÃO; 7,450 employees.

Delta Construções SA: Av. Rio Branco 156, 31° andar, Centro, 20040-003 Rio de Janeiro, RJ; tel. (21) 3974-2600; fax (21) 3974-2830; e-mail monica.paula@deltaconstrucao.com.br; internet www.deltaconstrucao.com.br; f. 1961; Pres. HUMBERTO JUNQUEIRA DE FARIAS; CEO DIONISIO JANONI TOLOMEI.

Food and Drink

AmBev (Companhia de Bebidas das Américas): Corporate Park, Renato Paes de Barros 1017, 4° andar, 04530-001 São Paulo, SP; tel. (11) 2122-1370; e-mail ci@ambev.com.br; internet www.ambev.com.br; f. 1999 following merger of Brahma and Antarctica beer producers; bought by InBev (Belgium) in 2004; beer and soft drinks maker, produces Brahma beer; CEO JOÃO MAURICIO GIFFONI DE CASTRO NEVES; Pres. (Latin America) LUIZ FERNANDO EDMOND; 13,000 employees.

BRF, SA (Brasil Foods, SA): Rua Hungria 1400, 1° andar, Jardim Europa, 01455-000 São Paulo, SP; tel. (11) 2322-5000; fax (11) 2322-5001; e-mail sac@brasilfoods.com; internet www.brasilfoods.com; f. 1934 as Perdigão; adopted present name in 2009 after merger with Sadia, SA; food-processing and packaging; Chair. ABILIO DINIZ (2013–15); 27,000 employees.

Sadia, SA: Rua Senador Attílio Fontana 86, Centro, 89700-000 Concórdia, SC; tel. (49) 3444-3000; fax (49) 3444-3001; e-mail ri@sadia.com.br; internet www.sadia.com.br; f. 1944; refrigeration, meat-packing, animal feeds; fully owned subsidiary of BRF, SA (q.v.) since 2009; CEO JOSÉ JULIO CARDOSO DE LUCENA; 40,000 employees.

Bunge Alimentos, SA: Rodovia Jorge Lacerda, Km 20, Poço Grande, 89110-000 Gaspar, SC; tel. (47) 3331-2222; fax (47) 3331-2005; internet www.bungealimentos.com.br; f. 2000 by merger of Santista Alimentos and Ceval Alimentos; agricultural processing; Pres. and CEO PEDRO PARENTE; 9,793 employees.

Carrefour Brasil: Rua George Eastman 213, São Paulo, SP; internet www.grupocarrefour.com.br; f. 1975 in Brazil; grocery sales, etc.; CEO GEORGES PLASSAT; 500 stores (2010); 70,000 employees.

Coca-Cola Andina Brasil: Rua André Rocha 2299, Taquara, 22710-561 Rio de Janeiro, RJ; tel. (21) 2429-1700; internet www.koandina.com; f. ; owned by Embotelladora Andina, SA; bottling co for Coca-Cola; Chair. JUAN CLARO GONZÁLEZ.

Companhia Brasileira de Distribuição/Grupo Pão de Açúcar: Av. Brig. Luís Antonio 3126, Jardim Paulista, 01402-901 São Paulo, SP; tel. (11) 3886-0533; fax (11) 3884-2677; e-mail cbd.ri@paodeacucar.com.br; internet www.grupopaodeacucar.com.br; f. 1948; supermarkets, hypermarkets and electrical stores; Chair. ABILIO DOS SANTOS DINIZ; CEO ENÉAS CÉSAR PESTANA NETO; 70,656 employees.

JBS, SA: Av. Marginal Direita do Tietê 500, Vila Jaguara, 05118-100 São Paulo, SP; tel. (11) 3144-4000; e-mail imprensa@jbs.com.br; internet www.jbs.com.br; f. 1953; food (particularly beef) and beverage producer; Pres. and CEO JOESLEY MENDONÇA BATISTA; 44,993 employees.

RENOSA (Refrigerantes do Noroeste, SA): Rod. Mário Andreazza 1800, 78156-105 Várzea Grande, MT; tel. (65) 3619-1001; internet www.renosa.com.br; f. 1977; mfrs of Coca-Cola in Brazil; Pres. RICARDO MELLO; 5 factories.

Walmart: Av. Tucunaré 125, Alphaville, 06460-020 Barueri, SP; tel. (11) 2103-5800; fax (11) 2103-5776; e-mail imprensa@wal-mart.com; internet www.walmartbrasil.com.br; f. 1995; subsidiary cos incl. Bompreço, SA and Sonae Distribuição Brasil, SA; grocery sales, etc.; Pres. GUILHERME LOUREIRO; 21,000 employees.

Pharmaceuticals

Aché Laboratórios Farmacêuticos, SA: Rodovia Presidente Dutra, Km 222.2, Porto da Igreja, 07034-904 Guarulhos, SP; tel. (11) 2608-6000; fax (11) 2608-6178; e-mail cac@ache.com.br; internet www.ache.com.br; f. 1966 as Prodoctor Produtos Farmacêuticos; CEO JOSÉ RICARDO MENDES DA SILVA; 2,600 employees.

Biosintética: Av. das Nações Unidas 22428, Jurubatuba, 04795-916 São Paulo, SP; tel. (11) 5546-6822; fax (11) 5546-6800; e-mail cac@ache.com.br; internet www.biosintetica.com.br; acquired by Aché in 2005; cardiovascular medication and other products; Nat. Man. MIRIAM FERREIRA OLIVEIRA.

Copersucar, SA: Av. Paulista 287, 1°–3° andares, 01311-000 São Paulo, SP; tel. (11) 2618-8166; fax (11) 2618-8355; internet www.copersucar.com.br; f. 2008; sugar and ethanol trader and exporter; Chair. LUÍS ROBERTO POGETTI; CEO PAULO ROBERTO DE SOUZA.

EMS Indústria Farmacêutica, Ltda: Rodovia Jornalista Francisco Aguirre Proença, Km 08, Bairro Chacara Assay, 13186-481 Hortolândia, SP; tel. (19) 3887-9800; fax (19) 3887-9515; e-mail sac@ems.com.br; internet www.ems.com.br; f. 1964.

Eurofarma: Av. das Nações Unidas 22215, Jurubatuba, 04795-100 São Paulo, SP; tel. and fax (11) 5521-0232; e-mail euroatende@eurofarma.com.br; internet www.eurofarma.com.br; f. 1972 as Billi Farmacêutica; products include prescription and oncological medications; Pres. MAURIZIO BILLI.

JP Indústria Farmacêutica, SA: Av. Presidente Castelo Branco 999, Lagoinha, 14095-000 Ribeirão Preto, SP; tel. (16) 3512-3500; fax (16) 3512-3510; e-mail sac@jpfarma.com.br; internet www.jpfarma.com.br; f. 1966; hospital supplies and medications; Exec. Pres. ANDRÉ ALI MERE.

Libbs: Rua Josef Kryss 250, Barra Funda, 01140-050 São Paulo, SP; tel. (11) 3879-2500; fax (11) 3879-0957; e-mail heloisio.rodrigues@libbs.com.br; internet www.libbs.com.br; f. 1958; general pharmaceutical products; Pres. ALCEBÍADES DE MENDONÇA ATHAYDE; 1,050 employees.

Medley, SA, Indústria Farmacêutica: Rua Macedo Costa 55, Jardim Santa Genebra, 13080-180 Campinas, SP; tel. (19) 3708-8222; fax (19) 3708-8227; internet www.medley.com.br; subsidiary of Sanofi, France; brand and generic products; Dir-Gen. WILSON BORGES.

Miscellaneous

Duratex, SA: Av. Paulista 1938, 5° andar, Bela Vista, 01310-942 São Paulo, SP; tel. (11) 3179-7733; fax (11) 3179-7355; internet www.duratex.com.br; f. 1951; mfrs of hardboard and plywood, ceramic products and bathroom fixtures; part of Itaúsa Group; Chair. SALO DAVI SEIBEL; CEO ANTÔNIO JOAQUIM DE OLIVEIRA; 6,785 employees.

Electrolux do Brasil, SA: Rua Ministro Gabriel Passos 360, Guabirotuba, 81520-620 Curitiba, PR; tel. (41) 2108-6700; fax (41) 0371-7541; e-mail eluxfct@electrolux.com.br; internet www .electrolux.com.br; f. 1926; makers of refrigerators, freezers and vacuum cleaners; CEO RUY HIRSCHHEIMER; 431 employees.

Elevadores Atlas Schindler, SA: Av. do Estado 6116, Cambuci, 01516-900 São Paulo, SP; tel. (11) 2020-5100; fax (11) 2020-5478; e-mail sac.brasil@br.schindler.com; internet www.schindler.com/br; f. 1918; produces and maintains lifts and escalators; Pres. LUIS DEL BARRIO RUIZ; 4,500 employees.

Empresa Brasileira de Correios e Telégrafos (Correios): Edif. Sede dos Correios, SBN, Quadra 1, Bloco A, 15° andar, 70002-900 Brasília, DF; tel. (61) 3426-2450; fax (61) 3327-5455; e-mail presidencia@correios.com.br; internet www.correios.com.br; f. 1969; state-owned; postal and telegraph services; Chair. PAULO BERNARDO SILVA; Exec. Pres. WAGNER PINHEIRO DE OLIVEIRA; 108,000 employees.

Itaú Tecnologia, SA (Itautec): Av. Paulista 2028, 15° andar, Bela Vista, 01310-200 São Paulo, SP; tel. (11) 3543-3000; e-mail ri@itautec .com; internet www.itautec.com.br; f. 1979; part of Itaúsa Group; mfrs of computer hardware; Chair. RICARDO EGYDIO SETUBAL; CEO HENRI PENCHAS; 5,347 employees.

Lojas Americanas, SA: Rua Coelho e Castro 60, Saúde, 20081-260 Rio de Janeiro, RJ; tel. (21) 3723-8080; internet ri.lasa.com.br; f. 1929; retail chain; part of the Carrefour Group; Pres. CARLOS ALBERTO DA VEIGA SICUPIRA; CEO MIGUEL GOMES PEREIRA SARMIENTO GUTIERREZ; 8,490 employees.

Repsol Sinopec Brasil, SA: Praia de Botafogo 300, 7° andar, 22250-040, Rio de Janeiro, RJ; tel. (21) 2559-7000; fax (21) 2552-8552; e-mail mritter.re@repsol.com; internet www.repsol.com/br_pt; f. 1987; 40% stake owned by Sinopec, China; Chair. ANTONIO BRUFAO; CEO JOSÉ MARIA MORENO.

Saint-Gobain Vidros, SA: Av. Santa Marina 482, Agua Blanca, 05036-903 São Paulo, SP; tel. (11) 2246-7600; fax (11) 3611-0299; internet www.saint-gobain.com.br; f. 1937; subsidiary of Groupe Saint-Gobain (France); glass mfrs; CEO JOSÉ LUIZ REDONDO; 3,120 employees.

Souza Cruz, SA: Rua Candelária 66, Centro, 20091-900 Rio de Janeiro, RJ; tel. (21) 3849-9000; fax (21) 3849-9643; e-mail sac@scruz .com.br; internet www.souzacruz.com.br; f. 1903; mfrs of cigarettes and tobacco; subsidiary of British American Tobacco; Pres. ANDREA MARTINI; 5,955 employees.

Via Varejo, SA: Rua Joao Pessoa 83, Centro, 09520-010 São Caetano do Sul, SP; tel. (21) 3886-0421; fax (21) 3884-2677; internet www .viavarejo.com.br; f. 1946 as Globex Utilidades, SA, present name adopted 2012; household goods retail; owns Casas Bahia, Pontofrio and Bartira brands; Chair. MICHAEL KLEIN; CEO LIBANO MIRANDA BARROSO; 8,300 employees.

Votorantim Participações: Rua Amauri 255, 01448-000 São Paulo, SP; tel. (11) 3071-1633; fax (11) 3167-1550; internet www .votorantim.com.br; f. 1918; part of Votorantim Group; holding co with interests in cement, paper, metals, chemicals and financial services; Chair. JOSÉ ROBERTO ERMÍRIO DE MORAES; CEO RAÚL CALFAT; 28,000 employees.

Whirlpool, SA: Edif. Plaza Centenário, Av. das Nações Unidas 12995, 32° andar, 04578-000 São Paulo, SP; tel. (11) 6940-1000; e-mail ana.paiva@cdn.com.br; internet www.whirlpool.com.br; f. 2006; with the re-organization of Multibrás, SA Eletrodomésticos and Empresa Brasileira de Compressores, SA-Embraco; retail of household appliances; Pres. (Latin America) JOÃO CARLOS BREGA; 8,000 employees.

Xerox Brasil: Av. Rodrigues Alves 261, 20220-360 Rio de Janeiro, RJ; tel. (21) 4009-1212; fax (21) 4009-2749; e-mail webmaster@xerox .com.br; internet www.xerox.com.br; office equipment, technology; Pres. RICARDO KARBAGE.

UTILITIES

Regulatory Agencies

Agência Nacional de Energia Elétrica (ANEEL): SGAN 603, Módulo I-J, 70830-110 Brasília, DF; tel. (61) 2192-8600; e-mail aneel@aneel.gov.br; internet www.aneel.gov.br; f. 1939 as Conselho Nacional de Aguas e Energia Elétrica, present name adopted 1996; Dir-Gen. ROMEU DONIZETE RUFINO.

Comissão Nacional de Energia Nuclear (CNEN): Rua General Severiano 90, Botafogo, 22290-901 Rio de Janeiro, RJ; tel. (21) 2173-2000; fax (21) 2173-2003; e-mail corin@cnen.gov.br; internet www .cnen.gov.br; f. 1956; management of nuclear power programme; Pres. CRISTÓVÃO ARARIPE MARINHO.

Operador Nacional do Sistema Elétrico (ONS): Rua Júlio do Carmo 251, Cidade Nova 20211-160, Rio de Janeiro, RJ; tel. (21) 3444-9400; internet www.ons.org.br; operates national electricity grid; regulated by ANEEL; Dir-Gen. HERMES CHIPP.

Electricity

Ampla Energia e Serviços, SA (Ampla): Praça Leoni Ramos 1, Bloco 1, 7° andar, São Domingos, 24210-205 Niterói, RJ; tel. (21) 2613-7000; fax (21) 2613-7153; e-mail ampla@ampla.com; internet www.ampla.com; f. 1907, privatized in 2004; fmrly Companhia de Eletricidade do Estado do Rio de Janeiro-CERJ; Pres. MARCELO ANDRÉS LLÉVENES REBOLLEDO.

CPFL Energia, SA (Companhia Paulista de Força e Luz): Rua Gomes de Carvalho 1510, 14° andar, Conj. 1402, 04547-005 Vila Olímpia, SP; tel. (19) 3756-8018; fax (19) 3252-7644; internet www .cpfl.com.br; provides electricity through govt concessions; operates 21 subsidiaries; Exec. Dir WILSON PINTO FERREIRA JÚNIOR.

Centrais Elétricas Brasileiras, SA (Eletrobras): Av. Presidente Vargas 409, 13° andar, Centro, 20071-003 Rio de Janeiro, RJ; tel. (21) 2514-5151; fax (21) 2514-6479; e-mail pr@eletrobras.gov.br; internet www.eletrobras.com; f. 1962; 54% govt-owned; Pres. JOSÉ DA COSTA CARVALHO NETO; controls 6 electricity generation and transmission subsidiaries and 6 distribution subsidiaries:

Eletrobras Amazonas Energia: Av. Sete de Setembro 2414, Cachoeirinha, 69005-141 Manaus, AM; tel. (92) 3621-1201; fax (92) 3633-2406; internet www.amazonasenergia.gov.br; f. 1895; name changed as above in 2010; distribution; Exec. Dir RADYR GOMES DE OLIVEIRA.

Eletrobras CGTEE (Companhia de Geração Térmica de Energia Elétrica): Rua Sete de Setembro 539, 90010-190 Porto Alegre, RS; tel. (51) 3287-1500; fax (51) 3287-1566; internet www.cgtee.gov.br; f. 1997; became part of Eletrobras in 2000; generation and transmission; Pres. VALTER LUIZ CARDEAL DE SOUZA; Exec. Dir SERENO CHAISE.

Eletrobras Chesf (Companhia Hidro Eléctrica do São Francisco): 333 Bongi, Rua Delmiro Golveia, 50761-901 Recife, PE; tel. (81) 3229-2000; fax (81) 3229-2390; e-mail chesf@chesf.com.br; internet www.chesf.gov.br; f. 1948; generation and transmission; Pres. ARMANDO CASADO DE ARAÚJO; Exec. Dir ANTÔNIO VAREJÃO DE GODOY.

Eletrobras Distribuição Acre (ELETROACRE): Rua Valério Magalhães 226, Bairro do Bosque, 69909-710 Rio Branco, AC; tel. (68) 3212-5700; fax (68) 3223-1142; e-mail ouvidoria@eletroacre .com.br; internet www.eletroacre.com.br; f. 1965; distribution; Exec. Dir JOAQUIM CALDAS ROLIM DE OLIVEIRA.

Eletrobras Distribuição Alagoas (CEAL): Av. Fernandes Lima 3349, Gruta de Lourdes, 57057-900 Maceió, AL; tel. (82) 2126-9247; fax (82) 2126-9326; e-mail ape@ceal.com.br; internet www .ceal.com.br; f. 1961; electricity distribution; Exec. Dir CÍCERO VLADIMIR DE ABREU.

Eletrobras Distribuição Piauí (CEPISA): Av. Maranhão 759, Sul, 64001-010 Teresina, PI; tel. (86) 3228-8000; internet www .cepisa.com.br; f. 1962, bought by Eletrobras in 1997; distribution; Exec. Dir MARCELINO DA CUNHA MACHADO NETO.

Eletrobras Distribuição Rondônia, SA (CERON): Av. Imigrantes 4137, Industrial, 76821-063 Porto Velho, RO; tel. (69) 3216-4000; internet www.ceron.com.br; f. 1968; distribution; Exec. Dir LUIZ MARCELO REIS DE CARVALHO.

Eletrobras Distribuição Roraima (Boa Vista Energia): Av. Capitão Ene Garcêz 691, Centro, 69310-160 Boa Vista, RR; tel. (95) 2621-1400; e-mail frvcarvalho@boavistaenergia.gov.br; internet www.boavistaenergia.gov.br; f. 1997; distribution; Exec. Dir ANTONIO PERREIRA CARRAMILO NETO.

Eletrobras Eletronorte: SCN, Quadra 6, Conj. A, Blocos B e C, Entrada Norte 2, Asa Norte, 70716-901 Brasília, DF; tel. (61) 3429-5151; fax (61) 3328-1463; e-mail ouvidoria@eln.gov.br; internet www.eln.gov.br; f. 1973; generation and transmission; serves Amapá, Acre, Amazonas, Maranhão, Mato Grosso, Pará, Rondônia, Roraima and Tocantins; Pres. JOSÉ ANTONIO MUNIZ LOPES; Exec. Dir TITO CARDOSO DE OLIVEIRA NETO.

Eletrobras Eletronuclear: Rua da Candelária 65, Centro, 20091-906 Rio de Janeiro, RJ; tel. (21) 2588-7000; fax (21) 2588-7200; internet www.eletronuclear.gov.br; f. 1997 by merger of the nuclear br. of Furnas with Nuclebrás Engenharia (NUCLEN); operates 2 nuclear facilities, Angra I, II and III; Exec. Dir OTHON LUIZ PINHEIRO DA SILVA.

Eletrobras Eletrosul: Rua Deputado Antônio Edu Vieira 999, Pantanal, 88040-901 Florianópolis, SC; tel. (48) 3231-7000; fax (48) 3234-4040; internet www.eletrosul.gov.br; f. 1968; generation and transmission; Pres. VALTER LUIZ CARDEAL DE SOUZA; Exec. Dir EURIDES LUIZ MESCOLOTTO.

Eletrobras Furnas: Rua Real Grandeza 219, Bloco A, 16° andar, Botafogo, 22281-900 Rio de Janeiro, RJ; tel. (21) 2528-3112; fax (21) 2528-5858; e-mail webfurnas@furnas.com.br; internet www .furnas.com.br; f. 1957; generation and transmission; Pres. JOSÉ DA COSTA CARVALHO NETO; Exec. Dir FLAVIO DECAT DE MOURA.

Companhia de Eletricidade do Estado da Bahia (COELBA): Av. Edgard Santos 300, 300 Narandiba, 41186-900 Salvador, BA; tel. (71) 3370-5130; fax (71) 3370-5135; internet www.coelba.com.br; f. 1960; Pres. MARCO GEOVANNE TOBIAS DA SILVA; Exec. Dir MOISÉS AFONSO SALES FILHO.

Companhia Energética de Brasília (CEB): SIA/SAPS, Trecho 01, Lotes C, Asa Sul, 71215-000 Brasília, DF; tel. (61) 3363-4011; fax (61) 3363-2657; e-mail info@ceb.com.br; internet www.ceb.com.br; generation and distribution of electricity in Distrito Federal; also operates gas distribution co CEBGAS; Pres. and CEO RUBEM FONSECA FILHO.

Companhia Energética do Ceará (COELCE): Rua Padre Valdevino 150, 1° andar, Joaquim Távora, 60135-040 Fortaleza, CE; tel. (85) 3247-1444; fax (85) 3216-4088; e-mail gercom@coelce.com.br; internet www.coelce.com.br; f. 1971; part of Endesa (Spain); Pres. MÁRIO FERNANDO DE MELO SANTOS.

Companhia Energética do Maranhão (CEMAR): Alameda A, SQS, Quadra 100, Loteamento Quitandinha, Altos do Calhau. 65071-680 São Luís, MA; tel. (98) 3217-8000; fax (98) 3321-7161; e-mail corporativo@cemar-ma.com.br; internet www.cemar-ma.com.br; f. 1958 as Centrais Elétricas do Maranhão; changed name as above in 1984; owned by PPL Global, Inc (USA); Pres. AUGUSTO MIRANDA DA PAZ JÚNIOR.

Companhia Energética de Minas Gerais (CEMIG): Av. Barbacena 1200, 5° andar, Ala B1, Bairro Santo Agostinho, 30161-970 Belo Horizonte, MG; tel. (31) 3299-4900; fax (31) 3299-3700; e-mail atendimento@cemig.com.br; internet www.cemig.com.br; f. 1952; 51% state-owned, 33% owned by Southern Electric Brasil Partipações, Ltda; Exec. Dir DJALMA BASTOS DE MORAIS.

Companhia Energética de Pernambuco (CELPE): Av. João de Barros 111, Sala 301, Boa Vista, 50050-902 Recife, PE; tel. (81) 3217-5168; e-mail rodrigo.carvalho@celpe.com.br; internet www.celpe.com.br; Pres. JOILSON RODRIGUES FERREIRA; Exec. Dir LUIZ ANTÔNIO CIARLINI.

Companhia Energética de São Paulo (CESP): Av. Nossa Senhora do Sabará 5312, Bairro Pedreira, 04447-011 São Paulo, SP; tel. (11) 5613-2100; fax (11) 3262-5545; e-mail inform@cesp.com.br; internet www.cesp.com.br; f. 1966; Pres. MARCO ANTONIO MROZ; Exec. Dir VILSON DANIEL CHRISTOFARI.

Companhia Paranaense de Energia (COPEL): Rua Coronel Dulcídio 800, 80420-170 Curitiba, PR; tel. (41) 3331-5050; fax (41) 3331-4376; e-mail copel@copel.com; internet www.copel.com; f. 1954; Pres. LÉO DE ALMEIDA NEVES; Exec. Dir LINDOLFO ZIMMER.

Eletropaulo Metropolitana Eletricidade de São Paulo, SA (AES Eletropaulo): Av. Lourenço Marques 158, 3° andar, Vila Olímpia, 04547-100 São Paulo, SP; tel. (11) 2195-2000; fax (11) 2195-2511; e-mail administracao@eletropaulo.com.br; internet www.aeseletropaulo.com.br; f. 1899; acquired by AES in 2001; Pres. VINCENT WINSLOW MATHIS; Exec. Dir BRITALDO PEDROSA SOARES.

Energisa Minas Gerais: Praça Rui Barbosa 80, Centro, 36770-901 Cataguases, MG; tel. (32) 3429-6000; fax (32) 3429-6317; e-mail secretaria@energisa.com.br; internet www.minasgerais.energisa.com.br; f. 1905 as Companhia Força e Luz Cataguazes-Leopoldina, adopted present name in 2008; subsidiary of Grupo Energisa, SA; Pres. IVAN MÜLLER BOTELHO; Exec. Dir RICARDO PERÉZ BOTELHO.

Espírito Santo Centrais Elétricas, SA (EDP Escelsa): Rua José Alexandre Buaiz 160, 8° andar, Enseada do Suá, 29050-955 Vitória, ES; tel. (27) 3321-9000; fax (27) 3322-9109; e-mail escelsa@enbr.com.br; internet www.escelsa.com.br; f. 1968; subsidiary of EDB; Pres. ANA MARÍA MACHADO FERNANDES; Exec. Dir MIGUEL NUNO FERREIRA SETAS.

Indústrias Nucleares do Brasil, SA (INB): Av. João Cabral de Mello Netto 400, 101 a 304 Barra da Tijuca, 22775-057 Rio de Janeiro, RJ; tel. (21) 3797-1600; fax (21) 3793-1757; e-mail inbrio@inb.gov.br; internet www.inb.gov.br; f. 1988; Pres. AQUILINO SENRA MARTINEZ.

Itaipu Binacional: Av. Tancredo Neves 6731, 85866-900 Foz de Iguaçu, PR; tel. (45) 3520-5252; fax (45) 3520-3015; e-mail itaipu@itaipu.gov.br; internet www.itaipu.gov.br; f. 1974; hydroelectric power station on Brazilian–Paraguayan border; jtly owned by Brazil and Paraguay; 98,630 GWh produced in 2013; Dir-Gen. (Brazil) JORGE MIGUEL SAMEK; Dir-Gen. (Paraguay) JAMES EDWARD CLIFTON SPALDING HELLMERS.

LIGHT—Serviços de Eletricidade, SA: Av. Marechal Floriano 168, CP 0571, 20080-002 Rio de Janeiro, RJ; tel. (21) 2211-7171; fax (21) 2233-1249; e-mail light@lightrio.com.br; internet www.lightrio.com.br; f. 1905; electricity generation and distribution in Rio de Janeiro; fmrly state-owned, sold in 1996; 79.4% owned by Rio Minas Energia Participacoes, SA (RME), 10% by EDF (France); generating capacity of 850 MW; Pres. SÉRGIO ALAIR BARROSO; Exec. Dir PAULO ROBERTO RIBEIRO PINTO.

Gas

Ceg Rio Gas Natural Fenosa: Av. Pedro II 68, Prédio 24, São Cristóvão, 20941-070 Rio de Janeiro, RJ; tel. (21) 3115-6565; fax (21) 2585-7070; internet www.ceg.com.br; f. 1969, privatized in 1997; fmrly Companhia Distribuidora de Gás do Rio de Janeiro; adopted present name in 2011; Pres. SERGIO ARANDA MORENO; Exec. Dir BRUNO ARMBRUST.

Companhia de Gás de Alagoas, SA (ALGÁS): Rua Artur Vital da Silva, 04, Gruta de Lourdes, 57052-790 Maceió, AL; tel. (82) 3218-7767; fax (82) 3218-7742; e-mail algas@algas.com.br; internet www.algas.com.br; 51% state-owned; Pres. IÁSNAIA POLIANA LEMOS SANTANA; Exec. Dir GEOBERTO ESPÍRITO SANTO.

Companhia de Gás de Bahia (BAHIAGÁS): Av. Tancredo Neves 450, Edif. Suarez Trade, 20° andar, Caminho das Arvores, 41820-901 Salvador, BA; tel. (71) 3206-6000; fax (71) 3206-6001; e-mail atendimento@bahiagas.com.br; internet www.bahiagas.com.br; f. 1991; 51% state-owned; Exec. Dir LUIZ RAIMUNDO BARREIROS GAVAZZA.

Companhia de Gás do Ceará (CEGÁS): Edif. Empresarial Iguatemi, 11° andar, Av. Washington Soares 55, Bairro Cocó, 60811-341 Fortaleza, CE; tel. (85) 3266-6900; fax (85) 3265-2026; e-mail ouvidoria@cegas.com.br; internet www.cegas.com.br; 51% owned by the state of Amazonas; Exec. Dir ANTONIO ELBANO CAMBRAIA.

Companhia de Gás de Minas Gerais (GASMIG): Av. do Contorno 6594, 10° andar, Lourdes, 30110-044 Belo Horizonte, MG; tel. (31) 3265-1000; fax (31) 3265-1100; e-mail gasmig@gasmig.com.br; internet www.gasmig.com.br; Exec. Dir JOSÉ CARLOS DE MATTOS.

Companhia de Gás de Pernambuco (COPERGÁS): Av. Mal. Mascarenhas de Morais 533, Imbiribeira, 51150-904 Recife, PE; tel. (81) 3184-2000; e-mail copergas@copergas.com.br; internet www.copergas.com.br; 51% state-owned; Exec. Dir ALDO GUEDES.

Companhia de Gás do Rio Grande do Sul (SULGÁS): Edif. Santa Cruz, 5° andar, Rua 7 de Setembro 1069, Centro, 90010-190 Porto Alegre, RS; tel. (51) 3287-2200; fax (51) 3287-2205; internet www.sulgas.rs.gov.br; f. 1993; 51% state-owned; 49% owned by Petrobras; Pres. JOÃO LUIS DE MATOS; Exec. Dir ROBERTO DA SILVA TEJADAS.

Companhia de Gás de Santa Catarina (SCGÁS): Rua Antônia Luz 255, Centro Empresarial Hoepcke, 88010-410 Florianópolis, SC; tel. (48) 3229-1200; fax (48) 3229-1230; internet www.scgas.com.br; f. 1994; 51% state-owned; Exec. Dir COSME POLÊSE.

Companhia de Gás de São Paulo (COMGÁS): Av. Pres. Juscelino Kubitschek 1327, 14° andar, Vila Nova Conceição, 04543-011 São Paulo, SP; tel. (11) 4504-5000; fax (11) 4504-5027; e-mail investidores@comgas.com.br; internet www.comgas.com.br; f. 1872; owned by Cosan Group and Royal Dutch Shell Group; Chair. RUBENS OMETTO SILVEIRA MELLO; Exec. Dir LUIS HENRIQUE GUIMARÃES.

Companhia Paraibana de Gás (PBGÁS): Av. Presidente Epitácio Pessoa 4756, Cabo Branco, 58045-000 João Pessoa, PB; tel. (83) 3219–1700; fax (83) 3247-2244; e-mail cicero@pbgas.com.br; internet www.pbgas.com.br; f. 1995; 51% state-owned; Exec. Dir GEORGE VENTURA MORAIS.

Companhia Paranaense de Gás (COMPAGÁS): Rua Hasdrúbal Bellegard 1177, Cidade Industrial, 81460-120 Curitiba, PR; tel. (41) 3312-1900; fax (41) 3312-1922; e-mail compagas@compagas.com.br; internet www.compagas.com.br; f. 1998; 51.0% owned by Copel Participaçoes, SA, 24.5% by Gaspetro and 24.5% by Mitsui Gás e Energia do Brasil; Exec. Dir LUCIANO PIZZATTO.

Companhia Potiguar de Gás (POTIGÁS): Av. Brancas Dunas 485, Lojas 1 e 2, Salas 101 a 106, Candelária, 59064-720 Natal, RN; tel. (84) 3204-8500; fax (84) 3206-8504; e-mail mauricio@potigas.com.br; internet www.potigas.com.br; 17% state-owned; Pres. CARLOS AUGUSTO DE ROSADO; Exec. Dir FRANCISCO ISALTINO GUEDES DO REGO.

Companhia Rondoniense de Gás, SA (RONGÁS): Av. Carlos Gomes 1223, Sala 403, 4° andar, Centro, 76801-123 Porto Velho, RO; tel. and fax (69) 3229-0333; e-mail rongas@rongas.com.br; internet www.rongas.com.br; f. 1997; 17% state-owned; Exec. Dir MARIA AUXILIADORA DE OLIVEIRA SILVA.

Empresa Sergipana de Gás, SA (EMSERGÁS): Av. Heráclito Rollemberg 2482, Conj. Augusto Franco, Bairro Farolândia, 49030-640 Aracaju, SE; tel. (79) 3243-8500; fax (79) 3243-8508; e-mail emsergas@infonet.com.br; internet www.sergipegas.com.br; f. 1993; 51% state-owned; Exec. Dir MAURÍCIO ARAÚJO RAMOS.

Water

Águas e Esgotos do Piauí (AGESPISA): Av. Marechal Castelo Branco 101, Norte, Cabral, 64000-810 Teresina, PI; tel. (86) 3216-6300; fax (86) 3216-8182; e-mail marcosvenicius@agespisa.com.br; internet www.agespisa.com.br; f. 1962; state-owned; Exec. Dir JOSÉ AUGUSTO NUNES.

Companhia de Agua e Esgosto de Ceará (CAGECE): Av. Dr Lauro Vieira Chaves 1030, Vila União, 60420-280 Fortaleza, CE; tel.

(85) 3101-1805; fax (85) 3101-1834; e-mail asimp-cagece@cagece.com
.br; internet www.cagece.com.br; f. 1971; state-owned; Pres. CARLO
FERRENTINI SAMPAIO; Exec. Dir ANDRÉ MACÊDO FACÓ.

Companhia Algoas Industrial (CINAL): Rodovia Divaldo Sur-
uagy, BR 424, Km 12, 57160-000 Marechal Deodoro, AL; tel. (82)
3218-2500; fax (82) 3269-1199; e-mail airton@cinal.com.br; internet
www.cinal.com.br; f. 1982; Pres. ROBERTO PRISCO PARAÍSO RAMOS;
Exec. Dir FRANCISCO CARLOS RUGA.

Companhia Espírito Santense de Saneamento (CESAN): Av.
Governador Bley 186, Edif. BEMGE, 3° andar, Centro, 29010-150
Vitória, ES; tel. (27) 2127-5353; fax (27) 2127-5000; e-mail
comunica@cesan.com.br; internet www.cesan.com.br; f. 1968; state-
owned; Exec. Dir PAULO RUY VALIM CARNELLI.

Companhia Estadual de Aguas e Esgotos (CEDAE): Rua Saca-
dura Cabral 103, 9° andar, 20081-260 Rio de Janeiro, RJ; tel. (21)
2332-3600; fax (21) 2296-0416; internet www.cedae.com.br; f. 1975;
state-owned; Pres. LEONARDO ESPÍNDOLA DÍAS; Exec. Dir WAGNER
GRANJA VICTER.

Companhia Pernambucana de Saneamento (COMPESA): Rua
da Aurora 777, Boa Vista, 50040-905 Recife, PE; tel. (81) 3412-9693;
fax (81) 3412-9181; internet www.compesa.com.br; state-owned;
Exec. Dir ROBERTO CAVALCANTI TAVARES.

Companhia Riograndense de Saneamento (CORSAN): Rua
Caldas Júnior 120, 18° andar, 90010-260 Porto Alegre, RS; tel. (51)
3215-5600; e-mail ascom@corsan.com.br; internet www.corsan.com
.br; f. 1965; state-owned; Exec. Dir ARNALDO DUTRA.

**Companhia de Saneamento Básico do Estado de São Paulo
(SABESP):** Rua Costa Carvalho 300, Pinheiros, 05429-000 São
Paulo, SP; tel. (11) 3388-8200; fax (11) 3813-0254; internet www
.sabesp.com.br; f. 1973; state-owned; Pres. MAURO GUILHERME
JARDIM ARCE; Exec. Dir DILMA SELI PENA.

TRADE UNIONS

Central Unica dos Trabalhadores (CUT): Rua Caetano Pinto
575, Brás, 03041-000 São Paulo, SP; tel. (11) 2108-9200; fax (11)
2108-9310; e-mail duvaier@cut.org.br; internet www.cut.org.br;
f. 1983; central union confederation; left-wing; 3.5m. mems; Pres.
VAGNER FREITAS DE MORAES; Gen. Sec. SÉRGIO NOBRE.

Confederação Nacional dos Metalúrgicos (Metal Workers): Av.
Antártico, 480-Jardim do Mar, São Bernardo do Campo, 09726-150
São Paulo, SP; tel. (11) 4122-7700; fax (11) 3523-1449; e-mail
cnmcut@cnmcut.org.br; internet www.cnmcut.org.br; f. 1992; Pres.
PAULO CAYRES; Gen. Sec. JOÃO CAYRES.

Confederação Nacional das Profissões Liberais (CNPL) (Liberal Professions): SCS, Quadra 02, Bloco D, Edif. Oscar Niemeyer, 9°
andar, 70316-900 Brasília, DF; tel. (61) 2103-1683; fax (61) 2103-
1684; e-mail secretaria@cnpl.org.br; internet www.cnpl.org.br;
f. 1953; 260,000 mems (2007); Pres. CARLOS ALBERTO SCHMITT DE
AZEVEDO; Sec.-Gen. JOSÉ ALBERTO ROSSI.

**Confederação Nacional dos Trabalhadores na Indústria
(CNTI)** (Industrial Workers): SEP/NORTE, Quadra 505, Conj. A,
70730-540 Brasília, DF; tel. (61) 3448-9900; fax (61) 3448-9956;
e-mail cnti@cnti.org.br; internet www.cnti.org.br; f. 1946; Pres.
JOSÉ CALIXTO RAMOS; Sec.-Gen. APRÍGIO GUIMARÃES.

**Confederação Nacional dos Trabalhadores no Comércio
(CNTC)** (Commercial Workers): Av. W/5 Sul, SGAS Quadra 902,
Bloco C, 70390-020 Brasília, DF; tel. (61) 3217-7100; fax (61) 3217-
7122; e-mail cntc@cntc.org.br; internet www.cntc.com.br; f. 1946;
Pres. LEVI FERNANDES PINTO.

**Confederação Nacional dos Trabalhadores em Transportes
Aquaviários e Aéreos, na Pesca e nos Portos (CONTTMAF)**
(Maritime, River and Air Transport Workers): SDS, Edif. Venâncio
V, Grupos 501/503, 70393-900 Brasília, DF; tel. (61) 3226-5263; fax
(61) 3322-6383; e-mail conttmaf@conttmaf.org.br; internet www
.conttmaf.org.br; f. 1957; Pres. SEVERINO ALMEIDA FILHO; Sec.-Gen.
ODILON DOS SANTOS BRAGA.

**Confederação Nacional dos Trabalhadores em Comunica-
ções e Publicidade (CONTCOP)** (Communications and Advertising Workers): SCS, Quadra 02, Edif. Serra Dourada, Sala 705–709,
70300-902 Brasília, DF; tel. (61) 3224-7926; fax (61) 3224-5686;
e-mail faleconosco@contcop.org.br; internet www.contcop.org.br;
f. 1964; 350,000 mems; Pres. ANTÔNIO MARIA THAUMATURGO CORTIZO;
Sec.-Gen. BENEDITO ANTONIO MARCELLO.

**Confederação Nacional dos Trabalhadores nas Empresas de
Crédito (CONTEC)** (Workers in Credit Institutions): SEP-SUL,
Av. W/4, EQ 707/907, Conj. A/B, 70390-078 Brasília, DF; tel. (61)
3244-5833; fax (61) 3224-2743; e-mail contec@contec.org.br; internet
www.contec.org.br; f. 1958; Pres. LOURENÇO FERREIRA DO PRADO; Sec.-
Gen. GILBERTO ANTONIO VIEIRA.

**Confederação Nacional dos Trabalhadores em Estabelec-
imentos de Educação e Cultura (CNTEEC)** (Workers in Education and Culture): SAS, Quadra 04, Bloco B, 70070-908 Brasília, DF;

tel. (61) 3321-4140; fax (61) 3321-2704; internet www.cnteec.org.br;
f. 1966; Pres. MIGUEL ABRÃO NETO.

**Confederação Nacional dos Trabalhadores na Agricultura
(CONTAG)** (Agricultural Workers): SMPW, Quadra 01, Conj. 02,
Lote 02, Núcleo Bandeirante, 71735-102 Brasília, DF; tel. (61) 2102-
2288; fax (61) 2102-2299; e-mail contag@contag.org.br; internet www
.contag.org.br; f. 1964; represents 25 state feds and 3,630 syndicates,
15m. mems; Pres. ALBERTO ERCÍLIO BROCH; Sec.-Gen. DAVID
WYLKERSON RODRIGUES DE SOUZA.

**Federação Nacional dos Trabalhadores em Empresas dos
Correios e Similares (FENTECT)** (Postal Workers): SDS, Edif.
Venâncio V, Bloco R, Loja 60, 70393-900 Brasília, DF; tel. and fax (61)
3323-8810; e-mail fentect@fentect.org.br; internet www.fentect.org
.br; f. 1989; Sec.-Gen. JOSÉ RODRIGUES DOS SANTOS NETO.

Força Sindical (FS): Rua Rocha Pombo, 94 Liberdade, 01525-010
São Paulo, SP; tel. and fax (11) 3348-9000; e-mail secgeral@fsindical
.org.br; internet www.fsindical.org.br; f. 1991; 2.1m. mems (2007);
Pres. PAULO PEREIRA DA SILVA; Sec.-Gen. JOÃO CARLOS GONÇALVES.

União Geral dos Trabalhadores (UGT): Rua Aguiar de Barrios,
144 Bela Vista, 01316-020 São Paulo, SP; tel. (11) 2111-7300; fax (11)
2111-7501; e-mail ugt@ugt.org.br; internet www.ugt.org.br; f. 2007
by merger of Confederação Geral dos Trabalhadores with 2 other
unions; Pres. RICARDO PATAH; Sec.-Gen. FRANCISCO CANINDÉ PEGADO
DO NASCIMENTO.

Transport

Ministry of Transport: see The Government—Ministries.

Agência Nacional de Transportes Terrestres (ANTT): Edif.
Phenícia, SBN, Quadra 02, Bloco C, Lote 17, 70040-020 Brasília, DF;
tel. (61) 3410-8100; fax (61) 3410-1189; e-mail ouvidoria@antt.gov.br;
internet www.antt.gov.br; f. 2002; govt agency; oversees road and
rail infrastructure; Dir-Gen. JORGE LUIZ MACEDO BASTOS.

RAILWAYS

In 2013 there were 30,051 km of railway lines. There were also
railways owned by state governments and several privately owned
railways. Construction of a new high-speed rail link connecting Rio
de Janeiro, São Paulo and Campinas was originally scheduled to
begin in 2010, but this was postponed until 2013. The estimated cost
of the project was R $38,000m. In addition, the first part of a 24-km
urban transit system was scheduled to begin operations in São Paulo
in early 2014, with completion of the monorail system by the end of
2016. Construction of a metro system in Salvador, originally begun in
2000, was finally under way in 2014. In 2012 the federal Government
announced an additional US $63,600m. in expenditure on transport
infrastructure.

América Latina Logística do Brasil, SA (ALL): Rua Emilio
Bertolini 100, Vila Oficinas, Cajuru, Curitiba, PR; tel. (41) 2141-
7555; e-mail caall@all-logistica.com; internet www.all-logistica.com;
f. 1997; 6,586 km in 2003; acquired Ferrovia Novoeste, SA in 2006;
Pres. WILSON FERRO DE LARA; Dir-Gen. PAULO LUIZ ARAÚJO BASÍLIO.

> **Ferrovia Bandeirante, SA (Ferroban):** Av. Paulista 1.499, 17°
> andar, Sala 5, São Paulo, SP; tel. (11) 3138-2048; fax (11) 3138-
> 2054; f. 1971 by merger of five railways operated by São Paulo
> State; transferred to private ownership in 1998; fmrly Ferrovia
> Paulista; 4,236 km open in 2003; Dir JOÃO GOUVEIA FERRÃO NETO.

Associação Brasileira da Indústria Ferroviáia (ABIFER): Av.
Paulista 1313, 8° andar conjunto 801, 01311-923 São Paulo, SP; tel.
(11) 3289-1667; fax (11) 3171-2286; e-mail abifer@abifer.org.br;
internet www.abifer.org.br; f. 1977; rail industry asscn; Pres.
VICENTE ABATE.

**Associação Nacional dos Transportadores Ferroviários
(ANTF):** Edif. CNT, Torre A, 6° andar, Sala 605, Quadra 01, Bloco
J, 70070-010 Brasília, DF; tel. (61) 3226-5434; fax (61) 3221-0135;
e-mail imprensa@antf.org.br; internet www.antf.org.br; promotes
railway devt; 11 mem. cos; Exec. Dir GUSTAVO BAMBINI.

Cia Brasileira de Trens Urbanos (CBTU): Estrada Velha da
Tijuca 77, Usina, 20531-080 Rio de Janeiro, RJ; tel. (21) 2575-3399;
fax (21) 2571-6149; e-mail imprensa@cbtu.gov.br; internet www.cbtu
.gov.br; f. 1984; fmrly responsible for suburban networks and metro
systems throughout Brazil; operates 5 metro systems; Pres. PEDRO
GHERARDI NETO.

> **Metrô BH** (Superintendência de Trens Urbanos de Belo Hori-
> zonte): Rua Janúaria 181m, 31110-060 Belo Horizonte, MG; tel.
> (31) 3250-3900; fax (31) 3250-4053; e-mail decombh@cbtu.gov.br;
> internet www.metrobh.gov.br; f. 1981 as DEMETRÔ; present
> name adopted 2003; operates 3 lines; Supt JOSÉ DÓRIA.

METROREC (Superintendência de Trens Urbanos de Recife):
Rua José Natário 478, Areias, 50900-000 Recife, PE; tel. (81) 2102-
8500; fax (81) 3455-4422; e-mail ouvidoria@metrorec.com.br;

internet www2.cbtumetrorec.gov.br; f. 1985; 71 km open in 2010;
Supt JOSÉ MARQUES DE LIMA.

**Superintendência de Trens Urbanos de João Pessoa (GTU/
JOP):** Praça Napoleão Laureano 1, Varadouro, 58010-040 João
Pessoa, PB; tel. (83) 3241-4240; fax (83) 3241-6388; e-mail
gecomjp@cbtu.gov.br; internet joaopessoa.cbtu.gov.br; 30 km;
Supt LUCÉLIO CARTAXO.

Superintendência de Trens Urbanos de Maceió (STU/MAC):
Rua Barão de Anadia 121, Centro, 57020-630 Maceió, AL; tel. (82)
2123-1700; fax (82) 2123-1445; e-mail orleanes@cbtu.gov.br;
internet www.cbtu.gov.br; f. 1996; 32 km; Supt MARCELO DE
AGUIAR GOMES.

Superintendência de Trens Urbanos de Natal (STU/NAT):
Praça Augusto Severo, 302 Ribeira, 59012-380 Natal, RN; tel. (84)
3221-3355; fax (84) 3211-3546; e-mail stunat@cbtu.gov.br;
internet natal.cbtu.gov.br; f. 1984; 56 km; Supt JOÃO MARIA
CAVALCANTI.

Cia Cearense de Transportes Metropolitanos, SA (Metrofor):
Rua 24 de Maio 60, 60020-001 Fortaleza, CE; tel. (85) 3101-7100; fax
(85) 3101-4744; e-mail metrofor@metrofor.ce.gov.br; internet www
.metrofor.ce.gov.br; f. 1997; 46 km; Pres. RÔMULO DOS SANTOS FORTES.

Cia do Metropolitano de São Paulo: Rua Boa Vista 175, 01014-
001, São Paulo, SP; tel. (11) 3291-7800; fax (11) 3371-7329; e-mail
ouvidoria@metrosp.com.br; internet www.metro.sp.gov.br; f. 1968;
4-line metro system, 61.3 km open in 2007; Dir-Gen. SÉRGIO
HENRIQUE PASSOS AVELLEDA.

Cia Paulista de Trens Metropolitanos (CPTM): Av. Paulista
402, 5° andar, 01310-000 São Paulo, SP; tel. (11) 3371-1530; fax (11)
3285-0323; e-mail usuario@cptm.sp.gov.br; internet www.cptm.sp
.gov.br; f. 1992 to incorporate suburban lines fmrly operated by the
CBTU and FEPASA; 286 km; Pres. Dr JURANDIR FERNANDES; Dir-
Gen. MARIO MANUEL SEABRA RODRIGUES BANDEIRA.

Empresa de Trens Urbanos de Porto Alegre, SA: Av. Ernesto
Neugebauer 1985, 6° andar, Humaitá, 90250-140 Porto Alegre, RS;
tel. (51) 3363-8000; fax (51) 3363-8166; e-mail atendimento@
trensurb.com.br; internet www.trensurb.gov.br; f. 1985; Pres.
ROBERTO DE OLIVEIRA MUNIZ; Dir-Gen. HUMBERTO KASPER.

Estrada de Ferro do Amapá (EFA): Av. Santana 429, Porto de
Santana, 68925-000 Macapá, AP; tel. (96) 281-1845; fax (96) 281-
1175; f. 1957; operated by Indústria e Comércio de Minérios, SA;
194 km open in 2007; Dir Supt JOSÉ LUIZ ORTIZ VERGULINO.

Estrada de Ferro Campos do Jordão: Rua Martin Cabral 87, CP
11, 12400-020 Pindamonhangaba, SP; tel. (12) 3642-3233; fax (12)
242-2499; internet www.efcj.sp.gov.br; f. 1914; operated by the
Tourism Secretariat of the State of São Paulo; Dir SILVIO CAMARGO.

Estrada de Ferro Carajás: Av. Graça Aranha 26, 20030-000 RJ;
tel. (21) 3814-4477; fax (21) 3814-4040; f. 1985 for movement of
minerals from the Serra do Carajás to the port at Ponta da Madeira;
operated by Vale, SA (CVRD); Supt JUARES SALIBRA.

Estrada de Ferro do Jari: Vila Munguba s/n, Monte Dourado,
68230-000 Pará, PA; tel. (91) 3736-6526; fax (91) 3736-6490; e-mail
ascarvalho@jari.com.br; f. 1979; transportation of timber; 70 km
open; Operations Man. PABLO ASSIS GUZZO.

Estrada de Ferro Paraná-Oeste, SA (FERROESTE): Av. Iguaçu
420, 7° andar, Rebouças, 80230-902 Curitiba, PR; tel. (41) 3281-9800;
fax (41) 3233-2147; e-mail ferroest@pr.gov.br; internet www
.ferroeste.pr.gov.br; f. 1988; serves the grain-producing regions in
Paraná and Mato Grosso do Sul; Pres. MAURICIO QUERINO THEODORO.

Estrada de Ferro Vitória-Minas: Av. Aarão Reis 423, Centro, Belo
Horizonte, MG; tel. (31) 273-5976; fax (31) 3279-4676; f. 1942; operated by Vale, SA (CVRD); transport of iron ore, general cargo and
passengers; Dir ALVARO ALBERGARIA.

Ferrovia Centro Atlântica, SA: Rua Sapucaí 383, Floresta 30150-
904, Belo Horizonte, MG; tel. (31) 3279-5323; fax (31) 3279-5709;
e-mail thiers@centro-atlantica.com.br; internet www.fcasa.com.br;
f. 1996 following the privatization of Rede Ferroviária Federal, SA;
owned by Vale, SA (CVRD) since 2003; industrial freight; 8,000 km;
Dir-Gen. MARCELLO SPINELLI.

Ferrovia de Integração Oeste-Leste (FIOL): Av. Soares Lopes,
956 Casa, Centro, 45653-005 Ilhéus, BA; tel. (73) 3231-5769; internet
www.valec.gov.br; 1,527 km from Bahia to Tocantins; Supt NEVILLE
BARBOSA.

Ferrovia Norte-Sul: Av. Marechal Floriano 45, Centro, 20080-003
Rio de Janeiro, RJ; tel. (21) 2291-2185; fax (21) 2263-9119; e-mail
valecascom@ferrovianortesul.com.br; 2,066 km from Belém to
Goiânia; Dir JOSÉ FRANCISCO DAS NEVES.

Ferrovia Tereza Cristina, SA (FTC): Rua dos Ferroviários 100,
Bairro Oficinas, 88702-230 Tubarão, SC; tel. (48) 3621-7724; fax (48)
3621-7747; e-mail comunicacao@ftc.com.br; internet www.ftc.com
.br; 164 km in 2007; Man. Dir BENONY SCHMITZ FILHO.

Metrô-DF (Cia do Metropolitano do Distrito Federal): Av. Jequitibá,
lote 155, Águas Claras, 71929-540 Brasília, DF; tel. (61) 3353-7373;

fax (61) 3352-1472; e-mail atendimentoaousuario@metro.df.gov.br;
internet www.metro.df.gov.br; f. 1991; Pres. IVELISE MARIA LONGHI
PEREIRA DA SILVA.

Metrô Rio: Av. Presidente Vargas 2000, Col. Centro, 20210-031 Rio
de Janeiro, RJ; tel. (21) 3211-6300; e-mail sac@metrorio.com.br;
internet www.metrorio.com.br; 2-line metro system; operated by
Opportans Concessão Metroviária, SA.

MRS Logística, SA: Praia de Botafogo 228, Sala 1201E, Ala B,
Botafogo, 22359-900 Rio de Janeiro, RJ; tel. (21) 2559-4610; e-mail
daf@mrs.com.br; internet www.mrs.com.br; f. 1996; CEO EDUARDO
PARENTE.

SuperVia, SA: Rua da América 210, Santo Cristo, 20220-590 Rio de
Janeiro, RJ; tel. (21) 2111-9646; internet www.supervia.com.br;
f. 1998; operates commuter trains in Rio de Janeiro; Pres. CARLOS
JOSÉ CUNHA.

Transnordestina Logística, SA: Av. Francisco de Sá 4829, Bairro
Carlito Pamplona, 60310-002 Fortaleza, CE; tel. (85) 4008-2500; fax
(85) 4008-2525; e-mail kerley@cfn.com.br; internet www.cfn.com.br;
fmrly Cia Ferroviária do Nordeste; changed name as above in 2008;
subsidiary of Grupo CSN (Cia Siderúrgica Nacional); 4,534 km in
2003; Dir-Gen. TUFI DAHER FILHO.

Transporte Urbano do Distrito Federal (DFTRANS): SAIN,
Estação Rodoferroviária, Ala Sul, Sobreloja, 70631-900 Brasília, DF;
tel. (61) 3043-0401; e-mail ouvidoriadftrans@yahoo.com.br; internet
www.dftrans.df.gov.br; the first section of the Brasília metro, linking
the capital with the western suburb of Samambaia, was inaugurated
in 1994; Dir MARCO ANTONIO CAMPANELLA.

ROADS

In 2010 there were 1,580,964 km of roads in Brazil, of which 13.5%
were paved. Of the total, 99,220 km were part of the national road
network and 219,999 km formed the regional road network. Brasília
has been a focal point for inter-regional development, and paved
roads link the capital with every region of Brazil. Major projects
include the Interportos Highway, linking the ports of Paraná,
Paranaguá, Antonina and the future port terminals of Pontal and
Emboguaçu. A 3.5-km bridge linking Manaus with Iranduba over the
Rio Negro, a tributary of the Amazon, was inaugurated in 2011. In
the same year a 2,600-km road, linking Rio Branco, the capital of
Acre, with Nazca on the coast of Peru, was opened.

**Departamento Nacional de Infra-Estrutura de Transportes
(DNIT)** (National Roads Development): Edif. Núcleo dos Transportes, SAN, Quadra 3, Bloco A, Lote A, 70040-902 Brasília, DF;
tel. (61) 3315-4000; fax (61) 3315-4050; e-mail diretoria.geral@dnit
.gov.br; internet www.dnit.gov.br; f. 1945 to plan and execute federal
road policy and to supervise state and municipal roads in order to
integrate them into the national network; Dir-Gen. JORGE ERNESTO
PINTO FRAXE; Exec. Dir TARCÍSIO GOMES DE FREITAS.

INLAND WATERWAYS

River transport plays only a minor part in the movement of goods.
There are three major river systems, the Amazon, the Paraná and the
São Francisco, with a total of 28,000 km of waterways. The Amazon is
navigable for 3,680 km, as far as Iquitos in Peru, and ocean-going
ships can reach Manaus, 1,600 km upstream.

Agência Nacional de Transportes Aquaviários (ANTAQ): Edif.
ANTAQ, SEPN, Quadra 514, Conj. E, 70760-545 Brasília, DF; tel.
(61) 2029-6500; fax (61) 3447-1040; e-mail asc@antaq.gov.br;
internet www.antaq.gov.br; Dir-Gen. FERNANDO ANTÔNIO BRITO
FIALHO.

**Administração das Hidrovias da Amazônia Ocidental (AHI-
MOC):** Rua Marquês de Santa Cruz 264, Centro, 69005-050 Manaus,
AM; tel. (92) 3633-3061; fax (92) 3232-5156; e-mail ahimoc@ahimoc
.com.br; internet www.ahimoc.com.br; Supt SEBASTIÃO DA SILVA REIS.

**Administração das Hidrovias da Amazônia Oriental (AHI-
MOR):** Rua Joaquim Nabuco 8, Nazaré, 66055-300 Belém, PA; tel.
(91) 3039-7700; fax (91) 3039-7721; e-mail ahimor@ahimor.gov.br;
internet www.ahimor.gov.br; Supt ALBERTINO DE OLIVEIRA E SILVA.

Administração das Hidrovias do Nordeste (AHINOR): Rua da
Paz 561, Centro, 65020-450 São Luiz, MA; tel. and fax (98) 3231-5122;
fax (98) 3232-6707; e-mail ahinor@elo.com.br; internet www.ahinor
.gov.br; Pres. JOSÉ OSCAR FRAZÃO FROTA.

Administração da Hidrovia do Paraguai (AHIPAR): Rua Treze
de Junho 960, 79300-040 Corumbá, MS; tel. (67) 3234-3200; fax (67)
3231-2661; internet www.ahipar.gov.br; Supt ANTÔNIO PAULO DE
BARROS LEITE.

Administração da Hidrovia do Paraná (AHRANA): Av. Brig.
Faria Lima 1912, 16° andar, Jardim Paulistano, 01451-000 São
Paulo, SP; tel. (11) 2106-1600; fax (11) 3815-5435; e-mail ahrana@
ahrana.gov.br; internet www.ahrana.gov.br; Supt ANTONIO BADIH
CHENIN.

Administração da Hidrovia do São Francisco (AHSFRA):
Praça do Porto 70, Distrito Industrial, 39270-000 Pirapora, MG;

tel. (38) 3741-2555; fax (38) 3741-3046; e-mail superint@ahsfra.gov
.br; internet www.ahsfra.gov.br; Supt SEBASTIÃO JOSÉ MARQUES DE
OLIVEIRA.

Administração das Hidrovias do Sul (AHSUL): Praça Oswaldo
Cruz 15, 3° andar, Sala 311–314, 90030-160 Porto Alegre, RS; tel. (51)
3225-0700; fax (51) 3226-9068; e-mail ahsul@uol.com.br; internet
www.ahsul.com.br; Supt JOSÉ LUIZ FAY DE AZAMBUJA.

**Administração das Hidrovias do Tocantins e Araguaia (AHI-
TAR):** ACSE Conj. 02, Lote 33, 1° andar, Sala 02, 77020-024 Palmas,
TO; tel. (62) 3215-3171; fax (62) 3213-1904; e-mail ahitar@terra.com
.br; internet www.ahitar.gov.br; Supt TARLES JUNQUEIRA CALEMAN.

SHIPPING

There are more than 40 deep-water ports in Brazil, all but one of
which (Imbituba) are directly or indirectly administered by the
Government. The majority of ports are operated by state-owned
concerns (Cia Docas do Pará, Estado de Ceará, Estado do Rio Grande
do Norte, Bahia, Paraíba, Espírito Santo, Rio de Janeiro and Estado
de São Paulo), while a smaller number (including Suape, Cabedelo,
São Sebastião, Paranaguá, Antonina, São Francisco do Sul, Porto
Alegre, Itajaí, Pelotas and Rio Grande) are administered by state
governments. The Government was seeking some US $26,000m.
investment in the ports in 2013 in order to improve efficiency and
upgrade facilities.

The ports of Santos, Rio de Janeiro and Rio Grande have specialized container terminals handling more than 1,200,000 TEUs (20-ft
equivalent units of containerized cargo) per year. Santos is the major
container port in Brazil, accounting for 800,000 TEUs annually. The
ports of Paranaguá, Itajaí, São Francisco do Sul, Salvador, Vitória
and Imbituba cater for containerized cargo to a lesser extent.

Brazil's flag registered fleet comprised 823 vessels in 2013, with a
combined aggregate displacement of some 3,156,535 grt.

Departamento de Marinha Mercante: Coordenação Geral de
Transporte Maritimo, Av. Rio Branco 103, 6° e 8° andar, 20040-004
Rio de Janeiro, RJ; tel. (21) 2221-4014; fax (21) 2221-5929; Dir
DÉBORA TEIXEIRA.

Secretariat of Ports: see The Government—Ministries.

Port Authorities

Administração do Porto de Manaus (SNPH): Rua Marquês de
Santa Cruz 25, Centro, 69005-050 Manaus, AM; tel. (92) 2123-4350;
fax (92) 2123-4358; e-mail falecom@portodemanaus.com.br; internet
www.portodemanaus.com.br; private; operates the port of Manaus;
Dir ALESSANDRO BRONZE.

Administração dos Portos de Paranaguá e Antonina (APPA):
Av. Conde Matarazzo 2500, 83370-000 Antonina, PR; Av. Ayrton
Senna da Silva 161D, Pedro II, 83203-800 Paranaguá, PR; tel. (41)
3420-1100; fax (41) 3423-4252; e-mail superintendencia@appa.pr
.gov.br; internet www.portosdoparana.pr.gov.br; Supt AIRTON VIDAL
MARON.

Administração do Porto de São Francisco do Sul (APSFS): Av.
Eng. Leite Ribeiro 782, CP 71, 89240-000 São Francisco do Sul, SC;
tel. (47) 3471-1200; fax (47) 3471-1211; e-mail porto@apsfs.sc.gov.br;
internet www.apsfs.sc.gov.br; Pres. PAULO CÉSAR CORTES CORSI.

Cia Docas do Espírito Santo (CODESA): Av. Getúlio Vargas 556,
Centro, 29010-945 Vitória, ES; tel. (27) 3132-7360; fax (27) 3132-
7311; e-mail dirpre@codesa.gov.br; internet www.portodevitoria
.com.br; f. 1983; Dir-Gen. CLOVIS LASCOSQUE.

Cia das Docas do Estado de Bahia (CODEBA): Av. da França
1551, Comércio, 40010-000 Salvador, BA; tel. (71) 3320-1100; fax (71)
3320-1375; e-mail business@codeba.com.br; internet www.codeba
.com.br; f. 1977; port authority of state of Bahia and administers the
ports of Salvador, Aratu and Ilhéus; CEO JOSÉ MUNIZ REBOUÇAS.

Cia Docas do Estado de Ceará (CDC): Praça Amigos da Marinha
s/n, Mucuripe, 60182-640 Fortaleza, CE; tel. (85) 3266-8800; internet
www.docasdoceara.com.br; administers the port of Fortaleza; Dir-
Gen. PAULO ANDRÉ DE CASTRO HOLANDA.

Cia Docas do Estado de São Paulo (CODESP): Av. Conselheiro
Rodrigues Alves s/n, Macuco, 11015-900 Santos, SP; tel. (13) 3202-
6565; fax (13) 3202-6411; internet www.portodesantos.com; admin-
isters the ports of Santos, Charqueadas, Estrela, Cáceres and
Corumbá/Ladário, and the waterways of Paraná (AHRANA),
Paraguai (AHIPAR) and the South (AHSUL); Dir-Gen. JOSÉ ROBERTO
CORREIA SERRA.

Cia Docas de Imbituba (CDI): Av. Presidente Vargas 100, CP 01,
88780-000 Imbituba, SC; tel. (48) 3355-8900; fax (48) 3255-0701;
e-mail docas@cdiport.com.br; internet www.cdiport.com.br; private
sector concession; Pres. NILTON GARCIA DE ARAUJO; Port Administrator JEZIEL PAMATO DE SOUZA.

Cia Docas do Pará (CDP): Av. Presidente Vargas 41, 2° andar,
Centro, 66010-000 Belém, PA; tel. (91) 3182-9029; fax (91) 3182-9139;
e-mail asscom@cdp.com.br; internet www.cdp.com.br; f. 1967;
administers the ports of Belém, Miramar, Santarém Obidos,

Altamira, São Francisco, Marabá and Vila do Conde; Dir-Gen.
CARLOS J. PONCIANO DA SILVA.

Cia Docas da Paraíba (DOCAS-PB): Porto de Cabedelo, Rua
Presidente João Pessoa s/n, Centro, 58310-000 Cabedelo, PB; tel. (83)
3250-3000; fax (83) 3250-3001; e-mail gvp@docaspb.com.br; internet
www.docaspb.com.br; administers the port of Cabedelo; Dir-Gen.
WILBUR JÁCOME.

Cia Docas do Rio de Janeiro (CDRJ): Rua do Acre 21, Centro,
20081-000 Rio de Janeiro, RJ; tel. (21) 2219-8617; fax (21) 2253-0528;
e-mail aleconosco@portosrio.gov.br; internet www.portosrio.gov.br;
administers the ports of Rio de Janeiro, Niterói, Itaguaí and Angra
dos Reis; Dir-Gen. JORGE LUZ DE MELLO.

Cia Docas do Rio Grande do Norte (CODERN): Av. Hildebrando
de Góis 220, Ribeira, 59010-700 Natal, RN; tel. (84) 4005-5311; e-mail
administrativo@codern.com.br; internet www.codern.com.br;
administers the ports of Areia Branca, Natal and Maceió; Dir-Gen.
PEDRO TERCEIRO DE MELO.

Empresa Maranhense de Administração Portuária (EMAP):
Av. dos Portugueses s/n, Itaquí, 65085-370 São Luís, MA; tel. (98)
3216-6000; fax (98) 3216-6060; e-mail csl@emap.ma.gov.br; internet
www.emap.ma.gov.br; f. 2001 to administer port of Itaquí as
concession from the state of Maranhão; Pres. LUIZ CARLOS FOSSATI.

**Sociedade de Portos e Hidrovias do Estado de Rondônia
(SOPH):** Rua Terminal dos Milagres 400, Bairro da Balsa, 78900-
750 Porto Velho, RO; tel. (69) 3229-2134; fax (69) 3229-3904; e-mail
soph@soph.ro.gov.br; internet www.soph.ro.gov.br; operates the
port of Porto Velho; Dir-Gen. MATEUS SANTOS COSTA.

**SUAPE—Complexo Industrial Portuário Governador Eraldo
Gueiros:** Rodovia PE-060, Km 10, Engenho Massangana, 55590-972
Ipojuca, PE; tel. (81) 3527-5000; fax (81) 3527-5066; e-mail
presidencia@suape.pe.gov.br; internet www.suape.pe.gov.br;
administers the port of Suape; Pres. MÁRCIO STEFANNI MONTEIRO.

Superintendência do Porto de Itajaí: Rua Blumenau 5, Centro,
88305-101 Itajaí, SC; tel. (47) 3341-8000; fax (47) 3341-8075; e-mail
atendimento@portoitajai.com.br; internet www.portoitajai.com.br;
Supt ANTÔNIO AYRES DOS SANTOS, Jr.

Superintendência do Porto de Rio Grande (SUPRG): Av.
Honório Bicalho s/n, CP 198, 96201-020 Rio Grande do Sul, RS;
tel. (53) 3231-1366; fax (53) 3231-1857; e-mail dirceu.lopes@
portoriogrande.com.br; internet www.portoriogrande.com.br;
f. 1996; Supt DIRCEU DA SILVA LOPES.

Superintendência do Porto de Tubarão: Ponta de Tubarão, CP
1078, 29072-970 Vitória, ES; tel. (27) 3335-4666; fax (27) 3335-3535;
operated by Vale, SA (CVRD); handles iron ore cargoes; Exec. Dir
TITO MARTINS.

**Superintendência de Portos e Hidrovias do Estado do Rio
Grande do Sul (SPH):** Av. Mauá 1050, 4° andar, 90010-110 Porto
Alegre, RS; tel. and fax (51) 3288-9200; e-mail executiva@sph.rs.gov
.br; internet www.sph.rs.gov.br; f. 1921; administers the ports of
Porto Alegre, Porto Pelotas, Porto Cachoeira, the São Gonçalo canal
and other waterways; Dir-Supt PEDRO HOMERO FLORES OBELAR.

Private Companies

Aliança Navegação e Logística, Ltda: Rua Verbo Divino 1547,
Bairro Chácara Santo Antônio, 04719-002 São Paulo, SP; tel. (11)
5185-3100; fax (11) 5185-5624; e-mail alianca@sao.alianca.com.br;
internet www.alianca.com.br; f. 1951; cargo services to Argentina,
Uruguay, European and North Atlantic ports; Pres. ARSÉNIO CARLOS
NÓBREGA.

Cia Libra de Navegação: Av. Rio Branco, 4, 6° e 7° andares, 20090-
000 Rio de Janeiro; tel. and fax (21) 2213-9700; e-mail atendimento
.brasil@csavgroup.com; internet www.libra.com.br.

Cia de Navegação da Amazônia (CNA): Edif. Vieiralves Business
Center, Rua Salvador 120, 11° andar, Adrianópolis, Manaus, AM; tel.
(92) 2125-1200; fax (92) 2125-1212; internet www.cnamazon.com.br;
f. 1942; Exec. Pres. RENÉ LEVY AGUIAR.

Cia de Navegação Norsul: Av. Augusto Severo 8, 8° andar, 20021-
040 Rio de Janeiro, RJ; tel. (21) 2139-0505; fax (21) 2507-1547; e-mail
norsul@norsul.com; internet www.norsul.com; f. 1963; largest private fleet, more than 28 vessels; Pres. CARLOS TEMKE.

Petrobras Transporte, SA (TRANSPETRO): Edif. Visconde de
Itaboraí, Av. Presidente Vargas 328, 20091-060 Rio de Janeiro, RJ;
tel. (21) 3211-7848; e-mail ouvidoria@transpetro.com.br; internet
www.transpetro.com.br; f. 1998; absorbed the Frota Nacional de
Petroleiros (FRONAPE) in 1999; transport of petroleum and related
products; 53 vessels; Pres. JOSÉ SERGIO DE OLIVEIRA MACHADO.

Wilson Sons Agência Marítima: Rua Jardim Botânico 518, 3°
andar, 22461-000 Rio de Janeiro, RJ; tel. (21) 2126-4222; fax (21)
2126-4190; e-mail box@wilsonsons.com.br; internet www.wilsonsons
.com.br; f. 1837; shipping agency, port operations, towage, small
shipyard; CEO AUGUSTO CEZAR TAVARES BAIÃO.

CIVIL AVIATION

Of the 67 principal airports, 22 are international, although most international traffic is handled by the two airports at Rio de Janeiro and two at São Paulo. In 2012 the Government reached agreement with foreign consortia to expand or upgrade the two São Paulo airports and the airport at Brasília.

Agência Nacional de Aviação Civil: Edif. Parque Cidade Corporate Torre A, SCS, Quadra 09, Lote C, 70308-200 Brasília, DF; tel. (61) 3314-4105; internet www.anac.gov.br; f. 2006; Dir-Pres. MARCELO PACHECO DOS GUARANYS.

Empresa Brasileira de Infra-Estrutura Aeroportuária (Infraero): Estrada do Aeroporto, Setor de Concessionárias, Lote 5, Edif. Sede, 71608-900 Brasília, DF; tel. (61) 3312-3222; fax (61) 3321-0512; e-mail webmaster@infraero.gov.br; internet www.infraero.gov.br; Pres. GUSTAVO DO VALE.

Secretariat of Civil Aviation: see The Government—Ministries.

Principal Airlines

Avianca: Av. Marechal Câmara 160, Sala 1532, Centro, 20020-080 Rio de Janeiro, RJ; tel. (21) 2544-2181; fax (21) 2215-7181; e-mail reservas@avianca.com.br; internet www.avianca.com.br; f. 1998 as Oceanair Linhas Aéreas, Ltda; changed name as above 2010; domestic services; Pres. JOSÉ EFROMOVICH.

Azul Linhas Aéreas Brasileiras: São Paulo, SP; tel. (11) 4831-1245; e-mail imprensa@voeazul.com.br; internet www.voeazul.com .br; f. 2009; merge with TRIP in 2012; Pres. DAVID NEELEMAN.

GOL Transportes Aéreos, SA: Rua Tamios 246, Jardim Aeropuerto, 04630-000 São Paulo, SP; tel. (11) 5033-4200; e-mail faleconosco@golnaweb.com.br; internet www.voegol.com.br; f. 2001; low-cost airline, acquired VARIG, SA in 2007; Man. Dir CONSTANTINO OLIVEIRA JÚNIOR.

Líder Aviação, SA: Av. Santa Rosa 123, São Luiz, 31270-750 Belo Horizonte, MG; tel. (31) 3490-4500; fax (31) 3490-4600; internet www .lideraviacao.com.br; f. 1958 as Líder Táxi Aéreo; changed name 2005; helicopters and small jets; Pres. JOSÉ AFONSO ASSUMPÇÃO.

TAM Linhas Aéreas, SA (TAM Airlines—TAM): Av. Jurandir 856, Jardim Aeroporto, 04072-000 São Paulo, SP; tel. (11) 5582-8811; e-mail relacoesinstitucionais@tam.com.br; internet www.tam.com .br; f. 1976; part of LATAM Airlines Group, SA following a merger with LAN Airlines, SA (Chile) in 2012, although still operates under TAM brand; scheduled passenger and cargo services from São Paulo to destinations throughout Brazil and in Argentina, Paraguay, Europe and the USA; CEO, LATAM Airlines ENRIQUE CUETO PLAZA; CEO, TAM Airlines MARCO ANTONIO BOLOGNA.

Tourism

In 2012 some 5.7m. tourists visited Brazil and in 2013 receipts from tourism totalled US $6,711m., according to provisional figures. Rio de Janeiro, with its famous beaches, is the centre of the tourist trade.

Like Salvador, Recife and other towns, it has excellent examples of Portuguese colonial and modern architecture. Other attractions include the modern capital, Brasília, the Iguaçu Falls, the seventh largest (by volume) in the world, the tropical forests of the Amazon basin and the wildlife of the Pantanal.

Associação Brasileira da Indústria de Hotéis (ABIH): Edif. América Office Tower, 17° andar, Salas 1712 e 1713, SCN, Quadra 01, Bloco F, 70711-905 Brasília, DF; tel. and fax (61) 3326-1177; e-mail secretariaabih@abih.com.br; internet www.abih.com.br; f. 1936; hoteliers' asscn; Pres. ENRICO FERMI TORQUATO.

Federação Nacional de Turismo (FENACTUR): Largo do Arouche 290, 6° andar, São Paulo, SP; tel. (11) 3331-4590; fax (11) 3221-6947; e-mail fenactur@uol.com.br; internet www.fenactur.com .br; f. 1990; Pres. MICHEL TUMA NESS.

Instituto Brasileiro de Turismo (EMBRATUR): Edif. Embratur, 3° andar, SCN, Quadra 02, Bloco G, 70712-907 Brasília, DF; tel. (61) 3429-7777; fax (61) 3429-7710; e-mail presidencia@embratur .gov.br; internet www.embratur.gov.br; f. 1966; Pres. VICENTE JOSÉ DE LIMA NETO.

Defence

As assessed at November 2013, Brazil's armed forces numbered 318,500: army 190,000 (including 70,000 conscripts); navy 59,000 (including at least 3,200 conscripts; also including 2,500 in the naval air force and 15,000 marines); and air force 69,500. Reserves numbered 1,340,000 and there were some 395,000 in the paramilitary Public Security Forces, state militias under army control. Military service lasts for 12 months and is compulsory for men between 18 and 45 years of age.

Defence Budget: R $67,800m. in 2013.

Chief of Staff of the Air Forces: Gen. JUNITI SAITO.

Chief of Staff of the Army: Gen. ENZO MARTINS PERI.

Chief of Staff of the Navy: Adm. JÚLIO SOARES DE MOURA NETO.

Education

Education is free in official schools at primary and secondary level. Primary education is compulsory between the ages of six and 14 years and lasts for nine years. Secondary education begins at 15 years of age and lasts for three years. In 2008 enrolment in primary schools included 94% of children in the relevant age-group, while enrolment in secondary schools included 82% of those in the relevant age-group. The federal Government is responsible for higher education, and in 2011 there were 190 universities, of which 102 were state-administered. Numerous private institutions exist at all levels of education. Federal government expenditure on education was R $7,746.2m. in 2010.

Bibliography

For works on South America generally, see Select Bibliography (Books)

Amann, E., Baer, W., and Coes, D. (Eds). *Energy, Bio Fuels and Development: Comparing Brazil and the United States.* Abingdon, Routledge, 2010.

Arestis, P., and Saad-Filho, A. (Eds). *Political Economy of Brazil: Recent Economic Performance.* Basingstoke, Palgrave Macmillan, 2007.

Arias, E. D. *Drugs and Democracy in Rio de Janeiro: Trafficking, Social Networks, and Public Security.* Chapel Hill, NC, University of North Carolina Press, 2006.

Bailey, S. R. *Legacies of Race: Identities, Attitudes, and Politics in Brazil.* Palo Alto, CA, Stanford University Press, 2009.

Baiocchi, G. *Militants and Citizens: The Politics of Participatory Democracy in Porto Alegre.* Palo Alto, CA, Stanford University Press, 2005.

Bourne, R. *Lula of Brazil: The Story So Far.* London, Zed Books, 2008.

Brainard, Lael and Martinez, Leonard *Brazil As an Economic Superpower?: Understanding Brazil's Changing Role in the Global Economy.* Washington, DC, Brookings Institution Press, 2009.

Branford, S., and Rocha, J. *Cutting the Wire: The Story of the Landless Movement in Brazil.* London, Latin America Bureau, 2002.

Bruhn, K. *Urban Protest in Mexico and Brazil.* Cambridge, Cambridge University Press, 2008.

Cardoso, F. H. *The Accidental President of Brazil: A Memoir.* New York, Public Affairs, 2006.

Castro, P. F. *Fronteras Abiertas: Expansionismo y Geopolítica en el Brasil Contemporáneo.* Madrid, Editores Siglo XXI, 2002.

de Paula, L. F. *Financial Liberalization and Economic Performance: Brazil at the Crossroads.* Abingdon, Routledge, 2010.

Dillon Soares, G. A. *A Democracia Interrompida.* Rio de Janeiro, RJ, Editora FGV, 2001.

Font, M. A., Spanakos, A., and Bordin, C. *Reforming Brazil (Western Hemisphere Studies).* Lanham, MD, Lexington Books, 2004.

Freyre, G. *The Masters and the Slaves: A Study in the Development of Brazilian Civilization.* New York, Alfred A. Knopf, 1946.

Gómez Bruera, Hernán F. *Lula, the Workers' Party and the Governability Dilemma in Brazil.* Abingdon, Routledge, 2013.

Graham, Lawrence S. and Wilson, Robert H. (Eds) *The Political Economy of Brazil: Public Policies in an Era of Transition.* Austin, TX, University of Texas Press, 2012.

Hunter, W. *The Transformation of the Workers' Party in Brazil, 1989–2009.* New York, Cambridge University Press, 2010.

Ioris, Rafael R. *Transforming Brazil: A History of National Development in the Postwar Era*. Abingdon, Routledge, 2014.

Johnson, O. A., III. *Brazilian Party Politics and the Coup of 1964*. Gainesville, FL, University Press of Florida, 2001.

Matos, C. *Journalism and Political Democracy in Brazil*. Lanham, MD, Lexington Books, 2008.

Mendes, C. *Fight for the Forest: Chico Mendes in his own Words*. London, Latin America Bureau, 1989.

Montero, A. *Brazilian Politics: Reforming a Democratic State in a Changing World*. Cambridge, Polity Press, 2006.

Newitt, M. (Ed.). *The First Portuguese Colonial Empire*. Exeter, University of Exeter Press, 2002.

Perlman, J. *Favela: Four Decades of Living on the Edge in Rio de Janeiro*. New York, Oxford University Press, 2010.

Platt, D., and Neate, P. *Bolado: Life, Death and Survival Strategies in the Favelas*. London, Latin America Bureau, 2006.

Power, T. J. and Taylor, M. (Eds) *Corruption and Democracy in Brazil: The Struggle for Accountability*. Notre Dame, IN, University of Notre Dame Press, 2011.

Reiter, B. *Negotiating Democracy in Brazil: The Politics of Exclusion*. Boulder, CO, FirstForum Press, 2008.

Reiter, B., and Mitchell, G. L. (Eds) *Brazil's New Racial Politics*. Boulder, CO, Lynne Rienner Publrs, 2009.

Revkin, A. *The Burning Season: The Murder of Chico Mendes and the Fight for the Amazon Rain Forest*. Washington, DC, Shearwater Books, 2004.

Rocha, S. *Pobreza no Brasil: Afinal de que se trata?* Rio de Janeiro, RJ, Editora, FGV, 2003.

Rohter, L. *Brazil on the Rise: The Story of a Country Reformed*. Basingstoke, Palgrave Macmillan, 2010.

Sluyter-Beltrão, J. *Rise and Decline of Brazil's New Unionism (Trade Unions Past, Present and Future)*. New York, Peter Lang, 2010.

Smith, J. *A History of Brazil*. Harlow, Longman, 2002.

Brazil and the United States: Convergence and Divergence. Athens, GA, University of Georgia Press, 2010.

Telles, E. E. *Race in Another America: The Significance of Skin Color in Brazil*. Princeton, NJ, Princeton University Press, 2006.

Trebat, T. J., and Knight, A. (Ed.). *Brazil's State-Owned Enterprises: A Case Study of the State as Entrepreneur*. Cambridge, Cambridge University Press, 2007.

Wolfe, J. *Autos and Progress: The Brazilian Search for Modernity*. New York, Oxford University Press, 2010.

Wolford, W. *The Land is Ours Now: Social Mobilization and the Meanings of Land in Brazil*. Durham, NC, Duke University Press, 2010.

Woodard, J. P. *A Place in Politics: Sao Paulo, Brazil, from Seigneurial Republicanism to Regionalist Revolt*. Durham, NC, Duke University Press, 2009.

THE BRITISH VIRGIN ISLANDS

Geography

PHYSICAL FEATURES

The British Virgin Islands is an Overseas Territory of the United Kingdom in the West Indies. The Virgin Islands lie at the north-western end of the Lesser Antilles, the chain that defines the edge of the Caribbean Sea, north and east of which is the Atlantic Ocean. To the east of the British Virgin Islands, beyond the shipping lane known as the Anegada Passage, Anguilla (another British dependency) and the other Leeward Islands continue the arc of the Lesser Antilles southeastwards, while to the west of the US Virgin Islands (formerly the Danish West Indies) is Puerto Rico, and the other Greater Antilles. The Virgin Islands themselves are divided between two sovereignties, the smaller, eastern group being British, the rest constituting a Territory of the USA. South-west from Tortola, the main island of the British Virgin Islands, across a narrow sea channel, is the US Virgin Island of St John. The main island of Puerto Rico (another US Territory) is almost 100 km (60 miles) to the west. The British Virgin Islands has a total area of 153 sq km (59 sq miles).

The British Virgin Islands consists of between 40 and 60 islands, islets and cays (with only about 80 km of coastline between them) strewn over almost 3,450 sq km of sea. Of the main islands, 16 are inhabited and 20 uninhabited. The largest island is Tortola (54 sq km), where the capital is located. The next in size are Anegada (39 sq km), Virgin Gorda (21 sq km) and Jost Van Dyke (9 sq km). The last is west of Tortola, while Virgin Gorda is to the east (beyond the small clump of the Dog Islands), and the more isolated Anegada is north of Virgin Gorda. At the centre of the archipelago is the 30-km Sir Francis Drake Channel, which runs north-eastwards from St John to Virgin Gorda, flanked by Tortola (on the northern side) and by a string of islands including Norman, Peter, Salt, Cooper and Ginger (to the south). Most of the main islands are hilly and steep (the highest point is Mt Sage on Tortola, at 521 m or 1,710 ft), the result of long-past volcanic activity, which has made the islands fertile and lush with tropical greenery. Only on Tortola are there open streams, and these are seasonal. However, there are also extensive coral reefs, most notably in the northern island of Anegada. South of Anegada is the 18-km Horseshoe Reef, one of the largest reefs in the world. The complicated island geography has, historically, attracted pirates, but it is now tourists, particularly yachters, who are drawn to the scattered islands. Some tree species can only be found on the Virgin Islands, as can one of the two smallest lizards in the world, the cotton ginner or Virgin Islands dwarf gecko, while Anegada, by contrast, shelters the last survivors of an endemic variety of rock iguana (Cyclura pinguis), which can grow to over 1.5 m.

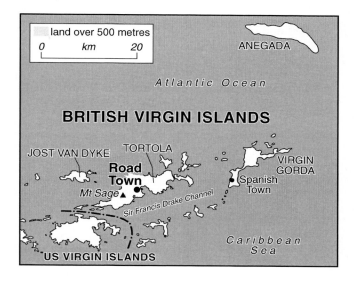

CLIMATE

The climate is subtropical and humid, moderated by the trade winds off the Atlantic. The hilly terrain helps capture some of the 1,350 mm (53 ins) of rainfall received in an average year. However, the British Virgin Islands are in the hurricane belt, which can strike to devastating effect. Temperature variations are relatively mild, ranging between 22°C–28°C (72°F–82°F) in winter (December–March) and 26°C–32°C (79°F–90°F) in summer.

POPULATION

Most of the population is black and Christian (33% Methodist, 20% from other Protestant denominations, 17% Anglican—Episcopal—and 10% Roman Catholic). English is the official and most widely spoken language. Links with the neighbouring US Virgin Islands are strong.

The total population was projected at 29,537 in mid-2010. It is reckoned to have almost doubled in the last 20 years of the 20th century, with only about one-half of the present population judged to be of British Virgin Islands origin, the rest being drawn by opportunities in tourism and construction. The capital is Road Town, on the south coast of Tortola, the most populous (83% of the total) as well as the largest island. Fifteen other islands are also inhabited, although most of the rest of the population is on Virgin Gorda (itself once the centre of population), the chief settlement of which is Spanish Town.

History

MARK WILSON

The British Virgin Islands is a United Kingdom Overseas Territory. A Governor, who is the representative of the British monarch, has important reserve powers, including responsibility for national security and defence, the civil service, the judiciary and certain financial matters. In accordance with constitutional reforms agreed in May 2007 and approved by the United Kingdom Privy Council in June, a Premier chairs a Cabinet, and is responsible to the House of Assembly, similar in function to a parliament, which contains a majority of elected members; nine represent constituencies, while four 'at large' members are elected by an overall vote. The Governor attends Cabinet, and shares responsibility for setting its agenda. A national security council allows advice from senior local politicians on issues relating to the police and other security issues. These changes follow a constitutional review submitted to the Chief Minister and the Governor for consideration in April 2005, with a total of 116 recommendations, but with the overall conclusion that the people of the Territory preferred the sharing of responsibilities between the Government of the Virgin Islands and the Government of the United Kingdom to be continued. A charter of human rights has also been agreed, and there is provision for a sixth ministerial position. The Virgin Islands Constitutional Order 2007 became effective on 15 June following the dissolution of the Legislative Council (which became the House of Assembly). With a headquarters building completed in 2009, the British Virgin Islands was host to a commercial court which served the islands participating in the Eastern Caribbean court system.

Few traces remain of the original Amerindian inhabitants. The Virgin Islands were named by Christopher Columbus in 1493. The first European settlers were from the Netherlands, but the islands were British from 1666. There was an elected Assembly from 1773. From 1871 to 1956 the British Virgin Islands formed part of the Leeward Islands Federation. From 1951 the local Legislative Council was given four elected representatives, equal in number to the nominated members, with the franchise extended to adults passing a literacy test. The islands did not join the Federation of the West Indies in 1958, possibly because islanders saw their future as more closely linked to the neighbouring US Virgin Islands. Instead they were, from 1960, a separate British Dependent Territory, first under an Administrator, then under a Governor. From February 1998 they were, along with the United Kingdom's other remaining dependencies, designated a United Kingdom Overseas Territory.

In 1967 a new Constitution established the office of Chief Minister. For most of the succeeding period, the Virgin Islands Party (VIP) held office, led by H. Lavity Stoutt until his death in 1995, and then by Ralph T. O'Neal. The United Party (UP) formed a coalition during 1983–86, with an independent member, Cyril Romney, as Chief Minister.

In 1986 the VIP then returned to office, winning a further election in 1989, but losing its absolute majority in a general election in February 1995. Four 'at large' members had been added to the nine constituency representatives, against the wishes of the VIP; with the composition of the Legislative Council altered in this way, the VIP took six seats, with two for the UP, two for the Concerned Citizens' Movement (CCM), and three independents. However, one of the independents joined the VIP, which was thus able to form an administration with a majority of a single seat. At the general election of 17 May 1999 the VIP retained its single-seat majority in spite of a strong challenge from the recently formed National Democratic Party (NDP).

A brief political crisis ensued in July 2000, when the appointment of Eileene L. Parsons as Minister for Health, Education, Culture and Welfare was revoked. Parsons then joined the NDP, a move that would have deprived the VIP of its majority, had not the single CCM member, Ethlyn E. Smith, defected to join the Government. O'Neal's support was increased from seven to eight seats in February 2001 when another opposition member, Mark Vanterpool, joined the VIP.

Reported corruption on an airport-improvement project precipitated a serious political crisis in 2001–02. Following a report presented to the Governor in November 2001, several people were arrested, including the Government's financial secretary Allen Wheatley, the budget co-ordinator and the former head of the telephone services management unit. In March 2002 they were charged with conspiracy to defraud the Government and related offences; they received sentences of between six and nine months in January 2004. A report by the Government's chief auditor in September 2003 expressed concern over the neglect of established procedures for the award of government contracts. An opposition-proposed motion of no confidence in the Legislative Council was defeated in May 2004, with O'Neal expressing a lack of concern about the issue. The standing of the Government, however, was severely weakened and, with a constitutional review in progress, strong pressure for stricter financial management was expected from the British authorities. However, the Chief Minister argued for greater local autonomy and a reduction in the Governor's reserve powers, while a report by the United Kingdom's Centre for Management and Policy Studies commented on the 'almost total breakdown' in the relationship between elected ministers and senior civil servants.

In May 2002 the British Overseas Territories Act, having received royal assent in the United Kingdom in February, came into force and granted British citizenship to the people of its Overseas Territories, including the British Virgin Islands. Under the new law, British Virgin Islanders would be able to hold British passports and work in the United Kingdom and anywhere else in the European Union.

After 17 years in office, the VIP relinquished control of the legislature after a general election on 16 June 2003. The NDP secured eight seats compared with the VIP's five after a campaign that was dominated by the issues of alleged corruption, management of public sector capital projects and relations with the United Kingdom. The VIP, which claimed returning officers failed to account for all ballots issued and votes cast, demanded a recount in two constituencies; however, the complaint was rejected by the High Court. The new Chief Minister, Orlando Smith, appointed Ronnie Skelton as Minister of Finance, Health and Welfare, Paul Wattley as Minister of Communications and Works, Lloyd Black as Minister of Education and Culture, and J. Alvin Christopher as Minister of Natural Resources and Labour. In an effort to improve strategic planning for public sector capital spending, the new Government decided to reappraise a controversial US $77m. hospital project, and ended a dispute with the Caribbean Development Bank over the appointment of contractors to complete an airport-improvement project; work was completed in May 2004. A contract was signed for a modified $64m. hospital project in December 2006.

The Minister of Communications and Works, Paul Wattley, died in July 2003. The NDP won the ensuing by-election with 54% of the votes cast, increasing its legislative representation to nine seats; J. Alvin Christopher became Wattley's successor in September, while Eileene Parsons replaced Christopher as Minister for Natural Resources and Labour. Christopher was removed from his tenure at the Ministry of Communications and Works in May 2006, after disagreeing with his colleagues over proposals for the liberalization of the telecommunications sector, in place of the monopoly still held by Cable & Wireless. However, he remained a member of the NDP, having broken with the former VIP Government in 2002, in the ministerial portfolio by Elmore Stoutt.

A new Constitution negotiated with the United Kingdom after broad public consultations was agreed by the Legislative Council in May 2007. A Cabinet chaired by a Premier replaced the Executive Council chaired by the Governor. Police and security remained the Governor's responsibility, but with advice from a new National Security Council in which elected politicians were to participate. A United Kingdom White Paper published in June 2012 set out a strategy of greater British involvement in the governance of the remaining 14 United Kingdom Overseas Territories, and stated that the present was not a suitable time to initiate further constitutional reform.

At a general election on 20 August 2007, the VIP returned to office, taking 10 of the 13 seats, with Ralph O'Neal as Premier. A former Deputy Governor, Dancia Penn Sallah, was appointed Deputy Premier and Minister of Health and Social Development. The NDP held only two seats, and Christopher, running as an independent, took one. The NDP had presided over a period of strong economic growth, with completion of several infrastructural projects, and its period in office had been largely free of accusations of corruption. However, there was widespread public concern over the rapid pace of economic development, led mainly by investors from outside the British Virgin Islands. As during his previous administration, O'Neal developed a difficult relationship with the British-appointed Governor, whom he accused in February 2008 of favouring the NDP opposition. O'Neal also objected to the appointment in August of Inez Archibald, who was Speaker of the Legislative Council before the 2007 general election, as Deputy Governor.

In the British Virgin Islands, as in most of the Caribbean, there is concern over violent crime; the prison, which was designed for up to 60 inmates, held 113 in 2011. There were six murders in the territory in 2007 and eight in 2008, resulting in a murder rate of 31 per 100,000 inhabitants, more than five times that of the USA. However, the number of murders decreased from 2009; there was only one murder in 2013. Most killings appear to be directly or indirectly drugs-related; suspects were identified for only six of the 32 murders committed in the years from 2000 to 2011. The islands are a short distance from the US Virgin Islands, which are within the US customs and immigration area, and are therefore an attractive staging post for drugs- and human-trafficking. A police Drug and Violent Crime Task Force was formed in 2005 and a new visa regime implemented by the Government in 2007; the latter required that, in order to enter the Territory, Jamaican nationals without residency or 'belonger' status obtain a visa, in an effort to enhance immigration-monitoring and curb the numbers of non-British Virgin Islanders residing in the country illegally. There have also been several instances of serious fraud, some of which have involved the offshore financial sector. Assets to the value of US $45m. held in the British Virgin Islands by three International Business Company subsidiaries of a Bermuda-registered entity, the IPOC International Growth Fund, were confiscated in 2007 following a guilty plea on charges of perverting the course of justice during

a money-laundering investigation linked to the Russian telecommunications industry. Reports in June 2013 indicated that North Korea was conducting some of its international operations through companies registered in the British Virgin Islands. The US Department of State classes the British Virgin Islands as a country 'of primary concern' in relation to money-laundering and terrorist-financing.

Indicating a history of weak public sector management, the Governor, David Pearey, in March 2009 appointed a commission of inquiry into alleged evasion of stamp duty in 2000–06, headed by a former Eastern Caribbean Chief Justice, Brian Alleyne. A report was submitted to the Governor in March 2010. The opposition in June called for an inquiry into the Government's relations with a British company, Biwater Holdings Ltd, after agreements to purchase a generator and to operate a Build-Own-Operate-Transfer desalination, water supply and sewerage contract were both reportedly negotiated without tender; the Minister of Education and Culture, Andrew Fahie, in November also expressed concerns. The incoming NDP Government (see below) was unable to fulfil an election pledge to hold a review of the tendering process. Work on the plant finally got under way in November 2012, and was scheduled for completion in late 2014.

A new Governor, William Boyd McCleary, was inaugurated in August 2010. A further election was held on 7 November 2011. The NDP was returned to office, with 52.5% of the popular vote and nine of the 15 seats. O'Neal, who turned 78 shortly after the poll, again led his party and won his seat; however, the VIP retained only 39.0% of the popular vote. Smith was reappointed Premier. Relations with the United Kingdom have since been more cordial than those of other British Overseas Territories in the Caribbean. Differences which emerged in mid-2013 over international sharing of tax information and related matters appeared to have been resolved by 2014 following the Government's endorsement of the Organisation for Economic Co-operation and Development's Multilateral Convention on Mutual Administrative Assistance in Tax Matters, which came into effect in March. Following publication of leaked information on offshore companies in 2013, the House of Assembly in the same month approved legislation purportedly with worldwide reach aiming to impose fines of up to US $500,000 and prison sentences of up to 20 years for unauthorized publication of information about British Virgin Island companies. After widespread local and international criticism, however, this legislation had not been brought into effect by the Governor by June.

Economy

MARK WILSON

The British Virgin Islands is situated in the Eastern Caribbean and had an estimated population of 29,537 in 2010, occupying 153 sq km of territory. Immigration resulting from economic prosperity led to an average annual population growth of 2.7% in 2001–10. Of the total population, 83% lived on the island of Tortola. Virgin Gorda, with 14%, is developing rapidly, and there is 1% each on Anegada and Jost Van Dyke.

The British Virgin Islands is an associate member of the Caribbean Community and Common Market, or CARICOM, whose members formed a single market and economy in 2006. It is also a member of the Organisation of Eastern Caribbean States, which links nine of the smaller Caribbean territories. However, the islands do not participate in the Eastern Caribbean Central Bank and have no separate central banking arrangements, using US currency for all purposes.

The islands have an extremely prosperous economy, with an estimated per-head gross domestic product (GDP) of US $32,375 for 2012, according to UN estimates, when GDP totalled $873m., and an unemployment rate of an estimated 3.1% in 2008.

The economy slowed in 2000–03, largely reflecting an international downturn in tourism. A brisk pace of growth was

resumed from 2004; growth averaged 4.3% in 2004–07, although GDP contracted by 0.6% in 2008 as investment and tourism demand fell. The economy of the British Virgin Islands suffered in 2008 and 2009 as the international economic downturn adversely affected international financial services, tourism and hotel construction. GDP contracted by 1.9% in 2008 and by a further 11.6% in 2009; the Government estimated growth at a modest 2.0% for 2010 and 2.4% in 2011, driven in part by a recovery in financial services, with 4.0% growth projected for 2012. However, according to UN figures, GDP contracted by 1.6% in 2011 and by a further 4.5% in 2012. Public debt was US $127.7m. at the end of 2013, or less than 15% of GDP. The 2014 budget projected revenue of $301.7m. Capital projects included a runway extension at the main Terrance B. Lettsome International Airport. A medium term fiscal plan for 2014–16 was approved in 2013.

Financial and business services and real estate made up 33.3% of GDP in 2009. The very large offshore financial sector, administered by an independent Financial Services Commission, specializes in the registration of International Business Companies, with a cumulative total of 482,087 active companies by March 2014. British Virgin Island companies may be listed on the New York, Nasdaq, Toronto, Singapore or Hong Kong stock exchanges, or on the London stock exchange's AIM international market for smaller and growing companies. There were 2,215 active licensed mutual funds in 2014. Offshore banking is not well developed, a deliberate choice by the authorities who are hesitant to take on the regulatory problems involved; however, there were 237 licensed banks in 2014. Legislation on trusts introduced in 2003 was designed to broaden the basis of the offshore sector, and to control possible abuse of existing regulations. Fees from the offshore sector were projected at US $188m. for 2012, or just over 63% of total government revenue. Following international pressure, in particular from the Organisation for Economic Co-operation and Development (OECD), legislation to improve transparency in the financial sector was introduced. In 2002 the Government committed itself to improving the islands' financial sector to meet OECD guidelines. A Tax Information Exchange Treaty with the USA was signed, followed, in 2008, by tax information exchange agreements with the United Kingdom and Australia. In 2004 further legislation was introduced, eliminating the distinction between onshore and offshore taxation regimes, specifically in order to correspond to OECD and European Union standards; however, 40% of offshore business was by 2013 derived from Asia.

The US Department of State in 2014 still listed the British Virgin Islands as of 'primary concern' for money-laundering, demanding tougher penalties, stricter reporting requirements and additional regulatory staff. The USA noted that there is no requirement to file a statement of ownership or of authorized capital, while the use of the US dollar as currency, proximity to the US Virgin Islands and location on major drugs-transshipment routes all posed additional risks. Although OECD in 2009 placed the British Virgin Islands on a so-called 'grey list' of countries that had not yet done enough to implement tax transparency, the territory was removed from the list later that year after signing sufficient tax information exchange agreements. The offshore sector also suffered from the sharp downturn in international economic activity from 2008, with major professional practices laying off staff. A recovery in the offshore financial sector was reported from 2010. However, with continuing international concern over the use of offshore jurisdictions to avoid tax liability, confidence in the sector was shaken slightly in April 2013 with the leakage and publication of a large quantity of data by the International Consortium of Investigative Journalists. The resulting publicity was blamed in part for a decrease in new company registrations, which were 15% fewer in the first three quarters of 2013 than in January–September 2012. There were concerns also over the listing of the islands by France as a 'non-co-operative' jurisdiction in August 2013.

Tourism is the other mainstay of the economy, with the sector accounting for 27.0% of GDP in 2014, according to the World Travel and Tourism Council. On the smaller islands in the group, there is the added benefit of near-complete privacy. The number of stop-over tourists reached 358,056 in 2007, but fell sharply to 308,800 in 2009 as international demand weakened, before rebounding to 355,677 in 2013. Creating some concerns, the main international carrier, American Airlines, reduced flights to the British Virgin Islands in 2008. A new carrier, BVI Airways, began services to nearby islands from 2010, but a large number of international passengers flew to the US Virgin Islands and made the last leg of their journey by ferry. The Government proposed in 2012 to increase the length of the main airport runway by 2,500 feet to take direct flights to North America; at present, it cannot accommodate even large private jets. Yachting is an important segment of the tourism industry. Most tourists stay in luxury accommodation; their high spending power per head is of further economic benefit. Although there were complaints that cruise ship traffic was diluting the islands' 'exclusive' image, proposals for a US $75m. cruise pier expansion were announced in 2012 (there were some 367,362 cruise ship passengers in 2013). Visitor expenditure totalled some US $397m. in 2012.

Residential, commercial, public sector and tourism-related investment has resulted in a high level of construction activity, making up 5.6% of GDP in 2012. Mismanagement and alleged corruption in public sector capital projects was a major concern until 2003, when the incoming National Democratic Party (NDP) Government attempted to address this issue, reappraising a US $77m. hospital project, and reaching an agreement with the Caribbean Development Bank that allowed a long-delayed airport runway improvement to be completed. The NDP was defeated in the 2007 general election, but there was no clear indication of renewed corrupt activities following the return to office of the Virgin Islands Party, or that of the NDP in 2011. Transport and communications contributed 11.3% of GDP in 2012.

Agriculture (including fishing) comprised only 1.0% of GDP in 2012, with a few farmers keeping livestock and growing food crops. Manufacturing (2.9% of GDP in 2012) is limited to activities such as printing and the blending and bottling of rum. Electric power supply has been a problem, in spite of the addition of new generating capacity. The BVI Electricity Corporation in 2005 borrowed US $32m. for its capital programme and repayment of existing debt. In 2006 the Chief Minister stressed the importance of economic diversification; in conjunction with this policy, the Government established a guarantee facility to enable small businesses lacking collateral to secure financial loans.

The territory is in the heart of the hurricane belt, and has been damaged by several storms in recent years. There is, however, no volcanic risk, although earthquakes have been known to occur.

Statistical Survey

Source: Development Planning Unit, Central Administrative Complex, Road Town, Tortola VG1110; tel. 494-3701; fax 494-3947; e-mail dpu@dpu.org; internet dpu.gov.vg.

AREA AND POPULATION

Area: 153 sq km (59 sq miles). *Principal Islands* (sq km): Tortola 54.4; Anegada 38.8; Virgin Gorda 21.4; Jost Van Dyke 9.1.

Population: 16,115 at census of 12 May 1991; 23,161 (males 11,436, females 11,725) at census of 21 May 2001. *By Island* (2001 census): Tortola 19,282; Virgin Gorda 3,203; Anegada 250; Jost Van Dyke 244; Other 182 (Other islands 86, Boats 96); Total 23,161. *2010* (official estimate): 29,537.

Density (2010): 193.1 per sq km.

Population by Age (official projections, 2010): *0–14 years:* 7,404; *15–64 years:* 20,368; *65 years and over:* 1,765; *Total* 29,537.

Principal Town: Road Town (capital), population 13,102 (UN estimate, incl. suburbs, mid-2014). Source: UN, *World Urbanization Prospects: The 2014 Revision.*

Births, Marriages and Deaths (2007 unless otherwise indicated): 279 live births (birth rate 10.1 per 1,000); 419 marriages (marriage rate 15.2 per 1,000); 109 deaths (2008—death rate 3.9 per 1,000). *2013:* Crude birth rate 10.8 per 1,000; Crude death rate 4.9 per 1,000 (Source: Pan American Health Organization).

Life Expectancy (years at birth, estimates): 78.1 (males 76.9; females 79.5) in 2013. Source: Pan American Health Organization.

Employment (2005): Agriculture, hunting and forestry 78; Fishing 14; Mining and quarrying 37; Manufacturing 404; Electricity, gas and water supply 145; Construction 1,260; Wholesale and retail trade 1,624; Hotels and restaurants 2,573; Transport, storage and communications 454; Financial intermediation 797; Real estate, renting and business activities 1,307; Public administration and social security 5,142; Education 1,119; Health and social work 141; Other community, social and personal service activities 724; Private households with employed persons 404; *Sub-total* 16,223; Not classifiable by economic activity 9; *Total* 16,232. *2010:* Total employed 18,796.

HEALTH AND WELFARE

Total Fertility Rate (children per woman, 2013): 1.2.

Physicians (per 1,000 head, 1999): 1.15.

Hospital Beds (per 1,000 head, 2006): 1.8.

Health Expenditure (% of GDP, 1995): 3.9. *2004* (public expenditure only): 2.3.

Health Expenditure (public, % of total, 1995): 36.5.

Source: Pan American Health Organization.

For definitions, see explanatory note on p. vi.

AGRICULTURE, ETC.

Livestock ('000 head, 2012, FAO estimates): Cattle 2.4; Sheep 6.1; Goats 10.0; Pigs 1.5.

Fishing (metric tons, live weight, 2012, FAO estimates): Snappers 70; Boxfishes 30; Jacks and crevalles 25; Caribbean spiny lobster 40; Marine fishes 770; Total catch (incl. others) 1,200.

Source: FAO.

INDUSTRY

Electric Energy (production, million kWh): 50 in 2008; 52 in 2009; 54 in 2010. Source: UN Industrial Commodity Statistics Database.

FINANCE

Currency and Exchange Rate: United States currency is used: 100 cents = 1 US dollar ($). *Sterling and Euro Equivalents* (30 May 2014): £1 sterling = US $1.682; €1 = US $1.361; US $100 = £59.45 = €73.47.

Budget (US $ million, 2014, projections): *Revenue:* Tax revenue 282.7; Other revenue 19.7; Total revenue 302.3. *Expenditure:* Recurrent expenditure 246.8; Capital expenditure 54.4; Total expenditure 301.2.

Cost of Living (Consumer Price Index at August; base: March 1995 = 100): All items 161.8 in 2010; 166.4 in 2011.

Gross Domestic Product (US $ million at constant 2005 prices): 929.1 in 2010; 914.4 in 2011; 872.9 in 2012. Source: UN Statistics Division, National Accounts Main Aggregates Database.

Expenditure on the Gross Domestic Product (US $ million at current prices, 2012): Government final consumption expenditure 76; Private final consumption expenditure 317; Gross fixed capital formation 217; Changes in inventories –18; *Total domestic expenditure* 592; Exports of goods and services 1,017; *Less* Imports of goods and services 701; *GDP in purchasers' values* 909. Source: UN Statistics Division, National Accounts Main Aggregates Database.

Gross Domestic Product by Economic Activity (US $ million at current prices, 2012): Agriculture, hunting, forestry and fishing 9; Mining, manufacturing and utilities 50 (Manufacturing 27); Construction 52; Wholesale, retail trade, restaurants and hotels 251; Transport, storage and communication 104; Other activities 455; *Total gross value added* 921; Net taxes on products –12 (figure obtained as a residual); *GDP in purchasers' values* 909 (Source: UN Statistics Division, National Accounts Main Aggregates Database).

EXTERNAL TRADE

Principal Commodities (US $ '000): *Imports c.i.f.* (1997): Food and live animals 31,515; Beverages and tobacco 8,797; Crude materials (inedible) except fuels 1,168; Mineral fuels, lubricants, etc. 9,847; Chemicals 8,816; Basic manufactures 31,715; Machinery and transport equipment 47,019; Total (incl. others) 116,379. *Exports f.o.b.* (1996): Food and live animals 368; Beverages and tobacco 3,967; Crude materials (inedible) except fuels 1,334; Total (incl. others) 5,862. *2001* (exports, US $ million): Animals 0.1; Fresh fish 0.7; Gravel and sand 1.4; Rum 3.6; Total 28.13.

Principal Trading Partners (US $ '000): *Imports c.i.f.* (1997): Antigua and Barbuda 1,807; Trinidad and Tobago 2,555; United Kingdom 406; USA 94,651; Total (incl. others) 166,379. *Exports f.o.b.* (1996): USA and Puerto Rico 1,077; US Virgin Islands 2,001; Total (incl. others) 5,862. *1999:* Imports 208,419; Exports 2,081.

Source: mainly UN, *International Trade Statistics Yearbook.*

TRANSPORT

Road Traffic (motor vehicles registered and licensed, 2005): 13,392 (Private vehicles 9,201, Commercial vehicles 2,102, Rental vehicles 1,196, Taxis 483, Government 275, Motorcycles 135).

Shipping: *Flag Registered Fleet* (at 31 December 2013): Number of vessels 84; Total displacement 26,545 grt. Source: Lloyd's List Intelligence (www.lloydslistintelligence.com).

Civil Aviation (passenger arrivals): 153,391 in 2003; 220,239 in 2004 (estimate); 220,116 in 2005 (estimate).

TOURISM

Visitor Arrivals ('000): 345.9 stop-over visitors, 571.7 cruise ship passengers in 2008; 308.8 stop-over visitors, 530.3 cruise ship passengers in 2009; 330.3 stop-over visitors, 501.5 cruise ship passengers in 2010. *Total Arrivals:* 338 in 2011; 351 in 2012 (provisional) (Source: World Tourism Organization).

Tourism Revenue (US $ million, incl. passenger transport): 389 in 2010; 388 in 2011; 397 in 2012. Source: World Tourism Organization.

COMMUNICATIONS MEDIA

Telephones (2013): 12,080 main lines in use.

Mobile Cellular Telephones (2013): 53,406 subscribers.

Internet Subscribers (2010): 10,900.

Broadband Subscribers (2013): 6,182.

Source: International Telecommunication Union.

EDUCATION

Pre-primary (2010/11 unless otherwise indicated): 5 schools (1994/95); 78 teachers; 853 pupils.

Primary (2010/11 unless otherwise indicated): 21 schools (2006); 263 teachers; 3,138 pupils.

Secondary (2010/11 unless otherwise indicated): 7 schools (2006); 239 teachers; 1,923 pupils.

Tertiary (2008/09): 105 teachers; 1,211 pupils.

Pupil-teacher Ratio (primary education, UNESCO estimate): 11.9 in 2010/11.

Sources: UNESCO Institute for Statistics; Caribbean Development Bank, *Social and Economic Indicators.*

Directory

The Constitution

The British Virgin Islands have had a representative assembly since 1774. Following a United Kingdom Government invitation in 2001 for its Overseas Territories to institute programmes of constitutional reform, a new Constitution for the British Virgin Islands was finalized in May 2007 and formally ratified by the Privy Council of the United Kingdom in June. The Virgin Islands Constitutional Order 2007 became effective (largely—see below) from 15 June and represented the first comprehensive revision of the territory's Constitution since the revision that had precipitated the 1977 Constitution, which it replaced. Under the terms of the 2007 Constitution, the Governor is responsible for defence and internal security (includ-

ing the police force), external affairs, terms and conditions of service of public officers, and the administration of the Courts. The Governor also possesses reserved legislative powers in respect of legislation necessary in the interests of his special responsibilities and fulfils the role of Presiding Officer at meetings of the Cabinet (formerly the 'Executive Council'). The Cabinet comprises the Premier (formerly 'Chief Minister'), one ex officio member (the Attorney-General), and four other ministers (appointed by the Governor on the advice of the Premier); a Cabinet Secretary sets the Cabinet's agenda under consultation with the Premier. The House of Assembly (formerly 'Legislative Council') consists of a Speaker, chosen from among the elected members of—or those eligible for election to—the Assembly, one ex officio member (the Attorney-General) and 13 elected members (nine members from one-member electoral districts and four members representing the territory 'at large').

The new Constitution also makes provision for the formation of a sixth government ministry, while a National Security Council, comprised of the Governor, Premier, Attorney-General, Commissioner of Police and a named government minister, advises the Governor upon matters of internal security and policing of the territory. A Fundamental Rights Chapter, ensuring the protection of citizens' human rights and freedoms, is also in effect. By mid-2009 a Public Service Commission and Judicial and Legal Services Commission had been instituted, while preparations for a Human Rights Commission were ongoing.

The division of the islands into nine electoral districts, instead of seven, came into effect at the 1979 general election. The four 'at large' seats were introduced at the 1995 general election. The minimum voting age was lowered from 21 years to 18 years.

Under the British Overseas Territories Act, which entered into effect in May 2002, British Virgin Islanders have the right to United Kingdom citizenship and the right of abode in the United Kingdom. British citizens do not enjoy reciprocal rights.

The Government

HEAD OF STATE

Queen: HM Queen ELIZABETH II.

Governor: JOHN S. DUNCAN (assumed office 15 Aug. 2014).

Deputy Governor: INEZ ARCHIBALD.

CABINET
(September 2014)

The Government is formed by the National Democratic Party.

Premier and Minister of Finance: D. ORLANDO SMITH.

Deputy Premier and Minister of Natural Resources and Labour: KEDRICK PICKERING.

Minister of Health and Social Development: RONNIE W. SKELTON.

Minister of Education and Culture: MYRON V. WALWYN.

Minister of Communications and Works: MARK VANTERPOOL.

Attorney-General: Dr CHRISTOPHER PHILLIP MALCOLM.

MINISTRIES

Office of the Governor: 20 Waterfront Dr., POB 702, Road Town, Tortola VG1110; tel. 494-2345; fax 494-5582; e-mail bvigovernor@gov.vg; internet www.bvi.gov.vg.

Office of the Deputy Governor: Central Administration Bldg, West Wing, 33 Admin Dr., Road Town, Tortola VG1110; tel. 494-3701; fax 494-6481; e-mail webmaster@dgo.gov.vg; internet www.dgo.gov.vg.

Office of the Premier: 33 Admin Dr., Wickham's Cay 1, Road Town, Tortola VG1110; tel. 468-3701; fax 494-6413; e-mail premieroffice@gov.vg.

Ministry of Communications and Works: 33 Admin Dr., Wickham's Cay 1, Road Town, Tortola VG1110; tel. 468-2183; fax 494-3873; e-mail mcw@gov.vg.

Ministry of Education and Culture: 33 Admin Dr., Wickham's Cay 1, Road Town, Tortola VG1110; tel. 468-3358; fax 468-0021; e-mail mec@gov.vg.

Ministry of Finance: 33 Admin Dr., Wickham's Cay 1, Road Town, Tortola VG1110; tel. 494-3701; fax 494-6413; e-mail finance@gov.vg; internet www.finance.gov.vg.

Ministry of Health and Social Development: 33 Admin Dr., Wickham's Cay 1, Road Town, Tortola VG1110; tel. 468-3701; fax 468-4412; e-mail ministryofhealth@gov.vg.

Ministry of Natural Resources and Labour: 33 Admin Dr., Wickham's Cay 1, Road Town, Tortola VG1110; tel. 468-0675; fax 494-4283; e-mail nrl@gov.vg.

Legislature

HOUSE OF ASSEMBLY

Speaker: INGRID MOSES-SCATLIFFE.

Clerk: PHYLLIS EVANS, Richard C. Stoutt Bldg, Wickham's Cay I, POB 2390, Road Town, Tortola VG1110; tel. 494-4757; fax 494-4544; e-mail JHodge@gov.vg; internet www.legco.gov.vg.

General Election, 7 November 2011

Party	Seats
National Democratic Party (NDP)	9
Virgin Islands Party (VIP)	4
Total	**13**

Election Commission

Office of the Supervisor of Elections: Ulric Dawson Bldg, 6 Russell Hill Rd, Road Town, Tortola VG1110; tel. 468-4380; fax 468-2779; e-mail electionsoffice@gov.vg; Supervisor of Elections JULIETTE PENN.

Political Organizations

National Democratic Party (NDP): Wickham Cay, Tortola VG1110; e-mail bvindp@gmail.com; internet bvindp.com; f. 1998; Chair. EILEEN PARSONS; Pres. D. ORLANDO SMITH.

People's Empowerment Party: Road Town, Tortola; f. 2014; Leader J. ALVIN CHRISTOPHER; Pres. NATALIO WHEATLEY.

People's Party (POP): Road Town, Tortola; f. 2011; Leader ALLEN WHEATLEY.

United Party (UP): POB 3068, Road Town, Tortola VG1110; tel. 495-2656; fax 494-1808; e-mail liberatebvi@msn.com; f. 1967; Chair. CONRAD MADURO.

Virgin Islands Party (VIP): Road Town, Tortola VG1110; e-mail info@viparty.com; Chair. RALPH T. O'NEAL.

Judicial System

Justice is administered by the Eastern Caribbean Supreme Court (ECSC), based in Saint Lucia, which consists of two divisions: the High Court of Justice and the Court of Appeal. There are two resident High Court Judges, as well as an Acting High Court Judge. A visiting Court of Appeal, comprised of the Chief Justice and two Judges of Appeal, sits twice a year in the British Virgin Islands. There is also a Magistrates' Court, which hears prescribed civil and criminal cases. The final Court of Appeal is the Privy Council in the United Kingdom. Under the terms of the 2007 Constitution, a Judicial and Legal Services Commission, chaired by the Chief Justice, was established to counsel the Governor in matters relating to judicial appointments and regulation of the territory's legal system. In 2009 the ECSC established a new division of the court, based on Tortola, to preside over all stages of litigation concerning major domestic, international or cross-border commercial claims.

High Court Judges: EDWARD BANNISTER (acting), VICKI ANN ELLIS, ALBERT REDHEAD.

Registrar: PAULA AJARIE.

Magistrate's Office: Magistrates Court, POB 140, Road Town, Tortola VG1110; tel. 468-3701; fax 468-4302; e-mail magistrate@vigilate.org; Magistrate TAMIA RICHARDS.

Attorney-General: Dr CHRISTOPHER PHILLIP MALCOLM.

Religion

CHRISTIANITY

The Roman Catholic Church

The diocese of St John's-Basseterre, suffragan to the archdiocese of Castries (Saint Lucia), includes Anguilla, Antigua and Barbuda, the British Virgin Islands, Montserrat and Saint Christopher and Nevis. The Bishop is resident in St John's, Antigua. According to official estimates from 2005, 10% of the population are Roman Catholics.

The Anglican Communion

The British and US Virgin Islands form a single, missionary diocese of the Episcopal Church of the United States of America. The Bishop of the Diocese of the Virgin Islands is resident on St Thomas in the US Virgin Islands. According to official estimates from 2005, 17% of the population are Anglicans.

Protestant Churches

Various Protestant denominations are represented, principally the Methodist Church (an estimated 33% of the population in 2005).

Others include the Church of God (9%), Seventh-day Adventist (6%), and Baptist Churches (5%).

The Press

The BVI Beacon: 10 Russell Hill Rd, POB 3030, Road Town, Tortola VG1110; tel. 494-3434; fax 494-6267; e-mail bvibeacn@surfbvi.com; internet www.bvibeacon.com; f. 1984; Thur.; local and international news; also operates from the US Virgin Islands; Publr and CEO RUSSELL HARRIGAN; Editor FREEMAN ROGERS; circ. 3,400.

The Island Sun: 112 Main St, POB 21, Road Town, Tortola VG1110; tel. 494-2476; fax 494-5854; e-mail islandsun@surfbvi.com; internet www.islandsun.com; f. 1962; publ. by Sun Enterprises (BVI) Ltd.

Just 4 Health: Relyon Marketing Group, Wickham's Cay, Road Town, Tortola VG1110; f. 2013; quarterly; health issues; Publr ELTON CALLWOOD.

Virgin Islands Platinum News: Road Town, Tortola; tel. 442-3663; e-mail editorial@bviplatinum.com; internet www.bviplatinum.com; online; Sr Reporter MELISSA EDWARDS.

The Welcome (The Welcome Guide to the British Virgin Islands): POB 133, Road Town, Tortola; tel. 494-2413; fax 494-4413; e-mail info@bviwelcome.com; internet www.bviwelcome.com; f. 1971; every 2 months; general, tourist information; Publr and Editor CLAUDIA COLLI; circ. 165,000.

Publishers

aLookingGlass: 7 Road Reef Plaza, POB 3895, Sea Cow's Bay, Tortola, VG1110; tel. 494-7788; fax 494-8777; e-mail info@alookingglass.com; internet alookingglass.com; f. 2002; publishes *The BVI Property & Yacht* monthly; Man. Dir OWEN WATERS; Gen. Man. COLIN RATHBUN.

Global Directories (BVI) Ltd: Wickham's Cay 1, POB 3403, Road Town, Tortola VG1110; tel. 494-2060; fax 494-3060; e-mail bvi-sales@globaldirectories.com; internet bviyp.com; fmrly Caribbean Publishing Co (BVI) Ltd; subsidiary of MediaHouse Ltd, Bermuda; telephone directories, Caribbean Yellow Pages; Gen. Man. MICHAEL ARNOLD.

Island Publishing Services Ltd: Blackburn Hwy, POB 133, Road Town, Tortola VG1110; tel. 494-2413; fax 494-6589; e-mail info@bviwelcome.com; internet www.bviwelcome.com; publishes *The Welcome* (q.v.), *BVI Restaurant and Food Guide* (annual), *The Limin' Times* (weekly entertainment guide), and *The British Virgin Islands Cruise Ship Visitors' Guide* (annual); Gen. Man. KAREN BELL; Publr and CEO CLAUDIA COLLI.

Broadcasting and Communications

TELECOMMUNICATIONS

A Telecommunications Liberalization Act was ratified by the Government in 2007.

Caribbean Cellular Telephone (CCT Global Communications): Geneva Pl., 333 Waterfront Dr., POB 267, Road Town, Tortola VG1110; tel. 494-3825; fax 494-4933; internet www.cctwireless.com; f. 1986 as CCT Boatphone; mobile cellular telephone operator; Gen. Man. JOSE LUIS FERNANDEZ.

Digicel: POB 4168, Road Town, Tortola VG1110; tel. 494-2048; fax 494-0111; e-mail bvicustomercare@digicelgroup.com; internet www.digicelbvi.com; granted licence to operate mobile cellular telephone network in British Virgin Islands in Dec. 2007; mobile telecommunications and internet services provider; CEO DECLAN CASSIDY (British Virgin Islands).

LIME: Cutlass Bldg, Wickham's Cay 1, POB 440, Road Town, Tortola VG1110; tel. 494-4444; fax 494-2506; internet www.lime.com; f. 1967 as Cable & Wireless (WI) Ltd; name changed as above 2008; Group CEO TONY RICE; Regional CEO GERARD BORELY.

Regulatory Bodies

Telecommunications Regulatory Commission: LM Business Centre, 3rd Floor, 27 Fish Lock Rd, Road Town, POB 4401, Tortola; tel. 468-4165; fax 494-6786; e-mail contact@trc.vg; internet www.trc.vg; f. 2006; regulatory body; Chair. AYANA HULL-BRATHWAITE; CEO GUY L. MALONE.

Telephone Services Management Unit: Deputy Governor's Office, Central Administration Bldg, 2nd Floor, West Atrium, Road Town, Tortola VG1110; tel. 494-4728; fax 494-6551; e-mail tsmu@bvigovernment.org; govt agency; Man. REYNELL FRASER.

BROADCASTING

Radio

Virgin Islands Broadcasting Ltd—Radio ZBVI: Baughers Bay, POB 78, Road Town, Tortola VG1110; tel. 494-2250; fax 494-1139; e-mail zbvi@caribsurf.com; internet www.zbvi.vi; f. 1965; commercial; Gen. Man. HARVEY HERBERT; Operations Man. SANDRA POTTER WARRICAN.

Television

BVI Cable TV: Fishlock Rd, POB 644, Road Town, Tortola VG1110; tel. 494-3831; fax 494-3205; operated by Innovative Communication Corporation, based in the US Virgin Islands; programmes from US Virgin Islands and Puerto Rico; 53 channels; Gen. Man. LUANNE HODGE.

Finance

BANKING

Commercial Banks

Banco Popular de Puerto Rico: POB 67, Road Town, Tortola VG1110; tel. 494-2117; fax 494-5294; e-mail internet@bppr.com; internet www.bancopopular.com; Pres. and CEO RICHARD L. CARRIÓN; Man. SANDRA SCATLIFFE.

CIBC FirstCaribbean International Bank: Wickham's Cay 1, POB 70, Road Town, Tortola VG1110; tel. 852-9900; fax 495-2361; e-mail barcbvi@surfbvi.com; internet www.cibcfcib.com; f. 2003 following merger of Caribbean operations of Barclays Bank PLC and CIBC; Barclays relinquished its stake in 2006; CEO RIK PARKHILL; 3 brs.

First Bank Virgin Islands: Road Town Business Centre, Wickham's Cay 1, Road Town, POB 435, Tortola VG1110; tel. 494-8899; fax 494-3863; e-mail e-firstbank@firstbankpr.com; internet www.firstbankvi.com; f. 1994; est. as a commercial bank in Puerto Rico; Pres. and CEO AURELIO ALEMÁN-BERMÚDEZ.

Scotiabank (Canada): Wickham's Cay 1, POB 434, Road Town, Tortola VG1110; tel. 494-2526; fax 494-4657; e-mail joycelyn.murraine@scotiabank.com; internet www.scotiabank.com/vg/en; f. 1998; Chair. and Dir JOYCELYN MURRAINE; 2 brs.

VP Bank (BVI) Ltd: 3076 Sir Francis Drake's Highway, POB 3463, Road Town, Tortola VG1110; tel. 494-1100; fax 494-1144; e-mail info.bvi@vpbank.com; internet www.vpbank.vg; Chair. FREDY YOGT; CEO SIEGBERT NÄSCHER.

Development Bank

National Bank of the Virgin Islands Ltd: New Social Security Bldg, Wickham's Cay 1, POB 275, Road Town, Tortola VG1110; tel. 494-3737; fax 494-3119; e-mail admin@natbankvi.com; internet www.natbankvi.com; f. 1976; fmrly Development Bank of the British Virgin Islands; state-owned; Chair. KENNETH HODGE.

REGULATORY AUTHORITY

Financial Services Commission: Pasea Estate, POB 418, Road Town, Tortola VG1110; tel. 494-1324; fax 494-5016; e-mail enquiries@bvifsc.vg; internet www.bvifsc.vg; f. 2002; independent financial services regulator; Chair. ROBIN GAUL; Man. Dir and CEO ROBERT MATHAVIOUS.

TRUST COMPANIES

Abacus Trust and Management Services Ltd: 333 Waterfront Dr., Road Town, Tortola VG1110; tel. 494-4388; fax 494-3088; e-mail info@mwmabacus.com; internet www.mwmabacus.com; f. 1994; Man. MEADE MALONE.

AMS Trustees Ltd: Sea Meadow House, POB 116, Road Town, Tortola VG1110; tel. 494-3399; fax 494-3041; e-mail enquiries@amsbvi.com; internet www.amsbvi.com; f. 1985; privately owned; subsidiary of the AMS Group (British Virgin Islands); Man. Dir NICHOLAS CLARK.

ATU General Trust (BVI) Ltd: 3076 Sir Francis Drake's Hwy, POB 3463, Road Town, Tortola; tel. 494-1122; fax 494-1199; e-mail info@atubvi.com; internet www.atubvi.com.

Belmont Trust Ltd: Belmont Chambers, Tropic Isle Bldg, Nibbs St, POB 3443, Road Town, Tortola VG1110; tel. 494-5800; fax 494-2545; e-mail info@belmontbvi.net; internet www.belmontbvi.com; Man. Dir ANDREA DOUGLAS.

CCP Financial Consultants Ltd: Ellen Skelton Bldg, Fishers Lane, POB 681, Road Town, Tortola VG1110; tel. 494-6777; fax 494-6787; e-mail info@ccpbvi.com; internet www.ccpbvi.com; Dir JOSEPH ROBERTS.

Citco BVI Ltd: Wickham's Cay, POB 662, Road Town, Tortola VG1110; tel. 494-2217; fax 494-3917; e-mail bvi-trust@citco.com; internet www.citco.com.

HSBC International Trustee (BVI) Ltd: Woodbourne Hall, POB 916, Road Town, Tortola VG1110; tel. 494-5414; fax 494-2417; e-mail kenneth.morgan@htvg.vg; Dir KENNETH MORGAN.

Hunte & Co Services Ltd: Yamraj Bldg, 2nd Floor, POB 3504, Road Town, Tortola; tel. 495-0232; fax 495-0229; e-mail laura.arthur@hunteandco.com; internet www.hunteandco.com; f. 2004.

Intertrust BVI: Main St 171, POB 4041, Road Town, Tortola; tel. 394-9100; fax 494-9101; e-mail bvi@intertrustgroup.com; internet www.intertrustgroup.com; Sr Vice-Pres. SABINAH CLEMENT.

Maples and Calder BVI: Sea Meadow House, POB 173, Road Town, Tortola VG1110; tel. 852-3000; fax 852-3097; e-mail bviinfo@maplesandcalder.com; internet www.maplesandcalder.com; Man. Partner ARABELLA DI LORIO.

Midocean Management and Trust Services (BVI) Ltd: 9 Columbus Centre, Pelican Dr., POB 805, Road Town, Tortola VG1110; tel. 494-4567; fax 494-4568; e-mail midocean@maitlandgroup.com; owned by Maitland Group; Man. ELIZABETH WILKINSON.

Moore Stephens International Services (BVI) Ltd: Palm Grove House, Wickham's Cay I, POB 3186, Road Town, Tortola VG1110; tel. 494-3503; fax 494-3592; e-mail moorestephens@moorestephensbvi.com; internet www.moorestephens.com; Partner NICHOLAS LANE.

TMF (BVI) Ltd: Palm Grove House, 4th Floor, POB 438, Road Town, Tortola VG1110; tel. 494-2616; fax 494-2704; e-mail bvi@tmf-group.com; internet www.tmf-group.com; Dir GRAHAM COOK.

Totalserve Trust Company Ltd: 197 Main St, POB 3540, Road Town, Tortola VG1110; tel. 494-6900; fax 494-6990; e-mail bvi@totalserve.eu; internet www.totalservetrust.eu; f. 2003; Man. DENESHAR MEADE.

Tricor Services (BVI) Ltd: Palm Grove House, Wickham's Cay, POB 3340, Road Town, Tortola VG1110; tel. 494-6004; fax 494-6404; e-mail info@bvi.tricorglobal.com; internet www.bvi.tricorglobal.com; f. 2000; Man. PATRICK A. NICHOLAS.

Trident Trust Company (BVI) Ltd: Trident Chambers, Wickham's Cay, POB 146, Road Town, Tortola VG1110; tel. 494-2434; fax 494-3754; e-mail bvi@tridenttrust.com; internet www.tridenttrust.com; Man. BARRY R. GOODMAN.

In March 2014 there were 2,215 active licensed mutual funds, according to the Financial Services Commission.

INSURANCE

ALTA Insurance Management (BVI) Ltd: POB 4623, Road Town, Tortola VG1110; tel. 494-9670; fax 494-9690; e-mail gtaylor@altaholdings.com; internet www.altaholdings.com; Pres. DONALD B. ROUSSO; Man. Dir GREGORY M. TAYLOR.

AMS Insurance Management Services Ltd: Sea Meadow House, POB 116, Road Town, Tortola VG1110; tel. 494-4078; fax 494-8589; e-mail enquiries@amsbvi.com; internet www.amsbvi.com; f. 1982; Man. Dir NICHOLAS CLARK; Dir (Insurance) DEREK LLOYD.

Belmont Insurance Management Ltd: Belmont Chambers, Tropic Isle Bldg, Nibbs St, POB 3443, Road Town, Tortola VG1110; tel. 494-5800; fax 494-2545; e-mail info@belmontbvi.com; internet www.belmontbvi.com; Man. Dir ANDREA DOUGLAS.

Caledonian Global Insurance Services (BVI) Ltd: Harbour House, Waterfront Dr., Road Town, Tortola VG1110; tel. 949-0050; fax 814-4875; e-mail insurance@caledonian.com; internet www.caledonian.com; f. 2005; acquired by New World Holdings Inc in 2011; Dir DAVE SIMS.

Captiva Managers (BVI) Ltd: Caribbean Chambers, POB 4428, Road Town, Tortola VG1110; tel. 494-4111; fax 494-4222; e-mail info@captivagroup.net; internet www.captiva.vg; Dir NOELLA M. THOMPSON; Man. Dir HARRY J. THOMPSON.

Caribbean Insurers Ltd (CIL): Mirage Bldg, POB 129, Road Town, Tortola VG1110; tel. 494-2728; fax 494-4393; e-mail pl@caribbins.com; internet www.caribbeaninsurers.com; f. 1973; part of the Caribbean Insurers Group; Chair. JOHN WILLIAMS; Man. Dir BRIAN JERMYN.

Colonial Insurance (BVI) Ltd: Palm Grove House, POB 2377, Road Town, Tortola; tel. 494-8450; fax 494-8559; internet bvi.cgigroup.com; owned by Colonial Group International (Bermuda).

HWR Insurance Management Services Ltd (Harneys Insurance): Craigmuir Chambers, POB 71, Road Town, Tortola VG1110; tel. 494-2233; fax 494-3547; e-mail bvi@harneys.com; internet www.harneys.com; Man. Dir DAVID SPYER.

Marine Insurance Office (BVI) Ltd (MIO): Mill Mall, Wickham's Cay 1, POB 874, Road Town, Tortola VG1110; tel. 494-3795; fax 494-4540; e-mail info@mioinsurance.com; f. 1985; Man. WESLEY WOOLHOUSE.

Osiris Insurance Management Ltd: Coastal Bldg, Wickham's Cay 11, POB 2221, Road Town, Tortola VG1110; tel. 494-9820; fax 494-6934; e-mail miles@osiristrust.com; internet osiristrust.com; Man. Dir MILES WALTON.

Trident Insurance Management (BVI) Ltd: Trident Chambers, Wickham's Cay, POB 146, Road Town, Tortola VG1110; tel. 494-2434; fax 494-3754; e-mail bvi@tridenttrust.com.

USA Risk Group (BVI) Inc: Harbour House, 2nd Floor, POB 4428, Road Town, Tortola; tel. 872-7475; fax 229-6280; e-mail rleadbetter@usarisk.ky; internet www.usarisk.com; Pres. GARY H. OSBORNE; Man. ROB LEADBETTER.

Several US and other foreign companies have agents in the British Virgin Islands. At the end of 2013 there were 147 'captive' insurance companies registered in the British Virgin Islands.

Trade and Industry
GOVERNMENT AGENCY

Trade and Investment Promotion Department: Chief Minister's Office, Central Administration Bldg, 33 Administration Dr., Road Town, Tortola VG1110; tel. 494-5007; fax 494-5657; e-mail trade@bvigovernment.org.

CHAMBER OF COMMERCE

British Virgin Islands Chamber of Commerce and Hotel Association: Tropic Aisle Bldg, Wickham's Cay 1, POB 376, Road Town, Tortola VG1110; tel. 494-3514; fax 494-6179; e-mail info@bviccha.org; internet www.bviccha.org; f. 1986; Chair. LOUIS POTTER; Pres. (Business) TROY CHRISTOPHER; Pres. (Hospitality) WILBURT MASON; 250 mems.

UTILITIES
Electricity

British Virgin Islands Electricity Corpn (BVIEC): Long Bush, POB 268, Road Town, Tortola VG1110; tel. 494-3911; fax 494-4291; e-mail bviecgm@bvielectricity.com; internet www.bvielectricity.com; f. 1978; privatization pending; Chair. RON POTTER; Gen. Man. LEROY ABRAHAM.

Water

Water and Sewerage Dept: Water & Sewerage Compound, Baughers Bay, Road Town, POB 130, Tortola VG1110; tel. 494-3416; fax 494-6746; e-mail wsd@gov.vg; f. 1980; Dir PERLINE SCATLIFFE-LEONARD.

Transport
ROADS

In 2002 there were 132 km (82 miles) of access roads, 77 km of primary roads, 37 km of secondary roads and 90 km of tertiary roads.

Public Works Department: Baughers Bay, POB 284, Tortola VG1110; tel. 494-2722; fax 494-4740; e-mail pwd@bvigovernment.org; responsible for road maintenance; Dir JEFFREY SKELTON.

SHIPPING

There are two direct steamship services, one from the United Kingdom and one from the USA. Motor launches maintain daily mail and passenger services with St Thomas and St John, US Virgin Islands. Expansion of the cruise ship pier in Road Town was completed in 2008.

British Virgin Islands Ports Authority: Port Purcell, POB 4, Road Town, Tortola VG1110; tel. 494-3435; fax 494-2642; e-mail bviports@bviports.org; internet www.bviports.org; f. 1991; Chair. GREGORY ADAMS; Man. Dir VINCENT VICTOR O'NEAL.

Island Shipping & Trading Co Ltd: POB 61, Road Town, Tortola VG1110; tel. 494-2268; fax 494-4708; e-mail operations@islandshipping.com; internet www.islandshipping.com; Chair. PETER HAYCRAFT; Man. Dir CHRISTOPHER HAYCRAFT.

Tropical Shipping: Port Purcell Seaport, Island Shipping and Trading, POB 250, Road Town, Tortola VG1110; tel. 494-2674; fax 494-3505; e-mail lmoses@tropical.com; internet www.tropical.com; Pres. MIKE PELLICCI; Man. LEROY MOSES.

CIVIL AVIATION

Terrance B. Lettsome (formerly Beef Island) International Airport, about 16 km (10 miles) from Road Town, has a runway with a length of 1,500 m (4,921 ft). Captain Auguste George Airport on Anegada has been designated an international point of entry. In 2010 the airport on Virgin Gorda underwent major renovation, including an extension to the runway to allow larger aircraft to land. The Government in 2014 was planning an expansion of the Terrance B. Lettsome Airport.

British Virgin Islands Airports Authority: POB 4416, Road Town, Tortola VG1110; tel. 852-9000; fax 852-9045; internet www.bviaa.com; f. 2005; Chair. DEBRA ROMNEY-HODGE (acting); Man. Dir DENNISTON FRASER.

BVI Airways: Suite 234, Terrance B. Lettsome International Airport, Beef Island, Tortola VG1120; e-mail customerservice@bviairways.com; internet www.gobvi.com; f. 2010; flights to St Maarten, Dominica and Antigua; Pres. and CEO JERRY WILLOUGHBY.

Tourism

The main attraction of the islands is their tranquillity and clear waters, which provide excellent facilities for sailing, fishing, diving and other water sports. In 2010 there were an estimated 2,353 hotel rooms. There are also many charter yachts offering overnight accommodation. There were an estimated 351,000 arrivals to the islands in 2012. The majority of tourists are from the USA. Receipts from tourism totalled some US $397m. in 2012.

British Virgin Islands Chamber of Commerce and Hotel Association: see Chamber of Commerce.

British Virgin Islands Tourist Board: AKARA Bldg, 2nd Floor, DeCastro St, Road Town, Tortola VG1110; tel. 494-3134; fax 494-3866; e-mail info@bvitourism.com; internet www.bvitourism.com; Chair. RUSSEL HARRIGAN; Dir SHARON FLAX-MARS.

Defence

The United Kingdom is responsible for the defence of the islands.

Education

Primary education is free, universal and compulsory between the ages of five and 11 years. Secondary education is also free and lasts from 12 to 16 years of age. In 2010/11 some 853 pupils were attending pre-primary schools; in 2011, according to UNESCO estimates, enrolment at primary schools included 81% of children in the relevant age-group, while enrolment at secondary schools was equivalent to 97% of pupils in the relevant age category. Some 3,138 pupils attended primary schools in 2010/11, while 1,923 students attended secondary schools. Higher education is available at the University of the Virgin Islands (St Thomas, US Virgin Islands) and elsewhere in the Caribbean, in North America and in the United Kingdom. The 2014 budget allocated US $53.9m. to the Ministry of Education and Culture, some 17.8% of total recurrent expenditure.

THE CAYMAN ISLANDS

Geography

PHYSICAL FEATURES

The Cayman Islands is a United Kingdom Overseas Territory in the Caribbean Sea, mid-way between Cuba and Honduras. The islands are located about 240 km (150 miles) south of Cuba and some 290 km north-west of Jamaica, upon which the Territory was once dependent (before Jamaican independence). The Caymans are separated from Jamaica by the Cayman Trench, the deepest part of the Caribbean. The territory covers an area of only 262 sq km (102 sq miles).

The three islands are low, limestone-and-coral formations, largely surrounded by coral reef, and with shorelines ill-defined by mangrove swamps. The largest island is Grand Cayman (about 35 km—22 miles—long, with an average width of some 6 km), which constitutes three-quarters of the territory's land area, although about one-half of it is wetland. The island is aligned along an east–west axis, tapering in the south-west before a northward-extending spit defines the western shore of the 110-sq-km shallow lagoon, the North Sound, as well as the sheltered west coast of the whole island (notably the West Bay and its Seven Mile Beach). The other two islands are long and narrow, aligned more to the north-east, end to end and separated by an 8-km channel. They lie 128 km to the east of Grand Cayman, and a little north, slightly closer to both Cuba and Jamaica than the largest island. Low-lying and swampy Little Cayman (26 sq km) is about 16 km long and seldom more than 1.5 km wide. Cayman Brac (39 sq km) is the most easterly of the islands. It is about 19 km long and about 2 km wide, but reaches the highest point in the territory, where a huge limestone outcrop, called The Bluff (43 m—a Gaelic word for a bluff is brac), rises along the centre of the island. The islands' land and marine environments are extensively protected, in an effort to preserve the bird and animal life, some of it unique (a species of orchid on Grand Cayman, for instance, trees on Cayman Brac and Cayman parrots). The islands were originally named, and, indeed, settled for the large turtle population, although they have long been named with the Carib word for the marine crocodile that also lived here.

CLIMATE

The climate is subtropical marine, with warm, wet summers between May and October (in the latter part of this season hurricanes occasionally occur) and milder, dryer winters. Rain is essential to the freshwater supply. Average annual rainfall

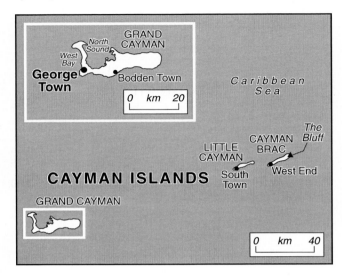

is about 1,290 mm (50 ins), and the average annual temperature is 28.5°C (83.3°F).

POPULATION

A mixed-race population (40%) is balanced by roughly equal black and white communities (each about 20%), as well as expatriates of various ethnic groups. About one-third of the population are foreign workers. The islanders are predominantly Christian and English-speaking (91% in 2010), although there are some Spanish and Filipino speakers.

According to official estimates, the population was 55,691 in December 2013. The vast majority of the population lived on Grand Cayman. The capital is George Town in the south-west of Grand Cayman, which had a population of 29,144 in December 2013. West Bay (to the north of the capital) and Bodden Town (on the central southern coast) are the other main centres on Grand Cayman. The main settlements on the other two islands are West End on Cayman Brac and South Town on Little Cayman. The territory is divided into eight administrative districts.

History

The Cayman Islands constitute a United Kingdom Overseas Territory, with a Cabinet (known as the Executive Council until 2003) headed by the Governor, who is the representative of the British monarch.

Grand Cayman became a British colony in 1670, with the two smaller islands settled only in 1833. Until 1959 all three islands were a dependency of Jamaica. In 1962 a separate Administrator for the islands was appointed (redesignated Governor in 1971).

In the absence of formal political parties, elections to the Assembly were contested every four years by independents and by individuals standing as 'teams'. In 1991, however, the territory's first formal political organization since the 1960s was formed, the Progressive Democratic Party. It opposed various provisions of the proposed constitutional reforms. It developed into a broad coalition and was renamed the National Team, and then won 12 of the 15 elective seats at the general election of November 1992. At a general election in November

1996 the National Team remained in power, winning nine seats in the Legislative Assembly.

A serious problem for the Cayman Islands in recent years has been drugs-related crime. The Mutual Legal Assistance Treaty (ratified by the US Senate in 1990) between the Cayman Islands and the USA provides for the mutual exchange of information for use in combating crime (particularly drugs-trafficking and money-laundering). Further legislation relating to the abuse of the financial sector by criminal organizations was approved in 1996.

In March 1999 the British Government published draft legislation confirming that its Dependencies were to be referred to as United Kingdom Overseas Territories; the document stated that all such territories would be required to comply with European standards on human rights and financial regulation. In May 2002 the British Overseas Territories Act, having received royal assent in the United Kingdom in February, came into force and granted British citizenship to the people of its Overseas Territories, including the Cayman Islands. Under the new law, Caymanians would be able to hold British passports and work in the United Kingdom and elsewhere in the European Union.

The governing National Team suffered a heavy defeat in the general election of November 2000. It lost six of its nine seats, including that held by Truman Bodden, the Leader of Government Business. The newly elected Legislative Assembly chose Kurt Tibbetts of the Democratic Alliance to be Leader of Government Business.

In November 2001 several members of the Legislative Assembly formed the United Democratic Party (UDP). McKeeva Bush, the leader of the new party, claimed that at least 10 members of the 15-member Assembly were UDP supporters. Subsequently, the approval of a motion of no confidence (by nine votes to five, with one abstention) against the Leader of Government Business resulted in Tibbetts and Edna Moyle, the Minister of Community Development, Women's Affairs, Youth and Sport, leaving the Executive Council. Bush became the new Leader of Government Business, while two other UDP legislators joined the Cabinet. Bush was formally elected leader of the party in May 2002. In the same month it was announced that the five opposition members of the Legislative Assembly had formed a new political party, the People's Progressive Movement (PPM), led by Tibbetts.

In March 2002 a three-member Constitutional Review Commission submitted a new draft constitution. The proposed document had to be debated by the Legislative Assembly and then approved by the British Parliament before being formally adopted. The draft constitution included the creation of the office of Chief Minister, proposed a full ministerial government, and incorporated a bill of rights. The opposition demanded a referendum on the recommendations, on the grounds that the UDP had rejected several of the proposals, despite strong public support for the changes, but Bush forwarded the proposals to the British Foreign and Commonwealth Office (FCO), via the Governor's office. Consensus, however, proved impossible to achieve.

In January 2003 Bush accused the United Kingdom of undermining the course of Cayman Islands' justice, after a routine money-laundering case was dismissed amid allegations of espionage and obstruction of justice by British intelligence agents. The trial collapsed after it was alleged that the Director of the Cayman Islands Financial Reporting Unit and a key witness in the trial had passed information about the case to an unnamed agency of the British Government, understood to be the Secret Intelligence Service (MI6). It was claimed that MI6 wished to protect the names of its sources within the Caribbean offshore banking community. Bush demanded that the British Government pay for the failed trial, estimated to have cost some US $5m., and for any negative repercussions the affair might have for the reputation of the territory's banking sector. The United Kingdom, however, refused to compensate the Cayman Islands and maintained that although its intelligence agencies might have helped in the investigation, they had never interfered in the case. In March the Attorney-General, David Ballantyne, resigned amid accusations that he was aware that British intelligence agents were working covertly in the Cayman Islands.

The legislative election scheduled to take place in November 2004 was postponed by six months following the devastation caused by Hurricane Ivan in September. In response to the hurricane Governor Bruce Dinwiddy enacted the Emergency Powers Act, allowing him to extend the remit of his authority and impose a curfew until the restoration of full electricity supplies, as a deterrent to looting. The opposition PPM secured nine of the 15 seats available in the ballot that was held in May 2005; the UDP won only five mandates and the remaining seat was occupied by an independent candidate. The outgoing UDP Government had been criticized for its management of the aftermath of the hurricane and also for the decision to grant Caymanian 'belonger' status to 3,000 residents in 2003, which was interpreted by many as an attempt to increase in the party's favour the number of those eligible to vote. The leader of the PPM, Kurt Tibbetts, once again became the Leader of

Government Business and committed the administration to holding a referendum on increased autonomy in the territory.

Informal talks on constitutional modernization were held between the Government and representatives of the FCO in March 2006. The establishment of a Constitutional Review Secretariat, to initiate renewed efforts towards constitutional reform in the territory, was announced by the Government in February 2007. In January 2008 the Government launched a series of public consultations ahead of a referendum scheduled to be held in May. The FCO affirmed in April that the new constitution must include a bill of rights and, in response, the Government postponed the referendum to allow a longer period of public deliberation. The UDP voiced strong objections to the revised date for the ballot of 30 July, contending that this did not allow for a sufficient period of preparation and discussion, and in June the Government postponed the referendum once more until May 2009 in order for it to be held concurrently with a general election. This was to allow for the finalization of a draft constitution following the conclusion of discussions with the United Kingdom.

In an effort to enhance constitutional democracy, Tibbetts announced in November 2006 that a Freedom of Information Bill—intended to promote government transparency and accountability—was to be debated in the Legislative Assembly, prior to a public consultation exercise. A National Archives and Public Records Bill, governing the preservation of government records was approved in March 2007, as a preparatory step towards examination of the Freedom of Information Bill, which had been subject to delays. The legislation was finally approved in August, and in the following month the Freedom of Information Unit was officially opened. The law eventually became effective on 5 January 2009.

The general election was held on 20 May 2009, at which the opposition UDP defeated the incumbent PPM, securing nine of the 15 available seats. The PPM secured five seats and the remaining one was taken by an independent candidate. McKeeva Bush was sworn in as Leader of Government Business on 27 May.

In the concurrent referendum on the draft constitution some 62% of voters supported the changes (the votes of 50% plus one were required for the result to be binding). As a result, on 10 June 2009 the Privy Council approved the new charter, which came into force on 6 November. The new Constitution gave greater autonomy to the Cabinet, replacing the Governor-appointed Financial Secretary with an elected Minister of Finance—a portfolio assumed by Bush, whose post of Leader of Government Business was also redesignated Premier. Under the Constitution, the Premier was limited to serving a maximum of two consecutive four-year terms in office. Juliana O'Connor-Connolly, the Minister of District Administration, Works and Gender Affairs, was additionally appointed to the newly created post of Deputy Premier. Although the Governor retained overall control of foreign affairs, certain aspects of external dealings were delegated to the Cabinet. A Bill of Rights, Freedom and Responsibilities came into effect in November 2012.

Tibbetts resigned as leader of the opposition and PPM leader in February 2011. He was succeeded by Alden McLaughlin.

In May 2011 the British Government declared that approval of the 2011/12 budget would only be granted after the Cayman authorities agreed to reduce their expenditure projections; a revised budget received British endorsement in the following month. Bush agreed to abide by new fiscal responsibility guidelines, as delineated in the Framework for Fiscal Responsibility (FFR) in November. The United Kingdom finally approved the territory's 2012/13 budget in August 2012 after Bush pledged to implement further austerity measures and to enact the FFR. However, in October, in spite of vehement opposition from the British Government, Bush announced his intention to modify certain clauses within the FFR; nevertheless, in the following month Bush submitted the FFR to the legislature unaltered, and the document was approved later in that month.

In July 2011 the Governor confirmed that a police investigation was under way into alleged financial irregularities in 2004 by Premier Bush. It had been alleged that the then Leader of Government Business had requested funds from a development corporation in exchange for cabinet approval for redevelopment projects in the aftermath of Hurricane Ivan. Moreover, in April 2012 it was revealed that a second investigation into Bush's financial affairs had begun, and later that month details emerged of a third police inquiry, which was examining the Premier's alleged connection to an illegal shipment of dynamite. McLaughlin urged Bush to resign and threatened to organize a vote of no confidence in the Government. Bush protested his innocence and accused the opposition of colluding with British officials to end his premiership, precipitating a deterioration in relations with the United Kingdom (see above), which strongly denied that the police investigations were politically motivated.

Following pressure from opposition-supported campaigners, Bush agreed to hold a referendum on electoral reform on 18 July 2012. Voters were presented with the question 'Do you support an electoral system of single member constituencies with each elector being entitled to cast only one vote?' Bush claimed that a single member constituency system would be costly, divisive and more susceptible to fraud than the existing multi-member constituency framework, while proponents contended that the current electoral rules were undemocratic. The constitutional requirement was that 50% or more of the entire electorate must vote 'yes' for the result to be binding. Although more than 65% of the 8,677 who took part in the poll voted in favour of the proposal, the result was considered merely advisory, as the positive votes made up only 37% of the electorate.

Bush was arrested on 11 December 2012 on charges of financial irregularities and was granted bail on the following day. In response, a no confidence motion against Bush was adopted by the Legislative Assembly on 18 December, and he was duly replaced as Premier by Juliana O'Connor-Connolly, the erstwhile Deputy Premier, the following day. O'Connor-Connolly formed a minority Government comprised of those UDP members who had endorsed the motion of no confidence, all of whom resigned from the party on 29 December. In June 2013 Bush was charged with misconduct and breach of trust; his trial was expected to begin in September 2014. It subsequently emerged that the police were also conducting an investigation into unrelated corruption allegations against Attorney-General Samuel Bulgin, former Governor Stuart Jack and FCO official Larry Covington.

A general election was held on 22 May 2013. The PPM won nine of the 18 elected seats in the enlarged Legislative Assembly, while Bush's UDP's parliamentary representation was reduced to four. The People's National Alliance, formed by O'Connor-Connolly to contest the election, secured one seat. Turnout was recorded at 79.9%. Following the election, O'Connor-Connolly announced she was joining the PPM, giving that party the majority necessary to form a government. PPM leader Alden McLaughlin was appointed Premier on 29 May; his new Cabinet comprised eight PPM members and two independents. Independent candidates had secured four seats in the new Parliament. Former Premier Bush was sworn in as opposition leader. McLaughlin declared that his main priorities were economic diversification and the improvement of relations with the British Government. In September Helen Kilpatrick became the territory's new Governor. Meanwhile, UDP officials announced in December that the party was to be renamed the Cayman Islands Democratic Party.

Following criticism, by the Organisation for Economic Co-operation and Development (OECD) and the IMF, of the regulatory mechanisms governing operations in the Cayman Islands financial services sector, the territory renewed efforts to bolster its international reputation as a legitimate and prestigious financial centre. In 2006 the Cayman Islands Monetary Authority (CIMA) announced amendments to the Mutual Funds Law, including new, more stringent requirements for the administration of funds and raising the minimum subscription for registered funds from US $50,000 to $100,000. However, in 2007 the US Senate Finance Committee reported that it had identified some 18,000 registered companies purportedly maintaining headquarters at a single address in the Caribbean island nation, and subsequently commissioned an inquiry into the anomaly by the Government Accountability Office, which concluded that US companies were using the haven to hide illegal activity or evade income tax payment. It was estimated that evasion of US tax obligations by such entities—achieved by establishing offshore subsidiaries on the islands—had resulted in a $100,000m. shortfall in tax-based revenue and precipitated a growing sentiment of hostility between the two nations' respective regulatory authorities. In 2008 the United Kingdom's Select Committee on Public Accounts reported that there had been a considerable expansion of the capacity of financial regulators on the islands since 2000, allowing more successful investigative activities in relation to suspicious activity reports. Nevertheless, the collapse in 2008 of several Cayman Island-based hedge funds, exacerbating the global financial crisis, caused increased attention to be focused on the territory's financial institutions. US President Barack Obama in 2009 called for more transparency from the offshore sector. In the same year OECD included the territory on its 'grey list' of 'unco-operative tax havens', namely those that had committed to an internationally agreed standard of transparency but had yet to implement it. The territory was removed from the list later in the year after signing sufficient bilateral tax information sharing agreements. In 2010 (and again in 2013) the territory received a broadly favourable assessment under OECD's Global Forum on Transparency and Exchange of Information for Tax Purposes peer review mechanism, although the need for further reform was highlighted. A new task force to address money-laundering was established by the Government in March 2012, and in June 2013 the British Government reached agreement on new banking transparency laws for the territory as part of efforts to combat international tax evasion. The PPM Government that took office in the previous month pledged to defend the Cayman Islands' financial sector from further regulation, although it did announce that it would adhere to OECD's Multilateral Convention on Mutual Administrative Assistance in Tax Matters.

Economy

Following the introduction of secrecy laws in respect of bank accounts and other professional information in the late 1960s, and the easing of foreign exchange regulations in the 1970s (finally abandoned entirely in 1980), the islands developed as one of the world's major offshore financial markets. In 2012 the finance and insurance sector contributed some 36.7% of gross domestic product (GDP), while financial services employed 9.2% of the total labour force in 2013. There were 213 licensed banks and trusts and 11,379 mutual funds on the islands in 2013. The absence of any form of direct taxation has also made the islands notorious as a tax haven.

In 1986 a treaty of mutual assistance was signed with the USA, providing access for US law-enforcement agencies to the financial records of Cayman Islands banks, in cases where serious criminal activity is suspected. In 1996 the powers of the authorities to investigate such cases were augmented. The Cayman Islands Monetary Authority (CIMA), responsible for managing the islands' currency and reserves and for regulating the financial sector, began operations in 1997.

In 2000 the Cayman Islands were included on a list, compiled by the Financial Action Task Force on Money Laundering (FATF, based in Paris, France), of those jurisdictions considered to be 'non-co-operative' in international efforts to combat money-laundering. The Government's prompt response in addressing the FATF's concerns resulted in the Cayman Islands' removal from the list in 2001. The CIMA was given increased powers, and efforts were made to eliminate so-called 'shell banks' on the islands (those banks registered in the jurisdiction but with no staff or offices).

In anticipation of the publication by the Organisation for Economic Co-operation and Development (OECD) of a blacklist of 'unco-operative tax havens', in early 2000 the Government of the Cayman Islands made a commitment to the elimination of harmful tax practices. In 2001, in a further move to increase international confidence in its financial regulation, the Government signed a tax information exchange agreement with the USA.

From late 2002 the financial sector faced further disruption when the United Kingdom, under pressure from a European Union (EU) investigation into tax evasion, demanded that the Cayman Islands disclose the identities and account details of Europeans holding private savings accounts on the islands. The Cayman Islands, along with some other United Kingdom Overseas Territories facing similar demands, claimed it was being treated unfairly compared with more powerful European countries, such as Switzerland and Luxembourg, and refused to make any concessions. The British Paymaster-General demanded that the Cayman Islands enact the necessary legislation to implement the EU's Savings Tax Directive. The Legislative Assembly, after the British Government pledged to safeguard the territory's interests, voted to accept British/EU demands by 1 January 2005. However, the implementation of the regulations was delayed until July and the Cayman Islands authorities were able to negotiate some exemptions. In 2009 OECD included the Cayman Islands on its so-called 'grey list' of territories that had committed to but not yet implemented an internationally agreed standard of transparency measures, but the conclusion of a 12th bilateral tax information sharing agreement later that year enabled its removal from the list. (By early 2014 the Cayman Islands had signed a further 22 accords.) In October 2010 the territory received a broadly favourable assessment under OECD's Global Forum on Transparency and Exchange of Information for Tax Purposes peer review mechanism, although the need for further reform was highlighted. The Government created a task force to address money-laundering in March 2012. After discussions with the British Government, in November 2013 an accord was formalized in which the Cayman Islands agreed to share information with the United Kingdom about bank accounts held in the territory. (A similar accord was also concluded with the US Administration later that month.) In June, meanwhile, British Prime Minister David Cameron met with government officials from the Cayman Islands and other United Kingdom Overseas Territories to discuss the further restructuring of their offshore financial sectors. Following the meeting, Cameron announced that the territories had pledged to maintain company ownership registers and to adopt OECD's Multilateral Convention on Mutual Administrative Assistance in Tax Matters. The Cayman Islands acceded to the OECD Convention in September, and the instrument entered into force in January 2014.

In addition to offshore financial services, the tourism sector contributes strongly to the economy. Both of these sectors benefit from the Cayman Islands' political stability, good infrastructure and extensive development. According to the World Travel and Tourism Council, in 2013 the tourism industry, directly or indirectly, accounted for 25.4% of GDP and 27.3% of employment. Most tourists are from the USA (76.8% of stop-over arrivals in 2013). The industry is marketed towards the wealthier visitor and the Government limits the number of cruise ship passengers. The Cayman Islands also maintains the largest registry of luxury yachts of over 100 ft in length in the world. With North America and Europe accounting for the vast majority of total air arrivals, the recession in those regions from 2009 was detrimental to tourism in the Cayman Islands, and a decline of 10.2% in air arrival numbers was recorded in 2009. Nevertheless, the sector quickly recovered: numbers rose by 6.0% in 2010, 7.1% in 2011, 4.1% in 2012 and 7.4% in 2013. The recovery in cruise ship passenger numbers was not so clear cut: totals declined in 2008 and in 2009, but a rise of 5.1% was recorded in 2010 before a further decline, of 12.3%, occurred in 2011. The sector recovered by 7.6% in 2012, but declined once again in 2013, by 8.7%. In June 2013 the Government announced its intention to move forward with plans for a cruise port, intended to increase future cruise ship passenger numbers.

There is also an active construction sector (contributing 2.9% of GDP in 2012), owing to expansion of the tourism and commercial sectors. Industry as a whole accounted for 7.5% of GDP in that year and engaged 14.5% of the total workforce in 2013. The restaurant and hotel sector contributed 5.2% of GDP in 2012. According to official estimates, only 56.8% of the population of the islands were Caymanian in 2012 (compared with 79% in 1980). Some 6.3% of the labour force were unemployed in 2013.

More than 90% of the islands' food needs are imported. Agriculture is limited by infertile soil, low rainfall and high labour costs. Traditional fishing activities, chiefly of turtles, declined from 1970, particularly after the USA imposed an import ban on turtle products in 1979 (the islands possess the world's only commercial turtle farm). Agriculture and fishing contributed just 0.3% of GDP in 2012 and 0.8% of the total workforce in 2013.

The economy recovered well from Hurricane Ivan in 2004 and the territory recorded economic growth of 6.6% in 2005. GDP growth declined thereafter, however, while rising food costs led to increases in the inflation rate. The economy contracted by 7.0% in 2009, owing to the adverse effect of the global downturn on its principal sectors (tourism, financial services and construction), and consumer prices declined by an annual average of 1.5% in the year overall, as domestic demand weakened. In 2010 GDP decreased by a further 2.9%. In spite of mixed results in the tourism and financial industries, as well as another year of negative growth in the construction sector, real GDP expanded by 0.9% in 2011. Although financial services and construction continued to struggle during 2012, rising tourist arrivals supported real GDP growth of 1.4% in that year. The economy expanded by a further 1.2% in 2013, driven primarily by an upturn in stay-over tourist arrivals. However, the cruise sector registered a contraction in that year, and activity in the financial and construction industries remained relatively subdued. The inflation rate stood at 2.2% in 2013. The Government forecast real GDP growth of 1.9% in 2014, predicated on an improvement in the territory's key economic sectors.

Statistical Survey

Sources: Government Information Services, Cricket Sq., Elgin Ave, George Town, Grand Cayman; tel. 949-8092; fax 949-5936; The Information Centre, Economic and Statistics Office, Government Administration Bldg, Grand Cayman; tel. 949-0940; fax 949-8782; e-mail infostats@gov.ky; internet www.eso.ky.

AREA AND POPULATION

Area: 262 sq km (102 sq miles). The main island of Grand Cayman is about 197 sq km (76 sq miles), about one-half of which is swamp. Cayman Brac is 39 sq km (15 sq miles); Little Cayman is 26 sq km (11 sq miles).

Population: 39,410 at census of 10 October 1999; 55,036 (males 27,218, females 27,818) at census of 10 October 2010 (Grand Cayman 52,740, Cayman Brac 2,098, Little Cayman 198). *2013* (official estimate at 31 December): 55,691.

Density (at 31 December 2013): 212.6 per sq km.

Population by Age and Sex (official estimates at 31 December 2012): *0–14 years:* 10,357 (males 5,302, females 5,055); *15–64 years:* 43,032 (males 21,009; females 22,023); *65 years and over:* 3,343 (males 1,442, females 1,901); *Total* 56,732 (males 27,753, females 28,979).

Principal Towns (official estimates at 31 December 2013): George Town (capital) 29,144; Bodden Town 11,243; West Bay 10,728.

Births, Marriages and Deaths (2012): Live births 759 (birth rate 13.4 per 1,000, preliminary); Marriages 473 (marriage rate 8.3 per 1,000); Deaths 172 (death rate 3.0 per 1,000, preliminary).

Life Expectancy (years at birth, 2013): 80.9 (males 78.2; females 83.6). Source: Pan American Health Organization.

Economically Active Population (sample survey, persons aged 15 years and over, 2013): Agriculture and fishing 299; Manufacturing, mining, printing and publishing 978; Construction 4,164; Electricity, gas and water supply 450; Wholesale and retail trade 4,920; Restaurants and hotels 3,407; Transport, post and telecommunication 2,289; Financial services 3,536; Public administration, education, health and social work 6,736; Other community, social and personal service activities 790; Private households with employed persons 3,109; Real estate, renting and business services 5,332; Other 39; *Sub-total* 36,049; Not classifiable by economic activity 21; *Total employed* 36,070; Unemployed 2,413; *Total labour force* 38,483 (Caymanian 19,317, non-Caymanian 19,165).

HEALTH AND WELFARE

Total Fertility Rate (children per woman, 2013): 1.9.

Physicians (per 1,000 head, 2012): 1.9.

Health Expenditure: % of GDP (1997): 4.2.

Health Expenditure: public (% of total, 1997): 53.2.

Total Carbon Dioxide Emissions ('000 metric tons, 2010): 590.4.

Total Carbon Dioxide Emissions Per Head (metric tons, 2010): 10.6.

Source: mainly Pan American Health Organization.

For definitions, see explanatory note on p. vi.

AGRICULTURE, ETC.

Livestock ('000 head, 2012, FAO estimates): Cattle 2.0; Goats 2.1; Pigs 1.1; Chickens 6.

Fishing (metric tons, live weight, 2012): Total catch 125 (all marine fishes).

Source: FAO.

INDUSTRY

Electric Energy (production, million kWh): 605.1 in 2010; 606.5 in 2011; 587.1 in 2012.

FINANCE

Currency and Exchange Rates: 100 cents = 1 Cayman Islands dollar (CI $). *Sterling, US Dollar and Euro Equivalents* (30 May 2014): £1 sterling = CI $1.402; US $1 = 0.833 CI cents; €1 = CI $1.134; CI $100 = £71.34 = US $120.00 = €88.16. *Exchange rate:* Fixed at CI $1 = US $1.20.

Budget (CI $ million, 2012): *Revenue:* Taxes on international trade and transactions 167.2; Taxes on other domestic goods and services 296.6; Taxes on property 36.7; Other tax revenue 4.4; Non-coercive revenue 59.7 (Sales of goods and services 55.0); Total 564.5. *Expenditure:* Current expenditure 547.2 (Personnel costs 226.5, Supplies and consumable goods 94.1, Subsidies 23.4, Transfer payments 131.7, Interest payments 30.5, Extraordinary expenses 33.8; Other 7.1); Capital expenditure and net lending 68.5; Total 615.6.

Cost of Living (Consumer Price Index; base: June 2008 = 100): All items 100.2 in 2011; 101.4 in 2012; 103.6 in 2013.

Gross Domestic Product (CI $ million at constant 2007 prices): 2,562.0 in 2010; 2,584.2 in 2011; 2,620.0 in 2012.

Gross Domestic Product by Economic Activity (CI $ million in current prices, 2012): Agriculture and fishing 9.5; Mining and quarrying 19.3; Manufacturing 24.7; Electricity and water supply 91.1; Construction 85.7; Wholesale and retail trade 218.8; Hotels and restaurants 152.8; Transport, storage and communication 206.1; Finance and insurance 1,082.1; Real estate, renting and business services 636.8; Public administration and defence 185.8; Education

67.9; Health and social work 84.2; Other services 83.6; *Sub-total* 2,948.4; *Less* Financial intermediation services indirectly measured 372.4; *GDP in basic prices* 2,575.9; Tax less subsidies on products 201.0; *GDP in purchasers' values* 2,776.9.

EXTERNAL TRADE

Principal Commodities (CI $ million, 2013): *Imports c.i.f.:* Food and live animals 137.9; Beverages and tobacco 30.0; Petroleum products and gas 170.9; Chemicals and related products 38.4; Basic manufactures 94.5; Machinery and transport equipment 117.3; Miscellaneous manufactured articles 120.9; Total (incl. others) 774.5. *Exports f.o.b.:* Crude materials 0.7; Basic manufactures 0.4; Machinery and transport equipment 0.6; Miscellaneous manufactured articles 0.5; Total (incl. others) 25.3.

Principal Trading Partners (CI $ million, 2013): *Imports c.i.f.:* Jamaica 7.9; Japan 3.0; United Kingdom 6.3; USA 714.9; Total (incl. others) 774.5. *Exports f.o.b.:* Total 25.3.

TRANSPORT

Road Traffic ('000 motor vehicles in use, 2002): Passenger cars 23.8; Commercial vehicles 6.4.

Shipping: *Cargo Vessels* (2012): Vessels 60; Calls at port 486. *Flag Registered Fleet* (at 31 December 2013): Number of vessels 861; Total displacement 3,833,934 grt. (Source: Lloyd's List Intelligence—www.lloydslistintelligence.com).

Civil Aviation (traffic at Owen Roberts International Airport and Gerrard Smith International Airport, 2011): Aircraft movements 29,100; Freight carried (metric tons) 2,061.6 (loaded 311.1, unloaded 1,750.5); Passengers carried 1,151,500 (arriving 577,600, departing 573,900).

TOURISM

Visitor Arrivals ('000): 1,710.6 (arrivals by air 309.1, cruise ship passengers 1,401.5) in 2011; 1,829.1 (arrivals by air 321.7, cruise ship passengers 1,507.4) in 2012; 1,721.3 (arrivals by air 345.4, cruise ship passengers 1,375.9) in 2013.

Stay-over Arrivals by Place of Origin ('000, 2013): Canada 23.6; Europe 27.8; USA 265.4; Total (incl. others) 345.4. Source: Cayman Islands Tourism Department, George Town.

Tourism Receipts (US $ million, excl. passenger transport unless otherwise indicated): 485 in 2010; 491 in 2011; 480 in 2012. Source: World Tourism Organization.

COMMUNICATIONS MEDIA

Telephones: 36,717 main lines in use in 2013.

Mobile Cellular Telephones (subscribers): 98,036 in 2013.

Fixed and Mobile Telecommunication Lines (number in service): 133,684 in 2012.

Broadband Subscribers: 20,335 in 2013.

Internet Users: 24,000 in 2009.

Source: mainly International Telecommunication Union.

EDUCATION

(at 30 September 2012 unless otherwise indicated)

Institutions (excl. Lighthouse School): Government 17; Private 10; *Total* 27.

Enrolment (at 30 September 2010): *Government:* Primary 2,553; Middle 1,198; Secondary 1,111; Total 4,862. *Private:* Total 2,881. *Total:* 7,743 (excl. Lighthouse School 86). *2011:* Government 4,890 (primary 2,509, secondary 2,381); Private 2,756 (primary 1,655, secondary 1,101); Total 7,646. *2012:* Government 4,956 (primary 2,426, secondary 2,530); Private 2,787 (primary 1,537, secondary 1,250); Total 7,743.

Pupil-teacher Ratio (primary education, UNESCO estimate): 12.1 in 2010/11. Source: UNESCO Institute for Statistics.

Adult Literacy Rate: 98.9% in 2007 (males 98.7%, females 99.0%). Source: UNESCO Institute for Statistics.

Directory

The Constitution

A new Constitution was enacted in 2009. Although it afforded Cayman Islanders more autonomy, the new Constitution extended many of the terms of the previous 1959 charter: the Governor, who is appointed for four years, is responsible for defence and internal security, external affairs, and the public service. The Governor appoints the Premier. As well as the Chairman (the Governor) and the Premier, the Cabinet comprises the Deputy Premier, the Attorney-General and the Cabinet Secretary (all of whom are appointed by the Governor in consultation with the Premier) and five other Ministers elected by the Legislative Assembly from their own number. The Governor assigns ministerial portfolios to the elected members of the Cabinet, in consultation with the Premier. There are 18 elected members of the Legislative Assembly (elected by direct, universal adult suffrage for a term of four years) and two official members (the Attorney-General and the Deputy Governor), appointed by the Governor. The Speaker presides over the Assembly. The new Constitution establishes a National Security Council, to advise the Governor on internal security policy. The United Kingdom retains full control over foreign affairs. A Bill of Rights, Freedom and Responsibilities came into effect in November 2012.

BILL OF RIGHTS, FREEDOM AND RESPONSIBILITIES

The Bill of Rights implemented from 6 November 2012 upheld a list of rights to be exercised by the citizens of The Cayman Islands. Some of these include the right to life, to a free and fair trial under the rule of law, to personal liberty and expression, to non-discrimination on account of sex, race, colour, language, religion, political or other opinion and birth, or other status. The rights to education, to marriage, to children, to own property, to practise religion and to free movement within the islands are also guaranteed.

The Government

HEAD OF STATE

Queen: HM Queen ELIZABETH II.

Governor: HELEN KILPATRICK (took office 6 Sept. 2013).

CABINET
(September 2014)

The Government is formed by members of the People's Progressive Movement and Independents.

Chairman: HELEN KILPATRICK (The Governor).

Premier and Minister of Home and Community Affairs: ALDEN M. McLAUGHLIN.

Deputy Governor and Head of the Civil Service*: FRANZ MANDERSON.

Attorney-General*: SAMUEL BULGIN.

Deputy Premier and Minister of District Administration, Tourism and Transport: MOSES KIRKCONNELL.

Minister of Finance and Economic Development: MARCO ARCHER.

Minister of Financial Services, Commerce and Environment: WAYNE PANTON.

Minister of Health, Sports, Youth and Culture: OSBOURNE BODDEN.

Minister of Planning, Lands, Agriculture, Housing and Infrastructure: D. KURT TIBBETTS.

Minister of Education, Employment and Gender Affairs: TARA RIVERS.

Cabinet Secretary: SAMUEL ROSE.
* Appointed by the Governor.

GOVERNMENT OFFICES

Office of the Governor: Govt Admin. Bldg, 133 Elgin Ave, George Town, Grand Cayman KY1-9000; tel. 244-2401; fax 945-4131; e-mail staffoff@candw.ky; internet www.ukincayman.fco.gov.uk.

All official government offices and ministries, unless otherwise stated, are located in the Government Administration Building, Elgin Ave, George Town, Grand Cayman.

Legislature

LEGISLATIVE ASSEMBLY

Legislative Assembly: 33 Fort St, POB 890, George Town, Grand Cayman KY1-1103; tel. 949-4236; fax 949-9514; internet www.legislativeassembly.ky; Clerk ZENA MERREN-CHIN.

Speaker: JULIANA O'CONNOR-CONNELLY.

Election, 22 May 2013

Party	Seats
People's Progressive Movement (PPM) . . .	9
United Democratic Party (UDP)*	4
People's National Alliance (PNA)†	1
Independents	4
Total	**18**

In addition to the 18 elected members, there are two official members, appointed by the Governor.
* The UDP was renamed the Cayman Islands Democratic Party in December 2013.
† The PNA candidate, Juliana O'Connor-Connelly, joined the PPM following the election.

Election Commission

Elections Office: Smith Road Centre, 2nd Floor, 150 Smith Rd, George Town, Grand Cayman; tel. 949-8047; fax 946-2977; e-mail electionsoffice@candw.ky; internet www.electionsoffice.ky; Supervisor of Elections KEARNEY SIDNEY GOMEZ.

Political Organizations

Cayman Islands Democratic Party (CDP): Unit 15, 2nd Floor, Rankin's Plaza, Eastern Ave, POB 12417, Grand Cayman; tel. 943-3338; fax 943-3339; f. 2001 as United Democratic Party, name changed 2013; Leader W. McKEEVA BUSH; Chair. TESSA BODDEN.

Coalition for Cayman: tel. 943-0242; e-mail team@coalitionforcayman.ky; internet www.coalitionforcayman.ky; f. 2012; contested the 2013 general election; Chair. JAMES BERGSTROM.

People's Progressive Movement (PPM): 488 Crewe Rd, George Town, POB 10526, Grand Cayman; tel. 945-1776; fax 946-0184; e-mail info@ppm.ky; internet www.theprogressives.ky; f. 2002; Leader ALDEN McLAUGHLIN; Gen. Sec. RAYBURN FARRINGTON.

Judicial System

There is a Grand Court of the Islands (with Supreme Court status), a Summary Court, a Youth Court and a Coroner's Court. The Grand Court has jurisdiction in all civil matters, admiralty matters, and in trials on indictment. Appeals lie to the Court of Appeal of the Cayman Islands (comprised of eight members) and beyond that to the Privy Council in the United Kingdom. The Summary Courts deal with criminal and civil matters (up to a certain limit defined by law) and appeals lie to the Grand Court.

The Grand Court: Edward St, George Town, POB 495, Grand Cayman KY1-1106; tel. 949-4296; fax 949-9856; internet www.judicial.ky; Chief Justice ANTHONY SMELLIE; Chief Magistrate NOVA G. A. HALL.

President of the Court of Appeal: Sir JOHN CHADWICK.

Registrar of the Court of Appeal: AUDREY BODDEN.

Attorney-General: SAMUEL BULGIN.

Religion

CHRISTIANITY

The oldest established denominations are (on Grand Cayman) the United Church of Jamaica and Grand Cayman (Presbyterian), and (on Cayman Brac) the Baptist Church. Anglicans are adherents of the Church in the Province of the West Indies (Grand Cayman forms part of the diocese of Jamaica). Within the Roman Catholic Church, the Cayman Islands forms part of the archdiocese of Kingston in

Jamaica. According to 2010 census figures, some 23% of the population are adherents of the Church of God, 14% are Roman Catholics, 9% are Seventh-day Adventists, 9% belong to the Presbyterian or United Church, 8% are Baptists, 7% are Pentecostalists and 4% are Anglicans.

The Press

Cayman Compass: The Compass Centre, Shedden Rd, POB 1365, George Town, Grand Cayman; tel. 949-5111; fax 949-7675; e-mail newsdesk@pinnaclemedialtd.com; internet www.caymancompass.com; f. 1965; publ. by Pinnacle Media Ltd; 5 a week; Publr DAVID LEGGE; circ. 10,000.

The Cayman Islands Journal: The Compass Centre, Shedden Rd, POB 1365, George Town, Grand Cayman; tel. 949-5111; fax 949-7675; internet www.compasscayman.com/journal; publ. by Cayman Free Press; monthly; broadsheet business newspaper; Publr BRIAN UZZELL.

Cayman Net News: Mirco Centre, 85 North Sound Rd, Alissta Towers, POB 11063, Grand Cayman KY1-1008; tel. 623-6060; fax 949-0679; e-mail info@caymannetnews.com; internet www.caymannetnews.com; internet news service; publishes weekly newspaper (f. 2006); Publr and Editor-in-Chief DEON EBANKS.

The Chamber: POB 1000, George Town, Grand Cayman; tel. 949-8090; fax 949-0220; e-mail info@caymanchamber.ky; internet www.caymanchamber.ky; f. 1965; monthly; newsletter of the Cayman Islands Chamber of Commerce; Editor WIL PINEAU; circ. 5,000.

Christian Lifestyle: Bldg G, Unit 3, Countryside Shopping Village, POB 1217, Grand Cayman KY1-1108; tel. 926-2507; fax 946-1737; e-mail editor@cstylemagazine.com; internet www.cstylemagazine.com; f. 2008; publ. every 2 months; Editor KAREN CHIN.

Gazette: Government Information Services, 2nd Floor, Govt Admin. Bldg, George Town, Grand Cayman; tel. 949-8092; fax 949-5936; e-mail caymangazette@gov.ky; internet www.gazettes.gov.ky; official govt newspaper; fortnightly; Editor-in-Chief PATRICIA EBANKS.

Key to Cayman: The Compass Centre, Shedden Rd, POB 1365, George Town, Grand Cayman KY1-1108; tel. 949-5111; fax 949-7675; e-mail cfp@candw.ky; internet keytocayman.com; 2 a year; free tourist magazine; publ. by the Cayman Free Press; Cayman Free Press also publs *Caymanian Compass* newspaper and accompanying supplements, *Cayman Islands Journal*, *Cayman Islands Yearbook & Business Directory*, *Cayman Islands Map*, and *Inside Out*, a home and living magazine; Editor NATASHA WERE.

Publishers

Acorn Publishing Co: Alissta Towers, North Sound Rd, Seven Mile Beach, POB 31403, Grand Cayman KY1-1206; tel. 916-2413; fax 946-2830; e-mail info@acorn.ky; internet caymanyp.com/Cayman-Islands/Publishers-Book; Publishes Good Taste Magazine, Explore Cayman.

Cayman Free Press Ltd: The Compass Centre, Shedden Rd, POB 1365, George Town, Grand Cayman, KY1-1108; tel. 949-5111; fax 949-7675; e-mail info@cfp.ky; internet www.caymanfreepress.com; f. 1965; publishes *Caymanian Compass, The Journal, Observer on Sunday, Cayman Financial Review, What's Hot, Cayman Buzz Directory, Inside Out, Cayman Ashore, Hurricane Supplement*; Gen. Man. BRIAN UZZELL.

CLM Publishing: POB 1217, Grand Cayman, KY1-1108; tel. 926-2507; e-mail clmpublishing@gmail.com; internet www.clmpublsihing.webs.com; publishes *Christian Lifestyle Magazine* ; Chair. and CEO KAREN E. CHIN.

Global Directories (Cayman) Ltd: 62 Form Lane, 3rd Floor, Camana Bay, POB 688, George Town, Grand Cayman; tel. 949-7027; fax 949-8366; e-mail caysales@globaldirectories.com; internet caymanislandsyp.com; f. 1978; fmrly Caribbean Publishing Co (Cayman) Ltd; Dir LESTER GARNETT.

Government Information Services: Gazette Office, Government Information Services, 2nd Floor, Govt Admin. Bldg, George Town, Grand Cayman; tel. 949-8092; fax 949-5936; e-mail caymangazette@gov.ky; internet www.gazettes.gov.ky; publr of official govt releases, *Gazette*.

Tower Marketing: Grand Cayman; tel. 623-6700; fax 769-6700; e-mail lynne@tower.com.ky; internet www.tower.com.ky; f. 1999; Man. Dir LYNNE BYLES.

Broadcasting and Communications

REGULATORY AUTHORITY

Information and Communications Technology Authority (ICTA): Alissta Towers, 3rd Floor, 85 North Sound Rd, POB 2502, Grand Cayman KY1-1104; tel. 946-4282; fax 945-8284; e-mail info@icta.ky; internet www.icta.ky; f. 2002; responsible for the regulation and licensing of telecommunications, broadcasting, and all forms of radio which includes ship, aircraft, mobile and amateur radio and the management of the Cayman Islands internet domain; Chair. DALE CRIGHTON; Man. Dir ALEE FA'AMOE.

TELECOMMUNICATIONS

Digicel Cayman: Cayman Financial Centre, 36A Roys Dr., 3rd Floor, POB 700, George Town, Grand Cayman; tel. 623-3444; fax 623-3329; e-mail caycustomercare@digicelgroup.com; internet www.digicelcayman.com; f. 2003; owned by an Irish consortium; acquired the operations of Cingular Wireless (fmrly those of AT&T Wireless) in the country in 2005 (www.cingular.ky); Chair. DENIS O'BRIEN; CEO CHRIS HAYMAN.

LIME: Anderson Sq. Bldg, Anderson Sq., Shedden Rd, POB 293, George Town, Grand Cayman; tel. 949-7800; fax 949-7962; internet www.lime.com; f. 1966 as Cable & Wireless (Cayman Islands) Ltd; name changed as above 2008; Cable & Wireless' monopoly over the telecommunications market ended in 2004; CEO TONY RICE; CEO (Jamaica and the Cayman Islands) GARRY SINCLAIR.

Logic Communications: Governors Sq., West Bay Rd, Seven Mile Beach, POB 31112, Grand Cayman, KY1-1205; tel. 743-4300; fax 743-4301; e-mail support@logic.ky; internet www.logic.ky; f. 2003 as WestTel Ltd; name changed as above in 2010; wholly owned subsidiary of KeyTech Ltd, Bermuda; provides telephone and internet services; CEO MICHAEL EDENHOLM.

TeleCayman: Cayman Corporate Centre, 27 Hospital Rd, 4th Floor, POB 704 GT, Grand Cayman; tel. 769-1000; fax 769-0999; e-mail customer@telecayman.com; internet www.telecayman.com; f. 2003; provides telephone and internet services; Business Man. CHRIS HAYDON.

BROADCASTING

Radio

Radio Cayman: Elgin Ave, POB 1110 GT, George Town, Grand Cayman KY1-1102; tel. 949-7799; fax 949-6536; e-mail radiocayman@gov.ky; internet www.radiocayman.gov.ky; started full-time broadcasting 1976; govt-owned commercial radio station; service in English; operates Radio Cayman One and Breeze FM; Dir NORMA MCFIELD.

Radio Heaven 97 FM: Hurst Rd, Newlands, POB 31481, Grand Cayman, KY1-1206; tel. and fax 938-1082; e-mail pam@heaven97.com; internet www.heaven97.com; f. 1997; owned by Christian Communications Asscn; commercial station; Christian broadcasting, music and news; Man. Dir STEPHEN FAUCETTE.

Radio ICCI-FM: International College of the Cayman Islands, 595 Hirst Rd, POB 136, Grand Cayman KY1-1501; tel. 947-1100; fax 947-1210; e-mail info@myicci.com; internet www.icci.edu.ky; f. 1973; radio station of the International College of the Cayman Islands; educational and cultural; Pres. TASHA EBANKS GARCIA.

Radio Vibe: 21 Eclipse Dr., POB 10236, George Town, Grand Cayman KY1-1002; tel. 949-8423; fax 946-9867; e-mail info@paramountmedia.ky; internet www.vibefm.ky; operated by Paramount Media Services, in addition to Spin FM; Man. KENNETH G. RANKINE.

Radio Z99.9 FM: Grand Harbour, Suite 21 and 22, Shamrock Rd, POB 30110, George Town, Grand Cayman KY1-1201; tel. 945-1166; fax 945-1006; e-mail info@z99.ky; internet www.z99.ky; owned by Hurley's Entertainment Corpn Ltd; Programs Dir JASON HOWARD.

Television

Cayman Adventist Television Network (CATN/TV): 209 Walkers Rd, POB 515, George Town, Grand Cayman KY1-1106; tel. 949-8167; fax 949-6167; e-mail mission@candw.ky; internet caymanadventist.org; f. 1996; local and international programmes, mainly religious; Pres. SHIAN O'CONNOR; Exec. Sec. AL POWELL.

Cayman Christian TV Ltd: POB 964, Grand Cayman KY1-1102; tel. 947-2599; relays Christian broadcasting from the USA; Vice-Pres. FRED RUTTY.

CITN Cayman 27: 45 Eclipse Way, POB 30563, Grand Cayman KY1-1203; tel. 745-2739; fax 749-1002; e-mail hlofters@weststartv.com; internet www.cayman27.com.ky; f. 1992 as Cayman International Television Network; 24 hrs daily; local and international news and US entertainment; 10-channel cable service of international programmes by subscription; Gen. Man. APRIL CUMMINGS; News Dir BEN MEADE.

WestStar TV Ltd: 45 Eclipse Way, POB 31117, Grand Cayman KY1-1205; tel. 745-5555; fax 745-5554; e-mail support@weststartv.ky; internet www.weststar.com; f. 1993; owned by British Overseas Territory Cable and Telecommunications Ltd (BOTCAT); affiliated to WestTel Ltd; cable television service; CEO BOB TAYLOR; Operations Man. TRACI BRADLEY.

Finance

(cap. = capital; res = reserves; dep. = deposits; m. = million; brs = branches)

Banking facilities are provided by commercial banks. The islands have become an important centre for offshore companies and trusts. At the end of 2013 there were 213 banks, 140 active trust companies and 11,379 mutual funds on the islands. The islands are well known as a tax haven owing to the absence of any form of direct taxation. In June 2013 assets held by banks registered in the Cayman Islands totalled US \$1,503,000m.

Cayman Islands Monetary Authority (CIMA): 80E Shedden Rd, Elizabethan Sq., POB 10052 APO, George Town, Grand Cayman KY1-1001; tel. 949-7089; fax 946-4230; e-mail contactpublicrelations@cimoney.com.ky; internet www.cimoney.com.ky; f. 1997; responsible for managing the territory's currency and reserves and for regulating the financial services sector; cap. CI \$2.3m., res CI \$21m., dep. CI \$87.2m. (June 2013); Chair. GEORGE MCCARTHY; Man. Dir CINDY SCOTLAND.

PRINCIPAL BANKS AND TRUST COMPANIES

Appleby Trust (Cayman) Ltd: Clifton House, 75 Fort St, POB 1350, Grand Cayman KY1-1108; tel. 949-4900; fax 949-4901; e-mail cayman@applebyglobal.com; internet www.applebyglobal.com; f. 2006 following acquisition of business interests of Ansbacher (Cayman) Ltd; offices in Bermuda; Man. Dir. BRYAN HUNTER.

Atlantic Security Bank: 190 Elgin Ave, POB 1034, George Town 1097, Grand Cayman; internet www.asbnet.com; f. 1981 as Banco de Crédito del Perú, name changed as above 1986; cap. US \$70m. res US \$18.9m. dep. US \$1,444.6m. (Dec. 2013); Pres. DIONISIO ROMERO.

Banco Safra (Cayman Islands) Ltd: 190 Elgin Ave, POB 1034, George Town, Grand Cayman; tel. 814-1574; fax 949-9512; f. 1993; res US \$101.1m., dep. US \$195.7m. (Dec. 2012); Pres. CARLOS ALBERTO VIEIRA.

BNP Paribas Fortis Bank (Cayman) Ltd: Grand Pavilion Commercial Centre, 802 West Bay Rd, POB 2003, George Town, Grand Cayman; tel. 949-7942; fax 949-8340; e-mail phil.brown@ky.fortisbank.com; internet www.bnpparibas.com; f. 1984 as Pierson, Heldring & Pierson (Cayman) Ltd; name changed to Mees Pierson (Cayman) Ltd in 1993; present name adopted in 2000; Chair. BAUDOUIN PROT; CEO JEAN-LAURENT BONNAFÉ.

Butterfield Bank (Cayman) Ltd: Butterfield House, 68 Fort St, POB 705, George Town, Grand Cayman KY1-1107; tel. 949-7055; fax 949-7004; e-mail info@ky.butterfieldbank.com; internet www.ky.butterfieldgroup.com; f. 1967; name changed as above in 2004, fmrly Bank of Butterfield International (Cayman) Ltd; subsidiary of Bank of N. T. Butterfield & Son Ltd, Bermuda; cap. US \$16.4m., res US \$10.88m., dep. US \$1,915.6m. (Dec. 2012); Chair. SOPHIA HARRIS; 3 brs.

Caledonian Bank Ltd: Caledonian House, 69 Dr Roy's Dr., POB 1043, George Town, Grand Cayman KY1-1102; tel. 949-0050; fax 949-8062; e-mail info@caledonian.com; internet www.caledonian.com; f. 1970; Man. Dir. DAVID SARGISON.

Cayman National Bank Ltd: Cayman National Bank Bldg, 4th Floor, 200 Elgin Ave, POB 1097, George Town, Grand Cayman; tel. 949-4655; fax 949-7506; e-mail cnb@caymannational.com; internet www.caymannational.com; f. 1974; subsidiary of Cayman National Corpn; cap. CI \$2.4m., res CI \$41.5m., dep. CI \$882.9m. (Sept. 2013); Chair. STUART J. DACK; Pres. ORMOND A. WILLIAMS; 7 brs.

CIBC FirstCaribbean International Bank: POB 68, 25 Main St, George Town, Grand Cayman KY1-1102; tel. 949-7300; fax 949-7179; e-mail care@cibcfcib.com; internet www.cibcfcib.com; f. 2002 following merger of Caribbean operations of Barclays Bank PLC and CIBC; Barclays relinquished its stake to CIBC in 2006, adopted present name in 2011; CEO RIK PARKHILL; Man. Dir (Caymans) MARK MCINTYRE; 3 brs.

CIBC Bank and Trust Co (Cayman) Ltd: CIBC Financial Centre, 11 Dr Roy's Dr., POB 694, George Town, Grand Cayman; tel. 949-8666; fax 949-0626; internet www.cibc.com; f. 1967; subsidiary of CIBC FirstCaribbean International Bank; CEO MICHAEL FRANCIS BENEDICT GILLOOLY.

CITCO Bank and Trust Co Ltd: 89 Nexus Way, 2nd Floor, Camana Bay, POB 31105, Grand Cayman KY1-1205; tel. 945-3838; fax 945-3888; e-mail cayman-bank@citco.com; internet www.citco.com; Pres. MIKE MCWATT.

Deutsche Bank (Cayman) Ltd: Boundary Hall, Cricket Sq., 171 Elgin Ave, POB 1984, George Town, Grand Cayman KY1-1104; tel. 949-8244; fax 949-8178; e-mail dmg-cay@candw.ky; internet www.db-ci.com; f. 1983 as Morgan Grenfell (Cayman) Ltd; name changed to Deutsche Morgan Grenfell (Cayman) Ltd in 1996; name changed as above in 1998; Chair. Dr PAUL ACHLEITNER; Co CEO JÜRGEN FITSCHEN, ANSHU JAIN.

Fidelity Bank (Cayman) Ltd: POB 914, Dr Roy's Dr., George Town, Grand Cayman KY1-1103; tel. 949-7822; fax 949-4079; e-mail info@royalfidelity.com; internet www.fidelitycayman.com; f. 1979; Pres. LEONARD EBANKS.

HSBC Bank Cayman: HSBC House, 68 West Bay Rd, POB 1109, George Town, Grand Cayman KY1-1102; tel. 949-7755; fax 949-7634; e-mail hbky.information@ky.hsbc.com; internet www.hsbc.ky; f. 1982; CEO JONATHAN COOPER; Head of Corporate Banking ANTHONY RIKER.

Intertrust Bank (Cayman) Ltd: 190 Elgin Ave, George Town, Grand Cayman KY1-9005; tel. 949-8455; fax 949-9717; e-mail cayman@intertrustgroup.com; internet www.intertrustgroup.com; f. 1952 (Intertrust); took over operations of Close Bank (Cayman) Ltd in Aug. 2011; Man. Dir LESLEY CONNOLLY.

Merrill Lynch Bank and Trust Co (Cayman) Ltd: Harbour Centre, 4th Floor, North Church St, George Town, Grand Cayman; tel. 637-7455; fax 949-8895; internet www.ml.com.

Royal Bank of Canada: 24 Shedden Rd, POB 245, Grand Cayman KY1-1104; tel. 949-4600; fax 949-7396; internet www.royalbank.com; Vice-Pres. and Country Head JASON K. WATERS.

Royal Bank of Canada Trust Co (Cayman) Ltd: 24 Shedden Rd, POB 1586 GT, Grand Cayman KY1-1110; tel. 949-9107; fax 949-5777; internet www.rbcwminternational.com; Man. Dir DEANNA BIDWELL.

Scotiabank and Trust (Cayman) Ltd: Scotia Centre, 6 Cardinal Ave, POB 689, George Town, Grand Cayman KY1-1107; tel. 949-7666; fax 949-0020; e-mail scotiaci@candw.ky; internet www.cayman.scotiabank.com; f. 1968; fmrly Bank of Nova Scotia Trust Co (Cayman) Ltd; present name adopted 2003; Man. Dir DOUG COCHRANE; 4 brs.

UBS Fund Services (Cayman Islands) Ltd: UBS House, 227 Elgin Ave, POB 852, George Town, Grand Cayman KY1-1103; tel. 914-1060; fax 914-4060; internet www.ubs.com/fundservices; Man. Dir MONETTE WINDSOR.

Development Bank

Cayman Islands Development Bank: Cayman Financial Centre, 36B Dr Roy's Dr., POB 2576 GT, George Town, Grand Cayman; tel. 949-7511; fax 949-6168; e-mail cidb.manager@cidb.ky; internet cidb.ky; f. 2002; replaced the Housing Devt Corpn and the Agricultural and Industrial Devt Bd; under the jurisdiction of the Ministry of Financial Services, Commerce and Environment; Gen. Man and CEO TRACY EBANKS.

Banking Association

Cayman Islands Bankers' Association: Caledonian House, 69 Dr Roy Dr., POB 676, George Town, Grand Cayman; tel. 949-0330; fax 945-1448; e-mail ciba@cibankers.org; internet www.cibankers.org; Pres. MARK I. MCINTYRE; COO CECIL CHAN-A-SUE; 78 full mems, 200 assoc. mems.

STOCK EXCHANGE

Cayman Islands Stock Exchange (CSX): 4th Floor, Elizabethan Sq., POB 2408, George Town, Grand Cayman KY1-1105; tel. 945-6060; fax 945-6061; e-mail csx@csx.com.ky; internet www.csx.com.ky; f. 1996; more than 3,000 cos listed (Feb. 2011); govt-owned; Chair. ANTHONY B. TRAVERS; CEO VALIA THEODORAKI.

INSURANCE

Several foreign companies have agents in the islands. A total of 761 insurance companies were registered as of December 2013. In particular, the islands are a leading international market for health insurance. Locally incorporated companies include the following:

BAF Insurance Co (Cayman) Ltd: Dorcy Dr., POB 10389, Grand Cayman KY1-1004; tel. 949-5089; fax 949-7192; e-mail bafcayman@mybafsolutions.com; internet www.cayman.mybafsolutions.com; Chair. HARVEY STEPHENSON; Gen. Man. TERENCE SPENCER.

British Caymanian Insurance Agency Ltd: BritCay House, 236 Eastern Ave, POB 74, Georgetown, Grand Cayman KY1-1102; tel. 949-8699; fax 949-8411; internet cayman.cgigroup.com; owned by Colonial Group International (Bermuda).

Captiva Managers Ltd: Governors Sq., 23 Lime Tree Bay Ave, POB 32315, Grand Cayman KY1-1209; tel. 946-4111; fax 946-4222; e-mail info@captivamanagers.com; internet www.captivamanagers.com; Group Dir HARRY J. THOMPSON; Man. Dir CONOR JENNINGS.

Cayman First Insurance Co Ltd: 3rd Floor, Harbour Pl., 103 South Church St, POB 2171, Grand Cayman KY1-1105; tel. 949-7028; fax 949-7457; e-mail askus@caymanfirst.com; internet www.caymanfirst.com; Gen. Man. MICHAEL GAYLE.

Cayman Islands National Insurance Co Ltd (CINICO): Cayman Centre, 1st Floor, Dorcy Dr., Airport Rd, George Town, POB 10112, Grand Cayman KY1-1001; tel. 949-8101; fax 949-8226; e-mail ltibbetts@cinico.ky; internet www.cinico.ky; govt-owned; Chair. SCOTT CUMMINGS; CEO LONNY TIBBETTS.

Insurance Company of the West Indies (Cayman) Ltd (ICWI): 150 Smith Rd, POB 461, Grand Cayman KY1-1106; tel. 949-6970; fax 949-6929; e-mail cayman@icwi.com; internet www.icwi.com/cayman; subsidiary of Insurance Co of the West Indies, Jamaica; Chair. and CEO DENNIS LALOR; Gen. Man. HEATHER LANIGAN.

Island Heritage Insurance Co Ltd: Island Heritage House, 128 Lawrence Blvd, POB 2501, Grand Cayman KY1-1104; tel. 949-7280; fax 945-6765; e-mail info@islandheritage.com.ky; internet www.islandheritageinsurance.com; general insurance; acquired by BF&M (Bermuda) in 2012; CEO MARC SHIRRA.

Pan-American International Insurance Corpn: Unit 221, Mirco Centre, North Sound Rd, Grand Cayman; tel. 949-8304; fax 949-8305; internet www.palig.com; f. 2012; part of Pan-American Life Insurance Group (USA); Pres. and CEO BRUCE PARKER; Man. LESTER ROUSE.

Sagicor Life of the Cayman Islands Ltd: 103 South Church St, POB 1087, George Town, Grand Cayman KY1-1102; tel. 949-8211; fax 949-8262; e-mail customerservicecayman@sagicor.com; internet www.sagicorcayman.com; wholly owned subsidiary of Sagicor Life Jamaica Ltd; Chair. RICHARD O. BYLES; Pres. and CEO MICHAEL A. FRASER.

Trade and Industry

GOVERNMENT AGENCY

National Investment Council: Cayman Corporate Centre, 1st Floor, Hospital Rd, POB 10087 APO, Grand Cayman KY1-1001; tel. 945-0943; fax 945-0941; e-mail investment@dci.gov.ky; internet www.investcayman.ky; f. 2003 as Cayman Islands Investment Bureau; renamed 2010 and merged into Dept of Commerce and Investment; CEO RYAN RAJKUMARSINGH.

CHAMBER OF COMMERCE

Cayman Islands Chamber of Commerce: Unit 4-107, Governors Sq., 23 Lime Tree Bay Ave, West Bay Rd, POB 1000, West Bay, Grand Cayman KY1-1102; tel. 949-8090; fax 949-0220; e-mail info@caymanchamber.ky; internet www.caymanchamber.ky; f. 1965; Pres. JOHANN MOXAM; CEO WIL PINEAU; 594 corporate mems and 78 assocs.

TRADE ASSOCIATION

Cayman Finance: 94 Shedden Rd, Suite 2, POB 11048, Grand Cayman KY1-1008; tel. 946-6000; fax 946-6001; e-mail info@caymanfinances.com; internet www.caymanfinances.com; f. 2003 as Cayman Islands Financial Services Asscn; name changed as above in Oct. 2009; aims to promote the integrity and transparency of the financial services sector; Chair. RICHARD COLES; CEO GONZALO JALLES.

UTILITIES

Electricity

Electricity Regulatory Authority: Grand Pavilion Commercial Centre, Suite 14, 2nd Floor, Hibiscus Way Entrance, West Bay Rd, POB 10189, Grand Cayman KY1-1002; tel. 949-8372; fax 947-9598; e-mail foi.era@gov.ky; internet caymanera.com; f. 2005; Chair. SHERRI BODDEN-COWAN; Man. Dir CHARLES FARRINGTON.

Caribbean Utilities Co Ltd (CUC): Corporate HQ & Plant, 457 North Sound Rd, POB 38, George Town, Grand Cayman KY1-1101; tel. 949-5200; fax 949-5203; e-mail service@cuc.ky; internet www.cuc-cayman.com; Pres. and CEO J. F. RICHARD HEW; Chair. DAVID RITCH.

Cayman Brac Power and Light Co Ltd (CBP&L): Kirkconnell Market Plaza, Stake Bay Rd, POB 95, Stake Bay, Cayman Brac KY2-2101; tel. 948-2224; fax 948-2204; e-mail info@cbpl.ky; internet www.caymanera.com/cbpal; f. 1956; Gen. Man. JONATHAN TIBBETTS.

Water

Cayman Islands Water Authority: 13G Red Gate Rd, POB 1104 GT, George Town, Grand Cayman KY1-1102; tel. 949-2837; fax 949-0094; e-mail info@waterauthority.ky; internet www.waterauthority

.ky; Man. Dir Dr GELIA FREDERICK-VAN GENDEREN; Chair. JOHN LEMUEL HURLSTON.

Consolidated Water Co Ltd (CWCO): Windward 3, 4th Floor, Regatta Office Park, POB 1114, George Town, Grand Cayman KY1-1102; tel. 945-4277; fax 949-2957; e-mail info@cwco.com; internet www.cwco.com; f. 1973; Pres. and CEO FREDERICK W. MCTAGGART; Dir and Chair. WILMER F. PERGANDE.

Transport

ROADS

There are some 406 km (252 miles) of motorable roads, of which 304 km are surfaced with tarmac. The road network connects all districts on Grand Cayman and Cayman Brac (which has 76 km of motorable roads), and there are 43 km of motorable roads on Little Cayman (of which about 18 km are paved). According to the 2012/13 budget address, US $1.6m. was to be allocated for ongoing improvements to the islands' road network and also for the planning and development of new public roads.

SHIPPING

George Town is the principal port. An agreement to build a new port facility in George Town was signed in 2010. Cruise liners, container ships and smaller cargo vessels ply between the Cayman Islands, Florida, Jamaica and Costa Rica. There is no cruise ship dock in the Cayman Islands. Ships anchor off George Town and ferry passengers ashore to the North or South Dock Terminals in George Town. The number of cruise ship passengers is limited to 6,000 per day. The port of Cayman Brac is Creek; there are limited facilities on Little Cayman. In December 2013 the shipping register comprised 861 vessels, with combined displacement totalling 3,833,934 grt, of which 18 were bulk carriers and 16 were general cargo ships.

Maritime Authority of Cayman Islands (MACI): Strathvale House, 2nd Floor, 90 North Church St, POB 2256, Grand Cayman KY1-1107; tel. 949-8831; fax 949-8849; e-mail maci.consulting@cishipping.com; internet www.cishipping.com; f. 2005; wholly govt-owned; legal entity responsible for enforcement of international maritime laws and conventions; implementation of maritime safety and security, Cayman Islands marine environment laws; formation of national maritime policy; representation and protection of national maritime interests at international forums; also undertakes vessel and mortgage registration, advisory and marine survey and audit services fmrly administered by Cayman Islands Shipping Registry; Chair. PHILLIP A. BARNES; CEO A. JOEL WALTON.

Port Authority of the Cayman Islands: Harbour Dr., POB 1358 GT, George Town, Grand Cayman KY1-1108; tel. 949-2055; fax 949-5820; e-mail support@caymanport.com; internet www.caymanport.com; Chair. ERROL BUSH.

Principal Shipping Companies

Cayman Islands Shipping Registry: Govt Administration Bldg, 3rd Floor, 133 Elgin Ave, POB 2256, Grand Cayman KY1-110; tel. 949-8831; fax 949-8849; e-mail cisrky@cishipping.com; internet www.cishipping.com; f. 1993; division of Maritime Authority of Cayman Islands (MACI); CEO A. JOEL WALTON.

Seaboard Marine (Cayman): Mirco Commerce Centre, 2nd Floor, Industrial Park, POB 1372, George Town, Grand Cayman KY1-1108; tel. 949-4977; fax 949-8402; e-mail info@seaboardcayman.com; internet www.seaboardcayman.com; Man. Dir ROBERT FOSTER.

Thompson Shipping Co Ltd: 10 Shipping Lane, off Portland Rd, Industrial Park, POB 188, George Town, Grand Cayman KY1-1104; tel. 949-8044; fax 949-8349; e-mail info@thompsonshipping.com; internet www.thompsonshipping.com; f. 1977; agent for Thompson Line, a div. of Tropical Shipping; Contact Person SUSAN GABRUCH.

CIVIL AVIATION

There are two international airports in the territory: Owen Roberts International Airport, 3.5 km (2 miles) from George Town, and Gerrard Smith International Airport on Cayman Brac. Both are capable of handling jet-engined aircraft. In 2012 the Government announced a project to expand terminal facilities at Gerrard Smith to accommodate long-haul international flights and in 2014 a feasibility study on an expansion of Owen Roberts Airport was in its initial stages.

Cayman Islands Airport Authority (CIAA): 298 Owen Roberts Dr., POB 10098, Grand Cayman KY1-1001; tel. 943-7070; fax 943-7071; e-mail ciaa@caymanairports.com; internet www.caymanairports.com; operates both international airports; CEO ALBERT ANDERSON; Chair. KIRKLAND NIXON.

Civil Aviation Authority of the Cayman Islands (CAACI): Unit 2, Cayman Grand Harbour Complex, Shamrock Rd, POB 10277, George Town, Grand Cayman KY1-1003; tel. 949-7811; fax 949-0761;

e-mail civil.aviation@caacayman.com; internet www.caacayman.com; f. 1987; Dir-Gen. P. H. RICHARD SMITH; Chair. IAN PAIRAUDEAU.

Cayman Airways Ltd: 91 Owen Roberts Dr., POB 10092, Grand Cayman KY1-1001; tel. 949-8200; fax 949-7607; e-mail customerrelations@caymanairways.net; internet www.caymanairways.com; f. 1968; wholly govt-owned since 1977; operates local services and scheduled flights to Jamaica, Honduras and the USA; Chair. PHILLIP RANKIN (acting); Pres. and CEO FABIAN WHORMS.

Cubano Airtours: Shedden Rd, George Town; tel. 623-0765; e-mail sales@cubanoairtours.com; internet www.cubanoairtours.com; f. 2013; flights to Cuba; Man. Dir ALEJANDRO MATIENZO.

Island Air: Airport Rd, POB 2433, George Town, Grand Cayman KY1-1105; tel. 949-5252; fax 949-1073; e-mail res@islandair.ky; internet islandair.ky; f. 1987; operates daily scheduled services between Grand Cayman, Cayman Brac and Little Cayman; Man. Dir MARCUS CUMBER.

Tourism

The Cayman Islands are a major tourist destination, the majority of visitors coming from North America. The beaches and opportunities for diving in the offshore reefs form the main attraction for most tourists. In 2013 there were 345,400 arrivals by air (compared with 321,700 in 2012) and some 1,375,900 cruise visitors (compared with 1,507,400 in 2012). The USA remained the core market for stay-over visitors to the islands (76.8% in 2013). In 2010 there were an estimated 4,587 hotel rooms. In 2012 the tourism industry earned an estimated US $480m.

Cayman Islands Department of Tourism (CIDOT): Govt Admin. Bldg, 133 Elgin Ave, POB 134, Grand Cayman KY1-9000; tel. 949-0623; fax 949-4053; e-mail pr@caymanislands.ky; internet www.caymanislands.ky; f. 1965; Dir ROSA HARRIS.

Cayman Islands Tourism Association (CITA): 1320 West Bay Rd, POB 31086 SMB, Grand Cayman KY1-1205; tel. 949-8522; fax 946-8522; e-mail info@cita.ky; internet www.cita.ky; f. 2001 as a result of the amalgamation of the Cayman Tourism Alliance and the Cayman Islands Hotel and Condominium Asscn; Pres. KENNETH HYDES; Exec. Dir JANE VAN DER BOL.

Sister Islands Tourism Association (SITA): POB 187, Cayman Brac KY2-2101; tel. and fax 916-4874; e-mail sita@candw.ky; internet www.sisterislands.com; Pres. NEIL VAN NIEKERK; Exec. Sec. CHEVALA BURKE.

Defence

The United Kingdom is responsible for the defence of the Cayman Islands.

Education

Schooling is compulsory for children between the ages of five and 17 years. It is provided free in 11 government-run primary schools and three secondary schools. There are also 10 private schools. Primary education, from five years of age, lasts for six years; in 2007/08 enrolment at primary schools included an estimated 90% of pupils in the relevant age-group. Secondary education is for seven years; enrolment at secondary-level institutions in 2007/08 included an estimated 83% of students in the relevant age-group. The Cayman Islands Law School, Community College of the Cayman Islands, University College of the Cayman Islands and the International College of the Cayman Islands number among providers of tertiary-level education in the territory. In 2013 the Government set out a five-year strategy for improving education. Budgetary spending on education in 2012/13 was approved at US $66.9m.

CHILE

Geography

PHYSICAL FEATURES

The Republic of Chile occupies the narrow strip of territory between the Andes and the Pacific in the southern part of South America. The country is 4,329 km (2,688 miles) in length, but never more than 180 km in width, and its border along the mountainous Continental Divide is primarily with Argentina (5,150 km in extent). The north of the country (Atacama was gained from Bolivia in the 1880s, although that country still pursues a claim for a sovereign corridor to the Pacific through Chile) has a western frontier with landlocked Bolivia (861 km of border) and a short northern one with Peru (160 km). Chile has an issue with Peru over maritime economic boundaries, otherwise its only other territorial dispute concerns its claim in Antarctica (which conflicts with Argentine and British claims). Chile has a total area of 756,096 sq km (291,930 sq miles—excluding the 1.25m. sq km of the Antarctic claim).

Chile includes many of the clustered islands into which the continent disintegrates in the south-west and in the eastward flick of its tail, as well as an often deeply indented shore, so that it has a total coastline of 6,435 km. The country also includes a number of islands in the Pacific proper—notably Isla de Pascua (Easter Island or Rapa Nui—the most distant, at 3,790 km west of the north-central mainland), but also Sala y Gómez, Islas de los Desventurados and Archipiélago Juan Fernández. The first is famous for the isolated Polynesian civilization that flourished here long before the arrival of Europeans and erected the great stone statues (moai), and the last includes one island named for a shipwrecked sailor (Alexander Selkirk) and another for the fictional character he inspired (Robinson Crusoe).

Chile itself consists of the narrow lands west of the Andes, from the Atacama Desert in the north to the Patagonian icefields. It is a geologically unstable area, with earthquakes common and volcanoes active in the mountains, and the coasts are sometimes struck by tsunamis. The arid north is dominated by some of Chile's highest mountains, where the main Andean cordillera is at its widest and includes broad plateaux and soaring peaks (including the country's highest, Ojos del Salado—6,893 m or 22,615 ft—on the border with Argentina). Here the country forms the Atacama Desert, reputedly the driest in the world, but also rich in minerals and, especially, nitrates. Central Chile, with its more Mediterranean-type climate, sees a clear definition between the main line of the Andes and the lower coastal range, with an intervening Central Valley. The Andes are lower and narrower here, pierced by the best passes to the east, and the coast has many good harbours. Between is the Central Valley, some 40–80 km in width, with fertile, deep alluvial soils, particularly between the Aconcagua and Bío-Bío rivers (from just north of Santiago, the capital, south to Concepción). South of Puerto Montt the interior valley or plateau between the Andean and coastal ranges disappears beneath the sea, the coastal mountains continuing as a mass of islands off shore, itself studded with fjords and inlets. Archipelagic Chile extends from Chiloé all the way down to Tierra del Fuego (of which Argentina has the eastern part) and the Isla Hornos, with its famous Cabo de Hornos (Cape Horn). On the mainland, the Andes are lower than in the north (seldom more than 1,800 m), the lowlands forming the desolate, undulating plains of Patagonia that sweep down to the tip of the continent and over into Argentina. Apart from areas of permanent ice (the Patagonian ice cap is reckoned to be the largest after those of Antarctica and Greenland), this is a steppe country of coarse grasses and shrubs, while the north of Chile is a true desert, with very little vegetation at all. The vegetation of the central regions ranges, however, from cacti and scrub in the north to some dense rainforest south of Valdivia. Flora and fauna are not as rich in Chile as it is beyond the high Andes, although the coastal waters are teeming with life. The rivers, all short and steep

(vital to irrigation and electricity generation), have few fish (mainly the introduced trout) and few of the larger birds common on the continent are found here. However, there is a Chilean pine (with edible nuts), and animal species include the llama, the alpaca, the chinchilla, the Andean wolf, the puma, the huemal (a large deer) and the pudu (a small deer).

CLIMATE

The climate is very varied across such a long country, but is generally moderated by oceanic influences. The northern region is one of the driest areas of the world, although temperatures are moderated by the cold offshore Humboldt or Peru Current. Average temperatures at Antofagasta range from 12°–16°C (54°–61°F) in July up to 18°–23°C (64°–73°F) in January, but rainfall is only 2 mm (barely 0.1 ins) per year. Rainfall increases southwards, reaching 360 mm (14 ins) at Santiago in the Central Valley, where it falls mainly in the winter months of May–August. The winters, apart from being fairly wet, are mild, and the summers are cool. The average temperatures range from 3°–15°C (37°–59°F) in July to 12°–29°C (54°–84°F) in January. In the south it is a temperate marine climate, cooler and still wetter, with rain falling fairly evenly throughout the year and reaching levels of, at most, about 5,000 mm (much falling as snow) near the Straits of Magellan. Strong winds and cyclonic storms are common. The annual average temperature at Punta Arenas is 7°C (45°F).

POPULATION

The early, mainly Spanish, settlers from Europe intermarried with the local Amerindians (predominantly the Araucanian Mapuche tribes, who boast of never having succumbed to the Quechua-speaking Incas), and over 90% of the population is of mixed race. Subsequent European immigration was not as important to Chile as to many other South American countries, although immigration by Germans to the Valdivia–Puerto Montt area was influential, and other groups to make a significant contribution were from the United Kingdom, France, Italy, Switzerland, Austria and the former Yugoslavia.

According to the 2002 census, 4.6% of the total population identified as Amerindian. Of these, the overwhelming majority are Mapuche (87% of the ethnic minority total), who survive mainly in the south, with some Aimará in the north (7%), Atacameño (3%) and the Polynesian-descended Rapa Nui (1%) on Easter Island. There are a few other groups, including the aboriginal peoples of Patagonia and Tierra del Fuego. The official language, however, and that in almost total use is Spanish. Some of the other European-descended groups retain some use of their ancestral languages, but the aboriginal languages, including the seven Araucanian dialects, are struggling to survive. Most of the population is Roman Catholic, with about 70% acknowledging adherence, but Evangelical Christians claimed 15%. There is a relatively high figure of 8% given for those expressing no religious affiliation.

According to official estimates, the total population was 17.7m. in mid-2014. Some 90% of the population lived in the central region. About one-third of the total population lived in and around the capital city alone. Gran Santiago had a population of 6.7m. according to the 2012 census. The next largest city in population terms is Puente Alto, part of metropolitan Santiago, which had a population of 583,471 in 2012, followed by Antofagasta, in the north, with 348,669 in 2012. Other major population centres are Viña del Mar and Valparaíso, both to the north-west of Santiago. The country is divided into 15 regions.

History

SANDY MARKWICK

In 1536, when Diego de Almagro arrived to pave the way for the Spanish colony of Santiago, an indigenous population of around 500,000 inhabited the land that was to become Chile. The Inca empire had extended its reach as far south from Cusco (Cuzco) as the Maule river in the centre of modern Chile, but could not overcome fiercely resistant Mapuche Indian communities. The Mapuche resisted European colonialism too, but as occurred elsewhere in the Americas, indigenous Indians (Amerindians) were subjugated by disease and superior military force. Intermittent armed conflict with central government forces in post-colonial Chile persisted into the late 19th century. Colonial Chile, a distant and geographically isolated territory of the Spanish crown, had a minor economic role, principally focused on producing fruit and grains for export by sea to Lima, Peru.

INDEPENDENCE

War in Europe unleashed the forces of independence in Chile. Napoleon Bonaparte's invasion of Spain led landowning oligarchs in Chile to forge self-government while ostensibly remaining loyal to the imprisoned Spanish King, Ferdinand VII. Modern Chileans commemorate independence on 18 September, although the events of that day in 1810 were less decisive: a junta of Criollo (Creole) leaders issued a declaration of self-government and simultaneously declared loyalty to the ousted Spanish King.

Self-rule escalated into demands for permanent, full-scale independence. Internecine conflict among local élites stemmed from regional tensions, personal rivalries and arguments between conservatives and liberals over the role of the Roman Catholic Church. Conflict descended into civil war between the forces of José Miguel Carrera and Bernardo O'Higgins Riquelme, whose fragile truce could not resist Spanish royalist forces from the Viceroyalty of Peru resuming control following the Battle of Rancagua in 1814.

Independence forces exiled in Argentina came under the command of José de San Martín, who led an expedition over the Andes in early 1817 and dealt a decisive blow for independence at Maipú in April 1818. O'Higgins assumed dictatorial powers in Chile and focused on restoring order in remaining royalist strongholds and eradicating support for rivals. O'Higgins' authoritarian tendencies alienated liberals within the oligarchy, while his attempts to restrict the powers of the Church and to reform the system of land tenure aroused the opposition of conservative and landowning interests. In 1823, with the state virtually bankrupt, troops loyal to rival oligarchic interests both north and south forced his resignation. Instability and intermittent civil war continued thereafter as rival élite factions dominated by anticlerical liberals competed for control with conservatives and regional military leaders (*caudillos*).

AUTOCRATIC REPUBLIC, 1831–91

Conservative Domination, 1831–61

Following a military defeat of forces loyal to the liberal President Ramón Freire Serrano at Lircay in 1830, an era of domination by conservative factions commenced, which lasted until 1861. A merchant from Valparaíso, Diego Portales, although never assuming the presidency, was the power behind the scenes until his assassination in 1837.

Portales brokered a new Constitution in 1833, which centralized government by granting sweeping powers to the President over elections, the legislature, judiciary and public appointments throughout the country. The military was brought under civilian control and its successes in a war against the Peruvian-Bolivian Confederation in 1836–39 instilled in the young country a sense of national identity. Meanwhile, Portales repealed liberal reforms that had targeted Church privileges, thereby reinforcing its loyalty and underpinning the Church's role as an institution of social control.

Divisions within Chile's ruling classes centred on the degree of power centralized in the office of the President in Santiago and the privileged role of the Church. Despite abortive attempts by liberals to remove conservatives from power in 1835, 1851 and 1859, the Constitution of 1833 gave Chile a period of relative stability in 19th century South America. The Constitution survived until 1925, albeit with amendments reducing presidential powers in 1891. Fundamental to Chile's relative stability was the small and homogeneous ruling class, interconnected by ties of family and commerce. Regional, church-state and, to a lesser extent, ethnic tensions were less acute in Chile than elsewhere in South America. Stability during this period proved to be a springboard for territorial expansion and economic development.

Liberal Domination, 1861–91

A realignment of political forces saw a succession of liberal Presidents from the middle of the century to 1891. Reforms were introduced gradually. Church control was reduced in education and with the introduction of civil registrations of births, marriages and deaths. Power transferred peacefully between successive liberal Presidents serving a single term: Federico Errázuriz Zañartu (1871–76); Aníbal Pinto Garmendia (1876–81); and Domingo Santa María González (1881–86).

During the 19th century mining, not agriculture, was the leading force in the economy. Agricultural exports suffered from the long distances to key markets and from competition from Argentina. Silver and copper production grew rapidly from the 1840s, and by 1870 Chile controlled approximately 25% of the world copper market.

Tensions with Chile's northern neighbours over the activities of Chilean nitrate mining operations in disputed territory led to the War of the Pacific (1879–83). Chile was victorious and gained territory in the north from Peru and Bolivia. Chile also acquired valuable deposits of nitrates, which became the country's leading export, used for fertilizer and explosives, and the main driver of the economy until the First World War. Foreign investors, mostly European, owned two-thirds of nitrate fields by 1884.

The pattern of peaceful transitions of power ended dramatically with civil war during the term of President José Manuel Balmaceda. The Congreso (Congress), which had gradually claimed increased authority over the budgets and ministerial appointments, led a rebellion against the President's attempts to bypass congressional influence. Balmaceda had proposed that a public works programme be paid for using taxes raised from the nitrate industry. His plans were met with opposition in the Congress from northern mining interests allied to the Catholic hierarchy and landowning and merchant élites controlling parliament.

Opposition in the Congress received support from most of the navy, under Capt. Jorge Montt Alvarez, while the army was predominantly loyal to Balmaceda. Northern rebel forces supported by foreign-dominated mining interests mobilized to sail south to depose the President and defeated the army near Valparaíso before taking Santiago. Balmaceda sought refuge in the Argentine embassy, where he committed suicide.

PARLIAMENTARY REPUBLIC, 1891–1925

The new President, Jorge Montt, took office with the Congress now strengthened in its powers over the executive, particularly in relation to its authority over cabinet appointees. This period in Chilean history was characterized by the expansion of suffrage and the growing importance of new parties representing a more urbanized electorate of middle-class and skilled workers and provincial élites. Despite this, the Congress remained largely dominated by landowning élites, who controlled local elections through patronage, corruption and intimidation of rural voters.

After 1900 workers became more militant as they made demands for wages to protect them from inflation. Labour unrest peaked in 1917–20. The system of government was increasingly under strain as Chile transformed into an urbanized society whose population was suffering under the strains of spiralling inflation and the country's dependence on volatile nitrate exports, which had declined markedly with the outbreak of the First World War in 1914.

In this context, President Arturo Alessandri Palma took office in 1920, representing an alliance of reformist liberals, radicals and democrats. However, a conservative Congress blocked his legislative agenda, which featured a proposed labour code and social welfare reform. The deadlock led to agitation by military officers and demands for improvements in military salaries. Alessandri left the country and thus a long period of civilian government was interrupted by the military junta that took charge. The junta was divided, however, and in January 1925 a faction favouring the restoration of Alessandri took control. Alessandri's return to office in March was short-lived (he was deposed again by the military), but during his tenure the Constitution of 1925 was ratified, which made official the separation of Church and state and gave workers the legal right to organize. The President was to be directly elected and the power to select cabinet appointees was shifted from the legislature, now bi-cameral, to the executive.

CIVILIAN DEMOCRACY, 1925–73

Col Carlos Ibáñez del Campo, the most powerful political figure during this time, formally assumed the presidency in 1927. He expanded the role of the state, promoting industry and the modernization of infrastructure. The economy initially expanded as a result, until the Great Depression of 1929–31. Ibáñez's orthodox economic response to the crisis and his use of repression led to widespread unrest and his eventual exile in Argentina in 1931.

A period of short-lived Governments, including a 12-day 'Socialist Republic' led by Marmaduke Grove, eventually led to a third period in power for Arturo Alessandri after his victory in the 1932 elections. Economic recovery followed increased public spending, expansion of the money supply, a shift to import tariffs to nurture domestic industry and a revival of copper exports.

Alessandri's presidency marked the beginning of one of the longest periods of stable civilian government in South America. The fragmentation of the party system led to highly competitive elections and effective government required participation in coalitions. Electoral participation was high and results respected. Initially it was a restricted democracy, with only middle- and upper-class males enfranchised. Voting was extended to women in 1949, and to landless rural labourers and the urban poor with the introduction of universal suffrage in 1970.

Once the reforming alternative to the forces of conservatism, Alessandri turned the powers of the state to control the threat posed by organized labour and leftist parties. The Frente Popular, a coalition of communists, radicals, socialists and unions, united in opposition to the Government and in 1938 its candidate, Pedro Aguirre Cerda, won a narrow victory in the presidential election, with 50.3% of the vote.

In power, the Frente Popular Government pursued the development of a mixed economy and a goal of national industrial expansion, using high tariffs for imports to make domestic manufacturing viable and provide government credit to new enterprises. Modernization rather than radical redistribution was the priority.

The Frente Popular was a heterogeneous coalition, which proved difficult to maintain. After it disbanded, its followers supported two Radical Party presidencies, namely those of Juan Antonio Ríos Morales (1942–46) and Gabriel González Videla (1946–52). These Governments were pragmatic in balancing demands for radical social reform from left-wing groups with a need to appease landowning interests in the Congress. However, divisions widened with the onset of economic stagnation and high inflation.

Jorge Alessandri Rodríguez, the son of former President Alessandri, was elected to the presidency in 1958, representing a conservative-liberal alliance. Salvador Allende Gossens, the candidate of the Frente de Acción Popular (FRAP—Popular Action Front), a coalition of socialists and communists, came second, and Eduardo Frei Montalva of the Partido Demócrata Cristiano (PDC—Christian Democratic Party) came third. The PDC promoted economic and social reform, but stood against liberalism's emphasis on the individual and the collectivism and atheism of Marxism. The PDC displaced the Radical Party as the party of the centre.

The PDC won the 1964 elections, with Frei once again as its presidential candidate, by persuading the conservative-liberal alliance to support it in order to prevent a Marxist victory; Frei received 55.7% of the votes to Allende's 38.6%. However, the electoral coalition with the conservative-liberal alliance did not survive into government, and Frei encountered an opposition-dominated legislature. Frei's programme involved popular expansionary measures to increase consumption and production. However, he was forced into a retreat when confronted with inflation and increasing militancy on the part of the unions.

Frei was the first Chilean President to implement an agrarian reform bill. Despite its agricultural potential, Chile imported substantial volumes of food produce. Land distribution was uneven and land use inefficient, and the difficulties of sustaining an existence in the countryside had led many rural poor to move to the cities during the 1950s. Under the new law, which came into effect in 1967, large estates were to be divided and expropriated lands given to rural workers; by 1970, however, only 21,000 landless peasant families had benefited from the reform, far short of the 100,000 target. This was the result of a combination of bureaucracy, technical problems and obstructionism by landowners. The resultant disappointment assisted Allende in attracting the votes of the rural poor in 1970, while alienating conservative élites.

The Frei Government also undertook the 'Chileanization' of the mining sector, a centrist option falling short of the outright nationalization of mines, which were owned and operated predominantly by foreign companies. The mining law introduced by Frei in 1969 authorized the Government to buy 51% of the shares of the largest mine owned by the US Braden Copper Co. In his care not to deter foreign investors, Frei was criticized heavily by left-wing interests for being too moderate.

The Presidency of Salvador Allende

The PDC nominated Radomiro Tomic as its presidential candidate in 1970. The conservative-liberal alliance had formed a single party, the Partido Nacional (PN—National Party), in 1966, and nominated Jorge Alessandri as its candidate. Allende again represented the left, whose Unidad Popular (UP—Popular Unity) coalition had supplanted the FRAP. With the PN and the PDC fighting separately, Allende secured the presidency, winning 36.6% of the votes cast.

Allende's objectives centred on creating a mixed economy, placing major enterprises under state control while leaving small retail operations and companies untouched. Allende's intention was to build an alliance of the middle and working classes by expanding the state sector and increasing mass consumption while targeting the privileges of the élite. Against a background of growing nationalist sentiment, the UP Government nationalized certain foreign-owned operations, sometimes without compensation.

Chile became a highly politicized society. Workers mobilized independently of the Government to occupy firms, demanding nationalization and thereby accelerating the process. Nationalizations alienated the PDC as well as the USA under President Richard Nixon, who used his considerable influence to isolate Chile from the international economy. The USA halted new credit to Chile in a bid to force Allende to request moratoriums on debt repayments (which he did in 1971) and to undermine the country's credit rating. A severe shortage of financing ensued as loans from multilateral institutions stopped and direct investment from overseas receded.

Allende accelerated and widened the agrarian reform that Frei had initiated, partly prompted by a wave of land seizures. Meanwhile, an initial series of populist measures, including price freezes and substantial wage increases, led to a consumer boom and a short-term redistribution of wealth. Gross domestic product (GDP) grew rapidly and there was full employment, while inflation fell. During this early phase the UP attained its greatest popularity, winning nearly one-half of the votes cast in the 1971 local elections. However, problems began to appear from 1972. GDP declined by 5% as private firms responded negatively to price controls and the threat of expropriation, while the state lacked resources to invest. In response to a widening fiscal deficit, Allende increased the money supply. Consumer prices rose rapidly in 1972 and increased by 190% in the first nine months of 1973.

There was a huge voter turnout in the March 1973 congressional elections. The PN and the PDC sought to win two-thirds of the seats to allow them to impeach Allende. In fact, the UP increased its share of the national vote to 43%, the first time in Chile that a governing party had increased its vote mid-term, but its gains were not sufficient to win majority control in the Cámara de Diputados (lower house) or in the Senado (upper house).

The Nixon Administration, implacably opposed to Allende's regime, gave significant sums of aid to the Chilean military and provided covert assistance to opposition groups in a bid to destabilize the Government. Opposition groups mobilized protests, strikes and workplace lockouts from 1972, paralysing the Chilean economy. As Chile became increasingly polarized and tensions rose, so too did the threat of military intervention.

THE PINOCHET DICTATORSHIP

On 11 September 1973, in a well-planned military overthrow, the air force attacked the presidential palace, where Allende was making a last stand, having refused offers of exile. Allende died inside the palace, where he is widely believed to have committed suicide. The coup was organized by a military junta, featuring the army, navy, national police and the air force. The Commander-in-Chief of the Army, Gen. Augusto Pinochet Ugarte, soon emerged as the dominant figure.

On assuming control, the military began purging government and civilian institutions of UP sympathizers. The junta closed the Congress, censored the media, ousted suspected opponents from positions in educational establishments and banned union and political party activities. Institutions were dismantled and replaced, thenceforth under the direct authority of the military. The goal was stabilization through brutal repression and the imposition of a bureaucratic-authoritarian regime intent on remaining in power for an indefinite period. The most egregious human rights abuses took place in the first four years of the dictatorship, when thousands were murdered, jailed, tortured and exiled.

Pinochet consolidated his position by assuming dictatorial powers. He declared himself head of state and commander-in-chief of the armed forces, improved pay and conditions in the military to secure its loyalty and controlled all military appointments.

The economic goals of the Pinochet regime represented a radical shift from the past. From 1975 neo-liberal policies were accelerated and deepened under the control of a cadre of civilian radical advocates of free market reform. The regime determined to reduce the role of the state through privatizations, tariff reductions and reduced public spending. Until 1981 this resulted in notable economic success, which nevertheless came at the cost of high unemployment and regressive redistribution of wealth, while foreign debt increased massively as the Government sought capital from international organizations and bilateral aid.

By 1982 the initial success of growth and declining inflation was over and in its place came recession and bankruptcies. The problems were compounded by a decline in international copper prices and by the international debt crisis. Recovery during the late 1980s was based on an export boom encouraged by a highly competitive real exchange rate and low tariffs. Chile diversified exports and markets, which contributed to the country achieving one of the highest GDP growth rates in Latin America.

A new Constitution, implemented in 1981, was designed to re-establish a semblance of civilian government while simultaneously entrenching the military's position by giving it a supervisory role in government and creating a weak legislature. Notably, the Constitution limited the power of the Congress by preventing it from initiating legislation that required budgetary approval, and ensured that further constitutional reform was virtually impossible by creating nine seats in the Senate (one-third of the total) for nominees of the regime. The Constitution provided for a referendum in 1988 on whether Pinochet would remain in charge for a further eight years, and also stipulated that Pinochet would remain Commander-in-Chief of the Army for a period of eight years after relinquishing the presidency.

The regime took steps to control any future transition to civilian government and attempted to ensure that the military would retain significant power and influence to protect its members from prosecution. Among these were the amnesty law of 1978, preventing prosecution for human rights crimes committed between 1973 and 1978, and Pinochet's own continued position as head of the army. A protracted return to civilian rule ensued for much of the 1980s. Civil society and political activity slowly became more openly active as support for authoritarianism diminished with the economic crisis and international pressure for a return to democracy.

RESTORATION OF CIVILIAN GOVERNMENT

In the referendum held in October 1988, in accordance with the 1981 Constitution, 55% of the electorate voted for a return to civilian democracy, obliging the regime to hold elections within one year. In 1989 consensus was reached between the right-wing Renovación Nacional (RN—National Renewal) and the Concertación de Partidos por la Democracia (CPD—Coalition of Parties for Democracy), a centre-left coalition of 17 anti-Pinochet groups, regarding further constitutional reform. These reforms would reduce the presidential term to four years, increase the number of senators from 26 to 38 (thereby diminishing the influence of the nine non-elected senators) and require a two-thirds' majority in the Congress for constitutional amendments. The reforms were endorsed in a referendum later that year.

THE GOVERNMENT OF PRESIDENT AYLWIN

In the presidential election of December 1989 Patricio Aylwin Azócar, representing the CPD, was the victor. Aylwin was a member of the PDC, which, along with the Partido Socialista de

Chile (PS—Chilean Socialist Party), was the dominant party within the coalition. He took office on 11 March 1990.

While his predecessors in the PDC had advocated price controls, high tariff barriers and economic nationalism, Aylwin's presidency was to mark the start of a new consensus in civilian politics towards a social democratic model of moderately redistributive policies allied to macroeconomic prudence and trade liberalism. Aylwin placed emphasis on the market, not the state, as the key driver of the economy. To this end, he maintained the broad thrust of the economic policies of the military regime's later years, although increases in public spending were funded through tax rises rather than financed by deficits.

How best to remove the vestiges of military rule was an issue for Aylwin and his successors, as was the best way to tackle unsolved human rights crimes. Aylwin created the Truth and Reconciliation Commission (Comisión Nacional de Verdad y Reconciliación) to investigate human rights abuses by the military. The exercise was a compromise designed to establish the facts and to identify victims entitled to compensation, but which was not intended to lead to prosecutions. The Commission documented nearly 3,000 deaths at the hands of the regime. Pinochet resisted attempts to force his resignation as head of the army and the armed forces remained loyal to him. The Commission was limited in its scope from the outset, its main success being that it ended the legal limbo in which families of the 'disappeared' found themselves and that it undermined the military's interpretation of this period of Chilean history, forcing it to defend its actions. Aylwin declared the period of reconciliation over in 1991, although the scars in Chilean society remained visible for many years.

THE GOVERNMENT OF PRESIDENT FREI

The presidential election of December 1993 resulted in a convincing victory, with 58% of the votes cast, for another CPD candidate, Eduardo Frei Ruiz-Tagle, a PDC senator and son of former President Frei. In concurrent congressional elections, however, the CPD failed to win the two-thirds' majority required to amend Pinochet's 1981 Constitution.

While progress towards full civilian democracy was secure, tensions with the military persisted over its autonomy and budgets, its influence in government institutions and investigations into human rights crimes. Pinochet retired from the army at 83 years of age in March 1998 and assumed his seat as senator-for-life, which granted him immunity from prosecution. This was to be tested in October when, on a private visit to the United Kingdom, Pinochet was arrested following an extradition request from a Spanish judge investigating human rights abuses against Spanish citizens during Pinochet's regime. The Chilean Government protested against the arrest on the grounds that he was protected by diplomatic immunity. Following protracted legal and diplomatic deliberations, the British judicial authorities released Pinochet in March 2000, citing ill health as preventing the former dictator from undergoing trial proceedings.

THE GOVERNMENT OF PRESIDENT LAGOS

CPD candidate Ricardo Lagos Escobar narrowly defeated Joaquín Lavín Infante of the right-wing Alianza por Chile (APC—Alliance for Chile), formed in 1999 as a successor to the Unión por Chile, in a second-round ballot for the presidency in January 2000. It was illustrative of the strength of civilian government in Chile that victory for Lagos, a member of the PS, did not raise fears of military intervention. Like Frei before him, Lagos pursued pragmatic liberal economic management and consensus. He maintained a policy of fiscal prudence, signed numerous bilateral free trade agreements (FTAs) and sought private investment to upgrade basic infrastructure. The contentious issue of military privileges was settled during the Lagos presidency. A Supreme Court ruling revoked Pinochet's parliamentary immunity in August 2000, shortly after his return from detention in the United Kingdom. Pinochet faced charges of tax evasion, kidnapping and murder, although claims and counterclaims about whether he was fit to stand trial were protracted. Pinochet resigned as senator-for-life in 2002. Residual institutionalized military authority over civil-

ian government was brought to an end when, in 2004, the Supreme Court overturned the amnesty law of 1978, which had protected members of the armed forces, a move that opened the way for investigations into multiple human rights abuses. Finally, Chile's transition to full democracy was completed with the constitutional reform of 2005, which eliminated seats for non-elected senators and senators-for-life.

THE GOVERNMENT OF PRESIDENT BACHELET

Strong economic growth boosted the popularity of the Lagos Government and helped ensure the CPD was victorious in the presidential election in December 2005, the coalition's fourth consecutive victory. The CPD candidate, Michelle Bachelet Jeria, won 46.0% of the votes cast, while the right-wing vote was split between the candidates of two of the constituent parties of the APC—Sebastián Piñera Echeñique of the RN, who secured 25.4% of the vote, and Joaquín Lavín of the Unión Demócrata Independiente (UDI—Independent Democratic Union), with 23.2%. Bachelet won a second-round contest in January 2006, winning 53.5% of the votes. Bachelet, the first female President of Chile, was inaugurated in March for a newly reduced four-year term of office. Congressional elections held simultaneously with the first ballot for the presidency secured majorities for the CPD in both the Chamber of Deputies, with 65 out of 120 seats, and the Senate, where it won 11 seats, bringing its total to 20 out of 38 seats. Bachelet was the first of the post-Pinochet civilian Presidents to benefit from a majority in the Congress, partly a consequence of the abolition of seats for non-elected senators. However, she had to deal with a more fractious alliance than her predecessors.

Following a strike and the occupation of schools by secondary school students in May 2006, the Government announced a series of immediate measures to enhance education infrastructure and promised further reform to improve funding and the quality of teaching. The protest was the largest popular mobilization since the return of civilian democracy.

Further pressure on the Bachelet Government stemmed from a series of corruption scandals involving CPD politicians under the Lagos administration, which only came to light at the end of 2006. President Bachelet responded by swiftly announcing measures to improve transparency in public administration.

In September 2006 a new fiscal responsibility law was approved, designed to increase transparency in the rules for managing the fiscal surplus. In 2006, aided by burgeoning copper exports as a result of high global prices, the surplus was equivalent to 7.7% of GDP, affording the Government room for manoeuvre in social investment. The budget for 2007, approved by the Congress in November 2006, was the most expansionary since the restoration of civilian democracy. In December the Government published a significant pension reform bill, increasing benefits to the poor and less affluent by providing a universal minimum pension and subsidies for workers' pension contributions. Bachelet continued the free trade outlook of her predecessors, signing numerous FTAs and making Chile one of the most open trading nations in the world.

Gen. Pinochet died in December 2006. President Bachelet precluded a state funeral normally given to former Presidents; Pinochet was, however, buried with full military honours as a former Commander-in-Chief. The death of the former dictator was expected to improve the electoral prospects of the opposition APC, which had suffered as a result of the close relations between Pinochet and the UDI.

In January 2008 the ruling coalition was left with a minority in both legislative chambers, following the PDC's decision in December 2007 to expel a senator who had sided with the opposition on an important vote and the subsequent defection of five PDC deputies from the lower house. The Government's declining popularity, in part owing to high prices, energy shortages and crime, and in the face of a resurgent opposition, was evidenced in municipal elections in October 2008, in which the APC made strong gains, receiving the largest share of votes and taking control of a number of mayoralties previously considered CPD strongholds.

The Government's response to the global economic downturn from early 2009 helped to boost President Bachelet's approval ratings in the middle of that year to their highest level since the start of her administration. Popular discontent over the Government's conservative approach to spending windfall earnings from copper exports gave way to appreciation of the fact that strong public finances in 2009 allowed the Government to increase spending significantly, and thus offset the effects of the decline in demand.

In May 2009 the APC formally joined forces with a number of independent politicians, regional groupings and splinter groups previously aligned with the ruling CPD to form the Coalición por el Cambio (Coalition for Change). In an apparent realignment of the Chilean political landscape, the conservative opposition increasingly occupied the centre ground, assisted by the high approval ratings of Piñera, the former leader of the RN and now the candidate of the Coalición por el Cambio for the forthcoming presidential election.

PRESIDENT PIÑERA ENDS CENTRE-LEFT DOMINANCE

Piñera secured the highest number of votes in the presidential poll held on 13 December 2009, garnering 44.1% of the ballot, ahead of the CPD candidate, former President Eduardo Frei Ruiz-Tagle, who won 29.6%, and the independent Marco Enríquez-Ominami Gumucio (formerly of the PS), who gained 20.1%. In a run-off election, held on 17 January 2010, Piñera defeated Frei, attracting 51.6% of the total votes.

The result brought to an end 20 years of centre-left government since the restoration of democracy. However, the new Government's freedom of manoeuvre was constrained by a Congress finely balanced between Piñera's Coalición por el Cambio and the CPD. In congressional elections held simultaneously with the first ballot for the presidency in December 2009, the Coalición became the largest group in the Chamber of Deputies, securing 58 seats—three short of a majority and one more than the CPD. An agreement with the centrist Partido Regionalista de los Independientes (PRI—Independent Regionalist Party) gave Piñera's Government a narrow majority in the lower house. In the Senate, the CPD secured 19 of the 38 seats; of the remainder, 16 were won by the Coalición.

The new Government was further constrained by an urgent requirement to lead a reconstruction programme in the aftermath of a devastating earthquake that struck Chile's central region in February 2010. Homes and infrastructure in the Maule and Bíobío regions, and particularly the city of Concepción, were destroyed, with damage estimated at US $29,700m. The disaster prompted a large-scale humanitarian response. Outgoing President Bachelet declared a state of emergency and deployed 10,000 troops to assist in the relief effort. The disaster forced the new Government's original spending programme to be sidelined even before Piñera had taken office and ensured that reconstruction efforts would dominate expenditure plans into 2011.

Divisions between the two main components of the governing Coalición—the UDI and the President's party, the RN—damaged the Government's approval ratings. Divisions were highlighted in the wake of separate corruption controversies which resulted in the resignations of the Governor of Bíobío and the Minister of Housing and Urban Development in April 2011.

POPULAR PROTESTS

In mid-2012, halfway through his term of office, President Piñera's approval ratings were at their lowest since coming to power and lower than those experienced by any preceding Government since the return of democracy. The most vociferous opposition came from student protesters demanding greater public spending, a reduction in levels of inequality and, in particular, free university education and an end to the activities of commercial education providers in the further education sector. Students were required to supplement government grants with state-guaranteed bank loans, which were more costly at a new breed of private further education institution, and the burden of interest on loans threatened to exclude poorer people from universities. Students claimed the initiative was expanding commercial opportunities for private companies and raising costs for students. A series of government concessions in mid-2011, including a reduction in student loan rates, a pledge of further investment in education, and an improvement in the regulation of underperforming institutions, succeeded in easing tensions. However, unrest persisted with a broader focus on the high level of inequality across Chilean society, which continued despite a trend of impressive economic growth. Students allied themselves with regional social movements, the most important of which emerged in the isolated Aisén del Gen. Carlos Ibáñez del Campo region of southern Chile. A contentious decision in May 2011 to approve a large hydroelectric project, HidroAysén, in the area provoked widespread national opposition and was a catalyst for the ensuing and prolonged student unrest. Local protest groups around Aisén launched a campaign of roadblocks and broadened their campaign away from a focus on the hydroelectric project to demand increased fuel subsidies and improved transportation infrastructure and to protest against a new fishing law. The Aisén demonstrations led to the departure of four Ministers of Energy and accusations that the Government had mishandled the affair.

BACHELET RE-ELECTED FOR A SECOND TERM

With approval ratings for the Government at a very low level, the ruling Coalición por el Cambio held primary elections (the first by any party in Chile) to choose candidates for municipal elections scheduled for October 2012, in an attempt to modernize and to connect with the electorate. The exercise generated reasonable levels of participation, but it also deepened divisions within the CPD, which were exacerbated by losses in the municipal polls.

Approval ratings for the Piñera Government recovered in 2013, helped by its success in overseeing an economy that had exceeded growth expectations following the earthquake and tsunami of 2010 and the prolonged global economic crisis. The Government could also cite the record growth in job creation, which had raised real wages. Criticism of the Government focused on its management of education, crime and health care, and on the perceived arrogance of Piñera. Despite the restored approval ratings, however, the most popular politician was former President Michelle Bachelet, who returned from her UN post to announce her intention to contest the presidential election in November 2013.

In the first round of the presidential elections held on 17 November 2013 Bachelet, representing a new leftist alliance Nueva Mayoría (NM—New Majority) received 46.7% of the votes cast, just short of the majority required for an outright victory. Her closest rival was Evelyn Matthei of the UDI, representing the Alianza Por Chile, who received 25.0% of votes. Bachelet comfortably won the second round run-off held in the following month with 62.2% of votes. The victorious NM was the result of a pact between the members of the centrist CPD, the Partido Comunista (PC—Communist Party) and some smaller leftist parties.

The NM was also successful in congressional elections held concurrently with the first round presidential ballot, securing outright majorities in both houses (67 seats in the 120-seat Chamber of Deputies and 21 of 38 contested seats in the Senate).

While the results afforded Bachelet a clear mandate, the broader coalition of leftist interests represented by the NM suggested that Bachelet would face a more difficult challenge in maintaining unity across the alliance, than across a traditional CPD centre-left coalition. Bachelet pledged to introduce redistributive tax reform and to increase spending on public education. However, she was expected to pursue broadly moderate and pragmatic policies, thereby disappointing those on the left of the NM, who were making more radical demands. Although the Government was able to pass tax reforms with a simple legislative majority, the final bill was set to take into consideration demands from the right to water down the measures. The RN and the business community claimed that the original proposals would adversely affect levels of investment. The reforms were designed to help fund changes to the education system that would include free university education and the abolition of state subsidies for private profit-making schools. The Government was also expected to introduce constitutional reform to scale back the current binomial electoral system, in which parties contest two seats in the Senate or the Chamber of Deputies to represent an electoral district. The system favoured the two broad coalitions of left and right and was seen as a legacy of the Pinochet era, designed to shore up support for the right under a democratic system. Unlike with the tax reforms, the Government would need to build alliances to pass education and constitutional reforms, which required larger majorities. A Government proposal to reform Chile's outright prohibition of abortion, allowing the

practice in cases of rape, where the woman's life is at risk or where the foetus is non-viable was expected to face opposition from conservatives. However, polls suggested significant popular support for the reform. Chile was one of only a very few countries in the world with an outright ban on abortion in all cases.

President Bachelet's Government took a significant decision early in her presidency to cancel the permit of the HidroAysén dam project, following a ministerial review into the environmental impact of the development.

Economy

SANDY MARKWICK

Chile's landmass of 756,096 sq km occupies a distinctive geographic position, extending 4,329 km from the Atacama desert, bordering Peru in the north, to the icecaps of southern Patagonia. The breadth of the country does not exceed 180 km between the Pacific Ocean to the west and the Andes to the east. The fertile Central Valley extends north–south between the Andes and the lower coastal range. Additionally, the Pacific islands of Rapa Nui (Easter Island) and Juan Fernández form part of Chile. The extension of Chile over close to 40° of latitudinal spread and its variation in topography partly account for its mineral wealth and climate diversity, with heavy rainfall in the south distinct from the temperate Central Valley and the extremely arid north.

Chile is located on a fault line dividing the Nazca and South American tectonic plates, rendering it prone to earthquakes. In February 2010 an earthquake with a magnitude of 8.8 struck off the coast of the central Maule region, causing serious damage throughout central Chile (home to 80% of the population). The worst-hit area was the city of Concepción. Hundreds of people were killed, with many more injured or made homeless. In addition to the direct human casualties, the earthquake had a devastating impact on the Chilean economy. The cost of the damages was estimated at US $29,700m., with estimated losses in Chilean gross domestic product (GDP) of $7,600m.

The population in 2014 was estimated at 17.7m., with a growth rate of less than 1.0% per year, down from 2.1% in the 1960s. Chile's population is ageing as a result of a slowing population growth rate and an increase in life expectancy. Chileans over 40 years of age accounted for an estimated 41.1% of the total population in mid-2014, compared with 27.7% in 1992. Life expectancy at birth was 79.1 years in 2014, up from 63.4 years in 1975. Meanwhile, the rate of infant mortality per 1,000 live births had declined to 6.5 by 2014, from 78 in 1970. The re-establishment of civilian democracy and a robust economy slowed emigration rates from the 1990s, and in 2014 there was a small net inflow of migrants to Chile.

Economic activity is concentrated in a central region between the Aconcagua and Bío-Bío rivers, where around two-thirds of the population live and which includes the capital, Santiago, and Chile's other main cities. In 2014 just over 50% of the population lived in the greater Santiago area and in the neighbouring Valparaíso region. The country has become increasingly urbanized, with 87.0% of the population estimated to be living in towns, compared with 60% in 1960. In recent decades a centralizing tendency has been slowed by strong growth in mining, concentrated in the north, and tourism and non-traditional exports, such as salmon farming and methanol production, in the south.

Standards of living are high in Chile in comparison with the rest of Latin America. GDP per head, at US $15,7914 in 2013, ranked first in the region. According to official figures, unemployment declined to an average of 6.0% in 2013 (compared with 9.7% in 2009), reflecting Chile's emergence from recession. The rate increased slightly, however, to 6.5% in March 2014. Educational standards are high in comparison with the rest of South America. Compulsory school education

for a period of eight years reached 98.5% of the population and helped to reduce the adult illiteracy rate to 1.0%. Enrolment rates in further education in Chile compare favourably with the South American regional average. In 2012 some 22.9% of all students achieved further education qualifications. Attainment of higher education qualifications in Chile compared favourably with the average among members of the Organisation for Economic Co-operation and Development.

ECONOMIC STRUCTURE, SIZE AND PERFORMANCE

For most of its history, primary exports have been the key component fuelling Chile's economy. With the fertile Central Valley, a long Pacific Ocean coastline and abundant mineral wealth, exports traditionally focused on wheat and leather, fish and mining products. Chile is the world's largest copper producer (since the early 1980s) and a significant producer of gold, silver, molybdenum and nitrates.

Following severe recession in the 1980s, a period of sustained recovery ensued that continued into the 21st century. Increasingly open markets gave a boost to traditional exports and encouraged the development of newer commodities such as fruit, wine and wood products as well as transport and other export services.

An increasingly diversified export sector was the principal driver of economic growth from the 1980s. Higher growth rates after 2004 were primarily a result of dramatic increases in international copper prices. Growth slowed to 3.2% in 2008, a result of reduced domestic demand stemming from declining consumer confidence amid a downturn in the global economy, higher credit costs and depreciation of the peso.

The decline continued into 2009 as Chile followed most economies into recession, leading to a decrease of 1.7% for 2009 as a whole, despite positive economic growth returning mid-year. In April 2010 year-on-year GDP growth stood at 3.8%. However, the massive earthquake that struck central Chile in February of that year threatened the economic recovery, although the relatively minor extent of the damage inflicted on major industrial infrastructure meant that any lasting economic impact was minimized. Chile's major ports and airports escaped largely unscathed, as did the key mining sector, located primarily in the far north of the country. The incoming Government of President Sebastián Piñera Echeñique was forced to discard its economic plans in favour of a massive reconstruction programme. Piñera announced a reallocation of funds from the 2010 budget to tackle immediate issues arising from the aftermath of the earthquake, including the provision of housing and temporary employment. The economy recovered strongly in the course of 2010, with an overall annual GDP growth rate of 6.1%. Growth averaged 5.7% in 2011–12, but slowed to 4.1% in 2013 when total GDP amounted to an estimated US $268,300m. In that year, services contributed 61.2% of GDP, industry, including mining, construction and utilities, accounted for 35.6% and agriculture (including fishing) for 3.2%.

Successive governments have targeted consumer price control as a principal pillar of economic policy. Annual average inflation increased to 8.7% during 2008, as a result of rising international food and energy prices and a harsh winter that affected domestic harvests. However, the rate declined in 2009: weak domestic demand and cheaper imports resulting from an appreciation of the peso, combined with low electricity and food prices and a reduction in interest rates, leading consumer prices to rise by an average of 1.4% in 2009–10, and further to 3.4% in 2011, before falling to 3.0% in 2012 and 1.8% in 2013. However, by May 2014 the rate had increased to 4.3%.

Total external debt increased steadily, from US $25,700m. in 1995 to $130,900m. in March 2014, with the increase principally comprised of private sector debt. Nevertheless, successive governments have prudently managed debt repayments, incurring no penalties on principal arrears. Of the total debt, an estimated 94.4% was private sector debt in 2014, while 85.0% was due for maturity in the long term. The 12.8% public debt-to-GDP ratio in 2013 compared favourably with the rest of Latin America.

MANUFACTURING AND CONSTRUCTION

Adjustment to a new competitive environment after protective tariff barriers were dismantled in the 1970s proved difficult for some domestic industries, notably textiles, and, with low levels of investment, the contribution of industry to GDP declined. Recovery from the mid-1990s resulted in annual growth in manufacturing until 2006, when output stalled across all subsectors. Growth, of 3.1%, was restored in 2007, led by the print and paper sub-sector, a result of two large cellulose plants starting operations, and capital goods manufacturing. The global economic downturn reduced demand in 2008, leading to static output in the manufacturing sector that year and a 6.7% contraction in 2009, with consumer goods the worst performing category. Manufacturing growth returned in 2010, although the 3.8% increase in output was less than the rest of the economy as a whole. An increase of 6.6% was recorded in the sector in 2011. Growth fell back to 2.6% in 2012 and stagnated in 2013 with a slight contraction during the year (down 0.3%), in part a result of the completion of a large mining project, leading to reduced demand for metal products. Manufacturing accounted for 11.3% of the employed labour force and contributed an estimated 10.1% of GDP in 2013, compared with 15.0% in 2008. Construction output grew by an average annual rate of 3.8% during 2003–10, led by investments in the mining and energy sectors, and following a brief decline during 2009 increased by an impressive average of 9.6% in 2011–12. Modest growth of 3.2% was recorded in 2013. Some 8.7% of the employed labour force was engaged in construction in 2013, while the industry's contribution to total GDP in that year was 6.9%.

MINING

Northern Chile is rich in minerals. Chile has approximately 30% of the world's proven reserves of copper, as well as significant reserves of nitrates, molybdenum, selenium, iodine and gold. Deposits are of high quality and close to the surface, making exploitation relatively easy, while the short distances to the coastal ports facilitate exports of mining products.

Chile is the largest copper producer in the world. In 2013 the country produced 5.7m. metric tons of refined copper, equivalent to 17% of global output (although production had contributed 32% of global output in the previous year). A three-fold increase in output since 1990 was the result of large-scale investment, dominated by the private sector, although the Corporación Nacional del Cobre de Chile (Codelco), the state copper concern, also expanded its operations. La Escondida in the northern Atacama desert is the world's largest copper mine with an annual capacity of 1.2m. tons of fine copper, and is owned mostly by British and Australian interests (Rio Tinto and BHP Billiton, respectively). In 2013 the mining sector contributed an estimated 12.1% to total GDP, accounted for 57.3% of total exports and engaged 3.2% of the employed labour force.

A copper boom from 2003 was fuelled by demand from the USA and the People's Republic of China. In 2003 the average price of copper rose by 14.1%; it reached record highs over the next three years, rising at an average annual rate of 57.4%. Prices reached a new record high of US $4.63 per pound in 2011. High copper prices and a strong currency raised concerns that aluminium and plastic alternatives to copper would be developed more quickly, fears that recalled the decline of Chile's nitrate industry in the early 20th century. Nevertheless, copper prices had decreased to an average $3.32 per pound in 2013.

An increase in international copper prices led to copper export revenues of US $28,222m. in 2010. Despite a stagnation in production in 2011, primarily owing to declining ore grade, Chile earned revenues of $44,438m., owing to continued price rises. Production increased by 6.6% in 2013; however, export earnings declined to $42,184m., owing to a fall in copper prices. In that year copper accounted for 91.4% of mining exports and 52.4% of total merchandise exports. Total mining exports earned $43,937m. in 2013, representing a historically high level, although down from the preceding three years and some 10.5% lower than the 2011 figure. Codelco announced record investment of $4,300m. in 2012 to develop copper deposits and improve mining infrastructure.

ENERGY SUPPLY

Chile is a significant net energy importer, a consequence of having modest hydrocarbon reserves estimated at 155m. metric tons of low quality coal, 98,000m. cu m of natural gas and 150m. 42-gallon barrels of petroleum, located off shore in the extreme south. Thermoelectricity, largely using imported fuel, accounted for approximately two-thirds of installed energy capacity and electricity generation in 2013, with hydroelectricity making up the remainder. Alternative energy generation, including wind power, was statistically insignificant. Thermoelectricity generation relied mostly on natural gas, and to a lesser extent coal and diesel fuel. Heavy rainfall and mountainous topography in the south provides huge potential to generate energy from hydroelectricity. However, installed power-generating capacity from hydroelectric installations in 2011, at some 5,000 MW, was just 21% of its potential as estimated by the National Energy Commission (Comisión Nacional de Energía—CNE). There were plans by HidroAysén, a joint venture between Spanish-owned energy company Endesa and Colbun of Chile, to build five hydroelectric dams in the southern Aisén region, which would provide a total capacity of 2,430 MW. The project, located in an area of exceptional natural wilderness, attracted strong opposition from local communities and environmental groups. The Supreme Court rejected a series of injunctions filed by opponents of the scheme in April 2012; however, in June 2014 the new Government of President Michelle Bachelet cancelled HidroAysén's licence, following a ministerial review of the environmental impact of the project. Lengthy legal proceedings were expected to ensue, as the interests behind the venture appealed the decision or altered the plans to secure its approval.

The Ministry of Energy estimated that Chile needed an additional 8,000 MW of new generating capacity to keep pace with demand up to 2020. Reliance on hydroelectricity and imported fuel makes power supplies vulnerable to periods of low rainfall and external forces. In 2007, in response to Chile's energy insecurity, the CNE announced a schedule of investment in new generation and transmission capacity up to 2015. The plan included increasing generating capacity by 2,000 MW through new coal-based installations and by 1,905 MW through plants fuelled by liquefied natural gas (LNG). An LNG port terminal at Quintero, near Santiago, with a daily capacity to convert LNG back into gas of 10m. cu m, began operations in 2009. The Government was expected to accelerate plans for investment in additional LNG terminals, as well as in solar power development in the Atacama desert and in increased energy efficiency. The GDP of the electricity, gas and water sector increased at an average annual rate of 124% in 2009–12. The rate of growth in the sector slowed to 7.2% in 2013.

SERVICES

In 2013 some 66.5% of the employed labour force was engaged in the service sector, principally in tourism, retail and financial services. The retail sector is modern, highly competitive and dominated by domestic chains that have expanded into operations in other Latin American countries. Chile's diverse range of scenery, particularly the unspoiled lakes and fjords in the south, along with opportunities for skiing, beach and mountaineering holidays, attract large numbers of visitors and support a robust tourism sector. There were 3.6m. tourist visits from abroad in 2013, representing an average annual increase of 6.4% since 2008. Overseas tourists spent an estimated US $2,219m. in Chile in 2013, equivalent to 2.9% of merchandise exports. European visitors accounted for 10.6% of all overseas tourists, compared with 6.2% from North America and 58.1% from neighbouring countries.

The country's sophisticated financial services sub-sector expanded by an average of 5.3% per year in 2001–08 before contracting by 1.7% in 2009 in line with the economy as a whole. Growth, measured at 7.6%, was restored in 2010, accelerated to 10.0% in 2012 and slowed to 4.4% in 2013. Around 655,000 people, or 8.4% of the employed labour force, were engaged in financial services, including property, in 2013.

Banks in Chile are prudently capitalized under the supervision of the Superintendencia de Bancos e Instituciones Financieras. Many foreign and national banks operate in the country, holding total deposits at the beginning of 2014 estimated at 97,695,000m. pesos. Total stock market capitalization in 2012 averaged US $313,325.3m.

Financial deregulation has helped nurture dynamic capital markets, with a wide range of financial services available. Deregulation of capital markets was implemented in 2001 to increase liquidity and encourage savings and investment. Further reforms, approved by the Congreso in 2007, included measures to promote the development of a risk capital industry through tax incentives and greater flexibility in investment regulations. The reforms also targeted deregulation to help develop mutual funds and markets in derivatives and bonds.

TRANSPORT AND COMMUNICATIONS

Transport infrastructure and internal transport services are well developed. Private investment through build-operate-transfer (BOT) concessions has led to a modern motorway network serving the central region where most of the population lives, as well as urban toll roads. There were approximately 18,000 km of paved roads in 2012.

The state railway company, Empresa de los Ferrocarriles del Estado (EFE), formerly managed a rail network extending from Iquique in the far north to Puerto Montt in the south. Shorter lines extended west–east connecting main towns. New investment was limited. Freight services were privatized in 1995, as was Ferronor, the northern railway division, in 1996, but plans to sell other parts of the network were abandoned under President Ricardo Lagos, who increased funds for EFE to modernize central and southern services.

A large network of airports complements the road and rail infrastructure and is particularly useful to shorten travel times, given Chile's considerable distances and mountainous terrain. Foreign investment increased the capacity of Santiago's international airport terminal three-fold following a BOT concession in 1997. A second runway was added in 2005. BOT concessions were also awarded to expand the most important regional airports, thus releasing government funds for investment in smaller airports.

There were 38 ports handling cargo in Chile, with a mixture of private and state ownership after the sector was opened to private operators in the 1990s. Investment in port infrastructure resulted in annual handling volumes increasing to 95m. metric tons in 2011, from 28m. tons in 2002. The busiest ports in terms of volume of cargo loaded and unloaded were San Antonio and Quintero which, respectively, accounted for 12.0% and 11.6% of the national total in 2011. While San Antonio was diversified in the commodities it handled, Quintero was almost exclusively focused on handling imported oil. Other important ports were Valparaíso, which handled 9.0% of the total national volume of cargo, Patillos (5.8% of the total and largely focused on salt exports), San Vicente (5.4%) and Lirquén (4.6%). The port handling the largest share of copper exports was Angames, accounting for 37.1% of the total, followed by Antofagasta with 28.6%. Chile has an important merchant marine dominated by Compañía Sud Americana de Vapores (CSAV), which was the principal shipping company in South America with acquisitions of smaller, competitor companies in Brazil and Uruguay.

Telecommunications are the most advanced in the region. The ratio of mobile cellular telephone handsets to the population surpassed 100% in 2010. Fixed-line penetration declined after 2001 (when it reached 22.3%). There were 3.2m. fixed lines in service in 2013, representing 18.2% penetration. The incumbent operator, Telefónica CTC Chile, operating under the Movistar brand, encountered increased competition from new cable television entrants to the market providing 'triple play' services that featured fixed-line telephony and broadband internet access as well as television services. At 12.4 subscriptions per 100 inhabitants in 2012, Chile had the second highest broadband internet access rates in Latin America after Uruguay. The transport and communications sub-sector accounted for 7.1% of the employed labour force in 2012.

AGRICULTURE

Diversity in climate and soil type ensures that there is considerable agricultural potential. Furthermore, natural barriers in the form of desert to the north, the Andes to the east and the ocean to the west protect crops and livestock from disease and pests. Since the 1990s free trade agreements (FTAs) have boosted agriculture and encouraged modern and efficient production processes. However, agricultural performance was severely affected by the earthquake of February 2010, which caused extensive damage to irrigation infrastructure and to fishing and forestry production plants. Chile barely registered any growth across agriculture, hunting, forestry and fishing in 2010 (0.3%), but saw output increase by 11.8% in 2011. A contraction of 1.1% followed in 2012, before growth was restored at 2.3% in 2013. The sector engaged 9.6% of the employed labour force.

Chile is one of the most important suppliers of fruit to world markets. Total fruit exports were valued at US $4,738m. in 2013, more than twice the value in 2005. The main fruit export is grapes, which earned $1,605m. in export earnings in 2013. Other important fruit exports were apples, blueberries and cherries. Olive oil production has risen significantly since 2003, when the domestic market was supplied by imports and there was only a marginal export business. Access to new markets via FTAs has helped to boost the fruit industry, supported by investment in new plantations. Chile was one of the most important suppliers of fresh fruit to China following an FTA in 2005. China issued permits to Chilean suppliers to export cranberries, kiwis, apples, plums, grapes, pears, cherries and citrus fruit.

The valleys of central Chile provide excellent conditions for vineyards. Planting and wine-making capacity increased rapidly from the 1980s. The area of land covered by vineyards almost doubled in the 10 years to 2006, and increased further thereafter, to stand at 205,000 ha in 2012. In that year Chile was the sixth largest producer of wine in the world, with an annual output of 1,255m. litres. Earnings from wine exports increased to US $1,560m. in 2013, from $1,166m. in 2009.

Although exports of meat are modest, this sub-sector is growing in importance, fuelled by new FTAs. Chile produced 1.5m. metric tons in 2013, up from 1.3m. tons in 2010. Meat exports earned US $730m. in 2013, a slight decrease compared with the previous year. Pork remains the most important product, although its relative share of meat exports has diminished owing to the introduction in 2006 of quotas for the export of beef and poultry to the USA under a bilateral FTA.

Chile is one of the world's largest suppliers of fish and fish products, although it ranks behind its northern neighbour, Peru. The performance of the fishing industry is volatile and depends on the annual catch. Southern Chile's extensive network of lakes and fjords is rich in salmon. Since the mid-1980s a salmon-farming industry has emerged and, at over 35% of the world market share, it now rivals Norway's. The most important markets for Chilean salmon are the USA and Japan. In 2009 a decline in export volumes, although partly offset by higher prices, led to a 17% decrease in revenues. Export revenues declined further in 2010, following large-scale damage to tinning and freezing plants in the 2010 earthquake, but recovered with growth of 61.0% in 2011, underpinned by reconstruction efforts. Exports grew by a further 6.9% in 2012 and by 3.9% in 2013 to US $2,772m.

There is an abundance of temperate rainforests, with over 10.5m. ha of protected natural forest and 2.7m. ha planted and managed for wood and wood products. Increased investment at the end of the last century, supported by government subsidies and a benign tax regime, led to an expansion of the sector and a shift away from the primary resource towards higher value processed products, including cellulose. Processing capacity rose from 2004 with the construction of new cellulose plants in Valdivia, Nueva Aldea and Santa Fe. Cellulose product exports rose consistently during 2003–08, reaching US $3,250m. Exports declined by 17.3% in 2009, before recovering in 2010–11 to reach $3,625m. in the later year. Exports declined by 9.0% in 2012 before rising to $3,607m. in 2013. Meanwhile, investment in forestry brought the industry into conflict with environmental groups and with Mapuche Indians over land rights.

FOREIGN TRADE

From its colonial origins until the 1930s Chile was a trading nation whose economy relied on exports. Primary resources or products with minimal processing dominated exports. Fish, wheat and leather products were significant, but the most important exports were minerals (particularly nitrates until the First World War), copper and gold.

From the 1930s successive governments introduced protective import tariffs to create a domestic market for Chilean manufacturing and to nurture a domestic industrial base. Chile reverted to an export-led growth model in the mid-1970s, resulting in merchandise trade surpluses, which continued into the 21st century. Various governments have expanded free trade with a succession of bilateral FTAs, including with the European Union (implemented in 2003), the USA (2004), China (2006), Japan (2007), Australia (2008), Malaysia (2009), Turkey (2010) and Viet Nam (2011), making Chile one of the most open countries in the world economy. Traditional exports, notably copper, dominated and further outstripped other commodities following a boom in copper prices from 2003. Copper accounted for more than 52.4% of merchandise export earnings in 2013. Despite the enduring importance of copper, however, there has been a long-term trend towards diversifying exports. Significant non-traditional exports include cellulose, wood and wood products, fruit, salmon, wine, methanol, meat, seeds and metal-processing equipment.

An increase in imports accompanied economic growth and a rise in foreign direct investment (FDI) in the 1990s. In 2013 imports of intermediate goods, including petroleum, represented 53.5% of total imports, while 27.2% of total imports were consumer products and 19.3% were capital goods.

China, which overtook the USA as Chile's largest single market in 2007, purchased 24.9% of Chilean exports in 2013 (up from 8.8% in 2006), followed by the USA with 12.1% (down from 16.1% in 2006) and Japan with 10.6%. The Netherlands was the most important primary European destination for Chile's exports, taking 3.5% of the total in 2013, although much of this was transported to other European markets. Imports are generally less diversified, with Latin America supplying 28.0% of all goods and services entering Chile in 2012. The USA was the largest single source of imports for Chile in 2012, accounting for 22.6% of the total, followed by China with 18.2%, Argentina (6.7%) and Brazil (6.5%).

In 2013 the surplus in the country's merchandise trade balance, of US $2,117m., was down from $15,182m. in 2010, which had resulted largely from increases in export prices. Chile recorded trade surpluses of $22,947m. and $24,132m. in 2006 and 2007, respectively, underpinned by record copper prices.

CURRENT ACCOUNT

Chile traditionally had current account deficits resulting from deficits in the services account and, more significantly, in the income account associated with profit remittances sent overseas by foreign companies. Remittances tended to correlate positively with export performance. During 2004–07 Chile reported current account surpluses, stimulated by demand for Chilean exports, particularly copper, from fast-growing China, which resulted in high international prices. In 2008 the current account went into deficit, equivalent to 2.0% of GDP, as improvements in the services and income balance were offset by a declining trade surplus. In 2009 a 31% contraction in the value of imports ensured the restoration of a current account surplus, despite a concomitant decrease in export earnings. The current account stayed in surplus in 2010, totalling $3,581m. In 2011, however, Chile recorded a deficit on the current account of $3,069m., and this deficit widened to $9,083m. in 2012 and further to $9,486m. in 2013.

FOREIGN DIRECT INVESTMENT

Foreign investors were significant protagonists in the economic development of Chile in the 19th century, notably focusing on the nitrate industry. From the 1930s to 1973 a shifting popular consensus increasingly favoured restricting the terms of engagement governing foreign investors' participation in the economy. Antagonism towards foreign investors reached a head during the presidency of Salvador Allende (1970–73), whose socialist experiment included nationalizing several (mainly US) foreign companies, including some without compensation. The confiscation of US-owned assets contributed to the US Government of President Richard Nixon undertaking a campaign to destabilize the Allende regime, to which it was already implacably opposed.

The military dictatorship that took charge in 1973 ushered in an era of free market reform that persisted following the restoration of civilian democracy in 1990. FDI inflows peaked in the late 1990s, but inflows recovered strongly after 2003, mainly driven by investment in copper (encouraged by high international prices). In the 2000s foreign investment continued to be encouraged by a liberal and stable environment as well as dynamism in the economy. Chile's stock of FDI amounted to US $215,452m. in 2013, with the mining and financial services sectors the main focal points. Direct investment in Chile amounted to US $20,258m. in 2013, representing a decline of 29% compared with the previous year, although still a historically high level.

OUTLOOK

The Chilean economy remains one of the most developed in Latin America, with living standards among the highest. However, an open, liberal economy ensured that Chile was vulnerable to a decline in global demand for its exports, and the country, therefore, did not escape the global recession that afflicted most economies in 2008–10. In particular, an easing of growth rates in China was expected to have an impact on Chile through lower import earnings. Nevertheless, the country's sound fiscal position, political and institutional stability and strong banking system ensured that the downturn was relatively mild compared with other regional economies. A conservative approach to windfall earnings from exceptionally high copper prices meant that the Government had significant international reserves of approximately US $40,970m., as well as savings in sovereign wealth funds, to support stimulus initiatives. Investment in reconstruction following the 2010 earthquake also provided a stimulus to economic growth in 2010–12. A new centre-left Government under President Michelle Bachelet, which took office in March 2014, was expected to increase public spending funded by a higher corporate tax rate, although she was widely predicted to pursue policies of pragmatic, moderate economic management.

Statistical Survey

Sources (unless otherwise stated): Instituto Nacional de Estadísticas (INE), Avda Bulnes 418, Casilla 498-3, Correo 3, Santiago; tel. (2) 2366-7777; fax (2) 2671-2169; e-mail inesdadm@reuna.cl; internet www.ine.cl; Banco Central de Chile, Agustinas 1180, Santiago; tel. (2) 2696-2281; fax (2) 2698-4847; e-mail bcch@bcentral.cl; internet www.bcentral.cl.

Area and Population

AREA, POPULATION AND DENSITY*

Area (sq km)	756,096†
Population (census results)‡	
24 April 2002	15,116,435
9 April 2012§	
Males	8,101,890
Females	8,532,713
Total	16,634,603
Population (official estimates at mid-year)‖	
2013	17,556,815
2014	17,711,004
Density (per sq km) at mid-2014	23.4

* Excluding Chilean Antarctic Territory (approximately 1,250,000 sq km).
† 291,930 sq miles.
‡ Excluding adjustment for underenumeration.
§ In November 2013 a government commission investigating claims that the 2012 census results contained compromising irregularities rejected earlier demands that the census should be annulled, but recommended that the published results should be revised with expanded documentation of the irregularities.
‖ Estimates not adjusted to take account of the 2012 census.

POPULATION BY AGE AND SEX
(at 2012 census)

	Males	Females	Total
0–14 years	1,829,199	1,759,524	3,588,723
15–64 years	5,534,705	5,791,414	11,326,119
65 years and over	737,986	981,775	1,719,761
Total	**8,101,890**	**8,532,713**	**16,634,603**

REGIONS
(population at 2012 census)*

	Area (sq km)	Population	Density (per sq km)	Capital
Tarapacá . . .	42,225.8	300,021	7.1	Iquique
Antofagasta . .	126,049.1	547,463	4.3	Antofagasta
Atacama . . .	75,176.2	292,054	3.9	Copiapó
Coquimbo . . .	40,579.9	707,654	17.4	La Serena
Valparaíso . . .	16,396.1	1,734,917	105.8	Valparaíso
El Libertador Gen. Bernardo O'Higgins . .	16,387.0	877,784	53.6	Rancagua
Maule	30,296.1	968,336	32.0	Talca
Biíobío . . .	37,068.7	1,971,998	53.2	Concepción
La Araucanía . .	31,842.3	913,065	28.7	Temuco
Los Lagos . . .	48,583.6	798,141	16.4	Puerto Montt
Aisén del Gen. Carlos Ibáñez del Campo . . .	108,494.4	99,609	0.9	Coyhaique
Magallanes y Antártica Chilena* . .	1,382,291.1	159,468	0.1	Punta Arenas
Metropolitan Region (Santiago) . .	15,403.2	6,685,685	434.0	—
Los Ríos . . .	18,429.5	364,592	19.8	Valdivia
Arica y Parinacota .	16,873.3	213,816	12.7	Arica
Total	**2,006,096.3**	**16,634,603**	**8.3**	**—**

* Including Chilean Antarctic Territory (approximately 1,250,000 sq km).

PRINCIPAL TOWNS
(2012 census)

Gran Santiago (capital) . .	6,685,685		Arica	210,936
Puente Alto . .	583,471		Coquimbo . .	202,441
Antofagasta . .	348,669		Talca	201,142
Viña del Mar . .	331,399		Los Angeles . .	187,494
Valparaíso . .	294,848		Iquique . . .	184,953
San Bernardo . .	277,802		Chillán . . .	175,869
Temuco . . .	269,992		Valdivia . . .	154,445
Puerto Montt . .	238,455		Osorno . . .	154,137
Rancagua . . .	232,524		Talcahuano . . .	151,524
Concepción . .	214,926		Calama	138,722
La Serena . . .	211,275			

BIRTHS, MARRIAGES AND DEATHS

	Registered live births*		Registered marriages		Registered deaths	
	Number	Rate (per 1,000)	Number	Rate (per 1,000)	Number	Rate (per 1,000)
2004 . .	230,352	14.5	53,403	3.3	86,138	5.4
2005 . .	230,831	14.3	53,842	3.3	86,102	5.3
2006 . .	231,383	14.2	58,155	3.5	85,639	5.2
2007 . .	240,569	14.6	57,792	3.5	93,000	5.6
2008 . .	246,581	14.8	56,112	3.3	90,168	5.4
2009 . .	252,240	15.0	56,127	3.3	91,965	5.4
2010 . .	250,643	14.7	60,362	3.5	97,930	5.7
2011 . .	247,358	14.4	64,768	3.8	94,985	5.5

* Adjusted for underenumeration.

Life expectancy (years at birth): 79.6 (males 76.8; females 82.5) in 2012 (Source: World Bank, World Development Indicators database).

ECONOMICALLY ACTIVE POPULATION*
(labour force survey October—December, '000 persons aged 15 years and over, preliminary)

	2011	2012	2013
Agriculture, hunting, forestry and fishing	784.0	800.7	726.3
Mining and quarrying	221.5	260.3	249.4
Manufacturing	842.4	873.4	891.5
Electricity, gas and water	57.9	55.9	52.8
Construction	620.3	649.8	682.2
Trade, restaurants and hotels .	1,816.7	1,799.3	1,889.5
Transport, storage and communications	535.9	544.5	576.9
Financing, insurance, real estate and business services	622.8	599.2	668.3
Public administration and defence; compulsory social security . .	432.3	446.5	433.5
Education	530.2	600.3	645.8
Health and social services . . .	332.0	338.4	345.8
Community, social and personal services	244.8	239.0	253.8
Private households with employed persons	521.5	490.0	483.8
Extraterritorial organizations and bodies	2.2	2.1	4.4
Total employed	**7,564.3**	**7,699.4**	**7,904.0**
Unemployed	534.4	496.2	474.8
Total labour force	**8,098.7**	**8,195.6**	**8,378.9**

* Figures are based on sample surveys, covering 36,000 households, and exclude members of the armed forces. Estimates are made independently, therefore totals are not always the sum of the component parts.

Health and Welfare

KEY INDICATORS

Total fertility rate (children per woman, 2012)	1.8
Under-5 mortality rate (per 1,000 live births, 2012) . . .	9
HIV/AIDS (% of persons aged 15–49, 2012)	0.4
Physicians (per 1,000 head, 2009)	1.0
Hospital beds (per 1,000 head, 2010)	2.1
Health expenditure (2011): US $ per head (PPP)	1,478
Health expenditure (2011): % of GDP	7.1
Health expenditure (2011): public (% of total)	48.4
Access to water (% of persons, 2012)	99
Access to sanitation (% of persons, 2012)	99
Total carbon dioxide emissions ('000 metric tons, 2010) . .	72,258.2
Carbon dioxide emissions per head (metric tons, 2010) . .	4.2
Human Development Index (2013): ranking	41
Human Development Index (2013): value	0.822

For sources and definitions, see explanatory note on p. vi.

Agriculture

PRINCIPAL CROPS
('000 metric tons)

	2010	2011	2012
Wheat	1,524	1,576	1,213
Rice, paddy	95	130	150
Barley	97	123	76
Maize	1,358	1,438	1,493
Oats	381	564	451
Potatoes	1,081	1,676	1,093
Sugar beet	1,420	1,951	1,824
Beans, dry	23	24	11
Rapeseed	44	71	114
Cabbages and other brassicas* .	44	38	45
Lettuce and chicory* . . .	94	102	99
Tomatoes*	738	726	400
Pumpkins, squash and gourds* .	137	141	142
Chillies and peppers, green* . .	50	46	51
Onions, dry*	297	295	300
Carrots and turnips* . . .	150	161	165
Maize, green*	176	177	180
Watermelons*	52	53	55
Cantaloupes and other melons* .	49	49	50
Oranges*	134	141	145
Lemons and limes*	155	153	160
Apples	1,624	1,588	1,625*
Pears*	180	190	191
Peaches and nectarines* . . .	357	320	325
Plums and sloes*	298	293	300
Grapes*	2,904	3,149	3,200
Avocados	166	156	160*
Kiwi fruit*	229	237	240

* FAO estimate(s).

Aggregate production ('000 metric tons, may include official, semi-official or estimated data): Total cereals 3,588 in 2010, 3,950 in 2011, 3,465 in 2012; Total roots and tubers 1,094 in 2010, 1,690 in 2011, 1,107 in 2012; Total vegetables (incl. melons) 2,107 in 2010, 2,123 in 2011, 1,827 in 2012; Total fruits (excl. melons) 6,184 in 2010, 6,391 in 2011, 6,514 in 2012.

Source: FAO.

LIVESTOCK
('000 head, year ending September)

	2010	2011	2012*
Horses	308†	310†	311
Cattle	3,830*	3,759	3,750
Pigs	2,706	2,824	2,940
Sheep	3,644†	3,600*	3,650
Goats*	750	745	747
Chickens	47,479	47,479	48,000
Turkeys*	30,000	32,000	32,000

* FAO estimate(s).
† Unofficial figure.
Source: FAO.

LIVESTOCK PRODUCTS
('000 metric tons)

	2010	2011	2012*
Cattle meat	210.7	191.0	195.0
Sheep meat	10.5	11.2	11.6
Pig meat	498.5	527.9	540.0
Horse meat	7.4	8.3	9.2
Chicken meat	503.8	562.1	572.0
Cows' milk	2,530	2,620	2,650
Goats' milk*	10.3	9.7	10.0
Hen eggs	190.8	198.3	200.0
Wool, greasy	7.8	7.8*	8.0

* FAO estimate(s).
Source: FAO.

Forestry

ROUNDWOOD REMOVALS
('000 cubic metres, excluding bark)

	2009	2010	2011
Sawlogs, veneer logs and logs for sleepers	13,962	14,905	16,147
Pulpwood	22,279	19,424	22,722
Other industrial wood	161	231	281
Fuel wood	14,621	12,655	15,998
Total	51,023	47,215	55,148

2012: Figures are assumed to be unchanged from 2011 (FAO estimates).
Source: FAO.

SAWNWOOD PRODUCTION
('000 cubic metres, including railway sleepers)

	2009	2010	2011
Coniferous (softwood)	5,566	6,050	6,507
Broadleaved (hardwood) . . .	271	304	278
Total	5,837	6,354	6,785

2012: Figures are assumed to be unchanged from 2011 (FAO estimates).
Source: FAO.

Fishing

('000 metric tons, live weight)

	2010	2011	2012
Capture	2,679.7	3,063.4	2,572.9
Patagonian grenadier . . .	74.3	70.1	62.2
Araucanian herring	750.8	887.3	848.5
Anchoveta (Peruvian anchovy) .	755.4	1,191.4	903.9
Chilean jack mackerel . . .	464.8	247.3	227.5
Chub mackerel	95.7	26.1	24.3
Jumbo flying squid	200.4	163.5	145.0
Aquaculture	701.1	954.8	1,071.4
Atlantic salmon	123.2*	264.3	399.7
Coho (silver) salmon . . .	122.7*	159.6	162.0
Rainbow trout	220.2*	224.4	254.4
Total catch	3,380.8*	4,018.3	3,644.3

* FAO estimate.

Note: Figures exclude aquatic plants ('000 metric tons): 380.8 (capture 368.6, aquaculture 12.2) in 2010; 418.2 (capture 403.5, aquaculture 14.5) in 2011; 436.4 (capture 436.0, aquaculture 0.4) in 2012.
Source: FAO.

Mining

('000 metric tons unless otherwise indicated)

	2009	2010	2011
Copper (metal content) . . .	5,394	5,419	5,263
Coal	636	619	654
Iron ore*	8,242	9,130	12,625
Calcium carbonate	6,012	6,518	6,270
Zinc—metal content (metric tons) .	27,801	27,662	36,602
Molybdenum—metal content (metric tons) . . .	34,925	37,186	40,889
Manganese (metric tons)† . . .	5,722	—	—
Gold (kg)	40,834	39,494	45,137
Silver (kg)	1,301	1,287	1,291
Crude petroleum	1,355	1,536	1,741

* Gross weight. The estimated iron content is 61%.
† Gross weight. The estimated metal content is 32%.

Source: US Geological Survey.

Industry

SELECTED PRODUCTS
('000 metric tons unless otherwise indicated)

	2008	2009	2010
Beer ('000 hl)	7,091	6,678	5,583
Wine*	868.3	1,000.1	1,307.5
Soft drinks ('000 hl)	19,744	19,314	20,402
Cigarettes (million)	19,498	17,359	n.a.
Non-rubber footwear ('000 pairs) .	2,821	2,503	2,400
Mattresses ('000)	2,031	1,896	1,694
Jet fuel	511	610	585
Motor spirit (petrol)	2,230	2,445	2,028
Kerosene	77	60	58
Distillate fuel oils	3,811	3,442	2,920
Residual fuel oils	1,906	1,802	1,401
Cement	4,620	2,579	3,417
Tyres ('000)	5,036	n.a.	n.a.
Blister copper	2,134	2,131	n.a.
Refined copper, unwrought . .	98	2,407	n.a.
Electric energy (million kWh) .	59,704	60,722	60,434

* Source: FAO.

Wine ('000 metric tons unless otherwise indicated): 1,518.3 in 2011; 1,086.5 in 2012 (Source: FAO).

Source (unless otherwise indicated): UN Industrial Commodity Statistics Database.

Finance

CURRENCY AND EXCHANGE RATES

Monetary Units
100 centavos = 1 Chilean peso.

Sterling, Dollar and Euro Equivalents (30 May 2014)
£1 sterling = 932.006 pesos;
US $1 = 554.040 pesos;
€1 = 754.104 pesos;
10,000 Chilean pesos = £10.73 = $18.05 = €13.26.

Average Exchange Rate (pesos per US $)
2011   483.668
2012   486.471
2013   495.273

GOVERNMENT FINANCE
(general government transactions, non-cash basis, million pesos)

Summary of Balances

	2010	2011	2012
Revenue	25,577,517	29,508,700	30,890,972
Less Expense	21,523,119	22,729,390	24,702,986
Net operating balance . . .	4,054,398	6,779,310	6,187,986
Less Net acquisition of non-financial assets	4,460,201	5,075,938	5,302,470
Net lending/borrowing . . .	−405,803	1,703,372	885,516

Revenue

	2010	2011	2012
Net tax revenue	19,042,371	22,770,751	24,614,798
Gross copper revenue . . .	3,042,010	2,765,411	1,963,870
Social security contributions .	1,493,987	1,623,817	1,802,468
Grants	81,691	156,050	126,288
Property income	481,798	558,816	622,777
Operating revenue	587,285	611,146	702,913
Other revenue	848,376	1,022,709	1,057,859
Total	25,577,517	29,508,700	30,890,972

Expense

Expense by economic type	2010	2011	2012
Compensation of employees . .	6,339,591	6,745,129	7,405,419
Use of goods and services . .	3,202,605	3,602,327	3,718,668
Interest	537,523	676,690	765,405
Subsidies and grants . . .	6,364,756	6,435,691	7,284,077
Social benefits	5,027,790	5,207,538	5,448,996
Other expense	50,853	62,016	80,421
Total	21,523,119	22,729,390	24,702,986

Source: Dirección de Presupuestos, Santiago.

INTERNATIONAL RESERVES
(US $ million at 31 December)

	2011	2012	2013
Gold (national valuation) . . .	12.2	13.1	9.6
IMF special drawing rights . .	1,214.1	1,211.4	1,146.9
Reserve position in IMF . . .	601.1	691.7	640.6
Foreign exchange	40,116.6	39,733.0	39,296.2
Total	41,944.0	41,649.1	41,093.3

Source: IMF, *International Financial Statistics*.

MONEY SUPPLY
('000 million pesos at 31 December)

	2011	2012	2013
Currency outside depository corporations	3,892.3	4,480.0	4,985.5
Transferable deposits . . .	17,536.5	19,954.8	22,086.1
Other deposits	34,704.2	39,738.9	46,226.3
Securities other than shares . .	35,337.8	36,719.4	39,443.0
Broad money	91,470.8	100,893.0	112,740.8

Source: IMF, *International Financial Statistics*.

COST OF LIVING
(Consumer Price Index; base: 2009 = 100)

	2011	2012	2013
Food (incl. non-alcoholic beverages)	109.0	117.4	122.6
Rent, fuel and light . . .	108.1	108.5	111.3
Clothing (incl. footwear) . . .	73.1	68.0	59.8
All items (incl. others) . . .	104.8	108.0	109.9

NATIONAL ACCOUNTS
('000 million pesos at current prices)

Expenditure on the Gross Domestic Product

	2011	2012	2013
Government final consumption expenditure	14,690.6	15,679.5	16,994.6
Private final consumption expenditure	74,091.7	81,327.3	87,872.1
Increase in stocks	1,652.6	1,429.4	423.2
Gross fixed capital formation	27,132.0	31,093.3	32,394.5
Total domestic expenditure	117,566.9	129,529.5	137,684.4
Exports of goods and services	46,162.8	44,374.9	44,672.5
Less Imports of goods and services	42,326.9	44,303.5	45,145.0
GDP in purchasers' values	121,402.8	129,600.8	137,212.1

Gross Domestic Product by Economic Activity

	2011	2012	2013
Agriculture and forestry	3,357.5	3,346.4	3,758.6
Fishing	631.4	669.0	556.1
Mining and quarrying	18,070.6	16,620.6	15,283.9
Copper	16,113.9	14,761.6	13,390.6
Manufacturing	13,295.3	13,545.9	14,400.9
Electricity, gas and water	3,375.4	3,350.9	3,886.5
Construction	8,370.4	9,533.1	10,712.9
Trade, restaurants and hotels	11,477.9	12,931.4	13,923.8
Transport	4,679.5	5,340.0	5,316.3
Communications	2,381.0	2,647.5	2,774.3
Financial services*	21,524.5	24,155.5	26,198.9
Sale of real estate	5,946.6	6,666.0	7,029.9
Personal services†	13,109.8	14,122.1	15,446.5
Public administration	5,184.1	5,619.2	6,203.8
Sub-total	111,404.0	118,547.6	125,492.4
Value-added tax	9,347.6	10,360.6	11,041.6
Import duties	651.2	692.7	677.9
GDP in purchasers' values	121,402.8	129,600.8	137,212.1

* Including insurance, renting of property and business loans.
† Including education.

BALANCE OF PAYMENTS
(US $ million)

	2011	2012	2013
Exports of goods	81,437.8	77,965.4	76,684.3
Imports of goods	−70,398.2	−75,457.7	−74,567.8
Balance on goods	11,039.6	2,507.6	2,116.5
Exports of services	13,105.3	12,455.6	12,786.7
Imports of services	−16,158.3	−14,731.9	−15,694.5
Balance on goods and services	7,986.6	231.3	−791.3
Primary income received	7,007.1	7,141.2	7,809.3
Primary income paid	−20,928.4	−18,646.2	−18,912.3
Balance on goods, services and primary income	−5,934.8	−11,273.7	−11,894.3
Secondary income received	4,350.6	3,890.2	4,224.9
Secondary income paid	−1,485.7	−1,699.2	−1,816.5
Current balance	−3,069.9	−9,082.7	−9,485.9
Capital account (net)	11.9	11.7	11.4
Direct investment assets	−20,251.9	−22,330.2	−10,922.9
Direct investment liabilities	23,443.9	28,541.7	20,258.2
Portfolio investment assets	798.4	−13,130.6	−10,699.0
Portfolio investment liabilities	10,685.3	10,911.9	15,740.6
Financial derivatives and employee stock options assets	12,270.2	9,674.4	7,279.4
Financial derivatives and employee stock options liabilities	−14,688.4	−9,663.9	−8,057.7
Other investment assets	662.0	2,514.6	992.3
Other investment liabilities	4,908.6	2,521.9	−3,311.2
Net errors and omissions	−578.3	−334.7	−1,493.2
Reserves and related items	14,191.8	−365.9	312.0

Source: IMF, *International Financial Statistics*.

External Trade

PRINCIPAL COMMODITIES
(distribution by SITC, US $ million)

Imports c.i.f.	2011	2012	2013
Food and live animals	4,796	5,175	5,250
Mineral fuels, lubricants, etc.	15,933	17,990	16,963
Petroleum, petroleum products, etc.	12,386	14,589	13,961
Gas, natural and manufactured	2,388	2,250	1,901
Chemicals and related products	7,315	8,055	8,183
Basic manufactures	7,170	8,894	8,773
Machinery and transport equipment	22,542	29,110	29,737
Machinery specialized for particular industries	3,385	3,972	3,540
General industrial machinery equipment and parts	3,188	3,666	3,970
Telecommunications and sound equipment	2,697	3,441	3,692
Other electrical machinery apparatus, etc.	2,080	2,687	1,912
Road vehicles and parts*	7,717	9,251	9,759
Miscellaneous manufactured articles	6,042	7,939	8,450
Footwear	2,005	2,706	2,871
Total (incl. others)	74,199	79,468	79,621

* Data on parts exclude tyres, engines and electrical parts.

Exports f.o.b.	2011	2012	2013
Food and live animals	12,088	12,300	13,643
Fish, crustaceans and molluscs and preparations thereof	3,932	3,788	4,446
Vegetables and fruit	5,612	5,803	6,438
Crude materials (inedible) except fuels	23,002	24,454	25,784
Pulp and waste paper	2,899	2,534	2,805
Metalliferous ores and metal scrap	17,930	19,684	20,617
Chemicals and related products	3,516	3,852	3,502
Basic manufactures	33,666	29,735	26,380
Non-ferrous metals	30,461	26,580	23,334
Machinery and transport equipment	1,342	2,316	2,458
Total (incl. others)	80,586	78,277	77,368

PRINCIPAL TRADING PARTNERS
(US $ million)

Imports c.i.f.	2011	2012	2013
Argentina	4,728	5,283	3,934
Brazil	6,196	5,186	5,111
Canada	876	1,032	1,544
China, People's Republic	10,686	14,432	15,702
Colombia	2,186	2,185	1,721
Ecuador	1,297	2,155	2,515
France	1,045	1,555	2,428
Germany	2,682	2,862	3,202
Italy	1,138	1,264	1,281
Japan	2,408	2,596	2,495
Korea, Republic	2,564	2,604	2,771
Mexico	2,438	2,608	2,543
Peru	2,018	2,072	1,758
Spain	1,050	1,394	1,757
Trinidad and Tobago	656	1,450	1,050
United Kingdom	1,352	892	1,468
USA	13,948	18,188	16,088
Total (incl. others)	74,199	79,468	79,621

Exports f.o.b.	2011	2012	2013
Argentina	1,175	1,070	1,046
Australia	878	1,250	801
Belgium	1,364	1,249	1,385
Bolivia	370	1,550	1,705
Brazil	4,382	4,294	4,434
Canada	1,468	1,283	1,418
China, People's Republic	17,923	18,218	19,219
Colombia	939	914	869
France	1,418	1,222	1,109
Germany	1,182	941	1,013
India	1,873	2,586	2,304
Italy	2,731	2,013	1,658
Japan	8,826	8,384	7,661
Korea, Republic	4,330	4,551	4,272
Mexico	1,922	1,346	1,321
Netherlands	3,788	2,739	2,542
Peru	1,492	1,813	1,963
Spain	1,579	1,616	1,379
Switzerland	767	1,077	1,041
Taiwan	2,110	1,818	1,646
United Kingdom	727	715	706
USA	9,012	9,580	9,756
Total (incl. others)	80,586	78,277	77,368

Transport

PRINCIPAL RAILWAYS

	2011	2012	2013
Passenger journeys ('000)	26,859	29,463	28,624
Passenger-km ('000)	851,582	933,999	861,780
Freight ('000 metric tons)	27,374	27,537	26,036
Freight ton-km (million)	4,123	4,090	3,981

ROAD TRAFFIC
(motor vehicles in use)

	2010	2011	2012
Passenger cars and jeeps (excl. taxis)	2,070,060	2,262,436	2,479,813
Minibuses and vans	164,195	174,203	188,941
Light trucks	608,507	653,691	703,616
Motorcycles and mopeds	102,314	112,806	133,640

SHIPPING
Flag Registered Fleet
(at 31 December)

	2011	2012	2013
Number of vessels	596	601	614
Total displacement ('000 grt)	881	800	908

Source: Lloyd's List Intelligence (www.lloydslistintelligence.com).

International Seaborne Shipping
(freight traffic, '000 metric tons)

	2008	2009	2010
Goods loaded	46,386	48,002	48,770
Goods unloaded	40,904	35,101	41,610

CIVIL AVIATION
(traffic on scheduled services)

	2010	2011	2012
Kilometres flown (million)	153.6	173.2	188.2
Passengers carried ('000)	11,064.5	12,989.3	15,234.0
Passenger-km (million)	25,096.5	28,320.5	31,412.0
Freight carried ('000 metric tons)	295.8	298.5	318.2
Freight ton-km (million)	5,306.2	6,367.0	6,647.7

Tourism

ARRIVALS BY NATIONALITY

	2011	2012	2013
Argentina	1,118,767	1,377,645	1,360,654
Bolivia	321,488	355,758	383,545
Brazil	324,594	373,840	360,900
France	60,993	60,220	60,832
Germany	58,202	62,891	63,595
Peru	338,916	338,026	328,082
Spain	55,643	62,646	70,963
USA	52,446	158,493	154,012
Total (incl. others)	3,137,285	3,554,279	3,569,744

Source: Servicio Nacional de Turismo.

Tourism receipts (US $ million, excl. passenger transport): 1,889 in 2011; 2,150 in 2012; 2,219 in 2013 (provisional) (Source: World Tourism Organization).

Communications Media

	2011	2012	2013
Telephones ('000 main lines in use)	3,366.3	3,280.5	3,203.3
Mobile cellular telephones ('000 subscribers)	22,315.2	23,941.0	23,659.4
Internet subscribers ('000)	2,025.1	n.a.	n.a.
Broadband subscribers ('000)	1,998.1	2,154.2	2,158.6

Source: International Telecommunication Union.

Education

(2012 unless otherwise indicated)

	Institutions	Teachers	Students
Pre-primary		16,528†	348,495
Special primary		7,673†	159,078
Primary	n.a.*	75,854†	1,976,176
Secondary		49,144†	1,044,233
Adult		1,897‡	131,237†
Higher (incl. universities)	226‡	n.a.	1,127,181

* Many schools offer more than one level of education; a detailed breakdown is given below.
† 2004 figure.
‡ 2003 figure.

Schools (2004): Pre-primary: 640; Special 766; Primary 3,679; Secondary 517; Adult 292; Pre-primary and special 10; Pre-primary and primary 3,172; Pre-primary and secondary 1; Special and primary 22; Special and adult 3; Primary and secondary 380; Primary and adult 82; Secondary and adult 156; Pre-primary, special and primary 52; Pre-primary, primary and secondary 1,070; Pre-primary, primary and adult 261; Special, primary and secondary 2; Primary, secondary and adult 49; Pre-primary, special, primary and secondary 13; Pre-primary, special, primary and adult 7; Pre-primary, primary, secondary and adult 106; Pre-primary, special, primary, secondary and adult 5.

2010/11: *Teachers:* Pre-primary 57,404; Primary 69,191; Secondary 70,903; Tertiary 70,248 (Source: UNESCO Institute for Statistics).

2011/12: *Students:* Pre-primary 555,046; Primary 1,503,898; Secondary 1,443,554; Tertiary 1,118,773 (Source: UNESCO Institute for Statistics).

Pupil-teacher ratio (primary education, UNESCO estimate): 21.2 in 2011/12 (Source: UNESCO Institute for Statistics).

Adult literacy rate (UNESCO estimates): 98.6% (males 98.6%; females 98.5%) in 2009 (Source: UNESCO Institute for Statistics).

Directory

The Constitution

The 1981 Constitution, described as a 'transition to democracy', separated the presidency from the Junta and provided for presidential elections and for the re-establishment of the bicameral legislature, consisting of Senado (Senate) of both elected and appointed senators, who are to serve an eight-year term, and a Cámara de Diputados (Chamber of Deputies) of 120 deputies elected for a four-year term. There is a National Security Council consisting of the President of the Republic, the heads of the Armed Forces and the police, and the Presidents of the Supreme Court and the Senate.

In July 1989 a national referendum approved 54 reforms to the Constitution, including 47 proposed by the Government and seven by the Military Junta. Among provisions made within the articles were an increase in the number of directly elected senators from 26 to 38, the abolition of the need for the approval of two successive Congresses for constitutional amendments (the support of two-thirds of the Chamber of Deputies and the Senate being sufficient), the reduction in term of office for the President to be elected in 1989 from eight to four years, with no immediate re-election possible, and the redrafting of the provision that outlawed Marxist groups so as to ensure 'true and responsible political pluralism'. The President's right to dismiss the Congress and sentence its members to internal exile was eliminated.

In November 1991 the Congress approved constitutional changes to local government. The amendments provided for the replacement of centrally appointed local officials with directly elected representatives.

In February 1994 an amendment to the Constitution was approved whereby the length of the presidential term was reduced from eight to six years.

In September 2005 constitutional reforms came into force reducing the presidential term from six to four years, abolishing the positions of senators-for-life and appointed senators and providing for a presidential prerogative to dismiss the Commanders-in-Chief of the Armed Forces.

The Government

HEAD OF STATE

President: MICHELLE BACHELET JERIA (took office 11 March 2014).

THE CABINET
(September 2014)

The Government was comprised of members of the Nueva Mayoría coalition and independents.

Minister of the Interior and Public Security: RODRIGO PEÑAILILLO (PPD).

Minister of Foreign Affairs: HERALDO MUÑOZ (PPD).

Minister of National Defence: JORGE BURGOS (PDC).

Minister of Finance: ALBERTO ARENAS (PS).

Minister, Secretary-General of the Presidency: XIMENA RINCÓN (PDC).

Minister, Secretary-General of the Government: ALVARO ELIZALDE (PS).

Minister of the Economy, Development and Tourism: LUIS FELIPE CÉSPEDES (PDC).

Minister of Social Development: FERNANDA VILLEGAS (PS).

Minister of Education: NICOLÁS EYZAGUIRRE (PPD).

Minister of Justice: JOSÉ ANTONIO GÓMEZ (PRSD).

Minister of Labour and Social Security: JAVIERA BLANCO (Ind.).

Minister of Public Works: ALBERTO UNDURRAGA (PDC).

Minister of Health: HELIA MOLINA (PPD).

Minister of Housing and Urban Development: PAULINA SABALL (PS).

Minister of Agriculture: CARLOS FURCHE (PS).

Minister of Mining: AURORA WILLIAMS (PRSD).

Minister of Transport and Telecommunications: ANDRÉS GÓMEZ-LOBO (PPD).

Minister of National Property: VÍCTOR OSORIO (IC).

Minister of Energy: MÁXIMO PACHECO MATTE (PS).

Minister of the Environment: PABLO BADENIER (PDC).

Minister of Sport: NATALIA RIFFO (MAS).

Minister of the National Women's Service (Sernam): CLAUDIA PASCUAL (PC).

Minister of the National Commission for Culture and the Arts: CLAUDIA BARATTINI (Ind.).

MINISTRIES

Ministry of Agriculture: Teatinos 40, 1°, Santiago; tel. (2) 2393-5000; fax (2) 2393-5135; internet www.minagri.gob.cl.

Ministry of the Economy, Development and Tourism: Avda Libertador Bernardo O'Higgins 1449, Santiago Downtown Torre II, CP 8340487, Santiago; tel. (2) 2473-3400; fax (2) 2473-3403; e-mail economia@economia.cl; internet www.economia.cl.

Ministry of Education: Alameda 1371, 7°, Santiago; tel. (2) 2406-6000; fax (2) 2380-0317; e-mail consultas@mineduc.cl; internet www.mineduc.cl.

Ministry of Energy: Edif. Santiago Downtown II, 13° y 14°, Alameda 1449, Santiago; tel. (2) 2365-6800; internet www.minenergia.cl.

Ministry of the Environment: Teatinos 254/258, Santiago; tel. (2) 2240-5600; fax (2) 2240-5758; internet www.mma.gob.cl.

Ministry of Finance: Teatinos 120, 12°, Santiago; tel. (2) 2828-2000; internet www.minhda.cl.

Ministry of Foreign Affairs: Teatinos 180, Santiago; tel. (2) 2827-4200; internet www.minrel.gov.cl.

Ministry of Health: Enrique MacIver 541, 3°, Santiago; tel. (2) 2574-0100; e-mail consulta@minsal.cl; internet www.minsal.cl.

Ministry of Housing and Urban Development: Alameda 924, CP 6513482, Santiago; tel. (2) 2351-3000; fax (2) 2633-7830; e-mail contactenos@minvu.cl; internet www.minvu.cl.

Ministry of the Interior and Public Security: Palacio de la Moneda, Santiago; tel. (2) 2690-4000; fax (2) 2699-2165; internet www.interior.cl.

Ministry of Justice: Morandé 107, Santiago; tel. (2) 2674-3100; fax (2) 2698-7098; internet www.minjusticia.cl.

Ministry of Labour and Social Security: Huérfanos 1273, 6°, Santiago; tel. (2) 2753-0400; fax (2) 2753-0401; e-mail mintrab@mintrab.gob.cl; internet www.mintrab.gob.cl.

Ministry of Mining: Teatinos 120, 9°, Santiago; tel. (2) 2473-3000; fax (2) 2687-9339; internet www.minmineria.cl.

Ministry of National Defence: Edif. Diego Portales, 22°, Villavicencio 364, Santiago; tel. (2) 2222-1202; fax (2) 2633-0568; e-mail correo@defensa.cl; internet www.defensa.cl.

Ministry of National Property: Avda Libertador Bernardo O'Higgins 720, Santiago; tel. (2) 2937-5100; fax (2) 2351-2160; e-mail consultas@mbienes.cl; internet www.bienesnacionales.cl.

Ministry of Public Works: Morandé 59, Of. 545, 2°, Santiago; tel. (2) 2449-4000; fax (2) 2441-0914; e-mail dv.secretariatecnica@mop.gov.cl; internet www.vialidad.cl.

Ministry of Social Development: Ahumada 48, 7°, Santiago; tel. (2) 2675-1400; fax (2) 2672-1879; internet www.ministeriodesarrollosocial.gob.cl.

Ministry of Sport: Fidel Oteíza 1956, 3°, Providencia, Santiago; tel. (2) 754-0200; fax (2) 368-9685; internet www.ind.cl.

Ministry of Transport and Telecommunications: Amunátegui 139, 3°, Santiago; tel. (2) 2421-3000; fax (2) 2421-3552; internet www.mtt.cl.

National Commission for Culture and the Arts: Paseo Ahumada 11, 9°-11°, Santiago; tel. (2) 2618-9000; e-mail oirs@cultura.gob.cl; internet www.consejodelacultura.cl.

National Women's Service (Sernam): Huérfanos 1219, Santiago Centro, Santiago; tel. (2) 2549-6100; fax (2) 2549-6247; e-mail sernam@sernam.gov.cl; internet www.sernam.gov.cl.

Office of the Minister, Secretary-General of the Government: Palacio de la Moneda, Santiago; tel. (2) 2690-4000; fax (2) 2697-1756; e-mail cmladini@segegob.cl; internet www.segegob.cl.

Office of the Minister, Secretary-General of the Presidency: Moneda 1160, Entrepiso, Santiago; tel. (2) 2690-4000; fax (2) 2694-5888; e-mail contactenos@minsegpres.gob.cl; internet www.minsegpres.gob.cl.

President and Legislature

PRESIDENT

Election, First Round, 17 November 2013

Candidate	Valid votes	% of valid votes
Michelle Bachelet Jeria (Nueva Mayoría)*	3,075,839	46.70
Evelyn Matthei Fornet (Alianza)† . .	1,648,481	25.03
Marco Enríquez-Ominami Gumucio (PRO)	723,542	10.99
Franco Aldo Parisi Fernández (Ind.) .	666,015	10.11
Marcel Claude Reyes (Partido Humanista)	185,072	2.81
Alfredo Sfeir Younis (PEV) . . .	154,648	2.35
Roxana Miranda Meneses (Partido Igualdad)	81,873	1.24
Others	50,338	0.76
Total valid votes‡	**6,585,808**	**100.00**

* Comprising the Concertación de Partidos por la Democracia coalition, the Partido Comunista de Chile, the Izquierda Ciudadana and the Movimiento Amplio Social.
† Comprising the Renovación Nacional and the Unión Demócrata Independiente.
‡ In addition, there were 46,268 blank and 66,935 spoiled votes.

Election, Second Round, 15 December 2013

Candidate	Valid votes	% of valid votes
Michelle Bachelet Jeria (Nueva Mayoría)*	3,470,379	62.17
Evelyn Matthei Fornet (Alianza)† . .	2,111, 891	37.83
Total valid votes‡	**5,582,270**	**100.00**

* Comprising the Concertación de Partidos por la Democracia coalition, the Partido Comunista de Chile, the Izquierda Ciudadana and the Movimiento Amplio Social.
† Comprising the Renovación Nacional and the Unión Demócrata Independiente.
‡ In addition, there were 32,565 blank and 82,916 spoiled votes.

NATIONAL CONGRESS
(Congreso Nacional)

Senate

President: ISABEL ALLENDE BUSSI.

The Senate has 38 members, who hold office for an eight-year term, with approximately one-half of the seats renewable every four years. The last election, to renew 20 of the 38 seats, was held on 17 November 2013. The table below shows the composition of the Senate following that election.

Distribution of Seats by Legislative Bloc, November 2013

	Seats
Nueva Mayoría	21
Partido Socialista	7
Partido por la Democracia	6
Partido Demócrata Cristiano	6
Independents	2
Alianza	16
Unión Demócrata Independiente . . .	8
Renovación Nacional	8
Independent	1
Total	**38**

Chamber of Deputies

President: ALDO CORNEJO GONZÁLEZ (PDC).

General Election, 17 November 2013

Legislative bloc	% of valid votes	Seats
Nueva Mayoría	47.73	67
Partido Demócrata Cristiano . .	—	21
Partido Socialista de Chile . . .	—	15
Partido por la Democracia . . .	—	15
Partido Radical Socialdemócrata . .	—	6
Partido Comunista de Chile . .	—	6
Independents	—	4
Alianza	36.17	49
Unión Demócrata Independiente .	—	29
Renovación Nacional	—	19
Independent	—	1
Si Tú Quieres, Chile Cambia* . . .	5.45	1
Independents	3.31	3
Partido Humanista	3.36	—
Nueva Constitución para Chile† . .	2.78	—
Partido Regionalista de los Independientes	1.16	—
Total valid votes	**100.00**	**120**

* Electoral alliance comprising the Partido Liberal de Chile, the Partido Progresista and Independents.
† Electoral alliance comprising the Partido Igualdad, the Partido Ecologista Verde and Independents.

Election Commissions

Servicio Electoral: Esmeralda 611/615, Santiago; tel. (2) 2731-5500; fax (2) 2639-7296; e-mail direnac@servel.cl; internet www.servel.cl; f. 1986; Dir ELIZABETH CABRERA.

Tribunal Calificador de Elecciones (TCE): Calle Compañía de Jesús 1288, Santiago; tel. (2) 2733-9300; fax (2) 2699-4464; e-mail tce@tribunalcalificador.cl; internet www.tribunalcalificador.cl; f. 1980; Pres. PATRICIO VALDÉS ALDUNATE.

Political Organizations

Alianza: f. 1999 as the Alianza por Chile, known as the Coalición por el Cambio in 2009–12, adopted present name to contest the 2013 elections; right-wing alliance; comprises the following parties:

Renovación Nacional (RN): Antonio Varas 454, Providencia, Santiago; tel. (2) 2799-4200; fax (2) 2799-4212; e-mail clarrain@rn.cl; internet www.rn.cl; f. 1988; right-wing; Pres. CRISTIÁN MONCKEBERG; Sec.-Gen. MARIO DESBORDES.

Unión Demócrata Independiente (UDI): Avda Suecia 286, Providencia, Santiago; tel. (2) 2241-4200; fax (2) 2233-6189; e-mail contacto@udi.cl; internet www.udi.cl; f. 1989; right-wing; Pres. ERNESTO SILVA MÉNDEZ; Sec.-Gen. JAVIER MACAYA DANÚS.

Concertación de Partidos por la Democracia (CPD): Londres 57, Santiago; tel. and fax (2) 2639-7170; f. 1988 as the Comando por el No, an opposition front to campaign against the military regime in the plebiscite of 5 Oct. 1988; adopted present name following plebiscite; contested the 2013 elections as the Nueva Mayoría coalition with the Partido Comunista de Chile (q.v.); Nat. Co-ordinator DOMINGO NAMUNCURA.

Partido Demócrata Cristiano (PDC): Alameda 1460, 2°, Santiago; tel. and fax (2) 2376-0136; e-mail info@pdc.cl; internet www.pdc.cl; f. 1957; Pres. IGNACIO WALKER PRIETO; Sec. VÍCTOR MALDONADO ROLDÁN.

Partido por la Democracia (PPD): Santo Domingo 1828, Santiago; tel. and fax (2) 2671-2320; e-mail presidencia@ppd.cl; internet www.ppd.cl; f. 1987; Pres. JAIME DANIEL QUINTANA LEAL; Sec.-Gen. LUIS GONZALO NAVARRETE MUÑOZ.

Partido Radical Socialdemócrata (PRSD): Londres 57, Santiago; tel. and fax (2) 2633-6928; fax (2) 2638-3353; e-mail ernestov@123mail.cl; internet www.partidoradical.cl; centre-left; Pres. JOSÉ ANTONIO GÓMEZ URRUTIA; Sec.-Gen. ERNESTO VELASCO RODRÍGUEZ.

Partido Socialista de Chile (PS): París 873, Santiago; tel. (2) 2549-9900; e-mail pschile@pschile.cl; internet www.pschile.cl; f. 1933; left-wing; mem. of Socialist International; Pres. OSVALDO ANDRADE LARA; Sec.-Gen. ALVARO ELIZALDE SOTO.

Izquierda Ciudadana (IC): Santiago; internet www.izquierdaciudadanadechile.cl; f. 1971 as Izquierda Cristiana de Chile, present name adopted 2013; mem. of the Nueva Mayoría coalition; Pres. CRISTIAN MÉNDEZ; Sec.-Gen. BERNARDA PÉREZ.

Movimiento Amplio Social (MAS): Calle Padre Alonso de Ovalle 726, Santiago; f. 2008; mem. of the Nueva Mayoría coalition; Pres. ALEJANDRO NAVARRO BRAIN; Sec.-Gen. FERNANDO ZAMORANO FERNÁNDEZ.

Partido Comunista de Chile (PC): Avda Vicuña Mackenna 31, Santiago; tel. and fax (2) 2222-2750; e-mail www@pcchile.cl; internet www.pcchile.cl; f. 1912; achieved legal status in 1990; contested the 2013 elections as mem. of the Nueva Mayoría coalition with the Concertación de Partidos por la Democracia (q.v.); Pres. GUILLERMO TEILLIER; Sec.-Gen. LAUTARO CARMONA.

Partido Ecologista Verde (PEV): O'Higgins 1104, Concepción; e-mail admin@partidoecologista.cl; internet partidoecologista.cl; f. 2002 as Partido Ecologista; Pres. FÉLIX GONZÁLEZ GATICA.

Partido Humanista (PH): Condell 860, Providencia, Santiago; tel. (2) 2634-7562; e-mail danilo.monteverde.reyes@gmail.com; internet www.partidohumanista.cl; f. 1984; Pres. OCTAVIO GONZÁLEZ; Sec.-Gen. EFRÉN OSORIO.

Partido Igualdad: Pasaje Huérfanos 1460, Of. 3B4, Santiago; tel. (2) 5792-3426; e-mail contacto@roxanamiranda.cl; internet partidoigualdad.cl; f. 2009; left-wing; Leader ROXANA MIRANDA MENESES.

Partido Liberal de Chile: Of. 613, Paseo Huérfanos 886, Santiago; tel. (2) 2638-0551; e-mail contacto@losliberales.cl; internet www .losliberales.cl; f. 2007 as Chile Primero by fmr mems of the Partido por la Democracia (q.v.), reconstituted in 2012; contested the 2013 legislative elections in alliance with the Partido Progresista; Pres. VLADO MIROSEVIC; Sec.-Gen. IVÁN MORÁN.

Partido Progresista (PRO): Salvador 1029, Providencia; tel. (2) 2204-5274; e-mail cwarner@losprogresistas.cl; internet losprogresistas.cl; f. 2010; Pres. PATRICIA MORALES ERRÁZURIZ; Sec.-Gen. CAMILO LAGOS.

Partido Regionalista de los Independientes (PRI): Avda Miraflores 133, Of. 33, Santiago; tel. (2) 2664-8772; fax (2) 2664-8773; e-mail pri@pricentro.cl; internet www.pricentro.cl; f. 2006 following merger of Alianza National de Independientes and Partido de Acción Regionalista de Chile; Pres. HUMBERTO DE LA MAZA MAILLET; Sec.-Gen. EDUARDO SALAS CERDA.

Wallmapuwen (Partido Nacionalista Mapuche): e-mail wallmapuwen@gmail.com; internet www.wallmapuwen.cl; f. 2005; campaigns for Mapuche rights; not officially registered; Pres. GUSTAVO QUILAQUEO BUSTOS; Sec.-Gen. CLAUDIO CARIHUENTRU MILLALEO.

Diplomatic Representation

EMBASSIES IN CHILE

Algeria: Monseñor Nuncio Sotero Sanz 221, Providencia, Santiago; tel. (2) 2820-2100; fax (2) 2820-2121; e-mail embajadargelia.cl@gmail .com; Ambassador NOURREDINE YAZID.

Argentina: Miraflores 285, Santiago; tel. (2) 2582-2500; fax (2) 2639-3321; e-mail ehile@cancilleria.gov.ar; internet ehile.cancilleria.gov .ar; Ambassador GINÉS GONZÁLEZ GARCÍA.

Australia: Isidora Goyenechea 3621, El Golf Torre B, 12° y 13°, Casilla 33, Correo 10 Las Condes, Santiago; tel. (2) 2550-3500; fax (2) 2331-5960; e-mail dima-santiago@dfat.gov.au; internet www.chile .embassy.gov.au; Ambassador TIMOTHY KANE.

Austria: Barros Errazuriz 1968, 3°, Santiago; tel. (2) 2223-4774; fax (2) 2204-9382; e-mail santiago-de-chile-ob@bmaa.gv.at; internet www.chile-embajadadeaustria.at; Ambassador DOROTHEA AUER.

Belgium: Edif. Forum, Avda Providencia 2653, 11°, Of. 1103, Santiago; tel. (2) 2232-1070; fax (2) 2232-1073; e-mail santiago@ diplobel.org; internet www.diplomatie.be/santiago; Ambassador BEATRIX VAN HEMELDONCK.

Brazil: Padre Alonso Ovalle 1665, Casilla 1497, Santiago; tel. (2) 2698-2486; fax (2) 2671-5961; e-mail embrasil@brasembsantiago.cl; internet www.brasembsantiago.cl; Ambassador GEORGES LAMAZIERE.

Canada: Edif. World Trade Center, Torre Norte, 12°, Nueva Tajamar 481, Santiago; tel. (2) 2652-3800; fax (2) 2652-3912; e-mail stago@international.gc.ca; internet www.canadainternational.gc .ca/chile-chili; Ambassador PATRICIA FULLER.

China, People's Republic: Pedro de Valdivia 550, Santiago; tel. (2) 2233-9880; fax (2) 2335-2755; e-mail embajadachina@entelchile.net; internet cl.china-embassy.org; Ambassador YANG WANMING.

Colombia: Los Militares 5885, 3°, Las Condes, Santiago; tel. (2) 2220-6273; fax (2) 2224-3585; e-mail echile@cancilleria.gov.co; internet chile.embajada.gov.co; Ambassador MAURICIO ECHEVERRY GUTIÉRREZ.

Costa Rica: Zurich 255, Of. 85, Las Condes, Santiago; tel. (2) 2334-9486; fax (2) 2334-9490; e-mail embacostarica@adsl.tie.cl; Ambassador JAN RUGE MOYA.

Croatia: Ezequias Alliende 2370, Providencia, Santiago; tel. (2) 2269-6141; fax (2) 2269-6092; e-mail croemb.santiago@mvep.hr; Ambassador NIVES MALENICA.

Cuba: Avda Los Leones 1346, Providencia, Santiago; tel. (2) 2596-8553; fax (2) 2596-8584; e-mail emcuchil@embacuba.cl; internet www.embacuba.cl; Ambassador ADOLFO CURBELO CASTELLANOS.

Czech Republic: Avda El Golf 254, Santiago; tel. (2) 2232-1066; fax (2) 2232-0707; e-mail santiago@embassy.mzv.cz; internet www.mfa .cz/santiago; Ambassador ZDENÉK KUBÁNEK.

Denmark: Jacques Cazotte 5531, Casilla 18, Centro Cívico, Vitacura, Santiago; tel. (2) 2941-5100; fax (2) 2218-1736; e-mail sclamb@ um.dk; internet chile.um.dk; Ambassador JESPER FERSLØV.

Dominican Republic: Candelaria Goyenechea 4153, Vitacura, Santiago; tel. (2) 2953-5750; fax (2) 2953-5758; e-mail embrepdom@erd.co.cl; Ambassador PABLO ARTURO MARIÑEZ ALVAREZ.

Ecuador: Avda Providencia 1979 y Pedro Valdivia, 5°, Casilla 16007, Correo 9, Santiago; tel. (2) 2231-5073; fax (2) 2232-5833; e-mail embajadaecuador@adsl.tie.cl; internet www .embajadaecuador.cl; Ambassador HOMERO ARELLANO.

Egypt: Roberto del Río 1871, Providencia, Santiago; tel. (2) 2274-8881; fax (2) 2274-6334; e-mail embassy.santiago@mfa.gov.eg; Ambassador OSAMA MOHAMED AHMED ELSAYED.

El Salvador: Coronel 2330, 5°, Of. 51, Casilla 16863, Correo 9, Santiago; tel. (2) 2233-8324; fax (2) 2231-0960; e-mail embasalva@ adsl.tie.cl; internet www.rree.gob.sv/embajadas/chile.nsf; Ambassador AIDA ELENA MINERO REYES.

Finland: Alcántara 200, Of. 201, Las Condes, Casilla 16657, Correo 9, Santiago; tel. (2) 2263-4917; fax (2) 2263-4701; e-mail sanomat .snt@formin.fi; internet www.finland.cl; Ambassador ILKKA HEISKANEN.

France: Avda Condell 65, Casilla 38D, Providencia, Santiago; tel. (2) 2470-8000; fax (2) 2470-8050; e-mail ambassade@ambafrance-cl.org; internet www.france.cl; Ambassador MARC GIACOMINI.

Germany: Las Hualtatas 5677, Vitacura, Santiago; tel. (2) 2463-2500; fax (2) 2463-2525; e-mail info@santiago-de-chile.diplo.de; internet www.santiago.diplo.de; Ambassador HANS-HENNING BLOMEYER-BARTENSTEIN.

Greece: Jorge Sexto 306, Las Condes, Santiago; tel. (2) 2212-7900; fax (2) 2212-8048; e-mail secretaria@mfa.gr; internet www.mfa.gr/ santiago; Ambassador AGLAIA BALTA.

Guatemala: Zurich 255, Of. 55, Las Condes, Santiago; tel. (2) 2326-8133; fax (2) 2326-8142; e-mail embajada@guatemala.cl; internet www.guatemala.cl; Ambassador GUISELA ATALIDA GODINEZ SAZO.

Haiti: Zurich 255, Of. 21, Las Condes, Santiago; tel. (2) 2231-3364; fax (2) 2231-0967; e-mail embajada@embajadahaiti.cl; Ambassador JEAN-VICTOR HARVEL JEAN-BAPTISTE.

Holy See: Nuncio Sótero Sanz 200, Casilla 16836, Correo 9, Santiago (Apostolic Nunciature); tel. (2) 2231-2020; fax (2) 2231-0868; e-mail nunciatura@iglesia.cl; Apostolic Nuncio Most Rev. IVO SCAPOLO (Titular Archbishop of Thagaste).

Honduras: Zurich 255, Of. 51, Las Condes, Santiago; tel. (2) 2234-4069; fax (2) 2334-7946; e-mail secretaria@embajadadehonduras.cl; Ambassador MARÍA DEL CARMEN NASSER DE RAMOS.

Hungary: Avda Los Leones 2279, Providencia, Santiago; tel. (2) 2274-2210; fax (2) 2234-1227; e-mail huembstg@entelchile.net; Ambassador PÁL VARGA KORITÁR.

India: Alcantara 971, Casilla 10433, Las Condes, Santiago; tel. (2) 2228-4141; fax (2) 2321-7217; e-mail info@embajadaindia.cl; internet www.embajadaindia.cl; Ambassador DEBRAJ PRADHAN.

Indonesia: Avda Nueva Costanera 3318, Vitacura, Santiago; tel. (2) 2207-6266; fax (2) 2207-9901; e-mail kbristgo@mi.cl; Ambassador ALOYSIUS LELE MADHAAS.

Iran: Estoril 755, Las Condes, Santiago; tel. (2) 2723-3623; fax (2) 2723-3632; e-mail embiranchile@mail.com; internet www .embiranchile.com; Ambassador HOUSHANG KARIMI ABHARI.

Iraq: Enrique Fosters Sur 369, Santiago; tel. (2) 2984-5147; fax (2) 2982-5189; e-mail sanemb@iraqmfamail.com; internet www .mofamission.gov.iq/chl/ab/articles.aspx; Chargé d'affaires a.i. AMER ABDUL HUSSEIN ABBAS AL-FATLAWI.

Israel: San Sebastián 2812, 5°, Las Condes, Santiago; tel. (2) 2750-0500; fax (2) 2750-0555; e-mail amb.sec@santiago.mfa.gov.il; internet santiago.mfa.gov.il; Ambassador DAVID DADONN.

Italy: Clemente Fabres 1050, Providencia, Santiago; tel. (2) 2470-8400; fax (2) 2223-2467; e-mail info.santiago@esteri.it; internet www .ambsantiago.esteri.it; Ambassador MARCO RICCI.

Japan: Avda Ricardo Lyon 520, Santiago; tel. (2) 2232-1807; fax (2) 2232-1812; e-mail contactoembajadajapon@sg.mofa.go.jp; internet www.cl.emb-japan.go.jp; Ambassador HIDENORI MURAKAMI.

Jordan: Of. 1307, Calle Pio X 2460, Providencia, Santiago; tel. (2) 2975-6187; fax (2) 2975-6178; e-mail embajadadejordania@manquehue.net; Ambassador SUHEIL HADDAD.

Korea, Republic: Alcántara 74, Casilla 1301, Santiago; tel. (2) 2228-4214; fax (2) 2206-2355; e-mail coremb@tie.cl; internet chl.mofat.go.kr; Ambassador HWANG EUI-SEUNG.

Kuwait: San José de la Sierra 479, Las Condes, Santiago; tel. (2) 2883-9800; e-mail embajadadekuwaitchile@gmail.com; Ambassador REEM M. AL-KHALED.

Lebanon: Fray Montalva 292, Las Condes, Santiago; tel. (2) 2218-2835; fax (2) 2219-3502; e-mail info@embajadadellibano.cl; internet www.embajadadellibano.cl; Chargé d'affaires a.i. BRIGITTA AL-OJEIL.

Malaysia: Tajamar 183, 10°, Of. 1002, Correo 35, Las Condes, Santiago; tel. (2) 2233-6698; fax (2) 2234-3853; e-mail mwstg@embdemalasia.cl; internet www.kln.gov.my/perwakilan/santiago; Ambassador GANESON SIVAGURUNATHAN.

Mexico: Félix de Amesti 128, Las Condes, Santiago; tel. (2) 2583-8400; fax (2) 2583-8484; e-mail info@emexico.cl; internet www.emexico.cl; Ambassador OTTO RENÉ GRANADOS ROLDÁN.

Morocco: Avda Jorge VI 375, Las Condes, Santiago; tel. (2) 2212-1766; fax (2) 2212-1747; e-mail embamarruecos@yahoo.es; Ambassador ABDELKADER CHAUI LUDIE.

Netherlands: Apoquinado 3500, 13°, Las Condes, Santiago; tel. (2) 2756-9200; fax (2) 2756-9226; e-mail stg@minbuza.nl; internet chile.nlembajada.org; Ambassador MARION S. KAPPEYNE VAN DE COPPELLO.

New Zealand: Avda Isidora Goyenechea 3000, 12°, Las Condes, Santiago; tel. (2) 2616-3000; fax (2) 2951-6138; e-mail embajada@nzembassy.cl; internet www.nzembassy.cl; Ambassador JOHN CAPPER.

Nicaragua: Zurich 255, Of. 111, Las Condes, Santiago; tel. (2) 2234-1808; fax (2) 2234-5170; e-mail embanic@embajadadenicaragua.tie.cl; Ambassador MARÍA LUISA ROBLETO AGUILAR.

Norway: Los Militares 5001, 7°, Las Condes, Santiago; tel. (2) 2234-2888; fax (2) 2234-2201; e-mail emb.santiago@mfa.no; internet www.noruega.cl; Ambassador HEGE ARALDSEN.

Panama: Latadía 5930, Las Condes, Santiago; tel. (2) 2228-1687; e-mail embajadapanamachile@vtr.net; internet www.panamaenelexterior.gob.pa/chile; Ambassador MERCEDES ALFARO DE LÓPEZ.

Paraguay: Carmen Sylva 2437, Providencia, Santiago; tel. (2) 2963-6380; fax (2) 2963-6381; e-mail epychemb@entelchile.net; Ambassador TERUMI MATSUO DE CLAVEROL.

Peru: Avda Andrés Bello 1751, Casilla 16277, Providencia, Santiago; tel. (2) 2339-2600; fax (2) 2235-2053; e-mail embstgo@entelchile.net; Ambassador CARLOS PAREJA RÍOS.

Philippines: Félix de Amesti 367, Las Condes, Santiago; tel. (2) 2208-1313; fax (2) 2208-1400; e-mail embassyphil@vtr.net; Ambassador MARÍA CONSUELO PUYAT-REYES.

Poland: Mar del Plata 2055, Providencia, Santiago; tel. (2) 2204-1213; fax (2) 2204-9332; e-mail santiagodechile.embajada@msz.gov.pl; internet santiagodechile.msz.gov.pl; Ambassador ALEKSANDRA PIATKOWSKA.

Portugal: Nueva Tajamar 555, Torre Costanera 16°, Las Condes, Santiago; tel. (2) 2203-0542; fax (2) 2203-4004; e-mail embajada@embportugal.tie.cl; Ambassador LUIS JOÃO DE SOUSA LORVÃO.

Romania: Benjamín 2955, Las Condes, Santiago; tel. (2) 2231-1893; fax (2) 2232-2325; e-mail embajada@rumania.tie.cl; internet www.rumania.cl; Ambassador FLORIN ANGELO FLORIAN.

Russia: Avda Américo Vespucio 2127, Vitacura, Santiago; tel. (2) 2208-6254; fax (2) 2206-8892; e-mail embajada@rusia.tie.cl; internet www.chile.mid.ru; Ambassador MIKHAIL ORLOVETS.

South Africa: Avda 11 de Septiembre 2353, 17°, Torre San Ramón, Santiago; tel. (2) 2820-0300; fax (2) 2231-3185; e-mail info.chile@dirco.gov.za; internet www.embajada-sudafrica.cl; Ambassador HILTON FISHER.

Spain: Avda Andrés Bello 1895, Casilla 16456, Providencia, Santiago; tel. (2) 2235-2755; fax (2) 2235-1049; e-mail emb.santiagodechile@mae.es; internet www.mae.es/embajadas/santiagodechile; Ambassador CARLOS ROBLES FRAGA.

Sweden: Avda 11 de Septiembre 2353, 4°, Providencia, Santiago; tel. (2) 2940-1700; fax (2) 2940-1730; e-mail ambassaden.santiago-de-chile@foreign.ministry.se; internet www.embajadasuecia.cl; Ambassador EVA ZETTERBERG.

Switzerland: Avda Américo Vespucio Sur 100, 14°, Las Condes, Santiago; tel. (2) 2928-0100; fax (2) 2928-0135; e-mail san.vertretung@eda.admin.ch; internet www.eda.admin.ch/santiago; Ambassador YVONNEE BAUMANN.

Syria: Carmencita 111, Casilla 12, Correo 10, Santiago; tel. (2) 2232-7471; fax (2) 2231-1825; e-mail embajadasiria@tie.cl; Chargé d'affaires a.i. KALIL BITAR.

Thailand: Avda Américo Vespucio 100, 15°, Las Condes, Santiago; tel. (2) 2717-3959; fax (2) 2717-3758; e-mail rte.santiago@vtr.net; internet www.thaiembassychile.org; Ambassador SURAPON PETCH-VRA.

Turkey: Edif. Montolin, Of. 71, Monseñor Sotero Sanz 55, Providencia, Santiago; tel. (2) 2231-8952; fax (2) 2231-7762; e-mail embturquia@123.cl; Ambassador NACIYE GÖKÇEN KAYA.

United Arab Emirates: Avda Apoquindo 3039, 7°, Las Condes, Santiago; tel. (2) 2790-0000; fax (2) 2790-0033; e-mail archive.santiago@mofa.gov.ae; Ambassador ABDULLAH MOHAMMED AL MU'INA.

United Kingdom: Avda el Bosque Norte 0125, Santiago; tel. (2) 2370-4100; fax (2) 2370-4160; e-mail embsan@britemb.cl; internet ukinchile.fco.gov.uk; Ambassador FIONA CLOUDER.

USA: Avda Andrés Bello 2800, Las Condes, Santiago; tel. (2) 2232-2600; fax (2) 2330-3710; internet chile.usembassy.gov; Ambassador MICHAEL A. HAMMER.

Uruguay: Avda Pedro de Valdivia 711, Santiago; tel. (2) 2204-7988; fax (2) 2204-7772; e-mail urusgo@uruguay.cl; internet www.uruguay.cl; Ambassador RODOLFO CAMAROSANO BERSANI.

Venezuela: Bustos 2021, Providencia, Santiago; tel. (2) 2365-8700; fax (2) 2981-9087; e-mail embve.chile@mppre.gob.ve; internet chile.embajada.gob.ve; Ambassador ARÉVALO ENRIQUE MÉNDEZ ROMERO.

Viet Nam: Eliodoro Yañez 2897, Providencia, Santiago; tel. (2) 2244-3633; fax (2) 2244-3799; e-mail sqvnchile@yahoo.com; Ambassador HA THI NGOC HA.

Judicial System

There are Courts of Appeal throughout the country whose members are appointed from a list submitted to the President of the Republic by the Supreme Court. The number of members of each court varies. Judges and ministers of the Supreme Court do not continue in office beyond the age of 75 years.

Corte Suprema: Compañía 1140, 2°, Santiago; tel. (2) 2873-5000; fax (2) 2873-5276; e-mail mgonzalezp@poderjudicial.cl; internet www.poderjudicial.cl; 21 mems; Pres. SERGIO MUÑOZ GAJARDO.

Attorney-General: SABAS CHAHUÁN.

Religion

CHRISTIANITY

The Roman Catholic Church

According to the latest available census figures (2002), some 70% of the population aged 15 years and above are Roman Catholics. Chile comprises five archdioceses, 19 dioceses, two territorial prelatures and one apostolic vicariate.

Bishops' Conference: Conferencia Episcopal de Chile, Echaurren 4, 6°, Casilla 517-V, Correo 21, Santiago; tel. (2) 2671-7733; fax (2) 2698-1416; e-mail prensa@episcopado.cl; internet www.iglesia.cl; f. 1955 (statutes approved 2000); Pres. Cardinal RICARDO EZZATI ANDRELLO (Archbishop of Santiago).

Archbishop of Antofagasta: PABLO LIZAMA RIQUELME, San Martín 2628, Casilla E, Antofagasta; tel. and fax (55) 226-8856; e-mail antofagasta@episcopado.cl; internet www.iglesiadeantofagasta.cl.

Archbishop of Concepción: FERNANDO CHOMALI GARIB, Calle Barros Arana 544, Casilla 65-C, Concepción; tel. (41) 262-6100; fax (41) 223-2844; e-mail amoreno@episcopado.cl; internet www.arzobispadodeconcepcion.cl.

Archbishop of La Serena: RENE OSVALDO REBOLLEDO SALINAS, Los Carrera 450, Casilla 613, La Serena; tel. (51) 222-5658; fax (51) 222-5291; e-mail laserena@episcopado.cl; internet www.arzobispadodelaserena.cl.

Archbishop of Puerto Montt: CRISTIÁN CARO CORDERO, Calle Benavente 385, Casilla 17, Puerto Montt; tel. (65) 225-2215; fax (65) 227-1861; e-mail puertomontt@episcopado.cl; internet www.arzobispadodepuertomontt.cl.

Archbishop of Santiago de Chile: Cardinal RICARDO EZZATI ANDRELLO, Erasmo Escala 1872, Casilla 30-D, Santiago; tel. (2) 2787-5600; fax (2) 2787-5664; e-mail curiasantiago@arzobispado.tie.cl; internet www.iglesiadesantiago.cl.

The Anglican Communion

Anglicans in Chile come within the Diocese of Chile, which forms part of the Anglican Church of the Southern Cone of America, covering Argentina, Bolivia, Chile, Paraguay, Peru and Uruguay.

Bishop of Chile: Rt Rev. HECTOR F. ZAVALA, Corporación Anglicana de Chile, Victoria Subercaseaux 41, Of. 301, Casilla 50675, Correo Central, Santiago; tel. (2) 2638-3009; fax (2) 2639-4581; e-mail diocesis@iach.cl; internet www.iach.cl.

Other Christian Churches

According to the 2002 census, 15% of the population are Evangelical Christians, 1% are Jehovah's Witnesses and 1% are Mormons.

Church of Jesus Christ of Latter-Day Saints (Mormons): Pocuro 1940, Providencia 664-1404, Santiago; tel. (2) 340-5070; internet www.lds.org; 577,716 mems.

Iglesia Católica Apostólica Ortodoxa de la Santísima Virgen María (Orthodox Church of the Patriarch of Antioch): Avda Pedro de Valdivia 92, Providencia, Santiago; tel. (2) 2231-7284; fax (2) 2232-0860; e-mail iglesia@iglesiaortodoxa.cl; internet www .iglesiaortodoxa.cl; Archbishop Mgr SERGIO ABAD.

Iglesia Evangélica Luterana en Chile: Juan Enrique Concha 121, Nuñoa, Casilla 167–11, Santiago; tel. (2) 2223-3195; fax (2) 2205-2193; e-mail secretaria@ielch.cl; internet www.ielch.cl; f. 1937; Pres. Dr LUIS ALVAREZ FIGUEROA; 3,000 mems.

Iglesia Luterana en Chile: Avda Lota 2330, POB 16067, Correo 9, Santiago; tel. (2) 2231-7222; fax (2) 2231-3913; e-mail obispo@ iglesialuterana.cl; internet www.iglesialuterana.cl; Bishop SIEG-FRIED SANDER; 10,280 mems.

Iglesia Metodista de Chile: Sargento Aldea 1041, Casilla 67, Santiago; tel. (2) 2556-6074; fax (2) 2554-1763; e-mail imech .chile@metodista.cl; internet www.metodistachile.cl; autonomous since 1969; Bishop MARIO MARTÍNEZ TAPIA; 9,882 mems.

Iglesia Pentecostal de Chile: Manuel Rodríguez 1155, Curicó; tel. (75) 231-8640; e-mail iglesia@pentecostaldechile.cl; internet www .pentecostaldechile.cl; f. 1947; Pres. Rev. SERGIO VELOSO TOLOSA; Bishop Rev. LUIS ULISES MUÑOZ MORAGA; 125,000 mems.

Jehovah's Witnesses: Avda Concha y Toro 3456, Casilla 267, Puente Alto; tel. (2) 2428-2600; fax (2) 2428-2609; Dir PEDRO J. LOVATO GROSSO.

Unión de Iglesias Evangélicas Bautistas de Chile: Miguel Claro 755, Providencia, Santiago; tel. (2) 2264-1208; fax (2) 2431-8012; e-mail centrobautista@ubach.cl; internet www.ubach.cl; f. 1908; Pres. Pastor MAURICIO REYES.

JUDAISM

There is a small Jewish community in Chile, numbering 14,976 at the 2002 census (less than 1% of the population).

Círculo Israelita de Santiago: Comandante Malbec 13210, Lo Barnechea, Santiago; tel. (2) 2240-5000; fax (2) 2243-6244; e-mail socios@cis.cl; internet www.cis.cl; f. 1982; Rabbi EDUARDO WAINGOR-TIN.

Comunidad Israelita Sefardi de Chile: Avda Las Condes 8361, Providencia, Santiago; tel. (2) 2202-0330; fax (2) 2204-7382; e-mail contacto@sefaradies.cl; internet www.sefaradies.cl; Rabbi ANGEL KREIMAN.

ISLAM

There is a small Muslim community in Chile, numbering 2,894 at the 2002 census (less than 1% of the population).

Centro Islámico de Chile: Mezquita As-Salam, Campoamor 2975, esq. Chile-España, Nuñoa, Santiago; tel. (2) 2343-1376; fax (2) 2343-1378; e-mail contacto@islamenchile.cl; internet www.islamenchile .cl; f. 1925 as the Sociedad Unión Musulmana; Sec. MOHAMED RUMIE.

BAHÁ'Í FAITH

National Spiritual Assembly: Manuel de Salas 356, Casilla 3731, Nuñoa, Santiago; tel. (2) 2752-3999; fax (2) 2752-3999; e-mail secretaria@bahai.cl; internet www.bahai.cl.

The Press

DAILIES

Santiago

La Cuarta: Diagonal Vicuña Mackenna 1870, Casilla 2795, Santiago; tel. (2) 2551-7067; fax (2) 2555-7071; e-mail contacto@lacuarta .cl; internet www.lacuarta.cl; f. 1984; morning; popular; Dir SERGIO MARABOLÍ TRIVIÑO; circ. 146,000.

Diario Financiero: Avda Apoquindo 3885, 1°, Las Condes, Santiago; tel. (2) 2339-1000; fax (2) 2231-3340; e-mail ventas@df.cl;

internet www.df.cl; f. 1988; morning; Gen. Man. PAULA URENDA WARREN; circ. 20,000.

Diario Oficial de la República de Chile: Dr Torres Boonen 511, Providencia, Santiago; tel. (2) 2486-3600; fax (2) 2698-1059; e-mail consultasdof@interior.gob.cl; internet www.diariooficial.interior.gob .cl; f. 1877; Dir CARMEN CECILIA POWER HELFMANN; circ. 2,000.

Estrategia: Luis Carrera 1289, Vitacura, Santiago; tel. (2) 2655-6100; fax (2) 2655-6439; e-mail estrategia@estrategia.cl; internet www.estrategia.cl; f. 1978; morning; business news; Dir VÍCTOR MANUEL OJEDA MÉNDEZ; circ. 33,000.

La Hora: Avda Vicuña Mackenna 1870, Santiago; tel. (2) 2550-7000; fax (2) 2550-7770; e-mail contacto@lahora.cl; internet www.lahora .cl; f. 1997; Mon.–Fri; distributed free of charge; Editor SALVADOR CARMONA SCHÖNFFELDT; circ. 106,000.

El Mercurio: Avda Santa María 5542, Casilla 13-D, Santiago; tel. (2) 2330-1111; fax (2) 2242-6965; e-mail elmercurio@mercurio.cl; internet www.elmercurio.cl; f. 1900; morning; conservative; Dir CRISTIÁN ZEGERS ARIZTÍA; circ. 154,000 (Mon.–Fri.), 232,000 (weekends).

La Nación: Serrano 14, Casilla 81-D, Santiago; tel. (2) 2787-0100; fax (2) 2698-1059; e-mail contactoln@lanacion.cl; internet www .lanacion.cl; f. 1917 to replace govt-subsidized El Cronista; online only from Dec. 2010; owned by Soc. Periodística La Nación; Dir SAMUEL ROMO; circ. 11,000.

Santiago Times: Avda Santa María 227, Of. 12, Santiago; tel. (2) 2735-9044; fax (2) 2777-5376; e-mail editor@santiagotimes.cl; internet www.santiagotimes.cl; f. 1991; daily; national news in English; Publr STEVE ANDERSON; Editor-in-Chief DAVID PEDIGO; 10,000 subscribers.

La Segunda: Avda Santa María 5542, Casilla 13-D, Santiago; tel. (2) 2330-1111; fax (2) 2242-6965; e-mail cartas@lasegunda.cl; internet www.lasegunda.com; f. 1931; owned by proprs of *El Mercurio*; evening; Dir VÍCTOR CARVAJAL; circ. 40,000.

La Tercera: Avda Vicuña Mackenna 1870, Nuñoa, Santiago; tel. (2) 2550-7000; fax (2) 2555-7071; e-mail contactoweb@grupocopesa.cl; internet www.latercera.cl; f. 1950; morning; Dir ANDRÉS AZÓCAR ZAMUDIO; circ. 91,000 (Mon.–Fri.), 201,000 (weekends).

Las Ultimas Noticias: Bellavista 0112, Providencia, Santiago; tel. (2) 2730-3000; fax (2) 2730-3331; e-mail ultimas.noticias@lun.cl; internet www.lun.cl; f. 1902; owned by the proprs of *El Mercurio*; morning; Dir AGUSTÍN EDWARDS DEL RÍO; circ. 133,000 (Mon.–Fri.), 176,000 (weekends).

Antofagasta

La Estrella del Norte: Manuel Antonio Matta 2112, Antofagasta; tel. (55) 245-3672; fax (55) 245-3671; e-mail cronicanorte@ estrellanorte.cl; internet www.estrellanorte.cl; f. 1966; evening; Dir SERGIO MERCADO RICHARDS; circ. 5,000.

El Mercurio de Antofagasta: Manuel Antonio Matta 2112, Antofagasta; tel. (55) 2425-3600; fax (55) 2425-3612; e-mail cartas@ mercurioantofagasta.cl; internet www.mercurioantofagasta.cl; f. 1906; morning; conservative ind; owned by Soc. Chilena de Publicaciones; Dir VÍCTOR TOLOZA JIMÉNEZ; circ. 9,000.

Arica

La Estrella de Arica: San Marcos 580, Arica; tel. (58) 235-2828; fax (58) 235-2841; e-mail cronica@estrellaarica.cl; internet www .estrellaarica.cl; f. 1976; Dir EDUARDO CAMPOS CORREA; circ. 10,000.

Atacama

Chañarcillo: Maipú 849, Casilla 198, Copiapó, Atacama; tel. and fax (52) 224-0948; fax (52) 221-9044; internet www.chanarcillo.cl; f. 1992; morning; Dir ALBERTO BICHARA NICOLÁS.

Calama

El Mercurio de Calama: Abaroa 2051, Calama; tel. (55) 245-8571; fax (55) 245-8172; e-mail cronicacalama@mercurio.cl; internet www .mercuriocalama.cl; f. 1968; owned by Soc. Chilena de Publicaciones; Dir JAVIER ORELLANA VERA; circ. 4,500 (weekdays), 7,000 (Sun.).

Chillán

La Discusión: 18 de Septiembre 721, Casilla 479, Chillán; tel. (42) 220-1200; fax (42) 221-3578; e-mail diario@ladiscusion.cl; internet www.diarioladiscusion.cl; f. 1870; morning; ind; Dir FRANCISCO MARTINIC FIGUEROA; circ. 5,000.

Concepción

El Sur: Caupolicán 518, 8°, Casilla 8-C, Concepción; tel. (41) 279-4760; fax (41) 279-4761; e-mail buzon@diarioelsur.cl; internet www .elsur.cl; f. 1882; morning; ind; Dir MAURICIO RIVAS ALVEAR; circ. 28,000 (weekdays), 45,000 (Sun.).

Copiapó

El Diario de Atacama: Atacama 725A, Copiapó; tel. (52) 221-8509; fax (52) 223-2212; e-mail ddoll@diarioatacama.cl; internet www.diarioatacama.cl; f. 1970; morning; ind.; Dir DAVID DOLL PINTO; circ. 6,500.

Coyhaique

El Diario de Aysén: 21 de Mayo 410, Coyhaique; tel. (67) 2234-850; fax (67) 2232-318; e-mail contacto@diarioaysen.cl; internet www.diarioaysen.cl; f. 1981; Dir GABRIELA VICENTINI ROGEL.

Curicó

La Prensa: Sargento Aldea 632, Curicó; tel. (75) 231-0132; fax (75) 231-1924; e-mail correo@diariolaprensa.cl; internet diariolaprensa.cl; f. 1898; morning; right-wing; Dir MANUEL MASSA MAUTINO; circ. 6,000.

Iquique

La Estrella de Iquique: Luis Uribe 452, Iquique; tel. (57) 239-9311; fax (57) 242-7975; e-mail cronica@estrellaiquique.cl; internet www.estrellaiquique.cl; f. 1966; evening; Dir CAUPOLICÁN MÁRQUEZ VERGARA; circ. 10,000.

La Serena

El Día: Brasil 431, La Serena; tel. (51) 220-0400; fax (51) 221-9599; e-mail azenteno@eldia.la; internet diarioeldia.cl; f. 1944; morning; Editor ELEAZAR GARVISO GÁLVEZ; Dir FRANCISCO PUGA VERGARA; circ. 10,800.

Los Angeles

La Tribuna: Colo Colo 464, Casilla 15-D, Los Angeles; tel. (43) 231-3315; fax (43) 231-4987; e-mail gerencia@diariolatribuna.cl; internet www.diariolatribuna.cl; f. 1958; ind; Dir DANIA PINCHEIRA PASCAL; circ. 4,200.

Osorno

El Austral–El Diario de Osorno: O'Higgins 870, Osorno; tel. (64) 222-2300; fax (64) 222-2316; e-mail cronica@australosorno.cl; internet www.australosorno.cl; f. 1982; Dir GUIDO RODRÍGUEZ AVÍLES; circ. 6,500 (weekdays), 7,300 (Sun.).

Ovalle

El Ovallino: Vicuña Mackenna 473, Ovalle; tel. (53) 243-3430; fax (53) 243-3429; e-mail contacto@elovallino.cl; internet www.elovallino.cl; f. 1989; Editor DAVID FLORES BARRIOS.

Puerto Montt

El Llanquíhue: Antonio Varas 167, Puerto Montt; tel. (65) 243-2400; fax (65) 243-2401; e-mail cartasdirector@diariollanquihue.cl; internet www.diariollanquihue.cl; f. 1885; Dir ROBERTO GAETE PARRAGUEZ; circ. 4,800 (weekdays), 5,700 (Sun.).

Punta Arenas

La Prensa Austral: Waldo Seguel 636, Casilla 9-D, Punta Arenas; tel. (61) 220-4000; fax (61) 224-7406; e-mail redaccion@laprensaaustral.cl; internet www.laprensaaustral.cl; f. 1941; morning; ind.; Gen. Editor POLY RAÍN HARO; Dir FRANCISCO KARELOVIC CAR; circ. 8,000 (Mon.–Sat.); *El Magallanes*; f. 1894, circ. 9,500.

Quillota

El Observador: La Concepción 277, Casilla 1-D, Quillota; tel. (33) 234-2209; fax (33) 231-1417; e-mail elobser@entelchile.net; internet www.diarioelobservador.cl; f. 1970; Man. Dir ROBERTO SILVA BIJIT.

Rancagua

El Rancagüino: O'Carroll 518, Casilla 50, Rancagua; tel. (72) 232-7400; e-mail web@elrancaguino.cl; internet www.elrancaguino.cl; f. 1915; ind; Dir ALEJANDRO GONZÁLEZ PINO; circ. 10,000.

Talca

El Centro: Casa Matriz, Avda Lircay 3030, Talca; tel. (71) 251-5300; fax (71) 251-0310; e-mail diario@diarioelcentro.cl; internet www.diarioelcentro.cl; f. 1989; Dir JOSÉ ALVAREZ ESPINOZA.

Temuco

El Austral–El Diario de la Araucanía: Antonio Varas 945, Casilla 1-D, Temuco; tel. (45) 229-2727; fax (45) 223-7765; e-mail cronica@australtemuco.cl; internet www.australtemuco.cl; f. 1916; owned by Soc. Periodística Araucanía; morning; commercial, industrial and agricultural interests; Dir MARCO SALAZAR PARDO; circ. 15,100 (weekdays), 23,500 (Sun.).

Tocopilla

La Estrella de Tocopilla: Bolívar 1244, Tocopilla; tel. (83) 281-3036; e-mail prensa@prensatocopilla.cl; internet www.prensatocopilla.cl; f. 1924; morning; ind; Dir SERGIO MERCADO RICHARDS; circ. 3,000.

Valdivia

El Diario Austral de Valdivia: Yungay 499, Valdivia; tel. (63) 224-2200; fax (63) 224-2209; e-mail cartasdirector@australvaldivia.cl; internet www.australvaldivia.cl; f. 1982; Dir VERÓNICA MORENO AGUILERA; circ. 5,600.

Valparaíso

La Estrella: Esmeralda 1002, Casilla 57-V, Valparaíso; tel. (32) 226-4264; fax (32) 226-4108; e-mail cartasdirector@estrellavalpo.cl; internet www.estrellavalpo.cl; f. 1921; evening; owned by the proprs of *El Mercurio*; Dir CARLOS VERGARA EHRENBERG; circ. 28,000 (weekdays), 35,000 (Sat.).

El Mercurio de Valparaíso: Esmeralda 1002, Casilla 57-V, Valparaíso; tel. (32) 226-4264; fax (32) 226-4248; e-mail sclientevalpo@mercuriovalpo.cl; internet www.mercuriovalpo.cl; f. 1827; owned by the proprs of *El Mercurio*; morning; Dir PEDRO URZÚA BAZIN; circ. 65,000.

PERIODICALS

América Economía: tel. (2) 2290-9400; fax (2) 2206-6005; e-mail rferro@aeconomia.cl; internet www.americaeconomia.com; f. 1986; monthly; business; Publr and Editor ELÍAS SELMAN; Gen. Man. EDUARDO ALBORNOZ.

CA (Ciudad/Arquitectura) Revista Oficial del Colegio de Arquitectos de Chile AG: Avda Libertador Bernardo O'Higgins 115, Santiago; tel. (2) 2353-2321; fax (2) 2353-2355; e-mail revistaca@colegioarquitectos.com; internet www.revistaca.cl; f. 1968; 4 a year; architecture; Dir HUGO MONDRAGÓN L.; circ. 4,000.

Caras: Rosario Norte 555, 18°, Santiago; tel. (2) 2595-5000; e-mail revista@caras.cl; internet www.caras.cl; f. 1988; women's interest; Dir CAROLINA GARCÍA-HUIDOBRO; Editor LORRAINE THOMSON.

Chile Forestal: Paseo Bulnes 265, Of. 601, Santiago; tel. (2) 2663-0208; fax (2) 2696-6724; e-mail mariela.espejo@conaf.cl; internet www.conaf.cl/conaf/seccion-revista-chile-forestal.html; f. 1974; 6 a year; state-owned; technical information and features on forestry sector; Dir RICARDO SAN MARTÍN; Editor MARIELA ESPEJO SUAZO; circ. 4,000.

Cinegrama: Avda Holanda 279, Providencia, Santiago; tel. (2) 2422-8500; fax (2) 2422-8570; e-mail cinegrama@cinegrama.cl; internet www.cinegrama.cl; f. 1987; monthly; cinema; Dir JUAN IGNACIO OTO; Editor LEYLA LÓPEZ.

The Clinic: Santo Domingo 550, Of. 601, Santiago; tel. (2) 2633-9584; fax (2) 2639-6584; e-mail theclinic@theclinic.cl; internet www.theclinic.cl; fortnightly; political and social satire; Editor PABLO BASADRE; Dir PATRICIO FERNÁNDEZ CHADWICK.

Conozca Más: Rosario Norte 555, 18°, Las Condes, Santiago; tel. (2) 2366-7100; fax (2) 2246-2810; e-mail viamail@conozcamas.cl; internet www.conozcamas.cl; monthly; science; Dir PAULA AVILÉS VILLAGRA; circ. 90,000.

Cosas: Almirante Pastene 259, Providencia, Santiago; tel. (2) 2364-5100; fax (2) 2235-8331; e-mail info@cosas.com; internet www.cosas.com; f. 1976; fortnightly; entertainment and lifestyle; Editor OSCAR SEPÚLVEDA PACHECO; Dir MÓNICA COMANDARI KAISER; circ. 40,000.

Ercilla: Avda Holanda 279, Providencia, Santiago; tel. (2) 2422-8500; fax (2) 2422-8570; e-mail ercilla@holanda.cl; internet www.ercilla.cl; f. 1936; weekly; general interest; conservative; Dir JUAN IGNACIO OTO; circ. 28,000.

El Gráfico: Avda Kennedy 5735, Of. 701, Torre Poniente Hotel Marriott, Las Condes, Santiago; tel. (2) 2434-4900; fax (2) 2421-5900; e-mail deportes@publimetro.cl; internet www.elgraficochile.cl; monthly; sport, illustrated; Editor MATÍAS CARVAJAL.

Paula: Vicuña Mackenna 1962, Ñuñoa, Santiago; tel. (2) 2550-7000; fax (2) 2550-7195; e-mail cartas@paula.cl; internet www.paula.cl; f. 1967; monthly; women's interest; Dir MILENA VODANOVIC; Editor CAROLINA DÍAZ; circ. 85,000.

Punto Final: San Diego 31, Of. 606, Casilla 13954, Correo 21, Santiago; tel. and fax (2) 2697-0615; e-mail revistapuntofinal@movistar.cl; internet www.puntofinal.cl; f. 1965; fortnightly; politics; left-wing; Dir MANUEL CABIESES DONOSO; circ. 15,000.

¿Qué Pasa?: Vicuña Mackenna 1870, Ñuñoa, Santiago; tel. (2) 2550-7523; fax (2) 2550-7529; e-mail quepasa@copesa.cl; internet www

.quepasa.cl; f. 1971; weekly; general interest; Editor Francisco Aravena; Dir José Luis Santa María; circ. 30,000.

Revista Agrícola: O'Higgin 870, Osorno; tel. (63) 222-2300; e-mail contacto@revistaagricola.cl; internet www.revistaagricola.cl; agricultural research; Dir Guido Rodríguez Avíles.

Revista Mensaje: Cienfuegos 21, Santiago; tel. (2) 2698-0617; fax (2) 2671-7030; e-mail rrpp@mensaje.cl; internet www.mensaje.cl; f. 1951; monthly; national, church and international affairs; Dir Antonio Delfau; circ. 6,000.

Vea: Avda Holanda 279, Providencia, Santiago; tel. (2) 2422-8500; fax (2) 2422-8572; e-mail vea@holanda.cl; internet www.vea.cl; f. 1939; weekly; general interest, illustrated; Dir Martha Beltrán; circ. 150,000.

PRESS ASSOCIATION

Asociación Nacional de la Prensa: Carlos Antúnez 2048, Providencia, Santiago; tel. (2) 2232-1004; fax (2) 2232-1006; e-mail info@anp.cl; internet www.anp.cl; f. 1951; Pres. Alvaro Caviedes Barahona; Sec.-Gen. Sebastián Zárate Rojas.

NEWS AGENCIES

Agencia Chile Noticias (ACN): Carlos Antúnez 1884, Of. 104, Providencia, Santiago; tel. and fax (2) 2717-9121; e-mail prensa@chilenoticias.cl; internet www.chilenoticias.cl; f. 1993; Editor Norberto Parra Hidalgo.

Agencia Orbe: Avda Phillips 56, Of. 66, Santiago; tel. (2) 2251-7800; fax (2) 2251-7801; e-mail prensa@orbe.cl; internet www.orbe.cl; f. 1955; Bureau Chief Patricia Escalona Cáceres.

Business News Americas: San Patricio 2944, Las Condes, Santiago; tel. (2) 2941-0300; fax (2) 2232-9376; e-mail info@bnamericas.com; internet www.bnamericas.com; internet-based business information; CEO Gregory Barton.

UPI Chile Ltd: Avda Nataniel Cox 47, 9°, Santiago; tel. (2) 2657-0874; fax (2) 2698-6605; e-mail prensa@upi.com; internet www.upi.cl; Gen. Man. Jorgeq Iribarren Espejo.

Publishers

Carlos Quiroga Editorial: La Concepción 56, Of. 202, Providencia, Santiago; tel. and fax (2) 2202-9825; e-mail cquiroga@carlosquiroga.cl; internet www.carlosquiroga.cl; children's and educational; Gen. Man. Marianella Medina.

Edebé—Editorial Don Bosco: Avda Gen. Bulnes 35, Santiago; tel. (2) 2437-8050; e-mail contacto@edebe.cl; internet www.edebe.cl; f. 1904 as Editorial Salesiana; adopted present name in 1996; general, political, biography, religious, children's; Chair. Aldo Moltedo; Gen. Man. Pablo Marinkovic.

Ediciones B Chile: Avda Las Torres 1375A, Huechuraba, Santiago; tel. (2) 2729-5400; fax (2) 2231-6300; e-mail mansieta@edicionesbchile.cl; internet www.edicionesbchile.cl; f. 1986; part of Grupo Zeta; children's and fiction; Gen. Man. Marilén Wood.

Ediciones Mil Hojas: Avda Antonio Varas 1480, Providencia, Santiago; tel. (2) 2274-3172; fax (2) 2223-7544; e-mail milhojas@terra.cl; internet www.milhojas.cl; educational and reference; Dir Julieta Melo Cabello.

Ediciones Universitarias de Valparaíso: Universidad Católica de Valparaíso, Calle 12 de Febrero 187, Casilla 1415, Valparaíso; tel. (32) 227-3087; fax (32) 227-3429; e-mail euvsa@ucv.cl; internet www.euv.cl; f. 1970; literature, social and general sciences, engineering, education, music, arts, textbooks; Chair. Patricio Arana Espina; Gen. Man. María Teresa Vega Segovia.

Ediciones Urano: Avda Francisco Bilbao 2790, CP 7510745, Providencia, Santiago; tel. (2) 2341-7493; fax (2) 2225-3896; e-mail info@edicionesurano.cl; internet www.edicionesurano.cl; f. 1983 in Spain, f. 1996 in Chile; self-help, mystical and scholarly; Gen. Man. Ricardo Vlastelica Vega.

Editec (Ediciones Técnicas Ltda): El Condor 844, Of. 205, Ciudad Empresarial, Huechuraba, Santiago; tel. (2) 2757-4200; fax (2) 2757-4201; e-mail editec@editec.cl; internet www.editec.cl; Pres. Ricardo Cortes Donoso; Gen. Man. Roly Solis Sepúlveda.

Editorial Antártica, SA: San Francisco 116, Santiago; tel. (2) 2639-3476; fax (2) 2633-3402; e-mail consulta@antartica.cl; internet www.antartica.cl; f. 1978; Gen. Man. Paul Laborde U.

Editorial Borlando: Avda Victoria 155, Santiago; tel. (2) 2555-9566; fax (2) 2556-7100; e-mail ventas@editorialborlando.cl; internet www.editorialborlando.cl; f. 1984; scholarly, juvenile, educational and reference; Dir-Gen. Sergio Borlando Portales.

Editorial Cuatro Vientos Ltda: Maturana 19, Metro República, entre Brasil y Cumming, Santiago; tel. (2) 2672-9226; fax (2) 2673-2153; e-mail editorial@cuatrovientos.cl; internet cuatrovientos.cl; f. 1980; Man. Editor Juan Francisco Huneeus Cox.

Editorial y Distribuidora Lenguaje y Pensamiento Ltda: Avda 11 de Septiembre 1881, Of. 324, Metro Pedro de Valdivia, Santiago; tel. (2) 2335-2347; e-mail contacto@lenguajeypensamiento.cl; internet www.editoriallenguajeypensamiento.cl; children's, educational; Gen. Man. María Lorena Terán.

Editorial Evolución, SA: Ministro Carvajal 6, Providencia, Santiago; tel. (2) 2681-8072; fax (2) 2236-2071; e-mail info@evolucion.cl; internet www.evolucion.cl; business and management; Dir Juan Bravo Carrasco.

Editorial Fondo de Cultura Económica Chile, SA: Paseo Bulnes 152, Metro Moneda, Santiago; tel. (2) 2594-4100; fax (2) 2594-4101; e-mail info@fcechile.cl; internet fcechile.cl; f. 1954; Gen. Man. Oscar Bravo.

Editorial Jurídica de Chile: Ahumada 131, 4°, Santiago; tel. (2) 2461-9500; fax (2) 2461-9501; e-mail covalle@editorialjuridica.cl; internet www.editorialjuridica.cl; f. 1945; law; Gen. Man. Patricio Rojas.

Editorial Patris: José Manuel Infante 132, Providencia, Santiago; tel. (2) 2235-1343; fax (2) 2235-8674; e-mail gerencia@entelchile.net; internet www.patris.cl; f. 1982; Catholic; Dir José Luis Correa Lira.

Editorial Renacimiento: Amunátegui 458, Santiago; tel. (2) 2345-8300; fax (2) 2345-8320; e-mail pedidos@editorialrenacimiento.com; internet www.editorialrenacimiento.com; f. 1977; Gen. Man. Alberto Aldea.

Editorial San Pablo: Avda Libertador Bernardo O'Higgins 1626, Casilla 3746, Santiago; tel. (2) 2720-0300; fax (2) 2672-8469; e-mail alameda@san-pablo.cl; internet www.sanpablochile.cl; f. 1914; Catholic texts; Dir-Gen. Bruno Bressan.

Editorial Tiempo Presente Ltda: Almirante Pastene 345, Providencia, Santiago; tel. (2) 2364-5100; fax (2) 2235-8331; e-mail info@cosas.com; internet www.cosas.com; Gen. Man. Matías Pfingsthorn Olivares.

Editorial Universitaria, SA: Avda Libertador Bernardo O'Higgins 1050, Santiago; tel. (2) 2487-0700; fax (2) 2487-0702; e-mail comunicaciones@universitaria.cl; internet www.universitaria.cl; f. 1947; general literature, social science, technical, textbooks; Man. Dir Rodrigo Fuentes.

Empresa Editora Zig-Zag SA: Los Conquistadores 1700, 10°, Providencia, Santiago; tel. (2) 2810-7400; fax (2) 2810-7452; e-mail zigzag@zigzag.cl; internet www.zigzag.cl; f. 1905; general publrs of literary works, reference books and magazines; Pres. Alfredo Vercelli; Gen. Man. Ramón Olaciregui.

Grupo Planeta: Avda 11 de Septiembre 2353, 16°, CP 7510058, Providencia, Santiago; tel. (2) 2652-2927; fax (2) 2652-2912; e-mail info@planeta.cl; internet www.editorialplaneta.cl; f. 1968; nonfiction, philosophy, psychology; Gen. Man. Elsy Salazar Campo.

Liberalia Ediciones: Avda Italia 2016, Nuñoa, Santiago; tel. (2) 2432-8003; fax (2) 2326-8805; e-mail liberalia@liberalia.cl; internet www.liberalia.cl; f. 1997; Dir Jaime Oxley Muñoz.

McGraw-Hill/Interamericana de Chile Ltda: Evaristo Lillo 112, 7°, Las Condes, Santiago; tel. (2) 2661-3000; fax (2) 2661-3020; e-mail info_chile@mcgraw-hill.com; internet www.mcgraw-hill.cl; educational and technical; Gen. Man. José Aberg Cobo.

Norma de Chile, SA: Monjitas 527, 17°, Centro, Santiago; tel. (2) 2731-7500; fax (2) 2632-2079; e-mail david.malhue@norma.com; internet www.librerianorma.com; f. 1960; part of Editorial Norma of Colombia; Gen. Man. David Malhue.

Pearson Educación de Chile: José Ananias 505, Macul, Santiago; tel. (2) 2237-2387; fax (2) 2237-2397; e-mail infopear@pearsoned.cl; Gen. Man. Eduardo Guzmán Barros.

Pehuen Editores, SA: Brown Norte 417, Nuñoa, Santiago; tel. (2) 2795-7131; fax (2) 2795-7133; e-mail editorial@pehuen.cl; internet www.pehuen.cl; f. 1983; literature, sociology, photography and illustrated children's books; Pres. Sebastián Barros Cerda; Gen. Man. Juan Manuel Galán.

RIL Editores (Red Internacional del Libro Ltda): Los Leones 2258, Providencia, CP 751-1055, Santiago; tel. (2) 2223-8100; fax (2) 2225-4269; e-mail ril@rileditores.com; internet www.rileditores.com; literature, poetry, scholarly and political; f. 1991 as Red Internacional del Libro Ltda; Dir Eleonora Finkelstein; Dir of Publications Daniel Calabrese.

Tajamar Editores: Avda Mariano Sánchez Fontecilla 352, Las Condes, Santiago; tel. (2) 2245-7026; e-mail info@tajamar-editores.cl; internet www.tajamar-editores.cl; f. 2002; literature; Gen. Man. María Paz Gaete Silva.

PUBLISHERS' ASSOCIATIONS

Asociación de Editores de Chile (Asociación de Editores Independientes, Universitarios y Autónomos): Maturana 19, Santiago; tel. (2) 2632-9210; e-mail contacto@editoresdechile.cl; internet www

.editoresdechile.cl; Pres. PAULO SLACHEVSKY CHONCHOL; Exec. Dir CARMEN GLORIA ARCE.

Cámara Chilena del Libro, AG: Avda Libertador Bernardo O'Higgins 1370, Of. 502, Casilla 13526, Santiago; tel. (2) 2672-0348; fax (2) 2687-4271; e-mail prolibro@tie.cl; internet www.camaradellibro.cl; f. 1950; Pres. EDUARDO CASTILLO GARCÍA.

Broadcasting and Communications

REGULATORY AUTHORITY

Subsecretaría de Telecomunicaciones (Subtel): Amunátegui 139, 5°, Casilla 120, Correo 21, Santiago; tel. (2) 2421-3500; fax (2) 2421-3553; e-mail subtel@subtel.cl; internet www.subtel.cl; f. 1977; part of the Ministry of Transport and Telecommunications; Under-Sec. JORGE ATTON PALMA.

TELECOMMUNICATIONS

Claro Chile, SA: Avda del Cóndor 820, Ciudad Empresarial, Comuna de Huechuraba, Santiago; tel. (2) 2444-5000; fax (2) 2444-5170; internet www.clarochile.cl; fmrly Smartcom; acquired in 2005 by América Móvil, SA de CV (Mexico); merged with Telmex Chile in 2010; Gen. Man. GERARDO MUÑOZ.

CMET Telecomunicaciones: Avda Los Leones 1412, Providencia, Santiago; tel. (2) 2250-0105; fax (2) 2274-9573; internet www.cmet.cl; f. 1978.

Empresa Nacional de Telecomunicaciones, SA—ENTEL Chile, SA: Andrés Bello 2687, 14°, Casilla 4254, Las Condes, Santiago; tel. (2) 2360-0123; fax (2) 2360-3424; internet www.entel.cl; f. 1964; operates the Chilean land satellite stations of Longovilo, Punta Arenas and Coyhaique, linked to INTELSAT system; 52% owned by Telecom Italia; Pres. JUAN JOSÉ HURTADO VICUÑA; Gen. Man. ANTONIO BÜCHI BUC.

Grupo GTD: Moneda 920, 11°, CP 2099, Santiago; tel. (2) 2413-9400; fax (2) 2413-9100; e-mail soporte@gtdinternet.com; internet www.grupogtd.cl; f. 1979; internet and telephone service provider; Pres. JUAN MANUEL CASANUEVA PRÉNDEZ; Gen. Man. MARIO RAÚL DOMÍNGUEZ ROJAS.

Movistar: Providencia 111, CP 16-D, Santiago; tel. (2) 2691-2020; fax (2) 2691-7881; internet www.movistar.cl; f. 1996 as Telefónica Móvil de Chile, present name adopted in 2005 following merger of Telefónica Móviles de Chile with BellSouth Communications (USA); mobile cellular telephone services; Pres. CLAUDIO MUÑOZ ZÚÑIGA; Gen. Man. FERNANDO SAIZ MAREGATTI.

VTR GlobalCom: Reyes Lavalle 3340, 9°, Las Condes, Santiago; tel. (2) 2310-1000; fax (2) 2310-1560; internet www.vtr.cl; f. 1928 as Vía Transradio Chilena; present name adopted in 1999; 80% owned by Liberty Global Inc (USA), 20% owned by Cristalerías Chile of the Claro group; Exec. Pres. MAURICIO RAMOS BORRERO.

BROADCASTING

Radio

Agricultura (AM y FM): Avda Manuel Rodríguez 15, Santiago; tel. (2) 2392-3000; fax (2) 2392-3072; internet www.radioagricultura.cl; owned by Sociedad Nacional de Agricultura; Pres. DOMINGO ROMERO CORTÉS; Gen. Man. LUIS LANGLOIS DIAZ.

Beethoven FM: Avda. Santa María 2670, 2°, Providencia, Santiago; tel. (2) 2571-7056; fax (2) 2274-3323; e-mail director@redfm.cl; internet www.beethovenfm.cl; f. 1981; mainly classical music; affiliate stations in Viña del Mar and Temuco; Dir ADOLFO FLORES.

Bío Bío La Radio: Avda Libertador Bernardo O'Higgins 680, Concepción; tel. (41) 262-0620; fax (41) 222-6742; e-mail internet@laradio.cl; internet www.radiobiobio.cl; affiliate stations in Concepción, Los Angeles, Temuco, Ancud, Castro, Osorno, Puerto Montt, Santiago and Valdivia; Man. PATRICIO ANDRADE.

Duna FM: Avda Santa María 2670, 2°, Providencia, Santiago; tel. (2) 2225-5494; fax (2) 2225-6013; e-mail aholuigue@duna.cl; internet www.duna.cl; affiliate stations in Viña del Mar and Concepción; Pres. FELIPE LAMARCA CLARO; Dir A. HOLUIGUE.

Estrella del Mar AM: Eleuterio Ramírez 207, Ancud, Isla de Chiloé; tel. and fax (65) 262-2722; e-mail secretariaestrelladelmar@gmail.com; internet www.radioestrelladelmar.cl; f. 1982; station of the Roman Catholic diocese of San Carlos de Ancud; affiliate stations in Castro, Quellón, Melinka, Achao, Futaleufú, Palena and Chaitén; Exec. Dir PABLO DURÁN LEIVA.

Festival AM: Quinta 124A, 2°, Casilla 337, Viña del Mar; tel. (32) 268-4251; fax (32) 268-0266; e-mail servicios@festival.cl; internet www.festival.cl; f. 1976; Dir-Gen. ROSSANA CHIESA VENEGAS.

Horizonte: Avda Pocuro 2151, Providencia, Santiago; tel. (2) 2410-5400; fax (2) 2410-5460; internet www.horizonte.cl; f. 1985; affiliate stations in Arica, Antofagasta, Iquique, La Serena, Viña del Mar,

Concepción, San Antonio, Temuco, Villarrica, Puerto Montt, Punta Arenas and Osorno; Dir RODRIGO HURTADO.

IberoAmericana Radio Chile: Eliodoro Yáñez 1783, Providencia, Santiago; tel. (2) 2390-2000; fax (2) 2390-2047; e-mail aaguirre@iarc.cl; internet www.iarc.cl; part of Prisa Radio; Exec. Dir MARCELO ZÚÑIGA VETTIGER; Communications Man. JAVIERA BALLACEY T.; the media group operates 11 radio stations.

40 Principales 101.7 FM: e-mail radio@los40.cl; internet www.los40.cl.

ADN Radio Chile 91.7 FM: e-mail radio@adnradio.cl; internet www.adnradio.cl; general and sports news.

Concierto 88.5 FM: e-mail radio@concierto.cl; internet www.concierto.cl; f. 1999; 1980s music; Gen. Man. JAIME VEGA DE KUYPER.

Corazón 101.3 FM: e-mail radio@corazon.cl; internet www.corazon.cl; f. 1997.

FMDos 98.5 FM: e-mail radio@fmdos.cl; internet www.fm2.cl; popular music.

Futuro 88.9 FM: e-mail radio@futuro.cl; internet www.futuro.cl; rock music.

Imagina 88.1 FM: e-mail radio@radioimagina.cl; internet www.radioimagina.cl; women's radio.

Pudahuel 90.5 FM: e-mail radio@pudahuel.cl; internet www.pudahuel.cl; f. 1966; Pres. SUSANA MUTINELLI ANCHUBIDART; Gen. Man. JOAQUÍN BLAYA BARRIOS.

Radioactiva 92.5 FM: e-mail info@radioactiva.cl; internet www.radioactiva.cl; dance music.

Rock & Pop 94.1 FM: e-mail contacto@rockandpop.cl; internet www.rockandpop.cl; retro classics and 1990s music.

Uno 97.1 FM: e-mail contacto@radiounochile.cl; internet www.radiounochile.cl; Chilean national music.

Infinita FM: Avda Los Leones 1285, Providencia, Santiago; tel. (2) 2754-4400; fax (2) 2341-6727; internet www.infinita.cl; f. 1977; affiliate stations in Santiago, Viña del Mar, Concepción and Valdivia; Gen. Man. CARLOS ALBERTO PEÑAFIEL GUARACHI.

Para Ti FM: Vial 775, Puerto Montt, Santiago; tel. (65) 2317-003; internet www.radioparati.cl; 16 affiliate stations throughout Chile; Gen. Man. PATRICIO COROMINAS.

Play FM: Alcalde Dávalos 164, Providencia, Santiago; tel. (2) 2630-2600; fax (2) 2630-2264; e-mail asanchez@13.cl; internet www.playfm.cl; f. 2006; Dir GABRIEL POLGATI; Gen. Man. XIMENA CALLEJÓN.

Radio Carolina: Avda Santa Maria 2670, 2°, Providence, Santiago; tel. (2) 2571-7000; fax (2) 2571-7002; internet www.carolina.cl; f. 1975; owned by COPESA, SA; Contact HÉCTOR CABRERA.

Radio El Conquistador FM: El Conquistador del Monte 4644, Huechuraba, Santiago; tel. (2) 2580-2000; e-mail radio@elconquistadorfm.cl; internet www.elconquistadorfm.cl; f. 1962; affiliate stations in Santiago, Iquique, Antofagasta, La Serena, Viña del Mar, Rancagua, Talca, Chillán, Concepción, Talcahuano, Pucón, Temuco, Villarrica, Lago Llanquihue, Osorno, Puerto Montt, Puerto Varas, Valdivia and Punta Arenas; Pres. JOAQUÍN MOLFINO.

Radio Cooperativa (AM y FM): Antonio Bellet 353, Casilla 16367, Correo 9, Santiago; tel. (2) 2364-8000; fax (2) 2236-0535; e-mail info@cooperativa.cl; internet www.cooperativa.cl; f. 1936; affiliate stations in Copiapó, Arica, Coquimbo, La Serena, Valparaíso, Concepción, Calama, Temuco and Castro; Gen. Man. LUIS AJENJO ISASI.

Radio Nacional de Chile: Roca 931, 2°, Santiago; tel. (61) 222-2957; fax (61) 222-2304; e-mail radionacional@123.cl; internet www.radio-nacional.cl; f. 1974; Gen. Man. SOFIA MANSILLA ALVARADO.

Radio Nueva Belén FM: Benavente 385, 3°, Puerto Montt; tel. (65) 225-8042; fax (65) 225-8084; e-mail nuevabelen@gmail.com; internet www.radionuevabelen.cl; f. 2005; owned by Archbishopric of Puerto Montt; Dir HÉCTOR ASENJO REYES; Gen. Man. CARLOS WAGNER CATALÁN.

Radio Polar: Bories 871, 2° y 3°, Punta Arenas; tel. (61) 224-1417; fax (61) 224-9001; e-mail secretaria@radiopolar.com; internet www.radiopolar.com; f. 1940; Pres. RENÉ VENEGAS OLMEDO.

Superandina FM: Avda Chacabuco 281, Los Andes; tel. (34) 242-2515; fax (34) 290-4091; e-mail radio@superandina.cl; internet www.superandina.cl; f. 1987; Dir JOSÉ ANDRÉS GÁLVEZ VALENZUELA.

Universo FM: Antonio Bellet 223, Providencia, Santiago; tel. (2) 2364-8000; e-mail alfredo@universo.cl; internet www.universo.cl; affiliate stations in 18 cities; Commercial Man. RODRIGO LIU L.

Television

Corporación de Televisión de la Universidad Católica de Chile—Canal 13: Inés Matte Urrejola 0848, Providencia, Santiago; tel. (2) 2251-4000; fax (2) 2630-2683; internet www.canal13.cl;

f. 1959; non-commercial; Pres. Nicolás Eyzaguirre; Exec. Dir David Belmar.

Corporación de Televisión de la Pontificia Universidad Católica de Valparaíso (UCV TV): Edif. Panorámico, Torre A, Of. 1402, Avda 11 Septiembre 2155, Santiago; tel. (2) 2586-4350; fax (2) 2586-4351; e-mail direccion@ucvtv.cl; internet www.ucvtv.cl; f. 1957; Pres. Bernardo Donoso Riveros; Exec. Dir Enrique Aimone García.

Red de Televisión SA/Chilevisión—Canal 11: Inés Matte Urrejola 0825, Casilla 16547, Correo 9, Providencia, Santiago; tel. (2) 2461-5100; fax (2) 2461-5371; e-mail contactoweb@chilevision.cl; internet www.chilevision.cl; Exec. Dir Jaime de Aguirre Hoffa; Gen. Man. Alicia Zaldívar Peralta.

La Red Televisión TV: Manquehue Sur 1201, Las Condes, Santiago; tel. (2) 2385-4000; fax (2) 2385-4020; e-mail administracion@lared.cl; internet www.redtv.cl; f. 1991; Dir-Gen. José Manuel Larraín; Exec. Dir Javier Urrutia.

Red Televisiva Megavisión, SA—Canal 9: Avda Vicuña Mackenna 1348, Nuñoa, Santiago; tel. (2) 2810-8000; fax (2) 2551-8369; e-mail mega@mcl.cl; internet www.mega.cl; f. 1990; Pres. Ricardo Claro Valdés; Gen. Man. Cristóbal Bulnes Serrano.

Televisión Nacional de Chile—Canal 7: Bellavista 0990, Casilla 16104, Providencia, Santiago; tel. (2) 2707-7777; fax (2) 2707-7766; e-mail relaciones.publicas@tvn.cl; internet www.tvn.cl; f. 1969; govt network of 140 stations and an international satellite signal; Chair. Mauro Valdés; Exec. Dir Daniel Fernández Koprich.

Regulatory Authority

Consejo Nacional de Televisión (CNTV): Mar del Plata 2147, Providencia, Santiago; tel. (2) 2592-2700; internet www.cntv.cl; f. 1989; Pres. Herman Chadwick Piñera.

Broadcasting Associations

Asociación Nacional de Televisión (ANATEL): Lota 2257, Of. 501, Providencia, Santiago; tel. (2) 2231-3755; fax (2) 2331-9803; e-mail contacto@anatel.cl; internet www.anatel.cl; 7 mem. networks; Pres. Ernesto Corona Bozzo; Sec.-Gen. Hernán Triviño Oyarzun.

Asociación de Radiodifusores de Chile (ARCHI): Pasaje Matte 956, 8°, Of. 801, Casilla 10476, Santiago; tel. (2) 2639-8755; fax (2) 2639-4205; e-mail archi@archiradios.cl; internet www.archi.cl; f. 1933; more than 1,000 affiliated stations; Nat. Pres. Carlos Alberto Peñafiel; Sec.-Gen. Fernando Ocaranza Yñesta.

Finance

(cap. = capital; res = reserves; dep. = deposits; m. = million; brs = branches; amounts in pesos, unless otherwise specified)

BANKING

Supervisory Authority

Superintendencia de Bancos e Instituciones Financieras: Moneda 1123, 6°, Casilla 15-D, Santiago; tel. (2) 2887-9200; fax (2) 2381-0410; e-mail superintendente@sbif.cl; internet www.sbif.cl; f. 1925; affiliated to Ministry of Finance; Supt Eric Parrado Herrera.

Central Bank

Banco Central de Chile: Agustinas 1180, Santiago; tel. (2) 2670-2000; fax (2) 2670-2099; e-mail bcch@bcentral.cl; internet www.bcentral.cl; f. 1925; autonomous from 1989; bank of issue; cap. and res 806,560.9m., dep. 15,274,011.2m. (Dec. 2009); Pres. Rodrigo Vergara Montes; Gen. Man Alejandro Zurbuchen Silva.

State Bank

Banco del Estado de Chile (BancoEstado): Avda Libertador Bernardo O'Higgins 1111, Casilla 240V, Santiago; tel. (2) 2970-7000; fax (2) 2970-5711; internet www.bancoestado.cl; f. 1953; state bank; cap. 278,497m., res 798,805m., dep. 18,087,570m. (Dec. 2013); Pres. Segismundo Schulin-Zeuthen Serrano; CEO Pablo Piñera Echenique; 344 brs.

Commercial Banks

Banco BICE: Teatinos 220, Santiago; tel. (2) 2692-2000; fax (2) 2696-5324; e-mail webmaster@bice.cl; internet www.bice.cl; f. 1979 as Banco Industrial y de Comercio Exterior; adopted present name 1988; cap. 32,142m., res −9,265m., dep. 2,759,549m. (Dec. 2013); Pres. and Chair. Bernardo Matte Larraín; CEO Alberto Schiling Redlich; 26 brs.

Banco Bilbao Vizcaya Argentaria Chile: Pedro de Valdivia 100, 17°, Providencia, Santiago; tel. (2) 2692-1000; fax (2) 2698-5640; e-mail ascarito@bbva.cl; internet www.bbva.cl; f. 1883 as Banco Hipotecario de Fomento Nacional; controlling interest acquired by Banco Bilbao Vizcaya (Spain) in 1998; adopted current name 2003; cap. 275,795m., res 340,120m., dep. 6,077,181m. (Dec. 2013); Chair. José Said Saffie; Gen. Man. and CEO Manuel Olivares Rossetti; 155 brs.

Banco de Chile: Ahumada 251, Casilla 151-D, Santiago; tel. (2) 2468-9624; fax (2) 2637-3434; internet www.bancochile.cl; f. 1894; 35.6% owned by SAOS, SA; cap. 1,436,083m., res −142,094m., dep. 14,344,330m. (Dec. 2011); Pres. and Chair. Pablo Granifo Lavín; 422 brs.

Banco de Crédito e Inversiones (Bci): Avda El Golf 125, Las Condes, Santiago; tel. (2) 2692-7000; fax (2) 2695-3775; e-mail webmaster@bci.cl; internet www.bci.cl; f. 1937; cap. 1,381,371m., res −9,978m., dep. 12,570,331m. (Dec. 2013); Pres. and Chair. Luis Enrique Yarur Rey; Gen. Man. Lionel Olavarría; 258 brs.

Banco Internacional: Moneda 818, Casilla 135-D, Santiago; tel. (2) 2369-7000; fax (2) 2369-7367; e-mail banco@binter.cl; internet www.bancointernacional.cl; f. 1944; cap. 57,545m., res 5,794m., dep. 805,139m. (Dec. 2013); Pres. Julio Jaraquemada Ledoux; Gen. Man. Carlos Ibañez.

Banco Itaú Chile: Avda Apoquindo 3457, Las Condes, Santiago; tel. (2) 2686-0000; internet www.itau.cl; cap. 290,697m., res 251,329m., dep. 4,441,867m. (Dec. 2013); Pres. Ricardo Villela Marino; Gen. Man. Jaime Uribe Hidalgo.

Banco Penta: Avda El Bosque Norte 440, 1°, Las Condes, Santiago; tel. (2) 2873-3062; internet www.bancopenta.cl; cap. 113,754m., res −1,663m., dep. 725,124m. (Dec. 2013); Pres. Carlos Alberto Délano Abbott; Gen. Man. Andrés Chechilnitzky Rodríguez.

Banco Santander Chile: Bandera 150, 2°, Casilla 57-D, Santiago; tel. (2) 2647-4341; fax (2) 2631-2009; e-mail webmaster@santander.cl; internet www.santander.cl; f. 1926; cap. 891,303m., res 992,449m., dep. 17,176,343m. (Dec. 2013); subsidiary of Banco Santander (Spain); Chair. Mauricio Larraín Garces; CEO Claudio Melandri; 72 brs.

Banco Security: Apoquindo 3150, Las Condes, Santiago; tel. (2) 2584-4000; fax (2) 2584-4058; e-mail banco@security.cl; internet www.bancosecurity.cl; f. 1981; fmrly Banco Urquijo de Chile; cap. 215,207m., res 9,331m., dep. 2,853,570m. (Dec. 2013); Pres. and Chair. Francisco Silva S.; Gen. Man. Bonifacio Bilbao; 28 brs.

Corpbanca: Rosario Norte 660, Las Condes, Casilla 80-D, Santiago; tel. (2) 2660-2240; fax (2) 2660-2206; e-mail corpbanca@corpbanca.cl; internet www.corpbanca.cl; f. 1871 as Banco de Concepción, current name adopted in 1997; bought by Itaú Unibanco (Brazil) in 2014; cap. 781,559m., res 414,649m., dep. 10,923,523m. (Dec. 2013); Chair. Jorge Andrés Saieh Guzmán; 70 brs.

HSBC Bank (Chile): Avda Isidora Goyenechea 2800, 23°, Santiago; tel. (2) 2299-7200; fax (2) 2299-7395; e-mail camilo.jimenez@cl.hsbc.com; internet www.hsbc.cl; f. 2003 as HSBC Bank Chile; present name adopted in 2004; cap. 92,032m., res 2,062m., dep. 815,070m. (Dec. 2013); Pres. José Manuel Dominguez; CEO and Gen. Man. Gustavo Costa.

Scotiabank Chile (Canada): Morandé 226, Casilla 90-D, Santiago; tel. (2) 2675-7776; fax (2) 2698-6008; e-mail scotiabank@scotiabank.cl; internet www.scotiabank.cl; f. 1983; fmrly Banco del Desarrollo, renamed as above in 2009; cap. 390,158m., res 39,165m., dep. 5,269,050m. (Dec. 2013); Pres. Peter Cardinal; 155 brs.

Banking Association

Asociación de Bancos e Instituciones Financieras de Chile AG: Avda Nueva Costanera 4091, 4°, Vitacura; tel. (8) 292-2800; fax (8) 292-2826; e-mail general@abif.cl; internet www.abif.cl; f. 1945; Pres. Jorge Awad M.; Gen. Man. Ricardo Matte E.

Other Financial Supervisory Bodies

Superintendencia de Administradoras de Fondos de Pensiones (SAFP) (Superintendency of Pension Funds): Avda Libertador Bernardo O'Higgins 1449, 1°, Local 8, Santiago; tel. (2) 2753-0100; fax (2) 2753-0122; internet www.safp.cl; f. 1981; Supt Alvaro Gallegos Alfonso.

Superintendencia de Seguridad Social (Superintendency of Social Security): Huérfanos 1376, 5°, Santiago; tel. (2) 2620-4500; fax (2) 2696-4672; e-mail contacto@suseso.cl; internet www.suseso.gov.cl; f. 1927; Supt Claudio Ibáñez González.

STOCK EXCHANGES

Bolsa de Comercio de Santiago: La Bolsa 64, Casilla 123-D, Santiago; tel. (2) 2399-3000; fax (2) 2318-1961; e-mail chathaway@bolsadesantiago.com; internet www.bolsadesantiago.com; f. 1893; 32 mems; Pres. Juan Andrés Camus Camus; Gen. Man. José Antonio Martínez Zugarramurdi.

Bolsa de Corredores—Valores de Valparaíso: Prat 798, Casilla 218-V, Valparaíso; tel. (32) 225-0677; fax (32) 221-2764; e-mail bolsadec.orred001@chilnet.cl; internet www.bovalpo.cl; f. 1905;

Pres. CARLOS F. MARÍN ORREGO; Man. ARIE JOEL GELFENSTEIN FREUNDLICH.

Bolsa Electrónica de Chile: Huérfanos 770, 14°, Santiago; tel. (2) 2484-0110; fax (2) 2484-0101; e-mail contactoweb@bolchile.cl; internet www.bolchile.cl; f. 1989; Pres. FERNANDO CAÑAS BERKOWITZ; Gen. Man. JUAN CARLOS SPENCER OSSA.

INSURANCE
Supervisory Authority

Superintendencia de Valores y Seguros: Avda Libertador Bernardo O'Higgins 1449, Casilla 834-0518, Santiago; tel. (2) 2617-4000; fax (2) 2617-4101; internet www.svs.cl; f. 1931; under Ministry of Finance; Supt CARLOS PAVEZ TOULOUSE.

Principal Companies

ACE Seguros, SA: Miraflores 222, 17°, Centro, Santiago; tel. (2) 2549-8300; fax (2) 2632-8289; e-mail contact.la@acegroup.com; internet www.aceseguros.cl; f. 1999; Chair. EVAN G. GREENBERG.

Aseguradora Magallanes, SA: Avda Alonso de Córdova 5151, 17° y 18°, Of. 1801, Las Condes, Santiago; tel. (2) 2715-4605; fax (2) 2715-4860; e-mail fvarela@magallanes.cl; internet www.magallanes.cl; f. 1957; general; Pres. EDUARDO DOMINGUEZ COVARRUBIAS; Gen. Man. FERNANDO VARELA VILLARROEL.

Axa Asistencia Chile: Josué Smith Solar 390, 6650378 Providencia, Santiago; tel. (2) 2941-8900; fax (2) 2941-8951; e-mail asistencia@axa-assistance.cl; internet www.axa-assistance.cl; f. 1994; general; CEO SARA GONZÁLEZ.

Cardif Chile: Vitacura 2670, 13°, Las Condes, Santiago; tel. (2) 2370-4800; fax (2) 2370-4910; e-mail cardif@cardif.cl; internet www.cardif.cl; f. 1997; owned by BNP Paribas (France); Pres. FRANCISCO VALENZUELA; Gen. Man. ALESSANDRO DEODATO.

Chilena Consolidada Seguros, SA: Avda Pedro de Valdivia 195, Casilla 16587, Correo 9, Providencia, Santiago; tel. (2) 2200-7000; fax (2) 2274-9933; internet www.chilena.cl; f. 1853; owned by Zurich group; general and life; Pres. HERNÁN FELIPE ERRÁZURIZ CORREA; Gen. Man. JOSÉ MANUEL CAMPOSANO LARRAECHEA.

Chubb de Chile Compañía de Seguros Generales, SA: Américo Vespucio Sur 100, 5°, Of. 501, Las Condes, Santiago; tel. (2) 2398-7000; fax (2) 2398-7090; e-mail chileinfo@chubb.com; internet www.chubb.com/chile; f. 1992; general; Gen. Man. CLAUDIO MARCELO ROSSI.

Cía de Seguros de Crédito Continental, SA: Avda Isidora Goyenechea 3162, 6°, Edif. Parque 1 Golf, Santiago; tel. (2) 2636-4000; fax (2) 2636-4001; e-mail seguros@continental.cl; internet www.continental.cl; f. 1990; general; Pres. VICENTE DE LA FUENTE MONTANÉ; Gen. Man. ANDRÉS MENDIETA VALENZUELA.

Cía de Seguros de Vida Cruz del Sur, SA: Avda El Golf 150, Las Condes, Santiago; tel. (2) 2461-8000; fax (2) 2461-8334; internet www.cruzdelsur.cl; f. 1992; life; CFO CARLOS MONTIGLIA.

Consorcio, SA: Edif. Consorcio, Avda El Bosque Sur 180, Las Condes, Santiago; tel. (2) 2230-4000; fax (2) 2230-4050; internet www.consorcio.cl; f. 1916; life and general insurance; Pres. JUAN BILBAO HORMAECHE; Gen. Man. NICOLÁS GELLONA AMUNATEGUI.

Euroamérica Seguros de Vida, SA: Apoquindo 3885, 20°, Las Condes, Santiago; tel. (2) 2582-3000; fax (2) 2581-7722; internet www.euroamerica.cl; f. 1962; life; Pres. NICHOLAS DAVIS LECAROS; Gen. Man. CLAUDIO ASECIO FULGERI.

HDI Seguros, SA: Encomenderos 113, Casilla 185-D, Centro 192, Las Condes, Santiago; tel. (2) 2422-9000; fax (2) 2246-7567; e-mail contacto@hdi.cl; internet www.hdi.cl; f. 1989 in Chile; general; CEO PATRICIO ALDUNATE.

ING Seguros de Vida, SA: Avda Suecia 211, 7°, Providencia, Santiago; tel. (2) 2252-1464; fax (2) 2364-2060; e-mail centro.solucionwm@ing.cl; internet www.ingvida.cl; f. 1989; life; CEO ANDRÉS CASTRO.

Mapfre Seguros: Isidora Goyenechea 3520, 14°, Casilla 7550071, Las Condes, Santiago; tel. (2) 2700-4000; fax (2) 2694-7566; internet www.mapfreseguros.cl; f. 1991; general; Gen. Man. JULIO DOMINGO SOUTO.

MetLife Chile Seguros de Vida, SA: Agustinas 640, 9°, Casilla 111, Correo Central, Santiago; tel. (2) 2640-1000; fax (2) 2640-1100; internet www.metlife.cl; f. 1980 as Seguros Interamericana; subsidiary of MetLife Inc. since 2002; Pres. OSCAR SCHMIDT; Gen. Man. ANDRÉS MERINO CANGAS.

Renta Nacional Compañías de Seguros, SA: Amunátegui 178, 2°, Centro, Santiago; tel. (2) 2670-0200; fax (2) 2670-0039; e-mail renta@rentanac.cl; internet www.rentanac.cl; f. 1982; life; Pres. FRANCISCO JAVIER ERRÁZURIZ TALAVERA.

RSA Chile (United Kingdom): Providencia 1760, 4°, Santiago; tel. (2) 2396-1000; fax (2) 2396-1291; e-mail servicioaclientes@cl.rsagroup.com; internet www.rsagroup.com; f. 2000; fmrly known as Royal & Sun Alliance Seguros; Pres. VÍCTOR MANUEL JARPA RIVEROS; Group CEO STEPHEN HESTER.

Vida Security, SA: Apoquindo 3150, 8°, Las Condes, Santiago; tel. (2) 2584-2400; internet www.vidasecurity.cl; f. 2002 through merger of Seguros Security and Seguros Previsión Vida; Pres. FRANCISCO SILVA SILVA; CEO RENATO PEÑAFIEL MUÑOZ.

Insurance Association

Asociación de Aseguradores de Chile, AG: La Concepción 322, Of. 501, Casilla 2630, Providencia, Santiago; tel. (2) 2834-4900; fax (2) 2834-4920; e-mail seguros@aach.cl; internet www.aach.cl; f. 1931; Pres. JOSÉ MANUEL L. CAMPOSANO.

Trade and Industry
GOVERNMENT AGENCIES

Comisión Nacional de Energía (CNE): Miraflores 222, 10°, Santiago; tel. (2) 2797-2600; fax (2) 2797-2627; internet www.cne.cl; Exec. Sec. JUAN MANUEL CONTRERAS SEPÚLVEDA.

Corporación de Fomento de la Producción (CORFO): Moneda 921, Casilla 3886, Santiago; tel. (2) 2631-8200; e-mail info@corfo.cl; internet www.corfo.cl; f. 1939; holding group of principal state enterprises; grants loans and guarantees to private sector; responsible for sale of non-strategic state enterprises; promotes entrepreneurship; Pres. LUIS FELIPE CÉSPEDES (Minister of the Economy, Development and Tourism); Exec. Vice-Pres. HERNÁN CHEYRE VALENZUELA; 13 brs.

PROCHILE (Dirección General de Relaciones Económicas Internacionales): Teatinos 180, Santiago; tel. (2) 2827-5100; fax (2) 2696-0639; e-mail info@prochile.cl; internet www.prochile.cl; f. 1974; bureau of international economic affairs; Dir (vacant).

Servicio Nacional de Capacitación y Empleo (SENCE) (National Training and Employment Service): Teatinos 333, 8°, Santiago; tel. (2) 2870-6222; fax (2) 2696-7103; internet www.sence.cl; attached to Ministry of Labour and Social Security; Nat. Dir JOSÉ JUAN BENNETT URRUTIA.

STATE CORPORATIONS

Corporación Nacional del Cobre de Chile (Codelco): Huérfanos 1270, Casilla 150-D, Santiago; tel. (2) 2690-3000; fax (2) 2690-3059; e-mail comunica@codelco.cl; internet www.codelco.com; f. 1976 as a state-owned enterprise with copper-producing operational divisions at Chuquicamata, Radomiro Tomić, Salvador, Andina, Talleres Rancagua and El Teniente; attached to Ministry of Mining; Chair. OSCAR LANDERRETCHE; CEO OCTAVIO ARANEDA (acting); 18,496 employees.

Empresa Nacional de Petróleo (ENAP): Vitacura 2736, 10°, Las Condes, Santiago; tel. (2) 2280-3000; fax (2) 2280-3199; e-mail webenap@enap.cl; internet www.enap.cl; f. 1950; state-owned petroleum and gas exploration and production corpn; subsidiaries include Enap Sipetrol and Enap Refinerías; Pres. MÁXIMO PACHECO MATTE (Minister of Energy); Gen. Man. RICARDO CRUZAT OCHAGAVÍA; 3,286 employees.

DEVELOPMENT ORGANIZATIONS

Comisión Chilena de Energía Nuclear: Amunátegui 95, Santiago; tel. (2) 2470-2500; fax (2) 2470-2570; e-mail oirs@cchen.cl; internet www.cchen.cl; f. 1965; govt body to develop peaceful uses of atomic energy; concentrates, regulates and controls all matters related to nuclear energy; Pres. RENATO AGURTO COLIMA; Exec. Dir JAIME SALAS KURTE.

Corporación Nacional de Desarrollo Indígena (Conadi): Aldunate 285, Temuco, Chile; tel. (45) 2641-500; fax (45) 2641-520; e-mail ctranamil@conadi.gov.cl; internet www.conadi.cl; promotes the economic and social development of indigenous communities; Nat. Dir JORGE RUBIO RETAMAL.

Corporación Nacional Forestal (CONAF): Paseo Bulnes 285, Santiago; tel. (2) 2663-0000; fax (2) 2225-0641; e-mail consulta@conaf.cl; internet www.conaf.cl; f. 1970 to promote forestry activities, enforce forestry law, promote afforestation, administer subsidies for afforestation projects and to increase and preserve forest resources; manages 13.97m. ha designated as National Parks, Natural Monuments and National Reserves; under Ministry of Agriculture; Exec. Dir EDUARDO VIAL RUIZ-TAGLE.

Empresa Nacional de Minería (ENAMI): MacIver 459, 2°, Casilla 100-D, Santiago; tel. (2) 2637-5278; fax (2) 2637-5452; e-mail eiturra@enami.cl; internet www.enami.cl; promotes the devt of small and medium-sized mines; attached to Ministry of Mining; partially privatized; Exec. Vice-Pres. FELIPE BARROS.

CHAMBERS OF COMMERCE

Cámara Chileno China de Comercio, Industria y Turismo: Morandé 322, Of. 502, Santiago; tel. (2) 2673-0304; fax (2) 2697-1510; e-mail camara@chicit.cl; internet www.chicit.cl; f. 1997; Pres. JUAN ESTEBAN MUSALEM AIACH.

Cámara de Comercio de Santiago: Edif. Del Comercio, Monjitas 392, Santiago; tel. (2) 2360-7000; fax (2) 2633-3595; e-mail cpn@ccs.cl; internet www.ccs.cl; f. 1919; 1,300 mems; Pres. PETER HILL D.; Sec.-Gen. CRISTIAN GARCÍA-HUIDOBRO.

Cámara de Comercio, Servicios y Turismo de Antofagasta: Latorre 2580, 3°, Of. 21, Antofagasta; tel. (55) 2225-175; fax (55) 2222-053; e-mail info@ccantof.cl; internet www.ccantof.cl; f. 1924; Pres. GIANCARLO CORONATO MACKENZIE; Co-ordinator Gen. MARCELA REY LEVA.

Cámara de Comercio, Servicios y Turismo de Temuco, AG: Vicuña Mackenna 396, Temuco; tel. (45) 221-0556; fax (45) 223-7047; e-mail secretaria@camaratemuco.cl; internet www.camaratemuco.cl; Pres. JORGE ARGANDOÑA RAMOS; Gen. Man. RUBÉN RIOS ROJAS.

Cámara Nacional de Comercio, Servicios y Turismo de Chile: Merced 230, Santiago; tel. (2) 2365-4000; fax (2) 2365-4001; internet www.cnc.cl; f. 1858; Pres. RICARDO MEWES; Sec.-Gen. JAIME ALÉ YARAD; 120 mems.

Cámara de la Producción y del Comercio de Concepción: Cauplicán 567, 2°, Concepción; tel. (41) 224-1121; fax (41) 224-1440; e-mail lmandiola@cpcc.cl; internet www.cpcc.cl; f. 1927; Pres. ALBERTO MIRANDA GUERRA; Gen. Man. LEONCIO TORO ARAYA.

INDUSTRIAL AND TRADE ASSOCIATIONS

Asociación de Exportadores de Frutas de Chile, AG (ASOEX): Cruz del Sur 133, Of. 904, Las Condes, Santiago; tel. (2) 2472-4778; internet www.asoex.cl; f. 1935; Pres. RONALD BOWN.

Servicio Agrícola y Ganadero (SAG): Avda Bulnes 140, 8°, Santiago; tel. (2) 2345-1100; fax (2) 2345-1102; e-mail dirnac@sag.gob.cl; internet www.sag.cl; under Ministry of Agriculture; responsible for the protection and devt of safe practice in the sector; Nat. Dir ANÍBAL ARIZTÍA REYES.

Servicio Nacional de Pesca y Acuicultura (SERNAPESCA): Victoria 2832, Valparaíso; tel. (32) 281-9100; fax (32) 225-6311; e-mail informaciones@sernapesca.cl; internet www.sernapesca.cl; f. 1978; govt regulator of the fishing industry; Nat. Dir JUAN LUIS ANSOLEAGA BENGOECHEA.

Sociedad Agrícola y Servicios Isla de Pascua (SASIPA): Hotu Matu'a s/n, Hanga Roa, Isla de Pascua; tel. (32) 210-0212; e-mail atencion@sasipa.cl; internet www.sasipa.cl; f. 1966; administers agriculture and public services on Easter Island; Pres. DANIEL TOMÁS PLATOVSKY TUREK; Gen. Man. PEDRO HEY ICKA.

EMPLOYERS' ORGANIZATIONS

Confederación del Comercio Detallista y Turismo de Chile, AG (CONFEDECH): Merced 380, 8°, Of. 74, Santiago; tel. (2) 2639-1264; fax (2) 2638-0338; e-mail comerciodetallista@confedech.cl; internet www.confedech.cl; f. 1938; retail trade; Nat. Pres. RAFAEL CUMSILLE ZAPAPA; Sec.-Gen. PEDRO ZAMORANO PIÑATS.

Confederación Nacional de Dueños de Camiones de Chile (CNDC): Santiago; internet www.cndc.cl; represents 39,000 truck cos; Pres. JUAN ARAYA JOFRÉ.

Confederación de la Producción y del Comercio: Monseñor Sótero Sanz 182, Providencia, Santiago; tel. (2) 2231-9764; fax (2) 2231-9808; e-mail procomer@entelchile.net; internet www.cpc.cl; f. 1936; Pres. ANDRÉS SANTA CRUZ LÓPEZ; Gen. Man. FERNANDO ALVEAR ARTAZA.

Affiliated organizations:

Asociación de Bancos e Instituciones Financieras de Chile AG: see Finance (Banking Association).

Cámara Nacional de Comercio, Servicios y Turismo de Chile: see Chambers of Commerce.

Cámara Chilena de la Construcción (CChC): Marchant Pereira 10, 3°, Providencia, CP 6640721, Santiago; tel. (2) 2376-3300; fax (2) 2371-3430; internet www.cchc.cl; f. 1951; Pres. DANIEL HURTADO PAROT; 17,442 mems.

Sociedad de Fomento Fabril, FG (SOFOFA): Avda Andrés Bello 2777, 3°, Las Condes, Santiago; tel. (2) 2391-3100; fax (2) 2391-3200; e-mail sofofa@sofofa.cl; internet www.sofofa.cl; f. 1883; largest employers' org.; Pres. HERMAN VON MÜHLENBROCK SOTO; Sec.-Gen. CRISTÓBAL PHILIPPI IRARRAZÁVAL; 2,500 mems.

Sociedad Nacional de Agricultura—Federación Gremial (SNA): Tenderini 187, 2°, CP 6500978, Santiago; tel. (2) 2639-6710; fax (2) 2633-7771; e-mail comunicaciones@sna.cl; internet www.sna.cl; f. 1838; landowners' asscn; controls Radio Stations CB 57 and XQB8 (FM) in Santiago, CB-97 in Valparaíso, CD-120 in

Los Angeles, CA-144 in La Serena, CD-127 in Temuco; Pres. PATRICIO CRESPO URETA; Sec.-Gen. JUAN PABLO MATTE FUENTES.

Sociedad Nacional de Minería (SONAMI): Avda Apoquindo 3000, 5°, Santiago; tel. (2) 2335-9300; fax (2) 2334-9700; e-mail monica.cavallini@sonami.cl; internet www.sonami.cl; f. 1883; Pres. ALBERTO SALAS MUÑOZ; Gen. Man. FELIPE CELEDÓN MARDONES; 48 mem. cos.

CONUPIA (Confederación Gremial Nacional Unida de la Mediana y Pequeña Industria, Servicios y Artesanado): Phillips 40, 6°, Of. 63, Providencia, Santiago; tel. (2) 2633-1492; e-mail secgeneral@conupia.cl; internet www.conupia.cl; f. 1966; small and medium-sized industries and crafts; Pres. PEDRO DAVIS URZÚA; Sec.-Gen. JOSÉ LUIS RAMÍREZ ZAMORANO.

MAJOR COMPANIES

Petroleum and Mining

Antofagasta Minerals, SA: Avda Apoquindo 4001, 18°, Las Condes, Santiago; tel. (2) 2798-7000; fax (2) 2798-7402; e-mail contacto@aminerals.cl; internet www.aminerals.cl; subsidiary of Antofagasta PLC, United Kingdom; copper mining; operations in Michilla, El Tesoro, Esperanza and Los Pelambres; Chair. JEAN-PAUL LUKSIC; CEO DIEGO HERNÁNDEZ; 1,736 employees.

Cía de Petróleos de Chile, SA (COPEC): Agustinas 1382, 1°–7°, Casilla 9391, Santiago 6500586; tel. (2) 2690-7000; fax (2) 2672-5119; e-mail icontact@copec.cl; internet www.copec.cl; f. 1934; mfrs of petroleum products; owned by Angelini group following privatization in 1986; Pres. ROBERTO ANGELINI ROSSI; Gen. Man. LORENZO GAZMURI SCHLEYER; 8,500 employees.

Minera Escondida Ltda: Avda Américo Vespucio Sur 100, 9°, Las Condes, Santiago; tel. (2) 2330-5000; fax (2) 2207-6520; internet www.escondida.cl; f. 1985; 57.5% owned by BHP Billiton (Australia), 30% owned by Rio Tinto PLC (United Kingdom); copper mining and cathodes production; Pres. EDGAR BASTO; 2,189 employees.

Sociedad Punta del Cobre, SA (PUCOBRE): Avda El Bosque Sur 130, 14°, Las Condes, Santiago; tel. (2) 2379-4560; fax (2) 2379-4570; e-mail info@pucobre.cl; internet www.pucobre.cl; f. 1989; copper processing; Chair. JUAN HURTADO VICUÑA; Gen. Man. SEBASTIAN RÍOS RIVAS; 360 employees.

Sociedad Química y Minera de Chile, SA (SQM, SA): El Trovador 4285, Las Condes, Santiago; tel. (2) 2425-2000; fax (2) 2425-2060; e-mail admin_web@sqm.cl; internet www.sqm.cl; f. 1968; mining co; nitrates, etc.; Pres. JULIO PONCE LEROU; CEO PATRICIO CONTESSE GONZÁLEZ; 3,418 employees.

Soprocal, Calerías e Industrias, SA: Avda Pedro de Valdivia 0193, Of. 31, Providencia, Santiago; tel. (2) 2231-8874; fax (2) 2233-3396; e-mail info@soprocal.cl; internet www.soprocal.cl; f. 1940; producers of lime; Exec. Chair. ALFONSO ROZAS OSSA; Gen. Man. ALFONSO ROZAS RODRÍGUEZ; 72 employees.

Food and Beverages

Agrícola Nacional, SACEI (ANASAC): Almirante Pastene 300, Providencia, Santiago; tel. (2) 2470-6800; fax (2) 2470-6860; e-mail info@anasac.cl; internet www.anasac.cl; f. 1948; food, agricultural chemicals and pest control; Chair. FERNANDO MARTÍNEZ PÉREZ-CANTO; CEO LUIS MARCELO BECONI; 553 employees.

Blumar, SA: Avda Presidente Riesco 5711, Of. 1201, Las Condes, Santiago; tel. (2) 2782-5400; fax (2) 2231-0973; e-mail info@blumar.com; internet www.blumar.com; f. 1948; fmrly Pesquera Itata; name changed as above 2012 following merger between Itata and El Golfo; fish and fish products; Pres. RODRIGO SARQUIS SAID; Gen. Man. GERARDO BALBONTÍN; 307 employees.

Cervecera CCU Chile Ltda: Vitacura 2670, 20°-27°, Las Condes, Santiago; tel. (2) 2427-3000; fax (2) 2427-3333; e-mail ccuir@ccu-sa.com; internet www.ccu.cl; f. 1902; part of Quiñenco conglomerate; 20% owned by Anheuser Busch of the USA; beverages; Gen. Man. PATRICIO JOTTAR; 4,500 employees.

Coca-Cola Embonor, SA: Santa María 2652, Arica; tel. (5) 2820-2400; internet www.embonor.cl; f. 1943; bottling co for Coca-Cola; Chair. ANDRÉS VICUÑA GARCÍA-HUIDOBRO; Gen. Man. JOSE DOMINGO JARAMILLO JIMENEZ; 4,193 employees.

Concha y Toro, SA: Avda Nueva Tajamar 481, Torre Norte, 15°, Santiago; tel. (2) 2476-5000; fax (2) 2203-6740; e-mail conchaytoro@banfivintners.com; internet www.conchaytoro.com; f. 1883; vintners; Chair. ALFONSO LARRAÍN; CEO EDUARDO GUILISASTI GANA.

Copefrut, SA: Panamericana Sur, Km 185, Curicó; tel. (2) 2209-220; fax (2) 2380-905; e-mail copefrut@copefrut.cl; internet www.copefrut.cl; f. 1955; fruit producers and exporters; Chair. JOSÉ LUIS SOLER RUIZ; Gen. Man. FERNANDO CISTERNAS LIRA; 309 employees.

CORPESCA, SA: Avda El Golf 150, 15°, Las Condes, Santiago; tel. (2) 2476-4000; internet www.corpesca.cl; f. 1955; fish oil and flour producers; Chair. ROBERTO ANGELINI ROSSI; Gen. Man. ARTURO NATHO GAMBOA; 600 employees.

Dos en Uno, SA: Placer 1324, Santiago; tel. (2) 2520-8700; e-mail arcor@dosenuno.cl; internet www.dosenuno.cl; f. 1989; part of Grupo Arcor (Argentina); makers of biscuits, cakes, etc.; CEO JOSÉ MIGUEL LECUMBERRI B.; 1,700 employees.

Embotelladora Andina, SA (Coca-Cola Andina Chile): Avda Carlos Valdovinos 560, San Joaquín, Santiago; tel. (2) 2462-2486; e-mail andina.ir@koandina.com; internet www.koandina.com; f. 1946; bottling co for Coca-Cola; Chair. JUAN CLARO GONZÁLEZ; Gen. Man. JOSÉ LUIS SOLORZANO; 1,732 employees.

Empresas Iansa, SA: Rosario Norte 615, 23°, Las Condes, Santiago; tel. (2) 2571-5400; fax (2) 2565-5525; e-mail iansa@iansa.cl; internet www.empresasiansa.cl; f. 1953; sugar production, frozen fruit and vegetables, fruit juices, animal feed; fmrly known as Industria Azucarera Nacional, SA; Chair. JOAQUÍN NOGUERA WILSON; CEO JOSÉ LUIS IRARRÁZAVAL OVALLE; 1,255 employees (Dec. 2004).

Iansagro, SA: Km 385 Panamericana Sur, San Carlos, Chillán; tel. (42) 2454-300; fax (42) 2454-338; internet www.iansagro.cl; agricultural produce and animal feed; owned by Empresas Iansa, SA; Gen. Man. ALVARO PRIETO; 2,173 employees.

Empresas Santa Carolina, SA: Rodrigo de Araya 1431, Macul, Santiago; tel. (2) 2450-3000; fax (2) 2238-0307; internet www.santacarolina.cl; f. 1874; wine producers; part of Watts, SA, group; Gen. Man. SANTIAGO LARRAÍN CRUZAT; 1,117 employees.

Fruticola Viconto, SA: Avda Apoquindo 4775, 16°, Las Condes, Santiago; tel. (2) 2707-4200; fax (2) 2707-4250; e-mail viconto@viconto.cl; internet www.viconto.cl; f. 1986; wholesale fruit exporters; Pres. CARLOS GUILLERMO SOUPER URRA; Gen. Man. JOSÉ ANTONIO RODRÍGUEZ; 200 employees.

Industrias Alimentícias Carozzi, SA: Camino Longitudinal Sur 5201, Km 23, Casilla 70, San Bernardo, Santiago; tel. (2) 2377-6400; fax (2) 2377-6635; internet www.carozzi.cl; f. 1898; food-processing; Pres. GONZALO BOFILL VELARDE; Gen. Man. JOSÉ JUAN LLUGANY RIGORIGHY; 5,584 employees.

LDC Trading & Services Chile Ltda: Cerro El Plomo 5420, Of. 1102, 11°, Las Condes, Santiago; tel. (2) 361-0474; e-mail SAN-Metals@ldccom.com; internet www.ldc.com.ar/ldc_chile.php; f. 2008; Group Chair. MARGARITA LOUIS-DREYFUS; Man. (Latin America) GONZALO RAMIREZ MARTIARENA.

Sociedad Pesquera Coloso, SA: Avda El Bosque Norte 0440, 9°, Las Condes, Santiago; tel. (2) 2371-2600; fax (2) 2203-5001; e-mail caracena@coloso.cl; internet www.coloso.cl; processed fish exporters; owners of Pesquera San José, SA; Pres. SERGIO LECAROS MENÉNDEZ; CEO RAFAEL LEONARDO SEPULVEDA RUIZ; 731 employees.

Viña Errázuriz, SA: Avda Nueva Tajamar 481, Torre Sur, Of. 503, Torre Sur, Las Condes, Santiago; tel. (2) 2339-9100; fax (2) 2203-6690; e-mail wine.report@errazuriz.cl; internet www.errazuriz.com; f. 1870; wine producers; Pres. EDUARDO CHADWICK; CEO ANDRÉS IZQUIERDO; 180 employees.

Viña San Pedro, SA: Avda Vitacura 4380, 16°, Vitacura, Santiago; tel. (2) 2477-5300; fax (2) 2477-5307; e-mail info@vsptwines.com; internet www.sanpedro.cl; f. 1865; wine producers; part of Grupo San Pedro Tarapacá; Pres. PABLO GRANIFO LAVÍN; Gen. Man. PEDRO HERANE AGUADO; 347 employees.

Viña Undurraga, SA: Camino A, Melipilla, Km 34, Talagante; tel. (2) 2372-2900; fax (2) 2372-2956; e-mail info@undurraga.cl; internet www.undurraga.cl; f. 1885; wine producers; Pres. MAURICIO PICCIOTTO KASSIN; Gen. Man. ERNESTO MÜLLER AGUADO; 576 employees.

Viñedos Emiliana, SA: Edif. World Trade Center, Avda Nueva Tajamar 481, Las Condes, Santiago; tel. (2) 2353-9130; fax (2) 2203-6936; e-mail info@emiliana.cl; internet www.emiliana.cl; f. 1986; wines and spirits producers; Chair. RAFAEL GUILISASATI GANA; Gen. Man JOSÉ GUILISASTI GANA; 508 employees.

Wood, Pulp and Paper

Celulosa Arauco y Constitución, SA (ARAUCO): El Golf 150, 14°, Las Condes, Santiago; tel. (2) 2461-7200; fax (2) 2698-5967; internet www.arauco.cl; f. 1967; wood pulp and timber group; operations in Argentina and Brazil; CEO MANUEL ENRIQUE BEZANILLA; Pres. CRISTIÁN INFANTE; 35,000 employees.

Empresas CMPC, SA: Agustinas 1343, Santiago; tel. (2) 2441-2000; fax (2) 2672-1115; e-mail pfriedl@gerencia.cmpc.cl; internet www.cmpc.cl; f. 1920; paper and packaging mfrs, cellulose, wood products and pulp; Chair. ELIODORO MATTE; Gen. Man. HERNÁN RODRÍGUEZ WILSON; 11,919 employees.

Industrias Forestales, SA: Agustinas 1357, 9°, Santiago; tel. (2) 2441-2050; fax (2) 2695-7809; internet www.inforsa.cl; f. 1956; paper producers; acquired by Empresas CMPC in 2011; Pres. EDUARDO SERRANO SPOERER; 372 employees.

Construction Materials

Besalco, SA: Ebro 2705, Las Condes, Santiago; tel. (2) 2338-0800; fax (2) 2334-4031; e-mail besalco@besalco.cl; internet www.besalco

.cl; f. 1944; civil engineering and construction; Pres. VICTOR BEZANILLA SAAVEDRA; Gen. Man. PAULO BEZANILLA SAAVEDRA; 7,200 employees.

Cementos Bío-Bío, SA: Barros Errazuriz 1968, 4°, Casilla 16603, Providencia, Santiago; tel. (2) 2560-7000; fax (2) 2560-7051; internet www.cbb.cl; f. 1957; cement, forestry and raw materials; Pres. HERNÁN BRIANES GOICH; CEO JORGE MATUS CAMPOS; 1,128 employees.

Cerámicas Cordillera, SA: Avda Lo Boza 120A, Pudahuel, Santiago; tel. (2) 2387-4200; fax (2) 2387-4321; e-mail cemento@melon.lafarge.cl; internet www.cordillera.cl; f. 1984; tiles, building materials; owned by Empresas Pizarreño, SA; Pres. JORGE BENNETT URRUTIA; Gen. Man. ROBERTO CALCAGNI GONZÁLEZ; 243 employees.

Cía Industrial El Volcán, SA: Agustinas 1357, 10°, Santiago; tel. (2) 2483-0500; fax (2) 2380-9710; internet www.volcan.cl; f. 1916; makers of insulation and gypsum products; Pres. BERNARDO MATTE LARRAÍN; Gen. Man. ANTONIO SABUGAL ARMIJO; 287 employees.

Edelpa, SA (Envases del Pacífico, SA): Camino a Melipilla 13320, Maipú, Santiago 45; tel. (2) 2385-4500; fax (2) 2385-4600; e-mail comercial@edelpa.cl; internet www.edelpa.cl; f. 1984; plastic packaging and bottling producers; owners of Italprint, SA; Chair. RENATO RAMÍREZ FERNÁNDEZ; Gen. Man. JAIME SILVACRUZ; 506 employees.

Empresas Pizarreño, SA: Camino a Melipilla 10803, Maipú, Santiago; tel. (2) 2391-2401; fax (2) 2391-2402; e-mail info@pizarreno.cl; internet www.pizarreno.cl; f. 1935; owned by Etex of Belgium; plastic building materials; controls Cerámica Cordillera, SA; Chair. CANIO CORBO LIOI; Gen. Man. RODRIGO PALACIOS; 2,553 employees.

Grupo Polpaico, SA: Avda El Bosque Norte 0177, Las Condes, Santiago; tel. (2) 2696-9039; fax (2) 2699-4597; internet www.holcim.cl; f. 1948; jtly owned by GASCO and Holcim of Switzerland; Gen. Man. MAURICIO ECHEVERRI; 1,213 employees.

Melón SA: Vitacura 2939, Las Condes, Santiago; tel. (2) 2280-0000; fax (2) 2280-0412; internet www.melon.cl; f. 1908 as Empresas Melón, SA; renamed Lafarge Chile in 2007; acquired by Grupo Brescia (Perú) and adopted present name in 2009; mfrs of cement; Pres. ALEX PAUL BRESCIA; Gen. Man. JORGE EUGENÍN ULLOA; 77,000 employees (group).

Metals and Chemicals

Aceros Chile, SA: Avda Diego Portales Oriente 3499-A, Casilla 808-0776, San Bernardo, Santiago; tel. (2) 2483-8700; fax (2) 2483-8701; e-mail web@aceroschile.cl; internet www.aceroschile.cl; f. 1980; steelmakers; Gen. Man. HUGO GAIDO; 188 employees.

CAP, SA: Gertrudis Echeñique 220, Las Condes, Santiago; tel. (2) 2818-6000; fax (2) 2818-6116; e-mail webmaster@cap.cl; internet www.cap.cl; f. 1946; steel producer and exporter; Pres. ROBERTO DE ANDRACA; CEO FERNANDO REITICH; 4,746 employees.

Enaex, SA: El Trovador 4253, Las Condes, Santiago; tel. (2) 2837-7600; fax (2) 2206-6752; e-mail enaex@enaex.cl; internet www.enaex.cl; f. 1920; industrial chemicals, incl. explosives; Chair. JUAN EDUARDO ERRÁRUIZ OSSA; Gen. Man. JUAN ANDRÉS ERRÁZURIZ DOMÍNGUEZ; 863 employees.

Instituto Sanitas, SA: Avda Américo Vespucio Norte 01260, Quilicura, Santiago; tel. (2) 2444-6600; fax (2) 2444-6651; e-mail sanitas@sanitas.cl; internet www.sanitas.cl; f. 1920; medicines and vaccines; Chair. JOAQUÍN BARROS FONTAINE; 171 employees.

Laboratorio Chile, SA: Avda Maratón 1315, Nuñoa, Santiago; tel. (2) 2365-5000; fax (2) 2365-5100; e-mail pilar.rodriguez@labchile.cl; internet www.labchile.cl; f. 1896; pharmaceutical co; mem. of the Teva Group (Israel); CEO HERNÁN PFEIFER FRENZ; 1,000 employees.

Madeco, SA: Avda Presidente Eduardo Frei Montalva 9160, Quilicura, Santiago; tel. (2) 2679-3200; fax (2) 2520-1140; e-mail cgt@madeco.cl; internet www.madeco.cl; f. 1944; metallurgy and packaging; part of Quiñenco conglomerate; Chair. FELIPE JOANNON VERGARA; Gen. Man. CLAUDIO INGLESI NIETO; 2,949 employees.

ME Elecmetal, SA (Cía Electro Metalúrgica-Elecmetal): Avda Vicuña Mackenna 1570, Nuñoa, Santiago; tel. (2) 2361-4020; fax (2) 2361-4021; e-mail ventas@elecmetal.com; internet www.me-elecmetal.com; f. 1917; metal foundry, manufactures parts for heavy machinery; part of Cristalchile group; Chair. JAIME ARTURO CLARO VALDES; Gen. Man. ROLANDO MEDEIROS SOUX; 3,653 employees.

Molymet, SA (Molibdenos y Metales, SA): Camino nos a los Morros 66, San Bernardo, Santiago; tel. (2) 2937-6600; fax (2) 2937-6653; e-mail info@molymet.cl; internet www.molymet.cl; f. 1975; producers of industrial chemicals and ferroalloy ores; Chair. CARLOS HURTADO RUIZ-TAGLE; CEO JOHN GRAELL MOORE; 602 employees.

Tricolor, SA: Avda Claudio Arrau 9440, Pudahuel, Santiago; tel. (2) 2290-8700; fax (2) 2601-0055; e-mail sac@tricolor.cl; internet www.tricolor.cl; part of Grupo CB conglomerate; paint; f. 1937; Gen. Man. ROBERTO LEHMANN COSOI; 606 employees.

Textiles

Bata Chile, SA: Camino a Melipilla 9460, Maipú, Santiago; tel. (2) 2560-4200; fax (2) 2533-2931; e-mail bsochile@bata.cl; internet www .bata.cl; f. 1939; mfrs and distributors of sportswear and shoes; Chair. FERNANDO RIVERA JIMÉNEZ; Gen. Man. LUIS ERNESTO ROJAS; 2,132 employees.

Retail

Cencosud, SA: Avda Kennedy 9001, 6°, Las Condes, Santiago; tel. (2) 2959-0000; fax (2) 2212-1469; e-mail contactoscl@cencosud.cl; internet www.cencosud.cl; f. 1952; retail conglomerate; Chilean concerns incl. Jumbo (hypermarkets), Santa Isabel (supermarkets), Easy (home improvement stores) and Paris (dept stores); operations in Argentina, Brazil, Colombia and Peru; Chair. HORST PAULMANN KEMNA; CEO DANIEL RODRÍGUEZ COFRÉ.

Falabella, SACI: Rosas 1665, Santiago; tel. (2) 2620-2000; fax (2) 2620-2000; internet www.falabella.cl; f. 1889; dept stores and textiles; Pres. JUAN CUNEO SOLARI; CEO SANDRO SOLARI DONAGGIO; 13,935 employees.

Sodimac, SA: Avda Presidente Eduardo Frei 3092, Renca, Casilla 3110, Santiago; tel. (2) 2738-1000; fax (2) 2641-8271; internet www .sodimac.cl; f. 1982; home improvement products retailers; Chair. JUAN PABLO DEL RÍO GOUDIE; CEO ENRIQUE GUNDERMANN; 20,000 employees.

Walmart Chile, SA: Avda Eduardo Frei Montalva 8301, Quilicura, Santiago 7490562; tel. (2) 2200-5000; fax (2) 2200-5100; e-mail info@ dys.cl; internet www.dys.cl; f. 1893; fmrly Distribución y Servicio, SA; supermarket group, owns Ekono and Líder chains; Chair. FELIPE IBÁÑEZ SCOTT; Gen. Man. GIAN CARLO NUCCI; 17,000 employees.

Information Technology

Adexus, SA: Miraflores 383, 8°, Santiago; tel. (2) 2686-1000; fax (2) 2686-1201; e-mail adexus@adexus.cl; internet www.adexus.com; information technology systems contractors; f. 1990 as Tandem Chile, SA; name changed 1998; CEO CARLOS BUSSO VYHMEISTER; 500 employees.

Sonda, SA: Teatinos 500, Santiago; tel. (2) 2657-5000; fax (2) 2657-5410; e-mail info@sonda.com; internet www.sonda.com; f. 1974; information technology services; Pres. ANDRÉS NAVARRO HAEUSSLER; Gen. Man RAÚL VÉJAR OLEA; 2,400 employees.

Miscellaneous

Cía Chilena de Fósforos, SA: Los Conquistadores 1700, 15°, Providencia, Santiago; tel. (2) 2707-6200; fax (2) 2231-5072; e-mail ventas@fosforos.cl; internet www.fosforos.cl; f. 1913; makers of safety matches and producers of wine; Pres. JOSÉ LUIS VENDER BRESCIANI; Gen. Man. VIVIANA HORTA POMETTO; 1,776 employees.

Cía Chilena de Tabacos, SA (Chiletabacos): Avda Suiza 244, Cerrillos, Santiago; tel. (2) 2464-6000; fax (2) 2464-6241; internet www.chiletabacos.cl; f. 1909; subsidiary of British American Tobacco Co Ltd, United Kingdom; tobacco co; Pres. CARLOS FRANCISCO CÁCERES CONTRERAS; Gen. Man. FABIO LIMA; 752 employees.

Cía Tecno Industrial, SA (CTI, SA): Alberto Llona 777, Maipú, Santiago; tel. (2) 2837-6000; fax (2) 2532-8773; e-mail wadm@cti.cl; internet www.cti.cl; f. 1905; mfrs of domestic electrical appliances; Chair. JUAN EDUARDO ERRÁZURIZ OSSA; CEO MARIO RODRIGO OPORTUS MORALES; 1,254 employees.

Cías CIC, SA: Avda Esquina Blanca 960, Maipú, Santiago; tel. (2) 2530-4000; fax (2) 2530-4558; e-mail servicio@cic.cl; internet www .cic.cl; f. 1912; exporters of wooden furniture, mattresses, etc.; Chair. LEONIDAS VIAL ECHEVERRÍA; Gen. Man. MIGUEL VALENZUELA LAGOS; 994 employees.

Cristalerías de Chile, SA (Cristalchile, SA): Apoquindo 3669, 16°, Las Condes, Santiago; tel. (2) 2787-8888; fax (2) 2787-8800; e-mail gerencia@cristalchile.cl; internet www.cristalchile.cl; f. 1904; bottle and packaging producers; the group also controls winemakers Santa Rita, the *Diario Financiero* newspaper and the Megavisión television network; Chair. BALTAZAR SÁNCHEZ GUZMÁN; CEO CIRILO ELTON GONZÁLEZ; 700 employees.

Sociedad El Tattersall, SA: Isidora Goyenechea 3600, 5°, Las Condes, Santiago; tel. (2) 2362-3005; fax (2) 2362-3002; e-mail sociedad@tattersall.cl; internet www.tattersall.cl; f. 1913; distributors of agricultural machinery; also represent Budget car rentals in Chile; Chair. TOMÁS BÖTTIGER MÜLLER; Gen. Man. JORGE RODRÍGUEZ CIFUENTES; 501 employees.

Somela, SA: Avda Escobar Williams 600, Cerillos, Santiago; tel. (2) 2837-6600; fax (2) 2557-5667; e-mail contacto@somela.cl; internet www.somela.cl; f. 1950; mfrs of domestic appliances; Chair. JOAO CLAUDIO GUETTER; Gen. Man. PABLO ARRIAGADA CASTILLO; 183 employees.

UTILITIES

Comisión Nacional de Energía: see Government Agencies.

Superintendencia de Electricidad y Combustibles (SEC): Avda Libertador Bernardo O'Higgins 1449, 13°, Torre 1, Santiago; tel. (2) 2756-5149; fax (2) 2756-5155; e-mail pchotzen@sec.cl; internet www.sec.cl; Supt LUIS AVILA BRAVO.

Electricity

AES Gener, SA: Mariano Sánchez Fontecilla 310, 3°, Las Condes, Santiago; tel. (2) 2686-8900; fax (2) 2686-8991; e-mail gener@gener .cl; internet www.gener.cl; f. 1981 as Chilectra Generación, SA; privatized in 1988; current name adopted in 1998; owned by AES Corpn (USA); responsible for operation of power plants at Renca, Ventanas, Laguna Verde, El Indio, Altalfal, Maitenes, Queltehues and Volcán; Pres. ANDRÉS RICARDO GLUSKI WEILERT; Gen. Man. LUIS FELIPE CERÓN CERÓN; 1,121 employees (group).

Eléctrica Santiago: Jorge Hirmas 2964, Renca, Santiago; tel. (2) 2680-4760; fax (2) 2680-4743; e-mail electricasantiago@aes.com; internet www.electricasantiago.cl; f. 1994; operates the Renca and the Nueva Renca thermoelectric plants in Santiago; installed capacity of 379 MW; Pres. VICENTE JAVIER GIORGIO; Gen. Man. RODRIGO OSORIO BÓRQUEZ.

Empresa Eléctrica Guacolda, SA: Avda Apoquindo 3885, 10°, Las Condes, Santiago; tel. (2) 2362-4000; fax (2) 2464-3560; internet www.guacolda.cl; operates a thermoelectric power station in Huasco; installed capacity of 304 MW; Pres. JORGE RODRÍGUEZ GROSSI; Gen. Man. MARCO ARRÓSPIDE RIVERA.

Energía Verde: Mariano Sánchez Fontecilla 310, 3°, Las Condes, Santiago; tel. (43) 2402-700; fax (43) 2402-709; internet www .energiaverde.cl; operates 2 co-generation power stations at Constitución and Laja and a steam plant at Nacimiento; supplies the Cabrero industrial plant; CEO ARIEL ARMAN LAPUS.

Norgener, SA: Jorge Hirmas 2960, Renca, Santiago; tel. (2) 2680-4710; fax (2) 2680-4868; northern subsidiary supplying the mining industry; Exec. Dir JUAN CARLOS OLMEDO HIDALGO.

Arauco Generación: El Golf 150, 14°, Las Condes, Santiago; tel. (2) 2461-7200; fax (2) 2698-5967; e-mail gic@arauco.cl; internet www .arauco.cl; f. 1994 to commercialize surplus power from pulp processing facility; Pres. MANUEL ENRIQUE BEZANILLA; Gen. Man. CRISTIÁN INFANTE.

Chilquinta Energía, SA: Avda Argentina 1, 9°, Casilla 12v, Valparaíso; tel. (32) 245-2000; fax (32) 245-2820; e-mail contactoweb@chilquinta.cl; internet www.chilquinta.cl; f. 1997 as Energas, SA; present name adopted in 2001; owned by Inversiones Sempra and PSEG of the USA; Pres. LUIS EDUARDO PAUWLUSZEK; Gen. Man. FRANCISCO MUALIM TIETZ.

Compañía Eléctrica del Litoral, SA: Avda Peñablanca 540, Algarrobo, Casilla 14454, Santiago; tel. (2) 2481-195; fax (2) 2483-313; e-mail fmartine@litoral.cl; internet www.litoral.cl; f. 1949; Gen. Man. JUAN CARLOS BAEZA.

Compañía General de Electricidad, SA (CGE): Teatinos 280, Santiago; tel. (2) 2680-7000; fax (2) 2680-7104; e-mail contacto@cge .cl; internet www.cge.cl; installed capacity of 662 MW; Pres. JORGE EDUARDO MARÍN CORREA; Gen. Man. EDUARDO MORANDÉ.

Compañía Nacional de Fuerza Eléctrica, SA (CONAFE): Norte 13, Of. 810, Viña del Mar; tel. (32) 220-6100; fax (32) 227-1593; e-mail serviciocliente@conafe.cl; internet www.conafe.cl; f. 1945; Pres. JOSÉ LUIS HORNAUER HERRMANN; Gen. Man. ALFONSO TORO.

E-CL, SA (Energía Esencial): El Bosque Norte 500, 9°, Vitacura, Santiago; tel. (2) 2353-3200; fax (2) 2353-3210; e-mail contacto@ edelnor.cl; internet www.e-cl.cl; f. 1981; acquired by Codelco and Tractebel, SA (Belgium) in 2002; fmrly Edelnor, changed name as above in 2010 following merger with Electroandina; Pres. JUAN CLAVERÍA; Gen. Man. LODEWIJK VERDEYEN.

Empresa Eléctrica de Magallanes, SA (Edelmag, SA): Croacia 444, Punta Arenas; tel. (71) 271-4000; fax (71) 271-4077; e-mail edelmag@edelmag.cl; internet www.edelmag.cl; f. 1981; 55% owned by CGE; Pres. JORGE JORDAN FRANULIC; Gen. Man. CARLOS YÁNEZ ANTONUCCI.

Empresas Emel, SA: Avda Libertador Bernardo O'Higgins 886, 10°, Santiago; tel. (2) 2344-8000; fax (2) 2344-8001; internet www.emel.cl; holding co for the Emel group of electricity cos, bought by CGE in 2007; Gen. Man. ANDRÉS SWETT; Emel group includes:

ELECDA (Empresa Eléctrica de Antofagasta, SA): José Miguel Carrera 1587, Antofagasta 1250; tel. (55) 268-1401; internet www .elecda.cl; Regional Man. ORLANDO ASSAD MANRÍQUEZ.

ELIQSA (Empresa Eléctrica de Iquique, SA): Zegeres 469, Iquique; tel. (57) 240-5400; fax (57) 242-7181; e-mail eliqsa@eliqsa.cl; internet www.eliqsa.cl; Pres. PABLO GUARDA BARROS; Regional Man. JUAN CARLOS GÓMEZ GAMBOA.

EMELARI (Empresa Eléctrica de Arica, SA): Baquedano 731, Arica; tel. (58) 2201-100; fax (58) 223-1105; internet www.emelari .cl; Gen Man. IVÁN MELÉNDEZ VARGAS.

EMELAT (Empresa Eléctrica Atacama, SA): Circunvalación Ignacio Carrera Pinto 51, Copiapó; tel. (52) 220-5111; fax (52) 220-5103; internet www.emelat.cl; f. 1981; distribution co; Gen. Man. CLAUDIO JACQUES VERGARA.

EMELECTRIC (Empresa Eléctrica de Melipilla, Colchagua y Maule): Ortúzar N° 376, Melipilla; internet www.emelectric.cl; Pres. FRANCISCO JAVIER MARÍN ESTÉVEZ; Regional Mans NOLBERTO PÉREZ PEÑA (Melipilla), JUAN CARLOS OLIVER PÉREZ (Colchagua), JUAN MANUEL ORTEGA MUÑOZ (Maule).

ENERSIS, SA: Santa Rosa 76, Casilla 1557, Vitacura, Santiago; tel. (2) 2353-4400; fax (2) 2378-4788; e-mail comunicacion@e.enersis.cl; internet www.enersis.cl; f. 1981; holding co for Spanish group generating and distributing electricity through its subsidiaries throughout South America; 60.62% owned by Endesa Chile; Pres. PABLO YRARRÁZAVAL VALDÉS; Gen. Man. IGNACIO ANTOÑANZAS ALVEAR; 10,957 employees.

Chilectra, SA: Santo Domingo 789, Casilla 1557, Santiago; tel. (2) 2632-2000; fax (2) 2639-3280; e-mail rrpp@chilectra.cl; internet www.chilectra.cl; f. 1921; transmission and distribution arm of ENERSIS; supplies distribution cos, including the Empresa Eléctrica Municipal de Lo Barnechea, Empresa Municipal de Til-Til, and the Empresa Eléctrica de Colina, SA; holds overseas distribution concessions in Argentina, Peru and Brazil; acquired by ENERSIS of Spain in 1999; Pres. JUAN MARÍA MORENO MELLADO; Gen. Man. CRISTIÁN FIERRO MONTES.

Endesa Chile: Santa Rosa 76, Casilla 1392, Santiago; tel. (2) 2630-9000; fax (2) 2635-4720; e-mail comunicacion@endesa.cl; internet www.endesa.cl; f. 1943; installed capacity 4,035 MW (2002); ENERSIS obtained majority control of Endesa Chile in 1999; operates subsidiaries in Pehuenche, Pangue, San Isidro y Celta; Pres. JORGE ROSENBLUT; Gen. Man. JOAQUÍN GALINDO VÉLEZ.

SAESA (Sociedad Austral de Electricidad, SA): Manuel Bulnes 441, Casilla 21-0, Osorno; tel. (64) 220-6200; fax (64) 220-6309; e-mail saesa@saesa.cl; internet www.saesa.cl; owned by PSEG Corpn of the USA; Pres. JORGE LESSER GARCÍA-HUIDOBRO; Gen. Man. FRANCISCO ALLIENDE ARRIAGADA.

Gas

Abastible, SA (Abastecedora de Combustible): Avda Vicuña Mackenna 55, Providencia, Santiago; tel. (2) 2693-9000; fax (2) 2693-9304; internet www.abastible.cl; f. 1956; owned by COPEC; Pres. EDUARDO NAVARRO; Gen. Man. JOSÉ ODONE.

Compañía de Consumidores de Gas de Santiago (GASCO, SA): 1061 Santo Domingo, Casilla 8-D, Santiago; tel. (2) 2694-4444; fax (2) 2694-4370; e-mail info@gasco.cl; internet www.gasco.cl; natural gas utility; supplies Santiago and Punta Arenas regions; owned by CGE; Pres. CLAUDIO HORNAUER HERRMANN; Gen. Man. RICARDO CRUZAT OCHOGAVÍA.

Electrogas: Alonso de Cordova 5900, Of. 401, Las Condes, Santiago; tel. (2) 2299-3400; fax (2) 2299-3490; e-mail carlos.andreani@ electrogas.cl; internet www.electrogas.cl/default.asp; f. 1998; subsidiary of Endesa Chile; CEO CARLOS ANDREANI LUCO.

Empresas Lipigas: Las Urbinas 53, 13°, Of. 131, Providencia, Santiago; tel. (2) 2650-3582; e-mail info@empresaslipigas.cl; internet www.lipigas.cl; f. 1950; liquid gas supplier; also operates Agrogas, Enagas and Industrias Codigas; Pres. JUAN MANUEL SANTA CRUZ MUNIZAGA; Gen. Man. ANGEL MAFUCCI SOLIMANO.

GasAndes: Avda Chena 11650, Parque Industrial Puerta Sur, San Bernardo, Santiago; tel. (2) 2366-5960; fax (2) 2366-5942; internet www.gasandes.com; distributes natural gas transported from the Argentine province of Mendoza via a 463-km pipeline; Gen. Man. RAÚL MONTALVA.

GasAtacama Generación: Isidora Goyenechea 3365, 8°, Las Condes, Santiago; tel. (2) 2366-3800; fax (2) 2366-3802; e-mail info@ gasatacama.cl; internet www.gasatacama.cl; natural gas producer and transporter; subsidiary of Endesa Chile; Pres. JOAQUÍN GALINDO VÉLEZ; Gen. Man. EDUARDO SOTO TRINCADO.

GasValpo, SA: Camino Internacional 1420, Viña del Mar; tel. (32) 227-7000; fax (32) 221-3092; e-mail info@gasvalpo.cl; internet www .gasvalpo.cl; f. 1853; owned by AGL of Australia; Pres. GREG MARTIN; Gen. Man. LUIS KIPREOS.

Linde Chile: Paseo Presidente, Errázuriz Echaurren 2631, Casilla 16953, Providencia, Santiago; tel. (2) 2330-8000; fax (2) 2231-8009; e-mail callcentre@cl.aga.com; internet www.linde.cl; f. 1920 as AGA Chile, SA; owned by Linde Gas Corpn of Germany; natural and industrial gases utility; Gen. Man. IGNACIO VIÑUELA.

Water

Aguas Andinas, SA: Avda Presidente Balmaceda 1398, Santiago; tel. (2) 2688-1000; fax (2) 2698-5871; e-mail info@aguasandinas.cl; internet www.aguasandinas.cl; water supply and sanitation services to Santiago and the surrounding area; sold to a French-Spanish consortium in June 1999; Pres. FELIPE LARRAIN ASPILLAGA; Gen. Man. JORDI VALLS.

Empresa de Obras Sanitarias de Valparaíso, SA (Esval): Cochrane 751, Valparaíso; tel. (32) 220-9000; fax (32) 220-9502; e-mail infoesval@esval.cl; internet www.esval.cl; f. 1989; sanitation and irrigation co serving Valparaíso; Pres. JORGE ADOLFO GARCÍA HUIDOBRO; Gen. Man. JOSÉ LUIS MURILLO C.; 377 employees.

Sigsig Ltda (Tecnagent) (Servicios de Ingeniería Sigren y Sigren Ltda): Presidente Errázuriz 3262, Casilla 7550295, Las Condes, Santiago; tel. (2) 2335-2001; fax (2) 2334-8466; e-mail tecnagent@ tecnagent.cl; internet www.tecnagent.cl; f. 1986; Pres. RAÚL B. SIGREN BINDHOFF; Gen. Man. RAÚL A. SIGREN ORFILA.

TRADE UNIONS

Central Unions

Central Autónoma de Trabajadores (CAT): Sazié 1761, Santiago; tel. and fax (2) 2657-8533; e-mail catchile@catchile.cl; internet www.catchile.cl; 107,000 mems (2007); Pres. OSCAR OLIVOS MADARIAGA; Sec.-Gen. ALFONSO PASTENE URIBE.

Central Unitaria de Trabajadores de Chile (CUT): Alameda 1346, Centro, Santiago; tel. (2) 2352-7600; fax (2) 2672-0112; e-mail cutorganizacion@gmail.com; internet www.cutchile.cl; f. 1988; affiliated orgs: 20 asscns, 28 confederations, 64 federations, 35 unions; 670,000 mems (2009); Pres. BÁRBARA FIGUEROA; Gen. Sec. ARTURO MARTÍNEZ.

Unión Nacional de Trabajadores: Moneda 1447, Santiago; tel. (2) 2688-6344; e-mail info@untchile.cl; internet untchile.cl; Pres. DIEGO OLIVARES ARAVENA; Gen. Sec. LUIS PALOMINOS LIZAM.

Union Confederations

Agrupación Nacional de Empleados Fiscales (ANEF): Edif. Tucapel Jiménez, Alameda 1603, Santiago; tel. (2) 2696-2957; fax (2) 2697-9764; e-mail info@anef.cl; internet www.anef.cl; f. 1943; affiliated to CUT; public service workers; Pres. RAÚL DE LA PUENTE PEÑA; Sec.-Gen. BERNARDO JORQUERA ROJAS.

Colegio de Profesores de Chile: Moneda 2394, Santiago; tel. (2) 2470-4200; fax (2) 2470-4290; e-mail contacto@colegiodeprofesores .cl; internet www.colegiodeprofesores.cl; f. 1974; 100,000 mems; Pres. JAIME GAJARDO ORELLANA; Sec.-Gen. DARÍO VÁSQUEZ SALAZAR.

Confederación Nacional Campesina: Eleuterio Ramírez 1471, Santiago; tel. and fax (2) 2696-2673; affiliated to CUT; Pres. SEGUNDO STEILEN NAVARRO; Sec.-Gen. RENÉ ASTUDILLO R.

Confederación Nacional de Federaciones y Sindicatos de Gente de Mar, Portuarios y Pesqueros de Chile (CONGEMAR): José Tomás Ramos 170, Valparaíso; tel. (32) 225-7580; e-mail congemar@tie.cl; internet www.congemar.cl; affiliated to CUT; Pres. JORGE MOISES BUSTOS B.; Sec.-Gen. MARIANO VILLA PERÉZ.

Confederación Nacional de Funcionarios Municipales (ASEMUCH): Curicó 176, Santiago; tel. (2) 222-9414; fax (2) 222-8185; e-mail asemuchchile@gmail.com; internet www.asemuch.cl; f. 1946 as Asociación Nacional de Empleados Municipales de Chile; reconstituted in 1996 under present name; municipal workers' union; Pres. OSCAR HUMBERTO YÁÑEZ POL; Sec.-Gen. MANUEL JUVENAL BRAVO MUÑOZ.

Confederación Nacional de Sindicatos Agrícolas—Unidad Obrero Campesina (UOC): Eleuterio Ramírez 1463, Centro, Santiago; tel. and fax (2) 2696-6342; e-mail confe.uocchile@uocchile.cl; internet www.uocchile.cl; affiliated to CUT; Pres. OLGA GUTIÉRREZ.

Confederación Nacional de Sindicatos, Federaciones y Asociaciones de Trabajadores del Sector Privado de Chile (CEPCH): Valentín Letelier 18, Centro, Santiago; tel. (2) 2673-5221; e-mail convocatoriacepch@gmail.com; internet cepch.org; trade union for workers in private sector; affiliated to CUT; Pres. RUBEN VILLANUEVA LARA; Sec.-Gen. MAURICIO OLIVA CARCAMO.

Confederación Nacional de Sindicatos de Trabajadores de la Construcción, Maderas, Materiales de Edificación y Actividades Conexas (CNTC): Almirante Hurtado 2069, Centro, Santiago; tel. (2) 2632-3913; fax (2) 2632-2579; e-mail cntc@chile.com; internet www.cntc.cl; f. 1936; affiliated to CUT; Pres. JOSÉ SANTOS HERNANDEZ; Sec.-Gen. HECTOR VILLEGAS AREVALO.

Confederación Nacional de Sindicatos de Trabajadores Textiles, de la Confección y Vestuario (CONTEVECH): Agustinas 2349, Dpto 0555, Centro, Santiago; tel. (2) 2688-2008; e-mail contevech@hotmail.es; internet contevech.blogspot.com; affiliated to CUT; Pres. JOSÉ GERMÁN SAN MARTÍN PÉREZ.

Confederación Nacional de Suplementeros de Chile (CONASUCH): Tucapel Jiménez 26, Centro, Santiago; tel. (2) 2784-3444; fax (2) 2784-3449; e-mail conasuch1942@gmail.com; internet conasuch.hostoi.com; f. 1942; trade union for newspaper vendors; Pres. IVÁN ENSINA CARO.

Confederación Nacional de Trabajadores del Comercio, Oficinas, Industrias y Servicios (CONSFETRACOSI): Almirante Simpson 70, Providencia, Santiago; tel. (2) 2655-0301; fax (2) 2222-7804; e-mail consfetracosi@gmail.com; internet consfetracosi .blogspot.com; f. 1995; affiliated to CAT; Sec.-Gen. MAGDALENA CASTILLO D.

Confederación Nacional de Trabajadores Electrometalúrgicos, Mineros y Automotrices de Chile (CONSFETEMA): Vicuña Mackenna 3101, San Joaquín, Santiago; tel. (2) 2238-1732; fax (2) 2553-6494; e-mail consfetema@123mail.cl; Pres. LUIS SEPÚLVEDA DEL RÍO.

Confederación Nacional de Trabajadores Forestales de Chile (CTF): Concepción; tel. and fax (41) 220-0407; internet ctf-chile .blogspot.com; f. 1988; 45,000 mems; Pres. JORGE GONZÁLEZ CASTILLO; Sec.-Gen. SERGIO GATICA ORTIZ.

Confederación Nacional de Trabajadores Metalúrgicos (CONSTRAMET): Santa Rosa 101, esq. Alonso Ovalle, Santiago; tel. (2) 2664-8581; fax (2) 2638-3694; e-mail secretaria@constramet .cl; internet www.constramet.cl; affiliated to CUT and the International Metalworkers' Federation; Pres. HORACIO FUENTES GONZALEZ; Sec.-Gen. ROBERTO BUSTAMENTE ROJAS.

Confederación Nacional de Trabajadores de Salud (Fenats): Santa Rosa 3453, San Miguel, Santiago; internet www .fenatsmetropolitana.cl; health workers' union; Pres. OSCAR RIVEROS.

Confederación de Sindicatos Bancarios y Afines: Agustinas 814, Of. 606, Santiago; tel. (2) 2481-6122; fax (2) 2481-6123; e-mail confederacionbancaria@gmail.com; internet www.bancariachile.cl; affiliated to CUT; Pres. ANDREA RIQUELME BELTRÁN; Sec.-Gen. LUIS MESINA MARÍN.

Confederación de Trabajadores del Cobre (CTC): Santiago; e-mail secretariageneral@confederaciondelcobre.cl; internet www .confederaciondelcobre.cl; f. 2007; copper workers' union; Pres. CRISTIÁN CUEVAS ZAMBRANO; Sec.-Gen. JEDRY VELIS PALMA.

Transport

RAILWAYS

In 2010 there were 6,188 km of railway lines in the country.

State Railways

Empresa de los Ferrocarriles del Estado (EFE): Morandé 115, 6°, Santiago; tel. (2) 2376-8500; fax (2) 2776-2609; e-mail principios@ efe.cl; internet www.efe.cl; f. 1851; 2,072 km of track in use (2006); Pres. JORGE INOSTROZA SÁNCHEZ; Gen. Man. CECILIA ARAYA CATALÁN.

Ferrocarriles Suburbanos de Concepción (FESUB): Avda Padre Hurtado 570, 4°, Concepción; tel. (41) 286-8015; e-mail contacto@biotren.cl; internet www.fesub.cl; f. 2008; serves Corto Laja and Regional Victoria Temuco; Pres. JOAQUÍN BRAHM BARRIL; Gen. Man. NELSON HERNÁNDEZ ROLDÁN.

Servicio de Trenes Regionales Terra, SA (TerraSur): Avda Libertador Bernardo O'Higgins 3170, andén 6, 2°, Santiago; tel. (2) 2585-5000; fax (2) 2585-5914; e-mail comunicaciones@terrasur.cl; internet www.tmsa.cl/link.cgi/servicios/terrasur; operated by Trenes Metropolitanos, SA; Gen. Man. JOSÉ MIGUEL OBANDO.

Transporte Ferroviario Andrés Pirazolli, SA (Transap): Exterminal Ferroviario Los Lirios, Rancagua; tel. (67) 2222-2242; fax (67) 2222-2039; e-mail contacto@transap.cl; internet www.transap.cl; f. 2000; freight services; Pres. MARCELO PIRAZZOLI; Gen. Man. NABIL KUNCAR.

Private Railways

Empresa de Transporte Ferroviario, SA (Ferronor): Huérfanos 587, Ofs 301 y 302, Santiago; tel. (2) 2938-3170; fax (2) 2638-0464; e-mail ferronor@ferronor.cl; internet www.ferronor.cl; 2,412 km of track (2009); operates cargo services only; interconnected with Argentina, Bolivia, Brazil and Paraguay; Pres. ROBERTO PIRAZZOLI; Gen. Man. MARÍO VILLALÓN.

Ferrocarril de Antofagasta (FCAB): Bolívar 255, Casillas ST, Antofagasta; tel. (55) 220-6100; fax (55) 220-6220; e-mail fcab .cl; internet www.fcab.cl; f. 1888; subsidiary of Grupo Antofagasta PLC (United Kingdom); operates an international railway to Bolivia and Argentina; cargo-forwarding services; track length in use 1,000 km (2011); Gen. Man. MIGUEL V. SEPÚLVEDA.

Ferrocarril del Pacífico, SA (FEPASA): Málaga 120, 5°, Las Condes, Santiago; tel. (2) 2837-8000; fax (2) 2837-8005; e-mail oguevara@fepasa.cl; internet www.fepasa.cl; f. 1993; privatized

freight services on EFE track; 19.83% owned by EFE; Pres. OSCAR GUILLERMO GARRETÓN PURCELL; Gen. Man. CLAUDIO GONZÁLEZ OTAZO.

Association

Asociación Chilena de Conservación de Patrimonio Ferroviario (ACCPF): Casilla 51996, Correo Central, Santiago; tel. (2) 2699-4607; fax (2) 2280-0252; e-mail info@accpf.cl; internet www .accpf.cl; f. 1986; railway preservation asscn; Pres. JOSÉ TOMÁS BRETÓN JARA; Sec.-Gen. EUGENIO TUEVE RIVERA.

METROPOLITAN TRANSPORT

Metro de Santiago: Avda Libertador Bernardo O'Higgins 1414, Santiago; tel. (2) 2250-3000; fax (2) 2937-2000; e-mail comunicaciones@metro.cl; internet www.metrosantiago.cl; f. 1975; 5 lines, 103 km (2012); extension to 140 km scheduled for completion in 2017; Pres. ALDO GONZÁLEZ TISSINETTI; Gen. Man. HERNÁN VEGA MOLINA.

Metro Valparaíso, SA (MERVAL): Viana 1685, Viña del Mar, V Región, Valparaíso; tel. (32) 252-7511; fax (32) 252-7509; e-mail jmobando@metro-valparaiso.cl; internet www.metro-valparaiso.cl; f. 1995; Pres. JOSÉ LUIS DOMÍNGUEZ; Gen. Man. MARISA KAUSEL CONTADOR.

Transantiago: Nueva York 9, 10°, Santiago; tel. (2) 2428-7900; fax (2) 2428-7926; internet www.transantiago.cl; f. 2005; govt scheme to co-ordinate public transport in Santiago; comprises 10 bus networks and the Metro de Santiago; Gen. Man. JUAN MANUEL VARGAS.

Trenes Metropolitanos, SA: Avda Libertador Bernardo O'Higgins 3170, Andén 6 de Estación Central, Santiago; tel. (2) 2585-5000; fax (2) 2776-3304; e-mail contacto@tmsa.cl; internet www.tmsa.cl; f. 1990; subsidiary of Empresa de los Ferrocarriles del Estado (EFE); connects Santiago with several communities near San Fernando; operates Metrotren, TerraSur and Buscarril; Pres. JORGE IVÁN INOSTROZA SÁNCHEZ.

ROADS

In 2010 the road network comprised 77,764 km of roads, of which 23% were paved. Of the total, 9,041 km were part of the national road network and some 14,139 km formed the provincial road network. The road system includes the entirely paved Pan-American Highway, extending 3,455 km from north to south.

Dirección de Vialidad: Morandé 59, 2°, Santiago; tel. (2) 2449-4000; fax (2) 2441-0914; internet www.vialidad.cl; f. 1953; supervising authority; Dir MARIO FERNÁNDEZ RODRÍGUEZ.

SHIPPING

As a consequence of Chile's difficult topography, maritime transport is of particular importance. The principal state and privately owned ports are San Antonio, Quintero, Valparaíso, Lirquén, San Vicente, Patillos, Mejillones, Ventanas, Huasco, Iquique, Tocopilla and Antofagasta. Chile's flag registered fleet comprised 614 vessels, totalling 907,989 grt at December 2013.

Supervisory Authorities

Asociación Nacional de Armadores: Blanco 869, 3°, Valparaíso; tel. (32) 221-2057; fax (32) 221-2017; e-mail info@armadores-chile.cl; internet www.armadores-chile.cl; f. 1931; shipowners' asscn; Pres. ROBERTO HETZ VORPAHL; Gen. Man. ARTURO SIERRA MERINO.

Cámara Marítima y Portuaria de Chile, AG: Blanco 869, 2°, Valparaíso; tel. (32) 225-0313; fax (32) 225-0231; e-mail info@ camport.cl; internet www.camport.cl; Pres. JORGE MARSHALL RIVERA; Exec. Vice-Pres. RODOLFO GARCÍA SÁNCHEZ.

Dirección General de Territorio Marítimo y Marina Mercante (DIRECTEMAR): Errázuriz 537, 4°, Valparaíso; tel. (32) 220-8000; fax (32) 225-2539; e-mail transparencia@directemar.cl; internet www.directemar.cl; maritime admin. of the coast and national waters, control of the merchant navy; ship registry; Dir-Gen. Rear-Adm. HUMBERTO RAMÍREZ NAVARRO.

Cargo-handling Companies

Empresa Portuaria Antofagasta (EPA): Avda Grecia s/n, Puerto Antofagasta, Casilla 190, Antofagasta; tel. (55) 256-3756; fax (55) 256-3735; e-mail epa@anfport.cl; internet www.anfport.cl; f. 1998; Pres. FERNANDO FUENTES HÉRNANDEZ; Gen. Man. CARLOS ESCOBAR OLGUIN.

Empresa Portuaria Arica: Máximo Lira 389, Arica; tel. (58) 220-2080; fax (58) 220-2090; e-mail puertoarica@puertoarica.cl; internet www.puertoarica.cl; f. 1998; Pres. FRANCISCO JAVIER GONZÁLEZ SILVA; Gen. Man. RODOLFO BARBOSA BARRIOS.

Empresa Portuaria Austral: Avda Bernardo O'Higgins 1385, Punta Arenas; tel. (61) 271-1200; fax (61) 271-1231; e-mail info@ australport.cl; internet www.australport.cl; Pres. MARIO JOSÉ MATURANA JAMAN; Gen. Man. IGNACIO FUGELLIE.

Empresa Portuaria Chacabuco (EMPORCHA): Avda Bernardo O'Higgins s/n, Puerto Chacabuco, XI Región; tel. (67) 235-1139; fax (67) 235-1174; e-mail info@chacabucoport.cl; internet www .chacabucoport.cl; f. 1998; Pres. CARLOS SACKEL BAHAMONDES; Gen. Man. ENRIQUE RUNÍN ZUÑIGA.

Empresa Portuaria Coquimbo: Melgarejo 676, Casilla 10D, Coquimbo; tel. (51) 231-3606; fax (51) 232-6146; e-mail gerenciag@ entelchile.net; internet www.puertocoquimbo.cl; Pres. HUGO GRI-SANTI ABOGABIR.

Empresa Portuaria Iquique: Avda Jorge Barrera 62, Casilla 47D, Iquique; tel. (57) 240-0100; fax (57) 241-3176; e-mail epi@epi.cl; internet www.epi.cl; f. 1998; Pres. CLAUDIO AGOSTINI GONZÁLEZ; Gen. Man. LUIS ALFREDO LEITON ARBEA.

Empresa Portuaria Puerto Montt: Avda Angelmó 1673, Puerto Montt, Región de los Lagos; tel. (65) 236-4500; fax (65) 236-4517; e-mail gerencia@empormontt.cl; internet www.empormontt.cl; Pres. CARLOS GUILLERMO GEISSE MACEVOY; Gen. Man. ALEX WINKLER RIETZSCH.

Empresa Portuaria San Antonio (EPSA): Alan Macowan 0245, San Antonio; tel. (35) 258-6000; fax (35) 258-6015; e-mail correo@ saiport.cl; internet www.sanantonioport.cc.cl; f. 1998; Pres. JOSÉ LUIS MARDONES SANTANDER; Gen. Man. ALDO SIGNORELLI BONOMO.

Empresa Portuaria Talcahuano-San Vicente: Calle La Vega 491, Santa Leonor, Talcahuano; tel. (41) 272-0300; fax (41) 272-0326; e-mail eportuaria@puertotalcahuano.cl; internet www .puertotalcahuano.cl; Pres. ALVARO DÍAZ PÉREZ; Gen. Man. LUIS ALBERTO ROSENBERG NESBET.

Empresa Portuaria Valparaíso: Avda Errázuriz 25, 4°, Of. 1, Valparaíso; tel. (2) 2244-8800; fax (2) 2222-4190; e-mail comercial@ epv.cl; internet www.epv.cl; Pres. RAÚL URZÚA MARAMBIO; Gen. Man. HARALD JAEGER KARL.

Principal Shipping Companies
Santiago

Agencias Universales, SA (AGUNSA): Edif. del Pacífico, 15°, Avda Andrés Bello 2687, Casilla 2511, Las Condes, Santiago; tel. (2) 2460-2700; fax (2) 2203-9009; e-mail agunsascl@agunsa.cl; internet www.agunsa.cl; f. 1960; maritime transportation and shipping, port and docking services; owned by Empresas Navieras, SA; Chair. JOSÉ MANUEL URENDA SALAMANCA; Gen. Man. LUIS MANCILLA PÉREZ.

Empresa Marítima, SA (Empremar Chile): Encomenderos 260, Piso 7°, Las Condes, Santiago; tel. (2) 2469-6100; fax (2) 2469-6199; internet www.empremar.cl; f. 1953; international and coastal services; Gen. Man. CRISTIÁN BERNALES PENSA.

Navimag Ferries, SA (NAVIMAG): Avda El Bosque, Norte 0440, 11°, Of. 1103/1104, Las Condes, Santiago; tel. (2) 2442-3120; fax (2) 2203-4025; e-mail sales@navimag.cl; internet www.navimag.cl; f. 1979; part of Nisa Navegación, SA; Gen. Man. HÉCTOR HENRÍQUEZ NEGRÓN.

Ultranav: Avda El Bosque Norte 500, 20°, Las Condes, Santiago; tel. (2) 2630-1009; fax (2) 2232-8856; e-mail ultragas@ultragas.cl; internet www.ultragasgroup.com; f. 1960; part of Ultramar Group; tanker services; Chair. DAG VON APPEN BUROSE; CEO ENRIQUE IDE.

Valparaíso

Broom Valparaíso: Almirante Señoret 70, 10°, Valparaíso; tel. (32) 226-8200; fax (32) 221-3308; e-mail info@broomgroup.cl; internet www.broomgroup.com; f. 1920; shipowners and brokers; Pres. JAMES C. WELLS M.; CEO ANDRÉS NUÑEZ SORENSEN.

Cía Chilena de Navegación Interoceánica, SA (CCNI): Plaza de la Justicia 59, Valparaíso; tel. (32) 227-5500; fax (32) 225-5949; e-mail info@ccni.cl; internet www.ccni.cl; f. 1930; regular sailings to Japan, Republic of Korea, Taiwan, Hong Kong, USA, Mexico, South Pacific, South Africa and Europe; bulk and dry cargo services; owned by Empresas Navieras, SA; Chair. BELTRÁN FELIPE URENDA SALAMANCA; CEO JOSÉ LUIS CHANES.

Cía Sud Americana de Vapores (CSAV): Plaza Sotomayor 50, Casilla 49v, Valparaíso; tel. (32) 220-3000; fax (32) 320-3333; e-mail info@csav.com; internet www.csav.com; f. 1872; regular services worldwide; bulk and container carriers, tramp and reefer services; Chair. FRANCISCO PÉREZ MACKENNA; Gen. Man. JUAN ANTONIO ALVAREZ AVENDAÑO.

Naviera Chilena del Pacífico, SA (Nachipa): Almirante Señoret 70, 6°, Casilla 370, Valparaíso; tel. (32) 250-0300; e-mail valparaiso@ nachipa.com; internet www.nachipa.cl; cargo; Pres. PABLO SIMIAN ZAMORANO; Gen. Man. FELIPE SIMIAN FERNÁNDEZ.

Sudamericana Agencias Aéreas y Marítimas, SA (SAAM): Blanco 895, Valparaíso; tel. (32) 220-1000; fax (32) 220-1481; e-mail servicioalcliente@saamsa.com; internet www.saam.cl; f. 1961; cargo services; Pres. FELIPE JOANNON V.; Gen. Man. JAVIER BITAR H.

Punta Arenas

Transbordadora Austral Broom, SA: Avda Juan Williams 06450, Punta Arenas; tel. (61) 272-8100; fax (61) 272-8109; e-mail correo@ tabsa.cl; internet www.tabsa.cl; f. 1968; ferry services in Chilean Antarctica; Pres. PEDRO LECAROS; Gen. Man. ALEJANDRO KUSANOVIC.

Puerto Montt

Transmarchilay, SA (Transporte Marítimo Chiloé-Aysén): Angelmo 2187, Puerto Montt; tel. (65) 227-0700; fax (65) 227-0730; e-mail transporte@tmc.cl; internet www.transmarchilay.cl; f. 1971; Pres. HARALD ROSENQVIST; Gen. Man. ALVARO CONTRERAS.

CIVIL AVIATION

There are 330 airfields in the country, of which eight have long runways. Arturo Merino Benítez, 20 km north-east of Santiago, and Chacalluta, 14 km north-east of Arica, are the principal international airports.

Regulatory Authority

Dirección General de Aeronática Civil (DGAC): Miguel Claro 1314, Providencia, Santiago; tel. (2) 2439-2000; fax (2) 2436-8143; internet www.dgac.gob.cl; f. 1930; Dir-Gen. Brig.-Gen. ROLANDO MERCADO ZAMORA.

Principal Airlines

Aerocardal: Aeropuerto Internacional Arturo Merino Benítez, Avda Diego Barros Ortiz 2065, Pudahuel, Santiago; tel. (2) 2377-7400; fax (2) 2377-7405; e-mail ventas@aerocardal.com; internet www.aerocardal.com; f. 1990; executive, charter and tourist services; Gen. Man. RICARDO REAL.

Aerovías DAP: Avda Bernardo O'Higgins 891, Casilla 406, Punta Arenas; tel. (61) 261-6100; fax (61) 261-6159; e-mail ventas@ aeroviasdap.cl; internet www.aeroviasdap.cl; f. 1980; domestic services; CEO ALEX PISCEVIC.

LAN Airlines (Línea Aérea Nacional de Chile): Avda Presidente Riesco 5711, 20°, Las Condes, Santiago; tel. (2) 2565-2525; fax (2) 2565-3890; internet www.lan.com; f. 1929; merged with TAM Linhas Aéreas, SA in 2012 to form LATAM Airlines Group, SA, although still operates under LAN brand; operates scheduled domestic and international passenger and cargo (LAN Cargo) services; CEO, LATAM Airlines ENRIQUE CUETO PLAZA; CEO, LAN Airlines ENRIQUE ELSACA.

Tourism

Chile has a wide variety of attractions for the tourist, including fine beaches, ski resorts in the Andes, lakes, rivers and desert scenery. Isla de Pascua (Easter Island) may also be visited by tourists. In 2013 there were 3,569,744 tourist arrivals and receipts from tourism totalled US $2,219m.

Servicio Nacional de Turismo (SERNATUR): Avda Providencia 1550, 2°, CP 7500548, Santiago; tel. (2) 2731-8419; fax (2) 2236-1417; e-mail contacto@sernatur.cl; internet www.sernatur.cl; f. 1975; Nat. Dir NICOLÁS MENA.

Asociación Chilena de Empresas de Turismo (ACHET): Avda Providencia 2019, Of. 42B, Santiago; tel. (2) 2439-9100; fax (2) 2439-9118; e-mail achet@achet.cl; internet www.achet.cl; f. 1945; 155 mems; Pres. GUILLERMO CORREA SANFUENTES; Sec.-Gen. LORENA ARRIAGADA GÁLVEZ.

Defence

As assessed at November 2013, Chile's armed forces numbered 61,400: army 34,650, navy 18,700 and air force 8,050. There were also paramilitary forces of 44,700 *carabineros*. Reserve troops numbered 40,000. Compulsory military service was ended in 2005.

Defence Expenditure: Expenditure was budgeted at 2,250,000m. pesos in 2013.

Chief of Staff of National Defence: Rear-Adm. JOSÉ MIGUEL ROMERO AGUIRRE.

Commander-in-Chief of the Army: Gen. HUMBERTO OVIEDO ARRIAGADA.

Commander-in-Chief of the Navy: Adm. ENRIQUE LARRAÑAGA MARTÍN.

Commander-in-Chief of the Air Force: Gen. JORGE ROJAS AVILA.

Education

Primary education in Chile is free and compulsory for eight years, beginning at six or seven years of age. It is divided into two cycles: the first lasts for four years and provides a general education; the second cycle offers a more specialized schooling. There were 1,976,176 pupils in primary education in 2012. Secondary education is divided into the humanities-science programme (lasting four years), with the emphasis on general education and possible entrance to university, and the technical-professional programme (lasting for up to six years). In 2012 there were 1,044,233 students in secondary education. There are three types of higher education institution: universities, professional institutes and centres of technical information. In 2012 there were 1,127,181 students in higher education. The 2013 central government budget allocated 6,712,290m. pesos to the Ministry of Education.

Bibliography

For works on South America generally, see Select Bibliography (Books)

Aguilera, P., and Fredes, R. (Eds). *Chile—The Other September 11: Reflections and Commentaries on the 1973 Coup in Chile*. New York, Ocean Press, 2006.

Angell, A. *Democracy after Pinochet: Politics, Parties and Elections in Chile*. London, Institute for the Study of the Americas, 2007.

Aroca, P. A., and Hewings, G. J. D. (Eds). *Structure and Structural Change in the Chilean Economy*. Basingstoke, Palgrave Macmillan, 2006.

Barr-Melej, P. *Reforming Chile: Cultural Politics, Nationalism and the Rise of the Middle Class*. Chapel Hill, NC, University of North Carolina Press, 2001.

Beckett, A. *Pinochet in Piccadilly: Britain and Chile's Hidden History*. London, Faber and Faber, 2002.

Berg, J. *Miracle for Whom?: Chilean Workers Under Free Trade*. Abingdon, Routledge, 2013.

Borzutzky, S. *Vital Connections: Politics, Social Security, and Inequality in Chile*. Notre Dame, IN, University of Notre Dame Press, 2002.

Borzutzky, S., and Oppenheim, L. (Eds). *After Pinochet: The Chilean Road to Democracy and the Market*. Gainesville, FL, University Press of Florida, 2006.

Borzutzky, S., and Weeks, G. B. (Eds). *The Bachelet Government: Conflict and Consensus in Post-Pinochet Chile*. Gainesville, FL, University Press of Florida, 2010.

Collier, S., and Sater, W. *A History of Chile, 1808–2002*. Cambridge, Cambridge University Press, Cambridge Latin American Studies, 2004 (2nd edn, Ed. Knight, A.).

Faundez, J. *Democratization, Development and Legality: Chile, 1831–1973*. Basingstoke, Palgrave Macmillan, 2007.

French-Davis, R. *Economic Reforms in Chile: From Dictatorship to Democracy*. 2nd edn, Michigan, MI, University of Michigan Press, 2010.

Haughney, D. *Neoliberal Economics, Democratic Transition and Mapuche Demands for Rights in Chile*. Gainesville, FL, University Press of Florida, 2006.

Hilbink, L. *Judges beyond Politics in Democracy and Dictatorship: Lessons from Chile (Cambridge Studies in Law and Society)*. Revised edn, Cambridge, Cambridge University Press, 2011.

Lagos, R., *The Southern Tiger: Chile's Fight for a Democratic and Prosperous Future*. New York, Palgrave Macmillan, 2012.

Meller, P. *The Unidad Popular and the Pinochet Dictatorship: A Political Analysis*. New York, St Martins Press, 2000.

Nuñéz, R. C. *The Politics of Social Policy Change in Chile and Uruguay: Retrenchment versus Maintenance, 1973–1998*. London, Routledge, 2005.

O'Shaughnessy, H. *Pinochet: The Politics of Torture*. London, Latin America Bureau, 1999.

Power, M. *Right-Wing Women in Chile: Feminine Power and the Struggle Against Allende*. Pennsylvania, PA, Penn State University Press, 2002.

Report of the National Commission on Political Imprisonment and Torture. Santiago, 2004.

Roht-Arriaza, N. *The Pinochet Effect: Transnational Justice in the Age of Human Rights*. Philadelphia, PA, University of Pennsylvania Press, 2006.

Rosemblatt, K. A. *Gendered Compromises: Political Cultures and the State in Chile, 1920–1950*. Chapel Hill, NC, University of North Carolina Press, 2000.

Sehnbruch, K. *The Chilean Labour Market: A Key to Understanding Latin American Labour Markets*. Basingstoke, Palgrave Macmillan, 2007.

Silva, P. *In the Name of Reason: Technocrats and Politics in Chile*. University Park, PA, Pennsylvania State University Press, 2009.

Spooner, M. H. *The General's Slow Retreat: Chile after Pinochet*. Los Angeles, CA, University of California Press, 2011.

Stern, S. J. *Reckoning with Pinochet: The Memory Question in Democratic Chile, 1989-2006*. Durham, NC, Duke University Press, 2010.

Taylor, M. *From Pinochet to the Third Way: Neoliberalism and Social Transformation in Chile*. London, Pluto Press, 2006.

Tinsman, H. *Partners in Conflict: The Politics of Gender, Sexuality and Labor in the Chilean Agrarian Reform, 1950–1973*. Durham, NC, Duke University Press, 2002.

Verdugo, P. *Chile, Pinochet and the Caravan of Death*. Boulder, CO, Lynne Rienner Publrs, 2001.

Vergara, A. *Copper Workers, International Business and Domestic Politics in Cold War Chile*. University Park, PA, Pennsylvania State University Press, 2008.

Wright, T. C. *State Terrorism in Latin America: Chile, Argentina, and International Human Rights*. Lanham, MD, Rowman & Littlefield Publrs, 2007.

COLOMBIA

Geography

PHYSICAL FEATURES

The Republic of Colombia is in north-western South America, the only country on that continent to have coastlines on both the Pacific Ocean and the Caribbean Sea, separated mid-way by the westward-heading Isthmus of Panama. The country's shortest land border (225 km or 140 miles), therefore, is with Panama, to the west, across the start of the Central American land bridge (until 1903 Panama was a province of Colombia). To the south lie Ecuador and Peru, the former on the coast beyond a 590-km frontier and the latter inland, the border extending for 1,496 km onto the Amazonian plains. Here Colombia also meets Brazil, which lies east and south of a 1,643-km border in the south-east of the country. The longest border, however, is with Venezuela, which lies to the east. Central Colombia thrusts further east than the rest of the country, while in the north Venezuela encroaches into the west. However, Colombia still has 1,760 km of north-west-facing shores on the Caribbean (1,448 km on the Pacific), giving it the right to maintain its possession of a number of islands and islets off shore. These are grouped in a single administrative unit, the smallest department in the country (44 sq km or 17 sq miles), San Andrés y Providencia Islands, which also has jurisdiction over Roncador Cay and the Quita Sueño, Serrana and Serranilla Banks. However, Colombian possession of this territory impelled Nicaragua in 2001 to pursue a claim with the International Court of Justice (based in The Hague, Netherlands) involving 50,000 sq km of territorial waters—San Andrés is only 180 km east of Nicaragua, whereas it is some 700 km north of the Colombian mainland. Providencia is a further 80 km north. The still more distant Serranilla Bank is claimed by the USA (which recognized Colombian possession of Roncador, Serrana and Quita Sueño in 1981, when a 1972 treaty took effect) and, on occasion, by Honduras. Colombia also has a dispute over maritime boundaries in the Gulf of Venezuela, with Venezuela. The Pacific coast involves fewer formal international problems—Isla de Malpelo is the only Pacific island to be included in Colombian territory, although it adds little area to the overall national territory of 1,141,748 sq km (making the country a little bigger than Bolivia).

The western two-fifths of Colombia are dominated by the Andes and the coastal lowlands, with the east and south dominated, respectively, by the Llanos (the grassland plains of the Orinoco basin) and by the Selvas (the flat rainforest region typical of the Amazon basin). These torrid lowlands of the east are sparsely inhabited and little explored, watered by rivers that drain into the Atlantic—the Llanos by the Meta and other tributaries of the Orinoco, and the Selvas by the Caquetá and other Amazon tributaries. The most important river of Colombia, however, is the Magdalena, which cuts north through the Andes for about 1,540 km, through the most settled parts of the country, to empty into the Caribbean. The great Andean chain enters the country in the south-west, then splits into three cordilleras, the western, the lowest, the central, the highest, and the eastern. Like the coast, the volcanic ranges run slightly north of a south-west to north-east course. The region consists of soaring ranges separated by high plateaux, broad upland basins and deep, fertile valleys carrying powerful rivers. The Cordillera Occidental is a sheer wall of barren peaks rising to some 3,700 m (over 12,000 ft). The Cordillera Central has peaks over 5,500 m, the Cordillera Oriental some that are not much less, and both are under permanent snow at their summits. This, and a timberline at about 3,000 m, contrasts dramatically with the swampy tropical jungle the mountains descend to some 240 km short of the Caribbean coast. The Cordillera Oriental is distinguished by its densely populated plateaux and basins, usually between 2,400 m and 2,700 m, in one of which is the capital city, although there are also large centres in the Cordillera Central.

Between the two ranges clefts the mighty Magdalena, serving as a transport conduit to the Atlantic (Caribbean) coast.

On the other side of the Cordillera Central, to the west, is the Cauca, a tributary of the Magdalena, joining it some 320 km before it reaches the sea. These rivers link the highlands and the Atlantic lowlands, which are often marshy, but long settled. These lowlands are separated from Venezuela by a north-ward extension of the Cordillera Oriental, the Sierra de Perijá, and, on the north-western coast, the flat, semi-arid Gujaira peninsula (which forms the western bluff of the Gulf of Venezuela) to the east and the isolated mountain mass of the Sierra Nevada de Santa Marta to the west. This range on the Caribbean includes the country's highest point, Pico Cristóbal Colón (5,776 m or 18,957 ft)—named, like the country, for Christopher Columbus, the Genoese (Italian) navigator who claimed much of the continent for Spain. The nearby Pico Simón Bolívar, named for the great liberator of South America, has a similar elevation. In the south the Atlantic plains narrow, and the densely forested region on the border with Panama leads onto the Pacific coast, first the Serranía del Baudó and then the jungles and swamps of the coastal plains, watered by relatively short Andean rivers, such as the Patía in the south. This varied terrain gives Colombia a biodiversity reckoned to be second only to Brazil, sheltering in forests that cover almost one-half of the country and on pastureland that covers about two-fifths (although some of this is on the bleak high moors, *páramo*, between the mountain basins). The forest is densest in the tropical east, but deforestation is probably a greater threat in the north and west. There is also a problem with illegal smuggling of animals, which can have a severe effect on endangered populations—particularly threatened species include the yellow-eared parrot, the condor, the giant armadillo, the cotton-top marmoset, the white-footed tamarin, tapir and some alligators. Other fauna that flourish in the natural conditions of Colombia include hummingbirds, toucans, storks, pumas, jaguars, red deer, sloths and monkeys. The country's flora ranges from coconut and mangrove, through mahogany, oak, pine, balsam, rubber, ginger, tonka beans, etc., to the extensive (illegal) cultivation of coca (Colombia is the world's leading producer), opium poppies and cannabis.

CLIMATE

The Equator passes through the far south-east of Colombia, so most of the country lies within the Tropic of Cancer, but elevation makes a dramatic difference to the climate. The coastal lowlands and the deep Magdalena and Patía valleys, for instance, are very hot, with average annual temperatures of 24°C–27°C (75°F–81°F). From about 500 m the climate becomes subtropical, and then from about 2,300 m temperate (many people live at this level). It is only cold above 3,000 m (average temperatures ranging from –18°C to 13°C, 0°F to 55°F). Seasonal variation, however, is slight—the capital, Bogotá, has average high temperatures of 19°C (66°F) in July and of 20°C (68°F) in January. The main seasons are the wet and dry seasons, the two periods of rain being in March–May and September–November, except on the Atlantic coast, where there is one long wet season, in May–October. Rain is heaviest on the Pacific coast, and it is drier in the north and on the slopes of the Cordillera Oriental. At Bogotá the average annual rainfall is 1,050 mm (41 ins), but at Barranquilla, on the Caribbean, it is 800 mm.

POPULATION

Before the advent of Europeans, there was a large Amerindian population in what is now Colombia, notably of the Chibcha (Muisca) people. There remain about 60 tribes scattered throughout the country. The Spanish settlement and long years of colonial rule, as an imperial centre moreover, engrained a socially rigid class stratification. The extremes of poverty in the country have not helped with widespread problems of social and political violence. According to the 2005 census, most of the population (86%) did not identify with any ethnic grouping. Some 10% of the population were Afro-Colombian, and 3% were indigenous or Amerindian. The official language is Spanish, with Colombian Spanish said to be the purest in Latin America, but some native languages are still spoken by remoter groups and now have recognition under the Constitution. The Roman Catholic Church (which claims the nominal adherence of 87% of the population) also enjoys some official sanction, although it is not, formally, the state religion. There are small Protestant and Jewish minorities, with some even smaller Arab communities (in which there are some Muslims).

According to official projections, the total population was 47.7m. in mid-2014. About three-quarters live in urban centres, most above the courses of the Magdalena and the Cauca and on the Atlantic coast. The national capital is Bogotá. It is located in the centre of the country, towards the southern end of the Cordillera Oriental, and is the largest city in Colombia (an estimated 7.8m. in mid-2014). The cities of Medellín (2.4m.), in the north of the Cordillera Central, and Cali (2.3m.), in the southern Cauca valley, are next in size, followed by the Caribbean cities of Barranquilla, at the mouth of the Magdalena, and Cartagena, south-west along the coast. Colombia is a unitary republic consisting of 32 departments and one capital district (distrito capital—Bogotá).

History

Sir KEITH MORRIS

Colombia shares many features with the other Latin American countries and particularly with its Andean neighbours. However, its geography, and pre-Columbian and colonial history gave the country distinctive characteristics that were accentuated following independence and became increasingly marked in the 20th century. The 60% of the country to the east of the Andes is divided between the Llanos (savannah, much of which is flooded for nine months of the year) and Amazonian jungle. Many places are only accessible by air. With its capital at Bogotá (500 miles from the Caribbean ports of entry and 8,600 ft high in the Cordillera Oriental), the country was inevitably inward-looking and regional.

The regionalism was reinforced by the country's Amerindian heritage. Although Colombia had many different civilizations before the Spanish conquest in the 16th century (they reached a high level of sophistication, producing the finest gold work in the Americas), they were never united in a large state like the Inca or Aztec empires. Few of them have survived as distinct groups, and most were hispanicized, unlike those in Ecuador, Peru and Bolivia to the south. By the end of the colonial period the majority of Colombians were Mestizos (of mixed European and Amerindian descent) with significant European and mulatto minorities—the latter descended from the African slaves imported to work in the gold mines. The resulting lack of communal identity added individualism to the regionalism and localism, which geography and pre-colonial history had encouraged.

INDEPENDENCE AND THE 19TH CENTURY

Nueva Granada became a Viceroyalty in 1739. Simón Bolívar made Santa Fe de Bogotá, as it was called in colonial times, the target of his great independence campaign of 1819 and there established the capital of Gran Colombia, comprising present-day Colombia, Venezuela, Ecuador and Panama. However, Gran Colombia broke up amid much bitterness in 1830, leaving the Colombians with a strong preference for civilian government after their experience with Bolívar and his largely Venezuelan generals.

Following independence, Colombia's politics underwent a turbulent period with nine civil wars. These were essentially struggles for power between the two main currents of national political life that had, by the middle of the century, emerged as the Partido Liberal (PL—Liberal Party) and the Partido Conservador (PC—Conservative Party). The only issue that consistently divided them was the greater or lesser role of the Roman Catholic Church: the PL contained anti-clerical elements. Both parties were at times federalist, at times centralist, though the Liberals inclined more towards the former. However, party allegiance was often decided as much by family and locality as by doctrine.

The collapse of Gran Colombia had other lasting effects. It left Colombia with the largest share of the Gran Colombian debt. The Colombian state's finances were therefore poor from the beginning. The country remained poor for the rest of the century, first because of the lack of large commodity discoveries and, second, owing to a poor external sector. As a result, the state was chronically weak with an army of only 2,000–3,000 men, which was frequently incapable of maintaining public order. No Colombian President could exercise the sort of authority that later enabled the Venezuelan leader, Gen. Juan Vicente Gómez (1908–35), effectively to disarm the Venezuelan population in the early 1900s. The Colombian Constitution alternated between extreme federalism (1863) and excessive centralism (1886). The latter was confirmed by the War of the Thousand Days (1899–1902), although the centralism was more policy than practice.

EARLY 20TH CENTURY

Colombia's story in the 20th century was to diverge greatly from that of its neighbours. It was to have much greater constitutional stability (only one four-year military regime) and steadier economic development, but, paradoxically, more violence. A consequence of the difficult geography and the poverty of the state was the development of a frontier tradition. Colombia became a land of many internal frontiers as *colonos* (colonists) cleared the river valleys, as well as opening up the Llanos and the jungle. As the state was absent in most of these areas, traditions of private justice prevailed. The rural conflicts that afflicted Colombia in the late 20th and early 21st centuries led to many *colonos* taking their weapons and their frontier customs to the cities.

From the end of the War of the Thousand Days until the mid-1940s, Colombia enjoyed relative tranquillity. The Conservatives remained in power until 1930. The coffee and textile industries developed greatly, the latter mainly in Medellín. In 1930 the Conservatives divided into factions, which allowed a moderate Liberal, Enrique Olaya Herrera, to govern in coalition with Conservatives. An attack by Peru on Colombia's Amazonian territories in 1931 ensured wide support for the new Government. President Alfonso López Pumarejo, who succeeded Olaya in 1934, introduced 'New Deal' type reforms, consolidating the Liberals' popular support. His successor, Eduardo Santos Montejo (1938–42), slowed the pace of reform.

Divisions within the PL led to a Conservative victory in 1946. However, by 1948 the Liberals had reunited behind the popular figure of Jorge Eliécer Gaitán, the dissident Liberal candidate in the 1946 elections who had been expected to regain the presidency for the Liberals in 1950. The assassination of Gaitán in Bogotá on 9 April 1948 led to an outbreak of civil unrest, the Bogotazo, with days of rioting, leaving several thousand dead. The Government managed to restore order in the cities, but the conflict spread to the rural areas. 'La Violencia', as the period became known, continued until 1958 and may have claimed the lives of as many as 200,000 people.

FRENTE NACIONAL, 1958–74

The military, led by Gen. Gustavo Rojas Pinilla, took power in 1953. The coup, the only one in the 20th century, initially enjoyed popular support; this, however, waned as it became clear that Rojas did not intend to restore constitutional government and corruption became rampant. A military junta removed Rojas in 1957 and, in the following year, power was transferred to a Frente Nacional (National Front). This power-sharing agreement between the two traditional political parties provided for them to alternate in the presidency for four terms and to have an equal number of seats in the Cabinet and the Congreso (Congress). As under the Colombian system anyone could claim to be a Liberal or Conservative, the seats on both sides were strongly contested, with Communists winning some Liberal seats and Rojas's movement, the Alianza Nacional Popular (ANAPO), well represented on both sides.

Violence declined under the Frente Nacional as most of the remaining armed groups relinquished violence or were suppressed. However, the success of the Cuban revolution in 1959 gave fresh impetus to guerrilla activity. One of the surviving groups of Liberal guerrillas relaunched itself in the mid-1960s as the Fuerzas Armadas Revolucionarias de Colombia (FARC), the military wing of the pro-Soviet Communist Party, with strong support in some rural areas. The Ejército de Liberación Nacional (ELN), a Cuban-orientated movement, was founded at the same time. The Ejército Popular de Liberación (EPL), a smaller, Maoist guerrilla movement, followed in 1969.

Generally, the Frente Nacional's period of rule, which formally ended in 1974, was one of good economic growth and social progress, especially under Carlos Lleras Restrepo (1966–70), who gave much impetus to agrarian and administrative reform. In the 1970 presidential election, the narrow victory of the official Conservative candidate, Misael Pastrana, was challenged by the second-placed candidate, Gen. Rojas, representing ANAPO. When Pastrana's victory was confirmed there were mass protests, as the result reinforced the popularly held view that the system was unfair and could not produce change peacefully. One consequence was the founding by some ANAPO supporters in 1974 of the Movimiento 19 de Abril (M-19), a non-Marxist guerrilla group, which, unlike the others, was initially city-based.

RETURN TO LIBERAL GOVERNMENT, 1974–82

In the presidential election of 1974 the Liberal candidate, Alfonso López Michelsen, won a decisive victory over the Conservative Alvaro Gómez and the ANAPO contender, María Eugenia Rojas de Moreno Díaz. Curiously, the fathers of all three were former Presidents. The expectations aroused by López Michelsen's victory were great. He was the first Liberal to win a fully competitive election since his father, whose name still symbolized progressive liberalism. However, he was committed to continue to govern in coalition with the Conservatives, and any attempt at constitutional reform faced formidable opposition in the Congress and the Supreme Court. In fact, the López Michelsen administration's most lasting achievement was probably the introduction of association contracts for oil exploration, at a time when other Latin American countries were nationalizing their oil industries. This led to the great discoveries at Caño Limón in 1982 and at Cusiana in 1991.

President López Michelsen's successor was Julio César Turbay Ayala, who sought to solve the problems of urban terrorism and drugs-trafficking. His efforts met with some success, although his counter-insurgency campaign against guerrillas in 1982 provoked many allegations of human rights abuses by the armed forces.

THE DRUGS TRADE

The illegal drugs trade became a key factor in Colombia from the late 20th century. It began quietly in the 1970s with the cultivation and export of marijuana. Then, some Colombians saw the opportunity to gain a dominant role in the cocaine business. The coca paste was produced largely in Peru and Bolivia, which was flown to Colombia, which was strategically placed to process it into cocaine and ship it to the USA. By the early 1980s two groups in Medellín and Cali controlled most of the trade. When challenged by the Government, they retaliated and unleashed a cycle of violence that has continued to the present. In the case of the Medellín cartel under Pablo Escobar, violence escalated into 'narco-terrorism' (a direct assault on the state to force it to abandon the policy of extradition to the USA). The traffickers also hired paramilitaries to defend their newly acquired ranches from attack by the guerrillas. These paramilitary groups, often originally formed by the army, went increasingly on the offensive and killed many civilians in their counter-guerrilla war. Many cocaine laboratories and much of the coca cultivation were situated in the jungle in south-east Colombia, a stronghold of the FARC. (In 1982 the FARC added Ejército del Pueblo to its title, becoming FARC—EP for official purposes, although it remained commonly known by its shorter acronym.) The drugs cartels paid the FARC 'protection' money, which rapidly made it the world's richest guerrilla group. The advent of opium poppy cultivation in the early 1990s and the increase in coca cultivation from 1995 made the FARC and their paramilitary enemies in the Autodefensas Unidas de Colombia (AUC) even richer. From 2001 'Plan Colombia' (see below) led to a significant reduction in coca production, but the trend was temporarily reversed in 2005 as cultivation was switched to more inaccessible areas and smaller plots. However, the total of 68,000 ha under coca cultivation in 2009 represented a 60% fall over 10 years. Total acreage declined further to 57,000 ha in 2010 and stabilized at about 48,000 ha in subsequent years. Cocaine production totalled 290 metric tons in 2013, down from 333 tons in 2012 and 640 tons in 2005. Meanwhile, in Peru, coca cultivation increased to 60,000 ha in 2012 and, despite a decrease to 50,000 ha in 2013, the country remained the largest coca producer. It appeared that in Colombia a significant reduction in the trade and its profits was finally being made. In May 2014 the Government and FARC agreed to measures to help end drug production through greater support for crop substitution and voluntary eradication, with FARC ending its involvement in the trade and clearing mines in an attempt to make manual eradication safer.

The impact of the drugs trade on Colombia went much further than the direct effects described above. It diverted and weakened the judicial system and security forces, allowing common criminality greater impunity and creating a culture of violence and contempt for any legal or moral restraints. This led President Juan Manuel Santos in November 2011 to call for a serious debate on the UN drugs regime, including the possibility of legalization. The Organization of American States (OAS), at the Summit of the Americas in the city of Cartagena in April 2012, agreed to undertake a study of the issue (see below). The study, released in May 2013, did not issue recommendations but was highly critical of existing policies. In September 2012 the UN General Assembly agreed to hold a Special Session on drugs policy in 2016, at the request of the Presidents of Colombia, Mexico and Guatemala.

REFORM, PEACE AND NARCO-TERRORISM, 1982–90

In May 1982 the Conservative candidate, Belisario Betancur Cuartas, was elected to the presidency, mainly owing to divisions within the PL. Betancur had moved from the right of the party to its far left. However, with a Liberal majority in the Congress he had to continue the tradition of coalition government. Like his predecessors, he followed a prudent economic policy and encouraged foreign investment. Under his leadership, Colombia, traditionally a loyal US ally, became a member of the Non-Aligned Movement as well as the Contadora Group, which assisted efforts to find a peaceful solution to the conflicts in Central America.

Betancur attempted to resolve Colombia's internal conflict by agreement. He granted an amnesty to guerrilla prisoners and concluded ceasefires with the FARC, M-19 and the EPL. The FARC founded a political party, the Unión Patriótica (UP), which contested the 1986 elections. However, the ceasefires with both M-19 and the EPL broke down and in November 1985 the M-19 seized the Palace of Justice. In the ensuing recapture of the building by the army about 100 people were killed, including 11 judges, leading to strong public criticism of both the Government and the army. Betancur also faced the beginnings of narco-terrorism when, in 1984, drugs-traffickers from Medellín assassinated the justice minister, Rodrigo Lara Bonilla, who had taken the first serious measures to combat their activities. Betancur concluded that extradition to the USA was the only effective means of addressing the problem.

The drugs-trafficking problem dominated the presidency of the Liberal Virgilio Barco Vargas, elected in 1986 by a decisive majority. His offer to the Conservatives of a limited participation in government was refused, which resulted in the first single-party Government since 1953. Barco shared Betancur's belief in extradition, but the Supreme Court twice ruled that such a treaty with the USA was unconstitutional. Barco, however, used emergency decrees to proceed with extraditions. The Medellín cartel began a campaign of terror to force the Government to abandon this policy. In August 1989 it assassinated Luis Carlos Galán, the favourite to win the PL's presidential nomination in 1990. The M-19 and UP presidential candidates were also assassinated in early 1990. An aeroplane belonging to the national airline Avianca was blown up as were government offices, and in the first seven months of 1990 more than 200 police officers were killed in Medellín. Barco refused to be intimidated and appealed successfully for international support to counter the cartel's threat.

Barco also continued the peace process with the guerrillas. The ceasefire with the FARC broke down in 1987, but in 1989 a settlement was reached with the M-19. They regrouped as the Alianza Democrática—M-19 (AD—M-19) and participated in the 1990 elections. Their presidential candidate, Carlos Pizarro, was assassinated by paramilitaries. Successful negotiations with the EPL, the Partido Revolucionario de Trabajadores (PRT) and the Comando Quintín Lame were also concluded in 1990. Sadly, hopes that the FARC and the ELN might also enter into peaceful dialogue were reduced by the killing of over 2,000 members of the UP, largely by paramilitaries linked to the Medellín cartel. Although many of the paramilitary groups had been set up by the army, as they fell increasingly under the control of drugs cartels they were declared illegal in 1989.

CÉSAR GAVIRIA TRUJILLO: THE REFORM PROJECT

César Gaviria Trujillo, the Liberal candidate elected President in May 1990, was determined to accelerate political reform and the liberalization of the economy, a policy known as *apertura* (opening). After decades in which the Congress and the Supreme Court had opposed almost all constitutional change, an informal referendum, held at the time of the presidential election in 1990, produced a huge majority in favour of the election of a Constituent Assembly. It was elected in December, and the AD—M-19 and the Liberals received the largest share of the vote. Seats were also allocated to the EPL, the PRT and the Comando Quintín Lame as part of those groupings' peace settlements.

The Constituent Assembly drafted a new Constitution in 1991. It guaranteed every conceivable human right and took decentralization further, through the election of governors and the transfer of functions and central funds to departments and municipalities. It weakened the presidency by limiting emergency powers and providing for censure of ministers. A Constitutional Court was created, as was a prosecution service. Citizens were given the right to challenge almost any measure through an injunction (*tutela*), and extradition was prohibited. The Medellín cartel had halted its mass terrorist attacks when Gaviria took office, but had kidnapped several prominent figures. Gaviria offered the cartel the possibility of avoiding extradition if they released their hostages and surrendered, an offer that several prominent cartel members, including its leader, Pablo Escobar, accepted.

In his first year in office Gaviria liberalized labour markets, improved terms for foreign investment and promoted rapid integration within the Andean community, especially with Venezuela and Ecuador. However, the liberalization of the political system was not completed by a peace settlement with the FARC and the ELN. Negotiations with both groups failed in Caracas, Venezuela, in 1991 and in Tlaxcala, Mexico, in 1992. This was followed in April 1992 by a drought, which, in a country that was 80% dependent on hydroelectric power, resulted in 13 months of power cuts. In July the Government was humiliated when Pablo Escobar escaped from his luxurious prison outside Medellín and returned to narco-terrorism. However, his organization was gradually dismantled and he was killed by the police in Medellín in December 1993. Gaviria's determination to persist with his reforms was admired, and when he left office in 1994 his popularity was higher than that of any previous retiring President.

ERNESTO SAMPER PIZANO: SOCIAL REFORM AND POLITICAL CRISIS

In June 1994 the PL's Ernesto Samper Pizano was elected by a narrow margin in Colombia's first two-round presidential election. Two days later his defeated Conservative opponent, Andrés Pastrana Arango, disclosed the existence of taped conversations suggesting that the Cali drugs cartel had partly financed Samper's campaign. An initial investigation cleared Samper, but one year later the case was reopened when his treasurer, Santiago Medina, and then his campaign manager (at the time his Minister of Defence) accused him of personal involvement. The Cámara de Representantes (House of Representatives) finally voted to clear him of any wrongdoing in June 1996, but this was perceived by many as a political, rather than a legal, verdict. This long-running political crisis, which was exacerbated by US policy (see below), made it difficult for Samper to carry out the social reform programme on which he had been elected. Samper had made clear his reservations about the rapid pace of *apertura* pursued by Gaviria (under whom he had served as Minister of Economic Development until late 1991), and, as President, had aimed to moderate this policy.

Samper's domestic problems were exacerbated by the response of the USA. Initially, the US Administration stated that Samper would be judged on the results of his anti-narcotics policy, which proved to be quite successful, with the leaders of the Cali cartel captured in 1995. However, following Medina's accusations against Samper in mid-1995, US policy shifted, and the Administration of President Bill

Clinton (1993–2001) openly expressed its lack of confidence in Samper and demanded that further anti-narcotics legislation be adopted (seizure of assets, stricter penalties and even the reintroduction of extradition). Samper eventually succeeded in getting these measures approved by the Congress. Colombia was, meanwhile, refused certification for its anti-narcotic efforts in both 1996 and 1997 and only received a conditional certification in 1998. The consequences of decertification were severe: Colombia received no US export credits and the USA voted against loans to Colombia from multilateral banks. The confidence of both domestic and foreign investors inevitably declined. The fiscal deficit and foreign debt rose and economic growth slowed. The FARC and the ELN were correspondingly encouraged and saw no reason to negotiate with a President whom the USA considered corrupt. Foreign pressure, however, undoubtedly helped Samper to maintain a considerable level of popular support, as many Colombians resented such blatant US interference.

ANDRÉS PASTRANA ARANGO: THE PEACE PROCESS AND THE 'PLAN COLOMBIA'

The 1998 presidential contest was one of the closest fought in Colombian history. In the first round the Liberal candidate, Horacio Serpa Uribe, was less than one percentage point ahead of Pastrana, the defeated 1994 Conservative candidate. In the second round, however, Pastrana won by 500,000 votes. Many leading Liberals had supported Pastrana, believing him better placed to end Colombia's isolation, restore confidence in the economy and restart the peace process.

Unfortunately, the means to achieving the last two goals were often in conflict. Restoring economic confidence meant reducing the fiscal deficit sharply by cutting public expenditure and raising taxes. In the short term this worsened the recession and made it very difficult to maintain popular support for the peace process, which required greater military spending and increased social spending to mitigate rising unemployment.

Pastrana launched the peace process by taking the dramatic step of meeting Manuel Marulanda Vélez, leader of the FARC, in his jungle hide-out. Relations with the USA immediately improved following the President's stated commitment to orthodox financial management. The USA granted Colombia full certification in March 1999 and in 2000 gave US $1,300m. over two years to help restore security and stability and reduce the drugs trade. This funding formed the initial US portion of Plan Colombia (see below). To persuade the rebels to negotiate, Pastrana ceded them, temporarily, 41,000 sq km in south-east Colombia, from which all government troops were withdrawn. Public support soon disappeared when it became clear the FARC was using the demilitarized zone as a safe haven and was keeping military prisoners and kidnapped civilians there. Moreover, there was widespread public disquiet when both the FARC and the ELN began to kidnap more indiscriminately, particularly by taking more child victims.

President Pastrana's support for firmer military action against the FARC, while negotiating, and his success in winning substantially increased US aid for the armed forces ensured that military discontent with the peace process was contained. From 1998 the armed forces won all major engagements against the FARC, which contrasted with the last two years of the Samper administration when the army suffered several humiliating defeats. However, the FARC's capacity to launch guerrilla attacks was not affected and the number of kidnappings close to large cities rose. This led to increased support for the paramilitary AUC, whose numbers rose faster than those of the FARC. The AUC put the ELN under great pressure, which in turn exerted pressure with periodic mass kidnappings.

Central to Pastrana's strategy from 2000 was Plan Colombia. Its aims included increasing the efficiency of the security forces and the judicial system, eliminating drugs production through both eradication and crop substitution, and reducing unemployment. The international community was to fund almost 50% of the US $7,500m. Plan. The initial US contribution of $1,300m. included a military component of $1,000m. and in 2001 it provided a further $882m. under the new Andean Region Initiative, introduced following criticism of the Plan by worried neighbouring countries. The member states of the European Union (EU) also agreed to provide $300m., which was to be devoted to economic and social projects; the EU made it clear that its aid was not linked to Plan Colombia, owing to its differences over the project's military emphasis.

However, the slow progress of peace negotiations frustrated the Colombian public. Some degree of international involvement from February 2001 raised hopes that the peace process would succeed, but, following the hijacking of an aeroplane and the kidnapping of a prominent senator by the FARC, an utterly disillusioned Pastrana ended the peace process on 20 February 2002 and ordered the armed forces to regain control of the demilitarized zone. The FARC responded by resorting to urban terrorism in an attempt to intimidate the public into demanding peace again. The result was the election of Alvaro Uribe Vélez to the presidency in May, with 54% of the votes cast. The Liberal Horacio Serpa won 32%, while the Conservatives did not even field an official candidate, preferring to support Uribe. Uribe was a dissident Liberal candidate who had been a strong critic of Pastrana's peace process, and he proposed a dramatic increase in the security forces.

ALVARO URIBE VÉLEZ: TOWARDS DEMOCRATIC SECURITY

Colombian voters entered new territory in electing Alvaro Uribe to the presidency in 2002. For the first time, they elected someone who was not the official candidate of one of the two traditional parties. A dissident Liberal, Uribe ran as an independent, without even the support of a faction within the PL. He was also the first President committed to ensuring the state's control of Colombia's entire territory, and protecting the lives of all Colombians became the central tenet of his election manifesto. His success in improving security was to be a decisive factor in both the rapid economic recovery and in a dramatic political shift: constitutional change to allow presidential re-election, and his own subsequent re-election. Uribe's Democratic Security Policy faced an immense challenge. The illegal groups had grown to unprecedented levels, and the FARC saw him as a serious threat. Uribe increased the security forces by one-third during his first term. However, the economic restraints were considerable following the slow recovery from the 1999 recession, and Colombia's foreign debt neared the limits of sustainability.

Nevertheless, the new President had two factors in his favour. First, the security forces had been modernized under Pastrana and the military equipment and training provided by the USA under Plan Colombia were starting to show results. Second, the Uribe Government enjoyed high levels of public support, with an approval rating averaging some 70% during his first term. On taking office, Uribe declared a state of emergency, under which he levied a wealth tax to finance increased security. The expansion of the army and the police force was supplemented by the recruitment of 'peasant soldiers', who would serve in their own districts. A network of 'informers' was also established to help protect the roads. Within months the main roads were largely safe during daytime. Police began moving back to the 160 or so municipalities whence they had been withdrawn following guerrilla pressure, and by the end of 2003 all had a police presence again.

The FARC responded to the Government's measures by escalating its campaign of urban terrorism and attacks on the country's infrastructure; however, the group was increasingly on the defensive, and by 2004, under strong pressure from the security forces, it had withdrawn from the area around Bogotá towards its bases in the jungles of the southeast. The FARC rejected the President's terms for negotiations, which included discussions under UN auspices, on condition of a ceasefire.

Meanwhile, the majority of the AUC in July 2003 committed itself to a ceasefire, to be followed by negotiations and a phased demobilization. Over 30,000 paramilitaries were demobilized by March 2006 under the Justice and Peace Act (Ley de Justicia y Paz) passed in the previous year. When the provisions of the law for punishing crimes committed by the paramilitaries were strengthened by the Constitutional Court in 2006, AUC leaders threatened to remobilize the group. The task of integrating the rank-and-file members back into society strained government resources. A significant minority either became common criminals or, in some cases, joined new groups working for drugs-traffickers.

In addition to gaining congressional approval for unpopular tax, pension and labour reforms in late 2002, Uribe attempted to introduce further reforms, including a reduction in the size of the Congress, which were put to a referendum in October 2003. The results were disqualified, however, owing to a low turn-out and Uribe had to return to the Congress for further tax increases in 2005 and 2006. A further proposal to amend the Constitution to allow presidential re-election, which had failed to receive congressional approval in 2003, was revived in 2004 and approved by the Congress at the end of the year and by the Constitutional Court in October 2005. The measure had been opposed strongly by the PL and by a recently formed left-wing party, the Polo Democrático Independiente (which in 2006 merged with another group to become the Polo Democrático Alternativo—PDA).

The congressional elections of March 2006 gave majorities in both the House and the Senate to pro-Uribe parties: the newly formed Partido Social de la Unidad Nacional (Partido de la U) and the PC both did well. The PL came third in the elections to the Senate, but secured the most seats in the House.

Uribe's victory in the first round of the presidential election in May 2006 was expected, but its scale was not: with 63.6% of the valid ballot, it was more than any presidential candidate had received in Colombian history. Equally surprising was the impressive 22.5% of the vote secured by the PDA candidate, Carlos Gaviria Díaz, who came second. The 12.1% vote for the PL candidate, Horacio Serpa Uribe, contesting his third presidential election, was an extraordinary humiliation. Finally, it seemed, the established political dominance of the PL and PC had ended.

The decisive electoral victory did not bring the results expected of it. The economy prospered at first, with growth rates at their highest levels for nearly 30 years. Security continued to improve, although less rapidly than before, and reducing the drugs trade remained difficult. An investigation by the Supreme Court into links between congressmen and paramilitaries, which began in 2006, had by mid-2014 led to the arrest of or investigations into over 100 congressmen, as well as a large number of local politicians. The majority of those involved came from Uribista parties and generally represented departments on the Caribbean coast, where paramilitary influence had been strong. The 'parapolitical' scandal, as it was called, damaged the President's standing and soured relations with the Congress and the Supreme Court. The flow of public confessions by the main paramilitary leaders in Itagüí prison from late 2006 (although in May 2008 some 14 of the most prominent were extradited to the USA) continued to bring to light new allegations against congressmen, officials and officers, with many convicted including a cousin of the President.

Pressure increased during 2006 and 2007 for a humanitarian agreement under which about 50 prominent hostages of the FARC, including former presidential candidate Ingrid Betancourt and three US contractors, would be exchanged for the 500 or so FARC prisoners in Colombian gaols. In September 2007 Uribe asked the Venezuelan President, Lt-Col (retd) Hugo Chávez Frías, to use his good offices. This he did with enthusiasm until Uribe decided that he was intervening in Colombian internal affairs and abruptly ended his mandate in November. Chávez, nevertheless, persevered, and the FARC released two small groups of prisoners to him in early 2008 with the co-operation of the Colombian authorities. Colombians reacted with a demonstration in February 2008 by millions for the liberty of all the 700 or so hostages held by the FARC. In March 2008 Colombian forces bombed and briefly occupied a FARC camp inside Ecuador. Raúl Reyes, the FARC second-in-command and chief negotiator, was killed, and three computers were seized. Chávez broke off diplomatic relations with Colombia. President Rafael Correa of Ecuador also severed relations. Following an apology, Venezuela subsequently restored relations with Colombia. The Colombian

authorities' possession of more than 30,000 computer files, the authenticity of which was confirmed by Interpol, may have influenced Chávez's decision, as well as food shortages in Venezuela, which made Colombian food imports vital at that time.

Inside Colombia the FARC suffered further blows. Iván Ríos, one of its seven-member Secretariat, was killed by his own men in March 2008, and Manuel Marulanda, its founder and undisputed leader, died shortly afterwards. Moreover, in July 2008 a FARC commander was tricked into boarding a helicopter with 15 prisoners, including Ingrid Betancourt and the three US contractors, supposedly for transfer to the headquarters of Guillermo León Sáenz (alias Alfonso Cano), the new FARC leader, for negotiations for their release. The helicopter in fact belonged to the Colombian army, and the hostages were released without a shot being fired. There was general rejoicing in Colombia, and the incident, known as Operación Jaque, received highly favourable coverage around the world. The euphoria did not last long. The army's reputation was damaged by allegations in October 2008 that, in order to meet body count targets, unemployed youths from near Bogotá had been recruited to work in Cúcuta, where they had been shot while dressed as guerrillas. It became clear that it had been far from the sole case of 'false positives'. Uribe acted swiftly and dismissed three generals and 24 other commissioned and non-commissioned officers. Investigations were started against several of them, but strong criticism continued to be voiced by human rights organizations, both domestic and international.

The global financial crisis made Uribe's final year in office difficult. Minimal gross domestic product (GDP) growth in 2009 caused a rise in unemployment, and although growth resumed in the first quarter of 2010, the administration found it hard to deal with the effective bankruptcy of the public health system.

In the Congress the passage of a political reform bill to correct the faults exposed by the 'parapolitical' scandal, and of legislation to provide for a referendum on a constitutional amendment to allow the President to serve a third term (for which 5m. signatures had been collected), occupied the first nine months of 2009. Both measures were finally approved, but in February 2010 the Constitutional Court decided that the referendum could not take place, to the surprise of many observers. At the congressional elections on 14 March the Partido de la U came first in both houses with increased representation. The PC also made gains and came second. Although it only lost one seat in the House, the PL dropped from first to third place. The PDA lost seats in both houses, its representation decreasing from 10 to four in the lower house. The Cambio Radical (CR) also lost seven of its 15 seats in the Senate. The new entrants were a striking contrast: the Partido de Integración Nacional (PIN), which won nine seats in the Senate and 11 in the House, was a merger of several small Uribista parties whose candidates were usually relatives or close associates of congressmen condemned or under investigation for their participation in the 'parapolitical' scandal. The Partido Verde (PV—Green Party), from which five senators and three representatives were elected, had significantly gained in influence. Former mayor of Bogotá, Antanas Mockus Sivickas, was elected to the leadership of the party, and was subsequently selected as the PV's presidential candidate.

The presidential campaign saw Juan Manuel Santos Calderón of the Partido de la U, believed to be Uribe's favoured candidate, take an early lead, with Noemí Sanín (PC) in second place. However, the situation changed when an independent candidate, Sergio Fajardo, the ex-mayor of Medellín, realized that his chances were poor and joined Mockus's ticket as vice-presidential candidate, greatly improving Mockus's ratings. On 30 May 2010 Santos won 47% of the votes cast. Mockus came second with 22%, followed by Vargas Lleras (CR) with 10%, Gustavo Petro Urrego (PDA) 9%, Sanín 6% and Rafael Pardo Rueda (PL) 4%. In the second round on 20 June Santos was elected with 69% of the vote; Mockus secured 27%. The result of the election showed popular support for continuity but also for the 'cleaner' government that Mockus advocated.

JUAN MANUEL SANTOS, 2010–

Santos's election was greeted with relief by most Colombians. It was emphatic and put an end to the uncertainties of the previous two years. The PL, which had opposed Uribe strongly, joined a Government of National Unity, alongside the Partido de la U, the Conservatives and the CR. Germán Vargas Lleras, the CR leader who had been an increasingly harsh critic of Uribe, became Minister of the Interior. Consensus and conciliation rather than confrontation became the leitmotiv of the Santos administration. Santos's decision to restore the Ministry of Justice, which Uribe had merged with the Ministry of the Interior, found favour with the judiciary. Moreover, radical reform measures, especially a law to compensate victims of violence and restore land to the dispossessed, which was approved in June 2011 and signed by Santos in the presence of the UN Secretary-General, were widely welcomed, except by Uribe and his close followers, who objected to victims of the security forces being included. However, many had private doubts about the capacity of the administration to implement such an ambitious and controversial scheme.

Indeed, despite protestations of mutual respect between Santos and Uribe, Uribe seemed more and more to be the real opposition, with the formal opposition parties, the PV and the PDA, both disunited and ineffective. (In July 2011 the PV decided to support the Government, although without accepting office.) Uribe was highly critical of Santos's foreign policy. Negotiations on outstanding issues with Venezuela led to the eventual restoration of formal relations. Relations with Ecuador were also restored in January 2011. The ending of what had been seen as Colombia's isolation in the region added to Santos's popularity. Other foreign policy successes included the ratification of the free trade agreement (FTA) by the USA in 2011, and his appeal for a debate on UN drugs policy, which was taken up by the OAS in April 2012 and the UN General Assembly in October, the latter agreeing to hold a Special Session on drugs policy in 2016 (see above).

The killing of Mono Jojoy (Víctor Julio Suárez Rojas), the military commander of the FARC, in September 2010 was a major blow to the FARC. The FARC leader, Alfonso Cano, who had held out in south-west Colombia, was eventually killed in November 2011. Despite these setbacks, the FARC continued to mount frequent actions, which together with the increased activity of drugs-related gangs, usually formed of ex-paramilitaries, known as BACRIM (Bandas Criminales Emergentes—Emerging Criminal Gangs), in north-west and south-west Colombia, led to charges that the Santos administration was softening its approach. The Government increased its efforts against the BACRIM and killed or captured many of their known leaders, but in mid-2014 they still remained a significant problem, especially on the Caribbean coast.

After the death of Cano, Santos stated his determination to bring the armed conflict to an end during his presidency. Legislation, the Marco Jurídico para la Paz (Legal Framework for Peace), which provided a constitutional basis for the Government to put specific proposals to the Congress to offer special treatment to FARC or ELN members if there was a peace agreement, was passed in June 2012, despite much criticism from human rights organizations. However, the FARC remained publicly scornful.

Santos maintained very high approval ratings through most of his first two years. However, his ratings fell below 50% for first time in mid-2012 when he himself had to call on the Congress to abandon the major legal reform that he had proposed. In negotiations between the Senate and the House clauses were added, which would have allowed up to 1,500 prisoners facing trial for links with the paramilitaries (including a hundred ex-congressmen) to go free as the new arrangements to prosecute them would not have been in place. As these reforms took the form of constitutional amendments Santos did not have the right of veto but he persuaded the Congress to vote again to abandon the whole project.

This episode damaged the reputation not only of the Congress, which was already low, but of the higher courts whose justices had insisted on extended terms and later retirement as the price of their agreement. Doubts were raised about Santos's style of governance. Critics also stated that the reform measures had been too wide-reaching and complex. The failure meant that the slowness of justice and the high incidence of impunity, one of Colombia's most urgent problems, would yet again not be addressed.

Santos restored his reputation for decisiveness by unexpectedly announcing the start of peace negotiations with the FARC in September 2012. They had been prepared in complete secrecy in Havana, Cuba, by a government delegation led by the national security adviser, Sergio Jaramillo Caro. The talks opened formally in Oslo in October and negotiations started in Havana in November. Public opinion was favourable. The efforts were also praised by the international community for the apparently professional manner in which they had been prepared and for the decision to involve Norway and Cuba as guarantors, with Venezuela and Chile as supporters, but without external mediation. The fact that the talks would concentrate on ending the conflict, with no ceasefire until a deal was struck also received approval. In other words, there would be no repeat of the demilitarized zone project of 1999–02.

Doubts about the possibility of success, however, soon arose as dialogue on the first item of six (rural development) continued until May 2013. The second item (political participation) was not concluded until November 2013, which had been Santos's original target date for a deal. Agreement on the third item (drug policy) was reached only in May 2014. The fourth item (victims) was concluded in June 2014 just before the second round of the presidential elections. This slow progress weakened support for the process, and political grandstanding by the FARC, combined with persistent low level attacks by the FARC and ELN, exacerbated the criticism. In early June 2014 it was announced that preparatory talks had been held with the ELN and progress had been made on an agenda. It was thought likely that the negotiations would take place in Ecuador.

Uribe was very critical of the peace process, and, increasingly, of Santos personally and of his handling of security. In July 2012 he launched a new movement, the Centro Democrático (CD), to field a candidate against Santos if he sought re-election. In early 2013 Santos's standing suffered heavily from a series of strikes and demonstrations (paros) by coffee, dairy and potato farmers against low prices and imports under the FTA with the USA. The protesters' grievances were real although, according to some reports, the CD and the FARC had fomented some of the unrest. Santos, initially dismissive, was forced to buy off the protesters with subsidies, which would be unsustainable in the long term. The paros were repeated on a smaller scale in May 2014 during the presidential campaign.

THE RE-ELECTION OF SANTOS

At congressional elections in March 2014 Santos's governing coalition retained its majorities in both houses, although a strong opposition emerged in the Senate, where the CD under Uribe's leadership won 20 seats. The Partido de la U secured 21 seats, the PC won 18 and the PL 17. In the House of Representatives the PL led with 39 seats, followed by the Partido de la U led with 37 seats, the PC with 27, the CD with 19 and the CR with 16.

The success of the CD transformed prospects for the presidential election in May 2014. The re-election of Santos had seemed assured, despite a majority in the polls against re-election in principle and the impact of the paros. Moreover, the CD's success in the congressional elections provided a great boost to their candidate, Oscar Iván Zuluaga, who secured 29.3% of votes in the first round against Santos's 25.7%. The PC candidate, Marta Lucía Ramírez, won 15.5%, the PDA candidate, Clara López, won 15.2%, while the Green candidate, Enrique Peñalosa, secured 8.3%.

In the second round, on 15 June 2014, Santos, who had received the support of Clara López, as well as Mayor of Bogotá Gustavo Petro and other leftist leaders, won 51% of the vote, to Zuluaga's 45%. The turnout was recorded at 48%. Santos's vote increased decisively in Bogotá where the Left's support was critical, and on the Caribbean and Pacific coasts where the PL's support had historically been strongest.

INTERNATIONAL POLICY

Given Colombia's association in the popular mind with violence, it is worth stressing that the country has an admirable record in international matters. Colombia has never attacked another country, and lost Panama through US intervention in 1903. Colombia has been a consistent opponent of the use of force to settle disputes and condemned the Argentine invasion of the Falkland Islands (Islas Malvinas) in 1982, despite pressure from most other Latin American countries. The country has contributed to UN peacekeeping operations since their inception.

A founder of the Andean Pact in 1969, Colombia under President Gaviria played a leading role in the 1990s in making economic integration a reality, initially with Venezuela and Ecuador. This was followed by the formation of a free trade area with Venezuela and Mexico in 1994—the G-3. Colombia concluded FTAs with Chile and, in 2004, with the Mercado Común del Sur (MERCOSUR). In June 2004 Colombia, together with Ecuador and Peru, began negotiations for an FTA with the USA, which Colombia concluded in February 2006. The Congress ratified the FTA in June 2007, but the US Congress repeatedly postponed consideration of the accord until the outcome of the investigations into the 'parapolitical' scandal was known and measures were taken to protect trade unionists. The FTA was finally ratified in October 2011 and entered into force in May 2012. Colombia signed an FTA with the EU in June 2012, which was ratified by the European Parliament in December and by the Congress in June 2013. It entered into force in 2014, following ratification by all EU member state parliaments.

In 2007 Venezuela denounced the agreements as submission to US 'imperialism', having withdrawn from the Andean Community of Nations and G-3. Relations with Venezuela deteriorated further when President Uribe ended President Chávez's mandate as a negotiator with the FARC for hostage release (see above). They reached their lowest point when Chávez broke off relations after the Colombian attack on the FARC camp in Ecuador in March 2008 (see above). Relations were restored after the Rio Group summit days later, and, despite ideological differences, Uribe and Chávez resumed a working relationship. Ecuador also severed relations at this time, which were not fully restored until 2011. Relations with Venezuela worsened again in mid-2009 when Colombia agreed to allow US forces to use seven Colombian military bases for counter-terrorist and counter-narcotics operations. Chávez denounced the move as part of a US plan to intervene in Venezuela and imposed severe trade sanctions against Colombia. These caused a sharp fall in Colombian exports to Venezuela in 2009. Ironically, in 2010 the Constitutional Court ruled that the agreement was unconstitutional. Relations were restored under Santos and Venezuela paid some of its debts to Colombian exporters. A close diplomatic collaboration developed, which helped to resolve the Honduran dispute and led to the two countries taking turns to hold the post of Secretary-General of the Union of South American Nations (Unión de Naciones Suramericanas—UNASUR). Venezuela became one of the countries to support the peace process in 2012. The newly elected Venezuelan President, Nicolás Maduro, threatened to withdraw this support when President Santos received his defeated opponent, Henrique Capriles, in May 2013. He did not do so, but Colombia's willingness to act as one of three observers at talks between the Maduro administration and the opposition in early 2014 was intended to reduce the likelihood of future tensions.

Traditionally, Colombia has been a loyal US ally, although its role in the Non-aligned Movement from the 1980s led to some more independent stands. Close collaboration with the USA on anti-narcotics policy was established under President Barco and continued thereafter, albeit with difficulties under President Samper (see above). Under the Uribe administration, the relationship became even closer, and Colombia supported the US-led coalition against the regime of Saddam Hussein in Iraq in 2003. There were signs of disillusionment in Colombia about US policy, and the Santos administration looked increasingly to Europe and to Asia. The People's Republic of China had replaced Venezuela as Colombia's second most important market in 2010. In June 2012 Colombia signed an FTA with the EU (see above), concluded negotiations for one with the Republic of Korea (South Korea) and formed the Pacific Alliance with Mexico, Peru and Chile, which aimed at increasing trade between them and with Asia.

Santos's appeal in November 2011 for a serious debate on the UN drug regime was a clear sign of increased Colombian confidence. The subject was discussed at the Summit of the Americas in Cartagena in April 2012 and a study by the OAS was agreed and reported in May 2013 (see above). The UN General Assembly in October 2012 agreed at the request of Colombia, Mexico and Guatemala to hold a Special Session on drugs policy in 2016.

In November 2012 the International Court of Justice issued a judgment in a case brought by Nicaragua, which awarded sovereignty of disputed islands to the west of the San Andrés archipelago to Colombia, but established a maritime boundary between the two countries in favour of Nicaragua. This was widely regarded as a serious blow to Colombian diplomacy, as well as to the livelihoods of San Andrés fishermen, and the Uribe and Pastrana administrations were held responsible. The Santos administration claimed no change to Colombia's boundaries could be made except by treaty.

OUTLOOK

Colombia in mid-2014 was seen as one of the most promising economies in the developing world. All three leading rating agencies had awarded it investment grade status. The turn-around from 2002 under Uribe and then Santos had taken Colombia from talk of becoming a failed state, to a country highly favoured by foreign investors. This success was reflected in the robustness of the Colombian economy in the financial crisis, recording significant growth, despite the slowing of the world economy and falling commodity prices. It had become, however, an economy for the first time primarily dependent on oil and mining, which produced large revenues but severe environmental problems, and few jobs and an overvalued currency. Foreign investment was also much more significant than previously. The Colombian state could no longer plead poverty and the public was increasingly frustrated by the country's poor infrastructure and slow progress in improving it, although ambitious projects were under way and more were planned. Although now considered an upper-middle income country by the IMF, in 2014 it still had high, although declining, levels of poverty and inequality.

The prospect of a successful peace process had made Colombia even more attractive to investors, but politically it had created uncertainty. Santos's victory gave him a mandate to complete the process, but success was by no means assured. The two remaining items (victims and disarmament and implementation of the agreement) would not be settled easily. Delays, accompanied by continued FARC attacks, would erode public support. Uribe would continue to criticize bitterly. In mid-2014 the FARC still seemed committed to an agreement. There was, however, a risk that by having played politics with the *paros* and delaying a deal until after the election, Santos had been weakened to the point where the far Left could claim to have contributed significantly to his victory, and the best chance of securing public approval of an agreement might have been missed.

The most critical point was that the FARC were likely to resist the imprisonment of any of their leaders or their illegibility to run for elected office. Santos, who was committed to avoiding impunity, hoped that under the Legal Framework for Peace (see above), a transitional justice formula could be found—a Commission on Truth and Justice, suspended sentences, community service—which the FARC could accept. It was far from certain that they would do so. If it passed the various legal hurdles it would need to be approved by a referendum. A majority had been in favour of an agreement throughout, (although disinclined to believe that the FARC would deliver), but only on condition the FARC leaders served time. Santos would find it a great challenge to square this circle. The 45% of votes won by Zuluaga in the presidential election means a referendum victory would be hard to achieve, especially if Uribe decided to lead the 'no' campaign himself.

One problem would be turnout, as under the Constitution 25% is required for validity.

The failure of the peace process would be a serious setback for Colombia. It was estimated that a fully implemented peace process would be worth an additional 2% of GDP, not to mention the number of lives saved. However, as there had not been a cessation of the conflict, it would be more a loss of expectations than a change on the ground. The security forces would be fully capable of keeping FARC activity to much its present level and of weakening the organization gradually over time. It would, of course, be a considerable blow to Santos's own position, as he had staked his presidency on achieving peace.

The future of the peace process will not be the only source of political uncertainty over the next four years. The role of the CD as a powerful opposition from the Right was a new and unpredictable factor. It had become more so by virtue of Zuluaga's strong showing in the presidential race and also because of the bitterness of the campaign. There were allegations of criminal activity by campaign advisers from both campaigns. The Santos campaign portrayed the Zuluaga campaigners as extreme rightists who would insist on a military solution to the country's conflict, while the Zuluaga team suggested that a Santos victory would hand the country over to Castro-Chavismo. While Zuluaga accepted defeat gracefully, Uribe claimed that there had been extensive vote-buying and also intimidation by FARC and ELN. The country, or at least its political mainstream, seemed polarized as it had not been since the 1950s. Fortunately, the public no longer followed their leaders with the same passion.

Santos has his mandate and retains the power of patronage but might find it difficult to meet the demands of the heterogeneous coalition that re-elected him. His vote in the second round ballot fell from 69% in 2010 to 51% in 2014 and his 47% in the first round in 2010 came from very much the same voters who had provided Zuluaga's 45% in the second round in 2014. With the various factions of the Left expecting his support in holding on to power in Bogotá and the old-guard politicians from the coasts demanding additional public spending in their fiefs, as well as a larger share of posts, life would not be easy. Faced by determined opposition from the CD and the Left, except on peace in the latter case, Santos would have difficulty in reforming the judiciary and the health system, which he had failed to achieve in his first term. Other unresolved issues were the new mining code and the problem of environmental licensing and community consultation, which had seriously slowed mining, energy and infrastructure projects, and the lack of any coherent agricultural policy.

Santos added another element of uncertainty by proposing that re-election should be dropped and the presidential term lengthened to five or six years. The change had wide support, as re-election had become associated with heightened corruption. The prospect of an extended term made the 2018 presidential election particularly tempting. The main political beneficiary of a successful peace process was likely to be Santos's new Vice-President, Germán Vargas Lleras, who would be a strong candidate, having been Santos's most successful minister and having considerable experience, both in the Congress and as a campaigner. The democratic left could, however, be the long-term winner. The existence of the FARC (and the ELN) had blighted the chances of the democratic left for 50 years. The control of Bogotá by the Left since 2003 had shown its electoral potential. A centre-left candidate should logically be a leading contender in 2018, with a better chance of victory in 2023 or 2024. What could stop such a realignment of Colombian politics would be the traditional factionalism of the Colombian left (the PDA had split in 2011—see above) and the fear of Bolivarianism from the neighbouring country. Only a leftist candidate, untainted by Bolivarianism, could hope to win in the second round of a presidential election. The present Governor of Antioquia, Sergio Fajardo, who was a successful Mayor of Medellín, could attract significant support as a modernizer outside the main parties. Additionally, of course, there would be a strong CD challenge, even with a peace deal. Implementation would necessarily be difficult, as Northern Ireland showed, and the CD could benefit as the Democratic Ulster Party did there. If the peace process were to fail, the CD's chances would be even greater and the Left's would be reduced.

Colombian foreign policy under the second Santos administration would continue to be pragmatic with trade being the top priority. With FTAs with both the USA and EU in place, Colombia was looking to Asia. Its membership of the Pacific Alliance (Alianza del Pacífico), comprising Mexico, Colombia, Peru and Chile, which was established in June 2012, was key to this strategy. These countries shared Colombia's liberal, reformist approach. There would be competition not confrontation with the Venezuelan-led Bolivarian Alliance for the Peoples of our America-People's Trade Treaty (Alianza Bolivariana para los Pueblos de Nuestra América-Tratado de Comercio de los Pueblos—ALBA-TCP). Trying to avoid conflict with Venezuela, in contrast with the Uribe administration, would continue to be a priority, especially since Venezuela's support was vital to the peace process. Colombia's role as one of the three countries accompanying the talks between the Maduro administration and the opposition in 2014 was an effort to reduce the risk that Venezuela's internal crisis would spill over into Colombia. It involved ignoring the FARC presence there, which Uribe was quick to criticize. A successful peace process would remove this constant cause of tension.

Seeking a new approach on international drugs policy would also continue to be a priority. Santos had put it firmly on the agenda and would want Colombia to play a leading role at the UN General Assembly Special Session in 2016. Colombia would continue to have higher than normal levels of violence, even after a successful peace process, as long as the illegal drugs trade remained a hugely profitable business.

Economy

JEREMY THORP

INTRODUCTION

Colombia has the fourth largest economy in Latin America. Its gross domestic product (GDP) in 2012 was US $369,789m., according to the IMF, and it is the third largest country in terms of population (47.6m. in 2014, according to Colombia's Departamento Administrativo Nacional de Estadística—DANE). According to IMF estimates, Colombia is the 29th largest economy in the world, adjusted for purchasing power parity. The economy has weathered global financial turbulence in recent years and has grown strongly since 2003, changing over the past decade from a basically agricultural to an oil- and mineral-exporting country.

Colombia is classified by the World Bank as an upper middle-income country, with substantial potential, yet with high rates of poverty and inequality. This reflects Colombia's history. As both a Spanish colony and an independent state, Colombia has been impoverished. Economic development was hampered by the country's challenging geography and a lack of a major export commodity, which constrained successive governments from raising the revenue from customs duties needed either to maintain law and order or to build infrastructure. These factors and the small size of the market deterred both foreign investors and also immigrants.

A brief coffee-led period of prosperity in the 1920s was ended by the Great Depression in the 1930s. This led to a policy of import substitution, with the aim of both promoting local industry and insulating the country against the world economy. With this policy in place, Colombia grew steadily, if unspectacularly, until the 1990s, and it became a rare model of economic and financial stability in Latin America, especially during the turbulent 1970s and 1980s. GDP grew at an average annual rate of about 4% throughout the 1970s, 1980s and most of the 1990s.

The Government of President César Gaviria Trujillo (1990–94) changed the direction of Colombia's economy, opening it up to global competition by reducing tariffs, abolishing many import restrictions, inviting foreign investment, embarking on a privatization programme and allowing the Colombian peso to float relatively freely. However, the economy weakened in the second half of the 1990s. Although the administration of President Ernesto Samper Pizano (1994–98) largely maintained the free market policies implemented by Gaviria, a steep increase in central government and regional spending, and the increasing cost of the civil conflict, weakened economic performance and sharply increased the fiscal deficit and inflation. Average annual GDP growth during Samper's presidency was just over 2.5%.

The incoming Government of President Andrés Pastrana Arango (1998–2002) faced an incipient recession, sharp declines in international commodity prices and prevailing instability in emerging markets. Despite the Pastrana Government pursuing a fiscally conservative, orthodox economic programme for recovery, the economy suffered from adverse external factors, a banking crisis and the growing internal conflict. Colombia lost its investment-grade sovereign debt rating. Inflation fell, but GDP growth remained sluggish; average annual growth during the Pastrana administration, at 0.5%, continued the decline of previous years.

The administration of President Alvaro Uribe Vélez took office in 2002 and implemented significant tax, pension and labour reforms. The new Government's success in improving the security situation, together with rising commodity prices, made a major impact in restoring business and international confidence. The result was higher GDP growth rates and sharply increased investment (total investment was 22% of GDP in 2010, according to the IMF). A favourable economic conjuncture helped secure President Uribe a second term in office in 2006. Thereafter, foreign direct investment (FDI) continued to rise sharply. In 2008–13 FDI totalled about US $70,200m., compared with $22,100m. in 2000–05, according to Banco de la República. The conservative economic policies implemented by successive governments resulted in a gradual reduction in the rate of consumer price inflation, from a 15.3% average annual rate in 1993–2002 to about 2.7% in 2011–13 (according to Banco de la República). Unemployment remained high, and above the regional average, at about 9.6% in 2013 (according to the IMF), but compared favourably with a rate of 20% recorded in 2000.

The improvement in Colombia's economy in recent years is encapsulated by the change from the 2.5% average annual increase in real GDP in 1993–2002, to 4.8% in 2010–13 (according to the IMF). The IMF's current forecast for 2014 is an increase of 4.5%. Per caput GDP rose from US $6,476 in 2003 (adjusted for purchasing power parity, in current dollars) to around $11,188 in 2013, an increase of about 72%, according to the IMF. However, the economy is one of the poorest, and the level of income inequality one of the highest, of the larger economies in the region with a Gini coefficient of 0.539 in 2013, according to DANE. About 33% of the population were below the poverty line in 2012 (of which about 9% were in extreme poverty), although this compares with 42% in 2008. About one-half of workers are in the informal sector. Poverty and income inequality remain a challenge and a major priority for the current administration, as well as a constraint on the economy.

AGRICULTURE

Until the 1990s Colombia relied heavily on agriculture, a sector of the economy that was immensely diverse, owing to the country's varied topography. In 1960 agriculture (including forestry, fishing and hunting) employed over one-half of Colombia's total workforce, and in 1976 it accounted for 26% of GDP. By 2012 agricultural employment had fallen to 16.9% of total employment (according to the World Bank), and nearly four-fifths of the population lived in urban areas. The contribution of the sector to GDP was about 6.1% in 2012 (according

to DANE). The long-term decline in agricultural employment sharply accelerated during the economic liberalization of the early 1990s, as reduced tariffs made imports affordable. After 1994 the sector became more stable, despite the continuing violence in many of Colombia's rural areas. Production, measured at constant prices, grew slowly (by an average of 1.5%) in 2006–12. Widespread flooding, as a result of the weather phenomenon La Niña, had a negative impact on output in 2010 and 2011. However, output recovered in 2013, despite strikes in the agricultural sector, which resulted from fears that the US-Colombia Free Trade Agreement (FTA) was having an adverse impact on domestic agricultural production. Much land in Colombia is either not cultivated or under-cultivated, with long-term potential for increased production.

Coffee

Coffee is Colombia's leading legal cash and export crop, although 2012 was one of the worst for coffee output for many years and prices have fluctuated widely in recent years. Colombian coffee enjoys an excellent reputation around the world and Colombia was ranked in 2012 as the world's fourth largest producer after Brazil, Viet Nam and Indonesia (according to the International Coffee Organization). In the early 1980s coffee accounted for roughly one-half of total export earnings, but with the growth of oil and minerals exports this figure had fallen to about 3.2% by 2013 (according to Banco de la República). With almost 800,000 employees coffee still accounted for about one-half of employment in agriculture. Some 560,000 families in Colombia worked in coffee plantations at this time, of whom 95% owned less than 5 ha, creating a rural middle class unusual in Latin America (according to the Federación Nacional de Cafeteros de Colombia—FNC—National Federation of Coffee Growers).

The coffee sector was well regulated. Policy was set by the semi-official FNC. The Fondo Nacional del Café (National Coffee Fund) was established to help producers overcome sharp fluctuations in world prices. However, not even the Fund could cope with the fall in the coffee price following the collapse of the International Coffee Agreement in 1989. Colombia's response was to increase production, relying on its reputation as a high-quality producer of Arabica coffees. Prices fluctuated during much of the 1990s and fell to a 100-year low, in real terms, by the turn of the century owing, in part, to the dramatic entry of relatively low-quality Vietnamese Robusta coffee into the market. Colombia's small farmers could not compete on cost with large-scale Brazilian producers or the Vietnamese with their extremely low labour costs. The average price of Colombian coffees reached a low of US $0.64 in 2002, but with increasing demand and better marketing of high quality specialist brands it began to recover strongly and reached $2.83 in 2011, before falling back as low as US $1.25 at the end of 2013 as a result of oversupply, and picking up again to $2.20 in April 2014 (according to the International Coffee Organization). The area under coffee cultivation (about 974,000 ha in 2013, according to the FNC) has increased since the low in 2002, as have the number of growers. Coffee exports in 2013 were valued at $1,883m., a fall of about one-quarter compared with 2011 ($2,608m., according to DANE).

Bananas

Bananas were Colombia's most contentious legal export, the subject of long-standing trade disputes. The banana is a traditional Colombian crop and became part of the country's drive towards agricultural diversification designed to protect the economy from the fluctuations of the coffee market. Most of the bananas exported were grown in Uraba, in the north-west of the country, and Santa Marta in the central north. About 69,000 people were directly employed in the industry. The long-running dispute between the USA and the European Union (EU) about the latter's banana quotas was finally resolved at the end of 2009. The EU's FTA with Colombia, which entered into force in 2013, reduced the tariff on Colombian bananas from 12.5% to zero and promised substantial benefit to Colombia, with total exports of around US $764m. in 2013 (according to DANE), equivalent to about 1.3% of total exports. The EU was Colombia's biggest export market for bananas at this time.

Production was significantly affected by bacterial diseases in 2011 and a strike in 2013.

Flowers

The cut-flower industry was the biggest success story of Colombia's agricultural diversification. The industry is largely concentrated on the plain surrounding Bogotá, a choice influenced both by the climate and the presence of the international airport, vital for rapid movement of the flowers, mostly to the USA. The industry successfully coped with the overvalued peso of the mid-1990s and with increasing international competition. According to the industry, cut-flower production employed about 92,000 directly and 80,000 indirectly in 2010. Production appeared to suffer from the widespread flooding that affected Colombia in 2010–11, and the appreciation of the peso against the dollar. Exports were US $1,335m. in 2013, a 5% increase compared with the previous year and equivalent to about 2.27% of total exports.

Palm Oil

In 2013 Colombia, with about 1.025m. metric tons production, was the world's fifth largest producer of palm oil, although its market share was very small when compared with Malaysia and Indonesia. Palm oil production has increased steadily: exports in 2013 earned some US $180m. About 130,000 people are employed in palm oil production; in 2012 344,643 ha were under cultivation (according to the Ministry of Agriculture). The sector was encouraged by successive governments. The industry had considerable potential because the yields per hectare were some of the highest in the world and only a small proportion of the suitable land has yet been utilized. High costs, particularly of transportation from the interior, deterred expansion in the past, but total acreage sown for all palm production increased by over 90% in 2002–08, much of it near the Caribbean coast. However, the environmental and social impact of palm oil production is contentious; many large scale purchasers are now requiring growers to adopt more sustainable methods. There is also considerable potential for the export of the exotic fruits native to Colombia, such as star fruit and guanabana, although volumes will inevitably remain modest.

Staples

The traditional elements of the Colombian diet—apart from meat—are potatoes, maize, beans, rice, plantains, cassava and citrus. Domestic production of these crops was inevitably affected by the import liberalization of the early 1990s. Production stabilized thereafter. Colombia was the fourth largest rice producer in the Americas, with about 432,000 ha under cultivation. Rice production totalled about 1.9m. metric tons in 2013 (according to the US Department of Agriculture). Sugar production (raw and milled) was about 2.4m. tons in 2013, while potato output stood at around 2.6m. tons in 2012, according to FAO.

Livestock

Government initiatives to promote the supply of meat and dairy products through the use of subsidies led to an expansion in the amount of arable land dedicated to livestock. Almost 80% of the cattle population was based in the north-eastern pasture land of the Llanos. Cattle meat production in terms of animals slaughtered has fluctuated between 3.4m. and 4.4m. from 1995 to 2013. A problem facing many ranchers was endemic guerrilla violence in cattle-raising areas. Wealthy ranch owners, particularly those with connections to the drugs trade, could afford to defend their landholdings, but the threat of guerrilla and paramilitary violence, although reduced in many areas, continued to depress levels of rural investment and discourage foreign involvement in the sector.

Agrarian Reform

Land reform is a high priority of, and its implementation a major challenge for, the current administration. It is a key issue in the current talks between the Government and the FARC guerrillas. About one-quarter of Colombians live on the land. According to a frequently quoted statistic, 52% of land is owned by 1.1% of the population. Estimates of the numbers of Colombians forcibly displaced vary from nearly 4m. since 1997 (the Government's estimate) to 5.3m. (that of non-official

sources), and displacement is still occurring in parts of the country, particularly the south-west. Estimates of illegally expropriated land vary likewise, from 4m. to 6.6m. ha. Successive governments have attempted to improve economic and social infrastructure in rural areas. Since the introduction of the first agrarian reform law in 1961, Colombia's progress in this field has been intermittent and, while progress is being made it has been slow, notwithstanding the practical difficulties. Under President Uribe some 250,000 ha were to be subject to redistribution in 2006–10; 88,000 ha, about one-third of this objective, had been achieved by 2010, according to the Instituto Colombiano de Desarrollo Rural. In 2011 the Congreso (Congress) adopted wide-ranging legislation to restore the rights of millions of people forced off their land. It was hoped that the implementation of this legislation would help remove a major cause of social tension in rural areas. As part of a 10-year programme, with an estimated cost of about US $30,000m., the aim is to make restitution of 2m. ha by 2014; in 2013 official sources said that this target had been met. It is unclear what proportion of displaced people will return to the countryside when security is established and assistance to relocate is available.

The pattern of landholding varies greatly from region to region. The highlands of the Cordillera Oriental are mainly cultivated by smallholders, the majority of whom are often subsistence farmers. The coffee zone in the Cordillera Central is farmed in family-size commercial farms. The country's large cattle ranches are situated on the Caribbean coast and the Llanos. A longstanding obstacle to reforming the agricultural sector has been the question of legal title, as many internal migrants, or *colonos*, occupied land on Colombia's many internal frontiers. The legal position of these holdings has often remained obscure.

Drugs

The illicit drugs trade has both contributed to Colombia's economic growth and hindered it. Marijuana and coca have long been grown in the country, but the drugs trade really took off with the processing of cocaine from the late 1970s. Until the mid-1990s most of the coca paste used came from Peru and Bolivia, but when the supply, largely by light aircraft, was disrupted, coca cultivation in Colombia increased five-fold to replace it. Increased aerial spraying under 'Plan Colombia' reduced the overall area under cultivation (102,000 ha in 2002) by almost one-half between 2001 and 2004, despite considerable replanting, according to UN figures (US figures were much higher). In 2013, according to revised estimates from the UN Office on Drugs and Crime (UNODC), the area under coca cultivation in Colombia remained stable, at about 48,000 ha, compared with 2012. The production of coca leaves decreased by 14% owing to a lower yield per ha. The total farm gate value of the coca leaf crop and its derivatives (coca paste and cocaine base) was US $313m., 18% less than in 2012 and equivalent to about 0.2% of GDP. The number of households involved in coca production fell by 6% compared to 2012, according to UNODC. Since the market price of cocaine showed little change between the two years, the proportion of income from cocaine sales that was repatriated to Colombia may also have fallen. While Colombia remained the world's largest producer (accounting for some 50% of production), its share of global coca output was observed to be declining. In the 1990s there was an expansion, mainly in the south-west of the country, in the cultivation of the opium poppy—used to make heroin—and Colombia became the main supplier to the US market. However, acreage declined from 4,100 ha in 2003 to an insignificant level by 2011. The benefits or otherwise of this hidden input from drugs were disputed, as, by its nature, the trade resisted quantification, and many conflicting and extravagant estimates have been made. One reputable study estimated that Colombian traffickers' net profits averaged between US $1,500m. and $2,500m. from 1982 to 1998, and that two-thirds of this was brought back to Colombia. This would represent an average of 3.8% of GDP per year. Government estimates have put the figure at closer to $1,000m. per year, representing an average of 1.5%–2.0% of GDP, which seemed more likely, given that, for obvious reasons, a high proportion of drugs money is kept outside the country. The takeover by Mexican cartels of important drug supply routes to the USA that were previously controlled by Colombians may also have reduced net profits further in recent years. In May 2014 the Colombian Government and the Revolutionary Armed Forces of Colombia (FARC) reached an agreement on the subject of illicit drugs. A key aspect of the agreement is to help farmers switch from coca cultivation to legal activities in regions plagued by illicit crops.

The Colombian Government has always argued that the cost in terms of extra security expenditure, corruption and lost foreign investment was much higher than any gains. Certainly, the extra drugs-related crime—the guerrilla group FARC was believed to derive significant income from drugs-related activities in Colombia—and violence in rural areas, along with associated environmental damage, had a major negative impact. The Colombian Minister of Finance and Public Credit estimated in 2011 that between 1980 and 2005 Colombia's GDP had been reduced by about 1% annually as a result of violence and drugs-trafficking; others believe that the loss may have been higher. The World Bank has estimated that average income in Colombia would be some 50% higher than present levels had Colombia resolved drugs-fuelled and guerrilla violence 20 years ago. Violence in rural areas has also resulted in massive displacement from the countryside. This has, in part, resulted in about 75% of Colombians residing in urban areas, a proportion that is considerably higher than the regional average.

MINING AND ENERGY

Colombia had a long history of oil production, the largest coal reserves in Latin America, the world's largest emerald deposits and much gold, as well as great hydraulic resources. Mining and energy accounted for 11% of GDP in 2013 (of which oil and mining (coal and nickel) contributed about 8%, according to DANE, but represented about 70% of exports (Banco de la República). In 2013 Colombia's primary energy consumption was the equivalent of 38.0m. metric tons of oil, of which oil constituted the largest share (36.5%), followed by hydroelectricity (26.3%), gas (25.2%) and coal (11.3%), according to the BP *Statistical Review of World Energy 2014*. By 2012 the energy sector contributed about 25% of total government revenues (oil royalties alone were over US $5,000m.), about 70% of total exports and some 55% of FDI.

Coal

With the largest coal reserves in Latin America, according to the BP *Statistical Review of World Energy*, Colombia's proven recoverable coal reserves were about 6,746m. metric tons in 2013 (equivalent to 76 years at current production levels). In 2013 it was the world's 11th largest producer and in the previous year its fifth largest exporter, with over 90% of domestic production exported (according to BP and World Coal Association). Production has expanded rapidly, from 65.6m. tons oil equivalent in 2006 to 89.0m. in 2012 (according to BP). Coal exports in 2013 were US $6,687m., a fall from $7,805m. in the previous year, according to Banco de la República. The volume of production was about 3.5% lower in 2013 than in the previous year, reflecting the impact of strikes and environmental problems. The leading coal producer was the El Cerrejón open-cast mine in the Guajira, one of the largest mines in the world. It is currently owned in equal shares by an international consortium of BHP Billiton PLC, Anglo-American PLC and Xstrata. El Cerrejón produced 32.6m. tons of coal in 2013. The second largest producer in Colombia was the US company Drummond Ltd mining at La Loma in César department, with output of around 26m. tons in 2012, in a joint venture with Japanese trading house Itochu that was formed in 2011.

Petroleum and Gas

Colombia was a modest oil producer, usually producing a small surplus for export, from early in the 20th century until the major discoveries in the 1980s and 1990s. These followed the introduction of association contracts for oil exploration in the mid-1970s, which kept Colombia open to foreign companies just when most other developing countries were nationalizing their oil industries. The largest field in the country is the Rubiales field, located in Meta department. Other large oil fields include Caño Limón, Castilla, and Cupiagua. In the past, the Cusiana/Cupaigua complex (which BP sold to the largely state-owned Empresa Colombiana de Petróleos—Ecopetrol—in 2011) and Caño Limón represented the bulk of Colombia's oil production, but steep declines have reduced production at each to less than 50,000 barrels per day (b/d). Colombia's current oil production is more diffuse, with a large number of relatively small oilfields. According to industry analysts, the country is relatively under-appraised. Total Colombian petroleum production in 2012 was 1,004,000 b/d, over 6% higher than in 2012 (according to BP), following a period of static or declining production in 2003–07. Proven crude petroleum reserves stood at about 2,400m. barrels at the end of 2013, an increase of about 9% year-on-year, and equivalent to about 7.1 years' production (according to BP). The Colombian authorities recognize that the reserves to production ratio remains a challenge. Shale and offshore oil potential have yet to be fully explored.

A tightening of the terms of the association contracts in 1989 led to a sharp fall in new exploration in the 1990s. The creation in 2003 of the Agencia Nacional de Hidrocarburos (ANH) to take over the regulatory side of the activities of Ecopetrol and the new, improved terms that the ANH introduced in 2004, the most attractive in Latin America, were welcomed by the international oil industry. Furthermore, the exploration of blocks off the Caribbean coast had already attracted interest from leading companies. The ANH signed an increasing number of contracts (some 45 in 2012) and 115 exploratory wells were sunk in 2013 (and 131 in 2012). The oil sector has also benefited from recent improvements in security, which has improved access to remote areas previously dominated by the FARC (see History).

Colombia's gas potential has never received the same investment as oil, owing largely to low local demand. However, there were important stand-alone natural gas fields off the Caribbean coast and a great deal of associated gas in the main oilfields. In recent years production has increased rapidly, from an average of 6,100m. cu m in 2001 to 12,600m. cu. m (11.4m. tons of oil equivalent) in 2013, a 5.6% increase on 2012. Proven gas reserves were estimated at about 200,000m. cu m at the end of 2013, about the same as in the previous year (according to BP).

Minerals

Despite Colombia's position as a leading producer of gold, the country's mines were not only small scale and technologically unsophisticated, but also located in remote areas heavily affected by guerrilla activity in the late 1990s. However, after 2000 the volume of production increased rapidly, by about 70% by 2010. In 2013 gold production fell by 16% compared with the previous year, to 1.79m. troy ounces (55.7 tons). Exports were US $2,226m. in 2013, equivalent to about 3.7% of total exports (Banco de la República), a fall from the 2012 level, partly reflecting the fall in the gold price. Potentially large deposits have been found in the north of the country. Gold (and other) mining is increasingly controversial, mainly on environmental grounds, and licensing arrangements for new projects are expected to to be tightened. The nickel industry, accounting for about 1.16% of total exports ($680m. in 2013), is concentrated at the Cerromatoso plant, which is the world's second largest producer of ferronickel and has one of the lowest costs. Colombia produces about 60% of the world's emeralds; however, large-scale smuggling and fluctuations in quality made measurement exceptionally difficult. Emerald exports were officially valued at about $122m. in 2012 and $125m. in 2013. Colombia's mineral potential has not been fully explored; a medium term aim of the current administration is to diversify production in order to reduce reliance on oil and coal.

Power

Colombia made a massive investment in large hydroelectric projects in the 1970s and 1980s, and in 2012 this sector represented 64% of generating capacity with the remainder coming from thermal plants. The average effective electricity generating capacity in 2013 was 14,485 MW (Unidad de Planeación Minero-Energética). Following a severe drought in 1992–93, which exposed the economy's vulnerability to this over-reliance on hydroelectric power, a rapid expansion of thermal power stations was undertaken. Net generation reached an estimated 61,822m. kWh and domestic consumption averaged 60,287m. kWh in 2012, according to the International Energy Agency. According to the *BP Statistical Yearbook 2014*, hydroelectricity consumption was 44.4 terawatt hours in 2013, 6.6% lower than in 2012. During the mid-1990s there was a major privatization programme, with the sale of eight companies for more than US $5,000m., largely to Spanish electricity concerns. The privatization process of ISAGEN, the third largest generator in which the Government holds a 58% stake, was announced in 2013, suspended in March 2014, but resumed subsequently.

MANUFACTURING

Manufacturing, which accounted for 11.2% of GDP in 2013, representing a fall of around 1% compared with 12.0% in 2012 and 12.3% in 2011 (according to Banco de la República), grew steadily under import substitution policies from the 1930s to 1990. The drastic reduction in tariffs and removal of import controls in 1991 under President Gaviria's policy of economic liberalization, the *apertura* (opening), led to an average annual contraction in the sector of 0.8% in 1995–2004. As well as facing increased international competition, manufacturing had to cope with an overvalued currency for most of the decade and large-scale smuggling, which drugs-traffickers often used for money-laundering. None the less, manufacturing grew strongly (by some 20%) in the boom years of 2004–08. Thereafter, the sector experienced volatility and weakened in 2012 and 2013. The appreciation of the peso, volatility in neighbouring Venezuela and growth in imports from the People's Republic of China and Mexico were contributory factors. Food and beverages, the largest sector, was adversely affected by increased import penetration; growing by about 2% in both 2012 and 2013 (according to Banco de la República). The industry accounted for about 2.2% of GDP in 2011. The chemicals industry prospered, owing to major investment by multinational companies. The value of chemical exports increased from US $318.2m. in 1990 to $3,525m. in 2012 and 3.813m. in 2013, about 6.4% of total exports and 20 times greater than in 2010 (according to Banco de la República). The automobile industry is largely foreign owned. Eight car and motorcycle assembly plants produced about 139,000 units in 2012 and about 7% fewer in 2013. About 60% of all new units were imported. The textiles sector, based largely in Medellín, drove Colombia's industrialization from the beginning of the 20th century; in recent years production has declined slightly due to foreign competition. The industry contributed some 1.2% of GDP and about 1.6% of exports in 2013. Textile exports earned some $979.6m. in 2013 (according to Banco de la República).

CONSTRUCTION

As in many countries, the construction industry in Colombia is highly cyclical. The industry expanded by about 15% in 2012 and by a similar rate in 2013 (according to DANE), and in the latter year represented about 8.6% of GDP (according to Banco de la República).

TELECOMMUNICATIONS

Telecommunications, formerly the exclusive monopoly of the state communications company, were deregulated in the 1990s. Mobile licences were opened to international competition, and competition to the state concern for long-distance calls, the Empresa Nacional de Telecomunicaciones (TELECOM), was introduced. In 2003 TELECOM itself, which was heavily indebted, was dissolved by the Government and reconstituted as Colombia Telecomunicaciones, SA. A 50% stake in the firm was acquired by Telefónica of Spain in 2006 for US $370m. The industry as a whole expanded rapidly, outpacing the rest of the official economy. In 2013 there were an estimated 105 mobile telephones per 100 inhabitants (according to the Ministry of Telecommunications). In addition, there were about 7.1m. landlines in use, and 49 broadband internet users per 100 people in 2012.

FINANCIAL SERVICES

Colombia's financial services sector and its regulation are well developed by regional standards, particularly in banking. It is unique in Latin America in that a majority of its banks are locally and privately owned, and the sector is highly concentrated (about 50% of banking assets are controlled by two domestic financial entities). Only one-third of the population has access to the banking system, reflecting in part the large informal sector. The Colombian regulatory authorities maintain strict anti-money-laundering practices, according to the IMF. After banking crises in 1982 and 1998 banks' policies were more prudent and banking supervision was notably strengthened. Subsequently, the financial system recovered strongly and Colombian banks weathered the global financial crisis well. Assets of the financial sector increased by about 11% (9% in real terms) in 2013, (according to the Superintendencia Financiera de Colombia). The expansion of consumer credit (11.5%) continued to moderate in 2013 (according to Banco de la República). Return on assets and equity in 2013 was about 2.6% and 19.5%, respectively (according to the IMF). In March 2012 the capital asset ratio of credit institutions relative to risk-weighted assets was 16.3% in February 2014, with a regulatory minimum of 9%. In 2012 the authorities issued a decree to phase in by August 2013 a new capital adequacy regime that, according to the IMF, would significantly enhance the loss-absorbing capacity of bank capital. Overall the non-performing loan ratio was 2.8% at the end of 2013, the same level as in 2012, with provisions covering 186% of total non-performing loans, according to the IMF. Despite recent increases, total credit was equivalent to about 41% of GDP at the end of 2013 (according to Superintendencia) and gross household debt at mid-2012 amounted to about 13% of GDP (IMF). The stock exchanges in Bogotá, Cali and Medellín grew rapidly in the early 2000s (compound annual growth rate in 2003–09 was about 40%) as a result of privatization and deregulation measures undertaken. The assets of Colombian banks' subsidiaries abroad reached US $54,000m. (of which $44, 000m. was in Central America, particularly Panama), accounting for about 26.8% of the total assets of the Colombian banking system. The Colombian stock exchange index fell by about 12% throughout 2013 following the collapse of a brokerage firm the previous year. At the end of 2013 the market capitalization was about US $215,294m. (according to the Bolsa de Valores de Colombia). In 2011 Colombia, Chile and Peru formally combined the operations of their stock markets to form the Latin American Integrated Market, with a total market capitalization of about $601,953m. at the end of 2013. One aim is to diversify the constituent economies from their historic commodities exports. The Mexican stock exchange is expected to be incorporated into MILA in mid-2014, which would make the latter the largest exchange in Latin America.

PRIVATIZATION

The Gaviria administration made a modest start to privatizing Colombia's inadequate infrastructure by transferring ports, railways and some power stations to the private sector. Concessions were let for construction or modernization of airports, roads and water utilities, and several banks were also sold. The Samper administration privatized a major part of the power-generation industry, as well as several other banks. The Pastrana administration was forced to cancel its plans to sell the remainder of the power sector, however, owing to changed market conditions, but the state coal company, CARBOCOL, was sold in 2000. In 2004 the Uribe administration announced plans to privatize US $10,000m. of state assets over a five-year period. Sold first were two banks, Bancafe ($937m.) and Megabanco ($342m.). Ecogás was sold in 2006 to the Empresa de Energía de Bogotá, SA, for $1,410m., and a 50% stake in the state telecommunications firm was sold to Telefónica for $370m., also in 2006. In 2007 52% of steel company Acerías Paz del Río was bought by Votorantim Metais of Brazil for $850m. Equity offerings in the state oil company Ecopetrol reduced the state's ownership to 88.5% and a sale of an additional 8.3% has been mooted. The Government sold several regional power distributors in 2007, but plans by the Government of President Juan Manuel Santos to sell its stake in a major electricity company, ISAGEN, have been delayed (see above). Widespread strikes in Colombia in 2013 were partly aimed at privatizations.

INFRASTRUCTURE

Because of Colombia's daunting geography and history of under-investment, existing infrastructure does not match the needs of an expanding and modernizing economy. The quality of its roads was rated 126th in the world, according to a World Economic Forum global competitiveness report. A programme of infrastructure expenditure totalling some US $50,000m. was approved for 2012–20. Its aim was to increase transport investment to 3% of GDP (equivalent to some $10,000m.) by 2014. About $25,000m. was to be spent on roads, with additional major expenditures on railways, ports and airports and the recovery of the river Magdalena's navigability. About $10,000m. is allocated to increase power generation capacity from about 14,450 MW to 19,000 MW in 2019. Implementing these massive programmes is a major challenge; progress has been slower than had been hoped. The Government has taken steps to speed up compulsory purchases and environmental licensing, and a significant number of prequalification procedures have begun and contracts let.

FOREIGN TRADE AND BALANCE OF PAYMENTS

Colombia's foreign trade balance is dominated by increasing exports of oil and minerals, principally coal. Total exports recovered rapidly from the global market convulsions that had begun in 2008. Petroleum exports were estimated at US $32,009m. in 2013, equivalent to about 55% of total exports of goods, compared with 41% in 2010. The small increase in value (of 1.6%) compared with 2012 reflected increased volume, which compensated for a decline in the oil price (according to Banco de la República). Colombia exports about three-quarters of its oil production, mostly to the USA (according to the US Energy Information Administration). Coal exports have also risen steadily, from $2,558m. in 2005 to $6,688 in 2013, a decrease of 14% compared with $7,805m. in 2012, equivalent to about 11% of total exports; the decline reflected falls in both volume and price. Other major exports in 2012 included gold, cut flowers, nickel and bananas. Helped by favourable commodity prices and robust international economic activity, total exports had grown rapidly, from $21,200m. in 2005 to a near tripling in earnings (and a doubling in volume) of $58,923m. in 2012. However, they fell by about 3% in 2013 to $58,030m., resulting from lower commodity prices and volume. Workers' remittances were running at about $4,071m. in 2013 (equivalent to about 1.1% of GDP according to Banco de la República). The *apertura* of the early 1990s and a steadily growing economy saw Colombia's imports of goods—which had traditionally been fairly modest—grow rapidly, reaching $55,031m. in 2013, an increase of 0.7% compared with 2012. Colombia was able to report positive balances in trade in goods in most years from 1999, amounting to $6,189m. in 2012. Recent growth in imports resulted from strong consumption growth and investment-related imports and (on the services account) large profit repatriations by firms. The current account deficit totalled some $12,722m. in 2013, broadly equivalent to about 3.4% of GDP. However, the deficit continued to be more than offset by large FDI inflows (see below). The overall surplus was around $6,957m. in 2013. The exchange rate depreciated by about 9%.

Colombia's largest export market in 2013 was the USA (40% of the total), followed by the EU (15%), Venezuela (4%, still below the level before the latter's 2009 embargo) and China (5%). Colombia's main suppliers of imports in 2013 were the USA (about 30%), Mexico (10%), China (11%), the EU (12%) and Brazil (about 5%), according to DANE.

TRADE AGREEMENTS

Colombia's total trade in goods (exports and imports) with the rest of the world has risen from 25% of GDP in 2000 to 31% of GDP in 2013, according to the IMF. Increasing Colombia's network of trade agreements has been a major priority in recent years. Colombia enjoyed temporary trade preferences with the USA under the 2002 Andean Trade Promotion and Drug Eradication Act, covering about 80% of Colombian exports. The US-Colombian Free Trade Promotion Agreement (FTA) entered into force in May 2012, made those preferences permanent and extended them to almost all Colombian exports to the USA, as well as allowing, over a timetable, US agricultural, machinery and textile products into Colombia. An FTA with Canada entered into force in 2011. FTAs with the Republic of Korea (South Korea, 2012), Israel and Panama (both in 2013) have been signed, and negotiations for an FTA agreement with Japan continued in 2014. An EU-Colombia FTA, agreed in 2011, became effective in 2013, and was expected to eliminate tariffs on almost all Colombian industrial goods immediately; those on EU goods entering Colombia will be eliminated gradually by 2024. The agreement will also eliminate tariffs on agricultural trade in both directions. In June 2012 the Presidents of Colombia, Peru, Chile and Mexico launched the Pacific Alliance, to deepen the integration of their markets and provide a stronger platform for trade with Asian countries. The plan is to eliminate over 90% of tariffs between them by 2015; the remainder in the agricultural sector are to be gradually eliminated. Panama and Costa Rica have shown interest in joining the Alliance. Colombia has also established bilateral investment treaties with China, the United Kingdom and India, in addition to existing ones with Peru, Spain and Switzerland.

FOREIGN DIRECT INVESTMENT

FDI increased greatly during the 1990s, after the Andean Pact's abolition of limits on foreign holdings in 1990. Much European money went into the petroleum industry and then into banks and power generation when these were privatized. The level of foreign investment increased even further after 2004. In 2001–05 total FDI was US $19,700m.; during 2009–13 it was $59,598m., of which about $16,772m. was in 2013), equivalent to about 4.3% of GDP. About 47% of FDI in the latter period was in the oil and mining sectors. Other important recipients of FDI are manufacturing (17%), financial services, telecommunications, and the retail, restaurants and hotels sectors. The USA, Europe (notably the United Kingdom and Spain) and Mexico are the biggest investors in Colombia; Chilean firms also have a significant presence.

INDEBTEDNESS

Colombia was the only Latin American country that avoided major debt rescheduling in the 1980s. External debt grew slowly; from US $17,000m. in 1986, it reached $20,832m. in 2005 (from 46% of GDP to 27%). Total external borrowings increased thereafter, to about $91,879m. in 2013, equivalent to about 24% of GDP, of which public external debt was 13.8%, according to the Banco de la República. The external debt service to exports ratio was about 17% in 2013, of which public sector debt was about 10.3%. The Colombian authorities had little difficulty in financing the debt. Colombia's international reserves were equivalent to 10 months of imports at the end of 2013, when they stood at $43,632m., nearly 18% higher than at the end of 2012, and $45,036m. at end of May 2014, a further rise of 3% (according to the Banco de la República). Net public sector debt in 2013 was equivalent to about 41% of GDP, compared with about 46% in 2010 (according to the IMF). The public sector primary balance (before debt service interest payments) was estimated at 2.9% and 1.2% of GDP in 2012 and 2013, respectively. The combined public sector balance was a surplus in 2012 of 0.4% of GDP in 2012 and a deficit of 1% in 2013 (IMF). The establishment of fiscal rules and other reforms are expected further to reduce the deficit in the medium term.

At the beginning of 2011 the credit rating agencies raised their foreign currency rating on Colombia to investment grade status. This should reduce the cost of borrowing for both the Government and the private sector, and, after the loss of investment grade status for a decade, may prove a benchmark for future economic strategy.

OUTLOOK

The considerable economic successes under President Uribe's two terms in office owed more to improved domestic security, the benign international economic environment, at least until 2009, strong demand for oil and minerals, and continued conservative fiscal and monetary policies than to economic reforms. Colombia weathered the global economic and financial crisis of 2008–09 well. Volatility in financial markets and a slowdown in economic activity resulting from a reduced demand for exports, a fall in commodity prices, lower investment, reduced workers' remittances, and a drop in consumer confidence resulted in a sharp fall in GDP growth from 6.9% in 2007 to 1.5% in 2009 (according to Banco de la República). However, the economy recovered rapidly in 2010. Helped by strong exports, high FDI and robust domestic demand, growth was 4.0% in that year and 6.6% in 2011. However, the unemployment rate, which had fallen from around 15% at the beginning of the decade to 10%–11% in 2004, has since fallen only gradually. Consumer price inflation fell to 2.5% in 2012, at the lower end of the central bank's 2%–4% target range. The rate of growth moderated in 2012, to 4.0%, reflecting counter-cyclical policies, some supply interruptions and weaker demand for Colombia's exports. Following a reduction in the growth rate, in April 2013 the authorities published a stimulus plan with an estimated value of US $5,000m. The central bank's policy interest rate was held at 3.25% between April 2013 and April 2014. Since April 2014 the central bank increased its policy rate to 3.75% in the light of an acceleration in growth and inflation in the second half of 2013. Strong exports and FDI inflows (as well as monetary developments in developed countries) have caused the peso to appreciate since mid-2009. At the end of 2008 the peso stood at 2,243 to the US dollar; in mid-2011 it had strengthened to 1,750, an appreciation of 19%, but subsequently it has gradually weakened, to 1,884 in mid-June 2014. Inflows of external funds have created a dilemma for policy-makers; the appreciation has helped moderate inflation and the prices of capital goods, but could make the economy uncompetitive. The central bank undertook a number of measures to mitigate the rise in the peso, including a programme of foreign exchange purchases. This appears to have had some effect.

The incoming Santos administration faced a relatively benign economic outlook in August 2010. However, the Government was confronted with a number of challenges: a rate of growth that has not helped job creation and reduce unemployment; poverty reduction; inadequate infrastructure, particularly in the transport sector; an overvalued peso according to *The Economist'* s 'Big Mac' criteria; and improved but still unresolved security and drugs-trafficking issues. The new administration continued the basic elements of its predecessor's policies, maintaining and strengthening macroeconomic stability and high FDI inflows, and fostering a more business-friendly environment. Key 'engines of growth' have been identified as agriculture, housing, mining and energy, infrastructure, and innovation. The objective is to increase the trend growth rate and to reduce unemployment and underemployment. As part of a wide-ranging reform agenda, in 2011 the Congress approved a new fiscal rule, requiring that the structural balance of the central Government may not exceed an annual deficit of 1.0% of GDP effective from 2022 (it was just over 1% in 2013). Counter-cyclical spending, for which $970m. is being allocated to a stabilization fund, would be allowed if growth is two percentage points below the potential rate. Another law enacted in 2011 aimed to ensure that royalties from the petroleum and minerals sectors are distributed more evenly throughout Colombia rather than concentrated on a few regions. Royalties will also be used to finance science and technology and improve the quality of education. Draft legislation to facilitate formal job creation, improve finance for the housing sector, reduce tariff levels and reform health care has also been presented to the Congress. The Government aimed to reduce inequality via land redistribution, including to victims of the armed conflict, and establishing public services in remote areas. The Victims and Land Restitution Law, approved in June 2011, was likely to improve land distribution. A longer-term aim of the administration was to develop at least 5m. ha of under-used agricultural land, mainly adjacent to the Orinoco river in the Llanos region. Reducing Colombia's high income inequality is a policy priority. The National Development Plan targets a reduction of 1 percentage point per year in the Gini coefficient, which measures income inequality, between 2010 and 2014; the coefficient was calculated as 0.539 in 2012 and has been falling gradually. A 2010 tax reform increased the rate and base of the wealth tax paid by corporations and individuals, but was a temporary measure until 2014. The Government was making progress in phasing in universal and equal access to health services.

GDP in real terms grew by 4.3% in 2013 (about 4.9% at current prices), following 4.0% growth in 2012. The IMF's April 2014 *World Economic Forecast* predicted that growth in 2014 and over the medium term would be around 4.5%; Government forecasts for the year are a little higher. The external environment became less favourable in 2013, with lower commodity prices. However, growth recovered sharply during 2013 and does not seem to have been affected by the tighter financing conditions experienced elsewhere in Latin America; GDP growth in the first quarter of 2014 is provisionally estimated at 6.4%. Inflation remained towards the bottom of the authorities 2%–4% target range, although it rose to nearly 3% in the first quarter of 2014. Unemployment declined slightly, but is still high compared with other countries in the region. Barring major external shocks, the economy should continue to grow steadily. The re-election of President Santos for a second term in June 2014 is unlikely to alter the authorities' prudent fiscal and financial policies. Remaining challenges include the reform of pensions and health care, improvements to the quality of education, the implementation of a massive infrastructure programme and of major tax reforms, which hitherto has proved elusive. However, a robust policy framework, low levels of debt, increased expenditure on infrastructure, growing private and public consumption put Colombia in a strong position to weather any future storms. The currency appreciation seen in 2013 reduces but does not eliminate the risk that the economy could become uncompetitive. Colombia is also more vulnerable than hitherto to commodity price shocks; commodity exports contributed about 75% of export revenues in 2013, and FDI inflows were mainly linked to commodities. Stricter global financing conditions could also affect private capital inflows and public external financing. Perhaps in view of this, in June 2013 Colombia agreed with the IMF a fourth, two-year flexible credit line, of about US $5,840m., which the authorities regarded as a precautionary measure (none of the previous credit lines have been drawn upon). In June 2014 the IMF confirmed that Colombia continued to meet the qualification criteria for eligibility of credit line resources. Increased royalties from oil and minerals should help finance a successful outcome and implementation of a settlement, the subject of ongoing negotiations, to end the long-running internal conflict. This could provide a significant longer-term boost to the economy.

Statistical Survey

Sources (unless otherwise stated): Departamento Administrativo Nacional de Estadística (DANE), Transversal 45 No 26-70, Interior I-CAN, Bogotá, DC; tel. (1) 597-8300; fax (1) 597-8399; e-mail dane@dane.gov.co; internet www.dane.gov.co; Banco de la República, Carrera 7A, No 14-78, 5°, Apdo Aéreo 3551, Bogotá, DC; tel. (1) 343-1111; fax (1) 286-1686; e-mail wbanco@banrep.gov.co; internet www.banrep.gov.co.

Area and Population

AREA, POPULATION AND DENSITY

Area (sq km)	1,141,748*
Population (census results)	
24 October 1993†	37,635,094
30 June 2005‡	
Males	21,169,835
Females	21,718,757
Total	42,888,592
Population (official projections at mid-year)	
2012	46,581,823
2013	47,121,089
2014	47,661,787
Density (per sq km) at mid-2014	41.7

* 440,831 sq miles.
† Revised figure, including adjustment for underenumeration. The enumerated total was 33,109,840 (males 16,296,539, females 16,813,301) in 1993.
‡ A 'census year' was conducted between 22 May 2005 and 22 May 2006, and a 'conciliated' total for 30 June 2005 was finally published in May 2007 (the original enumerated total was 41,298,706) incorporating adjustments for underenumeration, geographical undercoverage and underlying natural growth trends.

POPULATION BY AGE AND SEX
(official projections at mid-2014)

	Males	Females	Total
0–14 years	6,579,899	6,292,690	12,872,589
15–64 years	15,390,911	15,911,272	31,302,183
65 years and over	1,560,860	1,926,155	3,487,015
Total	23,531,670	24,130,117	47,661,787

DEPARTMENTS
(official population projections at mid-2014)

Department	Area (sq km)	Population	Density (per sq km)	Capital (with population)
Amazonas . .	109,665	75,388	0.7	Leticia (41,000)
Antioquia . .	63,612	6,378,132	100.3	Medellín (2,441,123)
Arauca . . .	23,818	259,447	10.9	Arauca (87,242)
Atlántico . .	3,388	2,432,003	717.8	Barranquilla (1,212,943)
Bolívar . . .	25,978	2,073,004	79.8	Cartagena (990,179)
Boyacá . . .	23,189	1,274,615	55.0	Tunja (184,864)
Caldas . .	7,888	986,042	125.0	Manizales (394,627)
Caquetá . .	88,965	471,541	5.3	Florencia (169,336)
Casanare . .	44,640	350,239	7.8	Yopal (136,484)
Cauca . . .	29,308	1,366,984	46.6	Popayán (275,129)
César . . .	22,905	1,016,533	44.4	Valledupar (443,210)
Chocó . . .	46,530	495,151	10.6	Quibdó (115,517)
Córdoba . .	25,020	1,683,782	67.3	Montería (434,950)
Cundinamarca	22,623	2,639,059	116.7	Bogotá* (see note)
Guainía . .	72,238	40,839	0.6	Puerto Inírida (19,641)
La Guajira .	20,848	930,143	44.6	Riohacha (250,236)
Guaviare . .	42,327	109,490	2.6	San José del Guaviare (63,493)
Huila . . .	19,890	1,140,539	57.3	Neiva (340,046)
Magdalena .	23,188	1,247,514	53.8	Santa Marta (476,385)
Meta . . .	85,635	943,072	11.0	Villavicencio (473,766)

Department—*continued*	Area (sq km)	Population	Density (per sq km)	Capital (with population)
Nariño . . .	33,268	1,722,945	51.8	Pasto (434,486)
Norte de Santander .	21,658	1,344,038	62.1	Cúcuta (643,666)
Putumayo . .	24,885	341,034	13.7	Mocoa (41,304)
Quindío . .	1,845	562,114	304.7	Armenia (295,143)
Risaralda . .	4,140	946,632	228.7	Pereira (467,185)
San Andrés y Providencia Islands . .	44	75,801	1,722.8	San Andrés (70,684)
Santander del Sur . . .	30,537	2,051,022	67.2	Bucaramanga (527,451)
Sucre . . .	10,917	843,202	77.2	Sincelejo (271,375)
Tolima . . .	23,562	1,404,262	59.6	Ibagué (548,209)
Valle del Cauca	22,140	4,566,875	206.3	Cali (2,344,734)
Vaupés . .	65,268	43,240	0.7	Mitú (31,265)
Vichada . .	100,242	70,260	0.7	Puerto Carreño (15,505)
Capital District				
Bogotá, DC . .	1,587	7,776,845	4,900.3	—
Total . . .	1,141,748	47,661,787	41.7	—

* The capital city, Bogotá, exists as the capital of Cundinamarca department as well as the Capital District. The city's population is included here only in Bogotá, DC.

PRINCIPAL TOWNS
(official projected population estimates at mid-2014)

Bogotá, DC (capital)	7,776,845	Bello	447,185
Medellín . .	2,441,123	Valledupar . .	443,210
Cali . . .	2,344,734	Montería . .	434,950
Barranquilla .	1,212,943	Pasto . . .	434,486
Cartagena . .	990,179	Manizales . .	394,627
Cúcuta . . .	643,666	Buenaventura . .	392,054
Soledad . .	599,012	Neiva . . .	340,046
Ibagué . .	548,209	Palmira . .	302,727
Bucaramanga .	527,451	Armenia . .	295,143
Soacha . .	500,097	Popayán . .	275,129
Santa Marta .	476,385	Sincelejo . .	271,375
Villavicencio .	473,766	Itagüí . .	264,775
Pereira . . .	467,185	Floridablanca . .	264,695

BIRTHS, MARRIAGES AND DEATHS*

	Registered live births	Registered deaths
2006	714,450	192,814
2007	709,253	193,936
2008	715,453	196,943
2009	699,775	196,933
2010	654,627	200,524
2011	665,499	195,823
2012†	676,471	199,151
2013†	649,742	191,880

* Data are tabulated by year of registration rather than by year of occurrence, although registration is incomplete. According to UN estimates, the average annual rates in 1995–2000 were: births 24.0 per 1,000, deaths 5.8 per 1,000; in 2000–05: births 22.0 per 1,000, deaths 5.6 per 1,000; and in 2005–10: births 20.6 per 1,000, deaths 5.5 per 1,000 (Source: UN, *World Population Prospects: The 2012 Revision*).
† Preliminary figures.

Life expectancy (years at birth): 73.8 (males 70.2; females 77.5) in 2012 (Source: World Bank, World Development Indicators database).

ECONOMICALLY ACTIVE POPULATION

(integrated household survey February–April, '000 persons aged 10 years and over)

	2012	2013	2014
Agriculture, hunting, forestry and fishing	3,679.8	3,508.8	3,322.0
Mining and quarrying	181.0	206.6	207.4
Manufacturing	2,760.9	2,511.4	2,559.6
Electricity, gas and water	103.3	110.5	126.9
Construction	1,283.7	1,121.9	1,251.8
Trade, restaurants and hotels	5,301.5	5,634.7	5,752.8
Transport, storage and communications	1,719.1	1,789.6	1,765.9
Financial intermediation	268.2	256.5	290.8
Real estate, renting and business activities	1,248.1	1,440.7	1,487.0
Community, social and personal services	3,841.4	3,863.4	4,156.7
Sub-total	20,387.0	20,444.1	20,920.9
Activities not adequately described	8.0	3.6	1.5
Total employed	20,395.1	20,447.6	20,922.3
Unemployed	2,529.2	2,456.6	2,270.2
Total labour force	22,924.3	22,904.1	23,192.5

Note: Totals may not be equal to the sum of components, owing to rounding.

Health and Welfare

KEY INDICATORS

Total fertility rate (children per woman, 2012)	2.3
Under-5 mortality rate (per 1,000 live births, 2012)	18
HIV/AIDS (% of persons aged 15–49, 2012)	0.5
Physicians (per 1,000 head, 2010)	1.5
Hospital beds (per 1,000 head, 2007)	1.0
Health expenditure (2011): US $ per head (PPP)	657
Health expenditure (2011): % of GDP	6.5
Health expenditure (2011): public (% of total)	75.2
Access to water (% of persons, 2012)	91
Access to sanitation (% of persons, 2012)	80
Total carbon dioxide emissions ('000 metric tons, 2010)	75,679.5
Carbon dioxide emissions per head (metric tons, 2010)	1.6
Human Development Index (2013): ranking	98
Human Development Index (2013): value	0.711

For sources and definitions, see explanatory note on p. vi.

Agriculture

PRINCIPAL CROPS

('000 metric tons)

	2010	2011	2012
Rice, paddy	2,011	2,034	1,957
Maize	1,422	1,681	1,826
Sorghum	99	50	30
Potatoes	1,868	1,710	1,847
Cassava (Manioc)	2,082	2,165	2,274
Yams	394	397	361
Sugar cane*	37,000	42,000	38,000
Beans, dry	137	130	133
Soybeans (Soya beans)	54	75	87
Coconuts	101†	102†	102*
Oil palm fruit*	3,100	3,780	3,820
Cabbages and other brassicas*	145	136	135
Tomatoes	513	595	647
Chillies and peppers, green*	50	52	n.a.
Onions, dry	459	379	377
Carrots and turnips	263	264	261
Watermelons	100	93	117
Bananas	2,020	2,043	1,983
Plantains	2,978	2,946	3,327

—continued	2010	2011	2012
Oranges	228	260	269
Mangoes, mangosteens and guavas	201	221	235
Avocados	205	215	219
Pineapples	444	512	551
Papayas	158	153	164
Coffee, green	535	468	464

* FAO estimate(s).
† Unofficial figure.

Aggregate production ('000 metric tons, may include official, semi-official or estimated data): Total cereals 3,564 in 2010, 3,783 in 2011, 3,827 in 2012; Total roots and tubers 4,398 in 2010, 4,348 in 2011, 4,556 in 2012; Total vegetables (incl. melons) 1,854 in 2010, 1,850 in 2011, 1,965 in 2012; Total fruits (excl. melons) 7,936 in 2010, 8,097 in 2011, 8,527 in 2012.

Source: FAO.

LIVESTOCK

('000 head, year ending September)

	2010	2011	2012
Horses	2,126	851	900
Asses	172	134	111
Mules	310	147	183
Cattle	27,329	25,156	23,494
Pigs	5,162	5,127	5,527
Sheep	1,792	1,549	1,045
Goats	2,564	1,694	804
Chickens*	158,000	160,000	160,000

* FAO estimates.

Source: FAO.

LIVESTOCK PRODUCTS

('000 metric tons)

	2010	2011	2012
Cattle meat	766.6	821.0	854.2
Sheep meat*	5.8	11.6	7.7
Goat meat*	14.1	14.2	14.2
Pig meat	196.6	216.2	238.5
Horse meat*	6.7	6.8	6.8
Chicken meat	1,066.9	1,075.1	1,112.2
Cows' milk	6,285	6,284	6,483
Hen eggs	585	640	636

* FAO estimates.

Source: FAO.

Forestry

ROUNDWOOD REMOVALS

('000 cu metres, excl. bark)

	2008	2009	2010
Sawlogs, veneer logs and logs for sleepers	1,062	1,500	1,029
Pulpwood	746	825	932
Other industrial wood	503	1,421	1,589
Fuel wood	8,826	8,826	8,826
Total	11,137	12,572	12,376

2011–12: Production assumed to be unchanged from 2010 (FAO estimates).

Source: FAO.

SAWNWOOD PRODUCTION

('000 cu metres, incl. railway sleepers)

	2008	2009	2010
Coniferous (softwood)	115	163	166
Broadleaved (hardwood)	366	517	527
Total	481	680	693

2011–12: Production assumed to be unchanged from 2010 (unofficial figures).

Source: FAO.

Fishing

('000 metric tons, live weight)

	2010	2011	2012
Capture	81.2	87.5	78.0*
Bigeye tuna	2.0	2.2	1.4
Characins	6.7	10.6	10.0*
Freshwater siluroids	11.3	10.5	9.9*
Other freshwater fishes	3.1	3.8	4.1
Pacific anchoveta	8.2	7.8	7.2*
Skipjack tuna	12.7	23.7	15.8
Yellowfin tuna	23.7	20.0	22.1
Aquaculture	80.4	83.7	89.7
Tilapias	41.0	38.4	41.6
Pirapatinga	10.7	14.8	16.0
Rainbow trout	2.9	5.6	6.1
Whiteleg shrimp	12.6	9.4	8.9
Total catch	161.5	171.2	167.7*

* FAO estimate.

Note: Figures exclude crocodiles, recorded by number rather than by weight. The number of spectacled caimans caught was: 647,565 in 2010; 638,903 in 2011; 623,596 in 2012. The number of American crocodiles caught was: 200 in 2010; 1,192 in 2011; 1,618 in 2012.

Source: FAO.

Mining

('000 metric tons unless otherwise indicated)

	2009	2010	2011
Gold (kg)	47,838	53,606	55,908
Silver (kg)	10,827	15,300	24,045
Salt	612	645	428
Hard coal	72,807	74,350	85,803
Iron ore*	281	77	174

* Figures refer to the gross weight of ore. The estimated iron content was 46%.

Source: US Geological Survey.

Crude petroleum ('000 metric tons, estimates): 35,320 in 2009; 41,391 in 2010; 48,206 in 2011; 49,863 in 2012 (Source: BP, *Statistical Review of World Energy*).

Natural gas ('000 million cu m): 10.5 in 2009; 11.3 in 2010; 11.0 in 2011; 12.0 in 2012 (Source: BP, *Statistical Review of World Energy*).

Industry

SELECTED PRODUCTS

('000 metric tons unless otherwise indicated)

	2008	2009	2010
Sugar	2,036	2,598	2,078
Cement*	10,456	9,100	9,488
Crude steel ingots (incl. steel for casting)*	1,125	1,053	1,213
Semi-manufactures of iron and steel (hot-rolled)*	1,435	1,454	1,614
Gas-diesel (distillate fuel) oils	4,395	3,570	3,501
Residual fuel oils	3,318	3,251	3,871
Motor spirit (petrol)	3,164	2,964	3,113

* Source: US Geological Survey.

Source: mostly UN Industrial Commodity Statistics Database.

2011 ('000 metric tons): Cement 10,777; Crude steel ingots (incl. steel for casting) 1,290; Semi-manufactures of iron and steel (hot-rolled) 1,500 (estimate) (Source: US Geological Survey).

Finance

CURRENCY AND EXCHANGE RATES

Monetary Units
100 centavos = 1 Colombian peso.

Sterling, Dollar and Euro Equivalents (30 May 2014)
£1 sterling = 3,205.5 pesos;
US $1 = 1,905.5 pesos;
€1 = 2,593.6 pesos;
10,000 Colombian pesos = £3.12 = $5.25 = €3.86.

Average Exchange Rate (pesos per US $)
2011   1,848.14
2012   1,796.90
2013   1,868.79

GOVERNMENT FINANCE

(budgetary central government transactions, non-cash basis, '000 million pesos, provisional figures)

Summary of Balances

	2010	2011	2012
Revenue	82,319	106,031	148,185
Less Expense	97,497	103,500	145,542
Net operating balance	−15,178	2,531	2,644
Less Net acquisition of non-financial assets	7,348	625	−16,003
Net lending/borrowing	−22,526	1,906	18,646

Revenue

	2010	2011	2012
Taxes	61,730	85,397	87,257
Taxes on income, profits and capital gains	20,539	23,325	33,447
Individuals	20,502	23,325	33,447
Taxes on goods and services	29,777	33,754	35,740
Social contributions	405	439	12,932
Grants	185	214	−274
Other revenue	19,999	19,980	48,270
Total	82,319	106,031	148,185

Expense/Outlays

Expense by economic type	2010	2011	2012
Compensation of employees	7,113	7,609	16,165
Use of goods and services	6,871	6,923	17,478
Consumption of fixed capital	832	998	1,088
Interest	15,189	16,106	16,088
Subsidies	1,836	1,660	1,902
Grants	31,737	38,331	52,825
Social benefits	23,533	15,112	17,816
Other expense	10,385	16,761	22,180
Total	97,497	103,500	145,542

Source: IMF, *Government Finance Statistics Yearbook*.

2013 (budgetary central government transactions, '000 million pesos, 2013, preliminary): *Revenue* Tax revenue 101,685; Non-tax revenue 519; Funds 1,552; Capital revenue 14,559; Total 118,315. *Expenditure* Interest payments 19,019; Investment 20,269; Operational expense 94,808; Total 134,096 (excl. net lending 146) (Source: Ministry of Finance and Public Credit, Bogotá, DC).

Public sector account ('000 million pesos): *Revenue:* 146,913.1 in 2010; 171,229.7 in 2011 (preliminary); 193,798.4 in 2012 (preliminary). *Expenditure (incl. interest payments):* 163,847.1 in 2010; 182,548.1 in 2011 (preliminary); 190,809.2 in 2012 (preliminary).

INTERNATIONAL RESERVES
(US $ million at 31 December)

	2011	2012	2013
Gold (national valuation) . . .	524	554	400
IMF special drawing rights . .	1,140	1,131	1,132
Reserve position in IMF . . .	370	392	435
Foreign exchange	29,876	34,920	41,823
Total	31,910	36,997	43,790

Source: IMF, *International Financial Statistics*.

MONEY SUPPLY
('000 million pesos at 31 December)

	2011	2012	2013
Currency outside banks . . .	33,366.9	35,063.3	39,751.0
Transferable deposits	33,177.0	36,694.8	43,914.5
Other deposits	95,573.2	109,695.5	128,805.0
Securities other than shares . .	83,340.9	103,453.4	111,567.9
Broad money	245,457.9	284,907.0	324,038.3

Source: IMF, *International Financial Statistics*.

COST OF LIVING
(Consumer Price Index for low-income families; base: 2000 = 100)

	2011	2012	2013
Food and beverages	201.0	209.2	211.0
All items (incl. others) . . .	184.2	190.7	194.3

Source: ILO.

NATIONAL ACCOUNTS
('000 million pesos at current prices, provisional figures)

Expenditure on the Gross Domestic Product

	2011	2012	2013
Final consumption expenditure .	479,304	517,320	549,255
Households*	379,532	407,193	431,175
General government	99,772	110,127	118,080
Gross capital formation . . .	148,008	159,176	171,065
Gross fixed capital formation .	146,318	157,742	170,291
Change in inventories . . .	1,690	1,434	774
Total domestic expenditure .	627,312	676,496	720,320
Exports of goods and services . .	116,144	121,496	125,418
Less Imports of goods and services	123,562	132,551	139,061
GDP in market prices . . .	619,894	665,441	706,677
GDP at constant 2005 prices .	452,578	470,903	490,950

* Including non-profit institutions serving households.

Gross Domestic Product by Economic Activity

	2011	2012	2013
Agriculture, hunting, forestry and fishing	38,722	38,368	39,098
Mining and quarrying . . .	68,943	73,343	75,726
Manufacturing	76,497	79,973	79,605
Electricity, gas and water . .	21,146	22,399	23,980
Construction	45,866	52,856	61,007
Wholesale and retail trade; repair of motor vehicles, motorcycles, and personal and household goods; hotels and restaurants .	70,332	75,663	80,718
Transport, storage and communications	36,199	38,018	40,113
Financial intermediation, insurance, real estate, renting and business activities . .	113,878	123,852	132,856
Other community, social and personal service activities .	93,796	103,681	112,952
Gross value added in basic prices	565,379	608,153	646,055
Taxes on products	55,407	58,294	61,687
Less Subsidies on products . .	892	1,006	1,065
GDP in market prices . . .	619,894	665,441	706,677

BALANCE OF PAYMENTS
(US $ million)

	2010	2011	2012
Exports of goods	40,655.1	58,176.1	61,355.6
Imports of goods	−38,405.8	−52,127.0	−56,648.3
Balance on goods	2,249.3	6,049.1	4,707.3
Exports of services	4,251.5	4,676.0	5,168.8
Imports of services	−7,843.8	−9,358.0	−10,610.7
Balance on goods and services	−1,343.0	1,367.1	−734.6
Primary income received . .	1,439.2	2,708.9	3,813.5
Primary income paid	−13,463.0	−18,750.6	−19,781.8
Balance on goods, services and primary income	−13,366.8	−14,674.6	−16,702.9
Secondary income received . .	5,315.5	5,569.6	5,394.4
Secondary income paid . . .	−867.9	−735.4	−815.1
Current balance	−8,919.3	−9,840.4	−12,123.6
Direct investment assets . .	−6,892.8	−8,304.4	302.9
Direct investment liabilities .	6,746.2	13,405.5	15,650.0
Portfolio investment assets . .	−2,290.0	−2,111.3	−1,666.1
Portfolio investment liabilities .	3,262.6	8,201.7	7,355.7
Other investment assets . .	1,187.4	−3,512.3	−2,068.6
Other investment liabilities . .	9,743.4	5,288.2	−2,432.2
Net errors and omissions . . .	279.8	609.5	303.2
Reserves and related items .	3,117.2	3,736.6	5,321.4

Source: IMF, *International Financial Statistics*.

External Trade

PRINCIPAL COMMODITIES
(US $ million)

Imports c.i.f.	2011	2012	2013
Agricultural, livestock, hunting and forestry products . . .	2,543	2,685	2,563
Prepared foodstuffs, beverages and tobacco	2,873	3,624	3,609
Textiles, clothing and leather products	2,556	2,922	2,753
Chemical products	9,130	9,783	10,074
Rubber and plastic goods . . .	1,842	2,062	2,066
Metals and metal manufactures .	4,558	4,572	4,218
Mechanical, electrical, office, telecommunications and medical equipment	14,206	15,534	15,723
Vehicles and transport equipment	9,720	9,005	8,810
Total (incl. others)	54,233	59,048	59,381

Exports f.o.b.	2011	2012	2013
Coffee	2,608	1,910	1,884
Coal	8,397	7,805	6,688
Petroleum and its derivatives .	28,421	31,559	32,483
Prepared foodstuffs, beverages and tobacco	4,775	3,988	4,019
Textiles, clothing and leather products	1,364	1,389	1,242
Paper and publishing	736	727	669
Chemicals	3,053	3,149	3,419
Metal manufactures	4,682	5,412	3,994
Mechanical, electrical and office equipment	735	836	872
Vehicles and transport equipment	457	618	910
Total (incl. others)	56,915	60,125	58,824

PRINCIPAL TRADING PARTNERS
(US $ million)

Imports c.i.f.	2011	2012	2013
Argentina	1,872	2,396	1,734
Brazil	2,740	2,851	2,590
Canada	960	1,142	1,001
Chile	902	966	904
China, People's Republic	8,176	9,822	10,363
Ecuador	1,066	1,090	882
France	1,477	1,129	1,433
Germany	2,147	2,267	2,207
India	976	1,146	1,144
Italy	794	961	1,011
Japan	1,438	1,677	1,479
Korea, Republic	1,234	1,313	1,296
Mexico	6,059	6,453	5,496
Peru	1,025	929	870
Spain	614	789	963
USA	13,549	14,178	16,337
Venezuela	563	533	431
Total (incl. others)	54,233	59,048	59,381

Exports f.o.b.	2011	2012	2013
Belgium	621	488	495
Ecuador	1,909	1,910	1,975
Germany	420	395	780
Japan	528	360	388
Mexico	705	835	864
Peru	1,323	1,582	1,274
USA	21,969	21,833	18,459
Venezuela	1,725	2,556	2,256
Total (incl. others)	56,915	60,125	58,824

Transport

RAILWAYS
(traffic)

	1996	1997	1998
Freight ('000 metric tons)	321	348	281
Freight ton-km ('000)	746,544	736,427	657,585

Source: Sociedad de Transporte Ferroviario, SA.

ROAD TRAFFIC
(motor vehicles in use at 31 December)

	2007	2008	2009
Passenger cars	1,674,441	1,849,962	2,397,716
Vans and lorries	1,064,513	554,064	619,136
Buses	148,537	197,285	203,938
Motorcycles and mopeds	1,930,978	2,311,652	2,630,391

Source: IRF, *World Road Statistics*.

SHIPPING
Flag Registered Fleet
(at 31 December)

	2011	2012	2013
Number of vessels	569	575	593
Total displacement ('000 grt)	164.9	158.3	176.7

Source: Lloyd's List Intelligence (www.lloydslistintelligence.com).

CIVIL AVIATION
(traffic)

	2010	2011
Kilometres flown (million)	163	174
Passengers carried ('000)	16,932	18,769
Passenger-km (million)	16,723	17,832
Total ton-km (million)	2,555	2,687

Source: UN, *Statistical Yearbook*.

Passengers carried ('000): 20,945 in 2012 (Source: World Bank, World Development Indicators database).

Tourism

TOURIST ARRIVALS

Country of origin	2010	2011	2012
Argentina	77,499	86,365	103,370
Brazil	63,794	90,646	83,112
Canada	30,389	35,848	41,878
Chile	42,976	53,732	73,869
Costa Rica	22,589	23,394	24,068
Ecuador	116,359	101,512	107,452
France	29,898	33,105	32,948
Germany	24,134	36,010	36,568
Italy	22,706	22,699	22,098
Mexico	64,886	75,011	80,865
Netherlands	12,064	13,721	14,285
Panama	37,822	37,166	36,588
Peru	74,093	71,488	82,797
Spain	76,485	83,761	87,052
United Kingdom	20,055	23,102	22,117
USA	357,464	328,663	328,949
Venezuela	187,619	215,007	230,212
Total (incl. others)	1,404,452	2,042,196	2,174,587

Total tourist arrivals ('000): 2,288 in 2013 (provisional).

Tourism receipts (US $ million, excl. passenger transport): 2,201 in 2011; 2,354 in 2012; 2,491 in 2013 (provisional).

Source: World Tourism Organization.

Communications Media

	2011	2012	2013
Telephones ('000 main lines in use)	7,126.7	7,134.1	7,141.5
Mobile cellular telephones ('000 subscribers)	46,200.4	49,066.4	50,295.1
Internet subscribers ('000)	3,297.0	n.a.	n.a.
Broadband subscribers ('000)	3,297.2	3,893.7	4,486.8

Source: International Telecommunication Union.

Education

(2012)

	Institutions	Teachers	Students ('000) Males	Females	Total
Pre-primary	46,016	55,123	565.8	542.0	1,107.8
Primary	54,826	185,997	2,375.9	2,180.3	4,556.2
Secondary*	33,704	214,433	2,107.7	2,199.3	4,307.0
Youth and adult education	n.a.	n.a.	319.7	325.1	644.8

* Inclusive of technical and vocational education.

Sources: Ministerio de Educación Nacional.

Higher (incl. universities) (2011/12 unless otherwise indicated): 32 institutions (2001/02); 110,488 teachers (2008/09); 1,958.4 pupils (males 935.2, females 1,023.2) (Source: UNESCO Institute for Statistics).

Pupil-teacher ratio (primary education, UNESCO estimate): 25.0 in 2011/12 (Source: UNESCO Institute for Statistics).

Adult literacy rate (UNESCO estimates): 93.6% (males 93.5%; females 93.7%) in 2011 (Source: UNESCO Institute for Statistics).

Directory

The Constitution

A new, 380-article Constitution, drafted by a 74-member National Constituent Assembly, took effect from 6 July 1991. The new Constitution retained the institutional framework of a directly elected President with a non-renewable four-year term of office, together with a bicameral legislature composed of an upper house or Senate (with 102 directly elected members) and a lower house or House of Representatives (to include at least two representatives of each national department). In December 2004 the legislature approved a constitutional amendment to allow re-election of the President for a second term in office. The reform took force prior to the May 2006 presidential election. A Vice-President is elected at the same time as the President, and also holds office for a term of four years.

The new Constitution also contained comprehensive provisions for the recognition and protection of civil rights, and for the reform of the structures and procedures of political participation and of the judiciary.

The fundamental principles upon which the new Constitution is based are embodied in articles 1–10.

Article 1: Colombia is a lawful state, organized as a single Republic, decentralized, with autonomous territorial entities, democratic, participatory and pluralist, founded on respect for human dignity, on the labour and solidarity of its people and on the prevalence of the general interest.

Article 2: The essential aims of the State are: to serve the community, to promote general prosperity, to guarantee the effectiveness of the principles, rights and obligations embodied in the Constitution, to facilitate the participation of all in the decisions which affect them and in the economic, political, administrative and cultural life of the nation, to defend national independence, to maintain territorial integrity and to ensure peaceful coexistence and the validity of the law.

The authorities of the Republic are instituted to protect the residents of Colombia, in regard to their life, honour, goods, beliefs and other rights and liberties, and to ensure the fulfilment of the obligations of the State and of the individual.

Article 3: Sovereignty rests exclusively with the people, from whom public power emanates. The people exercise power directly or through their representatives in the manner established by the Constitution.

Article 4: The Constitution is the highest authority. In all cases of incompatability between the Constitution and the law or other juridical rules, constitutional dispositions will apply.

It is the duty of nationals and foreigners in Colombia to observe the Constitution and the law, and to respect and obey the authorities.

Article 5: The State recognizes, without discrimination, the primacy of the inalienable rights of the individual and protects the family as the basic institution of society.

Article 6: Individuals are solely responsible to the authorities for infringements of the Constitution and of the law. Public servants are equally accountable and are responsible to the authorities for failure to fulfil their function or abuse of their position.

Article 7: The State recognizes and protects the ethnic diversity of the Colombian nation.

Article 8: It is an obligation of the State and of the people to protect the cultural and natural riches of the nation.

Article 9: The foreign relations of the State are based on national sovereignty, with respect for self-determination of people and with recognition of the principles of international law accepted by Colombia.

Similarly, Colombia's external politics will be directed towards Caribbean and Latin American integration.

Article 10: Spanish (Castilian) is the official language of Colombia. The languages and dialects of ethnic groups are officially recognized within their territories. Education in communities with their own linguistic traditions will be bilingual. (A constitutional amendment approved in January 2010 granted official status to other native languages.)

The Government

HEAD OF STATE

President: JUAN MANUEL SANTOS CALDERÓN (took office on 7 August 2010, re-elected 15 June 2014).

Vice-President: GERMÁN VARGAS LLERAS.

CABINET
(September 2014)

The Government is formed by a coalition led by the Partido Social de la Unidad Nacional.

Minister of the Interior: JUAN FERNANDO CRISTO BUSTOS.

Minister of Foreign Affairs: MARÍA ANGELA HOLGUÍN CUÉLLAR.

Minister of Finance and Public Credit: MAURICIO CÁRDENAS SANTAMARÍA.

Minister of National Defence: JUAN CARLOS PINZÓN BUENO.

Minister of Justice and Law: YESID REYES ALVARADO.

Minister of Agriculture and Rural Development: AURELIO IRAGORRI VALENCIA.

Minister of Health and Social Protection: ALEJANDRO GAVIRIA URIBE.

Minister of Labour: LUIS EDUARDO GARZÓN.

Minister of Mines and Energy: TOMÁS GONZÁLEZ ESTRADA.

Minister of Trade, Industry and Tourism: CECILIA ALVAREZ-CORREA GLEN.

Minister of National Education: GINA PARODY.

Minister of Housing, Cities and Territorial Development: LUIS FELIPE HENAO CARDONA.

Minister of the Environment and Sustainable Development: GABRIEL VALLEJO LÓPEZ.

Minister of Information Technology and Communications: DIEGO MOLANO VEGA.

Minister of Transport: NATALIA ABELLO VIVES.

Minister of Culture: MARIANA GARCÉS CÓRDOBA.

Minister of the Presidency: NÉSTOR HUMBERTO MARTÍNEZ.

In addition, there were five Minister-Counsellors (on post-conflict issues, human rights, national security, government and the private sector, and communications), with ministerial rank.

MINISTRIES

Office of the President: Palacio de Nariño, Carrera 8, No 7-26, Bogotá, DC; tel. (1) 562-9300; fax (1) 286-8063; internet www .presidencia.gov.co.

Ministry of Agriculture and Rural Development: Avda Jiménez, No 7A-17, Bogotá, DC; tel. (1) 334-1199; fax (1) 284-1775; e-mail despachoministro@minagricultura.gov.co; internet www .minagricultura.gov.co.

Ministry of Culture: Carrera 8, No 8-43, Bogotá, DC; tel. (1) 342-4100; fax (1) 381-6353; e-mail servicioalcliente@mincultura.gov.co; internet www.mincultura.gov.co.

Ministry of the Environment and Sustainable Development: Calle 37, No 8-40, Bogotá, DC; tel. (1) 332-3400; fax (1) 332-3400; e-mail servicioalciudadano@minambiente.gov.co; internet www .minambiente.gov.co.

Ministry of Finance and Public Credit: Carrera 8, No 6C-38, Of. 305, Bogotá, DC; tel. (1) 381-1700; fax (1) 381-2863; e-mail atencioncliente@minhacienda.gov.co; internet www.minhacienda .gov.co.

Ministry of Foreign Affairs: Palacio de San Carlos, Calle 10, No 5-51, Bogotá, DC; tel. (1) 381-4000; fax (1) 381-4747; e-mail cancilleria@ cancilleria.gov.co; internet www.cancilleria.gov.co.

Ministry of Health and Social Protection: Carrera 13, No 32-76, Bogotá, DC; tel. (1) 330-5000; fax (1) 330-5050; e-mail atencionalciudadano@minproteccionsocial.gov.co; internet www .minproteccionsocial.gov.co.

Ministry of Housing, Cities and Territorial Development: Calle 18, No 7-59, Bogotá, DC; tel. (1) 332-3434; fax (1) 281-7327; e-mail correspondencia@minvivienda.gov.co; internet www .minvivienda.gov.co.

Ministry of Information Technology and Communications: Edif. Murillo Toro, Carrera 8A entre, Calle 12 y 13, Apdo Aéreo 111711, Bogotá, DC; tel. (1) 344-3460; fax (1) 344-2293; e-mail info@ mintic.gov.co; internet www.mintic.gov.co.

Ministry of the Interior: La Giralda, Carrera 8, No 7-83, Bogotá, DC; tel. (1) 242-7400; fax (1) 341-9583; e-mail servicioalciudadano@ mininterior.gov.co; internet www.mininterior.gov.co.

Ministry of Justice and Law: Carrera 9, No 12C-10, Bogotá, DC; tel. (1) 444-3100; e-mail reclamos.minjusticia@minjusticia.gov.co; internet www.minjusticia.gov.co.

Ministry of Labour: Carrera 14, No 99-33, Bogotá, DC; tel. (1) 489-3900; fax (1) 489-3100; e-mail contactenostlc@mintrabajo.gov.co; internet www.mintrabajo.gov.co.

Ministry of Mines and Energy: Calle 43, No 57-31, Centro Administrativo Nacional (CAN), Bogotá, DC; tel. (1) 220-0300; fax (1) 222-3651; e-mail menergia@minminas.gov.co; internet www.minminas.gov.co.

Ministry of National Defence: Carrera 54, No 26-25, Centro Administrativo Nacional (CAN), Bogotá, DC; tel. (1) 266-0296; fax (1) 315-0111; e-mail usuarios@mindefensa.gov.co; internet www.mindefensa.gov.co.

Ministry of National Education: Calle 43, No 57-14, Centro Administrativo Nacional (CAN), Bogotá, DC; tel. (1) 222-2800; fax (1) 222-4953; e-mail dci@mineducacion.gov.co; internet www.mineducacion.gov.co.

Ministry of Trade, Industry and Tourism: Edif. Centro de Comercio Internacional, Calle 28, No 13A-15, 18°, Bogotá, DC; tel. (1) 606-7676; fax (1) 606-7522; e-mail info@mincomercio.gov.co; internet www.mincomercio.gov.co.

Ministry of Transport: Centro Administrativo Nacional (CAN), Of. 409, Avda El Dorado, Transversal 45, No 47-14, Bogotá, DC; tel. (1) 324-0800; fax (1) 428-7054; e-mail mintrans@mintransporte.gov.co; internet www.mintransporte.gov.co.

President and Legislature

PRESIDENT

Presidential Election, First Round, 25 May 2014

	Valid votes	% of votes cast
Oscar Iván Zuluaga (Centro Democrático) .	3,759,971	29.25
Juan Manuel Santos Calderón (Unidad Nacional*)	3,301,815	25.69
Marta Lucía Ramírez (Partido Conservador Colombiano)	1,995,698	15.52
Clara López Obregón (Polo Democrático Alternativo)	1,958,414	15.23
Enrique Peñalosa (Partido Alianza Verde) .	1,065,142	8.28
Votos en blanco†	770,610	5.99
Total‡	12,851,650	100.00

* Coalition formed by the Partido de la U and comprising the Partido Liberal Colombiano and the Cambio Radical.
† Blank, valid votes.
‡ In addition, there were 311,758 invalid and 52,994 blank votes.

Presidential Election, Second Round, 15 June 2014

	Valid votes	% of votes cast
Juan Manuel Santos Calderón (Unidad Nacional*)	7,816,986	50.95
Oscar Iván Zuluaga (Centro Democrático) .	6,905,001	45.00
Votos en blanco†	619,396	4.03
Total valid votes‡	15,341,383	100.00

* Coalition formed by the Partido de la U and comprising the Partido Liberal Colombiano and the Cambio Radical.
† Blank, valid votes.
‡ In addition, there were 403,405 invalid and 50,152 blank votes.

CONGRESS

Senate
(Senado)

President: José David Name Cardoso.
General Election, 9 March 2014

	Seats
Partido Social de la Unidad Nacional (Partido de la U)	21
Centro Democrático (CD)	20
Partido Conservador Colombiano (PC) . . .	18
Partido Liberal Colombiano (PL)	17
Cambio Radical (CR)	9
Alianza Partido Verde (PV)	5
Polo Democrático Alternativo (PDA) . . .	5
Opción Ciudadana	5
Indigenous groups*	2
Total	102

* Under the terms of the Constitution, at least two Senate seats are reserved for indigenous groups.

House of Representatives
(Cámara de Representantes)

President: Fabio Amin.
General Election, 9 March 2014

	Seats
Partido Liberal Colombiano (PL)	39
Partido Social de la Unidad Nacional (Partido de la U)	37
Partido Conservador Colombiano (PC)	27
Centro Democrático (CD)	19
Cambio Radical (CR)	16
Alianza Partido Verde (PV)	6
Opción Ciudadana	6
Polo Democrático Alternativo (PDA) . . .	3
Movimiento MIRA	3
Movimiento Cien por Ciento por Colombia . .	3
Movimiento Autoridades Indígenas de Colombia .	2
Indigenous groups*	2
Others†	3
Total	166

* Under the terms of the Constitution, at least two lower house seats are reserved for indigenous groups.
† The Alianza Social Independiente, the Movimiento de Integración Regional and the Por Un Huila Mejor each gained a seat.

Governors

DEPARTMENTS
(September 2014)

Amazonas: Carlos Arturo Rodríguez Celis.
Antioquia: Sergio Fajardo Valderrama.
Arauca: José Facundo Castillo Cisnero.
Atlántico: José Antonio Segebre Berardinelli.
Bolívar: Juan Carlos Gossaín Rognini.
Boyacá: Juan Carlos Granados Becerra.
Caldas: Julián Gutiérrez Botero.
Caquetá: Víctor Isidro Ramírez Loaiza.
Casanare: Marco Tulio Ruiz Riaño.
Cauca: Temístocles Ortega Narváez.
César: Luis Alberto Monsalvo Gnecco.
Chocó: Efrén Palacios Serna.
Córdoba: Alejandro Lyons Muskus.
Cundinamarca: Alvaro Cruz Vargas.
Guainía: Oscar Armando Rodríguez Sánchez.
La Guajira: José María Ballesteros Valdivieso.
Guaviare: José Octaviano Rivera Moncada.
Huila: Carlos Mauricio Iriarte Barrios.
Magdalena: Luís Miguel Cotes Habeych.
Meta: Alán Jesús Edmundo Jara Urzola.
Nariño: Raúl Delgado Guerrero.
Norte de Santander: Edgar Jesús Díaz Contreras.
Putumayo: Jimmy Harold Díaz Burbano.
Quindío: Sandra Paola Hurtado Palacio.
Risaralda: Carlos Alberto Botero López.
San Andrés y Providencia Islands: Aury Guerrero Bowie.
Santander del Sur: Richard Alfonso Aguilar Villa.
Sucre: Julio César Guerra Tulena.
Tolima: Luís Carlos Delgado Peñón.
Valle del Cauca: Ubeimar Delgado Blandón.
Vaupés: Roberto Jaramillo García.
Vichada: Sergio Andrés Espinosa Flores.
Bogotá, DC: Gustavo Francisco Petro Urrego.

Election Commissions

Consejo Nacional Electoral (CNE): Edif. Organización Electoral (CAN), Avda Calle 26 No 51-50, Bogotá, DC; tel. (1) 220-0800; e-mail contactenos.cne@registraduria.gov.co; internet www.cne.gov.co; f. 1888 as Gran Consejo Electoral; refounded under current name in 1985; Pres. Pablo Guillermo Gil de la Hoz.

Registraduría Nacional del Estado Civil: Avda Calle 26, No 51-50, Bogotá, DC; tel. (1) 220-2880; internet www.registraduria.gov.co;

f. 1948; ensures electoral transparency; Registrar CARLOS ARIEL SÁNCHEZ TORRES.

Political Organizations

Alianza Social Independiente (ASI): Calle 17, No 5-43, 8°, Bogotá, DC; tel. (1) 283-0616; fax (1) 282-7474; e-mail alianzasocialindependiente@gmail.com; internet www.asicolombia.com; f. 1991; fmrly Alianza Social Indígena; Leader ALONSO TOBON.

Cambio Radical (CR): Carrera 7, No 26-20, 26°, Bogotá, DC; tel. (1) 327-9696; fax (1) 210-6800; e-mail cambioradical@cable.net.co; internet www.partidocambioradical.org; f. 1998; contested the 2014 elections as mem. of the Unidad Nacional coalition with the Partido de la U; Pres. CARLOS FERNANDO GALÁN; Sec.-Gen. ANTONIO ALVAREZ LLERAS.

Centro Democrático (CD) (Centro Democrático Mano Firme Corazón Grande): Bogotá, DC; internet centrodemocratico.com.co; f. 2013 by supporters of fmr Pres. Alvaro Uribe; right-wing; Pres. OSCAR IVÁN ZULUAGA.

Compromiso Ciudadano por Colombia: Carrera 36, 8A-46, Of. 201, Medellín; tel. (4) 448-6048; fax (4) 312-7014; e-mail info@sergiofajardo.com; internet www.sergiofajardo.com; f. 2008; Leader SERGIO FAJARDO.

Fundación Ebano de Colombia Funeco: internet fundacionebanocolombia.jimdo.com; f. 1998; represents those of African descent; Leader CASSIANI HERRERA ALEXI.

Marcha Patriótica: internet www.marchapatriotica.org; f. 2012; left-wing, supports the Fuerzas Armadas Revolucionarias de Colombia—Ejército del Pueblo (q.v.).

Movimiento Apertura Liberal: Avda 3B, 5-70B, Latino, Cúcuta, Norte de Santander; tel. (7) 571-3729; e-mail info@aperturaliberal.com; f. 1993; Nat. Dir Dr MIGUEL ANGEL FLÓREZ RIVERA.

Movimiento Autoridades Indígenas de Colombia (AICO): Calle 23, No 7-61, Of. 302, Bogotá, DC; tel. (1) 286-8233; fax (1) 341-8930; e-mail aico@aicocolombia.org; internet www.aicocolombia.org; f. 1990; Pres. LUIS HUMBERTO CUASPUD.

Movimiento Cien por Ciento por Colombia (M100%C): Carretera 18, No 28-79, Sincelejo, Sucre; tel. (5) 282-2886; e-mail cienporcientoporcolombia@hotmail.com; Pres. EVELYN DEL TORO CARDALES; Sec.-Gen. JESÚS MARÍA BERTEL.

Movimiento de Integración Regional: Bogotá, DC.

Movimiento MIRA (Movimiento Independiente de Renovación Absoluta): Transversal 29, No 36-40, Bogotá, DC; tel. (1) 369-3222; fax 369-3210; e-mail contacto@movimientomira.com; internet www.movimientomira.com; f. 2000; Pres. CARLOS ALBERTO BAENA LÓPEZ.

Movimiento Progresista Colombiano: Carrera 15, No 44-18, CP 11001, Bogotá, DC; tel. (1) 289-7895; e-mail progresistascolombia@etb.net.co; internet www.colombiaprogresistas.com; f. 2011; Leader GUSTAVO FRANCISCO PETRO URREGO.

Opción Ciudadana: Calle 39, No 28A–26, Bogotá, DC; tel. (1) 340-8120; fax (1) 244-0189; internet www.partidoopcionciudadana.com; f. 2009; Sec.-Gen. EDISON BIOSCAR RUIZ VALENCIA.

Partido Colombia Democrática: Calle 41, No 13A-07, 2°, Bogotá, DC; tel. (1) 338-3624; fax (1) 338-2310; e-mail contactenos@colombiademocratica.com; f. 2003; conservative; Nat. Dir MARIO URIBE ESCOBAR; Sec.-Gen. GABRIEL SIERRA.

Partido Comunista Colombiano: Calle 18A, No 14-56, Apdo Aéreo 2523, Bogotá, DC; tel. (1) 334-1947; fax (1) 281-8259; e-mail notipaco@pacocol.org; internet www.pacocol.org; f. 1930; Marxist-Leninist; Sec.-Gen. JAIME CAYCEDO TURRIAGO.

Partido Conservador Colombiano (PC): Avda Carrera 24, No 37-09, La Soledad, Bogotá, DC; tel. (1) 597-9630; fax (1) 369-0053; e-mail presidencia@partidoconservador.com; internet www.partidoconservador.com; f. 1849; contesting the 2014 elections in coalition with the Partido de la U; 2.9m. mems; Pres. OMAR YEPES ALZATE; Sec.-Gen. JUAN CARLOS WILLS OSPINA.

Partido Liberal Colombiano (PL): Avda Caracas, No 36-01, Bogotá, DC; tel. (1) 593-4500; fax (1) 323-1070; e-mail direcciondecomunicaciones@partidoliberal.org.co; internet www.partidoliberal.org.co; f. 1848; contested the 2014 elections as mem. of the Unidad Nacional coalition with the Partido de la U; Pres. SIMÓN GAVIRIA MUÑOZ; Sec.-Gen. HÉCTOR OLIMPO ESPINOSA.

Partido de la U (Partido Social de la Unidad Nacional): Carrera 7, No 32-16, 21°, Bogotá, DC; tel. and fax (1) 350-0215; internet www.partidodelau.com; f. 2005; conservative; formed the Unidad Nacional coalition to contest the 2014 elections; Pres. SERGIO DÍAZ-GRANADOS.

Partido Alianza Verde (PV): Calle 66, No 7–69, Bogotá, DC; tel. (1) 606-7888; fax (1) 608-1312; e-mail movilizacion@partidoverde.org.co; internet www.partidoverde.org.co; Nat. Dir CARLOS RAMÓN GONZÁLEZ; Sec.-Gen. NÉSTOR DANIEL GARCÍA COLORADO.

Polo Democrático Alternativo (PDA): Carrera 17A, No 37-27, Bogotá, DC; tel. (1) 288-6188; e-mail info@polodemocratico.net; internet www.polodemocratico.net; f. 2002 as electoral alliance, constituted as a political party in July 2003; founded by fmr mems of the Movimiento 19 de Abril; fmrly Polo Democrático Independiente; adopted current name 2006; left-wing; Pres. CLARA LÓPEZ OBREGÓN; Sec.-Gen. GUSTAVO TRIANA SUÁREZ.

Por Un Huila Mejor: Neiva, Huila; regional coalition.

Unión Patriótica (UP): Carrera 13A, No 38-32, Of. 204, Bogota, DC; fax (1) 570-4400; f. 1985; Marxist party formed by the Fuerzas Armadas Revolucionarias de Colombia—Ejército del Pueblo (q.v.); declared illegal in 2002; legal status reinstated in 2013; Pres. OMER CALDERÓN.

The following are the principal guerrilla groups in operation in Colombia:

Ejército de Liberación Nacional (ELN): internet www.eln-voces.com; Castroite guerrilla movt; f. 1964; 1,500 mems; political status recognized by the Govt in 1998; Leader NICOLÁS RODRÍGUEZ BAUTISTA (alias Gabino).

Fuerzas Armadas Revolucionarias de Colombia—Ejército del Pueblo (FARC—EP): internet www.farc-ep.co; f. 1964, although mems active from 1949; name changed from Fuerzas Armadas Revolucionarias de Colombia to the above in 1982; fmrly military wing of the Communist Party; composed of 39 armed fronts and 8,000 mems; political status recognized by the Govt in 1998; mem. of the Coordinadora Nacional Guerrilla Simón Bolívar; C-in-C RODRIGO LONDOÑO ECHEVERRI (alias Timochenko).

Diplomatic Representation

EMBASSIES IN COLOMBIA

Algeria: Carrera 11, No 93-53, Of. 302, Bogotá, DC; tel. (1) 635-0520; fax (1) 635-0531; e-mail admin@embargelia-colombia.org; internet www.embargelia-colombia.org; Ambassador MOHAMED ZIANE HASSENI.

Argentina: Carrera 12, 97-80, 5°, Bogotá, DC; tel. (1) 288-0900; fax (1) 384-9488; e-mail embargentina@etb.net.co; internet www.ecolo.mrecic.gov.ar; Ambassador CELSO ALEJANDRO JAQUE.

Belgium: Calle 26, No 4A-45, 7°, Apdo Aéreo 3564, Bogotá, DC; tel. (1) 380-0370; fax (1) 380-0340; e-mail bogota@diplobel.fed.be; internet www.diplomatie.be/bogota; Ambassador SADI PAUL BRANCART.

Bolivia: Carrera 10, No 113-36, Santa Bárbara Central, Bogotá, DC; tel. (1) 619-4701; fax (1) 619-6050; e-mail central@embajadaboliviacolombia.org; internet www.embajadaboliviacolombia.org; Ambassador MARÍO CARVAJAL LOZANO.

Brazil: Calle 93, No 14-20, 8°, Apdo 90540, Bogotá, DC; tel. (1) 218-0800; fax (1) 218-8393; e-mail embaixada@brasil.org.co; internet bogota.itamaraty.gov.br; Ambassador MARIA ELISA BERENGUER.

Canada: Carretera 7, No 114-33, 14°, Apdo Aéreo 110067, Bogotá, DC; tel. (1) 657-9800; fax (1) 657-9912; e-mail bgota@international.gc.ca; internet www.canadainternational.gc.ca/colombia-colombie; Chargé d'affaires a.i. IAN MCKINLEY.

Chile: Calle 100, No 11B-44, Apdo Aéreo 90061, Bogotá, DC; tel. (1) 742-0136; fax (1) 744-1469; e-mail echile.colombia@minrel.gov.cl; internet chileabroad.gov.cl/colombia; Chargé d'affaires a.i. RICARDO GUSTAVO ROJAS GONZÁLEZ.

China, People's Republic: Carrera 16, No 98-30, Bogotá, DC; tel. (1) 622-3215; fax (1) 622-3114; e-mail chinaemb_co@mfa.gov.cn; internet co.china-embassy.org; Ambassador WANG XIAOYUAN.

Costa Rica: Carrera 12, No 114-37, Santa Bárbara Central, Bogotá, DC; tel. (1) 629-5095; fax (1) 691-8558; e-mail embacosta@etb.net.co; internet www.embajadadecostarica.org; Ambassador CIRCE MILENA VILLANUEVA MONGE.

Cuba: Carrera 9, No 92-54, Bogotá, DC; tel. (1) 621-7054; fax (1) 611-4382; e-mail embacuba@cable.net.co; internet www.cubadiplomatica.cu/colombia; Ambassador JORGE IVÁN MORA GODOY.

Dominican Republic: Carrera 18, No 123-43, Bogotá, DC; tel. (1) 601-1670; fax (1) 620-7597; e-mail embajado@cable.net.co; Ambassador BRIUNNY GARABITO.

Ecuador: Edif. Fernando Mazuera, 7°, Calle 72, No 6-30, Bogotá, DC; tel. (1) 212-6512; fax (1) 212-6536; e-mail eecucolombia@mmrree.gov.ec; internet www.ecuadorencolombia.net; Ambassador CÉSAR RAUL VALLEJO CORRAL.

Egypt: Carrera 16, No 101-51, Bogotá, DC; tel. (1) 236-9917; fax (1) 236-9914; e-mail embajadadeegipto@telmex.net.co; internet bogotamiciudad.com; Ambassador TAREK MAHMOUD ELKOUNY.

El Salvador: Edif. El Nogal, Of. 503, Carrera 9, No 80-15, Bogotá, DC; tel. (1) 349-6771; fax (1) 349-6670; e-mail elsalvador@supercable .net.co; Ambassador MARCOS GREGORIO SÁNCHEZ TREJO.

France: Carrera 11, No 93-12, Bogotá, DC; tel. (1) 638-1400; fax (1) 638-1430; e-mail amfrabog@andinet.com; internet www .ambafrance-co.org; Ambassador JEAN-MARC LAFORÊT.

Germany: Edif. Torre Empresarial Pacífic, 11°, Calle 110, No 9-25, Bogotá, DC; tel. (1) 423-2600; fax (1) 423-2615; e-mail info@bogota .diplo.de; internet www.bogota.diplo.de; Ambassador GÜNTER KNIESS.

Guatemala: Calle 87, No 20-27, Of. 302, Bogotá, DC; tel. (1) 257-6133; fax (1) 610-1449; e-mail embcolombia@minex.gob.gt; Ambassador MANILO FERNANDO SESENNA OLIVERO.

Holy See: Carrera 15, No 36-33, Apdo Aéreo 3740, Bogotá, DC (Apostolic Nunciature); tel. (1) 705-4545; fax (1) 285-1817; e-mail nunciatura@cable.net.co; Apostolic Nuncio ETTORE BALESTRERO (Titular Archbishop of Victoriana).

Honduras: Carrera 12, No 119-52, Barrio Multicentro, Bogotá, DC; tel. (1) 629-3302; fax (1) 217-1457; e-mail info@embajadadehonduras .org.co; internet www.embajadadehonduras.org.co; Ambassador FRANCISCO RAMÓN ZEPEDA ANDINO.

India: Calle 116, No 301, Torre Cusezar, Bogotá, DC; tel. (1) 637-3259; fax (1) 637-3451; e-mail central@embajadaindia.org; internet www.embajadaindia.org; Chargé d'affaires a.i. SAJEEV BABU KURUP.

Indonesia: Carrera 11, No 75-27, Bogotá, DC; tel. (1) 217-2404; fax (1) 326-2165; e-mail eindones@colomsat.net.co; internet bogota .kemlu.go.id; Ambassador TRIE EDI MULYANI.

Iran: Calle 96, No 11A-20, Apdo 93854, Bogotá, DC; tel. (1) 256-2862; fax (1) 256-2842; e-mail emiracol@gmail.com; Ambassador MANOU-CHEHR SOBHANI FIROUZABAD.

Israel: Calle 35, No 7-25, 14°, Bogotá, DC; tel. (1) 327-7500; fax (1) 327-7555; e-mail info@bogota.mfa.gov.il; internet bogota.mfa.gov.il; Ambassador YOED MAGEN.

Italy: Calle 93B, No 9-92, Apdo Aéreo 50901, Bogotá, DC; tel. (1) 218-7206; fax (1) 610-5886; e-mail ambbogo.mail@esteri.it; internet www .ambbogota.esteri.it; Ambassador GIANNI BARDINI.

Jamaica: Avda 19, No 106A-83, Of. 304, Apdo Aéreo 102428, Bogotá, DC; tel. (1) 612-3389; fax (1) 612-3479; e-mail emjacol@cable.net .com; Chargé d'affaires ELAINE TOWNSEND DE SÁNCHEZ.

Japan: Carrera 7A, No 71-21, 11°, Torre B, Bogotá, DC; tel. (1) 317-5001; fax (1) 317-4989; e-mail info@embjp-colombia.com; internet www.colombia.emb-japan.go.jp; Ambassador KAZUO WATANABE.

Korea, Republic: Calle 94, No 9-39, Bogotá, DC; tel. (1) 616-7200; fax (1) 610-0338; e-mail embcorea@mofat.go.kr; internet col.mofat.go .kr/index.jsp; Ambassador CHOO JONG-YOUN.

Lebanon: Calle 74, No 11-88, CP 51084, Bogotá, DC; tel. (1) 348-1781; fax (1) 347-9106; e-mail info@embajadadellibano.org.co; internet www.embajadadellibano.org.co; Ambassador HASSAN MUS-LIMANI.

Mexico: Edif. Teleport Business Park, Calle 113, No 7-21, Of. 204, Torre A, Barrio Santa Ana, Bogotá, DC; tel. (1) 629-4989; fax (1) 629-5121; e-mail emcolmex@etb.net.co; internet www.sre.gob.mx/ colombia; Ambassador ARNULFO VALDIVIA MACHUCA.

Morocco: Carrera 23, No 104A-34, Bogotá, DC; tel. (1) 619-3681; fax (1) 619-3685; e-mail embamarruecos@etb.net.co; internet www .embajadamarruecosbogota.com; Ambassador NOUREDDINE KHALIFA.

Netherlands: Carrera 13, No 93-40, 5°, Apdo Aéreo 43585, Bogotá, DC; tel. (1) 638-4200; fax (1) 623-3020; e-mail bog@minbuza.nl; internet colombia.nlembajada.org; Ambassador ROBERT VAN EMB-DEN.

Nicaragua: Calle 108A, No 25-42, Bogotá, DC; tel. (1) 703-6450; fax (1) 612-6050; e-mail embnicaragua@007mundo.com; Ambassador JULIO JOSÉ CALERO REYES.

Norway: OXO Centre, Of. 904, Carrera 11A, No 94-45, Bogotá, DC; tel. (1) 651-5500; fax (1) 2395-6902; e-mail emb.bogota@mfa.no; internet colombia.norway.info; Ambassador LARS OLE VAAGEN.

Panama: Calle 92, No 7A-40, Bogotá, DC; tel. (1) 257-5068; fax (1) 257-5067; e-mail embpacol@cable.net.co; internet www.empacol.org; Ambassador RICARDO ANGUIZOLA.

Paraguay: Calle 72, No 10-51, 10°, Of. 1001, Bogotá, DC; tel. (1) 235-6987; fax (1) 212-7552; e-mail embparaguaycol@gmail.com; internet www.mre.gov.py/embaparcolombia; Ambassador RICARDO LAVIERO SCAVONE YEGROS.

Peru: Calle 80A, No 6-50, Bogotá, DC; tel. (1) 257-0505; fax (1) 249-8581; e-mail embaperu@embajadadelperu.org.co; internet www .embajadadelperu.org.co; Ambassador NESTOR FRANCISCO POPOLIZIO BARDALES.

Poland: Carrera 21, Calle 104A, No 23-48, Apdó Aéreo 101363, Bogotá, DC; tel. (1) 214-0400; fax (1) 214-0854; e-mail bogota.amb .sekretariat@msz.gov.pl; internet www.bogota.polemb.net; Ambassador MACIEJ ZIĘTARA.

Portugal: Carrera 2, No 109-92, Barrio Santa Ana, Bogotá, DC; tel. (1) 215-6430; fax (1) 637-0042; e-mail embporbog@cable.net.co; Ambassador JOÃO MANUEL RIBEIRO DE ALMEIDA.

Romania: Carrera 7A, No 92-58, Chico, Bogotá, DC; tel. (1) 256-6438; fax (1) 256-6158; e-mail ambrombogota@etb.net.co; internet bogota .mae.ro; Chargé d'affaires a.i. RADU SARBU.

Russia: Carrera 4, No 75-02, Apdo Aéreo 90600, Bogotá, DC; tel. (1) 212-1881; fax (1) 210-4694; e-mail embajadaderusiaencolombia@ gmail.com; internet www.colombia.mid.ru; Ambassador PÁVEL SÉRGIEV.

Spain: Calle 92, No 12-68, Apdo 90355, Bogotá, DC; tel. (1) 593-0370; fax (1) 621-0809; e-mail informae@maec.es; internet www.mae.es/ embajadas/bogota; Ambassador NICOLÁS MARTIN CINTO.

Sweden: Edif. Avenida Chile, 8°, Calle 72, No 5-83, Apdo Aéreo 52966, Bogotá, DC; tel. (1) 325-6100; fax (1) 325-6101; e-mail embsueca@cable.net.co; internet www.swedenabroad.com/bogota; Ambassador MARIE ANDERSSON DE FRUTOS.

Switzerland: Carrera 9, No 74-08, Of. 1101, 11°, Apdo Aéreo 251957, Bogotá, DC; tel. (1) 349-7230; fax (1) 349-7195; e-mail bog .vertretung@eda.admin.ch; internet www.eda.admin.ch/bogota; Ambassador DORA RAPOLD.

Turkey: Calle 76, No 8-47, Bogotá, DC; tel. (1) 321-0073; fax (1) 321-0076; e-mail turkemb.bogota@hotmail.com; Ambassador ENGIN YÜRUR.

United Kingdom: Edif. ING Barings, Carrera 9, No 76-49, 9°, Bogotá, DC; tel. (1) 326-8300; fax (1) 326-8302; e-mail ppa.bogota@fco .gov.uk; internet ukincolombia.fco.gov.uk; Ambassador LINDSAY CROISDALE-APPLEBY.

USA: Calle 24-bis, No 48-50, Apdo Aéreo 3831, Bogotá, DC; tel. (1) 275-2000; fax (1) 275-4600; e-mail AmbassadorB@state.gov; internet bogota.usembassy.gov; Ambassador KEVIN WHITAKER.

Uruguay: Edif. El Nogal, Carrera 9A, No 80-15, 11°, Apdo Aéreo 101466, Bogotá, DC; tel. (1) 235-2748; fax (1) 248-3734; e-mail urucolom@etb.net.co; Ambassador DUNCAN CAYRÚS CROCI DE MULA.

Venezuela: Edif. Horizonte, 5°, Carrera 11, No 87-51, 5°, Bogotá, DC; tel. (1) 644-5555; fax (1) 640-1242; e-mail correspondencia .colombia@mppre.gob.ve; internet colombia.embajada.gob.ve; Ambassador IVÁN GUILLERMO RINCÓN URDANETA.

Judicial System

CONSTITUTIONAL COURT

The constitutional integrity of the State is ensured by the Constitutional Court. The Constitutional Court is composed of nine judges who are elected by the Senate for eight years. Judges of the Constitutional Court are not eligible for re-election.

Corte Constitucional: Edif. del Palacio de Justicia, Calle 12, No 7-65, Bogotá, DC; tel. (1) 350-6200; fax (1) 336-6822; internet www .corteconstitucional.gov.co; f. 1991; Pres. JORGE IVÁN PALACIO PALACIO.

SUPREME COURT OF JUSTICE

The ordinary judicial integrity of the State is ensured by the Supreme Court of Justice. The Supreme Court of Justice is composed of the Courts of Civil and Agrarian, Penal, and Labour Cassation. Judges of the Supreme Court of Justice, of which there are 23, are selected from the nominees of the Higher Council of Justice and serve an eight-year term of office, which is not renewable.

Corte Suprema de Justicia: Edif. de Palacio de Justicia, Calle 12, No 7-65, Bogotá, DC; tel. (1) 562-2000; internet www.cortesuprema .gov.co; Pres. Dr LUÍS GABRIEL MIRANDA BUELVAS.

Court of Civil Cassation (seven judges): Pres. Dr JESÚS VALL DE RUTEN RUIZ.

Court of Penal Cassation (nine judges): Pres. Dr FERNANDO ALBERTO CASTRO CABALLERO.

Court of Labour Cassation (seven judges): Pres. Dr RIGOBERTO ECHEVERRI BUENO.

Attorney-General: EDUARDO MONTEALEGRE LYNETT.

COUNCIL OF STATE

The Council of State serves as the supreme consultative body to the Government in matters of legislation and administration. It also serves as the supreme tribunal for administrative litigation (*Contencioso Administrativo*). It is composed of 27 magistrates, including a President.

Council of State: Edif. del Palacio de Justicia, Calle 12, No 7-65, Bogotá, DC; tel. (1) 350-6700; internet www.consejodeestado.gov.co; Pres. Dr Maria Claudia Rojas Lasso.

Religion

CHRISTIANITY

The Roman Catholic Church

Colombia comprises 13 archdioceses, 52 dioceses and 10 apostolic vicariates. Some 87% of the population are Roman Catholics.

Bishops' Conference: Conferencia Episcopal de Colombia, Carrera 58, No 80-87, Apdo Aéreo 7448, Bogotá, DC; tel. (1) 437-5540; fax (1) 311-5575; e-mail colcec@cec.org.co; internet www.cec.org.co; f. 1978; statutes approved 1996; Pres. Cardinal Jesús Rubén Salazar Gómez (Archbishop of Bogotá).

Archbishop of Barranquilla: Jairo Jaramillo Monsalve, Carrera 45, No 53-122, Apdo Aéreo 1160, Barranquilla 4, Atlántico; tel. (5) 360-0047; fax (5) 349-1530; e-mail contactenos@arquidiocesisbaq.org; internet www.arquidiocesisbaq.org.

Archbishop of Bogotá: Cardinal Jesús Rubén Salazar Gómez, Carrera 7a, No 10-20, Bogotá, DC; tel. (1) 350-5511; fax (1) 350-7290; e-mail sistemas@arquidiocesisbogota.org.co; internet www.arquidiocesisbogota.org.co.

Archbishop of Bucaramanga: Ismael Rueda Sierra, Calle 33, No 21-18, Bucaramanga, Santander del Sur; tel. (7) 630-4698; fax (7) 642-1361; e-mail sarqdbu@col1.telecom.com; internet www.arquidiocesisbucaramanga.com.

Archbishop of Cali: Darjío de Jesús Monsalve Mejía, Carrera 4, No 7-17, Apdo Aéreo 8924, Cali, Valle del Cauca; tel. (2) 889-0562; fax (2) 883-7980; e-mail jsarasti@andinet.com; internet www.arquidiocesiscali.org.

Archbishop of Cartagena: Jorge Enrique Jiménez Carvajal, Carrera 5, No 34–55, Apdo Aéreo 400, Cartagena; tel. (5) 664-5308; fax (5) 664-4974; e-mail buzonvirtual@arquicartagenadeindias.org; internet www.arquicartagenadeindias.org.

Archbishop of Ibagué: Flavio Calle Zapata, Calle 10, No 2-58, Plaza de Bolivar, Ibagué, Tolima; tel. (8) 261-1680; fax (8) 263-2681; e-mail info@arquidiocesisdeibague.org; internet www.arquidiocesisdeibague.org.

Archbishop of Manizales: Gonzalo Restrepo Restrepo, Carrera 23, No 19-22, Manizales, Caldas; tel. (6) 884-2933; fax (6) 884-3344; e-mail administrador@arquidiocesisdemanizales.com; internet www.arquidiocesisdemanizales.com.

Archbishop of Medellín: Ricardo Antonio Tobón Restrepo, Calle 57, No 49-44, 3°, Medellín; tel. (4) 251-7700; fax (4) 251-9395; e-mail arquidiomed@epm.net.co; internet www.arqmedellin.com.

Archbishop of Nueva Pamplona: Luis Madrid Merlano, Carrera 5, No 4-87, Nueva Pamplona; tel. (7) 568-2816; fax (7) 568-4540; e-mail gumafri@hotmail.com; internet www.arquipamplona.org.

Archbishop of Popayán: Iván Antonio Marín López, Calle 5, No 6-71, Apdo Aéreo 593, Popayán; tel. (2) 824-1710; fax (2) 824-0101; e-mail ivanarzo@emtel.net.co; internet www.arquidiocesisdepopayan.org.

Archbishop of Santa Fe de Antioquia: Orlando Antonio Corrales García, Plazuela Martínez Pardo, No 12-11, Santa Fe de Antioquia; tel. (4) 853-1155; fax (4) 853-1144; e-mail arquistafe@edatel.net.co; internet www.arquisantioquia.org.co.

Archbishop of Tunja: Luis Augusto Castro Quiroga, Carrera 2, No 59-390, Apdo Aéreo 1019, Tunja, Boyacá; tel. (8) 742-2093; fax (8) 743-3130; e-mail arquidio@telecom.com.co; internet www.arquidiocesisdetunja.org.

Archbishop of Villavicencio: Oscar Urbina Ortega, Carrera 39, No 34-19, Apdo Aéreo 2401, Villavicencio, Meta; tel. (8) 663-0337; fax (8) 665-3200; e-mail diocesisvillavicencio@andinet.com.

The Anglican Communion

Anglicans in Colombia are members of the Episcopal Church in the USA.

Bishop of Colombia: Rt Rev. Francisco José Duque Gómez, Carrera 6, No 49-85, 2°, Apdo Aéreo 52964, Bogotá, DC; tel. (1) 288-3187; fax (1) 288-3248; e-mail iec@iglesiaepiscopal.org.co; internet www.iglesiaepiscopal.org.co.

Other Christian Churches

Church of Jesus Christ of Latter-Day Saints (Mormons): Carrera 46, 127-45, Bogotá, DC; tel. (1) 625-8000; internet www.lds.org; 180,526 mems.

Iglesia Evangélica Luterana de Colombia: Calle 75, No 20-54, Apdo Aéreo 51538, Bogotá, DC; tel. (1) 212-5735; fax (1) 212-5714; e-mail ofcentral@ielco.org; internet www.ielco.org; 2,615 mems; Pres. Bishop Eduardo Martinez.

BAHÁ'Í FAITH

National Spiritual Assembly of the Bahá'ís of Colombia (Comunidad Bahá'í de Colombia): Apdo Aéreo 51387, Bogotá, DC; tel. and fax (1) 268-1658; internet www.bahai.org.co; Gen. Sec. Ximena Osorio V.; adherents in 1,013 localities.

JUDAISM

There is a community of about 4,200 Jews.

The Press

DAILIES

Bogotá, DC

El Espectador: Avda El Dorado 69-76, Bogotá, DC; tel. and fax (1) 423-2300; e-mail servicioalcliente@elespectador.com; internet www.elespectador.com; f. 1887; Editor Leonardo Rodríguez.

El Nuevo Siglo: Calle 25b, No 101-04, Apdo Aéreo 5452, Bogotá, DC; tel. (1) 413-9200; fax (1) 413-8547; e-mail contacto@elnuevosiglo.com.co; internet www.elnuevosiglo.com.co; f. 1936; conservative; Dir Juan Gabriel Uribe; Editor Alberto Abello; circ. 68,000.

Portafolio: Avda Calle 26, No 68b-70, Apdo Aéreo 3633, Bogotá, DC; tel. (1) 294-0100; e-mail sugerenciasysolicitudes@portafolio.co; internet www.portafolio.co; f. 1993; economics and business; Dir Ricardo Avila Pinto.

La República: Calle 25d Bis, 102a-63, Bogotá, DC; tel. (1) 422-7600; fax (1) 413-3725; e-mail diario@larepublica.com.co; internet www.larepublica.com.co; f. 1954; morning; finance and economics; Dir Fernando Quijano; circ. 55,000.

El Tiempo: Avda Calle 26, No 68b-70, Bogotá, DC; tel. (1) 294-0100; fax (1) 410-5088; e-mail servicioalcliente@eltiempo.com; internet www.eltiempo.com; f. 1911; morning; liberal; Editor Ernesto Cortés; Dir Roberto Pombo; circ. 265,118 (weekdays), 536,377 (Sun.).

Barranquilla, Atlántico

El Heraldo: Calle 53b, No 46-25, Barranquilla, Atlántico; tel. (5) 371-5000; fax (5) 371-5091; internet www.elheraldo.com.co; f. 1933; morning; liberal; Dir Marco Schwartz; circ. 70,000.

La Libertad: Carrera 53, No 55-166, Barranquilla, Atlántico; tel. (5) 349-1175; fax (5) 349-1298; e-mail libertad@lalibertad.com.co; internet www.lalibertad.com.co; f. 1979; liberal; Dir Roberto Esper Rebaje; Editor Luz Marina Esper Fayad; circ. 25,000.

Bucaramanga, Santander del Sur

Vanguardia Liberal: Calle 34, No 13-42, Bucaramanga, Santander del Sur; tel. (7) 680-0700; fax (7) 630-2443; e-mail ogonzalez@vanguardialiberal.com.co; internet www.vanguardia.com; f. 1919; morning; liberal; Sunday illustrated literary supplement and women's supplement; Editor Pablo Buitraga; circ. 48,000.

Cali, Valle del Cauca

Diario Occidente: Calle 8, No 5-70, 2°, Apdo Aéreo 5262, Cali, Valle del Cauca; tel. (2) 486-0555; e-mail opinion@diariooccidente.com.co; internet www.diariooccidente.com.co; f. 1961; morning; conservative; Editor Rosa María Agudelo Ayerbe; Dir Luis Oswaldo Venegas Cabrera; circ. 25,000.

El País: Carrera 2a, No 24-46, Apdo Aéreo 4766, Cali, Valle del Cauca; tel. (2) 898-7000; e-mail diario@elpais.com.co; internet www.elpais.com.co; f. 1950; conservative; Dir and Gen. Man. María Elvira Domínguez; circ. 60,000 (weekdays), 120,000 (Sat.), 108,304 (Sun.).

Cartagena, Bolívar

El Universal: Pie del Cerro Calle 30, No 17-36, Cartagena, Bolívar; tel. (5) 650-1050; fax (5) 650-1057; e-mail director@eluniversal.com.co; internet www.eluniversal.com.co; f. 1948; daily; liberal; Editor Germán Mendoza; Dir Pedro Luis Mogollón Vélez; circ. 167,000.

Cúcuta, Norte de Santander

La Opinión: Avda 4, No 16-12, Cúcuta, Norte de Santander; tel. (7) 582-9999; fax (7) 571-7869; e-mail gerencia@laopinion.com.co; internet www.laopinion.com.co; f. 1960; morning; Editor Dr José Eustorgio Colmenares Ossa; circ. 16,000.

Manizales, Caldas

La Patria: Carrera 20, No 46-35, Manizales, Caldas; tel. (6) 878-1700; e-mail lapatria@lapatria.com; internet www.lapatria.com; f. 1921; morning; ind; Dir NICOLÁS RESTREPO ESCOBAR; circ. 22,000.

Medellín, Antioquia

El Colombiano: Carrera 48, No 30 sur-119, Apdo Aéreo 80636, Medellín, Antioquia; tel. (4) 331-5252; fax (4) 331-4858; e-mail elcolombiano@elcolombiano.com.co; internet www.elcolombiano .com; f. 1912; morning; conservative; Dir ANA MERCEDES GÓMEZ MARTÍNEZ; circ. 90,000.

El Mundo: Calle 53, No 74-50, Apdo Aéreo 53874, Medellín, Antioquia; tel. (4) 264-2800; fax (4) 264-3729; e-mail elmundo@elmundo .com; internet www.elmundo.com; f. 1979; Dir GUILLERMO GAVIRIA ECHEVERRI; Editor IRENE GAVIRIA CORREA; circ. 37,200 (Mon.–Sat.), 55,000 (Sun.).

Neiva, Huila

Diario del Huila: Calle 8A, No 6-30, Neiva, Huila; tel. (8) 871-2458; fax (8) 871-2543; e-mail prensa@diariodelhuila.com; internet www .diariodelhuila.com; f. 1966; Dir MARÍA PÍA DUQUE RENGIFO; Editor GERMÁN HERNÁNDEZ VERA; circ. 12,000.

Pasto, Nariño

Diario del Sur: Calle 18, No 47-160, Torobajo, San Juan de Pasto, Nariño; tel. (2) 731-0048; e-mail diariodelsur@diariodelsur.com.co; internet www.diariodelsur.com.co; f. 1983; Dir HERNANDO SUÁREZ BURGOS.

Pereira, Risaralda

El Diario del Otún: Carrera 8A, No 22-75, Apdo Aéreo 2533, Pereira, Risaralda; tel. (6) 335-1313; fax (6) 325-4878; e-mail luiscramirez@eldiario.com.co; internet www.eldiario.com.co; f. 1982; Administrative Dir JAVIER IGNACIO RAMÍREZ MÚNERA; Editor-in-Chief JOHANNA MOLANO; circ. 30,000.

La Tarde: Parque Empresarial La Tarde, Km 3, Vía Armenia, Pereira, Risaralda; tel. (6) 313-7676; fax (6) 335-5187; internet www.latarde.com; f. 1975; morning; Dir SONIA DÍAZ MANTILLA; circ. 30,000.

Popayán, Cauca

El Liberal: Carrera 3, No 2-60, Apdo Aéreo 538, Popayán, Cauca; tel. (28) 24-2418; fax (28) 23-3888; e-mail gerencia@elliberal.com.co; internet www.elliberal.com.co; f. 1938; Man. ANA MARIA LONDOÑO R.; Dir ISMENIA ARDILA DÍAZ; circ. 6,500.

Santa Marta, Magdalena

El Informador: Avda Libertador 12A-37, Santa Marta, Magdalena; tel. (5) 421-7736; e-mail mensajes@elinformador.com.co; internet www.elinformador.com.co; f. 1958; liberal; Dir ALFONSO VIVES CAMPO; circ. 26,000.

PERIODICALS

ART NEXUS/Arte en Colombia: Carrera 5, No 67-19, Apdo Aéreo 90193, Bogotá, DC; tel. (1) 312-9435; fax (1) 312-9252; e-mail info@ artnexus.com; internet www.artnexus.com; f. 1976; quarterly; Latin American art, photography, visual arts; editions in English and Spanish; Pres. and Chief Editor CELIA SREDNI DE BIRBRAGHER; CEO SUSANNE BIRBRAGHER; circ. 26,000.

Coyuntura Económica: Calle 78, No 9-91, Apdo Aéreo 75074, Bogotá, DC; tel. (1) 325-9777; fax (1) 325-9770; e-mail coyuntura@ fedesarrollo.org.co; internet www.fedesarrollo.org.co; f. 1971; twice yearly; economics; published by Fundación para Educación Superior y el Desarrollo; Editor DANIEL GÓMEZ GAVIRIA; circ. 300.

Cromos Magazine: Avda El Dorado 69-76, Bogotá, DC; tel. (1) 423-2300; fax (1) 423-7641; e-mail internet@cromos.com.co; internet www.cromos.com.co; f. 1916; weekly; illustrated; general news; Dir JAIRO DUEÑAS VILLAMIL; circ. 102,000.

Dinero: Calle 93B, No 13-47, Bogotá, DC; tel. (1) 646-8400; fax (1) 621-9526; e-mail correo@dinero.com; internet www.dinero.com; f. 1993; fortnightly; economics and business; Dir SANTIAGO GUTIÉRREZ VIANA.

Gerente: Edif. Oficenter, Carrera 16, No 96-64, Santa Fe de Bogotá, DC; tel. (1) 636-9136; fax (1) 636-9638; e-mail ndelahoz@gmail.com; internet www.gerente.com; current affairs; Editor NARCISO DE LA HOZ.

El Malpensante: Calle 35, No 14-27, Bogotá, DC; tel. (1) 320-0120; fax (1) 340-2808; e-mail info@elmalpensante.com; internet www .elmalpensante.com; f. 1996; monthly; literature; Dir MARIO JURSICH DURÁN; Editor ANGEL UNFRIED.

Revista Credencial: Carrera 10, No 28-49, 23°, Bogotá, DC; tel. (1) 353-8307; fax (1) 353-8320; e-mail direccionrc@revistacredencial .com; internet www.revistacredencial.com; current affairs; Dir MARÍA ISABEL RUEDA; Editor ANDRÉS ARIAS.

Revista Escala: Calle 30, No 17-752, Bogotá, DC; tel. (1) 287-8200; fax (1) 285-9882; e-mail escala@revistaescala.com; internet www .revistaescala.com; f. 1962; fortnightly; architecture; Dir DAVID SERNA CÁRDENAS; circ. 18,000.

Revista Fucsia: Calle 93B, No 13-47, Bogotá, DC; tel. (1) 646-8400; fax (1) 621-9526; e-mail correo@fucsia.com; internet www .revistafucsia.com; fortnightly; women's interest; Dir LILA OCHOA.

Semana: Calle 93B, No 13-47, Bogotá, DC; tel. (1) 646-8400; fax (1) 621-9526; e-mail director@semana.com; internet www.semana.com; f. 1982; general; weekly; Dir ALEJANDRO SANTOS RUBINO; Editor ALVARO SIERRA RESTREPO.

Tribuna Médica: Calle 8B, No 68A-41, y Calle 123, No 8-20, Bogotá, DC; tel. (1) 262-6085; fax (1) 262-4459; e-mail editor@tribunamedica .com; internet www.tribunamedica.com; f. 1961; monthly; medical and scientific; Dir JOSÉ RIOS RODRIGUEZ; circ. 50,000.

Tribuna Roja: Calle 39, No 21-30, Bogotá, DC; tel. (1) 245-9647; e-mail tribojar@moir.org.co; internet tribunaroja.moir.org.co; f. 1971; quarterly; organ of the MOIR (pro-Maoist Communist party); Dir CARLOS NARANJO; circ. 300,000.

PRESS ASSOCIATIONS

Asociación Nacional de Diarios Colombianos (ANDIARIOS): Calle 61, No 5-20, Apdo Aéreo 13663, Bogotá, DC; tel. (1) 345-8011; fax (1) 212-7894; e-mail andiarios@andiarios.com; internet www .andiarios.com; f. 1962; 32 affiliated newspapers; Pres. JON RUIZ ITUARTE; Exec. Dir NORA SANÍN DE SAFFON.

Asociación Nacional de Medios de Comunicación (ASO-MEDIOS): see Broadcasting and Communications.

Círculo de Periodistas de Bogotá (CPB): Diagonal 33A, Bis No 16-56, Bogotá, DC; tel. (1) 340-0883; e-mail contactenos@ circulodeperiodistasdebogota.com; internet circulodeperiodistasdebogota.com; f. 1946; Pres. WILLIAM GIRALDO CEBALLOS; Sec.-Gen. MARTHA LUCÍA DÍAZ.

Publishers

Cengage Learning de Colombia, SA: Edif. Seguros Aurora, 8°, Carrera 7, No 74-21, Bogotá, DC; tel. (1) 212-3340; fax (1) 211-3995; e-mail clientes.pactoandino@cengage.com; internet www.cengage .com.co; Country Man. LILIANA GUTIERREZ.

Ecoe Ediciones Ltda: Carrera 19, No 63C-32, Bogotá, DC; tel. (1) 248-1449; fax (1) 346-1741; e-mail oswaldo@ecoeediciones.com; internet www.ecoeediciones.com; science, medical and general interest; Gen. Man. OSWALDO PEÑUELA CARRIÓN.

Ediciones Gaviota: Carrera 62, No 98B-13, Bogotá, DC; tel. (1) 613-6650; fax (1) 613-9117; e-mail gaviotalibros@edicionesgaviota.com .co; internet www.edicionesgaviota.com.co; Rep. FABIOLA RAMOS MONDRAGÓN.

Ediciones Modernas: Carrera 41A, No 22F-22, Bogotá, DC; tel. (1) 269-0072; fax (1) 244-0706; e-mail edimodernas@edimodernas.com .co; internet www.empresario.com.co/edimodernas; f. 1991; juvenile; Gen. Man. JORGE SERRANO GARCES.

Editorial Cypres Ltda: Carrera 15, No 80-36, Of. 301, Bogotá, DC; tel. (1) 618-0657; fax (1) 691-0578; e-mail cypresad@etb.net.co; general interest and educational; Gen. Man. JOHANNA VALENZUELA GONZÁLEZ.

Editorial El Globo, SA: Calle 25D, Bis 102A-63, Bogotá, DC; tel. (1) 606-1290; fax (1) 210-4900; e-mail rhumanos@larepublica.com.co; Gen. Man. OLGA LUCIA LONDOÑO M.

Editorial Kinesis: Carrera 25, No 18-12, Armenia; tel. (6) 740-9155; fax (6) 740-1584; e-mail informacion@kinesis.com.co; internet www .kinesis.com.co; physical education, recreation and sport; Dir DIÓGENES VERGARA LARA.

Editorial Leyer Ltda: Carrera 4, No 16-51, Bogotá, DC; tel. (1) 282-1903; fax (1) 282-2373; e-mail contacto@edileyer.com; internet www .edileyer.com; f. 1991; law; Dir HILDEBRANDO LEAL PÉREZ.

Editorial Paulinas: Calle 161A, No 15-50, Bogotá, DC; tel. (1) 528-7444; fax (1) 671-0992; e-mail comunicaciones@paulinas.org.co; internet www.paulinas.org.co; Christian and self-help.

Editorial San Pablo (Sociedad de San Pablo): Carrera 46, No 22A-90, Quintaparedes, Apdo Aéreo 080152, Bogotá, DC; tel. (1) 368-2099; fax (1) 244-4383; e-mail editorial@sanpablo.com.co; internet www .sanpablo.com.co; f. 1914; religion (Catholic); Editorial Dir Fr VICENTE MIOTTO; Editor AMPARO MAHECHA.

Editorial Temis, SA: Calle 17, No 68D, Apdo Aéreo 46, Bogotá, DC; tel. (1) 424-7855; fax (1) 292-5801; e-mail editorial@editorialtemis

.com; internet www.editorialtemis.com; f. 1951; law, sociology, politics; Gen. Man. ERWIN GUERRERO PINZÓN.

Editorial Voluntad, SA: Avda El Dorado, No 90-10, Bogotá, DC; tel. (1) 410-6355; fax (1) 295-2994; e-mail voluntad@voluntad.com.co; internet www.voluntad.com.co; f. 1930; school books; Pres. GASTÓN DE BEDOUT.

Fondo de Cultura Económica: Calle de la Enseñanza 11, No 5–60, La Candelaria, Zona C, Bogotá, DC; tel. (1) 283-2200; fax (1) 337-4289; e-mail caguilar@fce.com.co; internet www.fce.com.co; f. 1934; academic; Gen. Man. CÉSAR ANGEL AGUILAR ASIAIN.

Fundación Centro de Investigación y Educación Popular (CINEP): Carrera 5A, No 33B -02, Apdo Aéreo 25916, Bogotá, DC; tel. (1) 245-6181; fax (1) 287-9089; e-mail cinep@cinep.org.co; internet www.cinep.org.co; f. 1972; education and social sciences; Exec. Dir LUIS GUILLERMO GUERRERO GUEVARA.

Instituto Caro y Cuervo: Calle 10, No 4-69, Bogotá, DC; tel. (1) 342-2121; fax (1) 284-1248; e-mail direcciongeneral@caroycuervo.gov.co; internet www.caroycuervo.gov.co; f. 1942; philology, general linguistics and reference; Dir-Gen. GENOVEVA IRIARTE.

Inversiones Cromos, SA: Avda El Dorado, No 69-76, Bogotá, DC; tel. (1) 423-2300; fax (1) 423-7641; e-mail jduenas@cromos.com.co; internet www.cromos.com.co; f. 1916; Dir JAIRO DUEÑAS VILLAMIL; Editor LEONARDO RODRÍGUEZ.

Legis, SA: Avda Calle 26, No 82–70, Apdo Aéreo 98888, Bogotá, DC; tel. (1) 425-5200; e-mail servicio@legis.com.co; internet www.legis .com.co; f. 1952; economics, law, general; Pres. LUIS ALFREDO MOTTA VENEGAS.

McGraw Hill Interamericana, SA: Carrera 85D, No 46A–65, Bodegas 9, 10 y 11, Complejo Logístico San Cayetano, Urb. San Cayetano Norte, Bogotá, DC; tel. (1) 600-3800; fax (1) 600-3855; e-mail info_colombia@mcgraw-hill.com; internet www.mcgraw-hill .com.co; university textbooks; Dir-Gen. MARTÍN RENÉ CHUECO.

Publicar, SA: Avda 68, No 75A-50, 2°, 3° y 4°, Centro Comercial Metrópolis, Apdo Aéreo 8010, Bogotá, DC; tel. (1) 646-5555; fax (1) 646-5523; e-mail e-hamburger@publicar.com; internet www .publicar.com; f. 1959; owned by the Carvajal Group; directories; Pres. ERIC HAMBURGER.

Siglo del Hombre Editores, SA: Carrera 31A, No 25B-50, Bogotá, DC; tel. (1) 337-7700; fax (1) 337-7665; e-mail info@siglodelhombre .com; internet www.siglodelhombre.com; f. 1992; arts, politics, anthropology, history, humanities; Gen. Man. EMILIA FRANCO DE ARCILA.

Tercer Mundo Editores, SA: Grupo TM, SA, Calle 25B, No 31A-34, Bogotá, DC; tel. (1) 368-8645; e-mail grupotmsa@etb.net.co; internet grupotmsa.blogspot.com; f. 1963; social sciences.

Thomson PLM: Calle 106, No 54–81, Apdo Aéreo 52998, Barrio Puente Largo, Bogotá, DC; tel. (1) 613-1111; fax (1) 624-2335; e-mail contactoco@plmlatina.com; internet www.plmlatina.com; medical; Regional Dir CONSTANZA RIAÑO RODRÍGUEZ.

Tragaluz Editores: Edif. Lugo, Of. 108, Calle 6 Sur, No 43A-200, Medellín, Antioquia; tel. (4) 312-0295; fax (4) 268-4366; e-mail info@ tragaluzeditores.com; internet tragaluzeditores.com; literature and graphics; Editorial Dir PILAR GUTIÉRREZ LLANO.

Villegas Editores: Avda 82, No 11-50, Interior 3, Bogotá, DC; tel. (1) 616-1788; fax (1) 616-0020; e-mail informacion@villegaseditores .com; internet www.villegaseditores.com; f. 1986; illustrated and scholarly; Pres. BENJAMÍN VILLEGAS JIMÉNEZ.

ASSOCIATIONS

Asociación de Editoriales Universitarias de Colombia (ASEUC): Carrera 13A, No 38-82, Of. 901, Bogotá, DC; tel. (1) 805-2357; fax (1) 287-9257; e-mail asistente@aseuc.org.co; internet www.aseuc.org.co; Pres. NICOLÁS MORALES THOMAS; Sec.-Gen. LORENA RUIZ SERNA.

Cámara Colombiana del Libro: Calle 35, No 5A-05, Bogotá, DC; tel. (1) 323-0111; fax (1) 285-1082; e-mail camlibro@camlibro.com.co; internet www.camlibro.com.co; f. 1951; Pres. GUSTAVO RODRÍGUEZ GARCÍA; Exec. Dir ENRIQUE GONZÁLEZ VILLA; 95 mems.

Fundalectura: Avda Diagonal 40A Bis, No 16-46, Bogotá, DC; tel. (1) 320-1511; fax (1) 287-7071; e-mail contactenos@fundalectura.org.co; internet www.fundalectura.org; f. 1990; Pres. ALFONSO OCAMPO GAVIRIA; Exec. Dir CARMEN BARVO.

Broadcasting and Communications

TELECOMMUNICATIONS

Avantel, SAS: Carrera 11, No 93-92, Bogotá, DC; tel. (1) 634-3434; e-mail contactenos@avantel.com.co; internet www.avantel.com.co; f. 1996; telecom operator, wireless broadband; subsidiary of Axtel (Mexico); Pres. JORGE ANDRÉS PALACIO BECERRA.

Claro Colombia: Calle 90, No 14-37, Bogotá, DC; tel. (1) 616-9797; fax (1) 256-0538; e-mail servicioalcliente@claro.com.co; internet www.claro.com.co; f. 1994 as Occidente y Caribe Celular, SA (Occel); present name adopted in 2012 following the merger of Comcel and Telmex; owned by América Móvil, SA de CV (Mexico); cellular mobile telephone operator; Pres. JUAN CARLOS ARCHILA.

Colombia Móvil, SA (Tigo): Edif. Citibank, 5°, Carrera 9A, No 99-02, Bogotá, DC; tel. (1) 330-3000; fax (1) 618-2712; internet www.tigo .com.co; f. 2003; subsidiary of Millicom International Cellular, SA since 2006; mobile telephone services; Pres. ESTEBAN IRIARTE.

Empresa de Telecomunicaciones de Bogotá, SA (ETB): Carrera 8, No 20-56, 3°–9°, Bogotá, DC; tel. (1) 242-3483; fax (1) 242-2127; e-mail adrimara@etb.com.co; internet www.etb.com.co; Bogotá telephone co; partially privatized in 2003; Pres. SAÚL KATTAN COHEN; Sec.-Gen. JAVIER GUTIÉRREZ AFANADOR.

Telefónica Móviles Colombia (Movistar): Edif. Capital Tower, 17°, Calle 100, No 7-33, Bogotá, DC; tel. (1) 650-0000; fax (1) 650-1852; internet www.movistar.co; f. 2004 following acquisition of BellSouth's operations in Colombia by Telefónica Móviles, subsidiary of Telefónica, SA of Spain; CEO ARIEL PONTÓN.

Telefónica Telecom: Carrera 70, No 108-84, Bogotá, DC; tel. (1) 593-5399; fax (1) 593-1252; internet www.telefonica.co; f. 2003 following dissolution of state-owned Empresa Nacional de Telecomunicaciones (TELECOM, f. 1947); subsidiary of Telefónica, SA (Spain); Pres. ALFONSO GÓMEZ PALACIO.

UNE EPM Telecomunicaciones, SA (Une): Edif. EEPPM, Carrera 16, No 11, Sur 100, Medellín; tel. (4) 382-2020; fax (4) 515-5050; e-mail une@une.com.co; internet www.une.com.co; broadband and telecom services provider; Pres. MARC EICHMANN PERRET.

Regulatory Authority

Comisión de Regulación de Comunicaciones (CRC): Edif. LINK Siete Sesenta, 9°, Calle 59A bis, No 5-53, Bogotá, DC; tel. (1) 319-8300; fax (1) 319-8314; e-mail atencioncliente@crcom.gov.co; internet www.crcom.gov.co; f. 2000; regulatory body; Exec. Dir CARLOS PABLO MÁRQUEZ.

BROADCASTING

Radio

Cadena Melodía de Colombia: Calle 45, No 13-70, Bogotá, DC; tel. (1) 323-1500; fax (1) 288-4020; e-mail presidencia@cadenamelodia .com; internet www.cadenamelodia.com; Pres. EFRAÍN PÁEZ ESPITIA; Gen. Man. ELVIRA MEJÍA DE PÁEZ.

CARACOL, SA (Primera Cadena Radial Colombiana, SA): Edif. Caracol Radio, Calle 67, No 7-37, Bogotá, DC; tel. (1) 348-7600; fax (1) 337-7126; internet www.caracol.com.co; f. 1948; 107 stations; Pres. JOSÉ MANUEL RESTREPO FERNÁNDEZ DE SOTO.

Circuito Todelar de Colombia: Avda 13, No 84-42, Apdo Aéreo 27344, Bogotá, DC; tel. (1) 616-1011; fax (1) 616-0056; e-mail dircomercial@todelar.com; internet www.todelar.com; f. 1953; 74 stations; Dir SANDRA PATRICIA BARBOSA.

Colmundo Radio, SA ('La Cadena de la Paz'): Diagonal 61D, No 26A-29, Apdo Aéreo 36750, Bogotá, DC; tel. (1) 217-9220; fax (1) 348-2746; e-mail direcciongeneral@colmundoradio.com.co; internet colmundoradio.com.co; f. 1989; Pres. ZAIDY MORA QUINTERO; Dir-Gen. MIRIAM QUINTERO.

Organización Radial Olímpica, SA (ORO, SA): Calle 72, No 48-37, 2°, Apdo Aéreo 51266, Barranquilla; tel. (5) 358-0500; fax (5) 345-9080; e-mail ventasbarranquila@oro.com.co; internet www.oro.com .co; programmes for the Antioquia and Atlantic coast regions; Pres. MIGUEL CHAR; Production Dir RAFAEL PÁEZ.

Radio Cadena Nacional, SA (RCN Radio): Calle 37, No 13A-19, Apdo Aéreo 4984, Bogotá, DC; tel. (1) 314-7070; fax (1) 288-6130; e-mail rcn@impsat.net.co; internet www.rcn.com.co; 116 stations; official network; Pres. FERNANDO MOLINA SOTO.

Radio Nacional de Colombia: Carrera 45, No 26-33, Bogotá, DC; tel. (1) 597-8111; fax (1) 597-8011; e-mail contactoradionacional@rtvc .gov.co; internet www.radionacionaldecolombia.gov.co; f. 1940; national public radio; Dir GABRIEL GÓMEZ MEJÍA.

Radio Regional Independiente: Carrera 19A, No 98-12, Of. 801, Bogotá, DC; tel. (1) 691-9724; fax (1) 691-9725; e-mail info@reiltda .com; internet www.reiltda.com; f. 1995; Gen. Man. JUAN MANUEL ORTIZ NOGUERA.

Sistema Super de Columbia: Calle 39A, No 18-12, Bogotá, DC; tel. (1) 234-7777; fax (1) 287-8678; e-mail gerencia@cadenasuper.com; internet www.cadenasuper.com; f. 1971; stations include Radio Super and Super Stereo FM; Gen. Man. JUAN CARLOS PAVA CAMELO.

Television

Canal Institutional: Avda El Dorado, Carrera 45, No 26-33, Bogotá, DC; tel. (1) 597-8000; fax (1) 597-8011; e-mail

contactoinstitucional@rtvc.gov.co; internet www.institucional.gov
.co; f. 2004; govt-owned; Co-ordinator LENNART RODRÍGUEZ.

Canal RCN Televisión: Avda Américas, No 65-82, Bogotá, DC; tel.
(1) 426-9292; e-mail quienessomos@canalrcn.com; internet www
.canalrcnmsn.com; f. 1998; Pres. GABRIEL REYES.

Caracol Televisión, SA: Calle 103, No 69B-43, Apdo Aéreo 26484,
Bogotá, DC; tel. (1) 643-0430; fax (1) 643-0444; internet www
.caracoltv.com; f. 1969; Pres. PAULO LASERNA PHILLIPS.

Fox Telecolombia: Carrera 50, No 17-77, Bogotá, DC; tel. (1) 417-
4200; fax (1) 341-6198; e-mail john.ahumada@foxtelecolombia.com;
internet www.foxtelecolombia.com; formerly Cadena Uno; f. 1992;
acquired by Fox International Channels and changed name as above
in 2007; Pres. SAMUEL DUQUE ROZO.

Señal Colombia: Avda El Dorado, Carrera 45, No 26-33, Bogotá,
DC; tel. (1) 597-8132; fax (1) 597-8062; e-mail senalencontacto@rtvc
.gov.co; internet www.senalcolombia.tv; govt-owned; Co-ordinator
ADRIAN FRANCISCO COMAS.

Teleantioquia: Calle 44, No 53A–11, Apdo Aéreo 8183, Medellín,
Antioquia; tel. (4) 356-9900; fax (4) 356-9909; e-mail
comunicaciones@teleantioquia.com.co; internet www.teleantioquia
.com.co; f. 1985; Gen. Man. SELENE BOTERO GIRALDO.

Telecafé: Carrera 19A, Calle 43, Barrio Sacatín contiguo Universidad Autónoma, Manizales, Caldas; tel. (6) 872-7100; fax (6) 872-7610;
e-mail info@telecafe.tv; internet www.telecafe.tv; f. 1986; govt-
owned; broadcasts to the 'Eje Cafetero' (departments of Caldas,
Quindío and Risaralda); Gen. Man. JORGE EDUARDO URREA GIRALDO.

TeleCaribe: Carrera 54, No 72-142, 4°, Barranquilla, Atlántico; tel.
(5) 368-0184; fax (5) 360-7300; e-mail info@telecaribe.com.co;
internet www.telecaribe.com.co; f. 1986; Pres. ARTURO SARMIENTO;
Gen. Man. IVÁN GUILLERMO BARRIOS MASS.

Telepacífico (Sociedad de Televisión del Pacifico Ltda): Calle 5, No
38A-14, 3°, esq. Centro Comercial Imbanaco, Cali, Valle del Cauca;
tel. (2) 518-4000; fax (2) 588-281; e-mail gerenciatp@telepacifico.com;
internet www.telepacifico.com; Gen. Man. LORENA IVETTE MENDOZA
MARMOLEJO.

TV Cúcuta: tel. (7) 574-7874; fax (7) 575-2922; f. 1992; Pres. JOSÉ A.
ARMELLA.

Regulatory Authority

Autoridad Nacional de Televisión: Edif. Link Siete Sesenta, Of.
405, Calle 59A Bis, No 5–53, Bogotá, DC; tel. (1) 795-7000; e-mail
informacion@antv.gov.co; internet www.antv.gov.co; f. 2012; successor to Comisión Nacional de Televisión; Dir TATIANA ANDREA
RUBIO L.

Association

**Asociación Nacional de Medios de Comunicación (ASO-
MEDIOS):** Carrera 19C, No 85-72, Bogotá, DC; tel. (1) 611-1300;
fax (1) 621-6292; e-mail asomedios@asomedios.com; internet www
.asomedios.com; f. 1978; Exec. Pres. TITULO ANGEL ARBELAEZ.

Finance

(cap. = capital; res = reserves; dep. = deposits; m. = million;
brs = branches; amounts in pesos unless otherwise indicated)

Contraloría General de la República: Edif. Gran Estación II,
Carrera 60, No 24-09, Bogotá, DC; tel. (1) 647-7000; fax (1) 647-1852;
e-mail cgr@contraloria.gov.co; internet www.contraloriagen.gov.co;
f. 1923; Comptroller-Gen. SANDRA MORELLI RICO.

BANKING

Supervisory Authority

Superintendencia Financiera de Colombia: Calle 7, No 4-49,
11°, Apdo Aéreo 3460, Bogotá, DC; tel. (1) 594-0200; fax (1) 350-5707;
e-mail super@superfinanciera.gov.co; internet www.superfinanciera
.gov.co; f. 2006 following merger of the Superintendencia Bancaria
and the Superintendencia de Valores; Supt GERARDO HERNÁNDEZ
CORREA.

Central Bank

Banco de la República: Carrera 7A, No 14-78, 5°, Apdo Aéreo 3551,
Bogotá, DC; tel. (1) 343-1111; fax (1) 286-1686; e-mail wbanco@
banrep.gov.co; internet www.banrep.gov.co; f. 1923; sole bank of
issue; cap. 12,711m., res 13,671,591.5m., dep. 11,092,426.6m. (Dec.
2009); Gov. JOSÉ DARÍO URIBE ESCOBAR; 17 brs.

Commercial Banks

Banco Agrario de Colombia (Banagrario): Carrera 8, No 15-43,
Bogotá, DC; tel. (1) 382-1400; fax (1) 345-2279; e-mail attnclie@

bancoagrario.gov.co; internet www.bancoagrario.gov.co; f. 1999;
state-owned; Pres. DAVID GUERRO PÉREZ; 732 brs.

Banco de Bogotá: Calle 36, No 7-47, 13°, Apdo Aéreo 3436, Bogotá,
DC; tel. (1) 332-0032; fax (1) 332-4694; internet www.bancodebogota
.com.co; f. 1870; cap. 2,868m., res 6,885,748m., dep. 55,144,280m.
(Dec. 2012); Pres. Dr ALEJANDRO AUGUSTO FIGUEROA JARAMILLO; 556
brs.

Banco Colpatria Multibanca Colpatria SA: Torre Colpatria,
Carrera 7A, No 24-89, 10°, Bogotá, DC; tel. (1) 745-6300; e-mail
serviciocliente@colpatria.com; internet www.colpatria.com; f. 1969
as Banco Colpatria; name changed as above in 1998; merged with
Scotiabank Colombia SA (Canada) in 2012 following Scotiabank's
purchase of 51% of shares; cap. 233,885.5m., res 942,546.5m., dep.
12,370,752.3m. (Dec. 2013); Pres. LUIS SANTIAGO PERDOMO MAL-
DONADO.

Banco de Comercio Exterior de Colombia, SA (BANCOLDEX):
Calle 28, No 13A-15, 38°–42°, Apdo Aéreo 240092, Bogotá, DC; tel. (1)
486-3000; fax (1) 286-0237; e-mail contactenos@bancoldex.com;
internet www.bancoldex.com; f. 1992; provides financing alternatives for Colombian exporters; affiliate trust co FIDUCOLDEX, SA,
manages PROEXPORT (Export Promotion Trust); cap.
1,062,556.8m., res 320,733.2m., dep. 2,666,804.9m. (Dec. 2012);
Gen. Man. LUIS FERNANDO CASTRO.

Banco Davivienda, SA: Edif. Torre Bolívar, 68B-31, 10°, Avda El
Dorado, Bogotá, DC; tel. (1) 330-0000; fax (1) 285-7961; e-mail
cvirtual@davivienda.com; internet www.davivienda.com; f. 1972 as
Corporación Colombiana de Ahorro y Vivienda (Coldeahorro),
current name adopted in 1997; merged with Banco Superior in
2006, with Bancafé in 2010; cap. 62,190m., res 5,145,532.9m., dep.
36,286,120m. (Dec 2013); Pres. EFRAÍN ENRIQUE FORERO FONSECA;
550 brs.

Banco GNB Colombia, SA: Carrera 7, No 71-21, Of. 1601, Torre B,
16°, Apdo Aéreo 3532, Bogotá, DC; tel. (1) 334-5088; fax (1) 317-5169;
e-mail colombia.contactenos@bancognb.com.co; internet www
.bancognb.com.co; f. 1920 as a br. of Banco de Londres y Río de la
Plata; name changed to Banco de Londres y América del Sur in 1936,
then to Banco Anglo Colombiano in 1976; became HSBC Colombia in
2007, present name adopted in 2012 following sale to Banco GNB
Sudameris (q.v.); cap. 268,657m., res 18,220m., dep. 1,605,554m.
(Dec. 2012); Chair. FRANCISCO JAVIER VALADEZ ZAMORA; 20 brs.

Banco GNB Sudameris, SA: Carrera 7, No 71-52, 19°, Torre B,
Bogotá, DC; tel. (1) 325-5000; fax (1) 313-3259; internet www
.sudameris.com.co; f. 2005 following merger of Banco Sudameris
Colombia, SA and Banco Tequendama; cap. 60,459m., res 792,886m.,
dep. 7,426,956m. (Dec. 2012); Pres. and Chair. CAMILO VERÁSTEGUI
CARVAJAL; 6 brs.

Banco de Occidente: Carrera 4, No 7-61, 12°, Apdo Aéreo 7607,
Cali, Valle del Cauca; tel. (2) 886-1111; fax (2) 886-1298; e-mail
dinternacional@bancodeoccidente.com.co; internet www
.bancodeoccidente.com.co; f. 1965; cap. 4,676.9m., res 2,798,947.2m.,
dep. 12,422,643.9m. (Dec. 2011); 78.2% owned by Grupo Aval
Acciones y Valores; Pres. EFRAÍN OTERO ÁLVAREZ; 194 brs.

Banco Popular, SA: Calle 17, No 7-43, 3°, Bogotá, DC; tel. (1) 339-
5449; fax (1) 281-9448; e-mail vpinternacional@bancopopular.com
.co; internet www.bancopopular.com.co; f. 1951; cap. 77,253m., res
1,938,847m., dep. 11,217,190m. (Dec. 2013); Pres. JOSÉ HERNÁN
RINCÓN GÓMEZ; 216 brs.

Bancolombia, SA: Carrera 48, Avda Los Industriales 26-85, Medellín, Antioquia; tel. (4) 511-5516; fax (4) 576-3510; e-mail angospin@
bancolombia.com.co; internet www.bancolombia.com; f. 1998 by
merger of Banco Industrial Colombiano and Banco de Colombia; cap.
425,914m., res 10,616,293m., dep. 86,556,579m. (Dec. 2013); Chair.
DAVID EMILIO BOJANINI GARCÍA; Pres. CARLOS RAÚL YEPES JIMÉNEZ;
727 brs.

BBVA Colombia (Banco Bilbao Vizcaya Argentaria Colombia, SA):
Carrera 9, No 72-21, 11°, Bogotá, DC; tel. (1) 312-4666; fax (1) 347-
1600; internet www.bbva.com.co; f. 1956 as Banco Ganadero;
assumed current name 2004; 95.2% owned by Banco Bilbao Vizcaya
Argentaria, SA (Spain); cap. 89,779m., res 2,298,510m., dep.
24,261,983m. (Dec. 2012); Exec. Pres. OSCAR CABRERA IZQUIERDO;
279 brs.

Citibank Colombia, SA: Carrera 9A, No 99-02, 3°, Bogotá, DC; tel.
(1) 618-4099; fax (1) 618-2505; internet www.citibank.com.co; wholly
owned subsidiary of Citibank (USA); cap. 144,123m., res
1,191,839m., dep. 5,525,947m. (Dec. 2012); Pres. BERNARDO NOREÑA
OCAMPO; 23 brs.

Corpbanca Colombia: Carrera 7, No 99-53, Bogotá, DC; tel. (1)
644-8500; fax (1) 644-8430; internet www.bancocorpbanca.com.co;
f. 1961 as Banco Comercial Antioqueño; bought by Grupo Santander
(Spain) in 1997 and name changed to Banco Santander Colombia,
present name adopted 2011 following acquisition by Corpbanca
(Chile), which was bought by Itaú Unibanco (Brazil) in 2014; cap.
218,731m., res 589,577m., dep. 6,554,132m. (Dec. 2012); Pres. JAIME
MUNITA; 74 brs.

Helm Bank SA: Carrera 7, No 27-18, 19°, Bogotá, DC; tel. (1) 581-8181; e-mail servicio.empresarial@grupohelm.com; internet www .grupohelm.com; f. 1963 as Banco de Crédito; renamed Banco de Credito—Helm Financial Services in 2000; present name adopted in 2009; bought by Corpbanca in 2012; cap. 218,623.1m., res 912,991.6m., dep. 7,945,649.8m. (Dec. 2011); Pres. CARMIÑA FERRO IRIARTE; 26 brs.

Development Bank

Banco Caja Social: Torre BCSC, Carrera 7, No 77-65, 11°, Bogotá, DC; tel. (1) 313-8000; fax (1) 313-7150; e-mail csgarzon@ fundacion-social.com.co; internet www.bancocajasocial.com; f. 1911; cap. 204,678m., res 510,445m., dep. 6,300,449m. (Dec. 2009); Pres. DIEGO FERNANDO PRIETO RIVERA; 260 brs.

Banking Associations

Asociación Bancaria y de Entidades Financieras de Colombia (Asobancaria): Carrera 9A, No 74-08, 9°, Bogotá, DC; tel. (1) 326-6600; fax (1) 326-6604; e-mail eventos@asobancaria.com; internet www.asobancaria.com; f. 1936; 56 mem. banks; Pres. MARÍA MERCEDES CUÉLLAR LÓPEZ.

Asociación Nacional de Instituciones Financieras (ANIF): Calle 70A, No 7-86, Bogotá, DC; tel. (1) 310-1500; fax (1) 235-5947; e-mail anif@anif.com.co; internet anif.co; f. 1974; Pres. Dr SERGIO CLAVIJO.

STOCK EXCHANGE

Bolsa de Valores de Colombia: Edif. Bancafé, Torre B, Of. 1201, Carrera 7, No 71-21, Bogotá, DC; tel. (1) 313-9800; fax (1) 243-7327; internet www.bvc.com.co; f. 2001 following merger of stock exchanges of Bogotá, Medellín and Occidente; Pres. JUAN PABLO CÓRDOBA GARCÉS; CEO MAURICIO MOSSERI ESTRADA.

INSURANCE

Principal Companies

ACE Seguros, SA: Calle 72, No 10-51, 7°, Apdo Aéreo 29782, Bogotá, DC; tel. (1) 319-0300; fax (1) 319-0340; e-mail ace.servicioalcliente@ acegroup.com; internet www.acelatinamerica.com; fmrly Cigna Seguros de Colombia, SA; Regional Pres. (Latin America) JORGE LUIS CAZAR.

Aseguradora Colseguros, SA: Carrera 13A, No 29-24, Parque Central Bavaria, Apdo Aéreo 3537, Bogotá, DC; tel. (1) 560-0600; fax (1) 561-6695; internet www.colseguros.com; subsidiary of Allianz AG, Germany; f. 1874; Pres. ALBA LUCIA GALLEGO NIETO.

Aseguradora Solidaria de Colombia: Calle 100, No 9A-45, 8° y 12°, Bogotá, DC; tel. (1) 646-4330; fax (1) 296-1527; e-mail eguzman@ solidaria.com.co; internet www.aseguradorasolidaria.com.co; Pres. CARLOS ARTURO GUZMÁN PÉREZ.

BBVA Seguros: Carrera 11, No 87-51, Bogotá, DC; tel. (1) 219-1100; fax (1) 640-7995; internet www.bbvaseguros.com.co; f. 1994; Sec.-Gen. HERNÁN FELIPE GUZMÁN ALDANA.

Chartis Seguros Colombia, SA: Calle 78, No 9–57, Apdo Aéreo 9281, Bogotá, DC; tel. (1) 317-2193; fax (1) 310-1014; e-mail servicial .cliente@chartisinsurance.com; internet www.chartisinsurance .com; fmrly AIG Colombia Seguros Generales, SA; Chair. ANDRES HÉCTOR BOULLÓN.

Chubb de Colombia Cía de Seguros, SA: Calle 26 59–51, Torre 3, 7°, Bogotá, DC; tel. (1) 795-7777; fax (1) 795-7770; e-mail informaciongeneral@chubb.com; internet www.chubb.com.co; f. 1972; Pres. MANUEL OBREGÓN; 4 brs.

Cía Aseguradora de Fianzas, SA (Confianza): Calle 82, No 11-37, 7°, Apdo Aéreo 056965, Bogotá, DC; tel. (1) 644-4690; fax (1) 610-8866; e-mail correos@confianza.com.co; internet www.confianza.com .co; f. 1979; Pres. LUIS ALEJANDRO RUEDA RODRÍGUEZ.

Cía Mundial de Seguros, SA: Calle 33, No 6B-24, 2° y 3°, Bogotá, DC; tel. (1) 285-5600; fax (1) 285-1220; e-mail mundial@ mundialseguros.com.co; internet www.mundialseguros.com.co; f. 1995; Gen. Man. ALBERTO MISHAAN.

Cía de Seguros Bolívar, SA: Avda El Dorado, No 68B-31, 10°, Casilla 4421 y 6406, Bogotá, DC; tel. (1) 341-0077; fax (1) 283-0799; internet www.segurosbolivar.com.co; f. 1939; Pres. JORGE ENRIQUE URIBE MONTAÑO.

Cía de Seguros Colmena, SA: Calle 26, No 69C-03, Torre A, 4°–6°, Apdo Aéreo 5050, Bogotá, DC; tel. (1) 324-1111; fax (1) 324-0866; internet www.colmena-arl.com.co; Pres. SILVIA CAMARGO.

Cía de Seguros de Vida Aurora, SA: Carrera 9, No 70-69, Bogotá, DC; tel. (1) 319-2930; fax (1) 345-5980; e-mail soporte@segurosaurora .com; internet www.segurosaurora.com; f. 1967; Pres. LUIS ZARAZA CARRILLO.

Condor, SA, Cía de Seguros Generales: Carrera 7, No 74-21, 2°, Bogotá, DC; tel. (1) 319-2930; fax (1) 345-4980; e-mail orlandolugo@ condorsa.com.co; internet www.seguroscondor.com.co; f. 1957 as Cía de Seguros del Pacífico, SA; changed name as above as above 1983; Pres. JOSÉ ANCÍZAR JIMÉNEZ GUITIÉRREZ.

La Equidad Seguros, Organización Cooperativa: Calle 100 9A-45, Local 2, Apdo Aéreo 5922929, Bogotá, DC; tel. (1) 592-2929; fax (1) 520-0169; e-mail equidad@laequidadseguros.coop; internet www .laequidadseguros.coop; Pres. CARLOS AUGUSTO VILLA.

Generali Colombia—Seguros Generales, SA: Edif. Generali, Carrera 7A, No 72-13, 8°, Apdo Aéreo 076478, Bogotá, DC; tel. (1) 346-8888; fax (1) 319-8280; e-mail generali_colombia@generali.com .co; internet www.generali.com.co; f. 1937; Pres. EDUARDO SARMIENTO PULIDO.

Global Seguros, SA: Carrera 9, No 74-62, Bogotá, DC; tel. (1) 313-9200; fax (1) 317-5376; e-mail rodrigo.uribe@globalseguroscolombia .com; internet www.globalseguroscolombia.com; Pres. ALVARO HERNÁN VÉLEZ MILLÁN.

Liberty Seguros, SA: Calle 72, No 10-07, 6°–8°, Apdo Aéreo 57227 y 57243, Bogotá, DC; tel. (1) 376-5330; fax (1) 217-9917; e-mail lhernandez@impsat.net.co; internet www.libertycolombia.com.co; f. 1954; fmrly Latinoamericana de Seguros, SA; Pres. MAURICIO GARCÍA ORTIZ.

Mapfre Seguros de Crédito, SA (Mapfre Crediseguro, SA): Edif. Forum II, 8°, Calle 7 Sur, No 42-70, Antioquia; tel. (4) 444-0145; fax (4) 314-1990; e-mail adritoac@crediseguro.com.co; internet www .crediseguro.com.co; f. 1999; subsidiary of Mapfre; Exec. Pres. RAÚL FERNÁNDEZ MASEDA.

Mapfre Seguros Generales de Colombia, SA: Carrera 14, No 96-34, Bogotá, DC; tel. (1) 650-3300; fax (1) 650-3400; e-mail mapfre@ mapfre.com.co; internet www.mapfre.com.co; f. 1995; Pres. VICTORIA EUGENIA BEJARANO DE LA TORRE.

Metlife Colombia Seguros de Vida, SA: Carrera 7, No 99-53, 17°, Bogotá, DC; tel. (14) 358-1258; fax (14) 638-1299; e-mail cliente@ metlife.com.co; internet www.metlife.com.co; fmrly American Life Insurance Co (Alico); sold to MetLife in 2010; Pres. SANTIAGO OSORIO; Sec.-Gen. CONSUELO GONZÁLEZ.

Pan American de Colombia Cía de Seguros de Vida, SA: Carrera 7A, No 75-09, Apdo Aéreo 76000, Bogotá, DC; tel. (1) 326-7400; fax (1) 326-7390; e-mail servicioalclienteco@panamericanlife .com; internet www.panamericanlife.com; f. 1974; Gen. Man. MANUEL LEMUS.

La Previsora, SA, Cía de Seguros: Calle 57, No 9-07, Apdo Aéreo 52946, Bogotá, DC; tel. (1) 348-5757; fax (1) 540-5294; e-mail contactenos@previsora.gov.co; internet www.previsora.gov.co; f. 1914; Exec. Pres. ALEJANDRO SAMPER CARREÑO.

QBE Seguros, SA: Carrera 7, No 76-35, 7°–9°, Apdo Aéreo 265063, Bogotá, DC; tel. (1) 319-0730; fax (1) 319-0749; e-mail sylvia.rincon@ qbe.com.co; internet www.qbe.com.co; subsidiary of QBE Insurance Group, Australia; Pres. NICOLÁS DELGADO GONZÁLEZ.

RSA Colombia: Edif. Royal & Sun Alliance, Avda 19, No 104-37, Apdo Aéreo 4225, Bogotá, DC; tel. (1) 488-1000; fax (1) 214-0440; e-mail servicioalcliente@co.rsagroup.com; internet www.rsagroup .com.co; fmrly Seguros Fénix, SA, then Royal and Sun Alliance Seguros; Pres. LILIAN PEREA RONCO.

Segurexpo de Colombia, SA: Calle 72, No 6-44, 12°, Apdo Aéreo 75140, Bogotá, DC; tel. (1) 326-6969; fax (1) 211-0218; e-mail segurexpo@segurexpo.com; internet www.segurexpo.com; f. 1993; Gen. Man. JESÚS URDANGARAY LÓPEZ.

Seguros Alfa, SA: Carrera 13, No 27-47, 22° y 23°, Apdo Aéreo 27718, Bogotá, DC; tel. (1) 743-5333; fax (1) 344-6770; e-mail presidencia@segurosalfa.com.co; internet www.segurosalfa.com.co; Pres. ROBERTO VERGARA ORTIZ.

Seguros Colpatria, SA: Carrera 7A, No 24-89, 27°, Apdo Aéreo 7762, Bogotá, DC; tel. (1) 423-5757; fax (1) 286-9998; e-mail servicioalcliente@ui.colpatria.com; internet www.seguroscolpatria .com; f. 1955; Pres. FERNANDO QUINTERO ARTURO.

Seguros del Estado, SA: Carrera 13, No 96-66, Apdo Aéreo 6810, Bogotá, DC; tel. (1) 218-0903; fax (1) 218-0913; e-mail luis.correa@ segurosdelestado.com; internet www.segurosdelestado.com; f. 1956 as Cía Aliadas de Seguros, SA; changed name as above in 1973; Pres. JORGE MORA SÁNCHEZ.

Seguros Generales Suramericana, SA (Sura): Centro Suramericana, Carrera 64B, No 49A-30, Apdo Aéreo 780, Medellín, Antioquia; tel. (4) 260-2100; fax (4) 260-3194; e-mail contactenos@suramericana .com; internet www.sura.com; f. 1944; Group Pres. DAVID BOJANINI G.

Seguros de Riesgos Profesionales Suramericana, SA (ARP Sura): Centro Suramericana, Edif. Torre Suramericana, 7°, Calle 49A, No 63-55, Medellín, Antioquia; tel. (4) 430-7100; fax (4) 231-8080; e-mail scliente@sura.com.co; internet www.arlsura.com; f. 1996; fmrly SURATEP; name changed as above in 2009; subsidiary of Cía Suramericana de Seguros (Sura); CEO IVÁN IGNACIO ZULUAGA LATORRE.

Skandia Seguros de Vida, SA: Avda 19, No 109A-30, Apdo Aéreo 100327, Bogotá, DC; tel. (1) 658-4000; fax (1) 658-4123; e-mail servicioempresa@skandia.com.co; internet www.skandia.com.co; Pres. MARÍA CLAUDIA CORREA ORDÓÑEZ.

Insurance Association

Federación de Aseguradores Colombianos (FASECOLDA): Carrera 7A, No 26-20, 11° y 12°, Apdo Aéreo 5233, Bogotá, DC; tel. (1) 344-3080; fax (1) 210-7041; e-mail fasecolda@fasecolda.com; internet www.fasecolda.com; f. 1976; 32 mems; Chair. FERNANDO QUINTERO ARTURO.

Trade and Industry

GOVERNMENT AGENCIES

Agencia Nacional de Hidrocarburos (ANH): Edif. Cámara Colombiana de Infraestructura, Calle 26, No 59-65, 2°, Bogotá, DC; tel. (1) 593-1717; fax (1) 593-1718; e-mail info@anh.gov.co; internet www.anh.gov.co; f. 2003; govt agency responsible for regulation of the petroleum industry; Pres. JAVIER BETANCOURT VALLE.

Departamento Nacional de Planeación: Edif. Fonade, Calle 26, No 13-19, 14°, Bogotá, DC; tel. (1) 381-5000; fax (1) 282-7080; e-mail tmendoza@dnp.gov.co; internet www.dnp.gov.co; f. 1958; supervises and administers devt projects; approves foreign investments; Dir-Gen. TATIANA OROZCO DE LA CRUZ; Sec.-Gen TATIANA MILENA MENDOZA LARA.

Superintendencia de Industria y Comercio (SUPERINDUSTRIA): Carrera 13, No 27-00, 5°, Bogotá, DC; tel. (1) 382-0840; fax (1) 382-2696; e-mail contactenos@sic.gov.co; internet www.sic.gov.co; supervises chambers of commerce; controls standards and prices; Supt PABLO FELIPE ROBLEDO DEL CASTILLO.

Superintendencia de Sociedades (SUPERSOCIEDADES): Avda El Dorado, No 51-80, Apdo Aéreo 4188, Bogotá, DC; tel. (1) 324-5777; fax (1) 324-5000; e-mail webmaster@supersociedades.gov.co; internet www.supersociedades.gov.co; f. 1931; oversees activities of local and foreign corpns; Supt LUIS GUILLERMO VÉLEZ CABRERA.

DEVELOPMENT AGENCIES

Agencia Presidencial para la Acción Social y la Cooperación Internacional: Calle 7, No 6-54, Bogotá, DC; tel. (1) 352-6666; fax (1) 284-4120; e-mail cooperacionapc@apccolombia.gov.co; internet www.apccolombia.gov.co; f. 2005 following merger of Red de Solidaridad Social (RSS) and Agencia Colombiana de Cooperación Internacional (ACCI); govt agency intended to channel domestic and international funds into social programmes; Dir-Gen. SANDRA BESSUDO LIÓN.

Asociación Colombiana de Ingeniería Sanitaria y Ambiental (ACODAL): Calle 39, No 14-75, Bogotá, DC; tel. (1) 245-9539; fax (1) 323-1408; e-mail gerencia@acodal.org.co; internet www.acodal.org.co; f. 1956 as Asociación Colombiana de Acueductos y Alcantarillados; asscn promoting sanitary and environmental engineering projects; Pres. MARYLUZ MEJÍA DE PUMAREJO; Man. ALBERTO VALENCIA MONSALVE.

Asociación Colombiana de las Micro, Pequeñas y Medianas Empresas (ACOPI): Carrera 15, No 36-70, Bogotá, DC; tel. and fax (1) 320-4783; e-mail prensa@acopi.org.co; internet www.acopi.org.co; f. 1951; promotes small and medium-sized industries; Exec. Pres. MIGUEL ANGEL ECHEVERRI CHAVARRÍA.

Centro Internacional de Educación y Desarrollo Humano (CINDE): Calle 77, Sur 43A-27 Sabaneta, Antioquia, Medellín; tel. (4) 444-8424; fax (4) 288-3991; e-mail cinde@cinde.org.co; internet www.cinde.org.co; education and social devt; f. 1977; Dir-Gen. ALEJANDRO ACOSTA AYERBE.

Corporación para la Investigación Socioeconómica y Tecnológica de Colombia (CINSET): Carrera 48, No 91-94, La Castellana, Bogotá, DC; tel. (1) 256-0961; fax (1) 218-6416; e-mail cinset@cinset.org.co; internet www.cinset.org.co; f. 1987; social, economic and technical devt projects; Pres. RAFAEL DARIO ARIAS DURÁN; Exec. Dir JUAN CARLOS GUTIÉRREZ ARIAS.

Corporación Región: Calle 55, No 41-10, Medellín; tel. (4) 216-6822; fax (4) 239-5544; e-mail admonregion@region.org.co; internet www.region.org.co; f. 1989; environmental, political and social devt; Exec. Dir MAX YURI GIL RAMÍREZ.

Fondo Financiero de Proyectos de Desarrollo (FONADE): Calle 26, No 13-19, 19°-22°, Apdo Aéreo 24110, Bogotá, DC; tel. (1) 594-0407; fax (1) 282-6018; e-mail fonade@fonade.gov.co; internet www.fonade.gov.co; f. 1968; responsible for channelling loans towards economic devt projects; administered by a cttee under the head of the Departamento Nacional de Planeación; FONADE works

in close asscn with other official planning orgs; Gen. Man. NATALIA ARIAS ECHEVERRY.

Instituto Colombiano de Desarrollo Rural: Centro Administrativo Nacional (CAN), Avda El Dorado, Calle 43, No 57-41, Bogotá, DC; tel. (1) 383-0444; e-mail incoder@incoder.gov.co; internet www.incoder.gov.co; rural devt agency; Gen. Man. ARIEL BORBÓN ARDILA.

CHAMBERS OF COMMERCE

Confederación Colombiana de Cámaras de Comercio (CONFECAMARAS): Edif. Banco de Occidente, Of. 502, Carrera 13, No 27-47, Apdo Aéreo 29750, Bogotá, DC; tel. (1) 381-4100; fax (1) 346-7026; e-mail confecamaras@confecamaras.org.co; internet www.confecamaras.org.co; f. 1969; 56 mem. orgs; Exec. Pres. JULIO CÉSAR SILVA B.

Cámara Colombo China de Inversión y Comercio: Of. 214, Carrera 10, No 96-25, Bogotá, DC; tel. (1) 616-6164; e-mail info@camaracolombochina.com; internet www.camaracolombochina.com; f. 2010; Pres. RICARDO DUARTE.

Cámara Colombo Japonesa de Comercio e Industria: Calle 72, No 7-82, 7°, Bogotá, DC; tel. (1) 210-0383; fax (1) 349-0736; e-mail camcoljapon@etb.net.co; internet camaracolombojaponesa.org; f. 1988; Colombian-Japanese trade asscn; Pres. JUAN CARLOS MONDRAGÓN A.

Cámara Colombo Venezolana: Edif. Suramericana, Of. 503, Calle 72, No 8-24, Bogotá, DC; tel. (1) 211-6224; fax (1) 211-6089; e-mail info@comvenezuela.com; internet www.comvenezuela.com; f. 1977; Colombian-Venezuelan trade asscn; 19 mem. cos; Exec. Pres. MAGDALENA PARDO DE SERRANO.

Cámara de Comercio de Bogotá: Avda Eldorado, 68D-35, Bogotá, DC; tel. (1) 383-0300; fax (1) 284-7735; e-mail webmaster@ccb.org.co; internet www.ccb.org.co; f. 1878; 3,650 mem. orgs; Pres. FRANCISCO DURÁN CASAS.

Cámara de Comercio Colombo Americano: Of. 1209, Calle 98, No 22-64, Bogotá, DC; tel. (1) 587-7828; fax (1) 621-6838; e-mail website@amchamcolombia.com.co; internet www.amchamcolombia.com.co; f. 1955; Colombian-US trade asscn; Exec. Dir CAMILO REYES RODRÍGUEZ.

Cámara de Comercio Colombo Británica: Of. 301, Calle 104, No 14A-45, Bogotá, DC; tel. (1) 256-2833; fax (1) 256-3026; e-mail comunicaciones@colombobritanica.com; internet www.colombobritanica.com; Colombian-British trade asscn; Pres. SANTIAGO ECHAVARRIA; Dir PATRICIA TOVAR.

INDUSTRIAL AND TRADE ASSOCIATIONS

Corporación de la Industria Aeronáutica Colombiana, SA (CIAC SA): Avda Calle 26, No 103-08, Entrada 1, Bogotá, DC; tel. (1) 413-8312; e-mail atencion@ciac.gov.co; internet www.ciac.gov.co; Gen. Man. FLAVIO ENRIQUE ULLOA ECHEVERRY.

Industria Militar (INDUMIL): Calle 44, No 51-11, Apdo Aéreo 7272, Bogotá, DC; tel. (1) 220-7800; fax (1) 222-4889; e-mail indumil@indumil.gov.co; internet www.indumil.gov.co; attached to Ministry of National Defence; Gen. Man. Gen. (retd) GUSTAVO MATAMOROS CAMACHO.

Instituto Colombiano Agropecuario (ICA): Carrera 41, No 17-81, Bogotá, DC; tel. (1) 288-4800; fax (1) 332-3700; e-mail info@ica.gov.co; internet www.ica.gov.co; f. 1962; attached to the Ministry of Agriculture and Rural Devt; institute for promotion, co-ordination and implementation of research into and teaching and devt of agriculture and animal husbandry; Gen. Man. LUIS HUMBERTO MARTÍNEZ LACOUTURE.

Servicio Geológico Colombiano (SGC): Diagonal 53, No 34-53, Apdo Aéreo 4865, Bogotá, DC; tel. (1) 220-0200; fax (1) 220-0797; e-mail cliente@sgc.gov.co; internet www.sgc.gov.co; f. 1968; fmrly Instituto Colombiano de Geología y Minería (INGEOMINAS); adopted present name in 2011; responsible for mineral research, geological mapping and research including hydrogeology, remote sensing, geochemistry, geophysics and geological hazards; attached to the Ministry of Mines and Energy; Dir OSCAR PAREDES ZAPATA.

EMPLOYERS' AND PRODUCERS' ORGANIZATIONS

Asociación Colombiana de Cooperativos (ASCOOP): Transversal 29, No 36-29, Bogotá, DC; tel. (1) 368-3500; fax (1) 369-5475; e-mail ascoop@ascoop.coop; internet www.ascoop.coop; promotes co-operatives; Pres. CARLOS MARIO ZULUAGA PÉREZ; Exec. Dir CARLOS ERNESTO ACERO SÁNCHEZ.

Asociación de Cultivadores de Caña de Azúcar de Colombia (ASOCAÑA): Calle 58N, No 3N-15, Apdo Aéreo 4448, Cali, Valle del Cauca; tel. (2) 664-7902; fax (2) 664-5888; e-mail contactenos@asocana.org; internet www.asocana.org; f. 1959; sugar planters' asscn; Pres. LUIS FERNANDO LONDOÑO CAPURRO.

Asociación Nacional de Comercio Exterior (ANALDEX): Edif. UGI, Calle 40, No 13-09, 10°, Bogotá, DC; tel. (1) 570-0600; fax (1)

284-6911; e-mail analdex@analdex.org; internet www.analdex.org; exporters' asscn; Pres. JAVIER DÍAZ MOLINA.

Asociación Nacional de Empresarios de Colombia (ANDI): Carrera 43A, No 1-50, San Fernando Plaza, Torre 2, 9°, Apdo Aéreo 997, Medellín, Antioquia; tel. (4) 326-5100; fax (4) 326-0068; e-mail servicioalcliente@andi.com.co; internet www.andi.com.co; f. 1944; Pres. LUIS CARLOS VILLEGAS ECHEVERRI; 9 brs; 756 mems.

Asociación Nacional de Exportadores de Café de Colombia (Asoexport): Carrera 7, No 73-47, Of. 802, Bogotá, DC; tel. (1) 347-8419; fax (1) 347-9523; e-mail asoexport@asoexport.org; internet www.asoexport.org; f. 1933; private asscn of coffee exporters; Exec. Pres. CARLOS IGNACIO ROJAS GAITÁN.

Federación Colombiana de Ganaderos (FEDEGAN): Calle 37, No 14-31, Apdo Aéreo 9709, Bogotá, DC; tel. (1) 245-3041; fax (1) 578-2020; e-mail fedegan@fedegan.org.co; internet www.fedegan.org.co; f. 1963; cattle raisers' asscn; about 350,000 affiliates; Exec. Pres. JOSÉ FÉLIX LAFAURIE RIVERA.

Federación Nacional de Cacaoteros: Carrera 17, No 30-39, Apdo Aéreo 17736, Bogotá, DC; tel. (1) 327-3000; fax (1) 288-4424; e-mail info@fedecacao.com.co; internet www.fedecacao.com.co; fed. of cocoa growers; Exec. Pres. Dr EDUARD BAQUERO LÓPEZ.

Federación Nacional de Cafeteros de Colombia (FEDERA-CAFE) (National Federation of Coffee Growers): Calle 73, No 8-13, Apdo Aéreo 57534, Bogotá, DC; tel. (1) 217-0600; fax (1) 217-1021; internet www.federaciondecafeteros.org; f. 1927; totally responsible for fostering and regulating the coffee economy; Gen. Man. LUIS GENARO MUÑOZ ORTEGA; 203,000 mems.

Federación Nacional de Comerciantes (FENALCO): Carrera 4, No 19-85, 7°, Bogotá, DC; tel. (1) 350-0600; fax (1) 350-9424; e-mail fenalco@fenalco.com.co; internet www.fenalco.com.co; Pres. GUILLERMO BOTERO NIETO.

Federación Nacional de Cultivadores de Cereales y Leguminosas (FENALCE): Km 1, Via Cota Siberia, vereda El Abra Cota, Bogotá, Cundinamarca; tel. (1) 592-1092; fax (1) 592-1098; e-mail fenalce@cable.net.co; internet www.fenalce.org; f. 1960; fed. of grain growers; Pres. JAMES ORTEGA MELLO; Gen. Man. HENRY VANEGAS ANGARITA; 30,000 mems.

Sociedad de Agricultores de Colombia (SAC) (Colombian Farmers' Society): Carrera 7, No 24-89, Of. 4402, Bogotá, DC; tel. (1) 281-0263; fax (1) 284-4572; e-mail sac@sac.org.co; internet www.sac.org.co; f. 1871; Pres. RAFAEL MEJÍA LÓPEZ.

MAJOR COMPANIES

The following are some of the leading industrial and commercial companies operating in Colombia:

Acerías Paz del Río, SA: Calle 100, No 13-21, 6°, Bogotá, DC; tel. (1) 651-7300; fax (1) 341-6497; e-mail presidenciaapdr@hotmail.com; internet www.pazdelrio.com.co; f. 1948; 52% bought by Votorantim Metais (Brazil) in 2007; mining and processing of iron ores; Pres. VICENTE NOERO ARANGO.

Almacenes Exito, SA: Avda Las Vegas, Carrera 48, 32B Sur, Apdo Aéreo 139, Envigado, Antioquia; tel. (4) 339-6509; fax (4) 331-4792; e-mail fundacion.exito@group-exito.com; internet www.grupoexito.com.co; f. 1949; wholesaling and retailing; Chair. GONZALO RESTREPO LÓPEZ; CEO Dr CARLOS MARIO GIRALDO MORENO; 37,000 employees.

Alpina Productos Alimenticios, SA: Carrera 63, No 15-61, Bogotá, DC; tel. (1) 571-8609; e-mail alpina@alpina.com; internet www.alpina.com.co; f. 1978; food and food-processing; Pres. ERNESTO FAJARDO; 2,800 employees.

Alumina (Aluminio Nacional, SA): Carretera 32, No 11-101, Acopi Yumbo, Cali, Valle del Cauca; tel. (2) 370-5600; fax (2) 371-7503; internet www.alumina.com.co; f. 1960 as Alumina Alcan de Colombia, present name adopted 1985; aluminium production; Pres. JOSÉ E. MUÑOZ.

AngloGold Ashanti Colombia, SA: Edif. Cusezar, 8°, Calle 116, No 7-15, Bogotá, DC; tel. (1) 657-9100; e-mail comunicacionescolombia@anglogoldashanti.com; internet www.anglogoldashanti.com.co; f. 1917; subsidiary of AngloGold Ashanti Ltd, South Africa; gold exploration and mining at La Colosa and Gramalote; Pres. KEN KLUKSDAHL.

Bavaria, SA: Calle 53A, 127–35, Bogotá, DC; tel. (1) 638-9000; fax (1) 638-9344; e-mail bavaria@bavaria.com.co; internet www.bavaria.com.co; f. 1889; acquired by SABMiller (United Kingdom and South Africa) in 2005; holding co with principal interests in brewing and the manufacture of soft drinks; also transport, telecommunications, construction, forestry and fishing; Pres. and CEO RICHARD MARK RUSHTON; 18,895 employees.

> **Cerveza Aguila, SA:** Calle 10, No 38-280, Barranquilla; tel. (5) 350-4000; fax (5) 344-8815; internet www.cervezaaguila.com; f. 1913; brewery; parent co is Bavaria, SA; 980 employees.

Carvajal, SA: Calle 29 Norte, No 6A-40, Apdo Aéreo 46, Cali; tel. (2) 667-5011; fax (2) 668-7644; internet www.carvajal.com.co; f. 1941; holding co with principal interests in printing and publishing; also construction, electronic components, telecommunications, trade, personal credit and the manufacture of office furniture; Chair. BERNARDO QUINTERO BALCÁZAR; 10,000 employees.

Cementos Argos, SA: Calle 7D, No 43A-99, Medellín; tel. (4) 319-8712; e-mail rsierra@argos.com.co; internet www.argos.co; f. 1934; subsidiary of Grupo Argos; Pres. JOSÉ ALBERTO VÉLEZ CADAVID; CEO JORGE MARIO VELÁSQUEZ.

Cerrejón: Calle 100, No 19-54, 12°, Bogotá, DC; tel. (1) 595-5555; internet www.cerrejon.com; f. 1976 as jt venture between state-owned Carbocol, SA and Intercor (USA); govt sold its share in 2002 to int. consortium; owned by BHP Billiton Plc (Australia), Anglo American Plc (South Africa) and Xstrata (Switzerland); coal mining and export; CEO ROBERTO JUNGUITO POMBO.

Cerro Matoso, SA: Calle 114, No 9-01, Torre A, Edif. Teleport Park, Montelíbano, Córdoba; tel. (5) 629-1570; fax (5) 629-1593; internet www.bhpbilliton.com; f. 1979; mining of ferrous ores; owned by BHP Billiton; Chair. JACQUES NASSER; CEO ANDREW MACKENZIE; 950 employees.

Cía Colombiana Automotriz, SA (CCA): Calle 13, No 38-54, Bogotá, DC; tel. (1) 605-9400; fax (1) 201-1836; e-mail cca@mazda.com.co; internet www.mazda.com.co; f. 1973; automobile mfrs; majority of shares held by Mazda Ltd and Mitsubishi Corpn of Japan; Pres. FABIO SÁNCHEZ FORERO; 1,169 employees.

Cía Colombiana de Tabaco (COLTABACO): Carrera 12, No 93-08, Bogotá; tel. 639-9090; internet www.pmi.com; f. 1919; bought by Philip Morris (USA) in 2005; cigarette manufacturer; Gen. Man. LUC GERARD; 900 employees.

Cía Colombiana de Tejidos, SA (COLTEJER): Carretera 42, No 54A-161, Itagüí, Antioquia; tel. (4) 375-7500; fax (4) 372-8585; e-mail coltemed@coltejer.com.co; internet www.coltejer.com.co; f. 1907; textile mfrs; Pres. RAFAEL KALACH MIRZRAHI; 5,922 employees.

Colombiana de Artículos para Vapor (COLVAPOR, Ltda): Carrera 1, No 3-52, Barrio El Lucero, Parque Industrial Tecplas, Mosquera, Cundinamarca; e-mail ginah@colvapor.com; internet colvapor.com; f. 1975; imports and trades steel products for industry; brs in Cartagena and Houston, TX (USA).

Colombina, SA: Carrera 1, No 24-56, Cali; tel. (2) 886-1999; fax (2) 886-1713; internet www.colombina.com; f. 1927; confectionery; Exec. Pres. CÉSAR A. CAICEDO.

Cristalería Peldar, SA: Calle 39 Sur, No 48-180, Apdo Aéreo 215, Envigado, Antioquia; tel. (4) 378-8000; fax (4) 270-4225; e-mail pedidospeldar@o-i.com; internet www.o-i.com; f. 1962; subsidiary of Owens-Illinois Inc, USA; manufacture of glass products; Pres. ANDRÉS LÓPEZ; 1,800 employees.

Ecopetrol, SA: Edif. Ecopetrol, Carrera 13, No 36-24, 8°, Apdo Aéreo 5938, Bogotá, DC; tel. (1) 234-4000; fax (1) 234-4099; e-mail webmaster@ecopetrol.com.co; internet www.ecopetrol.com.co; f. 1951; state-owned co for the exploration, production, refining and transportation of petroleum; 10.1% sold to private ownership in 2007; Pres. JAVIER GUTIÉRREZ PEMBERTHY; 6,720 employees.

Enka de Colombia, SA: Of. 901, Carrera 37A, No 8-43, Apdo Aéreo 5233, Medellín; tel. (4) 405-5055; fax (4) 319-5155; e-mail ventasymercadeo@enka.com.co; internet www.enka.com.co; f. 1964; manufacture of synthetic fibres; Pres. ALVARO HINCAPIÉ VÉLEZ; 1,450 employees.

ExxonMobil de Colombia, SA: Calle 90, No 21-32, Bogotá, DC; tel. 628-3455; internet www.mobil.com.co; f. 2001 following the merger of Esso Colombiana with ExxonMobil; petroleum and gas exploration and extraction; Pres. CAMILO DURÁN.

Fabricato Tejicondor: Carrera 50, No 38-320, Bello, Antioquia; tel. (4) 448-3500; fax (4) 454-3407; e-mail contactenos@fabricato.com.co; internet www.fabricato.com; f. 1923; manufacture and export of cotton, textiles and synthetic fibre goods; CEO JUAN CARLOS CADAVID GÓMEZ; 4,325 employees.

GM Colmotores: Avda Boyacá, No 36A-03 Sur, Bogotá, DC; tel. (1) 710-1111; fax (1) 270-8382; internet www.chevrolet.com.co; f. 1957; subsidiary of General Motors Corpn, USA; producers of passenger and commercial vehicles, spare parts and accessories; Pres. JORGE MEJÍA GONZÁLEZ; 1,254 employees.

Grupo Nutresa: Carrera 43A, No 1A Sur 143, Medellín; tel. (4) 325-8711; fax (4) 268-1868; internet www.nutresa.com; f. 1920 as Cía Nacional de Chocolates Cruz Roja, underwent various name changes, incl. Grupo Nacional de Chocolates SA, present name adopted 2011; processed food producer; many subsidiaries, incl. Cía de Galletas Noel, SA, and Industrias Aliadas; Pres. and CEO CARLOS PIEDRAHITA; 29,000 employees.

Incauca, SA: Carrera 9, No 28-103, Cali, Valle del Cauca; tel. (2) 418-3000; fax (2) 438-4909; e-mail incauca@incauca.com; internet www.incauca.com; f. 1963; cultivation and processing of sugar cane; 5,109 employees.

Ingenio Providencia, SA: Carrera 28, No 28-103, Palmira; tel. (2) 318-4500; fax (2) 438-4929; e-mail ingprovidencia@ingprovidencia .com; internet www.ingprovidencia.com; f. 1926; cultivation and wholesale of sugar cane; Gen. Man. GONZALO ORTIZ ARISTIZABA; 2,700 employees.

Leonisa Internacional: Carrera 51, No 13-158, Medellín; tel. (4) 350-6100; fax (4) 265-0617; e-mail info@leonisa.com; internet www .leonisa.com/co; f. 1956; mfrs of men's and women's clothing; Man. LINA MARÍA ESCOBAR; 2,000 employees.

Occidental Petroleum Corpn: Calle 77A, No 11-32, Apdo 92171, Bogotá, DC; tel. (1) 346-0111; fax (1) 211-6820; internet www.oxy .com; f. 1977; principal shareholder Occidental Petroleum Corpn of the USA; petroleum and gas exploration and production; Chair. EDWARD DJEREJIAN; 681 employees.

Pacific Rubiales Energy Corpn: Torre Empresarial Pacific, Calle 110, No 9-25, Bogotá, DC; tel. (1) 511-2000; fax (1) 745-1001; e-mail accionistas@pacificrubiales.com.co; internet www.pacificrubiales .com; f. 2007; oil and gas exploration and production; owns oil & gas operators Pacific Stratus and Meta Petroleum Ltd; Pres. JOSÉ FRANCISCO ARATA; CEO RONALD PANTIN.

Papeles Nacionales, SA: Paraje La Marina, Vía Cartago, Valle; tel. (52) 214-7500; e-mail servicio.cliente@papelesnacionales.com; internet www.papelesnacionales.com; f. 1960; paper products; owns subsidiary Fibras Nacionales Ltda, a recycling plant; Gen. Man. JAIME EDUARDO MARTINEZ MADRIÑAN; 6 brs.

Petrobras Colombia: Carrera 7, No 71-21, Torre B, 17°, Bogotá, DC; tel. (1) 313-5000; fax (1) 313-5070; internet www.petrobras.com; f. 1972; subsidiary of Petróleo Brasileiro, SA (Petrobras), Brazil; oil exploration and production; Pres. NILO AZEVEDO DUARTE.

Prodeco, SA: Centro Empresarial Las Americas II, Calle 77B, No 59-61, Barranquilla, Atlántico; tel. (5) 369-5500; fax (5) 358-2825; e-mail salua.mrad@prodeco.com.co; internet www.prodeco.com.co; Swiss-owned co; mining and natural resources; subsidiary of Glencore International Plc; Exec. Pres. MARK MCMANUS; 5,617 employees.

Promigas: Calle 66, No 67-123, Barranquilla; tel. (95) 371-3444; fax (95) 368-0515; e-mail promigas@promigas.com; internet www .promigas.com; f. 1974; natural gas distributor, network covers 60% of the country; CEO ANTONIO MARIO APARICIO; Pres. JOSÉ ELÍAS MELO ACOSTA.

Smurfit Kappa Cartón de Colombia, SA: Calle 15, No 18-109, Puerto Isaacs, Yumbo; tel. (2) 691-4000; fax (2) 691-4199; e-mail comunicaciones@smurfitkappa.com.co; internet www.smurfitkappa .com.co; f. 1944; mfrs of paper and packaging materials; subsidiary of Smurfit Kappa Group of Ireland; Pres. ALVARO JOSÉ RAMOS; 1,500 employees.

Sociedad de Fabricación de Automotores, SA (Sofasa Renault): Carretera Central del Norte, Km 17, Chía, Cundinamarca; tel. (1) 676-0108; e-mail servicioalcliente@sofasa.com.co; internet www.renault.com.co; f. 1973; manufacture of motor vehicles and spare parts; Pres. LUIS FERNANDO PELÁEZ GAMBOA; 873 employees.

Tecnoquímicas, SA: Calle 23, No 7-39, Cali; tel. (2) 882-5555; fax (2) 684-5959; e-mail rpacifico@tecnoquimicas.com.co; internet www .tecnoquimicas.com.co; f. 1934; manufacture of pharmaceuticals; Pres. FRANCISCO JOSÉ BARBERI OSPINA; 1,670 employees.

UTILITIES
Regulatory Agencies

Comisión de Regulación de Agua Potable y Saneamiento Básico (CRA): Carrera 12, No 97-80, 2°, CP 110221, Bogotá DC; tel. (1) 487-3820; fax (1) 489-7650; e-mail correo@cra.gov.co; internet www.cra.gov.co; regulation of public utilities, granting subsidies and setting rates; Exec. Dir JULIO CÉSAR AGUILERA WILCHES.

Comisión de Regulación de Energía y Gas (CREG): Edifico Cusezar Int. 2 Oficina 901, Av. Calle 116 No. 7-15, Bogotá, DC; tel. (1) 603-2020; fax (1) 603-2100; e-mail creg@creg.gov.co; internet www .creg.gov.co; f. 1994; Exec. Dir CARLOS FERNANDO ERASO CALERO.

Superintendencia de Servicios Públicos Domiciliarios: Carrera 18, No 84-35, Bogotá, DC; tel. (1) 691-3005; fax (1) 691-3142; e-mail sspd@superservicios.gov.co; internet www.superservicios.gov .co; Supt PATRICIA DUQUE CRUZ.

Electricity

Electrificadora del Caribe, SA ESP (Electricaribe): Carrera 55, No 72-109, El Prado, Barranquilla; tel. (55) 361-1000; internet www .electricaribe.com; f. 1998; owned by Gas Natural Fenosa (Spain); distributes electricity in 6 depts of the Caribbean Coast Region; Dir-Gen. JOSE GARCÍA SANLEANDRO.

Empresa de Energía de Bogotá, SA ESP (EEB): Of. Principal, 6°, Carrera 9A, No 73-44, Bogotá, DC; tel. (1) 326-8000; fax (1) 226-8010; e-mail webmaster@eeb.com.co; internet www.eeb.com.co; provides electricity for Bogotá area by generating capacity of 680 MW, mainly

hydroelectric; Pres. SANDRA STELLA FONSECA ARENAS; Man. Dir ASTRID MARTÍNEZ ORTIZ.

Instituto de Planificación y Promoción de Soluciones Energéticas para las Zonas No Interconectadas (IPSE): Edif. 100 Street, 14°, Torre 3, Calle 99, No 9A, Bogotá, DC; tel. (1) 639-7899; fax (1) 639-7888; e-mail ipse@IPSE.gov.co; internet www.ipse.gov.co; f. 1999; attached to the Ministry of Mines and Energy; co-ordinates and develops energy supply in rural areas; Dir-Gen. ELKIN EDUARDO RAMÍREZ PRIETO.

Interconexión Eléctrica, SA (ISA): Calle 12 Sur, No 18-168, El Poblado, Apdo Aéreo 8915, Medellín, Antioquia; tel. (4) 325-2270; fax (4) 317-0848; e-mail isa@isa.com.co; internet www.isa.com.co; f. 1967; created by Colombia's principal electricity production and distribution cos to form a national network; operations in Brazil, Ecuador, Peru, Bolivia and Central America; 52.9% state-owned; Pres. Dr SANTIAGO MONTENEGRO TRUJILLO; Gen. Man. LUIS FERNANDO ALARCÓN MANTILLA.

ISAGEN: Avda El Poblado, Carrera 43A, No 11A-80, Apdo Aéreo 8762, Medellín, Antioquia; tel. (4) 316-5000; fax (4) 268-4646; e-mail isagen@isagen.com.co; internet www.isagen.com.co; f. 1995 following division of ISA (q.v.); 58% state-owned; generates electricity from 3 hydraulic and 2 thermal power plants; Gen. Man. LUIS FERNANDO RICO PINZÓN.

Gas

Empresa Colombiana de Gas (Ecogás): Of. 209, Centro Internacional de Negocios La Triada, Calle 35, No 19-41, Bucaramanga, Santander del Sur; tel. (7) 642-1000; fax (7) 642-6446; e-mail correspondencia@ecogas.com.co; internet www.ecogas.com.co; f. 1997; operation and maintenance of gas distribution network; sold in 2006 to Empresa de Energía de Bogotá, SA; Dir GERONIMO MANUEL GUERRA CÁRDENAS.

Gas Natural, SA ESP: Calle 71A, No 5-38, Bogotá, DC; tel. (1) 338-1199; fax (1) 288-0807; internet gasnaturalfenosa.com.co; f. 1987; owned by Gas Natural Fenosa (Spain); distributes natural gas in Bogotá and Soacha; Dir-Gen. (Latin America) SERGIO ARANDA MORENO; Exec. Pres. MARÍA EUGENIA CORONADO ORJUELA.

Surtigas: Avda Pedro de Heredia, Calle 31, No 47-30, Apdo Aereo 317, Cartagena, Bolívar; tel. (5) 672-3200; fax (5) 662-5676; internet www.surtigas.com.co; f. 1968; natural gas distribution in the depts of Bolívar, Sucre, Córdoba, Antioquia and Magdalena; Gen. Man. MAGÍN ORTIGA PAREJA.

TRADE UNIONS

Asociacion Colombiana de Camioneros (ACC): Avda Boyaca, No 21-19, Plaza Comercial Montevideo, Local 8, Bogotá, DC; tel. (1) 404-3760; e-mail informativocamionero@yahoo.com; Pres. PEDRO AGUILAR RODRIÍGUEZ.

Central Unitaria de Trabajadores de Colombia (CUT): Calle 35, No 7-25, 9°, Apdo Aéreo 221, Bogotá, DC; tel. and fax (1) 323-7550; e-mail comunicaciones@cut.org.co; internet www.cut.org.co; f. 1986; comprises 50 feds and 80% of all trade union members; Pres. TARCISIO HORA GODOY; Sec.-Gen. DOMINGO TOVAR ARRIETA.

Federación Colombiana de Educadores (FECODE): Carrera 13A, No 34-54, Bogotá, DC; tel. (1) 338-1711; fax (1) 285-3245; internet fecode.edu.co; Pres. SENÉN NIÑO AVENDAÑO; Sec.-Gen. LUIS EDUARDO VARELA.

Federación de Loterías de Colombia (FEDELCO): Carrera 6, No 26–85, 8°, Bogotá, DC; tel. (1) 282-5874; fax (1) 282-5894; e-mail info@fedelco.com.co; internet www.fedelco.com.co; f. 1970; lottery ticket sellers' union; Pres. LUZ STELLA CARDONA MEZA.

Federación Nacional Sindical Unitaria Agropecuaria (FENSUAGRO): Calle 17, No 10-16, Of. 104, Bogotá, DC; tel. (1) 286-7794; fax (1) 282-8871; e-mail fensuagro@hotmail.com; internet www.fensuagro.org; f. 1976 as Federación Nacional Sindical Agropecuaria (FENSA); comprises 37 unions, 7 peasant asscns, with 80,000 mems; Pres. EBERTO DÍAZ MONTES; Sec.-Gen. PARMENIO POVEDA.

Federación Nacional Sindicatos Bancarios Colombianos (FENASIBANCOL): Calle 30A, No 6-22, Of. 1601, Bogotá, DC; tel. (1) 287-5728; fax (1) 288-0235; e-mail fenasibancol@telecom.com .co; internet www.fenasibancol.org; Pres. ROBERTO MORENO SERNA; Sec.-Gen. CESAR AUGUSTO CÁRDENAS.

Federación Nacional de Trabajadores de Alimentación, Bebidas, Afines y Similar (Fentralimentación): Calle 8 sur, 68B-60, Bogotá, DC; tel. (1) 414-6505; fax (1) 290-0390; e-mail fentralimentacion@hotmail.com; represents the food and drink industry; Pres. ALFONSO LÓPEZ FREYLE.

Federación Nacional de Trabajadores al Servicio del Estado (FENALTRASE): Calle 17, No 5-21, Of. 502, Bogotá, DC; tel. (1) 334-4815; e-mail fenaltrese@hotmail.com; f. 1960; Pres. ROBERTO CHAMUCERO.

FUNTRAENERGETICA: Calle 16, No 13-49, Of. 201, Bogotá, DC; tel. (1) 334-0447; fax (1) 286-5259; e-mail funtraenergetica@colombia.com; f. 2001 following merger of Funtrammetal and Fedepetrol; represents workers in the energy sector; Pres. JOAQUÍN ROMERO.

Sindicato Nacional de los Trabajadores de la Industria del Carbón (SINTRACARBON): Carrera 6, No 9-20, Barrancas, Riohacha, Guajira; tel. (5) 774-8126; internet www.sintracarbon.com; f. 1996; Pres. IGOR DÍAZ LÓPEZ.

Unión Sindical Obrera de la Indústria del Petróleo (USO): Calle 38, No 13-37, Of. 302, Bogotá, DC; tel. (1) 234-4074; fax (1) 234-4399; e-mail prensa@usofrenteobrero.org; internet www.usofrenteobrero.org; f. 1922; petroleum workers' union; affiliated to CUT; Pres. RODOLFO VECINO ACEVEDO; Sec.-Gen. ISNARDO LOZANO GÓMEZ; 3,200 mems.

Confederación General del Trabajo (CGT): Calle 39A, No 14-52, Bogotá, DC; tel. (1) 288-1504; fax (1) 573-4021; e-mail cgtprensa2010@gmail.com; internet www.cgtcolombia.org; Pres. JULIO ROBERTO GÓMEZ ESGUERRA; Sec.-Gen. MIRYAM LUZ TRIANA ALVIS.

Confederación de Trabajadores de Colombia (CTC) (Colombian Confederation of Workers): Calle 39, No 26A-23, Barrio La Soledad, Apdo Aéreo 4780, Bogotá, DC; tel. (1) 269-7117; fax (7) 268-8576; e-mail ctc1@etb.net.co; internet www.ctc-colombia.com.co; f. 1934; mainly liberal; 600 affiliates, including 6 national orgs and 20 regional feds; admitted to the International Trade Union Confederation; Pres. LUIS MIGUEL MORANTES ALFONSO; Sec.-Gen. ROSA ELENA FLÉREZ; 400,000 mems.

Transport

Land transport in Colombia is rendered difficult by high mountains, so the principal means of long-distance transport is by air.

Superintendencia de Puertos y Transporte: Ministerio de Transporte, Edif. Estación de la Sabana, 2° y 3°, Calle 63, No 9A-45, Bogotá, DC; tel. and fax (2) 352-6700; e-mail atencionciudadano@supertransporte.gov.co; internet www.supertransporte.gov.co; f. 1992 as Superintendencia General de Puertos, present name adopted in 1998; part of the Ministry of Transport; oversees transport sector; Supt Dr JUAN MIGUEL DURÁN PRIETO.

Agencia Nacional de Infraestructura (ANI): Edif. Ministerio de Transporte, Centro Administrativo Nacional (CAN), 3°, Avda El Dorado, Bogotá, DC; tel. (1) 379-1720; fax (1) 324-0800; e-mail contactenos@ani.gov.co; internet www.ani.gov.co; fmrly Instituto Nacional de Concesiones; changed name as above in 2011; govt agency charged with contracting devt of transport infrastructure to private operators; part of the Ministry of Transport; Pres. LUIS FERNANDO ANDRADE MORENO.

Instituto Nacional de Vías (INVIAS): Edif. INVIAS, Centro Administrativo Nacional (CAN), Carrera 59, No 26-60, Bogotá, DC; tel. and fax (1) 705-6000; e-mail atencionciudadano@invias.gov.co; internet www.invias.gov.co; govt agency responsible for non-contracted transport infrastructure; Dir-Gen. LEONIDAS NARVÁEZ MORALES.

RAILWAYS

In 2008 there were 1,663 km of track. The Agencia Nacional de Infraestructura (q.v.) operates the Red Férrea del Atlántico and the Red Férrea del Pacífico. Construction of Ferrocarril del Carare, which would connect mining sites in the departments of Santander del Sur, Boyacá and Cundinamarca with ports on the Atlantic coast, was proceeding in 2013. The cost of the proposed project was US $2,700m.

El Cerrejón Mine Railway: Cerrejón, Calle 100, No 19-54, Bogotá, DC; tel. (1) 595-5555; e-mail comunica@cerrejon.com; internet www.cerrejon.com; f. 1989 to link the mine and the port at Puerto Bolívar; 150 km.

Ferrocarriles del Norte de Colombia, SA (FENOCO, SA): Calle 94A, No 11A-27, 3°, Bogotá, DC; tel. (1) 622-0505; fax (1) 622-0440; e-mail contactenos@fenoco.com.co; internet www.fenoco.com.co; f. 1999; operates the Concesión de la Red Férrea del Atlántico; 226 kms; Pres. TONY MARQUIS.

Metro de Medellín (Empresa de Transporte Masivo del Valle de Aburrá Ltda): Calle 44, No 46-001, Apdo Aéreo 9128, Bello, Medellín, Antioquia; tel. (4) 444-9598; fax (4) 452-4450; e-mail contactenos@metrodemedellin.gov.co; internet www.metrodemedellin.gov.co; f. 1995; 5-line metro system; Gen. Man. RAMIRO MÁRQUEZ RAMÍREZ.

Tren de Occidente, SA: Avda Vásquez Cobo, No 23N-27, Of. 308, Santiago de Cali, Valle del Cauca; tel. (2) 667-7733; e-mail contacto.cali@trendeoccidente.com; internet www.trendeoccidente.com; f. 1998; operates la Concesión de la Red Férrea del Pacífico; Gen. Man. ALFONSO PATIÑO FAJARDO.

ROADS

In 2009 there were 129,485 km of roads, of which 13,386 km were under the national road network and 27,577 km formed the regional road network. A part of the Pan-American Highway, the Western Trunk Highway, connects the country with Ecuador. Other major highways include the Buenaventura Transverse and the Caribbean Transverse which connects major cities and ports with the Venezuelan highway network. In 2013 the Government initiated an ambitious US $7,200m. project to build more than 1,000 km of roads.

Instituto Nacional de Vías (INVIAS): Edif. INVIAS, Carrera 59, No 26-60, Bogotá, DC; tel. (1) 705-6000; fax (1) 315-6713; e-mail lnarvaezm@invias.gov.co; internet www.invias.gov.co; f. 1966; reorganized 1994; responsible to the Ministry of Transport; maintenance and construction of national road network; Gen. Man. JOSÉ LEONIDAS NARVÁEZ MORALES.

Transmilenio: Edif. Ministerio de Transporte, Centro Administrativo Nacional (CAN), 3°, Avda El Dorado, No 66-63, Bogotá, DC; tel. (1) 220-3000; fax (1) 324-9870; e-mail marthal.gutierrez@transmilenio.gov.co; internet www.transmilenio.gov.co; f. 2000; bus-based mass transit system in Bogotá; Gen. Man. FERNANDO SANCLEMENTE ALZATE.

INLAND WATERWAYS

The Magdalena–Cauca river system is the centre of river traffic and is navigable for 1,500 km, while the Atrato is navigable for 687 km. The Orinoco system has more than five navigable rivers, which total more than 4,000 km of potential navigation (mainly through Venezuela); the Amazon system has four main rivers, which total 3,000 navigable km (mainly through Brazil).

SHIPPING

The four most important ocean terminals are Buenaventura on the Pacific coast and Santa Marta, Barranquilla and Cartagena on the Atlantic coast. The port of Tumaco on the Pacific coast is gaining in importance and there are plans for construction of a deep-water port at Bahía Solano. In December 2013 Colombia's flag registered fleet comprised 593 vessels, with a total displacement of some 176,739 grt.

Port Authorities

Sociedad Portuaria Regional de Barranquilla: Carrera 38, Calle 1A, Barranquilla, Atlántico; tel. (5) 371-6200; fax (5) 371-6310; e-mail servicioalcliente@sprb.com.co; internet www.sprb.com.co; privatized in 1993; Pres. RENE F. PUCHE RESTREPO.

Sociedad Portuaria Regional de Buenaventura: Edif. de Administración, Avda Portuaria, Apdo 478-10765, Buenaventura; tel. 241-0700; fax 242-2700; e-mail servicioalaccionista@sprbun.com; internet www.puertobuenaventura.com; Pres. BARTOLO VALENCIA RAMOS; Gen. Man. DOMINGO CHINEA BARRERA.

Sociedad Portuaria Regional de Cartagena: Manga, Terminal Marítimo, Cartagena, Bolívar; tel. (5) 660-7781; fax (5) 650-2239; e-mail comercial@sprc.com.co; internet www.puertocartagena.com; f. 1993; Gen. Man. ALFONSO SALAS TRUJILLO.

Sociedad Portuaria de Santa Marta: Carrera 1, 10A-12, Apdo 655, Santa Marta; tel. (5) 421-7970; fax (5) 421-2161; e-mail spsm@spsm.com.co; internet www.spsm.com.co; Gen. Man. MAURICIO SUÁREZ.

Private shipping companies include the following:

NAVESCO, SA: Torre Cusezar, No 7-15, 17°, Avda Calle 116, Bogotá, DC; tel. (1) 657-5868; fax (1) 657-5869; e-mail gsolano@navesco.com.co; internet www.navesco.com.co; f. 1980; Pres. RUBEN ESCOBAR; Gen. Man. GUILLERMO SOLANO.

CIVIL AVIATION

Colombia has 11 international airports: Bogotá, DC (El Dorado International Airport), Medellín, Cali, Barranquilla, Bucaramanga, Cartagena, Cúcuta, Leticia, Pereira, San Andrés and Santa Marta.

Regulatory Authority

Aeronáutica Civil (Aerocivil): Nuevo Edif. Aerocivil, Avda El Dorado 103–15, 4°, Bogotá, DC; tel. (1) 425-1000; fax (1) 413-5000; e-mail quejasyreclamos@aerocivil.gov.co; internet www.aerocivil.gov.co; f. 1967 as Departamento Administrativo de Aeronáutica Civil, reorganized in 1992; part of the Ministry of Transport; develops and regulates the civil aviation industry; Dir-Gen. GUSTAVO ALBERTO LENIS STEFFENS.

National Airlines

Avianca (Aerovías Nacionales de Colombia, SA): Avda El Dorado, No 93-30, 5°, Bogotá, DC; tel. (1) 413-9862; fax (1) 413-8716; internet www.avianca.com/es-co; f. 1919; operates domestic services to all cities in Colombia and international services to the USA, France, Spain, and throughout Central and Southern America; allied with

TACA of El Salvador (q.v.) in 2009; Exec. Pres. FABIO VILLEGAS RAMÍREZ.

Avianca Cargo, SA: Aeropuerto José María Córdova, Terminal Internacional de Carga, Rionegro, Medellín, Antioquia; tel. (4) 569-9200; fax (4) 562-2847; e-mail laura.herzberg@aviancataca.com; internet www.aviancacargo.com; f. 1973; fmrly Tampa Cargo; operates international cargo services to destinations throughout the Americas; acquired by AviancaTaca Holdings in 2010; adopted present name in 2013; Dir LUÍS FELIPE GOMÉZ TORO.

Copa Airlines Colombia: Edif. Citibank, Calle 100, Carrera 9A, No 99–02, Bogotá, DC; tel. (1) 320-9090; fax (1) 320-9095; internet www.copaair.com; f. 1992 as Aero República; changed name as above in 2010; subsidiary of Copa Holdings (Panama); CEO EDUARDO LOMBANA.

LAN Colombia (Aires Colombia): El Dorado International Airport, Bogotá, DC; internet www.lan.com; f. 1980 as Aerovías de Integración Regional (AIRES); acquired by LAN Airlines, SA (Chile) and rebranded as above in 2010; domestic and international passenger services, domestic cargo services; CEO NICOLÁS CORTÁZAR.

Líneas Aéreas Suramericanas (LAS): Avda El Dorado, No 103-22, Entrada 2, Interior 7, Bogotá, DC; tel. (1) 413-9515; fax (1) 413-5356; internet www.lascargo.com; f. 1972 as AeroNorte, present name adopted 1986; charter cargo services.

Satena (Servicio de Aeronavegación a Territorios Nacionales): Avda El Dorado, No 103-08, Apdo Aéreo 11163, Bogotá, DC; tel. (1) 423-8530; e-mail info@satena.com; internet www.satena.com; f. 1962; commercial enterprise attached to the Ministry of National Defence; internal services; Pres. Maj.-Gen. JUAN CARLOS RAMIREZ MEJÍA.

Tourism

The principal tourist attractions are the Caribbean coast (including the island of San Andrés), the 16th-century walled city of Cartagena, the Amazonian town of Leticia, the Andes mountains, the extensive forests and jungles, pre-Columbian relics and monuments of colonial art. In 2013 there were a provisional 2,288,000 visitors, most of whom came from the USA and Venezuela. In the same year tourism receipts totalled a provisional US $2,491m.

Asociación Colombiana de Agencias de Viajes y Turismo (ANATO): Carrera 19B, No 83-49, 4°, Apdo Aéreo 7088, Bogotá, DC; tel. (1) 610-7099; fax (1) 236-2424; e-mail anato@anato.org; internet www.anato.org; f. 1949; Pres. ALONSO MONSALVE GÓMEZ; Exec. Dir JULIÁN TORRES SARRIA.

Defence

As assessed at November 2013, Colombia's armed forces numbered 281,400, of whom the army comprised 221,500, the navy 46,150 (including 27,000 marines and 7,200 conscripts) and the air force 13,750. In addition, there were some 61,900 reservists, of whom 54,700 were in the army, 4,800 in the navy, 1,200 in the air force and 1,200 in the joint services. There was also a paramilitary National Police Force numbering 159,000. Military service is compulsory for men (except for students) and lasts for 12–24 months.

Defence Budget: 12,600,000m. pesos in 2013.

Commander of the Armed Forces: Maj.-Gen. JUAN PABLO RODRÍGUEZ BARRAGÁN.

Chief of Staff of the Armed Forces: Maj.-Gen. JAVIER ALBERTO FLÓREZ ARISTIZÁBAL.

Commander of the Army: Maj.-Gen. JAIME ALFONSO LASPRILLA VILLAMIZAR.

Commander of the Navy: Rear-Adm. HERNANDO WILLS VÉLEZ.

Commander of the Air Force: Maj.-Gen. GUILLERMO LEÓN.

Education

Education in Colombia commences at nursery level for children under six years of age. Primary education is free and compulsory for five years. Admission to secondary school is conditional upon the successful completion of these five years. Secondary education is for four years. Following completion of this period, pupils may pursue a further two years of vocational study. In 2011/12 a total of 4,742,500 students were in primary education and some 4,584,900 attended secondary schools. In 2012 enrolment at primary and secondary schools included 84% and 74% of the school-age population, respectively. In 2013 there were 32 public universities in Colombia. The proposed central Government expenditure on education for 2013 was 24.9m. pesos.

Bibliography

For works on South America generally, see Select Bibliography (Books)

Alesina, A. *Institutional Reforms: The Case of Colombia*. Cambridge, MA, MIT Press, 2005.

Aviles, W. *Global Capitalism, Democracy, and Civil-Military Relations in Colombia*. Albany, NY, State University of New York Press, 2007.

Bergquist, C. W. *Violence in Colombia, 1990–2000: Waging War and Negotiating Peace*. Wilmington, DC, Scholarly Resources Inc, 2001.

Bouvier, V. M. *Colombia: Building Peace in a Time of War*. Washington, DC, United States Institute of Peace Press, 2009.

Brittain, J. J. *Revolutionary Social Change in Colombia: The Origin and Direction of the FARC–EP*. London, Pluto Press, 2010.

Bruce, V. and Hayes, K. *Hostage Nation: Colombia's Guerrilla Army and the Failed War on Drugs*. New York, Alfred A. Knopf, 2010.

Carroll, L. A. *Violent Democratization: Social Movements, Elites, and Politics in Colombia's Rural War Zones, 1984-2008*. Notre Dame, IN, University of Notre Dame Press, 2011.

Crandall, R. *Driven by Drugs: US Policy Toward Colombia*. 2nd Edn, Boulder, CO, Lynne Rienner Publrs, 2008.

Croce, E. *Programación Financiera: Métodos y Aplicación al caso de Colombia*. Washington, DC, IMF Publications, 2002.

Dudley, S. *Walking Ghosts: Murder and Guerrilla Politics in Colombia*. London, Routledge, 2004.

Earle, R. A. *Spain and the Independence of Colombia, 1808–1825*. Exeter, University of Exeter Press, 2000.

Gow, D. G. *Countering Development: Indigenous Modernity and the Moral Imagination*. Durham, NC, Duke University Press, 2008.

Hartlyn, J. *The Politics of Coalition Rule in Colombia*. Cambridge, Cambridge University Press, 2008.

Henderson, J. *Modernization in Colombia: The Laureano Gómez Years, 1889–1965*. Gainesville, FL, University Press of Florida, 2001.

Hernández Gamarra, A. *A Monetary History of Colombia*. Bogotá, DC, Villegas Editores, 2002.

Hinojosa, V. J. *Domestic Politics and International Narcotics Control*. London, Taylor & Francis, 2007.

Jaramillo, F. *Liberalization and Crisis in Colombian Agriculture*. Boulder, CO, Westview Press, 1998.

Kirk, R. *More Terrible Than Death: Drugs, Violence, and America's War in Colombia*. Jackson, TN, Perseus Books, 2004.

Kline, H. F. *Chronicle of a Failure Foretold: The Peace Process of Colombian President Andrés Pastrana*. Tuscaloosa, AL, University of Alabama Press, 2007.

Livingstone, G. *Inside Colombia: Drugs, Democracy and War*. London, Latin America Bureau, 2002.

Londoño-Vega, P. *Religion, Society and Culture in Colombia: Antioquia and Medellín, 1850–1930*. Oxford, Clarendon Press, 2002.

McFarlane, A. *Colombia Before Independence*. Cambridge, Cambridge University Press, 2002.

Posada-Carbó, E. *Colombia: The Politics of Reforming the State*. Basingstoke, Palgrave Macmillan, 1997.

Rausch, J. *Colombia: Territorial Rule and the Llanos Frontier*. Gainesville, FL, University Press of Florida, 1999.

Richani, N. *Systems of Violence: The Political Economy of War and Peace in Colombia*. Albany, NY, State University of New York Press, 2002.

Ruiz, B. *The Colombian Civil War*. Jefferson, NC, McFarland & Co, 2001.

Safford, F., and Palacios, M. *Colombia: Fragmented Land, Divided Society*. Oxford, Oxford University Press, 2001.

Sanchez, G., and Meertens, D. *Bandits, Peasants and Politics: The Case of 'La Violencia' in Colombia*. Austin, TX, University of Texas Press, 2001.

Schott, J. J. (Ed.). *Trade Relations between Colombia and the United States*. Washington, DC, Peterson Institute for International Economics, 2006.

Simons, G. *Colombia: A Brutal History*. London, Saqi Books, 2004.

Uribe Velez, Alvaro *Showing Teeth to the Dragons*. Tuscaloosa, AL, University of Alabama Press, 2009.

No Lost Causes. New York, NY, Celebra (Penguin Group), 2012.

Welna, C., and Galón, G. (Eds). *Peace, Democracy, and Human Rights in Colombia*. Notre Dame, IN, University of Notre Dame Press, 2007.

COSTA RICA

Geography

PHYSICAL FEATURES

The Republic of Costa Rica is the southernmost of the Central American countries, with Panama beyond the southern frontier (330 km or 205 miles in length). Nicaragua lies to the north (309 km). Although the border with Panama is across a narrower part of the isthmus, it is more convoluted and, therefore, longer. The country has coasts on both the Pacific (1,015 km) and the Caribbean (usually referred to as the Atlantic coast— 212 km). The territory of the country includes the rugged Isla del Coco (Cocos Island), some 480 km south-west of continental Costa Rica. The country has a dispute with Nicaragua over navigational rights on the San Juan river on the border, exacerbated by the presence of many illegal Nicaraguan immigrants in the country. Costa Rica has a total area of 51,100 sq km (19,730 sq miles).

The San Juan, the outflow of Lake Nicaragua, flows into the Caribbean Sea and forms much of the north-eastern border. In the north-west the border skirts the south-western edges of Lake Nicaragua, to the east of the Cordillera de Guanacaste, on the Pacific side of which is the Nicoya peninsula. These mountains head inland eventually to join the higher, central ranges, culminating in the Cordillera de Talamanca, which thrusts up the spine of the country from the south. The region is also volcanic, with four volcanoes near San José, the capital, two of them active: Irazu last erupted destructively in the mid-1960s. The highest point is south of here at Cerro Chirripo (3,810 m or 12,504 ft), in the rugged Talamanca range. The capital city is located in a fertile, upland basin, the Meseta Central Valley, at an altitude of about 1,170 m. On either side of the mountains are coastal plains, the Pacific coast being more irregular in outline and the Atlantic coast lower, swampier and heavily forested (almost one-third of the country is wooded). Costa Rica is about 460 km at its maximum length, its axis running from south-east to north-west, with the northern border the widest part of the country (260 km). The country is very fertile and rich in biodiversity, among the most intense in the world, with a massive range of flora and fauna, notably bird life, flourishing in a huge range of ecosystems. Thirty nature reserves cover some 11% of the territory, with about twice as much again also gaining some form of protection, sheltering more than 200 species of mammals (including six species of wild cat), over 850 species of birds (including endemic species, such as two types of hummingbird and a tanager), 1,000 butterfly types and almost 200 amphibians and 220 reptiles. The country is reckoned to contain up to 13,000 varieties of flowering plant and 10% of the world's birds and butterflies. The isolation of the Isla del Coco has created another unspoilt natural haven for both land and marine life (here alone are three endemic bird species: the Cocos finch, flycatcher and cuckoo). In 2014 UNESCO added four pre-Columbian sites in the south of the country to its World Heritage List.

CLIMATE

The climate is tropical and subtropical, varied by the highlands and the competing weather systems of the Pacific and the Caribbean. The dry season is December–April. The onset of the rainy (or green) season can bring flooding in the coastal lowlands and, later, landslides in the mountainous interior, in a topography complicated by earthquakes and active volcanoes.

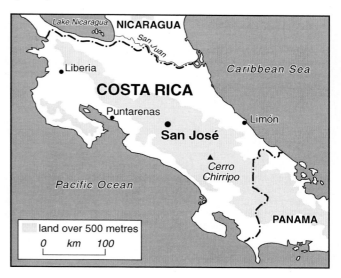

Hurricanes are likely along the Caribbean coast, where rainfall is greater than on the Pacific coast. Rainfall is also greater in the mountains. Annual precipitation varies enormously according to location, some places recording a remarkable 6,000 mm (234 ins), others as relatively little as 1,500 mm. The average for the whole country is 3,300 mm. Temperatures vary mainly with altitude, the coast experiencing thermometer readings between about 27°C and 32°C (81°–90°F) and the Central Valley around 22°C (72°F) with the mountains being cooler still.

POPULATION

The white and mixed-race population, mainly of Spanish descent, accounted for 84% of the total, according to the 2011 census, with a further 7% identifying as mulatto, 2% as indigenous or Amerindian, and 1% as black. Traditionally a Roman Catholic country, the denomination still enjoys the adherence of about four-fifths of the population; however, evangelical Christian groups have gained many new followers, and non-Catholic Christians now represent more than one-sixth of the population. Spanish is the official language, but some English is spoken around Puerto Limón, which is the heart of black Creole culture, on the Caribbean. The Amerindian languages spoken in Costa Rica are all of the Chibcha group. Costa Ricans refer to themselves informally as Ticos.

About one-half of the total population of 4.8m. (according to official mid-year estimates in 2014) live in the central plateau (Meseta Central) around San José, the capital. There are several other large population centres in that region, but the principal cities of the Pacific coast are Puntarenas, on the Gulf of Nicoya, in the north-west, and further north, inland, Liberia. The main city of the Atlantic coast is Limón. Another important demographic statistic is the large number of foreign tourists who visit annually; these totalled 2.3m. in 2012. The country consists of seven provinces.

History

Dr DAVID DÍAZ ARIAS

A SUCCESSFUL NATION-STATE

Costa Rica secured independence from Spain in 1821 as part of the Kingdom of Guatemala. Between 1824 and 1835 Costa Rica was part of the Federal Republic of Central America, which disappeared in 1839 owing to economic and political problems. At that time Costa Rica had enjoyed a period of some political stability and had become involved in two brief civil wars, in 1823 and 1835. By the end of the 1830s some entrepreneurs started to plant and export coffee, and during the 1840s and the 1850s this product became the most important factor in Costa Rica's economy. The coffee industry gave rise to an élite who gained political power and developed political institutions to consolidate a modern state. Costa Rica officially became a republic in 1848.

In 1856–57 Costa Rica joined the Central American armies in Nicaragua to battle US filibuster William Walker, who sought to create a personal empire in Central America by conquering it. Costa Rica played an important role in defeating Walker. During 1859–70 the country experienced some political instability but it was able to fortify state institutions by centralizing political power. In 1870 Gen. Tomás Guardia overthrew the Government and ruled until 1882, giving power to a young generation of liberal politicians, known as El Olimpo (the Olympians).

In the late 19th century major cultural and social transformations took place in Costa Rica. The coffee economy boom after the 1840s produced several changes in the cultural patterns of consumption. During the 1850s, for the first time, newspapers advertised goods, new public services, the building of shops and workshops, and the spread of lawyers' and doctors' offices, as well as published advertisements about craft classes. This publicity increased from 1850–1900 and was accompanied by a tremendous cultural differentiation between the social classes.

The last 30 years of the 19th century were marked by the consolidation of El Olimpo. They initiated a series of reforms, based on a new perception about the role of the state and rooted in a commitment to transform Costa Rican society. The most important events associated with this group were the 1884 liberal reforms, which attempted to reduce the Catholic Church's influence on the popular classes and to expand scientific and secular visions of life and nature among those sections of society.

Electoral inclusion began during the 1880s, allowing adult males to vote and creating a measure of popular political participation. Liberal politicians focused on policies advancing public education and public health. Figures on Costa Rica's literacy rates demonstrate the success of liberal politicians in improving public education. In 1864 the total literacy rate reached 38.4% in urban areas, while rural areas had a literate population of just above 10.5%. In 1927 total literacy for all children above nine years of age reached 85.7% in urban areas, 66.8% in small cities, and 56.4% in rural areas.

From the 1870s Costa Rican liberals began to create a new national identity for the country based on liberal political concepts. Fundamental ideas that related to this national discourse involved cultural differentiations in ethnicity (a country of 'white' people), politics (democracy and social peace) and history. In the construction of a suitable past, Costa Rican liberal historians embraced the image of a poor country in the colonial era that progressed rapidly because of the coffee economy boom after the 1840s. At the same time, liberal historians and politicians reconstructed the war against William Walker as the most important part of Costa Rican history and transformed one of its participants—soldier Juan Santamaría—into Costa Rica's most important national hero. Therefore, liberal politicians succeeded in constructing a strong national identity defined by Santamaría, the war of 1856–57, and the vision of Costa Rican society as a white and peaceful community. There is enough evidence to assert that labourers and sectors within the urban popular class had received and assimilated this discourse about their national identity by the beginning of the 20th century. For example, in a census carried out in 1904, San José residents (labourers included) answered the question 'nationality' with the response: 'Costa Rican, fortunately'.

During the first part of the 20th century Costa Rica experienced the most tremendous social transformation. Urban workers became organized securing labour rights, promoting strikes during different periods and founding some unions during the 1930s. In the 1920s political discussion began to include new points of view such as reformism, while some intellectuals and workers founded a Communist Party in 1931. The Partido Republicano Nacional (PRN) ruled during the 1930s by investing in public works and consolidating democratic elections.

Costa Rica experienced tremendous social tensions during 1940–48. President Rafael Angel Calderón Guardia, who won the 1940 presidential election with almost 85% of the votes, organized the first and clearest instance of a populist movement in this country's history, which mobilized thousands of people. As had happened during the 1940s in countries such as Argentina, Brazil, Mexico, Venezuela, Colombia, and Nicaragua, Calderón Guardia's populism embraced and propelled workers' unionist activities, through which he transformed himself into a *caudillo* (an indisputable, indispensable leader, implicitly chosen by God). Calderón Guardia's administration brought about what is known as the Social Reform, which was progressive legislation that created a wide social system of health insurance (the Caja Costarricense de Seguro Social) and the University of Costa Rica, as well as a chapter of social guarantees to the Constitution, and a Labour Code. The Social Reform of 1940–43 created some of the most important institutions that produced the social progress that Costa Rica enjoyed during the second half of the 20th century. Certainly, that legislation was only possible thanks to a tradition of state investment, since the end of the 19th century, in public education and public health. More clearly, however, that reform was possible due to an unusual alliance between the 'bourgeois' PRN, the Communist Party of Costa Rica, the Roman Catholic Church, and the working class. In several ways, as it motivated a strong counter-populist group, Calderón Guardia's populism drove the country to an extremely violent civil war in 1948. José Figueres Ferrer, the leader of the revolutionary movement that confronted Calderón Guardia, became the President of a junta controlling the country during 1948–49. In 1951 he founded the social-democratic Partido Liberación Nacional (PLN).

CONTEMPORARY COSTA RICA

After the civil war, the victorious junta outlawed the Costa Rican Communist Party. Between 1948 and 1973 the Constitution forbade the participation of communist parties in elections. This was a concession to the anti-communist group that had opposed the Governments of the period 1940–48 and which had sought to destroy the Left's influence and its union activities. However, in several ways, the new party, Figueres's PLN, played an important role in balancing power by serving as a centre-left electoral option. Indeed, the PLN declared itself to be a social-democratic party, which meant that it supported the state's control of economics and the enactment of legislation to launch the state-initiated enterprises for national farmers, peasants, and the extension of a social security system similar to that in some European countries such as France. In that sense, the PLN continued to fortify the social legislation enacted in the 1940s, the very legislation that gave Costa Rica its high standards in health, education, life expectancy and the economy. Thanks to such policies, Costa Rica developed strong and high social indexes in health and education.

Thus, although the Costa Rican Communist Party was not able to recuperate its pre-1948 power and then, during the

1980s, fell apart, further reducing its chance to fight electorally, the PLN offered a model of social-democracy that the Costa Rican right was not able to defeat. Between 1953 and 1990 the PLN won six of a total of nine elections. However, in the 1980s the PLN began to renounce its centre-left ideals and embraced the neo-liberal dogma and the 'Washington Consensus' of economic policies prescribing financial liberalization and deregulation, producing a reform that was designed to decimate state control in economics and society. It seems that during the first administration of Oscar Arias Sánchez (1986–90), the PLN began to divide into two factions: the neo-liberal group, which advocated state reform, and the social-democratic group, which aimed to return to the 1960s–70s period. Although the PLN candidate, José María Figueres Olsen (the son of the founder of the PLN), won the presidential election of 1994 by promising to return to the PLN's founding principles, Figueres Olsen very soon had to renounce that plan, and continued to use shock therapy to apply the neo-liberal reform. Analysts began to talk about the PLUSC, an alliance between the PLN and the Partido Unidad Social Cristiana (PUSC, a centre-right party founded in 1983 which became the second electoral force), which was to promote the neo-liberal reform.

Owing to social mobilizations between 1986 and 2001, however, the neo-liberals were not able to transform totally the Costa Rican state. People, especially peasants and middle class urban groups, rejected the attempt to decimate the welfare state that they knew. The biggest mobilization took place in 2001, when a heterogeneous social movement impeded President Miguel Angel Rodríguez from adopting legislation that would have allowed the end of the state monopoly on telecommunications. Rodríguez's defeat seems to have been a lesson for neo-liberals, who began to plan a way to continue their reform. Such an opportunity appeared with the negotiation of the Dominican Republic-Central American Free Trade Agreement (CAFTA-DR, also comprising Costa Rica, El Salvador, Guatemala, Honduras and Nicaragua) with the USA, which was finally approved after a difficult popular plebiscite in 2007.

The approbation of CAFTA-DR took place in a polarized social environment. This polarization was already manifest in the presidential election of 2006, which Oscar Arias contested against Ottón Solís Fallas and won with only 1% more of the vote than Solís. In several ways, the contest between Arias and Solís was a clash between the PLN's neo-liberal and social-democratic wings. Solís had abandoned the PLN in 1998, along with other PLN members, founding the Partido Acción Ciudadana (PAC) as a way to keep social-democracy alive. For many scholars and intellectuals, Solís therefore represented the heir to the centre-left tradition that would halt the neo-liberal reform. Thus, Solís and the PAC opposed CAFTA-DR. By the end of 2009 the PAC clearly appeared to have a good chance of winning the 2010 elections. However, in the event the PLN easily defeated it.

LAURA CHINCHILLA'S ADMINISTRATION, 2010–14

On 7 February 2010 Costa Ricans chose Laura Chinchilla Miranda as the new President. Chinchilla (the candidate of the PLN) won the election with 46.9% of the vote, while her principal challengers Ottón Solís (of the PAC) and Otto Guevara Guth (of the Movimiento Libertario—ML) received 25.1% and 20.9%, respectively. What attracted most attention was that Chinchilla's election was overwhelming, even though many Costa Rican scholars and intellectuals had been expecting a political sea-change. Such wishful thinking was rooted in memories of the impressive social mobilization against CAFTA-DR, which resulted in well-attended demonstrations all over Costa Rica during 2006–07. By associating that popular mobilization with Arias's opposition, and based on the results of the presidential election of 2006, centre-leftist parties really believed that Costa Rica would turn to a different electoral option at the presidential election of 2010. The illusion, however, was over as soon as Chinchilla's victory was announced.

However, Chinchilla's new Government rapidly lost popular support. By July 2013 some 60% of Costa Ricans evaluated Chinchilla's administration as bad or very bad, while 31% of respondents considered that it was a regular administration and just 9% of them qualified it as good. How did Chinchilla reach those levels of disapprobation? Her Government suffered as a result of several scandals. Chinchilla tried to secure the adoption of tax reform legislation, which was presented as crucial for the Government to address the fiscal deficit. In March 2012, however, the Sala IV (the Constitutional Chamber of the Supreme Court) declared the tax reform bill unconstitutional. Chinchilla publicly stated that this decision was disastrous for Costa Rica. Yet, at the same time that the Government was asking people to accept increased taxes, newspaper *La Nación* reported that the Minister of Finance, Fernando Herrero, was not paying the appropriate amount of taxes on two of his properties. Herrero submitted his resignation, but the scandal also involved other members of the Chinchilla administration.

Furthermore, in 2010 the Nicaraguan Government sent forces to occupy some islands in Costa Rica's maritime border area with Nicaragua. Costa Rica claimed that Nicaragua had invaded its national territory, while Nicaragua asserted that the region fell within its own maritime territory. At that time, Chinchilla announced the construction of a roadway stretching 150 km in north Costa Rica. This highway, popularly known as La Trocha, was presented as a nationalistic strategy to protect Costa Rican sovereignty against Nicaragua. The Government hired a private construction company to build the road at a cost of some US $40m. However, in 2012 press reports indicated that La Trocha was still an incomplete mud road. The press also claimed to have evidence of corruption among public officials who had allegedly accepted bribes in order to approve the road contract. A major scandal ensued, as a result of which the Minister of Public Works and Transport, Francisco Jiménez, resigned.

Problems continued with the Government's concession to the Brazilian company OAS for the reconstruction of a highway between San José and the city of San Ramón (in Alajuela). After rehabilitating the highway, the company was to charge US $8 in round-trip tolls on the highway for the next 30 years. Following the La Trocha scandal, Costa Ricans decided to combat this concession with calls for nationwide protest. On 11 April 2013, when Chinchilla visited Alajuela to celebrate a national holiday, local residents took to the streets to protest. Similar protests were held all over the country and Chinchilla was obliged to withdraw from the agreement with OAS, announcing on 22 April in a televised message that the concession would be cancelled.

Chinchilla continued to be beset by controversy. In May 2013 it was claimed that a private jet used by the President to attend a wedding in Peru was owned by a Colombian with alleged links to drugs-trafficking organizations. Pressure from the press and social networks subsequently forced Chinchilla to request the resignation of the head of intelligence and security and that of the Minister of Communications and Public Relations. Chinchilla also faced difficulties with the Caja Costarricense de Seguro Social, one of the country's most significant public institutions, owing to a crisis in its finances. By July Oscar Arias, who had supported Chinchilla's presidential candidacy in 2010, publicly criticized her on television.

Chinchilla's administration, no doubt, confronted a period of social transformation. The President, recognized as close to the Roman Catholic Church, experienced pressure from different activist groups to approve legislation permitting gay marriage, abortion, and in vitro fertilization (IVF). Chinchilla was also the first Costa Rican President who has been constantly evaluated on social networks.

Chinchilla's administration also confronted an economic paradigm that clearly did not benefit the poor. Costa Rica, once recognized as a leading country in social terms, is facing an increase in social inequality. Between 2000 and 2010 Costa Rica, Uruguay, and Honduras became the three Latin American countries in which inequality grew. In 2012 Costa Rica registered good economic results, but the index of poverty remained the same as in 1994, at about 20% of the population. This means that social inequality is increasing between the 20% wealthiest and the 20% poorest sections of the population. The gap between the rich and the poor has not ended. On the contrary, the benefits of the economic bonanza have essentially focused on the rich.

In terms of foreign relations, Costa Rica remained a close ally of the USA. During the 1980s Costa Rica confronted US President Ronald Reagan's foreign policy on the 1978–79 Sandinista revolution in Nicaragua by organizing a peace agreement among Central American Presidents. During the 1990s and at the beginning of the 21st century Costa Rica proved to be very close to the USA by supporting every US policy, including the invasion of Iraq in 2003. Costa Rica has received US support for police training and the legislature has authorized the deployment of US army ships in Costa Rican waters to confront drugs-trafficking. Moreover, in 2009 the US Government asked Costa Rica to act as an intermediary during the coup in Honduras. In May 2013 Chinchilla received US President Barack Obama as part of an official visit to the region.

Nevertheless, the country's foreign relations are shifting; shortly after Obama's visit, in June 2013, the President of the People's Republic of China, Xi Jinping, visited Costa Rica to announce a range of economic co-operation agreements between the two countries. Until 2007 Costa Rica had supported Taiwan in international forums, but in that year President Arias suspended diplomatic relations with Taiwan and established close links with China. Arias subsequently visited China and the Chinese Government financed the construction of a football stadium in San José as a gesture of co-operation. President Xi Jinping's visit appeared to demonstrate a further strengthening of its relations between the two countries.

THE PRESIDENTIAL ELECTION OF 2014

As early as 2010 Oscar Arias's brother, Rodrigo Arias, began a public campaign to be the PLN presidential candidate. Yet he was not alone; Johnny Araya Monge, the long-standing mayor of San José, also presented himself as a potential candidate for the party. However, owing to Rodrigo Arias's association with Chinchilla's administration problems, he was subject to negative campaigning on social networks, and consequently was unable to run a successful campaign for nomination. He renounced his candidacy aspirations in 2013, thereby allowing Araya to be declared the official PLN candidate for the election scheduled for 2 February 2014. Araya tried to distance himself from the Chinchilla administration as much as possible. By mid-2013 opinion polls presented Araya as virtually undefeatable, although by the end of that year he had begun to lose support, while other candidates gained popularity, notably José María Villalta of the leftist party Frente Amplio (FA).

Villalta was the only FA congressman during Chinchilla's administration, and he came to prominence presenting various issues to the legislature, such as the protection of natural resources, especially water, and the role of public institutions and of minorities. The FA, the PAC, and other small parties discussed the possibility of creating a coalition to challenge the PLN, but failed to reach agreement and, therefore, ran for office separately. At the end of 2013 and the beginning of 2014, Villalta confounded expectations by performing better in opinion polls than any leftist candidate had ever done. As Villalta led the polls, Araya's PLN focused its attention on attacking the FA's young candidate, denouncing him as a communist and a *chavista* (in the style of the late Venezuelan President Hugo Chávez), and claiming that the FA represented a serious danger to Costa Rica's democracy. This electoral strategy may have influenced voters by invoking Costa Rica's traditional fear of communism and the low opinion of *chavismo* among most Costa Ricans. Moreover, other parties, such as the ML—the third option according to opinion polls—attempted to attract conservative voters by accusing Villalta of wanting to legalize abortion and gay marriage if elected. Villalta and the FA confronted the PLN's and the ML's propaganda, publicly stating that he was part of a communist tradition, but was neither communist nor *chavista*.

The PAC also experienced an internal dispute. Its long-time leader, Ottón Solís, had announced in 2010 that he would not run for office again. Several PAC militants subsequently presented themselves as potential candidates: Luis Guillermo Solís, Epsy Campbell, Juan Carlos Mendoza, and Ronald Solís. In July 2013 Luis Guillermo Solís, an academic not widely known to the electorate, secured the party's presidential nomination. The PAC did not appear in opinion polls as a potential challenger to the PLN or the FA. The electoral struggle between the PLN, the FA and the ML conspicuously ignored Solís. However, Solís and the PAC ran an effective campaign, while their propaganda focused on promoting themselves as a serious alternative to the neo-liberal PLN and the inexperienced FA. By mid-January 2014 Solís was concentrating on presenting his party as part of a social-democratic tradition, appearing as a college professor who could create the political transformation that Costa Rica needed. In public debates, he showed his knowledge of Costa Rican society and presented specific solutions to the main problems. He demonstrated he was serious and prepared to rule the country. He also demonstrated some charisma during his 'rutas de la alegría' (tours of local communities during the campaign).

The PUSC had recovered some popularity with the selection as its presidential candidate of Dr Rodolfo Hernández, a paediatrician who served for many years as the director of the National Children's Hospital. Hernández gained support in opinion polls, thereby practically reviving his party after almost 12 years of electoral losses. However, in early October 2013 Hernández unexpectedly renounced his nomination and accused PUSC's traditional leaders of a conspiracy against him. The PUSC elected to replace him with Rodolfo Piza, a well-known lawyer. Piza made great efforts to rescue the PUSC's image, and was a credible participant in the many debates leading up to the election. However, he did not appear to capture the public imagination.

The outcome of the presidential election, which took place on 2 February 2014 came as a complete surprise to analysts. The PAC received 30.6% of the votes, the largest share of the vote, although less than the necessary 40% required to avoid a subsequent round of voting. The PLN received 29.7% of the valid votes cast, the FA 17.3%, the ML 11.3%, and the PUSC 6.0%. The remaining votes went to eight smaller political parties. Faced with the likelihood of defeat, on 6 March Araya announced his withdrawal from the second round election. However, the electoral authorities subsequently declared this to be unconstitutional and Araya's name appeared on the run-off ballot papers. At the second round of voting on 6 April Solís secured 77.8% of votes and Araya received 22.2%, giving the PAC its first election victory.

THE FIRST DAYS OF LUIS GUILLERMO SOLÍS'S ADMINISTRATION

On 8 May 2014 Luis Guillermo Solís assumed presidential power in a ceremony at the Estadio Nacional. As promised, he appointed many scholars, women, and young politicians to head key public institutions and departments. President Solís announced that his appointees would have 100 days to evaluate their institutions and to present a plan to improve them. Solís's inaugural address was celebrated as a sign of hope for a new Costa Rica.

The new President, however, must confront several challenges. First, even though he won the presidential election, the Legislative Assembly remained completely divided and the PAC lacked a governing majority. Indeed, out of 57 deputies, the PLN won 18, the PAC 14, the FA nine, the PUSC eight, and the ML three, with the remainder divided among the smaller parties. Within this divided Assembly, Solís would have to create a coalition to secure approval for his legislative initiatives. The FA announced the conditional support of its deputies for the Solís administration in those projects that they share, while the PUSC deputies supported the appointment of a PAC deputy as legislative speaker for the 12 months from May 2014. The PAC will depend on building similar alliances in order to be able to advance its legislative programme.

Solís will also have to find new ways of responding to the demands of social movements following the Chinchilla administration. The President is considered to be part of a political party that helped to organize people and support demonstrations against PLN administrations. However, immediately after his inauguration, he was confronted by striking teachers, many of whom had not been paid since March 2014, when the Department of Education (still under the PLN at that time) changed its payroll software. The teachers claimed that some of them had not received wages for three months and that they needed a fast and immediate solution. Solís asked the teachers to return to work while a solution was found, reminding them that it was a problem caused by the previous administration. However, the teachers did not comply, and indeed intensified their protests, leading to accusations of intransigence by Solís. The strike was finally ended in early June following an agreement on a resolution and payment schedule.

Solís will also have to confront economic problems. In April 2014 microprocessor manufacturer Intel, which established a presence in the country in 1998, announced plans to transfer its Costa Rican operations to Malaysia, involving the loss of some 1,500 jobs. The impact of this on the country's economy was expected to be significant, considering that Intel's operations in Costa Rica are worth about US $2,000m. per year, equivalent to some 20% of the country's total export earnings. However, in August 2014 Intel announced its intention to open a laboratory in the country in mid-2015 that would eventually employ 200 people.

Compared to his predecessor, Solís has adopted a more inclusive understanding of sexual identities and minorities. On 17 May 2014, just days after taking office, Solís gave a strong indication of the progressive intentions of his Government by raising the rainbow flag of the lesbian, gay, bisexual and transgender (LGBT) movement above the presidential residence. Solís asserted before a crowd of LGBT leaders: 'This is the house of all Costa Ricans. When we say all Costa Ricans we mean all, without exclusion, without violence, without harassment in absolute respect for the rights of each one'. In the same month Solís visited the La Trocha site and announced renewed efforts to finish the project. In recognition of the various unresolved and outstanding problems facing his administration, Solís made a plea for patience from the electorate. It was apparent, however, that some who voted for Solís were not prepared to wait for too long. As the first President of a PAC administration and the individual who embodies the hopes of so many Costa Ricans, Solís faces considerable pressures, both in meeting his own objectives and retaining popular support.

Economy

Dr RONNY VIALES-HURTADO

Based on an earlier article by DIEGO SÁNCHEZ-ANCOCHEA

Costa Rica's new Government was inaugurated on 8 May 2014. The new President, Luis Guillermo Solís Rivera of the Partido Acción Ciudadana won the election with 77.8% of the vote. The election removed the Partido Liberación Nacional from power following eight years governing the country. Solís does not, however, have a majority in the Legislative Assembly. This new political context could signify either the transformation or the continuity of the Costa Rican development model of the last 30 years.

Costa Rica has one of the highest levels of human development in Latin America. In 2013 it was ranked 68th in the UN Human Development Index (a fall of six places from the previous year), below Chile, Argentina, Uruguay, Cuba and Panama in the region. Life expectancy at birth stood at 79.7 years in 2012 and the under-five mortality rate at only 10 per 1,000 live births in the same year. The literacy rate was 96% in 2013 and Costa Rica was ranked 11th out of all non-Organisation for Economic Co-operation and Development (OECD) countries in the UN Human Poverty Index in 2009. This reflects a long-term commitment to social stability, political accountability and public spending in health and education. Costa Rica has one of the highest levels of social spending in Latin America and the Caribbean (22.9% of gross domestic product—GDP—in 2010). The economy has been historically stable. According to the World Bank, gross national income per head was US $8,740 in 2012, the highest in Central America, despite a reduced flow of remittances in the region (totalling, according to the Inter-American Development Bank, US $561m. in 2013).

STAGES OF ECONOMIC DEVELOPMENT

During the 16th century the conquest of Costa Rica by Spaniard conquistadors exploited native labour and few indigenous people survived this exploitation. During the colonial period, Costa Rica experienced the commercialization of cacao and snuff, which was limited by the Spanish monopoly system. However, illegal trade flourished in the Caribbean Sea, much of which was carried out by British pirates. Thus, subsistence agriculture and smallholder farming coexisted with limited trade flows until the introduction of large-scale cultivation of first coffee and then bananas from the early 19th century. From then on, Costa Rica's development outpaced the rest of Central America. It was first to export coffee (in 1832), to establish a commercial bank (in 1864) and to build a railway (in 1890). After the 1948 civil war, Costa Rica departed even further from its Central American neighbours. Large sectors of the economy were nationalized and considerable state support given to smallholders, who made up the backbone of the agricultural economy and underpinned its commitment to democracy. A welfare state was established and public utilities expanded quickly under state ownership.

In the 1960s the Government sought to diversify the economy and promote new exports through industrial import substitution within the Central American Common Market (CACM), attempting to build a domestic manufacturing industry through protectionist tariffs and export subsidies. This process also involved an increase in dairy farming for domestic consumption and meat export, particularly to the US market. Yet it was not until the 1990s, when the tourism sector expanded and extensive foreign investment fostered first a textile, then a high-technology sector, that Costa Rica reduced its reliance on coffee and bananas. It sought to transform itself into a diversified exporter with world-class companies through a mixture of government incentives and a network of free trade agreements. However, success in the export sector was accompanied by problems in other spheres. By the 1980s high debt threatened to swamp the country, which also suffered the negative impact of the difficulties of the CACM, as well as the armed conflict in the region. The Government was forced to pursue a series of unpopular structural adjustment programmes with multilateral lending institutions. Successive governments also sought to develop non-traditional exports with incentive schemes. Nevertheless, large deficits had to be funded by heavy domestic and overseas borrowing, and in 1988 the country was forced to apply for IMF and World Bank help to reschedule its debts. While it gained temporary relief, progress over the subsequent 15 years was painstakingly slow because of public opposition to a diminution of the welfare state and an increase in taxes. The debt restructuring of 1988–89, better borrowing terms and more careful policy management reduced public external debt, from 43.7% of GDP in 1990 to an estimated 7.8% of GDP in 2012. However, public internal debt grew rapidly, and, according to the IMF, was equivalent to an estimated 30.3% of GDP in 2012 (compared with 26.8% in 2011). The IMF expected this ratio to decrease slightly to 30.2% by 2013.

From the mid-1980s Costa Rica followed an at times inconsistent path towards a neo-liberal policy model. Significant reforms were introduced, including changes to the pensions and tax systems and measures to promote foreign investment and to facilitate private sector involvement in banking and power generation. At the same time, however, other reforms such as the deregulation of the telecommunications industry failed, owing to the active opposition of a majority of the population. Costa Rica's economy expanded at an average annual rate of 5.5% between 2000 and 2008, one of the highest rates in Latin America. However, the economic model remained dependent on external forces and especially on ties with the USA, a problem that became evident after the advent of the global financial crisis in 2008. The USA was Costa Rica's main export partner in 2013, accounting for 37.0% of all exports, as well as the main source of imports, accounting for 49.2% of the total. This relationship and the global recession directly contributed to low economic growth of 2.7% in 2008 (less than any other country in Central America) and to an economic contraction of 1.0% in 2009. The recession in Costa Rica was mild, however, with real GDP growth of 5.0% registered in 2010, 4.5% in 2011 and 5.1% in 2012. However, in 2013 GDP growth showed signs of a slowdown at 3.5%. The IMF predicted growth of 3.8% in 2014. None the less, in the context of the region, where overall GDP increased by 2.5% in 2013 and was forecast to grow by 2.9% in 2014 (according to the World Bank), these figures were positive. Costa Rica's unemployment rate, however, increased to 7.8% in 2009 (from 4.8% in 2008), before declining slightly to 7.3% in 2010. Rates of 7.7% and 7.8% were recorded in 2011 and 2012, respectively, and by 2013 this figure had increased to 8.5%. The departure, announced in mid-2014, of telecommunications company Intel from the country, with the loss of 1,500 jobs, was likely to lead to an increase in this figure (although in August Intel announced it was planning to open a laboratory in mid-2015 that will eventually employ 200 people).

These indicators show the impact of the global recession on Costa Rica. The export-led model has created a dual economy and questioned the survival of the former institutional structure. While export sectors performed well, traditional producers faced the loss of government subsidies and protective measures. Poverty has been gradually decreasing in the last decade, from 20.3% of the population living in poverty in 2002 to 18.5% in 2009; in recent years, poverty levels have been similar to those of the early 21st century: 21.3% in 2010, 21.6% in 2011 and 20.3% in 2012. Extreme poverty, or indigence, declined from 8.2% in 2002 to 4.2% in 2009, but increased to 6.4% in 2011, according to the World Bank. International poverty lines are favourable compared with the rest of Latin America, with 6.0% of the population living on less than US $2 per day and only 3.1% living on less than $1.25 in 2009, according to the same source. Income inequality continued its worsening trend. Inequality has increased, with the poorest 20% of the population receiving just 3.9% of the national income compared to the richest 20%, who received 55.9%. Plan Escudo, a social and economic protection programme introduced by President Oscar Arias Sánchez in 2009, aimed to protect Costa Rican businesses, the financial sector, workers and families from the worst effects of the global financial crisis. President Laura Chinchilla Miranda's administration continued these policies by approving a national development plan for the 2011–14 period.

AGRICULTURE

Agriculture, hunting, forestry and fishing contributed an estimated 5.4% of GDP and engaged 12.7% of the employed population in 2013. In 2008 the agricultural sector experienced a significant crisis, with negative growth of 2.3%. This continued in 2009 with a contraction of 2.5%, although there was a return to positive growth in the following year. Agricultural GDP expanded an estimated 1.1% in 2011. The major agricultural commodities were coffee, bananas, pineapples, sugar and beef for export, and rice for domestic consumption. The Government's attempt to encourage non-traditional export crops meant that the country was no longer self-sufficient in staples and imported large quantities of maize, beans, rice and soy-

beans. The recovery of coffee prices, together with an increased demand for pineapple and other non-traditional crops for export, contributed to a rise in agricultural export earnings to US $2,993m. in 2012, although this fell slightly to $2,923m. in 2013, when food and live animals contributed 25.5% of the value of total exports.

PINEAPPLES

Pineapple cultivation has expanded significantly in the last 20 years owing to the increase of international demand. Costa Rica is now the leading exporter of pineapples. In 2011 a total of some 45,000 ha were cultivated with the crop. Environmental groups, however, have expressed concern at the contamination of aquifers and rivers through the use of associated pesticides. Pressure from these groups resulted in better environmental practices by some producers. Between 2009 and 2013 the volume of exports increased by 42%, with a slight decrease in production between 2012 and 2013. Export earnings from the crop rose from US $571m. in 2009 to $718m. in 2011, and to $793m. in 2012. In 2013 this figure reached $821m., when exports represented 7.3% of total exports, thus becoming the most important of the country's agricultural exports. Some 50% of pineapple exports are purchased by the USA, while 47% are purchased by the European Union (EU). In 2011 there were about 1,300 pineapple growers—96% of them are considered to be small growers and 67% of the production was made by independent growers.

BANANAS

Apart from a brief period in the mid-1980s, bananas, cultivation of which was concentrated on the Pacific and Caribbean coasts, have consistently been Costa Rica's main export commodity. In 1985 the closure and diversification of the Pacific coast operations of Chiquita brought widespread economic depression to the region, since many of its towns were wholly dependent on the company's fortunes. Consequently, the Government purchased 1,700 ha of the abandoned plantations (which totalled 2,300 ha) and converted them to the cultivation of cocoa. Elsewhere, bananas were replaced by more profitable crops such as African palm, sugar cane and exotic fruits, especially pineapples.

The Costa Rican banana industry recovered gradually with incentives from the Government, but faced a new threat from the EU quota system from 1993. The quota system, designed to protect banana production in the former European colonies, placed an annual limit of 2.0m. metric tons on banana imports from Latin American countries. This led to the flooding of non-EU markets and a significant decrease in banana prices in Costa Rica. There was also increasing competition from Ecuador, which rapidly became a bigger banana producer than Costa Rica. While Costa Rica had the world's highest productivity levels, it also had higher costs: the average worker earned US $18 per day, compared with $2 in Ecuador. In 2001 the EU and the USA settled the banana dispute. Under the terms of the deal, the EU was to initiate a transitional system, issuing licences according to historical trade patterns, before a tariff-only system was introduced from 2006. Nevertheless, a world banana surfeit continued, leading to the closure of four plantations and the loss of some 1,200 jobs, as well as the cancellation of contracts in Costa Rica by the three principal exporters, Chiquita Brands, the Banana Development Corporation and the Standard Fruit Company. From 2002 banana exports slowly recuperated, but still constituted a small share of total exports. In 2012 banana exports totalled $705m. (just 6.3% of total export revenues), up from $221m. in 1988. In 2013 exports earned $778m. and accounted for nearly 7% of the value of total exports.

COFFEE

Costa Rica grows only Arabic highland coffee, which commands a premium on the world market, and uses technology to achieve some of the highest yields in the world. Sharp falls in the international price of coffee in 1992 caused bankruptcies and led many coffee growers to diversify into other crops. International prices reached a 30-year low in early 2001 and coffee production suffered, amounting to only 150,289 metric tons in that year. Prices declined by two-thirds between 1998 and 2002, but recovered in 2002–07, growing by a combined 140%. This contributed to the gradual recovery of coffee export earnings, which increased from US $194m. in 2003 to $417m. in 2012. Nevertheless, production declined overall from 2.1m. bags in 2001/02 to 1.6m. bags in 2012. Earnings were estimated at $301m. in 2013, equivalent to 2.6% of total export revenue, and making the crop Costa Rica's third most important agricultural export. Production in 2013–14 was adversely affected by an outbreak of rust disease, leading to a decline of almost 10% in coffee exports during the first two months of 2014. The authorities expected that about 18% of that year's production would be lost as a result of the disease, although coffee growers received government support totalling some $40m. to assist them during the emergency. International coffee prices, which had declined in recent years, were expected to recover in 2014–15 to an estimated $200 per quintal.

SUGAR

Sugar production began to increase at the end of the 1990s, in spite of a reduction in the annual US sugar quota. Production stabilized at around 340,000 metric tons in the mid-2000s. Owing to the international price increase, export earnings grew by 64% between 2005 and 2007; however, they decreased by 44% in the following year. The sector was expected to expand somewhat after the Dominican Republic-Central America Free Trade Agreement (CAFTA-DR) came into force in January 2009, particularly because the USA granted Costa Rica a tariff-free import quota in June 2010. Costa Rica's sugar exports earned US $26m. in 2009, before rising to $67m. in 2010. Export revenues totalled $69m. in 2012. The USA and the EU together purchased $47.2m. of Costa Rica's sugar exports in 2012, equivalent to 68.5% of the total, although the USA has consistently been the main market for the country's sugar exports.

A partnership agreement between Costa Rica and the EU was implemented on 1 January 2014. A total export quota of sugar for Central America of 150,000 metric tons was set for the first year. Costa Rica is able to export 19,464 tons. The main challenge for the region is to meet the assessed contributions or transfer them to the other partners.

OTHER CROPS

Crops for domestic consumption included maize, beans and rice, which were grown mainly on small farms with low yields, although advances were being made in rice cultivation, and the size of the units of production was also increasing. The Government gave priority for export incentives on traditional crops such as cocoa, African oil palm, cotton, vegetables, cut flowers, macadamia nuts, coconuts and tropical fruit. Although the EU imposed an 8.8% tariff on most of Costa Rica's fruit and vegetable exports in 2004 after ruling that it was too wealthy to continue to benefit from the General System of Preferences, non-traditional primary exports grew by a combined 55% between 2004 and 2008. Between 2010 and 2011 exports of non-traditional agricultural products grew by 78%.

FORESTRY AND FISHING

Costa Rica has considerable forestry resources, but the Government imposed strict controls on their exploitation because of high historical rates of deforestation. A 20-year US $275m. programme to maintain and develop the forestry resource was announced in 1990. A 1996 forestry law introduced incentives for reforestation and a law of biodiversity in 1998 ensured the protection of natural resources. More than 26% of the country lies in 186 protected areas, which include national parks, biological reserves, forest reserves and wildlife refuges. Costa Rica was a pioneer in the use of 'debt-for-nature' swaps, introduced in the late 1980s, (where a creditor nation forgives debt in return for environmental pledges) to protect its rainforest. Between 2005 and 2007 the proportion of forest area increased slightly, from 46.8% to 46.9%. However, the reforested area decreased from 150,000 ha in the 1990s to less than 75,000 ha in 2013. Costa Rica has also been active in selling carbon credit offsets for the clean air its forests produce. Costa Rica was ranked fifth globally and first within the Americas in terms of the 2012 Environmental Performance Index, which measures the environmental performance of a country's policies.

Costa Rica earned US $85m. from exports of wood and wooden furniture in 2012, but this declined to $72.6m. in 2013, according to the National Forest Office. Teak wood is the main timber exported and three countries (Singapore, India and Viet Nam) import 86% of Costa Rica's teak exports.

Exports of fresh and frozen fish reached US $89.2m. in 2002, but decreased each year thereafter until 2008, when export revenues experienced a small recuperation, totalling $97.1m. By 2012 exports had increased to $121.6m. In that year fish exports contributed some 40% of export earnings from livestock and fisheries, and 1.1% of total export revenue.

MINING AND POWER

Costa Rica has deposits of iron ore, bauxite, sulphur, manganese, mercury, gold and silver. However, by the beginning of the 21st century only the last two were mined. Canadian companies were most active, but mining remained a tiny industry because of strong environmental protection; in 2013 it accounted for just 0.1% of GDP. A mining code adopted in 2001 reduced taxes and improved the legal environment for mining operations. However, a law banning open-cast operations was enacted in 2002. In 2006 the Constitutional Court confirmed the ban in a ruling regarding the gold-mining exploitation of Las Crucitas. In 2008 the Arias Government reversed a moratorium on mining and gave permission for the Las Crucitas project to proceed, leading to protests from social groups and the Nicaraguan Government. In May 2010 incoming President Chinchilla banned all gold mining in the country except in Las Crucitas. However, owing to environmental concerns, the Las Crucitas concession was also revoked in November of that year.

The country also has substantial reserves of petroleum, but they have remained largely unexploited. In 1998 Costa Rica offered exploration concessions in the Caribbean to international companies. However, in 2002 the state environmental regulator refused foreign oil companies licences to prospect on environmental grounds. As a result of the state's refusal to allow the exploitation of petroleum reserves, Costa Rica has been compelled to import all its oil, mostly from Venezuela, under the Caracas Accord of 2000, which provided concessional financing for some of the cost. The petroleum refinery at Puerto Limón processes up to 25,000 barrels per day.

Costa Rica has virtually eliminated the need for petroleum products for electricity generation through its development of hydroelectric power resources and the use of fuel wood, bagasse (vegetable waste) and sugar cane alcohol. Geothermal energy from volcanoes was also developed, and investment in the national grid ensured that 95% of the population was covered by 2002. In 2007 an estimated 75% of all the annual electricity generated was hydroelectric, 14% geothermal, 6% gas and 3% wind power. By 2009 the proportion of electrical energy from clean sources increased to 99%, with the aim of becoming carbon neutral by 2021. Although the state electricity company, the Instituto Costarricense de Electricidad (ICE), generated the bulk of power, private producers generated 17.2% of the country's electricity in 2006. The Sistema de Interconexión Eléctrica de los Países de América Central, a US $500m. programme to connect the electricity networks of the region, was expected to be completed in 2014. It was hoped that the project would reduce consumer electricity bills and improve the reliability of Costa Rica's national grid.

MANUFACTURING

With the manufacturing sector generating an estimated 15.3% of GDP and industry as a whole representing 24.0% of GDP in 2013, Costa Rica was the most industrialized country in Central America. Rapid growth in this sector during the 1960s and 1970s owing to the creation of the CACM resulted in a high level of diversification. Industrial GDP increased in real terms by an average annual rate of 6% between 1990 and 2006.

However, there was a contraction of 3.1% in 2009 before a recovery in the sector of 2.2% in 2010 and 2.5% in 2011.

Manufacturing is dominated by the free trade zones, representing 41% of the total value added in 2006 (second was food, beverages and tobacco, with a share of 20%). At the end of 2009 the Government adopted a law to encourage companies to establish themselves in free trade zones outside the central valley and capital region. By 2010 the electronics industry was the focus of manufacturing, with the previously significant textile industry unable to compete globally, especially relative to the People's Republic of China. Free trade zones accounted for 50%–53% of total exports annually in 2008–12, of which electrical goods alone contributed 27% in 2012. A total of 256 businesses were active in free trade zones in 2010.

In 2012 industrial exports contributed 75.2% of total export earnings, of which electronic goods accounted for 27.1%, precision and medical equipment for 13.2% and food-related manufactured goods for 12.3%. Industrial exports increased from US $6,679.7m. in 2009 to $7,700.7m. and $8,528.8m. in 2011 and 2012, respectively.

TOURISM

Tourism became Costa Rica's largest single source of foreign exchange earnings in the 1990s following significant investment in the sector, with revenue increasing to US $2,427m. in 2013. In that year travel and tourism contributed 4.9% of GDP. In 2013 the total number of tourists was 2.42m. (an increase of 3.4%, compared with the previous year). The country's reputation for political stability and relatively low crime attracts tourists to its fine beaches and extensive system of national parks and protected areas. The rainforest is accessible and bird-watching and trekking are popular. Costa Rica is home to an impressive variety of flora and fauna and is estimated to have 5% of the world's biodiversity, which has encouraged an important ecotourism sector.

The Government aimed to diversify from its dependence on North American visitors, and by 2012 some 39.3% of all foreign tourists came from the USA (down from 51% in 2006). In the first quarter of 2014 there was a total of 802,437 visitor arrivals, of whom some 40% were from the USA. The Government also encouraged a shift from small operators catering to independent tourists to large resorts, built around San José and the northern Pacific coast. In 2013 Costa Rica ranked 47th in the world (out of 140) and sixth in the Americas in the World Economic Forum's 2013 *Travel and Tourism Competitiveness Report*, which measures the attractiveness of a country as a place to establish a tourism business.

INFRASTRUCTURE

Costa Rica has an estimated 39,018 km of roads, of which 26% were paved, in 2010. The main road is the Pan-American Highway, which runs north–south and is fully paved. Public investment in roads increased by more than 37% in real terms in 2003, following the implementation of an extensive maintenance programme to improve the quality of some existing roads. However, since then public investment in transportation has been erratic due to fiscal constraints: in 2004 and 2005 it declined by a combined 43% in real terms, while in 2007 it increased by 88%. A new highway connecting San José to Puntarenas was opened in January 2010.

There are five international ports in Costa Rica. Four are on the Pacific coast—Puntarenas, Calderas, Quepos and Golfito—and one on the Atlantic Coast at Limón/Moín. The latter accounts for over 80% of cargo handled. The Pacific ports were leased to a private operator in 2001. Trade unions prevented such a move on the Atlantic coast until an agreement in 2010 to allow the ports of Limón and Moín to be opened for bidding from the private sector. Plans to fund a new container terminal, expanding existing refinery capacity at Moín, were agreed through a joint partnership between Recope (Refinadora Costarricense de Petróleo), the national oil refinery company, and the Chinese National Petroleum Corporation. Construction of the facility had been scheduled to commence in September 2013, but in June of that year, owing to uncertainty in the feasibility report, the Contraloría General de la

República halted the project; any decision on the project was pending for the new Solís Government in mid-2014.

In 1995 the state railway company, Instituto Costarricense de Ferrocarriles (INCOFER), suspended operations indefinitely, pending privatization, although the transport of cargo continued. In 2008 INCOFER bought trains and technical assistance from a Spanish company, FEVE, and by mid-2009 a wide range of rail lines had reopened.

Costa Rica has four international airports, two of which are located in San José: Juan Santamaría, which is one of the busiest in Central America, transporting an average of 1.5m. passengers per year, and the Tobías Bolaños International Airport in the Pavas area of San José. The other two are the Daniel Oduber Quirós International Airport in Liberia serving the Pacific coast and the Limón International Airport on the Caribbean coast. There are a further 38 small airports with paved runways located throughout the country.

The state electricity company ICE is also responsible for telecommunications and built an impressive land network. There were 33 telephone lines per 100 inhabitants in 2009, although this had declined to 21 by 2012. Investments led to an increase in the number of cellular subscribers from 26 per 100 inhabitants in 2005 to 128 in 2012. Secure internet servers per million people also increased considerably, from 62 in 2005 to 98 in 2009. The number of broadband internet subscribers in the country increased from 107,400 in 2008 to 481,300 in 2012. The approval of the General Telecommunications Law—precipitated by the signing of CAFTA-DR—allowed private participation in network, internet and wireless services from 2008, and the ICE monopoly over the telecommunications market was abrogated in November 2011. Claro and Movistar, two new private companies, have a combined 20% share of the market, and use of mobile internet services increased to 17% of subscribers in 2012.

Construction of a long-awaited bridge linking the borders of Costa Rica and Nicaragua across the San Juan river began in 2012, despite an ongoing diplomatic dispute between the two countries relating to alleged violations of the border in this region (see History). The project, which had cost US $30m., and had received funding from the Japanese Government, was completed in early 2014.

FINANCE AND INVESTMENT

Adverse economic conditions and a lack of fiscal reform precipitated a crisis in Costa Rica's public finances in the early 1980s, necessitating the implementation of a stabilization plan. By the early 1990s the Government was focused on reducing inflation through strict monetary control. Inflation has long been a problem for Costa Rica, although it was brought under control from 20.8% in 1988 to 4.0% in 2009. A rate of 5.8% was recorded in 2010, although this fell again to 4.7% and 4.5% in 2011 and 2012, respectively, but rose to 5.3% in 2013. The fiscal deficit also preoccupied successive governments, in view of the general commitment to public spending. However, budget reductions and tax measures have been politically very difficult to pursue and have faced concerted opposition from labour organizations and civil society to maintain the welfare regime. The deficit was transformed into a surplus under the Arias administration in 2007. The surplus was short-lived and a deficit was recorded again in 2008. The Chinchilla Government committed to maintain the social and economic stimulus measures, resulting in a continuation of a fiscal deficit of 5.4% of GDP in 2010 (from 3.6% in 2009), 4.3% in 2011, 4.4% in 2012 and 5.4% in 2013. The Ministry of Finance had projected a deficit equivalent to 6.0% of GDP for 2014. Public expenditure rose to 18.9% of GDP in 2010 (an increase from 17.6% in 2009) and stood at 18.0% in 2011, 18.3% in 2012, 19.2% in 2013, and an estimated 19.8% in 2014.

There was an increase in foreign direct investment (FDI) in the 1990s, as Costa Rica moved from being predominantly an exporter of coffee and bananas to an advanced technology and *maquila* (offshore assembly) exporter with a successful tourism industry. Total annual FDI increased from US $172m. in 1991 to $662m. in 2002. FDI reached a new record in 2008 in absolute terms ($2,072m.—equivalent to 6.9% of GDP), before declining to $1,339m. (4.6% of GDP) in 2009. In 2008 US companies accounted for 60% of incoming investment. In particular, call centres expanded rapidly, with 20 companies establishing such centres by the end of 2009, generating approximately 12,000 direct jobs. Total FDI reached $1,465m. (4.0% of GDP) in 2010, exceeding the target set by the new Government, which envisaged FDI of $9,000m. during 2010–14. The figure reached $2,682m. in 2013.

BALANCE OF PAYMENTS AND EXTERNAL DEBT

The reduction of import tariffs in 1993 contributed to a dramatic increase in the trade deficit in the 1990s. While this was partially offset by increased tourism revenues and the operations of the free trade zones, it necessitated high levels of external borrowing. The trade deficit totalled US $538.8m. in 2000, increasing to $5,013m. in 2008. This was partly compensated by the tourism sector, giving rise to a current account deficit of $2,787m.—more than double that of two years earlier. Following a decline in 2009, the trade deficit increased in 2010, to $5,362m., and the current account deficit also expanded sharply, to $1,281m. The trade deficit reached $6,935m. in 2011 and $7,427m. in 2012, while the deficit in the current account was recorded at $2,203m. in 2011 and $2,376m. in 2012. Between 2000 and 2005 public external debt remained at around 19% of GDP. According to IMF estimates, in 2012 the consolidated public external debt was equivalent to 7.8% of GDP and interest payments on the total public debt were equivalent to 2.3% of GDP.

OUTLOOK

Costa Rica illustrates as well as any other country in Latin America and the Caribbean both the opportunities and the threats that the current process of market globalization can bring. On the positive side, Costa Rica succeeded in increasing total exports and diversifying its export base. The arrival of multinational corporations in the high technology and service sectors led to the creation of new, well-paid jobs, demonstrating the long-term importance of public investment in education. In the mid-2000s the country benefited from a new round of foreign investment and the expansion of non-traditional exports, partly as a result of closer economic and political ties with China. However, repeated efforts by different administrations to deepen the process of neo-liberal reforms were met with significant public opposition. Dissatisfaction with an economic model that had resulted in greater inequality was increasing. The global financial crisis of 2008 highlighted the contradictions of the Costa Rican model: dependence on external markets, especially the USA, resulted in a recession. However, Costa Rica dealt with the effects of the global financial crisis better than anticipated, influenced partly by an effective social and economic stimulus and protection measures in the form of the Plan Escudo. Although real GDP growth resumed in 2010 and medium-term economic projections were favourable, the fiscal deficit was a cause for concern, and implementation of a comprehensive reform of the tax system was urgently required to restore fiscal stability. However, the Chinchilla administration was unable to secure legislative support for its economic agenda, owing to the absence of a majority in the Asamblea Legislativa (Legislative Assembly) and internal divisions within the ruling party. Economic growth remained strong at 4.5% in 2011 and 5.1% in 2012, supported by robust levels of domestic demand and increased activity in the tourism and manufacturing sectors. Furthermore, although Chinchilla's expansive fiscal reform plans were rejected by the Constitutional Court in April 2012, smaller-scale measures were implemented later that year, thus stabilizing the Government's near-term financial position. The IMF estimated real GDP growth of 3.5% in 2013 and a projected rate of 3.8% in 2014, with domestic demand and manufacturing output expected to moderate.

Economic priorities for the Government of Luis Solís that took office in May 2014 are likely to include the development of a new social contract that allows it to keep funding social policies, as well as development of the welfare state and export-led growth, a reduction in inflation, tax reform, and introduction of a new energy policy that protects the environment. Corruption and tax evasion will also need to be addressed. Intel's departure from the country is an indicator of the limitations of relying on foreign investment as a major economic policy. According to official sources, Costa Rica's exports increased by an annual average of 6.6% between 2000 and 2012 and diversified considerably over the same period. Exports to China and Hong Kong have increased significantly, while the US market's share of total exports declined from 52% to 37% in 2006–13. The service sector has expanded, as have imports from the USA, contributing to the new role of Costa Rica as a technological *maquila*. For this reason, many economic analysts have recommended increased investment in science, technology and innovation, and stronger policies relating to production chains.

Statistical Survey

Sources (unless otherwise stated): Instituto Nacional de Estadística y Censos, Edif. Ana Lorena, Calle Los Negritos, de la Rotonda de la Bandera 450 m oeste, Mercedes de Montes de Oca, San José; tel. 2280-9280; fax 2224-2221; e-mail informacion@inec.go.cr; internet www.inec.go.cr; Banco Central de Costa Rica, Avdas Central y Primera, Calles 2 y 4, Apdo 10058, 1000 San José; tel. 2233-4233; fax 2223-4658; internet www.bccr.fi.cr.

Area and Population

AREA, POPULATION AND DENSITY

Area (sq km)	
Land	51,060
Inland water	40
Total	51,100*
Population (census results)	
28 June 2000	3,810,179
30 May–3 June 2011	
Males	2,106,188
Females	2,195,524
Total	4,301,712
Population (official estimates at mid-year)	
2012	4,652,459
2013	4,713,168
2014	4,773,130
Density (per sq km) at mid-2014	93.4

* 19,730 sq miles.

POPULATION BY AGE AND SEX
('000 persons, official estimates at mid-2014)

	Males	Females	Total
0–14 years	573.2	544.7	1,117.9
15–64 years	1,676.1	1,637.9	3,314.1
65 years and over	161.0	180.1	341.1
Total	**2,410.3**	**2,362.8**	**4,773.1**

Note: Totals may not be equivalent to components, owing to rounding.

PROVINCES
(population at 2011 census)

	Area (sq km)	Population	Density (per sq km)	Capital (with population)
Alajuela . .	9,757.5	847,660	86.9	Alajuela (254,567)
Cartago . .	3,124.7	491,425	157.3	Cartago (147,882)
Guanacaste .	10,140.7	326,821	32.2	Liberia (62,987)
Heredia . .	2,657.0	433,975	163.3	Heredia (123,067)
Limón . .	9,188.5	386,954	42.1	Limón (94,420)
Puntarenas .	11,265.7	410,914	36.5	Puntarenas (115,009)
San José . .	4,965.9	1,403,963	282.7	San José (287,619)
Total . .	51,100.0	4,301,712	84.2	—

PRINCIPAL TOWNS
(population at 2011 census)

San José . . .	287,619	Pérez Zeledón . .	135,429
Alajuela . . .	254,567	Pococí . . .	125,847
Desamparados .	207,082	Heredia . . .	123,067
San Carlos .	163,751	Puntarenas . . .	115,009
Cartago . . .	147,882	Goicoechea . . .	114,736

BIRTHS, MARRIAGES AND DEATHS

	Registered live births		Registered marriages		Registered deaths	
	Number	Rate (per 1,000)	Number	Rate (per 1,000)	Number	Rate (per 1,000)
2005	71,548	16.8	25,631	6.0	16,139	3.8
2006	71,291	16.5	26,575	6.1	16,766	3.9
2007	73,144	16.7	26,010	5.9	17,071	3.9
2008	75,187	16.9	25,034	5.6	18,021	4.1
2009	75,000	16.6	23,920	5.3	18,560	4.1
2010	70,922	15.5	23,955	5.3	19,077	4.2
2011	73,459	17.1	25,013	5.8	18,801	4.4
2012*	73,326	15.7	26,112	5.6	19,200	4.1

* Preliminary.

Life expectancy (years at birth): 79.7 (males 77.5; females 82.0) in 2012 (Source: World Bank, World Development Indicators database).

ECONOMICALLY ACTIVE POPULATION*
(household survey at July, '000 persons aged 12 years and over)

	2011	2012	2013
Agriculture, hunting, forestry and fishing	271.49	269.54	256.43
Mining and manufacturing . .	237.36	228.00	235.31
Electricity, gas and water supply .	40.08	36.90	33.98
Construction	118.95	127.25	114.64
Wholesale and retail trade . .	361.20	354.75	364.27
Hotels and restaurants . .	88.21	98.04	96.86
Transport, storage and communications	125.94	142.17	140.41
Financial intermediation . . .	52.37	51.99	48.04
Real estate, renting and business activities	149.55	174.71	186.10
Public administration activities .	102.97	93.63	110.18
Education	128.11	132.50	129.78
Health and social work . . .	67.35	66.34	71.02
Other community, social and personal service activities . .	86.51	89.48	100.67
Private households with employed persons	150.28	139.84	131.20
Extraterritorial organizations and bodies	2.73	2.93	0.91
Sub-total	1,983.12	2,008.10	2,019.79
Not classifiable by economic activity	6.41	4.15	2.68
Total employed	1,989.53	2,012.25	2,022.47
Unemployed	165.02	169.49	188.10
Total labour force	2,154.55	2,181.75	2,210.57

* Figures for activities are rounded to the nearest 10 persons, and totals may not be equivalent to the sum of component parts as a result.

Health and Welfare

KEY INDICATORS

Total fertility rate (children per woman, 2012)	1.8
Under-5 mortality rate (per 1,000 live births, 2012) . . .	10
HIV/AIDS (% of persons aged 15–49, 2012) . . .	0.3
Physicians (per 1,000 head, 2000)	1.3
Hospital beds (per 1,000 head, 2010)	1.2
Health expenditure (2011): US $ per head (PPP)	1,243
Health expenditure (2011): % of GDP	10.2
Health expenditure (2011): public (% of total)	74.7
Access to water (% of persons, 2011)	96
Access to sanitation (% of persons, 2011)	94
Total carbon dioxide emissions ('000 metric tons, 2010) . .	7,770.4
Carbon dioxide emissions per head (metric tons, 2010) . .	1.7
Human Development Index (2013): ranking	68
Human Development Index (2013): value	0.763

For sources and definitions, see explanatory note on p. vi.

Agriculture

PRINCIPAL CROPS
('000 metric tons)

	2010	2011	2012
Rice, paddy	267.8	279.0	214.3
Potatoes	55.8	60.0	69.3
Cassava (Manioc)*	529.1	788.0	560.0
Sugar cane	4,150.0*	4,000.0*	4,005.8
Watermelons	49.7	44.4	52.4
Cantaloupes and other melons .	198.9	160.8	132.0
Oil palm fruit	985.8	1,050.0	1,111.3
Bananas†	2,020	2,125	2,136
Plantains	90.0	90.0	80.0
Oranges	252.0	170.0*	280.0
Pineapples	1,976.8	2,269.0	2,484.7
Coffee, green	97.2	100.1	125.1

* FAO estimate(s).
† Unofficial figures.

Aggregate production ('000 metric tons, may include official, semi-official or estimated data): Total cereals 286.5 in 2010, 297.5 in 2011, 231.6 in 2012; Total roots and tubers 653.9 in 2010, 919.6 in 2011, 694.1 in 2012; Total vegetables (incl. melons) 431.1 in 2010, 394.0 in 2011, 366.2 in 2012; Total fruits (excl. melons) 4,732.9 in 2010, 5,078.5 in 2011, 5,435.3 in 2012.

Source: FAO.

LIVESTOCK
('000 head, year ending September, FAO estimates)

	2010	2011	2012
Horses	124	125	126
Asses	8	8	8
Cattle	1,350	1,380	1,400
Pigs	438	432	436
Sheep	3	3	3
Goats	5	5	5
Chickens	23,900	22,900	23,600

Source: FAO.

LIVESTOCK PRODUCTS
('000 metric tons)

	2010	2011	2012
Cattle meat	97.5	96.0	87.5
Pig meat	46.1	51.8	55.4
Chicken meat	105.1	100.2	103.9
Cows' milk	951.7	966.3	1,014.6
Hen eggs	53.5	50.8	59.2
Honey*	1.1	1.1	1.2

* FAO estimates.

Source: FAO.

Forestry

ROUNDWOOD REMOVALS
('000 cubic metres, excl. bark)

	2010	2011	2012
Sawlogs, veneer logs and logs for sleepers	1,080*	919	1,058
Other industrial wood†	246	246	246
Fuel wood†	3,377	3,364	3,352
Total†	4,703	4,529	4,656

* Unofficial figure.
† FAO estimates.
Source: FAO.

SAWNWOOD PRODUCTION
('000 cubic metres, incl. railway sleepers)

	2010*	2011	2012
Broadleaved (hardwood)	540	459	529
Total	540	459	529

* Unofficial figures.
Source: FAO.

Fishing

('000 metric tons, live weight)

	2010	2011	2012
Capture*	21.0	20.5	20.5
Clupeoids*	2.6	2.6	2.6
Tuna-like fishes*	1.4	1.4	1.4
Common dolphinfish*	3.9	3.8	3.8
Sharks, rays, skates, etc.*	2.9	2.6	2.6
Other marine fishes	4.2*	4.1*	n.a.
Aquaculture	26.8	27.8*	27.2*
Tilapias	23.0	24.0	23.4
Whiteleg shrimp	3.2	3.0	3.0
Total catch*	47.8	48.3	47.7

* FAO estimate(s).
Source: FAO.

Industry

SELECTED PRODUCTS
('000 metric tons unless otherwise indicated)

	2008	2009	2010
Raw sugar	351	305	392
Kerosene	2	2	2
Distillate fuel oils	244	127	147
Residual fuel oils	201	91	196
Bitumen	8	14	2
Electric energy (million kWh)	9,474	9,290	9,583

Source: UN Industrial Commodity Statistics Database.

Cement ('000 metric tons, estimates): 1,276 in 2010; 1,600 in 2011; 1,500 in 2012 (Source: US Geological Survey).

Finance

CURRENCY AND EXCHANGE RATES

Monetary Units
100 céntimos = 1 Costa Rican colón.

Sterling, Dollar and Euro Equivalents (30 April 2014)
£1 sterling = 922.489 colones;
US $1 = 548.415 colones;
€1 = 759.555 colones;
10,000 Costa Rican colones = £10.84 = $18.23 = €13.17.

Average Exchange Rate (colones per US $)
2011 505.664
2012 502.901
2013 499.767

GOVERNMENT FINANCE
(central government operations, '000 million colones)

Revenue	2011	2012	2013
Current revenue	3,024.1	3,270.4	3,536.2
Taxation	2,836.1	3,082.0	3,348.6
Income tax	828.7	891.7	1,014.4
Taxes on property	121.0	161.3	199.4
Taxes on goods and services	1,626.4	1,752.6	1,872.8
Taxes on international trade	187.7	197.6	205.5
Non-tax revenue	22.7	22.2	20.8
Current transfers	165.3	166.2	166.8
Capital revenue	0.3	3.9	1.1
Total	3,024.4	3,274.3	3,537.3

Expenditure	2011	2012	2013
Current expenditure	3,566.6	3,943.9	4,471.8
Wages and salaries	1,268.2	1,380.1	1,523.3
Social security contribution	172.6	188.8	203.5
Goods and services	135.6	142.9	158.4
Current transfers	1,540.8	1,760.4	1,955.3
Interest payments	449.4	471.8	631.4
Domestic	390.9	424.8	568.9
External	58.5	47.0	62.5
Capital expenditure	303.2	331.6	400.5
Real investment	65.3	50.2	80.0
Financial investment	6.8	1.3	1.4
Capital transfers	231.1	280.1	319.1
Total	3,869.8	4,275.5	4,872.3

Source: Ministry of Finance, San José.

Public Sector Accounts ('000 million colones): *Total revenue:* 6,275.7 in 2010; 7,039.1 in 2011; 7,675.0 in 2012. *Total expenditure:* 7,199.1 in 2010; 7,783.7 in 2011; 8,550.3 in 2012.

INTERNATIONAL RESERVES
(excl. gold, US $ million at 31 December)

	2011	2012	2013
IMF special drawing rights	203.49	203.68	204.07
Reserve position in IMF	30.73	30.77	30.83
Foreign exchange	4,521.58	6,622.22	7,095.96
Total	4,755.81	6,856.67	7,330.86

Source: IMF, *International Financial Statistics*.

MONEY SUPPLY
('000 million colones at 31 December)

	2011	2012	2013
Currency outside depository corporations	545.7	590.9	640.2
Transferable deposits	4,731.5	5,013.6	5,496.3
Other deposits	78.9	98.6	114.6
Securities other than shares	4,927.7	5,512.1	5,941.9
Broad money	10,283.8	11,215.2	12,193.1

Source: IMF, *International Financial Statistics*.

COST OF LIVING
(Consumer Price Index; base: July 2006 = 100)

	2011	2012	2013
Food and non-alcoholic beverages .	171.6	177.7	184.5
Clothing and footwear	103.4	103.3	102.6
Housing	160.1	171.4	200.2
All items (incl. others) . . .	146.8	153.4	161.5

NATIONAL ACCOUNTS
('000 million colones at current prices)

National Income and Product

	2011	2012*	2013*
GDP in purchasers' values .	20,852.2	22,819.0	24,799.0
Net primary incomes from abroad .	−507.7	−655.6	−729.8
Gross national income . . .	20,344.5	22,163.5	24,069.2
Less consumption of fixed capital .	1,220.7	1,284.1	1,395.5
Net national income . . .	19,123.8	20,879.4	22,673.7
Net current transfers	163.2	167.5	169.7
Gross national disposable income	19,287.0	21,046.8	22,843.3

* Preliminary figures.

Expenditure on the Gross Domestic Product

	2011	2012*	2013*
Government final consumption expenditure	3,730.9	4,035.4	4,446.8
Private final consumption expenditure	13,582.3	14,822.5	15,963.8
Increase in stocks	388.6	305.8	82.7
Gross fixed capital formation .	4,167.8	4,647.0	5,200.8
Total domestic expenditure .	21,869.6	23,810.7	25,694.1
Exports of goods and services .	7,753.5	8,489.2	8,714.1
Less Imports of goods and services	8,770.9	9,480.7	9,609.2
GDP in purchasers' values .	20,852.2	22,819.0	24,799.0
GDP at constant 1991 prices .	2,277.4	2,394.4	2,478.1

* Preliminary figures.

Gross Domestic Product by Economic Activity

	2011	2012*	2013*
Agriculture, hunting, forestry and fishing	1,212.9	1,260.8	1,276.3
Mining and quarrying	29.2	31.9	31.0
Manufacturing	3,286.0	3,517.5	3,636.4
Electricity, gas and water . .	462.2	547.6	768.5
Construction	1,028.1	1,167.2	1,272.3
Trade, restaurants and hotels .	3,288.4	3,563.8	3,798.0
Transport, storage and communications	1,912.0	2,131.8	2,351.3
Finance and insurance . .	1,298.0	1,452.3	1,537.7
Real estate	580.2	634.4	693.5
Other business services . .	1,434.9	1,650.8	1,868.9
Public administration . . .	955.5	1,053.6	1,170.0
Other community, social and personal services	4,437.5	4,856.8	5,372.6
Sub-total	19,924.9	21,868.5	23,776.5
Less Imputed bank service charge	972.8	1,081.1	1,128.1
GDP at basic prices	18,952.1	20,787.4	22,648.1
Taxes on products	1,949.0	2,083.6	2,203.8
Less Subsidies	48.8	51.9	52.9
GDP in purchasers' values .	20,852.2	22,819.0	24,799.0

* Preliminary figures.

BALANCE OF PAYMENTS
(US $ million)

	2010	2011	2012
Exports of goods	4,457.1	4,932.3	5,314.0
Imports of goods	−9,819.1	−11,867.7	−12,741.1
Balance on goods . . .	−5,362.0	−6,935.4	−7,427.2
Exports of services	6,140.7	6,644.4	7,418.6
Imports of services	−1,681.1	−1,668.3	−1,886.0
Balance on goods and services	−902.5	−1,958.8	−1,894.6
Primary income received . . .	199.3	484.1	664.3
Primary income paid . . .	−944.5	−1,051.1	−1,479.1
Balance on goods, services and primary income	−1,647.6	−2,525.8	−2,709.4
Secondary income received . .	605.7	593.5	628.5
Secondary income paid . .	−239.3	−270.6	−295.3
Current balance	−1,281.2	−2,202.9	−2,376.2
Capital account (net) . .	53.5	21.6	37.5
Direct investment assets . .	−24.8	−57.8	−776.8
Direct investment liabilities .	1,465.6	2,155.6	2,636.2
Portfolio investment assets . .	218.6	258.9	192.5
Portfolio investment liabilities .	—	−102.2	1,180.6
Other investment assets . .	−376.5	−243.8	−324.4
Other investment liabilities . .	495.4	417.2	548.7
Net errors and omissions . .	−144.0	−220.8	244.0
Reserves and related items .	406.7	25.7	1,362.2

Source: IMF, *International Financial Statistics*.

External Trade

PRINCIPAL COMMODITIES
(US $ million)

Imports c.i.f.	2011	2012	2013
Food and live animals	959.3	955.8	950.0
Mineral products	2,338.8	2,358.2	2,353.1
Basic manufactures . . .	688.5	1,106.6	1,021.8
Chemicals and related products .	1,792.4	1,861.0	1,821.4
Plastic materials and manufactures	1,380.0	1,259.6	1,304.0
Leather, hides and furs . . .	59.2	44.8	45.0
Paper, paperboard and manufactures	125.2	81.0	77.5
Wood pulp and other fibrous materials	727.7	690.8	751.1
Silk, cotton and textile fibres . .	609.1	628.0	570.5
Footwear, hats, umbrellas, etc. .	143.8	155.4	164.7
Stone manufactures, etc. . .	204.1	192.4	197.2
Natural and cultured pearls . .	46.5	54.6	58.5
Common metals and manufactures	1,521.7	1,512.9	1,407.7
Machinery and electrical equipment	5,201.1	5,098.5	5,207.9
Transport equipment . . .	1,556.4	1,402.5	1,312.1
Optical and topographical apparatus and instruments, etc. .	537.4	635.8	546.2
Total (incl. others)	18,263.8	18,357.2	18,126.9

Exports f.o.b.	2011	2012	2013
Food and live animals	2,821.5	2,993.3	2,922.5
Mineral products	66.4	39.7	36.6
Basic manufactures	966.3	1,043.3	1,255.2
Chemicals and related products	640.0	567.5	569.5
Plastic materials and manufactures	563.6	596.4	627.8
Leather, hides and furs	34.7	23.9	23.8
Paper, paperboard and manufactures	73.6	86.8	65.2
Wood pulp and other fibrous materials	240.7	161.4	131.2
Silk, cotton and textile fibres	220.7	269.1	170.5
Stone manufactures, etc.	101.5	164.5	117.1
Natural and cultured pearls	90.6	105.8	3.0
Common metals and manufactures	404.4	538.6	406.6
Machinery and electrical equipment	2,652.2	2,987.4	3,277.2
Transport equipment	74.9	122.0	86.7
Optical and topographical apparatus and instruments, etc.	1,198.0	1,364.7	1,517.1
Total (incl. others)	10,223.5	11,266.0	11,479.9

PRINCIPAL TRADING PARTNERS
(US $ million)

Imports c.i.f.	2011	2012	2013
Brazil	351.7	424.2	383.4
China, People's Rep.	1,528.5	1,446.0	1,748.4
Colombia	655.9	342.7	358.5
Germany	421.3	318.4	339.8
Guatemala	457.3	416.9	387.4
Japan	688.7	560.6	525.8
Korea, Republic	n.a.	n.a.	329.6
Mexico	1,220.6	1,187.1	1,155.0
USA	8,296.6	9,493.7	9,041.2
Total (incl. others)	18,263.8	18,357.2	18, 126.9

Exports f.o.b.	2011	2012	2013
China, People's Rep.	n.a.	326.7	377.8
El Salvador	285.8	305.0	311.7
Guatemala	407.5	432.5	451.0
Honduras	336.2	349.4	322.8
Hong Kong	517.0	533.4	648.0
Mexico	307.1	314.9	n.a.
Netherlands	686.2	850.0	829.7
Nicaragua	455.8	501.3	498.3
Panama	560.0	584.0	580.1
USA	3,764.4	4,167.0	4,248.5
Total (incl. others)	10,223.5	11,266.0	11,479.9

Transport

ROAD TRAFFIC
(motor vehicles in use at 31 December)

	2009	2010	2011
Passenger cars	594,192	598,021	611,175
Buses and coaches	13,999	14,182	13,969
Lorries and vans	153,492	175,380	174,017
Motorcycles and mopeds	141,470	144,681	130,500

SHIPPING
Flag Registered Fleet
(at 31 December)

	2011	2012	2013
Number of vessels	6	6	8
Total displacement (grt)	2,760	2,760	6,977

Source: Lloyd's List Intelligence (www.lloydslistintelligence.com).

CIVIL AVIATION
(scheduled services)

	2010	2011
Kilometres flown (million)	28	31
Passengers carried ('000)	1,678	1,862
Passenger-km (million)	2,761	2,950
Total ton-km (million)	251	268

Source: UN, *Statistical Yearbook*.

Passengers carried ('000): 1,905 in 2012 (Source: World Bank, World Development Indicators database).

Tourism

FOREIGN TOURIST ARRIVALS BY COUNTRY OF ORIGIN

	2010	2011	2012
Canada	119,654	133,033	151,568
El Salvador	53,669	61,257	64,923
Germany	44,539	49,225	50,938
Guatemala	48,682	54,759	55,334
Mexico	54,662	52,707	66,959
Nicaragua	427,362	432,766	474,011
Panama	77,918	n.a.	90,899
Spain	48,492	47,782	47,505
USA	830,993	858,829	921,097
Total (incl. others)	2,099,829	2,192,059	2,343,213

Tourism receipts (US $ million, excl. passenger transport): 1,999 in 2010; 2,152 in 2011; 2,425 in 2012 (provisional) (Source: World Tourism Organization).

Communications Media

	2011	2012	2013
Telephones ('000 main lines in use)	1,031.6	995.9	967.5
Mobile cellular telephones ('000 subscribers)	4,153.1	5,378.1	7,112.0
Internet subscribers ('000)	452.9	n.a.	n.a.
Broadband subscribers ('000)	413.7	448.1	473.6

Source: International Telecommunication Union.

Education

(2012/13 unless otherwise indicated)

	Institutions	Teachers	Students Males	Females	Total
Pre-primary	2,862	7,693*	60,097	57,233	117,330
Primary	4,069	29,233*	247,085	233,040	480,125
Secondary	951	28,111*	222,801	226,234	449,035
Special	2,420	n.a	8,843	5,911	14,754
Tertiary	52†	4,494‡	92,353§	110,822§	203,175§

* 2005.
† 1999.
‡ 2002/03.
§ 2011/12.

Source: mainly Ministry of Public Education, San José.

Pupil-teacher ratio (primary education, UNESCO estimate): 17.3 in 2010/11 (Source: UNESCO Institute for Statistics).

Adult literacy rate (UNESCO estimates): 97.4% (males 97.3%; females 97.5%) in 2011 (Source: UNESCO Institute for Statistics).

Directory

The Constitution

The present Constitution of Costa Rica was promulgated in November 1949. Its main provisions are summarized below:

GOVERNMENT

The government is unitary: provincial and local bodies derive their authority from the national Government. The country is divided into seven provinces, each administered by a Governor who is appointed by the President. The provinces are divided into cantons, and each canton into districts. There is an elected Municipal Council in the chief city of each canton, the number of its members being related to the population of the canton. The Municipal Council supervises the affairs of the canton. Municipal government is closely regulated by national law, particularly in matters of finance.

LEGISLATURE

The government consists of three branches: legislative, executive and judicial. Legislative power is vested in a single chamber, the Legislative Assembly (Asamblea Legislativa), which meets in regular session twice a year—from 1 May to 31 July, and from 1 September to 30 November. Special sessions may be convoked by the President to consider specified business. The Assembly is composed of 57 deputies elected for four years. The chief powers of the Assembly are to enact laws, levy taxes, authorize declarations of war and, by a two-thirds' majority, suspend, in cases of civil disorder, certain civil liberties guaranteed in the Constitution.

Bills may be initiated by the Assembly or by the Executive and must have three readings, in at least two different legislative periods, before they become law. The Assembly may override the presidential vote by a two-thirds' majority.

EXECUTIVE

The executive branch is headed by the President, who is assisted by the Cabinet. If the President should resign or be incapacitated, the executive power is entrusted to the First Vice-President; next in line to succeed to executive power are the Second Vice-President and the President of the Legislative Assembly.

The President sees that the laws and the provisions of the Constitution are carried out, and maintains order; has power to appoint and remove cabinet ministers and diplomatic representatives, and to negotiate treaties with foreign nations (which are, however, subject to ratification by the Legislative Assembly). The President is assisted in these duties by a Cabinet, each member of which is head of an executive department.

ELECTORATE

Suffrage is universal, compulsory and secret for persons over the age of 18 years.

DEFENCE

The Costa Rican Constitution has a clause outlawing a national army. Only by a continental convention or for the purpose of national defence may a military force be organized.

The Government

HEAD OF STATE

President: LUIS GUILLERMO SOLÍS RIVERA (assumed office 8 May 2014).
First Vice-President: HELIO FALLAS VENEGAS.
Second Vice-President: ANA HELENA CHACÓN ECHEVERRÍA.

THE CABINET
(September 2014)

The Government was formed by members of the Partido Acción Ciudadana.
Minister of the Presidency: MELVIN JIMÉNEZ MARÍN.
Minister of Justice and Peace: CRISTINA RAMÍREZ CHAVARRÍA.
Minister of National Planning and Economic Policy: OLGA MARTA SÁNCHEZ OVIEDO.
Minister of Finance: HELIO FALLAS VENEGAS.
Minister of Foreign Affairs and Worship: MANUEL GONZÁLEZ SANZ.
Minister of Foreign Trade: ALEXANDER MORA DELGADO.
Minister of Public Security, Governance and Police: CELSO GAMBOA SÁNCHEZ.
Minister of Economy, Industry and Commerce: WELMER RAMOS GONZÁLEZ.

Minister of the Environment and Energy: EDGAR GUTIÉRREZ ESPELETA.
Minister of Labour and Social Security: VÍCTOR MANUEL MORALES MORA.
Minister of Public Education: SONIA MARTA MORA ESCALANTE.
Minister of Health: MARÍA ELENA LÓPEZ NÚÑEZ.
Minister of Housing and Settlements: ROSENDO PUJOL MESALLES.
Minister of Public Works and Transport: CARLOS SEGNINI VILLALOBOS.
Minister of Science, Technology and Telecommunications: GISELA KOPPER ARGUEDAS.
Minister of Culture and Youth: ELIZABETH FONSECA CORRALES.
Minister of Tourism: WILHELM VON BREYMANN BARQUERO.
Minister of Agriculture and Livestock: LUIS FELIPE ARAUZ CAVALLINI.
Minister of Human Development and Social Inclusion and President of the Mixed Institute for Social Assistance: CARLOS ALVARADO QUESADA.
Minister of Sport and President of the Costa Rican Institute of Sport and Recreation: CAROLINA MAURI CARABAGUÍAZ.
President of the National Women's Institute: ALEJANDRA MORA MORA.

MINISTRIES

Ministry of Agriculture and Livestock: Antigüo Colegio La Salle, Sabana Sur, Apdo 10094, 1000 San José; tel. 2231-2344; fax 2232-2103; e-mail sunii@mag.go.cr; internet www.mag.go.cr.
Ministry of Culture and Youth: Avdas 3 y 7, Calles 11 y 15, frente al parque España, San José; tel. 2255-3188; fax 2233-7066; e-mail mincjd@mcjd.go.cr; internet www.mcjdcr.go.cr.
Ministry of Economy, Industry and Commerce: 400 m oeste de la Contraloría General de la República, Sabana Sur, Apdo 10216-1000, San José; tel. 2249-1400; fax 2291-2059; e-mail informacion@meic.go.cr; internet www.meic.go.cr.
Ministry of the Environment and Energy: Edif. Vista Palace, Avdas 8 y 10, Calle 25, Apdo 10104, 1000 San José; tel. 2233-4533; fax 2257-0697; e-mail dgpcc.dir@gmail.com; internet www.minae.go.cr.
Ministry of Finance: Edif. Antigüo Banco Anglo, Avda 2a, Calle 3a, San José; tel. 2284-5000; fax 2255-4874; e-mail webmaster1@hacienda.go.cr; internet www.hacienda.go.cr.
Ministry of Foreign Affairs and Worship: Avda 7 y 9, Calle 11 y 13, Apdo 10027, 1000 San José; tel. 2223-7555; fax 2257-6597; e-mail despacho.ministro@rree.go.cr; internet www.rree.go.cr.
Ministry of Foreign Trade: Edif. Centro Comercio Exterior, Avda 1 y 3, Calle 40, Apdo 297, 1007 Centro Colón, San José; tel. 2299-4700; fax 2255-3281; e-mail pep@comex.go.cr; internet www.comex.go.cr.
Ministry of Public Security: Barrio Córdoba, frente al Liceo Castro Madriz, San José; tel. 2586-4000; internet www.seguridadpublica.go.cr.
Ministry of Health: Calle 16, Avda 6 y 8, Apdo 10123, 1000 San José; tel. 2223-0333; fax 2255-2636; e-mail prensams@netsalud.sa.cr; internet www.ministeriodesalud.go.cr.
Ministry of Housing and Settlements: Of. Mall San Pedro, 7°, Costado Norte, Apdo 1753, 2050 San Pedro de Montes de Oca; tel. 2202-7900; fax 2202-7910; e-mail info@mivah.go.cr; internet www.mivah.go.cr.
Ministry of Justice and Peace: 50 m norte de la Clínica Bíblica, frente a la Escuela M. García Flamenco, 1000 San José; tel. 2256-6700; fax 2234-7959; e-mail justicia@gobnet.go.cr; internet www.mjp.go.cr.
Ministry of Labour and Social Security: Edif. Benjamín Núñez, 4°, Barrio Tournón, Apdo 10133, 1000 San José; tel. 2542-0000; fax 2256-2061; e-mail walter.villalobos@mtss.go.cr; internet www.mtss.go.cr.
Ministry of National Planning and Economic Policy: De Autos Subarú 200 m al norte, Barrio Dent, San Pedro de Montes de Oca, Apdo 10127, 1000 San José; tel. 2281-2700; fax 2253-6243; e-mail despacho@mideplan.go.cr; internet www.mideplan.go.cr.
Ministry of the Presidency: Casa Presidencial, Zapote, Apdo 520, 2010 San José; tel. 2207-9100; fax 2253-9078; e-mail sugerencias@presidencia.go.cr; internet www.presidencia.go.cr.
Ministry of Public Education: Edif. Rofas, frente al Hospital San Juan de Dios, Apdo 10087, 1000 San José; tel. 2258-3745; fax 2248-1763; e-mail contraloriaservicios@mep.go.cr; internet www.mep.go.cr.
Ministry of Public Security: Barrio Córdoba, frente al Liceo Castro Madriz, San José; tel. 2586-4000; internet www.seguridadpublica.go.cr.

Ministry of Public Works and Transport: Plaza González Víquez, Calles 9 y 11, Avda 20 y 22, Apdo 10176, 1000 San José; tel. 2523-2000; fax 2257-7405; e-mail ofprensa@mopt.go.cr; internet www.mopt.go.cr.

Ministry of Science, Technology and Telecommunications: 50 m Este del Museo Nacional, Avda Segunda, Calles 19 y 17, Apdo 5589, 1000 San José; tel. 2248-1515; fax 2257-8895; e-mail micit@micit.go.cr; internet www.micit.go.cr.

Ministry of Social Welfare: San José; tel. 2202-4000; fax 2202-4069; e-mail informatica@imas.go.cr; internet www.imas.go.cr.

Costa Rican Institute of Sport and Recreation (ICODER): Parque Metropolitano, La Sabana, Estadio Nacional, Apdo 5009, 1000 San José; tel. 2549-0700; e-mail gabriela.azofeifa@icoder.go.cr; internet www.icoder.go.cr.

Costa Rican Institute of Tourism (ICT): see Tourism.

Mixed Institute for Social Assistance (IMAS): see Trade and Industry—Government Agencies.

National Women's Institute (Instituto Nacional de las Mujeres—INAMU): Edif. SIGMA, detrás del Mall, San Pedro de Montes de Oca, San José; tel. (506) 2527-8405; fax (506) 2253-9772; e-mail despacho@inamu.go.cr; internet www.inamu.go.cr.

President and Legislature

PRESIDENT

Election, First Round, 2 February 2014

Candidate	Valid votes cast	% of valid votes
Luis Guillermo Solís Rivera (PAC)	629,866	30.64
Johnny Araya Monge (PLN)	610,634	29.71
José María Villalta Florez-Estrada (FA)	354,479	17.25
Otto Guevara Guth (ML)	233,064	11.34
Rodolfo Piza Rocafort (PUSC)	123,653	6.02
José Miguel Corrales Bolaños (PPN)	30,816	1.50
Carlos Luis Avendaño Calvo (PRN)	27,691	1.35
Others	45,269	2.20
Total valid votes*	2,055,472	100.00

* In addition there were 43,747 invalid or blank votes.

Election, Second Round, 6 April 2014

Candidate	Valid votes cast	% of valid votes
Luis Guillermo Solís Rivera (PAC)	1,338,321	77.77
Johnny Araya Monge (PLN)	382,600	22.23
Total valid votes*	1,720,921	100.00

* In addition there were 18,314 invalid or blank votes.

LEGISLATIVE ASSEMBLY

President: HENRY MORA JIMÉNEZ (PAC).
General Election, 2 February 2014

Party	Votes cast	% of votes cast	Seats
Partido Liberación Nacional (PLN)	526,531	25.71	18
Partido Acción Ciudadana (PAC)	480,969	23.48	14
Frente Amplio (FA)	269,178	13.14	9
Partido Unidad Social Cristiana (PUSC)	205,247	10.02	8
Movimiento Libertario (ML)	162,559	7.94	3
Partido Renovación Costarricense (PRC)	83,083	4.06	2
Partido Restauración Nacional (PRN)	84,265	4.11	1
Partido Accesibilidad Sin Exclusión (PASE)	81,291	3.97	1
Alianza Demócrata Cristiana (ADC)	23,886	1.17	1
Partido Patria Nueva (PPN)	42,234	2.06	—
Partido Nueva Generación (PNG)	25,060	1.22	—
Others	63,998	3.12	—
Total valid votes	2,048,301	100.00	57

Election Commission

Tribunal Supremo de Elecciones (TSE): Avda 1 y 3, Calle 15, Apdo 2163, 1000 San José; tel. 2287-5555; fax 2255-0213; e-mail secretariatse@tse.go.cr; internet www.tse.go.cr; f. 1949; independent; Pres. LUIS ANTONIO SOBRADO GONZÁLEZ; Sec.-Gen. ERICK ADRIÁN GUZMÁN VARGAS.

Political Organizations

Alianza Demócrata Cristiana (ADC): San José; tel. 2591-9105; e-mail info@alianzademocratacristiana.com; internet alianzademocratacristiana.com; Leader MARIO REDONDO POVEDA.

Alianza Patriótica: Edif. Rojo, 2°, de la esquina sureste del Museo Nacional, 1 cuadra este a mano derecha, San José; tel. 2223-9595; fax 2223-9596; e-mail adrianj.zuniga@gmail.com; Pres. MARIANO FIGUERES OLSEN; Sec.-Gen. ARNOLDO MORA VAGLIO.

Avance Nacional: Barrio Colonia del Río, detrás del Centro Comercial Guadalupe, Guadalupe, Goicoechea, San José; tel. 2256-7375; fax 2223-6714; e-mail contactenos@partidoavancenacional.com; internet partidoavancenacional.com; Pres. JOSÉ MANUEL ECHANDI MEZA; Sec.-Gen. SHIRLEY MARÍA ARAYA CASTILLO.

Centro Democrático y Social: 75 m sur del Restaurante Rostipollos, Barrio Jiménez, Goicoechea, Guadalupe, San José; tel. 2245-7522; fax 2256-6274; e-mail guivarsa@gmail.com; f. 2012; Pres. GUILLERMO VARGAS SALAZAR; Sec.-Gen. JUAN RAFAEL LIZANO SÁENZ.

Frente Amplio (FA): Barrio Amón, costado suroeste del INVU, 25 m sur, Apdo 11481, Moravia, San José; tel. 2258-5641; fax 2010-8467; e-mail info@frenteamplio.org; internet www.frenteamplio.org; f. 2004; Pres. PATRICIA MORA CASTELLANOS; Sec.-Gen. RODOLFO ULLOA BONILLA.

Movimiento Libertario (ML): Of. de Cabinas San Isidro, Barrio Los Yoses Sur, Apdo 4674, 1000 San José; tel. 2283-8600; fax 2283-9600; internet www.movimientolibertario.com; f. 1994; Pres. OTTO GUEVARA GUTH; Sec.-Gen. VÍCTOR DANILO CUBERO CORRALES.

Partido Accesibilidad Sin Exclusión (PASE): San José; tel. 2214-6110; internet partidopase.blogspot.in; f. 2004; Leader OSCAR LÓPEZ ARIAS; Sec. ERIC RAMÓN CHACÓN VALERIO.

Partido Acción Ciudadana (PAC): 25 San Pedro, 425 m sur del Templo Parroquial, San José; tel. 2281-2727; fax 2280-6640; e-mail accionciudadana@pac.or.cr; internet www.pac.or.cr; f. 2000; centre party; Pres. (vacant); Sec.-Gen. MARÍA GABRIELA SABORÍO DE LA ESPRIELLA.

Partido Integración Nacional (PIN): Edif. de Imágenes Médicas, 2°, Apdo 219, 2050 San Pedro de Montes de Oca, San José; tel. 2221-3300; fax 2500-0729; e-mail partidointegracionnacionalcr@gmail.com; f. 1996; Pres. Dr WALTER MUÑOZ CÉSPEDES; Sec.-Gen. HEINER ALBERTO LEMAITRE ZAMORA.

Partido Liberación Nacional (PLN): Mata Redonda, 125 m oeste del Ministerio de Agricultura y Ganadería, Casa Liberacionista José Figueres Ferrer, Apdo 10051, 1000 San José; tel. 2232-5133; fax 2231-4097; e-mail secregeneralpln@ice.co.cr; internet www.pln.co.cr; f. 1952; social democratic party; affiliated to the Socialist International; 500,000 mems; Pres. BERNAL JIMÉNEZ MONGE; Sec.-Gen. ANTONIO CALDERÓN CASTRO.

Partido Nueva Generación (PNG): 250 m al este y 125 m norte de la POPs, contiguo al Parque Infantil, Cinco Esquinas, Llorente, Tibás, San José; tel. 2253-3193; fax 2253-3180; e-mail contacto@partidonuevageneracion.net; internet www.partidonuevageneracion.net; f. 2010; Pres. SERGIO MENA DÍAZ; Sec.-Gen. LUZ MARY ALPÍZAR LOAIZA.

Partido Patria Nueva (PPN): Edif. Amalia, 3°, Of. 4B, del Templo de la Música del Parque Morazán, 100 m sur y 25 m oeste, San José; tel. 2256-3298; e-mail partidopatrianueva@gmail.com; f. 2012; Pres. ALVARO EDUARDO MONTERO MEJÍA; Sec.-Gen. CÉLIMO GUIDO CRUZ.

Partido Renovación Costarricense (PRC): Centro Educativo Instituto de Desarrollo de Inteligencia, Hatillo 1, Avda Villanea, Apdo 31, 1300 San José; tel. 2254-3651; fax 2252-3270; e-mail jimmysos@costarricense.cr; f. 1995; Pres. JUSTO OROZCO ALVAREZ; Sec. JIMMY SOTO SOLANO.

Partido Restauración Nacional (PRN): Del Restaurante la Princesa Marina, 75 m norte, portón amarillo, casa al fondo, contiguo al local de pinturas Protecto, Moravia, San Vicente; tel. 2243-2851; fax 2243-2855; e-mail restauracion.sol@gmail.com; f. 2005; provincial party; Pres. CARLOS LUIS AVENDAÑO CALVO; Sec.-Gen. CÉSAR ALEXANDER ZÚÑIGA RAMÍREZ.

Partido de los Trabajadores (PT): Edif. de Ladrillos en medio de la cuadra, Avda 10, entre Calle 1 y 3, San José; tel. 2222-0442; e-mail secretariado@ptcostarica.org; internet ptcostarica.org; Pres. HÉCTOR ENRIQUE MONESTEL HERRERA; Sec. JAVIER FERNÁNDEZ BARRERO.

Partido Unidad Social Cristiana (PUSC): 100 m al oeste del Hospital de Niños, Paseo Colón, Apdo 10095, 1000 San José; tel. 2280-2920; fax 2248-3678; e-mail alvarado-w@hotmail.com; internet www.pusc.cr; f. 1983; Pres. GERARDO VARGAS ROJAS; Sec.-Gen. WILLIAM ALVARADO BOGANTES.

Unión Nacional: Frente a la Asociación China, Barrio Francisco Peralta, San José; tel. 2289-4670; fax 2234-3207; e-mail partidounionnacional@yahoo.com; f. 2004; Pres. ARTURO ACOSTA MORA; Sec.-Gen. HERNÁN RICARDO ZAMORA ROJAS.

Diplomatic Representation

EMBASSIES IN COSTA RICA

Argentina: McDonald's de Curridabat, 700 m sur y 25 m este, Apdo 1963, 1000 San José; tel. 2234-6520; fax 2283-9983; e-mail erica@mrecic.gov.ar; Ambassador MARTÍN ANTONIO BALZA.

Bolivia: Del Centro Comercial Plaza del Sol, 200 m al sur y 50 metros al este, Curridabat, San José; tel. 2524-3491; fax 2280-0320; e-mail embocr@racsa.co.cr; Chargé d'affaires a.i. JOSÉ ENRRIQUE COLODRO BALDIVIEZO.

Brazil: Edif. Torre Mercedes, 6°, Paseo Colón, Apdo 10132, 1000 San José; tel. 2295-6875; fax 2295-6874; e-mail brasemb.saojose@itamaraty.gov.br; internet www.brasilcostarica.tk; Ambassador MARIA DULCE SILVA BARROS.

Canada: Oficentro Ejecutivo La Sabana, Edif. 5, 3°, detrás de la Contraloría, Centro Colón, Apdo 351, 1007 San José; tel. 2242-4400; fax 2242-4410; e-mail sjcra@international.gc.ca; internet www.canadainternational.gc.ca/costa_rica; Ambassador WENDY DRUKIER.

Chile: Casa 225, Los Yoses, del Automercado Los Yoses 225 m sur, Calle 39, Avdas 10 y 12, Apdo 10102, 1000 San José; tel. 2280-0037; fax 2253-7016; e-mail infocr@minrel,gov.cl; internet chileabroad.gov.cl/costa-rica; Ambassador MIGUEL ÁNGEL GONZÁLEZ MORALES.

China, People's Republic: De la casa de Don Oscar Arias, 100 m sur y 50 m este, Rohrmoser, Pavas, Apdo 1518, 1200 San José; tel. 2291-4811; fax 2291-4820; e-mail embchina_costarica@yahoo.com.cn; internet cr.chineseembassy.org/esp; Ambassador SONG YANBIN.

Colombia: Barrio Dent de Taco Bell, San Pedro, Apdo 3154, 1000 San José; tel. 2283-6871; fax 2283-6818; e-mail esanjose@cancilleria.gov.co; internet www.embajadaencostarica.gov.co; Ambassador HERNANDO HERRERA VERGARA.

Cuba: Sabana Norte, del restaurante El Chicote 100 norte, 50 este y 200 norte, Casa esquinera, costado izquierdo, San José; tel. 2231-6812; fax 2232-2985; e-mail oficinapolitica@consulcubacr.com; internet www.cubadiplomatica.cu/costarica; Ambassador LEDA ELVIRA PEÑA HERNÁNDEZ.

Dominican Republic: McDonald's de Curridabat 400 sur, 100 m este, Apdo 4746, 1000 San José; tel. 2283-8103; fax 2280-7604; e-mail embdominicanacr@ice.co.cr; Ambassador NESTOR JUAN CERÓN SUERO.

Ecuador: Sabana sur de la Contraloría-General de la República, 400 m sur y 75 m este, San José; tel. and fax 2232-1562; e-mail eecucostarica@mmrree.gov.ec; internet www.consuladoecuadorsj.com; Ambassador DAISY TULA ESPINEL DE ALVARADO.

El Salvador: Del Restaurante McDonald's de Plaza del Sol, 7 c. sur y 50 m. este, Curridabat, San José; tel. 2257-7855; fax 2258-1234; e-mail embasacr@amnet.co.cr; internet embajadacostarica.rree.gob.sv/; Ambassador SEBASTIÁN VAQUERANO LÓPEZ.

France: Carretera a Curridabat, de Mitsubishi 200 m sur y 25 m oeste, Apdo 10177, 1000 San José; tel. 2234-4167; fax 2234-4195; e-mail sjfrance@sol.racsa.co.cr; internet www.ambafrance-cr.org; Ambassador JEAN-BAPTISTE CHAUVIN.

Germany: Edif. Torre la Sabana, 8°, Sabana Norte, Apdo 4017, 1000 San José; tel. 2290-9091; fax 2231-6403; e-mail info@san-jose.diplo.de; internet www.san-jose.diplo.de; Ambassador Dr ERNST MARTENS.

Guatemala: De Sabana Sur, del Gimnasio Fitsimons 100 sur y 50 m oeste, Apdo 328, 1000 San José; tel. 2291-6172; fax 2290-4111; e-mail embaguat@ice.co.cr; Ambassador HECTOR ROLANDO PALACIOS LIMA.

Holy See: Barrio Rohrmoser, Centro Colón, Apdo 992, 1007 San José (Apostolic Nunciature); tel. 2232-2128; fax 2231-2557; e-mail nuncio@nunciocr.org; Apostolic Nuncio Rt Most Rev. ANTONIO ARCARI (Titular Archbishop of Caeciri).

Honduras: De la esq. norte de Telética, 175 m. oeste, por el Estadio Nacional, Sabana Oeste, San José; tel. 2232-9506; fax 2291-5147; e-mail embhoncr@embajadahonduras.co.cr; internet www.embajadahonduras.co.cr; Ambassador JUAN ALBERTO LARA BUESO.

Israel: Edif. Centro Colón, 11°, Calle 38 Paseo Colón, Apdo 5147, 1000 San José; tel. 2221-6444; fax 2257-0867; e-mail admin-sec@sanjose.mfa.gov.il; internet sanjose.mfa.gov.il; Ambassador ABRAHAM HADDAD.

Italy: Los Yoses, 5a entrada, Apdo 1729, 1000 San José; tel. 2225-6396; fax 2225-8200; e-mail ambasciata.sanjose@esteri.it; internet www.ambsanjose.esteri.it; Ambassador FRANCESCO CALOGERO.

Japan: Edif. Torre La Sabana, 10°, Sabana Norte, Apdo 501, 1000 San José; tel. 2232-1255; fax 2231-3140; e-mail embjapon@racsa.co.cr; internet www.cr.emb-japan.go.jp; Ambassador MAMORU SHINOHARA.

Korea, Republic: 400 m. norte y 200 m. oeste del Restaurante Rostipollos, Urb. Trejos Montealegre, San Rafael de Escazú, San José; tel. 2220-3160; fax 2220-3168; e-mail koco@mofat.go.kr; internet cri.mofat.go.kr; Ambassador HONG JO CHUN.

Mexico: Avda 7A, No 1371, Apdo 10107, 1000 San José; tel. 2257-0633; fax 2258-2437; e-mail rmision@embamexico.or.cr; internet embamex.sre.gob.mx/costarica; Ambassador FERNANDO BAEZA MELÉNDEZ.

Netherlands: Oficentro Ejecutivo La Sabana (detrás de la Contraloría), Edif. 3, 3°, Sabana Sur, Apdo 10285, 1000 San José; tel. 2296-1490; fax 2296-2933; e-mail sjo@minbuza.nl; internet costarica.nlembajada.org; Ambassador METTE GONGGRIJP.

Nicaragua: Avda Central 2540, Calle 25 bis, Barrio la California, Apdo 1382, 1000 San José; tel. 2233-8747; fax 2221-3036; e-mail embanic@racsa.co.cr; Ambassador HAROLD FERNANDO RIVAS REYES.

Panama: Del Antigüo Higuerón de San Pedro 200 m sur y 25 m este, Barrio La Granja, San Pedro de Montes de Oca, Apdo 103, 2050 San José; tel. 2280-1570; fax 2281-2161; e-mail panaembacr@racsa.co.cr; internet www.embajadadepanamaencostarica.org; Ambassador JOSÉ JAVIER MULINO QUINTERO.

Paraguay: De la Kentucky de Plaza del Sol 600 m al sur y 50 m al este, 12 Curridabat, San Pedro de Montes de Oca, Apdo 2420, 2050 San José; tel. 2234-2932; fax 2234-0891; e-mail embapar@racsa.co.cr; Ambassador OSCAR BUENAVENTURA LLANES TORRES.

Peru: De McDonald's de Plaza del Sol, 500 m al sur y 175 m al este, Curridabat, San José; tel. 2225-9145; fax 2253-0457; e-mail embaperu@amnet.co.cr; Ambassador LUIS WILFREDO SANDIGA CABRERA.

Russia: Barrio Escalante, 100 m norte y 150 m este de la Iglesia Santa Teresita, Apdo 6340, 1000 San José; tel. 2256-9181; fax 2221-2054; e-mail rusemb.costarica@mail.ru; internet www.costarica.mid.ru; Ambassador ALEXANDER DOGADIN.

Spain: Calle 32, entre Paseo Colón y Avda 2, Apdo 10150, 1000 San José; tel. 2222-1933; fax 2257-5126; e-mail Emb.SanJose@maec.es; internet www.maec.es/subwebs/embajadas/sanjosecostarica; Ambassador ELENA MADRAZO HEGEWISCH.

Switzerland: Edif. Centro Colón, 10°, Paseo Colón, Apdo 895, 1007 San José; tel. 2221-4829; fax 2255-2831; e-mail sjc.vertretung@eda.admin.ch; internet www.eda.admin.ch/sanjose; Ambassador YASMINE CHATILA ZWAHLEN.

United Kingdom: Edif. Centro Colón, 11°, Paseo Colón, Apdo 815, 1007 San José; tel. 2258-2025; fax 2233-9938; e-mail britemb@racsa.co.cr; internet www.ukincostarica.fco.gov.uk; Ambassador SHARON ISABEL CAMPBELL.

Uruguay: Trejos Monte Alegre, Escazú, del Vivero Exótica 900 m oeste y 100 m sur, Apdo 3448, 1000 San José; tel. 2288-3424; fax 2288-3070; e-mail embajrou@sol.racsa.co.cr; Ambassador FERNANDO DANIEL ALEJANDRO MARR MERELLO.

USA: Calle 98, Vía 104, Pavas, San José; tel. 2519-2000; fax 2220-2305; e-mail info@usembassy.or.cr; internet sanjose.usembassy.gov; Ambassador S. FITZGERALD HANLEY (designate).

Venezuela: De la Casa de Don Oscar Arias, 100 m al sur, 400 m al oeste y 25 m al sur, Barrio Rohrmoser, Apdo 10230, 1000 San José; tel. 2220-3102; fax 2290-3806; e-mail embve.crsjo@mre.gob.ve; internet embavenezuelacr.org; Ambassador JESÚS JAVIER ARIAS FUENMAYOR.

Judicial System

Ultimate judicial power is vested in the Supreme Court, the justices of which are elected by the Legislative Assembly for a term of eight years, and are automatically re-elected for an equal period, unless the Assembly decides to the contrary by a two-thirds' vote. The Supreme Court justices sit in four courts: the First Court (civil, administrative, agrarian and commercial matters), the Second Court (employment and family), the Third Court (penal) and the Fourth, or Constitutional, Court. There are, in addition, appellate courts, criminal courts, civil courts and special courts. The jury system is not used.

Supreme Court: Sala Constitucional de la Corte Suprema de Justicia, Apdo 5, 1003 San José; tel. 2295-3000; fax 2295-3712;

e-mail sala4-informacion@poder-judicial.go.cr; internet www
.poder-judicial.go.cr; Pres. ZARELA VILLANUEVA.

Attorney-General: JORGE CHAVARRÍA.

Religion

Under the Constitution, all forms of worship are tolerated. Roman
Catholicism is the official religion of the country. Various Protestant
churches are also represented.

CHRISTIANITY
The Roman Catholic Church

Costa Rica comprises one archdiocese and seven dioceses. Roman
Catholics represent some 82% of the total population.

Bishops' Conference: Conferencia Episcopal de Costa Rica, Apdo
7288, 1000 San José; tel. 2221-3053; fax 2221-6662; e-mail seccecor@
racsa.co.cr; internet www.iglesiacr.org; f. 1977; Pres. Most Rev. JOSÉ
RAFAEL QUIROS QUIROS (Archbishop of San José de Costa Rica).

Archbishop of San José de Costa Rica: Most Rev. JOSÉ RAFAEL
QUIROS QUIROS, Arzobispado, Apdo 497, 1000 San José; tel. 2258-
1015; fax 2221-2427; e-mail arzobispo@arquisanjose.org; internet
www.arquisanjose.org.

The Anglican Communion

Costa Rica comprises one of the five dioceses of the Iglesia Anglicana
de la Región Central de América.

Bishop of Costa Rica: Rt Rev. HÉCTOR MONTERROSO GONZALEZ,
Apdo 10520, 1000 San José; tel. 2225-0790; fax 2253-8331; e-mail
hmonterroso@episcopalcostarica.org; internet www
.episcopalcostarica.org.

Other Churches

Church of Jesus Christ of Latter-Day Saints (Mormons): Del
Hotel Marriott, 600m oeste, La Ribera de Belén, 40702 Heredia, San
José; tel. 2293-6681; internet www.lds.org; Bishop SAAVEDRA
BRIONES; 41,353 mems.

Federación de Asociaciones Bautistas de Costa Rica: Apdo
1631, del Banco Nacional en Guadalupe centro, 100 norte y 75 este,
San José; tel. 2253-5820; fax 2253-4723; e-mail fabcr@fabcr.com;
internet www.fabcr.com; f. 1946; represents Baptist churches; Pres.
NIDIA RODRÍGUEZ JIMÉNEZ.

Iglesia Evangélica Metodista de Costa Rica (Evangelical Methodist Church of Costa Rica): Apdo 5481, 1000 San José; tel. 2227-
3321; fax 2227-3243; e-mail oficinacentral@iglesiametodistacr.org;
internet iglesiametodistacr.org; autonomous since 1973; affiliated to
the United Methodist Church; 6,000 mems; Pres. Bishop LUIS F.
PALOMO.

Iglesia Luterana Costarricense (Lutheran Church of Costa Rica):
Apdo 1890, Paseo de los Estudiantes, 1002 San José; tel. 2226-1792;
fax 2227-1984; e-mail direccionejecutiva@ilco.cr; f. 1955; German
congregation; 220 mems; Bishop MELVIN JIMÉNEZ; Exec. Dir XINIA
CHACÓN RODRÍGUEZ.

BAHÁ'Í FAITH

National Spiritual Assembly of the Bahá'ís of Costa Rica: Apdo
553, 1150 La Uruca; tel. 2520-2127; fax 2296-1033; e-mail info@
bahaicr.org; internet www.bahaicr.org; f. 1942.

The Press
DAILIES

Al Día: Llorente de Tibás, Apdo 10138, 1000 San José; tel. 2247-4647;
fax 2247-4665; e-mail redaccionad@aldia.co.cr; internet www.aldia
.co.cr; f. 1992; morning; independent; Dir GUSTAVO JIMÉNEZ; Editor
ANTONIO ALFARO; circ. 60,000.

Diario Extra: Edif. de La Prensa Libre, Calle 4, Avda 4, Apdo 177,
1009 San José; tel. 2223-6666; fax 2223-6101; e-mail redaccion@
diarioextra.com; internet www.diarioextra.com; f. 1978; morning;
independent; Dir IARY GOMÉZ; circ. 157,000.

La Gaceta: La Uruca, Apdo 5024, San José; tel. 2296-9570; e-mail
direccion@imprenta.go.cr; internet www.gaceta.go.cr; f. 1878; official gazette; Dir JORGE LUIS VARGAS ESPINOZA; circ. 5,300.

La Nación: Llorente de Tibás, Apdo 10138, 1000 San José; tel. 2247-
4747; fax 2247-5022; e-mail agonzales@nacion.com; internet www
.nacion.com; f. 1946; morning; independent; Dir YANANCY NOGUERA;
Editor ARMANDO MAYORGA; circ. 90,000.

La Nueva Prensa: San José; tel. 8537-3219; e-mail
lanuevaprensacr@gmail.com; internet www.lanuevaprensacr.com;

f. 2007; aimed at Nicaraguans living in Costa Rica; Editor ALONSO
MEJÍA.

La Prensa Libre: Edif. Borrasé, Calle 4, Avda 4, Apdo 10121, 1000
San José; tel. 2547-9300; fax 2223-4671; e-mail plibre@prensalibre
.cr; internet www.prensalibre.cr; f. 1889; evening; independent; Dir
WILLIAM GÓMEZ VARGAS; Editor SANDRA GONZALEZ VARGAS; circ.
56,000.

La República: Barrio Tournón, Guadalupe, Apdo 2130, 1000 San
José; tel. 2522-3300; fax 2257-0401; e-mail redaccion@larepublica
.net; internet www.larepublica.net; f. 1950; reorganized 1967;
morning; independent; Editor DANIEL CHACÓN; circ. 61,000.

PERIODICALS

Abanico: Calle 4, Avda 4, Apdo 10121, 1000 San José; tel. 2223-6666;
fax 2223-4671; e-mail abanico@prensalibre.co.cr; internet www
.prensalibre.cr; weekly supplement of La Prensa Libre; women's
interests; Editor EFRÉN LÓPEZ; circ. 50,000.

Actualidad Económica: San José; tel. 2226-6483; fax 2224-1528;
e-mail contacto@actualidad.co.cr; internet www.actualidad.co.cr;
Dir NORA RUIZ.

Eco Católico: Calle 22, Avdas 3 y 5, Apdo 1064, San José; tel. 2222-
8391; fax 2256-0407; e-mail info@ecocatolico.org; internet www
.ecocatolico.org; f. 1883; Catholic weekly; Dir MARTÍN RODRÍGUEZ
GONZÁLEZ; circ. 20,000.

El Financiero: Grupo Nación, Edif. Subsidiarias, Llorente de Tibás,
185-2120 Guadalupe; tel. 2247-5555; fax 2247-5177; e-mail
redaccion@elfinancierocr.com; internet www.elfinancierocr.com;
f. 1995; Dir JOSÉ DAVID GUEVARA MUÑOZ.

INCAE Business Review: Apdo 960-4050, Alajuela; tel. 2258-6834;
fax 2258-2874; e-mail info@revistaincae.com; internet www
.revistaincae.com; f. 1982; publ. by INCAE business school; Dir
MARLENE DE ESTRELLA LÓPEZ; circ. 18,000.

Perfil: Llorente de Tibás, Apdo 1517, 1100 San José; tel. 2247-4345;
fax 2247-5110; e-mail perfil@nacion.co.cr; internet www.perfilcr
.com; f. 1984; fortnightly; women's interests; Dir ISABEL OVARES;
Man. Editor THAIS AGUILAR ZÚÑIGA; circ. 16,000.

The Tico Times: Calle 15, Avda 8, Apdo 4632, 1000 San José; tel.
2258-1558; fax 2223-6378; e-mail info@ticotimes.net; internet www
.ticotimes.net; f. 1956; weekly; in English; Editor STEVE MACK; circ.
15,210.

PRESS ASSOCIATIONS

Colegio de Periodistas de Costa Rica: Sabana Este, Calle 42,
Avda 4, Apdo 5416, San José; tel. 2233-5850; fax 2223-8669; e-mail
direccion@colper.or.cr; internet www.colper.or.cr; f. 1969; 1,447
mems; Pres. Dr MARLON MORA JIMÉNEZ; Exec. Dir CLARIBET MORERA.

Sindicato Nacional de Periodistas de Costa Rica: Edif. Colegio
de Periodistas de Costa Rica, 2°, diagonal al Gimnasio Nacional, San
José; tel. 2222-7589; fax 2258-3229; e-mail info@
sindicatodeperiodistas.org; internet sindicatodeperiodistas.org;
f. 1970; 220 mems; Sec.-Gen. SANTIAGO ORTÍZ.

Publishers

Caribe-Betania Editores: Apdo 1.307, San José; tel. 2222-7244;
e-mail info@editorialcaribe.com; internet www.caribebetania.com;
f. 1949 as Editorial Caribe; present name adopted 1992; division of
Thomas Nelson Publrs; religious textbooks; Exec. Vice-Pres. TAMARA
L. HEIM; Dir JOHN STROWEL.

Editorial Costa Rica: Calle 1, entre avda 8 y 10, esq. suroeste del
Banco Popular, 250 m al sur, Apdo 10010-1000, San José; tel. 2233-
0812; fax 2233-1949; e-mail difusion@editorialcostarica.com;
internet www.editorialcostarica.com; f. 1959; govt-owned; cultural;
Pres. LUIS ENRIQUE ARCE NAVARRO; Gen. Man. MARÍA ISABEL BRENES
ALVARADO.

Editorial Fernández Arce: 50 este de Sterling Products, la
Paulina de Montes de Oca, Apdo 2410, 1000 San José; tel. 2224-
5201; fax 2225-6109; e-mail ventas@fernandez-arce.com; internet
www.fernandez-arce.com; f. 1967; textbooks for primary, secondary
and university education; Dir Dr MARIO FERNÁNDEZ ARCE.

Editorial INBio de Costa Rica: San José; tel. 2507-8183; e-mail
editorial@inbio.ac.cr; internet www.inbio.ac.cr/editorial; f. 2000;
part of Instituto Nacional de Biodiversidad; Man. FABIO ROJAS.

Editorial Legado: Apdo 2160, 2050 San José; tel. 2280-8007; fax
2280-0945; e-mail legado@editlegado.com; internet www.editlegado
.com; f. 1976; Gen. Man. SEBASTIÁN VAQUERANO.

Editorial Tecnológica de Costa Rica: 1 km al sur de la Basílica de
Los Angeles, Apdo 159-7050, Cartago; tel. 2550-2297; fax 2552-5354;
e-mail editorial@tec.ac.cr; internet www.tec.ac.cr; f. 1978; Dir ANA
RUTH VÍLCHEZ RODRÍGUEZ.

Editorial de la Universidad Autónoma de Centro América (UACA): Apdo 7637, 1000 San José; tel. 2272-9100; fax 2271-2046; e-mail info@uaca.ac.cr; internet www.uaca.ac.cr; f. 1981; Editor JULISSA MÉNDEZ MARÍN.

Editorial Universidad de Costa Rica: Ciudad Universitaria Rodrigo Facio, San Pedro, Montes de Oca, 2060 San José; tel. 2511-5310; fax 2511-5257; e-mail direccion.siedin@ucr.ac.cr; internet www.editorial.ucr.ac.cr; Dir ALBERTO MURILLO-HERRERA.

Editorial de la Universidad Estatal a Distancia (EUNED): Mercedes de Montes de Oca, Apdo 474-2050, San José; tel. 2527-2440; fax 2234-9138; e-mail euned@uned.ac.cr; internet www.uned.ac.cr/editorial; f. 1979; Pres. Dr LUIS ALBERTO CAÑAS ESCALANTE; Dir RENÉ MUIÑOS GUAL.

Editorial Universidad Nacional: Campus Universitario, Frente Escuela de Ciencias Ambientales, Apdo 86, 3000 Heredia; tel. 2277-3204; fax 2277-3825; e-mail editoria@una.ac.cr; internet www.una.ac.cr/euna; f. 1976; Pres. CARLOS FRANCISCO MONGE.

Grupo Editorial Norma: Zona Franca Metropolitana Local 7B, Barreal de Heredia, Heredia, Apdo 592, 1200 Pavas; tel. 2293-1333; fax 2239-3947; e-mail gerencia@farben.co.cr; internet www.norma.com; fmrly Ediciones Farben; Man. Editor ALEXANDER OBONAGA.

Grupo Santillana: La Uruca 78, 1150 San José; tel. 2220-4242; fax 2220-1320; e-mail santilla@santillana.co.cr; internet www.gruposantillana.co.cr; f. 1993; Editorial Dir ELSA MORALES CORDERO.

Imprenta Nacional: La Uruca, San José; tel. 2296-9570; e-mail direccion@imprenta.go.cr; internet www.imprentanacional.go.cr; Dir-Gen. JORGE VARGAS ESPINOZA.

Librería Lehmann, Imprenta y Litografía, Ltda: Calles 1 y 3, Avda Central, Apdo 10011, 1000 San José; tel. 2522-4848; fax 2233-0713; e-mail servicio@librerialehmann.com; internet www.librerialehmann.com; f. 1896; general fiction, educational, textbooks; Man. Dir ANTONIO LEHMANN GUTIÉRREZ.

Océcor de CR: Edif. Océano, Sabana Norte, del ICE 300m al Noreste, San José; tel. 2210-2000; fax 2210-2061; e-mail ocecor@racsa.co.cr; internet www.oceano.com; Gen. Man. JORGE ROJAS.

PUBLISHING ASSOCIATION

Cámara Costarricense del Libro: Paseo de los Estudiantes, Apdo 1571, 1002 San José; tel. 2225-1363; fax 2253-4297; e-mail ccl@libroscr.com; internet www.libroscr.com; f. 1978; Pres. DUNIA SOLANO AGUILAR.

Broadcasting and Communications

TELECOMMUNICATIONS

Cabletica: Sabana Oeste, 25 m al sur del Estadio Nacional, contiguo a Canal 7, San José; tel. 2210-1450; fax 2520-7777; e-mail servicioalcliente@cabletica.com; internet www.cabletica.com; cable television and internet services; Gen. Man. HILDA MORENO.

Claro CR Telecomunicaciones, SA: Ruta 27, Salida de Santa Ana hacia Lindora, 500 m norte y 400 m este, Pozos de Santa Ana, San José; tel. 2296-3136; e-mail clientes@claro.cr; internet www.claro.cr; f. 2011; subsidiary of América Móvil, Mexico; Exec. Dir RICARDO TAYLOR.

Instituto Costarricense de Electricidad (ICE): govt agency for power and telecommunications (see Utilities)

Kölbi: Sabana Norte, San José; tel. 2000-7720; e-mail tuserviciokolbi@ice.go.cr; cellular and internet services; owned by ICE; Gen. Man. CARLOS MECUTCHEN AGUILAR.

Radiográfica Costarricense, SA (RACSA): Avda 5, Calle 1, frente al Edif. Numar, Apdo 54, 1000 San José; tel. 2287-0087; fax 2287-0379; e-mail racsaenlinea@racsa.co.cr; internet www.racsa.co.cr; f. 1921; state telecommunications co, owned by ICE; Gen. Man. ORLANDO CASCANTE.

Movistar (Telefónica de Costa Rica TC, SA): Edif. Los Balcones, 4°, Centro de Negocios Plaza Roble, Escazú, San José; internet www.movistar.co.cr; f. 2011 in Costa Rica; subsidiary of Telefónica, Spain; Dir-Gen. JORGE ABADÍA.

Tigo: Edif. Sabana Real, Sabana Sur, del MAG 200 m este, San José; tel. 4030-9000; internet www.tigo.cr; f. 2004 as Amnet Cable; adopted present name in 2012; cable television, cellular and internet services; subsidiary of Millicom International Cellular (Luxembourg); Gen. Man. ANGELO IANNUZZELLI.

Regulatory Authority

Superintendencia de Telecomunicaciones (SUTEL): Edif. Tapantí, 3°, Complejo Multipark, 100 m norte Construplaza, Guachipelín de Escazú, San José; tel. 4000-0000; fax 2215-6821; e-mail info@sutel.go.cr; internet www.sutel.go.cr; f. 2008; regulatory body; forms part of the Autoridad Reguladora de los Servicios Públicos

(ARESEP—see Trade and Industry—Utilities); Pres. MARYLEANA MÉNDEZ.

BROADCASTING

Radio

Cadena Radial Costarricense: 75 m oeste de la Pozuelo, La Uruca, San José; tel. 2220-1001; fax 2255-4483; e-mail aguevara@crc.cr; internet www.crc.cr; operates nine AM and FM radio stations; Dir ANDRÉS QUINTANA CAVALLINI.

Central de Radios Costa Rica: Costado sur oeste, Puente Juan Pablo II, La Uruca, San José; tel. 2296-6093; fax 2296-0413; e-mail ventas@monumental.co.cr; internet www.cdr.cr; f. 1929; operates Radio Monumental, Radio ZFM, Momentos Reloj, Best FM, EXA FM, La Mejor FM, Radio Disney and 4 AM; Gen. Man. HERNAN AZOFEIFA.

Faro del Caribe: Apdo 2710, 1000 San José; tel. 2286-1755; fax 2227-1725; e-mail info@farodelcaribe.org; internet www.farodelcaribe.org; f. 1948; religious and cultural programmes in Spanish and English; non-commercial; Dir LUIS SERRANO.

FCN Radio Internacional (Family Christian Network): Apdo 60-2020, Zapote, San José; tel. 2209-8000; fax 2293-7993; e-mail info@fcnradio.com; internet www.fcnradio.com; non-commercial; Dir Dr DeCAROL WILLIAMSON.

Grupo Centro: Tibás, 100 norte y 125 oeste de la Municipalidad, Apdo 6133, 1000 San José; tel. 2240-7591; fax 2236-3672; e-mail info@radiocentrocr.com; internet www.radiocentrocr.com; f. 1971; operates Radio Centro 96.3 FM, Radio 820 AM, Televisora Guanacasteca Channels 16 and 28; Dir ROBERTO HERNÁNDEZ RAMÍREZ.

Grupo Columbia: 400 m oeste de la Casa Presidencial, Zapote, Apdo 168-2020, San José; tel. 2224-0707; fax 2225-9275; e-mail columbia@columbia.co.cr; internet www.columbia.co.cr; operates Radio Columbia, Radio Dos, Radio 955 Jazz; Dir YASHÍN QUESADA ARAYA; Gen. Man. MIGUEL MONGE.

Radio 16: Centro Comercial San Francisco, Calle 5 y 6, Grecia 16-4100, Alajuela; tel. 2494-5356; fax 2494-2031; e-mail gerencia@radio16.com; internet www.radio16.com; Dir LUIS GUSTAVO JIMÉNEZ RAMÍREZ.

Radio América: Sociedad Periódistica Extra Ltda, Edif. Borrasé de la Prensa Libre, Calle 4, Avda 4, Fecosa 177, 1009 San José; tel. 2223-6666; fax 2255-3712; e-mail radioamerica@780am.com; internet www.780america.com; f. 1948 as Radio América Latina; changed name as above in 1996; Dir ADRIÁN MARRERO REDONDO.

Radio Chorotega: Conferencia Episcopal de Costa Rica, Casa Cural de Santa Cruz, Apdo 92, 5175 Guanacaste; tel. and fax 2680-0447; e-mail ugiocr@hotmail.com; internet www.radiochorotega1100am.com; f. 1983; Roman Catholic station; Co-ordinator-Gen. JOSÉ MARCELINO MAYORGA CASTILLO.

Radio Emaús: Edif. CENAP, contiguo a la Of. Parroquial, Parroquia de Nuestra Señora de Lourdes, San Vito, Coto Brus; tel. and fax 2773-3101; fax 2773-4035; e-mail radioemaus@racsa.co.cr; internet radioemaus.org; f. 1962; Roman Catholic station; religious programmes; Dir Rev. WILLIAM RODRGUEZ LÉON.

Radio Fides: Avda 4, 2°, costado sur de la Catedral Metropolitana, Curia Metropolitana, Apdo 5079, 1000 San José; tel. 2258-1415; fax 2233-2387; e-mail programas@radiofides.co.cr; internet www.radiofides.co.cr; f. 1952; Roman Catholic station; non-commercial; Dir JASON GRANADOS SÁNCHEZ.

Radio Musical: 1 km al este Hipermás, Carretera a 3 Ríos, Apdo 854, 1000 San José; tel. 2518-2290; fax 2518-2270; e-mail cabina@radiomusical.com; internet www.radiomusical.com; f. 1951; Gen. Man. JAVIER CASTRO.

Radio Nacional: 1 km oeste del Parque Nacional de Diversiones, La Uruca, Apdo 7, 1980 San José; tel. 2231-3331; fax 2220-0070; e-mail sdiaz@sinart.go.cr; internet www.sinart.go.cr; f. 1978; non-commercial; Dir FREDDY GÓMEZ HERNÁNDEZ.

Radio Santa Clara: Edif. CENCO, Santa Clara, San Carlos, Apdo 221, Ciudad Quesada, Alajuela; tel. 2460-6666; fax 2460-2151; e-mail radio@radiosantaclara.org; internet www.radiosantaclara.org; f. 1984; Roman Catholic station; non-commercial; Dir Rev. MARCO ANTONIO SOLÍS V.

Sistema Radiofónico de la Universidad de Costa Rica: Ciudad Universitaria Rodrigo Facio, San Pedro, Montes de Oca, Apdo 2060, 1000 San José; tel. 2511-6850; fax 2511-4832; e-mail radiosucr@gmail.com; internet radios.ucr.ac.cr; f. 1949; stations include Radio Universidad (96.7 FM), Radio U (101.9 FM) and Radio 870 UCR (870 AM); Dir GISELLE BOZA SOLANO.

Television

Cablevision de Costa Rica, SA: Edif. CableVision, Calle Privada, esq. noreste del colegio San Francis, 75 m este y 25 m sur, Moravia, San José; tel. 2545-1111; fax 2236-8801; e-mail mbarboza@

cablevision.co.cr; internet www.cablevision.co.cr; more than 100 channels; digital television; Gen. Man. LEYDA ELIZABETH LOMBANA.

Representaciones Televisivas Repretel (Canales 4, 6 y 11): Edif. Repretel, La Uruca del Hospital México, 300 m al oeste, Apdo 2860, 1000 San José; tel. 2299-7200; fax 2232-4203; e-mail info@ repretel.com; internet www.repretel.com; f. 1993; Pres. FERNANDO CONTRERAS LÓPEZ; News Dir MARCELA ANGULO.

Sistema Nacional de Radio y Televisión Cultural (SINART): 1 km al oeste del Parque Nacional de Diversiones La Uruca, Apdo 7, 1980 San José; tel. 2231-3333; fax 2231-6604; e-mail secretariapresidencia@sinart.go.cr; internet www.sinart.go.cr; f. 1977; cultural; Dir-Gen. RODRIGO ARIAS CAMACHO.

Telefides (Canal 40): detrás de la Imprenta Nacional, de La Kia Motors, 200 m sur y 200 m oeste, La Uruca, San José; tel. 2520-1112; fax 2290-5346; e-mail info@telefides.com; internet www.telefides .com; f. 1992; Man. SARAY AMADOR.

Televisora de Costa Rica (Canal 7), SA (Teletica): Costado oeste Estadio Nacional, Apdo 3876, San José; tel. 2290-6245; fax 2231-6258; e-mail escribanos@teletica.com; internet www.teletica.com; f. 1960; operates Channel 7; Pres. OLGA COZZA DE PICADO; Gen. Man. RENÉ PICADO COZZA.

Regulatory Authorities

Asociación Costarricense de Información y Cultura (ACIC): Apdo 365, 1009 San José; tel. 2227-4694; f. 1983; independent body; controls private radio stations; Pres. MIGUEL ANGEL AGÜERO ALFARO.

Cámara Nacional de Radio (CANARA): Paseo de los Estudiantes, Apdo 1583, 1002 San José; tel. 2256-2338; fax 2255-4483; e-mail info@canara.org; internet www.canara.org; f. 1947; Pres. GUSTAVO PIEDRA GUZMÁN; Sec. CARLOS LAFUENTE CHRYSSOPOULOS.

Control Nacional de Radio (CNR): Edif. García Pinto, 2°, Calle 33, Avdas Central y Primera, Barrio Escalante, Apdo 1344, 1011 San José; tel. 2524-0455; fax 2524-0454; e-mail controlderadio@ice.co.cr; internet www.controlderadio.go.cr; f. 1954; governmental supervisory department; Dir FERNANDO VÍCTOR.

Finance

(cap. = capital; res = reserves; dep. = deposits; m. = million; brs = branches; amounts in colones, unless otherwise indicated)

BANKING

Central Bank

Banco Central de Costa Rica: Avdas Central y Primera, Calles 2 y 4, Apdo 10058, 1000 San José; tel. 2243-3333; fax 2243-4566; internet www.bccr.fi.cr; f. 1950; cap. and res −1,276,176.5m., dep. 3,991,482.1m. (Dec. 2009); state-owned; Pres. OLIVIER CASTRO PÉREZ; Gen. Man. (vacant).

State-owned Banks

Banco de Costa Rica (BCR): Avdas Central y 2da, Calles 4 y 6, Apdo 10035,1000 San José; tel. 2287-9000; fax 2255-0911; e-mail bancobcr@bancobcr.com; internet www.bancobcr.com; f. 1877; responsible for industry; cap. 112,052.8m., res 201,514.4m., dep. 3,299,840.5m. (Dec. 2013); Pres. RONALD SOLÍS BOLAÑOS; Gen. Man. MARIO RIVERO TURCIOS; 136 brs.

Banco Crédito Agrícola de Cartago (BANCREDITO): Costado sur de la Catedral de Cartago (Iglesia del Carmen), 7050 Cartago; tel. 2550-0202; fax 2551-8538; e-mail zailyn.espinoza@bancreditocr .com; internet www.bancreditocr.com; f. 1918; cap. 4,372.4m., res 43,126.4m., dep. 459,057.9m. (Dec. 2013); Pres. THELVIN CABEZAS GARITA; CEO GERARDO PORRAS SANABRIA.

Banco Nacional de Costa Rica: Avda 1–3, Calles 2 y 4, Apdo 10015, 1000 San José; tel. 2212-2000; fax 2233-6356; e-mail bncr@ bncr.fi.cr; internet www.bncr.fi.cr; f. 1914; responsible for the agricultural sector; cap. 118,130.3m., res 271,774.5m., dep. 4,080,227.3m. (Dec. 2013); Pres. ALFREDO VOLIO PÉREZ; Gen. Man. FERNANDO NARANJO VILLALOBOS; 150 brs.

Banco Popular y de Desarrollo Comunal: Calle 1, Avda 2, Apdo 10190, 1000 San José; tel. 2211-7000; fax 2255-1966; e-mail popularenlinea@bp.fi.cr; internet www.bancopopular.fi.cr; f. 1969; cap. 130,000m., res 103,998.7m., dep. 1,352,769.9m. (Dec. 2012); Pres. Dr FRANCISCO ANTONIO PACHECO; Gen. Man. GERARDO PORRAS SANABRIA.

Private Banks

Banca Promérica de Costa Rica, SA: Centro Corporativo El Cedral, Trejos Montealegre, Escazú, Costado Oeste del Hipermás, Apdo 1289, 1200 San José; tel. 2505-7000; fax 2505-7081; e-mail solucion@promerica.fi.cr; internet www.promerica.fi.cr; cap.

25,930.1m., res 6,456.3m., dep. 269,273.9m. (Dec. 2013); Pres. EDGAR ZURCHER GURDIÁN; 21 brs.

Banco BAC San José, SA: Calle Central, Avdas 3 y 5, Apdo 5445, 1000 San José; tel. 295-9797; fax 2222-7103; e-mail info@bacsanjose .com; internet www.bacsanjose.com; f. 1986; fmrly Bank of America, SA; cap. 140,245.9m., res 23,647.6m., dep. 1,267,779.3m. (Dec. 2013); Pres. ERNESTO CASTEGNARO ODIO; Gen. Man. GERARDO CORRALES BRENES; 38 brs.

Banco BCT, SA: 150 m norte de la Catedral Metropolitana, San José; tel. 2212-8000; fax 2222-3706; e-mail info@corporacionbct.com; internet www.bancobct.com; f. 1984; cap. 15,500m., res 2,204.6m., dep. 147,498.6m. (Dec. 2013); merged with Banco del Comercio, SA, in 2000; Gen. Man. ALVARO SABORIO DE ROCAFORT.

Banco Citibank de Costa Rica, SA: De La Rotonda Juan Pablo II, 150 m norte, Contiguo, La Uruca, Apdo 6531, 1000 San José; tel. 2299-0299; fax 2296-0027; e-mail cuscatlan@cuscatlancr.com; internet www.citibank.co.cr; f. 1984 as Banco de Fomento Agrícola; changed name to Banco BFA in 1994 and became Cuscatlan in 2000; current name adopted in 2008 after acquisition by Citi; Banco CMB (Costa Rica) SA merged in Oct.2012; cap. 51,763.8m., res 7,734.5m., dep. 352,063.5m. (Dec. 2013); Pres. RAÚL ARMANDO ANAYA E.; Gen. Man. JAIME ALBERTO MARTINEZ ALVAREZ.

Banco Davivienda (Costa Rica), SA: Barrio Tournón, Diagonal a Ulacit, Apdo 7983, 1000 San José; tel. 2588-9000; fax 2287-1020; internet www.davivienda.cr; f. 1981 as Banco Agroindustrial y de Exportaciones, SA; became Banco Banex SA in 1987; incorporated Banco Metropolitano in 2001 and Banco Bancrecen in 2002, became Banco HSBC in 2007; bought by Banco Davivienda (Colombia) in 2012; cap. 57,597.2m., res 9,295.4m., dep. 457,431.6m. (Dec. 2013); Pres. PEDRO URIBE TORRES; 31 brs.

Banco Improsa, SA: Barrio Tournón, costado sur del Periódico La República, San José; tel. 2284-4000; fax 2284-4009; e-mail banimpro@sol.racsa.co.cr; internet www.improsa.com; cap. 19,943.2m., res 3,706.7m, dep. 134,846.7m. (Dec. 2013); Pres. MARIANELA ORTUÑO PINTO; Gen. Man. FÉLIX ALPÍZAR LOBO.

Banco Lafise: Fuente de la Hispanidad 50 m este, San Pedro, Montes de Oca; tel. 2246-0800; fax 2280-5090; e-mail info@lafise.fi.cr; internet www.lafise.fi.cr; f. 1974; owned by Grupo Lafise; cap. 15,505.7m., res 7,590m., dep. 234,943.5m. (Dec. 2013); Pres. ROBERTO J. ZAMORA LLANES; Gen. Man. GILBERTO SERRANO.

Bansol (Banco de Soluciones de Costa Rica, SA): Montes de Oca, frente al costado norte del Mall San Pedro, Apdo 10882, 1000 San José; tel. 2528-1800; fax 2528-1880; e-mail info@bansol.fi.cr; internet www.bansol.fi.cr; f. 2010; owned by Grupo Financiera Acobo; internet banking; cap. 10,839.4m., res 167.8m, dep. 105,836.4m. (Dec. 2013); Pres. JACK LOEB CASANOVA; Gen. Man. CARLOS FERNÁNDEZ; 5 brs.

Scotiabank de Costa Rica (Canada): Frente a la esquina noroeste de La Sabana, Edif. Scotiabank, Apdo 5395, 1000, San José; tel. 2210-4000; fax 2210-4510; e-mail servicioalcliente@scotiabank.com; internet www.scotiabankcr.com; f. 1995; cap. 64,314.2m., res 41,878.2m, dep. 713,868m. (Dec. 2012); Pres. JUAN CARLOS GARCÍA VIZCAÍNO; Gen. Man. BRIAN W. BRADY; 13 brs.

Banking Associations

Asociación Bancaria Costarricense: Apdo 7-0810, 1000 San José; tel. 2253-2898; fax 2225-0987; e-mail ejecutiva@abc.fi.cr; internet www.abc.fi.cr; Pres. GILBERTO SERRANO G.; Exec. Dir MARÍA ISABEL CORTÉS C.

Cámara de Bancos e Instituciones Financieras de Costa Rica (CBF): Edif. Torre Mercedes, 2°, Paseo Colón, San José; tel. 2256-4652; fax 2221-9444; e-mail info@camaradebancos.fi.cr; internet www.camaradebancos.fi.cr; f. 1968; Pres. GUILLERMO QUESADA O.; Exec. Dir ANNABELLE ORTEGA A.

STOCK EXCHANGE

Bolsa Nacional de Valores, SA: Parque Empresarial FORUM (Autopista Próspero Fernández), Santa Ana, Apdo 03-6155, 1000 San José; tel. 2204-4848; fax 2204-4749; e-mail servicioalcliente@bolsacr .com; internet www.bolsacr.com; f. 1976; Pres. Dr GILBERTO SERRANO GUTIÉRREZ; Gen. Man. JOSÉ RAFAEL BRENES.

INSURANCE

State monopoly of the insurance sector was ended in 2008.

Supervisory Authorities

Instituto Nacional de Seguros: Avdas 7 y 9, Calles 9 y 9B, Apdo 10061, 1000 San José; tel. 2287-6000; fax 2255-3381; e-mail contactenos@ins-cr.com; internet www.ins-cr.com; f. 1924; Exec. Pres. SERGIO IVÁN ALFARO SALAS; Vice-Pres. LUIS ALBERTO CASAFONT FLORES.

Superintendencia General de Seguros (SUGESE): Edif. Torre del Este, 8°, San Pedro de Montes de Oca, San José; tel. 2243-5108; fax 2243-5151; e-mail sugese@sugese.fi.cr; internet www.sugese.fi.cr; f. 2010; regulates the insurance sector; Supt TOMÁS SOLEY PÉREZ.

Principal Companies

ALICO Costa Rica, SA (American Life Insurance Co): Santa Ana Forum 1, Torre 1, 2°, San José; tel. 2204-6300; fax 2288-0931; e-mail servicioalclientecr@palig.com; internet www.alico.co.cr; f. 2010; part of MetLife Inc; Pres. JOSÉ S. SUQUET; Exec. Vice-Pres. EUGENIO MAGDALENA.

Aseguradora del Istmo (ADISA), SA: Edif. Stewart Title, 4°, San Rafael de Escazú, San José; tel. 2228-4850; fax 2228-0483; e-mail info@adisa.cr; internet www.adisa.cr; f. 2010; Gen. Man. KEVIN MARK LUCAS.

ASSA Cía de Seguros, SA: Edif. F, Centro Empresarial Fórum I, 1°, Santa Ana, San José; tel. 2503-2700; fax 2503-2797; e-mail contacto@assanet.com; internet www.assanet.cr; f. 2009; subsidiary of Grupo ASSA, Argentina; Pres. STANLEY MOTTA; Gen. Man. SERGIO RUÍZ.

Caja Costarricense de Seguro Social: Avda 2da, entre calles 5 y 7, Apdo 10105, San José; tel. 2539-0000; fax 2222-1217; e-mail webmaster@ccss.sa.cr; internet www.info.ccss.sa.cr; accident and health insurance; state-owned; Pres. MARÍA DEL ROCÍO MADRIGAL.

Mapfre Seguros Costa Rica, SA: Edif. Alvasa, 2°, Barrio Tournón, Ruta 32, San José; tel. 2010-3000; e-mail servicioalcliente@mapfre.co.cr; internet www.mapfrecr.com; f. 2010; fmrly Aseguradora Mundial, SA; Pres. JOSÉ ANTONIO ARIAS BERMÚDEZ; Gen. Man. CARLOS GRANGEL LOIRA.

Pan-American Life Insurance de Costa Rica, SA: Santa Ana Forum 1, Torre 1, 2°, San José; tel. 2505-3600; e-mail servicioalclientecr@palig.com; internet www.palig.com; f. 2010; acquired Alico operations in Costa Rica; CEO JOSÉ S. SUQUET.

Sociedad de Seguros de Vida del Magisterio Nacional, SA: Costado Sur de la Sociedad de Seguros del Vida del Magisterio Nacional, Calle 1, Avda 10, San José; tel. 2523-6767; fax 2222-5332; e-mail ssvmnseg@racsa.co.cr; internet www.segurosdelmagisterio.com; f. 1920; insurance for teachers; Pres. RUTH CHAVES CASCANTE; Gen. Man. RAFAEL MONGE CHINCHILLA.

Trade and Industry

GOVERNMENT AGENCIES

Instituto Mixto de Ayuda Social (IMAS): Calle 29, Avdas 2 y 4, Apdo 6213, San José; tel. 2202-4066; fax 2224-8930; e-mail gerencia_general@imas.go.cr; internet www.imas.go.cr; Exec. Pres. CARLOS ALVARADO QUESADA (Minister of Human Development and Social Inclusion); Gen. Man. MARGARITA FERNÁNDEZ GARITA.

Instituto Nacional de Vivienda y Urbanismo (INVU): Avda 9, Calles 3 bis y 5, Apdo 2534-1000, San José; tel. 2256-5265; fax 2223-4006; internet www.invu.go.cr; housing and town planning institute; Exec. Pres. ALVARO GONZÁLEZ ALFARO; Gen. Man. MARÍA DEL CARMEN REDONDO SOLÍS.

Promotora del Comercio Exterior de Costa Rica (PROCOMER): Edif. Centro de Comercio Exterior, Avdas 3, Calle 40, Centro Colón, Apdo 1278, 1007 San José; tel. 2299-4700; fax 2233-5755; e-mail info@procomer.com; internet www.procomer.com; f. 1997 to improve international competitiveness by providing services aimed at increasing, diversifying and expediting international trade; Pres. ALEXANDER MORA DELGADO (Minister of Foreign Trade); Gen. Man. JORGE SEQUEIRA.

DEVELOPMENT ORGANIZATIONS

Cámara de Azucareros: Calle 3, Avda Fernández Güell, Apdo 1577, 1000 San José; tel. 2221-2103; fax 2222-1358; e-mail crazucar@racsa.co.cr; internet www.laica.co.cr; f. 1949; sugar growers; 16 mems; Pres. FEDERICO CHAVARRÍA K; Exec. Dir EDGAR HERRERA ECHANDI.

Cámara Nacional de Bananeros: Edif. Urcha, 3°, Calle 11, Avda 6, Apdo 10273, 1000 San José; tel. 2222-7891; fax 2233-1268; e-mail canaba@ice.co.cr; internet canabacr.com; f. 1967; banana growers; Pres. LUIS UMAÑA; Exec. Dir MARÍA DE LOS ANGELES VINDAS.

Cámara Nacional de Cafetaleros: Condominio Oroki 4D, La Uruca, Apdo 1310, San José; tel. and fax 2296-8334; fax 2296-8334; e-mail camcafe@ice.co.cr; f. 1948; 30 mems; coffee millers and growers; Pres. RODRIGO VARGAS RUÍZ; Exec. Dir GABRIELA LOBO H.

Coalición Costarricense de Iniciativas de Desarrollo (CINDE) (Costa Rican Investment Promotion Agency): Edif. Los Balcones, Plaza Roble, 4°, Guachipelin, Ezcazú; tel. 2201-2800; fax 2201-2867; e-mail invest@cinde.org; internet www.cinde.org; f. 1983; coalition for development of initiatives to attract foreign investment for production and export of new products; Pres. JOSÉ ROSSI; CEO GABRIELA LLOBET.

Corporación Bananera Nacional, SA (CORBANA): Zapote frente Casa Presidencial, Apdo 6504-1000 San José; tel. 2202-4700; fax 2234-9421; e-mail corbana@racsa.co.cr; internet www.corbana.co.cr; f. 1971; public co; cultivation and wholesale of agricultural produce, incl. bananas; Pres. EDUARDO GÓMEZ BODDEN; Gen. Man. JORGE SAUMA.

InfoAgro (Sistema de Información del Sector Agropecuario): Ministerio de Agricultura y Ganadería, Antigüo Colegio La Salle, Sabana Sur, San José; tel. 2296-2579; fax 2296-1652; e-mail infoagro@mag.go.cr; internet www.infoagro.go.cr; state agency; dissemination of information to promote the agricultural sector; Nat. Co-ordinator ANA ISABEL GÓMEZ DE MIGUEL.

Instituto del Café de Costa Rica: Calle 1, Avdas 18 y 20, Apdo 37, 1000 San José; tel. 2222-6411; fax 2222-2838; internet www.icafe.go.cr; e-mail promo@icafe.cr; internet www.icafe.cr; f. 1933 to develop the coffee industry, to control production and to regulate marketing; Exec. Dir RONALD PETERS SEEVERS.

CHAMBERS OF COMMERCE

Cámara de Comercio de Costa Rica: Urb. Tournón, 125 m noroeste del parqueo del Centro Comercial El Pueblo, Goicoechea, Apdo 1114, 1000 San José; tel. 2221-0005; fax 2223-1157; e-mail camara@camara-comercio.com; internet www.camara-comercio.com; f. 1915; 900 mems; Pres. FRANCISCO LLOBET RODRÍGUEZ; Exec. Dir ALONSO ELIZONDO BOLAÑOS.

Cámara de Industrias de Costa Rica: 350 m sur de la Fuente de la Hispanidad, San Pedro de Montes de Oca, Apdo 10003, San José; tel. 2202-5600; fax 2234-6163; e-mail cicr@cicr.com; internet www.cicr.com; Pres. JUAN RAMÓN RIVERA RODRÍGUEZ; Exec. Vice-Pres. MARTHA CASTILLO DÍAZ.

Costa Rican–American Chamber of Commerce (AMCHAM): 300 m noreste del ICE, Sabana Norte, POB 4946, 1000 San José; tel. 2220-2200; fax 2220-2300; e-mail chamber@amcham.co.cr; internet www.amcham.co.cr; Pres. HUMBERTO PACHECO A.; Exec. Dir CATHERINE REUBEN.

Unión Costarricense de Cámaras y Asociaciones de la Empresa Privada (UCCAEP): De McDonald's en Sabana Sur, 400 m al sur, 10 m al este, 25 m al sur, San José; tel. 2290-5595; fax 2290-5596; e-mail uccaep@uccaep.or.cr; internet www.uccaep.or.cr; f. 1974; business fed; Pres. RONALD JIMÉNEZ LARA; Exec. Dir SHIRLEY SABORÍO MARCHENA.

INDUSTRIAL AND TRADE ASSOCIATIONS

Asociación de Empresas de Zonas Francas (AZOFRAS): Plaza Mayor, 2°, Pavas, San José; tel. 2520-1635; fax 2520-1636; e-mail azofras@racsa.co.cr; internet www.azofras.com; f. 1990; Pres. JORGE BRENES; Exec. Dir ALVARO VALVERDE PALAVICINI.

Cámara Nacional de Agricultura y Agroindustria: 300 m sur y 50 m este de McDonald's, Plaza del Sol, Curridabat, Apdo 1671, 1000 San José; tel. 2280-0996; fax 2280-0969; e-mail camaradeagricultura@cnaacr.com; internet www.cnaacr.com; f. 1947; Pres. JUAN RAFAEL LIZANO; Exec. Dir MARTÍN CALDERÓN CHAVES; 23 mems.

Cámara de Tecnología de Información y Comunicación (CAMTIC): Apdo 2101, San Pedro de Montes de Oca, 2050 San José; tel. 2283-2205; fax 2280-4691; e-mail info@camtic.org; internet www.camtic.org; Pres. ALEXANDER MORA DELGADO; Exec. Dir OTTO RIVERA VALLE.

Consejo Nacional de Producción: Avda 10, Calle 36, Apdo 2205, San José; tel. 2257-9355; fax 2256-9625; e-mail soporte@cnp.go.cr; internet www.cnp.go.cr; f. 1948 to encourage agricultural and fish production and to regulate production and distribution of basic commodities; state-run; Exec. Pres. CARLOS ENRIQUE MONGE MONGE.

Instituto de Desarrollo Agrario (IDA): Ofs Centrales IDA, Moravia, Residencial Los Colegios, frente al IFAM, Apdo 5054, 1000 San José; tel. 2247-7400; fax 2241-4891; internet www.ida.go.cr; Exec. Pres. ROLANDO GONZÁLEZ ULLOA; Gen. Man. VÍCTOR JULIO CARVAJAL GARRO.

Instituto Nacional de Fomento Cooperativo: Avdas 5 y 7, Calle 20 Norte, Apdo 10103, 1000 San José; tel. 2256-2944; fax 2255-3835; e-mail info@infocoop.go.cr; internet www.infocoop.go.cr; f. 1973 to encourage the establishment of co-operatives and to provide technical assistance and credit facilities; Pres. GERALD CALDERÓN SÁNCHEZ; Exec. Dir RONALD FONSECA VARGAS (acting).

MAJOR COMPANIES

Agrosuperior, SA (Agromec, Abonos Superior): La Uruca, Apdo 10116-1000, San José; tel. 2210-5300; fax 2231-1811; e-mail info@agromec.co.cr; internet www.agromec.co.cr; holding co with interests in the fertilizer, utilities and industrial machinery sectors; Gen. Man. RICARDO FOURNIER VARGAS.

ArtinSoft: Torre La Sabana, 6°, 300 m oeste del Edif. del ICE, San José; tel. 2519-1000; fax 2519-1010; e-mail info@artinsoft.com; internet www.artinsoft.com; f. 1993; producer of computer software; partially owned by Intel (USA); Chair. MANUEL PARRA; CEO ROBERTO LEITÓN.

Atlas Eléctrica, SA: Carretera a Heredia, Km 12, Apdo 2166, 1000 San José; tel. 2277-2000; fax 2277-2101; e-mail atlaselectrica@atlas.co.cr; internet www.atlas.co.cr; f. 1961; acquired by Mabe in 2006; manufacturers of domestic cooking and refrigeration appliances; Chair. LUIS GAMBOA ARGUEDAS; Man. DIEGO ARTIÑANO FERRIS; 750 employees.

BASF de Costa Rica, SA: Edif. Los Balcones, Sección A, 1°, Plaza Roble Escazú, San 1000 José; tel. 2201-1900; fax 2201-8221; e-mail jose.chacon@basf.com; internet www.centroamerica.basf-cc.com; f. 1975; chemicals; owned by BASF, AG (Germany); Dir ANDREAS KREIMEYER.

Bayer Costa Rica, SA: Eurocenter II, Barreal de Heredia, San José; tel. 2589-8600; fax 2589-8900; e-mail bayer.costarica.bc@bayer-ca.com; internet www.bayer-ca.com; f. 1978; chemicals; Country Head ANNETTE ROSENOW.

BDF Costa Rica, SA: Edif. El Pórtico, 1°, Centro Corporativo, Plaza Roble, Blvd Multiplaza, San José; tel. 2201-8020; fax 2201-8023; internet www.beiersdorf.co.cr; manufacturer of pharmaceuticals and toiletries; owned by Beiersdorf, AG (Germany); CEO STEFAN F. HEIDENREICH.

Bticino Costa Rica, SA: Frente al Cenada, Parque Industrial Heredia, Apdo 6563, 1000 San José; tel. 2298-5600; fax 2239-0472; e-mail bticino@racsa.co.cr; internet www.bticino.co.cr; f. 1975; manufacturer of electrical apparatus; Gen. Man. FEDERICO CALDERÓN.

CAMtronics, SA: Edif. 50, Parque Industrial Zona Franca Cartago, Cartago; tel. 2573-7366; fax 2573-7225; e-mail business@camtronicscr.com; internet www.camtronicscr.com; f. 1985; manufacturers of electronic equipment; Pres. and CEO MARK WELLMAN.

Cemex Costa Rica: Edif. El Pórtico, 3°, Plaza Roble, Guachipelín de Escazú, Apdo 6558, 1000 San José; tel. and fax 2201-2000; fax 2201-8202; internet www.cemexcostarica.com; subsidiary of Cemex, SA de CV (Mexico); cement manufacturers; Country Dir ROBERTO PONGUTÁ URQUIJO.

Cibertec International, SA: 100 m este de Fuente de Hispanidad, Calle Privada, San Pedro de Montes de Oca, POB 149-2300, San José; tel. 2524-0002; fax 2280-5957; e-mail info@cibertec.com; internet www.cibertec.com; f. 1979; telecommunications equipment; Dir JULIO CÁRDENAS.

Colgate Palmolive (Costa Rica), SA: 400 m oeste, 400 m norte de la Plaza de Deportes, Barreal de Heredia, POB 10040-1000, San José; tel. 2298-4600; fax 2293-7171; e-mail juanita_espinoza@colpal.com; internet www.colgatecentralamerica.com; manufacturers of toiletries; Pres. (Latin America) NOEL WALLACE.

Compañía Costarricense del Café, SA (CAFESA): La Uruca, Apdo 4588, 1000 San José; tel. 2232-2255; fax 2231-3640; e-mail cafesa@racsa.co.cr; f. 1956; manufacturer of agrochemicals, fertilizers; Pres. CARLOS ABREU MCDONOUGH; Man. MARCO ANTONIO PINTO.

Componentes Intel de Costa Rica, SA: Centro de Ciencia y Tecnologia Ultrapark, Ultra Park, Bldg 1B, La Aurora, Heredia; tel. 2298-6000; fax 2298-7206; e-mail intel.public.affairs@intel.com; internet www.intel.com/costarica; f. 1998; microprocessor support; closed assembly operations in 2014 although finance and human resource dept still operating; Group CEO BRIAN M. KRZANICH; Chair ANDY D. BRYANT.

Cooperativa Agrícola Industrial Victoria, RL (CoopeVictoria): Apdo 176-4100, San Isidro, Grecia, 41000 Alajuela; tel. 2494-1866; fax 2444-6346; e-mail victoria@coopevictoria.com; internet www.coopevictoria.com; f. 1949; co-operative of local coffee and sugar growers and processors; Pres. BERNARDO PERALTA CORDERO; Gen. Man. WENCESLAO RODRÍGUEZ; 345 employees.

Cooperativa de Productores de Leche Dos Pinos, RL: Apdo 179-4060, Alajuela; tel. 2437-3000; fax 2437-3010; e-mail centrodecontactos@dospinos.com; internet www.dospinos.com; f. 1948; manufacturers of dairy products and fruit juices; Gen. Man. MILAGRO MORA ARAYA; 2,526 employees.

Corporación de Desarrollo Pinero de Costa Rica, SA (Pineapple Development Corporation—PINDECO): Apdo 4084-1000 San José; tel. 2222-9211; fax 2233-7808; f. 1971; subsidiary of Del Monte Fresh; cultivation and wholesale of pineapples; Dir-Gen. RODRIGO JIMÉNEZ; 4,800 employees.

Corporación Fischel: Edif. Club Unión, Calle 2, Avda 3, Frente al Correo, Apdo 410300, 1000 San José; tel. 2248-1692; fax 2248-1682; e-mail regente-s00@fischel.co.cr; internet www.fischel.cr; subsidiary of Corporación CEFA; pharmaceutical manufacturers; Pres. WALTER REICHE; Gen. Man. EMILIO JIMÉNEZ.

Corporación Pipasa, SA: 1.5 km al oeste de la Firestone, La Ribera de Belén, Apdo 22-4005, San Antonio Belén; tel. 2293-4801; fax 2293-0479; e-mail pipasa@sol.racsa.co.cr; internet www.crica.com/biz/pipcorp.html; f. 1969; owned by Rica Foods Inc, USA; production of meat products and animal feed; owns the As de Oro brand; Exec. Pres. VÍCTOR OCONITRILLO CONEJO; 1,670 employees.

Corrugados Belén, SA (CORBEL): Contiguo a Fábrica Firestone, Autopista General Cañas, Apdo 100-4005, Heredia; tel. 2239-0122; fax 2239-1023; e-mail adascoli@corbel.co.cr; internet www.corbel.co.cr; manufacturers of corrugated cardboard boxes; Gen. Man. ALFREDO DASCOLI.

DEMASA (Derivados de Maíz Alimenticios, SA): 2 km al oeste de la Embajada Norteamericana, Pavas, Apdo 1071-1000 San José; tel. 2543-1300; fax 2231-1935; e-mail scliente@demasa.com; internet www.grumacentroamerica.com; f. 1986; subsidiary of Gruma, Mexico; food processing; Pres. HANS J. BÜCHER CHÉVES; 2,500 employees.

Dole Fresh Fruit International Ltd: Centro Colón, POB 12, 1000 San José; tel. 2287-2170; fax 2287-2172; e-mail frans.wielemaker@dole.com; internet www.doleorganic.com; div. of Dole Food Co Inc; fmrly Standard Fruit Company; Vice-Pres. MICHAEL CARTER; 3,250 employees.

Durman Esquivel, SA: 1 km al este del cruce de cinco esqs de Tibás, Calle Blancos, Apdo 6139-1000, San José; tel. 256-7176; e-mail costarica@durman.com; internet www.durman.com; f. 1959; subsidiary of Aliaxis, SA; manufacturer of plastic products; Pres. FRANCIS DURMAN.

Fábrica Nacional de Licores (FANAL): 800 m oeste del Puente sobre Río Rosales, Autopista Bernardo Soto, Apdo 184-4100 Grecia, Alajuela; tel. 2494-0100; fax 2494-3652; e-mail info@fanal.co.cr; internet www.fanal.co.cr; f. 1853; state distillery; Gen. Man. MAX CARRANZA ARCE.

Fertilizantes de Centroamérica, SA (FERTICA): De las Ofs de Pizza Hut, 150 m este, Oficentro Mediterráneo Of. 1, Pavas, 1000 San José; tel. 2231-2555; fax 2290-7571; e-mail ventas@fertica.com; internet www.fertica.com; f. 1961; manufacturers of chemical fertilizers; Pres. OSCAR HENRIQUEZ; 360 employees.

Florida Ice and Farm Company, SA: Apdo 2046-3000 Heredia; tel. 2437-6700; fax 2437-7000; e-mail info@florida.co.cr; internet www.florida.co.cr; f. 1966; 3 main subsidiaries: Florida Inmobiliaria, SA, Florida Capitales, SA, and Florida Bebidas, SA; Pres. WILHELM STEINVORTH HERRERA; CEO RAMÓN MENDIOLA; 1,465 employees.

Holcim (Costa Rica), SA: Edif. Administrativo, Centro Industrial Holcim, 200 m este y 100 m sur de la Cruz Roja de San Rafael de Alajuela, Apdo 4301-1000, Alajuela; tel. 2205-2900; fax 2205-3100; e-mail contactenos-cri@holcim.com; internet www.holcim.cr; f. 1960 as Industria Nacional de Cemento (INCSA); owned by Holcim Ltd (Switzerland); manufacturers of cement; Chair. JEAN PIERRE RATTON CARBONNEL; CEO MANRIQUE ARREA; 924 employees.

Hultec Terramix, SA: 150 m norte de La Cañada, Apdo 84140, 1000 San José; tel. 2205-1800; fax 2282-7559; e-mail hultec@hultec.com; internet www.hulteccr.com; f. 1976 as Hules Técnicos; manufacturers of rubber seals for PVC tubes; Pres. ALVARO GUTIÉRREZ; 673 employees.

Instituto Costarricense de Acueductos y Alcantarillados: Edif. La Llacuna, 9°, Costado de los Bomberos, Pavos, Apdo 5120-1000 San José; tel. 2242-5090; fax 2256-5642; e-mail administrador@aya.go.cr; internet www.aya.go.cr; f. 1961; construction and operation of water and sewerage services; Exec. Pres. YESSENIA CALDERÓN; Gen. Man. HEIBEL ANTONIO RODRÍGUEZ ARAYA; 2,975 employees.

Nestlé Costa Rica, SA: 300 m oeste de Cenada en Barreal de Heredia, Apdo 1349, 1000 San José; tel. 2209-6600; fax 2239-2678; e-mail nestlecr@sol.racsa.co.cr; internet www.nestle-centroamerica.com; chocolate producers; Exec. Vice-Pres. LUIS CANTARELL.

Productos Ujarras, SA: 600 m oeste de la Plaza, San Diego, Apdo 2622-1000 Tres Ríos, Cartago; tel. 2278-2770; fax 2278-2774; e-mail info@ujarras.com; internet www.ujarras.com; f. 1962; food products; Gen. Man. EDGARDO RODRÍGUEZ SOTO.

Refinadora Costarricense de Petróleo (Recope): Goicoechea, San Francisco de Guadalupe de la Iglesia 200 m oeste, Apdo 4351-1000 San José; tel. 2284-2700; fax 2255-4993; internet www.recope.go.cr; f. 1961; state petroleum co; Pres. LITLETON BOLTON JONES; Gen. Man. JORGE ROJAS; 1,100 employees.

Roche Servicios, SA: Edif. 6A, 1 km noreste de Real Cariari, Zona Franca Ultrapark, Apdo 3438-1000, La Aurora, Heredia; tel. 2298-1500; fax 2298-1607; internet www.roche.com; medication and diagnostic instruments; Group CEO SEVERIN SCHWAN.

Siemens, SA: La Uruca, de la Plaza de Deportes 200 m al este, Apdo 1002-1000 San José; tel. 2287-5050; fax 2221-5050; e-mail siemens@racsa.co.cr; internet www.siemens-centram.com/index_costarica.shtml; electronic systems, telecommunications equipment; Gen. Man. ERWIN ELLER.

Telefónica de Promociones de San José, SA: Edif. 5D, Zona Franca Metropolitana, Barreal de Heredia; tel. 2239-9370; internet www.qualfon.com; owned by Qualfon (Mexico); call centre; CEO MICHAEL P. MARROW.

UTILITIES

Regulatory Body

Autoridad Reguladora de los Servicios Públicos (ARESEP): Edif. Turrubares, Complejo Multipark, 100 m norte Construplaza, Guachipelín de Escazú, Apdo 936, 1000 San José; tel. 2506-3200; fax 2215-6052; e-mail cmora@aresep.go.cr; internet www.aresep.go.cr; f. 1996; oversees telecommunications, public utilities and transport sectors; Regulator Gen. DENNIS MELÉNDEZ HOWELL.

Electricity

Instituto Costarricense de Electricidad (ICE): Apdo 10032, 1000 San José; tel. 2220-7720; fax 2220-1555; e-mail ice-si@ice.co.cr; internet www.ice.co.cr; f. 1949; govt agency for power and telecommunications; Exec. Pres. CARLOS MANUEL OBREGÓN QUESADA; Gen. Man. MARTÍN VINDAS GARITA.

Cía Nacional de Fuerza y Luz, SA (CNFL): Calle Central y 1, Avda 5, Apdo 10026, 1000 San José; tel. 2296-4608; fax 2296-3950; e-mail info@cnfl.go.cr; internet www.cnfl.go.cr; f. 1941; electricity co; mem. of ICE Group; Pres. LUIS PACHECO MORGAN; Gen. Man. VÍCTOR SOLÍS RODRÍGUEZ.

JASEC (Junta Administrativa del Servicio Eléctrico Municipal de Cartago): Apdo 179, 7050 Cartago; tel. 2550-6800; fax 2551-1683; e-mail agomez@jasec.co.cr; internet www.jasec.co.cr; f. 1964; Pres. LILLIAM CALDERÓN MONTOYA; Gen. Man. OSCAR MENESES QUESADA.

Water

Instituto Costarricense de Acueductos y Alcantarillados: Edif. Central, Pavas, 1000 San José; tel. 2242-5591; fax 2222-2259; e-mail centrodoc@aya.go.cr; internet www.aya.go.cr; f. 1961; water and sewerage; Pres. YAMILETH ASTORGA ESPELETA; Gen. Man. HEIBEL ANTONIO RODRÍGUEZ ARAYA.

TRADE UNIONS

Asociación Nacional de Educadores (ANDE): Avda 5a, Calle O y 2, Apdo 2938, 1000 San José; tel. 2257-9898; fax 2233-1930; e-mail info@ande.cr; internet www.ande.cr; teachers' union; Pres. GILBERTO CASCANTE MONTERO.

Asociación Nacional de Empleados Públicos (ANEP): Casa Sindical, Calle 20 norte, 300 N Hospital Nacional de Niños, frente a Coopeservidores, Apdo 5152, 1000 San José; tel. 2257-8233; fax 2257-8859; e-mail info@anep.or.cr; internet www.anep.or.cr; f. 1958; Sec.-Gen. ALBINO VARGAS BARRANTES.

Central del Movimiento de Trabajadores Costarricenses (CMTC) (Costa Rican Workers' Union): Calle 20, 200 m norte del Hospital de Niños, 1000 San José; tel. 2221-7701; fax 2221-3353; e-mail info@cmtccr.org; internet www.cmtccr.org; f. 1994; Pres. OLMAN CHINCILLA; 108,000 mems (2011).

Confederación de Trabajadores Rerum Novarum (CTRN): Barrio Escalante, de la Rotonda el Farolito 250 m este, Apdo 31100, San José; tel. 2283-4244; fax 2234-2282; e-mail ctrn@ice.co.cr; internet www.rerumnovarum.or.cr; Pres. RODRIGO AGUILAR ARCE; Sec.-Gen. SERGIO SABORÍO BRENES.

Unión Nacional de Empleados de la Caja y la Seguridad Social (UNDECA): 350m norte del Hospital Nacional de Niños, Calle 20 Norte, 1000 San José; tel. 2233-6538; fax 2221-1138; internet www.undeca.cr; represents workers in the social security institute; Sec.-Gen. LUIS CHAVARRÍA VEGA.

Transport

Autoridad Reguladora de los Servicios Públicos (ARESEP): regulatory body for the telecommunications industry, public utilities and transport (see Trade and Industry—Utilities).

RAILWAYS

AmericaTravel: Edif. INCOFER, Estación al Pacífico, Avda 20, Calle 2, Apdo 246, 1009 San José; tel. 2233-3300; fax 2223-3311; e-mail americatravel@ice.co.cr; operates weekend tourist trains between San José and Caldera; Gen. Man. JUAN PANIAGUA ZELEDÓN.

Instituto Costarricense de Ferrocarriles (INCOFER): Calle Central, Avda 22 y 24, Apdo 1, 1009 San José; tel. 2222-8857; fax 2222-6998; e-mail incofer@sol.racsa.co.cr; internet www.incofer.go.cr; f. 1985; govt-owned; 471 km, of which 388 km are electrified; in 1995 INCOFER suspended most operations, pending privatization, although some cargo transport continued; by 2012 a wide range of rail lines had reopened; Exec. Pres. GUILLERMO SANTANA BARBOZA.

ROADS

In 2010 there were 39,018 km of roads, of which 26% were paved. In 2009 the Government and the Andean Promotion Corporation signed a US $60m. loan agreement for the Atlantic Corridor Investment Program. The project included construction of a new highway between the Atlantic ports of Costa Rica and Nicaragua, as well as a new bridge over the Sixaola river on the border with Panama. In 2010 the Central American Bank for Economic Integration approved a loan of $140m. for the San José–San Carlos highway, intended to improve access between the capital and the north of the country.

Consejo Nacional de Vialidad (CONAVI): 50 m este y 10 m norte de la Rotonda Betania, Apdo 616, Zapote, 2010 San José; tel. 2202-5300; e-mail contraloria@conavi.go.cr; internet www.conavi.go.cr; f. 1998; Exec. Dir CARLOS ACOSTA MONGE.

SHIPPING

Local services operate between the Costa Rican ports of Puntarenas and Limón and those of Colón and Cristóbal in Panama and other Central American ports. Caldera on the Gulf of Nicoya is the main Pacific port. The Caribbean coast is served by the port complex of Limón/Moín, which was being expanded in 2014. In December 2013 the flag registered fleet comprised eight vessels, with a total displacement of some 6,977 grt.

Instituto Costarricense de Puertos del Pacífico (INCOP): Calle 36, Avda 3, Apdo 543, 1000 San José; tel. 2634-9100; fax 2634-9101; e-mail info@incop.go.cr; internet www.incop.go.cr; f. 1972; state agency for the development of Pacific ports; Exec. Pres. JORGE LUIS LORÍA; Gen. Man. WITMAN CRUZ MÉNDEZ.

Junta de Administración Portuaria y de Desarrollo Económico de la Vertiente Atlántica (JAPDEVA): Calle 17, Avda 7, Apdo 5.330, 1000 San José; tel. 2795-4747; fax 2795-0728; e-mail cthomas@japdeva.go.cr; internet www.japdeva.go.cr; f. 1963; state agency for the devt of Atlantic ports; Exec. Pres. ALLAN HIDALGO CAMPOS; Gen. Man. CARLOS THOMAS ARROYO.

Principal Shipping Companies

Inter-Moves SG Global de Costa Rica: Apdo 11990, 1000 San José; tel. 2241-2147; fax 2241-2260; e-mail info@intermoves-sgcr.com; internet www.intermoves-sgcr.com; shipping, freight forwarding and logistics; Gen. Man. JOSÉ ANTONIO SUEIRAS.

Maersk Costa Rica, SA: Oficentro La Virgen, Edif. Prisma, 3°, Pavas, Apdo 12187, 1000 San José; tel. 2543-5100; fax 2543-5150; e-mail crics@maersk.com; internet www.maerskline.com/es-cr; f. 1994; subsidiary of Maersk Line (Denmark); Man. Dir RODRIGO ARTAVIA.

Puerto Limón Agency: 800 este y 100 sur Plaza del Sol, San José; tel. 2758-2062; fax 2758-2022; e-mail info@limonagency.com; internet www.limonagency.com.

CIVIL AVIATION

Costa Rica has four international airports: Juan Santamaría Airport, the largest, 16 km from San José at El Coco, Tobías Bolaños Airport in Pavas, Daniel Oduber Quirós Airport, at Liberia, and Limón International.

Nature Air: Juan Santamaría Main Airport, San José; tel. 2299-6000; fax 2232-2516; e-mail info@natureair.com; internet www.natureair.com; f. 2000; flights from San José to 13 domestic destinations; international destinations include Nicaragua and Panama; carbon-neutral airline; CEO ALEX KHAJAVI.

Servicios Aéreos Nacionales, SA (SANSA): Edif. TACA, La Uruca, San José; tel. 2290-3543; fax 2290-3538; e-mail infosansa@taca.com; internet www.flysansa.com; subsidiary of TACA; international, regional and domestic scheduled passenger and cargo services; Man. Dir CARLOS MANUEL DELGADO AGUILAR.

Tourism

Costa Rica boasts a system of nature reserves and national parks unique in the world, covering one-third of the country. Some 2,343,213 tourists visited Costa Rica in 2012, while tourism receipts totalled a provisional US $2,425m. Most visitors came from the USA (39% in 2012).

Cámara Nacional de Turismo de Costa Rica (CANATUR): Zapote, de la Universidad Veritas, 200 m hacia el este, San José; tel. 2234-6222; fax 2253-8102; e-mail supervisor@canatur.org; internet www.canatur.org; f. 1974; Pres. PABLO ABARCA MORA; Exec. Dir TATIANA CASCANTE ROJAS.

Instituto Costarricense de Turismo (ICT): La Uruca, Costado Este del Puente Juan Pablo II, Apdo 777, 1000 San José; tel. 2299-5876; fax 2220-3559; e-mail info@visitcostarica.com; internet www.visitcostarica.com; f. 1931; Pres. WILHELM VON BREYMANN BARQUERO (Minister of Tourism); Gen. Man. JUAN CARLOS BORBÓN MARKS.

Defence

Costa Rica has had no armed forces since 1948. As assessed at November 2013, Rural and Civil Guards totalled 2,000 and 4,500 men and women, respectively. In addition, there were 2,500 Border Security Police. There was also a Coast Guard Unit numbering 400 and an Air Surveillance Unit of 400.

Security Budget: an estimated 202,000m. colones in 2013.

Minister of Public Security, Governance and Police: CELSO GAMBOA SÁNCHEZ.

Education

Education in Costa Rica is free, and is compulsory between six and 13 years of age. Primary education begins at the age of six and lasts for six years. Official secondary education consists of a three-year basic course, followed by a more specialized course lasting two years in academic schools and three years in technical schools. In 2012/13 a total of 480,125 students attended primary schools and 449,035 attended secondary schools. In 2013 there were 57 universities, of which five were state-run, with, in 2011/12, 203,175 students. The provision for education in the 2013 government budget was US $3,479m., equivalent to 9.3% of total government spending.

Bibliography

For works on Central America generally, see Select Bibliography (Books)

Berigan, Y. *Performing Costa Rica: 'El Tico' and National Identity.* Saarbrüchen, VDM Verlag Dr. Müller, 2011.

Chamberlain, A. B. *Privatization in Costa Rica: A Multi-Dimensional Analysis.* Lanham, MD, University Press of America, 2007.

Cruz, C. *Political Culture and Institutional Development in Costa Rica and Nicaragua: World-Making in the Tropics.* Cambridge, Cambridge University Press, 2005.

Evans, S. *The Green Republic: A Conservation History of Costa Rica.* Austin, TX, University of Texas Press, 1999.

Foreign Investment in Latin America and the Caribbean. Santiago, Economic Commission for Latin America and the Caribbean, 2004.

Lehoucq, F. E., and Molina, I. *Stuffing the Ballot Box: Fraud, Electoral Reform, and Democratization in Costa Rica.* Cambridge, Cambridge University Press, 2006.

Luetchford, P. *Fair Trade and a Global Commodity: Coffee in Costa Rica.* London, Pluto Press, 2007.

Palmer, S., and Molina, I. (Eds). *The Costa Rica Reader: History, Culture, Politics.* Durham, NC, Duke University Press, 2004.

Paus, E. *Foreign Investment, Development, and Globalization: Can Costa Rica Become Ireland?* Basingstoke, Palgrave Macmillan, 2005.

Sandoval-García, C. *Threatening Others: Nicaraguans and the Formation of National Identities in Costa Rica (Latin America S.).* Athens, OH, Ohio University Press, 2004.

Shattering Myths on Immigration and Emigration in Costa Rica. Plymouth, Lexington Books, 2011.

Yashar, D. J. *Demanding Democracy: Reform and Reaction in Costa Rica and Guatemala, 1870s–1950s.* Stanford, CA, Stanford University Press, 1997.

CUBA

Geography

PHYSICAL FEATURES

The Republic of Cuba consists of the island of Cuba (the largest and westernmost of the Greater Antilles), the Isla de la Juventud (Isle of Youth, until 1978 the Isle of Pines—Isla de Pinos) and 1,600 small offshore islands. Cuba is the largest island in the West Indies, lying at the entrance to the Gulf of Mexico (to the north-west), and is washed by the Caribbean Sea to the south and west and by the Atlantic Ocean to the north-east. Cuba lies only 145 km (90 miles) north of Jamaica and, at the other, north-western end of the island, a similar distance south of Key West in Florida, USA. However, some of the more remote cays of the Bahamas lie much closer, and that country stretches across the north-eastern approaches to Cuba. Haiti is only 80 km to the east. The Yucatán peninsula of Mexico lies about 210 km to the west and the British dependency of the Cayman Islands some 240 km to the south. Cuba also has a 29-km land border in the south-east, where the USA has a lease on the area around its naval base on Guantánamo Bay, but Cuba retains sovereignty. Cuba, the largest country of the insular Caribbean, in terms of both extent and population, covers an area of 109,886 sq km (42,427 sq miles) or about 45% of the total surface area of the Antilles.

The island of Cuba, which is roughly the same size as the North Island of New Zealand or Newfoundland (Canada), is about 1,250 km long and between 32 km and 191 km wide. From a flattened, southern head of mountainous terrain, the island of Cuba extends back north-westwards into a narrowing tail that begins to turn towards the south-west when the island ends. This tail is attempting to encompass the 2,200-sq km Isla de la Juventud, which lies about 100 km to the south (north of a large, bisecting swamp, this island, famed for its citrus fruits, is generally dry and flat, although there are some hills). The Isla de la Juventud is by far the largest of the myriad offshore islands and cays that, together with extensive coral reefs, further complicate the heavily indented, 3,735-km coastline. In the north old coral and limestone has lifted into a steep shore of cliffs and bluffs, sheltering some fine harbours, while the south subsides into a low and often marshy littoral. Much of the terrain of this predominantly limestone island is flat or undulating plain, with wide and fertile valleys, and highlands of any significance only in the south-east. About one-quarter of Cuba's territory is mountainous, with three main ranges: the Cordillera de Guaniguanico (including the distinctive steep-sided, flat-topped mountains of the Sierra de los Organos and the more easterly Sierra del Rosario) at the north-western end of the island; the centre-west highlands, such as the Escambray; and the geologically more recent Sierra Maestra (largely volcanic in origin) in the far south-east, where Pico Turquino reaches 2,005 m (6,580 ft). Rivers tend to be short and fall steeply. The longest is the Cauto, in the east, at only 240 km, and the Toa (110 km long) is the widest river in Cuba.

Rivers and plentiful rainfall water an island still rich in biodiversity, although the almost entirely wooded island that the Spanish first settled on is now three-quarters savannah or plains (there are two main areas of savannah). About 4% of the island is swampy wetland, and a reforestation programme aims to increase the area under trees to 27% of the total. Meanwhile, Cuba is home to an extraordinary range of terrains and vegetation types, with the eastern end of the south-east being particularly rich in biodiversity (it claims to be the most diverse in the Caribbean, with almost one-third of the endemic species of the island). Over 7,000 species of flora have been identified on Cuba, of which about 3,000 are endemic. However, almost 1,000 have been made extinct, rare or endangered since the 17th century. Examples of native plants include the world's only carnivorous epiphyte (plants that live on other plants, but are not parasitic, like moss or orchids), about 100 types of palm (90 of which are endemic) and one of nature's largest flowers. Cuba might be more generally associated with

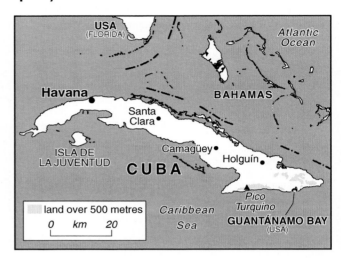

claims of the world's smallest products of nature, however, particularly in the animal kingdom: the smallest frog, the Cuban pygmy frog, which is 12 mm (0.5 ins); the smallest mammal, the 55-mm butterfly bat (*mariposa*); the smallest scorpion, the 10-mm dwarf scorpion; and the smallest bird, the 63-mm bee hummingbird (*zunzuncito*). There is also a pygmy owl, tiny salamanders and the insect-eating rodent, the *almiquí*, which is a long-surviving species, a 'living fossil' (like the cork palm, the Cuban or rhombifer crocodile and the Cuban alligator). In all, there are almost 14,000 species of fauna, although about 1,500 are said to be near extinction. Many of the species have diversified into distinctly Cuban varieties—40% of mammal species (including some of the larger ones, such as manatees or sea cows and hutias), 85% of reptiles, 90% of amphibians and 96% of molluscs are said to be endemic. Protected areas cover 30% of Cuba, including its marine platform and four UNESCO biosphere reserves, although enforcement sometimes lacks infrastructure.

CLIMATE

The climate is subtropical, warm and humid, with the Atlantic trade winds alleviating extremes. A rainy season falls from May to October. During this time hurricanes occasionally trouble the eastern coasts. Drought is a more usual and general problem. Average annual rainfall in Havana (La Habana—the capital, in the north-west) is 1,730 mm (67 ins), but 860 mm in the east. The average annual temperature in Cuba is 25°C (77°F), but readings can rise to 33°C (91°F) in the shade even in Havana (the south-eastern city of Santiago de Cuba is hotter and drier) during the summer. The drier, winter months of December–April see temperatures nearer 20°C (68°F), but they can occasionally fall to as low as 8°C (46°F) in a north wind.

POPULATION

According to the 2012 census, 64% of the population identified themselves as white, a further 27% defined themselves as of mixed race, and 9% were black. Numerous influxes have influenced Cuba and its culture, notably in the south-east, where the French fled from revolution in Haiti in the early 19th century and, more recently, Jamaicans have settled. The oldest influences to modify Spanish colonial settlers, however, came from West Africa with the slaves brought to work the plantations. The most numerous group was of Yoruba speakers from south-western Nigeria, Benin (formerly Dahomey) and Togo. They are known in Cuba as *Lucumí*. The descendants of the

Bantu-speaking peoples brought from the Congo basin are known as the *Congos*, while those from the Calabar region of southern Nigeria and Cameroon are known as the *Carabalí*. The Yoruba pantheon and legends were syncretized by the early *Lucumí* with the saints of the Christian religion they were formally required to adopt, forming the basis of the Regla de Ocha cult, or *Santería*. It is a religion without sects or missionaries and can co-exist without complication with both Christianity or the similarly syncretic cult of the *Congos*, the Regla Conga or Palo Monte. Some practise all three belief systems at once. The *Carabalí* originated not a cult, but a sort of masonic closed sect, the Abakuá Secret Society, which is open to men only and upholds values traditionally associated with masculinity (it is also known as *ñañiguismo*). Ostensibly, however, the predominant religion remains Roman Catholic

Christianity and some 85% of the population were at least nominally Roman Catholic. In 2005 some 53% of the population were open adherents of Roman Catholicism (with another 10% belonging to other Christian denominations). There are also some Jews and a few that practise other faiths. Spanish is the official language.

The population totalled 11.2m., according to official estimates at December 2013. About three-quarters of the population are urbanized and some 2.1m. (in 2012) live in Havana, on the north coast. The capital is one of 16 provinces. The second city is Santiago de Cuba (with a population of over 506,037 in 2012), in the south-east, followed by Holguín, Camagüey, Santa Clara and Bayamo. There is a high level of illicit emigration from Cuba, particularly to the USA.

History
Prof. ANTONI KAPCIA

PRE-COLUMBIAN AND COLONIAL CUBA

When Christopher Columbus arrived in 1492, Cuba's indigenous population numbered about 60,000 Siboney in the west and more agriculturally advanced Arawaks (or Taínos) in the east. After Sebastián de Ocampo proved Cuba to be an island, in 1508, a period of exploration and rapid conquest followed. Between 1512 and 1515 the Spanish founded seven defined *villas* (settlements): Baracoa, Bayamo, Trinidad, Sancti Spíritus, Havana, Puerto Príncipe and Santiago de Cuba, the last serving as the capital city until it was replaced by Havana in the 1550s.

Thereafter, Cuba's colonial experience was unusual. First, the rapid decline of the indigenous population (to around 1,000 persons within 50 years), with few Spanish settlers, made Cuba initially one of Spain's 'whitest' colonies. Second, from 1561 Cuba's imperial significance came from its role as a port of call for Spanish-bound fleets transporting silver from the Americas, making Havana an economic hub, as well as a prime target for piracy, requiring a strong military presence.

In 1762–63 a brief but pivotal British occupation opened up trade with North America, changing the perspectives of locally born whites (*criollos*); about 5,000 slaves were imported during this period to develop sugar, establishing a historic nexus between sugar, slavery and colonialism. While *criollos* elsewhere saw decreasing incentives to remain Spanish, for those in Cuba there was every reason. Once the British Empire abolished, in 1807, the slave trade, only Spain could guarantee the *criollos* a significant slave supply, which was required for the development of Cuba's burgeoning sugar trade. Moreover, a violent slave rebellion in 1791 in the nearby French territory of Saint Domingue (now Haiti), coupled with the rising number of blacks owing to slave imports, increased fears among the whites of the possibility of revolt; as a result, the *criollos* welcomed Spain's military might.

However, as the Spanish excluded *criollos* politically and denied them access to capital, slave-based *criollo* planters were not able to modernize. Hence, while Spanish planters flourished, *criollo* production declined, pushing them towards separatism; however, fearful of the United Kingdom and the black majority, the *criollos* preferred annexation by the USA, which at that time imported about 40% of Cuba's sugar. This produced several revolts, supported by southern US interests, and three US Governments tried to purchase Cuba.

THE WARS OF INDEPENDENCE

When the US Civil War made annexation impossible, some *criollos* opted for independence; on 10 October 1868 Carlos Manuel de Céspedes launched a rebellion. The rebel ranks swelled with thousands of black guerrillas (*mambises*) equating political liberation with racial equality. However, with increased Spanish numbers, the war was confined to the east (Oriente), and, fearful of the implications of a largely black

rebellion, the white rebels finally surrendered in 1878. The recalcitrant and popular *mulato* leader, Antonio Maceo, then led a second Oriente revolt, the 'Little War', in 1879–80.

By then, slavery was no longer a prominent issue; Spain had abolished slavery in 1817, although it was not effectively abolished until 1886. Henceforth, *criollo* planters were replaced by large modern US-owned sugar mills, and Spanish repression forced many to leave. One exile was the poet José Martí, who left Cuba in 1871, devoting his journalistic and political skills to campaigning for independence and founding the Cuban Revolutionary Party in 1892. In February 1895 Martí led an invasion of Oriente; although he was killed in May, the *mambises*' Liberation Army soon increased (to around 40,000) and reached the west.

Having been driven by a press campaign against alleged Spanish atrocities, by US companies' pleas, by an expansionist lobby, and by the unexplained explosion in Havana of the *USS Maine* in February 1889, the US Government declared war on Spain in April. Thus, the Cuban War of Independence became the Spanish–American War.

US INTERVENTION AND CONTROL

The war lasted until August 1898. The Treaty of Paris, signed by Spain and the USA in December of that year, established US control over Cuba, which lasted until Cuba was granted independence on 20 May 1902. During that period, social provision improved but US economic interests increased. Most controversially, the new Cuban Constitution included clauses from the so-called Platt Amendment, limiting the Cubans' right to sign treaties or contract loans, leasing territory on the island for US military bases and allowing unilateral US intervention in Cuba to quell unrest. Codified in a 1903 treaty, this legitimized neo-colonial control (and gave the USA Guantánamo Bay), provoking ongoing resentment. A 1903 Reciprocity Treaty, signed by Tomás Estrada Palma, the first President of the new Republic, confirmed economic dependence, while a second treaty signed by Estrada Palma incorporated the Platt Amendment. Under the terms of this second agreement, there was another period of US intervention in 1906–09, and again in 1912, when a protest staged by the Independent Party of Colour against the marginalization of black Cubans was forcefully repressed, resulting in the death of 3,000 people. A fourth period of US intervention occurred in 1917.

In 1920 collapsing sugar prices undermined political stability and faith in the neo-colonial system, producing a decade of union militancy (increasingly led by the Communist Party, founded in 1925), student radicalism and the election in 1924 of Gerardo Machado, whose presidency degenerated into corruption and authoritarianism.

The 1929 Wall Street Crash and ensuing Great Depression caused sugar prices to plummet still further, and resulted in more protests and a virtual labour insurrection, with student radicalism metamorphosing into armed conflict. US pressure led the army, in August 1933, to depose President Machado, whose interim replacement, Carlos Manuel de Céspedes (the younger), was overthrown in the following month by an alliance of students and mutinying non-commissioned officers under Sgt (later Gen.) Fulgencio Batista Zaldivar. Ramón Grau San Martín replaced Céspedes as President. However, Céspedes was denied recognition by the new non-interventionist US President, Franklin Roosevelt, and was unable to control the continuing unrest on all sides. Meanwhile, his Minister of the Interior, Antonio Guiteras, led appeals for a deeper social revolution.

Sustained US pressure led Batista to seize power in January 1934, upon which he ruled dictatorially via 'puppet' Presidents until 1940, during which time he also enacted a populist programme giving farmers and entrepreneurs greater economic space, secured the end of the Platt Amendment and introduced various social reforms. In 1938 he legalized the Communist Party (subsequently renamed the People's Socialist Party—PSP—in 1944), allowing them to control the trade unions, in exchange for electoral support. That alliance ensured the approval of a progressive new Constitution in 1940, as well as facilitating his victory in the presidential election in the same year.

Batista retired in 1944, his presidency having overseen rampant corruption (through patronage, links with US crime and the degeneration of student radicalism into gangsterism). Grau, leader of the Authentic Cuban Revolutionary Party (Auténticos), was elected in his stead later that year, and was in turn replaced by Carlos Prío Socarrá, a fellow Auténtico, in 1948. Prío's rule was increasingly conservative and corrupt, and his term was brought to a premature end when Batista seized power on 10 March 1952, thereby preventing the electoral victory of the Cuban People's Party (Ortodoxos), led by the charismatic Eduardo Chibás. A strong candidate for the presidency, Chibás publicly committed suicide during a live radio broadcast in 1951, in a personal protest against the social injustice and political corruption that he deemed to be rife in Cuba.

The coup remained largely unchallenged, except for a protest movement among students, led by a former student activist, Fidel Castro Ruz. On 26 July 1953 a group of 132 rebels attacked two eastern military barracks, with the force of their assault concentrated on the Moncada garrison in Santiago de Cuba. Intended to spark a rebellion, the attack failed, resulting in the death of seven rebels (with a further 54 killed after arrest). Among those surviving were Castro and his younger brother, Raúl Castro Ruz, both of whom were captured, tried, and subsequently sentenced to 15 and 13 years' imprisonment, respectively, for their roles in the attack. Fidel Castro's defence speech at his trial was later published as 'History Will Absolve Me'.

In prison, the Castro brothers organized the 26 July Movement. Released as part of a general amnesty of political prisoners in 1955, they headed to Mexico, where they prepared for an invasion and guerrilla resistance against Batista, and met the Argentine radical Ernesto ('Che') Guevara. In November 1956 82 rebels sailed for eastern Cuba aboard the yacht *Granma*. However, they landed late, at the wrong place, missing by a couple of days a Santiago uprising that had been supposed to distract attention, and were dispersed under air attack. Two weeks later, around two dozen rebels regrouped in the nearby Sierra Maestra mountains.

Two years of guerrilla warfare followed, the rebels benefiting from mobility, growth, skilful publicity, peasant support and military prowess (especially the Castro brothers and Guevara). Meanwhile, the Batista regime faced economic stagnation, dissent, urban violence (provoking a repression that embarrassed the US Government into withholding arms in 1958), the guerrillas' superiority and the army's falling morale. By 1958 all alternatives to the 26 July Movement had disappeared or fallen into line, including the small Revolutionary Directorate (Directorio Revolucionario), the leader of which—José Antonio Echevarría—had been killed in an attack on Batista's palace in March 1957, and the PSP, which, having criticized Castro, joined the rebel alliance in 1958. The guerrilla movement's rapid westward advance from mid-1958 culminated in victory

under Guevara in Santa Clara on 30 December 1958. The next day Batista fled, and Guevara entered Havana on 1 January 1959, a general strike ensuring control.

THE RADICALIZATION OF THE REVOLUTIONARY PROCESS

The first Government was a coalition combining representatives of the 26 July Movement, liberals and social democrats, under the presidency of a respected judge, Manuel Urrutia Lleó; Fidel Castro assumed the position of Prime Minister, with Raúl as his deputy. While they agreed on their main objectives (diversification of the economy, improved social welfare and better Cuban-US relations), they differed over their preferred means of attaining these ends, for the rebels had radicalized since 1953 through contact with the peasantry and the influence of radicals such as Guevara and the PSP.

The PSP's role led Urrutia to resign in July 1959, whereupon he was replaced by Osvaldo Dorticós Torrado. Fears of communism prompted US concern, and caution soon turned to opposition, with the US Government and press criticizing the public trials of supporters of Batista. After a goodwill visit to the USA by Castro in April 1959, US Vice-President Richard Nixon's concerns about the 'Communist threat' led him to approve plans by the US Central Intelligence Agency (CIA) to train Cuban exiles. In reality, although the PSP was involved in early planning of reforms, its presence was often resented by those critical of its former alliance with Batista.

The most significant of those reforms—land reform legislation adopted in May 1959—outlawed large landholdings and guaranteed a minimum stake for farmers, prompting concern among US corporations, which feared expropriation, the implications of the establishment of a National Institute for Agrarian Reform, and the trend towards co-operatives and 'people's farms'.

Other reforms abolished urban renting (later giving title to former tenants and rehousing the homeless and slum-dwellers in empty middle-class properties), expanded education and health, and banned racial discrimination. Meanwhile, from 1960–61 Cubans were mobilized in new 'mass organizations', the first of which were the citizens' militia, established in 1959, and the neighbourhood Committees for the Defence of the Revolution (CDR), set up in the following year; other organizations subsequently sprang up for women, private farmers, students and others. One existing organization, the Central de Trabajadores de Cuba trade union, soon came under radical leadership, including PSP activists, fuelling fears of communism.

Looming fears of a US invasion were intensified, in February 1960, by a Cuban-Soviet agreement to exchange sugar (500,000 metric tons annually) for oil, sparking a rapid deterioration in US-Cuban relations: when US-owned refineries in Cuba refused to refine the oil, they were nationalized, beginning a process of gradual elimination of the US quota for Cuban sugar, an increase in economic sanctions imposed by the USA against Cuba, steady nationalization of US enterprises within Cuba, and the increasing Soviet purchase of unsold Cuban sugar.

The USA severed diplomatic relations with Cuba in January 1961. In April the CIA-trained Cuban exile forces launched an ill-fated attack on the southern Bay of Pigs (known locally as Playa Girón), with the support of the US Administration. The invasion was an unmitigated disaster for the USA: the 1,480 invaders were resisted by peasant militias; the Cuban army and air force lost 87 personnel, but took 1,180 prisoners; and the CDRs detained thousands of alleged collaborators.

The episode was a turning point. It discredited the USA and drew a clear line between the Revolution and the old Cuba. It led to the expulsion of clergy and the nationalization of private schools; it established the CDRs as an ideal mechanism for the mobilization, involvement and politicization of Cubans; and it confirmed the shift towards socialism. In response to a shortage of private capital, upon Soviet advice, Cuba began to industrialize, centralize and nationalize; 70% of land was seized by the state in 1963. The middle classes now left in droves, fearing expropriation and rationing, and, in 1965, the US and Cuban Governments agreed to a regular airlifting of disgruntled Cubans off the island. By 1971 some 700,000 had left, removing valuable professional expertise but also a considerable source of potential unrest.

Meanwhile, two key processes were initiated in 1961. First, a high-profile literacy campaign enlisted 270,000 young volunteers to reduce illiteracy from around 23% to just 3% within a year. Besides its educational value, the campaign integrated and politicized both the 707,000 newly literate and their educators. Second, the 26 July Movement, PSP and CDR were merged to form the Organizaciones Revolucionarias Integradas (ORI—Integrated Revolutionary Organizations); following widespread criticism, ORI was restyled in 1962 as the Partido Unido de la Revolución Socialista Cubana (PURSC—United Party of the Socialist Revolution of Cuba).

The growing mistrust between Cuba and the USA led to an incident in October 1962 commonly referred to as the Cuban Missile Crisis. Cuban fears and Soviet misjudgements led to the stationing of nuclear missiles in Cuba. A US ultimatum secured their withdrawal, following a tense 13 days, but, although the USA agreed (secretly) not to invade Cuba, the Soviet climb-down angered Castro.

That displeasure, coupled with other Cuban dissatisfactions, led to a growing distance between Cuba and the USSR, a distance that was exacerbated by a crisis in March 1962. Aníbal Escalante, an ORI co-ordinator, was accused of using his position to enhance the PSP's power, leading to the demotion of many PSP activists within the newly formed PURSC. Thereafter, the former guerrillas pursued their own definition of socialist revolution, rejecting Soviet dictates. In 1965 the PURSC was replaced by the Partido Comunista de Cuba (PCC—Communist Party of Cuba).

Bitter theoretical differences finally led, in the mid-1960s, to a 'moral economy', maximizing sugar production but, following Guevara's advice, emphasizing centralization and consciousness. This strategy reflected Cuba's isolation, which was formalized in 1962 by its suspension, in January, from the Organization of American States (OAS) and the imposition, in February, of a near-total trade embargo by the USA; the resulting 'siege mentality' and austerity led some to see Cuba's resources in its human capital and land, now the focus of all investment. In 1968, as part of the 'Revolutionary Offensive', all remaining non-agricultural private enterprises, numbering some 55,000, were nationalized in an attempt to combat declining production and increasing levels of absenteeism.

Independence was also true abroad. From 1962 Cuba actively supported guerrillas in the region and in Africa. Guevara left the country in 1965 and, after an abortive Congo campaign, began a struggle in Bolivia in 1966, until he was captured and killed in October 1967. By 1968 Cuba was fighting 'US imperialism' and challenging the Soviet policy of 'peaceful coexistence'.

POST-1970 INSTITUTIONALIZATION

A disastrous harvest in 1970 provoked a reassessment, as a result of which the 1960s strategy was replaced by an Eastern Bloc orthodoxy, which persuaded the Bloc's trading organization (the Council for Mutual Economic Assistance—CMEA) to admit Cuba as a full member in 1972, having previously refused. This gave Cuba economic stability, together with a reliable market (for diversified exports), manufactured imports, a more rational wage structure, rising standards and a move away from rationing.

The rethink also rehabilitated the former PSP members, now given economic and political responsibility in a strengthened PCC, which had its first party congress in 1975; party membership expanded from about 55,000 in 1975 to 500,000 in 1985. The first Constitution of the Revolution, implemented in 1976, created a Soviet-style 'people's power' system, with directly elected municipal assemblies subsequently electing the Government and other higher bodies. Cuba increasingly resembled the Socialist Bloc, with growing professional, military and educational links.

Relations with the USA also improved during the presidency of Jimmy Carter (1977–81). In 1977 'interest sections' were opened in third-country embassies in Havana and Washington, DC, and Latin American countries could recognize and trade with Cuba. In 1979 Cuban-American emigrants returned on family visits, although protests (at Cubans' relative poverty) then led to an invasion of the Peruvian embassy by some 10,000 people wishing to emigrate. When the violence escalated, the Government allowed would-be emigrants to be collected by boat from Mariel, west of Havana; some 121,000 left the island.

Apparent 'Sovietization' was, however, misleading. Even Castro's 1968 endorsement of the Soviet invasion of Czechoslovakia was more complex than it seemed, and when, in 1975, Cuban troops arrived in Angola to defend the Movimento Popular de Libertação de Angola (MPLA—People's Movement for the Liberation of Angola) Government against South Africa, Cuba was simply continuing old links, and the Cuban action forced the USSR to supply and transport the operation. This popular involvement (halting the South Africans and then defeating them in 1988) opened a new overseas strategy: internationalism. This meant sending thousands of volunteer professionals to developing countries, supporting successful revolutions in Nicaragua and Grenada, and collaborating with sympathetic Latin American, Caribbean and African governments. This strategy, besides allowing young Cubans to travel, usually to poorer countries, gave Cuba international leverage and support against the US trade embargo.

In the 1980s, however, the influence of the CMEA began to decline, and the Cold War prompted the Soviet President, Mikhail Gorbachev, to implement a series of reforms that directly affected Cuba: with trade and aid in crisis, urgent action was needed. This led to another strategic reassessment, at the 1986 PCC party congress, which led to a campaign of 'rectification' (which was also in part a reaction to the bureaucratization and opportunism that had originated from the recent rapid expansion of the party); rectification meant purging membership, economic streamlining and a return to some of the principles of the 1960s.

THE SPECIAL PERIOD

During 1989–91 the Eastern Bloc disintegrated, the CMEA was dissolved and the USSR imploded, all in quick succession. Suddenly, Cuba had lost 80% of its trade and faced a hostile USA alone and militarily weakened, the armed forces having been cut by one-half. In August 1990 Fidel Castro declared a war footing, the start of a 'special period in time of peace'. In 1992 the US Congress tightened the trade embargo against Cuba in the Cuban Democracy Act.

The scale of the crisis threatened the Revolution's existence. The economy shrank by 35% by 1994, with hitherto unthinkable levels of unemployment; oil supplies collapsed, affecting energy production and transport and worsening daily life and economic activity, and sugar output plummeted to less than 4m. metric tons annually.

The social effects were traumatic, total collapse being mitigated by rationing. Despite sustained spending, health and education standards fell, and people's expectations collapsed, with thousands leaving the PCC, and thousands more leaving Cuba illegally, as *balseros* (rafters). In August 1994 ferry hijackings produced clashes, deaths and unprecedented disturbances in Havana; when would-be emigrants were again allowed to leave by boat, some 35,000 left immediately, with a significant side-effect: since 1966 illegal Cuban immigrants had uniquely been allowed permanent US residence and eventual citizenship; now the USA and Cuba agreed to distinguish between those migrants caught at sea by the US Coastguard ('wet foot'), who were to be repatriated, and those migrants, who, if they reached US soil, could enjoy the 1966 rights ('dry foot').

Then, with the Revolution teetering on the brink of ruin, the economy began to recover, responding to a programme of unprecedented measures adopted at the PCC congress in 1991. Most significantly, the holding of US dollars was decriminalized in 1993; although this produced a new inequality between the dollar economy and the peso economy, dollar-denominated income from family remittances and tourism was crucial in facilitating the economic recovery. Tourism replaced sugar as Cuba's principal industry (one-half of Cuba's sugar mills were closed in 2003–04 alone), and annual tourist arrivals rose rapidly, reaching 2m. in 2000 and generating satellite economies, employment and revenue. Limited self-employment was tolerated in small-scale activities, allowing for the creation of private restaurants and rented accommodation, both geared towards the tourism market. More fundamentally, in 1993 state lands became co-operatives, to incentivize farmers, who were now given titles and allowed to sell surplus produce commercially, as was the military.

These unprecedented reforms had no political parallel, but there were further, lesser changes. A political broadening included Cuba's churches, which, sharing leaders' concerns about social collapse, were now allowed greater autonomy to practise and publish, members being welcomed into the PCC. The National Assembly became directly elected in 1992, and workplace-based assemblies debated measures and reforms. Finally, one response to the collapse—the revitalization of barrio-level life, filling gaps left by the state—was formalized, through local regenerative 'workshops' and People's Councils.

However, for most Cubans, the daily preoccupation was on economic and social conditions, as the disintegration wrought by the combination of economic collapse and tourism undermined the old morality of collective solidarity and encouraged individualism, a vast 'black' market and a rise in petty criminality. Tourism, in particular, resurrected long-banished problems: hustling and prostitution; racism, as black Cubans benefited less from remittances than their white compatriots; illegal internal migration, worsening an already overcrowded Havana and creating shanties; and a 'brain drain' from sectors such as education and health.

Meanwhile, the USA loomed large. Although the trade embargo remained in place, the 'twin track' policy of the Administration of US President Bill Clinton (1993–2001) advocated contacts with 'civil society' in Cuba. However, this partial opening angered émigrés, and, in February 1996, two aircraft from Brothers to the Rescue—a US-based activist organization formed by Cuban exiles—violated Cuban airspace to provoke a reaction; when the aircraft were shot down by the Cuban air force, resulting in the deaths of several US citizens, Clinton responded by signing the previously vetoed Cuban Liberty and Solidarity Act (commonly known as the Helms-Burton Act), allowing the embargo to be extended to include other countries that traded with, or invested in, Cuba, and giving it the force of a treaty, able to be repealed only by a two-thirds' congressional majority.

One window of Cuban opportunity opened in late 1999. Elián González, a six-year old boy whose mother died while attempting to take him illegally to Florida, USA, was rescued at sea, and thus was due to be deported. However, his US relatives refused to hand him over to the authorities. When, in April 2000, armed immigration officers seized him, flag-burning protests in Florida demonstrated public opinion. However, with the US presidential election approaching, the embargo could not be changed, and in November the Cuban-Americans in Florida were pivotal in electing George W. Bush (2001–09), who, determined to end the Cuban regime, revived the old hostility.

After the terrorist attacks against the USA on 11 September 2001, the Bush Administration implicitly included Cuba in its new 'axis of evil', campaigning to isolate Cuba and wean the European Union (EU) from its long-standing policy of engaging in dialogue and trade with the country. The US Interests Section began supporting dissidents materially, provoking the Cuban authorities, which, in April 2003, arrested and imprisoned 75 activists. This persuaded the EU to impose diplomatic sanctions for a two-year period, pragmatism and Spanish pressure shifting them back to their 'common position'. In 2004 the Bush Administration restricted remittances and family visits to Cuba, in an attempt to starve the Cuban economy of US dollars, although the Cuban Government's response (banning the dollar as legal currency and replacing it with the convertible peso—thereby swelling the state coffers as Cubans exchanged their worthless dollars—and charging 10% for all dollar exchanges) led many Cuban-Americans to criticize the original measures.

Elsewhere, foreign relations improved dramatically, especially in Latin America, where the election of leftist governments created more sympathy for Cuba, especially in Venezuela, whose President, Hugo Chávez, developed a close

relationship with Fidel Castro. In 2002 the Cuban and Venezuelan Governments established what became known as the Bolivarian Alliance for the Peoples of our America-People's Trade Treaty (Alianza Bolivariana para los Pueblos de Nuestra América-Tratado de Comercio de los Pueblos—ALBA-TCP), intended as an alternative to the Free Trade Area of the Americas. The two Governments also agreed to an exchange of Cuban expertise for Venezuelan oil. Other governments also moved closer to Cuba, and the Caribbean Common Market (CARICOM), and even the OAS in 2009, voted to admit Cuba (although Cuba declined the latter invitation).

The Elián González affair also changed Cuban politics, leaders regarding it as an opportunity to revive political mobilization and target youth. Both were urgently needed. Mobilization had suffered from institutionalization and a crisis that left no time, means or inclination to engage in campaigning. Cuba's leaders reasoned that, having regained the ability to mobilize large numbers effectively owing to the incident, they should target the young; activists had long feared that young Cubans lacked ideological commitment and that, born during relative material security, they had developed unrealistic expectations and responded less to the discourse of an ageing leadership. However, from January 2000 it was Cuba's youth organizations that led six months of daily national campaigning, and, once Elián returned to Cuba, in June, the campaign's mechanisms and enthusiasm were marshalled in a broader campaign.

The youth organizations' campaigning began a new 'battle of ideas', which, recognizing that ideological commitment had suffered during the Special Period, urged Cubans to revive ideological fervour, resist capitalism and address the 'internet threat', rebuilding the ideological basis of a shattered nation. Internationally, this meant supporting both Latin America's struggle against globalization and the left-wing Government of Venezuela. Nationally, it reinvigorated debate and revived the spirit of the literacy campaign (see above), which had been a casualty of the Special Period. Above all, through intensive schools it trained particular groups of young people (e.g., those who had missed out on access to university), specifically to meet new social needs and shortages: the first schools produced social workers to work in the slums while studying at university, while similar schools addressed the primary teaching and nursing sectors depleted by the dual-currency 'brain drain'. To meet this new demand, in 2002 university branches were opened in each of Cuba's 169 municipalities, while a wider educational campaign developed televised university courses.

By 2005 the 'battle of ideas' was leading to absenteeism, exhaustion and inefficiency. This now coincided with a new development: namely, the increasing frailty of Fidel Castro, now almost 80 and losing his old vigour. On 1 August 2006 he announced that he was temporarily ceding power to his brother, Raúl, while he underwent urgent surgery (for diverticulitis). The Cuban population seemed neither surprised nor disappointed, many seeing Raúl Castro as a legitimate historic leader, who, known for his efficiency and pragmatism, might bring economic change.

While uncertainty reigned, few major decisions were taken. However, in July 2007 Raúl Castro voiced public criticisms of Cuba's economic, political and social failings, and then launched a nationwide consultation. However, despite the urgency of change (expectations being high), Raúl was limited in his scope. First, Fidel might either return or undermine reforms; second, Raúl recognized the need for balance. Finally, in January 2008, on the eve of Assembly elections, Fidel resigned as head of state, Raúl being then elected to the presidency in February.

CUBA UNDER RAÚL CASTRO

Raúl Castro reshaped his Government, emphasizing efficiency and relying on the military and former guerrillas, notably José Ramón Machado Ventura (elected First Vice-President in February 2008) and Ramiro Valdés (given an oversight role). However, in March 2009 he also summarily dismissed two rising stars, the Secretary of the Council of Ministers, Carlos Lage Dávila, and Minister of Foreign Relations Felipe Pérez

Roque, both of whom, lacking the same guerrilla pedigree, had also perhaps overplayed their succession ambitions.

Raúl's priority was clear: economic reforms to ensure public confidence and bolster the Revolution's legitimacy. However, in 2008 three hurricanes and the global economic crisis (affecting import prices and export income) slowed down change: in 2008–09 farmers were allowed access to unused public land, and measures were taken to incentivize production and improve efficiency, accompanied by a campaign against pilfering, absenteeism and inefficient work practices, as well as higher level corruption. In 2010 Raúl shocked Cubans by his five-year plan to shed up to 1.3m. jobs from an overstaffed state sector, one-half in the first six months. The intention was that the resulting surplus labour would expand the self-employed sector, since the proposed cuts would formalize what was already happening informally, i.e., widespread 'moonlighting' by state employees. Ultimately, this plan was slowed in the face of trade union objections.

Another obstacle to reform came from resistance within the PCC, whose Sixth Congress had failed to materialize since 2002 (its due date). Hence, one of Raúl's first acts in 2008 was to seek to convene it for 2009, but continuing resistance and delay led him to threaten a Special Conference, to make 'personnel changes'. This broke the deadlock, the Congress eventually meeting in April 2011. That gathering (preceded by months of debate at different levels of the Party) approved major reform proposals, including extensions of self-employment, limited freedom to buy and sell housing, and greater freedom of movement of labour. It also confirmed Raúl as party leader, once Fidel confirmed his 2008 resignation. The threatened Special Conference actually took place in January 2012, but, while not making significant personnel changes, did reduce the Party's ability to interfere in government. A further, widely popular, reform began in January 2013: the easing of 50-year-old restrictions on foreign travel (previously requiring an exit visa and US $150, this now was replaced by a passport and appropriate entry visa). The massive take-up of these opportunities, by Cubans on the island, in 2013–14, confirmed the measure's popularity.

Meanwhile, another priority was to ease US–Cuban relations. Barack Obama's 2008 election to the US presidency had aroused expectations that were high and often unrealistic, given the trade embargo's legal status and Florida's continued electoral importance; indeed, these factors limited Obama to reversing the 2004 measures, softening open hostility and resuming Clinton's 'twin track' policy, e.g. easing regulations on US citizens' travel to Cuba. However, as Cuba's dissidents, inactive since 2006, revived activity in 2009–10 (including hunger strikes and an increased activism by the 'Ladies in White', the wives of the remaining 2003 prisoners), the Cuban authorities' response forced a return to the traditional US opposition. From late 2010, however, the Cuban leadership's growing rapprochement with the Roman Catholic Church led to an agreement to release a large number of prisoners, including all remaining prisoners from 2003, most agreeing

to leave Cuba, usually for Spain. However, surprisingly, the new travel freedom extended to many prominent dissidents, now allowed to campaign abroad against Cuba's human rights' record. Another slight shift in US–Cuban relations came in May 2013, when one of the five Cubans sentenced in the USA in 2000 for spying was allowed to return and then remain in Cuba (through a legal loophole, whereby he renounced his US citizenship), leading to hopes that Cuba would, in return, announce concessions on Alan Gross, the US citizen sentenced in 2011 for spying in Cuba. Another of the five was also released in February 2014, but any such deal remained as a hope rather than expectation. However, this latter case was complicated in April, when it emerged in the US press that, since 2010, USAID (for whom Gross had been working when arrested) had been financing a covert operation to create a social media site in Cuba, Zunzuneo, with the explicit aim of fostering active and even violent dissent; this not only cast serious doubt on Gross's innocence, but suggested that the Obama Administration's gestures of dialogue had not replaced the traditional measures to undermine the Cuban system.

The main event of 2013 was the general election to the National Assembly in February. While showing familiar levels of support (91% turnout and 75% accepting the 'full slate' of approved candidates), the outcome was doubly significant. First, members of the resulting (National and Provincial) Assemblies and the subsequently elected Council of State were all noticeably younger than before (average age 48, 47 and 57, respectively), and the Council's 31 members included 13 women and 12 black or mixed-race members. Second, the Council elections surprisingly resulted in Machado Ventura being replaced as senior Vice-President by 53-year old Miguel Díaz-Canel Bermúdez, formerly Minister of Higher Education. This was taken generally as indicating Raúl's preference for the future shape of government (he had effectively already announced his determination to stand down in 2018): a younger, less overtly political administration that would be recognized for its effectiveness. Therefore, although there was still no prospect of real change in the US embargo, Raúl Castro was not only more decidedly in control of the Government and of the Party, but had indicated the likely 'succession'. The only remaining uncertainty was the success of his economic reforms.

In fact, the following year saw those reforms continue steadily, following Castro's motto of 'sin pausa, sin prisa' (without stopping, but without hurrying)—an important principle for the system's stability, given the need to avoid either destabilization, through over-rapid or over-extensive change (remembering the fate of Gorbachev's USSR), or frustration arising from any delays. With around half a million Cubans working in the self-employed sector legally, many of them now allowed to employ people beyond the family, the artisan and small-business sector seemed clearly to be taking off as planned, and 2014 saw greater moves to extend the process of creating business and artisan co-operatives, closer ideologically to the traditional principles.

Economy

Dr EMILY MORRIS

The structure of the Cuban economy is very unusual, with the state owning most enterprises, a dual exchange rate system, many prices set by the state, and public services (particularly health and education) accounting for an exceptionally large proportion of national income and employment. These characteristics make it difficult to determine the relative size of the economy. Estimates of Cuba's gross domestic product (GDP) range from US $71,000m. in 2013 (World Bank estimate for purchasing power parity US dollar GDP at current prices in 2011, adjusted for GDP growth and US dollar inflation) to $104,000m. (UN Human Development Index 2013 estimate for 2005, adjusted for GDP growth and US dollar inflation). The middle of this range would put Cuban national income at

around $88,000m. With a population of 11.2m., this would suggest that national income per head is around $7,800—within the range defined as 'middle income' and slightly below the average for the Latin American and Caribbean region.

There is also some uncertainty surrounding estimates of real (inflation-adjusted) GDP growth performance. Although Cuba has an extensive and effective system for collecting physical production data, it is likely that there are some distortions in terms of the weightings used due to problems of aggregating different sets of prices and the degree of structural change that has occurred since the 1997 base year. None the less, the overall trend reported in the official figures appears plausible. It shows real GDP growth performance broadly in line with the average for the region over the past decade, which is not sufficient to restore Cuba's relative position to its 1990 level. The legacy of the economic recession of the 1990s remains, with continued severe economic hardship for many Cubans, far greater inequality than before, and severely decapitalized infrastructure and productive capacity. To understand the recent performance and current challenges, it is necessary to trace the evolution of Cuba's economic structure and performance since it lost the support of the Soviet bloc.

ECONOMIC CRISIS AND RESPONSE IN THE 1990s

Cuba's integration into the Council for Mutual Economic Assistance (the Soviet economic bloc) had created an economic structure that was highly dependent on exports of sugar at very favourable prices in exchange for petroleum and other imports, and generous grants or concessional loans to cover any trade deficits. The direct result of the loss of those favourable prices and financing arrangements when the Soviet bloc collapsed was a 70% decline in total foreign exchange inflows, which in turn caused a 35% decrease in national income between 1990 and 1994.

Unlike the other countries of the former Soviet bloc, Cuba's recovery has been hampered by restricted access to international markets and finance. It had no access to support from multilateral financial institutions such as the European Bank for Reconstruction and Development that aided the countries of Central and Eastern Europe, and was hindered by US sanctions that not only blocked access to most other sources of international finance but also prohibited trade with its natural partner, the USA, and deterred trade partners from other countries.

These US sanctions were tightened during the worst years of hardship, first with the Cuban Democracy Act (also known as the Torricelli Act) in 1992, and then the wide-ranging Cuban Liberty and Solidarity Act (commonly known as the Helms-Burton Act) in 1996, which created additional deterrents to third country businesses considering Cuban trade or investments. US restrictions on Cuban trade and financing, together with an unorthodox approach to economic adjustment, have contributed to the development of an unusual and unbalanced economic structure.

With import deliveries interrupted, the central planning system stalled in 1990–91. The Cuban Government responded by appealing for mass mobilization as if the country were experiencing war conditions, in the hope that it could pre-empt unrest and preserve the social safety net and universal health and education services. The planning authorities still had a monopoly on international transactions and sought to prioritize essential food imports, but despite reducing oil imports by 70% and other products by more than 80%, they still had only enough foreign exchange to purchase half as much food as before. A 'food programme' sought to encourage self-provisioning and innovative methods, while the Government attempted to minimize economic and social disruption by maintaining fixed salaries and prices for basic goods, and keeping state employees (90% of the total labour force) in work. Inevitably, as output declined, productivity per worker decreased sharply, the cost of subsidies rose and the fiscal deficit increased dramatically. The deficit was monetized, with the result that the black market value of the Cuban peso collapsed, from around seven pesos per US dollar in 1990 to beyond 100 pesos in 1993.

For Cuban state employees, the decline in living standards was experienced as the emergence of acute shortages of all but the most essential goods, as the decline in the black market value of the Cuban peso meant that imported goods were priced beyond their means. However, most jobs were secure, nominal incomes remained unchanged, and all Cubans still had access to a basic food ration, utilities and public services. The legalization of the US dollar and the establishment of an official exchange market for personal transactions, together with a stabilization programme launched in 1994, halted the Cuban peso's decline but only partially restored its value; the domestic currency had strengthened to 25 pesos per US dollar by the end of 1995, and remained around that level for the next two decades. Meanwhile, the official rate of exchange, used for

official transactions and accounting purposes, remained at one peso per dollar.

This policy succeeded in its main objectives: social protection was broadly achieved—as reflected in the fact that Cuban mortality rates remained relatively unaffected during the deprivations of the 'transition recession' (unlike many of the other countries of the former Soviet bloc, which saw national income declines during those years)—and, after the deep recession of 1990–93, the economy began to recover from 1994. However, the legacy of the crisis years remains, including an economic structure that has remained over-specialized and distorted, along with deep monetary imbalances, growing income inequality, and flourishing black markets that have hampered economic efficiency and dynamism.

UNBALANCED GROWTH

With the crisis of the 1990s having clearly been caused by the acute shortage of foreign exchange, Cuban recovery efforts were focused on seeking new sources of international earnings. A constitutional reform of 1992 and foreign investment law of 1995 opened the Cuban economy to new sources of financing, management skills and marketing, in the sectors with the most potential for rapid foreign exchange earnings. This policy of channelling resources into a few areas has resulted in a recovery built around the growth of only a small number of industries: tourism, nickel, professional services and petroleum-processing.

Tourism was the first new industry to emerge in the post-Soviet years. Since the 1960s US sanctions had forbidden tourist travel from the USA, so the once-thriving industry had been neglected for 30 years. As a result, in 1990 Cuba had a wealth of underexploited resources that provided a high return for relatively little investment. By opening the industry up to foreign companies, it was possible to accelerate the process of upgrading old hotels, building new establishments, training managers and workers, and developing new markets. Tourist arrivals grew by an average of 18% a year in the 1990s, rising from 340,000 in 1990 to 1.7m. by 2000. Gross tourism receipts overtook sugar earnings in 1994, and by 2000 they were more than four times as large, totalling US $1,900m. Since 2000 the industry has matured and the average annual growth rate has moderated to 4%, with 2.8m. arrivals in 2013 bringing in gross revenue of $2,600m.

Nickel was the second industry to expand. The key foreign investment was a joint venture deal with Sherritt International, a Canadian mining company, which brought new financing that increased nickel production from 27,000 metric tons in 1994 to 77,000 tons by 2001, yielding a rise in export earnings from US $200m. to $465m. The agreement gave Cuba a share in a Canadian nickel-processing plant, as well as granting Sherritt a stake in a Cuban mine. Since 2001 production has stabilized at around 70,000 tons per year. A surge in world market prices pushed earnings up to a peak of over $2,000m. in 2007, but softer prices reduced revenues to $1,000m. by 2012.

Since 2005 the broad range of activities grouped together as 'non-tourism services' has dominated Cuba's international earnings, according to official balance of payments accounts. The increase was sudden: in 2004 the accounts showed total earnings from the sector of US $1,300m.; in the following year the figure had doubled to $2,600m.; and by 2010 it had grown to $5,000m.—twice as much as tourism receipts. Although the accounts provide no breakdown of components within this category, most of the increase can be attributed to a Cuban-Venezuelan agreement that provides for Cuba to import Venezuelan oil in return for the sale of the services of Cuban professionals, mainly public health workers.

Petroleum-refining is the most recent addition to the list of growth industries. Earnings from exports of oil products rose from under US $200m. in 2007 to over $800m. in 2008, as a new refinery in the coastal city of Cienfuegos came on stream. The project was undertaken by a joint venture between the Cuban and Venezuelan state oil companies, which raised Cuba's annual output of refined petroleum products from 2.3m. tons to around 5m. tons. The refinery supplies oil products to Cuba's domestic market, as well as exporting them. Strong international prices helped to increase the industry's export earnings to $1,900m. by 2010, the latest year for which data are available.

Biotechnology is another important industry. State investment in the sector was maintained even during the worst years of the economic crisis of the 1990s, and, after a slow start due to the long process of intellectual property registration and difficulties of penetrating a global market, its export earnings rose 10-fold in the decade to 2012, to reach around US $500m., equivalent to 4% of total export revenues. In addition, earnings from the licensing of overseas production of Cuban-patented medicines may account for some of the growth of 'non-tourism services' income. Cuba's exceptional capacity in this area suggests the potential for the sector to become a major contributor to economic growth in the future.

While Cuba's success in rebuilding international earnings has been impressive—by 2005 total import capacity had returned to its 1990 level of US $8,000m., and by 2014 the country was able to pay for imports of $14,000m.—the focus of policy and investment on the development of such a narrow range of 'strategic' industry enclaves, and the persistence of a dual currency system, has created an over-specialized and distorted pattern of development.

Cuba's external accounts reveal the extent of specialization. By 2012 the five industries listed above accounted for 90% of the country's US $16,000m. foreign exchange earnings. The economy's vulnerability to external shocks resulting from such export product concentration is compounded by a high dependence on a single trade partner. For the past decade all of Cuba's oil imports, which accounted for nearly one-half of all import spending in 2012, have come from Venezuela. These are paid for by Cuban earnings from the sale of professional services to Venezuela, leaving Cuba very exposed to political changes in that country that might end the favourable trade relationship. With heightened political uncertainty in Venezuela since the death of President Lt-Col (retd) Hugo Rafael Chávez Frías in early 2013, Cuba has been urgently seeking new markets for its medical services. South Africa and Brazil have emerged as important customers.

RAÚL CASTRO'S CHALLENGE: INJECTING ECONOMIC DYNAMISM

Beyond this handful of export industries, there are few other areas of economic activity that have recovered to their 1990 levels. Most analysts agree that the task of reversing the severe decapitalization that occurred during the economic recession of the 1990s is incomplete. The process has been hampered by a chronic shortage of investment finance and very restricted access to foreign exchange. The favourable trade agreement with Venezuela produced a brief surge in economic performance in 2005–07, with average annual real GDP growth rising above 10%, but it soon petered out. Average annual growth in 2009–13 moderated to 2.5%, and the aggregate level of investment remains at only around 10% of GDP—less than one-half the average for the Latin American and Caribbean region, and a level too low to prevent further erosion of the national capital base.

The dual currency system has not only continued to obstruct the integration of the external and internal economies, but has also contributed to increasing real income inequality. For Cubans who receive incomes in convertible currencies, and some of those who are self-employed (either formally or informally), living standards have improved substantially since the crisis of the 1990s. However, for the rest, whose incomes are in the undervalued Cuban peso, living standards are still worse than they were in 1990, with the prices of the many goods and services that are denominated in convertible currency or sold at market prices completely out of reach. Low productivity remains a burden for the state budget, which continues to subsidize production and prices, while wide income inequality, with continued hardships and shortages, is providing poor incentives for work and fertile ground for corruption.

This is the context for the economic reforms introduced by Cuban President Gen. Raúl Castro Ruz. To bolster support for the process, he initiated a national consultation in 2010 to identify and confront economic weaknesses and to develop a

strategy to lift the economy out of stagnation. A government team drafted a document on *Economic and Social Policy Guidelines for the Party and the Revolution*, which was circulated to thousands of meetings of members of the ruling Partido Comunista de Cuba (PCC—Communist Party of Cuba) and other 'mass organizations' for discussion and proposed amendments. The result was a revised draft, which was approved by the 6th Congress of the PCC in April 2011.

The strategy outline, known as *lineamientos* (guidelines), is providing the framework for a far-reaching five-year process of 'updating' the economy. It involves the liberalization of some markets, within the framework of an economy in which most production remains state owned, with continued strict regulation of economic activity and a government commitment to social protection and universal health and education services. The aim is to introduce a new dynamism into the parts of the economy that have been languishing.

The agricultural sector has been subject to a series of reforms designed to improve productivity over the past two decades, but 'updating' is still badly needed. According to national income accounts, total output in 2013 was still only around two-thirds of its 1990 level—an improvement since the worst years of the crisis (when output contracted to only one-half the 1990 amount), but a disappointment none the less.

One of the reasons for the low figure is the decline in the sugar crop: a sudden collapse when favourable Soviet prices ended, from 8.4m. metric tons in the harvest completed in 1990 to 4m. tons in 1994; then a rationalization process that further reduced production to below 2m. tons by 2005. Sugar exports in 2012 accounted for only 3% of total shipments, down from more than 70% in 1990. The focus of policy has shifted from meeting crop targets to improving productivity and diversifying production, including generating electricity from burning bagasse. The industry has been reorganized, with the abolition of the Ministry of Sugar and the establishment of semi-autonomous enterprises under a national holding company. Each of these is empowered to sign contracts with foreign investors, who are now being actively invited to help to provide the finance and technology required to modernize sugar agriculture and associated industries.

Although there are some other agricultural export products (led by citrus), the sector's strategic importance now lies in its capacity to produce food. Food imports account for around 10% of all import spending, making food supplies vulnerable to foreign exchange availability and fluctuations in world market prices. A series of policy initiatives have transformed the pattern of land tenure (with state farming now limited only to the largest plantations and new private farms established) to improve incentives, and, having assessed the reasons for the slow pace of improvement, the Government is now working to improve credit facilities and the availability of inputs and equipment, and to secure financing for investment in infrastructure and distribution networks.

Manufacturing output, according to official figures, only recovered to its 1990 level in 2007, and since then its annual rate of growth has been only 1.6%. The sector's recovery has been severely hampered by the dual currency system, which has made it difficult for state enterprises to compete internationally, either to develop export markets or to build domestic businesses to substitute for imports. One of the key measures included among the *lineamientos* is the unification of the currencies.

The *lineamientos* document does not state how and when the exchange rate reform is to be conducted, but a document published in the *Gaceta Oficial* in early March 2014 provided some clues. In a single day (referred to as *dia cero*—day zero), the convertible peso will be withdrawn from circulation. In preparation for the change, accountants in every enterprise and public entity are being trained in the rules for measuring the value of assets and liabilities, and setting prices. There remains great uncertainty about the date of the change and the rate of exchange for the Cuban peso, which in mid-2014 was valued at 24 Cuban pesos = 1 convertible peso at the 'Cadeca' rate used for personal transactions and for the private sector. State enterprises are starting to move away from use of the official 1 Cuban peso = 1 convertible peso rate, and use variable rates of around 10 Cuban pesos = 1 convertible peso. The convertible peso is valued at 1 convertible peso = US $1. If the central bank were to leave the value at 24 Cuban pesos = 1 convertible peso, it is likely that Cuban enterprises would continue to use a different rate, and this new form of dualism would be phased out gradually, as the two rates progressively moved closer.

It is the manufacturing sector that the Government hopes will benefit most from a new foreign investment law, which was approved in March 2014 and implemented in June. The new law retains most of the key principles of its 1995 predecessor, including the need for Cuban government approval for all major projects, but offers more attractive tax concessions and a clearer legal framework. The Government has emphasized that it would welcome US investors if and when US sanctions prohibiting them were lifted. Another recent economic reform intended to attract more foreign investors, announced in late 2013, is the creation of a new 'special development zone' at the port of Mariel.

Construction activity has more than doubled since the mid-1990s, but remains at only around two-thirds of its pre-crisis level. According to official statistics, the sector, which had contracted over the previous five years, grew by an average of more than 12% in 2012 and 2013. It received a strong boost from the legalization of a free, albeit still regulated, market in housing in 2011 and an increase in production and sales of building materials and new fittings. After decades of being unable to obtain materials to undertake home improvements, Cubans—especially those receiving remittances or earning more money from private sector activity—now have both the means and incentive to carry out remedial work. With most of the home improvements carried out in the informal sector, the official statistics probably understate the growth of house-building activity.

Construction activity also includes building work to expand productive capacity and is therefore closely linked with the amount of aggregate investment, for which new sources of financing are being sought. Infrastructure investment, which has traditionally been mainly financed from tax revenue and therefore severely restricted by fiscal constraints since 1990, has now started to increase. A huge port infrastructure upgrade, inaugurated on schedule in January 2014 at Mariel, has set a precedent for external funding for major projects. The scheme received financing of almost US $1,000m. from the Brazilian state-owned development Bank, the Banco Nacional do Desenvolvimento Econômico e Social, and will be managed by a Singaporean company, PSA International. The Cuban Ministry of Foreign Trade and Investment is now actively seeking new international partners for other infrastructure projects, as well as for new investments in manufacturing, agriculture and energy.

Energy has long been a priority sector due to Cuba's heavy dependence on imports. In the 1990s it was the only sector supplying the domestic economy that was able to attract international partners. This was thanks to an innovative financing arrangement under which the Government paid the foreign partner in hard currency for domestically produced oil. Foreign investment lifted total output from 1.5m. metric tons of oil equivalent in 1997 to a peak of 4.3m. tons in 2003. This oil was from Cuba's existing fields, on the north coast of the island. Output from these reserves is now diminishing, as they become exhausted.

Foreign investors have also been involved in exploration for petroleum in Cuba's deep-water territory in the Gulf of Mexico. Four exploration wells have been sunk, but so far none have yielded petroleum in commercial quantities. Investor interest in the Cuban exploration blocs has been dampened by US sanctions, which not only block the prospect of selling oil to the USA if any were found, but also raise costs due to restrictions on the use of technology or supplies from the USA. Recent talks with the US environmental protection authorities achieved a breakthrough in terms of the use of some US technology in the Cuban oil sector.

Cuba's policy guidelines also stress the need to explore the potential for renewable energy. In recent years there have been substantial investments in solar, wind and biomass technologies, although renewable sources still account for only around 1% of total electricity generation. The use of bagasse to power sugar mills accounts for most of the 22% of all primary energy production produced by renewables. With sugar output expected to grow strongly from its current low level, and investments to improve the efficiency of sugar mill boilers, biomass is expected to make an increasing contribution to Cuban energy and electricity production over the coming decade.

Services still dominate the Cuban economy, but their composition and role is changing. According to official national income statistics, they account for 63% of total employment and more than 70% of national income. The 'services' category of national income covers a huge range of activities, but in Cuba's case the main employers are the unusually extensive public services (particularly health and education) and tourism-related activities. During the crisis of the 1990s the services sector contracted less than others (with a 25% decline, compared with 35% for the economy as a whole). This is because the tourism industry was growing strongly during those years and public services remained a government priority.

The priority given to health and education, and the expansion of the export of medical services, ensured that there was a strongly rising trend in employment in health and education between 2000 and 2008: the proportion of the total working population who were employed in 'community and social' services rose from 34% to 42% in those years. However, since then, a process of rationalization throughout the public sector has halted the rising trend in both spending and employment in health and education. At the same time, the Government is seeking to expand other sectors and create new opportunities for work in the non-state sector. The result is that government spending, which peaked at 78% of GDP in 2008, declined to 60% in 2013. This trend is expected to continue. The fiscal deficit, which widened to 6.7% of GDP in 2008, narrowed to just 1.2% in 2013.

The results of Raúl Castro's economic reforms have so far been modest in terms of economic performance, with average annual real GDP growth of just 2.7% in 2008–13. However, their effects have been profound in terms of shifting the role of the state and the pattern of economic development. Many of the changes described in the *lineamientos*, which provide an outline of priorities for the five years to 2016, have already been implemented, including the growth of the non-state sector, rationalization of the state sector (involving the removal of job security) and decentralization of economic decision-making. Of those measures still pending, one of the most important will be exchange rate unification, as it will pave the way for further fundamental changes in the way the economy functions. The process of adjustment carries risks, but if it is achieved without major economic disruption, it will be a major step towards the achievement of greater economic efficiency and dynamism. By 2016 prices and markets will be playing a greater role in the allocation of resources, as the Government withdraws from the direct control of economic activity and becomes focused more on monitoring, providing key public services and welfare, strategic planning, and regulation. There will be greater space for non-state economic activity, including a wider opening to foreign investment. Any relaxation of US sanctions would increase both the degree of integration of the Cuban economy into the global market and its rate of economic growth, but the possibility of such an outcome will depend on domestic US politics as the 2016 presidential and congressional elections there approach.

Statistical Survey

Sources (unless otherwise stated): Cámara de Comercio de la República de Cuba, Calle 21, No 661/701, esq. Calle A, Apdo 4237, Vedado, Havana; tel. (7) 830-4436; fax (7) 833-3042; e-mail pdcia@camara.com.cu; internet www.camaracuba.cu; Oficina Nacional de Estadísticas, Calle Paseo 60, entre 3 y 5, Plaza de la Revolución, Vedado, Havana, CP 10400; tel. (7) 830-0053; fax (7) 833-3083; e-mail oneweb@one.gov.cu; internet www.one.cu.

Area and Population

AREA, POPULATION AND DENSITY

Area (sq km)	109,884*
Population (census results)	
7–16 September 2002	11,177,743
15–24 September 2012	
Males	5,570,825
Females	5,596,500
Total	11,167,325
Population (official estimate at 31 December)†	
2013	11,210,064
Density (per sq km) at 31 December 2013	102.0

* 42,426 sq miles.
† Preliminary figure.

POPULATION BY AGE AND SEX
(population at 2012 census)

	Males	Females	Total
0–14 years	989,346	933,216	1,922,562
15–64 years	3,891,012	3,876,994	7,768,006
65 years and over	690,467	786,290	1,476,757
Total	5,570,825	5,596,500	11,167,325

PROVINCES
(population at 2012 census)

	Area (sq km)	Population	Density (per sq km)	Capital (population)
Artemisa . . .	4,003.2	494,631	123.6	Artemisa (82,873)
Camagüey . .	15,386.2	771,905	50.2	Camagüey (323,309)
Ciego de Avila .	6,971.6	426,054	61.1	Ciego de Avila (147,745)
Cienfuegos . .	4,188.6	404,228	96.5	Cienfuegos (171,946)
Granma . . .	8,374.2	834,380	99.6	Bayamo (235,107)
Guantánamo .	6,168.0	515,428	83.6	Guantánamo (228,436)
La Habana . .	728.3	2,106,146	2,891.9	—
Holguín . . .	9,215.7	1,035,072	112.3	Holguín (346,195)
Isla de la Juventud . .	2,419.3	84,751	35.0	Nueva Gerona (56,214)*
Matanzas . .	11,791.8	694,476	58.9	Matanzas (151,624)
Mayabeque .	3,743.8	376,825	100.7	San Jose de las Lajas (73,136)
Pinar del Río .	8,883.7	587,026	66.1	Pinar del Río (188,614)
Sancti Spíritus .	6,777.3	463,458	68.4	Sancti Spíritus (138,504)
Santiago de Cuba.	6,227.8	1,049,084	168.5	Santiago de Cuba (506,037)
Las Tunas . .	6,592.7	532,645	80.8	Las Tunas (202,105)
Villa Clara . .	8,411.8	791,216	94.1	Santa Clara (240,543)
Total . . .	109,884.0	11,167,325	101.6	—

* Preliminary figure.

PRINCIPAL TOWNS
(population at 2012 census)

La Habana (Havana, capital) . . .	2,106,146	Guantánamo . .	228,436
Santiago de Cuba .	506,037	Las Tunas . . .	202,105
Holguín . . .	346,195	Pinar del Río . .	188,614
Camagüey . . .	323,309	Cienfuegos . . .	171,946
Santa Clara . .	240,543	Matanzas . . .	151,624
Bayamo	235,107	Ciego de Avila . .	147,745

BIRTHS, MARRIAGES AND DEATHS*

	Registered live births†		Registered marriages‡		Registered deaths	
	Number	Rate (per 1,000)	Number	Rate (per 1,000)	Number	Rate (per 1,000)
2006 . .	111,323	9.9	56,377	5.0	80,831	7.2
2007 . .	112,472	10.0	56,781	5.1	81,927	7.3
2008 . .	122,569	10.9	61,852	5.5	86,423	7.7
2009 . .	130,036	11.6	54,969	4.9	86,940	7.7
2010 . .	127,746	11.4	58,490	5.2	91,065	8.1
2011 . .	133,067	11.8	59,676	5.3	87,040	7.7
2012 . .	125,674	11.3	55,759	5.0	89,368	4.6
2013§ . .	125,880	11.2	n.a.	n.a.	92,269	4.2

* Data are tabulated by year of registration rather than by year of occurrence.
† Births registered in the National Consumers Register, established on 31 December 1964.
‡ Including consensual unions formalized in response to special legislation.
§ Preliminary figures.

Life expectancy (years at birth): 79.1 (males 77.1; females 81.1) in 2012 (Source: World Bank, World Development Indicators database).

ECONOMICALLY ACTIVE POPULATION
('000 persons aged 15 years and over, official estimates)

	2010	2011	2012
Agriculture, hunting, forestry and fishing	921.5	986.5	944.2
Mining and quarrying	33.7	40.2	39.0
Manufacturing	486.6	507.9	608.5
Electricity, gas and water . . .	101.6	91.5	83.1
Construction	224.5	219.2	210.0
Trade, restaurants and hotels .	641.9	647.3	683.3
Transport, storage and communications	304.5	310.1	286.3
Financing, insurance, real estate and business services . . .	116.2	125.2	103.1
Community, social and personal services	2,154.0	2,082.3	1,944.7
Total employed	4,984.5	5,010.2	4,902.2
Unemployed	128.0	164.3	175.7
Total labour force	5,112.5	5,174.5	5,077.9

Health and Welfare

KEY INDICATORS

Total fertility rate (children per woman, 2012)	1.5
Under-5 mortality rate (per 1,000 live births, 2012) . . .	6
HIV/AIDS (% of persons aged 15–49, 2012)	<0.1
Physicians (per 1,000 head, 2010)	6.7
Hospital beds (per 1,000 head, 2010)	5.9
Health expenditure (2011): US $ per head (PPP)	429
Health expenditure (2011): % of GDP	10.0
Health expenditure (2011): public (% of total)	94.7
Access to water (% of persons, 2012)	94
Access to sanitation (% of persons, 2012)	93
Total carbon dioxide emissions ('000 metric tons, 2010) . .	38,364.2
Carbon dioxide emissions per head (metric tons, 2010) . .	3.4
Human Development Index (2013): ranking	44
Human Development Index (2013): value	0.815

For sources and definitions, see explanatory note on p. vi.

Agriculture

PRINCIPAL CROPS
('000 metric tons)

	2010	2011	2012
Rice, paddy	454.4	566.4	641.6
Maize	324.5	354.0	360.4
Potatoes	191.5	165.6	130.9
Sweet potatoes	384.7	311.9	335.3
Cassava (Manioc)	405.9	485.7	465.8
Yautia (Cocoyam)	137.4	132.1	153.8
Sugar cane	11,500.0	15,800.0	14,400.0
Beans, dry	80.4	133.0	127.1
Groundnuts, in shell* . . .	5.8	5.3	5.8
Coconuts	72.1	65.5	70.9
Cabbages and other brassicas .	134.6	162.9	123.3
Tomatoes	517.0	601.0	494.4
Pumpkins, squash and gourds .	347.1	340.3	361.4
Cucumbers and gherkins . .	92.7	94.1	95.5
Chillies and peppers, green . .	44.5	55.1	62.2
Onions, dry	111.7	143.5	118.2
Garlic	33.8	26.0	21.8
Watermelons	52.0	53.1	48.9
Cantaloupes and other melons* .	46.8	48.1	50.0
Bananas	249.2	250.0	195.5
Plantains	485.8	585.0	689.5
Oranges	178.3	122.9	93.8
Tangerines, mandarins, clementines and satsumas . .	23.0	23.0	18.6
Lemons and limes	6.1	6.6	6.5
Grapefruit and pomelos . .	137.7	112.0	84.7
Guavas, mangoes and mangosteens	275.2	270.0	389.6
Pineapples	64.8	76.9	84.1
Papayas	135.7	135.0	178.6
Coffee, green	8.4†	10.2†	11.0*
Tobacco, unmanufactured . .	20.5	19.9	19.5

* FAO estimate(s).
† Unofficial figure.

Aggregate production ('000 metric tons, may include official, semi-official or estimated data): Total cereals 779.1 in 2010, 920.7 in 2011, 1,002.3 in 2012; Total roots and tubers 1,515.0 in 2010, 1,445.0 in 2011, 1,452.0 in 2012; Total vegetables (incl. melons) 2,187.8 in 2010, 2,248.1 in 2011, 2162.0 in 2012; Total fruits (excl. melons) 1,870.5 in 2010, 1,966.4 in 2011, 2,014.3 in 2012.

Source: FAO.

LIVESTOCK
('000 head, year ending September)

	2010	2011	2012
Cattle	3,992.5	4,059.1	4,084.0
Horses	613.6	642.7	681.9
Mules	20.3	20.0	20.3
Pigs	1,591.0	1,518.0	1,545.1
Sheep	2,361.9	2,125.7	2,102.3
Goats	938.1	844.3	651.0
Chickens	30,950	33,663	30,182

Source: FAO.

LIVESTOCK PRODUCTS
('000 metric tons)

	2010	2011	2012
Cattle meat	63.5	66.5	67.1
Pig meat	172.3	176.2	166.3
Chicken meat	33.6	35.4	35.0
Cows' milk	629.5	599.5	604.3
Hen eggs	106.9	115.3	110.5
Honey	4.7	6.7	6.8

Source: FAO.

Forestry

ROUNDWOOD REMOVALS
('000 cubic metres, excl. bark, FAO estimates)

	2010	2011	2012
Sawlogs, veneer logs and logs for sleepers	229	230	200
Other industrial wood	361	361	361
Fuel wood	1,141	1,141	1,141
Total	1,731	1,732	1,702

Source: FAO.

SAWNWOOD PRODUCTION
('000 cubic metres, incl. railway sleepers)

	2010	2011	2012
Coniferous (softwood)	125	105	91
Broadleaved (hardwood) . . .	32	46	39
Total	157	151	130

Source: FAO.

Fishing

('000 metric tons, live weight)

	2010	2011	2012
Capture	24.0	24.0	22.3
Blue tilapia	2.0	1.3	1.6
Lane snapper	1.5	1.2	1.7
Caribbean spiny lobster . . .	4.5	5.0	4.5
Aquaculture*	31.4	24.6	26.2
Silver carp	16.2	14.6	14.4
Total catch*	55.4	48.6	48.5

* FAO estimates.

Note: Figures exclude sponges (metric tons): 45 in 2010; 49 in 2011; 29 in 2012.

Source: FAO.

Mining

('000 metric tons unless otherwise indicated)

	2009	2010	2011
Crude petroleum	2,731.3	3,024.8	3,011.7
Natural gas (million cu m) . .	1,155.3	1,072.5	1,019.8
Nickel (metal content)	3,949.0	2,511.0	2,442.8

2012: Natural gas 1,034.5 million cu m.

Industry

SELECTED PRODUCTS
('000 metric tons unless otherwise indicated)

	2010	2011	2012
Crude steel	277.6	282.1	277.0
Grey cement	1,631.4	1,730.7	1,824.8
Corrugated asbestos-cement tiles .	5,430.8	5,316.3	4,290.8
Colour television sets ('000) . .	46.5	57.2	7.0
Fuel oil	2,435.9	2,321.9	2,520.4
New tyres ('000)	57.4	58.3	49.3
Recapped tyres ('000)	90.2	111.1	119.4
Woven textile fabrics (million sq metres)	25.6	24.8	27.5
Cigarettes ('000 million) . . .	13.1	13.0	13.0
Cigars (million)	376.4	391.6	391.2
Alcoholic beverages (excl. wines, '000 litres)	1,102.8	1,111.2	1,146.8
Beer ('000 hectolitres) . . .	2,586.3	2,589.0	2,533.0
Soft drinks ('000 hectolitres) . .	3,669.9	3,781.3	3,773.1
Bicycles ('000)	28.2	54.3	61.0
Fishing vessels	14	4	12
Electric energy (million kWh) .	17,395.5	17,754.1	18,431.5

Finance

CURRENCY AND EXCHANGE RATES

Monetary Units
  100 centavos = 1 Cuban peso.
  1 Cuban peso = 1 convertible peso (official rate).

Sterling, Dollar and Euro Equivalents (30 May 2014)
  £1 sterling = 1.682 convertible pesos;
  US $1 = 1.000 convertible pesos;
  €1 = 1.361 convertible pesos;
  100 convertible pesos = £59.45 = $100.00 = €73.47.

Note: The foregoing information relates to official exchange rates. For the purposes of foreign trade, the peso was at par with the US dollar during each of the 10 years 1987–96. In addition, a 'convertible peso' was introduced in December 1994. Although officially at par with the Cuban peso, in March 2005 the 'unofficial' exchange rate prevailing in domestic exchange houses was adjusted to 24 pesos per convertible peso.

STATE BUDGET
(million pesos)

Revenue	2010	2011	2012
Tax revenue	24,201	26,508	29,068
Road and sales tax . . .	10,525	11,819	14,511
Taxes on services . . .	1,758	1,876	1,721
Taxes on utilities	3,049	3,742	3,662
Taxes on labour	4,414	4,235	4,108
Personal income tax . . .	554	762	873
Other taxes	927	1,078	1,150
Social security contributions .	2,974	2,996	3,043
Non-tax revenue	17,546	17,551	18,867
Transfers from state enterprises	2,886	4,664	5,629
Other non-tax revenue . .	14,660	12,887	13,238
Capital revenue	1,228	1,189	1,097
Restitution payments	−252	−388	−396
Total	42,723	44,861	48,635

Expenditure	2010	2011	2012
Current expenditure	41,118	42,048	44,876
Education	8,282	8,817	8,776
Public health and social assistance	6,930	7,314	6,236
Administration, defence and public order	3,586	5,148	5,566
Social security	4,886	5,074	5,346
Community services . . .	1,718	1,323	1,306
Industry	791	393	550
Culture, art and sport . .	2,117	1,970	1,664
Science and technology . .	613	212	188
Other activities	2,588	477	268
Subsidies, etc. to state enterprises	7,710	9,679	10,826
Financial operations	1,897	1,641	4,150
Investment expenditure . . .	3,895	3,966	6,430
Total	45,013	46,015	51,305

2013 (million pesos, estimates): *Revenue:* Tax revenue 28,500.0 (Road and sales tax 13,850.0, Taxes on services 1,515.0, Taxes on utilities 4,150.0, Taxes on labour 3,420.0, Personal income tax 1,045.0, Other taxes 1,370.0, Social security contributions 3,150.0); Non-tax revenue 16,277.2 (Transfers from state enterprises 4,861.0, Other non-tax revenue 11,416.2); Restitution payments −780.0; Total revenue 43,997.2. *Expenditure:* Current expenditure 42,043.9 (Education 8,545.4, Public health and social assistance 6,318.4, Administration, defence and public order 7,218.6, Social security 5,570.1, Community services 1,051.6, Industry 576.5, Culture, art and sport 1,666.8, Science and technology 149.6, Subsidies, etc. to state enterprises 10,046.9, Financial operations 900.0); Capital expenditure 5,358.6; Total expenditure 47,402.5.

2014 (million pesos, budget proposals): *Revenue:* Tax revenue 28,647.8 (Road and sales tax 14,745.7, Taxes on services 1,579.6, Taxes on utilities 4,067.0, Taxes on labour 2,760.0, Personal income tax 1,105.0, Other taxes 1,356.0, Social security contributions 3,034.5); Non-tax revenue 14,940.0 (Transfers from state enterprises 3,580.7, Other non-tax revenue 11,359.3); Restitution payments −330.0; Total revenue 43,257.8. *Expenditure:* Current expenditure 44,486.8 (Education 8,460.3, Public health and social assistance 7,421.0, Administration, defence and public order 7,184.3, Social security 5,122.7, Community services 1,219.6, Industry 582.4, Culture, art and sport 1,687.2, Science and technology 95.6, Subsidies, etc. to state enterprises 12,200.3, Financial operations 363.4, Provisions for disasters 150.0); Capital expenditure 2,461.0; Reserves 150.0; Development fund 50.0; Total expenditure 47,147.8.

MONEY SUPPLY
(million pesos)

	2011	2012	2013*
Currency in circulation . . .	10,646.0	12,480.4	13,719.2
Savings	16,436.1	17,567.6	18,476.7
Total	27,082.1	30,048.0	32,195.9

* Preliminary figures.

NATIONAL ACCOUNTS
(million pesos at current prices)

Composition of Gross National Product

	2008	2009	2010
Compensation of employees .	21,729.1	23,006.1	23,795.9
Operating surplus . . . }	25,077.8	25,514.2	26,794.2
Consumption of fixed capital . }			
Gross domestic product (GDP) at factor cost . .	46,806.9	48,520.3	50,590.1
Indirect taxes, less subsidies .	13,999.4	13,558.3	13,738.7
GDP in purchasers' values .	60,806.3	62,078.6	64,328.8
Less Factor income paid abroad (net)	1,055.2	1,643.0	1,432.0
Gross national product . .	59,751.1	60,435.6	62,896.8

Expenditure on the Gross Domestic Product

	2010	2011	2012
Government final consumption expenditure	22,359.6	24,436.3	23,341.6
Private final consumption expenditure	32,368.6	36,468.9	39,857.8
Increase in stocks	1,229.8	407.2	512.8
Gross fixed capital formation	5,561.4	5,319.6	5,758.4
Total domestic expenditure	61,519.4	66,632.0	69,470.6
Exports of goods and services	14,209.5	17,157.1	18,659.2
Less Imports of goods and services	11,400.6	14,799.0	14,887.9
GDP in purchasers' values	64,328.2	68,990.1	73,241.9
GDP at constant 1997 prices	47,459.0	48,789.3	50,259.7

Gross Domestic Product by Economic Activity

	2010	2011	2012
Agriculture, hunting, forestry and fishing	2,324.8	2,487.6	2,816.4
Mining and quarrying	861.3	895.1	955.3
Manufacturing	9,623.1	10,129.4	11,275.4
Electricity, gas and water	1,031.7	1,067.1	1,141.7
Construction	3,211.1	3,265.2	3,717.8
Wholesale and retail trade, restaurants and hotels	15,156.0	16,170.2	17,112.0
Transport, storage and communications	5,314.3	5,594.7	6,041.0
Finance, insurance, real estate and business services	2,802.2	2,854.5	3,081.2
Community, social and personal services	23,345.6	25,745.7	26,277.7
Sub-total	63,670.1	68,209.5	72,418.5
Import duties	658.1	780.6	823.4
Total	64,328.2	68,990.1	73,241.9

BALANCE OF PAYMENTS
(million pesos)

	1999	2000	2001
Exports of goods	1,456.1	1,676.8	1,661.5
Imports of goods	−4,365.4	−4,876.7	−4,838.3
Trade balance	−2,909.3	−3,117.2	−3,076.2
Services (net)	2,162.7	2,223.0	2,212.8
Balance on goods and services	−746.6	−894.2	−863.4
Other income (net)	−514.1	−622.2	−502.2
Balance on goods, services and income	−1,260.7	−1,516.4	−1,365.6
Current transfers (net)	798.9	740.4	812.9
Current balance	−461.8	−776.0	−552.7
Direct investment (net)	178.2	448.1	38.9
Other long-term capital (net)	31.7	570.3	328.3
Other capital (net)	275.0	−213.0	227.3
Overall balance	23.1	29.4	41.8

2008 (million pesos): Exports of goods 3,664.2; Imports of goods −14,234.1; Goods acquired at seaports and airports 197.2; *Trade balance* −10,372.7; Services (net) 8,637.2; *Balance on goods and services* −1,735.5; Income (net) −1,055.2; Current transfers (net) 481.9; *Current balance* −2,308.8.

2009 (million pesos): Exports of goods 2,863.0; Imports of goods −8,906.0; Goods acquired at seaports and airports 125.6; *Trade balance* −5,917.4; Services (net) 7,163.0; *Balance on goods and services* 1,245.6; Income (net) −1,643.0; Current transfers (net) 235.0; *Current balance* −162.4.

2010 (million pesos): Exports of goods 4,549.5; Imports of goods −10,644.3; Goods acquired at seaports and airports 159.5; *Trade balance* −5,935.3; Services (net) 9,053.7; *Balance on goods and services* 3,118.4; Income (net) −1,432.3; Current transfers (net) −196.2; *Current balance* 1,489.9.

External Trade

PRINCIPAL COMMODITIES
('000 pesos)

Imports c.i.f.	2010	2011	2012
Food and live animals	1,467,094	1,863,194	1,644,877
Cereals and cereal preparations	670,547	906,073	755,850
Mineral fuels, lubricants, etc.	4,529,660	6,369,886	6,475,033
Chemicals and related products	966,239	1,254,433	1,225,362
Basic manufactures	1,100,435	1,396,452	1,415,344
Manufactures of metal	245,328	297,530	320,507
Machinery and transport equipment	1,668,506	1,954,198	1,939,893
General industrial machinery and equipment and machine parts	372,870	543,631	495,864
Electrical machinery, appliances and apparatus	321,428	427,161	451,230
Miscellaneous manufactured articles	595,396	732,055	666,543
Total (incl. others)	10,644,338	13,952,403	13,800,851

Exports f.o.b.	2010	2011	2012
Food and live animals	355,850	482,568	570,329
Sugar, sugar preparations and honey	266,038	378,606	471,490
Beverages and tobacco	284,724	315,703	316,992
Tobacco and snuff products	202,070	222,987	224,381
Crude materials (inedible) except fuels	1,206,917	1,479,788	1,082,279
Metalliferous ores and metal scrap	1,198,538	1,465,513	1,060,178
Chemicals and related products	538,407	582,706	620,141
Medicinal and pharmaceutical products	489,574	523,281	553,676
Basic manufactures	123,347	145,148	144,599
Machinery and transport equipment	111,380	136,110	104,699
Total (incl. others)	4,549,533	5,870,090	5,577,268

PRINCIPAL TRADING PARTNERS
('000 pesos)

Imports c.i.f.	2010	2011	2012
Algeria	213,271	308,756	330,979
Argentina	129,110	148,613	119,539
Brazil	444,354	643,863	648,177
Canada	331,398	478,784	387,253
China, People's Republic	1,223,245	1,281,415	1,236,840
France	189,629	343,975	359,705
Germany	269,417	286,259	311,463
Italy	292,133	387,799	380,512
Korea, Republic	94,455	128,819	110,185
Mexico	359,970	449,711	486,694
Russia	227,220	224,366	251,674
Spain	785,376	1,019,560	1,006,294
USA	406,118	433,795	508,656
Venezuela	4,301,862	5,902,075	6,078,898
Viet Nam	266,260	308,747	190,459
Total (incl. others)	10,644,338	13,952,403	13,800,851

Exports f.o.b.	2010	2011	2012
Brazil	57,843	82,069	108,053
Canada	604,024	718,645	551,042
China, People's Republic	680,564	778,196	459,060
Côte d'Ivoire	93,465	n.a.	n.a.
Cyprus	28,669	39,400	n.a.
Dominican Republic	23,218	29,360	84,128
France	106,664	23,479	28,021
Netherlands	353,154	655,009	697,605
Nigeria	20,386	100,934	111,745
Panama	12,295	7,002	111,750
Russia	57,472	55,792	89,554
Singapore	186,227	26,553	31,913
Spain	160,746	164,868	149,792
Venezuela	1,716,739	2,273,109	2,483,951
Total (incl. others)	4,549,533	5,870,090	5,577,268

Transport

RAILWAYS

	2010	2011	2012
Passenger-kilometres (million)	925	934	922
Freight ton-kilometres (million)	1,852	1,913	2,714

ROAD TRAFFIC
(motor vehicles in use at 31 December)

	1996	1997
Passenger cars	216,575	172,574
Buses and coaches	28,089	28,861
Lorries and vans	246,105	156,634

2007–08: Passenger cars 236,881; Buses and coaches 197,740; Lorries and vans 171,081; Motorcycles and mopeds 217,141.

Source: IRF, *World Road Statistics*.

SHIPPING
Flag Registered Fleet
(at 31 December)

	2011	2012	2013
Number of vessels	66	65	66
Total displacement ('000 grt)	97	87	95

Source: Lloyd's List Intelligence (www.lloydslistintelligence.com).

International Seaborne Freight Traffic
('000 metric tons)

	2010	2011	2012
Goods loaded	2,521	2,336	2,297
Goods unloaded	8,348	7,782	7,314

CIVIL AVIATION
(traffic on scheduled services)

	2010	2011	2012
Passengers carried (million)	1.2	1.1	1.2
Passenger-kilometres (million)	2,574	2,545	2,610
Freight carried ('000 metric tons)	10.5	8.6	9.6
Total ton-kilometres (million)	50	43	33

Kilometres flown (million): 16 in 2010; 17 in 2011 (Source: UN, *Statistical Yearbook*).

Tourism

ARRIVALS BY COUNTRY OF RESIDENCE*

	2010	2011	2012
Argentina	58,612	75,968	94,691
Canada	945,248	1,002,318	1,071,696
France	80,470	94,370	101,522
Germany	93,136	95,124	108,712
Italy	112,298	110,432	103,290
Mexico	66,650	76,326	78,289
Russia	56,245	78,554	86,944
Spain	104,948	101,631	81,354
United Kingdom	174,343	175,822	153,737
USA	63,046	73,566	98,050
Total (incl. others)	2,531,745	2,716,317	2,838,607

* Figures include same-day visitors (excursionists).

2013 (preliminary): Canada, 1,105,729; Germany 115,984; Italy 95,542; Spain 73,056; United Kingdom 149,515; Total (incl. others) 2,852,572.

Tourism receipts (million pesos, incl. passenger transport): 2,503 in 2011: 2,613 in 2012; 2,627.0 in 2013 (preliminary).

Communications Media

	2011	2012	2013
Telephones ('000 main lines in use)	1,193.4	1,216.5	1,237.3
Mobile cellular telephones ('000 subscribers)	1,315.1	1,681.6	1,995.7
Internet subscribers ('000)	41.1	n.a.	n.a.
Broadband subscribers ('000)	4.4	5.0	5.4

Source: International Telecommunication Union.

Education

(2013/14 unless otherwise indicated)

	Institutions	Teachers	Students
Pre-primary*	1,086	7,645	106,629
Primary	6,842	84,126	826,893
Secondary	1,781	89,560	776,632
Tertiary	58	44,222	207,237

* 2012/13.

Pupil-teacher ratio (primary education, UNESCO estimate): 9.1 in 2011/12 (Source: UNESCO Institute for Statistics).

Adult literacy rate (UNESCO estimates): 99.8% (males 99.8%; females 99.8%) in 2011 (Source: UNESCO Institute for Statistics).

Directory

The Constitution

Following the assumption of power by the Castro regime, on 1 January 1959, the Constitution was suspended and a Fundamental Law of the Republic was instituted, with effect from 7 February 1959. In February 1976 Cuba's first socialist Constitution came into force after being submitted to the first Congress of the Communist Party of Cuba, in December 1975, and to popular referendum, in February 1976; it was amended in July 1992. The main provisions of the Constitution, as amended, are summarized below.

Note: On 27 July 2002 the Constitution was further amended to enshrine the socialist system as irrevocable and to ratify that economic, diplomatic and political relations with another state cannot be negotiated in the face of aggression, threat or pressure from a foreign power. A clause was also introduced making it impossible to remove these amendments from the Constitution.

POLITICAL, SOCIAL AND ECONOMIC PRINCIPLES

The Republic of Cuba is a socialist, independent and sovereign state, organized with all and for the sake of all as a unitary and democratic republic for the enjoyment of political freedom, social justice, collective and individual well-being, and human solidarity. Sovereignty rests with the people, from whom originates the power of the State. The Communist Party of Cuba is the leading force of society and the State. The State recognizes, respects and guarantees freedom of religion. Religious institutions are separate from the State. The socialist State carries out the will of the working people and guarantees work, medical care, education, food, clothing and housing. The Republic of Cuba bases its relations with other socialist countries on socialist internationalism, friendship, co-operation and mutual assistance. It reaffirms its willingness to integrate with and co-operate with the countries of Latin America and the Caribbean.

The State organizes and directs the economic life of the nation in accordance with a central social and economic development plan. The State directs and controls foreign trade. The State recognizes the right of small farmers to own their lands and other means of production and to sell that land. The State guarantees the right of citizens to ownership of personal property in the form of earnings, savings, place of residence, and other possessions and objects that serve to satisfy their material and cultural needs. The State also guarantees the right of inheritance.

Cuban citizenship is acquired by birth or through naturalization. The State protects the family, motherhood and matrimony, and directs and encourages all aspects of education, culture and science. All citizens have equal rights and are subject to equal duties.

The State guarantees the right to medical care, education, freedom of speech and press, assembly, demonstration, association, and privacy. In the socialist society work is the right and duty of, and a source of pride for, every citizen.

GOVERNMENT

National Assembly of People's Power

The National Assembly of People's Power (Asamblea Nacional del Poder Popular) is the supreme organ of the State and is the only organ with constituent and legislative authority. It is composed of deputies, over the age of 18, elected by free, direct and secret ballot, for a period of five years. All Cuban citizens aged 16 years or more, except those who are mentally incapacitated or who have committed a crime, are eligible to vote. The National Assembly of People's Power holds two ordinary sessions a year and a special session when requested by one-third of the deputies or by the Council of State. More than one-half of the total number of deputies must be present for a session to be held.

All decisions made by the Assembly, except those relating to constitutional reforms, are adopted by a simple majority of votes. The deputies may be recalled by their electors at any time.

The National Assembly of People's Power has the following functions:

to reform the Constitution;

to approve, modify and annul laws;

to supervise all organs of the State and government;

to decide on the constitutionality of laws and decrees;

to revoke decree-laws issued by the Council of State and the Council of Ministers;

to discuss and approve economic and social development plans, and the state budget, monetary and credit systems;

to approve the general outlines of foreign and domestic policy, to ratify and annul international treaties, and to declare war and approve peace treaties;

to approve the administrative division of the country;

to elect the President, First Vice-President, the Vice-Presidents and other members of the Council of State;

to elect the President, Vice-President and Secretary of the National Assembly;

to appoint the members of the Council of Ministers on the proposal of the President of the Council of State;

to elect the President, Vice-President and other judges of the People's Supreme Court;

to elect the Attorney-General and the Deputy Attorney-Generals;

to grant amnesty;

to call referendums.

The President of the National Assembly presides over sessions of the Assembly, calls ordinary sessions, proposes the draft agenda, signs the Official Gazette, organizes the work of the commissions appointed by the Assembly and attends the meetings of the Council of State.

Council of State

The Council of State is elected from the members of the National Assembly and represents that Assembly in the period between sessions. It comprises a President, one First Vice-President, five Vice-Presidents, one Secretary and 23 other members. Its mandate ends when a new Assembly meets. All decisions are adopted by a simple majority of votes. It is accountable for its actions to the National Assembly.

The Council of State has the following functions:

to call special sessions of the National Assembly;

to set the date for the election of a new Assembly;

to issue decree-laws in the period between the sessions of the National Assembly;

to decree mobilization in the event of war and to approve peace treaties when the Assembly is in recess;

to issue instructions to the courts and the Office of the Attorney-General of the Republic;

to appoint and remove ambassadors of Cuba abroad on the proposal of its President, and to grant or refuse recognition to diplomatic representatives of other countries to Cuba;

to suspend those provisions of the Council of Ministers that are not in accordance with the Constitution;

to revoke the resolutions of the Executive Committee of the local organs of People's Power that are contrary to the Constitution or laws and decrees formulated by other higher organs.

For all purposes, the Council of State is the highest representative of the Cuban state.

Head of State

The President of the Council of State is the Head of State and the Head of Government and has the following powers:

to represent the State and Government and conduct general policy;

to convene and preside over the sessions of the Council of State and the Council of Ministers;

to supervise the ministries and other administrative bodies;

to propose the members of the Council of Ministers to the National Assembly of People's Power;

to receive the credentials of the heads of foreign diplomatic missions;

to sign the decree-laws and other resolutions of the Council of State;

to exercise the Supreme Command of all armed institutions and determine their general organization;

to preside over the National Defence Council;

to declare a state of emergency in the cases outlined in the Constitution.

In the case of absence, illness or death of the President of the Council of State, the First Vice-President assumes the President's duties.

The Council of Ministers

The Council of Ministers is the highest-ranking executive and administrative organ. It is composed of the Head of State and Government, as its President, the First Vice-President, the Vice-Presidents, the Ministers, the Secretary and other members determined by law. Its Executive Committee is composed of the President, the First Vice-President, the Vice-Presidents and other members of the Council of Ministers determined by the President.

The Council of Ministers has the following powers:

to conduct political, economic, cultural, scientific, social and defence policy as outlined by the National Assembly;

to approve international treaties;

to propose projects for the general development plan and, if they are approved by the National Assembly, to supervise their implementation;

to conduct foreign policy and trade;

to draw up bills and submit them to the National Assembly;

to draw up the draft state budget;

to conduct general administration, implement laws, issue decrees, and supervise defence and national security.

The Council of Ministers is accountable to the National Assembly of People's Power.

LOCAL GOVERNMENT

The country is divided into 15 provinces (and one special municipality, Isla de la Juventud) and 168 municipalities. The provinces are: Pinar del Río, Artemisa, La Habana, Mayabeque, Matanzas, Villa Clara, Cienfuegos, Sancti Spíritus, Ciego de Avila, Camagüey, Las Tunas, Holguín, Granma, Santiago de Cuba and Guantánamo.

Voting for delegates to the municipal assemblies is direct, secret and voluntary. All citizens over 16 years of age are eligible to vote. The number of delegates to each assembly is proportionate to the number of people living in that area. A delegate must obtain more than one-half of the total number of votes cast in the constituency in order to be elected. The Municipal and Provincial Assemblies of People's Power are elected by free, direct and secret ballot. Nominations for Municipal and Provincial Executive Committees of People's Power are submitted to the relevant assembly by a commission presided over by a representative of the Communist Party's leading organ and consisting of representatives of youth, workers', farmers', revolutionary and women's organizations. The President and Secretary of each of the regional and the provincial assemblies are the only full-time members, the other delegates carrying out their functions in addition to their normal employment.

The regular and extraordinary sessions of the local Assemblies of People's Power are public. More than one-half of the total number of members must be present in order for agreements made to be valid. Agreements are adopted by simple majority.

JUDICIARY

Judicial power is exercised by the People's Supreme Court and all other competent tribunals and courts. The People's Supreme Court is the supreme judicial authority and is accountable only to the National Assembly of People's Power. It can propose laws and issue regulations through its Council of Government. Judges are independent, but the courts must inform the electorate of their activities at least once a year. Every accused person has the right to a defence and can be tried only by a tribunal.

The Office of the Attorney-General is subordinate only to the National Assembly and the Council of State, and is responsible for ensuring that the law is properly obeyed.

The Constitution may be totally or partially modified only by a two-thirds' majority vote in the National Assembly of People's Power. If the modification is total, or if it concerns the composition and powers of the National Assembly of People's Power or the Council of State, or the rights and duties contained in the Constitution, it also requires a positive vote by referendum.

The Government

Head of State: Gen. RAÚL CASTRO RUZ (took office 24 February 2008, re-elected 24 February 2013).

COUNCIL OF STATE

President: Gen. RAÚL CASTRO RUZ.

First Vice-President: MIGUEL DÍAZ-CANEL BERMÚDEZ.

Vice-Presidents: JOSÉ RAMÓN MACHADO VENTURA, RAMIRO VALDÉS MENÉNDEZ, GLADYS BEJERANO PORTELA, LÁZARA MERCEDES LÓPEZ ACEA, SALVADOR ANTONIO VALDÉS MESA.

Secretary: HOMERO ACOSTA ALVAREZ.

Members: INÉS MARÍA CHAPMAN WAUGH, Lt-Gen. LEOPOLDO CINTRA FRÍAS, ABELARDO COLOMÉ IBARRA, GUILLERMO GARCÍA FRÍAS, TANIA LEÓN SILVEIRA, Lt-Gen. ALVARO LÓPEZ MIERA, MARINO ALBERTO MURILLO JORGE, SERGIO JUAN RODRÍGIEZ MORALES, LESTER ALAIN ALEMÁN HURTADO, TERESA MARÍA AMARELLE BOUÉ, YARAMIS ARMENTEROS MEDINA, MIGUEL ANGEL BARNET LANZA, YUNIASKY CRESPO

BAQUERO, ILEANA AMPARO FLORES MORALES, FÉLIX GONZÁLEZ VIEGO, CARMEN ROSA LÓPEZ RODRÍGUEZ, MARTHA DEL CARMEN MESA VALENCIANO, CARLOS RAFAEL MIRANDA MARTÍNEZ, MIRIAM NICADO GARCÍA, MILADYS ORRACA CASTILLO, BRUNO RODRÍGUEZ PARILLA, LIZ BELKYS ROSABAL PONCE, ADEL ONOFRE YZQUIERDO RODRÍGUEZ.

COUNCIL OF MINISTERS
(September 2014)

The Government is formed by the Partido Comunista de Cuba.

President: Gen. RAÚL CASTRO RUZ.

Secretary: Brig.-Gen. JOSÉ AMADO RICARDO GUERRA.

First Vice-President: MIGUEL DÍAZ-CANEL BERMÚDEZ.

Vice-Presidents: RICARDO CABRISAS RUIZ, RAMIRO VALDÉS MENÉNDEZ, Gen. ULISES ROSALES DEL TORO, MARINO ALBERTO MURILLO JORGE, Gen. ANTONIO ENRIQUE LUSSÓN BATLLE, ADEL ONOFRE YZQUIERDO RODRÍGUEZ.

Minister of Agriculture: GUSTAVO RODRÍGUEZ ROLLERO.

Minister of Construction: RENÉ MESA VILLAFAÑA.

Minister of Culture: RAFAEL BERNAL ALEMANY.

Minister of Domestic Trade: MARY BLANCA ORTEGA BARREDO.

Minister of Economy and Planning: ADEL ONOFRE YZQUIERDO RODRÍGUEZ.

Minister of Education: ENA ELSA VELÁZQUEZ COBIELLA.

Minister of Energy and Mines: ALFREDO LÓPEZ VALDÉS.

Minister of Finance and Prices: LINA PEDRAZA RODRÍGUEZ.

Minister of the Food Industry: MARÍA DEL CARMEN CONCEPCIÓN GONZÁLEZ.

Minister of Foreign Relations: BRUNO EDUARDO RODRÍGUEZ PARILLA.

Minister of Foreign Trade and Investment: RODRIGO MALMIERCA DÍAZ.

Minister of Higher Education: RODOLFO ALARCON ORTIZ.

Minister of Industries: SALVADOR PARDO CRUZ.

Minister of Information Technology and Communications: MAIMIR MESA RAMOS.

Minister of the Interior: Lt-Gen. ABELARDO COLOMÉ IBARRA.

Minister of Justice: MARÍA ESTHER REUS GONZÁLEZ.

Minister of Labour and Social Security: MARGARITA MARLENE GONZÁLEZ FERNÁNDEZ.

Minister of Public Health: ROBERTO MORALES OJEDA.

Minister of the Revolutionary Armed Forces: Lt-Gen. LEOPOLDO CINTRA FRÍAS.

Minister of Science, Technology and the Environment: ELBA ROSA PEREZ MONTOYA.

Minister of Tourism: MANUEL MARRERO CRUZ.

Minister of Transportation: CÉSAR IGNACIO AROCHA MASID.

Minister, President of the Banco Central de Cuba: ERNESTO MEDINA VILLAVEIRÁN.

MINISTRIES

Ministry of Agriculture: Edif. MINAG, Avda Conill, esq. Carlos M. Céspedes, Nuevo Vedado, Plaza de la Revolución, 10600 Havana; tel. (7) 884-5370; fax (7) 881-2837; e-mail armando@minag.cu; internet www.minag.cu.

Ministry of Construction: Avda Carlos Manuel de Céspedes, Calle 35, Plaza de la Revolución, 10600 Havana; tel. (7) 881-4745; fax (7) 855-5303; e-mail sitio@micons.cu; internet www.micons.cu.

Ministry of Culture: Calle 2, No 258, entre 11 y 13, Plaza de la Revolución, Vedado, CP 10400, Havana; tel. (7) 838-2246; e-mail secretarias@min.cult.cu; internet www.min.cult.cu.

Ministry of Domestic Trade: Calle Habana 258, entre Empedrado y San Juan de Dios, Havana; tel. (7) 867-0133; fax (7) 867-0094; e-mail estadistica@cinet.cu.

Ministry of Economy and Planning: 20 de Mayo, entre Territorial y Ayestarán, Plaza de la Revolución, Havana; tel. (7) 881-9354; fax (7) 855-5371; e-mail mep@ceniai.inf.cu.

Ministry of Education: Calle 17, esq. O, Vedado, Havana; tel. (7) 838-2930; fax (7) 838-3105; e-mail despacho@mined.rimed.cu; internet www.rimed.cu.

Ministry of Energy and Mines: Avda Salvador Allende 666, entre Oquendo y Soledad, Havana; tel. (7) 878-7840; fax (7) 873-5345.

Ministry of Finance and Prices: Calle Obispo 211, esq. Cuba, Habana Vieja, Havana; tel. (7) 867-1800; fax (7) 833-8050; e-mail bhcifip@mfp.gov.cu; internet www.mfp.cu.

Ministry of the Food Industry: Avda 41, No 4455, entre 48 y 50, Playa, Havana; tel. (7) 203-6801; fax (7) 204-0517; e-mail minal@minal.get.cma.net; internet www.minal.cubaindustria.cu.

Ministry of Foreign Relations: Calzada 360, esq. G, Vedado, Plaza de la Revolución, Havana; tel. (7) 836-4500; e-mail cubaminrex@minrex.gov.cu; internet www.cubaminrex.cu.

Ministry of Foreign Trade and Investment: Infanta y 23, Plaza de la Revolución, Miramar, Havana; tel. (7) 838-0436; fax (7) 204-3496; e-mail secretariataller@mincex.cu; internet www.mincex.cu.

Ministry of Higher Education: Calle 23, No 565, esq. F, Vedado, Plaza de la Revolución, Havana; tel. (7) 830-3674; e-mail sitio_mes@reduniv.edu.cu; internet www.mes.edu.cu.

Ministry of Industries: Avda Independencia y Calle 100, Havana; tel. (7) 265-3606; fax (7) 267-0501.

Ministry of Information Technology and Communications: Avda Independencia No 2, entre 19 de Mayo y Aranguren, Plaza de la Revolución, Havana; tel. (7) 882-8000; fax (7) 885-4048; e-mail dircom@mic.cu; internet www.mic.gov.cu.

Ministry of the Interior: Sitio Minint, Plaza de la Revolución, Havana; tel. (7) 30-1566; fax (7) 855-6621; e-mail correominint@mn.mn.co.cu.

Ministry of Justice: Calle O, No 216, entre 23 y 25, Plaza de la Revolución, Apdo 10400, Havana 4; tel. (7) 838-3450; e-mail apoblacion@oc.minjus.cu; internet www.minjus.cu.

Ministry of Labour and Social Security: Calle 23, esq. Calles O y P, Vedado, Municipio Plaza de la Revolución, Havana; tel. (7) 838-0022; e-mail webmaster@mtss.cu; internet www.mtss.cu.

Ministry of Public Health: Calle 23, No 201, entre M y N, Vedado, Plaza de la Revolución, Havana; tel. (7) 835-2767; fax (7) 833-2195; e-mail apoblacion@infomed.sld.cu; internet www.sld.cu.

Ministry of the Revolutionary Armed Forces: Plaza de la Revolución, Havana; internet www.cubagob.cu/otras_info/minfar/far/minfar.htm.

Ministry of Science, Technology and the Environment: Industria y San José, Habana Vieja, Havana; tel. (7) 860-3411; fax (7) 866-8654; e-mail comunicacion@citma.cu.

Ministry of Tourism: Calle 3, No 6, entre F y G, Vedado, Plaza de la Revolución, Havana; tel. (7) 836-3245; fax (7) 836-4086; e-mail dircomunicacion@mintur.tur.cu; internet www.cubatravel.cu.

Ministry of Transportation: Avda Carlos Manuel de Céspedes s/n, entre Tulipán y Lombillo, Plaza de la Revolución, 10600 Havana; tel. (7) 855-5030; fax (7) 884-1105; e-mail mitrans@mitrans.transnet.cu; internet www.transporte.cu.

Legislature

NATIONAL ASSEMBLY OF PEOPLE'S POWER
(Asamblea Nacional del Poder Popular)

The National Assembly of People's Power was constituted on 2 December 1976. In 1992 the National Assembly adopted a constitutional amendment providing for legislative elections by direct vote. Only candidates nominated by the Partido Comunista de Cuba (PCC) were permitted to contest the elections. At elections to the National Assembly conducted on 3 February 2013, all 614 candidates succeeded in obtaining the requisite 50% of valid votes cast. Of the 8.7m. registered voters, 90.88% participated in the elections. Only 5.83% of votes cast were blank or spoiled.

President: JUAN ESTEBAN LAZO HERNÁNDEZ.

Vice-President: ANA MARÍA MARI MACHADO.

Secretary: MIRIAM BRITO SARROCA.

Political Organizations

Partido Comunista de Cuba (PCC) (Communist Party of Cuba): Havana; e-mail root@epol.cipcc.inf.cu; internet www.pcc.cu; f. 1961 as the Organizaciones Revolucionarias Integradas (ORI) from a fusion of the Partido Socialista Popular (Communist), Fidel Castro's Movimiento 26 de Julio and the Directorio Revolucionario 13 de Marzo; became the Partido Unido de la Revolución Socialista Cubana (PURSC) in 1962; adopted current name in 1965; youth wing, the Unión de Jóvenes Comunistas (Union of Young Communists, First Sec. YUNIASKI CRESPO), comprises c. 500,000 mems; 150-member Central Committee, Political Bureau, 12-member Secretariat and five Commissions.

Political Bureau

Gen. RAÚL CASTRO RUZ (First Sec.), JOSÉ RAMÓN MACHADO VENTURA (Second Sec.), RAMIRO VALDÉS MENÉNDEZ, JUAN ESTEBAN LAZO HERNÁNDEZ, Lt-Gen. ABELARDO COLOMÉ IBARRA, Lt-Gen. LEOPOLDO CINTRA FRÍAS, Lt-Gen. RAMÓN ESPINOSA MARTÍN, MIGUEL MARIO DÍAZ-CANEL BERMÚDEZ, SALVADOR ANTONIO VALDÉS MESA, Lt-Gen. ALVARO LÓPEZ MIERA, ADEL ONOFRE YZQUIERDO RODRÍGUEZ, MARINO ALBERTO

MURILLO JORGE, MERCEDES LÓPEZ ACEA, BRUNO EDUARDO RODRÍGUEZ PARILLA.

There are a number of dissident groups operating in Cuba. Among the most prominent of these are the following:

Arco Progresista: tel. 763-0912; e-mail arcoprogresista.gl@gmail.com; internet www.cuba-progresista.org; f. 2003 as an alliance of three social-democratic groups in and outside Cuba: Corriente Socialista Democrática, Partido del Pueblo and Coordinadora Socialdemócrata en el Exilio; merged into a single party in 2008; Spokesperson MANUEL CUESTA MORÚA.

Asamblea para Promover la Sociedad Civil en Cuba: e-mail asambleacivil@bellsouth.net; internet www.asambleasociedadcivilcuba.info; f. 2002; alliance of 365 civil society asscns; Leader MARTHA BEATRIZ ROQUE CABELLO.

Movimiento Cristiano Liberación (MCL): e-mail info@oswaldopaya.org; internet www.oswaldopaya.org; f. 1988; campaigns for peaceful democratic change and respect for human rights; associated with the Varela Project, established 1998 to petition the Govt for democratic freedoms; Leader OFELIA ACEVEDO.

Partido Demócrata Cristiano de Cuba (PDC): 1236 SW 22 Ave, Miami, FL 33135, USA; tel. (305) 644-3395; fax (305) 644-3311; e-mail miyares@pdc-cuba.org; internet www.pdc-cuba.org; f. 1959 as Movimiento Demócrata Cristiano; adopted current name in 1991; Pres. RENÉ HERNÁNDEZ; Vice-Pres ANDRÉS HERNÁNDEZ, EDUARDO MESA, YAXYS CIRES.

Partido Liberal de Cuba: 20 de Mayo 531, Apto B-14, entre Marta Abreu y Línea del Ferrocarril, Cerro, 10600 Havana; tel. and fax (7) 878-4010; f. 1991 as Partido Liberal Democrático de Cuba; mem. of Liberal International; Pres. HÉCTOR MASEDA GUTIÉRREZ; Sec. REINALDO HERNÁNDEZ CARDONA.

Partido Liberal Nacional Cubano (PLNC): Calle 148, No 4116 entre 41 y 43, Apto 1, La Lisa, Havana; tel. 3445927; e-mail fernandopalacio3@gmail.com; internet cubadesdeadentro.com; f. 2004 as Movimiento Liberal Cubano; adopted present name in 2009; part of Convergencia Liberal Cubana; Pres. FERNANDO EDGARDO PALACIO MOGAR; Exec. Nat. Sec. RONALDO MENDOZA MENDEZ.

Partido Pro-Derechos Humanos de Cuba (PPDHC): e-mail rene.montesdeoca@yahoo.es; internet www.partidoproderechoshumanosdecuba.com; f. 1988 to defend human rights in Cuba; Sec.-Gen. JULIÁN ENRIQUE MARTÍNEZ BÁEZ.

Partido Social Revolucionario Democrático de Cuba: 5900 Starlite Lane, Milton, FL 32570, USA; tel. and fax (305) 693-7543; e-mail psrdc@psrdc.org; internet www.psrdc.org; f. 1992; exec. cttee of 15 mems; Pres. JORGE VALLS; Exec. Sec. ROBERTO SIMEON.

Partido Solidaridad Democrática (PSD): Calle Trocadero 414 bajos, entre Galiano y San Nicolás, Municipio Pio-Centro, 10200 Havana; tel. (7) 866-8306; e-mail gladyperez@aol.com; f. 1993; mem. of Liberal International; Pres. FERNANDO SÁNCHEZ LÓPEZ.

Unión Liberal Cubana: Paseo de la Retama 97, 29600 Marbella, Spain; tel. (91) 4340201; fax (91) 5011342; e-mail cubaliberal@mercuryin.es; internet unionliberalcubana.com; mem. of Liberal International; Pres. ANTONIO GUEDES.

Diplomatic Representation

EMBASSIES IN CUBA

Algeria: Avda 5, No 2802, esq. 28, Miramar, Havana; tel. (7) 204-2835; fax (7) 204-2702; e-mail embhav@argelia.sytes.net; Ambassador ABDELLAH LAOUARI.

Angola: Avda 5, No 1012, entre 10 y 12, Miramar, Havana; tel. (7) 204-2474; fax (7) 204-0487; e-mail embangol@ceniai.inf.cu; Ambassador JOSÉ CÉSAR AUGUSTO.

Antigua and Barbuda: Avda 5, esq. 66, No 6407, Miramar, Havana; tel. (7) 207-9756; fax (7) 207-9757; e-mail anubarembassy@enet.cu; Ambassador BRUCE GOODWIN.

Argentina: Calle 36, No 511, entre 5 y 7, Miramar, Havana; tel. (7) 204-2565; fax (7) 204-2140; e-mail embajador@ecuba.co.cu; Ambassador JULIANA ISABEL MARINO.

Austria: Avda 5A, No 6617, esq. 70, Miramar, Havana; tel. (7) 204-2825; fax (7) 204-1235; e-mail havanna-ob@bmeia.gv.at; Ambassador ANDREAS RENDL.

Bahamas: Avda 5, No 3006, entre 30 y 32, Miramar, Playa, Havana; tel. (7) 206-9918; fax (7) 206-9921; e-mail embahamas@enet.cu; Ambassador ALMA ADAMS.

Belarus: Avda 5, No 6405, entre 64 y 66, Miramar, Havana; tel. (7) 204-7330; fax (7) 204-7332; e-mail cuba@mfa.gov.by; internet www.cuba.mfa.gov.by; Ambassador VLADZIMIR A. ASTAPENKA.

Belgium: Calle 8, No 309, entre 3 y 5, Miramar, Havana; tel. (7) 204-4806; fax (7) 204-6516; e-mail havana@diplobel.fed.be; internet www.diplomatie.be/havana; Ambassador LUC DEVOLDER.

Belize: Avda 5, No 3606, esq. 36 y 36A, Miramar, Havana; tel. (7) 204-3504; fax (7) 204-3506; e-mail belizecuba@yahoo.es; Chargé d'affaires a.i. EFRAIN RAVEY NOVELO.

Benin: Calle 20, No 119, entre 1 y 3, Miramar, Havana; tel. (7) 204-2179; fax (7) 204-2334; e-mail ambencub@ceniai.inf.cu; Ambassador ANTOINE DIMON AFOUDA.

Bolivia: Calle 36A, No 3601, entre Avdas 3 y 5, Miramar, Havana; tel. (7) 209-7513; fax (7) 204-2739; e-mail emboliviacuba@gmail.com; Ambassador PALMIRO LEÓN SORIA SAUCEDO.

Brazil: Centro de Negocios Miramar, Edif. Beijing, 2°, Of. 206, Calle 3, entre 76 y 79, Miramar, Havana; tel. (7) 214-4713; fax (7) 866-2912; e-mail brasemb.havana@itamaraty.gov.br; Ambassador JOSÉ E. MARTINS FELICIO.

Bulgaria: Calle B, No 252, entre 11 y 13, Vedado, Havana; tel. (7) 833-3125; fax (7) 833-3297; e-mail embassy.havana@mfa.bg; internet www.mfa.bg/embassies/kuba; Ambassador SVETLA T. STEFANOVA.

Burkina Faso: Calle 40, No 516, entre Avdas 5 y 7, Miramar, Havana; tel. (7) 204-2217; fax (7) 204-1942; e-mail ambfaso@ceniai.inf.cu; Ambassador DANIEL OUÉDRAOGO.

Cabo Verde: Calle 20, No 2001, esq. a 7, Miramar, Havana; tel. (7) 204-2979; fax (7) 204-1072; e-mail emb.caboverde.cuba@gmail.com; Ambassador MANUEL AVELINO COUTO DA SILVA MATOS.

Cambodia: Avda 5, No 7001, entre 70 y 72, Miramar, Havana; tel. (7) 204-1496; fax (7) 204-6400; e-mail cambohav@enet.cu; Ambassador HAY SONNARIN.

Canada: Calle 30, No 518, esq. 7, Miramar, Havana; tel. (7) 204-2516; fax (7) 204-2044; e-mail havan@international.gc.ca; internet www.canadainternational.gc.ca/cuba; Ambassador YVES GAGNON.

Chile: Calle 33, No 1423, entre 14 y 18, Miramar, Havana; tel. (7) 204-1222; fax (7) 204-1694; e-mail echile.cuba@minrel.gov.cl; Ambassador ROLANDO DRAGO RODRÍGUEZ.

China, People's Republic: Calle C, entre 13 y 15, Vedado, Havana; tel. (7) 833-3005; fax (7) 833-3092; e-mail chinaemb_cu@mfa.gov.cn; Ambassador ZHANG TUO.

Colombia: Calle 14, No 515, entre 5 y 7, Miramar, Havana; tel. (7) 204-1248; fax (7) 204-0464; e-mail ecuba@cancilleria.gov.co; internet cuba.embajada.gov.co; Ambassador GUSTAVO ADOLFO BELL LEMUS.

Congo, Republic: Avda 5, No 1003, Miramar, Havana; tel. and fax (7) 204-9055; fax (7) 204-9055; e-mail ambacohavane@yahoo.fr; Ambassador PASCAL ONGEMBY.

Costa Rica: Avda 5, No 6604, esq. 66 y 68, Miramar, Havana; tel. (7) 204-6938; fax (7) 204-6937; e-mail embajada@costaricacuba.org; Ambassador HUBERT GERARDO MÉNDEZ ACOSTA.

Cyprus: Avda 5, No 8409, entre 84 and 86, Miramar, Havana; tel. (7) 212-5229; fax (7) 212-5227; e-mail chancery@cyprusembassycuba.org; internet www.cyprusembassycuba.org; Ambassador STAVROS LOIZIDES.

Czech Republic: Avda Kohly, No 259, entre 41 y 43, Nuevo Vedado, CP 10600, Havana; tel. (7) 883-3201; fax (7) 883-3596; e-mail havana@embassy.mzv.cz; internet www.mzv.cz/havana; Chargé d'affaires a.i. JAROSLAV ZAJÍC.

Dominica: Calle 36, No 507, entre 5 y 7, Miramar, Havana; tel. (7) 214-1096; fax (7) 214-1097; e-mail embcwdom@enet.cu; Ambassador CHARLES J. CORBETTE.

Dominican Republic: Avda 5, No 9202, entre 92 y 94, Miramar, Havana; tel. (7) 204-8429; fax (7) 204-8431; e-mail edc@enet.cu; Ambassador JOSÉ MANUEL CASTILLO BETANCES.

Ecuador: Avda 7, No 3804, esq. a 40, Miramar, Havana; tel. (7) 204-2868; e-mail embecuador@yahoo.com; Ambassador EDGAR PONCE ITURRIAGA.

Egypt: Avda 5, No 1801, esq. 18, Miramar, Havana; tel. (7) 204-2441; fax (7) 204-0905; e-mail emegipto@enet.cu; Ambassador TAREK MOHEY ELDIN ELWASSIMY.

El Salvador: Calle 24, No 307, esq. 3ra y 5ta, Miramar, Havana; tel. (7) 212-5612; e-mail embajadaencuba@rree.gob.sv; Ambassador DOMINGO SANTACRUZ CASTRO.

Equatorial Guinea: Calle 20, No 713, entre 7 y 9, Miramar, Havana; tel. (7) 204-1720; fax (7) 204-1724; Ambassador LOURDES MBA AYECABA.

Ethiopia: Avda 5, No 6604, Apto 3, entre 66 y 68, Miramar, Havana; tel. (7) 206-9905; fax (7) 206-9907; e-mail info@embaethi.co.cu; Ambassador BOGALE TOLESSA MARU.

France: Calle 14, No 312, entre 3 y 5, Miramar, Havana; tel. (7) 201-3131; fax (7) 201-3107; e-mail internet.la-havane-amba@diplomatie.fr; internet www.ambafrance-cu.org; Ambassador JEAN MENDELSON.

The Gambia: Calle 40, No 155, 1ra y 3ra, Miramar, Havana; tel. and fax (7) 212-5626; e-mail gambia.secretariat@mail.com; Ambassador MASANSH NYUKU KINTEH.

Germany: Calle 13, No 652, esq. B, Vedado, Havana; tel. (7) 833-2569; fax (7) 833-1586; e-mail info@havanna.diplo.de; internet www.havanna.diplo.de; Ambassador PETER RUDOLF SCHOLZ.

Ghana: Avda 5, No 1808, esq. 20, Miramar, Havana; tel. (7) 204-2153; fax (7) 204-2317; e-mail embassyofghanahavgh@gmail.com; Ambassador JOHN AKOLOGU TIA.

Greece: Avda 5, No 7802, esq. 78, Miramar, Havana; tel. (7) 204-2995; fax (7) 204-9770; e-mail gremb@enet.cu; Ambassador APOSTOLOS-PAUL CHARALAMPOUS.

Grenada: Avda 5, No 2006, entre 20 y 22, Miramar, Havana; tel. (7) 204-6764; fax (7) 204-6765; e-mail embgranada@ip.etecsa.cu; Ambassador CLARICE CHARLES.

Guatemala: Calle 20, No 301, entre 3 y 5, Miramar, Havana; tel. (7) 204-3417; fax (7) 204-8173; e-mail cuba@minex.gob.gt; internet www.cuba.minex.gob.gt; Ambassador JUAN LEÓN ALVARADO.

Guinea: Calle 20, No 504, entre 5 y 7, Miramar, Havana; tel. (7) 292-9212; fax (7) 204-1894; e-mail ambaguineehav@yahoo.com; Ambassador HADIATOU SOW.

Guinea-Bissau: Avda 5, No 8203, entre 82 y 84, Miramar, Havana; tel. (7) 204-5742; fax (7) 204-2794; e-mail embaguib@enet.cu; Ambassador ABEL COELHO MENDONÇA.

Guyana: Calle 18, No 506, entre 5 y 7, Miramar, Havana; tel. (7) 204-2094; fax (7) 204-2867; e-mail embguyana@enet.cu; Ambassador MITRADEVI ALI.

Haiti: Avda 7, No 4402, esq. 44, Miramar, Havana; tel. (7) 204-5421; fax (7) 204-5423; e-mail embhaiti@enet.cu; Ambassador JEAN VICTOR GENEUS.

Holy See: Calle 12, No 514, entre 5 y 7, Miramar, Havana (Apostolic Nunciature); tel. (7) 204-2700; fax (7) 204-2257; e-mail csa@pcn.net; Apostolic Nuncio BRUNO MUSARÒ (Titular Archbishop of Abari).

Honduras: Edif. Santa Clara, 1°, Of. 121 Centro de Negocios Miramar, Calle 3a No 123, entre 78 y 80 Calles, Miramar, Havana; tel. (7) 204-5496; fax (7) 204-5497; e-mail embhondcuba@yahoo.com; Ambassador ALAMS ARMANDO ESPINAL ZUNIGA.

Hungary: Calle G, No 458, entre 19 y 21, Vedado, Havana; tel. (7) 833-3365; fax (7) 833-3286; e-mail mission.hav@kum.hu; internet www.mfa.gov.hu/kulkepviselet/cu/hu; Ambassador ANDRÁS GÁBOR DREXLER.

India: Calle 21, No 202, esq. K, Vedado, Havana; tel. (7) 833-3777; fax (7) 833-3287; e-mail hoc@indembassyhavana.cu; internet www.indembassyhavana.cu; Ambassador CHINTHAPALLY RAJASEKHAR.

Indonesia: Avda 5, No 1607, esq. 18, Miramar, Havana; tel. (7) 204-9618; fax (7) 204-9617; e-mail indonhav@ceniai.inf.cu; internet www.deplu.go.id/havana; Ambassador TEISERAN FOUN CORNELIS.

Iran: Avda 5, No 3002, esq. 30, Miramar, Havana; tel. (7) 204-2675; fax (7) 204-2770; e-mail embassy_iran_havana@yahoo.com; Ambassador ALI CHEGENI.

Italy: Avda 5, No 402, esq. 4, Miramar, Havana; tel. (7) 204-5615; fax (7) 204-5659; e-mail ambasciata.avana@esteri.it; internet www.amblavana.esteri.it; Ambassador CARMINE ROBUSTELLI.

Jamaica: Calle 22, No 503, entre 5 y 7, Miramar, Havana; tel. (7) 204-2908; fax (7) 204-2531; e-mail embjmcub@enet.cu; Ambassador A'DALE GEORGE ROBINSON.

Japan: Centro de Negocios Miramar, Avda 3, Edif. 1, 5°, esq. 80, Miramar, Havana; tel. (7) 204-3355; fax (7) 204-8902; e-mail taisi@ceniai.inf.cu; internet www.cu.emb-japan.go.jp; Ambassador HIROSHI SATO.

Korea, Democratic People's Republic: Calle 17 y Paseo, No 752, Vedado, Havana; tel. (7) 833-2313; fax (7) 833-3073; e-mail dprkorcuba@enet.cu; Ambassador PAK CHANG YUL.

Laos: Avda 5, No 2808, esq. 30, Miramar, Havana; tel. (7) 204-1057; fax (7) 204-9622; e-mail embalao@enet.cu; Ambassador KHAMPO KYAKHAMPHITOUNE.

Lebanon: Calle 17A, No 16403, entre 164 y 174, Siboney, Havana; tel. (7) 208-6220; fax (7) 208-6432; e-mail lbcunet@ceniai.inf.cu; Ambassador ROBERT NAOUM.

Libya: Avda 7, No 1402, esq. 14, Miramar, Havana; tel. (7) 204-2192; fax (7) 204-2991; e-mail oficinalibia@ip.etecsa.cu.

Malaysia: Avda 5, No 6612, entre 66 y 68, Miramar, Havana; tel. (7) 204-8883; fax (7) 204-6888; e-mail malhavana@kln.gov.my; internet www.kln.gov.my/perwakilan/havana; Ambassador JOJIE SAMUEL.

Mali: Calle 36A, No 704, entre 7 y 42, Miramar, Havana; tel. (7) 204-5321; fax (7) 204-5320; e-mail ambamali@ceniai.inf.cu; Ambassador MODIBO DIARRA.

Mexico: Calle 12, No 518, esq. Avda 7, Miramar, Playa, Havana; tel. (7) 204-2553; fax (7) 204-2717; e-mail embamex@embamexcuba.org; internet www.sre.gob.mx/cuba; Ambassador JUAN JOSÉ BREMER DE MARTINO.

Mongolia: Calle 66, No 505, esq. 5A, Miramar, Havana; tel. (7) 204-2763; fax (7) 204-0639; e-mail embahavana@ceniai.inf.cu; Ambassador Otgonbayaryn Davaasambuu.

Mozambique: Avda 7, No 2203, entre 22 y 24, Miramar, Havana; tel. (7) 204-2443; fax (7) 204-2232; e-mail tsocotsinha@gmail.com; Ambassador Miguel Costa Mkaima.

Namibia: Calle 36, No 504, entre 5 y 5A, Miramar, Havana; tel. (7) 204-1430; fax (7) 204-1431; e-mail namembassycuba@hotmail.com; Ambassador Jerobeam Shaanika.

Netherlands: Calle 8, No 307, entre 3 y 5, Miramar, Havana; tel. (7) 204-2511; fax (7) 204-2059; e-mail hav@minbuza.nl; internet cuba.nlambassade.org; Ambassador Norbert W.M. Braakhuis.

Nicaragua: Calle 20, No 709, entre 7 y 9, Miramar, Havana; tel. (7) 204-1025; fax (7) 204-5387; e-mail nicaragua@embnicc.co.cu; Ambassador Luis Cabrera González.

Nigeria: Avda 5, No 1401, entre 14 y 16, Miramar, Havana; tel. (7) 204-2898; fax (7) 204-2202; e-mail chancery@nigeria-havana.com; Ambassador Laraba Elsie Binta Bhutto.

Norway: Calle 30, No 315, entre 3 y 5, Miramar, Havana; tel. (7) 204-0696; fax (7) 204-0699; e-mail emb.havana@mfa.no; internet www.noruega-cuba.org; Ambassador John Petter Opdahl.

Pakistan: Avda 5, No 2606, entre 26 y 28, Miramar, Havana; tel. (7) 214-1151; fax (7) 214-1154; e-mail parephavana@hotmail.com; internet www.mofa.gov.pk/cuba; Ambassador Qazi M. Khalilullah.

Panama: Calle 26, No 109, entre 1 y 3, Miramar, Havana; tel. (7) 204-0858; fax (7) 204-1674; e-mail panaemba_cuba@panaemba.co.cu; Ambassador Mario Rafael Gálvez Evers.

Paraguay: Calle 34, No 503, entre 5 y 7, Miramar, Havana; tel. (7) 204-0884; fax (7) 204-0883; e-mail cgphav@enet.cu; Chargé d'affaires a.i. Víctor Benítez.

Peru: Calle 30, No 107, entre 1 y 3, Miramar, Havana; tel. (7) 204-2632; fax (7) 204-2636; e-mail embaperu@embaperu.org; Ambassador Víctor Ricardo Mayorga Miranda.

Philippines: Avda 5, No 2207, esq. 24, Miramar, Havana; tel. (7) 204-1372; fax (7) 204-2915; e-mail philhavpe@enet.cu; Ambassador Catalino R. Dilem.

Poland: Calle G, No 452, esq. 19, Vedado, Havana; tel. (7) 833-2439; fax (7) 833-2442; e-mail hawana.amb.sekretariat@msz.gov.pl; Ambassador Malgorzata Galinska-Tomaszewska.

Portugal: Avda 7, No 2207, esq. 24, Miramar, Havana; tel. (7) 204-0149; fax (7) 204-2593; e-mail embpthav@embporthavana.org; Ambassador Fernando Antonio Alberty Tavares de Carvalho.

Qatar: Avda 3, No 3407, entre 34 y 36, Miramar, Havana; tel. (7) 204-0587; fax (7) 204-0003; e-mail embajada@qatar.co.cu; Ambassador Rashid Mirza Al-Mulla.

Romania: Avda 5, No 4407, entre 44 y 46, Miramar, Havana; tel. (7) 214-4922; fax (7) 214-4949; e-mail havana@mae.ro; Ambassador Dumitru Preda.

Russia: Avda 5, No 6402, entre 62 y 66, Miramar, Havana; tel. (7) 204-2686; fax (7) 204-1038; e-mail embrusia@newmail.ru; internet www.cuba.mid.ru; Ambassador Mikhail L. Kamynin.

Saint Christopher and Nevis: Havana; Ambassador Kenneth Douglas (designate).

Saint Lucia: Centro de Negocios Miramar, Edif. Jerusalén, Calle 3, No 403, entre 78 y 80, Miramar, Havana; tel. (7) 206-9609; fax (7) 206-9610; Ambassador Charles Isaac.

Saint Vincent and the Grenadines: Centro de Negocios Miramar, Edif. Jerusalén, Of. 403, Avda 3 y Calle 80, Miramar, Havana; tel. (7) 206-9783; fax (7) 206-9782; e-mail embsvg@mtc.co.cu; Ambassador Dexter E. M. Rose.

Saudi Arabia: Avda 5, No 4605, Miramar, Havana; tel. (7) 214-4590; fax (7) 214-4587; e-mail haemb@mofa.gov.sa; Ambassador Saeed Hassan Saeed al-Jomae.

Serbia: Avda 5, No 4406, entre 44 y 46, Miramar, Havana; tel. (7) 204-2488; fax (7) 204-2982; e-mail ambsrbhav@embajadaserbia.co.cu; internet havana.mfa.gov.rs; Ambassador Marina Perović Petrović.

Slovakia: Calle 66, No 521, entre 5B y 7, Miramar, Havana; tel. (7) 204-1884; fax (7) 204-1883; e-mail embeslovaca@mzv.sk; Ambassador Zdenek Rozhold.

South Africa: Avda 5, No 4201, esq. 42, Miramar, Havana; tel. (7) 204-9671; fax (7) 204-1101; e-mail mision@sudafrica.cu; Ambassador Naphtal Manana.

Spain: Calle Cárcel No 51, esq. a Zulueta, Havana; tel. (7) 866-8025; fax (7) 866-8006; e-mail emb.lahabana@maec.es; Ambassador Juan Francisco Montalban Carrasco.

Sri Lanka: Avda 5, No 3004, entre 30 y 32, Miramar, Havana; tel. (7) 204-2562; fax (7) 204-2183; e-mail sri.lanka@enet.cu; Ambassador K. S. C. Dissanayake.

Suriname: Edif. Beijing, Of. 220, Centro de Negocios de Miramar, Calle 3, entre 76 y 78, Playa, Miramar, Havana; tel. (7) 207-9559; fax (7) 207-9561; e-mail secembsur@mtc.co.cu; Ambassador Ike Desmond Antonius.

Sweden: Calle 34, No 510, entre 5 y 7, Miramar, Havana; tel. (7) 204-2831; fax (7) 204-1194; e-mail ambassaden.havanna@foreign.ministry.se; internet www.swedenabroad.com/havanna; Ambassador Elisabeth Eklund.

Switzerland: Avda 5, No 2005, entre 20 y 22, Miramar, Havana; tel. (7) 204-2611; fax (7) 204-1148; e-mail hav.vertretung@eda.admin.ch; internet www.eda.admin.ch/havana; Ambassador Anne Pascale Krauer Müller.

Syria: Calle 20, No 514, entre 5 y 7, Miramar, Havana; tel. (7) 204-2266; fax (7) 204-9754; e-mail embsiria@ceniai.inf.cu; Ambassador (vacant).

Timor-Leste: Calle 40A, No 301, esq. 3, Miramar, Havana; tel. (7) 206-9911; e-mail embtimor@enet.cu; Ambassador Olimpio Branco.

Trinidad and Tobago: Avda 5, No 6603, entre 66 y 68, Miramar, Havana; tel. (7) 207-9603; fax (7) 207-9604; e-mail ttmissionscuba@enet.cu; Ambassador Jennifer Jones-Kernahan.

Turkey: Avda 5, No 3805, entre 36 y 40, Miramar, Havana; tel. (7) 204-1204; fax (7) 204-2899; e-mail turkemb@gmail.com; internet havana.be.mfa.gov.tr; Ambassador Hasan Servet Oktem.

Ukraine: Avda 5, No 4405, entre 44 y 46, Miramar, Havana; tel. (7) 204-2586; fax (7) 204-2341; e-mail emb_cub@mfa.gov.ua; internet www.mfa.gov.ua/cuba; Chargé d'affaires a.i. Volodymyr Kozlov.

United Kingdom: Calle 34, No 702/4, esq. 7 y 17, Miramar, Havana; tel. (7) 214-2200; fax (7) 214-2218; e-mail UKinCuba@fco.gov.uk; internet ukincuba.fco.gov.uk; Ambassador Tim Cole.

USA (Relations severed in 1961): Interests Section in the Embassy of Switzerland: Calzada, entre L y M, Vedado, Havana; tel. (7) 833-3551; fax (7) 833-1084; e-mail irchavana@state.org; internet havana.usint.gov; Principal Officer John Caulfield.

Uruguay: Calle 36, No 716, entre 7 y 17, Miramar, Havana; tel. (7) 204-2311; fax (7) 206-9683; e-mail urucub@rou.co.cu; Ambassador Ariel Arturo Bergamino Sosa.

Venezuela: Edif. Beijing, 2°, Centro de Negocios Miramar, Avda 3, entre 74 y 76, Miramar, Havana; tel. (7) 204-2612; fax (7) 204-9790; e-mail embajada@venezuela.co.cu; Ambassador Edgardo Antonio Ramírez.

Viet Nam: Avda 5, No 1802, esq. 18, Miramar, Havana; tel. (7) 204-1525; fax (7) 204-5333; e-mail embavina@embavicu.org; internet www.vietnamembassy-cuba.org; Ambassador Duong Mihn.

Yemen: Avda 5, No 8201, entre 82 y 84, Miramar, Havana; tel. (7) 204-1506; fax (7) 204-1131; e-mail gamdan-hav@enet.cu; Ambassador Yahya Mohamed Ahmed al-Syaghi.

Zimbabwe: Avda 3, No 1001, entre 10 y 12, Miramar, Havana; tel. (7) 204-2857; fax (7) 204-2720; e-mail zimhavan@enet.cu; Ambassador John Shumba Mvundura.

Judicial System

The judicial system comprises the People's Supreme Court, the People's Provincial Courts and the People's Municipal Courts. The People's Supreme Court exercises the highest judicial authority.

Tribunal Supremo Popular (TSP) (People's Supreme Court): Nuevo Veodad, CP 10600, Havana; tel. (7) 881-2124; fax (7) 881-2245; e-mail ravelo@tsp.cu; internet www.tsp.cu; comprises the Plenum, six Courts of Justice in joint session and the Council of Govt, which comprises the President and Vice-Presidents of the TSP, the Presidents of each Court of Justice, and the Attorney-General; Pres. Dr Rubén Remigio Ferro.

Religion

There is no established Church, and all religions are permitted, though Roman Catholicism predominates. The Afro-Cuban religions of Regla de Ocha (Santería) and Regla Conga (Palo Monte) also have numerous adherents.

CHRISTIANITY

Consejo de Iglesias de Cuba (CIC) (Cuban Council of Churches): Calle 14, No 304, entre 3 y 5, Miramar, Playa, Havana; tel. (7) 204-2878; fax (7) 204-1755; e-mail iglesias@enet.cu; internet www.consejodeiglesias.co.cu; f. 1941; 25 mem. churches; Pres. Rev. Joel Ortega Dopico.

The Roman Catholic Church

Cuba comprises three archdioceses and eight dioceses. Adherents represent some 53% of the total population.

Conferencia de Obispos Católicos de Cuba (COCC) (Bishops' Conference): Calle 26, No 314, entre 3 y 5, Miramar, Apdo 635, 11300 Havana; tel. (7) 204-0165; fax (7) 204-2168; e-mail cocc@iglesiacatolica.cu; internet www.iglesiacubana.org; f. 1983; Pres. DIONISIO GUILLERMO GARCÍA IBÁÑEZ (Archbishop of Santiago de Cuba).

Archbishop of Camagüey: JUAN DE LA CARIDAD GARCÍA RODRÍGUEZ, Calle Luaces, No 55, Apdo 105, 70100 Camagüey; tel. (32) 229-2268; fax (32) 228-7143; e-mail info@arzcamaguey.co.cu.

Archbishop of San Cristóbal de la Habana: Cardinal JAIME LUCAS ORTEGA Y ALAMINO, Calle Habana No 152, esq. a Chacón, Apdo 594, 10100 Havana; tel. (7) 862-4000; fax (7) 866-8109; e-mail info@arquidiocesisdelahabana.org; internet www.arquidiocesisdelahabana.org.

Archbishop of Santiago de Cuba: DIONISIO GUILLERMO GARCÍA IBÁÑEZ, Calle Sánchez Hechevarría 607, entre Barnada y Paraíso, Apdo 26, 90100 Santiago de Cuba; tel. (22) 62-5480; fax (22) 68-6186; e-mail info@arzsantiago.co.cu; internet www.arzobispadosantiagodecuba.org.

The Anglican Communion

Anglicans are adherents of the Iglesia Episcopal de Cuba (Episcopal Church of Cuba).

Bishop of Cuba: Rt Rev. MIGUEL TAMAYO ZALDÍVAR, Calle 6, No 273, entre 11 y 13, Vedado, 10400 Havana; tel. (7) 832-1120; fax (7) 834-3293; e-mail episcopal@ip.etecsa.cu; internet www.cuba.anglican.org.

Other Christian Churches

Iglesia Metodista en Cuba (Methodist Church in Cuba): Calle K, No 502, 25 y 27, Vedado, 10400 Havana; tel. (7) 832-2991; fax (7) 832-0770; e-mail imecu@enet.cu; internet www.imecu.com; autonomous since 1968; 215 churches, 17,000 mems (2005); Bishop RICARDO PEREIRA DÍAZ.

Iglesia Presbiteriana Reformada en Cuba (Presbyterian-Reformed Church in Cuba): Salud 222, entre Lealtad y Campanario, 10200 Havana; tel. (7) 862-1219; fax (7) 866-8819; e-mail presbit@enet.cu; internet www.prccuba.org; f. 1890; 8,000 mems; Moderator Rev. Dr HÉCTOR MÉNDEZ RODRÍGUEZ.

Other denominations active in Cuba include the Apostolic Church of Jesus Christ, the Bethel Evangelical Church, the Christian Pentecostal Church, the Church of God, the Church of the Nazarene, the Free Baptist Convention, the Holy Pentecost Church, the Pentecostal Congregational Church and the Salvation Army. Membership of evangelical churches increased from the late 20th century—in 2010 there were an estimated 800,000 adherents, according to the Consejo de Iglesias de Cuba.

The Press

DAILIES

Granma: Avda Gen. Suárez y Territorial, Plaza de la Revolución, Apdo 6187, CP 10699, Havana; tel. (7) 881-3333; fax (7) 881-9854; e-mail correo@granma.cip.cu; internet www.granma.cubaweb.cu; f. 1965, to replace *Hoy* and *Revolución*; official Communist Party organ; Editor-in-Chief PELAYO TERRY CUERVO; circ. 400,000.

Juventud Rebelde: Avda Territorial y Gen. Suárez, Plaza de la Revolución, Apdo 6344, CP 10600, Havana; tel. (7) 882-0155; fax (7) 883-8959; e-mail digital@jrebelde.cip.cu; internet www.juventudrebelde.cu; f. 1965; organ of the Young Communist League; Editor-in-Chief MARINA MENÉNDEZ; circ. 250,000.

PERIODICALS

Adelante: Salvador Cisneros Betancourt 306, entre Ignacio Agramonte y General Gómez, Camagüey; tel. (32) 284432; e-mail cip222@cip.enet.cu; internet www.adelante.cu; f. 1959; Dir Dr DAICAR SALADRIGAS GONZÁLEZ; Editor YANEXIS ESTRADA TORRES; circ. 42,000.

Ahora: Salida a San Germán y Circunvalación, Holguín; e-mail director@ahora.cu; internet www.ahora.cu; f. 1962; Dir JORGE LUIS CRUZ BERMÚDEZ; circ. 50,000.

Alma Mater: Prado 553, esq. Teniente Rey, Habana Vieja, Havana; e-mail almamater@editoraabril.co.cu; internet www.almamater.cu; f. 1922; aimed at a student readership; Dir YOERKY SÁNCHEZ CUÉLLAR.

Bohemia: Avda Independencia y San Pedro, Apdo 6000, Havana; tel. (7) 81-9213; fax (7) 33-5511; e-mail bohemia@bohemia.co.cu; internet www.bohemia.cu; f. 1908; fortnightly; politics; Dir JOSÉ FERNÁNDEZ VEGA; circ. 100,000.

El Caimán Barbudo: Casa Editora Abril, Prado 553, entre Dragones y Teniente Rey, Vedado, Havana; tel. (7) 860-4237; e-mail rgrillo@enet.cu; internet www.caimanbarbudo.cu; f. 1966; 6 a year; cultural; Dir FIDEL DÍAZ CASTRO; Editor RAFAEL GRILLO; circ. 20,000.

Cinco de Septiembre: Avda 54, No 3516, entre 35 y 37, CP 55100, Cienfuegos; tel. (43) 52-2144; e-mail arosell@enet.cu; internet www.5septiembre.cu; f. 1980; Dir ALINA ROSELL CHONG; circ. 18,000.

Cubadebate: Unión de Periodistas de Cuba, Avda 23, No 452, esq. I, Vedado, Havana; e-mail editor@cubadebate.cu; internet www.cubadebate.cu; Dir RANDY ALONSO FALCÓN.

Dedeté: Territorial y Gen. Suárez, Plaza de la Revolución, Apdo 6344, Havana; tel. (7) 882-0155; fax (7) 81-8621; e-mail contacto@dedete.cu; internet dedete.cu; f. 1969; weekly; humorous supplementary publ. of Juventud Rebelde; Dir ADÁN IGLESIAS TOLEDO; circ. 70,000.

La Demajagua: Amado Estévez, esq. Calle 10, Rpto R. Reyes, Bayamo; tel. (23) 42-4221; e-mail cip225@cip.enet.cu; internet www.lademajagua.co.cu; f. 1977; Dir LUIS CARLOS FRÓMETA AGÜERO; Editor GISLANIA TAMAYO CEDEÑO; circ. 21,000.

El Economista de Cuba: Asociación Nacional de Economistas y Contadores de Cuba, Calle 22, No 901 esq. a 901, Miramar, Havana; tel. (7) 209-3303; fax (7) 202-3456; e-mail eleconomist@cibercuba.com; internet www.eleconomista.cubaweb.cu; monthly; business; Dir-Gen. DANILO GUZMAN DOVAO; Editor MAGALI GARCÍA MORÉ.

Escambray: Adolfo del Castillo 10, Sancti Spíritus; tel. (41) 32-3003; e-mail cip220@cip.enet.cu; internet www.escambray.cu; f. 1979 as daily; weekly from 1992; serves Sancti Spíritus province; Dir JUAN ANTONIO BORREGO DÍAZ; circ. 21,000.

Espacio Laical: Casa Laical, Teniente Rey y Bernaza y Villegas, Habana Vieja, Havana; e-mail info@espaciolaical.org; internet www.espaciolaical.org; f. 2005; monthly; Roman Catholic; Editor MANUEL RODRÍGUEZ VALDÉS.

Girón: Avda Camilo Cienfuegos No 10505, P. Nuero, Matanzas; e-mail cip217@cip.enet.cu; internet www.giron.co.cu; f. 1960; organ of the Communist Party in Matanzas province; Dir CLOVIS ORTEGA CASTAÑEDA; circ. 25,000.

Guerrillero: Colón 12 entre Juan Gualberto Gómez y Adela Azcuy, CP 20100, Pinar del Río; e-mail cip216@cip.enet.cu; internet www.guerrillero.cu; f. 1969; organ of Communist Party in Pinar del Río province; Dir ERNESTO OSORIO ROQUE; Editor IDALMA MENÉNDEZ FEBLES; circ. 33,000.

Invasor: Avda de los Deportes s/n, Ciego de Avila; e-mail cip221@cip.enet.cu; internet www.invasor.cu; f. 1979; provincial periodical; Editor RIGOBERTO TRIANA MARTÍNEZ; circ. 10,500.

La Jiribilla: Havana; e-mail lajiribilla@enet.cu; internet www.lajiribilla.cu; f. 2001; cultural; weekly; Dir IROEL SÁNCHEZ ESPINOSA.

Juventud Técnica: Prado 553, esq. Teniente Rey, Habana Vieja, Havana; tel. (7) 862-9264; e-mail jtecnica@editoraabril.co.cu; internet www.juventudtecnica.cu; f. 1965; every 2 months; scientific-technical; Editor-in-Chief IRAMIS ALONSO PORRO; Editor BÁRBARA MASEDA; circ. 20,000.

Mar y Pesca: Calle Línea 10, esq. N, Vedado, Plaza de la Revolución, Havana; tel. (7) 835-0883; fax (7) 835-0084; e-mail revist@marypesca.cu; internet www.marypesca.cu; f. 1965; bi-monthly; fishing; Dir PEDRO E. PÉREZ BORDÓN; circ. 23,500.

Mujeres: Galiano 264, entre Neptuno y Concordia, CP 10200, Havana; tel. (7) 861-5919; e-mail mujeres@teleda.get.tur.cu; internet www.mujeres.co.cu; f. 1961; weekly; organ of the Federación de Mujeres Cubanas; Dir IVETTE VEGA HERNÁNDEZ; circ. 270,000.

El Nuevo Fenix: Independencia 52, esq. Honorato del Castillo, Sancti Spíritus; tel. (41) 327902; e-mail plss@ip.etecsa.cu; internet www.fenix.co.cu; f. 1999; published by Sancti Spíritus bureau of Prensa Latina (see News Agencies); Editor-in-Chief RAÚL I. GARCÍA ALVAREZ.

Opciones: Territorial esq. Gen. Suárez, Plaza de la Revolucíon, Havana; tel. (7) 881-8934; fax (7) 881-8621; e-mail chabela@opciones.cu; internet www.opciones.cu; f. 1994; weekly; finance, commerce and tourism; Chief Editor ISABEL FERNÁNDEZ GARRIDO.

Palante: Calle 21, No 954, entre 8 y 10, Vedado, Havana; tel. (7) 833-5098; e-mail cip319@cip.enet.cu; internet www.palante.co.cu; f. 1961; weekly; humorous; Dir MERCEDES AZCANO TORRES; circ. 235,000.

Periódico 26: Avda Carlos J. Finlay s/n, CP 75100, Las Tunas; e-mail cip224@cip.enet.cu; internet www.periodico26.cu; f. 2000; provincial periodical; Dir RAMIRO SEGURA GARCÍA; Editor MARYLA GARCÍA SANTOS.

Pionero: Calle 17, No 354, Havana; tel. (7) 32-4571; e-mail pionero@editoraabril.co.cu; internet www.pionero.cu; f. 1961; monthly; children's magazine; Dir LUCÍA SANZ ARAUJO; circ. 210,000.

Revista Casa: 3 y G, Vedado, CP 10400, Havana; tel. (7) 838-2706; fax (7) 834-4554; e-mail revista@casa.cult.cu; internet www.casa

.cult.cu/revistacasa.php; f. 1960; 6 a year; Latin American theatre; Dir ROBERTO FERNÁNDEZ RETAMAR; Editor XENIA RELOBA.

Sierra Maestra: Avda de Los Desfiles, Santiago de Cuba; e-mail cip226@cip.enet.cu; internet www.sierramaestra.cu; f. 1957; weekly; organ of the PCC in Santiago de Cuba; Dir OLGA THAUREAUX PUERTAS; circ. 45,000.

Somos Jóvenes: Calle Prado, esq. a Teniente Rey, Havana; tel. (7) 862-5031; e-mail abadell@gmail.com; internet www.somosjovenes .cu; f. 1977; weekly; Dir MARIETTA MANSO MARTÍN; Editor ALICIA CENTELLES; circ. 200,000.

Temas: Calle 23, No 1155, 5° entre 10 y 12, CP 10400, El Vedado, Havana; tel. and fax (7) 838-3010; e-mail temas@iciaic.cu; internet www.temas.cult.cu; f. 1995; quarterly; cultural, political; Dir RAFAEL HERNÁNDEZ; Chief Editor JUANA MARÍA MARTÍNEZ.

Trabajadores: Territorial esq. Gen. Suárez, Plaza de la Revolución, CP 10698, Havana; tel. (7) 79-0819; fax (7) 55-5927; e-mail editor@ trabaja.cip.cu; internet www.trabajadores.cu; f. 1970; organ of the trade union movt; Dir ALBERTO NÚÑEZ BETANCOURT; circ. 150,000.

Tribuna de la Habana: Territorial esq. Gen. Suárez, Plaza de la Revolución, Havana; tel. (7) 881-8021; e-mail redac@tribuna.cip.cu; internet www.tribuna.co.cu; f. 1980; weekly; Dir JESÚS ALVAREZ FERRER; circ. 90,000.

Vanguardia: Calle Céspedes 5, esq. Plácido, Santa Clara, CP 50100, Matanzas; e-mail contacto@vanguardia.cip.cu; internet www .vanguardia.co.cu; f. 1962; weekly; Dir F. A. CHANG L.; circ. 45,000.

Venceremos: Avda Ernesto Che Guevara, Km 1½, CP 95400, Guantánamo; tel. (7) 32-7398; e-mail cip227@cip.enet.cu; internet www.venceremos.co.cu; f. 1962; economic, political and social publ. for Guantánamo province; Dir YAMILKA ÁLVAREZ RAMOS; Editor-in-Chief ARIANNY TÉLLEZ LAMOTHE; circ. 33,500.

Victoria: Carretera de la Fe, Km 1½, Plaza de la Revolución, Nueva Gerona, Isla de la Juventud; tel. (46) 32-4210; e-mail cip228@cip.enet .cu; internet www.victoria.co.cu; f. 1967; Dir MATILDE CAMPOS JOA; Chief Editor OLGA L. MORALES VILAÚ; circ. 9,200.

Zunzún: Prado 553, CP 10500, Havana; e-mail zunzun@eabril .jovenclub.cu; internet www.zunzun.cu; f. 1980; children's magazine; Dir ADELA MORO; Chief Editor HÉCTOR QUINTERO.

PRESS ASSOCIATIONS

Unión de Escritores y Artistas de Cuba: Calle 17, No 354, entre G y H, Vedado, Havana; tel. (7) 838-3158; e-mail presidencia@uneac.co .cu; internet www.uneac.org.cu; f. 1961; Pres. MIGUEL BARNET LANZA.

Unión de Periodistas de Cuba (UPEC): Avda 23, No 452, esq. a I, Vedado, CP 10400, Havana; tel. (7) 832-4550; fax (7) 33-3079; e-mail vpetica@upec.co.cu; internet www.cubaperiodistas.cu; f. 1963; Pres. ANTONIO MOLTÓ MARTORELL.

NEWS AGENCIES

Agencia de Información Nacional (AIN): Calle 23, No 358, esq. J, Vedado, Havana; tel. (7) 881-6423; fax (7) 66-2049; e-mail edda@ain .cu; internet www.ain.cu; f. 1974; national news agency, publishes Agencia Cubana de Noticias (ACN) website; Gen. Man. EDDA DIZ GARCÉS.

Prensa Latina (Agencia Informativa Latinoamericana, SA): Calle 23, No 201, esq. N, Vedado, Havana; tel. (7) 838-3496; fax (7) 33-3068; e-mail difusion@prensa-latina.cu; internet www.prensa-latina .cu; f. 1959; Pres. LUIS ENRIQUE GONZÁLEZ.

Publishers

Artecubano Ediciones: Calle 3, No 1205, entre 12 y 14, Playa, Havana; tel. (7) 203-8581; fax (7) 204-2744; e-mail cnap@cubarte.cult .cu; attached to the Ministry of Culture; Dir RAFAEL ACOSTA DE ARRIBA.

Casa de las Américas: Calle 3 y Avda G, Plaza de la Revolución, Vedado, 10400 Havana; tel. (7) 838-2706; fax (7) 834-4554; e-mail presidencia@casa.cult.cu; internet www.casadelasamericas.com; f. 1959; Latin American literature and social sciences; Dir ROBERTO FERNÁNDEZ RETAMAR.

Casa Editora Abril: Prado 553, esq. Teniente Rey y Dragones, Habana Vieja, 10200 Havana; tel. (7) 862-5031; fax (7) 862-4330; e-mail webeditora@editoraabril.co.cu; internet www.editoraabril .cu/editora; f. 1980; attached to the Union of Young Communists; cultural, children's literature; Dir NIURKA DUMÉNIGO GARCÍA.

Ediciones Creart: Calle 4, No 205, entre Línea y 11, Plaza de la Revolución, Vedado, Havana; tel. (7) 55-3496; fax (7) 33-3069; e-mail creart@cubarte.cult.cu; f. 1994; Dir TOMÁS VALDÉS BECERRA.

Ediciones Unión: Calle 17, No 354, entre G y H, Plaza de la Revolución, Vedado, 10400 Havana; tel. (7) 55-3112; fax (7) 33-3158; e-mail editora@uneac.co.cu; internet www.uneac.org.cu;

f. 1962; publishing arm of the Unión de Escritores y Artistas de Cuba; Cuban literature, art; Dir OLGA MARTA PÉREZ RODRÍGUEZ.

Ediciones Vigía: Magdalena 1, Plaza de la Vigía, 40100 Matanzas; tel. (452) 44845; e-mail vigia@cult.cu; internet www.atenas.cult.cu/ ?q=editorialedicionesvigia; f. 1985; Dir AGUSTINA PONCE.

Editora Atril (Ediciones Musicales—ABDALA): Producciones Abdala, SA, Calle 32, No 318, esq. 5 Avda, Miramar, Playa, Havana; tel. (7) 204-5213; fax (7) 204-4006; e-mail atril.abdalal@cimex.com .cu; internet www.abdala.cu; Dir TERESA TORRES PÁEZ.

Editora Política: Belascoaín No 864, esq. Desagüe, Centro Habana, 10300 Havana; tel. (7) 879-8553; fax (7) 55-6836; e-mail editora@epol .cc.cu; internet www.editpolitica.cu; f. 1963; publishing institution of the Communist Party of Cuba; Dir SANTIAGO DÓRQUEZ PÉREZ.

Editorial Academia: Industria y Barcelona, Capitolio Nacional, 4°, Centro Habana, 10200 Havana; tel. and fax (7) 863-0315; e-mail editorial@gecyt.cu; f. 1962; attached to the Ministry of Science, Technology and the Environment; scientific and technical; Dir GLADYS HERNÁNDEZ HERRERA.

Editorial Arte y Literatura: Calle O'Reilly, No 4, esq. Tacón, Habana Vieja, 10100 Havana; tel. (7) 862-4326; fax (7) 833-8187; e-mail publicaciones@icl.cult.cu; internet www.cubaliteraria.cu/ editorial/Arte_y_Literatura; f. 1967; traditional Cuban literature and arts; Dir LOURDES GONZÁLEZ CASAS.

Editorial Ciencias Médicas: Edif. Soto, 2°, Calle 23, No 177, entre N y O, Plaza de la Revolución, Vedado, 10400 Havana; tel. (7) 833-0311; fax (7) 33-3063; e-mail ecimed@infomed.sld.cu; internet www .sld.cu/sitios/ecimed; f. 1988; publishing arm of the Centro Nacional de Información de Ciencias Médicas de Cuba; attached to the Ministry of Public Health; books and magazines specializing in the medical sciences; Dir DAMIANA MARTÍN LAURENCIO.

Editorial Félix Varela: San Miguel No 1011, entre Mazón y Basarrate, Plaza de la Revolución, Vedado, 10400 Havana; tel. (7) 877-5617; fax (7) 73-5419; e-mail elsa@enpses.co.cu; Dir ELSA RODRÍGUEZ.

Editorial Gente Nueva: Calle 2, No 58, entre 3 y 5, Plaza de la Revolución, Vedado, 10400 Havana; tel. (7) 833-7676; fax (7) 33-8187; e-mail gentenueva@icl.cult.cu; f. 1967; books for children; Dir ENRIQUE PÉREZ DÍAZ.

Editorial José Martí: Calzada 259, entre I y J, Apdo 4208, Plaza de la Revolución, Vedado, 10400 Havana; tel. (7) 835-1921; fax (7) 33-3441; e-mail editjmal@icl.cult.cu; internet www.cubaliteraria.cu/ editorial/editora_marti; f. 1982; attached to the Ministry of Culture; foreign-language publishing; Dir ANA MARÍA DÍAZ CANALS.

Editorial Letras Cubanas: Calle O'Reilly, No 4, esq. Tacón, Habana Vieja, 10100 Havana; tel. (7) 862-4378; fax (7) 66-8187; e-mail elc@icl.cult.cu; internet www.letrascubanas.cult.cu; f. 1977; attached to the Ministry of Culture; general, particularly classic and contemporary Cuban literature and arts; Dir ROGELIO RIVERÓN.

Editorial de la Mujer: Calle Galiano, No 264, esq. Neptuno, Havana; tel. (7) 862-4905; e-mail mujeres@enet.cu; f. 1995; female literature; publishing house of the Cuban Women's Fed; Dir-Gen. ISABEL MOYA RICHARD.

Editorial Nuevo Milenio: Calle 14, No 4104, entre 41 y 43, Playa, Havana; tel. (7) 203-6090; fax (7) 833-3441; e-mail nuevomil@cubarte .cult.cu; internet www.cubaliteraria.cu/editorial/Nuevo Milenio; f. 1967 as Editorial de Ciencias Sociales and Editorial Científico-Técnica; merged and name changed as above in 1999; attached to the Ministry of Culture; technical, scientific and social sciences literature; Dir SONIA ALMAGUER DARNA.

Editorial Oriente: Santa Lucía 356, 90100 Santiago de Cuba; tel. (226) 22496; fax (226) 86111; e-mail edoriente@cultstgo.cult.cu; internet www.editorialoriente.cult.cu; f. 1971; fiction, history, female literature and studies, art and culture, practical books, and books for children; Dir AIDA BAHR.

Editorial Pablo de la Torriente Brau: Calle 11, No 160, entre K y L, Plaza de la Revolución, Vedado, 10400 Havana; tel. (7) 832-7581; fax (7) 33-3079; e-mail pbagenda@ip.etecsa.cu; f. 1985; publishing arm of the Unión de Periodistas de Cuba; Dir IRMA DE ARMAS FONSECA.

Editorial Pueblo y Educación: Avda 3A, No 4601, entre 46 y 60, Playa, Havana; tel. (7) 202-1490; fax (7) 204-0844; e-mail epe@ceniai .inf.cu; f. 1971; textbooks and educational publs; publishes Revista Educación (3 a year, circ. 2,200); Dir CATALINA LAJUD HERRERO.

Editorial Sanlope: Calle Gonzalo de Quesada, No 121, entre Lico Cruz y Lucas Ortiz, Las Tunas; tel. (31) 48191; fax (31) 43180; e-mail librolt@tunet.cult.cu; internet www.tunet.cult.cu/pagsec/institut/ sanlope/index.html; f. 1991; attached to the Ministry of Culture; Dir VERENA GARCÍA MIRABAL.

GOVERNMENT PUBLISHING HOUSES

Instituto Cubano del Libro: Palacio del Segundo Cabo, Calle O'Reilly, No 4, esq. Tacón, Habana Vieja, Havana; tel. (7) 862-8091;

fax (7) 33-8187; e-mail promocion@icl.cult.cu; internet www .cubaliteraria.cu; f. 1967; printing and publishing org. attached to the Ministry of Culture, which combines several publishing houses and has direct links with others; presides over the National Editorial Council (CEN) organizes the annual Havana International Book Fair; Pres. ZULEICA ROMAY GUERRA.

Oficina Publicaciones del Consejo de Estado: Calle 17, No 552, esq. D, Plaza de la Revolución, Vedado, 10400 Havana; tel. (7) 55-1406; fax (7) 57-5258; e-mail palvarez@ip.etecsa.cu; f. 1972; attached to the Council of State; books, pamphlets and other printed media on historical and political matters; Dir PEDRO ALVAREZ TABÍO.

Broadcasting and Communications

TELECOMMUNICATIONS

Empresa de Telecomunicaciones de Cuba, SA (ETECSA): Edif. Beijing, 5°, Avda 3, entre 76 y 78, Centro de Negocios Miramar, 11300 Havana; tel. (7) 266-8500; fax (7) 860-5144; e-mail atencion_usuarios@etecsa.cu; internet www.etecsa.cu; f. 1991; merged with Empresa de Telecomunicaciones Celulares del Caribe, SA (C-Com) and Teléfonos Celulares de Cuba, SA (CUBACEL) in 2003; Exec. Pres. MAIMIR MESA RAMOS.

Instituto de Investigación y Desarrollo de Comunicaciones (LACETEL): Avda Independencia, No 34515, Km 14½, Reparto 1 de Mayo, Rancho Boyeros, CP 19210, Havana; tel. (7) 683-9180; fax (7) 649-5828; e-mail despacho@lacetel.cu; internet www.lacetel.cu; f. 1964; state-owned; Dir-Gen. GLAUCO GUILLÉN NIETO.

Telecomunicaciones Móviles, SA (MOVITEL): Avda 47, No 3405, Reparto Kohly, Playa, Havana; tel. (7) 204-8400; fax (7) 204-4264; e-mail movitel@movitel.co.cu; internet www.movitel.co.cu; mobile telecommunications; Dir-Gen. ASELA FERNÁNDEZ LORENZO.

Regulatory Authority

Ministerio de la Informática y las Comunicaciones (Dirección de Regulaciones y Normas): Avda Independencia y 19 de Mayo, Plaza de la Revolución, Havana; tel. (7) 81-7654; e-mail infosoc@mic.cu; internet www.mic.gov.cu; Dir WILFREDO REINALDO LÓPEZ RODRÍGUEZ.

BROADCASTING

Radio

In 2011 there were seven national networks and one international network, 16 provincial radio stations and 25 municipal radio stations.

Habana Radio: Edif. Lonja del Comercio, Lamparilla 2, Plaza de San Francisco de Asís, Habana Vieja, Havana; tel. (7) 866-2706; e-mail sitioweb@habradio.ohc.cu; internet www.habanaradio.cu; f. 1999; run by the Oficina del Historiador de la Ciudad de La Habana; cultural and factual programmes; Dir MAGDA RESIK.

Radio Cadena Agramonte: Calle Cisneros, No 310, entre Ignacio Agramonte y General Gómez, 70100 Camagüey; tel. (322) 29-8673; e-mail cip240@cip.enet.cu; internet www.cadenagramonte.cu; f. 1957; serves Camagüey; Dir ONELIO CASTILLO CORDERÍ.

Radio Cubana: Calle 23, No 258, entre L y M, 10°, Vedado, Plaza de la Revolución, Havana; tel. (7) 832-2477; e-mail pavon@radio.icrt.cu; internet www.radiocubana.cu; Vice-Pres. GUILLERMO PAVÓN PACHECO.

Radio Enciclopedia: Edif. N, Calle N, No 266, entre 21 y 23, Vedado, 10400 Havana; tel. (7) 838-4586; e-mail lmarquez@ renciclopedia.icrt.cu; internet www.radioenciclopedia.cu; f. 1962; national network; instrumental music programmes; 24 hours daily; Dir-Gen. LUISA MÇARQUEZ ECHEVARRIA.

Radio Habana Cuba: Infanta 105, Apdo 6240, Havana; tel. (7) 877-6628; e-mail radiohc@enet.cu; internet www.radiohc.cu; f. 1961; shortwave station; broadcasts in Spanish, English, French, Portuguese, Arabic, Esperanto, Quechua, Guaraní and Creole; Dir-Gen. ISIDRO FARDALES GONZÁLEZ.

Radio Musical Nacional (CBMF): Edif. N, Calle N, No 266, entre 21 y 23, Vedado, 10400 Havana; tel. (7) 832-8893; e-mail rmusical@ cmbf.icrt.cu; internet www.cmbfradio.cu; f. 1948; national network; classical music programmes; 17 hours daily; Dir OTTO BRAÑA GONZÁLEZ.

Radio Progreso: Infanta 105, esq. a 25, 6°, Apdo 3042, Havana; tel. (7) 877-5519; e-mail paginaweb@rprogreso.icrt.cu; internet www .radioprogreso.cu; f. 1929; national network; mainly entertainment and music; 24 hours daily; Dir-Gen. JOSÉ ANTONIO GUERRA GARCÍA.

Radio Rebelde: Calle 23, No 258, entre L y M, Plaza de la Revolución, Vedado, Apdo 6277, 10400 Havana; tel. (7) 838-4365; fax (7) 33-4270; e-mail smabel@radiorebelde.icrt.cu; internet www .radiorebelde.com.cu; f. 1958; merged with Radio Liberación in 1984;

national network; 24-hour news and cultural programmes, music and sports; Dir-Gen. SOFÍA MABEL MANSO DELGADO.

Radio Reloj: Edif. Radiocentro, Calle 23, No 258, entre L y M, Plaza de la Revolución, Vedado, 10400 Havana; tel. (7) 838-4185; fax (7) 838-4225; e-mail relojmailj@rreloj.icrt.cu; internet www.radioreloj .cu; f. 1947; national network; 24-hour news service; Dir OMAIDA ALONSO DIEZCABEZA.

Radio Revolución: Aguilera No 554, entre San Agustín y Barnada, 90100 Santiago de Cuba; tel. (226) 28038; e-mail cip233@cip.enet.cu; internet www.cmkc.cu; serves Santiago de Cuba; Dir ROSA ILEANA NAVARRO PUPO.

Radio Taino: Edif. Radiocentro, Calle 23, No 258, Plaza de la Revolución, entre L y M, Vedado, 10400 Havana; tel. (7) 838-4157; e-mail sitioweb@rtaino.icrt.cu; internet www.radiotaino.icrt.cu; f. 1985; broadcasts in English and Spanish; Dir FERNANDO PÉREZ RICARDO.

Television

The Cuban Government holds a 19% stake in the regional television channel Telesur, based in Caracas, Venezuela.

Televisión Cubana: Avda 23, No 258, entre L y M, Vedado, 10400 Havana; tel. (7) 55-4059; fax (7) 33-3107; e-mail tvcubana@icrt.cu; internet www.tvcubana.icrt.cu; f. 1950; broadcasts through five national channels—Canal Educativo, Canal Educativo 2, Cubavisión, Multivisión, Tele Rebelde—and 15 provincial channels; Pres. DANIEL SIRIO; Dir-Gen. FABIO FERNÁNDEZ QUEZZEL.

Canal Educativo: Calle P, entre Humbolt y 23, Plaza de la Revolución, Vedado, 10400 Havana; tel. (7) 831-4653; fax (7) 831-4654; e-mail canaleducativo@cedu.icrt.cu; internet www .canaleducativo.cu; f. 2002; broadcasts on channel 13; educational; Dir IVÁN BARRETO.**Cubavisión:** Calle M, No 313, Vedado, Havana; e-mail info@cubavision.icrt.cu; internet www.cubavision.cubaweb .cu; broadcasts on channel 6.

Multivisión: f. 2008; broadcasts programmes from foreign networks.

Tele Rebelde: Mazón, No 52, Vedado, Havana; tel. (7) 32-3369; broadcasts on channel 2; Dir MAURICIO NÚÑEZ RODRÍGUEZ.

Regulatory Authorities

Empresa de Radiocomunicación y Difusión de Cuba (RADIO-CUBA): Calle Habana 406, entre Obispo y Obrapía, Habana Vieja, Havana; tel. (7) 860-0796; fax (7) 860-3107; e-mail radiocuba@ radiocuba.cu; f. 1995; controls the domestic and international broadcast transmission networks; Dir-Gen. AMADO HERNÁNDEZ.

Instituto Cubano de Radio y Televisión (ICRT): Edif. Radiocentro, Avda 23, No 258, entre L y M, Vedado, Havana 4; tel. (7) 32-1568; fax (7) 33-3107; e-mail icrt@cecm.get.tur.cu; internet www .cubagob.cu/des_soc/icrt; f. 1962; Vice-Pres. OMAR OLAZÁBAL.

Finance

(cap. = capital; res = reserves; dep. = deposits; m. = million; brs = branches, amounts in convertible pesos unless otherwise stated)

BANKING

All banks were nationalized in 1960. Legislation establishing the national banking system was approved by the Council of State in 1984. A restructuring of the banking system to accommodate Cuba's transformation to a more market-orientated economy, was initiated in 1995. A new central bank, the Banco Central de Cuba (BCC), was created in 1997 to supersede the Banco Nacional de Cuba (BNC). The BCC was to be responsible for issuing currency, proposing and implementing monetary policy, and the regulation of financial institutions. The BNC was to continue functioning as a commercial bank and servicing the country's foreign debt. The restructuring of the banking system also allowed for the creation of an investment bank, the Banco de Inversiones, to provide medium- and long-term financing for investment, and the Banco Financiero Internacional, SA, to offer short-term financing. The banking system is under the control of Grupo Nueva Banca, which holds a majority share in each institution.

Central Bank

Banco Central de Cuba (BCC): Calle Cuba, No 402, Aguiar 411, Apdo 746, Habana Vieja, Havana; tel. (7) 860-4811; fax (7) 863-4061; e-mail cibe@bc.gov.cu; internet www.bc.gov.cu; f. 1997; sole bank of issue; Pres. ERNESTO MEDINA VILLAVEIRÁN.

Commercial Banks

Banco de Crédito y Comercio (BANDEC): Amargura 158, entre Cuba y Aguiar, Habana Vieja, Havana; tel. (7) 866-8967; fax (7) 863-

8803; e-mail rgallardo@oc.bandec.cu; f. 1997; cap. 790m., res 739.9m., dep. 15,853.4m. (Dec. 2012); Pres. ILEANA ESTÉVEZ; 209 brs.

Banco Exterior de Cuba: Calle 23, No 55, esq. P, Vedado, Municipio Plaza, Havana; tel. (7) 55-0795; fax (7) 55-0794; e-mail bec@bec.co.cu; f. 1999; cap. US $486m., res $22.7m., dep. $898.2m. (Dec. 2012); Pres. JACOBO PEISON WEINER.

Banco Financiero Internacional, SA: Avda 5, No 9009, esq. 92, Miramar, Municipio Playa, Havana; tel. (7) 267-5000; fax (7) 267-5002; e-mail bfi@bfi.com.cu; f. 1984; autonomous; finances Cuba's foreign trade; Chair. LUIS MARIO SALCES MOLINA; 29 brs.

Banco Industrial de Venezuela-Cuba, SA (BIVC): Edif. Jerusalén, 2°, Of. 202, Centro de Negocios Miramar, Sector Miramar, Havana; tel. (7) 206-9650; fax (2) 206-9651; f. 2005 as a subsidiary of state-owned Banco Industrial de Venezuela, SA; Pres. RODOLFO PORRO ALETTI.

Banco Internacional de Comercio, SA: 20 de Mayo y Ayestarán, Apdo 6113, 10600 Havana; tel. (7) 883-6038; fax (7) 883-6028; e-mail bicsa@bicsa.co.cu; f. 1993; cap. US $396.2m., res $61.2m., dep. $4,204.6m. (Dec. 2012); Chair. and Pres. JOSÉ JULIO RODRÍGUEZ FALCÓN.

Banco Metropolitano, SA: Avda 5 y Calle 112, Miramar, Municipio Habana Vieja, 11600 Havana; tel. (7) 866-6659; fax (7) 864-2916; e-mail bm@banco-metropolitano.com; internet www .banco-metropolitano.com; f. 1996; offers foreign currency and deposit account facilities; cap. 584.6m., res 85.9m., dep. 13,610.9m. (Dec. 2013); Pres. ORLANDO D. LÓPEZ GARCÉS; 90 brs.

Banco Nacional de Cuba (BNC): Aguiar 456, entre Amargura y Lamparilla, Habana Vieja, Havana; tel. (7) 862-8896; fax (7) 866-9390; e-mail bancuba@bnc.cu; internet www.cubagob.cu; f. 1948; reorganized 1997; Pres. RENÉ LAZO FERNÁNDEZ.

Savings Bank

Banco Popular de Ahorro: Calle 16, No 306, entre 3ra y 5ta, Playa, Miramar, Havana; tel. (7) 204-2545; fax (7) 204-1180; e-mail presidencia@mail.bpa.cu; internet www.bpa.cu; f. 1983; savings bank; cap. 271m., res 255.2m., dep. 12,139.5m. (Dec. 2012); Pres. JOSÉ LÁZARO ALARI MARTÍNEZ; 520 brs.

Investment Bank

Banco de Inversiones, SA: Avda 5, No 6802 esq. a 68, Miramar, Havana; tel. (7) 204-3374; fax (7) 204-3377; e-mail inversiones@bdi .cu; internet www.bdi.cu; f. 1996; cap. 31.5m., res 4.7m., dep. 33.1m. (Dec. 2010); Exec. Pres. ARMINDA GARCÍA GONZÁLEZ.

INSURANCE

The Superintendencia de Seguros (f. 1997) is the regulatory authority supervising the entities engaged in insurance, reinsurance and auxiliary services of brokers and insurance agents.

State Organizations

Grupo Caudal, SA (Grupo de Seguros y Servicios Financieros de Cuba): Calle 43, No 2210, entre 22 y 24, Playa, Havana; tel. (7) 204-8822; fax (7) 204-8813; e-mail caudal@caudal.cu; internet www.mfp .cu; management and development of insurance, brokerage and insurance auxiliary services; includes Agencia Internacional de Inspección, Ajuste de Averías y Otros Servicios Conexos (INTERMAR, SA), Asistencia al Turista (ASISTUR), Consultorías y Avalúos (CONAVANA, SA), Empresa Grafica de Finanzas y Precios (EGRAFIP) and INTERAUDIT, SA; Pres. JOSÉ M. ESCANDELL CÁMBARA.

Empresa del Seguro Estatal Nacional (ESEN): Calle 5, No 306, entre C y D, Vedado, Havana; tel. (7) 830-2509; fax (7) 832-5510; e-mail rfo@esen.com.cu; internet www.ain.cu/publicidad/ sitio esen/index.htm; f. 1978; motor and agricultural insurance; Dir-Gen. HUMBERTO BARRETO NARDO.

Seguros Internacionales de Cuba, SA (Esicuba): Cuba No 314, entre Obispo y Obrapía, Habana Vieja, Havana; tel. (7) 862-8031; fax (7) 866-8038; e-mail esicuba.clientes@esicuba.cu; internet www.esicuba.cu; f. 1963; reorganized 1986; all classes of insurance except life; Dir-Gen. JOSÉ CARLOS MEIJIDES ALFONSO.

Trade and Industry

GOVERNMENT AGENCIES

Centro para la Promoción del Comercio Exterior de Cuba (CEPEC): Infanta 16, esq. 23, 2°, Vedado, Municipio Plaza, Havana; tel. (7) 838-0428; fax (7) 833-2220; e-mail cepecdir@mincex.cu; internet www.cepec.cu; f. 1995; Dir-Gen. RAYSA COSTA BLANCO.

Grupo Empresarial de la Agroindustria Azucarera (AZCUBA): Óf. de Comunicación Institucional, Calle 23, No 171,

entre N y O, Vedado, Havana; tel. (7) 832-9356; e-mail liobel@ ocentral.minaz.cu; f. 2011 to replace the Ministry of Sugar; 13 provincial brs managing 56 sugar mills; Pres. ORLANDO CELSO GARCÍA.

CHAMBER OF COMMERCE

Cámara de Comercio de la República de Cuba: Calle 21, No 661/ 701, esq. Calle A, Apdo 4237, Vedado, Havana; tel. (7) 830-4436; fax (7) 833-3042; e-mail pdcia@camara.com.cu; internet www .camaracuba.cu; f. 1963; mems include all Cuban foreign trade enterprises and the most important agricultural and industrial enterprises; Pres. ORLANDO HERNÁNDEZ GUILLÉN; Sec.-Gen. OMAR DE JESÚS FERNÁNDEZ JIMÉNEZ.

AGRICULTURAL ORGANIZATION

Asociación Nacional de Agricultores Pequeños (ANAP) (National Association of Small Farmers): Calle I, No 206, entre Linea y 13, Vedado, Havana; tel. (7) 32-4541; fax (7) 33-4244; f. 1961; 200,000 mems; Pres. FÉLIX GONZÁLEZ VIEGO; 331,874 mems.

STATE IMPORT-EXPORT BOARDS

Alimport (Empresa Cubana Importadora de Alimentos): Infanta 16, 3°, Apdo 7006, Havana; tel. (7) 54-2501; fax (7) 33-3151; e-mail precios@alimport.com.cu; f. 1962; controls import of foodstuffs and liquors; Pres. IGOR MONTERO.

Aviaimport (Empresa Cubana Importadora y Exportadora de Aviación): Calle 182, No 126, entre 1 y 5, Rpto Flores, Playa, Havana; tel. (7) 273-0077; fax (7) 273-6365; e-mail dcom@aviaimport.avianet .cu; import and export of aircraft and components; Man. Dir MARCOS LAGO MARTÍNEZ.

Caribex (Empresa Comercial Caribe): Avda La Pesquera y Atarés, Puerto Pesquero de La Habana, 3°, Habana Vieja, Havana; tel. (7) 864-4135; fax (7) 864-4144; e-mail caribex@caribex.cu; internet www .caribex.cu; export of seafood and marine products; Dir ESTHER ALEJO.

Catec (Empresa Cubana Exportadora y Comercializadora de Productos y Servicios de la Ciencia y la Técnica Agraria): Calle 148, No 905, entre 9 y 9A, Rpto Cubanacán, Playa, Havana; tel. (7) 208-2164; fax (7) 204-6071; e-mail alina@catec.co.cu; internet www.catec.cu; exports, imports and markets scientific and technical products relating to the farming and forestry industries; Dir-Gen. OSVALDO CARVEJAL GABELA.

Construimport (Empresa Exportadora e Importadora de Equipos de Construcción): Carretera de Varona, Km 1½, Capdevila, Havana; tel. (7) 645-2567; fax (7) 646-8943; e-mail equipo@construimport.co .cu; internet www.construimport.cubaindustria.cu; f. 1969; controls the import and export of construction machinery and equipment; Gen. Dir DEYSI ROMAY.

Consumimport (Empresa Cubana Importadora de Artículos de Consumo General): Calle 23, No 55, 9°, Apdo 6427, Vedado, Plaza de Revolución, Havana; tel. (8) 36-7717; fax (8) 33-3847; e-mail comer@ consumimport.infocex.cu; f. 1962; imports and exports general consumer goods; Dir MERCEDES REY HECHAVARRÍA.

Copextel (Corporación Productora y Exportadora de Tecnología Electrónica): Avda 11, entre 222B y 222C, Siboney, Playa, Havana; tel. (7) 273-0820; fax (7) 273-6540; e-mail copextel@copextel.com.cu; internet www.copextel.com.cu; f. 1985; exports LTEL personal computers and micro-computer software; Dir ADOLFO CEPERO BARROSO.

Cubaexport (Empresa Cubana Exportadora de Alimentos y Productos Varios): Calle 23, No 55, entre Infanta y P, 8°, Vedado, Apdo 6719, Havana; tel. (7) 838-0595; fax (7) 833-3587; e-mail cubaexport@ cexport.mincex.cu; f. 1965; export of foodstuffs and industrial products; Man. Dir FRANCISCO SANTIAGO PICHARDO.

Cubahidráulica (Empresa Central de Equipos Hidráulicos): Carretera Vieja de Guanabacoa y Linea de Ferrocarril, Rpto Mañana, Guanabacoa, Havana; tel. (7) 797-0821; fax (7) 797-1627; e-mail cubahidraulica@enet.cu; internet www.cubahidraulica.com; f. 1995; imports and exports hydraulic and mechanical equipment, parts and accessories; Dir-Gen. OSMUNDO PAZ PAZ.

Cubametales (Empresa Cubana Importadora de Metales, Combustibles y Lubricantes): Infanta 16, 4°, entre 23 y Humboldt, Apdo 6917, Vedado, Havana; tel. (7) 838-0531; fax (7) 838-0530; e-mail mcarmen@cubametal.mincex.cu; f. 1962; controls import of metals (ferrous and non-ferrous), crude petroleum and petroleum products; also engaged in the export of petroleum products and ferrous and non-ferrous scrap; Dir-Gen. MARY CARMEN ARENCIBIA VÁZQUEZ.

Cubaniquel (Empresa Cubana Exportadora de Minerales y Metales): Carretera Moa, Sagua Km 1½, Moa, CP 83330, Holguín; tel. (24) 60-8283; fax (24) 60-2156; e-mail cceac@cubaniquel.moa .minbas.cu; f. 1961; sole exporter of minerals and metals; operates 2 nickel plants; Man. Dir ANGEL ROBERTO HERNÁNDEZ.

Cubatabaco (Empresa Cubana del Tabaco): Calle Nueva 75, entre Universidad y Pedroso, Cerro, Havana; tel. (7) 879-0253; fax (7) 33-8214; e-mail cubatabaco@cubatabaco.cu; internet www.cubatabaco.cu; f. 1962; controls export of leaf tobacco, cigars and cigarettes to France; Dir ALFREDO S. CALERO ACOSTA.

Ediciones Cubanas (Empresa de Comercio Exterior de Publicaciones): Obispo 527, esq. Bernaza, Apdo 47, Habana Vieja, Havana; tel. (7) 863-1989; fax (7) 33-8943; e-mail edicuba@cubarte.cult.cu; controls import and export of books and periodicals; Dir ROLANDO VERDÉS PINEDA.

Egrem (Estudios de Grabaciones y Ediciones Musicales): Calle 3, No 1008, entre 10 y 12, Miramar, Playa, Havana; tel. (7) 204-1925; fax (7) 204-2519; e-mail director@egrem.co.cu; internet www.egrem.com.cu; f. 1964; controls the import and export of CDs, printed music and musical instruments; Gen. Dir MARIO ESCALONA SERRANO.

Emiat (Empresa Importadora y Exportadora de Suministros Técnicos): Avda 47, No 2828, entre 28 y 34, Rpto Kohly, Havana; tel. (7) 203-0345; fax (7) 204-9353; e-mail emiat@enet.cu; f. 1983; imports technical materials, equipment and special products; exports furniture, kitchen utensils and accessories.

Emidict (Empresa Especializada Importadora, Exportadora y Distribuidora para la Ciencia y la Técnica): Calle 16, No 102, esq. Avda 1, Miramar, Playa, 13000 Havana; tel. (7) 203-5316; fax (7) 204-1768; e-mail emidict@ceniai.inf.cu; internet www.emidict.com.cu; f. 1982; controls import and export of scientific and technical products and equipment, live animals; scientific information; Dir-Gen. CALIXTO A. RODRÍGUEZ DIAGO.

Energoimport (Empresa Importadora de Objetivos Electro-energéticos): Amenidad No 124, entre Nueva y 20 de Mayo, Municipio Cerro, 10600 Havana; tel. (7) 70-2501; fax (7) 66-6079; f. 1977; controls import of equipment for electricity generation; Dir-Gen. RAFAEL ERNESTO.

Eprob (Empresa de Proyectos para las Industrias de la Básica): Avda 31A, No 1805, entre 18 y 20, Edif. Las Ursulinas, Miramar, Playa, Apdo 12100, Havana; tel. (7) 202-5562; fax (7) 204-2146; e-mail direccion@eprob.cu; f. 1967; exports consulting services, processing of engineering construction projects and supplies of complete industrial plants and turnkey projects; Chair. ORLANDO HERNÁNDEZ GUILLÉN.

Eproyiv (Empresa de Proyectos para Industrias Varias): Calle 31A, No 1815, entre 18 y 20, Playa, Havana; tel. (7) 202-7097; fax (7) 204-2149; e-mail dg-eproyiv@eproyiv.cu; internet www.eproyiv.cu; f. 1967; consulting services, feasibility studies, devt of basic and detailed engineering models, project management and turnkey projects; Dir MARTA ELENA HERNÁNDEZ DÍAZ.

Fondo Cubano de Bienes Culturales: Calle 36, No 4702, esq. Avda 47, Rpto Kohly, Playa, Havana; tel. (7) 204-6428; fax (7) 204-0391; e-mail fcbc@fcbc.cult.cu; f. 1978; controls export of fine handicrafts and works of art; Dir-Gen. GUILLERMO SOLENZAL MORALES.

Habanos, SA: Avda 3, No 2006, entre 20 y 22, Miramar, Havana; tel. (7) 204-0524; fax (7) 204-0491; e-mail habanos@habanos.cu; internet www.habanos.com; f. 1994; controls export of leaf and pipe tobacco, cigars and cigarettes to all markets; jt venture with Altadis, SA (Spain); Pres. JORGE LUIS FERNÁNDEZ MAIQUE.

ICAIC (Instituto Cubano del Arte e Industria Cinematográficos): Calle 23, No 1155, Vedado, Havana 4; tel. (7) 55-3128; fax (7) 33-3032; e-mail webmaster@icaic.cu; internet www.cubacine.cu; f. 1959; production, import and export of films and newsreel; Dir CAMILO VIVES PALLÉS.

Maprinter (Empresa Comercializadora de Materias Primas y Productos Intermedios): Edif. MINCEX, Calle 23, No 55, entre P e Infanta, 8°, Plaza de la Revolución, Vedado, Havana; tel. (7) 838-0645; fax (7) 833-3535; e-mail direccion@maprinter.mincex.cu; internet www.maprinter.cu; f. 1962; controls import and export of raw materials and intermediate products; Dir-Gen. ISABEL CRISTINA BLANCO PÉREZ.

Maquimport (Empresa Comercializadora de Objetivos Industriales, Maquinarias, Equipos y Artículos de Ferretería): Calle 23, No 55, 6°, entre P e Infanta, Vedado, Apdo 6052, Havana; tel. (7) 838-0635; fax (7) 838-0632; e-mail direccion@maquimport.mincex.cu; imports industrial goods and equipment; Dir ESTHER VERA GONZALEZ.

Medicuba (Empresa Cubana Importadora y Exportadora de Productos Médicos): Máximo Gómez 1, esq. Egido, Habana Vieja, Havana; tel. (7) 862-4061; fax (7) 866-8516; e-mail dirgeneral@medicuba.sld.cu; f. 1962; enterprise for the export and import of medical and pharmaceutical products; Dir-Gen. JORGE LUIS MECÍAS CUBILLA.

Quimimport (Empresa Cubana Importadora y Exportadora de Productos Químicos): Calle 23, No 55, entre Infanta y P, Apdo 6088, Vedado, Havana; tel. (7) 33-3394; fax (7) 33-3190; e-mail global@quimimport.infocex.cu; internet www.quimimport.cu; con-

trols import and export of chemical products; Dir ARMANDO BARRERA MARTÍNEZ.

Tecnoazúcar (Empresa de Servicios Técnicos e Ingeniería para la Agro-industria Azucarera): Calle 12, No 310, entre 3 y 5, Miramar, Playa, Havana; tel. (7) 29-5441; fax (7) 33-1218; e-mail tecno@tecnoazucar.cu; internet www.tecnoazucar.cu; imports machinery and equipment for the sugar industry; provides technical and engineering assistance for the sugar industry; exports equipment and spare parts for sugar machinery; provides engineering and technical assistance services for sugar-cane by-product industry; Dir-Gen. HÉCTOR COMPANIONI ECHEMENDÍA.

Tractoimport (Empresa Central de Abastecimiento y Venta de Maquinaria Agrícola y sus Piezas de Repuesto): Avda Rancho Boyeros y Calle 100, Apdo 7007, Havana; tel. (7) 45-2166; fax (7) 267-0786; e-mail direccion@tractoimport.co.cu; f. 1962; import of tractors and agricultural equipment; also exports pumps and agricultural implements; Dir-Gen. ABDEL GARCÍA GONZÁLEZ.

Transimport (Empresa Central de Abastecimiento y Venta de Equipos de Transporte Pesados y sus Piezas): Calle 102 y Avda 63, Marianao, Apdo 6665, 11500 Havana; tel. (7) 260-0329; fax (7) 267-9050; e-mail direccion@transimport.co.cu; internet www.transimport.co.cu; f. 1968; controls import and export of vehicles and transportation equipment; Dir-Gen. JESÚS JOSÉ DE HOMBRE MARCIAL.

OTHER MAJOR COMPANIES

Acinox (Grupo Industrial de la Sideurgica): Calle 1, No 3405, esq. 34, Miramar, Playa, Havana; tel. (7) 204-6723; fax (7) 204-6564; e-mail webmaster@acinox.co.cu; internet www.acinox.cu; Pres. EDISMAR SAAVEDRA YERO.

Biopower, SA: Ciro Redondo; e-mail oscar.vickerman@havana-energy.com; f. 2012; 51% stake owned by Zerus, SA; 49% stakes owned by Havana Energy, United Kingdom; produces renewable energy with cane refuse and other biomass vegetation.

BrasCuba Cigarrillos, SA: Calle Princesa, No 202, entre Reyes y San José, Luyanó, Havana; tel. (5) 866-9306; fax (5) 696-7522; e-mail afdezm@nfomed.sld.cu; internet www.brascuba.cu; f. 1995; manufactures and markets cigarettes; jt venture between TabaCuba (Grupo Empresarial del Tobaco) and Souza Cruz, SA (Brazil); Marketing Dir VÍCTOR SOUZA.

CariFin (Caribbean Finance Investments Ltd): Calle 22, No 313, entre 3 y 5, Miramar, Playa, Havana; tel. (7) 204-4468; fax (7) 204-5950; e-mail jcarracedo@carifin.cu; f. 1996 in the British Virgin Islands; started lending operations in Cuba in 1997; subsidiary of the Commonwealth Devt Corpn (United Kingdom) and Grupo Nueva Banca, SA (Cuba); financial services such as loans to businesses, international money transfers and leasing of equipment and machinery; Pres. PAUL NABAVI; 23 employees.

Corporación Cuba Ron, SA (CubaRon): Calle 200, No 1708, esq. 17, Rpto Atabey, Playa, Havana; tel. (7) 273-0102; fax (7) 273-6600; e-mail cubaron@cubaron.colombus.cu; internet www.cubaron.com; f. 1993; production, marketing and distribution of rum and other alcoholic beverages; Pres. LUIS PERDOMO.

Cubalub (Empresa Cubana de Lubricantes): Calle Oficios No 154, entre Amargura y Teniente Rey, 3°, Habana Vieja, 10100 Havana; tel. (7) 861-6512; fax (7) 867-9197; e-mail mabel@cubalub.cupet.cu; state-owned; manufactures and markets lubricants; Dir CESAR FAUSTINO LEÓN DÍAZ.

Cubapetróleo (Cupet): Oficios No 154, entre Amargura y Teniente Rey, Habana Vieja, 10100 Havana; tel. (7) 862-0551; fax (7) 862-7577; e-mail escobar@union.cupet.cu; state-owned; extraction and production of petroleum; Pres. FIDEL RIVERO PRIETO.

Grupo Industrial Refrigeración y Calderas: Calle 31, No 19811, entre 198 y 208, La Coronela, La Lisa, Havana; tel. (7) 33-0492; fax (7) 33-8501; e-mail gruporc@colombus.cu; f. 1985; manufacturer of refrigerators and air-conditioning appliances; Man. Dir EMILIO MARILL FREYRE DE ANDRADE; 2,200 employees.

Grupo Industrial Unecamoto: Calle 37, entre 208 y 212, La Coronela, La Lisa, Havana; tel. (7) 21-6665; fax (7) 33-6545; e-mail unecamoto@colombus.cu; produces automobile parts and accessories; Vice-Pres. ANA MARI LÓPEZ GARCÍA.

Havana Energy: Edif. Barcelona, 2°, Of. 204, Miramar Playa, Havana; tel. (7) 204-7710; fax (7) 204-7711; e-mail info@havana-energy.com; internet www.havana-energy.com; f. 2006; subsidiary of Esencia Group, United Kingdom; assists in the expansion of tourism and the renewable energy sector with development projects in both biomass and hydroelectricity; Chair. BRIAN WILSON.

Suchel Camacho, SA: Vía Blanca y Vía Monumental Berroa, Habana del Este, Havana; tel. (7) 795-9848; fax (7) 795-9844; e-mail suchelcamacho@suchelcamacho.cu; internet www.suchelcamacho.cu; f. 1977 as state-run enterprise, present status and name adopted 1995; jt venture between Unión Suchel and Manuel Camacho, SA (Spain); perfumery and cosmetics producers and distributors; Dir GEANNY BELLO CAMPO.

TabaCuba (Grupo Empresarial del Tabaco): Calle 19, esq. M, No 102, Vedado, Havana; tel. (7) 53-5665; fax (7) 53-5732; internet www .tabacuba.com.cu; f. 2000; state-owned; regulates tobacco cultivation and cigar production in Cuba; Pres. JORGE LUIS FERNÁNDEZ MAIQUE.

Unión de Empresas Constructoras Caribe, SA (UNECA, SA): Calle 7, esq. 41, No 701, entre 6 y 10, Miramar, Playa, CP 6020, Havana; tel. (7) 204-4582; fax (7) 209-6067; e-mail presidente@uneca .co.cu; internet www.uneca.com.cu; f. 1978; construction and engineering services; operates in South and Central America and the Caribbean and sub-Saharan Africa; est. turnover of US $12m. (2009); Chair. and CEO RICARDO DE JESÚS MENÉNDEZ CAMPOS.

Zerus, SA: Havana; f. 1997 as Quiminaz; changed name as above in 2005; subsidiary of AZCUBA; development and supervision of business and investment projects in the sugar sector; Dir-Gen. JOSÉ RIVERA ORTIZ.

UTILITIES
Electricity

Unión Nacional Eléctrica (UNE): Havana; public utility; Dir-Gen. RAÚL GARCÍA BARREIRO.

Water

Aguas de la Habana: Calle Fomento, esq. Recreo, Rpto Palatino, Cerro, Havana; tel. (7) 643-4950; fax (7) 642-4961; e-mail jmtura@ ahabana.co.cu; internet www.ahabana.co.cu; water supplier; Dir-Gen. JOSEP OLLER HERNÁNDEZ.

Instituto Nacional de Recursos Hidráulicos (INRH) (National Water Resources Institute): Calle Humbolt, No 106, esq. a P, Plaza de la Revolución, Vedado, Havana; tel. (7) 836-5571; e-mail gisel@hidro .cu; internet www.hidro.cu; regulatory body; Pres. INÉS MARÍA CHAPMAN WAUGH.

TRADE UNIONS

All workers have the right to become members of a national trade union according to their industry and economic branch.

The following industries and labour branches have their own unions: Agriculture, Chemistry and Energetics, Civil Workers of the Revolutionary Armed Forces, Commerce and Gastronomy, Communications, Construction, Culture, Defence, Education and Science, Food, Forestry, Health, Light Industry, Merchant Marine, Mining and Metallurgy, Ports and Fishing, Public Administration, Sugar, Tobacco, and Transport.

Central de Trabajadores de Cuba (CTC) (Confederation of Cuban Workers): Palacio de los Trabajadores, San Carlos y Peñalver, Havana; tel. (7) 78-4901; fax (7) 55-5927; e-mail cubasindical@ctc.cu; internet www.cubasindical.cu; f. 1939; 19 national trade unions affiliated; Gen. Sec. SALVADOR ANTONIO VALDÉS MESA.

Transport

RAILWAYS

The total length of railways in 2009 was 5,076 km.

Ferrocarriles de Cuba: Edif. Estación Central, Egido y Arsenal, Havana; tel. (7) 70-1076; fax (7) 33-1489; f. 1960; operates public services; Dir-Gen. MIGUEL ACUÑA FERNÁNDEZ; divided as follows:

División Camilo Cienfuegos: serves part of Havana province and Matanzas.

División Centro: serves Villa Clara, Cienfuegos and Sancti Spíritus.

División Centro-Este: serves Camagüey, Ciego de Avila and Las Tunas.

División Occidente: serves Pinar del Río, Ciudad de la Habana, Havana province and Matanzas.

División Oriente: serves Santiago de Cuba, Granma, Guantánamo and Holguín.

ROADS

There were an estimated 60,856 km of roads, of which 4,353 km were highways or main roads. Nearly 50% of the total road network is paved. The Central Highway runs from Pinar del Río in the west to Santiago de Cuba, for a length of 1,144 km. In addition to this highway, there are a number of secondary and 'farm-to-market' roads. Some of these secondary roads are paved, but many can be used by motor vehicles only during the dry season.

SHIPPING

Cuba's principal ports are Havana (which handles 60% of all cargo), Santiago de Cuba, Cienfuegos, Nuevitas, Matanzas, Antilla, Guayabal and Mariel. A US $800m. expansion of the Port of Mariel was completed in early 2014, funded by a loan from the Brazilian Government. The upgraded facilities would be able to handle 3m. containers annually. In 2010 a project to expand the port of Cienfuegos, including the construction of a super-freighter terminal, was announced. At December 2013 the flag registered fleet comprised 66 vessels, totalling 94,897 grt.

Regulatory Authority

Administración Portuaria Nacional (APN): Calle Oficios 170, entre Teniente Rey y Amargura, Habana Vieja, Havana; tel. (7) 860-5383; internet www.apn.transnet.cu; f. 2005; Dir LUIS MEDINA SOÑARA.

Principal Companies

Consignataria Marítima Caribeña, SA: Quinta Avda, No. 4001, entre 40 y 42, Miramar, Playa, Havana; tel. (7) 204-1226; fax (7) 204-1227; e-mail info@cmc.com.cu; internet www.cmc.com.cu; f. 1996; Pres. ALEJANDRO GONZÁLEZ NEIRA.

Coral Container Lines, SA: Of. 170, 1°, POB 6755, Habana Vieja, Havana; tel. (7) 33-8261; fax (7) 33-8970; e-mail info@coral.com.cu; internet fis.com/coralcontainer; f. 1994; liner services to Europe, Canada, Brazil and Mexico; 11 containers; Dir LUIS RODRÍGUEZ HERNÁNDEZ.

Empresa Consignataria Mambisa: San José No 65, entre Prado y Zulueta, Habana Vieja, Havana; tel. (7) 862-2061; fax (7) 66-8111; e-mail mercedes@mambisa.transnet.cu; shipping agent, bunker suppliers; Man. Dir MERCEDES PÉREZ NEWHALL.

Empresa de Navegación Caribe (Navecaribe): Calle San Martín, No 65, 4°, entre Agramonte y Pasco de Martí, Habana Vieja, Havana; tel. (7) 861-8611; fax (7) 866-8564; e-mail navcar@transnet .cu; f. 1966; operates Cuban coastal fleet; Dir LUIS IRENE RODRÍGUEZ HERNÁNDEZ.

Expedimar, SA: Avda 1, No 1205, entre Calle 12 y 14, Playa, Havana; tel. (7) 204-2440; fax (7) 204-0080; e-mail expedimar@ expedimar.cu; Dir-Gen. FRANCISCO A. PIEDRA SANSARIG.

Waterfront AUSA: Centro de Negocios AUSA, Of. 513, Desamparados 166, entre Habana y Compostela, Habana Vieja, Havana; tel. (7) 866-4976; fax (7) 863-5814; e-mail ariel@waterfrontshipping.com; internet www.waterfrontshipping.com; jt venture between Waterfront Shipping Ltd and Almacenes Universales, SA.

CIVIL AVIATION

There are a total of 21 civilian airports, with 11 international airports, including Havana, Santiago de Cuba, Camagüey, Varadero and Holguín. In 2003 the King's Gardens International Airport in Cayo Coco was opened. The airport formed part of a new tourist offshore centre. In 2013 Brazil agreed to finance a project to expand and modernize Cuba's airports.

Instituto de Aeronáutica Civil de Cuba (IACC): Calle 23, No 64, Plaza de la Revolución, Vedado, Havana; tel. (7) 834-4949; fax (7) 834-4553; e-mail webmaster@iacc.gov.cu; internet www.iacc.gov.cu; f. 1985; responsible for directing, implementing and monitoring air transport and other related services; Pres. RAMÓN MARTÍNEZ ECHEVARRÍA.

Aero Caribbean: Calle 23, No 64, esq. P, Vedado, Havana; tel. (7) 832-7584; fax (7) 336-5016; e-mail reserva@cacsa.avianet.cu; f. 1982; international and domestic scheduled and charter services; state-owned; Chair. JULIÁN ALVAREZ INFIESTA.

Aerogaviota: Aeropuerto de Playa Baracoa, Carretera Panamericana, Km 15 ½, Caimito, Artemisa; tel. (7) 203-0668; fax (7) 204-2621; e-mail vpcom@aerogaviota.avianet.cu; internet www .aerogaviota.com; f. 1994; Exec. Pres. VÍCTOR MANUEL AGUILAR OSORIA.

Empresa Consolidada Cubana de Aviación (Cubana): Aeropuerto Internacional José Martí, Terminal 1, Avda Rancho Boyeros, Havana; tel. (7) 266-4644; fax (7) 33-4056; e-mail comunicacion@ cubana.avianet.cu; internet www.cubana.cu; f. 1929; international services to North America, Central America, the Caribbean, South America and Europe; internal services from Havana to 14 other cities; Pres. RICARDO SANTILLÁN MIRANDA.

Tourism

Tourism began to develop after 1977, with the easing of travel restrictions by the USA, and Cuba subsequently attracted European tourists. In 2011 the number of hotel rooms had reached 65,878. In 2013 receipts from tourism totalled an estimated 2,627m. pesos. Tourist arrivals stood at an estimated 2,852,572 in 2013, compared with 2,838,607 in 2012.

Cubanacán: Calle 23, No 156, entre O y P, Vedado, 10400 Havana; tel. (7) 833-4090; fax (7) 22-8382; e-mail com_electronic@cubanacan .cyt.cu; internet www.cubanacan.cu; f. 1987; Pres. JUAN JOSÉ VEGA.

Empresa de Turismo Internacional (Cubatur): Calle 15, No 410, entre F y G, Plaza, Vedado, Havana; tel. (7) 836-2076; fax (7) 836-3170; e-mail casamatriz@cubatur.cu; internet www.cubatur.cu; f. 1963 as Empresa de Turismo Nacional e Internacional; changed name as above in 1969; Dir BÁRBARA CRUZ.

Minister of the Revolutionary Armed Forces: Lt-Gen. LEOPOLDO CINTRA FRÍAS.

Head of the Joint Chiefs of Staff: Lt-Gen. ALVARO LÓPEZ MIERA.

Defence

As assessed at November 2013, according to Western estimates, Cuba's Revolutionary Armed Forces numbered 49,000 (including ready reserves serving 45 days a year, to complete active and reserve units): Army 38,000, Navy 3,000 and Air Force 8,000. There were an additional 39,000 army reserves. Cuba's paramilitary forces included 20,000 State Security troops, 6,500 border guards, a civil defence force of 50,000 and a Youth Labour Army of some 70,000. There was also a Territorial Militia, comprising an estimated 1m. men and women. Conscription for military service is for a two-year period from 17 years of age, and conscripts also work on the land. Despite Cuban hostility, the USA maintains a base at Guantánamo Bay, which comprised 950 armed forces personnel.

Defence Expenditure: The proposed state budget for 2013 allocated 7,159.9m. pesos to administration, defence and public order.

Education

Education is universal and free at all levels. Education is based on Marxist-Leninist principles and combines study with manual work. Day nurseries are available for all children after their 45th day, and national schools at the pre-primary level are operated for children of five years of age. Primary education, from six to 11 years of age, is compulsory, and secondary education lasts from 12 to 17 years of age, comprising two cycles of three years each. In 2012 enrolment at primary and secondary schools included 96% and 87% of the school-age population, respectively. There were 261,468 students in higher education in 2012/13. Workers attending university courses receive a state subsidy to provide for their dependants. Courses at intermediate and higher levels lay an emphasis on technology, agriculture and teacher training. In 2013 proposed budgetary expenditure on education was 9,115.6m. pesos (18.1% of total spending).

Bibliography

For works on the Caribbean generally, see Select Bibliography (Books)

Abrahams, H. and Lopez-Levy, A. *Raul Castro and the New Cuba: A Close-Up View of Change.* Jefferson, NC, Mcfarland, 2011.

Ayorinde, C. *Afro-Cuban Religiosity, Revolution, and National Identity.* Gainesville, FL, University Press of Florida, 2004.

Azicri, M., and Deal, E. (Eds) *Cuban Socialism in a New Century: Adversity, Survival and Renewal.* Gainesville, FL, University Press of Florida, 2005.

Baez, A. C. *State Resistance to Globalisation in Cuba.* London, Pluto Press, 2004.

Basdeo, S., and Nicol, H. N. (Eds). *Canada, the United States, and Cuba: An Evolving Relationship.* Boulder, CO, Lynne Rienner Publrs, 2002.

Benjamin-Alvarado, J. (Ed.). *Cuba's Energy Future: Strategic Approaches to Cooperation.* Washington, DC, Brookings Institution Press, 2010.

Blight, J. A., and Welch, D. A. (Eds) *Intelligence and the Cuban Missile Crisis.* London, Frank Cass, 1998.

Calvo, H., and Declercq, K. *The Cuban Exile Movement: Dissidents or Mercenaries?* Melbourne, Ocean Press, 2000.

Campbell, A. (Ed.) *Cuban Economists on the Cuban Economy.* Gainesville, FL, University Press of Florida, 2013.

Chaffee, W. A., and Prevost, G. (Eds). *Cuba: A Different America.* Lanham, MD, Rowman & Littlefield Publrs, 2002.

Chomsky, A., Carr, B., and Smorkaloff, P. M. (Eds). *The Cuba Reader.* Durham, NC, Duke University Press, 2004.

Chrisp, P. *The Cuban Missile Crisis.* London, Hodder Wayland, 2001.

Cirules, E. *The Mafia in Havana: A Caribbean Mob Story.* Melbourne, Ocean Press, 2004.

Coltman, L. *The Real Fidel Castro.* New Haven, CT, Yale University Press, 2003.

Curry-Machado, J. *Cuban Sugar Industry: Transnational Networks and Engineering Migrants in Mid-Nineteenth Century Cuba.* New York, NY, Palgrave Macmillan, 2011.

Eckstein, S. E. *Back from the Future: Cuba Under Castro.* London, Routledge, 2003.

The Immigrant Divide: How Cuban Americans Changed the US and Their Homeland. Abingdon, Routledge, 2009.

Erisman, H. M., and Kirk, J. M. *Redefining Cuban Foreign Policy: The Impact of the 'Special Period'.* Gainesville, FL, University Press of Florida, 2006.

Escalante, F. *The Cuba Project: CIA Covert Operations against Cuba 1959–62.* St Paul, MN, Consortium, 2004.

Facio, E. (Ed.). *Cuba: Economic Challenges and the Globalization of Capitalism.* Lanham, MD, Rowman & Littlefield Publrs, 2007.

Falcoff, M. *Cuba the Morning After: Normalization and its Discontents.* Washington, DC, AEI Press, 2003.

Farber, S. *The Origins of the Cuban Revolution Reconsidered.* Chapel Hill, NC, University of North Carolina Press, 2006.

Feinberg, R. *The New Cuban Economy: What Roles for Foreign Direct Investment in the New Cuban Economy?* Washington, DC, The Brookings Institution, 2012.

Fernández, D. J. *Cuba Transitional.* Gainesville, FL, University Press of Florida, 2005.

Fernández, S. J. *Encumbered Cuba.* Gainesville, FL, University Press of Florida, 2002.

Ferrer, A. *Insurgent Cuba: Race, Nation, and Revolution, 1868–1898.* Chapel Hill, NC, University of North Carolina Press, 1999.

Fuente, A. de la. *A Nation for All: Race, Inequality, and Politics in Twentieth-Century Cuba (Envisioning Cuba).* Chapel Hill, NC, University of North Carolina Press, 2001.

García Luis, J. (Ed.). *Cuban Revolution Reader: A Documentary History of 40 Years of Revolution.* Melbourne, Ocean Press, 2000.

George, E. *The Cuban Intervention in Angola, 1965–1991: From Che Guevara to Cuito Cuanavale.* London, Routledge, 2005.

Gibbs, J. *US Policy Towards Cuba: Since the Cold War.* London, Routledge, 2010.

González, E., and McCarthy, K. *Cuba after Castro: Legacies, Challenges and Impediments.* Santa Monica, CA, RAND Corpn, 2004.

González, M. *Che Guevara and the Cuban Revolution.* London, Bookmarks Publications, 2004.

Afro-Cuban Theology: Religion, Race, Culture, and Identity. Gainesville, FL, University Press of Florida, 2006.

Gott, R. *Cuba: A New History.* New Haven, CT, Yale University Press, 2004.

Gray, A. I., and Kapcia, A. (Eds). *The Changing Dynamic of Cuban Civil Society.* Gainesville, FL, University Press of Florida, 2008.

Hirschfield, K. *Health, Politics and Revolution in Cuba since 1898.* Piscataway, NJ, Transaction Publrs, 2009.

Horowitz, I. L. (Ed.). *Cuban Communism, 1959–1995,* 10th edn. New Brunswick, NJ, Transaction Publrs, 2001.

Klepak, H. *Cuba's Military 1990–2005: Revolutionary Soldiers During Counter–Revolutionary Times.* London, Institute for the Study of the Americas, 2005.

Lambie, G. *The Cuban Revolution in the 21st Century.* London, Pluto Press, 2010.

Leonard, T. M. *Encyclopedia of Cuban-United States Relations.* Jefferson, NC, McFarland & Co, 2003.

Levine, R. *Secret Missions to Cuba.* Basingstoke, Palgrave Macmillan, 2002.

MacDonald, T. H. *The Education Revolution: Cuba's Alternative to Neoliberalism.* London, Manifesto Press, 2009.

McCoy, T. *Cuba on the Verge: An Island in Transition.* New York, Little, Brown USA, 2003.

Meso-Lago, C., and Pérez-López, J. *Cuba's Aborted Reform: Socioeconomic Effects, International Comparisons, and Transition Policies.* Gainesville, FL, University Press of Florida, 2005.

Morales Domínguez, E., and Prevost, G. *United States–Cuban Relations: A Critical History*. Lanham, MD, Lexington Books, 2008.

Morley, M., and McGillion, C. *Cuba, the United States, and the Post-Cold War World: The International Dimensions of the Washington–Havana Relationship*. Gainesville, FL, University Press of Florida, 2005.

Moses, C. *Real Life in Castro's Cuba (Latin American Silhouettes)*. Wilmington, DE, Scholarly Resources, 1999.

Oficina Nacional de Estadisticas. *Anuario Estadístico de Cuba 2010*, Edición 2011. Havana. www.one.cu/sitioone2006.asp.

Panorama Ambiental 2011. Edición 2012.

Paris, M. L. *Embracing America*. Gainesville, FL, University Press of Florida, 2002.

Pedraza, S. *Political Disaffection in Cuba's Revolution and Exodus (Cambridge Studies in Contentious Politics)*. Cambridge, Cambridge University Press, 2007.

Perales, J. R. *The Cuban Economy: Recent Trends*. Washington, DC, Woodrow Wilson International Center for Scholars, 2011.

Pérez, Jr, L. A. *Cuba: Between Reform and Revolution*, 4th edn. Oxford, Oxford University Press, 2010.

On Becoming Cuban: Identity, Nationality, and Culture. Chapel Hill, NC, University of North Carolina Press, 1999.

Winds of Change: Hurricanes and the Transformation of Nineteenth-Century Cuba. Chapel Hill, NC, University of North Carolina Press, 2001.

Pérez-López, J. F., and Alvarez, J. *Reinventing the Cuban Sugar Agroindustry*. Lanham, MD, Rowman and Littlefield Pblrs, 2005.

Pérez-Stable, M. *The United States and Cuba: Intimate Enemies*. Abingdon, Routledge, 2010.

Piñeiro, M. *Che Guevara and the Latin American Revolution*. Melbourne, Ocean Press, 2006.

Purcell, S. K., and Rothkopf, D. (Eds). *Cuba: The Contours of Change*. Boulder, CO, Lynne Rienner Publrs, 2000.

Ritter, A. R. M. (Ed.). *The Cuban Economy (Pitt Latin American Series)*. Pittsburgh, PA, University of Pittsburgh Press, 2004.

Robins, N. A. *The Culture of Conflict in Modern Cuba*. Jefferson, NC, McFarland and Co, 2002.

Robinson, E. *Last Dance in Havana: The Final Days of Fidel and the Start of the New Cuban Revolution*. New York, Free Press, 2004.

Roman, P. *People's Power: Cuba's Experience with Representative Government*. Lanham, MD, Rowman & Littlefield Publrs, 2003.

Roy, J. *The Cuban Revolution (1959–2009): Relations with Spain, the European Union and the United States*. Basingstoke, Palgrave Macmillan, 2009.

Sánchez, G. *Cuba y Venezuela: Reflecciones y Debates*. Melbourne, Ocean Press, 2006.

Sawyer, M. Q. *Racial Politics in Post-Revolutionary Cuba*. London, Cambridge University Press, 2011.

Shaffer, K. R. *Anarchism and Countercultural Politics in Early Twentieth-Century Cuba*. Gainesville, FL, University Press of Florida, 2005.

Sweig, J. E. *Inside the Cuban Revolution: Fidel Castro and the Urban Underground*. Cambridge, MA, Harvard University Press, 2004.

Cuba: What Everyone Needs to Know. New York, Oxford University Press, 2013.

Thomas, H. *Cuba or the Pursuit of Freedom*, revised edn. New York, First Da Capo Press, 1998.

Villafaña, F. R. *Expansionism: Its Effects on Cuba's Independence*. Piscataway, NJ, Transaction Publishers, 2011.

White, M. J. *Missiles in Cuba: Kennedy, Khrushchev, Castro, and the 1962 Crisis*. Chicago, IL, Ivan R. Dee, 1997.

Zebich-Knos, M., and Nicol, H. *Foreign Policy Toward Cuba: Isolation or Engagement?* Lanham, MD, Rowman and Littlefield Publrs, 2005.

CURAÇAO

Geography

PHYSICAL FEATURES

Curaçao, in the southern Caribbean sea, is part of the quadripartite Kingdom of the Netherlands. Between 1954 and 2010 the dependency formed part of the Netherlands Antilles, along with Bonaire, Sint (St) Maarten, Sint Eustatius (Statia—from the original Spanish name, St Anastasia) and Saba. Following the dissolution of the Netherlands Antilles in October 2010, Curaçao adopted the status of autonomous country within the Kingdom of the Netherlands. One of Curaçao's two Caribbean colleagues in the Kingdom, Aruba (the other is St Maarten), is 68 km (42 miles) to the west of Curaçao. These two islands, which, together with Bonaire are known as the ABC islands, lie off the coast of Venezuela, and are the westernmost extension of the southern Lesser Antilles. The Venezuelan mainland is about 55 km south of Curaçao. Curaçao and Bonaire, about 35 km apart, together with Aruba, are known as the Benedenwindse Eilands (Leeward Islands). Curaçao covers an area of 444 sq km (171 sq miles).

Curaçao is about 61 km long, undulating in width (at most, 14 km) south-eastwards from the north-western tip (North Point) to East Point. Volcanic in origin, reef development has added to the island, which remains surrounded by coral barriers. The northern coasts face the weather, while a complex littoral of drowned valleys and inlets, still home to some mangrove wetlands, is more characteristic of the leeward shore. The largest enclosed bay is the Schottegat, on the south coast, which is where the port of Willemstad, the capital, has its Annabaai harbour, inland from the original site of the city. The interior (cunucu) is hilly (the highest point being St Christoffelberg, at 345 m or 1,132 ft, in the north-west), but dry, with vegetation being scrubby and drought resistant. The natural environment is similar to that in Aruba and Bonaire, but has eroded more from human development, although it is distinguished by fauna such as the blue iguana and the small Curaçao deer (a white-tail deer believed to have been imported by the original Amerindian Arawaks in the 14th century).

CLIMATE

The climate of Curaçao is tropical. The island is south of the main hurricane belt and receives little rain, while the fairly constant Atlantic breezes contribute to a high evaporation rate, ensuring that the climate is defined as semi-arid. Average annual rainfall is 570 mm (22 ins), although this varies con-

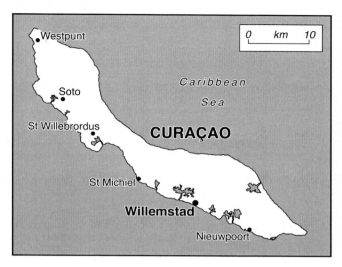

siderably from year to year, and there is more in November–December than in other months. The mean annual air temperature is 27.5°C (81.5°F), with a nocturnal minimum of about 26°C and a daytime maximum of 30°C. January is the coolest month.

POPULATION

Most of the population are of a mixed black descent (85%), including some claiming descent from the original Amerindians, while the rest are other mestizos, whites and Asians. Roman Catholicism is the predominant religion: some 73% of the population were adherents, according to the 2011 census. Curaçao (and Bonaire) is where the cosmopolitan islanders developed the native Papiamento dialect, an eclectic mix of Portuguese, Spanish, Dutch and English evolved from a slave pidgin. Papiamento and Dutch are the official languages of the dependency, although Spanish is also widely spoken.

The total population was 154,843 in January 2014. The capital is Willemstad, where most of the population lives (114,831 at mid-2011).

History

CHARLES ARTHUR

Revised for this edition by the editorial staff

The island, originally inhabited by Arawak Amerindians, was claimed by Spanish explorers in 1499. For over a century Curaçao was used by the Spanish mainly as a source of labour—Arawak people were rounded up and transported to work as slaves in Hispaniola—but also as a location for rearing livestock. The Dutch took control of Curaçao in 1634 and it soon became the hub of the Dutch Caribbean empire. It was a strategically important point for Dutch military and naval campaigns against the Spanish, and from 1648 it became the centre of the Dutch slave trade. By the end of the 17th century the majority of slaves transported from Africa to the Caribbean passed through Curaçao. The Dutch West-Indische Compagnie (WIC—West Indian Company) founded the capital, Willemstad, and the natural harbour at this location permitted a

flourishing trade in slaves, as well as a range of goods. Under the administration of the Dutch WIC Curaçao became immensely wealthy, and during the 18th century it attracted a range of immigrants from Europe, who set up small plantations despite the difficult terrain and climate. The majority came from the Protestant south-west of the Netherlands, but significant numbers of Jews escaping persecution in Spain and Portugal also migrated to Curaçao.

During the 18th and early 19th centuries control of the island changed hands several times as the British, the French, and the Dutch all tried to establish themselves. In 1815 the Dutch regained control from the British, who had held the island since 1807. Willemstad became the capital of the newly created colony of Curaçao and Dependencies, which, in time, came to include all six Caribbean islands colonized by the Dutch. The demise of the transatlantic slave trade during the first decades of the 19th century initiated a slow deterioration of the economy, and when slavery in the Dutch territories was finally abolished in 1863 the plantation system entered a further decline. Following the commercialization of sugar beet in Europe, the sugar cane sector went into decline in the colony, as it did across the Caribbean. The island's fortunes did not start to improve until the discovery of petroleum in the neighbouring South American country of Venezuela in 1914. The following year the Royal Dutch Shell Company established an oil refinery in Curaçao as a way of avoiding the consequences of expected political instability in Venezuela. The refinery, and the various businesses that sprang up to serve it, provided economic opportunities and jobs. There was further economic progress for Curaçao during the Second World War when an influx of US troops—sent to protect oil installations—created the basis for a tourism industry. Even more importantly, Dutch businesses, anticipating the German invasion of the Netherlands, transferred their assets to Curaçao, and gave the impetus to what became a thriving offshore finance industry.

In the aftermath of the Second World War, demands for independence from the Netherlands began to be heard, but greater autonomy was not granted until 1954 when the Dutch Government agreed to allow self-government except in relation to foreign affairs, defence, security and migration. The status of all six Dutch Caribbean islands was promoted from that of a colonial territory to part of the Kingdom of the Netherlands, as an associated state within a federation. Willemstad in Curaçao became the seat of government of the Netherlands Antilles. Aruba left the federation in 1986 and the status of the other islands in relation to the Netherlands has been the main political issue over recent decades. Referendums in the 1990s produced conclusive votes in favour of maintaining the federation. However, subsequent ballots produced markedly different results, and in 2004 a commission established by the Dutch and Antillean Governments recommended the dissolution of the federation on the grounds that public support for it had more or less evaporated. An interisland constitutional conference held in April 2005 recommended the abolition of the federation by July 2007, but negotiations concerning the details of the transition were marred by controversy, with opposition leaders, in particular in Curaçao, accusing the Dutch authorities of acting in bad faith. A new accord was signed in December 2008, stipulating that Curaçao and Sint (St) Maarten would become self-governing (except in matters of defence, foreign policy, judicial and financial matters), and the other three small 'BES' islands—Bonaire, St Eustatius and Saba—would gain a new status equivalent to that of Dutch municipalities.

The impetus for the dissolution of the federation was boosted by the results of a referendum in Curaçao in May 2009 when 52% of voters cast their ballot in support of autonomy for the island. However, while the process of preparing the BES islands for their new status progressed well, preparations for Curaçao and St Maarten proved much more difficult and another deadline for the dissolution of the federation was postponed.

Finally, on 10 October 2010 the Federation of the Netherlands Antilles was officially dissolved. Curaçao became an independent nation within the Kingdom of the Netherlands, making it a constitutionally equal partner with Aruba, St Maarten, and the Netherlands itself. The new country's first Government, installed in September, was a coalition between the Movementu Futuro Korsou (MFK—Movement for the Future of Curaçao), the Pueblo Soberano (PS—Sovereign People's Party) and the Movementu Antia Nobo (MAN—Movement for a New Antilles). In elections, held in the previous month, the Partido Antía Restrukturá (PAR—which was renamed the Partido Alternativo Real, Real Alternative Party,

in late 2010) had emerged as the largest party, gaining eight of the 21 seats in the new Curaçao parliament. However, with the PAR short of the majority needed to form a government without a coalition, the MFK with five seats, the PS with four and the MAN with two seized the opportunity to form a coalition. The MFK leader, Gerrit Schotte, became the country's first Prime Minister, and his Government focused on the restructuring of the energy sector and the development of stronger ties with regional allies and with the Netherlands.

The new country of Curaçao faced serious challenges. Economically, there was uncertainty over whether refinery activities would continue and whether the international financial services sector would remain one of the island's economic pillars. Curaçao faced integrity issues; names of high-ranking officials and ministers were mentioned in connection with money-laundering, abuse of power and favouritism. Intra-Kingdom relations deteriorated owing to these corruption allegations and to disagreements over the fiscal deficit. According to the 1954 Constitution, the Kingdom Government, in which the Netherlands had the majority vote, had to guarantee good governance on Curaçao. The Dutch Government made attempts to steer the island administration towards further transparency, but the Government in Curaçao viewed this as interference.

In early August 2012, following the withdrawal from the coalition of the PS and the MAN, Schotte tendered his resignation as Prime Minister, and that of the Council of Ministers. An interim Government, headed by Stanley Betrian, was inaugurated on 29 September, with a general election scheduled to take place on 19 October. The Netherlands recognized the interim authorities, although Schotte argued that he was entitled to remain in power until a new government was elected, claiming that his replacement by Betrian constituted a 'coup'. The PS attracted the most votes in the general election and gained control of five seats in the legislature. The MFK also won five seats, while the PAR and the Partido pa Adelanto i Inovashon Soshal (PAIS) each secured four seats, the MAN two, and the Partido Nashonal di Pueblo (PNP—People's National Party) one. Voter turnout was recorded at 74.5%. Following lengthy discussions, in mid-December the PS, the PAIS, the PNP and an independent deputy (formerly of the PAR) agreed that, after a transitional period of between three and six months, they would form a coalition government. Daniel Hodge of the PS was sworn in as transitional Prime Minister on 31 December, and his administration assumed office on 2 January 2013. Meanwhile, Goedgedrag resigned as Governor in November 2012; he was succeeded in an acting capacity by Adele van der Pluijm-Vrede.

Hodge and the transitional Council of Ministers resigned on 27 March 2013 but remained in office as a 'demissionary' administration while negotiations on the establishment of the coalition government continued. On 5 May, in an unprecedented act of political violence, PS leader Helmin Wiels was assassinated by two gunmen. (Several suspects were subsequently arrested, and legal and investigative proceedings were ongoing in mid-2014.) The coalition administration was finally inaugurated on 7 June 2013, with Ivar Asjes of the PS serving as Prime Minister. Lucille George-Wout took office as the territory's new Governor in November.

Former Prime Minister Schotte's home and offices were raided by the police in December 2013. It was subsequently reported that Schotte was under investigation for money-laundering and forgery, and in May 2014 the former premier was detained and questioned by the police in connection with these alleged crimes. Schotte claimed that the investigation, which was ongoing in mid-2014, was politically motivated.

Elections to the European Parliament took place in Curaçao on 22 May 2014. The Christen Democratisch Appèl (Christian Democrat Appeal) won the majority of the local ballot, although the rate of participation by the electorate was very low.

Economy

ROLAND VAN DEN BERGH

Based on an earlier article by CHARLES ARTHUR and subsequently revised by the editorial staff

During the late 17th and 18th centuries Curaçao's economy flourished as the hub of the Dutch slave trade in the Caribbean. The Dutch West-Indische Compagnie (WIC—West Indian Company) developed a lucrative commercial network based on the natural harbour in the capital, Willemstad. Some plantations were established on the island but, other than the slave trade and commerce, the only other notable economic activity during this era was the mining of salt. The demise of the slave trade during the early part of the 19th century and the final abolition of slavery by the Dutch in 1863 caused an economic downturn, and many inhabitants emigrated to other islands.

The discovery of petroleum in Venezuela in 1914 transformed the economic situation in Curaçao. In 1915 Royal Dutch Shell began the construction of an extensive oil refinery installation near Willemstad, and in 1918 the refining of Venezuelan oil began. From this time Curaçao's economy was transformed, as new employment opportunities brought immigrants and wealth to the island. By 1954, when Curaçao, as part of the Netherlands Antilles federation, gained autonomy within the Kingdom of the Netherlands, the oil refinery was at its peak, with approximately 12,600 employees. In the 1970s the oil-refining sector diversified into transshipment and oil storage. The transshipment sector revolved around the construction of terminals to handle the huge oil tankers that, because of their size, could not deliver directly to the USA. In the 1980s the terminal at Bullebaai in Curaçao, then one of the world's largest, made as much revenue as the refinery. However, in the mid-1980s the construction of large offshore terminals in the Gulf of Mexico and on the eastern US seaboard, the drop in oil prices, and the lowering of Venezuelan oil output made the oil-processing industry much less profitable. In 1985 the Government took ownership of the refinery, and it was eventually leased to the Venezuelan state oil producer, Petróleos de Venezuela, SA (PDVSA), which adapted it to process Venezuelan heavy crude petroleum. In the late 20th century the economy began to diversify and Curaçao reduced its dependence on the oil refinery.

In 2014 Curaçao had a diversified economy, based on four foreign-exchange earning pillars: oil, tourism, logistics and international financial services. By the end of the 20th century Curaçao had one of the highest standards of living in the Caribbean and a well-developed infrastructure. In 2011 per caput gross domestic product (GDP) was US $20,094. Inflation in 2003–13 was moderate, at an annual average of 2.9%. The island had a population of 154,843 at 1 January 2014.

The refinery, known as Refinería Isla, has succeeded in increasing efficiency in recent years through extensive reductions in the number of workers on the payroll, amounting to nearly 1,000 employees. Contractors also provide a further 400–600 labourers with employment. The refinery and oil terminal are leased by PDVSA until 2019. There is an urgent need for upgrading the refinery in order to keep it viable (in 2010 the refinery was forced to shut down for almost nine months, owing to a technical failure). In the near future it will become clear whether the refinery will continue its operations on the island, or will close and be dismantled. The oil terminal at Bullebaai is expected to continue operations.

Although Curaçao has little to offer in the way of marketable natural resources, tourists are attracted by the warm climate, the many beaches and extensive shopping opportunities. In recent years the tourism sector has benefited from major investment projects, including several large hotel complexes such as Hyatt and Renaissance, a 'mega-pier' at the entrance to the Willemstad harbour, and a new terminal at the Hato International Airport. Tourism gradually increased in the 2000s, from 191,000 visitors in 2000 to 409,000 in 2008. Stay-over tourist numbers decreased to 342,000 in 2010, owing to the world economic crisis, before recovering strongly to

420,000 in 2012 and 440,000 in 2013. Curaçao's main tourism markets, Europe (and in particular the Netherlands), North America and Latin America, all performed reasonably well during 2011–13. Although timeshare residences hardly exist on the island, second-home ownership for non-residents, mostly of Dutch nationality, increased dramatically during 2005–09. However, the economic crisis resulted in the suspension of further development of this sector. The number of cruise passengers visiting the island doubled between 2000 and 2013, from just over 300,000 to approximately 600,000.

The Second World War provided the stimulus for another new economic development as Dutch businesses, anticipating the German invasion of the Netherlands, transferred their assets to Curaçao. This move provided the impetus for what was to become a thriving international financial services industry. This sector took off in the early 1990s—driven partly by the deregulation of the financial services industry—and many foreign offshore banks set up in Curaçao to offer specialized international financial services for non-residents and foreign companies. As result of the worldwide focus on money-laundering, in particular in relation to the financing of terrorism, Curaçao opted to comply with international regulations in that area. In addition, it signed a number of bilateral tax information agreements, of which the one with the Netherlands was by far the most important. In response to the improved accountability and transparency of the financial services, in 2008 the Organisation for Economic Co-operation and Development (OECD) placed the Netherlands Antilles on its 'white list', a status that was retained after the constitutional changes in 2010. During the last decade Curaçao's international financial services sector registered a decline in activity, related mainly to the impact of the international financial crisis and increased competition. In an effort to halt the downward trend, a stock exchange was established and new financial incentives were developed.

The port of Willemstad is one of the largest harbours in the Caribbean, and it houses most of the shipping facilities available on the island. Cruise ships dock at various cruise terminals on the side of the bay, at the end of which lie the port's main facilities, including the oil refinery, a dry dock, an economic free zone area, a modern container terminal, cargo wharves and marine facilities for small yachts. It also houses the coast guard and the Dutch navy. Furthermore, the island has another deep-water port, located at Bullebaai, which in particular serves oil tankers. Most of the harbour-related activities have remained at a similar level during the last five years. Prospects for the state-owned ship-repair yard, Curaçao Dry-dock Company (CDM), are positive. However, to remain viable it requires significant investment to upgrade its facilities and an international partner to improve its operations and marketing.

Twelve economic (or free) zones have been established on Curaçao. The business focus within the zones has moved from servicing shoppers to import/export trade. A new free zone with an international data centre has been recently established.

The construction sector on Curaçao boomed during 2005–08, when many real estate projects were developed, and new hotels and houses constructed. Since 2008 the number of new project tenders has been limited, resulting in substantially less construction activity.

The market for retail outlets is saturated. Many shop owners face a difficult period as tourists (stay-over and cruise) have less to spend, and the purchasing power of local residents is also under pressure. However, the business-to-business (B2B) sector is still performing well, as a result of government reorganizations, adaptation to new legislation, and the execution of development co-operation projects financed by the Netherlands and the European Commission. Future developments within the international financial services sector will have a significant impact on turnover within the B2B sector.

In 2010 electricity production decreased by 1.2%, and that of water by 3.2%, as companies and domestic households began to save by reducing consumption of water and electricity. Nevertheless, water production rose by 3.3% in 2011 and 1.6% in 2012, while power output increased by 4.1% and 0.6% during those years. In 2013, however, production of water and electricity declined by 0.8% and 1.7%, respectively.

Private consumption decreased somewhat in 2009, but rose again in 2010–12, according to the IMF. This also explains, to some extent, the large current account deficit at this time. The growth in private investment has stabilized in Curaçao, whereas other Caribbean islands recorded substantial decreases. The share of net foreign direct investment as a percentage of GDP declined from 5.2% in 2008 to approximately 2% during 2009–11, before rising to an estimated 3.5% in 2012.

Figures from Curaçao's Central Bureau of Statistics indicated an increase in merchandise trade (excluding oil products) to NA Fl. 2,669m. in 2008 and a small decrease to around NA Fl. 2,500m. in 2009–10. Exports in 2010 amounted to NA Fl. 258m. This is also reflected by, and in line with, the balance of payments account. In 2011 imports totalled NA Fl. 2,299m. and exports NA Fl. 287m.

A debt relief programme funded by the Netherlands enabled the islands finally to break out of a chronic debt-accumulation cycle and obtain manageable public finances. As a result, the ratio of debt to GDP was reduced from 63.0% in 2007 to 34.6% in 2010. The newly autonomous Curaçao began with debt of NA Fl. 1,830m. This debt was financed by the Dutch Ministry of Finance against low interest rates. A common fiscal supervision agency was established, the Council for Financial Supervision (College Financieel Toezicht—CFT). The new fiscal framework prohibited current budget deficits, capped interest payments to 5% of fiscal revenues, and required medium-term budgeting. Borrowing by Curaçao is only allowed for capital expenditures. Initially, the 2011 budget was balanced; in practice, however, there was a deficit of NA Fl. 154m., equivalent to 2.8% of GDP. The budget deficit narrowed to NA Fl. 36m.

(0.6% of GDP) in 2012. Government debt totalled NA Fl. 1,858m. (33.2% of GDP) in that year.

Since 10 October 2010 Curaçao and St Maarten have formed a monetary union; both have the Netherlands Antilles guilder or florin as their legal tender, which is pegged to the US dollar at a rate of NA Fl. 1.79. Curaçao has a huge current account deficit, equivalent to 28.1% of GDP in 2012. In an effort to counteract this deficit, the island's Central Bank introduced a credit restriction, one of the factors causing monetary irritation between the two islands. Higher exports and lower domestic consumption would also be necessary to reduce the deficit. In the short term, the foreign exchange coverage of imports was sufficient, but in the longer term continuation of this current account deficit would put the value of the currency under pressure.

The international economic recession resulted in real GDP declining by 0.5% in 2009, and growth during 2010–11 was negligible. According to the Central Bank, in 2012 the economy contracted again, albeit by just 0.1%. Austerity measures, including an increase in the retirement age, reductions in health care expenditure, and a rise in sales and property taxes, were adopted in 2013 in an attempt to stabilize the island's public finances. Although these reforms bolstered the fiscal position, they contributed to a further economic contraction (estimated at 0.8%) in that year. The prospects for three of the economic pillars of the island were uncertain: with regard to refinery activities, uncertainty over whether the lease contract with PDVSA would be continued; uncertainty over whether the international financial services sector would be able to recover its former position as one of the world's leading financial centres; and uncertainty over whether the logistics sector (free zones, dry dock, transshipment, etc.) had the ability to increase its activities. However, tourism prospects for the island were positive owing to the gradual recovery in the global economy, and the Central Bank and the IMF both forecast real GDP growth of approximately 0.5% in 2014. Nevertheless, according to the IMF, the economy was facing risks related to the island's large current account deficit, weak business environment and inefficient labour market.

Statistical Survey

Note: The Netherlands Antilles was officially dissolved on 10 October 2010. The figures in this Statistical Survey refer to Curaçao only, unless otherwise indicated

Sources (unless otherwise stated): Centraal Bureau voor de Statistiek, Fort Amsterdam, Willemstad, Curaçao; tel. (9) 461-1031; fax (9) 461-1696; internet www.cbs.cw/; Centrale Bank van Curaçao en Sint Maarten, Simon Bolivar Plein 1, Willemstad, Curaçao; tel. (9) 434-5500; fax (9) 461-5004; e-mail info@centralbank.an; internet www.centralbank.cw.

AREA AND POPULATION

Area: 444 sq km (171.4 sq miles).

Population: 150,563 (males 68,848, females 81,715) at census of 26 March 2011; 154,843 (males 70,823, females 84,020) at 1 January 2014.

Density (at 1 January 2014): 348.7 per sq km.

Population by Age and Sex (official estimates at 1 January 2014): *0–14 years:* 29,447 (males 15,120, females 14,327); *15–64 years:* 102,272 (males 46,069, females 56,203); *65 years and over:* 23,124 (males 9,634, females 13,490); *Total* 154,843 (males 70,823, females 84,020).

Principal Town: Willemstad (capital), population (incl. suburbs, UN estimate) 144,730 at mid-2014. Source: UN, *World Urbanization Prospects: The 2014 Revision.*

Births, Marriages and Deaths (2013): Registered live births 1,959 (birth rate 13.4 per 1,000); Registered marriages 665 (marriage rate 4.3 per 1,000); Registered deaths 1,250 (death rate 8.2 per 1,000).

Life Expectancy (years at birth, 2012): Males 72.4; females 80.1.

Immigration and Emigration (2012): *Immigration:* Aruba 82; China, People's Republic 66; Colombia 166; Dominican Republic 187; Netherlands 3,292; Venezuela 174; Total (incl. others) 4,883. *Emigration:* Aruba 128; Netherlands 3,304; USA 39; Total (incl. others) 4,251.

Economically Active Population (persons aged 15 years and over, 2013): Agriculture, forestry and fishing 139; Mining and quarrying 102; Manufacturing 3,960; Electricity, gas and water 1,236; Construction 4,773; Wholesale and retail trade, repairs 11,994; Hotels and restaurants 6,108; Transport, storage and communications 5,060; Financial intermediation 4,495; Real estate, renting and business activities 6,586; Public administration, defence and social security 4,699; Education 3,520; Health and social work 5,308; Other community, social and personal services 2,814; Private households with employed persons 2,088; Extraterritorial organizations and bodies 116; *Sub-total* 62,998; Activities not adequately defined 495; *Total employed* 63,493 (males 31,350, females 32,143); Unemployed 9,512; *Total labour force* 73,005.

HEALTH AND WELFARE

(Data refer to Netherlands Antilles)

Total Fertility Rate (children per woman, 2013): 2.2.

Under-5 Mortality Rate (per 1,000 live births, 2010): 13.5.

Physicians (per 1,000 head, 1999): 1.4.

Hospital Beds (per 1,000 head, 2012): 3.4.

Health Expenditure (% of GDP, 2008): 14.0.

Total Carbon Dioxide Emissions ('000 metric tons, 2007): 6,232.5.

Total Carbon Dioxide Emissions Per Head (metric tons, 2007): 32.4.

Source: mostly Pan American Health Organization.

For other sources and definitions, see explanatory note on p. vi.

AGRICULTURE, ETC.

Livestock (Netherlands Antilles, '000 head, year ending September 2010, FAO estimates): Cattle 0.7; Pigs 2.7; Goats 13.7; Sheep 9.3; Chickens 165.

Livestock Products (Netherlands Antilles, metric tons, 2010, FAO estimates): Pig meat 203; Chicken meat 380; Cows' milk 460; Hen eggs 630.

Fishing (all capture, metric tons, live weight, 2012): Atlantic bonito 538; Frigate tuna 238; Skipjack tuna 12,779; Yellowfin tuna 6,792; Bigeye tuna 2,890; Total catch (incl. others) 23,800 (FAO estimate).

Source: FAO.

MINING

(Data refer to Netherlands Antilles)
Production ('000 metric tons, estimate): Salt 500 in 2003–08.
Source: US Geological Survey.

INDUSTRY

(Data refer to Netherlands Antilles unless otherwise indicated)
Production ('000 metric tons, 2008, unless otherwise indicated): Jet fuel 731; Kerosene 46 (2004); Residual fuel oils 3,789; Lubricating oils 327 (2007); Petroleum bitumen (asphalt) 1,128 (2007); Liquefied petroleum gas, refined 78; Motor spirit (petrol) 1,856; Aviation gasoline 17; Distillate fuel oils (gas-diesel oil) 2,195; Sulphur (recovered) 23; Electric energy (Curaçao only, million kWh, 2012) 910.3.

FINANCE

Currency and Exchange Rates: 100 cents = 1 Netherlands Antilles gulden (guilder) or florin (NA Fl.). *Sterling, Dollar and Euro Equivalents* (30 May 2014): £1 sterling = NA Fl. 3.011; US $1 = NA Fl. 1.790; €1 = NA Fl. 2.436; NA Fl. 100 = £33.21 = $55.87 = €41.04. *Exchange Rate:* In December 1971 the central bank's mid-point rate was fixed at US $1 = NA Fl. 1.80. In 1989 this was adjusted to $1 = NA Fl. 1.79. In December 2009 it was announced that the US dollar would replace the Netherlands Antilles guilder and florin in Bonaire, St Eustatius and Saba from 1 January 2011, following the dissolution of the previous federation of the Netherlands Antilles in October 2010. In Curaçao and St Maarten, the Netherlands Antilles guilder was expected to be replaced with a newly created Caribbean guilder, but negotiations on the introduction of the new currency appeared to have stalled by early 2014.

Central Government Budget (NA Fl. million, 2012): *Revenue:* Tax revenue 1,445.8 (Taxes on income 712.9, Taxes on property 43.9, Taxes on goods and services 516.4, Taxes on international trade and transactions 166.4, Other taxes 6.2); Non-tax revenue 208.9; Total 1,654.7. *Expenditure:* Current expenditure 1,675.6 (Wages and salaries 737.2, Other goods and services 391.3, Interest payments 50.0, Transfers and subsidies 497.1); Capital expenditure (incl. transfers and net lending) 89.4; Total 1,765.0.

International Reserves (Netherlands Antilles, US $ million at 31 December 2009): Gold (national valuation) 356; Foreign exchange 867; Total 1,223. Source: IMF, *International Financial Statistics*.

Money Supply (Curaçao and Sint Maarten, NA Fl. million at 31 December 2010): Currency outside banks 326; Demand deposits at commercial banks 2,811; Total (incl. others) 3,137 (Source: IMF, *2011 Article IV Consultation—Staff Report; Informational Annex; and Public Information Notice on the Executive Board Discussion* (December 2011)).

Cost of Living (Consumer Price Index; base: October 2006 = 100): All items 117.0 in 2011; 120.7 in 2012; 122.3 in 2013.

Gross Domestic Product (million NA Fl. at current prices): 5,282.9 in 2010; 5,439.3 in 2011; 5,604.7 in 2012.

Gross Domestic Product by Economic Activity (million NA Fl. at current prices, 2012): Agriculture, fishing and mining 29.6; Electricity, gas and water 193.2; Manufacturing 443.5; Construction 280.6; Trade 635.3; Hotels and restaurants 205.5; Transport, storage and communications 479.6; Real estate, renting and business activities 372.8; Education 27.9; Health and social welfare 224.8; Other non-financial service activities 182.1; Financial corporations 995.2; Government 634.5; Households and non-profit institutions 476.0; *Sub-total* 5,180.6; Net of indirect taxes 424.1; *GDP in purchasers' values* 5,604.7.

Balance of Payments (NA Fl. million, 2012): Exports of goods f.o.b. 1,697.0; Imports of goods f.o.b. –4,035.3; *Trade balance* –2,338.3; Services (net) 973.9; *Balance on goods and services* –1,364.4; Income (net) –68.6; *Balance on goods, services and income* –1,433.1; Current transfers (net) –139.6; *Current balance* –1,572.6; Capital account (net) 48.8; Direct investment (net) 81.0; Portfolio investment (net) 658.5; Other investment (net) 616.4; Net errors and omissions –37.3; *Overall balance* –205.3.

EXTERNAL TRADE

(Note: Although the import and export of petroleum and petroleum products, largely for refinery, transshipment and storage purposes, made a significant contribution to the economy of Curaçao, such transactions are not included in official trade statistics.)
Principal Commodities (NA Fl. million, 2011, excl. petroleum): *Imports c.i.f.:* Food and live animals 436; Beverages and tobacco 92; Chemical products 285; Manufactured goods 297; Machinery and transport equipment 756; Miscellaneous articles 376; Total (incl. others) 2,299. *Exports f.o.b.:* Food and live animals 47; Beverages and tobacco 18; Chemical products 32; Manufactured goods 29; Machinery and transport equipment 100; Miscellaneous articles 38; Total (incl. others) 287.

Principal Trading Partners (NA Fl. million, 2011, excl. petroleum): *Imports c.i.f.:* Netherlands 411; Panama 83; Puerto Rico 117; USA 949; Venezuela 91; Total (incl. others) 2,299. *Exports f.o.b.:* Aruba 46; Netherlands 41; USA 46; Total (incl. others) 287.

TRANSPORT

Road Traffic (motor vehicles registered, excl. government-owned vehicles, 2012): Passenger cars 69,035; Lorries 12,908; Buses 369; Taxis 159; Other cars 404; Motorcycles 1,300.

Shipping: *International Seaborne Freight Traffic* (TEUs moved, 2011): 94,097. *Flag Registered Fleet* (at 31 December 2013): Number of vessels 145; Total displacement 1,337,091 grt (Source: Lloyd's List Intelligence—www.lloydslistintelligence.com).

Civil Aviation (2012): Aircraft landings 23,551 (Commercial 17,516); Passenger movements 1,757,000.

TOURISM

Tourist Arrivals: *Stop-overs:* 390,282 (Netherlands 141,536; USA 63,268; Venezuela 61,582) in 2011; 419,810 (Netherlands 138,201; USA 62,262; Venezuela 83,148) in 2012; 440,063 (Netherlands 131,858; USA 61,747; Venezuela 92,123) in 2013. *Cruise ship passengers:* 400,596 in 2011; 436,068 in 2012; 583,994 in 2013.

Tourism Receipts (Netherlands Antilles, NA Fl. million, incl. passenger transport): 1,683.5 in 2002; 1,761.0 in 2003; 1,906.5 in 2004.

COMMUNICATIONS MEDIA

Telephones (December 2012): 71,995 main lines in use.

Mobile Cellular Telephones (December 2012): 204,702 subscribers.

EDUCATION

Students (2013/14 unless otherwise indicated): Primary 17,967; Secondary 11,024; Senior secondary vocational 3,779; University 224 (2013).

Pupil-teacher Ratio (Netherlands Antilles, primary education, UNESCO estimate): 19.8 in 2002/03.

Adult Literacy Rate (Netherlands Antilles, 2011, UNESCO estimates): 96.5% (males 96.6%; females 96.5%).

Source: partly UNESCO Institute for Statistics.

Directory

The Constitution

The Constitution (*Staatsregeling*) of Curaçao was adopted by the Island Council of Curaçao by a majority vote on 5 September 2010. Following the dissolution of the Netherlands Antilles on 10 October, the new Constitution entered into force.

The form of government for Curaçao is embodied in the Charter of the Kingdom of the Netherlands, which came into force on 20 December 1954. The Charter designated the Netherlands Antilles (comprising Curaçao, Sint (St) Maarten, Bonaire, Saba and St Eustatius) as a separate territory forming the Kingdom of the Netherlands with the Netherlands.

As a constituent country of the Kingdom of the Netherlands, Curaçao enjoys full autonomy in domestic and internal affairs. The Government of the Netherlands is responsible for foreign affairs and defence. The monarch of the Netherlands is represented in Curaçao by the Governor, appointed by the Dutch Crown for a term of six years. The central Government of Curaçao appoints a Minister Plenipotentiary to represent the island in the Government of the Kingdom.

Executive power in internal affairs is vested in the nominated Council of Ministers, responsible to the legislature, the Staten (States). The States consists of 21 members elected by universal adult suffrage for four years (subject to dissolution).

The Government

HEAD OF STATE

King of the Netherlands: HM King WILLEM-ALEXANDER.

Governor: LUCILLE A. GEORGE-WOUT (sworn in on 4 November 2013).

COUNCIL OF MINISTERS
(September 2014)

The Government is formed by the Pueblo Soberano, the Partido Adelanto i Inovashon Soshal and the Partido Nashonal di Pueblo.

Prime Minister and Minister of General Affairs: IVAR ASJES.

Minister of Economic Development: STANLEY PALM.

Minister of Finance: Dr JOSÉ MANUEL R. JARDIM.

Minister of Public Health, Environment and Nature: Dr BERNARD DENZIL WHITEMAN.

Minister of Education, Science, Culture and Sports: IRENE DICK.

Minister of Social Development, Labour and Welfare: RUTH-MILDA. D. LARMONIE-CECILIA.

Minister of Justice: NELSON GENARO NAVARRO.

Minister of Traffic, Transport and Urban Planning: EARL WINSTON BALBORDA.

Minister of Government Policy, Planning and Public Services: ETIENNE VAN DER HORST.

Minister Plenipotentiary of Curaçao in the Netherlands: MARVELYNE WIELS.

MINISTRIES

Office of the Governor: Fort Amsterdam 2, Willemstad; tel. (9) 461-2148; fax (9) 461-2045; e-mail adjudant@kgcur.org; internet www.gouverneurvancuracao.org.

Office of the Prime Minister: Fort Amsterdam 17, Willemstad; tel. (9) 463-0495; fax (9) 461-7199.

Ministry of Economic Development: Dienst Economische Zaken, Pietermaai 25B, Willemstad; tel. (9) 462-1444; fax (9) 462-7590; e-mail info.meo@gobiernu.cw.

Ministry of Education, Science, Culture and Sports: Scharloo-weg 102, Willemstad; tel. (9) 461-5133; fax (9) 461-5320; e-mail info.sae@gobiernu.cw.

Ministry of Finance: Pietermaai 17, Willemstad; tel. (9) 432-8000; fax (9) 461-3339; e-mail directie.financien@gobiernu.cw.

Ministry of General Affairs: Fort Amsterdam 17, Willemstad; tel. (9) 463-0495; e-mail info.gobierno@gobiernu.cw.

Ministry of Government Policy, Planning and Public Services: Breedestraat 39C, Punda, Willemstad; tel. (9) 433-3130; e-mail info.gobiernu@gobiernu.cw.

Ministry of Justice: Wilhelminaplein z/n, Willemstad; tel. (9) 463-0628; fax (9) 461-0598; e-mail Ministerie.Justitie@gobiernu.cw.

Ministry of Public Health, Environment and Nature: Dept of Health, Piscaderaweg 49, Willemstad; tel. (9) 432-5800; fax (9) 738-432-5805; e-mail info.ggd@gobiernu.cw; Dept of Environment and Nature, Straat Rosaweg 124, Willemstad; tel. (9) 736-9012; fax (9) 736-9195; e-mail info.mil@gobiernu.cw.

Ministry of Social Development, Labour and Welfare: Pietermaai Parking & Mall, Willemstad; tel. (9) 434-0300; fax (9) 461-0521; e-mail info.dwi@gobiernu.cw.

Ministry of Traffic, Transport and Urban Planning: Plasa Horacio Hoyer 19, Willemstad; tel. (9) 433-3200; fax (9) 433-3200; tel. info.rop@gobiernu.cw.

Office of the Minister Plenipotentiary for Curaçao in the Netherlands: Kabinet van de Gevolmachtigde Minister van de Curaçao, Badhuisweg 173–175, POB 90706, 2509 LS The Hague, Netherlands; tel. (70) 306-6111; fax (70) 306-6110; internet www.vertegenwoordigingcuracao.nl.

Legislature

STATES
(Staten)

President: MARCOLINO (MIKE) FRANCO (PAIS).

Vice-President: JAIME CORDOBA (PS).

Election, 19 October 2012

Party	Votes	% of votes	Seats
Pueblo Soberano (PS) .	19,716	22.65	5
Movementu Futuro Korsou (MFK) . . .	18,441	21.18	5
Partido Alternativo Real (PAR)* . . .	17,149	19.70	4
Partido pa Adelanto I Inovashon Soshal (PAIS) . . .	15,395	17.68	4
Movementu Antia Nobo (MAN) . . .	8,297	9.53	2
Partido Nashonal di Pueblo (PNP) . . .	5,136	5.89	1
Others . . .	2,924	3.36	—
Total†	87,058	100.00	21

* A PAR deputy, Glenn Sulvaran, subsequently declared he would sit in the States as an Independent, reducing the PAR's parliamentary representation to three.

† In addition, there were 370 invalid/blank votes.

Election Commission

Konseho Supremo Elektoral (KSE): Roodeweg 42, Willemstad; tel. (9) 434-1600; fax (9) 461-8166; e-mail info@kse.cw; internet www.kse.cw; Chair. GEOMALY MARTES.

Political Organizations

Democratische Partij—Curaçao (DP—C) (Democratic Party—Curaçao): Neptunusweg 28, Willemstad; f. 1944; Leader GEORGE HERNANDEZ.

Forsa Kòrsou: F. D. Rooseveltweg 347, Willemstad; tel. (9) 888-3041; fax (9) 888-3504; e-mail forsakorsou@onenet.an; Pres. NELSON NAVARRO; Leader GREGORY DAMOEN.

Frente Obrero i Liberashon 30 di mei (FOL) (Workers' Liberation Front of 30 May): Mayaguanaweg 16, Willemstad; tel. (9) 461-8105; f. 1969; socialist; Leader ANTHONY GODETT.

Movementu Antia Nobo (MAN) (Movement for a New Antilles): Landhuis Morgenster, Willemstad; tel. (9) 468-4781; internet www.new.partidoman.org; f. 1971; socialist; Pres. EUGENE CLEOPA; Leader HENSLEY KOEIMAN.

Movementu Futuro Korsou (MFK) (Movement for the Future of Curaçao): Salinja Lindbergweg z/n, Willemstad; tel. (9) 461-7766; e-mail info@mfk.an; internet www.gerritschotte.com; f. 2010; Leader GERRIT F. SCHOTTE.

Partido Adelanto i Inovashon Soshal (PAIS): Rozenweg 1, Willemstad; tel. (9) 518-8802; internet www.partidopais.com; f. 2010; Pres. MARCOLINO (MIKE) FRANCO; Leader ALEX ROSARIA.

Partido Alternativo Real (PAR) (Real Alternative Party): Fokkerweg 26, Unit 3, Willemstad; tel. (9) 465-2566; fax (9) 465-2622; internet www.partido-par.com; f. 1993 as the Partido Antiá Restrukturá, renamed as above in 2010; social-Christian ideology; Leader ZITA JESUS-LEITO.

Partido Nashonal di Pueblo (PNP) (National People's Party): Winston Churchillweg 133, Willemstad; tel. (9) 869-6777; fax (9) 869-6688; f. 1958; also known as Nationale Volkspartij; social-Christian party; Leader HUMPHREY DAVELAAR.

Pueblo Soberano (PS) (Sovereign People Party): Willemstad; internet www.pueblosoberano.org; pro-independence; Pres. EDWARD JOSEPH; Sec. GUSTAVO LAUFFER.

Judicial System

Legal authority is exercised by the Joint Court of Justice of Aruba, Curaçao and St Maarten, and of Bonaire, St Eustatius and Saba. The Court hears civil, criminal and administrative cases in the first instance and on appeal. The members of the Joint Court of Justice sit singly as judges in the Courts of First Instance and as a three-member panel in the appeals court. The Supreme Court of the Netherlands (based in The Hague) is the court of Final Instance for any appeal.

Joint Court of Justice: Wilhelminaplein 4, Willemstad; tel. (9) 463-4111; fax (9) 461-8341; e-mail curacao@caribjustitia.org; internet www.gemhofvanjustitie.org; Chief Justice LISBETH HOEFDRAAD.

Attorney-General: GUUS SCHRAM.

Religion

CHRISTIANITY

Most of the population are Christian, the predominant denomination being Roman Catholicism. There are also small communities of Jews, Muslims and Bahá'ís.

Curaçaose Raad van Kerken (Curaçao Council of Churches): Periclesstraat 6, Willemstad; tel. (9) 465-3207; fax (9) 461-0733; e-mail ddtic@yahoo.com; f. 1958; six mem. churches; Chair. Rev. PATMORE C. HENRY.

The Roman Catholic Church

Roman Catholics form the largest single group on Curaçao. According to the 2011 census, 73% of the population were Roman Catholic. Curaçao and the other former constituent territories of the Netherlands Antilles, together form the diocese of Willemstad, suffragan to the archdiocese of Port of Spain (Trinidad and Tobago). The Bishop participates in the Antilles Episcopal Conference, currently based in Trinidad and Tobago.

Bishop of Willemstad: Rt Rev. LUIS ANTONIO SECCO, Obispado Pietermaai, Julianaplein 5, Willemstad; tel. (9) 462-5876; fax (9) 462-7437; e-mail bisdomwstad@gmail.com; internet www.willemstaddiocese.org.

Other Christian Churches

The largest of the other churches in Curaçao, according to the 2011 census, were the Pentecostal (7% of the population), Protestant (3%), Seventh-day Adventist (3%), Jehovah's Witnesses (2%) and Evangelist (2%). Other denominations included Methodists, Anglican, Mormons and Baptists.

Iglesia Adventista di Shete Dia—Asosiashon Curaçao & Bonaire: Scalaweg 7, Willemstad; tel. (9) 737-1359; fax (9) 737-8201; e-mail sdaconference@adventcb.org; internet www.adventcb.org.

Iglesia Protestant Uni (United Protestant Church): Fortkerk, Fort Amsterdam, Willemstad; tel. (9) 461-1139; fax (9) 465-7481; e-mail vpg-cur@curlink.com; internet www.vpg-curacao.com; f. 1825 by union of Dutch Reformed and Evangelical Lutheran Churches; associated with the World Council of Churches and the Caribbean and North American Council for Mission (CANACOM); Pres. JOHANNES (HANCO) DE LIJSTER; 3 congregations; 11,280 adherents; 3,200 mems.

United Pentecostal Church of Curaçao: Willemstad; internet jrblack.info; Pastor J. R. BLACK.

OTHER RELIGIONS

According to the 2011 census, 0.8% of the population of Curaçao were Hindu, 0.5% were Muslim, and 0.2% were Jewish.

Congregation 'Shaarei Tsedek' Ashkenazi Orthodox Jewish Community: The Herman and Miriam Tauber Jewish Center, 37 Magdalenaweg, Willemstad; tel. (9) 510-5900; e-mail shaareitsedek

.shul@gmail.com; internet www.shaareitsedekcuracao.com; 140 mems; Rabbi ARIEL YESHURUN.

Reconstructionist Shephardi Congregation Mikvé Israel-Emanuel: Hanchi di Snoa 29, POB 322, Willemstad; tel. (9) 461-1067; fax (9) 465-4141; e-mail info@snoa.com; internet www.snoa.com; f. 1732 on present site; Rabbi GERALD ZELERMYER; about 150 mems.

The Press

Amigoe: Kaya Fraternan di Skèrpènè z/n, POB 577, Willemstad; tel. (9) 767-2000; fax (9) 767-4084; e-mail directie@amigoe.com; internet www.amigoe.com; f. 1884; Christian; daily; evening; Dutch; Dir ERNEST VOGES; Editor-in-Chief GINO BERNADINA; circ. 12,000.

Antilliaans Dagblad: ABCourant NV, Prof. Kernkampweg z/n, POB 725, Willemstad; tel. (9) 747-2200; fax (9) 747-2257; e-mail algemeen@antilliaansdagblad.com; internet www.antilliaansdagblad.com; f. 2003; daily; Dutch; privately owned; Publr MICHAEL WILLEMSE.

De Curaçaosche Courant: Saliña 147, Willemstad; tel. (9) 461-2766; fax (9) 461-6302; e-mail info@curcourant.com; internet www.curcourant.com; f. 1812; weekly; Dutch; Editor H. C. (PIM) ELISA-BETH.

Extra: Rector Zwijssenstraat 24, Willemstad; tel. (9) 462-4595; fax (9) 462-7575; e-mail redactie@extra.an; internet extra.cw; daily; morning; Papiamento; Man. R. YRAUSQUIN; Editor MIKE OEHLERS; circ. 20,000.

Nobo: Scherpenheuvel w/n, POB 323, Willemstad; tel. (9) 767-3500; fax (9) 767-3550; daily; evening; Papiamento; Editor CARLOS DAANTJE; circ. 15,000.

Notisia360: Kaya Shon Louis Perret 9, Willemstad; tel. (9) 738-4086; e-mail info@notisia360.com; internet www.notisia360.com; Dutch and Papiamento; Editor-in-Chief ROLAND PERRET GENTIL.

La Prensa: W. I. Compagniestraat 41, Willemstad; tel. (9) 462-3850; fax (9) 462-5983; e-mail webmaster@laprensacur.com; f. 1929; daily; evening; Papiamento; Man. R. YRAUSQUIN; Editor SIGFRIED RIGAUD; circ. 10,750.

De Telegraaf (Caribische Editie): ABCourant NV, Prof. Kernkampweg z/n, Willemstad; tel. (9) 747-2200; fax (9) 747-2257; e-mail algemeen@antilliaansdagblad.com; internet www.antilliaansdagblad.com; Caribbean edn of Dutch daily.

Ultimo Noticia: Frederikstraat 100, Willemstad; tel. (9) 462-3446; fax (9) 462-6535; e-mail redakshon@ultimo.cw; daily; morning; Papiamento; Editor CHICHO JONCKHEER.

Vigilante Korsou: Kaya Wilson Papa Godett 24, Pietermaai; tel. (9) 465-3596; fax (9) 465-6571; e-mail redakshon@vigilantekorsou.com; internet www.vigilantekorsou.com; f. 1994; Papiamento.

NEWS AGENCY

Algemeen Nederlands Persbureau (ANP) (Netherlands): Panoramaweg 5, POB 439, Willemstad; tel. (9) 461-2233; fax (9) 461-7431; Representative RONNIE RENS.

Publishers

Drukkerij Scherpenheuvel NV: Lindberghweg 28A, Willemstad; tel. (9) 465-6801.

Drukkerij de Stad NV: W. I. Compagniestraat 41, POB 3011, Willemstad; tel. (9) 462-3566; fax (9) 462-2175; e-mail management@destad.an; internet www.drukkerijdestad.com; f. 1929; Dir KENRICK A. YRAUSQUIN.

Broadcasting and Communications

TELECOMMUNICATIONS

Digicel Curaçao: Biesheuvel 24–25; tel. (9) 736-1056; fax (9) 736-1057; e-mail customercare@digicelcuracao.com; internet www.digicelcuracao.com; f. 1999 as Curaçao Telecom; bought by Digicel (Ireland) in 2005, present name adopted 2006; telephone and internet services; Chair. DENIS O'BRIEN; CEO (Dutch Caribbean) SANDER GIELEN.

Scarlet: Fokkerweg 26, Suite 106, Willemstad; tel. (9) 766-0000; fax (9) 461-8301; internet www.scarlet.an; telecommunications provider in Curaçao and St Maarten; CEO ERIC E. STAKLAND.

United Telecommunication Services, NV (UTS): UTS Headquarters, Rigelweg 2, Willemstad; tel. (9) 777-0101; fax (9) 777-1284; e-mail info@uts.cw; internet www.uts.cw; f. 1999 following merger of

Antelecom NV (f. 1908) and SETEL (f. 1979); Antelecom and SETEL still operate under own names; CEO PAUL DE GEUS.

Servicio de Telekomunikashon (UTS Wireless Curaçao) (SETEL): UTS Headquarters, Rigelweg 2, Willemstad; tel. (9) 777-0101; fax (9) 777-1284; e-mail info@uts.cw; internet www.uts .cw; f. 1979; forms part of UTS; state-owned, privatization pending; telecommunications equipment and network provider; Pres. ANGEL R. KOOK; Man. Dir JULIO CONSTANCIA; 400 employees.

BROADCASTING

Radio

Curom Broadcasting Inc: Roodeweg 64, POB 2169, Willemstad; tel. (9) 462-2020; fax (9) 462-5796; e-mail z86@curom.com; internet www.curom.com; f. 1933; broadcasts in English, Papiamento, Dutch and Spanish; Dir ORLANDO CUALES.

Mi 95: f. 1988; FM; music station, aimed at adults.

Z-86: news station.

88 Ròckòrsou: rock music station, aimed at young people.

Easy 97.9 FM: Arikokweg 19A, Willemstad; tel. (9) 462-3162; fax (9) 462-8712; e-mail radio@easyfm.com; internet www.easyfm.com; f. 1995; Dir KEVIN CARTHY.

Gold 91.5 FM Curaçao: De Rouvilleweg 7, Ingang Klipstraat, POB 6103, Willemstad; tel. (9) 426-1803; fax (9) 461-9103; e-mail info@ gold915.com; internet www.gold915.com; music station.

Paradise FM: De Rouvilleweg 7, Ingang Klipstraat, POB 6103, Willemstad; tel. (9) 426-1803; fax (9) 461-9103; e-mail studio@ paradisefm.an; internet paradisefm.an; news station.

Radio Caribe: Ledaweg 35, Brievengat, Willemstad; tel. (9) 736-9564; fax (9) 736-9569; f. 1955; commercial station; programmes in Dutch, English, Spanish and Papiamento; Dir-Gen. C. R. HEILLEGGER.

Radio Exito: Julianaplein 39, Willemstad; tel. (9) 462-5577; fax (9) 462-5580.

Radio Hoyer NV: Plasa Horacio Hoyer 21, Willemstad; tel. (9) 461-1678; fax (9) 461-6528; e-mail hoyer1@radiohoyer.com; internet www.radiohoyer.com; f. 1954; commercial; two stations: Radio Hoyer I (mainly Papiamento, also Spanish) and II (mainly Dutch, also English) in Curaçao; Man. Dir HELEN HOYER.

Radio Korsou FM: Bataljonweg 7, POB 3250, Willemstad; tel. (9) 737-3012; fax (9) 737-2888; e-mail studio@korsou.com; internet www .korsou.com; f. 1976; 24 hrs a day; programmes in Papiamento and Dutch; Gen. Man. ALAN H. EVERTSZ.

Radio Tropical: Kaya W. F. G. Mensing, Willemstad; tel. (9) 465-0190; fax (9) 465-2470; e-mail tropi@cura.net; Dir DWIGHT RUDOLPHINA.

Television

Antilliaanse Televisie Maatschappij NV (TeleCuraçao): Berg Ararat z/n, POB 415, Willemstad; tel. (9) 461-1288; fax (9) 461-4138; e-mail web@telecuracao.com; internet www.telecuracao.com; f. 1960; fmrly operated Tele-Aruba; commercial; owned by United Telecommunication Services; also operates cable service, offering programmes from US satellite television and two Venezuelan channels; Dir PAUL DE GEUS; Gen. Man. HUGO LEW JEN TAI.

Five television channels can be received on Curaçao in total. Curaçao has a publicly owned cable television service, TDS.

Finance

(cap. = capital; res = reserves; dep. = deposits; m. = million; br.(s) = branch(es); amounts in Netherlands Antilles guilders unless otherwise indicated)

BANKING

Regulatory Authority

College Financieel Toezicht (CFT): De Rouvilleweg 39, Willemstad; tel. (9) 461-9081; fax (9) 461-9088; e-mail info@cft.an; internet www.cft.an; f. 2008; board of financial supervision; office on Sint Maarten (q.v.); Chair. AGE BAKKER.

Central Bank

Centrale Bank van Curaçao en Sint Maarten: Simon Bolivar Plein 1, Willemstad; tel. (9) 434-5500; fax (9) 461-5004; e-mail info@ centralbank.cw; internet centralbank.cw; f. 1828 as Curaçaosche Bank, renamed Bank van de Nederlandse Antillen in 1962, present name adopted in 2010; cap. 30.0m., res 610.5m., dep. 2,520.9m. (Dec. 2009); Pres. Dr EMSLEY D. TROMP; br. on St Maarten.

Commercial Banks

Banco di Caribe NV: Schottegatweg Oost 205, POB 3785, Saliña, Willemstad; tel. (9) 432-3000; fax (9) 461-5220; e-mail info@ bancodicaribe.com; internet www.bancodicaribe.com; f. 1973; cap. 20.6m., res 108.1m., dep. 1,371.5m. (Dec. 2013); Chair. R. GIBSON; CEO and Gen. Man. Dir IDEFONS D. SIMON; 5 brs.

CIBC FirstCaribbean International Bank: De Ruyterkade 61, POB 3144, Willemstad; tel. (9) 433-8000; fax (9) 433-8198; e-mail bank.curacao@cibcfcib.com; internet www.cibcfcib.com; f. 1964 as ABN AMRO Bank NV; adopted present name in 2002 following merger of Caribbean operations of CIBC and Barclays Bank PLC; Barclays relinquished its stake in 2006, present name adopted 2011; CEO RIK PARKHILL; Man. Dir (Dutch Caribbean) PIM VAN DER BURG; 1 br.

CITCO Banking Corporation NV: De Ruyterkade 62, POB 707, Willemstad; tel. (9) 732-2322; fax (9) 732-2330; e-mail curacao-bank@ citco.com; internet www.citco.com; f. 1980 as Curaçao Banking Corpn NV; Man. Dir and Gen. Man. RONALD IRAUSQUIN; Man. Dirs GLENDA E. C. LALLJEE-TRAPENBERG, NIHAILA TH FANEYTE.

Girobank NV: Scharlooweg 35, Willemstad; tel. (9) 433-9999; fax (9) 461-7861; e-mail info@gironet.com; internet www.girobank.net; cap. 46.5m., res 49.2m., dep. 1,236m. (Dec. 2011); Pres. ÉRIC GARCIA; Man. Dirs STEPHAN CAPELLA, RICHARD RAJACK.

Maduro & Curiel's Bank NV: Plaza Jojo Correa 2–4, POB 305, Willemstad; tel. (9) 466-1100; fax (9) 466-1122; e-mail info@ mcb-bank.com; internet www.mcb-bank.com; f. 1916 as NV Maduro's Bank; merged with Curiel's Bank in 1931; affiliated with Bank of Nova Scotia NV, Toronto, Canada; br. in Bonaire; cap. 51m., res 190.6m., dep. 5,243.7m. (Dec. 2013); Pres. and CEO LIONEL CAPRILES; Man. Dirs RONALD GOMES CASSERES, JOE VAN DONGEN; 15 brs.

Orco Bank NV: Schottegatweg Oost, POB 4928, Landhuis Cerrito, Willemstad; tel. (9) 732-7000; fax (9) 737-6425; e-mail info@orcobank .com; internet www.orcobank.com; f. 1986; cap. 7.8m., res 17.4m., dep. 600.1m. (Dec. 2011); Man. Dirs M. N. S. SPROCK, M. M. S. BOSKALJON-ROMER; CEO K. R. CANWORD; 3 brs.

Rabobank Curaçao NV: Zeelandia Office Park, Kaya W. F. G. (Jombi), Mensing 14, POB 3876, Willemstad; tel. (9) 465-2011; fax (9) 465-2066; e-mail l.an.curacao.ops@rabobank.com; internet www .rabobank.com; f. 1978; cap. US $53.0m., res $17.8m., dep. $4,535.2m. (Dec. 2003); Chair. R. VAN ZADELHOFF; Gen. Man. T. STEVENS.

RBC Royal Bank NV: Kaya Flamboyan 1, Rooi Catootje, POB 763, Willemstad; tel. (9) 763-8438; fax (9) 737-0620; e-mail tt-info@rbc .com; internet www.rbc.com/caribbean; f. 1997 as Antilles Banking Corpn; name changed to RBTT Bank NV in 2002; name changed as above in 2012; cap. 114.5m., res 139m., dep. 3,553.2m. (Dec. 2010); Pres. and Country Head (Curaçao) ROBERT DA SILVA; 4 brs.

SFT Bank NV: Schottegatweg Oost 44, POB 707, Willemstad, Curaçao; tel. (9) 732-2900; fax (9) 732-2902; e-mail info@sftbank .com; internet www.sftbank.com; f. 1982 as Curaçao Banking Corpn; restructured as CITCO Bank Antilles in 1984; changed name as above in 1995; total assets 453.2m. (Dec. 2011); Man. Dir LEO RIGAUD.

Offshore Banks

Abu Dhabi International Bank NV: Kaya W. F. G. (Jombi), Mensing 36, POB 3141, Willemstad; tel. (9) 461-1299; fax (9) 461-5392; e-mail info@ant-trust.com; internet www.nbad.com; f. 1981; cap. US $20.0m., res $30.0m., dep. $112.2m. (Dec. 2006); Pres. NAGY KOLTA.

DVB Bank America NV: Zeelandia Office Park, Kaya W. F. G. (Jombi) Mensing 14, POB 3107, Willemstad; tel. (9) 431-8700; fax (9) 465-2366; e-mail sandra.sponselee@dvbbank.com; internet www .dvbbank.com; Gen. Man. SANDRA SPONSELEE.

Van Lanschot Bankiers (Curaçao) NV: Schottegatweg Oost 32, POB 4799, Willemstad; tel. (9) 737-1011; fax (9) 737-1086; e-mail info@vanlanschot.com; internet www.vanlanschot.com; f. 1962; wholly owned by F. Van Lanschot Bankiers NV (Netherlands); Man. A. VAN GEEST.

Savings Bank

Curaçaose Postspaarbank (PSB Bank): Schottegatweg Noord 24 Units M-N-O, Willemstad; tel. (9) 432-2000; fax (9) 737-2969; e-mail info@psbbanknv.com; internet www.psbbanknv.com; f. 1905; post office savings bank; Man. Dir GUIVERON WEERT; cap. 21m.; 20 brs.

Banking Associations

Association of International Bankers (IBA): A. M. Chumaceiro Blvd 3, POB 3369, Willemstad; tel. (9) 461-5367; fax (9) 461-5369; e-mail info@ibna.an; internet www.ibna.an; f. 1980; supervisory body for banks operating in Curaçao and Sint Maarten; 32 mems; Pres. ARTHUR ADAMS; Sec. ANTONIO TORRES.

Curaçao Bankers' Association (CBA): Plaza Jojo Correa 2–4, Willemstad; tel. (9) 466-1100; fax (9) 466-1122; e-mail florisela.bentoera@an.rbtt.com; f. 1972; Pres. LIONEL CAPRILES; Sec. FLORISELA BENTOERA.

Curaçao International Financial Services Association (CIFA): A. M. Chumaceiro Blvd 3, Willemstad; tel. (9) 461-5371; fax (9) 461-5378; e-mail info@cifa-curacao.com; internet www.cifa-curacao.com; representative association for the international financial services sector; Chair. ETIENNE YS.

INSURANCE

ASKA Holding NV (ASKA Levenverzekering NV/ASKA Schadeverzekering NV): Scharlooweg Oost 19, POB 3778, Willemstad; tel. (9) 734-5566; fax (9) 766-5588; e-mail info@askanv.com; internet www.askanv.com; f. 1995; accident and health, motor vehicle, property.

ENNIA Caribe Holding NV: J.B. Gorsiraweg 6, POB 581, Willemstad; tel. (9) 434-3800; fax (9) 434-3873; e-mail mail@ennia.com; internet www.ennia.com; f. 1948 as Nieuw Eerste Nederlandse Insurance Co; changed name as above in 1974; part of the Parman International BV (USA) since Jan. 2006; Pres. RALPH PALM.

> **Ennia Caribe Schaden NV:** J. B. Gorsiraweg 6, POB 581, Willemstad; tel. (9) 434-3800; fax (9) 434-3873; e-mail mail@ennia.com; f. 1948; general; life insurance as Ennia Caribe Leven NV.

> **Ennia Caribe Zorg NV:** John B. Gorsiraweg 6, POB 581, Willemstad; tel. (9) 461-6399; fax (9) 461-6709; fmrly De Amersfoortse Antillen NV; name changed as above in 2002; health care.

Fatum: Cas Coraweg 2, Roi Katochi, Willemstad; tel. (9) 777-7777; fax (9) 736-3333; e-mail info@dc.myguardiangroup.com; internet myguardiangroup.cw; f. 1904; owned by Guardian Holdings Ltd; bought Royal & Sun Alliance (Antilles) NV in 2012; Pres. and CEO STEVEN MARTINA.

Maduro & Curiel's Insurance Services NV: Lio Capriles Banking Center, Rooi Catootje, POB 305, Willemstad; tel. (9) 466-1855; fax (9) 466-1611; e-mail mcis@mcb-bank.com; internet www.mcb-insurance.com; Man. CHANTIENNE ALCENDOR.

NAA-Citizens Curaçao NV: Salinja 170, Willemstad; tel. (9) 465-7144; fax (9) 461-6269; e-mail rwawoe@citizens-ins.net; internet www.naa-curacao.com; fmrly Netherlands Antilles and Aruba Assurance Company (NA&A) NV; accident and health, motor vehicle, property.

Pan-American Life Insurance Co of Curaçao and Sint Maarten, NV: Pan-American Life Bldg, Schottegatweg Oost 104, Willemstad; tel. (9) 461-3232; fax (9) 461-3240; internet www.palig.com; f. 2012; part of Pan-American Life Insurance Group (USA); CEO and Man. Dir (Caribbean) WILLIAM R. SCHULZ, Jr; Gen. Man. VALERY SINOT.

United Insurance Company Ltd: c/o UNIRISK, Schottegatweg Oost 60, POB 609, Willemstad; tel. (9) 737-4005; fax (9) 737-4006; e-mail info@united.cw; internet www.united.cw.

Trade and Industry

DEVELOPMENT ORGANIZATIONS

Curaçao Industrial and International Trade Development Company NV (CURINDE): Emancipatie Blvd 7, Landhuis Koningsplein; tel. (9) 737-6000; fax (9) 737-1336; e-mail info@curinde.com; internet www.curinde.com; f. 1980; state-owned; manages the harbour free zone, the airport free zone and the industrial zone; Man. Dir J. JANSEN (acting).

World Trade Center Curaçao (WTCC): POB 6005, Piscadera Bay; tel. (9) 463-6132; fax (9) 463-6573; e-mail ceo@wtccuracao.com; internet www.worldtradecentercuracao.com; CEO CARMELO DE STEFANO.

CHAMBER OF COMMERCE

Curaçao Chamber of Commerce and Industry: Kaya Junior Salas 1, Pietermaai, World Trade Centre Bldg, POB 10, Piscadera Bay; tel. (9) 461-1451; fax (9) 461-5652; e-mail management@curacao-chamber.cw; internet www.curacao-chamber.cw; f. 1884; Chair. WILLIAM JONCKHEER; Exec. Dir JOHN H. JACOBS.

INDUSTRIAL AND TRADE ASSOCIATIONS

Curaçao Exporters' Association (CEA): c/o Seawings NV, Maduro Plaza z/n CEA, POB 6049, Willemstad; tel. (9) 733-1585; fax (9) 733-1599; e-mail seawings@madurosons.com; f. 1993; Dir ALBERT ELENS.

Curaçao International Financial Services Association (CIFA): Chumaceiro Blvd 3, POB 220, Willemstad; tel. (9) 461-

5371; fax (9) 461-5378; e-mail info@cifa-curacao.com; internet www.cifa-curacao.com; f. 1980; represents financial services companies, over 100 mems; Chair. ETIENNE YS.

Curaçao Trade and Industry Association (Vereniging Bedrijfsleven Curaçao—VBC): Kaya Junior Salas 1, POB 49, Willemstad; tel. (9) 461-1410; fax (9) 461-5422; e-mail info@vbcuracao.com; internet www.vbcuracao.com; f. 1944; Pres. BASTIAN KOOYMAN; Exec. Dir JOHAN LIEUW.

STATE HYDROCARBON COMPANY

Refinería di Korsou NV: Ara Hilltop Office Complex, Pletterijweg 1, POB 3627, Willemstad; tel. (9) 461-1050; fax (9) 461-3377; e-mail info@refineriadikorsou.com; internet www.refineriadikorsou.com; f. 1915 by Royal Dutch Shell Co, taken over by Govt and leased to PDVSA of Venezuela in 1985; Man. Dir HERBERT MENSCHE; Pres. OSWALD VAN DER DIJS.

MAJOR COMPANIES

Antilliaanse Brouwerij NV: Rijkseenheid Blvd w/n, POB 465, Willemstad; tel. (9) 434-1500; fax (9) 434-1599; e-mail r_voorn@heineken.nl; f. 1958; manufacture and distribution of beer and soft drinks; acquired by Parera Group Holding NV in 2010; Man. YORICK GELDOLPH TEN HOUTE DE LANGE; 121 employees.

Antilliaanse Verffabriek NV: Asteroidenweg z/n, POB 3944, Willemstad; tel. (9) 736-5866; fax (9) 736-5048; e-mail info@avfpaint.com; internet www.avfpaint.com; f. 1960; manufactures paint products; Man. Dir FRANK BRANDAO; 40 employees.

Caribbean Bottling Co Ltd (CBC–Pepsi Curaçao): Kaminda André F. E. Kusters 6, Zeelandia, POB 302, Willemstad; tel. (9) 461-2488; fax (9) 465-1377; f. 1948; produces carbonated drinks; owned by Pepsi; Man. ALAN F. MADURO; 110 employees.

Carnefco Curaçao BV: Pletterijweg z/n, POB 3121, Willemstad; tel. (9) 465-0221; fax (9) 465-2586; e-mail info@carnefco.com; f. 1973; ship maintenance, grit-blasting, wet-blasting, high-pressure water blasting, internal coatings, etc.; part of Carnefco Group; Man. Dir ROBERT MATTHES; 60 employees.

Curaçao Beverage Bottling Co NV (Coca-Cola Curaçao): Rijkseenheid Blvd 1, POB 95, Willemstad; tel. (9) 461-3311; fax (9) 461-1310; f. 1938; bottlers and mfrs of soft drinks, many under licence; Man. Dir TIBOR LUCKMANN; 105 employees.

Curaçao Oil NV (CUROIL): Abraham Mendes Chumaceiro Blvd 15, POB 3927, Willemstad; tel. (9) 432-0000; fax (9) 461-3335; e-mail curoil@curoil.com; internet www.curoil.com; f. 1985; fuel and petroleum lubricants marketing company; supplies automotive, marine, aviation and industrial fuels and lubricants; Man. Dir YAMIL LASTEN; 80 employees.

CurAloe: Curaçao Ecocity Projects, Aloë Vera Plantage, Groot Sint Joris West z/n, Willemstad; tel. (9) 767-5577; fax (9) 767-5577; e-mail ecocity@cura.net; internet www.aloecuracao.com; f. 2002; jt venture between BioClin, Netherlands, and local shareholders; produces range of aloe vera skin-care and health products; Man. PIET VILJOEN.

Danella NV: Pletterijweg z/n, Willemstad; tel. (9) 461-6300; fax (9) 471-3727; e-mail info@danella-nv.com; internet www.danella-nv.com; f. 1973; manufactures scaffolding, galvanized pipes, steel fittings, valves and ductile iron; Man. LUCIEN P. LIEUW-SJONG.

Janssen de Jong Caribbean: Fort Nassauweg z/n, Willemstad; tel. (9) 433-8500; fax (9) 465-8500; e-mail info@info.jajo.com; internet www.janssendejongcaribbean.com; subsidiary of Janssen de Jong Group BV, Netherlands; mining, concrete industry, infrastructure, maritime and civil construction activities; Man. Dir PIETER VAN GULIK.

> **Beton Industrie Brievengat NV:** Kaya Playa Kanoa, Brievengat, Willemstad; tel. (9) 433-8533; fax (9) 737-5192; e-mail info@bib.an; internet www.bib.an; part of Janssen de Jong Caribbean; concrete products; Dir ROY VOOGT.

> **Curacaose Wegenbouw Maatschappij:** Fort Nassauweg z/n, Willemstad; tel. (9) 433-8500; fax (9) 465-8500; e-mail info@cwm.jajo.com; internet www.curacaosewegenbouw.com; f. 1953; part of Janssen de Jong Caribbean; infrastructure, road building and trenching; Operations Man. EDWIN SLIEKER.

> **Harbour and Civil Construction Curaçao (HCCC):** Parera, POB 431, Willemstad; tel. (9) 461-1807; fax (9) 461-1146; e-mail info@hccc.jajo.com; internet www.harbourcivil.com; part of Janssen de Jong Caribbean; construction of civil and marine devts.

> **Mijnmaatschappij Curaçao:** POB 3078, Newport, Willemstad; tel. (9) 767-3400; fax (9) 767-6721; e-mail info@mmc.jajo.com; internet www.miningcompanycuracao.com; part of Janssen de Jong Caribbean; 70 employees.

Kooyman NV: Kaya W. F. G. (Jombi) Mensing 44, POB 3062, Zeelandia, Willemstad; tel. (9) 461-3333; fax (9) 465-5428; e-mail info-headoffice@kooymanbv.com; internet www.kooymanbv.com; f. 1939; building supplies, hardware, steel/aluminium goods, glass, timber goods, etc.; Pres. BASTIAAN KOOIJMAN; CEO HERBERT VAN DER WOUDE; over 400 employees.

Lovers Industrial Corporation NV: Industrial Park Brievengat JII 1–2, Willemstad; tel. (9) 737-0499; fax (9) 737-1747; e-mail lovers@loversglobal.com; internet www.loversglobal.com; f. 1984; produces fruit juices, ice cream, frozen yoghurt; purchased Otto Senior ('Ritz') juice and dairy business in 2003; Pres. OSWALD C. VAN DER DIJS; 180 employees.

Plastico NV: Pletterijweg z/n, Parera; tel. (9) 461-6300; fax (9) 461-9329; e-mail pipe@plastico-nv.com; internet www.plastico-nv.com; f. 1985; manufactures polythene pipes for water-distribution and irrigation purposes; Man. L. LIEUW-SJONG; 10 employees.

Softex Products NV: Industrial Park Brievengat, POB 3795, Willemstad; tel. (9) 737-7811; fax (9) 737-7903; e-mail softex@cura.net; f. 1976; produces paper towels, napkins, etc.; Man. PAUL L. M. LIEUW; 40 employees.

West India Mercantile Co (WIMCO): Saliña, POB 74, Willemstad; tel. (9) 461-1833; fax (9) 461-1627; e-mail info@wimco-nv.com; internet www.wimco-nv.com; f. 1928; wholesale and retail of electrical household and commercial appliances; Man. Dir ANTHONY COHEN HENRÍQUEZ; 90 employees.

UTILITY

Electricity and Water

Aqualectra Production NV (KAE): Rector Zwijsenstraat 1, POB 2097; tel. (9) 463-2200; fax (9) 463-2228; e-mail info@aqualectra.com; internet www.aqualectra.com; present name adopted in 2001 following the restructuring of Curaçao's energy sector; CEO DARICK JONIS (acting).

TRADE UNIONS

Algemene Bond van Overheidspersoneel (ABVO) (General Union of Civil Servants): Kaya Thomas Henriquez 21, POB 3604, Willemstad; tel. (9) 737-6097; fax (9) 737-3145; e-mail abvona@cura.net; f. 1936; Chair. WENDY CALMES; 4,000 mems.

Central General di Trahadonan di Corsow (CGTC) (General Headquarters for Workers of Curaçao): POB 2078, Otrobanda, Willemstad; tel. (9) 737-6097; fax (9) 737-3145; e-mail cgtc.curacao@gmail.com; f. 1949; Sec.-Gen. ROLAND (NACHO) IGNACIO.

Curaçaosche Federatie van Werknemers (Curaçao Federation of Workers): Schouwburgweg 44, POB 4327, Willemstad; tel. (9) 737-0390; fax (9) 737-1403; e-mail curafed@yahoo.com; f. 1964; Pres. WILFRED SPENCER; Sec.-Gen. GILBERT POULINA; 204 affiliated unions; about 2,000 mems.

Petroleum Workers' Federation of Curaçao: Willemstad; tel. (9) 737-0255; fax (9) 737-5250; affiliated to Int. Petroleum and Chemical Workers' Federation; f. 1955; Pres. ANGELO MEYER; approx. 1,500 mems.

Sentral di Sindikatonan di Korsou (SSK) (Central Trade Unions of Curaçao): Schouwburgweg 44, POB 3036, Willemstad; tel. (9) 737-0255; fax (9) 737-5250; e-mail ssk@cura.net; Pres. ALCIDES COVA; 6,000 mems.

Sindikato di Trahado den Edukashon na Korsou (SITEK) (Curaçao Schoolteachers' Trade Union): Landhuis Stenen Koraal, Kaya Maestronan di Skol s/n, POB 3545, Willemstad; tel. (9) 468-2902; fax (9) 469-0552; Pres. SIDNEY JUSTIANA; Sec. DARIUS (LIO) PLANTIJN; 1,234 mems.

Transport

RAILWAYS

There are no railways.

ROADS

Curaçao has a good system of all-weather roads.

Autobusbedrijf Curaçao NV (ABC): Industrieterrein Buena Vista, Willemstad; tel. (9) 868-4733; fax (9) 868-3026; internet autobusbedrijf.com; f. 1943; bus services.

SHIPPING

Curaçao is an important centre for the refining and transshipment of Venezuelan and Middle Eastern petroleum. Willemstad is served by the Schottegat harbour, set in a wide bay with a long channel and deep water. There are a further six ports on the island. A 'mega cruise' facility, with capacity for the largest cruise ships, has been constructed on the Otrobanda side of St Anna Bay. Ports at Bullen Bay and Caracas Bay also serve Curaçao. At December 2013 the flag registered fleet comprised 145 vessels, totalling 1,337,091 grt.

Curaçao Ports Authority: Werf de Wilde z/n, POB 689, Willemstad; tel. (9) 434-5999; fax (9) 461-3907; e-mail info@curports.com; internet curports.com; Man. Dir HUMBERTO DE CASTRO.

Principal Shipping Companies

Caribbean Cargo Services NV: Caracasbaaiweg 328, POB 442, Willemstad; tel. (9) 767-2588; fax 747-1155; internet www.ccs.an; Man. Dir LOES VAN DER WOUDE.

Curaçao Drydock Company (CDM): POB 3012; tel. (9) 733-0000; fax (9) 736-5580; f. 1958; state-owned; ship repair yard.

Dammers Ship Agencies Inc: Dammers Bldg, Kaya Flamboyan 11, POB 3018, Willemstad; tel. (9) 737-0600; fax (9) 737-3875; e-mail directorate@dammers-curacao.com; internet www.dammers-curacao.com; f. 1964; fmrly Dammers & van der Heide, Shipping and Trading (Antilles) Inc; Man. Dir MARLON MANUEL.

Gomez Shipping NV: Landhuis Zeelandia z/n, Willemstad; tel. (9) 461-5900; fax (9) 461-3358; e-mail info@gomezshipping.ibm.net; Man. FERNANDO DA COSTA GÓMEZ.

S. E. L. Maduro Shipping: Dokweg 19, Maduro Plaza, POB 3304, Willemstad; tel. (9) 733-1510; fax (9) 733-1538; e-mail maduroship@madurosons.com; internet www.madurosons.com; f. 1837; Man. Dir H. MEIJER.

VR Shipping NV: Scarlet Bldg, Fokkerweg 26, POB 3677, Willemstad; tel. (9) 461-4700; fax (9) 461-2576; e-mail info@vrshipping.com; internet www.vrshipping.com; f. 1975 as Anthony Veder & Co NV; brs in Aruba and Bonaire.

CIVIL AVIATION

Curaçao International Airport is located at Hato, 12 km from Willemstad. In 2006 a new passenger terminal building was opened.

Civil Aviation Authority (CCAA): Seru Mahuma z/n, Willemstad; tel. (9) 839-3333; fax (9) 868-9924; e-mail civilair@gov.an; Dir Lt-Col (retd) OSCAR DERBY.

Curaçao Airline Association (CAA): Curaçao International Airport, Hato; tel. (9) 839-1111; fax (9) 839-1112; internet curacaoairlinesassociation.org; f. 2003; 42 mems; Pres. GERMAINE RICHIE; Sec. GERHARD GOSELINK.

InselAir: Curaçao International Airport, Hato; tel. (9) 737-0444; e-mail customerrelations@fly-inselair.com; internet www.fly-inselair.com; f. 2006; flights within Caribbean, to Venezuela and to USA (Charlotte, NC); CEO ALBERT J. KLUIJVER.

Tourism

Tourism is a major industry on Curaçao. The principal attractions for tourists are the white, sandy beaches, marine wildlife and diving facilities. Visitor arrivals to Curaçao totalled 440,063 in 2013. The majority of visitors were from the Netherlands (30%) and Venezuela (21%). Tourism receipts totalled US $453m. in 2011.

Curaçao Hospitality and Tourism Association (CHATA): Kaya Junior Salas 01, Willemstad; tel. (9) 465-1005; fax (9) 465-1052; e-mail info@chata.org; internet www.chata.org; f. 1967 as Curaçao Hotel Asscn; Pres. and CEO LIZANNE DINDIAL.

Curaçao Tourist Board: Pietermaai 19, POB 3266, Willemstad; tel. (9) 434-8200; fax (9) 461-5017; e-mail info@curacao.com; internet www.curacao.com; f. 1989; supervised by the Curaçao Tourism Development Bureau; CEO (vacant).

Defence

The Netherlands is responsible for the defence of Curaçao. The Dutch-appointed Governor is Commander-in-Chief of the armed forces on the island. A Dutch naval contingent is stationed in Curaçao and Aruba.

Flag Officer, Caribbean: Cdre HANS LODDER.

Education

Education was made compulsory in 1992. The island's educational facilities are generally of a high standard. The education system is the same as that of the Netherlands. Dutch is the principal language of instruction, although lessons are also taught in Papiamento in primary schools. Primary education begins at six years of age and lasts for six years. Secondary education lasts for a further five years.

DOMINICA

Geography

PHYSICAL FEATURES

The Commonwealth of Dominica is found in the central Lesser Antilles, the northernmost of the Windward Islands in the old British West Indies. Early colonization and rule by the French has left its mark on the island, reinforced by the continued French presence among Dominica's nearest neighbours. To the north are the main islands of Guadeloupe, an overseas department of the French Republic, and to the south the island of Martinique, another such department. Dominica is the largest of the anglophone islands in the Lesser Antilles (excluding Trinidad), covering an area of 751 sq km (290 sq miles).

Formed by volcanic activity, which is still prevalent on the island, Dominica is a mountainous land, lush and fertile, the most rugged of the Lesser Antilles. Its physical geography helped the long resistance of the native Carib Amerindians to European colonization. Dominica has the highest mountain in the eastern Caribbean, Morne Diablotins, at 1,447 m (4,749 ft). The high interior is covered by dense rainforest, which accounts for about 60% of the island and is protected by three national parks. The southernmost park, around Morne Trois Pitons (a UNESCO World Heritage Site), is considered to have the richest biodiversity in the Caribbean, but also contains five active volcanoes, fuelling about 50 fumaroles and hot springs, as well as Boiling Lake, one of the largest thermally active lakes in the world (its main rival is in New Zealand). Fertility has encouraged the wooded nature of the hills, and there is rich flora and fauna (including the endemic sisserou or imperial parrot, which features on the country's flag, the red-necked or jacquot parrot, the forest thrush, the blue-headed humming-bird, turtles, a rare iguana and the crapaud—eaten as 'mountain chicken'—this last a large frog, which has found its main haven in Dominica since the devastating volcanic activity on Montserrat in the 1990s). The steep terrain and wet climate also give rise to numerous rivers, streams and waterfalls, many of which are seasonal. Little of the landscape is farmed. There are 148 km (92 miles) of coastline, with reefs offshore, and the island itself is about 47 km long (north–south, the northern end of the island leaning more towards the north-west) and 26 km wide.

CLIMATE

The climate is subtropical and the mountains attract rain, making the island relatively rich in water resources and often humid. The wettest month is August, and the driest months are February–June. Average annual rainfall is high—in Roseau, the capital on the south-western coast, it is about 2,160 mm (85 ins), but in the mountains it is over some 8,640 mm (340 ins). The terrain makes the risk of flash flooding high, and the island also lies in the possible path of hurricanes, during June–October particularly. Daytime temperatures average between

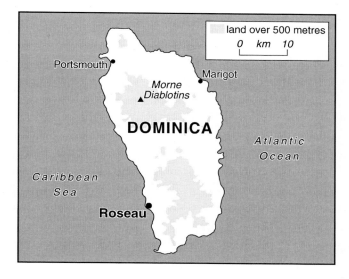

70°F and 85°F (21°C–29°C), the hottest month being August, but it is much cooler in the highlands, especially at night.

POPULATION

Ethnically, the island population is mainly black, but there are also whites and many of mixed race, as well as a more recent Syrian community. The legacy of previous rulers survives in the only extant Carib population of the West Indies (most living in the 15 sq km Carib Territory, or Waitukubuli Karifuna area, on the rugged Atlantic coast) and in a thriving French Creole patois, the most widely spoken local dialect. Spoken Carib has not survived. In the north-west an English patois, Kokay, is spoken by the Methodist descendants of freed slaves from Antigua. The official language, however, is English, which is widely spoken, and the main Christian denomination is Roman Catholic (about 62% of the population), with a further 20% adhering to a number of other Christian churches.

The total population was 71,293 according to preliminary results of the May 2011 census, with 15,035 living in the capital, Roseau, in the south-west, in one of the 10 parishes into which the country is divided. The second town, Portsmouth, is also on the western coast, but at the northern end. On the north-east Atlantic coast, Marigot, near to the airport, is the main town. As mentioned above, Dominica is the only island of the Caribbean to retain some of its pre-Columbian Amerindian population—about 3,000 Caribs, or those of mixed Carib descent, live on the north-eastern coast, just south of Marigot.

History

MARK WILSON

Dominica is a republic within the Commonwealth. It has a ceremonial President as head of state and a Prime Minister who leads the majority party in the unicameral House of Assembly, where elected representatives sit alongside appointed senators.

Dominica's original Carib Amerindian inhabitants, the Kalinago or Karifuna, knew the island as Waitukubuli—'tall is her body'—and survive in a small community at Salybia in the north-east with 3,000 inhabitants on an area of 15 sq km. The island was given its present name by the explorer Christopher Columbus, who sighted it on Sunday 3 November 1493. Its mountainous topography discouraged early settlement, and it was declared neutral by England and France in 1600 and again in 1686. With the islands of Martinique and Guadeloupe in close proximity, French settlers gradually moved in during the 17th and early 18th centuries. The island was first claimed by the United Kingdom in 1759, and changed hands several times before finally becoming a British possession in 1805. However, the French creole language, aspects of French culture and the Roman Catholic religion remain firmly established today; Dominica is a member of La Francophonie as well as of the Commonwealth.

Despite the island's high rainfall and fertile soil, its broken terrain and poor communications made large-scale plantation agriculture less profitable than on some neighbouring islands. Commercial crops during the colonial period included coffee, cocoa, coconuts (for copra) and limes, as well as sugar. The island remained something of a backwater, although one administrator, Hesketh Bell, initiated significant infrastructural improvements between 1899 and 1905. Dominica formed part of the Leeward Islands Federation from 1833 until 1940, when it was transferred to the (British) Territory of the Windward Islands, also a loose confederation of colonies.

The first elections with universal suffrage were held in 1951, with candidates supported by the Dominica Trade Union winning the majority of seats. In 1955 the Dominica Labour Party (DLP) was founded by Phyllis Shand Allfrey, a white Dominican and author of a well-known local novel, *The Orchid House*. However, an organized party system emerged more slowly than on most other islands. Dominica joined the Federation of the West Indies in 1958 along with nine other British colonies. When Jamaica and Trinidad and Tobago left in 1962, the Federation collapsed; an attempt to unite the remaining colonies as the 'little eight' was unsuccessful. Along with its neighbours, Dominica became a British Associated State in 1967. While it remained responsible for its internal affairs, the United Kingdom retained control of foreign relations and defence.

After winning an election held in 1971 the DLP was led from 1974 by Patrick John, who became the first Prime Minister upon the granting of independence on 3 November 1978. In February 1979 John announced that a 'Dominica Caribbean Free Port Authority' owned by Don Pierson, a developer from Texas, USA, would be given extensive rights over the northern third of the island. This proposal was abandoned owing to strong popular opposition. However, further disputes followed, including a strike by the civil service. In an attempt to disperse one large demonstration at the end of May, the Defence Force shot and killed one person and left 10 injured. A general strike by the private sector then led to the resignation of several cabinet ministers, while the President, Frederick Degazon, left the island in early June. The former Governor, Sir Louis Cools-Lartigue, was installed as acting President, but resigned after only one day in office. Following arson attacks on the Court House and Registry shortly afterwards, the political opposition formed a Committee for National Salvation (CNS), together with private sector, business, labour and agricultural organizations. On 21 June, in an improvised procedure, Jenner Armour was sworn in as acting President; he then appointed one of John's former ministers, Oliver Seraphin, as Prime Minister.

The interim Government led by Seraphin was not an unqualified success, not least owing to disputes over the management of hurricane reconstruction efforts. At a general election in July 1980, Seraphin's followers were soundly defeated by the Dominica Freedom Party (DFP), and Eugenia Charles (later Dame Eugenia Charles) became the Caribbean's first female Prime Minister. Premier Charles developed a strong reputation both within the island and internationally and was an articulate supporter of the invasion of Grenada in 1983.

In March 1981 the new Government stated that members of the small Defence Force were planning a coup to restore Patrick John to office, with the support of US and Canadian 'soldiers of fortune'—members of the extremist right-wing Ku Klux Klan. The Defence Force was disbanded in April 1982, while John was tried and acquitted of attempting to overthrow the Government in the same year. However, following a retrial in 1985, John was sentenced to a 12-year prison term; he was released before the expiry of his sentence. (He was later involved in the affairs of the Fédération Internationale de Football Association—FIFA—but was in November 2011 banned from taking part in any football-related activity for two years for his part in an alleged bribery scandal.) Meanwhile, in 1985 the DLP, the Democratic Labour Party, the United Dominica Labour Party and the Dominica Liberation Movement united to form the Labour Party of Dominica; however, the merged organization remains known as the DLP.

Although the DFP majority was reduced to a single seat in the general election of May 1990, Charles remained in office until 1995; she was replaced as leader of the DFP by Brian Alleyne, under whose leadership the party was defeated in a general election held in June of that year. The Dominica United Workers' Party (UWP), led by Edison James, won 11 of the 21 seats in the House of Assembly.

Troubles in the banana industry undermined support for the UWP Government, and there was considerable controversy over its spending proposals, including one for the development of an airport. In a general election in January 2000, the UWP's parliamentary representation was reduced to nine seats. The DLP, led by Roosevelt (Rosie) Douglas, won 10 seats and formed a coalition with the DFP, which won two seats. One UWP member subsequently defected from the party and joined the ruling coalition, strengthening the position of the new Government within the House of Assembly. Douglas died in October; he was succeeded by his deputy, Pierre Charles.

In 2001 Canada announced that Dominicans travelling to Canada would require visas. This reflected growing international concern over Dominica's 'economic citizenship' programme, under which passports were sold to non-citizens in return for an 'investment of US $100,000'. Following the terrorist attacks in the USA in September, Dominica came under increased pressure to abandon the programme; however, it continued, with approximately 3,000 believed to have been granted economic citizenship by 2013, and was to be expanded following that year's annual budget address. In 2014 the Government inaugurated an investment scheme as part of its economic citizenship programme.

In July 2002 the Dominica Public Service Union organized a large-scale demonstration in the capital, Roseau, to protest against controversial tax increases introduced in a budget intended to bring about economic recovery. In November Frederick Baron, one of the two DFP members of parliament, announced that he would no longer support the Government, leaving it with backing from 11 of the 21 elected members. With the economic situation remaining difficult, the Government was in a severely weakened condition in 2003, while the leadership of Charles was strongly questioned from within his own party. Charles died in January 2004 and was succeeded by the 31-year-old Roosevelt Skerrit, hitherto Minister of Education, Youth and Sports.

In spite of the country's economic difficulties and a stringent austerity programme, Skerrit re-established the Government's popularity. At a general election in May 2005 the DLP took 52% of the popular vote, compared with 43% at the elections in 2000. The party won 12 of the 21 seats, and a further seat was taken by a close ally of the DLP, who ran as an independent; the UWP secured the remaining eight seats (and 44% of the votes cast). The DFP was defeated in each of two constituencies in which it fielded a candidate; however, its leader, Charles Savarin, was appointed as a senator and retained his place in Skerrit's new administration as Minister of Foreign Affairs, Trade, Labour and the Public Service, and later as Minister of National Security; he was appointed by the majority in parliament to the post of ceremonial president in October 2013, in spite of opposition protests.

The former UWP deputy leader, and spokesperson for finance and planning, Julius Timothy, changed party allegiance in September 2006 to join the DLP Cabinet as Minister of Planning and Economic Development. This UWP defection increased the Government's strength to 13 of the 21 elected seats. However, there was some concern over Timothy's role in the previous UWP administration, which had borrowed heavily at commercial rates for an unrealistic airport project, and which had seriously mismanaged the offshore financial sector. Ambrose George was dismissed from the Cabinet (he was at that point responsible for works and infrastructure) in November 2008, reportedly after asking to be paid for assistance in establishing an offshore bank, the principal investor of which had previously been convicted of money-laundering.

The opposition team experienced its own troubles. Leader of the Opposition Edison James resigned from office in July 2007; Earl Williams, who had succeeded James as leader of the UWP the previous year, replaced him. However, Williams resigned as party leader in August 2008 after allegations that he had misappropriated the funds of legal clients. He was succeeded by Ronald Green. However, James returned to his former position as party leader in January 2012.

At a general election on 18 December 2009 the DLP won a third parliamentary term with 18 of the 21 elected seats and 61.2% of the popular vote, compared with three seats and 34.9% for the UWP, and 2.4% for the DFP. The new UWP leader Ronald Green lost his seat, and the party alleged irregularities, such as special flights being provided for nationals resident overseas returning home to vote. The party also claimed that Skerrit was not qualified to sit in parliament as he had acquired French nationality as a child, in addition to his Dominican citizenship. In protest, the opposition staged a boycott of the House of Assembly, although one opposition member put in a single token appearance. The seats of the remaining two were declared vacant by the Speaker in May 2010. In two by-elections in July the UWP retained both seats, declaring that having made its point about the 2009 poll, it would resume its active role as a parliamentary opposition. The High Court in January 2012 rejected election petitions from the opposition challenging the election to parliament in 2009 of Skerrit and another DLP member of parliament on the grounds that they held dual nationality. A general election is due by April 2015, but is expected to be held at an earlier date.

Dominica in July 2014 approved legislation to replace the Privy Council, which sits in London, as the final court of appeal, with the Caribbean Court of Justice (CCJ), based in Trinidad and Tobago. Dominica had been a signatory to the 2003 agreement establishing the CCJ, which was inaugurated in 2005, although the country had yet to adopt it as its final appellate court. In November 2013 Prime Minister Skerrit announced that his administration had officially informed the British Government of this objective and in January 2014 Skerrit disclosed that the British authorities had not objected to the move.

Dominica is a comparatively peaceful island. However, murders increased from seven in 2008 to 15 in 2010, the latter figure equivalent to 21 per 100,000 population, around four times the US murder rate. The rising crime rate placed increased demands on the police force, which has a strength of over 400. There were also reports of attacks on visiting yachts. The police estimated cocaine transshipment at 100 kg–200 kg weekly. Drugs-trafficking through the eastern Caribbean increased notably in 2013–14. Local sources estimated that 90% of drugs in transit move on to Guadeloupe, Antigua and Barbuda or Saint-Martin; an estimated 10% of the population use cocaine, and 25% use marijuana, with an estimated 210 acres under cultivation in 2011, according to the US Department of State. Although the small offshore financial sector had an uneven regulatory record, the island was not thought to be a major money-laundering risk. The Caribbean Financial Action Task Force noted serious deficiencies in Dominica's money-laundering control regime, and was monitoring implementation of an action plan from 2013; legislation was strengthened in that year with a civil asset forfeiture law.

INTERNATIONAL RELATIONS

In March 2004, following a visit to the Chinese capital, Beijing, Skerrit announced that Dominica would recognize the People's Republic of China in place of Taiwan. China had agreed to provide US $6m. in budgetary support, equivalent to around 8% of annual recurrent revenue, followed by EC $300m.–$330m. in grant aid for a road, the main hospital, a school and a sports stadium, equivalent in value to some 45% of one year's gross domestic product or 1.5 years' recurrent revenue; smaller aid projects have continued since. An embassy of the People's Republic of China was duly opened in Roseau in June. In 2005 Taiwan initiated legal action to recover US $12m. in debt contracted under assistance programmes in place before 2003.

Dominica's perceived attachment to so-called 'chequebook diplomacy' was criticized again in 2004 when Japan provided funding of some EC $33m. for the construction of a fisheries complex on the island, allegedly in return for supporting the Japanese Government's pro-whaling stance. Dominica was among other member states of the Organisation of Eastern Caribbean States criticized for voting in favour of the proposed lifting of a 20-year moratorium on commercial whaling—tendered by Japan—during the annual meeting of the International Whaling Commission (IWC) in 2006. In 2007 Prime Minister Skerrit made an official visit to Japan, following which he announced that Japanese funding for a further fisheries facility had been secured. Skerrit also stated his intention to renew Dominica's support for the Japanese Government's bid to resume commercial whaling. The President of the Caribbean Conservation Association and former Minister of the Environment in the Dominican Government, Atherton Martin, accused his country of behaving like 'an international prostitute' for agreeing to support Japan at the IWC while accepting financial assistance from the Japanese Government. However, UWP leader Edison James cautioned that the decision could adversely affect Dominica's tourism industry, a significant proportion of which came from whale-watching. As a result of increasing local and international concern, from 2008 Dominica moved to a position of abstention on whaling issues.

Dominica has developed friendly relations with Venezuela, although there was potential for a divisive dispute over maritime boundaries and the status of tiny Aves Island/Bird Rock 220 km to the west. Dominica benefits from Venezuela's Petrocaribe initiative, and in January 2008 ratified membership of the Bolivarian Alliance for the Peoples of our America-People's Trade Treaty (Alianza Bolivariana para los Pueblos de Nuestra América-Tratado de Comercio de los Pueblos—ALBA-TCP) group, along with Bolivia, Cuba and Nicaragua. Venezuela has provided substantial grant aid, and proposed in 2008 to build a small US $80m. petroleum refinery, a proposal which had obvious technical difficulties and has failed to materialize. At the same time Dominica maintained friendly relations with the USA, the United Kingdom, Canada and France, whose two overseas departments of Guadeloupe and Martinique are Dominica's nearest neighbours.

Economy

MARK WILSON

Dominica is the second smallest country in the Western hemisphere in terms of population, with 71,293 inhabitants living on its 751 sq km at the May 2011 census; the population has declined by more than 3,000 since 1981, with estimated net outward migration of 3,800 in the 10 years to 2011 offsetting the slow rate of natural increase. Accordingly, migrant remittances made up 11% of gross domestic product (GDP) in 2001–11, by far the highest figure in the Eastern Caribbean. The island has developed a modest middle-income economy, but the per-head GDP at market prices of US $6,776 in 2011 was the second lowest in the Eastern Caribbean. GDP has grown by an average of 2.5% since the early 1990s, compared with 3.5% for the wider Caribbean, as banana exports have contracted and tourism has grown only slowly. Overseas grants have played a significant role in the economy, and peaked at 6.4% of annual GDP in 2008, a figure which was reduced to 0.9% in 2012 and 0.8% in 2013. GDP grew at an average annual rate of 4.5% in 2003–08 as grant-funded projects mainly assisted by the People's Republic of China and other non-traditional donors stimulated the economy. However, with this stimulus reduced, the economy contracted by 1.5% in 2010, then grew by 1.7% in 2011, contracted by 0.2% in 2012, and grew by just 0.8% in 2013. Construction expanded by a cumulative 252% in 2002–11, then contracted by a cumulative 15% in 2012–13 as public sector investments slowed. Dominica was less immediately affected by the global economic recession from 2008 than most of its neighbours as tourism played a smaller role in its economy. A relatively favourable fiscal position and significant overseas grant aid allowed the Government to maintain some capital spending. According to the Caribbean Development Bank, unemployment fell from 25% in 2002 to 14% in 2009, while the proportion of the population living below the poverty line declined from 39% to 29% over the same period; however, inequality increased, and youth unemployment remained high, at 31%. Dominica faces difficulties in moving away from an agricultural economy, as tourism and other services have not grown fast enough to compensate for the loss of export banana markets.

A high debt ratio has been a significant problem, with high foreign commercial borrowing in the years around 2000. Donor agencies, including the European Union (EU), the IMF and the World Bank, were closely involved in the discussion of possible measures to stabilize the economy. Concessional borrowing of EC $30m. in 2002 included assistance from Barbados, Trinidad and Tobago, and Saint Vincent and the Grenadines, as well as from more obvious donor agencies. The IMF agreed a stand-by credit, with performance targets, although the island failed to meet these goals. New policy targets were set in 2003, and were followed by a US $11.4m. line of credit under the IMF's Poverty Reduction and Growth Facility (PRGF). An IMF mission in 2004 found that the new targets had been implemented. Public sector salary costs were reduced from 17% of GDP in 2002/03 to 13% by 2005/06. The fiscal outlook benefited significantly in 2004 from an agreement by China to provide substantial project grant aid in exchange for diplomatic recognition.

A third tranche of assistance was agreed with the IMF in 2004, by which time 60% of eligible debt was covered by a restructuring programme. In 2004/05 there was a recurrent surplus of EC $31m., while a primary surplus of 3% of GDP was achieved two years ahead of the target date, and maintained for some years afterwards; further improvements in revenue collection followed the introduction of a value-added tax in 2006 in accordance with IMF recommendations. Creditors holding 70% of Dominica's debt had reached restructuring agreements by November 2005, with outstanding debt down by the end of the year to 108% of GDP—still a very high figure by international standards, but a great improvement on earlier levels. With an increase in capital spending finance, mainly supported by development grant assistance, GDP began to grow again from 2004, and the Government was able in mid-2005 to reverse the public sector pay reduction, although a

salary 'freeze' remained in effect until 2006. Central government debt was an estimated 75% of GDP in June 2014.

The overall fiscal balance moved into a small surplus from 2005 to 2008. This represented a recovery in the Government's financial position, assisted by major grant inflows; however, the international recession had an adverse effect on the overall fiscal balance, with the primary balance moving back into a deficit averaging 2.4% of GDP in 2010–12, but was again in positive territory at 1.2% of GDP for the year ending in June 2014. The IMF in 2010 expressed concern over proposed borrowing, including a 'soft' loan from China of US $40m., equivalent to 8.6% of GDP; a further Chinese loan of US $60m. for hotel development was also under consideration. Points of concern in 2014 included increasing international commodity prices, and an expected decline in grants from non-traditional donors, principally Venezuela, China and Libya. The IMF called for fiscal consolidation, strengthening of the financial sector and structural reform.

Dominica is a member of the Caribbean Community and Common Market (CARICOM) and of the Caribbean Single Market and Economy (CSME). The regional development fund set aside US $250m. to bolster smaller market economies against the abolition of import taxes integral to the CSME, assuaging fears of unequal trading status and expediting the inauguration of the system. Dominica is also a member of the Organization of Eastern Caribbean States (OECS), which links nine of the smaller Caribbean territories, while its financial affairs are supervised by the Eastern Caribbean Central Bank, which has its headquarters in Saint Christopher and Nevis.

Agriculture accounted for a preliminary 16.1% of GDP in 2013, against an OECS average of 3.9%. The export of bananas to the United Kingdom had been the mainstay of the economy since the 1950s, and Dominica was more dependent on this activity than any other Caribbean country, although dependence on agriculture has decreased in recent years. In 1990 banana exports constituted 92.1% of total merchandise exports and generated 34.4% of foreign exchange earnings, while more than one-half of the country's workforce was involved to some extent with the industry. As a result of changes in the EU's import regime, banana exports decreased from 55,000 metric tons in 1993 to 6,236 tons in 2009, representing an estimated 15.6% of merchandise exports by value and 2.8% of foreign exchange earnings. Bananas made up only 8.1% of agricultural output and 1.25% of GDP in 2012. Significant EU grant aid was available for modernizing the banana industry and for enabling economic diversification, although the rate of disbursement was painfully slow, and there was further damage to the banana crop from Sigatoka disease from 2012. Small farmers produce a wide variety of fruits, vegetables and livestock products for the local market, with some produce exported to Barbados, Antigua and Barbuda, and the neighbouring French Overseas Departments of Martinique and Guadeloupe.

There is a small manufacturing sector, which in 2013 accounted for a preliminary 3.3% of GDP. The main exporter was Dominica Colgate Palmolive, which made soap from locally produced copra, as well as detergent and (until 2007) toothpaste, but the company downsized significantly in 2007–09.

The island's airport at Melville Hall is not capable of accommodating long-haul aeroplanes. Connections to Europe and North America are made through larger regional airports such as those in Antigua or Barbados. There has been Venezuelan and other assistance for airport improvements, and EU funding allowed for night flights from 2011, facilitating same-day connections on neighbouring islands for intercontinental travel, to the benefit of tourism; further airport improvements to accommodate larger aircraft were in progress. Upgrading of the airport road, via French funding, was completed in 2013. There was further discussion in 2013 of a proposal for a long-runway airport; however, the Government was unwilling to incur the debt required to finance construction.

There are few sandy beaches, and rainfall is much higher than on most Caribbean islands. These factors, as well as the lack of direct air access, have restricted the development of tourism, which makes up 10% of GDP compared with the 18% OECS average; hotels and restaurants comprised a preliminary 2.0% of GDP in 2013. However, Dominica's wildlife and natural beauty have attracted visitors interested in the island's flora and fauna. Visitor expenditure totalled US $82.0m. in 2013. Stop-over arrivals totalled 78,277 in 2013, according to the Caribbean Tourism Organization, a 6.8% decrease compared with the peak year of 2006, but 3.6% more than in 2011. In 2013 some 26.9% of arrivals were from North America and 17.3% were from Europe; the largest groups were business and family visitors from other Caribbean islands. Stop-over tourists were easily outnumbered by the 230,587 cruise ship passengers in 2013; however, this group spends little money ashore, and accordingly brings fewer economic benefits than the numbers would indicate, while changes in cruise ship routes bring about sudden fluctuations, such as the 49% two-year decline in arrivals recorded in 2010–12. Of some significance was the student and organizational spending of two US offshore medical schools, the Ross University School of Medicine in the north of the island and the smaller and more recently established All Saints University School of Medicine in the south.

The 2011 census reported 45% of households with internet access; there were 143 mobile telephone connections per 100 people.

There is a small offshore financial sector. Unfortunately, the country has been accused of failing to meet internationally acceptable financial standards. In 2000 Dominica was listed as a 'non-co-operative jurisdiction' on the issue of money-laundering by the Financial Action Task Force on Money Laundering (FATF, based in Paris, France) and as a harmful tax haven by the Organisation for Economic Co-operation and Development (OECD). Having made regulatory reforms, Dominica was conditionally de-listed by the FATF in 2002, and is now listed by the US Department of State under 'other jurisdictions monitored' rather than as a country of concern. OECD in 2008 included Dominica on a 'grey list' of countries that did not yet have a significant number of Tax Information Exchange Agreements in place. Dominica was removed from this list in 2010. Following a November 2011 assessment, the Caribbean Financial Action Task Force in May 2013 noted serious continuing deficiencies in Dominica's money-laundering control regime, but six months later reported significant progress in the implementation of an action plan. Like its neighbours, Dominica suffered in 2009 and afterwards from the collapse of a Trinidad-based insurance conglomerate, CL Financial, which posed risks to financial stability throughout the Eastern Caribbean, with an important subsidiary, the British American Insurance Company, declared insolvent. The IMF estimated net liabilities in Dominica at 11.5% of GDP, with the financial system and government likely to suffer large contingent losses. The IMF also stressed the importance of strengthening the recently established Financial Services Unit for improved financial sector supervision, and noted the risks attached to credit unions with a high non-performing loan ratio; credit unions account for one-third of financial system assets, with membership equivalent to 83% of the population, the highest ratio in the world.

The economic citizenship programme, under which Dominican nationality can be acquired in return for a cash investment, has been in place, under various guises, since independence. It is viewed with some suspicion internationally, as it is considered open to exploitation by criminals; recent data on the programme was not readily available. The programme was relaunched in 2002, with a fee of US $75,000 for individual applicants; 650 passports were sold in 1996–2002. Negotiations for visa-free travel for Dominicans to neighbouring Martinique and Guadeloupe collapsed in 2006; restrictions on immigration to those territories and to others that were party to the EU's Schengen Agreement on open borders remained in place.

Dominica is at risk from hurricanes, of which the most recent was Hurricane Dean in 2007. Tropical storms, while less violent, can cause serious damage to the fragile banana plants, most recently with Tropical Storm Chantal in 2013. The island is also at risk from earthquakes. There are several volcanic centres, which are currently inactive; regional geologists suggest there is a 25% chance of a major eruption within the next 25 years. In the absence of recent eruptions, however, volcanic features such as the Boiling Lake and Valley of Desolation are attractions for the more energetic tourists. An initial investigation of geothermal power potential was completed in 2009, and proposed an initial 5-MW plant to open by 2014, followed by a further four plants with a total capacity of up to 120 MW by 2017 if further investigations produced positive results. With peak demand currently at 18 MW, this programme would, if successfully completed, leave a substantial potential for export to neighbouring islands, particularly Martinique and Guadeloupe. This ambitious schedule was not met; however, France in 2014 offered to finance an initial 15 MW plant for completion in 2016.

Statistical Survey

Source (unless otherwise stated): Eastern Caribbean Central Bank; internet www.eccb-centralbank.org.

AREA AND POPULATION

Area: 751 sq km (290 sq miles).

Population: 71,727 at census of 12 May 2001; 71,293 (males 36,411, females 34,882) at census of 14 May 2011 (preliminary).

Density (at 2011 census): 94.9 per sq km.

Population by Age and Sex (31 December 2006): *0–14 years:* 20,976 (males 10,759, females 10,217); *15–64 years:* 42,979 (males 22,280, females 20,699); *65 years and over:* 7,226 (males 3,200, females 4,026); *Total* 71,180 (males 36,238, females 34,942) (Source: UN, *Demographic Yearbook*).

Principal Town (population at 2011 census, preliminary): Roseau (capital) 15,035.

Births, Marriages and Deaths (registrations, 2002 unless otherwise indicated): Live births 1,081 (birth rate 15.4 per 1,000); Marriages (1998) 336 (marriage rate 4.4 per 1,000); Deaths 594 (death rate 8.4 per 1,000) (Source: UN, *Demographic Yearbook*). *2010:* Live births 933; Deaths 588. *2013:* Birth rate 15.6 per 1,000; Death rate 8.0 per 1,000 (Source: Pan American Health Organization).

Life Expectancy (years at birth): 76.4 (males 73.4; females 79.5) in 2013. Source: Pan American Health Organization.

Economically Active Population ('000 persons aged 15 years and over, 2001): Agriculture, hunting, forestry and fishing 5.22; Manufacturing (incl. mining and quarrying) 2.10; Utilities 0.41; Construction 2.42; Wholesale and retail trade, restaurants and hotels 5.12; Transport, storage and communications 1.56; Financing, insurance, real estate and business services 1.14; Community, social and personal services 6.77; *Sub-total* 24.73; Activities not adequately defined 0.08; *Total employed* 24.81; Unemployed 3.05; *Total labour force* 27.86 (males 17.03, females 10.83) (Source: ILO). *Mid-2014* (estimates): Agriculture, etc. 6,000; Total labour force 32,000 (Source: FAO).

HEALTH AND WELFARE

Key Indicators

Total Fertility Rate (children per woman, 2012): 2.1.

Under-5 Mortality Rate (per 1,000 live births, 2012): 13.

Physicians (per 1,000 head, 2001): 1.6.

Hospital Beds (per 1,000 head, 2010): 3.8.

Health Expenditure (2011): US $ per head (PPP): 758.

Health Expenditure (2011): % of GDP: 6.0.

Health Expenditure (2011): public (% of total): 71.0.

Access to Water (% of persons, 2004): 97.

Access to Sanitation (% of persons, 2004): 84.

Total Carbon Dioxide Emissions ('000 metric tons, 2010): 135.7.

Total Carbon Dioxide Emissions Per Head (metric tons, 2010): 1.9.

Human Development Index (2013): ranking: 93.

Human Development Index (2013): value: 0.717.

For sources and definitions, see explanatory note on p. vi.

AGRICULTURE, ETC.

Principal Crops ('000 metric tons, 2012, FAO estimates): Sweet potatoes 2.2; Cassava 1.2; Yautia (Cocoyam) 5.0; Taro (Cocoyam) 13.0; Yams 14.0; Sugar cane 4.8; Coconuts 11.5; Cabbages 0.8; Pumpkins 0.9; Cucumbers 1.4; Carrots 0.8; Bananas 24.5; Plantains 5.7; Oranges 6.3; Lemons and limes 1.4; Grapefruit (incl. pomelos) 13.5; Guavas, mangoes and mangosteens 2.1; Avocados 0.4. *Aggregate Production* ('000 metric tons, may include official, semi-official or estimated data): Fruits (excl. melons) 55.0.

Livestock ('000 head, year ending September 2012, FAO estimates): Cattle 14.0; Pigs 5.0; Sheep 7.9; Goats 9.7; Chickens 200.

Livestock Products ('000 metric tons, 2012, FAO estimates): Cattle meat 0.6; Pig meat 0.4; Chicken meat 0.3; Cows' milk 7.6; Hen eggs 0.2.

Fishing (metric tons, live weight, 2012): Capture 561 (Yellowfin tuna 71; Marlins, sailfishes, etc. 54; Common dolphinfish 136); Aquaculture 35 (FAO estimate); *Total catch* 596 (FAO estimate).

Source: FAO.

MINING

Pumice ('000 metric tons, incl. volcanic ash): Estimated production 100 per year in 1988–2004. Source: US Geological Survey.

INDUSTRY

Production (2006, metric tons, unless otherwise indicated, preliminary): Laundry soap 3,605; Toilet soap 4,296; Dental cream 1,376; Liquid disinfectant 1,861; Crude coconut oil 855 (2001); Coconut meal 331 (2001); Electricity 99.0 million kWh (2010). Sources: IMF, *Dominica: Statistical Appendix* (September 2007), and UN Industrial Commodity Statistics Database.

FINANCE

Currency and Exchange Rates: 100 cents = 1 Eastern Caribbean dollar (EC $). *Sterling, US Dollar and Euro Equivalents* (30 May 2014): £1 sterling = EC $4.542; US $1 = EC $2.700; €1 = EC $3.675; EC $100 = £22.02 = US $37.04 = €27.21. *Exchange Rate:* Fixed at US $1 = EC $2.70 since July 1976.

Budget (EC $ million, 2013, preliminary): *Revenue:* Tax revenue 303.2 (Taxes on income and profits 58.5, Taxes on property 7.8, Taxes on domestic goods and services 180.2, Taxes on international trade and transactions 56.7); Other current revenue 79.6; Total 382.8, excl. grants received 11.7. *Expenditure:* Current expenditure 352.4 (Wages and salaries 149.8, Goods and services 107.4, Interest payments 28.1, Transfers and subsidies 67.1); Capital expenditure and net lending 160.7; Total 513.1.

International Reserves (US $ million at 31 December 2013): IMF special drawing rights 1.67; Reserve position in IMF 0.01; Foreign exchange 85.36; Total 87.05. Source: IMF, *International Financial Statistics*.

Money Supply (EC $ million at 31 December 2013): Currency outside depository corporations 41.59; Transferable deposits 199.57; Other deposits 1,058.86; *Broad money* 1,300.02. Source: IMF, *International Financial Statistics*.

Cost of Living (Retail Price Index, base: 2005 = 100): All items 119.0 in 2011, 120.8 in 2012, 120.3 in 2013. Source: IMF, *International Financial Statistics*.

Gross Domestic Product (EC $ million at constant 2006 prices): 1,181.72 in 2011; 1,167.54 in 2012; 1,158.96 in 2013 (preliminary).

Expenditure on the Gross Domestic Product (EC $ million at current prices, 2013, preliminary): Government final consumption expenditure 244.49; Private final consumption expenditure 1,186.58; Gross fixed capital formation 178.12; *Total domestic expenditure* 1,609.19; Exports of goods and services 420.25; *Less* Imports of goods and services 666.29; *GDP in purchasers' values* 1,363.15.

Gross Domestic Product by Economic Activity (EC $ million at current prices, 2013, preliminary): Agriculture, hunting, forestry and fishing 196.14; Mining and quarrying 15.68; Manufacturing 40.43; Electricity and water 61.53; Construction 50.56; Wholesale and retail trade 168.01; Restaurants and hotels 24.42; Transport, storage and communications 161.73; Finance and insurance 81.64; Real estate, housing and business activities 107.86; Public administration, defence and compulsory social security 96.87; Education 156.57; Health and social work 40.40; Other community, social and personal services 12.40; Private households with employed persons 3.24; *Sub-total* 1,217.48; *Less* Financial intermediation services indirectly measured (FISIM) 65.87; *Gross value added in basic prices* 1,151.60; Taxes, less subsidies, on products 211.55; *GDP in market prices* 1,363.15.

Balance of Payments (US $ million, 2012): Exports of goods 40.6; Imports of goods −182.7; *Balance on goods* −142.1; Services (net) 87.8; *Balance on goods and services* −54.3; Primary income (net) −17.2; *Balance on goods, services and primary income* −71.4; Secondary income (net) 16.5; *Current balance* −54.9; Capital transfers 16.5; Direct investment liabilities 19.6; Portfolio investment (net) 3.7; Other investment (net) 19.2; Net errors and omissions −1.3; *Reserves and related items* 2.7. Source: IMF, *International Financial Statistics*.

EXTERNAL TRADE

Principal Commodities (distribution by HS, US $ million, 2012): *Imports c.i.f.:* Live animals and animal products 13.5 (Meat and edible meat offal 6.7); Vegetables and vegetable products 8.5; Prepared foodstuff, beverages, spirits and vinegar, tobacco, etc. 26.5 (Beverages, spirits and vinegar 7.5); Mineral Products 51.3 (Mineral fuels, oils, distillation products, etc. 47.6); Chemicals and related products 15.3; Plastics, rubbers, and articles thereof 8.9; Pulp of wood, paper and paperboard, and articles thereof 9.2; Iron and steel, other base metals and articles of base metals 12.7; Machinery and mechanical appliances, electrical equipment and parts thereof 25.8 (Machinery, boilers, etc. 13.1); Electrical and electronic equipment 12.6); Vehicles, aircraft, vessels and associated transport equipment 10.0 (Vehicles other than railway, tramway 8.6); Total (incl. others) 211.9. *Exports f.o.b.:* Vegetables and vegetable products 3.3 (Vegetables and roots and tubers 1.3; Edible fruit, nuts, peel of citrus fruit, melons, etc. 1.9); Mineral products 3.5 (Salt, sulphur, earth, stone, plaster, lime and cement 3.5); Chemicals and related products 18.8 (Tanning, dyeing extracts, pigments, etc. 1.5; Soaps, lubricants, waxes, candles and modelling pastes, etc. 16.5); Pulp of wood, paper and paperboard, and articles thereof 4.5 (Printed books, newspapers and pictures 4.5); Machinery and mechanical appliances, electrical equipment and parts thereof 4.1 (Electrical and electronic equipment 3.8); Total (incl. others) 37.0.

Principal Trading Partners (US $ million, 2012): *Imports c.i.f.:* Antigua and Barbuda 4.5; Barbados 3.8; Brazil 2.2; Canada 4.9; China, People's Republic 5.2; Colombia 4.2; Dominican Republic 3.7; France (incl. Monaco) 4.2; Grenada 2.3; Guyana 2.2; Jamaica 3.8; Japan 5.0; Netherlands 2.7; Saint Lucia 3.5; Saint Vincent and the Grenadines 3.4; Trinidad and Tobago 36.0; United Kingdom 8.4; USA 77.9; Total (incl. others) 211.9. *Exports f.o.b.:* Antigua and Barbuda 2.0; Barbados 2.3; France (incl. Monaco) 3.2; Guyana 3.5; Jamaica 6.9; Saint Christopher and Nevis 5.3; Saint Lucia 0.9; Saint Vincent and the Grenadines 0.4; Suriname 0.7; Trinidad and Tobago 6.9; USA 1.6; Total (incl. others) 37.0.

Source: Trade Map-Trade Competitiveness Map, International Trade Centre, www.intracen.org/marketanalysis.

TRANSPORT

Road Traffic (motor vehicles licensed in 1994): Private cars 6,491; Taxis 90; Buses 559; Motorcycles 94; Trucks 2,266; Jeeps 461; Tractors 24; Total 9,985. *2000* (motor vehicles in use): Passenger cars 8,700; Commercial vehicles 3,400. Source: partly UN, *Statistical Yearbook*.

Shipping: *Flag Registered Fleet* (at 31 December 2013): 79 vessels (total displacement 698,019 grt). Source: Lloyd's List Intelligence (www.lloydslistintelligence.com).

Civil Aviation (1997): Aircraft arrivals and departures 18,672; Freight loaded 363 metric tons; Freight unloaded 575 metric tons.

TOURISM

Visitor Arrivals: 434,796 (82,193 stop-over visitors, 764 excursionists, 341,501 cruise ship passengers, 10,338 yacht passengers) in 2011; 366,025 (85,980 stop-over visitors, 2,104 excursionists, 266,178 cruise ship passengers, 11,763 yacht passengers) in 2012; 334,268 (86,136 stop-over visitors, 1,898 excursionists, 230,587 cruise ship passengers, 15,647 yacht passengers) in 2013.

Tourism Receipts (EC $ million, estimates): 285.95 in 2011, 205.54 in 2012; 221.32 in 2013.

COMMUNICATIONS MEDIA

Telephones (2013): 17,144 main lines in use.

Mobile Cellular Telephones (2013): 93,575 subscribers.

Internet Subscribers (2010): 8,600.

Broadband Subscribers (2013): 10,667.

Source: International Telecommunication Union.

EDUCATION

Institutions (1994/95 unless otherwise indicated): Pre-primary 72 (1992/93); Primary 64; Secondary 14; Tertiary 2.

Teachers (2011/12 unless otherwise indicated): Pre-primary 160; Primary 516; General secondary 503; Secondary vocational 22 (2010/11); Tertiary 34 (1992/93).

Pupils (2011/12 unless otherwise indicated): Pre-primary 1,734 (males 864, females 870); Primary 8,144 (males 4,186, females 3,958); General secondary 6,093 (males 3,090, females 3,003); Secondary vocational 302 (males 93, females 209) (2010/11); Tertiary 229 (males 55, females 174) (2007/08).

Sources: UNESCO, *Statistical Yearbook*, Institute for Statistics; Caribbean Development Bank, *Social and Economic Indicators*; UN Economic Commission for Latin America and the Caribbean, *Statistical Yearbook*.

Pupil-teacher Ratio (primary education, UNESCO estimate): 15.8 in 2011/12 (Source: UNESCO Institute for Statistics).

Adult Literacy Rate (2004): 88.0%. Source: UN Development Programme, *Human Development Report*.

Directory

The Constitution

The Constitution came into effect at the independence of Dominica on 3 November 1978. Its main provisions are summarized below:

FUNDAMENTAL RIGHTS AND FREEDOMS

The Constitution guarantees the rights of life, liberty, security of the person, the protection of the law and respect for private property. The individual is entitled to freedom of conscience, of expression and assembly and has the right to an existence free from slavery, forced labour and torture. Protection against discrimination on the grounds of sex, race, place of origin, political opinion, colour or creed is assured.

THE PRESIDENT

The President is elected by the House of Assembly for a term of five years. A presidential candidate is nominated jointly by the Prime Minister and the Leader of the Opposition and on their concurrence is declared elected without any vote being taken; in the case of disagreement the choice will be made by secret ballot in the House of Assembly. Candidates must be citizens of Dominica aged at least 40 who have been resident in Dominica for five years prior to their nomination. A President may not hold office for more than two terms.

PARLIAMENT

Parliament consists of the President and the House of Assembly, composed of 21 elected Representatives and nine Senators. According to the wishes of Parliament, the latter may be appointed by the President—five on the advice of the Prime Minister and four on the advice of the Leader of the Opposition—or elected. The life of Parliament is five years.

Parliament has the power to amend the Constitution. Each constituency returns one Representative to the House who is directly elected in accordance with the Constitution. Every citizen over the age of 18 is eligible to vote.

THE EXECUTIVE

Executive authority is vested in the President. The President appoints as Prime Minister the elected member of the House who commands the support of a majority of its elected members, and other ministers on the advice of the Prime Minister. Not more than three ministers may be from among the appointed Senators. The President has the power to remove the Prime Minister from office if a resolution expressing no confidence in the Government is adopted by the House and the Prime Minister does not resign within three days or advise the President to dissolve Parliament.

The Cabinet consists of the Prime Minister, other ministers and the Attorney-General in an ex officio capacity.

The Leader of the Opposition is appointed by the President as that elected member of the House who, in the President's judgement, is best able to command the support of a majority of the elected members who do not support the Government.

The Government

HEAD OF STATE

President: CHARLES ANGELO SAVARIN (assumed office 2 October 2013).

CABINET
(September 2014)

The Government is formed by the Dominica Labour Party.

Prime Minister and Minister of Finance, Foreign Affairs and Information Technology and of National Security, Labour and Immigration: ROOSEVELT SKERRIT.

Attorney-General: LEVI PETER.

Minister of Housing, Lands, Settlement and Water Resources: REGINALD AUSTRIE.

Minister of Agriculture and Forestry: MATTHEW WALTER.

Minister of Employment, Trade, Industry and Diaspora Affairs: Dr JOHN COLIN MCINTYRE.

Minister of the Environment, Natural Resources, Physical Planning and Fisheries: Dr KENNETH DARROUX.

Minister of Education and Human Resource Development: PETTER SAINT-JEAN.

Minister of Social Services, Community Development and Gender Affairs: GLORIA SHILLINGFORD.

Minister of Culture, Youth and Sports: JUSTINA CHARLES.

Minister of Tourism and Legal Affairs: IAN DOUGLAS.

Minister of Information, Telecommunications and Constituency Empowerment: AMBROSE GEORGE.

Minister of Health: JULIUS TIMOTHY.

Minister of Public Works, Energy and Ports: RAYBURN BLACKMORE.

Minister of Carib Affairs: ASHTON GRANEAU.

Minister of State in the Ministry of Foreign Affairs: ALVIN BERNARD.

Parliamentary Secretary in the Office of the Prime Minister, responsible for Information Technology: KELVAR DARROUX.

Parliamentary Secretary in the Ministry of Public Works: JOHNSON DRIGO.

Parliamentary Secretary in the Ministry of Housing, Lands, Settlement and Water Resources: IVOR STEPHENSON.

MINISTRIES

Office of the President: Morne Bruce, Roseau; tel. 4482054; fax 4498366; e-mail presidentoffice@cwdom.dm; internet presidentoffice.gov.dm.

Office of the Prime Minister: 6th Floor, Financial Centre, Roseau; tel. 2663300; fax 4488960; e-mail opm@dominica.gov.dm; internet opm.gov.dm.

All other ministries are at Government Headquarters, Kennedy Ave, Roseau; tel. 4482401.

CARIB TERRITORY

This reserve of the remaining Amerindian population is located on the central east coast of the island. The Caribs enjoy a measure of local government and elect their chief. The last election was held in July 2014.

Chief: CHARLES WILLIAMS.

Waitukubuli Karifuna Development Committee (WAIKADA): Salybia, Carib Territory; tel. 4457336; e-mail waikada@cwdom.dm.

Legislature

HOUSE OF ASSEMBLY

Speaker: ALIX BOYD-KNIGHT.

Clerk: VERNANDA RAYMOND.

Senators: 9.

Elected Members: 21.

General Election, 18 December 2009

Party	% of votes	Seats
Dominica Labour Party (DLP) . . .	61.2	18
Dominica United Workers' Party (UWP)	34.9	3
Dominica Freedom Party (DFP) . .	2.4	—
Others	1.5	—
Total	100.0	21

Election Commission

Electoral Office: Commission's Bldg, Jewel St, Roseau; tel. 2663336; fax 4483399; e-mail electoraloffice@dominica.gov.dm; internet electoraloffice.gov.dm; Chair. GERALD D. BURTON; Chief Elections Officer STEVEN LA ROCQUE (acting).

Political Organizations

Dominica Freedom Party (DFP): 37 Great George St, Roseau; tel. 4482104; fax 4481795; e-mail freedompar2@yahoo.com; internet www.thedominicafreedomparty.com; f. 1968; Leader MICHAEL ASTAPHAN.

Dominica Labour Party (DLP): 18 Hanover St, Roseau; tel. 4488511; e-mail dlp@cwdom.dm; internet www .dominicalabourparty.com; f. 1985 as a merger and reunification of left-wing groups, incl. the Dominica Labour Party (f. 1961); Leader ROOSEVELT SKERRIT; Deputy Leader AMBROSE GEORGE.

Dominica United Workers' Party (UWP): 37 Cork St, POB 00152, Roseau; tel. 6134508; fax 4498448; e-mail secretariat@ uwpdm.com; internet www.uwpdm.com; f. 1988; Leader LENNOX LINTON.

People's Democratic Movement (PDM): 22 Upper Lane, POB 2248, Roseau; tel. 2354171; e-mail para@cwdom.dm; internet www .dapdm.org; f. 2006; Leader Dr WILLIAM E. 'PARA' RIVIERE.

Diplomatic Representation

EMBASSIES IN DOMINICA

China, People's Republic: Ceckhall, Morne Daniel, POB 2247, Roseau; tel. 4490080; fax 4400088; e-mail chinaemb_dm@mfa.gov .cn; internet dm.chineseembassy.org; Ambassador LI JIANGNING.

Cuba: Morne Daniel, Canefield, POB 1170, Roseau; tel. 4490727; e-mail cubanembassy@cwdom.dm; internet www.cubadiplomatica .cu/dominica; Ambassador JUANA ELENA RAMOS RODRÍGUEZ.

Venezuela: 20 Bath Rd, 3rd Floor, POB 770, Roseau; tel. 4483348; fax 4486198; e-mail embven@cwdom.dm; Ambassador HAYDEN OWANDO PIRELA SÁNCHEZ.

Judicial System

Justice is administered by the Eastern Caribbean Supreme Court (based in Saint Lucia), consisting of the Court of Appeal and the High Court. The final appellate court is the Privy Council in the United Kingdom, although in July 2014 the House of Assembly approved legislation allowing for the Caribbean Court of Justice, based in Trinidad and Tobago, to become the country's final court of appeal. Two of the High Court Judges are resident in Dominica and preside over the Court of Summary Jurisdiction. The District Magistrate Courts deal with summary offences and civil offences involving limited sums of money (specified by law).

High Court Judges: ERROL THOMAS, M. E. BIRNIE STEPHENSON-BROOKS.

Registrar: OSSIE WALSH (acting).

Attorney-General: LEVI PETER.

Religion

Most of the population profess Christianity, but there are some Muslims, Bahá'ís and Jews. The largest denomination is the Roman Catholic Church.

CHRISTIANITY

The Roman Catholic Church

Dominica comprises the single diocese of Roseau, suffragan to the archdiocese of Castries (Saint Lucia). According to official figures from 2001, 62% of the population are Roman Catholics. The Bishop participates in the Antilles Episcopal Conference (currently based in Port of Spain, Trinidad and Tobago).

Bishop of Roseau: Rt Rev. GABRIEL MALZAIRE, Bishop Arnold Boghaert Catholic Centre, Turkey Lane, POB 790, Roseau; tel. 4482837; fax 4483404; e-mail bishop@cwdom.dm; internet www .dioceseofroseau.org.

The Anglican Communion

Anglicans in Dominica, representing less than 1% of the population in 2001, are adherents of the Church in the Province of the West Indies. The country forms part of the diocese of the North Eastern Caribbean and Aruba. The Bishop is resident in Antigua and Barbuda, and the Archbishop of the Province is currently the Bishop of Barbados.

Other Christian Churches

According to official figures from 2001, 6% of the population are Seventh-day Adventists, 6% are Pentecostalists, 4% are Baptists and 4% are Methodists. In addition to the Christian Union Church, other denominations include Church of God, Presbyterian, the Assemblies of Brethren and Moravian groups, and the Jehovah's Witnesses.

BAHÁ'Í FAITH

Bahá'ís of the Commonwealth of Dominica: 79 Victoria St, POB 136, Roseau; tel. 4483881; fax 4488460; e-mail monargedom@gmail .com; internet barbadosbahais.org; Sec. MONA GEORGE-DILL.

The Press

The Chronicle: Wallhouse, Loubiere, POB 1764, Roseau; tel. 4487887; fax 4480047; e-mail thechronicle@cwdom.dm; f. 1909; Friday; progressive independent; Man. Dir MICHAEL JONES; circ. 4,500.

Official Gazette: Office of the Prime Minister, Financial Centre, 6th Floor, Kennedy Ave, Roseau; tel. 2363300; fax 4488960; e-mail cabsec@cwdom.dm; weekly; circ. 550.

The Sun: Sun Inc, 50 Independence St, POB 2255, Roseau; tel. 4484501; e-mail info@sundominica.com; internet sundominica.com; f. 1998; weekly; Editor CHARLES JAMES.

Publisher

Andrews Publishing Co Ltd: 25 Independence St, Roseau; tel. 2753196; e-mail dominicanewsonline@gmail.com; internet www .dominicanewsonline.com; publishes Dominica News Online; Man. Dir MERRICK ANDREWS.

Broadcasting and Communications

TELECOMMUNICATIONS

Digicel Dominica: Wireless Ventures (Dominica) Ltd, POB 2236, Roseau; tel. 6161500; fax 4403189; e-mail customercare.dominica@ digicelgroup.com; internet www.digiceldominica.com; acquired Cingular Wireless's Caribbean operations and licences in 2005; owned by an Irish consortium; acquired Orange Dominica in 2009; Chair. DENIS O'BRIEN; Country Man. RICHARD STANTON.

LIME: Hanover St, POB 6, Roseau; tel. 2551000; fax 2551111; internet www.lime.com; frmrly Cable & Wireless Dominica; name changed as above 2008; Group CEO TONY RICE; Eastern Caribbean CEO GERARD BORELY; Gen. Man. JEFFREY BAPTISTE.

Marpin 2K4: 5–7 Great Marlborough St, POB 2381, Roseau; tel. 5004107; fax 5002965; e-mail manager@mtb.dm; f. 1982, present name adopted in 1996; jtly owned by WRB Enterprises and the Dominica Social Security; commercial; cable telephone, television and internet services; Man. PERICSON ISIDORE.

SAT Telecommunications: 20 Bath Rd, St George, Roseau; tel. 4485095; fax 4484956; internet www.sat.dm; f. 1999; internet services provider; CEO and Man. Dir MARLON ALEXANDER.

Regulatory Authority

National Telecommunications Regulatory Commission of Dominica (NTRC Dominica): 42-2 Kennedy Ave, POB 649, Roseau; tel. 4400627; fax 4400835; e-mail secretariat@ntrcdm.org; internet www.ectel.int/ntrcdm; f. 2000 as the Dominican subsidiary of the Eastern Caribbean Telecommunications Authority (ECTEL)—established simultaneously in Castries, St Lucia, to regulate telecommunications in Dominica, Grenada, St Christopher and Nevis, St Lucia and St Vincent and the Grenadines; Chair. JULIAN JOHNSON; Exec. Dir CRAIG NESTY.

BROADCASTING

Radio

Dominica Broadcasting Corporation: Victoria St, POB 148, Roseau; tel. 4483283; fax 4482918; e-mail dbsmanager@dbcradio .net; internet www.dbcradio.net; f. 1971; govt station; daily broadcasts in English; 2 hrs daily in French patois; 10 kW transmitter on the medium wave band; FM service; programmes received worldwide through live streaming; Chair. AURELIUS JOLLY.

Kairi FM: 42 Independence St, POB 931, Roseau; tel. 4487331; fax 4487332; e-mail hello@kairifmonline.com; internet www.kairifm .com; f. 1994; CEO FRANKIE BELLOT; Gen. Man. STEVE VIDAL.

Voice of Life Radio (ZGBC): Gospel Broadcasting Corpn, Loubiere, POB 205, Roseau; tel. 4487017; fax 4400551; e-mail volradio@ cwdom.dm; internet www.voiceofliferadio.dm; f. 1975; 24 hrs daily FM; Gen. Man. CLEMENTINA MUNRO.

Television

There is no national television service, although there is a cable television network serving 95% of the island.

Finance

(cap. = capital; res = reserves; dep. = deposits; m. = million;
brs = branches; amounts in East Caribbean dollars)

The Eastern Caribbean Central Bank, based in Saint Christopher, is the central issuing and monetary authority for Dominica.

Eastern Caribbean Central Bank—Dominica Office: Financial Centre, 3rd Floor, Kennedy Ave, POB 23, Roseau; tel. 4488001; fax 4488002; e-mail eccbdom@cwdom.dm; internet www .eccb-centralbank.org; Country Dir EDMUND ROBINSON.

Financial Services Unit: Ministry of Finance, Kennedy Ave, Roseau; tel. 2663514; fax 4480054; e-mail fsu@cwdom.dm; regulatory authority for banks and insurance cos; Man. AL MONELLE.

BANKS

CIBC FirstCaribbean International Bank: Old St, POB 4, Roseau; tel. 2557900; fax 4483471; internet www.cibcfcib.com; f. 2002 following merger of Caribbean operations of Barclays Bank PLC and CIBC; Barclays relinquished its stake to CIBC in 2006, present name adopted in 2011; CEO RIK PARKHILL.

National Bank of Dominica: 64 Hillsborough St, POB 271, Roseau; tel. 2552300; fax 4483982; e-mail customersupport@nbd .dm; internet www.nbdominica.com; f. 1978 as the National Commercial Bank of Dominica; name changed as above following privatization in 2003; cap. 11.0m., res 16.4m., dep. 850m. (June 2013); 49% govt-owned; Chair. ANTHONY JOHN; Man. Dir LINDA TOUSSAINT PETER; 4 brs.

Scotiabank (Canada): 28 Hillsborough St, POB 520, Roseau; tel. 4485800; fax 2551300; e-mail bns.dominica@scotiabank.com; f. 1988; Country Man. JIM ALSTON; 1 br.

DEVELOPMENT BANK

Dominica Agricultural, Industrial and Development Bank (AID Bank): cnr Charles Ave and Rawles Lane, Goodwill, POB 215, Roseau; tel. 4484903; fax 4484903; e-mail aidbank@cwdom.dm; internet www.aidbank.com; f. 1971; responsible to Ministry of Finance; provides finance for the agriculture, tourism, housing, education and manufacturing sectors; total assets 125.3m. (June 2006); Chair. MARTIN CHARLES; Gen. Man. EMALINE HARRIS-CHARLES.

STOCK EXCHANGE

Eastern Caribbean Securities Exchange: Bird Rock, POB 94, Basseterre, Saint Christopher and Nevis; tel. (869) 466-7192; fax (869) 465-3798; e-mail info@ecseonline.com; internet www .ecseonline.com; f. 2001; regional securities market designed to facilitate the buying and selling of financial products for the eight member territories—Anguilla, Antigua and Barbuda, Dominica, Grenada, Montserrat, St Kitts and Nevis, St Lucia and St Vincent and the Grenadines; Chair. Sir K. DWIGHT VENNER; Gen. Man. TREVOR E. BLAKE.

INSURANCE

First Domestic Insurance Co Ltd: 19–21 King George V St, POB 1931, Roseau; tel. 4498202; fax 4485778; e-mail insurance@cwdom .dm; internet www.firstdomestic.dm; f. 1993; privately owned; Man. Dir and CEO CURTIS TONGE; Gen. Man. ROBERT TONGE.

Pan-American Life Insurance Co of the Eastern Caribbean: 16 Kennedy Ave, Roseau; tel. 448-5501; fax 448–5497; internet www .palig.com; f. 2012; part of Pan-American Life Insurance Group (USA); CEO and Man. Dir (Caribbean) WILLIAM R. SCHULZ, Jr; Agent JOAN OSCAR.

Windward Islands Crop Insurance Co (Wincrop): Vanoulst House, Goodwill, POB 469, Roseau; tel. 4483955; fax 4484197; f. 1987; regional; coverage for weather destruction of, mainly, banana crops; Man. HERNICA FERREIRA; brs in Grenada, St Lucia and St Vincent.

Trade and Industry

DEVELOPMENT ORGANIZATIONS

Invest Dominica Authority: Financial Centre, 1st Floor, Roseau; tel. 4482045; fax 4485840; e-mail info@investdominica.dm; internet www.investdominica.dm; f. 1988 as National Development Corpn (NDC) by merger of Industrial Development Corpn (f. 1974) and Tourist Board; NDC disbanded in 2007 by act of parliament and replaced by two separate entities, Invest Dominica and Discover Dominica Authority; promotes local and foreign investment to increase employment, production and exports; Chair. PAUL MOSES; Exec. Dir RHODA JOSEPH.

Organisation of the Eastern Caribbean States Export Development Unit (OECS–EDU): Financial Centre, 4th Floor, Kennedy Ave, POB 769, Roseau; tel. 4482240; fax 4485554; e-mail edu@oecs .org; internet www.oecs.org/edu; f. 1997 as Eastern Caribbean States Export Development Agency and Agricultural Diversification Coordination Unit; reformed as above in 2000; OECS Sub Regional Trade Promotion Agency; Head of Unit VINCENT PHILBERT.

INDUSTRIAL AND TRADE ASSOCIATIONS

Dominica Agricultural Producers and Exporters Ltd (DAPEX): Fond Cole Hwy, Fond Cole, POB 1620, Roseau; tel. 4482671; fax 4486445; e-mail dapex@cwdom.dm; f. 1934 as Dominica Banana Growers' Asscn; restructured 1984 as the Dominica Banana Marketing Corpn; renamed Dominica Banana Producers Ltd in 2003; present name adopted in 2010; privatized; Chair. LUKE PREVOST; Gen. Man. ERROL EMANUEL.

Dominica Association of Industry and Commerce (DAIC): 17 Castle St, POB 85, Roseau; tel. and fax 4491962; e-mail daic@cwdom .dm; internet www.daic.dm; f. 1972 by a merger of the Manufacturers' Asscn and the Chamber of Commerce; represents the business sector, liaises with the Govt, and stimulates commerce and industry; 30 mems; Pres. ROBERT TONGE.

Dominica Export-Import Agency (DEXIA): Bay Front, POB 173, Roseau; tel. 4482780; fax 4486308; e-mail info@dexia.dm; internet www.dexia.dm; f. 1986; replaced the Dominica Agricultural Marketing Board and the External Trade Bureau; exporter of Dominican agricultural products, trade facilitator and importer of bulk rice and sugar; Gen. Man. GREGOIRE THOMAS.

EMPLOYERS' ORGANIZATION

Dominica Employers' Federation: 14 Church St, POB 1783, Roseau; tel. 4482314; fax 4484474; e-mail def@cwdom.dm; f. 1966; Pres. BENOIT BARDOUILLE.

UTILITIES

Regulatory Body

Independent Regulatory Commission (IRC): 42 Cork St, POB 1687, Roseau; tel. 4406634; fax 4406635; e-mail admin@ircdominica .org; internet www.ircdominica.org; f. 2006 to oversee the electricity sector; Chair. BERNADETTE LAMBERT; Exec. Dir LANCELOT MCCASKEY.

Electricity

Dominica Electricity Services Ltd (Domlec): 18 Castle St, POB 1593, Roseau; tel. 2256000; fax 4485397; e-mail support@domlec.dm; internet www.domlec.dm; national electricity service; 52% owned by

Light & Power Holdings (Barbados), 21% owned by Dominica Social Security; Chair. ROBERT BLANCHARD, Jr; Gen. Man. COLLIN GROVER.

Water

Dominica Water and Sewerage Co Ltd (DOWASCO): POB 185, Roseau; tel. 4484811; fax 4485813; e-mail dowasco@dowasco.dm; internet www.dowasco.dm; state-owned; Chair. LARRY BARDOUILLE; Gen. Man. BERNARD ETTINOFFE.

TRADE UNIONS

Dominica Amalgamated Workers' Union (DAWU): 43 Hillsborough St, POB 137, Roseau; tel. 4482343; fax 4480086; e-mail wawuunion@hotmail.com; f. 1960; Gen. Sec. ELIAS LEAH SHILLINGFORD (acting); 500 mems (1996).

Dominica Association of Teachers: 7 Boyd's Ave, POB 341, Roseau; tel. and fax 4488177; e-mail dat@cwdom.dm; internet dateachers.org; f. 1990; Pres. CELIA NICHOLAS; Gen. Sec. ISABELLA PRENTICE; 670 mems (2012).

Dominica Public Service Union (DPSU): cnr Valley Rd and Windsor Lane, POB 182, Roseau; tel. 4482102; fax 4488060; e-mail dcs@cwdom.dm; internet dpsu.org; f. 1940; registered as a trade union in 1960; representing all grades of civil servants, including firemen, prison officers, nurses, teachers and postal workers; Pres. STEVE JOSEPH; Gen. Sec. THOMAS LETANG; 1,400 mems.

Dominica Trade Union: 70–71 Independence St, Roseau; tel. 4498139; fax 4499060; e-mail domtradun@hotmail.com; f. 1945; Pres. HAROLD SEALEY; Gen. Sec. LEO J. BERNARD NICHOLAS; 400 mems (1995).

National Workers' Union: 102 Independence St, POB 387, Roseau; tel. 4485209; fax 4481934; e-mail icss@cwdom.dm; f. 1977; Pres.-Gen. RAWLINS JEMMOTT; Gen. Sec. FRANKLIN FABIEN; 450 mems (1996).

Waterfront and Allied Workers' Union (WAWU): 43 Hillsborough St, POB 181, Roseau; tel. 4482343; fax 4480086; e-mail wawuunion@hotmail.com; f. 1965; Sec.-Treas. KERTISTE AUGUSTUS; 1,500 mems.

Transport

ROADS

In 2010 there were an estimated 1,512 km (940 miles) of roads. The West Coast Road Project, a 45.2 km highway linking Roseau and Portsmouth, estimated to cost some EC $100m. and partly financed by the Government of the People's Republic of China, was completed in 2012. There were also plans to improve the Wotten Waven Road, to be financed by the Caribbean Development Bank.

SHIPPING

A deep-water harbour at Woodbridge Bay serves Roseau, which is the principal port. Several foreign shipping lines call at Roseau, and there is a high-speed ferry service between Martinique and Guadeloupe, which calls at Roseau. A ferry service between Dominica and Guadeloupe, Martinique and Saint Lucia began operations in 2011. Ships of the Geest Line call at Prince Rupert's Bay, Portsmouth, to collect bananas, and there are also cruise ship facilities there. There are other specialized berthing facilities on the west coast. In December 2013 Dominica's flag registered fleet comprised 79 vessels, with an aggregate displacement of some 698,019 grt.

Dominica Air and Seaport Authority (DASPA): Woodbridge Bay, Fond Cole, POB 243, Roseau; tel. 4484131; fax 4486131; e-mail daspa@cwdom.dm; f. 1972; air transit, pilotage and cargo handling; Chair. DERMOT SOUTHWELL; Gen. Man. BENOIT BARDOUILLE.

CIVIL AVIATION

Melville Hall Airport, 64 km (40 miles) from Roseau, is the main airport on the island. The regional airline LIAT (based in Antigua and Barbuda, and in which Dominica is a shareholder) provides daily services and, together with Air Caraïbes, connects Dominica with all the islands of the Eastern Caribbean. Seaborne Airlines (based in the US Virgin Islands) began services from Puerto Rico to Melville Hall in 2013.

Tourism

The Government has designated areas of the island as nature reserves to preserve the beautiful, lush scenery and the rich, natural heritage that constitute Dominica's main tourist attractions. Bird life is particularly prolific, and includes several rare and endangered species, such as the imperial parrot. There are also two marine reserves. Tourism is not as developed as it is among Dominica's neighbours, but the country is being promoted as an eco-tourism and cruise destination. There were an estimated 354,189 visitors in 2012 (of whom 266,178 were cruise ship passengers). Efforts were also made to promote tourism to the Carib Territory. Receipts from tourism totalled an estimated EC $307.2m. in 2012.

Discover Dominica Authority: Financial Centre, 1st Floor, Roseau; tel. 4482045; fax 4485840; e-mail tourism@dominica.dm; internet www.discoverdominica.com; f. 1988 following merger of Tourist Board with Industrial Devt Corpn; CEO and Dir of Tourism COLIN PIPER.

Dominica Hotel and Tourism Association (DHTA): 17 Castle St, POB 384, Roseau; tel. 6161055; fax 4403433; e-mail dhta@cwdom.dm; internet www.dhta.org; Pres. RENEE WHITCHURCH AIRD-DOUGLAS (acting); Sec. DARYL AARON (acting); 98 mems.

Defence

The Dominican Defence Force was officially disbanded in 1982. There is a police force of about 325, which includes a coastguard service. The country participates in the US-sponsored Regional Security System.

Education

Education is free and is provided by both government and denominational schools. There are also a number of schools for the mentally and physically handicapped. Education is compulsory for 10 years between five and 15 years of age. Primary education begins at the age of five and lasts for seven years. Secondary education, beginning at 12 years of age, lasts for five years. In 2011/12, according to UNESCO estimates, a total of 6,093 pupils were enrolled at secondary schools in the relevant age-group. The Dominica State College is the main provider of higher education. There is also a branch of the University of the West Indies on the island. The Ross University School of Medicine has a campus at Picard for overseas medical students and there is also the All Saints University School of Medicine in the south of the island. The 2013/14 budget allocated EC $59.7m. to the Ministry of Education and Human Resource Development (equivalent to 16% of total recurrent expenditure).

Bibliography

For works on the Caribbean generally, see Select Bibliography (Books)

Baker, P. L. *Centring the Periphery: Chaos, Order and the Ethnohistory of Dominica*. Kingston, University of the West Indies Press, 1996.

Barriteau, E., and Cobley, A. (Eds). *Enjoying Power: Eugenia Charles and Political Leadership in the Commonwealth Caribbean*. Kingston, University of the West Indies Press, 2006.

Honychurch, L. *The Dominica Story: A History of the Island*. Oxford, Macmillan Caribbean, 1995.

Lestrade, S. (Ed.). *Continuing the Journey: Dominica's Development Challenges and Responses Going Forward*. Charlston, SC, BookSurge Publishing, 2010.

Paravisini-Gebert, L. *Phyllis Shand Allfrey: A Caribbean Life*. Piscataway, NJ, Rutgers University Press, 1996.

THE DOMINICAN REPUBLIC

Geography

PHYSICAL FEATURES

The Dominican Republic comprises almost two-thirds of the island of Hispaniola (Isla Española) in the Greater Antilles. It lies at the eastern end of the island, with Haiti to the west of the land border that runs for 360 km (224 miles), from north to south, across the widest part of Hispaniola. The next nearest neighbours are Puerto Rico, a US Commonwealth territory 120 km to the east (across the Mona Passage), and the Turks and Caicos Islands, a British territory 145 km to the north. The country has 1,288 km of coastline and a total area of 48,734 sq km (18,816 sq miles), including 597 sq km of inland waters. Although less than one-half the size of Cuba, the Dominican Republic is the second largest country of the insular Caribbean and about the same size as Costa Rica.

The Dominican Republic occupies that part of Hispaniola that tapers eastwards—in the south, this is from the Pedernales peninsula, which is just east of the border with Haiti and thrusts southwards to culminate in Cabo Beata. Like Haiti, the Dominican Republic is very rugged and mountainous (80%), but, unlike its neighbour, its hillsides have not been denuded of woodland. The highlands are cleft by fertile valleys, many of them broad, and there is one fairly extensive range of coastal plain, named for the capital, Santo Domingo, narrow to the west of the city, but broad and running to the end of the island in the east. The northern boundary of this plain is the range of hills called the Cordillera Oriental, which parallels the Atlantic coast, like the higher, north-western range, the Cordillera Septentrional. The highest mountains of the island and, indeed, of the West Indies are found in the Cordillera Central, where rise Pico Duarte (3,175 m or 10,420 ft) and its near twin, La Pelona. The Cordillera Central occupies the centre of the island, running eastwards out of the Massif du Nord in Haiti and eventually curving southwards to the Caribbean. A mere 85 km to the south-west of Pico Duarte is the lowest point in the Caribbean, where, 46 m below sea level, is the bitter lake, the 200-sq km Lago Enriquillo, in hot, arid surroundings between the rocky dryness of the remaining two mountain ranges, the Sierra de Neiba and, to the south of Enriquillo, the Sierra de Baharuco (a continuation of the Massif du Selle, in Haiti). The high, forested mountains of the Dominican Republic attract good rainfall, though the Cordillera Central tends to shadow the south-west of the country, but there are also some important rivers. The longest river of the Dominican Republic, watering the Ceiba Valley, is the north-westward-flowing Yaque del Norte, which exits into the sea near the border with Haiti. Other major rivers are the westward-flowing Yuna, the southward-flowing Yaque del Sur and, running into Haiti, the Artibonite. The main offshore islands, which are not significant in territorial extent, are Saona (south of the southeastern end of the island) and the uninhabited Beata (off Cabo Beata). To the west of each is a smaller island, Catalina and Alto Velo, respectively. There are also three lacustrine islands in Enriquillo and some sandy cays off the northern coast. The range of the terrain and weather conditions makes for a wide variety of environments, ranging from the arid tropical forests of the west, for instance, to the pine woodland of the highlands. Native mammals are few and endangered, notably the hutia (*jutía*), a small rodent, the solenodon, an insectivore, and the manatee or sea cow. Birds are more numerous and include the endemic Hispaniolan woodpecker. There is a variety of parrots, parakeets and hummingbirds.

CLIMATE

The climate is subtropical maritime, experiencing little seasonal variation in temperature and with exposure to hurricanes for some months from the middle of the year, but particularly in September. The Dominican Republic suffers occasional flooding and more regular droughts, but generally

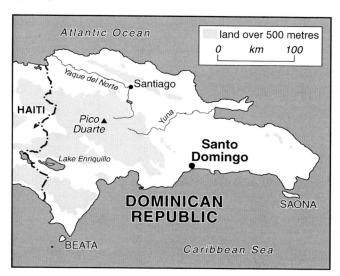

has good rainfall, although it is very affected by the geography of the island. Rainfall is greater with altitude and with exposure to the north-eastern trade winds off the Atlantic, so the Cordillera Septentrional can receive more than 2,500 mm (98 ins) per year, on average, but the valleys between ranges can be much drier. The average annual temperature is about 25°C (77°F), with little seasonal variation, but, again, altitude has a major influence (below-freezing temperatures have been recorded atop Pico Duarte) and the north can be noticeably cooler under the influence of weather fronts coming out of the north.

POPULATION

Santo Domingo was the first Spanish capital in the Americas and the centre of early colonial expansion. African slaves began to arrive in the city in the 1520s, to replace the disappearing Amerindian population as labour. The proportion of black slaves in what is now called the Dominican Republic was never as high as in the French part of Hispaniola (Saint-Domingue, now Haiti); however, they still constituted an important part of the population and were later the object of 'liberating' incursions by their free western neighbours. The majority of the population is mixed race (65%), although social conditions have ensured that colour has remained an important issue into the present, with a complex vocabulary for skin colour and ethnic identity evolving. Whites and blacks each account for about 15% of the population now, because, although many of the descendants of the original Spanish settlers fled at the time of independence amid fears of Haitian aggression, the ruling class considered it important to encourage new white immigration. Thus, groups of settlers from the Canary Islands (Spain) and Italy settled in the country, although there were also Syrians (known locally as Turcos), who came to establish businesses, and sugar plantation workers from the anglophone Virgin and Leeward Islands (known as Cocolos). However, Spanish is the official language and the population remains overwhelmingly Roman Catholic, at least in nominal adherence. African traditions are also practised, usually in parallel to more orthodox ecclesiastical practice. There is also an element of reconstructed *Taíno* (Amerindian) belief systems (the perceived legitimacy of which can also be observed in racial claims), all of which contribute to the local voodoo (*vodú dominicana*).

The total population of the Dominican Republic, according to official projections, was 10.4m. in mid-2014. Social conditions are marked by income inequality and the fact that 30% of the population is under 15 years of age. There is a large immigrant Haitian population, most of whom have entered the country for work and often illegally. The capital and largest city, Santo Domingo (with a population of 2.8m. at the 2010 census), which is located midway along the southern coast, is constituted as a special National District (Distrito Nacional), in addition to the 31 provinces into which the country is divided. The second city of the republic is Santiago de los Caballeros (691,262 in 2010), in the north-west, in the fertile and productive Ceiba Valley.

History

DAVID HOWARD

Revised for this edition by the editorial staff

The original inhabitants of the island on which Christopher Columbus landed in 1492 were the indigenous Tainos. They called their land Quisqueya, but, in honour of the Spanish monarchs who sponsored his voyage, Columbus named it La Isla Española (Hispaniola). The Taino population, estimated to number 500,000 in 1492, was drastically reduced by disease and the brutal treatment administered by the Spanish. By the mid-16th century the genocide was effectively complete and, in need of an alternative source of labour, the colonists established the transatlantic system of slavery, relying on the trade of enslaved labourers from West Africa.

The first Spanish settlements were founded on the north coast, but as the colonists spread out in search of gold, they soon discovered the fertile plains in the centre of the country, an area known as the Cibao. A capital, Santo Domingo, was established on the south coast, and developed into the first European-style city in Latin America. With gold discoveries proving disappointingly small, Spanish colonial attentions turned instead to Mexico and Peru. Although the city of Santo Domingo remained an important staging post between Europe and the mainland of Central and South America, within a few decades of its establishment, the colony itself was receiving little attention.

During the 17th century European adventurers, many of French origin, began to settle and cultivate the coastal plains of the largely abandoned western part of the island. In 1697 Spain ceded these lands to France, and the French colony of Saint-Domingue quickly developed into a prosperous sugar-exporting slave economy, overshadowing its neighbour. The Spanish colony, Santo Domingo, as it was known, remained sparsely populated. The slave revolt that began in French Saint-Domingue in August 1791 initiated a chaotic and violent period, during which Spanish, French and British armies, and rebellious slaves, fought for control of the island. In 1795 Spain surrendered control of its colony to France, and then, between 1801 and 1803, Toussaint Louverture, leader of the slave insurrection, took control of the whole island. In 1803 the French regained control of Santo Domingo, but the same year suffered a final defeat in the west. Saint-Domingue became the independent black republic of Haiti in early 1804. Five years later the French abandoned their interest in the island, and Santo Domingo was handed back to Spain. In 1822 Haiti occupied its eastern neighbour, remaining until the declaration of Dominican independence in 1844. The new Dominican Republic was, however, plagued by political strife and violence, and in 1861 Spain granted a request to recolonize. This remarkable move proved a dismal failure, and after a 'War of Restoration' between Dominican nationalists and Spanish sympathizers, independence was regained in 1865.

The late 19th and early 20th centuries were periods of political and economic instability, broken only by the dictatorship of Ulises Heureaux (1882–99), and the 1916–24 occupation by the USA. During the late 1920s the head of the Dominican Army, Rafael Leonidas Trujillo Molina, established political control, and in May 1930 was elected President.

Trujillo's rule quickly developed into a dictatorship that was to last until 1961. Holding power direct as President or via 'puppet' leaders, Trujillo used coercion, bribery and blackmail to ensure the loyalty of his supporters, and torture and murder to repress his opponents. The regime was propped up by an ideology that endlessly stressed the nation's Hispanic, Catholic and white roots, and portrayed neighbouring Haiti and its people as a primitive, black, African threat. In 1937 a notorious episode in Trujillo's nation-building campaign saw the deployment of the Dominican armed forces into the previously barely governed regions near the border with Haiti, and the massacre of over 20,000 black people suspected of being Haitians.

Over time, the dictator and his family came to control 80% of the country's industrial production, including two-thirds of a booming sugar industry. Administrations in the USA viewed Trujillo with a mixture of admiration and distrust, but generally tolerated a regime that came to be regarded as an ally. However, following the 1959 Cuban revolution, US strategists decided that the dictator's excesses were making the country vulnerable to a Communist takeover. The traditional Dominican oligarchy had grown increasingly resentful of the Trujillo family's monopoly of economic and political power, and in May 1961 a group of middle-class Dominicans, acting with US intelligence support, had Trujillo assassinated.

Elections were held in December 1962, and Juan Bosch Gaviño, leader of the social democratic Partido Revolucionario Dominicano (PRD—Dominican Revolutionary Party), promising land reform and job creation, won an overwhelming victory and was inaugurated in February 1963. However, Bosch achieved little, and after only seven months was overthrown by a military coup. The military appointed a civilian junta, but it failed to establish any form of stability, and in 1965 armed conflict broke out between supporters and opponents of the exiled Bosch. In April, using the pretext of a looming Communist takeover, the USA deployed a large force of marines to side with the anti-Bosch faction. The Organization of American States (OAS) oversaw the establishment of a provisional Government, and new elections were held in June 1966. In the months preceding the deeply flawed elections, hundreds of PRD supporters were assassinated, and a strong military presence at polling stations ensured an easy victory for Joaquín Balaguer, leader of the Partido Reformista (PR—Reformist Party), the candidate favoured by the USA and the Dominican élite.

Balaguer established an authoritarian regime that carried out a brutal campaign of repression against PRD activists. As a result, the main opposition party boycotted elections in 1970 and 1974, handing Balaguer two further victories. The opposition's disarray deepened in 1973 when Bosch resigned from the PRD and formed his own new party, the Partido de la Liberación Dominicana (PLD—Party of Dominican Liberation). For three consecutive terms, Balaguer opened the country to foreign investment and enjoyed significant development assistance from the USA. A period of economic prosperity saw diversification into tourism and industrial free trade zones.

Pressure from the USA prompted a much more open electoral contest in 1978, and the PRD's Silvestre Antonio Guzmán Fernández was elected President. Guzmán's Government had some success with its efforts to weaken the armed forces' influence by dismantling the officer hierarchy that had supported Trujillo and Balaguer, but it failed either to deliver the benefits expected by its supporters or efficiently to manage the economy. Despite its failings, the PRD won a second term in 1982, with its leader Salvador Jorge Blanco defeating the challenge of Balaguer, who had merged his party with the Partido Revolucionario Social Cristiano (Social Christian

Revolutionary Party) to form the Partido Reformista Social Cristiano (PRSC—Reformist Social Christian Party). However, the new Government proved even more corrupt and incompetent than its predecessor. When an economic crisis prompted the application of austerity measures in 1984, popular protests against the Government degenerated into riots and military repression. With the left wing of the PRD fiercely criticizing the Government, elections held in May 1986 were won again by the PRSC.

The second period of Balaguer government was one of instability and contestation. Economic problems fuelled increasing conflict between the authorities and a growing popular movement for social and political change. During 1988 a wave of strikes and anti-Government protests were met with fierce repression by the police and military. Balaguer was able to win yet another election in 1990 only because the opposition vote, although a majority, was divided between José Francisco Peña Gómez's PRD and Bosch's PLD.

The economy continued to falter, and in 1991 Balaguer was obliged to negotiate a new anti-inflationary austerity agreement with the IMF. Price controls and reductions in government expenditure led to more strikes and public protests. The 1994 elections saw Balaguer again facing the challenge of the PRD's Peña Gómez. The election campaign was dominated by racist slurs against Peña Gómez, with suggestions that his alleged Haitian ancestry made him unfit to govern. Amid allegations of widespread fraud, Balaguer was adjudged to have won a very narrow victory. In the face of deep popular discontent over what many felt was a stolen victory, Balaguer reached agreement with the PRD to limit his term of office to 18 months (later extended to two years) and to prohibit future Presidents from seeking consecutive terms in office.

The next presidential election was held in May 1996, and for the first time in three decades, Balaguer was not a candidate. His influence on the outcome was, none the less, profound, as he refused to support the PRSC's candidate, who polled just 15% of the votes, and instead courted the PLD. None of the candidates achieved the 50% or more votes required for an outright victory according to a new voting system, and the two leading candidates, the PRD's Peña Gómez and the PLD's Leonel Fernández Reyna, entered a second round contest. A remarkable political alliance between lifetime foes, Balaguer and Bosch, resulted in PRSC and PLD supporters uniting in support of Fernández, ensuring his victory over Peña Gómez.

There were high expectations that the 43-year-old, US-educated Fernández would bring an end to the dominance of vested political and economic interests. However, his party, the PLD, was barely represented in the legislature, the Congreso Nacional (Congress), and the new President struggled to gain approval for intended reforms. Legislative elections in 1998 improved the PLD's position in the Congress, but the party remained well short of a majority. The PRD's grip on the legislature allowed it to obstruct Fernández's initiatives. Stymied at home, Fernández focused on building up the country's links in the region, travelling extensively on diplomatic visits, and in 1998 negotiating free trade agreements with the Central American republics and the Caribbean Community and Common Market (CARICOM).

By the 2000 presidential election there had been a rapprochement between Balaguer and his party, and the veteran politician stood as the PRSC candidate, while the PLD, unable to field the incumbent, Fernández, nominated Danilo Medina Sánchez as its nominee. The PRD's long-serving leader, Peña Gómez, had died in 1998, and its candidate was Rafael Hipólito Mejía Domínguez. Mejía won 49.9% of the vote, against Medina's 24.9% and Balaguer's 24.6%. After Medina conceded defeat, the election commission, the Junta Central Electoral, awarded victory to Mejía, even though he had just failed to secure more than one-half of the votes cast.

The Mejía presidency proved immensely controversial. Public discontent grew rapidly as the country plunged into an economic crisis from 2002. Prices increased exponentially, salaries stagnated and jobs were lost. Persistent power cuts provoked public protests that frequently degenerated into violent clashes with the security services.

The Mejía administration responded by tightening monetary policy and implementing austerity measures, but only

succeeded in pushing the economy into recession. The Government's standing fell further in April 2003 when it was forced to take over the country's second largest commercial bank, Banco Intercontinental (Baninter), after it collapsed because of widespread fraud. The Baninter rescue provoked public outrage when it was revealed that many leading politicians in previous administrations, including Mejía (a former Minister of Agriculture), had received illicit payments.

In foreign policy, Mejía was more successful, developing good relations with the US Administration of President George W. Bush by supporting US policy, in particular by contributing Dominican troops to the US-led international force that invaded Iraq in 2003. In 2004 the President also negotiated the inclusion of the Dominican Republic in a planned Central American Free Trade Agreement (which became known as CAFTA-DR) with the USA.

During the latter half of 2003 rising prices and the effects of further austerity measures led to a series of violent protests across the country. Clashes between protesters and police resulted in a number of deaths and hundreds of injuries. Anti-Government feeling increased when energy generators cut electricity supplies after the Government and distributors failed to pay their debts, and Mejía deployed the military to suppress efforts to mount a general strike.

In 2002 a constitutional amendment had been adopted allowing a President to serve two consecutive terms, and in early 2003 Mejía announced he would seek the PRD's candidacy for the 2004 presidential election. His re-election bid was not only unpopular with the public, but also met fierce opposition from within his own party.

In the months preceding the election Mejía attempted to recoup some of his lost support among the public by spending heavily on public works projects. Further street protests and anti-Government strikes indicated that this largesse failed to change public perceptions, and this was confirmed by the election result. The PLD's Fernández won an outright victory in the first round, held on 16 May 2004, polling 57.1% of the vote against Mejía's 33.7%. The PRSC's Rafael Eduardo Estrella Virella polled just 8.7%, a disastrous result for a party that had dominated Dominican politics for decades under Balaguer.

On taking office in August 2004, Fernández immediately fulfilled a campaign promise to reduce the size of the armed forces. In a move designed to break the close ties that existed between his predecessor and the senior officer corps, 130 generals were given early retirement. Fernández was more hesitant about taking action on another pre-election pledge, combating government corruption, and caused controversy by selecting a number of officials for his new administration who had allegedly been involved in dubious dealings during his first presidency. Nor did he authorize judicial investigations into officials from the Mejía administration widely believed to have engaged in corruption. The reluctance to pursue PRD leaders was a tacit recognition of that party's strong position in the Congress, and the need to avoid open conflict with it if his Government were to advance its planned legislation. In the Senado (Senate) the PRD held an overwhelming majority, with 29 of the 32 seats, while Fernández's PLD held only one. In the lower house, the Cámara de Diputados (Chamber of Deputies), the PLD was better placed, with 42 seats, but still lagged far behind the PRD, which held 72 of the 150 seats. A major priority for the new Government was securing congressional approval for CAFTA-DR. The Agreement had been brokered by the Mejía administration, but was strongly supported by the new administration. It was ratified by the Congress in September 2005, but final implementation did not begin until March 2007.

The new Government struggled to resolve a number of issues that had undermined its predecessor. A crime wave, variously attributed to the economic crisis, the influence of drugs-traffickers and the impact of criminal deportees from the USA, continued to rage during the first year of Fernández's second presidency. Impeded by a weak and often corrupt police force, the authorities finally took decisive action in July 2005 when large numbers of police officers were deployed in marginalized neighbourhoods in Santo Domingo and the second largest city, Santiago. Criminal activity declined in these areas, but increased in previously relatively safe middle-class residential areas.

Fernández also faced difficulties in trying to overcome the country's chronic electricity crisis. In mid-2006 a heat wave prompted increased demand for electricity for air-conditioning and refrigeration, and the country was once again beset by power cuts lasting between eight and 16 hours a day. With energy generation heavily dependent on oil imports, soaring prices in 2006 created further problems. The electricity sector remained one of the economy's key structural weaknesses. The new Government had more success with other aspects of the economy, making significant advances to counter the mismanagement and overspending of the Mejía presidency. An austerity budget was accepted by the Congress, and at the beginning of 2005 negotiations with the IMF produced a crucial stand-by agreement, opening the way for additional multilateral disbursements.

The steps taken by the administration restored confidence in the economy and produced a strong recovery from the crisis of 2003–04. Public approval of this performance was reflected by the results of the legislative elections held in May 2006. Fernández's party, the PLD, won a major victory, securing comfortable working majorities in both chambers. In the months preceding the elections there had been speculation that a tentative electoral alliance between the main opposition parties, the PRD and the PRSC, would prevail. In response, the PLD had concluded a tactical alliance with a group of small parties, including the right-wing nationalist Fuerza Nacional Progresista (FNP), a move that showed how far the PLD had departed from its leftist origins.

Relations with Haiti became increasingly strained from 2006 as the neighbouring country's dire economic situation continued to prompt large numbers of Haitians to cross the border in search of a livelihood. Although Dominican employers were content to hire Haitian labour when necessary, the influx of Haitians was regarded by right-wing Dominicans as a threat that would fundamentally alter the country's ethnic composition. With the FNP stoking anti-Haitian prejudice, there were numerous incidents of violence against Haitians in the border regions, and the Dominican Army was repeatedly deployed to arrest and deport Haitian immigrants; nearly 20,000 Haitians were deported in 2006 and a further 17,000 in 2007. During 2008 poverty in Haiti was exacerbated by a series of natural disasters and continuing economic woes. At the same time, there was increased hardship in the Dominican Republic, prompting increased tensions around the perennially thorny issue of illegal Haitian immigrants.

In the months leading up to the May 2008 presidential election the Government faced a number of difficulties, including a series of corruption scandals and continuing labour unrest. However, despite these problems, Fernández's personal charisma and his success in restoring economic stability allowed him to retain his popularity. The main opposition candidate, the PRD's Miguel Vargas Maldonado, failed to dispel public perception that he had a strong connection to former President Mejía, for whom he served as Secretary of State for Public Works and Communications. Many Dominicans appeared to regard the Mejía Government as more corrupt than its successor, and remained distrustful of a party that had led the country into a financial crisis and profound economic instability in 2003–04. Heavy state spending, including increased subsidies and increases in the state payroll, and major public works such as the hastily completed Santo Domingo metro, shored up Fernández's election bid. In the first round, held on 16 May 2008, he secured an outright victory, with 53.8% of the valid votes cast against Vargas' 40.5%.

Fernández was inaugurated for his second consecutive term in August 2008. Public criticism of the new Government grew during 2009, with education, health and crime the prime areas of concern. During the year the Government's inability to provide regular electricity, an adequate water supply, and security against crime sparked increasing public anger. These omissions, in tandem with a failure to execute necessary infrastructural projects at the municipal level, provoked daily demonstrations in several cities.

In October 2009 the Chamber of Deputies adopted amendments to more than 40 articles of the Constitution, despite public protests and criticism from civil society groups that opposed the more socially conservative provisions. The reforms stipulated a complete ban on abortion and defined marriage as being solely between a man and a woman. An unlimited number of non-consecutive presidential terms was to be permitted, thus allowing Fernández to contest the presidency again in 2016, following a term out of office. Among other provisions, administrative corruption of public officials was made a constitutional offence, while trade unionism, strikes, public education, and swift justice with the presumption of innocence were established as constitutional rights. The revised Constitution came into force on 26 January 2010.

An earthquake with a magnitude of 7.0 devastated Haiti in January 2010, killing more than 200,000 people. In response, the Dominican Government waived visa restrictions for Haitians seeking emergency medical care, authorized nearly 300 flights carrying aid, donated US $11m., and despatched more than 100 soldiers to aid UN forces in stabilizing the country. The economic dislocation and subsequent worsening of social conditions caused by the earthquake prompted further emigration from Haiti into the Dominican Republic. Although cordial and outwardly supportive relations were maintained at the intergovernmental level, the influx of Haitian immigrants was popularly perceived to have placed additional stresses on local communities, particularly in terms of the provision of basic health care.

The PLD achieved a decisive victory in legislative and municipal elections conducted on 16 May 2010, securing 31 of the Senate's 32 seats and 105 of the 183 seats in the enlarged Chamber of Deputies. The PRSC, which had formed an alliance with the PLD, took the remaining seat in the upper chamber and three seats in the lower chamber, where the PRD won 75 seats. The PLD also secured control of 92 of the 155 municipalities (20 more than in the 2006 elections). Turnout was low, at 56.4%, while polling was also marred by violence, in which five people were reportedly killed, and opposition accusations of voting irregularities and misuse of state funds by the PLD. The PLD's strong performance was attributed to signs of recovery in the economy and the popularity of social welfare programmes introduced by Fernández, as well as the failure of the divided PRD to present itself as a viable alternative. Under the amended Constitution, the newly elected legislators, mayors and councillors were to serve an exceptional term of six years (rather than four) to enable legislative, municipal and presidential elections to be held concurrently from 2016.

The political scene in 2010 and 2011 was dominated by speculation concerning the possibility that Fernández would hold a referendum on amending the Constitution to allow him to run for a consecutive term in the presidential election due in May 2012. In October 2010 24 of the 32 senators published a letter pledging their support should he decide to run. After hinting on several occasions that he wanted to seek re-election, eventually, in April 2011, he abandoned this plan. The move averted a threat to political stability, as there had been widespread opposition to the idea of Fernández perpetuating himself in power. However, concerns that Fernández hoped to maintain his influence after his term ended did not evaporate completely because the President backed his wife, Margarita Cedeño, as a candidate for the party's presidential nomination.

The candidate finally elected to represent the PLD in the presidential election in May 2012 was Danilo Medina Sánchez, with Cedeño as the vice-presidential candidate. They were victorious after a vigorously contested election against former President Mejía, who had previously defeated the PRD leader Vargas in a poll to secure the party's presidential nomination. Popular dissatisfaction with the Fernández Government, due to rising crime and corruption, and to high levels of unemployment, inequality and poverty despite rapid economic growth, caused the poll to be closely contested. Medina won 51.2% of the votes in the first round of the presidential election on 20 May, with Mejía receiving 47.0%, thus avoiding the necessity of a second ballot.

Under the amended Constitution of 2010, the presidential poll incorporated the election of Overseas Deputies for the first time, with Dominican expatriates contesting seven new seats in the Chamber of Deputies. The 300,000 eligible Dominican expatriates constituted 5% of the electorate, one-third of whom were living in the US state of New York, and who provided key additional votes for the PLD. Medina's term of office began in August 2012, with the PLD holding the majority of seats in both the Senate (31 of the total 32) and the Chamber of Deputies (108 of 190). Despite commanding control of the two chambers, Medina faced ongoing popular concerns about the rising levels of unemployment and poverty. The beginning of 2013 was marked by uncertainty and conflict between the Government and Barrick Gold Corporation, the Canadian mining alliance that operated one of the world's largest gold-mining projects at Pueblo Viejo in the centre of the country. The Government sought to renegotiate the terms of operation, raising the threat of additional taxes on the mine's profits. An agreement was reached in May that would increase the state's share of benefits from the Pueblo Viejo gold mine by an estimated US $1,500m. over the lifetime of the mine.

Although this was a significant victory, the Government's ongoing discussions with the IMF over renewal of the stand-by agreement continued to shadow its economic plans. Medina, however, made a robust start to addressing fiscal reform, which was welcomed by the IMF. While IMF negotiations were ongoing, the Government's economic strategy in 2013–14 would largely follow that laid out in the country's National Development Plan 2010–30, with the President stating his specific commitment to raising tax revenues, improving education and increasing electricity production. The Government committed to fulfilling a constitutional mandate to raise education spending to the equivalent of 4% of gross domestic product. The PLD administration also reaffirmed a campaign pledge to end illiteracy. The lack of a regular electricity supply for most Dominicans and the ineffective implementation of privatized production and supply during the last decade remained a central concern, and perhaps the most significant obstacle facing Medina in terms of securing wider popular electoral support in 2016.

In an attempt to improve the security situation, in early 2013 the Government announced that the police force, which had frequently been accused of corruption and human rights abuses, would be restructured. A number of senior officers were replaced during that year, but by mid-2014 the Government had made no substantive progress with regard to its broader objective of effecting a major structural reorganization of the police service. Meanwhile, in a controversial move, soldiers were deployed in mid-2013 to assist the police in their patrols.

The Constitutional Court generated considerable controversy in September 2013, when it ruled that children born in the Dominican Republic to undocumented migrants before 2010 were not eligible to attain Dominican citizenship. Although this premise had been enshrined in the 2010 Constitution, it had been widely assumed that it would not be applied retroactively. Consequently, many thousands of ethnic Haitians residing in the Dominican Republic were effectively rendered 'stateless'. The Court's ruling was censured by, *inter alia*, the Office of the United Nations High Commissioner for Human Rights, the OAS Inter-American Commission on Human Rights, CARICOM and the Organisation of Eastern Caribbean States. In spite of this negative international attention, the Dominican Government declared that it would abide by the Court's judgment. Under increasing regional pressure, however, the Dominican Republic entered into negotiations with Haiti in November 2013 in an attempt to resolve the crisis. Following further bilateral discussions, in May 2014 the Congress adopted legislation to normalize the immigration status of the relatively small number of residents affected by the September 2013 ruling who could prove that they had been born in the Dominican Republic. The Haitian Government responded positively to this development, although human rights organizations continued to demand a more comprehensive solution. A regularization programme for undocumented migrants was implemented in June 2014 in conjunction with the new immigration law, but the precise scope of this initiative was unclear.

The PRD, which had been beset by often violent factional infighting since Mejía's electoral defeat in 2012, was confronted with a new crisis in July 2014, when Mejía's faction revealed that it intended to form a new party, the Partido Revolucionario Mayoritario. Also in that month, the PRSC announced that it was terminating its alliance with the ruling PLD owing to concerns about the potential erosion of its political independence.

Economy

DAVID HOWARD

Revised for this edition by the editorial staff

As a Spanish colony until the mid-19th century, the economy of the Dominican Republic had languished, and cattle-rearing was the most important economic activity. Following independence, the growth of a sugar cane industry helped to improve economic performance, but, despite a diversification into coffee and tobacco production, it contracted again in the early part of the 20th century. In the late 1960s and 1970s there was a period of economic expansion driven by international loans, high sugar prices on the world market, and President Joaquín Balaguer's extravagant public works programmes. During the 1980s loans ceased, and the economy struggled under the burdens of trade and budget deficits and heavy debts. Free trade zone manufacturing, tourism and services overtook agriculture as the dominant sectors of the economy.

Economic growth in the early 1990s was erratic, reflecting bouts of government austerity policies, varying trends in the manufacturing-for-export free zone, construction and tourism sectors, as well as problems with the country's electricity supply. The economy grew in the late 1990s, based on increased activity in the tourism, construction, energy and manufacturing sectors. By 2003 though there was negative growth, reflecting the Government of Rafael Mejía's mismanagement and corruption, and lower US demand for Dominican manufactured goods.

The macroeconomic situation showed dramatic improvements following the election of Leonel Fernández: inflation fell sharply, and the Fernández administration successfully renegotiated debt repayments with the international community. Fiscal and financial targets of a stand-by agreement with the IMF were met, and in 2005 real gross domestic product (GDP) growth of 9.3% was recorded. In 2006 GDP grew by 10.7%, as a strong rise in US demand supported the recovery from the 2003–04 crisis. In subsequent years, however, real GDP growth slowed, and had fallen to 3.5% by 2009, partly as a consequence of the increase in international competition arising from trade liberalization under the Dominican Republic-Central American Free Trade Agreement (CAFTA-DR), which came into force in 2007. The GDP growth rate was also negatively affected by the reduced performance of the export-oriented sectors of the economy, notably mining and free trade zone manufacturing, both of which suffered the effects of the global downturn. Average growth, however, has remained at almost 4% per year since 2000, revealing a significant level of macroeconomic and political stability.

In November 2009 the IMF approved a 28-month stand-by arrangement, worth approximately US $1,700m., to support the Government's strategy to stabilize the economy. There was a positive impact on real GDP, which rose by 7.8% in 2010.

There was growth in all sectors, particularly construction, financial services and commerce, which were boosted by low interest rates and high consumer demand. (The stand-by arrangement expired in March 2012 and had not been renewed by mid-2014.) Since taking office in August 2012, President Danilo Medina Sánchez has endorsed austerity and fiscal reform measures. Tax reforms introduced in late 2012 raised value-added tax from 16% to 18%, and increased duties on cigarettes and alcohol. While not receiving popular support, these measures were welcomed by the IMF.

In the early years of the 21st century the population grew at around 1.5% per year. It numbered 10.4m. in 2014, according to official projections. The population density of 213.0 per sq km was one of the lowest in the Caribbean region. The composition of the Dominican labour force has undergone a profound shift over the last 50 years. In 1960 the agricultural sector employed 73% of the labour force; by the end of the 1980s it accounted for 35%, and in October 2013 the figure was just 14%. According to official estimates, the number of Dominicans in employment totalled 4,051,800 in October 2013. A 2013 report by the International Labour Organization and the IMF noted the ongoing 'Dominican paradox' of relatively high economic growth in the regional context, allied with declining real wages, persistent poverty and dependence on the informal economy. The report further raised concerns about the limited creation of skilled, formal employment. The World Bank noted the poor level of public service delivery in the country and the ongoing reliance of the Dominican middle classes on private education, health and electricity provision, underpinned by a low supply of service and lack of trust in state institutions. In October 2013 27.1% of employed workers were engaged in the commerce and the hotel and catering sectors, while 9.9% of the employed labour force worked in manufacturing, 5.9% in the construction industry and 0.3% in mining. The successful completion of tense negotiations with the Barrick Gold Corporation in 2013 over the Government's share of profits from the Pueblo Viejo gold mine was expected to generate an additional US $1,500m. for the state's coffers.

Some 7.8% of those employed in October 2013 worked in transport and communications, with a further 2.6% in the finance and real estate sector. According to the central bank, the unemployment rate stood at an estimated 15.0% in 2013, although this was notably higher among 15–24-year-olds. Approximately 55.9% of the employed labour force worked in the informal sector in that year. The World Bank indicated that, while the macroeconomic context and outlook for the Dominican Republic remained satisfactory, the problems of unemployment and increasing rates of poverty left many Dominicans increasingly vulnerable to the social and health effects of low incomes.

Estimates show that between 650,000 and 1m. Haitians and people of Haitian descent live and work in the Dominican Republic, many without access to formal documentation or residency. Haitian labour underpinned the sugar industry throughout the 20th century, when workers were contracted for the duration of the cane harvest. Over recent decades tens of thousands of undocumented Haitians have crossed the border in search of employment or were informally recruited, and they provide an important source of informal and skilled or unskilled labour in all forms of agriculture, as well as in the construction and tourism sectors. In April 2013 a new and potentially ground-breaking accord was signed by the Haitian and Dominican Governments, which proposed that the Dominican Republic would more actively assist in the provision of temporary working visas and identity cards for Haitian migrant workers, and would begin to formalize the residential status of legal Haitian-Dominican residents in the country. The Dominican Government implemented a regularization programme for undocumented migrants in mid-2014.

Official and unofficial emigration created a large expatriate population in the USA, predominantly in the New York City metropolitan area. These migrants provided an important contribution to the general economic health of their homeland by regularly sending remittances to family members in the Dominican Republic. According to the Inter-American Development Bank (IDB), the value of remittances stood at US $3,333m. in 2013, an increase of 5.5% compared with the previous year. Remittances from Dominicans working abroad in 2013 were ranked as the fifth largest in Latin America. The Dominican Republic was the only Caribbean state to record a significant growth rate in remittances in 2013.

Since colonial times, the largest and most productive agricultural region has been the Cibao valley, situated in the north of the country. The main sugar-producing areas have been on the plains in the east and south-east. Traditional agriculture (i.e., the cultivation of sugar, coffee, cocoa and tobacco) has been declining since the 1980s under the weight of several adverse factors, including price controls, lack of investment, the subsidized sale by the Government of imported agricultural products, foreign competition, and tariffs on imported inputs. Agricultural exports have long ceased to be of critical importance to the economy. Since the late 1980s non-traditional crops, such as pineapples, oranges, bananas, vegetables and flowers, have increased in importance, and this diversification has boosted the ailing agricultural sector. None the less, the sector's contribution to GDP has declined in recent years, falling from 15% in 1990 to stabilize at around 6% during the current decade. In 2013 the agricultural sector registered an increase in value of 9.3%.

The once dominant sugar industry has generally been in decline for many years. The state-owned Consejo Estatal del Azúcar (CEA) suffered from a lack of investment under successive governments, and its percentage of the total annual sugar output decreased consistently. In 1999 the first Fernández Government sold off some CEA properties to a Mexican consortium. To compensate for the reduced yields produced by the state-owned enterprise, private companies, including the Central Romana Corporation and the Grupo Vicini, have increased their output to meet demand both for export and for domestic consumption. However, in 2004 output was so low that it was insufficient to meet domestic demand. Owing to the increased use of mechanized harvesting techniques, the sugar sector has since made a partial recovery, with production of sugar cane and refined sugar rising by 4.8% and 5.1%, respectively, in 2012. A possible lifeline for the sugar sector has been provided by the recent interest in biofuels as an alternative to increasingly expensive petroleum. Both foreign and local investors are exploring the possibilities of producing sugar cane in the Dominican Republic, with a view to transforming it into ethanol for local use and for export to the potentially vast US market.

Sugar remained the most important traditional agricultural export until 2009, when it was overtaken by cocoa, exports of which rose by 57%. In 2012 cocoa increased by 30% in terms of production, while tobacco output also rose by 30% and coffee cultivation by 23%. Coffee was an important traditional agricultural crop from the mid-18th century, but towards the end of the 20th century the value of coffee exports decreased, and in the late 2000s its contribution to the country's exports was a mere 0.4% of the total value, despite improving production levels.

Manufacturing is the largest sector in the Dominican economy, accounting for 21.9% of GDP in 2013. This sector is divided into two main sub-sectors: domestic manufacturing and free trade zone export manufacturing. Domestic manufacturing, which is the most significant in terms of profit margins, consists largely of food-processing operations, clothing and footwear, leather goods, and cement. Growth has been moderate in recent years, but accounted for 18.6% of GDP in 2013. Manufacturing in free trade zones developed rapidly from the 1980s, mainly as a result of tax exemption incentives and a devaluation of the peso that made Dominican labour relatively cheap for foreign assembly companies. The most common product is garments, but footwear, electronic goods, jewellery, pharmaceuticals and cigars are also manufactured. For much of the current decade, the free trade zone sector has been struggling, losing its market share in the USA, its main market, particularly in the garments sector, which traditionally accounts for around 50% of merchandise exports. This trend accelerated following the phasing out of global quotas in 2005, and Asian producers, particularly those in the People's Republic of China, gained a greater share of the US market. In 2007 the GDP of the free trade zone sector fell by 10%.

Subsequent years have showed consecutive increases, however. The sector provided 3.3% of GDP in 2013.

A recovery in the construction industry began in 2005, when private, and to a lesser extent public, investment resumed. In 2006 the sector grew by 24.6% compared with the previous year. An additional boost was provided by the central Government's spending on the initial phase of the underground subway system in Santo Domingo. However, in 2007, despite increased public spending on construction during the year and consistent growth in property services and prices, the level of construction activity rose by a modest 3.2%. By 2008 a slowdown in the property market had negatively affected the construction industry and the sector declined (by 0.4%). A further contraction, of 3.9%, was registered in 2009, but the sector subsequently recovered, increasing by 11.0% in 2010, 1.4% in 2011, 3.5% in 2012 and 6.9% in 2013. Construction contributed 5.2% of GDP in 2013.

The mining sector, dominated by ferro-nickel, is subject to wildly fluctuating international prices for the metal. In 2007 a rise in the international price boosted export earnings by 54.8%, to US $1,098.9m. However, in 2008 earnings declined to $492.3m., after the international price crashed as slowing global economic activity dampened demand for the metal. Prices and earnings fell further in 2009, the latter amounting to only $4.1m. There was significant foreign investment in the mining sector in 2009, however, and the sector registered growth of 2.9% in 2010, which soared to a substantial 79.7% in 2011, as nickel production continued to increase and gold exports began. In 2011 export earnings from ferro-alloys recovered to $277.3m., before registering a slight fall, to $270.1m., in 2012. In 2013, however, the Medina Government declined to pursue a major nickel-mining proposal owing to environmental damage concerns outlined by the UN Development Programme. Export earnings declined to $157.0m. in that year.

The tourism trade is primarily focused on the country's beaches, which comprise about one-third of a 1,400-km coastline. The leading resort is Puerto Plata on the north coast, but Punta Cana and Romana-Bayahibe are also popular destinations with significant hotel construction being focused on these coastlines over the last decade. Tourism is the Dominican Republic's largest earner of foreign exchange, and a major source of employment, with 248,600 people employed in hotels, bars and restaurants in October 2013. The number of tourist arrivals increased steadily during 2002–07, but declined in 2008 as a result of the global economic downturn. Nevertheless, arrival numbers resumed their upward trajectory from 2009, reaching 5.2m. in 2013. Income from tourism has also been rising steadily, with the sector generating US $5,118m. in 2013. Tourist arrivals from North America accounted for 44.5% of visitors in 2013, with 21.9% coming from Europe. The generally rapid growth of the tourism sector in recent decades has given a boost to other sectors, notably the construction industry, but also to transport and commerce. Until now the focus has been on the budget end of the market, and all-inclusive package tours for holidaymakers from North America and Europe have become very popular. However, the structure of the Dominican tourism market is changing from the mass market model to a more high-end niche, emphasized by the construction of several luxury, non-all inclusive, five-star hotels during the last five years.

In spite of recent years of growth and strong investment, the tourism sector is struggling to remain competitive as a result of challenges such as inadequate infrastructure, inefficient and costly electricity supply, and less frequent flights. There are international airports at Santo Domingo, Puerto Plata, Punta Cana, La Romana, Barahona, Samaná and Santiago. Punta Cana remained the principal arrival destination for tourists, receiving 48% of the country's total passenger arrivals in 2012. The main seaports are Santo Domingo, Haina, Boca Chica and San Pedro de Macorís on the south coast, and Puerto Plata in the north. Traffic congestion increasingly brings gridlock to the capital, which has persisted despite the completion in 2009 of a north–south underground railway system in the city. Communications has been one of the fastest growing economic sectors in recent years. In 2013 there were 9.2m. mobile telephone subscribers, compared with just 705,431 in 2000.

The spiralling growth in mobile use contrasted with a relatively stagnant growth in residential line connections. In 2013 there were 1.2m. main lines in use, up from 894,200 in 2000. Some 46% of Dominicans had an internet connection in 2013, up from 11% in 2005.

The Dominican Republic has no oil resources and, aside from power supplied by a small hydroelectric sector, relies entirely on imported petroleum for its energy needs. This dependence has left the energy sector extremely vulnerable to movements in international oil prices. In 2012 90% of power output was produced by thermal (oil-fired) generators, nearly all of them running on imported fuel. Most oil imports were supplied by Mexico and Venezuela on preferential terms. The country was a member of Venezuela's Petrocaribe agreement, under which Venezuela would meet all of the Dominican Republic's oil needs on beneficial terms. The Medina Government responded enthusiastically to the prospects for developing biofuel production, exploring initiatives to produce biofuel from sugar cane and jatropha plants.

Nevertheless, concern remained focused on the worsening general production of electricity for residential and industrial usage. The World Bank has stated that the revitalization of the Dominican economy remains dependent on the successful resolution of the supply and demand problems of electricity. The sector has long been undermined by inadequate investment, high costs, theft and low collection rates, including recurrent payment arrears accumulated by the public sector. There have been frequent blackouts, obliging companies and households to turn to their own small-scale generators. In 2007 the authorities criminalized electricity theft, a move intended to help reduce the need for budgetary support for the electricity sector, and in 2008 the authorities initiated a further attempt to reform the electricity supply sector. However, these schemes were not successfully implemented, and the industry has continued to provide an unreliable service and customers have continued to experience extended blackouts. As part of the stand-by arrangement agreed with the IMF, the Government committed itself to the reform of the electricity sector, developing a strategy in conjunction with the IDB and the World Bank. Conscious of the failure of these agreements to have brought significant improvement, in 2012 Medina specifically set out better electricity provision as a key goal. The Government pledged to generate 25% of electricity from renewable sources by 2025, and has supported a metering provision to encourage the use of solar photovoltaic energy to reduce electricity bills. Furthermore, a new law reduced import duties for renewable energy equipment, with additional tax incentives implemented. A revision of electricity pricing mechanisms and collection methods has been proposed to address more effectively the sector's increasing debt, indexing prices to the cost of the generating fuel.

Government finances have fluctuated since the early 2000s. Following two consecutive years of deficits in 2004 and 2005, in 2006 the Government was obliged to prepare another tax reform. In 2007 there was a sharp improvement, largely as a result of a strong increase in revenue collection. However, loosening of fiscal policy in 2008, as a result of election spending and the international oil price shock, led to a deficit of 61,208m. pesos. Although much lower oil prices removed one significant source of pressure in 2009, the Government still struggled to fund stimulus spending on infrastructure and local public works, as well as social programmes, and the deficit fell only slightly in 2010, to 55,276m. pesos. Similar pre-election spending led to the deficit increasing to 59,926m. pesos in 2011 and a preliminary 156,674m. pesos in 2012, although the deficit narrowed to an estimated 81,865m. pesos in 2013. Total foreign debt also increased to US $14,920m. in 2013, over four times the total debt in 2000. The national debt rose from 13.6% of GDP in 2000 to 38.5% in 2013.

Foreign investment also fluctuated in the 2000s. Foreign direct investment (FDI) inflows increased to US $1,123m. in 2005, reflecting a boost to business confidence brought about by the restoration of stability and economic recovery. In 2007 FDI rose by 54%, to reach $1,667m., partly as a consequence of the entry into force of the CAFTA-DR agreement in March, and the recent Economic Partnership Agreement with the European Union. Inflows increased further in 2008, to a record $2,870m.

After moderating somewhat during 2009–11, FDI rose again to a record $3,142m. in 2012. FDI inflows stood at an estimated $1,991m. in 2013. The leading receiving sector in that year was electricity, followed by wholesale and retail trade. The tourism and real estate sectors also attracted a significant share of FDI. The main sources of FDI inflows are the USA, Canada, Spain and Mexico.

The Dominican Republic's most important trading partner is the USA. Other important export markets included Haiti, Canada and China. During the first years of the 21st century exports have continued to grow. The current account deficit widened from US $2,096m. in 2007 to a record $4,519m. in 2008, driven by rising import costs and declining earnings from nickel and free zone exports. The deficit was halved in 2009 as the value of imports declined at a faster rate than remittances from abroad and the value of exports. However, in 2010 the deficit surged again, to $4,330m., increasing to $4,379m. in 2011. The deficit narrowed to $4,037m. in 2012.

CONCLUSION

While impressive GDP growth rates in 2005 and 2006 reflected a strong recovery, growth has since slowed, as a result of the collapse in global trade, a US recession and a sharp contraction in consumption. The fiscal deficit meanwhile has increased substantially and remained a major problem for President Medina. The deterioration in the fiscal situation prompted the Government to seek assistance from the IMF in November 2009, although the stand-by arrangement was suspended in

2012 and has not yet been renewed. Nevertheless, the IMF has continued to welcome stable management of the economy, reflecting a continuation of existing policies from the previous administration, as well as the Medina Government's more visible efforts to improve tax collection and bank supervision. According to the IMF, real GDP rose by 4.5% in 2011, 3.9% in 2012 and an estimated 4.1% in 2013, continuing the 'Dominican paradox' of relatively high economic growth with high levels of formal unemployment. This remained a major concern for the Government and the economy.

The key economic challenge facing the Medina Government was the negotiation of a renewed stand-by agreement with the IMF. The President's endorsement of austerity and fiscal reform measures has been viewed positively, but Medina will be aware that to ensure macroeconomic stability and reduce vulnerability to external economic shocks, more sustained corporate confidence in capital investment, in addition to further financial assistance from international donors, will be necessary. In 2013 Medina expressed his Government's desire to join the Caribbean Community and Common Market, which would usefully strengthen the country's political relationships with other Caribbean states and provide a platform for wider economic engagement in the region. The Government will continue the economic policies of recent years, but Medina has specifically targeted the education and electricity sectors as key areas of concern. While immediate results are not anticipated, continued failings in both sectors will be highly visible and contentious.

Statistical Survey

Sources (unless otherwise stated): Oficina Nacional de Estadística, Edif. de Oficinas Gubernamentales, 9°, Avda México, esq. Leopoldo Navarro, Santo Domingo, DN; tel. 682-7777; fax 685-4424; e-mail info@one.gob.do; internet www.one.gob.do; Banco Central de la República Dominicana, Calle Pedro Henríquez Ureña, esq. Leopoldo Navarro, Apdo 1347, Santo Domingo, DN; tel. 221-9111; fax 686-7488; e-mail info@bancentral.gov.do; internet www.bancentral.gov.do.

Area and Population

AREA, POPULATION AND DENSITY

Area (sq km)	
Land	48,137
Inland water	597
Total	48,734*
Population (census results)	
18–20 October 2002	8,562,541
1–7 December 2010	
Males	4,739,038
Females	4,706,243
Total	9,445,281
Population (official projections)†	
2012	10,135,105
2013	10,257,724
2014	10,378,267
Density (per sq km) at 2014 . . .	213.0

* 18,816 sq miles.

† Not adjusted to take account of results of 2010 census.

POPULATION BY AGE AND SEX
(official projections, 2014)

	Males	Females	Total
0–14 years	1,597,320	1,540,016	3,137,336
15–64 years	3,262,061	3,317,186	6,579,247
65 years and over . . .	315,293	346,391	661,684
Total	**5,174,674**	**5,203,593**	**10,378,267**

PROVINCES
(official population projections, 2014)

	Area (sq km)	Population	Density (per sq km)
Distrito Nacional Region			
Distrito Nacional	104.4	1,168,629	11,193.8
Santo Domingo	1,296.4	2,347,968	1,811.1
Valdesia Region			
Peravia	997.6	213,809	214.3
Monte Plata	2,632.1	220,231	83.7
San Cristóbal	1,265.8	711,209	561.9
San José de Ocoa . . .	650.2	69,366	106.7
Norcentral Region			
Espaillat	839.0	243,505	290.2
Puerto Plata	1,856.9	336,825	181.4
Santiago	2,839.0	1,102,840	388.5
Nordeste Region			
Duarte	1,605.4	305,347	190.2
Hermanas Mirabal . . .	440.4	104,364	237.0
María Trinidad Sánchez . .	1,271.7	144,183	113.4
Samaná	853.7	102,473	120.0
Enriquillo Region			
Baoruco	1,282.2	120,724	94.2
Barahona	1,739.4	206,980	119.0
Independencia	2,006.4	58,442	29.1
Pedernales	2,074.5	26,980	13.0
Este Region			
El Seibo	1,786.8	110,960	62.1
Hato Mayor	1,329.3	92,613	69.7
La Altagracia	2,474.3	250,665	101.3
La Romana	654.0	258,619	395.4
San Pedro de Macorís . .	1,255.5	355,646	283.3

—continued	Area (sq km)	Population	Density (per sq km)
El Valle Region			
Azua	2,531.8	252,590	99.8
Elías Piña	1,426.2	74,490	52.2
San Juan	3,569.4	243,463	68.2
Noroeste Region			
Dajabón	1,020.7	68,531	67.1
Monte Cristi	1,924.4	125,265	65.1
Santiago Rodríguez	1,111.1	54,242	48.8
Valverde	823.4	200,061	243.0
Cibao Central Region			
La Vega	2,287.0	445,406	194.8
Monseñor Nouel	992.4	204,175	205.7
Sánchez Ramírez	1,196.1	157,666	131.8
Total	48,137.0*	10,378,267	215.6*

* Land area only.

PRINCIPAL TOWNS
(population at census of October 2010)

Santo Domingo DN (capital)	2,806,636	Moca	179,829
Santiago de los Caballeros	691,262	Higuey	168,501
Concepción de la Vega	248,089	Monseñor Nouel	165,224
San Cristóbal	232,769	San Felipe de Puerto Plata	158,756
La Romana	228,875	Baní	157,316
San Pedro de Macorís	195,037	San Juan de la Maguana	132,177
San Francisco de Macorís	188,118	Bajos de Haina	124,193

BIRTHS, MARRIAGES AND DEATHS
(year of registration)

	Registered live births Number	Rate (per 1,000)	Registered marriages Number	Rate (per 1,000)	Registered deaths Number	Rate (per 1,000)
2005	183,819	19.9	39,439	4.3	33,949	3.7
2006	174,575	18.7	42,375	4.5	33,060	3.5
2007	193,978	20.4	39,993	4.2	33,009	3.5
2008	196,387	20.4	38,310	4.0	32,991	3.4
2009	210,098	21.5	40,040	4.1	32,826	3.4
2010	196,253	19.9	43,797	4.4	35,244	3.6
2011	194,641	19.4	44,253	4.4	33,995	3.4
2012	193,241	19.1	43,307	4.3	34,198	3.4

Life expectancy (years at birth): 73.2 (males 70.2; females 76.5) in 2012 (Source: World Bank, World Development Indicators database).

ECONOMICALLY ACTIVE POPULATION
(official estimates at October 2013, '000 persons aged 10 years and over)

	Males	Females	Total
Agriculture, hunting, forestry and fishing	543.5	28.7	572.2
Mining and quarrying	12.0	0.7	12.7
Manufacturing	300.5	99.0	399.5
Electricity, gas and water supply	27.7	8.0	35.8
Construction	232.7	4.6	237.3
Wholesale and retail trade	535.3	315.2	850.5
Hotels and restaurants	117.9	130.7	248.6
Transport, storage and communications	280.2	37.4	317.6
Financial intermediation			
Real estate, renting and business activities	48.0	58.0	106.0
Public administration and defence	133.0	64.1	197.1
Education			
Health and social work			
Other community, social and personal service activities	360.5	714.0	1,074.5
Total employed	2,591.3	1,460.4	4,051.8
Unemployed	271.8	445.9	717.7
Total labour force	2,863.2	1,906.3	4,769.5

Health and Welfare

KEY INDICATORS

Total fertility rate (children per woman, 2012)	2.5
Under-5 mortality rate (per 1,000 live births, 2012)	27
HIV/AIDS (% of persons aged 15–49, 2012)	0.7
Physicians (per 1,000 head, 2011)	1.49
Hospital beds (per 1,000 head, 2010)	1.6
Health expenditure (2011): US $ per head (PPP)	521
Health expenditure (2011): % of GDP	5.4
Health expenditure (2011): public (% of total)	49.3
Access to water (% of persons, 2012)	81
Access to sanitation (% of persons, 2012)	82
Total carbon dioxide emissions ('000 metric tons, 2010)	20,964.2
Carbon dioxide emissions per head (metric tons, 2010)	2.1
Human Development Index (2013): ranking	102
Human Development Index (2013): value	0.700

For sources and definitions, see explanatory note on p. vi.

Agriculture

PRINCIPAL CROPS
('000 metric tons)

	2010	2011	2012
Rice, paddy	850.2	874.7	849.7
Maize	36.7	35.4	41.6
Potatoes	51.4	53.6	60.6
Sweet potatoes	53.6	46.5	44.5
Cassava (Manioc)	211.1	184.8	170.0
Yautia (Cocoyam)	30.3	32.9	32.6
Sugar cane	4,577.1	4,644.5	4,865.6
Beans, dry	33.0	34.4	32.4
Coconuts	129.7	150.5	162.5
Oil palm fruit*	236.0	258.5	262.0
Tomatoes	240.3	290.2	258.8
Pumpkins, squash and gourds	40.6	38.3	41.9
Chillies and peppers, green	37.2	36.8	35.6
Onions, dry	48.4	76.4	55.8
Garlic	2.0	3.1	4.3
Carrots and turnips	24.7	44.8	48.0*
Cantaloupes and other melons	18.3	25.1	26.5*

—continued				2010	2011	2012
Bananas	.	.	.	735.0	829.8	871.9
Plantains	.	.	.	491.5	503.5	543.5
Oranges	.	.	.	138.0	139.4	170.9
Guavas, mangoes and						
mangosteens	.	.	.	7.9	9.0	10.0*
Avocados	.	.	.	288.7	295.1	290.0
Pineapples	.	.	.	157.4	221.7	447.4
Papayas	.	.	.	908.5	891.7	815.5
Coffee, green	.	.	.	21.9	27.3	27.0
Cocoa beans	.	.	.	58.3	54.3	72.2
Tobacco, unmanufactured	.	.	8.1	10.2	9.1

* FAO estimate(s).

Aggregate production ('000 metric tons, may include official, semi-official or estimated data): Total cereals 888.3 in 2010, 912.4 in 2011, 893.3 in 2012; Total roots and tubers 374.1 in 2010, 346.0 in 2011, 336.3 in 2012; Total vegetables (incl. melons) 527.7 in 2010, 625.5 in 2011, 585.5 in 2012; Total fruits (excl. melons) 2,818.9 in 2010, 2,990.7 in 2011, 3,255.2 in 2012.

Source: FAO.

LIVESTOCK
('000 head, year ending September)

				2010	2011	2012
Horses*	.	.	.	350	350	352
Asses*	.	.	.	151	151	151
Cattle*	.	.	.	2,900.0	2,950.0	3,000.0
Pigs*	.	.	.	620	625	628
Sheep*	.	.	.	240.0	245.0	246.5
Goats*	.	.	.	225.0	230.0	232.0
Chickens	.	.	.	178,433	174,791	173,000*

* FAO estimate(s).

Source: FAO.

LIVESTOCK PRODUCTS
('000 metric tons)

				2010	2011	2012
Cattle meat	.	.	.	113.0	102.0	95.9
Pig meat	.	.	.	89.5	103.8	103.2
Chicken meat	.	.	.	331.8	324.7	299.3*
Cows' milk	.	.	.	521.0	501.6	573.4
Hen eggs*	.	.	.	105.7	97.4	98.1
Honey†	.	.	.	4.9	4.9	5.0

* Unofficial figure(s).
† FAO estimates.

Source: FAO.

Forestry

ROUNDWOOD REMOVALS
('000 cubic metres, excl. bark, FAO estimates)

				2010	2011	2012
Sawlogs, veneer logs and logs for						
sleepers	.	.	.	7	7	7
Other industrial wood	.	.	.	3	3	3
Fuel wood	.	.	.	913	920	928
Total	.	.	.	922	930	937

Source: FAO.

Fishing
('000 metric tons, live weight)

				2010	2011	2012
Capture	.	.	.	14.5	14.0	13.7
Tilapia	.	.	.	0.1	0.2	0.2
Groupers, seabasses	.	.	1.5	0.7	0.7
Common carp	.	.	.	0.1	0.2	0.2
Snappers and jobfishes	.	.	1.3	1.1	1.0
King mackerel	.	.	.	0.8	0.1	0.1
Blackfin tuna	.	.	.	1.0	0.6	0.6
Caribbean spiny lobster	.	.	1.0	2.6	2.5
Stromboid conchs	.	.	.	0.3	1.9	2.2
Aquaculture	.	.	.	1.3*	2.1	1.0*
Penaeus shrimps	.	.	.	0.5*	—	—
Total catch	.	.	.	15.8*	16.2	14.7*

* FAO estimate.

Source: FAO.

Mining
('000 metric tons)

				2010	2011	2012
Ferro-nickel	.	.	.	—	13.5	15.2
Nickel (metal content of laterite						
ore)	.	.	.	—	1,143.0	1,301.7
Gypsum	.	.	.	53.8	31.2	102.1

Source: US Geological Survey.

Industry

SELECTED PRODUCTS
('000 metric tons, preliminary, unless otherwise indicated)

				2010	2011	2012
Flour and derivatives ('000						
quintales*)	.	.	.	3,714.4	4,747.8	3,538.4
Refined sugar	.	.	.	147.7	157.8	165.8
Cement	.	.	.	4,105.7	3,996.5	4,129.7
Beer ('000 hl)	.	.	.	4,838.0	4,886.9	4,703.3
Cigarettes (million)	.	.	.	2,154.1	2,222.0	2,058.0
Motor spirit (petrol)†‡	.	.	3,000	3,000	n.a.
Jet fuel†‡	.	.	.	1,900	2,000	n.a.
Distillate fuel†‡	.	.	.	2,900	3,000	n.a.
Residual fuel oil†‡	.	.	.	4,600	5,000	n.a.
Electric energy (million kWh)	.	12,271.7	12,960.5	13,848.5

* 1 quintale is equivalent to 46 kg.
† Estimated production, '000 barrels.
‡ Source: US Geological Survey.

Finance

CURRENCY AND EXCHANGE RATES

Monetary Units
100 centavos = 1 Dominican Republic peso (RD $ or peso oro).

Sterling, Dollar and Euro Equivalents (30 April 2014)
£1 sterling = 72.776 pesos;
US $1 = 43.265 pesos;
€1 = 59.922 pesos;
1,000 Dominican Republic pesos = £13.74 = $23.11 = €16.69.

Average Exchange Rate (RD $ per US $)
2011   38.232
2012   39.336
2013   41.808

BUDGET
(RD $ million)

Revenue	2011	2012*	2013*
Tax revenue	273,132.0	312,064.1	355,314.0
Taxes on income and profits .	65,204.9	92,274.4	108,248.5
Taxes on goods and services .	167,941.4	175,892.5	199,152.2
Taxes on international trade and transactions	23,003.3	23,444.1	23,795.5
Other current revenue . . .	7,318.2	6,480.7	14,098.2
Capital revenue	6.7	13.9	0.4
Total	280,456.9	318,558.8	369,412.6

Expenditure	2011	2012*	2013*
Current expenditure . . .	263,928.7	323,722.2	357,564.9
Wages and salaries . . .	79,113.7	87,846.0	105,286.5
Other goods and services . .	33,468.7	44,254.5	39,305.4
Current transfers . . .	106,515.5	134,936.7	153,414.8
Interest payments . . .	44,830.6	56,219.3	59,218.9
Capital expenditure . . .	76,454.0	151,510.7	93,712.2
Capital transfers . . .	21,807.1	34,699.4	22,212.2
Total	340,382.7	475,232.9	451,277.1

* Preliminary figures.

INTERNATIONAL RESERVES
(US $ million at 31 December)

	2011	2012	2013
Gold*	28.0	30.3	22.0
IMF special drawing rights . .	18.6	20.3	2.1
Foreign exchange	4,070.4	3,528.2	4,678.6
Total	4,117.0	3,578.8	4,702.7

* Valued at market-related prices.

Source: IMF, *International Financial Statistics*.

MONEY SUPPLY
(RD $ million at 31 December)

	2011	2012	2013
Currency outside depository corporations	61,463	65,374	72,243
Transferable deposits . . .	113,917	125,866	149,462
Other deposits	327,857	359,755	426,444
Securities other than shares . .	205,631	225,552	241,734
Broad money	708,868	776,547	889,883

Source: IMF, *International Financial Statistics*.

COST OF LIVING
(Consumer Price Index; base: December 2010 = 100)

	2011	2012	2013
Food and non-alcoholic beverages .	106.8	112.2	117.4
Clothing	100.8	100.6	99.0
Housing	106.9	109.0	112.1
All items (incl. others) . . .	105.6	109.5	114.8

NATIONAL ACCOUNTS
(RD $ million at current prices)

Expenditure on the Gross Domestic Product

	2011	2012	2013
Final consumption expenditure .	1,989,712.5	2,140,512.0	2,303,779.6
Households			
Non-profit institutions serving households	1,833,738.8	1,952,642.2	2,109,619.0
General government . . .	155,973.5	187,869.9	194,160.6
Gross capital formation . . .	348,270.3	379,873.9	369,430.6
Gross fixed capital formation .	345,404.1	376,738.8	366,005.8
Changes in inventories . .			
Acquisitions, less disposals, of valuables	2,866.1	3,135.1	3,424.7
Total domestic expenditure .	2,337,982.8	2,520,385.9	2,673,210.2
Exports of goods and services .	530,803.4	582,359.9	659,952.0
Less Imports of goods and services	749,484.4	785,962.3	799,094.5
GDP in market prices . .	2,119,301.8	2,316,783.7	2,534,067.8

Gross Domestic Product by Economic Activity

	2011	2012	2013
Agriculture, hunting, forestry and fishing	118,040.3	130,860.4	143,043.8
Mining and quarrying . . .	7,528.4	10,197.8	23,662.5
Manufacturing	487,207.0	508,189.4	535,235.1
Local manufacturing . .	418,444.0	436,114.9	454,233.4
Free trade zones . . .	68,763.0	72,074.5	81,001.7
Electricity and water . . .	44,375.6	48,176.1	49,304.8
Construction	115,921.2	119,956.0	128,225.1
Wholesale and retail trade . .	194,212.6	212,467.7	218,927.5
Restaurants and hotels . . .	192,250.7	206,338.1	232,015.7
Transport and storage . . .	177,252.9	195,487.9	214,591.1
Communications	53,063.7	54,940.1	58,403.6
Finance, insurance and business activities	142,616.4	170,374.6	194,194.4
Real estate	175,205.5	187,104.2	199,421.6
General government services (incl. defence)	59,666.7	71,123.0	78,505.2
Education	75,496.5	93,159.7	115,347.1
Health	42,757.3	45,008.5	49,304.7
Other services	162,236.2	183,480.0	204,702.3
Sub-total	2,047,831.0	2,236,863.5	2,444,884.5
Less Financial intermediation services indirectly measured .	67,614.4	74,235.3	82,123.8
Gross value added in basic prices	1,980,216.9	2,162,628.2	2,362,760.6
Taxes, *less* subsidies . . .	139,084.9	154,155.4	171,307.2
GDP in market prices . .	2,119,301.8	2,316,783.7	2,534,067.8

BALANCE OF PAYMENTS
(US $ million)

	2010	2011	2012
Exports of goods	2,536.1	3,678.0	4,091.4
Imports of goods	−13,025.3	−14,537.3	−14,965.5
Balance on goods	−10,489.2	−10,859.3	−10,874.1
Exports of services	6,907.5	7,372.7	7,959.9
Imports of services	−2,185.0	−2,235.0	−2,283.5
Balance on goods and services	−5,766.7	−5,721.6	−5,197.7
Primary income received . . .	496.6	505.7	512.6
Primary income paid	−2,183.0	−2,596.3	−2,724.9
Balance on goods, services and primary income	−7,453.1	−7,812.2	−7,410.0
Secondary income received . .	3,476.1	3,755.5	3,732.8
Secondary income paid . . .	−352.5	−322.2	−359.9

—continued	2010	2011	2012
Current balance	−4,329.5	−4,378.9	−4,037.1
Capital account (net)	81.9	57.8	54.8
Direct investment assets . .	203.5	79.2	−273.5
Direct investment liabilities .	1,692.8	2,195.8	3,857.1
Portfolio investment assets . .	−10.6	36.9	−800.1
Portfolio investment liabilities .	770.1	709.0	−196.1
Other investment assets . .	694.0	−40.0	−354.3
Other investment liabilities .	2,109.7	1,000.4	1,702.5
Net errors and omissions . . .	−1,139.6	501.5	−393.9
Reserves and related items .	72.3	161.7	−440.6

Source: IMF, *International Financial Statistics*.

External Trade

PRINCIPAL COMMODITIES
(distribution by HS, US $ million)

Imports f.o.b.	2011	2012	2013
Vegetables and vegetable products	937.7	781.4	807.5
Cereals	563.0	498.1	500.8
Prepared foodstuffs, beverages, spirits, tobacco, etc.	1,005.3	1,142.7	1,163.8
Mineral products	4,734.2	4,471.6	5,450.8
Mineral fuels, oils, distillation products, etc.	4,669.8	4,407.4	5,388.7
Crude petroleum oils . .	979.5	1,030.3	1,235.3
Petroleum oils, not crude .	2,508.6	2,233.0	2,977.4
Petroleum gases	801.4	838.4	886.2
Chemicals and related products	1,453.8	1,884.5	1,697.1
Pharmaceutical products . .	486.1	507.2	591.9
Plastics, rubber and articles thereof	1,228.9	1,395.5	1,376.5
Plastics and articles thereof .	1,053.5	1,168.9	1,186.7
Pulp of wood, paper and paperboard, and articles thereof	559.8	483.4	512.1
Textiles and textile articles .	1,254.0	1,275.2	1,201.0
Cotton	664.7	573.3	544.2
Iron and steel, other base metals and articles of base metal	1,324.2	1,180.7	1,060.1
Iron and steel	677.1	505.6	492.4
Machinery and mechanical appliances, electrical equipment	2,599.3	2,958.5	2,667.7
Machinery, boilers, etc. . . .	1,184.5	1,273.9	1,259.9
Electrical and electronic equipment	1,414.9	1,684.6	1,407.7
Vehicles, aircraft, vessels and associated transport equipment	708.3	1,054.6	976.8
Vehicles other than railway, tramway	686.4	942.0	960.5
Total (incl. others)	18,156.1	19,200.5	19,349.8

Exports f.o.b.	2011	2012	2013
Vegetables and vegetable products	428.2	312.8	428.7
Edible fruit, nuts, peel of citrus fruit, melons	208.0	120.7	233.9
Prepared foodstuffs, beverages, spirits, tobacco, etc.	1,023.4	1,103.1	1,282.0
Tobacco and manufactured tobacco substitutes	407.5	514.2	594.7
Cigars, cheroots, cigarillos and cigarettes	324.4	408.3	510.5
Mineral products	270.9	219.3	367.0
Chemicals and related products	284.3	554.0	531.7
Pharmaceutical products . .	125.2	350.5	322.2
Pharmaceutical goods and specified sterile products, sutures	3.3	314.5	278.2
Plastics, rubber and articles thereof	354.9	307.1	296.8
Plastics and articles thereof . .	342.8	294.5	282.0
Textiles and textile articles .	980.1	1,095.9	1,084.1
Cotton	279.8	234.2	379.7
Woven cotton fabrics . .	276.1	0.8	—
Articles of apparel, accessories, knitted or crocheted	348.1	463.5	305.4
T-shirts, singlets and other vests	149.0	354.7	204.6
Articles of apparel, accessories, not knitted or crocheted	283.8	285.2	267.8
Footwear, headgear, umbrellas, walking sticks, etc.	259.1	316.4	323.8
Footwear, gaiters, etc. . . .	251.6	307.5	317.0
Footwear	184.9	99.6	72.2
Pearls, precious stones, metals, coins, etc.	223.2	322.2	1,478.5
Gold	6.7	169.5	1,198.4
Articles of jewellery and parts thereof	197.0	137.5	194.8
Base metals and articles thereof	783.0	604.2	523.7
Iron and steel	584.6	458.2	355.0
Ferro-alloys	277.3	270.1	157.0
Machinery and mechanical appliances, electrical equipment	501.7	615.5	593.7
Electrical and electronic equipment	471.9	513.2	499.0
Electrical apparatus for switching, exceeding 1,000 volts	212.3	5.5	4.9
Electrical apparatus for switching, not exceeding 1,000 volts	40.5	368.4	367.0
Optical, photo, cinema, measuring, checking precision equipment . .	676.0	712.5	802.9
Optical, photo, technical, medical apparatus, etc.	675.5	711.8	801.6
Electro-medical apparatus . .	662.4	690.0	752.7
Total (incl. others)	6,112.5	6,902.5	7,961.0

Source: Trade Map-Trade Competitiveness Map, International Trade Centre, www.intracen.org/marketanalysis.

PRINCIPAL TRADING PARTNERS
(US $ million)

Imports c.i.f.	2011	2012	2013
Argentina	243.6	278.6	288.0
Bahamas	161.3	359.2	410.1
Brazil	419.2	524.7	482.1
China, People's Republic	1,787.2	1,928.3	2,050.5
Colombia	725.1	397.9	409.4
Costa Rica	241.7	253.6	260.9
Germany	287.3	299.7	344.4
Italy	213.4	277.6	227.8
Japan	214.1	347.9	359.6
Korea, Republic	114.0	167.0	260.0
Mexico	1,084.9	998.0	1,177.2
Spain	422.7	559.0	440.0
Trinidad and Tobago	835.3	1,165.8	883.1
USA	7,555.2	7,405.9	7,440.0
Venezuela	1,237.2	1,217.5	1,276.1
Total (incl. others)	18,156.1	19,200.5	19,349.8

Exports f.o.b.	2011	2012	2013
Belgium	84.8	52.0	88.1
Canada	48.1	64.0	974.1
China, People's Republic	330.3	355.8	231.7
Germany	59.1	81.5	106.3
Guatemala	47.4	130.0	64.1
Haiti	1,013.6	986.9	1,042.9
Honduras	54.4	108.2	43.1
Korea, Democratic People's Republic	41.5	82.1	5.3
Netherlands	128.3	120.0	129.4
Nigeria	73.8	61.0	31.9
Spain	0.4	50.3	102.1
United Kingdom	117.4	63.6	114.6
USA	3,330.9	3,867.9	4,070.5
Venezuela	80.2	37.6	76.6
Total (incl. others)	6,112.5	6,902.5	7,961.0

Source: Trade Map-Trade Competitiveness Map, International Trade Centre, www.intracen.org/marketanalysis.

Transport

ROAD TRAFFIC
(motor vehicles in use)

	2011	2012	2013
Passenger cars	953,542	991,081	1,029,257
Buses and coaches	76,300	78,888	81,660
Vans and lorries	373,987	382,380	391,403
Motorcycles and mopeds	1,481,255	1,566,815	1,678,979
Total (incl. others)	2,917,573	3,052,686	3,215,773

SHIPPING

Flag Registered Fleet
(at 31 December)

	2011	2012	2013
Number of vessels	34	35	38
Total displacement ('000 grt)	13.2	13.4	14.4

Source: Lloyd's List Intelligence (www.lloydslistintelligence.com).

International Seaborne Freight Traffic
('000 metric tons)

	2010	2011	2012
Goods loaded	2,420	3,570	4,242
Goods unloaded	13,129	15,722	13,766

CIVIL AVIATION
(traffic on scheduled services)

	1997	1998	1999
Kilometres flown (million)	1	1	0
Passengers carried ('000)	34	34	10
Passenger-km (million)	16	16	5
Total ton-km (million)	1	1	0

Source: UN, *Statistical Yearbook*.

Passengers carried ('000): 19,167 in 2010; 28,232 in 2011; 28,442 in 2012 (Source: World Bank, World Development Indicators database).

Tourism

ARRIVALS BY NATIONALITY

	2011	2012	2013
Argentina	99,618	103,389	107,305
Brazil	78,083	81,501	92,870
Canada	665,640	685,889	684,071
France	260,289	259,991	232,754
Germany	182,529	183,887	232,754
Italy	104,852	95,030	80,112
Russia	124,319	167,700	188,110
Spain	171,353	157,214	142,207
United Kingdom*	138,816	98,288	108,236
USA	1,286,161	1,456,671	1,587,404
Total (incl. others)	4,776,473	5,047,021	5,163,682

* Includes arrivals from England and Scotland only.

Tourism receipts (US $ million, excl. passenger transport): 4,436 in 2011; 4,736 in 2012; 5,118 in 2013 (provisional) (Source: World Tourism Organization).

Communications Media

	2011	2012	2013
Telephones ('000 main lines in use)	1,099.8	1,128.9	1,171.0
Mobile cellular telephones ('000 subscribers)	8,770.8	8,934.2	9,200.4
Internet subscribers ('000)	436.1	n.a.	n.a.
Broadband subscribers ('000)	403.7	446.7	484.9

Source: International Telecommunication Union.

Education

(public and private sectors, 2011/12)

	Institutions	Students Males	Females	Total
Pre-primary	272	126,707	126,346	253,053
Primary	1,544	854,424	768,728	1,623,152
Secondary	1,145	266,189	304,630	570,819
General	n.a.	250,032	279,144	529,176
Vocational	n.a.	16,157	25,486	41,643
Adult	821	87,612	96,808	184,420

Teaching staff: (public sector only, May 2013) 70,670 (males 18,969, females 51,701).

Source: Ministry of Education, Santo Domingo.

Pupil-teacher ratio (primary education, estimate): 23.6 in 2011/12 (Source: UNESCO Institute for Statistics).

Adult literacy rate (estimates): 90.9% (males 90.5%; females 91.3%) in 2013 (Source: UNESCO Institute for Statistics).

Directory

The Constitution

The Constitution of the Dominican Republic was promulgated on 26 January 2010, replacing the charter of 28 November 1966. Amendments were also made in 1994 and 2002. The Constitution contains 273 articles. Its main provisions are summarized below:

The Dominican Republic is a sovereign, free, independent state; no organizations set up by the state can bring about any act which might cause direct or indirect intervention in the internal or foreign affairs of the state or which might threaten the integrity of the state. The Dominican Republic recognizes and applies the norms of general and American international law and is in favour of and will support any initiative towards economic integration for the countries of America. The civil, republican, democratic, representative Government is divided into three independent powers: legislative, executive and judicial.

The territory of the Dominican Republic is as laid down in the Frontier Treaty of 1929 and its Protocol of Revision of 1936.

The life and property of the individual citizen are inviolable; there can be no sentence of death, torture nor any sentence which might cause physical harm to the individual. There is freedom of thought, of conscience, of religion, freedom to publish, and freedom of unarmed association, provided that there is no subversion against public order, national security or decency. The right to life is inviolable from conception to death. There is freedom of labour and trade unions; and freedom to strike, except in the case of public services, according to the dispositions of the law.

The state will undertake agrarian reform, dedicating the land to useful interests and gradually eliminating the latifundios (large estates). The state will do all in its power to support all aspects of family life. Marriage is defined as being between a man and a woman. Primary education is compulsory and all education is free. Social security services will be developed. Every Dominican has the duty to give what civil and military service the state may require. Every legally entitled citizen must exercise the right to vote, i.e. all persons over 18 years of age and all who are or have been married even if they are not yet 18. Children born in the Dominican Republic to foreign parents in transit or in the country illegally will not automatically be granted Dominican citizenship.

GOVERNMENT

Legislative power is exercised by Congress which is made up of the Senate and Chamber of Deputies, elected by direct vote. Senators, one for each of the 31 Provinces and one for the Distrito Nacional, are elected for four years; they must be Dominicans in full exercise of their citizen's rights, and at least 25 years of age. Their duties are to elect the President and other members of the Electoral and Accounts Councils, and to approve the nomination of diplomats. Deputies, one for every 50,000 inhabitants or fraction over 25,000 in each Province and the Distrito Nacional, are elected for four years and must fulfil the same conditions for election as Senators.

Decisions of Congress are taken by absolute majority of at least one-half of the members of each house; urgent matters require a two-thirds' majority. Both houses normally meet on 27 February and 16 August each year for sessions of 90 days, which can be extended for a further 60 days. Any amendments to the Constitution must be approved by referendum.

Executive power is exercised by the President of the Republic, who is elected by direct vote for a four-year term. The President may not serve a consecutive term, although an unlimited number of non-consecutive terms are permitted. The successful presidential candidate must obtain an overall majority of the votes cast; if necessary, a second round of voting is held 45 days later, with the participation of the two parties that obtained the highest number of votes. The President must be a Dominican citizen by birth or origin, over 30 years of age and in full exercise of citizen's rights. The President must not have engaged in any active military or police service for at least one year prior to election. The President takes office on 16 August following the election. The President of the Republic is Head of the Public Administration and Supreme Chief of the armed forces and police forces. The President's duties include nominating Ministers and Deputy Ministers and other public officials, promulgating and publishing laws and resolutions of Congress and seeing to their faithful execution, watching over the collection and just investment of national income, nominating, with the approval of the Senate, members of the Diplomatic Corps, receiving foreign Heads of State, presiding at national functions, and decreeing a State of Siege or Emergency or any other measures necessary during a public crisis. The President may not leave the country for more than 15 days without authorization from Congress. In the absence of the President, the Vice-President will assume power, or failing him or her, the President of the Supreme Court of Justice. From 2016 presidential elections are to be held at the same time as legislative and municipal elections, every four years.

LOCAL GOVERNMENT

Government in the Distrito Nacional and the Municipalities is in the hands of local councils, with members elected proportionally to the number of inhabitants, but numbering at least five. Each Province has a civil Governor, designated by the Executive.

JUDICIARY

Judicial power is exercised by the Supreme Court of Justice and the other Tribunals; no judicial official may hold another public office or employment, other than honorary or teaching. The Supreme Court is made up of at least 11 judges, who must be Dominican citizens by birth or origin, at least 35 years old, in full exercise of their citizen's rights, graduates in law and have practised professionally for at least 12 years. All Supreme Court judges must retire at the age of 75. The National Judiciary Council appoints the members of the Supreme Court, who in turn appoint judges at all other levels of the judicial system. There are nine Courts of Appeal, a Lands Tribunal and a Court of the First Instance in each judicial district; in each Municipality and in the Distrito Nacional there are also Justices of the Peace. Under the terms of the 2010 constitutional amendments, a Constitutional Court was to be established.

OTHER PROVISIONS

Elections are directed by the Central Electoral Board. The armed forces are essentially obedient and apolitical, created for the defence of national independence and the maintenance of public order and the Constitution and Laws.

The artistic and historical riches of the country, whoever owns them, are part of the cultural heritage of the country and are under the safe-keeping of the state. All beaches, rivers and water sources are part of the national heritage and belong to the people, respecting the rights of private property. Mineral deposits belong to the state. There is freedom to form political parties, provided they conform to the principles laid down in the Constitution. Justice is administered without charge throughout the Republic.

This Constitution can be reformed if the proposal for reform is supported in Congress by one-third of the members of either house or by the Executive. A special session of Congress must be called and any resolutions must have a two-thirds' majority. There can be no reform of the method of government, which must always be civil, republican, democratic and representative.

The Government

HEAD OF STATE

President: DANILO MEDINA SÁNCHEZ (took office 16 August 2012).
Vice-President: MARGARITA CEDEÑO LIZARDO.

CABINET
(September 2014)

The Government is formed by the Partido de la Liberación Dominicana.

Minister of the Presidency: GUSTAVO MONTALVO.
Minister of Foreign Affairs: ANDRÉS NAVARRO.
Minister of the Interior and Police: JOSÉ RAMÓN FADUL.
Minister of the Armed Forces: Maj.-Gen. MAXIMILIANO WILLIAM MUÑOZ DELGADO.
Minister of Finance: SIMÓN LIZARDO MÉZQUITA.
Minister of Education: CARLOS AMARANTE BARET.
Minister of Agriculture: ANGEL ESTÉVEZ.
Minister of Public Works and Communications: GONZALO CASTILLO.
Minister of Public Health and Social Welfare: LORENZO WILFREDO HIDALGO NÚÑEZ.
Minister of Industry and Commerce: JOSÉ DEL CASTILLO SAVIÑÓN.
Minister of Labour: MARITZA HERNÁNDEZ.
Minister of Tourism: FRANCISCO JAVIER GARCÍA.
Minister of Sport and Recreation: JAIME DAVID FERNÁNDEZ MIRABAL.
Minister of Culture: JOSÉ ANTONIO RODRÍGUEZ.
Minister of Higher Education, Science and Technology: LIGIA AMADA DE MELO.
Minister of Women: ALEJANDRINA GERMÁN.

Minister of Youth: JORGE MINAYA.

Minister of the Environment and Natural Resources: Dr BAUTISTA ROJAS GÓMEZ.

Minister of the Economy, Planning and Development: JUAN TEMÍSTOCLES MONTÁS.

Minister of Public Administration: RAMÓN VENTURA CAMEJO.

Minister of Energy and Mines: PELEGRÍN CASTILLO SEMÁN.

Administrative Secretary to the Presidency: JOSÉ RAMÓN PERALTA.

MINISTRIES

Office of the President: Palacio Nacional, Avda México, esq. Dr Delgado, Gazcue, Santo Domingo, DN; tel. 695-8000; fax 682-4558; e-mail info@presidencia.gob.do; internet www.presidencia.gob.do.

Ministry of Agriculture: Autopista Duarte, Km 6.5, Los Jardines del Norte, Santo Domingo, DN; tel. 547-3888; fax 227-1268; e-mail agricultura@agricultura.gob.do; internet www.agricultura.gob.do.

Ministry of the Armed Forces: Plaza de la Bandera, Avda 27 de Febrero, esq. Avda Luperón, Santo Domingo, DN; tel. 530-5149; fax 531-0461; e-mail directorrev@j2.mil.do; internet www.fuerzasarmadas.mil.do.

Ministry of Culture: Centro de Eventos y Exposiciones, Avda George Washington, esq. Presidente Vicini Burgos, Santo Domingo, DN; tel. 221-4141; fax 688-2908; e-mail accesoainfo@sec.gob.do; internet www.cultura.gob.do.

Ministry of the Economy, Planning and Development: Palacio Nacional, Avda México, esq. Dr Delgado, Bloque B, 2°, Santo Domingo, DN; tel. 688-7000; fax 221-8627; e-mail informacion@economia.gob.do; internet www.economia.gob.do.

Ministry of Education: Avda Máximo Gómez, esq. Santiago 2, Gazcue, Santo Domingo, DN; tel. 688-9700; fax 689-8688; e-mail mlibreacceso@see.gob.do; internet www.see.gob.do.

Ministry of Energy and Mines: Santo Domingo, DN.

Ministry of the Environment and Natural Resources: Avda Luperón, Santo Domingo, DN; tel. 567-4300; fax 683-4774; e-mail contacto@medioambiente.gob.do; internet www.ambiente.gob.do.

Ministry of Finance: Avda México 45, esq. Leopoldo Navarro, Apdo 1478, Santo Domingo, DN; tel. 687-5131; fax 682-0498; e-mail info@hacienda.gov.do; internet www.hacienda.gov.do.

Ministry of Foreign Affairs: Avda Independencia 752, Estancia San Gerónimo, Santo Domingo, DN; tel. 987-7001; fax 987-7002; e-mail relexteriores@serex.gob.do; internet www.serex.gov.do.

Ministry of Higher Education, Science and Technology: Avda Máximo Gómez 31, esq. Pedro Henríquez Ureña, Santo Domingo, DN; tel. 731-1100; fax 535-4694; e-mail info@seescyt.gob.do; internet www.seescyt.gov.do.

Ministry of Industry and Commerce: Edif. de Ofs Gubernamentales Juan Pablo Duarte, 7°, Avda México, esq. Leopoldo Navarro, Apdo 9876, Santo Domingo, DN; tel. 685-5171; fax 686-1973; e-mail info@seic.gob.do; internet www.seic.gov.do.

Ministry of the Interior and Police: Edif. de Ofs Gubernamentales Juan Pablo Duarte, 13°, Avda México, esq. Leopoldo Navarro, Santo Domingo, DN; tel. 686-6251; fax 689-6599; e-mail info@mip.gob.do; internet www.seip.gob.do.

Ministry of Labour: Centro de los Héroes, Avda Jiménez Moya 9, La Feria, Santo Domingo, DN; tel. 535-4404; fax 535-4833; e-mail info@mt.gob.do; internet www.ministeriodetrabajo.gob.do.

Ministry of Public Administration: Edif. de Ofs Gubernamentales Juan Pablo Duarte, 12°, Avda México, esq. Leopoldo Navarro, Apdo 20031, Santo Domingo, DN; tel. 682-3298; fax 686-6652; e-mail seap@seap.gob.do; internet www.map.gob.do.

Ministry of Public Health and Social Welfare: Avda Héctor Homero Hernández, esq. Tiradentes, Ensanche La Fe, Santo Domingo, DN; tel. 541-3121; fax 540-6445; e-mail correo@salud.gob.do; internet www.msp.gov.do.

Ministry of Public Works and Communications: Avda Héctor Homero Hernández, esq. Avda Tiradentes, Ensanche La Fe, Santo Domingo, DN; tel. 565-2811; fax 562-3382; e-mail contacto@mopc.gob.do; internet www.seopc.gov.do.

Ministry of Sport and Recreation: Avda Correa y Cidrón, esq. John F. Kennedy, Estadio Olímpico, Centro Olímpico Juan Pablo Duarte, Santo Domingo, DN; tel. 565-3325; fax 563-6586; e-mail juliomonnadal@miderec.gov.do; internet www.miderec.gov.do.

Ministry of Tourism: Edif. de Ofs Gubernamentales, Bloque D, Avda México, esq. 30 de Marzo, Apdo 497, Santo Domingo, DN; tel. 221-4660; fax 682-3806; e-mail info@sectur.gob.do; internet www.sectur.gob.do.

Ministry of Women: Edif. de Ofs Gubernamentales, Bloque D, 2°, Avda México, esq. 30 de Marzo, Santo Domingo, DN; tel. 685-3755; fax 685-8040; e-mail info@mujer.gob.do; internet www.mujer.gob.do.

Ministry of Youth: Avda Jiménez de Moya 71, esq. Calle Desiderio Arias, Ensanche La Julia, Santo Domingo, DN; tel. 508-7227; fax 508-6686; e-mail info@juventud.gob.do; internet www.juventud.gob.do.

President and Legislature

PRESIDENT

Election, 20 May 2012

Candidate	Votes	% of valid votes cast
Danilo Medina Sánchez (PLD)	2,323,461	51.21
Rafael Hipólito Mejía Domínguez (PRD) .	2,130,187	46.95
Guillermo Moreno (ALPAIS)	62,296	1.37
Others	20,962	0.46
Total	4,536,906	100.00

NATIONAL CONGRESS

The Congress comprises a Senate and a Chamber of Deputies.

President of the Senate: Dr CRISTINA LIZARDO (PLD).

President of the Chamber of Deputies: ABEL MARTÍNEZ DURÁN (PLD).

General Election, 16 May 2010

	Seats	
	Senate	Chamber of Deputies
Partido de la Liberación Dominicana (PLD)	31	105
Partido Revolucionario Dominicano (PRD)	—	75
Partido Reformista Social Cristiano (PRSC)	1	3
Total	32	183*

* A further seven deputies were elected by overseas voters in an election held on 20 May 2012, increasing the total number of deputies to 190. Of these seven seats, four were won by the PRD and three were secured by the PLD.

Election Commission

Junta Central Electoral (JCE): Avda 27 de Febrero, esq. Gregorio Luperón, Santo Domingo, DN; tel. 539-5419; e-mail webmaster@jce.gob.do; internet www.jce.gob.do; f. 1923; govt-appointed body; Pres. Dr ROBERTO ROSARIO MÁRQUEZ.

Political Organizations

Alianza País (ALPAIS): Calle Pasteur 55, 2°, Gazcue, Santo Domingo, DN; tel. 238-5409; e-mail participa@alianzapais.com.do; internet www.alianzapais.com.do; Pres. GUILLERMO MORENO.

Alianza por la Democracia (APD): Benito Mención 10, Gazcue, Santo Domingo, DN; tel. 687-0337; fax 687-0360; f. 1992 by breakaway group of the PLD; Pres. MAXIMILIANO PUIG; Sec.-Gen. CARLOS LUIS SÁNCHEZ S.

Bloque Institucional Socialdemócrata (BIS): Avda Bolívar 24, esq. Uruguay, Ensanche Lugo, Apdo 5413, Santo Domingo, DN; tel. 682-3232; fax 682-3375; e-mail bloque.institucionalsocialdemocrata@hotmail.com; internet bis.org.do; f. 1989 by breakaway group of the PRD; Leader JOSÉ FRANCISCO PEÑA TAVAREZ.

Fuerza Nacional Progresista (FNP): Calle Emilio A. Morel 17, Ensanche La Fe, Santo Domingo, DN; tel. 732-0849; e-mail fuerza_nacional_progresista@hotmail.com; internet fuerzanacionalprogresista.blogspot.com; right-wing; Pres. MARINO VINICIO CASTILLO (alias Vincho); Sec.-Gen. JOSÉ RICARDO TAVERAS BLANCO.

Partido de la Liberación Dominicana (PLD): Avda Independencia 401, Santo Domingo, DN; tel. 685-3540; fax 687-5569; e-mail pldorg@pld.org.do; internet www.pld.org.do; f. 1973 by breakaway group of the PRD; left-wing; Leader LEONEL FERNÁNDEZ REYNA; Sec.-Gen. REINALDO PARED PÉREZ.

Partido Reformista Social Cristiano (PRSC): Avda Tiradentes, esq. San Cristóbal, Ensanche La Fe, Apdo 1332, Santo Domingo, DN; tel. 621-7772; fax 476-9361; e-mail s.seliman@codetel.net.do; internet www.prsc.com.do; f. 1964; centre-right party; Pres. FEDER-ICO ANTÚN BATLLE; Sec.-Gen. RAMÓN ROGELIO GENAO.

Partido Revolucionario Dominicano (PRD): Avda Dr Comandante Enrique Jiménez Moya 14, Bella Vista, Santo Domingo, DN; tel. 687-2193; e-mail prensa_tribunalp.r.d@hotmail.com; internet www.prd.org.do; f. 1939; democratic socialist; Pres. MIGUEL VARGAS MALDONADO; Sec.-Gen. ORLANDO JORGE MERA.

Partido Revolucionario Independiente (PRI): Edif. Galerías Comerciales, Avda 57, Apdo 509, Santo Domingo, DN; tel. 221-8286; e-mail trajano.s@codetel.net.do; f. 1985 after split by the PRD's right-wing faction; Pres. Dr TRAJANO SANTANA; Sec.-Gen. DR JORGE MONTES DE OCA.

Partido de los Trabajadores Dominicanos (PTD): Avda Bolívar 101, esq. Dr Báez, Gazcue, Santo Domingo, DN; tel. 685-7705; fax 333-6443; e-mail contacto@ptd.org.do; internet www.ptd.org.do; f. 1979; Communist; Pres. JOSÉ GONZÁLEZ ESPINOZA; Sec.-Gen. ANTONIO FLORIÁN.

Diplomatic Representation

EMBASSIES IN THE DOMINICAN REPUBLIC

Argentina: Avda Máximo Gómez 10, Apdo 1302, Santo Domingo, DN; tel. 682-2977; fax 221-2206; e-mail edomi@mreic.gov.ar; Ambassador NOEMI MARCÍA GOMEZ.

Belize: Carretera La Isabela, Calle Proyecto 3, Arroyo Manzano 1, Santo Domingo, DN; tel. 567-7146; fax 567-7159; e-mail embassy@embelize.org; internet www.embelize.org; Ambassador R. EDUARDO LAMA S.

Brazil: Eduardo Vicioso 46A, esq. Avda Winston Churchill, Ensanche Bella Vista, Apdo 1655, Santo Domingo, DN; tel. 532-4200; fax 532-0917; e-mail contacto@embajadadebrasil.org.do; internet www.embajadadebrasil.org.do; Ambassador JOSÉ MARCUS VINICIUS DE SOUSA.

Canada: Avda Winston Churchill 1099, Torre Citigroup en Acrópolis Center, 18°, Ensanche Piantini, Apdo 2054, Santo Domingo, DN; tel. 262-3100; fax 262-3108; e-mail sdmgo@international.gc.ca; internet www.canadainternational.gc.ca/dominican_republic-republique_dominicaine; Ambassador GEORGES BOISSÉ.

Chile: Avda Anacaona 11, Mirador del Sur, Santo Domingo, DN; tel. 532-7800; fax 530-8310; e-mail embachile1@claro.net.do; internet chileabroad.gov.cl/republica-dominicana; Ambassador FERNANDO BARRERA ROBINSON.

Colombia: Calle Andrés Julio Aybar 27, casi esq. Avda Abraham Lincoln, Ensanche Piantini, Santo Domingo, DN; tel. 562-1670; fax 562-3253; e-mail erdomini@cancilleria.gov.co; Ambassador Adm. (retd) ROBERTO GARCÍA MÁRQUEZ.

Costa Rica: Calle Malaquías Gil 11 Altos, entre Abraham Lincoln y Lope de Vega, Ensanche Serralles, Santo Domingo, DN; tel. 683-7209; fax 565-6467; e-mail emb.costarica@codetel.net; Ambassador JOSÉ RAFAEL TORRES CASTRO.

Cuba: Francisco Prats Ramírez 808, El Millón, Santo Domingo, DN; tel. 537-2113; fax 537-9820; e-mail embadom@codetel.net.do; internet www.cubadiplomatica.cu/republicadominicana; Ambassador ALEXIS BANDRICH VEGA.

Ecuador: Edif. Optica Félix, Penthouse 601, Avda Abraham Lincoln 1007, Ensanche Piantini, Santo Domingo, DN; tel. 563-8363; fax 563-8153; e-mail mecuador@verizon.net.do; Ambassador CARLOS LÓPEZ DAMM.

El Salvador: Calle 2da, No 2, esq. Calle Central, Ensanche Bella Vista, Santo Domingo, DN; tel. 565-4311; fax 541-7503; e-mail EmbajadaDominicana@rree.gob.sv; Ambassador CARLOS ALBERTO CALLES CASTILLO.

France: Calle Las Damas 42, esq. El Conde, Zona Colonial, Santo Domingo, DN; tel. 695-4300; fax 695-4311; e-mail ambafrance@ambafrance-do.org; internet www.ambafrance.org.do; Ambassador BLANDINE KREISS.

Germany: Edif. Torre Piantini, 16° y 17°, Calle Gustavo Mejía Ricart 196, esq. Avda Abraham Lincoln, Ensanche Piantini, Santo Domingo, DN; tel. 542-8949; fax 542-8955; e-mail info@santo-domingo.diplo.de; internet www.santo-domingo.diplo.de; Ambassador VICTORIA ZIMMERMANN VON SIEFART.

Guatemala: Edif. Corominas Pepín, 9°, Avda 27 de Febrero 233, Santo Domingo, DN; tel. 381-0249; fax 381-0278; e-mail embrepdominicana@minex.gob.gt; Ambassador ALEJANDRO JOSÉ BUITRÓN PORRAS.

Haiti: Calle Juan Sánchez Ramírez 33, esq. Desiderio Valdez 33, Zona Universitaria, Santo Domingo, DN; tel. 686-8185; fax 686-6096; e-mail embajadahaiti@yahoo.com; Ambassador Dr FRITZ N. CINEAS.

Holy See: Avda Máximo Gómez 27, esq. César Nicolás Penson, Apdo 312, Santo Domingo, DN (Apostolic Nunciature); tel. 682-3773; fax 687-0287; Apostolic Nuncio Most Rev. JUDE THADDEUS OKOLO (Titular Archbishop of Novica).

Honduras: Calle Arístides García Mella, esq. Rodríguez Objío, Edif. El Buen Pastor VI, Apt 1B, 1°, Mirador del Sur, Santo Domingo, DN; tel. 482-7992; fax 482-7505; e-mail e.honduras@codetel.net.do; Ambassador MARÍA EUGENIA BARRIOS ALEMÁN.

Israel: Calle Pedro Henríquez Ureña 80, La Esperilla, Santo Domingo, DN; tel. 920-1500; fax 472-1785; e-mail info@santodomingo.mfa.gov.il; internet santodomingo.mfa.gov.il; Ambassador BAHIJ MANSOUR.

Italy: Calle Rodríguez Objío 4, Gazcue, Santo Domingo, DN; tel. 682-0830; fax 682-8296; e-mail ambsdom.mail@esteri.it; internet www.ambsantodomingo.esteri.it; Chargé d'affaires a.i. OLINDO D'AGOSTINO.

Jamaica: Avda Sarasota 36, Bella Vista, Plaza Kury, Suite 304, Santo Domingo, DN; tel. 567-7770; fax 620-2497; e-mail embjamaica.info@correo.tricom.net; internet www.embajadadejamaica-rd.com; Chargé d'affaires a.i. THOMAS F. ALLAN MARLEY.

Japan: Torre BHD, 8°, Avda Winston Churchill, esq. Luis F. Thomén, Ensanche Evaristo Morales, Apdo 9825, Santo Domingo, DN; tel. 567-3365; fax 566-8013; e-mail embjpn@codetel.net.do; internet www.do.emb-japan.go.jp; Ambassador TAKASHI FUCHIGAMI.

Korea, Republic: Torre Forum, 14°, Avda 27 de Febrero 495, Santo Domingo, DN; tel. 482-6505; fax 482-6504; e-mail embcod@mofa.go.kr; internet dom.mofa.go.kr; Ambassador OH HANGU.

Mexico: Arzobispo Meriño 265, esq. Las Mercedes, Zona Colonial, Santo Domingo, DN; tel. 687-7793; fax 687-7872; e-mail embamex@codetel.net.do; Ambassador JOSÉ IGNACIO PIÑA ROJAS.

Morocco: Avda Abraham Lincoln 1009, Edif. Profesional EFA, 6°, Ensanche Piantini, Santo Domingo, DN; tel. 732-0409; fax 732-1703; e-mail sifamasdomingo@codetel.net.do; Ambassador IBRAHIM HOUSSEIN MOUSSA.

Netherlands: Max Henríquez Ureña 50, entre Avda Winston Churchill y Abraham Lincoln, Ensanche Piantini, Apdo 855, Santo Domingo, DN; tel. 262-0320; fax 565-4685; e-mail std@minbuza.nl; internet www.holanda.org.do; Ambassador MARIJKE A. VAN DRUNEN LITTEL.

Nicaragua: Avda Helios, Calle Corozal, No 6, Bella Vista, Santo Domingo, DN; tel. 535-1120; fax 535-1230; e-mail embanic-rd@codetel.net.do; Ambassador NELSON ARTOLA ESCOBAR.

Panama: Benito Monción 255, Gazcue, Santo Domingo, DN; tel. 688-3789; fax 685-3665; e-mail emb.panam@codetel.net.do; Ambassador ALBERTO MAGNO CASTILLERO PINILLA.

Peru: Calle Mayreni 31, Urb. Los Cacicazgos, Santo Domingo, DN; tel. 482-3300; fax 482-3334; e-mail embaperu@verizon.net.do; Ambassador ENRIQUE ALEJANDRO PALACIOS REYES.

Qatar: Avda Sarasota 7, Santo Domingo, DN; tel. 535-7600; fax 535-7900; internet www.qataremb.com; Ambassador KHAMIS BUTTI AL-SAHOUTI.

Spain: Avda Independencia 1205, Apdo 1468, Santo Domingo, DN; tel. 535-6500; fax 535-1595; e-mail informae@maec.es; internet www.exteriores.gob.es/embajadas/santodomingo; Ambassador JAIME LACADENA HIGUERA.

Switzerland: Edif. Aeromar, 2°, Avda Winston Churchill 71, esq. Desiderio Arias, Bella Vista, Apdo 3626, Santo Domingo, DN; tel. 533-3781; fax 532-3781; e-mail sdd.vertretung@eda.admin.ch; internet www.eda.admin.ch/santodomingo; Ambassador LINE LEON-PERNET.

Taiwan (Republic of China): Avda Rómulo Betancourt 1360, Secto Bella Vista, Santo Domingo, DN; tel. 508-6200; fax 508-6335; e-mail dom@mofa.gov.tw; internet www.taiwanembassy.org/DO; Ambassador TOMÁS PING FU HOU.

United Kingdom: Edif. Corominas Pepin, 7°, Avda 27 de Febrero 233, Santo Domingo, DN; tel. 472-7111; fax 472-7574; e-mail brit.emb.sadom@codetel.net.do; internet ukindominicanrepublic.fco.gov.uk; Ambassador STEVEN FISHER.

USA: Avda República de Colombia 57, Altos de Arroyo Hondo, Santo Domingo, DN; tel. 567-7775; fax 686-7437; e-mail reference@embajadausa.gov.do; internet santodomingo.usembassy.gov; Ambassador JAMES (WALLY) BREWSTER.

Uruguay: Edif. Gapo, Local 401, Avda Luis F. Thomen 110, Ensanche Evaristo Morales, Santo Domingo, DN; tel. 227-3475; fax 472-4231; e-mail urudominicana@mrree.gub.uy; Ambassador RAÚL JUAN POLLAK GIAMPIETRO.

Venezuela: Avda Anacaona 7, Mirador del Sur, Santo Domingo, DN; tel. 537-8882; fax 537-8780; e-mail embvenezuela@codetel.net.do;

internet www.embajadavenezuelard.org; Ambassador ALBERTO EFRAÍN CASTELLAR PADILLA.

Judicial System

The Judicial Power resides in the Supreme Court of Justice, the Courts of Appeal, the Tribunals of First Instance, and the municipal courts. The Supreme Court is composed of 16 judges and the Attorney-General, and exercises disciplinary authority over all the members of the judiciary. The National Judiciary Council appoints the members of the Supreme Court, which in turn appoints judges at all other levels of the judicial system.

Suprema Corte de Justicia: Centro de los Héroes, Calle Juan de Dios Ventura Simó, esq. Enrique Jiménez Moya, Apdo 1485, Santo Domingo, DN; tel. 533-3191; fax 532-2906; e-mail suprema.corte@verizon.net.do; internet www.suprema.gov.do; Pres. Dr MARIANO GERMAN MEJÍA.

Attorney-General: FRANCISCO DOMÍNGUEZ BRITO.

Religion

The majority of the inhabitants belong to the Roman Catholic Church, but freedom of worship exists for all denominations. The Baptist, Evangelist, Seventh-day Adventist and Mormon churches and the Jewish faith are also represented.

CHRISTIANITY

The Roman Catholic Church

The Dominican Republic comprises two archdioceses and nine dioceses. Roman Catholics represent about 87% of the population.

Bishops' Conference: Isabel la Católica 55, Apdo 186, Santo Domingo, DN; tel. 685-3141; fax 685-0227; e-mail nicolas.clr@codetel.net.do; internet www.ced.org.do; f. 1985; Pres. Cardinal NICOLÁS DE JESÚS LÓPEZ RODRÍGUEZ (Archbishop of Santo Domingo).

Archbishop of Santiago de los Caballeros: Most Rev. RAMÓN BENITO DE LA ROSA Y CARPIO, Arzobispado, Duvergé 14, Apdo 679, Santiago de los Caballeros; tel. 582-2094; fax 581-3580; e-mail arzobisp.stgo@verizon.net.do.

Archbishop of Santo Domingo: Cardinal NICOLÁS DE JESÚS LÓPEZ RODRÍGUEZ, Arzobispado, Isabel la Católica 55, Apdo 186, Santo Domingo, DN; tel. 685-3141; fax 688-7270; e-mail nicolas.clr@codetel.net.do.

The Anglican Communion

Anglicans in the Dominican Republic are under the jurisdiction of the Episcopal Church in the USA. The country is classified as a missionary diocese, in Province IX.

Bishop of the Dominican Republic: Rt Rev. JULIO CÉSAR HOLGUÍN KHOURY, Santiago 114, Apdo 764, Santo Domingo, DN; tel. 688-6016; fax 686-6364; e-mail iglepidom@verizon.net.do; internet episcopaldominican.org.

Other Christian Churches

Church of Jesus Christ of Latter-Day Saints (Mormons): Avda Bolívar 825, Los Robles, Santo Domingo, DN; tel. 731-2078; internet www.lds.org; 124,435 mems.

BAHÁ'Í FAITH

Bahá'í Community of the Dominican Republic: Cambronal 152, esq. Beller, Santo Domingo, DN; tel. 687-1726; fax 687-7606; e-mail bahai.rd.aen@verizon.net.do; internet www.bahai.org.do; f. 1961; 402 localities.

The Press

DAILIES

El Caribe: Calle Doctor Defilló 4, Los Prados, Apdo 416, Santo Domingo, DN; tel. 683-8100; fax 544-4003; e-mail editora@elcaribe.com.do; internet www.elcaribe.com.do; f. 1948; morning; Pres. FÉLIX M. GARCÍA; Dir OSVALDO SANTANA; circ. 32,000.

El Día: Avda San Martín 236, Santo Domingo, DN; tel. 565-5581; fax 540-1697; e-mail eldia@eldia.com.do; internet www.eldia.com.do; f. 2002; Dir RAFAEL MOLINA MORILLO; Editor FRANKLIN PUELLO.

Diario Libre: Avda Abraham Lincoln, esq. Max Henríquez Ureña, Apdo 20313, Santo Domingo, DN; tel. 476-7200; fax 616-1520; internet www.diariolibre.com; Dir ADRIANO MIGUEL TEJADA.

Dominican Today: Avda Abraham Lincoln 452, Local 220B, Plaza La Francesa, Piantini, Santo Domingo, DN; tel. 334-6386; e-mail jorge.pineda@dominicantoday.com; internet www.dominicantoday.com; online, English language; Editor-in-Chief JORGE PINEDA.

Hoy: Avda San Martín 236, Santo Domingo, DN; tel. 565-5581; fax 567-2424; e-mail periodicohoy@hoy.com.do; internet www.hoy.com.do; f. 1981; morning; Dir ALVAREZ VEGA; Man. Editors CLAUDIO ACOSTA, MARIEN CAPITÁN; circ. 40,000.

La Información: Carretera Licey, Km 3, Santiago de los Caballeros; tel. 581-1915; fax 581-7770; e-mail lainformacion@lainformacion.com.do; internet lainformacion.com.do; f. 1915; morning; Dir EMMANUEL CASTILLO; Editor-in-Chief SERVIO CEPEDA; circ. 15,000.

Listín Diario: Paseo de los Periodistas 52, Ensanche Miraflores, Santo Domingo, DN; tel. 686-6688; fax 686-6595; e-mail info@listindiario.com.do; internet www.listin.com.do; f. 1889; morning; bought in mid-2010; Dir-Gen. MIGUEL FRANJUL; Editor-in-Chief FABIO CABRAL; circ. 60,000.

El Nacional: Avda San Martín 236, Santo Domingo, DN; tel. 565-5581; fax 565-4190; e-mail elnacional@elnacional.com.do; internet www.elnacional.com.do; f. 1966; evening and Sun.; Dir RADHAMÉS GÓMEZ PEPÍN; circ. 45,000.

El Nuevo Diario: Avda Francia 41, Santo Domingo, DN; tel. 687-7450; fax 687-3205; e-mail redaccionnd@gmail.com; internet www.elnuevodiario.com.do; f. 1981; morning; Exec. Dir COSETTE BONNELLY; Editor LUIS BRITO.

PERIODICALS

Arquitexto: Gustavo Mejía Ricart 37, 6°, Ensanche Naco, Apdo 560, Santo Domingo, DN; tel. 732-7674; e-mail arquitexto@arquitexto.com; internet arquitexto.com; f. 1985; 4 a year; architecture; Editor CARMEN ORTEGA.

La Casa: Avda Abraham Lincoln 708, esq. Max Henríquez Ureña, Ensanche Piantini, Apdo 20313, Santo Domingo, DN; tel. 476-3022; e-mail lacasa@revistalacasa.com; internet www.revistalacasa.com; f. 1998; architecture and interior design; Dir BEATRIZ BIENZOBAS.

Gestión: Torre Piantini, Suite 903, Avda Abraham Lincoln, esq. Gustavo Mejía Ricart, Santo Domingo, DN; tel. 542-0126; fax 540-1982; e-mail info@gestion.com.do; internet www.gestion.com.do; f. 2008; Dir-Gen. NEY DIAZ; Editor VIRGINIA DE MOYA.

Novus Dominicana: Calle Gaspar Polanco, 258 Torre Malaquias II, Suite 5-B-Bella Vista, Santo Domingo, DN; tel. 289-2022; fax 341-8877; e-mail info@novusmagazine.com; internet www.novusdominicana.com; Gen. Man DAVIDE VIANELLO.

Pandora: Calle Doctor Defilló 4, Los Prados, Apdo 416, Santo Domingo, DN; tel. 683-8504; fax 544-4003; e-mail pandora@elcaribe.com.do; internet www.pandora.com.do; f. 2003; 2 a month; Dir and Editor AIRAM TORIBIO.

Refugios: Edif. Tres Robles, Calle Freddy Prestol Castillo 23, Apto 1-C, Piantini, Santo Domingo, DN; tel. and fax 732-0421; e-mail info@coralcomunicaciones.com; internet www.refugiosmagazine.com; f. 2007; 6 a year; travel; Pres. LAURA DE LA NUEZ.

Revista Social Sports: Avda Imbert, esq. Pedro Casado, La Vega; tel. 242-4887; e-mail revistasocialsports@gmail.com; internet www.revistasocialsports.com; monthly; Exec. Dir JOSÉ LUIS BAUTISTA.

Visión Agropecuaria: Autopista Duarte, Km 6.5, Los Jardines del Norte, Santo Domingo, DN; tel. 547-1193; e-mail visionagropecuaria27@gmail.com; newsletter of the Ministry of Agriculture; 6 a year; Dir WILFREDO POLANCO; Editor ANTONIO CÁCERES.

Publishers

Editora Alfa y Omega: José Contreras 69, Santo Domingo, DN; tel. 532-5578; e-mail alfayomega.editora@gmail.com; f. 1976.

Editora El Caribe, C por A: Calle Doctor Defilló 4, Los Prados, Apdo 416, Santo Domingo, DN; tel. 683-8100; fax 544-4003; e-mail editora@elcaribe.com.do; internet www.elcaribe.com.do; f. 1948; Pres. FÉLIX GARCÍA.

Editora Hoy, C por A: Avda San Martín 436, Santo Domingo, DN; tel. 566-1147.

Editorama, SA: Calle Eugenio Contreras, No 54, Los Trinitarios, Apdo 2074, Santo Domingo, DN; tel. 596-6669; fax 594-1421; e-mail editorama@editorama.com; internet www.editorama.com; f. 1970; Pres. JUAN ANTONIO QUIÑONES MARTE.

Grupo Editorial Norma: Calle D, Zona Industrial de Herrera, Santo Domingo, DN; tel. 274-3333; e-mail editoranorma@codetel.net.do; internet www.norma.com.do.

Grupo Editorial Oceano: Edif. Calidad a Tiempo, 2°, Calle J, esq. Calle L, Zona Industrial de Herrera, Santo Domingo, DN; tel. 537-

0832; fax 537-5187; e-mail info@oceano.com.do; internet www
.oceano.com; Pres. JOSÉ LLUIS MONREAL.

Publicaciones Ahora, C por A: Avda San Martín 236, Apdo 1402,
Santo Domingo, DN; tel. 565-5580; fax 565-4190; Pres. JULIO A.
MORENO.

ASSOCIATIONS

Asociación Dominicana de Libreros y Afines (Asodolibro):
Calle Espaillat 201, entre El Conde y Arzobispo Nou, Santo Domingo,
DN; tel. 688-8425; fax 689-3865; e-mail asodolibro@codetel.net.do;
Pres. DENNIS PEÑA.

Cámara Dominicana del Libro, Inc: Arzobispo Nouel 160, Santo
Domingo, DN; tel. 682-1032; fax 686-6110; e-mail
camaradominicanadellibro@hotmail.com; internet www
.camaradominicanadellibro.com; f. 1970; Pres. URIBE VIRTUES; Sec.
JACQUELINE DÍAZ.

Broadcasting and Communications

REGULATORY AUTHORITY

**Instituto Dominicano de las Telecomunicaciones (INDO-
TEL):** Avda Abraham Lincoln, No 962, Edif. Osiris, CP 10148, Santo
Domingo, DN; tel. 732-5555; fax 732-3904; e-mail info@indotel.gob
.do; internet www.indotel.org.do; f. 1998; Chair. GEDEÓN SANTOS;
Exec. Dir TERESITA BENCOSME DE UREÑA.

TELECOMMUNICATIONS

**Compañía Dominicana de Teléfonos, C por A (Claro—Code-
tel):** Avda John F. Kennedy 54, Apdo 1377, Santo Domingo, DN; tel.
220-1111; fax 543-1301; e-mail servicioalcliente@codetel.net.do;
internet www.codetel.net.do; f. 1930; owned by América Móvil, SA
de CV (Mexico); operates mobile services as Claro and fixed-line
services as Codetel; 51% of mobile market; Pres. OSCAR PEÑA CHACÓN.

Orange Dominicana, SA: Calle Víctor Garrido Puello 23, Edif.
Orange, Ensanche Piantini, Santo Domingo, DN; tel. 859-1000; fax
539-8454; e-mail servicio.cliente@orange.com.do; internet www
.orange.com.do; f. 2000; mobile cellular telephone operator; subsidiary of Orange, SA (France); 38% of mobile market; Pres. JEAN MARC
HARION.

Tricom Telecomunicaciones de Voz, Data y Video: Avda Lope
de Vega 95, Ensanche Naco, Santo Domingo, DN; tel. 476-6000; fax
476-6700; e-mail sc@tricom.com.do; internet www.tricom.net;
f. 1992; 3% of mobile market; Pres. and CEO HÉCTOR CASTRO NOBOA;
Gen. Man. CARLOS ESCOBAR.

VIVA (Trilogy Dominicana, SA): Edif. Carib Alico, 3°, Avda Abraham
Lincoln 295, Sector La Julia, Santo Domingo, DN; internet www.viva
.com.do; f. 2008; mobile cellular telephone network and internet
provider; 7.4% of mobile market.

BROADCASTING

Radio

The government-owned broadcasting network, Corporación Estatal
de Radio y Televisión, operates three radio stations. There were some
130 commercial stations in the Dominican Republic.

Asociación Dominicana de Radiodifusoras Inc (ADORA):
Calle Paul Harris 3, Centro de los Héroes, Santo Domingo, DN;
tel. 535-4057; fax 535-4058; e-mail adora.org.do@gmail.com; internet
adora-do.blogspot.com; f. 1967; Pres. SANDRA PONS.

Cadena de Noticias (CDN) Radio: Calle Doctor Defilló 4, Los
Prados, Apdo 416, Santo Domingo, DN; tel. 683-8100; fax 544-4003;
e-mail inforadio@cdn.com.do; internet www.cdn.com.do.

Zulu Radio: Isabel La Católica 7, Santo Domingo 10210, DN; tel.
686-0757; internet www.zulurd.com; f. 2010; Co-owners AURO
LOVILUZ, JUAN CARLOS GARCÍA.

Television

Antena Latina, Canal 7: Avda Gustavo Mejía Ricart 45, Ensanche
Naco, Santo Domingo, DN; tel. 412-0707; fax 333-0707; e-mail
contacto@antenalatina7.com; internet www.antenalatina7.com;
f. 1999; owned by Grupo Sin; Pres. JOSÉ MIGUEL BONETTI.

Cadena de Noticias (CDN) Televisión: Calle Doctor Defilló 4, Los
Prados, Apdo 416, Santo Domingo, DN; tel. 262-2100; fax 567-2671;
e-mail direccion@cdn.com.do; internet www.cdn.com.do; broadcasts
news on Channel 37; Dir FERNANDO HASBÚN.

Color Visión, Canal 9: Emilio A. Morel, esq. Luis Pérez, Ensanche
La Fe, Apdo 30043, Santo Domingo, DN; tel. 566-5875; fax 732-9347;
e-mail color.vision@colorvision.com.do; internet www.colorvision
.com.do; f. 1969; majority-owned by Corporación Dominicana de
Radio y Televisión; commercial station; Dir-Gen. DOMINGO OCTAVIO
BERMUDEZ MADERA.

Corporación Estatal de Radio y Televisión (CERTV): Dr
Tejada Florentino 8, Apdo 869, Santo Domingo, DN; tel. 689-2120;
e-mail rm.colombo@codetel.net.do; internet www.certvdominicana
.com; f. 1952; fmrly Radio Televisión Dominicana, Canal 4; changed
name as above in 2003; govt station; Channel 4; Pres. ELISEO PÉREZ;
Dir-Gen. PEDRO J. BATISTA CABA.

Teleantillas, Canal 2: Autopista Duarte, Km 7½, Los Prados, Apdo
30404, Santo Domingo, DN; tel. 567-7751; fax 540-4912; e-mail
webmaster@tele-antillas.tv; internet www.tele-antillas.tv; f. 1979;
Gen. Man. HÉCTOR VALENTÍN BÁEZ.

Telecentro, Canal 13: Avda Luperón 25, Herrera, Santo Domingo,
DN; tel. 334-3040; fax 274-0599; e-mail info@rnn.com.do; internet
www.telecentro.com.do; f. 1986; Santo Domingo and east region;
Pres. NELSON GUILLÉN.

Telemedios Dominicanos, Canal 25: 16 de Agosto, Santo Domingo, DN; tel. 583-2525; internet www.canal25net.tv; f. 1999; Dir
CÉSAR HERNÁNDEZ.

Telemicro, Canal 5: Edif. Telemicro, Calle Mariano Cestero, esq.
Enrique Henríquez 1, Gazcue, Santo Domingo, DN; tel. 689-0555; fax
686-6528; e-mail programacion@telemicro.com.do; internet www
.telemicro.com.do; f. 1982; Dir DOMINGO DEL PILLAR.

Telesistema, Canal 11: Avda 27 de Febrero 52, esq. Máximo
Gómez, Sector Bergel, Santo Domingo, DN; tel. 563-6661; fax 472-
1754; e-mail info@telesistema11.tv; internet www.telesistema11.tv;
Pres. JOSÉ L. CORREPIO ESTRADA.

Finance

(cap. = capital; res = reserves; dep. = deposits; m. = million;
brs = branches; amounts in pesos)

BANKING

Supervisory Body

Superintendencia de Bancos: 52 Avda México, esq. Leopoldo
Navarro, Apdo 1326, Santo Domingo, DN; tel. 685-8141; fax 685-
0859; e-mail nmolina@supbanco.gov.do; internet www.supbanco.gov
.do; f. 1947; Supt RAFAEL CAMILO ABREU.

Central Bank

Banco Central de la República Dominicana: Calle Pedro Henríquez Ureña, esq. Leopoldo Navarro, Apdo 1347, Santo Domingo,
DN; tel. 221-9111; fax 687-7488; e-mail info@bancentral.gov.do;
internet www.bancentral.gov.do; f. 1947; cap. 2,371.3m., res 1.0m.,
dep. 312,156.4m. (Dec. 2009); Gov. HÉCTOR VALDEZ ALBIZU; Man.
ERVIN NOVAS BELLO.

Commercial Banks

Banco Dominicano del Progreso, SA (Progreso): Avda John F.
Kennedy 3, Apdo 1329, Santo Domingo, DN; tel. 378-3233; fax 227-
3107; e-mail informacion@progreso.com.do; internet www.progreso
.com.do; f. 1975; merged with Banco Metropolitano, SA, and Banco de
Desarrollo Dominicano, SA, in 2000; cap. 4,428.6m., res 658.6m., dep.
34,786.2m. (Dec. 2012); Pres. MARK SILVERMAN; 56 brs.

Banco Múltiple BHD León, SA: Avda 27 de Febrero, esq. Avda
Winston Churchill, Santo Domingo, DN; tel. 243-3232; fax 809-
5676747; e-mail servicio@bhd.com.do; internet www.bhd.com.do;
f. 1972; cap. 9,940.4m., res 1,658.7m., dep. 94,614.8m. (Dec. 2013);
Pres. LUIS EUGENIO MOLINA ACHÉCAR; Dir JAIME SUED; 4 brs.

Banco Popular Dominicano Banco Múltiple, SA: Avda John F.
Kennedy 20, Torre Popular, Apdo 1441, Santo Domingo, DN; tel. 544-
5000; fax 544-5899; e-mail contactenos@bpd.com.do; internet www
.bpd.com.do; f. 1963; cap. 12,697.4m., res 5,066.4m., dep. 177,043.4m.
(Dec. 2013); Pres., Chair. and Gen. Man. MANUEL ALEJANDRO
GRULLÓN; 205 brs.

**Banco de Reservas de la República Dominicana (Banreser-
vas):** Isabel la Católica 201, Apdo 1353, Santo Domingo, DN; tel. 960-
4000; fax 689-2305; e-mail mensajeadministrador@banreservas
.com; internet www.banreservas.com.do; f. 1941; state-owned; cap.
3,500.0m., res 11,240.6m., dep. 236,305.5m. (Dec. 2013); Pres. SIMÓN
LIZARDO MÉZQUITA (Minister of Finance); Administrator VICENTE
BENGOA ALBIZU; 195 brs.

Scotiabank (Canada): Avda John F. Kennedy, esq. Lope de Vega,
Apdo 1494, Santo Domingo, DN; tel. 567-7268; e-mail drinfo@
scotiabank.com; internet www.scotiabank.com.do; f. 1920; Vice-
Pres. and Gen. Man. CHIARA BORRELLI; 74 brs.

Development Banks

Banco Agrícola de la República Dominicana: Avda G. Washington 601, Apdo 1057, Santo Domingo, DN; tel. 535-8088; fax 508-6212;
e-mail bagricola@bagricola.gov.do; internet www.bagricola.gov.do;

f. 1945; govt agricultural devt bank; Gen. Man. and Chair. CARLOS ANTONIO SEGURA FOSTER.

Banco Múltiple ADEMI, SA: Avda Pedro Henríquez Ureña 78, La Esperilla, Santo Domingo, DN; tel. 683-0853; internet www .bancoademi.com.do; f. 1997 by Asociación para el Desarrollo de Microempresas (ADEMI); Pres. GUILLERMO RONDÓN J.

Banco Múltiple BDI, SA: Avda Sarasota 27, esq. La Julia, Santo Domingo, DN; tel. 535-8586; fax 535-8692; internet www.bdi.com.do; f. 1974; cap. 700m., res 165.8m., dep. 8,592.2m. (Dec. 2013); Pres. JUAN CARLOS RODRIGUEZ COPELLO; 10 brs.

STOCK EXCHANGE

Bolsa de Valores de la República Dominicana, SA: Edif. BVRD, 2°, Calle José Brea Peña 14, Evaristo Morales, Santo Domingo, DN; tel. 567-6694; fax 567-6697; e-mail info@bolsard.com; internet www .bolsard.com; Pres. MARÍA ANTONIA ESTEVA DE BISONO; Gen. Man. DARYS ESTRELLA.

INSURANCE

Supervisory Body

Superintendencia de Seguros: Ministerio de Finanzas, Avda México 54, esq. Leopoldo Navarro, Apdo 2207, Santo Domingo, DN; tel. 221-2606; fax 685-5096; e-mail info@superseguros.gob.do; internet www.superseguros.gob.do; f. 1969; Supt EUCLIDES GUTIÉRREZ FÉLIX.

Companies

Angloamericana de Seguros, SA: Avda Gustavo Mejía Ricard 8, esq. Hermanos Roque Martínez, Ensanche El Millón, Santo Domingo, DN; tel. 227-1002; fax 227-6005; e-mail angloseguros@ angloamericana.com.do; internet www.angloamericana.com.do; f. 1996; Pres. NELSON HEDI HERNÁNDEZ P.; Vice-Pres. ESTEBAN BETANCES FABRÉ.

ARS Palic Salud: Edif. ARS Palic Salud, Avda 27 de Febrero 50, Urb. El Vergel, Santo Domingo, DN; tel. 381-5000; fax 381-4646; e-mail servicios@arspalic.com.do; internet www.arspalic.com.do; fmrly Cía de Seguros Palic, SA; acquired by Centro Financiero BHD in 1998; changed name as above in 2003; Exec. Vice-Pres. ANDRÉS MEJÍA.

Aseguradora Agropecuaria Dominicana, SA (AGRODOSA): Avda Independencia 455, Gazcue, Santo Domingo, DN; tel. 562-6849; fax 687-4790; e-mail agrodosa@claro.net.do; agricultural sector; Exec. Dir AGRON EMILIO OLIVO TORIBIO.

Atlántica Insurance, SA: Avda 27 de Febrero 365A, 2°, Apdo 826, Santo Domingo, DN; tel. 565-5591; fax 565-4343; e-mail atlanticains@codetel.net.do; Pres. RHINA RAMIREZ; Gen. Man. Lic. GERARDO PERALTA.

BMI Compañía de Seguros, SA: Edif. Alfonso Comercial, Avda Tiradentes 14, Apdo 916, Ensanche Naco, Santo Domingo, DN; tel. 562-6660; fax 562-6849; e-mail reclamos@bmi.com.do; internet www .bmi.com.do; f. 1998; Pres. FRANCISCO GARCÍA; Gen. Man. EFRÉN ORTIZ.

Bupa Dominicana, SA: Avda Lope de Vega 13, casi esq. Avda Roberto Pastoriza, Plaza Progreso Business Center, Suite 310, Santo Domingo, DN; tel. 566-7759; fax 565-6451; e-mail dr@ bupalatinamerica.com; internet www.bupalatinamerica.com; fmrly Amedex Insurance Co; Gen. Man. INGRID REYNOSO.

Cía Dominicana De Seguros, C por A: Avda 27 de Febrero 302, Bella Vista, Santo Domingo, DN; tel. 535-1030; fax 533-2576; e-mail dominicana.seg@codetel.net.do; internet www .dominicanadeseguros.com; f. 1960; Pres. RAMÓN MOLINA; CEO VÍCTOR J. ROJAS.

La Colonial, SA: Avda Sarasota 75, Bella Vista, Santo Domingo, DN; tel. 508-8000; fax 508-0608; e-mail luis.guerrero@lacolonial.com .do; internet www.lacolonial.com.do; f. 1971; general; Pres. Dr MIGUEL FERIS IGLESIAS; Exec. Vice-Pres. LUIS EDUARDO GUERRERO ROMÁN.

Confederación del Canadá Dominicana: Calle Salvador Sturla 17, Ensanche Naco, Apdo 30088, Santo Domingo, DN; tel. 544-4144; fax 540-4740; e-mail confedom@codetel.net.do; internet www .confedom.com; f. 1988; Pres. Lic. MOISES A. FRANCO LLENAS.

Cooperativa Nacional De Seguros, Inc (COOP-SEGUROS): Calle Hermanos Deligne 156, Gazcue, Santo Domingo, DN; tel. 682-6118; fax 682-6313; e-mail contacto@coopseguros.coop; internet coopseguros.coop; f. 1990; functions as a co-operative; general and life; Pres. Dr IGNACION VALENZUELA.

Cuna Mutual Insurance Society Dominicana, C. por A: Edif. AIRAC, Avda Aristides Fiallo Cabral 258, Zona Universitaria, Santo Domingo, DN; tel. 682-2862; fax 687-2862; internet www .cunamutual.com.pr/rd; f. 2010; Regional Man. FRANCISCO ANTONIO ESTEPAN GRISANTY.

General de Seguros, SA: Avda Sarasota 55, esq. Pedro A. Bobea, Apdo 2183, Santo Domingo, DN; tel. 535-8888; fax 532-4451; e-mail info@gs.com.do; internet www.lageneraldeseguros.com; f. 1981; general; Pres. Dr FERNANDO A. BALLISTA DÍAZ.

Progreso Compañía de Seguros, SA (PROSEGUROS): Avda John F. Kennedy 1, Ensanche Miraflores, Santo Domingo, DN; tel. 985-5000; fax 985-5187; e-mail carlosro@progreso.com.do; internet www.proseguros.com.do; Pres. GONZALO ALBERTO PÉREZ ROJAS; CEO CARLOS ROMERO.

REHSA Compañía de Seguros y Reaseguros: Avda Gustavo Mejía Ricart, esq. Hermanas Roques Martínez, Ensanche El Millón, Santo Domingo, DN; tel. 548-7171; fax 584-7222; e-mail info@rehsa .com.do; internet www.rehsa.com.do; Pres. NELSON HERNÁNDEZ.

Scotia Seguros: Avda Francia No 141, esq. Máximo Gómez, 3°, Sección 2, Gazcue, Santo Domingo, DN; tel. 730-4031; fax 686-2165; e-mail info@scotiaseguros.com.do; internet www.scotiaseguros.com .do; f. 2006; fmrly BBVA Seguros; Gen. Man. DENIS LISANDRO BERROCAL.

Seguros BanReservas: Avda Jiménez Moya, esq. Calle 4, Centro Technológico Banreservas, Ensanche La Paz, Santo Domingo, DN; tel. 960-7200; fax 960-5148; e-mail serviseguros@segbanreservas .com; internet www.segurosbanreservas.com; Pres. VICENTE BENGOA ALBIZU; Vice-Pres. RAFAEL MEDINA.

Seguros Constitución: Calle Seminario 55, Ensanche Piantini, Santo Domingo, DN; tel. 620-0765; fax 412-2358; e-mail info@ segurosconstitucion.com.do; internet www.segurosconstitucion.com .do; fmrly El Sol de Seguros; changed name as above in 2008; Exec. Vice-Pres. SIMÓN MAHFOUD MIGUEL; Gen. Man. JUAN JOSÉ GUERRERO GRILLASCA.

Seguros Pepín, SA: Edif. Corp. Corominas Pepín, Avda 27 de Febrero 233, Ensanche Naco, Santo Domingo, DN; tel. 472-1006; fax 565-9176; e-mail info@segurospepin.com; internet www .segurospepin.com; general; Pres. HÉCTOR COROMINAS PEÑA.

Seguros Universal: Avda Winston Churchill 1100, Evaristo Morales, Apdo 1242, Santo Domingo, DN; tel. 544-7200; fax 544-7999; e-mail servicioalcliente@universal.com.do; internet www.universal .com.do; f. 1964 as La Universal de Seguros; merged with Grupo Asegurador América in 2000; name changed as above in 2006; general; Pres. ERNESTO M. IZQUIERDO; Vice-Pres. MARINO GINEBRA.

Unión de Seguros, C por A: Edif. B 101, Avda John F. Kennedy, Apartamental Proesa, Santo Domingo, DN; tel. 566-2191; fax 542-0065; e-mail r.sanabia@uniondeseguros.com; internet uniondeseguros.com; f. 1964; Pres. JOSÉ A. PADILLA ORTIZ; Exec. Vice-Pres. FERNANDO R. HERNÁNDEZ.

Insurance Association

Cámara Dominicana de Aseguradores y Reaseguradores, Inc: Edif. Torre BHD, 5°, Luis F. Thomen, esq. Winston Churchill, Apdo 601, Santo Domingo, DN; tel. 566-0014; fax 566-2600; e-mail cadoar@codetel.net.do; internet www.cadoar.org.do; f. 1972; Pres. ERNESTO M. IZQUIERDO; Exec. Vice-Pres. MIGUEL VILLAMÁN.

Trade and Industry

GOVERNMENT AGENCIES

Comisión Nacional de Energía (CNE): Avda Rómulo Betancourt 361, Bella Vista, CP 10112, Santo Domingo, DN; tel. 540-9002; fax 547-2073; e-mail info@cne.gov.do; internet www.cne.gov.do; f. 2001; responsible for regulation and devt of energy sector; Pres. ENRIQUE RAMIREZ.

Comisión para la Reforma de la Empresa Pública: Edif. Gubernamental Dr Rafael Kasse Acta, 6°, Gustavo Mejía Ricart 73, esq. Agustín Lara, Ensanche Serrallés, Santo Domingo, DN; tel. 683-3591; fax 683-3114; e-mail info@fonper.gov.do; internet www .fonper.gov.do; commission charged with divestment and restructuring of state enterprises; Pres. FERNANDO ROSA.

Consejo Estatal del Azúcar (CEA) (State Sugar Council): Calle Fray Cipriano de Utrera, Centro de los Héroes, Apdo 1256/1258, Santo Domingo, DN; tel. 533-1161; fax 533-1305; f. 1966; Dir-Gen. JOSÉ JOAQUÍN DOMÍNGUEZ PEÑA.

Instituto de Estabilización de Precios (INESPRE): Plaza de la Bandera, Apdo 86-2, Santo Domingo, DN; tel. 621-0020; fax 620-2588; e-mail informacion@inespre.gov.do; internet www.inespre.gov .do; f. 1969; price commission; Exec. Dir JORGE RADHAMÈS ZORRILLA OZUNA.

Instituto Nacional de la Vivienda: Avda Pedro Henríquez Ureña, esq. Avda Alma Mater, Santo Domingo, DN; tel. 732-0600; fax 227-5803; e-mail invi@verizon.net.do; internet www.invi.gob.do; f. 1962; low-cost housing institute; Dir-Gen. ALMA FERNÁNADEZ DURÁN.

DEVELOPMENT ORGANIZATIONS

Centro para el Desarrollo Agropecuario y Forestal, Inc (CEDAF): Calle José Amado Soler 50, Ensanche Paraíso, CP 567-2, Santo Domingo, DN; tel. 565-5603; fax 544-4727; e-mail cedaf@cedaf.org.do; internet www.cedaf.org.do; f. 1987 to encourage the devt of agriculture, livestock and forestry; fmrly Fundación de Desarrollo Agropecuario, Inc; Pres. MARCIAL NAJRI; Exec. Dir JUAN JOSÉ ESPINAL.

Centro de Desarrollo y Competitividad Industrial (PROINDUSTRIA): Avda 27 de Febrero, esq. Avda Luperón, Plaza de las Banderas, Apdo 1462, Santo Domingo, DN; tel. 530-0010; fax 530-1303; e-mail info@proindustria.gov.do; internet www.proindustria.gov.do; f. 1962 as Corporación de Fomento Industrial; restructured and name changed as above in 2007; industrial sector regulator; Dir-Gen. ALEXANDRA IZQUIERDO.

Fundación Dominicana de Desarrollo (Dominican Development Foundation): Mercedes No 4, Apdo 857, Santo Domingo, DN; tel. 688-8101; fax 686-0430; e-mail info@fdd.org.do; internet fdd.org.do; f. 1962 to mobilize private resources for collaboration in financing small-scale devt programmes; 384 mems; Pres. ERNESTO ARMENTEROS CALAC; Exec. Dir FRANCISCO J. ABATE F.

Instituto de Desarrollo y Crédito Cooperativo (IDECOOP): Avda Héroes de Luperón 1, Centro de los Héroes, Apdo 1371, Santo Domingo, DN; tel. 533-8131; fax 533-5149; e-mail idecoop@codetel.net.do; internet idecoop.gov.do; f. 1963 to encourage the devt of co-operatives; Pres. PEDRO CORPORÁN CABRERA; Dir CARLOS JUNIOR ESPINAL.

CHAMBERS OF COMMERCE

Cámara Americana de Comercio de la República Dominicana: Torre Empresarial, 6°, Avda Sarasota 20, Apdo 99999, Santo Domingo, DN; tel. 381-0777; fax 381-0286; e-mail amcham@codetel.net.do; internet www.amcham.org.do; Pres. MÁXIMO VIDAL; Exec. Vice-Pres. WILLIAM M. MALAMUD.

Cámara de Comercio y Producción de Santo Domingo: Avda 27 de Febrero 228, Torre Friusa, Sector La Esperilla, CP 10106, Santo Domingo, DN; tel. 682-2688; fax 685-2228; e-mail info@camarasantodomingo.do; internet www.camarasantodomingo.org.do; f. 1910; 1,500 active mems; Pres. PEDRO PEREZ GONZALEZ; Exec. Vice-Pres. FERNANDO FERRAN BRU.

INDUSTRIAL AND TRADE ASSOCIATIONS

Asociación Dominicana de Exportadores (ADOEXPO): Calle Virgilio Díaz Ordóñez 42, esq. Viriato Fiallo, Ensanche Julieta, Santo Domingo, DN; tel. 567-6779; fax 563-1926; internet adoexpo.org/es/; f. 1972; Pres. SADALA KHOURY.

Asociación Dominicana de Hacendados y Agricultores (ADHA): 265 Avda 27 de Febrero, al lado de Plaza Central, Santo Domingo, DN; tel. 565-0542; fax 565-8696; farming and agricultural org.; Pres. RICARDO BARCELÓ.

Asociación Dominicana de la Industria Eléctrica (ADIE): Calle Gustavo Mejía Ricart, esq. Avda Abraham Lincoln, Torre Piantini, 5°, Local 502-B, Ensanche Piantini, Santo Domingo, DN; tel. 547-2109; e-mail info@adie.org.do; internet www.adie.org.do; f. 2009; electrical industry asscn; Pres. MARCOS COCHÓN.

Asociación Dominicana de Zonas Francas Inc (ADOZONA): Avda Sarasota 20, 4°, Torre Empresarial AIRD, Apdo 3184, Santo Domingo, DN; tel. 472-0251; fax 472-0256; e-mail info@adozona.org; internet www.adozona.org; f. 1988; Pres. AQUÍLES BERMÚDEZ; Exec. Vice-Pres. JOSÉ MANUEL TORRES.

Asociación de Industrias de la República Dominicana, Inc: Avda Sarasota 20, Torre Empresarial AIRD, Santo Domingo, DN; tel. 472-0000; fax 472-0303; e-mail aird@verizon.net.do; internet www.aird.org.do; f. 1962; industrial org.; Pres. LIGIA BONETTI DE VALIENTE; Exec. Vice-Pres. CIRCE ALMÁNZAR MELGÉN.

Centro de Exportacióne e Inversión de la República Dominicana (CEI-RD): Avda 27 de Febrero, esq. Avda Gregorio Luperón, frente a La Plaza de la Bandera, Apdo 199-2, Santo Domingo, DN; tel. 530-5505; fax 530-8208; e-mail webmaster@cei-rd.gov.do; internet www.cei-rd.gov.do; fmrly Centro Dominicano de Promoción de Exportaciones (CEDOPEX); merged with Oficina para la Promoción de Inversiónes de la República Dominicana (OPI-RD) and changed name as above in 2003; promotion of exports and investments; Exec. Dir JEAN ALAIN RODRÍGUEZ.

Consejo Nacional de la Empresa Privada (CONEP): Avda Sarasota 20, Torre Empresarial, 12°, Ensanche La Julia, Santo Domingo, DN; tel. 472-7101; fax 472-7850; e-mail conep@conep.org.do; internet www.conep.org.do; Pres. MANUEL DIEZ CABRAL; Exec. Dir RAFAEL PAZ FAMILIA.

Consejo Nacional de Zonas Francas de Exportación (CNZFE): Edif. San Rafael, 5°, Avda Leopoldo Navarro 61, Apdo 21430, Santo Domingo, DN; tel. 686-8077; fax 686-8079; e-mail e.castillo@cnzfe.gob.do; internet www.cnzfe.gov.do; co-ordinating body for the free trade zones; Exec. Dir LUISA FERNÁNDEZ DURÁN.

Corporación Zona Franca Industrial de Santiago: Avda Mirador del Yaque, Santiago; tel. 575-1290; fax 575-1778; e-mail czfistgo@codetel.net.do; internet www.zonafrancasantiago.com; free zone park; Pres. MIGUEL LAMA.

Dirección General de Minería: Edif. de Ofs Gubernamentales, 10°, Avda México, esq. Leopoldo Navarro, Santo Domingo, DN; tel. 685-8191; fax 686-8327; e-mail direc.mineria@verizon.net.do; internet www.dgm.gov.do; f. 1947; govt mining and hydrocarbon org.; Dir-Gen. ALEXANDER MEDINA HERASME.

Instituto Agrario Dominicano (IAD): Avda 27 de Febrero, Plaza la Bandera, Santo Domingo, DN; tel. 620-6585; fax 620-1537; e-mail info@iad.gob.do; internet www.iad.gob.do; Exec. Dir ALFONSO RADHAMES VALENZUELA.

Instituto Azúcarero Dominicano (INAZUCAR): Avda Jiménez Moya, Apdo 667, Santo Domingo, DN; tel. 532-5571; fax 533-2402; e-mail inst.azucar2@codetel.net.do; internet www.inazucar.gov.do; f. 1965; sugar institute; Exec. Dir JOSÉ CASIMIRO RAMOS CALDERÓN.

Instituto de Innovación en Biotecnología e Industria (IIBI): Calle Olof Palme, esq. Núñez de Cáceres, San Gerónimo, Apdo 392-2, Santo Domingo, DN; tel. 566-8121; fax 227-8808; e-mail servicio@iibi.gov.do; internet www.iibi.gov.do; fmrly Instituto Dominicano de Tecnología Industrial (INDOTEC); name changed as above in 2005; Pres. JUAN ANTONIO OVALLES PÉREZ; Exec. Dir Dr BERNARDA A. CASTILLO.

EMPLOYERS' ORGANIZATIONS

Confederación Patronal de la República Dominicana (COPARDOM): Avda Abraham Lincoln, esq. Avda Gustavo Mejía Ricart 1003, Torre Profesional Biltmore I, Suite 501, Santo Domingo, DN; tel. 683-0013; fax 566-0879; e-mail copardom@copardom.org; internet www.copardom.org; f. 1946; Pres. JAIME O. GONZÁLEZ; Exec. Dir PEDRO R. RODRÍGUEZ VELÁZQUEZ.

Federación Dominicana de Comerciantes: Carretera Sánchez Km 10, Santo Domingo, DN; tel. 533-2666; Pres. IVAN DE JESÚS GARCÍA.

MAJOR COMPANIES

Abbott Laboratories International: Avda Monumental, esq. Republica de Colombia, Los Peralejos, Apdo 846, CP 10702, Santo Domingo, DN; tel. 542-7181; fax 922-8041; e-mail mirian.zapata@abbott.com; internet www.abbott.com; manufacturers of nutritional and pharmaceutical products; Chair. and CEO MILES D. WHITE; Man. MIRIAM ZAPATA.

Americana Departamentos, C por A: Avda John F. Kennedy, Km 5.5, Santo Domingo, DN; tel. 549-7777; fax 567-7063; e-mail atencionalcliente@americanadepartamentos.com; internet www.americana.com.do; f. 1944; distributors of hardware, houseware, animal food and construction materials; Pres. LUIS GARCÍA SAN MIGUEL; 400 employees.

Brugal & Co, C por A: Avda John F. Kennedy 57, Santo Domingo, DN; tel. 566-5651; e-mail contacto@edrington.co.uk; internet www.brugal.es/home.php; f. 1888; owned by Edrington Group (United Kingdom); rum production; Chair. GEORGE ARZENO BRUGAL; CEO FRANKLIN BÁEZ BRUGAL; c. 1,000 employees.

Cartonera Rierba, SA: Anibal de Espinosa 366, Apdo 1162, CP 10409, Santo Domingo, DN; tel. 695-4000; fax 695-4111; e-mail todocarton@cartonerarierba.com.do; internet www.cartonerarierba.com.do; f. 1946; fmrly Cartonajes Hernández, SA; mfrs of cardboard and packaging materials; Exec. Pres. and CEO RICARDO HERNÁNDEZ MARCHENA; 285 employees.

Cementos Cibao, C por A: Carretera Baitoa Km 8.5, Palo Amarillo, Apdo 571, Santiago de los Caballeros; tel. 233-7111; fax 242-7135; e-mail madelynn@cementoscibao.com; internet www.cementoscibao.com; f. 1964; mfrs of concrete and cement blocks; Pres. DENISSE RODRÍGUEZ DE FERNÁNDEZ; 516 employees.

Cemex Dominicana, C por A: Torre Acrópolis, 20°, Avda Winston Churchill 67, Ensanche Piantini, Santo Domingo, DN; tel. 683-4901; fax 683-4949; e-mail contactanos@cemexdominicana.com; internet www.cemexdominicana.com; f. 1976 as Cementos Nacionales, SA; name changed as above in 2000, following acquisition by Cemex, SA de CV (Mexico) in 1995; mfrs of cement and cement products; Dir-Gen. CARLOS GONZÁLEZ.

Central Romana Corporación: Apdo 891, La Romana, DN; tel. 730-1017; e-mail alburquerque@crcltd.com.do; internet www.centralromana.com.do; f. 1912; agro-industrial and tourism devt; CEO ALFONSO FANJUL; 25,000 employees.

Cervecería Nacional Dominicana, C por A: Avda Independencia, Santo Domingo, DN; tel. 487-3802; fax 533-5815; e-mail atencionalcliente@eli.com.do; internet www.cnd.com.do; f. 1929; part of Grupo León Jimenes; manufacturers of beer and malt liquor;

41% bought by Ambev (Brazil) in 2012; Pres. FRANKLIN LEÓN; 2,500 employees.

Delta Comercial, C por A: Avda Luperón, esq. Rómulo Betancourt, Apdo 1376, Santo Domingo, DN; tel. 620-3000; fax 518-1202; e-mail info@deltacomercial.com.do; internet www.deltacomercial.com.do; f. 1962; importers and distributors of Toyota and Lexus cars; Pres. JOSÉ ANTONIO NAJRI; Gen. Man. ALFREDO NAJRI; 675 employees.

DuBar & Co, C por A: Avda Ulises Heureaux 20, Villa Duarte, Santo Domingo, DN; tel. 592-2223; fax 593-4209; e-mail info@dubar.com.do; internet www.dubar.com.do; f. 1926 as Barceló & Co, present name adopted 2010; mfrs of distilled alcoholic drinks; Pres. JOSÉ ANTONIO BARCELÓ; 145 employees.

Falcondo Xstrata Nickel, C por A: Avda Máximo Gómez 30, Apdo 1343, Santo Domingo, DN; tel. 682-6041; fax 730-2679; e-mail falcondoinfo@xstratanickel.com.do; internet www.falcondo.com.do; f. 1971; subsidiary of Xstrata PLC; nickel mining and smelting; Gen. Man. ANTONIO GARCÍA; 600 employees.

Grupo León Jimenes: Avda Gustavo Mejía Ricart, esq. Avda Abraham Lincoln 304, Torre Piantini, Santo Domingo, DN; tel. 565-1234; fax 533-5845; e-mail info@elj.com.do; internet www.elj.com.do; f. 1985; mfrs of beer and cigars; Pres. JOSÉ LEÓN ASENCIO; 1,000 employees.

Grupo M: Caribbean Industrial Park, Santiago de los Caballeros; tel. 241-7171; fax 242-7022; e-mail info@grupom.com.do; internet www.grupom.com.do; f. 1986; mfrs of clothing; Pres. FERNANDO CAPPELLÁN; approx. 12,000 employees.

Grupo Vicini: Isabel la Católica 158, Zona Colonial, Santo Domingo, DN; tel. 541-5400; fax 735-2005; e-mail c.moya@codetel.net.do; internet www.grupovicini.com; f. 1883; sugar-cane cultivation and processing; Pres. FELIPE VICINI LLUBERES; Vice-Pres. CAMPOS DE MOYA FERNÁNDEZ.

Induban, C por A (Industrias Banilejas): Avda Máximo Gómez 118, Apdo 942, Santo Domingo, DN; tel. 565-3121; fax 541-5465; e-mail i.banilejas@verizon.net.do; internet www.induban.com; f. 1962; coffee roasting and processing; Pres. RAFAEL PERELLÓ; 877 employees.

Induveca: Avda Máximo Gómez, No 182, Santo Domingo, DN; tel. 793-3000; fax 541-2627; e-mail dist.universal@codetel.net.do; internet www.induveca.com.do; f. 2000 by merger of Industrias Vegas and Mercasid; producer of meat products and edible oils; Dir, Operations RÚBEN SANTANA.

El Mundo Hidraulico, SRL: Calle Tunti Cáceres 224, entre Summer Wells y Alonzo Espinosa, Santo Domingo, DN; tel. 549-5497; fax 567-8180; e-mail info@elmundohidraulico.com; internet www.elmundohidraulico.com; f. 2005; hydraulic equipment; Pres. VAMNY JOEL BAUTISTA.

Padilla, C por A: Avda 27 de Febrero, esq. Carretera Manoguayabo, Santo Domingo, DN; tel. 379-1550; fax 379-2631; e-mail info@padilla.com.do; internet www.editorialpadilla.com.do; f. 1964; graphic design and printing, particularly food labels; Pres. FERNANDO ARTURO DE LEÓN HERBERT.

Pueblo Viejo Dominicana Corpn: Santo Domingo, DN; internet barrick.com; gold mining; 60% owned by Barrick Gold Corpn (Canada), 40% owned by Goldcorp Inc (Canada); commercial production commenced 2013; Pres. and CEO JAMIE C. SOKALSKY.

Refinería Dominicana de Petroleo, SA (Refidomsa): Antigua Carretera Sánchez, Km 17.5, Zona Industrial de Haina, Apdo 1439, Santo Domingo, DN; tel. 472-9800; fax 957-3566; e-mail contacto@refidomsa.com.do; internet www.refidomsa.com.do; f. 1973; petroleum refinery; state-owned; sale of 49% stake to PDVSA Petróleo, SA, Venezuela, agreed in mid-2010; Pres. FELIX JIMÉNEZ; Gen. Man. HÉCTOR GRULLÓN.

Ron Bermúdez: Calle J, esq. K, Zona Industrial de Herrera, Santo Domingo, DN; tel. 620-1852; fax 947-4200; e-mail administracion@bermudez.com.do; internet www.ronbermudez.com; f. 1852; rum production.

La Tabacalera, C por A: Calle Numa Silverio 1, Villa González, Apdo 758, Santiago de los Caballeros; tel. 535-4448; fax 581-3019; e-mail info@latabacalera.com; internet www.latabacalera.com; f. 1902 as La Habanera; adopted current name 2000; mfrs of cigarettes and tobacco products; Pres. FRANCISCO DURÁN; 1,300 employees.

UTILITIES

Regulatory Authority

Superintendencia de Electricidad: Avda John F. Kennedy 3, esq. Erick Leonard Eckman, Arroyo Hondo, Santo Domingo, DN; tel. 683-2500; fax 544-1637; e-mail sie@sie.gov.do; internet www.sie.gov.do; f. 2001; Pres. EDUARDO QUINCOCES BATISTA.

Electricity

AES Dominicana: Avda Winston Churchill 1099, Torre Citigroup, en la plaza Acrópolis, 23°, Ensanche Piantini, Santo Domingo, DN; tel. 955–2223; e-mail infoaesdominicana@aes.com; internet www.aesdominicana.com.do; f. 1997; subsidiary of AES Corpn, USA; largest private electricity generator in the Dominican Republic (300 MW); Pres. EDWIN DE LOS SANTOS.

Corporación Dominicana de Empresas Eléctricas Estatales (CDEEE): Edif. Principal CDE, Centro de los Héroes, Avda Independencia, esq. Fray C. de Utrera, Apdo 1428, Santo Domingo, DN; tel. 535-9098; fax 533-7204; e-mail mediossociales@cdeee.gob.do; internet www.cdeee.gob.do; f. 1955; state electricity co; partially privatized in 1999, renationalized in 2003; Pres. JOSÉ RAFAEL SANTANA CEDEÑO; Exec. Vice-Pres. JERGES RUBÉN JIMÉNEZ BICHARA.

EDE Este, SA (Empresa Distribuidora de Electricidad del Este): Avda Sábana Larga 1, esq. San Lorenzo, Los Mina, Santo Domingo, DN; tel. 788-2373; fax 788-2595; e-mail infoedeeste@edeeste.com.do; internet www.edeeste.com.do; f. 1999; state-owned electricity distributor; Pres. MARÍA LUISA CARBONELL MORETA; Gen. Man. LUIS ERNESTO DE LEÓN.

EDENORTE Dominicana, SA (Empresa Distribuidora de Electricidad del Norte): Avda Juan Pablo Duarte 74, Santiago; tel. 241-9090; e-mail webmaster@edenorte.com.do; internet www.edenorte.com.do; f. 1999; state-owned electricity distributor; Gen. Man. JULIO CÉSAR CORREA.

EDESUR Dominicana, SA (Empresa Distribuidora de Electricidad del Sur): Calle Carlos Sánchez y Sánchez, esq. Avda Tiradentes, Torre Serrano, Santo Domingo, DN; tel. 683-9292; e-mail info@edesur.com.do; internet www.edesur.com.do; f. 1999; state-owned electricity distributor; Pres. JUAN CARLOS SEGURA; Gen. Man. RUBÉN MONTÁS.

Empresa de Generación Hidroeléctrica Dominicana (EGEHID): Avda Rómulo Betancourt 303, Bella Vista, Santo Domingo, DN; tel. 533-5555; fax 535-7472; e-mail administrador@hidroelectrica.gob.do; internet www.hidroelectrica.gob.do; distributor of hydroelectricity; Pres. MARIO FERNÁNDEZ SAVIÑON; Gen. Man. DEMETRIO LLUBERES VIZCAÍNO.

Unidad de Electrificación Rural y Suburbana (UERS): Avda José Andrés Aybar Castellanos 136, Ensanche La Esperilla, Santo Domingo, DN; tel. 227-7666; e-mail info@uers.gov.do; internet www.uers.gov.do; f. 2006; manages supply of electricity to rural areas; Pres. JULIO CÉSAR BERROA ESPAILLAT; Dir-Gen. THELMA MARÍA EUSEBIO DE LÓPEZ.

Gas

AES Andrés: Santo Domingo, DN; internet www.aes.com; f. 2003; subsidiary of AES Corpn (USA); 3 generation facilities; 1 gas-fired plant and 1 liquefied natural gas terminal, 319-MW in Andrés and 236-MW in Los Mina; 1 coal-fired plant in Itabo; Pres. ANDREW VESEY.

Water

Corporación del Acueducto y Alcantarillado de Santo Domingo: Calle Euclides Morillo 65, Arroyo Hondo, Santo Domingo, DN; tel. 562-3500; fax 541-4121; e-mail info@caasd.gov.do; internet www.caasd.gov.do; f. 1973; Dir ALEJANDRO MONTÁS.

Instituto Nacional de Aguas Potables y Alcantarillado (INAPA): Edif. Inapa, Centro Comercial El Millón, Calle Guarocuya, Apdo 1503, Santo Domingo, DN; tel. 567-1241; fax 567-8972; e-mail info@inapa.gob.do; internet www.inapa.gob.do; Exec. Dir ALBERTO HOLGUÍN.

Instituto Nacional de Recursos Hidráulicos: Avda Jiménez de Moya, Centro de los Héroes, Santo Domingo, DN; tel. 532-3271; fax 532-2321; internet www.indrhi.gov.do; f. 1965; Exec. Dir OLGO FERNÁNDEZ.

TRADE UNIONS

Asociación Dominicana de Profesores (ADP): Avda Cervantes 57, Gazcue, Santo Domingo, DN; tel. 687-3268; fax 687-5800; e-mail adpinstitucion@gmail.com; internet adpmagisterio.org; f. 1972; Pres. EDUARDO HIDALGO.

Confederación Autónoma de Sindicatos Clasistas (CASC) (Autonomous Confederation of Trade Unions): Juan Erazo 14, Villa Juana, 4°, Santo Domingo, DN; tel. 687-8533; fax 689-1439; e-mail cascnacional@codetel.net.do; f. 1962; supports PRSC; Sec.-Gen. GABRIEL DEL RÍO DOÑÉ.

Confederación Nacional de Trabajadores Dominicanos (CNTD) (National Confederation of Dominican Workers): Calle José de Jesús Ravelo 56, Villa Juana, 2°, Santo Domingo, DN; tel. 221-2117; fax 221-3217; e-mail cntd@codetel.net.do; f. 1988 by merger; 11 provincial federations totalling 150 unions are affiliated; Sec.-Gen. JACOBO RAMOS; c. 188,000 mems.

Confederación Nacional de Unidad Sindical (CNUS): Edif. Centrales Sindicales, Calle Juan Erazo 14, Villa Juana, Santo Domingo, DN; tel. 221-2158; fax 689-1248; e-mail cnus@verizon.net.do; internet www.cnus.org.do; Pres. RAFAEL (PEPE) ABREAU.

Federación Dominicana de Trabajadores de Zona Francas, Industrias Diversas y de Servicios (FEDOTRAZONAS): Edif. Centrales Sindicales, 1°, Calle Juan Erazo 14, Villa Juana, Santo Domingo, DN; tel. 686-8140; fax 685-2476; e-mail info@fedotrazonas.org; internet fedotrazonas.org; f. 2002; 10 affiliate trade unions; Sec.-Gen. YGNACIO HERNÁNDEZ HICIANO.

Confederación de Trabajadores Unitaria (CTU) (United Workers' Confederation): Edif. de las Centrales Sindicales, Luis Manuel Caceres (Tunti) 222, 3°, Villa Juana, Santo Domingo, DN; tel. 565-0881; e-mail ctu01@codetel.net.do; internet ctu.com.do; f. 1991; Sec.-Gen. EUGENIO PÉREZ CÉSPEDES.

Unión General de Trabajadores Dominicanos (UGTD): Santo Domingo, DN; e-mail uniongeneraldetrabajadoresdominicanos ugtd@hotmail.com; Pres. CRISTÓBAL MANZANILLO.

Transport

Oficina por la Reordenamiento de Transporte (OPRET): Avda Máximo Gómez esq. Reyes Católicos, Antigua Cementera, Santo Domingo, DN; tel. 732-2670; fax 563-0199; e-mail accesoalainformacion@opret.gob.do; internet www.opret.gob.do; f. 2005 to oversee devt and modernization of the transport system; Dir DIANDINO ADRIANO PEÑA CRIQUE.

RAILWAYS

The Government invested US $50m.–$100m. in the installation of an underground railway system in Santo Domingo. The first line—14.5 km in length, between Villa Mella and Centro de los Héroes—entered into service in 2009. The completed network was to have a total length of some 60 km. In 2011 the legislature approved funding for a second line, to run for 32 km between Los Alcarrizos and the Francisco del Rosario Sánchez bridge.

Metro de Santo Domingo: Edif. RS, 1°, Avda 27 de Febrero 328, Santo Domingo, DN; internet metrodesantodomingo.wordpress .com; f. 2008; 1 line currently in operation, north–south between Villa Mella and Centro de los Héroes; second line, east–west between Los Alcarrizos and the Francisco del Rosario Sánchez bridge, under construction; Dir LEONEL CARRASCO.

ROADS

In 2005 there were an estimated 17,000 km of roads, of which about 6,225 km were paved. There is a direct route from Santo Domingo to Port-au-Prince in Haiti. The Coral Highway, a four-lane motorway linking Santo Domingo with Punta Cana, was inaugurated in 2012, at an estimated cost of US $400m. A further 22-km highway between San Pedro and La Romana was opened in late 2013.

Autoridad Metropolitana de Transporte (AMET): Avda Expreso V Centenario, esq. Avda San Martín, Santo Domingo, DN; tel. 686-8469; fax 686-6766; e-mail info@amet.gov.do; internet www.amet.gov.do; Dir-Gen. Brig.-Gen. PABLO ARTURO PUJOLS (designate).

Dirección General de Carreteras y Caminos Vecinales: Avda San Cristóbal, esq. Avda Tiradentes, Ensanche la Fe, Santo Domingo, DN; tel. 565-2811; fax 567-5470; f. 1987; operated by the Ministry of Public Works and Communications.

SHIPPING

The Dominican Republic has 14 ports, of which Río Haina is by far the largest, handling about 80% of imports. Other important ports are Boca Chica, Santo Domingo and San Pedro de Macorís on the south coast, and Puerto Plata in the north. The Caucedo port and transshipment centre was specifically for use by free trade zone businesses. In December 2013 the Dominican Republic's flag registered fleet comprised 38 vessels, with an aggregate displacement of some 14,435 grt.

Agencias Navieras B&R, SA: Avda Abraham Lincoln 504, Apdo 1221, Santo Domingo, DN; tel. 793-7000; fax 562-3383; e-mail ops@navierasbr.com; internet www.navierasbr.com; f. 1919; shipping agents and export services; Man. JEFFREY RANNIK.

Autoridad Portuaria Dominicana: Avda Máximo Gómez, Santo Domingo, DN; tel. 687-4772; fax 687-2661; internet www.apordom .gov.do; Pres. VÍCTOR DÍAZ RÚA; Exec. Dir RAMÓN RIVAS.

Frederic Schad, Inc: Calle José Gabriel García 26, Apdo 941, Santo Domingo, DN; tel. 221-8000; fax 688-7696; e-mail mail@schad.do; internet www.schad.do; f. 1922; logistics and shipping agent; Pres. FEDERICO SCHAD.

Maersk Dominicana, SA: Calle J. A. Soler 49, Santo Domingo, DN; tel. 732-1234; fax 566-5950; e-mail crbcsegen@maersk.com; internet www.maerskline.com/es-do; f. 1995; Gen. Man. MANUEL ALEJANDRO TERRERO.

Naviera Ebenezer, C por A: Los Charamicos, Sosua, Puerto Plata; tel. 875-9704; fax 571-4258; e-mail navieraebenezer@hotmail.com; Pres. MIGUEL A. DÌAZ.

CIVIL AVIATION

There are eight international airports, two at Santo Domingo, and one each at Puerto Plata, Punta Cana, Santiago, La Romana, Samaná and Barahona. The regional airline LIAT (see Antigua and Barbuda) provides scheduled services. Air Europe increased its services to Santo Domingo from mid-2013.

Instituto Dominicano de Aviación Civil: Avda México, esq. Avda 30 de Marzo, Apdo 1180, Santo Domingo, DN; tel. 221-7909; fax 221-6220; e-mail info@idac.gov.do; internet www.idac.gov.do; f. 1955 as Dirección General de Aeronáutica Civil; govt supervisory body; Dir-Gen. Dr ALEJANDRO HERRERA RODRIGUEZ.

Aerodomca (Aeronaves Dominicanas): Joaquín Balaguer Int. Airport, El Higuero La Isabela, Santo Domingo, DN; tel. 826-4141; fax 826-4065; e-mail ventas@aerodomca.com; internet www.aerodomca .com; f. 1980; charter flights within the Caribbean.

Caribair (Caribbean Atlantic Airlines): Aeropuerto Internacional La Isabela, Santo Domingo, DN; tel. 826-4444; fax 826-4063; e-mail info@caribair.com.do; internet www.caribair.com.do; f. 1983; scheduled flights to Aruba, Haiti, and domestic and regional charter flights; CEO RAFAEL ROSADO FERMIN.

Helidosa: Aeropuerto Internacional La Isabela, Santo Domingo, DN; tel. 826-4100; internet www.helidosa.com; f. 1992; chartered helicopter services; Man. Dir GONZALO CASTILLO.

Lineas Aereas Inter Islas, SA (Air Inter Island): Avda Rómulo Betancourt 483, casi esq. Núñez de Cáceres, Plaza Violeta, Local 22, 2°, Ensanche Mirador Norte, Santo Domingo, DN; e-mail info@airinterisland.com; internet www.airinterisland.com; f. 2003; services between the Dominican Republic and Haiti; CEO MARTÍN MALDONADO FROMETA.

Servicios Aéreos Profesionales (SAP): Dr Joaquín Balaguer International Airport, La Isabela, Santo Domingo, DN; tel. 826-4117; fax 372-8817; e-mail comercial@sapair.com; internet www .sapair.com; f. 1981; charter flights to Central America, the Caribbean and the USA; Pres. JOSÉ MIGUEL PATIN.

Tropical Aero Servicios, SRL (TAS): Avda Winston Churchill 557, Plaza Paseo de la Churchill 18B, Ensanche Piantini, Santo Domingo; tel. 826-4135; internet www.tas.com.do; f. 2011; passenger and cargo services in the Caribbean region; Man. Dir A. HENRÍQUEZ.

Tourism

The total number of visitors to the Dominican Republic in 2013 was 5,163,682. In that year receipts from tourism, excluding passenger transport, totalled a provisional US $5,118m.

Asociación Dominicana de Agencias de Viajes y Turismo (ADAVIT): Calle Padre Billini 263, Apdo 2097, Santo Domingo, DN; tel. 221-4343; fax 685-2577; e-mail adavit@codetel.net.do; f. 1963; Pres. EDISON UREÑA; Sec. ANA KATINGO SANTELISES DE LATOUR; 126 mems.

Asociación de Hoteles y Turismo de la República Dominicana, Inc (ASONAHORES): Edif. La Cumbre, 8°, Calle Presidente González, esq. Avda Tiradentes, Ensanche Naco, Santo Domingo, DN; tel. 368-4676; fax 368-5566; e-mail asonahores@asonahores .com; internet www.asonahores.com; f. 1962; asscn of private orgs; includes the Consejo de Promoción Turística; Pres. SIMON SUAREZ.

Corporación de Fomento de la Industria Hotelera y Desarrollo del Turismo (CORPHOTELS): Avda México, esq. 30 de Marzo, Ofs Gubernamentales, Santo Domingo, DN; tel. 688-3417; fax 689-3907; e-mail info@corphotels.gob.do; internet ch.corphotels.gob .do; f. 1969; promotes the hotel industry and tourism in general; state-run; Dir BIENVENIDO PÉREZ.

Defence

As assessed at November 2013, the Dominican Republic's armed forces numbered an estimated 46,000: army 26,000, navy 10,000 (including naval infantry), air force 10,000. There were also paramilitary forces numbering 15,000. Military service is voluntary and lasts for four years. In February 2012 it was announced that a US naval station was to be constructed on the island of Saona.

Defence Expenditure: The budget allocation for 2013 was an estimated RD $15,100m.

Minister of the Armed Forces and General Chief of Staff: Maj.-Gen. MAXIMILIANO WILLIAM MUÑOZ DELGADO.

Commander-Gen. of the Army: Brig.-Gen. JOSÉ EUGENIO MATOS DE LA CRUZ.

Commander-Gen. of the Navy: Vice-Adm. EDMUNDO FÉLIX PIMEN-TEL.

Commander-Gen. of the Air Force: Maj.-Gen. ELVIS M. FELIZ PÉREZ.

Education

Education is, where possible, compulsory for children between the ages of six and 14 years. Primary education commences at the age of six and lasts for eight years. Secondary education lasts for four years. In 2012 enrolment at primary level included 87% of children in the relevant age-group, while secondary enrolment included 62% of children in the relevant age-group (males 58%, females 66%). In 2010/11 some 1,310,199 pupils attended primary schools and 898,690 students attended secondary schools. There were 31 higher education institutions recognized by the National Council for Higher Education, Science and Technology. Budgetary expenditure on education in 2012 was RD $43,217m. (9.7% of total expenditure).

Bibliography

For works on the Caribbean generally, see Select Bibliography (Books)

Atkins, G. P., and Wilson, L. C. *The Dominican Republic and the United States: From Imperialism to Transnationalism*. Athens, GA, University of Georgia Press, 1998.

Betances, E. *The Catholic Church and Power Politics in Latin America: The Dominican Case in Comparative Perspective*. Lanham, MD, Rowman & Littlefield Publrs, 2007.

Carruyo, L. *Producing Knowledge, Protecting Forests: Rural Encounters with Gender, Ecotourism, and International Aid in the Dominican Republic*. University Park, PA, Pennsylvania State University Press, 2008.

Chester, E. T. *Rag-tags, Scum, Riff–raff, and Commies: The US Intervention in the Dominican Republic, 1965–1966*. New York, Monthly Review Press, 2001.

Derby, L. *The Dictator's Seduction: Politics and the Popular Imagination in the Era of Trujillo*. Durham, NC, Duke University Press, 2009.

Diederich, B. *Trujillo: The Death of the Dictator*. Princeton, NJ, Markus Wiener Publrs, 2000.

Gregory, S. *The Devil Behind the Mirror: Globalization and Politics in the Dominican Republic*. Berkeley, CA, University of California Press, 2006.

Hall, M. R. *Sugar and Power in the Dominican Republic: Eisenhower, Kennedy and the Trujillos (1958–62)*. Westport, CT, Greenwood Press, 2000.

Hartlyn, J. *The Struggle for Democratic Politics in the Dominican Republic*. Chapel Hill, NC, University of North Carolina Press, 1998.

Hernández, R. *The Mobility of Workers Under Advanced Capitalism: Dominican Migration to the United States*. New York, Columbia University Press, 2002.

Hillman, R. S., and D'Agostino, T. J. *Distant Neighbors: The Dominican Republic and Jamaica in Comparative Perspectives*. New York, Praeger Publrs, 1992.

Hoffnung-Garskof, J. *A Tale of Two Cities: Santo Domingo and New York after 1950*. Princeton, NJ, Princeton University Press, 2010.

Howard, D. *Dominican Republic in Focus: A Guide to the People, Politics and Culture*. London, Latin America Bureau, 1999.

Coloring the Nation: Race and Ethnicity in the Dominican Republic. Oxford, Signal Books, 2001.

Itzigsohn, J. *Developing Poverty: The State, Labor Market Deregulation, and the Informal Economy in Costa Rica and the Dominican Republic*. University Park, PA, Pennsylvania State University Press, 2000.

Martinez-Vergne, T. *Nation and Citizen in the Dominican Republic, 1880–1916*. Chapel Hill, NC, University of North Carolina Press, 2005.

Moya Pons, F. *The Dominican Republic: A National History*. Princeton, NJ, Markus Wiener Publrs, 1998.

Peguero, V., and Crawford, L. *Immigration and Politics in the Caribbean: Japanese and Other Immigrants in the Dominican Republic*. Coconut Creek, FL, Caribbean Studies Press, 2008.

Peguero, V., Maslowski, P., and Grimsley, M. (Eds). *Militarization of Culture in the Dominican Republic: From the Captains General to General Trujillo (Studies in War, Society & the Military)*. Lincoln, NE, University of Nebraska Press, 2004.

Roorda, E. P. *The Dictator Next Door: The Good Neighbor Policy and the Trujillo Regime in the Dominican Republic, 1930–1945*. Durham, NC, Duke University Press, 1998.

San Miguel, P. L. *The Imagined Island: History, Identity, and Utopia in Hispaniola*. Chapel Hill, NC, University of North Carolina Press, 2005.

Simmons, K. E. *Reconstructing Racial Identity and the African Past in the Dominican Republic*. Gainesville, FL, University Press of Florida, 2011.

Turits, R. L. *Foundations of Despotism: Peasants, the Trujillo Regime and Modernity in Dominican History*. Revised edn. Palo Alto, CA, Stanford University Press, 2004.

Veeser, C. *Improving Paradise: American Capitalists and US Intervention in the Dominican Republic, 1890–1908*. New York, Columbia University Press, 2003.

Vega, B. (Ed.). *Dominican Cultures: The Making of a Caribbean Society*. Princeton, NJ, Markus Wiener Publishing, 2008.

ECUADOR

Geography

PHYSICAL FEATURES

The Republic of Ecuador is in western South America, straddling the Equator, which gives the country its name. Some 965 km (about 600 miles) to the west of the mainland, but also on the Equator, is the country's Pacific territory on the Islas Galápagos (Galápagos Islands—the observation of whose unique ecosystem was important to the development of the theory of evolution by the 19th-century British scientist Charles Darwin). Continental Ecuador was once rather more extensive, but border disputes and adverse military encounters have reduced Ecuador's territory considerably (notably in 1904–42). There have been occasional clashes subsequently, mainly with Peru—most recently in 1995, although this was resolved in 1999. Ecuador's main border concerns are now not so much territorial as preventing any extension of the conflicts in Colombia. The border with Peru, to the east and south, has been settled at some 1,420 km in extent, and that with Colombia, to the north, is 590 km, giving Ecuador a total area of 272,045 sq km (105,037 sq miles).

Ecuador stretches for 2,237 km along the west coast of South America, extending over the Andes and, in the north-east, down onto the edge of the great Amazonian plains. The country is divided, therefore, into the Costa or coastal plains, the Sierra or central highlands and the Oriente, the forested eastern slopes of the Andes descending to alluvial plains. The Costa covers about one-quarter of the country and is a rich agricultural region, with rolling, forested hills in the north and, generally, a broad lowland basin descending from the Andes to the sea. There is also tropical jungle in the south, climbing the mountain sides as wet, mossy woodland. The Sierra itself is where the chain of the Andes, the Continental Divide, forms a double range of mountains flanking a narrow, inhabited upland plateau. The great cordilleras, Occidental and Oriental, include 22 massive volcanoes among their peaks, including the highest active volcano in the world, Cotopaxi (5,897 m or 19,354 ft), signalling the seismic instability of the region. The highest point in the country is at the summit of Chimborazo (6,310 m or 20,702 ft), which is also distinguished as being the point on the surface of the earth furthest from its centre (owing to the globe being wider around the Equator). The Oriente, or eastern jungles, consists of the eastern, forested slopes of the Andes and the gently undulating plains, thick with tropical rainforest. In fact, trees cover over one-half of the country, with 15% classed as pastureland. The mountain heights above 3,000 m or so tend to be grassland. Wildlife includes bears, jaguars, otters, skunks and crocodiles, with a huge variety of birds, including a number of North American species that winter here. Perhaps more unique is the isolated ecosystem of the Galápagos (officially, the Archipiélago de Colón), the six larger and nine smaller islands of which (mostly extinct volcanic peaks) have been declared a UNESCO World Heritage Site.

CLIMATE

The climate is tropical at sea level, the Costa being hot and humid, with an average annual temperature of 78°F (26°C). Being on the Equator, there is little seasonal variation in temperature, although there is a wet season from December to April, with particularly heavy rains, but there is no dry season as such. On the Sierra the average temperatures range from 45°F to 70°F (7°C–21°C), depending on the elevation, with Quito at 2,850 m above sea level averaging 13°C (55°F). How-

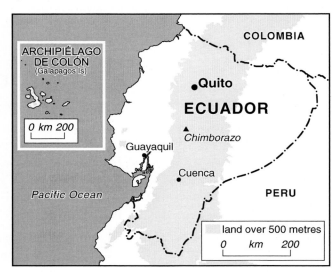

ever, average figures can obscure the contrast of warm days and chilly nights. The Oriente is even hotter and more humid than the Costa. Temperatures approach nearer 40°C (104°F) and average annual rainfall is about 2,050 mm (80 ins), falling all year round.

POPULATION

The majority of the population, over four-fifths, is either Amerindian or of mixed Amerindian descent. Figures vary as to the exact proportions, but indigenous peoples could make up anywhere upward of one-fifth of the entire population. The white population, predominantly of Spanish descent, account for little more than 10% of the total, and black Ecuadoreans amount to about one-half of that, with even smaller groups of Arabs and Asians. The official language, however, is Spanish, although many speak Quechua, the language of the Incas, in daily life. There are about 700 tribes, the main ones being the Otavalos, the Salasacas, the Saraguros, the Colorados, the Cayapas, the Jivaros, the Aucas, the Yumbos, the Zaparos and the Cofan. Many retain the use of their own dialects or languages. The ancient religions, by contrast, now only persist in the more remote parts of the Oriente, although elements have been maintained in conjunction with the dominant Roman Catholic Christianity (which claims the adherence of about 80% of the population). There is a small, but growing, Evangelical Christian (11%) minority.

According to UN mid-year estimates, the total population was 16,027,466 in 2014. Almost one-half of the population lives on the Costa, and only slightly less on the Sierra (where most people are Amerindians). The capital is Quito, at 2,850 m the second highest capital in South America, but the largest city is Guayaquil, the main port (2.6m. according official estimates in 2014—compared to Quito's 2.5m.). Guayaquil is in the south, on the gulf that bears its name, while Quito is in the Sierra, towards the north. The third city, Cuenca, is also in the mountains, but in the south. The country is divided into 24 provinces.

History

SANDY MARKWICK

Archaeologists date the existence of ancient civilization in the area comprising modern-day Ecuador as far back as 3500 BC. Evidence, though limited, points to the presence of numerous distinct tribal peoples often in conflict with each other. The Esmeralda, Manta, Huancavilca and Puná peoples farmed the coastal lowlands and were also hunters, fishermen and traders. Indigenous peoples in the Andean Sierra were more tied to the land and organized in dispersed communities growing maize, beans, potatoes and squash.

In the late 15th century these various tribes were subsumed into the Inca Empire of Tahuantinsuyo as it expanded north from modern-day Peru. The Incas introduced new crops, new agricultural methods and imposed new systems of land ownership. Internal migration spread the use of Quechua at the expense of local languages and established Quito as the most important city in the Inca Empire after Cusco (Cuzco), Peru. A standing army, a clergy and a bureaucracy reinforced Inca control.

By the time the first Spanish conquistadores arrived in search of land, wealth and power in 1526, the Inca Empire was already disintegrating and crucially weakened by civil war following the death of the Inca Emperor Huayna Cápac.

SPANISH COLONIAL RULE AND INDEPENDENCE

The Spanish Crown sponsored several exploratory voyages southwards along the Pacific coast of South America. Francisco Pizarro led the forces that conquered the Inca territory for the Spanish Crown, and in 1534 Quito was captured by Sebastián de Belalcázar. In 1540 Pizarro appointed his brother Gonzalo as Governor of Quito, as the colony was named.

As a result of infighting among rival Spanish conquistadores, the Spanish crown intervened to establish order by incorporating the territory into the Viceroyalty of Peru in 1544, although it was briefly transferred to the Viceroyalty of Nueva Granada in 1717. Spanish dominance was not uniform as significant areas, particularly of the coastal region and jungle lowlands, remained unconquered.

In Ecuador, the movement for independence from Spain was part of a pan-continental struggle between criollos (the local élite of Spanish descent) and the demands of the Spanish crown and the privileges of its local representatives. Following decades of revolts, successfully contained, colonial rule ended when Simón Bolívar's forces, under the command of Venezuelan Gen. José Antonio de Sucre, defeated the Spanish at the battle of Pichincha in 1822. Ecuador was then incorporated into the short-lived Confederación de Gran Colombia. In 1830 Ecuador seceded from the Confederación and attained independence. Gen. Juan José Flores became the country's first President and dominated the politics of the new republic for the first 15 years.

LIBERALISM VERSUS CONSERVATISM

Throughout the 19th century Ecuador endured political instability. In 1851 Gen. José María Urbina seized power. A defining characteristic of Ecuadorean politics began to emerge during his rule, which lasted until 1856: a persistent power struggle between the forces of liberalism, largely based in Guayaquil, and conservatism, based in the Sierra. This bipartisan dichotomy continued to resonate in the modern era.

Liberalism as represented by Urbina and his successor, Gen. Francisco Robles, was a modernizing, anti-clerical and pro-business influence. Urbina ended slavery, and Robles partially abolished the feudal annual tributes that the indigenous population had been required to pay to landowners for centuries. Regional interests reinforced the ideological division, with modern business and trading interests concentrated in the port city of Guayaquil, while Quito was the centre of the old landowning élites of the Sierra. The liberal direction of the Urbina-Robles era provoked regional opposition from local caudillos (provincial rulers), which threatened to undermine the territorial integrity of Ecuador.

In response to the liberal influence of Urbina and Robles emerged the controversial figure of Gabriel García Moreno (President in 1861–65 and 1869–75), the founder of conservatism in Ecuador. He suppressed local rebellions and expelled the Peruvian army from southern Ecuador. The conservatism of García Moreno was rooted in a fanatical adherence to contemporary Catholic theology, which emphasized personal self-discipline, hierarchy and order. In 1869 he founded the Partido Conservador (PC—Conservative Party) and attempted to install a theocratic state. His nation-building vision also took the form of a major road- and railway-building exercise linking the capital Quito with Guayaquil.

Between 1852 and 1890 the value of exports grew from US $1m. to $10m., partly because Ecuador took advantage of trading opportunities that arose while Ecuador's main trading rivals—Peru, Chile and Bolivia—were engaged in the War of the Pacific (1879–83). The economic boom strengthened the Guayaquil business élite, which was then reflected in a period of power for the Liberals between 1895 and 1925.

If García Moreno was the founder of conservatism in Ecuador, Gen. José Eloy Alfaro Delgado was the principal figure behind Ecuadorean liberalism. He seized power and founded the Partido Liberal Radical (PLR—Radical Liberal Party) in 1895, and quickly commenced stripping the Roman Catholic Church of the powers and privileges it had enjoyed under the García Moreno regime. The Government tried to implement social reform to help the poor, but progress was undermined by unfavourable economic conditions. Liberal rule also failed to build and strengthen democratic institutions, and the period was noted for its violent instability, stemming largely from disunity within the PLR.

Political power during the early 20th century was dominated by an oligarchy of agricultural and banking interests based in the coastal region. A spendthrift attitude among money-printing bankers and agriculturalists within this liberal élite (known as la argolla—the ring) led to spiralling inflation. Economic conditions were exacerbated by competition from overseas cocoa producers. The authorities ruthlessly suppressed a general strike in Guayaquil in 1922 and a peasant rebellion in the Sierra in 1923. In 1925, with unrest growing, a group of military social reformers, the League of Young Officers, overthrew the Government with the stated aim of ending the corruption of liberal rule.

The post-liberal era proved to be equally unstable. From 1925 to 1948 Ecuador had 22 Governments, each one terminated by unconstitutional means. A new Constitution was introduced in 1929, which shifted the balance of power away from the executive to the legislature, thereby encouraging a plethora of minor political parties and groupings that, in combination with the Wall Street Crash of 1929 and the ensuing Great Depression, increased instability. Nationalist opinion was inflamed by the signing of the Rio Protocol in 1942, in which Ecuador renounced claims to 200,000 sq km of territory to Peru. In 1948 Galo Plaza Lasso came to power at the head of a coalition of liberals and socialists. His victory began an era of 12 years of unbroken constitutional rule.

CONSTITUTIONAL RULE, 1948–60

Plaza aligned himself closely to the USA, which proved a frequent source of tension between the Government and populist opposition politicians. He was credited with attempts to deepen democratic rights and institutions even though the opposition largely frustrated his attempts to reform economic and development policy along pragmatic and technocratic lines. Political frustration was the price for relative stability, which was undoubtedly helped by a banana boom during which revenue from exports grew from US $2m. in 1948 to $20m. in 1952. During this time the Government succeeded in balancing budgets and slowing inflation.

José María Velasco Ibarra, elected President for the third time (previously in 1934 and 1944), succeeded Plaza in 1952. Encouraged by the relatively healthy state of the economy, Velasco raised public spending on infrastructure projects and the military, but his Government became increasingly authoritarian. He was succeeded by Camilo Ponce Enríquez in 1956, but won another term of office in 1960. However, after 14 months in office and amid a general strike and violent unrest precipitated by worsening economic conditions, the military deposed Velasco and installed Carlos Julio Arosemena Monroy as President. Nevertheless, the military was concerned about Arosemena's pro-Cuban rhetoric and, fearing the emergence of domestic left-wing insurgency, ousted the President in 1963.

MILITARY RULE, 1963–79

The new military Government, led by a four-man junta, intended to stay in power for as long as it took to implement unpopular economic policies while defeating left-wing political activity. However, in 1966, confronted with continued economic problems and growing unrest, the military stepped down. Interim Governments took office while an elected constituent assembly drafted a new constitution. In 1968 the first elections under the new Constitution returned 75-year-old Velasco to the presidency for the fifth time, although he received just one-third of the votes cast. The last Velasco Government was hampered by a weak mandate, which fuelled instability and led to an autogolpe (coup) in 1970, in which Velasco disbanded the Congreso Nacional (Congress) and the Supreme Court and assumed direct powers himself with the support of the military. Velasco implemented various unpopular measures, including a devaluation of the sucre. In 1972 he was deposed by a military coup led by Gen. Guillermo Rodríguez Lara, who became head of state.

The military regime had a nationalist outlook that underpinned its heavy investment in infrastructure and industry and the founding of the state petroleum company, Estatal Petrolera Ecuatoriana (which was replaced by PETROECUA-DOR—Empresa Estatal Petróleos del Ecuador—in 1989). The Government's nationalism was reflected in its petroleum policy: it took Ecuador into the Organization of the Petroleum Exporting Countries (OPEC) in 1973 and renegotiated contracts to develop petroleum concessions with foreign oil companies on more favourable terms.

The military Government tried to control inflation with low tariffs to encourage imports and absorb the spending power of the small, but growing, middle class. However, the strategy fuelled balance of payments problems. When the regime changed policy and imposed a 60% duty on luxury imports it provoked fierce opposition from Ecuador's élite, which had grown accustomed to cheap luxury goods. In 1976 a military faction led a successful and bloodless transfer of power to a three-man military junta, appointed to oversee the return to civilian rule. In 1978 voters approved a new, more progressive Constitution in a referendum. The Constitution acknowledged the role of the state in socio-economic development, established a single-chamber legislature, disallowed immediate re-election for serving presidents and ended the literacy standards for voter eligibility (effectively enfranchising a large proportion of the indigenous population).

In 1979 Jaime Roldós Aguilera, from the Concentración de Fuerzas Populares (CFP—Concentration of Popular Forces), was elected President with over 68% of the second-round votes cast. Doubts that the military would permit Roldós to take office were dispelled when he assumed the presidency in August, although the military had put in place safeguards to prevent any investigations into human rights violations during its period in power.

CIVILIAN GOVERNMENT RESTORED

Many of the weaknesses of civilian politics in Ecuador re-emerged when democracy was restored. Regional and personal rivalries were expressed in the high number of small political parties, groupings and shifting alliances. President Roldós, who came to power with an agenda to promote socio-economic reform, encountered opposition not only from the traditional right, but also from within his own CFP. In May 1981 the President, his wife and the Minister of Defence were killed in a plane crash in the southern province of Loja. The Vice-President, Osvaldo Hurtado, the leader of the Partido Demócratico Cristiano (PDC—Christian Democratic Party), assumed the presidency amid a deteriorating economic situation occasioned by the end of the petroleum boom. Foreign debt totalled some US $7,000m. Despite Hurtado's left-of-centre credentials, his response was to pursue IMF-approved austerity measures. He reduced government subsidies and devalued the sucre. In the 1984 presidential election right-wing interests united behind León Febres Cordero, a Guayaquil businessman of the Partido Social Cristiano (PSC—Social Christian Party), who narrowly defeated Rodrigo Borja Cevallos, who had defected from the PLR to form the Izquierda Democrática (ID—Democratic Left).

Conflict between the executive and the legislature threatened a number of constitutional crises. Febres Cordero's use of executive power was consistent with the long tradition in Ecuador of the caudillo rather than the constitutionally elected politician, and he attempted to implement changes that would grant him additional powers and postpone legislative elections. The President's relationship with the military was tense. His dismissal of the chief of the armed forces, Lt-Gen. Frank Vargas Pazzos, for allegations of corruption he had made against senior defence staff, led to a military revolt at an air base and at Quito's international airport in 1986. Vargas was arrested and Febres Cordero subsequently ignored an amnesty granted to Vargas by the Congress. In January 1987 paratroopers loyal to Vargas abducted the President. Vargas was given an amnesty in exchange for Febres Cordero's release.

In May 1988 Rodrigo Borja Cevallos won the presidential election, defeating Abdalá Bucaram Ortiz of the Partido Roldosista Ecuatoriano (PRE—Ecuadorean Roldosist Party) in the second round of voting. Both candidates had proposed economic nationalism and import substitution. Borja's ID also won the largest number of seats in the Congress and entered into an alliance with fringe leftist and populist parties, thus securing a strong base in the legislature. Borja pledged to defend human rights and introduce moderate socio-economic reforms while balancing the conflicting interests of the labour movement and Guayaquil's business élite. However, a concurrent programme of economic austerity provoked large public demonstrations and led to disillusion among the electorate. In mid-term legislative elections in June 1990 the ID-led coalition lost its majority in the Congress, resulting in legislative paralysis for the remainder of Borja's term of office.

During the Borja presidency there was a greater mobilization of social groups representing the indigenous population. Particularly active was the Confederación de Nacionalidades Indígenas del Ecuador (CONAIE—Confederation of Indigenous Nationalities of Ecuador). CONAIE led an uprising in seven Andean provinces in 1990, during which they blocked roads and brought the countryside to a virtual standstill. The trade union movement joined the protests of the increasingly powerful indigenous organization, which fuelled conservative fears of the Borja administration, particularly after the Government had made overtures to left-wing insurgents to end their violent struggle. In 1989 the President had successfully concluded negotiations with Alfaro Vive ¡Carajo! (Alfaro Lives, Damn It!), a small guerrilla movement, after it agreed to abandon the armed struggle and enter the legal political arena.

PRESIDENT DURÁN BALLÉN, 1992–96

These fears helped the conservative Sixto Durán Ballén of the Partido Unitario Republicano (PUR—Unitary Republican Party) to victory in the second round of the presidential election in July 1992. Durán Ballén defeated another right-wing candidate, Jaime Nebot Saadi of the PSC, with 58% of the ballot. The ID candidate was humiliated, receiving just 8.2% of the votes cast in the first round in May as those associated with the labour unrest and the incumbent Government were unequivocally rejected. Durán Ballén, having promised to accelerate free market reforms and encourage foreign investment, introduced a series of structural reforms within two months of assuming power, including taking Ecuador into the Andean Pact free trade area. In November 1992 Ecuador withdrew from OPEC to allow it greater freedom in the production and export of oil. Negotiations to restructure the foreign debt led to improved relations with international creditors and a stand-by facility from the IMF in 1994.

During the first half of Durán Ballén's term of office the Government depended on an alliance of the PUR and the PC, with additional ad hoc support from the PSC, to secure a majority in the Congress. However, this period of relative legislative consensus was short-lived as corruption charges levelled at cabinet members undermined the fragile support of the PSC. In May 1994 the opposition parties effectively took control of the Congress, following an emphatic defeat for the PUR and PC in legislative mid-term elections.

Renewed military skirmishes along the border with Peru in January 1995 temporarily stifled domestic political opposition. However, normal political discourse resumed in February after a ceasefire agreement was reached and following revelations that government representatives had paid legislators and judges to help to ease the path of legislative proposals. The President survived the scandal, but it highlighted the existence of widespread corruption within the political and judicial élite. There was an increasing mobilization of the population against the policies and practices of the Durán Ballén administration in the wake of the scandal.

PRESIDENTS BUCARAM AND ALARCÓN, 1996–98

The presidential election of 1996 resulted in victory for the populist Abdalá Bucaram Ortiz, representing the PRE, who unexpectedly won the second round of voting, defeating Nebot Saadi of the PSC. His victory was fuelled both by a widespread disillusion with established party politics and a rejection of the structural adjustment economic programme initiated by Durán Ballén. Bucaram's electoral platform included anti-poverty measures, such as increased subsidies for basic commodities and wage rises for public sector workers. However, once in power, Bucaram raised the price of utilities as the Government tried to balance its budget. In early 1997 there was a general strike in response to commodity price increases, mass demonstrations and violent clashes between protesters and the security forces.

Charges of 'cronyism' were levelled against the President after family members and close friends were appointed to important cabinet positions. Eventually, Bucaram's undiplomatic style and unpredictable decision-making created such an atmosphere of instability that, on 6 February 1997, the Congress voted by simple majority to dismiss Bucaram on grounds of mental incapacity (thus avoiding impeachment proceedings, which required a two-thirds' majority). The Congress elected Fabián Alarcón Rivera to the presidency on 11 February, and scheduled new elections for August 1998.

Elections to a 70-member Asamblea Nacional (National Assembly) to consider constitutional reform were brought forward to November 1997 under considerable public pressure. In February 1998 the Assembly agreed a series of reforms designed to ensure greater government stability, including the enlargement of the Congress from 82 to 121 seats, the abolition of mid-term elections and more limited impeachment powers for the Congress. Elections to the newly enlarged Congress were held in May. The Democracia Popular (DP—People's Democracy) became the largest single party. In the second round of the presidential election in July, Quito mayor and DP candidate Jamil Mahuad Witt narrowly defeated the PRE's Alvaro Noboa Pontón. Mahuad took office in August and appointed a Cabinet largely composed of independents.

PRESIDENT MAHUAD, 1998–2000

A peace agreement with Peru in October 1998 increased Mahuad's popular standing. The treaty established a definitive border with Peru and granted Ecuador navigation rights on the Amazon river. Unlike previous agreements, this accord seemed to offer the opportunity of a permanent settlement, which would allow the two countries to normalize relations. However, the new administration quickly encountered Ecuador's familiar economic and political problems. The strength of the political opposition in the Congress ensured that there was little consensus, and any reforms required a tortuous process of

negotiation with a multitude of disparate parties, each aiming to extract policy concessions from the Government.

The introduction of austerity measures led to a general strike in October 1998, followed by a period of violent unrest. By 1999 the economic crisis was in danger of leading to a collapse of the banking system, default on debt repayments, hyperinflation and a rapid decline in investor confidence. Protests against a freeze on bank deposits, decreed in March by Mahuad in response to the decreasing value of the sucre, led to violent demonstrations and the declaration of a 60-day state of emergency. The military was deployed to maintain order while the Government, aiming to secure much-needed loans from international creditors, increased attempts to restructure the public sector in line with IMF prescriptions. However, in August Mahuad declared a moratorium on foreign debt repayments, making Ecuador the first country to default on its Brady bond and Eurobond commitments.

Popular protests continued despite the debt moratorium. The President's popularity declined precipitously. In January 2000 Mahuad announced the decision to adopt the US dollar in place of the sucre as the currency of Ecuador, provoking the resignation of the central bank President, Pablo Better. Further protests by indigenous groups received the tacit support of sections of the military, which allowed thousands of protesters to occupy the Congress building on 21 January. During the occupation, CONAIE leader Antonio Vargas, along with a group of army colonels (among them Lucio Gutiérrez Borbua, who would become President three years later), announced the overthrow of Mahuad. The military high command was divided, but the following day supported the transfer of power to Vice-President Gustavo Noboa Bejeramo, who was given the task of completing Mahuad's four-year term.

PRESIDENT NOBOA, 2000–03

Gustavo Noboa was an independent, although he was associated with the PSC and another right-leaning party, the Movimiento de Integración Nacional (MIN—National Integration Movement), which was formed following a split with former President Mahuad's DP. His Cabinet included representatives of several parties and had a strong business influence.

Noboa, as Mahuad before him, had to secure the approval of legislation with the help of ad hoc alliances to secure congressional approval. Ecuador's history of a political party system, only loosely based around ideology with regional and personal rivalries much in evidence, had produced a highly fragmented political landscape. However, popular weariness of political instability allowed Noboa to deepen the economic reform programme. High petroleum prices and pressure from the IMF in the early 21st century further encouraged neo-liberal reform.

In March 2000 Noboa secured congressional approval for the Ley de Transformación Económica (Economic Transformation Law). This latest attempt to introduce structural reforms included dollarization, increased labour market flexibility, and an extended policy of privatization, as well as reductions in government spending and tax reform. Additional measures, including a timetable for the adoption of the Basel standard of capital adequacy for the banking sector, persuaded the IMF in April to extend a one-year stand-by agreement, conditionally approving US $2,000m. in multilateral aid over the following two years. In the same month the Government formally began the process of replacing the sucre with the US dollar as Ecuador's unit of currency, which led to the stabilization of the exchange rate and reduced interest rates.

Opposition to economic liberalization persisted, led by the forces that had been so influential in removing Mahuad from office: CONAIE, trade unions and students. Anti-Government protests led by CONAIE escalated following fuel price rises in December 2000. Noboa's Government declared a national state of emergency, giving the security forces extra powers to control unrest. In contrast to Mahuad, however, Noboa maintained the support of most mainstream political parties, as well as the business community and the military.

PRESIDENT GUTIÉRREZ, 2003–05

Elections to the presidency and the legislature proceeded as scheduled in October 2002, with the two leading presidential candidates competing in a second round of voting in November. Lucio Gutiérrez Borbua, a former army colonel involved in the coup to oust President Mahuad, won 59% of the votes cast in the run-off ballot, defeating a wealthy banana magnate, Alvaro Noboa Pontón (of no relation to former President Gustavo Noboa). Gutiérrez's nationalist and leftist campaign rhetoric, targeting corruption within the political establishment in particular, earned him the support of a loose alliance of indigenous peoples' interests and left-wing groups. Principal among these was the Partido Sociedad Patriótica 21 de Enero (PSP—Patriotic Society Party), which Gutiérrez had formed with former army colleagues, the indigenous Pachakútik movement and the small left-wing Movimiento Popular Democrático (MPD—Popular Democratic Movement).

The new President confronted an opposition-dominated Congress. Parties of the ruling coalition accounted for just 20 of the Congress's 100 seats, a figure that had been reduced to 17 by mid-2003. The opposition included the larger established parties such as the PSC and ID, as well as the PRE, the DP and former presidential candidate Noboa's own Partido Renovador Institucional de Acción Nacional (PRIAN—National Action Institutional Renewal Party).

On taking office, President Gutiérrez moderated his rhetoric and quickly embarked on a largely orthodox programme of economic management, including public sector wage freezes and reduced fuel subsidies, intended to secure an IMF stand-by loan. Although not all IMF prescriptions were followed—notably, the politically sensitive subsidy on cooking gas was maintained—the Government's proposals damaged relations with its own supporters. Trade unions and popular and indigenous groups were dissatisfied with what they perceived to be broken promises, and the Government's ability to sustain its minority alliance in the Congress or its support in the country at large seemed doubtful.

In March 2003 the IMF approved a US $205m. stand-by loan, which paved the way for further lending. In May the World Bank announced a four-year programme of lending, worth a projected $1,050m. Ambivalence within the Congress led to several measures being diluted and falling short of IMF demands. The Government struggled to satisfy IMF requirements on the one hand, while attempting to avoid alienating its campaign supporters on the other.

Gutiérrez's political difficulties mounted towards the end of 2004. The ruling PSP won just 7% of the vote in local and provincial elections held in October of that year, while the PSC gained control of several coastal cities and the ID dominated in the Sierra. Emboldened by this strong electoral support the opposition began impeachment proceedings against Gutiérrez, accusing him of misappropriating public funds during October's elections. The President survived the attempt to depose him by engaging the support of exiled former President Bucaram of the PRE and the PRIAN's Alvaro Noboa, with additional support from smaller parties. In November allies of the new governing majority were appointed as justices to the Constitutional Tribunal and the Supreme Electoral Court. More controversial still, the Government called an extraordinary session of the Congress, during which it voted to expel 27 members of the Supreme Court alleged to be too closely associated with the PSC. They were replaced with new judges with links to the PRE, PRIAN and the Government. This purge was widely condemned as a gross violation of the judiciary's independence and of the Constitution.

In early 2005 the PSC called protest demonstrations against the Government, taking advantage of popular discontent over its record, especially in reducing crime and providing services in Guayaquil, in order to maintain pressure on the Government over its manipulation of the judiciary. Popular protest spread to Quito and elsewhere. As predicted by the opposition, in March the Supreme Court announced that all charges against exiled former President Bucaram had been dismissed. Polls indicated that support for Gutiérrez had declined to below 5%. Following a week of daily protests by thousands in the capital, on 15 April Gutiérrez declared a state of emergency and announced the dissolution of the Supreme Court; however,

by this time he had lost the support both of the Congress, which on 20 April voted to oust him for 'abandoning his post', and of the military, which had allowed protesters to reach the presidential palace on the same day. Gutiérrez (who fled to Brazil, where he claimed asylum) became the third elected President since 1997 to be removed following popular unrest.

INTERIM GOVERNMENT OF PRESIDENT PALACIO, 2005–07

Immediately following the removal of Gutiérrez, his Vice-President, Dr Alfredo Palacio González, was sworn in as President. Palacio, while nominally an independent, had associations with the PSC, and his cabinet appointees similarly had links with the traditional parties. There were doubts over the constitutional legitimacy of Palacio's accession because the vote to remove Gutiérrez from office had not been approved by the required minimum of 67 legislators in the Congress. Palacio secured initial support with an alliance of the PSC, ID, Pachakútik, DP, MPD and assorted independents. However, active support, beyond simple recognition of Palacio as head of an interim Government, was not forthcoming from any party or legislative bloc, making it difficult for him to govern effectively. Political weakness undermined the ability of the Palacio Government to impose its own legislative agenda. President Palacio's attempted reforms, including restoring a bicameral legislature and increasing regional autonomy, were rejected by the Congress in September 2005.

Meanwhile, the new Government had an important decision to make concerning the composition of the Supreme Court of Justice, which had been suspended since the state of emergency introduced by former President Gutiérrez in April 2005. Rather than reinstate the disbanded Supreme Court, an independent panel was appointed to select new justices and a new Supreme Court was established in December.

Relations with overseas investors deteriorated in April 2006 when Palacio signed a new hydrocarbons law imposing a windfall tax on foreign oil companies' earnings over a designated threshold. It was hoped that this tax would raise government revenues by some US $500m. Tensions increased in May after the Government announced that the US Occidental Petroleum Corpn (Oxy) had violated the terms of its contract by transferring 40% of its shares to the Canadian firm EnCana. The Government cancelled Oxy's exploration and production contract and transferred its operations to PETROECUADOR. The dispute halted negotiations for a free trade agreement with the USA, and damaged Ecuador's reputation among foreign investors.

PRESIDENT CORREA AND CONSTITUTIONAL REFORM, 2007–13

In November 2006 Rafael Correa Delgado, a radical candidate of the left, won a convincing presidential election run-off, with 56.7% of the vote, against Alvaro Noboa, the defeated candidate in the 2003 election and a populist right-wing businessman. The result was a surprise, as Correa had not won the largest share of the vote in the first round, and opinion polls had suggested that supporters of eliminated candidates would transfer their allegiance to Noboa. Correa moderated his rhetoric prior to the second ballot and underplayed his friendship with Venezuela's radical President, Hugo Chávez Frías.

Elections to the Congress were held concurrently with the first round of the presidential ballot in October 2006. Correa's Alianza País (AP—Country Alliance) did not campaign in the legislative elections, and the President sought to govern with the informal support of the PSP and smaller left-wing parties.

Correa took office in January 2007 with a programme of constitutional reform, increasing the state's participation in the oil sector and prioritizing public spending on social services over debt servicing. Correa's stated aim in securing constitutional reform was to depoliticize Ecuador's state institutions, which were controlled by entrenched interests, particularly within the powerful PSC, and to instil greater democracy in the country's party system. President Correa charged the Supreme Electoral Court with preparing a referendum on the establishment of a constituent assembly to rewrite the Constitution. For the referendum to be held, the support of both the Supreme Electoral Court and the Congress would be required. In March the Court approved a referendum by three votes to two and then expelled 57 legislators from the 100-member Congress who had voted for the head of the Court to be dismissed. It was his casting vote that had secured support for a referendum. The dismissal of the deputies, who were replaced by only 21 new representatives, helped to ensure that the Congress, aware of the risks of a potential public backlash, approved the referendum. With 81.7% of voters supporting the proposal, Correa secured an overwhelming victory in the referendum, which was held in April. In September an election to a 130-member Constituent Assembly, tasked with drafting a new constitution in 2008, resulted in a majority for the AP, which obtained a total of 80 seats. At its first session in November, the Constituent Assembly voted to dissolve the Congress until a further referendum on the new constitution was held. Meanwhile, Correa transferred the legislative powers of the Congress to a commission of the Constituent Assembly. The expulsion of opponents from the Congress, the referendum victory and the transfer of legislative powers to the commission bolstered Correa's position. The draft Constitution was approved by the Assembly on 24 July and in a referendum in September.

President Correa won a second term of office following elections in April 2009. In a comfortable victory, Correa won in the first round of voting with 52% of the vote, while his nearest rival, former President Gutiérrez, polled 28%, thereby satisfying the two conditions required for automatic first round victory: a more than 50% vote share for the winner and a minimum 10% margin of victory over the second-placed candidate. Correa's victory was the first time since the restoration of civilian democracy in 1979 that a second round had not been required in a presidential contest. Correa also became the first incumbent President to win re-election (President Velasco Ibarra was elected five times between 1934 and 1968, but failed to complete his term on each occasion). Correa benefited from a particularly weak and fragmented opposition. Neither of the traditionally powerful parties, the PSC from the right nor the ID from the left, put forward candidates.

President Correa enjoyed broad popular support for his spending increases on health, education, pensions and infrastructure. His defiance in the face of the perceived influence of the USA and international financial institutions garnered further support. Correa defaulted on some of the country's debt commitments in December 2008, claiming that they were 'illegitimate', and in early 2009 ended a lease arrangement with the USA to operate a military base at Manta. However, despite his clear popular mandate, Correa's ability to govern was hampered by a loss of legislative majority. Correa's AP had secured 59 seats in the new National Assembly, four short of a majority, requiring the Government to seek support from smaller parties on the left. The Government was frustrated in its attempt to introduce laws regulating strategic sectors including communications, hydrocarbons and water, while divisions within the AP further complicated the approval of legislation.

Financial constraints grew owing to the Government's difficulty in accessing international funding, which led Correa to embark on a round of spending cuts and provoked some popular opposition. In September 2010 a police protest against cuts in benefits escalated when President Correa was forcibly detained in a hospital where he was taken after being jostled and exposed to tear gas during an earlier attempt to negotiate with protesters. Police protesters continued to demonstrate sporadically across the country, while a contingent of rebel troops briefly occupied Quito's international airport in opposition to government austerity measures. Troops loyal to Correa stormed the hospital after 10 hours to release the President and suppress the protests. Correa denounced the incident as a coup attempt, although opponents accused him of taking advantage of the episode to denounce his opponents and consolidate power.

Correa held a referendum on a series of measures, including reform of the judiciary and media, in May 2011. Although all measures were passed, the margin of victory was narrower than in the 2008 referendum, indicating a decline in the President's popularity. The passage of the reforms paved the

way for 21 judges to be sworn in to the new Corte Nacional de Justicia (CNJ—National Court of Justice) in January 2012, tasked with overhauling the judiciary over an 18-month period.

In February 2012 the CNJ ruled in favour of the President and against two journalists whose book, published in 2010, reported claims by Correa's brother Fabricio that firms linked to him had benefited from an opaque bidding process to win US $120m. of federal construction contracts. The judge ordered the journalists each to pay $1m. in compensation for 'damages' to the President's name, despite the tacit admission that the bidding process in question was flawed as indicated by it subsequent reform. Also in February the CNJ upheld prison sentences and heavy fines against the directors of the national daily newspaper *El Universo* for accusing the President of abuse of powers during the police mutiny of September 2010. Correa was accused of exercising undue influence on the legal process by appearing in court along with several members of his Cabinet for the hearing, despite originally bringing the case as a private citizen.

Correa accused his opponents within the media of representing élite interests against his 'citizen's revolution'. The President drew on history in his battle with the modern media and in order to reinforce his own self-image, he took advantage of the centenary of the assassination of his political hero, Eloy Alfaro, during 2012. In addition to elaborate official celebrations to mark the centenary, Correa was at pains to draw direct parallels between Alfaro and himself as progressive leaders fighting the élite and their allies in the media. Correa was accused of crude historical revisionism in expressing strong views about the role of the press in the 1912 murder of Alfaro in order to justify the restrictions that he had imposed on the media. It appeared to be a thinly disguised attempt by Correa to identify himself alongside a progressive hero from Ecuador's history and to cast his opponents as 'unpatriotic'. This approach, along with tensions in the relationship with the USA, reinforced parallels with President Chávez in Venezuela.

Although tensions between the executive and legislature persisted, they did not seriously threaten Correa's Government during its first five years. Fears that Ecuador might be reverting to a familiar pattern of instability, prompted by the police mutiny of September 2010, proved premature. The period of relative political stability was in part achieved through his constitutional reforms, which consolidated his power relative to other government institutions. However, opponents criticized Correa of undermining democracy, in particular by attempting to bring the judiciary increasingly under the President's influence and by intimidating the media and undermining freedom of expression.

TENSIONS WITH THE USA

Under the Government of Correa, a history of conflict between successive Governments and the US oil firm Texaco (part of Chevron since 2001) over environmental damage came to a head. In 2011 an Ecuadorean court ordered Chevron to pay US $18,200m. in compensation. The company argued that its responsibilities were fulfilled following a settlement with the Government in 1998, which included a $40m. clean-up operation, and it filed a counter-claim that the legal case against the company was a violation of a 1997 US-Ecuador bilateral investment treaty. In February 2013 a tribunal under the jurisdiction of the Permanent Court of Arbitration in The Hague, Netherlands, ruled in the company's favour and warned that Ecuador might be liable for any attempted enforcement of the compensation payments. President Correa denounced the ruling and called on regional governments to back Ecuador's position. Ecuador's highest court, the Corte Nacional de Justicia (National Corte of Justice), upheld the Government's position that Chevron was responsible, but reduced its liabilities to $9,500m. Meanwhile, Chevron was suing the US lawyer representing the Government, alleging that the original ruling holding the company responsible had been corruptly obtained. The dispute was expected to continue to undermine Ecuador's relations with the USA.

Relations with the USA were further exacerbated in April 2011 when the WikiLeaks website (an organization releasing leaked private and classified content) published a confidential diplomatic cable from the US Ambassador, Heather Hodges, in which she claimed that police corruption in Ecuador was widespread and that President Correa was aware of the problem. Ecuador expelled Hodges and the USA retaliated by expelling Ecuador's ambassador in Washington, DC. Full diplomatic relations were restored in May 2012. However, relations remained difficult. US President Barack Obama criticized Correa's actions against the press while Ecuador's close alliance with Venezuela's President Chávez and its ties with Iran were other sources of dispute. Correa received an official visit from Iranian President Mahmoud Ahmadinejad in January 2012.

The granting of political asylum in August 2012 to Julian Assange, the Australian founder of WikiLeaks, increased Correa's international profile, as well as further straining relations with the USA, and with the United Kingdom. Assange had sought asylum in the Ecuadorean embassy in London in June in an attempt to avoid extradition to Sweden where he faced sexual assault charges. Assange feared that the Swedish authorities would transfer him to the USA where charges against him associated with WikiLeaks activities in publishing classified military and diplomatic communications carried the threat of the death penalty for those found guilty. At mid-2014 Assange remained at the Ecuadorean embassy, mired in diplomatic and legal deadlock.

PRESIDENT CORREA RE-ELECTED, 2013

At the presidential election held in February 2013, Correa was returned to office, having received an outright majority with 57% of the vote and thereby obviating the need for a second ballot. His main opponent, Guillermo Lasso of the newly formed Creating Opportunities (CREO), representing the pro-business, economically liberal right, garnered just 23% of the vote. In legislative elections, also held in February, voters strongly backed the governing AP, thus giving Correa the legislative majority that he previously lacked. The AP commanded 100 of the 137 seats in the new legislature, which convened for the first time in May.

The re-election of Correa, whose new term of office began in August 2013, confirmed a new era of relative stability in Ecuadorean politics. Despite polarizing public opinion, domestically as well as abroad, Correa had now become the longest-serving President in Ecuadorean history. (By contrast, there had been seven different Presidents in the decade prior to Correa's initial election in 2006.) Correa's enduring popularity was highest among low-income groups, largely owing to high levels of government expenditure on subsidies, social projects and other wealth transfer initiatives. Robust economic performance with a strong record in job creation, which has weakened opposition to public sector spending cuts, has aided this period of relative stability. Correa's position has also been assisted by high oil prices, as well as the provision by the People's Republic of China of credit and other finance (totalling US $7,250m.), secured against oil purchases. China's funding was free of policy prescriptions, unlike loans provided by multilateral institutions such as the IMF and the World Bank, and has assisted Correa's public spending plans.

However, a fragmented party system, based around personalities as well as regional and ethnic interests, continued to pose a threat to coherent government, rather than providing an effective balance to executive power. Correa has sought to improve the governability of the country by increasing his powers as President over the legislature. In February 2014 Correa suffered defeat in municipal elections, at which various opposition parties secured control of Ecuador's largest cities. Following the setback, Correa made significant ministerial changes in March in an effort to regain support.

Meanwhile, diplomatic relations between Ecuador and the USA deteriorated further in June 2013 following the leaking by former CIA contractor Edward Snowden of details of clandestine mass surveillance activities carried out by the US and British Governments. Speculation that Snowden, who was seeking a legal safe haven from the USA, might be granted asylum by Ecuador prompted members of the US Congress to warn that, in such an event, a system of trade preferences benefiting Ecuadorean exporters, which was due for renewal at the end of July 2013, would not be extended. The arrangements were part of the Andean Trade Promotion and Drug Eradication Act (ATPDEA) and gave duty-free access to the US market for a range of products from Ecuador and other Andean exporters. Correa responded by unilaterally renouncing ATPDEA, and offered US $23m. to the USA for human rights training, seemingly in response to recent criticism by the US Government of Ecuador's own human rights record. The dispute appeared to render the prospect of a revival of negotiations towards a US-Ecuadorean free trade agreement, suspended since 2006 (see above), ever more remote.

In April 2014, following 29 years of negotiations, Ecuador and Costa Rica signed a treaty to resolve an outstanding maritime border dispute. The agreement was the result of lengthy diplomatic efforts and was achieved without recourse to the International Court of Justice in The Hague, the most common route to seeking settlement of territorial disputes. The two sides followed the principles established in the UN Convention of the Law of the Sea to set the boundaries. As a result of the agreement, Ecuador had no remaining territorial disputes for the first time in its history.

In June 2014 the President of the National Assembly, Gabriela Rivadeneira of the governing AP, submitted a series of constitutional amendments to the Corte Constitucional (Constitutional Court), a body which replaced the Tribunal Constitucional (Constitutional Tribunal) in 2008 as the ultimate protector of the new Constitution. Among the proposals were several controversial reforms which opponents of President Correa claimed reflected his authoritarian, anti-democratic tendencies. The reforms included a provision to allow indefinite re-election of the President, a stipulation that media communications were a 'public service', and restrictions to the right of citizens to request referendums. The nine judges of the Constitutional Court were due to rule by August on whether a simple vote in the National Assembly was sufficient to pass the reforms or whether a referendum was required. An additional legislative proposal (which did not require a constitutional amendment) to establish a new monetary and financial code, which was expected to be passed into law in July, would result in the Government extending its powers over regulation of the private banking sector.

The proposed constitutional amendments were expected to be approved, thereby allowing Correa to seek re-election at the next presidential election in 2017. Correa had announced in May 2014 that he was seeking to abolish term limits for elected officials, while underlining his intention to prevent a reversal of his progressive policies by future governments. By imposing a public service remit on the media, critics claimed that the Government was using its powers further to curtail freedom of expression. Meanwhile, restrictions on referendums appeared counter to the Government's commitment to democratic participation, which it claimed was an important motivation for drafting the constitutional reforms. One such proposed referendum was over government plans to exploit two oilfields, Tiputini and Tambachocha, located in and around the Yasuni national park, which were estimated to hold up to US $1,000m. of recoverable oil reserves, equivalent to 20% of Ecuador's total current proven reserves. Opponents of the proposals included representatives of Amerindian communities in the location. The state oil firm Petroamazonas was awarded the licence to proceed in May; the project was expected to be operational within two years, and to provide windfall earnings to the Correa Government just in time for the 2017 election.

Economy

SANDY MARKWICK

Ecuador comprises a land mass of 272,045 sq km (105,037 sq miles), making it one of the smaller South American countries. Despite this, Ecuador has a richly diverse geography. The Andean Sierra runs north to south through the middle of the country forming a natural barrier between the tropical lowlands of the Amazon basin to the east, the Oriente region, and the coastal lowlands, the Costa, to the west. Meanwhile, the Galápagos Islands, 1,500 km off the Pacific coast, contribute a unique range of flora and fauna to the already rich biodiversity of mainland Ecuador.

Climate varies between regions. Most of the country is tropical or subtropical while some 20% is temperate. Ecuador has some 8.29m. ha of land with potential for agricultural use. The fertile soils of the coastal plains and Oriente can support a wide range of crops, while the coastlines, as well as freshwater rivers and lakes, provide abundant opportunity for commercial fishing and seafood production. Ecuador suffers from the regular occurrence of El Niño, a periodic warming of the tropical Pacific Ocean that brings heavy rains and damages agricultural output.

The population rose by approximately 1.7% annually in the first decade of the 21st century and reached an estimated 16.0m. in 2014. Net emigration increased from 1998 to the mid-2000s, which, along with improvements in family planning, slowed population growth. Job prospects at home and restrictions to immigration abroad slowed the pace of emigration subsequently, although it continued to have an important economic impact as growth in the formal economy struggled to absorb young entrants to the labour market. Most emigrants left for Spain, followed by the USA. Ecuador was also a destination and a transit point for migration from neighbouring Peru and Colombia. According to estimates, net emigration from Ecuador in 2013 took place at a rate of 0.25 per 1,000, down from nearly eight per 1,000 in 2008. In common with other developing countries, Ecuador has a large informal economy. Around two-thirds of the population lived in cities in 2013, compared with less than one-half in 1980. The three largest cities—Guayaquil, Quito and Cuenca—accounted for 35% of the population. Almost 50% of Ecuadoreans live in the coastal lowlands, and 45% in the Sierra, while only 4.5% live in the Oriente and less than 1% in the Galápagos Islands. Ecuador has a young population, with approximately 30.3% aged under 15 years.

Most social indicators show Ecuador to be among the poorest countries in South America. Gross domestic product (GDP) per head was an estimated US $5,957 in 2013. According to official estimates, the proportion of the population considered poor was 25.6% in 2013. In common with most of the region, income distribution was uneven, although Ecuador's Gini co-efficient, at 0.45 in 2013, compared with 0.63 in 2003, showed an improvement in this area. Indicators suggested that there had been advancements in living standards since 1980. Life expectancy increased to an estimated 76 years in 2012 from 63 years in 1980, and infant mortality declined significantly from 74 per 1,000 live births in 1980 to 20 per 1,000 in 2012. The proportion of the urban workforce considered unemployed or underemployed was estimated at 45.0% in May 2013. High rates of emigration and the Government's narrow definition of unemployment tended to restrain official unemployment figures, according to which 5.6% of the total urban labour force were out of work in March 2014, a decline from 9.1% in March 2010 as a result of economic growth.

The country's GDP grew by 4.5% in 2013, to US $94,135m., at nominal dollar rates, compared with 5.1% in 2012. Ecuador is the seventh largest economy in South America but is in eighth position in terms of GDP per head in the region. In 2013 agriculture and fisheries contributed an estimated 9.5% of GDP; industry, including mining, construction and utilities, accounted for 38.3%, and services for 52.2%. Since Ecuador began producing petroleum in the early 1970s, economic growth figures have closely mirrored the performance of the petroleum sector. Economic recovery in 2000 was helped by an increase in oil pipeline capacity and higher petroleum output. GDP increased by an average of 4.5% per year between 2001 and 2008. However, reduced expansion in the oil sector combined with the global economic slowdown precipitated a recession in 2009, when the economy grew by just 0.6%. Growth accelerated to 2.8% in 2010 and further to 7.8% in 2011, when the best performing sectors were construction and shrimp fishing.

Petroleum revenues in the 1970s stimulated domestic demand and inflationary pressures. Public sector spending increases led to budget deficits and currency weakness, fuelling inflation from the 1980s. Inflation in the 1990s averaged 37.4% a year, but increased to an annual average of 96.9% in 2000. The increase stemmed largely from the Government offering financial assistance to banks confronting liquidity crises, which in turn led to a decline in the value of the sucre, further fuelling inflation. Fears about hyperinflation led to the policy of 'dollarization', in which the sucre was replaced with the US dollar in 2000. The policy had the effect of stabilizing the economy in the long term: inflation declined to an annual average of 2.1% in 2005. However, annual inflation rose sharply during 2008–09, a result of higher prices for imports, particularly food and commodities and exacerbated by the weakness of the US dollar and poor weather conditions associated with the El Niño weather pattern. Price rises and a fixed exchange rate undermined the competitiveness of Ecuadorean producers. Attempts to increase productivity or to push for privatization or other structural reforms to boost competitiveness could expect opposition from entrenched business interests, as well as trade unions and left-wing groups. The annual inflation rate was 3.4% in May 2014, compared with 3.0% 12 months earlier.

Successive governments came under pressure to generate fiscal surpluses in order to meet burdensome debt obligations. The Ley Orgánica de Responsibilidad, Estabilización y Transparencia Fiscal (Fiscal Responsibility, Stability and Transparency Law), adopted in 2002, restricted the Government to annual spending increases of no more than 3.5% in real terms, and directed windfall profits from petroleum production towards debt buy-back. As a result, small fiscal surpluses were recorded from 2004. In 2003 the new Government of Lucio Gutiérrez Borbua addressed the fiscal shortfall by decreeing reductions in fuel subsidies and other public spending. A stand-by agreement with the IMF was an important first step in gaining access to credit from the other multilateral lending agencies and private creditors required to finance Ecuador's debt. President Alfredo Palacio Gonzáles (2005–07) relaxed fiscal rules by assigning petroleum revenues to social spending. Higher spending under Palacio's successor, President Rafael Correa Delgado, caused the fiscal surplus to decline, despite high oil prices and improvements in tax collection. In 2008 the fiscal balance was in deficit equivalent to 0.9% of GDP, stemming from sharp increases in spending. In 2013 the fiscal deficit widened to 3.0% of GDP from 0.9% in 2012, as earnings from stagnant oil prices struggled to support government public spending.

AGRICULTURE AND FISHERIES

Close to one-third of Ecuador's land mass is used for agricultural purposes. Sectoral output grew by an estimated 6.2% in 2013, following growth of 1.6% in 2012 and 4.6% in 2011. The contribution of agriculture (including fisheries) to GDP, at 9.5% in 2013, has been largely stable since the early 1990s. During the previous three decades, however, the importance of agriculture declined dramatically: agriculture accounted for 25% of total output in the 1960s. A combination of poor infrastructure, lack of mechanization, financing difficulties and the effects of El Niño limited productivity in the sector.

Ecuador's climatic and geographic diversity supports a wide range of crops and fisheries production. The coastal region features a modern agro-industry where land has been converted for production, largely for export, of bananas and other fruit, coffee, cocoa, rice and shrimps. Another important export is cut flowers, the cultivation of which is concentrated in the Sierra. Staple products for domestic consumption include rice, sugar cane and plantains, grown in coastal areas, while grains, vegetables and dairy products are produced in the Sierra.

Ecuador exports more bananas than any other country in the world, accounting for 30.2% of global export volumes in 2012, despite a decline in output of 5.6%, to 7.4m. metric tons, during the year, as a result of flooding. Bananas became the principal crop of Ecuador in the 1940s when disease and hurricanes damaged production in Central America. Banana plantations were principally located in the lowlands of Guayas province, although road construction and improved irrigation expanded the viable area of production. Global growth in demand in the 1990s led to heavy investment in technology. The disease-resistant and higher-yielding Cavendish variety of banana replaced the traditional Gros Michel. However, increased output and reduced demand saw prices decrease from 1997. The steady decline in exports was reversed from 2001, when exports earned US $847m. In 2013 bananas accounted for export revenues of $2,332m., though as a contribution to total exports, the banana sector declined between those dates from 18.2% in 2001 to 9.3% in 2013, as oil export revenue increased. The World Trade Organization (WTO) in 1999 ruled in favour of Ecuador in a dispute with the European Union (EU). Ecuador had long protested that the preference for trading with African, Caribbean and Pacific countries, with which parts of the EU maintained post-colonial ties, was contrary to trade regulations. The dispute was exacerbated by the EU's introduction in 2006 of a levy on banana imports from Latin America to replace a quota system, which imposed a lower tariff on imports over a quota limit. Ecuador and other Latin American producers complained that the new tariff was discriminatory and contrary to the spirit of the 1999 WTO ruling. The dispute was finally settled following an agreement in December 2009 in which the EU agreed to reduce gradually the tariffs on bananas from Latin America by up to one-third.

Before bananas took over in the 1940s, cocoa had been Ecuador's main export crop. In the 19th century coastal plantations had produced cocoa accounting for up to three-quarters of total export earnings. Decline followed disease and the emergence of alternative sources to satisfy global demand. The crop is vulnerable to adverse climatic conditions and fluctuations in demand. In 2013 Ecuador produced an estimated 133,323 metric tons of cocoa, down 40.7% compared with the previous year. Despite lower production volumes, export earnings benefited from favourable world prices. Ecuadorean cocoa and cocoa products earned an estimated US $532.4m. in 2013, a 17.1% recovery following a decline in earnings of 22.3% the previous year. Plans to focus on high-quality niche markets for cocoa were showing signs of success.

As with other commodities, the importance of coffee to the Ecuadorean economy varied with international prices, supply and climatic conditions. With more than 100,000 small family growers, coffee production is fragmented and inefficient. Production levels reached an historic low estimated at 37,800 metric tons in 2009. New planted areas and renovations of existing plantations from 2005 added 12,000 ha of land dedicated to coffee. This, along with higher international prices, arrested decline with production growing modestly to 39,000 tons in the year ending March 2011. Average prices for Ecuadorean coffee increased three-fold between 2001 and 2010. However, prices declined by an average of 43.2% during 2011–13. In 2013 coffee export revenues decreased by 16.0%, to US $219.4m. Coffee prices recovered during the first half of 2014.

New agricultural products, including cut flowers, melons, asparagus, artichokes and strawberries, boosted export earnings in the 2000s. Cut flowers earned export revenues estimated at US $837.3m. in 2013, a rise of 8.6% compared with the previous year. Ecuadorean producers took advantage of the appreciation of the Colombian peso, which ensured more competitive prices in international markets. Colombia was Ecuador's principal competitor in the flower industry. Both countries, however, were vulnerable to the strengthening real exchange rate.

Staple crops such as rice, sugar cane, potatoes, maize, soybeans, wheat, barley and cotton were important for domestic consumption, but contributed insignificant amounts to overall export earnings. Landholdings in the non-export sector tended to be smaller and had lower levels of productivity. Rice production increased significantly after 2007, a consequence of new varieties allowing for more harvests per year combined with increased government subsidies. In 2012–13 Ecuador produced 2.0m. metric tons of rice (milled and rough), a peak which represented a 24% increase compared with the previous harvest year. Production is concentrated in the Guayas lowlands. Ecuador relied on imports to satisfy requirements for wheat and barley. Patterns of land ownership, characterized by a predominance of subsistence smallholdings, contributed to the shortfall in wheat production.

Ecuador's shrimp-fishing sector earned US $1,795.0m. in 2013, a rise of 40.6% from the previous year, continuing a progressive increase from 2002, when revenues were $253m. Additional revenues came from tuna, sardines, mackerel, anchovies and fishmeal. Canned fish earned an estimated $1,337.9.m. in export revenues in 2013, compared with $601.3m. in 2010.

MINING AND ENERGY

Oil drilling in Ecuador began in 1917 in the Santa Elena peninsula, west of Guayaquil. However, large-scale production dates back to the late 1960s with the discovery of major reserves in Lago Agrio in the Oriente by the US consortium of Texaco-Gulf. The Trans-Andean pipeline was built linking the oilfields to a tanker terminal in the port of Esmeraldas, and exports began in 1972. Ecuador joined the Organization of the Petroleum Exporting Countries (OPEC) in 1973, but the required production quotas limited exploration and proven reserves.

The Government made it easier for foreign companies to operate in the petroleum sector in 1983, following which several foreign companies signed contracts with the state oil company Corporación Estatal Petrolera Ecuatoriana (CEPE). New reserves were found in the south-eastern Oriente. Ignoring OPEC production quotas, Ecuador increased production to maximize revenues when oil prices were declining. In 1989 President Rodrigo Borja Cevallos formed a new state oil company, Empresa Estatal Petróleos del Ecuador (PETRO-ECUADOR), to replace CEPE and assume greater state control over the process of production and distribution. PETROECUADOR took over the Trans-Andean pipeline, but a decline in export revenues led to a policy that encouraged greater levels of foreign investment. A more liberal foreign investment code was introduced in 1993. The changed rules led to eight new production-sharing agreements with petroleum companies in the mid-1990s.

In 1992 President Sixto Durán Ballén withdrew Ecuador from membership of OPEC owing to its refusal to authorize an increase in the country's production quota. In the mid-1990s petroleum discoveries almost tripled Ecuador's proven reserves, and the Government signed several contracts with foreign companies for drilling and exploration. Increased opposition and sensitivities to foreign participation in the petroleum sector slowed development and growth. Underinvestment during the administration of President Fabián Alarcón Rivera (1997–98) contributed to a decline in production that occurred concurrently with a decrease in international petroleum prices. Following expansion of the Sistema del Oleoducto Trans-Ecuatoriano (SOTE—Trans-Ecuadorean Oil Pipeline System), which added 60,000 barrels per day (b/d) to overall capacity, as well as the introduction of the Oleoducto de Crudos Pesados, a pipeline that doubled heavy crude petroleum transport capacity, average production in 2003 increased to 447,000 b/d. However, in 2004 oil shipments via the SOTE were suspended following a landslide, forcing PETROECUADOR to declare *force majeure* on its contractual obligations. A dispute with the US Occidental Petroleum Corporation (Oxy), which led the Government to cancel its exploration and production contract and take over its operations in May 2006, increased the state company's output relative to private sector output. However, the takeover undermined the planned expansion of petroleum production. The Oxy contract cancellation and tax disputes with foreign oil companies were precipitated by a history of conflict between successive Governments and the US oil firm Texaco (part of Chevron since 2001) over massive environmental damage. The company argued that its responsibilities were fulfilled following a settlement with the Government in 1998, which included a US $40m. clean-up operation. In 2011 an Ecuadorean court ordered Chevron to pay compensation; however, in February 2013 the company's position contesting liability was upheld by the Permanent Court of Arbitration in The Hague, Netherlands. The dispute was expected to continue to undermine relations with the USA (see History).

Relations with foreign oil companies deteriorated further under President Correa following the termination of a contract with French firm Perenco in 2009 and a demand by the Government that the company, along with Spain's Repsol, pay US $326m. and $444m., respectively, in disputed taxes. Meanwhile, in 2007 Correa restored Ecuador's status within OPEC after a 15-year hiatus. In July 2010 a new law came into effect which replaced production-sharing agreements with a flat fee and gave the state 100% ownership of the oil and gas produced. The Government claimed that it would come to a fair settlement to end contracts with any company choosing not to accept the new terms. In April 2010 the Government split PETROECUADOR with the creation of EP PETROECUADOR, responsible for exploration, refinery and commercial exploitation of oil, while PETROECUADOR was confined to downstream service stations. The Government created two other state oil companies to develop selected oilfields, Petroamazonas and Rio Napa, a joint venture with the Venezuela state oil company. In 2013 Ecuador produced an average of 526,000 b/d of petroleum, a 4.4% increase compared with the previous year, but down from a peak of 536,000 b/d in 2007.

Ecuador is heavily reliant on oil as a source of export revenues. Petroleum and petroleum derivatives were Ecuador's most important export commodities (comprising an estimated 56.5% of total export revenues in 2013), and the sector contributed 28.8% of total government revenues in that year. Ecuador exported 105.5m. barrels, earning US $14,108m., in 2013. Ecuador's crude oil varieties were largely stable in 2012–13, averaging $99.75 per barrel in 2012 and $99.6 in the first three quarters of 2013. During that period prices were almost those in mid-2009. The USA was the most significant destination for petroleum exports. Proven reserves were estimated at 8,240m. barrels in 2013. Most Ecuadorean petroleum was medium-heavy crude, although recent discoveries have been of heavy crude. Under President Correa, relations with Venezuela, under the leadership of President Hugo Chávez, became closer, leading to an agreement in May 2006 whereby Venezuela would help to finance the construction of a 300,000-b/d oil refinery at the port of Manta. Relations with Venezuela continued to be close, despite the death of Chávez in March 2013, and extended beyond financial assistance to close diplomatic alignment, underpinned by a shared resistance to the power and influence of the USA.

Most mining focuses on non-metals used in construction, including limestone, sand and clay, though there are reserves of metals such as gold, silver, copper, iron, lead, zinc, uranium and magnesium. The Government opened up mining to foreign investment in 1991 in a bid to develop the sector with a more liberal mining law. Subsequently, the bureaucracy associated with investment was reduced, and further reforms were introduced in 2000 granting stronger legal rights to mining companies. However, the risks surrounding exploration rights owing to changes in government policy and enforcement have deterred investment. The Government introduced reforms to the mining code in May 2013 that were designed to attract foreign investment to develop the sector. However, high tax rates on profits, which were focused on large projects in the sector, continued to deter investors.

The Government was proceeding with plans to exploit two oilfields, Tiputini and Tambachocha, located in and around the Yasuní national park, which were estimated to hold up to US $1,000m. of recoverable oil reserves, equivalent to 20% of Ecuador's total current proven reserves. Opponents of the plans included representatives of Amerindian communities in the location. The state oil firm Petroamazonas was awarded the licence to proceed in May 2014; the project was expected to be operational within two years, and to provide windfall earnings to the Correa Government.

MANUFACTURING AND CONSTRUCTION

Traditional manufacturing sectors were textiles, food and drink, tobacco, petroleum refining and cement production. Most industrial activity takes place in the Guayas and Pichincha provinces, though other areas occupied important roles in industry. Petroleum-refining and wood activity take place in Esmeraldas, iron and steel in Cotopaxi, while ceramics, furniture and tyres are produced in Azuay, and marine and agricultural products are manufactured in Manabí. Ecuador established *maquiladoras* (in-bond assembly plants) at the Guayas Free Zone near Guayaquil, and several other areas have been identified for further free zones.

The petroleum boom of the 1970s fuelled expansion in manufacturing, which the Government encouraged with protectionist trade initiatives. Industrial development was heavily dependent on the import of capital goods. The sector stagnated in the 1980s, but growth was restored in the 1990s. Manufacturing output increased by an average of 4.9% per year during 2000–09. After contraction of 1.5% in 2009, manufacturing output (excluding construction and oil refining) increased by an annual average of 4.0% during 2010–12 and by 3.6% in 2013. In that year the combined manufacturing (including oil refining) and construction sector's contribution to GDP was 24.6%. During the 1990s government policy shifted significantly away from protectionism towards a more liberal trade environment in line with regional and global developments. Membership of the WTO and Comunidad Andina de Naciones (CAN—Andean Community of Nations) reinforced this outlook. Exports to the CAN, in particular, led to an expansion in the chemicals, machinery, minerals, paper, printing and wood products industries. However, an underdeveloped stock market was an impediment to businesses seeking investment capital.

The construction sector grew during the recession of 2009 and continued to outpace the economy in 2010–12, with average annual growth of 13.5% during that period. The sector contributed 12.0% of GDP in 2013. The state sector accounted for most of the investment in construction, and major public sector infrastructure projects, such as new oil pipelines and highways, were an important source of employment.

TRANSPORT AND COMMUNICATIONS

Under-investment has left most of Ecuador's road network in poor condition. The standard of the road network was best near the coast, where large-scale reconstruction followed extensive damage caused by El Niño in 1997–98. In 2012 there were some 1.5m. registered vehicles, compared with just 76,000 in 1971. Roads were built to open up new areas in the Oriente and Costa regions for agriculture and settlement. Ecuador now has a 42,200-km road network.

The railway network, once nearly 1,000 km in length, fell into disrepair as a consequence of flooding and lack of investment. The main railway line runs between San Lorenzo, on the northern coast, through the Sierra to Cuenca and to the coast at Guayaquil. Limited sections of the track are operational and serve local and tourist traffic. In 2011 the Government restored a 30-km route between Salinas and Ibarra in the north largely to boost tourism. The line was reopened in 2012.

Quito and Guayaquil host Ecuador's two main international airports. In 2002 an international consortium won a 35-year concession to operate Quito's existing Mariscal Sucre airport and to build a new one 25 km east of the capital at Puembo. Construction, originally scheduled for completion in 2010, was delayed owing to a legal dispute between the investors and local state authorities over airport tariff entitlements which affected the financing of the project. An agreement was reached in February 2011 and the new airport began operations in 2013. The principal airline, TAME, Línea Aérea del Ecuador, served Latin American destinations as well as national routes. A new airline, LAN Ecuador, was launched in 2003. TAME and LAN, along with a third airline Aerogal, owned by Colombian airline Avianca, dominate domestic air travel.

Ecuador has seven deep water ports. Of these, Balao was the most significant in terms of cargo traffic measure in metric tons and as an oil export terminal. Guayaquil is the main port for non-oil trade. Puerto Bolívar (was the main route for banana exports. The other principal ports are Manta (through which most coffee and cocoa exports are distributed), El Salitral, La Libertad and Esmeraldas.

Ecuador had an average of just 14.7 fixed telephone lines for every 100 inhabitants in 2013—below average for South America. Installed lines are concentrated in urban areas. The underdevelopment of fixed-line telecommunications was partially offset by a rapid increase in mobile cellular telephone use which surpassed a 100% penetration rate by 2010. In 2008 the Government merged the two state telecommunications companies Andinatel and Pacifictel to form the Corporación Nacional de Telecomunicaciones (CNT—National Telecommunications Corporation) with a market share of fixed-line telephony in excess of 90%. The company committed to an estimated US $520m. in investment. Two foreign-controlled mobile network operators dominated the market: Conecel and Movistar, with majority ownership from Mexico and Spain, respectively. The generally undeveloped telecommunications infrastructure undermined the use of the internet as a tool for business, although measures to provide a legal framework for so-called e-commerce and fixed tariffs on internet connections helped to increase use.

TOURISM

Tourism became Ecuador's fourth largest earner of foreign exchange during the 1990s, behind petroleum, bananas and shrimps. Despite its significance as a foreign exchange earner, Ecuadoreans spent more outside Ecuador than visitors spent in the country. Ecuador's rich biodiversity and varied climate and landscape—Andean highlands, tropical rainforest, Pacific beaches and the Galápagos Islands—mostly within accessible journey times from main cities, make it a popular destination.

The number of tourists visiting Ecuador increased to 1.4m. in 2013, a rise of 7.4% compared with the previous year. Most international visitors were from Colombia, the USA and Peru. Resolution of the long-running border dispute with Peru led to direct air links between Peru's capital, Lima, and several destinations in Ecuador.

FOREIGN INVESTMENT

Regulations governing foreign investment were liberalized from the 1980s in line with global and regional trends. President León Febres Cordero (1984–88) relaxed ownership restrictions on foreign companies and raised limits on profit remittances. In 1991 President Borja opened up some sectors of the economy that had been restricted to sole or majority domestic ownership only. In 1993 President Durán Ballén opened further sectors of the economy to foreign capital. In 1998 the remaining restrictions on foreign investment in strategic sectors such as fishing, air transport and media were abolished.

Encouraged by these reforms, together with membership of the CAN, which restricted future governments' ability to return to a less liberal investment environment, foreign direct investment (FDI) increased. From an average annual rate of US $108m. in 1982–92, FDI rose to $589m. in 1993–99. Investment in the petroleum sector accounted for more than 90% of FDI. Under President Correa, Ecuador assumed a more radical profile in terms of relations with foreign investors and international financial institutions. Despite a perception of increased political risks to foreign investment in Ecuador under Correa, net FDI increased from $194.2m. in 2007 to $1,005.8m. in 2008. The mining sector largely accounted for the massive increase in FDI during 2008, although there were also significant increases in foreign investment in communications and manufacturing. FDI levels declined following the completion of the heavy crude pipeline, decreasing to $163.1m. in 2010, but increased to $639.3m. in 2011. FDI levels decreased to $586.5m. in 2012 before increasing by 20.2% to $702.8m. in 2013. Between 2007 and 2013 Mexico was the most

important source of FDI, followed by Canada, Panama, the People's Republic of China and Spain. In 2013 Uruguay was the largest source of FDI with $115.2m, (16.4%), followed by Mexico (12.9%), China (12.6%), Spain (9.6%) and Italy (8.4%). The USA accounted for a 5.9% share of FDI, having been historically the largest foreign investor; Ecuador's dispute with Chevron (see above) has damaged bilateral commercial relations with that country. The mining sector received 34.1% of total FDI in 2013, followed by manufacturing, which attracted 19.1%. The contribution of the stock market to the economy was insignificant, both as a source of investment funds for local business and as a destination for portfolio investment. Banks were the principal source of financing available. Net portfolio investment represented an outflow of funds.

DEBT

Ecuador rapidly accumulated sizeable debt in the 1970s to finance state-led industrial development. Petroleum reserves were used to finance the debt, but the country fell behind in repayments following a decrease in petroleum prices. Lending from both commercial banks and the 'Paris Club' of official creditors increased annually between 1987 and 1994 to unsustainable levels.

Persistent difficulties in debt repayment obligations led to the 1995 Brady Plan, in which US $7,580m. of debt with commercial banks was restructured to ensure that Ecuador had access to further commercial lending. However, a combination of a depreciating currency, low petroleum prices and a weak economy led to a further deterioration of the debt position. Total public external debt increased to more than 100% of GDP in 1999, making Ecuador the first country to default on Brady and Eurobond obligations. In 2000 the Noboa Government reached an agreement with the IMF and private sector creditors to restructure debt.

In 2003 the Gutiérrez Government secured a 13-month stand-by loan of US $205m. from the IMF, conditional upon a programme of structural reform and austerity measures, giving Ecuador access to further multilateral lending. In December 2008 the Correa Government announced that it was defaulting on $3,200m. of outstanding debt, in the form of global bonds. This was Ecuador's third debt default in 15 years, which made it more difficult for Ecuador to secure external funding to finance fiscal deficits. Ecuador secured finance from China estimated at $7,250m., which was not conditional on fiscal performance and helped the Government to fund its public spending plans. During 2009–13 China granted 10 separate loans to Ecuador amounting to $9,900m. In an effort to reduce dependency on China, President Correa issued a $2,000m. sovereign bond in June 2014, the first since its 2008 default. The Government planned to spend the funds on infrastructure projects and the financing of existing loans, while other bonds were due to mature in 2015. The success of the bond issue, which was oversubscribed, raised the prospect of Ecuador returning to the international debt markets. In 2014 the Government and the IMF opened up Article IV Consultations, which had been suspended after the 2008 debt default, with a view to restoring IMF economic assessments. Offsetting the positive developments with the IMF, however, ongoing tensions in relations with the USA led to the cancellation of $32m. in aid from the US Agency for International Development. Total foreign debt was estimated at $18,499m. in March 2014.

FOREIGN TRADE

Liberalization of trade policy progressively made Ecuador more open in the 1990s, beginning with a reform of the Tariff Law and the elimination of import quotas. Ecuador joined the WTO in 1996 and ratified the General Agreement on Trade in Services. Domestic manufacturing—with a few exceptions, such as vehicles, as permitted by the WTO—no longer enjoys the protection of high tariff barriers. Ecuador's standard tariff is below the CAN's agreed common external tariff, making it one of the most open in South America. Trade liberalization, including the burgeoning new CAN markets, encouraged diversification of exports. However, despite diversification,

Ecuador remained vulnerable to the volatility of international commodity markets, as exports remained dominated by primary products.

According to central bank figures, Ecuador registered a trade deficit of US \$1,090m. in 2013, a rise compared with \$440.6m. in 2012 and \$829.5m. in 2011, but lower than a deficit of \$1,978.7m. in 2010. The trade balance was affected by a dramatic collapse in petroleum prices in the second half of 2008. Monthly deficits continued into 2009, undermined further by recession in the USA, Ecuador's main export market. Before 2003 the trade account had been regularly in deficit. The shift into a positive trade balance on goods was led by increased volumes and prices of petroleum exports, which outpaced strong import growth. In 2013 consumer goods accounted for an estimated 20.6% of all imports, while capital goods comprised 26.7% and primary goods 30.9%. After oil, the most important exports were bananas, shrimps, canned fish, cut flowers and cocoa powder. The USA was Ecuador's largest export market, purchasing some 44.6% of total exports in 2013. Chile accounted for 9.9% of exports that year, followed by Peru and Colombia with shares of 7.5% and 3.7%, respectively. The largest European export destination was Spain, accounting for 3.1% of total exports. In 2013 the USA was also the largest source of imports (25.2%), followed by China (16.7%), Colombia (8.0%) and Panama (4.8%). High oil prices had offset repatriation of foreign investors' earnings abroad, as well as Ecuador's large interest obligations on its debt, allowing the country to record current account surpluses from 2005. Remittances from Ecuadoreans living abroad represented the largest source of foreign exchange earnings after petroleum, totalling an estimated \$2,449m. in 2013, marginally lower than the previous year, and a decrease compared with \$3,335.4m. in 2007. Remittances were vulnerable to economic slowdowns, particularly in the main host countries, the USA and Spain.

Talks between the USA and Ecuador over a proposed free trade agreement collapsed after the Government's takeover of the operations of Oxy in 2006 (see above). Relations with the USA worsened, following a diplomatic dispute over the publication of leaked diplomatic cables, distributed by the website WikiLeaks (an organization publishing leaked classified content), in 2011, when the founder of WikiLeaks, Julian Assange, sought to evade extradition to the USA by seeking political asylum in the Ecuadorean embassy in London, United Kingdom. In June 2013 President Correa announced the withdrawal of Ecuador from a system of trade preferences with the USA under the Andean Trade Promotion and Drug Eradication Act, pre-empting the possibility that the US Congress would not approve renewal of the arrangement which was due in July. The Government compensated some 650 companies exporting 166 products. By contrast, in 2012 Ecuador sought to renew trade talks with the EU, from which it had withdrawn in 2009, following claims that it was being pushed towards accepting liberal free trade principles rather than trade co-operation, along with provision for investment and aid. Trade representatives from the EU and Ecuador met in March 2014 to consider Ecuador joining an existing trade agreement between the EU and Ecuador's neighbours, Colombia and Peru. Discussions on the issue were ongoing in 2014.

CONCLUSION

President Correa came to power in 2007 on a radical platform opposed to IMF-prescribed structural reform designed to boost the non-oil economy, including changes to the tax regime, the introduction of private management in public sector utilities and greater flexibility in labour markets. Once in power, Correa used increased oil revenues to expand social investment significantly. Despite generally high oil prices the Government was confronted by an increased fiscal deficit, prompting speculation that it might abandon dollarization, and leading to further economic uncertainty. The fiscal challenge facing President Correa was exacerbated by difficulties in securing external credit, a legacy of his 2008 default on global bonds and his heterodox policy mix.

Public finances were boosted by record earnings from oil exports, a consequence of high international prices, and by lending from China. Windfall oil earnings eased pressure to reverse the policy of dollarization, with its concomitant restrictions on monetary policy, despite hesitancy from international investors, which was attributed in part to President Correa's apparent unpredictability and confrontational style. Dollarization protected Ecuador from hyperinflationary tendencies and underpinned broad macroeconomic stability. Ecuador remained vulnerable to decreases in international oil prices and was reliant on high oil prices to permit state spending to compensate for low investment rates. Despite a degree of controversy surrounding President Correa, he presided over a period of relative political stability. Correa became the longest-serving President in modern Ecuadorean history by securing a second four-year term in office in February 2013. The President planned to imbed his leftist programme, and to that end sought reform of the Constitution to allow him to stand for re-election again in 2017. Correa's position was strengthened by a overall majority in the Congreso Nacional (National Congress), following concurrent legislative elections, improving the prospects for stability under his Government.

Statistical Survey

Sources (unless otherwise stated): Instituto Nacional de Estadística y Censos, Juan Larrea 534 y Riofrío, Quito; tel. (2) 252-9858; e-mail inec1@ecnet.ec; internet www.inec.gob.ec; Banco Central del Ecuador, Casilla 339, Quito; tel. (2) 257-2522; fax (2) 295-5458; internet www.bce.fin.ec; Ministerio de Industrias y Competitividad, Avda Eloy Alfaro y Amazonas, Quito; tel. (2) 254-6690; fax (2) 250-3818; e-mail info@mic.gov.ec; internet www.mic.gov.ec.

Area and Population

AREA, POPULATION AND DENSITY

Area (sq km)	272,045*
Population (census results)	
25 November 2001	12,156,608
28 November 2010	
Males	7,177,683
Females	7,305,816
Total	14,483,499
Population (official estimates)	
2012	15,520,973
2013	15,774,749
2014	16,027,466
Density (per sq km) at 2014	58.9

* 105,037 sq miles.

POPULATION BY AGE AND SEX
(UN estimates at mid-2014)

	Males	Females	Total
0–14 years	2,414,440	2,318,794	4,733,234
15–64 years	5,076,536	5,107,125	10,183,661
65 years and over	497,961	567,695	1,065,656
Total	**7,988,937**	**7,993,614**	**15,982,551**

Source: UN, *World Population Prospects: The 2012 Revision.*

2014 (official population estimates): *0–14 years:* 4,982,359; *15–64 years:* 9,967,520; *65 years and over:* 1,077,587; *Total* 16,027,466 (males 7,939,552, females 8,087,914).

REGIONS AND PROVINCES
(projected population estimates at mid-2007)

	Area (sq km)	Population	Density (per sq km)	Capital
Sierra . . .	63,269	6,111,542	96.6	—
Azuay . . .	8,125	678,746	83.5	Cuenca
Bolívar . . .	3,940	180,293	45.8	Guaranda
Cañar . . .	3,122	226,021	72.4	Azogues
Carchi . . .	3,605	166,116	46.1	Tulcán
Chimborazo . .	6,072	443,522	73.0	Riobamba
Cotopaxi . .	6,569	400,411	61.0	Latacunga
Imbabura . .	4,559	397,704	87.2	Ibarra
Loja . . .	11,027	434,020	39.4	Loja
Pichincha . .	12,915	2,683,272	207.8	Quito
Tungurahua . .	3,335	501,437	150.4	Ambato
Costa . . .	67,646	6,720,798	99.4	—
El Oro . . .	5,850	608,032	103.9	Machala
Esmeraldas . .	15,239	438,576	28.8	Esmeraldas
Guayas . . .	20,503	3,617,504	176.4	Guayaquil
Los Ríos . .	7,175	742,241	103.4	Babahoyo
Manabí . . .	18,879	1,314,445	69.6	Portoviejo
Amazónica . .	130,834	662,948	5.1	—
Morona Santiago .	25,690	131,337	5.1	Macas
Napo . . .	11,431	96,029	8.4	Tena
Orellana . . .	22,500	110,782	4.9	Puerto Francisco de Orellana (Coca)
Pastaza . . .	29,774	75,782	2.5	Puyo
Sucumbíos . .	18,328	163,447	8.9	Nueva Loja
Zamora Chinchipe .	23,111	85,571	3.7	Zamora
Insular . . .	8,010	22,678	2.8	—
Archipiélago de Colón				Puerto Baquerizo (Isla San Cristóbal)
(Galápagos) .	8,010	22,678	2.8	
Uncharted areas .	2,289	87,519	38.2	—
Total . . .	272,045	13,605,485	50.0	

Note: Two new provinces, Santo Domingo de los Tsáchilas and Santa Elena, were created in late 2007.

Source: partly Stefan Helders, *World Gazetteer*.

PRINCIPAL TOWNS
(official population estimates, 2014)

Guayaquil . .	2,560,505	Manta . . .		247,463
Quito (capital) .	2,505,344	Riobamba . .		246,861
Cuenca . .	569,416	Loja . . .		243,321
Santo Domingo de los Colorados .	411,009	Esmeraldas . .		206,298
Ambato . . .	360,544	Ibarra . . .		201,237
Portoviejo . .	304,227	Quevedo . .		193,308
Eloy Alfaro (Durán).	271,085	Latacunga . .		188,627
Machala . . .	270,047			

BIRTHS, MARRIAGES AND DEATHS
(excluding nomadic Indian tribes)*

	Registered live births†		Registered marriages		Registered deaths	
	Number	Rate (per 1,000)	Number	Rate (per 1,000)	Number	Rate (per 1,000)
2004 . . .	254,362	19.5	63,299	4.9	54,729	4.2
2005 . . .	252,725	19.1	66,612	5.0	56,825	4.3
2006 . . .	278,591	20.8	74,036	5.5	57,940	4.3
2007 . . .	283,984	20.9	76,154	5.6	58,016	4.3
2008 . . .	291,055	21.1	76,354	5.5	60,023	4.3
2009 . . .	298,337	21.3	76,892	5.5	59,714	4.3
2010 . . .	292,375	19.5	74,800	5.3	61,681	4.3
2011 . . .	n.a.	n.a.	73,579	4.8	62,304	4.1

* Registrations incomplete.

† Figures include registrations of large numbers of births occurring in previous years. The number of births registered in the year of occurrence was: 168,893 in 2004; 168,324 in 2005; 185,056 in 2006; 195,051 in 2007; 206,215 in 2008; 215,906 in 2009; 219,162 in 2010; 229,780 in 2011.

Life expectancy (years at birth): 76.2 (males 73.4; females 79.2) in 2012 (Source: World Bank, World Development Indicators database).

ECONOMICALLY ACTIVE POPULATION
(ISIC major divisions, December of each year, '000 persons aged 15 years and over)

	2011	2012
Agriculture, hunting and forestry	1,687.6	1,694.8
Fishing	68.6	63.3
Mining and quarrying	32.7	32.3
Manufacturing	672.9	689.6
Electricity, gas and water	27.7	27.7
Construction	382.4	403.2
Wholesale and retail trade; repair of motor vehicles, motorcycles and personal and household goods	1,319.0	1,311.2
Hotels and restaurants	310.7	328.4
Transport, storage and communications . .	393.6	400.7
Financial intermediation	67.2	58.3
Real estate, renting and business activities .	282.7	340.1
Public administration and defence; compulsory social security	237.8	240.2
Education	325.6	338.0
Health and social work	176.2	177.4
Other community, social and personal service activities	171.7	159.3
Private households with employed persons .	147.6	158.0
Extraterritorial organizations and bodies . .	0.6	2.6
Total employed	6,304.8	6,425.1
Unemployed	276.8	276.2
Total labour force	6,581.6	6,701.3
Males	3,976.3	4,038.5
Females	2,605.4	2,662.8

Source: ILO.

2014 (labour force survey at March, '000 persons aged 15 years and over): Total employed 6,706.3; Unemployed 342.1; Total labour force 7,048.4.

Health and Welfare

KEY INDICATORS

Total fertility rate (children per woman, 2012) . . .	2.6
Under-5 mortality rate (per 1,000 live births, 2012) . . .	23
HIV/AIDS (% of persons aged 15–49, 2012)	0.6
Physicians (per 1,000 head, 2009)	1.7
Hospital beds (per 1,000 head, 2009)	1.5
Health expenditure (2011): US $ per head (PPP) . . .	665
Health expenditure (2011): % of GDP	6.9
Health expenditure (2011): public (% of total) . . .	36.1
Access to water (% of persons, 2012)	86
Access to sanitation (% of persons, 2012)	83
Total carbon dioxide emissions ('000 metric tons, 2010) .	32,636.3
Carbon dioxide emissions per head (metric tons, 2010) . .	2.2
Human Development Index (2013): ranking	98
Human Development Index (2013): value	0.711

For sources and definitions, see explanatory note on p. vi.

Agriculture

PRINCIPAL CROPS
('000 metric tons)

	2010	2011	2012
Rice, paddy	1,706	1,478	1,566
Barley	19	25	11
Maize	906	864	1,243
Potatoes	387	339	285
Cassava (Manioc)	54	52	71
Sugar cane	8,347	8,132	7,379
Beans, dry	15	13	10
Soybeans (Soya beans) . . .	70*	71*	75†
Oil palm fruit	2,850	2,097	2,350†
Tomatoes	54	36	63
Onions and shallots, green† . .	111	100	105
Carrots and turnips†	28	30	35

—continued				2010	2011	2012
Watermelons†	.	.	.	58	60	63
Bananas	.	.	.	7,931	7,428	7,012
Plantains	.	.	.	547	592	559
Oranges	.	.	.	47	37	48
Mangoes†	.	.	.	212	201	202
Pineapples†	.	.	.	124	117	120
Papayas†	.	.	.	41	39	40
Coffee, green	.	.	.	31	24	7
Cocoa beans	.	.	.	132	224	133
Abaca (Manila hemp)†	.	.	.	31	35	35

* Unofficial figure.
† FAO estimate(s).

Aggregate production ('000 metric tons, may include official, semi-official or estimated data): Total cereals 2,654 in 2010, 2,388 in 2011, 2,843 in 2012; Total roots and tubers 465 in 2010, 420 in 2011, 384 in 2012; Total vegetables (incl. melons) 477 in 2010, 447 in 2011, 453 in 2012; Total fruits (excl. melons) 9,325 in 2010, 8,794 in 2011, 8,375 in 2012.

Source: FAO.

LIVESTOCK
('000 head, year ending September)

				2010	2011	2012
Cattle	.	.	.	5,254	5,359	5,236
Sheep	.	.	.	792	743	750*
Pigs	.	.	.	1,490	1,831	1,162
Horses	.	.	.	367	344	338
Goats	.	.	.	135	112	109
Asses	.	.	.	139	131	121
Mules	.	.	.	125	119	120
Chickens	.	.	.	152,926	140,000*	140,000*

* FAO estimate.
Source: FAO.

LIVESTOCK PRODUCTS
('000 metric tons)

				2010	2011	2012
Cattle meat*	.	.	.	260.0	268.0	265.0
Sheep meat*	.	.	.	5.6	5.6	5.6
Pig meat*	.	.	.	184.7	200.0	205.0
Goat meat*	.	.	.	1.2	1.0	1.1
Chicken meat*	.	.	.	340.0	330.0	330.0
Cows' milk	.	.	.	5,709.5	6,375.3	5,675.1
Sheep's milk*	.	.	.	7.1	6.9	7.1
Goats' milk*	.	.	.	2.9	2.9	3.0
Hen eggs*	.	.	.	110.0	130.0	140.0
Wool, greasy*	.	.	.	1.4	1.4	1.4

* FAO estimates.
Source: FAO.

Forestry

ROUNDWOOD REMOVALS
('000 cubic metres, excluding bark, FAO estimates)

		2010	2011	2012
Sawlogs, veneer logs and logs for sleepers	.	1,280	1,280	1,280
Pulpwood		481	481	481
Other industrial wood	.	330	330	330
Fuel wood	.	4,940	4,952	4,965
Total	.	7,031	7,043	7,056

Source: FAO.

SAWNWOOD PRODUCTION
('000 cubic metres, including railway sleepers)

			2008	2009	2010
Coniferous (softwood)*	.	.	107	118	118
Broadleaved (hardwood)	.	.	310	310*	401
Total	.	.	417	428*	519

* Estimate(s).

2011–12: Production assumed to be unchanged from 2010 (FAO estimates).

Source: FAO.

Fishing

('000 metric tons, live weight)

		2010	2011	2012
Capture	.	399.9	506.4	513.4
Pacific thread herring	.	29.4	20.3	33.1
Anchoveta (Peruvian anchovy)	.	n.a.	3.0	12.1
Pacific anchoveta	.	0.7	13.0	2.8
Frigate and bullet tunas	.	37.7	43.8	56.4
Skipjack tuna	.	110.1	178.8	186.9
Yellowfin tuna	.	28.9	33.9	32.8
Bigeye tuna	.	32.8	32.1	47.1
Chub mackerel	.	52.8	31.8	51.8
Aquaculture	.	271.9	308.9*	321.9
Whiteleg shrimp	.	223.3	260.0*	281.1
Nile tilapia	.	47.7	48.0*	39.8
Total catch	.	671.8	815.3*	835.3

* Estimate.
Source: FAO.

Mining

		2010	2011	2012*
Natural gas (gross, million cu m)	.	1,275	1,300	1,300
Gold (kg)†	.	4,593	4,149	4,000

* Estimates.
† Metal content of ore only.

Source: US Geological Survey.

Crude petroleum ('000 metric tons, estimates): 26,809 in 2011; 27,097 in 2012; 28,243 in 2013 (Source: BP, *Statistical Review of World Energy*).

Industry

SELECTED PRODUCTS
('000 barrels unless otherwise indicated)

		2010	2011	2012
Motor spirit (gasoline)	.	12,486	15,416	17,133*
Distillate fuel oils	.	8,472	9,918	9,048*
Residual fuel oils	.	9,447	10,754	8,238*
Liquefied petroleum gas	.	2,004	3,046	2,674*
Crude steel ('000 metric tons)	.	372	525	536
Cement ('000 metric tons)	.	5,280	5,700	6,025

* Estimated figures.

Jet fuels ('000 barrels): 2,913 in 2007.

Source: US Geological Survey.

Electric energy (million kWh): 19,010 in 2008; 18,022 in 2009; 17,688 in 2010 (Source: UN Industrial Commodity Statistics Database).

Finance

CURRENCY AND EXCHANGE RATES

Monetary Units
    United States currency is used: 100 cents = 1 US dollar ($).

Sterling and Euro Equivalents (30 May 2014)
    £1 sterling = US $1.682;
    €1 = US $1.361;
    US $100 = £59.45 = €73.50.

Note: Ecuador's national currency was formerly the sucre. From 13 March 2000 the sucre was replaced by the US dollar, at an exchange rate of $1 = 25,000 sucres. Both currencies were officially in use for a transitional period of 180 days, but from 9 September sucres were withdrawn from circulation and the dollar became the sole legal tender.

BUDGET
(consolidated central government accounts, US $ million, provisional)

Revenue	2011	2012	2013
Petroleum revenue	5,971.4	6,085.6	4,676.8
Non-petroleum revenue . . .	11,227.0	13,437.3	15,723.2
Taxation	9,765.3	12,254.7	13,667.6
Taxes on goods and services .	4,818.3	6,099.5	6,799.7
Value-added tax . . .	4,200.4	5,415.0	6,056.1
Taxes on income . . .	3,030.2	3,312.9	3,847.4
Import duties	1,156.0	1,261.1	1,352.2
Other non-petroleum revenue .	1,209.9	1,128.2	1,960.5
Transfers	251.8	54.4	95.1
Total	17,198.4	19,522.8	20,400.0

Expenditure	2011	2012	2013
Wages and salaries	6,466.2	7,352.9	7,897.1
Purchases of goods and services .	1,279.2	1,657.6	2,034.8
Interest payments	673.0	827.9	1,168.6
Transfers	997.8	1,242.9	1,511.4
Other current expenditure . .	983.2	884.1	1,663.7
Capital expenditure	8,035.5	9,260.2	11,585.7
Total	18,434.8	21,225.6	25,861.3

Public Sector Accounts (US $ million, preliminary): *Total revenue:* 31,189.8 in 2011; 34,529.6 in 2012; 37,168.7 in 2013. *Total expenditure:* 31,194.9 in 2011; 35,478.9 in 2012; 41,607.3 in 2013.

INTERNATIONAL RESERVES
(US $ million at 31 December)

	2011	2012	2013
Gold (national valuation) . . .	1,293.3	1,402.6	1,023.5
IMF special drawing rights . .	23.1	24.2	27.9
Reserve position in IMF . . .	43.8	43.8	43.9
Foreign exchange	1,597.4	1,011.9	3,256.2
Total	2,957.6	2,482.5	4,351.5

Source: IMF, *International Financial Statistics*.

MONEY SUPPLY
(US $ million at 31 December)

	2011	2012	2013
Currency outside depository corporations	83.2	84.5	87.3
Transferable deposits . . .	7,931.4	9,623.9	10,815.0
Other deposits	14,888.2	16,856.1	19,308.0
Broad money	22,902.8	26,564.5	30,210.4

Source: IMF, *International Financial Statistics*.

COST OF LIVING
(Consumer Price Index; base: 2004 = 100)

	2011	2012	2013
Food (incl. non-alcoholic beverages)	155.4	164.4	167.4
Housing, fuel (excl. light) . . .	123.4	126.5	129.3
All items (incl. others) . . .	133.0	139.8	143.6

NATIONAL ACCOUNTS
(US $ million at current prices)

Expenditure on the Gross Domestic Product

	2011	2012	2013
Government final consumption expenditure	10,092.5	11,507.7	12,425.4
Private final consumption expenditure	48,781.0	53,047.1	56,798.7
Changes in stocks	2,341.5	992.9	1,193.8
Gross fixed capital formation . .	20,769.2	23,779.3	25,600.4
Total domestic expenditure . .	81,984.2	89,327.0	96,018.3
Exports of goods and services . .	24,214.3	25,994.3	27,482.2
Less Imports of goods and services	26,418.7	27,822.8	29,754.1
GDP in market prices . . .	79,779.8	87,498.6	93,746.4
GDP in constant 2007 prices .	60,882.6	64,009.5	66,879.4

Gross Domestic Product by Economic Activity

	2011	2012	2013
Agriculture, hunting, forestry and fishing	7,544.5	7,846.3	8,459.1
Petroleum and other mining . .	9,622.0	10,480.0	11,171.8
Manufacturing (excl. petroleum-refining)	9,654.1	10,420.2	11,137.8
Manufacture of petroleum derivatives	711.2	367.1	142.0
Electricity, gas and water . . .	998.5	1,066.2	1,103.6
Construction	8,347.1	9,833.0	10,714.7
Wholesale and retail trade . .	8,201.4	8,711.3	9,275.2
Hotels and restaurants . . .	1,576.7	1,852.2	2,078.9
Transport, storage and communications	5,900.4	6,549.5	7,009.7
Financial intermediation . . .	2,318.7	2,557.7	2,624.4
Professional, technical and administrative activities . .	4,686.5	5,178.5	5,610.1
Public administration, defence and other social services	4,967.4	5,708.4	6,099.4
Education, health and social work	6,336.2	7,170.4	7,818.8
Other services	5,149.3	5,584.5	5,890.6
Private households with domestic services	348.6	337.5	370.2
Gross value added in basic prices	76,362.7	83,662.8	89,506.3
Taxes, less subsidies, on products	3,417.2	3,835.8	4,240.1
GDP in market prices . . .	79,779.8	87,498.6	93,746.4

BALANCE OF PAYMENTS
(US $ million)

	2010	2011	2012
Exports of goods	18,131	23,077	24,648
Imports of goods	−19,635	−23,237	−24,577
Balance on goods	−1,504	−160	69
Exports of services	1,479	1,594	1,816
Imports of services	−3,004	−3,156	−3,223
Balance on goods and services	−3,030	−1,723	−1,338
Primary income received . . .	76	85	105
Primary income paid	−1,118	−1,307	−1,430
Balance on goods, services and primary income	−4,071	−2,946	−2,662
Secondary income received . .	2,895	2,983	2,762
Secondary income paid . . .	−447	−262	−276
Current balance	−1,623	−225	−177

—continued		2010	2011	2012
Capital account (net) . . .		65	82	130
Direct investment liabilities . .		167	641	591
Portfolio investment assets .		−721	48	139
Portfolio investment liabilities .		−10	−7	−72
Other investment assets . .		83	−2,511	−1,343
Other investment liabilities . .		703	2,174	253
Net errors and omissions . . .		125	72	−149
Reserves and related items .		−1,211	273	−627

Source: IMF, *International Financial Statistics*.

External Trade

PRINCIPAL COMMODITIES
(distribution by HS, US $ million)

Imports f.o.b.	2011	2012	2013
Vegetables and vegetable products	697.6	632.8	610.2
Prepared foodstuffs; beverages, spirits, vinegar; tobacco and articles thereof .	895.0	960.2	1,055.7
Mineral products	5,507.2	5,748.6	6,439.6
Mineral fuels, oils, distillation products, etc.	5,406.6	5,642.6	6,302.5
Oil and other distillation products, etc.	1,533.7	2,052.8	2,113.4
Non-crude petroleum oils . .	2,857.3	2,887.1	3,403.9
Petroleum gases	858.6	644.5	657.8
Chemicals and related products	2,874.2	3,046.3	3,155.9
Pharmaceutical products . . .	953.1	981.8	1,025.9
Medicament mixtures put in dosage	762.0	788.8	803.1
Plastics, rubber, and articles thereof	1,467.5	1,496.0	1,533.8
Plastics and articles thereof . .	1,063.6	1,047.3	1,138.1
Textiles and textile articles .	764.7	741.9	839.1
Iron and steel, other base metals and articles of base metal	2,047.5	1,969.0	2,195.7
Iron and steel	901.0	767.0	946.1
Machinery and mechanical appliances; electrical equipment; parts thereof .	5,072.2	5,618.3	6,125.6
Boilers, machinery, etc. . . .	2,861.2	3,345.6	3,423.3
Electrical, electronic equipment .	2,211.0	2,272.7	2,702.3
Vehicles, aircraft, vessels and associated transport equipment	2,352.3	2,348.0	2,309.5
Vehicles other than railway, tramway	2,225.5	2,260.8	2,229.0
Cars, station wagon, etc. . .	876.9	764.5	784.5
Total (incl. others)	24,286.1	25,196.5	27,064.5

Exports f.o.b.	2011	2012	2013
Live animals and animal products	1,507.5	1,657.1	2,104.0
Fish, crustaceans, molluscs, aquatic invertebrates . . .	1,480.8	1,617.9	2,093.2
Crustaceans	1,176.5	1,279.8	1,795.0
Vegetables and vegetable products	3,314.3	3,187.2	3,508.6
Live trees, plants, bulbs, roots, cut flowers, etc.	684.3	776.2	841.2
Cut flowers and flower buds for bouquets, etc.	679.9	771.3	837.3
Edible fruit, nuts, peel of citrus fruit, melons	2,344.3	2,185.6	2,471.7
Bananas and plantains . .	2,246.4	2,082.0	2,332.2
Prepared foodstuffs; beverages, spirits, vinegar; tobacco and articles thereof .	2,158.9	2,283.9	2,634.0
Food preparations of meat, fish and seafood	880.0	1,125.8	1,352.1
Prepared or preserved fish, caviar, etc.	870.3	1,112.8	1,337.9
Mineral products	12,945.8	13,847.6	14,194.0
Mineral fuels, oils, distillation products, etc.	12,909.4	13,797.5	14,106.4
Crude petroleum oils . .	11,800.0	12,711.2	13,411.8
Non-crude petroleum oils . .	1,033.9	863.7	551.9
Total (incl. others)	22,342.5	23,852.0	24,957.6

Source: Trade Map-Trade Competitiveness Map, International Trade Centre, www.intracen.org/marketanalysis.

PRINCIPAL TRADING PARTNERS
(US $ million)

Imports c.i.f.	2011	2012	2013
Argentina	559.2	477.6	421.4
Belgium and Luxembourg . . .	116.2	325.5	135.5
Brazil	949.9	925.3	907.8
Canada	313.8	307.0	316.0
Chile	529.1	625.1	562.6
China, People's Republic . . .	3,327.0	2,810.7	4,508.4
Colombia	2,108.1	2,190.2	2,162.9
Germany	650.3	589.2	666.0
India	258.3	442.5	607.9
Italy	331.6	282.3	341.9
Japan	900.9	727.7	867.8
Korea, Republic	946.7	789.9	1,057.3
Mexico	1,070.9	888.3	1,168.2
Panama	1,471.6	1,663.0	1,293.8
Peru	915.1	1,128.0	995.2
Spain	322.1	610.8	698.5
Thailand	256.5	313.1	236.9
United Kingdom	188.3	485.7	409.9
USA	5,138.4	6,774.0	6,808.0
Venezuela	962.1	239.3	73.5
Total (incl. others)	24,286.1	25,196.5	27,064.5

Exports f.o.b.	2011	2012	2013
Belgium and Luxembourg . . .	265.0	208.4	233.8
Chile	1,105.5	1,993.8	2,464.2
China, People's Republic . . .	191.9	391.5	568.8
Colombia	1,023.2	1,059.1	921.7
El Salvador	225.7	147.2	94.1
France	211.8	239.8	318.7
Germany	491.9	378.4	415.1
Italy	580.4	489.3	422.2
Japan	348.9	653.7	570.4
Netherlands	349.2	333.5	430.5
Netherlands Antilles	470.7	40.3	0.9
Panama	1,041.4	923.5	628.4
Peru	1,764.6	1,991.6	1,882.9
Russia	699.9	706.8	817.4
Spain	467.7	444.0	781.8
USA	9,725.7	10,662.6	11,131.0
Venezuela	1,473.9	1,007.9	464.2
Viet Nam	50.2	143.7	325.5
Total (incl. others)	22,342.5	23,852.0	24,957.6

Source: Trade Map-Trade Competitiveness Map, International Trade Centre, www.intracen.org/marketanalysis.

Transport

RAILWAYS
(traffic)

	2002	2003	2004
Passenger-km (million) . . .	33	4	2

Source: UN, *Statistical Yearbook*.

ROAD TRAFFIC
(motor vehicles in use at 31 December)

	2007	2009*	2010
Passenger cars	507,469	487,199	597,427
Buses and coaches	10,925	6,518	20,261
Lorries and vans	323,480	285,640	413,073
Motorcycles and mopeds . . .	78,323	106,979	179,855

* Data for 2008 were not available.

Source: IRF, *World Road Statistics*.

SHIPPING

Flag Registered Fleet
(at 31 December)

	2011	2012	2013
Number of vessels	170	176	184
Total displacement ('000 grt) . .	326.3	331.3	330.6

Source: Lloyd's List Intelligence (www.lloydslistintelligence.com).

International Seaborne Freight Traffic
('000 metric tons; estimates derived from monthly averages)

	2010	2011	2012
Goods loaded	19,944	54,636	33,036
Goods unloaded	10,380	10,680	14,712

Note: For goods unloaded, data include freight movement at ports of El Salitral, Esmeraldas, Guayaquil, La Libertad, Manta and Puerto Bolívar; data for goods loaded also include movements at the port of Balao.

Source: UN, *Monthly Bulletin of Statistics*.

CIVIL AVIATION
(traffic on scheduled services)

	2010	2011
Kilometres flown (million)	44	45
Passengers carried ('000)	4,818	5,094
Passenger-km (million)	5,421	5,720
Total ton-km (million)	615	63

Source: UN, *Statistical Yearbook*.

Passengers carried ('000): 5,512 in 2012 (Source: World Bank, World Development Indicators database).

Tourism

FOREIGN VISITOR ARRIVALS*

Country of residence	2010	2011	2012
Argentina	30,653	37,465	46,203
Canada	23,867	24,834	26,980
Chile	28,478	34,864	41,647
Colombia	203,916	265,557	349,457
Cuba	27,001	24,064	21,482
Germany	25,011	26,669	29,582
Peru	154,216	144,905	137,096
Spain	59,030	60,666	65,765
United Kingdom	22,597	22,877	21,144
USA	249,081	241,605	248,064
Venezuela	31,558	38,308	45,704
Total (incl. others)	1,047,098	1,141,037	1,271,953

* Figures refer to total arrivals (including same-day visitors), except those of Ecuadorean nationals residing abroad.

Total visitor arrivals ('000): 1,366 in 2013 (provisional).

Tourism receipts (US $ million, excl. passenger transport): 843 in 2011; 1,033 in 2012; 1,246 in 2013 (provisional).

Source: World Tourism Organization.

Communications Media

	2011	2012	2013
Telephones ('000 main lines in use)	2,210.6	2,308.7	2,394.8
Mobile cellular telephones ('000 subscribers)	15,332.7	16,456.7	17,541.8
Internet subscribers ('000) . .	639.1	n.a.	n.a.
Broadband subscribers ('000) . .	618.9	818.8	997.6

Source: International Telecommunication Union.

Education

(2011/12 unless otherwise indicated)

	Institutions	Teachers	Students ('000) Males	Females	Total
Pre-primary . .	8,328	39,456	239.5	235.9	475.4
Primary . . .	10,326	116,411	1,079.8	1,038.1	2,117.9
Secondary . .	34,689	132,867	772.7	758.0	1,530.7
Lower secondary .	n.a.	70,605	443.9	414.2	858.1
Upper secondary .	n.a.	62,262	328.7	343.8	672.5
Tertiary* . .	n.a.	26,910	251.9	282.6	534.5

* 2007/08.

Sources: UNESCO Institute for Statistics; Ministerio de Educación.

Pupil-teacher ratio (primary education, UNESCO estimate): 18.2 in 2011/12 (Source: UNESCO Institute for Statistics).

Adult literacy rate: 93.3% (males 94.4%; females 92.2%) in 2013 (Source: UNESCO Institute for Statistics).

Directory

The Constitution

The Constitution of the Republic of Ecuador—the country's 20th—was promulgated on 20 October 2008 following its approval in a referendum held on 28 September. It replaced the Constitution of 1998, which retained many of the provisions of the 1979 Constitution that introduced democratic reforms following a period of military rule.

The first part of the Constitution enshrines certain rights and constitutional guarantees: these include rights relating to *sumak kawsay* ('good living'), disadvantaged people, political participation, freedom, the environment and justice. The other main provisions of the Constitution are summarized below:

LEGISLATIVE POWER

Legislative power is exercised by the unicameral National Assembly (Asamblea Nacional), whose members are elected for a four-year term. The National Assembly is composed of 15 members elected from a nationwide constituency and two from each province, plus one for every 200,000 inhabitants or the greater fraction thereof in each province. The functions of the National Assembly include: inaugurating the President and Vice-President of the Republic; enacting, codifying, reforming and repealing laws; levying taxes; approving international treaties; authorizing, by means of a two-thirds' majority, criminal proceedings against the President or Vice-President; approving the state budget; and granting amnesties and pardons. The Assembly convenes on 14 May of the year of its election.

The National Assembly may dismiss the President of the Republic for acting contrary to the Constitution (subject to approval by the Constitutional Court) or because of serious political crisis and internal commotion. The dismissal of the President requires a two-thirds' majority vote, and may be carried out once only during a legislative term and only in the first three years of the same. Early legislative and presidential elections shall subsequently be held to cover the remainder of the term. The Assembly may also dismiss government ministers and certain other officials—by means of a two-thirds' majority vote, in the case of ministers—for non-compliance of their functions as determined by the Constitution and the law.

EXECUTIVE POWER

Executive power is exercised by the President and Vice-President of the Republic, the Ministries of State and other bodies created to fulfil that function. The President must be Ecuadorean by birth and at least 35 years of age. The President and Vice-President are elected on the same ballot. If no candidate achieves an absolute majority, a second round of voting is contested by the two candidates with the most votes. A second round is not necessary if the winner achieves at least 40% of the valid votes and a difference of at least 10 percentage points over the votes cast for the second-placed candidate. The President serves a four-year term and may be re-elected only once.

The President's functions include: obeying and ensuring the obedience of the Constitution, the law, international treaties and other legal requirements; defining and directing the policies of the executive; presenting the National Development Plan for approval by the National Planning Council; creating, modifying or abolishing ministries and other such bodies, and appointing ministers; reporting the Government's achievements and objectives to the National Assembly once a year; presenting the state budget to the National Assembly for its approval; defining foreign policy; signing and ratifying international treaties; participating in the legislative process by initiating legislation; and exercising supreme authority over the armed forces and national police.

The President may dissolve the National Assembly for acting contrary to the Constitution (subject to approval by the Constitutional Court), or if it repeatedly and unjustifiably obstructs the execution of the National Development Plan, or because of serious political crisis and internal commotion. This right may be exercised once only during a legislative term and only in the first three years of the same. Legislative and presidential elections shall subsequently be held to cover the remainder of the term.

Ministers of state are freely appointed by the President, and represent him in the affairs pertaining to them. They are responsible for the actions they undertake in the exercise of their functions. Close relations of the President, those contracted by the state to undertake public works or services, and serving members of the armed forces and police may not be ministers.

JUDICIAL POWER

The authorities of indigenous communities exercise jurisdiction according to their ancestral traditions and within their territorial limits. They shall apply their own rules and procedures for the resolution of internal conflicts, providing these do not contravene the Constitution or internationally recognized human rights.

The judicial structure comprises the National Court of Justice (Corte Nacional de Justicia), provincial courts of justice, other courts and tribunals as established by law, and courts of the peace. The Council of the Judiciary (Consejo de la Judicatura) regulates and administers the judicial system and is responsible to the National Assembly.

TERRITORIAL ORGANIZATION

The state is organized into regions, provinces, cantons and rural parishes. Autonomous metropolitan districts, the province of Galápagos and indigenous territories constitute special regimes. Contiguous provinces meeting certain requirements of area and population may form an autonomous region, with an elected regional council and governor; similarly, one or more contiguous cantons containing a large conurbation may form an autonomous metropolitan district.

The Constitution defines the powers of the various levels of government. The exclusive powers of the state include: national defence and internal order; foreign relations; economic policy; education, health, social security and housing policy; and natural resources. The exclusive powers of autonomous regional governments, in addition to any other powers that may be granted by law, include: regional planning; the management of water catchment areas; regional transport; and the promotion of regional production and food security.

OTHER PROVISIONS

A part of the Constitution regulates economic affairs, while another concerns social affairs and environmental protection.

The foreign relations of Ecuador are based on principles that include the independence and equality of states, peaceful solutions to conflicts, the condemnation of intervention in the internal affairs of other states, universal citizenship, and the political, cultural and economic integration of the Andean region, South America and Latin America. Foreign military bases and installations are not permitted in Ecuador.

Amendments to one or more articles of the Constitution, providing they do not alter its fundamental structure, may be effected by referendum or by a two-thirds' majority vote of the National Assembly. Any constitutional reform of wider scope must be approved by the National Assembly and subsequently approved by a referendum. The formation of a constituent assembly must receive prior approval in a popular consultation, and the new constitution thereby drafted shall require approval by referendum.

The Government

HEAD OF STATE

President: RAFAEL CORREA DELGADO (took office 15 January 2007; re-elected 26 April 2009 and 17 February 2013).

Vice-President: JORGE DAVID GLAS ESPINEL.

CABINET
(September 2014)

The Government is comprised of members of the Alianza País.

Co-ordinating Ministers

Co-ordinating Minister for Social Development: CECILIA VACA.

Co-ordinating Minister for Strategic Sectors: RAFAEL POVEDA BONILLA.

Co-ordinating Minister for Economic Policy: PATRICIO RIVERA.

Co-ordinating Minister for Security: JUAN FERNANDO CORDERO CUEVA.

Co-ordinating Minister for Production, Competitiveness and Employment: Dr RICHARD ESPINOSA GUZMÁN.

Co-ordinating Minister for Knowledge and Human Resources: GUILLAUME LONG.

Ministers

Minister of Foreign Relations, Trade and Integration: RICARDO ARMANDO PATIÑO AROCA.

Minister of Finance: FAUSTO HERRERA.

Minister of the Interior: JOSÉ SERRANO.

Minister of National Defence: MARÍA FERNANDA ESPINOSA GARCÉS.

Minister of Electricity and Renewable Energy: ESTEBAN ALBORNOZ.

Minister of Transport and Public Works: PAOLA CARVAJAL AYALA.

Minister of Telecommunications and Information: AUGUSTO ESPÍN TOVAR.

Minister of Agriculture, Livestock, Aquaculture and Fishing: JAVIER PONCE CEVALLOS.

Minister of Education: AUGUSTO ESPINOSA ANDRADE.

Minister of Justice, Human Rights and Worship: LEDY ZÚÑIGA ROCHA.

Minister of Labour Relations: CARLOS MARX CARRASCO.

Minister of Economic and Social Inclusion: BETTY TOLA.

Minister of Public Health: Dr CARINA VANCE MAFLA.

Minister of Urban Development and Housing: DIEGO AULESTIA VALENCIA.

Minister of Culture and National Heritage: FRANCISCO BORJA CEVALLOS.

Minister of Sport: JOSÉ FRANCISCO CEVALLOS VILLAVICENCIO.

Minister of the Environment: LORENA TAPIA.

Minister of Tourism: SANDRA NARANJO.

Minister of Non-Renewable Natural Resources: PEDRO MERIZALDE.

Minister of Industry and Productivity: RAMIRO GONZÁLEZ JARAMILLO.

National Secretaries

National Secretary of Public Administration: VINICIO ALVARADO ESPINEL.

National Secretary of Communication: FERNANDO ALVARADO ESPINEL.

National Secretary of Policy Management: VIVIANA BONILLA SALCEDO.

National Secretary of Planning and Development: PABEL MUÑOZ LÓPEZ.

In addition, there were Secretaries of Water, Amazon Development, Higher Education, Science, Technology and Innovation, and Risk Management.

MINISTRIES

Office of the President: Palacio Nacional, García Moreno 10–43, entre Chile y Espejo, Quito; tel. (2) 382-7000; e-mail prensa.externa@ secom.gob.ec; internet www.presidencia.gob.ec.

Office of the Vice-President: Calle Benalcázar N4-40, entre Calles Espejo y Chile, Quito; tel. and fax (2) 258-4574; e-mail info@www .vicepresidencia.gob.ec; internet www.vicepresidencia.gob.ec.

Ministry of Agriculture, Livestock, Aquaculture and Fishing: Avda Eloy Alfaro y Amazonas, Quito; tel. (2) 396-0100; fax (2) 396-0200; e-mail webmaster@magap.gob.ec; internet www.magap.gob .ec.

Ministry of Culture and National Heritage: Avda Colón E5-34 y Juan León Mera, Quito; tel. (2) 381-4550; e-mail comunicacion@ ministeriodecultura.gob.ec; internet www.ministeriodecultura.gob .ec.

Ministry of Economic and Social Inclusion: Edif. Matríz, Robles E3-33 y Ulpiano Páez, Quito; tel. (2) 398-3000; fax (2) 250-9850; e-mail jantonio.egas@mies.gob.ec; internet www.inclusion.gob.ec.

Ministry of Education: Avda Amazonas N34-451 y Avda Atahualpa, Quito; tel. (2) 396-1300; e-mail info@educacion.gob.ec; internet www.educacion.gob.ec.

Ministry of Electricity and Renewable Energy: Edif. Correos del Ecuador, 6°, Eloy Alfaro N29-50 y 9 de Octubre, Edif. Correos del Ecuador, Quito; tel. (2) 397-6000; e-mail sylvia.abad@meer.gob.ec; internet www.energia.gob.ec.

Ministry of the Environment: Calle Madrid 1159 y Andalusía, Quito; tel. (2) 398-7600; fax (2) 256-3462; e-mail mma@ambiente.gob .ec; internet www.ambiente.gob.ec.

Ministry of Finance: Avda 10 de Agosto 1661 y Bolivia, Quito; tel. (2) 399-8300; fax (2) 250-5256; e-mail mefecuador@finanzas.gob.ec; internet www.finanzas.gob.ec.

Ministry of Foreign Relations, Trade and Integration: Avda 10 de Agosto y Carrión E1-76, Quito; tel. (2) 299-3200; fax (2) 299-3273; e-mail gabminis@mmrree.gob.ec; internet www.mmrree.gob.ec.

Ministry of Industry and Productivity: Avda Eloy Alfaro y Amazonas, Quito; tel. (2) 254-6690; fax (2) 250-3818; e-mail ragama@mipro.gob.ec; internet www.mipro.gob.ec.

Ministry of the Interior: Espejo y Benalcázar N4-24, Quito; tel. (2) 295-5666; fax (2) 295-8360; e-mail informacion@

ministeriodelinterior.gob.ec; internet www.ministeriodelinterior .gob.ec.

Ministry of Justice, Human Rights and Worship: Avda Colón, entre Diego de Almagro y Reina Victoria, Quito; tel. (2) 395-5840; fax (2) 246-4914; e-mail sindatos@minjusticia.gob.ec; internet www .justicia.gob.ec.

Ministry of Labour Relations: República del Salvador N34-183 y Suiza, Quito; tel. (2) 381-4000; fax (2) 254-2580; e-mail comunicacion_social@mrl.gob.ec; internet www.relacioneslaborales .gob.ec.

Ministry of National Defence: Calle Exposición S4-71 y Benigno Vela, Quito; tel. (2) 295-1951; fax (2) 258-0941; e-mail comunicacion@ midena.gob.ec; internet www.defensa.gob.ec.

Ministry of Non-Renewable Natural Resources: Edif. MTOP, Avda Orellana 26-220 y Juan León Mera (esq.), Quito; tel. (2) 297-7000; fax (2) 290-6350; e-mail Chrystiam_Cevallos@mrnnr.gob.ec; internet www.mrnnr.gob.ec.

Ministry of Public Health: República de El Salvador 36-64 y Suecia, Quito; tel. and fax (2) 381-4400; e-mail comunicacion.social@ msp.gob.ec; internet www.salud.gob.ec.

Ministry of Sport: Avda Gaspar de Villaroel E10-122 y 6 de Diciembre, Quito; tel. (2) 396-9200; fax (2) 245-4418; e-mail comunicacion@deporte.gob.ec; internet www.deporte.gob.ec.

Ministry of Telecommunications and Information: Avda 6 de Diciembre N25-75 y Avda Colón, Quito; tel. (2) 220-0200; fax (2) 222-8950; e-mail info@mintel.gob.ec; internet www.telecomunicaciones .gob.ec.

Ministry of Tourism: El Telégrafo E7-58, entre El Tiempo y Avda de los Shyris, Quito; tel. and fax (2) 399-9333; e-mail contactenos@ turismo.gob.ec; internet www.turismo.gob.ec.

Ministry of Transport and Public Works: Avda Juan León Mera N26-220 y Orellana, Quito; tel. (2) 397-4600; e-mail comunicacion@ mtop.gob.ec; internet www.mtop.gob.ec.

Ministry of Urban Development and Housing: Avda 10 de Agosto y Luis Cordero, Quito; tel. (2) 223-8060; fax (2) 256-6785; e-mail despacho@miduvi.gob.ec; internet www.miduvi.gob.ec.

President and Legislature

PRESIDENT

Election, 17 February 2013

Candidate	Valid votes	% of valid votes
Rafael Correa Delgado (Alianza País)	4,918,482	57.17
Guillermo Alberto Santiago Lasso Mendoza (CREO)	1,951,102	22.68
Lucio Gutiérrez Borbua (PSP) . .	578,875	6.73
Mauricio Esteban Rodas Espinel (Movimiento SUMA)	335,532	3.90
Alvaro Fernando Noboa Pontón (PRIAN)	319,956	3.72
Alberto Acosta Espinosa (Unidad Plurinacional de las Izquierdas) .	280,539	3.26
Others	218,117	2.54
Total*	8,602,603	100.00

* In addition, there were 179,230 blank and 684,027 invalid ballots.

NATIONAL ASSEMBLY
(Asamblea Nacional)

President: GABRIELA RIVADENEIRA.

Election, 17 February 2013

Political parties	Seats
Alianza País (AP)	97
CREO	12
Partido Social Cristiano (PSC)	6
Partido Sociedad Patriótica 21 de Enero (PSP) . .	6
Unidad Plurinacional de las Izquierdas (UPI) . .	6
Avanza	5
Independents	3
Partido Roldosista Ecuatoriano (PRE)	1
Sociedad Unida Más Acción (Movimiento SUMA) .	1
Total	**137**

Election Commission

Consejo Nacional Electoral (CNE): Avda 6 de Diciembre N33-122 y Bosmediano, Quito; tel. (2) 381-5410; internet www.cne.gob.ec; f. 2008 to replace the Tribunal Supremo Electoral; independent; Pres. DOMINGO PAREDES CASTILLO.

Political Organizations

Alianza País (Patria Altiva i Soberana—AP): Avda Los Shyris N34-368 y Portugal, Quito; tel. (2) 224-3299; fax (2) 600-1029; e-mail comunicacion@35pais.com.ec; internet movimientoalianzapais.com.ec; f. 2006; electoral alliance mainly comprising the Movimiento País; left-wing; Pres. RAFAEL CORREA DELGADO; Exec. Sec. DORIS SOLIZ CARRIÓN.

Avanza: Avda Naciones Unidas OE1–108, entre Avda 10 de Agosto y Barón de Carondelet, Quito; tel. (2) 603-6808; e-mail partidoavanza@gmail.com; internet www.avanza.ec; f. 2012; Pres. RAMIRO GONZÁLEZ.

CREO (Creando Oportunidades): Edif. Albra, 6°, Of. 601, Orellana E11-75 y Coruña, Quito; tel. (2) 382-6154; e-mail registro@creo.com.ec; internet creo.com.ec; f. 2012; supported the 2013 presidential election candidacy of Guillermo Alberto Santiago Lasso Mendoza; Nat. Pres. CÉSAR MONGE.

Movimiento Ruptura 25: Quito; f. 2004; left-wing; fmr mem. of Alianza País; Pres. MARÍA PAULA ROMO.

Movimiento SUMA (Sociedad Unida Más Acción): Quito; internet www.suma.ec; f. 2012; Leader MAURICIO ESTEBAN RODAS ESPINEL.

Partido Renovador Institucional Acción Nacional (PRIAN): Quito; internet www.prian.org.ec; right-wing, populist; Leader ALVARO FERNANDO NOBOA PONTÓN.

Partido Roldosista Ecuatoriano (PRE): 1 de Mayo 912 y Tulcán, Quito; tel. (2) 229-0542; fax (2) 269-0250; e-mail dalo-por-hecho@hotmail.com; internet www.dalo10.com; f. 1982; populist; Nat. Dir ABDALÁ BUCARAM PULLEY.

Partido Social Cristiano (PSC): Gerónimo Carrión E6-21 (entre Juan León Mera y Reina Victoria), Casilla 9454, Quito; internet www.la6.ec; f. 1951; centre right; Pres. PASCUAL EUGENIO DEL CIOPPO ARAGUNDI.

Partido Sociedad Patriótica 21 de Enero (PSP): Calle República del Salvador N34-107 y Suiza, Quito; e-mail faustolupera@yahoo.com; internet www.lucio3.com; f. 2002; Leader LUCIO GUTIÉRREZ BORBUA.

Unidad Plurinacional de las Izquierdas (UPI) (Coordinadora Plurinacional de las Izquierdas): Quito; f. 2011; leftist coalition; 2013 presidential election candidate Alberto Acosta Espinosa; constituent political parties and movts include Montecristi Vive, Movimiento Convocatoria por la Unidad Provincial, Poder Popular, Frente Popular and the following:

Movimiento Popular Democrático (MPD): Manuel Larrea N14-70 y Rio Frío, Quito; tel. (2) 250-3580; fax (2) 252-6111; e-mail info@mpd15.org.ec; internet www.mpd15.org.ec; f. 1978; attached to the PCMLE (q.v.); Dir LUIS VILLACÍS; Sec. MARCO CADENA.

Movimiento de Unidad Pluriacional Pachakútik—Nuevo País (MUPP—NP): Calle Lugo 13-40 y Avda Ladrón de Guevara, La Floresta, Quito; tel. (2) 322-7259; fax (2) 256-0422; e-mail info@pachakutik.org.ec; internet www.pachakutik.org.ec; f. 1995 as Movimiento Nuevo País—Pachakútik (MNPP); represents indigenous, environmental and social groups; Nat. Co-ordinator RAFAEL ANTUNI; Sec. PATRICIO QUEZADA ORTEGA.

Participación: Quito; f. 2011; Pres. MARCELO LARREA.

Partido Comunista Marxista-Leninista de Ecuador (PCMLE): e-mail pcmle@bigfoot.com; internet www.pcmle.org; f. 1964; contests elections as the MPD; Leader OSWALDO PALACIOS.

Partido Socialista—Frente Amplio (PS—FA): Avda Gran Colombia N15-201 y Yaguachi, Quito; tel. (2) 232-4417; fax (2) 222-2184; e-mail psecuador@andinanet.net; internet psfaecuador.org; f. 1926; Pres. ALEX FABIÁN SOLANO MORENO; Vice-Pres. BYRON CORRAL.

Red Etica y Democracia (RED): Edif. Alemania, 1°, Alemania y Guayanas, Quito; tel. (2) 222-3348; e-mail info@redeticaydemocracia.com; Leader MARTHA ROLDÓS.

Unión Demócrata Cristiana (UDC): Pradera N30-58 y San Salvador, Quito; tel. (2) 250-2995; e-mail cbonilla@udc.com.ec; internet www.udc.com.ec; f. 1978 as Democracia Popular-Unión Demócrata Cristiana (DP-UDC); adopted current name 2006; deregistered as a pol. party by the CNE in 2013; Pres. SANDRA ALARCÓN.

Confederación de las Nacionalidades Indígenas de la Amazonia Ecuatoriana (CONFENIAE): Union Base, Apdo 17-01-4180, Puyo; tel. (3) 227-644; fax (3) 227-644; e-mail info_confel@confeniae.org.ec; represents indigenous peoples; mem. of CONAIE; Pres. TITO PUANCHIR.

Confederación de Nacionalidades Indígenas del Ecuador (CONAIE): Avda Los Granados 2553 y 6 de Diciembre, Quito; tel. (2) 245-2335; fax (2) 244-4991; e-mail info@conaie.org; internet www.conaie.org; f. 1986; represents indigenous peoples; MUPP—NP represents CONAIE and related orgs in the legislature; Pres. HUMBERTO CHOLANGO; Vice-Pres. MIGUEL GUATEMAL.

Confederación de los Pueblos de Nacionalidad Kichua del Ecuador (Ecuarunari): Edif. El Conquistador, 1°, Julio Matovelle 128, entre Vargas y Pasaje San Luis, Quito; tel. (2) 258-0700; fax (2) 258-0713; e-mail ecuarunari@ecuarunari.org; internet www.ecuarunari.org; f. 1972; indigenous movt; Pres. DELFÍN TENESACA.

Coordinadora de las Organizaciones Indígenas de la Cuenca Amazónica (COICA): Sevilla N24-358 y Guipuzcoa, La Floresta, Quito; tel. (2) 322-6744; e-mail com@coica.org.ec; internet www.coica.org.ec; f. 1984 in Lima, Peru; moved to Quito in 1993; umbrella group of 9 orgs representing indigenous peoples of the Amazon Basin in Bolivia, Brazil, Colombia, Ecuador, French Guiana, Guyana, Suriname and Venezuela; Gen. Co-ordinator EGBERTO TABO CHIPUNAVI; Vice-Co-ordinator ROSA ALVORADO.

The following guerrilla organizations were reported to be active in the 2000s.

Ejército de Liberación Alfarista (ELA): f. 2001; extreme left-wing insurrectionist group; formed by fmr mems of disbanded armed groups Alfaro Vive ¡Carajo!, Montoneros Patria Libre and Sol Rojo; Spokesperson SEBASTIÁN SÁNCHEZ.

Grupos de Combatientes Populares (GCP): Cuenca; internet gcp-ecuador.blogspot.com; communist guerrilla grouping; active since 2000.

Izquierda Revolucionaria Armada (IRA): extreme left-wing revolutionary group opposed to international capitalism.

Milicias Revolucionarias del Pueblo (MRP): extreme left-wing grouping opposed to international capitalism.

Diplomatic Representation

EMBASSIES IN ECUADOR

Argentina: Avda Amazonas 447 y Roca, 8°, Apdo 17-12-937, Quito; tel. (2) 256-2292; fax (2) 256-8177; e-mail eecua@cancilleria.gob.ar; Ambassador ALBERTO ÁLVAREZ TUFILLO.

Bolivia: Avda Eloy Alfaro 2432 y Fernando Ayarza, Apdo 17-210003, Quito; tel. (2) 244-4830; fax (2) 224-4833; e-mail embajadabolivia@embajadabolivia.ec; internet www.embajadabolivia.ec; Ambassador RUSENA MARIBEL SANTAMARÍA MAMANI.

Brazil: Edif. Amazonas Plaza, Avda Amazonas, N39-123 y José Arízaga, 7°, Quito; tel. (2) 227-7300; fax (2) 250-4468; e-mail ebrasil@embajadadelbrasil.org.ec; internet quito.itamaraty.gov.br/pt-br; Ambassador FERNANDO SIMAS MAGALHÃES.

Canada: Edif. Eurocenter, 3°, Avda Amazonas 4153 y Unión Nacional de Periodistas, Apdo 17-11-6512, Quito; tel. (2) 245-5499; fax (2) 227-7672; e-mail quito@international.gc.ca; internet www.canadainternational.gc.ca/ecuador-equateur; Ambassador PAMELA O'DONNELL.

Chile: Edif. Xerox, 4°, Juan Pablo Sanz 3617 y Amazonas, Apdo 17-17-206, Quito; tel. (2) 245-3327; fax (2) 244-4470; e-mail echile.ecuador@minrel.gov.cl; internet chileabroad.gov.cl/ecuador/; Ambassador GABRIEL ASCENCIO.

China, People's Republic: Avda Atahualpa 349 y Amazonas, Quito; tel. (2) 244-4362; fax (2) 244-4364; e-mail embchina@uio.telconet.net; internet ec.china-embassy.org/chn/; Ambassador WANG SHIXIONG.

Colombia: Edif. World Trade Center, Torre B, 14°, Avda 12 de Octubre No 24-528 y Luis Cordero, Quito; tel. (2) 223-6463; fax (2) 222-1969; e-mail eecuador@cancilleria.gov.co; internet ecuador.embajada.gov.co/; Ambassador RICARDO LOZANO FORERO.

Costa Rica: Javier Aráuz 111 y Germán Alemán, Apdo 17-03-301, Quito; tel. (2) 225-2330; fax (2) 225-4087; e-mail embajcr@uio.satnet.net; Ambassador PAULA MARÍA MIRANDA.

Cuba: Mercurio 365, entre La Razón y El Vengador, Quito; tel. (2) 245-6936; fax (2) 243-0594; e-mail embajada@embacuba.ec; internet www.cubadiplomatica.cu/ecuador; Ambassador JORGE RODRIGUEZ HERNÁNDEZ.

Dominican Republic: German Alemán E12-80 y Juan Ramírez, Sector Megamaxi, Batan Alto, Quito; tel. (2) 243-4232; fax (2) 243-4275; e-mail info@embajadadominicanaecuador.com; internet www.embajadadominicanaecuador.com; Ambassador VÍCTOR REINALDO LORA DÍAZ.

Egypt: Avda Tarqui E4-56 y Avda 6 de Diciembre, Apdo 17-7-9355, Quito; tel. (2) 222-5240; fax (2) 256-3521; e-mail embassy.quito@mfa.gov.eg; internet www.mfa.gov.eg/Quito_Emb; Ambassador MEDHAT K. EL-MELIGY.

El Salvador: Edif. Banco del Litoral, 2°, Calle Japón E5-25 y Avda Amazonas, Quito; tel. (2) 225-4433; fax (2) 225-4431; e-mail embajada@elsalvador.com.ec; internet www.elsalvador.com.ec; Ambassador LUIS ALBERTO CORDOVA.

France: Calle Leonidas Plaza 107 y Avda Patria, Apdo 19-13-536, Quito; tel. (2) 294-3800; fax (2) 294-3809; e-mail chancellerie.quito@ifrance.com; internet www.ambafrance-ec.org; Ambassador FRANÇOIS GAUTHIER.

Germany: Edif. Citiplaza, 13° y 14°, Avda Naciones Unidas E10-44 y República de El Salvador, Apdo 17-17-536, Quito; tel. (2) 297-0820; fax (2) 297-0815; e-mail info@quito.diplo.de; internet www.quito.diplo.de; Ambassador ALEXANDER OLBRICH.

Guatemala: Edif. Gabriela III, 3°, Of. 301, Avda República de El Salvador 733 y Portugal, Apdo 17-03-294, Quito; tel. (2) 368-0397; fax (2) 368-0397; e-mail embecuador@minex.gob.gt; Ambassador IRMA MONZÓN.

Holy See: Avda Orellana 692 E10-03, Apdo 17-07-8980, Quito; tel. (2) 250-5200; fax (2) 256-4810; e-mail nunzec@uio.satnet.net; Apostolic Nuncio Most Rev. GIACOMO GUIDO OTTONELLO (Titular Archbishop of Sasabe).

Honduras: Edif. Suecia, Avda Shyris y calle Suecia 277, 5° Norte, Apdo 17-03-4753, Quito; tel. (2) 243-8820; fax (2) 244-2476; e-mail embhquito@yahoo.com; Ambassador MAYRA FALCK.

Indonesia: Avda Portugal E 12-33 y Francisco Cazanova, Quito; tel. (2) 224-7677; fax (2) 333-1967; e-mail lopezmar_indos@yahoo.com; internet www.kemlu.go.id/quito/Pages/default.aspx; Ambassador SAUT MARULI TUA GULTOM.

Iran: José Queri E14-43 y Avda Los Granados, Quito; tel. (2) 334-3450; fax (2) 245-2824; e-mail embiranecuador@gmail.com; Ambassador AHMAD PABARJA.

Israel: Edif. Altana Plaza, Avda La Coruña E25-58 y San Ignacio, Quito; tel. (2) 397-1500; fax (2) 397-1555; e-mail info@quito.mfa.gov.il; internet www.quito.mfa.gov.il; Ambassador ELIYAHU YERUSHALMI.

Italy: Calle La Isla 111 y Humberto Alborñoz, Apdo 17-03-72, Quito; tel. (2) 321-1647; fax (2) 321-0818; e-mail archivio.quito@esteri.it; internet www.ambquito.esteri.it; Ambassador GIANNI MICHELE PICCATO.

Japan: Edif. Amazonas Plaza, 11° y 12°, Avda Amazonas N39-123 y Arízaga, Apdo 17-21-01518, Quito; tel. (2) 227-8700; fax (2) 244-9399; e-mail embapon@qi.mofa.go.jp; internet www.ec.emb-japan.go.jp; Ambassador TORU KODAKI.

Korea, Republic: Edif. World Trade Center, Avda 12 de Octubre 1942 y Cordero, Torre B, 3°, Apdo 17-03-626, Quito; tel. (2) 290-9227; fax (2) 250-1190; e-mail ecuador@mofat.go.kr; internet ecu.mofat.go.kr; Ambassador IN GYUN CHUNG.

Mexico: Avda 6 de Diciembre N36-165 y Naciones Unidas, Apdo 17-11-6371, Quito; tel. (2) 292-3770; fax (2) 244-8245; e-mail embajadamexico@embamex.org.ec; internet www.sre.gob.mx/ecuador; Ambassador JAIME DEL ARENAL FENOCHIO.

Panama: Germán Alemán No E12-92 y Arroyo, Del Río en el sector Batán Bajo, Quito; tel. (2) 245-1806; fax (2) 245-1825; e-mail panaembaecuador@hotmail.com; internet www.embajadadepanamaecuador.com; Ambassador JOSÉ NORIEL ACOSTA RODRÍGUEZ.

Paraguay: Edif. Torre Sol Verde, 8°, Avda 12 de Octubre, esq. Salazar, Apdo 17-03-139, Quito; tel. (2) 290-9005; fax (2) 290-9006; e-mail embapar@uio.satnet.net; internet www.embajadadeparaguay.ec/; Ambassador JOSÉ MARÍA ARGANA MATEU.

Peru: Avda República de El Salvador N34-361 e Irlanda, Apdo 17-07-9380, Quito; tel. (2) 246-8410; fax (2) 225-2560; e-mail embaperu-quito@rree.gob.pe; internet www.embajadadelperu.org.ec; Ambassador ESTHER ELIZABETH ASTETE RODRÍGUEZ.

Russia: Reina Victoria 462 y Ramón Roca, Apdo 17-01-3868, Quito; tel. (2) 252-6361; fax (2) 256-5531; e-mail embrusia_ecuador@mail.ru; internet www.ecuador.mid.ru; Ambassador YAN A. BURLIAY.

Spain: General Francisco Salazar E12-73 y Toledo (Sector La Floresta), Apdo 17-01-9322, Quito; tel. (2) 322-6296; fax (2) 322-7805; e-mail emb.quito@mae.es; internet www.maec.es/embajadas/quito; Ambassador VÍCTOR FAGILDE GONZÁLEZ.

Switzerland: Edif. Xerox, 2°, Avda Amazonas 3617 y Juan Pablo Sanz, Apdo 17-11-4815, Quito; tel. (2) 243-4949; fax (2) 244-9314; e-mail qui.vertretung@eda.admin.ch; internet www.eda.admin.ch/quito; Ambassador ROLAND FISCHER.

Turkey: Calle Sebastián de Benalcázar 9-28, entre Oriente y Esmeraldas, Centro Histórico, Quito; tel. (2) 251-1490; fax 251-1493; e-mail embassy.quito@mfa.gov.tr; Ambassador KORKUT GÜNGEN.

United Kingdom: Edif. Citiplaza, 14°, Avda Naciones Unidas y República de El Salvador, Apdo 17-17-830, Quito; tel. (2) 297-0800; fax (2) 297-0809; e-mail britembq@uio.satnet.net; internet ukinecuador.fco.gov.uk; Ambassador PATRICK MULLEE.

USA: Avigiras 12-170 y Eloy Alfaro, Apdo 17-17-1538, Quito; tel. (2) 398-5000; fax (2) 398-5100; e-mail contacto.usembuio@state.gov; internet ecuador.usembassy.gov; Ambassador ADAM E. NAMM.

Uruguay: Edif. Josueth González, 9°, Avda 6 de Diciembre 2816 y Paul Rivet, Apdo 17-12-282, Quito; tel. (2) 256-3762; fax (2) 256-3763; e-mail uruecuador@mrree.gub.uy; Ambassador ENRIQUE DELGADO GENTA.

Venezuela: Edif. COMONSA, 8° y 9°, Avda Amazonas N30-240 y Eloy Alfaro, Apdo 17-01-688, Quito; tel. (2) 255-4032; fax (2) 252-0306; e-mail embve.ecqto@mre.gob.ve; internet ecuador.embajada.gob.ve; Ambassador MARÍA DE LOURDES URBANEJA DURANT.

Judicial System

CONSTITUTIONAL COURT

Tribunal Contencioso Electoral: José Manuel Abascal N37-499 y Portete, Apdo 17-17-949, Quito; tel. (2) 381-5000; e-mail servicio.ciudadano@tce.gob.ec; internet www.tce.gob.ec; f. 2008 by reform of fmr Tribunal Constitucional; Pres. Dr MARÍA CATALINA CASTRO LLERENA; Sec.-Gen. GUILLERMO FALCONÍ.

NATIONAL COURT OF JUSTICE

Corte Nacional de Justicia: Avda Amazonas N37-101, esq. Unión Nacional de Periodistas, Quito; tel. (2) 227-8396; e-mail ramaguai@funcionjudicial-pichincha.gov.ec; internet www.cortenacional.gob.ec; f. 1830 as Corte Suprema de Justicia; reconstituted in 2008 under new Constitution; 21 Justices, including the President; two penal law courts, one administrative litigation court, one fiscal law court, one civil law court and two employment law courts; Pres. Dr CARLOS RAMIREZ ROMERO.

Attorney-General: Dr DIEGO GARCÍA CARRIÓN.

TRANSITIONAL COUNCIL OF THE JUDICIARY

Consejo de la Judicatura: Jorge Washington E4-157, entre Juan León Mera y Avda Río Amazonas, Quito; e-mail webadmin@funcionjudicial.gob.ec; internet www.funcionjudicial.gob.ec; f. 1998; transitional council created by July 2011 referendum charged with reform of the judicial system; Pres. GUSTAVO JALKH.

Religion

There is no state religion, but the vast majority of the population are Roman Catholics. There are representatives of various Christian Churches and of the Jewish and Buddhist faiths in Quito and Guayaquil.

CHRISTIANITY

The Roman Catholic Church

Ecuador comprises four archdioceses, 12 dioceses and eight Apostolic Vicariates. Some 80% of the population are Roman Catholics, according to the 2010 census.

Bishops' Conference: Conferencia Episcopal Ecuatoriana, Avda América 24-59 y La Gasca, Apdo 17-01-1081, Quito; tel. (2) 222-3139; fax (2) 250-1429; e-mail info@iglesiacatolica.ec; internet www.iglesiacatolica.ec; f. 1939; statutes approved 1999; Pres. Most Rev. ANTONIO ARREGUI YARZA (Archbishop of Guayaquil).

Archbishop of Cuenca: LUIS GERARDO CABRERA HERRERA, Arzobispado, Manuel Vega 8-66 y Calle Bolívar, Apdo 01-01-0046, Cuenca; tel. (7) 284-7234; fax (7) 284-4436; e-mail jlcabrera@arquicuencaec.org; internet www.arquicuencaec.org.

Archbishop of Guayaquil: ANTONIO ARREGUI YARZA, Arzobispado, Edif. Promoción Humana, 3°, Of. 302, Diagonal a la Catedral de Guayaquil, Avda 10 de Agosto 541 y Boyacá, Guayaquil; tel. (4) 232-2778; fax (4) 232-9695; e-mail secretaria@rccguayaquil.com; internet www.rccguayaquil.com.

Archbishop of Portoviejo: LORENZO VOLTOLINI ESTI, Arzobispado, Avda Universitaria s/n, Entre Alajuela y Ramos y Duarte, Apdo 13-01-0024, Portoviejo; tel. (5) 263-0404; fax (5) 263-4428; e-mail arzobis@ecua.net.ec; internet arquidiocesisdeportoviejo.org.

Archbishop of Quito: Fausto Gabriel Trávez Trávez, Palacio Arzobispal, Calle Chile 1140, Apdo 17-01-106, Quito; tel. (2) 228-4429; fax (2) 252-7898; e-mail info@arquidiocesisdequito.ec; internet www.arquidiocesisdequito.ec.

The Anglican Communion

Anglicans in Ecuador are under the jurisdiction of Province IX of the Episcopal Church in the USA. The country is divided into two dioceses, one of which, Central Ecuador, is a missionary diocese.

Bishop of Central Ecuador: Rt Rev. Luis Fernando Ruiz Restrepo, Avda Francisco Sarmiento 39-54 y Portete, Apdo 17-03-353, Quito; tel. (2) 254-1735; internet www.episcopalchurch.org/diocese/central-ecuador.

Bishop of Littoral Ecuador: Rt Rev. Alfredo Morante, Amarilis Fuente 603, entre José Vicente Trujillo y la D, Apdo 0901-5250, Guayaquil; tel. (4) 244-6699; e-mail iedl@gu.pro.ec; internet www.episcopalchurch.org/diocese/litoral-ecuador.

Other Churches

Church of Jesus Christ of Latter-Day Saints (Mormons): Calle 6ta y Avda Rodrigo Chávez González, Principado de las Lomas Urdesa Norte, Guayaquil; tel. (4) 288-9388; internet www.lds.org; 211,165 mems.

Convención Bautista Ecuatoriana: Casilla 3236, Guayaquil; tel. (4) 237-5673; fax 245-2319; e-mail julxa@hotmail.com; internet bautistasec.com; f. 1950; Baptist; Pres. Rev. Julio Xavier Alvarado Silva.

Iglesia Evangélica Metodista Unida del Ecuador: Rumipamba 915, Apdo 17-03-236, Quito; tel. (2) 226-5158; fax (2) 243-9576; Methodist; Bishop Silvio Cevallos Parra; 800 mems, 2,000 adherents.

Sociedad de Estudiantes de la Biblia—Testigos de Jehová (Jehovah's Witnesses): Km 23.5, Via a la Costa, Apdo 09-01-1334, Guayaquil; tel. (4) 371-2720.

BAHÁ'Í FAITH

National Spiritual Assembly of the Bahá'ís: Calle García Moreno 135 y Calle Cumba, Cumbayá, Quito; tel. (2) 256-3484; fax (2) 252-3192; e-mail aelquito@gmail.com; internet www.bahaiecuador.org; mems resident in 1,121 localities.

The Press

PRINCIPAL DAILIES

Quito

El Comercio: Avda Pedro Vicente Maldonado 11515 y el Tablón, Apdo 17-01-57, Quito; tel. (2) 267-0999; fax (2) 267-0214; e-mail contactenos@elcomercio.com; internet www.elcomercio.com; f. 1906; morning; independent; Proprs Compañía Anónima El Comercio; Pres. Fabrizio Acquaviva Mantilla; Editor Fernando Larenas; circ. 160,000.

La Hora: Panamericana Norte km 3½, Quito; tel. (2) 247-5724; fax (2) 247-6085; e-mail nacional@lahora.com.ec; internet www.lahora.com.ec; f. 1982; 12 regional edns; Pres. Dr Francisco Vivanco Riofrío; Gen. Editor Juana López Sarmiento.

Hoy: Avda Mariscal Sucre Of. 6-116, Apdo 17-07-09069, Quito; tel. (2) 249-0888; fax (2) 249-1881; e-mail hoy@hoy.com.ec; internet www.hoy.com.ec; f. 1982; morning; independent; Dir Jaime Mantilla Anderson; Editor Juan Tibanlombo; circ. 72,000.

Ultimas Noticias: Avda Pedro Vicente Maldonado 11515 y el Tablón, Apdo 17-01-57, Quito; tel. (2) 267-0999; fax (2) 267-4923; e-mail mivoz@ultimasnoticias.ec; internet www.ultimasnoticias.ec; f. 1938; evening; independent; commercial; Proprs Compañía Anónima El Comercio; Dir Jorge Ribadeneira; Gen. Editor Carlos Mora; circ. 60,000.

Guayaquil

Expreso: Avda Carlos Julio Arosemena km 2½ y Las Mongas, Casilla 5890, Guayaquil; tel. (4) 220-1100; fax (4) 220-0291; e-mail editorgeneral@granasa.com.ec; internet www.diario-expreso.com; f. 1973; morning; independent; Dir Galo Martínez Merchán; Gen. Editor Rubén Darío Buitrón; circ. 60,000.

Extra: Avda Carlos Julio Arosemena km 2½, Casilla 5890, Guayaquil; tel. (4) 220-1100; fax (4) 220-0291; e-mail matriz@granasa.com.ec; internet www.diario-extra.com; f. 1974; morning; popular; Dir Nicolás Ulloa Figueroa; circ. 200,000.

La Razón: Avda Constitución y las Américas, Guayaquil; tel. (4) 228-0100; fax (4) 228-5110; e-mail cartas@larazonecuador.com; internet www.larazonecuador.com; f. 1965; morning; independent; circ. 35,000.

El Telégrafo: Avda Carlos Julio Arosemena, Km 1.5, Guayaquil; tel. (4) 259-5700; fax (4) 232-3265; e-mail info@telegrafo.com.ec; internet www.telegrafo.com.ec; f. 1884; acquired by the state in 2008 and refounded; morning; Dir Orlando Pérez; Chief Editor Omar Jaen.

El Universo: Avda Domingo Comín y Alban, Casilla 09-01-531, Guayaquil; tel. (4) 249-0000; fax (4) 249-1034; e-mail redaccion@eluniverso.com; internet www.eluniverso.com; f. 1921; morning; independent; Dir Carlos Pérez Barriga; Gen. Editor Gustavo Cortez; circ. 174,000 (weekdays), 290,000 (Sundays).

Cuenca

El Mercurio: Avda las Américas, Sector El Arenal, Casilla 60, Cuenca; tel. (7) 409-5682; fax (7) 409-5685; e-mail redaccion1@elmercurio.com.ec; internet www.elmercurio.com.ec; f. 1924; morning; Dir Nicanor Merchán Luco; Editor Jorge Durán Figueroa.

El Tiempo: Avda Loja y Rodrigo de Triana, Cuenca; tel. (7) 288-2551; fax (7) 288-2555; e-mail redaccion@eltiempo.com.ec; internet www.eltiempo.com.ec; f. 1955; morning; independent; Dir Dr René Toral Calle; Editor Margarita Toral Peña; circ. 35,000.

Portoviejo

El Diario: Avda Metropolitana Eloy Alfaro, Km 1½, Vía Manta, Casilla 13-01-050, Portoviejo; tel. (5) 293-3777; fax (5) 293-3151; e-mail redaccion@eldiario.ec; internet www.eldiario.ec; f. 1992; independent; Dir Pedro Zambrano Lapentti; Editor Jaime Ugalde Moreira.

Ibarra

El Norte: Avda Juan José Flores 11-55 y Avda Jaime Rivadeneira Imbabura, Ibarra; tel. (6) 295-5495; fax (6) 264-3873; e-mail info@elnorte.ec; internet www.elnorte.ec; Exec. Pres. Luis Mejía Montesdeoca; Editor Danilo Moreno.

PERIODICALS

Quito

Chasqui: Avda Diego de Almagro 32-133 y Andrade Marín, Apdo 17-01-584, Quito; tel. (2) 254-8011; fax (2) 250-2487; e-mail chasqui@ciespal.net; internet www.revistachasqui.org; f. 1997; quarterly; media studies; publ. of the Centro Internacional de Estudios Superiores de Comunicación para América Latina (CIESPAL); Dir Edgar Jaramillo; Editor Gustavo Abad.

Cosas: Avda 12 de Octubre N26-14 y Avda La Coruña, Quito; tel. and fax (2) 250-2444; e-mail redaccion@cosas.com.ec; internet www.cosas.com.ec; f. 1994; women's interest; Dir Patty Salame; Editor Martha Dubravcic.

Criterios: Edif. Las Cámaras, 4°, Avda Amazonas y República, Casilla 17-01-202, Quito; tel. (2) 244-3787; fax (2) 243-5862; e-mail criterios@lacamaradequito.com; internet www.lacamaradequito.com; f. 1996; monthly; organ of the Cámara de Comercio de Quito; commerce; Dir-Gen. Lolo Echeverría.

Gestión: Edif. Delta, 2°, Avda González Suárez N27-317 y San Ignacio, Quito; tel. (2) 255-9930; e-mail revistagestion@dinediciones.com; internet www.revistagestion.ec; f. 1994; monthly; economy and society; Dir Juanita Ordóñez; Editor Dr Gonzalo Ortiz; circ. 15,000.

Mundo Diners: Edif. Delta, 2°, Avda González Suárez N27-317 y San Ignacio, Quito; tel. (2) 250-5588; e-mail revistamundodiners@dinediciones.com; internet www.revistamundodiners.com; f. 1986; monthly; culture, politics, society, etc.; Pres. Fidel Egas Grijalva.

Guayaquil

El Agro: Adace Calle 11 y Calle A, Casilla 09-01-9686, Guayaquil; tel. (4) 269-0019; fax (4) 269-0555; e-mail elagro@uminasa.com; internet www.elagro.com.ec; f. 1991; monthly; agriculture; Pres. Eduardo Peña; Gen. Editor Alexandra Zambrano de Andriuoli.

Análisis Semanal: Edif. La Mirador, Of. 2, Plaza Lagos, Km. 6.5, Vía Puntilla, Samborondón, Guayaquil; tel. (4) 500-9343; e-mail info@ecuadoranalysis.com; internet www.ecuadoranalysis.com; weekly; economic and political affairs; Editor Walter Spurrier Baquerizo.

El Financiero: Avda Jorge Pérez Concha (Circunvalación Sur) 201 y Única, Casilla 6666, Guayaquil; tel. (4) 288-0203; fax (4) 288-2950; e-mail redaccion@elfinanciero.com; internet www.elfinanciero.com; weekly; business and economic news; f. 1990; Dir Xavier Pérez MacCollum.

Generación XXI: Aguirre 734 y García Avilés, Guayaquil; tel. (4) 232-7200; fax (4) 232-4870; e-mail g21@vistazo.com; internet www.generacion21.com; f. 1996; youth; Dir Sebastian Mélières; Editor Christian Kalil Carter.

Revista Estadio: Aguirre 734 y García Avilés, Casilla 09-01-1239, Guayaquil; tel. (4) 232-7200; fax (4) 232-0499; e-mail estadio@vistazo.com; internet www.revistaestadio.com; f. 1962; fortnightly; sport; Dir-Gen. Sebastian Mélières; Editor Fabricio Zavala García; circ. 40,000.

Revista Hogar: Aguirre 724 y Boyacá, Apdo 09-01-1239, Guayaquil; tel. (4) 232-7200; fax (4) 232-4870; e-mail rbustap@vistazo.com; internet www.revistahogar.com; f. 1964; monthly; women's interest; Dir-Gen. MARÍA GABRIELA GÁLVEZ VERA; Chief Editor WENDY SALAZAR GUILLÉN; circ. 47,000.

La Verdad: Malecón 502 y Tomás Martínez, Guayaquil; e-mail laverdad@telconet.net; internet www.revista-laverdad.com; f. 1988; monthly; politics and economics; associated with the Partido Renovador Institucional de Acción Nacional; Dir RODOLFO BAQUERIZO BLUM.

Vistazo: Aguirre 734 y García Avilés, Casilla 09-01-1239, Guayaquil; tel. (4) 232-7200; fax (4) 232-4870; e-mail vistazo@vistazo.com; internet www.vistazo.com; f. 1957; fortnightly; general; Gen. Editor PATRICIA ESTUPIÑÁN DE BURBANO; circ. 85,000.

PRESS ASSOCIATION

Asociación Ecuatoriana de Editores de Periódicos (AEDEP): Edif. World Trade Center, 14°, Of. 14-01, Avda 12 de Octubre y Cordero, Quito; tel. (2) 254-7457; fax (2) 254-7404; e-mail aedep@aedep.org.ec; internet www.aedep.org.ec; f. 1985; Pres. CÉSAR PÉREZ BARRIGA; Exec. Dir DIEGO CORNEJO MENACHO.

Publishers

Casa de la Cultura Ecuatoriana: Avdas 6 de Diciembre 16–224 y Patria, El Ejido, Quito; tel. (2) 290-2272; e-mail info@cce.org.ec; internet www.cce.org.ec; Pres. MARCO ANTONIO RODRÍGUEZ.

Centro Interamericano de Artesanías y Artes Populares (CIDAP): Hermano Miguel 3-23, Casilla 01-011-943, Cuenca; tel. (7) 282-9451; fax (7) 283-1450; e-mail cidapl@cidap.org.ec; internet www.cidap.org.ec; art, crafts, games, hobbies; Dir CLAUDIO MALO GONZÁLEZ.

Centro Internacional de Estudios Superiores de Comunicación para América Latina (CIESPAL): Avda Diego de Almagro 32-133 y Andrade Marín, Apdo 17-01-584, Quito; tel. (2) 254-8011; fax (2) 250-2487; e-mail ciespal@ciespal.net; internet www.ciespal.net; f. 1959; communications, technology; Dir FERNANDO CHECA MONTÚFAR.

Centro de Planificación y Estudios Sociales (CEPLAES): Sarmiento N39-198 y Hugo Moncayo, Apdo 17-11-6127, Quito; tel. (2) 225-0659; fax (2) 245-9417; e-mail ceplaes@andinanet.net; internet www.ceplaes.org.ec; f. 1978; agriculture, anthropology, education, health, social sciences, women's studies; Exec. Dir GLORIA CAMACHO.

Corporación Editora Nacional: Roca E9-59 y Tamayo, Apdo 17-12-886, Quito; tel. (2) 255-4358; fax (2) 256-6340; e-mail cen@cenlibrosecuador.org; internet www.cenlibrosecuador.org; f. 1977; archaeology, economics, education, geography, political science, history, law, literature, management, philosophy, social sciences; Pres. SIMÓN ESPINOSA CORDERO.

Corporación de Estudios y Publicaciones: Acuna E2-02 y Juan Agama, entre 10 de Agosto e Inglaterra, Casilla 17-21-00186, Quito; tel. (2) 222-1711; fax (2) 222-6256; e-mail editorial@cep.org.ec; internet www.cep.org.ec; f. 1963; law, public administration; Dir MAURICIO TROYA MENA.

Dinediciones: Avda 12 de Octubre N25-32 y Coruña, esq., Quito; tel. (2) 254-5209; fax (2) 254-5188; e-mail info@dinediciones.com; internet www.portal.dinediciones.com; magazines; Dir HERNÁN ALTAMIRANO.

Ediciones Abya-Yala: Avda 12 de Octubre 1430 y Wilson, Apdo 17-12-719, Quito; tel. (2) 250-6251; fax (2) 250-6255; e-mail editorial@abyayala.org; internet www.abyayala.org; f. 1975; anthropology, environmental studies, languages, education, theology; Pres. Fr JUAN BOTTASSO; Dir-Gen. P. XAVIER HERRÁN.

Edinun: Avda Occidental 10-65 y Manuel Valdivieso, Sector Pinar Alto, Quito; tel. (2) 227-0316; fax (2) 227-0699; e-mail edinun@edinun.com; internet www.edinun.com; f. 1982; Gen. Man. VICENTE VELÁSQUEZ.

Editorial Don Bosco: Vega Muñoz 10-68 y General Torres, Cuenca; tel. (7) 283-1745; fax (7) 284-2722; e-mail edibosco@bosco.org.ec; internet www.lns.com.ec; f. 1920; Gen. Man. MARCELO MEJIA MORALES.

Editorial El Conejo: Edif. Brother, 3°, Avda 6 de Diciembre N26-97 y La Niña, Apdo 17-03-4629, Quito; tel. (2) 222-7948; fax (2) 250-1066; e-mail editorialelconejo@editorialelconejo.com; internet www.editorialelconejo.com; f. 1979; non-profit publr of educational and literary texts; Dir ABDÓN UBIDIA.

Editorial Santillana: Avda Eloy Alfaro N33-347 y Avda 6 de Diciembre, Pichincha, Quito; tel. (2) 244-6656; fax (2) 244-8791; e-mail comunicaciones@santillana.com.ec; internet www.santillana.com.ec; f. 1994; part of Grupo Santillana, Spain; Gen. Man. FERNANDO REVILLA.

Eskeletra Editorial: Edif. Gayal, 1°, Of. 102, Roca 130 y 12 de Octubre, Quito; tel. (2) 255-6691; e-mail eskeletra@hotmail.com; internet www.eskeletra.com; f. 1990; Gen. Man. AZUCENA ROSERO JÁCOME.

Libresa, SA: Murgeón Oe 3–10 y Ulloa, Apdo 17-01-456, Quito; tel. (2) 223-0925; fax (2) 250-2992; e-mail libresa@libresa.com; internet www.libresa.com; f. 1979; education, literature, philosophy; Pres. FAUSTO COBA ESTRELLA; Man. JAIME PEÑA NOVOA.

Manthra Editores: Avda Coruña N31-70 y Whymper, Quito; tel. (2) 600-0998; fax (2) 255-8264; e-mail info@manthra.net; internet www.manthra.net; Gen. Man. JERÓNIMO VILLARREAL.

Maya Ediciones: Avda 6 de Diciembre N40-34 y Los Granados, Quito; tel. (2) 510-2447; e-mail servicioalcliente@mayaediciones.com; internet www.mayaediciones.com; f. 1992; children's books; Gen. Man. FANNY BUSTOS PEÑAHERRERA.

Pontificia Universidad Católica del Ecuador, Centro de Publicaciones: Avda 12 de Octubre, entre Patria y Veintimilla, Apdo 17-01-2184, Quito; tel. (2) 299-1700; fax (2) 256-7117; e-mail puce@edu.ec; internet www.puce.edu.ec; f. 1974; literature, natural science, law, anthropology, sociology, politics, economics, theology, philosophy, history, archaeology, linguistics, languages, business; Dir Dr PATRICIA CARRERA.

Trama Ediciones: Juan de Dios Martínez N34-367 y Portugal, El Batán, Quito; tel. (2) 224-6315; fax (2) 224-6317; e-mail info@trama.ec; internet www.trama.com.ec; f. 1977; architecture, design, art, tourism; Dir-Gen. ROLANDO MOYA TASQUER.

ASSOCIATIONS

Asociación Ecuatoriana de Editores de Libros de Texto: Quito; tel. (2) 227-0285; e-mail revistadidactica@gmail.com; internet www.revistadidactica.blogspot.com; f. 2004; publ. *Revista Didáctica*; Pres. VICENTE VELÁSQUEZ GUZMÁN.

Cámara Ecuatoriana del Libro: Edif. Eloy Alfaro, 9°, entre Inglaterra, Avda Eloy Alfaro 29-61, Quito; tel. (2) 255-3311; fax (2) 222-2150; e-mail celnp@uio.satnet.net; internet www.celibro.org.ec; f. 1978; Pres. FABIÁN LUZURIAGA.

Broadcasting and Communications

REGULATORY AUTHORITIES

Consejo Nacional de Telecomunicaciones (CONATEL): Avda Diego de Almagro 31-95, entre Whymper y Alpallana, Casilla 17-07-9777, Quito; tel. (2) 294-7800; fax (2) 250-5119; internet www.regulaciontelecomunicaciones.gob.ec/conatel/; f. 1942 as Instituto Ecuatoriano de Telecomunicaciones (IETEL); Pres. JAIME GUERRERO RUIZ (Minister of Telecommunications and Information).

Secretaría Nacional de Telecomunicaciones (SENATEL): Edif. SENATEL, Avda Diego de Almagro 31-95, entre Whymper y Alpallana, Casilla 17-07-9777, Quito; tel. (2) 294-7800; fax (2) 290-1010; e-mail comunicacion@conatel.gob.ec; internet www.conatel.gob.ec; Nat. Sec. RUBÉN LEÓN.

Superintendencia de Información y Comunicación: Quito; f. 2013; Supt CARLOS OCHOA HERNÁNDEZ.

Superintendencia de Telecomunicaciones (SUPERTEL): Edif. Matriz, Avda 9 de Octubre 1645 (N27-75) y Berlín, Casilla 17-21-1797, Quito; tel. (2) 294-6400; fax (2) 223-2115; e-mail info@supertel.gob.ec; internet www.supertel.gob.ec; f. 1992; Supt FABIÁN LEONARDO JARAMILLO PALACIOS.

TELECOMMUNICATIONS

Claro (CONECEL, SA): Edif. Centrum, Avda Francisco de Orellana y Alberto Borgues, Guayaquil; tel. (4) 269-3693; e-mail callcenter@conecel.com; internet www.claro.com.ec; f. 1993; fmrly Porta; subsidiary of América Móvil group (Mexico); mobile telecommunications provider; Pres. ALFREDO ESCOBAR SAN LUCAS.

Corporación Nacional de Telecomunicaciones EP (CNT): Edif. Estudio Zeta, Avda Veintimilla 1149 y Amazonas, Quito; tel. (2) 297-7100; fax (2) 256-2240; e-mail ventalinea@cnt.info.ec; internet www.cnt.gob.ec; f. 2008 by merger of Andinatel and Pacifictel; state-owned; absorbed all services provided by Alegro (Telecomunicaciones Móviles del Ecuador, SA—Telecsa) in 2010; Pres. RODRIGO LÓPEZ; Gen. Man. CÉSAR REGALADO IGLESIAS.

Movistar Ecuador: Avda República y esq. La Pradera, Quito; tel. (2) 222-7700; fax (2) 222-7597; internet www.movistar.com.ec; f. 1997; name changed from BellSouth Ecuador to above in 2004; owned by Telefónica Móviles, SA (Spain); mobile telephone services; CEO JUAN FEDERICO GOULÚ.

    Otecel, SA: f. 2004; subsidiary of Movistar Ecuador; mobile cellular telephone network provider.

BROADCASTING

Radio

Radio Católica Nacional: Avda América 1830 y Mercadillo, Casilla 17-03-540, Quito; tel. (2) 254-1557; fax (2) 256-7309; e-mail direccion@radiocatolica.org.ec; internet www.radiocatolica.org.ec; f. 1985; Dir-Gen. RENÉ BRITO.

Radio Centro: Carchi 702, entre 9 de Octubre y 1 de Mayo, 6°, Guayaquil; tel. and fax (4) 288-0500; e-mail noticiero_elobservador@hotmail.com; internet www.radiocentro.com.ec; f. 1979; Dir HERNÁN OVIEDO GUTIERREZ; Gen. Man. JUAN XAVIER BENEDETTI RIPALDA.

Radio CRE Satelital (CORTEL, SA): Edif. El Torreón, 8°, Avda Boyacá 642 y Padre Solano, Apdo 4144, Guayaquil; tel. (4) 256-4290; fax (4) 256-0386; e-mail cre@cre.com.ec; internet www.cre.com.ec; Pres. RAFAEL GUERRERO VALENZUELA; Gen. Man. ANTONIO GUERRERO GÓMEZ.

Radio FM Mundo: Edif. Argentum, 10°, Of. 1001–1002, Avda de los Shyris 1322 y Suecia, Quito; tel. (2) 333-0866; fax (2) 333-2975; e-mail fmmundo@fmmundo.com; internet www.fmmundo.com; Gen. Man. CRISTHIAN DEL ALCÁZAR.

Radio Latina: Quito; internet www.radiolatina.com.ec; f. 1990; Pres. RICARDO GUAMÁN.

Radio La Luna: Avda América 3584, Casilla 17-08-8604, Quito; tel. (2) 226-646; f. 1996; Owner PACO VELASCO; Gen. Man. ATAÚLFO REINALDO TOBAR BONILLA.

Radio Quito (Ecuadoradio, SA): Edif. Aragones, 9°, Avda Coruña 2104 y Whimper, Quito; tel. (2) 250-8301; fax (2) 250-3311; e-mail radioquito@ecuadoradio.com; internet www.ecuadoradio.ec; f. 1940; owned by *El Comercio* newspaper.

Radio Sonorama (RDSR): Moscú 378 y República del Salvador, Quito; tel. (2) 243-5355; fax (2) 227-1555; internet www.sonorama.com.ec; f. 1975; Gen. Man. MAURICIO RIVAS.

Radio Sucre: Ciudadela Albatros, Calle Fragata 203, atrás de la Sociedad Italiana Garibaldi, Guayaquil; tel. (4) 229-2109; fax (4) 229-2119; e-mail info@radiosucre.com.ec; internet www.radiosucre.com.ec; f. 1983; Dir VICENTE ARROBA DITO.

La Voz de los Andes (HCJB): Villalengua OE2-52 y Avda 10 de Agosto, Casilla 17-17-691, Quito; tel. (2) 226-6808; fax (2) 226-4765; e-mail radio@hcjb.org.ec; internet www.radiohcjb.org; f. 1931; operated by World Radio Missionary Fellowship; programmes in 11 languages (including Spanish and English) and 22 Quechua dialects; Evangelical; Dir TATIANA DE LA TORRE; Production Dir DUVAL RUEDA.

Television

EcuadorTV: Edif. Medios Públicos, San Salvador E6-49 y Eloy Alfaro, Quito; tel. (2) 397-0800; internet www.ecuadortv.ec; f. 2007; public service broadcaster; br. in Guayaquil; Gen. Man. ENRIQUE AROSEMANA.

Ecuavisa Guayaquil: Cerro El Carmen, Casilla 1239, Guayaquil; tel. (4) 256-2444; fax (4) 256-2432; e-mail contacto@ecuavisa.com; internet www.ecuavisa.com; f. 1967; Pres. XAVIER ALVARADO ROCA; Gen. Man. RICARDO VAZQUEZ DONOSO.

Ecuavisa Quito: Bosmediano 447 y José Carbo, Bellavista, Quito; tel. (2) 244-8101; fax (2) 244-5488; internet www.ecuavisa.com; commercial; f. 1970; Pres. PATRICIO JARAMILLO; Editor-in-Chief FREDDY BARROS.

GamaTV: Quito; internet www.gamatv.com.ec; f. 1977 as Telenacional, became Gamavisión in 1985, present name adopted in 2008; state-run.

TC Televisión: Avda de las Américas, frente al Aeropuerto, Casilla 09-01-673, Guayaquil; tel. (4) 239-7664; fax (4) 228-7544; internet www.tctelevision.com; f. 1969; commercial; seized by the Govt in 2008; Gen. Man. CARLOS COELLO BECEKE.

Teleamazonas Cratel, CA: Antonio Granda Centeno Oeste 429 y Brasil, Casilla 17-11-04844, Quito; tel. (2) 397-4444; fax (2) 244-1620; e-mail abravo@teleamazonas.com; internet www.teleamazonas.com; f. 1974; commercial; Exec. Dir LUIS CUCALÓN; Gen. Man. SEBASTIÁN CORRAL.

Association

Asociación Ecuatoriana de Radiodifusión (AER): Edif. Atlas, 8°, Of. 802, Calle Justino Cornejo con Francisco de Orellana, Guayaquil; tel. (4) 229-1795; fax (4) 229-1783; internet aer.ec; ind. asscn; Pres. ROBERTO MANCIATI ALARCÓN.

Finance

(cap. = capital; res = reserves; dep. = deposits; m. = million; brs = branches; amounts in US dollars unless otherwise indicated)

SUPERVISORY AUTHORITY

Superintendencia de Bancos y Seguros: Avda 12 de Octubre 1561 y Madrid, Casilla 17-17-770, Quito; tel. (2) 299-6100; fax (2) 250-6812; e-mail webmaster@sbs.gob.ec; internet www.sbs.gob.ec; f. 1927; supervises national banking system, including state and private banks and other financial institutions; Supt PEDRO SOLINES.

BANKING

Central Bank

Banco Central del Ecuador: Avda 10 de Agosto N11-409 y Briceño, Casilla 339, Quito; tel. (2) 257-2522; fax (2) 258-3059; e-mail info@bce.ec; internet www.bce.fin.ec; f. 1927; cap. 2.4m., res 724.9m., dep. 5,300m. (Dec. 2009); Pres. DIEGO MARTINEZ; Gen. Man. MATEO VILLALBA; 2 brs.

Other State Banks

Banco Ecuatoriano de la Vivienda: Avda 10 de Agosto 2270 y Luis Cordero, Casilla 3244, Quito; tel. and fax (2) 223-7114; fax (2) 250-4615; e-mail bevinfo@bev.fin.ec; internet www.bev.fin.ec; f. 1961; Pres. PEDRO JARAMILLO CASTILLO; Gen. Man. LUIS EFRAÍN CAZAR MONCAYO.

Banco del Estado (BDE): Avda Atahualpa 628 y Avda 10 de Agosto, Casilla 17-17-1728, Quito; tel. (2) 226-0723; fax (2) 226-0320; e-mail secretaria@bancoestado.com; internet www.bancoestado.com; f. 1976 as Banco de Desarrollo del Ecuador (BEDE); Gen. Man. VERÓNICA GALLARDO AGUIRRE.

Banco Nacional de Fomento: Antonio Ante Oeste 1–15 y Avda 10 de Agosto, Casilla 685, Quito; tel. (2) 294-6500; fax (2) 257-0286; e-mail sugerencias@bnf.fin.ec; internet www.bnf.fin.ec; f. 1928; cap. 254.2m., res 144.1m., dep. 621.9m. (Dec. 2009); Pres. JAVIER PONCE CEVALLOS; Gen. Man. NANCY ALICIA BONILLA YÁNEZ; 70 brs.

Corporación Financiera Nacional (CFN): Avda Juan León Mera 130 y Avda Patria, Casilla 17-21-01924, Quito; tel. (2) 256-4900; fax (2) 222-3823; e-mail informatica@q.cfn.fin.ec; internet www.cfn.fin.ec; f. 1964; state-owned bank providing export credits, etc.; Pres. CAMILO SAMÁN SALEM; Gen. Man. JORGE WATED.

Commercial Banks

Banco Amazonas, SA: Edif. Soroa, Avda Francisco Orellana 238, Guayaquil; tel. (4) 268-3600; fax (4) 268-3400; e-mail webmaster@bancoamazonas.com; internet www.bancoamazonas.com; f. 1975; cap. 13.5m., res 1.9m., dep. 128.1m. (Dec. 2012); affiliated to Banque Paribas; CEO SERGIO R. TORASSA; CFO JOSÉ PONCE; 3 brs.

Banco del Austro: Sucre y Borrero (esq.), Casilla 01-01-0167, Cuenca; tel. (7) 283-1646; fax (7) 283-2633; internet www.bancodelaustro.com; f. 1977; cap. 89m., res 22.6m., dep. 1,160.5m. (Dec. 2013); Pres. JUAN ELJURI ANTÓN; Gen. Man. GUILLERMO TÁLBOT DUEÑAS; 19 brs.

Banco Bolivariano, CA: Junín 200 y Panamá, Casilla 09-01-10184, Guayaquil; tel. (4) 230-5000; fax (4) 256-6707; e-mail info@bolivariano.com; internet www.bolivariano.com; f. 1979; cap. 102.5m., res 17.7m., dep. 1,402.3m. (Dec. 2010); Pres. JOSÉ SALAZAR BARRAGÁN; CEO FERNANDO SALAZAR ARRARTE; 12 brs.

Banco Comercial de Manabí, SA: Avda 10 de Agosto 600 y 18 de Octubre, Casilla 13-01-038, Portoviejo; tel. and fax (5) 263-2222; fax (5) 263-5527; e-mail info@bcmanabi.com; internet www.bcmanabi.com; f. 1979; Gen. Man. WALTER ANDRADE CASTRO.

Banco General Rumiñahui: Avda República E6-573 y Avda Eloy Alfaro, Quito; tel. (2) 250-9929; fax (2) 256-3786; e-mail mrodas@bgr.com.ec; internet www.bgr.com.ec; f. 1988; cap. 29.7m., res 4.3m., dep. 506.4m. (Dec. 2013); Gen. Man. ALEJANDRO RIBADENEIRA JARAMILLO.

Banco de Guayaquil, SA: Plaza Ycaza 105 y Pichincha, Casilla 09-01-1300, Guayaquil; tel. (4) 251-7100; fax (4) 251-4406; e-mail servicios@bankguay.com; internet www.bancoguayaquil.com; f. 1923; cap. 358m., dep. 3,119.6m. (Dec. 2013); Pres. DANILO CARRERA DROUET; Exec. Pres. GUILLERMO LASSO MENDOZA; 50 brs.

Banco Internacional, SA: Avda Patria E-421 y 9 de Octubre, Casilla 17-01-2114, Quito; tel. (2) 256-5547; fax (2) 256-5758; e-mail bancinteronline@bancointernacional.com.ec; internet www.bancointernacional.com.ec; f. 1973; cap. 122m., res 35.2m., dep. 1,838.1m. (Dec. 2012); Pres. JOSÉ ENRIQUE FUSTER CAMPS; CEO ENRIQUE BELTRÁN MATA; 58 brs.

Banco de Loja: esq. Bolívar y Rocafuerte, Casilla 11-01-300, Loja; tel. (7) 257-1682; fax (7) 257-3019; e-mail info@bancodeloja.fin.ec; internet www.bancodeloja.fin.ec; f. 1968; cap. 15m., res 3.8m., dep.

204.3m. (Dec. 2009); Pres. STEVE BROWN HIDALGO; Man. LEONARDO BURNEO MULLER.

Banco de Machala, SA: Avda 9 de Mayo y Rocafuerte, Casilla 711, Machala; tel. (7) 293-0100; fax (7) 292-2744; e-mail jorejuela@bmachala.com; internet www.bmachala.com; f. 1962; cap. 35.5m., res 7.1m., dep. 549.7m. (Dec. 2012); Chair. Dr ESTEBAN QUIROLA FIGUEROA; 2 brs.

Banco del Pacífico: Francisco de P. Ycaza 200, entre Pichincha y Pedro Carbo, Casilla 09-01-988, Guayaquil; tel. (4) 256-6010; fax (4) 232-8333; e-mail webadmin@pacifico.fin.ec; internet www.bancodelpacifico.com; f. 2000 by merger of Banco del Pacífico and Banco Continental; 100% owned by Banco Central del Ecuador; cap. 300.5m., res 117.7m., dep. 3,198.8m. (Dec. 2013); Exec. Pres. EFRAÍN VIEIRA; 131 brs.

Banco Pichincha, CA: Avda Amazonas 4600 y Pereira, Casilla 261, Quito; tel. (2) 298-0980; fax (2) 298-1153; e-mail sugerencias@pichincha.com; internet www.pichincha.com; f. 1906; cap. 530m., res 190.5m., dep. 7,552.6m. (Dec. 2013); 61.4% owned by Pres; Exec. Pres. and Chair. Dr FIDEL EGAS GRIJALVA; Gen. Man. AURELIO FERNANDO POZO CRESPO; 267 brs.

Banco Territorial, SA: P. Icaza 115, entre Malecón y Pichincha, Guayaquil; tel. (4) 256-1950; e-mail informacion@grupozunino.com; internet www.bancoterritorial.com; f. 1886; Pres. PIETRO FRANCESCO ZUÑINA ANDA; Gen. Man. RAÚL FERNANDO SÁNCHEZ RODRÍGUEZ.

Produbanco (Banco de la Producción, SA): Avda Amazonas N35-211 y Japón, Quito; tel. (2) 299-9000; fax (2) 244-7319; e-mail bancaenlinea@produbanco.com; internet www.produbanco.com; f. 1978 as Banco de la Producción; adopted current name in 1996; cap. 148m., res 30m., dep. 2,175m. (Dec. 2011); part of Grupo Financiero Producción; Pres. RODRIGO PAZ DELGADO; Exec. Pres. ABELARDO PACHANO BERTERO; 76 brs.

UniBanco (Banco Universal, SA): República 500 y Pasaje Carrión, Quito; tel. (2) 395-0600; internet unibanco.ec; f. 1964 as Banco de Cooperativas del Ecuador; adopted current name 1995; Pres. ANDRÉS JERVIS GONZÁLEZ.

Associations

Asociación de Bancos Privados del Ecuador: Edif. Delta 890, 7°, Avda República de El Salvador y Suecia, Casilla 17-11-6708, Quito; tel. (2) 246-6670; fax (2) 246-6702; e-mail abpe1@asobancos.org.ec; internet www.asobancos.org.ec; f. 1965; 36 mems; Pres. RICARDO CUESTA DELGADO; Exec. Pres. CÉSAR ROBALINO GONZAGA.

Asociación de Instituciones Financieras del Ecuador (AIFE): Edif. La Previsora, Torre B, 3°, Of. 308, Avda Naciones Unidas 1084 y Amazonas, Quito; tel. and fax (2) 246-6560; e-mail aife1@punto.net.ec; internet www.aife.com.ec; Pres. CARLOS CORONEL LOAYZA; Exec. Dir JULIO DOBRONSKY NAVARRO.

STOCK EXCHANGES

Bolsa de Valores de Guayaquil: Edif. TOUS, Pichincha 335, Guayaquil; tel. (4) 252-3523; fax (4) 252-3521; e-mail webmaster@bvg.fin.ec; internet www.mundobvg.com; Pres. RODOLFO KRONFLE AKEL; Dir-Gen. ARTURO BEJARANO ICAZA.

Bolsa de Valores de Quito: Edif. Londres, 8°, Avda Amazonas 21-252 y Carrión, Casilla 17-01-3772, Quito; tel. (2) 398-8500; fax (2) 398-8590; e-mail informacion@bolsadequito.com; internet www.bolsadequito.com; f. 1969; Gen. Man. PAUL MacEVOY; Chair. MÓNICA VILLAGÓMEZ DE ANDERSON.

INSURANCE
Principal Companies

Ace Seguros, SA: Edif. Antisana, 5°, Avdas Amazonas 3655 y Juan Pablo Sanz, Quito; tel. (2) 294-0400; fax (2) 244-5817; e-mail serviciocliente@ace-ina.com; internet www.acelatinamerica.com; Pres. EDWIN ASTUDILLO.

AIG Metropolitana Cía de Seguros y Reaseguros, SA: Edifc. IACA, 5°, Avda Brasil 293 y Antonio Granda Centeno, Quito; tel. (2) 395-5000; fax (2) 292-4434; e-mail servicio.cliente@aig.com; internet www.aig.com.ec; part of American International Group, Inc (USA); CEO BOB BENMOSCHE.

Alianza Cía de Seguros y Reaseguros, SA: Edif. Corporación Maresa, 4°, Avda de los Granados E 11-67 y Las Hiedras, Quito; tel. (2) 395-8545; fax (2) 256-4059; e-mail alianzauio@segurosalianza.com; internet www.segurosalianza.com; f. 1982; Gen. Man. EDUARDO BARQUET PENDÓN.

Bolívar Cía de Seguros del Ecuador, SA: Edif. Centro Empresarial Las Cámaras, Torre B, 3° y 12°, Planta Baja, Avda Francisco de Orellana, Calle Kennedy Norte, Guayaquil; tel. (2) 602-0700; fax (2) 268-3363; e-mail ssanmiguel@seguros-bolivar.com; internet www.seguros-bolivar.com; f. 1957; Pres. FABIÁN ORTEGA TRUJILLO.

Cía de Seguros Ecuatoriano Suiza, SA: Avda 9 de Octubre 2101 y Tulcán, Apdo 09-01-397, Guayaquil; tel. (4) 373-1515; fax (4) 245-

3229; e-mail ecuasuiza@ecuasuiza.com; internet www.ecuasuiza.com; f. 1954; Pres. JOSÉ SALAZAR BARRAGÁN; CEO ALEJANDRO AROSEMENA.

Cía Seguros Unidos, SA: Edif. Metrocar, 2°, Avda 10 de Agosto 31-162 y Avda Mariana de Jesús, Quito; tel. (2) 600-7700; fax (2) 245-0920; e-mail comercial@sunidos.fin.ec; internet www.segurosunidos.com.ec; f. 1994; part of Grupo Eljuri; Gen. Man. RAFAEL ALBERTO MATEUS PONCE.

Cóndor Cía de Seguros, SA: Edif. Seguros Cóndor, 6°, Francisco de Plaza Ycaza 302, Apdo 09-01-5007, Guayaquil; tel. (4) 256-5300; fax (4) 256-5041; e-mail ochavez@seguroscondor.com; internet www.seguroscondor.com; f. 1966; Gen. Man. OTÓN CHÁVEZ TORRES.

Coopseguros del Ecuador, SA: Edif. Coopseguros, Avda Noruega 210 y Suiza, Casilla 17-15-0084-B, Quito; tel. (2) 292-1669; fax (2) 292-1666; internet www.coopseguros.com; f. 1970; Gen. Man. FRANCISCO PRIETO SÁNCHEZ.

Liberty Seguros: Calle Portugal E-12-72 y Avda Eloy Alfaro, Quito; tel. (2) 298-9600; fax (2) 246-9650; e-mail auto.siniestros@liberty.ec; internet www.liberty.ec; f. 1973; fmrly Panamericana del Ecuador; changed name as above in 2012; Pres. CARLOS VANEGAS GARCÍA.

Mapfre Atlas Cía de Seguros, SA: Edif. Torre Atlas, 11°, Kennedy Norte, Justino Cornejo, entre Avda Francisco de Orellana y Avda Luis Orrantia, Casilla 09-04-491, Guayaquil; tel. (4) 222-3973; fax (4) 256-0673; e-mail noticiascorporativas@mapfreatlas.com.ec; internet www.mapfreatlas.com.ec; f. 1984; Exec. Chair. RAFAEL SUÁREZ LÓPEZ.

QBE Seguros Colonial: Avda. Eloy Alfaro 40-270 y José Queri, Quito; tel. (2) 398-9800; e-mail info@qbe.com.ec; internet www.qbe.com.ec; f. 1992 as Seguros Colonial, SA; acquired by Grupo QBE (Australia) and changed name as above in 2010; Chair. MARTY BECKER; CEO JOHN NEAL.

Seguros Rocafuerte, SA: Edif. Filanbanco, 14°-16°, Plaza Carbo 505 y Avda 9 de Octubre, Apdo 09-04-6491, Guayaquil; tel. (4) 232-6125; fax (4) 232-9353; e-mail segroca@gye.satnet.net; internet www.rocafuerte.com; f. 1967; life and medical; Pres. PEDRO SOLINES CHACON.

Seguros Sucre, SA: Edif. San Francisco 300, 6°, Pedro Carbo 422 y Avda 9 de Octubre, Apdo 09-01-480, Guayaquil; tel. (4) 256-3399; fax (4) 231-4163; e-mail pespinel@segurossucre.fin.ec; internet www.segurossucre.fin.ec; f. 1944; part of Grupo Banco del Pacífico; Gen. Man. MAXÍMILIANO DONOSO VALLEJO.

La Unión Cía Nacional de Seguros: Urb. Los Cedros Solares 1-2, Km 5½, Vía a la Costa, Apdo 09-01-1294, Guayaquil; tel. (4) 285-1500; fax (4) 285-1700; e-mail rgoldbaum@seguroslaunion.com; internet www.seguroslaunion.com; f. 1943; state-owned; Pres. ROBERTO GOLDBAUM; Dir DAVID GOLDBAUM.

ASSOCIATIONS

Asociación de Compañías de Seguros del Ecuador (ACOSE): Edif. Carolina Park, 2°, Calle Japón 230 y Avda Amazonas, Quito; tel. (2) 225-6182; fax (2) 246-3057; internet www.acose.org; f. 1978; affiliated to FEDESEG; 15 mems; Pres. RODRIGO CEVALLOS BREIHL; Gen. Man. PATRICIO SALAS GUZMÁN.

Federación Ecuatoriana de Empresas de Seguros (FEDESEG): Edif. Intercambio, 1°, Junín y Malecón Simón Bolivar 105, Guayaquil; tel. (4) 456-5340; fax (4) 430-6208; affiliated to Federación Interamericana de Empresas de Seguros (FIDES); CEO ANDRÉS CÓRDOVEZ.

Trade and Industry
GOVERNMENT AGENCIES

Instituto Ecuatoriano de Seguridad Social: Edif. Zarzuela, 6°, Avda 9 de Octubre 20-68 y Jorge Washington, Quito; tel. (2) 396-9300; fax (2) 256-3917; e-mail cdirectivo@iess.gob.ec; internet www.iess.gob.ec; f. 1928; directs the social security system; provides social benefits and medical service; Pres. HUGO VILLACRÉS; Gen. Man. ROBERTO MACHUCA.

Superintendencia de Compañías del Ecuador: Roca 660 y Amazonas, Casilla 687, Quito; tel. (2) 252-9960; fax (2) 256-6685; e-mail comunicacionuio@supercias.gob.ec; internet www.supercias.gob.ec; f. 1964; responsible for the legal and accounting control of commercial enterprises; Supt SUAD RAQUEL MANSSUR VILLAGRÁN; Sec.-Gen. JOSÉ LUIS CHEVASCO ESCOBAR.

CHAMBERS OF COMMERCE AND INDUSTRY

Cámara de Agricultura: Edif. La Previsora, Torre B, 8°, Of. 805, Avda Naciones Unidas 1084 y Amazonas, Casilla 17-21-322, Quito; tel. (2) 225-7618; fax (2) 227-4187; e-mail gremios@caiz.org.ec; internet www.agroecuador.com; Pres. VÍCTOR LÓPEZ.

Cámara de Comercio de Ambato: Edif. Las Cámaras, Montalvo 03-31, entre Bolívar y Rocafuerte, Ambato; tel. (3) 242-4773; fax (3) 242-1930; e-mail webmaster@ccomercioambato.org.ec; internet www.ccomercioambato.org.ec; Pres. MIGUEL SUÁREZ JARAMILLO.

Cámara de Comercio Ecuatoriano-Americana (Amcham Quito-Ecuador): Edif. Multicentro, 4°, Avda 6 de Diciembre y la Niña, Quito; tel. (2) 250-7450; fax (2) 250-4571; e-mail info@ecamcham.com; internet www.amchamec.org; f. 1974; promotes bilateral trade and investment between Ecuador and the USA; brs in Ambato, Cuenca and Manabí; Pres. MAURICIO DURANGO; Exec. Dir CRISTIAN ESPINOSA CAÑIZÁRES.

Cámara de Comercio Ecuatoriano Canadiense (Ecuadorean-Canadian Chamber of Commerce): Torre Centro Ejecutivo, Of. 201, 2°, Inglaterra 1373 y Avda Amazonas, Quito; tel. (2) 244-5972; fax (2) 246-8598; e-mail camara.canadiense@ecucanchamber.org; internet www.ecucanchamber.org; Pres. BARRY MOROCHO; Exec. Dir CECILIA PEÑA ODE.

Cámara de Comercio de Guayaquil: Edif. Centro Empresarial 'Las Cámaras', 2° y 3°, Avda Francisco de Orellana y Miguel H. Alcívar, Guayaquil; tel. (4) 268-2771; fax (4) 268-2766; e-mail info@lacamara.org; internet www.lacamara.org; f. 1889; 31,000 affiliates; Pres. PABLO AROSEMENA MARRIOTT.

Cámara de Comercio de Machala: Edif. Cámara de Comercio, 2°, Rocafuerte y Buenavista, CP 825, Machala, El Oro; tel. (7) 293-0640; fax (7) 293-4454; e-mail info@ccmachala.org.ec; Pres. FREDDY MONTALVO SALINAS.

Cámara de Comercio de Manta: Edif. Cámara de Comercio, Avda 2, entre Calles 10 y 11, Apdo 13-05-477, Manta; tel. (5) 262-1306; fax (5) 262-6516; e-mail direccion@ccm.org.ec; internet www.ccm.org.ec; f. 1927; Pres. LUCÍA FERNÁNDEZ DE DEGENNA; Exec. Dir AURORA VALLE.

Cámara de Comercio de Quito: Edif. Las Cámaras, 6°, Avda República y Amazonas, Casilla 17-01-202, Quito; tel. (2) 244-3787; fax (2) 243-5862; e-mail ccq@ccq.org.ec; internet www.ccq.org.ec; f. 1906; 12,000 mems; Pres. BLASCO PEÑAHERRERA SOLAH; Exec. Dir GUIDO TOLEDO ANDRADE.

Cámara de Industrias de Cuenca: Edif. Cámara de Industrias de Cuenca, 12° y 13°, Avda Florencia Astudillo y Alfonso Cordero, Cuenca; tel. (7) 284-5053; fax (7) 284-0107; internet www.industriascuenca.org.ec; f. 1936; Pres. AUGUSTO TOSI LEÓN; Exec. Vice-Pres. CAROLA RÍOS DE ANDRADE.

Cámara de Industrias de Guayaquil: Centro Empresarial Las Cámaras, Torre Institucional, 4° y 5°, Avda Francisco de Orellana y M. Alcívar, Casilla 09-01-4007, Guayaquil; tel. (4) 371-3390; fax (4) 268-2680; e-mail caindgye@industrias.ec; internet www.industrias.ec; f. 1936; Pres. HENRY KRONFLE KOZHAYA.

Federación Nacional de Cámaras de Comercio del Ecuador: Avda Amazonas y República, Edif. Las Cámaras, Quito; tel. (2) 244-3787; fax (2) 292-2084; Pres. BLASCO PEÑAHERRERA SOLAH; Vice-Pres. EDUARDO VEÑA.

Federación Nacional de Cámaras de Industrias del Ecuador: Avda República y Amazonas, 10°, Casilla 2438, Quito; tel. (2) 245-2992; fax (2) 244-8118; e-mail fedin@cip.org.ec; internet www.camindustriales.org.ec; f. 1972; Pres. Dr PABLO DÁVILA JARAMILLO.

INDUSTRIAL AND TRADE ASSOCIATIONS

Asociación de la Industria Hidrocarburífera del Ecuador (AIHE): Edif. Puerta del Sol, 8°, Avda Amazonas 4080 y Calle UNP, Quito; tel. (2) 226-1270; fax (2) 226-1272; e-mail aihe@aihe.org.ec; internet www.aihe.org.ec; f. 1997 as Asociación de Compañías Petroleras de Exploración y Explotación de Hidrocarburos del Ecuador (ASOPEC); name changed as above in 2002; asscn of 24 int. and domestic hydrocarbon cos; Exec. Pres. LUIS ERNESTO GRIJALVA HARO.

Corporación de Promoción de Exportaciones e Inversiones (CORPEI): Centro de Convenciones Simón Bolivar, 1°, Avda de las Américas 406, Guayaquil; tel. (4) 228-7123; fax (4) 229-2910; internet www.corpei.org; f. 1997 to promote exports and investment; CEO RICARDO ALFREDO ESTRADA.

Federación Ecuatoriana de Exportadores (FEDEXPOR): Edif. Colegio de Economistas, 4°, Iñaquito 3537 y Juan Pablo Sanz, Quito; tel. (2) 225-2426; e-mail fedexpor@fedexpor.com; internet www.fedexpor.com; f. 1976; Pres. FELIPE RIBADENEIRA.

EMPLOYERS' ORGANIZATIONS

Asociación Ecuatoriana de Industriales de la Madera: Edif. de las Cámaras, 7°, República y Amazonas, Quito; tel. (2) 226-0980; fax (2) 243-9560; e-mail info@aima.org.ec; internet www.aima.org.ec; f. 1976; wood mfrs' asscn; Pres. SEBASTIÁN ZUQUILANDA.

Asociación de Exportadores de Banano del Ecuador (AEBE): Edif. World Trade Center, Torre A, 9°, Of. 904, Avda Francisco de Orellana, Calle Kennedy Norte, Guayaquil; tel. (4) 263-1419; fax (4) 263-1485; e-mail eledesma@aebe.com.ec; internet www.aebe.com.ec; banana exporters' asscn; Pres. JORGE ALEX SERRANO; Exec. Dir EDUARDO LEDESMA.

Asociación de Industriales Gráficos: Edif. de las Cámaras, 8°, Amazonas y República, Quito; tel. (2) 292-3141; fax (2) 245-6664; e-mail aigquito@aig.org.ec; internet www.aig.org.ec; asscn of the graphic industry; Pres. MAURICIO MIRANDA; Exec. Dir KARINA CHÁVEZ.

Asociación de Industriales Textiles del Ecuador (AITE): Edif. Las Cámaras, 8°, Avda República y Amazonas, Casilla 2893, Quito; tel. (2) 224-9434; fax (2) 244-5159; e-mail aite@aite.org.ec; internet www.aite.com.ec; f. 1938; textile mfrs' asscn; 40 mems; Pres. JOSÉ MARÍA PONCE; CEO JAVIER DÍAZ CRESPO.

Asociación Nacional de Empresarios (ANDE): Edif. España, 6°, Of. 67, Avda Amazonas 25–23 y Colón, Casilla 17-01-3489, Quito; tel. (2) 290-2545; fax (2) 223-8507; e-mail info@ande.org.ec; internet www.ande.org.ec; national employers' asscn; Pres. PATRICIO DONOSO CHIRIBOGA; Vice-Pres. ALEJANDRO RIBADENEIRA.

Asociación Nacional de Exportadores de Cacao y Café (ANECAFE): Edif. Banco Pichincha, 10°, Of. 1001, Avda 2da entre calles 11 y 12, Manta; tel. (5) 261-3337; fax (5) 262-3315; e-mail info@anecafe.org.ec; internet www.anecafe.org.ec; f. 1983; cocoa and coffee exporters' asscn; Pres. ASKLEY DELGADO FLOR.

Cámara Ecuatoriana de Consultoría (CEC): Edif. Solamar, 4°, Of. 405, Avda Colón E4-105 y 9 de Octubre, Quito; tel. (2) 290-5515; fax (2) 290-5410; e-mail faguilar@icaconsultores.com.ec; internet www.acce.com.ec; fmrly Asociación de Compañías Consultoras del Ecuador; asscn of consulting cos; Pres. FERNANDO AGUILAR GARCÍA.

STATE HYDROCARBON COMPANY

EP PETROECUADOR (Empresa Pública de Hidrocarburos del Ecuador): Alpallana E8-86 y Avda 6 de Diciembre, Casilla 17-11-5007, Quito; tel. (2) 256-3060; fax (2) 250-3571; e-mail hramirez@petroecuador.com.ec; internet www.eppetroecuador.ec; f. 1989; state petroleum co; Exec. Pres. MARCO CALVOPIÑA.

MAJOR COMPANIES

Acero Comercial Ecuatoriano, SA: Avda La Prensa, No 45-14 y Telégrafo 1, Quito; tel. (2) 245-4333; fax (2) 245-4455; e-mail infouio@acerocomercial.com; internet www.acerocomercial.com; f. 1957; production of construction materials; Pres. RICHARD RODRÍGUEZ; 260 employees.

Cervecería Nacional, CA: Vía a Daule, Km 16½, Calle Cobre, entre Avda Río Daule y Avda Pascuales, Casilla 519, Guayaquil; tel. (4) 289-3088; fax (4) 289-3263; e-mail info@cervecerianacional.com.ec; internet www.cervecerianacional.com.ec; f. 1921; subsidiary of SABMiller PLC (United Kingdom); brewing; Exec. Pres. ROBERTO JARRÍN; 1,154 employees.

Compañía Azucarera Váldez, SA: Edif. Executive Center Mezanine 1, Avda Joaquín Orrantia y Avda Juan Tanca Marengo, Guayaquil; tel. (4) 256-3966; fax (4) 256-3248; internet www.azucaravaldez.com; f. 1884; processing and refining of sugar; Exec. Pres. RICARDO RIVADENEIRA; Gen. Man. RALF SCHNEIDEWIND SCHMITH; 3,100 employees.

Corporación El Rosado Cía Ltda: Avda 9 de Octubre 729, entre García Aviles y Boyacá, Casilla 0901-534, Guayaquil; tel. (4) 232-2000; fax (4) 232-8196; e-mail luchoweb@elrosado.com; internet www.elrosado.com; f. 1954; retailing; Dir-Gen. JOHNNY CZARNINSKI BAIER; 4,000 employees.

Hidalgo e Hidalgo, SA: Avda Galo Plaza Lasso, No 51-127 y Algarrobos, Quito; tel. (2) 240-0585; fax (2) 240-0541; e-mail hidalgo@hehconstructores.com.ec; internet www.hehconstructores.com.ec; f. 1969; civil engineering; Pres. JUAN FRANCISCO HIDALGO; Gen. Man. JULIO HIDALGO GONZÁLEZ; 1,000 employees.

Holcim Ecuador, SA: Edif. El Caimán, 2°, Avda Barcelona, Urb. San Eduardo I, Casilla 09-01-04243, Guayaquil; tel. (4) 370-9000; fax (4) 287-3482; internet www.holcim.com.ec; f. 1934; manufacture of cement; Exec. Pres. BERNARD FONTANA; 864 employees.

Industria Ecuatoriana Productora de Alimentos, CA (INEPACA): Calle Malecón, Casilla 4881, Manta; tel. (5) 262-4584; fax (5) 262-4870; e-mail inepaca@inepaca.net; internet www.inepaca.net; f. 1949; fishing and processing of fish; Gen. Man. CARLOS ENRIQUE ZÁRATE SANCHEZ; 987 employees.

Industrias Ales, CA: Avda Galo Plaza N51-23 y Rua Bustamente, Quito; tel. (2) 240-2600; fax (2) 240-8344; e-mail jmalo@ales.com.ec; internet www.ales.com.ec; f. 1943; manufacture of cooking oils, fats and soap; Gen. Man. JOSÉ MALO DONOSO.

Lafarge Cementos, SA: Edif. Banco La Previsora, 4°, Of. 402, Amazonas y Naciones Unidas, Casilla 6663, Quito; tel. (2) 245-9140; fax (2) 225-6091; e-mail comunicacion@lafarge.com; internet www.lafarge.com.ec; f. 1979; fmrly owned by Lafarge Group (France), bought by UNACEM (Peru) in 2014; manufacture of cement; Pres. FERNANDO SANTOS; Gen. Man. CHARLES LAW; 567 employees.

Lanafit, SA: Capitán Rafael Ramos E5-84 y Gonzalo Zaldumbide, Quito; tel. (2) 224-9311; fax (2) 246-7049; e-mail lanafit@textilanafit .com; internet www.textilanafit.com; f. 1953; part of Grupo Dassum; manufacture of clothing from synthetic fibres; Gen. Man. FUAD ALBERTO DASSUM ARMÉNDARIZ; 700 employees.

Sociedad Agrícola e Industrial San Carlos, SA: General Elizalde 114, Guayaquil; tel. (4) 232-1280; fax (4) 251-0377; e-mail xmarcos@gu.pro.ec; internet www.sancarlos.com.ec; f. 1897; agriculture, processing and refining of sugar; Pres. MARIANO GONZÁLEZ PORTÉS; Dir XAVIER MARCOS STAGG; 4,000 employees.

Supermercados La Favorita, CA (SUPERMAXI): Avda Gen. Enriquez s/n, Sangolquí, Quito; tel. (2) 299-6500; fax (2) 299-6502; e-mail favorita@favorita.com; internet www.supermaxi.com; f. 1952; Exec. Vice-Pres. RONALD WRIGHT DÚRAN BALLÉN; 2,475 employees.

Tejidos Pintex, SA: Avda de la Prensa Oeste 5-28 y Manuel Herrera, Quito; tel. (2) 600-1377; fax (2) 244-8335; e-mail pintex@ pintex.com.ec; internet www.pintex.com.ec; f. 1959; manufacture of textiles; Pres. CRISTINA PINTO MANCHENO; Gen. Man. SUSANA PINTO; 420 employees.

Textil San Pedro, SA: Avda Napo y Pedro Pinto Guzmán 709, Apdo 17-01-3002, Quito; tel. (2) 209-3999; fax (2) 209-3958; e-mail ppinto@ textilsanpedro.com; internet www.textilsanpedro.com; production of cotton textiles; f. 1948; Gen. Man. PEDRO PINTO.

Universal Sweet Industries, SA: Eloy Alfaro 1103, entre Gómez Rendón y Maldonada, Guayaquil; tel. and fax (4) 241-0222; fax (4) 241-0222; e-mail rponse@launiversal.com.ec; internet www .launiversal.com.ec; f. 1889 as La Universal (ceased trading 2001); relaunched under current name in 2005; manufacture of food products; Gen. Man. CÉSAR AUGUSTO GAVIÑO AGUILAR; 400 employees.

UTILITIES
Regulatory Authorities

Agencia de Control y Regulación Hidrocarburífera (ARCH): Calle Estadio, entre Manuela Cañizares y Lola Quintana, Sector La Armenia, Conocoto, Pichincha; tel. (2) 399-6500; e-mail lidia_acosta@arch.gob.ec; internet www.arch.gob.ec; f. 2010; responsible for the regulation and control of the hydrocarbons sector; Dir JOSÉ LUIS CORTÁZAR.

Centro Nacional de Control de Energía (CENACE): Panamericana Sur Km 17.5, Sector Santa Rosa de Cutuglagua, Casilla 17-21-1991, Quito; tel. (2) 299-2001; fax (2) 299-2031; e-mail pcorporativo@ cenace.org.ec; internet www.cenace.org.ec; f. 1999; co-ordinates and oversees national energy system; Exec. Dir GABRIEL ARGÜELLO RÍOS.

Consejo Nacional de Electricidad (CONELEC): Avda Naciones Unidas E7-71 y Avda De Los Shyris, Apdo 17-17-817, Quito; tel. (2) 226-8746; fax (2) 226-8737; e-mail conelec@conelec.gob.ec; internet www.conelec.gob.ec; f. 1999; supervises electricity industry following transfer of assets of the former Instituto Ecuatoriano de Electrificación (INECEL) to the Fondo de Solidaridad; pending privatization as 6 generating cos, 1 transmission co and 19 distribution cos; Exec. Dir Dr ANDRÉS CHÁVEZ (acting).

Secretaría del Agua (SENAGUA): Edif. Rigel, Yánez Pinzón 26-12, entre Avda Colón y La Niña, CP 170516, Quito; tel. (2) 381-5640; fax (2) 255-4251; internet www.agua.gob.ec; Sec. WALTER SOLÍS VALAREZO.

Secretaría de Hidrocarburos: Edif. Amazonas 4000, Avda Amazonas 35-89 y Juan Pablo Sanz, Quito; tel. (2) 395-5300; internet www.hidrocarburos.gob.ec; f. 2010; fmrly known as the Dirección Nacional de Hidrocarburos; part of the Ministry of Non-Renewable Natural Resources; supervision of the enforcement of laws regarding the exploration and devt of petroleum; also responsible for dispute resolution and imposition of sanctions against oil cos failing industry standards; Sec. Dr YVONNE FABARA.

Electricity

Corporación Nacional de Electricidad (CNEL EP): Edif. Onyx, 1°, Avda Nahim Isaías y Miguel H. Alcivar, Guayaquil; tel. (4) 268-3218; e-mail centrodecontacto@cnel.gob.ec; internet www.cnel.gob .ec; f. 2008 following the fusion of 10 electricity cos (Esmeraldas, Manabí, Santa Elena, Milagro, Guayas-Los Ríos, Los Ríos, EL Oro, Bolívar, Santo Domingo and Sucumbíos); Gen. Man. JORGE EDUARDO JARAMILLO MOGROVEJO.

Empresa Eléctrica Azogues, CA: Avda Aurelio Jaramillo y Bolívar, Azogues; tel. (7) 224-0377; internet www.electricaazogues .com.ec; f. 1972; Pres. Dr DARÍO TITO QUISHPI; Gen. Man. LUIS GERARDO GONZALEZ MEDINA.

Empresa Eléctrica Provincial Cotopaxi, SA (ELEPCO): Marquez de Maenza 5-44, entre Quijano y Ordoñez, Casilla 239, Latacunga, Cotopaxi; tel. (3) 281-2630; e-mail info@elepcosa.com;

internet www.elepcosa.com; f. 1983; Exec. Pres. EDGAR ALONSO JIMENEZ SARZOSA.

Empresa Eléctrica Provincial Galápagos, SA (ELECGALAPAGOS): Calle Española y Juan José Flores, San Cristóbal; tel. (52) 520-136; fax (52) 521-827; e-mail sistemas@elecgalapagos.com.ec; internet www.elecgalapagos.com.ec; Exec. Pres. MARCO PATRICIO SALAO BRAVO.

Empresa Eléctrica Pública de Guayaquil, EP: Urb. La Garzota, Sector 3, Manzana 47; tel. (4) 262-8600; fax (4) 262-1112; e-mail aloor@electricaguayaquil.gob.ec; internet www.electricaguayaquil .gob.ec; f. 2003, as Corporación para la Administración Temporal Eléctrica de Guayaquil (Categ) to administer activities of fmr state-owned Empresa Eléctrica del Ecuador (EMELEC); privatized and changed name as above in 2009; major producer and distributor of electricity, mostly using oil-fired or diesel generating capacity; Gen. Man. FRANCISCO ESTARELLAS.

Empresa Eléctrica Quito, SA (EEQ): Avda 10 de Agosto y Bartolomé de las Casas, Casilla 17-01-473, Quito; tel. (2) 396-4700; fax (2) 250-3817; e-mail portalweb@eeq.com.ec; internet www.eeq .com.ec; f. 1955; produces electricity for the region around Quito, mostly from hydroelectric plants; Gen. Man. IVÁN ESTUARDO VELÁSTEGUI RAMOS.

Empresa Eléctrica Regional Norte (EMELNORTE): Grijalva 6-54 y Olmedo, Ibarra; tel. (6) 299-7100; e-mail mmoreno@emelnorte .com; internet www.emelnorte.com; f. 1975; Exec. Pres. MARCELO PATRICIO MORENO.

Empresa Eléctrica Regional del Sur, SA (EERSSA): Avda Olmedo 08-84 y Rocafuerte, Loja; tel. (7) 370-0200; e-mail epinos@ eerssa.com; internet www.eerssa.com; f. 1973; electricity production and generation in Loja and Zamora Chinchipe provinces; Exec. Pres. WILSON JOAQUIN VIVANCO ARIAS.

Empresa Eléctrica Riobamba, SA: Larrea 2260 y Primera Constituyente, Riobamba; tel. (3) 296-0283; fax (3) 296-5257; e-mail e-mail@eersa.com.ec; internet www.eersa.com.ec/eersa.php; state-owned utility; Pres. MARIANO CURICAMA; Gen. Man. JOE RAFAEL RUALES PARREÑO.

TRADE UNIONS

Central Ecuatoriana de Organizaciones Clasistas (CEDOC-CLAT): Avda 24 de Mayo 344, Quito; tel. (2) 221-3704; internet www .cedoc-clat.org; f. 1938 as Confederación Ecuatoriana de Obreros Católicos (CEDOC); changed name as above in 2000; humanist; craft and manual workers, and intellectuals; affiliated to Confederación Sindical de Trabajadores y Trabajadoras de las Américas; Pres. FERNANDO IBARRA.

Confederación Sindical de Trabajadoras y Trabajadores del Ecuador (CSE): Pasaje Fray Gerundio E7-19 y el Tiempo (Tras Hotel Crown Plaza), Quito; tel. (2) 246-9547; e-mail cseecuador@ cse-ec.org; internet www.gye.cse-ec.org; f. 2010; formed by dissident members of Confederación Ecuatoriana de Organizaciones Sindicales Libres (CEOSL); Pres. JAIME ARCINIEGA.

Frente Unitario de los Trabajadores (FUT): f. 1971; left-wing; 300,000 mems; Pres. MESÍAS TATAMUEZ; comprises:

> **Confederación Ecuatoriana de Organizaciones Clasistas Unitarias de Trabajo (CEDOCUT):** Edif. Cedocut, 5°, Flores 846 y Manabí, Quito; tel. (2) 295-4551; fax 295-4013; e-mail presidcocut@cedocut.org; internet www.cedocut.org.ec; f. 1938; humanist; Pres. MESÍAS TATAMUEZ MORENO; 1,065 mem. orgs, 86,416 individual mems.

> **Confederación Ecuatoriana de Organizaciones Sindicales Libres (CEOSL):** Avda Tarqui 15-26 (785) y Estrada, 6°, Casilla 17-11-373, Quito; tel. (2) 252-2511; fax (2) 250-0836; e-mail presidencia@ceosl.net; internet ceosl.net; f. 1962; Pres. PABLO ANIBAL SERRANO CEPEDA; 110,000 mems (2007).

> **Confederación de Trabajadores del Ecuador (CTE)** (Confederation of Ecuadorean Workers): Avda 9 de Octubre 1248 y Marieta de Veintimilla, Casilla 17-01-4166, Quito; tel. (2) 252-0456; fax (2) 252-0446; e-mail presidencia@cte-ecuador.org; internet www.cte-ecuador.org; f. 1944; Pres. SANTIAGO YAGUAL YAGUAL; Vice-Pres. EDGAR SARANGO CORREA.

Unión General de Trabajadores del Ecuador (UGTE): Avda Arenas 3-22 y Juan Larrea, Quito; tel. (2) 254-8915; e-mail info@ ugtecuador.com; internet www.ugtecuador.com; f. 1982; Pres. NELSON ERAZO H.; Sec. WILSON ALBARRACÍN.

Transport

RAILWAYS

All railways are government-controlled. In 2000 the total length of track was 960 km. A programme for the rehabilitation of 456 km of disused lines was begun in 2008. By 2011 nine sections had been reopened.

Ferrocarriles del Ecuador Empresa Pública (FEEP): Quilotoa y Sangay, estación Eloy Alfaro (Chimbacalle), Quito; tel. (2) 399-2100; e-mail info@ferrocarrilesdelecuador.gob.ec; internet www .ferrocarrilesdelecuador.gob.ec; fmrly Empresa de Ferrocarriles Ecuatorianos (EFE); Gen. Man. JORGE EDUARDO CARRERA SÁNCHEZ.

ROADS

There were 42,200 km of roads in 2013. The Pan-American Highway runs north from Ambato to Quito and to the Colombian border at Tulcán, and south to Cuenca and Loja.

Agencia Nacional de Tránsito (ANT): Avda Antonio José de Sucre y José Sánchez, Quito; tel. (2) 382-8890; e-mail contactenos@ant.gob.ec; internet www.ant.gob.ec; govt body, regulates road transport; Exec. Dir MICHEL DOUMET CHEDRAUI.

Comisión de Tránsito del Ecuador: Chile 1710 y Brasil, Guayaquil; tel. (4) 241-1397; internet www.comisiontransito.gob.ec; state-run transit commission; Dir HÉCTOR SOLÓRZANO CAMACHO.

SHIPPING

There are four commercial state-owned ports, which are independently managed. At December 2013 the flag registered fleet comprised 184 vessels, totalling 330,576 grt.

Port Authorities

Autoridad Portuaria de Esmeraldas: Avda Jaime Roldós Aguilera (Recinto Portuario), Esmeraldas; tel. (6) 272-1352; fax (6) 272-1354; e-mail ape@puertoesmeraldas.gob.ec; internet www .puertoesmeraldas.gob.ec; f. 1970; 25-year operating concession awarded to private consortium in 2004; renationalized in 2010; Gen. Man. GABRIELA BANGUERA ORDOÑEZ.

Autoridad Portuaria de Guayaquil: Avda de la Marina, Vía Puerto Marítimo, Casilla 09-01-5739, Guayaquil; tel. (4) 248-0120; fax (4) 248-4728; e-mail juanjairala@apg.gob.ec; internet www.apg .gob.ec; f. 1958; Gen. Man. JUAN CARLOS JAIRALA REYES.

Autoridad Portuaria de Manta: Avda Malecón s/n, Manta; tel. (5) 262-7161; fax (5) 262-1861; e-mail info@puertodemanta.gob.ec; internet www.puertodemanta.gob.ec; f. 1966; Gen. Man. ERNESTO RODOLFO CANO MURE.

Autoridad Portuaria de Puerto Bolívar: Avda Bolívar Madero Vargas, Puerto Bolívar; tel. (7) 292-9999; e-mail appb@appb.gob.ec; internet www.puertobolivar.gob.ec; f. 1970; Pres. MONTGOMERY SÁNCHEZ REYES; Gen. Man. WILMER ENCALADA LUDEÑA.

Principal Shipping Companies

Andinave, SA: Edif. Previsora, 29°, Of. 2901, Avda 9 de Octubre 100 y Malecon Simon Bolivar, Guayaquil; tel. (4) 232-5555; fax (4) 232-5957; e-mail info@andinave.com; internet www.andinave.com; f. 1983; shipping and port agents, stevedoring and logistics; Pres. ANDRÉS RIZZO.

BBC Ecuador Andino Cía Ltda: Edif. San Luis, 3°, Suite 6, Avda Tulcán 809 y Hurtado, Casilla 3338, Guayaquil; tel. (4) 371-3255; fax (4) 604-1898; e-mail guayaquil@bbc-chartering.com; internet www .bbc-chartering.com; subsidiary of BBC Chartering & Logistic (Germany); Gen. Man. FEDERICO FERBER.

CMA CGM Ecuador, SA: Parque Empresarial Colón, Corporativo 2, Ofs 501 y 503, Avda Rodrigo Chávez s/n, Guayaquil; tel. (4) 213-6501; fax (4) 336-5626; e-mail gql.genmbox@cma-cgm.com; internet www.cma-cgm.com; Gen. Man. JAVIER MOREIRA CALDERÓN.

Flota Petrolera Ecuatoriana (FLOPEC): Edif. FLOPEC, Avda Amazonas No 24–196 y Cordero, Casilla 535-A, Quito; tel. (2) 398-3600; fax (2) 250-1428; e-mail planificacion@flopec.com.ec; internet www.flopec.com.ec; f. 1972; Gen. Man. Capt. RAÚL SAMANIEGO GRANJA.

Investamar, SA: Edif. Berlín, 4°, Las Monjas 10 y C. J. Arosemena, Guayaquil; tel. (4) 220-4000; fax (4) 220-6646; e-mail investamar@ grupoberlin.com; internet www.investamar.com.ec; Gen. Man. Capt. ROLF BENZ.

J. M. Palau Agencia de Vapores: Edif. Plaza, 6°, Of. 603-604, Baquierzo Moreno 1119 y Avda 9 de Octubre, POB 09019108, Guayaquil; tel. (4) 256-2178; fax (4) 256-3473; e-mail jmpav@ecua .net.ec; internet www.jmpalau-shipagency.com; f. 1956; Gen. Man. NAPOLEÓN CADENA.

Naviera Marnizam, SA: Edif. El Navio, Avda Malecon y Calle 19, Manta; tel. (5) 262-6445; fax (5) 262-4414; e-mail info@ marzam-online.com; internet www.marzam-online.com; f. 1985; Gen. Man. LUCÍA ZAMBRANO SEGOVIA.

CIVIL AVIATION

There are four international airports: Mariscal Sucre in Quito, José Joaquín de Olmedo in Guayaquil, Eloy Alfaro in Manta (Manabí) and Cotopaxi Internacional in Latacunga. In 2009 the total number of airports in Ecuador was 402, of which 103 had paved runways.

Dirección General de Aviación Civil: Avda Buenos Aires Oeste 1-53 y 10 de Agosto, Quito; tel. (2) 223-2184; fax (2) 255-2987; e-mail subdirector.subdac@dgac.gov.ec; internet www.dgac.gob.ec; f. 1946; Dir-Gen. Cmdre ROBERTO YEROVI DE LA CALLE.

Aerogal (Aerolíneas Galápagos): Amazonas 7797 y Juan Holguín, Quito; tel. (2) 396-0600; fax (2) 243-0487; e-mail customerservice@ aerogal.com.ec; internet www.aerogal.com.ec; f. 1985; owned by Avianca (Colombia); domestic flights and also flights to Colombia and USA; Exec. Pres. JULIO GAMERO.

LAN Ecuador, SA: Avda de las Américas s/n, Guayaquil; tel. (4) 269-2850; fax (4) 228-5433; internet www.lan.com; f. 2002; commenced operations in 2003 following acquisition of assets of Ecuatoriana by LAN Chile; scheduled daily flights to Quito, Guayaquil, and the USA; Gen. Man. MAXIMILIANO NARANJO ITURRALDE.

TAME Línea Aérea del Ecuador: Edif. TAME, Avda Amazonas No 24–260 y Avda Colón, 6°, Casilla 17-07-8736, Sucursal Almagro, Quito; tel. (2) 396-6300; fax (2) 255-4907; e-mail tamejefv@impsat .net.ec; internet www.tame.com.ec; f. 1962; fmrly Transportes Aéreos Mercantiles Ecuatorianos, SA; removed from military control in 1990; state-owned; domestic scheduled and charter services for passengers and freight; Pres. FERNANDO MARTÍNEZ DE LA VEGA.

Tourism

Tourism has become an increasingly important industry in Ecuador, with a wide variety of heritage sites, beaches, rainforest reserves and national parks. The main attractions include the Galápagos Islands and the Yasuní National Park. In 2013 foreign arrivals (including same-day visitors) numbered a provisional 1,366,000. In the same year receipts from the tourism industry amounted to a provisional US $1,246m.

Asociación Ecuatoriana de Agencias de Viajes, Operadores de Turismo y Mayoristas (ASECUT): Caldas 340 y Guayaquil, Edif. San Blas, 6°, Ofs 61–62, Quito; tel. (2) 250-0759; fax (2) 250-3669; e-mail asecut@pi.pro.ec; f. 1953; Pres. ALFONSO SEVILLA.

Federación Hotelera del Ecuador (AHOTEC): América No 38–80 y Diguja, Quito; tel. (2) 244-3425; fax (2) 245-3942; e-mail ahotec@ interactive.net.ec; internet www.hotelesecuador.com.ec; Pres. JOSÉ OCHOA GARCÍA; Exec. Dir DIEGO UTRERAS.

Defence

As assessed at November 2013, Ecuador's armed forces numbered 58,000: army 46,500, navy 7,300 (including 2,150 marines and 380 in the naval air force) and air force 4,200. Paramilitary forces included 500 coastguards. Military service lasts for one year and is selective for men at the age of 20.

Defence Budget: an estimated US $1,510m. in 2013.

Chief of the Joint Command of the Armed Forces: Gen. CARLOS ANTONIO LEONARDO BARREIRO MUÑOZ.

Chief of Staff of the Army: Gen. JORGE ANÍBAL PEÑA COBEÑA.

Chief of Staff of the Navy: Vice-Adm. LUIS AURELIO JARAMILLO ARIAS.

Chief of Staff of the Air Force: Lt-Gen. ENRIQUE VELASCO DÁVILA.

Education

Education in Ecuador is compulsory between five and 15 years of age. All public schools are free. Private schools feature prominently in the educational system. Primary education lasts for six years. Secondary education, in general and specialized technical or humanities schools, lasts for up to six years, comprising two equal cycles of three years each. In 2012 enrolment at primary schools included 95% of pupils in the relevant age-group, while the comparable ratio for secondary schools in 2012, according to UNESCO estimates, was 74%. In many rural areas, Quechua and other indigenous Amerindian languages are used in education. The total government expenditure on education was estimated at US $23.9m. for 2012.

Bibliography

For works on South America generally, see Select Bibliography (Books)

Acosta, A. M. *Informal Coalitions and Policymaking in Latin America: Ecuador in Comparative Perspective.* London, Routledge, 2009.

Dosh, P. *Demanding the Land: Urban Popular Movements in Peru and Ecuador, 1990–2005.* University Park, PA, Pennsylvania State University Press, 2010.

Gerlach, A. *Indians, Oil, and Politics: A Recent History of Ecuador (Latin American Silhouettes).* Wilmington, DE, Scholarly Resources Inc, 2003.

Giugale, M., Fretes-Cibils, F., and Somensatto, E. (Eds). *Revisiting Ecuador's Economic and Social Agenda in an Evolving Landscape.* Washington, DC, World Bank, 2008.

Herz, M., and João Pontes, N. *Ecuador vs Peru: Peacemaking Amid Rivalry.* Boulder, CO, Lynne Rienner Publrs, 2002.

Hurtado, O. *Portrait of a Nation: Culture and Progress in Ecuador.* Lanham, MD, Madison Books, 2010.

Lane, K. *Quito 1599: City and Colony in Transition.* Albuquerque, NM, University of New Mexico Press, 2002.

Mantilla, S., and Mejía, S. *Rafael Correa, Balance de la Revolución Ciudadana.* Quito, Editorial Planeta, 2012.

Pallares, A. *From Peasant Struggles to Indian Resistance: The Ecuadorian Andes in the Late Twentieth Century.* Norman, OK, University of Oklahoma Press, 2002.

Rival, L. *Trekking Through History: The Huaorani of Amazonian Ecuador.* New York, Columbia University Press, 2002.

Roitman, K. *Race, Ethnicity, and Power in Ecuador: The Manipulation of Mestizaje.* Boulder, CO, Lynne Rienner Publrs, 2009.

Sawyer, S. *Crude Chronicles: Indigenous Politics, Multinational Oil, and Neoliberalism in Ecuador.* Durham, NC, Duke University Press, 2004.

Striffler, S. *In the Shadows of State and Capital: The United Fruit Company, Popular Struggle, and Agrarian Restructuring in Ecuador, 1900–1995.* Durham, NC, Duke University Press, 2002.

Suarez-Cruz, E. *The Dollarization Process in Ecuador: Adoption History and Macroeconomic Performance till 2006.* Saarbrücken, VDM Verlag Dr. Müller, 2011.

Villavicencio, F. *Ecuador Made in China.* Quito, Interamerican Institute for Democracy, 2013.

Whitten, D., and Whitten, N. *Histories of the Present: People and Power in Ecuador.* Champaign, IL, University of Illinois Press, 2011.

EL SALVADOR

Geography

PHYSICAL FEATURES

The Republic of El Salvador is the smallest country in Central America and the only one without a Caribbean shore. It lies on the western or Pacific side of the Central American land bridge, but itself has a southern coast. Guatemala lies to the west, further up the isthmus, beyond a 203-km (126-mile) border. Honduras is to the north and east—a definitive border demarcation, along the 342 km of frontier, was only agreed in 1992, when an International Court of Justice (ICJ) decision was accepted, although the demarcation was not ratified by both countries until 2006. The ICJ referred the issue of the maritime boundary in the Gulf of Fonseca (a line was agreed in 1990 by the Honduras–Nicaragua Mixed Boundary Commission) to tripartite discussion—Nicaragua lies beyond the Gulf, in the south-east. The dispute in the Gulf is also complicated by the Salvadorean claim to the island of Conejo, currently held by Honduras. The country has a total area of 21,041 sq km (8,124 sq miles).

El Salvador is about 260 km in length (east–west) and 140 km wide, with 307 km of coast along the Pacific Ocean. It is a land of volcanoes, and is prone to sometimes devastating earthquakes. This can make the terrain unstable and dangerous, but has also given the country rich volcanic soil suitable for growing coffee, the basis of the Salvadorean economy. The uplands consist of a double row of volcanoes and mountains, the roughly parallel and east–west coastal chain and the further inland Cordillera Apeneca, which reach their highest point in the north-west, at Cerro El Pital (2,730 m or 8,960 ft). There is also a central plateau and, beneath the highlands, falling fairly steeply into the Pacific, is a narrow coastal plain. The three main topographical areas are, therefore: a flat, tropical region in the south, some of it wetlands; the central plateau of mountains, valleys and volcanoes; and the northern lowlands formed by the valleys of the Lempa river and the Sierra Madre. In all there are 150, usually fast-flowing, rivers and three lakes. The terrain still sustains much biological diversity, despite the pressures of the densely settled human population, with, for instance, more species of trees than in all of Western Europe. There are reckoned to be large numbers of species of plants (notably orchids), butterflies, birds and fish, but, nevertheless, there are fewer than in any other Central American country. Woodland covers 17% of El Salvador (only 3% of the country remains with its natural primary forest), most of it secondary forest and scrubland, but there is an additional 9% of territory planted with coffee bushes, which are also provided with trees for shade. El Salvador has the highest rate of deforestation (just over 3% per year) and the least amount of territory protected by national parks (0.5%) in Central America.

CLIMATE

The climate is tropical, but more temperate in the high country. The rainy season is during the summer, in May–October, the wettest month in San Salvador, the inland capital, being June. Rainfall is generally heavier on the coast, however, while the interior remains relatively dry. The average annual rainfall for the whole country is almost 1,800 mm (70 ins). Temperatures in the wet season average about 28°C (82°F), whereas in the

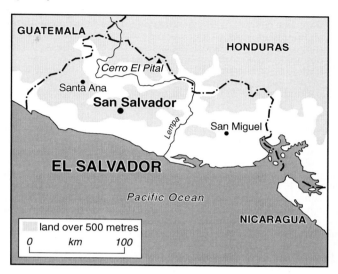

cooler dry season they range between 15°C and 23°C (59°F–73°F). Greater altitude, of course, moderates these temperatures. The country is susceptible to hurricanes from the Caribbean, as well as to the vagaries of the El Niño weather phenomenon.

POPULATION

The population is predominantly of mixed-race descent (86%, according to the 2007 census), the rest of the population consisting of those of European stock and of indigenous Amerindians (the latter consisting mainly of the Kakawira, the Nahua-Pipil, descendants of the Aztecs, and the Lenca). A number of nationalities have settled in El Salvador over the years, but nearly all of today's population is of Spanish descent. For this reason it is no surprise to find that around 76% of the country adheres to the Roman Catholic Church, although, as elsewhere in Latin America, evangelical Protestant groups have been very active and have made significant numbers of converts. The official language, and that used by nearly the entire population, is Spanish. Some speak Amerindian tongues, notably Nahua (Pipil). Informally, the people of El Salvador are sometimes known as Guanacos.

The total population was estimated at 6.3m. in 2014. The capital, San Salvador, is located in the highlands immediately above the western end of the coastal plains. The capital's population numbered 281,870 in 2014. There are a number of other large urban centres, but probably the two most eminent cities are Soyapango, within the department of San Salvador, Santa Ana, to the north-west of the capital, and San Miguel, in the south-east of El Salvador. Although it is the smallest country of Central America, El Salvador is the most densely populated country on the American mainland (300.8 people per sq km in 2014). For administrative purposes, the country is divided into 14 departments.

History

NICHOLAS WATSON

Based on an earlier article by DIEGO SÁNCHEZ-ANCOCHEA

El Salvador's history has been dominated by the land question. The country is the smallest and most densely populated on mainland America and has very few natural resources. For thousands of years before the conquest by Spain during 1524–35 indigenous (Amerindian) races populated the country. Following the conquest, Spanish settlers established large plantations of cocoa and then indigo for export, and the native population was forced on to ever smaller areas of common land where they grew traditional subsistence crops such as rice, beans and yucca. Competition for a limited land base and the practice of planting export crops over as great an area as possible shaped El Salvador's society, politics and economy.

El Salvador, which comprised part of the Captaincy-General of Guatemala, in 1821 achieved independence from Spanish rule. It then formed part of the United Provinces of Central America, which grouped it with Honduras, Guatemala, Nicaragua and Costa Rica. The United Provinces were recast as a Federal Republic in 1824, but the arrangement was never stable, and in 1841 El Salvador declared independence and drew up its own Constitution. From the mid-19th century a small group of local landowners and merchants transformed the country into a specialized producer of agricultural exports. After the collapse of world demand for indigo in the 1860s, coffee emerged as the mainstay of the national commercial economy, displacing traditional systems of local food production. In 1882 all common lands were abolished and three-quarters of all land passed into the ownership of families comprising only about 2% of El Salvador's inhabitants. The majority of the population, displaced from their traditional lands, became permanent wage labourers on the new plantations or migratory seasonal workers.

In contrast to other Central American countries, the agro-export economy of El Salvador was created by domestic, not foreign, capital and expertise. The economy was dominated by an interlocked élite of landowners and merchants (known as the 'Fourteen Families'), who controlled the state, land, capital and markets. The formal democratic procedures of a constitutional republic were maintained, but governments were effectively appointed by the oligarchy to administer power in its own interests.

MILITARY DOMINATION OF GOVERNMENT, 1932–82

The events of 1931–32 challenged the basis of this power structure. In 1931, against a background of national and international economic depression, relatively fair elections brought to office a reformist President, Arturo Araújo. The existence of widespread popular discontent and allegations that the Partido Comunista Salvadoreño (PCS—Salvadorean Communist Party), recently established under the leadership of Agustín Farabundo Martí, was promoting armed insurrection, provoked a conservative reaction. Araújo was deposed by a military coup in December 1931 and replaced by Gen. Maximiliano Hernández Martínez. A large-scale peasant uprising in January 1932 was violently suppressed; 10,000–30,000 people, among them many Amerindians, were killed in reprisals known as la matanza (the massacre). Farabundo Martí was arrested and executed. The landowning élite, shaken by these perceived threats to its economic interest, abdicated its control of political power to the army that had saved it.

For the next 50 years the relationship between the armed forces and the civilian oligarchy remained the central reality of the nation's power structure: the former guaranteed the privileges of the latter, while simultaneously promoting their own interests by establishing military rule as an institution. Shifts between 'conservative' and 'progressive' factions within the military led to a pattern of reform and repression. When abuses of presidential power threatened to provoke popular discon-

tent, incumbent presidents were removed by military coup: Gen. Hernández Martínez in 1944, Lt-Col José María Lemus in 1960 and Gen. Carlos Humberto Romero Mena in 1979. When reformist administrations were considered to be too radical, they were removed by counter-coup, as in the overthrow of the military-civilian juntas of 1944 and 1960.

Between 1961 and 1979 the military leadership attempted to present its own party, the Partido de Conciliación Nacional (PCN—Party of National Conciliation), as the country's unifying force. Other parties were tolerated, but repeated electoral manipulation ensured that PCN candidates—Lt-Col Julio Adalberto Rivera, Gen. Fidel Sánchez Hernández, Col Arturo Armando Molina Barraza and Gen. Romero—gained the presidency, and so retained power in the hands of the army. From 1960 the Partido Demócrata Cristiano (PDC—Christian Democratic Party), under the leadership of José Napoleón Duarte, consistently attracted the largest electoral support for any opposition party and steadily grew in strength.

In July 1969 a 13-day war with Honduras resulted in the deaths of 2,000 people. The catalyst for the so-called football war was a disputed decision in the third qualifying round of the football (soccer) World Cup, although the roots of the conflict were territorial disputes and migration pressures. Some 300,000 Salvadoreans had emigrated to Honduras to farm. Honduras decided to expel them as it pressed a boundary claim. The frontier dispute was settled in September 1972 when Honduras was awarded two-thirds of the disputed land by international arbitration.

The return of the emigrants, now refugees, put more pressure on El Salvador's land. The number of landless peasants grew from 30,500 in 1961 (12% of the rural population) to 167,000 in 1975 (41% of the rural population). This combined with an economic depression, caused partly by the 1973 oil shock and its global consequences and partly by the loss of the Honduran market, to put heavy pressure on the regime. In the 1972 presidential election the opposition parties united behind Duarte, but Col Molina unilaterally declared victory. Subsequent protests and an attempted coup were crushed and was Duarte exiled.

In 1970 Cayetano Carpio, Secretary-General of the PCS, broke from the party to pursue a campaign of armed insurrection. His lead was followed by a number of distinct guerrilla groups on the extreme left, and in Cuba in 1980 they co-ordinated to form the Frente Farabundo Martí para la Liberación Nacional (FMLN—Farabundo Martí National Liberation Front). The FMLN also established a political wing, the Frente Democrático Revolucionario (FDR—Democratic Revolutionary Front). Reforming politicians, previously strongly opposed to armed struggle, began to support the FMLN as the only available option for the pursuit of democratic change.

Gen. Romero's victory in the presidential election of 1977 followed a campaign characterized by intimidation, fraud and violent suppression of subsequent public protests. Alarmed by the implications of the overthrow of the dictatorship of Gen. Anastasio Somoza Debayle in Nicaragua in July 1979, the military ousted Romero in October. After a series of abortive civilian-military juntas, Duarte agreed to lead a provisional government, on the condition that fundamental reforms be introduced immediately and be guaranteed by the military and by the USA.

Duarte joined the junta in March 1980. In the same month the Government, assisted by the USA, expropriated one-quarter of all agricultural land, for conversion into peasant co-operatives, and nationalized the banks and major export institutions. This was the first stage of the most important change in the nation's economy since the abolition of common lands one century ago. However, civil war was already imminent. Army and 'death squad' human rights abuses were such that the population had little faith in the Government. At the end of March Oscar Romero, Archbishop of San Salvador, who had regularly expressed support for the cause of the poor and oppressed, was assassinated in the act of celebrating Mass. At his funeral, without provocation, soldiers fired into the crowd of mourners. The Government was also under pressure from the left, which, as in 1932, favoured revolution over reform.

THE CIVIL WAR

The Effects of the War

In January 1981 the FMLN launched its 'Final Offensive', intended to achieve victory before the inauguration of President Ronald Reagan of the USA. It failed, and the civil war continued at an increasing cost in human suffering and economic disruption. By 1992 more than 80,000 combatants and civilians had been killed, the vast majority by the armed forces; an estimated 550,000 (more than 10% of the population) had been displaced from their homes, while in excess of 500,000 had fled the country as refugees. There was military stalemate. The army, relying heavily on US support, was increased in size to 55,000 military and 15,000 paramilitary personnel. However, it was ill-led and relied on a strategy of sporadic infantry attacks, supported by aerial bombings across extensive 'free-fire' zones, thus alienating the civilian population.

The economic cost of the conflict was so high that the collapse of the economy was only averted by direct US economic assistance. One-half of government budgets were committed to defence spending. Unemployment and underemployment affected more than one-half of the adult population and per-head income decreased to levels of the 1960s. The crisis was exacerbated by two natural disasters: the 1986 earthquake that killed 1,500 people and a subsequent drought.

Elections for a constituent assembly in March 1982 divided power between the PDC and two major right-wing parties—the PCN and the Alianza Republicana Nacionalista (ARENA—Nationalist Republican Alliance), founded in 1981. In 1982 Alvaro Magaña Borja, a politically independent banker, was accepted by all parties as interim President. Under his guidance, in 1983 the major parties agreed to a new Constitution. This provided for a democratic political process and incorporated the essential principles of economic reform.

In May 1984 Duarte won the presidency in a direct electoral contest with the ARENA candidate, Maj. Roberto D'Aubuisson Arrieta. Elections in March 1985 gave the PDC an absolute majority in the Asamblea Legislativa (Legislative Assembly). However, Duarte failed to make progress towards a negotiated settlement of the war, or social and economic reforms. In the 1988 election ARENA won control of the Asamblea Legislativa and in 1989 its candidate, Alfredo Cristiani Burkard, was elected President.

Progress Towards Peace

Formal and informal contacts between the Government and the FDR-FMLN began as early as 1980. However, each attempt at a negotiated peace foundered on two key issues: the future role, control and structure of the military; and the integration of the FDR-FMLN into national political life. Despite his position as Commander-in-Chief of the Armed Forces, President Duarte did not control them and so could not guarantee the FDR-FMLN's conditions. His failure to do so was demonstrated by the terror tactics of the extreme right-wing death squads, which, aided by his senior officers, were responsible for the assassination of church leaders, trade unionists and political activists.

The FDR-FMLN also considered each of the six elections held between 1982 and 1989 as invalid. On each occasion the guerrillas disrupted balloting. From 1989 the FDR leaders accepted that there had been sufficient improvement in electoral conditions to allow them openly to participate in the election, as the Convergencia Democrática (CD—Democratic Convergence), but not until 1991 did one of its five constituent parties contest national elections.

The victory of ARENA in the elections of 1989 and 1991 caused widespread expectation that the conflict would escalate. Many of its senior members were openly committed to a military solution and there was a common belief that some

party leaders, such as Roberto D'Aubuisson, were involved in the death squads. Following President Cristiani's assumption of power in April 1989, the FMLN launched limited, but effective, offensives in May and June, accompanied by direct attacks against the ARENA leadership, notably the assassination of the Attorney-General in April and the Minister of the Presidency in July. The reaction of the right-wing extremists, orchestrated by groups within ARENA and the military, involved the assassination of trade union leaders and suspected FMLN sympathizers. FMLN–ARENA negotiations in September collapsed almost immediately and were followed by an FMLN nationwide offensive in November. The FMLN secured temporary occupation of large areas of the capital, while reprisals by right-wing extremists included the assassination of six Jesuit priests in 1989, the killings of alleged FDR-FMLN sympathizers, and the intimidation of church and human rights groups and of left-wing politicians. In April 1990, however, representatives of the Government and the FDR-FMLN met in Geneva, Switzerland, under the chairmanship of the UN Secretary-General. Following a series of negotiations, a comprehensive agreement was reached by 31 December 1991, leading to a ceasefire on 1 February 1992.

The ceasefire was brought about by both domestic and international factors. The end of the Cold War in 1989 put a stop to US–Soviet confrontation in Central America, and this allowed a regional solution by reviving the Esquípulas Accord, proposed by Costa Rica and endorsed by Central American presidents in 1987. The Accord committed all five countries to adopting specific measures to achieve regional peace. These measures included: dialogue between governments and insurgent groups; commitments to democratic and pluralistic political systems; and cessation of support for insurgent groups from whatever source. The end of the Cold War also allowed the UN to become actively involved in the task of conflict resolution in El Salvador: first, by sponsorship of negotiations; and second, by the establishment of a resident UN Observer Mission in El Salvador (ONUSAL), to verify compliance with negotiated agreements. Finally, within El Salvador, the Government, and especially the military, came under intense US pressure to reach a peace settlement.

This settlement was achieved in the UN-brokered agreement, announced in December 1991, and signed at Chapultepec castle in Mexico City on 16 January 1992. The Chapultepec Accords provided a framework for the reconstruction of Salvadorean society, focusing on the demilitarization and submission of the country to civilian control under the rule of law. On 1 February the formal ceasefire was implemented under the supervision of some 1,000 UN personnel, and the National Commission for the Consolidation of Peace was formally installed with representatives from government and guerrilla forces and all major political parties.

As well as the immediate measures for the disengagement and demobilization of FMLN guerrillas, and the reform and reduction of the Salvadorean military, the Accords established a range of new civilian institutions and programmes and included the participation of former FMLN members in a new national civilian police force (Policía Nacional Civil—PNC), which replaced the paramilitary national police. A new National Council for the Defence of Human Rights was to be supported by an independent National Judiciary Council. A Land Transfer Programme for demobilized combatants and displaced civilians envisaged the transfer of some 10% of El Salvador's agricultural land to a total beneficiary population of about 47,500 people.

Initial progress was made possible by a widespread desire for reconciliation and a willingness to seek consensus. However, mutual allegations of failure to comply with the terms of the Accords persisted throughout 1992 and resulted in the negotiation of a revised timetable for disarmament. Nevertheless, the ceasefire was observed by both sides and, on 15 December (declared National Reconciliation Day), the conflict was formally concluded. On the same day the FMLN was officially registered and recognized as a legitimate political party.

POST-ACCORDS POLITICS

Expectations over the Chapultepec Accords were only partially fulfilled. In November 1992 the Comisión de la Verdad (Truth Commission) released the names of 103 military personnel alleged to have participated in human rights abuses during the civil war. However, the Government was at first reluctant to remove from the armed forces those personnel identified by the Commission. The FMLN was prompted to delay the demobilization of its forces. The effective operation of the new civilian police was constrained by a lack of resources. A dramatic decline in political violence and human rights violations was accompanied by increasing criminal violence. The independence and security of the judiciary, reformed on the recommendations of the Commission's report, had not yet been tested. In late 1993, following international pressure, the military personnel identified by the Commission were dismissed.

These issues posed the principal themes in the campaign leading to national elections in March 1994, monitored by ONUSAL. In spite of problems in the organization of the polls, the people of El Salvador were provided with their first opportunity to express their political preferences in elections that were peaceful as well as free and fair. The three major contending parties were ARENA, the PDC and the FMLN, which in September 1993 had confirmed its political alliance with the CD, and later, in December, with the Movimiento Nacional Revolucionario (MNR—National Revolutionary Movement). Following a second round, Armando Calderón Sol, the ARENA candidate, was elected President. He took office on 1 June.

Despite its success, serious divisions emerged within the FMLN in 1994. In December two factions, the Resistencia Nacional (RN—National Resistance) and the Expresión Renovadora del Pueblo (ERP—Renewed Expression of the People), left the FMLN because of a difference in political interests. In March 1995 Joaquín Villalobos, the ERP Secretary-General, announced the formation of the Partido Demócrata (PD—Democrat Party), a centre-left grouping consisting of the ERP, the RN, the MNR and a dissident faction of the PDC. The PD co-operated with the ruling ARENA party initially, but later withdrew in protest at the coalition's neo-liberal policies.

Meanwhile, there was increasing dissatisfaction with the Government's failure to honour the terms of the Chapultepec Accords. Former soldiers alleged that they had not received financial compensation and other benefits promised in the 1992 agreement. In September 1994 retired soldiers occupied the parliament building and held a number of deputies hostage. The Government immediately pledged to enter into direct negotiations with the soldiers, and the siege ended peacefully. However, in January 1995 former soldiers again seized the Asamblea Legislativa and took a number of hostages; the occupation ended swiftly as the Government reiterated its promise to meet its obligations. However, the spectre of renewed armed conflict remained.

A reduced ONUSAL contingent, known as Misión de las Naciones Unidas en El Salvador, remained in El Salvador until the end of 1996. In March 1997, contrary to expectations, the ruling ARENA party lost seats to the FMLN in municipal and legislative elections. The FMLN also experienced a significant increase in support in the capital. However, the party was deeply divided and unable to present a coherent alternative to ARENA nationally. In the election in March 1999, Francisco Flores Pérez, the ARENA candidate, was elected President. The election was notable for an abstention rate of over 60% of registered voters.

Although in many respects the peace process in El Salvador had opened the country's political arena to wider participation, and judicial and political reforms were planned, most of the population remained more concerned with the daily struggle for economic survival and the continuing high level of violent crime in the country. The neo-liberal reforms adopted from the beginning of the 1990s had delivered neither high rates of growth nor a substantial improvement in general living standards.

THE FLORES AND SACA ADMINISTRATIONS

The presidency of Francisco Flores was dominated by dollarization, the response to natural disasters and growing security concerns. In November 2000 Flores unexpectedly announced that, from 1 January 2001, the US dollar would be introduced as an official currency alongside the colón, anchored to the latter at a fixed rate of exchange. The intention was to stabilize the economy, introduce lower interest rates, and encourage domestic and foreign investment.

Two severe earthquakes struck El Salvador in January and February 2001, presenting the country with its most serious test since the civil war. More than 1,100 people were killed and damage was estimated at US $1,900m., representing 14% of gross domestic product for that year. Around 1.5m. people (one-quarter of the population) were made homeless. The Government was initially overwhelmed; however, international and domestic criticism prompted President Flores to devolve much responsibility to the municipalities. Society became more cohesive through the national recovery effort and the efficient response of the police and army, both of which grew in popularity. In March the US immigration authorities granted a temporary protected status (TPS) to Salvadorean illegal immigrants residing in the USA, releasing those held in custody. This was subsequently extended a number of times and was to remain in force until at least March 2015.

The FMLN did unexpectedly well in regional and congressional elections held in March 2003 and won 31 seats in the Asamblea Legislativa, compared with ARENA's 27. However, ARENA renewed its alliance with the PCN, and Flores announced aggressive policies to reduce insecurity. He introduced the Mano Dura (Firm Hand) policy, imposing strict penalties on anyone convicted of being a member of a street gang, blamed by Salvadoreans for the rampant crime rate in the country. However, the law was ruled unconstitutional by the Supreme Court, and judges and lawyers generally declined to take on cases brought under it.

The presidential election of March 2004 pitted two sharply differing candidates against each other. The FMLN selected Schafik Jorge Handal, a 72-year-old committed Marxist and former guerrilla leader, as its candidate. In contrast, ARENA's candidate, Elías Antonio (Tony) Saca González, was a 39-year-old media entrepreneur of middle-class origins. His selection confirmed ARENA's transformation from a party of the old, coffee-producing élite to one dominated by businessmen from services such as banking and retailing. Saca won 57.7% of the vote against 35.7% for Handal. The turnout was a record high of 66.2%, the public having been galvanized by a fierce campaign.

Following his election, Saca announced plans to reduce unemployment, poverty and violence. The Government introduced legislation to combat organized crime, selected members for the National Commission for Public Security and Social Peace and created a new Ministry of Justice and Public Security. In 2007 there was a 13% reduction in violent crime, although there were still an average of nine murders per day, a higher number than at the beginning of the term (when there were six or seven per day). Despite higher rates of economic growth than in previous years, continued inequality and social polarization, together with insufficient expansion of social programmes, contributed to increasing public dissatisfaction.

Nevertheless, the opposition FMLN failed to benefit from Saca's ineffective Government, and in the legislative and municipal elections of March 2006 ARENA increased its representation in the Asamblea Legislativa from 27 deputies to 34, and its number of mayors from 111 to 147 (56% of the total in the country). The FMLN succeeded in retaining control of San Salvador's mayoralty, but by only 44 votes. Despite ARENA's new majority, low social spending, poor economic performance and high insecurity remained persistent problems for Saca's administration.

THE FUNES PRESIDENCY

Saca's relative ineffectiveness, in addition to deteriorating global economic conditions, contributed to the results of the legislative and presidential elections of January and March 2009, respectively. At legislative elections in January the FMLN became the largest party in the Asamblea Legislativa with 35 out of 84 deputies, followed by ARENA with 32 and the PCN with 11. In the concurrent municipal elections, ARENA lost 27 mayoralties, while the FMLN gained 35 (although it lost the capital).

The presidential election on 15 March 2009 was contested by Mauricio Funes of the FMLN and Rodrigo Avila Avilez of ARENA. A popular journalist, Funes marked a break from Handal, whose death in 2006 created the opportunity for a more moderate candidate to represent the party. Avila, the former Director-General of the police, was regarded by many as an uninspiring candidate. Despite a tense campaign and some concern about electoral fraud, the elections were relatively peaceful and the results historic. For the first time since the 1992 Chapultepec Accords, the candidate from the left-wing, former guerrilla movement FMLN won (with 51.3% of the vote, compared with 48.7% for his opponent). The extraordinary result was expected to open a new era in Salvadorean politics and to herald fresh progress towards the consolidation of democracy.

However, upon taking office on 1 June 2009 Funes was immediately confronted with a hostile legislature. ARENA, the PCN and the PDC had formed an opposition coalition with a combined majority over the FMLN in the Asamblea Legislativa, allowing the right-wing parties to block Funes' proposed legislation. As an early demonstration of this obstructive power, in July the new President was forced to compromise over the composition of the Supreme Court and the appointment of the Attorney-General, which preserved ARENA's domination of the judiciary, thereby undermining Funes' pledge to prosecute members of the previous administration for corruption. However, in a dramatic manifestation of the growing disharmony within ARENA, in October 12 deputies announced their withdrawal from the party and formed a new legislative bloc, the Gran Alianza por la Unidad Nacional (GANA). The loss of the right-wing coalition's majority in the legislature prompted vicious infighting within ARENA. In the following month GANA, the PCN and the PDC voted with the FMLN to approve Funes' budget, which allocated additional funding for health and education, leaving ARENA politically isolated. Moreover, a fiscal reform bill, approved with the help of the GANA deputies in December, was viewed as a significant victory for Funes. Continuing discord within ARENA led to the expulsion of former President Saca by party officials who blamed him for 'instigating the defection of the 12 ARENA deputies' and for selecting the lacklustre Avila as ARENA's unsuccessful candidate in the presidential election.

Tensions within the FMLN also became apparent during 2009 with Vice-President Salvador Sánchez Cerén making a number of public statements that appeared to depart from Funes's moderate, left-leaning, but business-friendly agenda. His pronouncements embarrassed Funes and revealed that the party was still dominated by a more radical core of activists. The divisions were made more apparent in January 2010 by the Asamblea Legislativa's adoption of populist, FMLN-led legislation that removed telephone tariffs, undermining the President's efforts to develop a business environment attractive to investors. By mid-2010 Funes' relationship with the FMLN had deteriorated to such an extent that he was regularly co-operating with right-wing parties in order to pass legislation. Moreover, WikiLeaks, an organization publishing leaked private and classified content, in December released confidential US diplomatic cables revealing Funes' concerns that he was being wire-tapped by members of his own party and excluded from key debates. In a further attempt to demonstrate his distinctiveness from the core of the FMLN, Funes launched an informal grouping, the Citizens' Movement for Change, in mid-2010.

The divisions within the FMLN, the economy's weak performance and concerns over the rising cost of living all combined to result in a minor upset for the FMLN in the March 2012 legislative elections. ARENA secured 33 of the 84 seats (representing a gain of one seat from the 2009 election), while the FMLN took 31 seats (a loss of four) and GANA obtained 11 (down from 16). Despite the decline in support for the FLMN, the latter was able to maintain a legislative majority with the continuing informal backing of GANA and a number of smaller parties in the Asamblea Legislativa. The results signalled the continuing dominance of the two main parties. A mid-2012 poll by the Universidad Centroamericana (UCA)

indicated that 52% of Salvadoreans believed that the change from a right-wing to a left-wing administration in 2009 had been 'positive'.

Subsequent events demonstrated how evenly divided the political situation stood prior to the 2014 election. An institutional dispute between the Supreme Court and the Asamblea Legislativa over the appointment of a new Attorney-General continued for much of 2012; the crisis, which had been precipitated by the inability of the FMLN and ARENA to agree on who should fill the post, was resolved with the FMLN eventually compromising on an ARENA-backed candidate. Then, in November 2012 ARENA expelled four of its own deputies, after they voted to approve the government budget. This was followed in April 2013 by the resignation from ARENA of another deputy, which reduced the party's representation to 28 deputies. Significantly, this effectively removed ARENA's ability to block Asamblea votes requiring a two-thirds' majority.

In addition to the signs of political polarization, the legacy of violence committed during the civil war (1980–92) continued to influence the political life of the country. In January 2010 President Funes made the first formal apology for human rights abuses committed by the state during that period. Meanwhile, human rights activists and organizations, including Amnesty International, used the 30th anniversary of the murder of Oscar Romero to urge the Government to repeal the controversial law, promulgated in 1992, which exempted all war crimes from prosecution. In March 2011, in a highly symbolic gesture that also harked back to the civil war, US President Barack Obama visited Romero's tomb in San Salvador. However, in an equally telling development that indicated the lingering repercussions of the civil war, Obama pointedly did not meet the then Minister of Justice and Public Security, Manuel Melgar, who was accused of complicity in the 1985 killing of four US marines by the FMLN.

THE 2014 PRESIDENTIAL ELECTION

The presidential election of 2 February 2014 saw Funes's Vice-President Salvador Sánchez Cerén pitted against ARENA's Norman Quijano, the mayor of San Salvador. The choice of former guerrilla Sánchez Cerén was controversial, with many suggesting that his radical past made him effectively unelectable. However, the FMLN candidate moderated his more radical rhetoric during the campaign, and his choice of Oscar Ortiz, the popular mayor of Santa Tecla, as running mate was astute. The FMLN also profited from ARENA's difficulties, in particular the inconsistencies in its security policies and in the corruption scandal that enveloped Quijano's campaign manager and former President Francisco Flores in late 2013. In addition, ARENA continued to lose ground to the GANA breakaway faction, led by former President Saca, which joined forces with the Partido de la Esperanza (Party of Hope, as the PDC had become) and Concertación Nacional (National Consensus, as the PCN had become) under the banner of the Unidad (Unity) movement to contest the election.

Sánchez Cerén comfortably won the first round of the election on 2 February 2014 with 48.9% of the vote, just short of the 50% plus one vote required to avoid a second-round run-off ballot, while Quijano won 39.0%. At the second round of voting on 9 March, contrary to expectations of a clear FMLN victory, Sánchez Cerén secured just 50.1% of the vote, defeating Quijano, who received 49.9%, a difference of fewer than 7,000 votes. The close result led Quijano to challenge the electoral authorities' declaration, alleging fraud, bias and double voting. However, after several days of tensions, ARENA's appeals for a recount were rejected and Sánchez Cerén was formally declared the winner. ARENA announced its recognition of the FMLN's victory, having exhausted the legal options to continue challenging the result. As the first former FMLN guerrilla to secure the presidency, Sánchez Cerén's victory was a personal triumph, even if the narrow margin by which he won demonstrated the continued polarization between right and left.

CRIME AND GANG TRUCE

In 2014 high rates of violent crime remained the most prominent issue of concern for most Salvadoreans and a key priority for Sánchez Céren. The gang truce that took effect from March 2012 began to fray in early 2014, having helped dramatically to reduce the number of murders from 4,362 in 2011 to 2,576 in 2012 and then to a 10-year low of 2,490 in 2013. However, the truce appeared to have run its course by the end of the Funes presidency, with violent crime undergoing a steady rise during his final months in office; the PNC reported 1,478 murders in the first six months of 2014. At his inauguration Sánchez Cerén did not clarify whether he would seek to revive the truce, referring only to the need to strengthen the PNC and address systemic problems within the prison system. The President also pledged to maintain troop deployments in anti-crime operations. Even if Sánchez Cerén were to reactivate some kind of gang truce, broader efforts to address the entrenched socio-economic factors associated with crime, as well as issues such as judicial impunity and police corruption clearly remain necessary.

RELATIONS WITH THE USA AND THE VENEZUELAN CONNECTION

Relations between El Salvador and the USA are close, and are underpinned by the contribution to El Salvador's economy made by remittances sent home from the approximately 2.5m. Salvadoreans resident in the USA, many of whom enjoy special TPS under US law. In order to strengthen relations with the USA and to ensure continued inflows of bilateral aid and assistance, in 2003 Flores signed up to the US-led 'coalition of the willing' in Iraq. Saca maintained the Salvadorean military commitment well after the disbandment of the Plus Ultra Brigade that included neighbours Honduras and Nicaragua; the deployment of Salvadorean troops only ended in February 2009. In addition, since 2000 the USA has operated a Forward Operating Location airbase to host US drug detection aircraft at Comalapa. El Salvador was the first country to implement the Dominican Republic-Central America Free Trade Agreement (CAFTA-DR) in early 2006. The FMLN assumed a more nationalistic stance, opposing both involvement in Iraq and the stationing of US military personnel in El Salvador, which had been regarded as an act of submission to the USA. However, in government, Funes fended off criticism of the continuing US presence at Comalapa, which was granted a five-year extension shortly before he took office in mid-2009, while maintaining El Salvador's CAFTA-DR membership. In 2011 Obama visited San Salvador and praised Funes's commitment to 'consensus-building' and 'wise leadership'. It was a measure of Funes's moderate policies and Sánchez Cerén's more prag-

matic stance that the spectre of a breakdown in bilateral relations with the USA gained little traction in the 2014 presidential campaign.

Under Funes, El Salvador re-established diplomatic ties with socialist Cuba, although relations with the leftist Government in Venezuela remained cordial rather than close. However, Sánchez Cerén appeared likely to develop closer relations with Venezuela after El Salvador was formally accepted into the Venezuelan-led Petrocaribe subsidized oil initiative. None the less, Venezuela's domestic economic difficulties have prompted doubts over how long Venezuelan largesse can last, despite pledges from Nicolás Maduro, the successor to the late Hugo Chávez, to maintain the status quo. With Venezuela mired in economic crisis and rocked by protests by early 2014, Sánchez Cerén increasingly compared himself to Uruguay's former guerrilla-turned-moderate President José 'Pepe' Mujica rather than Chávez or Maduro. Above all, with Venezuela's ability and willingness to sustain its foreign aid and subsidies in doubt, the USA's importance as El Salvador's key ally and trade partner remained irrefutable in 2014.

PROSPECTS FOR THE FUTURE

In the first years of the 21st century El Salvador consolidated an economic and political model based on the tenets of increasing political and economic links with the USA and the implementation of neo-liberal economic policies. Despite having contributed to the expansion of remittances and nontraditional exports, this model created numerous social tensions. The 2009 elections were a milestone for the consolidation of democracy in El Salvador, and proved that the political system could withstand the transfer of power between once-implacable civil war foes. Funes quashed fears that an FMLN administration would distance El Salvador from the USA and draw the country into Venezuela's political orbit, while he charted a moderate course for the economy that did not entail major structural changes. Whether Sánchez Cerén maintains Funes's moderate course or tacks significantly to the left remains to be seen. Clearly, the 2014 presidential election result shows that political polarization persists almost a quarter of a century after the end of the civil conflict, although it also showed that El Salvador has the institutional framework to resolve political disputes peacefully. The challenge ahead is to tackle insecurity and socio-economic inequalities while reviving the economy.

Economy

NICHOLAS WATSON

With a gross domestic product (GDP) per head of US $7,700, on an international purchasing-power parity basis, in 2012, El Salvador is a lower middle-income country, according to the World Bank classification. At the same time, however, El Salvador is one of the least developed countries in Latin America and the Caribbean: in 2014 the country was ranked 115th out of 187 countries in the UN Human Development Index (HDI), higher than neighbouring Guatemala and Honduras, but in the bottom one-third of Latin American countries.

In 2012 infant mortality was 13 per 1,000 live births, life expectancy at birth was 72.1 years and adult illiteracy was 15.5%. According to the 2013 HDI, the average Salvadorean spends just seven-and-a-half years in education. Human development is constrained by an unequal distribution of land and a high population density. El Salvador has a land area of only 20,721 sq km (8,003 sq miles) and an estimated population of 6.33m. in 2014, resulting in one of the highest population densities in the Western Hemisphere (301 people per sq km). A high level of violence is also a problem: El Salvador has one of the highest murder rates in the world.

PHASES OF ECONOMIC DEVELOPMENT

El Salvador, like many of its neighbours in Central America and the Caribbean, has slowly moved from a primary-based economy to one that depends on manufacturing exports from free trade zones and remittances from Salvadoreans abroad. This process of change has taken place in five different phases since independence in 1821. Initially, the dominant products were indigo and cotton. From the mid-19th century coffee superseded these commodities in importance. After the abolition of common land in 1882 vast haciendas (plantations) emerged, worked by a seasonal peasant workforce which had lost access to common land. Coffee 'barons' branched out into finance and commerce, and in the 1960s their capital helped to establish a manufacturing base that exported throughout Central America.

The new process of industrialization based on the Central American Common Market (CACM) contributed to the acceleration of economic growth and opened a third stage of development. However, deterioration in the price of coffee and other commodities, together with adverse international conditions and the crisis of the CACM, led to a severe downturn at the end of the 1970s. By 1983 GDP per head had fallen to levels comparable with those of the 1960s. From 1979 to 1982 investment, in real terms, decreased by 68% and consumption by 20%. Unemployment, combined with underemployment, was estimated to affect more than 40% of the total workforce. In an attempt to ease social tensions and avert a left-wing uprising, a new military Government nationalized the banks and the coffee industry and began breaking up large haciendas and handing them to worker co-operatives, initiating what can be considered the fourth phase of development. Nevertheless, these attempts failed to prevent a civil war that extended from 1980 to 1992. The war caused more than 80,000 deaths, the internal and external displacement of over 1m. people, a massive flight of capital, and economic damage estimated at more than US \$2,000m. During the war external financial assistance, mainly from the USA, helped to keep the economy from sliding into recession. Between 1980 and 1990 total external financial assistance to El Salvador exceeded \$5,000m., with approximately 90% from the USA. One of the main purposes of US assistance was to offset economic sabotage by the Frente Farabundo Martí para la Liberación Nacional (FMLN—Farabundo Martí National Liberation Front), which particularly affected the harvesting and export of the country's main export crop, coffee, and severely disrupted transport and power transmission.

The latest stage of economic development, which began in 1989, involved a full adoption of the so-called Washington Consensus. El Salvador was one of the most radical reformers in Latin America and the Caribbean, with policies ranging from external liberalization to privatization of key public companies, domestic deregulation and the dollarization of the economy. During the administration of Alfredo Cristiani (1989–94) important sectors of the economy were returned to private ownership, including sugar refineries, distilleries, textile mills, hotels and fish-processing plants, as well as most of the banks and financial institutions. Public spending was cut and price controls and subsidies reduced or abolished. The tax system was simplified and tariffs diminished.

Market reforms continued after the peace accords under successive Alianza Republicana Nacionalista (ARENA—Nationalist Republican Alliance) Governments. In 1998 the state telecommunications company, Administración Nacional de Telecomunicaciones, was privatized and in 1999 several electricity generating stations were sold. Although public protests prevented further privatization in the health and banking sectors in the period 1999–2002, other radical reforms were implemented during the administration of Francisco Flores Pérez (1999–2004). The most important of these was the dollarization of the economy, approved in November 2000. From 1 January 2001 the US dollar circulated freely with the colón at a fixed rate of \$1 = 8.75 colones. The World Bank and the IMF supported the move, which aimed to reduce real interest rates to close to US levels to encourage investment and integrate El Salvador into the global economy. The colón was phased out by 2003.

The election of ARENA's candidate Elías Antonio (Tony) Saca González in March 2004 did not change the direction of economic policy. El Salvador was the first country to approve the Dominican Republic-Central American Free Trade Agreement (CAFTA-DR) with the USA, in December of that year. Despite mass demonstrations, El Salvador was also the first country to implement the institutional changes required to be in full compliance with CAFTA-DR during the second half of 2005; the accord came into effect in El Salvador in March 2006. Mauricio Funes (from the left-wing FMLN), who became President in June 2009, emphasized the moderate nature of his agenda and his desire to develop a business environment attractive to investors. In January 2011, a decade after dollarization was first introduced, Funes reiterated his commitment to the policy, despite continuing opposition from within the FMLN.

Overall, the Funes Government offered a broad continuity of economic policy rather than any significant change to the neoliberal model, much to the chagrin of many within the FMLN. However, in March 2014 the FMLN's Salvador Sánchez Cerén, a former teacher and guerrilla from a working-class background, won the presidential election, taking office in June 2014. Despite his radical past, Sánchez Cerén struck a moderate policy stance in his campaign, and as of mid-2014 it remained to be seen whether he would tack to the left in economic policy or maintain Funes's brand of pragmatic centrism.

THE ECONOMY SINCE 1990

Cristiani's reforms and heightened demand after the end of the war led to a short-lived economic boom, partly facilitated by the expansion of remittances. Between 1990 and 1995 real GDP per head expanded rapidly, at an average annual rate of 4%. However, in 1995–2005 GDP per head stagnated, increasing at an average annual rate of only 0.7%. The economy did recuperate between 2006 and 2008, but the average annual rise in real GDP per head of 2.3% was less than in the rest of Central America (where it expanded at an average of 3.2% a year during this period). From 2008 the global financial crisis reduced the opportunities for growth and the economy contracted by 3.5% in 2009. Over the following years there was a moderate recovery, with GDP growing by 1.4% in 2010, 1.5% in 2011, 1.9% in 2012 and 1.7% in 2013. However, according to a 2013 report by the Central American Monetary Council, El Salvador has had the weakest GDP growth rates in the Central American region since 2006.

Frequent natural disasters were partly responsible for this uneven economic record. Hurricane Mitch, which struck Central America in 1998, resulted in the loss of an estimated 8% (about US \$1,760m.) of El Salvador's GDP in that year. In 2001 two severe earthquakes hit the country, killing more than 1,100 people and leaving 1.5m. people homeless. Reconstruction costs were estimated at \$1,900m., equivalent to 14% of GDP. The Government diverted \$150m. from the 2001 budget, and was also forced to borrow heavily to finance reconstruction over the following five years. External debt increased from a comparatively low 21.6% of GDP in 2000 to an estimated 29.3% of GDP in 2005. The debt burden continued to increase under both ARENA and FMLN Governments. The public debt-to-GDP ratio was equivalent to some 56.2% of GDP at the end of the Funes presidency in early 2014, compared with 39.7% when Funes came to power in 2009.

Low economic growth and ineffective economic reforms were instrumental in maintaining high levels of poverty. According to data from the UN Economic Commission for Latin America (ECLAC), the poverty rate decreased by 2.3% between 2001 and 2011, when it stood at 46.6%. During 2012 there was a heated political debate over the poverty rate in El Salvador; the local research institute Fundación Salvadoreña para el Desarrollo Económico y Social (El Salvadorean Foundation for Economic and Social Development) claimed that approximately 600,000 people lived below the poverty line between 2008 and 2012. However, the Funes Government claimed that the number of households living in poverty had fallen from 40.5% in 2011 to 34.5% in 2012. However, ECLAC reported a poverty rate of 45.3% by the end of 2013. Addressing poverty and socioeconomic inequalities remains a key challenge; ECLAC estimates that 10% of the population receive 30% of the national income, while the poorest 40% of the population receive just 18%.

Poor urban, as well as rural, households became increasingly dependent on remittances from family members who had migrated, especially to the USA. Remittances reached US \$3,787.7m. in 2008, covering almost four-fifths of the growing trade deficit. Recession in the USA led to a decline in remittances in 2009, although they subsequently revived, reaching \$3,910m. in 2012 and \$3,969m in 2013 (equivalent to 15.9% of GDP).

El Salvador's revenue from taxes is equivalent to just 13.6% of GDP, well below the Latin American average of 18%. The Funes Government introduced two separate tax reforms and proposed a third set of measures including new property taxes before the end of its term in 2014. However, the reforms failed to stem the growth of the deficit.

AGRICULTURE

Agriculture (including hunting, forestry and fishing) remains an important economic activity in the early 21st century, despite a contraction in the sector, owing to mass migration to the cities. By 2007 an estimated 60% of the population lived in urban areas, compared with 50% in 1995. Agricultural growth was stagnant between 1996 and 2003, during which time sectoral contribution to real GDP decreased from 13.5% to 11.4%. Agricultural performance improved in 2004–08, but growth was minimal in 2009–13, when the total revenue from the sector increased from US $1,130m. to $1,170m. There is still intense pressure for land in a country with an increasing population density. Uneven rainfall, some 84% of which occurs during May–October, is another problem, while severe weather takes its toll on the sector. A combination of heavy rains and drought have contributed to uneven agricultural performance in the last five years.

Inequality in the distribution of land is a long-standing problem. During the war the centrist Government attempted substantial, but flawed, agricultural reform. In 1980 all plantations of more than 500 ha (20% of all agricultural land) were expropriated by the state-owned Instituto Salvadoreño de Transformación Agraria (Salvadorean Institute of Agrarian Transformation), for transfer to peasant-run co-operatives. More than 35,000 peasants benefited from a programme of transfer of freehold titles to tenant smallholders between 1981 and 1985. In 1983 a statutory limit of 245 ha was placed upon the amount of land that could be owned by any Salvadorean national. The aim was to provide one-half of the landless rural population with land rights, though ultimately less than one-quarter received rights. As part of the 1992 peace settlement, an estimated 10% of agricultural land was to be distributed among 45,000 families of refugees and combatants. The programme was finally completed in 1998. Nevertheless, post-war administrations gave little assistance to the agriculture sector, with the exception of coffee, believing that progress lay in industrialization. Hence, land reform proved no panacea, with many new landowners lacking the capital and expertise necessary fully to exploit their land.

Production of arabica coffee was adversely affected by external and internal shocks in the 1990s and 2000s. Natural disasters together with low prices caused by rising exports from non-traditional growers such as Vietnam adversely affected the sector. Export income from coffee declined, owing to 40-year price lows in 2002–03, and was determined more by the fluctuations in international prices than by output. Coffee export revenues increased in subsequent years to reach US $122m. in 2007/08, only to dip again, to $191m., in 2009/10, following a record low harvest. However, a resurgence in world prices led to a substantial increase in coffee exports, which earned $464m. in 2010/11 (representing around three-quarters of export revenue from traditional exports). Revenue declined to $300m. in 2011/12 and to $234m in 2012/13, owing to a combination of poor weather conditions, pests such as the coffee rust fungus, and declining productivity.

Output of sugar cane, another important cash crop, also declined during the civil war, and a recovery in the sector in the late 1990s proved short-lived. The sugar sector accounted for around 2.4% of GDP in 2013, and provides employment for approximately 50,000 people, as well as a further 200,000 indirect jobs. Production increased by 39% in the five years preceding the 2012/13 harvest. Roughly two-thirds of output is for export and one-third is directed towards local consumption. Sugar export revenues have risen steadily from US $75m. in 2008 to $190m. in 2013. Expectations for the sugar sector were high in 2014 as local producers hoped to take advantage of tariff-free access to the European Union (EU) following Central America's Association Agreement with the bloc, which came into force in El Salvador in October 2013.

The commercial fishing industry expanded considerably after the 1960s. However, earthquakes, pollution and changes in weather associated with the El Niño phenomenon reduced the total catch to a low of 9,900 metric tons in 2000. Rapid expansion of industrial fishing of tuna and other pelagic fishes allowed for the recuperation of the sector in the following years. In 2012 the total catch amounted to 57,300 tons. The value of El Salvador's sea products has fluctuated over the last decade; it reached a peak of US $334m. in 2008, but decreased to $198m. in 2009, before recovering slightly to reach $211m. in 2010.

Non-traditional exports (including animal fodder, melons and pineapples) became more important at the end of the 20th century, particularly exports to the countries of the CACM. Food production for the domestic market is dominated by the cultivation of maize, sorghum, beans and rice, primarily on smallholdings. However, El Salvador imports around 30% of its basic food needs. Production of staples declined after 1979, owing mainly to the security situation and the displacement of the population. Nevertheless, substantial increases were achieved after 1982. The staple food of most Salvadoreans is maize (output of which totalled 926,000 metric tons in 2012), and beans (108,500 tons). For most of the 2000s dry weather affected rice production, which more than halved in 2000–05, from 47,204 tons to 17,100 tons, but increased by 21% between 2006 and 2008 owing to higher prices. However, according to the Ministry of Agriculture, between 2000 and 2011 rice output decreased by 45%. In 2012/13 rice output stood at 562,960 quintales, down from 758,536 quintales in 2010/11, mainly because of adverse weather conditions. El Salvador's reliance on food imports became a focus of attention amid the rise in global food prices in 2011, when it emerged that the country imported 30% of the beans and 70% of the rice it consumed. Subsequent efforts to increase domestic production have not fundamentally altered the country's vulnerabilities.

MINING AND POWER

Although El Salvador has mineral potential, mining is not as significant as in neighbouring Guatemala or Honduras, accounting for an estimated 0.4% of GDP in 2013, and employing less than 0.1% of the total workforce. The main minerals produced are limestone, gypsum and salt. A legal case brought by mining company Pacific Rim (subsequently taken over by Oceana Gold) against the Salvadorean state in 2009, which was ongoing as of mid-2014, is likely to curb further mining development until its resolution.

El Salvador still relies significantly on imported petroleum, despite a drive to exploit the hydroelectric and geothermal potential in its rugged terrain and volcanoes. In 2014 some 23% of the country's energy came from geothermal sources, 30% from hydroelectricity and the rest from fossil fuels. The sharp rise in world petroleum prices in 2008, and again in 2011, with a significant impact on consumers in El Salvador, served as a reminder of the huge benefits that would result from a reduction in the country's reliance on imported petroleum. The cost of petroleum imports increased by 32% from 2009 to 2010 alone, and continued to have a detrimental effect on El Salvador's trade balance in 2014. However, incoming President Salvador Sánchez Cerén's move to join the Venezuelan-led Petrocaribe subsidized oil initiative in June 2014 could be highly advantageous to El Salvador given the generous terms under which oil is supplied to member states.

The Government prioritized energy production as a motor of industrialization and economic recovery after the civil war. In 1998 some 75% of the shares were sold in four state-owned regional electricity distribution companies. The state still owns the nation's hydroelectric dams, but competition is allowed in thermal and geothermal production, in an effort to encourage investment. Modernization of the infrastructure for energy production and distribution received a boost when the Plan Puebla–Panamá (see Foreign Trade and Payments) devised the creation of the Sistema de Interconexión Eléctrica de Centroamérica (SIEPAC—Central American Electricity Interconnection System). The SIEPAC included the construction of 282 km of electrical transmission lines in El Salvador to connect the country with Honduras.

Efforts are under way to diversify El Salvador's energy matrix to include wind and other forms of renewable power, though advances have been few and far between. The El Chaparral hydroelectric project in San Miguel department has been in limbo since 2010 owing to disagreements between the Government and the project contractor; the project remained stalled in mid-2014 and faced a review by Vice-President Oscar Ortiz. A US $120m. project to install 28 wind turbines in Metapán (Santa Ana department) which could potentially supply power to 100,000 homes, was expected to be completed by 2015. The Funes Government attempted to promote solar power projects, although progress was slow; a $150m. solar power project in Tecoluca (San Vicente department) is expected to be operational by 2015. A round of bidding for 100 MW of solar and wind projects was held in mid-2014.

MANUFACTURING

The rapid growth of the manufacturing sector after 1960, within the CACM, increased the sector's contribution to 15% of GDP by 1979. Although the war reversed this trend temporarily, from 1983 a series of measures was adopted to revitalize the sector, including the promotion of exports within the regional market and the creation of credit lines for industrial companies in the context of the US Government's Caribbean Basin Initiative (CBI). The return of business confidence and the development of regional markets in Central America contributed to the recuperation of the manufacturing sector during the post-war period. Manufacturing production grew at an average annual rate of 4.2% in real terms between 1995 and 2004, making it the strongest performing sector in the economy. Although the sector underperformed, in comparison with the rest of the economy, during 2004–07, it has since then largely followed the fortunes of the wider economy. Manufacturing GDP decreased by 3.0% in 2009, but grew by 2.2% in 2010, 2% in 2011 and 2.7% in 2012.

The *maquila* plants, which mainly assemble apparel products for the US market, have played a central role in the promotion of manufacturing production, exports and jobs in the last two decades or so. The creation of the CBI, favourable access to the US market and tax incentives in El Salvador contributed to the *maquila* sector's rapid expansion during the 1990s. Between 1991 and 2000 *maquila* exports grew at an average annual rate of 32% and by 2003 the sector employed more than 89,000 people. Nevertheless, the sector suffered two significant limitations: the low level of value-added generated in free trade zones, and declining competitiveness in the US market despite improvements in market access. In 2000 the USA broadened the terms of the CBI to provide North American Free Trade Agreement parity to El Salvador and 23 other Latin American countries. The enhanced CBI provided duty-free access to the US market for a number of previously excluded categories of *maquila* garments. The CAFTA-DR agreement has been a boost for the *maquila* sector. According to the Cámara de la Industria Textil, Confección y Zonas Francas de El Salvador, *maquila* export revenues increased by 37% between 2005 and 2013, reaching US $2,394m.in the latter year, equivalent to 44% of total export earnings.

TRANSPORT AND TOURISM

There were some 6,545 km of roads in 2013, of which 3,600 km were paved; the road network is generally considered to be the best in Central America. The number of vehicles on the roads has almost doubled from 450,000 in 2001 to 795,000 in 2013. Improving the quality of existing roads through maintenance, rehabilitation and modernization was a major challenge for post-war El Salvador. Furthermore, the earthquakes of 2001 caused considerable damage to the road system. In 2002 the Government established a road maintenance fund (FOVIAL—Fondo de Conservacion Vial), financed by a tax on petrol, giving concessions to private companies to repair the roads.

The Comisión Ejecutiva Portuaria Autónoma (CEPA) is responsible for the administration of El Salvador's main ports, Acajutla and Cutuco, and the El Salvador International Airport at Comalapa, Cuscatlán. CEPA improved its financial situation in the 1990s, but faced the problem of recovering traffic lost during the civil war, as well as competing with other Central American ports, particularly Puerto Quetzal in Guatemala. In 2009 modernization of Cutuco port, renamed Puerto La Unión Centroamericana, on the Gulf of Fonseca was completed, with support from the Japanese Government. However, the operating concession was never successfully awarded and according to the CEPA, only 15 ships used the port facilities during the whole of 2013. As of mid-2014, the tender process remained open amid concerns about the cost of dredging access channels. The national railway system, which comprised some 555 km of track, stopped operating in 2005 owing to the high cost of maintenance. However, a limited passenger service was resumed in 2007, though the rehabilitation of further sections of track has not materialized as planned.

El Salvador's recent bloody history and high crime rate has stunted the growth of its tourism industry. Nevertheless, the country has much to offer, with Mayan temples and cities, volcanoes, mountain lakes and sandy beaches. President Saca prioritized the industry by creating a Ministry of Tourism when he took office in 2004. Tourist arrivals rose from 387,052 in 1997 to almost 1.4m. in 2008, and exceeded 1.8m. in 2013, according to official figures (although the World Tourism Organization put arrivals at 1.3m. in 2012). Approximately one-quarter of all visitors to El Salvador are Salvadoreans returning to visit families or their home towns. As a result of the expansion in the number of tourists, the foreign exchange generated by the tourism sector has increased steadily; in 2004 tourism became the second largest source of foreign exchange, after remittances. Earnings from the sector increased from US $75m. in 1997 to over $904m. in 2013, equivalent to 3% of GDP (figures from the World Tourism Organization were lower, at a provisional $613m., although this excluded passenger transport receipts). Nevertheless, the state tourism promotion agency, Corporación Salvadoreña de Turismo, still has a limited budget to promote El Salvador overseas, compared with Costa Rica, for example.

INVESTMENT AND FINANCE

In 2001 the public deficit rose to 3.6% of GDP as a result of post-earthquake reconstruction costs. However, the deficit narrowed in subsequent years—in 2007 the deficit was reduced to US $56m., equivalent to 0.6% of GDP—before rising again to reach 4.2% of GDP in 2013. Concerns about the long-term sustainability of the current pensions system and its impact on public finances remain at the fore.

In 2012 the Minister of Finance warned that, unless substantial reforms were undertaken, the state would be required to disburse over US $1,000m. per year by 2030. The country continues to depend on high levels of foreign aid and concessionary loans to finance much-needed infrastructural development. Public revenue rose from 12.5% of GDP in 2002 to an estimated 14.7% in 2008, following minor tax reform in 2006. The Government has increased incentives for foreign investment as part of its programme for economic reactivation and stabilization; however, high crime levels and a violent death rate, on a par with that experienced during the civil war, continue to deter foreign investors.

In the early 21st century the introduction of the US dollar as legal tender and the forging of closer links with Mexico contributed to an escalation of foreign direct investment (FDI), though external circumstances have caused significant fluctuations in FDI inflows in recent years. According to ECLAC, FDI totalled US $1,500m. in 2007, before declining dramatically, to just $72m., in 2010. The total recovered somewhat to reach $386m. in 2011 and $516m. in 2012. However, FDI dropped to a meagre $140m. in 2013, equivalent to just 1.4% of the total of $10,000m. in investment inflows to Central America that year.

The average annual rate of inflation was 3.7% in 2003–12. The rate increased to 5.5% in 2008, largely owing to rising oil and food prices. The rate declined to 0.9% in 2010, but rose once again to reach 5.0% in 2011, before decreasing to 1.7% in 2012 and to 0.7% in 2013. The relatively low inflation rate has been one of the key accomplishments of the dollarization process, particularly when compared with the situation in the 1980s (before dollarization), when accumulated inflation reached a staggering 468.5%.

FOREIGN TRADE AND PAYMENTS

The change in the Salvadorean economic model has been particularly reflected in the shift in the export structure. While in 1970 coffee and sugar constituted 91% of non-regional exports, they accounted for only an estimated 7.7% of total exports in 2013. Meanwhile, *maquilas*, tourism and, most importantly, remittances from abroad became the main generators of foreign exchange. The shift in the structure of exports coincided with an expansion of both exports and imports. Export receipts increased from US $4,490m. in

2010 to \$5,491m. in 2013, while the cost of imports rose at an even higher rate, from \$8,500m. in 2010 to \$10,772m. in 2013. The trade deficit increased by 7.4% between 2012 and 2013. The principal export partner is the USA, which in 2013 purchased 45% of El Salvador's exports and provided some 39% of its imports, according to the central bank.

The trade surplus that El Salvador had recorded during most of the 1970s gave way to a deficit from 1981, even though the declines in export revenues were accompanied by rigorous restrictions on 'non-essential' imports. After 1992 the deficit increased. Since the 1980s the deterioration in the trade balance has been offset by remittances from abroad and by capital inflows. As a result, international reserves steadily increased from a low of US \$72m. in 1981 to a total of \$2,745m. by December 2013.

Between 1990 and 2013 total external debt increased from US \$2,148m. to \$13,989m. (equivalent to 56.2% of GDP), as successive governments borrowed to finance reconstruction following earthquakes and to increase expenditure on selected social programmes. Almost all of this debt was incurred on a medium- to long-term basis at low interest rates, owing to El Salvador's high credit rating. El Salvador has been an active participant in recent processes of regional integration. In 2001 a free trade agreement (FTA) with Mexico, Guatemala and Honduras came into effect, which, it was hoped, would gradually open up markets for industrial and agricultural products over a 12-year period. In the same year the Central American countries, including El Salvador, reached the basis of a deal with Mexico, the Puebla–Panamá Plan (restyled the Proyecto de Integración y Desarrollo de Mesoamérica in 2008), to integrate the region through joint transport, industry and tourism projects. In March 2006 CAFTA-DR entered into force in El Salvador. El Salvador and Honduras also signed an FTA with Taiwan, a move that threatened to impede trade relations with the People's Republic of China. In addition, El Salvador was a leading proponent of the free trade Association Agreement between Central America and the EU. Negotiations on the agreement were concluded in May 2010 and a final accord was signed in June 2012. The agreement came into force in October 2013.

OUTLOOK

The economy of El Salvador was reasonably stable in 2014, although two decades of growth in which economic expansion averaged less than 2% annually points to structural problems that have yet to be addressed. The country had one of the most liberal economies in Latin America and had established strong links with the US economy. Despite all the reforms, many challenges remained. GDP per head grew slowly and was affected by repeated natural disasters. Poverty remained widespread and dollarization eroded some of the country's competitive advantages. High levels of poverty, exposure to agricultural price cycles, environmental damage, and increasing crime and violence were all issues that incoming President Salvador Sánchez Cerén would need to confront urgently in order to meet his pledge to achieve annual growth of 3%. External conditions helped El Salvador to expand its economy faster between 2006 and 2008 than at any time in the previous decade, but the financial crisis slowed this considerably, and exposed the country's vulnerability to high external food and energy prices. The recovery had yet to become established by 2014.

President Funes pledged to adopt a more progressive and redistributive policy approach in government. In the event, the Funes Government had little room for manoeuvre, owing to difficult external conditions. Funes can at least be credited with having steered El Salvador out of the worst of the financial crisis by 2012, even if he was able to deliver only marginal improvements in the country's economy during his mandate. Whether Sánchez Cerén can overcome entrenched political polarization to implement an economic agenda capable of tackling long-standing structural issues remains to be seen.

Statistical Survey

Sources (unless otherwise stated): Banco Central de Reserva de El Salvador, Alameda Juan Pablo II y 17 Avda Norte, Apdo 01-106, San Salvador; tel. 2281-8000; fax 2281-8011; internet www.bcr.gob.sv; Dirección General de Estadística y Censos, Edif. Centro de Gobierno, Alameda Juan Pablo II y Calle Guadalupe, San Salvador; tel. 2286-4260; fax 2286-2505; internet www.digestyc.gob.sv.

Area and Population

AREA, POPULATION AND DENSITY

Area (sq km)	
Land	20,721
Inland water	320
Total	21,041*
Population (census results)†	
27 September 1992	5,118,599
12 May 2007	
Males	2,719,371
Females	3,024,742
Total	5,744,113
Population (official estimates)	
2012	6,251,494
2013	6,288,899
2014	6,328,196
Density (per sq km) at 2014	300.8

* 8,124 sq miles.

† Excluding adjustments for underenumeration.

POPULATION BY AGE AND SEX
('000, official estimates at 2014)

	Males	Females	Total
0–14 years	933.5	893.7	1,827.2
15–64 years	1,822.5	2,191.7	4,014.2
65 years and over	211.4	275.4	486.7
Total	2,967.4	3,360.8	6,328.2

Note: Totals may not be equal to the sum of components, owing to rounding.

DEPARTMENTS

(official population estimates at 2014)

	Area (sq km)	Population ('000)	Density (per sq km)
Ahuachapán	1,239.6	337.3	272.1
Santa Ana	2,023.2	577.4	285.4
Sonsonate	1,225.8	464.9	379.2
Chalatenango	2,016.6	206.0	102.2
La Libertad	1,652.9	757.4	458.2
San Salvador	886.2	1,742.5	1,966.3
Cuscatlán	756.2	256.8	339.7
La Paz	1,223.6	330.5	270.1
Cabañas	1,103.5	165.9	150.3
San Vicente	1,184.0	175.7	148.4
Usulután	2,130.4	369.0	173.2
San Miguel	2,077.1	482.0	232.1
Morazán	1,447.4	201.0	138.9
La Unión	2,074.3	261.7	126.2
Total	21,040.8	6,328.2	300.8

PRINCIPAL TOWNS

(official population estimates at 2014)*

San Salvador (capital) . .	281,870	Santa Tecla† . .	135,483
Soyapango . .	275,868	Ciudad Delgado .	128,635
Santa Ana . .	265,518	Tonacatepeque . .	124,675
San Miguel . .	249,638	Ilopango . . .	124,522
Apopa . . .	165,897	Colón . . .	120,048
Mejicanos . .	146,915	Ahuachapán . .	118,164

* Figures refer to municipios, which may each contain rural areas as well as an urban centre.
† Formerly Nueva San Salvador.

BIRTHS, MARRIAGES AND DEATHS

	Registered live births		Registered marriages		Registered deaths	
	Number	Rate (per 1,000)	Number	Rate (per 1,000)	Number	Rate (per 1,000)
2002 . .	129,363	19.9	26,077	4.0	27,458	4.2
2003 . .	124,476	18.7	25,071	3.8	29,377	4.4
2004 . .	119,710	17.7	25,240	3.7	30,058	4.4
2005 . .	112,769	16.4	24,475	3.6	30,933	4.5
2006 . .	107,111	15.3	24,500	3.5	31,453	4.5
2007 . .	110,730	18.2	28,675	4.0	31,349	4.4
2008 . .	111,278	18.2	27,714	3.8	31,594	4.4
2009 . .	107,880	17.5	28,048	4.6	32,872	5.3

Crude birth rates (annual averages, official estimates): 21.9 per 1,000 in 2000–05; 20.4 per 1,000 in 2005–10.

Crude death rates (annual averages, official estimates): 6.8 per 1,000 in 2000–05; 6.9 per 1,000 in 2005–10.

Life expectancy (years at birth): 72.1 (males 67.5; females 76.9) in 2012 (Source: World Bank, World Development Indicators database).

ECONOMICALLY ACTIVE POPULATION

(sample household surveys, persons aged 16 years and over)

	2010	2011	2012
Agriculture, hunting and forestry .	482,195	514,272	518,563
Fishing	16,117	18,163	18,137
Mining and quarrying	1,368	1,068	1,716
Manufacturing	371,372	381,781	397,046
Electricity, gas and water . . .	11,067	13,720	10,921
Construction	129,038	127,875	129,918
Wholesale and retail trade; hotels and restaurants . . .	704,138	700,451	734,113
Transport, storage and communications	102,673	109,502	110,642
Financing, insurance, real estate and business services . .	128,078	136,920	137,588
Public administration, defence and social security	101,075	107,257	116,297
Education	77,056	76,269	81,379
Health and other community, social and personal services . . .	173,535	175,921	190,074
Private households with employed persons	100,062	102,510	112,688
Other services	704	666	233
Total employed	2,398,478	2,466,375	2,559,315
Unemployed	181,806	174,758	165,439
Total labour force	2,580,284	2,641,133	2,724,754
Males	1,514,123	1,568,675	1,607,819
Females	1,066,161	1,072,458	1,116,935

Health and Welfare

KEY INDICATORS

Total fertility rate (children per woman, 2012)	2.2
Under-5 mortality rate (per 1,000 live births, 2012) . . .	16
HIV/AIDS (% of persons aged 15–49, 2012)	0.6
Physicians (per 1,000 head, 2008)	1.6
Hospital beds (per 1,000 head, 2010)	1.0
Health expenditure (2011): US $ per head (PPP)	467
Health expenditure (2011): % of GDP	6.8
Health expenditure (2011): public (% of total)	63.6
Access to water (% of persons, 2012)	90
Access to sanitation (% of persons, 2012)	70
Total carbon dioxide emissions ('000 metric tons, 2010) . .	6,248.6
Carbon dioxide emissions per head (metric tons, 2010) . .	1.0
Human Development Index (2013): ranking	115
Human Development Index (2013): value	0.663

For sources and definitions, see explanatory note on p. vi.

Agriculture

PRINCIPAL CROPS

('000 metric tons)

	2010	2011	2012
Rice, paddy	34.5	25.6	28.3
Maize	768.1	756.4	925.8
Sorghum	106.5	142.0	136.6
Yautia (Cocoyam)*	40.4	43.0	43.0
Sugar cane	5,126.7	9,899.0	9,899.0*
Beans, dry	71.3	64.8	107.8
Coconuts	60.2†	60.3†	63.5*
Watermelons	49.3	52.0*	60.0
Bananas*	39.0	38.4	41.5
Plantains	20.0	11.7	36.8
Oranges	45.7	42.4	94.8
Coffee, green	112.6	82.1	89.5

* FAO estimate(s).
† Unofficial figure.

Aggregate production ('000 metric tons, may include official, semi-official or estimated data): Total cereals 909.1 in 2010, 923.9 in 2011, 1,090.7 in 2012; Total vegetables (incl. melons) 147.3 in 2010, 147.7 in 2011, 160.8 in 2012; Total fruits (excl. melons) 377.4 in 2010, 386.9 in 2011, 473.0 in 2012.

Source: FAO.

LIVESTOCK
('000 head, year ending September)

	2010	2011	2012
Horses*	96	96	98
Asses*	3	3	3
Mules*	24	24	24
Cattle	1,247	1,015	1,123
Pigs	427†	440†	445*
Sheep*	5	5	5
Goats*	15	15	15
Chickens	15,000†	15,500†	15,500*

* FAO estimate(s).
† Unofficial figure.
Source: FAO.

LIVESTOCK PRODUCTS
('000 metric tons)

	2010	2011	2012
Cattle meat	33.0	23.4	26.0
Pig meat	8.3	8.4	9.5
Chicken meat	104.5	108.5	109.5
Cows' milk	457.7	415.7	406.1
Hen eggs	64.7	59.7	62.3

Source: FAO.

Forestry

ROUNDWOOD REMOVALS
('000 cubic metres, excl. bark, estimates)

	2010	2011	2012
Sawlogs, veneer logs and logs for sleepers	682	682	682
Fuel wood	4,225	4,217	4,215
Total	4,907	4,899	4,897

Source: FAO.

SAWNWOOD PRODUCTION
('000 cubic metres, incl. railway sleepers, estimates)

	2002	2003	2004
Total (all broadleaved, hardwood)	68.0	68.0	16.3

2005–12: Figures assumed to be unchanged from 2004 (estimates).
Source: FAO.

Fishing

('000 metric tons, live weight)

	2010	2011	2012
Capture	39.0	54.3	52.0*
Skipjack tuna	14.3	22.2	20.8
Yellowfin tuna	3.7	9.9	9.4
Bigeye tuna	2.6	4.8	4.9
Other marine fishes	14.9	14.7	14.1
Pacific seabobs	0.9	0.3	0.3
Aquaculture*	4.5	4.9	5.3
Total catch*	43.5	59.2	57.3

* FAO estimate(s).
Source: FAO.

Mining

('000 metric tons unless otherwise indicated)

	2006	2007	2008
Gypsum*	5.5	5.5	5.5
Steel (crude)	72.0	73.0	71.0
Limestone*	1,200	1,200	1,200
Salt (marine)*	30.0	30.0	30.0

* Estimates.
2009–11: Limestone 1,200 (estimate).
Steel (crude): 56.0 in 2009 (estimate); 64.0 in 2010; 100.0 in 2011; 102.0 in 2012.
Source: US Geological Survey.

Industry

SELECTED PRODUCTS
('000 metric tons unless otherwise indicated)

	2008	2009	2010
Raw sugar	597	518	690
Motor gasoline (petrol)	111	105	100
Kerosene	2	2	2
Distillate fuel oil	186	197	132
Residual fuel oil	410	399	464
Liquefied petroleum gas (refined)	20	14	13
Cement	1,300	1,212	1,200
Electric energy (million kWh)	5,960	5,788	5,980

Cement ('000 metric tons): 1,200 in 2011–12.
Sources: US Geological Survey; UN Industrial Commodity Statistics Database.

Electric energy (million kWh): 5,722 in 2010; 5,812 in 2011; 5,946 in 2012.

Finance

CURRENCY AND EXCHANGE RATES
Monetary Units
    100 centavos = 1 Salvadorean colón.

Sterling, Dollar and Euro Equivalents (30 May 2014)
    £1 sterling = 14.719 colones;
    US $1 = 8.750 colones;
    €1 = 11.910 colones;
    100 Salvadorean colones = £6.79 = $11.43 = €8.40.

Note: The foregoing information refers to the principal exchange rate, applicable to official receipts and payments, imports of petroleum and exports of coffee. In addition, there is a market exchange rate, applicable to other transactions. The principal rate was maintained at 8.755 colones per US dollar from May 1995 to December 2000. However, in January 2001, with the introduction of legislation making the US dollar legal tender, the rate was adjusted to $1 = 8.750 colones; both currencies have circulated freely as parallel legal currencies since that date.

CENTRAL GOVERNMENT BUDGET
(US $ million)

Revenue*	2011	2012	2013
Current revenue	3,343.5	3,588.1	3,902.6
Tax revenue	3,193.3	3,433.8	3,746.3
Taxes on earnings	1,126.8	1,249.8	1,479.5
Import duties	167.3	179.6	199.2
Value-added tax	1,574.1	1,676.9	1,730.7
Non-tax revenue	150.2	154.3	156.3
Public enterprise transfers	3.3	7.7	9.8
Financial public enterprise transfers	43.0	44.9	35.6
Capital revenue	0.2	0.2	—
Total	3,343.6	3,588.3	3,902.6

Expenditure†	2011	2012	2013
Current expenditure	3,369.9	3,373.3	3,654.6
Remunerations	1,278.7	1,329.3	1,386.4
Goods and services	540.7	502.2	629.9
Interest payments	507.9	526.4	582.7
Transfers	1,042.7	1,015.4	1,055.6
To other government bodies .	513.8	526.5	607.4
To the private sector . . .	515.9	481.2	431.5
Capital expenditure	718.4	787.8	730.8
Gross investment	364.8	450.6	357.1
Total	**4,088.3**	**4,161.1**	**4,385.5**

* Excluding grants received (US $ million): 213.9 in 2011; 170.0 in 2012; 57.1 in 2013.

† Excluding lending minus repayments (US $ million): –6.6 in 2011; 3.9 in 2012; 10.2 in 2013.

INTERNATIONAL RESERVES
(US $ million at 31 December)

	2011	2012	2013
Gold (national valuation) . .	351.3	369.8	268.7
IMF special drawing rights . .	251.5	252.5	255.0
Foreign exchange	1,901.4	2,553.9	2,221.2
Total	**2,504.2**	**3,176.2**	**2,744.9**

Source: IMF, *International Financial Statistics*.

MONEY SUPPLY
(US $ million at 31 December)

	2011	2012	2013
Currency outside depository corporations	4.5	4.2	4.0
Transferable deposits	2,556.7	2,792.2	2,887.9
Other deposits	6,651.8	7,050.8	7,264.5
Securities other than shares . .	852.8	793.5	715.4
Broad money	**10,065.8**	**10,640.7**	**10,871.9**

Source: IMF, *International Financial Statistics*.

COST OF LIVING
(Consumer Price Index; base: December 2009 = 100)

	2011	2012	2013
Food and non-alcoholic beverages .	111.6	112.0	114.6
Clothing and footwear	101.7	102.8	102.7
Rent, water, electricity, gas and other fuels	112.3	116.5	116.6
All items (incl. others) . . .	**106.3**	**108.1**	**108.9**

NATIONAL ACCOUNTS
(US $ million at current prices, preliminary)

Expenditure on the Gross Domestic Product

	2011	2012	2013
Final consumption expenditure .	24,139.0	24,864.8	25,305.8
Households	21,580.8	22,190.9	22,406.8
General government	2,558.2	2,673.9	2,899.0
Gross capital formation . . .	3,323.2	3,367.8	3,663.9
Total domestic expenditure .	**27,462.2**	**28,232.6**	**28,969.7**
Exports of goods and services .	6,474.3	6,093.8	6,093.8
Less Imports of goods and services	10,797.4	10,512.7	11,113.2
Statistical discrepancy . . .	—	—	308.8
GDP in purchasers' values .	**23,139.0**	**23,813.6**	**24,259.1**
GDP at constant 1990 prices .	**9,277.2**	**9,451.7**	**9,610.1**

Gross Domestic Product by Economic Activity

	2011	2012	2013
Agriculture, hunting, forestry and fishing . .	2,651.4	2,597.4	2,402.6
Mining and quarrying . . .	65.9	} 4,466.1	4,539.2
Manufacturing	4,291.6		
Construction	898.4	925.1	940.9
Electricity, gas and water . .	479.1	518.9	534.8
Transport, storage and communications	1,814.8	1,871.7	1,925.1
Wholesale and retail trade, restaurants and hotels . .	4,610.9	4,818.4	4,964.9
Finance and insurance . .	1,054.1	1,042.7	1,090.6
Real estate and business services	1,022.6	1,068.1	1,106.2
Owner-occupied dwellings . .	1,500.4	1,524.3	1,542.2
Community, social, domestic and personal services	1,817.9	1,888.2	1,961.0
Government services	1,851.6	1,939.6	2,061.8
Sub-total	**22,058.7**	**22,660.4**	**23,069.3**
Import duties and value-added tax	1,950.7	2,030.7	2,102.5
Less Imputed bank service charge	870.3	877.8	912.7
GDP in purchasers' values .	**23,139.0**	**23,813.6**	**24,259.1**

BALANCE OF PAYMENTS
(US $ million)

	2010	2011	2012
Exports of goods	3,473.2	4,242.6	4,235.6
Imports of goods	–7,495.4	–9,014.8	–9,175.0
Balance on goods	**–4,022.2**	**–4,772.2**	**–4,939.4**
Exports of services	1,498.0	1,636.0	1,849.5
Imports of services	–1,099.7	–1,186.9	–1,239.3
Balance on goods and services	**–3,623.9**	**–4,323.1**	**–4,329.2**
Primary income received . . .	63.4	67.8	57.1
Primary income paid	–607.9	–722.5	–989.2
Balance on goods, services and primary income . . .	**–4,168.4**	**–4,977.8**	**–5,261.4**
Secondary income received . .	3,670.1	3,919.2	4,104.5
Secondary income paid . . .	–71.6	–78.2	–100.6
Current balance	**–569.7**	**–1,136.8**	**–1,257.4**
Capital account (net)	232.0	266.4	201.4
Direct investment assets . . .	–145.2	113.8	49.0
Direct investment liabilities . .	247.7	306.2	466.8
Portfolio investment assets . .	–118.2	99.4	47.0
Portfolio investment liabilities .	–3.2	1.0	836.3
Other investment assets . . .	109.1	–111.9	–112.4
Other investment liabilities . .	–266.5	284.5	604.5
Net errors and omissions . . .	217.6	–238.2	–185.1
Reserves and related items .	**–296.5**	**–415.6**	**650.1**

Source: IMF, *International Financial Statistics*.

External Trade

PRINCIPAL COMMODITIES
(US $ million, preliminary)

Imports c.i.f.*	2011	2012	2013
Live animals and animal products; vegetables, crops and related products, primary	812.2	774.1	729.0
Food, beverages (incl. alcoholic) and tobacco manufactures	682.9	714.2	756.4
Mineral products	1,769.8	1,977.9	2,058.8
Crude petroleum oils	565.7	409.4	—
Light oils (gasoline, etc.) . . .	319.4	405.9	548.2
Heavy oils (gas oil, diesel oil, fuel oil, etc.)	506.2	748.8	1,004.7

Imports c.i.f.*—continued	2011	2012	2013
Chemicals and related products	1,130.5	1,164.8	1,150.5
Therapeutic and preventative medicines	325.1	306.0	267.5
Plastics, artificial resins, rubbers, and articles thereof	661.7	663.3	703.1
Plastics, artificial resins, and articles thereof	566.9	564.3	603.2
Wood pulp, paper, paperboard and articles thereof	388.8	397.0	414.7
Textile materials and articles thereof	1,037.9	1,000.0	1,088.3
Base metals and manufactures thereof	586.0	568.4	611.8
Cast iron and steel	290.6	282.4	307.2
Mechanical and electrical machinery and apparatus	1,218.3	1,213.4	1,331.2
Mechanical machinery and apparatus	638.5	612.2	676.4
Electrical machinery and appliances	579.8	601.2	654.8
Radio and television transmitters and receivers, and parts thereof	226.0	244.1	254.9
Transport equipment	311.6	342.8	408.5
Total (incl. others)	9,327.7	9,552.4	7,573.7

* Excluding imports into *maquila* zones (US $ million, preliminary): 636.8 in 2011; 717.2 in 2012; 564.3 in 2013.

Exports f.o.b.*	2011	2012	2013
Vegetables, crops and related products, primary	580.8	419.7	350.6
Coffee, including roasted and decaffeinated	464.0	300.0	233.9
Food, beverages (incl. alcoholic) and tobacco manufactures	666.3	755.4	802.9
Unrefined sugar	132.6	166.7	190.1
Mineral products	184.9	194.5	139.5
Chemical products	240.4	245.9	252.0
Therapeutic and preventative medicines	104.6	107.1	109.5
Plastics, rubber, and articles thereof	276.5	302.8	316.4
Boxes, bags, bottles, stoppers and other plastic containers	149.2	165.6	169.7
Wood pulp, paper, paperboard and articles thereof	284.2	286.1	297.0
Textile materials and articles thereof	1,287.0	1,350.9	1,482.9
Clothing, inner wear	642.9	694.6	691.0
Clothing, outer wear	362.8	388.9	488.4
Base metals and manufactures thereof	294.9	282.1	290.4
Other iron and steel products	126.7	132.4	130.0
Miscellaneous manufactured articles	124.1	132.0	139.1
Total (incl. others)	4,239.6	4,233.1	4,332.9

* Excluding exports from *maquila* zones (US $ million, preliminary): 1,068.6 in 2011; 1,106.0 in 2012; 1,158.2 in 2013.

PRINCIPAL TRADING PARTNERS
(US $ million, preliminary)

Imports c.i.f.*	2011	2012	2013
Brazil	167.9	218.4	157.3
China, People's Republic	552.2	603.5	703.0
Colombia	182.7	328.9	170.3
Costa Rica	293.2	296.2	282.9
Ecuador	255.8	187.5	76.4
Germany	138.6	151.4	167.8
Guatemala	989.6	997.6	935.4
Honduras	467.3	463.7	560.5
Japan	210.0	172.9	178.0
Korea, Republic	121.4	149.1	202.5
Mexico	740.4	694.6	746.0
Netherlands Antilles	55.2	100.8	198.6
Nicaragua	195.7	209.8	202.8
Panama	203.0	179.4	159.3
Taiwan	139.8	157.4	168.8
USA	3,799.9	3,873.7	4,186.3
Venezuela	232.7	211.6	286.8
Total (incl. others)	9,964.5	10,258.1	10,772.0

* Including imports into *maquila* zones (mostly from USA) (US $ million, preliminary): 636.8 in 2011; 717.2 in 2012; 564.3 in 2013.

Exports f.o.b.*	2011	2012	2013
Canada	70.8	54.4	76.7
Costa Rica	213.6	230.5	229.2
Dominican Republic	68.3	80.0	74.8
Germany	140.3	69.8	57.8
Guatemala	736.3	714.7	721.8
Honduras	698.1	761.0	793.3
Mexico	86.1	83.4	81.9
Nicaragua	294.8	320.2	323.8
Panama	108.7	124.6	121.7
Spain	76.0	79.9	79.3
USA	2,425.4	2,469.9	2,490.3
Total (incl. others)	5,308.2	5,339.1	5,491.1

* Including exports from *maquila* zones (mostly to USA) (US $ million, preliminary): 1,068.6 in 2011; 1,106.0 in 2012; 1,158.2 in 2013.

Transport

RAILWAYS
(traffic)

	1999	2000
Number of passengers ('000)	543.3	687.3
Passenger-km (million)	8.4	10.7
Freight ('000 metric tons)	188.6	136.2
Freight ton-km (million)	19.4	13.1

Source: Ferrocarriles Nacionales de El Salvador.

ROAD TRAFFIC
(motor vehicles in use at 31 December)

	2007	2009*	2010
Passenger cars	283,787	302,802	305,856
Buses and coaches	6,306	10,148	26,445
Lorries and vans	n.a.	17,789	n.a.
Motorcycles and mopeds	44,145	51,835	53,637

* Data for 2008 were not available.

Source: IRF, *International Road Statistics*.

SHIPPING

Flag Registered Fleet
(at 31 December)

	2011	2012	2013
Number of vessels	5	6	6
Total displacement ('000 grt) . .	9.5	9.6	9.6

Source: Lloyd's List Intelligence (www.lloydslistintelligence.com).

CIVIL AVIATION

(traffic on scheduled services)

	2010	2011
Kilometres flown (million)	38	45
Passengers carried ('000)	2,137	2,530
Passenger-km (million)	3,593	4,222
Total ton-km (million)	319	378

Source: UN, *Statistical Yearbook*.

Passengers carried ('000): 1,414.3 (arrivals 702.6, departures 711.7) in 2010; 1,396.7 (arrivals 665.0, departures 731.6) in 2011; 1,461.9 (arrivals 701.1, departures 760.8) in 2012.

Tourism

TOURIST ARRIVALS BY NATIONALITY
(arrivals of non-resident tourists at national borders)

	2010	2011	2012
Canada	20,432	28,205	30,216
Costa Rica	18,443	20,300	20,306
Guatemala	518,957	535,246	537,612
Honduras	145,868	126,446	136,451
Mexico	17,607	19,699	15,950
Nicaragua	43,488	40,756	32,566
Panama	10,579	10,733	11,479
USA	318,569	320,736	396,909
Total (incl. others)	1,149,562	1,184,497	1,254,724

Receipts from tourism (US $ million, excl. passenger transport): 415 in 2011; 558 in 2012; 621 in 2013 (provisional).

Source: World Tourism Organization.

Communications Media

	2011	2012	2013
Telephones ('000 main lines in use)	1,029.7	1,059.0	949.7
Mobile cellular telephones ('000 subscribers)	8,316.2	8,649.0	8,634.9
Broadband subscribers ('000) . .	206.0	242.1	282.3

Internet subscribers ('000): 150.5 in 2009.

Source: International Telecommunication Union.

Education

(2011/12 unless otherwise indicated)

		Students		
	Teachers	Males	Females	Total
Pre-primary . . .	9,318*	113,089	110,316	223,405
Primary	30,755*	448,390	410,474	858,864
Secondary . . .	24,556*	309,893	301,622	611,515
Tertiary	9,567	79,376	90,484	169,860

* 2010/2011.

Institutions (2001/02): Pre-primary 4,838; Primary 5,414; Secondary 757; Tertiary 43.

Sources: Ministry of Education and UNESCO Institute for Statistics.

Pupil-teacher ratio (primary education, UNESCO estimate): 29.3 in 2010/11 (Source: UNESCO Institute for Statistics).

Adult literacy rate (UNESCO estimates): 85.5% (males 88.4%; females 83.0%) in 2011 (Source: UNESCO Institute for Statistics).

Directory

The Constitution

The Constitution of the Republic of El Salvador came into effect on 20 December 1983. It has been amended from time to time.

The Constitution provides for a republican, democratic and representative form of government, composed of three powers—legislative, executive, and judicial—which are to operate independently. Voting is a right and duty of all citizens over 18 years of age. Presidential and congressional elections may not be held simultaneously.

The Constitution binds the country, as part of the Central American Nation, to favour the total or partial reconstruction of the Republic of Central America. Integration in a unitary, federal or confederal form, provided that democratic and republican principles are respected and that basic rights of individuals are fully guaranteed, is subject to popular approval.

LEGISLATIVE ASSEMBLY

Legislative power is vested in a single chamber, the Asamblea Legislativa (Legislative Assembly), whose members are elected every three years and are eligible for re-election. The Assembly's term of office begins on 1 May. The Assembly's duties include the choosing of the President and Vice-President of the Republic from the two citizens who shall have gained the largest number of votes for each of these offices, if no candidate obtains an absolute majority in the election. It also selects the members of the Supreme and subsidiary courts; of the Elections Council; and the Accounts Court of the Republic. It deter-

mines taxes; ratifies treaties concluded by the Executive with other states and international organizations; sanctions the Budget; regulates the monetary system of the country; determines the conditions under which foreign currencies may circulate; and suspends and reimposes constitutional guarantees. The right to initiate legislation may be exercised by the Assembly (as well as by the President, through the Cabinet, and by the Supreme Court). The Assembly may override, with a two-thirds' majority, the President's objections to a bill that it has sent for presidential approval.

PRESIDENT

The President is elected for five years, the term beginning and expiring on 1 June. The principle of alternation in the presidential office is established in the Constitution, which states the action to be taken should this principle be violated. The Executive is responsible for the preparation of the Budget and its presentation to the Legislative Assembly; the direction of foreign affairs; the organization of the armed and security forces; and the convening of extraordinary sessions of the Assembly. In the event of the President's death, resignation, removal or other cause, the Vice-President takes office for the rest of the presidential term and, in case of necessity, the Vice-President may be replaced by one of the two Designates elected by the Assembly.

JUDICIARY

Judicial power is exercised by the Supreme Court and by other competent tribunals. The magistrates of the Supreme Court are elected by the Legislature, their number to be determined by law. The Supreme Court alone is competent to decide whether laws, decrees and regulations are constitutional or not.

The Government

HEAD OF STATE

President: SALVADOR SÁNCHEZ CERÉN (assumed office 1 June 2014).
Vice-President: OSCAR SAMUEL ORTIZ.

CABINET
(September 2014)

The Government is formed by the Frente Farabundo Martí para la Liberación Nacional.

Minister of Finance: JUAN RAMÓN CARLOS ENRIQUE CÁCERES CHÁVEZ.

Minister of Foreign Affairs: HUGO MARTÍNEZ BONILLA.

Minister of Internal Affairs: RAMÓN ARÍSTIDES VALENCIA.

Minister of Justice and Public Security: BENITO ANTONIO LARA.

Minister of the Economy: THARSIS SALOMÓN LÓPEZ.

Minister of Education: CARLOS MAURICIO CANJURA LINARES.

Minister of National Defence: Gen. (retd) DAVID VICTORIANO MUNGUÍA PAYÉS.

Minister of Labour and Social Security: SANDRA EDIBEL GUEVARA PÉREZ.

Minister of Public Health: ELVIA VIOLETA MENJÍVAR.

Minister of Agriculture and Livestock: ORESTES ORTEZ ANDRADE.

Minister of Public Works, Transport, Housing and Urban Development: GERSON MARTÍNEZ.

Minister of the Environment and Natural Resources: LINA DOLORES POHL ALFARO.

Minister of Tourism: JOSÉ NAPOLEÓN DUARTE DURÁN.

MINISTRIES

Office of the President: Alameda Dr Manuel Enrique Araujo 5500, San Salvador; tel. 2248-9000; fax 2248-9370; internet www .presidencia.gob.sv.

Ministry of Agriculture and Livestock: Final 1, Avda Norte, 13 Calle Poniente y Avda Manuel Gallardo, Santa Tecla; tel. 2210-1700; fax 2229-9271; e-mail info@mag.gob.sv; internet www.mag.gob.sv.

Ministry of the Economy: Edif. C1–C2, Centro de Gobierno, Alameda Juan Pablo II y Calle Guadalupe, San Salvador; tel. 2231-5600; fax 2221-5446; e-mail comunicaciones@minec.gob.sv; internet www.minec.gob.sv.

Ministry of Education: Edif. A, Centro de Gobierno, Alameda Juan Pablo II y Calle Guadalupe, San Salvador; tel. 2592-2122; fax 2281-0077; e-mail educacion@mined.gob.sv; internet www.mined.gob.sv.

Ministry of the Environment and Natural Resources: Edif. MARN 2, Calle y Col. Las Mercedes, Carretera a Santa Tecla, Km 5.5, San Salvador; tel. 2132-6276; fax 2132-9420; e-mail medioambiente@ marn.gob.sv; internet www.marn.gob.sv.

Ministry of Finance: Blvd Los Héroes 1231, San Salvador; tel. 2244-3000; fax 2244-6408; e-mail info@mh.gob.sv; internet www.mh .gob.sv.

Ministry of Foreign Affairs: Calle El Pedregal, Blvd Cancillería, Ciudad Merliot, Antiguo Cuscatlán; tel. 2231-1000; fax 2289-8016; e-mail webmaster@rree.gob.sv; internet www.rree.gob.sv.

Ministry of Internal Affairs: Centro de Gobierno, Calle Oriente 9 y Avda Norte 15, San Salvador; tel. 2527-7000; fax 2527-7972; e-mail oirmigob@gobernacion.gob.sv; internet www.gobernacion.gob.sv.

Ministry of Justice and Public Security: Complejo Plan Maestro, Edifs B1, B2 y B3, Alameda Juan Pablo II y 17 Avda Norte, San Salvador; tel. 2526-3000; fax 2526-3105; e-mail webmaster@ seguridad.gob.sv; internet www.seguridad.gob.sv.

Ministry of Labour and Social Security: Edifs 2 y 3, Alameda Juan Pablo II y 17 Avda Norte, San Salvador; tel. 2209-3700; fax 2209-3756; e-mail asesorialaboral@mtps.gob.sv; internet www.mtps .gob.sv.

Ministry of National Defence: Alameda Dr Manuel E. Araújo, Km 5, Carretera a Santa Tecla, San Salvador; tel. 2250-0100; e-mail oirmdn@faes.gob.sv; internet www.fuerzaarmada.gob.sv/index .html.

Ministry of Public Health: Calle Arce 827, San Salvador; tel. 2205-7000; fax 2221-0991; e-mail atencion@salud.gob.sv; internet www .salud.gob.sv.

Ministry of Public Works, Transport, Housing and Urban Development: Plantel la Lechuza, Carretera a Santa Tecla Km 5.5,

San Salvador; tel. 2528-3000; fax 2279-3723; e-mail info@mop.gob .sv; internet www.mop.gob.sv.

Ministry of Tourism: Edif. Carbonel 1, Alameda Dr Manuel Enrique Araujo y Pasaje Carbonel, Col. Roma, San Salvador; tel. 2243-7835; fax 2223-6120; e-mail info@mitur.gob.sv; internet www .mitur.gob.sv.

President and Legislature

PRESIDENT

Election, First Round, 2 February 2014

Candidates	Votes	% of votes
Salvador Sánchez Cerén (FMLN) . . .	1,315,768	48.93
Norman Quijano (ARENA)	1,047,592	38.96
Elías Antonio Saca González (Unidad)* .	307,603	11.44
René Rodríguez Hurtado (PSP) . . .	11,314	0.42
Oscar Lemus (FPS)	6,659	0.25
Total valid votes	2,688,936	100.00

* A coalition comprising the Gran Alianza por la Unidad Nacional, the Concertación Nacional and the Partido de la Esperanza.

Election, Second Round, 9 March 2014

Candidates	Votes	% of votes
Salvador Sánchez Cerén (FMLN) . . .	1,495,815	50.11
Norman Quijano (ARENA)	1,489,451	49.89
Total valid votes	2,985,266	100.00

LEGISLATIVE ASSEMBLY

President: OTHON SIGFRIDO REYES MORALES (FMLN).
General Election, 11 March 2012

Party	Valid votes cast	% of valid votes	Seats
Alianza Republicana Nacionalista (ARENA)	892,688	39.84	33
Frente Farabundo Martí para la Liberación Nacional (FMLN) .	824,686	36.80	31
Gran Alianza por la Unidad Nacional (GANA)	214,498	9.57	11
Concertación Nacional (CN) . .	162,083	7.23	6
Partido de la Esperanza (PES) .	60,641	2.71	1
Cambio Democrático (CD) . .	47,797	2.13	1
Coalición CN-PES*	17,580	0.78	1
Others	20,945	0.93	—
Total	2,240,918	100.00	84

* The Concertación Nacional (CN) and the Partido de la Esperanza (PES) formed a coalition in Chalatenango department.

Election Commission

Tribunal Supremo Electoral (TSE): 15 Calle Poniente 4223, Col. Escalón, San Salvador; tel. 2209-4000; fax 2263-4678; e-mail info@ tse.gob.sv; internet www.tse.gob.sv; f. 1992; Pres. JULIO OLIVO GRANADINO.

Political Organizations

Alianza Republicana Nacionalista (ARENA): Prolongación Calle Arce 2426, Col. Flor Banca, San Salvador; tel. 2260-4400; fax 2260-6260; e-mail infoparena@gmail.com; internet www.arena.com .sv; f. 1981; right-wing; Pres. JORGE VELADO; Exec. Dir ORLANDO CABRERA CANDRAY.

Cambio Democrático (CD): Casa 197, Calle Héctor Silva, Col. Médica, San Salvador; tel. 2225-5978; fax 2281-9636; e-mail comunicaciones@cambiodemocraticosv.org; internet www .cambiodemocraticosv.org; f. 1987 as Convergencia Democrática (CD); changed name as above in 2005; Sec.-Gen. DOUGLAS AVILÉS; Dep. Sec. JUAN JOSÉ MARTEL.

Fraternidad Patriota Salvadoreña (FPS): 13 Avda Norte, G29, Col. Santa Monica, Santa Tecla; tel. 2288-4211; e-mail fraternidadpatriota@hotmail.com; Pres. OSCAR LEMUS.

Frente Democrático Revolucionario (FDR): Avda Sierra Nevada 926, Col. Miramonte, San Salvador; tel. 2237-8844; fax 2260-1547; e-mail info@fdr.org.sv; internet www.fdr.org.sv; f. 2005; left-wing, reformist; breakaway faction of FMLN; Co-ordinator-Gen. JULIO HERNÁNDEZ.

Frente Farabundo Martí para la Liberación Nacional (FMLN): 27 Calle Poniente, Col. Layco 1316, San Salvador; tel. 2226-7183; e-mail comision.politica@fmln.org.sv; internet www .fmln.org.sv; f. 1980 as the FDR (Frente Democrático Revolucionario—FMLN) as a left-wing opposition front to the Govt; the FDR was the political wing and the FMLN was the guerrilla front; achieved legal recognition 1992; comprised various factions, including Communist (Leader SALVADOR SÁNCHEZ CERÉN), Renewalist (Leader OSCAR ORTIZ) and Terceristas (Leader GERSON MARTÍNEZ); Co-ordinator-Gen. MEDARDO GONZÁLEZ.

Partido Salvadoreño Progresista (PSP): Col. San Benito, Calle 2, Casa 280, entre Calle La Reforma y Avda Loma Linda, San Salvador; tel. 2223-3191; e-mail psppartidopolitico@gmail.com; internet www.psp.org.sv; Pres. RENÉ RODRÍGUEZ HURTADO.

Unidad: Calle Poniente entre 43 y 45, 6°, Avda Sur, Casa 2326, Col. Flor Blanca, San Salvador; tel. 2298-9638; e-mail info@unidad.org .sv; internet www.unidad.org.sv; f. 2013; electoral coalition; Leader ELÍAS ANTONIO (TONY) SACA GONZÁLEZ; comprises the following parties.

Concertación Nacional (CN): 15 Avda Norte y 3a Calle Poniente 244, San Salvador; tel. 2221-3752; fax 2281-9272; f. 2011 as successor party to the Partido de Conciliación Nacional (f. 1961); right-wing; Sec.-Gen. MANUEL RODRÍGUEZ.

Gran Alianza por la Unidad Nacional (GANA): 41 Avda Sur y 16 Calle Poniente 2143, Col. Flor Blanca, San Salvador; tel. 2279-0254; internet www.gana.org.sv; f. 2009 by fmr mems of ARENA (q.v.); Pres. JOSÉ ANDRÉS ROVIRA CANALES.

Partido de la Esperanza (PES): Centro de Gobierno, Alameda Juan Pablo II y 11 Avda Norte bis 507, San Salvador; tel. 2281-5498; fax 7998-1526; e-mail pdcsal@navegante.com.sv; f. 2011; successor to the disbanded Partido Demócrata Cristiano (f. 1960); 150,000 mems; advocates self-determination and Latin American integration; Sec.-Gen. RODOLFO ANTONIO PARKER SOTO.

Diplomatic Representation

EMBASSIES IN EL SALVADOR

Argentina: Calle La Sierra 3-I-B, Col. Escalón, San Salvador; tel. 2521-9400; fax 2521-9410; e-mail esalv@mrecic.gov.ar; Ambassador BETINA ALEJANDRA PASQUALI DE FONSECA.

Belize: Calle y Col. La Mascota, Residencial La Mascota 456, San Salvador; tel. and fax 2264-8024; e-mail embsalbel@yahoo.com; Ambassador CELIE PAZ MARIN.

Brazil: Blvd Sérgio Vieira de Mello 132, Col. San Benito, San Salvador; tel. 2298-3286; fax 2279-3934; e-mail embajada@brasil .org.sv; internet www.brasil.org.sv; Ambassador JOSÉ FIUZA NETO.

Canada: Centro Financiero Gigante, Torre A, Lobby 2, Alameda Roosevelt y 63 Avda Sur, Col. Escalón, San Salvador; tel. 2279-4655; fax 2279-0765; e-mail ssal@international.gc.ca; internet www .canadainternational.gc.ca/el_salvador-salvador; Ambassador PIERRE GIROUX.

Chile: Paseo Gen. Escalón 5355, Contiguo a Club Campestre, Col. Escalón, San Salvador; tel. 2263-4285; fax 2263-4308; e-mail embajadadechile@amnetsal.com; internet chileabroad.gov.cl/ el-salvador; Ambassador JOSÉ RENATO SEPÚLVEDA NEBEL.

Colombia: Calle El Mirador 5120, Col. Escalón, San Salvador; tel. 2263-1936; fax 2263-1942; e-mail elsalvador@minrelext.gov.co; internet elsalvador.embajada.gov.co; Ambassador JULIO ANÍBAL RIAÑO VELANDIA.

Costa Rica: 5453 Calle Arturo Ambrogi, Col. Escalón, San Salvador; tel. 2264-3863; fax 2264-3866; e-mail embajada@embajadacostarica .org.sv; internet www.embajadacostarica.org.sv; Ambassador ADRIANA PRADO CASTRO.

Cuba: Calle Arturo Ambrogui 530, esq. Avda el Mirador, Col. Escalón, San Salvador; tel. 2508-0446; fax 2508-0455; e-mail embajada@sv.embacuba.cu; internet www.cubadiplomatica.cu/ elsalvador; Ambassador ILIANA TERESA FONSECA LORENTE.

Dominican Republic: Edif. Colinas, 1°, Blvd El Hipódromo 253, Zona Rosa, Col. San Benito, San Salvador; tel. 2223-4036; fax 2223-3109; e-mail endosal@saltel.net; Ambassador VÍCTOR SÁNCHEZ PEÑA.

Ecuador: Pasaje Los Pinos 241, entre 77 y 79 Avda Norte, Col. Escalón, San Salvador; tel. 2263-5258; fax 2264-2973; e-mail ecuador@integra.com.sv; Ambassador SEGUNDO ANDRANGO.

France: 1a Calle Poniente 3718, Col. Escalón, Apdo 474, San Salvador; tel. 2521-9090; fax 2521-9092; e-mail info@

ambafrance-sv.org; internet www.ambafrance-sv.org; Ambassador PHILIPPE VINOGRADOFF.

Germany: 7a Calle Poniente 3972, esq. 77a Avda Norte, Col. Escalón, Apdo 693, San Salvador; tel. 2247-0000; fax 2247-0099; e-mail info@san-salvador.diplo.de; internet www.san-salvador.diplo .de; Ambassador HEINRICH HAUPT.

Guatemala: 15 Avda Norte 135, entre Calle Arce y 1a Calle Poniente, San Salvador; tel. 2271-2225; fax 2221-3019; e-mail embelsalvador@minex.gob.gt; Ambassador LUIS ROLANDO TORRES CASANOVA.

Holy See: 87 Avda Norte y 7a Calle Poniente, Col. Escalón, Apdo 01-95, San Salvador (Apostolic Nunciature); tel. 2263-2931; fax 2263-3010; e-mail nunels@integra.net; Apostolic Nuncio Most Rev. LUIGI PEZZUTO (Titular Archbishop of Torre di Proconsolare).

Honduras: 89 Avda Norte 561, entre 7a y 9a Calle Poniente, Col. Escalón, San Salvador; tel. 2263-2808; fax 2263-2296; e-mail embhon@integra.com.sv; internet www.sre.hn/elsalvador.html; Ambassador CÉSAR PINTO.

Israel: Centro Financiero Gigante, Torre B, 11°, Alameda Roosevelt y Avda Sur 63, San Salvador; tel. 2211-3434; fax 2211-3443; e-mail info@sansalvador.mfa.gov.il; internet sansalvador.mfa.gov.il; Ambassador SHMULIK ARIE BASS.

Italy: Calle la Reforma 158, Col. San Benito, Apdo 0199, San Salvador; tel. 2223-5184; fax 2298-3050; e-mail ambasciatore .sansalvador@esteri.it; internet www.ambsansalvador.esteri.it; Ambassador TOSCA BARUCCO.

Japan: World Trade Center, Torre 1, 6°, 89 Avda Norte y Calle El Mirador, Col. Escalón, Apdo 115, San Salvador; tel. 2528-1111; fax 2528-1110; internet www.sv.emb-japan.go.jp; Ambassador MASATAKA TARAHARA.

Korea, Republic: Edif. Torre Futura, 14°, Calle El Mirador y 87 Avda Norte, Local 5, Col. Escalón, San Salvador; tel. 2263-9145; fax 2263-0783; e-mail embcorea@mofat.go.kr; internet slv.mofat.go.kr; Ambassador MAENG DAL-YOUNG.

Mexico: Calle Circunvalación y Pasaje 12, Col. San Benito, Apdo 432, San Salvador; tel. 2248-9900; fax 2248-9906; e-mail embamex@ intercom.com.sv; internet portal.sre.gob.mx/elsalvador; Ambassador RAÚL LÓPEZ LIRA NAVA.

Nicaragua: 7 Calle Poniente Bis, No 5135, Col. Escalón, San Salvador; tel. 2263-8770; fax 2263-8849; e-mail embanicsv@ cancilleria.gob.ni; Ambassador GILDA MARÍA BOLT GONZÁLEZ.

Panama: Calle los Bambúes, Avda las Bugambilías 21, Col. San Francisco, San Salvador; tel. 2536-0601; fax 2536-0602; e-mail embpan@telesat.net; Ambassador ENRIQUE BERMÚDEZ MARTINELLI.

Peru: Avda Masferrer Norte 17P, Cumbres de la Escalafón, Col. Escalón, San Salvador; tel. 2523-9400; fax 2523-9401; e-mail embperu@telesal.net; internet www.embajadaperu.com.sv; Ambassador ERIC EDGARDO ANDERSON.

Qatar: Avda Boquerón, Lote 21, Poligono L, Urb. Cumbre de la Escalón, San Salvador; tel. 2562-1480; fax 2562-1883; e-mail eqatar .salvador@gmail.com; Ambassador ABDULRAHMAN MOHAMED HAMDAN AL-DOUSSARI.

Spain: Calle La Reforma 164 bis, Col. San Benito, San Salvador; tel. 2257-5700; fax 2257-5712; e-mail emb.sansalvador@maec.es; internet www.maec.es/embajadas/sansalvador; Ambassador FRANCISCO RABENA BARRACHINA.

Taiwan (Republic of China): Avda La Capilla 716, Blvd. del Hipódromo, Col. San Benito, Apdo 956, San Salvador; tel. 2263-1330; fax 2263-1329; e-mail sinoemb3@gmail.com; internet www .taiwanembassy.org/sv; Ambassador ANDREA SUNG YING LEE.

United Kingdom: Torre Futura, 14°, Plaza Futura, Calle El Mirador, Col. Escalón, San Salvador; tel. 2511-5757; e-mail britishembassy.elsalvador@fco.gov.uk; internet ukinelsalvador.fco .gov.uk; Ambassador LINDA MARY CROSS (until Dec. 2014), BERNHARD GARSIDE (from Jan. 2015).

USA: Blvd Santa Elena Sur, Antiguo Cuscatlán, San Salvador; tel. 2501-2999; fax 2501-2150; internet sansalvador.usembassy.gov; Ambassador MARI CARMEN APONTE.

Uruguay: Edif. Gran Plaza 405, Blvd del Hipódromo 111, Col. San Benito, San Salvador; tel. 2279-1626; fax 2279-1627; e-mail urusalva@telesal.net; Ambassador MARÍA CRISTINA FIGUEROA URSI.

Venezuela: 7a Calle Poniente 3921, entre 75 y 77 Avda Norte, Col. Escalón, San Salvador; tel. 2263-3977; fax 2211-0027; e-mail embajadadevenezuela@telesal.net; internet embavenez-elsalvador .com.sv; Ambassador NORA MARGARITA URIBE TRUJILLO.

Judicial System

The Supreme Court of Justice comprises 15 Justices. There are the Courts of Second Instance, Courts of Appeal and other trial courts

(Courts of Peace). The National Judiciary Council, an independent institution, is in charge of proposing candidates to serve as justices on the Supreme Court and judges for the courts of appeal and the trial courts.

Corte Suprema de Justicia: Frente a Plaza José Simeón Cañas, Centro de Gobierno, San Salvador; tel. 2271-8888; fax 2271-3767; internet www.csj.gob.sv; f. 1824; 15 magistrates, one of whom is its President; the Court is divided into 4 chambers: Constitutional Law, Civil Law, Criminal Law and Litigation; Pres. Armando Pineda Navas.

Attorney-General: Luis Antonio Martínez González.

Procurator-General for the Defence of Human Rights: Oscar Humberto Luna.

Religion

Roman Catholicism is the dominant religion, but other denominations are also permitted. The Baptist Church, Seventh-day Adventists and Jehovah's Witnesses are represented.

CHRISTIANITY

The Roman Catholic Church

El Salvador comprises one archdiocese and seven dioceses. Roman Catholics represent some 76% of the total population.

Bishops' Conference: Conferencia Episcopal de El Salvador, 15 Avda Norte 1420, Col. Layco, Apdo 1310, San Salvador; tel. 2225-8997; fax 2226-5330; e-mail cedes.casa@telesal.net; internet iglesia.org.sv; f. 1974; Pres. Most Rev. José Luis Escobar Alas (Archbishop of San Salvador).

Archbishop of San Salvador: Most Rev. José Luis Escobar Alas, Arzobispado, Col. Médica, Avda Dr Emilio Alvarez y Avda Dr Max Bloch, Apdo 2253, San Salvador; tel. 2226-0501; fax 2226-4979; e-mail info@arzobispadosansalvador.org; internet www.arzobispadosansalvador.org.

The Anglican Communion

El Salvador comprises one of the five dioceses of the Iglesia Anglicana de la Región Central de América. The Iglesia Anglicana has some 5,000 members.

Bishop of El Salvador: Rt Rev. Martín de Jesús Barahona Pascacio, 47 Avda Sur, 723 Col. Flor Blanca, Apdo 01-274, San Salvador; tel. 2223-2252; fax 2223-7952; e-mail anglican.sal@integra.com.sv.

The Baptist Church

Baptist Association of El Salvador: Avda Sierra Nevada 922, Col. Miramonte, Apdo 347, San Salvador; tel. 2260-2070; e-mail abes1911_2011@hotmail.com; internet ubla.net/paises/elsalvador.htm; f. 1933; Pres. Mauricio Salinas Sandoval; 4,427 mems.

Other Churches

Church of Jesus Christ of Latter-day Saints (Mormons): San Salvador Temple, Avda El Espino, Col. San Benito frente al Redondel Roberto D'Abuisson, Antiguo Cuscatlan, San Salvador; tel. 2520-2631; internet www.lds.org; 114,674 mems.

Sínodo Luterano Salvadoreño (Iglesia Luterana Salvadoreña) (Salvadorean Lutheran Synod): Final 49 Avda Sur, Calle Paralela al Bulevar de los Próceres, San Salvador; tel. 2225-2843; fax 2248-3451; e-mail lutomg@sls.org.sv; internet sls.org.sv; Pres. Bishop Medardo E. Gómez Soto; 20,000 mems.

The Press

DAILY NEWSPAPERS

Co Latino: 23 Avda Sur 225, Apdo 96, San Salvador; tel. 2222-1009; fax 2271-0822; e-mail info@diariocolatino.com; internet nuevaweb.diariocolatino.com; f. 1890; evening; Dir Francisco Elías Valencia Soriano; Editor Patricia Meza; circ. 15,000.

El Diario de Hoy: 11 Calle Oriente 271 y Avda Cuscatancingo 271, Apdo 495, San Salvador; tel. 2231-7777; fax 2231-7869; e-mail redaccion@elsalvador.com; internet www.elsalvador.com; f. 1936; morning; ind; also publishes *Diario de Occidente* and *Diario de Oriente* (f. 1910); Dir Enrique Altamirano Madriz; Editor Ricardo Chacón; circ. 115,000.

Diario Oficial: 4 Calle Poniente y 15 Avda Sur 829, San Salvador; tel. 2555-7829; fax 2222-4936; e-mail info@imprentanacional.gob.sv; internet www.imprentanacional.gob.sv; f. 1875; govt publ; Dir Edgar Antonio Mendoza Castro; circ. 1,000.

El Faro (Online newspaper): Calle El Mirador 138, Col. Escalón, San Salvador; tel. 2208-6685; internet www.elfaro.net; f. 1998; Editor Carlos Dada.

El Mundo: 15 Calle Poniente y 7a Avda Norte 521, San Salvador; tel. 2234-8000; fax 2222-8190; e-mail redaccion@elmundo.com.sv; internet www.elmundo.com.sv; f. 1967; morning; Exec. Dir Onno Wuelfers; Editor Alvaro Cruz Rojas; circ. 40,215.

La Página: Avda La Capilla 319, Col. San Benito, San Salvador; tel. 2243-8969; fax 2521-5718; e-mail redaccion@lapagina.com.sv; internet www.lapagina.com.sv.

La Prensa Gráfica: Final Blvd Santa Elena, frente Embajada de EUA, Antiguo Cuscatlán, La Libertad, San Salvador; tel. 2241-2000; fax 2271-4242; e-mail opinion@laprensagrafica.com; internet www.laprensagrafica.com; f. 1915; general information; conservative, independent; Dir José Dutriz; Editor Rodolfo Dutriz; circ. 97,312 (weekdays), 115,564 (Sundays).

PERIODICALS

Boletín Cultural Informativo: Universidad 'Dr José Matías Delgado', Km 8.5, Carretera Santa Tecla; tel. 2278-1011; fax 2289-5314; e-mail boculin@yahoo.es; internet www.ujmd.edu.sv; f. 2001; published by the Universidad 'Dr José Matías Delgado'; Dir Claudia Hérodier.

Cultura: Dirección de Publicaciones e Impresos, 17 Avda Sur 430, San Salvador; tel. 2510-5318; fax 2221-4415; e-mail revistacultura.sv@gmail.com; internet revista-cultura.com; f. 1955; 3 a year; publ. by the National Council for Culture and the Arts; Dir Mauricio Orellana Suárez; circ. 1,000.

El Economista: Grupo Dutriz, Blvd Santa Elena, Antiguo Cuscatlán, La Libertad; tel. 2241-2677; e-mail eleconomista@eleconomista.net; internet www.eleconomista.net; f. 2005; owned by Grupo Dutriz; monthly; business and economics; Editor Alfredo Hernández.

Ella: Final blvd Santa Elena, frente a embajada de EUA, Antiguo Cuscatlán, La Libertad; tel. 2241-2000; e-mail ella@laprensa.com.sv; internet ella.laprensagrafica.com; f. 1987; publ. by La Prensa Gráfica.

El Gráfico: Urb. y Blvd Santa Elena, Antiguo Cuscatlán, La Libertad; e-mail grafico@laprensa.com.sv; internet www.elgrafico.com; publ. by Grupo Dutriz; sports; fortnightly; Editor Daniel Herrera.

El Salvador Investiga: Proyección de Investigaciones, Edif. A5, 2°, Centro de Gobierno, San Salvador; tel. 2221-4439; e-mail direccion.investigaciones@concultura.gob.sv; internet www.concultura.gob.sv/revistainvestiga.htm; f. 2005; 2 a year; publ. by the National Council for Culture and the Arts; historical and cultural research; Editor Mario Colorado.

Motor City: Final blvd Santa Elena, frente a embajada de EUA, Antiguo Cuscatlán, La Libertad; tel. 2241-2000; e-mail motor@laprensa.com.sv; internet www.laprensagrafica.com; publ. by La Prensa Gráfica; Editor Roberto Flores Pinto.

PRESS ASSOCIATION

Asociación de Periodistas de El Salvador (Press Association of El Salvador): Edif. Casa del Periodista, Paseo Gen. Escalón 4130, San Salvador; tel. 2263-5335; e-mail info@apes.org.sv; internet www.apes.org.sv; Pres. José Luis Benitez; Sec.-Gen. Raquel Morán.

Publishers

Clásicos Roxsil, SA de CV: 4a Avda Sur 2–3, Nueva San Salvador; tel. 2228-1832; fax 2228-1212; e-mail roxanabe@navegante.com.sv; f. 1976; textbooks, literature; Dir Rosa Victoria Serrano de López; Editorial Dir Roxana Beatriz López.

Dirección de Publicaciones e Impresos (DPI): 17a Avda Sur 430, San Salvador; tel. 2271-1071; e-mail direcciondepublicaciones@cultura.gob.sv; internet www.dpi.gob.sv; f. 1953; literary, history and culture; Dir Róger Lindo.

Editorial Universidad Don Bosco: Calle Plan del Pino, Ciudadela Don Bosco, Soyapango, San Salvador; tel. 2251-8212; e-mail hflores@udb.edu.sv; internet www.udb.edu.sv/editorial/; f. 2005; academic periodicals and texts; Pres. Dr José Humberto Flores.

UCA Editores: Blvd Los Próceres, Apdo 01-575, San Salvador; tel. 2210-6600; fax 2210-6650; e-mail ucaeditores@gmail.com; internet www.ucaeditores.com.sv/uca; f. 1975; social sciences, religion, economy, literature and textbooks; Dir Andreu Oliva.

PUBLISHERS' ASSOCIATION

Cámara Salvadoreña del Libro: Edif. Forty Seven, Local 4, Col. Flor Blanca, 47 Avda Norte y 1a Calle Poniente, Apdo 3384, San

Salvador; tel. 2275-0293; fax 2261-2231; e-mail camsalibro@terra
.com.sv; internet www.camsalibro.com; f. 1974; Pres. ANA DOLORES
MOLINA DE FAUVET; Exec. Dir AMÉRICA DOMÍNGUEZ.

Broadcasting and Communications

TELECOMMUNICATIONS

Claro: Edif. F, 1°, Complejo Telecom Roma, Calle Liverpool y Final
Calle El Progreso, Col. Roma, San Salvador; tel. 2250-5555; fax 2221-
4849; e-mail clientes@claro.com.sv; internet www.claro.com.sv;
telecommunications network, fmrly part of Administración Nacional
de Telecomunicaciones (ANTEL), which was divested in 1998;
changed name from CTE Antel Telecom in 1999; acquired by América
Móvil, SA de CV (Mexico) in 2003; fixed line and mobile cellular
operations; Exec. Pres. ERIC BEHNER.

Digicel: Edif. Palic, 5°, Alameda Dr Manuel Enrique Araujo y Calle
Nueva No 1, Col. Escalón, San Salvador; tel. 2285-5100; fax 2285-
5585; e-mail servicioalcliente.sv@digicelgroup.com; internet www
.digicel.com.sv; owned by Digicel (USA); mobile telecommunications;
CEO JOSÉ ANTONIO RODRÍGUEZ.

Intelfon, SA de CV (RED): Centro Financiero Gigante, Torre A, 12°,
Of. 503, Alameda Roosevelt y 63 Avda Sur, San Salvador; tel. 2515-
0000; e-mail rtrujillo@red.com.sv; internet www.red.com.sv; f. 2005;
cellular and internet services; Dir JUAN JOSÉ BORJA PAPINI.

Telefónica Móviles El Salvador, SA de CV (Movistar): Torre
Telefónica (Torre B de Centro Financiero Gigante), Alameda Roosevelt y 63 Avda Sur, Col. Escalón, San Salvador; tel. 2244-0144;
e-mail telefonica.empresas@telefonica.com.sv; internet www
.movistar.com.sv; mobile telecommunications; 92% owned by Telefónica Móviles, SA (Spain); Exec. Dir HERNÁN OZÓN.

Tigo El Salvador: Centro Financiero, Gigante Torre D, 9°, Avda
Roosevelt, San Salvador; tel. 2246-9977; fax 2246-9999; e-mail
servicioalcliente@tigo.com.sv; internet www.tigo.com.sv; mobile
telecommunications and internet services; subsidiary of Millicom
International Cellular (Luxembourg); CEO MARCELO JULIO ALEMÁN.

Regulatory Authority

**Superintendencia General de Electricidad y Telecomunica-
ciones (SIGET):** 16 Calle Poniente y 37 Avda Sur 2001, Col. Flor
Blanca, San Salvador; tel. 2257-4438; fax 2257-4498; e-mail info@
siget.gob.sv; internet www.siget.gob.sv; f. 1996; Supt BLANCA COTO.

BROADCASTING

Radio

Radio Corporación FM: 69 Avda Norte, No 213, Col Escalón, San
Salvador; tel. 2283-2222; fax 2224-1212; e-mail mercadeo@
radiocorporacionfm.com.sv; internet www.radiocorporacionfm.com
.sv; f. 1988; owns and operates 6 radio stations; Pres. JOSÉ LUIS SACA
MELÉNDEZ.

Radio Nacional de El Salvador: Edif. Ministerio de Gobernación,
Cto. de Gobierno, 10°, Alameda Juan Pablo II, San Salvador; tel.
2527-7272; e-mail info@turadioelsalvador.com; internet www
.turadioelsalvador.com; f. 1926; non-commercial cultural station;
Dir-Gen. RICARDO ALBERTO MARTÍNEZ BARRERA.

Radio Paz: 1 Calle Poniente 3412, Col. Escalón, Contiguo al
Seminario San José de la Montaña, San Salvador; tel. 2245-2941;
fax 2245-1069; e-mail director@radiopaz.com.sv; internet www
.radiopaz.com.sv; f. 1998; operated by the Archdiocese of El Salvador;
Gen. Man. MARITZA VILLA.

Television

Canal 8 (Agape TV): Centro Comunicaciones AGAPE, 1511 Calle
Gerardo Barrios, Col. Cucumacuyán, San Salvador; tel. 2281-2828;
fax 2211-0799; e-mail info@agapetv8.com; internet www.agapetv8
.com; Catholic, family channel; Pres. FLAVIÁN MUCCI.

Canal 12: Blvd Santa Elena Sur 12, Antiguo Cuscatlán, La Libertad;
tel. 2560-1212; fax 2278-0722; e-mail mercadotecnia@canal12.com
.sv; internet www.canal12.com.sv; f. 1984; Dir ALEJANDRO GONZÁLEZ.

Grupo Megavisión: Calle Poniente entre 85 y 86 Avda Norte, Apdo
2789, San Salvador; tel. 2283-2121; e-mail serviciosmegavision@
salnet.net; internet www.megavision.com.sv; operates Canal 21;
Dir-Gen. FREDDY UNGO.

Grupo Televisivo Cuscatleco: 6a–10a Calle Poniente 2323, Col.
Flor Blanca, San Salvador; tel. 2559-8326; fax 2245-6142; e-mail info
.sv@tecoloco.com; internet www.tecoloco.com.sv; operates Canal 23,
25, 67 and 69 (in the west only).

Tecnovisión Canal 33: entre 75 y 77 Avda Nte, Istmania No 262,
San Salvador; tel. 2559-3333; e-mail info@canal33.tv; internet www
.canal33.tv; Pres. ENRIQUE RIBOBÓ.

Association

Asociación Salvadoreña de Radiodifusores (ASDER): Calle
Las Jacarandas, Pasaje 3 No 7K, Urb. Maquilishuat, San Salvador;
tel. 2563-5302; fax 2563-5304; e-mail informacionam@asder.com.sv;
internet www.asder.com.sv; f. 1964; Pres. PEDRO LEONEL MORENO
MONGE; Exec. Dir ANA MARÍA URRUTIA DE LARA.

Finance

(cap. = capital; res = reserves; dep. = deposits; m. = million;
brs = branches; amounts in US dollars)

BANKING

Supervisory Bodies

Superintendencia del Sistema Financiero: 7a Avda Norte 240,
Apdo 2942, San Salvador; tel. 2281-2444; fax 2281-1621; e-mail
internacional@ssf.gob.sv; internet www.ssf.gob.sv; Supt JOSÉ
RICARDO PERDOMO.

Superintendencia de Valores: Antiguo Edif. BCR, 2°, 1a Calle
Poniente y 7a Avda Norte, San Salvador; tel. 2281-8900; fax 2221-
3404; e-mail info@superval.gob.sv; internet www.superval.gob.sv;
Supt RENÉ MAURICIO GUARDADO RODRÍGUEZ.

Central Bank

Banco Central de Reserva de El Salvador: Alameda Juan Pablo
II, entre 15 y 17 Avda Norte, Apdo 01-106, San Salvador; tel. 2281-
8000; fax 2281-8011; e-mail info@bcr.gob.sv; internet www.bcr.gob
.sv; f. 1934; nationalized Dec. 1961; entered monetary integration
process 2001; cap. 115.0m., res 171.2m., dep. 2,017.3m. (Dec. 2009);
Pres. OSCAR CABRERA MELGAR; Vice-Pres. MARTA EVELYN DE RIVERA.

Commercial and Mortgage Banks

Banco Agrícola: Blvd Constitución 100, San Salvador; tel. 2267-
5000; fax 2267-5930; e-mail info@bancoagricola.com; internet www
.bancoagricola.com; f. 1955; merged with Banco Desarrollo in 2000;
acquired Banco Capital in 2001; bought by Bancolombia in 2012; cap.
297.5m., res 161.1m., dep. 2,793.2m. (Dec. 2013); Chair. RAFAEL
BARRAZA DOMINGUEZ; Pres. SERGIO RESTREPO ISAZA; 8 brs.

Banco Citibank de El Salvador, SA: Edif. Pirámide Cuscatlán,
Km 10, Carretera a Santa Tecla, Apdo 626, San Salvador; tel. 2212-
2000; fax 2228-5700; e-mail info@bancocuscatlan.com; internet www
.citi.com.sv; f. 1972; acquired by Citi (USA) in 2008; cap. 155.7m., res
168.9m., dep. 2,011.3m. (Dec. 2008); Pres. LUIS ALBERTO MARÍN; 25
brs.

Banco Davivienda Salvadoreño, SA (Bancosal): Edif. Centro
Financiero, Avda Manuel E. Araujo y Avda Olímpica 3550, Apdo
0673, San Salvador; tel. 2214-2000; fax 2214-2755; internet www
.davivienda.com.sv; f. 1885 as Banco Salvadoreño, SA; became Banco
HSBC Salvadoreño in 2007; bought by Banco Davivienda (Colombia)
in 2012 and present name adopted; cap. 150m., res 116.2m., dep.
1,339.6m. (Dec. 2013); Exec. Pres. (El Salvador) GERARDO JOSÉ SIMÁN
SIRI; 60 brs.

Banco Hipotecario de El Salvador: Pasaje Senda Florida Sur,
Col. Escalón, Apdo 999, San Salvador; tel. 2223-7713; fax 2298-2071;
e-mail servicio.cliente@hipotecario.com.sv; internet www
.bancohipotecario.com.sv; f. 1935; cap. 38.3m., res 10.8m., dep. 429m.
(Dec. 2011); Pres. NORA MERCEDES MIRANDA DE LÓPEZ; 16 brs.

Banco Promérica: Edif. Promérica, Centro Comercial La Gran Vía,
Antiguo Cuscatlán; tel. 2513-5000; fax 2211-4257; e-mail
soluciones@promerica.com.sv; internet www.promerica.com.sv;
f. 1996; privately owned; cap. 34.7m., res 6.5m., dep. 683.5m. (Dec.
2013); Chair. RAMIRO NORBERTO ORTIZ GUDÍAN; Exec. Pres. EDUARDO
ALBERTO QUEVEDO MORENO.

Scotiabank El Slavador, SA (Canada): Centro Financiero, 25
Avda Norte, No 1230, San Salvador; tel. 2250-1111; fax 2234-4577;
e-mail atencion.cliente@scotiabank.com.sv; internet www
.scotiabank.com.sv; f. 1997; cap. 114.1m., res 67.5m., dep. 1,280.4m.
(Dec. 2011); Pres. JEAN LUC RICH; Exec. Dir JUAN CARLOS GARCÍA
VIZCAÍNO.

Public Institutions

Banco de Desarrollo de El Salvador (BANDESAL): Edif. World
Trade Center II, 4°, San Salvador; tel. 2267-0000; fax 2267-0011;
e-mail karla.martinez@bandesal.gob.sv; internet www.bandesal.gob
.sv; f. 1994 as Banco Multisectorial de Inversiones; adopted present
name in 2011; Pres. MARÍA MÉLIDA MIRANDA.

Banco de Fomento Agropecuario: Km 10.5, Carretera al Puerto
de la Libertad, Santa Tecla, La Libertad, Nueva San Salvador; tel.
2241-0966; fax 2241-0800; internet www.bfa.gob.sv; f. 1973; state-
owned; cap. 17.8m., dep. 174.8m. (Dec. 2010); Pres. (vacant); Gen.
Man. JOSÉ ANTONIO PEÑATE; 27 brs.

Federación de Cajas de Crédito y Bancos de los Trabajadores (FEDECREDITO): 25 Avda Norte y 23 Calle Poniente, San Salvador; tel. 2209-9696; fax 2226-7059; e-mail informacion@fedecredito.com.sv; internet www.fedecredito.com.sv; f. 1943; Pres. MACARIO ARMANDO ROSALES ROSA.

Fondo Social para la Vivienda (FSV): Calle Rubén Darío 901, entre 15 y 17 Avda Sur, Apdo 2179, San Salvador; tel. 2231-2000; fax 2271-4011; e-mail comunicaciones@fsv.gob.sv; internet www.fsv.gob.sv; f. 1973; provides loans to workers for house purchases; Pres. JOSÉ TOMÁS CHÉVEZ; Gen. Man. MARIANO ARÍSTIDES BONILLA.

Banking Association

Asociación Bancaria Salvadoreña (ABANSA): Pasaje Senda, Florida Norte 140, Col. Escalón, San Salvador; tel. 2298-6959; fax 2223-1079; e-mail info@abansa.net; internet www.abansa.org.sv; f. 1965; Pres. ARMANDO ARIAS; Exec. Dir MARCELA DE JIMÉNEZ.

STOCK EXCHANGE

Bolsa de Valores de El Salvador, SA de CV: Blvd Merliot y Avda Las Carretas, Urb. Jardines de la Hacienda, Antiguo Cuscatlán, La Libertad, San Salvador; tel. 2212-6400; fax 2278-4377; e-mail info@bolsadevalores.com.sv; internet www.bolsadevalores.com.sv; f. 1992; Pres. ROLANDO ARTURO DUARTE SCHLAGETER.

INSURANCE

Aseguradora Agrícola Comercial, SA: Alameda Roosevelt 3104, Apdo 1855, San Salvador; tel. 2261-8200; fax 2260-5592; e-mail informacion@acsasal.com.sv; internet www.acsasal.com.sv; f. 1973; Pres. LUIS ALFREDO ESCALANTE SOL; Gen. Man. RAÚL ANTONIO GUEVARA.

Aseguradora Popular, SA: Paseo Gen. Escalón 5338, Col. Escalón, San Salvador; tel. 2263-0700; fax 2263-1246; e-mail info@aseguradorapopular.com; internet aseguradorapopular.com; f. 1975; Pres. Dr CARLOS ARMANDO LAHÚD.

Aseguradora Suiza Salvadoreña, SA (ASESUISA): Alameda Dr Manuel Enrique Araujo, Plaza Suiza, Apdo 1490, Col. San Benito, San Salvador; tel. 2209-5000; fax 2209-5001; e-mail info@asesuisa.com; internet www.asesuisa.com; f. 1969; acquired in 2001 by Inversiones Financieras Banco Agrícola (Panama); Pres. GONZALO PÉREZ; Dir ADELAIDA MARÍA TAMAYO.

La Central de Seguros y Fianzas, SA: Avda Olímpica 3333, Apdo 01-255, San Salvador; tel. 2268-6000; fax 2223-7647; e-mail gerenciaseguros@lacentral.com.sv; internet www.lacentral.com.sv; f. 1983; Pres. EDUARDO ENRIQUE CHACÓN BORJA; Man. (Insurance) FRANCISCO LOZANO.

Chartis Seguros El Salvador, SA: Calle Loma Linda 265, Col. San Benito, Apdo 92, San Salvador; tel. 2250-3200; fax 2250-3201; e-mail chartis.elsalvador@chartisinsurance.com; internet www.chartisinsurance.com; f. 1998 as AIG Unión y Desarrollo, SA; following merger of Unión y Desarrollo, SA and AIG; changed name as above in 2009; Pres. FRANCISCO R. R. DE SOLA.

Internacional de Seguros, SA (Interseguros): Edif. Plaza Credicorp Bank, Calle 50, 19°, 20° y 21°, San Salvador; tel. 2206-4000; fax 2210-1900; e-mail interseguros@interseguros.com.sv; internet isweb.iseguros.com/iseguros; f. 1910; merged with Seguros Universales in 2004; Pres. ROY ICAZA JIMÉNEZ.

Mapfre La Centro Americana, SA: Alameda Roosevelt 3107, Apdo 527, San Salvador; tel. 2257-6666; fax 2223-2687; e-mail lacentro@lacentro.com; internet www.lacentro.com; f. 1915; acquired by Mapfre, SA in 2000; Pres. JOSÉ ANTONIO ARIAS; Gen. Man. JOSÉ TULIO URRUTIA.

Pan-American Life Insurance Co: Edif. PALIC, Alameda Dr Manuel Enrique Araujo y Calle Nueva 1, Col. Escalón, Apdo 255, San Salvador; tel. 2209-2700; fax 2245-2792; e-mail servicioalclientesv@panamericanlife.com; internet www.palig.com/regions/el_salvador.aspx; f. 1928; Country Man. JEAN CARLO CALDERÓN.

Scotia Seguros, SA: Calle Loma Linda 223, Col. San Benito, Apdo 1004, San Salvador; tel. 2209-7003; fax 2223-0734; e-mail contactenos@scotiaseguros.com.sv; internet www.scotiaseguros.com.sv; f. 1955; fmrly Compañía General de Seguros, SA; changed name as above in 2005; Pres. SERGIO CRUZ FERNÁNDEZ.

Seguros e Inversiones, SA (SISA): Carretera Panamericana, 10.5 Km, Santa Tecla, La Libertad; tel. 2241-0000; fax 2241-1213; e-mail servicioalcliente@sisa.com.sv; internet www.sisa.com.sv; f. 1962; Pres. JOSÉ EDUARDO MONTENEGRO PALOMO.

Association

Asociación Salvadoreña de Empresas de Seguros (ASES): Calle Los Castaños 120, Col. San Francisco, San Salvador; tel. 2223-7169; fax 2223-8901; e-mail asesgeneral@ases.com.sv; internet www.ases.com.sv; f. 1970; Pres. EDUARDO MONTENEGRO PALOMO; Exec. Dir Dr RAÚL BETANCOURT MENÉNDEZ.

Trade and Industry

GOVERNMENT AGENCIES AND DEVELOPMENT ORGANIZATIONS

Comisión Nacional de la Micro y Pequeña Empresa (CONAMYPE): Edif. Gazzolo, 25 Avda Norte y 25 Calle Poniente, San Salvador; tel. 2121-1300; fax 2521-2274; e-mail conamype@conamype.gob.sv; internet www.conamype.gob.sv; f. 1996; micro and small industrial devt; Pres. THARSIS SALOMÓN LÓPEZ (Minister of the Economy); Exec. Dir ILIANA ROJEL.

Consejo Nacional de Ciencia y Tecnología (CONACYT): Avda Dr Emilio Alvarez, Pasaje Dr Guillermo Rodríguez Pacas 51, Col. Médica, San Salvador; tel. 2234-8400; fax 2225-6255; e-mail info@conacyt.gob.sv; internet www.conacyt.gob.sv; f. 1992; formulation and guidance of national policy on science and technology; Pres. ARMANDO FLORES; Exec. Dir CARLOS ROBERTO OCHOA CÓRDOBA.

Corporación de Exportadores de El Salvador (COEXPORT): Avda La Capilla 359A, Col. San Benito, San Salvador; tel. 2212-0200; fax 2243-3159; e-mail info@coexport.com.sv; internet www.coexport.com.sv; f. 1973 to promote Salvadorean exports; Pres. FRANCISCO BOLAÑOS; Exec. Dir SILVIA M. CUÉLLAR DE PAREDES.

Corporación Salvadoreña de Inversiones (CORSAIN): Avda Bunganbilias, Casa 14, Col. San Francisco, San Salvador; tel. 2224-6070; fax 2224-6877; e-mail info@corsain.gob.sv; internet www.corsain.gob.sv; Pres. VIOLETA ISABEL SACA DE RIVERA.

Fondo de Inversión Social para el Desarrollo Local (FISDL): Blvd Orden de Malta 470, Urb. Santa Elena, Antiguo Cuscatlán, La Libertad, San Salvador; tel. 2133-1200; fax 2133-1370; e-mail webmaster@fisdl.gob.sv; internet www.fisdl.gob.sv; f. 1990; poverty alleviation and development; Pres. CAROLINA AVALOS.

Instituto Salvadoreño de Fomento Cooperativo (INSAFO-COOP): Edif. Urrutia Abrego 2, Frente a INPEP, 15 Calle Poniente, No 402, San Salvador; tel. 2222-2563; fax 2222-4119; e-mail insafocoop@insafocoop.gob.sv; internet www.insafocoop.gob.sv; f. 1971; devt of co-operatives; Pres. FÉLIX CÁRCAMO.

Instituto Salvadoreño de Transformación Agraria (ISTA): Final Col. Las Mercedes, Km 5.5, Carretera a Santa Tecla, San Salvador; tel. 2527-2600; fax 2224-0259; e-mail info@ista.gob.sv; internet www.ista.gob.sv; f. 1976 to promote rural devt; empowered to buy inefficiently cultivated land; Pres. CARLA ALBÁNEZ AMAYA.

CHAMBER OF COMMERCE

Cámara de Comercio e Industria de El Salvador: 9a Avda Norte y 5a Calle Poniente, Apdo 1640, San Salvador; tel. 2231-3000; fax 2271-4461; e-mail camara@camarasal.com; internet www.camarasal.com; f. 1915; 2,000 mems; Pres. LUIS CARDENAL; brs in San Miguel, Santa Ana, Sonsonate and La Unión.

INDUSTRIAL AND TRADE ASSOCIATIONS

Asociación Azúcarera de El Salvador (AAES): 103 Avda Norte y Calle Arturo Ambrogi 145, Col. Escalón, San Salvador; tel. 2264-1226; fax 2263-0361; e-mail asosugar@sal.gbm.net; internet www.asociacionazucarera.com; national sugar asscn, fmrly Instituto Nacional del Azúcar; Pres. MARIO SALAVERRÍA; Dir JULIO ARROYO.

Asociación Cafetalera de El Salvador (ACES): 67 Avda Norte 116, Col. Escalón, San Salvador; tel. 2223-3024; fax 2298-6261; e-mail ascafes@telesal.net; f. 1930; coffee growers' asscn; Pres. JOSÉ ROBERTO INCLÁN ROBREDO; Exec. Dir AMIR SALVADOR ALABÍ.

Asociación Salvadoreña de Beneficiadores y Exportadores de Café (ABECAFE): 87 Avda Norte, Condominio Fountainblue 4, Col. Escalón, San Salvador; tel. 2263-2834; fax 2263-2833; e-mail abecafe@telesal.net; coffee producers' and exporters' asscn; Pres. CARLOS BORGONOVO.

Asociación Salvadoreña de Industriales: Calles Roma y Liverpool, Col. Roma, Apdo 48, San Salvador; tel. 2279-2488; fax 2267-9253; e-mail medios@asi.com.sv; internet www.industrialsalvador.com; f. 1958; 400 mems; manufacturers' asscn; Pres. JAVIER ERNESTO SIMAN; Exec. Dir JORGE ARRIAZA.

Cámara Agropecuaria y Agroindustrial de El Salvador (CAMAGRO): Calle El Lirio 19, Col. Maquilishuat, San Salvador; tel. 2264-4622; fax 2263-9448; e-mail contactenos@camagro.com; internet www.camagro.com; Pres. AGUSTÍN MARTÍNEZ.

Consejo Salvadoreño del Café (CSC) (Salvadorean Coffee Council): 1 Avda Norte y 13 Calle Poniente, Nueva San Salvador, La Libertad; tel. 2505-6600; fax 2505-6691; e-mail csc@consejocafe.org.sv; internet www.consejocafe.org; f. 1989 as successor to the

Instituto Nacional del Café; formulates policy and oversees the coffee industry; Exec. Dir José Hugo Hernández.

EMPLOYERS' ORGANIZATION

Asociación Nacional de Empresa Privada (ANEP) (National Private Enterprise Association): 1 Calle Poniente y 71 Avda Norte 204, Col. Escalón, Apdo 1204, San Salvador; tel. 2209-8300; fax 2209-8317; e-mail communicaciones@anep.org.sv; internet www.anep.org.sv; national private enterprise asscn; Pres. Jorge Daboub; Exec. Dir Arnoldo Jiménez.

MAJOR COMPANIES

Construction and Metals

Cilindros Zaragoza, SA de CV: Carretera de Santa Ana hacia Chalchuapa, Km 73½, San Juan Opico, La Libertad, San Salvador; tel. 2408-3686; fax 2241-0100; e-mail infocilza@cilindroszaragoza.com; internet www.cilindroszaragoza.com; f. 2006; mfrs of cylinders for transportation of liquid gas; operates in 4 countries; Man. Edwin Romero.

Condusal, SA (Conductores Eléctricos Salvadoreños): Autopista al Aeropuerto Internacional, Km 15, Santo Tómas, San Salvador; tel. 2213-5999; fax 2213-5998; e-mail nfo@condusal.com; internet www.condusal.com; f. 1988; manufactures electrical conductors; Pres. Jaime Mauricio Fuente García.

Corporación Industrial Centroamericana, SA de CV (COR-INCA): Edif Atrium Plaza, No 21-c, Blvd Santa Elena, Antiguo Cuscatlan, San Salvador; tel. 2310-2033; fax 2310-2234; internet www.corinca.com.sv; f. 1966; iron rods and wire, construction and building materials; Gen. Man. Carlos Francisco Alvarado; 350 employees.

Grupo Agrisal: Torre Futura, 20°, Calle El Mirador entre 87 y 89 Avda Norte, San Salvador; tel. 2500-9000; e-mail ag@agrisal.com; internet www.agrisal.com; f. 1905; Pres. Luis Rolando Alvarez Prunera.

Holcim El Salvador, SA de CV: Avda El Espino y Calle Holcim, Urb. Madreselva, Antiguo Cuscatlán, La Libertad; tel. 2505-0000; fax 2505-0777; e-mail cessamer@cessa.com.sv; internet www.holcim.com.sv; f. 1949 as Cemento de El Salvador; adopted present name in 2010 following acquisition of 90% stake by Holcim, Switzerland; mfrs of Portland cement; Pres. Rafael Alvarado Cano; CEO Ricardo Chávez Caparroso; 400 employees.

Food and Beverages

Industrias La Constancia, SA de CV (ILC): Avda Independencia 526, San Salvador; tel. 2209-7555; fax 2231-5152; e-mail servicioalcliente@ca.sabmiller.com; internet www.laconstancia.com; f. 1906; subsidiary of SABMiller PLC (United Kingdom); produces and sells beer; Pres. Carlos Habencio Fernández; 950 employees.

Molinos de El Salvador, SA: Blvd del Ejército Nacional y 50 Avda Norte, Apdo 327, San Salvador; tel. 2297-8900; fax 2293-1525; e-mail info@molsa.com.sv; internet www.molsa.com.sv; f. 1959; production of wheat flour and biscuits; Gen. Man. Jorge Armando Cardona; 121 employees.

Productos Alimenticios Diana, SA de CV: 12 Avda Sur 111, Col. Guadalupe, Apdo 117, Soyapango; tel. 2227-1233; fax 2277-0088; e-mail servicioalcliente@diana.com.sv; internet www.diana.com.sv; f. 1951; food-processing; Pres. Rosy de Paredes; 2,000 employees.

Sello de Oro, SA, Productos Alimenticios: Carretera a Jayaque, 2.5 Km, La Libertad, San Salvador; tel. 2317-7777; fax 2317-7704; e-mail info@sellodeoro.com.sv; internet www.sellodeoro.com.sv; f. 1967; food and food-processing; Pres. Carmen Elena del Sol; 1,285 employees.

Pharmaceuticals

Droguería Santa Lucía, SA de CV: Calle Roma 238, Col. Roma, Apdo 06-5, San Salvador; tel. 2250-6200; fax 2223-8033; e-mail administracion@drogueriasantalucia.com; internet www.drogueriasantalucia.com; owned by AstraZeneca PLC (United Kingdom); pharmaceutical products; Man. Dir Alfredo Cristiani.

Laboratorio López, SA de CV: Blvd del Ejército Nacional, Km 5.5, Jurisdicción de Soyapango, San Salvador; tel. 2277-6166; fax 2277-2783; e-mail laboratorioslopez@lablopez.com.sv; internet www.lablopez.com; f. 1948; mfrs of pharmaceutical products; Pres. Bernardo López.

Laboratorios Vijosa, SA de CV: Calle L-3, 10 Zona Industrial Merliot, Antiguo Cuscatlán; tel. 2251-9797; fax 2278-3121; e-mail info@vijosa.com; internet www.vijosa.com; mfrs of pharmaceutical products; Pres. Dr Víctor Jorge Saca; 130 employees.

Textiles and Clothing

Almacenes Simán, SA de CV: Centro Comercial Galerías, Paseo General Escalón 3700, Col. Escalón, San Salvador; tel. 2507-3000; fax 2245-4000; e-mail contacto@siman.com.sv; internet www.siman.com.sv; f. 1921; wholesale and retail sale of clothing; Exec. Pres. Ricardo Simán; Regional Man. Alvaro Corpiño; 1,100 employees.

Grupo Hilasal: Carretera a Santa Ana, Km 32, San Juan Opico, La Libertad, San Salvador; tel. 2319-1201; fax 2338-4064; e-mail cserviceinfo@hilasal.com; internet www.hilasal.com.sv; mfrs of cotton goods and towelling; Pres. and CEO Ricardo Sagrera, III; 1,000 employees.

Industrias Unidas, SA (IUSA): Carretera Panamericana Oriente, Km 11.5, Ilopango, Apdo 893, San Salvador; tel. 2250-9500; fax 2295-0846; e-mail ventas@iusa.com.sv; internet www.iusa.com.sv; f. 1955; owned by Toyobo-Itochu y Marubeni (Japan); mfrs of textiles; Pres. Eduardo Martínez; 1,600 employees.

INSINCA, SA (Industrias Sintéticas de Centroamérica): Carretera Troncal del Norte, Km 12.5, Apopa, San Salvador; tel. 2216-0055; fax 2216-0062; e-mail servicioalcliente@insinca.com; internet www.insinca.com; f. 1966; mfrs of synthetic fibres; Pres. Lorenzo Rivera; 1,000 employees.

Textufil, SA de CV: 12 Avda Sur, Soyapango, Apdo 1632, San Salvador; tel. 2277-0066; fax 2227-2308; e-mail info@textufil.com; internet www.textufil.com; f. 1972; mfrs of nylon and polyester textiles; Pres. Jorge Elías Bahaia.

Miscellaneous

Alba Petróleos de El Salvador, SEM de CV: Parque Industrial El Boquerón, Bloco A, No 1, Blvd Orden de Malta Sur, Urb. Santa Elena, La Libertad; tel. 2526-7700; e-mail contactenos@albapetroleos.com.sv; internet www.albapetroleos.com.sv; f. 2006; fuel distribution; 60% shares held by PDV Caribe and 40% shares held by ENEPASA; CEO Luis Beltrán Rivas Molina.

Distribuidora Unida Industrial, SA de CV (DUISA): 29 Calle Oriente 73, Col. La Rabida, San Salvador; tel. 2234-9600; fax 2225-8430; e-mail ventas@coquinsa.com; internet www.coquinsa.com; f. 1979; mfrs of adhesives, detergents, disinfectants, insecticides; Dir Alma Veronica Rodríguez Tejada.

Excel Automotriz: Avd Luis Poma y Blvd Juan Pablo II, San Salvador; tel. 2261-1133; fax 2260-3516; internet www.excelautomotriz.com/sv/inicio.html; f. 1919; known as DIDEA El Salvador until 2010; distributor of cars and car supplies; Pres. Ricardo Poma; 3,179 employees.

Grupo Monge: Calle El Boqueron 5, Urb. Santa Elena, Antiguo Cuscatlán, La Libertad; tel. 2212-1000; fax 2289-7105; e-mail naguirre@prado.com.sv; internet www.grupom.net; f. 1952 as Muebles Metálicos Prado, SA de CV; bought by Grupo Monge in 2006, name changed 2010; 355 stores in Central America under several brands: El Gallo más Gallo, Monge, Play, El Verdugo and Almacenes Prado; home appliances.

Grupo Unicomer: Edif. Unicomer, Escalón, San Salvador; internet www.regalforest.com; f. 2000; retail; owns Courts Caribbean, Almacenes Tropigas, among others; Pres. Mario Simán.

PricewaterhouseCoopers: Centro Profesional Presidente, Avda La Revolución y Calle Circunvalación, Col. San Benito, Apdo 695, San Salvador; tel. 2243-5844; fax 2243-3546; internet www.pwc.com/sv; accountancy and management consultancy; Pres. Mario Wilfredo Salgado; 150 employees.

Siemens, SA: Calle Siemens 43, Parque Industrial Santa Elena, Antiguo Cuscatlán, Apdo 1525, San Salvador; tel. 2248-7333; fax 2278-3334; e-mail siemens.elsalvador@siemens.co; internet www.siemens-centram.com/index_elsalvador.shtml; owned by Siemens AG (Germany); mfrs of electrical equipment and machinery; Gen. Man. Arturo Lara.

SIGMA/Q, SA: Blvd del Ejército, Km 8, Apdo 1096, San Salvador; tel. 2254-2500; fax 2424-3298; e-mail atencionalcliente@sigmaq.com; internet www.sigmaq.com; f. 1973; mfrs of collapsible packaging; Man. Corporate Affairs Carmen Aida de Meardi; 957 employees.

Tabacalera de El Salvador, SA de CV: 69 Avda Norte 213, Col. Escalón, San Salvador; tel. 2241-5200; fax 2241-5270; e-mail jorge.zablah@pmintl.com; f. 1976; subsidiary of Philip Morris Inc, USA; mfrs of cigarettes; Pres. Jorge Zablah Touché; 186 employees.

UTILITIES

Regulatory Authority

Superintendencia General de Electricidad y Telecomunicaciones (SIGET): see Broadcasting and Communications—Regulatory Authority.

Electricity

AES El Salvador: e-mail consultas@aes.com; internet www
.aeselsalvador.com; Exec. Pres. ABRAHAM BICHARA; operates 4
distribution cos in El Salvador:

CLESA: 23 Avda Sur y 5 Calle Oriente, Barrio San Rafael, Santa
Ana; tel. 2429-4000; f. 1892; distributes electricity in Santa Ana,
Sonsonate, Ahuachapán and La Libertad depts; Gen. Man. RAMÓN
MONTERROSA.

Compañía de Alumbrado Electric (CAESS): Calle El Bambú,
Col. San Antonio, Ayutuxtepeque, San Salvador; tel. 2529-9999;
f. 1890; distributes electricity in Chalatenango, Cuscatlán, Caba-
ñas and northern San Salvador depts; Gen.Man. HUMBERTO
LEMUS.

Distribuidora Eléctrica de Usulután (DEUSEM): Centro
Comercial Puerta de Oriente Local 2, Usulután; tel. 2622-4000;
f. 1957; Gen. Man. LUIS SOLÍS.

EEO: Final 8, Calle Poniente, Calle a Ciudad Pacífico, Plantel
Jalacatal, San Miguel; tel. 2606-8000; f. 1995; distributes electri-
city in the depts of San Miguel, Morazán, La Unión, and parts of
Usulután and San Vicente; Gen. Man. EDWIN GÁLVEZ.

Comisión Ejecutiva Hidroeléctrica del Río Lempa (CEL): 9
Calle Poniente 950, entre 15 y 17 Avda Norte, Centro de Gobierno,
San Salvador; tel. 2211-6000; fax 2207-1302; e-mail naguilar@cel.gob
.sv; internet www.cel.gob.sv; f. 1948; hydroelectric electricity gen-
eration; Pres. DAVID ANTONIO LÓPEZ VILLAFUERTE; Exec. Dir JAIME
CONTRERAS.

Distribuidora de Electricidad del Sur (DELSUR): Edif. Corporativo DELSUR, Unidad de Comunicaciones, Final 17 Avda Norte
y Calle El Boquerón, Santa Tecla, La Libertad; tel. 2233-5700; fax
2243-8662; e-mail informacion@delsur.com.sv; internet www.delsur
.com.sv; Gen. Man. ROBERTO GONZÁLEZ.

LaGeo SA de CV: Final 15, Avda Sur y Blvd Sur, Col. Utila, Santa
Tecla, La Libertad; tel. 2211-6700; fax 2211-6746; e-mail info@lageo
.com.sv; internet www.lageo.com.sv; f. 1999; owned by INE-ENEL;
25% share market; operates Ahuachapán and Berlin geothermal
fields; Pres. JULIO E. VALDIVIESO.

Water

**Administración Nacional de Acueductos y Alcantarillados
(ANDA):** Edif. ANDA, Final Avda Don Bosco, Col. Libertad, San
Salvador; tel. 2247-2700; fax 2225-3152; e-mail sugerencias@anda
.gob.sv; internet www.anda.gob.sv; f. 1961; maintenance of water
supply and sewerage systems; Pres. MARCO ANTONIO FORTÍN; Exec.
Dir CARLOS MANUEL DERAS BARILLAS.

TRADE UNIONS

Central Autónoma de Trabajadores Salvadoreños (CATS):
Calle Los Pinares 17, Col. Centroamérica, San Salvador; tel. 2211-
2570; e-mail cats@catselsalvador.org; internet www.catselsalvador
.org; Sec.-Gen. FRANCISCO QUIJANO; 30,000 mems (2010).

Central de Trabajadores Democráticos de El Salvador (CTD)
(Democratic Workers' Confederation): Avda Norte 19 y Calle
Poniente 17, No 135, Barrio San Miguelito, San Salvador; tel. and
fax 2235-8043; e-mail ctdelsalv_orit@navegante.com.sv; Sec.-Gen.
JOSÉ MARÍA AMAYA; 50,000 mems (2007).

Central de Trabajadores Salvadoreños (CTS) (Salvadorean
Workers' Confederation): Calle Darío González 616, San Jacinto,
San Salvador; tel. 2237-2315; fax 2270-1703; e-mail felixblancocts@
hotmail.com; f. 1966; Christian Democratic; Pres. MIGUEL ÁNGEL
VÁSQUEZ; 30,000 mems (2007).

Confederación General de Sindicatos (CGS) (General Confederation of Unions): Edif. Kury, 3a Calle Oriente 226, San Salvador;
tel. and fax 2222-3527; f. 1958; admitted to ITUC/ORIT; Sec.-Gen.
JOSÉ ISRAEL HUIZA CISNEROS; 27,000 mems.

**Confederación Sindical de Trabajadoras y Trabajadores
Salvadoreños (CSTS)** (Salvadorean Workers' Union Federation):
Blvd Universitario 2226, Col. San José, San Salvador; tel. 2225-2315;
fax 2225-5936; e-mail confederacioncsts@gmail.com; internet www
.cstsconfederacion.org; f. 2005; conglomerate of independent left-
wing trade unions; Sec.-Gen. JULIO CESAR FLORES.

**Confederación Unitaria de Trabajadores Salvadoreños
(CUTS)** (United Salvadorean Workers' Federation): 141 Avda A,
Col. San José, San Salvador; tel. and fax 2226-2100; e-mail
proyectocuts@salnet.net; internet www.cutselsalvador.org; left-
wing; Sec.-Gen. BÁRBARA FIGUEROA.

**Federación Nacional Sindical de Trabajadores Salvadoreños
(FENASTRAS)** (Salvadorean Workers' National Union Federation): 4 Calle Poniente, No 2438A, Col. Flor Blanca, San Salvador;
tel. 2298-2954; fax 2298-2953; e-mail fenastras@hotmail.com;
internet www.fenastras.org; f. 1972; left-wing; 35,000 mems in 16
affiliates; Sec.-Gen. JUAN JOSÉ HUEZO.

Transport

Comisión Ejecutiva Portuaria Autónoma (CEPA): Edif. Torre
Roble, Blvd de Los Héroes, Col. Miramonte, Centro Comercial
Metrocentro, San Salvador; tel. 2218-1300; fax 2121-1212; e-mail
info@cepa.gob.sv; internet www.cepa.gob.sv; f. 1952; operates and
administers the ports of Acajutla and Cutuco and the international
airport, as well as Ferrocarriles Nacionales de El Salvador; Pres.
NELSON EDGARDO VANEGAS; Gen. Man. SALVADOR VILLALOBOS.

RAILWAYS

In 2005 there were 554.8 km of railway track in the country. The
main track linked San Salvador with the ports of Acajutla and Cutuco
(also known as La Unión) and with Santa Ana. Operation of the
railway network was suspended in 2005; however, a passenger
service between San Salvador and Apopa (a distance of 12.5 km)
resumed in 2007, and the rehabilitation of further sections of track
was planned.

Ferrocarriles Nacionales de El Salvador (FENADESAL): Final
Avda Peralta 903, Apdo 2292, San Salvador; tel. 2530-1700; e-mail
salvador.sanabria@cepa.gob.sv; internet www.fenadesal.gob.sv;
555 km of track; administered by CEPA (q.v.); Pres. NELSON EDGARDO
VANEGAS RODRÍGUEZ.

ROADS

There were some 6,545 km of roads in 2013, of which 3,600 km were
paved. In 2012 the 216-km Carretera Longitudinal del Norte, connecting the north of El Salvador with the rest of the country, was
opened.

Fondo de Conservación Vial (FOVIAL): Carretera a La Libertad,
Km 10.5, Antiguo Cuscatlán, San Salvador; tel. 2257-8300; e-mail
info@fovial.com; internet www.fovial.com; f. 2000; responsible for
maintaining the road network; Exec. Dir ELIUD ULISES AYALA
ZAMORA.

SHIPPING

The port of Acajutla is administered by CEPA (see above). Services
are also provided by foreign lines. An expansion of the port of Cutuco
(Puerto La Unión Centroamericana) was completed in 2009. In
December 2013 El Salvador's flag registered fleet comprised six
vessels, with an aggregate displacement of some 9,643 grt.

Autoridad Portuaria de La Unión: Depto de La Unión; tel. 2623-
6100; e-mail info@launion.gob.sv; internet www.puertolaunion.gob
.sv; Gen. Man. MILTON LACAYO.

CIVIL AVIATION

El Salvador's international airport (renamed Monseñor Oscar
Arnulfo Romero International Airport in 2014) is located 40 km
(25 miles) from San Salvador in Comalapa. The former international
airport at Ilopango is used for military and private civilian aircraft;
there are an additional 88 private airports.

Autoridad de Aviación Civil: Km 9½, Aeropuerto Internacional
de Ilopango, Blvd del Ejercito, San Salvador; tel. 2565-4494; fax 2565-
4408; e-mail mmencos@aac.gob.sv; internet www.aac.gob.sv; f. 1962
as Dirección General de Aeronáutica Civil; reformed and adopted
present name in 2001; Pres. Col RENÉ ROBERTO LÓPEZ MORALES; Exec.
Dir ROGER ANTONIO MENÉNDEZ HERNÁNDEZ.

TACA International Airlines: Santa Elena, Antiguo Cuscatlán,
San Salvador; tel. 2267-8888; internet www.taca.com; f. 1931; allied
with Avianca of Colombia in 2009; passenger and cargo services to
Central America and the USA; Exec. Pres. FABIO VILLEGAS RAMÍREZ.

VECA Airlines (Vuelos Económicos Centroamericanos, SA): Monseñor Sscar Arnulfo Romero Internacional Aeropuerto, San Salvador; internet www.vecaairlines.com; f. 2013; low cost carrier; CEO
EDGAR HASBUN.

Tourism

In 2012 a total of 1,255,000 tourists visited the country. Tourism
receipts, excluding passenger transport, stood at a provisional
US $621m. in 2013.

Asociación Salvadoreña de Hoteles: Hotel Suites Las Palmas,
Blvd del Hipódromo, Col. San Benito, San Salvador; tel. 2298-5383;
fax 2298-5382; e-mail info@hoteles-elsalvador.com; internet www
.hoteles-elsalvador.com; f. 1996; Pres. ALBERTO ASCENCIO; Exec. Dir
MORENA TORRES; 33 mems.

Cámara Salvadoreña de Turismo (CASATUR): 63 Avda Sur,
Pasaje y Urb., Santa Mónica 12- A, Col. Escalón, San Salvador; tel.
2298-6011; fax 2279-2156; e-mail info@casatur.org; internet www
.casatur.org; f. 1978; non-profit org. concerned with promotion of
tourism in El Salvador; Pres. RAFAEL LARET CASTILLO; Gen. Man.
DALILA URRITIA.

Corporación Salvadoreña de Turismo (CORSATUR): Edif. Carbonel 1, Pasaje Carbonel, Alameda Doctor Manuel Enrique Araujo, Col. Roma, San Salvador; tel. 2243-7835; fax 2223-6120; e-mail info@corsatur.gob.sv; internet www.elsalvador.travel; f. 1996; Dir-Gen. ROBERTO VIERA.

Instituto Salvadoreño de Turismo (ISTU) (National Tourism Institute): 41 Avda Norte y Alameda Roosvelt 115, San Salvador; tel. 2260-9249; fax 2260-9254; e-mail informacion@istu.gob.sv; internet www.istu.gob.sv; f. 1950; Pres. MANUEL AVILÉS; Exec. Dir DOLORES EDUVIGES HENRÍQUEZ DE FUNES.

Defence

As assessed at November 2013, the armed forces totalled 15,300, of whom an estimated 13,850 (including 4,000 conscripts) were in the army, 700 were in the navy and 750 (including some 200 conscripts) were in the air force. There were also some 9,900 joint reserves. The Policía Nacional Civil numbered some 17,000. Military service is by compulsory selective conscription of males aged between 18 and 30 years and lasts for one year.

Defence Budget: an estimated US $154m. in 2013.

Chief of the Joint Command of the Armed Forces: Maj.-Gen. JAIME LEONARDO PARADA GONZÁLEZ.

Chief of Staff of the Army: Brig.-Gen. FRANCISCO EUGENIO DEL CID DÍAZ.

Chief of Staff of the Navy: Capt. GUILLERMO JIMÉNEZ VÁSQUEZ.

Chief of Staff of the Air Force: Col CARLOS JAIME MENA TORRES.

Education

Education in El Salvador is provided free of charge in state schools and there are also numerous private schools. Pre-primary education—beginning at four years of age and lasting for three years—and primary education—beginning at the age of seven years and lasting for nine years—are officially compulsory. In 2012 enrolment at primary schools included 93% of children in the relevant age-group. Secondary education, from the age of 16, lasts two years for an academic diploma or three years for a vocational one. In 2012 enrolment at secondary schools included 62% of students in the relevant age–group. Budget allocation for education was US $827m. in 2012.

Bibliography

For works on Central America generally, see Select Bibliography (Books)

Almeida, P. D. *Waves of Protest: Popular Struggle in El Salvador, 1925–2005 (Social Movements, Protest and Contention).* Minneapolis, MN, University of Minnesota Press, 2008.

Brockett, C. D. *Political Movements and Violence in Central America (Cambridge Studies in Contentious Politics).* Cambridge, Cambridge University Press, 2005.

Cavallaro, J. L., and Miller, S. *No Place to Hide: Gang, State, and Clandestine Violence in El Salvador.* Cambridge, MA, Human Rights Program, Harvard Law School, 2011.

La Comisión de la Verdad para El Salvador. *De la Locura a la Esperanza: La Guerra de 12 Años en El Salvador.* San Salvador, United Nations, 1993.

Consalvi, C. H. *Broadcasting the Civil War: A Memoir of Guerrilla Radio.* Austin, TX, University of Texas Press, 2010.

Cousens, E. M., et al. (Eds). *Peacebuilding as Politics.* Boulder, CO, Lynne Rienner Publrs, 2001.

DeLugan, R. M. *Reimagining National Belonging: Post-Civil War El Salvador in a Global Context.* Tucson, AZ, University of Arizona Press, 2012.

Eriksson, J. R., et al. *El Salvador: Post Conflict Reconstruction: Country Case Evaluation.* Washington, DC, World Bank, 2000.

Hume, M. *The Politics of Violence: Gender, Conflict and Community in El Salvador.* Hoboken, NJ, Wiley-Blackwell, 2009.

Juhn, T. *Negotiating Peace in El Salvador: Civil–Military Relations and the Conspiracy to End the War.* London, Macmillan, 1998.

Ladutke, L. M. *Freedom of Expression in El Salvador: The Struggle for Human Rights and Democracy.* Jefferson, NC, McFarland & Co Inc Publrs, 2004.

Lauria-Santiago, A. A. *An Agrarian Republic: Commercial Agriculture and the Politics of Peasant Communities in El Salvador, 1823–1914.* Pittsburgh, PA, University of Pittsburgh Press, 1999.

Lauria-Santiago A. A., and Binford, L. *Landscapes of Struggle: Politics, Society, and Community in El Salvador.* Pittsburgh, PA, University of Pittsburgh Press, 2004.

Lindo-Fuentes, H., and Ching, E. *Modernizing Minds in El Salvador: Education Reform and the Cold War, 1960–1980.* Albuquerque, NM, University of New Mexico Press, 2012.

MacLeod, L. *Constructing Peace: Lessons from UN Peacebuilding Operations in El Salvador and Cambodia.* Lanham, MD, Lexington Books, 2006.

Miller, A. P. *Military Disengagement and Democratic Consolidation in Post-Military Regimes: The Case of El Salvador.* Ceredigion, Edwin Mellen Press, 2006.

Moodie, E. *El Salvador in the Aftermath of Peace: Crime, Uncertainty and the Transition to Democracy.* Philadelphia, PA, University of Pennsylvania Press, 2012.

Negroponte, D. V. *Seeking Peace in El Salvador: The Struggle to Reconstruct a Nation at the End of the Cold War.* Basingstoke, Palgrave Macmillan, 2012.

Popkin, M. L. *Peace Without Justice: Obstacles to Building the Rule of Law in El Salvador.* University Park, PA, Pennsylvania University Press, 2000.

Reformas Económicas, Régimen Cambiario y Choques Externos: Efectos en el Desarrollo Económico, la Desigualdad y la Pobreza en Costa Rica, El Salvador y Honduras (Estudios y Perspectivas). New York, United Nations Educational, 2005.

Ross, D. G. *Development of Railroads in Guatemala and El Salvador, 1849–1929.* Lewiston, NY, Edwin Mellen Press, 2001.

Studemeister, M. S. *El Salvador: Implementation of the Peace Accords.* Washington, DC, US Institute of Peace, 2000.

Williams, P. J., and Walter, K. *Militarization and Demilitarization in El Salvador's Transition to Democracy.* Pittsburgh, PA, University of Pittsburgh Press, 1998.

THE FALKLAND ISLANDS

Geography

PHYSICAL FEATURES

The Falkland Islands is an Overseas Territory of the United Kingdom, claimed by Argentina as the Islas Malvinas. It is located in the South Atlantic, at the same latitude as southern Argentina and Chile, some 770 km (480 miles) north-east of Cape Horn, but 480 km from the nearest point on the South American mainland. The colony's authorities claim an economic zone around the islands and their waters, so as to regulate fishing and the exploitation of hydrocarbons, but the United Kingdom seeks agreement with Argentina on such issues. The islands cover an area more than one-half the size of Wales (United Kingdom), 12,173 sq km (4,700 sq miles).

There are several hundred islands and many more islets and rocks, with a combined area greater than that of Jamaica, but stretching over a distance of 238 km from east to west. The two main islands of East and West Falkland butterfly on either side of the intervening Falkland Sound. The coastline, 1,288 km in total length, is deeply indented and rugged. The windswept islands are hilly, clad in lichen-covered rocks, low-lying, scrubby vegetation or grassland dotted with heath and dwarf shrubs. There are some undulating and usually boggy plains. The islands reach their heights at Mt Usborne (705 m or 2,314 ft) on East Falkland and Mt Adam (700 m) on West Falkland. The natural environment is rich, despite the harsh conditions, although the last example of the only native mammal, the warrah or Falklands wolf, was killed in 1876. Introduced species of mammal, apart from sheep (of which there are more than 500,000), cattle, horses and, more recently, reindeer, include the Patagonian fox, rats, mice, cats, rabbits and, on Staats Island, the guanaco. There are also breeding colonies of the southern sea lion, leopard, elephant and fur seals, and rockhopper, king, macaroni, gentoo and Magellanic (or jackass) penguins. In fact, over 200 species of birds have been recorded in the islands, from the tiny tussac, through two endemic species, the Falkland flightless steamer duck (logger) and the Cobb's or rock wren, to the mighty black-browed albatross.

CLIMATE

The climate is a cold marine one, cloudy, humid, windy (there are strong westerlies) and seldom hot. Although the Falklands are at a similar latitude to the south as the British capital of London is to the north, there is no Gulf Stream to warm the islands, so temperatures range from –5°C (23°F) in July (winter) to 22°C (72°F) in January (summer). Average annual rainfall is low, but fairly evenly distributed throughout the

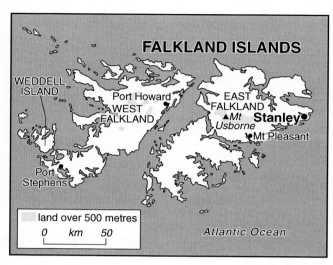

year, at 626 mm (24 ins). It can snow in any month except the main summer months of January and February.

POPULATION

The majority of the population are of British descent (there are also some descended from Scandinavian whalers), 92% hold British citizenship and English is the universal language. Spanish names and phrases in use stem from the mid-19th century, when farmers brought in gauchos from the South American mainland to help work the vast livestock holdings. The main religion is Christianity (Anglican, Roman Catholic and some Nonconformist Protestant denominations). Some 66% of the population were Christian, according to the 2012 census.

The total population at the 2012 census was 2,471, with most people (2,120) living in the capital, Stanley, in the east of northern East Falkland. There are obviously few people left in the small settlements scattered over the rest of the countryside (known locally as the 'Camp', from the Spanish for countryside). There were 127 people on West Falkland and 22 on other islands (apart from East Falkland). There were also some 369 military personnel located at the Mount Pleasant military base in that year.

History

The islands are a United Kingdom Overseas Territory. From February 1998 the British Dependent Territories were referred to as the United Kingdom Overseas Territories, following the announcement of the interim findings of a British Government review of the United Kingdom's relations with the Overseas Territories. The Governor of the islands, who is the representative of the British monarch, is advised by a six-member Executive Council; the separate post of Chief Executive (responsible to the Governor) was created in 1983. A new Constitution was introduced in 2009.

From the late 17th century the British, French and Spanish disputed sovereignty over the Falkland Islands (Islas Malvinas). Finally, in 1832 a British expedition expelled colonists from the recently independent Argentine Republic.

The Falkland Islands became a British Crown Colony in 1833. Argentina continued to claim sovereignty over the islands.

In 1966 negotiations between Argentina and the United Kingdom were opened. Limited progress was made, but on 2 April 1982 Argentine forces invaded the islands, expelled the Governor and established a military governorship. A British naval task force was dispatched and the Argentine forces formally surrendered on 14 June; in the conflict about 750 Argentines, 255 British soldiers and three Falkland Islanders were killed. A Civil Commissioner (later restored to the title of Governor) resumed authority in the dependency, and the British Government established a garrison of some 4,000 troops (later reduced).

www.europaworld.com

The Argentine military Government refused to declare a formal cessation of hostilities until the United Kingdom agreed to negotiations on sovereignty, while the United Kingdom maintained that sovereignty was not negotiable and that the wishes of the Falkland Islanders were paramount (the Constitution of 1985 guaranteed the islanders' right to self-determination). It was only in October 1989 that the formal cessation of hostilities and the re-establishment of diplomatic relations at consular level were agreed. In February 1990 it was announced that full diplomatic relations were to be re-established and the naval protection zone around the islands was to be ended. Disputes over fishing areas and exclusion zones continued into the 1990s, but did not prevent some agreement between the United Kingdom and Argentina on the allocation of marine resources and the exploitation of hydrocarbons reserves: a joint hydrocarbon exploratory contract was signed by the Argentine President, Carlos Saúl Menem, in 1995 and was regarded as recognizing the United Kingdom's claim to the sea floor surrounding the Falkland Islands.

In May 1999 delegations from the Falkland Islands and Argentina met in the United Kingdom for formal negotiations intended to improve relations. In July an agreement was signed by both Governments that ended a ban on Argentine citizens visiting the islands and re-established direct flights there from Chile. (In March Chile had ended its country's regular air services to the islands in protest at the British Government's continued detention of the former Chilean dictator Gen. Augusto Pinochet.) Furthermore, Argentina and the islands were to co-operate in fishing conservation and in the prevention of poaching in the South Atlantic. The agreement did not affect claims to sovereignty.

In 2000 the Government of Argentine President Fernando de la Rúa announced that it would not engage in any dialogue with Falkland Islands councillors that involved the British Government, and the Anglo-Argentine dialogue on joint petroleum and gas exploration was suspended by mutual agreement for an indefinite period of time.

In November 2003 Argentina began to demand that the increasingly frequent air charter services flying from the Falkland Islands to Chile obtain permission to use Argentine airspace. The decision was intended to exert pressure on the British Government into reversing its policy of not allowing Argentine airlines to fly to the Falkland Islands. The services were suspended in January 2004 after the British Government lodged objections to the Argentine demands. Appeals by Falkland Islands councillors to the UN's Special Committee on Decolonization in mid-2005 to be allowed to exercise the right to self-determination proved fruitless: at a Caribbean regional session of the Committee in mid-2007, it was determined that territories currently the subject of sovereignty disputes were excluded from self-determination rights on the basis of their contested status. The ruling meant that any ambition within the Falkland Islands for complete self-governance would have to wait until Argentina and the United Kingdom reached a peaceful solution.

The Argentine Government formed a Congressional Observatory in June 2006 with the express function of actively reclaiming the Falkland Islands, which it continued to refer to as Argentine territory. In July, in response to a recent policy change by the British Government in issuing fishing licences for up to 25 years (as opposed to just one, as had been the practice hitherto), the Government of Argentina threatened to adopt sanctions against businesses that engaged in the exploration or extraction of hydrocarbons or in fishing activities in the region. In February 2007 Argentina rejected an invitation by the British Government to participate in joint commemorative celebrations to mark the 25th anniversary of the conflict's end and, in the following month, suspended its 1995 joint hydrocarbon exploratory contract with the United Kingdom. Argentina accused the British of pursuing a 'unilateral' approach to oil exploration initiatives and declared that, until the United Kingdom had agreed to resume negotiations over the islands' sovereignty, the suspension would remain. New legislation was approved by the Argentine Government in April that effectively politicized the permit-issuing process for fishing companies wishing to operate in the maritime exclusion zone surrounding the islands; companies were now required to choose between Argentine and British issuing authorities, while commercial access to Argentine jurisdictional waters was restricted to holders of Argentine-issued permits. In response to further pressure from the Argentine administration for the British Government to engage in dialogue over the islands' future, the United Kingdom announced that no amendments to the governance or sovereign allegiance of the Falkland Islands would be considered unless and until a request to this effect was registered by the islanders.

The Argentine Government continued to seek a favourable resolution with regard to its claims of sovereignty over the Falkland Islands. The new President of Argentina, Cristina Fernández de Kirchner, stated in December 2007 that she was not prepared to make concessions in those claims, and her Government once again urged the United Kingdom to relaunch the negotiations process. Tensions between the two countries were exacerbated in May 2008 when Argentine foreign minister Jorge Taiana accused the British Government of 'illegitimately' issuing licences for hydrocarbon exploration and extraction activities in an area north of the Falkland Islands, part of the Argentine continental shelf. The British Government refused to concede to any of the claims made by its Argentine counterpart and maintained that it held sovereignty over the disputed area. In April 2009 Argentina lodged a hostile claim before the UN Commission to some 1.7m. sq km (660,000 sq miles) of seabed surrounding the territory, as well as an area north of Antarctica. This was formally countered by the United Kingdom, which presented its own claim to the disputed region in the following month. As a result, both claims were frozen, preventing either country from exploiting the areas beyond 200 nautical miles from its respective coastline.

Tensions between Argentina and the United Kingdom rose further in September 2009 after a British company, Desire Petroleum, announced plans to commence drilling in an area north of the Falklands in 2010. In the weeks preceding the start of the operation in February the Argentine Government asserted that the drilling was illegal, and reiterated its claim to the seabed surrounding the islands. In mid-February President Fernández de Kirchner decreed that all ships sailing through Argentine waters must hold a permit, effectively blockading the area around the islands, and later that month Taiana formally requested the UN to initiate negotiations with the United Kingdom over the sovereignty of the islands. At the end of February US Secretary of State Hillary Clinton appeared to support Argentina's position by pledging to help to 'resolve' the sovereignty issue. Despite the escalation of the dispute, drilling went ahead as planned, although only small deposits of hydrocarbons were found in the first well drilled. In May, however, the British company, Rockhopper Exploration, which was also involved in drilling north of the Falklands, announced that it had discovered oil in a second well in the area. After further analysis of the deposit, Rockhopper Exploration confirmed in March 2011 the presence of a 'significant' amount of petroleum, and details of a further major discovery were announced in September; Premier Oil, which took over from Rockhopper in 2013, announced in early 2014 that it anticipated production to commence by 2019, later than originally expected. Drilling by numerous oil firms was ongoing in early 2014, in spite of threats by Argentina to initiate legal action against the companies involved.

A Constitutional Select Committee was convened in February 2007 to complete discussions on a constitutional review, with the aim of according greater self-governance to the islands. Its final proposals were submitted to the United Kingdom's Foreign and Commonwealth Office (FCO) for deliberation in June. Following two rounds of talks between the Constitutional Select Committee and FCO officials, as well as further public consultation, the new Constitution came into force on 1 January 2009. It re-asserted the islanders' right to self-determination and contained amendments to the rules under which British citizens would be eligible for Falklands Islands status, as well as provisions for a Public Accounts Committee and a Complaints Commissioner to improve transparency in the territory. It also provided further clarification of the division of powers between the Executive Council and the Governor, stating that the Governor must abide by the advice of the Executive Council on domestic policies, though not in matters of external affairs, defence and the administration of justice.

An operation, begun in 2009, to remove some 1,250 land-mines from four minefields left on the islands following the 1982 conflict was completed successfully in June 2010. However, the British Government estimated in February 2011 that over 15,000 mines, in 83 minefields, were still deployed in the territory. A demining operation in Stanley concluded in March 2012, as a result of which an additional 3.5 sq km of land was made accessible to residents and tourists. A third clearance operation was completed in 2013.

In a symbolic move designed to pressure the British Government, in December 2011 the Mercado Común del Sur (MERCOSUR—Southern Common Market), of which Argentina is a prominent member, proclaimed that vessels registered in the Falkland Islands would be prohibited from docking at MERCOSUR ports; the United Kingdom censured the decision. The Unión de Naciones Suramericanas (Union of South American Nations) had imposed a similar ban in November 2010. Bilateral tensions had intensified during 2011 due to Argentina's assertive rhetoric regarding its claim over the islands, which British Prime Minister David Cameron denounced as akin to 'colonialism' in January 2012. Cameron repeatedly refused to engage in sovereignty negotiations, citing the overwhelming desire of the islanders to remain under British control. In the following month Argentina criticized the United Kingdom's alleged 'militarization' of the region after HRH Prince William, the Duke of Cambridge, was sent to the South Atlantic as part of a brief military tour of duty and following confirmation that a British destroyer would be deployed in the Falkland Islands to replace an older vessel.

The Argentine authorities also suspected that the United Kingdom had stationed a nuclear submarine in the region, but British officials rejected this claim. The British embassy in Argentina was attacked by protesters on 2 April, the 30th anniversary of the start of the Falklands conflict; British and Argentine officials condemned the violence. In June Gavin Short, the Chairman of the territory's Legislative Assembly, announced that a referendum on the islands' future status would be held in 2013; the electorate was widely expected to endorse the maintenance of the status quo. Later that month President Kirchner of Argentina gave a speech to the UN's Committee of 24 (Special Committee on Decolonization), an unprecedented move by a head of state, in which she strongly criticized the planned referendum and again appealed for sovereignty talks with the United Kingdom.

A British offer to host trilateral discussions with the Falkland Islands and Argentina was rejected by the latter in January 2013. In the referendum, which was held on 10–11 March, 99.8% of voters endorsed the continuation of the territory's existing relationship with the United Kingdom. The rate of participation by the electorate was 92%. Argentina refused to recognize the results, and President Kirchner insisted that the plebiscite had no legal validity.

Argentina adopted legislation in November 2013 that prescribed a variety of severe penalties for oil companies operating in the waters surrounding the Falkland Islands. The British Government denounced the new law and submitted a formal complaint to the Argentine authorities.

A poll was held on 7 November 2013 to elect the (politically independent) members of a new Legislative Assembly. Governor Nigel Haywood was succeeded by Colin Roberts in late April 2014.

Economy

The main economic activity of the Falkland Islands was fishing. The economy enjoyed a period of strong and sustained growth at the end of the 20th century, notably after the introduction of the fisheries licensing scheme in 1987. The annual income of the islands tripled following the introduction of a licensing system for foreign vessels fishing within a 150-nautical-mile conservation and management zone. The revenue, amounting to £20.0m. in 2011, funds social provisions and economic development programmes, including subsidies to the wool industry, which is in long-term decline, owing to the oversupply of that commodity on the international market. Stocks of squid, for which the waters around the islands are noted, can vary considerably from year to year owing to their one-year life cycle. Owing to the low stocks, companies with licences to fish for *illex* squid were reimbursed in 2009, resulting in a significant reduction in fishing revenue. However, the squid catch rose to 61,532 tons in 2010, according to FAO figures, falling to 35,525 tons in 2011, before increasing to 71,239 tons in 2012, when the total fishing catch was 96,000 tons.

The decline in revenues from the fishing licence sector in the 2000s increased hopes that exploitation of hydrocarbons in the waters around the islands would yield positive results. Licences for petroleum and gas exploration had been issued in 1996 under an Argentine-British agreement, although no commercial quantities of petroleum were found in the initial phase of drilling in 1998. In 2002 the Falkland Islands Government, without consultation with the Argentine Government, granted 10 petroleum exploration licences to the Falklands Hydrocarbon Consortium (comprising Global Petroleum Ltd, Hardman Resources Ltd and Falkland Islands Holdings)—now known as Falkland Oil and Gas Ltd (FOGL)—for an area covering 57,700 sq km to the south of the islands. In 2007 Argentina terminated a joint hydrocarbon exploration agreement with the United Kingdom. None the less, amid significant increases in the price of oil, the waters around the Falkland Islands became of increasing interest to oil exploration companies during 2008, with seismic surveys suggesting

that the area could yield as much as 18,000m. barrels of petroleum. A second phase of exploratory drilling commenced in 2010, with a well in the North Falkland Basin licensed to a British company, Desire Petroleum. Only small amounts of hydrocarbons were discovered in this first well. More encouraging was the discovery of oil in a well drilled by the British company, Rockhopper Exploration, also in the North Falkland Basin. After further analysis of the deposit, Rockhopper Exploration confirmed in March 2011 the presence of a 'significant' amount of petroleum, which was 'highly likely to prove commercially viable', and another major discovery was announced in September. However, in January 2014 Premier Oil (which had taken over Rockhopper) announced it anticipated production would begin in 2019, three years later than originally hoped. The renewed exploration of hydrocarbons in the area reignited the issue of the sovereignty of the islands (see History). Argentina imposed several economic sanctions on the Falklands, including a ban on oil companies working in that country from any involvement in oil exploration around the Falkland Islands; nevertheless, drilling operations were ongoing in 2014.

The services sector has expanded rapidly during the last decade, while the importance of the agricultural sector has decreased, not least because of its reliance on direct and indirect subsidies. There were some 85 farms on the islands in 2010/11. The Government has made efforts to diversify the agricultural sector in recent years: in 2001 the Government brought 100 reindeer from the South Georgia Islands (with the aim of increasing the number to 10,000 over the next 20 years) in order to export venison to Scandinavia and Chile. In 2011 there were 184 reindeer on the islands.

Tourism, and in particular eco-tourism, was developing rapidly in the early 21st century. During 2008/09 69,000 tourists visited the Falklands Islands, with around 62,600 of these arriving on cruise ships. However, the number of cruise ship visitors declined to 48,359 in 2009/10 and 40,542 in 2010/11. Tourism numbers had been expected to increase in 2012; however, several cruise lines cancelled their Falklands itineraries in 2012 after some vessels returning from the islands were subjected to harassment and obstruction while attempting to dock at Argentine ports. Poor weather conditions also led to further cancellations. Cruise ship arrivals consequently decreased by 16% in 2012/13. Nevertheless, there was an upturn in stay-over visitors in 2012 and preliminary data indicated that there was a substantial rise in cruise ship passengers during the 2013/14 season. The sale of postage stamps and coins also represents a significant source of income.

In 2000 the Falkland Islands recorded an estimated trade surplus of £28m. Fish, most of which is purchased by the United Kingdom, Spain and Chile, is the islands' most significant export. The annual rate of inflation averaged 2.5% in 1995–2003; consumer prices increased by 1.2% in 2003. Budgeted overall revenue totalled an estimated £46.5m. in 2011/12, while expenditure was estimated at £43.0m., leaving a surplus of £3.5m. According to government figures, the economy expanded by 5.3% in 2010. This followed a drastic contraction of about 9.0%, according to preliminary estimates, in 2009, mainly owing to the decrease in the squid catch and a reduction in tourist numbers.

Statistical Survey

Source (unless otherwise stated): The Treasury of the Falkland Islands Government, Stanley, FIQQ 1ZZ; tel. 27143; fax 27144; internet www.falklands.gov.fk.

AREA AND POPULATION

Area: approx. 12,173 sq km (4,700 sq miles): East Falkland and adjacent islands 6,760 sq km (2,610 sq miles); West Falkland and adjacent islands 5,413 sq km (2,090 sq miles).

Population*: 2,478 at census of 8 October 2006; 2,471 at census of 15 April 2012.
* Census data exclude military personnel. Data also exclude civilians based at Mount Pleasant military base (477 in 2006; 369 in 2012), and residents absent on census night (84 in 2006; 91 in 2012).

Density (at 2012 census): 0.20 per sq km.

Population by Age and Sex (at 2012 census): *0–14 years:* 455 (males 204, females 251); *15–64 years:* 1,703 (males 873, females 830); *65 years and over:* 298 (males 154, females 144); *Total* 2,456 (males 1,231, females 1,225). Note: Figures exclude 15 non-respondents.

Population by Place of Birth (incl. civilians based at Mount Pleasant military base, 2012 census): Argentina 38; Chile 181; Falkland Islands 1,339; Philippines 22; St Helena 295; United Kingdom (not elsewhere specified) 798; Other 167; *Total* 2,840.

Principal Town (population at 2012 census): Stanley (capital) 2,120.

Births and Deaths (2006): Live births 27; Deaths 20. Source: UN, *Population and Vital Statistics Report.*

Economically Active Population (persons aged 15 years and over, 2012 census): Agriculture and fishing 247; Mining and quarrying (incl. oil and gas exploration) 26; Manufacturing 30; Construction 143; Electricity, water and gas 74; Hospitality and tourism 179; Wholesale and retail trade 183; Transport, storage and communications 203; Finance 41; Business services 38; Administration and support service activities 117; Community, social and personal services 100; Public service (local government) 485; Public service (other) 25; Other services 16; *Total employed* 1,907.

AGRICULTURE, ETC.

Livestock (2011, official figures at 31 May): Sheep 488,395; Cattle 4,688; Goats 145; Reindeer 184; Horses 494; Poultry 2,070.

Livestock Products (metric tons, 2012, FAO estimates): Cattle meat 157; Sheep meat 810; Cows' milk 1,500; Wool, greasy 2,200. Source: FAO.

Fishing ('000 metric tons, live weight of capture, 2012): Southern blue whiting 0.4; Argentine hake 4.1; Patagonian grenadier 3.5; Patagonian squid 64.2; Argentine shortfin squid 7.0; Total catch (incl. others) 96.0. Source: FAO.

FINANCE

Currency and Exchange Rates: 100 pence (pennies) = 1 Falkland Islands pound (FI £). *Sterling, Dollar and Euro Equivalents (30 May* 2014): £1 sterling = FI £1.00; US $1 = 59.45 pence; €1 = 80.91 pence; FI £100 = £100.00 sterling = $168.22 = €123.59. *Average Exchange Rate* (FI £ per US dollar): 0.6241 in 2011; 0.6330 in 2012; 0.6397 in 2013. Note: The Falkland Islands pound is at par with the pound sterling.

Budget (FI £ million, 2009/10): *Revenue:* Sales and services 9.7; Fishing licences and transshipments 18.0; Investment income 4.5; Taxes and duties 10.2; Total 42.4. *Expenditure:* Operating expenditure 38.9 (Public works 8.5, Fisheries 5.2, Health care 7.5, Education 5.3, Aviation 2.5, Police and justice 1.5, Agriculture 1.0, Central administration 3.5, Other 3.9); Capital expenditure 8.7; Total 47.6. *2011/12:* Revenue 46.5; Operating expenditure 43.0.

Cost of Living (Consumer Price Index for Stanley; base: 2000 = 100): All items 101.3 in 2001; 102.0 in 2002; 103.2 in 2003. Source: ILO.

EXTERNAL TRADE

2000 (estimates): Total imports £18,958,103; Total exports £47,000,000. Fish is the principal export. Trade is mainly with the United Kingdom, Spain and Chile.

TRANSPORT

Shipping: *Flag Registered Fleet* (at 31 December 2013): Number of vessels 29; Total displacement 48,228 grt. Source: Lloyd's List Intelligence (www.lloydslistintelligence.com).

Road Traffic: 2,011 vehicles in use at 2012 census.

TOURISM

Day Visitors (country of origin of cruise ship excursionists, 2006/07 season): Canada 4,862; United Kingdom 6,736; USA 21,298; Total (incl. others) 51,282. *2008/09:* Total 62,600 (Source: Falkland Islands Tourist Board).

COMMUNICATIONS MEDIA

Telephones (fixed lines): 1,170 at 2012 census.

Mobile Cellular Telephones (handsets): 1,678 at 2012 census.

Personal Computers (incl. tablets): 1,702 at 2012 census.

Internet Access (households): 947 (of 1,316 respondents) at 2012 census.

EDUCATION

2003 (Stanley): *Primary:* Teachers 18; Pupils 203. *Secondary:* Teachers 18; Pupils 160.

Directory

The Constitution

The present Constitution of the Falkland Islands came into force on 1 January 2009 (replacing that of 1985). The Governor, who is the personal representative of the British monarch, is advised by the Executive Council, comprising six members: the Governor (presiding), three elected members of the Legislative Assembly and two ex officio members, the Chief Executive and the Financial Secretary of the Falkland Islands Government, who are non-voting. The Legislative Assembly is composed of the Governor, eight elected members and the same two (non-voting) ex officio members. One of the principal features of the Constitution is the reference in the preamble to the islanders' right to self-determination. The separate post of Chief Executive (responsible to the Governor) was created in 1983. The electoral principle was introduced, on the basis of universal adult suffrage, in 1949. The minimum voting age was lowered from 21 years to 18 years in 1977.

The Government

(September 2014)

HEAD OF STATE

Queen: HM Queen ELIZABETH II.

Governor: COLIN ROBERTS (assumed office 29 April 2014).

HEAD OF GOVERNMENT

Chief Executive of the Falkland Islands Government: KEITH PADGETT.

TERRITORIAL ADMINISTRATION

Government Secretary: PETER T. KING.

Attorney-General: PETER JUDGE.

Commander, British Forces South Atlantic Islands: Brig. BILL ALDRIDGE.

EXECUTIVE COUNCIL

The Council consists of three elected members and two ex officio members (the Chief Executive and the Financial Secretary, presided over by the Governor. In addition, the Attorney-General and the Commander, British Forces South Atlantic Islands, may speak on any matter.

GOVERNMENT OFFICES

Office of the Governor: Government House, Stanley, FIQQ 1ZZ; tel. 28200; fax 27434; e-mail gov.house@horizon.co.fk.

London Office: Falkland Islands Government Office, Falkland House, 14 Broadway, London, SW1H 0BH, United Kingdom; tel. (20) 7222-2542; fax (20) 7222-2375; e-mail reception@falklands.gov .fk; internet www.falklands.gov.fk; f. 1983.

LEGISLATIVE ASSEMBLY

Comprises the Governor, two ex officio members (the Chief Executive and the Financial Secretary) and eight elected members. Elections to the Legislative Assembly are held every four years. The last election was held on 7 November 2013.

Speaker: KEITH BILES.

Office of the Legislative Assembly: Legislature Dept, Gilbert House, Stanley, FIQQ 1ZZ; tel. 27451; e-mail assembly@sec.gov.fk; internet www.falklands.gov.fk.

Judicial System

The judicial system of the Falkland Islands is administered by the Supreme Court (presided over by the non-resident Chief Justice), the Magistrate's Court (presided over by the Senior Magistrate) and the Court of Summary Jurisdiction. The Court of Appeal for the territory sits in the United Kingdom and appeals therefrom may be heard by the Judicial Committee of the Privy Council.

Supreme Court: Town Hall, Ross Rd, Stanley, FIQQ 1ZZ; tel. 27271; fax 27270; Chief Justice CHRISTOPHER GARDNER, QC; Registrar and Courts Administrator JAN PARKE.

Court of Appeal: Stanley, FIQQ 1ZZ; Pres. Judge BRIAN APPLEBY; Registrar MICHAEL J. ELKS.

Attorney-General: PETER JUDGE.

Religion

CHRISTIANITY

The Anglican Communion, the Roman Catholic Church and the United Free Church predominate. Also represented are the Evangelist Church, Jehovah's Witnesses, the Lutheran Church and Seventh-day Adventists. Some 66% of the population considered themselves Christian in 2012.

The Anglican Communion

The Archbishop of Canterbury, the Primate of All England, exercises episcopal jurisdiction over the Falkland Islands and South Georgia.

Episcopal Commissary for the Falkland Islands: Rt. Rev. STEPHEN VENNER (Bishop of Dover, United Kingdom).

Rector: Rev. Dr RICHARD HINES, The Deanery, Christ Church Cathedral, Stanley, FIQQ 1ZZ; tel. 21100; fax 21842; e-mail deanery@horizon.co.fk.

The Roman Catholic Church

Prefect Apostolic of the Falkland Islands: Mgr MICHAEL McPARTLAND, St Mary's Presbytery, 12 Ross Rd, Stanley, FIQQ 1ZZ; tel. 21204; fax 22242; e-mail stmarys@horizon.co.fk; internet www.southatlanticrcchurch.com; f. 1764; 300 adherents (2010).

The Press

Falkland Islands Gazette: Attorney-General's Chambers, POB 587, Stanley, FIQQ 1ZZ; tel. 28464; fax 27276; e-mail bsteen@sec.gov .fk; internet www.falklands.gov.fk; govt publ; Editor BARBARA STEEN.

Falkland Islands News Network: POB 141, Stanley, FIQQ 1ZZ; tel. and fax 21182; e-mail finn@horizon.co.fk; internet www .falklandnews.com; relays news daily online and via fax as FINN(COM) Service; Man. JUAN BROCK; publishes *Teaberry Express* (weekly).

Penguin News: Ross Rd, Stanley, FIQQ 1ZZ; tel. 22709; fax 22238; e-mail adverts@penguinnews.co.fk; internet www.penguin-news .com; f. 1979; weekly (Fri.); independent newspaper; Man. FRAN BIGGS; Editor LISA WATSON; circ. 1,450.

Broadcasting and Communications

TELECOMMUNICATIONS

In 1989 Cable & Wireless PLC installed a digital telecommunications network covering the entire Falkland Islands. The system provides international services as well as a new domestic network. The first mobile telephone network was introduced in 2005 and a broadband internet service in 2006.

Sure South Atlantic Ltd: Ross Rd, POB 584, Stanley, FIQQ 1ZZ; tel. 20834; fax 20811; e-mail info@sure.co.fk; internet www.sure.co .fk; f. 1989; fmrly Cable & Wireless South Atlantic Ltd, name changed 2013; bought by Batelco Group in 2013; exclusive provider of national and international telecommunications and internet services in the Falkland Islands under a licence issued by the Falkland Islands Govt; CEO JUSTIN McPHEE.

BROADCASTING

Radio

British Forces Broadcasting Service (BFBS): BFBS Falkland Islands, Mount Pleasant, BFPO 655; tel. 32179; fax 32193; e-mail falklands@bfbs.com; internet www.bfbs-radio.com; 24-hour satellite service from the United Kingdom; Station Man. CHRIS PEARSON; Sr Engineer ADRIAN ALMOND.

Falkland Islands Radio Service: Broadcasting Studios, John St, Stanley, FIQQ 1ZZ; tel. 27277; fax 27279; e-mail jclifford@firs.co.fk; internet www.firs.co.fk; f. 1929; fmrly Falkland Islands Broadcasting Station; 24-hour service, partly financed by local Govt; broadcasts in English; Station Man. JOHN CLIFFORD (acting); Programme Controller LIZ ELLIOT.

Television

British Forces Broadcasting Service (BFBS): BFBS Falkland Islands, Mount Pleasant, BFPO 655; tel. 32179; fax 32193; internet www.bfbs.com/tv; daily 4-hour transmissions of taped broadcasts from BBC and ITV of London, United Kingdom; Technology Man. PETER NEALE.

KTV: Dean St, POB 68, Stanley, FIQQ 1ZZ; tel. 22349; fax 21049; e-mail kmzb@horizon.co.fk; internet www.ktv.co.fk; satellite television broadcasting services; Man. Dirs MARIO ZUVIC BULIC, SHARON ZUVIC BULIC.

Finance

BANK

Standard Chartered Bank: Ross Rd, POB 597, Stanley, FIQQ 1ZZ; tel. 22220; fax 22219; e-mail bank.info@sc.com; internet www .standardchartered.com/fk; br. opened in 1983; CEO BINOY KARIA.

INSURANCE

Consultancy Services Falklands Ltd: 44 John St, Stanley, FIQQ 1ZZ; tel. 22666; fax 22639; e-mail consultancy@horizon.co.fk; Man. ALISON BAKER.

Trade and Industry

DEVELOPMENT ORGANIZATION

Falkland Islands Development Corporation (FIDC): Shackleton House, West Hillside, Stanley, FIQQ 1ZZ; tel. 27211; fax 27210; e-mail dwaugh@fidc.co.fk; internet www.fidc.co.fk; f. 1983; provides loans and grants; encourages private sector investment, inward investment and technology transfer; Gen. Man. MARTIN SLATER (acting).

CHAMBER OF COMMERCE

Chamber of Commerce: West Hillside, POB 378, Stanley, FIQQ 1ZZ; tel. 22264; fax 22265; e-mail manager@commerce.co.fk; internet www.falklandislandschamberofcommerce.com; f. 1993; promotes private industry; operates DHL courier service; runs an employment agency; Pres. ROGER SPINK; 87 mems.

TRADING COMPANIES

Falkland Islands Co Ltd (FIC): Crozier Pl., Stanley, FIQQ 1ZZ; tel. 27600; fax 27603; e-mail fic@horizon.co.fk; internet www .the-falkland-islands-co.com; f. 1852; part of Falkland Islands Holding PLC; the largest trading co; retailing, wholesaling, shipping, insurance and Land Rover sales and servicing; operates as agent for Lloyd's of London and general shipping concerns; travel services; wharf owners and operators; Dir and Gen. Man. ROGER KENNETH SPINK.

Falkland Islands Meat Co Ltd: Sand Bay, East Falklands, FIQQ 1ZZ; tel. 27013; fax 27113; e-mail info@falklandmeat.co.fk; internet www.falklands-meat.com; exporters of lamb, mutton and beef meat; Gen. Man. JOHN FERGUSON.

Falkland Oil and Gas Ltd (FOGL): 56 John St, Stanley, F1QQ 1ZZ; e-mail info@fogl.com; internet www.fogl.co.uk; f. 2004; shareholders include Falkland Islands Holdings PLC (16%), Global Petroleum (14%) and RAB Capital PLC (33%); operates an offshore petroleum exploration programme with 8 licences covering 65,354 sq km; Chair. RICHARD LIDDELL; CEO TIM BUSHELL.

EMPLOYERS' ASSOCIATIONS

The Falkland Islands Sheep Owners' Association: Coast Ridge Farm, Fox Bay, FIQQ 1ZZ; tel. 42094; fax 42084; e-mail n.knight .coastridge@horizon.co.fk; f. 1967; asscn for sheep station owners; limited liability private co; Company Sec. N. KNIGHT.

Rural Business Association of the Falkland Islands: POB 296, Stanley, FIQQ 1ZZ; tel. 22432; fax 22660; e-mail secretary@rba.org .fk; internet www.rba.org.fk; f. 1999; farmers' org.; Chair. RICHARD EVANS.

TRADE UNION

Falkland Islands General Employees Union: Ross Rd, Stanley, FIQQ 1ZZ; tel. 21151; e-mail geu@horizon.co.fk; f. 1943; Chair. GAVIN SHORT; 400 mems.

Transport

RAILWAYS

There are no railways on the islands.

ROADS

There are 29 km (18 miles) of paved road in and around Stanley. There are 54 km of all-weather road linking Stanley and the Mount Pleasant airport (some of which has been surfaced with a bitumen substance), and a further 37 km of road as far as Goose Green. There are 300 km of arterial roads in the North Camp on East Falkland linking settlements, and a further 197 km of road on West Falkland. Where roads have still not been built, settlements are linked by tracks, which are passable by all-terrain motor vehicles or motorcycles except in the most severe weather conditions. Total expenditure on roads, improving the North Camp and Stanley road networks, was estimated at £1.13m. for the fiscal year 2011/12.

SHIPPING

There is a floating deep-water jetty in Stanley. There is a ship on charter to the Falkland Islands Co Ltd, which makes the round trip to the United Kingdom four or five times a year, carrying cargo. The British Ministry of Defence charters ships to the Falkland Islands once every three weeks. There are irregular cargo services between the islands and southern Chile and Uruguay. The Falkland Islands Development Corpn commissioned a development plan in 2007 for the upgrade of existing facilities to reflect growth in containerized traffic and cruise ship arrivals, and to accommodate proposed further oil exploration in territorial waters.

The Falkland Islands flag registered fleet numbered 29 vessels, with a total displacement of 48,228 grt, at December 2013; the majority of vessels registered are deep-sea fishing vessels.

Stanley Harbour: c/o Dept of Fisheries, POB 598, Stanley, FIQQ 1ZZ; tel. 27260; fax 27265; e-mail Mjamieson@fisheries.gov.fk; Marine Officer and Harbour Master MALCOLM JAMIESON.

Private Companies

Byron Marine Ltd: Byron House, 3 H Jones Rd, Stanley, FIQQ 1ZZ; tel. 22245; fax 22246; e-mail info@byronmarine.com; internet www .byronmarine.com; f. 1992; additional activites include offshore oil and gas exploration support services, deep-sea fishing and property; contracted managers of the Falkland Islands Government Port Facility; island-wide pilotage services; vessel and port agency; Man. Dir LEWIS CLIFTON.

Falkland Islands Shipping Ltd: Crozier Pl., Stanley, FIQQ 1ZZ; tel. 27629; fax 27601; e-mail stanleyoffice@falklandislandshipping .com; internet www.falklandislandshipping.com; subsidiary of the Falkland Islands Co Ltd (q.v.); Man. JIMMY FORSTER.

Seaview Ltd: 37 Fitzroy Rd, POB 215, Stanley, FIQQ 1ZZ; tel. 22669; fax 22670; e-mail seaview.agent@horizon.co.fk; internet www .fis.com/polar; operates subsidiary co, Polar Ltd (f. 1989); Man. Dir ALEX REID.

Sulivan Shipping Services Ltd: Davis St, POB 159, Stanley, FIQQ 1ZZ; tel. 22626; fax 22625; e-mail sulivan@horizon.co.fk; internet www.sulivanshipping.com; f. 1987; provides port agency and ground-handling services; Man. Dir JOHN POLLARD; Operations Man. RUSSELL MORRISON.

CIVIL AVIATION

There are airports at Stanley and Mount Pleasant; the latter has a runway of 2,590 m (8,497 ft), and is capable of receiving wide-bodied jet aircraft. The British Royal Air Force operates two weekly flights from the United Kingdom. The Chilean carrier LAN Airlines operates weekly return flights from Punta Arenas. An 'air bridge', operated by charter carriers subcontracted to the British Ministry of Defence, provides a link via Ascension Island between the Falkland Islands and the United Kingdom.

Falkland Islands Government Air Service (FIGAS): Stanley Airport, Airport Rd, Stanley, FIQQ 1ZZ; tel. 27219; fax 27302; e-mail operations@figas.gov.fk; internet www.visitorfalklands.com/ contents/view/116; f. 1948 to provide social, medical and postal services between the settlements and Stanley; aerial surveillance for Dept of Fisheries; operates 5 9-seater aircraft to over 35 landing strips across the islands; Gen. Man. MORGAN GOSS.

Tourism

In 2010/11 there were an estimated 40,452 cruise visitors to the islands. US citizens constitute the primary visitor group. Wildlife photography, bird-watching and hiking are popular tourist activities. The Falkland Islands Development Corpn plans to develop the sector in collaboration with the Government and tourism operators in the territory.

Falkland Islands Tourist Board: Jetty Visitor Centre, POB 618, Stanley, FIQQ 1ZZ; tel. 22215; fax 27020; e-mail info@ visitorfalklands.com; internet www.falklandislands.com; Man. Dir TONY MASON.

Defence

As assessed at November 2013, there were approximately 1,500 British troops stationed on the islands. The cost of maintaining the garrison totalled £75m. in 2010–11. There is a Falkland Islands Defence Force, composed of 75 islanders.

Education

Education is compulsory, and is provided free of charge, for children between the ages of five and 16 years. Facilities are available for further study beyond the statutory school-leaving age. In 2003 203 pupils were instructed by 18 teachers at the primary school in Stanley, while 160 pupils received instruction from 18 teachers at the secondary school in the capital; further facilities existed in rural areas, with six peripatetic teachers visiting younger children for two out of every six weeks (older children boarded in a hostel in Stanley). Total expenditure on education was estimated at £6.4m. for 2011/12 (equivalent to 14% of total government expenditure).

FRENCH GUIANA

Geography

PHYSICAL FEATURES

France's Overseas Department of Guiana is the easternmost and smallest of the three Guianas on the north coast of South America (until 1946 it was administered as a colony, under the name of its capital, Cayenne). Suriname (formerly Dutch Guiana) lies to the west, beyond a frontier of 510 km (317 miles), but it also claims territory in the south-east of the Department, beyond the border-marking Litani (Itany) river, as far as the Marouini (both headwaters of the Lawa and, later, the Maroni—Marowijne—which also help to delineate the western border). Brazil is to the south-east and south, beyond a border of 673 km, much of it along the course of the Oiapoque (Oyapock). There are 378 km of north-east-facing Atlantic coastline. French Guiana is the only place on the American mainland not to be independent, although it is an integral part of France. It covers an area of 83,534 sq km (32,253 sq miles).

Most of French Guiana is fairly low-lying, flat and sometimes marshy along the coast, which has a number of rocky islands off shore (notably the old penal camp of Ile du Diable—Devil's Island). The Department chiefly consists of rolling, fertile plains, reaching inland to the lower, northern foothills of the Serra Tumucumaque. Hills occasionally break the monotony of the landscape, with the Chaîne Granitique in the centre of the territory, and low mountains rising in the far south. The highest point is Bellevue de l'Inini, at 851 m (2,793 ft). Most of the terrain is wooded (83%), much of it rainforest, and few people live in the swathes of wilderness inland.

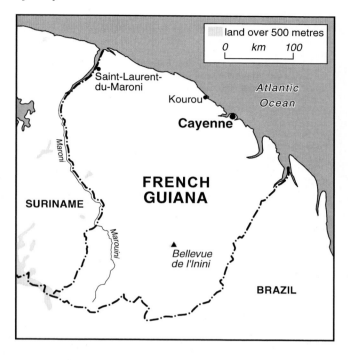

CLIMATE

The climate is tropical, hot and humid, with little seasonal variation in temperature. Average year-round temperatures in Cayenne, on the coast, range between 23°C and 33°C (73°F–91°F). The dry season is in August–October, the wet season December–June. Average annual rainfall is over 2,500 mm (around 100 ins), with frequent heavy showers and thunderstorms able to cause flooding in the generally flat countryside.

POPULATION

The people of the Department are French citizens, and approximately two-thirds are black—about 17% of the population are of Haitian extraction. Some 12% are white, while the rest are mainly native Amerindian, 'East' Indian or Chinese (the latter two groups arriving when labour was needed after the abolition of slavery in the 19th century). Although there are followers of native, tribal faith systems, as well as adherents of syncretic Afro-American spiritualist groups and some Muslims, the majority of the population are nominally Christians. About 80% are Roman Catholics and 4% Protestants. French is the official and most widely used language, but there are speakers of Amerindian tongues and of a local Creole patois.

The total population was estimated at 249,225 at mid-2013, according to UN estimates. The majority of the population live in the coastal areas, and about four-fifths in urban areas. The departmental headquarters and the largest city is Cayenne, a port on the east-central coast. To the west is Kourou, the launching centre for the European Space Agency. In the far north-west is the town of Saint-Laurent-du-Maroni. None of the inland towns is large.

History

JESSICA BYRON

Based on an earlier article by PHILLIP WEARNE

The land that is now French Guiana (Guyane) was first sighted by Europeans at the end of the 15th century. The French began to settle the territory in 1604, but rumours of its potential gold and diamond wealth led to frequent changes of ownership. The Dutch, British and Portuguese all occupied the area, and there were frequent border disputes before the colony was finally confirmed as French in 1817. Subsequent border disputes were settled by arbitration in 1891, 1899 and 1915. In March 1946 the colony, hitherto known as Cayenne, became an Overseas Department, like Guadeloupe and Martinique, with the same laws and administration as a Department of metropolitan France. The head of state is the President of France, represented locally by a Commissioner of the Republic. The Conseil Général (General Council) with 19 seats and the Conseil Régional (Regional Council) with 31 seats are the two local legislative houses. Both have Presidents, and the territory also sends two deputies to the French Assemblée Nationale (National Assembly), one senator to the Sénat (Senate) in Paris and one representative to the European Parliament in Strasbourg.

The discovery of gold in the basin of the Approuague river brought a brief period of prosperity in the mid-19th century, but French Guiana's chief notoriety, until 1937, was as a penal colony. After arriving, prisoners were distributed to camps scattered throughout the territory. Devil's Island became the most infamous. Prisoners mingled freely with other settlers and the indigenous population during a period of exile after serving their sentences, but few could afford to return to France.

The practice of imprisoning convicts and political prisoners in French Guiana ceased in 1937. However, the territory's reputation as a political and economic 'backwater' persisted until the 1970s, when separatist pressure and racial tension exploded in demonstrations against French rule and the deteriorating economic situation. The French Government responded with a combination of strict security measures and the allocation of more economic aid—the traditional prescription for disturbances in the Caribbean Overseas Departments. Leading trade unionists and separatist politicians were arrested, while the Minister for Overseas Departments and Territories introduced a wide-ranging plan for economic revitalization.

However, economic expansion failed to materialize and the rate of unemployment increased to over 30%. This prompted further demands for greater autonomy by the leading Parti Socialiste Guyanais (PSG), and for full independence by separatist groups, particularly the Parti National Populaire Guyanais (PNPG). In 1980 there were several bomb attacks on government offices and buildings, for which the left-wing group Fo nou Libéré la Guyane claimed responsibility. In 1983 several other small-scale bomb attacks were attributed to the Guadeloupe-based Alliance Révolutionnaire Caraïbe, which had frequently threatened to broaden its campaign to include France's other Caribbean possessions.

In elections to the Regional Council in 1983 the separatist vote reached 9% of the total—the highest ever recorded in any of France's Caribbean Departments. Moreover, the three separatist members of the Union des Travailleurs Guyanais (UTG) held the balance of power. However, at elections to the Regional Council in 1986 the separatists, now grouped together in the PNPG, had their proportion of the vote reduced by 60% to only 3.3% of the total votes polled. Thereafter, opinion polls repeatedly indicated a majority in favour of greater autonomy, with an average of about 5% of the population favouring complete independence.

In 1989 a split occurred in the PSG when Georges Othily, President of the Regional Council, was expelled from the party for unauthorized links with the opposition, along with five other senior party figures. Analysts believed that the revolt signified growing discontent with the PSG's increasingly partisan and corrupt 10-year domination of Guianese politics. The PSG split was at least partially responsible for the party's loss of support in the 1992 elections, although Elie Castor, leader of the PSG, remained President of the General Council and one of the territory's two representatives in the National Assembly. In the elections to the Regional Council, the PSG won 16 seats, but Othily supporters secured 10 seats.

Weakened by continued infighting, the decline of the PSG continued. In the 1993 elections to the National Assembly a political newcomer, Christiane Taubira-Delannon of the Walwari movement, a dissident Socialist who once favoured independence, defeated the PSG's candidate, Rodolfe Alexandre, for the Cayenne-Macouria seat. Léon Bertrand of the Rassemblement pour la République (RPR) won a convincing 52.5% of the vote in the election for the second constituency seat of Kourou-Saint-Laurent. PSG representation in the General Council decreased to eight seats after the 1994 elections. Castor left the party, but a PSG member, Stéphan Phinera-Horth, was elected President of the General Council. Taubira-Delannon was ousted by Antoine Karam, the PSG's Secretary-General.

Bertrand and Taubira-Delannon were both re-elected to the National Assembly in 1997, although candidates from pro-independence parties gained increased support. The high rate of abstention in the 1997 legislative and presidential elections and the re-emergence of separatist parties were symptoms of an increasing dissatisfaction with departmental politics and rising tension between the Department and metropolitan France. These developments precipitated, and were reinforced by, escalating social unrest. In November 1996 protests in Cayenne, in support of secondary school pupils who were boycotting classes to demand improved study conditions, degenerated into rioting and looting. Violent clashes between protesters and anti-riot police sent from metropolitan France provoked a one-day general strike in Cayenne, organized by the UTG. These tensions worsened as pupils' representatives and local politicians criticized the actions of the police, and local officials alleged that separatist groups were working to exploit the crisis for their own ends. The situation was temporarily resolved when the French Government announced administrative reform and additional funding for the education system.

In January 1999 representatives from 10 separatist organizations from French Guiana, Guadeloupe and Martinique, including the PNPG and the Mouvement pour la Décolonisation et l'Emancipation Sociale (MDES), signed a joint declaration denouncing 'French colonialism'. The political and constitutional future of the Overseas Departments generated considerable debate and controversy throughout that year, especially in French Guiana. In February members of the two Councils held a congress, which recommended the replacement of the two Councils with a single body to which added powers and responsibilities in areas such as economic development, health and education would be transferred. In October, however, the French Prime Minister, Lionel Jospin, ruled out the possibility of any such merger. In December Karam, along with the Presidents of the Regional Council in both Guadeloupe and Martinique, signed a declaration stating their intention to seek legislative and constitutional amendments aimed at creating a new status of Overseas Region (Région d'Outre-mer). The amendments would also provide for greater financial autonomy. The declaration and subsequent announcements by Karam and his counterparts were dismissed by Jean-Jack Queyranne, Secretary of State for Overseas Departments and Territories, in February 2000 as unconstitutional and exceeding the mandate of the politicians responsible. In March rioting broke out following Queyranne's refusal to meet a delegation of separatist organizations during an official visit to the Department. Later that month the Regional Council rejected a series of reforms proposed by Queyranne, which included the creation of a Congrès (Congress) in French Guiana, as well as the extension of the Departments' powers in areas such as regional co-operation. Nevertheless, the proposals were provisionally accepted by the National Assembly in May, and were subsequently adopted, by a narrow margin, by the Senate, following a number of modifications. In November the National Assembly approved the changes and in December they were ratified by the Constitutional Council.

In November 2000 riots took place in Cayenne. The demonstrations followed a march, organized by the UTG, demanding greater autonomy for French Guiana, as well as immediate negotiations with the new Secretary of State for Overseas Departments and Territories, Christian Paul. Discussions were held in the following month between Paul, senior politicians from French Guiana, and representatives from the PSG, the RPR, Walwari, and the Forces Démocratiques Guyanaises (FDG). It was agreed that further talks would be held between the General Council and the Regional Council of French Guiana before the end of 2001 to be followed by a referendum in the Department; however, no constitutional changes were to be effected before the 2002 presidential and parliamentary elections. Following a meeting of members of both councils in June 2001, a series of proposals on greater autonomy was drawn up. These included: the division of the territory into four districts; the creation of a Territorial Collectivity (Collectivité Territoriale), governed by a 41-member Assembly elected for a five-year term; and the establishment of an independent executive council. Furthermore, the proposals included a request that the territory assume control of legislative and administrative affairs, as well as legislative authority on matters of sole concern to French Guiana. In November the French Government announced itself to be in favour of the suggested constitutional developments, and in March 2003 the two houses of the French parliament approved constitutional changes that conferred the status of Overseas Region (Région d'Outre-mer) on French Guiana; the changes also allowed for a referendum on proposals for greater autonomy, as occurred in

Martinique and Guadeloupe. However, the electorate of French Guiana was not consulted in a referendum, a majority of 10 of the 19 members of the General Council voted against the proposal, provoking accusations that the MDES had behaved in an anti-democratic manner.

In September 2001 Christian Paul announced the establishment of a number of measures designed to improve security in the Department. Plans included a 20% increase in the police force, the creation of a small 'peace corps', and a continuous police presence in the town of Maripasoula and its surrounding region, following concerns over the security of gold prospectors in the area. In September the gendarmerie, in co-operation with the national police, launched Operation Anaconda in the south of the Department, aimed at stopping the illegal gold trade. Unlicensed gold-mining operations were a chief cause of illegal immigration, and a focus for other criminal activities, such as drugs-smuggling and gun-running. They also caused extensive environmental damage, destroying natural habitats and polluting watercourses. Official estimates of the total number of illegal immigrants in French Guiana were between 30,000 and 35,000, the majority from Brazil and Suriname. Operation Anaconda was followed by Operation Harpie 1 in February 2008, which involved 423 raids to interdict illegal gold mining and seize the proceeds. Operation Harpie 2 was launched in April 2009: it was reported in 2011 that the authorities had conducted 2,663 interdiction operations in 2009 and 2010, many in the Amazonian Park and the area of Haut Maroni. In March 2010 French President Nicolas Sarkozy announced that Operation Harpie would be institutionalized in French Guiana. In 2010 €260,000 was provided for helicopter surveillance, an increase of 73% compared with the previous year. There was a shift in tactics in 2011. While there was a 44% increase in seizures of illegal gold–mining proceeds in that year, Operation Harpie 2 focused also on the closure of illegal mines, with 172 such sites identified in 2011, up from 67 in 2010. Attempts were also made to foster closer co-operation with Brazil in the interdiction efforts. In April 2011 the National Assembly ratified a Franco-Brazilian border agreement, which aimed to strengthen judicial co-operation and to co-ordinate joint monitoring of gold-mining and -trading on both sides of the border.

In elections to the Regional Council held in March 2004 the PSG won 17 of the Council's 31 seats, while the FDG and the Union pour un Mouvement Populaire (UMP) each won seven seats. Antoine Karam was duly re-elected as President of the Regional Council.

In January 2006 a strike by dockers over working conditions, introduced the previous November, paralysed the port at Dégrad-des-Cannes for 12 days, causing a backlog of more than 200 shipping containers. An agreement was eventually reached with local employers' organizations, but the strike had a serious impact on the local economy, particularly on smaller companies and those dependent on primary materials. It was the fourth such strike since January 2005.

In December 2006 a week of industrial action by employees in the electricity sector led to long periods without power across the Department. The strike was in protest against proposed plans by the state-owned Eléctricité de France (EdF) to remodel its operations, which employees feared would result in at least a degree of privatization. The industrial action was suspended following an agreement by EdF to schedule negotiations in Paris with trade unions, including the UTG.

At elections to the National Assembly held on 10 and 17 June 2007, Taubira-Delannon, representing the Walwari party, was re-elected, as was the PSG nominee Chantal Berthelot. Following municipal elections held on 10 March 2008, Alain Tien-Liong replaced Pierre Désert as President of the General Council.

In November 2008 protests erupted against high fuel prices, and a damaging blockade was put in place. The strike and the blockade ended in early December after an agreement was signed between the prefect and local politicians that included a commitment to reduce the price of fuel. It was suggested that the two-week strike cost the economy between €143m. and €165m. Further protests, albeit on a more limited scale, took place in February and March 2009. These were largely inspired by events in Martinique and particularly Guadeloupe (q.v.), where serious labour and civil unrest occurred.

Later in 2009, in light of the perceived dissatisfaction with the existing governance arrangements, the French Government and local representatives agreed that a referendum should be held on the subject of whether French Guiana should become an autonomous territory governed by Article 74, which grants greater autonomy (rather than Article 73), of the French Constitution. The vote took place on 10 January 2010 and, contrary to expectations, some 69.8% of voters rejected the motion. Turnout was moderate, at 48.2% of the electorate. In a follow-up vote conducted two weeks later, 57.5% of voters cast their ballots in support of the less significant reform of merging the Regional Council and General Council into a single body. Turnout was disappointing, at 27.4%. The French Government accepted the results of both votes and suggested that a conclusion to the debate over French Guiana's constitutional relationship with France had thus been reached.

The referendum results of January 2010 were expected to lead to the reorganization of local administrative structures and the elimination of the system of two councils, with the present arrangements being replaced between 2012 and 2014 by one Collectivity with a single elected assembly. However, many aspects of the new administrative arrangements were unclear at that time. In July 2011 the National Assembly approved legislation delineating the future institutional arrangements for French Guiana. The Collectivity of French Guiana would have an assembly of 51 elected members, a permanent commission and a President. A council to address social, economic and environmental affairs would also be established. One section of the council would be in charge of economic and environmental matters, while the other would handle cultural matters, education and sport. The territory would have eight electoral divisions. In December 2012 the French Council of Ministers confirmed that elections to the new assembly would be held in March 2015. The Council of Ministers also approved two ordinances, the first of which concerned the transfer of regional and departmental staff and assets to the future Territorial Collectivity. The second ordinance concerned modifications to the budgetary, financial and accounting rules and procedures to facilitate the establishment of the new institutions.

In elections to the Regional Council held on 14 and 21 March 2010, Guyane 73, the UMP-supported list, secured 21 of the 31 seats, with 56.1% of the ballot, while Deux Ans: Un Marathon pour Bâtir, comprising various left-wing parties led by Walwari and the MDES, won the remaining 10 seats, with 43.9%. The UMP list's electoral prospects had been aided by the leadership of Rodolphe Alexandre, the mayor of Cayennes—formerly a member of the PSG but allied to Sarkozy since 2007—who had been one of the few politicians publicly to oppose greater autonomy prior to the referendum in January 2010. Disunity among the political left and the decision of Antoine Karam to retire from front-line politics had also facilitated the UMP's victory. Alexandre was elected President of the Regional Council on 26 March. In December 2010 the Regional Council approved a new development strategy, which posited the need to prepare new institutional structures. It defined three future administrative pillars: the French state; the Territorial Collectivity as the main local power; and the communes, reorganized as communities.

In the French presidential elections of May 2012 the Socialist candidate François Hollande won 62% of the vote in French Guiana with Nicolas Sarkozy securing only 38%. This was followed by new President Hollande naming Taubira-Delannon as the French Minister of Justice and Keeper of the Seals. Taubira-Delannon was the first national from the French Departments of the Americas and the first black woman to have held such a powerful ministerial post in the French Government.

In light of her appointment as Minister of Justice, Taubira-Delannon did not contest the French legislative elections of June 2012. At the elections two Socialist representatives were elected as Deputies to the National Assembly: Gabriel Serville was elected for the first time with 54.7% of the vote in Constituency One and Chantal Berthelot was re-elected with 61% of the vote in Constituency Two.

In 2012 and 2013 preparations continued for the institutional transition to a single Collectivity, scheduled for 2015. Debates were rekindled on contentious aspects of the 2011 legislation, which had not been supported by Guianese representatives in the French Senate. They had appealed for additional financial support to ease the institutional evolution and had criticized the single presidency and lack of an executive council. Guianese pressure had yielded amendments requiring consultations with the cultural councils of the Maroon and Amerindian communities. In 2013 concerns about economic support for the establishment of the new Collectivity intensified following the introduction of fiscal austerity measures throughout France. In May Berthelot urged the regional and departmental authorities to update the public on the arrangements for the Collectivity and also appealed for assurances that all necessary technical and administrative measures would be in place before the 2015 deadline.

Joint congresses of the Regional Council and the General Council were convened in December 2012 and in May 2013. The General Council proposed that, with effect from the end of 2013, it would cease to pay the salaries of 33 Catholic priests based in the territory. This was subsequently approved, but the Congress concluded that further study was needed on a second proposal to eliminate salary payments to traditional Amerindian and Maroon chiefs under the new institutional arrangements. This matter had first been raised in the December 2012 congress, when Tien-Liong had noted that there was no formal arrangement to incorporate the traditional chiefs into the local governance system. Several delegates argued that, since French Guiana had indigenous communities, there was a need to develop appropriate governance structures that suited the diversity and cultural characteristics of its population and that promoted inclusiveness and consultation with all communities in the territory.

The May 2013 Congress endorsed the institutional structures proposed by the National Assembly in 2011 for the Collectivity of French Guiana—a President, a permanent commission and a deliberative assembly, each with six-year terms of office from March 2015. The Congress also endorsed an appeal for additional economic assistance to support the establishment of the new Collectivity and to realize the territory's developmental objectives. In December 2013 French Guiana became the first Overseas Department to be visited by President Hollande, who travelled to the territory following a state visit to Brazil, where he had signed a new agreement with the Brazilian authorities to combat illegal gold-mining on both sides of the Brazil–French Guiana border. The President of the Regional Council used this opportunity to continue to lobby for increased development resources for the territory.

In mid-2013 steps were taken towards the establishment of the new Collectivity: the multinational accounting firm Ernst & Young was retained to provide consultancy assistance to the Regional and General Councils and to prepare a 'roadmap' for the creation of new governance structures. A steering committee composed of representatives of the Prefect's office and the Regional and General Council administrations began meeting every two weeks from mid-October. In April 2014 an initial information seminar on the establishment of the Collectivity was held for local government employees. In the context of a lacklustre economy and ongoing austerity measures, concerns increased about the economic viability of the new territorial entity and the projected costs of its creation. In June the overseas members of the National Assembly met in Paris and adopted a declaration that drew attention to the rising social welfare expenses of the Overseas Departments and the French state's reduced contribution to meeting these costs. The declaration made specific mention of French Guiana and Martinique, urging the French Government to approve a special grant for these territories to offset the transitional costs of their institutional changes. Finally, the representatives of the Overseas Departments expressed their desire to meet with the new French Prime Minister Manuel Valls in September to discuss these issues further.

Meanwhile, in February 2013 a new social movement was formed to oppose the adoption of the Amazonian Park Charter. The grouping included political parties such as the Parti Progressiste Guyanais, the PSG and Walwari, as well as several communal mayors and individual citizens. The Amazonian Park had been established in 2007 and was the largest French national park, encompassing 24% of the land expanse of French Guiana. In addition to Amazonian forest reserves, it incorporated a number of communes, which were expected to formulate sustainable development projects. There was an autonomous Administrative Council and a staff of some 89 persons to manage the park, while a development budget of €65m. was provided for 2007–13. A draft charter had been elaborated for the protection of the park's physical and cultural patrimony, for its management and regulation, and to assist the progress of sustainable development projects. Following public and institutional consultations, the charter was expected to be presented to the French Constitutional Council in the second half of 2013.

The anti-charter grouping criticized the timing of the public consultations in the territory, which had coincided with carnival festivities in January–February 2013. It also suspected that the charter would ultimately lead to the Amazonian Park being controlled by the French Ministry of Ecology, Sustainable Development and Energy, rather than by elected Guianese officials. Moreover, the group argued that the charter had major developmental implications for French Guiana, which needed to be carefully considered.

In September 2013 students from the Guianese branch of the Université des Antilles et de la Guyane commenced a six-week strike to protest against what they perceived to be the neglect of their campus and the unequal distribution of the regional university's resources. Their campaign was supported by Walwari, which appealed for the establishment of a full service university in French Guiana that could better address the educational development needs of the territory. The strike ended in November, when a protocol was signed by representatives of the state, the students and the university trade unions providing for the establishment of this new entity. The protocol included provisions that the campus in French Guiana would be allocated up to 60 new posts over the following three years and student facilities would be improved. The new Université de la Guyane was expected to be operational by 2014. There were many challenges for the development of the university, given that there were fewer than 3,000 students, the territory had low completion rates at the secondary education level, and there were shortages with respect to staffing and facilities.

Municipal elections were held on 22 and 29 March 2014. Mayors were elected in 22 communes. At least 13 of the mayors elected belonged to the Divers Gauche (a loose grouping of left-wing independents). In May European parliamentary elections took place, although a very low voter turnout rate was recorded in French Guiana (and the other French Departments in the Caribbean). Of the 10% of the electorate who participated, 41% supported Europe Écologie Les Verts, while the Socialists gained the second largest proportion of the vote.

Economy

JESSICA BYRON

French Guiana boasts the largest territory of any region in France. With an estimated population of 255,455 in mid-2014, it also features the lowest population density and, paradoxically, the highest population growth rate in France (2.5% in 2011). The population has increased by 25% since 1999. French Guiana also has the largest proportion of immigrants in its population (30%), with nationals of Brazil, Haiti and Suriname accounting for the majority. Some 44% of the population are below the age of 20, while 7% are over 60.

Approximately 76% of gross domestic product (GDP) and 56% of employment generation occurs in the sectors of commerce and public sector and commercial services. The main merchandise exports are gold, capital goods, fish, shrimps and rice. However, these account for a small proportion of French Guiana's value-added activity, given that its economy is so heavily oriented towards the tertiary sector, and that data for trade in services is not reported in the same way as merchandise trade. Mineral resources and hydroelectric potential remain underexploited, and, although the tourism sector has expanded, its growth is limited by the lack of infrastructure in the interior. Like Martinique and Guadeloupe, the Department is highly dependent on France for its foreign trade and for aid transfers, estimated at €982.6m. in 2009, to offset the balance of payments deficit. In 2012 French Guiana's GDP was €3,806m., according to official figures, equivalent to €15,900 per head. The rate of GDP growth was 3.3% in 2012. According to the central bank, the Institut d'Emission des Départements d'Outre-mer (IEDOM), the inflation rate in that year and in 2013 was 1.5%. French Guiana was the only Overseas Department to maintain positive growth in the midst of the global recession. However, economic growth has been outpaced by population growth.

In 2012 the Department recorded a trade deficit of €1,263.2m., an increase of 4.7% over 2011. IEDOM reported improved external trade flows in 2010, attributing this partly to rising international prices for gold and the strong performance of the European Union (EU)'s space industry, based in French Guiana. The value of exports in 2012 was €223.4m., an increase of 44.6% over the preceding year. Exports emanating from the space industry, while not produced in the domestic economy, represented 85% of the total value of exports in 2012. Gold-mining was the second most productive sector, while agricultural and agro-processed products declined by 4.7%. France remained French Guiana's principal trading partner in 2012, supplying 30% of its imports and receiving approximately 50% of its exports. Martinique and Guadeloupe supplied 13% of French Guiana's imports and purchased 8.1% of its exports, mainly in the form of fish products, gold and wood. Other major trading partners included Trinidad and Tobago (bilateral trade was valued at €20m. as a result of French Guiana's ongoing petroleum exploration efforts), some EU countries, the People's Republic of China and the USA. Road vehicles, refined petroleum products, pharmaceuticals, processed food products and industrial inputs for the space industry were among the Department's principal imports. French Guiana has had fairly insignificant trade flows with its South American neighbours to date. In 2012 trade with Brazil and Suriname was valued at, respectively, €7m. and €4m.

French Guiana's debt-to-GDP ratio increased to 107.9% in 2008 as many local authorities increasingly resorted to loans to finance capital projects. According to the 2009 departmental budget, expenditure totalled €1,075.2m., while revenue amounted only to €131m. The budget deficit totalled €982.6m. In addition to budgetary subventions from the French state, transfers from the EU in 2009 for public and private sector projects amounted to €41.9m. In 2011 €6.8m. of EU funds were used to finance public and private sector development projects. EU development support for the period 2007–13 totalled €506.2m.; by the end of 2012 €400.7m., or 79.2% of this amount, had been committed. The funds made available through the Contrat de Projets Etat-Région-Département (CPER—a joint investment scheme involving the French state, the territorial authorities and private financiers) for 2007–13 amounted to €170m., of which 80% was provided by the state. This was mostly programmed in co-ordination with the EU funding. The CPER programme's investment focus has mainly been on the improvement of the territory's physical infrastructure and on sustainable development. By the end of 2012 52% of this funding had been committed and €40.6m. (24%) actually disbursed. The emphasis was on water and electrification projects, training and certification, and the strengthening of productivity in the fishing sector. The Agence Française de Développement was also a major source of investment finance, making €62.5m. available to French Guiana in 2012, its highest commitment in the territory for 10 years.

Overall, the territorial authorities' gross savings improved after 2011. Although grants and subventions declined by 14.9% compared with 2010, there was an 11.7% increase in tax receipts in 2011, while expenditure only rose by 8.6%. The region registered receipts of €142.4m. in 2011, and its expenditure amounted to €126.2m. Operational costs accounted for 68% of this amount, including increases in personnel costs. The Department's receipts reached €336.8m., with grants and subventions providing 13.2% of the total and tax revenues 65.1%. Departmental expenditure in 2011 was €317.4m., up by 2.3% over 2010, mostly as a result of a 9.6% increase in operational costs. The communes' receipts increased by 13% in 2011 over the preceding year, to €317.6m., while their expenditure amounted to €297.5m. By January 2011 four intercommunal entities had been established, encompassing all of the communes in French Guiana—three Communities of Communes in the Western, Eastern and Savanna regions, and one Community of Agglomeration in the Central Coastal region. These intercommunal entities had receipts of €50.2m. in 2011 and spent €53.9m. By 2013 the departmental budget deficit had decreased to €34.1m.

The unemployment rate in 2010 and 2011 stood at 21% but rose in 2012 to 22.3%. Young people represented over 50% of the unemployed in 2012, while 45% of those out of work had been jobless for more than three years (the average duration of unemployment was 39 months). At the end of 2012 there were 18,850 job seekers registered. In light of the major employment concerns in all of the Overseas Departments, in June 2014 the new French Minister of Overseas Territories, George Pau-Langevin, proposed a Pact of Respect and Solidarity, a new fiscal initiative designed to create more jobs and improve consumers' purchasing power. The proposal aimed to make available €400m. through tax reductions. Initial analyses pointed to households and the private sector as the principal potential beneficiaries of the planned tax decreases. However, the Overseas Collectivities expressed some reservations about the possible impact on their tax revenues.

The agricultural sector, concentrated in forestry and fisheries, engaged less than 1% of the salaried labour force in 2013 and contributed 4% of GDP in 2007, according to official data. In 2013 agricultural products accounted for 4.0% of total export earnings. Fish and shrimps were the most important agricultural exports. Shrimp production in 2011 amounted to 1,037 metric tons, an increase of 9.9% over 2010, but output declined to 742 tons in 2012. This was mainly owing to the liquidation of a large production firm, but the catch was expected to increase again over subsequent years as new companies entered the market. The volume of snapper caught in 2012 was 1,580 tons, and overall fish exports in that year amounted to 1,573 tons, an annual increase of 3%. Most of these exports went to Martinique. While fish exports have been steadily increasing, shrimp exports declined significantly during the mid-2000s owing to increased competition from shrimp producers in Latin America and Asia and high fuel prices. French and EU support for shrimp production in 2010 amounted to €1,385 per ton. These funds were aimed at strengthening the production and export marketing infrastructure.

The main crops grown for local consumption were cassava, vegetables, rice and sugar cane, the last for use in the making of rum. Rum production was insignificant in comparison with Guadeloupe and Martinique, totalling 2,626 hl in 2012 and 1,359 hl in 2013. Approximately 1% of the volume of rum produced is exported. Livestock-rearing was also largely for subsistence. In 2012 Guianese abattoirs produced some 312 metric tons of beef and 359 tons of pork. These amounts represented 13% and 14%, respectively, of local consumption. Pineapples, citrus fruit and rice continued to be cultivated for export. Rice production, which had amounted to 9,481 tons in 2010, following a 47.7% increase in the volume exported in the previous year, had virtually collapsed by 2012. This was owing to the territory's inability to meet the EU's phytosanitary standards, as well as parasite attacks and marine erosion of rice acreage.

Timber exports declined steadily from the mid-1980s to 2001. In the latter year total wood extraction was 48,122 cu m, about one-half of the 1991 figure. However, the figure then stabilized and stood at 55,946 cu m in 2007. In 2008 extraction increased by 27% to reach 71,302 cu m, bolstered by higher demand from the construction sector. There were several sawmills, but exploitation of timber resources was hampered by the lack of infrastructure in the forest. Local mills produced plywood and veneers, while rosewood, satinwood and mahogany were the major hardwood products. The lumber yield has averaged 70,000 cu m per year since the mid-2000s. According to FAO, by 2012 roundwood removals totalled some 221,200 cu m, while sawnwood production (including railway sleepers) amounted to 31,500 cu m. The value of timber exports in 2011 was €2.3m.

The sector has seen the recent implementation of sustainable forestry management policies, which culminated in the adoption by the local authorities in 2010 of a Charter on Sustainable Forestry Exploitation. These new policies were expected to lead in the long term to a more environmentally friendly forestry industry, international certification according to sustainability standards and greater competitiveness of timber exports. French Guiana's forestry sector was programmed to receive €148m. in public investment between 2007 and 2013 for the sustainable development and greater competitiveness of the industry. The first phase of preparation for international certification for sustainable forestry exploitation was completed in 2010. In 2011 procedures for 'eco-labelling' began, and by the end of 2012 some two types of wood had been certified by the Programme for Endorsement for Certification. In 2010 €2.2m. was invested in the management and development of the forestry sector. The creation of forest trails has received 44% of total investment since 2007. In spite of the emphasis on the sustainable, technological upgrading of the forestry sector, only 2% appeared to have been allocated for training. The sector had 210 businesses registered and employed approximately 900 people.

Industry, including construction, engaged 16.1% of the salaried workforce in 2013, and contributed 20% of GDP in 2007, according to official sources. There is little manufacturing activity in French Guiana, except for the processing of agricultural or seafood products, mainly shrimp-freezing and rum distillation. The European Space Agency's satellite-launching centre at Kourou has provided a considerable stimulus to the economy, most notably to the construction sector (which engaged an estimated 7.8% of the salaried labour force in 2013). The space centre generated 15% of French Guiana's GDP in 2010. In 2011 it provided direct employment for 1,600 individuals, 75% of whom were locally recruited staff. In 2012 the centre hosted the inaugural launch of the Vega series of rockets, seven Ariane 5 rocket launches and two Soyuz rocket launches; 18 satellites were also placed into orbit. The space sector in 2012 accounted for 85% of French Guiana's export earnings. In addition to its direct economic contribution to GDP, the European Space Agency contributed €39.5m. to local development programmes in training, employment creation, and economic and cultural development between 2007 and 2013.

The mining sector is dominated by the extraction of gold, mostly in the Inini region, which involves small-scale alluvial operations and larger local and multinational mining concerns. Exploration activity intensified in the mid-1990s, and the proposed construction of a major new road into the interior

of the Department was expected to encourage further development. The first new concession in 70 years was awarded to Cambior in 2004 for a 25-year period. In 2003 exports of gold were worth €54.1m., accounting for some 49.9% of export earnings. By 2009, although gold still accounted for more than 20% of export earnings, the value of gold exports had declined to €25.3m. In 2010 gold exports were valued at €30.4m., an increase of some 20% in value, owing to higher gold prices. By 2012 gold exports generated €65.3m., an increase of 41% over the preceding year. Gold was the most productive export sector after the space industry.

The illegal gold trade has been a long-standing problem for French Guiana. It was estimated that there were between 4,000 and 10,000 illegal gold miners in the country, with many prospectors crossing the southern border from Brazil. The ongoing activities of Operation Anaconda and Operations Harpie (see History), stricter environmental regulation of the sector, and enhanced co-operation between the Governments of France, Brazil and Suriname placed limits on the expansion of the mining industry. In 2010 Brazil and France concluded a further agreement to prohibit illegal gold-mining activity. This agreement was adopted by the Assemblée Nationale (National Assembly) in April 2011. Moreover, in 2010 a law aimed at ensuring the traceability of gold products came into force in French Guiana.

In 2012 the authorities continued their efforts to combat illegal mining. A new administrative structure, the Schéma départemental d'orientation minière de la Guyane, was established, and new measures to regulate the mining sector were introduced. Mining was thenceforth prohibited on 45% of French Guiana's territory, particularly in the Parc Amazonien, and tougher environmental regulations were imposed to govern operations in the remaining 55%. In 2013 a public mining company was established by the Ministry of Overseas Territories, the Ministry of the Economy and Finance, and the Regional Council of French Guiana. The state held 51% of the equity of this company, while the regional and intercommunal authorities controlled 49%. Its purpose was to stimulate foreign investment in the sector, discourage illegal mining (particularly by placing multinational operators in areas seized from unauthorized producers), and increase the developmental impact of gold-mining activity.

Exports of all metals and metal products amounted to just €7.5m. in 2013, compared to €43.9m. in 2008, that figure itself a 20% decline compared to the previous year. Crushed rock for the construction industry was the only other mineral extracted in significant quantities, but exploratory drilling of known diamond deposits began in 1995. Bauxite, kaolin and columbo-tantalite were also present in commercial quantities, in particular on the Kaw plateau and near Saint-Laurent-du-Maroni. However, low market prices and the high cost of building the infrastructure necessary for the exploitation of such reserves hampered development.

Before the flooding of the Petit-Saut hydroelectric dam on the River Sinnamary in 1994 French Guiana depended heavily on imported fuels for the generation of energy (in 2013 imports of petroleum products alone accounted for 15% of total imports). Together with existing plants, the 116-MW dam was expected to supply the Department's energy for 30 years, annually generating around two-thirds of the Department's electricity. However, drought conditions in 2009 adversely affected hydroelectric generation and hydrocarbon fuel consumption increased by 30% over the preceding year. In response to increasing demand for electricity, plans have been put in place further to increase capacity, including the development of biofuels (mainly through the establishment of palm oil plantations) and other renewables (including biomass and solar power). By 2012 70% of French Guiana's energy generation was derived from renewable sources, predominantly hydroelectricity. The territory produced 870.2 GWh of electricity in that year. There was an average annual increase of 3.5% in electricity generated between 2000 and 2010.

In 2001 an Australian hydrocarbons company, Hardman Resources (now known as Tullow Oil), was awarded a 10-year exclusive exploration licence for French Guiana's offshore basin. In 2011 Tullow Oil (in partnership with the international oil companies Shell and Total) announced a major discovery of petroleum deposits off the coast of French Guiana, containing over 1,000m. barrels of oil according to preliminary estimates. The announcement aroused considerable interest in the possibility of further offshore oil finds in the Guianas region of South America. The consortium was due to make a decision on the exploitation of these reserves by 2015. The prospect of an oil industry had significant implications for the expansion of employment opportunities in French Guiana and for education and training policies in the short to medium term. In 2012 a commission was established to monitor further developments and to guide decisionmaking with respect to oil production. It is jointly chaired by the Prefect and the President of the Conseil Régional (Regional Council), and it shares information and engages in consultations with all stakeholders involved in the development of the petroleum sector.

French Guiana's economic development has been hindered by its location, its poor infrastructure away from the coast and the lack of a skilled indigenous workforce, which left the potential for growth in agriculture, fishing, tourism, forestry and the energy sector largely unexploited. Much agricultural and mining work has been carried out by undocumented migrants from Haiti, Suriname and Brazil. French Guiana's geographical characteristics, with large parts of the territory accessible only by river, have made it difficult to regulate key sections of the economy, such as gold-mining and forestry. Considerable concern has been voiced by environmentalists that this could have severe ecological consequences. In 2007 the Guiana Amazonian Park was established by the French Government. The central area of the park, in which the natural environment is fully protected, encompasses 7,840 sq miles (24% of the surface area of French Guiana), while the outer rim covers a further 5,250 sq miles. The park borders the Tumucumaque National Park in neighbouring Brazil, and together they constitute the largest area of protected rainforest in the world.

In 2003 the then French Minister of the Overseas Departments, Territories and Country announced plans to stimulate the economies of French Guiana, Guadeloupe and Martinique by introducing tax incentives for the hotel sector, to help it to remain competitive in the Caribbean region, and by creating jobs, for young people in particular. In 2007 the tourism sector contributed 2% of GDP, and hotels and restaurants employed 3.4% of salaried individuals in 2013. Several cultural and environmental heritage sites, such as the Guiana Zoo and the Amerindian Museum, were opened or refurbished in 2008–09, and the Space Centre remained a major tourist attraction. In 2010 French Guiana recorded its largest increase in visitor arrivals in the last 10 years; there were 423,849 air arrivals in that year. The average hotel occupancy rate fluctuated between 58% and 61% during 2009–12. Tourism companies made strong representations to the Government in 2012 about the negative impact on their sector of violent confrontations between security forces and illegal miners in July, resulting in the deaths of two French soldiers.

Much emphasis has been placed by the French Government and the local authorities on economic development projects. The CPER programme for 2007–13 prioritized maritime, river, air and road transport infrastructure, urban development, solid waste management, education, information technology, tourism development, and environmental protection. Infrastructural projects under this programme generated much of the dynamism in the construction sector and the wider economy in 2010 and 2011. The CPER scheme was also complemented by a new development strategy approved by the Regional Council in December 2010, which emphasized energy development, potable water, transport, low income housing, health, education, employment, endogenous development and administrative reorganization. Finally, it stressed the need for French Guiana to be better integrated into its geographical region. In this regard, French Guiana's Regional Council was charged with co-ordinating an Amazonian development co-operation programme with Brazil and Suriname, supported by €17m. of EU financing. A separate development co-operation programme had also been agreed with Suriname. In 2011 a joint Suriname–French Guiana Maroni River Council was convened. Numerous co-operation agreements were concluded with Brazil in 2008 and 2009, the most significant of which was construction of a bridge across the Oiapoque river, thereby providing the territory with road links to the Brazilian state of Amapá. It was hoped that this would stimulate trade and tourism between Brazil and French Guiana. Construction began in 2008 and was completed in 2011. The long-term impact on integration between the two countries is expected to be significant.

Statistical Survey

Sources (unless otherwise indicated): Institut National de la Statistique et des Etudes Economiques (INSEE), Service Régional de Guyane, ave Pasteur, BP 6017, 97306 Cayenne Cédex; tel. 5-94-29-73-00; fax 5-94-29-73-01; internet www.insee.fr/fr/insee_regions/guyane; Chambre de Commerce et d'Industrie de la Guyane (CCIG), Hôtel Consulaire, pl. de l'Esplanade, BP 49, 97321 Cayenne Cédex; tel. 5-94-29-96-00; fax 5-94-29-96-34; internet www.guyane.cci.fr.

AREA AND POPULATION

Area: 83,534 sq km (32,253 sq miles).

Population: 157,213 at census of 8 March 1999; 237,549 at census of 1 January 2011. Note: According to new census methodology, data in 2011 refer to median figures based on the collection of raw data over a five-year period (2009–13). *Mid-2014* (UN estimate): 255,455 (Source: UN, *World Population Prospects: The 2012 Revision*.

Density (at mid-2014): 3.1 per sq km.

Population by Age and Sex (UN estimates at mid-2014): *0–14 years:* 81,462 (males 41,506, females 39,956); *15–64 years:* 161,422 (males 80,121, females 81,301); *65 years and over:* 12,571 (males 6,115, females 6,456); *Total* 255,455 (males 127,742, females 127,713) (Source: UN, *World Population Prospects: The 2012 Revision*).

Principal Towns (population at 2010 census): Cayenne (capital) 55,753; Saint-Laurent-du-Maroni 38,367; Matoury 28,110; Kourou 25,189; Rémire-Montjoly 19,279.

Births, Marriages and Deaths (2012 unless otherwise indicated): Registered live births 6,609 (birth rate 26.8 per 1,000); Registered marriages 634 (marriage rate 2.7 per 1,000) (2011); Registered deaths 789 (death rate 3.2 per 1,000).

Life Expectancy (years at birth): 77.1 (males 73.9; females 80.9) in 2013. Source: Pan American Health Organization.

Employment (persons aged 15 years and over, provisional estimates at 31 December 2013): Agriculture, forestry and fishing 298; Mining, electricity, gas and water supply 1,445; Manufacturing 2,639; Construction 3,858; Wholesale and retail trade; repair of motor vehicles, motorcycles, etc. 4,633; Transport 2,421; Hotels and restaurants 1,668; Information and communication 625; Financial intermediation 564; Real estate, renting and business activities 4,644; Public administration and defence; education, health and social work 24,439; Other community, social and personal service activities 2,108; *Total employed* 49,342. Note: Data exclude 2,864 persons employed without salary.

HEALTH AND WELFARE

Key Indicators

Total Fertility Rate (children per woman, 2013): 3.1.

Under-5 Mortality Rate (per 1,000 live births, 2011): 15.0.

Physicians (per 1,000 head, c. 2010): 1.8.

Hospital Beds (per 1,000 head, 2012): 2.6.

Access to Water (% of persons, 2012): 90.

Access to Sanitation (% of persons, 2012): 90.

Source: mostly Pan American Health Organization.

For other sources and definitions, see explanatory note on p. vi.

AGRICULTURE, ETC.

Principal Crops ('000 metric tons, 2012, FAO estimates): Rice, paddy 2.0; Cassava 23.9; Sugar cane 3.6; Cabbages and other brassicas 5.3; Tomatoes 4.4; Cucumbers and gherkins 2.0; Beans, green 1.0; Bananas 9.0; Plantains 3.5. *Aggregate Production* ('000 metric tons, may include official, semi-official or estimated data): Total vegetables (incl. melons) 21.2; Total fruits (excl. melons) 23.9.

Livestock ('000 head, 2012, FAO estimates): Cattle 14.5; Pigs 8.9; Sheep 1.4.

Livestock Products (metric tons, 2012): Cattle meat 312; Pig meat 359; Chicken meat 470 (FAO estimates); Cows' milk 260 (FAO estimates); Hen eggs 1,036 (FAO estimates).

Forestry ('000 cubic metres, 2012, FAO estimates unless otherwise indicated): *Roundwood Removals* (excl. bark): Sawlogs, veneer logs and logs for sleepers 74.9 (unofficial figure); Other industrial wood 9.0; Fuel wood 137.3; Total 221.2. *Sawnwood Production* (incl. railway sleepers): Total 31.5.

Fishing (metric tons, live weight, 2012, FAO estimates): Capture 3,700 (Marine fishes 2,958; Shrimps 742); Aquaculture 35; *Total catch* 3,735.

Source: FAO.

MINING

Production ('000 metric tons unless otherwise indicated, 2011, estimates): Cement 62,000; Gold (metal content of ore, kilograms, reported figure) 1,300; Sand 500. Source: US Geological Survey.

INDUSTRY

Production (2013): Rum 1,359 hl; Electric energy 875 million kWh (Source: l'Institut d'Emission des Départements d'Outre-mer, *Rapport Annuel 2013*).

FINANCE

Currency and Exchange Rates: 100 cent = 1 euro (€). *Sterling and Dollar Equivalents* (30 May 2014): £1 sterling = €1.236; US $1 = €0.735; €10 = £8.09 = $13.61. *Average Exchange Rate* (euros per US dollar): 0.719 in 2011; 0.778 in 2012; 0.753 in 2013. Note: The national currency was formerly the French franc. From the introduction of the euro, with French participation, on 1 January 1999, a fixed exchange rate of €1 = 6.55957 French francs was in operation. Euro notes and coins were introduced on 1 January 2002. The euro and French currency circulated alongside each other until 17 February, after which the euro became the sole legal tender. Some of the figures in this Survey are still in terms of francs.

Budgets (excl. debt rescheduling, € million, 2013, preliminary): *Regional Government:* Current revenue 101.6 (Taxes 67.9, Grants 33.7); Capital revenue 46.2; Total 147.8. Current expenditure 85.6; Capital expenditure 62.2; Total 147.8. *Departmental Government:* Revenue 354.3 (Current revenue 312.7, Capital revenue 41.6); Expenditure 388.4 (Current expenditure 323.9, Capital expenditure 64.5). Source: Département des Etudes et des Statistiques Locales.

Cost of Living (Consumer Price Index; base: 2000 = 100): All items 121.6 in 2011; 123.4 in 2012; 125.2 in 2013. Source: ILO.

Expenditure on the Gross Domestic Product (€ million at current prices, 2012, estimates): Total final consumption expenditure 3,675 (General government and non-profit institutions serving households 1,862, Households 1,813); Gross capital formation 1,143; *Total domestic expenditure* 4,818; Exports of goods and services 1,239; *Less* Imports of goods and services 3,637; Statistical discrepancy 1,386; *GDP in purchasers' values* 3,806. Source: Institut d'Emission des Départements d'Outre-mer, *Guyane: Rapport Annuel 2013*.

Gross Domestic Product by Economic Activity (€ million at current prices, 2003): Agriculture, hunting, forestry and fishing 95; Food industries 39; Manufacturing 180; Energy 40; Construction 163; Services 1,564 (Restaurants and hotels 42, Transport −85, Commerce 223, Other market services 560; Non-market services 824); *Sub-total* 2,081; Financial intermediation services indirectly measured −42; Import duties, less subsidies 169; *GDP in purchasers' values* 2,207.

EXTERNAL TRADE

Principal Commodities (€ million, 2013): *Imports c.i.f.:* Agriculture, forestry and fishing 16.4; Products of agriculture and food industries 214.7; Consumer industry products 167.2 (Pharmaceuticals 57.6); Capital industry products 515.8 (Industrial and agricultural machinery 177.2; Transport equipment 188.1); Mineral products, rubber and plastic 66.2; Chemicals 241.0; Metal and metal products 102.2; Petroleum products 238.9; Total (incl. others) 1,589.0. *Exports f.o.b.:* Agriculture, forestry and fishing 0.6; Products of agriculture and food industries 11.2; Consumer industry products 0.9; Capital industry products 185.0 (Electronic goods and computer equipment 24.1; Industrial and agricultural machinery 80.0; Transport equipment 70.9); Mineral products, rubber and plastic 67.5; Metals and products thereof 7.5; Petroleum products 4.4; Total (incl. others) 292.6 (Source: Institut d'Emission des Départements d'Outre-mer, *Guyane: Rapport Annuel 2013*).

Principal Trading Partners (€ million, 2008): *Imports c.i.f.:* France (metropolitan) 485.4; Germany 31.9; Italy 17.6; Martinique 38.4; Netherlands 21.2; Spain 17.0; Trinidad and Tobago 51.4; Total (incl. others) 1,065.0. *Exports f.o.b.:* France (metropolitan) 37.3; Germany 11.4; Guadeloupe 7.7; Italy 9.5; Martinique 8.3; Spain 2.5; Switzerland 15.0; Total (incl. others) 96.3. *2010* (€ million): Total imports 1,081.8; Total exports 158.3. *2011* (€ million): Total imports 1,333.1; Total exports 154.4 (Source: Institut d'Emission des Départements d'Outre-mer, *Guyane: Rapport Annuel 2011*). *2012* (€ million): Total imports 1,486.5; Total exports 223.4 (Source: Institut d'Emission des Départements d'Outre-mer, *Guyane: Rapport Annuel 2012*). *2013* (€ million): Total imports 1 589.0; Total exports 292.6 (Source: Institut d'Emission des Départements d'Outre-mer, *Guyane: Rapport Annuel 2013*).

TRANSPORT

Road Traffic ('000 motor vehicles in use, 2001): Passenger cars 32.9; Commercial vehicles 11.9 (Source: UN, *Statistical Yearbook*). *2002:* 50,000 motor vehicles in use. *1 January 2010:* ('000 commercial motor vehicles in use): Buses 0.4; Vans and trucks 17.3.

Shipping: *Flag Registered Fleet* (at 31 December 2013): Vessels registered 2; Total displacement: 3,881 grt. Source: Lloyd's List Intelligence (www.lloydslistintelligence.com).

International Seaborne Shipping (traffic, 2013): Goods carried 656,282 metric tons in 2012; 653,941 metric tons in 2013. Source: Institut d'Emission des Départements d'Outre-mer, *Guyane: Rapport Annuel 2013*.

Civil Aviation (2013): Aircraft movements 10,415; Freight carried (incl. post) 5,843 metric tons; Passengers carried 436,991. Source: Institut d'Emission des Départements d'Outre-mer, *Guyane: Rapport Annuel 2013*.

TOURISM

Tourist Arrivals by Country (2007): France 62,016; Guadeloupe 14,362; Martinique 22,739; Total (incl. others) 108,801. *2009:* 83,000 tourist arrivals.

Receipts from Tourism (US $ million, incl. passenger transport): 49 in 2007.

Source: World Tourism Organization.

COMMUNICATIONS MEDIA

Telephones ('000 main lines in use): 45.5 in 2010.

Mobile Cellular Telephones ('000 subscribers): 217.7 in 2009.

Internet Users ('000): 58.0 in 2009.

Broadband Subscribers ('000): 30.2 in 2009.

Source: International Telecommunication Union.

EDUCATION

Pre-primary (2012/13): 43 institutions; 15,419 students (14,526 state, 893 private).

Primary (2012/13): 119 institutions (111 state, 8 private); 27,702 students (25,852 state, 1,850 private).

Specialized Pre-primary and Primary (2012/13): 435 students (435 state only).

Secondary (2012/13): 47 institutions (42 state, 5 private); 32,371 students (0,104 state, 2,267 private).

Higher (2012/13): 3,434 students.

Teachers (2008/09 unless otherwise indicated): *Primary:* 2,243 teachers (2,121 state, 122 private); *Secondary:* 2,433 teachers (2,285 state, 148 private); *Higher* (2004/05): 63 teachers. Source: Ministère de l'Education Nationale, *Repères et références statistiques. 2012/13* (state schools): 2,377 in primary; 2,571 in secondary.

Adult Literacy Rate: 83.0% (males 83.6%, females 82.3%) in 1998. Source: Pan American Health Organization.

Directory

The Government

(September 2014)

HEAD OF STATE

President: FRANÇOIS HOLLANDE.

Prefect: ERIC SPITZ, Préfecture, 1 rue Fiedmont, BP 7008, 97307 Cayenne Cédex; tel. 5-94-39-45-00; fax 5-94-30-02-77; e-mail courrier@guyane.pref.gouv.fr; internet www.guyane.pref.gouv.fr.

DEPARTMENTAL ADMINISTRATION

President of the General Council: ALAIN TIEN-LIONG, Hôtel du Département, pl. Léopold Héder, BP 5021, 97397 Cayenne Cédex; tel. 5-94-29-55-89; fax 5-94-29-55-25; e-mail atienliong@cg973.fr; internet www.cg973.fr.

President of the Regional Council: RODOLPHE ALEXANDRE (UMP), Cité Administrative Régionale, 4179 route de Montabo, Carrefour de Suzini, BP 7025, 97307 Cayenne Cédex; tel. 5-94-29-20-20; fax 5-94-31-95-22; e-mail cabcrg@cr-guyane.fr; internet www.cr-guyane.fr.

Elections, 14 and 21 March 2010

	Seats
Guyane 73*	21
Deux Ans: Un Marathon pour Bâtir†	10
Total	31

* Electoral list comprising the Union pour un Mouvement Populaire (UMP) and allies.
† Electoral list comprising various left-wing parties led by Walwari and the Mouvement de Décolinisation et d'Emancipation Sociale (MDES).

REPRESENTATIVES TO THE FRENCH PARLIAMENT

Deputies to the French National Assembly: GABRIEL SERVILLE (Gauche Démocrate et Républicaine), CHANTAL BERTHELOT (Socialiste, Républicain et Citoyen).

Representatives to the French Senate: GEORGES PATIENT (Groupe Socialiste), JEAN-ETIENNE ANTOINETTE (Groupe Socialiste).

GOVERNMENT OFFICE

Economic, Social and Environmental Regional Committee: 66 ave du Général de Gaulle, 97300 Cayenne; tel. 5-94-28-96-01; fax 5-94-30-73-65; e-mail info@ceser-guyane.fr; internet www.ceser-guyane.fr; Pres. ARIANE FLEURIVAL.

Political Organizations

Forces Démocratiques de Guyane (FDG): 41 rue du 14 Juillet, BP 403, 97300 Cayenne; tel. 5-94-28-96-79; fax 5-94-30-80-66; e-mail g.othily@senat.fr; f. 1989 by a split in the PSG; Sec.-Gen. GIL HORTH.

Mouvement de Décolonisation et d'Emancipation Sociale (MDES): 21 rue Maissin, 97300 Cayenne; tel. 5-94-30-55-97; fax 5-94-30-97-73; e-mail mdes.parti@wanadoo.org; f. 1991; pro-independence; Sec.-Gen. MAURICE PINDARD.

Parti Progressiste Guyanais (PPG): 1994 Route de Montabo, 97300 Cayenne; e-mail jmj_taubira@yahoo.fr; internet www.partiprogressisteguyanais.fr; f. 2013; Sec.-Gen. JEAN-MARIE TAUBIRA.

Parti Socialiste (PS): 7 rue de l'Adjudant Pindard, 97300 Cayenne Cédex; tel. 5-94-37-81-33; fax 5-94-37-81-56; e-mail fede973.partisocialiste@wanadoo.fr; internet guyane.parti-socialiste.fr; departmental br. of the metropolitan party; Leader LÉON JEAN BAPTISTE EDOUARD.

Parti Socialiste Guyanais (PSG): 1 Cité Césaire, BP 46, 97300 Cayenne; tel. 5-94-28-11-44; fax 5-94-28-46-92; e-mail partisocialisteguyanais@orange.fr; f. 1956; left-wing; Sec.-Gen. MARIE JOSÉ LALSIE.

Union pour un Mouvement Populaire (UMP): 42 rue du Docteur Barrat, 97300 Cayenne; tel. 5-94-28-80-74; fax 5-94-28-80-75; internet www.u-m-p.org; f. 2002 as Union pour la Majorité Presidentielle by mems of the fmr Rassemblement pour la République and Union pour la Démocratie Française; centre-right; departmental br. of the metropolitan party; Sec.-Gen. LUC CHATEL.

Les Verts Guyane: 64 rue Madame Payé, 97300 Cayenne; tel. 5-94-40-97-27; e-mail tamanoir.guyane@wanadoo.fr; internet guyane.lesverts.fr; ecologist; departmental br. of the metropolitan party; Regional Sec. JOSÉ GAILLOU.

Walwari: 35 rue Schoelcher, BP 803, 97300 Cayenne Cédex; tel. 5-94-30-31-00; fax 5-94-31-84-95; e-mail info@walwari.org; internet www.walwari.org; f. 1993; left-wing; Leader CHRISTIANE TAUBIRA-DELANNON; Sec.-Gen. JOËL PIED.

Judicial System

Court of Appeal: 1 rue Louis Blanc, 97300 Cayenne; tel. 5-94-27-48-48; fax 5-94-27-48-72; Pres. PIERRE GOUZENNE.

There is also a Tribunal de Grande Instance and a Tribunal d'Instance.

Religion

CHRISTIANITY

The Roman Catholic Church

French Guiana comprises the single diocese of Cayenne, suffragan to the archdiocese of Fort-de-France, Martinique. Some 80% of the population are Roman Catholics. French Guiana participates in the Antilles Episcopal Conference, currently based in Port of Spain, Trinidad and Tobago.

Bishop of Cayenne: Rt Rev. EMMANUEL M. P. L. LAFONT, Evêché, 24 rue Madame Payé, BP 378, 97328 Cayenne Cédex; tel. 5-94-28-98-48; fax 5-94-30-20-33; e-mail emmanuel.lafont@wanadoo.fr; internet www.guyane.catholique.fr.

The Anglican Communion

Within the Church in the Province of the West Indies, French Guiana forms part of the diocese of Guyana. The Bishop is resident in Georgetown, Guyana. There were fewer than 100 adherents in 2000.

Other Churches

In 2000 there were an estimated 7,000 Protestants and 7,200 adherents professing other forms of Christianity.

Assembly of God: 1051 route de Raban, 97300 Cayenne; tel. 5-94-35-23-04; fax 5-94-35-23-05; e-mail jacques.rhino@wanadoo.fr; internet www.addguyane.fr; Pres. JACQUES RHINO; c. 500 mems.

Church of Jesus Christ of Latter-day Saints (Mormons): Route de la Rocade, 97305 Cayenne; c. 362 mems.

Seventh-day Adventist Church: Mission Adventiste de la Guyane, 39 rue Schoëlcher, BP 169, 97324 Cayenne Cédex; tel. 5-94-25-64-26; fax 5-94-37-93-02; e-mail adventiste.mission@wanadoo.fr; f. 1949; Pres. and Chair. ALAIN LIBER; Sec.-Treas. DANIEL CARBIN; 2,299 mems.

The Jehovah's Witnesses are also represented.

The Press

France-Guyane: 17 rue Lallouette, BP 428, 97329 Cayenne; tel. 5-94-29-70-00; fax 5-94-29-70-02; e-mail infos@franceguyane.fr; internet www.franceguyane.fr; daily; Publishing Dir DENIS BERRIAT; Editor-in-Chief JÉRÔME RIGOLAGE; circ. 9,000.

Le Marron—Petit Journal de Kourou: BP 53, 97372 Kourou; tel. 5-94-32-49-54; fax 5-94-32-10-70; e-mail pjk@blada.com; internet www.blada.com; f. 2001; Dir ODILE FARJAT.

Ròt Kozé: 11 rue Maissin, 97300 Cayenne; tel. 5-94-30-55-97; fax 5-94-30-97-73; e-mail redacteur@rotkoze.com; internet www.rotkoze.com; f. 1990; left-wing organ of the MDES party; monthly; Dir MAURICE PINDARD.

La Semaine Guyanaise: 6 ave Louis Pasteur, 97300 Cayenne; tel. 5-94-31-09-83; fax 5-94-31-95-20; e-mail semaineguyanaise@nplus.gf; internet www.semaineguyanaise.com; weekly (Thur.); Dir ALAIN CHAUMET; Editor-in-Chief JÉRÔME VALLETTE.

Publishers

Editions Anne C.: 8 Lot Mapaou, route de Baduel, BP 212, 97325 Cayenne; tel. and fax 5-94-35-20-10; e-mail canne@nplus.gf; internet www.redris.pagesperso-orange.fr/HTML/Livres.htm; f. 1998; French-Creole children's and youth literature; Dir NICOLE PARFAIT-CHAUMET.

Ibis Rouge Editions: chemin de la Levée, BP 267, 97357 Matoury Cédex; tel. 5-94-35-95-66; fax 5-94-35-95-68; e-mail jlm@ibisrouge.fr; internet www.ibisrouge.fr; f. 1995; general literature, French-Creole, and academic; Publr JEAN-LOUIS MALHERBE; agencies in Guadeloupe and Martinique.

PUBLISHERS' ASSOCIATION

Promolivres Guyane: BP 96, 97394 Rémire-Montjoly Cédex; tel. 5-94-29-55-56; fax 5-94-38-52-82; e-mail promolivreguyane@wanadoo.fr; f. 1996; asscn mems incl. editors, booksellers, journalists and librarians; promotes French Guianese literature; Pres. TCHISSÉKA LOBELT.

Broadcasting and Communications

TELECOMMUNICATIONS

Digicel Antilles Françaises et Guyane: see Martinique—Telecommunications; Dir-Gen. FRANCK ROGIER.

France Telecom: 76 ave Voltaire, BP 8080, 97300 Cayenne; tel. 5-94-39-91-15; fax 5-94-39-91-00; e-mail eline.miranda@francetelecom.com.

Orange Caraïbe: see Guadeloupe—Telecommunications.

Outremer Telecom: 112 ave du Général de Gaulle, 97300 Cayenne; tel. 5-94-28-71-15; fax 5-94-23-93-59; e-mail communication@outremer-telecom.fr; internet www.outremer-telecom.fr; f. 1998; mobile telecommunications provider; Group CEO JEAN-MICHEL HEGESIPPE.

ONLY: 112 ave du Général de Gaulle, 97300 Cayenne; tel. 5-94-28-71-15; fax 5-94-23-93-59; e-mail contact@outremer-telecom.fr; internet www.only.fr; f. 2004 as Outremer Telecom Guyane; subsidiary of Outremer Telecom, France; present name adopted following merger of Volubis, ONLY and OOL in 2006; mobile and fixed telecommunications provider.

BROADCASTING

Guyane 1ère (Outre-mer Première): ave le Grand Boulevard, Z.A.D. Moulin à Vent, 97354 Rémire-Montjoly; tel. 5-94-25-67-00; fax 5-94-25-67-64; internet guyane.la1ere.fr; acquired by Groupe France Télévisions in 2004; fmrly Société Nationale de Radio-Télévision Française d'Outre-mer; name changed to Réseau France Outre-mer (RFO) in 1998; present name adopted in 2010; Radio-Guyane Inter accounts for 46.6% of listeners (2003); Télé Guyane/RFO1 and RFO (Tempo) account for 52.3% and 7.5% of viewers, respectively (2003); Dir-Gen. GENEVIÈVE GIARD; Regional Dir FRED AYANGMA.

Radio

KFM Guyane: 6 rue François Arago, 97300 Cayenne; tel. 5-94-31-30-38; fax 5-94-37-84-20; internet www.kfmguyane.skyrock.com; f. 1993 as Radio Kikiwi; present name adopted 2003.

Métis FM: Cayenne; internet www.metis.fm; popular music station.

Mig FM Guyane: 100 ave du Général de Gaulle, 97300 Cayenne; tel. 5-94-30-77-67; fax 5-94-31-86-81; f. 1995; Creole.

NRJ Guyane: 2 blvd de la République, 97300 Cayenne; tel. 5-94-39-54-88; fax 5-94-39-54-79; e-mail wladimir@nrjguyane.com; internet www.nrjguyane.com; f. 2006; commercial radio station; Man MARC HO-A-CHUCK.

Ouest FM Guyane: Cayenne; tel. 5-94-38-29-19; e-mail contact@ouestfm.net; internet www.ouestfm.net; commercial music station.

Radio Joie de Vivre: 39 rue Schoëlcher, 97324 Cayenne Cédex; BP 169, 97300 Cayenne; tel. 5-94-31-29-00; fax 5-94-29-47-26; f. 1993; operated by the Seventh-day Adventist church; Gen. Man. ESAÏE AUGUSTE.

Radio Littoméga (RLM): 24 blvd Malouet, BP 108, 97320 Saint-Laurent-du-Maroni; tel. 5-94-34-22-09; e-mail centre.cl@wanadoo.fr; internet www.rlm100.com; f. 1994; Dir ARIELLE BERTRAND.

Radio Mosaïque: 11 rue Sainte-Catherine, cité Brutus, 97300 Cayenne; tel. 5-94-30-94-76; e-mail guyanes@free.fr; commercial radio station; Man. BÉRIL BELVU.

Radio Ouassailles: rue Maurice Mongeot, 97360 Mana; tel. 5-94-34-80-96; fax 5-94-34-13-89; e-mail radio.ouassailles@wanadoo.fr; f. 1994; French and Creole; Man. RÉMY AUBERT.

Radio Saint-Gabriel: Salle Paul VI, Cité Mirza, 97300 Cayenne; tel. 5-94-31-17-11; fax 5-94-28-17-51; e-mail radiosaintgabriel@wanadoo.fr; f. 2001; Roman Catholic; Man. HENRI-CLAUDE ASSÉLOS.

Radio Toucan Fréquence International (TFI): 1 pl. du Vidé, BP 68, 97300 Kourou; tel. 5-94-32-96-11; fax 5-94-39-71-61; e-mail direction@tfifm.com; internet www.tfifm.com; f. 1983; part of Groupe I-Medias Antilles-Guyane; commercial radio station.

Radio UDL (Union de la Défense des Libertés): 7 rue Félix Eboué, BP 5, 97393 Saint-Laurent-du-Maroni; tel. 5-94-34-27-90; fax 5-94-34-04-78; e-mail radio.udl@wanadoo.fr; internet www.udlradio.com; f. 1982; Man. JEAN GONTRAND.

Radio Voix dans le Désert: 5 chemin du Château, 97300 Cayenne; tel. 5-94-31-73-95; fax 01-73-76-88-00; e-mail president@rvld.fr; internet www.rvld.fr; f. 1993; operated by the Assembly of God church; Pres. EDDY LAUTRIC.

Television

Antenne Créole Guyane: 31 ave Louis Pasteur, 97300 Cayenne; tel. 5-94-28-82-88; fax 5-94-29-13-08; e-mail acg@acg.gf; internet www.acg.gf; f. 1994; sole local private TV station; gen. interest with focus on music and sports; produces 30% of own programmes; received by 95% of the population, accounting for 25% of viewers (2003); Pres. MARC HO-A-CHUCK; Gen. Man. WLADIMIR MANGACHOFF.

Canal+ Guyane: 14 Lotissement Marengo, Z. I. de Collery, 97300 Cayenne; tel. 8-10-50-15-02; fax 5-94-30-53-35; internet www.canalplus-caraibes.com/guyane; f. 1996; subsidiary of Groupe Canal+, France; satellite TV station; Dir OLEG BACCOVICH.

Finance

(cap. = capital; res = reserves; dep. = deposits; m. = million; brs = branches)

BANKING

Central Bank

Institut d'Emission des Départements d'Outre-mer (IEDOM): 8 rue Christophe Colomb, BP 6016, 97306 Cayenne Cédex; tel. 5-94-29-36-50; fax 5-94-30-02-76; e-mail direction@iedom-guyane.fr; internet www.iedom.fr; f. 1959; Dir FABRICE DUFRESNE.

Commercial Banks

Banque Française Commerciale Antilles-Guyane (BFC Antilles-Guyane): 8 pl. des Palmistes, BP 111, 97345 Cayenne; tel. 5-94-29-11-11; fax 5-94-30-13-12; e-mail service-client@bfc-ag.com; internet www.bfc-ag.com; f. 1985; Pres. CHRISTIAN DUVILLET.

BNP Paribas Guyane SA: 2 pl. Victor Schoëlcher, BP 35, 97300 Cayenne; tel. 5-94-39-63-00; fax 5-94-30-23-08; e-mail bnpg@bnpparibas.com; internet www.bnpparibas.com; f. 1964 following purchase of BNP Guyane (f. 1855); name changed 2000; 94% owned by BNP Paribas SA, 3% by BNP Paribas Martinique and 3% by BNP Paribas Guadeloupe; Dir and CEO ANTOINE GARCIA; Gen. Sec. JACQUES SALGE; 2 brs.

Crédit Agricole: see Martinique—Finance.

Development Bank

Société Financière pour le Développement Economique de la Guyane (SOFIDEG): PK 3, 700 route de Baduel, BP 860, 97339 Cayenne Cédex; tel. 5-94-29-94-29; fax 5-94-30-60-44; e-mail sofideg@nplus.gf; f. 1982; bought from the Agence Française de Développement (AFD—q.v.) by BRED-BP in 2003; Dir FRANÇOIS CHEVILLOTTE.

Insurance

Allianz IARD: 34 rue Léopold Heder, BP 462, 97300 Cayenne Cédex; tel. 5-94-30-27-66; fax 5-94-30-69-09; e-mail agfguyana@wanadoo.fr; internet www.allianz.fr; life and short-term insurance; Dir (Latin America) Dr HELGA JUNG.

Groupama Antilles Guyane: see Martinique—Insurance.

Trade and Industry

GOVERNMENT AGENCIES

Direction de l'Agriculture et de la Forêt (DAF): Parc Rebard, BP 5002, 97305 Cayenne Cédex; tel. 5-94-29-63-74; fax 5-94-29-63-63; e-mail daf.guyane@agriculture.gouv.fr; internet daf.guyane.agriculture.gouv.fr; Dir FRANÇOIS CAZOTTES.

Direction Régionale et Départementale des Affaires Maritimes (DRAM): 2 bis, rue Mentel, BP 6008, 97306 Cayenne Cédex; tel. 5-94-29-36-15; fax 5-94-29-36-16; e-mail Dram-Guyane@developpement-durable.gouv.fr; responsible for shipping, fishing and other maritime issues at nat. and community level; Dir STÉPHANE GATTO.

Direction Régionale de l'Industrie, de la Recherche et de l'Environnement (DRIRE): Pointe Buzaré, BP 7001, 97307 Cayenne Cédex; tel. 5-94-29-75-30; fax 5-94-29-07-34; e-mail drire-antilles-guyane@industrie.gouv.fr; internet www.ggm.drire

.gouv.fr; active in industry, business services, transport, public works, tourism and distribution; Regional Dir JOEL DURANTON.

DEVELOPMENT ORGANIZATIONS

Agence de l'Environnement et de la Maîtrise de l'Energie (ADEME): 28 ave Léopold Heder, 97300 Cayenne Cédex; tel. 5-94-31-73-60; fax 5-94-30-76-69; e-mail ademe.guyane@ademe.fr; internet www.ademe-guyane.fr; Dir SUZANNE PONS.

Agence Française de Développement (AFD): Lotissement les Héliconias, route de Baduel, BP 1122, 97345 Cayenne Cédex; tel. 5-94-29-90-90; fax 5-94-30-63-32; e-mail afdcayenne@afd.fr; internet www.afd-guyane.org; fmrly Caisse Française de Développement; Dir ROBERT SATGE.

Agence Régionale de Développement Économique de la Guyane (ARD): 1 pl. Schoëlcher, BP 325, 97325 Cayenne Cédex; tel. 5-94-25-66-66; fax 5-94-25-43-19; e-mail ard.guyane-developpement@wanadoo.fr; f. 2009 to replace Agence pour la Création et le Développement des Entreprises en Guyane; Pres. CAROL OSTORERO; Dir PASCAL VELINORE.

Fédération des Organisations Amérindiennes de Guyane (FOAG): Centre des Cultures, rue Capt. Charles Claude, 97319 Awala Yalirnapo; tel. 6-94-42-27-76; fax 5-94-33-50-06; e-mail foag@nplus.gf; f. 1993; civil liberties org. representing the rights of the indigenous peoples of French Guiana; Pres. Chief JEAN AUBÉRIC CHARLES.

CHAMBERS OF COMMERCE

Chambre d'Agriculture: 8 ave du Général de Gaulle, BP 544, 97333 Cayenne Cédex; tel. 5-94-29-61-95; fax 5-94-31-00-01; e-mail chambre.agriculture.973@wanadoo.fr; internet www.chambres-agriculture.fr; Pres. CHRISTIAN EPAILLY; Dir THIERRY BASSO.

Chambre de Commerce et d'Industrie de la Guyane (CCIG): Hôtel Consulaire, pl. de l'Esplanade, BP 49, 97321 Cayenne Cédex; tel. 5-94-29-96-00; fax 5-94-29-96-34; e-mail contact@guyane.cci.fr; internet www.guyane.cci.fr; Pres. JEAN-PAUL LE PELLETIER.

Chambre de Métiers: 41 Lotissement, Artisanal Zone Galmot, 97300 Cayenne Cédex; tel. 5-94-25-24-70; fax 5-94-30-54-22; e-mail m.toulemonde@cm-guyane.fr; internet www.cm-guyane.fr; Pres. HARRY CONTOUT; Sec.-Gen. FRANCELINE MATHIAS-DANIEL.

Jeune Chambre Economique de Cayenne: 1 Cité A. Horth, route de Montabo, BP 1094, Cayenne; tel. 5-94-31-62-99; fax 5-94-31-76-13; internet www.jcicayenne.com; f. 1960; Pres. YÀSIMÎN VAUTOR; Gen. Sec. ANGÉLIQUE BOURGEOIS.

EMPLOYERS' ORGANIZATIONS

Groupement Régional des Agriculteurs de Guyane (GRAGE): PK 15 route nationale 1, Domaine de Soula, 97355 Macouria; tel. 5-94-38-71-26; e-mail 973@confederationpaysanne.fr; internet www.grage.gf; affiliated to the Confédération Paysanne; Pres. SYLVIE HORTH.

MEDEF Guyane: 27A Résidence Gustave Stanislas, Source de Baduel, BP 820, 97338 Cayenne Cédex; tel. 5-94-31-17-71; fax 5-94-30-32-13; e-mail updg@nplus.gf; internet medefguyane.fr; f. 2005; fmrly Union des Entreprises de Guyane; Pres. ALAIN CHAUMET.

Ordre des Pharmaciens du Département Guyane: 7 Avenue du Général de Gaulle, 97300 Cayenne; tel. 5-94-32-17-62; fax 5-94-32-17-66; e-mail delegation_guyane@ordre.pharmacien.fr; internet www.ordre.pharmacien.fr; Pres. ALINE ABAUL-BALUSTRE.

Syndicat des Transformateurs du Bois de Guyane (STBG): Menuiserie Cabassou, PK 4.5, route de Cabassou, 97354 Remire-Montjoly; tel. 5-94-31-34-49; fax 5-94-35-10-51; f. 2002; represents artisans using wood; Pres. YVES ELISE; Sec. FRANÇOIS AUGER.

MAJOR COMPANIES

Air Liquide Spatial Guyane (ALSG): Route de l'Espace, Ensemble de Lancement, BP 826, 97388 Kourou Cedex; tel. 5-94-33-75-69; fax 5-94-33-75-77; f. 1969; subsidiary of Air Liquide Group; mfrs of propellant gases for the space industry; CEO LAURENT DU HAYES; Dir FRANCOIS MOUTIEZ; c. 46 employees.

Arianespace: BP 809, 97388 Kourou Cedex; tel. 5-94-33-67-07; fax 5-94-33-62-66; e-mail info@arianespaceonline.com; internet www.arianespace.com; f. 1979; local br. of French-based co; satellite launch vehicle operators; 32.53% owned by CNES, France; 15.81% owned by Airbus, France; 10.87% owned by EADS ST Gmbh, Germany; Chair. and CEO STÉPHANE ISRAËL; 3 launch vehicles; c. 50 employees.

Auplata: 9 Lotissement Montjoyeux, 97300 Cayenne; tel. 5-94-29-54-40; fax 5-94-29-85-00; e-mail presse@auplata.fr; internet www.auplata.fr; f. 2004; gold-mining; Chair. JEAN-FRANÇOIS FOURT; CEO DIDIER TAMAGNO.

Bamyrag-Pétrole: 7 Lotissement Marengo, Z. I. Collery, 97300 Cayenne; tel. 5-94-35-21-03; fax 5-94-35-14-45; subsidiary of Groupe Bernard Hayot, Martinique; distribution of fuels, metal minerals and chemical products; Pres. BERNARD HAYOT.

Cegelec Space: Global Technologies, CIGMA Division, Immeuble Vercors, pl. Newton, 97310 Kourou; BP 819, 97388 Kourou; tel. 5-94-32-05-24; fax 5-94-32-31-39; e-mail space@cegelec.com; internet www.space.cegelec.com; f. 2001; supplier to the space industry; responsible for operation and maintenance of Guiana Space Centre ground infrastructure; subsidiary of Cegelec Germany and Cegelec France; Pres. MICHAEL MARTER; 350 employees.

Ciments Guyanais (CIGU): Z. I. Dégrad-des-Cannes, 97354 Rémire-Montjoly; tel. 5-94-35-54-98; fax 5-94-35-54-99; e-mail accueil@ciments-guyanais.com; f. 1989; owned by Holcim (Switzerland) and Lafarge (France); cement production; Gen. Man. PATRICK VANDRESSE; 25 employees.

Groupe Rubis Antilles-Guyane: Z. I. Pariacabo, BP 139, 97310 Kourou; tel. 5-94-32-05-00; fax 5-94-32-22-40; internet www.vito-ag.com; f. 2005; fmrly Shell SAGF; subsidiary of GPL Rubis, France; distribution of petroleum products; Dir M. SUVELOR.

Hardman Petroleum France SAS (HPF SAS): Parc d'Activite C. O. Soprim, 97354 Remire Montjoly; affiliate of Tullow Oil; CEO ALAN MARTIN.

Nofrayane: 9 Parc d'Activité Cognot Matoury, BP 1166, 97345 Cayenne; tel. 5-94-35-18-65; fax 5-94-35-18-60; e-mail nofrayane@nofrayane.fr; internet www.nofrayane.fr; subsidiary of Vinci Construction Grands Projets; construction and civil engineering; Dir OLIVIER MANTEZ; 98 employees.

Régulus (CSG): Centre Spatial Guyanais, BP 73, 97372 Cayenne; tel. 5-94-35-15-00; fax 5-94-32-49-42; f. 1991; space industry; jt subsidiary of Fiat Avio, Italy (60%) and SNPE, France (40%); Plant Dir JEAN-EMMANUEL QUEBRE.

SARA (Société Anonyme de la Raffinerie des Antilles): Dégrad-des-Cannes, BP 227, 97301 Cayenne; tel. 5-94-25-50-50; fax 5-94-35-41-79; internet www.sara.mq; f. 1982; second depot opened in Kourou in 2000; Chair. CHRISITAN CHAMMAS; Regional Gen. Man. FRANÇOIS NAHAN; c. 250 employees regionally (see entry in Martinique).

UTILITIES

Electricity

EDF Guyane: blvd Jubelin, BP 6002, 97306 Cayenne; tel. 5-94-39-64-00; fax 5-94-30-10-81; internet guyane.edf.com; electricity producer; Dir JEAN-PHILIPPE BLAVA.

Water

Société Guyanaise des Eaux: 2738 route de Montabo, BP 5027, 97306 Cayenne Cédex; tel. 5-94-25-59-26; fax 5-94-30-59-60; internet www.suez-environnement.fr; f. 1978; CEO JEAN-LOUIS CHAUSSADE; Gen. Man. RODOLPHE LELIEVRE.

TRADE UNIONS

Centrale Démocratique des Travailleurs Guyanais (CDTG): 99–100 Cité Césaire, BP 383, 97328 Cayenne Cédex; tel. 5-94-31-02-32; fax 5-94-31-81-05; e-mail sg.cdtg@wanadoo.fr; internet cdtg-guyane.com; affiliated to the Confédération Française Démocratique du Travail; Sec.-Gen. GÉRARD FAUBERT.

    SGEN-CFDT: 99–100 Cité Césaire, BP 383, 97328 Cayenne Cédex; tel. 5-94-31-02-32; fax 5-94-35-71-17; e-mail sgen@sgen.cfdt.fr; affiliated to the Fédération des Syndicats Généraux de l'Education Nationale et de la Recherche; represents teaching staff; Sec.-Gen. MARTINE NIVOIX.

Fédération Syndicale Unitaire Guyane (FSU): Mont Lucas, Bât G, No C37, 97300 Cayenne; tel. 5-94-30-05-69; fax 5-94-38-36-58; e-mail fsu973@fsu.fr; f. 1993; departmental br. of the Fédération Syndicale Unitaire; represents public sector employees in teaching, research and training, and also agriculture, justice, youth and sports, and culture; Sec. ALAIN BRAVO.

Union Départementale Confédération Française des Travailleurs Chrétiens Guyane (UD CFTC): 19 lot Gibelin 1, BP 763, 97351 Matoury Cédex; tel. 5-94-35-63-14; fax 5-94-90-59-05; e-mail lydie.leneveu@wanadoo.fr; Sec. LYDIE LENEVEU.

Union Départementale Force Ouvrière de Guyane (FO): 4 ave Pasteur, 97300 Cayenne; tel. and fax 5-94-31-79-66; e-mail force-ouvriere-guyane@orange.fr; internet guyane.force-ouvriere.org; Sec.-Gen. DOMINIQUE BONADEI.

Union des Travailleurs Guyanais (UTG): 40 ave Digue Ronjon, BP 265, 97326 Cayenne; tel. and fax 5-94-30-82-46; e-mail utg1@wanadoo.fr; Sec.-Gen. ALBERT DARNAL.

UNSA Education Guyane: 46 rue Vermont Polycarpe, BP 807, 97300 Cayenne Cédex; tel. 5-94-31-02-10; fax 5-94-31-30-08; e-mail

973@se-unsa.org; internet sections.se-unsa.org/973; Sec.-Gen. SAN-
DRINE MADERE.

Transport

RAILWAYS

There are no railways in French Guiana.

ROADS

In 2004 there were 1,300 km (808 miles) of roads in French Guiana, of
which 397 km were main roads. Much of the network is concentrated
along the coast, although proposals for a major new road into the
interior of the Department were under consideration.

SHIPPING

Grand Port Maritime de Guyane at Dégrad-des-Cannes, on the
estuary of the river Mahury, is the principal port, handling the
majority of maritime traffic. There are other ports at Le Larivot,
Saint-Laurent-du-Maroni and Kourou. Saint-Laurent is used primarily for the export of timber, and Le Larivot for fishing vessels.
There are river ports on the Oiapoque and on the Approuague. There
is a ferry service across the Maroni river between Saint-Laurent and
Albina, Suriname. The rivers provide the best means of access to the
interior, although numerous rapids prevent navigation by large
vessels. A bridge across the Oyapock river, linking the cities of
Oiapoque in Brazil and Saint-Georges de l'Oyapock in French
Guiana and funded by the Governments of France and Brazil, was
completed in 2011. In December 2013 French Guiana's flag registered fleet comprised two vessels, with an aggregate displacement of
some 3,881 grt.

Compagnie Maritime Marfret: Immeuble Face Scierie Patoz,
Z. I. Degrad-des-Cannes, 97354 Rémire-Montjoly; tel. 5-94-31-04-
04; fax 5-94-35-18-44; e-mail jccelse@marfret.fr; internet www
.marfret.fr; Gen. Man. JEAN-CHRISTIAN CELSE-L'HOSTE.

Grand Port Maritime de Guyane: Z. I. de Dégrad-des-Cannes,
Rémire-Montjoly, 97354 Cayenne Cédex; tel. 5-94-35-44-90; f. 1974
as Port International Dégrad-des-Cannes; under management of
Chambre de Commerce et de l'Industrie de la Guyane 1988–2012;
publicly owned entity with a supervisory board from 2013.

SOMARIG (Société Maritime et Industrielle de la Guyane): Z. I. de
Dégrad-des-Cannes, Rémire-Montjoly, BP 81, 97354 Cayenne
Cédex; tel. 5-94-35-42-00; fax 5-94-35-53-44; e-mail cay.genmbox@
cma-cgm.com; internet www.cma-cgm.com; f. 1960; owned by
Groupe CMA—GGM (France); Man. Dir HERVÉ ROUCHON.

CIVIL AVIATION

Rochambeau International Airport, situated 17.5 km (11 miles) from
Cayenne, is equipped to handle the largest jet aircraft. There are also
airports at Maripasoula, Saul and Saint Georges. Access to remote
inland areas is frequently by helicopter.

Air Guyane: Aéroport de Rochambeau, 97300 Matoury; tel. 5-94-29-
36-30; fax 5-94-30-54-37; e-mail reservations@airguyane.com;
internet www.airguyane.com; f. 1980; 46% owned by Guyane Aéro
Invest, 20% owned by Sodetraguy; operates domestic services; Pres.
CHRISTIAN MARCHAND.

Tourism

The main attractions are the natural beauty of the tropical scenery
and the Amerindian villages of the interior. In 2005 there were 27
hotels with some 1,184 rooms. Receipts from tourism in 2007 were
US $49m. while in 2009 tourist arrivals totalled an estimated 83,000.

Comité du Tourisme de la Guyane: 12 rue Lallouette, BP 801,
97338 Cayenne Cédex; tel. 5-94-29-65-00; fax 5-94-29-65-01; e-mail
ctginfo@tourisme-guyane.com; internet www.tourisme-guyane
.com; Pres. SYLVIE DESERT; Dir-Gen. ERIC MADELEINE.

**Délégation Régionale au Tourisme, au Commerce et à l'Arti-
sanat pour la Guyane:** 9 rue Louis Blanc, BP 7008, 97300 Cayenne
Cédex; tel. 5-94-28-92-90; fax 5-94-31-01-04; e-mail 973.pole3e@
dieccte.gouv.fr; Delegate DIDIER BIRONNEAU (acting).

L'Ensemble Culturel Régional (ENCRE): 82 ave du Général de
Gaulle, BP 6007, 97306 Cayenne Cédex; tel. 5-94-28-94-00; fax 5-94-
28-94-04; e-mail encre.crg@wanadoo.fr; f. 2004 by merger of Ecole
Nationale de Musique et de Danse and Office Culturel de la Région
Guyane; fmrly Asscn Régionale de Développement Culturel; Pres.
ANTOINE KARAM.

**Fédération des Offices du Tourisme et Syndicat d'Initiative
de la Guyane (FOTSIG):** 12 rue Lallouette, BP 702, 97301 Cayenne; tel. 5-94-30-96-29; fax 5-94-31-23-41; e-mail frguyane@fnotsi
.net; Pres. JULIETTE GOUSSET.

Defence

As assessed at November 2013, France maintained a military force of
2,200 in French Guiana, including a gendarmerie. The headquarters
is in Cayenne.

Education

Education is modelled on the French system and is compulsory and
free for children between six and 16 years of age. Primary education
begins at six years of age and lasts for five years. Secondary education, beginning at 11 years of age, lasts for up to seven years,
comprising a first cycle of four years and a second of three years.
In 2012/13 there were 43 pre-primary schools, 119 primary schools
and 47 secondary schools. In the same period there were 43,121
students in pre-primary and primary education, while in secondary
education there were 32,371 students, of whom some 93% were
educated in the state sector. Higher education in law, administration, French language and literature and teacher training is provided
by a branch of the Université des Antilles et de la Guyane in Cayenne,
although in December 2013 French Guiana withdrew from participation in this regional university; a new Université de la Guyane was
to be established. There is also a technical institute at Kourou and an
agricultural college. In 2012/13 some 3,434 students were enrolled in
higher education in French Guiana.

Bibliography

For works on the Caribbean generally, see Select Bibliography (Books)

Mam-Lam-Fouk, S. *Histoire générale de la Guyane française.*
Matoury, Ibis Rouge, 2002.
Plénet, C. *Les fonds structurels européens.* Matoury, Ibis Rouge,
2005.

Redfield, P. *Space in the Tropics: From Convicts to Rockets in French
Guiana.* Berkeley, CA, University of California Press, 2000.
Rodway, J. *Guiana: British, Dutch, and French.* Boston, MA, Elibron
Classics, 2005.

GRENADA

Geography

PHYSICAL FEATURES

Grenada is in the Windward Islands, in the Lesser Antilles, and is considered to be the most southerly island of the eastern Caribbean. It lies about 145 km (90 miles) north of Trinidad (Trinidad and Tobago). The country includes Carriacou, the largest island of the Grenadines, and a number of smaller islands in the chain that runs north and a little east of the main island. Off shore from Carriacou, to the east, is Petit (often spelled Petite) Martinique, the most northerly of the islands of Grenada and separated from Petit St Vincent (Saint Vincent and the Grenadines) by only a narrow sea channel. Grenada is the second smallest independent state in the Americas (after Saint Christopher and Nevis), with a total area of 344.5 sq km (133 sq miles).

The main island of Grenada is about 34 km long by 19 km wide, aligned along a north–south axis, apart from a southern tapering towards the south-west and a northern tendency to reach towards the chain of the Grenadines in the north-east. The wooded mountains march across the island following this diagonal, the land to the north and west rising (the highest point is at Mt St Catherine—840 m or 2,757 ft), the land to the south and east falling to an indented coast of rias (drowned valleys), which provide deep harbours. Grenada is volcanic in origin, demonstrated by its central highlands and its fertile soil, which give sustenance to tropical forests and mangrove swamps, as well as the crops that have earned it the moniker of the 'spice island of the Caribbean'. Birds and animals thrive, including armadillos and Mona monkeys originally imported from Africa, but the only unique species are the endangered hookbilled kite—a large hawk that eats tree snails and is now, globally, only found in the Levera National Park—and the native Grenada dove. A controversial amendment to the Grenada National Parks and Protected Areas Act in May 2007, however, allowed for the sale for development of the Mount Hartman National Park—the last sanctuary of the Grenada dove—threatening the imminent decline of the already critically endangered species. The 121-km coastline is largely protected by reefs, particularly in the Grenadines.

The southern Grenadines form part of the country of Grenada. These islands include a group around Ronde Island, then, further north, a smaller group located just to the south of the large island of Carriacou, which is 37 km north-east of Grenada itself. Carriacou is almost 34 sq km in extent, an island of low, green hills. About 4 km east of its northern end is the island of Petit Martinique, the next largest of the Grenadian Grenadines.

CLIMATE

The climate is subtropical, tempered by north-eastern trade winds off the Atlantic. Grenada can occasionally be affected by hurricanes, but the country is generally considered to lie just to the south of the hurricane belt (in 1999 a heavy swell from a hurricane to the north caused considerable damage, for instance). There is, though, a rainy season from June to

November, followed by the cooler months of December and January. Average annual rainfall is about 1,520 mm (60 ins), but in the high forest there can be over 4,000 mm per year. The average annual temperature along the coast is 28°C (82°F).

POPULATION

The population is 85% black, with 11% of mixed black-white ancestry and the rest consisting mainly of whites and 'East' Indians. Some claim to include in their ancestry traces of the original Carib and Arawak Amerindian inhabitants. Although most cultural evidence of early French rule has disappeared, almost one-half of the population is still Roman Catholic, with Non-conformist Protestant denominations (33%) and Anglicans (14%) making up the balance. The official language is English, but a French patois has survived in some areas.

According to UN estimates, the total population was 106,304 in mid-2014. About 4,000 live in the capital, the beautiful harbour city of St George's in the south-west, and almost 6,000 on the islands of Carriacou and Petit Martinique. The chief town of the Grenadines is Hillsborough, on the central western shore of Carriacou. Grenada island is divided into six parishes, with Carriacou and Petit Martinique described as a dependency.

History

MARK WILSON

Grenada is a constitutional monarchy within the Commonwealth. Queen Elizabeth II is Head of State, and is represented in Grenada by a Governor-General. There is a bicameral legislature with an elected chamber.

Grenada was known by its original Carib inhabitants as Camerhogue, but was named Concepción by Christopher Columbus on his third voyage in 1498, and later renamed La Grenade by the French, who colonized the island from 1650, meeting fierce resistance from the Caribs. The island was ceded to Great Britain by the Treaty of Paris in 1763, but was briefly recaptured by France in 1779–83. A slave revolt led by Julian Fedon in 1795–96 was the most successful in the Eastern Caribbean, gaining control of almost the entire island, but was bloodily suppressed. Slavery was abolished in 1834, as in the United Kingdom's other Caribbean colonies.

Eric (later Sir Eric) Gairy dominated the island's politics in the 1950s, 1960s and 1970s. He rose to prominence in 1950, as the founder of the Grenada Manual and Mental Workers' Union, which led a series of strikes the next year. Four people were killed in violent clashes with the authorities, and his Grenada People's Party, later renamed the Grenada United Labour Party (GULP), won the first universal suffrage election, which was fought on 10 October of that year, with 71% of the popular vote. Gairy became the first Chief Minister and was fiercely supported by the rural masses, who gave him credit for increased wages and improvements in education and welfare. At the same time, he was feared and despised by the urban middle class, most of whom supported Herbert Blaize's National Party (NP), which held office in 1957–61 and 1962–67.

Grenada joined the Federation of the West Indies in 1958 along with nine other British colonies. When Jamaica and Trinidad left in 1962 the Federation collapsed, and an attempt to unite the remaining colonies as the 'little eight' was unsuccessful, while a proposal for a union with Trinidad and Tobago was not followed through. Along with its neighbours to the north, Grenada became a British Associated State in 1967, responsible for its internal affairs, with the United Kingdom retaining control of external affairs and defence.

Young left-wing opponents of Gairy, led by Maurice Bishop, in 1973 formed the New Jewel Movement (NJM—Joint Endeavour for Welfare, Education and Liberation). Grenada was the first Associated State to gain independence, on 7 February 1974. Gairy's opponents were strongly opposed to separation from the United Kingdom under what they saw as a repressive regime, and the months before were marked by protracted strikes and widespread demonstrations; Bishop's father was shot dead by the police during a demonstration on 21 January.

In elections held in 1976 an opposition alliance won 48% of the popular vote; Bishop became leader of the opposition. On 13 March 1979 the NJM removed Gairy from power, installing a People's Revolutionary Government (PRG), with Bishop as Prime Minister, but retaining the Queen as Head of State. The PRG had close relations with Cuba and the USSR, while the USA regarded the regime as a potential security threat. Bishop, in particular, at first enjoyed strong popular support, but this was gradually eroded both by the refusal to call elections and by economic difficulties. An important policy initiative was the construction, with Cuban assistance, of the Point Salines International Airport. Although designed as a civilian facility, the USA feared that Point Salines could be used for military purposes.

In 1983 a militant wing of the NJM and the army became increasingly hostile to Bishop and his immediate supporters. In October these forces organized a coup, led by Gen. Hudson Austin. Bishop and several cabinet ministers were shot, as well as members of a crowd of demonstrators, which gathered in the capital, St George's. The USA led a military intervention, supported by seven Caribbean states, which installed an interim Government, led by Nicholas Brathwaite. In June 2006 Grenada's Truth and Reconciliation Commission submitted a report to Parliament that appealed for fresh trials to be held of 17 people convicted in relation to the 1983 killings. In February 2007 the Privy Council, based in the United Kingdom, ordered that the remaining 13 prisoners be resentenced (following the release of three of their original number in December 2006 on grounds of good behaviour, and the earlier discharge of Phyllis Coard in 2000 in order to seek life-saving medical treatment), and in June of that year a hearing in the Grenada High Court precipitated the immediate acquittal of a further three prisoners. Lawyers for the prosecution had recommended that consecutive fixed-term sentences, providing for eventual release, be considered in respect of the other 10 prisoners. The presiding judge, Justice Francis Belle of Barbados—whose suitability in such a capacity was officially contested by several of the victims' families—subsequently handed down sentences of up to 40 years, although most of the 10 had already served a majority of this term. National responses to the verdict were deeply divided, with many in government expressing incomprehension at the decision while declaring many of the local advocates for the defence to be affiliates of the opposition National Democratic Congress (NDC). Bernard Coard and the remaining prisoners were released in September 2009, having served 26 years in prison.

The NP, still led by Blaize, convincingly won the general election of December 1984. Blaize's Government completed the construction of the international airport and returned the country to a more stable path of development. None the less, splits and defections weakened the NP Government, as did the death of Blaize in 1989. Blaize's successor, Ben Jones, lost a general election in March 1990; the NDC, led by Brathwaite, gained a majority through the defection of individual members from other parties. However, the NP's main successor, the New National Party (NNP), led by Keith Mitchell, regained office in June 1995. After losing his parliamentary majority through further defections, Mitchell called fresh elections in January 1999, in which the NNP won all 15 parliamentary seats.

The NNP had at times been criticized over allegations of impropriety, including lax supervision of the offshore financial sector; moreover, several prominent overseas investors had proved to be undesirable, and departed in controversial circumstances. Four officers of the former First International Bank of Grenada in 2007 received prison sentences in the USA for fraud, after pleading guilty. The bank and its subsidiaries had in 1996–2000 operated a Ponzi scheme (a fraudulent investment scheme that promises investors high returns with little risk), with investors losing an estimated US $170m.

In late 2001 Canada announced that Grenadians travelling to Canada would require visas. This reflected growing international concern, which increased following the terrorist attacks on the USA in September, about Grenada's economic citizenship programme, under which passports were sold to non-citizens. Grenada eventually abandoned the programme in December 2002.

The NNP narrowly won a general election held on 27 November 2003, holding eight of the 15 seats in the House of Representatives; the NDC took the remaining seven seats. The results were contested, however, and the opposition pursued legal challenges to the election results, while in 2006 the Government attempted unsuccessfully to unseat an opposition Member of Parliament on the grounds that he had held dual Grenadian and Canadian citizenship at the time of the 2003 election. Mitchell appointed a new Cabinet in December 2003; the most significant change was the transferral of the agriculture portfolio to Gregory Bowen, the erstwhile Minister of Communications, Works and Public Utilities, as part of a wider plan to revitalize the ailing agricultural sector, in particular the nutmeg industry.

Hurricane Ivan struck Grenada in September 2004, causing widespread devastation. A further storm, Hurricane Emily, struck the island in July 2005. In spite of this, the political climate remained bitterly polarized. Lawyers and trade unions campaigned vigorously in February of that year against a proposal to appoint a controversial Jamaican lawyer, Hugh

Wildman, as Attorney-General, successfully persuading the Judicial and Legal Services Commission of the Organisation of Eastern Caribbean States (OECS) to oppose the appointment. The Government unwillingly accepted the ruling, and in March the position of Attorney-General was added to the other portfolios held by Elvin Nimrod, the Minister of Foreign Affairs and International Trade, of Carriacou and Petit Martinique Affairs, and of Legal Affairs. Wildman remained legal adviser to the Government and launched a legal challenge to the OECS legal commission's refusal to appoint him. A commission of inquiry was established in 2004 to investigate alleged corruption by Mitchell; however, it was unable to start work, as the opposition contested a refusal to grant it the right to examine witnesses, and the subsequent arrival of Hurricane Ivan visited further disruption upon proceedings.

Further controversy was caused by the switching of diplomatic recognition in January 2005 from Taiwan to the People's Republic of China. China had agreed in December 2004 to assist with the construction of a sports stadium, housing and other projects. A broadly similar package had previously been agreed with Taiwan, formerly the island's largest bilateral aid donor, but Mitchell argued that the destruction caused by Hurricane Ivan had forced the Government to reconsider its international relationships. A formal opening ceremony for the China-funded stadium was held in February 2007, ahead of the Cricket World Cup; however, the Grenadian police band caused some consternation by playing the Taiwanese national anthem. Two separate public inquiries were held into the incident. Taiwan's Export-Import Bank in 2011 attempted to recover US $28m. in loans made to Grenada before 2005, with court action in the USA requiring cruise lines and airlines from October 2011 to pay money due to Grenada into an escrow account; however, Grenada won a tactical victory in June 2012, with a US court ruling that the payments should again be made to the Grenadian seaport and airport authorities, pending a final resolution of the dispute.

Grenada is a centre for cocaine and marijuana transshipment, and is a minor marijuana producer. Close co-operation is reported with Trinidadian anti-trafficking organizations (and indeed, on the other side, with Trinidadian traffickers); 80% of cocaine transshipped from the island is believed to be destined for the British market. Cocaine seizures fell from 936 kg in 2007 to just 6 kg in 2009, rising slightly to 25 kg in 2010. However, there was an increase in cocaine transshipment through the eastern Caribbean for the US market from 2013. The drugs trade fosters the import of illegal weapons and gang violence. There were 14 murders in 2012, equivalent to a per head murder rate of 14 per 100,000, a high figure by international standards and three times that of the USA. The country's prison was designed for 198 inmates, but held 456 in 2013. The US Department of State lists Grenada as a 'country of concern' for money-laundering. New anti-corruption legislation was approved in 2013, but had not come into effect by 2014.

A general election was held on 8 July 2008, ahead of the April 2009 constitutional deadline. The NNP failed to secure an unprecedented fourth successive term in office, with the NDC winning 11 of the 15 legislative seats and 51% of the valid votes cast. The NNP won the remaining four seats and 48% of the vote. The United Labour Platform, a coalition of the GULP and the People's Labour Movement, failed to have an impact upon the result. Electoral turnout was high, with some 80.3% of eligible voters participating in the poll, and election observers from the Organization of American States reported positively upon the procedure of the election. Tillman Thomas was sworn in as Prime Minister and the new Cabinet was installed: notable appointments included Nazim Burke as Minister of Finance, Planning, Economy, Energy and Co-operatives, and Peter David as Minister of Tourism and then of Foreign Affairs.

One of the NDC Government's first priorities was to effect measures to counteract the rising cost of living: the party's election manifesto had included proposals to reduce import duties on selected essential goods and to increase the provision of affordable housing. There were clear indications of tensions within the NDC leadership from 2010; following a cabinet reshuffle in November, Peter David, who had been moved back to the tourism portfolio, stayed away from a swearing-in ceremony, as did two other ministers. Michael Church, formerly Minister of Environment, Foreign Trade and Export Development, who had been demoted to a junior portfolio, subsequently resigned; his successor, Joseph Gilbert, was dismissed in January 2012 after allegedly writing a letter to an overseas tourism developer stating that the Government would legalize casino gambling. Four NDC members of Parliament did not attend the vote on the March 2012 budget, resulting in a reduced government majority, while Peter David (who did vote for the budget) resigned in April, followed in May by the Minister of Foreign Affairs, Karl Hood. Hood and Church in July joined with the NNP to defeat the Government on a proposed levy on insurance premiums. To avert an expected motion of no confidence, Parliament was prorogued on 17 September. Government support had been further undermined by late payment of public service salaries for June and August, and a reported bailout from the Government of neighbouring Saint Vincent and the Grenadines.

In a general election held on 19 February 2013, Mitchell's NNP won all 15 seats with 58.8% of the popular vote on an 87.6% voter turnout. Mitchell was duly sworn in as Prime Minister. The Governor-General appointed three former NDC cabinet ministers, including former Minister of Finance Nazim Burke, to fill the three opposition seats in the Senate. In opposition, the NNP continued to be plagued by feuds and divisions; Burke was elected party leader in February 2014. In August 2013 Parliament approved controversial legislation allowing foreigners to become citizens of Grenada in return for financial investment in a National Transformation Fund.

The new Governor-General, Dame Cecile La Grenade, announced in her 2013 throne speech that a referendum would be held on a new constitution; proposed changes were to include the restructuring of Parliament and the replacement of the Privy Council as final appeal court with the Caribbean Court of Justice (CCJ), based in Trinidad and Tobago. In July 2014 the Government proposed a referendum to be held in February 2015 on the changes, including the switch to the CCJ and changing the country's official name to Grenada, Carriacou and Petit Martinique, but not any major changes to the legislature. The changes would require a two-thirds' majority in both a referendum and in the House of Representatives.

The International Centre for Settlement of Investment Disputes in Washington, DC, USA, ruled in 2009 in favour of Grenada in a dispute with petroleum company RSM Production over a 1996 agreement to issue an oil and gas exploration licence. Grenada subsequently announced that maritime boundary talks would be resumed with Trinidad and Tobago; these had been inactive since 1993. An agreed line was fixed by treaty and ratified in April 2010. An agreed south-eastern maritime boundary will allow bidding for oil and gas exploration in parts of Grenada's exclusive economic zone; however, the maritime boundary with other neighbouring states remained unclear. Grenada has observer status within the Venezuelan-led Bolivarian Alliance for the Peoples of our America-People's Trade Treaty (Alianza Bolivariana para los Pueblos de Nuestra América-Tratado de Comercio de los Pueblos) grouping, and applied in January 2014 for full membership, also declaring its support for Argentina's claim to the Falkland Islands; closer relations would be expected by some to assist in the negotiation of a maritime boundary, to which end, however, there had been no progress by mid-2014.

Economy

MARK WILSON

The three-island state of Grenada, Carriacou and Petit Martinique is the second smallest nation in the western hemisphere in area, with 345 sq km (133 sq miles) and 103,328 inhabitants at the 2011 census, of whom approximately 4,900 live on Carriacou and 800 on Petit Martinique; the number of inhabitants increased by only 696, or 0.7%, during the 10 years following the 2001 census, with a net annual emigration rate of three per 1,000; accordingly, migrant remittances made up 7% of gross domestic product (GDP) in 2001–11. The nation had developed a fairly prosperous middle-income economy, with a per head GDP at market prices of US $7,878 in 2011. The unemployment rate decreased from 17.0% to 11.5% in 2000–03; however, a labour force survey estimated unemployment at 34% in 2013, rising to 56% in the 15–24 age group. This was a source of serious concern and an indication of continuing economic weakness, which was to be addressed in part through public sector investment programmes. The Caribbean Development Bank in 2008 estimated the poverty rate at 38% of the population, up from 32% 10 years earlier and the highest figure in the Organisation of Eastern Caribbean States (OECS). Growth has been uneven in recent years: GDP grew by an average of 2.3% in 2000–04. A rapid rebuilding effort produced expansion of 12.5% in 2005, following Hurricane Ivan in 2004, with the construction sector expanding by 91%. Although GDP contracted by 4.4% in 2006 as reconstruction slowed, growth averaged 4.0% in 2007–08. There was then a contraction of 5.6% in 2009 as investment inflows, tourism and migrant remittances were negatively affected by the international financial crisis; the economy contracted by a further 2.0% in 2010, with weak growth of 0.8% in 2011, a contraction of 1.8% in 2012, and weak growth of 1.9% (according to Eastern Caribbean Central Bank—ECCB—estimates) in 2013.

Grenada is a member of the Caribbean Community and Common Market, or CARICOM, which formed a single market (the Caribbean Single Market and Economy) in 2006. Grenada is also a member of the Eastern Caribbean Securities Exchange (based in Saint Christopher and Nevis), while its financial affairs are supervised by the ECCB, also located in Saint Christopher and Nevis.

Agriculture made up some 3.9% of GDP in 2013, with a further 1.8% from fishing. The major export crops were nutmeg and its by-product, mace, of which, until recently, Grenada was the world's second most important producer, after Indonesia. However, these and other tree crops were devastated by Hurricane Ivan, with 70% or more of nutmeg trees destroyed. Production fell from 5,756 metric tons of 'green' unprocessed nutmeg in 2004 to an estimated 600 tons in 2011, and, with replanting proceeding slowly at best, and an outbreak of nutmeg wilt disease in 2011, output did not increase in 2012 and was expected to remain well below pre-2004 levels for the foreseeable future, while Grenada slipped to fourth place as exporter, behind India and Sri Lanka. There was some prospect of offshore petroleum or gas reserves, and the Government negotiated an exclusive economic zone boundary with Trinidad and Tobago, and intended to pursue similar agreements with Venezuela and other maritime neighbours. Grenada was also one of 13 states to subscribe to Venezuela's Petrocaribe initiative in 2006, receiving up to 340,000 barrels of gasoline, diesel and fuel oil annually, purchased on favourable terms.

The pleasant climate, white sand beaches and natural beauty of the islands have encouraged the growth of tourism, with the additional benefit of direct air connections to the United Kingdom and North America. Receipts from tourism increased from US $37.5m. in 1990 to US $119.8m. in 2013, as estimated by the ECCB. The number of stop-over tourists declined to 98,548 in 2005 following Hurricane Ivan; numbers recovered to 129,088 in 2007 after most hotels came back into operation (only 300 of the 1,700 hotel rooms were usable in the immediate aftermath of the hurricane), before slipping to 106,156 in 2010 as international demand slowed, and then recovering to 113,049 in 2013. There were also 197,308 cruise ship passengers in 2013, who made a smaller contribution to the economy as a result of limited onshore spending. Hotels' and restaurants' contribution to GDP was 4.0% in 2013, down from 7.1% in 2000. There are several proposals for major hotel developments. Progress was set back from 2008, owing to the worldwide recession and consequent fall in international tourism demand; an existing hotel was renovated and expanded as a Sandals resort, which opened in 2014 with the benefit of generous tax concessions and an agreed multi-year US $100m. investment programme.

St George's University, which includes an offshore medical school, had close to 6,000 resident students in 2013, most of them from the USA, and approximately 500 academic staff, with direct local spending estimated in 2009 at US $40m. Its expansion contributed to the growth in the education sector from 8.9% of GDP in 2000 to 23.1% in 2013.

Manufacturing made up some 3.6% of GDP in 2013. Industries such as the assembly of electronic components were oriented entirely to the export market, while others, such as beverages, were produced for the local market, with some exports to other Caribbean islands.

The Government stressed the importance of recent advances in technology for economic development. Grenada is a member of the Eastern Caribbean Telecommunications Authority, which liberalized the regime for local and international communications. Call centres and telemarketing operations have been a source of employment, but performance was uneven.

There is a small offshore financial sector. The sector, until the late 2000s, failed to meet internationally accepted regulatory standards; Grenada was listed as a 'non-co-operative jurisdiction' by the Organisation for Economic Co-operation and Development (OECD) in 2001, and also appeared on a comparable list compiled by the Financial Action Task Force on Money Laundering (FATF, based in Paris, France). Legislation and regulatory standards were subsequently tightened by the Grenada International Financial Services Authority; as a result, Grenada was delisted by the FATF in 2003. None the less, international monitoring of the sector remained strict, and Grenada was listed by the US Department of State as a country of concern, their intermediate category. OECD in 2008 included Grenada on a 'grey' list of countries that did not yet have a significant number of Tax Information Exchange Agreements in place; however, the country was removed from the list in 2010.

Like its neighbours, Grenada suffered in 2009 and afterwards from the collapse of a Trinidad-based insurance conglomerate, CL Financial, which posed risks to financial stability throughout the eastern Caribbean, with an important subsidiary, the British American Insurance Company, declared insolvent. The IMF estimated Grenada's exposure to the CL group at 3.9% of GDP. Meanwhile, the performance of the domestic financial sector has been weak, with the non-performing loans ratio of domestic banks rising to 14.1% in 2014.

The islands contain several volcanic centres, although the only one with a recent history of activity was the underwater volcano of Kick 'Em Jenny, to the north of the main island. Earthquakes also represent a threat. The Government proposes to develop geothermal energy, which would make a major contribution to its target of reducing carbon emissions from fossil fuels by 30% by 2020; wind energy is to become the primary source of electricity for the island of Carriacou. Energy concerns included electricity charges of 40 US cents per kWh, described by the Government as among the highest in the world.

Hurricane Ivan caused extensive damage to housing stock, infrastructure and public services. The OECS assessed damage at US $815m., equivalent to more than double the country's annual GDP in 2004. As a result, the construction sector expanded from 10.8% of GDP in 2004 to 19.4% in 2005, before contracting to 6.6% of GDP in 2013.

As a consequence of the hurricane, the burden on public finances was dramatically increased, while revenue was sharply reduced. Generous grant aid supported disaster relief and reconstruction efforts, with pledges totalling one-third of annual GDP. Most of the external creditors in 2005 agreed a debt restructuring programme, with interest reduced for the period to 2015 and the principal to be repaid in 2025. However, total debt stock increased from 96% of GDP in 2005 to 114% in 2006, in part because of substantial domestic borrowing. In 2006 the Government raised additional revenue from fuel and from a contentious 3% levy on salaries, while curtailing recurrent expenditure and obtaining additional development assistance. The target of moving from a primary deficit of 2.0% of GDP in 2005 to a primary surplus of 2.5% by 2008, while reducing debt to 60% of GDP by 2015, proved unattainable, with debt rising to 114% of GDP in 2009 amid an international recession. The IMF's three-year Poverty Reduction and Growth Facility approved a one-year extension to 2010 and granted a waiver for missed targets on the government primary balance. In 2010 the Fund completed a performance review and agreed a new three-year extended credit facility of US $13.3m. to mitigate the effects of the global financial crisis and support a reform programme designed to boost growth, reduce poverty, improve the business climate and reduce the vulnerability of the financial sector. A value-added tax was also introduced in 2010. However, the Fund characterized Grenada's performance under this programme as 'weak'.

Following four years of economic decline or stagnation, severe fiscal pressures in 2012 led to late payment of public service salaries, with the situation eased only by assistance from neighbouring Saint Vincent and the Grenadines. With delays in interest payments on a US $193m. bond in September, Standard and Poor's in October lowered Grenada's credit rating from B-/B to Selective Default, raising it, however, a few days later to CCC+/C when the payment was made within the 30-day grace period. If the Government did not pursue economic restructuring, pressures were expected to continue, as the interest rate increased to 6% in September 2013 and was forecast to rise in stages by 9% in 2018. With payment of the March 2013 instalment also missed, Standard and Poor's again reduced Grenada's rating to Selective Default, and the Government announced a 'comprehensive and collaborative' restructuring of public debt.

The fiscal deficit was estimated by the IMF at 5.4% of GDP in 2012 and at 7.1% of GDP for 2013, with total public sector debt (including government guaranteed debt) at 110% of GDP. The deficit was projected at 6.2% of GDP for 2014, with debt servicing accounting for 30% of government spending. In what the IMF called a 'deep fiscal crisis', the New National Party Government that took office in 2013 proposed to cut the size of the public service, maintain a salaries freeze, continue reductions in recurrent spending and restructure government debt, as part of a three-year 'home grown' IMF programme running from June 2014, to tighten income policies, reform the energy sector, put in place the legal structures for public private partnerships, restore fiscal sustainability, restructure debt, and strengthen the financial sector.

Statistical Survey

AREA AND POPULATION

Area: 344.5 sq km (133.0 sq miles).

Population: 102,632 at census of 25 May 2001; 103,328 (males 52,651, females 50,677) at census of 12 May 2011 (preliminary). *Mid-2014* (UN estimate) 106,304 (Source: UN, *World Population Prospects: The 2012 Revision*).

Density (mid-2014): 308.6 per sq km.

Population by Age and Sex (UN estimates at mid-2014): *0–14 years:* 28,297 (males 14,498, females 13,799); *15–64 years:* 70,481 (males 35,726, females 34,755); *65 years and over:* 7,526 (males 3,052, females 4,474); *Total* 106,304 (males 53,276, females 53,028) (Source: UN, *World Population Prospects: The 2012 Revision*).

Parishes (population at 2011 census, preliminary): Carriacou 5,354; St Andrew 25,722; St David 12,561; St George 36,823; St John 7,802; St Mark 4,086; St Patrick 10,980; *Total* 103,328.

Principal Town (population at 2011 census, preliminary): St George's (capital) 2,982. *Mid-2014* (UN estimate, incl. suburbs): St George's 37,822 (Source: UN, *World Urbanization Prospects: The 2014 Revision*).

Births and Deaths (registrations, 2001, provisional): Live births 1,899 (birth rate 18.8 per 1,000); Deaths 727 (death rate 7.2 per 1,000); *2013*: Birth rate 16.6 per 1,000; Death rate 8.0 per 1,000 (Source: Pan American Health Organization).

Life Expectancy (years at birth): 72.6 (males 70.2; females 75.2) in 2012. Source: World Bank, World Development Indicators database.

Employment (employees only, 1998): Agriculture, hunting, forestry and fishing 4,794; Mining and quarrying 58; Manufacturing 2,579; Electricity, gas and water 505; Construction 5,163; Wholesale and retail trade 6,324; Restaurants and hotels 1,974; Transport, storage and communications 2,043; Financing, insurance and real estate 1,312; Public administration, defence and social security 1,879; Community services 3,904; Other services 2,933; *Sub-total* 33,468; Activities not adequately defined 1,321; *Total employed* 34,789 (males 20,733, females 14,056). *Mid-2014* (estimates): Agriculture, etc. 9,000; Total labour force 47,000 (Source: FAO).

HEALTH AND WELFARE

Key Indicators

Total Fertility Rate (children per woman, 2012): 2.2.

Under-5 Mortality Rate (per 1,000 live births, 2012): 14.

Physicians (per 1,000 head, 2009): 0.8.

Hospital Beds (per 1,000 head, 2009): 2.4.

Health Expenditure (2011): US $ per head (PPP): 694.

Health Expenditure (2011): % of GDP: 6.5.

Health Expenditure (2011): public (% of total): 48.3.

Access to Water (% of persons, 2012): 97.

Access to Sanitation (% of persons, 2012): 98.

Total Carbon Dioxide Emissions ('000 metric tons, 2010): 260.4.

Total Carbon Dioxide Emissions Per Head (metric tons, 2010): 2.5.

Human Development Index (2013): ranking: 79.

Human Development Index (2013): value: 0.744.

For sources and definitions, see explanatory note on p. vi.

AGRICULTURE, ETC.

Principal Crops ('000 metric tons, 2012, FAO estimates unless otherwise indicated): Sugar cane 7.2; Pigeon peas 0.9; Coconuts 6.5; Bananas 3.4; Plantains 0.3; Oranges 0.6; Grapefruit and pomelos 1.5; Apples 0.6; Plums and sloes 0.7; Mangoes, mangosteens and guavas 1.2; Avocados 1.5; Cocoa beans 0.8 (unofficial figure); Nutmeg, mace and cardamom 0.6. *Aggregate Production* ('000 metric tons, may include official, semi-official or estimated data): Roots and tubers 2.4; Vegetables (incl. melons) 4.1 Fruits (excl. melons) 14.4.

Livestock ('000 head, year ending September 2012, FAO estimates): Cattle 4.6; Pigs 3.0; Sheep 13.2; Goats 7.2; Chickens 270.

Livestock Products ('000 metric tons, 2012, FAO estimates): Chicken meat 0.7; Cows' milk 0.7; Hen eggs 1.4.

Fishing (metric tons, live weight, 2012): Red hind 120; Coney 23; Snappers and jobfishes 95; Parrotfishes 111; Blackfin tuna 160; Yellowfin tuna 829; Atlantic sailfish 178; Swordfish 24; Common dolphinfish 183; *Total catch* (incl. others) 2,258.

Source: FAO.

INDUSTRY

Production (1994 unless otherwise indicated): Rum 300,000 litres; Beer 2,400,000 litres; Wheat flour 4,000 metric tons (1996); Cigarettes 15m.; Electricity 213.0 million kWh (2010). Source: UN, *Industrial Commodity Statistics Yearbook*.

FINANCE

Currency and Exchange Rates: 100 cents = 1 Eastern Caribbean dollar (EC $). *Sterling, US Dollar and Euro Equivalents* (30 May 2014): £1 sterling = EC $4.542; US $1 = EC $2.700; €1 = EC $3.675; EC $100 = £22.02 = US $37.04 = €27.21. *Exchange Rate:* Fixed at US $1 = EC $2.70 since July 1976.

Budget (EC $ million, 2013): *Revenue:* Tax revenue 410.8 (Taxes on income and profits 64.4, Taxes on property 13.5, Taxes on domestic goods and services 211.6, Taxes on international trade and transactions 121.3); Other current revenue 19.4; Total 430.2 (excluding grants received 26.5) *Expenditure:* Current expenditure 443.4 (Personal emoluments 242.3, Goods and services 74.2, Interest payments 55.8, Transfers and subsidies 71.0); Capital expenditure and net lending 134.9; Total 578.3. Source: Eastern Caribbean Central Bank.

International Reserves (US $ million at 31 December 2013): IMF special drawing rights 15.16; Foreign exchange 135.41; *Total* 150.57. Source: IMF, *International Financial Statistics.*

Money Supply (EC $ million at 31 December 2013): Currency outside depository corporations 115.69; Transferable deposits 376.73; Other deposits 1,556.44; *Broad money* 2,048.86. Source: IMF, *International Financial Statistics.*

Cost of Living (Consumer Price Index; base: 2005 = 100): 125.4 in 2011; 127.7 in 2012; 125.8 in 2013. Source: IMF, *International Financial Statistics.*

Gross Domestic Product (EC $ million at constant 2006 prices): 1,892.04 in 2011; 1,857.51 in 2012; 1,892.02 in 2013 (estimate). Source: Eastern Caribbean Central Bank.

Expenditure on the Gross Domestic Product (EC $ million at current prices, 2012): Government final consumption expenditure 347.67; Private final consumption expenditure 1,974.21; Gross capital formation 353.00; *Total domestic expenditure* 2,674.88; Exports of goods and services 557.53; *Less* Imports of goods and services 1,068.35; *GDP in purchasers' values* 2,164.06. Source: Eastern Caribbean Central Bank.

Gross Domestic Product by Economic Activity (EC $ million at current prices, 2012): Agriculture and fishing 104.77; Mining and quarrying 4.25; Manufacturing 67.27; Electricity and water 85.51; Construction 104.83; Wholesale and retail trade 152.69; Hotels and restaurants 81.60; Transport and communications 227.74; Housing, real estate and business activities 255.47; Financial services 132.02; Public administration and defence 156.21; Other services 521.22; *Sub-total* 1,893.58; *Less* Financial intermediation services indirectly measured (FISIM) 25.28; *GDP at factor cost* 1,868.30; Taxes on products, less subsidies 295.76; *GDP in market prices* 2,164.06. Source: Eastern Caribbean Central Bank.

Balance of Payments (EC $ million, 2013): Goods (net) –749.80; Services (net) 173.35; *Balance of goods and services* –576.45; Other income (net) –69.39; Current transfers (net) 71.16; *Current balance* –574.64; Capital account (net) 162.76; Direct investment 201.66; Portfolio investment 38.54; Other investments 177.12; Net errors and omissions 79.37; *Overall balance* 84.79. Source: Eastern Caribbean Central Bank.

EXTERNAL TRADE

Principal Commodities (distribution by SITC, EC $ million, 2013): *Imports c.i.f.:* Food and live animals 205.46; Mineral fuels and related materials 252.20; Chemicals and related products 68.69; Manufactured goods 138.82; Machinery and transport equipment 167.90; Miscellaneous manufactured articles 114.40; Total (incl. others) 994.78. *Exports f.o.b.:* Food and live animals 66.20; Chemicals and related products 4.90; Manufactured goods 10.38; Machinery and transport equipment 7.73; Miscellaneous manufactured articles

7.90; Total (incl. others) 101.52 (re-exports 14.08). Source: Eastern Caribbean Central Bank.

Principal Trading Partners (US $ million, 2008): *Imports c.i.f.:* Barbados 6.5; Brazil 9.2; Canada 10.1; China, People's Republic 12.0; France (incl. Monaco) 3.2; Germany 5.2; Guyana 3.9; Japan 13.0; Netherlands 4.8; Trinidad and Tobago 90.3; United Kingdom 16.1; USA 112.2; Venezuela 25.5; Total (incl. others) 363.3. *Exports f.o.b.:* Antigua and Barbuda 1.0; Barbados 2.9; Belgium 1.0; Canada 0.9; Dominica 5.0; France (incl. Monaco) 0.3; Guyana 0.6; Jamaica 0.5; Japan 6.5; Netherlands 1.1; Saint Christopher and Nevis 2.6; Saint Lucia 3.4; Saint Vincent and the Grenadines 1.0; Trinidad and Tobago 0.6; USA 5.0; Total (incl. others) 30.5. Source: Trade Map-Trade Competitiveness Map, International Trade Centre, www.intracen.org/marketanalysis. *2012* (EC $ million): Total imports 921.42; Total exports 93.43 (re-exports 11.42). (Source: Eastern Caribbean Central Bank).

TRANSPORT

Road Traffic ('000 motor vehicles in use, 2001): Passenger cars 15.8; Commercial vehicles 4.2. Source: UN, *Statistical Yearbook.*

Shipping: *Flag Registered Fleet* (at 31 December 2013): 8 vessels (total displacement 1,762 grt). Source: Lloyd's List Intelligence (www.lloydslistintelligence.com).

Civil Aviation (aircraft arrivals, 1995): 11,310.

TOURISM

Visitor Arrivals: 428,596 (incl. 113,947 stop-over visitors and 309,564 cruise ship passengers) in 2011; 361,673 (incl. 112,335 stop-over visitors and 242,757 cruise ship passengers) in 2012; 315,118 (incl. 113,049 stop-over visitors and 197,308 cruise ship passengers) in 2013.

Tourism Receipts (EC $ million): 315.3 in 2011; 328.3 in 2012; 324.4 in 2013 (estimate).

Source: Eastern Caribbean Central Bank.

COMMUNICATIONS MEDIA

Telephones (2013): 28,585 main lines in use.

Mobile Cellular Telephones (2013): 133,000 subscribers.

Internet Subscribers (2010): 14,400.

Broadband Subscribers (2013): 18,000.

Source: International Telecommunication Union.

EDUCATION

Pre-primary (2009/10 unless otherwise indicated): 74 schools (1994); 246 teachers; 3,562 pupils.

Primary (2009/10 unless otherwise indicated): 57 schools (1995); 851 teachers; 13,663 pupils.

Secondary (2009/10 unless otherwise indicated): 20 schools (2002); 566 teachers; 11,500 pupils.

Higher (excl. figures for the Grenada Teachers' Training College, 1993): 66 teachers; 651 students.

Source: partly UNESCO Institute for Statistics.

Pupil-teacher Ratio (primary education, UNESCO estimate): 16.1 in 2009/10 (Source: UNESCO Institute for Statistics).

Adult Literacy Rate: 96.0% in 2003. Source: UN Development Programme, *Human Development Report.*

Directory

The Constitution

The 1974 independence Constitution was suspended in March 1979, following the coup, and almost entirely restored between November 1983, after the overthrow of the Revolutionary Military Council, and the elections of December 1984. The main provisions of this Constitution are summarized below:

The Head of State is the British monarch, represented in Grenada by an appointed Governor-General. Legislative power is vested in the bicameral Parliament, comprising a Senate and a House of Representatives. The Senate consists of 13 Senators, seven of whom are appointed on the advice of the Prime Minister, three on the advice of

the Leader of the Opposition and three on the advice of the Prime Minister after he has consulted interests that he considers Senators should be selected to represent. The Constitution does not specify the number of members of the House of Representatives, but the country consists of 15 single-member constituencies, for which representatives are elected for up to five years, on the basis of universal adult suffrage.

The Cabinet consists of a Prime Minister, who must be a member of the House of Representatives, and such other ministers as the Governor-General may appoint on the advice of the Prime Minister.

There is a Supreme Court and, in certain cases, a further appeal lies to Her Majesty in Council.

The Government

HEAD OF STATE

Queen: HM Queen ELIZABETH II.

Governor-General: Dame CECILE LA GRENADE (took office 7 May 2013).

THE CABINET
(September 2014)

The Government was formed by the New National Party.

Prime Minister and Minister of Finance, National Security, Public Administration, Disaster Preparedness, Home Affairs, Implementation and Information: KEITH MITCHELL.

Deputy Prime Minister, and Minister of Legal Affairs, Labour, Carriacou and Petite Martinique Affairs and Local Government: ELVIN NIMROD.

Minister of Economic Development, Planning, Trade and Co-operatives: OLIVER JOSEPH.

Minister of Communications, Works, Physical Development, Public Utilities and Information Communication Technology: GREGORY BOWEN.

Minister of Culture: BRENDA HOOD.

Minister of Tourism and Civil Aviation: Dr ALEXANDRA OTWAY-NOEL.

Minister of Agriculture, Lands, Forestry, Fisheries and the Environment: ROLAND BHOLA.

Minister of Education and Human Resource Development: ANTHONY BOATSWAIN.

Minister of Health and Social Security: Dr CLARICE MODESTE-CURWEN.

Minister of Foreign Affairs and International Business: NICKOLAS STEELE.

Minister of Youth, Sports and Religious Affairs: EMMALIN PIERRE.

Minister of Social Development and Housing: DELMA THOMAS.

MINISTRIES

Office of the Governor-General: Government House, Bldg 5, Financial Complex, The Carenage, St George's; tel. 440-6639; fax 440-6688; e-mail pato@spiceisle.com.

Office of the Prime Minister: Ministerial Complex, 6th Floor, Botanical Gardens, Tanteen, St George's; tel. 440-2255; fax 440-4116; e-mail pmsec@gov.gd; internet www.gov.gd/ministries/opm.html.

Ministry of Agriculture, Lands, Forestry, Fisheries and the Environment: Ministerial Complex, 3rd Floor, Botanical Gardens, Tanteen, St George's; tel. 440-2708; fax 440-4191; e-mail agriculture@gov.gd; internet www.agriculture.gov.gd.

Ministry of Carriacou and Petit Martinique Affairs and Local Government: Beauséjour, Carriacou; tel. 443-6026; fax 443-6040; e-mail minccoupm@spiceisle.com.

Ministry of Communications, Works, Physical Development, Public Utilities and Information Communication Technology: Ministerial Complex, 4th Floor, Botanical Gardens, Tanteen, St George's; tel. 440-2271; fax 440-4122; e-mail ministryofworks@gov.gd.

Ministry of Culture: Ministerial Complex, 4th Floor, Botanical Gardens, Tanteen, St George's.

Ministry of Economic Development, Planning, Trade, Energy and Co-operatives: Financial Complex, The Carenage, St George's; tel. 440-2731; fax 440-4115.

Ministry of Education and Human Resource Development: Ministry of Education Bldg, Ministerial Complex, Botanical Gardens, Tanteen, St George's; tel. 440-2737; fax 440-6650; internet www.grenadaedu.com.

Ministry of Foreign Affairs and International Business: Ministerial Complex, 4th Floor, Botanical Gardens, Tanteen, St George's; tel. 440-2640; fax 440-4184; e-mail foreignaffairs@gov.gd.

Ministry of Health and Social Security: Ministerial Complex, Southern Wing, 1st and 2nd Floors, Botanical Gardens, Tanteen, St George's; tel. 440-2649; fax 440-4127; e-mail min-healthgrenada@spiceisle.com.

Ministry of Legal Affairs and Labour: Ministerial Complex, 3rd Floor, St George's; tel. 440-2532; fax 440-4923; e-mail ministry_labourga@hotmail.com.

Ministry of National Security, Public Administration, Disaster Preparedness, Home Affairs, Implementation and Information: Ministerial Complex, 6th Floor, Botanical Gardens, Tanteen, St George's; tel. 440-2265; fax 440-4116; e-mail pmsec@gov.gd.

Ministry of Social Development and Housing: Ministerial Complex, 2nd Floor, Botanical Gardens, Tanteen, St George's; tel. 440-2103; fax 435-5864; e-mail mofhlcd@gov.gd.

Ministry of Tourism and Civil Aviation: Ministerial Complex, 4th Floor, Botanical Gardens, Tanteen, St George's; tel. 440-0366; fax 440-0443; e-mail tourism@gov.gd; internet www.grenada.mot.gd.

Ministry of Youth, Sports and Religious Affairs: Ministerial Complex, 3rd Floor, Botanical Gardens, Tanteen, St George's; tel. 440-6917; fax 440-6924; e-mail sports@gov.gd.

Legislature

PARLIAMENT

Houses of Parliament: Office of the Houses of Parliament, Botanical Gardens, Tanteen, POB 315, St George's; tel. 440-2090; fax 440-4138; e-mail order.order@spiceisle.com.

Senate

President: LAWRENCE JOSEPH.

There are 13 appointed members.

House of Representatives

Speaker: GEORGE JAMES McGUIRE.

General Election, 19 February 2013

	Votes	%	Seats
New National Party (NNP) .	32,225	58.77	15
National Democratic Congress (NDC)	22,260	40.59	—
Others*	346	0.63	—
Total valid votes	54,831	100.00	15

* Comprising the Good Old Democracy Party (GOD), the Grenada Renaissance Party (GRP), the Grenada United Patriotic Movement (GUPM), the Movement for Independent Candidates (MIC), the National United Front (NUF) and the People's United Labor Party (PULP).

Political Organizations

Good Old Democracy Party (GOD): St George's; contested the 2013 elections; Leader JUSTIN McBURNIE.

Grenada Renaissance Party (GRP): St George's; contested the 2013 elections; Leader DESMOND CUTHBERT SANDY.

Grenada United Labour Party (GULP): St George's; tel. 438-1234; e-mail gulp@spiceisle.com; f. 1950; merged with United Labour Congress in 2001; right-wing; did not contest 2013 elections; Pres. and Acting Leader WILFRED HAYES.

Grenada United Patriotic Movement (GUPM): St George's; contested the 2013 elections.

National Democratic Congress (NDC): NDC Headquarters, Lucas St, St George's; tel. 440-3769; e-mail info@ndcgrenada.net; internet www.ndcgrenada.org; f. 1987 by fmr mems of the NNP and merger of Democratic Labour Congress and Grenada Democratic Labour Party; centrist; Leader NAZIM BURKE.

National United Front (NUF): St George's; e-mail info@nationalunitedfront.org; internet www.nationalunitedfront.org; f. 2012 by expelled mems of the NDP; Chair. SIDDIQUI SYLVESTER; Leader GLYNIS ROBERTS.

New National Party (NNP): Upper Lucas St, Mount Helicon, POB 646, St George's; tel. 440-1875; fax 440-1876; e-mail nnpadmin@spiceisle.com; internet www.nnpnews.com; f. 1984 following merger of Grenada Democratic Movt, Grenada National Party and National Democratic Party; centrist; Leader Dr KEITH MITCHELL; Dep. Leader GREGORY BOWEN.

People's United Labor Party (PULP): St George's; contested the 2013 elections; Leader WINSTON FREDERICK.

Diplomatic Representation

EMBASSIES IN GRENADA

Brazil: Mount Cinnamon Hill, Morne Rouge, POB 1226, Grand Anse, St George's; tel. 439-7162; fax 439-7165; e-mail brasemb

.saintgeorges@mre.gov.br; Ambassador RICARDO ANDRE VIEIRA DINIZ.

China, People's Republic: Azar Villa, Calliste, POB 1079, St George's; tel. 439-6228; fax 439-6231; e-mail chinaemb_gd@mfa .gov.cn; internet gd.china-embassy.org; Ambassador OU BOQIAN.

Cuba: L'Anse aux Epines, St George's; tel. 444-1884; fax 444-1877; e-mail embacubagranada@caribsurf.com; internet www .cubadiplomatica.cu/granada; Ambassador MARIA CARIDAD BALAGUER LABRADA.

USA: L'Anse aux Epines, POB 54, St George's; tel. 444-1173; fax 444-4820; e-mail usembgd@caribsurf.com; Ambassador LARRY LEON PALMER (resident in Barbados).

Venezuela: Upper Lucas St, Belmont, POB 201, St George's; tel. 440-1721; fax 440-6657; e-mail vennes@caribsurf.com; Ambassador JORGE ALFONZO GUERRERO VELOZ.

Judicial System

Justice is administered by the Eastern Caribbean Supreme Court, based in Saint Lucia, composed of a High Court of Justice and a Court of Appeal. The Itinerant Court of Appeal consists of three judges and sits three times a year; it hears appeals from the High Court and the Magistrates' Court. Three judges of the High Court are resident in Grenada. The Magistrates' Court administers summary jurisdiction.

High Court Judges: MARGARET MOHAMMED, PAULA GILFORD, MARGARET PRICE FINDLAY.

Registrar: COLIN MEADE.

Office of the Attorney-General: Communal House, 414 H. A. Blaize St, St George's; tel. 440-2050; fax 435-2964; e-mail legalaffairs@spiceisle.com; Attorney-Gen. CAJETON HOOD.

Religion

CHRISTIANITY

The Roman Catholic Church

Grenada comprises the single diocese of Saint George's, suffragan to the archdiocese of Castries (Saint Lucia). The Bishop participates in the Antilles Episcopal Conference (based in Port of Spain, Trinidad and Tobago). Some 45% of the population are Roman Catholics.

Bishop of St George's in Grenada: Rev. VINCENT DARIUS, Bishop's House, Morne Jaloux, POB 375, St George's; tel. 443-5299; fax 443-5758; e-mail bishopgrenada@spiceisle.com; internet www.stgdiocese .org.

The Anglican Communion

Anglicans in Grenada are adherents of the Church in the Province of the West Indies. The country forms part of the diocese of the Windward Islands. The Bishop resides in Kingstown, Saint Vincent.

Other Christian Churches

The Presbyterian, Methodist, Plymouth Brethren, Baptist, Salvation Army, Jehovah's Witness, Pentecostal and Seventh-day Adventist faiths are also represented.

The Press

NEWSPAPERS

Barnacle: Mt Parnassus, St George's 3530; tel. 435-0981; e-mail barnacle@spiceisle.com; internet www.barnaclegrenada.com; f. 1991; business journal; every 2 weeks; Editor IAN GEORGE.

The Grenada Informer: Market Hill, POB 622, St George's; tel. 440-1530; fax 440-4119; e-mail grenada.informer@yahoo.com; internet www.thegrenadainformer.com; f. 1985; weekly.

The Grenadian Voice: Frequente Industrial Park, Bldg 1B, Maurice Bishop Hwy, POB 633, St George's; tel. 440-1498; fax 440-4117; e-mail gvoice@spiceisle.com; weekly; Man. Editor LESLIE PIERRE; circ. 3,000.

The New Today: POB 1970, St George's; tel. 435-9363; e-mail newtoday@spiceisle.com; internet thenewtoday.gd.

PRESS ASSOCIATION

Media Workers Association of Grenada: Bruce St, POB 1995, St George's; e-mail secretary@mwaggrenada.org; Pres. SHERE-ANN NOEL.

Publishers

Anansi Publications: Woodlands, St George's; tel. 440-0800; e-mail aclouden@spiceisle.com; f. 1986; Man. Dir ALVIN CLOUDEN.

Caribbean Publishing Co: Suite 5, Le Marquis Complex, POB 1744, Grand Anse, St George's; tel. 439-5000; fax 439-5003; e-mail vcharlemagne@globaldirectories.com; internet www.grenadayp .com; print and online directories.

St George's University Publications: Office of University Publications, University Centre, St George's; tel. 444-4175; fax 444-1770; e-mail mlambert@sgu.edu; internet www.sgu.edu/university-communications; f. 2007; Dir MARGARET LAMBERT.

Broadcasting and Communications

TELECOMMUNICATIONS

Digicel Grenada Ltd: Point Salines, POB 1690, St George's; e-mail grenadacustomercare@digicelgroup.com; internet www .digicelgrenada.com; tel. 439-4463; fax 439-4464; f. 2003; owned by an Irish consortium; Chair. DENIS O'BRIEN; Man. (Grenada) PATRICIA MAHER.

Grenada Postal Corporation (GPC): Burns Point, St George's; tel. 440-2526; fax 440-4271; e-mail grenadapost@grenadapost.net; internet www.grenadapost.net; Chair. ADRIAN FRANCIS; Dir of Post LEO ROBERTS.

LIME: POB 119, The Carenage, St George's; tel. 440-1000; fax 440-4134; internet www.lime.com; f. 1989; fmrly Cable & Wireless Grenada Ltd; name adopted as above 2008; until 1998 known as Grenada Telecommunications Ltd (Grentel); 30% govt-owned; fixed lines, mobile telecommunications and internet services provider; CEO (Caribbean) MARTIN JOOS (acting).

Regulatory Authorities

Eastern Caribbean Telecommunications Authority: Vide Boutielle, Castries, POB 1886, Saint Lucia; tel. 458-1701; fax 458-1698; e-mail ectel@ectel.int; internet www.ectel.int; f. 2000 to regulate telecommunications in Grenada, Dominica, Saint Christopher and Nevis, Saint Lucia and Saint Vincent and the Grenadines.

National Telecommunications Regulatory Commission (NTRC): Maurice Bishop Highway, Grand Anse Shopping Centre, POB 854, St George's; tel. 435-6872; fax 435-2132; e-mail gntrc@ectel.int; internet www.ntrc.gd; Chair. Dr SPENCER THOMAS; Coordinator ALDWYN FERGUSON.

BROADCASTING

Radio

City Sound FM: River Rd, St George's; tel. 440-9616; e-mail citysound97i5@yahoo.com; internet www.citysoundfm.com; f. 1996.

Grenada Broadcasting Network (Radio): see Television.

HOTT FM: Observatory Rd, POB 535, St George's; tel. 444-5521; fax 440-4180; e-mail gbn@spiceisle.com; internet www .klassicgrenada.com; f. 1999 as Sun FM, present name adopted 2007; contemporary music.

Klassic AM: Observatory Rd, POB 535, St George's; tel. 444-5521; fax 440-4180; e-mail gbn@spiceisle.com; internet www .klassicgrenada.com.

Harbour Light of the Windwards: 400 Harbour Light Way, Tarleton Point, Carriacou; tel. and fax 443-7628; e-mail harbourlight@spiceisle.com; internet www.harbourlightradio.org; f. 1991; owned by Aviation Radio Missionary Services; Christian radio station; Man. Dir Dr RANDY CORNELIUS.

KYAK 106 FM: Church St, Hillsborough, Carriacou; tel. 443-6262; e-mail info@kyak106.com; internet www.kyak106.com; f. 1996; Office Man. DOREEN STANISLAUS.

Sister Isle Radio: Fort Hill, Hillsborough, Carriacou; tel. 443-8141; fax 443-8142; e-mail sisterisle@gmail.com; internet www .sisterisleradio.com; f. 2005.

Spice Capital Radio FM 90: Springs, St George's; tel. 440-3601.

WeeFM: Cross St, POB 555, St George's; tel. 440-4933; e-mail weefmradio@hotmail.com; internet www.weefmgrenada.com.

Television

Television programmes from Trinidad and Tobago and Barbados can be received on the island.

Grenada Broadcasting Network (GBN): Observatory Rd, POB 535, St George's; tel. 444-5521; fax 440-4180; e-mail gbn@spiceisle .com; internet www.klassicgrenada.com; f. 1972; 60% owned by One Caribbean Media Ltd, 40% govt-owned; 2 radio stations and 1 television station, GBN TV; Chair. CRAIG REYNALD; CEO VICTOR FERNANDES.

Finance

(cap. = capital; res = reserves; dep. = deposits; brs = branches; amounts in Eastern Caribbean dollars)

The Eastern Caribbean Central Bank, based in Saint Christopher and Nevis, is the central issuing and monetary authority for Grenada.

Eastern Caribbean Central Bank—Grenada Office: Monckton St, St George's; tel. 440-3016; fax 440-6721; e-mail eccbgnd@spiceisle .com; Country Dir LINDA FELIX-BERKLEY.

BANKING

Commercial Banks

CIBC FirstCaribbean International Bank: Church St, POB 37, St George's; tel. 440-3232; fax 440-4103; internet www.cibcfcib.com; f. 2002 as FirstCaribbean International Bank following merger of Barclays and Canadian Imperial Bank of Commerce (CIBC)'s Caribbean operations; Barclays relinquished its stake in 2006, present name adopted in 2011; CEO RIK PARKHILL; 4 brs.

Grenada Co-operative Bank Ltd: 8 Church St, POB 135, St George's; tel. 440-2111; fax 440-6600; e-mail co-opbank@caribsurf .com; internet www.grenadaco-opbank.com; f. 1932; cap. 24.8m., res 13m., dep. 568.7m. (Sept. 2013); Chair. DERICK STEELE; Man. Dir and Sec. RICHARD W. DUNCAN; brs in St Andrew's, St George's, St Patrick's and Hillsborough.

Grenada Development Bank: Cnr Young and Scott Sts, POB 2300, St George's; tel. 440-2382; fax 440-6610; e-mail gdbbank@ spiceisle.com; internet www.grenadadevelopmentbank.com; f. 1965; govt-owned; Chair. MICHAEL ARCHIBALD.

RBTT Bank Grenada Ltd: Grand Anse, POB 4, St George's; tel. 440-3521; fax 440-4153; e-mail RBTTLTD@caribsurf.com; internet www.rbtt.com; f. 1983 as Grenada Bank of Commerce; name changed as above 2002; 10% govt-owned; national insurance scheme 15%; public 13%; RBTT Bank Caribbean Ltd, Castries 62%; cap. 11.0m., res 11.1m., dep. 389m. (Oct. 2013); Chair. PATRICIA NARAYANSINGH; Regional CEO SURESH SOOKOO; 4 brs.

Republic Bank (Grenada) Ltd: Republic House, Maurice Bishop Hwy, Grand Anse, POB 857, St George's; tel. 444-2265; fax 444-5500; e-mail republichouse@republicgrenada.com; internet www .republicgrenada.com; f. 1979; fmrly National Commercial Bank of Grenada; name changed as above in 2006; 51% owned by Republic Bank Ltd, Port of Spain, Trinidad and Tobago; cap. 15.0m., res 19.5m., dep. 633.1m. (Sept. 2013); Chair. RONALD HARFORD; Man. Dir KEITH A. JOHNSON; 6 brs.

Scotiabank Grenada (Canada): Granby and Halifax Sts,POB 194, St George's; tel. 440-3274; fax 440-4173; e-mail bns.grenada@ scotiabank.com; internet www.scotiabank.com/gd/en; f. 1963; Country Man. ELIE BENDALY; 3 brs.

REGULATORY AUTHORITY

Grenada Authority for the Regulation of Financial Institutions (GARFIN): POB 3973, Queens Park, St George's; tel. 440-6575; fax 440-4780; e-mail angus.smith@garfin.org; internet www .garfingrenada.org; f. 1999 as Grenada International Financial Services Authority; name changed to above in 2007; regulates non-banking financial sector; Chair. TIMOTHY ANTOINE; Exec. Dir ANGUS SMITH.

STOCK EXCHANGE

Eastern Caribbean Securities Exchange: Bird Rock, Basseterre, Saint Christopher and Nevis; tel. (869) 466-7192; fax (869) 465-3798; e-mail info@ECSEonline.com; internet www.ecseonline.com; f. 2001; regional securities market designed to facilitate the buying and selling of financial products for the 8 mem. territories—Anguilla, Antigua and Barbuda, Dominica, Grenada, Montserrat, Saint Christopher and Nevis, Saint Lucia, and Saint Vincent and the Grenadines; Chair. Sir K. DWIGHT VENNER; Gen. Man. TREVOR E. BLAKE.

INSURANCE

Several foreign insurance companies operate in Grenada and the other islands of the group. Principal locally owned companies include the following:

Gittens Insurance Brokerage Co Ltd: Benoit Bldg, Grand Anse, POB 1695, St George's; tel. 439-4408; fax 439-4462; internet www .cisgrenada.com/gittensinsurance; f. 2003; Chair. PHILLIP MCLAW-RENCE GITTENS; CEO PHILLIP ARTHUR GITTENS.

Grenada Motor and General Insurance Co Ltd: Scott St, POB 152, St George's; tel. 440-3379; fax 440-7977; e-mail g500z@hotmail .com; Gen. Man. GABRIEL OLOUYNE.

Grenadian General Insurance Co Ltd: Cnr of Young and Scott Sts, POB 47, St George's; tel. 440-2434; fax 440-6618; e-mail ggicoltd@spiceisle.com; Dir KEITH RENWICK.

GTM Grenada (Guyana and Trinidad Mutual Group of Insurance Companies): Church St, St George's; tel. 440-2839; internet www .gtm-gy.com/grenada; f. 1909; headquarters in Guyana; Country Man. SHONETTE INNISS-HOYTE.

Pan-American Life Insurance Co of the Eastern Caribbean: Modern Photo Studio Bldg, St George's; tel. 435-0058; fax 435-0060; internet www.palig.com; f. 2012; part of Pan-American Life Insurance Group (USA); CEO and Man. Dir (Caribbean) WILLIAM R. SCHULZ, Jr; Man. PEARLY CHARLES.

Trade and Industry

CHAMBER OF COMMERCE

Grenada Chamber of Industry and Commerce, Inc (GCIC): Bldg 11, POB 129, Frequente, St George's; tel. 440-2937; fax 440-6627; e-mail gcic@grenadachamber.org; internet www .grenadachamber.org; f. 1921, incd 1947; 170 mems; Pres. AINE BRATHWAITE; Exec. Dir HAZELANN HUTCHINSON.

INDUSTRIAL AND TRADE ASSOCIATIONS

Grenada Cocoa Association (GCA): Kirani James Blvd, POB 3649, St George's; tel. 440-2234; fax 440-1470; e-mail gca@spiceisle .com; f. 1964; Chair. RAMSEY RUSH; Man. ANDREW HASTICK.

Grenada Co-operative Nutmeg Association (GCNA): Lagoon Rd, POB 160, St George's; tel. 440-2117; fax 440-6602; e-mail gcna .nutmeg@caribsurf.com; f. 1947; processes and markets all the nutmeg and mace grown on the island; includes the production of nutmeg oil; Chair. DENIS FELIX; Gen. Man. MARLON CLYNE.

Grenada Industrial Development Corporation (GIDC): Frequenté Industrial Park, Grand Anse, St George's; tel. 444-1035; fax 444-4828; e-mail invest@grenadaidc.com; internet www.grenadaidc .com; f. 1985; Chair. R. ANTHONY JOSEPH; Gen. Man. SONIA RODEN.

Marketing and National Importing Board (MNIB): Young St, POB 652, St George's; tel. 440-1791; fax 440-4152; e-mail mnib@ spiceisle.com; internet www.mnib.gd; f. 1974; govt-owned; imports basic food items, incl. sugar, rice and milk; also exports fresh produce; Chair. CLAUDIA ALEXIS; Gen. Man. FITZROY JAMES.

EMPLOYERS' ORGANIZATION

Grenada Employers' Federation: Bldg 11, Frequenté Industrial Park, Grand Anse, POB 129, St George's; tel. 440-6627; e-mail gef@spiceisle.com; internet www.grenadaemployers.com; f. 1962; Pres. MICHAEL PHILBERT; Exec. Dir CECIL EDWARDS; 60 mems.

UTILITIES

Electricity

Grenada Electricity Services Ltd (Grenlec): Halifax St, POB 381, St George's; tel. 440-2097; fax 440-4106; e-mail customersupport@grenlec.com; internet www.grenlec.com; f. 1960; generation and distribution; majority privately owned (61% by WRB Enterprises, USA), 10% govt-owned; Chair. G. ROBERT BLANCHARD, Jr; Man. Dir and CEO VERNON LAWRENCE.

Water

National Water and Sewerage Authority (NAWASA): The Carenage, POB 392, St George's; tel. 440-2155; fax 440-4107; f. 1969; Chair. TERRENCE SMITH; Gen. Man. CHRISTOPHER HUSBANDS.

TRADE UNIONS

Bank and General Workers' Union (BGWU): Bain's Alley, POB 329, St George's; tel. and fax 440-3563; e-mail bgwu@caribsurf.com; Pres. JUSTIN CAMPBELL; Gen. Sec. EDMOND CALLISTE.

Commercial and Industrial Workers' Union: Bain's Alley, Grand Anse, POB 1791, St George's; tel. and fax 440-3423; e-mail cominwu@caribsurf.com; Pres. GEORGE MASON; Gen. Sec. BARBARA FRASER; 492 mems.

Grenada Manual, Maritime and Intellectual Workers' Union (GMMIWU): c/o Birchgrove, POB 1927, St Andrew's; tel. and fax 442-7724; Pres. BERT LATOUCHE; Gen. Sec. OSCAR WILLIAMS.

Grenada Public Workers' Union (GPWU): Tanteen, POB 420, St George's; tel. 440-2203; fax 440-6615; e-mail gpwu@spiceisle.com;

f. 1931 as Civil Service Asscn; Pres. ADRIAN FRANCIS; Exec. Sec. AUGUSTINE DAVID.

Grenada Technical and Allied Workers' Union (GTAWU): Green St, POB 405, St George's; tel. 440-2231; fax 440-5878; e-mail tawu@gtawu.org; internet spicy-design.net/~gtawu; f. 1958; Pres.-Gen. Sen. CHESTER HUMPHREY; Gen. Sec. BERT PATERSON.

Grenada Trade Union Council (GTUC): Green St, POB 411, St George's; tel. and fax 440-3733; e-mail gtuc@caribsurf.com; Pres. MADONNA HARFORD; Gen. Sec. RAY ROBERTS; 8,000 mems (2011).

Grenada Union of Teachers (GUT): Marine Villa, POB 452, St George's; tel. 440-2992; fax 440-9019; e-mail gut@caribsurf.com; internet gutgrenada.org; f. 1913; Pres. KENNY A. M. JAMES; Gen. Sec. TESSA MCQUILKIN; 1,300 mems.

Media Workers' Association of Grenada (MWAG): St George's; e-mail mwagrenada@yahoo.com; f. 1999; Pres. RAWLE TITUS.

Seamen and Waterfront Workers' Union: Ottway House, POB 154, St George's; tel. 440-2573; fax 440-7199; e-mail swwu@caribsurf.com; f. 1952; Pres. ALBERT JULIEN; Gen. Sec. LYLE SAMUEL; 350 mems.

Transport

RAILWAYS

There are no railways in Grenada.

ROADS

There were approximately 1,127 km (700 miles) of roads, of which 61% were paved. Following the completion of the first phase of the Agricultural Feeder Roads Project, funded by the OPEC Fund for International Development, work on the second phase of the project, at a cost of EC $45.4m., began in May 2013. Funding for the second phase was provided by the Kuwait Fund for Arab Economic Development.

SHIPPING

The main port is St George's, with accommodation for two ocean-going vessels of up to 500 ft. A number of shipping lines call at St George's. The Melville Street Cruise Terminal became operational in 2004. Grenville, on Grenada, and Hillsborough, on Carriacou, are used mostly by small craft. An ambitious EC $1,600m. development at Port Louis, to include a 350-slipway marina with yachting facilities, was completed in 2009. In December 2013 Grenada's flag registered fleet comprised eight vessels, with an aggregate displacement of some 1,762 grt.

Grenada Ports Authority: POB 494, The Pier, St George's; tel. 440-7678; fax 440-3418; e-mail grenport@caribsurf.com; internet www.grenadaports.com; f. 1981; state-owned; Chair. NIGEL JOHN; Gen. Man. AMBROSE PHILLIP.

CIVIL AVIATION

Maurice Bishop International Airport (formerly Point Salines International Airport) is 10 km (6 miles) from St George's and has scheduled flights to most Eastern Caribbean destinations, including Venezuela, and to the United Kingdom and North America. There is an airfield at Pearls, 30 km (18 miles) from St George's, and Lauriston Airport, on the island of Carriacou, offers regular sched-uled services to Grenada, Saint Vincent and Palm Island (Grenadines).

Grenada is a shareholder in the regional airline LIAT (see chapter on Antigua and Barbuda).

Grenada Airports Authority: Maurice Bishop Int. Airport, POB 385, St George's; tel. 444-4101; fax 444-4838; e-mail gaa@mbiagrenada.com; e-mail www.mbiagrenada.com; f. 1985; Chair. JOAN GILBERT.

Tourism

Grenada has the attractions of white sandy beaches and a scenic, mountainous interior with an extensive rainforest. There are also sites of historical interest, and the capital, St George's, is a noted beauty spot. In 2013 there were 113,049 stop-over arrivals and 197,308 cruise ship passengers. In that year tourism earned EC $324.4m.

Grenada Hotel and Tourism Association Ltd: Ocean House Bldg, Morne Rouge Rd, Grand Anse, POB 440, St George's; tel. 444-1353; fax 444-4847; e-mail mail@ghta.org; internet www.ghta.org; f. 1961; Pres. IAN FIELDEN DA BREO; Exec. Dir PANCY CHANDLER CROSS.

Grenada Tourism Authority: Burns Point, POB 293, St George's; tel. 440-2279; fax 440-6637; e-mail gbt@spiceisle.com; internet www.grenadagrenadines.com; f. 1991 as Grenada Board of Tourism; upgraded to an authority in 2013; Chair. RICHARD STRACHAN.

Defence

A regional security unit was formed in 1983, modelled on the British police force and trained by British officers. A paramilitary element, known as the Special Service Unit and trained by US advisers, acts as the defence contingent and participates in the Regional Security System, a defence pact with other Eastern Caribbean states.

Commissioner of Police: WINSTON JAMES (acting).

Education

Education is free and compulsory for children between the ages of five and 16 years. Primary education begins at five years of age and lasts for seven years. Secondary education, beginning at the age of 12, lasts for a further five years. In 2009 enrolment at primary schools included 87% of children in the relevant age-group. In 2009/10 some 13,663 pupils attended primary school while 11,500 students attended secondary school. Enrolment at all secondary schools included 91% of pupils in the relevant age-group in 2008/09. In 2006 there were 2,710 full-time enrolled students at the T. A. Marryshow Community College. The Extra-Mural Department of the University of the West Indies has a branch in St George's and there is also St George's University, which had 5,880 students in 2012. The combined capital expenditure on education and human resources development was budgeted at EC $109.6m. in 2012 (equivalent to 10.7% of total capital expenditure).

Bibliography

For works on the Caribbean generally, see Select Bibliography (Books)

Brizan, G. I. *Grenada: Island of Conflict*. Grand Cayman, Caribbean Publishing, 1998.

Coley, K. 'Grenada Rebuilds: After the Hurricane', in *UN Chronicle*, Vol. 42, No. 3 (2005).

Heine, J. (Ed.). *A Revolution Aborted*. Pittsburgh, PA, University of Pittsburgh Press, 1991.

Lewis, P. *Social Policies in Grenada*. 2nd edn, Commonwealth Secretariat, 2010.

Raines, E. F. *The Rucksack War: U.S. Army Operational Logistics in Grenada, 1983*. United States Dept of the Army, Center of Military History, 2011.

Smith, C. A. *Socialist Transformation in Peripheral Economies*. Brookfield, VT, Avebury Publishing Co, 1995.

Steele, B. A. *Grenada: A History of its People*. Oxford, Macmillan Caribbean, 2003.

Williams, G. *US-Grenada Relations: Revolution and Intervention in the Backyard*. Basingstoke, Palgrave Macmillan, 2007.

GUADELOUPE

Geography

PHYSICAL FEATURES

The Overseas Department of Guadeloupe is an integral part of the French Republic, but lies in the Lesser Antilles. It includes the main islands of Guadeloupe itself (Basse-Terre and Grande-Terre) and a number of surrounding islands, which lie in the Windward Islands. Until 2007 it also included St-Barthélemy and the northern part of the island of St-Martin (Sint Maarten) in the Leewards. All these islands lie in the north-eastern Caribbean. Guadeloupe itself is flanked by two sea lanes from the Atlantic: the Dominica Passage to the south, beyond which lies the Commonwealth of Dominica; and the wider Guadeloupe Passage to the north, beyond which, some 64 km (40 miles) to the north-west, is the southernmost of the Leeward Islands, the British dependency of Montserrat. A similar distance directly north is Antigua and Barbuda, while about one-half that distance south of Marie-Galante is the island of Dominica.

Guadeloupe, a butterfly-shaped land mass is, technically, two islands, separated by a narrow channel, the Rivière Sallée. The name Guadeloupe originally applied only to the larger, mountainous western island, which is now known as Basse-Terre (like the first settlement and the administrative headquarters), after the only 'low shore', on the leeward side of the cliff-edged island. The broad, flat lands of the east, Grande-Terre, soon assumed commercial and agricultural significance and the name of Guadeloupe came to be applied to both 'wings'. Basse-Terre, the largest single island of Guadeloupe (848 sq km), is fertile, mountainous and volcanic, the densely forested central range reaching the highest point in the Department, at the desolate volcano of La Soufrière (1,354 m or 4,444 ft), in the south of the island. About two-thirds of the way up the eastern coast of Basse-Terre a broad peninsula reaches out to its sister island. The lower-lying Grande-Terre (about three-fifths the size of Basse-Terre), essentially a limestone plateau, extends mainly northwards, tapering from a west–east base between the near-isthmus to Basse-Terre and the eastward-pointing Pointe des Châteaux. There are some hills in the south and mangrove swamps along the west coast, but much of the land is given to sugar cane, fruit trees and livestock. The wealth of vegetation throughout Guadeloupe includes native and widely protected forests, but indigenous wildlife has largely been wiped out—a few racoons (*ratons laveurs*) and iguanas survive on the offshore islands. The only other island of any size in the Department is 22 km south of Grande-Terre—the flat, round Marie-Galante (158 sq km). Just east of Grande-Terre is La Désirade, to the south-west of which, mid-way to Marie-Galante, are the Iles de la Petite-Terre. West of Marie-Galante and just south of Basse-Terre are the Iles des Saintes (near which an important naval battle took place in 1782). These are the main offshore islands of Guadeloupe and most are hilly, though drier than the mainland.

CLIMATE

The climate is subtropical, tempered by trade winds. All the islands lie in the potential path of hurricanes, and Guadeloupe itself is fairly humid. The average temperatures on the coast of the main islands range between 22°C and 30°C (72°F–86°F), but it can be about 3°C cooler inland, particularly in the

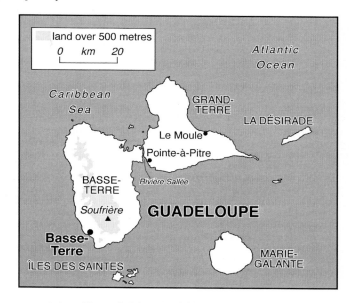

mountains. Most of this rain falls in September–November, although the wet season (*hivernage*) is reckoned to begin in July. The dry season (*carême*) falls in the cooler months of January–April.

POPULATION

Around 90% of the population is black or mixed race, with 5% white, and there are smaller communities of 'East' Indians, Chinese and Lebanese, similar to many places in the West Indies. Some 76% of the population is Roman Catholic, with only 1% Protestant, the rest being Hindu or espousing pagan African religions or syncretic versions thereof. The official language is French, which most people speak, but many people generally use the Creole patois that employs West African grammatical structures with a predominantly French-derived vocabulary.

The total population was estimated at 468,017 at mid-2014, according to UN estimates. The majority of the population live on Guadeloupe, with Grande-Terre being the more densely populated. The administrative capital, Basse-Terre, is not a large city—it is on the western coast, at the southern end, of the western wing of the main island. The largest city in the Department, the chief city of Grande-Terre and the commercial capital of Guadeloupe is Pointe-à-Pitre, on the south-west coast of the eastern wing, near the Rivière Sallée. There are about 100,000 people living in Pointe-à-Pitre and its environs. Other important centres include: Les Abymes, inland; Le Gosier, just to the south-east of Pointe-à-Pitre; and Le Moule, a former capital, on Grande-Terre, but on the east coast. Marie-Galante, with a total population of around 18,000, has three main settlements, the largest being Grand-Bourg, on the south-west coast.

History

JESSICA BYRON

Based on an earlier article by PHILLIP WEARNE

Named after the Spanish Virgin of Guadeloupe by the European navigator Christopher Columbus in 1493, the island was occupied by the French, almost without interruption, from 1635. Guadeloupe and its dependencies—Saint-Barthélemy, the northern part of Saint-Martin in the Leeward Islands, and the offshore islands of La Désirade, Marie-Galante and Iles des Saintes—became a French Overseas Department in March 1946, but achieved some degree of autonomy in 1983 as a result of the decentralization reforms of President François Mitterrand's Socialist Government. The island was administered by a Prefect, appointed by the French Ministry of the Interior. Local government was made up of a 42-seat Conseil Général (General Council), elected for a six-year term to oversee day-to-day activities such as social security, housing, primary education, health and urban management, and a 41-seat Conseil Régional (Regional Council), the main role of which was to promote the social, economic, cultural and scientific development of the region. The Regional Council consisted of local councillors and the two senators and four deputies Guadeloupe sends to the French Assemblée Nationale (National Assembly).

However, progress towards greater autonomy did not prevent an upsurge of nationalist sentiment during the 1980s, witnessed by the formation of several separatist groups, making Guadeloupe the most politicized of France's Caribbean territories. These groups comprised two broad categories: those that claimed responsibility for a series of bomb attacks on government offices and economic targets such as hotels and restaurants; and those that campaigned by lawful means. Among the former, the most active were the Alliance Révolutionnaire Caraïbe (ARC) and the Groupe Libération Armée. In 1984 the ARC merged with the Mouvement Populaire pour une Guadeloupe Indépendante (MPGI), but continued its bombing campaign, using the MPGI as a legitimate cover for its activities.

In 1989 the National Assembly granted an amnesty to those imprisoned or accused in connection with politically motivated crimes in the Overseas Departments. The amnesty, the failure of the independence groups at the polls and the Mitterrand administration's willingness to cede more autonomy to Guadeloupe's democratic left, formed the basis for a new political *modus vivendi* in Guadeloupe.

As in other French territories (such as New Caledonia, in the Pacific), nationalist pressure had a racial element. The original white planters represented only 5% of the population, yet they owned more than 80% of all land and property until 1945. The position of this group was consolidated, after 1946, by the arrival of French government officials and professionals. They not only altered the racial balance in favour of the whites, at a time when black national consciousness was growing, but also effectively blocked the advancement of people of African and mixed descent by monopolizing the most desirable jobs. The problems of change in the racial balance of the island were compounded by the influx of illegal immigrants from neighbouring islands, attracted by the relatively high standard of living, and by work opportunities in the agricultural sector. Salary levels were high by Caribbean standards, although many native islanders preferred to emigrate or to seek work in the services sector rather than accept wages below the legal minimum on the land. Emigration continued at a rate of nearly 20,000 per year, with the result that perhaps 40% of all Guadeloupeans lived abroad by the 1990s.

The belief that the separatists had an influence out of all proportion to their numbers was borne out by the Socialists' gains in the 1988 French presidential and parliamentary elections. In 1992 the Socialists suffered some reversals. In the elections to the Regional Council, the right-wing grouping, Objectif Guadeloupe, led by Lucette Michaux-Chévry, won 15 of the 41 seats, while two Socialist groups obtained 16 seats

between them. Taking advantage of the split on the Socialist side, Michaux-Chévry succeeded in ousting the Socialist Félix Proto from the presidency of the Regional Council. Objectif Guadeloupe took a further seven seats in elections to the Regional Council to push its tally up to 22, while the two left-wing parties retained only 10.

At elections to the French National Assembly in 1993 the local wing of the national Parti Socialiste (PS) lost more ground when an independent right-wing candidate, Edouard Chammougon, defeated Dominique Larifla. However, corruption charges led to Chammougon's membership of the National Assembly being revoked by the French Conseil Constitutionnel (Constitutional Council) in November 1994, following which Léo Andy of the 'dissident' PS was elected to his seat. In 1993 Michaux-Chévry retained her seat at the National Assembly, while a Socialist, Frédéric Jalton, and a dissident Communist, Ernest Moutoussamy, retained the other two seats.

At municipal elections in 1995 Michaux-Chévry defeated the Communist incumbent to become mayor of the capital, Basse-Terre. She and Larifla were elected to the French Sénat (Senate) in September, and Philippe Chaulet of the Rassemblement pour la République (RPR) was subsequently elected to her seat in the National Assembly. Jean Barfleur became Guadeloupe's first pro-independence mayor when he won Port-Louis.

At elections to the National Assembly in 1997, Moutoussamy, Andy and Chaulet all retained their seats, while Daniel Marsin, a candidate of the independent left, was elected in the Les Abymes–Pointe-à-Pitre constituency. In March 1998 the RPR won a majority of seats in the Regional Council, although the PS increased its representation. Michaux-Chévry was re-elected to the presidency of the Council. In concurrent elections to the General Council the Socialist-Communist coalition retained a majority, although the RPR increased its representation. Larifla was replaced as the President of the General Council by Marcellin Lubeth of the Parti Progressiste Démocratique Guadeloupéen (PPDG).

The issue of Guadeloupe's constitutional status arose in 1999 following a series of meetings between the Presidents of the Regional Councils of Guadeloupe, Martinique and French Guiana. In December Michaux-Chévry co-signed a declaration, stating the intention of the three Presidents to propose, to the French Government, legislative and constitutional amendments aimed at creating a new status of Overseas Region (Région d'Outre-mer) and providing for greater financial autonomy. The declaration was dismissed by Jean-Jack Queyranne, the French Secretary of State for Overseas Departments and Territories, in February 2000, as unconstitutional and exceeding the mandate of the politicians responsible. However, in May a number of proposals, including the extension of the Departments' powers in areas such as regional co-operation, were provisionally accepted by the National Assembly; a modified version of the proposals was subsequently adopted, by a narrow margin, by the Senate. In November the National Assembly approved the changes, and in December they were ratified by the Constitutional Council.

Michaux-Chévry was re-elected mayor of Basse-Terre in the 2001 municipal elections, but she relinquished the post to Pierre-Marti, owing to ongoing investigations into charges of corruption against her. Henri Bangou of the PPDG was also re-elected to the mayoralty of Pointe-à-Pitre. In the concurrently held election to the presidency of the General Council Jacques Gillot of Guadeloupe Unie, Socialisme et Réalité (GUSR) defeated Marcellin Lubeth of the PPDG.

In June 2001 riots took place in Pointe-à-Pitre in which a number of people were injured, in protest at the arrest of the leader of the UGTG, Michel Madassamy, who had been charged in May with vandalizing a number of shops that had remained open, in defiance of the UGTG's recommendations. A period of severe drought, necessitating the rationing of water supplies, served to exacerbate the deteriorating social situation on the island.

Following a meeting of members of the Regional Council and the General Council in late June 2001, a series of proposals on greater autonomy, to be presented to the French Government, was agreed upon. These included: the division of the territory into four districts; the creation of a Territorial Collectivity (Collectivité Territoriale), governed by a 41-member Assembly elected for a five-year term; and the establishment of an independent executive council. Furthermore, the proposals included a request that the territory be given control over legislative and administrative affairs, as well as legislative authority on matters concerning Guadeloupe alone. In November the French Government announced itself to be in favour of the suggested constitutional developments, and in March 2003 the two houses of the French parliament approved constitutional changes which would allow for a referendum on proposals for greater autonomy. In the same month the status of Overseas Region was conferred upon Guadeloupe.

At elections to the National Assembly in June 2002 Chaulet, Marsin, Moutoussamy and Andy were all defeated; Objectif Guadeloupe emerged as the most successful political grouping, with both Gabrielle Louis-Carabin and Joël Beaugendre being elected as deputies; Eric Jalton (son of Frédéric Jalton) of the Parti Communiste Guadeloupéen (PCG) and Victorin Lurel of the Gauche Plurielle grouping were also successful.

In December 2003 voting took place in the referendum to determine Guadeloupe's constitutional relationship with France. The proposed new arrangement, laid out by Jean-Pierre Raffarin's right-of-centre Government in Paris, foresaw the replacement of the General Council and Regional Council with a single elected council, with the aim of streamlining administrative and political processes. Despite the enthusiastic support of Michaux-Chévry, however, an overwhelming 73.0% voted against the proposal. Supporters of the 'yes' vote claimed that voters had been misled into believing that the new constitutional status would involve reductions in French subsidies and social security payments. In Saint-Barthélemy and Saint-Martin, however, the vote was in favour of the proposed change, by 95.5% and 76.2%, respectively, meaning that the islands would no longer be communes of Guadeloupe but separate Overseas Collectivities (Collectivités d'Outre-mer). The reorganization was subsequently approved by the French Senate and by the National Assembly. On 21 February Saint-Barthélemy and the French part of Saint-Martin were formally designated Overseas Collectivities. However, the existing forms of government continued until elections to a local legislative assembly—to be known as the Conseil Territorial (Territorial Council)—were held on 1 July, after which the two Overseas Collectivities acceded to administrative independence. Furthermore, each Overseas Collectivity was to elect one representative to the French Senate (in September 2008) and one deputy to the National Assembly (in 2012). (See the chapters on Saint-Barthélemy and Saint-Martin.)

In elections to the Regional Council in March 2004 Michaux-Chévry suffered a further defeat when Lurel's left-wing coalition, Guadeloupe pour Tous, won a majority of votes cast. Michaux-Chévry was forced to resign as President of the Regional Council.

Meanwhile, in October 2004 the arrest of Michel Madassamy on fresh charges of vandalism led to a deterioration in the social situation. Madassamy was accused of attacking two petrol tankers during the blockade of a service station in Pointe-à-Pitre in November 2003. In March 2004 he was found guilty and sentenced to 10 months' imprisonment. The UGTG challenged the legality of the arrest, and urged workers to strike in support of Madassamy's release; Madassamy began a hunger strike. While there was no appeal for a general strike, areas affected included the airport, local shops and service stations. Dock workers at the port of Jarry refused to load or unload containers and ships were diverted to other Caribbean ports. Madassamy was granted conditional release in November pending a further hearing in January 2005, when the judge ruled that he should serve a further eight months in prison.

At the first round of the national presidential election in April 2007, Nicolas Sarkozy of the Union pour un Mouvement Populaire (UMP) won 43% of the votes cast in Guadeloupe, ahead of PS candidate Ségolène Royal, who attracted 38% of the vote. At the second round, held in May, Royal gained 51% to Sarkozy's 49%, although Sarkozy emerged victorious overall. Meanwhile, at elections to the National Assembly in June, UMP candidate Gabrielle Louis-Carabin, PS representative Lurel and Eric Jalton of the PCG were re-elected, while Jeanny Marc-Matthiasin of the GUSR was also successful. At municipal elections in March 2008 Michaux-Chévry was again elected mayor of Basse-Terre. The Socialist parties retained control of the General Council, and Gillot was re-elected as its President.

In early 2009 Guadeloupe was severely disrupted by a six-week general strike. The unrest began with demands that the French authorities address growing inequality and social dislocation within Guadeloupean society. There was particular concern over the low wages of many workers, which were exacerbated by the increasing cost of living that was linked to the dependence on imports from the metropole. An 'umbrella' group, called the Liyannaj Kont Pwofitasyon (LKP), or 'Collective Against Exploitation', co-ordinated the demonstrations. This grouping contained a large number of trade unions and other civil society organizations, and provided an effective force in appealing for change. In the course of laying out their demands, the protesters directed some of their dissatisfaction against the *béké* class, the white descendants of colonial plantation owners, for allegedly exploiting their monopoly power in retail and construction in order to maintain high prices and therefore their privileged status. All aspects of society were affected by the general strike. Commercial activity was severely restricted, including at the main shipping and air ports, government business was disrupted, and schools were shut.

After a month of relatively peaceful protest the strike turned violent amid worsening economic and social conditions and growing frustration over the lack of progress in meeting the protesters' demands. Clashes took place between the police (several hundred of whom had been drafted in from mainland France) and demonstrators and on 18 February 2009 a union activist, Juan Bino, was shot and killed. Although the death appeared to be an accident, the incident highlighted to all sides the real risk of anarchy in the Department if a solution to the crisis were not found. Indeed, soon after Bino's death serious talks began between the French Government and the LKP. The negotiations were protracted, in large part owing to the Government's reluctance to accede to the central demands of the LKP. Nevertheless, on 4 March an accord was signed, prompting the LKP to call off the strike. The agreement included a pay rise for the lowest paid workers, a reduction in the cost of basic staples and commodities, and an increase in financial assistance for farmers, fishermen and small businesses.

President Sarkozy visited Guadeloupe and Martinique in June 2009. He was joined by his new Minister of the Overseas Departments and Territories, Marie-Luce Penchard, a native of Guadeloupe and the first holder of the office from outside metropolitan France. The intention of the visit was to hold talks with local politicians and members of civil society, and more broadly to assist the French Government's efforts to rebuild relations with the overseas territories. Sarkozy's visit came during a consultation process, initiated in April by the French Government, intended to address the underlying concerns within the Departments. Key issues considered included the development of local production, the pricing mechanisms for goods and services, and the ways in which social dialogue could be improved. A range of groups participated in the discussions, although most unions boycotted them. The LKP decreed 'a week of mobilization', with strikes and demonstrations to accompany Sarkozy's visit. In order to retain some calm during the presidential visit, some 900 extra police officers were drafted in from mainland France.

The situation remained tense in the ensuing months, and on 24–25 November 2009 the LKP staged a second general strike. A 10,000-strong demonstration was held in Pointe-à-Pitre, during which participants beseeched the French Government to honour the commitments of the March accord. However, there was a markedly lower level of support for widespread civil protest, suggesting that a degree of normality was returning to Guadeloupe. This notion was reinforced by elections to the Regional Council in March 2010. The PS-led list, Tous pour la Guadeloupe, retained power, securing 31 of the 41 council seats, with its share of the vote increasing to 57%. The Ensemble pour la Guadeloupe—comprising the UMP, led by Penchard, and other right-wing candidates—won just four seats, with 14% of the vote. The results highlighted Guadeloupeans' continued dissatisfaction with the French Government, but also a strong preference for more moderate and consensual leadership at home. During Sarkozy's 2009 visit Guadeloupe's elected representatives had been given a period of 18 months in which to hold consultations and to propose a formula for the reform of territorial institutions. In view of the fragile social consensus in the territory following the protests, they opted to defer change and not to request a referendum on the issue of greater autonomy (unlike Martinique and French Guiana). By contrast, Tous pour la Guadeloupe, with Lurel at the helm, determined that its focus should remain firmly on economic and social renewal. None the less, legislation was adopted by the French National Assembly on 17 November 2010 that decreed the implementation of institutional reform in all the Overseas Departments and Regions (as well as in metropolitan France) by 2014 (later delayed). Further legislation, approved in July 2011, specified that there would be 45 territorial councillors in the Guadeloupean Regional Council and General Council, a reduction of approximately 50%.

Following the March 2011 cantonal elections, Jacques Gillot was re-elected as President of the General Council for a fourth consecutive term. Later that year, Guadeloupe's political representatives announced that they were prepared to support modified proposals for institutional reform to come into effect by 2014. They proposed that the number of elected local government representatives should be 65 and that there should be scope for proportional representation. They were, however, advised by the Sarkozy administration that they would have to undertake a process of democratic consultation by referendum. There was no further action on this matter.

In May 2012 the fortunes of the Guadeloupean left continued to gain strength with the French presidential election. François Hollande, the Socialist candidate and overall winner of the election, gained 71.9% of the vote in Guadeloupe, while Nicholas Sarkozy secured just 28.1%. Voter turnout was 62.2%. Subsequently, Victorin Lurel, PS leader of Tous pour la Guadeloupe and former President of the Regional Council, was named as Minister of Overseas Territories in a new French cabinet with an unprecedented representation from the French Departments in the Americas (DFA). He was joined by two female ministers, Christiane Taubira-Delannon of French Guiana, who was appointed Minister of Justice, and George Pau-Langevin, who also originated from Guadeloupe but represented a Parisian constituency. She was appointed Junior Minister for National Education.

The first round of French legislative elections was held in Guadeloupe on 9 June 2012 and was contested by 33 candidates. (Voting in both the first and second rounds of the election took place 24 hours earlier in Guadeloupe than in mainland France in order that, despite the time difference, the results could be announced simultaneously.) There was a low voter turnout of 34.5%. Victorin Lurel, running in Constituency Four, won his seat in the first round with 67.2% of the vote. The remaining three constituencies went to a second round of voting. In that round, on 16 June Eric Jalton of the PS won 66.8% of the vote in Constituency One and Gabrielle Louis-Carabin won 71.8% of the vote in Constituency Two. Ary Chalus of the Divers Gauche (Miscellaneous Left) grouping was successful in the third constituency with 51.2% of the vote. The Guadeloupean electorate's strong swing to the left reflected its disaffection with the austerity measures and other programmes of the Sarkozy Government. There were hopes for policy changes by the new Socialist Government accompanied, however, by uncertainty concerning its room for manoeuvre in the current European and global economic climate. In Guadeloupe and the other French Caribbean Departments, there is equally a recognition that, although they have gained increased visibility and influence in the new Government in

Paris, their ministers will also be obliged to uphold the policies of the Hollande administration and follow the maxim that 'France speaks with one voice', rather than explore the limits of policy autonomy for the Overseas Departments.

In 2011–12 there were moves to deepen the formal structures for co-operation between Guadeloupe and neighbouring territories. Under the French Law on Overseas Departments (2000) the Regional Council in each of the Overseas Departments of the Americas had been given the authority to negotiate and conclude agreements with neighbouring states and regional organizations on matters within its area of constitutional competence, once such negotiations had been approved by the French state. The Overseas Departments could also apply for associate membership in certain regional groupings. Under this arrangement, and with the support of the French Ministry of Foreign Affairs, in December 2011 Guadeloupe and Martinique formally applied for associate membership in the Organisation of Eastern Caribbean States (OECS). The current Chair of the OECS, Prime Minister Kenny Anthony of Saint Lucia, in January 2012 welcomed their applications and announced that the organization would be exploring ways to deepen its relationship with Guadeloupe and Martinique. Guadeloupe and Martinique were already co-operating with the OECS territories on a range of socio-cultural, economic, environmental, law and order and disaster management projects. Relations with Dominica and Saint Lucia were particularly close and there was also increasing interaction with the rest of the group, which included Antigua and Barbuda, Grenada, Montserrat, Saint Kitts and Nevis, Saint Vincent and the Grenadines, and Anguilla and the British Virgin Islands as associate members. This development suggested an increased interest in the DFA and within the French Government in making further progress with the policy of decentralization and of integrating the DFA more firmly into their regional and hemispheric setting.

In late 2012 joint technical working groups were established by the OECS, Guadeloupe and Martinique to facilitate negotiations on the modalities of the French territories' associate membership in the grouping. However, it was recognized that talks with Martinique would proceed more quickly since Guadeloupe had not yet concluded its process of institutional reform and there remained many uncertainties about the ultimate configuration of its local institutions and their powers.

In August 2012 Guadeloupe, Martinique and French Guiana acceded to the UN Economic Commission for Latin America and the Caribbean as associate members. In 2013 Guadeloupe also presented an application to the Caribbean Community and Common Market for associate membership, while on 29 April, at the Fifth Summit of the Association of Caribbean States (ACS) in Pétionville, Haiti, Guadeloupe and Martinique were accepted as associate members. (They had participated in the work of the ACS since 1996 under the aegis of France's associate membership.) Their new membership status was ratified in February 2014.

Meanwhile, although the Sarkozy administration had given the Guadeloupean authorities until 2014 to conclude an agreement on a new territorial administration, the Hollande Government pursued a different approach to institutional reform. The French Minister of State Reform, Decentralization and Public Service, Marylise Lebranchu, was asked to draft new decentralization legislation for presentation to the National Assembly. It was expected that the new law would expand the economic powers of the Regional Councils, including the direct management of European Union funding, while the General Councils might become departmental councils with reduced powers and visibility. The Decentralization Law of 2010 was abrogated in November 2012 with the tabling of the preparatory documents for the replacement law.

Joint congresses of the Regional Council and the General Council were convened in December 2012 and March 2013 to debate a new institutional framework. Despite the broad support expressed by the Socialist Federation for a single representative assembly and expanded local powers, in 2013 different positions began to be voiced by the respective councils. The President of the Regional Council, Josette Borel-Lincertin, announced in January that council members wished to modify the appeal for new competences, arguing that they seemed to be extending beyond the limits of Article 73 of the French Constitution into the realm of Article 74, for which there was no popular mandate. The members of the Regional Council also expressed concerns about a proposed referendum on institutional change. They wished to clarify exactly which questions would be put to the electorate, stipulating that they should remain within the confines of Article 73. Borel-Lincertin argued that a new institutional framework was not the leading priority for Guadeloupe, and that elected officials should instead concentrate on the urgent social and economic problems confronting the territory.

In April 2013 the Permanent Commission of the General Council, led by President Gillot, adopted proposals for safeguards concerning the forthcoming transfers of competences, which they argued were required to meet Guadeloupe's special circumstances. The proposals specified which administrative and representative powers should be exercised at the regional, departmental and communal levels of government. It was also stipulated that all changes to competences should be supported by adequate funding, and an appeal was made for joint regional-departmental management of the territorial parliament and of all public policy formulation. The proposals were sent to the French Prime Minister for consideration while the new legislation on decentralization was being prepared.

Some indications of broader public opinion on institutional reform emerged through a Qualistat survey of a sample of 503 people over the age of 18 in February 2013. Approximately 95% of those surveyed indicated that they wanted to be consulted via a referendum on institutional changes. While 60% supported the idea of a single Territorial Collectivity, they wished to strengthen local powers but also to limit the powers of their local political representatives; 51% also supported increasing the powers of the French state. A large number of those surveyed agreed that institutional evolution was not their major preoccupation, indicating instead unemployment, social insecurity, education, housing, immigration and the environment. By June 2014, however, it appeared that the timeline for consultation and consensus among the local authorities, followed by a referendum, had been abandoned and that the structure and timing of the territory's institutional reform would instead be decided in by the metropolitan Government.

On 2 June 2014 President Hollande made a preliminary statement about his administration's forthcoming territorial reform initiative, aimed at modernizing the French state. He asserted that there were too many layers of territorial bureaucracy and that these should be simplified to rationalize the use of resources and to provide better quality services. The policy would therefore encourage intercommunality (i.e., the agglomeration of the communes and an increase in the size of administrative units). Each commune would have at least 20,000 inhabitants from January 2017, compared with the existing average of 5,000 inhabitants. The number of regions in France would be reduced from 22 to 14. These larger regions would be the major administrative authorities, and they would assume a wider range of responsibilities and be endowed with greater resources. They would be obliged to support industrial development, implement employment and training policies, and maintain the transport infrastructure. The regions would be governed by smaller assemblies with a reduced number of elected officials. The General Councils would gradually be phased out, taking into consideration their substantial role in administering social protection policies. It was envisaged that there would be a constitutional revision to eliminate the General Councils in 2020. Departments would remain an essential unit of the French state. However, their functions would be confined primarily to administering justice and protection, and many of their other powers would be assumed by the Territorial Collectivities. All of these proposals would be subject to parliamentary debate, which was expected to commence in late 2014.

Municipal elections were held throughout France on 23 and 30 March 2014 to select municipal and community councillors

and mayors. Since the Chevenement Law of 1999, introduced to facilitate co-operation and various types of mergers across the communes, intercommunal entities have become widespread. Intercommunality has been promoted as a new form of territorial organization that encourages investment in large-scale infrastructure projects, rationalizes resources and may enable the state to reduce its allocations to municipalities. In the French Caribbean, two types of intercommunality may exist: the Community of Communes, which is a looser arrangement and has two major mandates, that of economic development and the management of community spaces; and the Community of Agglomeration, which has four areas of responsibility, namely economic development, the management of community spaces, the organization of urban transport, and the implementation of urban policy and some areas of social policy. Municipal councils administer communes, while community councils administer intercommunalities. In March 2014, for the first time, in communes with more than 1,000 inhabitants, community councillors were not simply appointed from participating municipal councils, but were elected from party lists, similar to the system used to elect municipal councillors. Party lists on the ballots in each locality designated candidates for both municipal and community councils.

Although right-wing parties, particularly the Front National, made major gains throughout France in the municipal elections, in Guadeloupe the reverse was the case. Of the 29 mayors elected across the territory, more than 50% represented left-wing parties and groupings. The municipal polls were followed by European parliamentary elections on 23 May 2014. In Guadeloupe, there was a record abstention rate of 90% for the latter. One deputy from the French Caribbean was elected, Louis-Joseph Manscour of Martinique, who was on the PS list. The PS, nevertheless, registered heavy losses in the March municipal elections, which were generally regarded as a sign of popular dissatisfaction with the Hollande administration. The polls were followed immediately by the resignation of Prime Minister Jean-Marc Ayrault, the appointment of Manuel Valls as his successor and the reorganization of the Council of Ministers. Lurel resigned as Minister of Overseas Territories and was replaced by George Pau-Langevin. Following Lurel's return to Guadeloupe, Borel-Lincertin announced her resignation as President of the Regional Council, stating that she had agreed to serve in that capacity only during Lurel's absence. Lurel was re-elected as President of the Regional Council on 2 May 2014.

Crime and education continued to command major attention as public policy issues. The homicide rate had remained stable at 7.9 per 100,000 since 2009, which was regarded as low in the context of the Caribbean and Latin America. However, the police and the judiciary warned that burglaries and armed robberies had increased by approximately 8% in 2013, compared with the previous year. The future configuration of tertiary education in the DFA came into question after French Guiana withdrew from the regional university, the Université des Antilles et de la Guyane, in December 2013. This prompted widespread debate about the feasibility of maintaining a regional institution or establishing separate territorial universities. Guadeloupe's university trade unions appealed for a bigger role in the consultations on the university's future, and to be involved in direct negotiations with the Ministry of National Education, Higher Education and Research, as well as guarantees about the preservation of financial allocations and academic and administrative jobs at the Fouillole and Saint-Claude campuses in Guadeloupe. The university trade unions went on strike on 20 March 2014. Although the industrial action ended on 15 April, classes did not resume until 28 April. In the mean time, the French Government decided that the Université des Antilles et de la Guyane would be renamed the Université des Antilles and would continue to operate in Guadeloupe and Martinique, while French Guiana would establish its own university.

Economy

JESSICA BYRON

In mid-2014 Guadeloupe had an estimated population of 468,017. Between the censuses of 2000 and 2011, according to provisional figures, the population increased at an average annual rate of 0.3%. In 2009 foreign residents made up 4.3% of the population, 88.6% of whom originated from the Caribbean area; 74.2% were from Haiti and 21.2% from Dominica. The structure of Guadeloupe's economy helps to explain why the separatist movement has not commanded greater support. French and European Union (EU) aid and subsidies continue to provide substantial support and one of the highest standards of living in the Caribbean. In 2012 Guadeloupe's gross domestic product (GDP) amounted to €8,033m., equivalent to €19,884 per head. GDP growth in that year was 1.3% and the inflation rate was 1.9%. An official comparative study, published in 2011, concluded that consumer prices in Guadeloupe were 8.3% higher than those in metropolitan France.

Guadeloupe experienced a sustained period of economic growth between 1993 and 2008, averaging over 3% per year, but this was always accompanied by unemployment rates in excess of one-fifth of the total workforce. The economic situation began to weaken in 2006 and deteriorated sharply with the onset of the global economic crisis in the latter half of 2008, reaching a catastrophic low in 2009–10. GDP contracted by 4.8% in 2009. Between 2007 and 2013 the unemployment rate remained stable, at 23%. Despite a gradual economic recovery, in 2012 unemployment remained an issue of major concern and was high on the public policy agenda. In that year 59,660 job seekers were recorded, a 4.6% increase over 2011. The average duration of unemployment was 52 months, and 56% of job seekers were categorized as long-term unemployed. Women represented over 60% of the unemployed, while young people between 15 and 24 years of age accounted for 58% of the total. In 2013 the number of job seekers rose to 60,393.

In terms of overall economic activity, in 2012 the primary sector (agriculture, fishing and forestry) contributed 2.8% of GDP, the secondary sector (manufacturing, construction and utilities) contributed approximately 12.5%, and the tertiary sector (services, transport, communications and government services) approximately 84.7%. Compared with a decade earlier, the respective contributions of the primary and secondary sectors had declined slightly, while that of the tertiary sector had continued to increase, with the latter sector accounting for 86.2% of salaried employment. Guadeloupe's merchandise trade deficit rose steadily during the early 21st century. In 2008 the trade deficit stood at almost €2,200m., with exports representing 6.7% of imports. Food products, and fuels and combustibles have consistently been the main imports, followed by car industry products and pharmaceutical products. In 2009 the trade deficit contracted by 21.8%, but this was a result of the disruption to economic activity caused by the social upheavals of that year rather than increased exports. By 2012, with some degree of economic recovery evident, the value of imports increased to €2,662.9m., while exports amounted to €216.1m. Metropolitan France was the Department's most important trading partner in 2012, accounting for 53.6% of exports and 53.9% of imports. The other French Overseas Departments in the Caribbean accounted for 35.2% of exports, the rest of the EU for 5.7% of exports and 10.6% of imports, North America for 9.6% of imports, and Asia for 8.6% of imports. Other Caribbean markets accounted for 2.5% of Guadeloupe's exports and 5.8% of its imports.

Greater regional integration has been viewed as one possible solution to the island's deteriorating trade position. Closer co-operation with the Organisation of Eastern Caribbean States (OECS) and with other Caribbean Forum (CARIFORUM) countries has been explored tentatively, but only limited progress has been made in trade exchanges, compared with other forms of co-operation. According to the central bank, Guadeloupe's rate of 'trade openness' is about 40%, approximately one-half that of most of its Caribbean neighbours. It remained to be seen if the 2008 EU-CARIFORUM Economic Partnership Agreement would eventually stimulate increased economic exchanges and trade liberalization between the relatively protected French Caribbean territories and their neighbours. New efforts were subsequently made towards regional integration, with Guadeloupe and Martinique applying in December 2011 for associate membership of the OECS and in 2012–13 for associate membership of the Caribbean Community and Common Market and enhanced associate membership profiles in the Association of Caribbean States. The latter was approved in April 2013, although the other two applications were progressing more slowly.

Imports of mineral fuels increased from 2.1% of total imports in 1993 to 20.0% of the total in 2008. Much of the increase was owing to Guadeloupe's strong economic growth and the higher cost of oil (fossil fuels comprised 90% of the primary energy consumed by the Department); approximately one-third of imported fuel was destined for the production of electricity. After the social conflicts of 2009, a new fuel pricing policy, regulated by the Prefecture, was instituted in 2010. This resulted in a reduction in the price of fossil fuels and a 22.5% decline in the value of oil imports between 2009 and 2010. None the less, energy prices rose by 11.8% in 2011, with the cost of petroleum products increasing by 14%. In 2011 Guadeloupe was the only region in France to select energy management as one of its regional mandates and competencies. The territory had the authority to regulate energy policy and to develop strategies and plans for greater exploitation of renewable energy. The Government's target was to achieve 50% energy independence by 2020 and ultimately to be fully self-sufficient by 2050 through the exploitation of renewable energy resources. Guadeloupe generated 1,898 GWh of electricity in 2012, of which 86% was produced from fossil fuels. Total electricity consumption was 1,792 GWh, up by 2.8% from the preceding year. Renewable energy accounted for 14.2% of total energy production in 2012: 2.7% came from wind farms; 0.7% from hydroelectricity; 2.7% from geothermal sources; 4.8% from photovoltaic production; and 3.3% from biomass generated by cane bagasse. Overall, 20.3% of energy produced came from burning bagasse mixed with coal, which fuels the power plant at Le Moule. A new geothermal facility was under construction at Bouillante, and it was expected to enter into service in 2015, generating a further 30 MW of electricity. The neighbouring island of Dominica was also developing its geothermal energy potential, and there remained the possibility in the future of deepening regional energy co-operation.

As in other states in the region, the economy is based primarily on services with a minor contribution from agriculture and some light industry, mostly the processing of food and beverages. Agriculture employed 1.5% of the workforce in 2012. Bananas and raw sugar were traditionally Guadeloupe's principal exports. In 2011 banana exports rose by 41%, to 92,227 metric tons, stimulated by improved weather conditions and price increases in Europe. In 2012, however, banana exports declined to 66,923 tons. The liberalization of EU banana imports from 2006 onwards led many growers to abandon the crop, fearful of lower prices and increased competition. Since 1998 the number of banana farmers has dropped by about 80%. In 2008 there were only 212 active producers and 1,300 people directly employed by the industry. In conjunction with Martinique, Guadeloupe received €110m. in 2004, and a further €129m. in 2006, in EU aid as compensation for the low market price of bananas. EU assistance to the industry in 2012 amounted to €30.1m. The sector also benefited from higher banana prices on the European market in that year—€581 per ton as opposed to €486 per ton in 2011.

The decline in international sugar prices of the mid-1980s made the production of sugar cane in Guadeloupe uneconomic. A five-year plan to provide subsidies and price guarantees to growers was largely unsuccessful in maintaining production levels, as equipment deteriorated and growers voluntarily reduced production. Production recovered between 1998 and 2005, reaching almost 64,000 metric tons of raw sugar in the latter year from a harvest of around 855,400 tons of sugar cane.

EU reforms in 2006 led to a decline of 33% in the reference price, the sugar industry was entitled to a share of aid worth some €90m. as compensation for price reductions and the cost of restructuring. As a result, production increased to 73,700 tons in that year, according to official figures, despite a 5.2% decline in exports. Production increased once more in 2007, to 80,800 tons, and accounted for 29.8% of export earnings. Despite improved production, sugar's contribution to GDP remained low, at around 0.4%. In 2011 sugar output totalled 51,280 tons, 20% below the average production figure for the last 10 years. In 2012 53,499 tons of sugar were produced. However, the harvesting period was negatively affected by industrial disputes, which lasted for three weeks in April and may have cost the sector an estimated €800,000, according to the SICADEG agricultural co-operative. Output losses were, however, offset by an above average sucrose content in the harvested canes.

The 2010 census indicated that cultivated land acreage in Guadeloupe had diminished by 25% since 2000 and stood at 31,401 ha. The most promising agricultural sector remained non-traditional crops. In 2007, according to FAO estimates, melon (including cantaloupe) output reached an estimated 7,500 metric tons. Nevertheless, its importance remained limited, with production (along with that of pineapples) accounting for approximately 6% of total agricultural output. Melon exports were badly affected by ash falls from Montserrat in 2010, when they declined by 42%. In 2011 poor weather conditions adversely affected agricultural production, with rainfall at the beginning of the year about 2% higher than the average recorded during the last 30 years. Although melon exports reached 1,617 tons, a slight increase of 1% over the previous year, the total volume of fruit, vegetable and flower production contracted by 4.7% from 2010. In 2012 non-banana fruit and vegetable production amounted to 52,786 tons. Melon production rose to 2,910 tons in that year, although this was still below the output levels reached before the volcanic ash falls of 2010. Melons ranked fourth in value among Guadeloupe's exports, after rum, bananas and sugar. Output of aubergines, avocados, limes and cut flowers also increased from the 1980s, although many non-traditional sectors subsequently experienced problems. Yams, sweet potatoes and plantains were the main subsistence crops.

Meat production in 2011 covered 13.8% of local consumption. The livestock sector supplied 31% of local beef consumption and 35% of pork consumption in that year. In 2010 the fishing industry generated some 32% of the value added for the agricultural sector, amounting to €73.7m., and it fulfilled an estimated 60% of domestic requirements. Guadeloupe's fishing industry is classified as artisanal, and in 2010 there were 1,597 registered fishermen and a fleet of 978 boats. The total fishing catch in recent years has been estimated at 10,000 tons annually. In 2009 emergency support was made available to stimulate the agricultural sector and to provide short-term relief for farmers in difficulties. Some €40m. in EU funding, under the Programme d'Options Spécifiques à l'Eloignement et l'Insularité, was provided in 2010 to support agricultural diversification, and a further €2m. in 2011. In addition, between 2007 and 2009 more than €9m. was allocated for modernizing the fishing industry and by the end of 2010 the funds had assisted some 144 fishing projects. In 2012 the EU made €1.1m. available in assistance for the fishing sector.

The main industrial activity concerned the processing of the island's agricultural crops, particularly the refining of sugar and the distillation of rum, one of Guadeloupe's major manufactured exports. In 2003 sugar accounted for some 60% of processed agricultural products for consumption and rum some 20%. The rum sector received additional encouragement in 2007 when the EU announced that it would offer €60m. in aid through reduced excise duty on rum produced in the French Overseas Departments. Although in 2006 rum production had declined from a peak of 79,550 hl in 1989 to just 57,447 hl, in 2007 production recovered to 74,899 hl, and this level of production was maintained in 2008, with total production rising to 75,679 hl in 2009. Export volumes of rum have grown every year since 2003. Export earnings from rum remained stable in 2008 and 2009, at €17.3m. In 2010 a total of 64,832 hl of rum were produced, of which 80% was exported, resulting in

earnings of €19.6m. Rum production in 2012 rose to 81,950 hl, and rum exports increased by 22% in value over the preceding year. However, rum output fell to 73,938 hl in 2013. In 2011–12 agro-processing remained the most dynamic area of the manufacturing sector and made modest gains. In 2011 Guadeloupe's agricultural exports rose by 33% in value and its exports of agro-processed products registered an increase in value of 13%. Preliminary reports for 2012 indicated that agricultural exports increased by 18.4% and agro-processed products rose by 7.2%.

There was only limited activity in the textile, furniture, metal, cement, plastics and printing sub-sectors. Despite government efforts to expand the island's industrial base with the establishment of an industrial zone and free port at Jarry, and by the promotion of fiscal incentives, industry and construction continued to employ relatively few people. In 2012 some 12.3% of the salaried labour force were employed in the secondary sector, with the largest proportion working in construction. None the less, building activity was slow in 2011–12, although it was gradually re-emerging after the economic recession in spite of a dearth of large-scale public sector construction projects.

In December 2012 the French Institut National de la Statistique et des Études Économiques reported that there were 11,150 artisanal businesses in Guadeloupe, amounting to 280 per 100,000 inhabitants. Guadeloupe therefore had the second highest concentration of artisanal activity in France. This was linked to a new emphasis by the regional authorities on training and certification for various types of artisanal vocations. The Université Régionale des Métiers et de l'Artisanat was established in 2012 at a cost of €25.2m. In addition, the credit and insurance facilities available to small artisanal enterprises were reinforced.

Tourism remained the major source of foreign exchange. In 1988 tourism replaced sugar production as the Department's principal source of income, and the sector continued to expand rapidly in the 1990s. In the 2000s, however, the tourism sector suffered a steady slowdown, with overall passenger arrivals at the main airport declining from 773,400 in 2001 to 623,134 in 2006. Cruise ship passenger arrivals also decreased, from 361,700 in 2001 to 195,102 in 2006. As a consequence, tourism earnings declined from 7% of local GDP in 1995 to 3.4% in 2008. The hotel and restaurant sector employed some 6% of the salaried workforce in 2009 but was severely affected by the social unrest in that year: according to the central bank (Institut d'Emission des Départements d'Outre-mer—IEDOM), there were over 10,000 holiday cancellations during the first quarter of that year and a 30% decrease in the number of long-stay guests compared with 2008. Overall, cruise ship tourist traffic declined by 3.6% in 2009, and this negative trend continued into 2010. Hotel occupancy rates for 2009 stood at 50%, but improved in 2010 to 54% in the wake of a marketing campaign by the Guadeloupean tourism authority, which had cost some €5.34m. The sector demonstrated some degree of recovery by the end of 2010. In 2012 an eight-month marketing campaign, costing €1.2m., focused on the European and North American markets. There was an increase in low-cost holiday flights into Guadeloupe, and the cruise ship sector showed very encouraging growth. The number of ships docking in 2012 rose by 55%, with passenger arrivals totalling 158,288. Yacht visitors to Guadeloupe's three marinas also continued to increase steadily. The average hotel occupancy rate in 2012 was 57%.

The economy of Guadeloupe remained heavily underpinned by inflows of money from the French state. In 2008 public services—in health, education and social investment—accounted for 32.6% of GDP in Guadeloupe. In 2010 transfers from the state to Guadeloupe decreased by 5.7%, in line with a three-year freeze on state grants to the regions. Total spending by Guadeloupe in 2010 decreased by 7.6%. Overall state expenditure in 2011 amounted to €2,400m., an increase of 4.6%, mostly accounted for by personnel cost rises, while state receipts from the Department totalled €887m. State transfers to Guadeloupean administrative collectivities (the regional, departmental and communal authorities) in 2011 amounted to €650.9m. With an unemployment rate 2.5 times higher than in metropolitan France, an estimated 10% of the population was dependent on social security benefits in 2010–11. The Contrat de Projets Etat-région programme (CEPR), a major source of local development funding, was originally budgeted €332.7m. for 2007–13, with 51% of this amount provided by the French state and the remainder provided by local government and other local partnerships. However, in 2012 CEPR funding was reduced to €327.1m., with the state's contribution being reduced by €5.6m. By December 2012 38.6% of the CEPR allocation had been committed and 23.9% disbursed, mostly to fund research and education projects. EU financing is also important: allocated assistance from EU Structural Funds during 2007–13 amounted to €876.2m. By the end of 2012 84.4% of this amount had been programmed and 32.5% (€284.6m.) had actually been disbursed.

As the economy was heavily dependent on France, local commercial activity was largely dependent on the spending power of public sector employees and tourists. More than one-half of the total salary payments made on the island went to civil servants or the French Government's contractors. Civil servants received a 40% bonus on their basic metropolitan earnings, which further increased their economic importance to the Department, in terms of purchasing power. As a result, local investment interest has long been biased towards the import-export business or the commercial services sector (such as the discount stores that handled imported goods), rather than productive investment.

As a result of the global economic turbulence since 2008 and the eurozone crisis, several EU member countries, including France, were obliged to reduce spending. It was in this context of economic restructuring that French President Nicolas Sarkozy talked about decreasing the amount of central funding for the Departments and 'freeing' them from their dependency by giving them more autonomy and therefore a greater capacity for self-development, although this process was slowed by the outbreak of civil unrest in 2009 (see History). Nevertheless, that approach was built upon by Sarkozy's successor, François Hollande, and his administration's territorial reform proposals (see History) had clear cost reduction objectives. Direct and indirect tax receipts for 2010–11 amounted to 54% of total departmental revenues. While Guadeloupe had a narrow income tax base, with 72% of households recording income levels that were below the income tax threshold, indirect taxes were used to finance the transfer of competences from the French state to local authorities and they played an increasingly important role in fiscal receipts. In 2012 IEDOM estimated that the tax burden amounted to €923 per inhabitant, which was approximately 50% higher than that of most other Departments of comparable size.

Undoubtedly, the Guadeloupean economy suffered a major setback during 2008–09, which continued to affect the territory. The social unrest that erupted in early 2009 exacerbated the territory's economic challenges and was a symptom of a deeper economic malaise. Economic activity slowed significantly throughout the remainder of 2009, in spite of the agreement reached between the striking trade unions, government officials and private sector interests to reduce prices for petroleum products and basic foodstuffs, and to lower utility rates and bank charges. Other measures were put in place by the authorities to try to stimulate economic growth. These included the Law for the Development of Overseas Departments (Law no. 2009-594), adopted in May 2009, which authorized some new taxes and the creation of 'free zones' offering tax relief for certain types of businesses in order to strengthen their profitability and export potential. The activities of such enterprises had to fall into the categories of research and development, information technology, tourism, agri-business, environmental conservation or renewable energy. Businesses benefiting from such tax relief were required to invest in training programmes for their workers and in youth employment schemes. Such tax breaks were to be valid from 2009–15, declining thereafter until 2019. In general, local authorities' expenditure on education and training projects, competitiveness-building initiatives, and social interventions increased in 2009 and 2010. By 2010–11 there were cautious reports of a slightly improved business climate and a slow economic recovery. However, the revival subsequently faltered, and IEDOM in 2013 continued to describe the economy's progress as 'changeable and fragile', even though it gave positive assessments of the performance of the tourism sector and the banana industry.

Statistical Survey

Sources (unless otherwise indicated): Institut National de la Statistique et des Etudes Economiques (INSEE), Service Régional de la Guadeloupe, ave Paul Lacavé, BP 96, 97102 Basse-Terre; tel. 5-90-99-02-50; internet www.insee.fr/fr/regions/guadeloupe; Service de Presse et d'Information, Ministère des Départements et Territoires d'Outre-mer, 27 rue Oudinot, 75700 Paris 07 SP, France; tel. 1-53-69-20-00; fax 1-43-06-60-30; internet www.outre-mer.gouv.fr.

AREA AND POPULATION

(Note: In July 2007 Saint-Barthélemy and Saint-Martin seceded from Guadeloupe to become Overseas Collectivities.)

Area: 1,630 sq km (629.3 sq miles), comprising continental Guadeloupe 1,438 sq km (Basse-Terre à l'Ouest 848 sq km, Grande-Terre à l'Est 590 sq km) and dependencies 194 sq km (La Désirade 22 sq km, Iles des Saintes 14 sq km, Marie-Galante 158 sq km).

Population: 422,496 at census of 8 March 1999; 404,635 at census of 1 January 2011. Note: According to new census methodology, data in 2011 refer to median figures based on the collection of raw data over a five-year period (2009–13). *Mid-2014* (UN estimate): 468,017 (Source: UN, *World Population Prospects: The 2012 Revision*).

Density (at mid-2014): 287.1 per sq km.

Population by Age and Sex (UN estimates at mid-2014): *0–14:* 99,172 (males 50,572, females 48,600); *15–64:* 304,533 (males 142,436, females 162,097); *65 and over:* 64,312 (males 27,347, females 36,965); *Total* 468,017 (males 220,355, females 247,662). Source: UN, *World Population Prospects: The 2012 Revision*.

Principal Towns (population at 2010 census): Les Abymes 68,534; Baie-Mahault 30,251; Le Gosier 26,311; Sainte-Anne 24,192; Petit Bourg 23,199; Le Moule 22,381; Sainte-Rose 20,155; Capesterre-Belle-Eau 19,321; Pointe-à-Pitre 16,427; Basse-Terre (capital) 11,915.

Births, Marriages and Deaths (2012 unless otherwise indicated): Registered live births 5,233 (birth rate 12,9 per 1,000); Registered marriages 1,259 (marriage rate 3.1 per 1,000) (2011); Registered deaths 2,873 (death rate 7.1 per 1,000).

Life Expectancy (years at birth): 80.9 (males 77.5, females 84.1) in 2013. Source: Pan American Health Organization.

Employment (persons aged 15 years and over, provisional estimates at 31 December 2012): Agriculture, forestry and fishing 1,740; Mining and water supply 2,041; Manufacturing 6,156; Construction 6,295; Wholesale and retail trade; repair of motor vehicles, motorcycles, etc. 14,852; Transport, storage and communication 7,617; Hotels and restaurants 4,698; Financial intermediation 3,274; Real estate, renting and business activities 11,509; Public administration, health and social work 51,593; Other community, social and personal service activities 7,605; *Total employed* 117,380. Note: Data exclude 6,189 persons employed without salary.

HEALTH AND WELFARE

Key Indicators

Total Fertility Rate (children per woman, 2013): 2.1.

Under-5 Mortality Rate (per 1,000 live births, 2011): 7.6.

Physicians (per 1,000 head, c. 2010): 2.6.

Hospital Beds (per 1,000 head, 2011): 5.3.

Access to Water (% of persons, 2012): 99.

Access to Sanitation (% of persons, 2012): 97.

Source: mainly Pan American Health Organization.

For other sources and definitions, see explanatory note on p. vi.

AGRICULTURE, ETC.

Principal Crops ('000 metric tons, 2012, FAO estimates): Sweet potatoes 1.7; Sugar cane 1,000.0; Cabbages and other brassicas 2.5; Lettuce and chicory 3.9; Tomatoes 4.7; Cucumbers and gherkins 5.6; Bananas 60.0; Plantains 8.0. *Aggregate Production* ('000 metric tons, may include official, semi-official or estimated data): Total roots and tubers 15.2; Total vegetables (incl. melons) 50.5; Total fruits (excl. melons) 85.2.

Livestock ('000 head, year ending September 2012, FAO estimates): Cattle 75.0; Chickens 300.

Livestock Products ('000 metric tons, 2012, FAO estimates): Cattle meat 3.0; Pig meat 1.5; Chicken meat 1.4; Hen eggs 2.0.

Forestry ('000 cu m, 2012, FAO estimates): *Roundwood Removals* (excl. bark): Sawlogs, veneer logs and logs for sleepers 0.3; Fuel wood 15.0; Total 15.3. *Sawnwood Production* (incl. railway sleepers): Total 1.0.

Fishing (metric tons, live weight, 2012, FAO estimates): Capture 11,100 (Common dolphinfish 780; Other mackerel-like fishes 1,750; Marine fishes 8,180; Stromboid conchs 225); Aquaculture 12; *Total catch* 11,112.

Source: FAO.

MINING

Production ('000 metric tons, 2010, estimates): Cement 230; Pumice 210; Salt 49. Source: US Geological Survey.

INDUSTRY

Production (2013): Sugar 39,275 metric tons; Rum 73,938 hl; Electric energy 1,728 million kWh. Source: Institut d'Emission des Départements d'Outre-mer, *Guadeloupe: Rapport Annuel 2013*.

FINANCE

Currency and Exchange Rates: The French franc was used until the end of February 2002. Euro notes and coins were introduced on 1 January 2002, and the euro became the sole legal tender from 18 February. Some of the figures in this Survey are still in terms of francs. For details of exchange rates, see French Guiana.

Budget: *French Government* (€ million, 2005): Revenue 1,132; Expenditure 1,040. *Regional Budget* (€ million, 2012): Current revenue 266.1 (Taxes 171.6, Other current revenue 94.5); Capital revenues 149.8; Total 415.9. Current expenditure 237.6; Capital expenditure 180.6; Total 418.2 (Source: Institut d'Emission des Départements d'Outre-mer, *Guadeloupe: Rapport Annuel 2013*). *Departmental Budget* (excl. debt rescheduling, € million, 2013, preliminary): Revenue 676.9 (Current revenue 604.6, Capital revenue 72.4); Expenditure 676.9 (Current expenditure 583.9, Capital expenditure 93.0) (Source: Département des Etudes et des Statistiques Locales).

Money Supply (million French francs at 31 December 1996): Currency outside banks 1,148; Demand deposits at banks 6,187; Total money 7,335.

Cost of Living (Consumer Price Index; base: 2000 = 100): All items 125.1 in 2011; 127.5 in 2012; 128.6 in 2013. Source: ILO.

Expenditure on the Gross Domestic Product (€ million at current prices, 2012, estimates): Total final consumption expenditure 8,467 (General government and non-profit institutions serving households 3,572, Households 4,895); Gross fixed capital formation 1,419; *Total domestic expenditure* 9,886; Exports of goods and services 808; *Less* Imports of goods and services 2,686; Statistical discrepancy 25; *GDP in purchasers' values* 8,033. Source: Institut d'Emission des Départements d'Outre-mer, *Guadeloupe: Rapport Annuel 2013*.

Gross Domestic Product by Economic Activity (€ million at current prices, 2006): Agriculture, hunting, forestry and fishing 197; Food industries 87; Other manufacturing 265; Energy 37; Construction 713; Services 6,094 (Restaurants and hotels 253, Transport 249, Commerce 948, Other market services 2,269, Non-market services 2,375); *Sub-total* 7,393; Financial intermediation services indirectly measured (FISIM) –325; Import duties, less subsidies 690; *GDP in purchasers' values* 7,758.

EXTERNAL TRADE

Principal Commodities (€ million, 2013, provisional): *Imports c.i.f.:* Products of agriculture, fishing and food industries 463.6; Textiles, clothing, leather and footwear 123.4; Chemicals 126.7; Pharma-

ceutical products 154.4; Mineral products, rubber and plastic 141.5; Metal and metal products 164.0; Mechanical and electrical equipment 513.8; Transport equipment 237.3; Petroleum products 551.6; Miscellaneous manufactured goods 124.7; Total (incl. others) 2,747.4. *Exports f.o.b.:* Products of agriculture, fishing and food industries 99.7; Petroleum products 48.2; Chemicals 9.4; Mechanical and electrical equipment 25.8; Transport equipment 29.8; Metals and metallic products 9.4; Total (incl. others) 264.5. (Source: Institut d'Emission des Départements d'Outre-mer, *Guadeloupe: Rapport Annuel 2013*).

Principal Trading Partners (€ million, 2008): *Imports c.i.f.:* Aruba 98; China, People's Repub. 87; France (metropolitan) 1,355; Germany 110; Italy 65; Martinique 210; Spain 40; USA 146; Total (incl. others) 2,601. *Exports f.o.b.:* France (metropolitan) 79; French Guiana 40; Germany 3; Martinique 44; Poland 5; Portugal 4; USA 4; Total (incl. others) 205. *2010* (€ million): Total imports 2,232.6; Total exports 178.4. *2011* (€ million): Total imports 2,642.4; Total exports 234.8 (Source: Institut d'Emission des Départements d'Outre-mer, *Guadeloupe: Rapport Annuel 2011*). *2012* (€ million, provisional): Total imports 2,662.9; Total exports 216.1 (Source: Institut d'Emission des Départements d'Outre-mer, *Guadeloupe: Rapport Annuel 2012*). *2013* (€ million, provisional): Total imports 2,747.4; Total exports 264.5 (Source: Institut d'Emission des Départements d'Outre-mer, *Guadeloupe: Rapport Annuel 2013*).

TRANSPORT

Road Traffic ('000 motor vehicles in use, 2002): Passenger cars 117.7; Commercial vehicles 31.4 (Source: UN, *Statistical Yearbook*). *1 January 2010* ('000 commercial motor vehicles in use): Buses 0.8; Vans and trucks 39.6.

Shipping: *Flag Registered Fleet* (at 31 December 2013): Vessels 13; Total displacement 4,224 grt (Source: Lloyd's List Intelligence—www.lloydslistintelligence.com). *International Seaborne Traffic* (2010 unless otherwise indicated): Freight vessels entered 1,257 (1995); Freight vessels departed 1,253 (1995); Gross freight handled 3,156,160 metric tons; Containers handled 150,534 TEUs; Passengers carried 924,446 (2004).

Civil Aviation (2013): Aircraft movements 26,786; Freight carried (incl. post) 13,998 metric tons; Passengers carried 2,033,763. Source: Institut d'Emission des Départements d'Outre-mer, *Guadeloupe: Rapport Annuel 2013*.

TOURISM

Tourist Arrivals by Country (2009): Belgium 4,631; France 329,011; Germany 1,403; Italy 2,105; Martinique 936; Switzerland 1,778; United Kingdom 561; USA 281; Total (incl. others) 346,507. *2010:* Total 392,282 (France 370,482). *2011:* Total 418,000.

Receipts from Tourism (US $ million, excl. passenger transport): 510 in 2010; 583 in 2011.

Source: partly World Tourism Organization.

COMMUNICATIONS MEDIA

Telephones ('000 main lines in use): 255.7 in 2010.

Mobile Cellular Telephones ('000 subscribers): 314.7 in 2004.

Internet Users ('000): 109.0 in 2009.

Source: International Telecommunication Union.

EDUCATION

Pre-primary (2012/13): 134 institutions; 19,614 students (17,554 state, 2,060 private).

Primary (2012/13): 206 institutions; 35,584 students (31,648 state, 3,936 private).

Specialized Pre-primary and Primary (2012/13): 540 students (521 state, 19 private).

Secondary (2012/13): 94 institutions; 50,019 students (44,705 state, 5,314 private).

Higher (2012/13): 9,125 students.

Teachers (2007/08 unless otherwise indicated): *Primary:* 3,382 (3,139 state, 243 private); *Secondary:* 4,675 (4,223 state, 452 private); *Higher* (2004/05): 203 (Source: Ministère de l'Education Nationale, *Repères et références statistiques.*) *2012/13* (state schools): 2,931 in primary; 4,078 in secondary; 458 in higher.

Adult Literacy Rate: 90.1 (males 89.7; females 90.5) in 1998. Source: Pan American Health Organization.

Directory

The Government

(September 2014)

HEAD OF STATE

President: FRANÇOIS HOLLANDE.

Prefect: MARCELLE PIERROT, Préfecture, Palais d'Orléans, rue Lardenoy, 97109 Basse-Terre Cédex; tel. 5-90-99-39-00; fax 5-90-81-58-32; e-mail webmestre@guadeloupe.pref.gouv.fr; internet www.guadeloupe.pref.gouv.fr.

DEPARTMENTAL ADMINISTRATION

President of the General Council: Dr JACQUES GILLOT (Divers Gauche), Hôtel du Département, blvd Félix Eboué, 97109 Basse-Terre; tel. 5-90-99-77-77; fax 5-90-99-76-00; e-mail info@cg971.fr; internet www.cg971.fr.

President of the Regional Council: VICTORIN LUREL (PS), 1 rue Paul Lacavé, Petit-Paris, 97109 Basse-Terre; tel. 5-90-80-40-40; fax 5-90-81-34-19; internet www.cr-guadeloupe.fr.

Elections, 14 and 21 March 2010

	Seats
Tous pour la Guadeloupe*	31
Ensemble pour la Guadeloupe†	4
Région Autrement‡	4
Pou Gwadloup an nou ay	2
Total	41

* Comprising the Parti Socialiste (PS) and other left-wing candidates.

† Comprising the Union pour un Mouvement Populaire (UMP) and other right-wing candidates.

‡ Comprising smaller left-wing parties and dissident socialists.

REPRESENTATIVES TO THE FRENCH PARLIAMENT

Deputies to the French National Assembly: ERIC JALTON (Socialiste, Républicain et Citoyen), GABRIELLE LOUIS-CARABIN (Socialiste, Républicain et Citoyen), ARY CHALUS (Radical, Républicain, Démocrate et Progressiste), VICTORIN LUREL (Socialiste, Républicain et Citoyen).

Representatives to the French Senate: JACQUES CORNANO (Groupe Socialiste), FÉLIX DESPLAN (Groupe Socialiste), JACQUES GILLOT (Groupe Socialiste).

GOVERNMENT OFFICES

Directorate of the Culture, Education and Environment Committee: 16 rue Peynier, 97100 Basse-Terre; tel. 5-90-41-05-15; fax 5-90-41-05-23; e-mail cr-cesr-guadeloupe@wanadoo.fr; internet www.cr-guadeloupe.fr; Dir CAMILLUS RABIN.

Directorate of European Affairs and Co-operation: 16 rue Peynier, 97100 Basse-Terre; tel. 5-90-41-05-15; fax 5-90-41-05-23; e-mail cr-cesr-guadeloupe@wanadoo.fr; internet www.cr-guadeloupe.fr; Dir FRANCE-LISE FELIX-ISSORAT.

Directorate of the Regional Economic and Social Committee: 16 rue Peynier, 97100 Basse-Terre; tel. 5-90-41-05-15; fax 5-90-41-05-23; e-mail cr-cesr-guadeloupe@wanadoo.fr; internet www.cr-guadeloupe.fr; Dir GÉRARD LUREL.

General Directorate of Services: 16 rue Peynier, 97100 Basse-Terre; tel. 5-90-41-05-15; fax 5-90-41-05-23; e-mail cr-cesr-guadeloupe@wanadoo.fr; internet www.cr-guadeloupe.fr; Dir-Gen. DOMINIQUE LABAN.

Political Organizations

Combat Ouvrier: BP 213, 97156 Pointe-à-Pitre Cédex; tel. 5-90-26-23-58; e-mail menendez@wanadoo.fr; internet www.combat-ouvrier.net; Trotskyist; associated with national party Lutte Ouvrière; mem. of the Internationalist Communist Union; Leader JEAN-MARIE NOMERTIN.

Guadeloupe Unie, Socialisme et Réalité (GUSR): Pointe-à-Pitre; e-mail gusr@ais.gp; internet perso.mediaserv.net/gusr; 'dissident' faction of the Parti Socialiste; Pres. GUY LOSBAR.

Konvwa pou Liberasyon Nasyon Gwadloup (KLNG): Pointe-à-Pitre; f. 1997; pro-independence; Leader LUC REINETTE.

Parti Communiste Guadeloupéen (PCG): 119 rue Vatable, 97110 Pointe-à-Pitre; tel. 5-90-88-23-07; f. 1944; Sec.-Gen. FÉLIX FLÉMIN.

Parti Socialiste (PS): 8 Résidence Légitimus, blvd Légitimus, 97110 Pointe-à-Pitre; tel. and fax 5-90-21-65-72; fax 5-90-83-20-51; e-mail fede971@parti-socialiste.fr; internet www.parti-socialiste.fr; Regional Sec. MAX MATHIASIN.

Pou Gwadloup an nou ay: Pointe-à-Pitre; youth party; Leader CÉDRIC CORNET.

Union pour un Mouvement Populaire (UMP): Les Portes de Saint Martin Bellevue, 97150 Saint Martin; tel. and fax 5-90-87-50-01; fax 5-90-87-75-72; e-mail ump-sxm@laposte.net; internet www.u-m-p.org; f. 2002; centre-right; local br. of the metropolitan party; Pres., Departmental Cttee LAURENT BERNIER.

Les Verts Guadeloupe: 5 rue François Arago, 97110 Pointe-à-Pitre; tel. 5-90-35-41-90; fax 5-90-25-02-62; internet guadeloupe.lesverts.fr; ecologist; departmental br. of the metropolitan party; Regional spokespersons HARRY DURIMEL, JOCELYNE HATCHI.

Other political organizations included Mouvement pour la Démocratie et le Développement (MDDP), Union Populaire pour la Libération de la Guadeloupe (UPLG), Mouvman Gwadloupéyen (MG), Parti Progressiste Démocratique Guadeloupéen (PPDG), Renouveau Socialiste; and the coalitions Priorité à l'Education et à l'Environnement and Union pour une Guadeloupe Responsable.

Judicial System

Court of Appeal: Palais de Justice, 4 blvd Félix Eboué, 97100 Basse-Terre; tel. 5-90-80-63-36; fax 5-90-80-63-19; e-mail ca-basse-terre@justice.fr; First Pres. HENRY ROBERT; Procurator-Gen. CATHERINE CHAMPRENAULT.

There are two Tribunaux de Grande Instance and four Tribunaux d'Instance.

Religion

The majority of the population belong to the Roman Catholic Church.

CHRISTIANITY

The Roman Catholic Church

Guadeloupe comprises the single diocese of Basse-Terre, suffragan to the archdiocese of Fort-de-France, Martinique. Some 76% of the population are Roman Catholics. The Bishop participates in the Antilles Episcopal Conference, based in Port of Spain, Trinidad and Tobago.

Bishop of Basse-Terre: Mgr JEAN-YVES RIOCREUX, Evêché, pl. Saint-Françoise, BP 369, 97100 Basse-Terre Cédex; tel. 5-90-81-36-69; fax 5-90-81-98-23; e-mail eveche@catholique-guadeloupe.info; internet www.catholique-guadeloupe.info.

OTHER CHURCHES

Seventh-day Adventist Church: Eglise Adventiste de la Guadeloupe, BP 5, 97181 Les Abymes Cédex; tel. 5-90-82-79-76; fax 5-90-83-44-24; e-mail adventiste.federation@wanadoo.fr; internet www.adventiste-gp.org; f. 1931; Pres. ALAIN ANGERVILLE; Sec. JACQUES BIBRAC; 12,007 mems (2011).

Other denominations active in Guadeloupe include the Baptist Church and Jehovah's Witnesses.

The Press

Destination Guadeloupe: Pointe-à-Pitre; tel. 4-66-77-62-37; e-mail virginie@destination-guadeloupe.com; internet www.destination-guadeloupe.com; tourism; quarterly; Dir VIRGINIE LARNAC.

France Antilles: ZAC Moudong Sud, 97122 Baie-Mahault; tel. 5-90-90-25-25; fax 5-90-91-78-31; e-mail f.breland@media-antilles.fr; internet www.guadeloupe.franceantilles.fr; f. 1964; subsidiary of Groupe France Antilles; daily; Dir ALEXANDRE THEVENET; circ. 50,000.

Match: 35 rue Peynier, 97110 Pointe-à-Pitre; tel. 5-90-82-18-68; fax 5-90-82-01-87; f. 1943; fortnightly; Dir (vacant); circ. 6,000.

Nouvelles Etincelles: 119 rue Vatable, 97110 Pointe-à-Pitre; tel. 5-90-91-00-85; fax 5-90-91-06-53; e-mail nouvelles-etincelles@wanadoo.fr; internet nouvellesetincelles.com; f. 1944 as *l'Etincelle*, organ of the Parti Communiste Guadeloupéen (q.v.); present name adopted 2005; weekly; Dir CHRISTIAN CÉLESTE; circ. 5,000.

Publishers

Editions Exbrayat: 12 Allée des Marguerites, Les Jardins d'Arnouville, 97170 Petit-Bourg; tel. 5-90-26-32-33; fax 5-90-26-32-66; e-mail andre.exbrayat@exbrayat.com; internet commerce.ciel.com/exbrayat; Dir PAQUITA EXBRAYAT-SANCHEZ.

Editions Jasor: 46 rue Schoëlcher, 97110 Pointe-à-Pitre; tel. 5-90-91-18-48; fax 5-90-21-07-01; e-mail editionsjasor@wanadoo.fr; f. 1989; French-Creole culture, biography and language, and youth fiction; Dir RÉGINE JASOR.

PLB Editions: route de Mathurin, 97190 Gosier; tel. 5-90-89-91-17; fax 5-90-89-91-05; e-mail plbeditions@wanadoo.fr; internet www.plbeditions.com; f. 1997; regional natural history and French-Creole youth fiction; Dirs CHANTAL MATTET, THIERRY PETIT LE BRUN.

Broadcasting and Communications

TELECOMMUNICATIONS

CaribSat: 1406 rue Henri Becquerel, BP 2287, 97122 Baie-Mahault; internet www.caribsat.fr; internet service provider, providing satellite broadband services from late 2013; Man. MARYSE COPPET.

Digicel Antilles Françaises et Guyane: see Martinique—Telecommunications; Dir-Gen. (Guadeloupe) VINCENT VIENNET.

Orange Caraïbe: BP 2203, 97196 Jarry Cédex; tel. 5-90-38-45-55; fax 8-10-50-05-59; e-mail webmaster@orange.gp; internet www.orangecaraibe.com; f. 1996; subsidiary of Orange France; fixed lines, mobile telecommunications and internet services provider; network coverage incl. Martinique and French Guiana; Dir-Gen. JEAN-PHILIPPE GAY.

Outremer Telecom: SCI, Brand, voie Verte, Z. I. de Jarry, 97122 Baie-Mahault; e-mail communication@outremer-telecom.fr; internet www.outremer-telecom.fr; f. 1998; mobile telecommunications provider; Group CEO JEAN-MICHEL HEGESIPPE.

ONLY: SCI, Brand, voie Verte, Z. I. de Jarry, 97122 Baie-Mahault; e-mail communication@outremer-telecom.fr; internet www.outremer-telecom.fr; f. 1998 as Outremer Telecom Guadeloupe; present name adopted following merger of Volubis, ONLY and OOL in 2006; subsidiary of Outremer Telecom, France; fixed and mobile telecommunications provider.

BROADCASTING

Guadeloupe 1ère (Outre-mer Première): Morne Bernard Destrellan, BP 180, 97122 Baie-Mahault Cédex; tel. 5-90-60-96-96; fax 5-90-60-96-82; e-mail rfo@rfo.fr; internet guadeloupe.la1ere.fr; f. 1964; acquired by Groupe France Télévisions in 2004; fmrly Société Nationale de Radio-Télévision Française d'Outre-mer; name changed as Réseau France Outre-mer (RFO) in 1998; present name adopted in 2010; radio and TV; Dir-Gen. GENEVIÈVE GIARD; Regional Dir ROGER CESSY.

Radio

Kilti FM: Immeuble 573 rue de la Chapelle, Z. I. de Jarry 97122 Baie-Mahault; tel. 5-90-32-52-61; fax 5-90-25-66-03; e-mail kiltifm@wanadoo.fr; f. 2006; French and Creole; Man. ORTEZ SONGO.

NRJ Guadeloupe: 2 blvd de la Marne, 97200 Fort-de-France; tel. 5-96-63-63-63; fax 5-96-73-73-15; e-mail webmaster@nrjantilles.com; internet www.nrjantilles.com; Dir FRANCK FÉRANDIER-SICARD; Dir JEAN-CHRISTOPHE MARTINEZ.

Ouest FM: Immeuble Vivies, rue Thomas Edyson, Z. I. Jarry, 97122 Baie-Mahault; tel. 5-94-38-29-19; fax 5-90-26-02-97; e-mail contact@ouestfm.com; internet www.ouestfm.net; f. 2008; commercial radio station; French.

Radio Caraïbes International (RCI Guadeloupe): Carrefour Grand Camp, BP 40, 97151 Pointe-à-Pitre Cédex; tel. 5-90-83-96-96; fax 5-90-83-96-97; internet gp.rci.fm; f. 1962; Man. THIERRY FUNDÉRÉ.

Radio Contact: 40 bis, rue Lamartine, 97110 Pointe-à-Pitre; tel. 5-90-82-25-41; fax 5-96-91-56-77; internet www.radio-contact.net; operated by l'Asscn Citoyenne de Sauvegarde et de Défense des Intérêts des Guadeloupéens; Pres. OCTAVIE LOSIO; Man. HENRI YOYOTTE.

Radio Inter S'Cool (RIS): Lycée Ducharmoy, 97120 Saint-Claude; tel. and fax 5-90-80-38-40; e-mail contact@gupilvision.com; internet www.radiointerscool.net; educational and school-focused programmes; French and Creole; Pres. JAQUES REMUS.

Radio Tanbou: 153 résidence Espace, 97110 Pointe-à-Pitre; tel. 5-90-21-66-45; fax 5-90-21-66-48; e-mail kontak@radyotanbou.com; internet www.radyotanbou.com; French and Creole; operated by the l'Asscn pour le Développement de l'Information et de la Culture Guadeloupéenne.

RHT Guadeloupe (Radio Haute Tension): route de Petit Marquisat, Routhiers, 97130 Capesterre Belle Eau; tel. 5-90-99-08-12; e-mail ruddycornelie@radiohautetension.fr; internet www.radiohautetension.fr; f. 1986; Dir RUDDY CORNELIE.

Zouk Radio: Immeuble Général Bricolage, Petit Pérou, 97139 Les Abymes; tel. 5-90-89-25-80; fax 5-90-89-26-22; internet www.zoukradio.fr; commercial music station; French and Creole.

Television

Antilles Télévision (ATV): see Martinique—Television.

Archipel 4: Immeuble Debs-Montauban, 97190 Gosier; tel. 5-93-21-05-20; f. 2002; Chair. JEAN-CLAUDE THOMASEAU.

Canal Plus Antilles: Immeuble Canal Media, Moudong Centre Jarry, 97122 Baie-Mahault; tel. 5-90-38-09-00; fax 5-90-38-09-04; e-mail mrichol@canalantilles.gp; internet www.canalantilles.com; f. 1993; subsidiary of Groupe Canal Plus, France; satellite TV station; Pres. JEAN-NOËL TRONC.

Canal 10: Immeuble CCL, blvd de Houelbourg, ZI de Jarry, BP 2271, 97122 Baie-Mahault; tel. 5-90-26-73-03; fax 5-90-26-61-25; e-mail contact@canal10-tv.com; internet www.canal10-tv.com; f. 1990; focus on social, economic and cultural issues in Guadeloupe; produces 100% of its programmes; Dir MICHEL RODRIGUEZ.

Eclair TV (ETV): Basse-Terre Télévision, Pintade, 97100 Basse-Terre; tel. 5-90-60-15-30; fax 5-90-60-15-33; e-mail eclairfm.com@orange.fr; f. 1998; community station local to Basse-Terre; Pres. (vacant).

La Une Guadeloupe (L'A1): 20 rue Henri Becquerel, Z. I. de Jarry, 97122 Baie-Mahault; tel. 5-90-38-06-06; fax 5-90-38-06-07; f. 1998; fmrly TCI; gen. interest; purchases 65% of programmes from TF1, France (2003); Pres. JOSÉ GADDARKHAN.

Finance

(cap. = capital; res = reserves; dep. = deposits; m. = million; brs = branches; amounts in euros unless otherwise indicated)

BANKING

Central Bank

Institut d'Emission des Départements d'Outre-mer (IEDOM): Parc d'activité la Providence, ZAC de Dothémare, BP 196, 97139 Les Abymes; tel. 5-90-93-74-00; fax 5-90-93-74-25; e-mail iedom-pap-etudes@iedom-guadeloupe.fr; internet www.iedom.fr; f. 1959; Dir CHARLES APANON.

Commercial Banks

Banque des Antilles Françaises: Parc d'Activités de la Jaille, BP 46, Bâtiments 5 et 6, 97122 Baie-Mahault; tel. 5-90-60-42-00; fax 5-90-60-99-33; internet www.bdaf.fr; f. 1967 by merger of Banque de la Martinique and Banque de la Guadeloupe; subsidiary of Financière Océor, France; cap. 83.7m., res 7.7m., dep. 1,244.4m. (Dec. 2010); Pres. and Chair. PHILIPPE GARSUAULT; Gen. Man. DIDIER LOING; 19 brs.

Banque Française Commerciale Antilles-Guyane (BFC Antilles-Guyane): Immeuble BFC, Grand Camp-La Rocade, 97139 Pointe-à-Pitre; tel. 5-90-21-56-52; fax 5-90-21-56-62; e-mail f.aujoulat@bfc-ag.com; internet www.bfc-ag.com; f. 1976 as br. of Banque Française Commerciale, SA, separated 1984; cap. 51.1m., res 6.1m., dep. 661.6m. (Dec. 2012); Chair. CHRISTIAN DUVILLET; Dir-Gen. ALAIN STASSINET.

BNP Paribas Guadeloupe: pl. de la Rénovation, BP 161, 97155 Pointe-à-Pitre; tel. 5-90-90-58-58; fax 5-90-90-04-07; e-mail dg@bnp.gp; internet guadeloupe.bnpparibas.net; f. 1941; subsidiary of BNP Paribas, France; Gen. Man. DANIEL DELANIS; Gen. Sec. FRANCOIS PASETTI; 12 brs.

BRED Banque Populaire (BRED-BP): Immeuble Simcar, blvd Marquisat de Houelbourg, Z. I. Jarry, 97122 Baie-Mahault; tel. 5-90-82-65-46; internet www.bred.banquepopulaire.fr; cap. 242m. (Oct. 2005); Group Chair. STÈVE GENTILI.

Crédit Agricole de la Guadeloupe: Petit Pérou, 97176 Abymes Cédex; tel. 5-90-90-65-65; fax 5-90-90-65-89; e-mail catelnet@ca-guadeloupe.fr; internet www.ca-guadeloupe.fr; total assets 1,228.1m. (Dec. 2003); f. 1984; Pres. CHRISTIAN FLÉREAU; Gen. Man. ROGER WUNSCHEL; 30 brs.

Crédit Maritime de la Guadeloupe: 36 rue Achille René-Boisneuf, BP 292, 97175 Pointe-à-Pitre; tel. 5-90-21-08-40; fax 5-90-83-46-37; e-mail pointe-a-pitre-agence-cmm@creditmaritime.com; internet www.creditmaritime-outremer.com; Dir GÉRARD CADIC; 4 agencies.

Société Générale de Banque aux Antilles (SGBA): 30 rue Frébault, BP 55, 97152 Pointe-à-Pitre; tel. 5-90-25-49-77; fax 5-90-25-49-78; e-mail sgba@wanadoo.fr; internet www.sgba.fr; f. 1979;

cap. 32.6m., res −15.3m., dep. 360.5m. (Dec. 2009); Chair. ALEXANDRE MAYMAT; Man. Dir PHILIPPE RICHARD; 5 brs in Guadeloupe, 3 brs in Martinique.

Development Bank

Société de Crédit pour le Développement de Guadeloupe (SODEGA): Carrefour Raizet Baimbridge, BP 54, 97152 Pointe-à-Pitre; tel. 5-90-82-65-00; fax 5-90-90-17-91; e-mail credit@sodega.fr; internet www.sodega.fr; f. 1970; bought from the Agence Française de Développement (q.v.) by BRED Banque Populaire (q.v.) in 2003.

INSURANCE

Allianz Vie France: Le Patio de Grand Camp, BP 212, 97156 Pointe-à-Pitre Cédex; tel. 5-90-21-38-88; fax 5-90-82-78-25; e-mail agf.guavie@wanadoo.fr; internet www.allianz.fr; life insurance.

GAN Guadeloupe: 59–61 rue Achille René Boisneuf, BP 152, 97171 Pointe-à-Pitre Cédex; tel. 5-90-89-32-00; fax 5-90-04-43; internet www.groupama.es; subsidiary of Groupama, France; Dir-Gen. ALEXANDRE PASCAL; Man. GILLES CANO.

Mutuelle d'Assurance de Guadeloupe (MAG): Immeuble Capma & Capmi, blvd Légitimus, (face à Air France), 97110 Pointe-à-Pitre Cédex; tel. 5-90-82-22-71; fax 5-90-91-19-40; internet www.monceauassurances.com; fmrly Capma & Capmi; Chair. and Dir Gen. GILLES DUPIN.

Optimum Assurances: 3 bis rue Henri Bequerel, Jarry, 97122 Baie-Mahault; tel. 5-90-26-96-47; fax 5-90-26-81-27; internet www.assurances-guadeloupe.info; Dir-Gen. URBALD REINE.

WAB Assurances: Immeuble Stratégie, Moudong Sud, 97122 Baie-Mahault Cédex; tel. 5-90-32-66-66; fax 5-90-32-66-74; e-mail philippe.bech@wab-assu.com; internet www.wabassu.fr; f. 2005; Dir-Gen. PHILIPPE BECH.

Trade and Industry

GOVERNMENT AGENCIES

Direction de l'Alimentation, de l'Agriculture et de la Forêt (DAAF): Jardin Botanique, 97100 Basse-Terre; tel. 5-90-99-09-09; fax 5-90-99-09-10; e-mail daaf971@agriculture.gouv.fr; internet daaf971@agriculture.gouv.fr; Dir VINCENT FAUCHER.

Direction Régionale des Affaires Maritimes (DRAM): 20 rue Henri Becquerel, BP 2466, 97085 Jarry; tel. 5-90-41-95-50; fax 5-90-90-07-33; e-mail Dram-Guadeloupe@developpement-durable.gouv.fr; responsible for shipping, fishing and other maritime issues at national and community level; Dir FRÉDÉRIC BLUA.

Direction Régionale du Commerce Extérieur Antilles-Guyane (DRCE): see Martinique—Trade and Industry.

Direction Régionale de l'Industrie, de la Recherche et de l'Environnement (DRIRE): 552 rue de la Chapelle, Z. I. Jarry, 97122 Baie-Mahault; tel. 5-90-38-03-47; fax 5-90-38-03-50; e-mail pierre.juan@industrie.gouv.fr; internet www.ggm.drire.gouv.fr; active in industry, business services, transport, public works, tourism and distribution; Departmental Co-ordinator MICHEL MASSON.

DEVELOPMENT ORGANIZATIONS

Agence de l'Environnement et de la Maîtrise de l'Energie (ADEME): Immeuble Café Center, rue Ferdinand Forest, Z. I. Jarry, 97122 Baie-Mahault; tel. 5-90-26-78-05; fax 5-90-26-87-15; e-mail ademe.guadeloupe@ademe.fr; internet www.ademe.fr; developing energy and waste management; Man. CLAUDE COROSINE.

Agence Française de Développement (AFD): Parc d'activités de la Jaille, Bâtiment 7, BP 110, 97122 Baie-Mahault; tel. 5-90-89-65-65; fax 5-90-83-03-73; e-mail afdpointeaPitre@afd.fr; internet www.afd-guadeloupe.org; fmrly Caisse Française de Développement; Man. BERTRAND BOISSELET.

CHAMBERS OF COMMERCE

Chambre d'Agriculture de la Guadeloupe: Espace régional Agricole, Convenance BP 35, 97122 Baie-Mahault; tel. 5-90-25-17-17; fax 5-90-26-07-22; e-mail cda_direction@guadeloupe.chambagri.fr; Pres. ERIC NELSON; Dir JOËL PEDURAND.

Chambre de Commerce et d'Industrie de Région des Iles de Guadeloupe: Hôtel Consulaire, rue Félix Eboué, 97110 Pointe-à-Pitre Cédex; tel. 5-90-93-76-00; fax 5-90-90-21-87; e-mail contact@pointe-a-pitre.cci.fr; internet www.pointe-a-pitre.cci.fr; f. 1832; Pres. COLETTE KOURY; Sec. HENRI NAGAPIN; 34 full mems and 17 assoc. mems.

Chambre de Métiers et de l'Artisanat de la Guadeloupe (CMA): route Choisy, BP 61, 97120 Saint-Claude; tel. 5-90-80-23-33; fax 5-90-80-08-93; e-mail sgstc@cmguadeloupe.org; internet www.cmguadeloupe.org; Pres. JOËL LOBEAU; 11,630 mems (2005).

EMPLOYERS' ORGANIZATIONS

Association des Moyennes et Petites Industries (AMPI): rue Pierre et Marie Curie, Z.I. Jarry, BP 2325, 97187 Jarry Cédex; tel. 5-90-26-38-27; fax 5-90-95-52-57; e-mail mpi.guadeloupe@wanadoo.fr; internet www.industrieguadeloupe.com; f. 1974; Pres. FRANK DESALMA; Gen. Sec CHRISTOPHE WACHTER; 117 mem. cos.

Interprofession Guadeloupéenne pour la Canne à Sucre (IGUACANNE): Espace Régional Agricole de Convenance, 97122 Baie-Mahault; f. 2005; represents sugar cane growers, sugar producers and professional bodies; Pres. ATHANASE COQUIN.

Ordre des Pharmaciens du Département Guadeloupe: Immeuble Capital 16, 1°, ZAC de Houelbourg, SUD 2, 97122 Baie-Mahault; tel. 5-90-21-66-05; fax 5-90-21-66-07; e-mail delegation_guadeloupe@ordre.pharmacien.fr; Pres. MAGGY CHEVRY-NOL.

Syndicat des Producteurs-Exportateurs de Sucre et de Rhum de la Guadeloupe et Dépendances: Z. I. Jarry, 97122 Baie-Mahault; BP 2015, 97191 Pointe-à-Pitre; tel. 5-90-23-53-15; fax 5-90-23-52-34; f. 1937; Pres. M. VIGNERON; 4 mems.

Union des Entreprises-Mouvement des Entreprises de France (UDE-MEDEF): Immeuble SCI BTB, voie Principale de Jarry, Baie-Mahault; tel. 5-90-26-83-58; fax 5-90-26-83-67; e-mail ude.medef@medef-guadeloupe.com; Pres. WILLY ANGÈLE.

MAJOR COMPANIES

Barbotteau Distribution: impasse Jean-Marie Jacquard, 97122 Baie Mahault; tel. 5-90-32-56-78; fax 5-90-26-68-89; e-mail commercial.btb-distribution@barbotteau.fr; internet www.barbotteau-distribution.fr; subsidiary of Groupe Barbotteau et Cie, France; volume retail and distribution; Gen. Man. JEAN-MICHEL ABIDOS.

Chantiers Audebert et Cie, SARL: Z. I. Jarry, 97122 Baie-Mahault; tel. 5-90-26-75-40; fax 5-90-26-75-43; e-mail chantier@chantiers-audebert.com; internet www.chantiers-audebert.com; f. 1904; construction equipment; Chair. JEAN AUDEBERT; Gen. Man. DERRICK AUDEBERT; 100 employees.

Compagnie Frigorifique de la Guadeloupe, SARL (COFRIGO): Impasse Emile Dessout, Z. I. Jarry, 97122 Baie-Mahault; tel. 5-90-32-55-25; fax 5-90-26-80-91; e-mail info@cofrigo.fr; internet www.cofrigo.biz; f. 1973; manufacture of soft drinks; Pres. ALAIN HUYGHUES-DESPOINTES; Gen. Man. THIERRY HUYGHUES-DESPOINTES; 87 employees.

Coopérative des Marins-Pêcheurs de la Guadeloupe (COMAPEGA): Port de Pêche de Bergevin, 97110 Pointe-à-Pitre; tel. 5-90-21-46-60; fax 5-90-91-63-78; f. 1976; fishing co-operative; Pres. HENRI CICOFRAN.

Gardel SA: Usine de Gardel, 97160 Le Moule; tel. 5-90-23-87-87; fax 5-90-23-52-34; e-mail contact@gardel.fr; internet www.gardel.fr; f. 1870; 24.48% owned by Saint-Louis Sucre SNC, France; sole sugar refinery; Pres. MAXIME WOLFF; Dir-Gen. ERIC BOURRILLO; 350 employees.

Liquoristerie Madras (LIQUOMA): rue Eugene Freyssinet, 97122 Baie-Mahault; tel. 5-90-26-60-28; fax 5-90-26-76-69; f. 1983; production and bottling of cane syrup, rums and other beverages; Chair. CHRISTIAN BICHARA-JABOUR; 20 employees.

SARA (Société Anonyme de la Raffinerie des Antilles): BP 2039, 97191 Jarry Cédex; tel. 5-90-38-13-13; fax 5-90-26-70-98; e-mail francois.nahan@sara.mq; internet www.sara.gp; f. 1970; owned by TotalFinaElf 50%, Shell 24%, Esso 14.5%, Texaco 11.5%; Regional Gen. Man. FRANÇOIS NAHAN; c. 250 employees regionally (see entry in Martinique).

Severin Industrie SARL: Domaine de Séverin, Cadet, 97115 Sainte-Rose; tel. 5-90-28-91-86; fax 5-90-28-36-66; f. 1929; production of alcoholic beverages; Man. JOSÉ MARIE HENRI MARSOLLE.

Société Des Eaux Thermales Capes Dolé: Lieu-dit Dolé, 97113 Gourbeyre; tel. 5-90-92-10-92; fax 5-90-92-26-19; f. 1968; bottling of mineral water; 49 employees.

Somatco: Z. I. Jarry, impasse Augustin Fresnel, 97122 Baie-Mahault; tel. 5-90-26-71-67; fax 5-90-26-86-24; f. 1980; industrial manufacture of construction materials; Pres. CHRISTIAN BONNARDEL; 17 employees.

UTILITIES

Electricity

EDF Guadeloupe: BP 85, 97153 Pointe-à-Pitre; tel. 5-90-82-40-34; fax 5-90-83-30-02; e-mail marie-therese.fournier@edfgdf.fr; internet guadeloupe.edf.fr; electricity producer; Dir YVAN DELMAS; Man. MAX BORDELAIS.

Water

Veolia Water—Compagnie Générale des Eaux Guadeloupe:
18 ZAC de Houelbourg III, Voie verte de Jarry, 97122 Baie-Mahault;
tel. 5-90-89-76-76; fax 5-90-91-39-10; e-mail mail-elise@
gde-guadeloupe.com; internet www.generaledeseaux.gp; fmrly
SOGEA; Dir (Americas) AUGUSTE LAURENT.

TRADE UNIONS

Centrale des Travailleurs Unis de la Guadeloupe (CTU):
Logement Test 14, Bergevin, 97110 Pointe-à-Pitre; BP 120, 97153
Pointe-à-Pitre Cédex; tel. 5-90-28-96-36; fax 5-90-28-81-16; e-mail
ctu.gpe@wanadoo.fr; internet ctuguadeloupe.fr; f. 1999 by merger of
the FASU-G and Centrale Syndicale des Travailleurs de la
Guadeloupe; represents public and private sector workers; collegial
directorate of 11 Secs-Gen; Sec.-Gen. ALEX LOLLIA; 3,500 mems.

**Confédération Générale du Travail de la Guadeloupe
(CGTG):** 4 Cité Artisanale de Bergevin, BP 779, 97110 Pointe-à-
Pitre Cédex; tel. 5-90-82-34-61; fax 5-90-91-04-00; f. 1961; Sec.-Gen.
JEAN-MARIE NOMERTIN; 5,000 mems.

**Fédération Départementale des Syndicats d'Exploitants de
la Guadeloupe (FDSEA):** Chambre d'Agriculture, Rond-Point de
Destrellan, BP 150, 97122 Baie-Mahault; tel. 5-90-26-06-47; fax 5-90-
26-48-82; e-mail fdsea971@yahoo.fr; affiliated to the Fédération
Nationale des Syndicats d'Exploitants; Pres. ERIC NELSON.

**Fédération Syndicale Unitaire Guadeloupe (FSU Guade-
loupe):** BP 82, 97005 Pointe-à-Pitre Cedéx; tel. 5-90-23-13-66; fax
5-90-23-19-83; e-mail fsu971@fsu.fr; internet sd971.fsu.fr; f. 1993;
departmental br. of the Fédération Syndicale Unitaire; represents
public sector employees in teaching, research and training, and also
agriculture, justice, youth and sports, and culture; Sec.-Gen. EDDY
SÉGUR.

SE-UNSA Guadeloupe (Le Syndicat des Enseignants UNSA):
Immeuble Jabol, 5ème étage, 1 rue de la Clinique, 97139 Les Abymes;
tel. 5-90-82-22-04; fax 5-90-83-08-64; e-mail 971@se-unsa.org;
internet www.syndicat-enseignant-unsa-guadeloupe.fr; Sec.-Gen.
GIRARD PELAGE.

**Union Départementale de la Confédération Française des
Travailleurs Chrétiens (UD/UR CFTC):** BP 154, 97122 Baie-
Mahault Cédex; tel. 5-90-26-20-62; e-mail udurcftc.gpe@orange.fr;
f. 1937; Pres. SÉVERINE NOYER; 3,500 mems.

Union Départementale des Syndicats Force Ouvrière: 59 rue
Lamartine, BP 687, 97110 Pointe-à-Pitre; tel. 5-90-82-86-83; fax 5-
90-82-16-12; e-mail udfoguadeloupe@force-ouvriere.fr; internet
www.force-ouvriere.fr; Gen. Sec. MAX EVARISTE; 1,500 mems.

Union Générale des Travailleurs de la Guadeloupe (UGTG):
rue Paul Lacavé, 97110 Pointe-à-Pitre; tel. 5-90-83-10-07; fax 5-90-
89-08-70; e-mail ugtg@ugtg.org; internet www.ugtg.org; f. 1973;
confederation of pro-independence trade unions incl. Union des
Agents de la Sécurité Sociale (UNASS), l'Union des Employés du
Commerce (UEC), Union des Travailleurs de l'Etat et du Département (UTED), l'Union des Travailleurs des Collectivités (UTC),
l'Union des Travailleurs de l'Hôtellerie, du Tourisme et de la
Restauration (UTHTR), l'Union des Travailleurs des Produits
Pétroliers (UTPP), l'Union des Travailleurs de la Santé (UTS), and
l'Union des Travailleurs des Télécommunications (UTT); Gen. Sec.
ELIE DOMOTA; 4,000 mems.

**Union Interprofessionnelle Régionale CFDT de la Guade-
loupe (UIR CFDT):** 104 Immeuble Les Chicanes, 97139 Grand-
Camp Abymes; tel. 5-90-83-16-50; fax 5-90-20-42-61; e-mail cfdt
.gpe@wanadoo.fr; affiliated to the Fédération des Syndicats Gén-
éraux de l'Education Nationale et de la Recherche; represents
teaching staff.

**Union des Moyennes et Petites Entreprises de Guadeloupe
(UMPEG):** 17 Immeuble Coupole, Grand Camp, 97139 Abymes,
Pointe-à-Pitre; tel. 5-90-91-79-31; fax 5-90-93-09-18; Pres. EDOUARD
VAINQUEUR.

Transport

RAILWAYS

There are no railways in Guadeloupe.

ROADS

There were 2,069 km (1,286 miles) of roads in Guadeloupe, of which
323 km were Routes Nationales.

SHIPPING

The Guadeloupe Port Caraïbes (formerly Port Autonome de la
Guadeloupe) comprises five sites. The two principal seaports are
at Pointe-à-Pitre, which offers both cargo-handling and passenger
facilities, and the container terminal at Jarry (Baie-Mahault); the
smaller port of Basse-Terre caters to freight and inter-island pas-

senger traffic. There is also a sugar terminal at Folle-Anse (Saint-
Louis); and a marina at Bas-du-Fort with 1,000 berths for pleasure
craft. In December 2013 Guadeloupe's flag registered fleet comprised
13 vessels, with an aggregate displacement of some 4,224 grt.

Agence Petrelluzzi Transit et Maritime: 17 rue de la Chapelle,
97122 Baie Mahault; tel. 5-90-38-12-12; fax 5-90-26-69-26; e-mail
info@transitpetrelluzzi.com; internet transitpetrelluzzi.com; f. 1896;
Dir PATRICK PETRELLUZZI.

Compagnie Générale Maritime Antilles-Guyane: Route du
WTC, Zone Portuaire, BP 92, 97122 Baie-Mahault; tel. 5-90-25-57-
00; fax 5-90-25-57-81; e-mail ptp.mbellemare@cma-cgm.com;
internet www.cma-cgm.com; subsidiary of CMA-CGM, France;
shipping agents, stevedoring; Gen. Man. MARLÈNE BELLEMARE.

Guadeloupe Port Caraïbes: Quai Ferdinand de Lesseps, BP 485,
97165 Pointe-à-Pitre Cédex; tel. 5-90-68-61-70; fax 5-90-68-61-71;
e-mail contact@port-guadeloupe.com; internet
guadeloupe-portcaraibes.com; port authority; fmrly Port Autonome
de la Guadeloupe; became a Grand Port Maritime, a publicly owned
entity administered by a supervisory board, following adoption of
legislation in 2013; Dir-Gen. LAURENT MARTENS.

Compagnie Générale Portuaire: Marina Bas-du-Fort, 97110
Pointe-à-Pitre; tel. 5-90-93-66-20; fax 5-90-90-81-53; e-mail
marina@marina-pap.com; internet www.marina-pap.com; port
authority; Man. PHILIPPE CHEVALLIER; Harbour Master TONY
BRESLAU; 1,000 berths for non-commercial traffic.

**Société Guadeloupéenne de Consignation et Manutention
(SGCM):** 8 rue de la Chapelle, BP 2360, 97001 Jarry Cédex; tel. 5-90-
38-05-55; fax 5-90-26-95-39; e-mail gerard.petrelluzzi@sgcm.fr;
f. 1994; shipping agents, stevedoring; also operates Navimar Cruises
inter-island tour co; Gen. Man. GERARD PETRELLUZZI; 17 berths.

Transcaraïbes S.A.: BP 2453, 97085 Pointe-à-Pitre; tel. 5-90-26-63-
27; fax 5-90-26-67-49; e-mail transcaraibes.gpe@wanadoo.fr; f. 1976;
shipping agents, stevedoring; office in Martinique; Gen. Man. ERIK
URGIN.

CIVIL AVIATION

Raizet International Airport is situated 3 km (2 miles) from Pointe-à-
Pitre and is equipped to handle jet-engined aircraft. There are
smaller airports on the islands of Marie-Galante, La Désirade and
Saint-Barthélémy. The island is served by a number of regional
airlines, including LIAT (see Antigua and Barbuda). In 2013 American Airlines began a direct service from Miami, FL, USA, to Pointe-à-
Pitre.

Air Antilles Express: Aeroport Pôle Caraibes, Point-à-Pitre; tel. 5-
90-21-14-47; e-mail ar@media-caraibes.com; internet www
.airantilles.com; f. 2002; subsidiary of Compagnie Aerienne Inter
Regionale Express, France; serves Guadeloupe, Martinique, St-
Barthélémy, St-Martin, St Maarten and the Dominican Republic;
seasonal flights to San Juan, La Romana, Antigua and St Lucia; Dir
CHRISTIAN MARCHAND.

Air Caraïbes (CAT): Aéroport International Guadeloupe, Pôle
Caraïbes, 97139 Abymes; tel. 5-90-82-47-41; fax 5-90-82-47-49;
e-mail drh@aircaraibes.com; internet www.aircaraibes.com;
f. 2000 following merger of Air St Martin, Air St Barts, Air
Guadeloupe and Air Martinique; owned by Groupe Dubreuil;
operates daily inter-island, regional and international services
within the Caribbean, and flights to Brazil, French Guiana and
Paris; CEO SERGE TSYGALNITZKY; 16 aircraft; 800,000 passengers
(2006).

Air Caraïbes Atlantique: Aéroport, 97232 Le Lamentin; f. 2003;
subsidiary of Air Caraïbes; services between Pointe-à-Pitre, Fort-
de-France (Martinique) and Paris; Pres. FRANÇOIS HERSEN.

Tourism

Guadeloupe is a popular tourist destination, especially for visitors
from metropolitan France (who account for some 89% of tourists) and
the USA. The main attractions are the beaches, the mountainous
scenery and the unspoilt beauty of the island dependencies. In 2011
some 418,000 tourists visited Guadeloupe. Receipts from tourism
totalled US $583m. in the same year.

Comité du Tourisme: 5 sq. de la Banque, BP 555, 97166 Pointe-à-
Pitre Cédex; tel. 5-90-82-09-30; fax 5-90-83-89-22; e-mail info@
lesilesdeguadeloupe.com; internet www.lesilesdeguadeloupe.com;
Pres. JOSETTE BOREL-LINCERTIN; Dir THIERRY GARGAR.

**Délégation Régionale au Tourisme, au Commerce et l'Arti-
sanat:** 5 rue Victor Hugues, 97100 Basse-Terre; tel. 5-90-81-10-44;
fax 5-90-81-94-82; e-mail drtourisme.guadeloupe@wanadoo.fr; Dir
CHRISTIAN FOURCRIER.

Syndicat d'Initiative de Pointe-à-Pitre: Centre Commercial de
la Marina, 97110 Pointe-à-Pitre; tel. 5-90-90-70-02; fax 5-90-74-
70; e-mail syndicatinitiativedepap@wanadoo.fr; internet www.sivap
.gp; Pres. DENYS FORTUNE; Man. NADIA DEGLAS.

Defence

As assessed at November 2013, France maintained a military force of about 1,250 in Fort-de-France (Martinique).

Education

The education system is similar to that of metropolitan France (see the chapter on French Guiana). In 2012/13 there were 134 pre-primary and 206 primary schools. Secondary education was provided at 94 institutions in that year. In 2012/13 there were 19,614 students in pre-primary and 35,584 in primary education (a further 540 pupils attended specialized pre-primary and primary schools), while in secondary education there were 50,019 students, of whom some 89% attended state schools. A branch of the Université des Antilles et de la Guyane, at Pointe-à-Pitre, has faculties of law and economics, sciences, medicine, teacher training, sports science and humanities. In addition, there are colleges of agriculture, fisheries, hotel management, nursing, midwifery and childcare. In 2012/13 there was a total of 9,125 students in higher education.

Bibliography

For works on the Caribbean generally, see Select Bibliography (Books)

Bangou, H. (Ed.). *La Guadeloupe et sa décolonisation ou un demi-siècle d'enfantement*. Paris, Editions L'Harmattan, 2003.

Belenus, R. *L'esclave en Guadeloupe et en Martinique du XVIIe au XIXe siècles*. Pointe-à-Pitre, Editions Jasor, 1998.

Destouches, D. *Du statut colonial au statut départemental: L'administration révolutionnaire en Guadeloupe (1787-An X)*. Aix-en-Provence, Presses Universitaires d'Aix-Marseille, 2007.

Jeangoudoux, A. *Français de Souches*. Pointe-à-Pitre, Editions Jasor, 2005.

Lefort, J. *Chronique intempestive de la télévision de proximité en Guadeloupe*. Pointe-à-Pitre, Editions Jasor, 2003.

Orizio, R. *Lost White Tribes: The End of Privilege and the Last Colonials in Sri Lanka, Jamaica, Brazil, Haiti, Namibia and Guadeloupe*. Mississauga, ON, Random House of Canada, 2001.

Smeralda, J. *Peau noire, cheveu crépu*. Pointe-à-Pitre, Editions Jasor, 2005.

Valérius, R. *La Guadeloupe d'en-France*. Pointe-à-Pitre, Editions Jasor, 2005.

GUATEMALA

Geography

PHYSICAL FEATURES

The Republic of Guatemala is in Central America; apart from Belize it is the country furthest north on the isthmus, its territory abutting into the Yucatán peninsula. Its longest border (962 km or 597 miles), therefore, is with the North American country of Mexico, which lies to the north and the north-west (Campeche is to the north, Tabasco in the north-west and Chiapas stretches west). To the south-east, further down the trunk of Central America, are El Salvador (beyond a 203-km frontier) on the Pacific Ocean and, further north, Honduras (with a 256-km border). The long Pacific coast faces south and south-west. Apart from a relatively short, north-facing shore with no natural harbours at the marshy head of the Gulf of Honduras, the country is isolated from the Caribbean coast by Belize, which lies to the east of northern Guatemala. The border with Belize is 266 km long, but Guatemala maintains claims on territory in the south of Belize, as well as rights of access to the Caribbean. The area of Guatemala is 108,889 sq km (42,042 sq miles).

The extent of the country is about 450 km (north–south) by 430 km, and it has about 400 km of coastline, mainly on the Pacific. Guatemala is mostly mountainous (66%), with narrow coastal plains and a rolling limestone plateau in the north. It is heavily forested (62%), woodland types varying from warm and humid, through cool and humid to warm and dry, which, together with the altitude and two coasts, contributes to the variety of flora and fauna. The most spectacular of the many bird species in the country is the national bird, the quetzal, but another noteworthy example might be the ocellated turkey, while the largest native mammal is a freshwater sea cow (manatee) found in Lake Izabal, in the east. There are volcanoes in the mountains, indicating that the country is an area prone to seismic activity. A volcano is actually the highest point not only in Guatemala, but in all of Central America—Tajumulco, at 4,211 m or 13,821 ft—and is found at the western end of the main mountain chain, in the south-west of the country. The main mountain range of the high plateau of the south-west is the Sierra Madre, it runs roughly east–west above the Pacific coast. There is a branching range, the Sierra de los Chuchumatanes, which thrusts more to the north-west, and other highlands in this area include the Sierra Chaucus, the Montañas del Mico and the Sierra de Chama. Most of the country's volcanoes are on the central plateau. The three other topographical regions are less lofty. South of the mountains is the Pacific coast, which consists of tropical savannah plains and lagoons, and is traversed by 18 short rivers. North of the central plateau and in the east of the country are the lower slopes and more easterly out-thrusts of the Continental Divide (such as the Sierra de las Minas), giving way to the often swampy Caribbean flatlands. This region is dominated by three deep river valleys (of the Motagua, the Polochic and the Sarstun). Finally, north of here, occupying most of northern Guatemala and mainly beyond the Maya Mountains, is the water-eroded limestone plateau of El Petén, dotted with lakes and densely cloaked in tropical forest, watered by heavy, year-round rain. The largest lakes are not in this area, however, with the 800-sq-km Izabal (also known as the Dulce gulf) in the Caribbean lowlands and the famously beautiful, 126-sq-km Atitlán in the central highlands.

CLIMATE

The climate is tropical, hot and humid, especially on the Caribbean coast and in the El Petén lowlands, but it is cooler in the highlands. The Caribbean coast is also prone to hurricanes and other tropical storms. Average annual rainfall varies from as low as 510 mm (20 ins) in the eastern highlands to 2,540 mm (100 ins) in the north. The average maximum and minimum temperatures in Guatemala City, the capital, which is

located on the central plateau, range from 12°C–23°C (54°F–73°F) in January to 16°C–29°C (61°C–84°F) in May. May is the end of the dry season and the start of the rainy season.

POPULATION

Guatemala has the largest surviving indigenous population in Central America. The normally dominant population of mixed-Spanish descent (including assimilated Amerindians), here known as Ladino, accounts for barely 55% of the total. Often included with the Ladinos are the small populations of more purely Spanish descent and of other non-indigenous origins, such as Syrians and Lebanese, Asians and Garifuna (Black Caribs, mainly of African descent, with some Amerindian ancestry, settled on the Caribbean coast). Amerindian peoples, however, account for 43% of the population. That they are concentrated in the countryside may obscure the veracity of the figure, with some claiming that the Amerindians, the Mayas, account for almost two-thirds of the population. Spanish is the official language and is spoken by 60% of the population, but there is some official status for Garifuna (Carib) and around 20 of the 50 or so Mayan languages spoken in the country. The main Mayan language groups spoken in Guatemala are Quiché (Kiche), Cakchiquel, Mam and Kelchi. It is not only language that survives among the Maya, but also some traditional religious beliefs and practices, although usually syncretized with the dominant Roman Catholic Christianity. About 60% of the population are Roman Catholics. There are also small groups of Orthodox Catholics ('Uniates'), Buddhists, Jews, Muslims and 'Moonies' (followers of the Unification Church).

At mid-2014 the people of Guatemala numbered 15.8m., according to official estimates, making Guatemala the most populous nation in Central America. The majority of the population live in the temperate valleys of the highlands, in the south-centre of the country, around the capital. The capital is Guatemala City (which numbered some 993,815 residents at mid-2014. The other chief cities in terms of population are Villa Nueva and Mixco. The country is divided into 22 departments.

History

DANIEL SACHS

Based on an earlier article by DIEGO SÁNCHEZ-ANCOCHEA

PRE-HISPANIC, COLONY AND EARLY REPUBLIC

The territory of modern-day Guatemala was occupied as early as 2000 BC by fishing and farming villages. These gave rise to the Maya civilization, which became one of the most important in the continent. Extending to what is now southern Mexico, Honduras, Belize and El Salvador, the Maya civilization reached its height between AD 600 and AD 900. When Spanish conquistadors arrived in the early 16th century, they encountered fragmented ethnic groups, dispersed between different kingdoms, fighting for political and economic domination. Military superiority, exploitation of political differences, and the devastating effect of diseases of European origin on the indigenous population provided the invaders with the opportunity to secure a swift and decisive victory. Spanish settlers subsequently appropriated both land and labour, which were ruthlessly exploited.

The so-called Capitanía General del Reino de Guatemala—which included the five current Central American countries and Chiapas (now a state of Mexico)—attained independence from Spain peacefully in September 1821. The move towards independent statehood was led by wealthy landowners and businessmen, mainly of Spanish origin (Creoles). The resultant new federal, political and administrative entity, the United Provinces of Central America, was dissolved in 1839, owing to internal conflicts. The current geographical territory of Guatemala was established later in the century, following the loss of Belize to the United Kingdom and Chiapas to Mexico. From the mid-19th century onwards Guatemala invested heavily in the development of coffee plantations, which had become the main source of national income by the end of the century. After the 'Liberal Revolution' of 1871, the country was integrated into the global market by the rapid expansion of agro-exports. As a result of the introduction of new legislation and the creation of a national army, Liberal governments institutionalized a more coercive role for the state in promoting agrarian capitalism. Indigenous peoples lost huge swathes of their communal lands, which were incorporated into large landholdings dedicated to the production of coffee exports. Hundreds of European settlers, particularly Germans, were attracted by the prospect of favourable grants of land and labour to aid in the development of agro-exports. During the first two decades of the 20th century the Government of Manuel Estrada Cabrera opened the country to capital investment from the USA. This monopolized services such as railways, ports, electricity and maritime transport, as well as the international mail service. US monopoly capital was also used to acquire significant land holdings, as the United Fruit Company procured large tracts for the development of banana plantations.

In 1944, after 14 years in power, Gen. Jorge Ubico, the last representative of the Liberal reforms of 1871, was overthrown by a popular uprising led by nationalist members of the army and progressive intellectuals, who were inspired by US President Franklin Delano Roosevelt's 'Four Freedoms' address to the US Congress in 1941. The so-called October Revolution led to a presidential election, which was won by a civilian, Juan José Arévalo. Arévalo introduced a series of economic and social reforms, including universal male suffrage, the establishment of a social security system for state employees and a new labour code. His successor, Col Jacobo Arbenz Guzmán, who acceded to the presidency in 1950, enhanced these measures and initiated a radical agrarian reform, which encouraged the organization of peasant leagues throughout the countryside and benefited some 100,000 families by expropriating uncultivated lands from large landowners and the United Fruit Company. At the height of the Cold War, concerned about the influence of the communist Partido Guatemalteco del Trabajo (PGT—Guatemalan Labour Party) within the Arbenz administration, the recently created US Central Intelligence Agency exploited discontent within the Guatemalan army and private sector and organized a military invasion from Honduras, which overthrew the Arbenz Government in June 1954. The counter-revolution reversed most of the reforms of the previous decades, began a systematic process of political persecution of government supporters, and installed a series of anti-communist regimes dominated by the armed forces. During the late 1970s the ability of these military regimes to govern deteriorated, as a result of both internecine divisions and their lack of popular legitimacy. Elections held in 1974, 1978 and 1982 were openly fraudulent.

GUERRILLA WARFARE AND COUNTER-INSURGENCY

Beginning in the early 1960s an armed opposition developed, originating from a schism within the army, but later garnering widespread indigenous support in the rural areas. Guerrilla and anti-guerrilla warfare ensued for more than three decades. Some 200,000 Guatemalans were either killed or 'disappeared' during this period, largely as a result of state military operations against civilians, particularly rural Mayan communities suspected of supporting the insurgency. Mass violations of human rights under the military Government of Gen. Fernando Romeo Lucas García (1978–82) led the US Administration of Jimmy Carter (1977–81) to suspend military aid to Guatemala (resumed only in 1985 under President Ronald Reagan). In February 1982 three different guerrilla organizations and the PGT formed a guerrilla coalition, the Unidad Revolucionaria Nacional Guatemalteca (URNG—Guatemalan National Revolutionary Unity). At their height, the guerrillas were operating in 18 of the country's 22 departments. Divisions within the army over the prosecution of the war also facilitated two military coups during this period. The first took place on 23 March 1982 and was led by Gen. Efraín Ríos Montt, a former Christian Democrat presidential candidate and, latterly, evangelical preacher, who was denied the presidency in 1974, owing to electoral fraud. Gen. Ríos Montt's 15 months in office are widely regarded as having been the most violent in the country's modern history. Hundreds of villages were eradicated, destroyed by systematic army massacres. In the rural areas all men between the ages of 16 and 60 years were forced to participate in paramilitary civil defence patrols, which, at their height, comprised some 1m. peasants. 'Model villages', under strict army control, were established as detention centres for those across the country who had been displaced by war. The military operations of the guerrilla movement declined dramatically during this period, overwhelmed by the superior firepower and ruthless tactics of the army. In August 1983 Gen. Ríos Montt was overthrown by his Minister of Defence, Gen. Oscar Humberto Mejía Víctores. The new military regime restored the promotional hierarchy that had been disrupted by the former Government, and promised a swift return to constitutional rule, while enforcing a continued programme of counter-insurgency and political repression.

CIVILIAN RULE AND PEACE PROCESS

By the mid-1980s there was a consensus within the higher echelons of the military that Guatemala should shift to civilian rule if it was to change its international status as a pariah. On 1 July 1984 a Constituent Assembly was elected; the promulgation of a new Constitution in 1985 and the holding of general elections in the same year ushered in a period of elected civilian rule and a limited relaxation of the military's control over national affairs. However, the key institutions of the counter-insurgency, such as the civil patrols, were legalized by the new Constitution, which provided a framework for civilian government throughout the 1980s. Although the URNG boycotted the presidential election held in November 1985, the centre-right Christian Democrat candidate, Vinicio Cerezo, won it by an ample margin. Despite high hopes for the new civilian Government, Cerezo did not challenge the dominance of the military or address the country's acute socio-economic problems. This led to the re-emergence of social movements and civic protests, despite the harsh repressive measures that this evinced from the military. Nevertheless, on 30 March 1990 the guerrilla movement and the Government agreed to a framework for negotiations. However, within months the peace talks had stalled, owing to the army's insistence upon a full demobilization of the URNG prior to a final settlement and an amnesty on human rights violations.

In January 1991 Jorge Serrano Elías, an evangelical leader and former member of the 1982–83 Ríos Montt Government, won the presidential election. The new Government reinitiated peace negotiations with the guerrilla movement, and meetings were held in Cuernavaca, Mexico, in April. Meanwhile, the domestic political situation deteriorated; human rights organizations reported some 1,750 human rights violations, including 650 extrajudicial executions, during the first nine months of the Serrano Government. The USA once again suspended military aid to Guatemala and, together with the World Bank and the European Parliament, exerted pressure upon the Government to bring an end to the political violence. In October 1992 Rigoberta Menchú, a Guatemalan Maya-K'iche' woman and indigenous human rights activist, won the Nobel Peace Prize, focusing global attention on the ongoing human rights violations in the country, and also signalling the emergence of an increasingly organized Mayan popular movement. Facing a mounting crisis of legitimacy, President Serrano, supported by a faction of the military, mounted a so-called autogolpe 'self-coup' in May 1993, attempting to suspend significant constitutional guarantees and dissolve the Congreso (Congress) and the Supreme Court. However, in the face of domestic and international opposition, the coup ultimately proved unsuccessful, and a few days later Serrano abandoned the country for exile in Panama.

The then ombudsman for human rights, Ramiro de León Carpio, was designated interim President by Congress on 6 June 1993 to enable the completion of Serrano's presidential term. His cousin, Jorge Carpio Nicolle, a political leader and newspaper tycoon who had been defeated by Serrano in the second round of the 1991 election, was assassinated shortly after de León assumed power. The hard-line, populist Frente Republicano Guatemalteco (FRG—Guatemalan Republican Front), headed by the former de facto chief of state, Gen. (retd) Ríos Montt, obtained a congressional majority in elections held in 1994. In January the Government and the guerrilla movement signed a framework agreement for the resumption of peace talks in Mexico. In March a comprehensive agreement on human rights was signed following discussions held in Oslo, Norway, which was to enter into immediate effect and was to be verified by the UN. Before the end of the year the guerrilla movement and the Government had signed an agreement, with UN verification, for the protection of human rights. A further agreement established conditions for the resettlement of displaced populations. Most controversial was the June accord that delineated the terms of a Commission for Historical Clarification, or 'truth commission', to investigate human rights violations committed during the armed conflict. Despite the efforts of domestic and international human rights organizations, the final agreement stated that the commission's report would not individualize responsibility for gross violations—this was widely interpreted as being a concession to the hard-line element within the military. By mid-1995 peace negotiations had stalled again, a consequence of the declining strength of the de León Government and a lack of political will on the part of military and civilian élites.

The presidential election conducted in November 1995 led to the holding of a second round of voting, in January 1996, won by Alvaro Enrique Arzú Irigoyen of the Partido de Avanzada Nacional (PAN—National Advancement Party), a party representing the interests of the private sector. Arzú, a businessman, former mayor of Guatemala City and Minister of Foreign Affairs during the first months of Serrano's Government, won a close electoral race against Alfonso Portillo Cabrera of the FRG. The new administration advanced the peace process and gave new impetus to its development. Arzú appointed prominent business leaders to key government posts, securing the private sector's commitment to the peace negotiations. New peace accords, arguably some of the most controversial to date, were signed in 1996, before a final settlement was reached in December. The accords included an agreement on socio-economic issues and the agrarian situation, committing the Government to increase social spending and to fund a land bank through which landless peasants could acquire land. Another strengthened civilian rule and defined the function of the army in a democratic society, specifying the terms by which military power would be gradually reduced. A number of enabling accords were signed in December, including those referring to constitutional reform and the electoral regime; the legalization of the URNG; the conclusion of a definitive cease-fire; and the final accord for a firm and lasting peace, which was signed in Guatemala City on 29 December in the presence of UN Secretary-General Dr Boutros Boutros-Ghali. The rebels disarmed shortly afterwards, under UN supervision, and the URNG subsequently became a legal political party.

POST-ACCORD POLITICS

The period immediately following the achievement of the negotiated settlement was dominated by attempts to implement the reforms promised in the various accords, and by efforts to investigate past violations of human rights. In February 1999 the UN Report of Historical Clarification, based on over 9,000 testimonies, attributed 93% of wartime atrocities to the army and 3% to the URNG. The UN report demonstrated that the army had committed acts of genocide (as defined by international law) legitimated by state policy during the 1981–83 period. However, the costs of such investigations were high—Juan José Gerardi Conadera, the bishop in charge of a 1998 report on human rights violations, formulated by the Catholic Church's Oficina de Derechos Humanos del Arzobispado (Archbishopric's Human Rights Office), was murdered just days after its publication. It took three years and the exertion of immense international pressure for domestic courts to find three army officers guilty of his extrajudicial execution. Guatemalan human rights organizations attempting to secure the prosecution of former army officers in domestic and international courts for gross violations of human rights were subject to continuing intimidation and violence.

In March 1999 the peace settlement suffered a serious reverse when a referendum on a package of constitutional reforms agreed by the legislature to implement the peace agreements was rejected with a turnout of less than 25%, slowing implementation of the settlement almost to a standstill.

The FRG candidate, Alfonso Portillo, won the 1999 presidential election held in December. Although the FRG was formally committed to the implementation of the peace agreements (a key feature of the prevailing conditions by which international aid was granted), the party lacked the commitment of the Arzú administration to the process, divided as it was between moderates and hardliners, the latter allied with party founder Ríos Montt, who maintained a powerful position as the President of the Congreso. The weakness of the public security and justice systems and the growth of organized crime meant that the increasing problem of crime and public insecurity had reached unprecedented levels by the end of the decade. The state-orchestrated violence of the 1980s was replaced by a wave of kidnappings, armed assaults and robberies, leading to escalating public alarm about law and order and demands for more stringent penal measures (such as the introduction of the death penalty for kidnappers, which was approved in 1996). Meanwhile, the implementation of the demilitarization agreed in the September 1996 accord met with numerous obstacles; although the size of the armed forces was reduced by one-third as stipulated, the reform of military intelligence institutions was slow. Consistently high levels of violence and crime with impunity led the population to resort to private justice; levels of gun ownership and homicide continued to increase and suspected criminals were subjected to mob lynchings.

The Portillo administration was characterized by growing conflict between the Government and the private sector, which opposed the former's attempts to raise taxes—a key demand of the IMF and bilateral donors. Discontent over the Portillo administration's lacklustre record in office, multiple corruption scandals involving high-ranking government officials, and poor fiscal management became increasingly manifest. Relations with the USA were also strained, largely owing to the growth in drugs-trafficking, which was often linked to government officials. Fiscal weakness and divisions between the Portillo Government and Ríos Montt's faction of the FRG continued to undermine the administration's coherence. Until 2004 the country remained on the so-called 'black list' of countries considered to be unco-operative in the fight against money-laundering, drawn up by the Financial Action Task Force on Money Laundering, based in Paris, France.

THE GOVERNMENT OF OSCAR BERGER PERDOMO

Oscar Berger Perdomo of the centre-right Gran Alianza Nacional (GANA—Great National Alliance) won the 2003 presidential election, defeating Alvaro Colom Caballeros of the centre-left Unidad Nacional de la Esperanza (UNE—National Unity of Hope) in the second round.

Confidence in state institutions had been severely eroded during the Portillo Government, and on assuming office in January 2004 Berger launched a widely popular anti-corruption campaign, giving rise to dozens of investigations into alleged illicit activities and corrupt practices by former government officials. However, the new Government was based on an unstable coalition and lacked a congressional majority. As a result, Berger's Government pursued a minimalist agenda and made little progress in addressing social and economic inequalities, as mandated by the peace accords.

The Berger Government also witnessed rising social discontent in response to increases in rates of inflation, unemployment and poverty, as well as to worsening domestic security. The rapid rise in violent crime continued to be a major public—and international—concern, threatening to undermine the development agenda. A special UN Commission to investigate illegal and clandestine groups involved in organized crime (sometimes referred to as 'parallel powers'), the Comisión Internacional contra la Impunidad en Guatemala (CICIG—International Commission against Impunity in Guatemala), was approved by the UN and the Government in December 2006. Despite considerable domestic political opposition, legislation to establish the Commission was overwhelmingly approved by Congress in August 2007, and the new body was formally constituted in September.

THE ADMINISTRATION OF ALVARO COLOM CABALLEROS

More than 40 people were killed in the months preceding the presidential and legislative elections of 9 September 2007, including candidates, their relatives and party activists, in the most violent electoral campaign since the end of the civil war. In the presidential ballot the UNE's Alvaro Colom—contesting his third consecutive presidential election—secured 28.3% of the valid votes cast, followed by Gen. (retd) Otto Fernando Pérez Molina, the candidate of the right-wing Partido Patriota (PP—Patriot Party), with 23.5%, and former prison chief Alejandro Eduardo Giammattei Falla, representing the ruling business-friendly GANA alliance, who received 17.2%. A second round of voting resulted in the election of Colom as President, with 52.8% of the valid votes cast, defeating Pérez Molina.

The global financial crisis impeded progress during much of Colom's centre-left administration, although it was his inability to address effectively a deteriorating security environment, particularly the continued rise in organized crime and associated violence, which defined the majority of his time in office. Crime reached levels among the highest in Latin America, while gangs became increasingly powerful. The Colom administration was unable to prevent the growing presence of

Mexican drugs-trafficking organizations inside Guatemala. Following the Mexican Government's military-led crackdown, the cartels, most notably the Los Zetas group and the Sinaloa cartel, increasingly sought to expand their operations into Guatemala, taking advantage of the state's weak territorial control and institutional deficiencies to secure new drugs-trafficking routes. Colom attempted to challenge the widespread perception that his Government was powerless to tackle the cartels, declaring a two-month 'state of siege' in the northern department of Alta Verapaz, in December 2010 and January 2011, followed by another in May 2011, in response to the discovery of 29 decapitated farm labourers on a ranch in Petén department. In both cases the army was given special powers of arrest to combat cartel activity in the area, although the measures had only a limited impact.

In April 2009 the Government signed the Security and Justice Agreement, committing it to 101 separate measures aimed at improving security and justice by tackling corruption and impunity. However, neither the Government nor CICIG, which had been mandated by the UN to oversee institutional improvements to the judiciary, proved capable of addressing the chronic levels of impunity (estimated at 98% in 2009, according to the UN, with only two out of every 100 crimes going to court—a key factor in the high crime levels).

Meanwhile, in May 2009 the murder of a prominent lawyer, Rodrigo Rosenberg, resulted in one of the most serious political crises since the peace accords. After his death a video recording was released in which Rosenberg, filmed days earlier, accused Colom, and others, of plotting his murder. Rosenberg also made allegations concerning widespread corruption in the Government, and in the Banco de Desarrollo Rural. Street protests ensued to demand the resignation of the President, while others demonstrated in his support. By June Colom was under intense pressure from the press to resign. In January 2010, however, CICIG exonerated Colom, concluding that Rosenberg had orchestrated his own assassination, although the commission was to continue examining other claims made by Rosenberg, including alleged corruption at the Banco de Desarrollo Rural.

The Colom administration was hindered by a lack of a congressional majority as well as by persistent conflict with the powerful private sector (representing the traditional business élite), which was suspicious of the Government's social agenda. Congress rejected the Government's proposed budget for 2010, resulting in the 2009 budget being used again. Much-needed fiscal reforms, to raise tax revenues in order to address pressing social and security issues, were repeatedly resisted by legislators allied to private sector interests throughout Colom's tenure.

Although he presided over continued sluggish growth, Colom was praised by international institutions for maintaining macroeconomic stability during the global downturn and subsequent recovery. The introduction in 2008 of the Mi Familia Progresa social cohesion programme, which predominantly provided housing and food assistance to some 470,000 poor rural citizens, was also viewed as a significant achievement.

THE GOVERNMENT OF OTTO PÉREZ MOLINA

General (retd) Otto Pérez Molina of the PP assumed the presidency in January 2012 after winning the second round of the country's presidential election on 6 November 2011. Pérez Molina secured 53.7% of the vote, compared with 46.3% for Manuel Baldizón of the Libertad Democrática Renovada (LIDER—Renewed Democratic Freedom). Pérez Molina's victory ended a protracted voting process that at times appeared closer to fiction than reality. While Pérez Molina had long been depicted as the clear favourite, he faced a late challenge from Baldizón, a relative newcomer, before eventually emerging as the winner with a comfortable majority. Sandra Torres of the UNE divorced her husband, the outgoing President Colom, to contest the presidency, only for the Constitutional Court to bar her from doing so.

Pérez Molina's victory reflected a number of key factors, including the support of much of the powerful private sector, as well as access to the largest campaign funds. Baldizón, for his part, was ultimately unable to translate strategic alliances with other political parties into actual votes. Above all, Pérez Molina's military background and hard-line approach to security were ultimately well received by voters.

Although there were only isolated bouts of unrest and little evidence of fraud during the election, some concerns were expressed nevertheless. First, both the PP and LIDER appeared to breach campaign-financing laws by exceeding a spending limit stipulated by the Supreme Electoral Tribunal, as well as failing to declare their sources of funding; criminal elements were widely thought to have made substantial contributions to campaign finances in both the presidential and legislative elections. Meanwhile, the numerous alliances that Baldizón formed after the first round of voting emphasized the lack of ideological differences between the main political parties. Parties on the right almost exclusively dominate the political landscape, a situation civil rights groups have described as denying voters genuine choice.

During the first months of Pérez Molina's administration the President prioritized the implementation of his hard-line approach to tackling the increasingly complex security environment—known as Mano Dura (Firm Hand)—under which the military was to be the primary enforcer of domestic security. Upon assuming office he pledged to spend 70% of his time addressing crime, including reducing the murder rate by 40%. In January 2012 Pérez Molina confirmed the appointment of Col Ulises Noé Anzueto Girón, a former member of the country's élite special forces unit, the Kaibiles, as Minister of National Defence. Soldiers were deployed to patrol the streets, particularly in Guatemala City, the most violent area of the country.

However, Pérez Molina was simultaneously at the forefront of the regional push to consider alternative security policies. In April 2012 the Guatemalan President hosted a Central American summit to discuss counter-narcotics strategies in the region, and to debate the possibility of decriminalizing drugs as a means of combating high levels of insecurity. The focus on the decriminalization debate was thought, at least in part, to be an attempt by Pérez Molina to deflect attention from the lack of domestic progress on the underlying causes of drugs-related crime—weak institutions, social inequality and the lack of education.

Pérez Molina defied critics who predicted that, given his military background, he would move to block ongoing investigations into military atrocities committed during the country's civil war. Pérez Molina himself had long been accused by human rights groups of having been involved in abuses during his tenure as head of the country's military intelligence service. The President, however, has appeared to allow CICIG to work unimpeded; on 28 January 2012 a judge ruled that former military dictator Ríos Montt could stand trial for genocide and crimes against humanity (his immunity from prosecution having expired with the inauguration of the new Congress). Although Pérez Molina was believed privately to be against such action, he was also thought likely to be sensitive to international pressure to co-operate with efforts to bring those responsible for civil war atrocities to justice. Ríos Montt persistently pleaded his innocence during the genocide trial that commenced in March 2013 after a series of delays. The former dictator was accused of ordering the massacre of over 1,700 members of the indigenous Ixil Maya people in 1982–83. From the outset, the trial was tense and at times controversial. Court proceedings were temporarily suspended on 19 April over a dispute between two judges regarding who should preside over the case, but were resumed two weeks later following the intervention of Attorney-General Claudia Paz y Paz. Although Ríos Montt was convicted (by three votes to two) on 20 May, the verdict was almost immediately annulled by the Constitutional Court. The ruling followed a 10-day examination of the trial in response to an appeal by Ríos Montt's defence team (one of four separate appeals presented), which argued that proceedings after 19 April 2013—when the dispute broke out over which judge should preside over the case—should be disregarded. Despite its annulment of the verdict, however, according to the judgment of the Constitutional Court, the proceedings of the trial itself, including any evidence submitted before 19 April, remained valid. Indeed, the majority of the

proceedings—including the entirety of the prosecution's arguments and witness statements—would not have to be repeated, thus facilitating any future legal process. By mid-2014 the retrial, made necessary by the annulment decision, had not been scheduled, with court officials stating publicly that it was unlikely to resume until the start of 2015 at the earliest, owing to case backlogs.

PROSPECTS FOR THE FUTURE

Despite significant international support for the peace process, progress in Guatemala's development has been disappointing. The country has advanced in some areas (notably social spending and the greater participation of indigenous groups in the political debate), but its problems are still immense. Guatemala's population and economy are the largest in Central America, yet growth rates have remained sluggish. The country has also suffered from the region's lowest public investment in social services and worst tax collection base from which to support these investments. Massive inequality in incomes, as well as in access to health care and education, reflect the urban/rural, non-indigenous/indigenous divide. The lack of available economic alternatives for the poor majority has resulted in increased emigration and dependence on remittances from Guatemalans working abroad. Organized crime and associated violence, as well as endemic cross-sector corruption, have continued to hamper institution-building and economic development. Furthermore, a strongly polarized political system has prevented the Government from raising taxes to a level necessary to address many of the country's most pressing problems.

Pérez Molina's ability to implement his policy agenda on key issues beyond the realm of security has proven limited thus far, since the PP, despite being the largest grouping in Congress, lacks the majority required to pass legislation. This was clearly demonstrated by the failure of Congress to approve the 2014 national budget in November 2013, which has placed a strain on government efforts to increase spending on sectors such as education. Although Pérez Molina has called for Congress to approve the additional supplements to the budget, his party's lack of legislative majority is hindering the adoption of critical bills. Moreover, the more social democratic UNE, which is the second largest grouping in Congress, has different legislative priorities from those of the PP. In particular, the UNE continues to favour poverty reduction and social spending over security. Serious questions also persist over whether Pérez Molina seeks anything beyond nominal fiscal reform, particularly as the private sector—from which he derives much of his support—remains largely opposed to such reform.

International institutions have praised Guatemala in recent years for maintaining broad levels of macroeconomic stability; Colom sought to avoid risking fiscal instability and provoking higher inflation by spending within the country's means. Pérez Molina has continued to implement a broadly business-friendly agenda characterized by cautious fiscal and monetary policies. However, the country remains highly vulnerable to external shocks, largely because of its over-dependence on the US economy and a lack of diversity in exports. Furthermore, inflation has increased beyond target rates.

Pérez Molina's presidency has also been characterized by a substantial increase in social unrest as his Government has sought to expand the extractive sector. The administration's efforts to develop the nascent sector were principally aimed at diversifying the economy and boosting the state's woefully low levels of income. The Government hoped to take advantage of large reserves of gold, nickel, zinc, iron and copper to develop the faltering mining sector, which—despite the considerable mineral potential—contributed only an estimated 2.2% of gross domestic product in 2012. Increasingly well-organized anti-mining activism, however, is likely to have a significant negative effect on the Government's attempts to develop the extractive sector. Mining revenue reportedly declined substantially in 2012, partly owing to growing community activism. The situation was exacerbated by the authorities' reliance on force to curb the anti-mining movement, culminating in a series of violent incidents at a number of mines. In May 2013 the Government declared a state of emergency in four south-eastern towns following of the outbreak of unrest at the Escobal silver mine, located near the town of San Rafael Las Flores. It was reported that, as a result of the violent unrest, a number of protesters were injured, one police officer was killed and another 23 police officers were temporarily kidnapped by local villagers. Earlier that year, on 12 January, two private security personnel had been killed and seven other people injured during violent protests by local residents at the Escobal mine. In March the UN Office of the High Commissioner for Human Rights publicly raised its concerns about mining-related violence in Guatemala.

There was also an increase in social unrest as a result of growing community anger over perceived high electricity prices and the poor quality of utilities services. Tensions with indigenous communities were further compounded by the Government's reliance on the armed forces to deal with protests. On 4 October 2012 at least six indigenous activists were killed in clashes with the security forces on the Pan-American Highway in Totonicapán department during a demonstration over energy prices and unpopular proposed education reforms. In addition, seven soldiers and 30 civilians were injured in the fighting. The Government claimed that the troops that had been dispatched to reinforce the anti-riot police had come under attack from the indigenous activists. On 30 October security forces clashed with members of a rural indigenous community in the north-western department of San Marcos. The villagers had earlier taken eight people hostage to demand the release of a community leader who had been arrested over his involvement in protests against high electricity prices in September. Pérez Molina was criticized for appearing to favour a strong-armed approach to social problems rather than tackling their underlying causes, such as poverty and lack of education.

By mid-2014 the effectiveness of Pérez Molina's hard-line security strategy—the reason that many people had voted for him in 2011—was, for the first time, beginning to be widely questioned. A study released in March by the National Economic Investigations Centre (Centro de Investigaciones Económicas Nacionales—CIEN), found that there were 7,553 recorded cases of extortion in 2013, an increase from 6,513 in 2012. A total of 507 kidnappings were reported in 2013 compared with 642 in 2012, while 5,253 homicides were reported in 2013 compared with 5,155 in 2012. The Government's military-led approach, involving the militarization of policing and the deployment of the armed forces alongside the police to tackle crime, has largely failed to address the underlying causes of insecurity. These include social inequalities, the widespread availability of weapons and chronic institutional deficiencies. Mexican drug cartels such as Los Zetas had by mid-2013 developed a significant presence and a growing influence as they sought to establish new trafficking routes, exacerbating the existing insecurity generated by local street gangs.

By mid-2014 Pérez Molina was also facing growing pressure regarding his commitment to democracy, having long been criticized in this respect by civil rights groups, given his alleged role in civil war abuses. On 15 April he publicly called for a 'national debate' on the contentious issue of re-election for government ministers. Under current constitutional arrangements, government ministers are elected for a period of four years and cannot be re-elected. Although Pérez Molina stopped short of calling for a referendum on the issue, his comments are likely to add to growing concerns over the erosion of democracy under his leadership. Pérez Molina has prompted criticism from civil society groups owing to the increased influence of the military over civil policing since he came to power, as well as a continuing dispute between his government and daily newspaper *Siglo Veintiuno*. With two years of his presidency to go, Pérez Molina is unlikely to attempt to conduct a referendum on ministerial re-election or to introduce a constitutional reform bill on the issue. He lacks the legislative majority to pass a constitutional reform, while the majority of the population is unlikely to support any formal changes to ministerial terms, given the country's long and relatively recent history of dictatorship.

Despite strict constitutional limits on ministerial re-election, a range of other factors continue to undermine the country's democracy more broadly. The military continues to wield disproportionate influence over the Government through both official and unofficial channels, while the judiciary is subject to significant pressure from criminal and business interests. In addition, unions, civil society groups and the media face harassment from state security forces.

Pérez Molina has also faced criticism regarding his failure publicly to support Attorney-General Claudia Paz y Paz, who was ousted by the Constitutional Court in May 2014. The Constitutional Court on 6 February had upheld a ruling that Paz y Paz should resign in May, seven months before her four-year term was due to end in December. On 11 February Congress formed a commission to select a replacement for Paz y Paz. The decision to uphold the ruling to remove Paz y Paz (who had led the prosecution of Ríos Montt on charges of genocide) highlights the judiciary's lack of independence. The lawyer who brought the original case, on which the Constitutional Court ruled, to remove Paz y Paz ahead of the end of her tenure is known to have strong links to Ríos Montt. The development also highlights broader impunity issues. Certain sections of society that benefit from the climate of pervasive impunity have impeded the efforts of the Attorney-General and CICIG to curb high-level corruption. Corrupt politicians, members of the military and the judiciary have used their influence to resist the commission's attempts to address impunity or investigate human rights abuses from the civil war.

Pérez Molina's limited success in social and security issues, in particular, has resulted in a sharp reduction in approval ratings for his Government; in a January 2014 *Prensa Libre* newspaper poll he received a 44% rating, compared with 56% in the same poll in January 2013 and 1% above that of Colom during the same period in his presidency. Although Guatemala is still two years away from its next presidential election, a number of political figures are emerging as likely contenders. Manuel Baldizón of LIDER, who narrowly lost to Pérez Molina in the second round of the 2011 presidential election and is widely considered likely to run again, is rated by all recent opinion polls as the clear front-runner. While he has strong economic credentials, he was linked during the 2011 election period to receiving illicit party funds from drugs-trafficking. At the same time, Sandra Torres of the UNE party is likely to remain a powerful figure in opposition, despite having been barred from contesting the presidency in 2011. As a prominent member of the UNE, she is likely to consider appealing again to the courts in an attempt to seek the presidency in 2016.

Economy

DANIEL SACHS

INTRODUCTION

Despite being the largest economy in Central America in terms of population and output, Guatemala has one of the lowest levels of human development in the region. In 2013 gross domestic product (GDP) per capita was estimated by the World Bank to be just US $3,478, while the country was ranked 133rd out of 187 in the 2013 UN Human Development Index, the second lowest in Latin America (after Haiti). Social indicators are poor: according to official UN figures, in 2012 Guatemala had an adult literacy rate of 78.3%, life expectancy of 71.7 years and an under-five mortality rate of 32 per 1,000 live births. Despite some economic growth in the 1990s, Guatemala's economic development has been severely constrained by over-dependence on the agricultural sector (which, in 2013, contributed an estimated 11.0% of real GDP, according to preliminary figures) and by primary exports, low levels of human capital and one of the most unequal wealth distributions in the world—the richest 20% of the population accounted for 51% of the country's overall consumption in 2011. According to the World Food Programme, some 49.8% of children under five years of age were chronically malnourished in 2012, the fourth highest malnutrition rate in the world and the highest in the region. In addition, Guatemala is one of the 36 countries that account for 90% of all global stunting and chronic under-nutrition in indigenous areas stood at 69.5% in that year.

OVERALL ECONOMIC PERFORMANCE

Economic growth declined in the late 1970s after two decades of expansion, and the economy stagnated in the 1980s as war and violence escalated in Guatemala and the rest of Central America. In 1980–90 annual growth in real quetzales averaged 0.9%, while per head GDP decreased at an average annual rate of 0.8%, in real terms. From 1990 better international conditions and a more stable domestic environment contributed to greater economic expansion. Average annual growth in real quetzales in 1990–2006 was 3.6%, reaching its peak in 1998 at 5.0%, while GDP per head grew at an average annual rate of 1.4% during the same period. In 2007 and 2008 strong growth rates of 5.7% and 4.3%, respectively, were recorded. However, the country was badly affected by the global economic downturn in 2008–09 and by its over-dependence on the US economy. Growth declined in 2009 to 0.6% as export demand and foreign investment slowed amid the global recession. However, the economy has since recovered, registering GDP growth of 2.2%, 3.8% and 3.0% in 2010, 2011 and 2012, respectively. The slight deceleration in 2012 was a result of lower levels of consumption and exports as the US economy lost some momentum, amid increasing risks and continued crisis in the eurozone. The economy grew by an estimated 3.5% in 2013, as a result of economic recovery in the eurozone and the USA.

From 1990 growth was stimulated by a sharp rise in infrastructure development and by an increase in non-traditional exports, which in 1990 outperformed the principal traditional export, coffee. Nevertheless, Guatemala continues to show a large trade deficit, which increased from US $521m. in 1991 to $6,212m. in 2011 and further to $7,015m. in 2012, according to the Banco de Guatemala. The same source reported a trade deficit of $7,484m. in 2013. A weak manufacturing base and the failure to diversify its export base as rapidly as other Central American countries are partly responsible for the growing dependence of the Guatemalan economy.

According to UNICEF, 13.5% of the total population lived below the international poverty line of US $1.25 per day in 2011. Among indigenous groups, which constitute some 38% of the population, the rate living in poverty was thought to be much higher, at an estimated 73%, with approximately 28% living in extreme poverty. It is estimated that sustained annual GDP growth of at least 6% is required to address the problem of poverty. The country remains highly reliant on remittances, particularly from Guatemalans living in the USA, and is the leading recipient of remittances in Central America. From 1996 remittances increased annually, becoming Guatemala's second largest hard currency inflow after commodity exports. In 2007 remittances reached a record $4,314.7m. (more than seven times higher than in 2001), equivalent to 87% of the total exports of goods. Remittances decreased to $3,910m. in 2009 from $4,310m. in 2008, according to the central bank, although levels recovered somewhat in 2010 to reach $4,130m. According to the Banco de Guatemala, the country received $4,370m. in remittances in 2011 and $4,782m. in 2012. Remittances continued to rise, to $5,105m., in 2013, owing to economic recovery in the USA (the main source of remittances).

AGRICULTURE

Coffee, bananas, sugar and cardamom are the major agricultural exports; however, fluctuating international prices from the 1990s had an adverse effect on primary exports until the mid-2000s. Cardamom prices, for example, declined by more than 50% between 2002 and 2005, leading to a 25% reduction in export earnings from this product during this period. The situation reversed between 2006 and 2008, when exports of cardamom, bananas and coffee increased rapidly: exports of bananas grew by 47% during this period, while those of cardamom grew by 149% and coffee by 39%. Other exported agricultural products include vegetables, plants (including seeds and flowers) and fish.

Although the suspension of the International Coffee Organization quota system in 1989 was initially beneficial to Guatemala, it severely affected coffee exports in the early 1990s. There was some recovery during the mid-1990s, although Hurricane Mitch, which struck Central America in 1998, contributed to a decline in coffee exports in that year. Revenue from coffee exports decreased from US $586.5m. in 1998 to $261.8m. in 2002, partly as a result of low coffee prices. Small-scale producers, representing around 100,000 families and contributing 30% of overall national production, were particularly badly affected. Coffee prices recuperated in 2004 and exports earned $327.8m. in that year. However, in recent years the value of coffee exports has fallen, as a result of decreasing grain prices. According to the Banco de Guatemala, revenue from coffee exports declined from an impressive $1,174.2m. in 2011 to $958.1m. in 2012. Coffee exports were recorded by the same source at $714.5m. in 2013, equivalent to 7.1% of total exports.

The question of how best to sustain international coffee prices preoccupied all exporters following the collapse of the International Coffee Agreement. The Asociación Nacional del Café (Anacafé) adopted a 'hedged' loan programme, under which producers received financial support by selling coffee beans at or above a set minimum price, which would then cover the loan in the event of depressed market conditions. In 2001, with prices at an all-time low, Guatemala joined an agreement negotiated by Mexico, Colombia and the Central American nations to withhold 5% of their lowest quality beans from export and put them to other uses, for example, fertilizer or fuel for industry. The plan coincided with an international scheme to withhold 20% of the export goods that had failed to prevent the plunge in coffee prices. Meanwhile, some of the nation's growers held internet auctions of quality beans.

From the 1980s there was a substantial decline in the area planted with cotton, a trend accelerated by the guerrilla war and high production costs, compounded by competition from other regions and from a rise in the production of synthetic fibres. Conversely, the area planted with sugar cane expanded, and production of sugar rose slowly. Sugar exports in 1999 were worth US $192.1m., compared with $316.6m. in the previous year. Exports fluctuated thereafter, declining to $188.0m. in 2004, then recovering steadily to reach $507.7m. in 2009. Sugar cane production was badly affected by unfavourable weather conditions in 2010, although it gradually recovered over the following two years, with exports rising to $803.0m. in 2012, according to the Banco de Guatemala.

According to the same source, revenue from sugar exports amounted to $941.9m. in 2013.

Central bank data showed that banana export revenues increased to a high of US $414.6m. in 2009 before decreasing to $353.3m. in 2010. Banana exports rebounded strongly in 2011, as a result of more favourable weather conditions, and, according to the Banco de Guatemala, exports for that year reached $475.3m. and rose further, to $499.9m., in 2012. Revenue from banana exports rose to $601.5m. in 2013.

MINING AND POWER

The mining sector remains small, contributing only an estimated 1.9% of GDP in 2013, according to preliminary central bank figures. The largest operation is a copper mine in Alta Verapaz department, which began production in 1975, but has an unrealized potential of 150,000 metric tons per year. Lead and zinc output have decreased drastically and a nickel-mining project was suspended in 1980, after only three years of production, owing to low world prices and high production costs. Antimony and tungsten are mined and Guatemala has exploitable reserves of sulphur and marble. In 1996 the Government began attempts to attract foreign investment to the mining sector. Australia's Broken Hill Proprietary (BHP) Co was granted a concession to explore for copper, lead, zinc and silver in Quiché and Alta Verapaz in 1996. As in other sectors, mining production has also experienced an erratic trend in recent years. In 2005 it decreased by 1.3%, before increasing by a combined 31% in 2006 and 2007, due to a significant expansion in the output of sand and higher commodity prices. Owing to lower demand resulting from the global downturn, in 2009 mineral extraction accounted for 1.5% of GDP, compared with approximately 1.8% of GDP in 2008. The US Geological Survey reported that the value of mineral production (extraction only) in Guatemala decreased to US $560m. in 2009 from about $711m. in 2008. Although central bank data showed a significant rebound over the next two years, owing to higher commodity prices—with revenue from the sector totalling $523.7m. in 2010 and $941.6m. in 2011—exports declined by 34.9% in 2012 (to $612.9m.).

Mining revenues have been significantly disrupted in recent years, as a result of community activism. Indigenous communities have opposed extractives projects on environmental and cultural grounds, and have pursued legal and direct action measures, many of which have led to violence and operational disruption. The Government has also generated considerable uncertainty for investors in the mining sector. In July 2013 an appeals court ordered the suspension of US-based Tahoe Resources' Escobal silver mine's exploitation licence, following legal claims by local communities that the project violated their constitutional rights. The revocation of its exploitation licence followed serious social unrest at the Escobal mine. In the most recent incident in May, the Government declared a state of emergency in a number of municipalities surrounding the mine, after unrest in which a number of protesters were injured, one policeman was killed and another 20 were temporarily abducted by the local community. The court's decision generated legal concerns among existing mining investors. Extractives companies already operating in the country that have faced social unrest at their mines in the past are likely to be concerned by the legal precedent set by the court ruling and by the prospect of other communities seeking similar legal action.

The main reserves of petroleum are found in the north of the country, across the border from Mexico's south-eastern Tabasco production area, in Petén department. In January 2000 proven reserves totalled 526m. barrels, while potential reserves were believed to be 800m.–1,000m. barrels. Earnings from exports increased during the 1990s, reaching some 25,000 barrels per day (b/d) in 1997, worth US $98.7m. (equivalent to 4.2% of total export earnings). Greater political stability following the signing of the final peace accord in December 1996 raised hopes that more foreign petroleum companies could be encouraged to become active in Guatemala. Plans for the petroleum sector were, however, confounded by the decline in oil prices in 1998 (from $14.4 to $6.8 per barrel) and the withdrawal of foreign investors. Subsequently, exports increased as global prices rose dramatically. As a result, exports of petroleum increased steadily in value, from $58.3m. in 1998 to $249m. in 2007 and to $374m. in 2008 (4.8% of the total value of exports). Nevertheless, petroleum exports decreased in 2009 to $179m. as a result of lower demand during the global downturn. According to the central bank, petroleum exports recovered in 2010 to reach $247m. and further to $335m. in 2011 as the improvement in global economic conditions precipitated higher demand. Although exports declined to $292m. in 2012, it was hoped that the launch of a government-backed licensing round in February 2013 would significantly boost the sector in the coming years. The round focused on the northern jungle region of Petén where the majority of deposits are believed to be located. Guatemala's current petroleum production averages 14,000 b/d, 90% of which comes from the North and South Petén basins. The energy sector has experienced significant transformations in recent years and has been affected by government policy reversals. The privatization of the energy sector was a major objective of the Government of Alvaro Enrique Arzú Irigoyen (1996–2000): in July 1998 some 80% of the capital of the state-owned Empresa Eléctrica de Guatemala, SA, was sold to foreign investors for $520m., and in December the Instituto Nacional de Electrificación was sold for $100m. However, the Government of Alfonso Antonio Portillo Cabrera (2000–04) did much to reverse the privatization policy. The Chixoy watershed is the country's main source of hydroelectric power, and the Portillo Government promoted the creation of a new hydroelectric dam in Quiché department. In May 2007 the communities affected voted against the Xacbal dam's construction, although the Government successfully appealed against the decision (and the dam commenced operations in 2010). In 2008 the Government of Alvaro Colom Caballeros (2008–12) launched an ambitious plan to expand hydroelectric production and reduce the country's dependence on oil. The Government hoped to attract foreign investment to build five new hydroelectric plants and several carbon-based electric generating plants before 2014. The contribution of hydroelectric power to total power output decreased from 57.6% of electricity generation in 1997 to 23.3% in 2009 (while petroleum provided 34.5% in the latter year). Meanwhile, in 2009 Guatemala and Mexico linked their electricity grids. The programme was subsequently expanded to incorporate the creation of an integrated system to connect Central American electricity grids (the Sistema de Interconexión Eléctrica de los Países de América Central—SIEPAC), although progress was slow. Guatemala's electricity production totalled 8,146m. kWh in 2011.

MANUFACTURING

As in the rest of Central America, the manufacturing sector in Guatemala experienced rapid expansion in the 1960s and 1970s, under the stimulus of the Central America Common Market and sustained foreign investment. In the 1980s manufacturing output was adversely affected by the contraction in demand from other Central American countries as a result of the civil wars in the region and a shortage of domestic credit. Real manufacturing output decreased at an average annual rate of 1.7% during 1980–86. Some recovery was experienced during 1987–2001, but the manufacturing sector continued to expand at a slower rate than the rest of the economy (by 2.5% per year as opposed to 3.9% for the economy as a whole). According to the central bank, the total value of the country's manufacturing shipments was valued at an estimated US $3,120m. in 2013, compared with $3,147m. in 2012.

The clothing assembly, or *maquila*, plants contributed to an increase in non-traditional exports from the late 1980s. The sector's dynamism depended considerably on special government incentives to investors and low wages for a non-unionized labour force. The *maquila* sector expanded rapidly throughout the 1990s and into 2000. Following a period of contraction in 2001, apparel exports to the USA (most of which came from *maquilas*) resumed their growth and Guatemala gained market share in the USA. By the mid-2000s, however, increasing Chinese competition led to a reversal of this trend, as in the rest of Central America and Mexico. The approval of the Dominican

Republic-Central American Free Trade Agreement (CAFTA-DR), which entered into force in July 2006, did little to halt this downward trend: between 2007 and 2008 Guatemalan exports of textiles and apparel to the USA decreased by 17% and the market share in 2008 was just 1.5%, compared with 2.4% in 2004. The downward trend was also compounded by the global economic downturn. According to Central America Data, 78.1% of textile exports were purchased by the USA in 2010, while 17% were exported to countries within Central America. According to the Banco de Guatemala, exports of articles of clothing accounted for 11.7% of total export revenue in 2011, 11.9% in 2012 and 12.5% in 2013. The construction sector underwent a period of rapid expansion during the 1990s, although there were suspicions that the sector was partly funded by money raised from the illegal drugs trade. However, since then the sector's performance has been rather erratic. In 2002–04 construction GDP contracted dramatically. After a recuperation in 2005–07 (when construction grew at an average annual rate of 9.8%), the sector again experienced a contraction, of 3.6%, in 2008. The lack of state resources to pay contractors resulted in many public works projects stalling; in addition, with fewer houses being built, the private sector contracted by 12.2% in 2010, according to the Economic Commission for Latin America and the Caribbean. Construction GDP declined by an estimated 11.5% overall in 2010. The industry recovered somewhat in 2011, expanding by an estimated 1.6%, before rebounding strongly, to achieve growth of 7.7%, in 2012, according to official statistics. The construction sector grew by 0.6% in 2013. This recovery was largely owing to increased optimism in the housing market and a return of confidence following the economic downturn of 2009. In 2012 some 348,395 people were directly employed by the construction sector (5.8% of the total employed labour force) and it contributed an estimated 4.1% of that year's GDP.

TRANSPORT AND COMMUNICATIONS

The road system has experienced a significant modernization since 1990 (although Hurricane Mitch destroyed 60% of the road network and 98 bridges in 1998), with an increase in kilometres of paved roads of 5% per year during 1990–2005. According to Jane's Information Group (JIG), Guatemala possessed a road network of 14,118 km in 2010, unevenly distributed within the country, of which just over 6,500 km was paved (including 140 km of highways). JIG also noted that high-quality roads were restricted to the area around Guatemala City, intercity routes, the Pan-American Highway and the Inter-Ocean Highway, which connects the Atlantic and Pacific coasts. The Guatemalan section of the Pan-American Highway is 518.7 km long and totally asphalted. There are several airports, the main international airport being La Aurora, near Guatemala City.

Guatemala had 885 km of rail lines in 2007. The Arzú Government placed much emphasis on the modernization of the country's infrastructure, which included the sale of the Ferrocarriles de Guatemala rail network in 1997 and the sale of a 50-year concession of the railways to the Railroad Development Corporation (USA) in 1998. The Portillo Government also attempted to improve Guatemala's infrastructure, announcing several proposals in 2002, including plans to expand La Aurora airport and to construct a new international airport on the outskirts of Guatemala City. The modernization of La Aurora finally began in early 2006, delayed by conflicts between national and local government. However, the plans to build a new international airport for the capital city did not come to fruition.

In 1998 some 95% of the state telecommunications company, Empresa Guatemalteca de Telecomunicaciones (Guatel), was sold for US $700m. to a group of mostly domestic investors and the Mexican operator Teléfonos de México (Telmex). While the telecommunications service in the country has improved dramatically, with the number of main telephone lines per 100 people increasing from 2.9 in 1995 to 12 in 2013, and the number of mobile cellular subscribers per 100 people rising from just 0.3 in 1995 to 137 in 2013, it nevertheless remains inadequate.

In July 2013 the Guatemalan Government finally announced concrete plans for the creation of a dry canal. The project involved the construction of a 372-km dry canal with two ports on the Atlantic and Pacific coasts, five oil and gas pipelines, two rail lines, industrial parks along the length of the corridor and a highway. The two ports were to have the capacity to unload six vessels simultaneously and receive vessels of up to 22,000 20-foot equivalent units.

The project was being developed by Odepal Internacional, which holds 5% of Holding Corredor Interoceánico de Guatemala, the holding company that will own and build the project. The remaining 95% of the holding company is owned by locally constituted companies that will be responsible for awarding the private concessions for the land, on which the project will be built. While the land required for the project was believed to have been secured by the developers at mid-2014, project construction had not commenced, with a clear date for the commencement of works unknown.

INVESTMENT AND FINANCE

Following the transfer of power to the civilian Government of President Vinicio Cerezo in 1986, a programme of austerity measures and financial reform was implemented. As a result, the economy began to show signs of revival after several years of decline. However, these positive developments were adversely affected by the decrease in coffee prices in the late 1980s and the decline in international reserves. A single exchange rate was introduced to deal with the latter in February 1989, followed in November by the flotation of the Guatemalan currency unit, the quetzal. Inflationary pressures increased in the economy as the quetzal was devalued several times, and a series of austerity measures was introduced. Although the general value of the quetzal stabilized, the rate of inflation continued to rise. The Government of Jorge Serrano Elías (1991–93) succeeded in stabilizing the currency and in increasing international reserves. A more stable economy and better economic conditions resulted in higher rates of investment. Worsening external conditions, together with several natural disasters, resulted in a deterioration in investment levels during 2001–04, when total real gross capital formation decreased. However, during 2005–07 gross capital formation recovered, increasing at an average annual rate of 9.1%, owing to the improvement in global conditions and the reconstruction effort following Hurricane Stan (in October 2005). The rate of inflation averaged 7.0% annually in 1998–2005. Strict monetary policy in 2006 led to a significant reduction of the annual rate of inflation, to 5.8%, but high international oil and food prices resulted in an acceleration of inflation in 2007 and 2008, to 8.7% and 9.4%, respectively. However, during 2009 the recessionary pressures had a profound impact on the inflation rate, which contracted to 1.9%, according to the World Bank. The central bank reported that, with the economic recovery, the rate of inflation had increased to 6.2% in 2011. Inflation declined to an estimated 3.4% in 2012, below the Government's target inflation limit of 4.0%. It rose to an estimated 4.4% in 2013 following accelerating GDP growth, although it remained likely that interest rates would be raised by the central bank to lower inflation.

With the signing of the final peace accord in December 1996, Guatemala was able to attract international aid for reconstruction. A sum of around US $1,900m. in grants and loans was finally agreed. The Inter-American Development Bank (IDB) promised $800m., the World Bank $400m. and the European Union (EU) $250m. The Government committed itself to raising the shortfall of the estimated $2,500m. needed to implement the peace accords by raising tax revenues to 50% above the 1995 levels by 2000. However, failure to meet this commitment prompted increasing pressure on the Government from international organizations; the EU gave an explicit warning in June 2001. Guatemala's tax revenues slowly increased from that year onwards (see Public Revenue).

In an attempt to reduce the fragility of the banking sector, in mid-2001 the Guatemalan Monetary Board initiated a thorough review of the banking system. As a result, the courts were requested to liquidate the three banks that had been subjected to state intervention earlier in the year (following a corruption scandal), as well as two finance companies. Further reforms were enabled in that year when Congreso (Congress) approved four bills creating a legislative framework through which the central bank would be able to exercise more effective control over the banking sector. The new legislation also allowed for the supervision of offshore banks, for which previous banking laws had made no provision. The World Bank granted Guatemala two US \$155m. loans to strengthen the newly created framework. In addition, a licensing system was introduced. Despite all these efforts, the country experienced a new scandal in October 2006, when the central bank closed Banco del Café, the country's fourth largest bank. Moreover, in January 2007 Banco de Comercio was suspended, confirming the weakness of the Guatemalan banking sector.

FOREIGN TRADE AND THE BALANCE OF PAYMENTS

Central bank data showed that in 2013 traditional primary exports (sugar, coffee and bananas) accounted for approximately 22.5% of total exports, while textiles alone represented 12.7%. Between 2002 and 2008 growth in exports lagged behind growth in imports, and, according to UN figures, the trade deficit was equivalent to an estimated 11.3% of GDP in 2010. However, largely owing to remittances from citizens working abroad, the deficit on the current account of the balance of payments remained significantly lower as a proportion of GDP. With an increase of 20.9% in the trade deficit in 2011, the balance of payments current account deficit edged up, from 3.1% of GDP in 2011 to 3.6% in 2012. In 2013, according to the IMF, the current account deficit stood at US \$1,514.4m. According to the Banco de Guatemala, the primary export destinations in 2013 were the USA (accounting for 37.7% of the total), El Salvador, Honduras, Nicaragua, Mexico and the eurozone. In terms of imports, in 2013 the principal source of imports (37.0%) was the USA; other major suppliers were Mexico and the People's Republic of China.

At the end of the 1990s imports from Mexico far exceeded exports in terms of value. In April 2000 El Salvador, Guatemala and Honduras (the so-called CA-3 countries) signed a free trade agreement with Mexico, which promised greater access to the Mexican market for Guatemala, with increased bilateral trade in the future. The agreement became operational in March 2001. As predicted, however, the agreement initially benefited the Mexican economy to the detriment of Guatemala, as in 2001 Guatemalan exports to Mexico decreased by about one-third, while Mexican exports to Guatemala increased. By 2003, however, bilateral trade increased to the benefit of both countries. In 2002 Guatemala also agreed with Costa Rica, El Salvador, Honduras and Nicaragua to eliminate all regional trade barriers. Negotiations on the establishment of a Central American Free Trade Agreement with the USA were concluded in late 2003; the agreement (renamed the CAFTA-DR following the inclusion of the Dominican Republic in negotiations in 2004) was ratified by Congress in March 2005 and entered into force in July 2006. CAFTA-DR was intended to boost manufacturing exports to the USA, but the first years proved disappointing. In May 2004 President Oscar Berger Perdomo, together with the Presidents of El Salvador, Honduras and Nicaragua, signed an agreement creating a Central American customs union. A free trade agreement between Guatemala and Taiwan came into effect in early 2006. Negotiations between Central America and the EU regarding an association agreement were concluded in May 2010, while free trade discussions with Canada have been ongoing since 2001. A further free trade agreement between the countries of Central America and Mexico entered into force in September 2013.

In May 2001 the Central American countries, including Guatemala, reached an agreement with Mexico, called the Puebla-Panamá Plan (restyled the Proyecto de Integración y Desarrollo de Mesoamérica in 2008), to establish a series of joint transport, industry and tourism projects intended to integrate the region. In December Guatemala and Mexico agreed that they would link their electricity grids under the terms of the Plan, as part of its initiative on energy integration. Officials from the two nations agreed to co-operate on a project to construct an 80-km power line that would link a substation in Tapachula, Mexico, with a Guatemalan substation situated in Los Brillantes; the cost would be an estimated US \$30m. The 400-kV interconnection line was commissioned in April 2009, with an estimated transmission capacity of 200 MW from Mexico to Guatemala and 70 MW in the opposite direction. In 2006 construction began on SIEPAC via a transmission line that would span 1,830 km (281 km in Guatemala), linking 15 substations in Costa Rica, El Salvador, Guatemala, Honduras, Nicaragua and Panama. The IDB was partially financing the 230-kV project, with loans amounting to \$170m. towards the estimated total cost of \$385m. SIEPAC was completed in March 2014.

PUBLIC REVENUE

In 1998, as part of the socio-economic component of the peace accords, President Arzú proposed a Fiscal Pact, envisaged as a multi-sectoral, long-term consensus between the principal political, economic and social bodies of Guatemala over the future tax regime and fiscal policies. To this end, a Fiscal Pact Preparatory Committee (CPPF) was established to organize a national debate on tax policy. The CPPF's report, presented in late 1999, argued that increasing tax collection was the only means for Guatemala to meet peace accord goals and advance infrastructure development plans; the report contained 66 recommendations to be implemented by 2004. Its proposals included the establishment of mechanisms to audit the Superintendency for Tax Administration, and the creation of a body to curb tax evasion and strengthen the judiciary's capacity to process cases of tax evasion and fraud.

The Government of President Portillo also cited the signing of the Fiscal Pact to be one of its priorities, and in 2001 controversially raised the rate of value-added tax (VAT) to this end. In early 2003 Portillo implemented by decree further unpopular tax rises on fuel, wheat and a number of other items. In 2007 newly elected President Colom appointed as an active proponent of tax reform, Juan Alberto Fuentes, as Minister of Finance, and negotiations for further tax expansion began. Nevertheless, deteriorating economic conditions resulted in a reduction of tax revenues in 2008 and 2009. Low income from tax revenue resulted in increased levels of public debt, which rose from 5.6% of GDP in 2003 to 24.1% in 2011. Moreover, attempts to introduce fiscal reforms that would raise the Government's tax receipts were repeatedly opposed by private sector interests in Congress. After lengthy negotiation, Congress finally approved the tax reforms in February 2012. While the long-awaited reforms principally comprised new income tax legislation, the package also included a motor vehicle registration tax, a national customs law, amendments to the VAT law and to the land vehicle, vessel and aircraft circulation tax law, and adjustments to the law on revenue stamps and stamped paper to bring it in line with VAT provisions on the purchase of property. In addition, a new anti-evasion law was also approved to strengthen tax administration. Following the eventual implementation of the fiscal reforms in 2012, tax revenue reached 12.3% of GDP in 2013 (compared with 10.8% in 2012).

OUTLOOK

Guatemala encountered significant obstacles in adapting to globalization and achieving economic recovery after the civil war, despite an expansion of non-traditional exports and the increasing role of remittances as a source of income. The Portillo administration implemented a number of neo-liberal reforms, but corruption and institutional weakness were endemic. Furthermore, in 2003 a report by the Consultative Group of donor countries was highly critical of the Government's failure to implement the terms of the peace accords. The election of Berger of the centre-right Gran Alianza Nacional (GANA—Great National Alliance) to the presidency in November of that year gave rise to optimism that the change of government would prompt inflows of much-needed foreign investment; Berger's determination to address corruption at all levels of public office was welcomed by investors, as was the new Cabinet, largely comprising businessmen. However, the performance of the Berger administration in its four years of government was disappointing. GANA did not obtain a majority in Congress, thus impeding attempts to implement promised economic reforms, while tax reforms failed to increase revenues to the required level.

Colom of the Unidad Nacional de la Esperanza, who was elected to the presidency in November 2007, had pledged to introduce more progressive reforms, particularly in the tax system and social spending. Yet, the Colom administration had to contend with growing internal and external challenges. Persistent problems with institutionalized corruption and violent crime diminished the Government's ability to promote its economic agenda. Furthermore, continued opposition from Congress and the private sector to much-needed fiscal reform prevented the Government from raising the revenues required to meet its ambitious social policy objectives. In terms of external pressures, the global financial crisis created additional problems for the country, with a decline in revenue from exports and remittances precipitating a reduction in economic growth and an increase in poverty, from which it did not begin to recover until 2010.

During the first two and a half years of his tenure, President Pérez Molina proved successful in terms of adhering to the prudent fiscal policies of his predecessor that had produced broad macroeconomic stability. Nevertheless, he was largely unable to address the country's long-standing and deep-rooted underlying economic problems of poverty and crime, the major factors inhibiting higher levels of growth and foreign investment. With the failure to adopt meaningful fiscal reform, he was unable to increase state resources to requisite levels to address crime and poverty levels. While the moderate reforms that were introduced in 2012 were welcome, they remained insufficient in themselves, with tax revenue as a percentage of GDP remaining among the lowest in the region. In June 2014 the World Bank approved a 25-year loan of US $340m. to help Guatemala to improve the effectiveness and efficiency of public spending, and to reinforce the country's tax policy. Specifically, the loan is intended to support government measures to increase the amount of income tax raised as a proportion of Guatemala's GDP from 2.7% to 3.2%. That in itself is unlikely to be able to bring state income to levels that would address effectively the underlying issues in the economy.

Overall, Pérez Molina will continue to struggle to introduce serious fiscal reforms for the remainder of his presidency. First, representing much of the powerful business élite, which is vehemently opposed to the measures, he most likely lacks the political will to bring about such reforms. Second, the President lacks the congressional majority required to introduce meaningful fiscal reforms. The Government expected GDP to show continued steady growth in 2014, of around 4%.

Statistical Survey

Sources (unless otherwise stated): Banco de Guatemala, 7a Avda 22-01, Zona 1, Apdo 365, Guatemala City; tel. 2429-6000; fax 2253-4035; internet www.banguat .gob.gt; Instituto Nacional de Estadística, Edif. América, 4°, 8a Calle 9-55, Zona 1, Guatemala City; tel. 2232-6212; e-mail info-ine@ine.gob.gt; internet www.ine .gob.gt.

Area and Population

AREA, POPULATION AND DENSITY

Area (sq km)	
Land	108,429
Inland water	460
Total	108,889*
Population (census results)†	
17 April 1994	8,322,051
24 November 2002	
Males	5,496,839
Females	5,740,357
Total	11,237,196
Population (official estimates at mid-year)	
2012	15,073,375
2013	15,438,384
2014	15,806,675
Density (per sq km) at mid-2014	145.8

* 42,042 sq miles.
† Excluding adjustments for underenumeration.

POPULATION BY AGE AND SEX
(official estimates, '000 persons at mid-2013)

	Males	Females	Total
0–14 years	3,167.6	3,067.9	6,235.5
15–64 years	4,044.5	4,468.9	8,513.5
65 years and over	323.1	366.3	689.4
Total	7,535.2	7,903.1	15,438.4

Totals may not be equal to the sum of components, owing to rounding.

DEPARTMENTS
(official estimates at mid-2014)

Alta Verapaz .	1,219,585		Quetzaltenango .	844,906
Baja Verapaz .	291,903		Quiché . .	1,053,737
Chimaltenango .	666,938		Retalhuleu . . .	325,556
Chiquimula . .	397,202		Sacatepéquez . .	336,606
El Progreso . .	166,397		San Marcos . . .	1,095,997
Escuintla . .	746,309		Santa Rosa . .	367,569
Guatemala . .	3,306,397		Sololá . . .	477,705
Huehuetenango .	1,234,593		Suchitepéquez . .	555,261
Izabal . . .	445,125		Totonicapán . .	521,995
Jalapa . . .	345,926		Zacapa	232,667
Jutiapa . . .	462,714			
Petén	711,585		**Total**	15,806,675

PRINCIPAL TOWNS
(official population estimates at mid-2014)

			San Juan	
Guatemala City .	993,815		Sacatepéquez .	231,721
Villa Nueva . . .	552,535		Escuintla . . .	158,456
Mixco	491,619		Quetzaltenango .	157,559
Cobán	250,675		Jalapa	156,419
San Pedro Carcha .	235,213		Totonicapán . .	141,751

BIRTHS, MARRIAGES AND DEATHS

	Registered live births Number	Rate (per 1,000)	Registered marriages Number	Rate (per 1,000)	Registered deaths Number	Rate (per 1,000)
2005	374,066	29.5	52,186	4.1	71,039	5.6
2006	368,399	28.3	57,505	4.4	69,756	5.4
2007	366,128	26.8	57,003	4.3	70,030	5.2
2008	369,769	26.4	52,315	3.8	70,233	5.1
2009	351,628	25.1	62,104	4.4	67,284	4.8
2010	361,906	25.2	73,124	5.1	72,748	5.1
2011	373,692	25.4	78,286	5.3	72,354	4.9
2012	388,613	25.8	84,253	5.6	72,657	4.8

Sources: partly UN, *Demographic Yearbook* and *Population and Vital Statistics Report*.

Life expectancy (years at birth): 71.7 (males 68.2; females 75.3) in 2012 (Source: World Bank, World Development Indicators database).

ECONOMICALLY ACTIVE POPULATION
(population aged 15 years and over, March 2014)

	Males	Females	Total
Agriculture, forestry, hunting and fishing	1,611,479	209,930	1,821,409
Mining and quarrying; manufacturing	380,327	280,997	661,324
Construction	336,783	8,161	344,944
Wholesale and retail trade; transport and storage; hotels and restaurants	859,526	803,909	1,663,435
Information and communications	30,294	29,925	60,219
Financial and insurance services	31,682	21,854	53,536
Real estate activities	8,931	2,482	11,413
Professional, scientific, administrative and support services	121,284	43,951	165,235
Public administration and defence; education; health; social assistance	242,926	315,767	558,693
Other services	126,867	344,118	470,985
Total employed	3,750,099	2,061,094	5,811,193
Unemployed	118,067	61,176	179,243
Total labour force	3,868,166	2,122,270	5,990,436

Health and Welfare

KEY INDICATORS

Total fertility rate (children per woman, 2012)	3.8
Under-5 mortality rate (per 1,000 live births, 2012)	32
HIV/AIDS (% of persons aged 15–49, 2012)	0.7
Physicians (per 1,000 head, 2009)	0.9
Hospital beds (per 1,000 head, 2010)	0.6
Health expenditure (2011): US $ per head (PPP)	329
Health expenditure (2011): % of GDP	6.7
Health expenditure (2011): public (% of total)	35.4
Access to water (% of persons, 2012)	94
Access to sanitation (% of persons, 2012)	80
Total carbon dioxide emissions ('000 metric tons, 2010)	11,118.3
Carbon dioxide emissions per head (metric tons, 2010)	0.8
Human Development Index (2013): ranking	125
Human Development Index (2013): value	0.628

For sources and definitions, see explanatory note on p. vi.

Agriculture

PRINCIPAL CROPS
('000 metric tons)

	2010	2011	2012
Maize	1,634.0	1,672.2	1,690.0*
Potatoes	481.0	493.0	500.0†
Sugar cane	22,313.8	20,586.1	21,800.0†
Oil palm fruit†	1,213.0	1,653.0	2,067.0
Tomatoes	300.8	305.4	315.0
Watermelons†	125.2	128.3	130.0
Cantaloupes and other melons	480.4	497.2	500.0
Bananas	2,637.1	2,679.9	2,700.0
Plantains	192.6	188.8	195.0
Lemons and limes	107.8	109.1	112.0†
Guavas, mangoes and mangosteens	105.9	108.5	112.0
Pineapples	234.3	234.5	240.0†
Coffee, green	247.5	242.8	248.0†
Tobacco, unmanufactured†	18.6	22.4	24.0

* Unofficial figure.
† FAO estimate(s).

Aggregate production ('000 metric tons, may include official, semi-official or estimated data): Total cereals 1,723.6 in 2010, 1,760.3 in 2011, 1,771.4 in 2012; Total pulses 240.0 in 2010, 244.4 in 2011, 246.5 in 2012; Total roots and tubers 499.0 in 2010, 511.5 in 2011, 520.1 in 2012; Total vegetables (incl. melons) 1,553.9 in 2010, 1,592.0 in 2011, 1,626.0 in 2012; Total fruits (excl. melons) 3,968.4 in 2010, 4,013.3 in 2011, 4,069.1 in 2012.

Source: FAO.

LIVESTOCK
('000 head, year ending September)

	2010	2011	2012
Horses*	127	128	130
Asses*	9.9	9.9	10.0
Mules*	38.7	38.7	39.0
Cattle	3,306	3,388	3,400*
Sheep*	600	612	614
Pigs	2,733	2,799	2,800*
Goats*	128	130	132
Chickens*	33,000	34,000	35,000

* FAO estimate(s).

LIVESTOCK PRODUCTS
('000 metric tons)

	2010	2011	2012*
Cattle meat*	79.0	81.0	83.0
Pig meat*	58.7	60.0	61.5
Chicken meat	183.8	185.9	188.0
Cows' milk	463.1	463.1	465.0
Hen eggs	219.7†	224.6†	226.0
Honey*	3.5	3.5	3.6

* FAO estimate(s).
† Unofficial figure.

Source: FAO.

Forestry

ROUNDWOOD REMOVALS
('000 cubic metres, excl. bark, FAO estimates)

	2010	2011	2012
Sawlogs, veneer logs and logs for sleepers	677	837	705
Other industrial wood	15	15	15
Fuel wood	18,059	18,410	18,768
Total	18,751	19,262	19,488

Source: FAO.

SAWNWOOD PRODUCTION
('000 cubic metres, incl. railway sleepers, FAO estimates)

	2010	2011	2012
Coniferous (softwood) . . .	43	40	39
Broadleaved (hardwood) . . .	91	62	55
Total	134	102	94

Source: FAO.

Fishing

('000 metric tons, live weight)

	2010	2011	2012
Capture*	21.9	19.7	19.6
Freshwater fishes* . . .	2.3	2.3	2.3
Skipjack tuna	7.0	6.7	7.3*
Yellowfin tuna . . .	5.6	6.3	6.2*
Bigeye tuna	3.7	2.0*	2.0*
Penaeus shrimps . . .	0.7	0.6	0.3
Pacific seabobs . . .	1.3	0.9	0.5
Aquaculture	22.8	21.5*	17.7*
Other tilapias . . .	0.8	5.5	5.4
Penaeus shrimps . . .	21.9	15.9	12.3
Total catch*	44.7	41.2	37.3

* FAO estimate(s).

Source: FAO.

Mining

('000 metric tons, unless otherwise indicated)

	2010	2011	2012
Crude petroleum ('000 barrels) .	4,363	3,995	4,000*
Gold (kg)	9,213	11,898	6,473
Silver (kg)	194,683	272,771	204,555
Limestone	4,910	n.a.	2,000*
Sand and gravel ('000 cu m) . .	88	81	261

* Estimated figure.

Source: US Geological Survey.

Industry

SELECTED PRODUCTS
('000 metric tons unless otherwise indicated)

	2008	2009	2010
Sugar (raw)	2,145	2,382	2,495
Cement*	2,500	1,500	1,500
Electric energy (million kWh) .	8,717	9,039	8,832

* Estimates from US Geological Survey.

Cement ('000 metric tons, US Geological Survey estimates): 1,600 in 2011; 1,700 in 2012.

Source (unless otherwise indicated): UN Industrial Commodity Statistics Database.

Finance

CURRENCY AND EXCHANGE RATES

Monetary Units
100 centavos = 1 quetzal.

Sterling, Dollar and Euro Equivalents (30 May 2014)
£1 sterling = 13.093 quetzales;
US $1 = 7.783 quetzales;
€1 = 10.594 quetzales;
1,000 quetzales = £76.38 = $128.48 = €94.40.

Average Exchange Rate (quetzales per US dollar)
2011   7.7854
2012   7.8336
2013   7.8568

Note: In December 2000 legislation was approved to allow the circulation of the US dollar and other convertible currencies, for use in a wide range of transactions, from 1 May 2001.

BUDGET
(central government operations, million quetzales)

Revenue	2011	2012	2013*
Current revenue	43,165.2	45,855.1	49,250.3
Tax revenue	40,292.2	42,819.8	46,335.5
Direct taxes	12,710.5	13,453.7	16,052.8
Excise taxes	27,581.7	29,366.1	30,282.7
Non-tax revenue	2,873.0	3,035.3	2,914.8
Social Security . . .	1,214.4	1,273.6	1,273.6
Current transfers . . .	587.8	587.8	587.8
Capital revenue	12.9	18.7	8.8
Total	43,178.1	45,873.8	49,259.2

Expenditure	2011	2012	2013*
Current expenditure	38,774.2	42,307.5	45,555.3
Wages and salaries . . .	14,155.7	15,080.6	16,967.9
Use of goods and services . .	7,218.2	8,760.5	8,709.6
Interest	5,475.7	6,022.3	6,569.0
Discounts and rewards . . .	184.9	170.8	228.5
Transfers	8,592.6	8,967.5	9,499.4
Social benefits	3,147.1	3,305.9	3,580.9
Capital expenditure	14,736.8	13,012.0	12,713.7
Total	53,511.0	55,319.6	58,269.0

* Preliminary figures.

Source: Ministry of Finance, Guatemala City.

INTERNATIONAL RESERVES
(US $ million at 31 December)

	2011	2012	2013
Gold (national valuation) . . .	348.9	368.8	266.3
IMF special drawing rights . .	266.4	267.6	270.5
Foreign exchange	5,568.5	6,057.4	6,731.8
Total	6,183.8	6,693.8	7,268.6

Source: IMF, *International Financial Statistics*.

MONEY SUPPLY
(million quetzales at 31 December)

	2011	2012	2013
Currency outside depository corporations	20,510.5	21,227.0	21,964.9
Transferable deposits	52,138.2	56,655.2	60,706.0
Other deposits	88,477.4	98,176.5	110,332.2
Securities other than shares . .	5,135.4	5,766.0	6,179.7
Broad money	166,261.5	181,824.7	199,182.8

Source: IMF, *International Financial Statistics*.

COST OF LIVING
(Consumer Price Index at December; base: December 2010 = 100)

	2011	2012	2013
Food and non-alcoholic beverages .	112.1	118.8	129.3
Housing, water, electricity and gas	105.8	105.6	110.4
Clothing and footwear	103.0	106.2	108.2
All items (incl. others) . . .	106.2	109.9	114.7

All items (Consumer Price Index, annual averages; base: December 2010 = 100) (104.2 in 2011; 108.2 in 2012; 112.9 in 2013): .

NATIONAL ACCOUNTS
(million quetzales at current prices)

Expenditure on the Gross Domestic Product

	2011	2012*	2013*
Government final consumption expenditure	37,803.2	40,844.9	44,290.5
Private final consumption expenditure	316,528.2	339,236.0	366,075.1
Increase in stocks	1,592.1	649.6	–322.2
Gross fixed capital formation .	54,910.0	58,379.5	60,449.2
Total domestic expenditure	410,833.5	439,110.0	470,492.6
Exports of goods and services .	98,783.4	98,162.5	100,016.7
Less Imports of goods and services	138,605.4	142,549.4	147,839.3
GDP in purchasers' values .	371,011.6	394,723.0	422,670.0
GDP at constant 2001 prices .	207,776.0	213,946.6	221,842.3

Gross Domestic Product by Economic Activity

	2011	2012*	2013*
Agriculture, hunting, forestry and fishing	41,088.7	41,657.8	44,980.2
Mining and quarrying	10,512.2	8,604.2	7,817.4
Manufacturing	69,183.1	75,472.7	80,521.4
Electricity, gas and water . .	7,546.0	8,736.3	9,790.7
Construction	14,738.8	16,446.1	17,283.1
Trade, restaurants and hotels .	67,107.9	73,792.7	82,417.5
Transport, storage and communications	29,105.0	30,515.0	31,820.0
Finance, insurance and real estate	11,518.9	12,953.7	14,301.0
Ownership of dwellings . . .	30,448.4	31,712.8	33,018.4
General government services .	26,487.9	28,458.9	31,449.9
Other community, social and personal services	50,567.9	53,832.2	57,253.5
Sub-total	358,304.8	382,182.4	410,653.1
Less Financial intermediation services indirectly measured (FISIM)	10,646.4	11,591.4	12,829.9
Gross value added in basic prices	347,658.4	370,591.0	397,823.2
Taxes on imports, less subsidies .	23,353.3	24,131.9	24,846.8
GDP in purchasers' values .	371,011.6	394,723.0	422,670.0

* Preliminary figures.

BALANCE OF PAYMENTS
(US $ million)

	2011	2012	2013
Exports of goods	10,518.7	10,102.7	10,190.3
Imports of goods	–15,482.1	–15,837.7	–16,355.6
Balance on goods	–4,963.5	–5,735.0	–6,165.2
Exports of services	2,238.8	2,435.0	2,523.9
Imports of services	–2,516.8	–2,539.4	–2,725.4
Balance on goods and services	–5,241.4	–5,839.5	–6,366.7
Primary income received . .	413.6	447.0	453.5
Primary income paid . . .	–1,904.7	–1,562.2	–1,550.2
Balance on goods, services and primary income	–6,732.5	–6,954.7	–7,463.4
Secondary income received . .	5,092.6	5,632.7	5,988.3
Secondary income paid . . .	–32.0	–29.6	–39.3
Current balance	–1,671.8	–1,351.5	–1,514.4
Capital account (net) . . .	2.6	—	—
Direct investment assets . .	–130.8	–58.1	–75.1
Direct investment liabilities . .	1,139.7	1,263.6	1,350.1
Portfolio investment assets . .	–143.4	–8.7	5.9
Portfolio investment liabilities .	–297.7	–1.5	11.0
Other investment assets . .	–648.7	78.0	–282.1
Other investment liabilities . .	2,058.7	256.4	1,091.9
Net errors and omissions . .	–224.4	–453.5	–349.5
Reserves and related items .	84.1	–275.3	237.7

Source: IMF, *International Financial Statistics*.

External Trade

PRINCIPAL COMMODITIES
(US $ million)

Imports c.i.f.	2011	2012	2013
Textile materials	667.0	635.7	640.5
Gas-diesel (distillate fuel) oil . .	1,178.2	1,248.6	1,252.7
Motor spirit (gasoline)	991.1	1,029.0	1,067.5
Other petroleum derivatives . .	622.4	599.4	494.3
Chemical products	625.7	661.2	684.1
Pharmaceutical products . . .	503.2	528.3	595.9
Plastics and manufactures thereof	959.7	922.3	998.6
Transmitting and receiving apparatus	442.4	421.5	491.4
Electrical machinery and apparatus	1,405.1	1,531.4	1,621.3
Vehicles and transport equipment	1,133.7	1,273.7	1,190.6
Total (incl. others)	16,613.0	16,994.0	17,514.7

Exports f.o.b.	2011	2012	2013
Coffee	1,174.2	958.1	714.5
Bananas	475.3	499.9	601.5
Beverages, spirits and vinegar .	222.9	321.5	337.5
Sugar	648.8	803.0	941.9
Edible fats and oils	330.9	361.0	361.8
Natural rubber	397.4	295.0	239.5
Crude petroleum	335.4	291.7	277.3
Articles of clothing	1,216.4	1,189.5	1,270.8
Plastics and manufactures thereof	270.7	299.2	290.4
Precious metals and stones . .	941.6	612.9	482.7
Total (incl. others)	10,400.9	9,978.7	10,031.2

PRINCIPAL TRADING PARTNERS
(US $ million)

Imports c.i.f.	2011	2012	2013*
Argentina	91.4	162.5	186.9
Brazil	274.7	250.8	249.3
China, People's Republic	1,144.2	1,265.0	1,438.5
Colombia	596.8	551.4	767.6
Costa Rica	455.5	476.8	519.8
Ecuador	184.0	224.2	134.7
El Salvador	820.4	777.0	820.0
Germany	256.1	278.1	289.4
Honduras	344.7	367.1	394.8
Hong Kong	169.4	193.7	194.1
India	162.1	242.7	241.0
Japan	303.9	276.3	255.1
Korea, Republic	369.0	427.2	405.0
Mexico	1,858.9	1,915.7	1,860.3
Panama	476.8	544.4	584.9
Spain	171.9	186.5	222.1
USA	6,508.6	6,460.4	6,488.8
Total (incl. others)	16,613.0	16,994.0	17,514.7

Exports f.o.b.	2011	2012	2013*
Belgium	110.2	75.1	62.2
Canada	158.7	149.4	159.5
Chile	135.6	130.1	107.7
China, People's Republic	28.8	34.7	167.2
Costa Rica	404.3	424.5	396.2
Dominican Republic	127.2	115.5	127.6
El Salvador	1,132.3	1,110.7	1,108.8
Germany	145.2	119.6	88.1
Honduras	814.7	795.5	791.0
Italy	106.5	84.6	61.4
Japan	212.2	176.7	188.7
Korea, Republic	125.0	53.1	151.5
Mexico	512.3	550.1	469.6
Netherlands	136.2	169.2	252.6
Nicaragua	459.1	473.4	486.9
Panama	247.4	246.4	237.3
USA	4,307.5	3,955.0	3,786.1
Total (incl. others)	10,400.9	9,977.6	10,031.2

* Preliminary figures.

Transport

ROAD TRAFFIC
(motor vehicles in use)

	2008	2009	2010
Passenger cars	476,739	505,782	529,593
Buses and coaches	86,124	90,526	94,541
Lorries and vans	315,469	342,058	366,025
Motorcycles and mopeds	447,068	508,999	570,799
Total (incl. others)	1,760,013	1,912,469	2,051,945

SHIPPING

Flag Registered Fleet
(at 31 December)

	2011	2012	2013
Number of vessels	6	6	6
Total displacement ('000 grt)	3.0	3.0	3.0

Source: Lloyd's List Intelligence (www.lloydslistintelligence.com).

CIVIL AVIATION
(traffic on scheduled services)

	1997	1998	1999
Kilometres flown (million)	5	7	5
Passengers carried ('000)	508	794	506
Passenger-km (million)	368	480	342
Total ton-km (million)	77	50	33

Source: UN, *Statistical Yearbook*.
Passengers carried ('000): 313.9 in 2010; 326.1 in 2011; 288.0 in 2012 (Source: World Bank, World Development Indicators database).

Tourism

TOURIST ARRIVALS BY COUNTRY OF ORIGIN

	2011	2012	2013
Belize	35,960	35,481	40,303
Canada	42,719	53,696	52,955
Costa Rica	42,039	44,984	46,417
El Salvador	542,316	604,871	638,058
Honduras	223,010	235,680	220,497
Mexico	132,661	144,076	152,506
Nicaragua	74,362	77,238	77,691
USA	429,216	434,175	446,814
Total (incl. others)	1,822,663	1,951,173	2,000,126

Tourism receipts (US $ million, excl. passenger transport): 937.2 in 2011; 986.8 in 2012; 1,020.6 in 2013.

Source: Guatemalan Institute of Tourism.

Communications Media

	2011	2012	2013
Telephones ('000 main lines in use)	1,626.3	1,743.8	1,863.1
Mobile cellular telephones ('000 subscribers)	19,479.1	20,787.1	21,716.4
Broadband subscribers ('000)	n.a.	273.7	278.8

Internet users ('000) 2,279.4 in 2009.

Source: International Telecommunication Union.

Education

(2010/11 unless otherwise indicated)

	Institutions	Teachers	Students
Pre-primary	11,859*	26,126	537,265
Primary	17,499*	100,600	2,644,683
Secondary	4,874*	76,850	1,113,881
Tertiary	1,946†	3,843*	233,885‡

* 2005/06.
† 2003/04.
‡ 2006/07.

Source: mainly UNESCO Institute for Statistics.

Pupil-teacher ratio (primary education, UNESCO estimate): 26.3 in 2010/11 (Source: UNESCO Institute for Statistics).

Adult literacy rate (UNESCO estimates): 78.3% (males 84.8%; females 72.4%) in 2012 (Source: UNESCO Institute for Statistics).

Directory

The Constitution

A new Constitution (based on that of 1965) came into effect in January 1986. A series of amendments to the Constitution were approved by referendum in January 1994 and came into effect in April 1994. The Constitution's main provisions are summarized below:

Guatemala has a republican, representative, democratic system of government and power is exercised equally by the legislative, executive and judicial bodies. The official language is Spanish. Suffrage is universal and secret, obligatory for those who can read and write and optional for those who are illiterate. The free formation and growth of political parties, with democratic aims, are guaranteed. There is no discrimination on grounds of race, colour, sex, religion, birth, economic or social position, or political opinions.

The state will give protection to capital and private enterprise in order to develop sources of labour and stimulate creative activity.

Monopolies are forbidden and the state will limit any enterprise that might prejudice the development of the community. The right to social security is recognized and it shall be on a national, unitary and obligatory basis.

Constitutional guarantees may be suspended in certain circumstances for up to 30 days (unlimited in the case of war).

CONGRESS

Legislative power rests with Congress (Congreso de la República), which is made up of 158 deputies, elected according to a combination of departmental and proportional representation. Congress meets on 15 January each year and ordinary sessions last four months; extraordinary sessions can be called by the Permanent Commission or the Executive. All Congressional decisions must be taken by absolute majority of the members, except in special cases laid down by law. Deputies are elected for four years; they may be re-elected after a lapse of one session, but only once. Congress is responsible for all matters concerning the President and Vice-President and the execution of their offices; for all electoral matters; for all matters concerning the laws of the Republic; for approving the budget and decreeing taxes; for declaring war; for conferring honours, both civil and military; for fixing the coinage and the system of weights and measures; and for approving, by a two-thirds' majority, any international treaty or agreement affecting the law, sovereignty, financial status or security of the country.

PRESIDENT

The President is elected by universal suffrage, by absolute majority, for a non-extendable period of four years. Re-election or prolongation of the presidential term of office are punishable by law. The President is responsible for national defence and security, fulfilling the Constitution, leading the armed forces, taking any necessary steps in time of national emergency, passing and executing laws, international policy, and nominating and removing ministers, officials and diplomats. The Vice-President's duties include co-ordinating the actions of Ministers of State and taking part in the discussions of the Council of Ministers.

ARMY

The Guatemalan Army is intended to maintain national independence, sovereignty and honour, and territorial integrity. It is an indivisible, apolitical, non-deliberating body and is made up of land, sea and air forces.

LOCAL ADMINISTRATIVE DIVISIONS

For the purposes of administration, the territory of the Republic is divided into 22 departments and these into 330 municipalities, but this division can be modified by Congress to suit the interests and general development of the nation without loss of municipal autonomy. Municipal authorities are elected every four years.

JUDICIARY

Justice is exercised exclusively by the Supreme Court of Justice and other tribunals. Administration of justice is obligatory, free and independent of the other functions of state. The President of the judiciary, judges and other officials are elected by Congress for five years. The Supreme Court of Justice is made up of 13 judges. The President of the judiciary is also President of the Supreme Court. The Supreme Court nominates all other judges. Under the Supreme Court come the Court of Appeal, the Administrative Disputes Tribunal, the Tribunal of Second Instance of Accounts, Jurisdiction Conflicts, First Instance and Military, and the Extraordinary Tribunal of Protection. There is a Court of Constitutionality presided over by the President of the Supreme Court.

The Government

HEAD OF STATE

President: Gen. (retd) Otto Fernando Pérez Molina (took office 14 January 2012).
Vice-President: Ingrid Roxana Baldetti Elías.

CABINET
(September 2014)

The Government is formed by the Partido Patriota (PP) and the Visión con Valores-Encuentro por Guatemala (VIVA-EG) coalition.

Minister of Foreign Affairs: Carlos Raúl Morales Moscoso.

Minister of the Interior: Mauricio López Bonilla (PP).

Minister of National Defence: Brig.-Gen. Manuel Augusto López Ambrosio (PP).

Minister of Public Finance: Dorval Carías.

Minister of the Economy: Sergio de la Torre (PP).

Minister of Public Health and Social Welfare: Jorge Alejandro Villavicencio Alvarez (Ind.).

Minister of Communications, Infrastructure, Transport and Housing: Víctor Corado.

Minister of Agriculture, Livestock and Food: Elmer Alberto López Rodríguez (Ind.).

Minister of Education: Cynthia del Aguila (PP).

Minister of Energy and Mines: Erick Archila (PP).

Minister of Culture and Sport: Carlos Batzín (PP).

Minister of the Environment and Natural Resources: Michelle Martínez.

Minister of Social Development: Edgar Leonel Rodríguez Lara (PP).

Minister of Labour and Social Security: Carlos Contreras Solórzano (PP).

MINISTRIES

Ministry of Agriculture, Livestock and Food: Edif. Monja Blanca, Of. 306, 3°, 7a Avda 12-90, Zona 13, Guatemala City; tel. 2413-7000; fax 2413-7352; e-mail infoagro@maga.gob.gt; internet www.maga.gob.gt.

Ministry of Communications, Infrastructure, Transport and Housing: Edif. Antiguo Cocesna, 8a Avda y 15 Calle, Zona 13, Guatemala City; tel. 2223-4000; fax 2362-6059; e-mail relpublicas@micivi.gob.gt; internet www.civ.gob.gt.

Ministry of Culture and Sport: Calle 7, entre Avda 6 y 7, Centro Histórico, Palacio Nacional de la Cultura, Zona 1, Guatemala City; tel. 2239-5000; fax 2253-0540; e-mail info@mcd.gob.gt; internet www.mcd.gob.gt.

Ministry of the Economy: 8a Avda 10-43, Zona 1, Guatemala City; tel. 2412-0439; fax 2412-0200; e-mail infonegocios@mineco.gob.gt; internet www.mineco.gob.gt.

Ministry of Education: 6a Calle 1-87, Zona 10, Guatemala City; tel. 2411-9595; fax 2361-0350; e-mail info@mineduc.gob.gt; internet www.mineduc.gob.gt.

Ministry of Energy and Mines: Diagonal 17, 29-78, Zona 11, Las Charcas, Guatemala City; tel. 2419-6464; fax 2476-2007; e-mail informatica@mem.gob.gt; internet www.mem.gob.gt.

Ministry of the Environment and Natural Resources: Edif. MARN, 20 Calle 28-58, Zona 10, Guatemala City; tel. 2423-0500; e-mail sip@marn.gob.gt; internet www.marn.gob.gt.

Ministry of Foreign Affairs: 2a Avda La Reforma 4-17, Zona 10, Guatemala City; tel. 2410-0010; fax 2410-0011; e-mail webmaster@minex.gob.gt; internet www.minex.gob.gt.

Ministry of the Interior: Antiguo Palacio de la Policía Nacional Civil, 6a Avda 13-71, Zona 1, Guatemala City; tel. 2413-8888; fax 2413-8587; e-mail info@mingob.gob.gt; internet www.mingob.gob.gt.

Ministry of Labour and Social Security: Edif. Torre Empresarial, 7 Avda 3-33, Zona 9, Guatemala City; tel. 2422-2500; fax 2422-2503; e-mail ministro@mintrabajo.gob.gt; internet www.mintrabajo.gob.gt.

Ministry of National Defence: Antiguas Escuela Politécnica, Avda La Reforma 1-45, Zona 10, Guatemala City; tel. 2269-4924; fax 2360-9919; e-mail dip@mindef.mil.gt; internet www.mindef.mil.gt.

Ministry of Public Finance: Centro Cívico, 8a Avda y 21 Calle, Zona 1, Guatemala City; tel. 2248-5005; fax 2248-5054; e-mail info@minfin.gob.gt; internet www.minfin.gob.gt.

Ministry of Public Health and Social Welfare: Escuela de Enfermería, 3°, 6a Avda 3-45, Zona 1, Guatemala City; tel. 2475-2121; fax 2475-1125; e-mail info@mspas.gob.gt; internet www.mspas.gob.gt.

Ministry of Social Development: 3a Avda 6-44, Zona 1, Guatemala City; tel. 2491-0900; internet www.mides.gob.gt.

President and Legislature

PRESIDENT

Presidential Election, 11 September and 6 November 2011

Candidate	First round % of votes	Second round % of votes
Gen. (retd) Otto Fernando Pérez Molina (PP)	36.10	53.74
Manuel Antonio Baldizón Méndez (LIDER)	22.68	46.26
José Eduardo Suger Cofiño (CREO)	16.62	—
Mario Amilcar Estrada Orellana (UCN)	8.72	—
Harold Osberto Caballeros López (VIVA-EG)	6.24	—
Rigoberta Menchú Tum (WINAQ-URNG—MAIZ-ANN)	3.22	—
Juan Guillermo Gutiérrez Strauss (PAN)	2.76	—
Patricia de Arzú (Partido Unionista)	2.19	—
Alejandro Eduardo Giammattei Falla (CASA)	1.05	—
Adela Camacho de Torrebiarte (ADN)	0.42	—
Total valid votes	100.00	100.00

CONGRESS
(Congreso de la República)

President: Arístides Crespo.

General Election, 11 September 2011

	% of votes	Seats*
Partido Patriota (PP)	26.37	56
Unidad Nacional de la Esperanza-Gran Alianza Nacional (UNE-GANA)	22.24	48
Unión del Cambio Nacional (UCN)	9.48	14
Libertad Democrática Renovada (LIDER)	8.66	14
Compromiso, Renovación y Orden (CREO)	8.77	12
Visión con Valores-Encuentro por Guatemala (VIVA)	7.84	6
WINAQ-Unidad Revolucionaria Nacional Guatemalteca—Movimiento Amplio de Izquierdas-Alternativa Nueva Nación	3.20	3
Partido de Avanzada Nacional (PAN)	3.08	2
Frente Republicano Guatemalteco (FRG)†	2.72	1
Partido Unionista	2.67	1
VICTORIA	1.62	1
Centro de Acción Social	1.10	—
Acción de Desarrollo Nacional (ADN)	0.88	—
Frente de Convergencia Nacional (FCN)	0.53	—
Total valid votes (incl. others)	100.00	158

* Seats are distributed according to a combination of national lists and departmental and proportional representation.
† Succeeded by the Partido Republicano Institucional in 2013.

Election Commission

Tribunal Supremo Electoral: 6a Avda 0-32, Zona 2, Guatemala City; tel. 2413-0303; e-mail tse@tse.org.gt; internet www.tse.org.gt; f. 1983; independent; Pres. Rudy Marlón Pineda Ramírez.

Political Organizations

Acción de Desarrollo Nacional (ADN): Vía 7, 5-33 Zona 4, Guatemala City; tel. 2339-4000; internet www.adn.com.gt; registration cancelled by the Tribunal Supremo Electoral in May 2012; Sec.-Gen. Adela Camacho de Torrebiarte.

Alternativa Nueva Nación (ANN): Avda 1-31, 8°, Zona 1, Guatemala City; tel. 2251-2514; e-mail corriente@intelnet.net.gt; contested the 2011 elections in coalition with the URNG—MAIZ (q.v.) and the Movimiento Político WINAQ (q.v.); Sec.-Gen. Pablo Monsanto.

Bienestar Nacional (BIEN): 8a Avda 6-40, Zona 2, Guatemala City; tel. 2254-1458; internet www.bienestarnacional.org; Sec.-Gen. Fidel Reyes Lee.

Compromiso, Renovación y Orden (CREO): Vía 3, 5–27 Zona 4, Antiguo Edif. Manuel, Guatemala City; tel. 2339-4942; internet creo.org.gt; Sec.-Gen. Roberto González Díaz-Durán.

Encuentro por Guatemala (EG): 9 Avda 0-71, Zona 4, Guatemala City; tel. 2231-9859; fax 2230-6463; e-mail izaveliz@yahoo.es; internet encuentro.gt; f. 2006; centre-left; promotes indigenous interests; contested the 2011 elections in coalition with Visión con Valores (q.v.); Sec.-Gen. Nineth Verenca Montenegro Cottom.

Frente de Convergencia Nacional (FCN): Avda Centroamérica 13-45, Zona 1, Guatemala City; tel. 5908-7848; e-mail soporte@partidofcn.com; internet www.partidofcn.com; Sec.-Gen. Jimmy Morales Cabrera.

Gran Alianza Nacional (GANA): 6a Avda, 3-44, Zona 9, Guatemala City; tel. 2331-4811; fax 2362-7512; e-mail info@gana.com.gt; internet www.gana.com.gt; f. 2003 as electoral alliance of PP, Movimiento Reformador and Partido Solidaridad Nacional; registered as a party in 2005 following withdrawal of PP; Sec.-Gen. Jaime Antonio Martínez Lohayza.

Libertad Democrática Renovada (LIDER): 13 Calle, 2-52 Zona 1, Guatemala City; tel. 2463-4942; internet www.baldizon.com; f. 2010; Sec.-Gen. Manuel Baldizón.

Movimiento Político WINAQ: 33 Avda 3-57, Zona 4 de Mixco Bosques de San Nicolás, Guatemala City; tel. 2436-0939; internet winaq.org.gt; promotes indigenous interests; contested the 2011 elections in coalition with the URNG—MAIZ (q.v.) and the Alternativa Nueva Nación (q.v.); Sec.-Gen. Amilcar Pop.

Partido de Avanzada Nacional (PAN): 3a Avda 18-28, Zona 14, Guatemala City; tel. 2366-1509; fax 2337-2001; e-mail pan.partidodeavanzadanacional@gmail.com; internet www.pan-gt.com; Sec.-Gen. Juan Guillermo Gutiérrez Strauss.

Partido Patriota (PP): 11 Calle 11-54, Zona 1, Guatemala City; tel. 2311-6886; e-mail comunicacion@partidopatriota.org; internet www.partidopatriota.com; f. 2002; contested 2003 elections as part of GANA (q.v.); withdrew from GANA in May 2004; right-wing; Leader Gen. (retd) Otto Fernando Pérez Molina; Sec.-Gen. Ingrid Roxana Baldetti Elías.

Partido Republicano Institucional (PRI): Avda Las Américas 19-60, Zona 13, Guatemala City; tel. 2319-000; internet pri.gt; f. 2013 as successor party to Frente Republicano Guatemalteco (f. 1988); right-wing; Sec.-Gen. Luis Fernando Pérez Martínez.

Partido Unionista: 5a Avda 'A' 13-43, Zona 9, Guatemala City; tel. 2331-7468; fax 2331-6141; e-mail info@unionistas.com; internet www.unionistas.org; f. 1917; Sec.-Gen. Alvaro Enrique Arzú Irigoyen.

Unidad Nacional de la Esperanza (UNE): 6a Avda 8-72, Zona 9, Guatemala City; tel. 2334-3451; e-mail ideas@une.org.gt; internet www.une.org.gt; f. 2001 following a split within the PAN; centre-left; Sec.-Gen. Sandra Torres de Colom.

Unidad Revolucionaria Nacional Guatemalteca—Movimiento Amplio de Izquierdas (URNG—MAIZ): 12a Avda 'B' 6-00, Zona 2, Guatemala City; tel. 2254-0704; fax 2254-7062; e-mail debate@urng-maiz.org.gt; internet www.urng-maiz.org.gt; f. 1982 following unification of principal guerrilla groups engaged in the civil war; formally registered as a political party in 1998; contested the 2011 elections in coalition with the Movimiento Político WINAQ (q.v.) and the Alternativa Nueva Nación (q.v.); Sec.-Gen. Angel Sánchez Viesca.

Unión del Cambio Nacional (UCN): 5a Calle 5-27, Zone 9, Guatemala City; tel. 2361-6729; e-mail administracion.ucn@gmai.com; f. 2006; Sec.-Gen. Mario Amilcar Estrada Orellana.

Unión Democrática (UD): Casa 9, 5 Calle 12-00, Zona 14, Guatemala City; tel. 2363-5013; fax 2369-3062; e-mail info@uniondemocratica.info; f. 1983; Sec.-Gen. Manuel Eduardo Conde Orellana.

Los Verdes (LV): 3a Avda 3-72, Zona 1, Guatemala City; tel. 570-3420; e-mail losverdesguatemala@gmail.com; Sec.-Gen. Rodolfo Rosales García Salas.

VICTORIA: Edif. Crece Condado el Naranjo, Of. 607, 6°, 23 Calle 14-58, Zona 4 de Mixco, Guatemala City; Sec.-Gen. Edgar Abraham Rivera Sagastume.

Visión con Valores (VIVA): 41 Calle 3-45, Zona 8, Guatemala City; tel. 2243-2999; e-mail contacto@visionconvalores.com; internet www.visionconvalores.com; contested the 2011 elections in coalition with

Encuentro por Guatemala (q.v.); Sec.-Gen. HAROLD OSBERTO CABALLEROS LÓPEZ.

Diplomatic Representation

EMBASSIES IN GUATEMALA

Argentina: 5a Avda 6-50, Zona 14, Apdo 120, Guatemala City; tel. and fax 2464-5900; fax 2367-1091; e-mail eguat@mrecic.gov.ar; Ambassador ERNESTO JUSTO LÓPEZ.

Belize: Edif. Europlaza Torre II, Of. 1502, 5a Avda 5-55, Zona 14, Guatemala City; tel. 2207-4000; fax 2207-4001; e-mail infobelice@ embajadadebelice.org; internet www.embajadadebelice.org; Ambassador ALFREDO MARTÍN MARTÍNEZ.

Brazil: Edif. Los Arcos, 2a Avda 20-13, Zona 10, Apdo 196-A, Guatemala City; tel. 2321-6800; fax 2366-1762; e-mail brascom@ intelnet.net.gt; internet guatemala.itamaraty.gov.br; Ambassador JOSÉ ROBERTO DE ALMEIDA PINTO.

Canada: Edif. Edyma Plaza, 8°, 13a Calle 8-44, Zona 10, Apdo 400, Guatemala City; tel. 2363-4348; fax 2365-1210; e-mail gtmla@ international.gc.ca; internet www.canadainternational.gc.ca/ guatemala; Ambassador HUGUES RÉAL ROUSSEAU.

Chile: 3a Avda 14-33, Zona 14, Guatemala City; tel. 2490-2323; fax 2334-8276; e-mail echilegu@intelnet.net.gt; Ambassador DOMINGO NAMUNCURA.

Colombia: Edif. Europlaza, Torre I, Of. 1603, 5a Avda 5-55, Zona 14, Guatemala City; tel. 2385-3432; fax 2385-3438; e-mail embacolombia@intelett.com; internet www.embajadaenguatemala .gov.co; Ambassador FRANCISCO JOSÉ SANCLEMENTE MOLINA.

Costa Rica: 5a Avda 9-33, Zona 14, Guatemala City; tel. 2366-4215; fax 2337-1969; e-mail embacosta.gt@gmail.com; internet www .embajadacostaricaguatemala.com; Ambassador JAVIER DÍAZ CARMONA.

Cuba: Avda las Américas 20-72, Zona 13, Guatemala City; tel. 2332-5521; fax 2332-5525; e-mail embajador@gt.embacuba.cu; internet www.cubadiplomatica.cu/guatemala; Ambassador ROBERTO BLANCO DOMÍNGUEZ.

Dominican Republic: Centro Empresarial 'Zona Pradera', Torre II, Of. 1606, 18 Calle 24-69, Zona 10, Guatemala City; tel. 2261-7016; fax 2261-7017; e-mail embardgt@gmail.com; Ambassador RENÉ BIENVENIDO SANTANA GONZÁLEZ.

Ecuador: 4a Avda 12-04, Zona 14, Guatemala City; tel. 2368-0397; fax 2368-0397; e-mail embecuad@itelgua.com; Ambassador GALO ANDRÉS YÉPEZ HOLGUÍN.

Egypt: Edif. Cobella, 5°, 5a Avda 10-84, Zona 14, Apdo 502, Guatemala City; tel. 2333-6296; fax 2368-2808; e-mail embassy .guatemala@mfa.gov.eg; internet www.mfa.gov.eg/ Guatemala_Emb; Ambassador MOSTAFA MAHMOUD MAHER ELREMALY.

El Salvador: Avda las Américas 16-40, Zona 13, Guatemala City; tel. 2360-7660; fax 2332-1228; e-mail emsalva@intelnet.net.gt; Ambassador JORGE ALBERTO PALENCIA MENA.

France: Edif. Cogefar, 5a Avda 8-59, Zona 14, Apdo 971-A, 01014 Guatemala City; tel. 2421-7370; fax 2421-7372; e-mail courrier@ ambafrance-gt.org; internet www.ambafrance-gt.org; Ambassador PHILIPPE FRANC.

Germany: Edif. Reforma 10, 10°, Avda La Reforma 9-55, Zona 10, Guatemala City; tel. 2364-6700; fax 2365-2270; e-mail info@guat .diplo.de; internet www.guatemala.diplo.de; Ambassador MATTHIAS SONN.

Holy See: 10a Calle 4-47, Zona 9, Apdo 3041, Guatemala City (Apostolic Nunciature); tel. 2332-4274; fax 2334-1918; e-mail nuntius@itelgua.com; Apostolic Nuncio Most Rev. NICOLAS THEVENIN (Titular Archbishop of Aeclanum).

Honduras: 19 Avda A 20-19, Zona 10, Guatemala City; tel. 2366-5640; fax 2368-0062; e-mail embhond@intelnet.net.gt; Ambassador JORGE MIGUEL GABRIE LAGOS.

Israel: 13a Avda 14-07, Zona 10, Guatemala City; tel. 2333-6951; fax 2333-6950; e-mail info@guatemala.mfa.gov.il; internet guatemala .mfa.gov.il; Ambassador MOSHÉ BACHAR.

Italy: Edif. Santa Bárbara, 12a Calle 6-49, Zona 14, Guatemala City; tel. 2366-9271; fax 2367-3916; e-mail ambasciata.guatemala@esteri .it; internet www.ambguatemala.esteri.it; Ambassador FABRIZIO PIGNATELLI DELLA LEONESSA.

Japan: Edif. Torre Internacional, 10°, Avda de la Reforma 16-85, Zona 10, Guatemala City; tel. 2382-7300; fax 2382-7310; e-mail info@ japon.net.gt; internet www.gt.emb-japan.go.jp; Ambassador EIICHI KAWAHARA.

Korea, Republic: Edif. Europlaza, Torre III, 7°, 5a Avda 5-55, Zona 14, Guatemala City; tel. 2382-4051; fax 2382-4057; e-mail korembsy@mofat.go.kr; internet gtm.mofat.go.kr; Ambassador CHOO YEON-GON.

Mexico: 2a Avda 7-57, Zona 10, Apdo 1455, Guatemala City; tel. 2420-3400; fax 2420-3410; e-mail embamexguat@itelgua.com; internet www.sre.gob.mx/guatemala; Ambassador CARLOS TIRADA ZAVALA.

Nicaragua: 13 Avda 14-54, Zona 10, Guatemala City; tel. 2333-4636; fax 2368-2284; e-mail embaguat@terra.com.gt; Ambassador SILVIO MORA MORA.

Norway: Edif. Murano Center, 15°, Of. 1501, 14 Calle 3-51, Zona 10, Apdo 1764, Guatemala City; tel. 2506-4000; fax 2366-5823; e-mail emb.guatemala@mfa.no; internet www.noruega.org.gt; Ambassador JAN GERHARD LASSEN.

Panama: 12a Calle 2-65, Zona 14, Apdo 929-A, Guatemala City; tel. 2366-3336; fax 2366-3338; e-mail panaguate@hotmail.com; internet www.panamaenelexterior.gob.pa/guatemala; Ambassador IRVING ORLANDO CENTENO SANSON.

Peru: 15a Avda A 20-16, Zona 13, Guatemala City; tel. 2339-1060; e-mail embajadadelperu@yahoo.com; Ambassador NILO JÉSUS FIGUEROA CORTAVARRIA.

Russia: 2a Avda 12-85, Zona 14, Guatemala City; tel. 2367-2765; fax 2367-2766; e-mail embajadarusa@gmail.com; internet www.guat .mid.ru; Ambassador NIKOLAY Y. BÁBICH.

Spain: 6a Calle 6-48, Zona 9, Guatemala City; tel. 2379-3530; fax 2379-3533; e-mail emb.guatemala@maec.es; internet www.maec.es/ embajadas/guatemala; Ambassador MANUEL MARÍA LEJARRETA LOBO.

Sweden: Edif. Reforma 10, 11°, Avda de la Reforma 9-55, Zona 10, Apdo 966-A, Guatemala City; tel. 2384-7300; fax 2384-7350; e-mail ambassaden.guatemala@foreign.ministry.se; internet www .swedenabroad.com/guatemala; Ambassador JAN ANDERS MICHAEL FRUHLING.

Switzerland: Edif. Torre Internacional, 14°, 16a Calle 0-55, Zona 10, Apdo 1426, Guatemala City; tel. 2367-5520; fax 2367-5811; e-mail gua.vertretung@eda.admin.ch; internet www.eda.admin.ch/ guatemala; Ambassador JÜRG BENZ.

Taiwan (Republic of China): 4a Avda A 13-25, Zona 9, Apdo 897, Guatemala City; tel. 2322-0168; fax 2332-2668; e-mail gtm@mofa .gov.tw; internet www.taiwanembassy.org/gt; Ambassador ADOLFO SUN.

United Kingdom: Edif. Torre Internacional, 11°, Avda de la Reforma, 16a Calle, Zona 10, Guatemala City; tel. 2380-7300; fax 2380-7339; e-mail embassy@intelnett.com; internet ukinguatemala .fco.gov.uk; Ambassador SARAH DICKSON.

USA: Avda de la Reforma 7-01, Zona 10, Guatemala City; tel. 2326-4000; fax 2326-4654; internet guatemala.usembassy.gov; Ambassador TODD D. ROBINSON.

Uruguay: Centro Empresarial Pradera Torre IV, Of. 701, 18 Calle 24-69, Zona 10, Guatemala City; tel. 2261-8001; fax 2261-8003; e-mail uruguatemala@mrree.gub.uy; Ambassador ALFREDO LAFONE RAGGIO.

Venezuela: Edif. Atlantis, Of. 601, 13a Calle 3-40, Zona 10, Apdo 152, Guatemala City; tel. 2317-0703; fax 2317-0705; e-mail embavene@concyt.gob.gt; internet guatemala.embajada.gob.ve; Ambassador ORLANDO TORREALBA JÍMENEZ.

Judicial System

The judiciary comprises the Supreme Court, the Courts of Appeal, the Courts of the First Instance and the Justices of Peace. The Supreme Court is the highest court and is responsible for the administration of the judiciary. There are 20 Courts of Appeal throughout the country. There are 10 civil and 12 penal Courts of the First Instance in Guatemala City, and at least one civil and one penal in each of the 21 remaining departments.

Corte Suprema de Justicia: Centro Cívico, 21 Calle 7-70, Zona 1, Guatemala City; tel. 2426-7000; internet www.oj.gob.gt/csj; mems are appointed by Congress; Pres. JOSÉ ANTONIO SIERRA GONZÁLEZ.

Attorney-General: THELMA ESPERANZA ALDANA HERNÁNDEZ.

Religion

Almost all of the inhabitants profess Christianity, with a majority belonging to the Roman Catholic Church. In recent years the Protestant churches have attracted a growing number of converts.

CHRISTIANITY

The Roman Catholic Church

For ecclesiastical purposes, Guatemala comprises two archdioceses, 10 dioceses and the Apostolic Vicariates of El Petén and Izabal. Some 60% of the population are Roman Catholics.

Bishops' Conference: Conferencia Episcopal de Guatemala, Secretariado General del Episcopado, Km 15, Calzada Roosevelt 4-54, Zona 7, Mixco, Apdo 1698, Guatemala City; tel. 2433-1832; fax 2433-1834; e-mail ceguatemala@gmail.com; internet www.iglesiacatolica.org.gt; f. 1973; Pres. Rev. RODOLFO VALENZUELA NÚÑEZ (Bishop of La Verapaz).

Archbishop of Guatemala City: OSCAR JULIO VIAN MORALES, Palacio Arzobispal, 7a Avda 6-21, Zona 1, Apdo 723, Guatemala City; tel. 2231-9707; fax 2251-5068; e-mail arzobispadodeguatemala@gmail.com; internet www.arzobispadodeguatemala.com.

Archbishop of Los Altos, Quetzaltenango-Totonicapán: MARIO ALBERTO MOLINA PALMA, Arzobispado, 11 Avda 6-27, Zona 1, Apdo 11, 09001 Quetzaltenango; tel. 7761-2840; fax 7761-6049.

The Anglican Communion

Guatemala comprises one of the five dioceses of the Iglesia Anglicana de la Región Central de América.

Bishop of Guatemala: Rt Rev. ARMANDO ROMÁN GUERRA SORIA, Avda Castellana 40-06, Zona 8, Apdo 58, Guatemala City; tel. 2473-6828; fax 2472-0764; e-mail agepiscopal@yahoo.com; diocese founded 1967.

Protestant Churches

The largest Protestant denomination in Guatemala is the Full Gospel Church, followed by the Assembly of God, the Central American Church, and the Prince of Peace Church. The Baptist, Presbyterian, Lutheran and Episcopalian churches are also represented.

Convención de Iglesias Bautista de Guatemala (CIBG): Convention of Baptist Churches of Guatemala, 12 Calle 9-54, Zona 1, Apdo 322, 01901 Guatemala City; tel. and fax 2253-9194; e-mail convencion@cibg.org; internet cibg.org; f. 1946; Pres. OTTO ECHEVERRÍA VELÁSQUEZ; 43,876 mems.

Church of Jesus Christ of Latter-day Saints: 12a Calle 3-37, Zona 9, Guatemala City; e-mail contactos@mormones.org.gt; internet www.mormones.org.gt; 17 bishoprics, 9 chapels; Pres. THOMAS S. MONSON.

Conferencia de Iglesias Evangélicas de Guatemala (CIEDEG) (Conference of Protestant Churches in Guatemala): 7a Avda 1-11, Zona 2, Guatemala City; tel. 2232-3724; fax 2232-1609; internet www.nuevociedeg.org; f. 1987; Pres. VITALINO SIMILOX.

Congregación Luterana La Epifanía (Evangelisch-Lutherische Epiphanias-Gemeinde): 2a Avda 15-31, Zona 10, 01010 Guatemala City; tel. 2333-3697; fax 2366-4968; e-mail pfarrer@laepifania.org; internet www.laepifania.org; mem. of Lutheran World Federation; Pres. MARKUS BÖTTCHER; 200 mems.

Iglesia Evangélica Nacional Presbiteriana de Guatemala: Avda Simeón Cañas 7-13, Zona 2, Apdo 655, Guatemala City; tel. 2288-4441; fax 2254-1242; e-mail ienpg@yahoo.com; internet www.ienpg.org.gt; f. 1962; mem. of World Alliance of Reformed Churches; Pres. BENJAMIN YAC POZ; Sec. Pastor LAURENCE ELI BARRIOS CIFUENTES; 17,000 mems.

Iglesia Luterana Castillo Fuerte: 19 Avda 6-64, Zona 11, Guatemala City; tel. 2472-0186; fax 2384-0703; e-mail castillofuerte@lycos.com; f. 2000.

Iglesia Luterana El Divino Salvador de Zacapa: 4a Calle, 9-34, Zona 1, Barrio San Marcos, Zacapa; tel. 7941-0574; e-mail hogarluterano@hotmail.com; f. 1946; Pastors GERARDO VENANCIO VÁSQUEZ SALGUERO, ARED RODRÍGUEZ.

Iglesia Nacional Evangélica Menonita Guatemalteca: Guatemala City; tel. 2339-0606; e-mail AlvaradoJE@ldschurch.org; Pres. ALFREDO SIQUIC ACTÉ; 12,000 mems.

Union Church: 12a Calle 7-37, Zona 9, 01009 Guatemala City; tel. 2361-2037; fax 2362-3961; e-mail unionchurchguatemala@gmail.com; internet www.unionchurchguatemala.com; f. 1943; English-speaking church; Pastor JOHN CONNER.

The Press

PRINCIPAL DAILIES

Diario de Centro América: Casa Editora Tipografía Nacional, 18 Calle 6-72, Zona 1, Guatemala City; tel. 2414-9600; e-mail lector@dca.gob.gt; internet www.dca.gob.gt; f. 1880; morning; official; Dir-Gen. HÉCTOR SALVATIERRA; Editor-in-Chief JUAN CARLOS RUIZ CALDERÓN.

Guía Interamericana de Turismo: Edif. Plaza los Arcos, 3°, 20 Calle 5-35, Zona 10, Guatemala City; tel. 2450-6431; e-mail info@guiainter.org; internet www.guiainter.org; f. 1989; online journal; Dir-Gen. MARIO ORINI; Editor ALFREDO MAYORGA.

La Hora: 9 Calle A 1-56, Zona 1, Apdo 1593, Guatemala City; tel. 2423-1800; fax 2423-1837; e-mail lahora@lahora.com.gt; internet www.lahora.com.gt; f. 1920; evening; ind; Dir-Gen. OSCAR CLEMENTE MARROQUÍN; Editor-in-Chief JAVIER ESTRADA TOBAR; circ. 18,000.

Nuestro Diario: 15 Avda 24-27, Zona 13, Guatemala City; tel. and fax 2379-1600; fax 2379-1621; e-mail opinion@nuestrodiario.com.gt; internet www.nuestrodiario.com; Gen. Man. FERNANDO FAHSEN; Gen. Editor MARIO RECINOS.

El Periódico: 15 Avda 24-51, Zona 13, Guatemala City; tel. 2427-2300; fax 2427-2361; e-mail redaccion@elperiodico.com.gt; internet www.elperiodico.com.gt; f. 1996; morning; ind; Pres. JOSÉ RUBÉN ZAMORA MARROQUÍN; Editor TULIO JUÁREZ; circ. 30,000.

Prensa Libre: 13 Calle 9-31, Zona 1, Apdo 2063, Guatemala City; tel. 2230-5096; fax 2251-8768; e-mail nacionales@prensalibre.com.gt; internet www.prensalibre.com.gt; f. 1951; morning; ind; Gen. Man. LUIS ENRIQUE SOLÓRZANO; Editor GONZALO MARROQUÍN GODOY; circ. 120,000.

Siglo Veintiuno: 14 Avda 4-33, Zona 1, Guatemala City; tel. 2423-6100; fax 2423-6346; e-mail suscripciones@siglo21.com.gt; internet www.s21.com.gt; f. 1990; morning; Dir GUILLERMO FERNÁNDEZ; circ. 65,000.

PERIODICALS

Amiga: 13 Calle 9-31, Zona 1, Guatemala City; tel. 2412-5000; fax 2220-5123; e-mail revistas@prensalibre.com.gt; internet www.revistaamiga.com; f. 1988; health; Dir CAROLINA VÁSQUEZ ARAYA; Editor SILVIA LANUZA.

Gerencia: Torre Citigroup, Of. 402, 3a Avda 13-78, Zona 14, Guatemala City; tel. 2427-4900; fax 2427-4971; e-mail jaqueline@agg.org.gt; internet www.agg.org.gt/revista-gerencia-b; f. 1967; monthly; official organ of the Asscn of Guatemalan Managers; Man. ILEANA LÓPEZ ÁVILA.

El Metropolitano: Plaza Morumbi 7 y 8, 2°, 3a Calle 15-29, Zona 8, San Cristóbal, Guatemala City; e-mail info@elmetropolitano.net; internet www.elmetropolitano.net; Editor JORGE GARCÍA MONTENEGRO.

Mundo Motor: 13a Calle 9-31, Zona 1, Guatemala City; tel. 2412-5000; fax 2220-5123; e-mail evasquez@prensalibre.com.gt; internet www.mundoymotor.com; Dir CAROLINA VÁSQUEZ; Editor NÉSTOR A. LARRAZÁBAL B.

Revista Data Export: 15 Avda 14-72, Zona 13, Guatemala City; tel. 2422-3431; fax 2422-3434; e-mail portal@export.com.gt; internet revistadata.export.com.gt; monthly; foreign trade affairs; organ of the Asociacíon Guatemalteca de Exportadores; Editor FULVIA DONIS.

Revista Industria y Negocios: 6a Ruta 9-21, Zona 4, Guatemala City; tel. 2380-9000; e-mail contactemos@industriaguate.com; internet www.revistaindustria.com; monthly; official organ of the Chamber of Industry; Dir JAVIER ZAPEDA.

Revista Mundo Comercial: 10a Calle 3-80, Zona 1, 01001 Guatemala City; e-mail jbalcarcel@camaradecomercio.org.gt; internet www.negociosenguatemala.com; monthly; business; official organ of the Chamber of Commerce; Gen. Man. JEANNETTE BALCARCEL; circ. 11,000.

Viaje a Guatemala: 13 Calle 9-31, Zona 1, Guatemala City; tel. 2412-5000; fax 2220-5123; internet www.viajeaguatemala.com; Dir-Gen. CAROLINA VÁSQUEZ; Editor-in-Chief SILVIA LANUZA.

PRESS ASSOCIATION

Asociación de Periodistas de Guatemala (APG): 14 Calle 3-29, Zona 1, Guatemala City; tel. 2232-1813; fax 2238-2781; e-mail apege@intelnet.net.gt; internet www.apg-gt.org; f. 1947; affiliated to International Freedom of Expression Exchange and Fed. Latinoamericana de Periodistas; Pres. HUGO ROLANDO LÓPEZ; Sec. RAFAEL CAÑAS CASTILLO.

NEWS AGENCY

Inforpress Centroamericana: Calle Mariscal o Diagonal 21, 6-58, Zona 11, 0100 Guatemala City; tel. and fax 2473-1704; e-mail inforpre@guate.net; internet www.inforpressca.com; f. 1972; ind; publishes 2 weekly news bulletins, in English and Spanish; Dir NURIA VILLANOVA.

Publishers

Cholsamaj: Calle 5, 2-58, Zona 1, Iximulew, Guatemala City; tel. 2232-5402; fax 2232-5959; e-mail editorialcholsamaj@yahoo.com;

internet www.cholsamaj.org; Mayan language publs; Pres. KIKAB' GERBER MUX; Exec. Dir ULMIL JOEL MEJÍA.

Ediciones Legales Comercio e Industria: 12a Avda 14-78, Zone 1, Guatemala City; tel. 2253-5725; fax 2220-7592; Man. Dir LUIS EMILIO BARRIOS.

Editorial Cultura: Avda 12 11-11, Zona 1, Guatemala City; tel. 2232-5667; fax 2230-0591; e-mail kaxin@tutopia.com; internet www .mcd.gob.gt/editorial-cultura; f. 1987; part of the Ministry of Culture and Sport; Chief Editor FRANCISCO MORALES SANTOS.

Editorial Palo de Hormigo: 0 Calle 16-40, Zona 15, Col. El Maestro, Guatemala City; tel. 2369-3089; fax 2369-8858; e-mail eph_info@palodehormigo.com; f. 1990; Man. Dir RICARDO ULYSSES CIFUENTES.

Editorial Santillana, SA: 7 Avda 11-11, Zona 9, Guatemala City; tel. 2429-4300; fax 2429-4301; e-mail santillana@santillana.com.gt; internet www.gruposantillana.com/gr_gu.htm; f. 1995; subsidiary of Grupo Santillana (Spain); Dir-Gen. ALBERTO POLANCO.

Editorial Universitaria: Universidad de San Carlos de Guatemala, Ciudad Universitaria, Zona 12, Guatemala City; tel. and fax 2418-8070; e-mail editorialusac@usac.edu.gt; internet editorial.usac .edu.gt; literature, social sciences, health, pure and technical sciences, humanities, secondary and university educational textbooks; Dir ANACLETO MEDINA GÓMEZ.

F & G Editores: 31a Avda 'C' 5-54, Zona 7, 01007 Guatemala City; tel. and fax 2439-8358; e-mail informacion@fygeditores.com; internet www.fygeditores.com; f. 1990 as Figueroa y Gallardo; changed name in 1993; law, literature and social sciences; Editor RAÚL FIGUEROA SARTI.

Piedra Santa: 37 Avda 1-26, Zona 7, Guatemala City; tel. 2422-7676; fax 2422-7610; e-mail info@piedrasanta.com; internet www .piedrasanta.com; f. 1947; education, culture; Man. Dir IRENE PIEDRA SANTA.

PUBLISHERS' ASSOCIATION

Consejo Nacional del Libro (CONALIBRO): 11 Avda 11-07, Zona 1, Guatemala City; tel. 2253-0536; fax 2253-0544; e-mail conalibro@ gmail.com; f. 1989; Pres. LUIS EDUARDO MORALES.

Broadcasting and Communications

TELECOMMUNICATIONS

Comcel Guatemala (Tigo): Edif. Plaza Tigo, 3°, Km 9.5, Carretera al Salvador, Guatemala City; tel. 2428-0000; fax 2428-1140; e-mail servicioalcliente@tigo.com.gt; internet www.tigo.com.gt; f. 1990; provider of mobile telecommunications; 55% owned by Millicom International Cellular (Luxembourg); CEO VICTOR UNDA.

Telecomunicaciones de Guatemala, SA (Claro): Edif. Central Telgua, 7a Avda 12-39, Zona 1, Guatemala City; tel. 2230-2098; fax 2251-1799; e-mail clientes@claro.com.gt; internet www.claro.com.gt; fmrly state-owned Empresa Guatemalteca de Telecomunicaciones (Guatel); name changed as above to facilitate privatization; 95% share sold in 1998; owned by América Móvil, SA de CV (Mexico); Dir ANA BEATRIZ GODÍNEZ.

Telefónica Guatemala, SA (Movistar): Edif. Iberoplaza, 1°, Blvd Los Próceres 20-09, Zona 10, Guatemala City; tel. 2379-7979; e-mail servicioalcliente@telefonica.com.gt; internet www.movistar.com.gt; owned by TelefónicaMóviles, SA (Spain); acquired BellSouth Guatemala in 2004; wireless, wireline and radio paging communications services; 298,000 customers; Dir SALVADOR MONTES DE OCA.

Regulatory Authority

Superintendencia de Telecomunicaciones de Guatemala: 4 Avda 15-51, Zona 10, Guatemala City; tel. 2321-1000; fax 2321-1074; e-mail informacion@sit.gob.gt; internet www.sit.gob.gt; f. 1996; Supt EDDIE PADILLA.

BROADCASTING

Radio

Central de Radio, SA: Edif. Canal 3, 30 Avda 3-40, Zona 11, Guatemala City; tel. 2410-3150; internet www.centralderadio.com .gt; owns and operates 7 radio stations; Pres. FERNANDO VILLANUEVA CARRERA.

Emisoras Unidas de Guatemala: 4a Calle 6-84, Zona 13, Guatemala City; tel. 2421-5353; fax 2475-3870; e-mail patrullajeinformativo@emisorasunidas.com; internet www .emisorasunidas.com; f. 1964; 6 stations: Yo Sí Sideral, Emisoras-Unidas, Kiss, Atmósfera, Fabustereo and La Grande; Pres. EDGAR ARCHILA MARROQUÍN.

La Marca: 30a Avda 3-40, Zona 11, Guatemala City; tel. 2410-3150; fax 2410-3151; e-mail lamarca@94fm.com.gt; internet www.94fm .com.gt.

Metro Stereo: 14a Avda 14-78, Zona 10, Guatemala City; tel. 2277-7686; fax 2368-2040; e-mail metrored@metrostereo.net; internet www.metrostereo.net; f. 1980; Dir RUGGIERO MAURO-RHODIO.

Radio Corporación Nacional (RCN): Torre Profesional I, Of. 903, 6 Avda 0-60, Centro Comercial Zona 4, Guatemala City; tel. 2411-2000; tel. 2411-2005; internet www.rcn.com.gt; owns and operates 12 radio stations; Pres. SERGIO ROBERTO ALCÁZAR SOLÍS.

Radio Cultural TGN: 4a Avda 30-09 Zona 3, Apdo 601, 01901 Guatemala City; tel. 2207-7700; fax 2207-7600; e-mail tgn@ radiocultural.com; internet www.radiocultural.com; f. 1950; religious and cultural station; programmes in Spanish and English, Cakchiquel, Kekchi, Quiché and Aguacateco; Dir ESTEBAN SYWULKA.

Radio Grupo Alius, SA: Torre Profesional II, 10°, 6 Avda 0-60, Zona 4, Guatemala City; tel. 2412-8484; fax 2412-8448; e-mail exa@ grupoalius.com; internet www.grupoalius.com; owns and operates 5 radio stations; Pres. EDUARDO ALFONSO LIU.

Radio Nacional TGW (La Voz de Guatemala): 18a Calle 6-72, Zona 1, Guatemala City; tel. 2323-8282; fax 2323-8310; e-mail info@ radiotgw.gob.gt; internet www.radiotgw.gob.gt; f. 1930; govt station; Dir (vacant).

Television

Azteca Guatemala: 12 Avda 1-96, Zona 2 de Mixco, Col. Alvarado, Guatemala City; tel. 2411-1231; e-mail festrada@tvaguatemala.tv; internet www.azteca.com.gt; f. 2008; subsidiary by the merger of Televisión Azteca (Mexico) and Latitud TV; commercial; general; Dir-Gen. MARIO SAN ROMÁN.

Canal Antigua: Of. 12c, 12°, Avda Reforma 13-70, Zona 9, 01009 Guatemala City; tel. 2222-8800; e-mail info@canalantigua.com; internet www.canalantigua.com; f. 2009; commercial; news and opinions; Exec. Dir ANABEL BONAMI.

Guatevisión: Edif. Tikal Futura, Torre Sol, 4°, Calz Roosevelt 22-43, Zona 11, Guatemala City; tel. 2328-6000; e-mail info@guatevision .com; internet www.guatevision.com; f. 2000; Dir HAROLDO SÁNCHEZ.

Radio-Televisión Guatemala, SA: Edif. Canal 3, 30 Avda 3-40, Zona 11, Apdo 1367, Guatemala City; tel. 2410-3000; e-mail telediario@canal3.com.gt; internet www.canal3.com.gt; f. 1956; commercial; part of Albavisión; Pres. MAXIMILIANO KESTLER FARNÉS; Vice-Pres. J. F. VILLANUEVA; operates the following channels:

> **Teleonce:** 20 Calle 5-02, Zona 10, Guatemala City; tel. 2469-0900; fax 5203-8455; e-mail jcof@canalonce.tv; internet canales11y13 .blogspot.in; f. 1968; commercial; channel 11; Gen. Dir JUAN CARLOS ORTIZ.

> **Televisiete, SA:** 30 Avda 3-40, Zona 11, Apdo 1242, Guatemala City; tel. 2410-3000; fax 2369-1393; internet www.canal7.com.gt; f. 1988; commercial; channel 7; Dir LUIS RABBÉ.

> **Trecevisión, SA:** 20 Calle 5-02, Zona 10, Guatemala City; tel. 2368-2221; e-mail escribanos@canal7.com.gt; internet www .canaltrece.tv; f. 1978; commercial; channel 13; f. 1978; Dir FERNANDO VILLANUEVA.

Regulatory Authority

Dirección General de Radiodifusión y Televisión Nacional: Edif. Tipografía Nacional, 3°, 18 Calle 6-72, Zona 1, Guatemala City; tel. 2323-8282; e-mail contacto@radiotgw.gob.gt; internet www .radiotgw.gob.gt; f. 1931; govt supervisory body; Dir-Gen. JUAN JOSÉ RÍOS.

Finance

(cap. = capital; res = reserves; dep. = deposits; m. = million; brs = branches; amounts in quetzales)

BANKING

Superintendencia de Bancos: 9a Avda 22-00, Zona 1, Apdo 2306, Guatemala City; tel. 2429-5000; fax 2232-0002; e-mail info@sib.gob .gt; internet www.sib.gob.gt; f. 1946; Supt RAMÓN BENJAMÍN TOBAR MORALES.

Central Bank

Banco de Guatemala: 7a Avda 22-01, Zona 1, Apdo 365, Guatemala City; tel. 2429-6000; fax 2253-6086; e-mail webmaster@banguat.gob .gt; internet www.banguat.gob.gt; f. 1946; state-owned; cap. and res 504.1m., dep. 34,384.7m. (Dec. 2009); Pres. EDGAR BALTAZAR BARQUÍN DURÁN; Gen. Man. SERGIO FRANCISCO RECINOS RIVERA.

State Commercial Bank

Crédito Hipotecario Nacional de Guatemala (CHN): 7a Avda 22-77, Zona 1, Apdo 242, Guatemala City; tel. 2223-0333; fax 2238-2041; e-mail mercadeo@chn.com.gt; internet www.chn.com.gt; f. 1930; govt-owned; cap. 15m., res 594m., dep. 2,402.6m. (Dec. 2013); Pres. Wenceslao De Manuel Lemus; Gen. Man. Gustavo Adolfo Díaz León; 44 agencies.

Private Commercial Banks

Banco Agromercantil de Guatemala, SA: 7a Avda 7-30, Zona 9, 01009 Guatemala City; tel. 2338-6565; fax 2388-6566; e-mail info@bam.com.gt; internet www.bam.com.gt; f. 1926; changed name to Banco Agrícola Mercantil in 1948; cap. 1,339m., res 931.2m., dep. 16,781.1m. (Dec. 2013); Pres. José Luis Valdés O'Connell; Man. Christian Roberto Schneider Will; 237 brs.

Banco de América Central, SA (BAC): Local 6-12, 1°, 7a Avda 6-26, Zona 9, Guatemala City; tel. 2360-9440; fax 2331-8720; internet www.bac.net; f. 1997; Pres. Luis Fernando Samayoa Delgado; Gen. Man. Juan José Viaud Pérez; 20 brs.

Banco Citibank de Guatemala, SA: Torre Citibank, 1°, 3a Avda 13-78, Zona 10, 01010 Guatemala City; tel. 2333-6574; fax 2333-6860; internet www.citibank.com.gt; Citi acquired Banco Cuscatlan and Banco Uno in 2007; Pres. Constantino Gotsis; 37 brs.

Banco de Desarrollo Rural, SA: Avda La Reforma 9-30, Zona 9, Guatemala City; tel. 2339-8888; fax 2360-9740; e-mail internacional4@banrural.com.gt; internet www.banrural.com.gt; f. 1971 as Banco de Desarrollo Agrícola; name changed as above in 1998; cap. 1,168.2m., res 1,984.9m., dep. 31,627.3m. (Dec. 2012); Pres. Adolfo Fernando Peña Pérez; 640 brs.

Banco G & T Continental, SA: Plaza Continental, 6a Avda 9-08, Zona 9, Guatemala City; tel. 2338-6801; fax 2332-2682; e-mail subanco@gytcontinental.com.gt; internet www.gytcontinental.com.gt; f. 2000 following merger of Banco Continental and Banco Granai y Townson; total assets 11.4m. (2000); Gen. Man. Flavio Montenegro; 151 brs.

Banco Industrial, SA (BAINSA): Edif. Centro Financiero, Torre 1, 7a Avda 5-10, Zona 4, Apdo 744, Guatemala City; tel. 2420-3000; fax 2420-3118; e-mail webmaster@bi.com.gt; internet www.bi.com.gt; f. 1968 to promote industrial devt; merged with Banco del Quetzal in 2007; cap. 2,257.7m., res 1,366.9m., dep. 48,188.4m. (Dec. 2013); CEO Diego Pulido Aragón; 1,404 brs.

Banco Inmobilario, SA: Edif. Galerias España, 7a Avda 11-59, Zona 9, Apdo 1181, Guatemala City; tel. 2339-3777; fax 2332-1418; e-mail info@bcoinmob.com.gt; internet www.bancoinmobiliario.com.gt; f. 1958; cap. 77.6m., res 0.4m., dep. 738.6m. (Dec. 2002); Pres. Adel Abed Anton Turjuman; 44 brs.

Banco Promerica: Edif. Reforma 10, 2°, Avda 9-55Z, 01010 Guatemala City; tel. 2413-9400; e-mail servicio@bancopromerica.com.gt; internet www.bancopromerica.com.gt; f. 1991 as Banco de la Producción, SA (BANPRO), adopted present name in 2007 following merger with Bancasol; Pres. Ramiro Norberto Ortiz Gurdián.

Banco Reformador, SA: 7a Avda 7-24, Zona 9, 01009 Guatemala City; tel. 2362-0888; fax 2332-9595; internet www.bancoreformador.com; cap. 432.5m., res 294.5m., dep. 7,838.7m. (Dec. 2012); merged with Banco de la Construcción in 2000, acquired Banco SCI in 2007; Pres. Ernesto Castegnaro Odio; Gen. Man. Rolando Lucero; 100 brs.

Banco de los Trabajadores: Avda Reforma 6-20, Zona 9, 01001 Guatemala City; tel. 2410-2600; fax 2339-4750; e-mail webmaster@bantrab.net.gt; internet www.bantrab.com.gt; f. 1966; deals with loans for establishing and improving small industries as well as normal banking business; cap. 460.4m., dep. 2,119.5m., total assets 2,897.6m. (Dec. 2005); Pres. Sergio Hernández; Gen. Man. Ronald Giovanni García Navarijo; 33 brs.

Inter Banco, SA: Torre Internacional, Avda Reforma 15-85, Zona 10, Apdo 2588, Guatemala City; tel. 2277-3666; fax 2366-6743; e-mail info@bco.inter.com; internet www.interbanco.com.gt; f. 1976; cap. 217.7m., res 91m., dep. 3,545.8m. (Dec. 2011); Pres. César José Antonio Corrales Aguilar; Gen. Man. Francisco Naranjo Martínez; 44 brs.

Banking Association

Asociación Bancaria de Guatemala: Edif. Margarita 2, Torre II, 5°, Of. 502, Diagonal 6, No 10-11, Zona 10, Guatemala City; tel. 2382-7200; fax 2382-7201; internet www.abg.org.gt; f. 1961; represents all state and private banks; Pres. Luis Fernando Delgado.

STOCK EXCHANGE

Bolsa de Valores Nacional, SA: Centro Financiero, Torre 2, 9°, 7a Avda 5-10, Zona 4, Guatemala City; tel. 2338-4400; fax 2332-1721; e-mail info@bvnsa.com.gt; internet www.bvnsa.com.gt; f. 1987; the exchange is commonly owned (1 share per assoc.) and trades stocks from private cos, govt bonds, letters of credit and other securities; CEO Rolando San Román.

INSURANCE

National Companies

Aseguradora La Ceiba, SA: 20 Calle 15-20, Zona 13, Guatemala City; tel. 2379-1800; fax 2334-8167; e-mail aceiba@aceiba.com.gt; internet www.aceiba.com.gt; f. 1978; Man. Alejandro Beltranena.

Aseguradora General, SA: 10a Calle 3-71, Zona 10, Guatemala City; tel. 2285-7200; fax 2334-2093; e-mail servicio@generali.com.gt; internet www.aseguresemejor.com; f. 1968; subsidiary of Grupo Generali, Trieste, Italy; Pres. Enrique Neutze Aycinena; Man. Enrique Neutze Toriello.

Chartis Seguros Guatemala, SA: Edif. Etisa, 7a Avda 12-23, 3°, Plazuela España, Zona 9, Guatemala City; tel. 2285-5900; fax 2361-3032; e-mail cmg.servicios@aig.com; internet www.chartisinsurance.com; f. 1967 as La Seguridad de Centroamérica; present name adopted 2010; Pres. James W. Dwane.

Cía de Seguros El Roble, SA: Torre 2, 7a Avda 5-10, Zona 4, Guatemala City; tel. 2420-3333; fax 2361-1191; e-mail rerales@elroble.com; internet www.elroble.com; f. 1973; Gen. Man. Hermann Giron.

Departamento de Seguros y Previsión del Crédito Hipotecario Nacional: Centro Cívico, 7a Avda 22-77, Zona 1, Guatemala City; tel. 2223-0333; fax 2253-8584; e-mail vjsc@chn.com.gt; internet www.chn.com.gt; f. 1942; Pres. Oscar Erasmo Velasquez Rivera; Man. Gustavo Adolfo Díaz León.

Mapfre Seguros Guatemala, SA: Edif. Reforma 10, Avda 9-55, Zona 10, Guatemala City; tel. 2328-5000; fax 2328-5001; e-mail roberto.ewel@mapfre.com.gt; internet www.mapfre.com.gt; Gen. Man. José Tulio Urrutia.

Pan-American Life Insurance de Guatemala Cía de Seguros, SA: Edif. Plaza Panamericana, 10°, Avda la Reforma 9-00, Zona 9, Guatemala City; tel. 2338-9800; e-mail servicioalclientegt@panamericanlife.com; internet www.palig.com/Regions/guatemala; f. 1968; Country Man. Salvador Leiva Madrid.

Seguros Columna, SA: 5a. Calle 0-55, Zona 9, Apdo 01009, Guatemala City; tel. 2419-2020; e-mail info@seguroscolumna.com; internet www.seguroscolumna.com; f. 1994; part of Corporación Financiera Cooperativa FENACOAC; Pres. José Guillermo Peralta Rosa.

Seguros G & T, SA: Edif. Mini, 6a Avda 1-73, Zona 4, Guatemala City; tel. 2338-5778; e-mail tcontacto@gyt.com.gt; internet www.segurosgyt.com.gt; f. 1947; Pres. Marío Granai Andrino; Gen. Man. Enrique Rodríguez.

Seguros de Occidente, SA: Edif. Corporación de Occidente, 7a Avda 7-33, Zona 9, Guatemala City; tel. 2279-7000; e-mail seguros@occidentecorp.com.gt; internet www.occidente.com.gt/cdo; f. 1979; Gen. Man. Mario Roberto Valdeavellano Muñoz.

Seguros Universales, SA: 4a Calle 7-73, Zona 9, Apdo 01009, Guatemala City; tel. 2384-7400; fax 2332-3372; e-mail info@segurosuniversales.net; internet www.segurosuniversales.net; f. 1962; Pres. Pedro Nolasco Sicilia Valls; Gen. Man. Felipe Sicilia.

Insurance Association

Asociación Guatemalteca de Instituciones de Seguros (AGIS): Edif. Reforma 10, Of. 905, Avda La Reforma 9-55, Zona 10, Guatemala City; tel. 2361-7067; fax 2335-2357; e-mail info@agis.com.gt; internet www.agis.com.gt; f. 1953; 12 mems; Pres. Salvador Leiva Madrid; Exec. Dir Enrique Murillo C.

Trade and Industry

DEVELOPMENT ORGANIZATIONS

Instituto de Fomento de Hipotecas Aseguradas (FHA): Edif. Aristos Reforma, 2°, Of. 207, Avda Reforma 7-62, Zona 9, Guatemala City; tel. 2323-5656; fax 2362-9491; e-mail promocion@fha.gob.gt; internet www.fha.gob.gt; f. 1961; insured mortgage institution; Pres. Edin Homero Velasquez Escobedo; Man. Sergio Armando Irungaray Suárez.

Instituto Nacional de Administración Pública (INAP): Blvd Los Próceres 16-40, Zona 10, Apdo 2753, Guatemala City; tel. 2419-8181; fax 2419-8126; e-mail informacion@inap.gob.gt; internet www.inap.gob.gt; f. 1964; provides technical experts to assist in administrative reform programmes; provides training for govt staff; research programmes in administration, sociology, politics and economics; Pres. Fernando Fuentes Mohr; Man. Héctor Hugo Vásquez Barreda.

Secretaría de Planificación y Programación (SEGEPLAN): 9a Calle 10-44, Zona 1, Guatemala City; tel. 2232-6212; fax 2253-3127; e-mail segeplan@segeplan.gob.gt; internet www.segeplan.gob.gt; f. 1954; oversees implementation of the national economic devt plan; Sec. LUIS FERNANDO CARRERA CASTRO.

CHAMBERS OF COMMERCE AND INDUSTRY

Cámara de Comercio de Guatemala: 10a Calle 3-80, Zona 1, Guatemala City; tel. 2417-2700; fax 2220-9393; e-mail camaradecomercio.org.gt; internet www.negociosenguatemala.com; f. 1894; Pres. JORGE EDUARDO BRIZ ABULARACH; Exec. Dir JUAN JOSÉ CABRERA.

Cámara Empresarial de Comercio y Servicios (Cecoms): Guatemala City; Pres. GUILLERMO GONZÁLEZ.

Cámara de Industria de Guatemala: 6a Ruta 9-21, 12°, Zona 4, Apdo 214, Guatemala City; tel. 2380-9000; e-mail info@ industriaguate.com; internet www.industriaguate.com; f. 1959; Pres. ANDRÉS CASTILLO; Exec. Dir JAVIER ZEPEDA.

Cámara Oficial Española de Comercio de Guatemala: Edif. Paladium, 14°, 4 Avda 15-70, Zona 10, Guatemala City; tel. 2470-3301; fax 2470-3304; e-mail gerencia@camacoes.org.gt; internet www.camacoes.org.gt; f. 1928; Pres. Dr RAFAEL BRIZ; Gen. Man. SILVIA CAROLINA TAMAYAC MÁRQUEZ.

Comité Coordinador de Asociaciones Agrícolas, Comerciales, Industriales y Financieras (CACIF): Edif. Cámara de Industria de Guatemala, 6a Ruta 9-21, Zona 4, Guatemala City; tel. 2231-0651; fax 2334-7025; e-mail informacion@cacif.org.gt; internet www.cacif.org.gt; 6 mem. chambers; Pres. ANDRÉS CASTILLO; Exec. Dir ROBERTO ARDÓN.

INDUSTRIAL AND TRADE ASSOCIATIONS

Asociación de Azucareros de Guatemala (ASAZGUA): Edif. Europlaza, 178°, 5a Avda 5-55, Zona 14, Guatemala City; tel. 2386-2299; fax 2386-2020; e-mail asazgua@azucar.com.gt; internet www.azucar.com.gt; f. 1957; sugar producers' asscn; 15 mems; Pres. MARCO AUGUSTO GARCÍA; Gen. Man. ARMANDO BOESCHE.

Asociación General de Agricultores (AGA): Edif. Rodseguros, 6°, Via 1, 1-67, Zona 4, Guatemala City; tel. 2361-0654; fax 2332-4817; e-mail asistente@aga.org.gt; internet www.aga.org.gt; f. 1920; general farmers' asscn; Pres. PETER FRANK; 350 mems.

Asociación Guatemalteca de Exportadores (AGEXPORT): 15a Avda 14-72, Zona 13, Guatemala City; tel. 2422-3400; fax 2422-3434; e-mail portal@export.com.gt; internet www.export.com.gt; f. 1982; exporters' asscn; Pres. FRANCISCO MENENDEZ; Dir-Gen. LUIS GODOY.

Asociación Nacional de Avicultores (ANAVI): Edif. El Reformador, 4°, Of. 401, Avda La Reforma 1-50, Zona 9, Guatemala City; tel. 2360-3384; fax 2360-3161; e-mail anavi@anaviguatemala.org; internet www.anaviguatemala.com; f. 1964; national asscn of poultry farmers; 60 mems; Pres. MARIA DEL ROSARIO DE FALLA; Gen. Man. PEGGY CONTRERAS.

Asociación Nacional del Café—Anacafé: 5a Calle 0-50, Zona 14, Guatemala City; tel. 2421-3700; e-mail info@email.anacafe.org; internet www.anacafe.org; f. 1960; national coffee asscn; Pres. RICARDO VILLANUEVA CARRERA; Sec. MARTÍN ARÉVALO DE LEÓN.

Cámara del Agro: Edif. Géminis 10, Torre Norte, 9°, Of. 909, 12 Calle, 1-25, Zona 10, Guatemala City; tel. 2219-9021; e-mail camagro@intelnet.net.gt; internet www.camaradelagro.org; f. 1973; Pres. OTTO KUSIEK; Exec. Dir CARLA CABALLEROS.

Gremial de Empresarios Indígenas de Guatemala (Guate-Maya): f. 2012; private sector org. representing 190 indigenous cos; mem. of CACIF (q.v.); Pres. LUIS TEPEU.

Gremial de Huleros de Guatemala: 6a Avda A 12-37, Zona 9, Guatemala City; tel. 2339-1752; fax 2339-1755; e-mail gremhuleger@ guate.net.gt; internet www.gremialdehuleros.org; f. 1970; rubber producers' guild; 125 mems; Pres. JOSÉ MIGUEL EIZAGUIRRE; Gen. Man. CARLOS ALFREDO NÁJERA CASTILLO.

MAJOR COMPANIES

Construction

Cementos Progreso, SA: Centro Gerencial Las Margaritas, Torre II, 19°, Zona 10, Guatemala City; tel. 2338-9100; fax 2338-9110; e-mail info@cempro.com; internet www.cempro.com; f. 1899; cement mfrs; sold to the Swiss Holderbank Financiere Glaris Ltd in 2000; Gen. Man. JORGE LEMCKE; 1,550 employees.

Ingenieria De Construcción, SA (IDC): 14 Avda 14-50, Zona 10, Oakland, Guatemala City; tel. 5368-1974; fax 5333-4994; e-mail gerencia@idcguatemala.com; internet www.idcguatemala.com; commercial and residential constructions.

Food and Beverages

Central America Beverage Corporation (CABCORP): Guatemala City; f. 1885; mfr and distributor of Pepsi-Cola products; Pres. CARLOS ENRIQUE MATA CASTILLO.

Cervecería Centro Americana, SA: 3a Avda Norte Final, Finca El Zapote, Zona 2, Guatemala City; tel. 2289-1555; fax 2289-1716; internet www.cerveceria.com.gt; f. 1886; brewery; Pres. JORGE CASTILLO LOVE; 440 employees.

Industrias Alimenticias Kerns y CIA, SA: Km 7, Carretera al Atlántico, Zona 18, Guatemala City; tel. 2323-7100; fax 2256-2378; e-mail info@alimentoskerns.com; internet www.alikerns.com; f. 1959; mfrs of canned fruit juices and fruit products; Gen. Man. RICARDO SANTIZO; 550 employees.

Industrias Licoreras de Guatemala (ILG): Km 16.5, Carretera Roosevelt 4-81, Zona 1, Mixco; tel. 2470-9696; fax 2470-9508; e-mail info@ronesdeguatemala.com; internet industriaslicorerasdeguatemala.com; f. 1982; production and distribution of alcoholic beverages; subsidiaries incl. Ingenio Tululá, SA, and DARSA; Pres. ROBERTO GARCÍA BOTRÁN; 1,600 employees.

Pantaleon: Diagonal 6, 10-31, Centro Gerencial Las Margaritas, Zona 10, 01010 Guatemala City; tel. 2277-5100; fax 2334-7238; internet www.pantaleon.com; f. 1973; sugar producers; factories in Honduras, Nicaragua, Mexico and Brazil.

Pollo Campero: Guatemala City; tel. 2333-7233; e-mail ebarillas@ campero.com.gt; internet campero.gt; f. 1971; restaurant franchise; Pres. JUAN JOSÉ GUTIÉRREZ.

Metals and Rubber

Grupo Cobán: 24 Calle 20-56, Zona 12, Guatemala City; tel. 2421-6900; fax 2476-6335; e-mail info@grupocoban.com.gt; internet www.grupocoban.com.gt; f. 1914; mfrs of rubber goods; Gen. Man. JOSÉ CARMELO TORREBIARTE; 250 employees.

Llantas Vifrio, SA: 42 Calle 20-64, Zona 12, Guatemala City; tel. 2476-1212; fax 2479-3017; e-mail llantas@vifrio.com; internet www.vifrio.com; f. 1967; repair and retreading of tyres; Pres. HUMBERTO SUÁREZ VALDEZ.

SIDASA (Servicios Industriales y Agrícolas, SA): 10a Calle 0-52, Zona 9, Guatemala City; tel. 2323-5555; fax 2334-7149; e-mail info@ sidasa.net; internet www.sidasa.net; f. 1979; mfrs of industrial and agro-industrial equipment.

Pharmaceuticals

Abbott Laboratórios, SA: Edif. Europlaza, Torre I, 10°, 5 Avda 5-55, Zona 14, 01014 Guatemala City; tel. 2420-9797; fax 2420-9818; internet www.abbott.com; medical equipment mfrs; Group Chair. MILES D. WHITE.

Colgate Palmolive Central America, SA: Avda Ferrocarril 49-65, Zona 12, Guatemala City; tel. 2423-9200; fax 2423-9500; internet www.colgatecentralamerica.com; f. 1971; pharmaceuticals and consumer products; Pres. IAN M. COOK; Pres. (Latin America) NOEL WALLACE; 465 employees.

Miscellaneous

Alcatel-Lucent Tecnologías Guatemala, SA: Edif. Lucent, 9a Calle 15-45, Zona 13, Guatemala City; tel. 5278-7098; e-mail lizbeth .ulett@alcatel-lucent.com; subsidiary of Alcatel-Lucent (France); mfr of telecommunications equipment; Group CEO MICHEL COMBES.

British American Tobacco Central America (BATCA): 24 Avda 35-81, Zona 120, Calzada Atanacio Tzul, Apdo 316, Guatemala City; tel. 2410-3737; fax 2366-8785; internet www.batca.com; f. 1928; subsidiary of BAT Industries PLC (United Kingdom); cigarette mfrs; Man. SOFÍA OLIVA; 345 employees.

Entre Mares de Guatemala, SA: Europlaza World Business Center, Torre I, 6°, Of. 601, 5 Avda, 5-55, Zona 14, Guatemala City; tel. 2329-2600; fax 2329-2610; internet goldcorpguatemala.com; f. 1997; gold and silver mining; subsidiary of Goldcorp Inc (Canada); operations in the Cerro Blanco mine situated in Asunción Mita, Jutiapa (reported to be suspended in Aug. 2013); Vice-Pres. EDUARDO VILLACORTA.

Excel Automotriz: Guatemala City; tel. 2277-8200; internet www.excelautomotriz.com/gt/inicio.html; known as Grupo Central Automotriz until 2010; part of the Grupo POMA; distributor of cars and car parts; Exec. Vice-Pres. (Group) CARLOS BOZA.

Industria La Popular, SA: Vía 3 5-42, Zona 4, Guatemala City; tel. 2420-0202; fax 2331-0381; e-mail atencionalcliente@ilpsa.com; internet www.industrialapopular.com; f. 1920; producers of soap and detergents; Pres. FEDERICO KONG VIELMAN; 555 employees.

Inyectores de Plástico: Avda Petapa 8-95, Calle 56, Zona 21, Guatemala City; tel. 2326-5700; fax 2326-5710; e-mail ventasipsa@ icasa.com.gt; internet www.ipsa.com.gt; f. 1974; subsidiary of Grupo Industrial EEC; mfrs of plastic packaging; Gen. Man. JON ZABALA.

KPMG Guatemala: 7a Avda 5-10, Zona 4, Centro Financiero, Torre 1, 16°, Guatemala City; tel. 2334-2628; fax 2331-5477; e-mail kpmg@guate.net; internet www.kpmg.com/kca; accountants and management consultants; Pres. (Central America) CARLOS KARAMAÑITES; Country Dir FELIPE GÓMEZ.

PricewaterhouseCoopers: Edif. Tívoli Plaza, 6a Calle 6-38, Zona 9, Apdo 868, Guatemala City; tel. 2420-7800; fax 2331-8345; internet www.pwc.com/gt; accountants and management consultants; Partners DORA ORIZABAL, RICARDO MOLINA.

Proquirsa: Edif. Proquirsa, 19 Avda 12-57, Zona 11, Guatemala City; tel. 2310-6717; fax 2474-5761; e-mail ventas@proquirsa.com; internet www.proquirsa.com; distributors of industrial chemicals.

Sacos del Atlántico: 15 Avda 18-01, Zona 6, La Pedrera, Guatemala City; tel. 7929-0000; fax 2286-4153; internet www.sacosdelatlantico.com; paper products; Gen. Man. ESTUARDO FIGUEROA.

Vidriera Guatemalteca (VIGUA): Avda Petapa 48-01, Zona 12, Apdo 1759, Guatemala City; tel. 2422-6400; fax 2422-6500; e-mail vigua@grupovical.com; internet www.grupovical.com; f. 1964; subsidiary of Grupo Vidriero Centroamericano (VICAL); producers of glass bottles and containers.

UTILITIES

Regulatory Authority

Comisión Nacional de Energía Eléctrica (CNEE): Edif. Paladium, 12°, 4 Avda 15-70, Zona 10, Guatemala City; tel. 2321-8000; fax 2321-8002; e-mail cnee@cnee.gob.gt; internet www.cnee.gob.gt; f. 1996; Pres. CARMEN URÍZAR.

Electricity

Empresa Eléctrica de Guatemala, SA: 6 Avda 8-14, Zona 1, Guatemala City; tel. 2277-7000; e-mail consultas@eegsa.net; internet www.eegsa.com; f. 1972; state electricity producer; 80% privatized in 1998; Gen. Man. JORGE ALONZO; subsidiaries include:

Comercializadora Eléctrica de Guatemala, SA (COMEGSA): Avda 6, 8-14, Zona 1, Guatemala City; tel. 2420-4200; fax 2230-5628; e-mail info@comegsa.net; internet www.comegsa.com.gt; f. 1998; Gen. Man. ANGEL GARCÍA.

Trelec, SA: 2 Avda 9-27, Zona 1, Guatemala City; tel. 2420-4235; fax 2420-0409; e-mail trelec@trelec.net; f. 1999; Gen. Man. EDUARDO MANUEL ARITA.

Instituto Nacional de Electrificación (INDE): Edif. La Torre, 7a Avda 2-29, Zona 9, Guatemala City; tel. (2) 2422-1800; e-mail gerencia.general@inde.gob.gt; internet www.inde.gob.gt; f. 1959; fmr state agency for the generation and distribution of hydroelectric power; principal electricity producer; privatized in 1998; Pres. ERICK ESTUARDO ARCHILA DEHESA; Gen. Man. MARINUS ARIE BOER JOHANNESSEN.

CO-OPERATIVE

Instituto Nacional de Cooperativas (INACOP): Via 6, 6-72, Zona 4, Guatemala City; tel. 2339-1627; fax 2339-1648; e-mail gerentegeneral@inacop.gob.gt; internet www.inacop.gob.gt; technical and financial assistance in planning and devt of co-operatives; Gen. Man. LUIS ALBERTO MONTENEGRO.

TRADE UNIONS

Asamblea Nacional del Magisterio (ANM): Guatemala City; teachers' union; Co-ordinator JOVIEL ACEVEDO.

Central de Trabajadores del Campo y la Ciudad (CTC): 12a Calle 'A' 12-44, Zona 1, Guatemala City; tel. and fax 2232-6947; e-mail centracampo@yahoo.com; Sec.-Gen. MIGUEL ANGEL LUCAS GÓMEZ.

Confederación General de Trabajadores de Guatemala (CGTG): 3 Avda 12-22, Zona 1, Guatemala City; tel. 2232-1010; fax 2251-3212; e-mail info@confederacioncgtg.org; internet www.confederacioncgtg.org; f. 1987; fmrly Central Nacional de Trabajadores (CNT); Sec.-Gen. JOSÉ E. PINZÓN SALAZAR; 60,000 mems (2007).

Federación Sindical de Trabajadores de la Alimentación Agro-Industrias y Similares de Guatemala (FESTRAS): 16 Avda 13-52, Zona 1, Guatemala City; tel. and fax 2251-8091; e-mail festras@gmail.com; internet festras.blogspot.in; f. 1991; Sec.-Gen. JOSÉ DAVID MORALES C.

Sindicato Nacional de Trabajadores de Salud de Guatemala (SNTSG): Guatemala City; internet sindicatonacionaldesaludsntsg.blogspot.co.uk/2011/12/blog-post.html; health workers' union; Sec.-Gen. LUIS ALBERTO LARA.

Unidad de Acción Sindical y Popular (UASP): 10 Avda A 5-40, Zona 1, Guatemala City; tel. 2230-5423; fax 2230-3004; e-mail uaspgt@yahoo.com; internet www.uaspgt.es.tl; f. 1988; broad coalition of leading labour and peasant orgs; Co-ordinator NERY ROBERTO BARRIOS DE LEÓN; Sec. NÉLIDA CORADO; includes:

Comité de la Unidad Campesina (CUC) (Committee of Peasants' Unity): 31a Avda A 14-46, Zona 7, Ciudad de Plata II, Apdo 1002, Guatemala City; tel. 2434-9754; fax 2438-1424; e-mail cuc@intelnett.com; internet www.cuc.org.gt; f. 1978; Sec.-Gen. DANIEL PASCUAL HERNÁNDEZ.

Confederación de Unidad Sindical de Guatemala (CUSG): 12 Calle A, 0-66, Zona 1, Guatemala City; tel. and fax 2220-7875; fax 2238-3654; e-mail info@cusg.com.gt; internet www.cusg.com.gt; f. 1983; Sec.-Gen. CARLOS ENRIQUE MANCILLA GARCÍA; 30,000 mems (2011).

Federación Nacional de Sindicatos de Trabajadores del Estado de Guatemala (FENASTEG): 10a Avda 5-40, Zona 1, Guatemala City; tel. and fax 2232-2772; Sec. NÉSTOR DE LEÓN.

Unión Sindical de Trabajadores de Guatemala (UNSITRAGUA): 9a Avda 1-43, Zona 1, Guatemala City; tel. 2220-4121; fax 2238-2272; e-mail unsitragua02@yahoo.com; f. 1985; Sec.-Gen. AMPARO LOCÁN; 17,500 mems (2011).

Unión Guatemalteca de Trabajadores (UGT): 13a Calle 11-40, Zona 1, Guatemala City; tel. and fax 2251-1686; e-mail ugt.guatemala@yahoo.com; Sec.-Gen. ADOLFO LACS.

Transport

RAILWAYS

In 2007 there were 885 km of railway track in Guatemala.

Ferrovías Guatemala: 24 Avda 35-91, Zona 12, 01012 Guatemala City; tel. 2412-7200; fax 2412-7205; e-mail info@ferroviasgt.com; internet www.rrdc.com/op_guatemala_fvg.html; f. 1968 as Ferrocarriles de Guatemala (FEGUA); 50-year concession awarded in 1997 to the US Railroad Devt Corpn (RDC); 784 km from Puerto Barrios and Santo Tomás de Castilla on the Atlantic coast to Tecún Umán on the Mexican border, via Zacapa, Guatemala City and Santa María; in 2007 services were suspended after arbitration claim filed by the RDC under the terms of the Dominican Republic-Central American Free Trade Agreement; claim resolved in 2013, but the services remained suspended in 2014; Pres. WILLIAM J. DUGGAN.

ROADS

In 2010 there were 14,118 km of roads, of which just over one-half were paved. The Guatemalan section of the Pan-American highway is 518.7 km long and totally asphalted. In 2009 construction began of the 362-km Franja Transversal del Norte highway, linking the departments of Huehuetenango and Izabal. The Banco Centroamericano de Integración Económica approved a US $203m. loan for the project.

SHIPPING

Guatemala's major ports are Puerto Barrios and Santo Tomás de Castilla on the Gulf of Mexico, San José and Champerico on the Pacific Ocean, and Puerto Quetzal. At 31 December 2013 the flag registered fleet comprised six vessels, totalling 2,990 grt.

Comisión Portuaria Nacional: 6 Avda A 8-66, Zona 9, Apdo 01009, Guatemala City; tel. 2419-4800; fax 2360-5457; e-mail info@cpn.gob.gt; internet www.cpn.gob.gt; f. 1972; Pres. VIOLETA LUNA; Exec. Dir CARLOS ENRIQUE DE LA CERDA.

Dacotrans de Centroamerica, SA: 24 Avda 41-81, Zona 12, Interior Almacenadora Integrada, Apdo 40, Guatemala City; tel. 2381-1200; fax 2381-1244; e-mail dacotrans@dacotrans.com.gt; internet www.dacotrans.com.gt; f. 1969; part of Grupo Dacotrans Grosskopf GMBH & Co (Germany); Gen. Man. MATHIAS REHE.

Empresa Portuaria Nacional de Champerico: Avda del Ferrocarril, frente a la playa, 1000101 Champerico, Retalhuleu; tel. 7773-7223; fax 7773-7221; e-mail vallejo.l@gmail.com; internet www.epnac.blogspot.com; f. 1955; Pres. LUIS ENRIQUE PRADO LUARCA; Man. MARGARITO FLORIAN ESCOBEDO.

Empresa Portuaria Nacional Santo Tomás de Castilla (EMPORNAC): Calle Real de la Villa, 17 Calle 16-43, Zona 10, Guatemala City; tel. 7720-4040; fax 7960-0584; e-mail mercadeo@santotomasport.com.gt; internet www.santotomasport.com.gt; Pres. JOSÉ ROBERTO DÍAZ-DÚRAN QUEZADA; Gen. Man. EDGARDO LÓPEZ.

Empresa Portuaria Quetzal: Edif. Torre Azul, 1°, Of. 105, 4 Calle 7-53, Zona 9, 01009 Guatemala City; tel. 2312-5000; fax 2334-8172; e-mail mercadeo@puerto-quetzal.com; internet www.puerto-quetzal.com; port and shipping co; Pres. FELIPE CASTAÑEDA; Gen. Man. RODOLFO KUSHIEK.

Seaboard Marine Ltda: Edif. Galerias Reforma, 4°, Of. 411, Avda La Reforma 8-60, Zona 9, Guatemala City; tel. 2384-3900; fax 2334-0077; e-mail Guillermo_Ortiz@seaboardmarine.com.gt; internet www.seaboardmarine.com; subsidiary of Seaboard Corpn (USA); Rep. GUILLERMO ORTIZ.

Transmares, SA: Torre 2, 8°, Centro Gerencial Las Margaritas, Diagonal 6, 10-01, Zona 10, 01010 Guatemala City; tel. 2429-8100; fax 2429-8148; e-mail henneke.sieveking@transmares.net; internet www.transmares.org; ocean liner and cargo shipping; logistics services under Translogística, SA; Gen. Man. HENNEKE SIEVEKING.

CIVIL AVIATION

There are two international airports, La Aurora in Guatemala City and Mundo Maya in Santa Elena, El Petén.

Dirección General de Aeronáutica Civil: Aeropuerto La Aurora, Zona 13, 01013 Guatemala City; tel. 2362-0216; e-mail direccion@dgac.gob.gt; internet www.dgacguate.com; f. 1929; administers and regulates aviation services; Dir JUAN JOSÉ CARLOS SUÁREZ.

Aviones Comerciales de Guatemala (Avcom): Aeropuerto 'La Aurora', Avda Hincapié 18, Zona 13, Guatemala City; tel. 2331-5821; fax 2332-4946; domestic charter passenger services.

TACA: Aeropuerto 'La Aurora', Avda Hincapié 12-22, Zona 13, Guatemala City; tel. 2470-8222; e-mail scastillo@taca.com; internet www.taca.com; f. 1945 as Aerolíneas de Guatemala (AVIATECA); privatized in 1989; domestic services and services to the USA, Mexico, and within Central America; Gen. Man. MYNOR CORDON.

Transportes Aéreos Guatemaltecos, SA (TAG): Avda Hinapie y 18 Calle, Zona 13, Guatemala City; tel. 2380-9494; fax 2334-7205; e-mail tagsa@tag.com.gt; internet www.tag.com.gt; f. 1969; domestic and int. charter services; Gen. Man. JONATHAN LAYTON.

Tourism

Guatemala's main attraction lies in the ancient Mayan ruins. Other tourism highlights include its active steaming volcanos, mountain lakes, pristine beaches and a rich indigenous culture. The number of tourist arrivals rose steadily following the end of the civil war in 1996.

By 2013 arrivals had reached 2.0m. In the same year receipts from tourism, excluding passenger transport, were US $1,020.6m.

Instituto Guatemalteco de Turismo (INGUAT) (Guatemala Tourist Institute): Centro Cívico, 7a Avda 1-17, Zona 4, Guatemala City; tel. 2421-2800; fax 2331-4416; e-mail informacion@inguat.gob.gt; internet www.inguat.gob.gt; f. 1967; policy and planning council: 11 mems representing the public and private sectors; Dir PEDRO PABLO DUCHEZ.

Defence

As assessed in November 2013, Guatemala's active armed forces numbered an estimated 17,300: army 15,550, navy 900 and air force 850. Reserve forces totalled 63,850. In addition, there were paramilitary forces of 25,000. Military service is by selective conscription for 30 months.

Defence Budget: an estimated 2,040m. quetzales in 2013.

Chief of Staff of National Defence: Gen. CARLOS EDUARDO ESTRADA PERÉZ.

Education

Elementary education is free and compulsory between seven and 14 years of age. Primary education begins at the age of seven and lasts for six years. Secondary education, beginning at 13 years of age, lasts for up to six years, comprising two cycles of three years each. Enrolment at primary schools in 2011 included 93% of children in the relevant age-group. The comparable ratio for secondary education in that year was 46%. There are 12 universities, of which 11 are privately run. In 2012 expenditure on education by the central Government was projected at 11,097.7m. quetzales, equivalent to 18.6% of total spending.

Bibliography

For works on Central America generally, see Select Bibliography (Books)

Adams, A. E., and Smith, T. J. (Eds). *After the Coup: An Ethnographic Reframing of Guatemala 1954*. Champaign, IL, University of Illinois Press, 2011.

Afflitto, F., and Jesilow, P. *The Quiet Revolutionaries: Seeking Justice in Guatemala*. Austin, TX, University of Texas Press, 2007.

Barrie, L., and Anson, R. (Eds). *Prospects for the Textile and Clothing Industry in Guatemala*. Wilmslow, Textiles Intelligence, 2005.

Burrell, J. L. *Maya after War: Conflict, Power, and Politics in Guatemala* Austin, TX, University of Texas Press, 2013.

Cullather, N., and Gleijeses, P. *Secret History: The CIA's Classified Account of its Operations in Guatemala, 1952–1954*. Stanford, CA, Stanford University Press, 1999.

Dosal, P. J. *Doing Business with the Dictators: A Political History of United Fruits in Guatemala, 1899–1944*. Wilmington, DE, Scholarly Resources, 1993.

Forster, C. *The Time of Freedom: Campesino Workers in Guatemala's October Revolution*. Pittsburgh, PA, University of Pittsburgh Press, 2001.

Gaitan, H. *Los Presidentes de Guatemala: Historia y Anecdotas*. Guatemala City, Ediciones Artemis-Edinter, 2009.

Garrard-Burnett, V. *Terror in the Land of the Holy Spirit: Guatemala under General Efraín Ríos Montt 1982–1983*. New York, OUP USA, 2010.

Glebbeek, M.-L. 'In the Crossfire of Democracy: Police Reform and Police Practice', in *Post-Civil War Guatemala* (Thela Latin America Series). Amsterdam, Rozenberg, 2003.

Goldin, L. R. *Global Maya: Work and Ideology in Rural Guatemala*. Tucson, AZ, University of Arizona Press, 2011.

Haertle, J. *Retributive Genocide in the Highlands: Guatemala's Military Response to a Nationalized Indigenous Identity*. Lambert Academic Publishing, 2010.

Hawkins, T. *José de Bustamante and Central American Independence: Colonial Administration in an Age of Imperial Crisis*. Tuscaloosa, AL, University of Alabama Press, 2004.

Konefal, B. *For Every Indio Who Falls: A History of Maya Activism in Guatemala, 1960–1990*. Sante Fe, NM, University of New Mexico Press, 2010.

Little, W. E., and Smith, T. J. (Eds). *Mayas in Postwar Guatemala: Harvest of Violence Revisited (Contemporary American Indians)*. Tuscaloosa, AL, University of Alabama Press, 2009.

Levenson, D. T. *Adiós Niño: The Gangs of Guatemala City and the Politics of Death*. Durham, NC, Duke University Press, 2013.

Lovell, W. G. *A Beauty that Hurts: Life and Death in Guatemala*. 2nd edn, Austin, TX, University of Texas Press, 2010.

Neier, A. *Paradise in Ashes: A Guatemalan Journey of Courage, Terror, and Hope*. Berkeley, CA, University of California Press, 2004.

Nolin, C. *Transnational Ruptures: Gender and Forced Migration (Gender in a Global / Local World)*. Stanford, CA, Stanford University Press, 2006.

O'Neill, K. L., and Thomas, K. (Eds). *Securing the City: Neoliberalism, Space, and Insecurity in Postwar Guatemala*. Durham, NC, Duke University Press Books, 2011.

Sanford, V. *Buried Secrets: Truth and Human Rights in Guatemala*. New York, Palgrave Macmillan, 2003.

Schlesinger, S., and Kinzer, S. *Bitter Fruit: The Story of the American Coup in Guatemala*. Cambridge, MA, Harvard University Press, 1999.

Short, N. *The International Politics of Post-Conflict Reconstruction in Guatemala*. Basingstoke, Palgrave Macmillan, 2008.

Siekmeier, J. F. *Aid, Nationalism and Inter-American Relations— Guatemala, Bolivia and the United States 1945–1961*. Lewiston, NY, Edwin Mellen Press, 1999.

Stolen, K. A. *Guatemalans in the Aftermath of Violence: The Refugees' Return* (Ethnography of Political Violence Series). Philadelphia, PA, University of Pennsylvania Press, 2007.

Stoll, D. *Rigoberta Menchú and the Story of All Poor Guatemalans*. Boulder, CO, Westview Press, 1999.

GUYANA

Geography

PHYSICAL FEATURES

The Co-operative Republic of Guyana is the westernmost and largest of the three Guianas that occupy that part of the north-eastern coast of South America between the Serra Tumucu-maque and the Atlantic Ocean. Formerly the United King-dom's colony of British Guiana, Guyana is bordered to the east by Suriname (formerly Dutch Guiana). The two countries share a border along the Corentyne (Corantijn) river, although Suriname disputes possession of territory between the upper reaches of the Corentyne (or Kutari) and the New River (Upper Corentyne), in the south-eastern corner of Guyana. Venezuela, which lies to the west, claims most of northern Guyana by arguing that its border should run along the Essequibo river. Brazil lies beyond the longer, southern part of the western border and in the south (Brazil has 1,119 km—695 miles—of frontier with Guyana, Venezuela has 743 km and Suriname 600 km). Guyana is the third smallest country in South America (after Suriname and Uruguay), with an area of 214,969 sq km (83,000 sq miles).

Guyana consists of a northern block, longer along the coast, with a narrower southern extension into Brazil and along the border with Suriname. Guyana's Atlantic coast, which extends for 459 km, faces north-east. Behind it, protected by a complex system of dams and dykes (except in the east, where more than just a coastal strip is still swampy), is a rich plain of alluvial mud, deposited by the Amazon and other rivers. These coastal plains vary between 8 km and 65 km in width, and are mostly below sea level. Most of the agriculture and population of the country is located here. Inland are rolling highlands, most of it clad in dense woodland. The forest region, which accounts for four-fifths of the country, covers an eroded plateau. From this, in the south-west of northern Guyana, are the Pakaraima Mountains, including the country's highest, Roraima (2,835 m or 9,304 ft), which is on the Venezuelan border, and also just north of the border with Brazil. The forest region extends into the highlands, reaching as far as where the land rises again in the far south. Here, forest tends to be displaced by savannah grasslands, such as in the Rupununi valley in the far south-west. The country is 84% wooded, and has rich farmland along the coast, all of this watered by a number of rivers (Guyana means 'land of many waters'), the main ones being the Esse-quibo, in the centre of the country, and its tributaries, the Demerara, the Berbice and the Corentyne.

CLIMATE

Although the climate is characteristically hot and humid, it is relatively mild for such a low-lying area in the tropics, being moderated by the north-eastern trade winds off the Atlantic. There are two rainy seasons (May–August and November–January), during which flash floods are always a risk. The average annual rainfall in Georgetown, the capital, on the coast, is 2,280 mm (almost 90 ins). There is less rain on the higher plateau regions, with the savannah of the far south receiving about 1,525 mm per year. The average temperatures in Georgetown range from 23°C (73°F) to 31°C (88°F) all year round.

POPULATION

Guyana has a varied and complex ethnic constitution, the result of different solutions to labour demand during the

colonial period. There are some Amerindian peoples (about 9% according to the latest available (2002) census—mainly Caribs) in the interior still, but most of the population (43%) is 'East' Indian, descended from indentured workers brought from the Indian subcontinent in the 19th century. Some 30% are black, descended from the African slaves whose freedom had required new labour solutions. There are also the des-cendants of Chinese and Portuguese workers (the latter mainly from Madeira, but who have not maintained the use of their original language), who together comprise less than 1% of the total population. About 17% of the total population are of mixed race. English is the official language and the one most widely used by all these communities, but an English-based Creole is also spoken, as is (particularly among the older generations) Hindi, Urdu and Chinese. The Amerindians have their own languages too. Almost one-half of the popula-tion is Christian, 28% Hindu and 7% Muslim.

The total population, according to UN estimates, was 803,677 in mid-2014. Around 90% of the population lives on the coast and just over three-fifths reside in rural areas. In mid-2014 the UN estimated that some 124,000 people lived in and around the capital, Georgetown, which is located just to the east of the mouth of the Demerara. To the east of the capital is the port of New Amsterdam, another important town, and inland is the mining town of Linden, with the nearby centres of Wismar and Christianborg. The country is divided into 10 regions for administrative purposes.

History

MARK WILSON

Based on an earlier article by CHARLES ARTHUR

EARLY OCCUPATION

The region of present-day Guyana was originally inhabited by Carib, Arawak, Warao and other Amerindian peoples, and its name derives from Amerindian words meaning '[land of] many waters', owing to the numerous rivers and the extensive swamps in the coastal areas. The Dutch were the first Europeans to settle when, in 1616, traders established the fort and settlement of Kyk-Over-Al 25 km upstream from the mouth of the Essequibo river. In 1621 the Government of the Netherlands gave the newly formed Dutch West India Company control of this trading post, which subsequently developed into a colony known as Essequibo. The company established a second colony on the Berbice river, south-east of Essequibo, in 1627, and a third—Demerara, situated between Essequibo and Berbice—was settled in 1741 and recognized as a separate Dutch West India Company colony in 1773. The Dutch West India Company established tobacco and sugar cane plantations using the labour of Amerindian slaves. However, as the agricultural production of the colonies increased, a labour shortage emerged, and in the 1650s the first large-scale importation of African slaves began. By the 1660s the slave population numbered about 2,500, while the number of indigenous people had declined to an estimated 50,000 as a result of disease and poor treatment at the hands of the Dutch. Most of those who survived the encounter with the Europeans retreated into the interior of the territory. During the 18th and early 19th centuries more African slaves were brought to the territory to labour on sugar, cotton and coffee estates, most of them on reclaimed wetlands in the coastal plain. The working conditions were brutal, and there were several slave rebellions. One of the most famous took place in 1763, when slaves led by Cuffy (today the national hero of Guyana) rose up and forced more than one-half of the European population to flee. The rebel force of 3,000 slaves was eventually defeated with the assistance of troops from the neighbouring French and British colonies.

At various times control of the three colonies fell to the British and the French, while British planters settled in the Guianas even under Dutch rule. The British took permanent control in 1796, and in 1814 British rule was formally recognized by the Netherlands through the London Convention. In 1831 the colonies were consolidated as one administrative unit, named British Guiana. Slavery was abolished in 1834. It was succeeded by a system of 'apprenticeship', originally intended to last for six years; however, this was ended ahead of schedule in 1838, largely because of rebellions, including one in Guyana. From this date, the British began to bring in indentured (contract) labour from other sources, principally from India, but also from China and Madeira. The original intention was that the Indian labourers would return to their homeland once two five-year periods of service had ended, but the authorities were keen to retain labour. Many were asked to pay a proportion of their return passage, while some were offered land. Most stayed in Guyana, and by the end of indentured immigration in 1917, they formed the majority of the rural population of British Guiana, which was often referred to as the land of six peoples, with descendants of African, Chinese, Indian and Portuguese slaves and workers, and of the mainly British colonists, as well as the continuing presence of the Amerindians.

Indo-Guyanese, now universally English-speaking but retaining many of their cultural traditions, made up the largest ethnic group, with 43% of the population at the time of the 2002 census, and formed a clear majority in most of the coastal agricultural belt, particularly in eastern Guyana (Berbice). Most Indo-Guyanese are Hindu, but significant numbers are either Muslim or Christian. However, their proportion of the population has decreased from 52% in 1980, when Indo-Guyanese formed an absolute majority. Afro-Guyanese com-

prised 30% of the total in 2002, and formed the largest group in the capital, Georgetown, and in the bauxite-mining town of Linden, while 17% of Guyanese were of mixed race, an increase from 11% in 1980. Amerindians made up 9% of the population, a proportion that had increased from 5% in 1980 as a result of a higher birth rate and lower rate of emigration; most lived in the interior, or in coastal districts of north-western Guyana. Minorities of Chinese, Madeiran Portuguese, British and other European origin formed less than 1% of the total, but played a significant role in business and the professions.

THE BIRTH OF ETHNIC POLITICS

During the 19th century the political system was dominated by the white—mainly British and Dutch—sugar planters, but other groups increasingly pressed for constitutional reform and a more representative political system. Towards the end of the century disenfranchised elements began to organize themselves to demand greater participation in the colony's affairs. These organizations were mainly composed of members of the small, but articulate, emerging middle class. The demands of the working class were sometimes expressed in the form of protests and riots, as in the Ruimveldt riots around Georgetown in 1905. After the First World War, economic changes brought renewed pressure for political change. With less dependence on sugar, and the growing importance of rice and bauxite, the political dominance of the sugar planters was increasingly questioned. However, the drive for an expansion of democracy was impeded when the British announced a new Constitution in 1928. It made British Guiana a Crown Colony, with an increased role for the Governor and the appointed members of the Executive Council, and a reduced role for representatives who had been elected, albeit on the basis of a restricted franchise. During the Great Depression of the 1930s all of the colony's major exports—sugar, rice and bauxite—were affected by lower international prices. Unemployment increased rapidly, and, as in the rest of the British Caribbean, British Guiana experienced serious labour unrest and violent demonstrations. From 1943 the property qualification for voters was reduced, and elected members formed a majority in the Legislative Council. However, it was not until after the Second World War that political parties were formed that represented the majority of the population and the extension of universal suffrage opened up the possibility of significant political change.

The first modern political party in the colony's history was the People's Progressive Party (PPP), established in January 1950 by Dr Cheddi Jagan, a US-educated Indo-Guyanese dentist. Jagan had been a leading figure in the Political Affairs Committee, a left-wing discussion group that, through its outspoken criticism of the colony's poor living standards, had developed strong support, particularly from Indo-Guyanese workers. A turning point came in 1948, when five Indo-Guyanese sugar workers were shot by police at Enmore, close to Georgetown, during a strike and demonstration. The PPP aimed to win support from both the Afro-Guyanese and Indo-Guyanese communities, and its initial leadership was multi-ethnic. Forbes Burnham, a British-trained Afro-Guyanese lawyer, was the party's Chairman. In the run-up to the country's first general election held under universal adult suffrage, Jagan and Burnham proposed an anti-imperialist agenda. At the election in April 1953 the PPP won a resounding victory, taking 18 out of the 24 contested seats. However, the PPP's first administration was brief. Conservative forces in the business community were alarmed by the new Government's programme to expand the role of the state, and by its prompt moves to introduce reforms. At the same time, the British Conservative Government viewed the party's Labour Relations Act, which strengthened the position of the Guiana Industrial Workers' Union (GIWU), as a direct challenge to the Governor and to the Constitution. The day the Act was introduced to the legislature, the GIWU went on strike in support of the proposed law. The very next day, 9 October 1953, the British suspended the colony's Constitution and, under pretext of quelling disturbances, sent in troops. Jagan was removed from office and an interim Government was appointed. The demise of the PPP Government exposed and deepened cracks in the party's previously harmonious ethnic relations. Many Afro-Guyanese had viewed Jagan's proposals to overhaul the civil service as a threat to their established dominance of public administration, and in general perceived Jagan's radical approach as detrimental to the drive towards independence from Britain. In 1955 Jagan and Burnham formed rival wings of the PPP, with support for each leader largely, but not totally, divided along ethnic lines. Burnham's wing of the PPP, supported by the Africans, moved to the right, leaving Jagan's wing, supported mainly by the Indians, on the left. Elections were held in 1957 for 15 members of the Legislative Council, with the remaining nine either appointed or sitting ex officio; Jagan's wing of the PPP won a clear majority of elected seats with 48% of the vote. Burnham's move towards the right was confirmed when his faction of the PPP broke away and formed what eventually became the People's National Congress (PNC).

At elections in 1961, Jagan's PPP, strongly supported by the Indian population, won 20 of the 35 seats in a wholly elected Legislative Assembly; the PNC took 11, and The United Force (TUF), supported by business interests and some Amerindian communities, the remaining four. Ethnic tensions grew as the two main parties vied for power in the run-up to expected independence from the United Kingdom. Riots and demonstrations against the PPP administration were frequent, and during disturbances in 1962–63 mobs destroyed part of the capital, Georgetown. The PNC's efforts to destabilize the Government were encouraged by TUF. Following the success of the revolution led by Fidel Castro in Cuba in 1959, the USA as well as the British colonial authorities and local conservative forces feared that independence under the PPP would lead to a second Cuba on the South American mainland. The conflict between the parties was mirrored in the struggle for control of the labour movement. In an attempt to counter the PNC's strong links with organized labour, the PPP formed the Guianese Agricultural and General Workers' Union (GAWU) to organize among Indian sugar cane field workers. In March 1963 the PPP Government published a new Labour Relations Bill favouring the GAWU, and opponents responded with protests and rallies in Georgetown. The anti-PPP movement—encouraged by the US Central Intelligence Agency—increased the intensity of its campaign with a general strike and violent riots, which eventually forced the Government to withdraw the Bill.

At this delicate stage, the colonial authorities in the United Kingdom agreed to opposition parties' demands for a pre-independence election based on proportional representation, rather than the first-past-the-post system traditionally used in the Caribbean colonies. The opposition believed that this system would reduce the number of seats won by the PPP, and prevent it from obtaining a clear majority in parliament. In response the GAWU, which was sympathetic towards the PPP, appealed to sugar workers to strike in January 1964, and Jagan led a protest march by sugar workers from the interior of the country to Georgetown. The protest movement ignited outbursts of violence, and in May the Governor declared a state of emergency. As the situation worsened, in June the Governor assumed full powers, rushed in British troops to restore order, and banned all political activity. During six months of political turmoil more than 160 people were killed, thousands were injured and more than 1,000 homes were destroyed. When order was finally restored, elections were held in October 1964, and, just as the PPP had feared, the new system allowed the opposition to take power. The PPP won 24 seats, which made it the largest party, but the PNC, which won 22 seats, and TUF, with seven seats, formed a coalition. Jagan refused to resign as Prime Minister, but the Constitution was amended to allow the British Governor to remove Jagan from office, and the PNC's leader Forbes Burnham became Prime Minister in December.

BURNHAM'S RULE OF INDEPENDENT GUYANA

In the early years of the Burnham Government, economic conditions began to improve, with an end to the riots and disturbances, as the coalition administration implemented policies that favoured local investors and foreign industry. Two years of economic growth and relative domestic peace culminated in independence: on 26 May 1966 the colony of British Guiana became the independent nation of Guyana. In a move to ingratiate his Government with the US Administration, Burnham cut trade relations with Cuba, and Western aid money began to flow in. At elections held in 1968, which were, however, marred by fraud and coercion, the PNC won 30 seats to the PPP's 19 and TUF's four. Thereafter, governing without the need for a coalition with TUF, Burnham's rule became increasingly statist and authoritarian, and in February 1970 Guyana removed Queen Elizabeth II as head of state and declared itself a Co-operative Republic, initially under a largely ceremonial President, Arthur Chung. Relations with Cuba improved, and Guyana became a voice in the Non-aligned Movement (NAM). From the early 1970s electoral fraud became increasingly prevalent and overt. The police and military intimidated the Indo-Guyanese population, and the army was accused of tampering with ballot boxes. Although some Afro-Guyanese voters, especially among the middle class, were uneasy with Burnham's leanings to the left, they continued to support the PNC, viewing it as a bulwark against Indo-Guyanese dominance.

In 1975 the PPP—still under the control of Cheddi Jagan—tried to shift from confrontation to critical support of the PNC Government, but when overtures intended to bring about new elections and PPP participation in the Government were rejected, the largely Indo-Guyanese sugar workforce went on a bitter strike. The strike was broken, and sugar production declined steeply from 1976 to 1977. At the same time a new political force, the Working People's Alliance (WPA), was established with the aim of breaking the pattern of ethnic-based factionalism. The WPA opposed the PNC's authoritarian rule and promoted racial harmony and democratic socialism. When the PNC postponed the 1978 elections, and instead organized a referendum on a proposed new constitution in which an Executive President would hold wide-ranging powers, the WPA joined the PPP and other opposition forces in organizing a boycott, ensuring a low rate of participation of around 10% of the electorate. By 1979 the WPA found itself the target of increasing repression. When one of the party's leaders, Walter Rodney, and several academics at the University of Guyana were arrested on apparently unfounded arson charges, WPA leaders turned the organization into Guyana's most vocal opposition party. In June 1980 Rodney was killed by a bomb allegedly planted by agents of the Burnham regime. Two years later than scheduled, a general election was held in December 1980, with Burnham elected as Executive President. The PNC took 41 seats, while the PPP and TUF won 10 and two seats, respectively. The WPA refused to participate in an electoral contest it regarded as fraudulent. International observers upheld opposition claims of extensive electoral fraud. Christian church groups and human rights organizations took up the protest against Burnham, but he clung onto power despite the worsening economic situation in the early 1980s. With sugar, bauxite and many other sectors of the economy in state ownership, the country was plagued by blatant corruption and mismanagement, while relations with potential aid donors were soured both by Burnham's largely pro-Soviet foreign policy and his record of reneging on debt service. Petty economic controls were tightened, while large numbers of professionals, managers and business people emigrated to the USA, Canada, other Caribbean nations or elsewhere. Many imported consumer goods were banned or in short supply, to conserve foreign exchange; by 1984 wheat flour, bread and cheese were unobtainable through legal channels. Smuggling and the parallel economy thrived. Controls over newsprint imports were used to create a virtual press monopoly for the state-owned *Guyana Chronicle*. Domestic and international confidence in the regime had been further shaken in November 1978, when a US evangelist Jim Jones, welcomed to Guyana by Burnham in 1975, led a mass suicide at his Jonestown agricultural settlement in a remote district in north-western Guyana, in which more than 900 people died. Then, in August 1985 Burnham unexpectedly died while recovering from minor surgery for a throat ailment.

THE HOYTE PRESIDENCY, 1985–92

Following Burnham's death, Prime Minister Hugh Desmond Hoyte acceded to the presidency and led the PNC to claim another victory in a general election in December 1985. The party won 42 of the 53 directly elected seats. Eight seats were given to the PPP, two to TUF and one to the WPA. However, faced with no alternative as the economic collapse continued, Hoyte responded to international pressure and gradually reversed many of Burnham's policies, moving from state socialism and one-party control towards a market economy, and from 1986 allowing publication of an opposition weekly, *Stabroek News*, which later became a daily newspaper. Under pressure from the USA, Britain and Canada (the ABC group), the Hoyte Government took important steps to clean up the tarnished electoral process by abolishing overseas voting and the provisions for widespread proxy and postal voting, all of them subject to abuse. In 1988 Hoyte launched an Economic Recovery Programme, and made a televised address in which he declared that Guyana's economy and foreign policy would be pro-capitalist, noting that the strengthening of Guyana's relations with the USA was 'imperative'. He renewed relations with the IMF and the World Bank, and in return for implementing policies to promote the private sector and reduce the role of the state, Guyana started to receive loans from the international financial institutions. In the early 1990s Hoyte gradually opened up the political system. After a visit to Guyana by former US President Jimmy Carter in 1990, Hoyte made changes to the electoral rules, appointed an independent chairman for the Elections Commission, and endorsed the compilation of new voters' lists; this was also seen as a reason to delay elections, which had been due in 1990. Conditions of daily life, meanwhile, remained extremely difficult, with real wages eroded by devaluation and rapid price inflation, and daily power and water outages throughout the country.

THE CHEDDI JAGAN PRESIDENCY, 1992–97

At a general election in October 1992, the PPP finally returned to power after 28 years in opposition. In the ballot, deemed free and fair by international observers, the PPP in coalition with Civic, a movement created by members of the private sector, won 28 seats to the PNC's 23; minor parties secured two seats. PPP leader Jagan, by then 74 years old, was named President and the Civic leader, Samuel Hinds, was appointed Prime Minister. Over the years, Jagan had moderated his Marxist-Leninist leanings, and on becoming President, he followed a pro-Western foreign policy, adopted free market policies, and pursued sustainable development for Guyana's environment, presiding over a period of steady economic growth and social stability.

THE JANET JAGAN PRESIDENCY, 1997–99

Cheddi Jagan died in March 1997, and was succeeded as President by Hinds. At national elections held in December 1997, the PPP/Civic alliance won 29 of the 53 seats in the National Assembly to the PNC's 22, with two seats again going to minor parties. The PPP's candidate—Cheddi Jagan's widow, the US-born Janet Jagan—was declared President. Janet Jagan had been General Secretary of the PPP from 1950 to 1970 and had held several cabinet posts since the 1950s. However, the PNC disputed the results of the election, and racial slurs were aimed at the new, white President. There were large demonstrations by PNC supporters, and the situation only partly stabilized when mediators from the Caribbean Community and Common Market came to Georgetown to broker an accord between the two parties. The Herdmanston Accord in January 1998 followed by the St Lucia Accord in June provided for an international audit of the election results, a redrafting of the Constitution (which had by 2009 produced only minor reforms), and new elections within three years rather than five. In August 1999, as arguments continued about the legitimacy of the PPP/Civic Government, and after a

protracted strike by the largely Afro-Guyanese public sector trade unions, which resulted in substantial salary increases, Janet Jagan suffered a mild heart attack and relinquished her role as President. She was replaced by the Minister of Finance, Bharrat Jagdeo, who had been hastily appointed Prime Minister in place of Hinds so that the latter could assume the presidency. Once in office, Jagdeo reappointed Hinds as Prime Minister. Janet Jagan remained a prominent figure in Guyanese life until her death in March 2009, at the age of 88.

THE BHARRAT JAGDEO PRESIDENCY, 1999–2011

While controversy over the electoral process continued, new elections took place in March 2001. The PPP/Civic alliance won 34 of the 65 parliamentary seats, while the PNC—with independent supporters allied as the Reform group—won 27 seats. Smaller parties took four. The election results were contested by the PNCReform, but although international observers noted some protests, arson and street violence during the election, the process was deemed free and fair, and the nation's High Court upheld the results. As in 1997, the election result sparked numerous public demonstrations and some rioting among the minority Afro-Guyanese community, who claimed that there had been widespread election fraud. The Jagdeo administration immediately initiated moves to improve its relationship with the PNCReform, and Hoyte agreed to a process of dialogue that aimed to develop a more inclusive system of governance. However, within a year the dialogue broke down, with the PNCReform claiming that it was failing to produce any results. On the death of Desmond Hoyte following a heart attack in December 2002, the new PNCReform leader, Robert Corbin, agreed to resume the dialogue with the Government. As a result, Jagdeo and Corbin agreed on a number of confidence-building measures, including the appointment of an Ethnic Relations Committee and a commission to investigate the Disciplined Forces (police and army), which reported in 2004, making recommendations that in 2010 remained under consideration by a parliamentary select committee.

Against the backdrop of simmering ethnic tensions between the Indo- and Afro-Guyanese sections of the population, social tensions were further exacerbated by a sharp increase in violent crime during the early years of the 21st century. After the escape of five high-profile Afro-Guyanese prisoners in February 2002, the number of murders rose by 56% compared with the previous year, and there was a spate of robberies and attacks on businesses, particularly in the area around the capital and around the village of Buxton, which spans the only road connection to eastern Guyana. Human rights groups criticized the police force's heavy-handed response, while the reaction of some prominent PNCReform supporters to the upsurge in violence appeared ambivalent. Adding to the tensions were accusations that the Government was linked to a so-called 'death squad', allegedly responsible for more than 40 extrajudicial killings in 2003. New appointments to the leadership of both the police force and the army in early 2004 failed to ease public concerns. An official inquiry found no evidence of wrongdoing by the Minister of Home Affairs Ronald Gajraj, but he resigned in April 2005.

After some delays, a general election was held on 28 August 2006. The PPP/Civic increased its seats in the parliament from 34 to 36. The PNCReform lost five seats but remained the second largest political party. Although tensions had been raised in the pre-election period by a continuing crime wave and by the assassination of the Minister of Agriculture, Satyadeow Sawh, in April 2006, the campaign was largely peaceful, but the rate of participation was low at just 69% of the electorate. A new party, the Alliance for Change (AFC), founded prior to the elections by disaffected members of the PPP/Civic and PNCReform, campaigned to end the ethnic divide, and won 8.3% of the vote, securing just five seats; this was the best showing by a third party since the 1960s. Minor parties took two seats.

In early 2008 ethnic tensions were again inflamed by a series of killings carried out by members of armed groups in different parts of the country. Eleven Indo-Guyanese, including five children, were shot dead in January in the coastal village of

Lusignan, close to Buxton. In a subsequent statement, the authorities claimed that the attack had been an attempt to exacerbate tensions between the Afro- and Indo-Guyanese communities. Angry residents blocked streets and burned tyres after the massacre, venting anger against leading PPP/Civic politicians who were seen as ineffective in controlling violence. Then, in mid-February, armed gunmen attacked a police station and other buildings in the village of Bartica, killing three police officers and nine civilians, while eight diamond miners were massacred at a remote camp in June. Rondell 'Fineman' Rawlins, the last remaining 2002 prison escapee and held responsible for the massacres, was killed in a gun battle with police in August 2008. Ethnic tensions and violent crime remained two of the more urgent issues confronting the authorities. At 18 per 100,000 in 2012, the murder rate in Guyana is not particularly high by Caribbean standards, but it is more than three times that of the USA. Many murders are associated with domestic violence, with small scale gold-mining in the interior, or with the drugs trade. Assistance has been offered by the United Kingdom, the USA and the Organization of American States (OAS) for strengthening community security, but implementation of proposed programmes has been delayed by disagreements over policy issues. Counter to international advice, Guyana in 2007 appointed Bernard Kerik, a former police commissioner in New York, USA, as security adviser to the President; he was soon afterwards charged in the USA with tax evasion and corruption, and following his conviction was sentenced in February 2010 to four years' imprisonment. A proposal for a £4.9m. security reform programme, to be implemented with British funding, was agreed in outline in 2007, but the plans were abandoned in 2009 owing to disagreement regarding appropriate management and strategy, and to a lack of progress made by Guyana on key project requirements. The Inter-American Development Bank was in mid-2013 investigating allegations of misappropriation of funds allocated to its US $19m. Citizens' Security Programme.

THE DONALD RAMOTAR PRESIDENCY, 2011–

Inter-party hostility and mistrust remained strong, while entrenched ethnic voting brought little prospect of a change in political control, and institutions intended to promote consensus instead led to further disagreement. The leadership of both main parties remained intolerant of internal criticism and debate. Jagdeo, meanwhile, was limited under the Constitution to two terms in office, and did not therefore stand in the next election, which was held on 28 November 2011. The Central Committee of the PPP/Civic on 4 April 2011 chose Donald Ramotar as presidential candidate. Born on 22 October 1950, Ramotar began working at the party headquarters at the age of 15, and had been General Secretary since the death of Cheddi Jagan in 1997. He had trained as an economist in the former USSR, and worked in Czechoslovakia from 1983 to 1988 as a member of the editorial council of a Marxist magazine. He was seen as the choice of the immediate presidential circle; three rival candidates stood down, obviating the need for a Central Committee vote. Ethnic voting patterns were expected to guarantee him an easy victory. However, the PNCReform broadened its base of support by bringing in a number of minor parties, including the Working People's Alliance (WPA), the Guyana Action Party and the National Front Alliance, forming an alliance grouping that contested the election as A Partnership for National Unity (APNU), with Rupert Roopnarine of the WPA as candidate for Prime Minister. The PNCReform leader, Robert Corbin, was not the presidential candidate; instead, a special party congress in February 2011 nominated a retired army commander, David Granger. At the same time, the AFC fought a vigorous campaign; its candidate was Khemraj Ramjattan, and it secured the support of Moses Nagamootoo, a former PPP/Civic cabinet minister with a strong personal following in eastern Guyana, who had been sidelined by the current party leadership. In the event, Ramotar won the presidency, which is secured on a first-past-the-post basis, but the PPP/Civic narrowly failed to gain an absolute majority in the National Assembly, taking 48.6% of the popular vote and 32 of the 65 seats. APNU took 40.8% of the poll

and 26 seats, while the AFC took 10.3% with seven seats. Observers from the OAS, the Commonwealth and the Caribbean Community pronounced the election free and fair, but noted that the Government had excluded opposition views from the radio, which remained a state monopoly. Ramotar in February 2012 said that the PPP/Civic had in fact won more than 52% of the poll, and accused opposition parties of rigging the election, but did not provide any evidence to support this allegation.

APNU and the AFC proved able to co-operate in parliament on most issues. Accordingly, Raphael Trotman of the AFC was elected Speaker, with Deborah Backer of APNU as Deputy Speaker and David Granger as Leader of the Opposition. Despite initial declarations of an intention of fostering inter-party co-operation, with a PPP/Civic President and opposition control of the National Assembly, the political atmosphere remained polarized and confrontational. The Government in March 2012 attempted to initiate legal action to challenge the opposition's majority membership on parliamentary committees, while Ramotar said in June that he would veto any legislation initiated by the parliamentary opposition—a stance he has maintained since. The opposition was able to amend the 2012 budget, limiting government expenditure in some key areas. Three men were shot dead by police on 18 July 2012 during a peaceful protest in the mainly Afro-Guyanese bauxite mining town of Linden over proposals to increase electricity rates, which have traditionally been subsidised by the mining company. Protests continued until 21 August, when agreements were reached to establish a committee to discuss electricity rates and proposals to revive Linden's depressed economy, and to allow the local community to run a television channel from September. Neither agreement had been implemented by mid-2014, although an official inquiry reported in February that the police were responsible for the deaths, and proposed compensation of US $10,000–$15,000 for the victims' families. Amendments to the 2013 budget reduced proposed spending by 18%, refusing authorization of several government projects, including the proposed Amaila Falls hydroelectric plant. In January 2014 the Government obtained a court ruling that parliament had no power to amend the budget, but could only accept or reject it as a whole. The opposition immediately filed an appeal, which had not been heard by mid-2014. In the event, the opposition voted against 17% of the proposed spending. In order to avert the crisis which would have resulted had the whole budget been voted down, the Government then introduced an amended budget which was accepted by parliament and signed into law just ahead of the constitutional deadline, allowing the business of government to continue. However, the Minister of Finance, Dr Ashni Singh, proceeded to spend $ G4,400m. of the $ G37,400m. which had been cut, and was expected to seek retrospective parliamentary authorization. The opposition responded by threatening a parliamentary motion of no confidence, which, if passed, would force the Government to call a fresh general election within 90 days.

Local elections, due since 1997, have been repeatedly postponed. The Government stated that they would be held in 2013; however, as in previous years, this pledge went unobserved. The Government rejected opposition-sponsored legislation which would have required the elections to be held by 1 August 2014, stating that, as a result of changes in the voting system, there had not been sufficient time to prepare for the polls.

INTERNATIONAL RELATIONS

Relations with the USA and the United Kingdom were difficult during the Burnham presidency, when Guyana had friendly relations with the former USSR and was an active member of the NAM. There followed a rapprochement with the main Western countries during the Hoyte presidency, when the ABC group (the USA, Britain and Canada) pressed for free and fair elections, and for the restoration of good relations with the IMF and World Bank. However, relations with the USA and the United Kingdom deteriorated sharply during the Jagdeo and Ramotar presidencies. In 2009 Guyana broke off negotiations with the United Kingdom concerning a security sector reform programme (see above), citing the 'outrageous and insulting' proposals. Diplomatic cables made public by the WikiLeaks organization in 2011 showed the rising irritation of successive US ambassadors at the lack of political will on the part of the Guyanese authorities to pursue counter-narcotics initiatives and economic policy reform. At a farewell function held to mark the USA's Independence Day in July 2014, a sharply worded speech by the Guyanese acting Minister of Foreign Affairs, Priya Manickchand, scripted at cabinet level, sharply criticized the departing ambassador for 'totally unacceptable' behaviour in pressing for local government elections. Guyana has meanwhile developed a close relationship with the People's Republic of China, which has been a major source of funding for infrastructural projects in recent years.

Guyana has been involved in long-running border disputes with two of its neighbours, Venezuela and Suriname. In 1962 Venezuela renewed its claim to 130,000 sq km (50,000 sq miles) of land west of the Essequibo river (more than two-thirds of Guyanese territory). This dispute was unlikely to lead to open conflict, and day-to-day relations were often friendly. However, it delayed offshore petroleum exploration in the large area of Guyana's Exclusive Economic Zone that is claimed by Venezuela, as international oil companies have been threatened with retaliation for activities in the area. The land area claimed by Venezuela was accorded to Guyana in 1899, on the decision of an international tribunal, but Venezuela held that this award resulted from improper pressure by Britain. After Guyanese independence, Venezuela occupied the Guyanese portion of Ankoko island on the Cuyuni river, but the Port of Spain Protocol of 1970 put the issue in abeyance until 1982. Guyana and Venezuela referred the dispute to the UN in 1983, and in 1989 the two countries agreed to a mutually acceptable intermediary ('good officer') suggested by the UN Secretary-General; a Jamaican academic, Norman Girvan, was appointed to the post in 2010; he died in April 2014, but a successor had not been appointed by July. In 1999 Guyana and Venezuela established a joint commission, the High Level Binational Commission, to expedite resolution of the dispute. However, Venezuela's new Constitution, adopted in December of that year, reasserted the Venezuelan claim. In 2005 Guyana signed the Petrocaribe energy accord with Venezuela, which offered favourable terms for oil imports, while Venezuela in 2007 cancelled US $12.5m. in Guyanese debt. However, there have been serious border incidents; the Venezuelan national guard arrested six Guyanese on the Cuyuni river, within Guyanese territory, in 2006, killing one of them, while in 2007 a Venezuelan army unit with helicopter support destroyed two Guyanese gold dredges. Venezuela apologized for the latter incident. Meanwhile, in a more positive development, five bilateral energy and trade agreements were signed between the two countries in 2005. Guyana in 2011 put forward a claim to an extended continental shelf under the UN Convention on the Law of the Sea, extending into waters claimed by Venezuela. Although Venezuela objected, both sides reaffirmed their commitment to the UN 'good officer' process. However, the Venezuelan navy in October 2013 arrested a ship chartered by US oil company Anadarko to complete a sea floor survey well within internationally recognized Guyanese waters, forcing it to sail 400 km to the Venezuelan island of Margarita.

Relations with Suriname have been hampered by two significant disputes. A disagreement over the maritime boundary became critical in 2000, when a Surinamese gunboat prevented a rig operated by a small Canadian oil company, CGX Energy, from drilling an exploratory well in waters claimed by both parties. After repeated attempts to negotiate a settlement failed, in 2004 Guyana referred the dispute to arbitration at the UN's International Tribunal for the Law of the Sea. The Tribunal ruled in favour of Guyana in 2007, granting sovereignty over 33,152 sq km (12,800 sq miles) including the most promising geological structures for petroleum and gas; Suriname was awarded 17,891 sq km (6,900 sq miles). The second dispute over the 'New River Triangle', an area of uninhabited forest close to the southern border with Brazil, remained unresolved, and hinged on a debate as to which of two tributaries forms the true upstream continuation of the Corentyne border river. Surinamese irregulars built a border camp in the disputed area in 1967 (Post Tigri). This was

swiftly taken by Guyana, and remained an army post today as Camp Jaguar. Guyana's relations with Brazil remained amicable, aided by a long-standing border settlement. A bridge across the Takutu river between the two countries was opened to vehicular traffic in 2009.

Guyana is a centre for the transshipment of cocaine travelling from Colombia through Venezuela, and onwards, often through the Caribbean, to Europe and North America. There was little police or army presence in the sparsely populated interior, and most of the country's land and river borders were unguarded, while the coastguard in 2014 had only one offshore patrol boat, which had been out of action for extended periods, and controls over money-laundering remained weak. Onward drugs shipments have been found in consignments of almost every export commodity, from timber and sugar to rice and vegetables. The economic impact of the drugs trade was thought to be substantial, and there were concerns over the influence of trafficking organizations on Guyanese society. US Department of State analysts believed that counter-narcotics efforts were being hindered by inadequate resources and poor co-ordination among law enforcement agencies, an overburdened and inefficient judiciary, and the lack of a coherent national security strategy. US analysts also contended that drugs-trafficking organizations in Guyana eluded law enforcement through bribes and coercion, with arrests limited mainly to small-scale users and low-level couriers held at the airport, and suggested that North American law enforcement agencies were doing more to combat the problem of Guyanese drugs-trafficking than the authorities in Guyana itself. A leaked US diplomatic cable from 2007 refers to senior cabinet ministers and the heads of the defence force and police as 'the four horsemen of inertia'; however, the USA announced plans in 2014 to open an office of the Drug Enforcement Administration at its Georgetown embassy, with Guyanese political support. Illustrating the difficulty of monitoring financial transfers in an economy with a substantial small-scale gold and diamond mining sector, gold bars worth US $11.5m. were in November 2012 stolen from a small Guyanese fishing boat moored in Curaçao. Seven suspects were apprehended but later released, the crew were placed in a witness protection programme, and some gold had been recovered in Puerto Rico. However, by mid-2014 there was no apparent progress with the case, and no clear indication of why such a substantial amount of gold had been exported by such an insecure and irregular route. The US Department of State classed Guyana as a 'country of concern' on money-laundering, an intermediate category. However, the Caribbean Financial Action Task Force (CFATF) in May 2013 warned Guyana that it could face counter-measures from November, including 'enhanced scrutiny' of international financial transactions if it failed to tighten its money-laundering controls, which had been found wanting by a mutual evaluation report in July 2011. The Government proposed new legislation; however, the opposition blocked this in parliament, holding out for amendments to the draft legislation as well as for action by the Government to activate a commission to oversee public sector procurement, which is provided for under a 2002 constitutional amendment but has not been appointed or brought into operation. Accordingly, in May 2014 the CFATF called on its members to take measures to protect their financial systems against risks emanating from Guyana, and referred Guyana to the worldwide Financial Action Task Force, based in Paris, France.

Guyana has been vocal in pushing for countries with substantial areas of tropical forest to be compensated for conservation efforts that limit international carbon emissions. As early as 1989 Guyana made 3,600 sq km of remote forest available for sustainable management as the Iwokrama International Centre for Rainforest Conservation and Development. Jagdeo was one of three world leaders invited by the UN Secretary-General, Ban Ki-Moon, to participate in an Advisory Group on Climate Change Financing in 2010. Meanwhile, Guyana secured an environmental agreement with Norway in 2009, under the terms of which Norway was to provide up to US $280m. in return for an agreement that allowed Guyana to increase the rate of deforestation, but within agreed maximum limits, in a scheme linked to the World Bank's Forest Carbon Partnership Facility. Norway was to invest $30m. initially, and would disburse as much as an additional $250m. if this initial investment were to yield a tangible reduction in both emissions and poverty. Jagdeo expressed his 'delight' at Guyana's involvement in the search for 'solutions that align the development aspirations of our people with the urgent need to protect the world's tropical forests'. However, monitoring issues remained unresolved, and some environmental non-governmental organizations have expressed concerns. By July 2014 Norway had paid $115m. into the Guyana REDD+ Investment Fund, which is administered by the World Bank, although Guyana complained about the slow pace of disbursement. On the other side, there were concerns that deforestation had, since 2012, increased beyond the agreed benchmark level.

Economy

MARK WILSON

Based on an earlier article by CHARLES ARTHUR

Guyana has a small economy in a country rich in natural resources, yet it remains one of the poorest nations in the western hemisphere. In 2014 it ranked 121st out of 187 countries in the UN Development Programme's Human Development Index, the lowest ranking in the English-speaking Caribbean. In 2012, according to figures published by the IMF, Guyana had an estimated per caput gross domestic product (GDP) of US $3,596, also the lowest in the region and 21% below the next lowest, Belize. In recent decades the economic situation has been variable. A severe economic crisis in the late 1970s and 1980s was accompanied by a rapid deterioration in public services, infrastructure and overall quality of life, with basic consumer goods unavailable except on the illegal market, and real wages in steep decline. There was then a period of rapid growth in the 1990s, followed by almost 20 years of relative stagnation. The population totalled 747,884 at the 2012 census, and was heavily concentrated in the central and eastern parts of the coastal belt, with large areas of the north-west and interior almost uninhabited. The population declined by 3,339 in the 10 years following the 2002 census, with estimated migration of 124,800, mainly to North America.

After years of a state-dominated economy, concerted international pressure and the lack of any viable alternative forced President Hugh Desmond Hoyte in 1987 to launch an Economic Recovery Programme incorporating market-orientated reforms and liberalization. The move towards an open economy continued after free elections in 1992 resulted in a change in government, with Cheddi Jagan taking office after 28 years in opposition. In 1991–97 average annual growth reached 7%. Reforms introduced by both administrations reduced the state's role in the economy, encouraged foreign investment, enabled the Government to clear arrears on loan repayments to foreign governments and the multilateral banks, and led to the sale of 15 of the 41 state-owned businesses. A British firm, Booker Tate, was hired to manage the huge state sugar company, Guyana Sugar Corpn Inc (GuySuCo). Furthermore, a US company was allowed to open a bauxite mine, and two Canadian companies were permitted to develop the Omai gold mine, the largest open-pit gold mine in Latin America. The majority of price controls were removed, the laws regarding mining and petroleum exploration were improved, and an investment policy receptive to foreign investment was announced. Inflation declined to single digits from 1995, and the currency stabilized, while fiscal and external imbalances were reduced. However, by 1998 the recovery was exhausted and long-term structural vulnerabilities made themselves felt, while investor confidence was damaged by political disturbances following the 1997 election. Growth in the economy was also hindered by a lack of private sector activity, the ongoing migration of professionals to North America, large fiscal and external imbalances, and problems with the implementation of structural reforms. While financial stability was broadly maintained, annual growth averaged a meagre 0.3% from 1998 to 2005, with the economy contracting in four of these eight years. In early 2005 extensive flooding in the coastal areas, where the majority of the population lives, caused considerable damage. Sugar and rice production was badly affected, and GDP contracted by 2.0%.

Emerging from this unpromising environment, the economy made a recovery in 2006 and 2007, with GDP growth of 5.1% and 5.4%, respectively. After receiving debt relief totalling US $585m. in 2003 under the Enhanced Heavily Indebted Poor Countries (HIPC) Initiative, Guyana qualified for an additional $189m. under the Multilateral Debt Relief Initiative in 2006. GDP growth slackened to 3.1% in 2008. The economy achieved positive growth, which averaged 4.5% in 2009–12 and reached 5.2% in 2013, years in which many Caribbean and international economies contracted owing to the effects of the global economic downturn; this relative strength was attributable in part to high gold prices and the lack of dependence on leisure-based tourism, unlike many other Caribbean economies. However, the central Government's overall financial deficit was equivalent to 4.4% of GDP in 2013, representing an increase from 2.9% in 2010. Furthermore, the external current account deficit rose again, to 15.1% of GDP in 2013, compared with 8.8% in 2009 and 11.0% in 2010, owing in part to higher international oil prices. The Guyana dollar has remained broadly stable, depreciating by only 6.5% since 2003, with an exchange rate of $ G207.2 = US $1 in July 2014. Inflation was moderate, at 3.4% in 2012 and 0.9% in 2012. The IMF viewed the economic outlook for Guyana in 2012 as broadly positive, but noted several areas of concern, including rapid credit growth and the need for fiscal consolidation and structural reforms to strengthen debt sustainability.

AGRICULTURE, FORESTRY AND FISHING

Nearly all of Guyana's agricultural production takes place along the country's coastal plains. Originally swamp lands, these areas were reclaimed and converted into fertile estates by the Dutch during the colonial period. Since independence in 1966, successive governments have committed considerable resources to maintaining the sea defences and drainage systems in order to guarantee the continuation of one of Guyana's most important economic activities. In 2013 agriculture contributed 15.1% of total GDP, with a further 2.1% from fishing and 2.9% from forestry. Agricultural output expanded at an annual average rate of 2.4% in 2009–13, largely as a result of more favourable weather conditions; however, growth was restricted by high input costs and difficulties including labour unrest in the sugar industry.

GuySuCo was formed in 1976 as a single state-owned company and grows sugar cane in eight large estates, each with its own factory; four are located close to Georgetown, and four are in the eastern part of the coastal belt. Some cane is also grown by independent farmers for sale to GuySuCo. In contrast to the rest of the Caribbean, the climate allows two annual sugar crops, while canals are used for drainage, irrigation and the transport of cane. In 2012 and 2013 sugar output declined by a cumulative 21.0%, compared with 2011, to 186,777 metric tons, owing to poor weather, industrial unrest and technical difficulties at the sugar factories. However, the value of exports was reduced by only 7.5%, as the European Union (EU) export price improved. Total export earnings from sugar in 2013 amounted to US $114.2m., representing 8.3% of total export receipts. In addition, a further US $2.8m. in export revenue was provided by the sale of molasses. Traditionally, the main export market for Guyana's sugar has been the United Kingdom, owing to a preferential agreement between the EU and the former colonies of the African, Caribbean and Pacific (ACP) group of states. With the ending of the EU sugar protocol in 2009 and the phasing out of guaranteed sugar prices, export prices declined, although the reduction in the sugar price was offset in the years to 2008 by the appreciation of the euro against the US dollar, to which the Guyanese currency is closely linked. As a result of relatively low production costs and the Government's significant investments, Guyana was one of the few sugar producers in the Caribbean region thought able to survive the changes in the trading relationship with the EU. In 2013 some 84.1% of sugar exports went to the EU, while 6.8% of exports went to the Caribbean Community and Common Market (CARICOM) member states. Efforts are currently under way to restructure the sugar sector in order to maintain its competitiveness; the EU provided grants totalling €165m. to aid the restructuring process during 2007–13. Central to the initiative was the construction by Chinese contractors of a new US $110m sugar factory at Skeldon in Berbice, eastern Guyana, which commenced production in 2009 with a co-generation plant producing 30 MW of electricity from sugar cane waste (bagasse) and additional land for large-scale cane cultivation. The target was to produce 110,000 tons of sugar annually by 2013; however, the factory was still experiencing ongoing problems in the first half of 2014, and both sugar output and cane supply were far short of target levels. GuySuCo now also exports packaged and branded sugar, at a much higher price than the bulk commodity, and planned to increase the proportion of the harvest that is fully mechanized from 4% in 2008 to 47% in 2016, eventually phasing out the cutting of cane by hand. However, at mid-2014 the mechanization programme was far behind schedule, with GuySuCo heavily in debt and in arrears with current payments, and with production costs more than double the world market price for sugar. GuySuCo also intended to build a small-scale demonstration ethanol plant, and there has been some preliminary interest in large-scale ethanol production from overseas investors, such as the ANSA McAL conglomerate of Trinidad and Tobago.

The other main component of Guyana's agricultural sector is the rice industry, traditionally dominated by independent farmers. Rice farms are distributed throughout the coastlands, and, as with sugar, there are two annual harvests. Guyana remains the largest rice producer in the Caribbean. With increased acreage and investment in 2013, rice production increased by 26.9%, compared with the previous year, to 535,439 metric tons, while export prices rose by 3.4%. The volume of rice exported increased by 18.2% in 2013, and export earnings rose by 22.2%, to US $239.8m., or 17.4% of total exports, as international prices improved. Rice was formerly sold predominantly to the EU and CARICOM, markets in which Guyana had a tariff advantage. However, the tariff advantage in the European market has since been eroded, and in 2013 only 13% of rice exports went to Europe and 19% went to CARICOM, while 68% went to Latin American and other international markets, with significant sales to Venezuela under agreements linked to the Petrocaribe initiative.

In the late 2000s the Government implemented several initiatives to encourage farmers to increase production in the non-traditional sectors of agriculture. These measures achieved some positive results, with sales of fresh fruits and vegetables to Caribbean and North American markets reaching US $7.0m. in 2011; however, this revenue was reduced to US $4.2m. in 2013. Despite government efforts to promote aquaculture, the sector stagnated, mainly as a consequence of the rising cost of fuel, the risk of piracy and the depletion of fishing grounds. The shrimp catch has declined in recent years, but recovered to some extent by 2013. Export sales of shrimp and fish totalled US $76.0m., or 5.5% of total exports in 2013.

The exploitation of the tropical rainforest that covers approximately 75% of the country's land area increased in the 1990s and 2000s with the granting of concessions to Asian companies. Exports of 112,970 cu m of timber earned US $38.5m. in 2013, and constituted 2.8% of total exports. Forestry policy remained controversial, with loggers pressing for the export of unprocessed timber, and the Government for value-added production of sawn timber and other forest prod-

ucts, while there was an increasing emphasis in official policy statements on conservation objectives. Guyana has lobbied vigorously for substantial international compensation for countries that preserve their standing forests, thus reducing global carbon emissions. As early as 1989, Guyana made 3,600 sq km of remote forest available for sustainable management as the Iwokrama International Centre for Rainforest Conservation and Development. Most forests in the southern third of the country are still untouched by commercial forestry. In December 2009 Guyana and Norway signed an agreement under the terms of which Norway would invest up to US $280m. in grant aid during 2010–15, then almost 20% of annual GDP, in return for an agreement that allowed Guyana to increase the rate of deforestation, but within agreed maximum limits. This was a pioneer REDD+ scheme, linked to the World Bank's Forest Carbon Partnership Facility. Guyana has expressed concern over the administrative and verification processes, which had resulted in the slow disbursement of funds. A disbursement mechanism was agreed, with a Multi-Stakeholder Steering Committee and the World Bank acting as trustees for a Guyana REDD+ Investment Fund, but monitoring issues remained unresolved, and some environmental non-governmental organizations expressed concerns. By July 2014 Norway had paid US $115m. into the Fund, although Guyana remained concerned about the pace of disbursement. On the other side, there were concerns that deforestation had from 2012 increased beyond the agreed level. However, successful completion of the scheme would result in a substantial improvement to the balance of payments capital account, the fiscal deficit and Guyana's overall economic outlook.

MINING AND ENERGY

Mining, mainly of bauxite, gold and diamonds, was responsible for 18.0% of GDP in 2013. Substantial investment in and restructuring of the bauxite industry, and increases in the world prices for bauxite and gold, helped the mining sector to register growth of 22% in 2007 and 6% in 2008; however, growth slowed to 0.7% in 2009 and the sector contracted by 6.9% in 2010, as the continued prosperity of gold was outweighed by reduced diamond production and a decline in the bauxite industry owing to low international prices. The mining sector experienced strong recovery in 2011, 2012 and 2013, recording growth of 19.2%, 14.8% and 8.0%, respectively, owing mainly to continuing expansion in the gold industry.

Bauxite is mined around Linden on the Demerara river, and around Aroaima on the Berbice river. In addition to metal-grade bauxite, Guyana is one of the few producers of high-value, refractory-grade bauxite (used in the manufacture of firebricks, electrical insulators and anti-skid surfacing) and chemical-grade bauxite (for aluminium sulphate, used in water purification). Since 2007 the Linden mines have been operated by a Chinese company, Bosai Minerals Group, with the Government retaining a 30% stake, and the Aroaima mines have been operated since 2005 by United Company RUSAL. Although bauxite production declined by 48.3% in 2010 to 1.08m. metric tons, an unsteady recovery took it to 1.71m tons in 2013 as world market conditions for metal-grade bauxite recovered, with exports of US $134.6m. accounting for 9.8% of Guyana's total exports.

Guyanese gold miners operate on a small scale by international standards, using dredges to extract gold from gravel along the rivers of western Guyana. Diamond miners use similar methods. A Canadian-owned mine at Omai was a much larger operation, producing gold from crushed rock and accounting for up to three-quarters of Guyana's total gold production, but it closed in 2005 following the depletion of its ore resources. With gold prices high, the smaller-scale miners expanded their operations in the late 2000s, and in 2013 produced 481,087 oz, a 46.3% increase over 2010. Gold exports earned US $648.5m. in 2013 and accounted for 47.1% of Guyanese exports. A number of Canadian and other overseas companies have been prospecting for gold in recent years, and have been preparing to start mining operations. However, a decrease in gold prices from the first half of 2012 made prospective returns less attractive, and these projects were likely to be delayed or shelved. During 2006–12 diamond production declined by 88%, as miners switched their attention to gold. In 2012 diamond production amounted to 40,763 metric carats (the lowest figure since 1998); however it recovered in part to 63,961 metric carats in 2013 with exports totalling US $12.2m, or 09.% of total exports. Canadian company Reunion Manganese intended to open a manganese mine at Matthew's Ridge in north-western Guyana, with a planned investment of US $250m; however, there was no clear timetable for this project by mid-2014. In 2012 another Canadian company, U308, reported the discovery of large uranium deposits at Kurupung.

Guyana was dependent for most of its energy needs on imported refinery products from Trinidad and Tobago and from Venezuela. Electricity is generated and distributed by Guyana Power and Light Inc, which moved back into the state sector after an unsuccessful partnership with the Commonwealth Development Corporation and Ireland's Electricity Supply Board from 1999 to 2003. Problems in the energy sector include high generating costs, some antiquated plants, and the loss of up to 45% of power generated in some years (32% in 2012), either through theft of power from illegal connections or through losses incurred by the inadequate transmission and distribution system; an estimated 30% of households have illegal electricity connections. Most electricity is generated from petroleum products, but some is now supplied by the Skeldon co-generation plant and there are small hydroelectric plants in the interior. The high cost and poor reliability of electricity continues to constrain profitability and efficient business operations in Guyana and is an ongoing problem for all households. There is potential for very large-scale hydroelectric power production in the interior, which could supply existing general demand as well as an alumina plant and aluminium smelter, while also providing a surplus for export to neighbouring countries. However, the capital cost of development would be high. The construction of a 165-MW generating station at Amaila Falls was proposed, with a framework agreement signed in July 2010 by Guyana Power and Light, the China Development Bank, the China Railway First Group Co Ltd and Sithe Global Amaila Holdings Ltd (a subsidiary of Sithe Global, a power company majority owned by the Blackstone Group). However, finalization of the project was delayed; in 2011 the World Bank decided not to participate in the project. The scheme, the total cost of which was projected at an estimated US $840m. (then 31% of GDP), was to include 65 km of transmission lines, 195 km of new or improved access roads and other infrastructure. Development of the Amaila Falls site has been under discussion for more than a decade, with proposals mooted for further expansion, which would increase capacity eventually to 1,060 MW. The project was to be financed in part by the Guyana REDD+ Investment Fund, and would substitute hydroelectric power for imported hydrocarbons, although at some cost in terms of rainforest disturbance. Other concerns included escalating cost estimates and the 19% return on equity proposed for investors. Opposition parties, which held a majority in the National Assembly, voted against the project in 2013, although the Government had not at mid-2014 abandoned plans to proceed with it. Power generated nationally in 2011 was an estimated 690 GWh, a 5.7% increase compared with the previous year.

Despite their border dispute (see History), in 2005 Guyana was one of 13 Caribbean countries that signed the Petrocaribe agreement, under which Venezuela provides low-interest loans to finance a proportion of oil purchases. The cumulative total had reached US $364m. by the end of 2012, at which point it represented 27% of total external debt, while a further US $115.2m. was disbursed in 2013. However, the debt stock was also reduced through earnings from rice exports to Venezuela.

There is strong potential for petroleum exploration, mainly within the Exclusive Economic Zone, but also onshore. A study by the US Geological Survey suggested that Guyana may have offshore reserves of up to 2,200m. barrels of oil and 6,000,000m. cu ft of natural gas. Although seismic surveys appeared positive, initial exploration wells drilled in 2012 by Canadian company CGX Energy and by Repsol of Spain proved disappointing. Onshore prospects with more modest potential were explored by smaller oil companies; however, a Canadian company, Groundstar, abandoned drilling in the Takutu basin of southern Guyana in 2011 after failing to find petroleum in commercial quantities. Exploration of the western part of Guyana's Exclusive Economic Zone is complicated by the border claim of Venezuela, whose navy in October 2013 arrested a ship chartered by US oil company Anadarko to complete a sea floor survey within internationally recognized Guyanese waters, forcing it to sail 400 km to the Venezuelan island of Margarita.

MANUFACTURING AND CONSTRUCTION

The processing of sugar, rice, and other primary products accounts for some 42% of Guyana's manufacturing activity. A small manufacturing sector producing for the domestic market is confronted by serious constraints in the form of competition from cheap imports, high energy costs and inadequate infrastructure. The domestic sector's contribution to GDP had declined by 2013 to just 3.7%. One of the main remaining industries is the production of beverages, including beer, soft drinks and rum; local firms have in recent years competed effectively with imports, and in the case of rum have been able to develop export markets (earning revenue of US $32.4m. in 2013, or 2.4% of Guyana's exports) for branded premium products, while the Banks DIH brewery now has a mutual shareholding with Banks (Barbados) Breweries Ltd. The engineering and construction sector expanded by 22.6% in 2013, recovering from a contraction in the previous year. Construction has benefited from an increase in public sector investment, much of it funded with international assistance, in the construction of roads, housing, drainage and irrigation, and private sector investment in housing and other areas.

TOURISM

Despite government attempts to develop the sector, tourism facilities remain limited. The Guyana Tourism Authority was established in 2003 to market Guyana as a tourist destination, and focus has been placed on efforts to exploit the country's potential for 'eco-tourism'. However, a high proportion of travellers are business visitors or overseas Guyanese on family visits, and most hotel accommodation is in Georgetown. With a low proportion of visitors being leisure tourists, travel to Guyana remained largely unaffected by the global economic downturn that took hold in the second half of 2008. According to the Caribbean Tourism Organization, in 2012 the total number of visitors was 176,642, a 12.6% increase over the previous year; of these, 56% were from the USA, 15% from Canada and 5% from Europe (primarily the United Kingdom). Of the remaining 24%, the majority were from the English-speaking Caribbean. In 2011 the Shanghai Construction Group of the People's Republic of China held a launch ceremony for a US $58m. hotel in Georgetown which was to be managed by Marriott International of the USA; this was under construction in mid-2014, amid some controversy over the use of state land and equity participation in the project. With much of the existing capacity under-occupied and further new hotel construction proposed, there are concerns over the future profitability of the sector.

TRANSPORT AND INFRASTRUCTURE

The poor condition of Guyana's internal transport infrastructure poses a major impediment to the country's economic development. Paved roads connect the settlements of the coastal belt, and run inland to the bauxite-mining town of Linden and some other points. There are bridges over the Demerara and Berbice rivers, but the Essequibo and the Corentyne (the latter of which forms the border with Suriname and lies within Surinamese territory) must be crossed by ferry. An unpaved road connects Georgetown to the border with Brazil. A bridge over the Takutu river at the border with Brazil was completed in 2009, providing a continuous road connection to Boa Vista and the Brazilian highway network.

Guyana's main port is Georgetown, which can accommodate vessels with a draft of up to 6 m and up to 10,000 metric tons of cargo. There are specialized facilities elsewhere for bauxite and sugar, also with draft limitations, and a number of small river and sea ports. Guyana has around 120 airstrips, catering for light aircraft. The country's main international airport, the Cheddi Jagan International Airport, is located at Timehri, 42 km outside Georgetown. In 2011 the China Exim Bank agreed to provide US $138m. in funding for an improvement programme to be carried out on the airport by China Harbour Engineering Company; the opposition used its parliamentary majority to vote down funding for this project in April 2013, but the Government, none the less, planned to continue with it, a stance which was maintained in mid-2014. The Ogle airport just east of Georgetown was upgraded to take regional flights, providing services to Suriname, from 2010; a further upgrade of the runway, which allowed scheduled flights to Caribbean islands, was completed in 2013. Commercial railway services for both passengers and goods were operated until 1974, but were then closed, with some mineral lines in the interior operating until the 2000s.

SERVICES

In 2013 the services sector grew by 5.5% and accounted for 49.4% of GDP (excluding construction and utilities, which comprises 11.0% of GDP). Transport and storage expanded by 18.9% in 2012, assisted by an increase in vehicle imports. Wholesale and retail trade grew by 6.7%, with higher consumer demand for imports. There has been strong growth since 2008 in information and communications, as an Irish-owned provider, Digicel, which entered the market in 2006, continued its initial investment programme. There has been some recent growth in call centres, led by a Mexican company, Qualfon, which employed 1,200 staff in 2010. Public administration grew by only 1.4% in 2012 and 2.5% in 2013. Financial services and insurance grew by 11.2% in 2013, with expanding private sector credit to individuals and private sector businesses. Concerns over the standard of financial regulation and the ineffectiveness of money-laundering controls have been repeatedly expressed by the US Department of State and other international observers. The Caribbean Financial Action Task Force (CFATF) in May 2013 warned Guyana of countermeasures if it did not move decisively to comply, by November, with the recommendations of a 2011 mutual evaluation report that highlighted serious weaknesses. In May 2014 the CFATF urged its members to take measures to protect their financial systems against risks emanating from Guyana, and referred Guyana to the worldwide Financial Action Task Force, based in Paris, France.

INVESTMENT AND FINANCE

Guyana was heavily in debt in the 1970s and 1980s, and was unable to access further finance after repeated defaults. The Economic Recovery Programme from 1989 brought debt relief through the 'Paris Club' of major international donors, and renewed access to borrowing. Further debt relief of US $529m. was agreed in 1996 by the 'Paris Club', and by Trinidad and Tobago, which was also a major creditor. From 1998 Guyana qualified for additional debt relief under the HIPC programme of the IMF and World Bank, supplemented from 2000 by the Enhanced HIPC programme, with Guyana making a commitment to agreed macroeconomic targets and a Poverty Reduction and Growth Facility providing further assistance; however, waivers on some targets were granted, in view of a challenging political and economic environment. In 2007 Guyana's principal donor, the Inter-American Development Bank (IDB), agreed to 100% debt relief on loans outstanding at the end of 2004, with a total value of $467m., equivalent to 41% of GDP. This brought Guyana's cumulative debt relief since the mid-1990s to $1,300m. Total debt was dramatically reduced from 184% of GDP in 2005 to 58% in 2013, according to central bank estimates, at which point external debt was down to 42% of GDP. However, debt continued to be an area of macroeconomic concern. Investment was equivalent to some 18.6% of GDP in 2013, declining from 27% in 2010. Of total investment in 2013, just short of one-half was public sector investment

(much of it donor-funded) in roads, bridges, sea defence, drainage and irrigation, and the remainder was private investment, mainly in agriculture, manufacturing and information and communications technology.

TRADE AND BALANCE OF PAYMENTS

Guyana has a persistently large current account balance of payments deficit, which in 2013 was US $425m. (equivalent to 6.9% of GDP). Gold contributed 47% of total exports in 2013, with a further 41% provided by rice, bauxite, sugar and shrimps. Fuel imports accounted for 31.1% of the import bill in 2013, in a period of high oil prices. Exports in 2012 covered 74% of the value of imports, with a resulting merchandise trade deficit of US $471m., equivalent to 15.7% of GDP. Non-factor services were a net outflow item, at US $307m. in 2013. However, there was a positive flow of US $328m. (with an additional US $250.5m. in bank transfers) in family remittances from overseas Guyanese, equivalent to 11% of GDP. As in most recent years, the current account deficit was in large part covered by a capital surplus (of US $315m. in 2013), with foreign direct investment inflow of US $214m., and US $221m. in official development assistance, which included disbursements of US $34m. by the IDB, US $115m. from Petrocaribe, US $19m. from China and US $44m. in balance of payments support. Net international reserves at the end of 2013 amounted to US $784m.

In 2012 Guyana's main trading partners for exports were Canada (taking 35.9% of total exports), the USA (21.2%) and the United Kingdom (8.5%), and for imports the USA (providing 24.7% of total imports), Trinidad and Tobago (13.7%) and Venezuela (17.1%).

OUTLOOK

In spite of an unfavourable international economic environment, Guyana was able to maintain macroeconomic stability in the first half of 2014, with growth continuing, albeit at a relatively slow pace. This was in part the result of recent debt forgiveness, as well as continuing development assistance, arising from good relations with major aid donors. Capital spending and assistance programmes stimulated the construction sector, and helped to maintain reserves at comfortable levels in spite of persistent current account balance of payments deficits. There were continuing forward commitments for grants and loan assistance from the IDB, the EU and other agencies, as well as from Petrocaribe. However, the economic base remained narrow, with four commodities making up the bulk of export revenue, and gold alone providing more than half. This situation left Guyana vulnerable to price fluctuations and weather-related risks; there were also concerns in mid-2014 over the decline in international gold prices. Large-scale mining investments appear to be on hold, in part because of uncertain commodity prices. The US Department of State has also noted the clear influence of drugs-transshipment on the economy, but the exact extent of its impact remained unclear. In spite of recent investment, the vital sugar industry has only a fair prospect of survival, particularly with the ending of the EU sugar protocol and the scheduled removal in 2017 of sugar quotas for traditional importers; difficulties remained and good management would be of great importance. In the long term, there remained a reasonably good prospect of significant petroleum finds, which would be of great benefit to the economy, and of development of the large hydroelectric potential in the interior. Substantial grant aid flowing from participation in the REDD+ scheme would bring significant macroeconomic benefits, but only if the transparency issues were successfully addressed. In the public sector, there was a continuing need to address issues of management efficiency, transparency and good governance. With the opposition narrowly in control of parliament, political polarization and lack of trust severely hampered the ability of the Government to move forward with controversial large-scale investment projects.

Statistical Survey

Sources (unless otherwise stated): Bank of Guyana, 1 Church St and Ave of the Republic, POB 1003, Georgetown; tel. 226-3250; fax 227-2965; e-mail communications@bankofguyana.org.gy; internet www.bankofguyana.org.gy; Bureau of Statistics, Ministry of Finance, Main and Urquhart Sts, Georgetown; tel. 227-1114; fax 226-1284; internet www.statisticsguyana.gov.gy.

AREA AND POPULATION

Area: 214,969 sq km (83,000 sq miles).

Population: 723,673 at census of 12 May 1991; 751,223 (males 376,034, females 375,189) at census of 15 September 2002. *2010* (official estimate): 778,099 (males 390,827, females 387,272). *2014* (UN estimate at mid-year): 803,677 (Source: UN, *World Population Prospects: The 2012 Revision*).

Density (at mid-2014): 3.7 per sq km.

Population by Age and Sex (UN estimates at mid-2014): *0–14 years:* 284,060 (males 149,836, females 134,224); *15–64 years:* 491,777 (males 248,913, females 242,864); *65 years and over:* 27,840 (males 9,517, females 18,323); *Total* 803,677 (males 408,266, females 395,411) (Source: UN, *World Population Prospects: The 2012 Revision*).

Population by Ethnic Group (self-declaration at 2002 census): 'East' Indians 326,277; Africans 227,062; Mixed 125,727; Amerindians 68,675; Portuguese 1,497; Chinese 1,396; White 477; Total (incl. others) 751,223. Note: Classification of ethnicity reflects national census methodology.

Regions (population at 2002 census): Barima–Waini 24,275; Pomeroon–Supenaam 49,253; Essequibo Islands–West Demerara 103,061; Demerara–Mahaica 310,320; Mahaica–Berbice 52,428; East Berbice–Corentyne 123,695; Cuyuni–Mazaruni 17,597; Potaro–Siparuni 10,095; Upper Takutu–Upper Essequibo 19,387; Upper Demerara–Berbice 41,112; Total 751,223.

Principal Towns (population at 2002 census): Georgetown (capital) 134,497; Linden 29,298; New Amsterdam 17,033; Corriverton 11,494. *Mid-2014* ('000, incl. suburbs, UN estimate): Georgetown 124 (Source: UN, *World Urbanization Prospects: The 2014 Revision*).

Births, Marriages and Deaths (2013): Birth rate 18.5 per 1,000; Marriages 4,667 (marriage rate 6.3 per 1,000); Deaths 4,527 (death rate 6.6 per 1,000).

Life Expectancy (years at birth): 66.0 (males 63.5; females 68.7) in 2012. Source: World Bank, World Development Indicators database.

Economically Active Population (persons aged 15 years and over, census of 2002): Agriculture, hunting and forestry 45,378; Fishing 5,533; Mining and quarrying 9,374; Manufacturing 30,483; Electricity, gas and water 2,246; Construction 16,100; Trade, repair of motor vehicles and personal and household goods 37,690; Restaurants and hotels 5,558; Transport, storage and communications 16,790; Financial intermediation 3,074; Real estate, renting and business services 7,384; Public administration, defence and social security 14,995; Education 13,015; Health and social work 5,513; Other community, social and personal service activities 9,599; Private households with employed persons 6,156; Extraterritorial organizations and bodies 477; *Sub-total* 229,365; Activities not adequately defined 1,489; *Total employed* 230,854 (males 162,596, females 68,258); Unemployed 30,533; *Total labour force* 261,387 (males 180,946, females 80,441). *2013:* Central government 12,056; Rest of the public sector 16,941; Total public sector employment 28,997. *Mid-2014* ('000, estimates): Agriculture, etc. 48; Total labour force 357 (Source: FAO).

HEALTH AND WELFARE

Key Indicators

Total Fertility Rate (children per woman, 2012): 2.6.

Under-5 Mortality Rate (per 1,000 live births, 2012): 35.

HIV/AIDS (% of persons aged 15–49, 2012): 1.3.

Physicians (per 1,000 head, 2010): 0.2.

Hospital Beds (per 1,000 head, 2009): 2.0.

Health Expenditure (2011): US $ per head (PPP): 217.

Health Expenditure (2011): % of GDP: 6.8.

Health Expenditure (2011): public (% of total): 67.3.

Access to Water (% of persons, 2012): 98.

Access to Sanitation (% of persons, 2012): 84.

Total Carbon Dioxide Emissions ('000 metric tons, 2010): 1,701.5.

Total Carbon Dioxide Emissions Per Head (metric tons, 2010): 2.2.

Human Development Index (2013): ranking: 121.

Human Development Index (2013): value: 0.638.

For sources and definitions, see explanatory note on p. vi.

AGRICULTURE, ETC.

Principal Crops ('000 metric tons, 2012): Rice, paddy 600 (unofficial figure); Cassava (Manioc) 4 (FAO estimate); Sugar cane 2,900 (FAO estimate); Coconuts 80 (FAO estimate); Bananas 7; Plantains 5. *Aggregate Production* ('000 metric tons, may include official, semiofficial or estimated data): Total cereals 605.0; Vegetables (incl. melons) 44.4; Fruits (excl. melons) 36.2.

Livestock ('000 head, year ending September 2012, FAO estimates): Horses 2.4; Asses 1.0; Cattle 113; Sheep 131; Pigs 14; Goats 82; Chickens 26,000.

Livestock Products ('000 metric tons, 2012, FAO estimates unless otherwise indicated): Cattle meat 1.9; Sheep meat 0.6; Pig meat 0.8; Chicken meat 30.4; Cows' milk 44.0; Hen eggs 1.1 (unofficial figure).

Forestry ('000 cubic metres, 2012, FAO estimates): *Roundwood Removals:* Sawlogs, veneer logs and logs for sleepers 370, Pulpwood 100, Other industrial wood 17, Fuel wood 843; Total 1,330. *Sawnwood Production:* Total (all broadleaved) 76.

Fishing ('000 metric tons, live weight, 2012): Capture 53.8 (Marine fishes 24.9; Atlantic seabob 24.8; Whitebelly prawn 0.6); Aquaculture 0.3; *Total catch* 54.1. Note: Figures exclude crocodiles: the number of spectacled caimans caught in 2012 was 18,920.

Source: FAO.

MINING

Production (2013): Bauxite 1,713,242 metric tons; Gold 14,964 kg; Diamonds 63,961 metric carats.

INDUSTRY

Selected Products (2013): Raw sugar 186,771 metric tons; Rice 535,439 metric tons; Rum 40,835 hl; Beer and stout 173,612 hl; Logs 304,601 cu m; Margarine 2,318 metric tons; Biscuits 1,211,100 kg; Paint 26,949 hl; Electricity 711m. kWh.

FINANCE

Currency and Exchange Rates: 100 cents = 1 Guyana dollar ($ G). *Sterling, US Dollar and Euro Equivalents* (30 April 2014): £1 sterling = $ G347.354; US $1 = $ G206.500; €1 = $ G286.003; $ G1,000 = £2.88 = US $4.84 = €3.50. *Average Exchange Rate* ($ G per US $): 204.018 in 2011; 204.358 in 2012; 205.386 in 2013.

Budget ($ G million, 2013): *Revenue:* Tax revenue 126,509.7 (Income tax 46,393.9; Value-added tax 34,388.0; Trade taxes 13,411.8); Other current revenue 9,985.0; Capital revenue (incl. grants) 8,671.7; Total 145,166.4. *Expenditure:* Current expenditure 122,053.5 (Personnel emoluments 38,489.0; Other goods and services 77,458.2; Interest 6,106.3); Capital expenditure 50,144.5; Total 172,198.0.

International Reserves (US $ million at 31 December 2013): IMF special drawing rights 6.73; Foreign exchange 776.89; *Total* 783.62. Source: IMF, *International Financial Statistics*.

Money Supply ($ G million at 31 December 2013): Currency outside depository corporations 60,616; Transferable deposits 75,805; Other deposits 275,914; *Broad money* 412,335. Source: IMF, *International Financial Statistics*.

Cost of Living (Urban Consumer Price Index for Georgetown; base: December 2009 = 100): All items 107.7 in 2011; 109.7 in 2012; 111.8 in 2013.

Expenditure on the Gross Domestic Product ($ G million at current prices, 2013): Government final consumption expenditure 87,236; Private final consumption expenditure 578,782; Gross capital formation 114,211; *Total domestic expenditure* 780,228; Net imports of goods and services –166,099; *GDP in purchasers' values* 614,130.

Gross Domestic Product by Economic Activity ($ G million at current prices, 2013): Agriculture, forestry and fishing 101,553 (Sugar 17,384); Mining and quarrying 96,922; Manufacturing 36,166; Construction 48,037; Electricity, gas and water 11,316; Wholesale and retail trade 77,090; Transport, storage, information and communications 61,424; Finance and insurance 25,986; Real estate and renting 5,632; Public administration 47,592; Education 18,847; Health and social welfare 8,829; Other services 19,866; *Subtotal* 559,260; *Less* Financial intermediation services indirectly measured 21,833; *Gross value added in basic prices* 537,428; Indirect taxes, less subsidies 76,702; *GDP in purchasers' values* 614,130.

Balance of Payments (US $ million, 2013): Exports of goods f.o.b. 1,375.9; Imports of goods f.o.b. −1,847.3; *Trade balance* −471.4; Services (net) −307.1; *Balance on goods and services* −778.5; Transfers (net) 353.2; *Current balance* −425.3; Capital account (net) 314.8; Net errors and omissions −8.9; *Overall balance* −119.5.

EXTERNAL TRADE

Principal Commodities (US $ million, 2013): *Imports c.i.f.:* Agricultural machinery 87.8; Building materials 90.7; Chemicals 76.9; Fuel and lubricants 574.7; Industrial machinery 84.5; Transport machinery 70.0; Motor cars 39.4; Total (incl. others) 1,838.3. *Exports f.o.b.:* Fish and shrimps 76.0; Rice 239.8; Sugar 114.2; Timber 38.5; Bauxite 134.6; Gold 648.5; Total (incl. others, incl. re-exports) 1,375.9.

Principal Trading Partners (US $ million, 2012): *Imports:* Canada 43.0; China, People's Republic 194.5; Japan 77.9; Suriname 143.8; Trinidad and Tobago 269.4; United Kingdom 118.5; USA 486.0; Venezuela 336.0; Total (incl. others) 1,969.7. *Exports:* Canada 501.3; Germany 60.0; Jamaica 42.7; Trinidad and Tobago 54.8; Ukraine 23.4; United Kingdom 118.8; USA 295.2; Venezuela 145.9; Total (incl. others) 1,395.7. *2013* (US $ million): Total imports 1,838.3; Total exports 1,375.9.

TRANSPORT

Road Traffic (vehicles in use, 2008): Passenger cars 44,739; Lorries and vans 28,122; Motorcycles and mopeds 37,069. Source: IRF, *World Road Statistics*.

Shipping: *Flag Registered Fleet* (at 31 December 2013): Vessels 60; Total displacement 32,127 grt. Source: Lloyd's List Intelligence (www.lloydslistintelligence.com).

Civil Aviation ('000, 2012): Passengers carried 247.8. Source: World Bank, World Development Indicators database.

TOURISM

Tourist Arrivals: 152,000 in 2010; 157,000 in 2011; 177,000 in 2012.

Tourism Receipts (US $ million, excl. passenger transport): 80 in 2010; 95 in 2011; 64 in 2012.

Source: World Tourism Organization.

COMMUNICATIONS MEDIA

Telephones (2013): 156,805 main lines in use.

Mobile Cellular Telephones (2013): 555,035 subscribers.

Internet Subscribers (2010): 16,400.

Broadband Subscribers (2013): 36,900.

Source: International Telecommunication Union.

EDUCATION

Pre-primary (2011/12): Institutions 442; Teachers 1,601 (males 4, females 1,597); Students 25,543 (males 13,003, females 12,540).

Primary (2011/12): Institutions 436; Teachers 3,635 (males 418, females 3,217); Students 88,106 (males 44,737, females 43,369).

General Secondary (2011/12): Institutions 110; Teachers 3,204 (males 791, females 2,413); Students 67,548 (males 32,791, females 34,757).

Special Education (2011/12): Institutions 6; Teachers 36 (males 2, females 34); Students 647 (males 407, females 240).

Technical and Vocational (2011/12): Institutions 8; Teachers 239 (males 147, females 92); Students 4,548 (males 2,663, females 1,885).

Teacher Training (2011/12): Institutions 1; Teachers 184 (males 67, females 117); Students 1,795 (males 253, females 1,542).

University (2011/12): Institutions 1; Teachers 491 (males 288, females 203); Students 7,338 (males 2,783, females 4,555).

Private Education (2011/12 unless otherwise indicated): Institutions 58 (2009/10); Teachers 1,113 (males 249, females 864); Students 15,777 (males 7,668, females 8,109).

Source: Ministry of Education.

Pupil-Teacher Ratio (primary education, UNESCO estimate): 23.2 in 2011/12 (Source: UNESCO Institute for Statistics).

Adult Literacy Rate (UNESCO estimates): 85.0% (males 82.4%; females 87.3%) in 2009. Source: UN Development Programme, *Human Development Report*.

Directory

The Constitution

Guyana became a republic, within the Commonwealth, on 23 February 1970. A new Constitution was promulgated on 6 October 1980, and amended in 1998, 2000 and 2001. Its main provisions are summarized below:

The Constitution declares the Co-operative Republic of Guyana to be an indivisible, secular, democratic sovereign state in the course of transition from capitalism to socialism. The bases of the political, economic and social system are political and economic independence, involvement of citizens and socio-economic groups, such as co-operatives and trade unions, in the decision-making processes of the state and in management, social ownership of the means of production, national economic planning and co-operativism as the principle of socialist transformation. Personal property, inheritance, the right to work, with equal pay for men and women engaged in equal work, free medical attention, free education and social benefits for old age and disability are guaranteed. Additional rights include equality before the law, the right to strike and to demonstrate peacefully, the right of indigenous peoples to the protection and preservation of their culture, and a variety of gender and work-related rights. Individual political rights are subject to the principles of national sovereignty and democracy, and freedom of expression to the state's duty to ensure fairness and balance in the dissemination of information to the public. Relations with other countries are guided by respect for human rights, territorial integrity and non-intervention.

THE PRESIDENT

The President is the supreme executive authority, head of state and Commander-in-Chief of the armed forces, elected for a five-year term of office, with no limit on re-election. The successful presidential candidate is the nominee of the party with the largest number of votes in the legislative elections. The President may prorogue or dissolve the National Assembly (in the case of dissolution, fresh elections must be held immediately) and has discretionary powers to postpone elections for up to one year at a time for up to five years. The President may be removed from office on medical grounds, or for violation of the Constitution (with a two-thirds' majority vote of the Assembly), or for gross misconduct (with a three-quarters' majority vote of the Assembly if allegations are upheld by a tribunal).

The President appoints a First Vice-President and Prime Minister, who must be an elected member of the National Assembly, and a Cabinet of Ministers, which may include four non-elected members and is collectively responsible to the legislature. The President also appoints a Leader of the Opposition, who is the elected member of the Assembly deemed by the President most able to command the support of the opposition.

THE LEGISLATURE

The legislative body is a unicameral National Assembly of 65 members (66 in special circumstances), elected by universal adult suffrage in a system of proportional representation; 40 members are elected at national level, and a further 25 are elected from regional constituency lists. The Assembly passes bills, which are then presented to the President, and may pass constitutional amendments.

LOCAL GOVERNMENT

Guyana is divided into 10 regions, each having a Regional Democratic Council elected for a term of up to five years and four months, although it may be prematurely dissolved by the President.

OTHER PROVISIONS

Impartial commissions exist for the judiciary, the public service and the police service. An Ombudsman is appointed, after consultation between the President and the Leader of the Opposition, to hold office for four years.

The Government

HEAD OF STATE

President: DONALD RAMOTAR (sworn in 3 December 2011).

CABINET

(September 2014)

The PPP/Civic alliance forms the Government.

Prime Minister and Minister of Parliamentary Affairs and Energy: SAMUEL A. HINDS.

Minister of Foreign Affairs: Dr CAROLYN RODRIGUES-BIRKETT.

Minister of Finance: Dr ASHNI K. SINGH.

Minister of Agriculture: Dr LESLIE RAMSAMMY.

Minister of Amerindian Affairs: PAULINE CAMPBELL-SUKHAI.

Minister of Home Affairs: CLEMENT J. ROHEE.

Minister of Legal Affairs and Attorney-General: ANIL NANDLALL.

Minister of Education: PRIYA DEVI MANICKCHAND.

Minister of Health: Dr BHERI S. RAMSARAN.

Minister of Housing and Water: IRFAAN ALI.

Minister of Labour: Dr NANDA K. GOPAUL.

Minister of Human Services and Social Security: JENNIFER I. M. WEBSTER.

Minister of Local Government and Regional Development: NORMAN WHITTAKER.

Minister of Public Service: Dr JENNIFER WESTFORD.

Minister of Public Works: ROBESON BENN.

Minister of Culture, Youth and Sport: Dr FRANK C. S. ANTHONY.

Minister of Natural Resources and the Environment: ROBERT M. PERSAUD.

Minister of Tourism, Industry and Commerce: IRFAAN ALI (acting).

Head of the Presidential Secretariat: Dr ROGER LUNCHEON.

Minister in the Ministry of Finance: JUAN A. EDGHILL.

Minister in the Ministry of Agriculture: ALLI BAKSH.

MINISTRIES

Office of the President: New Garden St, Bourda, Georgetown; tel. 225-7051; fax 226-3395; e-mail opmed@op.gov.gy; internet www.op .gov.gy.

Office of the Prime Minister: Oranapai Towers, Wights Lane, Kingston, Georgetown; tel. 226-6955; fax 226-7573; e-mail opm@ networksgy.gy.

Ministry of Agriculture: Regent Rd and Shiv Chanderpaul Dr., POB 1001, Bourda, Georgetown; tel. 227-5049; fax 227-2978; e-mail info@agriculture.gov.gy; internet www.agriculture.gov.gy.

Ministry of Amerindian Affairs: 251–252 Thomas and Quamina Sts, South Cummingsburg, Georgetown; tel. 227-5067; fax 223-1616; e-mail ministryofamerindian@networksgy.com; internet www .amerindian.gov.gy.

Ministry of Culture, Youth and Sport: 71 Main St, North Cummingsburg, Georgetown; tel. 227-7860; fax 225-5067; e-mail mincys@guyana.net.gy; internet www.mcys.gov.gy.

Ministry of Education: 26 Brickdam, Stabroek, POB 1014, Georgetown; tel. 226-3094; fax 225-5570; e-mail moegyweb@yahoo .com; internet www.education.gov.gy.

Ministry of Finance: 49 Main and Urquhart Sts, Kingston, Georgetown; tel. 225-6088; fax 226-1284; e-mail minister@finance.gov.gy; internet www.finance.gov.gy.

Ministry of Foreign Affairs: 254 South Rd and Shiv Chanderpaul Dr., Bourda, Georgetown; tel. 226-1606; fax 225-9192; e-mail minfor@guyana.net.gy; internet www.minfor.gov.gy.

Ministry of Health: Brickdam, Stabroek, Georgetown; tel. 226-5861; fax 225-4505; e-mail moh@sdnp.org.gy; internet www.health .gov.gy.

Ministry of Home Affairs: 6 Brickdam, Stabroek, Georgetown; tel. 225-7270; fax 227-4806; e-mail info@moha.gov.gy; internet moha.gov .gy.

Ministry of Housing and Water: 41 Brickdam and United Nations Pl., Stabroek, Georgetown; tel. 225-7192; fax 227-3455; e-mail minister_housing@yahoo.com; internet www.chpa.gov.gy.

Ministry of Labour, Human Services and Social Security: 1 Water St and Corhill St, Stabroek, Georgetown; tel. 225-0655; fax 227-1308; e-mail psmlhsss@yahoo.com; internet www.mlhsss.gov .gy.

Ministry of Legal Affairs and Office of the Attorney-General: 95 Carmichael St, North Cummingsburg, Georgetown; tel. 226-2616; fax 225-4809; e-mail legalaffairsps@yahoo.com; internet legalaffairs .gov.gy.

Ministry of Local Government and Regional Development: De Winkle Bldg, Fort St, Kingston, Georgetown; tel. 225-8621; fax 226-5070; e-mail mlgrdps@telsnetgy.net.

Ministry of Natural Resources and the Environment: Shiv Chanderpaul Dr., Bourda, Georgetown; tel. 225-5285; fax 223-0969; e-mail minister@nre.gov.gy; internet www.nre.gov.gy.

Ministry of Public Service: 164 Waterloo St, North Cummingsburg, Georgetown; tel. 227-1193; fax 227-2700; e-mail psm@sdnp.org .gy.

Ministry of Public Works: Wights Lane, Kingston, Georgetown; tel. 226-1875; fax 225-6954; e-mail minoth@networksgy.com.

Ministry of Tourism, Industry and Commerce: 229 South Rd, Lacytown, Georgetown; tel. 226-2505; fax 225-9898; e-mail ministry@mintic.gov.gy; internet www.mintic.gov.gy.

President and Legislature

NATIONAL ASSEMBLY

Speaker: RAPHAEL TROTMAN.

Deputy Speaker: DEBORAH BACKER.

Clerk: SHERLOCK ISAACS.

Election, 28 November 2011

Party	% of votes	Seats
People's Progressive Party/Civic . . .	48.6	32
A Partnership for National Unity* . .	40.8	26
Alliance for Change	10.3	7
The United Force	0.2	—
Total	100.0	65

* A coalition comprising the Guyana Action Party, the National Front Alliance, the People's National Congress Reform and the Working People's Alliance.

Under Guyana's system of proportional representation, the nominated candidate of the party receiving the most number of votes is elected to the presidency. Thus, on 3 December 2011 the candidate of the PPP/Civic alliance, DONALD RAMOTAR, was inaugurated as President.

Election Commission

Guyana Elections Commission (GECOM): 41 High and Cowan Sts, Kingston, Georgetown; tel. 225-0277; fax 226-0924; e-mail gecomfeedback@webworksgy.com; internet www.gecom.org.gy; f. 2000; appointed by the Pres., partly in consultation with the leader of the opposition; Chair. Dr STEVE SURUJBALLY; Chief Elections Officer KEITH LOWENFIELD.

Political Organizations

Alliance for Change (AFC): 77 Hadfield St, Werk-en-Rust, Georgetown; tel. 231-8183; fax 225-0455; e-mail office@voteafc .com; internet www.afcguyana.com; f. 2005; Leader KHEMRAJ RAMJATTAN; Chair. NIGEL HUGHES.

Justice For All Party (JFAP): 43 Robb and Wellington Sts, Lacytown, Georgetown; tel. 226-5462; fax 227-3050; e-mail cnsharma@guyana.net.gy; Leader CHANDRANARINE SHARMA.

A Partnership for National Unity (APNU): 121 Regent Rd, Bourda, Georgetown; e-mail info@apnuguyana.com; internet www .apnuguyana.com; f. 2011; fmrly the Jt Opposition of Political Parties (JOPP); Leader Brig.-Gen. (retd) DAVID GRANGER; comprises the following parties:

Guyana Action Party (GAP): Georgetown; Leader PAUL HARDY.

National Front Alliance: Georgetown; f. 2000; comprises the National Democratic Movt and National Republican Party; Leader KEITH SCOTT.

People's National Congress Reform (PNCR): Congress Pl., Sophia, POB 10330, Georgetown; tel. 225-7852; fax 225-2704; e-mail pnc@guyana-pnc.org; internet www.guyanapnc.org; f. 1957 as People's National Congress following split with the PPP; present name adopted in 2006; Leader ROBERT H. O. CORBIN; Chair. BISHWAISHWAR RAMSAROOP; Gen. Sec. OSCAR E. CLARKE.

Working People's Alliance (WPA): Walter Rodney House, 80 Croal St, Stabroek, Georgetown; tel. and fax 225-3679; originally popular pressure group, became political party 1979; independent Marxist; Leaders Dr CLIVE THOMAS, Dr RUPERT ROOPNARINE.

People's Progressive Party/Civic (PPP/Civic): Freedom House, 41 Robb St, Lacytown, Georgetown; tel. 227-2095; fax 227-2096; e-mail pr@ppp-civic.org; internet www.ppp-civic.org; f. 1950; Marxist-Leninist; Gen. Sec. CLEMENT ROHEE.

The United Force (TUF): Unity House, 95 Robb and New Garden Sts, Bourda, Georgetown; tel. 226-2596; fax 225-2973; f. 1960; right-wing; Dep. Leader MICHAEL ANTHONY ABRAHAM.

Diplomatic Representation

EMBASSIES AND HIGH COMMISSIONS IN GUYANA

Argentina: 66 Brummel Pl., Stabroek, Georgetown; tel. 231-9521; fax 231-9505; e-mail eguya@mrecic.gov.ar; Ambassador LUIS MARTINO.

Brazil: 308 Church St, Queenstown, POB 10489, Georgetown; tel. 225-7970; fax 226-9063; e-mail brasemb@networksgy.com; Ambassador LINEU PUPO DE PAULA.

Canada: High and Young Sts, POB 10880, Georgetown; tel. 227-2081; fax 225-8380; e-mail grgtn@international.gc.ca; internet www.canadainternational.gc.ca/guyana; High Commissioner NICOLE GILES.

China, People's Republic: Lot 2, Botanic Gardens, Mandela Ave, Georgetown; tel. 227-1651; fax 225-9228; e-mail prcemb@networks.gy.com; internet gy.china-embassy.org/eng; Ambassador ZHANG LIMIN.

Cuba: 46 High St, POB 10268, Kingston, Georgetown; tel. 225-1883; fax 226-1824; e-mail emguyana@networksgy.com; internet www.cubadiplomatica.cu/guyana; Ambassador JULIO CÉSAR GONZÁLES MARCHANTE.

India: 307 Church St, Queenstown, Georgetown; tel. 226-3996; fax 225-7012; e-mail hoc.georgetown@mea.gov.in; internet www.hcigeorgetown.org.gy; High Commissioner VENKATACHALAM MAHALINGAM.

Mexico: 44 Brickdam, Stabroek, Georgetown; tel. 226-3987; fax 226-3722; e-mail mexicoembassygy@gmail.com; internet embamex.sre.gob.mx/guyana; Ambassador FRANCISCO OLGUIN.

Russia: 3 Public Rd, Kitty, Georgetown; tel. 226-9773; fax 227-2975; e-mail embrus.guyana@mail.ru; internet www.guyana.mid.ru; Ambassador NIKOLAY SMIRNOV.

Suriname: 171 Peter Rose and Crown Sts, Queenstown, Georgetown; tel. 226-7844; fax 225-0759; e-mail surnmemb@gol.net.gy; Ambassador NISHA KURBAN-BABU.

United Kingdom: 44 Main St, POB 10849, Georgetown; tel. 226-5881; fax 225-3555; e-mail bhcguyana@networksgy.com; internet ukinguyana.fco.gov.uk; High Commissioner ANDREW AYRE.

USA: 100 Young and Duke Sts, POB 10507, Kingston, Georgetown; tel. 225-4900; fax 225-8497; e-mail usembassy@hotmail.com; internet georgetown.usembassy.gov; Chargé d'affaires a.i. BRYAN D. HUNT.

Venezuela: 296 Thomas St, South Cummingsburg, Georgetown; tel. 226-1543; fax 225-3241; e-mail embveguy@gol.net.gy; Ambassador REINA MARGARITA ARRATIA DIAZ.

Judicial System

The Judicature of Guyana comprises the Supreme Court of Judicature, which consists of the Court of Appeal and the High Court (both of which are superior courts of record), and a number of Courts of Summary Jurisdiction.

The Court of Appeal consists of the Chancellor as President, the Chief Justice, and such number of Justices of Appeal as may be prescribed by the National Assembly.

The High Court of the Supreme Court consists of the Chief Justice as President of the Court and Puisne Judges. Its jurisdiction is both original and appellate. It has criminal jurisdiction in matters brought before it on indictment. The High Court of the Supreme Court has unlimited jurisdiction in civil matters and exclusive jurisdiction in probate, divorce and admiralty and certain other matters. In April 2005 the Caribbean Court of Justice was inaugurated, in Port of Spain, Trinidad and Tobago, as Guyana's highest court of appeal.

A magistrate has jurisdiction to determine claims where the amount involved does not exceed a certain sum of money, specified by law. Appeal lies to the Full Court.

Chancellor of the Judiciary: CARL SINGH (acting).

Chief Justice: IAN CHANG (acting).

Attorney-General: ANIL NANDLALL.

Religion

CHRISTIANITY

Guyana Council of Churches: 26 Durban St, Lodge, Georgetown; tel. 227-5126; e-mail bishopedghill@hotmail.com; f. 1967 by merger of the Christian Social Council (f. 1937) and the Evangelical Council (f. 1960); 15 mem. churches, 1 assoc. mem.; Chair. Rev. FRANCIS DEAN ALLEYNE.

The Anglican Communion

Anglicans in Guyana are adherents of the Church in the Province of the West Indies, comprising eight dioceses. The Archbishop of the Province is the Bishop of the North Eastern Caribbean and Aruba, resident in St John's, Antigua and Barbuda. The diocese of Guyana also includes French Guiana and Suriname. According to the latest available census figures, Anglicans constitute 7% of the population.

Bishop of Guyana: Rt Rev. CORNELL JEROME MOSS, Church House, 49 Barrack St, POB 10949, Georgetown 1; tel. and fax 226-4183; e-mail dioofguy@networksgy.com.

The Baptist Church

Baptist Convention of Guyana: POB 10149, Georgetown; tel. 226-0428; 33 mem. churches, 1,823 mems.

The Lutheran Church

Evangelical Lutheran Church in Guyana: Lutheran Courts, Berbice, POB 40, New Amsterdam; tel. and fax 333-6479; e-mail sjgoolsarran@gmail.com; internet www.elcguyana.org; f. 1947; 13,000 mems; Pres. Rev. MOSES PRASHAD.

The Roman Catholic Church

Guyana comprises the single diocese of Georgetown, suffragan to the archdiocese of Port of Spain, Trinidad and Tobago. According to the latest available census (2002), some 8% of the population are Roman Catholics. The Bishop participates in the Antilles Episcopal Conference Secretariat, currently based in Port of Spain, Trinidad.

Bishop of Georgetown: FRANCIS DEAN ALLEYNE, Bishop's House, 27 Brickdam, POB 101488, Stabroek, Georgetown; tel. 226-4469; fax 225-8519; e-mail rcbishop@networksgy.com; internet www.rcdiocesegy.org.

Seventh-day Adventists

According to the 2002 census, 5% of the population are Seventh-day Adventists. The Guyana Conference is a member of the Caribbean Union Conference and comprises two congregations and 137 churches.

Guyana Conference: 222 Peter Rose and Lance Gibbs Sts, Queenstown, POB 10191, Georgetown; tel. 226-3313; fax 223-8142; e-mail info@guyanaconference.org; internet guyanaconference.org; 50,291 mems in 2007; 173 churches in 23 pastoral districts; Pres. Pastor RICHARD JAMES.

Other Christian Churches

According to the 2002 census, 17% of the population are Pentecostal Christians. Other denominations active in Guyana include the African Methodist Episcopal Church, the African Methodist Episcopal Zion Church, the Church of God, the Church of the Nazarene, the Ethiopian Orthodox Church, the Guyana Baptist Mission, the Guyana Congregational Union, the Guyana Presbyterian Church, the Hallelujah Church, the Methodist Church in the Caribbean and the Americas, the Moravian Church, and the Presbytery of Guyana.

HINDUISM

According to the 2002 census, Hindus constitute 28% of the population.

Guyana Hindu Dharmic Sabha (Hindu Religious Centre): 392–393 Ganges St, Prashad Nagar, Demerara-Mahaica; tel. 227-6181; e-mail ghds@ymail.com; f. 1974; Pres. VINDHYA VASINI PERSAUD.

ISLAM

Muslims in Guyana comprise 7% of the population, according to the 2002 census.

Central Islamic Organization of Guyana (CIOG): M.Y.O. Bldg, Woolford Ave, Thomas Lands, POB 10245, Georgetown; tel. 225-8654; fax 227-2475; e-mail contact@ciog.org.gy; internet www.ciog.org.gy; Pres. Haji S. M. NASIR; Dir of Education QAYS ARTHUR.

Guyana United Sad'r Islamic Anjuman: 157 Alexander St, Kitty, POB 10715, Georgetown; tel. 226-9620; e-mail khalid@gusia.org; f. 1936; 120,000 mems; Pres. Haji A. HAFIZ RAHAMAN.

BAHÁ'Í FAITH

National Spiritual Assembly: 220 Charlotte St, Bourda, Georgetown; tel. and fax 226-5952; e-mail secretariat@gy.bahai.org; internet gy.bahai.org; incorporated in 1976; National Sec. KALA SEEGOPAUL.

The Press

DAILIES

Guyana Chronicle: 2A Lama Ave, Bel Air Park, POB 11, Georgetown; tel. 227-5204; fax 227-5208; e-mail gm@guyanachronicle.com; internet www.guyanachronicleonline.com; f. 1881; govt-owned; also produces weekly *Sunday Chronicle* (tel. 226-3243); Gen. Man. MICHAEL GORDON; Editor-in-Chief MAHENDRA (MARK) RAMOTAR; circ. 23,000 (weekdays), 43,000 (Sun.).

Guyana Times: 238 Camp and Quamina Sts, Georgetown; tel. 225-5128; fax 225-5134; e-mail news@guyanatimesgy.com; internet www.guyanatimesgy.com; f. 2008; owned by Queen's Atlantic Investment Inc; Editor NIGEL WILLIAMS.

Kaieteur News: 24 Saffon St, Charlestown, Georgetown; tel. 225-8465; fax 225-8473; e-mail kaieteurnews@yahoo.com; internet www.kaieteurnewsonline.com; f. 1994; independent; Editor-in-Chief ADAM HARRIS; Publr GLENN LALL; daily circ. 19,000, Fri. 25,000, Sun. 32,000.

Stabroek News: E1/2 46–47 Robb St, Lacytown, Georgetown; tel. 227-5197; fax 226-2549; e-mail stabroeknews@stabroeknews.com; internet www.stabroeknews.com; f. 1986; also produces weekly *Sunday Stabroek*; liberal independent; Editor-in-Chief ANAND PERSAUD; circ. 14,100 (weekdays), 26,400 (Sun.).

WEEKLIES AND PERIODICALS

The Catholic Standard: 222 South and Wellington Sts, Queenstown, POB 10720, Georgetown; tel. 226-2195; fax 226-2292; e-mail catholicstandardgy@gmail.com; f. 1905; organ of the Roman Catholic church; weekly; Editor COLIN SMITH; circ. 4,000.

The Official Gazette of Guyana: Guyana National Printers Ltd, Lot 1, Public Rd, La Penitence, Georgetown; tel. 226-2616; fax 225-4809; internet www.officialgazette.gov.gy; govt-owned; weekly; circ. 450.

PRESS ASSOCIATION

Guyana Press Association (GPA): 82c Duke St, Kingston, Georgetown; tel. 623-5430; fax 223-6625; e-mail gpaexecutive@gmail.com; f. 1945; affiliated with the Asscn of Caribbean Media Workers; Pres. GORDON MOSELEY.

NEWS AGENCY

Guyana Government Information Agency: Area B, Homestretch Ave, D'Urban Backlands, Georgetown; tel. 226-6715; fax 226-4003; e-mail gina@gina.gov.gy; internet www.gina.gov.gy; f. 1993; Dir NEAZ SUBHAN.

Publishers

Guyana National Printers Ltd: 1 Public Rd, La Penitence, POB 10256, Greater Georgetown; tel. 225-3623; e-mail gnpl@guyana.net.gy; f. 1939; govt-owned.

Guyana Publications Inc: E 1/2 46–47 Robb St, Lacytown, Georgetown; tel. 226-5197; fax 226-3237; e-mail info@stabroeknews.com; internet www.stabroeknews.com; publrs of *Stabroek News* and *Sunday Stabroek*; Chair. Dr IAN MCDONALD.

Broadcasting and Communications

TELECOMMUNICATIONS

Broadband Inc: Georgetown; tel. 226-4114; e-mail support@bbgy.com; internet www.bbgy.com; f. 2002; internet service provider; Exec. Dir NAVINDRA NARINE.

Digicel Guyana: Fort & Barrack St, Kingston, Georgetown; tel. 669-2677; fax 227-8184; e-mail guy_ccfrontoffice@digicelgroup.com; internet www.digicelguyana.com; f. 1999 as Trans-World Telecom; acquired Cel Star Guyana in 2003; acquired by Digicel Group in 2006; GSM cellular telecommunications network; operates Celstar and U-Mobile brands; CEO GREGORY DEAN.

E-Networks Inc: 220 Camp St, North Cummingsburg, Georgetown; tel. 225-1461; fax 225-1412; e-mail info@ewirelessgy.com; internet www.ewirelessgy.com; f. 2004; internet service provider; Man. Dir VISHOK PERSAUD.

Guyana Telephones and Telegraph Company (GT & T): 79 Brickdam, POB 10628, Georgetown; tel. 226-0053; fax 226-7269; e-mail pubcomm@gtt.co.gy; internet www.gtt.co.gy; f. 1991; fmrly state-owned Guyana Telecommunications Corpn; 80% ownership by Atlantic Tele-Network (USA); CEO JOSEPH GOVINDA SINGH.

Regulatory Authority

National Frequency Management Unit (NFMU): 68 Hadfield St, D'Urban Park, Georgetown; tel. 226-2233; fax 226-7661; e-mail info@nfmu.gov.gy; internet www.nfmu.gov.gy; f. 1990; following the Telecommunications Amendment Bill 2011, a new regulatory body, the Telecommunication Agency, was scheduled to be created; Man. Dir VALMIKKI SINGH.

BROADCASTING

Radio

Hits and Jams 94.1 Boom FM: 206 Lance Gibbs St, Queenstown, Georgetown; tel. 227-0580; f. 2013; part of the HJ Entertainment Group; Dirs RAWLE FERGUSON, KERWIN BOLLERS.

National Communications Network (NCN): see Television; operates 3 channels: Hot FM, Radio Roraima and Voice of Guyana.

Radio Guyana Inc. (RGI): TVG, Camp and Quamina St, South Cummingsburg, Georgetown; internet radioguyanafm89.com; f. 2012; part of Queens Atlantic Investment Inc (QAII); Pres. Dr RANJISINGHI (BOBBY) RAMROOP.

Television

CNS Television Six (CNS6): 43 Robb and Wellington Sts, Lacytown, Georgetown; tel. 226-5462; fax 227-3050; e-mail sharma@cns6.tv; internet www.cns6.tv; f. 1992; privately owned; Man. Dir CHANDRANARINE SHARMA.

Multi Technology Vision Inc (Channel 14/Cable 65): 218 Upper Oronoque and Charlotte Sts, Georgetown; tel. 226-3593; f. 2012; Gen. Man. MARTIN GOOLSARRAN.

National Communications Network (NCN): Homestretch Ave, D'Urban Park, Georgetown; tel. 227-1566; fax 226-2253; e-mail feedback@ncnguyana.com; internet www.ncnguyana.com; f. 2004 following merger of Guyana Broadcasting Corpn (f. 1979) and Guyana Television and Broadcasting Co (f. 1993); govt-owned; operates 3 radio channels and 6 TV channels; CEO RAYMOND AZEEZ (acting).

Regulatory Authority

Guyana National Broadcast Authority (GNBA): Georgetown; f. 2012; licensing authority; Chair. BIBI SAFORA SHADICK.

Finance

(cap. = capital; res = reserves; dep. = deposits; m. = million; brs = branches; amounts in Guyana dollars)

BANKING

Central Bank

Bank of Guyana: 1 Church St and Ave of the Republic, POB 1003, Georgetown; tel. 226-3250; fax 227-2965; e-mail communications@bankofguyana.org.gy; internet www.bankofguyana.org.gy; f. 1965; cap. 1,000m., res 1,125.8m., dep. 140,694.3m. (Dec. 2009); central bank of issue; acts as regulatory authority for the banking sector; Gov. Dr GOBIND GANGA (acting).

Commercial Banks

Bank of Baroda (Guyana) Inc (India): 10 Ave of the Republic and Regent St, POB 10768, Georgetown; tel. 226-4005; fax 225-1691; e-mail bobinc@networksgy.com; internet www.bankofbaroda.com; f. 1966; Man. Dir RAJENDRA KUMAR.

Citizens' Bank Guyana Inc (CBGI): 201 Camp St and Charlotte St, Lacytown, Georgetown; tel. 226-1705; fax 226-1719; e-mail info@citizensbankgy.com; internet www.citizensbankgy.com; f. 1994; 51% owned by Banks DIH; total assets 18,773m. (Sept. 2007); Chair. CLIFFORD B. REIS; Man. Dir ETON M. CHESTER; 4 brs.

Demerara Bank Ltd: 230 Camp and South Sts, POB 12133, Georgetown; tel. 225-0610; fax 225-0601; e-mail banking@demerarabank.com; internet www.demerarabank.com; f. 1994; cap. 450.0m., res 345.7m., dep. 17,899.9m. (Sept. 2007); Chair. YESU PERSAUD; CEO PRAVINCHANDRA S. DAVE.

Guyana Bank for Trade and Industry Ltd (GBTI): High and Young Sts, Kingston, POB 10280, Georgetown; tel. 231-4401; fax 231-4411; e-mail banking@gbtibank.com; internet www.gbtibank

.com; f. 1987 to absorb the operations of Barclays Bank; cap. 800m., res 486.9m., dep. 84,348m. (Dec. 2013); Chair. ROBIN STOBY; CEO JOHN TRACEY; 9 brs.

Republic Bank (Guyana): Promenade Court, 155–156 New Market St, North Cummingsburg, Georgetown; tel. 223-7938; fax 227-2921; e-mail email@republicguyana.com; internet www .republicguyana.com; f. 1984; 51% owned by Republic Bank Ltd, Port of Spain, Trinidad and Tobago; acquired Guyana National Co-operative Bank in 2003; name changed from National Bank of Industry and Commerce in 2006; cap. 300m., res 1,531.3m., dep. 117,307m. (Sept. 2013); Chair. NIGEL M. BAPTISTE; Man. Dir JOHN N. ALVES; 10 brs.

Scotiabank (Canada): 104 Carmichael St, POB 10631, Georgetown; Georgetown; tel. 225-9222; fax 225-9309; e-mail bns.guyana@ scotiabank.com; internet www.guyana.scotiabank.com; f. 1968; Country Man. AMANDA ST AUBYN; 5 brs.

Merchant Bank

Guyana Americas Merchant Bank Inc (GAMBI): GBTI Bldg, 138 Regent St, Lacytown, Georgetown; tel. 223-5193; fax 223-5195; e-mail gambi@networksgy.com; f. 2001; fmrly known as Guyana Finance Corpn Ltd; Man. Dir RICHARD ISAVA.

STOCK EXCHANGE

Guyana Association of Securities Companies and Intermediaries Inc (GASCI): Hand-in-Hand Bldg, 1 Ave of the Republic, Georgetown; tel. 223-6176; fax 223-6175; e-mail info@gasci.com; internet www.gasci.com; f. 2001; Chair. NIKHIL RAMKARRAN; Gen. Man. CHANDRA GAJRAJ.

INSURANCE

Caricom General Insurance Co Inc: Lot A, Ocean View Dr., Ruimzeight Gardens, Ruimzeight, West Coast Demerara; tel. 269-0020; fax 269-0022; e-mail mail@guyanainsurance.com; internet www.caricominsurance.com; f. 1997; fmrly Guyana Fire, Life & General Insurance Co Ltd; CEO SAISNARINE KOWLESSAR; Pres. KULWANTIE SOOKRAM.

Demerara Mutual Life Assurance Society Ltd: 61–62 Robb St and Ave of the Republic, Georgetown; tel. 225-8991; fax 225-8995; e-mail demlife@demeraramutual.com; internet demeraramutual .net; f. 1891; Chair. RICHARD B. FIELDS; CEO KEITH CHOLMONDELEY.

Diamond Fire and General Insurance Inc: 44B High St, Kingston, Georgetown; tel. 223-9771; fax 223-9770; e-mail diamondins@ solutions2000.net; f. 2000; privately owned; Asst Man. RABINDRA-NAUTH BASIL.

Guyana Co-operative Insurance Service (GCIS): 47 Main St, Georgetown; tel. 225-9153; f. 1976; 67% owned by the Hand-in-Hand Group.

Guyana and Trinidad Mutual Group of Insurance Companies (GTM): 27–29 Robb and Hinck St, Georgetown; tel. 225-7910; fax 225-9397; e-mail gtmgroup@gtm-gy.com; internet www.gtm-gy.com; f. 1880; Chair. HAROLD DAVIS; Man. Dir ROGER YEE.

Hand-in-Hand Mutual Fire and Life Group: Hand-in-Hand Bldg, 1–4 Ave of the Republic, POB 10188, Georgetown; tel. 225-1865; fax 225-7519; e-mail info@hihgy.com; internet www.hihgy .com; f. 1865; fire and life insurance; Chair. JOHN G. CARPENTER; CEO KEITH EVELYN.

Association

Insurance Association of Guyana: South 0.5, 14 Pere St, Kitty, Georgetown; tel. 226-3514; f. 1968.

Trade and Industry

GOVERNMENT AGENCIES

Environmental Protection Agency, Guyana: Ganges St, Sophia, Georgetown; tel. 225-5467; fax 225-5481; e-mail epa@epaguyana .org; internet www.epaguyana.org; f. 1988 as Guyana Agency for the Environment; renamed 1996; formulates, implements and monitors policies on the environment; Exec. Dir INDARJIT RAMDASS.

Guyana Energy Agency (GEA): 295 Quamina St, POB 903, South Cummingsburg, Georgetown; tel. 226-0394; fax 226-5227; e-mail gea@gea.gov.gy; internet www.gea.gov.gy; f. 1998 as successor to Guyana National Energy Authority; CEO MAHENDRA SHARMA.

Guyana Marketing Corporation: 87 Robb and Alexander Sts, Lacytown, Georgetown; tel. 226-8255; fax 227-4114; e-mail info@ newgmc.com; internet www.newgmc.com; Gen. Man. NIZAM HASSAN.

Guyana Office for Investment (Go-Invest): 190 Camp and Church Sts, Georgetown; tel. 225-0653; fax 225-0655; e-mail goinvest@goinvest.gov.gy; internet www.goinvest.gov.gy; f. 1994; CEO GEOFFREY DA SILVA.

National Industrial and Commercial Investment Ltd (NICIL): 126 Barrack St, Kingston, Georgetown; tel. 226-0576; e-mail winston.brassington@gmail.com; internet www .privatisation.gov.gy; f. 1991; state-run privatization unit; Exec. Dir WINSTON BRASSINGTON.

DEVELOPMENT ORGANIZATION

Institute of Private Enterprise Development (IPED): 253–254 South Rd, Bourda, Georgetown; tel. 225-8949; fax 226-4675; e-mail iped@solutions2000.net; internet www.ipedgy.com; f. 1986; total loans provided $ G1,400m. (2007); Chair. YESU PERSAUD; Exec. Dir RAMESH PERSAUD.

CHAMBER OF COMMERCE

Georgetown Chamber of Commerce and Industry (GCCI): 156 Waterloo St, North Cummingsburg, Georgetown; tel. 225-5846; fax 226-3519; e-mail info@gcci.gy; internet www .georgetownchamberofcommerce.org; f. 1889; Pres. CLINTON URLING; 90 mems.

INDUSTRIAL AND TRADE ASSOCIATIONS

Guyana Rice Development Board: 116–17 Cowan St, Kingston, Georgetown; tel. 225-8717; fax 225-6486; internet www.grdb.gy; f. 1994 to assume operations of Guyana Rice Export Board and Guyana Rice Grading Centre; Gen. Man. JAGNARINE SINGH.

National Dairy and Development Programme (NDDP): c/o Lands and Surveys Bldg, 22 Upper Hadfield St, Durban Backlands, POB 10367, Georgetown; tel. 225-7107; fax 226-3020; e-mail nddp@ sdnp.org.gy; f. 1984; aims to increase domestic milk and beef production; Programme Dir MEER BACCHUS.

EMPLOYERS' ASSOCIATIONS

Consultative Association of Guyanese Industry Ltd: 157 Waterloo St, POB 10730, North Cummingsburg, Georgetown; tel. 225-7170; fax 227-0725; e-mail info@cagi.org.gy; internet www.cagi .org.gy; f. 1962; Chair. YESU PERSAUD; Exec. Dir SAMUEL JERRY GOOLSARRAN; 54 mems.

Forest Products Association of Guyana: 157 Waterloo St, Cummingsburg, Georgetown; tel. 226-9848; fax 226-2832; e-mail fpasect@guyana.net.gy; internet www.fpaguyana.org; f. 1944; 62 mem. cos; Pres. KHALAWAN CORT; Exec. Officer JANICE CRAWFORD.

Guyana Manufacturing and Services Association Ltd (GMSA): National Exhibition Centre, Sophia, Georgetown; tel. 219-0072; fax 219-0073; e-mail gma_guyana@yahoo.com; f. 1967 as the Guyana Mfrs' Asscn; name changed in 2005 to reflect growth in services sector; 190 mems; Pres. CLINTON WILLIAMS.

Guyana Rice Producers' Association (GRPA): 126 Parade and Barrack St, Georgetown; tel. 226-4411; fax 223-7249; e-mail grpa .riceproducers@networksgy.com; f. 1946; non-govt org.; 18,500 mems; Pres. LEEKHA RAMBRICH; Gen. Sec. DHARAMKUMAR SEERAJ.

MAJOR COMPANIES
Food and Beverages

Banks DIH Ltd: Thirst Park, POB 10194, Georgetown; tel. 225-0910; fax 226-6523; e-mail banks@banksdih.com; internet www .banksdih.com; f. 1848; brewers and soft drinks and snacks mfrs; Chair. and Man. Dir CLIFFORD BARRINGTON REIS; 1,500 employees.

Demerara Distillers Ltd: Plantation Diamond, East Bank, Demerara; tel. 265-5019; internet www.theeldoradorum.com; f. 1952; rum distillers; Pres. and Chair. KOMAL SAMARRO; 1,165 employees.

Edward B. Beharry & Co Ltd (EBB): 191 Charlotte St, Lacytown, Georgetown; tel. 227-0632; fax 225-6231; e-mail ebbsales@ beharrygroup.com; internet www.beharrygroup.com; f. 1937; producer of confectionery, condiments and pasta; Chair. EDWARD ANAND BEHARRY.

GuySuCo (Guyana Sugar Corpn Inc): Ogle Estate, POB 10547, East Coast, Demerara; tel. 222-6030; fax 222-6048; e-mail info@guysuco .com; internet www.guysuco.com; f. 1976; sugar production; scheduled for privatization; CEO PAUL BHIM; Chair. RAJENDRA SINGH (acting).

National Milling Co of Guyana Inc (NAMILCO): Agricola, East Bank, Demerara; tel. 233-2462; fax 233-2464; e-mail namilco@ namilcoflour.com; internet www.namilcoflour.com; f. 1969; subsidiary of Seaboard Corporation (USA); flour millers; Man. Dir BERT SUKHAI.

Forestry and Timber

Barama Co Ltd: Land of Canaan, East Bank, Demerara; tel. 266-5633; fax 266-5634; e-mail barama@samling.com; internet www

.baramaguyana.com; f. 1991; subsidiary of Samling Global Ltd (Malaysia); forestry concession; CEO CLEMENT OOI; c. 1,000 employees.

Demerara Timbers Ltd (DTL): 1 Water St and Battery Rd, Kingston, Georgetown; tel. 225-9382; fax 2269-5387; e-mail demtim@solutions2000.net; owned by Prime Group Holdings Ltd (British Virgin Islands); CEO LU KUI SAN.

Toolsie Persaud Ltd: 10–12 Lombard St, Georgetown; tel. 226-4071; fax 226-0793; e-mail tpl@tpl-gy.com; internet www.tpl-gy.com; f. 1949; logging and quarrying co and manufacturer of construction materials; Chair. TOOLSIE PERSAUD; Man. Dir DAVID PERSAUD; 2,000 employees.

Mining

Bauxite Company of Guyana Inc (BCGI): 274 Peter Rose St, Queenstown, Georgetown; tel. 225-0231; e-mail norma.pooran@rusal.ru; internet www.rusal.ru; f. 2004 as jt venture between Govt and Russian Aluminium Company (RUSAL); 90% owned by RUSAL subsidiary, the Bauxite and Alumina Mining Venture (BAMV); acquired assets of the state-owned Aroaima Mining Co on 31 March 2006; commenced devt of bauxite deposit at Kurubuku 22 in Aroaima area in 2007 following agreement with indigenous community and Hururu tribe regarding the territory; CEO OLEG DERIPASKA; 506 employees.

Bosai Minerals Group (Guyana) Inc.: Washer Pond Rd, POB 32217, Linden; tel. 444-6415; fax 444-6103; f. 1992; fmrly state-owned Linden Mining Enterprises Ltd, name changed to Omai Bauxite Mining Inc upon privatization in 2004; name changed as above upon 70% acquisition by Bosai Minerals Group Co Ltd (China) in 2006; remaining 30% shares held by the Guyana Govt; mining of bauxite; Dir STEVEN MA; Gen. Man. GEORGE ZHAO; 300 employees.

Guyana Goldfields Inc: Georgetown; e-mail info@guygold.com; internet www.guygold.com; f. 1966; gold mining; based in Canada; Pres. and CEO A. SCOTT CALDWELL; Country Man. VIOLET SMITH.

Guyana Oil Company (GUYOIL): 191 Camp St, South Cummingsburg, Georgetown; tel. 225-1595; fax 226-7379; e-mail guyoil@guyoil.com; internet www.guyoil.com; f. 1976; state-owned; petroleum exploration and production; Man. Dir BADRIE PERSAUD.

Miscellaneous

A. H. & L. Kissoon Group of Companies: Lot 2, Strand, New Amsterdam, Berbice; tel. 333-2538; fax 333-4174; e-mail sales@kissoon-furniture.com; internet www.kissoon-furniture.com; construction of wooden furniture and housing, rice cultivation, cattle rearing; Man. Dir HEMRAJ KISSOON.

Courts Guyana Inc: 25–26 Main St, POB 10481, Georgetown; tel. 225-5886; fax 227-8751; e-mail fcollins@courtsguyana.com; internet www.courtsguyana.com; f. 1993 as Geddes Grant (Home Furnishers) Ltd; owned by Unicomer group (El Salvador); furniture stores.

Demerara Tobacco Co Ltd: 90 Carmichael St, South Cummingsburg, Georgetown; tel. 225-1900; fax 226-9322; internet www.batcentralamerica.com; f. 1975; subsidiary co of British American Tobacco PLC; importer of cigarettes; Chair. AMANDA CAVILL DE ZAVALEY; Man. Dir MALISSA SYLVESTER; 200 employees.

Denmor Garments (Manufacturers) Inc: 7–9 Coldingen Industrial Estate, East Bank, Demerara; tel. 270-4512; fax 270-4500; e-mail denmor@guyana.net.gy; clothing manufacturer; Man. Dir DENNIS MORGAN MUDLIER; 1,000 employees.

Gafsons Industries Ltd: Lot 1–2, Area X, Plantation Houston, Georgetown; tel. 227-5887; fax 266-5320; e-mail nil@guyana.net.gy; f. 1956; part of the Gafsons Group of Cos; manufacturer and wholesaler of PVC products and construction materials; Chair ABDOOL SATTAUR GAFOOR.

Guyana National Industrial Company (GNIC): 1-9 Lombard St, Charlestown, POB 10520, Georgetown, Demerara-Mahaica; tel. 226-0882; fax 226-0432; e-mail gnicadmin@futurenetgy.com; privatized in 1995; 70% owned by Laparkan Holdings Ltd and 30% owned by National Engineering Company; ship repairs, ship building, aluminium castings, wharf operations, machinery sales; CEO CLINTON WILLIAMS; 1,150 employees.

Laparkan Holdings Ltd: 2–9 Lombard St, Georgetown; tel. 226-1095; fax 227-6808; e-mail guyanaffd@laparkan.com; internet www.laparkan.com; Chair. and CEO GLEN KHAN; Man. Dir AVINAISH BHAGWANDIN; Gen. Man. OSCAR PHILLIPS.

National Hardware (Guyana) Ltd: 17–19A Water St, South Cummingsburg, Georgetown; tel. 227-1961; fax 226-5280; e-mail natware@guyana.net.gy; internet www.nationalhardwareguyana.com; f. 1971; CEO EDWARD BOYER; Man. Dir MOHAMMED OMAR RAZACK.

New GPC Inc: Al Farm, East Bank, Demerara; tel. 265-4261; fax 265-2229; e-mail limacol@newgpc.com; internet www.newgpc.com; fmrly Guyana Pharmaceutical Corpn Ltd, privatized Dec. 1999; manufacturer of pharmaceuticals and cosmetics; Exec. Chair. Dr RANJISINGHI RAMROOP; Company Sec. ROMEO SEENJAN.

Qualfon Guyana, Inc: 64 Industrial Site, Beterverwagting, East Coast Demerara, Georgetown; tel. 220-0401; internet www.qualfon.com; f. 2005; head office in Mexico; call centre; CEO MICHAEL P. MARROW.

Ram & MacRae: 157C Waterloo St, North Cummingsburg, POB 10148, Georgetown; tel. 227-6141; fax 225-4221; e-mail info@ramandmcrae.com; internet www.ramandmcrae.com; f. 1985; chartered accountants; Man. Partner CHRISTOPHER L. RAM.

G & C Sanata Company Inc: Industrial Site, Ruimveldt, Georgetown; tel. 231-7273-6; fax 227-8197; e-mail sanata@networksgy.com; fabrics manufacturer; Man. Dir CHEN RONG.

Sol Guyana Inc: Lot BB Rome, Agricola, East Bank, Demerara; tel. 431-4800; fax 426-9839; e-mail info.guyana@solpetroleum.com; internet solpetroleum.com; f. 1960; acquired Shell's petroleum distribution and marketing businesses in 2005; distributor of fuels, lubricants, bitumen and LPG; Gen. Man. ORLANDO BOXILL.

Torginol Paints Inc: 9–12 Industrial Site, Ruimveldt, East Bank, Demerara; tel. 226-4041; fax 225-3568; e-mail supports@torginolpaints.com; internet www.torginolpaints.com; manufacturer of paints; owned by The Continental Group of Companies.

UTILITIES

Electricity

Guyana Power and Light Inc (GPL): 40 Main St, POB 10390, Georgetown; tel. 224-4618; fax 227-1978; e-mail bharat.dindyal@gplinc.com; internet www.gplinc.com; f. 1999; fmrly Guyana Electricity Corpn; state-owned; Chair. WINSTON BRASSINGTON; CEO BHARAT DINDYAL; 1,200 employees.

Water

Guyana Water Inc (GWI): Vllissengen Rd and Church St, Bel Air Park, Georgetown; tel. 227-8701; fax 227-8718; e-mail customercallcentre@gwi.gy; internet www.gwiguyana.com; f. 2002 following merger of Guyana Water Authority and Georgetown Sewerage and Water Comm.; operated by Severn Trent Water International (United Kingdom); Chair. Dr RAMESH DOOKHOO; CEO SHAIK BAKSH.

TRADE UNIONS

Federation of Independent Trade Unions of Guyana (FITUG): Georgetown; f. 1988; c. 35,000 mems; Pres. CARVIL DUNCAN; Gen. Sec. KENNETH JOSEPH.

Clerical and Commercial Workers' Union (CCWU): Clerico House, 140 Quamina St, South Cummingsburg, POB 101045, Georgetown; tel. 225-2822; fax 227-2618; e-mail ccwu@guyana.net.gy; Pres. ROY HUGHES; Gen. Sec. ANN ANDERSON.

Guyana Agricultural and General Workers' Union (GAWU): 59 High St and Wights Lane, Kingston, Georgetown; tel. 227-2091; fax 227-2093; e-mail gawu@bbgy.com; internet www.gawu.net; f. 1977; Pres. KOMAL CHAND; Gen. Sec. SEEPAUL NARINE; 20,000 mems.

Guyana Labour Union (GLU): 198 Camp St, Cummingsburg, Georgetown; tel. 227-1196; fax 225-0820; e-mail glu@solutions2000.net; Pres. CARVIL DUNCAN; Gen. Sec. ROBERT WILLIAMS; 6,000 mems. **National Association of Agricultural, Commercial and Industrial Employees (NAACIE):** 64 High St, Kingston, Georgetown; tel. 227-2301; e-mail verbeke@networksgy.com; f. 1946; Gen. Sec. KENNETH JOSEPH; c. 2,000 mems.

Guyana Public Service Union (GPSU): 160 Regent Rd and Shiv Chanderpaul Dr., Bourda, Georgetown; tel. 225-0518; fax 226-5322; e-mail gpsu@networksgy.com; internet gpsu.org; f. 1923; Pres. PATRICK YARDE; Gen. Sec. DEBORAH MURPHY; 11,600 mems.

Guyana Trades Union Congress (GTUC): Critchlow Labour College, Woolford Ave, Non-pareil Park, Georgetown; tel. 226-2481; fax 227-0254; e-mail gtucorg@yahoo.com; f. 1940; national trade union body; 13 affiliated unions; c. 15,000 mems; affiliated to the International Trade Union Confederation; Pres. LESLIE GONSALVES; Gen. Sec. LINCOLN LEWIS.

Guyana Bauxite and General Workers' Union: 180 Charlotte St, Georgetown; tel. 225-4654; Pres. LINCOLN LEWIS; Gen. Sec. LESLIE GONSALVES.

Guyana Local Government Officers' Union (GLGOU): Woolford Ave, Georgetown; tel. 227-7209; fax 227-7376; e-mail daleantford@yahoo.com; f. 1954; Pres. ANDREW GARNETT; Gen. Sec. WENDY DECUNA.

Guyana Postal and Telecommunication Workers' Union: Postal House, 310 East St, POB 10352, Georgetown; tel. 226-7920; fax 225-1633; Pres. HAROLD SHEPHERD; Gen. Sec. GILLIAN BURTON.

Guyana Teachers' Union: Woolford Ave, POB 738, Georgetown; tel. 226-3183; fax 227-0403; Pres. COLLIN BYNOE; Gen. Sec. CORETTA MCDONALD.

Transport

RAILWAY

There are no public railways in Guyana. Until the early 21st century the 15-km Linmine Railway was used for the transportation of bauxite from Linden to Coomaka.

ROADS

The coastal strip has a well-developed road system. There were an estimated 7,970 km (4,952 miles) of paved and good-weather roads and trails. A bridge across the Takutu river, linking Guyana to Brazil, was inaugurated in 2009, while a bridge over the Berbice river was completed in the previous year. In 2012 Guyana and Suriname asked the Inter-American Development Bank (IDB) to fund a feasibility study of a bridge across the Corentyne river. The IDB approved another US $66m. for a road network upgrade and expansion programme in the same year.

SHIPPING

Guyana's principal ports are at Georgetown and New Amsterdam. The port at Linden serves for the transportation of bauxite products. A ferry service is operated between Guyana and Suriname. Communications with the interior are chiefly by river, although access is hindered by rapids and falls. There are 1,077 km (607 miles) of navigable rivers. At 31 December 2013 the flag registered fleet comprised 60 vessels, totalling 32,127 grt.

Transport and Harbours Department: Water St, Stabroek, Georgetown; tel. 225-9350; fax 227-8445; e-mail t&hd@solutions2000.net; Gen. Man. MARCLENE MERCHANT.

Shipping Association of Guyana Inc (SAG): 10–11 Lombard St, Werk-en-Rust, Georgetown; tel. 226-2169; fax 226-9656; e-mail saginc@networksgy.com; internet www.shipping.org.gy; f. 1952; non-governmental forum; Chair. ANDREW ASTWOOD; Sec. IAN D'ANJOU; members:

Guyana National Industrial Company Inc (GNIC): 1–9 Lombard St, Charlestown, POB 10520, Georgetown; tel. 225-5398; fax 226-0432; e-mail gnicadmin@futurenetgy.com; metal foundry, ship building and repair, agents for a number of international transport cos; privatized in 1995; CEO CLINTON WILLIAMS; Port Man. ALBERT SMITH.

Guyana National Shipping Corporation Ltd: 5–9 Lombard St, La Penitence, POB 10988, Georgetown; tel. 226-1840; fax 225-3815; e-mail agencydivision@gnsc.com; internet www.gnsc.com; fmrly Bookers Shipping Transport and Wharves Ltd; govt-owned since 1976; Man. Dir ANDREW ASTWOOD (acting).

John Fernandes Ltd: 24 Water St, POB 10211, Georgetown; tel. 227-3344; fax 226-1881; e-mail philip@jf-ltd.com; internet www.jf-ltd.com; f. 1959; ship agents, pier operators and stevedore contractors; part of the John Fernandes Group of Cos; Chair. and CEO CHRIS FERNANDES.

CIVIL AVIATION

The main airport, Cheddi Jaggan International Airport, is at Timehri, 42 km (26 miles) from Georgetown. Ogle International Airport, six miles east of Georgetown, also accepts international flights;

construction of a 4,000-ft runway was completed in 2013. The regional airline LIAT (based in Antigua and Barbuda, and in which Guyana is a shareholder) provides scheduled passenger and cargo services.

Roraima Airways: R8 Epring Ave, Bel Air Park, Georgetown; tel. 225-9650; fax 225-9648; e-mail ral@roraimaairways.com; internet www.roraimaairways.com; f. 1992; flights to Venezuela and 4 domestic destinations; Man. Dir Capt. GERALD GOUVEIA.

Trans Guyana Airways: Ogle Aerodrome, Ogle, East Coast Demerara; tel. 222-2525; e-mail commercial@transguyana.net; internet www.transguyana.net; f. 1956; internal flights to 22 destinations; Dir Capt. GERARD GONSALVES.

Tourism

Despite the beautiful scenery in the interior of the country, Guyana has limited tourist facilities, although during the 1990s the country began to develop its considerable potential as an eco-tourism destination. The total number of visitors to Guyana in 2012 was 177,000. Expenditure by tourists amounted to some US $64m. in the same year.

Guyana Tourism Authority: National Exhibition Centre, Sophia, Georgetown; tel. 219-0094; fax 219-0093; e-mail info@guyana-tourism.com; internet www.guyana-tourism.com; f. 2003; state-owned; Dir INDRANAUTH HARALSINGH.

Tourism and Hospitality Association of Guyana (THAG): 157 Waterloo St, Georgetown; tel. 225-0807; fax 225-0817; e-mail thag@networksgy.com; internet www.exploreguyana.com; f. 1992; Pres. PAUL STEPHENSON; Exec. Dir TREINA BUTTS.

Defence

The armed forces are united in a single service, the Combined Guyana Defence Force, which consisted of some 1,100 men (of whom 900 were in the army, 100 in the air force and about 100 in the navy), as assessed at November 2013. In addition there were reserve forces numbering some 670 (army 500, navy 170). The Guyana People's Militia, a paramilitary reserve force, totalled about 1,500. The President is the Commander-in-Chief.

Defence Budget: An estimated $ G7,390m. (US $35m.) in 2013.

Chief-of-Staff: Brig.-Gen. MARK PHILLIPS.

Education

Education is free and compulsory for children aged between five years and 15 years of age. Children receive primary education for a period of six years; enrolment at primary schools in 2012 included 72% of children in the relevant age-group. Secondary education, beginning at 12 years of age, lasts for up to seven years in a general secondary school. In 2011/12 an estimated 67,548 pupils were enrolled in state secondary schools. Higher education is provided by eight technical and vocational schools and one teacher training college, in all of which 6,343 students were enrolled in 2011/12. The state-run University of Guyana offers degrees, as does the private GreenHeart Medical University. An estimated $ G32,200m. was allocated to the education sector in 2014.

Bibliography

Bartilow, H. A. *The Debt Dilemma: IMF Negotiations in Jamaica, Grenada and Guyana*. Warwick, Warwick University Caribbean Studies, 1997.

Colchester, M. *Guyana: Fragile Frontier*. Kingston, Ian Randle Publrs, 1997.

Egoume-Bossogo, P., Faal, E., Nallari, R., and Weisman, E. *Guyana: Experience With Macroeconomic Stabilization, Structural Adjustment, and Poverty Reduction*. Ottowa, ON, Renouf Publishing Co Ltd, 2003.

Felix, W. *Issues in Guyana's Development*. Raleigh, NC, LuLu/McGraw-Hill Open Publishing, 2012.

Gafar, J. *Guyana: From State Control to Free Markets*. Hauppauge, NY, Nova Science Publrs Inc, 2003.

Goolsarran, S. A. *Improving Public Accountability: The Guyana Experience 1985–2007*. Denver, CO, Outskirts Press, 2010.

Graham Burnett, D. *Masters of All They Surveyed: Exploration, Geography and a British El Dorado*. Chicago, IL, University of Chicago Press, 2001.

Granger, D. G. (Ed.). *Emancipation*. Georgetown, Guyana Free Press, 1999.

Guyana's Military Veterans: Promises, Problems and Prospects. Georgetown, Guyana Free Press, 1999.

Guyana General and Regional Elections, 19 March 2001: The Report of the Commonwealth Observer Group. London, Commonwealth Secretariat Group, 2001.

Hinds, D. *Ethnopolitics and Power Sharing in Guyana: History and Discourse*. Washington, DC, New Academia Publishing, 2011.

Hintzen, P. C., and Campbell, E. Q. (Eds). *Costs of Regime Survival: Racial Mobilization, Elite Domination and Control of the State in*

Guyana and Trinidad. Cambridge, Cambridge University Press, 2007.

Irving, B. *Guyana: A Composite Monograph*. Hato Rey, Puerto Rico, Inter American University Press, 1972.

Joseph, C. L. *Anglo-American Diplomacy and the Re-Opening of the Guyana—Venezuela Boundary Controversy, 1961–66*. Georgetown, Guyana Free Press, 1998.

Josiah, B. P. *Migration, Mining, and the African Diaspora: Guyana in the Nineteenth and Twentieth Centuries*. Basingstoke, Palgrave Macmillan, 2011.

McGowan, W. F., et al. (Eds). *Themes in African-Guyanese History*. Georgetown, Guyana Free Press, 1998.

   The Demerara Revolt, 1823. Georgetown, Guyana Free Press, 1998.

Mars, J. R. *Deadly Force, Colonialism and the Rule of Law*. Westport, CT, Greenwood Press, 2002.

Mars, P., and Young, A. L. *Caribbean Labor and Politics: Legacies of Cheddi Jagan and Michael Manley*. Detroit, MI, Wayne State University Press, 2004.

Misir, P. *Racial Ethnic Imbalance in Guyana Public Bureaucracies: The Tension Between Exclusion and Representation*. Lewiston, NY, Edwin Mellen Press, 2010.

Mitchell, W. B., Bibbiana, W. A., DuPre, C. E., et al. *Area Handbook for Guyana*. Washington, DC, US Government Printing Office, 1969.

Mohamed, I. A. *Guyana's Approach: From Singapore to Seattle: World Trade Negotiations: Pushing for a Development Round of Negotiations through Process of Review, Repair and Reform of the World Trade Organization*. Georgetown, Ministry of Foreign Affairs, 2000.

Morrison, A. *Justice: The Struggle for Democracy in Guyana 1952–1992*. Georgetown, Red Thread Women's Press, 1998.

Munslow, B. *Guyana: Microcosm of Sustainable Development Challenges*. Aldershot, Ashgate, 1998.

Palmer, C. *Cheddi Jagan and the Politics of Power: British Guiana's Struggle for Independence*. Raleigh, NC, University of North Carolina Press, 2010.

Peake, L., and Peake, A. *Gender, Ethnicity and Poverty in Guyana*. London, Routledge, 1999.

Rabe, S. G. *U.S. Intervention in British Guiana: A Cold War Story (The New Cold War History)*. Chapel Hill, NC, University of North Carolina Press, 2005.

Ramcharan, B. G. *The Guyana Court of Appeal: The Challenges of the Rule in a Developing Country*. London, Routledge-Cavendish, 2002.

Scott, M. *Guyana's Public Policy and Post-Colonial Transformation in Perspective: The Politics of Radical Nationalism and the Sugar and Bauxite Industries*. Lambert Academic Publishing, 2010.

Seecomar, J. *Democratic Advance and Conflict Resolution in Post-Colonial Guyana*. Leeds, Peepal Tree Press, 2009.

Seetahal, D. S. *Commonwealth Caribbean Criminal Practice and Procedure: 2nd edn*. London, Routledge-Cavendish, 2006.

Singh, J. N. *Guyana: Democracy Betrayed*. Kingston, Jamaica, Kingston Publrs, 1996.

Sukhram, B. L. *Divide and Conquer: The Split in the People's Progressive Party of Guyana and the Cold War*. London, Hansib Publications, 2013.

HAITI

Geography

PHYSICAL FEATURES

The Republic of Haiti lies at the western end of the island of Hispaniola, which it shares with the larger Dominican Republic (beyond a 360-km or 224-mile eastern border, partly along the Pedernales river in the south and the Massacre in the north). The land border was first set by treaty between France and Spain at Ryswick (Rijswijk, Netherlands) in 1697, and most recently revised in 1936. Cuba lies 80 km beyond the Windward Passage in the north-west and Jamaica twice that distance to the west of the south-western peninsula. The country includes a number of offshore islands, but also claims Navassa Island. This is a scrubby, uninhabited, 5-sq km (2-sq mile), coral and limestone rock, some 65 km west of Haiti and 160 km south of the USA's Guantánamo Bay naval base in southern Cuba. Navassa is currently administered as an unincorporated territory and wildlife reserve by the USA. To the north, Haiti is less than 100 km from the southernmost Bahamas and about 140 km from the Turks and Caicos Islands, a British Overseas Territory. Haiti includes only 190 sq km of inland waters, but has 1,771 km of coastline. At 27,065 sq km (10,450 sq miles), the country is the same size as the US state of Massachusetts and somewhat smaller than Belgium.

Mainland Haiti has a long, westward-extending peninsula in the south of the country, while the centre and the north broaden north-westwards to form the other arm of the Gulf of Gonâve. At the head of the Gulf, in the south-east, lies the capital, Port-au-Prince. The Gulf embraces the barren island of Gonâve, at some 60 km in length and 15 km in width, the largest of Haiti's offshore territories. The next largest is the Ile de la Tortue, or Tortuga, 40 km in length and 12 km off Port-de-Paix on the north coast (it was the main Caribbean pirate centre in the 17th century, then the base for the French acquisition of western Hispaniola). Stretching east of here run the northern coastal plains (about 150 km in length, 30 km wide and covering some 2,000 sq km), the main area of flat land in the country, apart from the drier Cul-de-Sac in the south, which extends eastwards from Port-au-Prince to brackish Lake Saumâtre (20 km long and 6 km–14 km wide) in the south-east. The fertile, well-watered northern plains had attracted the original colonial plantations and, earlier, piratical outcasts and renegades, who hunted the wild cattle roaming the plains, cooking over wood fires known as *boucans*—hence the word buccaneer. The other main areas of flat land in Haiti are in the valley of the Artibonite, and on the south coast, the densely populated Léogâne plains. However, it is the highlands that are more typical of the country. Most of Haiti is mountainous and, in fact, it is considered the most mountainous country in the Caribbean. The Massif du Nord lies behind the coastal plains of the north, running north-westwards into the dry and drought-afflicted peninsula and, in the other direction, over the border of the Dominican Republic as the Cordillera Central. The highest point in the country, however, is Morne de la Selle (2,680 m or 8,796 ft), which rises from the south-eastern massif—the mountains then continue westwards, along the peninsula, where, towards the end, is the Massif de la Hotte. The centre of Haiti is dominated by the elevated eastern central plateau and a number of other ranges, extensions of the Massif du Nord or the Dominican Sierra de Neibe. Cleaving through the central highlands is the valley of the Artibonite (some 800 sq km of plains land), the main river of Haiti and the trunk of the largest drainage system. The river, 400 km in length, enters the country from the Dominican Republic (it also forms part of the border), but it arose in Haiti as the Libón. Although deep and strong, and prone to flooding in the wet seasons, at drier times of the year the river can shrink dramatically and even cease to flow in some places. The most important tributary of the Artibonite is the 95-km Guayamouc. The main river of the north, at 150 km in length, is the oddly named Trois Rivières. Flooding of the often swift-

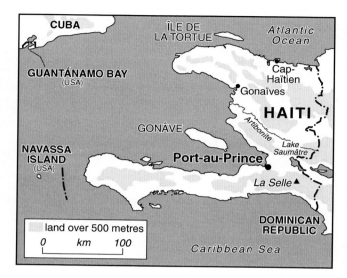

flowing rivers in steep terrain is made worse by the extensive soil erosion caused by deforestation. The widespread poverty in the country has contributed to the wiping out of Haiti's once-extensive tree cover. There are only really two places where woodland survives, both high and inaccessible (one on the Massif de la Selle, the other around the Pic de Macaya, at the end of the south-western peninsula). These places shelter some remnant riches of Haiti's devastated environment, which has been denuded of forest and rendered prone to soil erosion and drought.

CLIMATE

The climate is subtropical, but parts of Haiti are semi-arid, owing to the eastern mountains shadowing the rain brought by the Atlantic trade winds. The northern plains, the mountains of the north-east and the highlands of the south-western peninsula receive the most rain. The driest and most barren areas are the coastal strip east of Port-au-Prince and the north-western peninsula. The recurring problem of drought does not preclude severe storms during the June–October hurricane season, which can bring flooding, and the country also suffers from occasional earthquakes. There are two rainy seasons, April–May and September–October, with average annual rainfall, unevenly distributed, ranging between 1,400 mm (55 ins) and 2,000 mm (79 ins). It is humid on the coast, but the heat is made bearable by morning and evening breezes. Temperatures on the coast vary between about 20°C (68°F) and 35°C (95°F), being slightly hotter in April–September and cooler in the hills at any time of year.

POPULATION

The majority of Haitians are black (95%), the inheritors of the world's only successful slave revolt, which drove out or killed most of its white, planter aristocracy in the early 19th century (the French colony was known as Saint-Domingue). However, there is still a white and mulatto minority, most of whom remain disproportionately wealthy and powerful. Although race and colour have remained important prejudices bedevilling Haitian society, it is language that has had the widest effect. The élite continued to use French after the revolution, and to disparage the 'lower' classes' constant use of Creole (créole or kreyòl), perpetuating the old colonial tongue as the speech of formal use and as the official language into the present. However, only about 15% of the population speak

French and, although they usually also speak Creole, only about 5% can speak both fluently, crippling a society that has long permitted education and advancement solely on the basis of French. Only since the 1990s has Creole begun to make official advances, the culmination of a movement to dignify the native culture that began in the 1920s. Creole, now also an official language, is a tongue that shares many words with French, but has a very different (West African) grammatical structure, having its origins either in a pidgin used between slaves of various African nationalities and their French masters or in a French maritime-trade dialect. Another influence imported from West Africa into Haitian culture is in the field of religion, with Voodoo (vodou), as it is labelled, practised by over one-half of the population. This does not preclude continued adherence to the official religion, Roman Catholic Christianity, as Voodoo adapted the African veneration of family and ancestral spirits with local conditions under the French. The Roman Catholic Church is the main official religious affiliation, and still claims the loyalty of 55% of the population. However, its identity with the ruling establishment facilitated the growth of other churches, mainly Baptists—15% of the population, and Pentecostalists—8%. The Protestants, in contrast to the uneasy, de facto accommodation by the Roman Catholic Church, tend to be fierce in their rejection of Voodoo.

The population of Haiti totalled approximately 10.5m. in mid-2014, according to UN estimates. However, it was estimated that about 220,000 people were killed as a result of the earthquake of January 2010, and no reliable official population estimates have been made since then. About four-fifths of the population live in considerable poverty and Haiti is described as the poorest country in the Western Hemisphere (and one of the poorest in the world) under many definitions. Port-au-Prince and surrounding districts had an estimated population of 2.4m. in mid-2014. The second city of Haiti, and the largest port, is Cap-Haïtien (usually referred to as Cap or, in Creole, Okap), on the central northern coast. The third city, Gonaïves (known as the 'city of independence'), is also on the Gulf, but in the north-eastern corner. The fourth city is Les Cayes (Okay), on the south coast, towards the end of the south-western peninsula. Haiti is administered as 10 departments.

History

Prof. ROBERT E. LOONEY

Based on an earlier article by CHARLES ARTHUR

INTRODUCTION

The independent Republic of Haiti was born out of a 12-year revolutionary struggle for freedom from slavery, and against the colonial ambitions of France, Spain and the United Kingdom. The final victory for the revolutionaries came in late 1803 when the united black and mulatto forces defeated the French army, and the new Republic was declared on 1 January 1804. Although the 1791–1804 revolution brought an end to slavery and made both blacks and mulattos free and theoretically equal, racial, social and economic divisions deriving from the colonial regime exerted strong influences on the shaping of post-independence society.

The black former slaves, who composed the vast majority of the population, refused to return to work as labourers on the plantations and instead occupied idle or abandoned land or carved new plots out of marginal land on the hillsides. As a result, a minority élite—comprising both mulatto landowners and black officers from the revolutionary armies—was obliged to look for new ways to perpetuate their wealth. They turned away from investment in agricultural production, and instead focused on the distribution and export of the produce grown by peasant farmers and the control of state revenue, in particular the levying of taxes. Within a few decades the new nation of Haiti emerged, deeply divided between a rural population of smallholding peasants and an economic and political élite located in a few coastal towns.

The mostly black and poor peasants (and later shanty town dwellers) communicated in the Creole language, maintained certain African traditions and developed the rituals and ceremonies to serve the spirits of Voodoo (vodou). Meanwhile, a mainly mulatto, urban-based, élite minority wrote and spoke French, regarded itself as European, and professed spiritual allegiance to the Roman Catholic Church.

Throughout the 19th century competing élite factions manoeuvred to secure the power of government, giving rise to countless insurrections and coups. A US occupation from 1915–34 failed to alter the fundamental structure of Haitian society but did establish a basic infrastructure and, more significantly, a standing army. Formal politics continued to be marked by the almost complete exclusion of the majority population.

THE DUVALIER ERA

In 1957 Dr François ('Papa Doc') Duvalier proposed an alliance between the emerging black middle class and the poor black majority and subsequently won election as President. He swiftly countered the power of the army by creating his own militia force, popularly known as the Tontons Macoutes. Employing indiscriminate violence against all opposition, whether real, potential or imagined, Duvalier established a brutal dictatorship. All major institutions in civil society, including political parties, workers' unions, peasant co-operatives and student associations, were abolished and as many as 30,000 of his opponents were killed. Tens of thousands of educated Haitians chose to go into exile to North America, Europe and Africa.

Following Duvalier's death in 1971, his son, Jean-Claude, continued the dictatorship. Although some members of the black middle and lower-middle classes prospered through their association with the dictators' power structure, the majority of the population suffered from the exploitation and corruption on which the regime was based. In the mid-1980s, encouraged by the emerging liberation theology branch of the Roman Catholic Church, the increasingly poverty-stricken population began to organize in opposition to the dictatorship. Fearing a descent into revolution, the USA and the Haitian military decided to withdraw their support for the regime and, consequently, on 7 February 1986 Jean-Claude Duvalier and his family went into exile in France.

THE POST-DUVALIER ERA

Successive military governments countered an emerging movement for democracy and social change with repression. Elections in November 1987 were abandoned when soldiers and resurgent Tontons Macoutes gunned down voters at polling stations. Free elections, monitored by the UN, were finally held in December 1990, and were won convincingly by the radical Roman Catholic priest Jean-Bertrand Aristide. His campaign, which he called 'Lavalas'—Creole for an avalanche or flood—promised to cleanse Haiti of Duvalier's legacy, bringing justice, governmental accountability and the opportunity for the populace to determine the nation's future.

President Aristide's programme challenged vested interests, and after less than eight months in office his Government was overthrown by a military coup. Aristide was forced into exile and a military regime embarked on a campaign of repression targeting the country's pro-Lavalas grass-roots organizations. From late 1993, much of the repression was carried out by the army-sponsored paramilitary group Front Révolutionnaire pour l'Avancement et le Progrès d'Haïti (FRAPH).

The UN imposed economic sanctions in an attempt to unseat the military regime, but senior military officers and their élite supporters refused to yield and even prospered through the control of a thriving contraband trade. Continuing political instability and concerns about the continuing refugee exodus finally resulted in decisive action in September 1994 when 20,000 US troops, acting with UN authorization, were dispatched to Haiti. The invasion was unopposed and within four weeks the three principal military leaders went into exile, allowing Aristide to return to serve out the remaining 16 months of his presidency. One of his most significant acts in that short time was to disband the much detested army.

At the end of March 1995 the US occupation force was succeeded by a UN peacekeeping mission. Later that year parliamentary and local government elections were held, and the result was an overwhelming victory for a three-party coalition dominated by the Organisation Politique Lavalas (OPL). At the presidential election in December, Aristide's ally and former Prime Minister, René Garcia Préval, stood as the pro-Lavalas candidate and won convincingly.

The new OPL-led Government began to implement the programme of neo-liberal reforms suggested by the IMF and the World Bank. The ensuing austerity resulted in significant civil unrest. In late 1996 political tensions were exacerbated by Aristide's creation of a new party, La Fanmi Lavalas (FL), and his criticism of the Government's IMF/World Bank structural adjustment programme.

After many delays, elections for a new legislature, urban mayors and local administrative councils were eventually held in May 2000. Aristide's FL won a landslide victory. Although the elections were largely peaceful and well organized, the unsuccessful parties claimed the results were fraudulent. Despite threats by the USA and the European Union that future development aid would be withheld if the votes were not recounted, the Préval Government—under pressure from Aristide and his supporters—refused to back down. The main opposition parties denounced what they termed a totally flawed election process and joined together to form the Convergence Démocratique (CD) coalition. In August, amid continuing protests from the CD and the international community, a new legislature, dominated by the FL, was inaugurated.

In November 2000 a further round of elections for a new President and a third of the Sénat (Senate) went ahead, despite the opposition parties' refusal to participate and in the absence of international observers. Aristide won the presidency with 92% of the vote, and in the Senate his FL party now held 26 of the 27 seats in addition to all but 10 of the 83 seats in the Chambre des Députés (Chamber of Deputies). However, the CD refused to recognize the legitimacy of the legislature or of Aristide's presidency.

With the political impasse continuing, tensions increased when former soldiers mounted sporadic attacks on police stations in remote border areas and even briefly occupied the presidential palace in December 2001. The Government responded by using the police to harass opposition leaders and mobilizing its supporters among the urban youth to repress meetings of opposition parties, credit union members' organizations, women's groups, trade unions and university students. The Government attempted to secure the resumption of foreign aid by implementing the economic reform programme long demanded by international financial institutions. The harsh austerity programme included measures to reduce the public sector deficit by decreasing expenditure in areas such as education. The combination of heavy-handed repression with neo-liberal austerity rapidly alienated the small, urban middle class.

Although the Government maintained strong support among the inhabitants of the shanty towns in and around Port-au-Prince, it found itself increasingly isolated nationally and internationally. Aristide rejected all suggestions that he resign before the end of his mandate in February 2006; however, in the final days of February 2004 the USA and France withdrew their lingering support for the FL Government, ending hopes of a mediated settlement to the crisis. In the early hours of 29 February Aristide and his family left Haiti on a US Air Force plane in disputed circumstances.

The UN authorized US and French troops to take control of strategic points in the capital and deter any attempted takeover by the armed insurgents. With the collapse of the Government, Gérard Latortue, a career diplomat, was asked to assume the office of Prime Minister, and he selected a Cabinet composed of technocrats and leading figures from the anti-FL movement.

Latortue's Government, tasked with running the country on an interim basis pending new elections, courted the support of the armed insurgents and the private sector. It ordered the police to arrest a large number of high-ranking FL members, and incorporated several hundred former soldiers into the police force—moves that quickly alienated the still significant sector of the population that remained loyal to the ousted Aristide.

In June 2004 the UN deployed a peacekeeping force, the UN Stabilization Mission in Haiti (MINUSTAH), predominantly composed of troops from Brazil and other South American countries. The mission initially restricted its operations to patrols in Port-au-Prince, while in many other parts of the country former insurgents and former soldiers assumed responsibility for law and order. Supporters of the ousted Government claimed that they were victims of a wave of repression. At the beginning of October tense relations between the new Government and FL supporters in the capital erupted into violent conflicts.

After many delays caused by concerns over security and poor organization of voter registration, a general election was finally held on 7 February 2006. The FL was divided over whether to participate in the elections: one faction supported a boycott while another fielded candidates for legislative seats and backed the presidential bid of established politician Marc Bazin. The FL position was further complicated by Aristide's endorsement of the presidential candidacy of Catholic priest Gérard Jean-Juste, who had been detained in prison as a result of dubious allegations of involvement in acts of violence. The party was left in disarray when Jean-Juste was prevented from registering his candidacy from prison. Much FL support was subsequently transferred to former President René Préval, who was standing as the candidate for the newly formed party, Lespwa (l'Espoir). Préval won by far the largest share of votes in the presidential poll (51%), attracting support not only from FL supporters but also from a range of social sectors, including some of the more progressive members of the private sector.

In the legislative elections, Lespwa won the largest number of seats in both the upper and lower houses, but failed to obtain a majority in either. In May 2006 Préval nominated the Lespwa leader, Jacques-Edouard Alexis, as Prime Minister, and he in turn named a consensus Cabinet with ministers representing six different parties, including the FL.

Préval and Alexis stressed the need for political dialogue and reconciliation, and reached out to the core FL supporters by ordering the release from prison of FL members who had been detained without trial. The new Government moved to address the serious problem of violence and crime in the capital by negotiating with a number of gang leaders, who indicated that they would lay down their weapons if social welfare projects to improve the lives of slum residents were implemented. At the same time, Alexis announced that his Government would spend US $1,200m. over five years to strengthen the police force, increasing it in size from 5,000 to 12,000 officers. In the first few months after Préval's election victory there was a marked improvement in the security situation. However, by mid-2006 incidents of gang violence in the capital had begun to rise again.

Towards the end of 2007 as the number of kidnappings for ransom in Port-au-Prince surged, there was criticism of MINUSTAH's inability to combat organized crime. There was growing criticism too of the Government's failure to rebuild the economy, despite high levels of international assistance, and Alexis became the focus of accusations of government inefficiency and corruption. In early 2008 sharp increases in the cost of fuel and food caused public disenchantment with the Government to grow rapidly. In early April street protests spread from provincial towns to Port-au-Prince, where thousands of protesters erected roadblocks, ransacked several businesses and banks, and attempted to tear down the gates of the presidential palace. The fragile stability that had been growing steadily since Préval took office was reversed in the course of just a few days. On 12 April the Senate approved a motion of no confidence in Alexis on the grounds that he had failed to meet the basic demands of the population.

In August 2008 the legislature accepted Préval's nominee as new Prime Minister, Michèle Duvivier Pierre-Louis, an economist and the director of a charitable foundation. A new Government was formed in early September. However, just as one crisis was resolved, another, and much more serious, one developed. In August and early September a series of powerful hurricanes inflicted widespread damage and flooding across the country. More than 800 people were killed during the storms. Emergency relief agencies estimated that nationwide around 800,000 people had been left homeless or unable to feed themselves. There was also extensive damage to the country's rudimentary infrastructure and communications networks, and to thousands of buildings, including hospitals and schools.

During its first four months in office the new Pierre-Louis Government was obliged to focus on trying to provide relief and co-ordinating repairs and reconstruction in the wake of the weather catastrophe. Meanwhile, although the security situation improved, the Government, international agencies and diplomats of countries involved in Haiti warned that the country's hard-won stability remained in jeopardy because of its precarious socio-economic situation.

Growing public disenchantment with the political process was reflected in the long-delayed election for 11 Senate seats held in April 2009. Participation in this poll was low following the disqualification of all 16 FL candidates by the Conseil Electoral Provisoire (CEP—Provisional Electoral Council), on the grounds that the party's national representative, Aristide, who remained in exile in South Africa, had not sanctioned any of them. The decision was widely viewed as a political manoeuvre to remove the FL from the contest, and the party appealed to the electorate to boycott the ballot. Official figures recorded a voter participation rate of just 12%, but even this was probably an exaggeration.

In October 2009 a rare period of political stability was brought to an abrupt end when the Senate approved a vote of no confidence in Prime Minister Pierre-Louis, ostensibly because she had failed to account for the Government's use of US $197m. allocated to hurricane relief and repair projects. Some senators had further accused her administration of failing to combat poverty and revive the economy. Préval promptly nominated Minister of Planning and External Co-operation Jean-Max Bellerive, an architect of the poverty reduction strategy that underpinned the Government's economic policies, as Prime Minister.

In late 2009 Lespwa was disbanded by its leaders, including Préval, and a new party, Inite (Creole for 'unity'), was created in its stead. As well as including many of the leading figures from Lespwa, the new party also co-opted a number of prominent members of other parties, including dissidents from the FL.

THE 2010 EARTHQUAKE AND AFTERMATH

On 12 January 2010 a massive earthquake struck southern Haiti, causing extensive damage, claiming the lives of more than 200,000 people, injuring 250,000 more, destroying much of Port-au-Prince and many provincial towns and villages, and leaving around 1.2m. people homeless or displaced. The Haitian authorities were overwhelmed by the scale of the disaster. The parliament building, the presidential palace, the main police station and most government ministry buildings were all seriously damaged or destroyed by the earthquake.

International humanitarian relief groups were quickly mobilized, but rescue teams and medical aid were slow to arrive in the capital owing to the chaos and damage to transport routes and infrastructure. The collapse of the MINUSTAH headquarters also hampered the UN's initial relief efforts. In response, the US Administration of President Barack Obama deployed thousands of US marines in order to secure the airport infrastructure and establish security for the deployment of international aid workers and the distribution of medical and food assistance.

Thousands of those made homeless established 'tent cities' throughout the Port-au-Prince area. In February 2010 Haiti's Directorate of Civil Protection reported that at least 1,000 camps for displaced persons had been created around the country, and that nearly 600,000 displaced persons had migrated from Port-au-Prince and its environs to the countryside.

In the aftermath of the earthquake, there was a massive international response to the disaster, but it suffered from poor co-ordination. By early March 2010 the International Federation of Red Cross and Red Crescent Societies, which was responsible for co-ordinating the effort to provide shelter for earthquake survivors, announced that only around 40% of the estimated 1.2m. homeless and displaced persons had received any sort of shelter materials.

While the Government remained in ostensible control of the country, real authority resided with the UN, owing to the work of its various agencies and the presence of MINUSTAH, and with the USA, as a result of the large number of US troops deployed in Haiti and its position as the largest international aid donor. MINUSTAH's presence was increased, and by mid-2010 it comprised more than 11,500 soldiers and police officers. Former US President, Bill Clinton (1993–2001), was named as a co-Chairman, with Bellerive, of the Commission Intérimaire pour la Reconstruction d'Haïti (CIRH—Interim Haiti Reconstruction Committee), the body tasked with organizing Haiti's reconstruction and official aid distribution.

However, the CIRH struggled to galvanize the relief effort. By mid-July 2010, six months after the earthquake, only 2% of a promised US $5,300m. in reconstruction aid had materialized. Of the $1,100m. collected by 23 major charities in response to the earthquake, only 2% had been released. The main reasons given for the lack of progress were the very slow disbursements of foreign aid pledged for reconstruction, the campaign for the general election scheduled for November and the devastated state of government bureaucracy. In the temporary tent camps around Port-au-Prince, where at least 1m. people made homeless by the earthquake were living, conditions remained dire.

Haiti's difficulties worsened in October 2010 when there was an outbreak of cholera. During the first six months of the epidemic, several thousand people died, and, as the infection spread across the country, more than 300,000 were diagnosed with cholera. There was no history of cholera in Haiti and speculation among Haitians about how the deadly disease arrived in such remote rural areas focused on the UN base in the central town of Mirebalais and its contingent of Nepalese soldiers.

Subsequent scientific evidence appeared to support the Haitian contention that MINUSTAH troops introduced cholera to the country. However, in February 2013 the UN said it would not compensate cholera victims, citing diplomatic immunity.

Election day on 28 November 2010 was marked by disorganization and chaos, with many voters turned away from the polling stations on technical grounds. As the accusations of fraud spread, supporters of a popular singer, Michel Martelly, who was the presidential candidate for a new party, Repons Peyizan (RP), rioted in various parts of Port-au-Prince. Initially, all the presidential candidates apart from Jude Célestin, the former head of the state public works company, who was standing as the candidate for Inite, demanded that the voting be halted. However, within days, as early indications of the result began to be revealed, Martelly and another front-runner, Mirlande Manigat, the candidate of the Rassemblement des Démocrates Nationaux et Progressistes reversed their positions.

On 7 December 2010 the CEP announced that, with no candidate winning more than 50% of the vote, a run-off would take place between Manigat (who won 31.4% of the vote) and Célestin (with 22.5%). According to the CEP, Martelly had come third in the poll (with 21.8%). Protests by Martelly supporters erupted shortly after the announcement. As rioting continued (leading to five deaths), the USA began to exert pressure for the results to be reassessed. In mid-January 2011 President Préval received an Organization of American States (OAS) report on the November ballot recommending that, because of voting irregularities, Célestin should not proceed to the second round of voting. In late January, under intense diplomatic pressure, Inite officials finally announced that they would withdraw Célestin as a presidential candidate. It was agreed to hold a second round, pitting Martelly against Manigat, on 20 March.

The result of the second round of the presidential election, a decisive victory for Martelly (with 67.6% of the vote), marked a clear break with recent political history. With the exception of a two-year interim government (2004–06), Haiti had been governed over the preceding two decades only by Préval or Jean-Bertrand Aristide (1991, 1994–96 and 2001–04). Martelly, whose candidacy proved very popular among the country's youth, and whose campaign mixed populist and centre-right elements, represented the end of an era dominated by the political movement that drove Jean-Claude Duvalier from power in February 1986.

MARTELLY IN OFFICE

President Martelly, who assumed office on 14 May 2011, was a political novice and lacked a majority in a legislature dominated by the Inite party. Following the legislative elections that took place at the same time as the presidential contest, Inite held 15 of the 30 seats in the Senate and 46 of the 99 seats in the Chamber of Deputies while the RP held only three seats in the lower house and won no representation at all in the upper house. Consequently, the President needed the support of parliament to approve his choice of Prime Minister and to pass legislation, but it was far from clear that Inite would co-operate with Martelly.

Although he received strong initial support from the USA—a key player in Haiti—the new President faced a difficult political, economic and social situation. An estimated 1m. Haitians remained in tent camps and other improvised shelter. Government institutions, already extremely weak before the disaster, were not even yet functioning at pre-earthquake levels of competence, and health conditions remained precarious.

On taking office, President Martelly promised to boost reconstruction efforts, to address the cholera epidemic and to restore security. Rather controversially, he also proposed the re-establishment of the armed forces, which had been disbanded by Aristide in 1995, and suggested granting amnesty to Aristide and Duvalier.

On the day after his inauguration Martelly designated businessman Daniel-Gérard Rouzier as premier, but this was rejected in June 2011 by the lower house, in which Inite had joined with other parties to form the Groupe des Parlementaires pour le Renouveau, an informal alliance reportedly composed of around 70 deputies; the opposition alleged that Rouzier had connections with the former regime of Jean-Claude Duvalier.

The President's second nominee, Bernard Gousse, a former Minister of Justice in the mid-2000s, although having earlier been approved by the Chamber of Deputies, was rejected by the Senate in early August 2011. As tensions rose between the President and the legislature, the OAS and other international donors expressed concern over the persistent political stalemate. Finally, on 4 October, the appointment of Martelly's third nominee, Garry Conille, a medical doctor and former UN official, was endorsed by the Senate, having been unanimously approved by the Chamber of Deputies in mid-September; a new Cabinet, which included three members of the parliamentary alliance headed by Inite, was duly sworn in on 18 October.

In September 2011 President Martelly appointed a civilian commission tasked with considering the issue of the re-establishment of the military. In January 2012 Martelly announced that the commission had recommended the restoration of the army with a mandate to protect territorial integrity, respond to natural disasters and combat drugs-trafficking and terrorism. However, concerns remained within the opposition and the international community with regard to the financial burden involved (estimated at some US $95m.) and the poor human rights record of the previous armed forces. Many observers were of the belief that establishing a new civilian police force was the best option.

The mandate of the CIRH expired in October 2011, and, although Martelly and Conille favoured an extension, the renewal of its mandate was not subsequently approved by parliament. In September, meanwhile, Martelly announced the establishment of a Presidential Advisory Council on Economic Growth and Investment, including a number of former heads of state of various countries, as well as business executives; co-chaired by Bill Clinton, the aim of the Council was to help attract foreign investment to Haiti and to revive the country's economy.

With the security situation gradually stabilizing, Martelly began working with the UN on a plan for the eventual withdrawal of MINUSTAH. The plan involved training and equipping the country's police force, the Police Nationale d'Haïti (PNH), to the point that it could assume full responsibility for the country's security. In the mean time, in October 2013 the UN renewed MINUSTAH's mandate for another year, until October 2014 (although the size of the force will be cut gradually). The UN, along with other outside observers, contended that the PNH should fill the country's security needs and that the President's suggestion that a reconstituted Haitian army play a role was costly and unnecessary.

Following a deterioration in Conille's relations with Martelly and with the legislature, the Prime Minister resigned from office on 24 February 2012; in December 2011 the Senate had set up a committee of inquiry into the nationality of Martelly and members of his Government, following allegations that the President and several ministers (including Conille) held dual citizenship, in contravention of the Constitution. The President nominated close ally and Minister of Foreign Affairs and Religion Laurent Lamothe to succeed Conille; Lamothe's nomination was approved by the Senate in April 2012, and was overwhelmingly endorsed by the Chamber of Deputies in early May. The following month President Martelly yielded to international pressure and finally agreed to sign the amended Constitution that had been approved by parliament a year earlier.

In addition to the granting of dual citizenship to Haitians resident abroad, the constitutional amendments provided for the establishment of a permanent electoral council (Martelly had dismissed all nine members of the discredited CEP in December 2011 and had not replaced them), a Conseil Supérieur du Pouvoir Judiciaire (CSPJ—Supreme Council of Judicial Power) and a constitutional court, and the requirement that 30% of government employees be female. The enfranchisement of the Haitian diaspora was expected to have a major political impact, given their sheer numbers. The CSPJ, which was headed by the President of the Supreme Court, commenced operations in July 2012.

On 30 October 2012 the Government declared a 30-day state of emergency after Hurricane Sandy wreaked devastation that resulted in the deaths of more than 50 people and the destruction of food crops. The emergency followed a series of protests against President Martelly and his Government over the rising cost of living, as well as allegations of corruption, inefficient governance, inadequate social provision and the wasteful use of scarce resources on foreign travel and luxury items for government officials.

In addition to mounting criticism from within the country, the Government of President Martelly also came under pressure from the international community to ensure greater progress in establishing and institutionalizing the rule of law. Some measures were implemented, notably the creation of the CSPJ in 2012. However, much remained to be done, as foreign investors continued to bemoan the absence of transparency and fairness in the business environment, including legal protection of property rights and a code of company law. In 2013 Haiti's relationship with the Dominican Republic became severely strained. In September the Dominican Constitutional Court ruled that children born to parents who were considered 'in transit' in the country were no longer considered citizens of the Dominican Republic. The ruling, which was irrevocable, could render thousands of Dominican-Haitians stateless and, therefore, ineligible for all social benefits, including formal employment, education or health care, and, potentially, subject to deportation. Most of these individuals were born and raised in the Dominican Republic, and many were granted Dominican nationality at the time of their birth.

Following the Dominican court decision, representatives of the two countries have held a series of monthly meetings to resolve this and other issues of bilateral contention. There has been some flexibility over citizenship on the Dominican side: in January 2014 the Dominican Republic committed to enact measures to safeguard the rights of Haitians living in the Dominican Republic, and in May the Dominican Senate unanimously approved a bill providing a path to citizenship to hundreds of thousands of Dominican-born children of migrants. Progress has also been made in several other areas. In February representatives from both countries signed agreements related to agriculture, the environment, security and drugs-trafficking. Advances were also made in commercial matters, including the lifting of a Haitian ban on the importation and sale of Dominican poultry and egg products.

ELECTORAL ACCORD

Haiti was facing increasing domestic and international pressure to hold long-delayed elections. These were originally scheduled to take place toward the end of 2011 for two-thirds of the country's Senate, the entire Chamber of Deputies, and local and municipal officials, such as mayors. After a series of political stalemates, significant progress towards new elec-

tions was finally achieved in early 2014 following a series of negotiations held in Pétionville, mediated by the Bishop of Les Cayes, Cardinal Chibly Langlois. At that time, a national dialogue culminating in the so-called 'El Rancho' Accord (named after the hotel where talks were held) in March provided the guidelines for local, municipal, and legislative elections to take place no later than 26 October. Among the key provisions of the Accord were the amendment of the electoral law, the renaming of the Transitional College of the Permanent Electoral Council (formed in December 2012) as the Provisional Electoral Council (CEP), and an 'open government', one that could inspire trust to organize the elections. The Accord was approved by the Chamber of Deputies on 1 April. The CEP was officially inaugurated in May. In early June the 26 October was confirmed as the date elections would be held.

The UN hailed the country's progress towards elections as an 'unprecedented step in Haitian political history'. In a March 2014 speech before the UN Security Council, MINUSTAH Head of Mission Sandra Honoré noted that, 'the long-awaited adoption and promulgation of the Electoral Law in December 2013, along with the March 14th Accord emanating from the inter-Haitian dialogue, have prepared a path toward inclusive and transparent elections to be held later this year—a *sine qua non* for the continuous functioning of Parliament in January 2015.'

Economy

Prof. ROBERT E. LOONEY

Based on an earlier article by CHARLES ARTHUR

INTRODUCTION

Since the fall of the Duvalier dictatorship in 1986, Haiti has struggled to overcome its centuries-long legacy of authoritarianism, extreme poverty, and underdevelopment. During that time, economic and social stability began to improve. Unfortunately, Haiti's development was set back by a massive earthquake in January 2010 that devastated much of the capital of Port-au-Prince and other parts of the country.

Approximately 220,000 people were killed, including one in every three civil servants (many in middle management), 1,200 teachers, and over 500 health personnel. In addition, 300,000 houses, 13 out of 15 ministerial buildings, 4,200 schools, and more than 60% of the country's hospitals were damaged or destroyed. Total damage caused by the earthquake was estimated at about US $9,000m., equivalent to 120% of gross domestic product (GDP) in 2009.

Four years after the earthquake some aspects of life are slowly returning to normal. Still many Haitians and international donors acknowledge that the recovery has fallen far short of what was promised. Low levels of employment and agricultural output mean that food security and fulfilment of basic needs are still pressing concerns for many Haitians. Institutions such as the courts and judicial system are still very weak, and international drugs trafficking feeds criminal and corrupt activity. A cholera epidemic and forced eviction from tent encampments continue to be the reality. Delayed elections have left Haiti without a functioning Senate and with 130 (of 140) presidential appointees in what should be elected mayoral positions. Government revenue still comes from two main sources—international donor assistance and remittances—and not from domestic sources. Promises to restore education, housing, and other critical services have not been met.

While economic recovery is under way, the country continues to suffer setbacks stemming from subsequent natural disasters. Two hurricanes adversely affected agricultural output in 2012, causing growth to decline to 2.9%, compared with 5.6% in the previous year. However there are bright spots. With strong production in 2013, overall growth recovered to 4.3%. Non-farm real output increased by 4.2%, as services saw strong growth. In addition, public investment continued to

support construction, and increased apparel exports have facilitated a recovery in the manufacturing sector. The economy remains very fragile, however, with a number of factors potentially derailing the nascent recovery. A certain amount of donor aid fatigue has set in and future aid flows are in jeopardy due to impatience over the slow progress in improving governance and transparency. Official flows and remittances could also suffer if the recovery in advanced economies falters. Haiti has received considerable assistance from Venezuela through that country's subsidized oil delivery programme Petrocaribe. However, instability in that country combined with declining rates of oil production may result in the cancellation of the programme. The country is also a major importer of food and extremely vulnerable to price increases in basic commodities.

Adding to these challenges are the effects of climate change. According to Haitian government figures, average temperatures have risen significantly since the early 1970s. Moreover, rainfall patterns have become erratic, with precipitation arriving much later than usual, or not all, as illustrated by the 2013–14 drought in the north-west, where 43% of households were suffering from food insecurity and high rates of chronic malnutrition.

Despite the recovery, poverty remains massive and deep, and economic disparity is pervasive: Haiti continues to be the poorest country in the western hemisphere. According to the World Bank, in 2012 real per capita GDP was about US $460 (at constant 2005 prices), compared with $502 in 1999. Almost 80% of the population lived on less than $2 per day (classified as extreme poverty) and living standards are very low. Rural areas are the most affected, with nearly four-fifths of Haiti's extreme poor living outside cities. Rates of unemployment have been high for years. In 2010 the unemployment rate was estimated to be slightly more than 40%, with 62% unemployment among young people (aged between 15 and 19 years). More than two-thirds of the labour force do not have formal jobs.

In 2014 the country ranked 168 out of 187 countries, according to the UN Development Programme's (UNDP) Human Development Index. One of Latin America's biggest slums is situated in Port-au-Prince, with an estimated 500,000 people living in dire conditions and suffering from high rates of criminality. The income distribution inequality is very high, with a Gini coefficient rating (an international measure of inequality) of 0.59 in 2012. Even before the earthquake Haiti had one of the highest rates of hunger and malnutrition in the western hemisphere, with 45% of the population undernourished and 30% of children under five suffering from chronic malnutrition.

The state as a provider of basic functions is nearly non-existent. Some 8m. (out of an estimated population of 10.5m.) live without electricity, while some 5m. cannot read or write. Gender differences are high in education; only 39% of women are literate, compared with 53% of men. Access to health services is limited and worsened with the outbreak of cholera in 2010. More than 7,000 people died in this epidemic because there was insufficient or non-existent access to health care or clean water. Infant and maternal mortality in Haiti is the highest in the Americas, with about 60 deaths per 1,000 live births.

The country's poverty has deep historical roots. Through years of neglect and underinvestment Haiti's limited resource base has been depleted to the extent that it is barely able to support the country's growing population. Deepening poverty in the countryside, and the prospect—however remote—of finding employment in the city, spurred a rural exodus that is still continuing. An estimated 100,000 people relocate each year, most of them to the capital, Port-au-Prince. Nearly all of the new arrivals join the estimated 1m. people working in the so-called informal sector, a term that covers a multitude of occupations ranging from self-employed traders and artisans to casual labourers, porters, shoe-shiners and gardeners. By far the most common activities are the buying and re-selling of tiny quantities of everyday goods and the provision of basic services.

While the country has often attracted vast sums of aid and relief efforts there have been few signs of tangible improvements in the lives of the majority of the population. The country has suffered negative economic growth in three of the last four decades. The inability of poor Haitians to exploit growth-promoting opportunities for investment in physical and human capital has created a vicious circle of weak economic growth, high unemployment, persistent poverty, increased inequality and the mass emigration of skilled workers. Roughly 82% of Haitians with a college education have left the country. It is estimated that 37% of Haitians in the USA have a university degree.

Even when economic growth has taken place, it has not been sustained. Haiti has never developed 'inclusive' institutions, such as well-enforced property rights and contract enforcement necessary to create incentives for investment and development. Instead 'extractive' exclusionary institutions antithetical to progress have become entrenched. Institutional deficiency is reflected in the country's income distribution. Haiti has the second largest income disparity in the world. Over 68% of the total national income accrues to the wealthiest 20% of the population, while less than 1.5% of Haiti's national income is accumulated by the poorest 20% of the population.

Hoping to combat the country's many problems, the authorities have adopted a medium-term poverty reduction strategy, with special emphasis on job creation in manufacturing, tourism and agriculture, social inclusion, and improved governance. If successful, this programme would create an environment conducive to economic growth and to reducing Haiti's dependence on foreign assistance.

AGRICULTURE

Haiti's geography is mountainous (80% of the surface area) and does not lend itself to field crop production. Although only one-fifth of the land is considered suitable for agriculture, more than two-fifths are under cultivation. Major problems include soil erosion (particularly on mountain slopes, which are seldom terraced), recurrent drought, and an absence of irrigation. None the less, the primary productive sector in Haiti is agriculture and livestock (especially mangoes, coffee, bananas, cocoa, manioc, yam and avocado). Between 66% and 80% of

Haitians are dependent on small-scale agriculture production for their livelihoods and the sector constitutes approximately 20% of GDP.

Many farmers concentrate on subsistence crops, including cassava (manioc), plantains and bananas, corn (maize), yams and sweet potatoes, and rice. Some foodstuffs are sold in rural markets and along roads. A mild arabica coffee is Haiti's main cash crop. Haitian farmers sell it through a system of intermediaries, speculators, and merchant houses.

Over the last 100 years or so, agricultural output has suffered from a growing population farming a finite area of land. The result has been the division of cultivated land into smaller and smaller holdings. On these tiny plots, the soil has become progressively exhausted and less productive. This problem has been compounded by extensive deforestation, which has in turn led to severe erosion of the fertile topsoil. As yields have declined, peasant farmers have found themselves locked into a self-destructive cycle, in which the felling of trees for charcoal production, and the farming of land higher up the mountains, has staved off short-term financial disaster, but only created greater problems in the long term.

None the less, until the 1950s, crops grown by peasant farmers were sufficient to satisfy most of the country's food requirements, but since then the agricultural sector has experienced a deepening crisis. Agro-exports, once the mainstay of the national economy, declined throughout the latter half of the 20th century. Sugar cane is the second most important cash crop, but since the late 1970s Haiti has been a net importer of sugar. Productivity losses resulting from depleted natural resources, limited access to agricultural services, absence of secure property rights, high costs for market access, extreme vulnerability to climate change and natural disasters, as well as weak public institutions have all contributed to a downward economic spiral that accelerated during the late 20th century.

By the early 2000s the most significant agricultural exports were mangoes, cacao and essential oils. Export earnings from mangoes have increased each year since 2002, totalling US $10.1m. in 2011/12. Haiti is the biggest mango exporter in the Caribbean region, and the sixth largest source of mango imports to the USA. There is also an informal export trade to the Dominican Republic, where Haitian mangoes are used in the production of chutney for the European market.

Typically, a small peasant farm produces maize, millet, bananas and plantains, beans, yams and sweet potato. Rice is grown principally in the central Artibonite valley and a few other areas of the country where irrigation systems have been introduced.

Although it has undergone a massive decline, agriculture remains the mainstay of the economy. Agriculture is still Haiti's largest productive sector, contributing 23% of GDP in 2012/13. Approximately 70% of the population live in rural areas, and 65% of the economically active population depend directly or indirectly on the agricultural sector. As expected, poverty and extreme poverty are far more prevalent in rural areas, where 88% live below the poverty level and 59% earn less than US $1 a day.

Fishing supplements the diet of those peasant farmers who live on Haiti's 1,771 km-long coastline, but, like agriculture, this economic sector is facing serious problems. In the absence of the capital needed to purchase outboard motors and modern fishing boats, all fishing occurs in shallow coastal waters. Over the years, fish stocks in these waters have dwindled as fishermen have used nets with smaller and smaller mesh in an effort to make a catch. However, overfishing is not the only problem. Just as serious are the effects of the vast quantities of eroded topsoil washed into the sea at times of heavy rainfall. This silt destroys most sea life, including potentially fish-rich coral reefs.

The demise of the agricultural sector has had a number of repercussions. The central Government, which has long relied on customs charges on exports, has seen its revenue reduced dramatically. Because the country must import more than one-half of the food that is consumed, severe balance of payments pressures have occurred from time to time. The social and political ramifications of such dependence were starkly highlighted in early 2008 when a sudden increase in international food prices made many food items too expensive for poor Haitian families. The resultant demonstrations and riots across the country brought down the Government.

Also reflective of the decline of agriculture is a marked increase in the percentage of the population prone to food insecurity. According to a survey conducted by Haiti's National Food Security Coordination Agency in March 2012, food insecurity affects 39.5% of the population (around 3.8m. people), distributed as follows: 29.9% (2,993,557 people) are moderately food insecure; 8.1% (810,969 people) are affected by high transitory food insecurity; while 1.5% (150,179 people) suffer from high chronic food insecurity.

The Northern and Artibonite regions have potential for further agricultural development. Both regions have fertile soils, diversified ecosystems favourable to a wide range of crops and existing irrigation systems, as well as a high potential for additional irrigation development fed by rivers and groundwater. The location of the two regions also means easy access to the Dominican market with its demand for fresh agricultural products. There is also great potential for these regions to develop competitive exports to other Caribbean Community and Common Market (CARICOM) partners and other Caribbean islands, and to meet an anticipated increased urban food demand.

After the earthquake of 2010, the Haitian Government developed a National Agricultural Investment Plan (NAIP) to co-ordinate efforts to revitalize agriculture in Haiti. However, by late 2012 donors had only funded 47% of the US $790m. promised to implement the NAIP. President Michel Martelly's administration's most ambitious project, Aba Grangou (Alliance against Hunger), is also focused on the agricultural sector, but is more comprehensive. It aims to halve the number of people suffering from hunger by 2016 and to eradicate hunger and malnutrition in Haiti by 2020. The Aba Grangou initiative comprises a social safety net programme designed to improve the most vulnerable population's access to food, agricultural investment programmes designed to increase national food production and measures to improve basic service provision. For the short term (2012–16), Aba Grangou's specific goals are: 2.2m. school children to receive school meals; 1m. mothers and vulnerable people to receive money and food transfers; 1m. children under five years of age to benefit from nutrition programmes; 1m. small-scale farmers to benefit from agricultural programmes, crop storage facilities, and water tanks; and 200 medium-scale private investors to develop agricultural value chains on idle state-owned land.

MINING

Haiti has limited reserves of minerals. Gold and copper are found in small quantities in the north of the country. Limited deposits of bauxite (aluminium ore) are found on the southern peninsula, but large-scale mining there was discontinued in 1983.

At mid-2014 the most important extractive enterprises were those quarrying stone, gravel and sand for use in road-building and construction. According to the Government's Office of Mines and Energy, this sector provided employment for 3,000–4,000 people, and central bank data shows that it continues to exhibit remarkable growth, reflecting the continuing boom in the construction sector, particularly in the greater Port-au-Prince region. Following the earthquake, the construction sector expanded further; the sector's GDP increased by an estimated 5.9% in 2012/13.

Haiti's mineral industry may undergo change in the near future. In 2012 US and Canadian companies conducted exploratory drilling operations and reported finds beneath Haiti's north-eastern mountains of gold, copper and silver, potentially worth US $20,000m.

In addition to environmental impacts, the main concern over the sector's development is the absence of a sound governance framework needed to prevent many of the excesses that have plagued other developing countries. To this end, the Government recently cancelled all current mining licences, pending a review of contracts signed by the previous Government and a revision (the first since 1976) of its mining law.

ENERGY

Haiti has been unsuccessful in discovering hydrocarbons and is therefore heavily dependent on energy imports (petroleum and petroleum products). Hydroelectricity provides roughly one-half of the power generated in the country, the remainder coming from thermal (mainly coal-fired) plants, especially in Port-au-Prince. However, the power supply is insufficient to satisfy current needs, and the main sources of energy for cooking are firewood and charcoal. Venezuela erased Haiti's oil debt after the 2010 earthquake, but following the death of Hugo Chávez, it is unlikely that the country will be able to import Venezuelan oil at rates as favourable as it has enjoyed in the past. Under Chávez's Petrocaribe programme countries including Haiti needed to pay for only one-half of the oil they received, with the remainder being repaid over 25 years at 1%.

The challenges facing the energy sector, particularly those related to electricity generation, transmission and distribution and the associated institutional framework, have impeded Haiti's national development for over two decades. The high cost and unreliability of electricity severely restricts Haiti's economic growth. The 2010 earthquake caused substantial damage to energy sector infrastructure, and disrupted the commercial operations of Electricité d'Haïti (EDH). The direct damage to the power system was estimated at approximately US $20m. More than 60% of the population have no access to power, and those who do receive about 10 hours of service daily. In rural areas, just 5% have access to electricity. High levels of technical and commercial losses combined with an ingrained non-payment culture mean EDH is insolvent. EDH continues to operate thanks to annual transfers from the Treasury of more than $100m., which represents a serious drain on public finances. Specifically, transfers to the electricity sector (either in the form of subsidies or loans) represented nearly 2.5% of GDP in 2012/13, equivalent to 20% of total domestic revenue.

At the root of EDH's weak operational and financial situation and poor electricity service is deficient governance, including a lack of formal independent regulatory and oversight mechanisms. The complete lack of strategic planning capabilities have left the country with nine separate small local grids, but no national grid, and an installed generation capacity of 150 MW when national demand is estimated to be more than 500 MW.

The substitution of more sustainable energy sources for firewood and charcoal as the major source of energy for cooking and industrial heating continues as a major challenge, and the reduction of biomass usage to prevent the exhaustion of Haiti's forest area is also a high priority.

MANUFACTURING

Haiti's small domestic market, the lack of natural resources and internal instability have constrained the growth of manufacturing. Most manufacturing is of processed foods, beverages, textiles, and footwear. Other manufactures include chemical and rubber products, tobacco products, essential oils, and alcoholic beverages. Much of the country's sugar cane is processed in rural distilleries that produce a cheap rum, although Haiti also produces Barbancourt rum, one of the world's finest brands. Non-traditional exports such as ornamental flowers and sugar snap peas have increased in recent years. The manufacturing sector has been in decline since it peaked in the early 1980s. At that time it accounted for more than 18% of GDP, but by 2012/13 it had fallen to 8.8%.

Haitian manufacturing has also ventured into the export markets, largely through the establishment of assembly plants in special export zones. Assembly factories were originally introduced over 30 years ago by then President Jean-Claude 'Baby Doc' Duvalier. Duvalier envisioned Haiti becoming the 'Taiwan of the Caribbean', a vast factory complex where foreign firms could assemble textiles, electronics and baseballs for the nearby US market. The assembly industry for export thrived for a few years but was then decimated during the three years of military rule after the 1991 coup, when political upheaval, power supply problems and economic sanctions forced the closure of nearly all the assembly plants. During the second half of the 1990s the garment assembly sub-sector experienced a slight recovery, employing around 20,000 workers in Port-au-

Prince on extremely low wages to assemble pyjamas and t-shirts for the North American market.

In 2003 a new free trade zone in the north-eastern border town of Ouanaminthe opened, and over 1,000 workers were employed by the Dominican Grupo M company to assemble jeans and T-shirts. Political and criminal violence in Port-au-Prince in 2004–05 forced many garment assembly plants to close, and, with the expiry of the duty-free quota system under the Agreement on Textiles and Clothing at the beginning of 2005, there were serious concerns about the viability of the subsector. Already lagging far behind the Central American republics and the Dominican Republic in terms of a share of the US market, the removal of the duty-free quotas was a serious blow to Haitian manufacturers who were unable to compete with Chinese and other East Asian producers.

Government officials and operators in the garment assembly sector expected that the Haitian Hemispheric Opportunity through Partnership Encouragement (HOPE) Act, which was enacted by the US Congress in December 2006, would provide a significant boost to foreign investment and job creation in the industry. The legislation, which provided duty-free access to the US market for clothing assembled in Haiti from materials sourced from countries with which the USA had free trade agreements or regional preference programme partnerships, was predicted to create some 20,000 new jobs. However, only around 3,000 more workers had been taken on by late 2007, and the total labour force of the garment sector in Haiti still stood at just 20,000. In response to lobbying by the Haitian Government and the garment assembly sector, the US Congress approved the HOPE II Act in mid-2008, allowing for increased duty-free access to the USA and extending the life of the preference until 2018.

Local manufacturing was badly affected by the earthquake with the private sector suffering around 70% of the total estimated damages, amounting to a US $3,400m. equity loss. Smaller enterprises were particularly affected with an estimated 75% of small and micro firms rendered non-operational, while micro, small and medium-sized enterprises (SMEs) suffered 65% of productive sector losses.

The challenge for developing the private sector, particularly SMEs, is resolving institutional shortcomings and market failures. These include a lack of governance and a poor business environment with a weak framework for private investment and business activity, limited access to investment loans and an overall lack of capitalization of enterprises, insufficient human capital characterized by an unskilled labour force and weak management skills, and centralized economic activity. These factors elevate the risk perception (political, social, sector and natural) of the economy hindering foreign and local investment.

A major element of US aid to Haiti has been the development of the Caracol Industrial Park in Haiti's northern region. Although the region was not affected by the earthquake, the project is part of an effort—begun before the earthquake—to 'decentralize' development, stimulating the economy and creating jobs outside of the overcrowded capital. The park is expected to create 20,000 permanent jobs initially, with the potential for up to 65,000 jobs. By October 2012 about 1,000 Haitians were employed there.

With labour costs rising in China and Mexico, Haiti is very well positioned to capture a share of the rapidly expanding US supply-chain 'near-shoring' business. However, investor concerns over the country's political instability, violence and deficient infrastructure continue to place Haiti at a significant disadvantage compared with many rapidly growing locations in the region, such as Nicaragua.

In an effort to make Haiti's export zones more attractive to US, as well as other, investors, President Barack Obama signed the Haiti Economic Lift Program Act (HELP) in May 2010. The HELP Act has expanded duty-free access to the US market for certain Haitian textile and apparel exports and will extend until 2020 existing trade preference programmes for certain imported knitted articles made in Haiti from yarns wholly spun in the USA. The law also provides duty-free treatment for additional textile and apparel products that are wholly assembled or knit-to-shape in Haiti, regardless of the origin of the fabric or yarns from which the articles are made. Duty-free quotas for Haiti exports have also almost tripled to 200m. sq-m equivalents. Yet, the project has met with more than its share of scepticism. Previous export zones failed the country because they became enclaves without any links to the national economy. In addition, more often than not, they became a source of exploitation of local labour and farmers. Such endeavours in the country have also been rejected by the population at large, because of displacement of agricultural production and environmental destruction.

Fortunately, there are a number of model cases from the experiences of Ireland in the late 1980s, Costa Rica in the 1990s, and Uruguay in the 2000s that offer valuable lessons on how to overcome many of these concerns. These countries have also demonstrated the steps that must be taken to link free trade zones to the rest of the economy rather than to let them become enclaves within the country. The experiences of these countries lay out a clear blueprint as to what the Haitian authorities need in terms of a legal and regulatory framework to maximize the potential economic benefits of these ventures.

In general, successful strategies have been built on a combination of both export and local production zones. The idea is to focus reconstruction and aid efforts towards the economic zones as a way of replacing the current haphazard system of allocating foreign aid. Haiti's new strategy is beginning to be structured along these lines.

While the country's manufacturing sector is facing a much more favourable external environment than previously, there are still many obstacles that have to be overcome, specifically the country's lack of competitiveness. In the World Economic Forum's Competitiveness Report for 2013–14 Haiti ranked 143 out of 148 countries. The country was severely deficient in all the key sub-components of the index: institutions 146, infrastructure 142, health and primary education 133, higher education and training 128, goods market efficiency 144, financial market development 142, technological readiness 135, business sophistication 145, and innovation 144.

SERVICES

In Haiti services consist mainly of tourism, national and local government, finance, and trade. Services contributed almost 59% of GDP in 2012/13, according to provisional figures, although services provide only one-10th the number of jobs as agriculture.

As with agriculture and manufacturing, tourism has experienced major difficulties over the past several decades. The sector, which was once a principal source of foreign exchange, declined during the 1980s and 1990s owing to political instability. However, since around 2000 the Government has been making efforts to restore the sector in order to be competitive with other Caribbean destinations.

The Dominican Republic received 4.56m. visitors in 2012. The Caribbean region as a whole had nearly 25m. visitors in that year, who spent a total of US $27,500m. There is no reason why Haiti should not aim to receive a higher share of this market in the decades to come. Given Haiti's natural environment, which offers ample sites of interest for tourists, its proximity to the USA, and its increasing stability and accessibility to visitors, the tourism sector has great potential, and is showing signs of expanding. The country had 299,646 stop-over arrivals in the first nine months of 2013, a 17.9% increase over the same period in 2012. The country's main attractions are its unique colonial architecture, pristine beaches and gambling casinos. Haiti's tourist industry, however, has suffered from a range of problems, including prostitution, an influx of cultural imports (at the expense of local arts and customs), and the need to import costly foods and luxury items. Cap-Haïtien and Port-au-Prince have been the traditional tourist hubs. Cap-Haïtien provides access to Haiti's 19th-century citadel, Ramiers fortifications, and Sans Souci Palace—the three locations collectively designated a UNESCO World Heritage site in 1982.

Despite the slowdown of the US and European economies, tourism in the Caribbean has recovered somewhat from its sharp decline during the 2008–09 global financial crisis. For the Caribbean as a whole, tourism accounts for some 16% of GDP, and Haiti has the potential to equal or exceed that figure.

The aim of the Martelly Government is to give the country a fresh image. This implies providing additional attractions, as well as the traditional Caribbean offering of sun and sand, by exploiting Haiti's rich artistic culture and heritage. It also means improving transport and communications, and modernizing tourist accommodation, both by bringing traditional, locally owned hotels up to international standards and by attracting foreign investment into big new resorts.

The country has had some success in attracting investment for several major new hotels in Port-au-Prince. However, the obstacles to overcome if the country is to become an attractive destination for wealthy foreign tourists are formidable. Deficient public services, poor infrastructure, continuing security concerns and a shortage of trained personnel are among the main problems.

TRANSPORTATION

Haiti's road system is rudimentary, constrained by mountainous terrain, soil erosion and torrential rains. Nevertheless, road transport is the predominant transportation mode, even though the national road network offers limited coverage and is inadequately maintained. The total road network of 3,608 km comprises 950 km of primary or trunk roads (linking the main cities), 1,315 km of departmental or secondary roads and 1,343 km of tertiary or rural roads. Barely 5% of the road network is in good condition, while 80% is in poor or very poor condition. Only 10% of the road network receives any form of maintenance. The earthquake caused losses and damages to the inter-urban road network particularly in the Ouest, Nippes and Sud-Est departments.

There is no railway service. The primary means by which the rural population travel are on foot, by bicycle, by public bus (known as a 'tap-tap' in Haiti), or by donkey. The latter mode is also commonly used to transport goods.

Maritime transport is mainly centred in the port of Port-au-Prince. Earthquake damage was significant; the north pier (the port's largest) was destroyed, while part of the smaller south pier sank. A temporary barge arrangement has restored cargo throughput, and should suffice until 2016, when it is hoped that a permanent solution will be constructed.

The earthquake caused substantial airport damage, reducing the annual capacity of Haiti's main airport (Toussaint Louverture International Airport) to 500,000 passengers per year, significantly below current demand levels. Degraded port and airport infrastructure is an economic burden, increasing logistical costs for imports and exports, inhibiting the smooth arrival of tourists and further perpetuating Haiti's relative isolation.

Compounding the country's transport problems, the Ministry of Public Works, Transport and Communications responsible for administration, management, control, regulation and planning of all transport infrastructure investment is experiencing major difficulties carrying out its duties effectively owing to budgetary and institutional constraints.

INVESTMENT AND FINANCE

The small amounts of foreign investment that Haiti has received in recent decades have been committed almost exclusively to the assembly sector. Most of this investment has come from US companies, although in recent years some Dominican, Canadian and South Korean companies have also set up operations in Haiti. National private sector investment has traditionally been at very low levels, with Haitian investors favouring the stability and lower risks on offer in the USA and the Dominican Republic. The attraction of foreign investment

was a key priority of President Michel Martelly, and the Government estimated that investments by South Korean companies would create some 20,000 jobs in Haiti in 2012, in addition to those at the Caracol Industrial Park.

One of the more encouraging signs for the future is the increasing willingness of Haiti's increasingly affluent diaspora in the USA and Canada to play a more active role in the Haitian economy. In recent years remittances from this group have averaged around US $2,000m. annually, equivalent to approximately 20% of Haiti's GDP. This amounts to 90% of Haiti's federal budget and represents a figure three times greater than the value of its exports.

The diaspora is increasingly involved in directing funds toward local microfinance institutions. Many of these grassroots groups and organizations are committed to helping the poor and eliminating poverty. Two of the more rapidly growing organizations are Zafen and Fonkoze. Zafen provides interest-free loans to Haitian entrepreneurs in parts of the country that lack access to conventional banking services.

OUTLOOK

Haiti's dire situation will not improve dramatically in the short term as aid donors continue to fail to meet commitments. In addition, austerity programmes in the USA and Europe will curtail major efforts from these sources to rebuild the economy quickly.

The Haitian Government's strategy for the near term is laid out in its Post-Disaster Needs Assessment (PDNA). The PDNA is partly based on a 2007 poverty reduction strategy paper, which is focused on enhancing human development, strengthening democratic governance and promoting agriculture, rural development and tourism. Producing tangible results, such as building permanent housing for the remaining displaced people, will remain a key challenge. In 2012 the Government introduced a new cash transfer programme for mothers (called 'Ti manman cheri', or Dear Mother) to help those Haitians living in extreme poverty.

While these programmes are encouraging, it may take years for the national Government to achieve the levels of governance and effectiveness necessary to guide the economy out of poverty through a traditional top-down strategy. None the less, there is reason for optimism regarding Haiti's future. The country's unique social networks represent a grassroots force that is gaining increased traction in providing a better standard of living for large segments of the population.

The country's community-based assistance strategies are well established in Haiti and functioned admirably during the days following the earthquake. These arrangements include: *konbit*, when community members gather to work on behalf of one family (similar to a barn raising); *twòk*, referring to informal exchange or bartering; *sol* and *sabotaj*, two types of rotating pay-out funds that serve as savings mechanisms; and *men ansanm*, a community-based loans mechanism. Such co-operation within communities provides a basis for self-organization with the aim of reconstruction and development, as well as for increasing local trade and commerce.

In addition, it is likely that the country's increasingly affluent diaspora will play a greater role in providing a pool of remittances. Through more efficient and less expensive means of communication with successful relatives and friends in the USA and Canada, many Haitians are realizing for the first time what is possible. They are beginning to understand what needs to be done to make the country's Government more efficient and accountable.

Statistical Survey

Sources (unless otherwise stated): Banque de la République d'Haïti, angle rues du Pavée et du Quai, BP 1570, Port-au-Prince; tel. 2299-1202; fax 2299-1145; e-mail brh@brh.net; internet www.brh.net; Institut Haitien de Statistique et d'Informatique, Ministère de l'Economie et des Finances, 1 angle rue Joseph Janvier et boulevard Harry S Truman, Port-au-Prince; tel. 2514-3789; fax 2221-5812; e-mail info@ihsi.ht; internet www.ihsi.ht.

Area and Population

AREA, POPULATION AND DENSITY

Area (sq km)	27,065*
Population (census results)	
30 August 1982†	5,053,792
7 July 2003	
Males	4,039,272
Females	4,334,478
Total	8,373,750
Population (UN estimates at mid-year)‡	
2012	10,173,774
2013	10,317,461
2014	10,461,408
Density (per sq km) at mid-2014	386.5

* 10,450 sq miles.
† Excluding adjustment for underenumeration.
‡ Source: UN, *World Population Prospects: The 2012 Revision*.

Note: It was estimated that approximately 220,000 people were killed as a result of a powerful earthquake that devastated the country's capital, Port-au-Prince, in January 2010. No reliable official estimates of total population have been published since the earthquake.

POPULATION BY AGE AND SEX
(UN estimates at mid-2014)

	Males	Females	Total
0–14 years	1,839,968	1,775,057	3,615,025
15–64 years	3,117,053	3,254,578	6,371,631
65 years and over	212,031	262,721	474,752
Total	5,169,052	5,292,356	10,461,408

Source: UN, *World Population Prospects: The 2012 Revision*.

DEPARTMENTS
(official population projections at mid-2009)

	Area (sq km)	Population	Density (per sq km)	Capital
L'Artibonit				
(Artibonite) . .	4,886.9	1,571,020	321.5	Gonaïves
Centre . . .	3,487.4	678,626	194.6	Hinche
Grand'Anse . .	1,911.9	425,878	222.8	Jérémie
Nippes . . .	1,267.8	311,497	245.7	Miragoâne
Nord . . .	2,115.2	970,495	458.8	Cap-Haïtien
Nord-Est . .	1,622.9	358,277	220.8	Fort Liberté
Nord-Ouest . .	2,102.9	662,777	315.2	Port-de-Paix
Ouest . . .	4,982.6	3,664,620	735.5	Port-au-Prince
Sud . . .	2,653.6	704,760	265.6	Les Cayes
Sud-Est . .	2,034.1	575,293	282.8	Jacmel
Total . . .	27,065.3	9,923,243	366.6	—

PRINCIPAL TOWNS
(official projected population at mid-2009)

Port-au-Prince				
(capital) . .	897,859	Delmas	359,451	
Carrefour . . .	465,019			

Mid-2014 (urban agglomeration, UN estimate): Port-au-Prince (incl. Carrefour and Delmas) 2,375,910 (Source: UN, *World Urbanization Prospects: The 2014 Revision*).

BIRTHS AND DEATHS
(UN estimates)

	1995–2000	2000–05	2005–10
Crude birth rate (per 1,000) . .	32.7	29.7	27.7
Crude death rate (per 1,000) . .	11.3	10.6	9.4

Source: UN, *World Population Prospects: The 2012 Revision*.

Life expectancy (years at birth): 62.7 (males 60.9; females 64.6) in 2012 (Source: World Bank, World Development Indicators database).

ECONOMICALLY ACTIVE POPULATION
('000, FAO estimates at mid-year)

	2012	2013	2014
Agriculture, etc.	2,299	2,323	2,346
Total labour force (incl. others) .	3,984	4,064	4,144

Source: FAO.

2007/08 (national survey of employment and the informal economy, sample survey of persons aged 10 years and over, primary occupation, percentage distribution): Agriculture 36.8; Fishing 1.3; Mining and quarrying 0.3; Manufacturing 7.7; Electricity, gas and water 0.2; Construction 3.3; Wholesale and retail trade, vehicle repairs 27.2; Hotels and restaurants 3.8; Transport, storage and communications 3.0; Financial intermediation 0.6; Real estate, renting and other business activities 1.0; Public administration and compulsory social security 1.1; Education 4.8; Health and social welfare 1.9; Other community, social and personal services 2.3; Other services 4.7; Total employed 100.0.

Health and Welfare

KEY INDICATORS

Total fertility rate (children per woman, 2012) . . .	3.2
Under-5 mortality rate (per 1,000 live births, 2012) . . .	76
HIV/AIDS (% of persons aged 15–49, 2012)	2.1
Physicians (per 1,000 head, 1998)	0.3
Hospital beds (per 1,000 head, 2007)	1.3
Health expenditure (2011): US $ per head (PPP)	101
Health expenditure (2011): % of GDP	8.5
Health expenditure (2011): public (% of total)	21.5
Access to water (% of persons, 2012)	62
Access to sanitation (% of persons, 2012)	24
Total carbon dioxide emissions ('000 metric tons, 2010) . .	2,119.5
Carbon dioxide emissions per head (metric tons, 2010) . .	0.2
Human Development Index (2013): ranking	168
Human Development Index (2013): value	0.471

For sources and definitions, see explanatory note on p. vi.

Agriculture

PRINCIPAL CROPS
('000 metric tons)

	2010	2011	2012
Rice, paddy*	118	115	106
Maize†	340	360	202
Sorghum	116*	126*	92†
Sweet potatoes*	248	240	215
Cassava (Manioc)*	600	652	652
Yams*	353	323	323
Sugar cane*	1,110	1,150	1,200
Avocados*	49	52	53
Bananas*	255	265	270
Plantains*	239	265	267
Guavas, mangoes and mangosteens*	218	199	205

* FAO estimate(s).
† Unofficial figure(s).

Aggregate production ('000 metric tons, may include official, semi-official or estimated data): Total cereals 573 in 2010, 60 in 2011, 400 in 2012; Total roots and tubers 1,264 in 2010, 1,286 in 2011, 1,264 in 2012; Total vegetables (incl. melons) 158 in 2010, 149 in 2011, 155 in 2012; Total fruits (excl. melons) 901 in 2010, 930 in 2011, 950 in 2012.

Source: FAO.

LIVESTOCK
('000 head, year ending September, FAO estimates)

	2010	2011	2012
Horses	500	500	500
Asses	210	210	210
Mules	80	80	80
Cattle	1,455	1,460	1,465
Pigs	1,000	1,001	1,001
Sheep	153	153	154
Goats	1,910	1,920	1,950
Chickens	5,600	5,650	5,700
Turkeys	195	195	195
Ducks	190	190	190

Source: FAO.

LIVESTOCK PRODUCTS
('000 metric tons, FAO estimates)

	2010	2011	2012
Cattle meat	45.0	45.5	46.5
Goat meat	5.5	5.5	5.5
Pig meat	35.0	35.0	35.0
Horse meat	5.6	5.6	5.6
Chicken meat	8.0	8.0	8.0
Cows' milk	63.4	64.0	65.0
Goats' milk	28.1	28.1	28.2
Hen eggs	5.0	5.0	5.0

Source: FAO.

Forestry

ROUNDWOOD REMOVALS
('000 cubic metres, excl. bark, FAO estimates)

	2010	2011	2012
Sawlogs, veneer logs and logs for sleepers*	224	224	224
Other industrial wood*	15	15	15
Fuel wood	2,041	2,050	2,060
Total	2,280	2,289	2,299

* Production assumed to be unchanged since 1971.

Source: FAO.

SAWNWOOD PRODUCTION
('000 cubic metres, incl. railway sleepers, FAO estimates)

	2010	2011	2012
Coniferous (softwood)	5	8	8
Broadleaved (hardwood)	10	5	6
Total	14	13	14

Source: FAO.

Fishing

('000 metric tons, live weight)

	2010*	2011	2012*
Capture	13.7	16.5*	16.5
Freshwater fishes	0.5	0.6*	0.6
Marine fishes	12.5	15.2*	15.1
Marine crabs	0.1	0.2*	0.2
Caribbean spiny lobster	0.4	0.3	0.3
Natantian decapods	0.1	0.1*	0.1
Stromboid conchs	0.2	0.2*	0.2
Aquaculture	0.4	0.6	0.7
Total catch	14.1	17.1*	17.2

* FAO estimate(s).

Note: Figures exclude corals and madrepores (FAO estimates, metric tons): 10 in 2010–12.

Source: FAO.

Industry

SELECTED PRODUCTS
(estimates)

	2008	2009	2010
Cement ('000 metric tons)	290.0	290.0	290.0
Electric energy (million kWh)	486	721	587

Sources: US Geological Survey; UN Industrial Commodity Statistics Database.

Finance

CURRENCY AND EXCHANGE RATES

Monetary Units
100 centimes = 1 gourde.

Sterling, Dollar and Euro Equivalents (28 February 2014)
£1 sterling = 73.911 gourdes;
US $1 = 44.290 gourdes;
€1 = 61.178 gourdes;
1,000 gourdes = £13.53 = $22.58 = €16.35.

Average Exchange Rate (gourdes per US $)
2011   40.523
2012   41.950
2013   43.463

Note: The official rate of exchange was maintained at US $1 = 5 gourdes until September 1991, when the central bank ceased all operations at the official rate, thereby unifying the exchange system at the 'floating' free market rate.

BUDGET
(million gourdes, year ending 30 September)

Revenue	2011	2012*	2013†
Current revenue	38,893	41,970	46,475
Domestic taxes	24,460	28,076	29,242
Customs duties	13,672	13,721	14,230
Other current revenue . . .	761	174	3,002
Grants	27,428	34,803	29,380
Total	**66,321**	**76,774**	**75,855**

Expenditure	2011	2012*	2013†
Current expenditure	35,232	39,006	43,158
Wages and salaries . . .	14,809	16,706	20,007
Goods and services . . .	7,525	11,406	11,320
Interest payments . . .	1,272	1,359	1,711
Transfers and subsidies . .	11,626	9,534	10,120
Capital expenditure . . .	42,120	53,484	57,051
Domestically financed . .	17,642	19,252	31,190
Foreign-financed	24,478	34,232	25,861
Total	**77,352**	**92,490**	**100,208**

* Provisional figures.
† Estimates.

Source: IMF, *Haiti: Seventh Review Under the Extended Credit Facility, Requests for Waiver of Nonobservance of Performance Criterion, and Modification of Performance Criteria-Staff Report; Press Release; and Statement by the Executive Director for Haiti* (April 2014).

2014 (million gourdes, year ending 30 September, budget figures): *Imports:* Direct taxes 12,509; Indirect taxes 37,233 (Taxes on production 7,756, Taxes on international trade 25,171, Taxes on petroleum products 4,306); Other domestic taxes 2,260; Total revenue 52,002 (excl. grants 45,582). *Expenditure:* Current expenditure 41,426 (Wages and salaries 22,388, Goods and services 12,416, Transfers and subsidies 5,406, Interest payments 1,217); Capital expenditure 88,097; Total expenditure 129,523 (Source: Ministry of Economy and Finance, Port-au-Prince).

INTERNATIONAL RESERVES
(US $ million at 31 December)

	2011	2012	2013
IMF special drawing rights . .	105.7	105.8	106.0
Reserve position in IMF . . .	0.1	0.1	0.1
Foreign exchange	1,088.9	1,178.6	1,617.5
Total	**1,194.7**	**1,284.5**	**1,723.6**

Source: IMF, *International Financial Statistics*.

MONEY SUPPLY
(million gourdes at 31 December)

	2011	2012	2013
Currency outside depository corporations	21,701.5	23,263.3	25,055.4
Transferable deposits . . .	51,487.1	56,449.7	61,340.5
Other deposits	67,360.0	70,875.0	75,609.1
Broad money	**140,548.6**	**150,588.0**	**162,005.0**

Source: IMF, *International Financial Statistics*.

COST OF LIVING
(Consumer Price Index for metropolitan areas, base: 2000 = 100)

	2010	2011	2012
Food	397.4	438.1	467.3
All items (incl. others) . . .	380.1	411.9	431.9

Source: ILO.

All items (Consumer Price Index; base: August 2004 = 100): 185.2 in 2011; 196.9 in 2012; 208.4 in 2013.

NATIONAL ACCOUNTS
(million gourdes, year ending 30 September)

Expenditure on the Gross Domestic Product
(at current prices)

	2010/11	2011/12*	2012/13†
Final consumption expenditure .	344,247	350,070	381,652
Gross capital formation . . .	84,364	96,925	109,585
Total domestic expenditure .	**428,611**	**446,995**	**491,237**
Exports of goods and services .	52,848	55,466	66,544
Less Imports of goods and services	178,605	174,400	192,970
GDP in purchasers' values .	**302,854**	**328,061**	**364,811**
GDP at constant 1986/87 prices	**14,003**	**14,407**	**15,026**

Gross Domestic Product by Economic Activity
(at constant 1986/87 prices)

	2010/11	2011/12*	2012/13†
Agriculture, hunting, forestry and fishing	3,262	3,220	3,366
Mining and quarrying	20	17	18
Manufacturing	1,074	1,150	1,175
Electricity and water	91	69	69
Construction	1,275	1,345	1,470
Trade, restaurants and hotels .	3,765	3,954	4,147
Transport, storage and communications	1,092	1,078	1,117
Business services	1,577	1,638	1,692
Other services	1,584	1,629	1,672
Sub-total	**13,740**	**14,100**	**14,726**
Less Imputed bank service charge	810	853	910
Taxes, less subsidies, on products.	1,073	1,161	1,209
GDP in purchasers' values .	**14,003**	**14,407**	**15,026**

* Provisional figures.
† Estimates.

BALANCE OF PAYMENTS
(US $ million, year ending 30 September)

	2009/10	2010/11	2011/12
Exports of goods	563.4	768.1	785.0
Imports of goods	−2,810.1	−3,014.0	−2,679.3
Balance on goods	**−2,246.7**	**−2,245.9**	**−1,894.4**
Exports of services	239.0	249.2	257.0
Imports of services	−1,277.3	−1,140.2	−1,170.1
Balance on goods and services	**−3,284.9**	**−3,136.9**	**−2,807.5**
Primary income received . . .	32.7	44.2	72.4
Primary income paid	−10.4	−3.2	−3.7
Balance on goods, services and primary income	**−3,262.6**	**−3,095.9**	**−2,738.8**
Secondary income received . .	1,473.8	1,551.4	1,612.3
Secondary income paid . . .	−167.0	−240.2	−231.9
Current balance	**−1,955.8**	**−1,784.8**	**−1,358.4**
Capital account (net)	658.0	170.0	75.7
Direct investment liabilities . .	150.0	181.0	178.8
Other investment assets . . .	−334.7	−85.6	−69.7
Other investment liabilities . .	−595.6	−229.8	357.9
Net errors and omissions . . .	461.6	−64.9	67.6
Reserves and related items .	**−1,616.6**	**−1,814.1**	**−748.2**

Source: IMF, *International Financial Statistics*.

External Trade

PRINCIPAL COMMODITIES
(US $ million, year ending 30 September, provisional figures)

Imports c.i.f.	2010/11	2011/12	2012/13
Food products	551.3	523.0	622.5
Mineral fuels, lubricants, etc. .	770.4	820.5	951.0
Chemical products . . .	129.6	106.6	220.4
Basic manufactures . . .	843.1	673.1	643.2
Machinery and transport equipment	292.5	224.4	543.7
Miscellaneous manufactured goods	502.3	434.3	410.9
Total (incl. others)	3,240.9	2,881.1	3,579.8

Exports f.o.b.*	2010/11	2011/12	2012/13
Coffee	7.0	8.4	1.3
Cocoa	6.9	9.3	4.9
Mangoes	10.6	10.1	—
Essential oils	16.4	14.3	15.7
Manufactured goods . . .	267.8	273.7	314.4
Total (incl. others)	321.7	328.7	359.2

* Excluding re-export of assembled goods to the USA (US $ million, year ending 30 September, provisional figures): 686.3 in 2010/11; 706.0 in 2011/12; 802.9 in 2012/13.

PRINCIPAL TRADING PARTNERS
(US $ million, year ending 30 September)*

Imports c.i.f.	1989/90	1990/91	1991/92
Belgium	3.4	3.7	2.9
Canada	22.0	31.9	15.2
France	24.5	32.4	17.2
Germany, Federal Republic . .	14.6	19.2	10.0
Japan	23.6	31.2	17.7
Netherlands	11.2	13.9	8.7
United Kingdom	5.6	6.7	4.2
USA	153.1	203.2	126.7
Total (incl. others)	332.2	400.5	277.2

Exports f.o.b.†	1989/90	1990/91	1991/92
Belgium	15.9	19.5	6.0
Canada	4.5	4.7	2.3
France	17.4	21.6	6.1
Germany, Federal Republic . .	5.4	6.6	2.4
Italy	16.5	20.7	8.7
Japan	2.4	2.9	0.9
Netherlands	3.4	4.3	1.4
United Kingdom	2.3	2.3	0.7
USA	78.3	96.3	39.7
Total (incl. others)	163.7	198.7	74.7

* Provisional figures.

† Excluding re-exports.

Source: Administration Générale des Douanes, Port-au-Prince.

Transport

SHIPPING

Flag Registered Fleet
(at 31 December)

	2011	2012	2013
Number of vessels	4	4	4
Total displacement ('000 grt) . .	1.4	1.4	1.4

Source: Lloyd's List Intelligence (www.lloydslistintelligence.com).

CIVIL AVIATION

Traffic (international flights, 2012): Passengers arriving 615,191; Passengers departing 639,946.

Tourism

TOURIST ARRIVALS BY COUNTRY OF ORIGIN

	2009	2010	2011
Canada	31,017	20,119	19,568
Dominican Republic	9,910	3,168	4,487
France	12,508	14,261	18,432
USA	268,224	183,243	267,422
Total (incl. others)	387,218	254,732	348,755

Total tourist arrivals ('000): 349 in 2012; 420 in 2013 (provisional).

Receipts from tourism (US $ million, excl. passenger transport): 169 in 2010; 162 in 2011; 170 in 2012.

Source: World Tourism Organization.

Communications Media

	2011	2012	2013
Telephones ('000 main lines in use)	50.0	50.0	41.0
Mobile cellular telephones ('000 subscribers)	4,200.0	6,094.9	7,160.2
Broadband subscribers ('000) . .	16.7	n.a.	n.a.

Internet users ('000): 1,000 in 2009.

Source: International Telecommunication Union.

Education

(1994/95)

	Institutions	Teachers	Students
Pre-primary	n.a.	n.a.	230,391*
Primary	10,071	30,205	1,110,398
Secondary	1,038	15,275	195,418
Tertiary	n.a.	654*	6,288*

* 1990/91 figure.

Adult literacy rate (UNESCO estimates): 62.1% (males 60.1%; females 64.0%) in 2007 (Source: UNESCO Institute for Statistics).

Directory

The Constitution

The Constitution of the Republic of Haiti, which was amended in June 2012, was promulgated in March 1987. It provided for a system of power-sharing between a President (who may not serve two consecutive five-year terms), a Prime Minister, a bicameral legislature (comprising a Chamber of Deputies elected for four years and a Senate whose members serve six-year terms, one-third of whom are elected every two years) and regional assemblies. The army and the police were no longer to be a combined force. The death penalty was abolished. Official status was given to the Creole language spoken by Haitians and to the folk religion, Voodoo (vodou). In 2005 the number of seats in both chambers was increased, from 27 to 30 in the Senate and from 83 to 99 in the Chamber of Deputies. The amendments to the Constitution in 2012 provided for the legalization of dual citizenship, introduced 30% reservation for women in government jobs, allowed Haitians abroad to run for public offices (with some exceptions, including the President and Prime Minister), and to own land in the country. The amendments also aimed to establish a constitutional court to solve disputes between the legislature and the executive, and a new electoral council in place of the provisional body, the Conseil Electoral Provisoire (Provisional Electoral Council).

The Government

HEAD OF STATE

President: MICHEL JOSEPH MARTELLY (took office on 14 May 2011).

CABINET
(September 2014)

Prime Minister and Minister of Planning and External Co-operation: LAURENT SALVADOR LAMOTHE.
Minister of Foreign Affairs and Religion: DULY BRUTUS.
Minister of Justice and Public Security: JEAN RENEL SANON.
Minister of the Interior and Territorial Collectivities: RÉGINALD DELVA.
Minister of the Economy and Finance: MARIE-CARMELLE JEAN-MARIE.
Minister of Public Works, Transport and Communications: JACQUES ROUSSEAU.
Minister of Agriculture, Natural Resources and Rural Development: THOMAS JACQUES.
Minister of Trade and Industry: WILSON LALEAU.
Minister of Tourism: STÉPHANIE BALMIR VILLEDROUIN.
Minister of National Education and Vocational Training: NESMY MANIGAT.
Minister of Public Health and the Population: Dr FLORENCE DUPERVAL GUILLAUME.
Minister of Social Affairs and Labour: CHARLES JEAN-JACQUES.
Minister of Culture: MONIQUE ROCOURT.
Minister of Communication: RUDY HÉRIVEAUX.
Minister of Women's Affairs and Women's Rights: YANNICK MÉZILE.
Minister of National Defence: LENER RENAULD.
Minister of Youth, Sports and Civic Action: Col (retd) HIMLER RÉBU.
Minister of the Environment: JEAN FRANÇOIS THOMAS.
Minister of Haitians Residing Abroad: FRANÇOIS GUILLAUME, II.
Minister-delegate to the Prime Minister, in charge of Human Rights and the Fight Against Extreme Poverty: ROSE ANNE AUGUSTE.
Minister-delegate to the Prime Minister, in charge of Promoting the Peasantry: MARIE MIMOSE FÉLIX.
Minister-delegate to the Prime Minister, in charge of Energy Security: RENÉ JEAN-JUMEAU.
Minister-delegate to the Prime Minister, in charge of Strengthening Political Parties: PATRICK SULLY JOSEPH.
Minister-delegate to the Prime Minister, in charge of Parliamentary Relations: PHELITO DORAN.

MINISTRIES

Office of the President: Palais National, ave de la République, Champs de Mars, Port-au-Prince; tel. 2222-3024; e-mail webmestre@palaisnational.info; internet www.lapresidence.ht.
Office of the Prime Minister: 33 blvd Harry S Truman, BP 6114, Port-au-Prince; tel. 2221-0013; e-mail primature@primature.gouv.ht; internet www.primature.gouv.ht.
Ministry of Agriculture, Natural Resources and Rural Development: Route Nationale 1, Damien, BP 1441, Port-au-Prince; tel. 2510-3916; fax 2222-3591; internet www.agriculture.gouv.ht.
Ministry of Communication: 4 rue Magny, Port-au-Prince; tel. 2223-5514.
Ministry of Culture: angle des rues de la République et Geffrard 509, Port-au-Prince; tel. 2221-3238; fax 2221-7318; e-mail contact4@ministereculture.gouv.ht; internet www.ministereculture.gouv.ht.
Ministry of the Economy and Finance: Palais des Ministères, rue Mgr Guilloux, Port-au-Prince; tel. 2223-7113; fax 2223-1247; e-mail mef@mefhaiti.gouv.ht; internet www.mefhaiti.gouv.ht.
Ministry of the Environment: 11 rue Pacot, Port-au-Prince; tel. 2943-0520; fax 2943-0521; e-mail scmde.gouv.ht@hotmail.com; internet www.mde-h.gouv.ht.
Ministry of Foreign Affairs and Religion: blvd Harry S Truman, Cité de l'Exposition, Port-au-Prince; tel. 2222-8482; fax 2223-1668; e-mail webmaster@maehaitiinfo.org; internet www.mae.gouv.ht.

Ministry of Haitians Residing Abroad: 87 ave Jean-Paul II, Turgeau, BP 6113, Port-au-Prince; tel. 2245-1116; fax 2245-0287; e-mail info@mhave.gouv.ht; internet www.mhave.gouv.ht.
Ministry of the Interior and Territorial Collectivities: Palais des Ministères, Champs de Mars, Port-au-Prince; tel. 2223-0204; fax 2222-8057; e-mail info@mict.gouv.ht; internet www.mict.gouv.ht.
Ministry of Justice and Public Security: 19 ave Charles Summer, Port-au-Prince; tel. 2245-9737; fax 2245-0474; internet www.mjsp.gouv.ht.
Ministry of National Defence: 2 rue Bazelais, Delmas 60, BP 1106, Pétionville; tel. 3454-0501; e-mail haitidefense@gmail.com.
Ministry of National Education and Vocational Training: rue Dr Audain, Port-au-Prince; tel. 2222-1036; fax 2245-3400; e-mail menfp_info@eduhaiti.gouv.ht; internet www.eduhaiti.gouv.ht.
Ministry of Planning and External Co-operation: ave John Brown, route de Bourdon 347, Port-au-Prince; tel. 2228-2512; fax 2222-0226; e-mail info@mpce.gouv.ht; internet www.mpce.gouv.ht.
Ministry of Public Health and the Population: 111 rue Saint Honoré, Port-au-Prince; tel. 2223-6248; fax 2222-4066; e-mail info@mspp.gouv.ht; internet www.mspp.gouv.ht.
Ministry of Public Works, Transport and Communications: rue Toussaint Louverture, Delmas 33, Port-au-Prince; tel. 2222-2528; fax 2223-4519; e-mail secretariat.communications@mtptc.gouv.ht; internet www.mtptc.gouv.ht.
Ministry of Social Affairs and Labour: 16 rue de la Révolution, Port-au-Prince; tel. 2222-1244; fax 2221-0717.
Ministry of Tourism: 8 rue Légitime, Champs de Mars, Port-au-Prince; tel. 2949-2010; fax 2949-2011; e-mail info@haititourisme.gouv.ht; internet www.haititourisme.gouv.ht.
Ministry of Trade and Industry: Bureau du Ministre, 23 ave l'Amartinière, BP 6114, Port-au-Prince; tel. 2943-4488; fax 2943-1868; e-mail secretariatdumiistre@mci.gouv.ht; internet www.mci.gouv.ht.
Ministry of Women's Affairs and Women's Rights: ave Magny 4, Port-au-Prince; tel. 2224-9152; e-mail contact@mcfdf.ht; internet www.mcfdf.ht.
Ministry of Youth, Sports and Civic Action: Ranch de la Croix-des-Bouquets, route de Meyer, route Nationale 3, 18 route de Frères, Pétionville; tel. 2813-0268; internet www.jeunessetsports.gouv.ht.
Office of the Minister-delegate to the Prime Minister, in charge of Parliamentary Relations: Delmas 48, 5 rue François, Port-au-Prince; tel. 2246-9912.

President and Legislature

PRESIDENT

Election, first round, 28 November 2010*

Candidates	Valid votes cast	%
Mirlande Manigat (RDNP)	336,878	31.37
Jude Célestin (Inite)	241,462	22.48
Michel Joseph Martelly (Repons Peyizan)	234,617	21.84
Jean Henry Ceant (Renmen Ayiti)	87,834	8.18
Jacques-Edouard Alexis (MPH)	32,932	3.07
Charles Henri Baker (Respè)	25,512	2.38
Total (incl. others)	1,074,056	100.00

* Preliminary results from the Provisional Electoral Council. A report issued by the Organization of American States in January 2011 stated that Martelly, not Célestin, was the second-placed candidate. In February the Provisional Electoral Council announced that Manigat would face Martelly in the run-off ballot, held on 20 March.

Election, second round, 20 March 2011

Candidates	Valid votes cast	%
Michel Joseph Martelly (Repons Peyizan)	716,986	67.57
Mirlande Manigat (RDNP)	336,747	31.74
Total*	1,061,089	100.00

* Including 7,356 blank ballots.

LEGISLATURE

Senate
(Sénat)

President: Simon Dieuseul Desras (Oganizasyon Lavni).

Distribution of Seats, August 2012*

	Seats
Inite	15
Alternative pour le Progrès et la Democratie (Altenativ)	5
Fusion des Sociaux-Démocrates Haïtiens	3
Ayiti an Aksyon (AAA)	2
Konbit pou Bati Ayiti (KONBA)	1
Pou Nou Tout (PONT)	1
Organisation du Peuple en Lutte (OPL)	1
La Fanmi Lavalas (FL)	1
Oganizasyon Lavni (LAVNI)	1
Total	**30**

* The Senate has 30 members, three from each province. One-third of these seats are renewable every two years. The last elections to the Senate were held on 28 November 2010 and 20 March 2011.

Chamber of Deputies
(Chambre des Députés)

President: Stevenson Jacques Timoléon.

Elections, 28 November 2010 and 20 March 2011

	Seats
Inite	32
Alternative pour le Progrès et la Democratie (Altenativ)	11
Ansanm Nou Fò	10
Ayiti an Aksyon (AAA)	8
Oganizasyon Lavni (LAVNI)	7
Rasanble	4
Repons Peyizan	3
Konbit pou Refè Haïti (KONBIT)	3
Pou Nou Tout (PONT)	3
Mouvement Chrétien pour une Nouvelle Haïti (MOCHRENHA)	3
Plateforme Liberation	2
Plateforme des Patriotes Haïtiens (PLAPH)	2
Mouvement Action Socialiste (MAS)	2
Mouvement Démocratique pour la Libération d'Haïti-Parti Revolutionnaire Démocratique d'Haïti (MODELH-PRDH)	1
Respè	1
Veye Yo	1
Independent	2
Vacant	4
Total	**99**

Election Commission

The Provisional Electoral Council was dissolved on 29 December 2011. A constitutional amendment of 19 June 2012 allowed for the formation of a new electoral body, the Permanent Electoral Council. According to the Constitution, the nine-member commission would comprise three representatives from each of the three branches of government. A Memorandum of Understanding on 24 December 2012 formed the Transitional College of the Permanent Electoral Council to organize the next elections. The mandate for the Transitional College was to expire following the publication of the final election results. In May 2014 the Permanent Electoral Council was renamed the Provisional Electoral Council and in July the nine members of the Council were appointed.

President: Max Mathurin.

Political Organizations

Action Démocratique pour Bâtir Haïti (ADEBHA): 509 route de Delmas, entre Delmas 103 et 105, Port-au-Prince; tel. 2256-6739; fax 3446-6161; e-mail versun_etatdedroit@yahoo.fr; internet www.adebha.populus.org; f. 2004; Pres. René Julien.

Alliance Chrétienne Citoyenne pour la Reconstruction d'Haïti (ACCRHA): Port-au-Prince; Leader Jean Chavannes Jeune.

Alliance pour la Libération et l'Avancement d'Haïti (ALAH): Haut Turgeau 95, BP 13350, Port-au-Prince; tel. 2245-0446; fax 2257-4804; e-mail reynoldgeorges@yahoo.com; f. 1975; Leader Reynold Georges.

Alternative pour le Progrès et la Democratie (Altenativ): f. 2010 to contest the legislative elections; grouping of more than 70 legislative candidates; Mems of Exec. Cttee Rosny Smart, Edgard Leblanc Fils, Victor Benoît, Serge Gilles, Evans Paul.

Alyans (Alliance Démocratique): Port-au-Prince; centre-left coalition of Konvansyon Inite Demokratik (KID) and Popular Party for the Renewal of Haïti (PPRH); formed an alliance with the Fusion des Sociaux-Démocrates Haïtiens and the OPL in late 2009 to contest the 2010 legislative elections; Leader Evans Paul.

Ansanm Nou Fò: contested the 2010 elections; Leader Leslie Voltaire.

Ayisyen pou Ayiti: Port-au-Prince; contested the 2010 presidential election; Leader Yvon Néptune.

Ayiti an Aksyon (AAA): Port-au-Prince; internet ayitianaksyon.net; contested the 2010 legislative elections; Pres. Youri Latortue.

Congrès National des Mouvements Démocratiques (KONAKOM): Bois Verna, Port-au-Prince; tel. 2245-6228; f. 1987; social democratic; Leader Victor Benoît.

La Fanmi Lavalas (FL): blvd 15 Octobre, Tabarre, Port-au-Prince; tel. 2256-7208; internet www.hayti.net; f. 1996 by Jean-Bertrand Aristide; barred from contesting the 2010 elections.

Fòs 2010 (Force 2010): Delmas; f. 2010; contested the 2010 presidential election; Leader Wilson Jeudi.

Fòs Patriotik ou Respè Konstitsyon an (FOPARK) (Patriotic Force for the Respect of the Constitution): Port-au-Prince; opposition coalition; Nat. Dir Biron Odige.

Front pour la Reconstruction Nationale (FRN): Gonaïves; f. 2004; Sec.-Gen. Guy Philippe.

Fusion des Sociaux-Démocrates Haïtiens: POB 381056, Miami, FL 33138, USA; e-mail fusion@pfsdh.org; internet www.pfsdh.org; formed an alliance with Alyans and the OPL in late 2009 to contest the 2010 legislative elections; Leader Serge Gilles.

Grand Rassemblement pour l'Evolution d'Haïti (GREH): Port-au-Prince; f. 2003; Leader Col (retd) Himler Rébu.

Konbit pou Bati Ayiti (KONBA): Port-au-Prince; f. 2005.

Konbit pou Refè Haïti (KONBIT): Port-au-Prince; contested the 2010 legislative elections.

Konfyans: Port-au-Prince; centre-left; Leader Rudy Hériveaux.

Mobilisation pour le Progrès Haïtien (MPH): Port-au-Prince; contested the 2010 presidential election; Leader Jacques-Edouard Alexis.

Mouvement Action Socialiste (MAS): Hinche; contested the 2010 legislative elections.

Mouvement Chrétien pour une Nouvelle Haïti (MOCHRENHA): rue M 7 Turgeau, Carrefour, Port-au-Prince; tel. 3443-3120; e-mail mochrenha@hotmail.com; f. 1998; contested the 2010 legislative elections; Leaders Luc Mésadieu, Gilbert N. Léger.

Mouvement Démocratique pour la Libération d'Haïti-Parti Revolutionnaire Démocratique d'Haïti (MODELH-PRDH): contested the 2010 legislative elections; Leader François Latortue.

Mouvement Indépendant pour la Réconciliation Nationale (MIRN): Port-au-Prince; mem. of Inite; Leader Luc Fleurinord.

Mouvement pour l'Instauration de la Démocratie en Haïti (MIDH): 114 ave Jean Paul II, Port-au-Prince; tel. 2245-8377; f. 1986; centre-right; contested the 2010 legislative elections.

Mouvement Patriotique de l'Opposition Démocratique (MOPOD): Port-au-Prince; f. as umbrella opposition movt, registered as political party in 2014; Gen. Co-ordinator Jean André Victor.

Nouveau Parti Communiste Haïtien (NPCH): Grand Rue 1, Nan Gonmye; e-mail vanialubin@yahoo.fr; internet www.npch.net; Marxist-Leninist.

Oganizasyon Lavni (LAVNI): contested the 2010 presidential election; Leader Yves Christalin.

Organisation du Peuple en Lutte (OPL): 105 ave L'Amartinière, Bois Verna, Port-au-Prince; tel. 2245-4214; f. 1991 as Organisation Politique Lavalas; name changed as above 1998; formed an alliance with Alyans and the Fusion des Sociaux-Démocrates Haïtiens in late 2009 to contest the 2010 legislative elections; Leader Sauveur Pierre Etienne; Nat. Co-ordinator Edgard Leblanc Fils.

Parti Agricole Industriel National (PAIN): f. 1956; Pres. Hébert Docteur.

Parti du Camp Patriotique et de l'Alliance Haïtienne (PACA-PALAH): Port-au-Prince; contested the 2010 legislative elections.

Parti pour l'Evolution Nationale d'Haïti (PENH): Port-au-Prince; contested the 2010 elections; Leader Eric Smarki Charles.

Parti des Industriels, Travailleurs, Agents du Développement et Commercants d'Haïti (PITACH): Port-au-Prince.

Parti Nationale Démocratique Progressiste d'Haïti (PNDPH): Port-au-Prince; reactivated 2014; Pres. TURNEB DELPÉ.

Parti Social Rénové (PSR): Port-au-Prince; Leader BONIVERT CLAUDE.

Plateforme Liberation: Port-au-Prince; contested the 2010 legislative elections.

Plateforme des Patriotes Haïtiens (PLAPH): Cap-Haïtien; contested the 2010 legislative elections.

Pou Nou Tout (PONT): Port-au-Prince; contested the 2010 legislative elections.

Rasanble: contested the 2010 legislative elections.

Rassemblement des Démocrates Nationaux et Progressistes (RDNP): 234 route de Delmas, Delmas, Port-au-Prince; tel. 2246-3313; f. 1979; centre party; Sec.-Gen. MIRLANDE MANIGAT.

Regwoupman Sitwayen pou Espwa (Respè): Port-au-Prince; f. 2009; centre party; Pres. CHARLES HENRI BAKER.

Renmen Ayiti: Port-au-Prince; e-mail info@renmenayiti.org; internet www.renmenayiti.org; Leader JEAN HENRY CEANT.

Repons Peyizan (Réponse des Paysans): Port-au-Prince; Leader MICHEL JOSEPH MARTELLY.

Solidarité: contested the 2010 elections; Leader GÉNARD JOSEPH.

Union de Citoyens Ayisyen pour la Démocratie, le Développement et l'Education (UCADDE): Miragoâne; contested the 2010 legislative elections.

Veye Yo: Cap-Haïtien; contested the 2010 legislative elections.

Viv Ansanm: Port-au-Prince; Leader DANIEL JEAN JACQUES.

Diplomatic Representation

EMBASSIES IN HAITI

Argentina: 48 rue Metellus, Pétionville, Port-au-Prince; tel. 2940-6711; fax 2940-6714; e-mail ehait@mrecic.gov.ar; internet ehait .mrecic.gov.ar; Ambassador ALEJANDRO GUILLERMO ESCOBAR.

Bahamas: 12 rue Boyer, Pétionville, Port-au-Prince; tel. 2257-8782; fax 2256-5759; e-mail bahamasembassy@hainet.net; Ambassador GODFREY GORDON ROLLE.

Brazil: Immeuble Héxagone, 3ème étage, angle des rues Clerveaux et Darguin, Pétionville, BP 15845, Port-au-Prince; tel. 2256-0900; fax 2510-6111; e-mail brasemb1@accesshaiti.com; internet portoprincipe.itamaraty.gov.br; Ambassador JOSÉ LUIZ MACHADO E COSTA.

Canada: route de Delmas, entre Delmas 71 et 75, BP 826, Port-au-Prince; tel. 2249-9000; fax 2249-9920; e-mail prnce@international.gc .ca; internet www.canadainternational.gc.ca/haiti; Ambassador HENRI-PAUL NORMANDIN.

Chile: 2 rue Coutilien et rue Delmas 60, Musseau, Port-au-Prince; tel. 2813-1613; fax 2813-1708; e-mail embajadachile_haiti@hotmail .com; internet chileabroad.gov.cl/haiti; Ambassador RAUL FERNÁNDEZ DAZA.

Cuba: 3 rue Marion, Peguy Ville, Pétionville, POB 15702, Port-au-Prince; tel. 2256-3503; fax 2257-8566; e-mail secretaria@ht .embacuba.cu; internet www.cubadiplomatica.cu/haiti; Ambassador RICARDO SOTERO GARCÍA NÁPOLES.

Dominican Republic: rue Panaméricaine 121, BP 56, Pétionville, Port-au-Prince; tel. 2813-0887; fax 3257-0383; e-mail embrepdomhai@yahoo.com; Ambassador RUBÉN SILIÉ VALDEZ.

France: 51 rue de Capois, BP 1312, Port-au-Prince; tel. 2999-9000; fax 2999-9001; e-mail ambafrance@hainet.net; internet www .ambafrance-ht.org; Ambassador PATRICK NICOLOSO.

Germany: 2 impasse Claudinette, Bois Moquette, Pétionville, BP 1147, Port-au-Prince; tel. 2949-0202; fax 2257-4131; e-mail info@ port-au-prince.diplo.de; internet www.port-au-prince.diplo.de; Ambassador KLAUS PETER SCHICK.

Holy See: rue Louis Pouget, Morne Calvaire, BP 326, Port-au-Prince; tel. 2257-6308; fax 2257-3411; e-mail nonciaturep@hughes .net; Apostolic Nuncio Most Rev. BERNARDITO CLEOPAS AUZA (Titular Archbishop of Suacia).

Japan: Hexagone, 2ème étage, angle rues Clerveaux et Darguin, Pétionville, Port-au-Prince; tel. 2256-3333; fax 2256-9444; internet www.ht.emb-japan.go.jp; Ambassador KENJI KURATOMI (resident in the Dominican Republic).

Mexico: rue Métélus 48, Pétionville, BP 327, Port-au-Prince; tel. 2813-0089; fax 2256-6528; e-mail embhaiti@sre.gob.mx; internet embamex.sre.gob.mx/haiti; Ambassador JOSÉ LUIS ALVARADO GONZÁLEZ.

Panama: 73 rue Grégoire, Pétionville, Port-au-Prince; tel. 2513-1844; fax 3864-4881; e-mail panaembahaiti@yahoo.com; internet www.panamaenelexterior.gob.pa/Haiti; Ambassador JOHN EVANS ATHERLEY.

Spain: 50 rue Metellus, Pétionville, BP 386, Port-au-Prince; tel. 2940-0952; e-mail Emb.PuertoPrincipe@maec.es; internet www .maec.es/embajadas/puertoprincipe; Ambassador MANUEL HERNÁNDEZ RUIGÓMEZ.

Taiwan (Republic of China): 22 rue Lucien Hubert, Morne Calvaire, Pétionville, Port-au-Prince; tel. 3775-0109; fax 2256-8067; e-mail haiti888@gmail.com; internet www.taiwanembassy .org/HT; Ambassador PETER HWANG.

United Kingdom: rue Delmas 73–75, Port-au-Prince; tel. 2812-9191; Ambassador STEVEN FISHER (resident in the Dominican Republic).

USA: Tabarre 41, blvd 15 Octobre, Port-au-Prince; tel. 2229-8000; fax 2229-8028; internet haiti.usembassy.gov; Ambassador PAMELA WHITE.

Venezuela: blvd Harry S Truman, Cité de l'Exposition, BP 2158, Port-au-Prince; tel. 3443-4127; fax 2223-7672; e-mail embavenezhaiti@hainet.net; Ambassador PEDRO ANTONIO CANINO GONZÁLEZ.

Judicial System

Law is based on the French Napoleonic Code, substantially modified during the presidency of François Duvalier.

Courts of Appeal and Civil Courts sit at Port-au-Prince and the three provincial capitals: Gonaïves, Cap-Haïtien and Port de Paix. In principle each commune has a Magistrates' Court. Judges of the Supreme Court and Courts of Appeal are appointed by the President. Constitutional amendments in 2012 created a Supreme Council of Judicial Power and a constitutional court (which was yet to be appointed in 2014).

Conseil Supérieur du Pouvoir Judiciaire (Supreme Council of Judicial Power): la route de Frères, Port-au-Prince; f. 2012 to oversee judicial system, ensure separation of powers; 9 mems; Pres. ANEL ALEXIS JOSEPH (Pres. of Supreme Court).

Cour de Cassation (Supreme Court): Port-au-Prince; Pres. ANEL ALEXIS JOSEPH; Vice-Pres. ANTOINE NORGAISSE.

Citizens' Rights Defender: FLORENCE ÉLIE.

Religion

Roman Catholicism and the folk religion Voodoo (vodou) are the official religions. There are various Protestant and other denominations.

CHRISTIANITY

The Roman Catholic Church

For ecclesiastical purposes, Haiti comprises two archdioceses and eight dioceses. Some 55% of the population are Roman Catholics, according to the 2003 census.

Bishops' Conference: Conférence Episcopale de Haïti, angle rues Piquant et Lammarre, BP 1572, Port-au-Prince; tel. 222-5194; fax 223-5318; e-mail ceh56@hotmail.com; internet ceh.ht; f. 1977; Pres. Cardinal CHIBLY LANGLOIS (Bishop of Les Cayes).

Archbishop of Cap-Haïtien: Most Rev. LOUIS KÉBREAU, Archevêché, rue 19–20 H, BP 22, Cap-Haïtien; tel. 262-0071; fax 262-1278.

Archbishop of Port-au-Prince: GUIRE POULARD, Archevêché, rue Dr Aubry, BP 538, Port-au-Prince; tel. 2943-4446; e-mail guypoulard@hotmail.com; internet archidiocesedepaup.org.

The Anglican Communion

Anglicans in Haiti fall under the jurisdiction of a missionary diocese of Province II of the Episcopal Church in the USA.

Bishop of Haiti: Rt Rev. JEAN ZACHÉ DURACIN, Eglise Episcopale d'Haïti, BP 1309, Port-au-Prince; tel. 2257-1624; fax 2257-3412; e-mail epihaiti@egliseepiscopaledhaiti.org; internet www .egliseepiscopaledhaiti.org.

Other Christian Churches

According to the 2003 census, some 15% of the population were Baptists and 8% were Pentecostalists.

Baptist Convention: Route Nationale 1, Cazeau BP 2601, Port-au-Prince; tel. 3195-4664; e-mail conventionbaptiste@yahoo.com; f. 1964; Gen. Sec. EMMANUEL PIERRE.

Evangelical Lutheran Church of Haiti: Eglise Evangélique Luthérienne d'Haiti, 29 Route de Frére, Impasse Perpignant 8,

Port-au-Prince; tel. 2947-2347; e-mail info@lutheranchurchofhaiti .org; internet www.lutheranchurchofhaiti.org; f. 1975; Pres. Rev. JOSEPH LIVENSON LAUVANUS; 9,000 mems.

Other denominations active in Haiti include Methodists, Church of the Latter-Day Saints (Mormons) and the Church of God 'Eben-Ezer'.

VOODOO

Konfederasyon Nasyonal Vodou Ayisyen (KNVA): Le Péristyle de Mariani, Mariani; tel. 3458-1500; f. 2008; Supreme Leader FRANÇOIS MAX GESNER BEAUVOIR.

The Press

DAILY

Le Nouvelliste: 198 rue du Centre, Port-au-Prince; tel. 2222-4754; fax 2224-2061; e-mail manigapier@lenouvelliste.com; internet www .lenouvelliste.com; f. 1898; evening; French; ind; Editor-in-Chief FRANTZ DUVAL; Publr JEAN MAX CHAUVET; circ. 10,000.

PERIODICALS

Ayiti Fanm: Centre National et International de Documentation, d'Information et de Défense des Droits des Femmes en Haïti, 16 rue de La Ligue Féminine, BP 6114, Port-au-Prince; tel. 2245-0346; fax 2244-1841; e-mail ayitifanm@enfofanm.net; internet www .ayitifanm.org; f. 1991; monthly; publ. by ENFOFANM; Creole; Founder and Editor-in-Chief CLORINDE ZÉPHIR; Dir MYRIAM MERLET.

Haïti en Marche: 74 bis, rue Capois, Port-au-Prince; tel. 3454-0126; e-mail melodiefm@gmail.com; internet www.haitienmarche.com; f. 1986; weekly; Editors MARC GARCIA, ELSIE ETHÉART.

Haïti Observateur: 98 ave John Brown, 3ème étage, Port-au-Prince; tel. 2223-0782; e-mail contact@haiti-observateur.net; internet www.haiti-observateur.net; f. 1971; weekly; Editor RAY-MOND JOSEPH; circ. 75,000.

Haïti Progrès: 61, Rue Capois, Port-au-Prince; tel. 3446-1957; fax 3680-9397; e-mail editor@haiti-progres.com; internet www .haiti-progres.com; f. 1983; weekly; French, English, Spanish and Creole; Dir MAUDE LEBLANC.

Le Matin: 3 rue Goulard, Pétionville, Port-au-Prince; tel. 4688-3876; e-mail lematinpublicite@gmail.com; internet www.lematinhaiti .com; f. 1907; French; publ. every other week from Jan. 2010; ind; Editor-in-Chief DALY VALET; Publr RÉGINALD BOULOS; circ. 5,000.

Le Moniteur: Presses Nationales d'Haïti, rue Hammerton Killick 231, BP 1746 bis, Port-au-Prince; tel. 2222-1744; fax 2223-1026; e-mail pndh-moniteur@hainet.net; f. 1845; 2 a week; French; official state gazette; Dir-Gen. WILLEMS EDOUARD; circ. 2,000.

Le Septentrion: Cap-Haïtien; weekly; ind; Editor NELSON BELL; circ. 2,000.

NEWS AGENCIES

Agence Haïtienne de Presse (AHP): 6 rue Fernand, Port-au-Prince; tel. 2245-7222; fax 2245-5836; e-mail ahp@yahoo.com; internet www.ahphaiti.org; f. 1989; publishes daily news bulletins in French and English; Dir-Gen. GEORGES VENEL REMARAIS.

AlterPresse: 38 Delmas 8, BP 19211, Port-au-Prince; tel. 2249-9493; e-mail alterpresse@medialternatif.org; internet www .alterpresse.org; f. 2001; independent; owned by Alternative Media Group; Dir GOTSON PIERRE.

Haiti Press Network: 14 rue Lamarre, Pétionville, Port-au-Prince; tel. 2511-6555; fax 2256-6197; e-mail hpnhaiti@yahoo.fr; internet www.hpnhaiti.com; Dir CLARENS RENOIS.

Publishers

Editions des Antilles: route de l'Aéroport, Delmas, Port-au-Prince; tel. 2940-0217; fax 2249-1225; e-mail editiondesantilles@yahoo.com.

Editions Caraïbes, SA: 57 rue Pavée, BP 2013, Port-au-Prince; tel. 2222-0032; e-mail piereli@yahoo.fr; Man. PIERRE J. ELIE.

Editions CUC-Université Caraïbe: 7, Delmas 29, Port-au-Prince; tel. 2246-5531; e-mail editions@universitecaraibe.com; internet www.editionsuniversitecaraibe.com.

Editions Les Presses Nationales d'Haïti: 223 rue du Centre, BP 1746, Port-au-Prince; tel. 2222-1744; fax 2223-1026; e-mail pnd-moniteur@hainet.net.

Imprimerie Roland Theodore, SA: Delmas 1A, No 19, Delmas; tel. 2940-7200; e-mail info@imprimerie-theodore.com; internet www .imprimerie-theodore.com; Gen. Man. HENRI THEODORE.

Maison Henri Deschamps—Les Entreprises Deschamps Frisch, SA: 25 rue Dr Martelly Seïde, BP 164, Port-au-Prince; tel. 2223-2215; fax 2223-4976; e-mail entdeschamps@gdfhaiti.com; internet www.maisonhenrideschamps.com; f. 1898; education and literature; divisions include Editions Hachette-Deschamps and Imprimerie Henri Deschamps; Man. Dir JACQUES DESCHAMPS, Jr; CEO HENRI R. DESCHAMPS.

Broadcasting and Communications

REGULATORY BODY

Conseil National des Télécommunications (CONATEL): 4 ave Christophe, BP 2002, Port-au-Prince; tel. 2511-3940; fax 2223-9229; e-mail info@conatel.gouv.ht; internet www.conatel.gouv.ht; f. 1969; govt communications licensing authority; Dir-Gen. JEAN MARIE GUILLAUME.

TELECOMMUNICATIONS

Digicel Haiti: 151 angle ave John Paul II et Impasse Duverger, BP 15516, Port-au-Prince; tel. 3711-3444; e-mail customercarehaiti@ digicelgroup.com; internet www.digicelhaiti.com; f. 2005; owned by Digicel (Ireland); mobile telephone network provider; Group Chair. DENIS O'BRIEN; CEO, Haiti DAMIAN BLACKBURN.

HaiTel (Haiti Telecommunications International, SA): 17 rue Darguin, 3ème étage, Pétionville, Port-au-Prince; tel. 3510-1201; fax 3510-6273; f. 1999; part-owned by US-based MCI WorldCom; mobile telecommunications provider; Pres. FRANCK CINÉ.

Multilink Haiti: Autoroute de Delmas, angle Delmas 18, 1er étage, Port-au-Prince; tel. 2813-0231; fax 2949-2929; e-mail info@multilink .ht; internet www.multilink.ht; f. 1999; internet service provider; Gen. Man. PAOLO CHILOSI.

Natcom (National Télécom, SA): angle ave Martin Luther King et rue Fernand, Pont-Morin, BP 814, Port-au-Prince; tel. 2222-8888; fax 3939-3939; e-mail info@haititeleco.com; internet www.natcom .com.ht; fmrly Télécommunications d'Haïti (Haiti Téléco); renamed as above in 2010; 60% owned by Viettel (Viet Nam), 40% govt-owned; landline provider; Dir YVES ARMAND.

BROADCASTING

Radio

La Brise FM 104.9: Camp Perrin, Les Cayes, Sud; tel. 3709-6021; e-mail contact@labrisefm.com; internet www.labrisefm.com; f. 2007; music station; Dir MAX ALAIN LOUIS.

Radio Antilles International: 75 rue du Centre, BP 2335, Port-au-Prince; tel. 3433-0712; fax 2222-0260; e-mail jacquessampeur@yahoo .com; f. 1984; independent; Dir-Gen. JACQUES SAMPEUR.

Radio Caraïbes: 45 rue Chavannes, Port-au-Prince; tel. 3558-9110; e-mail radiocaraibesfm@yahoo.fr; internet radiotelevisioncaraibes .com; f. 1949; owned by Moussignac Group; broadcasts in Port-au-Prince area; Dir PATRICK MOUSSIGNAC.

Radio Galaxie: 17 rue Pavée, Port-au-Prince; tel. 2432-4473; e-mail info@radiogalaxiehaiti.com; internet www.radiogalaxiehaiti.com; f. 1990; independent; Dir YVES JEAN-BART.

Radio Ginen: 28 bis, Delmas 31, BP 6120, Port-au-Prince; tel. 2249-9292; fax 2511-1737; e-mail info@rtghaiti.com; internet www .rtghaiti.com; f. 1994; Dir JEAN LUCIEN BORGES.

Radio Ibo: 51 route du Canapé-Vert, BP 15174, Pétionville, Port-au-Prince; tel. 3557-5214; fax 2245-9850; e-mail ibo@radioibo.net; internet radioibo.net; Dir HÉROLD JEAN FRANÇOIS.

Radio Kiskeya: 42 rue Villemenay, Boisverna, Port-au-Prince; tel. 2244-6605; e-mail admin@radiokiskeya.com; internet radiokiskeya .com; f. 1994; Dir MARVEL DANDIN.

Radio Lumière: Côte-Plage 16, Carrefour, BP 1050, Port-au-Prince; tel. 2234-0331; fax 2234-3708; e-mail rlumiere@ radiolumiere.org; internet www.radiolumiere.org; f. 1959; Protestant; independent; Dir VARNEL JEUNE.

Radio Mélodie: 74 bis, rue Capois, Port-au-Prince; tel. 2452-0428; e-mail melodiefm@gmail.com; internet radiomelodiehaiti.com; f. 1998; Dir MARCUS GARCIA.

Radio Metropole: 8 route de Delmas 52, BP 62, Port-au-Prince; tel. 2246-2626; fax 2249-2020; e-mail informations@naskita.com; internet www.metropolehaiti.com; f. 1970; independent; Pres. HERBERT WIDMAIER; Dir-Gen. RICHARD WIDMAIER.

Radio Nationale d'Haïti: see Télévision Nationale d'Haïti.

Radio Nirvana FM: Cap-Haïtien; tel. 2431-5784; e-mail pdg@ radionirvanafm.com; internet www.radionirvanafm.com; Dir-Gen. RAPHAEL ABRAHAM.

Radio Port-au-Prince Plus: Stade Sylvio Cator, BP 863, Port-au-Prince; tel. 3927-3182; e-mail contactus@radioportauprinceplus .com; internet www.radioportauprinceplus.com; f. 1979; independent; broadcasts in Creole and English; religious programming; Dir-Gen. MAX PRINCE.

Radio Superstar: Delmas 68, angle rues Safran et C. Henri, Pétionville, Port-au-Prince; tel. 3734-2254; fax 2257-3015; e-mail info@radiosuperstarhaiti.com; internet www.superstarhaiti.com; f. 1987; independent; Dir ALBERT CHANCY, Jr.

Radio Tele Megastar: 106 rue de la Réunion, Port-au-Prince; tel. 3711-1197; e-mail jcharleus0@yahoo.com; internet www .radiotelemegastar.com; f. 1991; Pres. and Dir-Gen. JEAN-EDDY CHARLEUS.

Radio Télé Venus: 106 rue 5 et 6 E, Cap-Haïtien; tel. 2262-2742; fax 3780-8053; internet www.radiotelevenushaiti.com; f. 1994.

Radio Vision 2000: 184 ave John Brown, BP 13247, Port-au-Prince; tel. 2813-1875; e-mail info@radiovision2000.com; internet www .radiovision2000haiti.net; f. 1991; Dir LÉOPOLD BERLANGER.

Sans Souci FM: 57, rue 26, blvd Carénage, Cap-Haïtien; tel. 2813-1874; fax 3701-5913; e-mail sanssoucifm@radiosanssouci.com; internet www.radiosanssouci.com; f. 1998; Dir IVES MARIE CHANEL.

Signal FM: 127 rue Louverture, Pétionville, BP 391, Port-au-Prince; tel. 2256-4368; fax 2256-4396; e-mail info@signalfmhaiti.com; internet www.signalfmhaiti.com; f. 1991; independent; Dir-Gen. MARIO VIAU.

Television

CanalSat Haïti: angle des rues Faustin 1er et Chériez, Canapé-Vert, Port-au-Prince; tel. 2946-4141; internet www.emitelsa.com; f. 2011; satellite broadcaster, 46 European channels and 10 radio stations, mostly in French; Exec. Dir RÉGINALD BAKER.

NU TV: 57 rue Clerveaux, Pétionville, Port-au-Prince; tel. 4438-1204; e-mail ialerte@nu-tv.com; internet www.nu-tv.com; f. 2012; 90 Haitian, European, North American and Spanish-language TV channels via satellite; CEO PATRICE TURNIER.

Télé Caraïbes: 45 rue Chavannes, Port-au-Prince; tel. 3558-9110; e-mail radiocaraibesfm@yahoo.fr; internet www .radiotelevisioncaraibes.com; broadcasts in Port-au-Prince area; owned by Moussignac Group; Dir PATRICK MOUSSIGNAC; Exec. Dir WEIBERT ARTHUS.

Télé Eclair: 526 route de Delmas, Port-au-Prince; tel. 2256-4505; fax 2256-3828; f. 1996; independent; Dir PATRICK ANDRÉ JOSEPH.

Télé Ginen: 28 bis, Delmas 31, BP 6120, Port-au-Prince; tel. 2949-2407; fax 2511-1737; e-mail info@rtghaiti.com; internet www .rtghaiti.com; nationwide transmission; Owner, Dir and Gen. Man. JEAN LUCIEN BORGES.

Télé Haïti (Société Haïtienne de Télévision par Satellites, SA): blvd Harry S Truman, Bicentenaire, BP 1126, Port-au-Prince; tel. 2222-3887; fax 2222-9140; e-mail info@telhaiti.com; internet www .telehaiti.net; f. 1959; bldg destroyed by 2010 earthquake, recommenced broadcasts in 2012; pay cable station with 128 international channels; broadcasts in French, Spanish and English; Pres. ALLEN BAYARD.

Télé Metropole: 8 route de Delmas 52, BP 62, Port-au-Prince; tel. 2246-2626; fax 2249-2020; e-mail informations@naskita.com; internet www.metropolehaiti.com; f. 2007; broadcasts to Port-au-Prince area, mainly in French; Pres. HERBERT WIDMAIER; Dir-Gen. RICHARD WIDMAIER.

Télémax: 3 Delmas 19, Port-au-Prince; tel. 246-2002; fax 2246-1155; f. 1994; independent; Dir ROBERT DENIS.

Télévision Nationale d'Haïti: Delmas 33, BP 13400, Port-au-Prince; tel. 2246-2325; fax 2246-0693; e-mail info@tnh.ht; internet www.tnhtv.ht; f. 1979; merged with Radio Nationale d'Haïti in 1987; govt-owned; cultural; 4 channels in Creole, French and Spanish; administered by 4-mem. board; Dir-Gen.(Television) EMMANUEL MÉNARD; Dir-Gen. (Radio) HARRISON ERNEST.

Finance

(cap. = capital; m. = million; res = reserves; dep. = deposits; brs = branches; amounts in gourdes)

BANKING

Central Bank

Banque de la République d'Haïti: angle rues du Pavée et du Quai, BP 1570, Port-au-Prince; tel. 2299-1202; fax 2299-1145; e-mail webmaster@brh.net; internet www.brh.net; f. 1911 as Banque Nationale de la République d'Haïti; name changed as above in 1979; bank of issue; administered by 5-mem. board; cap. 50m., res 3,053.4m., dep. 55,355.2m. (Sept. 2009); Gov. CHARLES CASTEL; Gen. Man. MARC HÉBERT IGNACE.

Commercial Banks

Banque Nationale de Crédit: angle rues du Quai et des Miracles, BP 1320, Port-au-Prince; tel. 2299-4081; fax 2299-4076; internet www.bnconline.com; f. 1979; cap. 25m., dep. 729.9m. (Sept. 1989); Pres. JEAN PHILIPPE VIXAMAR; Dir-Gen. JOSEPH EDY DUBUISSON.

Banque Populaire Haïtienne: angle rues Aubran et Gabart, Pétionville, Port-au-Prince; tel. 2299-6080; fax 2299-6076; e-mail bphinfo@brh.net; f. 1973; state-owned; cap. and res 72.9m., dep. 819m. (Mar. 2007); Dirs-Gen. JESLY LÉVÊQUE, MYRIAM SANON; 3 brs.

Banque de l'Union Haïtienne: angle rues du Quai et Bonne Foi, BP 275, Port-au-Prince; tel. 2299-8500; fax 2299-8517; e-mail contact@buhsa.com; internet www.buh.ht; f. 1973; cap. 30.1m., res 6.2m. (Sept. 1997), dep. 1,964.3m. (Sept. 2004); Pres. MARCEL FONTIN; 12 brs.

Capital Bank: 38 rue Flaubert, Pétionville, BP 2464, Port-au-Prince; tel. 2299-6700; fax 2299-6520; e-mail capitalbank@brh.net; internet www.capitalbankhaiti.com; f. 1985; fmrly Banque de Crédit Immobilier, SA; cap. 270m., res 141.9m., dep. 6,903.3m. (Sept. 2011); Pres. BERNARD ROY; Gen. Man. LILIANE C. DOMINIQUE.

Scotiabank Haiti (Canada): 360 blvd J. J. Dessalines, BP 686, Port-au-Prince; tel. 2941-3001; e-mail bns.haiti@scotiabank.com; f. 1972; Country Man. CHESTER A. S. HINKSON; 4 brs.

Sogebank, SA (Société Générale Haïtienne de Banque, SA): route de Delmas, BP 1315, Port-au-Prince; tel. 2229-5000; fax 2229-5022; e-mail sogebanking@sogebank.com; internet www.sogebank.com; f. 1986; part of Groupe Sogebank; cap. 1,050m., res. 1,252.4m., dep 38,539.5m. (Sept. 2013); CEO ROBERT MOSCOSO; 35 brs.

Unibank: 157 rue Flaubert, Pétionville, BP 46, Port-au-Prince; tel. 2299-2057; fax 2299-2069; e-mail info@unibankhaiti.com; internet www.unibankhaiti.com; f. 1993; cap. 2,093.4m., res 837.1m., dep. 43,280.6m. (Sept. 2013); Pres. F. CARL BRAUN; 20 brs.

INSURANCE

Principal Companies

Alternative Insurance, SA: 4 rue Jean Gilles, blvd Toussaint Louverture, Port-au-Prince; tel. 2229-6300; fax 2250-1461; e-mail info@aic.ht; internet www.aic.ht; Dir-Gen. OLIVIER BARREAU.

Les Assurances Léger, SA (ALSA): 40 rue Lamarre, BP 2120, Port-au-Prince; tel. 2816-8888; fax 2223-8634; e-mail alsa@ alsagroup.com; f. 1994; headquarters in France; Man. S. ABDALLAH.

Compagnie d'Assurances d'Haïti, SA (CAH): étage Dynamic Entreprise, route de l'Aéroport, BP 1489, Port-au-Prince; tel. 2250-0700; fax 2250-0236; e-mail info@groupedynamic.com; internet www .groupedynamic.com/cah.php; f. 1978; subsidiary of Groupe Dynamic SA; Group Chair. and CEO PHILIPPE R. ARMAND.

Excelsior Assurance, SA: rue 6, no 24, Port-au-Prince; tel. 2245-8881; fax 2245-8598; e-mail ingesanon@yahoo.fr; Dir-Gen. EMMANUEL SANON.

Haïti Sécurité Assurance, SA: 352 ave John Brown, BP 1754, Bourdon, Port-au-Prince; tel. 3489-3444; fax 3489-3423; e-mail admin@haiti-securite.com; internet www.haiti-securite.com; f. 1985; Dir-Gen. WILLIAM PHIPPS.

MAVSA Multi Assurances, SA: étage Dynamic Entreprise, route de l'Aéroport, BP 1489, Port-au-Prince; tel. 2250-0700; fax 2250-0236; e-mail info@groupedynamic.com; internet www .groupedynamic.com/mavsa.php; f. 1992; subsidiary of Groupe Dynamic SA; credit life insurance and pension plans; Group Chair. and CEO PHILIPPE R. ARMAND.

National d'Assurance, SA (NASSA): 25 rue Ferdinand Canapé-Vert, BP 532, Port-au-Prince, HT6115; tel. 2245-9800; fax 2245-9701; e-mail nassa@nassagroup.com; internet www.nassagroup.com; f. 1989; specializing in property, medical and life insurance; Pres. FRITZ DUPUY.

National Western Life Insurance: 13 rue Pie XII, Cité de l'Exposition, Port-au-Prince; tel. 2223-0734; e-mail intlmktg@globalnw .com; headquarters in USA; Chair. and CEO ROBERT L. MOODY; Pres. ROSS R. MOODY.

Office National d'Assurance Vieillesse (ONA): 21 angle des rue Gregoire et Villate, Pétionville, Port-au-Prince; tel. 2256-6272; fax 2256-6274; e-mail ona@ona.ht; internet www.ona.ht; f. 1965; Dir-Gen. EMMANUEL MÉNARD.

Société de Commercialisation d'Assurance, SA (SOCOMAS): étage Complexe STELO, 56 route de Delmas, BP 636, Port-au-Prince; tel. 2246-4768; fax 2246-4874; e-mail socomashaiti@hotmail.com; Dir-Gen. JEAN DIDIER GARDÈRE.

Association

Association des Assureurs d'Haïti: 153 rue des Miracles, Port-au-Prince; tel. 2223-0796; fax 2223-8634; e-mail harold.cadet@ alsagroup.com; Pres. FRITZ DECATALOGNE.

Trade and Industry

GOVERNMENT AGENCIES

Centre de Facilitation des Investissements (CFI): 8 rue Légitime, Champs de Mars, BP 6110, Port-au-Prince; tel. 2514-5792; fax 2224-8990; e-mail fihaiti@gmail.com; internet www.cfihaiti.net; f. 2006; foreign investment promotion; Dir-Gen. NORMA POWELL.

Centre National des Équipements (CNE): Port-au-Prince; state-run construction co; Dir-Gen. JUDE CÉLESTIN.

Conseil de Modernisation des Entreprises Publiques (CMEP): Palais National, Port-au-Prince; tel. 2222-4111; fax 2222-7761; internet www.cmep.gouv.ht; f. 1996; oversees modernization and privatization of state enterprises; Dir-Gen. YVES BASTIEN.

DEVELOPMENT ORGANIZATIONS

Fonds de Développement Industriel (FDI): 12 angle rue Butte et impasse Chabrier, BP 2597, Port-au-Prince; tel. 2244-9728; fax 2244-9727; e-mail fdi@fdihaiti.com; internet www.fdihaiti.com; f. 1981; Dir-Gen. LHERMITE FRANÇOIS.

Mouvman Peyizan Papay (MPP): Papaye, Hinche; internet www.mpphaiti.org; f. 1973; peasant org., chiefly concerned with food production and land protection; Leader CHAVANNES JEAN-BAPTISTE.

Société Financière Haïtienne de Développement, SA (SOFIHDES): 11 blvd Harry S Truman, BP 1399, Port-au-Prince; tel. 2250-1427; fax 2250-1436; e-mail info@sofihdes.com; internet www.sofihdes.com; f. 1983; industrial and agro-industrial project-financing; Chair. FRANTZ BERNARD CRAAN; Man. Dir THONY MOÏSE.

Société Nationale des Parcs Industriels (SONAPI) (National Society of Industrial Parks): Port-au-Prince; manages industrial parks for housing cos; owns the Caracol Industrial Park (PIC) and the Metropolitan Industrial Park (PIM); Dir-Gen. BERNARD SCHETTINI.

CHAMBERS OF COMMERCE

Chambre Américaine de Commerce en Haïti (AMCHAM): 18 rue Moïse, Pétionville, Delmas, BP 13486, Port-au-Prince; tel. 2511-3024; fax 2940-3024; e-mail psaintcyr@amchamhaiti.com; internet amchamhaiti.com; f. 1979; Pres. PHILIPPE ARMAND; Exec. Dir PHILIPPE SAINT-CYR.

Chambre de Commerce et d'Industrie d'Haïti (CCIH): blvd Harry S Truman, Cité de l'Exposition, BP 982, Port-au-Prince; tel. and fax 3512-5141; e-mail ccih@ccih.ht; internet www.ccih.org.ht; f. 1895; 10 departmental chambers; Pres. HERVÉ DENIS; Sec. JOVENEL MOISE.

Chambre de Commerce et d'Industrie Haitiano-Canadienne (CCIHC): rue des Nimes, Port-au-Prince; tel. 2813-0773; e-mail direction@ccihc.com; internet ccihc.com; Pres. NATHALIE PIERRE-LOUIS LAROCHE; Exec. Dir LAROCHE CHANDLER.

Chambre Franco-Haïtienne de Commerce et d'Industrie (CFHCI): 5 rue Goulard, Pétionville, 6140 Port-au-Prince; tel. and fax 2510-8965; e-mail cfhci@yahoo.fr; internet www.chambrefrancohaitienne.com; f. 1987; Pres. GRÉGORY BRANDT; Exec. Dir KETTLY FOURON; 109 mems.

INDUSTRIAL AND TRADE ORGANIZATIONS

Association des Exportateurs de Café (ASDEC): rue Barbancourt, BP 1334, Port-au-Prince; tel. 2249-2160; fax 2249-2142; e-mail asdec@primexsa.com; Pres. JULIEN ETIENNE.

Association Haïtienne pour le Développement des Technologies de l'Information et de la Communication (AHTIC): 18 rue Moise, Pétionville, Port-au-Prince; tel. 2454-1498; e-mail sbruno@websystems.ht; Pres. REYNOLD GUERRIER; Exec. Dir STÉPHANE BRUNO.

Association Haïtienne des Economistes (AHE): rue Lamarre, 26 étage, BP 15567, Pétionville; tel. 2512-4605; e-mail haiti_economistes@yahoo.fr; Pres. EDDY LABOSSIÈRE.

Association des Industries d'Haïti (ADIH): 21 rue Borno, Pétionville, BP 15199, Port-au-Prince; tel. 3776-1211; fax 2514-0184; e-mail administration@adih.ht; internet www.adih.ht; f. 1980; Pres. CARL-FRÉDÉRIC MADSEN; Exec. Dir MARIE-LOUISE AUGUSTIN RUSSO.

Association Nationale des Distributeurs de Produits Pétroliers (ANADIPP): Centre Commercial Dubois, route de Delmas, Bureau 401, BP 1379, Port-au-Prince; tel. 2246-1414; fax 2245-0698; e-mail moylafortune@hotmail.com; f. 1979; Pres. ALAIN MAX ROMAIN.

Association Nationale des Exporteurs de Mangues (ANEM): 5 Santo 20, Route Nationale 3, Croix des Bouquets; tel. 2510-2636; e-mail anem@mango-haiti.com; Pres. JEAN-MAURICE BUTEAU; Man. BERNARD CRAAN.

Association Nationale des Institutions de Microfinance d'Haïti (ANIMH): 87 rue Wallon, Plc Boyer, BP 15321, Pétionville; tel. 2257-3405; e-mail info@animhaiti.org; internet www.animhaiti.org; f. 2002; Pres. YVENS VARISTE; Exec. Dir SOPHIE VINCENT.

Association Professionnelles des Banques (APB): 133 rue Faubert, Pétionville; tel. 2299-3298; fax 2257-2374; e-mail apbhaiti@yahoo.com; Pres. MAXIME CHARLES; Exec. Dir VLADIMIR FRANÇOIS.

MAJOR COMPANIES

Acra Industries: Autoroute de Delmas, Delmas 32, Port-au-Prince; tel. 2940-0500; fax 2246-0861; e-mail info@acraindustries.com; internet acraindustries.com; mfrs of metal construction sheeting, paper and plastic bags and plastic plumbing pipes; also importers of sugar and rice; operates 4 factories; subsidiaries include Caribbean Grain Co, SA, Industries Metallurgiques d'Haiti, SA (Inmetal) and Solidex, SA; Dir MARC-ANTOINE ACRA.

AGA Corporation: 26 angle rue Jean-Gilles et blvd Toussaint Louverture, Port-au-Prince; tel. 3701-3696; fax 2246-1417; e-mail clifford@agacorp.com; f. 1952; mfrs of textiles; subsidiaries incl. GMC Global Manufacturers & Contractors, SA, and Premium Apparel, SA; Pres. CLIFFORD APAID; 7,500 employees.

BRANA, SA (Brasserie Nationale d'Haïti): ave Hailé Sélassié, BP 1334, Port-au-Prince; tel. 2246-1528; fax 2246-1302; e-mail brana@branahaiti.com; f. 1973; brewery and soft drinks bottler; 95% owned by Heineken (Netherlands); Pres. and CEO JOSÉ MATTHIJSSE; 900 employees.

Carifresh, SA: Santo 17, Croix-Des-Bouquets, Port-au-Prince; tel. 3814-4541; fax 3437-2800; e-mail creimers@hotmail.com; fruit packers and exporters; Pres. WILHELM REIMERS.

Cimenterie Nationale, SEM (CINA): Fond Mombin, Cabaret, POB 16273, Pétionville, Port-au-Prince; tel. 2513-9588; e-mail csantamaria@cinahaiti.com; internet www.cina.com.ht; f. 1952; owned by Cementos Argos (Colombia); packagers of imported cement; Pres. CARLOS ESTEBAN SANTA MARIA; 200 employees.

De La Sol Haiti: Plaisance; e-mail stephanie@delasolhaiti.com; internet www.delasolhaiti.com; coffee, cacao and vanilla producers; Owners ANNE REYNOLDS, ROB REYNOLDS.

Etablissement Raymond Flambert, SA: 6 rue Flemming, Cité Militaire, Port-au-Prince; tel. 2228-5856; fax 2246-4908; e-mail erf@erfhaiti.com; internet www.erfhaiti.com; f. 1940; mfrs of building materials; Pres. ALEX FLAMBERT; 245 employees.

Groupe Dynamic, SA: étage Dynamic Enterprise, route de l'Aéroport, BP 1489, Port-au-Prince; tel. 2250-0700; fax 468-6203; e-mail info@groupedynamic.com; internet www.groupedynamic.com; holding co with 12 subsidiaries across the financial, insurance, medical, tourism, transportation and building sectors; Chair. and CEO PHILIPPE R. ARMAND.

JMB, SA: route Nationale 1, entrée Seminaire de Cazeau, Port-au-Prince; tel. 2513-9135; e-mail jmbuteau@mango-haiti.com; internet www.mango-haiti.com; f. 1983; mango exporters; Pres. and CEO JEAN-MAURICE BUTEAU.

Laboratoires 4C: Delmas 71, BP 44, Port-au-Prince; tel. 2249-4000; fax 2249-0379; e-mail info@laboratoires4c.com; internet www.laboratoires4c.com; f. 1952; mfrs of pharmaceuticals and paper products; Pres. and Gen. Man. MAURICE ACRE; 450 employees.

Mima, SA: POB 462, Port-au-Prince; tel. 2949-8922; fax 2810-9999; e-mail info@mima-sa.com; internet www.mima-sa.com; f. 1993; industrial chemical and lubricant mfr and raw materials supplier; Gen. Man. RAPHAËL J. BOULOS.

Les Moulins d'Haïti, SEM: 1 route Nationale, Laffiteau, BP 15509, Pétionville (bldg destroyed in Jan. 2010 earthquake); tel. 2813-0118; fax 2298-3600; e-mail lmh@lmh-ht.com; internet www.lmh-ht.net; fmrly la Minoterie d'Haïti; privatized 1999; now a semi-public co; 70% owned by 2 US agribusiness cos, 30% state-owned; flour milling; Pres. JAMIE MARKS.

Pacific Sports Haiti, SA: Park Industrial Sonapi, Bldg 27, route de l'Aeropuerte, Port-au-Prince; tel. 2250-1001; fax 2250-1002; textile; Pres. ROSA LEE.

Port Morgan: Village Touristique Morgan, BP 118, Les Cayes; tel. 3921-0000; e-mail info@port-morgan.com; internet www.port-morgan.com; tel. 3921-0000; hotels; CEO DIDIER BOULARD.

SAFICO (SA Filature et Corderia d'Haïti): Diquini 63, Port-au-Prince; tel. 3421-7895; e-mail micama45@yahoo.com; internet www.micamasoley.com; f. 1952; sisal processor, mattress and foam mfr; also produces lighting products; sales US $4.5m. (2011); Dir-Gen. THOMAS ADAMSON; 150 employees.

ShuttleHT: Port-au-Prince; tel. 33881-6162; e-mail info@shuttleht.com; internet shuttleht.com; car rental services; Man. Dir ANTONY JEAN.

Société du Rhum Barbancourt: 16 rue Bonne Foi, BP 33, Port-au-Prince; tel. 2223-2457; fax 5402-8197; e-mail rhum@barbancourt

.com; internet www.barbancourt.net; f. 1862; rum distillery; production recommenced mid-2010 following Jan. earthquake; Dir-Gen. THIERRY GARDÈRE; 250 employees.

Sun Auto, SA: 45 blvd du 15 Octobre, route de Tabarre, Port-au-Prince; tel. 2513-4646; fax 2298-4646; e-mail info@sunauto.net; internet www.sunauto.net; f. 1996; car sales; Founder and Gen. Man. DANIEL GÉRARD ROUZIER.

UTILITIES
Electricity

Electricité d'Haïti (EDH): angle rue Charéron, blvd Harry S Truman, Cité de l'Exposition, Port-au-Prince; tel. 2813-1641; e-mail info@edh.ht; internet www.edh.ht; f. 1971; state energy co; 6 sub-stations; Dir-Gen. JEAN ERROL MOROSE.

Water

Direction Nationale d'Eau Potable et de l'Assainissement (DINEPA): angle rue Metellus et route Ibo lélé, No 4, Pétionville, 6140 Port-au-Prince; tel. 2256-4770; fax 2940-0873; e-mail communication@dinepa.gouv.ht; internet www.dinepa.gouv.ht; fmrly Service Nationale d'Eau Potable (SNEP); Dir-Gen. JOSEPH LIONEL DUVALSAINT.

TRADE UNIONS

Association des Journalistes Haïtiens (AJH): Port-au-Prince; e-mail haitidabord@hotmail.com; f. 1954; Sec.-Gen. JACQUES DESROSIERS.

Batay Ouvriye (Workers' Struggle): Delmas, BP 13326, Port-au-Prince; tel. 2222-6719; e-mail batay@batayouvriye.org; internet www.batayouvriye.org; f. 2002; independent umbrella org.; Co-ordinator YANNICK ETIENNE.

Centrale Autonome des Travailleurs Haïtiens (CATH): 93 rue des Casernes, Port-au-Prince; tel. 3875-1044; e-mail cath.cath17@yahoo.com; f. 1980; Sec.-Gen. LOUIS FIGNOLÉ SAINT-CYR.

Confédération Nationale des Educateurs d'Haïti (CNEH): impasse Noë 17, ave Magloire Ambroise, BP 482, Port-au-Prince; tel. 3421-5777; fax 3812-4576; e-mail cnehaiti@haitiworld.com; f. 1986; Sec.-Gen. LOURDES EDITH JOSEPH DÉLOUIS.

Confédération des Travailleurs Haïtiens (CTH): 138 route de Fréres, Pétionville; tel. 2223-9216; fax 2223-7430; e-mail cthhaiti@gmail.com; internet haiticth.org; f. 1989; comprises 11 federations; Sec.-Gen. LOULOU CHÉRY.

Fédération des Syndicats des Travailleurs de l'EDH (FES-TREDH): angle rue Charéron, blvd Harry S Truman, Cité de l'Exposition, Port-au-Prince; tel. 2813-1641; f. 1986; 864 mems; Syndicats des Travailleurs de l'EDH (f. 2008), Cellule de Réflexion des Cadres de l'EDH (f. 2008) and Syndicat Moderne des Ouvrier de l'EDH (f. 2010) also represent l'EDH workers.

Transport
RAILWAYS

The railway service closed in the early 1990s.

ROADS

The total road network of 3,608 km comprises 950 km of primary roads (linking the main cities), 1,315 km of secondary roads and 1,343 km of tertiary or rural roads. The Inter-American Development Bank in November 2013 approved a US $50m. grant for a five-year road improvement project.

SHIPPING

The two principal ports are Port-au-Prince and Cap-Haïtien. In December 2013 the flag registered fleet comprised four vessels, totalling 1,473 grt.

Autorité Portuaire Nationale: blvd La Saline, BP 616, Port-au-Prince; tel. 2223-2440; fax 2221-3479; e-mail apnpap@hotmail.com; internet www.apn.gouv.ht; f. 1978; Dir-Gen. JEAN EVENS CHARLES.

Adeko Enterprises: 33–35 blvd Harry S Truman, ave Marie-Jeanne, Port-au-Prince; tel. 3445-0617; e-mail info@adeko-ht.com; internet www.adeko-ht.com; air and sea freight forwarders and maritime agency; Pres. JEAN MARC ANTOINE; Gen. Man. MARC KINSON ANTOINE.

AI Shipping International: Apt No 1, Sonadim Bldg, blvd Toussaint Louverture and Patrice Lumumba, Port-au-Prince; tel. 2940-5476; fax 2941-5476; e-mail info@aishippingintl.com; internet www.aishippingintl.com; f. 1981; freight forwarder and maritime agency; Pres. ANTOINE ILANES.

CIVIL AVIATION

The Toussaint Louverture International airport, situated 8 km (5 miles) outside Port-au-Prince, is the country's principal airport. There is also an airport at Cap-Haïtien, which opened to international flights in 2013 following an upgrade. In the same year it renamed the Hugo Chávez International Airport after the late Venezuelan President. Antoine-Simon airport at Les Cayes opened in 2005 and, following an extension of the runway and the building of a new terminal in 2013, was also expected to open to international flights. Construction of a new airport on the island of Ile à Vache began in 2013. There are smaller airfields at Jacmel, Jérémie and Port-de-Paix.

Autorite Aéroportuaire Nationale (AAN): Aéroport International Toussaint Louverture, Port-au-Prince; tel. 3443-0250; fax 2250-5866; e-mail dgaan@haitiworld.com; internet papaeroportauthority.org; Dir-Gen. PIERRE ANDRÉ LAGUERRE.

Haiti Aviation: Aeroport Toussaint Louverture, Port-au-Prince; tel. 2812-2812; e-mail Info@Haitiaviation.com; internet haitiaviation.com.

Office National de l'Aviation Civile (OFNAC): Aéroport International Toussaint Louverture, Delmas, BP 1346, Port-au-Prince; tel. 2246-0052; fax 2246-0998; e-mail lpierre@ofnac.org; Dir-Gen. JEAN MARC FLAMBERT.

Sunrise Airways: 12 Impasse Besse, rue Panamericaine, Pétionville; tel. 2816-0616; fax 2811-2222; e-mail info@sunriseairways.net; internet sunriseairways.net; f. 2009 as charter carrier; began scheduled flights within Haiti in 2012, flights to the Turks and Caicos in 2013 and Jamaica in 2014; Pres. PHILIPPE BAYARD.

Tortug' Air: Port-au-Prince; tel. 2511-4613; e-mail info@tortugair.com; internet www.tortugair.com; f. 2003; operates in partnership with Aerodynamics, Inc (USA); Vice-Pres. NICOLAS NTAHIRAJA; 200 employees.

Vision Air Haiti: Aérogare Guy Malary, Port-au-Prince; tel. 3886-2420; internet visionairhaiti.com; f. 2010; domestic flights; Gen. Man. JEAN JIHA, Jr.

Tourism

Tourism was formerly Haiti's second largest source of foreign exchange. However, as a result of political instability, the number of cruise ships visiting Haiti declined considerably. In 2013 tourist arrivals totalled a provisional 420,000 and receipts from tourism totalled US $170m. in 2012. In 2013 Best Western International opened a $15m. hotel in Pétionville. Further hotels, including a 173-room Marriott hotel in Port-au-Prince, were also under construction.

Association Haïtienne des Agences de Voyages (ASHAV): 17 rue des Miracles, Port-au-Prince; tel. 3445-5903; fax 2511-2424; e-mail ashav@hainet.net; f. 1988; Pres. PIERRE CHAUVET, Fils.

Association Touristique d'Haïti (ATH): rue Moise 18, Pétionville, BP 2562, Port-au-Prince; tel. 2946-8484; fax 3906-8484; e-mail athaiti@gmail.com; internet www.haiticherie.ht; f. 1951; Pres. RICHARD BUTEAU; Exec. Dir VALERIE LOUIS.

Defence

The armed forces were effectively dissolved in 1995, although officially they remained in existence pending an amendment to the Constitution providing for their abolition. As assessed at November 2013, the national police force numbered an estimated 2,000. There was also a coastguard of 50. In 2004 the UN Stabilization Mission in Haiti (MINUSTAH) assumed peacekeeping responsibilities in the country. Following the 2010 earthquake, MINUSTAH's authorized capacity was increased. As of February 2014, MINUSTAH comprised 6,355 troops, 2,240 civilian police, 1,629 international and local civilian staff (as of 30 November 2013), and 164 UN Volunteers. The MINUSTAH budget for 2013/14 was an estimated US $576.6m. In 2012 the Governments of Brazil and Ecuador agreed to assist Haiti in the formation of a new army, to number 1,500, which, it was hoped, would eventually replace MINUSTAH. In 2013 Haiti inaugurated a naval base at Les Cayes, intended primarily to counter drugs-trafficking activities.

Director-General of the Police Nationale: GODSON AURÉLUS.

Education

Education is provided by the state, by the Roman Catholic Church and by other religious organizations. Teaching is based on the French model, and French is the language of instruction. Primary education, which normally begins at six years of age and lasts for six years, is officially compulsory. Secondary education usually begins at 12 years of age and lasts for a further six years, comprising two cycles of three years each. According to UNICEF estimates, in 2011 the primary attendance ratio included 48% of male and 52% of female children in the relevant age-group, while at secondary schools it included 18% of male and 21% of female students in the relevant age-group. Higher education is provided by 18 technical and vocational centres, 42 domestic science schools, by the Université d'Etat d'Haïti and by the Université Roi Henri Christophe (inaugurated in 2012). More than 1,300 educational institutions were destroyed in the 2010 earthquake. In 2011 the National Fund for Education (FNE) was launched to provide more than 500,000 children with access to education. Some US $70m. was made available in 2012 to the FNE. In 2010/11 an estimated 8,504m. gourdes was allocated to education, representing 8% of the total spending.

Bibliography

For works on the Caribbean generally, see Select Bibliography (Books)

Brown, G. S. *Toussaint's Clause: The Founding Fathers and the Haitian Revolution*. Jackson, MS, University Press of Mississippi, 2005.

Chin, P., Flounders, S., and Dunkel, G. (Eds). *Haiti: A Slave Revolution—200 Years After 1804*. New York, International Action Center, 2004.

Chomsky, N., Farmer, P., and Goodman, A. *Getting Haiti Right This Time: The US and the Coup*. Monroe, ME, Common Courage Press, 2004.

Dubois, L. *Avengers of the New World: The Story of the Haitian Revolution*. Cambridge, MA, Belknap Press, 2004.

Farmer, P. *Haiti After the Earthquake*. New York, PublicAffairs, 2011.

Fatton, Jr, R. *Haiti's Predatory Republic: The Unending Transition to Democracy*. Boulder, CO, Lynne Rienner Publrs, 2002.

The Roots of Haitian Despotism. Boulder, CO, Lynne Rienner Publrs, 2007.

Ferguson, J. *Papa Doc, Baby Doc*. Oxford, Blackwell Publrs, 1998.

Fischer, S. *Modernity Disavowed: Haiti and the Cultures of Slavery in the Age of Revolution*. Durham, NC, Duke University Press, 2004.

Girard, P. *Paradise Lost: Haiti's Tumultuous Journey from Pearl of the Caribbean to Third World Hotspot*. Basingstoke, Palgrave Macmillan, 2010.

Gros, J. *State Failure, Underdevelopment, and Foreign Intervention in Haiti*. London, Routledge, 2011.

James, E. *Democratic Insecurities: Violence, Trauma, and Intervention in Haiti*. Berkeley, CA, University of California Press, 2010.

Kovats-Bernat, J. C. *Sleeping Rough in Port-au-Prince: An Ethnography of Street Children and Violence in Haiti*. Gainesville, FL, University Press of Florida, 2006.

Munro, M. (Ed.). *Haiti Rising: Haitian History, Culture and the Earthquake of 2010*. Kingston, University of West Indies Press, 2011.

Pezzullo, R. *Plunging into Haiti: Clinton, Aristide, and the Defeat of Diplomacy*. Jackson, MS, University Press of Mississippi, 2010.

Podur, J. *Haiti's New Dictatorship: The Coup, the Earthquake and the UN Occupation*. London, Pluto Press, 2012.

Polyne, M. *From Douglass to Duvalier: U.S. African Americans, Haiti, and Pan Americanism, 1870–1964*. Gainesville, FL, University Press of Florida, 2011.

Quinn, K. and Sutton, P. (Eds). *Politics and Power in Haiti*. New York, Palgrave Macmillan, 2013.

Robinson, R. *An Unbroken Agony: Haiti, from Revolution to the Kidnapping of a President*. New York, Basic Civitas Books, 2007.

San Miguel, P. L. *The Imagined Island: History, Identity, and Utopia in Hispaniola*. Chapel Hill, NC, University of North Carolina Press, 2005.

Smith, M. J. *Red and Black in Haiti: Radicalism, Conflict and Political Change, 1934–1957*. Chapel Hill, NC, University of North Carolina Press, 2009.

Suárez, L. M. *The Tears of Hispaniola: Haitian and Dominican Diaspora Memory*. Gainesville, FL, University Press of Florida, 2006.

White, A. *Encountering Revolution: Haiti and the Making of the Early Republic*. Baltimore, MD, John Hopkins University Press, 2010.

World Bank Country Study. *Social Resilience and State Fragility in Haiti*. Washington, DC, World Bank Publications, 2007.

Zacair, P. *Haiti and the Haitian Diaspora in the Wider Caribbean*. Gainesville, FL, University Press of Florida, 2011.

HONDURAS

Geography

PHYSICAL FEATURES

The Republic of Honduras is a Central American country, which sits on a north-facing Caribbean coast and, on its east side, tapers southwards to a short Pacific coast, on the Gulf of Fonseca. Its territory includes a number of offshore islands and cays in the Caribbean, but also in the Gulf of Fonseca. El Salvador, which lies in the south-west of the country, occupying the Pacific coast west of the Gulf of Fonseca, has claims on the island of Conejo in the Gulf. Competing maritime claims in the Gulf have been referred to a tripartite commission with Nicaragua. The exact demarcation of the Honduras–El Salvador border (342 km or 212 miles) was the subject of a decision by the International Court of Justice (ICJ) in 1992, although this was not ratified by both countries until 2006. Guatemala lies beyond a 256-km border in the west and north-west. Belize also lies to the north-west, but beyond the Gulf of Honduras (its Sapodilla Cays are claimed by Honduras). The longest border, across the widest part of the country, running south-westwards from the Caribbean (Atlantic) to the Pacific coasts, is the 922-km frontier with Nicaragua, which lies to the south-east. The maritime boundary between the two countries has been the subject of dispute since Nicaragua filed claims with the ICJ in 1999. The demarcation of the maritime boundary with the Cayman Islands, a British dependency in the Caribbean, has not yet been settled. Honduras, which is slightly larger than Guatemala, is the second largest country in Central America (after Nicaragua), covering an area of 112,492 sq km (43,433 sq miles), including about 200 sq km of inland waters.

Honduras is dominated by its central highlands, widest and highest in the west, towering above the narrow Pacific coastal plains and above the broader northern lowlands and plains on the Caribbean. About three-quarters of the country is mountainous, largely consisting of extinct volcanoes and their out-flows (the whole country is prone to usually mild earthquakes), while the shores along the southern Gulf of Fonseca amount to only 124 km and the Caribbean coast extends for 644 km. The northern lowlands include out-thrust ranges from the Continental Divide and river valleys, notably those of the Ulua and the Aguan, running down to the coastal plains. The North Coast region is agricultural and well populated. Other important rivers include the Guayape and the Patuca, the latter dominating the second northern topographical region, the flat, hot and humid Mosquito Coast (the name a corruption of the local Miskito people), densely clad in rainforest and sparsely inhabited. This region, in the far north-east of the country, includes extensive wetlands, especially around the Caratasca lagoon. Honduras encompasses only the northern part of the Mosquito Coast (Mosquitia—the rest is Nicaragua's eastern shore), which begins at Cabo Gracias a Dios, named in gratitude by the Genoese (Italian) navigator exploring for the Spanish monarchy, Christopher Columbus, when he rounded it and escaped the 'deep waters' (in Spanish) that gave Honduras its name. The central highlands, crowded in the west and dominating the south, consist of two main ranges, the Central American Cordillera and the Volcanic Highlands. The highest point in Honduras is in the west, at Celaque, the loftiest peak of which is Cerro de las Minas (2,870 m or 9,419 ft). The far south, beneath the heights where the national capital, Tegucigalpa, sprawls, is the fertile strip of coastal plain (only about 24 km in width) along the Gulf of Fonseca. Offshore are a number of islands belonging to Honduras, including the disputed Conejo and volcanic cones of Tigre and Zacate Grande, for instance. Strewn over a wider area are the Caribbean islands and cays of Honduras, notably the Bay Islands (Islas de la Bahía—mostly jungle-clad volcanic cones), just off the North Coast, and, further out, the Swan Islands. This vast territory includes a varied natural environment, little of it free from risk, be it mining damage to part of the country's exten-

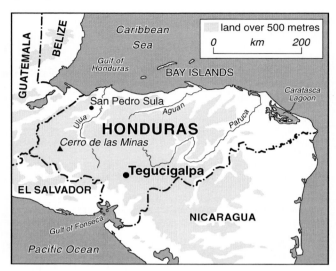

sive river system or to Lake Yojoa, an important source of fresh water, or the encroachments of urban expansion and agriculture. Deforestation throughout Honduras is a problem, with the accompanying hazards of soil erosion, etc., but just over one-half of the country is still wooded, more than anywhere else in Central America. The surviving forests host a huge variety of plant, bird and animal life, such as butterflies, jaguars, and white-faced, spider and howler monkeys. The insular environments are often more unusual, with the Bay Islands, for instance, noted for features such as its reef system (the most diverse in the Caribbean after Jamaica), the yellow-naped parrot or the spiny-tailed iguana found only on Utila.

CLIMATE

The climate is tropical in the lowlands and temperate in the mountainous interior. Both climatic zones have a wet season, which is in April–October. In the north of Honduras, on the North Coast and in the hill country between there and the highest uplands, average annual rainfall varies from 1,780 mm (70 ins) to about 2,550 mm, while along the Pacific coastal plains the range is around 1,550 mm–2,050 mm. The Caribbean coasts are very susceptible to hurricanes and flooding. The average minimum and maximum temperatures in Tegucigalpa range from 4°C–27°C (39°F–81°F) in February to 12°C–33°C (54°F–91°F) in May.

POPULATION

The people of Honduras, who refer to themselves as Catrachos, are mainly (90%) of mixed race (Ladino), with 7% Amerindian, 2% black and 1% white. Most Ladinos are of predominantly Spanish descent, and Spanish is the official and overwhelmingly the most widely spoken language. Some English is spoken on the North Coast and in the Bay Islands, by blacks and Anglo-Antilleans descended from those arriving in the country from elsewhere in the Caribbean about one century ago. Two centuries ago the main black population had arrived in this part of Central America, when the British deported the Black Caribs (mixed descendants of Amerindians and escaped slaves of African origin) from St Vincent (now part of Saint Vincent and the Grenadines); they speak Garifuna (Carib), originally an Amerindian tongue. Generally, however, such racial identities are preserved in cultural vestiges rather than language; the six dominant Amerindian language groups native to the region are Lenca, Jicaque or Tol, Paya, Chortí,

Miskito, and Sumo. Another legacy of the dominant Spanish influence in Honduras is that some 82% of the population still adhered to the Roman Catholic Church, although about 10% were Protestants.

Most of the 8.7m. (official estimate at mid-2014) population lives in central and western upland valleys, and on the North Coast. There are considerably fewer people in the north-east and in the south. The people of Honduras are poor—there are very pronounced levels of income inequality—and only two-fifths are urbanized. The capital is Tegucigalpa, in the centre-south of the country, in the highlands. The second city, in the north-west, is San Pedro Sula, which controls the important Ulea valley. La Ceiba, on the North Coast, was famous as the headquarters of the Standard Fruit Co, the US banana company that once dominated the country, whereas the Copán valley, in the far west, was the centre for the even earlier rule of the Mayas. Choluteca is the focus for southern Honduras, the Pacific coast. There are 18 departments.

History

SANDY MARKWICK

The history of Honduras has been strongly influenced by geography. The country has relatively few natural resources and is prone to natural disasters. In the 21st century Honduras was reckoned to be one of the poorest states in Latin America. It has suffered from endemic political instability, and despite many attempts at regional integration, Honduras has often come into conflict with its Central American neighbours. Its principal economic activity helped to earn it the epithet 'banana republic', and the cultivation of bananas also provided the basis for another major theme of the country's history in the 20th century, the dominant influence of the USA in the nation's internal politics and regional outlook. Major developments in the country's history have often been precipitated as much from events outside its borders as from internal politics.

Before the Spanish conquest Honduras lay on the southern edge of the Mayan civilization, which was already struggling with internal disturbances. Socio-economic pressures caused by famine, disease and soil erosion contributed to political divisions. After the Spanish adventurer Hernán Cortés had established power in Mexico City, he turned his attention south and arrived in Honduras in 1525, enticed by rumours of mineral wealth. The significant deposits of silver were largely exhausted by the 18th century, and the economic mainstay subsequently became subsistence farming. In 1549 Honduras became a province of the Kingdom of Guatemala, which was in turn part of the Viceroyalty of New Spain (Mexico). The existing rivalries between the provinces were fostered by Spain to help it retain its imperial power.

INDEPENDENCE

In 1822 the newly independent Mexico annexed Central America into its short-lived empire. The following year the provinces seceded and formed the Central American Federation. In 1827 internal conflict between the two main political factions, the Liberals, who supported the Federation, and the Conservatives, who opposed it, escalated into civil war. The liberal Honduran leader, Francisco Morazán, emerged as the President, but in 1838 a peasant revolt in Guatemala, led by the conservative Rafael Guerrera, brought the Federation to an end, and Honduras became an independent state.

The new country had internal divisions of its own, retaining the Liberal–Conservative divide, which continued to dominate political life throughout the 19th and 20th centuries. The Conservatives held power for most of the first few decades of independence, and the first national capital was the city of Comayagua. The Liberals returned to government in 1876 under Marco Aurelio Soto, and remained there for 56 years, consolidating their dominance by relocating the capital to Tegucigalpa. Despite the existence of the political tendencies (not yet fully formalized into parties), government was relatively weak, and was subject to considerable influence from other countries. Soto was both installed and removed in 1881 with the active participation of Guatemala, and in 1907 Nicaraguan forces helped to replace President Policarpo Bonilla with Miguel Dávila. The most powerful foreign influence, however, was that of the USA. In the late 19th and early 20th centuries vast tracts of land were granted to US companies, in particular the United Fruit Company (UFCO), on very advantageous terms, often in exchange for political support. By 1913 UFCO controlled two-thirds of Honduras's banana exports. A political crisis arose in 1911–12, in which President Dávila was overthrown and replaced by Manuel Bonilla in what was essentially a struggle between UFCO and another US banana enterprise.

DICTATORSHIP AND MILITARY RULE, 1932–80

The US Great Depression had a severe impact on the Honduran economy with its dependence on exports to the USA, and, as in Guatemala and El Salvador, contributed to the rise of dictatorship in the 1930s. Gen. Tiburcio Carías Andino, leader of the conservative Partido Nacional (PN), was elected President in 1932, and proceeded to hold office for 16 years without further election. He was persuaded to resign in 1948, and was succeeded by Dr Juan Manuel Gálvez of the PN, the sole candidate. After inconclusive elections in 1954, Vice-President Julio Lozano Díaz dissolved the Congreso Nacional (Congress), abrogated the Constitution and declared himself head of state. Lozano was in turn overthrown in a bloodless coup two years later. After constituent elections in which the Partido Liberal (PL) achieved a substantial majority, the PL leader, Dr José Ramón Villeda Morales, took office in 1957. His moderate social reforms aroused opposition from the traditional ruling class, and he was overthrown in 1963 in a military coup led by Gen. Oswaldo López Arellano. A new Constitution was approved in June 1965 and López Arellano was installed as President.

Elections were held again in 1971, and were won by the PN candidate, Dr Ramón Ernesto Cruz Uclés. This brief return to civilian rule followed a humiliating defeat for the Honduran military in the war against El Salvador in 1969. Triggered by events after two football World Cup qualifying matches, it became known as the 'Football War', although it had its roots in long-standing economic grievances between the two countries. Full-scale hostilities lasted less than two weeks, but a final peace agreement was not signed until 1980.

Gen. López Arellano returned to power in a coup in 1972, but in 1975 was overthrown by Col (later Gen.) Juan Melgar Castro. Only a few weeks before the coup López Arellano had been named in a bribery scandal involving United Brands Company (as UFCO had become in 1970), to which the company later admitted. Melgar Castro's attempts to introduce a comprehensive land reform programme provoked opposition from landed interests and he was removed from power in 1978, in a coup led by Gen. Policarpo Paz García.

RETURN TO CIVILIAN GOVERNMENT

During the 1980s Honduras became an important player in US policy in Central America. Ironically, the return to civilian government marked a sharp increase in actual military power, because the armed forces had greater, if not always overt, US support and were consequently better equipped than they had been previously. Under US encouragement, constituent elections were held in 1980, resulting in a surprise victory for the Liberals. PL leader Roberto Suazo Córdova was elected President in 1981 and a new Constitution was promulgated in January 1982; an amendment transferred the post of Commander-in-Chief from the President to the head of the armed forces (then Gen. Gustavo Adolfo Alvarez Martínez). Gen. Alvarez was widely regarded as the most powerful man in the country and, under his command, the army carried out a 'dirty war' against 'subversives'; the attendant allegations of human rights abuses would continue for the next two decades. (In 1993 a human rights commission attributed responsibility for 184 'disappearances' to special units directly answerable to Gen. Alvarez and his successors.) Alvarez was removed from power in 1984 by a group of junior officers disenchanted with his authoritarian policies, and he was assassinated in 1989.

The presidential election of November 1985 was won by José Simeón Azcona del Hoyo of the PL, under a new system that awarded victory to the leading candidate of the party with the greatest number of votes. (As each party fielded more than one candidate, the winner might not be the most popular individual candidate.) Azcona took office in January 1986, the first time for 55 years in which one freely elected president had succeeded another. The voting procedure was simplified for the 1989 elections, and the presidential ballot was won by Rafael Callejas Romero of the PN (who had polled the highest individual number of votes in 1985).

HUMAN RIGHTS AND SOCIAL ISSUES

Lacking a majority in the Congress, the Callejas administration also encountered opposition on many fronts. The armed forces, resenting attempts to prosecute some of its members for human rights abuses, continued to demonstrate that their influence outweighed the country's political and judicial institutions, and made unsuccessful coup attempts in 1991 and 1993. Meanwhile, the Government's economic structural adjustment programme raised vociferous protests not only from trade unions and peasant groups, but also from private business and the Roman Catholic Church. The Church was concerned principally with the matter of land distribution, and denounced the amassing of large estates by foreign companies, a development justified by the Government on the grounds of agricultural modernization. In addition, several indigenous Amerindian groups protested over the Government's failure to fulfil land rights agreements and to improve living and working conditions. A series of accords providing for the return of some 7,000 ha of land to the indigenous communities, along with many infrastructure projects on their land, was reached in 1994, but conflicted with vested interests.

Human rights was a prominent issue in the 1993 elections, with the two main parties accusing each other of complicity in past abuses. The campaign also exposed the regular practice of purchasing favourable press coverage. The PL retained its majority and its candidate, Carlos Roberto Reina Idiáquez, was elected President. Reina, a former President of the Inter-American Court of Human Rights (part of the Organization of American States—OAS), set out to reform the judicial system, curb the power of the army and combat political corruption. Under Reina the post of Commander-in-Chief was returned to the civilian authority (the minister responsible for defence), the Military High Council was abolished and a new national police force was created outside direct military control. Despite these measures, the armed forces generally managed to evade the judicial process, and in 1998 the independent Comité para la Defensa de Derechos Humanos en Honduras (CODEH—Committee for the Defence of Human Rights in Honduras) claimed that paramilitary 'death squad' activity had doubled since 1995.

The PL retained power in the 1997 elections and Carlos Roberto Flores Facussé became President. In 1999 he appointed Edgardo Dumas as the country's first civilian defence minister. Dumas opened an audit of the military pension fund, which had wide-ranging interests through the economy and allegedly operated an extensive network of corruption. The armed forces' economic penetration was so thorough that it constituted one of the principal business interests in the country. (In 2001 an investigation reported that five former Commanders-in-Chief had diverted some US $8m. in government revenues between 1986 and 1997.) The appointment of Dumas angered the military command, and President Flores

removed four senior officers and redeployed 33 others in an effort to reassert political supremacy over the armed forces. Tension between the civilian and military authorities increased with the discovery in August of a series of graves at a former US-built military base at El Aguacate. The camp had been used for training right-wing Nicaraguan counter-revolutionary guerrillas ('Contras') and allegedly for the detention and torture of suspected left-wing activists. The graves were estimated to contain about one-half of the 184 'disappeared'.

Protests against the land rights issue intensified, and were increasingly accompanied by demands from environmental groups. Regular demonstrations were staged in Tegucigalpa calling for a full investigation into the murders of more than 40 indigenous leaders, who had come into conflict with cattle ranchers, logging interests, energy companies and tourism developers.

The country also faced a range of socio-economic problems, and was ranked as one of the poorest in Central America. In 2001 a UN survey indicated that 79% of the population lived in poverty, and 56% were classified as destitute, with contingent poor standards of housing and health. The infant mortality rate was high, and 43% of children had no access to school education. Street children were at risk of summary brutality and execution, with more than 1,500 killed during 1998–2002, mostly by police and security forces. Many street children became involved in child prostitution. The country had a rising rate of violent crime, and the incidence of kidnapping increased sharply in 2001 and 2002, particularly targeted at the business community. The seriously overcrowded prisons often experienced violent riots by inmates, and some 90% of those in detention had not been convicted.

The country's socio-economic problems were compounded by frequent natural disasters, of which one of the most severe was Hurricane Mitch in 1998. There was major damage to infrastructure and the environment, as well as to health and job prospects, prompting an increase in illegal immigration to Mexico and the USA. Furthermore, the arrival of international aid focused attention on the country's inadequate provision of housing and services and on the high level of corruption.

THE GOVERNMENT OF RICARDO MADURO

The general election of 2001 resulted in a surprise victory for the PN. Its candidate, Ricardo Maduro Joest, was elected President and the party won the largest number of seats in the Congress for the first time since the restoration of civilian rule. A number of smaller parties, previously considered politically irrelevant, also made significant gains. In mid-2002 the Partido Demócrata Cristiano de Honduras (PDCH), which had won three seats in the elections, joined the government coalition to give the Maduro administration a majority in the legislature. Maduro, a prominent businessman and former Governor of the Central Bank, undertook to pursue the reforms advocated by the IMF, including the acceleration of the privatization programme and fiscal reform. Sales tax was introduced on a wider range of basic goods and income tax increased. President Maduro was also committed to reducing spending on public sector wages, a policy that led to strikes among teachers and health workers in 2005.

In 2003 the Government announced the formation of a special commission to investigate the murder of street children, and increased sentences for crimes committed by gang members were introduced. There had been a marked rise in violent gang conflict since 1997, when the USA had begun to deport convicted Honduran immigrants who were increasingly influenced by a gang culture fomented within the prison system of the USA. The most prominent gang was Mara 18, which had grown out of the civil wars of the 1980s and which operated throughout Central America and within the USA. The Honduran police force lacked training and resources and, at only 7,000 strong, proved unequal to combat the rising crime level. Since 2000 army units had been deployed to help them patrol the streets, a measure that alarmed many human rights groups. Many people died in gun battles between gang members and the police, and there were also numerous reports of innocent bystanders being arrested and killed. The authorities alleged that most of the street children killed by security forces were connected with gangs, but the human rights groups claimed many were shot indiscriminately. Criminal activity included extortion, with armed robberies in the streets and the levying of an illegal 'tax' to enter certain areas of the capital, as well as illegal drugs-trafficking. In order to counter the growing links between narcotics and political corruption, President Maduro announced restrictions on parliamentary immunity. There were renewed prison riots, and in April 2003, in a disturbance at La Ceiba prison, 69 inmates were shot dead (61 of whom were members of Mara 18) by security forces, some apparently after they had surrendered. Despite the Government's focus on crime, there was a continuing public perception that violence was on the increase. The problem of crime and insecurity was exacerbated further by the growth in the activities of Mexican drug cartels, particularly after 2006–07 when they took control of distribution routes through Central America.

THE GOVERNMENT OF MANUEL ZELAYA

Elections to the presidency and the Congress took place in November 2005. The PL candidate, José Manuel (Mel) Zelaya Rosales narrowly defeated PN nominee Porfirio Lobo Sosa, hitherto President of the Congress: Zelaya won 50% of the votes cast, compared with 46% obtained by Lobo. Constitutional rules had prevented Maduro from standing for a successive term of office. None the less, it was widely believed that corruption scandals during Maduro's administration damaged Lobo's chances. The result was also seen as a rejection of Lobo's draconian crime reduction proposals. The PL campaign focused on government accountability, addressing unemployment, improving rates of enrolment in schools and increasing popular participation in public life. However, there was broad consensus between the two leading candidates on continuing the economic programme agreed with the IMF.

The new administration was weakened by its position in the Congress. Having failed to garner a congressional majority, the Government had to rely on the support of other parties to pass legislative initiatives. Negotiating the selection of the President of the Congress was an early illustration of the political difficulties encountered by the new Government.

President Zelaya occupied centre-left territory within the PL, which, in addition to a populist style, raised doubts about the new Government's commitment to fiscal prudence. On taking office, Zelaya promised to create jobs, eliminate corruption and improve domestic security. However, combating crime required fundamental reform of the justice system to eradicate corruption among public officials, including the police, and Zelaya did not demonstrate sufficient political strength to suggest that such state reform was likely. Furthermore, the extra policing had minimal effect on crime levels. Zelaya also announced a package of social measures to increase employment and opportunities for young people in an attempt to promote internal security by reducing gang membership. In addition, the Government pursued campaign pledges to increase teachers' pay and fuel subsidies.

Economic growth and debt relief took some pressure off Zelaya in his bid to fulfil sometimes contradictory commitments to the IMF, on the one hand, and to reduce poverty and create jobs on the other. Zelaya oversaw the successful fulfilment of fiscal targets set out by the IMF. A new bridging agreement was signed with the IMF in 2008, committing the Government to reducing the fiscal deficit and shifting the emphasis of public spending towards longer-term investment. However, the Government faced a challenge in overcoming its weak position in the Congress while at the same time fulfilling its IMF commitments.

INTERNATIONAL RELATIONS

Honduras was drawn into the Central American conflicts of the 1980s when right-wing Nicaraguan Contras, with US support, began using its territory as a base for military operations and sabotage missions against Nicaragua, which had been ruled since 1979 by the left-wing Frente Sandinista de Liberación Nacional (FSLN—Sandinista National Liberation Front). The legacy of the conflict was a powerful, over-staffed and over-equipped armed forces, which needed to redefine its role, while also facing drastic cuts in US military aid. In addition, the virtual demise of the few and relatively small guerrilla groups formed in the 1980s eliminated an obvious internal threat. Another long-term consequence of the conflict was the presence of some 30,000 landmines along the country's border with Nicaragua, mostly planted by the Contras.

The advent of peace in Central America led to substantially improved relations between the Central American states, although the traditional sources of conflict resurfaced thereafter. Once again domestic troubles and the economic burdens imposed by natural disasters plagued renewed attempts at regional integration. One notable attempt was the formation of the Central American Integration System in 1991, which helped to foster a rapid expansion of the Central American Common Market.

The 1980 peace agreement with El Salvador (see above) had left territorial issues unresolved, both along the border and in the Gulf of Fonseca, causing intermittent tension. In 1992 the International Court of Justice (ICJ) in The Hague, Netherlands, awarded about two-thirds of the disputed territories to Honduras. In 1998 the two countries undertook to complete the border demarcation, but relations remained uneasy, and in 2001 Honduras expelled two Salvadorean diplomats, alleging that they had been involved in naval espionage. In 2006 the Congress voted to halt bilateral talks with El Salvador over a joint project to construct a hydroelectric dam on the countries' mutual border. The vote followed renewed tensions over the uninhabited island of Conejo, lying off the coast of Honduras and El Salvador in the Gulf of Fonseca, which did not form part of the 1992 ICJ ruling.

An ICJ ruling in 2007 delineating the maritime border between Honduras and Nicaragua ended almost a decade of tension between the two countries. The dispute began in 1999 after the Government asked the Congress to ratify an agreement with Colombia delineating maritime boundaries. The Nicaraguan Government protested that this threatened its national maritime claims, and both countries posted troops on their joint border. The border area was demilitarized in 2000 and, following OAS mediation, the two nations agreed to establish a maritime exclusion zone in the disputed area. Relations deteriorated in 2001 when Nicaragua accused Honduras of violating the agreement. Tensions continued for several years until the ICJ ruling, which awarded sovereignty of four small islands to Honduras.

Honduras maintained diplomatic relations with Taiwan, an important source of trade and investment, which was boosted by a bilateral free trade agreement signed in 2008. Ties with Taiwan have been a long-standing obstacle to the establishment of full diplomatic relations with the People's Republic of China. One of the challenges facing Honduras in the 21st century was how to forge stronger informal diplomatic ties with China, without damaging its relations with Taiwan, in order to maximize the vast investment potential of both.

Relations with the USA revolved chiefly around economic matters, among which was the question of the thousands of illegal Honduran immigrants living in the USA. Following the devastation caused by Hurricane Mitch in 1998, Honduran immigrants to the USA were granted Temporary Protected Status, which, in 2012, was renewed until January 2015. Under President Zelaya, diplomatic relations with the USA were strained as a result of the Government's warm relations with Venezuela's radical President, Hugo Chávez (offering the potential for cheap oil for Honduras), and by the nomination in 2007 of a Honduran ambassador to Cuba, the first since the suspension of diplomatic relations with that country in 1962.

CONSTITUTIONAL CRISIS

On 28 June 2009 the army seized President Zelaya and forced him into exile in Costa Rica. The ousting of Zelaya was the culmination of opposition from the Congress, including factions within the ruling PL, and the Supreme Court to the President's plans for a non-binding referendum, due to be held later that day, that would have sought public approval to hold a further referendum for the purpose of reforming the Constitution. Zelaya's opponents accused him of attempting to change the rules to allow him to remain in power after the end of his four-year term in January 2010, a charge that Zelaya denied. On the same day the Congress installed the speaker of the legislature, Roberto Micheletti Baín, as acting President. Micheletti was himself a member of the PL and a prospective candidate for the forthcoming presidential election, scheduled for 29 November 2009. Violence broke out in early July 2009 when President Zelaya attempted to fly to Tegucigalpa to retake power. The army refused to allow his aircraft to land and opened fire on a crowd of his supporters, killing at least two. The removal of President Zelaya differed from many previous coups in the country's history inasmuch as the army had no stated intention of assuming control of government. Nevertheless, the episode illustrated the fragile nature of Honduras's democratic institutions.

Strong international diplomatic efforts were launched in the immediate aftermath of the coup in an attempt to restore Zelaya to office. Despite Zelaya's strained relationship with the USA (see above), US President Barack Obama led demands from political leaders throughout the Americas for Zelaya's reinstatement. The USA, along with the OAS, the UN and the European Union (EU), refused to recognize Micheletti's de facto Government. The OAS suspended Honduras from the organization, the first time that it had suspended a member state since Cuba in 1962.

In September 2009 Zelaya returned to Honduras unnoticed by the authorities and immediately sought refuge in the Brazilian embassy. The embassy became a focal point for Zelaya's supporters, but the immediate area around the building was swiftly brought under the control of the security forces. While diplomatic attempts to resolve the crisis were under way, a microcosm of the constitutional crisis was played out in the form of a stand-off between Zelaya and his opponents. Talks between the two sides, brokered by the USA, led to the Tegucigalpa-San José Accord, under the terms of which both factions agreed to the establishment of a 'Government of Unity and National Reconciliation', which was to remain in force until the winner of the forthcoming presidential election took office. While important differences regarding interpretation of the Accord ensured a continuation of the dispute between the respective supporters of Zelaya and Micheletti, the agreement was a significant step towards Honduras restoring foreign diplomatic relations that had been broken since the June coup.

Presidential and legislative elections went ahead on 29 November 2009 as scheduled. Lobo was again the candidate of the PN. This time he was victorious, garnering 56% of the votes cast to defeat the PL candidate, Elvin Santos, who secured 36% of the ballot. Upon his inauguration on 27 January 2010, Lobo pledged to lead a government of national unity. Among his first acts as President was the signing of an amnesty for Zelaya and the military, and the supervision of the former's departure from the Brazilian embassy into exile in the Dominican Republic. Lobo's cabinet included members of the main opposition parties, while his Government was strengthened by a PN majority in the Congress, controlling 71 out of the 128 seats, and by the restoration of multilateral credit. A new 18-month stand-by agreement with the IMF in October 2010 consolidated Lobo's policies, which were more fiscally conservative than those of his predecessor.

THE END TO CRISIS: THE GOVERNMENT OF PORFIRIO LOBO SOSA

In May 2011 the Government of President Lobo and former President Zelaya reached an agreement, brokered by Colombia and Venezuela, which facilitated Zelaya's return to Honduras. The accord led to the restoration of full diplomatic relations with regional governments and the OAS, which in June formally reinstated Honduras following its suspension. The USA, satisfied with the process behind Lobo's assumption of power, had already restored relations with Honduras, while multilateral financial institutions had resumed credit lines to provide a firmer foundation for political and economic stability. An IMF review of Honduras's performance in April, as part of its stand-by agreement, concluded that the public sector deficit, debt-to-GDP (gross domestic product) ratio and international reserves were stable and manageable, while promoting the

importance of financial sector and pension reform, as well as measures to increase revenue from taxation. As part of the May agreement, arrest orders against Zelaya were annulled and Lobo pledged to consider a constitutional amendment permitting presidential re-election. Zelaya appeared intent on resuming political activity and enjoyed significant support, including from the teachers' union.

Honduras continued to face acute problems associated with crime, poverty and weak democratic institutions in 2013. President Lobo's initiatives to tackle crime were unsuccessful as violent crime rates continued to rise. There were an estimated 85.5 murders per 100,000 persons in 2012, one of the highest rates in the world. Lobo purged the Policía Nacional of a number of senior figures in a bid to root out corruption and increased the role of the military. A plot to assassinate public figures following the murder of a senior prosecutor in April 2013 showed that the threat to public security came from organized crime groups, not just street level gangs. Furthermore, the lack of public trust in the police reflected wider institutional weakness across the state.

Constitutional conflict still lingered in the form of tension between Lobo's Government and the legislature, on one hand, and the Supreme Court (Corte Suprema de Justicia) on the other. Despite a broad consensus among constitutionalists and the international community, the Supreme Court ruled in October 2011 that the ousting of President Zelaya in 2009 had been legal, absolving six senior generals for their part in the coup. A series of negative rulings by the Supreme Court against a number of government initiatives and legislative proposals further exacerbated these tensions. The Supreme Court ruled in October 2012 that government plans for 'model cities', special economic zones akin to Chinese Charter Cities, were a violation of sovereignty. In December, in the aftermath of another ruling by the Supreme Court, this time declaring the Government's police reform to be unconstitutional, Congress, with the support of President Lobo, voted to remove four members of the five-member Constitutional Committee of the Court. The change in the composition of the Supreme Court encouraged the Government to revisit its 'model cities' plan in 2013.

The failure of successive governments to implement land reform led to unrest in northern Honduras which threatened to have a significant political impact. In April 2012 thousands of peasant farmers occupied some 12,000 ha of land across six provinces. The occupations were organized by the Frente Nacional de Resistencia Popular on behalf of the estimated 300,000 landless farmers. Violent clashes between landless farmers and landowners led to dozens of deaths and raised the prospect of landowners employing armed security guards against the threat of land invasions which, together with the activities of drugs-traffickers, further threatened the stability of the area and increased the likelihood of militarization in the region. In October the Government signed an agreement through which close to 4,000 ha of land were transferred to 30 co-operative groups; however, violent conflict over land persisted in 2013.

THE NEW GOVERNMENT OF PRESIDENT JUAN ORLANDO HERNÁNDEZ

The presidential election took place as scheduled on 24 November 2013, the first since the coup of 2009 which had deposed President Zelaya. For the first time since the restoration of democracy in 1982, the election was contested by multiple parties, rather than just by the traditional PN and PL. PN presidential candidate Juan Orlando Hernández Alvarado, the former President of Congress, won the election with 36.9% of votes cast in a system requiring a plurality of votes for victory rather than a second round. Second placed was Xiomara Castro de Zelaya, wife of former President Zelaya, whose new party, Partido Libertad y Refundación (LIBRE, founded as a result of splits in the left following the 2009 coup), received 28.8% of the vote. Mauricio Villeda Bermúdez of the PL, a candidate from the centrist, pro-business wing of the party, was placed third, with 20.3% of votes cast. In fourth place, with 13.4% of votes, was television personality Salvador Nasralla, who had founded the Partido Anticorrupción (PAC) in 2011. The remaining votes were shared between four other candidates. Also on 24 November elections were held concurrently to the 128-seat Congress. President Hernández's PN won 48 seats, followed by LIBRE with 37, the PL with 27 and PAC with 13. The composition of Congress raised fears about governability, given the difficulties President Hernández, who took office in January 2014, would have in securing a majority. Hernández's ability to govern was made more difficult after LIBRE and PAC agreed to form an opposition bloc. The Government's attempts to attract PL support for its agenda were expected to be problematic, given historic enmity between the parties.

The principal challenges facing the new Government of President Hernández were the deep fiscal crisis and persistently very high levels of crime. The public sector deficit rose to an estimated 7.1% of GDP in 2013 from 4.2% in 2012 as spending increases outpaced tax income. The new Government targeted a 4.7% ratio in its budget for 2014, while seeking to restore the expired IMF stand-by agreement, but it faced political challenge in securing approval of the tax rises and wage cuts necessary to achieve this. An IMF delegation to Honduras in March–April 2014 welcomed the new Government's efforts to control public expenditure, but urged additional measures, including electricity sector reform and the facilitation of public-private partnerships, to relieve pressure on public finances.

Meanwhile, the Government revived the 'model cities' concept of the previous administration, proposing two areas for the renamed Zonas de Empleo y Desarrollo Económico (ZEDE—Economic Development and Employment Zones) to attract foreign direct investment. A constitutional amendment providing for the project had been approved in January 2013, when President Hernández was President of Congress. The concept was controversial, allowing not just separate regulatory environments, governing tax and investment incentives, but also separate legal jurisdictions and provision of public services on national territory. They were designed to attract foreign investment with tax incentives and an institutional environment more favourable to investors, as well as to provide a safer environment isolated from high crime rates in the rest of the country. In May 2014 the Supreme Court rejected an appeal by opponents of the ZEDE, who argued that they violated national sovereignty and were unconstitutional.

Economy

SANDY MARKWICK

With gross domestic product (GDP) estimated at just US $2,192 per head in 2012 ($3,946 at purchasing power parity, or PPP), Honduras remained one of the poorest and least developed nations in Latin America. Over one-half of the population was considered to be living below the poverty line and the country also posted one of the highest inequality ratings in the region. Acute socio-economic problems fuelled significant levels of crime and corruption. Despite some success in efforts to diversify the country's economic base, Honduras remained overly dependent on primary agricultural and fisheries exports such as coffee, bananas, meat, shrimp and lobster, as well as on large quantities of external finance. Dependence on agriculture also made the economy vulnerable in the wake of frequent natural disasters.

The country sustained steady rates of growth during most of the 2000s. GDP increased, in real terms, at an average annual rate of 4.3% in 2002–11. Growth was led by financial services, telecommunications, electricity and water, and was fuelled by a sharp increase in credit and foreign direct investment (FDI) built on confidence stemming from debt reduction and free trade agreements. The economy contracted by 2.4% in 2009, owing to a decline in investment resulting from the global liquidity crisis and political instability. Growth was restored in 2010 with a rate of 3.7% recorded that year, led by coffee, owing to higher international prices, forestry, and the textiles and drinks manufacturing sub-sectors. Growth continued at a similar pace in 2011 and 2012, at rates of 3.8% and 3.9%, respectively, with agriculture and communications the best performing sectors. In 2013 output slowed according to official estimates to growth of 2.6% supported by the expansion of 4G mobile telecommunications, as well as strong performances within financial services and agriculture.

The population growth rate was slowing progressively, decreasing to an annual rate of 2.0% in 2013 from 2.5% in 2001. The population stood at an estimated 8.7m. at mid-2014. The latest official figures on unemployment date from mid-2013 when it was measured at 3.9% of the economically active population, compared with 3.6% a year earlier. However, many more were underemployed. Pressure on land, the increased mechanization of export agriculture, and the seasonal nature of coffee, banana, sugar and fruit production led to high levels of underemployment among the agricultural workforce. Declining energy and food prices from late 2008, coupled with reduced demand owing to a contraction of economic activity and lower remittances sent by Hondurans overseas, led to an annual inflation rate of 3.0% in 2009, below a target range of 3.5%–5.5%. Inflation in 2010 rose to an average annual rate of 6.5% pushed up by reduced energy subsidies, rising commodity prices and a weaker currency, while remaining within the Banco Central's new target range of 5%–7%. Interest rates were increased by 1.0% during 2011, in an effort to control inflation and by a further 0.5% and 1.0% in January and May 2012, respectively. Average annual inflation rates in 2011 and 2012, at 5.6% and 5.4%, respectively, were below the target ranges set for each year. The downward trend continued in 2013, with inflation standing at 4.9% at the end of 2013, within a new target range of 4.5%–5.5%.

In the late 1980s imports soared, coffee prices fell drastically and the World Bank declared the country ineligible for further credits. This followed President José Simeón Azcona del Hoyo's (1986–90) unilateral suspension of all interest payments on the country's foreign debt. The Government of President Rafael Leonardo Callejas Romero (1990–94) steadily recovered the situation, adhering to the economic prescriptions of the US Agency for International Development.

The credibility of the new Government was rewarded by a stand-by agreement with the IMF, a second structural adjustment accord with the World Bank and a bridging loan. In 1992 Honduras signed an Extended Structural Adjustment Facility (ESAF) loan agreement with the IMF, but deterioration in the fiscal accounts meant that the Government of President Carlos Roberto Reina Idiáquez (1994–98) was forced to repeat the initial measures of its predecessor. The Inter-American Development Bank (IDB) and the World Bank both made funds available in 1996 and in the following year the IMF announced a partial agreement for the third-year disbursement of funds under its ESAF agreement.

Following Hurricane Mitch in 1998, the IMF approved a Poverty Reduction and Growth Facility (PRGF) to aid economic reconstruction. Honduras was supported further by a three-year deferral of bilateral debt service payments to the 'Paris Club' of Western creditor countries. Subsequently, the country was formally approved for debt relief under the IMF and World Bank's initiative for heavily indebted poor countries (HIPC). Under this programme, in 2000 the IMF and the World Bank announced a reduction in debt service payments, contingent on the Government's economic management. In 2004 the IMF approved a three-year PRGF, while at the same time maintaining pressure on the Government to extend reform. The IDB also approved funding totalling almost US $600m. In 2005 the IMF announced that Honduras had reached 'completion point' within the HIPC initiative, entitling the country to immediate debt relief worth $1,200m. over 10 years.

The fiscal deficit fluctuated, generally within the PRGF targets, declining to 1.1% of GDP in 2006, but rising to 6.1% in 2009. The deficit was kept down by GDP growth, higher aggregate demand, particularly consumer demand which boosted sales tax revenues, and improved tax collection, but also by the Government's failure to meet capital investment targets. Financing from multilateral organizations was threatened by the political instability that followed the forced removal from office of President José Manuel Zelaya Rosales by the army in 2009 (see History), which was widely denounced internationally as a coup.

The World Bank, the IDB and the US Government restored credit lines to Honduras following the inauguration of President Porfirio Lobo Sosa in January 2010. The renewal of multilateral financing was of paramount importance to the Government's management of the fiscal deficit and paved the way for congressional approval of a budget that was designed to improve the fiscal position. A new stand-by agreement was reached with the IMF in September to disburse US $196m. over a period of 18 months.

The prospects for stability improved with the restoration of diplomatic relations and economic growth. An IMF mission in late 2012 called for further reductions in the central government deficit. Much of the focus of government policy was to satisfy IMF concerns in order to secure a renewal of the stand-by agreement which had expired in March 2012. President Lobo's ability to obtain more funding was made more difficult by the approaching elections of November 2013, which put pressure on the Government to increase spending. The new President Juan Orlando Hernández, also of the centre-right Partido Nacional (PN), who took office in January 2014, faced deep fiscal challenges, including the necessity of securing the support of the IMF. The public sector deficit as a percentage of GDP was 7.1% at the end of 2013, compared with 4.2% in 2012, as spending increases exceeded tax income. An IMF delegation returned to Honduras in March–April 2014, after which it noted a weakened economic performance in 2013, but welcomed the new Government's efforts to control public expenditure. The IMF urged additional measures, including electricity sector reform and the facilitation of public-private partnerships, to relieve pressure on public finances.

AGRICULTURE

Agriculture remained the most important sector of the economy. In 2012 the sector (including hunting, forestry and fishing) employed 37.4% of the economically active population. Agriculture and fisheries accounted for an estimated 14.1% of GDP in 2013, compared with 23% in 1997, a decline that reflected long-term trends and the lasting impact of the devastation caused by Hurricane Mitch. The sector remained underdeveloped—of a total land area of 11.2m. ha, only an estimated 3.2m. ha were used for farming and livestock. Despite the country's relatively low density of population, land shortages were a persistent problem. As a result, disturbances caused by the unofficial occupation of unused or underutilized agricultural land had become a marked feature of life in rural Honduras.

The rapid development of cash crop farming, most notably coffee and bananas, as well as relatively stable world commodity prices, allowed for consistent annual growth in agricultural production during the 1960s and 1970s. A combination of adverse weather conditions, falling commodity prices, scarce credit facilities and the onset of world recession reduced the growth rate markedly during the 1980s. The sector began to recover in the 1990s, but Hurricane Mitch ended the revival. The sector's output during the 2000s was volatile. However, output grew by 6.5% in 2011 and by 9.9% in 2012, led by coffee, African palm, banana and fish products. Agricultural output increased by 4.0% in 2013.

In 1983 the effective control of the banana industry by two US conglomerates, United Brands Company (formerly the United Fruit Company) and Standard Fruit Company, was broken when agreements were reached for the sale of a large proportion of the national crop to local trading companies. This, combined with a government export incentive scheme, an increase in demand following the collapse of the Communist bloc in Eastern Europe in the early 1990s, and the implementation of the free market within the European Union (EU) in 1992, acted as a stimulant to banana production. In 1990 the Anglo-Irish banana company, Fyffes, began financing new, independent banana co-operatives, in a further challenge to the monopoly of the two US companies. Nevertheless, Chiquita Brands International Inc (formerly United Brands Company) and Dole Food Company (formerly Standard Fruit Company) remained the dominant forces in the industry. Banana exports from Honduras earned US $458.5m. in 2013, up from $335.4m. in 2010, a result of increasing prices and volumes.

Coffee earnings increased steadily to an estimated US $638.6m. in 2013, less than one-half of earnings in 2012 ($1,431.9m.), as both volumes and prices declined (by 21.9% and 30.2%, respectively). The prevalence of rust fungus adversely affected production in 2013. Prices recovered in early 2014. Poor prices and the consequent lower production caused the sugar, cotton and tobacco sectors to decrease dramatically in importance from the 1980s. By 2003 sugar exports were worth a mere $13.2m. Subsequent erratic recovery saw exports increase to $44.4m. in 2010, stemming from higher volume and higher prices. Volume rebounded in 2012, after declining in 2011, leading to revenue of $56.2m., boosted by a small increase in average prices. A 33.4% increase in volume in 2013 offset a decline in prices, producing revenue of $57.4m.

In 2013 wood exports were valued at US $20.7m., less than one-half of the value of a decade earlier. Almost all timber exports consisted of pine and other softwoods. An estimated 2.5m. ha of Honduras were believed to be in need of reforestation, following the loss of more than 30% of the country's forests since 1970.

MINING AND POWER

Although no comprehensive geological survey has been undertaken, Honduras is reported to have substantial reserves of tin, iron ore, coal, pitchblende and antimony, and exploitable reserves of gold. In recent years there has been an increase in interest in the sector from foreign companies, following the liberalization of the mining code. Commodity prices declined in 2009, contributing to a significant reduction in earnings from mining to US $69.4m. in that year, which was followed by a rebound to $113.0m. in 2010. Activity focused on the extraction of lead, zinc and silver. Significant shifts in the relative performance of different minerals reflected the limited extent of mineral exploitation in Honduras. Earnings decreased to $89.6m. in 2012, with a fall in zinc prices being the primary contributor to the decline. Mining exports amounted to $90.7m. in 2013, assisted by increased volume of zinc exports. Mining and quarrying accounted for only 1.0% of GDP in 2013.

Honduras has no exploited oil reserves. Minerals imports, largely composed of petroleum, accounted for 24.7% of imports in 2012. A combination of underinvestment, mismanagement and natural disasters had brought the sector into crisis in the 1990s. Declining levels of water in both hydroelectric systems were blamed on deforestation, caused by logging and the clearing of woodland for agriculture in order to cope with the country's growing land crisis. Successive governments attempted, with some success, to resolve the problems of the power sector. Electricity prices were increased several times, and the state-owned Empresa Nacional de Energía Eléctrica (ENEE—National Electrical Energy Company) intensified efforts to collect more than 120m. lempiras in debts. However, continued underinvestment in the transmission network meant that more than 20% of the power generated was lost. The damage caused by Hurricane Mitch proved a major obstacle to efforts to overhaul the distribution network to major cities. In 1999 the Governments of Honduras and El Salvador agreed to construct a regional electricity grid using a grant of US $30m. from the IDB. The transmission cable came into operation in 2002. In 2012 the country generated some 7,503 GWh of electricity, up 5.2% over the previous year. Hydroelectric plants accounted for 29.9% of the total electricity generating capacity, with thermal plants, largely in the private sector, accounting for 56.8%. All electricity generation was produced for the domestic market. Rising demand prompted the ENEE to arrange for additional supplies to be imported from neighbouring countries to ease the strain on domestic supplies. Installation of Patuca III, a 104-MW hydroelectricity plant, the first of three stations planned along the Patuca River in eastern Honduras was delayed because of lack of public funds in 2013, before the Government secured a $298m. loan from the Industrial and Commercial Bank of China. The final stage of Patuca III was expected to be completed in 2014. Completion of the whole Patuca River hydroelectricity project, which was funded by investment from the Chinese state firm, Sinohydro, was planned for 2020 and was expected to add 524 MW to the country's generating capacity. Other hydroelectricity projects were planned in Los Llanitos and Jicatuya in the department of Santa Bárbara.

MANUFACTURING

Owing to the establishment of *maquila* (offshore assembly) plants producing goods for re-export, the Honduran manufacturing sector underwent a substantial transformation in the 1980s and 1990s. The *maquila* industry was boosted in 2000 by the extension of the North American Free Trade Agreement (NAFTA) import duty parity to Honduran-assembled goods, which allowed import tariffs to be reduced by 15% on such goods entering the US market and allowed the sector to diversify into textile operations such as dyeing and cutting. The move encouraged the Government to target US $700m. in new investment into the sector over the subsequent five years. The *maquila* sub-sector was further boosted by the Dominican Republic-Central American Free Trade Agreement (CAFTA-DR) with the USA, ratified in 2005. While privileged access to North American markets encouraged growth, Honduras's *maquila* industry was particularly sensitive to demand from the USA, the country's major export market. According to the central bank, value-added earnings from *maquila* plants contracted by 14.8% during 2009, significantly more than for the economy as a whole, as a result of falling demand from the USA. The sector benefited from renewed demand in 2010, as well as from some companies moving production to Honduras following the earthquake in Haiti. With the slow return of international demand from 2010, and a further boost from the association agreement in that year between the EU and six countries of Central America to encourage trade between the regions, the forecast was for the Honduran *maquila* sector to become one of the economy's most dynamic. In 2012 value added earnings from *maquila* plants increased by 2.7%, much lower growth than in the rates of 20.2% registered in 2011 and 31.1% in 2010. The sector employed around 118,000 people in 2012 working in 330 companies. The overall manufacturing sector's contribution to GDP remained relatively stable as the decline in traditional industries offset the growth in the offshore assembly plants. Output growth in manufacturing was consistent during 2002–11, averaging 3.3% per year. The sector expanded by an average 3.1% in 2011–12. Growth slowed to 1.4% in 2013. The sector's contribution to overall GDP in that year was 18.9%.

Traditional manufacturing activity was based largely on agro-forestry products for both export and domestic consumption and included food processing, beverages, textiles, furniture making, cigarettes, sugar refining, seafood and meat processing, and paper and pulp processing. Cement, textile fabric, beer, soft drinks, wheat flour and rum were some of the major products. Much of the domestic manufacturing sector benefited substantially as a result of the reconstruction programme after Hurricane Mitch. Cement production, for example, increased from 28.8m. 42.5-kg bags in 2002 to 40.3m. bags in 2012.

FOREIGN TRADE AND PAYMENTS

Honduras recorded a persistent current account deficit in recent decades rising to US $2,127.9m. in 2008, equivalent to 15.3% of GDP. The current account deficit decreased in 2009 to $515.6m., 3.6% of GDP, as reduced demand caused the decline in the imports bill to exceed the fall in exports. The deficit increased to $682.1m. in 2010. Rises were registered in both import costs and export earnings in 2011, as well as a widened services deficit and growth in remittances from

abroad, with a net result that the current account deficit for that year increased to $1,408.3m., equivalent to 8.8% of GDP.

The trade deficit has always fluctuated in line with the prices of major exports and the demand for imports. According to the central bank, the trade deficit in goods and services rose throughout the 2000s, reaching US $3,572.3m. in 2011. The trade deficit contracted marginally to $3,546.4m. in 2012, as increased revenues from exports outpaced rises in the import bill and services deficit. In 2013 total exports were valued at $7,856.6m., falling by 5.0% during that year, following increases since 2010. A decline in imports of 2.6% and a widened services deficit resulted in a 5.3% rise in the overall trade deficit, amounting to $3,733.5m., in 2013.

The fiscal situation deteriorated in the 1990s, and the lempira was devalued in 1994 in order to secure a US $500m. loan agreement from the World Bank and the IMF. Multilateral and bilateral creditor support subsequently remained strong, despite the significant weakening of government finances in the wake of Hurricane Mitch. The most obvious demonstration of this was the country's achievement of HIPC status in 2000. The agreement promised debt service relief of some $900m. in return for continued economic reform and adherence to an IMF- and World Bank-agreed PRGF programme. The programme allowed for an increase in social spending, subject to a rise in national revenue. The debt relief secured by the Government after reducing the fiscal deficit and reaching 'completion point' within the HIPC initiative in 2005 enabled further investment in poverty reduction.

Improved terms from creditors in the 1990s were contingent upon investment liberalization, which helped dramatically to increase foreign investment inflows during that decade. FDI increased each year in the 2000s, reaching an estimated US $1,006.4m. in 2008, driven by loans to the private sector in order to exploit opportunities in mobile telecommunications, financial services and the *maquila* sub-sector of manufacturing. With the onset of a tightening of credit in the global economy, direct investment in Honduras contracted significantly, to $523.9m. in 2009. FDI levels increased to $1,032.7m. in 2013, led by transport, warehousing and telecommunications, which accounted for 28.0% of the total, followed by manufacturing (including the *maquila* sub-sector), which accounted for 24.8% of the total. The *maquila* sub-sector of manufacturing received 15.7% of FDI.

Total external debt declined from US $5,793m. in 2004 to an estimated $4,844.1m. in 2013, after the Government successfully met targets agreed in the PRGF. Public sector debt accounted for 77.1% of the total. The debt-to-GDP ratio increased to 53.8% in 2013, representing an increase from 31.9% in 2008, but less than the high of 83.0% in 2002.

Successive Honduran Governments enjoyed some success in their efforts to diversify the economy and the country's sources of foreign exchange. Non-traditional agricultural and fishery exports soared in the mid-2000s; earnings from the *maquila* industry exceeded those from both coffee and bananas; and invisibles, such as tourism and remittances from Hondurans living abroad, were making increasingly important contributions to the current account. Remittances totalled US $3,120.5m. in 2013. Meanwhile, Temporary Protected Status, covering undocumented Hondurans living in the USA, was renewed in 2013 until January 2015. Revenues from tourism amounted to an estimated $711m. in 2013. The vast majority of visitors were from other Central American countries and the USA.

There was less success in the diversification of the direction of trade, with dependence on the USA, the country's principal market, remaining strong. The proportion of exports purchased by the USA was 35.1% in 2013, compared with an average of 54% a decade earlier. This decline was partly explained by competition with Chinese exporters to the USA, particularly in textiles. Intra-regional trade was important to Honduras; other Central American countries, principally El Salvador and Guatemala, collectively purchased 22.8% of Honduran exports in 2013, while Latin America as a whole received 32.8% of Honduran exports. Reliance on US imports has been historically strong. In 2013 some 42.4% of the country's total imports came from the USA. Other important suppliers in that year were regional neighbours in Central

America, which together accounted for 19.8% of the total in 2013.

Additionally, the CAFTA-DR came into effect in 2006 following ratification by the USA, which consolidated Honduran trade privileges, particularly access to the US market. In 2011 a CAFTA-DR Commission, reviewing the agreement for the first time, claimed that it had resulted in an increase of 37% in trade between the USA and the region between 2005 and 2010, and an increase in intra-regional trade from US $4.2m. to $6.3m. during the same period. The Commission also highlighted an increase of 123% in average annual foreign investment inflows in the first four years of the agreement, relative to 2000–05. The Commission made recommendations to improve the effectiveness of the agreement focusing on initiatives to help small and medium-sized businesses. An agreement signed between the EU and the Sistema de la Integración Centroamericana (Central American Integration System) in June 2012 was expected to boost trade between Honduras and Europe.

The new Government of President Hernández introduced measures to improve fiscal discipline, after a significant package of measures focused on increasing revenue was approved by the outgoing Congress in December 2013. This was followed by the approval of legislation to implement electricity sector and pension reforms, as well as by measures to strengthen tax administration and improve discipline in the budget process. In the long term, Honduras had a critical need to strengthen institutions and improve infrastructure in order to support development and address widespread poverty.

Statistical Survey

Sources (unless otherwise stated): Department of Economic Studies, Banco Central de Honduras, Avda Juan Ramón Molina, 1a Calle, 7a Avda, Apdo 3165, Tegucigalpa; tel. 2237-2270; fax 2237-1876; e-mail jreyes@bch.hn; internet www.bch.hn; Instituto Nacional de Estadística, Edif. Plaza Guijarro, 5°, Lomas de Guijarro, Tegucigalpa; e-mail info@ine.hn.org; internet www.ine.gob.hn.

Note: The metric system is in force, although some old Spanish measures are used, including: 25 libras = 1 arroba; 4 arrobas = 1 quintal (46 kg).

Area and Population

AREA, POPULATION AND DENSITY

Area (sq km)	112,492*
Population (census results)†	
29 May 1988	4,614,377
1 August 2001	
Males	3,230,958
Females	3,304,386
Total	6,535,344
Population (official estimates at mid-year)	
2012	8,385,072
2013	8,555,072
2014	8,725,111
Density (per sq km) at mid-2014	77.6

* 43,433 sq miles.
† Excluding adjustments for underenumeration, estimated to have been 10% at the 1974 census.

POPULATION BY AGE AND SEX
(UN estimates at mid-2014)

	Males	Females	Total
0–14 years	1,465,038	1,405,441	2,870,479
15–64 years	2,494,032	2,523,090	5,017,122
65 years and over	174,480	198,667	373,147
Total	4,133,550	4,127,198	8,260,748

Source: UN, *World Population Prospects: The 2012 Revision*.

PRINCIPAL TOWNS
('000, official population estimates in 2013)

Tegucigalpa—Distrito			
Central (capital) .	1,195.6	Juticalpa	129.4
San Pedro Sula . .	753.9	Comayagua . . .	127.0
Choloma	320.0	Catacamas . . .	122.6
El Progreso . . .	223.1	Puerto Cortés . .	117.8
La Ceiba	201.8	Olanchito	99.9
Danlí	194.5	Siguatepeque . . .	92.8
Choluteca	183.6	Tela	87.7
Villanueva . . .	155.3	Tocoa	86.0

BIRTHS AND DEATHS
(UN estimates)

	1995–2000	2000–05	2005–10
Birth rate (per 1,000)	33.4	30.0	27.7
Death rate (per 1,000)	5.6	5.3	5.1

Source: UN, *World Population Prospects: The 2012 Revision*.

Life expectancy (years at birth): 73.5 (males 71.2; females 76.0) in 2012 (Source: World Bank, World Development Indicators database).

EMPLOYMENT
('000 persons)

	2011	2012	2013
Agriculture, hunting, forestry and fishing	1,180	1,240	1,248
Mining and quarrying	7	12	9
Manufacturing	433	434	443
Electricity, gas and water . . .	16	14	17
Construction	169	174	185
Trade, restaurants and hotels .	732	710	842
Transport, storage and communications	98	107	118
Financing, insurance, real estate and business services . . .	101	95	105
Community, social, personal and other services	491	459	521
Total employed	3,226	3,244	3,487

Health and Welfare

KEY INDICATORS

Total fertility rate (children per woman, 2012)	3.1
Under-5 mortality rate (per 1,000 live births, 2012) . . .	23
HIV/AIDS (% of persons aged 15–49, 2011)	0.5
Physicians (per 1,000 head, 2005)	0.4
Hospital beds (per 1,000 head, 2010)	0.8
Health expenditure (2011): US $ per head (PPP) . . .	335
Health expenditure (2011): % of GDP	8.4
Health expenditure (2011): public (% of total)	49.4
Access to water (% of persons, 2012)	90
Access to sanitation (% of persons, 2012)	80
Total carbon dioxide emissions ('000 metric tons, 2010) . .	8,107.7
Carbon dioxide emissions per head (metric tons, 2010) . .	1.1
Human Development Index (2013): ranking	129
Human Development Index (2013): value	0.617

For sources and definitions, see explanatory note on p. vi.

Agriculture

PRINCIPAL CROPS
('000 metric tons)

	2010	2011	2012
Maize	509	583	600*
Sorghum	63	37*	40*
Sugar cane	7,819	7,671†	8,600†
Beans, dry	69	91	100†
Oil palm fruit	1,556	1,265	1,414
Tomatoes	158	153†	155†
Melons†	333	385	396
Bananas	751	755†	765†
Plantains	82	84†	86†
Oranges	266	280†	285†
Pineapples	125	138†	142†
Coffee, green	229	282	300†

* Unofficial figure.
† FAO estimate(s).

Aggregate production ('000 metric tons, may include official, semi-official or estimated data): Total cereals 607.9 in 2010, 670.0 in 2011, 688.0 in 2012; Total vegetables (incl. melons) 735.8 in 2010, 786.5 in 2011, 812.3 in 2012; Total fruits (excl. melons) 1,361.3 in 2010, 1,400.5 in 2011, 1,424.2 in 2012.

Source: FAO.

LIVESTOCK
('000 head, year ending September)

	2010	2011*	2012*
Cattle	2,695	2,650	2,660
Sheep*	16	16	16
Goats*	25	25	25
Pigs	470	478	480
Horses*	181	181	182
Mules*	70	70	70
Chickens	40,590	39,500	40,000

* FAO estimates.
Source: FAO.

LIVESTOCK PRODUCTS
('000 metric tons)

	2010	2011*	2012*
Cattle meat	58.6	60.0	62.0
Pig meat	9.6	12.0	13.0
Chicken meat	152.5	158.7	160.0
Cows' milk	739.4	825.0	830.0
Hen eggs	44.2	45.0	45.6

* FAO estimates.
Source: FAO.

Forestry

ROUNDWOOD REMOVALS
('000 cubic metres, excl. bark)

	2010	2011	2012
Sawlogs, veneer logs and logs for sleepers	424	485	386
Other industrial wood	10	14	14
Fuel wood*	8,575	8,535	8,497
Total	9,009	9,034	8,897

* FAO estimates.
Source: FAO.

SAWNWOOD PRODUCTION
('000 cubic metres, incl. railway sleepers)

	2009	2010	2011
Coniferous (softwood)	267	225	230
Broadleaved (hardwood)	10	4	4
Total	277	229	234

2012: Production assumed to be unchanged from 2011 (FAO estimates).
Source: FAO.

Fishing

('000 metric tons, live weight)

	2010	2011	2012
Capture*	11.1	9.2	8.4
Marine fishes*	2.0	2.1	2.1
Caribbean spiny lobster	3.2	3.3	1.6
Penaeus shrimps	2.1	2.0	1.1
Stromboid conchs	1.6	1.6	1.6
Aquaculture*	27.5	37.0*	34.9
Nile tilapia	16.5	20.0*	7.8
Penaeus shrimps	11.1	17.0	27.0
Total catch*	38.6	46.1	43.3

* FAO estimate(s).
Source: FAO.

Mining

(metal content)

	2010	2011	2012
Lead (metric tons)	16,944	16,954	12,400
Zinc (metric tons)	33,839	26,000	26,000
Silver (kg)	58,158	53,167	50,605
Gold (kg)	2,197	1,893	1,858

Source: US Geological Survey.

Industry

SELECTED PRODUCTS

	2011	2012	2013
Raw sugar ('000 quintales)	9,410	10,657	11,084
Cement ('000 bags of 42.5 kg)	40,255	40,337	38,838
Cigarettes ('000 packets of 20)	286,568	267,605	232,951
Beer ('000 12 oz bottles)	257,031	256,198	273,631
Soft drinks ('000 12 oz bottles)	2,065,687	2,154,163	2,277,755
Wheat flour ('000 quintales)	3,319	3,624	3,687
Fabric ('000 sq m)	1,210,844	1,155,006	1,100,741
Liquor and spirits ('000 litres)	18,628	18,723	18,555
Vegetable oil and butter ('000 libras)	405,399	514,903	512,342
Electric energy (million kWh)	7,122	7,503	7,833

Finance

CURRENCY AND EXCHANGE RATES

Monetary Units
100 centavos = 1 lempira.

Sterling, Dollar and Euro Equivalents (31 March 2014)
£1 sterling = 34.536 lempiras;
US $1 = 20.751 lempiras;
€1 = 28.612 lempiras;
1,000 lempiras = £28.96 = $48.19 = €34.95.

Average Exchange Rate (lempiras per US $)
2010   18.895
2011   18.917
2012   19.502

GOVERNMENT FINANCE

(general government transactions, non-cash basis, million lempiras, preliminary)

Summary of Balances

	2010	2011	2012
Revenue	69,351.7	77,473.7	83,887.8
Less Expense	68,561.8	74,687.9	84,386.7
Gross operating balance . .	789.9	2,785.7	−499.0
Less Net acquisition of non-financial assets	10,880.1	12,644.4	12,087.1
Net lending/borrowing . . .	−10,090.2	−9,858.6	−12,586.1

Revenue

	2010	2011	2012
Taxes	45,388.6	51,808.7	55,493.8
Taxes of income, profits and capital gains	13,241.3	16,677.7	17,300.8
Taxes of goods and services .	26,432.2	29,640.1	32,498.7
Social contributions	8,671.1	9,653.5	10,934.2
Grants	4,162.6	3,676.7	3,550.2
Other revenue	11,129.4	12,334.8	13,909.5
Total	69,351.7	77,473.7	83,887.8

Expense by economic type*

	2010	2011	2012
Compensation of employees . .	39,585.8	39,971.7	42,630.1
Wages and salaries . . .	36,232.2	37,097.6	39,352.5
Social contributions . . .	3,353.6	2,874.1	3,277.6
Use of goods and services . .	10,961.8	12,183.9	14,904.0
Interest	2,560.5	4,072.4	5,538.9
Subsidies	318.2	557.5	1,091.4
Social benefits	406.3	364.8	226.8
Other expense	14,561.3	17,337.2	19,707.4
Grants	167.9	200.4	288.2
Total (incl. others)	68,561.8	74,687.9	84,386.7

*Including purchases of non-financial assets.

Source: IMF, *Government Finance Statistics Yearbook*.

2012 (general government budget, million lempiras, projections): *Revenue:* Current 60,316.4 (Taxes on profits and income 55,495.4); Other revenue 200.0; Grants 3,204.3; Total revenue 63,720.7; *Expenditure:* Current 64,879.4 (Wages and Salaries 34,974.0, Goods and services 8,931.7, Interest 6,466.6, Transfers and subsidies 14,507.1); Capital 15,004.0; Total expenditure 79,883.4 (excl. net lending −25.7).

2013 (general government budget, million lempiras, budget figures): *Revenue:* Current 63,603.7 (Taxes on profits and income 61,247.7); Other revenue 500.0; Grants 2,644.8; Total revenue 66,748.5; *Expenditure:* Current 67,394.8 (Wages and Salaries 36,651.1, Goods and services 9,268.2, Interest 8,391.5, Transfers and subsidies 13,084.0); Capital 13,010.7; Total expenditure 80,405.5 (excl. net lending −25.8).

CENTRAL BANK RESERVES

(US $ million at 31 December)

	2011	2012	2013
Gold (national valuation) . . .	35.02	38.79	26.57
IMF special drawing rights . .	154.20	148.08	142.08
Foreign exchange	2,582.30	2,333.90	2,826.50
Reserve position in IMF . .	13.24	13.26	13.28
Total	2,784.76	2,534.03	3,008.43

Source: IMF, *International Financial Statistics*.

MONEY SUPPLY

(million lempiras at 31 December)

	2011	2012	2013
Currency outside depository corporations	16,199	16,426	17,062
Transferable deposits . . .	30,804	29,102	29,795
Other deposits	122,947	136,336	150,672
Securities other than shares . .	2,222	2,411	2,458
Broad money	172,172	184,275	199,988

Source: IMF, *International Financial Statistics*.

COST OF LIVING

(Consumer Price Index, base: 1999 = 100)

	2011	2012	2013
Food and non-alcoholic beverages .	216.2	222.7	233.9
Rent, water, fuel and power . .	274.0	288.2	303.5
Clothing and footwear	208.1	218.9	232.0
All items (incl. others) . . .	235.1	247.3	260.1

NATIONAL ACCOUNTS

(million lempiras at current prices)

Expenditure on the Gross Domestic Product

	2011	2012*	2013*
Government final consumption expenditure	53,820	58,306	62,641
Private final consumption expenditure	260,106	281,802	305,828
Changes in inventories . . .	5,224	5,730	−1,623
Gross fixed capital formation .	81,883	87,889	92,413
Total domestic expenditure .	401,034	433,727	459,259
Exports of goods and services .	171,728	182,441	181,010
Less Imports of goods and services	237,733	254,123	262,639
GDP in purchasers' values .	335,028	362,044	377,630
GDP at constant 2000 prices .	165,958	172,370	176,789

Gross Domestic Product by Economic Activity

	2011	2012*	2013*
Agriculture, hunting, forestry and fishing	47,640	49,725	47,051
Mining and quarrying	3,329	3,290	3,342
Manufacturing	57,606	64,388	66,092
Electricity, gas and water . .	5,044	5,009	4,630
Construction	20,506	21,214	21,800
Wholesale and retail trade . .	46,247	50,036	53,193
Hotels and restaurants . . .	9,874	10,820	11,597
Transport and storage . . .	10,127	11,342	12,583
Communications	10,527	11,624	12,817
Finance and insurance . . .	20,253	22,054	24,427
Owner-occupied dwellings . .	17,361	18,571	20,165

—continued	2011	2012*	2013*
Business activities	15,247	16,905	18,360
Education services	23,692	26,029	27,623
Health	11,474	12,727	13,638
Public administration and defence	20,638	22,246	24,413
Other services	9,568	10,368	11,176
Sub-total	329,132	356,348	372,907
Less Financial intermediation services indirectly measured .	17,745	19,697	21,581
GDP at factor cost	311,388	336,651	351,326
Indirect taxes, *less* subsidies . .	23,640	25,393	26,305
GDP in purchasers' values .	335,028	362,044	377,630

* Preliminary.

BALANCE OF PAYMENTS
(US $ million)

	2010	2011	2012
Exports of goods	2,831.7	3,977.6	4,409.1
Imports of goods	−6,605.7	−8,355.9	−8,698.0
Balance on goods	−3,774.0	−4,378.4	−4,288.9
Exports of services	2,107.6	2,254.0	2,257.5
Imports of services	−1,169.5	−1,447.8	−1,515.0
Balance on goods and services	−2,835.9	−3,572.3	−3,546.4
Primary income received . . .	53.6	58.6	80.3
Primary income paid	−781.4	−1,032.3	−1,355.5
Balance on goods, services and primary income	−3,563.8	−4,545.9	−4,821.5
Secondary income received . .	2,949.3	3,220.5	3,315.9
Secondary income paid . . .	−67.7	−82.8	−81.3
Current balance	−682.1	−1,408.3	−1,586.9
Capital account (net)	84.7	166.2	101.2
Direct investment assets . . .	363.2	−30.3	−63.7
Direct investment liabilities . .	484.8	1,042.6	1,067.6
Portfolio investment assets . .	−18.9	45.8	−11.8
Portfolio investment liabilities .	−22.1	41.9	12.9
Other investment assets . . .	65.8	−436.6	137.3
Other investment liabilities . .	468.9	428.1	315.6
Net errors and omissions . . .	−174.8	184.4	−242.8
Reserves and related items .	569.5	33.8	−270.6

Source: IMF, *International Financial Statistics*.

External Trade

PRINCIPAL COMMODITIES
(US $ million)

Imports c.i.f.*	2011	2012	2013
Vegetables and fruit	434.8	414.1	410.1
Food products	812.2	907.9	950.2
Mineral products	2,155.5	2,284.0	2,305.9
Fuels and lubricants . . .	2,103.9	2,242.2	2,264.3
Chemicals and related products .	1,227.8	1,281.9	1,179.5
Plastic and manufactures . . .	508.2	558.6	533.1
Paper, paperboard and manufactures	395.5	352.7	394.3
Metal and manufactures . . .	614.6	611.4	556.0
Machinery and electrical appliances	1,380.8	1,359.5	1,342.6
Transport equipment . . .	497.3	573.4	483.9
Total (incl. others)	9,016.2	9,385.3	9,152.3

* Excluding imports destined for the *maquila* sector (US $ million): 2,879.7 in 2011; 2,780.8 in 2012; 2,698.8 in 2013.

Exports f.o.b.*	2011	2012	2013
Bananas	397.8	442.4	490.1
Cigars and cigarettes . . .	81.4	92.2	92.6
Coffee	1,358.4	1,402.4	749.8
Lead and zinc	65.3	51.6	44.4
Melons and watermelons . .	54.0	50.9	58.8
Palm oil	270.1	304.2	286.4
Lobsters and prawns . . .	205.8	211.5	268.8
Soaps and detergents . . .	68.9	82.1	97.0
Tilapia	62.8	61.7	65.2
Paper and paperboard . . .	63.7	148.7	138.3
Plastics and articles thereof . .	78.4	94.7	90.1
Total (incl. others)	3,866.4	4,281.3	3,830.9

* Excluding exports of gold, and of *maquila* goods (US $ million): 4,092.6 in 2011; 3,974.1 in 2012; 3,981.2 in 2013.

PRINCIPAL TRADING PARTNERS
(US $ million, excluding *maquila* goods)

Imports c.i.f.	2011	2012	2013
Brazil	83.9	95.5	86.5
China, People's Republic . . .	337.2	436.1	452.8
Colombia	317.0	272.2	331.2
Costa Rica	364.5	384.8	355.5
Ecuador	226.8	238.3	182.5
El Salvador	485.7	554.9	521.3
Germany	143.0	132.2	152.0
Guatemala	798.4	801.0	827.7
Japan	111.1	119.0	85.6
Korea, Republic	85.8	90.0	75.7
Mexico	488.8	538.0	514.5
Panama	346.9	359.6	336.2
Peru	27.5	75.2	101.2
Spain	80.4	95.7	80.1
USA	4,207.2	4,131.1	3,969.3
Total (incl. others)	9,016.2	9,385.3	9,152.3

Exports f.o.b.*	2011	2012	2013
Belgium	251.8	296.1	135.8
Canada	100.8	67.9	82.3
China, People's Republic . . .	102.6	113.7	130.0
Costa Rica	116.3	103.4	109.4
Dominican Republic . . .	40.7	46.2	51.1
El Salvador	298.5	293.7	334.5
France	61.2	53.2	43.7
Germany	416.1	498.4	273.9
Guatemala	235.4	218.5	259.9
Italy	68.2	80.5	42.2
Japan	52.5	34.2	27.7
Mexico	133.9	122.4	136.7
Netherlands	61.4	137.2	111.8
Nicaragua	157.2	202.3	204.3
Panama	24.8	52.8	61.8
Spain	39.1	55.1	44.9
United Kingdom	92.2	76.4	69.8
USA	1,269.1	1,494.8	1,404.8
Total (incl. others)	3,959.8	4,391.1	3,929.4

* Including exports of gold (US $ million): 93.4 in 2011; 109.7 in 2012; 98.5 in 2013.

Transport

ROAD TRAFFIC
(licensed vehicles in use)

	2001	2002	2003
Passenger cars	345,931	369,303	386,468
Buses and coaches	20,380	21,814	22,514
Lorries and vans	81,192	86,893	91,230
Motorcycles and bicycles . . .	36,828	39,245	41,852

2008 (vehicles in use): Passenger cars 213,643; Buses and coaches 51,233; Vans and lorries 427,503; Motorcycles and mopeds 122,397 (Source: IRF, *World Road Statistics*).

SHIPPING

Flag Registered Fleet
(at 31 December)

	2011	2012	2013
Number of vessels	690	677	664
Total displacement ('000 grt) . .	730.4	665.3	755.1

Source: Lloyd's List Intelligence (www.lloydslistintelligence.com).

CIVIL AVIATION
('000)

	2010	2011	2012
Passengers carried	501	424	421

Source: World Bank, World Development Indicators database.

Tourism

TOURIST ARRIVALS BY COUNTRY OF ORIGIN

	2010	2011	2012
Canada	16,838	18,530	17,086
Costa Rica	24,073	22,825	21,629
El Salvador	159,755	150,343	142,961
Guatemala	122,641	115,768	110,230
Italy	20,773	20,977	27,739
Mexico	20,613	22,968	21,045
Nicaragua	117,342	110,299	104,904
Panama	8,810	8,350	7,877
Spain	15,229	15,459	20,821
USA	248,137	275,117	253,887
Total (incl. others)	862,548	871,468	894,677

Total tourist arrivals ('000): 943 in 2013 (provisional).

Receipts from tourism (US $ million, excl. passenger transport): 639 in 2011; 661 in 2012; 711 in 2013 (provisional).

Source: World Tourism Organization.

Communications Media

	2011	2012	2013
Telephones ('000 main lines in use)	614.3	610.5	619.1
Mobile cellular telephones ('000 subscribers)	8,062.2	7,370.0	7,767.2
Broadband subscribers ('000) . .	57.9	61.3	68.1

Internet subscribers: 72,400 in 2009.

Education
(2013)

	Institutions	Students
Pre-primary	11,336	237,944
Primary	12,573	1,297,804
Secondary	1,699	547,419
Adult	253	10,512
Total	25,861	2,093,679

Teachers (2009/10 unless otherwise indicated): Pre-primary 8,837 (2008/09); Primary 37,370 (2008/09); Secondary 16,667 (2003/04); Higher (incl. university) 8,593 (Source: UNESCO Institute for Statistics).

Pupil-teacher ratio (primary education, UNESCO estimate): 33.9 in 2008/09 (Source: UNESCO Institute for Statistics).

Adult literacy rate (UNESCO estimates): 85.4% (males 85.7%; females 85.1%) in 2012 (Source: UNESCO Institute for Statistics).

Directory

The Constitution

Following the elections of April 1980, the 1965 Constitution was revised. The new Constitution was approved by the Congreso Nacional (National Congress) in November 1982, and amended in 1995 and 2011. The following are some of its main provisions:

Honduras is constituted as a democratic Republic. All Hondurans over 18 years of age are citizens.

THE SUFFRAGE AND POLITICAL PARTIES

The vote is direct and secret. Any political party that proclaims or practises doctrines contrary to the democratic spirit is forbidden. A National Electoral Council will be set up at the end of each presidential term. Its general function will be to supervise all elections and to register political parties. A proportional system of voting will be adopted for the election of municipal corporations.

INDIVIDUAL RIGHTS AND GUARANTEES

The right to life is declared inviolable; the death penalty is abolished. The Constitution recognizes the right of habeas corpus and arrests may be made only by judicial order. Remand for interrogation may not last more than six days, and no-one may be held incommunicado for more than 24 hours. The Constitution recognizes the rights of free expression of thought and opinion, the free circulation of information, of peaceful, unarmed association, of free movement within and out of the country, of political asylum and of religious and educational freedom. Civil marriage and divorce are recognized.

WORKERS' WELFARE

All have a right to work. Day work shall not exceed eight hours per day or 44 hours per week; night work shall not exceed six hours per night or 36 hours per week. Equal pay shall be given for equal work. The legality of trade unions and the right to strike are recognized.

EDUCATION

The state is responsible for education, which shall be free, lay, and, in the primary stage, compulsory. Private education is liable to inspection and regulation by the state.

LEGISLATIVE POWER

Deputies are obliged to vote, for or against, on any measure at the discussion of which they are present. The National Congress has power to grant amnesties to political prisoners; approve or disapprove of the actions of the Executive; declare part or the whole of the republic subject to a state of siege; declare war; approve or withhold approval of treaties; withhold approval of the accounts of public expenditure when these exceed the sums fixed in the budget; decree, interpret, repeal and amend laws, and pass legislation fixing the rate of exchange or stabilizing the national currency. The National Congress may suspend certain guarantees in all or part of the Republic for 60 days in the case of grave danger from civil or foreign war, epidemics or any other calamity. Deputies are elected in the proportion of one deputy and one substitute for every 35,000 inhabitants, or fraction over 15,000. Congress may amend the basis in the light of increasing population.

EXECUTIVE POWER

Executive power is exercised by the President of the Republic, who is elected for four years by a simple majority of the people. No President may serve more than one term.

JUDICIAL POWER

The Judiciary consists of the Supreme Court, the Courts of Appeal and various lesser tribunals. The nine judges and seven substitute judges of the Supreme Court are elected by the National Congress for a period of four years. The Supreme Court is empowered to declare laws unconstitutional.

THE ARMED FORCES

The Armed Forces are declared by the Constitution to be essentially professional and non-political. The President exercises direct authority over the military.

LOCAL ADMINISTRATION

The country is divided into 18 departments for purposes of local administration, and these are subdivided into 298 autonomous municipalities; the functions of local offices shall be only economic and administrative.

The Government

HEAD OF STATE

President: JUAN ORLANDO HERNÁNDEZ ALVARADO (took office 27 January 2014).

CABINET
(September 2014)

The Government is comprised of members of the Partido Nacional. In addition to the ministers listed below, there are seven sectoral ministries, responsible for the following areas: governability and decentralization, development and social inclusion, economic development, infrastructure, security and defence, competition and economic regulation, and foreign affairs.

Co-ordinator-General of the Government: JORGE RAMÓN HERNÁNDEZ ALCERRO.

Secretary of Human Rights, Justice, Government and Decentralization: RIGOBERTO CHANG CASTILLO.

Secretary of the Presidency: REINALDO SÁNCHEZ.

Secretary of Finance: WILFREDO CERRATO.

Secretary of Health: YOLANI BATRES.

Secretary of Public Security: ARTURO CORRALES ALVAREZ.

Secretary of National Defence: SAMUEL ARMANDO REYES RENDÓN.

Secretary of Foreign Affairs: MIREYA AGÜERO DE CORRALES.

Secretary of Infrastructure and Public Services: ROBERTO ORDÓÑEZ.

Secretary of Economic Development: ALDEN RIVERA.

Secretary of Education: MARLON ESCOTO.

Secretary of Energy, Natural Resources, Environment and Mines: JOSÉ ANTONIO GALDÁMEZ.

Secretary of Agriculture and Livestock: JACOBO PAZ BODDEN.

Secretary of Development and Social Inclusion: LISANDRO ROSALES.

Secretary of Communications and Strategy in the Office of the President: HILDA HERNÁNDEZ.

MINISTRIES

Office of the President: Palacio José Cecilio del Valle, Blvd Francisco Morazán, Tegucigalpa; tel. 2290-5010; fax 2231-0097; e-mail diseloalpresidente@presidencia.gob.hn; internet www.presidencia.gob.hn.

Secretariat of Agriculture and Livestock: Avda La FAO, Blvd Centroamérica, Col. Loma Linda, Tegucigalpa; tel. 2232-5029; fax 2231-0051; e-mail infoagro@infoagro.hn; internet www.sag.gob.hn.

Secretariat of Development and Social Inclusion: Edif. Ejecutivo, Las Lomas Anexo II, frente a Ferretería INDUFESA, Blvd Juan Pablo II, Tegucigalpa; tel. 2239-8005; internet sedis.gob.hn.

Secretariat of Economic Development: Edif. San José, Col. Humuya, Blvd José Cecilio del Valle, Tegucigalpa; tel. 2235-3699; fax 2235-3686.

Secretariat of Education: 1 Avda, entre 2 y 3 Calle, Comayagüela, Tegucigalpa; tel. 2238-4325; fax 2222-8571; e-mail webmaster@se.gob.hn; internet www.se.gob.hn.

Secretariat of Energy, Natural Resources, Environment and Mines: 100 m al sur del Estadio Nacional, Apdo 1389, Tegucigalpa; tel. 2232-1386; fax 2232-6250; e-mail sdespacho@yahoo.com; internet www.serna.gob.hn.

Secretariat of Finance: Edif. SEFIN, Avda Cervantes, Barrio El Jazmín, Tegucigalpa; tel. 2222-0112; fax 2238-2309; e-mail sgeneral@sefin.gob.hn; internet www.sefin.gob.hn.

Secretariat of Foreign Affairs: Centro Cívico Gubernamental, Antigua Casa Presidencial, Blvd Kuwait, Contiguo a la Corte Suprema de Justicia, Tegucigalpa; tel. 2230-4156; fax 2230-5664; e-mail cancilleria.honduras@gmail.com; internet www.sre.gob.hn.

Secretariat of Health: 2 Calle, Avda Cervantes, Tegucigalpa; tel. 2222-8518; fax 2238-6787; e-mail comunicacionessalud@yahoo.com; internet www.salud.gob.hn.

Secretariat of Human Rights, Justice, Government and Decentralization: Residencia La Hacienda, Calle La Estancia, Tegucigalpa; tel. 2232-5995; fax 2232-0226; e-mail francis.caceres@seip.gob.hn; internet www.seip.gob.hn.

Secretariat of Infrastructure and Public Services: Barrio La Bolsa, Comayagüela, Tegucigalpa; tel. 2225-2690; fax 2225-5003.

Secretariat of National Defence: Blvd Suyapa, Col. Florencia Sur, frente a Iglesia Colegio Episcopal, Tegucigalpa; tel. 2239-2330; e-mail transparencia@sedena.gob.hn; internet www.sedena.gob.hn.

Secretariat of Public Security: Cuartel General de Casamata, subida al Picacho, Tegucigalpa; tel. 2220-4298; fax 2220-1711; e-mail info@seguridad.gob.hn; internet www.seguridad.gob.hn.

President and Legislature

PRESIDENT

Election, 24 November 2013

Candidate	Valid votes cast	% of valid votes
Juan Orlando Hernández Alvarado (PN)	1,149,302	36.89
Xiomara Castro de Zelaya (LIBRE)	896,498	28.78
Mauricio Villeda (PL)	632, 320	20.30
Salvador Nasralla (PAC)	418,443	13.43
Others	18,885	0.61
Total*	3,115,448	100.00

*In addition, there were 108,171 spoiled votes and 51,727 blank votes.

NATIONAL CONGRESS
(Congreso Nacional)

President: MAURICIO OLIVA.

General Election, 24 November 2013

	Seats
Partido Nacional (PN)	48
Partido Libertad y Refundación (LIBRE)	37
Partido Liberal (PL)	27
Partido Anticorrupción (PAC)	13
Partido Innovación y Unidad—Social Demócrata (PINU—SD)	1
Partido de Unificación Democrática (PUD)	1
Partido Demócrata Cristiano de Honduras (PDCH)	1
Total	128

Election Commission

Tribunal Supremo Electoral (TSE): Col. El Prado, frente a Edif. Syre, Tegucigalpa; tel. 2239-1058; fax 2239-3060; e-mail centroinformacion@tse.hn; internet www.tse.hn; f. 2004 as successor to Tribunal Nacional de Elecciones; Pres. DAVID ANDRÉS MATAMOROS BATSÓN.

Political Organizations

Alianza Patriótica Hondureña (La Alianza): Tegucigalpa; tel. 2213-8091; fax 2213-2367; e-mail contacto@laalianza.hn; internet www.laalianza.hn; f. 2011; right-wing; Pres. Gen. (retd) ROMEO VÁSQUEZ VELÁSQUEZ.

Frente Amplio Político Electoral en Resistencia (FAPER): Tegucigalpa; internet partido-faper.blogspot.co.uk; f. 2012; contested the 2013 elections; Pres. ANDRÉS PAVÓN.

Partido Anticorrupción (PAC): Tegucigalpa; e-mail honduras@salvadornasralla.com; internet www.salvadornasralla.com; f. 2011; centre-left; Pres. SALVADOR NASRALLA.

Partido Demócrata Cristiano de Honduras (PDCH): Col. San Carlos, Tegucigalpa; tel. 2236-5969; fax 2236-9941; e-mail pdch@

hondutel.hn; internet www.pdch.hn; legally recognized in 1980; Pres. LUCAS EVANGELISTO AGUILERA PINEDA; Sec.-Gen. ARNOLD AMAYA.

Partido Innovación y Unidad—Social Demócrata (PINU—SD): 2a Avda, entre 9 y 10 calles, Apdo 105, Comayagüela, Tegucigalpa; tel. 2220-4224; fax 2220-4232; e-mail pinusd@amnettgu.com; internet pinusd.hn; f. 1970; legally recognized in 1978; Pres. JORGE RAFAEL AGUILAR PAREDES; Sec. IRIS ELIZABETH VIGIL.

Partido Liberal (PL): Col. Miramontes, atrás de Supermercado la Col. No 1, Tegucigalpa; tel. 2232-0822; e-mail info@partidoliberaldehonduras.hn; f. 1891; Pres. ELVIN SANTOS.

Partido Libertad y Refundación (LIBRE): Tegucigalpa; internet libertadyrefundacion.tumblr.com; f. 2011; party of 2013 presidential candidate Xiomara Castro de Zelaya; Pres. JOSÉ MANUEL ZELAYA ROSALES.

Partido Nacional (PN): Paseo el Obelisco, Comayagüela, Tegucigalpa; tel. 2237-7310; fax 2237-7365; e-mail partidonacional@partidonacional.net; internet www.partidonacional.net; f. 1902; traditional right-wing party; Pres. JUAN ORLANDO HERNÁNDEZ ALVARADO; Sec.-Gen. REINALDO SÁNCHEZ.

Partido de Unificación Democrática (PUD): Col. los Almendros, Blvd Morazón, atrás del Restaurante Las Reses, Tegucigalpa; tel. and fax 2236-6868; e-mail partidoudhonduras@yahoo.es; internet www.partidoud.com; f. 1992 following merger of Partido Revolucionario Hondureño, Partido Renovación Patriótica, Partido para la Transformación de Honduras and Partido Morazanista; left-wing; Pres. DAVID ADOLFO CÉSAR HAM PEÑA; Sec. MARTÍN PIÑEDA ENGELS.

Diplomatic Representation

EMBASSIES IN HONDURAS

Argentina: Calle Palermo 302, Col. Rubén Darío, Apdo 3208, Tegucigalpa; tel. 2232-3376; fax 2231-0376; e-mail ehond@mrecic.gov.ar; Ambassador GUILLERMO ROBERTO ROSSI.

Belize: Area Comercial del Hotel Honduras Maya, Col. Palmira, Tegucigalpa; tel. 2238-4614; fax 2238-4617; e-mail vesahonduras@gmail.com; Chargé d'affaires a.i. RICHARD CLARK VINELLI REISMAN.

Brazil: Col. Palmira, Calle República del Brasil, Apdo 341, Tegucigalpa; tel. 2221-4432; fax 2236-5873; e-mail brastegu@clarotv.com.hn; internet tegucigalpa.itamaraty.gov.br; Ambassador ZENIK KRAWCTSCHUK.

Chile: Torres Metrópolis 1, 16°, Of. 11608, Blvd Suyapa, Tegucigalpa; tel. 2232-4106; fax 2232-2114; e-mail embachilehonduras@clarotv.com.hn; internet chileabroad.gov.cl/honduras; Ambassador RODRIGO PÉREZ MANRÍQUEZ.

Colombia: Edif. Palmira, 3°, Col. Palmira, Apdo 468, Tegucigalpa; tel. 2239-9709; fax 2232-9324; e-mail ehonduras@cancilleria.gov.co; internet www.embajadaenhonduras.gov.co; Ambassador FRANCISCO CANOSSA GUERRERO.

Costa Rica: Residencial El Triángulo, Calle 3451, Lomas del Guijarro, Apdo 512, Tegucigalpa; tel. 2232-1768; fax 2232-1054; e-mail embacori@amnettgu.com; Ambassador MARÍA GUTIÉRREZ VARGAS.

Cuba: Col. Lomas del Guijarro, Calle Los Eucaliptos, No 3720, Tegucigalpa; tel. 2235-3349; fax 2235-7624; e-mail admon@hn.embacuba.cu; internet www.cubadiplomatica.cu/honduras; Chargé d'affaires a.i. SERGIO OLIVA GUERRA.

Dominican Republic: Plaza Miramontes, 2°, Local No 6, Col. Miramontes, Tegucigalpa; tel. 2239-0130; fax 2239-1594; e-mail joacosta@serex.gov.do; Ambassador JOSÉ OSVALDO LEGER AQUINO.

Ecuador: Bloque F, Casa 2968, Sendero Senecio, Col. Lomas del Castaños Sur, Apdo 358, Tegucigalpa; tel. 2221-4906; fax 2221-1049; e-mail mecuahon@multivisionhn.net; Chargé d'affaires a.i. CRISTINA GRANDA MENDOZA.

El Salvador: Col. Altos de Miramontes, Casa 2952, Diagonal Aguan, Tegucigalpa; tel. 2239-7015; fax 2239-6556; e-mail embasalhonduras@rree.gob.sv; internet embajadahonduras.rree.gob.sv; Ambassador CARLOS POZO.

France: Col. Palmira, Avda Juan Lindo, Callejón Batres 337, Apdo 3441, Tegucigalpa; tel. 2236-6800; fax 2236-8051; e-mail info@ambafrance-hn.org; internet www.ambafrance-hn.org; Ambassador PHILIPPE ARDANAZ.

Germany: Avda República Dominicana 925, Sendero Santo Domingo, Col. Lomas del Guijarro, Apdo 3145, Tegucigalpa; tel. 2232-3161; fax 2239-9018; e-mail info@tegucigalpa.diplo.de; internet www.tegucigalpa.diplo.de; Ambassador Dr JOHANNES TROMMER.

Guatemala: Casa No 0440, Bloque B, Calle Londres, Col. Lomas del Guijarro Sur, Tegucigalpa; tel. 2232-5018; fax 2239-9809; e-mail embhondurasgt@gmail.com; Ambassador HUGO RENÉ HEMMERLING GONZÁLEZ.

Holy See: Palacio de la Nunciatura Apostólica, Col. Palmira, Avda Santa Sede 401, Apdo 324, Tegucigalpa; tel. 2238-6013; fax 2238-6257; e-mail nunziohn@hotmail.com; Apostolic Nuncio (vacant).

Italy: Torre Lafise, 3°, Avda Los Próceres, Centro Corporativo, Col. San Carlos, Tegucigalpa; tel. 2221–4963; fax 2221–4953; e-mail ambasciata.tegucigalpa@esteri.it; internet www.ambtegucigalpa.esteri.it; Ambassador GIOVANNI ADORNI BRACCESI CHIASSI.

Japan: Col. San Carlos, Calzada Rep. Paraguay, Apdo 3232, Tegucigalpa; tel. 2236-5511; fax 2236-6100; e-mail keikyo1@multivisionhn.net; internet www.hn.emb-japan.go.jp; Ambassador KENJI OKADA.

Korea, Republic: Edif. Plaza Azul, 5°, Col. Lomas del Guijarro Sur, Tegucigalpa; tel. 2235-5561; fax 2235-5564; e-mail coreaembajada@mofat.go.kr; internet hnd.mofat.go.kr; Ambassador KIM RAI-HYUG.

Mexico: Col. Lomas del Guijarro, Avda Eucalipto 1001, Tegucigalpa; tel. 2232-4039; fax 2232-4719; e-mail embamexhonduras@gmail.com; internet www.sre.gob.mx/honduras; Ambassador VÍCTOR HUGO MORALES.

Nicaragua: Col. Tepeyac, Bloque M-1, Avda Choluteca 1130, Apdo 392, Tegucigalpa; tel. 2231-1966; fax 2231-1412; e-mail embanic@amnettgu.com; Ambassador MARIO JOSÉ DUARTE ZAMORA.

Panama: Edif. Palmira, 3°, Col. Palmira, Apdo 397, Tegucigalpa; tel. 2239-5508; fax 2232-8147; e-mail ephon@multivisionhn.net; Ambassador MARIO RUÍZ DOLANDE.

Peru: Col. Linda Vista, Calle Principal 3301, Tegucigalpa; tel. 2236-7994; fax 2221-4596; e-mail embajadadelperu@cablecolor.hn; Ambassador GUILLERMO GONZÁLEZ ARICA.

Spain: Col. Matamoros, Calle Santander 801, Apdo 3221, Tegucigalpa; tel. 2236-6875; fax 2236-8682; e-mail emb.tegucigalpa@maec.es; internet www.maec.es/Embajadas/Tegucigalpa; Ambassador MIGUEL ALBERO SUÁREZ.

Taiwan (Republic of China): Col. Lomas del Guijarro, Calle Eucaliptos 3750, Apdo 3433, Tegucigalpa; tel. 2239-5837; fax 2232-0532; e-mail hnd@mofa.gov.tw; internet www.taiwanembassy.org/hn; Ambassador JOSEPH Y. L. KUO.

USA: Avda La Paz, Apdo 3453, Tegucigalpa; tel. 2236-9320; fax 2236-9037; internet honduras.usembassy.gov; Ambassador LISA KUBISKE.

Venezuela: Col. Rubén Darío, 2116 Circuito Choluteca, Apdo 775, Tegucigalpa; tel. 2232-1879; fax 2232-1016; e-mail info@venezuelalabolivariana.com; internet venezuelalabolivariana.com; Chargé d'affaires a.i. ARIEL NICOLAS VARGAS ARDENCO.

Judicial System

Justice is administered by the Supreme Court, five Courts of Appeal, and departmental courts (which have their own local jurisdiction).

Tegucigalpa has two Courts of Appeal, the first of which has jurisdiction in the department of Francisco Morazán, and the second of which has jurisdiction in the departments of Choluteca Valle, El Paraíso and Olancho.

The Appeal Court of San Pedro Sula has jurisdiction in the department of Cortés; that of Comayagua has jurisdiction in the departments of Comayagua, La Paz and Intibucá; and that of Santa Bárbara in the departments of Santa Bárbara, Lempira and Copán.

Supreme Court: Edif. Palacio de Justicia, contiguo Col. Miraflores, Centro Cívico Gubernamental, Tegucigalpa; tel. 2275-7183; fax 2233-6784; e-mail comunicaciones@poderjudicial.gob.hn; internet www.poderjudicial.gob.hn; comprises 4 courts: constitutional, labour, civil and penal; Pres. JORGE RIVERA AVILÉS.

Attorney-General: OSCAR FERNANDO CHINCHILLA.

Religion

The majority of the population are Roman Catholics; the Constitution guarantees toleration of all forms of religious belief.

CHRISTIANITY

The Roman Catholic Church

Honduras comprises one archdiocese and seven dioceses. Some 82% of the population are Roman Catholics.

Bishops' Conference: Conferencia Episcopal de Honduras, Blvd Estadio Suyapa, Apdo 3121, Tegucigalpa; tel. 2229-1111; fax 2229-1144; e-mail ceh@unicah.edu; internet www.iglesiahn.org; f. 1929; Pres. Cardinal OSCAR ANDRÉS RODRÍGUEZ MARADIAGA (Archbishop of Tegucigalpa).

Archbishop of Tegucigalpa: Cardinal OSCAR ANDRÉS RODRÍGUEZ MARADIAGA, Arzobispado, 3a y 2a Avda 1113, Apdo 106, Tegucigalpa; tel. 2236-2849; fax 2236-2967; e-mail oficina@arquitegucigalpa.org; internet www.arquitegucigalpa.org.

The Anglican Communion

Honduras comprises a single missionary diocese, in Province IX of the Episcopal Church in the USA.

Bishop of Honduras: Rt Rev. LLOYD EMMANUEL ALLEN, Diócesis de Honduras, 23 Avda C, 21 St Colony Trejo, San Pedro Sula; tel. 2556-6155; fax 2556-6467; e-mail obispoallen@yahoo.com; internet honduras.fedigitales.org.

The Baptist Church

Convención Nacional de Iglesias Bautistas de Honduras (CONIBAH): Apdo 2176, Tegucigalpa; tel. and fax 2221-4024; e-mail conibah@sigmanet.hn; internet www.ublaonline.org/paises/honduras.htm; Pres. Pastor TOMÁS MONTOYA; 24,142 mems.

Other Churches

Church of Jesus Christ of Latter-Day Saints (Mormons): Residenciales Roble Oeste, Blvd Roble Oeste, 3ra Calle Sur, Comayagüela; tel. 2264-1212; internet www.lds.org; 154,207 mems.

Iglesia Cristiana Luterana de Honduras (Lutheran): Barrio Villa Adela, 19 Calle entre 5a y 6a Avda, Apdo 2861, Tegucigalpa; tel. 2225-4464; fax 2225-4893; e-mail iclh@cablecolor.hn; internet iclh.wordpress.com; Pres. Rev. JOSÉ MARTIN GIRÓN; 1,500 mems.

BAHÁ'Í FAITH

National Spiritual Assembly: Sendero de los Naranjos 2801, Col. Castaños, Apdo 273, Tegucigalpa; tel. 2232-6124; fax 2231-1343; e-mail sdooki@tropicohn.com; internet www.bahaihonduras.net; Co-ordinator SOHEIL DOOKI; 40,000 mems resident in more than 500 localities.

The Press

DAILIES

La Gaceta: Empresa Nacional de Artes Gráficas, Col. Miraflores, Tegucigalpa; tel. 2230-1339; fax 2230-3026; internet www.lagaceta.hn; f. 1830; morning; official govt paper; Gen. Man. MARTHA ALICIA GARCÍA CASCO; Co-ordinator MARCO ANTONIO RODRÍGUEZ CASTILLO; circ. 3,000.

El Heraldo: Avda los Próceres, Frente al Pani, Barrio San Felipe, Apdo 1938, Tegucigalpa; tel. 2236-6000; e-mail contactos@elheraldo.hn; internet www.elheraldo.hn; f. 1979; morning; independent; Editor FERNANDO BERRÍOS; circ. 50,000.

La Prensa: Guamilito, 3a Avda, 6–7 Calles No 34, Apdo 143, San Pedro Sula; tel. 2553-3101; fax 2553-0778; e-mail redaccion@laprensa.hn; internet www.laprensa.hn; f. 1964; morning; independent; Editor NELSON GARCÍA; Exec. Dir MARÍA ANTONIA MARTÍNEZ DE FUENTES; circ. 50,000.

El Tiempo: 1 Calle, 5a Avda 102, Barrio Santa Anita, Cortés, Apdo 450, San Pedro Sula; tel. 2553-3388; fax 2553-4590; e-mail web.tiempo@continental.hn; internet www.tiempo.hn; f. 1960; morning; left-of-centre; Pres. JAIME ROSENTHAL OLIVA; circ. 35,000.

La Tribuna: Col. Santa Bárbara, Carretera al Primer Batallón de Infantería, Comayagüela, Apdo 1501, Tegucigalpa; tel. 2234-3206; fax 2234-3050; e-mail tribuna@latribuna.hn; internet www.latribuna.hn; f. 1976; morning; independent; Dir ADÁN ELVIR FLORES; Editor OLMAN MANZANO; circ. 45,000.

PERIODICALS

Comercio Global: Cámara de Comercio e Industrias de Tegucigalpa, Blvd Centroamérica, Apdo 3444, Tegucigalpa; tel. 2232-4200; fax 2232-0759; e-mail mercadeo@ccit.hn; internet www.ccit.hn; f. 1970; 4 a year; commercial and industrial news; Publr DANIELA ZELAYA.

Cromos: Torre Libertad, Blvd Suyapa, Tegucigalpa; tel. 2239-3916; fax 2239-7008; e-mail editor@cromos.hn; internet www.cromos.hn; f. 1999; society; monthly; publishes specialized edns *Cromos Gourmet*, *Cromos Bodas*, *Cromos Seniors*, *Cromos Hogar*, *Cromos Fashion* and *Cromos Ellos* annually; Publr REGINA MARÍA WONG; Editors ALEJANDRA PAREDES, EMMA MIDENCE.

Estilo: Tegucigalpa; tel. 2553-3101; fax 2558-1273; e-mail revista@estilo.hn; internet www.estilo.hn; f. 1996; lifestyle; monthly; Pres. JORGE CANAHUATI LARACH; Editor BLANCA BENDECK.

Hablemos Claro: Edif. Torre Libertad, Blvd Suyapa, Residencial La Hacienda, Tegucigalpa; tel. 2232-8058; fax 2239-7008; e-mail rwa@hablemosclaro.com; internet www.hablemosclaro.com; f. 1990; weekly; Editor RODRIGO WONG ARÉVALO; circ. 9,000.

Honduras Weekly: Centro Comercial Villa Mare, Blvd Morazán, Apdo 1323, Tegucigalpa; tel. 2239-0285; fax 2232-2300; e-mail editor@hondurasweekly.com; internet www.hondurasweekly.com;

f. 1988; weekly; English language; tourism, culture and the environment; Bureau Chief NICOLE MUÑOZ; Editor MARCO CÁCERES.

El Libertador: Tegucigalpa; internet www.ellibertador.hn; Dir JHONNY LAGOS; Editor DELMER MEMBREÑO.

PRESS ASSOCIATION

Asociación de Prensa Hondureña: Casa del Periodista, Avda Gutemberg 1525, Calle 6, Barrio El Guanacaste, Apdo 893, Tegucigalpa; tel. 2239-2970; fax 2237-8102; f. 1930; Pres. CARLOS ORTIZ; Sec.-Gen. FELA ISABEL DUARTE.

Publishers

Centro Editorial: Apdo 1683, San Pedro Sula; tel. and fax 2558-6282; e-mail centroeditorialhn@gmail.com; f. 1987; Dir JULIO ESCOTO.

Ediciones Ramses: Edif. Chiminike, 2°, Blvr Fuerzas Armadas de Honduras, Tegucigalpa; tel. 2225-6630; fax 2225-6633; e-mail servicioalcliente@edicionesramses.hn; internet www.edicionesramses.hn; educational material.

Editorial Coello: Avda 9, Calle 4, 64a, Barrio El Benque, San Pedro Sula; tel. 2553-1680; fax 2557-4362; e-mail tcoello@globalnet.hn; Dir AUGUSTO C. COELLO.

Editorial Pez Dulce: 143 Paseo La Leona, Barrio La Leona, Tegucigalpa; tel. and fax 222-1220; e-mail pezdulce@yahoo.com; Dir RUBÉN IZAGUIRRE.

Editorial Universitaria de la Universidad Nacional Autónoma de Honduras: Blvd Suyapa, Tegucigalpa; tel. and fax 2232-4772; f. 1847; Dir SEGISFREDO INFANTE.

Guaymuras: Avda Zaragoza, Apdo 1843, Barrio La Leona, Tegucigalpa; tel. 2237-5433; fax 2238-4578; e-mail ediguay@123.hn; internet www.guaymuras.hn; f. 1980; Dir ISOLDA ARITA MELZER.

Broadcasting and Communications

REGULATORY AUTHORITY

Comisión Nacional de Telecomunicaciones (Conatel): Edif. Conatel, Col. Modelo, 6 Avda Suroeste, Comayagüela, Apdo 15012, Tegucigalpa; tel. 2232-9600; fax 2234-8611; e-mail info@conatel.gob.hn; internet www.conatel.gob.hn; f. 1995; Pres. RICARDO CARDONA.

TELECOMMUNICATIONS

The monopoly of the telecommunications sector by Hondutel ceased at the end of 2005, when the fixed line and international services market was opened to domestic and foreign investment.

Claro Honduras: Col. San Carlos, Avda República de Colombia, Tegucigalpa; tel. 2205-4222; fax 2205-4337; e-mail clientes@claro.com.hn; internet www.claro.com.hn; f. 2003; operated by Servicios de Comunicaciones de Honduras (Sercom Honduras), a subsidiary of América Móvil, SA de CV (Mexico) since 2004; mobile cellular telephone operator; Gen. Man. LUIS DEL SID.

Empresa Hondureña de Telecomunicaciones (Hondutel): Edif. Gerencia Los Almendros, Residencial Montecarlo, Tegucigalpa; tel. 2221-0411; fax 2216-7800; e-mail miguel.velez@hondutelnet.hn; internet www.hondutel.hn; f. 1976; scheduled for privatization; Gen. Man. Gen. (retd) ROMEO VÁSQUEZ VELÁSQUEZ.

Multifon: Tegucigalpa; tel. 206-0607; e-mail sac@multifon.net; f. 2003; subsidiary of MultiData; awarded govt contract with UT Starcom (q.v.) for fixed telephone lines in 2003; Pres. JOSÉ RAFAEL FERRARI; CEO JOSÉ LUIS RIVERA.

Telefónica Celular (CELTEL) (Tigo): Edif. Celtel, contiguo a la Iglesia Episcopal, Blvd Suyapa, Col. Florencia Norte Hondureña, Tegucigalpa; tel. 2235-7966; fax 2220-7060; e-mail info@mail.celtel.net; internet www.tigo.com.hn; f. 1996; mobile cellular telephone company; wholly owned subsidiary of Millicom International Cellular (Luxembourg); Pres. ANTONIO TAVEL OTERO.

UT Starcom (USA): Edif. Plaza Azul, 6°, Calle Viena, Avda Berlin, Col. Lomas del Guijarro Sur, Tegucigalpa; tel. 2239-8289; fax 2239-9161; e-mail services@utstar.com; internet www.utstar.com; awarded govt contract with Multifon (q.v.) for fixed telephone lines in 2003; Pres. and CEO JACK LU.

BROADCASTING

Radio

HRN, La Voz de Honduras: Blvd Suyapa, contiguo a Televicentro, Apdo 642, Tegucigalpa; tel. 2232-5100; fax 2232-5109; e-mail contacto@radiohrn.hn; internet www.radiohrn.hn; commercial station; f. 1933; part of Grupo Emisoras Unidas; broadcasts 12 channels; 23 relay stations; Gen. Man. NAHÚN EFRAÍN VALLADARES.

Power FM: Edif. Power FM, Blvd del Norte Costado Sur, 105 Brigada, Apdo 868, San Pedro Sula; tel. 2564-0500; fax 2564-0529; e-mail info@powerfm.hn; internet www.powerfm.hn; Gen. Man. XAVIER SIERRA.

Radio América: Col. Alameda, frente a la Droguería Mandofer, Apdo 259, Tegucigalpa; tel. 2290-4950; fax 2232-1009; e-mail info@ americamultimedios.net; internet www.radioamericahn.net; commercial station; broadcasts Radio San Pedro, Radio Continental, Radio Modermna, Radio Universal, Cadena Radial Sonora, Super Cien Stereo, Momentos FM Stereo and 3 regional channels; f. 1948; 13 relay stations; Gen. Man. JULIO ARÉVALO.

Radio Club Honduras: Salida Chamelecon, Apdo 273, San Pedro Sula; tel. 2556-6173; fax 2617-1151; e-mail hr2rch@yahoo.com; internet www.hr2rch.com; f. 1958; amateur radio club; Pres. NOE OLIVA.

Radio Juticalpa: Juticalpa, Olancho; tel. 2785-2277; fax 2785-5063; internet www.radiojuticalpa.com; Gen. Man. MARTHA ELENA RUBÍ H.

Radio Nacional de Honduras: Avda La Paz, Col. Lomas Del Mayab, detras del edif. del Ministerio de la Presidencia, Tegucigalpa; tel. 2235-6723; fax 2235-6678; e-mail radio@rnh.hn; internet www .rnh.hn; f. 1976; official station, operated by the Govt; Exec. Dir GUSTAVO BLANCO.

Radio la Voz del Atlántico: 12 Calle, 2–3 Avda, Barrio Copen, Apdo 21301, Puerto Cortés; tel. 2665-5166; fax 2665-2401; e-mail administracion@lavozdelatlantico.com; internet www .lavozdelatlantico.com; f. 1955; Dir FRANCISCO ANDRÉS GRIFFIN BOQUIN.

Super K: Entrada Principal, Barrio La Ceiba, San Lorenzo del Valle; tel. 2781-2001; e-mail superk_895fm@yahoo.com; internet www .lasuperkfm.com; f. 2008; Dir MARVIN ESTRADA.

Television

Televicentro: Edif. Televicentro, Blvd Suyapa, Col. Florencia, Apdo 734, Tegucigalpa; tel. 2207-5514; fax 2232-5514; e-mail tvcoperaciones@televicentro.hn; internet www.televicentrotv.net; f. 1987; 11 stations, including Telecadena 7 y 4 (f. 1985), Telesistema Hondureño, Canal 3 y 7 (f. 1967) and Megatv; Pres. JOSÉ RAFAEL FERRARI SAGASTUME.

Canal 5: tel. 2232-7835; fax 2232-0097; f. 1959; Gen. Man. RENATO ALVAREZ.

Televisión Nacional de Honduras (TNH): Edif. Ejecutivo 2, 4°, Frente Casa Presidencial, Tegucigalpa; e-mail info@tnh.gob.hn; internet www.tnh.gob.hn; f. 1962; channels include TVN–8, Telenacional, Cadena 1, Primera Cadena and TNH–8; Dir ARMANDO VALDÉZ.

VICA Television: 9a Calle, 10a Avda 64, Barrio Guamilito, Apdo 120, San Pedro Sula; tel. 2552-4478; fax 2557-3257; e-mail info@ mayanet.hn; internet www.vicatv.hn; f. 1986; operates regional channels 2, 9 and 13; Pres. RIGEL SIERRA.

Finance

(cap. = capital; res = reserves; dep. = deposits; m. = million; brs = branches; amounts in lempiras unless otherwise stated)

BANKING

Central Bank

Banco Central de Honduras (BANTRAL): Avda Juan Ramón Molina, 7a Avda y 1a Calle, Apdo 3165, Tegucigalpa; tel. 2237-2270; fax 2237-1876; e-mail Carlos.Espinoza@bch.hn; internet www.bch .hn; f. 1950; bank of issue; cap. 212.5m., res 1,192m., dep. 39,232.9m. (Dec. 2009); Pres. MARÍA MONDRAGÓN; Gen. Man. HÉCTOR MENDÉZ; 4 brs.

Commercial Banks

BAC Honduras: Blvd Suyapa, frente a Emisoras Unidas, Apdo 116, Tegucigalpa; tel. 2216-0200; fax 2239-4509; internet www.bac.net/ honduras; bought by Grupo Aval de Colombia in Dec. 2010; fmrly Banco Mercantil, SA, then BAC BAMER; Gen. Man. JACOBO ATALA.

Banco Atlántida, SA (BANCATLAN): Plaza Bancatlán, Blvd Centroamérica, Apdo 3164, Tegucigalpa; tel. 2280-0000; fax 2232-6120; e-mail webmaster@bancatlan.hn; internet www.bancatlan.hn; f. 1913; cap. 4,500m., res 22.7m. dep. 37,043.5m. (Dec. 2013); Pres. GILBERTO GOLDSTEIN RUBINSTEIN; 186 brs.

Banco Continental, SA (BANCON): Centro Comercial Novaprisa, 9–10 Avda NO, Blvd Morazán, San Pedro Sula; tel. 2550-0880; fax 2550-2750; e-mail imontoya@continental.hn; internet www.bancon

.hn; f. 1974; cap. 500m., res 19.5m., dep. 5,541.8m. (Dec. 2012); Pres. JAIME ROSENTHAL OLIVA; 77 brs.

Banco Davivienda Honduras, SA: Intersección Blvd Suyapa y Blvd Juan Pablo II, Apdo 344, Tegucigalpa; tel. 2240-0909; fax 2240-4873; internet www.davivienda.com.hn; f. 1947 as Capitalizadora Hondureña, became BANCAHSA in 1968; known as Banco HSBC from 2007 until 2012, when it was bought by Banco Davivienda (Colombia); part of the Grupo Financiero Bolívar Honduras, SA; cap. 1,280m., res 254.5m., dep. 13,694.8m. (Dec. 2013); CEO JONATHAN HARTLEY; 78 brs.

Banco Financiera Comercial Hondureña (Banco FICOHSA): Edif. Plaza Victoria, Col. Las Colinas, Blvd Francia, Tegucigalpa; tel. 2239-6410; fax 2239-6420; e-mail ficobanc@ficohsa.hn; internet www .ficohsa.com; Pres. JAVIER ATALA; 101 brs.

Banco de Honduras, SA: Blvd Suyapa, Col. Loma Linda Sur, Tegucigalpa; tel. 2232-6122; fax 2290-0123; internet www .bancodehonduras.citibank.com; f. 1889; subsidiary of Citibank NA (USA); cap. 250.0m., res 6.8m., dep. 1,940.9m. (2008); Gen. Man. CONSTANTINO GOTSIS; 2 brs.

Banco de Occidente, SA (BANCOCCI): Calle Centenario, 1 Avda sur este, esq. opuesta al Parque Central, Santa Rosa de Copán, Apdo 208, Copán; tel. 2662-0159; fax 2662-0692; e-mail info@bancocci.hn; internet www.bancocci.hn; f. 1951; cap. 1,600m., res 493.1m., dep. 29,907.9m. (Dec. 2012); Pres. and Gen. Man. JORGE BUESO ARIAS; Vice-Pres. EMILIO MEDINA R.; 158 brs.

Banco del País (BANPAIS): Edif. Torre del País, Blvd José Antonio Peraza, Calle Banpais esq., San Pedro Sula; tel. 2566-2020; fax 2566-2040; internet www.banpais.hn; f. 1969; acquired Banco Sogerin and client portfolio of Banco de las Fuerzas Armadas in 2003; cap. 1,400m., res 101.3m., dep. 13,072m. (Dec. 2010); Pres. JUAN MIGUEL TORREBIARTE; 109 brs.

Banco de los Trabajadores, SA (BANCOTRAB): 3a Avda, 13a Calle, Comayagüela, Apdo 3246, Tegucigalpa; tel. 2238-4421; fax 2238-0077; internet www.btrab.com; f. 1967; cap. 204.8m. (Dec. 2002); Pres. JOSÉ ADONIS LAVAIRE; Gen. Man. GUSTAVO ADOLFO ZELAYA CHÁVEZ; 34 brs.

Development Banks

Banco Centroamericano de Integración Económica: Edif. Sede BCIE, Blvd Suyapa, Apdo 772, Tegucigalpa; tel. 2240-2231; fax 2240-2185; e-mail echinchi@bcie.hn; internet www.bcie.org; f. 1960 to finance the economic devt of the Central American Common Market and its mem. countries; mems: Costa Rica, El Salvador, Guatemala, Honduras, Nicaragua; cap. and res US $1,020.0m. (June 2003); Gov. WILFREDO RODRÍGUEZ.

Banco Financiera Centroamericana, SA (FICENSA): Edif. FICENSA, Blvd Morazán, Apdo 1432, Tegucigalpa; tel. 2238-1661; fax 2221-3855; e-mail webmaster@ficensa.com; internet www .ficensa.com; f. 1974; private org. providing finance for industry, commerce and transport; Exec. Vice-Pres. and Gen. Man. ROQUE RIVERA RÍBAS; 41 brs.

Banco Hondureño del Café, SA (BANHCAFE): Calle República de Costa Rica, Blvd Juan Pablo II, Col. Lomas del Mayab, Apdo 583, Tegucigalpa; tel. 2232-8370; fax 2232-8782; e-mail banhcafe@ banhcafe.hn; internet www.banhcafe.com; f. 1981 to help finance coffee production; owned principally by private coffee producers; cap. 425m., res 69.1m., dep. 2,507.4m. (Dec. 2013); Pres. MIGUEL ALFONSO FERNÁNDEZ RÁPALO; Gen. Man. CÉSAR A. ZAVALA L.; 41 brs.

Banco Nacional de Desarrollo Agrícola (BANADESA): 4 Avda y 5 Avda, 13 Calle, contiguo al Estado Mayor, Barrio el Obelisco, Apdo 212, Comayagüela; tel. 2237-2201; fax 2237-5187; e-mail banadesa@ banadesa.hn; internet www.banadesa.hn; f. 1980; govt devt bank; loans to agricultural sector; cap. 9m., res 811.7m., dep. 1,095.8m. (Dec. 2012); Pres. JORGE JOHNY HANDAL HAWIT; 37 brs.

Banking Associations

Asociación Hondureña de Instituciones Bancarias (AHIBA): Edif. AHIBA, Blvd Suyapa, Apdo 1344, Tegucigalpa; tel. 2235-6770; fax 2239-0191; e-mail ahiba@ahiba.hn; internet www.ahiba.hn; f. 1957; 21 mem. banks; Pres. ROQUE RIBERA RIVAS; Exec. Dir MARÍA LYDIA SOLANO.

Comisión Nacional de Bancos y Seguros (CNBS): Edif. Santa Fé, Col. Castaño Sur, Paseo Virgilio Zelaya Rubí, Bloque C, Apdo 20074, Tegucigalpa; tel. 2290-4500; fax 2237-6232; e-mail rbarahona@cnbs.gov.hn; internet www.cnbs.gov.hn; Dir JOSÉ ADONIS LAVAIRE.

STOCK EXCHANGE

Bolsa Centroamericana de Valores: Edif. Torre Alianza 2, 5°, Frente a Gasolinera Puma, Blvd San Juan Bosco, Col. Lomas del Guijarro Sur, Apdo 3885, Tegucigalpa; tel. 2271-0400; fax 2271-0403; internet www.bcv.hn; Pres. JOSÉ ARTURO ALVARADO.

INSURANCE

American Home Assurance Co (Chartis Honduras): Edif. Los Castaños, 4°, Blvd Morazán, Apdo 3220, Tegucigalpa; tel. 2202-8300; fax 2239-9169; e-mail honduras.sugerencias@aig.com; internet www.chartisinsurance.com; f. 1958; Gen. Man. JOSÉ EDGARDO FLORES RIVEIRO.

Ficohsa Seguros, SA: Edif. Plaza Victoria, Torre II, Col. Las Colinas, Blvd Francia, Tegucigalpa; tel. 2232-4747; fax 2232-2255; internet www.ficohsaseguros.com; f. 1957; fmrly Interamericana de Seguros, SA; part of Grupo Financiero Ficohsa; Pres. LEONEL GIANNINI; Gen. Man. LUIS ALBERTO ATALA FARAJ.

Mapfre Honduras, SA: Edif. El Planetario, 4°, Avda París, Col. Lomas del Guijarro Sur, Calle Madrid, Apdo 312, Tegucigalpa; tel. 2216-2672; fax 2216-2680; e-mail info@mapfre.com.hn; internet www.mapfre.com.hn; f. 1954; fmrly Aseguradora Hondureña, SA; Gen. Man. GERARDO CORRALES.

Pan American Life Insurance Co (PALIC): Edif. PALIC, Avda República de Chile 804, Col. Palmira, Apdo 123, Tegucigalpa; tel. 2216-0909; fax 2239-3437; e-mail servicioalclientehn@panamericanlife.com; internet www.palig.com/Regions/honduras; f. 1944; Pres. SALVADOR ORTEGA (Central America); CEO JOSÉ S. SUQUET.

Seguros Atlántida: Edif. Sonisa, Costado Este de Plaza Bancatlan, Tegucigalpa; tel. 2232-4014; fax 2232-3688; e-mail info@seatlan.com; internet www.segurosatlantida.com; f. 1985; Pres. ROBERT VINELLI; Gen. Man. JUAN MIGUEL ORELLANA.

Seguros Continental, SA: Edif. Continental, 4°, 3a Avda SO, 2a y 3a Calle, Apdo 605, San Pedro Sula; tel. 2550-0880; fax 2550-2750; e-mail seguros@continental.hn; internet www.seguros.continental.hn; f. 1968; Pres. JAIME ROLANDO ROSENTHAL OLIVA; Gen. Man. MARIO ROBERTO SOLÍS DACOSTA.

Seguros Crefisa: Edif. Banco Ficensa, 1°, Blvd Morazán, Apdo 3774, Tegucigalpa; tel. 2238-1750; fax 2238-1714; e-mail info@crefisa.com; internet www.crefisa.com; f. 1993; Gen. Man. MARIO BATRES PINEDA.

Seguros del País: Edif. IPM Anexo, 4°, Blvd Centroamérica, Tegucigalpa; tel. 2239-7077; fax 2232-4216; internet www.segpais.com; f. 2000; Pres. JUAN MIGUEL TORREBIARTE.

Insurance Association

Cámara Hondureña de Aseguradores (CAHDA): Edif. Casa Metromedia, 3°, Col. San Carlos, Apdo 3290, Tegucigalpa; tel. 2545-1212; fax 2221-5356; e-mail info@cahda.org; internet www.cahda.org; f. 1974; Pres. PEDRO BARQUERO; Gen. Man. TETHEY MARTINEZ.

Trade and Industry

GOVERNMENT AGENCY

Fondo Hondureño de Inversión Social (FHIS): Antiguo Edif. I.P.M., Col. Godoy, Comayagüela, Apdo 3581, Tegucigalpa; tel. 2234-5231; fax 2534-5255; e-mail dgarcia@fhis.hn; internet www.fhis.hn; social investment fund; Exec. Dir GUNTHER BUSTAMENTE.

DEVELOPMENT ORGANIZATIONS

Dirección Ejecutiva de Fomento a la Minería (DEFOMIN): Edif. DEFOMIN, 3°, Blvd Miraflores, Avda la FAO, Apdo 981, Tegucigalpa; tel. 2232-6721; fax 2232-6044; e-mail miguel.mejia@defomin.gob.hn; internet www.defomin.gob.hn; promotes the mining sector; Exec. Dir ALDO SANTOS.

Instituto Hondureño del Café (IHCAFE): Edif. El Faro, Col. Las Minitas, Apdo 40-C, Tegucigalpa; tel. 2237-3130; fax 2238-2368; e-mail gerencia@ihcafe.2hn.com; internet www.cafedehonduras.org; f. 1970; coffee devt programme; Pres. ASTERIO REYES; Gen. Man. VICTOR HUGO MOLINA.

Instituto Hondureño de Mercadeo Agrícola (IHMA): Apdo 727, Tegucigalpa; tel. 2235-3193; fax 2235-5719; e-mail yohanyleticia@yahoo.com; internet www.ihma.gob.hn; f. 1978; agricultural devt agency; Gen. Man. JOSÉ CARLOS ARÍSTIDES GIRÓN AYALA.

Instituto Nacional Agrario (INA): Col. La Almeda, 4a Avda, entre 10a y 11a Calles, No 1009, Apdo 3391, Tegucigalpa; tel. 2232-4893; fax 2232-7398; e-mail transparencia@ina.hn; internet www.ina.hn; agricultural devt programmes; Minister of the INA NEPTALÍ MEDINA AGURCIA.

Instituto Nacional de Conservación Forestal (INCF): Salida Carretera del Norte, Zona El Carrizal, Col. Brisas de Olancho, Comayagüela, Apdo 1378, Tegucigalpa; tel. 2223-8587; e-mail direccion@icf.gob.hn; internet www.icf.gob.hn; f. 2008 to replace Corporación Hondureña de Desarrollo Forestal (f. 1974);

control of the forestry industry and conservation of forest resources; Dir JOSÉ TRINIDAD SUAZO BULNES.

CHAMBERS OF COMMERCE

Cámara de Comercio e Industrias de Copán: Edif. Comercial Romero, 2°, Barrio Mercedes, Santa Rosa de Copán; tel. 2662-0843; fax 2662-1783; e-mail info@camaracopan.com; internet www.camaracopan.com; f. 1940; Pres. RAMÓN DE JESÚS FLORES.

Cámara de Comercio e Industrias de Cortés (CCIC): Barrio Las Brisas, 22 y 24 Calle, Apdo Postal 14, San Pedro Sula; tel. 2561-6100; fax 2566-0344; e-mail cie@ccichonduras.org; internet www.ccichonduras.org; f. 1931; Pres. EMÍN JORGE ABUFELE.

Cámara de Comercio e Industrias de Tegucigalpa (CCIT): Blvd Centroamérica, Apdo 3444, Tegucigalpa; tel. 2232-4200; fax 2232-5764; e-mail asuservicio@ccit.hn; internet www.ccit.hn; Pres. MIGUEL R. MOURRA; Exec. Dir MARIO BUSTILLO.

Cámara Hondureña de la Industria de la Construcción (Chico): Casa 2525, 2da Calle, entre 1era y 2da Avda, al par de Kinder Happy Faces, Col. Florencia Sur, Tegucigalpa; tel. 2239-2039; internet www.chicoorg.org; f. 1968; Pres. JOSÉ ALEJANDRO ALVAREZ ALVARADO; Gen. Man. SILVIO LARIOS BONES.

Federación de Cámaras de Comercio e Industrias de Honduras (FEDECAMARA): Edif. Castañito, 2°, 6a Avda, Col. Los Castaños, Apdo 3393, Tegucigalpa; tel. 2232-1870; fax 2232-6083; e-mail fedecamara.direccion@amnettgu.com; internet www.fedecamara.org; f. 1948; 1,200 mems; Pres. AMÍLCAR BULNES; Coordinator JUAN FERRERA LÓPEZ.

Fundación para la Inversión y Desarrollo de Exportaciones (FIDE) (Foundation for Investment and Development of Exports): Col. La Estancia, Plaza Marte, final del Blvd Morazán, Apdo 2029, Tegucigalpa; tel. 2221-6304; fax 2221-6316; e-mail vsierra@fidehonduras.com; internet www.hondurasinfo.hn; f. 1984; non-profit; Exec. Pres. VILMA SIERRA DE FONSECA.

Honduran American Chamber of Commerce (Amcham Honduras): Commercial Area Hotel Honduras Maya, POB 1838, Tegucigalpa; tel. 2232-6035; fax 2232-2031; e-mail amcham@amchanhonduras.org; internet www.amchamhonduras.org; f. 1981; Pres. JOSÉ EDUARDO ATALA; Exec. Dir ARACELY BATRES.

INDUSTRIAL AND TRADE ASSOCIATIONS

Asociación Hondureña de Maquiladores (AHM): Altia Business Park, 12°, Blvd Armenta, San Pedro Sula; tel. 2516-9100; internet www.ahm-honduras.com; f. 1991; non-profit asscn for the *maquila* industry; Pres. DANIEL FACUSSÉ.

Consejo Hondureño de la Empresa Privada (COHEP): Edif. 8, Calle Yoro, Col. Tepeyac, Apdo 3240, Tegucigalpa; tel. 2235-3336; fax 2235-3345; e-mail consejo@cohep.com; internet www.cohep.com; f. 1968; represents 52 private sector trade asscns; Pres. ALINE FLORES PAVÓN; Exec. Dir ARMANDO URTECHO.

Asociación Hondureña de Productores de Café (AHPROCAFE) (Coffee Producers' Association): Edif. AHPROCAFE, Avda La Paz, Apdo 959, Tegucigalpa; tel. 2236-8286; fax 2236-8310; e-mail ahprocafe@amnet.tgu.com; Pres. ASTERIO REYES.

Asociación Nacional de Acuicultores de Honduras (ANDAH) (Aquaculture Association of Honduras): Empacadora San Lorenzo, Puerto Viejo, contiguo a Banco de Occidente, San Lorenzo, Valle; tel. 2782-0986; fax 2782-3848; e-mail andah@hondutel.hn; f. 1986; 136 mems; Pres. MARCO POLO MICHELETTI.

Asociación Nacional de Exportadores de Honduras (ANEXHON) (National Association of Exporters): Industrias Panavisión, salida nueva a la Lima Frente a Sigmanet, San Pedro Sula; tel. 2553-3029; fax 2557-0203; e-mail roberto@ipsa.hn; comprises 104 private enterprises; Pres. ROBERTO PANAYOTTI.

Asociación Nacional de Industriales (ANDI) (National Association of Manufacturers): Torre Alliance, 10°, Col. Lomas del Guijarro Sur, Blvd San Juan Bosco, Apdo 3447, Tegucigalpa; tel. 2271-0084; fax 2271-0085; e-mail andi@andi.hn; internet www.andi.hn; f. 1958; Pres. ADOLFO FACUSSÉ; Exec. Dir FERNANDO GARCÍA MERINO.

Asociación de Productores de Azúcar de Honduras (APAH): Edif. Palmira, 5°, Módulo E y B, Tegucigalpa; tel. 2239-4933; fax 2239-4934; e-mail apah@cablecolor.hn; internet www.azucar.hn; Pres. CARLOS MELARA.

Federación Nacional de Agricultores y Ganaderos de Honduras (FENAGH) (Farmers' and Livestock Breeders' Association): Col. Miramontes, Avda Principal, 7a Calle 1557, Tegucigalpa; tel. 2239-1303; fax 2231-1392; e-mail jlizardo@fenagh.net; internet www.fenagh.net; f. 1978; Pres. LEOPOLDO DÚRAN; Exec. Dir JOSÉ LIZARDO REYES.

MAJOR COMPANIES

Azucarera La Grecia, SA de CV: Municipio de Marcovia, Dept de Choluteca, Apdo 32, Choluteca; tel. 2787-3201; fax 2887-3203; e-mail grecia_admon@lagrecia.hn; f. 1976 as Azucarera Central; processing and refining of sugar cane; acquired by Grupo Panataleón in 2008; Gen. Man. ENRIQUE PALLAIS.

Cementos del Norte, SA de CV (CENOSA): Río Bijao, Choloma, Apdo 132, Cortés; tel. 2669-1407; fax 2669-1411; internet www .cenosa.hn; f. 1958; cement producers; Pres. YANI ROSENTHAL HIDALGO; Gen. Man. EDWIN ARGUETA; 265 employees.

Cervecería Hondureña, SA: Blvd. del Norte, Carretera a Puerto Cortés, Apdo 86, San Pedro Sula; tel. 2553-3310; fax 2552-2845; e-mail centroinformacion@ca.sabmiller.com; internet www .cerveceriahondurena.com; f. 1915; brewery and soft drink mfrs; subsidiary of SABMiller PLC (United Kingdom); Pres. BOYCE LLOYD; 1,150 employees.

Compañía Azucarera Choluteca, SA de CV: Municipio de Marcovia, Zona de los Mangos, Apdo 15, Choluteca; tel. 2882-0530; fax 2882-0554; e-mail achsa@hondudata.hn; f. 1967; sugar cane refining; Gen. Man. BRAULIO MIGUEL CRUZ ASCENCIO; 180 employees.

Compañía Azucarera Hondureña, SA: 3 Avda 36, Municipio de Villanueva, Búfalo, Apdo 552, Cortés; tel. 2574-8092; fax 2574-8093; e-mail epadilla@cahsa.hn; internet www.cahsa.hn; f. 1938; cultivation and refining of sugar cane; Gen. Man. CHARLES HEYER; 560 employees.

Corporación Lady Lee: Centro Comercial Megaplaza 2km, Autopista al Aeropuerto, Apdo 948, San Pedro Sula; tel. 2545-1919; fax 2580-6161; e-mail info@corporacionladylee.com; internet www .ladylee.com; department stores; COO ELIAS EL HAYEK; Gen. Man. RAYMOND MAALOUF.

Droguería Pharma Internacional: Edif. Pharma Internacional, Col. Los Ángeles, antiguo local de Golds Gym, Tegucigalpa; tel. 2234-8989; fax 2234-9292; e-mail info@pharmainternacional.com; internet www.pharmainternacional.com; f. 1994; mfrs of pharmaceutical products; Gen. Man. AURELIO NEMBRINI.

Excel Automotriz: Blvd La Hacienda, Tegucigalpa; tel. 2208-4250; e-mail hflores@excelautomotriz.com; internet www .mitsubishihonduras.com; known as Autoexcel until 2010; part of the Grupo DIDEA; distributor of cars and car parts; Exec. Vice-Pres. (Group) CARLOS BOZA.

Gabriel Kafati, SA: Barrio La Bolsa, Comayagüela, POB 37, Tegucigalpa; tel. 2225-1675; fax 2225-3792; e-mail sales@ cafeelindio.com; internet www.cafeelindio.com; f. 1933; coffee producer; Gen. Man. MIGUEL OSCAR KAFATI.

Hilos y Mechas, SA de CV: Carretera a Puerto Cortés, Apdo 118, San Pedro Sula; tel. 2558-8141; fax 2558-8142; e-mail himesa@ himesa.hn; internet www.himesa.hn; f. 1953; mfrs of cotton fabrics, twine and thread; Gen. Man. EDUARDO HANDAL; 856 employees.

Lácteos de Honduras, SA de CV (LACTHOSA): Carretera a Puerto Cortés, Apdo 140, San Pedro Sula; tel. 2566-3828; fax 2566-3917; e-mail servicioalcliente@lacthosa.com; internet www.lacthosa .com; mfr of dairy products and fruit juices under the Sula brand; Gen. Man. SHUKRI KAFIE; 1,000 employees.

Leche y Derivados, SA (LEYDE): 8km Carretera salida Ceiba a Tela, Apdo 90, La Ceiba; tel. 2442-4152; fax 2442-4857; e-mail rrhh@ leyde.hn; internet www.leyde.hn; f. 1973; milk and dairy products; Pres. JOSEPH BONANNO; 1,200 employees.

Nyrstar El Mochito: Edif. Torre Alianza II, 7°, Local 701, Blvd San Juan Bosco, Col. Lomas del Guijarro Sur, Tegucigalpa; tel. 2271-0284; e-mail communications@nyrstar.com; internet www.nyrstar .com; f. 1948; Nyrstar (Belgium) is owner/operator of the zinc, lead and silver mine at El Mochito, Las Vegas; owned by Breakwater Resources (Canada) until 2011; Chair. JULIEN DE WILDE; CEO ROLAND JUNCK; 882 employees.

Químicas Handal de Centroamérica, SA de CV: Km 2.6 Autopista a Puerto Cortés, Choloma, Apdo 559, Cortés; tel. 2617-8700; fax 2565-2909; e-mail info@quimicashandal.com; internet www .quimicashandal.com; f. 1968; mfr of household and home care products; Gen. Man. FUAD HANDAL.

Seajoy Honduras: Empacadora Deli SA, Carretera a Orocuina, desvío a Linaca, Apdo 181/255, Choluteca; tel. 2782-0099; fax 2782-2579; e-mail ismael@seajoy.com; internet www.seajoy.com; f. 1985; seafood exporters; owned by Seajoy, Miami, FL, USA; Gen. Man. ISMAEL WONG C.

Tabacalera Hondureña, SA: Blvd del Sur, Zona El Cacao, Apdo 64, San Pedro Sula; tel. 2545-3200; fax 2545-3232; e-mail graco .paredes@bat.com; internet www.batcentralamerica.com; f. 1928; subsidiary of British-American Tobacco Ltd, United Kingdom; cigarette mfrs; 280 employees.

Unilever de Centroamérica, Operación Honduras: Tegucigalpa; internet www.unilever-ancam.com; f. 2000 after Unilever bought Corporación Cressida; mfrs of detergents, soaps, fats and vegetable oils; subsidiary of Unilever (United Kingdom/Netherlands); CEO PAUL POLMAN; Gen. Man. OTTO PINEDA; 600 employees.

UTILITIES

Electricity

Empresa Nacional de Energía Eléctrica (ENEE) (National Electrical Energy Co): Edif. EMAS, 4°, Bo El Trapiche, Tegucigalpa; tel. 2235-2934; fax 2235-2969; e-mail informatica@enee.hn; internet www.enee.hn; f. 1957; state-owned electricity co; Pres. RIGOBERTO CUELLAR; Man. EMIL HAWIT.

Luz y Fuerza de San Lorenzo, SA (LUFUSSA): Edif. Comercial Los Próceres, Final Avda Los Próceres 3917, Tegucigalpa; tel. 2236-6545; fax 2236-5826; e-mail lufussa@lufussa.com; internet www .lufussa.com; f. 1994; generates thermoelectric power; Pres. EDUARDO KAFIE.

TRADE UNIONS

Central General de Trabajadores de Honduras (CGTH) (General Confederation of Labour of Honduras): Barrio La Granja, antiguo Local CONADI, Apdo 1236, Comayagüela, Tegucigalpa; tel. 2239-7383; fax 2225-2525; e-mail cgt@123.hn; f. 1970; legally recognized from 1982; attached to Partido Demócrata Cristiano de Honduras; Sec.-Gen. DANIEL A. DURÓN; 250,000 mems (2011).

> **Federación Auténtica Sindical de Honduras (FASH):** Barrio La Granja, antiguo Local CONADI, Apdo 1236, Comayagüela, Tegucigalpa; tel. 2225-2509; Sec.-Gen. HUMBERTO LARA.

> **Federación Sindical del Sur (FESISUR):** Barrio La Ceiba, 1 c. al norte del Instituto Santa María Goretti, Apdo 256, Choluteca; tel. 2882-0328; Pres. ALFONSO DE MONTOYA FLORES.

> **Unión Nacional de Campesinos (UNC)** (National Union of Farmworkers): antiguo Local CONADI, Barrio La Granja, Comayagüela, Tegucigalpa; tel. 2225-1005; Sec.-Gen. MARCIAL REYES CABALLERO.

Confederación Hondureña de Cooperativas (CHC): Edif. I.F.C., 3001 Blvd Morazán, Apdo 3265, Tegucigalpa; tel. 2232-2890; fax 2231-1024; f. 1971; Pres. JOSÉ FRANCISCO ORDÓÑEZ.

Confederación de Trabajadores de Honduras (CTH) (Workers' Confederation of Honduras): Edif. Beige, 2°, Avda Juan Ramón Molina, Barrio El Olvido, Apdo 720, Tegucigalpa; tel. 2220-1757; fax 2237-8575; e-mail organizacioncth@yahoo.es; f. 1964; Sec.-Gen. JOSÉ HILARIO ESPINOZA; 55,000 mems (2007).

> **Asociación Nacional de Campesinos Hondureños (ANACH)** (National Association of Honduran Farmworkers): Edif. Chávez Mejía, 2°, Calle Juan Ramón Molina, Barrio El Olvido, Tegucigalpa; tel. 2238-0558; f. 1962; Pres. RAMÓN NAVARRO; 80,000 mems.

> **Federación Central de Sindicatos de Trabajadores Libres de Honduras (FECESITLIH)** (Honduran Federation of Free Trade Unions): antiguo Edif. EUKZKADI, 3a Avda, 3a y 4a Calle No 336, Comayagüela, Tegucigalpa; tel. 2237-3955; Pres. HILARIO ESPINOZA.

> **Federación Sindical de Trabajadores Nacionales de Honduras (FESITRANH)** (Honduran Federation of Farmworkers): 10a Avda, 11a Calle, Barrio Los Andes, Apdo 245, Cortés, San Pedro Sula; tel. 2557-2539; f. 1957; Sec.-Gen. JOSÉ DOLORES VALENZUELA.

> **Sindicato Nacional de Motoristas de Equipo Pesado de Honduras (SINAMEQUIPH)** (National Union of HGV Drivers): Avda Juan Ramón Molina, Barrio El Olvido, Tegucigalpa; tel. 2237-4415; Pres. ERASMO FLORES.

Confederación Unitaria de Trabajadores de Honduras (CUTH): Barrio Bella Vista, 10a Calle, 8a y 9a Avda, Casa 829, Tegucigalpa; tel. and fax 2220-4732; e-mail sgeneral@cuth.hn; f. 1992; Sec.-Gen. JOSÉ LUIS BAQUEDANO; 295,000 mems (2011).

> **Asociación Nacional de Empleados Públicos de Honduras (ANDEPH)** (National Association of Public Employees of Honduras): Barrio Los Dolores, Avda Paulino Valladares, frente Panadería Italiana, atrás Iglesia Los Dolores, Tegucigalpa; tel. 2237-4393; Pres. DULCE MARÍA ZAVALA.

> **Federación Unitaria de Trabajadores de Honduras (FUTH):** Barrio La Granja, contiguo Banco Atlántida, Casa 3047, frente a mercadito La Granja, Apdo 1663, Comayagüela, Tegucigalpa; tel. 2225-1010; f. 1981; Pres. JUAN ALBERTO BARAHONA MEJÍA; 45,000 mems.

Federación de Cooperativas de la Reforma Agraria de Honduras (FECORAH): Casa 2223, antiguo Local de COAPALMA, Col. Rubén Darío, Tegucigalpa; tel. 2232-0547; fax 2225-2525; f. 1970; legally recognized 1974; Pres. ELÍAS VILLALTA.

Federación de Organizaciones Magisteriales (FOMH): Tegucigalpa; teachers' union; Sec.-Gen. EDWIN OLIVA.

Transport

RAILWAYS

The railway network is confined to the north of the country and most lines are used for fruit cargo. There are 995 km of railway track in Honduras, of which 349 km are narrow gauge. In 2010 the Government allocated 15m. lempiras to revive three railway routes serving San Pedro Sula, Choloma, Villanueva and Puerto Cortés. There are plans to restructure the train stations and coaches, as well as to set up additional railway routes to serve banana plantations.

Ferrocarril Nacional de Honduras (National Railway of Honduras): 1a Avda entre 1a y 2a Calle, Apdo 496, San Pedro Sula; tel. and fax 2552-8001; f. 1870; govt-owned; Gen. Man. LESTER AGUILAR.

ROADS

According to Fondo Vial de Honduras, in 2011 there were an estimated 14,044 km of roads in Honduras, of which only 21.2% were paved. A further 3,156 km of roads have been constructed by the Fondo Cafetero Nacional, and some routes have been built by the Corporación Hondureña de Desarrollo Forestal to facilitate access to coffee plantations and forestry development areas. In 2010 the Inter-American Development Bank (IDB) approved a US $30m. loan for a rapid bus transit system in Tegucigalpa. The IDB approved a further $17m. loan in 2013 to improve the main highway.

Dirección General de Carreteras: Barrio La Bolsa, Comayagüela, Tegucigalpa; tel. 2225-1703; fax 2225-2469; e-mail dgc@soptravi.gob.hn; internet www.soptravi.gob.hn/Carreteras; f. 1915; highways board; Dir WALTER MALDONADO.

SHIPPING

The principal port is Puerto Cortés on the Caribbean coast, which is the largest and best-equipped port in Central America. Other ports include Tela, La Ceiba, Trujillo/Castilla, Roatán, Amapala and San Lorenzo; all are operated by the Empresa Nacional Portuaria. There are several minor shipping companies. A number of foreign shipping lines call at Honduran ports. In December 2013 the flag registered fleet comprised 664 vessels, totalling 755,065 grt, of which three were gas tankers and 294 were general cargo ships.

Empresa Nacional Portuaria (National Port Authority): Apdo 18, Puerto Cortés; tel. 665-0987; fax 665-1402; e-mail gerencia@enp.hn; internet www.enp.hn; f. 1965; has jurisdiction over all ports in Honduras; a network of paved roads connects Puerto Cortés and San Lorenzo with the main cities of Honduras, and with the principal cities of Central America; Gen. Man. JOSÉ DARÍO GÁMEZ PANCHAMÉ.

CIVIL AVIATION

Local airlines in Honduras compensate for the deficiencies of road and rail transport, linking together small towns and inaccessible districts. There are four international airports: Golosón airport in La Ceiba, Ramón Villeda Morales airport in San Pedro Sula, Toncontín airport in Tegucigalpa and Juan Manuel Gálvaz airport in Roatán. A new airport at Río Amarillo, Copán, near the Copán Ruinas archaeological park, commenced operations in 2011.

Dirección General Aeronáutica Civil: Apdo 30145, Tegucigalpa; tel. 2234-0263; fax 2233-0258; e-mail contactos@dgachn.org; internet www.dgachn.org; airport infrastructure and security; Dir-Gen. MANUEL ENRIQUE CÁCERES.

Isleña Airlines: Edif. Taragon, 2°, Avda Circunvalacion, San Pedro Sula; tel. 2552-9910; fax 2552-9964; e-mail info.islena@taca.com; internet www.flyislena.com; subsidiary of TACA, El Salvador; domestic service and service to the Cayman Islands; Pres. and CEO ARTURO ALVARADO WOOD.

Tourism

Tourists are attracted by the Mayan ruins, the fishing and boating facilities in Trujillo Bay and Lake Yojoa, near San Pedro Sula, and the beaches on the northern coast. According to provisional figures, Honduras received 943,000 tourists in 2013, when tourism receipts (excluding passenger transport) totalled US $711m.

Asociación Hotelera y Afines de Honduras (AHAH): Hotel Escuela Madrid, Suite 402, Col. 21 de Octubre-Los Girasoles, Tegucigalpa; tel. 2221-5805; fax 2221-4789; e-mail asociacionhotelerahn@yahoo.com; Pres. LUZ MEJÍA AMADOR; Exec. Dir NORMA MENDOZA.

Asociación Nacional de Agencias de Viajes y Turismo de Honduras: Blvd Morazán, frente a McDonald's, Tegucigalpa; tel. 2232-2308; e-mail scarlethmoncada@yahoo.com; Pres. SCARLETH DE MONCADA.

Asociación de Operadores de Turismo Receptivo de Honduras (OPTURH): Col. San Carlos, Avda Ramon E. Cruz, Tegucigalpa; tel. 2236-9704; e-mail secretaria@opturh.com; internet www.opturh.com; f. 1996; Pres. ROBERTO BANDES.

Cámara Nacional de Turismo de Honduras: Calle Paris, Avda Niza, Casa 1233, Col. Lomas del Guijarro Sur, Tegucigalpa; tel. 2232-1937; fax 2235-8355; e-mail canaturh@canaturh.org; internet www.canaturh.org; f. 1976; Pres. EPAMINONDAS MARINAKYS.

Instituto Hondureño de Turismo: Edif. Europa, 5°, Col. San Carlos, Apdo 3261, Tegucigalpa; tel. and fax 2222-2124; e-mail tourisminfo@iht.hn; internet www.iht.hn; f. 1972; Exec. Vice-Pres. SYNTIA BENNETT SALOMON; Sec.-Gen. MÓNICA HÍDALGO.

Defence

Military service is voluntary. Active service lasts eight months, with subsequent reserve training. As assessed at November 2013, the armed forces numbered 12,000: army 8,300, navy 1,400 and air force some 2,300. Paramilitary public security and defence forces numbered 8,000. There were also 60,000 joint reserves. In addition, some 360 US troops were based in Honduras.

Defence Budget: 3,650m. lempiras (US $177m.) in 2013.

Chairman of the Joint Chiefs of Staff: Gen. FREDY SANTIAGO DÍAZ ZELAYA.

Commander-General of the Army: Col FRANCISCO ISAÍAS ALVAREZ URBINA.

Commander-General of the Air Force: Col JORGE ALBERTO FERNÁNDEZ LÓPEZ.

Commander-General of the Navy: Capt. HÉCTOR ORLANDO CABALLERO ESPINOZA.

Education

Primary education, beginning at six years of age and comprising three cycles of three years, is officially compulsory and is provided free of charge. Secondary education, which is not compulsory, begins at the age of 15 and lasts for three years. In 2012 enrolment at primary schools included 94% of children in the relevant age-group, while enrolment at secondary schools in 2012 was equivalent to 73% of children (66% of boys; 80% of girls) in the appropriate age-group. There are three universities, including the Autonomous National University in Tegucigalpa. Estimated spending on education in 2012 was 23,000m. lempiras, representing 15.9% of the total budget.

Bibliography

For works on Central America generally, see Select Bibliography (Books)

Bradshaw, S., and Linneker, B. *Challenging Women's Poverty: Perspectives on Gender and Poverty Reduction Strategies from Nicaragua and Honduras (CIIR Briefing)*. London, Catholic Institute for International Relations, 2004.

Caceres di Iorio, M. *The Good Coup: The Overthrow of Manuel Zelaya in Honduras*. British Columbia, CCB Publishing, 2010.

Chambers, G. A. *Race, Nation and West Indian Immigration to Honduras, 1890–1940*. Baton Rouge, LA, Louisiana State University Press, 2010.

Euraque, D. A. *Reinterpreting the Banana Republic: Region and State in Honduras, 1870–1972*. Chapel Hill, NC, University of North Carolina Press, 1996.

Gutiérrez Rivera, L. *Territories of Violence: State, Marginal Youth, and Public Security in Honduras*. New York, Palgrave Macmillan, 2013.

Leonard, T. M. *The History of Honduras*. London, Greenwood Press, 2011.

Loker, W. M. *Changing Places: Environment, Development and Social Change in Rural Honduras*. Durham, NC, Carolina Academic Press, 2004.

Reformas económicas, régimen cambiario y choques externos: efectos en el desarrollo económico, la desigualdad y la pobreza en Costa Rica, El Salvador y Honduras (Estudios y Perspectivas). New York, United Nations Educational, 2005.

Soluri, J. *Banana Cultures: Agriculture, Consumption, and Environmental Change in Honduras and the United States*. Austin, TX, University of Texas Press, 2006.

Tucker, C. M. *Changing Forests: Collective Action, Common Property, and Coffee in Honduras*. 2nd edn, Bloomington, IN, Springer, 2010.

USA Ibp. *Honduras Foreign Policy and Government Guide*. Milton Keynes, Lightning Source UK Ltd, 2003.

Honduras Customs, Trade Regulations and Procedures Handbook. Milton Keynes, Lightning Source UK Ltd, 2005.

JAMAICA

Geography

PHYSICAL FEATURES

Jamaica is in the Caribbean Sea, about 145 km (90 miles) south of eastern Cuba and 160 km west of south-western Haiti. The small, uninhabited US island of Navassa falls midway between Jamaica and Haiti, and the Cayman Islands, a British dependency, lies 290 km (180 miles) to the north-west. Jamaica lies between two of the main sea lanes to Panama, the Cayman Trench to the north and the Jamaica Channel to the east. Jamaica has an area of 10,991 sq km (4,244 sq miles), contained within 1,022 km of coastline and including 160 sq km of inland waters.

Jamaica is the third largest island of the Greater Antilles (after Cuba and Hispaniola), being 235 km from east to west and 82 km from north to south at its widest. The length of the island is dominated by ranges of mountains, reaching their height at Blue Mountain Peak (2,256 m or 7,404 ft) in the east, but falling away in the west. The mountains stretch north and south in a series of spurs and gullies, and the heights are luxuriantly forested. The terrain is, therefore, mainly mountainous, relieved only by narrow and discontinuous coastal plains. The soil is fertile and, although cultivation has made an impact, there are still vast tracts of native vegetation—for instance, some 3,000 species of flowering plant (827 of which are endemic) and 550 varieties of fern. There are several species of reptile (including the crocodile, the Jamaican iguana, which was thought to be extinct until 1990, and five types of snake, all harmless and rare, such as the yellow snake or Jamaican boa) and few large mammals (the mongoose, an introduced pest, wild boar in the mountains and the endangered hutia or coney, as well as the Pedro seal and a small number of sea cows or manatees). Life in the air is obviously more adaptable on Jamaica, with at least 25 species of bat (including a fish-eating one) and many butterflies and birds. There are a number of indigenous creatures, such as the extremely rare Jamaican butterfly (a black-and-yellow swallowtail, the largest butterfly of the Americas and the second largest in the world), the red-billed streamertail hummingbird or doctor bird (the national bird) and some parrots.

CLIMATE

The climate is subtropical, hot and humid on the coast, particularly, but more temperate inland, mainly owing to elevation. The average, annual temperature on the coast is 27°C (81°F). The thermometer can sometimes reach readings of 32°C (90°F) in the height of summer (July–August), but never falls below 20°C (68°F). However, in the mountains winter temperatures can fall as low as 7°C (45°F). The hurricane season is July–November and the rainy season October–November, although rain need not be uncommon from May onwards (average annual rainfall is 78 inches or 1,980 mm) and is more copious in the mountains.

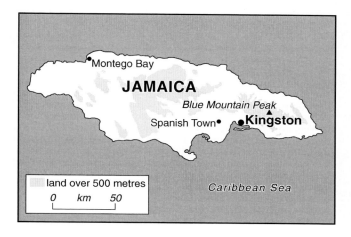

POPULATION

The population is mostly black, 91% being of African descent. The original settlers from Europe, who displaced the Taino Amerindians, were soon outnumbered by the slaves they brought in as agricultural labour, whose descendants are now Jamaica's dominant ethnic group. The vast majority of these slaves were brought in by the British, the main colonial power, but some earlier groups joined the original Spanish settlers in resisting the British occupation of the island. Some of their descendants still maintain a distinct identity in the west. British institutions and culture have, therefore, been influenced by other traditions, notably West African. English is the official language, but an English patois is generally spoken (using many Ashanti words) and, while most people are Christian, there are influences of other traditions in religion too. Protestant denominations have the largest number of followers (the Church of God claims 24% of the total population, Adventists 11% and Pentecostalists 10%), but there are also Anglicans, Roman Catholics and Ethiopian Orthodox adherents, and 35% of people profess other religions (apart from some Jews, Muslims and followers of various Asian belief systems, these are mainly spiritualist cults or the indigenous Rastafarian religion, a pan-Africanist movement). Some adaptations of Christianity, such as Pocomania and Revival, are also found.

UN estimates for mid-2014 put the total population of Jamaica at 2.8m., but there are far more people of Jamaican descent living abroad. About 0.6m. people live in the capital, Kingston, which is found at the eastern end of the southern coast. The second city is Montego Bay, right across the island, in the north-west. For administrative purposes, Jamaica is divided into 14 parishes.

History

MARK WILSON

Based on an earlier article by CHARLES ARTHUR

Prior to the arrival of Christopher Columbus in 1494, the island now known as Jamaica was inhabited by the indigenous Amerindians, who lived in simple communities based on fishing, hunting, and the small-scale cultivation of cassava and other crops. They called the island Xaymaca, meaning 'land of wood and springs'. The Spanish began colonizing in 1510, and within 70 years the effects of new diseases, warfare, and enslavement had decimated the Arawak population. Although the Spanish brought the first African slaves to Jamaica in 1517 and tried to build up a sugar and cotton plantation economy, the colony remained underpopulated and undeveloped. For nearly 150 years, its main importance was as a stopping point for galleons travelling to and from the more prosperous Spanish colonies on the Latin American mainland. In 1655 an English naval force sent by Oliver Cromwell seized the island. Cromwell increased the island's 3,000-strong white population by transporting indentured servants and prisoners captured in battles with the Irish and Scots, as well as some common criminals, to the territory. Great Britain gained formal possession of Jamaica in 1670, and the introduction of large numbers of African slaves over the following two centuries transformed the colony. At the beginning of the 18th century, the slave population stood at approximately 45,000, but, as the sugar plantation economy boomed, their number rose dramatically, and by 1800 had increased to in excess of 300,000. Over the years escaped slaves—known as Maroons—established communities in remote areas of the interior, and, for several decades during the 18th century, Maroon fighters inflicted heavy casualties on the British troops and local militia despatched to attack them, winning an autonomy from the colonial Government, which the community of Accompong retains to this day.

With the abolition of the slave trade in 1808, followed by that of slavery itself in 1834, the island's slave-based economy faltered. Immigrants from Europe and indentured servants from Africa and Asia were introduced in an attempt to bolster a dwindling plantation labour force, but these were far fewer than in Trinidad or Guyana. Then, in 1846, Jamaican planters, still reeling from the loss of slave labour, suffered a further crushing blow when the United Kingdom adopted legislation eliminating the tariff advantage previously given to its Caribbean colonies. The once immensely rich planter class saw its livelihood undercut by producers in Brazil and Cuba. In 1865 racial and political tensions erupted with the Morant Bay Rebellion, a peasant uprising over land rights. Although the rebellion was violently suppressed, the ensuing instability prompted the British Government to impose direct rule, with a temporary end to the island's assembly, elected on a limited franchise of propertied voters. As a Crown Colony, although elections for nine members of the executive council were restored from 1883, the island's white and mixed-race propertied class continued to hold dominant positions in every societal domain, while the vast majority of the black population remained poor and disenfranchised. Between the world wars the established élite and an emerging middle class grew increasingly dissatisfied with Crown Colony rule, and began to agitate for self-government.

At the same time, in the wake of the worldwide economic depression that began in 1929, economic and political tensions deepened. In 1938 a sugar workers' strike led to serious social unrest. During this period the two political parties that came to dominate Jamaica's modern political scene were formed. In September 1938 Norman Manley founded the People's National Party (PNP), based on the support of members of the mixed-race middle class and the liberal sector of the business community. The PNP reacted to the 1938 riots by trying to organize workers both in urban areas and in banana-growing rural parishes. In 1942 Manley's cousin, Alexander Bustamante, the founder of the first major Jamaican trade union—that had since evolved into the Bustamante Industrial Trade Union (BITU)—established a rival party, the Jamaica Labour Party (JLP). Although both parties sought the support of the general populace, and both advocated independence from the United Kingdom, there were significant differences between them. The JLP was supported by conservative businessmen and BITU members, mainly dock and sugar plantation workers and other unskilled urban labourers, and over time adopted a strong anti-communist, pro-USA position. By contrast, Manley's PNP embraced the social democratic model espoused by many Western European politicians. Although the PNP developed close links with the National Workers' Union that formed in the 1950s, it was less focused on union organizing and more interested in access to control over state power and political rights.

In 1944 a new Constitution, inaugurating limited self-government (based on the Westminster model) and universal adult suffrage, was introduced. The JLP, promising to create jobs and distribute public funds, won the 1944 elections and in the following year Bustamante took office as Jamaica's first premier. During the late 1940s and early 1950s the JLP and PNP vied for the uncommitted votes. The JLP narrowly won the general election in 1949, while the PNP won the 1955 election, having abandoned most of its socialist rhetoric. Moves towards independence gathered pace, with the British promoting the idea of a West Indian federation. Manley backed this proposal, believing it would expedite the achievement of independence, whereas Bustamante doubted the benefit for Jamaica of merging with many smaller and (at that time) poorer island states. In 1958 Jamaica joined nine other British territories in the West Indies Federation. Although the union was not popular with the Jamaican public, Manley won a second term as premier when the PNP secured a decisive victory in the general election of 1959. Bustamante continued to demand Jamaica's withdrawal from the Federation; a referendum on the issue was held in 1961, when 54% of the electorate voted to withdraw. Jamaica subsequently left the Federation, which collapsed in 1962 when Trinidad and Tobago also seceded. The JLP narrowly won the election of early 1962, and Bustamante assumed the premiership. Jamaica's transition to independence was formalized on 6 August 1962, although it retained its membership of the Commonwealth and the British monarch as head of state.

Bustamante retired from politics in 1964; his successor, Donald Sangster, led the JLP to a further narrow victory in the 1967 election. Political violence had already emerged at this early stage in Jamaica's independent history, with a state of emergency imposed in western areas of the capital, Kingston, in 1966. Sangster died two months later, and was replaced by Hugh Shearer, the leader of the BITU. The Shearer Government was beset by allegations of corruption and mismanagement, and its conservative positions and policies generated a growing discontent. Following the death of Norman Manley in 1969, his son Michael took over as leader of the PNP; with new leadership, the party built support among the disenchanted middle class, but also placed renewed emphasis on the PNP's socialist roots. Under the eloquent and charismatic Michael Manley, the PNP triumphed in the 1972 election. The victory owed something to Manley's courting of the Rastafarian and youth vote through frequent reference to the revered black nationalist leader Marcus Garvey. Rastafarianism, a 'return to Africa' religious current, had grown in popularity since its foundation in the 1940s.

Michael Manley's PNP Government set out to honour campaign pledges to protect the weaker sections of the population and promote the welfare of those on low incomes. It also attempted to increase the ability of the state to intervene in the economy, and tried to reduce the influence exerted by foreign and local capital. In 1974 the Government imposed a bauxite levy in an effort to extract a better deal from the foreign mining companies operating in Jamaica. However, these initiatives foundered in the unfavourable context of an international economic recession, and, as foreign investment declined, unemployment increased. Another important feature of Manley's move to the left was a new alignment with non-capitalist countries, and a particular emphasis on closer relations with Cuba.

Despite the Government's economic problems, the PNP won the 1976 election. Although it had lost much support among the upper and middle classes, the PNP increased its share of the votes cast by manual labourers and the unemployed. With the voting age for this election reduced from 21 to 18, the PNP also benefited from the youth vote. During Manley's second term he guided the party further to the left, appointing a number of leading left-wingers to cabinet positions, and forging close relations with the new communist Workers Party of Jamaica (WPJ). These developments caused serious rifts in diplomatic relations with the USA. In 1978 a balance of payments crisis obliged the Government to appeal to the IMF for financial assistance. Loans were conditional upon the Government reducing public spending and social service provisions. By the end of the 1970s economic problems, particularly growing unemployment, had begun to damage the PNP Government's popularity.

During the 1970s the rivalry between the two main parties grew increasingly bitter, and in the slum districts of Kingston gunmen acting in the name of the political parties fought for control of territory; a state of emergency was imposed prior to the 1976 election, and maintained during the succeeding years. In 1978, against a backdrop of politically motivated gang warfare, the reggae music icon Bob Marley staged a reconciliation concert in Kingston; however, the violence continued to intensify.

New elections in 1980 took place in the context of a foreign exchange crisis that translated into shortages in shops and industry. The JLP—now under the leadership of Edward Seaga—had moved away from its union-based origins and enjoyed strong support in the business community. Under Seaga the JLP took a pro-USA, pro-free enterprise line, portraying the PNP Government as inept in terms of its administration of the economy and dangerously close to communist Cuba. An extremely violent election campaign, in a year when the total number of murders reached close to 900, then an all-time high, ended with a landslide victory for the JLP.

Under Seaga, the new JLP Government announced a complete reversal of the country's economic policy, espousing the virtues of the free market, emphasizing the role of the private sector and encouraging foreign investment. A major realignment in foreign policy was also effected, involving the severing of relations with Cuba and the forging of close ties with the US Administration of President Ronald Reagan (1981–89). In October 1983 Jamaican forces participated in the US-led invasion to overthrow the left-wing Government in Grenada. Seaga took advantage of the initiative's popularity to hold an early election. The PNP, unable to nominate candidates within the four days allowed, boycotted the ballot, and, as a result, the JLP won all 60 seats in the House of Representatives. Despite enjoying complete control of the legislature and substantial financial support from the USA and the IMF, the JLP Government struggled to revive the economy: progress was further hindered by a recession in the USA, and the application of austerity measures, demanded by the IMF and the World Bank, failed to produce the expected improvements. The sale of many state-owned enterprises contributed to a rising rate of unemployment, while the removal of price controls on basic food items caused considerable hardship for the poor. In the general election of February 1989 the opposition PNP soundly defeated the JLP, winning 45 of the 60 seats in the House of Representatives.

Following his defeat in 1980, Manley had sought to moderate the PNP's political image. On returning to power in 1989, Manley cultivated cordial relations with the USA, and honoured existing agreements with the IMF. His Government instituted a number of neo-liberal economic reforms in return for further loans from international financial institutions; however, these measures failed to revitalize the economy. In 1992 deteriorating health obliged Manley to step down as Prime Minister, and his deputy, P. J. Patterson, was appointed as his successor. Under Patterson, the economy showed some signs of recovery, and in March 1993 he called an early election. The result was an easy victory for the PNP. A second defeat for the JLP generated increased internal criticism of Seaga's leadership, and in 1995 the former JLP chairman, Bruce Golding, resigned to form a new centre-right party, the National Democratic Movement. The split in the JLP helped the PNP to return to power for an unprecedented third consecutive term following an election in December 1997.

The country continued to confront economic and social difficulties throughout the remainder of the decade. There were violent protests in response to a 30% increase in fuel prices in April 1999, and in July of that year the army patrolled the streets of Kingston following a significant increase in crime. Industrial output continued to dwindle and the Government borrowed heavily, but the continuing growth of the tourism industry, particularly in northern coastal towns such as Ocho Rios and Montego Bay, provided some respite.

In legislative elections in October 2002 the PNP recorded yet another victory, taking 34 of the 60 seats. The PNP's success was facilitated by several years of economic growth, and by the public's continued lack of confidence in the JLP. The efforts of civil society organizations and the presence of international observers helped to reduce the violence that had plagued earlier elections, but the process was marred by a low turnout.

During its fourth consecutive term in office, the PNP Government confronted considerable economic difficulties, and struggled to cope with an increase in violent crime. Divisions among the JLP leadership impeded the party's attempts to capitalize on growing public dissatisfaction with the Government's performance. Edward Seaga finally stepped down at the end of 2004, and was replaced by Bruce Golding, who had rejoined the party in 2001. There was also a change of leadership for the PNP, when Patterson retired in 2005; Portia Simpson Miller assumed command of the PNP. Simpson Miller, a veteran politician with strong grass-roots appeal, became Jamaica's first female Prime Minister in March 2006.

On entering office Prime Minister Simpson Miller confronted heightened expectations from the electorate, but her Government was restricted in its ability to fund social programmes as a result of large-scale debts accumulated over previous years, and efforts to expedite economic growth faltered. The JLP rallied support in advance of a general election in August 2007 with a focus on boosting the island's economy, tackling national debt, and fighting crime and corruption. The election campaign was marked by violent incidents, and political tensions mounted when the planned voting date was postponed for a week after Hurricane Dean ravaged the island. Turnout was low, with some 60.5% of the registered electorate participating in the ballot: this partly was due to the chaos and damage caused by Hurricane Dean and concerns about another hurricane. The result was extremely close; after recounts the JLP, which secured 32 seats compared with the PNP's 28, emerged victorious. The result brought an end to 18 years of PNP government.

The new Prime Minister, Bruce Golding, confronted immediate difficulties caused by rising international oil and food prices. Another cloud over the incoming Government was the court challenge against four JLP members of Parliament accused of holding dual nationality. Court rulings forced two of the members affected to contest by-elections in 2009; both held their seats with increased margins, to the discomfort of the PNP. Corruption allegations damaged the governing JLP, however; the junior transport minister, Joseph Hibbert, resigned in July 2009 after allegations that he had, while a civil servant in the 1990s, received bribes from a British bridge construction company. James Robertson, the Minister of Energy and Mining, resigned in May 2011 after his US visa was revoked, a move which he attributed to allegations in a Florida court (vigorously denied by Robertson) that he was linked to criminal activities.

In August 2009 the USA requested the extradition of Christopher 'Dudus' Coke, the alleged leader of a large and powerful gang based in the Kingston slum district of Tivoli Gardens. Although Jamaica usually responded promptly to extradition requests, there were delays in this case, and an arrest warrant was not issued until May 2010, by which time Coke was preparing to barricade his Tivoli stronghold. After attacks on six police stations by supporters of Coke in late May the Government declared a state of emergency, and an estimated 2,000 soldiers and police officers moved into Tivoli Gardens, in the event meeting little resistance. At least 73 residents were killed before or during the operation, as well as three members of the security forces. Coke surrendered to police in late June and was extradited to New York; in June 2012 he was sentenced to 23 years in prison. During the clashes over 4,000 people were detained, and 16 were charged with serious offences; the PNP Government (see below) in May 2013 announced a commission of inquiry into the Tivoli incursion and associated events. The Government in 2014 also appointed a commission of inquiry into allegations that there had been a large number of extra-judicial killings during the incursion; in July, it was still to begin work. Partly because of the defeat of the Tivoli Gardens gang and its associates, the number of murders was reduced to 1,124 in 2011, the first full year after the confrontation, or one-third fewer than in 2009, and was reduced again to 1,083 in 2012. With renewed gang warfare, there were 1,198 homicides in 2013; the murder rate of 44 per 100,000 persons was again the highest in the English-speaking Caribbean. According to UN statistics for 2012, it was then the sixth highest in the world.

There was continuing criticism of Golding for his delay in moving against Coke, which may have played a factor in his unexpected decision in September 2011 to stand down as Prime Minister. He was succeeded by the Minister of Education, Andrew Holness, at 39 the youngest of the alternative candidates. Holness called an early election for 29 December, one year ahead of the constitutional deadline, in order to secure an independent mandate. The PNP ran a strong campaign, in which Simpson Miller surprised many observers by promising, if elected, a review of the island's antiquated laws against homosexuality. The PNP took 42 of the 63 seats with just 53.4% of the popular vote. At 52.8%, the turnout appeared to be low; however, this represented increased voter registration, and the number of votes cast was 5.9% greater than in 2007. Simpson Miller chose her long-standing party rival Peter Phillips to be Minister of Finance and Planning in her new Government. Phillips had been responsible for the equally challenging portfolio of national security in her previous administration.

The PNP consolidated its power in local elections in March 2012, in which the party took control of 13 of the 14 local authorities. The Cabinet proposed in June of that year to decriminalize the possession of up to two ounces of marijuana; this appeared to receive broad support. However, reform of Jamaica's 'anti-buggery' law remained an extremely remote possibility, in spite of the PNP campaign promise for a review, with a homophobic campaign in the media in May and June 2014 leading to a mass anti-homosexual rally in Kingston on 29 June, whose organisers claimed attendance of 25,000.

Since the beginning of the 21st century a variety of initiatives have been implemented to address the problem of crime and curtail its disruptive impact on daily life for the majority of Jamaicans, as well as on investor confidence, the development of tourism and the country's image abroad, with costs on some estimates equivalent to 5% of gross domestic product. The British Government was at the forefront of international efforts to enhance the strength and capacity of the local police, the Jamaica Constabulary Force, in order that it might more effectively combat the illegal drugs-trafficking business and related gang feuds in the deprived inner city areas of Kingston, Spanish Town and elsewhere, while the USA has provided significant assistance, most recently through the Caribbean

Basin Security Initiative, which was established in September 2010. Neighbourhood gangs were also involved in extortion and financial scams; many had links to the two main political parties, particularly in the inner-city 'garrison constituencies', originating in some cases from the time of the bitter inter-party conflicts of the 1970s. At the same time, Jamaica was a hub for Caribbean cocaine transshipment towards the United Kingdom and North America, with close links between local and overseas drugs gangs, and a lively 'guns for drugs' trade with Haiti. The island also remained a fairly important producer and exporter of marijuana. There was concern over links between popular entertainers, gang violence and drugs-trafficking, which were highlighted by the conviction in February 2011 of Mark Myrie (known as Buju Banton) in a Florida court for trafficking 5 kg of cocaine. Murder charges were laid in October 2011 against another popular performer, Adijah Palmer (known professionally as Vybz Kartel), who was in April 2014 sentenced to life in prison with no possibility of parole for 35 years. With several other entertainers charged with serious offences, Parliament on 7 March passed legislation prohibiting any 'audio, visual or audiovisual communication' that 'promotes killing or violence.'

International human rights organizations, including Amnesty International, have criticized the police force's aggressive approach to the crime problem, in particular raising concerns over the high number of people killed by police officers: in 2013 the Jamaican Constabulary Force killed 258 people, 245 of them in alleged gun battles; this was broadly in line with the annual average of 262 killed in 2007–12. This was equivalent to a rate of 9.5 per 100,000 population, or approximately twice the per head rate for all murders by criminals in the USA. The police anti-corruption branch was headed from its inception in 2008 until August 2012 by a British police officer, Justin Felice (who then moved to the Financial Investigation Unit). From 2008 to 2011 some 319 officers were dismissed for unethical or corrupt behaviour. Since 2010, police killings and other allegations of wrongdoing have been the responsibility of the Independent Commission of Investigations (INDECOM), which has had an uneasy and sometimes hostile relationship with the police, which was burdened with more than 1,300 ongoing investigations at the start of 2014.

The PNP has in general been more supportive of regional co-operation than the JLP, and during its four terms of office before 2007 spearheaded efforts to enhance regional integration by supporting the Caribbean Community and Common Market. Jamaica, together with Barbados, Belize, Guyana, Suriname, and Trinidad and Tobago, joined the Caribbean Single Market and Economy (CSME), the single market component of which was inaugurated on 1 January 2006. The CSME sought to remove most trade barriers and allow increased intra-regional migration. Simpson Miller stated within days of taking office that she would move to replace the Queen as head of state with a president. She also proposed to replace the Privy Council (based in the United Kingdom) with the Caribbean Court of Justice, based in Trinidad, as the country's highest appellate body. A similar proposal had been made by the former PNP Government, but had failed. The proposal to replace the Privy Council would require a two-thirds' majority in the Senate, and hence the support of at least one opposition Senator, while proposals to move to a republic would, in most views, require a referendum. There had been no apparent progress on either proposal by mid-2014. The economy remained a pressing concern for the Simpson Miller Government, which in May 2013 had finalized a US $932m. extended fund facility with the IMF; in spite of this, the Jamaica dollar continued to depreciate against the US currency, and the level of concern remained high.

Economy

MARK WILSON

Based on an earlier article by CHARLES ARTHUR

Jamaica's economy has changed considerably since its heyday as a colony producing sugar and other tropical crops. Tourism, bauxite and remittances from overseas migrants are now the main sources of foreign exchange. However, the island was faced with a problematic outlook in the early years of the 21st century, after decades of economic reversal or slow growth. The protracted decline of the island's sugar cane industry during the 19th century was a painful process, and it was only with the development of the banana as an export crop from the 1870s that an economic recovery began. The advent of refrigerated shipping helped the banana industry to prosper, and foreign fruit companies developed substantial interests in Jamaica. Peasant farmers came to rely on the crop as a steady, albeit modest, source of income, supplementing subsistence production and proceeds from the sale of coffee and citrus fruit. In the mid-20th century significant deposits of bauxite, the ore that is used to produce aluminium, were discovered, and when bauxite-mining began in 1952 the economy further diversified. In the period leading up to and following independence in 1962, efforts to develop a manufacturing base both for the domestic market and for export had some success, creating many new jobs and shifting the economy away from reliance on agro-industry. At the same time, with the advent of mass tourism, Jamaica's climate, coastline and natural beauty made it a popular destination. A tourism industry composed of resorts, hotels, restaurants and bars serving foreign visitors quickly developed into an economic mainstay. During the 1960s Jamaica's gross domestic product (GDP) grew by an average of almost 6% per year in real terms, mainly as a result of high prices for bauxite exports and substantial foreign investment. Despite this progress, the economy was vulnerable to external economic factors, such as decreases in international commodity prices, and sudden shifts in patterns of foreign investment. In the 1970s Michael Manley's People's National Party (PNP) Government tried to develop the country's human capital by increasing public expenditure on social services such as education and health. The aim was to try to establish the foundations for an economy less dependent on foreign capital and foreign markets. This attempt to reorientate the economy proved a general failure owing to an international economic recession and the hostility of the USA and the international financial institutions, as well as much of the local business community. From 1974 to 1980 the economy contracted sharply, with GDP declining by 16% overall.

From the 1970s international lending agencies insisted on neo-liberal reforms, including the privatization of state-owned industries, the reduction of public sector employment, the removal of price controls and subsidies, and the liberalization of the financial system, involving the privatization of banks. During the 1980s the Jamaica Labour Party (JLP) Government championed the free market and private sector-led growth, and received extensive international loans. However, overall average annual growth in 1980–90 was 1.6%, a minimal growth rate that left the Government ill-equipped to meet substantial and rising debt repayments. The PNP had during this period abandoned its earlier socialist orientation, and returned to government in 1989, but the overall economic outlook remained bleak. GDP growth averaged only 0.3% a year during the 1990s (3% cumulative growth over the decade), and agricultural and manufacturing output contracted. The Government responded to rapid inflation, peaking at 80% in the early part of the decade, with fiscal and monetary stringency. This stabilized the exchange rate for the Jamaican dollar, and brought inflation under control, but led to severe problems for most of the real economy, and a period of rapid and unsustainable growth for the financial sector. From 1994 mainstream financial institutions were in obvious difficulties, with growing liquidity problems and an expanding portfolio of non-performing loans, and in 1997 the state was forced to intervene in the sector. By 2002 the accumulated costs of the state rescue of the financial sector were equivalent to 40% of annual GDP.

After reaching 148% of GDP in 2003, the public debt ratio—although remaining very substantial—declined. However, general government gross debt was J \$1,952,518m. in 2012, equivalent to 146.1% of GDP. Contracting per head GDP during most of the last 25 years of the 20th century and the early part of the 21st century meant that average incomes in Jamaica failed to improve for close to four decades. Annual GDP growth averaged a weak 0.8% in 2002–11. GDP contracted by 3.1% in 2009 and 1.4% in 2010 as the global financial crisis unfolded. Bauxite exports declined by 70% in 2009, remittances decreased and hotels were forced to discount room rates heavily to maintain occupancy, while the fiscal deficit widened and the exchange rate depreciated. GDP grew by 1.7% in 2011, and contracted by 0.5% in 2012.

The high debt burden created severe difficulties in developing an effective countercyclical response to the economic crisis through further domestic or commercial borrowing. However, the IMF in February 2010 agreed an economic programme supported by a US \$1,270m. stand-by loan, of which US \$610m. was immediately disbursed, and which was expected to release a further US \$1,100m. in funding from other multilateral institutions. The programme covered public finance and public sector reform, financial sector regulation and a strategy for reduction of debt interest. Other aims included increased resources for investment in education and infrastructure, and higher levels of social spending.

A 'Jamaica Debt Exchange' package agreed in January 2010 aimed to lower debt interest payments by 3% of GDP and reduce repayment of maturing debt in 2010–13 by 65%. A total of J \$722,000m. in domestic debt, equivalent to 55% of total debt, and carrying interest rates of up to 28%, was swapped for new bonds with maximum interest rates of 13.25% and longer maturities, saving J \$40,000m. a year in interest costs. Financial institutions were able to absorb losses stemming from the debt exchange, and the Government's treasury bill borrowing rates were reduced to their lowest levels for 24 years, while the exchange rate appreciated by 4.3% in the first half of 2010. The satisfactory completion of three initial IMF reviews allowed disbursement of a further US \$230m. by January 2011. However, there were problems with subsequent reviews; one concern was a July 2011 salary award for public sector staff, which in the view of the IMF jeopardized agreed fiscal targets. The Government's difficulties in meeting targets were exacerbated as a general election approached, with the need to retain popular support. While in opposition, the PNP demanded the renegotiation of the IMF programme; having been returned to power in early 2012, the new Government began negotiations with the IMF to draw up a new three-year agreement. In February 2013 the Government announced a new restructuring for domestic debt, with lower interest rates and longer maturities, to reduce total interest payments by one-third. At the same time, the Minister of Finance and Planning proposed tax increases; the IMF then announced a staff-level agreement. Following the April budget, the IMF on 1 May approved a US \$932m. four-year arrangement. Aims included a primary surplus equivalent to 7.5% of GDP, and measures to boost growth and employment and to improve competitiveness. The IMF's Managing Director commented on a June 2014 visit to Jamaica that the economic outlook was improving, with growth picking up and debt on a downward course, although with pain felt by many Jamaicans, and many necessary reforms still to be implemented. Local observers count 13 IMF agreements since 1977, of which three were completed with no problems and two with special waivers of performance tests.

The 2011 census reported a population of 2,697,983, of whom 25% lived in the capital district of Kingston and St Andrew. A further 19% lived in the parish of St Catherine, which included the rapidly growing suburb of Portmore and the former capital of Spanish Town, now a satellite town. Other large centres were Montego Bay, situated on the north-west coast, which is a hub of tourism activity, and Mandeville, to the west of Kingston. The UN's official population estimate was 2,798,835 in mid-2014.

Despite Jamaica's poor track record of economic growth over recent decades, many of the country's social indicators are fairly good, and recent trends indicate declining poverty. In 2014 Jamaica ranked 96th out of 187 countries in the UN Development Programme's Human Development index. Life expectancy at birth, which has been rising gradually, was 73.3 years in 2012. Access to safe water and sanitary facilities has been increasing. At the national level, in 2011 93% of households had access to piped water, while 80% had access to sanitation facilities in 2012. At January 2014 the labour force totalled 1,305,500 people. During the economic troubles of the late 20th century unemployment was often extremely high, reaching levels of between 20% and 30%, but during the early years of the 21st century economic growth helped to reduce the rate. By 2010 the rate of unemployment had fallen to 11.6%, although it was 13.4% in January 2014, at which point youth unemployment (14–24 years of age) was 33%.

Despite consistently high levels of unemployment, the Jamaica Survey of Living Conditions calculated that the percentage of Jamaicans defined as living in poverty decreased from 28.0% in 1990 to a low of 9.9% in 2007, before increasing again, to between 18.5% and 20.3% in 2010, with all indicators pointing to a further deterioration since that date. These oscillations were in part attributable to changes in the relative price of food, the rate of inflation, the size of the informal sector and the level of remittances sent back by Jamaicans living abroad. Tens of thousands of Jamaicans earn a living in the unregulated informal sector, either as casual labourers in the agriculture or services sector, or as street merchants buying and selling tiny quantities of everyday goods. In 2005 the informal sector was estimated to be equivalent to 43% of GDP. Remittance inflows stood at US $2,065m. in 2013, a level exceeding earnings from either tourism or bauxite and equivalent to 15% of GDP. This reflected both the success of some emigrants and the high level of emigration during the previous four decades of economic stagnation. The main source of the remittances was the USA (59%), with the United Kingdom second (16%), followed by Canada (12%) and the Cayman Islands (6%). An estimated 80% of Jamaicans with university degrees lived overseas. Approximately as many Jamaicans live abroad as in Jamaica (depending on definitions used).

The once dominant agricultural sector (including fishing and forestry) is no longer a significant pillar of the economy, although it still provided employment to 18.4% of the labour force in 2014. Agriculture's decline gathered pace during the 1990s, and the sector suffered greatly from a series of weather-related shocks. Both larger-scale farming enterprises and smallholding peasant farmers were affected by the extreme weather. Peasant farmers grow a great variety of crops for the local market, but in terms of quantity the main ones are beans, plantains, sweet potatoes, yams and cassava. An additional pressure on domestic farming has been the reduction in import tariffs, which resulted in a large influx of cheaper foreign foodstuffs that have undercut local producers. Agriculture, including forestry and fishing, accounted for just 6.8% of GDP in 2013.

After experiencing decades of decline, the sugar industry, historically the most important sector of Jamaica's economy, shrank even further in the 2000s. The privatization of part of the state-owned sugar industry in 1993 proved to be a disaster, and the Government was in 1998 obliged to resume control of loss-making enterprises. Annual sugar production totalled 506,500 metric tons in 1965, but was only 121,100 tons in 2013. Export earnings from the 103,100 tons of sugar sold overseas in 2012 totalled US $94.1m., equivalent to a mere 1.3% of goods and services exports. Sugar export earnings were for many decades maintained by agreements guaranteeing preferential access to European markets, but with the expiry in 2009 of the European Union's (EU) sugar protocol, and the planned end to EU sugar quotas from 2017, the future for the industry looked bleak. The Jamaican sugar industry, which employed 40,000 persons in 2007, was uncompetitive, with production costs that were over three times those of the world's principal sugar exporters. While Jamaica's two private sector firms were still profitable and could possibly survive with lower preferences, the five state-owned companies could not survive without government subsidies or new investment. The Government therefore sold two enterprises to local investors in 2009, while Chinese company COMPLANT International Sugar Industry Company Ltd in 2011 bought the three remaining sugar factories for US $9m., with a 50-year lease on 300 sq km of cane lands; the arrangement also involved an ambitious US $156m. field and factory four-year investment programme.

The other main traditional agricultural export crop, bananas, also experienced serious difficulties, with the value of exports declining from US $45m. in 1996 to US $9m. in 2007, and export production coming to a halt in 2008 (although some bananas were still grown for the domestic market and for processed snack production). Problems included the high cost of the local industry, repeated hurricane damage, plant disease outbreaks, and most significantly the reduced protection given to traditional African, Caribbean and Pacific suppliers against Latin American rivals in the formerly protected European market. Tropical Storm Gustav in 2008 delivered a final blow to the industry, destroying 79% of the standing crop a year after the passage of Hurricane Dean. Another export crop for both small- and large-scale farmers is coffee. The two main varieties grown in Jamaica are lowland coffee, which is generally grown on small farms, and the connoisseur's Blue Mountain coffee, grown on highland farms in the island's three eastern parishes, with the majority exported in recent years to Japan. Production volumes have been in decline since 1996; exports of coffee were valued at US $17.3m. in 2012. In common with other agricultural products, the coffee sector suffers greatly from adverse weather and hurricane damage, as well as pest infestation and price fluctuations. Other export crops are citrus, cocoa and pimento (allspice).

Jamaica's most significant mineral resource is bauxite, mined mainly in the parishes of Clarendon, St Elizabeth, St Ann and Trelawny, in west-central Jamaica. Most Jamaican bauxite is processed locally for alumina, or pure aluminium oxide; this is then exported to overseas smelters to produce aluminium. Some bauxite is exported in its raw form to overseas alumina plants. Mining costs are high, as the bauxite is found in scattered pockets, rather than as a continuous deposit. Mining and quarrying comprised 1.2% of GDP in 2013 following the closure in 2009 of a number of bauxite mines and three alumina processing plants and a sharp decrease in commodity prices owing to the international recession. With sectoral productivity recorded at four times the average for the national economy, mining employed only 0.6% of the labour force in 2014. World aluminium demand and prices increased in the early years of the 21st century, and earnings from alumina exports were US $1,235m. in 2008, with an additional US $115m. from unprocessed bauxite, making up 49% of merchandise exports. However, export earnings from alumina and bauxite declined to US $453m. in 2009, with only a partial recovery, to US $638.4m., in 2012. Mining GDP contracted by 50.4% in 2009. Following another year of negative growth in 2010, the sector made a partial recovery in 2011 after the reopening of a bauxite/alumina plant contributed to growth of 19.4% in the first full year of renewed production. However, mining lapsed again in 2012, contracting by 9.1%, then recovered by an anaemic 3.8% in 2013, at which point output remained 46.4% below 2008 levels.

The three main bauxite-extracting and alumina-producing companies in Jamaica have been Jamalco, formerly a joint venture between the Jamaican Government and the US company Alcoa, which in June 2014 announced the sale of its Jamaican operations to the Noble Group of Hong Kong; the West Indies Alumina Co (WINDALCO), since 2007 a joint venture between the Jamaican Government and the Russian-Swiss concern United Company RUSAL; and Alumina Partners of Jamaica (Alpart), also owned by RUSAL. RUSAL suspended operations at both companies in 2009. Although the WINDALCO Ewarton plant reopened in 2010, the WIND-ALCO Kirkvine and Alpart plants remained out of operation in 2014; the Minister of Science, Technology, Energy and Mining, Phillip Paulwell, in July threatened to cancel RUSAL's mining licence at these two plants unless they reopened by January 2015.

Jamaica is heavily dependent on the import of petroleum products, which made up 35.6% of goods imports in 2013. There are fair geological prospects offshore, and several small overseas companies were exploring offshore blocks in the exclusive economic zone in 2014, but with no positive results. In 2012 a total of 4,136m. kWh of electricity was generated, slightly less than in each of the previous two years. In 2009 total generating capacity was 820 MW, with peak demand of 638 MW in 2010. The Jamaica Public Service Co (JPSCo), which is the sole distributor and main generator of electricity, has since 2011 been owned by the Marubeni Corporation of Japan (40%), Korea East-West Power (40%) and the Jamaican Government (19.9%). However, in 2012 the Government argued for the liberalized supply and distribution of electricity, while private citizens initiated legal action, according to which the courts were asked to rule that the 20-year exclusive licence granted to JPSCo in 2001 was invalid; there had been no final legal ruling by mid-2014. In 2010 JPSCo accounted for 68% of total electricity generated, and in addition to four large fossil fuel plants there were eight small hydroelectric plants, and a 39-MW wind farm complex, which provided 4.5% of national generating capacity. JPSCo also bought power from four smaller, independent generating companies. The reliability of the power supply improved in the 2000s, but electricity costs were higher than in many countries, with an average cost of 42 US cents per kWh in 2014. There have been several proposals to add substantial generating capacity, using either 'clean' coal or liquefied natural gas; however, none had been finalized by mid-2014.

Approximately 2.59m. metric tons of crude petroleum and petroleum products were imported in 2012. About one-third of the fuel was used for bauxite- and alumina-processing. Taking an opportunity to reduce the economic cost of imported petroleum, in 2005 the Government signed the Petrocaribe energy accord with Venezuela. Under the terms of the accord, Jamaica and other Caribbean nations received petrol imports from Venezuela at normal prices, but under preferential terms, allowing the importer to finance a proportion of the cost with long-term, low-interest loans; this resulted in accumulated borrowing of an estimated US $2,400m. by March 2013; however, this was offset in part by Jamaican exports to Venezuela of clinker for cement manufacturing. In 2006 Venezuela bought a 49% stake in the refinery operated by the state-owned Petroleum Corporation of Jamaica. However, a US $1,200m. investment and expansion programme, originally intended for completion in 2009, was subject to delays and rising cost estimates, and was not completed.

The export-orientated manufacturing sector grew rapidly in the mid-1980s, especially within the free trade zones established in Kingston, Montego Bay and Spanish Town. The free trade zones stimulated foreign investment in garment assembly, light manufacturing and data entry. However, from the late 1980s the manufacturing sector declined in importance, with its share of GDP decreasing from 19.6% in 1988 to 9.0% in 2013. Manufacturing output contracted by a cumulative 8.5% in 2008–13; the sector employed 6.4% of the labour force in 2014. At its height in the mid-1990s, Jamaica's apparel industry, which primarily assembled garments cut in the USA for re-export to that country, employed about 25,000 people and earned around an annual US $550m. in exports. With the advent of the North American Free Trade Agreement in 1994, and the end of the Multi-fibre Agreement 10 years later, it became increasingly difficult for Jamaica to compete with countries such as the People's Republic of China, which had lower wages and lower operating costs. Annual export earnings from assembled garments declined from US $149m. in 2000, to just US $9.4m. in 2005, and have since virtually ceased.

As the economy decelerated, the contribution of the construction sector fell from 10.9% of GDP in 2005 to 7.0% in 2013. The construction industry employed 7.2% of the labour force in 2014. The sector contracted by a cumulative 11.5% in 2008–13, as public sector, tourism-related and residential investment slowed.

Transport infrastructure is fairly well developed by regional standards, particularly with regard to seaports and airports. The principal port at Kingston is a major transshipment centre for the Caribbean region, and the natural harbour is the seventh largest in the world. Since 2000 investment in ports and the privately run airport at Montego Bay has continued and facilities have improved. However, shipping was affected by the international recession and the steep decline in alumina exports. Nevertheless, the Government sees shipping services as an important potential area of growth. Kingston, however, does not yet have sufficient draft to accommodate post-Panamax vessels with the expansion of the Panama canal in 2015, and plans for port development are complicated by proposals for privatization, which had not been finalized by mid-2014. China Harbour Construction Ltd has controversially proposed development of a logistics hub at the nature reserve of Goat Island to the west of Kingston, possibly linked to a redeveloped airport on a former US base at Vernamfield.

For a country of its size, the national road network is extensive (22,121 km in 2010), but, although the whole network is paved with asphalt, only 50% of it is in good condition. Insufficient maintenance, rising traffic volumes, increased overloading of commercial vehicles and, particularly over the past few years, damage caused by flooding associated with the increasing intensity of the hurricane seasons have all taken their toll. A highway along the north coast was completed in the late 2000s, and construction of Highway 2000, a toll road to connect Kingston, Ocho Rios and Montego Bay, was under way in 2014, with the section from Kingston to Spanish Town already open. Construction of the section from Spanish Town to Ocho Rios was being undertaken by the China Harbour Engineering Company. The public passenger railway service ceased operations in 1992, although private freight transport continued from the alumina plants to the export-shipping facilities. In 2008 the Minister of Transport and Works announced that China had agreed to help Jamaica to revive its rail network as a way of offsetting rising fuel costs by financing 85% of a US $354m. project through a loan with the state-owned Jamaica Railway Corporation. However, no progress had been made regarding these proposals by mid-2014.

Privatization and liberalization of the telecommunications sector from 2000 encouraged significant private sector investment which, in turn, resulted in improvements in coverage and access. Mobile cellular telephone penetration is very high; in 2013 there were 100 mobile and 9.6 fixed-line subscriptions per 100 people. The cellular sector is dominated by Irish-owned Digicel Jamaica, which in 2011 bought the local operations of Claro Jamaica (owned by América Móvil of Mexico). Digicel's main rival is LIME, a subsidiary of British firm Cable & Wireless and historically the main supplier of fixed lines, with an estimated market share of 16% of the cellular market. There were 4.7 fixed broadband subscriptions per 100 people in 2013. At least 37.8% of Jamaican residents used the internet in 2013. Call centres have been a successful growth industry, and employed approximately 10,000 people in 2012.

The health of the financial sector improved to some extent after restructuring in 1997–2002. Interest rates declined, although they remained very high by international standards. In April 2014 commercial bank loan rates averaged 17.7%, down from 43.6% in 1996. Treasury bill rates decreased after the debt restructuring of early 2010, and were close to 6.9% in July 2014, down from 21.1% in June 2009. Weaknesses in supervision were indicated by the ability of several high-profile unregulated foreign exchange trading and investment schemes to flourish in the early years of the 21st century, offering very high purported rates of return, taking on the characteristics of Ponzi schemes (fraudulent investment opportunities that promise high returns, supposedly with little risk to investors), and accumulating deposits estimated at between 12.5% and 25% of GDP. Most of these schemes collapsed in 2008, with a large number of depositors losing their funds. The US authorities, meanwhile, noted weaknesses in the Financial Investigations Division, which was responsible for controls on money-laundering within the Ministry of

Finance and Planning. Other areas of concern include the 'Lotto Scam', in which Jamaicans use skills and information acquired in the telemarketing industry to carry out financial fraud, with elderly US residents among their principal targets. There have been proposals since the late 2000s to establish an international financial centre in Jamaica, a move that would appear unwise and unlikely to succeed in view of the country's weak regulatory environment, the international financial crisis and the high level of regional competition. However, financial regulations were improved as part of the 2010 and 2013 IMF reform programmes.

Tourism began to grow in economic importance in the 1950s, and, with the advent of the long-haul charter flight and the popular package holiday in the late 1960s, the sector made rapid advances. Stop-over tourist arrivals rose from 840,777 in 1990 to 2.0m. in 2013. Cruise ships also brought visitors to the island, albeit for short visits and with only 8% of the average spend of stop-over tourists. Cruise ship arrivals increased from 133,400 in 1980 to 1.34m. in 2006, but had decreased to 909,619 by 2010, as cruise lines moved to other destinations. However, cruise ship arrivals recovered to 1.29m. in 2013, in part owing to the opening of a new cruise port at Falmouth. Partly because of the high crime rate and visitor harassment, Jamaica pioneered the 'all-inclusive' resort, and two locally owned companies, Sandals and SuperClubs, operate successfully across the island and in other Caribbean and overseas markets. In the early years of the 21st century several Spanish companies built large resorts in Jamaica, and room stock expanded by 13.8% in 2006–09, reaching a total of 30,347. This led to a further increase in tourist arrivals, in contrast to most other Caribbean markets, albeit with decreased percentage of room occupancy and following steep discounts in room rates. Hotels and restaurants employed 7.2% of the labour force in 2014. Tourism is heavily dependent on the US market, which accounted for 63% of arrivals in 2013, with 20% from Canada and 12% from Europe, most of whom were British.

Beginning in the 1970s, successive governments have struggled with fiscal deficits and mounting debts, largely as a consequence of overspending and low levels of tax collection. Despite numerous reform programmes recommended and monitored by the IMF, the situation had barely improved by the early years of the 21st century. The fiscal deficit narrowed to 3.5% of GDP in 2004/05, but then rose again, to 7.3%, in 2008/09. With revenue affected by the economic recession and with interest payments and other spending commitments increasing, the deficit rose to 10.9% in 2009/10, although there was a primary surplus of J $68,000m. In accordance with the IMF programme, the Government increased income tax for high earners and raised the rate of the General Consumption Tax (a value-added tax—VAT) from 2010, to accumulate revenue equivalent to 2% of GDP, while a two-year public sector wage freeze was introduced, after three years in which public sector salary costs had expanded by 54%. The Jamaica Debt Exchange was intended to bring the cost of debt-servicing down to 47% of total spending, from 60% in 2009/10. Accordingly, the budget for 2010/11 projected a deficit of 6.5% of GDP, of which two-thirds was to be financed by domestic borrowing; the medium-term target was to achieve a balanced budget by 2013/14. However, the IMF programme became contentious in the context of the December 2011 general election, with the incoming PNP Government calling initially for renegotiation, and then for improved terms in a new agreement to run from the expiry of the existing accord. In 2011/12 public finance fell significantly short of IMF targets, with a primary surplus of 3.2% of GDP, against a target of 6.8%, as a result of cuts in fuel taxes, weaker tax administration and widespread tax incentives and waivers (which increased by 55% in 2011, in spite of the stated aim of a freeze). The fiscal deficit in 2011/12 was 6.4% of GDP, and total public debt exceeded the IMF target by 6% of GDP. However, the budget for 2012/13 projected a primary surplus of 5.4% of GDP, rising to 7.5% in 2013/14. Targets set for 2015/16 included a balanced budget, public sector salary costs equivalent to no more than 9% of GDP, and a decrease in debt to 100% of GDP. In the mean time, the Government continued its divestment programme, selling the loss-making national airline Air Jamaica to Caribbean Airlines of Trinidad and Tobago in 2011. In that year the French shipping company

CMA CGM agreed to invest US $100m. to develop the state-owned Port of Kingston under a 35-year lease. However, the state's holdings in the bauxite industry had not been divested by mid-2014.

Efforts to improve on existing low rates of tax collection have been complicated by the difficulties posed by the existence of a growing informal sector and a culture of tax evasion. Following a comprehensive review of the tax system, in 2005 the Government pursued improvements in revenue collection. The reforms aimed to simplify tax administration and improve compliance, and included the modification of personal and corporate income tax, as well as bringing a number of indirect taxes into the VAT system. The IMF programmes and recent budgets have also proposed further reforms in tax administration.

The rate of the Jamaican dollar against the US dollar declined in the 2000s, down from J $47 = US $1 at the end of 2002, to J $89 = US $1 in April 2009. However, external support and debt restructuring prompted a recovery to J $86 = US $1 in June 2010. The exchange rate then declined further, to J $112 = US $1 by July 2014, with a continuing loss of confidence in the economy, in spite of the previous year's IMF agreement.

Monetary tightening resulted in relative currency stability, but at severe cost to the economy. After a period of double-digit price rises in 2003–05, inflation was reduced to a low point of 5.7% in 2006. Prices again rose rapidly, with inflation recorded at 16.8% in both 2007 and 2008, in part because of higher import costs for oil, basic foods and other commodities. However, inflation decreased to 6.0% in 2011, as a result of the stabilizing impact from mid-2009 of a steady exchange rate on the price of imports. The rate rose to 8.6% in 2012 and to 9.4% in 2013, in part because of the effect of currency depreciation on import prices. With public sector salaries largely frozen, this placed severe pressure on the living standards of those in work.

Jamaica's foreign trade balance has been in deficit since the mid-20th century. Although the level fluctuated when world prices for exports such as bauxite, alumina and sugar and for oil imports changed, the overall trend has been negative, as imports increased more than two-and-a-half times as fast as exports in 1994–2008. The deficit in merchandise trade was US $3,976m. in 2013, a 26.4% increase compared with 2010, with higher oil prices only partly offset by falling consumer demand. Tourism produced net earnings of US $1,903m. in 2013. However, a negative balance for other services meant that the net services balance of US $599m. covered only 15% of the trade deficit. Inward remittances of US $2,065m. were offset by outflows including interest payments on foreign debt. There was a resulting current account balance of payments deficit of US $1,385.6m., equivalent to 13% of GDP. Capital and investment inflows did not fully cover the current deficit. Reserves were down by US $78m. over the calendar year, and stood at US $1,048m. at the end of 2013, having reached a low point of US $836m., in November. Reserves increased to US $1,376m in June 2014 as the new IMF programme took effect.

CONCLUSION

Jamaica's economy has undergone a profound reorientation over the last 60 years or so, shifting from reliance on agricultural production for the local and export markets to dependence on bauxite and alumina, tourism, call centres, the informal sector and remittances from Jamaicans living abroad. However, Jamaica's economy grew only by a cumulative 25% between 1970 and 2008, while that of its Caribbean neighbours expanded on average by 174%, and the world economy by 216%; Jamaica has since lagged further behind. Jamaica currently has the third lowest per head GDP in the English-speaking Caribbean. Jamaica has more than twice the population of Trinidad and Tobago, but an economy that is one-half the size. The Jamaican economy remains vulnerable to fluctuating international commodity prices both for exports of bauxite and alumina, and for imports of petroleum, as well as to the international borrowing environment and international demand for tourism. After confronting the economic difficulties of 2008–09 and with earlier reform efforts interrupted in 2011, debt restructuring and an IMF programme appeared to provide a possible basis for stabilizing the economy in 2014, if agreed targets were maintained. However, the underlying structural problems that had produced the historically anaemic growth rate remained to be addressed. Structural problems included high energy prices, the high costs of the tourism industry at a time when it is increasingly challenged by competition from cruise ships and other destinations, the finite extent of remaining bauxite reserves and the great expense required to exploit them, and the apparent lack of growth or new enterprise in manufacturing or agriculture. However, the

Government envisaged growth potential in areas such as agriculture, tourism, shipping, logistics and business process outsourcing. Meanwhile, relations with international lending agencies remained, in general, fairly good. With social and political stability clearly necessary for economic growth, the continued existence of high levels of crime and youth unemployment underscored the need to translate macroeconomic progress into tangible improvements to the living standards of the poorer sectors of the population.

Statistical Survey

Sources (unless otherwise stated): Statistical Institute of Jamaica, 7 Cecelio Ave, Kingston 10; tel. 926-5311; fax 926-1138; e-mail info@statinja.gov.jm; internet www.statinja.gov.jm; Jamaica Information Service, 58A Half Way Tree Rd, POB 2222, Kingston 10; tel. 926-3740; fax 926-6715; e-mail jis@jis.gov.jm; internet www.jis.gov.jm; Bank of Jamaica, Nethersole Pl., POB 621, Kingston; tel. 922-0750; fax 922-0854; e-mail info@boj.org.jm; internet www.boj.org.jm.

Area and Population

AREA, POPULATION AND DENSITY

Area (sq km)	10,991*
Population (census results)	
10 September 2001	2,607,632
5 April 2011	
Males	1,334,533
Females	1,363,450
Total	2,697,983
Population (UN estimates at mid-year)†	
2012	2,768,942
2013	2,783,890
2014	2,798,835
Density (per sq km) at mid-2014	254.6

* 4,243.6 sq miles.
† Source: UN, *World Population Prospects: The 2012 Revision*.

POPULATION BY AGE AND SEX
(UN estimates at mid–2014)

	Males	Females	Total
0–14 years	376,750	365,443	742,193
15–64 years	899,322	933,824	1,833,146
65 years and over	101,973	121,523	223,496
Total	1,378,045	1,420,790	2,798,835

Source: UN, *World Population Prospects: The 2012 Revision*.

PARISHES
(population at 2011 census)

	Area (sq km)	Population	Density (per sq km)
Clarendon	1,196	245,103	204.9
Hanover	450	69,533	154.5
Kingston and St Andrew . . .	453*	662,426	1,462.3
Manchester	830	189,797	228.7
Portland	814	81,744	100.4
St Ann	1,213	172,362	142.1
St Catherine	1,192	516,218	433.1
St Elizabeth	1,212	150,205	123.9
St James	595	183,811	308.9
St Mary	611	113,615	185.9
St Thomas	743	93,902	126.4
Trelawny	875	75,164	85.9
Westmoreland	807	144,103	178.6
Total	10,991	2,697,983	245.5

* Kingston 22 sq km, St Andrew 431 sq km.

PRINCIPAL TOWNS
(population at 2011 census)

Kingston (capital) .	584,627		Montego Bay . .	110,115
Portmore . . .	182,153		May Pen . . .	61,548
Spanish Town . .	147,152		Mandeville . . .	49,695

Mid-2014 (incl. suburbs, UN estimate): Kingston 587,702 (Source: UN, *World Urbanization Prospects: The 2014 Revision*).

BIRTHS, MARRIAGES AND DEATHS*

	Registered live births		Registered marriages		Registered deaths	
	Number	Rate (per 1,000)	Number	Rate (per 1,000)	Number	Rate (per 1,000)
2006 . . .	43,243	16.3	18,960	7.2	23,181	8.7
2007 . . .	43,385	16.3	20,550	7.7	20,250	7.6
2008 . . .	43,112	16.1	19,966	7.5	22,152	8.3
2009 . . .	42,782	16.0	18,855	7.0	21,692	8.1
2010 . . .	40,508	15.1	21,503	8.0	20,910	7.8
2011 . . .	39,673	14.7	16,926	6.3	20,685	7.6
2012 . . .	39,553	14.5	16,998	6.3	16,998	6.3
2013 . . .	36,746†	13.5†	18,835†	9.9†	15,427†	5.7†

* Data are tabulated by year of registration rather than by year of occurrence.
† Provisional.

Life expectancy (years at birth): 73.3 (males 70.8; females 75.9) in 2012 (Source: World Bank, World Development Indicators database).

ECONOMICALLY ACTIVE POPULATION
('000 persons aged 14 years and over, January 2014)

	Males	Females	Total
Agriculture, forestry and fishing .	168.1	39.0	207.1
Mining and quarrying	6.4	0.5	6.9
Manufacturing	47.9	23.8	71.7
Electricity, gas and water . . .	6.8	1.2	8.0
Construction	78.8	2.7	81.5
Wholesale and retail, repair of motor vehicles and equipment .	106.2	127.0	233.2
Hotels and restaurants . . .	31.2	49.5	80.7
Transport, storage and communications	58.1	13.7	71.8
Financial intermediation . . .	9.3	16.9	26.2
Real estate, renting and business activities	37.7	33.0	70.7

—continued	Males	Females	Total
Public administration and defence; compulsory social security . .	26.7	30.5	57.2
Education	17.3	52.7	70.0
Health and social work . . .	8.1	24.5	32.6
Community, social and personal services	26.5	27.7	54.2
Private households with employed persons	12.6	43.0	55.6
Sub-total	641.7	485.7	1,127.4
Activities not adequately defined .	2.3	0.8	3.1
Total employed	644.0	486.5	1,130.5
Unemployed	72.7	102.4	175.1
Total labour force	716.7	588.8	1,305.5

Health and Welfare

KEY INDICATORS

Total fertility rate (children per woman, 2012)	2.3
Under-5 mortality rate (per 1,000 live births, 2012) . . .	17
HIV/AIDS (% of persons aged 15–49, 2012)	1.7
Physicians (per 1,000 head, 2008)	0.4
Hospital beds (per 1,000 head, 2010)	1.9
Health expenditure (2011): US $ per head (PPP)	395
Health expenditure (2011): % of GDP	5.2
Health expenditure (2011): public (% of total)	53.6
Access to water (% of persons, 2012)	93
Access to sanitation (% of persons, 2012)	80
Total carbon dioxide emissions ('000 metric tons, 2010) . .	7,158.0
Carbon dioxide emissions per head (metric tons, 2010) . .	2.6
Human Development Index (2013): ranking	96
Human Development Index (2013): value	0.715

For sources and definitions, see explanatory note on p. vi.

Agriculture

PRINCIPAL CROPS

('000 metric tons)

	2010	2011	2012
Sweet potatoes	35	42	42
Yams	137	135	145
Sugar cane	1,390	1,518	1,475
Coconuts	290*	290*	315†
Cabbages and other brassicas .	25	33	33
Tomatoes	19	27	27
Pumpkins, squash and gourds .	41	49	52
Carrots and turnips	21	32	30
Bananas	54	47	47
Plantains	30	35	36
Oranges	108	100	92
Lemons and limes†	24	26	27
Grapefruit and pomelos . . .	1	—	—
Pineapples	20	18	20

* Unofficial figure.
† FAO estimate(s).

Pimento, allspice ('000 metric tons): 10 in 2005.

Aggregate production ('000 metric tons, may include official, semi-official or estimated data): Total cereals 2.6 in 2010, 3.0 in 2011, 3.1 in 2012; Total roots and tubers 224.7 in 2010, 240.5 in 2011, 248.3 in 2012; Total vegetables (incl. melons) 202.7 in 2010, 267.7 in 2011, 273.5 in 2012; Total fruits (excl. melons) 287.6 in 2010, 280.5 in 2011, 277.1 in 2012.

Source: FAO.

LIVESTOCK

('000 head, year ending September, FAO estimates unless otherwise indicated)

	2010	2011	2012
Horses	4	4	4
Mules	10	10	10
Asses	23	23	23
Cattle	170	170	170
Pigs	197*	200	205
Sheep	1.6	1.4	1.4
Goats	490	500	520
Poultry	13,500	13,000	13,500

* Unofficial figure.

Source: FAO.

LIVESTOCK PRODUCTS

('000 metric tons)

	2010	2011	2012
Cattle meat	5.3	5.6	5.8
Goat meat	0.9	1.3	1.1
Pig meat	8.0	7.1	9.5
Chicken meat	100.6	101.5	102.2
Cows' milk	12.5	12.4	12.8
Hen eggs*	6.0	7.5	6.2
Honey*	0.7	0.8	0.8

* FAO estimates.

Source: FAO.

Forestry

ROUNDWOOD REMOVALS

('000 cubic metres, excl. bark, FAO estimates)

	2010	2011	2012
Sawlogs, veneer logs and logs for sleepers	4	1	1
Other industrial wood	151	151	151
Fuel wood	545	541	537
Total	700	693	689

Source: FAO.

SAWNWOOD PRODUCTION

('000 cubic metres, incl. railway sleepers, FAO estimates)

	2010	2011	2012
Coniferous (softwood)	3	3	3
Broadleaved (hardwood)	63	63	63
Total	66	66	66

Note: Annual production assumed to be unchanged from 1998.

Source: FAO.

Fishing

('000 metric tons, live weight)

	2010	2011*	2012
Capture	15.4	15.1	15.0*
Marine fishes	11.4	11.4	11.3*
Freshwater fishes	0.4	0.4	0.4*
Aquaculture*	4.1	1.2	0.6
Nile tilapia	3.9	1.1	0.6
Total catch*	19.5	16.3	15.6

* FAO estimate(s).

Source: FAO.

Mining

('000 metric tons)

	2010	2011	2012
Bauxite*	8,540	10,190	9,339
Alumina	1,591	1,960	1,758
Crude gypsum	230	96	100†
Lime	300†	300	n.a.
Salt	19.0†	n.a.	n.a.

* Dried equivalent of crude ore.
† Estimated figure.
Source: US Geological Survey.

Industry

SELECTED PRODUCTS

	2011	2012	2013
Sugar ('000 metric tons)	143.2	136.2	121.1
Rum ('000 litres)	17,627	24,508	31,259
Diesel and fuel oil (million litres)	987.8	982.8	937.1
Motor spirit (petrol, million litres)	194.3	181.2	167.1
Kerosene, turbo and jet fuel (million litres)	114.8	122.8	121.3
Cement ('000 metric tons)	717.3	760.3	824.9

Electrical energy (million kWh): 6,008 in 2008; 5,533 in 2009; 4,157 in 2010 (Source: UN Industrial Commodity Statistics Database).

Finance

CURRENCY AND EXCHANGE RATES

Monetary Units
100 cents = 1 Jamaican dollar (J $).

Sterling, US Dollar and Euro Equivalents (30 May 2014)
£1 sterling = J $186.899;
US $1 = J $111.104;
€1 = J $151.223;
J $1,000 = £5.35 = US $9.00 = €6.61.

Average Exchange Rate (J $ per US $)
2011	85.892
2012	88.751
2013	100.241

GOVERNMENT FINANCE
(budgetary central government, non-cash basis, J $ million, year ending 31 March)

Summary of Balances

	2010	2011*	2012*
Revenue	309,231	308,468	346,164
Less Expense	375,703	387,215	402,867
Gross operating balance	−66,472	−78,746	−56,703
Less Net acquisition of non-financial assets	26,752	24,149	25,040
Net lending/borrowing	−93,224	−102,895	−81,743

Revenue

	2010	2011*	2012*
Tax revenue	274,493	286,196	321,672
Taxes on income, profits and capital gains	116,954	121,427	138,513
Taxes on goods and services	124,799	129,990	142,744
Grants	9,669	3,347	1,123
Other revenue	25,069	18,925	23,370
Total	309,231	308,468	346,164

Expense/Outlays

Expense by economic type	2010	2011*	2012*
Compensation of employees	59,231	66,115	66,062
Use of goods and services	20,312	21,734	22,339
Interest	128,355	120,704	136,534
Social benefits	16,762	21,796	24,141
Other expense	151,043	156,866	153,792
Total	375,703	387,215	402,867

Outlays by functions of government†	2010	2011*	2012*
General public services	173,781	183,238	193,256
Defence	10,138	11,926	12,312
Public order and safety	34,805	40,060	42,959
Economic affairs	61,976	49,437	37,984
Environmental protection	712	937	1,103
Housing and community amenities	7,112	8,326	8,590
Health	34,627	37,384	36,365
Recreation, culture and religion	3,441	3,810	4,623
Education	71,288	76,601	82,080
Social protection	7,071	7,259	7,285
Statistical discrepancy	−2,496	−7,614	1,350
Total	402,455	411,364	427,907

* Preliminary.
† Including net acquisition of non-financial assets.
Source: IMF, *Government Finance Statistics Yearbook*.

2012/13 (central government operations, J $ million): *Revenue:* Tax revenue 319,764.9; Non-tax revenue 18,765.1; Other revenue 1,163.7; Capital revenue 1,015.8; Grants 3,968.3; Total 344,677.7. *Expenditure:* Current expenditure 361,521.0 (Programmes 87,201.5, Wages and salaries 147,381.8, Interest 126,937.7); Capital expenditure (incl. net lending) 37,757.9; Total 399,278.9 (Source: Ministry of Finance and Planning, Kingston).

2013/14 (central government operations, J $ million, estimates): *Revenue:* Tax revenue 343,836.1; Non-tax revenue 41,047.1; Other revenue 1,009.5; Capital revenue 658.1; Grants 10,627.4; Total 397,178.2. *Expenditure:* Current expenditure 360,248.9 (Programmes 93,967.7, Wages and salaries 156,361.7, Interest 109,919.5); Capital expenditure (incl. net lending) 35,171.8; Total 395,420.7 (Source: Ministry of Finance and Planning, Kingston).

2014/15 (central government operations, J $ million, projections): *Revenue:* Tax revenue 384,286.0; Non-tax revenue 34,186.4; Other revenue 17.9; Capital revenue 753.3; Grants 8,644.9; Total 427,888.5. *Expenditure:* Current expenditure 404,654.5 (Programmes 110,281.1, Wages and salaries 161,704.3, Interest 132,669.1); Capital expenditure (incl. net lending) 34,628.1; Total 439,282.6 (Source: Ministry of Finance and Planning, Kingston).

INTERNATIONAL RESERVES
(excl. gold, US $ million at 31 December)

	2011	2012	2013
IMF special drawing rights	315.9	306.5	296.1
Foreign exchange	1,966.1	1,674.3	1,522.3
Total	2,281.9	1,980.8	1,818.4

Source: IMF, *International Financial Statistics*.

MONEY SUPPLY
(J $ million at 31 December)

	2011	2012	2013
Currency outside depository corporations	51,505	53,502	57,038
Transferable deposits	117,908	105,951	145,006
Other deposits	391,282	418,009	480,061
Securities other than shares . .	70,567	40,837	42,328
Broad money	631,262	618,299	724,433

Source: IMF, *International Financial Statistics*.

COST OF LIVING
(Consumer Price Index; base: December 2006 = 100)

	2011	2012	2013
Food (incl. non-alcoholic beverages)	190.7	211.3	237.8
Clothing and footwear	166.1	183.3	204.0
Housing, utilities and fuel . .	190.4	201.6	218.9
All items (incl. others) . . .	172.8	184.7	202.0

NATIONAL ACCOUNTS
(J $ million at current prices)

Expenditure on the Gross Domestic Product

	2010	2011	2012
Government final consumption expenditure	185,669	196,091	214,210
Private final consumption expenditure	945,552	1,064,716	1,133,785
Increase in stocks	3,429	5,535	3,069
Gross fixed capital formation . .	229,408	259,834	258,093
Total domestic expenditure .	1,364,058	1,526,176	1,609,157
Exports of goods and services .	361,227	376,784	399,555
Less Imports of goods and services	571,608	663,195	695,660
GDP in purchasers' values .	1,153,678	1,239,766	1,313,052

Gross Domestic Product by Economic Activity

	2011	2012	2013
Agriculture, forestry and fishing .	70,438	75,465	86,258
Mining and quarrying	15,487	14,811	15,525
Manufacturing	96,566	103,554	113,349
Electricity and water	35,867	35,236	40,049
Construction	77,921	80,330	87,987
Wholesale and retail trade; repairs and installation of machinery .	201,491	214,156	233,935
Hotels and restaurants . .	45,481	48,175	53,222
Transport, storage and communication	104,330	101,388	105,551
Finance and insurance services .	111,869	117,281	123,411
Real estate, renting and business services	130,771	138,684	145,784
Producers of government services .	152,708	167,043	176,446
Other services	69,803	74,995	81,104
Sub-total	1,112,732	1,171,118	1,262,621
Less Financial intermediation services indirectly measured .	45,755	47,792	49,579
Gross value added in basic prices	1,066,975	1,123,327	1,213,041
Taxes, less subsidies, on products .	172,790	189,725	217,382
GDP in market prices . . .	1,239,766	1,313,052	1,430,423

BALANCE OF PAYMENTS
(US $ million)

	2011	2012	2013
Exports of goods	1,666.1	1,746.7	1,597.3
Imports of goods	−5,881.4	−5,904.7	−5,573.4
Balance on goods	−4,215.3	−4,158.0	−3,976.2
Exports of services	2,620.2	2,673.8	2,755.7
Imports of services	−1,946.0	−2,034.9	−2,156.6
Balance on goods and services	−3,541.2	−3,519.1	−3,377.1
Primary income received . . .	221.5	283.8	303.7
Primary income paid . . .	−739.9	−717.3	−529.0
Balance on goods, services and primary income	−4,059.6	−3,952.6	−3,602.3
Secondary income received . .	2,284.0	2,337.6	2,460.4
Secondary income paid . . .	−287.6	−289.8	−243.7
Current balance	−2,063.2	−1,904.8	−1,385.6
Capital account (net)	−9.1	−26.2	36.0
Direct investment assets . .	−29.1	24.2	1.6
Direct investment liabilities . .	172.8	228.8	534.3
Portfolio investment assets . .	−70.8	285.3	−154.3
Portfolio investment liabilities . .	240.5	−138.6	154.7
Other investment assets . .	−274.4	−369.7	−78.0
Other investment liabilities . .	1,270.8	245.8	553.5
Net errors and omissions . . .	494.9	818.2	161.0
Reserves and related items .	−267.8	−839.3	−179.4

Source: IMF, *International Financial Statistics*.

External Trade

PRINCIPAL COMMODITIES
(US $ million)

Imports c.i.f.	2011	2012	2013
Foods	938.7	959.2	962.1
Beverages and tobacco . . .	77.4	81.1	77.1
Crude materials (excl. fuels) . .	62.8	47.5	55.9
Mineral fuels and lubricants . .	2,310.9	2,390.3	2,251.6
Animal and vegetable oils and fats	58.6	51.6	42.9
Chemicals	873.4	924.0	773.1
Manufactured goods . . .	645.7	623.7	599.9
Machinery and transport equipment	932.1	919.4	898.4
Miscellaneous manufactured articles	471.4	480.0	443.3
Total (incl. others)	6,547.7	6,594.9	6,331.6

Exports f.o.b.	2011	2012	2013
Foods	232.3	274.0	243.1
Beverages and tobacco	113.2	104.3	83.3
Crude materials (excl. fuels) . .	767.9	665.4	685.5
Mineral fuels and lubricants . .	186.6	200.8	169.1
Chemicals	46.8	209.7	113.4
Machinery and transport equipment	50.4	22.8	38.9
Miscellaneous manufactured articles	19.1	18.5	24.0
Total (incl. others)	1,662.9	1,747.3	1,597.3

PRINCIPAL TRADING PARTNERS
(US $ million)

Imports c.i.f.	2010	2011	2012
Belgium	62.4	65.6	53.5
Brazil	203.2	323.7	241.9
Canada	91.7	117.7	101.3
China, People's Republic	242.9	282.3	310.5
Colombia	56.4	70.5	54.6
Costa Rica	52.8	54.7	56.9
Dominican Republic	54.8	66.5	47.7
Germany	47.8	64.1	70.5
Japan	121.0	148.7	208.4
Mexico	77.2	242.6	264.1
Trinidad and Tobago	721.0	831.3	699.0
United Kingdom	80.9	85.1	83.7
USA	1,875.1	2,163.3	2,349.2
Venezuela	732.8	958.8	1,013.9
Total (incl. others)	5,225.2	6,436.6	6,580.4

Exports f.o.b.	2010	2011	2012
Bahamas	3.3	2.1	21.8
Barbados	8.9	9.2	23.8
Bulgaria	0.0	0.0	18.3
Canada	163.4	263.7	121.6
China, People's Republic	1.8	21.4	11.4
France	16.1	7.0	16.5
Georgia	8.0	9.1	36.2
Iceland	18.3	7.8	27.2
Italy	1.0	1.2	37.9
Japan	15.8	13.7	10.6
Latvia	0.0	0.0	59.9
Netherlands	68.3	91.4	70.6
Norway	68.5	41.8	0.1
Poland	0.0	0.0	18.6
Russia	37.3	10.7	59.2
Slovenia	0.0	51.5	71.4
Trinidad and Tobago	19.1	21.0	18.3
Ukraine	13.5	0.0	0.0
United Arab Emirates	13.9	1.7	69.2
United Kingdom	83.9	111.6	44.9
USA	659.1	839.3	823.5
Total (incl. others)	1,327.6	1,622.9	1,711.8

Source: Trade Map-Trade Competitiveness Map, International Trade Centre, www.intracen.org/marketanalysis.

Transport

ROAD TRAFFIC
(motor vehicles in use at 31 December)

	2005	2006	2008*
Passenger cars	357,810	373,742	224,520
Motorcycles	27,038	29,061	6,249

* Data for 2007 were not available.

2010: Passenger cars 388,449; Buses 115,221; Lorries 3,095; Motorcycles 12,253.

Source: IRF, *World Road Statistics*.

SHIPPING

Flag Registered Fleet
(at 31 December)

	2011	2012	2013
Number of vessels	29	27	40
Total displacement ('000 grt)	157.3	123.1	168.4

Source: Lloyd's List Intelligence (www.lloydslistintelligence.com).

International Seaborne Freight Traffic
('000 metric tons, estimates)

	2011	2012	2013
Goods loaded	16,570	12,951	12,514
Goods unloaded	13,844	11,013	9,911

Source: Port Authority of Jamaica.

CIVIL AVIATION
(traffic on scheduled services)

	2007	2008	2009
Kilometres flown (million)	57	27	26
Passengers carried ('000)	1,618	1,500	1,380
Passenger-km (million)	3,959	3,027	2,839
Total ton-km (million)	380	315	295

Source: UN, *Statistical Yearbook*.

2010: Passengers carried ('000) 978 (Source: World Bank, World Development Indicators database).

Tourism

VISITOR ARRIVALS BY COUNTRY OF ORIGIN

	2011	2012	2013
Canada	378,938	403,200	399,331
USA	1,225,565	1,257,669	1,271,262
Total (incl. others)	1,951,752	1,986,082	2,008,409

Tourism revenue (US $ million): 2,012.5 in 2011; 2,046.3 in 2012; 2,073.9 in 2013.

Communications Media

	2011	2012	2013
Telephones ('000 main lines in use)	272.1	264.5	247.9
Mobile cellular telephones ('000 subscribers)	2,974.7	2,665.7	2,795.7
Broadband subscribers ('000)	106.5	119.7	132.5

Source: International Telecommunication Union.

Education

(2012/13 unless otherwise indicated)

	Institutions	Teachers	Students
Pre-primary	2,936	10,269	138,124
Primary	933	11,704	264,862
Secondary	387	13,914	236,002
Special schools	30	425	3,748
Tertiary	15	1,162	16,171
University*	2	1,049	26,295

* Figures for 2011/12.

Source: Ministry of Education, Kingston.

Pupil-teacher ratio (primary education, UNESCO estimate): 20.6 in 2009/10 (Source: UNESCO Institute for Statistics).

Adult literacy rate (UNESCO estimates): 87.0% (males 82.1%; females 91.8%) in 2011 (Source: UNESCO Institute for Statistics).

Directory

The Constitution

The Constitution came into force at the independence of Jamaica on 6 August 1962. Amendments to the Constitution are enacted by Parliament, but certain entrenched provisions require ratification by a two-thirds' majority in both chambers of the legislature, and some (such as a change of the head of state) require the additional approval of a national referendum.

HEAD OF STATE

The head of state is the British monarch, who is locally represented by a Governor-General, appointed by the British monarch, on the recommendation of the Jamaican Prime Minister in consultation with the Leader of the Opposition.

THE LEGISLATURE

The Senate consists of 21 Senators, of whom 13 will be appointed by the Governor-General on the advice of the Prime Minister and eight by the Governor-General on the advice of the Leader of the Opposition. (Legislation enacted in 1984 provided for eight independent Senators to be appointed, after consultations with the Prime Minister, in the eventuality of there being no Leader of the Opposition.) The House of Representatives consists of elected members called Members of Parliament.

A person is qualified for appointment to the Senate or for election to the House of Representatives if he or she is a citizen of Jamaica or another Commonwealth country, of the age of 21 or more and has been ordinarily resident in Jamaica for the immediately preceding 12 months.

THE PRIVY COUNCIL

The Privy Council consists of six members appointed by the Governor-General after consultation with the Prime Minister, of whom at least two are persons who hold or who have held public office. The functions of the Council are to advise the Governor-General on the exercise of the Prerogative of Mercy and on appeals on disciplinary matters from the three Service Commissions.

THE EXECUTIVE

The Prime Minister is appointed from the House of Representatives by the Governor-General, and is the leader of the party that holds the majority of seats in the House of Representatives. The Leader of the party is voted in by the members of that party. The Leader of the Opposition is voted in by the members of the Opposition party.

The Cabinet consists of the Prime Minister and not fewer than 11 other ministers, not more than four of whom may sit in the Senate. The members of the Cabinet are appointed by the Governor-General on the advice of the Prime Minister.

THE JUDICATURE

The judicature consists of a Supreme Court, a Court of Appeal and minor courts. Judicial matters, notably advice to the Governor-General on appointments, are considered by a Judicial Service Commission, the Chairman of which is the Chief Justice, members being the President of the Court of Appeal, the Chairman of the Public Service Commission and three others.

CITIZENSHIP

All persons born in Jamaica after independence automatically acquire Jamaican citizenship and there is also provision for the acquisition of citizenship by persons born outside Jamaica of Jamaican parents. Persons born in Jamaica (or persons born outside Jamaica of Jamaican parents) before independence who immediately prior to independence were citizens of the United Kingdom and colonies also automatically become citizens of Jamaica.

Appropriate provision is made which permits persons who do not automatically become citizens of Jamaica to be registered as such.

FUNDAMENTAL RIGHTS AND FREEDOMS

The Constitution includes provisions safeguarding the fundamental freedoms of the individual, irrespective of race, place of origin, political opinions, colour, creed or sex, subject only to respect for the rights and freedoms of others and for the public interest. The fundamental freedoms include the rights of life, liberty, security of the person and protection from arbitrary arrest or restriction of movement, the enjoyment of property and the protection of the law, freedom of conscience, of expression and of peaceful assembly and association, and respect for private and family life.

The Government

HEAD OF STATE

Queen: HM Queen ELIZABETH II.

Governor-General: Sir PATRICK LINTON ALLEN (took office 26 February 2009).

CABINET
(September 2014)

The Government is formed by the People's National Party.

Prime Minister and Minister of Defence, Development, Information and Sports: PORTIA SIMPSON MILLER.

Minister of Foreign Affairs and Foreign Trade: ARNOLD NICHOLSON.

Minister of Finance and Planning: Dr PETER PHILLIPS.

Minister of National Security: PETER BUNTING.

Minister of Education: Rev. RONALD THWAITES.

Minister of Water, Land, Environment and Climate Change: ROBERT PICKERSGILL.

Minister of Tourism and Entertainment: Dr WYKEHAM MCNEIL.

Minister of Justice: MARK GOLDING.

Minister of Industry, Commerce and Investment: ANTHONY HYLTON.

Minister of Local Government and Community Development: NOEL ASCOTT.

Minister of Labour and Social Security and Acting Minister of Agriculture and Fisheries: DERRICK KELLIER.

Minister of Health: Dr FENTON FERGUSON.

Minister of Youth and Culture: LISA HANNAH.

Minister of Transport, Works and Housing: Dr OMAR DAVIES.

Minister of Science, Technology, Energy and Mining: PHILLIP PAULWELL.

Minister without Portfolio in the Office of the Prime Minister with responsibility for Information: SANDREA FALCONER.

Minister without Portfolio in the Ministry of Finance and Planning with responsibility for the Public Service: HORACE DALLEY.

Minister without Portfolio in the Ministry of Transport, Works and Housing with responsibility for Housing: Dr MORAIS GUY.

Minister without Portfolio in the Office of the Prime Minister with responsibility for Sports: NATALIE NEITA-HEADLEY.

There are also eight Ministers of State.

MINISTRIES

Office of the Governor-General: King's House, Hope Rd, Kingston 6; tel. 927-6424; fax 927-4561; e-mail kingshouse@kingshouse.gov.jm; internet www.kingshousejamaica.gov.jm.

Office of the Prime Minister: Jamaica House, 1 Devon Rd, POB 272, Kingston 6; tel. 927-9941; fax 968-8229; e-mail pmo@opm.gov.jm; internet www.opm.gov.jm.

Ministry of Agriculture and Fisheries: Hope Gardens, POB 480, Kingston 6; tel. 927-1731; fax 927-1904; e-mail webmaster@moa.gov.jm; internet www.moa.gov.jm.

Ministry of Education: 2 National Heroes Circle, Kingston 4; tel. 922-1400; fax 967-1837; e-mail webmaster@moec.gov.jm; internet www.moec.gov.jm.

Ministry of Finance and Planning: 30 National Heroes Circle, Kingston 4; tel. 922-8600; fax 922-7097; e-mail info@mof.gov.jm; internet www.mof.gov.jm.

Ministry of Foreign Affairs and Foreign Trade: 21 Dominica Dr., POB 624, Kingston 5; tel. 926-4220; fax 929-5112; e-mail mfaftjam@cwjamaica.com; internet www.mfaft.gov.jm.

Ministry of Health: Oceana Hotel Complex, 2–4 King St, Kingston 10; tel. 967-1100; fax 967-1643; e-mail webmaster@moh.gov.jm; internet www.moh.gov.jm.

Ministry of Industry, Commerce and Investment (MITEC): 4 St Lucia Ave, Kingston 5; tel. 968-7116; fax 960-7422; e-mail communications@miic.gov.jm; internet www.miic.gov.jm.

Ministry of Justice: Mutual Life Bldg, NCB South Tower, 2 Oxford Rd, Kingston 5; tel. 906-4923; fax 906-1712; e-mail customerservice@moj.gov.jm; internet www.moj.gov.jm.

Ministry of Labour and Social Security: 1F North St, POB 10, Kingston; tel. 922-9500; fax 922-6902; e-mail mlss_perm_sect@yahoo .com; internet www.mlss.gov.jm.

Ministry of Local Government and Community Development: 85 Hagley Park Rd, Kingston 11; tel. 754-0992; fax 754-1000; e-mail communications@mlge.gov.jm; internet www .localgovjamaica.gov.jm.

Ministry of National Security: NCB North Tower, 2 Oxford Rd, Kingston 5; tel. 906-4908; fax 754-3601; e-mail information@mns.gov .jm; internet www.mns.gov.jm.

Ministry of Science, Technology, Energy and Mining: PCJ Bldg, 36 Trafalgar Rd, Kingston 10; tel. 929-8990; fax 960-1623; e-mail info@mem.gov.jm; internet www.mem.gov.jm.

Ministry of Tourism and Entertainment: 64 Knutsford Blvd, Kingston 5; tel. 929-9200; fax 929-9375; e-mail info@visitjamaica .com; internet www.tourismja.com.

Ministry of Transport, Works and Housing: 138H Maxfield Ave, Kingston 10; tel. 754-1900; fax 960-2886; e-mail ps@mtw.gov.jm; internet www.mtw.gov.jm.

Ministry of Water, Land, Environment and Climate Change: 25 Dominica Dr., Kingston 5; tel. 926-1690; fax 926-0543; e-mail info@mwh.gov.jm; internet www.mwh.gov.jm.

Ministry of Youth and Culture: 4–6 Trafalgar Rd, Kingston 5; tel. 978-7654; fax 968-4511; e-mail info@micys.gov.jm; internet www .micys.gov.jm.

Legislature

PARLIAMENT

Houses of Parliament: Gordon House, 81 Duke St, POB 636, Kingston; tel. 922-0202; fax 967-1708; e-mail clerk@japarliament .gov.jm; internet www.japarliament.gov.jm.

Senate

President: FLOYD MORRIS.

The Senate has a total of 21 members, including the President; 13 members are appointed on the advice of the Prime Minister and eight on the recommendation of the Leader of the Opposition.

House of Representatives

Speaker: MICHAEL PEART.
General Election, 29 December 2011

	Seats
People's National Party (PNP)	42
Jamaica Labour Party (JLP)	21
Total	63

Election Commission

Electoral Office of Jamaica (EOJ): 43 Duke St, Kingston; tel. 922-0425; fax 967-4058; e-mail eojinfo@eoj.com.jm; internet www.ecj.com .jm; f. 1943; Dir ORRETTE FISHER.

Political Organizations

Jamaica Alliance Movement (JAM): Flamingo Beach, Falmouth, Trelawny, Kingston; tel. 861-5233; e-mail nowjam@gmail.com; internet www.nowjam.org; f. 2001; Rastafarian; Pres. ASTOR BLACK.

Jamaica Labour Party (JLP): 20 Belmont Rd, Kingston 5; tel. 929-1183; e-mail join@jamaicalabourparty.com; internet www .jamaicalabourparty.com; f. 1943; supports free enterprise in a mixed economy and close co-operation with the USA; Leader ANDREW HOLNESS; Gen. Sec. HORACE CHANG.

National Democratic Movement (NDM): The Trade Centre, Unit 9, 30-32 Red Hills Rd, Kingston 10; tel. 906-8485; fax 922-7874; e-mail ndmjamaica@yahoo.com; internet www.ndmj.org; f. 1995; advocates a clear separation of powers between the central executive and elected representatives; supports private investment and a market economy; mem. of the New Jamaica Alliance; Pres. PETER TOWNSEND; Chair. MICHAEL WILLIAMS.

People's National Party (PNP): 89 Old Hope Rd, Kingston 6; tel. 978-1337; fax 927-4389; e-mail information@pnpjamaica.com; internet www.pnpjamaica.com; f. 1938; socialist principles; affiliated

with the National Workers' Union; Pres. PORTIA SIMPSON MILLER; Chair. ROBERT PICKERSGILL; Gen. Sec. PETER BUNTING.

Diplomatic Representation

EMBASSIES AND HIGH COMMISSIONS IN JAMAICA

Argentina: Dyoll Life Bldg, 6th Floor, 40 Knutsford Blvd, Kingston 5; tel. 926-5588; fax 926-0580; e-mail embargen@cwjamaica.com; Ambassador ARIEL FERNÁNDEZ.

Belgium: 6 St Lucia Ave, Kingston 5; tel. 754-7903; fax 906-5943; e-mail kingston@diplobel.fed.be; internet www.diplomatie.be/ kingston; Ambassador GODELIEVE VAN DEN BERGH.

Brazil: 23 Millsborough Crescent, Kingston 6; tel. 946-9812; fax 927-5897; e-mail brasemb.kingston@itamaraty.gov.br; internet kingston .itamaraty.gov.br; Ambassador ANTÔNIO FRANCISCO DA COSTA E SILVA NETO.

Canada: 3 West Kings House Rd, POB 1500, Kingston 10; tel. 926-1500; fax 511-3493; e-mail kngtn@international.gc.ca; internet www .canadainternational.gc.ca/jamaica-jamaique; High Commissioner ROBERT READY.

Chile: Courtleigh Corporate Centre, 5th Floor, South Sixth St, Lucia Ave, Kingston 5; tel. 968-0260; fax 968-0265; e-mail echile.jamaica@ minrel.gov.cl; internet chileabroad.gov.cl/jamaica; Ambassador EDUARDO BONILLA MENCHACA.

China, People's Republic: 8 Seaview Ave, POB 232, Kingston 10; tel. 927-3871; fax 927-6920; e-mail chinaemb_jm@mfa.gov.cn; internet jm.china-embassy.org; Ambassador DONG XIAOJUN.

Colombia: Victoria Mutual Bldg, 4th Floor, 53 Knutsford Blvd, Kingston 5; tel. 929-1701; fax 968-0577; e-mail ekingston@cancilleria .gov.co; internet www.embajadaenjamaica.gov.co; Ambassador LUÍS GUILLERMO MARTÍNEZ FERNÁNDEZ.

Costa Rica: 58 Hope Rd, Kingston 6; tel. 978-5210; e-mail embacostaricajamaica@gmail.com; Chargé d'affaires a.i. TANISHIA ELOÍSA ELLIS HAYLES.

Cuba: 9 Trafalgar Rd, Kingston 5; tel. 978-0931; fax 978-5372; e-mail embacubajam@cwjamaica.com; internet www.cubadiplomatica.cu/ jamaica; Ambassador BERNARDO GUANCHE HERNÁNDEZ.

Dominican Republic: Townhouse, 12 Norbrook Views, 13 Norbrook Cres., Kingston 8; tel. 931-0044; fax 925-1057; e-mail domemb@cwjamaica.com; Ambassador Dr JOSÉ TOMÁS ARES GERMÁN.

France: 13 Hillcrest Ave, POB 93, Kingston 6; tel. 946-4000; fax 946-4020; e-mail frenchembassyjamaica@gmail.com; Ambassador GINETTE DE MATHA.

Germany: 10 Waterloo Rd, POB 444, Kingston 10; tel. 926-6728; fax 620-5457; e-mail germanembassa.kingston@gmail.com; internet www.kingston.diplo.de; Ambassador JOSEF BECK.

Haiti: 2 Munroe Rd, Kingston 6; tel. 927-7595; fax 978-7638; Chargé d'affaires a.i. MAX ALCE.

India: 27 Seymour Ave, POB 446, Kingston 6; tel. 927-4270; fax 978-2801; e-mail hicomindkin@cwjamaica.com; internet www .hcikingston.com; High Commissioner PRATAP SINGH.

Japan: NCB Towers, North Tower, 6th Floor, 2 Oxford Rd, POB 8104, Kingston 5; tel. 929-3338; fax 968-1373; internet www.jamaica .emb-japan.go.jp; Ambassador YASUO TAKASE.

Korea, Republic: 5 Oakridge, Kingston 8; tel. 924-2731; fax 924-7325; e-mail jamaica@mofat.go.kr; internet jam.mofat.go.kr; Chargé d'affaires a.i. KI-MO LIM.

Mexico: PCJ Bldg, 36 Trafalgar Rd, Kingston 10; tel. 926-4242; fax 929-7995; e-mail embamexj@cwjamaica.com; internet embamex.sre .gob.mx/jamaica; Ambassador GERARDO LOZANO ARREDONDO.

Nicaragua: 2 Ottawa Ave, Kingston 6; tel. 285-9200; fax 631-7357; e-mail rhooker@cancilleria.gob.ni; Ambassador DAVID SIDNEY MCFIELD.

Nigeria: 5 Waterloo Rd, POB 94, Kingston 10; tel. 968-3732; fax 968-7371; e-mail nhckingston@mail.infochan.com; High Commissioner OLATOKUNBO KAMSON.

Panama: 34 Annette Cres., Suite 103, Kingston 10; tel. 924-5235; fax 924-3428; e-mail panaemba@hotmail.com; Chargé d'affaires a.i. ERICK CAJAR GRIMAS.

Peru: 23 Barbados Ave, POB 1818, Kingston 5; tel. 920-5027; fax 920-4360; e-mail embaperu-kingston@rree.gob.pe; Ambassador LUIS SÁNDIGA CABRERA.

Russia: 22 Norbrook Dr., Kingston 8; tel. 924-1048; fax 925-8290; e-mail rusembja@colis.com; internet en.rejamaica.ru; Ambassador VLADIMIR POLENOV.

Saint Christopher and Nevis: 11A Opal Ave, Golden Acres, Red Hills, St Andrew; tel. 944-3861; e-mail clrharper@yahoo.com; fax 945-0105; High Commissioner CEDRIC HARPER.

Senegal: Courtleigh Corporate Centre, 6–8 St Lucia Ave, Kingston 5; tel. 906-2919; fax 622-5758; e-mail senegalembassyjamaica@gmail.com; Ambassador Dr NAFISSATOU DIAGNE.

South Africa: 15 Hillcrest Ave, Kingston 6; tel. 620-4840; fax 978-0339; e-mail jamaicak@dirco.gov.za; High Commissioner MATHU JOYINI.

Spain: Courtleigh Corporate Centre, 6th Floor, 6–8 St Lucia Ave, Kingston 5; tel. 929-5555; fax 929-8965; e-mail emb.kingston@mae.es; Ambassador ANÍBAL JULIO JIMÉNEZ.

Trinidad and Tobago: 25 Windsor Ave, Kingston 5; tel. 926-5730; fax 926-5801; e-mail kgnhctt@cwjamaica.com; internet www.kgnhctt.org; High Commissioner Dr IVA CAMILLE GLOUDON.

United Kingdom: 28 Trafalgar Rd, POB 575, Kingston 10; tel. 936-0700; fax 936-0737; e-mail PPA.Kingston@fco.gov.uk; internet www.gov.uk/government/world/jamaica; High Commissioner DAVID FITTON.

USA: 142 Old Hope Rd, Kingston 6; tel. 702-6000; e-mail kingstonirc@state.gov; internet kingston.usembassy.gov; Chargé d'affaires a.i. ELIZABETH LEE MARTINEZ.

Venezuela: PCJ Bldg, 3rd Floor, 36 Trafalgar Rd, POB 26, Kingston 10; tel. 926-5510; fax 926-7442; e-mail embavene@n5.com.jm; Ambassador MARÍA JACQUELINE MENDOZA ORTEGA.

Judicial System

The judicial system is based on English common law and practice. Final appeal is to the Judicial Committee of the Privy Council in the United Kingdom.

Justice is administered by the Privy Council, Court of Appeal, Supreme Court, Resident Magistrates' Court (which includes the Traffic Court), two Family Courts and the Courts of Petty Sessions. The Caribbean Court of Justice, based in Trinidad and Tobago, is the court with jurisdiction for trade disputes.

Judicial Service Commission: Office of the Services Commissions, 30 National Heroes Circle, Kingston 4; tel. 922-8600; fax 924-9764; e-mail communications@osc.gov.jm; internet www.osc.gov.jm; advises the Governor-General on judicial appointments, etc.; Chief Justice ZAILA ROWENA MCCALLA.

Supreme Court: Public Bldg E, 134 Tower St, POB 491, Kingston; tel. 922-8300; fax 967-0669; e-mail webmaster@sc.gov.jm; internet supremecourt.gov.jm; Chief Justice ZAILA MCCALLA.

Court of Appeal: Public Bldg West, King St, POB 629, Kingston; tel. 922-8300; fax 967-1843; e-mail info@courtofappeal.gov.jm; internet www.courtofappeal.gov.jm; Pres. SEYMOUR PANTON.

Attorney-General: PATRICK ATKINSON.

Religion

CHRISTIANITY

Jamaica Council of Churches: 14 South Ave, Kingston 10; tel. and fax 926-0974; e-mail jchurch@cwjamaica.com; internet jamaicacouncilofchurches.yolasite.com; f. 1941; 10 mem. churches and 3 agencies; Gen. Sec. GARY HARRIOT.

The Anglican Communion

Anglicans in Jamaica are adherents of the Church in the Province of the West Indies, comprising eight dioceses. The Archbishop of the Province is the Bishop of Barbados. The Bishop of Jamaica and the Cayman Islands is assisted by three suffragan Bishops (of Kingston, Mandeville and Montego Bay). According to the 2001 census, some 4% of the population are Anglicans.

Bishop of Jamaica and the Cayman Islands: Rt Rev. HOWARD KINGSLEY AINSWORTH GREGORY, Church House, 2 Caledonia Ave, Kingston 5; tel. 926-8925; fax 968-0618; e-mail info@anglicandiocese.com; internet anglicandiocese.dthost.com.

The Roman Catholic Church

Jamaica comprises the archdiocese of Kingston in Jamaica (which also includes the Cayman Islands), and the dioceses of Montego Bay and Mandeville. Some 3% of the population are Roman Catholics. The Archbishop and Bishops participate in the Antilles Episcopal Conference (currently based in Port of Spain, Trinidad and Tobago).

Archbishop of Kingston in Jamaica: Most Rev. CHARLES HENRY DUFOUR, Archbishop's Residence, 21 Hopefield Ave, POB 43, Kingston 6; tel. 927-9915; fax 927-4487; e-mail rcabkgn@cwjamaica.com; internet www.archdioceseofkingston.org.

Other Christian Churches

According to the 2001 census, the largest religious bodies are the Church of God (whose members represent 24% of the population), Seventh-day Adventists (11% of the population), Pentecostalists (10%) and Baptists (7%). Other denominations include Jehovah's Witnesses, the Methodist and Congregational Churches, United Church, the Church of the Brethren, the Ethiopian Orthodox Church, the Disciples of Christ, the Moravian Church, the Church of Latter-Day Saints (Mormons), the Salvation Army and the Religious Society of Friends (Quakers).

Jamaica Baptist Union: 2B Washington Blvd, Kingston 20; tel. 969-2223; fax 924-6296; e-mail info@jbu.org.jm; internet www.jbu.org.jm; f. 1849; 40,000 mems in 332 churches; Pres. Rev. MICHAEL SHIM-HUE; Gen. Sec. Rev. KARL JOHNSON.

Jamaica Union Conference of Seventh-day Adventists (JUCSDA): 125 Manchester Rd, Mandeville; tel. 962-2284; fax 962-3417; e-mail info@wiunion.org; internet jmunion.org; f. 1903; Communications Dir NIGEL COKE; 205,000 mems.

Methodist Church (Jamaica District): 143 Constant Spring Rd, POB 892, Kingston 8; tel. 925-6768; fax 924-2560; e-mail jamaicamethodist@cwjamaica.com; internet www.jamaicamethodist.org; f. 1789; 15,820 mems; District Pres. Rev. EVERALD GALBRAITH.

Moravian Church in Jamaica and the Cayman Islands: 3 Hector St, POB 8369, Kingston 5; tel. 619-1148; e-mail moravianchurch@cwjamaica.com; internet www.jamaicamoravian.com; f. 1754; 30,000 mems.

United Church in Jamaica and the Cayman Islands: 12 Carlton Cres., POB 359, Kingston 10; tel. 926-6059; fax 929-0826; e-mail synod@ucjci.com; internet www.ucjci.com; f. 1965 by merger of the Congregational Union of Jamaica (f. 1877) and the Presbyterian Church of Jamaica and Grand Cayman to become United Church of Jamaica and Grand Cayman; merged with Disciples of Christ in Jamaica in 1992 when name changed as above; 20,000 mems; Moderator Rt. Rev. J. OLIVER DALEY; Gen. Sec. Rev. NORBERT STEPHENS.

RASTAFARIANISM

Rastafarianism is an important influence in Jamaican culture. The cult is derived from Christianity and a belief in the divinity of Ras (Prince) Tafari Makonnen (later Emperor Haile Selassie) of Ethiopia. It advocates racial equality and non-violence, but causes controversy in its use of 'ganja' (marijuana) as a sacrament. According to the 2001 census, 1% of the population are Rastafarians. Although the religion is largely unorganized, there are some denominations.

Haile Selassie Jahrastafari Royal Ethiopian Judah Coptic Church: 11 Welcome Ave, Kingston 11; tel. 461-2721; fax 639-4173; e-mail royalethiopian@gmail.com; internet www.nationofjahrastafari.org; f. 1966; not officially incorporated; Head Pres. Dr MATT O'NEIL MYRIE HAILE SELASSIE I.

BAHÁ'Í FAITH

National Spiritual Assembly: 208 Mountain View Ave, Kingston 6; tel. 927-7051; fax 978-2344; internet www.jm.bahai.org; incorporated in 1970.

ISLAM

According to the 2001 census, there are an estimated 5,000 Muslims (less than 1% of the population).

JUDAISM

According to the 2001 census, there are some 350 Jews (less than 1% of the population).

United Congregation of Israelites: K. K. Shaare Shalom Synagogue, 92 Duke St, Kingston 6; tel. and fax 922-5931; e-mail info@ucija.org; internet www.ucija.org; f. 1655; 250 mems; Rabbi DANA EVAN KAPLAN.

The Press

DAILIES

The Gleaner: 7 North St, POB 40, Kingston; tel. 922-3400; fax 922-6223; e-mail feedback@jamaica-gleaner.com; internet www.jamaica-gleaner.com; f. 1834; morning; independent; Chair. and Man. Dir CHRISTOPHER BARNES; Editor-in-Chief GARFIELD GRANDISON; circ. 50,000.

Jamaica Observer: 40–42 1/2 Beechwood Ave, Kingston 5; tel. 920-8136; fax 926-7655; e-mail editorial@jamaicaobserver.com; internet www.jamaicaobserver.com; f. 1993; Chair. GORDON 'BUTCH' STEWART.

The Jamaica Star: 7 North St, POB 40, Kingston; tel. 922-3400; fax 922-6223; e-mail star@gleanerjm.com; internet jamaica-star.com;

f. 1951; evening; Editor-in-Chief GARFIELD GRANDISON; Editor DWAYNE GORDON; circ. 45,000.

PERIODICALS

All Woman: 40-42 1/2 Beechwood Ave, Kingston 5; tel. 920-8136; e-mail editorial@jamaicaobserver.com; internet www .jamaicaobserver.com/magazines/allwoman; beauty, health and wellness; published by the Jamaica Observer Ltd; other publs include *Sunday Observer* and *Western News*; Editor NOVIA MCDONALD-WHYTE.

The Anglican: 2 Caledonia Ave, Cross Roads, Kingston 5; tel. 920-2714; fax 968-0618; e-mail info@anglicandiocese.com; internet www .anglicandiocesejamaica.com; f. 2004 following cessation of *Jamaica Churchman*; quarterly; circ. 9,000.

Catholic Opinion: Roman Catholic Chancery Office, 21 Hopefield Ave, POB 43, Kingston 6; tel. 927-9915; fax 927-4487; e-mail rcabkgn@cwjamaica.com; internet www.archdioceseofkingston.org; 6 a year; religious; circulated in the *Sunday Gleaner*; Editor Mgr MICHAEL LEWIS; circ. 100,000.

Children's Own: 7 North St, POB 40, Kingston; tel. 922-3400; fax 922-6223; e-mail feedback@jamaica-gleaner.com; internet www .jamaica-gleaner.com; weekly during term-time; publ. by The Gleaner Co; other publs include *Sunday Gleaner* and *Weekend Star*; Editor-in-Chief GARFIELD GRANDISON; circ. 120,000.

HHG Magazine: 5–7 Dunrobin Ave, Kingston 10; tel. 924-4306; fax 924-4985; e-mail hhgmagazine@cwjamaica.com; internet www .hhgmagazine.com; f. 2001; published by Health, Home & Garden Promotions; 3 a year; Editor-in-Chief FAY WINT-SMITH.

Jamaica Journal: 10–16 East St, Kingston; tel. 922-0620; fax 922-1147; e-mail jamaicajournal@instituteofjamaica.org.jm; internet jj .instituteofjamaica.org.jm/ioj_wp; f. 1967; 2 a year; literary, historical and cultural review; publ. by Institute of Jamaica; Chair. of Editorial Cttee Dr KIM ROBINSON.

The Jamaican Magazine: POB 24, Kingston 7; tel. 977-3779; e-mail deeksdesigns@gmail.com; internet www .thejamaicanmagazine.com; f. 1986; art, culture and design; Editor LORRAINE MURRAY.

Mandeville Weekly: 29 Ward Ave, Mandeville, Manchester; tel. 961-0118; fax 961-0119; e-mail mandevilleweekly@flowja.com; internet www.mandevilleweekly.com; f. 1993; Chair. and Editor-in-Chief ANTHONY FRECKLETON; Man. Dir WENDY FRECKLETON.

North Coast Times: 130 Main St, Ocho Rios; tel. and fax 974-9306; e-mail sales@northcoasttimesja.com; internet www .northcoasttimesja.com; f. 1995; weekly; Publr FRANKLIN MCKNIGHT.

Panache Jamaica: 22B Old Hope Rd, Kingston; e-mail editor@ panachejamagazine.com; internet www.panachejamagazine.com; f. 2008; fashion and lifestyle; Editorial Dir TRICIA WILLIAMSON.

Tallawah: Kingston; e-mail tyronesreid@gmail.com; internet www .tallawahmagazine.com; celebrity and lifestyle; monthly; Editor TYRONE S. REID.

West Indian Medical Journal: Faculty of Medical Sciences, University of the West Indies, Mona, Kingston 7; tel. 927-1214; fax 927-1846; e-mail wimj@uwimona.edu.jm; internet myspot.mona.uwi .edu/fms/wimj; f. 1951; monthly; Editor-in-Chief EVERARD N. BARTON; circ. 2,000.

PRESS ASSOCIATION

The Press Association of Jamaica (PAJ): 5 East Ave, Kingston 8; tel. and fax 631-6390; internet pressassociationjamaica.org; f. 1943; Pres. JENNI CAMPBELL; Sec. INGRID BROWN.

Publishers

Jamaica Publishing House Ltd: 97B Church St, Kingston; tel. 967-3866; fax 922-5412; e-mail jph@cwjamaica.com; f. 1969; subsidiary of Jamaica Teachers' Asscn; English language and literature, mathematics, history, geography, social sciences, music; Chair. WOODBURN MILLER; Man. ELAINE R. STENNETT.

LMH Publishing Ltd: 7 Norman Rd, Suite 10–11, Sagicor Industrial Park, POB 8296, Kingston CSO; tel. 938-0005; fax 759-8752; e-mail lmhbookpublishing@cwjamaica.com; internet www .lmhpublishing.com; f. 1970; educational textbooks, general, travel, fiction; Chair. L. MICHAEL HENRY; Man. Dir DAWN CHAMBERS-HENRY.

Ian Randle Publishers (IRP): 11 Cunningham Ave, POB 686, Kingston 6; tel. 978-0745; fax 978-1156; e-mail clp@ ianrandlepublishers.com; internet www.ianrandlepublishers.com; f. 1991; history, biography, politics, sociology, law, cooking and music; Chair. IAN RANDLE; Man. Dir CHRISTINE RANDLE.

University of the West Indies Press (UWI Press): 7A Gibraltar Hall Rd, Mona, Kingston 7; tel. 977-2659; fax 977-2660; internet www.uwipress.com; f. 1992; Caribbean history, culture and literature, gender studies, education and political science; Man. Editor SHIVAUN HEARNE; Gen. Man. LINDA SPETH.

Western Publishers Ltd: 4 Cottage Rd, POB 1258, Montego Bay; tel. 952-5253; fax 952-6513; e-mail westernmirror@mail.infochan .com; internet westernmirror.com; f. 1980; CEO and Editor-in-Chief LLOYD B. SMITH.

GOVERNMENT PUBLISHING HOUSE

Jamaica Printing Services: 77 1/2 Duke St, Kingston; tel. 967-2250; fax 967-2225; e-mail jps_1992@yahoo.com; internet jps1992 .org; Gen. Man. BLONDELL WYNDHAM.

ASSOCIATION

Caribbean Publishers' Network (CAPNET): 11 Cunningham Ave, Kingston 6; e-mail info@capnetonline.net; internet www .capnetonline.net; non-profit regional asscn; Pres. NEYSHA SOODEEN.

Broadcasting and Communications

TELECOMMUNICATIONS

Anbell Telecommunications Ltd: 51 Knutsford Blvd, Kingston 5; tel. 906-8479; fax 906-8487; e-mail support@anbell.net; internet anbell.net/telecom.htm; internet service provider; Man. GARFIELD BOLT.

Columbus Communications Jamaica Ltd (Flow): 6–8 St Lucia Ave, Kingston 5; tel. 620-3000; e-mail mediainquires@flowjamaica .com; internet discoverflow.co/jamaica; f. 2006; cable, internet and telephone service provider; Pres. and COO MICHELLE ENGLISH.

Digicel Jamaica: 14 Ocean Blvd, Kingston 5; tel. 619-5000; fax 920-0948; e-mail customercare@digicelgroup.com; internet www .digiceljamaica.com; f. 2001; mobile cellular telephone operator; owned by Irish consortium, Mossel (Jamaica) Ltd; absorbed all operations and subscribers of Claro Jamaica in 2012; Chair. DENIS O'BRIEN; CEO (Caribbean and Central America) ANDY THORBURN.

LIME: 7 Cecilio Ave, Kingston 10; tel. 926-9700; fax 929-9530; e-mail customer.services@lime.com; internet www.lime.com/jm; f. 1989; name changed as above in 2008; 79% owned by Cable & Wireless (UK); landline, internet and mobile services; CEO TONY RICE; Man. Dir (Jamaica and the Cayman Islands) GARRY SINCLAIR.

Noble Wi-Fi: Montego; tel. 410-8532; e-mail Sales-WiFi@noblecoms .com; internet noblecoms.com; f. 2014; internet service provider in north Jamaica; Dir RYAN FERNANDEZ.

Regulatory Authority

The sector is regulated by the Office of Utilities Regulation (see Utilities).

BROADCASTING

Radio

Independent Radio: 6 Bradley Ave, Kingston 10; tel. 968-4880; fax 968-9165; commercial; broadcasts 24 hrs a day on FM; Man. Dir NEWTON JAMES.

  Power 106: 6 Bradley Ave, Kingston 10; tel. 968-4880; fax 968-9165; e-mail power106@cwjamaica.com; internet www.go-jamaica .com/power; f. 1992; talk and sports programmes.

IRIE FM: 1B Coconut Grove, Ocho Rios, St Ann; tel. 968-5023; fax 968-8332; e-mail customerservice@iriefm.net; internet www.iriefm .net; f. 1990; owned by Grove Broadcasting Co; reggae music; Man. BRIAN SCHMIDT.

KLAS Sports FM 89: 17 Haining Rd, Kingston 5; tel. 929-1344; fax 960-0572; e-mail admin@klassportsradio.com; internet www .klassportsradio.com; f. 1991; sports broadcasting.

Kool 97 FM: 1 Braemar Ave, Kingston 10; tel. 978-4037; fax 978-3346; e-mail contact@kool97fm.com; internet www.kool97fm.com; f. 2001; music, news and tourism information.

Linkz 96 FM: 8 Beckford St, Savanna La Mar, Westmoreland; tel. 955-3686; fax 955-9523; e-mail linkz96fm@yahoo.com; internet www .linkzfm.com; f. 2004; Chair ROGER ALLEN.

Love FM: 81 Hagley Park Rd, Kingston 10; tel. 968-9596; e-mail webmaster@love101.org; internet love101.org; f. 1993; commercial radio station, religious programming on FM; owned by National Religious Media Ltd; Gen. Man. Rt Rev. HERRO BLAIR (acting).

Radio Jamaica Ltd (RJR): Broadcasting House, 32 Lyndhurst Rd, POB 23, Kingston 5; tel. 926-1100; fax 929-7467; e-mail rjr@ radiojamaica.com; internet www.radiojamaica.com; f. 1947; commercial, public service; 3 channels; Man. Dir GARY ALLEN; Gen. Man. Radio Services FRANCOIS ST JUSTE.

FAME 95 FM: 32 Lyndhurst Rd, Kingston 5; tel. 18763567406 (mobile); internet www.fame95fm.com; e-mail famefm@rjrgroup .com; f. 1984; broadcasts on FM, island-wide 24 hrs a day; Gen. Man. FRANCOIS ST JUSTE.

Hitz 92 FM: internet www.radiohitz92fm.com; broadcasts on FM, island-wide 24 hrs a day; youth station.

RJR 94 FM: internet rjr94fm.com; broadcasts on AM and FM, island-wide 24 hrs a day; Exec. Producer NORMA BROWN-BELL.

Roots FM: Mustard Seed Communities, POB 267, Kingston 10; tel. 923-2165; fax 923-6000; e-mail roots.fm@mustardseed.com; internet www.mustardseed.com; Chair TREVOR GORDON-SOMERS.

Stylz FM: 4 Boundbrook Ave, Port Antonio, Portland; tel. 993-3358; fax 993-3814; e-mail hueljacks@hotmail.com; internet www .rudelikedat.com/stylzfm; CEO HUEL JACKSON.

TBC FM: 51 Molynes Rd, Kingston 10; tel. 754-5120; fax 968-9159; e-mail gcallam@tbcradio.org; internet www.tbcradio.org; Gen. Man. GARY CALLAM.

ZIP 103 FM: 1B Courtney Walsh Dr., Kingston 10, Jamaica; tel. 929-6233; fax 929-4691; e-mail zip103fm@cwjamaica.com; internet www .zipfm.net; f. 2002; commercial radio station; Dir D'ADRA WILLIAMS.

104.9 FM: Shop 10, R.T. Plaza, Off Port Henderson Rd, Portmore, St Catherine; tel. 740-5087; e-mail motherincrisis@yahoo.com; internet www.suncityradio.fm; CEO DOREEN BILLINGS.

Television

Creative TV (CTV): Caenwood Campus, 37 Arnold Rd, Kingston 5; tel. 967-4482; fax 924-9432; internet www.creativetvjamaica.com; operated by Creative Production & Training Centre Ltd (CPTC); local cable channel; regional cultural, educational and historical programming; CEO Dr HOPETON DUNN.

CVM Television: 69 Constant Sprint Rd, Kingston 10; tel. 931-9400; fax 931-9417; e-mail contact@cvmtv.com; internet www.cvmtv .com; Pres. and CEO DAVID MCBEAN.

Love Television: Kingston; internet www.love101.org; f. 1997; religious programming; owned by National Religious Media Ltd.

Television Jamaica Limited (TVJ): 32 Lyndhurst Rd, Kingston 5; tel. 926-1100; fax 929-1029; e-mail tvjadmin@cwjamaica.com; internet www.televisionjamaica.com; f. 1959 as Jamaica Broadcasting Corpn; privatized and adopted current name in 1997; subsidiary of RJR Communications Group; island-wide VHF transmission 24 hrs a day; Chair. MILTON SAMUDA; Gen. Man. GARY ALLEN.

Regulatory Authorities

Broadcasting Commission of Jamaica: 5th Floor, Victoria Mutual Bldg, 53 Knutsford Blvd, Kingston 5; tel. 929-1998; fax 929-1997; e-mail info@broadcom.org; internet www .broadcastingcommission.org; f. 1986; Chair. Prof. HOPETON DUNN.

Spectrum Management Authority: 13–19 Harbour St, Kingston; tel. 967-7948; fax 922-4093; e-mail info@sma.gov.jm; internet www .sma.gov.jm; f. 2000; national regulator for radio frequency spectrum; govt-run; Chair. CHRISTOPHER HONEYWELL.

Finance

(cap. = capital; res = reserves; dep. = deposits; m. = million; brs = branches; amounts in Jamaican dollars)

REGULATORY AUTHORITY

Jamaica International Financial Services Authority: Kingston; f. 2011 following an Act of Parliament; Chair. ERIC CRAWFORD.

BANKING

Central Bank

Bank of Jamaica: Nethersole Pl., POB 621, Kingston; tel. 922-0750; fax 922-0854; e-mail info@boj.org.jm; internet www.boj.org.jm; f. 1960; cap. 4.0m., res 8,831.2m., dep. 198,440.4m. (Dec. 2009); Gov. and Chair. BRIAN HECTOR WYNTER.

Commercial Banks

CIBC FirstCaribbean International Bank: CIBC Centre, 23-27 Knutsford Blvd, Kingston 5; tel. 929-9310; fax 926-7751; internet www.firstcaribbeanbank.com; FirstCaribbean f. in 2002 following merger of Caribbean operations of CIBC and Barclays Bank PLC; Barclays relinquished its stake in 2006, present name adopted in 2011; cap. 1,396.7m., res 5,671m., dep. 42,595.3m. (Oct. 2011); CEO RIK PARKHILL; Man. Dir NIGEL HOLNESS; 13 brs.

Citibank, NA: 19 Hillcrest Ave, Kingston 6; tel. 926-3270; fax 978-8889; e-mail peter.moses@citi.com; internet www.citibank.com/ jamaica; owned by Citifinance Ltd; cap. 25.7m., res 128.4m., dep. 87.2m. (Dec. 2003); Man. Dir PETER MOSES.

National Commercial Bank Jamaica Ltd: 'The Atrium', 32 Trafalgar Rd, POB 88, Kingston 10; tel. 929-9050; fax 929-8399; tel. ncbinfo@jncb.com; internet www.jncb.com; f. 1837; merged with Mutual Security Bank in 1996; cap. 6,465.7m., res 32,191.8m., dep. 180,628.2m. (Sept. 2013); Chair. MICHAEL LEE-CHIN; Man. Dir PATRICK HYLTON; 37 brs.

RBC Royal Bank (Jamaica) Limited: 17 Dominica Dr., Kingston 5; tel. 960-2340; fax 960-5120; e-mail rbtt@cwjamaica.com; internet www.rbtt.com/jm; f. 1993 as Jamaica Citizens Bank Ltd; acquired by Royal Bank of Trinidad and Tobago in 2001 and name changed to RBTT Bank Jamaica Ltd; present name adopted 2011; to be sold to Sagicor Ltd in 2014; cap. 8,167.8m., res 2,764.5m., dep. 40,986m. (Dec. 2010); Chair. SURESH SOOKOO; 23 brs.

Scotiabank Jamaica Ltd (Canada): Scotiabank Centre Bldg, cnr Duke and Port Royal Sts, POB 709, Kingston; tel. 922-1000; fax 924-9294; e-mail customercare-jam@scotiabank.com; internet www .scotiabank.com.jm; f. 1967 subsidiary of Bank of Nova Scotia (Canada); cap. 2,927.2m., res 18,264.3m., dep. 151,668.4m. (Oct. 2010); Chair. SYLVIA CHROMINSKA; Pres. and CEO JACQUELINE SHARP; 35 brs.

Development Banks

Development Bank of Jamaica Ltd: 11A–15 Oxford Rd, POB 466, Kingston 5; tel. 929-4000; fax 929-6055; e-mail mail@dbankjm.com; internet www.dbankjm.com; f. 2000 following merger of Agricultural Credit Bank of Jamaica and the National Devt Bank of Jamaica; provides funds for medium- and long-term devt-orientated projects; Chair. JOSEPH M. MATALON; Man. Dir MILVERTON REYNOLDS.

Jamaica Mortgage Bank: 33 Tobago Ave, POB 950, Kingston 5; tel. 929-6350; fax 968-5428; e-mail info@jmb.gov.jm; internet www .jmb.gov.jm; f. 1971 by the Jamaican Govt and the US Agency for Int. Devt; govt-owned statutory org. since 1973; functions primarily as a secondary market facility for home mortgages and to mobilize long-term funds for housing devts in Jamaica; also insures home mortgage loans made by approved financial institutions, thus transferring risk of default on a loan to the Govt; Chair. HOWARD MOLLISON; Gen. Man. PATRICK THELWALL.

Sagicor Investments Jamaica Ltd: 60 Knutsford Blvd, Kingston 5; tel. 929-5583; fax 926-4385; e-mail options@sagicor.com; internet www.sagicor.com; fmrly Trafalgar Devt Bank, name changed as Pan Caribbean Financial Services in Dec. 2002; present name adopted in 2012; Chair. RICHARD O. BYLES; Pres. and CEO DONOVAN H. PERKINS.

Other Banks

National Export-Import Bank of Jamaica Ltd: 11 Oxford Rd, Kingston 5; tel. 960-9690; fax 960-9115; e-mail info@eximbankja .com; internet www.eximbankja.com; f. 1986; govt-owned; replaced Jamaica Export Credit Insurance Corpn; finances import and export of goods and services; Chair. WILLIAM CLARKE; Man. Dir LISA BELL.

Banking Association

Jamaica Bankers' Association: PSOJ Bldg, 39 Hope Rd, POB 1079, Kingston 10; tel. 927-6238; fax 927-5137; e-mail jbainfo@jba .org.jm; internet www.jba.org.jm; f. 1973; Pres. BRUCE BOWEN.

STOCK EXCHANGE

Jamaica Stock Exchange Ltd: 40 Harbour St, POB 1084, Kingston; tel. 967-3271; fax 967-3277; internet www.jamstockex.com; f. 1968; Chair. DONOVAN H. PERKINS; Gen. Man. MARLENE STREET-FORREST.

INSURANCE

Financial Services Commission: 39–43 Barbados Ave, Kingston 5; tel. 906-3010; fax 906-3018; e-mail inquiry@fscjamaica.org; internet www.fscjamaica.org; f. 2001; succeeded the Office of the Superintendent of Insurance; regulatory body; Chair. COLIN BULLOCK; Exec. Dir JANICE P. HOLNESS.

Principal Companies

Advantage General Insurance Co Ltd: 4-6 Trafalgar Rd, Kingston 5; tel. 978-3690; fax 978-3718; internet www.advantagegeneral .com; f. 1964; general; Chair. DENNIS G. COHEN; Pres. and CEO MARK THOMPSON.

British Caribbean Insurance Co Ltd (BCIC): 36 Duke St, POB 170, Kingston; tel. 922-1260; fax 922-4475; e-mail dsales@bcic-jm .com; internet www.bciconline.com; f. 1962; affiliate of Victoria Mutual Insurance Co; general; Chair. JOSEPH M. MATALON; Man. Dir PETER LEVY.

General Accident Insurance Co Jamaica Ltd: 58 Half Way Tree Rd, Kingston 10; tel. 929-8451; fax 929-1074; e-mail info@genac.com; internet www.genac.com; f. 1981; general; Chair. PAUL B. SCOTT; Man. Dir SHARON DONALDSON.

Globe Insurance Co of Jamaica Ltd: 19 Dominica Dr., POB 401, Kingston 5; tel. 926-3720; fax 929-2727; e-mail info@globeins.com; internet www.globeins.com; f. 1963; fmr subsidiary of Lascelles deMercado, bought by Guardian Holdings Ltd in Sept. 2012; general; Man. Dir EVAN THWAITES.

Guardian General Insurance Jamaica Ltd: 19 Dominica Dr., Kingston 5; tel. 929-8080; fax 929-2727; e-mail insure@wia.com.jm; internet www.guardiangroup.com; f. 1969; subsidiary of Guardian Holdings Ltd (Trinidad and Tobago); general; Pres. KAREN BHOOR-ASINGH.

Guardian Life: 12 Trafalgar Rd, Kingston 5; tel. 978-8815; fax 978-4225; e-mail guardian@ghl.com.jm; internet www.guardianlife.com .jm; subsidiary of Guardian Holdings Ltd (Trinidad and Tobago); pension and life policies; Pres. and CEO ERIC HOSIN.

Insurance Co of the West Indies Ltd (ICWI): 2 St Lucia Ave, POB 306, Kingston 5; tel. 926-9040; fax 929-6641; e-mail direct@icwi.com; internet icwi.com/jamaica; general; Chair. and CEO DENNIS LALOR.

Jamaica General Insurance Co Ltd: 19–21 Knutsford Blvd, New Kingston; tel. 926-3204; fax 968-1920; e-mail info@jiiconline.com; internet www.jiiconline.com; f. 1981; subsidiary of GraceKennedy Ltd; general; Chair. PETER MOSS-SOLOMON; Man. Dir GRACE BURNETT.

JN General Insurance Company Ltd (JNGI): NEM House, 9 King St, Kingston; tel. 922-1460; fax 922-4045; e-mail info@nemjam .com; internet www.nemjam.com; f. 1934; fmr NEM Insurance, present name adopted 2012; subsidiary of Jamaica National Bldg Soc; general; Chair. OLIVER CLARKE; Gen. Man. CHRISTOPHER HIND.

NCB Insurance Co Ltd (NCBIC): 32 Trafalgar Rd, Kingston 10; tel. 935-2730; fax 929-7301; e-mail ncbic@jncb.com; internet www .ncbinsurance.com; f. 1989; fmrly OMNI Insurance Services Ltd; life; Chair. WAYNE CHEN; Gen. Man. VERNON JAMES.

Sagicor Life Jamaica Ltd: 28–48 Barbados Ave, Kingston 5; tel. 960-8920; fax 960-1927; internet www.sagicorjamaica.com; f. 1970; owned by Sagicor Group (Barbados); merged with Island Life Insurance Co Ltd in 2001; renamed as above in 2009; life; Chair. R. DANNY WILLIAMS; Pres. and CEO RICHARD O. BYLES.

Scotia Jamaica Life Insurance Co Ltd (SJLIC): Duke and Port Royal Sts, Kingston; tel. 922-3765; e-mail sjlic.service@scotiabank .com; internet www.scotiabank.com; f. 1995; life; Pres. HUGH REID.

Association

Insurance Association of Jamaica (IAJ): 3–3A Richmond Ave, Kingston 10; tel. 929-8404; fax 906-1804; e-mail iaj@cwjamaica.com; internet www.iaj-online.com; f. 2005 by merger of the Jamaica Asscn of General Insurance Cos (JAGIC) and the Life Insurance Cos Asscn of Jamaica (LICA); Pres. HUGH REID; Exec. Dir ORVILLE JOHNSON.

Trade and Industry

GOVERNMENT AGENCY

Jamaica Information Service (JIS): 58A Half Way Tree Rd, POB 2222, Kingston 10; tel. 926-3740; fax 926-6715; e-mail jis@jis.gov.jm; internet www.jis.gov.jm; f. 1963; govt agency; CEO DONNA-MARIE ROWE.

DEVELOPMENT ORGANIZATIONS

Agro-Investment Corpn: Ministry of Agriculture and Fisheries, 188 Spanish Town Rd, Kingston 11; tel. 764-8071; fax 758-7160; e-mail agricultural@cwjamaica.com; internet www.assp.gov.jm; f. 2009; following the merger of Agricultural Devt Corp (ADC) and Agricultural Support Services Productive Projects Fund Ltd (ASSPPFL); agricultural devt, investment facilitation, promotion and management; Chair. DAVID LOWE; CEO HERSHELL BROWN.

JAMPRO Trade and Invest, Jamaica (JAMPRO): 18 Trafalgar Rd, Kingston 10; tel. 978-7755; fax 946-0090; e-mail info@jamprocorp .com; internet www.jamaicatradeandinvest.org; f. 1988 by merger of Jamaica Industrial Development Corpn, Jamaica National Export Corpn and Jamaica Investment Promotion Ltd; trade and investment promotion agency; Chair. MILTON SAMUDA; Pres. DIANE EDWARDS.

Planning Institute of Jamaica: 16 Oxford Rd, Kingston 5; tel. 960-9339; fax 906-5011; e-mail info@pioj.gov.jm; internet www.pioj.gov .jm; f. 1955 as the Central Planning Unit; adopted current name in 1984; formulates policy on and monitors performance in the fields of the economy and social, environmental and trade issues; publishing and analysis of social and economic performance data; Chair. and Dir-Gen. Dr GLADSTONE HUTCHINSON.

Urban Development Corpn: The Office Centre, 8th Floor, 12 Ocean Blvd, Kingston; tel. 922-8310; fax 922-9326; e-mail info@ udcja.com; internet www.udcja.com; f. 1968; responsibility for urban renewal and devt within designated areas; Chair. WAYNE CHEN; Gen. Man. DESMOND YOUNG.

CHAMBERS OF COMMERCE

American Chamber of Commerce of Jamaica: The Jamaica Pegasus, 81 Knutsford Blvd, Kingston 5; tel. 929-7866; fax 929-8597; e-mail amcham.ja@gmail.com; internet www.amchamjamaica.com; f. 1986; affiliated to the Chamber of Commerce of the USA; Pres. DERRICK NEMBHARD; Exec. Dir BECKY STOCKHAUSEN.

Jamaica Chamber of Commerce: UDC Office Centre, Suites 13–15, 12 Ocean Blvd, Kingston 10; tel. 922-0150; fax 924-9056; e-mail info@jamaicachamber.org.jm; internet www.jamaicachamber.org .jm; f. 1779; Pres. MILTON JEFFERSON SAMUDA; Gen. Man PATRICIA PEART; 450 mems.

INDUSTRIAL AND TRADE ASSOCIATIONS

Cocoa Industry Board: Marcus Garvey Dr., POB 1039, Kingston 15; tel. 923-6411; fax 923-5837; e-mail cocoajam@cwjamaica.com; f. 1957; has statutory powers to regulate and develop the industry; owns and operates 4 central fermentaries; Chair. FRANK PHIPPS; Man. and Sec. STEVE WATSON.

Coconut Industry Board: 18 Waterloo Rd, Kingston 10; tel. 926-1770; fax 968-1360; e-mail info@coconutindustryboard.org.jm; internet www.coconutindustryboard.org.jm; f. 1945; 9 mems; Chair. RICHARD A. JONES; Gen. Man. YVONNE BURNS.

Coffee Industry Board: 1 Willie Henry Dr., POB 508, Kingston 13; tel. 758-1259; fax 758-3907; e-mail datacoordinator@ciboj.org; internet www.ciboj.org; f. 1950; 9 mems; has wide statutory powers to regulate and develop the industry; Chair. HOWARD MITCHELL; Dir-Gen. CHRISTOPHER GENTLES.

Jamaica Bauxite Institute: Hope Gardens, POB 355, Kingston 6; tel. 927-2073; fax 927-1159; f. 1975; adviser to the Govt in the negotiation of agreements, consultancy services to clients in the bauxite/alumina and related industries, laboratory services for mineral and soil-related services, pilot plant services for materials and equipment-testing, research and devt; Chair. GARY PEART; Exec. Dir PARRIS LYEW-AYEE.

Jamaica Exporters' Association (JEA): 1 Winchester Rd, Kingston 10; tel. 960-4908; fax 960-9869; e-mail info@exportja.org; internet www.exportjamaica.org; f. 1966; promotes devt of export sector; Pres. VITUS EVANS; Gen. Man. JEAN SMITH.

Jamaica Manufacturers' Association Ltd (JMA): 85A Duke St, Kingston; tel. 922-8880; fax 922-9205; e-mail jma@cwjamaica.com; internet www.jma.com.jm; f. 1947; 340 mems; Pres. BRIAN PENGELLEY.

Sugar Industry Authority: 5 Trevennion Park Rd, POB 127, Kingston 5; tel. 926-5930; fax 926-6149; e-mail sia@cwjamaica .com; internet www.jamaicasugar.org; f. 1970; statutory body under portfolio of Min. of Agriculture and Fisheries; responsible for regulation and control of sugar industry and sugar-marketing; conducts research through Sugar Industry Research Institute; Exec. Chair. DERICK HEAVEN.

Trade Board Ltd: Air Jamaica Bldg, 10th Floor, 72 Harbour St, Kingston; tel. 967-0507; fax 948-5441; e-mail info@tradeboard.gov .jm; internet www.tradeboard.gov.jm; Trade Admin. DOUGLAS WEBSTER.

EMPLOYERS' ORGANIZATIONS

All-Island Banana Growers' Association Ltd: Banana Industry Bldg, 10 South Ave, Kingston 4; tel. 922-5497; fax 922-5497; e-mail aibga@cwjamaica.com; f. 1946; 1,500 mems (1997); Chair. GRETEL SESSING; Sec. I. CHANG.

Citrus Growers' Association Ltd: Bog Walk, St Catherine; tel. 708-2150; fax 708-2538; internet www.jcgja.com; f. 1944; 13,000 mems; Chair. JOHN THOMPSON; Gen. Man. DENNIS BOOTH.

Jamaica Association of Sugar Technologists: c/o Sugar Industry Research Institute, Kendal Rd, Mandeville; tel. 962-2241; fax 962-1288; e-mail jast@jamaicasugar.org; f. 1936; 275 mems; Chair. EARLE ROBERTS; Pres. IAN MAXWELL.

Jamaica Gasoline Retailers' Association (JGRA): Kings Plaza, POB 156, Kingston 10; tel. 929-2998; fax 929-8281; e-mail jgra@ cwjamaica.com; internet jgrajm.org; f. 1951; Pres. DERRICK THOMPSON.

Jamaica Livestock Association: Newport East, POB 36, Kingston; tel. 922-7130; fax 922-8934; internet www.jlaltd.com; f. 1941; 7,584 mems; Man. Dir and CEO HENRY J. RAINFORD.

Jamaica Sugar Cane Growers' Association (JSCGA): 4 North Ave, Kingston Gardens, Kingston 4; tel. 922-3010; fax 922-2077; e-mail allcane@cwjamaica.com; f. 1941; registered cane farmers; 27,000 mems; fmrly All-Island Cane Farmers' Asscn; name changed as above in 2008; Pres. ALLAN RICKARDS; Gen. Man. KARL JAMES.

Private Sector Organization of Jamaica (PSOJ): The Carlton Alexander Bldg, 39 Hope Rd, POB 236, Kingston 10; tel. 927-6957; fax 927-5137; e-mail psojinfo@psoj.org; internet www.psoj.org; f. 1976; federative body of private business individuals, cos and asscns; Pres. CHRISTOPHER ZACCA; CEO SANDRA GLASGOW.

Small Businesses' Association of Jamaica (SBAJ): 2 Trafalgar Rd, Kingston 5; tel. 978-0168; fax 927-7071; e-mail sbaj1org@yahoo.com; internet sbaj.org.jm; f. 1974; Pres. Dr MEREDITH DERBY.

Sugar Manufacturing Corpn of Jamaica Ltd: 5 Trevennion Park Rd, Kingston 5; tel. 925-3650; fax 926-6746; est. to represent sugar mfrs in Jamaica; deals with all aspects of the sugar industry and its by-products; provides liaison between the Govt, the Sugar Industry Authority and the Jamaica Sugar Cane Growers' Asscn; 9 mems; Gen. Man. DERYCK T. BROWN.

MAJOR COMPANIES

Food and Beverages

Dairy Industries (Jamaica) Ltd: 111 Washington Blvd, Kingston 20; tel. 934-8272; fax 934-1793; e-mail dairy@cwjamaica.com; internet dairyindustriesjamaica.com; f. 1964; 50% owned by Grace-Kennedy and Co PLC and 50% owned by Fonterra Co-op Group Ltd (New Zealand); mfr of dairy products, contract packer of powdered drinks; Chair. GORDON SHIRLEY; Group CEO DON WEHBY; 100 employees.

Desnoes and Geddes Ltd: 214 Spanish Town Rd, POB 190, Kingston 11; tel. 923-9291; fax 675-2029; f. 1918; part of Diageo Corpn; brewery and soft drinks bottlers; producers of Red Stripe lager and Dragon Stout; Chair. RICHARD BYLES; Man. Dir CEDRIC BLAIR; 624 employees (2011).

GraceKennedy Ltd: 73 Harbour St, POB 86, Kingston; tel. 922-3440; fax 948-3073; e-mail gracekennedy@gkco.com; internet www.gracekennedy.com; f. 1922; holding co concerned with food-processing and wholesale distribution, manufacturing, financial services, maritime activities, hardware, information technology; over 65 subsidiaries and related cos, incl. GK Investments and GK Foods; Chair. DOUGLAS ORANE; CEO DON WEHBY; 2,200 employees.

Island Spice: 21–23 Bell Rd, Kingston 11; tel. 757-8520; fax 757-8523; e-mail islandspice@cwjamaica.com; internet islandspice.com; f. 1987; producers of spices, flavourings, sauces and coffee; Contact LAWRENCE SHADEED.

Jamaica Broilers Group Ltd: McCook's Pen, St Catherine, C.S.O; tel. 943-4370; fax 943-4322; internet www.jamaicabroilersgroup.com; f. 1958; mfr of animal feed, producer of poultry, beef, tilapia and hatching eggs; operates an ethanol distillery; cap. J $762m.; Chair. ROBERT E. LEVY; Pres. and CEO CHRISTOPHER LEVY; 1,500 employees.

Jamaica Flour Mills Ltd: 209 Windward Rd, POB 28, Kingston 2; tel. 928-7221; fax 928-7348; e-mail jfmcustomerservice@adm.com; f. 1966; subsidiary of Archer Daniels Midland Co; milling of grain, incl. flour; Man. Dir DERRICK NEMBHARD; 104 employees.

Jamaica Producers' Group Ltd: Producers House, 6A Oxford Rd, POB 237, Kingston 5; tel. 926-3503; fax 926-3636; internet www.jpjamaica.com; f. 1929 as Jamaica Banana Producers Asscn Ltd; owns Eastern Banana Estates Ltd, St Mary Banana Estates Ltd, JP Fresh Produce, JP Snacks, Sunjuice Ltd, Jamaica Producers Shipping Co Ltd and A. L. Hoogesteger Fresh Specialist BV (Netherlands); producers and exporters of bananas and other foodstuffs; Chair. CHARLES H. JOHNSTON; CEO JEFFREY HALL.

Jamaica Standard Products Co Ltd: POB 2, Williamsfield, Manchester; tel. 963-4211; e-mail admin@jspcoffee.com; internet www.jamaicastandardproducts.com; f. 1942; production and export of coffee, coffee liqueurs, sauces and spices; Man. Dir JOHN O. MINOTT, Sr; 232 employees.

National Rums of Jamaica Ltd: The Towers, 10th Floor, 25 Dominica Dr., POB 174, Kingston 10; tel. 929-6484; fax 926-7499; e-mail info@monymuskrums.com; f. 1980 by jt venture between the Govt and Seagram Co Ltd; 51% state-owned, 49% owned by Diageo Group; mfr of distilled alcoholic drinks; Man. Dir R. EVAN BROWN; 139 employees.

Nestlé-JMP Jamaica Ltd: Pan Jamaican Bldg, 60 Knutsford Blvd, POB 281, Kingston 5; tel. 926-1300; fax 926-7388; e-mail donna-kaye.sharpe@jm.nestle.com; f. 1986; subsidiary of Nestlé (Switzerland); mfr of milk products; Gen. Man. JAMES RAWLE; 456 employees.

Pan-Caribbean Sugar Co: Kingston; internet www.complant.com; f. 1993 as Sugar Co of Jamaica, public-private consortium; owned by Complant International (China); bought 3 remaining state-owned sugar factories in 2011; CEO HUAIXIANG WU.

Pepsi-Cola Jamaica Bottling Co Ltd: 214 Spanish Town Rd, Kingston 11; tel. 757-3839; fax 937-8595; e-mail andrew.reid@pepsiamericas.com; bottling co for PepsiCo Beverages Americas soft drink mfrs; CEO GUSTAVO FLAMENCO; Dir ANDREW REID.

Salada Foods: 20 Bell Rd, POB 71, Kingston 11; tel. 923-7114; fax 923-5336; e-mail info@saladafoodsja.com; internet www.saladafoodsja.com; coffee production and processing; Chair. JOHN BELL; Man. Dir JOHN ROSEN.

Walkerswood Group: 38 Beechwood Ave, Kingston 5; tel. 926-6449; fax 926-6264; e-mail info@walkerswood.com; internet www.walkerswood.com; f. 1978; dissolved in 2009 but bought by New Castle Co in 2010 and reformed; mfr of food products.

Wisynco Group Ltd: White Marl, St Catherine; internet www.wisynco.com; mfr and distributor of food, drink and paper products; Man. Dir WILLIAM MAHFOOD.

J. Wray and Nephew Ltd: 234 Spanish Town Rd, POB 39, Kingston 11; tel. 923-6141; fax 923-6981; e-mail info@appletonestate.com; internet www.appletonestate.com; f. 1960; part-owned by Campari group; sugar plantation and rum distillery; owns Appleton Estates; Man. Dir PAUL HENRIQUES; Gen. Man. GRETA BOGUES; 2,400 employees.

Mining and Power

The Antilles Group Limited: 236 Windward Rd, Rockfort, Kingston 2; tel. 928-7301; fax 928-6045; e-mail info@tagjamaica.com; internet www.theantillesgroup.com; f. 2005; fmrly known as Cool Petroleum Holdings, present name adopted in 2012 after Blue Equity (USA) acquired a controlling interest; distributor of Shell bulk fuels and lubricants to retail, chemical and liquefied petroleum gas sectors; CEO JONATHAN BLUE; Man. Dir STEVEN WHITTINGHAM.

Jamalco: Clarendon Parish, Clarendon; tel. 986-2561; fax 986-9637; internet www.alcoa.com/Jamaica; f. 1959 as Alcoa Minerals of Jamaica; 45% owned by the Govt of Jamaica (as Clarendon Alumina Co) and 55% by Noble Resources Ltd (Hong Kong); alumina and bauxite mining; Man. Dir JEROME T. MAXWELL.

Noranda Bauxite Ltd: Discovery Bay Post Office, Kingston; tel. 973-2221; fax 973-2568; f. 1953 as Reynolds Jamaica Mines Ltd; name later changed to Kaiser Jamaica Bauxite Co; 51% owned by Century Aluminum and 49% by Noranda Aluminum Holding Corpn; bauxite mining; annual output of 4.5m. metric tons of bauxite; Pres. PANSY JOHNSON; 589 employees.

Petroleum Corpn of Jamaica (PCJ): 36 Trafalgar Rd, POB 579, Kingston 10; tel. 929-5380; fax 929-2409; e-mail ica@pcj.com; internet www.pcj.com; f. 1979; state-owned; owns and operates petroleum refinery; holds exploration rights to local petroleum and gas reserves; Chair. CHRISTOPHER CARGILL; Man. Dir WINSTON WATSON (acting).

Petrojam Ltd: 96 Marcus Garvey Dr., POB 241, Kingston 15; tel. 923-8611; e-mail mdoffice@petrojam.com; internet www.petrojam.com; f. 1964 by Esso, bought by Govt in 1982; 51% owned by PCJ, 49% by PDVSA of Venezuela; operates sole oil refinery in Jamaica; modernization planned in 2014; Chair. ERWIN JONES; Gen. Man. WINSTON WATSON; 145 employees.

Petroleum Co of Jamaica Ltd (PETCOM): 695 Spanish Town Rd, Kingston 11; tel. 934-6682; fax 934-6690; e-mail petcom@cwjamaica.com; internet www.pcj.com/petcom; f. 1984; wholly owned subsidiary of PCJ; markets gasoline, lubricants and petrochemicals and operates service stations; Chair. ANTHONY GRAHAM.

West Indies Alumina Co (WINDALCO): Kirkvine PO, Manchester; tel. 962-3141; fax 962-0606; internet www.windalco.com; f. 1943 as Alcan Jamaica; bought by United Company RUSAL (Russia/Switzerland) in 2007; bauxite mining, production of calcinated alumina; ended bauxite production in March 2010; operates Kirkvine and Ewarton refineries; Man. Dir LEONID STAVITSKY.

Miscellaneous

Alkali Group of Cos: 259 Spanish Town Rd, POB 200, Kingston 11; tel. 923-6131; fax 923-4947; f. 1960; holding co comprising Powertrac, Industrial Chemical Company, Leder Mode Ltd and Tanners Ltd; 800 employees.

Ashtrom International Ltd Jamaica: Twickenham Park, Spanish Town, St Catherine; tel. 984-2395; fax 984-3210; e-mail info@ashtromja.com; internet www.ashtromja.com; f. 1970; part of Ashtrom Group Ltd (Israel); production and installation of pre-constructed commercial buildings; Chair. HOWARD HAMILTON; Man. Dir YAIR SEGAL; 455 employees.

Berger Paints Jamaica Ltd: 256 Spanish Town Rd, POB 8, Kingston 11; tel. 923-6226; fax 923-5129; e-mail bergerja@infochan.com; internet www.bergeronline.com/caribbean; f. 1952; subsidiary of UB International Ltd (United Kingdom); mfr of paints; Man. Dir MUSTAFA TURRA; 125 employees.

Caribbean Cement Co Ltd: Rockfort, POB 448, Kingston 5; tel. 928-6232; fax 928-7381; e-mail info@caribcement.com; internet www.caribcement.com; f. 1947; mfr of cement; subsidiary of Trinidad Cement Ltd (TCL); Chair. BRIAN YOUNG; Gen. Man. FRANCIS L. A. HAYNES; 300 employees.

Courts Jamaica: 79–81A Slipe Rd, Cross Roads, Kingston 5; tel. 926-2110; fax 929-0887; internet www.courts.com.jm; owned by Unicomer group (El Salvador); furniture retailers.

Goodyear (Jamaica) Ltd: 230 Spanish Town Rd, Kingston 11; internet www.goodyear.com.jm; f. 1945; subsidiary of Goodyear Tire and Rubber Co (USA); mfr of automobile tyres; Chair. EDUARDO FORTUNATO; Gen. Man. STEVEN MILLER; 223 employees.

Kingston Wharves Ltd (KWL): Third St, New Port West, Kingston; tel. 923-9211; fax 923-5361; e-mail kingstonwharves@kwljm.com; internet www.kingstonwharves.com.jm; f. 1945; port terminal operators; subsidiaries include Harbour Cold Stores Ltd and Security Administrators Ltd; Chair. and CEO GRANTLEY STEPHENSON.

Multi-Media Jamaica Ltd: 32 Lyndhurst Rd, Kingston 5; tel. 926-1100; fax 929-2576; e-mail info@multimediajamaica.com; internet www.multimediajamaica.com; f. 2000; wholly owned subsidiary of Radio Jamaica Ltd (RJR); technology-related products and services; Gen. Man. MAURICE MILLER.

The Original Bamboo Factory: Windsor House, Caymanas Estate, Spanish Town, St Catherine; tel. 746-9906; fax 746-9905; e-mail hamilton1@cwjamaica.com; internet www.originalbamboofactory.com; f. 1990; CEO JOHN HAMILTON.

Seprod Group of Companies: 3 Felix Fox Blvd, Kingston; tel. 922-1220; fax 922-6948; e-mail corporate@seprod.com; internet www.seprod.com; f. 1940; owned by Musson Jamaica Ltd; mfr and distributor of soap, detergents, edible oils and fats, animal feeds; processors of grain, cereals, glycerine, etc.; Chair. PAUL B. SCOTT; CEO and Man. Dir BRYON E. THOMPSON; 370 employees.

Supreme Ventures Group: Sagicor Centre, 4th Floor, 28–48 Barbados Ave, Kingston 5; tel. 754-6526; fax 754-2143; internet www.supremeventures.com; f. 1995, granted lottery licence in 2001; owns the following subsidiaries: Supreme Ventures Lotteries Ltd, Prime Sports (Jamaica) Ltd and Supreme Ventures Financial Services Ltd; Chair. PAUL HOO; Pres. and CEO BRIAN GEORGE.

UTILITIES

Regulatory Authority

Office of Utilities Regulation (OUR): PCJ Resource Centre, 3rd Floor, 36 Trafalgar Rd, Kingston 10; tel. 968-6053; fax 929-3635; e-mail consumer@our.org.jm; internet www.our.org.jm; f. 1997; regulates provision of services in the following sectors: water and sewerage, electricity, telecommunications, public passenger transportation; Dir-Gen. ALBERT GORDON.

Electricity

Jamaica Energy Partners (JEP): Wikip Pl., Marcus Garvey Dr., Kingston 5; tel. 937-7915; fax 937-7937; e-mail info@jamenergy.com; internet jamenergy.com; f. 1995; owned by Conduit Capital Partners (USA); owns and operates 2 power barges at Old Harbour Bay, St Catherine; sells electricity to JPSCo; Gen. Man. and CEO WAYNE MCKENZIE.

Jamaica Public Service Co (JPSCo): Dominion Life Bldg, 6 Knutsford Blvd, POB 54, Kingston 5; tel. 926-3190; fax 968-5341; e-mail calljps@jpsco.com; internet www.myjpsco.com; responsible for the generation and supply of electricity to the island; the JPSCo operating licence due to expire in 2027; Pres. and CEO KELLY TOMBLIN.

South Jamaica Power Co (SJPC): Kingston; jtly owned by Japan's Marubeni Corpn (40%), East West Power Korea (40%) and JPSCo (20%); Man. Dir VALENTINE FAGAN.

Water

National Water Commission: LOJ Centre, 5th Floor, 28–48 Barbados Ave, Kingston 5; tel. 929-5430; fax 926-1329; e-mail pr@nwc.com.jm; internet www.nwcjamaica.com; f. 1980; statutory body; provides potable water and waste water services; Chair. Dr LEARY MYERS.

Water Resources Authority: Hope Gardens, POB 91, Kingston 7; tel. 927-0077; fax 977-0179; e-mail info@wra.gov.jm; internet www.wra.gov.jm; f. 1996; manages, protects and controls allocation and use of water supplies; Man. Dir BASIL FERNANDEZ.

TRADE UNIONS

Bustamante Industrial Trade Union (BITU): 98 Duke St, Kingston; tel. 922-2443; fax 967-0120; e-mail bitu@cwjamaica.com; f. 1938; Pres. KAVAN GAYLE; Gen. Sec. GEORGE FYFFE; 60,000 mems.

Caribbean Union of Teachers: 97 Church St, Kingston; tel. 922-1385; fax 922-3257; e-mail cut@caribbeanteachers.com; internet www.caribbeanteachers.com; f. 1935; umbrella org.; affiliates in 21 Caribbean countries; Pres. MARVIN ANDALL; Gen. Sec. Dr ADOLPH CAMERON.

Jamaica Confederation of Trade Unions (JCTU): 1A Hope Blvd, Kingston 6; tel. 927-2468; fax 977-4575; e-mail jctu@cwjamaica.com; Pres. LLOYD GOODLEIGH.

National Workers' Union of Jamaica (NWU): 130–132 East St, POB 344, Kingston 16; tel. 922-1150; fax 922-6608; e-mail nwyou@cwjamaica.com; f. 1952; affiliated to the International Trade Union Confederation; Pres. VINCENT MORRISON; Vice. Pres. HOWARD DUNCAN; 10,000 mems.

Principal Independent Unions

Jamaica Association of Local Government Officers: 15A Old Hope Rd, Kingston 5; tel. 929-5123; fax 960-4403; e-mail admin@jalgo.org; internet www.jalgo.org; Pres. STANLEY THOMAS; Gen. Sec. HELENE DAVIS-WHITE.

Jamaica Civil Service Association: 10 Caledonia Ave and 46 Market St, POB 106, Kingston 5; tel. 968-7087; fax 926-2042; e-mail jacisera@cwjamaica.com; internet www.jacisera.org; f. 1919; Pres. O'NEIL GRANT; Sec. CHELSIE SHELLIE VERNON.

Jamaica Federation of Musicians and Affiliated Artistes Union: 5 Balmoral Ave, Kingston 10; tel. 926-8029; fax 929-0485; e-mail jafedmusic@cwjamaica.com; internet jafedmusic.tripod.com; f. 1958; Pres. DESMOND YOUNG; Sec. CHARMAINE BOWMAN; 2,000 mems.

Jamaica Police Federation: Office Centre Bldg, 4th Floor, Kingston Mall, 12 Ocean Blvd, Kingston; tel. 922-4983; fax 922-3799; e-mail general@jampolicefed.org; internet www.jampolicefed.org; f. 1944; Chair. FRANZ MORRISON; Gen. Sec. DAVID WHITE.

Jamaica Teachers' Association: 97B Church St, Kingston; tel. 922-1385; fax 922-3257; e-mail jta@cwjamaica.com; internet www.jamaicateachers.org.jm; Pres. PAUL ADAMS; Sec.-Gen. Dr ADOLPH CAMERON.

Jamaica Workers' Union: 3 West Ave, Kingston 4; tel. 922-3222; fax 967-3128; e-mail jamaicaworkersunion@yahoo.com; Pres. CLIFTON BROWN.

Jamaican Airline Pilots' Association (JALPA): Unit 4, 2 Seymour Ave, Seymour Park, Kingston 10; tel. 927-6627; fax 978-2815; e-mail jalpajamaica@jalpa.org; internet www.jalpa.org; f. 1971; Pres. PATRICK BARNES; Sec. ALICE TABOIS.

Medical Association of Jamaica (MAJ): 19A Windsor Ave, Kingston 5; tel. 946-1105; fax 946-1107; e-mail majdoctors@cwjamaica.com; internet www.doctorsja.com; f. 1877; 18 affiliates; Pres. Dr AGGREY IRONS; 2,000 mems.

Nurses Association of Jamaica (NAJ): 4 Trevennion Park Rd, POB 277, Kingston 5; tel. 929-5213; fax 968-2200; e-mail najtrevennion@hotmail.com; Pres. ANTOINETTE LEANA PATTERSON; Sec. PRUDENCE GRANDISON.

Union of Schools, Agricultural and Allied Workers (USAAW): 2 Wildman St, Kingston; tel. 967-2970; fax 922-6770; e-mail usaaw_trade_union@yahoo.com; f. 1978; Gen. Sec. KEITH COMRIE.

Union of Technical, Administrative and Supervisory Personnel (UTASP): 108 Church St, Kingston; tel. 922-2086; Pres. ANTHONY DAWKINS; Gen. Sec. ST PATRICE ENNIS.

University and Allied Workers' Union (UAWU): 50 Lady Musgrave Rd, Kingston 10; tel. 927-6658; fax 927-9931; e-mail labpoyh@yahoo.com; Pres. LAMBERT BROWN.

Transport

RAILWAYS

There are about 339 km of railway, all standard gauge, in Jamaica. Passenger services ceased in 1992. In 2008 the Government announced that the People's Republic of China was to provide assistance in the reconstruction of the railway system between Kingston and Montego Bay, and Spanish Town and Ewarton.

Jamaica Railway Corpn (JRC): 142 Barry St, POB 489, Kingston; tel. 922-6443; fax 922-4539; e-mail odcrooks@cwjamaica.com; internet www.mtw.gov.jm/dep_agencies/ja_rail.aspx; f. 1845 as Jamaica Railway Co, the earliest British colonial railway; transferred to JRC in 1960; govt-owned; autonomous, statutory corpn until 1990, when it was partly leased to Alcan Jamaica Co Ltd (subsequently West Indies Alumina Co); planned privatization announced 2012; 215 km of railway; Chair. JOSEPH A. MATALON; Gen. Man. OWEN CROOKS.

ROADS

Jamaica has a good network of tar-surfaced and metalled motoring roads. In 2010 there were 22,121 km of roads in Jamaica. In 2004 the Export-Import Bank of China loaned US $340m. for the Jamaica Road Development Infrastructure Programme, a five-year project to rehabilitate more than 570 km of roads across the island. Development of a 66-km highway, the North–South Link, began in 2013.

Work on the US $610m. project by the China Harbour Engineering Company was expected to be completed by December 2015.

Jamaica Urban Transit Company (JUTC): 1 Michael Manley Dr., Twickenham Park, Spanish Town, St Catherine; tel. 749-3192; fax 924-8158; e-mail marketing@jutc.com.jm; internet www.jutc .com; f. 1999; operates public transport in Kingston metropolitan region; Chair. Rev. GARNETT ROPER; Man. Dir Rear-Adm. HARDLEY LEWIN.

Transport Authority: 119 Maxfield Ave, Kingston 10; tel. 926-8912; fax 929-4178; e-mail customerservice@ta.org.jm; internet www .ta.org.jm; regulatory body; administers the licensing of public and commercial vehicles; Chair. NORTON HINDS; Man. Dir DANIEL DAWES.

SHIPPING

The principal ports are Kingston, Montego Bay and Port Antonio. The port at Kingston is a major transshipment terminal for the Caribbean area. In 2008 the fifth phase of an expansion project in Kingston was completed, doubling the port's handling capacity. Further plans for the expansion of Jamaica's port facilities, to include the construction of three additional berths and a second terminal at Montego Bay, were under way. A new cruise ship pier at Falmouth opened in 2011. At December 2013 the flag registered fleet comprised 40 vessels, totalling 168,417 grt.

Port Authority of Jamaica: 15–17 Duke St, Kingston; tel. 922-0290; fax 948-3575; e-mail paj@portjam.com; internet www.portjam .com; f. 1966; Govt's principal maritime agency; responsible for monitoring and regulating the navigation of all vessels berthing at Jamaican ports, for regulating the tariffs on public wharves, and for the devt of industrial free zones in Jamaica; Pres. and Chair. NOEL A. HYLTON.

Kingston Free Zone Co Ltd: 27 Shannon Dr., POB 1025, Kingston 15; tel. 923-6021; fax 923-6023; e-mail blee@portjam .com; internet www.pajfz.com; f. 1976; subsidiary of Port Authority of Jamaica; management and promotion of an export-orientated industrial free trade zone for cos from various countries; Gen. Man. KARLA HUIE.

Montego Bay Free Zone: POB 1377, Montego Bay; tel. 979-8696; fax 979-8088; e-mail gchenry@portjam.com; internet www .mbfz-jamaica.com; Vice-Pres. GLORIA HENRY.

Shipping Association of Jamaica: 4 Fourth Ave, Newport West, POB 1050, Kingston 13; tel. 923-3491; fax 923-3421; e-mail saj@ jamports.com; internet www.jamports.com; f. 1939; 78 mems; regulates the supply and management of stevedoring labour in Kingston; represents mems in negotiations with govt and trade bodies; Pres. KIM CLARKE; Gen. Man. TREVOR RILEY.

Principal Shipping Company

Jamaica Freight and Shipping Co Ltd (JFS): 80–82 Second St, Newport West, Kingston 12; tel. 656-8629; fax 923-4091; e-mail jfs@ jashipco.com; internet www.jashipco.com; f. 1976; liner and port agents, stevedoring services; Exec. Chair. CHARLES JOHNSTON.

CIVIL AVIATION

There are three international airports linking Jamaica with North America, Europe, and other Caribbean islands. The Norman Manley International Airport is situated 22.5 km outside Kingston. Sangster International Airport is 5 km from Montego Bay. A J $800m. programme to expand and improve the latter was completed in 2009. The Ian Fleming International Airport at Boscobel, 10 km from Ocho Rios, opened in 2011.

Airports Authority of Jamaica: Norman Manley International Airport, Palisadoes; tel. 924-8452; fax 924-8419; e-mail aaj@aaj.com .jm; internet www.airportsauthorityjamaica.aero; Chair. MARK HART; Pres. EARL ANTHONY RICHARDS.

Civil Aviation Authority: 4 Winchester Rd, POB 8998, Kingston 10; tel. 960-3948; fax 920-0194; e-mail info@jcaa.gov.jm; internet www.jcaa.gov.jm; f. 1996; Dir-Gen. Lt Col OSCAR DERBY.

Air Jamaica Ltd: 72–76 Harbour St, Kingston; tel. 922-3460; fax 967-3125; internet www.airjamaica.com; f. 1968; privatized in 1994, reacquired by Govt in 2004; sold to Caribbean Airlines (Trinidad and Tobago) in 2011; Govt of Jamaica retained 16% share; services within the Caribbean and to Canada (in asscn with Air Canada), the USA and the United Kingdom; Chair. GEORGE M. NICHOLAS, III; CEO ROBERT CORBIE (acting).

Exec Direct Aviation (EDA): Bldg II, Suite 11, 1 Ripon Rd, Kingston 5; tel. 618-5884; fax 618-5888; internet www .flyexecdirect.com; f. 2011; cargo services to Caribbean, Central and South American destinations; COO KAMAL CLARKE.

Fly Jamaica Airways: 2 Holborn Rd, Kingston 10; tel. 632-7300; fax 908-3069; e-mail info@fly-jamaica.com; internet www .fly-jamaica.com; f. 2013; Chair. and CEO Capt. PAUL RONALD REECE; Sec. Capt. LLOYD TAI.

Jamaica Air Shuttle: Tinson Pen Aerodrome, Marcus Garvey Dr., Kingston 11; tel. 923-0371; fax 506-9071; e-mail reservations@ jamaicaairshuttle.com; internet www.jamaicaairshuttle.com; f. 2005; domestic and regional charter services to the Cayman Islands, Cuba, Dominican Republic and Haiti; Chair. CHRISTOPHER READ.

TimAir Ltd: Sangster International Airport, Montego Bay; tel. 952-2516; fax 979-1113; e-mail timair@usa.net; internet www.timair .com; f. 1983; charter services; Pres. FRASER MCCONNELL; Man. COLLEEN MCCONNELL.

Tourism

Tourists, mainly from the USA, visit Jamaica for its beaches, mountains, historic buildings and cultural heritage. In 2013 there were 2,008,409 visitor arrivals. Tourism receipts totalled US $2,073.9m. in that year.

Jamaica Hotel and Tourist Association (JHTA): 2 Ardenne Rd, Kingston 10; tel. 926-3635-6; fax 929-1054; e-mail info@jhta.org; internet www.jhta.org; f. 1961; trade asscn for hoteliers and other cos involved in Jamaican tourism; Pres. NICOLA MADDEN-GREIG; Exec. Dir CAMILLE NEEDHAM.

Jamaica Tourist Board (JTB): 64 Knutsford Blvd, Kingston 5; tel. 929-9200; fax 929-9375; e-mail info@visitjamaica.com; internet www .visitjamaica.com; f. 1955; a statutory body set up by the Govt to promote all aspects of the tourism industry; Chair. DENNIS MORRISON; Dir of Tourism PAUL PENNICOOK.

Defence

As assessed at November 2013, the total strength of the Jamaican Defence Force was 2,830. This included an army of 2,500, a coast-guard of 190 and an air wing of 140 members on active service. There were some 980 reservists.

Defence Budget: an estimated J $12,100m. (US $129m.) in 2013.

Chief of Defence Staff: Maj.-Gen. ANTONY BERTRAM ANDERSON.

Education

Primary education is compulsory in certain districts, and free education is ensured. The education system consists of a primary cycle of six years, followed by two secondary cycles of three and four years, respectively. In 2009/10 enrolment at primary schools included 82% of children in the relevant age-group. In the same year enrolment at secondary schools included 84% of children in the relevant age-group. Higher education was provided by four institutions, including the University of the West Indies, which has two campuses, at Mona and Montego Bay. Government spending on education in 2012/13 was budgeted at some J $73,829m.

Bibliography

For works on the Caribbean generally, see Select Bibliography (Books)

Clarke, C. *Decolonizing the Colonial City: Urbanization and Stratification in Kingston, Jamaica (Oxford Geographical & Environmental Studies)*. Oxford, Oxford University Press, 2006.

Delle, J. A. *Out of Many, One People: The Historical Archaeology of Colonial Jamaica*. Tuscaloosa, AL, University Alabama Press, 2011.

Harriott, A. *Understanding Crime in Jamaica*. Kingston, University of the West Indies Press, 2004.

  Organizational Crime and Politics in Jamaica. Kingston, University of the West Indies Press, 2007.

Harrison, M. *King Sugar: Jamaica, the Caribbean and the World Sugar Industry*. New York, New York University Press, 2001.

Haughton, S. *Drugged Out: Globalisation and Jamaica's Resilience to Drug Trafficking*. Lanham, MD, University Press of America, 2011.

Higman, B. W. *Plantation Jamaica, 1750-1850: Capital and Control in a Colonial Economy*. Kingston, University of the West Indies Press, 2005.

Manderson, P., *et al. The Story of the Jamaican People*. Kingston, Ian Randle Publrs, 1997.

Mars, P., and Young, A. L. *Caribbean Labor and Politics: Legacies of Cheddi Jagan and Michael Manley*. Detroit, MI, Wayne State University Press, 2004.

Miller, E. *Jamaica in the Twenty-First Century: Contending Issues*. Kingston, Grace Kennedy Foundation, 2001.

Monteith, K., and Richards, G. (Eds). *Jamaica in Slavery and Freedom: History, Heritage and Culture*. Kingston, University of the West Indies Press, 2001.

Patterson, P. J. *A Jamaica Voice in Caribbean and World Politics*. Kingston, Ian Randle Publrs, 2002.

Sives, A. *Elections, Violence and the Democratic Process in Jamaica 1944-2007*. Kingston, Ian Randle Publrs, 2010.

Tafari-Ama, I. *Blood, Bullets and Bodies: Sexual Politics Below Jamaica's Poverty Line (Caribbean Cultural Studies)*. Kingston, University of the West Indies Press, 2006.

Thomas, D. A. *Modern Blackness: Nationalism, Globalization, and the Politics of Culture in Jamaica*. Durham, NC, Duke University Press Books, 2004.

  Exceptional Violence: Embodied Citizenship in Transnational Jamaica. Durham, NC, Duke University Press Books, 2011.

Thomson, I. *The Dead Yard: A Story of Modern Jamaica*. New York, Nation Books, 2011.

MARTINIQUE
Geography

PHYSICAL FEATURES

The Overseas Department of Martinique is an integral part of France, but is located in the Windward Islands, in the Lesser Antilles, 6,856 km (4,261 miles) from the French capital, Paris. Its immediate neighbours are the two anglophone Windward nations of Dominica (25 km to the north—the islands of Guadeloupe, which are also French, lie beyond that) and Saint Lucia (37 km to the south). The Department, comprising the island of Martinique and its few offshore islets, covers an area of 1,100 sq km (425 sq miles), including 40 sq km of inland waters. This makes Martinique the largest single island of the Windwards or the Leewards (though smaller than the combined island of Guadeloupe, Basse-Terre and Grande-Terre together).

Martinique is about 80 km in length and 32 km at its widest, aligned more towards the north-west than along a straight north–south axis, its long, thin shape, broader in the north, distorted by two peninsulas. In the south-west there is a broad abutment of land, the north littoral of which forms the southern shore of the main bay on the leeward coast. The bay is named after the capital, Fort-de-France, which is on the north shore. Further north, but on the more rugged, eastern coast, thrusting out into the Atlantic, is the thinner Caravelle peninsula. South of these two features, the coastline (350 km around the whole island) is deeply indented and eroded, whereas the north is less so, having been more recently added to by volcanic action. The great volcano of Mt Pelée (1,397 m or 4,585 ft) dominates the north, while to its south the twin peaks (*pitons*) of Carbet achieve heights just below its own. The mountains in the south are much lower, with the land tending to fall away southwards, from the central, raised Lamentin plain of low, rounded hills and gentle valleys. The soil is extremely fertile, the north dominated by extensive rainforest (and banana and pineapple plantations) and the Lamentin plain by sugar cane. Native fauna is now scarce, but the flora remains rich and varied (the Carib name for Martinique meant 'island of flowers'—see History), the rainforest consisting of mahogany trees, mountain palms, bamboo and many other types of tree, as well as fostering flowering plants and orchids, and over 1,000 species of fern. This luxuriance flourishes on the productive emissions of former eruptions by Mt Pelée: the last were in 1902, the one on 8 May being the most famously devastating, wiping out the then capital of St-Pierre and all but one of its 26,000 inhabitants.

CLIMATE

The climate is humid subtropical and moderated by the trade winds (*alizés*) from the Atlantic (Antilles means 'breezy islands'). Precipitation is higher in Martinique than in many of the Caribbean islands, owing to its mountains. There is a rainy season from June to November, brought by the same weather conditions that can bring hurricanes to the region—the latter only occasionally hit Martinique. A more usual natural hazard is the risk of flooding, while an unusual one is the volcano, which is now dormant. The average annual temperature is about 26°C (79°F), but it can be much cooler at altitude.

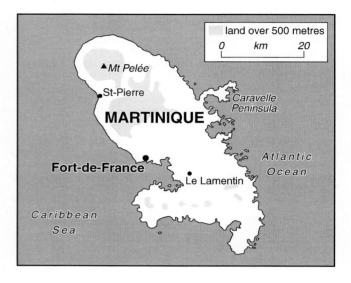

POPULATION

The majority of the population are of African descent, some 90% of the population being either black or of mixed descent (mainly black, white and Asian) and only 5% white. The remainder of the population is mainly Asian—Indian or Chinese. The Roman Catholic Church claims the adherence of 80% of the population, with the rest being mainly Hindu or practitioners of pagan rites adapted by those brought from Africa in the 17th and 18th centuries. Everyone speaks French, and many a Creole patois thereof. The hybrid culture, although increasingly French since Martinique became a Department, has always flourished and the island has long been considered the most sophisticated part of the French Antilles. Famous products and inhabitants of the island range from the rum invented by a Dominican monk, through the 'three queens' (Madame de Maintenon, mistress of Louis XIV; Marie Rose Tascher de la Pagerie, better known as Napoléon Bonaparte's Empress Josephine; and her cousin, Aimée Dubuc de Rivery, who married an Ottoman sultan and gave birth to his successor) to Aimé Césaire (politician, poet and a pioneer of the literary 'négritude' movement), one of the many writers from Martinique.

The total population was 404,705 in mid-2014, according to UN estimates. The capital and largest city is Fort-de-France (originally Fort-Royale, then République-Ville), on the west coast. The old administrative capital, St-Pierre, is further north up the coast. Inland from Fort-de-France, at the western end of the central plain of the same name, is Le Lamentin. There are also a number of other large towns not too far from Fort-de-France, and others on the east coast. Most people live in the capital or on the central plains.

History

JESSICA BYRON

Based on an earlier article by PHILLIP WEARNE

Martinique's name is either a corruption of the Amerindian (Kalinago/Carib) name of Madinina ('island of flowers') or a derivation of Saint Martin. The navigator Christopher Columbus sighted the island in 1493 or 1502—the date is disputed. It was first settled by the French in 1635, despite the hostility of the local Caribs, and was occupied with little interruption thereafter. Like Guadeloupe, Martinique was made a Département d'Outre-mer (Overseas Department) of France in 1946, its people becoming French citizens. The island's Governor was replaced with a Prefect and an elected Conseil Général (General Council) was constituted. Thereafter, the French Government's policy of assimilation created a strongly French society, bound by linguistic, cultural and economic ties to metropolitan France. The island enjoyed a better infrastructure and a higher standard of living than its immediate Caribbean neighbours, but in consequence it also became heavily dependent on France and more recently the European Union (EU). For many years economic power remained concentrated in the hands of the *békés* (descendants of white colonial settlers), who still owned most of the agricultural land and controlled the lucrative import-export market in the last decade of the 20th century. This led to little incentive for innovation or self-sufficiency and fostered resentment of lingering colonial attitudes.

The evolution of Martinique's political system was based on the French Government's response to the growth in nationalist sentiment during the latter half of the 20th century. In 1960 the mandate of the island's General Council was broadened, to permit discussion of political as well as administrative issues. In 1974 Martinique was granted regional status, as were Guadeloupe and French Guiana, and an indirectly elected Conseil Régional (Regional Council), the main role of which was to promote social, economic, cultural and scientific development of the region, was established. In the early 1980s the Socialist Government of President François Mitterrand tried to curb the continued growth of nationalist pressure and the threat of civil disturbances by instituting a policy of greater decentralization. The two local Councils were given increased control over taxation, the local police and the economy.

In the first direct election to the Regional Council in February 1983 the Department's left-wing parties, which articulated nationalist sentiments while supporting the French Government's policy of decentralization, gained 21 of the 41 seats. That success weakened the threat posed by militant separatist challengers inside and outside the left-wing parties. The most vocal of the separatist parties, the Mouvement Indépendantiste Martiniquais (MIM), won less than 3% of the votes cast.

The left wing secured control of the General Council in the 1988 elections with a one-seat majority. In 1992 the Parti Progressiste Martiniquais (PPM) candidate, Claude Lise became President of the General Council. The left-wing predominance in local politics was further enhanced by the results of elections to the Regional Council at the same time. Although the right-wing grouping was the largest single list, the parties of the left secured a working majority. Elections in 1994 brought little change in the composition of the General Council. However, at elections to the European Parliament later in the year, the Conservative government list secured the greatest proportion of the votes cast.

At elections to the French Assemblée Nationale (National Assembly) in 1997, Turinay and Petit of the Gaullist Rassemblement pour la République (RPR) were re-elected, together with Camille Darsières of the PPM. Alfred Marie-Jeanne, the First Secretary and a founding member of the MIM, was elected in the Le François-Le Robert constituency (hitherto held by the RPR). At elections to the Regional Council in 1998 the left retained a majority. Marie-Jeanne was elected to the presidency of the Regional Council. In concurrent elections to the General Council the parties of the left again performed

well, increasing their representation to 29 seats. Claude Lise was re-elected President of the General Council.

Martinique was adversely affected by industrial action in 1998 and 1999, with strikes occurring among banana and automobile sector workers. The crisis in the banana industry was caused by declining prices in the European market; however, a pay agreement was reached in January 1999. There was further conflict in the sector in October, however, when, prior to a visit by French Prime Minister Lionel Jospin, banana producers occupied the headquarters of the French naval forces, demanding the disbursement of exceptional aid to compensate for the adverse effect on their industry of a dramatic decline in prices on the European market. Marie-Jeanne, who was opposed to the limited nature of the Government's plans for institutional reform, refused to participate in the events organized for Jospin's visit. The Prime Minister announced an emergency plan for the banana sector and agreed, in principle, to a proposal for greater autonomy for the local authorities in conducting relations with neighbouring countries and territories. The dispute at the Toyota motor company, where workers were demanding substantial pay increases and a reduction in working hours, lasted five months and involved secondary action and blockades by trade unionists, but was eventually settled in November.

The issue of Martinique's constitutional status also arose in 1999, following a series of meetings between the Presidents of the Regional Councils of Martinique, Guadeloupe and French Guiana. In December Marie-Jeanne co-signed a declaration, stating the intention of the three Presidents to propose, to the French Government, legislative and constitutional amendments aimed at creating a new status of Région d'Outre-mer (Overseas Region). The declaration and subsequent announcements by Marie-Jeanne and his counterparts were dismissed by the Secretary of State for Overseas Affairs in February 2000 as unconstitutional and exceeding the mandate of the politicians responsible. However, in May a number of proposals, including the extension of the Departments' powers in areas such as regional co-operation, were provisionally accepted by the National Assembly; a modified version of the proposals was subsequently adopted by the Sénat (Senate). In November the National Assembly approved the proposals and in December they were ratified by the Conseil Constitutionnel (Constitutional Council). Following a meeting of members of the Regional Council and the General Council in June 2001, a series of proposals on greater autonomy, to be presented to the French Government, was agreed upon. These included: the division of the territory into four districts; the creation of a Collectivité Territoriale (Territorial Collectivity), governed by a 41-member assembly elected for a five-year term; and the establishment of an independent executive council. Furthermore, the proposals included a request that the territory be given control over legislative and administrative affairs, as well as legislative authority on matters concerning Martinique alone. In November the French Government announced that it was in favour of the suggested constitutional developments, and in March 2003 the two houses of the French parliament approved constitutional changes that would allow for a referendum on proposals for greater autonomy. In the same month the status of Overseas Region was conferred on Martinique.

At local elections held in March 2001 the PPM retained control of the majority of municipalities. In the concurrent election to the General Council, Claude Lise was re-elected as President. At elections to the National Assembly in June 2002 only the MIM candidate, Marie-Jeanne, was re-elected; the national Parti Socialiste (PS) representative, Louis-Joseph Manscour, Alfred Almont of the Union pour un Mouvement Populaire (UMP—the new grouping of the centre-right) and Pierre-Jean Samot of the left-wing Bâtir le Pays Martinique were also successful. Samot was ordered to resign by the

Constitutional Council in Paris, France, in 2003 for receiving campaign funds for the 2002 elections from his party, which was not officially registered at the time. Philippe Edmond-Mariette, also of Bâtir le Pays Martinique, won the ensuing by-election.

The referendum on Martinique's constitutional status and the proposed new Territorial Collectivity framework was held in December 2003. Despite the explicit support of Marie-Jeanne for the new arrangement, which would have replaced the General Council and Regional Council with a single elected council, 50.5% of those voting opposed the change. The rejection of the reform plan, proposed by the centre-right Government of Jean-Pierre Raffarin, was widely seen as symptomatic of fears that the French Government would seek to reduce subsidies and social security payments under any new constitutional arrangement.

In elections to the Regional Council held in March 2004 a joint list comprising Marie-Jeanne's MIM won 28 of the 41 seats, while the PPM and other left-wing candidates won only nine seats. Marie-Jeanne was subsequently elected President of the Regional Council.

In the national referendum on ratification of the proposed constitutional treaty of the EU, conducted on 29 May 2005, Martinique voted overwhelmingly in favour of the proposal (69.0%). At odds with the mainland French rejection of the proposed constitution, Martinique's endorsement was also overshadowed by a massive rate of abstention, with 71.6% of voters ignoring the poll.

In December 2005 it was reported that more than 1,000 protesters took part in demonstrations in Fort-de-France against a law that proposed changing the school syllabus to reflect the 'positive' role of French colonialism. The law had been quietly approved in the previous February, and attempts by left-wing representatives in the National Assembly to repeal it had been defeated. The French Minister of the Interior, Nicolas Sarkozy, a supporter of the law, was forced to cancel a planned visit to Martinique and Guadeloupe. President Chirac intervened, announcing later that month that the law was under review, and in January 2006 the law was removed in accordance with a ruling by the Constitutional Council that it lay outside the competence of the legislature.

At the first round of the national presidential election, in April 2007, Ségolène Royal of the PS won 49% of votes cast on the island, ahead of UMP candidate Sarkozy, who attracted 34% of the vote. At the second round in May, Royal won 60.5% of the vote in the Department, although Sarkozy emerged victorious nationally. Meanwhile, at elections to the National Assembly, held on 10 and 17 June, MIM candidate Marie-Jeanne, Manscour of the PS and Almont of the UMP were re-elected, while Serge Letchimy of the PPM was also successful. Following elections to the General Council in March 2008, Lise was again re-elected as the Conseil's President.

Martinique was affected by a period of serious labour unrest in February and March 2009. The trigger was a general strike that had begun two weeks earlier in Guadeloupe, which was experiencing the same social and economic problems as Martinique. In particular, there was concern over the low wages earned by many employees, exacerbated by the high cost of living that was linked to the significant dependence on imports from mainland France. The protests in Martinique, which also took the form of a general strike, were led by the February 5 Collective, a coalition of unions and other social groups. The protests centred largely on Fort-de-France but much of Martinique was affected. The demands of the Collective focused on the need to increase the minimum wage and to reduce the cost of key utilities such as water and electricity. As in Guadeloupe, protestors directed some of their dissatisfaction against the *béké* class for allegedly exploiting their monopoly power in retail and construction in order to maintain high prices and, therefore, their privileged status.

In an effort to defuse the worsening crisis, the French Government and local business leaders agreed to reduce the cost of a range of key commodities, including food staples. However, the general strike continued, and violent clashes took place between demonstrators and the police—some of whom had been drafted in from mainland France. However, in mid-March a deal was reached with the mainland Govern-

ment. The agreement gave an extra €200 per month to low-wage earners, and small increases to those with higher incomes. Despite a resolution to the dispute, much bitterness remained and more fundamentally the strike highlighted long-standing tensions in relation to the political, economic and social arrangements that operated both within Martinique and between Martinique and mainland France.

President Sarkozy visited Guadeloupe and Martinique in June 2009. He was joined by his new Minister of the Overseas Departments and Territories, Marie-Luce Penchard, a native of Guadeloupe and the first holder of the office from outside metropolitan France. The intention of the visit was to hold talks with local politicians and members of civil society, and more broadly to assist the French Government's efforts to rebuild relations with the Overseas Territories. Sarkozy's visit came during a consultation process, initiated in April by the French Government, intended to address the underlying concerns within the Departments. A range of groups participated in the discussions, although most unions boycotted them.

Later in 2009, in light of the perceived dissatisfaction with the existing governance arrangements, the French Government and local representatives agreed that a referendum should be held on the issue of greater autonomy for Martinique and whether or not it should become an autonomous territory governed by Article 74, which grants greater autonomy (rather than Article 73), of the French Constitution. The vote took place on 10 January 2010; contrary to expectations, 79.3% of voters rejected the motion. Turnout was 55.4%. In a follow-up vote conducted two weeks later, 68.3% of voters cast their ballots in support of the less significant reform of merging the Regional Council and General Council into a single body. Turnout was low, at 35.8%. The French Government accepted the results of both votes and suggested that a conclusion to the debate over Martinique's constitutional relationship with France had thus been reached. President Sarkozy, during a speech delivered in Fort-de-France in March, proposed a timeline for the preparation of a statute to bring into force new governance arrangements. Legislative discussions would begin after the regional elections were conducted later that month; the draft legislation would be presented in parliament by the end of the year and voted upon during the first half of 2011.

In elections to the Regional Council held on 14 and 21 March 2010, Letchimy's PPM secured a convincing victory, obtaining 48.4% of the ballot and 26 of the 41 seats. Marie-Jeanne's MIM won 12 seats, with 41.0% of the votes cast, while the UMP-led list attained only three seats, with 10.6%. On 23 March Marie-Jeanne announced that, after 18 years in the Regional Council, and 12 years as its leader, he was to relinquish his seat, with immediate effect. Letchimy was duly elected as the new President of the Regional Council. On 24 March 2011, following municipal elections four days earlier, Josette Manin—a member of the Bâtir le Pays Martinique party and candidate for a coalition led by the PPM—was elected as the territory's first female President of the General Council. She assumed office on 1 April, replacing Claude Lise (who had held that position for almost 20 years). A major task confronting the Presidents of both the General Council and the Regional Council was to forge a consensus on the details of the merger of their respective institutions. New administrative arrangements, which would entail a reduction in the overall number of councillors, were to be put in place between 2012 and 2014. Plans were also announced in February 2011 for the reform of the territorial administration, in order to enhance the performance and cost effectiveness of public agencies. Six regional directorates, to replace 20 existing agencies, were created: Culture; the Environment; the Economy; Agriculture; the Sea; and Social Cohesion. (The Departments of Education, Health and Public Finance were unchanged.) A new Prefect, Laurent Prévost, took office on 30 March.

The French presidential election took place in May 2012, and in Martinique with a voter turnout of 59.8%, the Parti Socialiste candidate François Hollande won 68.4% of the vote, while the incumbent Nicholas Sarkozy of the UMP secured 31.6%. A total of 45 candidates contested the first round of legislative elections on 9 June at which low voter turnout ranged from 30% to 35% across the four constituencies. The second round of voting took place on 16 June. (Voting in both the first and second rounds of the election took place 24 hours earlier in Martinique than in mainland France, in order that, despite the time difference, the results could be announced simultaneously.) In Constituency One veteran politician Alfred Marie-Jeanne was elected with 52.4% of the vote. In Constituency Two Bruno Azerot was elected with 55.5% of the vote, while in Constituency Three Serge Letchimy was elected with 70.2% of the total vote. In Constituency Four Jean-Philippe Nilor of the MIM secured 69.4% of the vote. The successful candidates from the first three constituencies were all from the miscellaneous left-wing grouping, Divers Gauche (DVG).

In late 2011 new efforts began to strengthen the formal structures for co-operation between Martinique and its neighbours. Under the French Law on Overseas Departments (2000), the Regional Council in each of the Overseas Departments had been given the authority to negotiate and conclude agreements with neighbouring states and regional organizations on matters within its area of constitutional competence, once such negotiations had been approved by the French state. The Overseas Departments could also apply for associate membership in certain regional groupings. Under this arrangement, and with the support of the French Ministry of Foreign Affairs, in December 2011 Martinique (and Guadeloupe) formally applied for associate membership of the Organisation of Eastern Caribbean States (OECS). In January 2012 the Chair of the OECS, Prime Minister Kenny Anthony of Saint Lucia, welcomed their applications and announced that the organization would be exploring ways to strengthen its relationship with them. Guadeloupe and Martinique were already co-operating with the OECS territories on a range of sociocultural, economic, environmental, law and order, and disaster management projects. Relations with Dominica and Saint Lucia were particularly close, and there was increasing interaction with the rest of the grouping, which included Antigua and Barbuda, Grenada, Montserrat, Saint Kitts and Nevis, Saint Vincent and the Grenadines, and Anguilla and the British Virgin Islands as associate members. A delegation of Martinican officials, led by Letchimy, attended the inaugural session of the OECS Assembly in St John's, Antigua, in August. In early 2013 talks began between OECS and Martinique technical teams on the modalities of associate membership; these negotiations were quite advanced by the end of 2013. Martinique also applied to the Caribbean Community and Common Market (CARICOM) for associate membership in 2013. Letchimy was a special guest at the 25th Intersessional Meeting of the Conference of Heads of Government of CARICOM in March 2014 in Saint Vincent and the Grenadines. At that meeting, CARICOM leaders endorsed procedures that would guide consideration of the five new applications for associate membership received from Curaçao, French Guiana, Guadeloupe, Martinique and Sint Maarten.

A French delegation, again headed by Letchimy, attended a meeting of the General Assembly of the UN Economic Commission for Latin America and the Caribbean in San Salvador, El Salvador, in August 2012, at which Martinique and Guadeloupe were accepted as associate members. In April 2013, at the Fifth Summit of the Association of Caribbean States (ACS) in Pétionville, Haiti, Martinique and Guadeloupe also became associate members of that regional organization in their own right. (They had participated in the activities of the ACS under the aegis of French associate membership since 1996.) Their new membership status was ratified in February 2014.

Law 2011-884, adopted in July 2011, had approved the future establishment of a Collectivité Unique (Single Collectivity) in Martinique under Article 73 of the French Constitution. The Collectivity would be governed by an assembly of 51 territorial councillors, elected for six-year terms and distributed among four electoral regions. A nine-member Executive Council would also be established. In December 2012 the French Council of Ministers confirmed that elections to this assembly, which would replace the Regional and General Councils, would be held in March 2015. The Council of Ministers also approved two ordinances, the first of which concerned the transfer of regional and departmental staff and assets to the future Collectivity. The second measure concerned modifications to the budgetary, financial and account-

ing rules and procedures to facilitate the establishment of the new institutions. Also in 2012, a Tripartite Commission was established—chaired by the Prefect and comprising representatives from the state, and the Regional and General Councils—to oversee the institutional transition. In April 2013 the French Constitutional Council ratified the decision to establish the Single Collectivity of Martinique in March 2015.

In 2012 the incoming Hollande administration had asked the Minister of State Reform, Decentralization and Public Service, Marylise Lebranchu, to draft new decentralization legislation for presentation to the National Assembly. It was expected that the new law would expand the economic powers of the Regional Councils, including the direct management of EU funding, while the General Councils may become departmental councils, possibly with reduced powers and visibility. This draft legislation was circulated to local government bodies for discussion in April 2013. In Martinique, this focused the debate on the expanded powers that may be required for the new Single Collectivity. The Regional Council and General Council held a joint congress in June to discuss the merger of their existing functions and any additional measures to strengthen the administration of the Collectivity. Areas of governance to be discussed included the protection of biodiversity, renewable energy development, land and maritime transport, employment generation, training, and capacity-building.

On 2 June 2014 President Hollande made a preliminary statement about his administration's forthcoming territorial reform initiative, aimed at modernizing the French state. He asserted that there were too many layers of territorial bureaucracy and that the administration should be simplified in order to rationalize the use of resources and to provide better quality services. The policy would therefore encourage intercommunality (i.e., the agglomeration of the communes and an increase in the size of administrative units). Each commune would have at least 20,000 inhabitants from January 2017, compared with the existing average of 5,000 inhabitants. The number of regions in France would be reduced from 22 to 14. These larger regions would be the major administrative authorities, and they would assume a wider range of responsibilities and be endowed with greater resources. They would be obliged to support industrial development, implement employment and training policies, and maintain the transport infrastructure. The regions would be governed by smaller assemblies with a reduced number of elected officials. The General Councils would be gradually phased out, taking into consideration their substantial role in administering social protection policies. It was envisaged that there would be a constitutional revision to eliminate the General Councils in 2020. Departments would remain an essential unit of the French state. However, their functions would be confined primarily to administering justice and protection, and many of their other powers would be assumed by the territorial Collectivities. All of these proposals would be subject to parliamentary debate, which was expected to commence in 2014.

The new territorial reform initiative introduced a degree of uncertainty into the process of establishing the Single Collectivity in Martinique. There was speculation that the election for the new territorial assembly would be postponed until the last quarter of 2015 and that, in the interim, the terms of Martinique's existing councillors would be extended. There was also some uncertainty surrounding the future powers of the new Collectivity, owing to the Hollande administration's emphasis on intercommunal entities, which would take on some of the functions of the General Councils. In Martinique there were three Communities of Agglomeration (see below): the Espace Sud for the south of the island; the Communauté d'Agglomération du Centre de la Martinique (CACEM) for central Martinique; and the Cap Nord for the northern communes.

Municipal elections were held throughout France on 23 and 30 March 2014 to select municipal and community councillors and mayors. Since the Chevenement Law of 1999, introduced to facilitate co-operation and various types of mergers across the communes, intercommunal entities have become widespread. Intercommunality has been promoted as a new form of territorial organization that encourages investment in large-scale infrastructure projects, rationalizes resources and may enable the state to reduce its allocations to municipalities. In the French Caribbean, two types of intercommunality may exist: the Community of Communes, which is a looser arrangement and has two major mandates, namely economic development and the management of community spaces; and the Community of Agglomeration, which has four areas of responsibility: economic development, the management of community spaces, the organization of urban transport, and the implementation of urban policy and some social policy. Municipal councils administer communes, while community councils administer intercommunalities. In March 2014, for the first time, in communes with more than 1,000 inhabitants, community councillors were not simply appointed from participating municipal councils, but were elected from party lists, similar to the system used to elect municipal councillors. Party lists on the ballots in each locality designated candidates for both municipal and community councils.

Although right-wing parties, particularly the Front National, made major gains throughout France in the municipal elections, in the French Caribbean the reverse tended to be the case. In Martinique 25 mayors were elected in the first round of voting, while the remaining nine were chosen in the second round. At least 20 of the 34 mayors were affiliated with left-wing parties. In April 2014 the Prefect of Martinique requested that the results of the municipal election for Saint-Pierre, in which Raphael Martine of the Rassemblement Démocratique pour la Martinique had been re-elected as mayor, be annulled on grounds of fraud. Also in April, the three Presidents of the Communities of Agglomeration were elected. On 24 May European parliamentary elections were held. Manscour of the PS was elected for the Atlantic Region and was expected to join the ranks of the Party of European Socialists. There was an abstention rate of 88.5% of the electorate in Martinique.

The future configuration of tertiary education in the French Caribbean became a major public policy issue in late 2013 after French Guiana withdrew from the regional university, the Université des Antilles et de la Guyane. This prompted widespread debate about the feasibility of maintaining a regional institution or establishing separate territorial universities. The French Government decided that the university would be renamed the Université des Antilles and would continue to operate in Guadeloupe and Martinique. This institution was given a transitional status in June 2014, while French Guiana would establish its own higher education institution.

Economy

JESSICA BYRON

Martinique's population in mid-2014 was, according to the UN, estimated at 404,705. Martinique was the most densely populated French Overseas Department in the Americas, with a population density of 368 persons per sq km in 2014. None the less, it had a negative population growth rate of –0.3%, and official figures for 2011 indicated that the territory was also the second most rapidly ageing region in France: 28.6% of its population were below 20 years of age, 52.8% were between 20 and 59 years, and 18.7% were over 60 years. According to the UN Development Programme, Martinique's Human Development Index was 0.814 in 2010, second only to Guadeloupe in the Caribbean region.

The territory's economy registered an average annual growth rate of 2.9% between 1997 and 2007, but it contracted by 0.3% in 2008 and more drastically by 6.5% in 2009. After two years of recession, real gross domestic product (GDP) grew by 4.6% in 2010, with growth slowing to 1.0% in 2011. Overall GDP in 2013 totalled €8,352m., while GDP per head amounted to €21,527, an increase of 1% over the preceding year. The rate of unemployment has remained high since 2009, fluctuating between 24% and 25% in 2010 and 2011, the highest rates recorded over the last decade. In 2012 Martinique had an unemployment rate of 21%. There were 43,426 job seekers registered at the end of that year, with the average duration of unemployment being 41 months; 22.6% of the female workforce and 19.2% of the male workforce were unemployed. For young people under the age of 25, the unemployment rate was 56.4%. Preliminary figures put the number of job seekers in 2013 at 52,860. In terms of overall economic activity, in 2012 the primary sector (agriculture) contributed 3% of value added; the secondary sector (industry, energy and construction) contributed 13.3%; and the tertiary sector (services, transport, communications and government services) contributed 83.7%.

Consumer prices increased at an average annual rate of 1.5% during 2003–12. The rate of inflation slowed to 0.8% in 2008 and to 0.6% in 2009, following significant price reductions after the social unrest in February and March 2009. In 2010, however, as the economy began to recover, consumer prices rose by 1.7%, driven upwards by higher fuel prices. The annual inflation rate was 1.4% in 2012 and 1.3% in 2013, predominantly driven again by rising energy costs.

Aid and subsidies, in various forms, are necessary to balance a huge deficit between visible exports and imports. In 2012 the value of exports amounted to €406.8m., while the value of imports was €2,765m. The external trade deficit narrowed to €2,358m. The increase in exports was mainly attributed to a 30.8% rise in petroleum product shipments, while rum and banana exports in total grew by 3.2%. The value of exports fell slightly in 2013, to €384m., while imports also decreased in value, to €2,641m.

In 2012 36% of exports, mainly agricultural and agri-processed products, went to metropolitan France. However, Guadeloupe and French Guiana were the most significant export markets, accounting for 54.8% of goods, mostly energy products. The main merchandise exports in that year were refined petroleum products (51%), primary agricultural products (21.5%) and agri-processed goods (12.4%). France was the single largest source of imports in 2012, accounting for 49.8% of their total value. Non-European Union (EU) European nations supplied 16.4%, and other EU countries and North America 11.8%. The principal imports included fuels and combustibles, processed food, car industry products, electrical and mechanical equipment, and pharmaceuticals. Martinique's most significant exports were refined petroleum products, which were mainly supplied to the French Caribbean islands and French Guiana.

Martinique has a small agricultural sector, which employed a provisional 3.6% of the labour force in 2013. Sugar, bananas, fruit, vegetables and some flowers are the principal crops. Martinique's oil refinery dominates industrial activity, but some light industry is also significant, with rum being one of the largest exports. The industrial and construction sectors employed a provisional 12.1% of the salaried workforce in 2013. Commercial services (including tourism) employed 43.6% of the salaried workforce in that year, while public sector services accounted for 40.7% of salaried employment.

AGRICULTURE

The sugar industry was Martinique's original source of prosperity. However, after the volcanic eruption of Mt Pelée in 1902, bananas became the major export. Banana exports reached 215,980 metric tons by 1990. From the 1990s the volume of exports fluctuated, owing to variable climatic conditions, a significant decline in prices on the European market, and an ongoing dispute between the USA and four Latin American countries and the EU over the latter's banana import regime. Following the destruction caused by Hurricane Dean in 2007, export volumes recovered somewhat to 180,000 tons in 2009. In 2010 the banana industry was affected by the passage of Hurricane Tomas, but 200,000 tons of the fruit were still produced in that year, of which 188,546 tons were exported. Sales of bananas represented 28% of the total value of exports. Also in 2010, the banana industry received €98.1m. in state and EU support.

In 2011 the banana industry did not fare as well. Rainfall levels were 42% above normal precipitation rates, and the crop was affected by an epidemic of Black Sigatoka disease. Banana production amounted to 185,000 metric tons, and exports totalled 175,829 tons, a decrease of 6.7% from the previous year. In November 2012 banana producers in Guadeloupe and Martinique entered into a technical co-operation agreement with the Empresa Brasileira de Pesquisa Agropecuária—an agricultural research institute owned by the Brazilian Government—on reducing the spread of Black Sigatoka disease. In 2012 exports increased to 187,029 tons, up 6.4% over 2011, while banana prices in the EU rose by 11%. However, the EU concluded an agreement with 11 Latin American countries in 2012, ending their trade disputes on market access for bananas. Consequently, between 2012 and 2017 the EU tariff on banana imports from third countries would be lowered from €176 per ton to €114 per ton, thereby exposing banana producers in the French Caribbean to greater competition. Financial support from the EU's Programme d'Options Spécifiques à l'Eloignement et l'Insularité (POSEI—which aimed to provide assistance to the 'outermost' regions of the EU) for banana cultivation in Martinique and Guadeloupe was therefore increased in late 2011 by €30m. In 2011 the banana sector in Martinique benefited from €98.2m. in EU funding.

Sugar cane remained a major agricultural crop, despite low world prices, underinvestment and the diversification of some cane-growing land to the cultivation of other crops. By 1982 local production proved insufficient to supply domestic demand, causing a reversal of the policy of neglect and a dramatic increase in the cane harvest, to 217,000 metric tons by 1989. However, by 2012 the harvest had declined to 175,305 tons, according to official figures, 31% less than the previous year (although FAO estimates put production at an estimated 325,000 tons in 2012). Moreover, cane farmers opted to sell more of their harvest to distilleries than to the island's sugar factory, resulting in only 2,920 tons of sugar being produced, 21.8% less than in 2011. This figure fell further in 2013, to 2,188 tons. Output of rum has historically varied according to the supply and the sucrose content of sugar cane. After years of decline in the 1990s, by 2002 production levels had recovered to 93,849 hl, but decreased again to around 74,500 hl by 2008. In 2010 Martinique produced 69,265 hl of pure alcohol (HAPs) of rhum agricole and 15,462 HAPs of rhum industriel. Of this volume, 79.2% was exported, mostly to France. Production totalled 83,033 HAPs in 2011, 78.3% of which was exported. In 2012 rum output increased to 85,366 HAPs, and the value of rum exports amounted to €34.5m. Output fell to 81,100 HAPs in 2013.

In the 1980s agricultural diversification became official government policy and it contributed to efforts to increase export earnings and reduce the cost of food imports. Pineapples, avocados and aubergines became significant export crops, and flowers and citrus fruits, particularly limes, were also shipped abroad. The most dramatic growth was in the cultivation of melons and pineapples; according to FAO estimates, output of the former reached an estimated 4,700 metric tons in 2010, and production of the latter was estimated at 17,000 tons in the same year. In 2011, however, fruit exports, with the exception of bananas, were insignificant. Only aromatic plant production appeared to be growing, with a 43.6% increase in output recorded over the last decade. One factor contributing to the stagnation of the sector was a lack of organization and representation, so a new umbrella association, the Interprofession Martiniquaise des Fruits, Legumes et Produits Horticoles (IMALFCHOR), was formed in 2010 by the growers to support and expand fruit, vegetable and horticultural production. In 2012 non-banana fruit and vegetable production amounted to 14,223 tons, according to official figures, most of which was destined for local consumption.

With less land available for pasture than on Guadeloupe, a significant proportion of the island's meat and dairy products had to be imported, although the local administration claimed

some success in boosting livestock production. In 2012 locally produced meat represented approximately 10.7% of the total consumed. Milk production continued to decline sharply, with 308,688 litres produced in that year, 23.9% less than in 2011. In 2009 local egg production met 80% of total domestic consumption. Government support to the livestock sector in 2010 amounted to €5.3m., of which poultry farmers received 29.3%, pig farmers 27.4% and cattle farmers 12.7%.

The total fishing catch declined sharply in the late 1980s, to only 3,314 metric tons in 1989, but recovered thereafter, reaching an estimated 7,924 tons in 2012, according to FAO estimates. However, this was insufficient to meet local consumption demand. In 2011 it was estimated that the local fishing sector provided 50% of the 16,000 tons of fish consumed. The aquaculture industry produced 24 tons of freshwater fish in 2012. The shortfall was covered by imports sourced from Europe, Guyana, Venezuela and neighbouring Caribbean islands.

Attempts have also been made to establish more sustainable and environmentally friendly forms of agriculture. Much emphasis has been placed since the social crisis of 2009 on encouraging the agricultural sector. EU funding under POSEI has financed schemes to improve livestock production, particularly chicken and pigs, to diversify vegetable production and to strengthen marketing. In 2011 Martinique received €121.4m. in POSEI funds, or 42.1% of all such funds destined for France. Some 70% of Martinique's funding under the EU's European Agricultural Fund for Rural Development has been committed to improving competitiveness and environmental management. The authorities also launched an emergency plan for support of the agricultural sector in 2010. This included €600,000 of credit for agricultural enterprises. Likewise, a further €600,000 was earmarked for the development of a 31 ha horticultural complex to strengthen the flower export industry. Work began on this project in December 2010. Martinique benefited from an allocation of €104.4m. in EU financing for the period 2007–13. By the end of 2012 77.6% of this amount had been programmed and 39.2% had been disbursed.

INDUSTRY

Industrial activity in the first quarter of 2011 was adversely affected by strikes at Electricité de France (EdF) and among port workers. Industry's contribution to the economy is dominated by the petroleum refinery, processing crude petroleum imported from Venezuela, Trinidad and Tobago, and Saudi Arabia. In 2011 it accounted for 47.8% of the sector's turnover and 22.6% of its salaried workers. Similarly, fuels and combustibles accounted for 42.9% of the total value of exports and 25.3% of the total value of imports. In 2009 the refinery's output contracted by 6.3%, owing largely to the impact of the social unrest in February and March. Following the protests, the prices of petroleum products were reduced, although these were driven upwards again in 2010–11. In 2013 the energy sector continued to dominate industrial activity, with refined petroleum products accounting for 47% of total exports. Energy is derived mainly from mineral fuels, with renewable energy accounting for 6.3% of total electricity generation in 2012. Renewable energy consisted primarily of solar photovoltaic power and biomass. Martinique consumed 1,590 GWh of electricity in 2012, 0.9% more than in 2011. By 2012 EdF had invested €450m. in a major project to extend and modernize the Bellefontaine power station in the north of Martinique. The new power station was inaugurated in June 2014 and was expected to improve generating efficiency by 20%, thereby reducing consumption levels.

Besides sugar-refining and the distillation of rum, industrial activity was concentrated on food- and drink-processing, in particular fish- and fruit-canning and soft drink manufacture. The food-processing industry accounted for 24% of the sector's turnover and 36.6% of its workforce in 2011. A polyethylene plant and a cement factory were in operation, the latter producing an estimated 261,725 metric tons of cement in 2008, virtually all of which was used locally. There were also producers of other construction materials, some small wood-furniture manufacturers and a paper-carton outlet. In 2011

35.1% of the firms in this sector were agri-processing enterprises, while 17.2% specialized in metal work and 16.4% in chemical production.

TOURISM

Martinique's tourist attractions are its beaches and coastal scenery, its mountainous interior, and the historic towns of Fort-de-France and St-Pierre. Tourism has remained one of the most important sources of foreign exchange. The hotel and restaurant sector directly accounted for a provisional 4.1% of the salaried labour force in 2013. There was considerable growth in the number of arrivals between the early 1990s and 2000. Most visitors are from France (79% in 2012). In recent years, however, the sector has shrunk, with visitor arrivals declining by an average of 3.9% per annum between 2000 and 2011. In 2012 the number of tourist arrivals totalled 642,115, of whom 487,769 were stay-over visitors. However, this was still 31% less than in 2000 when 928,197 tourists visited the islands. Hotel occupancy rates in 2012 were 56.3%. In 2012 tourism revenue was estimated at €462m. and the average amount spent per visitor was €511. In 2007 the hotel and restaurant sector generated approximately 3% of value added to the economy.

A significant decline has affected the cruise ship sub-sector. In 1995 there were 428,000 cruise visitors; by 2009 the figure had decreased to just 69,749. The primary reason for the decrease was a significant reduction in the number of visitors from the USA. By 2009 only 27.5% of cruise passenger arrivals were from North America while 66.7% were from Europe. The cruise market recovered somewhat in 2010, to reach 74,733 passengers, but contracted again in 2011. Yacht visitors in 2010 totalled 41,234, an increase of 2.9% over the preceding year. Cruise ship arrivals increased by 2.5% in 2012, reflecting the success of marketing campaigns in 2010–11.

Following the decline of 2009, the tourist board (Comité Martiniquais du Tourisme) launched a promotional campaign to improve the destination's image overseas, to increase the number of flights into Fort-de-France and to increase awareness among the local population of the role of the industry. In mid-2012 the Conseil Régional (Regional Council) presented tourism development proposals to the French Government aimed at further stimulation of the sector.

CONSTRUCTION

The construction industry employed a provisional 5.2% of the workforce in 2013. Sectoral activity declined in 2011 and 2012, as evidenced by a 7% reduction in cement sales in both years. However, some large public works projects were expected to commence in the near future, including an upgrade to the public transport infrastructure and a scheme to reinforce schools, medical facilities, social housing and transport infrastructure to withstand severe earthquakes: €547m. had been allocated in the 2007–13 budget for this purpose.

PUBLIC FINANCES

As in Guadeloupe, relatively high wages in Martinique—tied to those of metropolitan France—coupled with the high levels of aid and imports from France, have provided higher human development indices than in most of the rest of the Caribbean, but have simultaneously made the economy less competitive in terms of prices than many of its neighbours.

Unemployment remained a major cause for concern in Martinican society. According to official figures, in 2011 the authorities disbursed some €187.4m. in unemployment benefits to 23% of the active population. In 2009 69.2% of Martinican households were assessed as having earnings below the income tax threshold. Public services—in health, education, social investment and public administration—were a major contributor to economic activity, accounting for 34.1% of value added in 2007 and a provisional 40.7% of employment in 2013.

In 2010 Martinique's self-financing capacity was judged to be weak, but it improved slightly over the next two years. According to the regional budget, 23.7% of its operational receipts were internally generated. External grants (from the EU and the French state) accounted for 43% of total expenditure. Just 8.6% of the departmental operational budget was internally generated, and 36% of its expenditure relied on external grants. Municipal authorities were only able to generate 5.3% of their operational budget internally. External grants represented 20% of their total expenditure. Both the departmental and the municipal authorities were forced to resort to borrowing to cover financial shortfalls. By 2011 the region was perceived to be in reasonably good financial health with low levels of debt, although its operational expenses were increasing. The Department in 2011 had a total debt of €333m., an improvement over the preceding year. The municipal authorities (communes) were regarded as being in the most fragile budgetary situation, with a collective debt of €430m. and a limited capacity to make full repayments. New fiscal legislation adopted in 2011–12 included reductions in tax exemptions, subsidies and incentives.

In terms of development investment, for the period 2007–13 some €787m. had been allocated for 13 large-scale projects. The amount and its allocation underwent some revision in 2011, with the figure increasing to €793.3m. Of this amount, the EU and the French state would provide approximately 50%. EU development support for 2007–13 totalled €625.7m. By the end of 2012 77% of this financing had been committed and 39% had been disbursed.

CONCLUSION

In 2014 the Martinican economy was still trying to recuperate from the effects of the recession that began in 2008. In 2010 the Regional Council announced a three-year plan to boost the economy amounting to €345m., of which €148m. would be provided by the Region. This plan focused heavily on employment generation, especially through stimulating the construction sector by investments in low-cost housing and in infrastructure for the tourism industry. It also aimed to provide support for small and medium-sized enterprises and to strengthen the competitiveness of various economic sectors. The effects of the new investments were expected to be felt gradually after 2011. Martinique also benefited from the 2009 Law for the Economic Development of the Overseas Departments and its accompanying measures. In the first four months of 2011 economic growth was disrupted once again by three industrial disputes. These included the closure of the port of Fort-de-France for three weeks, industrial action at EdF and a 15-day strike by transport workers in the cement industry. The economy continued to stagnate during 2012, while 2013 was marked by uncertainty and a lack of sustained economic recovery.

Statistical Survey

Sources (unless otherwise indicated): Institut National de la Statistique et des Etudes Economiques (INSEE), Service Régional de Martinique, Centre Administratif Delgrès, blvd de la Pointe des Sables, Hauts de Dillon, BP 641, 97262 Fort-de-France Cédex; tel. 5-96-60-73-73; fax 5-96-60-73-50; e-mail antilles-guyane@insee.fr; internet www.insee.fr/fr/regions/martinique; Ministère des Départements et Territoires d'Outre-mer, 27 rue Oudinot, 75700 Paris 07 SP; tel. 1-53-69-20-00; fax 1-43-06-60-30; internet www.outre-mer.gouv.fr.

AREA AND POPULATION

Area: 1,100 sq km (424.7 sq miles).

Population: 381,427 at census of 8 March 1999; 392,291 at census of 1 January 2011. Note: According to new census methodology, data in 2011 refer to median figures based on the collection of raw data over a five-year period (2009–13). *Mid-2014* (UN estimate): 404,705 (Source: UN, *World Population Prospects: The 2012 Revision*).

Density (at mid-2014): 367.9 per sq km.

Population by Age and Sex (UN estimates at mid-2014): *0–14 years:* 73,529 (36,661 males, 36,868 females); *15–64 years:* 263,669 (120,459 males, 143,210 females); *65 years and over:* 67,507 (28,975 males, 38,532 females); *Total:* 404,705 (186,095 males, 218,610 females).

Principal Towns (at 2010 census): Fort-de-France (capital) 87,216; Le Lamentin 39,360; Le Robert 23,918; Schoelcher 20,814.

Births, Marriages and Deaths (2012 unless otherwise indicated): Registered births 4,458 (birth rate 11.5 per 1,000); Registered marriages 1,095 (marriage rate 2.8 per 1,000, 2012); Registered deaths 2,818 (death rate 7.3 per 1000).

Life Expectancy (years at birth): 81.4 (males 78.0; females 84.5) in 2013. Source: Pan American Health Organization.

Employment (persons aged 15 years and over at 31 December 2013, provisional): Agriculture, hunting, forestry and fishing 4,507; Mining, quarrying and utilities 2,319; Manufacturing 6,225; Construction 6,494; Trade 14,320; Hotels and restaurants 5,164; Transportation and storage 5,804; Communication 2,164; Finance and insurance 3,579; Real estate activities 835; Professional services 12,809; Public administration, education, health and other social services 50,715; Other services 9,579; *Total* 124,514. Note: Figures for employment exclude 6,757 persons employed without salary.

HEALTH AND WELFARE

Key Indicators

Total Fertility Rate (children per woman, 2012): 1.8.

Under-5 Mortality Rate (per 1,000 live births, 2011): 8.5.

Physicians (per 1,000 head, 2010): 26.2.

Hospital Beds (per 1,000 head, 2009): 4.1.

Source: mainly Pan American Health Organization.

For definitions and other sources, see explanatory note on p. vi.

AGRICULTURE, ETC.

Principal Crops ('000 metric tons, 2012, FAO estimates): Yams 1.4; Sugar cane 325.0; Lettuce and chicory 7.8; Tomatoes 6.5; Cucumbers and gherkins 6.2; Bananas 260.0; Plantains 14.0; Pineapples 2.2. *Aggregate Production* ('000 metric tons, may include official, semi-official or estimated data): Total vegetables (incl. melons) 34.8; Total fruits (excl. melons) 277.9.

Livestock ('000 head, year ending September 2012, FAO estimates): Cattle 18; Sheep 12; Pigs 12; Goats 6.

Livestock Products ('000 metric tons, 2012, FAO estimates): Cattle meat 1.1; Pig meat 1.1; Chicken meat 1.3; Cows' milk 2.8; Hen eggs 2.7.

Forestry ('000 cubic metres, 2012, FAO estimates): *Roundwood Removals* (excl. bark): Sawlogs, veneer logs and logs for sleepers 2.4; Fuel wood 10.0; Total 12.4. *Sawnwood Production* (incl. railway sleepers): 1.0.

Fishing (metric tons, live weight, 2012, FAO estimates): Capture 7,900 (Clupeoids 4,650; Common dolphinfish 147; Other marine fishes 1,800; Caribbean spiny lobster 180; Clams, etc. 715); Aquaculture 24; *Total catch* 7,924.

Source: FAO.

MINING

Production ('000 metric tons, 2010, estimates): Cement 221; Pumice 130; Salt 200. Source: US Geological Survey.

INDUSTRY

Production ('000 metric tons, 2010): Motor spirit (petrol) 139 (estimate); Kerosene 116 (estimate); Gas-diesel (distillate fuel) oils 198; Residual fuel oils 388; Liquefied petroleum gas 19 (estimate); Electric energy (million kWh) 1,778 (estimate) (Source: UN Industrial Commodity Statistics Database). *2013:* Raw sugar 2,188 metric tons; Rum (hl) 81,100. (Source: Institut d'Emission des Départements d'Outre-mer, *Martinique: Rapport Annuel 2013*).

FINANCE

Currency and Exchange Rates: The French franc was used until the end of 2001. Euro notes and coins were introduced on 1 January 2002, and the euro became the sole legal tender from 18 February. Some of the figures in this Survey are still in terms of francs. For details of exchange rates, see French Guiana.

Budget: *French Government* (million French francs, 1998): Revenue 4,757; Expenditure 8,309. *Regional Budget* (€ million, 2011): Current revenue 256.0 (Taxes 163.6, Grants 81.3; Other current revenue 11.1); Capital revenue 135.6; Total 391.6. Current expenditure 191.5 (Wages and salaries 44.1; Goods and services 18.5; Subsidies 106.8); Capital expenditure 217.8; Total 409.3. *Departmental Budget* (forecasts, million French francs, 2001): Tax revenue 836.9 (Departmental taxes 332.0, Fuel tax 295.0, Transfer taxes, etc. 58.0, Motor vehicle tax 68.0, Fiscal subsidy 53.0); Other current revenue 886.6 (Refunds of social assistance 65.0, Operational allowance 315.0, Decentralization allowance 477.0); Capital revenue 499.5 (EU development funds 71.0, Capital allowances 59.0, Other receipts 101.4, Borrowing 270.0); Total 2,223.0. Current expenditure 1,482.2 (Finance service 57.1, Permanent staff 394.7, General administration 65.1, Other indirect services 69.0, Administrative services 108.4, Public health 49.9, Social assistance 503.6, Support costs of minimum wage 99.8, Economic services 114.7); Capital expenditure 740.8 (Road system 139.5, Networks 47.9, Education and culture 111.5, Other departmental programmes 101.6, Other public bodies 83.7, Other programmes 96.3, Non-programme expenditure 162.3); Total 2,223.0. *2013* (€ million, excl. debt rescheduling, preliminary): Total revenue 644.5 (Current revenue 593.0, Capital revenue 51.4); Total expenditure 644.5 (Current expenditure 555.3, Capital expenditure 89.1) (Sources: partly Département des Etudes et des Statistiques Locales, Institut d'Emission des Départements d'Outre-mer, *Martinique: Rapport Annuel 2012*).

Cost of Living (Consumer Price Index; base: 2000 = 100): All items 124.5 in 2011; 126.3 in 2012; 127.9 in 2013. Source: ILO.

Gross Domestic Product (€ million at current prices, estimates): 8,128 in 2010; 8,291 in 2012; 8,352 in 2013. Source: Institut d'Emission des Départements d'Outre-mer, *Martinique: Rapport Annuel 2012*.

Expenditure on the Gross Domestic Product (€ million at current prices, 2012, estimates): Total final consumption expenditure 8,904 (General government and non-profit institutions serving households 3,701, Households 5,203); Changes in stocks –140; Gross fixed capital formation 1,507; *Total domestic expenditure* 10,271; Exports of goods and services 1,066; *Less* Imports of goods and services 2,985; *GDP in purchasers' values* 8,352. Source: Institut d'Emission des Départements d'Outre-mer, *Martinique: Rapport Annuel 2013*.

Gross Domestic Product by Economic Activity (€ million at current prices, 2006): Agriculture 160; Food industries 122; Other manufacturing 282; Energy 164; Construction 453; Services 6,088 (Restaurants and hotels 232, Transport 222, Commerce 852, Other market services 2,387, Non-market services 2,395); *Sub-total* 7,269; *Less* Financial intermediation services indirectly measured 298; Taxes, less subsidies 667; *GDP in purchasers' values* 7,638.

EXTERNAL TRADE

Principal Commodities (€ million, 2013): *Imports c.i.f.:* Agriculture, forestry and fishing 52.6; Natural hydrocarbons, etc. 309.7; Products of food industries 401.2; Textiles, clothing, leather and footwear 103.3; Petroleum products 446.8; Chemicals 120.9; Pharmaceutical products 142.2; Rubber, plastic and mineral products 132.7; Metal and metal products 107.9; Mechanical, electronics and electrical equipment 358.4; Transport equipment 257.7; Miscellaneous manufactured products 111.5; Total (incl. others) 2,641.1. *Exports f.o.b.:* Agriculture, forestry and fishing 77.1; Products of food industries 57.1; Petroleum products 179.7; Metal and metal products 9.9; Mechanical, electronics and electrical equipment 9.2; Transport equipment 20.4; Total (incl. others) 383.7. (Source: Institut d'Emission des Départements d'Outre-mer, *Martinique: Rapport Annuel 2013*).

Principal Trading Partners (€ million, 2008): *Imports c.i.f.:* Aruba 78; France (metropolitan) 1,519; Germany 72; Guadeloupe 44; Italy 45; Japan 36; Netherlands 54; Spain 26; United Kingdom 326; USA 199; Total (incl. others) 2,766. *Exports f.o.b.:* Antigua 4; France (metropolitan) 90; French Guiana 38; Guadeloupe 210; Netherlands Antilles 3; USA 9; Total (incl. others) 367. *2011* (€ million): Total imports 2,709.4; Total exports 308.3. *2012* (€ million): Total imports 2,764.8; Total exports 406.8. *2013* (€ million): Total imports 2,641.0; Total exports 383.7. (Source: Institut d'Emission des Départements d'Outre-mer, *Martinique: Rapport Annuel 2013*).

TRANSPORT

Road Traffic ('000 commercial motor vehicles in use, 1 January 2010): Buses 1.2; Vans and tractors 34.3.

Shipping: *Flag Registered Fleet* (at 31 December, 2013): Vessels 3; Total displacement 510 grt (Source: Lloyd's List Intelligence—www.lloydslistintelligence.com). *International Seaborne Traffic* (2011): Goods loaded 856,000 metric tons (petroleum products 359,000 metric tons); Goods unloaded 2,026,000 metric tons (petroleum products 923,000 metric tons).

Civil Aviation (2013 unless otherwise indicated): Freight (incl. 2,667 metric tons of post) carried 13,914 metric tons (2009); Passengers carried 1,623,870. Source: partly Institut d'Emission des Départements d'Outre-mer, *Martinique: Rapport Annuel 2013*.

TOURISM

Tourist Arrivals by Country (excl. same-day visitors and cruise ship arrivals, 2003): France (metropolitan) 357,726; Guadeloupe 40,668; French Guiana 10,619; Total (incl. others) 453,159. *2012* (excl. same-day visitors and cruise ship arrivals): Total 487,769 (Canada 9,154; France 384,526; French Guiana 13,626; Guadeloupe 45,556;). (Source: World Tourism Organization). *Total Arrivals* (excl. same-day visitors and cruise ship arrivals): 498,578 in 2011; 478,359 in 2012; 489,705 in 2013. (Source: partly Institut d'Emission des Départements d'Outre-mer, *Martinique: Rapport Annuel 2013*).

Receipts from Tourism (€ million, excl. passenger transport): 472 in 2010; 516 in 2011; 462 in 2012. Source: World Tourism Organization.

COMMUNICATIONS MEDIA

Telephones ('000 main lines in use): 172.0 in 2010.

Mobile Cellular Telephones ('000 subscribers): 295.4 in 2004.

Internet Users ('000): 170.0 in 2009.

Broadband Subscribers: 6,000 in 2010.

Source: International Telecommunication Union.

EDUCATION

Pre-primary (2013/14): 15,420 students (14,366 state, 1,054 private).

Primary (2012/13): 26,107 students (23,779 state, 2,328 private).

Specialized Pre-primary and Primary (2012/13): 334 students (334 state).

Secondary (2013/14): 38,615 students (34,843 state, 3,772 private).

Higher (2011/12): 7,829 students.

Teachers (2004/05): *Primary:* 3,031 (2,787 state, 244 private); *Secondary:* 4,553 (4,177 state, 376 private); *Higher:* 186. Source: Ministère de l'Education Nationale, *Repères et références statistiques—édition 2005. 2012/13* (state schools): 2,650 in primary; 3,510 in secondary.

Institutions (2003/04): 258 primary schools; 41 lower secondary schools; 22 state upper secondary schools; 24 private institutions. Source: Préfecture de Martinique, *Livret d'accueil des services de l'Etat en Martinique. 2012/13:* 72 pre-primary schools; 180 elementary and special schools; 80 secondary schools.

Adult Literacy Rate: 98.0% (males 97.6%, females 98.3%) in 2005. Source: Pan American Health Organization.

Directory

The Government

(September 2014)

HEAD OF STATE

President: FRANÇOIS HOLLANDE.

Prefect: LAURENT PRÉVOST, Préfecture, 82 rue Victor Sévère, BP 647–648, 97262 Fort-de-France Cédex; tel. 5-96-39-36-00; fax 5-96-71-40-29; e-mail contact.prefecture@martinique.pref.gouv.fr; internet www.martinique.pref.gouv.fr.

DEPARTMENTAL ADMINISTRATION

President of the General Council: JOSETTE MANIN (PPM), Conseil général de la Martinique, blvd Chevalier Sainte-Marthe, 97200 Fort-de-France Cédex; tel. 5-96-55-26-00; fax 5-96-73-59-32; internet www.cg972.fr.

President of the Regional Council: SERGE LETCHIMY, Hôtel de la Région, ave Gaston Deferre, BP 601, 97200 Fort-de-France Cédex; tel. 5-96-59-63-00; fax 5-96-72-68-10; e-mail service .communication@cr-martinique.fr; internet www.cr-martinique.fr.

Elections, 14 and 21 March 2010

	Seats
Parti Progressiste Martiniquais (PPM)	26
Mouvement Indépendantiste Martiniquais (MIM) . .	12
Rassembler la Martinique*	3
Total	41

* Electoral list comprising the Union pour un Mouvement Populaire (UMP) and allies.

REPRESENTATIVES TO THE FRENCH PARLIAMENT

Deputies to the French National Assembly: ALFRED MARIE-JEANNE (Gauche, Démocrate et Républicaine), BRUNO NESTOR AZEROT (Gauche, Démocrate et Républicaine), SERGE LETCHIMY (Socialiste, Républicain et Citoyen), JEAN-PHILIPPE NILOR (Gauche, Démocrate et Républicaine).

Representatives to the French Senate: SERGE LARCHER (Groupe Socialiste), MAURICE ANTISTE (Groupe Socialiste).

GOVERNMENT OFFICES

Culture, Education and Environment Committee: Hôtel de la Région, ave Gaston Deferre, Plateau Roy Cluny, BP 601, 97200 Fort-de-France; tel. 5-96-59-64-43; fax 5-96-59-63-21; e-mail ccee@cr-martinique.fr; internet www.cr-martinique.fr; Pres. GÉRARD LACOM.

Economic, Social and Environmental Regional Committee: Hôtel de la Région, ave Gaston Deferre, Plateau Roy Cluny, BP 601, 97200 Fort-de-France; tel. 5-96-59-63-00; fax 5-96-59-64-31; e-mail cesr-s@region-martinique.com; internet www.cr-martinique.fr; Pres. MICHEL CRISPIN.

Political Organizations

Bâtir le Pays Martinique: Fort-de-France; f. 1998; left-wing; split from the Parti Communiste Martiniquais; Leader PIERRE-JEAN SAMOT; Nat. Sec. DAVID ZOBDA.

Combat Ouvrier: BP 821, 97258 Fort-de-France Cédex; e-mail l .maugee972@orange.fr; internet www.combat-ouvrier.net; Trotskyist; mem. of the Communist Internationalist Union; Leader GHISLAINE JOACHIM-ARNAUD.

Conseil National des Comités Populaires (CNCP): 8 rue Pierre et Marie Curie, Terres Sainville, 97200 Fort-de-France; tel. 5-96-63-75-23; e-mail cncp@netcaraibes.com; internet www.m-apal.com; f. 1983; pro-independence party affiliated to the Union Général des Travailleurs de Martinique; contested the 2004 regional elections in alliance with the MIM; Pres. JOSETTE MASSOLIN; Spokesperson ROBERT SAÉ.

Fédération Socialiste de la Martinique (FSM): 52 rue du Capitaine Pierre-Rose, 97200 Fort-de-France; tel. 5-96-60-14-88;

fax 5-96-63-81-06; e-mail federation.socialiste-martinique@wanadoo
.fr; internet martinique.parti-socialiste.fr; local br. of the Parti
Socialiste (PS); Fed. Sec. LOUIS JOSEPH MANSCOUR; Spokesperson
FRÉDÉRIC BUVAL.

Forces Martiniquaises de Progrès (FMP): 12 rue Ernest
Deproge, 97200 Fort-de-France; tel. 5-96-57-74-10; fax 5-96-63-36-
19; e-mail miguel.laventure@fmp-regionales.org; internet www
.jrdmedias.com/laventure/index.html; f. 1998 to replace the local br.
of the Union pour la Démocratie Française; Pres. MIGUEL LAVENTURE.

**Mouvement des Démocrates et Écologistes pour une Marti-
nique Souveraine (MODEMAS):** Fort-de-France; f. 1992; left-
wing, pro-independence; Pres. GARCIN MALSA.

Mouvement Indépendantiste Martiniquais (MIM): Fort-de-
France; internet www.mim-matinik.org; f. 1978; pro-independence
party; First Sec. ALFRED MARIE-JEANNE.

Mouvement Populaire Franciscain: angle des rues Couturier et
Holo, 97240 Le François; tel. 5-96-54-20-40; e-mail direction@
pont-abel.fr; left-wing; Leader MAURICE ANTISTE.

Osons Oser: Fort-de-France; f. 1998; right-wing; affiliated with the
metropolitan Union pour un Mouvement Populaire (UMP); Pres.
PIERRE PETIT; Vice-Pres. JENNY DULYS-PETIT.

Parti Communiste Martiniquais (PCM): angle des rues A. Aliker
et E. Zola, Terres-Sainville, 97200 Fort-de-France; tel. 5-96-71-86-
83; fax 5-96-63-13-20; e-mail ed.justice@wanadoo.fr; internet
journal-justice-martinique.com; f. 1957; Sec.-Gen. GEORGES ERICHOT.

Parti Progressiste Martiniquais (PPM): Ancien Réservoir de
Trénelle, 97200 Fort-de-France; tel. 5-96-71-88-01; fax 5-96-72-68-
56; e-mail contact@ppm-martinique.fr; internet www
.ppm-martinique.fr; f. 1958; left-wing; Leader SERGE LETCHIMY; Sec.-
Gen. DIDIER LAGUERRE.

Parti Régionaliste Martiniquais: Fort-de-France; f. 2010 by fmr
mems of UMP (q.v.); right-wing; Pres. CHANTAL MAIGNAN; Sec.-Gen.
CHRISTIAN RAPHA.

Rassemblement Démocratique pour la Martinique (RDM):
Résidence Pichevin 2, Bâtiment Hildevert, Les Hauts du Port, 97200
Fort-de-France; tel. 5-96-71-89-97; internet rfdm.e-monsite.com;
f. 2006; Sec.-Gen. CLAUDE LISE.

Union pour un Mouvement Populaire (UMP): angle des rues de
la République et Vincent Allègre, 97212 Saint Joseph; tel. 5-96-57-
96-68; fax 5-96-57-32-68; internet www.u-m-p.org; centre-right; local
br. of the metropolitan party; Pres., Departmental Cttee MARC SEFIL.

Les Verts Martinique: Lotissement Donatien, 54 rue Madinina,
Cluny, 97200 Fort-de-France; tel. and fax 5-96-71-58-21; e-mail
louisleonce@wanadoo.fr; ecologist; departmental br. of the metropolitan party; Leader LOUIS-LÉONCE LECURIEUX-LAFFERONNAY.

Judicial System

Court of Appeal: ave St John Perse, Morne Tartenson, BP 634,
97262 Fort-de-France Cédex; tel. 5-96-70-62-62; fax 5-96-63-52-13;
e-mail ca-fort-de-france@justice.fr; highest court of appeal for
Martinique and French Guiana; First Pres. BRUNO STEINMANN;
Procurator-Gen. JEAN JACQUES BOSC.

There are two Tribunaux de Grande Instance, at Fort-de-France and
Cayenne (French Guiana), and three Tribunaux d'Instance (two in
Fort-de-France and one in Cayenne).

Religion

The majority of the population belong to the Roman Catholic Church.

CHRISTIANITY

The Roman Catholic Church

Some 80% of the population are Roman Catholics. Martinique comprises the single archdiocese of Fort-de-France. The Archbishop
participates in the Antilles Episcopal Conference, based in Port of
Spain, Trinidad and Tobago.

Archbishop of Fort-de-France and Saint-Pierre: Most Rev.
GILBERT MARIE MICHEL MÉRANVILLE, Archevêché, 5–7 rue du Rév-
érend Père Pinchon, BP 586, 97207 Fort-de-France Cédex; tel. 5-96-
63-70-70; fax 5-96-63-75-21; e-mail archeveche-martinique@
wanadoo.fr; internet martinique.catholique.fr.

Other Churches

Among the denominations active in Martinique are the Assembly of
God, the Evangelical Church of the Nazarene and the Seventh-day
Adventist Church.

The Press

Antilla: Le Lamentin, BP 46, 97281 Fort-de-France, Cédex 1; tel. 5-
96-75-48-68; fax 5-96-75-58-46; e-mail antilla@orange.fr; internet
www.antilla-blog.com; f. 1981; weekly; politics and economics; Publ.
Dir ALFRED FORTUNE; Editor-in-Chief TONY DELSHAM.

France Antilles: pl. François Mitterrand, 97207 Fort-de-France;
tel. 5-96-59-08-83; fax 5-96-60-29-96; e-mail redaction.fa@
media-antilles.fr; internet www.martinique.franceantilles.fr;
f. 1964; subsidiary of Groupe France Antilles; daily; Editor PAUL-
HENRI COSTE; circ. 30,000 (Martinique edn).

Journal Asé Pléré Annou Lité (Journal APAL): 8 rue Pierre et
Marie Curie, Terres Sainville, 97200 Fort-de-France; tel. 5-96-63-75-
23; fax 5-96-70-30-82; e-mail journ.apal@orange.fr; internet www
.m-apal.com; f. 1983; monthly; organ of the Conseil Nat. des Comités
Populaires (q.v.) and the Union Général des Travailleurs de
Martinique (q.v.); Dir ROBERT SAÉ.

Journal Combat Ouvriére: 1111 Rés Matéliane, L'Aiguille, 97128
Goyave; e-mail l.maugee972@orange.fr; internet www
.combat-ouvrier.net; f. 1970; fortnightly; communist; Publ. Dir
PHILIPPE ANAIS; circ. 14,000.

Justice: angle rue André Aliker et E. Zola, 97200 Fort-de-France;
tel. 5-96-71-86-83; fax 5-96-63-13-20; e-mail ed.justice@wanadoo.fr;
internet journal-justice-martinique.com; f. 1920; weekly; organ of
the Parti Communiste Martinique (q.v.); Dir FERNAND PAPAYA; circ.
8,000.

Le NAIF-Magazine: Résidence K, Pointe des Nègres, route Phare,
97200 Fort-de-France; tel. 5-96-61-62-55; fax 5-96-61-85-76; e-mail
docedouard@yahoo.fr; internet www.lenaif.net; weekly; publ. by
CIC; Owner CAMILLE CHAUVET.

Le Progressiste: c/o Parti Progressiste Martiniquais, Ancien Réservoir de Trénelle, 97200 Fort-de-France; tel. 5-96-71-88-01; e-mail d
.compere@ool.fr; internet www.ppm-martinique.fr; weekly; organ of
the PPM; Publ. Dir DANIEL COMPERE; circ. 13,000.

TV Magazine: pl. François Mitterrand, 97232 Lamentin; tel. 5-96-42-
51-28; fax 5-96-42-98-94; e-mail tv.mag@media-antilles.fr; f. 1989;
weekly; Editor-in-Chief LUCIENNE CHÉNARD.

Publishers

Editions Exbrayat: 5 rue des Oisillons, route de Balata, 97234
Fort-de-France; tel. 5-96-64-60-58; fax 5-96-64-70-42; e-mail editions
.exbrayat@exbrayat.com; internet commerce.ciel.com/exbrayat;
regional art, history, natural history, culinaria, maps and general
fiction; 2 brs in Guadeloupe; Commercial Dir PAQUITA EXBRAYAT-
SANCHEZ; Sec. HERMINIE MARIE-CLAIRE.

Editions Lafontaine: Bâtiment 12, Maniba, 97222 Case Pilote; tel.
and fax 5-96-78-87-98; e-mail info@editions-lafontaine.com; internet
www.editions-lafontaine.com; f. 1994; Creole, French and English
literature, general fiction, culture, history, youth and educational;
Dir JEANNINE 'JALA' LAFONTAINE.

Broadcasting and Communications

TELECOMMUNICATIONS

Digicel Antilles Françaises Guyane: Oasis, Quartier Bois Rouge,
97224 Ducos; tel. 8-10-63-56-35; fax 5-96-42-09-01; e-mail contact@
digicelgroup.fr; internet www.digicel.fr; f. 2000 as Bouygues Telecom
Caraïbe; acquired from Bouygues Telecom, France, in 2006; mobile
cellular telephone operator; network coverage incl. Guadeloupe and
French Guiana; CEO (French Caribbean) YANN KEREBEL; Dir-Gen.
(Martinique) SÉBASTIEN AUBÉ.

Orange Caraïbe: see Guadeloupe—Telecommunications.

Outremer Telecom: Z. I. la Jambette, BP 280, 97285 Lamentin
Cédex 2; e-mail communication@outremer-telecom.fr; internet www
.outremer-telecom.fr; f. 1998; mobile telecommunications provider;
CEO JEAN-MICHEL HEGESIPPE.

ONLY: Z. I. la Jambette, BP 280, 97285 Lamentin Cédex 2; e-mail
communication@outremer-telecom.fr; internet www
.outremer-telecom.fr; f. 1998 as Outremer Telecom Martinique;
present name adopted following merger of Volubis, ONLY and
OOL in 2006; telecommunications provider; subsidiary of
Outremer Telecom, France; Head of Operations (French West
Indies and French Guiana) FRÉDÉRIC HAYOT.

BROADCASTING

Atlantic FM Martinique: Lorrain; tel. 5-96-71-33-38; e-mail radio
.atlanticfm@yahoo.fr; internet www.atlanticfm.fr.

Martinique 1ère (Outre-mer Première): La Clairière, BP 662, 97263 Fort-de-France; tel. 5-96-59-52-00; fax 5-96-59-52-26; internet martinique.la1ere.fr; acquired by Groupe France Télévisions in 2004; fmrly Société Nationale de Radio-Télévision Française d'Outre-mer; name changed to Réseau France Outre-mer (RFO) in 1998; present name adopted in 2010; Dir-Gen. GENEVIÈVE GIARD; Regional Dir STÉPHANIE GAUMONT.

Radio

Radio Asé Pléré Annou Lité (Radio APAL) (Radio Pèp-la): 8 rue Pierre et Marie Curie, Terres Sainville, 97200 Fort-de-France; tel. 5-96-63-75-23; fax 5-96-70-30-82; e-mail radio.apal@orange.fr; internet www.m-apal.com; f. 1989; affiliated to the Conseil Nat. des Comités Populaires (q.v.) and the Union Général des Travailleurs de Martinique (q.v.); French and Creole; Dir MICHEL NE'DAN; Station Man. JEAN-CLAUDE LOUIS-SYDNEY.

Radio Banlieue Relax (RBR): 107 ave Léona Gabriel, Cité Dillon, 97200 Fort-de-France; tel. 5-96-60-00-90; fax 5-96-73-06-53; e-mail radio.br@orange.fr; internet www.rbrfm.com; f. 1981; regional social and cultural programmes; Pres. FRANTZ CLÉORON; Dir JOCELYN HERTÉ.

Radio Canal Antilles (RCA): plateau Fofo, 97233 Schoelcher; tel. 5-96-61-74-19; fax 5-96-61-23-58; internet membres.multimania.fr/canalantilles; f. 1980; fmrly Radio 105; regional social and cultural programmes; Radio France Internationale relay; Pres. SERGE POGNON.

Radio Caraïbes International (RCI Martinique): 2 blvd de la Marne, 97200 Fort-de-France Cédex; tel. 5-96-63-98-70; fax 5-96-63-26-59; internet www.rcimartinique.fm; commercial radio station; Dir JOSÉ ANELKA; Station Man. VINCENT CHRÉTIEN; Editor-in-Chief JEAN-PHILIPPE LUDON.

Radio Evangile Martinique (REM): 54 Route des Religieuses, 97200 Fort-de-France; tel. 5-96-70-68-48; fax 5-96-70-17-51; e-mail rem@evgi.net; internet rem.evgi.net; f. 1993; Pres. RAYMOND SORMAIN; Dir LUCIEN COIQUE.

Radio Fréquence Atlantique (RFA): 10 rue du Docteur Laveran, 97232 Le Lamentin; tel. 5-96-42-35-51; fax 5-96-51-04-26; e-mail r.f.a@wanadoo.fr; internet www.radiorfa.fr; operated by Société Martiniquaise de Communication; Dir JOSEPH LEVI.

Other radio stations include: Chérie FM (formerly Campêche FM); Difé Radio; Fun Radio (formerly Maxxi FM); Radio 22; Radio Actif Martinique; Radio Alizés; Radio Archipel; Radio Espérance; Radio Espoir; Radio Inter Tropicale; Radio Solidarité Rurale—La Voix des Mornes; and West Indies Radio.

Television

Antilles Télévision (ATV): 28 ave des Arawacks, Chateauboeuf, 97200 Fort-de-France; tel. 5-96-75-44-44; fax 5-96-75-55-65; e-mail contact@atvweb.fr; internet www.antillestelevision.com; f. 1993; general interest; accounts for 22% of viewers; also broadcasts to French Guiana and Guadeloupe; Chair. FABRICE JEAN-JEAN; Dir-Gen. DANIEL ROBIN; Editor-in-Chief KARL SIVATTE.

Canal Plus Antilles: see Guadeloupe—Television.

Kanal Martinique Télévision (KMT) (Kanal Matinik Télévision): voie 7, Renéville, 97200 Fort-de-France; tel. 5-96-63-64-85; e-mail webmaster@kmttelevision.com; internet kmttelevision.com; f. 2004; operated by l'Asscn pour le Développement des Techniques Modernes de Communication; Pres. ROLAND LAOUCHEZ.

Finance

(cap. = capital; res = reserves; dep. = deposits; m. = million; brs = branches; amounts in euros)

BANKING

Central Bank

Institut d'Emission des Départements d'Outre-mer (IEDOM): 1 blvd du Général de Gaulle, BP 512, 97206 Fort-de-France Cédex; tel. 5-96-59-44-00; fax 5-96-59-44-04; e-mail agence@iedom-martinique.fr; internet www.iedom.fr; Dir VICTOR-ROBERT NUGENT.

Commercial Banks

Banque des Antilles Françaises: see Guadeloupe—Finance.

BNP Paribas Martinique: 72 ave des Caraïbes, BP 588, 97200 Fort-de-France; tel. 5-96-59-46-00; fax 5-96-63-71-42; e-mail bnpm@bnp.mq; internet www.bnpparibas.mq; f. 1941; subsidiary of BNP Paribas, France; 12 brs; Chair. BAUDOUIN PROT.

BRED Banque Populaire: Z. I. la Jambette, 97232 Le Lamentin; tel. 5-96-63-77-63; e-mail courrier-direct@bred.fr; internet www.bred.banquepopulaire.fr; cap. 242m. (Oct. 2005); Regional Man. BRUNO DUVAL; brs in Martinique and French Guiana.

Crédit Agricole: rue Case Nègre, pl. d'Armes, BP 370, 97232 Le Lamentin Cédex 2; tel. 8-20-39-93-10; fax 5-96-51-37-12; internet www.ca-martinique.fr; f. 1950; total assets 1,263m. (Dec. 2004); Pres. XAVIER DELIN; Dir JEAN-MARIE CARLI; 30 brs in Martinique and French Guiana.

Société Générale de Banque aux Antilles (SGBA): see Guadeloupe—Finance.

INSURANCE

AGF Allianz Vie France: ZAC de l'Etang Z'Abricots, Bâtiment C, 97200 Fort-de-France; tel. 5-96-50-55-61; fax 5-96-50-55-71; e-mail marvie1@agfmar.com; internet www.allianz.fr; life insurance; subsidiary of Allianz Group.

Assurance Outre-mer: Hauts Dillon Delgres, Fort-de-France; tel. 5-96-73-09-70; fax 5-96-70-09-25; e-mail contact@assurance-outremer.fr; internet www.assurance-outremer.com; Dir-Gen. THIERRY COAT.

DPA Assurance: 126 route des Religieuses 97200 Fort de France; tel. 5-96-63-84-49; fax 5-96-63-09-52; e-mail dp.a@wanadoo.fr; internet www.dpa-assurances.com.

Groupama Antilles Guyane: 10 Lotissement Bardinet Dillon, BP 559, 97242 Fort-de-France Cédex; tel. 5-96-75-33-33; fax 5-96-75-06-78; internet www.groupama.fr; f. 1978; Group CEO THIERRY MARTEL; Dir-Gen. DIDIER COURIER; 6 brs in Martinique, 7 brs in Guadeloupe, 3 brs in French Guiana.

Groupement Français d'Assurances Caraïbes (GFA Caraïbes): 46–48 rue Ernest Desproges, 97205 Fort-de-France; tel. 5-96-59-04-04; fax 5-96-72-49-94; e-mail contact@gfa-caraibes.fr; internet www.gfacaraibes.fr; subsidiary of Gruppo Generali, Italy; Chair. JEAN-CLAUDE WULLENS; Man. Dir STÉPHANE COUDOUR.

Trade and Industry

GOVERNMENT AGENCIES

Direction Régionale du Commerce Extérieur Antilles-Guyane (DRCE): Bureaux 406 et 408, BP 647, 97262 Fort-de-France Cédex; tel. 5-96-39-49-90; fax 5-96-60-08-14; e-mail drceantilles@missioneco.org; internet www.tresor.economie.gouv.fr/region/antilles-guyane; Regional Dir MICHEL ROUSSELLIER; Regional Asst (Martinique) XAVIER BUCHOUX.

Direction Régionale de l'Industrie, de la Recherche et de l'Environnement (DRIRE): see French Guiana—Trade and Industry.

Direction de la Santé et du Développement Social (DSDS): Centre d'Affaires AGORA, l'Etang Z'abricots, Pointe des Grives, BP 658, 97263 Fort-de-France Cédex; tel. 5-96-39-42-43; fax 5-96-60-60-12; e-mail josiane.pinville@sante.gouv.fr; internet www.martinique.sante.gouv.fr; Dir CHRISTIAN URSULET.

DEVELOPMENT ORGANIZATIONS

Agence Française de Développement (AFD): 1 blvd du Général de Gaulle, BP 804, 97244 Fort-de-France Cédex; tel. 5-96-59-44-73; fax 5-96-59-44-88; e-mail afdfortdefrance@groupe-afd.org; internet www.afd.fr; fmrly Caisse Française de Développement; Man. ERIC BORDES.

Secrétariat Général pour les Affaires Régionales (SGAR)—Bureau de la Coopération Régionale: Préfecture, 97262 Fort-de-France; tel. 5-96-39-49-78; fax 5-96-39-49-59; e-mail jean-charles.barrus@martinique.pref.gouv.fr; successor to the Direction de l'Action Economique Régionale (DAER); research, documentation, and technical and administrative advice on investment in industry and commerce; Chief JEAN-CHARLES BARRUS.

CHAMBERS OF COMMERCE

Chambre d'Agriculture: pl. d'Armes, BP 312, 97286 Le Lamentin Cédex 2; tel. 5-96-51-75-75; fax 5-96-51-93-42; e-mail ca972@martinique.chambagri.fr; internet www.martinique.chambagri.fr; Pres. LOUIS-DANIEL BERTOME; Dir NICAISE MONROSE.

Chambre de Commerce et d'Industrie de la Martinique: 50 rue Ernest Desproge, BP 478, 97200 Fort-de-France Cédex; tel. 5-96-55-28-00; fax 5-96-60-66-68; e-mail dic@martinique.cci.fr; internet www.martinique.cci.fr; f. 1907; Pres. MANUEL BAUDOUIN; Dir-Gen. FRANTZ SABIN.

Chambre des Métiers et de l'Artisanat de la Martinique: 2 rue du Temple, Morne Tartenson, BP 1194, 97200 Fort-de-France; tel. 5-96-71-32-22; fax 5-96-70-47-30; e-mail cmm972@wanadoo.fr; internet www.cma-martinique.com; f. 1970; Pres. HERVÉ LAUREOTE; Sec.-Gen. HERVÉ ETILÉ; 8,000 mems.

INDUSTRIAL ORGANIZATION

Association Martiniquaise pour la Promotion de l'Industrie (AMPI): Centre d'Affaires de la Martinique, Bâtiment Pierre, 1er étage, Californie, BP 1042, 97232 Le Lamentin; tel. 5-96-50-74-00; fax 5-96-50-74-37; e-mail industrie@ampi.mq; internet www .industriemartinique.com; f. 1972 as Asscn des Moyennes et Petites Industries; 119 mem. cos; Pres. PIERRE MARIE-JOSEPH; Sec.-Gen. RICHARD CRESTOR.

EMPLOYERS' ORGANIZATIONS

Banalliance: Centre d'Affaires le Baobab, rue Léon Gontran Damas, 97232 Le Lamentin; tel. 5-96-57-42-42; fax 5-96-57-35-18; f. 1996; banana growers' alliance; Pres. DANIEL DISER; Dir-Gen. SANDRA ALEXIA; 220 mems.

Banamart: Quartier Bois Rouge, 97224 Ducos; tel. 5-96-42-43-44; fax 5-96-51-47-70; internet www.banamart.com; f. 2005 by merger of SICABAM and GIPAM; represents banana producers; Pres. NICOLAS MARRAUD DES GROTTES; Dir-Gen. PIERRE MONTEUX.

IMALFLHOR (Interprofession Martiniquaise des Fruits, Legumes et Produits Horticoles): Immeuble La Chapelle, Route du stade, Place d'Armes; tel. 5-96-59-70-56; fax 5-96-51-06-63; e-mail contact .imaflhor@gmail.com; internet sites.google.com/site/imaflhor/home; f. 2010; supports and develops agricultural production; Chair. FRANÇOIS DE MEILLAC.

Ordre des Médecins de la Martinique: 80 rue de la République, 97200 Fort-de-France; tel. 5-96-63-27-01; fax 5-96-60-58-00; e-mail martinique@972.medecin.fr; Pres. HELENON RAYMOND; Sec.-Gen. ELANA EMILE.

Ordre des Pharmaciens de la Martinique: Apt G-01, Immeuble Gaëlle, Résidence Studiotel-Grand Village, BP 587, 97233 Schoelcher; tel. 5-96-52-23-67; fax 5-96-52-20-92; e-mail delegation_martinique@ordre.pharmacien.fr; internet www.ordre .pharmacien.fr; Pres. JEAN BIGON.

MAJOR COMPANIES

Bellonie Bourdillon Successeurs (BBS): Z. I. Génipa, BP 35, 97224 Ducos; tel. 5-96-56-82-82; fax 5-96-56-82-83; e-mail info@ rhumdemartinique.com; internet www.rhumdemartinique.com; f. 1919; rum producer, markets other spirits and wines; Pres. XAVIER THIEBLIN; Dir-Gen. FRANÇOIS DE LAVIGNE; 161 employees.

Biometal, SA: Usine de Robert, Parc d'Activités, 97231 Le Robert; tel. 5-96-65-14-44; fax 5-96-65-45-12; e-mail biometal@biometal.com; internet www.biometalsa.com; f. 1979; manufacture of steel products; Pres. and Dir-Gen. LIONEL DE LAGUARIGUE; Man. GILLES DE REYNAL DE SAINT MICHEL; 70 employees.

Comptoir Martiniquais d'Industrie Alimentaire (COMIA): pl. d'Armes, BP 266, 97232 Le Lamentin; tel. 5-96-66-61-62; fax 5-96-51-40-21; e-mail info@comia.fr; f. 1978; cooked meats; Pres. MARCEL OSENAT; c. 40 employees.

Denel SAS: Usine Dénel, 97213 Gros-Morne; tel. 5-96-67-51-23; fax 5-96-67-67-56; e-mail info@denelmartinique.com; internet www .denelmartinique.com; f. 1932; subsidiary of Groupe Despointes; food processing, fruit juices and preserves; CEO ALAIN HUYGHUES-DESPOINTES; Gen. Man. LAURENT HUYGHUES-DESPOINTES; 49 employees.

Distillerie Dillon, SA: 9 route Chateauboeuf, BP 212, 97257 Fort-de-France Cédex; tel. 5-96-75-00-18; fax 5-96-75-30-33; e-mail info@ rhum-dillon.com; internet www.rhums-dillon.com; f. 1967; rum producer; Man. PASCAL RENARD; 45 employees; 80 planters.

Esso Antilles Guyane, SAS: pl. d'Armes, BP 272, 97285 Le Lamentin Cédex 2; tel. 5-96-66-90-82; fax 5-96-51-17-87; e-mail christian.l.porter@exxonmobil.com; f. 1965; distribution of petroleum and petroleum products; Pres. CÉDRIC BOUQUETY; 28 employees.

Groupe Bernard Hayot (GBH): Acajou, BP 423, 97232 Le Lamentin Cédex 02; tel. 5-96-50-37-56; fax 5-96-50-11-47; e-mail service .communication@gbh.fr; internet www.gbh.fr; f. 1960; volume retail and distribution; also operates in French Guiana and Guadeloupe; Chair. BERNARD HAYOT.

Groupe Ho Hio Hen: Hauts de Californie, 97232 Le Lamentin; tel. 5-96-75-71-24; fax 5-96-50-96-28; e-mail col@hiohen.com; internet www.groupehohiohen.com; f. 1972; volume retail and distribution; Chair. CHARLES HO HIO HEN; c. 800 employees in Martinique and Guadeloupe.

Groupe SEEN (Société d'Entretien et de Nettoyage): Z. I. de la Lézarde, 97232 Le Lamentin; tel. 5-96-66-65-66; fax 5-96-51-61-25; e-mail srh@groupeseen.com; internet www.groupeseen.com; f. 1979; commercial waste disposal and environmental services; Chair. YANN MONPLAISIR; Dir-Gen. LILIAN FANGET; 360 employees.

Prochimie, SA: Quartier Palmiste, BP 233, 97284 Le Lamentin Cédex 2; tel. 5-96-50-32-82; fax 5-96-50-22-48; e-mail contact@ prochimie.fr; internet www.prochimie.fr; f. 1972; domestic and sanitary products and paper; Man. ALEX DORMOY; 50 employees.

SAEM Le Galion (Société Anonyme d'Economie Mixte de Production Sucrière et Rhumière de La Martinique): Usine du Le Galion, 97220 La Trinité; tel. 5-96-58-20-65; fax 5-96-58-42-43; e-mail sucrerie@saem-legalion.net; f. 1984; sugar refinery; rum business managed by COFEPP; Man. PHILIPPE ANDRÉ; 91 employees.

SARA (Société Anonyme de la Raffinerie des Antilles): Z. I. Californie, BP 436, 97292 Le Lamentin Cédex 2; tel. 5-96-50-18-94; fax 5-96-50-00-15; e-mail christine.ransay@sara.mq; internet www.sara .mq; f. 1969; TotalFinaElf 50%, Shell 24%, Esso 14.5%, Texaco 11.5%; depots in French Guiana and Guadeloupe; processes 800,000 metric tons of crude oil annually; Dir-Gen. DAVID MARION; c. 260 employees regionally.

Siapoc, SA (Société Industrielle Antillaise de Peintures et de Produits Chimiques): Z. I. Californie, Acajou, 97232 Le Lamentin; tel. 5-96-50-54-14; fax 5-96-50-09-11; e-mail stesiapoc@siapoc.org; f. 1965; paints; Man. BRUNO MENCE; 65 employees.

SMPA: Z. I. pl. d'Armes, 97232 Le Lamentin; tel. 5-96-30-00-14; fax 5-96-51-70-43; e-mail eursulet@sasi.fr; f. 1987; industrial bakery products and frozen foods; Man. XAVIER SOCIRAT; 35 employees.

Socara, SARL (Société Caraïbe de Representation Importation Exportation): 2 ave des Arawaks, BP 560, 97242 Fort-de-France Cédex; tel. 5-96-75-04-04; fax 5-96-75-04-76; e-mail socara@wanadoo .fr; f. 1948; distribution of fruit juices, wines, beer, spirits; Dir NICOLAS CHABROL; 32 employees.

Société d'Embouteillage de l'Eau Minérale Didier (SEEMD): 9 km route de Didier, 97200 Fort-de-France; tel. 5-96-64-07-88; fax 5-96-64-01-69; e-mail seemd@fontainedidier.com; internet www .fontainedidier.com; mineral water; CEO JEAN-LUC GARCIN; 41 employees.

SOMES (Société Martiniquaise des Eaux de Source): Quartier Champflore, 97260 Morne Rouge; tel. 5-96-52-52-52; fax 5-96-52-30-55; e-mail somes@wanadoo.fr; f. 1976; carbonated drinks bottler and juice distributor; Pres. BERTRAND CLERC; 49 employees.

UTILITIES

Electricity

EDF Martinique (Electricité de France Martinique): Pointe des Carrières, BP 573, 97242 Fort-de-France Cédex 01; tel. 5-96-59-20-00; fax 5-96-60-29-76; e-mail edf-services-martinique@edfgdf.fr; internet www.edf.fr/martinique; f. 1975; electricity supplier; successor to Société de Production et de Distribution d'Electricité de la Martinique (SPDEM); Chair. and CEO HENRI PROGLIO; 174,753 customers (2006).

Water

Veolia Water-Société Martiniquaise des Eaux (SME): pl. d'Armes, BP 213, 97284 Le Lamentin Cédex 02; tel. 5-96-51-80-51; fax 5-96-51-80-55; e-mail sme@sme.mq; internet www.smeaux.fr; f. 1977 as Société Martiniquaise des Eaux; Dir-Gen. JEAN-PIERRE PIERRE.

TRADE UNIONS

Centrale Démocratique Martiniquaise du Travail (CDMT): Maison des Syndicats, Jardin Desclieux, 97200 Fort-de-France; tel. 5-96-70-19-86; fax 5-96-71-32-25; Sec.-Gen. PHILIPPE PIERRE-CHARLES.

Confédération Générale du Travail de la Martinique (CGTM): Maison des Syndicats, blvd Général de Gaulle, 97200 Fort-de-France; tel. 5-96-70-25-89; fax 5-96-63-80-10; e-mail contact@ cgt-martinique.fr; internet www.cgt-martinique.fr; f. 1961; affiliated to World Fed. of Trade Unions; Sec.-Gen. GHISLAINE JOACHIM-ARNAUD.

Fédération Départementale des Syndicats d'Exploitants Agricoles de la Martinique (FDSEA): Immeuble Chambre d'Agriculture, pl. d'Armes, 97232 Le Lamentin; tel. 5-96-51-61-46; fax 5-96-57-05-43; e-mail fdsea.martinique@wanadoo.fr; affiliated to the Fédération Nationale des Syndicats d'Exploitants Agricoles; Pres. BÉRARD CAPGRAS.

Fédération Syndicale Unitaire Martinique (FSU): route des Réligieuses, Bâtiment B, Cité Bon Air, 97200 Fort-de-France; tel. 5-96-63-63-27; fax 5-96-71-89-43; e-mail fsu@fsu-martinique.fr; internet www.fsu-martinique.fr; f. 1993; departmental br. of the Fédération Syndicale Unitaire; represents public sector employees in teaching, research and training, and also agriculture, justice, youth and sports, and culture; Sec.-Gen. BERNADETTE GROISON.

Union Départementale Confédération Française des Travailleurs Chrétiens Martinique (UD CFTC): Maison des Syndicats, Jardin Desclieux, 97200 Fort-de-France; tel. 5-96-71-95-10; fax 5-96-60-39-10; e-mail cftc972@wanadoo.fr; internet www.cftc.fr; Pres. PHILLIPE LOUIS; Sec.-Gen. PASCALE COTTON.

Union Départementale Force Ouvrière Martinique (UD-FO): rue Bouillé, BP 1114, 97248 Fort-de-France Cédex; tel. 5-96-70-07-

04; fax 5-96-70-18-20; e-mail udfomartinique@wanadoo.fr; internet www.force-ouvriere.fr; affiliated to the Int. Trade Union Confederation; Sec.-Gen. JEAN-CLAUDE MAILLY.

Union Générale des Travailleurs de Martinique (UGTM): 8 rue Pierre et Marie Curie, Terres Sainville, 97200 Fort-de-France; tel. 5-96-63-75-23; fax 5-96-70-30-82; e-mail ugtm.centrale@ wanadoo.fr; f. 1999; Pres. LÉON BERTIDE; Sec.-Gen. PATRICK DORÉ.

Union Régionale Martinique: Maison des Syndicats, rue de la Sécurité Jardin Desclieux, Salles 5–7, 97200 Fort-de-France; tel. 5-96-72-64-74; fax 5-96-70-16-80; e-mail ur-martinique@unsa.org; internet www.unsa.org.

UNSA Education Martinique (UE): Maison des Syndicats, Salles 4–5, Jardin Desclieux, 97200 Fort-de-France; tel. 5-96-72-64-74; fax 5-96-70-16-80; e-mail unsa-education972@orange.fr; internet www .unsa-education.org; 22-mem. fed; Sec.-Gen. MIREILLE JACQUES.

Transport

RAILWAYS

There are no railways in Martinique.

ROADS

There were 2,077 km (1,291 miles) of roads in 1998, of which 261 km were motorways and first-class roads.

SHIPPING

CMA-CGM CGM Antilles-Guyane: ZIP de la Pointe des Grives, BP 574, 97242 Fort-de-France Cédex; tel. 5-96-55-32-00; fax 5-96-63-08-87; e-mail fdf.jgourdin@cma-cgm.com; internet www.cma-cgm.com; subsidiary of CMA-CGM, France; also represents other passenger and freight lines; Pres. RODOLPHE SAADÉ; Man. Dir JACQUES GOURDIN.

Direction Régionale des Affaires Maritimes (DRAM): Centre de Sécurité des Navires, Fort-de-France Cédex; tel. 5-96-60-42-44; fax 5-96-63-67-30; e-mail affaires.maritimes.martinique@wanadoo .fr; Dir LUC NOSLIER.

Grand Port Maritime de la Martinique: quai de l'Hydro Base, BP 782, 97244 Fort-de-France Cédex; tel. 5-96-59-00-00; fax 5-96-71-35-73; e-mail contact@martinique.port.fr; internet www.martinique .port.fr; f. 1953 under management of Chambre de Commerce et de l'Industrie de la Martinique; present name adopted 2013 when port became publicly owned entity under supervisory body; Dir JEAN-RÉMY VILLAGEOIS.

CIVIL AVIATION

Aimé Césaire International Airport is located at Le Lamentin, 12 km from Fort-de-France and is equipped to handle jet-engined aircraft. Three scheduled airlines operate flights to Paris: Air France, Corsair and Air Caraïbes. Regional services are provided primarily by Air Caraïbes to Guadeloupe, St-Martin, St-Barthélemy, St Lucia and Guyana. Air France also provides a regular service to French Guiana. The regional airline LIAT (based in Antigua and Barbuda) provides scheduled services to all islands of the Eastern Caribbean. In 2013

American Airlines began a direct service from Miami, FL, USA, to Fort-de-France. Seaborne Airlines also was expected to launch a weekly service from San Juan to Martinique in 2013. Plans to upgrade the airport at Le Lamentin were agreed in June of that year.

Direction des Services Aéroportuaires: BP 279, 97285 Le Lamentin; tel. 5-96-42-16-00; fax 5-96-42-18-77; e-mail aeroport@ martinique.cci.fr; internet www.martinique.aeroport.fr; Dir FRANTZ THODIARD.

Air Caraïbes: see Guadeloupe—Transport.

Tourism

Martinique's tourist attractions are its beaches and coastal scenery, its mountainous interior, and the historic towns of Fort-de-France and Saint-Pierre. In 2013 the number of tourists who stayed on the island totalled 489,705. Receipts from tourism were €462m. in 2012.

Comité Martiniquais du Tourisme: Immeuble Beaupré, Pointe de Jaham, 97233 Schoelcher; tel. 5-96-61-61-77; fax 5-96-61-22-72; e-mail infos.cmt@martiniquetourisme.com; internet www .martiniquetourisme.com; Pres. KARINE ROY-CAMILLE.

Délégation Régionale au Tourisme: 41 rue Gabriel Périé, 97200 Fort-de-France; tel. 5-96-71-42-68; fax 5-96-73-00-96; e-mail drtmartinique.ndl@wanadoo.fr; Delegate VALÉRIE LEOTURE.

Fédération Martiniquaise des Offices de Tourisme et Syndicats d'Initiative (FMOTSI): Maison du Tourisme Vert, 9 blvd du Général de Gaulle, BP 491, 97207 Fort-de-France Cédex; tel. 5-96-63-18-54; fax 5-96-70-17-61; e-mail contact@fmotsi.net; internet www .fmotsi.net; f. 1984; Pres. JOSÉ REINETTE; Sec.-Gen. JEAN-MARC LUSBEC.

Defence

As assessed at November 2013, France maintained a military force of about 1,250. There was also a naval base, headquartered in Fort-de-France, and a gendarmerie.

Education

The educational system is similar to that of metropolitan France (see chapter on French Guiana). In 2012/13 there were 72 pre-primary schools, 180 elementary and special schools and 80 secondary schools. In 2012/13 there were 42,239 pupils in pre-primary and primary education, while in secondary education there were 39,362 students, of whom some 90% attended state schools. Higher education is provided by a branch of the Université des Antilles et de la Guyane. There are also colleges of agriculture, fisheries, hotel management, nursing, midwifery and childcare. In 2011/12 there were 7,829 students enrolled in higher education on the island. Departmental expenditure on education and culture was estimated at €44.1m. in 2006.

Bibliography

For works on the Caribbean generally, see Select Bibliography (Books)

Browne, K. *Creole Economics: Caribbean Cunning under the French Flag.* Austin, TX, University of Texas Press, 2005.

Darsières, C. *Des origines de la nation martiniquaise.* Fort-de-France, Editions Desormeaux, 1974.

Scarth, A. *La Catastrophe: The Eruption of Mount Pelée.* Oxford, Oxford University Press, 2002.

Schloss, R. H. *Sweet Liberty: The Final Days of Slavery in Martinique.* Philadelphia, PA, University of Pennsylvania Press, 2009.

MEXICO

Geography

PHYSICAL FEATURES

The United Mexican States is the southernmost of the three great federations of North America, a republic that narrows south and east towards the great land bridge of Central America. Mexico is the smallest of the continental North American countries, being about one-fifth the size of the USA or Canada, but it is the third largest country of Latin America (it is less than one-quarter the size of Brazil and 70% of Argentina, but the next country in area, Peru, is only two-thirds its size) and the most northerly. The longest border (3,152 km or 1,959 miles) is with the USA, which lies to the north and north-east, while its south-eastern frontier is with the Central American countries of Guatemala (956 km), on the Pacific side, and Belize (193 km), on the Caribbean side. The country's nearest insular Caribbean neighbour is Cuba, some 210 km to the east of the Yucatán peninsula, in the south. The eastern coast is along the Gulf of Mexico and on the Caribbean, while the western coast, almost double in length, is on the Pacific Ocean. In total, there are about 11,122 km of coastline. Mexico covers an area of 1,964,375 sq km (758,449 sq miles), including 5,127 sq km of islands (the latter an area almost equivalent in size to Trinidad and Tobago).

Mexico has a diverse and crumpled topography, covering a vast area (it is the 13th largest country in the world). It is at its widest in the north, along the US border, where it is about 2,000 km from east to west. It is at its narrowest, 210 km from north to south, on the Tehuantepec isthmus, where there is a break in the Continental Divide, just before the country broadens westwards into Central America. Some two-thirds of Mexico is mountainous and one-half of it above 1,500 m (about 5,000 ft). Most of it is dry and sere, although the extent and variety of the terrain makes for regional contrasts. The Pacific coast runs roughly from north-west to south-east, before curving in a south-facing shore and continuing into Guatemala. The more northerly section of this western coast is dominated by the lowlands of the Sonora Desert, shielded from the immediate presence of the Pacific by the 1,300-km peninsula of Baja California, joined to the rest of Mexico in the far north-west, then thrusting southwards, parallel to the main coast on the other shore of what is known in Mexico as the Sea of Cortez (Cortés—Gulf of California). On the other side of the country, the eastern coast curves out of the north-east, circling around the Gulf of Mexico and into the north-thrusting abutment of the Yucatán peninsula, which separates the Gulf from the Caribbean. The flat, forested Yucatán has a relatively short eastern coast on the Caribbean, below which is Belize. Much of the interior of the country is an elevated plateau, the Mesa Central, which occupies about 60% of the territory of Mexico and contains most of its mountains, population and historical remains. A number of other distinct regions can be identified— the narrow coastal plains of the Pacific and of the Gulf of Mexico, the peninsulas of Baja California and Yucatán, and two further areas of upland, the southern highlands and the Chiapas highlands.

The central plateau is flanked, to west and east, by two mountain ranges, each rising steeply from their respective coastal plains, the Sierra Madre Occidental and the Sierra Madre Oriental. The western (Occidental) mountains are generally higher, above narrower coastal plains. Both ranges continue the thrust of the Rockies from the north, and merge some 240 km south of Mexico City (Ciudad de México), the capital, in an area of towering, inactive volcanoes and some of the country's highest peaks—such as Potacatépetl and Ixaticcíhuatl (just south-east of Mexico City) or the highest, Orizaba (5,610 m or 18,412 ft), between there and the Gulf city of Veracruz. The average elevation of the central plateau itself is about 900 m in the north and 2,400 m in the south. The plateau is interrupted by heights and broad basins, consisting of desert in the north (*bolsones*) and areas of settlement amid the rolling

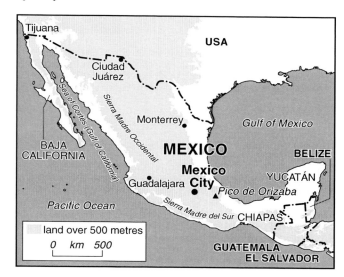

land over 500 metres

0 km 500

hills of the south. One such basin in the south of the plateau is the site of Mexico City and is known as the Valley of Mexico.

Just as the Sierra Madre is a part of the Continental Divide and a continuation of the Rockies, the mountainous interior of Baja (Lower) California is a continuation of the Coast Ranges in the USA. The northern connection to 'mainland' Mexico is interrupted by a deep cleft (continuing in the Sea of Cortez) in which the Laguna Salada is the lowest point in the country, being 10 m below sea level. Sparsely inhabited and arid, the peninsula most resembles the desert of the northern shores on the other side of the Sea of Cortez. Mid-way down the long inlet of the Pacific begin the coastal plains, about 50 km in width and extending southwards to just below Tepic (which lies north-west of Guadalajara). These plains are extensively irrigated and used for agriculture, being one of the limited fertile areas of the country (only 13% of the national territory is cultivated). Thereafter, the few patches of coastal plain are much narrower, as the southern highlands meet the sea, but widen again beyond Tehuantepec. The southern highlands are the Sierra Madre del Sur, which begin on the coast to the west of the Valley of Mexico and swing south of the central highlands, pushing south-eastwards to tail away at the Tehuantepec isthmus. The terrain consists of steep mountains, deep valleys (hot and dry inland) and high plateaux. The mountains often plunge straight into the Pacific, and the coast is rugged, and sometimes called the 'Mexican Riviera'. Beyond Tehuantepec, the Sierra Madre and the Continental Divide resume in the Chiapas highlands, continuing into Guatemala. The coastal plains also appear again at this point here, beneath the mountains, but the landscape is very different in the south. Chiapas receives more rainfall than anywhere else in Mexico and is thinly inhabited, leaving forest cover still extensive. Beyond the highlands, east of the central plateau, are the limestone lowlands and coastal plains along the Gulf of Mexico. In the north, near the US border along the Río Bravo del Norte (known as the Rio Grande in the USA), there are about 280 km between the sea and the steep mountain wall, but this narrows to only a few kilometres near Veracruz (which is east of Mexico City). Beyond here, the plains widen again into the lowlands of the Tehuantepec isthmus, before thrusting north and east beyond Tabasco into the Yucatán peninsula. Much of the plains immediately on the Gulf consist of lagoons and swampy lowlands. Yucatán itself is broad and flat, without surface rivers, being dry and scrubby in the north-west, but much wetter and covered in dense rainforest in the south, the jungle often cloaking the ruins of the old Maya civilization.

The country is largely dry and also has few large rivers. There are the Grijalva and the Usumacinta, for instance, which rise in Guatemala and empty into the Gulf of Mexico. The most important river system is that of the Grande de Santiago and the Lerma, which flow into the Pacific. The two rivers are interrupted by the country's largest lake, Chapala, which is 80 km long and 13 km wide—Mexico has relatively few lakes, although many lagoons and enclosed bodies of salt water contribute to inland waters of 49,510 sq km. This contributes to the variety of ecosystems to be found in the country, which still enjoys a diverse range of living species, both plant and animal. However, human settlement, in the north particularly, has had an adverse effect on the natural environment, with a continuing high rate of deforestation (this and the lack of clean water have both been declared national security issues by the Government: as an example of the seriousness of the situation, the depletion of groundwater reserves in the Valley of Mexico is causing subsidence). Nevertheless, about one-quarter of the country is forested (mainly in the south), and this helps to shelter the range of species found in Mexico—30,000 plants, 1,000 birds and 1,500 mammals, reptiles and amphibians. About 15% of these species are reckoned to be unique to Mexico. The human population being less numerous and less widespread in the south, the ecological damage here is considerably less than in the north, with the environment similar to Central America, still inhabited by animals such as tapirs, jaguars and monkeys. Even in the north, in the high Sierra Madre, animals such as bears, deer, coyotes and mountain lions can still be found. The ever rising population and the fact that most of Mexico's profitable natural resources are subsoil, however, represents a continuing threat to the environment, even in the hitherto neglected desert areas. It is the north of the country that is dominated by desert foliage, with extensive grasslands and hardwood forests in the highlands, while the wetter south is more typically rainforest.

CLIMATE

The climate is as varied as the topography, ranging from tropical to temperate, mainly depending on altitude. Most of the country is south of the Tropic of Cancer, which crosses the tip of the Baja California peninsula. It is also generally dry, particularly in the north-west, but the south receives copious rainfall. Mexico mostly experiences two seasons, wet and dry, the latter (November–May) being the cooler. The central plateau is milder than the rest of the country, the evenings being not only cool but even cold at times during the winter. Most rain falls between June and September, ranging from about 300 mm (12 ins) in the north to 500 mm–650 mm in the south. However, the deleterious effects human settlement can have even on weather is amply demonstrated in the disruption to the traditional rainfall patterns in the Valley of Mexico, owing to industrial pollution. The north-west of the country is the driest area, particularly on the Baja California peninsula. The northern part of the peninsula has a climate similar to that of southern California in the USA, with dry, warm summers and mild winters, while the south of the peninsula can get

extremely hot. Here and in the Sonora Desert are the areas of lowest rainfall (about 130 mm annually). The coastal plains of the Pacific tend to have a little more rain and rather stronger storm patterns. Further down this coast, on the Riviera region, there is a definite tropical monsoon climate, although the southern highlands hinterland tends to be drier. In Chiapas the tropical conditions are even more pronounced, with average annual rainfall reaching 2,030 mm, although many places receive as much as double that amount. The coast of the Gulf of Mexico is muggy, with average rainfall about twice that of Baja California and increasing significantly south of Tampico (midway between Veracruz and the US border). Summer temperatures are high, but rain in autumn and winter (September–February), a slightly different wet season, is helped by brisk, cold northerlies. Yucatán is hot and humid in its jungle interior, alleviated by proximity to the coasts. The north of the peninsula is dry, but precipitation levels in the south approach those of Chiapas. There are two main wet seasons, in April–May and September–January. September–October can bring hurricanes, to which Caribbean, Gulf and Pacific coasts are all prone (natural hazards also come from the earthquakes common in a volcanic region such as this, with tsunamis liable to hit the Pacific coast). The average maximum and minimum temperatures in Mexico City range from 6°C–19°C (43°F–66°F) in January to 12°C–26°C (54°F–79°F) in May.

POPULATION

The population of Mexico is predominantly (60%) of mixed Spanish and Amerindian descent, and Amerindian (anywhere between 15% and 30%, depending on which figures are given credence), the balance made up of whites (9%—of mixed descent from Spanish and other immigrant, mainly European, groups), with small black and Asian groups. The early adoption of Spanish and Roman Catholicism by the native Amerindians has made for a more uniform culture than might otherwise have been the case. Spanish remains the official language, although 7% of the population speak only one of at least 62 indigenous tongues (mainly Nahuatl or, in the south, Mayan languages). English is widely spoken along the northern border. About 83% of the population are at least nominally Roman Catholic, despite the official anti-clericalism of the regime for most of the 20th century, and 7% are Pentecostal or Evangelical Christians.

According to official estimates, the population of Mexico was 119.7m. in mid-2014. About three-quarters of this population is urbanized, with nearly one-fifth of the total living in or around Mexico City. The capital is just north of where the Sierra Madre Occidental and the Sierra Madre Oriental converge, in central Mexico. The population of Mexico City at the time of the 2010 census was 8.85m., although, in addition, some cities on its outskirts are virtually suburbs (such as Ecatepec—1.66m.—and Nezahualcóyotl—1.11m.). The third most populous city is Tijuana, in the far north-west, with 1.56m. people, followed by Puebla, not far to the south-east of Mexico City, with 1.54m. A further six cities had more than 1m. residents. Mexico is a federal republic, consisting of 31 states and the Federal District (Distrito Federal) encompassing Mexico City.

History

Prof. FRANCISCO E. GONZÁLEZ

INTRODUCTION

More than double the size of the USA in territory after its independence from Spain in 1821, Mexico experienced endemic political instability, social conflict, and economic decline during more than 50 years. By then, the country had repelled several attempted invasions by Spanish and French forces, had lost more than half its territory in a war against the USA (1846–48), had fought a bloody civil war between conservatives and liberals (Guerra de Reforma, 1857–61) and had endured French occupation and imperial rule under Maximilian of Habsburg (1863–37). It was far from a foregone conclusion that Mexico could become a viable modern nation state, which finally happened between the late 1860s and the early 1880s.

MEXICO'S DEEP-SEATED HISTORICAL FAULT LINES

Several economic, social, political and geopolitical fault lines help to explain why conflict and instability prevailed for so long after independence. Significantly, several of these fault lines continue to present structural impediments that are either present to different degrees, all or some of the time, or latent, but can become activated given the right conditions. Their operation or activation has militated against the country achieving sustained high economic growth, political stability, and social peace since the 1980s and into the second decade of the 21st century.

First, as the richest Spanish colony in the Americas, Mexico (alongside Peru), experienced longer, more destructive wars of independence (Mexico's, 1810–21) than other colonies because Spain's military forces dug in their heels and fought harder to retain their most profitable possessions. The end result was greater human, economic, and institutional destruction in these rich, mining-based societies than in less profitable colonies abandoned earlier by the Spaniards, such as what today are Paraguay, Chile and Argentina. From the very beginning, successive Mexican governments had to borrow capital from foreign banks, particularly British ones and later French and US ones, to make war reparations, reconstruct basic infrastructure, revive economic sources of production, and invest in state building. Thus, early on the country became dependent on foreign finance and good diplomatic relations to promote growth, order and stability. Dependence on foreign capital has remained a structural impediment to endogenous growth and development in Mexico.

Second, Mexico (like Peru) was not only the richest Spanish colony thanks to great deposits of precious minerals but, more importantly, was home to highly complex, advanced Amerindian societies with significant demographic weight before the Spaniards' arrival. Once defeated, the Aztec and Inca empires' human and social base provided some of the backbone of labour and services for production of food and raw materials used to advance the Spanish Empire. To achieve this, colonial societies were highly stratified by legally enshrined caste systems based on the level of miscegenation given white Europeans, Amerindians, and Africans imported as slaves. After the Spanish authorities were removed in the 1820s, and despite constitutions calling for the creation of individual citizens who would be equal under the law, the reality remained based on segregationist social rules and norms and high levels of socio-economic inequality, which correlated strongly with race and ethnicity. Mexico, like all other societies with a broad Amerindian base, was born deeply divided and unequal, and to a large extent remains so.

Third, the military leaders of the different sub-regions that made up a given colonial jurisdiction such as a vice-royalty or a general captaincy became the dispensers of law and order, patronage and promotion in their localities during the prolonged wars of independence and the vacuum of power left by the collapse of Spanish rule throughout Latin America. These regional strong men came to be known as *caudillos*, and the system of authoritarian rule by them, characterized by personality-based rather than rule-based decision making and exercise of power, became known as *caudillismo*. This political phenomenon has had a long tradition in Latin America, including in Mexico under Antonio López de Santa Anna, a quintessential 19th century *caudillo*. In parallel, both civilian and military strongmen and women, known as *caciques*, have controlled political and social life at the local level in a personal, rather than rule-based, fashion. They have traditionally been (and largely remain) in charge of patronage, distribution of resources and conflict management. The main long-term effect of these types of authoritarian exercise of power has been a permanent tension between formal, legal, institutional and informal, custom-based, personalized forms of political domination. Moreover, *caudillismo* has also contributed to create uncertainty and conflict in relationships between civil society and the military in Latin America, including in Mexico. Many *caudillos* started their ascent to power as military officers but later metamorphosed into paramilitary or civilian leaders, who then continued growing their base of mass support and the resources under their control. Even though Mexico has been considered a country with a clear predominance of civilians over the military—unlike most other Latin America countries—since the middle of the 20th century, charismatic, populist leaders have exploited a personalized style of leadership against established institutions on several occasions. Given high rates of socio-economic inequality and exclusion, such style has found fertile ground to mobilize the masses against the entrenched, privileged few. Such politics of kindling resentment and promising significant short-term redistribution remain alive and significant, although not dominant or majoritarian, in 21st century Mexico.

Fourth, the country was also deeply divided along ideological lines after independence. Liberals saw in the USA, and its republican, federal form of government, the model to follow. In contrast, conservatives saw the Spanish monarchical, unitary form of rule, which had established deep roots in Mexico, as the type of polity that the country should retain, in order that there was no brusque rupture with the past, and what they perceived as the imposition of a foreign form without local custom and practice behind it. Liberals tended to be anti-clerical and demanded a strict separation between Church and State, while conservatives argued, again, for keeping established practice on the ground, which meant a close relationship between the two. Liberals believed in decreeing the creation of individual citizens who would be equal before the law, while conservatives fought for the preservation of legal group privileges (i.e. *fueros*), which had structured colonial society. The conflicts that plagued the first two-thirds of the 19th century had such entrenched disputes at their heart, and were primarily responsible for the short life duration of governments, economic stagnation, regional allegiances that weakened national cohesion, the massive loss of territory and foreign occupation. While not as pronounced and irreconcilable as during the 19th century, the main political forces in Mexico have remained significantly divided, thereby creating strong left-wing, centre (catch-all or pragmatic), and right-wing movements and parties, which make the country home to a vibrant pluralism. While liable to escalating conflict, political pluralism has shown time and again since the 1990s that compromise and negotiation are possible, and that democratic government is possible. A more intractable problem that dominates Mexican politics is related to its federal structure, and the very significant differences in governance that this system allows. Of the country's 31 states, plus the capital (Distrito Federal or DF), some have economic and social indicators that are not far from those in developed countries while others are closer to poor countries in South Asia or Africa. The three levels of government (municipal—close to 2,500 municipalities, state and federal) create a complex, variegated tapestry of populations, natural resources, quality of institutions, and style of governance, making any generalizations about the country as a whole difficult. Alongside the president, governors have been the main powerbrokers in Mexico since the mid-1990s. Some commentators use the word 'feuderalist' to refer to the current system to highlight the extent to which governors have become a law unto themselves in their jurisdiction. In short, power in 21st century Mexico is significantly divided not only given checks and balances (i.e. the legislative and judicial powers have also become stronger in relation to the executive since the second half of the 1990s) but also the territorial division of power.

Fifth and last, Mexico's strategic geographic location as a meeting and transit point for global exchange (North and South America, Western Europe, West Africa and East Asia) and, crucially, its shared 2,000-mile (3,200-km) land border with the USA, the world's largest superpower, mean that the former country has played, and will continue to play, an important role in the calculations and actions that underpin international politics. Diplomatically, Mexico acted as an effective bridge during the Cold War, remaining a prominent member of the non-aligned nation states. It maintained good relations with the USA and its western allies, as well as with the Soviet Union, Cuba and the rest of Latin America, and other big non-aligned countries, such as India, as well as young independent countries in other parts of Asia and in Africa. Mexico's rich, multi-ethnic culture is depicted as potentially capable of mobilizing significant 'soft power' (i.e. cultural allegiance and influence) around the globe. With access to two oceans and the largest landmass south of the USA overlooking Central America and the Caribbean, Mexico's location is of strategic value for general trade and security. All types of trafficking targeting the USA or leaving that country can use Mexico as an obvious platform. Therefore, the most conspicuous feature of Mexico's geopolitical-economic location remains its relation with its northern neighbour. Mexico's economy has been very dependent on the USA and became even more so after the North American Free Trade Agreement (NAFTA) came into operation in 1994. US domestic politics and policies increasingly influence the constraints and opportunities that Mexican governments, private businesses, the middle classes, urban workers and rural populations face in the short and medium term. Of particular concern has been the emphasis that successive US and Mexican governments have placed on fighting drugs-trafficking through a warfare strategy that left more than 70,000 dead in Mexico between 2007 and 2012. Permanent tensions are likely to remain between the economic and security objectives (both of which are connected via legal exchange and illegal trafficking) of the two countries. Maximizing the benefits of both objectives rather than exacerbating their trade-offs will remain the key conundrum underlining this fault line.

CREATION OF A MODERN NATION STATE AND THE PORFIRIATO, 1867–1911

Two figures dominated the consolidation of the modern nation state in Mexico, Benito Juárez (presidencies between 1858 and 1872) and Porfirio Díaz (presidencies, 1876–80 and 1884–1911). The former was a civilian indigenous Zapotec who became the standard bearer of liberalism and its project to remake the country by destroying group privileges, consolidating the separation of Church and State, and creating self-reliant individual citizens, who like Thomas Jefferson's small, free farmers could become Mexico's backbone. Juárez and his adherents drafted the federalist, liberal 1857 Constitution to promote change to these ends. Conservatives resisted such far-reaching changes, and one decade of civil war, foreign occupation, and imperial rule culminated with the execution of Emperor Maximilian of Habsburg (his last words were 'Viva México!'), and Juárez and the liberals return to power in 1867. In spite of Juárez's rhetorical devotion to enlightened constitutionalism and the rule of law, his political practice tended toward authoritarianism and personalized rule. One of his maxims, 'To our friends, justice and grace; to our enemies, the law', illustrates this tension and the deep rooted political culture, which persists in today's Mexico, of using the law as a tool for the exercise of power rather than the dispensation of justice.

In contrast to Juárez, Porfirio Díaz was a military mestizo (i.e. of indigenous and Spanish descent). None the less, these two dominant figures shared important characteristics. They were both natives of the southern state of Oaxaca, who fought and resisted French occupation and Maximilian's empire, professed rhetorical support for liberal constitutionalism but exercised rule in a personalized, authoritarian fashion, and strongly resisted stepping down from the presidency. Gen. Díaz's reputation has been negative in official historiography, given his more than three decade dictatorial rule. Nevertheless, during his tenure annual economic growth rates averaged 7% (more than four times the annual average between 1821 and 1876); Mexico's population grew by 50% (from 10m. to 15m.); railways transformed economic and social life by integrating markets and allowing for faster, cheaper mobility of production factors; the country underwent industrialization (smelters, steel, textiles, paper, glass, shoes, beer, and food processing); concentration of land ownership created a capitalist agriculture that earned foreign currency for Mexico given growing exports; and Díaz diversified foreign investor sources to check overdependence on the USA.

However, fast-paced economic modernization also led to very significant dislocations that produced growing discontent, alienation, and conflict. Economic transformation depended heavily on foreign investors, who came to dominate opportunities for growth and prosperity. Not only the poor, but also the middle and upper classes, who were not part of the small, close-knit *porfirista* oligarchy, resented this exclusionary alliance. Inequality grew alarmingly and by 1911 around 90% of peasants were landless. Industrialization created a proletarian base who organized through middle-class intellectuals and activists. The regime responded to social demands time and again through armed repression. As the group in power aged, the perception of the need and possibility of ridding Mexico of what had become a gerontocracy was fed by Díaz himself, who declared to a US journalist in 1908 that he thought the country was ready for democracy given the approaching presidential elections in 1910.

To different degrees, the five fault lines discussed above operated during this period of nation state building and consolidation in Mexico. Of particular importance in precipitating conflicts that led to significant changes such as the rise and fall of governments, the authoritarian consolidation of power to impose stability, and the fast modernization that yielded sustained economic growth but at very high social costs, were: Mexico's dependence on foreign sources of capital and knowledge; high levels of socio-economic stratification based on race, ethnicity, and territorial location; the personalized exercise of power that trumped prescribed rules; the radicalization of ideological conflict as anarchist, socialist and communist ideas were added to the traditional liberal-conservative split; and the assertive role of the growing might of the USA, wary about potentially adverse changes to its interests south of its border.

THE MEXICAN REVOLUTION AND THE 1917 CONSTITUTION

Expectations and eventual frustration about a competitive election were not the only triggers of the revolution. The country's dependence on foreign capital and prices for its exports made Mexico's economy very liable to 'boom and bust' patterns of economic growth. The 1906–08 international financial crises and famines hit the country significantly. Repression of workers' strikes in mining and textiles became emblematic events that galvanized the opposition. In turn, the US Government reversed its support for Gen. Díaz given his diplomatic effort to help Nicaraguan President José Santos Zelaya, whom the USA wanted to depose, and also his preferential treatment of British petroleum investments.

Francisco I. Madero, the main opposition candidate in 1910, was arrested and imprisoned after questioning the legitimacy of Díaz's re-election. Madero fled to the USA and his summons were heard and acted upon by a surprisingly diverse number of groups who found a common objective in deposing Díaz, self-exiled in 1911. New elections resulted in Madero's triumph. The official pantheon of revolutionary heroes illustrates the multi-regional, multi-class force that dethroned Díaz. It includes Madero himself, a scion of one of the wealthiest families of the northern state of Coahuila, Emiliano Zapata, the poor community leader who fought for the restitution of peasant lands in the southern state of Morelos, and Doroteo Arango. Better known as Pancho Villa, Arango represented the poor and lower middle classes of the north, combining agricultural work with services associated with modernization and the links between cities and the countryside. The pantheon also includes Venustiano Carranza (President in 1917–20), Governor of the state of Coahuila who led the 'constitutionalist' resistance against the reactionary forces that deposed and assassinated Madero in 1913, and later convened the assembly that wrote the 1917 Constitution, as well as other northerners from the state of Sonora, such as Alvaro Obregón (President in 1920–24) and Plutarco Elías Calles (President in 1924–28). These last two fought for the centralization of power and creation of national institutions as a response to the proliferation of private armies and regional leaders unleashed by the revolution. Another revolutionary hero was Lázaro Cárdenas (President in 1934–40), the General from a modest background in the state of Michoacán who set in motion the progressive tenets of the revolution and nationalized the oil industry, creating Petróleos Mexicanos (PEMEX).

The Mexican Revolution morphed from a political movement against an aged, autocratic regime into a series of social movements that redefined citizen rights, property ownership, and the role of the state in the economy and society. The 1917 Constitution is considered a world pioneer in its wide provision of social rights and the power it gave to the state to alter the relationship between property and production. It created, at least on paper, strong checks and balances, and its golden rule, which is still in place, is the prohibition of presidential re-election. The diverse forces that participated in the conflict disagreed on many issues but they all shared basic tenets that tried to ameliorate the vulnerabilities Mexico had been repeatedly subjected to during its independent life, owing to the five fault lines discussed above. Thus, a more nationalist path in economic policy was decreed to try to reduce the country's dependence on foreign capital, and a point was made to at least rhetorically keep some distance from, but without antagonizing, the USA. The nationalist credo tried to disguise the deep racial, ethnic and socio-economic divisions by declaring Mexico's richly mixed population and culture to be a strength rather than a weakness. Of crucial importance were the institutionalization of political power (against the inheritance of *caudillismo*) and the development of a diffuse, pragmatic ideology which, under the banner of revolutionary nationalism forced political stability and social peace. Such innovations were imposed from the top and they were carried out under authoritarian rule.

RISE AND FALL OF POLITICAL HEGEMONY: MEXICO UNDER THE PRI, 1929–2000

The Partido Revolucionario Institucional (PRI) was born in 1929 under the name Partido Nacional Revolucionario (PNR). It was the child of outgoing President Calles, who confronted by the assassination of his elected successor, Obregón, brought together regional and state *caudillos* and *caciques* under the umbrella of a national party, whose mission would be to manage the distribution of power and, crucially, succession politics, under the peaceful rather than violent interaction of its leaders. Corporatism, the idea that society should be managed by political leaders through functional groups rather than the individualism expressed in the 'one person, one vote' principle of classical liberalism, was in vogue in Europe and other Latin American countries in the 1920s and 1930s. As a result, Calles and his allies were imbued with such ideas, and admired the way Mussolini had re-organized Italian politics. Calles remained the power behind the Mexican presidency until 1935.

Cárdenas destroyed Calles' power base, exiled him, and accelerated the corporatization of Mexican society. The PNR was renamed Partido de la Revolución Mexicana (PRM) and this was more than a change in label as the main sectors capable of wielding power in Mexican society—workers, peasants, and the military—were aggregated into organizations that became the main arms or sectors of the party. This type of linkage became very effective politically as the PRM leaders exercised mass control at the same time that organized social demands were channelled upward and, if not satisfied immediately, at least addressed gradually. Although Calles is considered a right-wing leader and Cárdenas a left-wing one, their politics were similarly authoritarian. A key distinction between the two is that the former, like the traditional *caudillos*, refused to relinquish power while once the latter stepped down in 1940 he played a less personal role in presidential politics.

After the end of the second world war, the PRM's leadership moved on to exclude the military as an official sector of the party although at the same time the top brass were given significant patronage and command of resources to retain their institutional loyalty. The party became the PRI in 1947, and civilians or at least officially retired military individuals came to dominate its positions. The end result of the transformation of the party between 1929 and 1947 was a self-reinforcing cycle between political control and the accommodation of mass demands.

This cycle gathered steam and led to a prolonged period of sustained high economic growth (6%–7% annually) under relatively low inflation (3%–4% annually) between the 1940s and the late 1960s. The period is known as the 'milagro mexicano' or Mexican miracle. The country experienced significant urbanization, industrialization and the spread of social services. A revolution of expectations took place as significant numbers of both men and women completed tertiary education. The economy was run under so-called import-substitution industrialization (ISI), an economic policy strategy that promoted domestic industrial activity to satisfy local needs through national production that could be either private or state-owned. The mixed economy produced not only material benefits to participants but also political ones, as a domestic entrepreneurial class, protected by the state, was able to incur losses without paying for them, inasmuch as the political regime considered that the maintenance of employment and capitalists' acquiescence was more important than productivity and profits. Moreover, the regime managed to portray itself as different from totalitarian communist regimes and military dictatorships because it held regular elections and allowed other parties to compete. Conservative forces coalesced around the Partido Acción Nacional (PAN) from its founding in 1939 and subsequently participated in local, state and federal elections. Likewise, the left also had important representatives, prominently the Partido Comunista Mexicano (PCM), founded in 1919, and the socialist Partido Popular (PP), later Partido Popular Socialista (PPS), founded in 1948. Under the guise of competitive elections, the PRI monopolized all key representative posts—President, all the Governors, all the Senate—and allowed some opposition representation in the lower chamber, some municipal governments and among city mayors.

The 'miracle' was not a stroll in the park for many Mexicans. Rural poverty and marginalization increased in relative terms, and organized labour, such as the railway workers or medical doctors in the public sector, who did not accept the PRI's carrots were given the stick. The regime preferred co-optation but selective repression was constantly present. The communist party was outlawed in 1946. The most infamous examples of regime repression were the student massacres of 2 October 1968 and 10 June 1971, by which time the rapid socio-economic modernization of the previous three decades had put growing pressures on the rigid, corporatist political system. Moreover, 1960s political activism went hand in hand with economic deceleration, which was a product of both the inherent contradictions of the low-productivity, *rentier*, protectionist economic model and the rise of international inflation, particularly in the early 1970s and as a consequence of the Arab oil-embargo of 1973–74.

Presidents Luis Echeverría (1970–76) and José López Portillo (1976–82) deepened the populist, public spending strategy to counteract the growth of political pluralism. Both governments ended up with problems because high spending depended on cheap foreign indebtedness, which was plentiful between 1974 and 1979–80, but then dried up in the wake of US Federal Reserve Chairman Paul Volcker's interest rate hikes aimed at taming inflation. Both Mexican governments ended up asking for help from the IMF, and the end result was austerity programmes which sapped energy and support for the PRI. López Portillo pursued the aggressive development of the petroleum industry, which turned PEMEX into a big oil exporter. Such large-scale transformation also created rampant corruption among the President and his close circle. In his last year in office and unable to meet debt obligations in the face of rising interest rates and growing shorter term loans, the López Portillo Government declared a moratorium in August 1982, which prompted a freeze in all lending, not only to Mexico but to all other highly indebted Latin American countries, and led to a great external debt crisis that sank the region into what came to be known as the 'lost decade' of growth and development.

The aftermath of the 1982 crisis, which included a presidential decree that nationalized the banking industry, broke the tacit understanding between the PRI regime and the Mexican capitalist class. As a consequence, business leaders started funding and joining the conservative PAN, elections were more fiercely contested, and PRI operators had to resort to blatant fraudulent methods to keep the party's hegemony. Likewise, confronted by an absence of growth, high inflation, and massive cuts to public services the middle classes and the poor turned against a closed political order whose legitimacy had rested on delivering gradual improvements in living conditions. An uncompromising debate broke out inside the PRI during the presidency of Miguel de la Madrid (1982–88). Aside from the externally imposed conditions of the IMF, which not only mandated austerity in public spending but also structural reforms to open up the Mexican economy, de la Madrid's Government contained both supporters of the continuation of the state-led, closed, nationalist economy and young, US-trained technocrats who supported dismantling protection and opening up to the international economy.

The two groups clashed in the run-up to the 1988 elections. The nationalist camp, led by Gen. Cárdenas' son, Cuauhtémoc, left the PRI after de la Madrid selected the young leader of the technocrats, Carlos Salinas, to succeed. The nationalists persuaded the many, small left-wing parties and movements to come together behind Cárdenas under a progressive front, which after the elections became the Partido de la Revolución Democrática (PRD). For the first time, the PRI faced both well-organized conservative, as well as left-wing, opposition in presidential elections. Facing potential defeat, the regime halted vote counting by alleging a computer system crash and declared Salinas the winner. Civil disobedience broke out and Salinas was only able to be confirmed thanks to an informal pact he struck with the PAN leaders, who were also in favour of embracing free market reforms and closer relations with the USA. Salinas was forced to declare the end of 'hegemony', and passed several electoral reforms. Political liberalization was selective as Salinas gave carrots to the PAN and the stick to the PRD. Carlos Salinas' Government (1988–94) carried out significant economic changes, including a large-scale privatization programme, liberalization of land ownership, and joining Mexico with the US and Canadian economies through NAFTA.

Mexico became a darling of foreign investors in the early 1990s, as Salinas and his supporters promised the country would join the 'first world' in a few years. However, the viability of the new, outward-oriented economic model rested on short-term financial flows and a combination of shocks derailed it. An indigenous revolt by the so-called Ejército Zapatista de Liberación Nacional (EZLN) broke out in January 1994. The PRI's presidential candidate for that year's elections, Luis Donaldo Colosio, was assassinated during a campaign rally in March. News about rampant corruption by Salinas and his close associates, given the privatization programmes and the liberalization of land ownership, plus a big credit binge incurred by the owners of newly privatized banks and their other industrial and service business interests, added to the climate of uncertainty. The Secretary-General of the PRI, José Francisco Ruiz Massieu, former brother-in-law of Salinas, was also murdered in October. Throughout the year, investors either fled Mexico or invested in bonds that were linked to the value of the dollar (so-called *Tesobonos*, which the Government issued to reassure

investors that Mexican taxpayers would cover their potential losses if the local currency, the peso, suffered a significant devaluation).

Salinas' successor, Ernesto Zedillo (1994–2000), tried to engineer a soft landing given the high financial stakes. The attempt failed as investors anticipated that a supposed modest broadening of the currency band that determined the relative value of Mexican pesos to US dollars would give way, given flailing Central Bank reserves, to a disorderly macro-devaluation. This became a self-fulfilling prophecy and Mexico plunged into another deep financial and economic crisis. The USA helped to put together a US $50,000m. bailout package in return for new austerity measures and a new round of privatizations. Zedillo was in a very weak position from the beginning of his term, and was forced to reach out to the opposition for support. Unlike Salinas, he offered a broad political opening by giving electoral authorities in the Instituto Federal Electoral (IFE), created by Salinas in 1990 but until 1996 under the control of the federal government, full autonomy. Thus, the 1996 political reforms, coupled with a new economic crisis and a dramatic fall in living conditions for a majority of Mexicans, dealt a mortal blow to the PRI's hegemony.

MEXICO SINCE ITS TRANSITION TO DEMOCRACY

It is hard to ascertain when a transition from authoritarian to democratic rule began in Mexico. Some authors identify the 1968 student bloodbath as the beginning of the end of PRI hegemony. Others mention the many electoral reforms that successive governments enacted between 1977 and 1996 to co-opt and negotiate with the opposition—more power and representation in exchange for support given during the recurrent financial crises (1976, 1982, 1987–88, and 1994–95)—as the catalyzers of change. Others highlight the rise of organized civil society during the 1980s to fight corruption in the face of growing inequality and poverty, demand free and fair elections, and denounce regime repression. Still others add international pressures, particularly coming from US governments and transnational non-governmental organizations (NGOs) after the end of the Cold War for Mexico to join the concert of democracies. All these factors made a contribution to the gradual erosion and final demise of PRI hegemony. The litmus test was the willingness of the PRI to accept defeat in a presidential election, which happened in 2000.

MEXICO UNDER THE PAN, 2000–12

The conservative PAN took over power and governed two consecutive terms under Presidents Vicente Fox (2000–06) and Felipe Calderón (2006–12). During their terms Mexico remained committed to conservative macroeconomic management, an open economy very close to the USA, and some social reforms to target poverty. The end of PRI hegemony did not mean its demise, however. It remained the dominant political force with the largest number of governorships, dominance in the Congreso (Congress—although it fell to third place in the lower chamber between 2006 and 2009), supporters in the judiciary, and many party stalwarts in the many public bureaucracies of local, state and federal governments. President Fox, while a very effective public communicator, showed poor political brinkmanship and was unable to negotiate with the PRI to push forward his government programme. Having promised high growth, law and order, an end to corruption and a closer partnership with the USA, he could not deliver on any of them. Major expectations of significant improvements once the PRI was kicked out of the presidency ended up in general frustration and cynicism.

Like the 1988 elections, the 2006 presidential contest was a very close race. Calderón officially beat the left-wing Andrés Manuel López Obrador (known popularly as AMLO) of the PRD by around half a percentage point. Civil disobedience broke out again and AMLO's supporters took over downtown Mexico City. Calderón assumed power on 1 December 2006 in the midst of general pushing and shoving in Congress and mass rallies against the supposed engineered electoral fraud. AMLO raised the stakes by carrying out his own inauguration and appointing a cabinet. During Calderón's early days in office, he was shadowed by hecklers questioning his legitimacy during public events. The new President decided to carry out a spectacular image coup to assert his power and bolster his authority, and less than two weeks after taking over he declared a 'war against drugs'.

Sure enough, the new strategy was very effective inasmuch as the controversies surrounding the elections and AMLO's actions disappeared from the headlines and military and police raids took over. The problem was that this became Calderón's signature policy, and he pursued it in an uncompromising fashion, in spite of the terrible human costs it entailed. Calderón reached out to his US counterpart, George W. Bush, who pledged support for the war. The US Congress appropriated around US $1,400m. to aid Calderón's Government under the Mérida Initiative. The bilateral relationship strengthened significantly in the areas of security and intelligence operations. However, the all-out assault on the drugs cartels did not stop narcotics trafficking. It did, however, spread corruption and impunity as more Mexican authorities came into contact with gang leaders. Violence spread and intensified as some cartels splintered into smaller, more ruthless outfits. Pressure exercised against their profits from the narcotics trade led to the diversification of activities by the organized criminal syndicates, and kidnappings, extortion, human- and weapons-trafficking, and mass robbery of oil and gasoline from PEMEX grew very significantly. When Calderón stepped down on 1 December 2012, estimates suggested that more than 70,000 individuals had been killed and thousands more 'disappeared'. Nothing approaching those numbers of deaths had occurred since the Mexican Revolution. The frustration and cynicism prompted by President Fox's inflated and unrealized promises were exacerbated by widespread fear and anger associated with Calderón's 'war on drugs'. A majority of Mexicans were disillusioned with the PAN and the PRI was returned to power in 2012.

RETURN OF THE PRI IN 2012

President Enrique Peña Nieto (2012–) represents a younger generation of PRI members. Their economic ideas follow the pro-foreign investment, open economy stance adopted during the de la Madrid, Salinas and Zedillo presidencies. While structural reforms to promote competition in areas such as labour, telecommunications, media, and energy remained stalled between 1997 and 2012, Peña Nieto forged an alliance with the PAN and PRD leaderships in the Congress, the so-called 'Pacto por México', which helped to break the deadlock. In only one year, his Government passed more structural reforms than any administration since that of Salinas. Such political brinkmanship was lauded by many analysts, including those who did not support the PRI. The informal congressional alliance proposed a total of 95 policies relating to the economy, to electoral changes, more government accountability and enhanced social welfare.

The PRI has been in an advantageous position to negotiate, because despite not having supermajorities in the Congress, it is the largest party in both federal chambers and controls more than one-half of the country's governorships and state legislatures. In addition, the PRI occupies the centre of the politico-ideological spectrum, which means that it can reach out either to the left-wing PRD, as it did to pass tax reforms, or to the right-wing PAN, as it did to pass energy reforms opening up the state monopoly on hydrocarbon exploration and production. Moreover, Peña Nieto's advisers were keen to create a sense of goodwill early on and therefore counselled the President to appoint a cabinet which included prominent PAN and PRD members. Thus, senior PRD leader, Rosario Robles Berlanga, was appointed Minister of Social Policy, while José Antonio Meade Kuribreña, a former finance minister in the PAN administration, assumed the role of foreign minister.

There has been a lively debate about the extent to which the younger *'priistas'* in government represent a 'new PRI,' meaning one whose modus operandi is not primarily based on graft, corruption, intimidation and outright violence against opponents. Early signs suggest that the PRI remains largely unchanged. If the public management style of Peña Nieto and his close associates can be gauged from their governing of México state (2005–11), then plenty of evidence has been

unearthed by journalists, civil society groups and political opponents about the preponderance of 'old PRI' practices. Critics highlight the fact that the huge infrastructure projects undertaken during Peña Nieto's governorship years translated into a 'graft-and-corruption' feast. Supporters retort that such projects created public benefits that will foster future growth in México state.

There has also been a paradoxical disconnect between Peña Nieto's popularity abroad and his growing unpopularity at home. Abroad, international financial institutions, banks, the US Government and pro-globalization groups such as the World Economic Forum at Davos, Switzerland, have hailed the Mexican President's ambitious economic reform agenda whose direction is pro-markets and pro-foreign investment. Among other things, he was featured on the cover of *Time* magazine as 'Man of the Year' in 2013. In contrast, having started with a domestic popularity rating of more than 50%, by mid-2014 this figure had fallen by around 20%. Such decline need not be permanent and might be reversed. However, the average Mexican believes that the Peña Nieto Government, aided by the giant media conglomerate Televisa, has been very good at presenting news and events in a positive light, which does not reflect the experience of many Mexicans. Of paramount importance are the continuation of violence and drugs-related killings in many states, despite the Government's claims about its new approach to the problem. A close second place in the public's priorities is the sluggish economic growth and the low rate of job creation since Peña Nieto assumed the presidency. Seasoned analysts highlight the importance of a 'political-business cycle,' according to which the Government raised taxes and balanced the books early on, in order that it can spend freely in the run-up to the 2015 mid-term elections, when the PRI will have to defend its current dominant position in the Congress.

A component of the 'Pacto por México' that is likely to remain salient for future politico-historical accounts is the electoral reform passed by the Congress in 2014. Both the PAN and the PRD lent their support for some of the economic structural reforms, on condition that the PRI agree to modify the current system of political competition. Given the framework of federalism, there is significant variation in terms of the freedom and fairness of elections in the 31 states plus the Federal District, because state authorities are in charge of their electoral processes. The opposition demanded that the electoral institution, the IFE, extend its jurisdiction to homogenize electoral competition standards throughout the country. The new institution, the Instituto Nacional Electoral (INE) will have more authority to regulate campaign financing and electoral propaganda, and to identify electoral crimes. The new law also allows independent candidacies (not allowed hitherto); mandates gender parity in political representation; elevates the threshold for parties to keep their charter to operate from 2%–3% of all votes (in an attempt to discourage small parties that frequently exist to sell their votes in exchange for a variety of benefits to their leaders); grants citizens the authority to participate in the law-making process through 'public consultation' and 'referendum'; and provides for a shorter period between a presidential election (early July) and the takeover by the newly elected Government from 1 December to 1 October.

Beyond any doubt the most important aspect of the politico-electoral reform is the change that will allow the re-election of federal and state legislators as well as mayors, although this will not apply to presidents or governors. This change is unprecedented since legislative re-election was banned in the early 1930s, while executive re-election was banned after the introduction of the 1917 Constitution. The creators of the Constitution were probably right in creating a single term for the executive branch, given the country's history of strongmen that tried, and in several cases were able, to stay in power for many years, creating personalized tyrannies. The re-election of legislators and mayors has been proposed as a way to build expertise and more representative-citizen accountability regarding the former as well as public management experience and capacity for the latter. These changes will not come into effect until 2018, but they will have the greatest impact on the behaviour of the Mexican political class, as well as the country's population and its relationship with politics. Mexico remains a young democracy. Wide-reaching constitutional reform, such as the changes that have been implemented during the early tenure of Peña Nieto, might end up contributing to the creation of a civic-minded political culture that holds power accountable at the same time as rewarding good administrations and punishing deficient, bad or corrupt ones. However, there is no guarantee that the original intentions written in the Constitution will translate into desired outcomes because human interaction is very complex and prone to react against attempts to control it through algorithmic rules and procedures.

CONCLUSION

Several of the deep-seated fault lines identified at the beginning of this essay will continue to make it difficult, though not impossible, for Mexico to grow at sustained, high rates and distribute the fruits of such growth less unequally at the same time that social peace and political stability are restored. The country's dependence on foreign investment is the Achilles heel of medium- to long-term growth. Mexico remains deeply divided along regional, ethnic, socio-economic, and in some localities even religious (Catholics against evangelical Christians) lines. Individuals and groups close to municipal, state and federal power enjoy impunity and are able to preserve and grow their power, influence and resources to the detriment of the rule of law and a fair allocation of justice. Levels of socioeconomic inequality put Mexico among the most unequal countries in the world, in spite of the growth of more middle class households in the 2000s. The temptation to resort to authoritarian rule is high given the climate of insecurity and violence that prevails in many parts of the country. Personalized styles of leadership can be fostered and rewarded in the context of a population living in fear and willing to give up degrees of freedom in return for more security. The demise of PRI hegemony brought governors to the forefront and standardization of governance will remain an uphill struggle with many jurisdictions ruled in autocratic, corrupt fashion. Lastly, Mexico's relationship with the USA will remain a factor of great significance in shaping future political and economic conditions in the former country. Continued emphasis on confronting the narcotics trade through armed means will translate into more violence and bloodshed in Mexico. The promise of an immigration reform in the USA, however far into the future, if fulfilled, could transform for the better the life opportunities of the more than 6m. Mexicans without documents living in the USA, and their families left behind in Mexico. More ambitious integration that contemplated not only the free movement of capital, as NAFTA does, but also of labour would result in more opportunities and prosperity in the medium to long term for both countries' populations. In spite of Mexico's autonomy given its status as a nation state, it is not possible to understand the country's past, present and future without bringing the USA into the equation, because the two countries are joined at the hip and their fates will remain intimately linked. Mexico is very dependent on the USA. The latter, while much less so, is also dependent on its southern neighbour. It remains its soft underbelly: the source of good nutrients for future growth or of disruptive pathogens that could slow it down and cause it serious discomfort.

Economy

Prof. FRANCISCO E. GONZÁLEZ*

INTRODUCTION

The relative size of Mexico's economy has fluctuated between the 11th and 14th largest in the world since the 1980s. In 2013, in purchasing-power parity (PPP) terms, gross domestic product (GDP) per head was around US $15,800, and the size of the economy around $1,700,000m. The World Bank classified Mexico as an upper-middle income country. In terms of the gross size of its economy, Mexico was one of only 15 countries with a GDP larger than $1,000,000m. With a population of around 115m., almost one-half of whom were under the age of 30, the country had significant potential to grow at high rates (5% or more per year) over the next two to three decades. Moreover, the country's geostrategic location in the middle of the Western hemisphere, with ports on both the Pacific and Atlantic Oceans and a 3,152-km border with the richest, most powerful country in the world, the USA, should also raise growth possibilities through trade. Mexico had the largest number of free trade agreements in the world, which included accords with 44 nations, and was the natural platform for goods that entered the US market free of charge owing to the North American Free Trade Agreement (NAFTA), which had been in operation since January 1994 and included Mexico, the USA and Canada. Furthermore, Mexico was a member of the most salient international groups that encompassed the largest (the Group of 20 leading industrialized nations—G20) and most advanced (the Organisation for Economic Co-operation and Development—OECD) economies.

Nevertheless, in spite of such a promising profile, Mexico's growth and development has disappointed economists, policy-makers and a majority of Mexicans themselves at least since the 1980s. Structural conditions that proved difficult to change, economic policy courses that led to inefficiency, high indebtedness, corruption, recurrent financial crises and an increasingly competitive international marketplace all contributed to keep Mexico on a low-growth trajectory during the last three decades. The political and economic consequences of long-term sluggish growth in the context of a fiscally weak state incapable of progressive redistribution included an intensified politicization of growing socioeconomic inequality (Mexico was ranked as one of the top 20 most unequal countries in the 2000s). Likewise, while successfully addressed by the country's world-renowned Oportunidades conditional cash transfer programme, poverty levels oscillated owing to the significant percentage of households that temporarily emerged above the poverty line only to fall back under it in the context of financial shocks, most recently demonstrated after the 2008–09 global financial crisis, which pushed some 50% of the population into poverty. The phenomenon of great inequality and poverty was historically rooted in race, ethnicity, region, urban–rural differences and, crucially, connections (or their absence) with politically and/or economically dominant individuals and groups. Mexico is an electoral democracy inasmuch as power has been contested more or less freely and fairly since the late 1990s (although this process remained inchoate). However, electoral competition on its own cannot create a fairly distributed, high-growth economic order.

In sum, the Mexican economy is characterized by deep contradictions: it is open to world competition, but its main domestic sectors remain heavily concentrated in monopolies or oligopolies; it is home to a sizeable number of highly educated, competent professionals, but its governments and businesses are run through cronyism rather than meritocracy; governments display the trappings of powerful, symbolically charged authority, but public finances are very weak and greatly dependent on oil export revenues; all of the institutions, rules and human resources are in place to enforce the rule of law, but justice is politicized, property rights are vulnerable and the criminal justice system is corrupt; and the formal economy includes global leaders in their fields, such as Petróleos Mexicanos—PEMEX (oil), América Móvil (telecommunications), Cemex (cement), Fomento Económico Mexicano (bev-

*The author acknowledges the superb research assistance of Daniel Rico Prieto.

erages), Grupo Bimbo (baking), Gruma (cornflour) and Tele-visa (multimedia), but an estimated 30%–50% of total economic activity takes place in the informal sector (including the highly profitable illegal narcotics trade).

HISTORICAL OVERVIEW

Mexico, alongside Peru, was the richest colony of the Spanish Empire. The vast majority of the silver and gold exported to Europe in the 16th and 17th centuries came from these two locations. Colonial society was highly stratified, and, while Spaniards born in Spain (*peninsulares*) occupied the main official positions in the state, Church and armed forces, and monopolized trade between the colonies and the metropolis, their children born in the Americas (*criollos*) became the owners and operators of the main economic activities, such as mining, agriculture and construction. A majority of the country's population was and remains the product of Amerindian and European mixing (*mestizos*), while a sizeable minority is Amerindian (15%–20% in the early 2010s).

Owing to its exports, vast territory and central geographical position, many Europeans imagined that Mexico was a cornucopia. The German polymath Alexander von Humboldt visited Mexico in 1803, and his lush and enthusiastic description contributed to this myth of natural abundance. In fact, unlike countries such as the USA, Canada and Argentina, arable land was relatively scarce in Mexico. The country did not possess large, navigable rivers, and more than one-half of its territory was comprised of desert-like landscape. No Great Plains, Prairies or Pampas for extensive cultivation and livestock-rearing existed. Instead, the country was traversed by three extensive mountain ranges, which made the integration of markets for the production and exchange of goods and services costly and time-consuming. Moreover, Mexico's war of independence against Spain (1810–21) resulted in the indiscriminate destruction of economic infrastructure and the incurrence of foreign debt. Independence did not precipitate an economic recovery because Mexico experienced half a century of political instability, civil and foreign wars, and occupation. As economic historians like John Coatsworth have shown, total and per caput income declined continuously until the late 1860s. National per caput income in Mexico was closer to that of the USA (almost one-half) and the United Kingdom (around one-third) in 1800 than any time afterward.

By the time political instability and economic stagnation had come to an end at the beginning of the long dictatorship of José de la Cruz Porfirio Díaz (1876–1911), Mexico's per caput income had declined to one-tenth of the advanced capitalist countries. Still, the Porfiriato oversaw fast, sustained growth. The gap between Mexico and the USA stopped growing, and the former embarked on industrialization. A key enabler of growth was the creation of a significant railway network, which joined regional markets and helped to create for the first time a proper national economy. Peace and growth under Díaz attracted large amounts of foreign investment, and the President made sure that Mexico's client portfolio remained diversified to impede the dominance of US businesses. There were significant British, French and German banking, mining, industrial and trading interests in Mexico during the so-called Belle Époque (1870s–1910). Alongside Brazil and Argentina, Mexico became an early industrializer in Latin America, with the development of smelters, steel, textiles and manufacturing.

The Porfiriato's economic success was very unevenly distributed, and growing industrial production and capitalist agriculture came at the price of very significant income and wealth concentration. Political activism, official repression, and financial and food shocks in 1906–08 led to a closely contested presidential election in 1910, which Díaz won through fraud, prompting a rebellion organized by a variety of worker, peasant, middle class and even élite forces. The end result was a revolution (1910–20) that severely disrupted population and economic growth. In 1917 a new Constitution, which espoused the principles of state intervention for the promotion of social justice via public education, communal landowning and robust labour rights, created the legal framework that still operates in Mexico today. After a turn towards capitalist accumulation in the 1920s under Presidents Álvaro Obregón and Plutarco Elías Calles, the country experienced a tilt towards socialism under President Lázaro Cárdenas (1934–40), who engaged in large-scale land redistribution via communally held *ejidos*, and nationalized the oil industry, creating PEMEX.

Mexico's political economy remained nominally under a political regime—based on the hegemonic Partido Revolucionario Institucional (PRI), founded as the Partido Nacional Revolucionario in 1929—that supported popular, progressive causes, was nationalistic, and relied on the state as the main propelling and steering force of the country's destiny. However, the economy relied primarily on domestic and international private investors. The PRI controlled organized workers, peasants, and the middle classes connected with the public sector. It crafted and retained an informal agreement with domestic and foreign investors to promote capital accumulation and growth, and to contain popular demands and dissidence by intellectuals and radical political activists, in exchange for the gradual satisfaction of social demands. The years 1940–70 came to be known as the 'Mexican miracle', given average annual growth rates of 6%–7% and inflation levels below 5%. The results were significant modernization (i.e., urbanization, industrialization, higher literacy rates and lower mortality rates) under an import substitution industrialization (ISI) framework, which had been adopted vigorously since the Second World War. However, this model of economic growth and development contained irreparable internal contradictions given that it was based on state protection, subsidies and central planning, which fostered favouritism, rent-seeking, corruption and low-productivity growth. The contemporary Mexican economy emerged in the early 1970s as the ISI model was foundering and the international economy was suffering from its most virulent shocks since the Second World War.

BIRTH AND GROWING PAINS OF MEXICO'S CONTEMPORARY ECONOMY, LATE 1960s TO EARLY 1980s

Economic and social modernization produced a revolution in expectations among urban dwellers, who demanded pluralism and placed increased pressure on the authoritarian, vertical command-and-control PRI administration. The regime suffered an existential crisis following the student massacres that it carried out in 1968 and 1971. It tried to regain the initiative by engaging in economic populism. The image of an overbearing, disorderly state that crowded out private initiative through nationalization (rising from 84 firms in 1970 to 1,155 in 1982), overspending and unsustainably expansive economic policies mostly applied to the 12 years that included the presidencies of Luis Echeverría (1970–76) and José López Portillo (1976–82). During this period economic policy became a tool to achieve political aims. The means to foster higher growth were foreign indebtedness (US $3,200m. in 1970 to $16,000m. in 1976), fiscal deficits (2.5% of GDP in 1971 to 9.3% in 1975) and higher inflation (5% in 1970 to 17% in 1976). These trends culminated in 1976, Echeverría's last year in office, with a balance of payments crisis, the first disorderly macro-devaluation of the Mexican peso since 1954 and an official request for a credit line from the IMF in exchange for austerity policies.

Despite this constraining inheritance, in 1978 López Portillo abandoned the internationally mandated austerity plan in the wake of seemingly favourable prospects. The large-scale development of Mexico's oil infrastructure and the availability of cheap international credit (resulting from the recycling of so-called 'petro-dollars' in the wake of the 1973–74 and 1979–81 global oil shocks) gave López Portillo a temporary window of opportunity to re-enact the personalized, state-led, expansionary economic policymaking style of his predecessor. Mexico became a major world oil producer, but the experiment ended in failure during the President's last year in office, 1982. The acceleration of foreign indebtedness (US $20,000m. in 1972 to $80,000m. in 1982), growing fiscal deficits (11% of GDP in 1975 to 18% in 1982), increasing inflation (17% in 1976 to 57% in 1982), and a twin process of rising international interest rates and declining oil prices created a crisis, in large part manufactured by López Portillo's imprudent, hubristic and one-sided policies. Relations between the Government and the private business class declined dramatically, as the President nationalized the banking industry in response to the massive capital flight that growing macroeconomic imbalances had precipitated, and which the regime considered unpatriotic. The magnitude of the crisis was such that it led to the so-called 'lost decade' of growth and development not only in Mexico but throughout Latin America.

ADOPTION OF NEO-LIBERALISM AND THE CONTINUATION OF ECONOMIC BUSTS, 1980s AND 1990s

Echoing the IMF's stance, the World Bank and the Inter-American Development Bank also made short-term financial help conditional on strict orthodox management (austerity-induced policies and the regular payment of interest and principal on foreign debts). The new Mexican administration led by President Miguel de la Madrid Hurtado (1982–88) had a cohesive core of young US-trained technocrats who embraced such orthodox external debt management. They precipitated the return to orthodox macroeconomic policies, which have dominated ever since. This group of young economists and public policy experts established a credible and robust presence both at home and abroad. Of particular relevance was their trusted operators' presence in the main multilateral economic agencies, as well as in the capitals of private financial markets (New York, USA, and London, United Kingdom).

In 1984–85 negotiations among the largest external debtors in Latin America, i.e. Brazil, Mexico and Argentina, might have led to the formation of a debtors' club to co-ordinate their actions and force the softening of creditors' conditions. Some members of de la Madrid's Cabinet supported this strategy, but the technocrats, led by future President Carlos Salinas de Gortari (1988–94), convinced the President to continue to pay the country's debt obligations, and to seek a unilateral rapprochement with the USA in an attempt to garner better paying conditions and fresh credit lines. Among other things, Mexico abandoned its long-term opposition to free trade by joining the 1986 round of negotiations under the General Agreement on Tariffs and Trade.

The triumph of this approach did not translate automatically into a return to growth and less stringent living conditions for the majority of Mexicans. Between the end of 1982 and the end of 1988, when de la Madrid stepped down, total GDP growth was 0.2%, average annual inflation was 87% and real wages contracted by 40%. Like his two predecessors, de la Madrid's last year in office also ended with a crisis of confidence, related in part to the global stock market collapse of October 1987, and uncertainty about future economic management. However, the commitment to maintain the neo-liberal approach (i.e., stabilize and adjust via stringent fiscal and monetary policies, and implement structural reforms to reorientate the economy in a free market direction) and the objective to forge a closer economic relationship with the USA meant that Salinas' presidency was welcomed and supported by the conservative Partido Acción Nacional (PAN), the US Government, US banks and other businesses, and the multilateral lending community. Conversely, there was significant opposition to the new administration from the left-wing Partido de la Revolución Democrática (PRD), which had been formed after the disputed 1988 presidential election.

The overall dynamic of financial flows changed for the first time as Mexico, having been a net capital exporter since the early 1980s, became a major recipient of fresh foreign capital (US $3,500m. in 1989 to $33,000m. in 1993) from investors searching for high yields. In the early 1990s Mexico's share of capital inflows into Latin America was around 40%. The confidence that Salinas' economic team inspired helped Mexico to become the first nation to undergo successful sovereign debt restructuring via the Brady bond scheme, whereby high-interest debt was sold at discounted prices and indebted countries were able to draw fresh resources from their creditors under advantageous conditions. Domestic and international élites also praised Salinas' policies of wholesale privatization, particularly returning banks to private owner-

ship; deregulation, capital account liberalization and pursuing trade liberalization by joining NAFTA; granting autonomy to the central bank (although the President still interfered in the bank's decision-making); and reuniting the public revenue-raising and spending functions, which López Portillo had separated, into a single ministry. A key short-term goal of the Salinas presidency was to combat inflation to restore confidence in the economy, and more specifically to force price change convergence between Mexico and the USA. He enacted an incomes policy and pegged the Mexican peso to the US dollar; both anchors were quite successful, although the latter, combined with the effects of trade liberalization since the mid-1980s and the enactment of free capital movements in 1989, led to currency appreciation, growing current account deficits, and eventually, as in the case of his three predecessors, a disorderly macro-devaluation and a financial crisis. (In Salinas' case, the devaluation occurred after he had left office, owing to his refusal to authorize this action.)

Salinas' successor, Ernesto Zedillo Ponce de León (1994–2000), also a US-trained technocrat who had been at the forefront of Mexico's external debt management, did not possess the political networks and support inside the PRI that his predecessor had exploited successfully to promote economic reforms. Moreover, having promised 'well-being for your family' during the election campaign, once in office he was challenged by a dramatic collapse in growth and a spike in inflation as a consequence of an ensuing sovereign and private debt crisis that came to be known as the 'tequila effect'. Large US banks, pension funds and hedge funds were perilously exposed to Mexico's so-called *Tesobonos* (US dollar-indexed bonds), and, having been refused help by the US Congress, US President Bill Clinton and his Secretary of the Treasury, Robert Rubin, engineered a Mexican bailout. Using US $20,000m. from the Economic Stabilization Fund, they persuaded the international financial institutions to contribute an additional $30,000m. The $50,000m. bailout helped to prevent further speculation and economic decline in Mexico.

Like the previous decade, living standards and levels of wellbeing declined for a majority of Mexicans during the 1990s. Per caput income in real terms continued to decrease as inflation outpaced growth throughout the decade. For a party whose main source of legitimacy had been gradual economic improvement, relative social peace and political stability, the four successive end-of-presidency crises (in 1976, 1982, 1987–88 and 1994–95) resulted in the long period of strong, centralized authority and vertical command-and-control exercise of power coming to an end. In order to garner broad support for renewed austerity policies imposed by the international financial institutions, in 1996 Zedillo ended the control of elections by the Secretary of the Interior, traditionally a sturdy PRI apparatchik. The effects of electoral autonomy were soon demonstrated, as voters punished the PRI in the mid-term elections of 1997 (the party lost its simple majority in the lower chamber) and later voted against the 71-year continuation of its rule by giving the presidential electoral victory to Vicente Fox Quesada (2000–06) of the PAN.

THE PAN IN POWER: ECONOMIC ORTHODOXY AND UNDERPERFORMANCE, 2000–12

The PAN inherited monetary and fiscal policies with a strong non-expansionary bias. On the monetary side, during the Zedillo presidency the Banco de México (the central bank) had adopted a policy of inflation-targeting (3% plus or minus 0.5% annual price change), which had helped to bring down the price increase spiral created by the 1994–95 macro-devaluation but at the cost of keeping credit scarce and expensive. On the fiscal side, the IMF-mandated austerity measures after that crisis resulted in reduced spending. In addition, the Fox Government pushed for the adoption of a fiscal rule in 2006 that established a zero target for the public sector balance given five-year projections that, among other factors, took into account fluctuations in the international price for oil, a key contributor (between 33% and 45%) to the annual federal budget.

Mexico's macroeconomic performance in the 2000s was mixed but on the whole was perceived by international and domestic observers as mediocre. The average annual growth rate was 2.2%, which was significantly lower than other large emerging markets, such as the BRIC countries (Brazil, Russia, India and the People's Republic of China), and, crucially, very sluggish regarding the creation of formal employment. More positively, inflation was under 7% year on year. Although the end results were disappointing, this was the first decade in which growth rates had outpaced inflation rates for several years; macroeconomic fundamentals remained solid; and the country's production structure and links, particularly with the USA, started to flourish, with strong, sustained growth of manufacturing exports, which were not limited to cheap, low value-added goods (as between the 1960s and 1990s), but included growing proportions of sophisticated high value-added goods owing to increased local sourcing in the vehicle and vehicle parts, electronics and microprocessors, and aeronautics industries. Aside from the orthodox macroeconomic management inheritance, the PAN Governments also inherited a targeted social policy inaugurated under Zedillo, known originally as *Progresa* and subsequently renamed *Oportunidades*. This so-called conditional cash transfer programme became a model for similar programmes around the world, as multilateral financial institutions identified such social policy as a new paradigm to further poverty reduction and development. While successful at helping to reduce the percentage of the population living below the national poverty line from around 69% in 1996 to 43% in 2006, this rate had increased to over 50% by 2010 owing to the impact of the 2008–09 global financial crisis.

Central political authority and the exercise of power by the executive continued to weaken during the PAN administrations despite an attempt by President Felipe Calderón (2006–12) to reverse this decline. Economically, his Government continued with the inherited orthodoxy but suffered several adverse shocks, some exogenous and others self-inflicted. The Calderón administration had to manage the effects of the 2008–09 global financial crisis, which—given that its epicentre was in the USA and given Mexico's deep economic integration with, and dependence on, that country—resulted in a very significant economic decline. The recession in 2009 was even deeper than that of 1994–95 following Mexico's own currency and banking crisis. The 2009 decline was compounded by the outbreak of the H1N1 flu pandemic, which devastated the country's tourism industry, a significant contributor to GDP (8%–10%). Moreover, Calderón launched a controversial 'war on drugs' shortly after coming into office in December 2006. The large-scale operations that ensued (involving the deployment of more than 50,000 military and police personnel), intended to combat drugs cartel violence, which had increased significantly since 2003–04, produced the opposite effect as leadership decapitation of some organized criminal groups led to splintering, fragmentation and the proliferation of indiscriminate violence in many cities and significant swathes of the country's territory. By the time Calderón had stepped down in late 2012, more than 70,000 individuals had been killed and thousands had disappeared as a consequence of the 'war'. Although the economic costs of insecurity and violence were impossible to quantify, Mexico's international image had suffered significant damage.

THE RETURN OF THE PRI IN 2012: CHALLENGES AND OPPORTUNITIES

After two successive PAN Governments, and with a generalized sense of fear and concern around the country, the Mexican electorate returned the PRI to power in the 2012 elections. Enrique Peña Nieto (2012–18), a representative of a younger generation of PRI members, took control of a US $2,100,000m. economy, with 115m. inhabitants, low growth, low inflation, the continuation of widespread organized criminal violence, and a wave of intense citizen expectations about the need for change. From the perspective of the international financial and economic analysis community, Mexico's economy was recovering and its prospects were favourable. During late 2010 and early 2011 the IMF, the World Bank, OECD, and commentary in *The Economist* and the *Financial Times* had noted the strong recuperation that Mexico's economy had experienced

after the 2008–09 global financial crisis, the dynamism of manufacturing exports, the decline in Mexicans seeking work in the USA, and the continued inflow of foreign investment into the country in spite of the unstable security situation. The financial media began to describe Mexico as a potential 'Aztec tiger'.

Mexico started to be compared favourably with Brazil; the loss of Mexico's market share, given the rapid growth in Chinese exports to the USA since the former had joined the World Trade Organization in 2001, began to reverse, particularly in sophisticated, bulkier, high value-added goods; a 20-year opportunity to raise growth rates—the so-called 'demographic bonus', whereby the country's dependency ratio would be lower until the 2030s—was identified; Mexico continued to be praised by the international financial institutions and the USA for its solid fundamentals, as more than a decade of orthodox macroeconomic policy had allowed the country to gain credibility and stature in the highly competitive world of foreign investment; and social policy, spearheaded by *Oportunidades*, was extolled as a model to combat poverty and create lower levels of socioeconomic exclusion.

There is a consensus that the Peña Nieto Government has been the boldest since Salinas' administration in enacting structural reforms owing to the establishment of the so-called 'Pacto por México', under which the PRI, the PRD and the PAN agreed to co-operate in the Congreso (Congress) in pursuit of such reforms. The principal changes have been in relation to the labour, education, telecommunications, fiscal, energy and financial sectors.

Labour reforms were adopted towards the end of President Calderón's presidency due to support pledged by President-elect Peña Nieto. Many articles of the Ley Federal de Trabajo (Federal Labour Law), which had traditionally established robust labour rights for workers, were amended. As with many other countries that had liberalized their economies since the 1980s, such strong worker protection laws had acted as a deterrent to investment because capital was allocated around the globe according to labour cost considerations. Consequently, countries with robust labour rights found it hard to generate formal employment, with young people forced to accept precarious, short-term positions with no benefits, or menial work in the informal sector. This phenomenon was recorded in both developed and developing countries. The labour reforms in Mexico were intended to increase the flexibility of Mexico's labour market by: validating and regulating outsourcing by companies; establishing training, and probationary, seasonal and part-time employment; instituting hourly wages; and limiting unpaid wages to 12 months in cases of unlawful dismissal. It was envisaged that this flexibility would encourage firms to hire individuals in formal employment, even though the latter would have fewer prerogatives than their predecessors. However, the reform has thus far not produced a turnaround in labour market conditions. In fact, a consensus is developing about why Mexico's economy has grown at such mediocre rates, and the labour market is at the centre of this interpretation. This view holds that there are 'two Mexicos'. One is made up of a modern, well-funded growth economy encompassing large corporations that are globally integrated. The other is a traditional, credit-starved, low productivity growth economy encompassing small and medium-sized firms and, crucially, the huge informal sector, which some economists estimate to include more than one-half of the economically active population. Shifting workers from the low to the high growth productivity sector, which was the aim of the reform, has not taken place, although it might take five to seven years after implementation to make a sound assessment of this reform.

The education reform was the first one passed after Peña Nieto assumed the presidency in December 2012. Primary and some secondary education were traditionally under the control of a powerful trade union, the Sindicato Nacional de Trabajadores de la Educación (SNTE), the largest union in Latin America. The SNTE used the education system as a machine for patronage and clientelistic practices to benefit the PRI until the early 2000s, when its leader, Elba Esther Gordillo, left the party to form her own political grouping to pledge her support in a strategic manner. The union's control was such that the

Government was unaware of how many teachers were employed in Mexico. Teaching posts were held as sinecures that could be bequeathed to family members, and there were thousands of teachers who had not taught for years, but were paid for conducting political work for the union. President Peña Nieto arrested Gordillo because of her resistance to sectoral reform. The changes intended to be effected by the new administration would transfer many of the prerogatives exercised by the union to the Government. The Professional Teaching Service was established to promote a meritocratic system. The main economic aim was to raise the level of human capital since more than 40% of the population were under the age of 30, and Mexico traditionally performed poorly in the standardized tests for literacy and maths carried out annually under the auspices of the OECD. The levels of primary and secondary school graduation in Mexico are high compared with other developing countries, but the quality of education, as these examinations show, is low. To move up the value-added chain, Mexico requires technicians and professionals, who remain in relatively short supply, although tertiary education (not a target of this reform) has grown considerably both in the public and private sectors, and the rate of growth of graduates in areas such as engineering, information technology and science accelerated in the 2000s.

Telecommunication and media reforms were approved in June 2013, modifying several articles of the Constitution. The conceptualization of freedom of expression and the right to information was updated and upgraded to include information and communication technologies as well as the state's responsibility to ensure that these services were provided to the public. A major, publicly funded infrastructure project to create a nationally integrated fibre optic network, which should be in operation by 2018, opened up the possibility for the growth of a telecommunications and internet services sector. In theory, the regulatory bodies were strengthened with the creation of IFETEL (Instituto Federal de Telecomunicaciones) and the state was granted the faculty to dismantle monopolies. Critics have pointed out that the process of appointment of the seven commissioners of IFETEL (proposed by the President and ratified by the Senate) will allow the executive branch to remain in control of the main new regulatory body. They add that the law does not include mechanisms to hold IFETEL accountable. This combination of features is dangerous because the sector is heavily concentrated in the hands of a few: Carlos Slim has a monopoly in telecommunications through Telmex and América Móvil, while the visual media is largely a duopoly comprised of Emilio Azcárraga's Televisa and Ricardo Salinas Pliego's Televisión Azteca. The tycoons are very influential, and it is easy to envisage how they could, with acquiescence from the President, control the regulatory body. The law has also been criticized for its apparent political bias. While the reform allowed unrestricted foreign investment in telecommunications firms, it established an upper limit of 49% in foreign ownership of the media. Critics point to President Peña Nieto's close relationship with Televisa, as well as to the 'blackmail power' that the media have over politicians, given their dominant role in shaping public opinion, in contrast to Slim's telecommunications empire, which lacks this power. Moreover, having been touted by *Forbes* magazine as the richest man in the world, in a country where more than 50% of the population live in poverty, Slim became a relatively easy target for the Government in trying to show that the authorities are as opposed to inequality as the general public. To compensate and show a semblance of equal treatment the Government decided to launch bids for two new channels that Televisa and Azteca were barred from participating in. It also ordered Televisa and Azteca to offer free-to-air programming free of charge to cable operators. Although Carlos Slim was seen as the main loser of this reform, he can now try to get into broadcasting with the comparative advantage of offering so-called 'triple play' (i.e. the supply of broadband, telephone and television). Another controversial aspect of the reform, which is expected to be watered down once secondary legislation is agreed upon, is the role of the state in patrolling information. Such guiding legislation contains what many civil society groups that support civil liberties and freedom of information regard as draconian measures that would give the state powers to intervene in communications, shut down webpages, and declare certain content as illegal. The backlash against such measures has been very considerable and highly visible, which suggests that the Government will reverse some of these 'authoritarian' provisions in exchange for allowing the main spirit of the reform (i.e. the total opening of telecommunications, the partial opening of the media, and the building of a national fibre optic network through public-private partnerships that might allow politicians and technocrats to pocket significant amounts of money) to go ahead.

The Peña Nieto Government's most important structural reforms have been those concerning fiscal policy and the energy sector. These two are seen as inextricably linked, given the federal Government's chronic dependence on oil revenue to make up the annual federal budget. During the last three decades, PEMEX, the state-owned oil and gas monopoly, has contributed some 30%–40% annually to that effect. The end result has been a fiscally weak state and a giant hydrocarbon producer that cannot reinvest to update technology, prospect, find or extract more fossil fuels. In contrast to the average fiscal intake to GDP of OECD countries, which oscillates around 30%–33% annually, Mexico's is the lowest with between 13%–17%. As a result, Peña Nieto initiated an ambitious fiscal reform during the last quarter of 2013. Strong pressure from well-organized, middle class groups succeeded in weakening the reforms. However, a few important, apparently progressive changes were enacted: higher income taxes between 31%–35% for top earners; elimination of various tax deductions that used to favour the wealthy; an 8% tax on 'junk' food and sugary drinks; a 10% tax on capital gains; an 8% tax on mining operations; an increase in value-added tax (VAT) in the six states that share a border with the USA from 11% to 16%, in line with the rest of the country. On the spending side, Peña Nieto enacted some of his principal campaign promises: a minimum universal pension for individuals 65 years and older and unemployment insurance. Many analysts remain sceptical about the possibility of balancing the books because the new revenues are only expected to contribute an additional 1%–2% in fiscal intake to GDP, while the outlays, given a growing proportion of older individuals in the future plus the uncertainty of what bad economic times might mean for the size of unemployment benefits, could force governments to incur unsustainable fiscal deficits.

Without a doubt the most significant reforms have concerned energy. This is the case because hitherto Mexico was the only country in the world where private sector participation in the exploration and production of oil was not permitted. The industry was nationalized in 1938 and has been a touchstone of Mexican pride and nationalism against the perceived arrogance and rapacious behaviour of foreign oil barons, especially US, British and Dutch companies. Liberalizing the sector was a decision forced on the Mexican authorities, rather than one chosen freely. Having reached peak oil production of close to 3m. barrels per day (b/d) in 2004, production has suffered a dramatic collapse, declining by more than 20% since then with the exhaustion of the Cantarell mega-field, which provided up to two-thirds of daily production. With PEMEX revenue plugging federal budget holes the company underinvested in exploration and production. Pessimistic predictions by both domestic and foreign analysts forecast that without new finds Mexico, hitherto a top ten world oil exporter, could become a net crude oil importer by the 2020s. Such alarming news led to the Government of Felipe Calderón to propose and enact a moderate reform of PEMEX in 2008. That event helped make Mexicans aware of the possibility of oil production ceasing and the consequences of this for domestic bills. With the PRI back in government, Peña Nieto and his team of technocrats launched an ambitious reform which opened up the sector. The notoriously corrupt oil workers' trade union (Sindicato de Trabajadores Petroleros de le República Mexicana) was stripped of its seats on PEMEX's board. Likewise, the electricity state monopoly under the Comisión Federal de Electricidad (CFE) was opened up. Now PEMEX and CFE are considered profit-making state enterprises, which if not meeting specific criteria can be penalized by, for example, giving loss-making areas and activities to the private sector, both domestic and foreign. Of greatest controversy was the issue of oil ownership, with energy multinationals keen to use reserves as a mean of increasing their market capitalization, which in turn allows them to borrow money in capital markets at lower rates. Because this issue remains socially and politically sensitive, the reform states that hydrocarbons under the ground will remain the property of the Mexican nation. However, once such hydrocarbons have been extracted their ownership can be assigned according to a variety of options. In effect, the reform established a menu of contract options measured through risk, technological, human and capital needs. Easy projects that PEMEX can continue to operate will remain as they are. PEMEX can continue to use service contracts to pay fees to private companies that participate in such projects or new profit-sharing contracts. When more complex projects are considered, production-sharing contracts or licences will be the vehicles used to entice private sector participation. Large oil interests prefer licences or concessions, whereby, once they have secured the right to operate, all the oil they find is theirs. Of course, they still pay royalties on extraction and taxes on their profits but the natural resource can be transferred to their balance sheet. In production-sharing agreements, the state oil firm and its private partners engage in exploration and production, pay costs to cover all operations, and then share the ownership of the remaining production known as 'profit oil.' Most oil-producing countries use one or more of these basic contracts to engage in exploration and production. The Mexican case seems to have followed a flexible approach that assigns contracts according to complexity. Such an approach has received a positive reaction in the industry, although details remain to be decided. With a potential 60,000m. barrels of oil and significant quantities of shale gas, Mexico could remain a major actor in the international energy scene. Currently, PEMEX has less than 10,000m. barrels of proven reserves. Tapping the great potential off shore in the Gulf of Mexico, as well as onshore in the north-east of the country, should be possible given the new framework, but secondary legislation, the quality of implementation, and the main results of new governance in the sector will determine the appetite that big multinationals develop for operating in Mexico.

Lastly, Peña Nieto also proposed a financial reform in January 2014 to release credit for investment and consumption, as well as to strengthen state development banks to promote the provision of public goods. This is an area that many economists highlight as a very significant drag on growth. The financial sector imploded during the so-called 'tequila crisis' (1994–95), and most banks went bust. The Mexican Government, aided by a US-led bailout, saved the banks and after 1997 sold them. The main buyers were large multinational banks such as Citibank, HSBC, BBVA, Santander, and Scotia Bank. Today, almost 90% of banking assets are controlled by foreign banks. The system is characterized by an oligopoly where competition is low, credit provision is scarce and fees for basic services are high. Private sector credit at around 25% of GDP places Mexico among the lowest emerging economies. Countries such as Brazil register around 55%, Chile is close to 80% and South Korea at 100%. The banks in Mexico have colluded to engage in credit underprovision and expensive services. This is the typical behaviour observed in markets that are rigged, owing to few participants who can underproduce and overcharge. As a result, micro, small and medium enterprises, agriculture, innovation, infrastructure, and housing have not had access to credit, which has contributed to the image of the 'two Mexicos.' In order to encourage increased lending, the Government has made it easier for banks to identify, evaluate, and collect collateral if interest payments are not met. The competition regulator (Comisión Federal de Competencia) will assess and demand greater competition among banks, and borrowers will be able to switch banks to those that offer the best deals. The central bank (Banco de México) will regulate lending rates and the fees and commissions banks charge for their services. There will also be significant government support for the state development bank sector. The Government has an ambitious plan to spend significant amounts of resources on infrastructure, and these banks will be at the forefront of such efforts.

The Peña Nieto Government cannot be accused of shyness regarding constitutional changes. If anything, the fear is that these early successes for Peña Nieto could lead to hubris and complacency, as happened under Salinas. These triumphs could founder without proper regulation, implementation and evaluation of the social and economic impact of the reforms. The Peña Nieto Government also needs to focus on addressing insecurity and violence, reforming the criminal justice system, establishing professional, non-corrupt law enforcement services, and redistributing resources and opportunities to reduce the high levels of inequality and poverty. In addition, reconstructing the state's capacity to exercise its authority effectively across the country's territory is essential if the 'Aztec tiger' appellation is to be realized. These tasks, although daunting, assist Mexico's demographic profile, geostrategic and economic location, and macroeconomic trends in achieving high growth in the future. In contrast, poor governance, violence and insecurity, microeconomic environments that face high base costs, scarce and expensive credit, and insecure property rights constitute disadvantages in realizing this high growth. Enacting dramatic legislative changes is only the first act of a play, to be concluded once secondary legislation for all the reforms are passed by the Congress. The next acts remain uncertain and observers are unaware if they are watching an epic or a tragic production.

Statistical Survey

Sources (unless otherwise stated): Instituto Nacional de Estadística, Geografía e Informática (INEGI), Edif. Sede, Avda Patriotismo 711, Torre A, 10°, Col. San Juan Mixcoac, Del. Benito Juárez, 03730 México, DF; tel. (55) 5278-1000 (ext. 1282); fax (55) 5278-1000 (ext. 1523); e-mail comunicacionsocial@inegi.org.mx; internet www.inegi.org.mx; Banco de México, Avda 5 de Mayo 1, Col. Centro, Del. Cuauhtémoc, 06059 México, DF; tel. (55) 5237-2000; fax (55) 5237-2370; internet www.banxico.org.mx.

Area and Population

AREA, POPULATION AND DENSITY

Area (sq km)	
Continental	1,959,248
Islands	5,127
Total	1,964,375*
Population (census and by-census results)	
29 October 2005	103,263,388
12 June 2010	
Males	54,855,231
Females	57,481,307
Total	112,336,538
Population (official estimates at mid-year)†	
2012	117,053,750
2013	118,395,054
2014	119,713,203
Density (per sq km) at mid-2014	61.1

* 758,449 sq miles.
† Source: Consejo Nacional de Población (CONAPO), México, DF.

POPULATION BY AGE AND SEX
('000, official estimates at mid-2014)

	Males	Females	Total
0–14 years	17,129.2	16,395.4	33,524.6
15–64 years	37,643.8	40,552.4	78,196.2
65 years and over	3,662.9	4,329.5	7,992.4
Total	58,435.9	61,277.3	119,713.2

Note: Totals may not be equal to the sum of components, owing to rounding.

Source: Consejo Nacional de Población (CONAPO), México, DF.

ADMINISTRATIVE DIVISIONS
(official estimates at mid-2014)

States	Area (sq km)*	Population†	Density (per sq km)	Capital
Aguascalientes (Ags) . .	5,623	1,270,174	225.9	Aguascalientes
Baja California (BC) . .	71,540	3,432,944	48.0	Mexicali
Baja California Sur (BCS) .	73,937	741,037	10.0	La Paz
Campeche (Camp.) . .	57,718	894,136	15.5	Campeche
Chiapas (Chis) .	73,680	5,186,572	70.4	Tuxtla Gutiérrez
Chihuahua (Chih.) . .	247,490	3,673,342	14.8	Chihuahua
Coahuila (de Zaragoza) (Coah.) . .	151,447	2,925,594	19.3	Saltillo
Colima (Col.) .	5,629	710,982	126.3	Colima
Distrito Federal (DF) . .	1,485	8,874,724	5,976.2	Mexico City
Durango (Dgo) .	123,364	1,746,805	14.2	Victoria de Durango
Guanajuato (Gto).	30,617	5,769,524	188.4	Guanajuato
Guerrero (Gro) .	63,618	3,546,710	55.8	Chilpancingo de los Bravos
Hidalgo (Hgo) .	20,855	2,842,784	136.3	Pachuca de Soto
Jalisco (Jal.) .	78,624	7,838,010	99.7	Guadalajara
México (Méx.) .	22,332	16,618,929	744.2	Toluca de Lerdo
Michoacán (de Ocampo) (Mich.) . .	58,672	4,563,849	77.8	Morelia
Morelos (Mor.) .	4,894	1,897,393	387.7	Cuernavaca
Nayarit (Nay.) .	27,861	1,201,202	43.1	Tepic
Nuevo León (NL).	64,206	5,013,589	78.1	Monterrey
Oaxaca (Oax.) .	93,348	3,986,206	42.7	Oaxaca de Juárez

States—continued	Area (sq km)*	Population†	Density (per sq km)	Capital
Puebla (Pue.) .	34,246	6,131,498	179.0	Heroica Puebla de Zaragoza
Querétaro (de Arteaga) (Qro) .	11,659	1,974,436	169.3	Querétaro
Quintana Roo (Q.Roo) . .	42,544	1,529,877	36.0	Ciudad Chetumal
San Luis Potosí (SLP) . . .	61,165	2,728,208	44.6	San Luis Potosí
Sinaloa (Sin.) .	57,334	2,958,691	51.6	Culiacán Rosales
Sonora (Son.) .	179,527	2,892,464	16.1	Hermosillo
Tabasco (Tab.) .	24,747	2,359,444	95.3	Villahermosa
Tamaulipas (Tamps) . .	80,155	3,502,721	43.7	Ciudad Victoria
Tlaxcala (Tlax.) .	3,988	1,260,628	316.1	Tlaxcala de Xicohténcatl
Veracruz-Llave (Ver.) . .	71,856	7,985,893	111.1	Jalapa Enríquez
Yucatán (Yuc.) .	39,675	2,091,513	52.7	Mérida
Zacatecas (Zac.) .	75,412	1,563,324	20.7	Zacatecas
Total . . .	**1,959,248**	**119,713,203**	**61.1**	—

* Excluding islands.
† Source: Consejo Nacional de Población (CONAPO), México, DF.

PRINCIPAL TOWNS
(population at census of June 2010)

Ciudad de México (Mexico City, capital) . .	8,851,080	Tlalnepantla de Baz (Tlalnepantla) .	664,225
Ecatepec de Morelos (Ecatepec) . .	1,656,107	Benito Juárez (Cancún) . . .	661,176
Tijuana . . .	1,559,683	Torreón	639,629
Heroica Puebla de Zaragoza (Puebla)	1,539,819	Santa María Chimalhuacán (Chimalhuacán) .	614,453
Guadalajara . .	1,495,189	Reynosa . . .	608,891
León	1,436,480	Tlaquepaque . .	608,114
Ciudad Juárez . .	1,332,131	Victoria de Durango (Durango) . .	582,267
Zapopan . . .	1,243,756	Tuxtla Gutiérrez .	553,374
Monterrey . . .	1,135,550	Veracruz Llave (Veracruz) . .	552,156
Nezahualcóyotl . .	1,110,565	Irapuato . . .	529,440
Mexicali . .	936,826	Tultitlán . . .	524,074
Culiacán Rosales (Culiacán) . .	858,638	Cuautitlán Izcalli .	511,675
Naucalpan de Juárez (Naucalpan) . .	833,779	Atizapán de Zaragoza . . .	489,937
Mérida . . .	830,732	Matamoros . . .	489,193
Toluca de Lerdo (Toluca) . .	819,561	Tonalá . . .	478,689
Chihuahua . . .	819,543	Iztapaluca . . .	467,361
Querétaro . . .	801,940	Ensenada . . .	466,814
Aguascalientes . .	797,010	Jalapa Enríquez (Xalapa) . . .	457,928
Acapulco de Juárez (Acapulco) . .	789,971	San Nicolás de los Garzas . . .	443,273
Hermosillo . .	784,342	Mazatlán . . .	438,434
San Luis Potosí .	772,604	Nuevo Laredo . .	384,033
Morelia . . .	729,279	Cuernavaca . . .	365,168
Saltillo . . .	725,123	Valle de Chalco (Xico)	357,645
Guadalupe . . .	678,006		

Mid-2014 (incl. suburbs, UN estimate): Ciudad de México (Mexico City, capital) 20,843,500 (Source: UN, *World Urbanization Prospects: The 2014 Revision*).

BIRTHS, MARRIAGES AND DEATHS

	Registered live births		Registered marriages		Registered deaths	
	Number	Rate (per 1,000)	Number	Rate (per 1,000)	Number	Rate (per 1,000)
2005	2,567,906	19.3	595,713	5.7	495,240	4.8
2006	2,505,939	19.0	586,978	5.6	494,471	4.8
2007	2,655,083	18.6	595,209	5.6	514,420	4.9
2008	2,636,110	18.3	589,352	5.5	539,530	4.9
2009	2,577,214	18.0	558,913	5.2	564,673	4.9
2010	2,643,908	17.8	568,632	5.2	592,018	5.0
2011	2,586,287	n.a.	570,954	4.9	590,693	n.a.
2012	2,498,880	n.a.	585,434	5.0	602,354	n.a.

2013 (official projections): Crude birth rate 19.0 per 1,000; Crude death rate 5.7 per 1,000.

2014 (official projections): Crude birth rate 18.7 per 1,000; Crude death rate 5.7 per 1,000.

Life expectancy (years at birth): 77.1 (males 74.8; females 79.6) in 2012 (Source: World Bank, World Development Indicators database).

ECONOMICALLY ACTIVE POPULATION

(sample surveys, '000 persons aged 14 years and over, January–March)

	2012	2013	2014
Agriculture, hunting, forestry and fishing	6,386.7	6,485.4	6,660.6
Mining, quarrying and electricity	385.8	428.1	441.4
Manufacturing	7,378.4	7,525.2	7,895.0
Construction	3,617.9	3,581.5	3,621.4
Trade	9,440.3	9,522.4	9,605.6
Hotels and restaurants	3,308.1	3,390.2	3,511.9
Transport and communications	2,346.2	2,430.7	2,446.1
Finance and business services	3,191.6	3,291.6	3,410.5
Social services	3,961.4	4,041.4	3,981.4
Other services	5,203.8	5,238.8	5,135.1
Public sector	2,402.7	2,332.5	2,329.6
Sub-total	47,622.9	48,267.8	49,039.0
Activities not adequately defined	348.1	297.2	267.0
Total employed	47,970.9	48,565.0	49,305.8
Unemployed	2,474.8	2,496.9	2,484.8
Total labour force	50,445.7	51,061.9	51,790.6
Males	31,443.3	31,776.6	32,171.2
Females	19,002.4	19,285.3	19,619.5

Health and Welfare

KEY INDICATORS

Total fertility rate (children per woman, 2012)	2.2
Under-5 mortality rate (per 1,000 live births, 2012)	16
HIV/AIDS (% of persons aged 15–49, 2012)	0.2
Physicians (per 1,000 head, 2011)	2.1
Hospital beds (per 1,000 head, 2009)	1.6
Health expenditure (2011): US $ per head (PPP)	1,004
Health expenditure (2011): % of GDP	6.0
Health expenditure (2011): public (% of total)	50.3
Access to water (% of persons, 2012)	95
Access to sanitation (% of persons, 2012)	85
Total carbon dioxide emissions ('000 metric tons, 2010)	443,674.0
Carbon dioxide emissions per head (metric tons, 2010)	3.8
Human Development Index (2013): ranking	71
Human Development Index (2013): value	0.756

For sources and definitions, see explanatory note on p. vi.

Agriculture

PRINCIPAL CROPS

('000 metric tons)

	2010	2011	2012
Wheat	3,677	3,628	3,274
Rice, paddy	217	173	179
Barley	672	487	1,032
Maize	23,302	17,635	22,069
Oats	111	51	84
Sorghum	6,940	6,429	6,970
Potatoes	1,537	1,433	1,802
Sugar cane	50,422	49,735	50,946
Beans, dry	1,156	568	1,081
Chick peas	132	72	272
Soybeans (Soya beans)	168	205	248
Groundnuts, with shell	81	80	115
Coconuts*	1,157	1,139	1,050
Safflower seed	97	131	257
Cabbages	222	239	224
Lettuce and chicory	341	370	335
Tomatoes	2,998	2,436	3,434
Cauliflower and broccoli	386	428	397
Pumpkins, squash and gourds	522	525	565
Cucumbers and gherkins	540*	545*	641
Chillies and peppers, green	2,336	2,132	2,380
Onions, dry	1,266	1,399	1,239
Carrots and turnips	346	405	337
Bananas	2,103	2,139	2,204
Oranges	4,052	4,080	3,668
Tangerines, mandarins, clementines and satsumas	409	406	450
Lemons and limes	1,891	2,148	2,071
Grapefruit and pomelos	401	397	415
Apples	585	631	375
Peaches and nectarines	227	167	163
Strawberries	227	229	360
Grapes	307	281	375
Watermelons	1,037	1,002	1,034
Cantaloupes and other melons	562	564	575
Guavas, mangoes and mangosteens	1,633	1,827	1,761
Avocados	1,107	1,264	1,316
Pineapples	702	743	760
Papayas	616	634	713
Coffee, green	245	237	246
Cocoa beans*	61	83	83
Tobacco, unmanufactured	7	10	15

* FAO estimate(s).

Aggregate production ('000 metric tons, may include official, semi-official or estimated data): Total cereals 34,922.5 in 2010, 28,405.9 in 2011, 33,610.7 in 2012; Total fruits (excl. melons) 15,430.3 in 2010, 16,231.4 in 2011, 15,917.8 in 2012; Total vegetables (incl. melons) 12,601.7 in 2010, 12,160.8 in 2011, 13,599.5 in 2012.

Source: FAO.

LIVESTOCK

('000 head, year ending September)

	2010	2011	2012
Horses*	6,355	6,355	6,356
Asses*	3,260	3,260	3,280
Mules*	3,280	3,280	3,285
Cattle	32,642	32,936	31,925
Pigs	15,435	15,547	15,858
Sheep	8,106	8,219	8,406
Goats	8,993	9,004	8,743
Chickens	506,256	510,133	516,711
Ducks*	8,300	8,350	8,350
Turkeys	4,030	4,078	4,015

* FAO estimates.

Source: FAO.

LIVESTOCK PRODUCTS
('000 metric tons)

	2010	2011	2012
Cattle meat	1,745	1,804	1,821
Sheep meat	55	57	58
Goat meat	44	44	41
Pig meat	1,175	1,202	1,239
Horse meat*	83	83	83
Chicken meat	2,681	2,765	2,792
Cows' milk	10,677	10,724	10,881
Goats' milk	162	162	156
Hen eggs	2,381	2,459	2,318
Honey	56	58	59

* FAO estimates.

Source: FAO.

Forestry

ROUNDWOOD REMOVALS
('000 cubic metres, excl. bark)

	2010	2011	2012
Sawlogs, veneer logs and logs for sleepers	4,470	4,133	3,812*
Pulpwood	423	417	805
Other industrial wood	148	330	330*
Fuel wood*	38,829	38,834	38,840
Total	43,870	43,714	43,787

* FAO estimate(s).

Source: FAO.

SAWNWOOD PRODUCTION
('000 cubic metres, incl. railway sleepers)

	2010	2011	2012
Coniferous (softwood)	2,136	2,068	1,892
Broadleaved (hardwood)	295	276	457
Total	2,431	2,344	2,349

Source: FAO.

Fishing

('000 metric tons, live weight)

	2010	2011	2012
Capture	1,526.5	1,566.1	1,575.4
Tilapias	62.4	64.9	55.8
California pilchard (sardine)	630.2	592.9	264.5
Yellowfin tuna	101.5	102.4	97.8
American cupped oyster	46.7	42.9	42.5
Jumbo flying squid	42.9	34.8	23.2
Aquaculture	126.2	137.1	143.7
Whiteleg shrimp	104.6	109.8	100.3
Total catch	1,652.7	1,703.2	1,719.1

Note: Figures exclude aquatic plants ('000 metric tons, capture only): 1.7 in 2010; 5.6 in 2011; 6.1 in 2012. Also excluded are aquatic mammals and crocodiles (recorded by number rather than by weight), shells and corals. The number of Morelet's crocodiles caught was: n.a. in 2010; 184 in 2011; 679 in 2012. The catch of marine shells and corals (metric tons) was: 648 in 2010; 523 in 2011; 444 in 2012.

Source: FAO.

Mining

(metric tons unless otherwise indicated)

	2010	2011	2012
Antimony*	71	5	—
Barytes	143,225	134,727	139,997
Bismuth*	982	935	800
Cadmium*	1,464	1,485	1,482
Celestite	31,429	40,669	46,190
Coal	11,246,639	13,718,159	13,656,051
Coke	2,105,000	2,121,866	2,166,046
Copper*	237,609	402,430	439,531
Crude petroleum ('000 barrels per day)†	2,577	2,553	2,548
Diatomite	91,710	84,231	84,537
Dolomite	1,499,744	2,785,314	2,111,114
Feldspar	398,849	382,497	380,441
Flourite	1,067,386	1,206,907	1,237,091
Gas (million cu ft per day)†	7,020	6,594	6,385
Gold (kg)*	72,596	84,118	96,650
Graphite	6,628	7,348	7,520
Gypsum	3,559,579	3,838,348	4,692,510
Iron*	7,931,194	7,763,048	8,047,183
Kaolin	120,094	120,003	163,148
Lead*	158,206	182,202	210,382
Manganese*	174,761	170,935	188,294
Molybdenum*	10,849	10,787	11,366
Salt	8,430,562	8,769,140	8,730,247
Silica	2,607,650	2,542,143	3,592,813
Silver*	3,499,470	4,150,347	4,496,393
Sulphur	991,802	959,488	1,010,875
Wollastonite	46,548	47,523	55,204
Zinc*	518,429	447,948	500,125

* Figures for metallic minerals refer to metal content of ores.
† Source: Petróleos Mexicanos, México, DF.

Industry

SELECTED PRODUCTS
('000 metric tons unless otherwise indicated)

	2008	2009	2010
Wheat flour	2,834	2,919	3,054
Maize (corn) flour	2,208	2,304	2,272
Raw sugar	5,041	4,470	4,185
Beer ('000 hl)	81,611	82,236	79,916
Soft drinks ('000 hl)	167,511	172,930	173,392
Cigarettes (million units)	45,907	45,059	44,090
Cotton yarn (pure and mixed)	40	n.a.	n.a.
Tyres ('000 units)*	14,192	13,540	16,429
Cement	42,275	40,902	39,065
Non-electric, cooking or heating appliances—household ('000 units)	3,678	3,179	3,373
Refrigerators—household ('000 units)	3,958	3,900	4,927
Washing machines—household ('000 units)	675	n.a.	n.a.
Lorries, buses, tractors, etc. ('000 units)	438	n.a.	n.a.
Passenger cars ('000 units)	1,389	1,033	1,464
Electric energy (million kWh)	258,913	261,018	270,968

* Tyres for road motor vehicles.

Source: UN Industrial Commodity Statistics Database.

Finance

CURRENCY AND EXCHANGE RATES

Monetary Units
100 centavos = 1 Mexican nuevo peso.

Sterling, Dollar and Euro Equivalents (30 May 2014)
£1 sterling = 21.643 nuevos pesos;
US $1 = 12.866 nuevos pesos;
€1 = 17.512 nuevos pesos;
1,000 Mexican nuevos pesos = £46.20 = $77.72 = €57.10.

Average Exchange Rate (nuevos pesos per US $)
2011   12.423
2012   13.169
2013   12.772

Note: Figures are given in terms of the nuevo (new) peso, introduced on 1 January 1993 and equivalent to 1,000 former pesos.

BUDGET*
(million new pesos)

Revenue	2011	2012	2013
Taxation	1,294,054.1	1,314,439.6	1,561,751.6
Income taxes . . .	720,445.3	758,912.4	905,298.6
Value-added tax . .	537,142.5	579,987.5	556,793.9
Excise tax . . .	−76,433.5	−130,131.4	−7,423.8
Import duties . . .	26,881.2	27,906.1	29,260.0
Other revenue . . .	1,026,187.6	1,138,094.2	1,141,823.6
Total revenue . . .	**2,320,241.7**	**2,452,533.8**	**2,703,575.2**

Expenditure	2011	2012	2013
Programmable expenditure . .	1,948,209.1	2,095,706.0	2,279,146.2
Current expenditure . .	400,215.6	429,106.6	407,835.3
Wages and salaries .	229,627.3	251,204.7	253,997.8
Acquisitions . . .	21,196.4	20,295.5	18,438.6
Other current expenditure .	149,391.9	157,606.4	135,398.9
Capital expenditure . . .	163,268.7	138,394.1	207,155.7
Transfers . . .	1,384,724.8	1,528,205.3	1,664,155.2
Non-programmable expenditure .	737,446.6	772,028.0	818,569.3
Interest and fees . . .	240,537.6	256,943.5	270,298.5
Revenue sharing . . .	477,256.2	494,264.5	532,455.5
Total expenditure . . .	**2,685,655.7**	**2,867,734.0**	**3,097,715.5**

* Figures refer to the consolidated accounts of the central Government, including government agencies and the national social security system. The budgets of state and local governments are excluded.

INTERNATIONAL RESERVES
(excl. gold, US $ million at 31 December)

	2011	2012	2013
IMF special drawing rights . .	4,084	4,134	4,111
Reserve position in the Fund . .	2,422	2,806	2,708
Foreign exchange . . .	137,485	153,473	168,613
Total	**143,991**	**160,413**	**175,432**

Source: IMF, *International Financial Statistics.*

MONEY SUPPLY
(million new pesos at 31 December)

	2011	2012	2013
Currency outside depository corporations	665,520	733,450	792,260
Transferable deposits . . .	1,452,298	1,560,182	1,734,497
Other deposits	2,372,420	2,655,909	2,832,151
Securities other than shares . .	11,791	6,732	7,724
Broad money	**4,502,029**	**4,956,274**	**5,366,632**

Source: IMF, *International Financial Statistics.*

COST OF LIVING
(Consumer Price Index; base: 2000 = 100)

	2010	2011	2012
Food, beverages and tobacco . .	174.0	183.0	196.9
All items (incl. others) . . .	157.9	163.3	170.0

Source: ILO.

All items (Consumer Price Index; base: 15–29 December 2010 = 100): 105.2 in 2012; 109.2 in 2013.

NATIONAL ACCOUNTS
('000 million new pesos at current prices)

Expenditure on the Gross Domestic Product

	2011	2012	2013
Government final consumption expenditure	1,683.8	1,839.1	1,936.3
Private final consumption expenditure	9,642.5	10,501.6	11,086.3
Increase in stocks	75.5	117.2	85.8
Gross fixed capital formation . .	3,163.3	3,493.7	3,383.0
Total domestic expenditure .	**14,565.1**	**15,951.6**	**16,491.4**
Exports of goods and services . .	4,549.0	5,100.6	5,115.3
Less Imports of goods and services	4,730.5	5,276.2	5,226.9
Statistical discrepancy . . .	166.4	−161.0	−275.5
GDP in purchasers' values .	**14,550.0**	**15,615.0**	**16,104.4**
GDP at constant 2008 prices .	**12,774.2**	**13,283.1**	**13,425.2**

Gross Domestic Product by Economic Activity

	2011	2012	2013
Agriculture, forestry and fishing .	470.8	532.5	540.3
Mining and quarrying	1,298.1	1,321.6	1,220.0
Manufacturing	2,393.8	2,701.5	2,754.8
Construction	1,152.5	1,231.1	1,165.3
Electricity, gas and water . .	256.6	251.1	258.0
Trade	2,172.9	2,356.3	2,513.9
Restaurants and hotels . . .	297.9	323.7	341.0
Transport, storage and communications	1,208.7	1,295.6	1,353.7
Finance, insurance, real estate and business services	2,978.8	3,152.8	3,289.0
Public administration . . .	578.3	631.3	661.8
Community, social and personal services	376.3	403.0	424.5
Education	567.7	623.6	663.4
Other activities	291.6	308.9	322.7
Gross value added in basic prices	**14,043.9**	**15,133.0**	**15,508.5**
Net taxes on products . . .	506.1	482.0	595.9
GDP in market prices . . .	**14,550.0**	**15,615.0**	**16,104.4**

BALANCE OF PAYMENTS
(US $ million)

	2011	2012	2013
Exports of goods	349,946	371,378	380,903
Imports of goods	−351,209	−371,151	−381,638
Balance on goods	**−1,263**	**227**	**−736**
Exports of services	15,582	16,146	19,586
Imports of services	−30,375	−30,708	−31,817
Balance on goods and services .	**−16,056**	**−14,335**	**−12,967**
Primary income received . . .	10,569	13,154	10,806
Primary income paid	−29,786	−36,144	−41,986
Balance on goods, services and primary income	**−35,274**	**−37,325**	**−44,147**
Secondary income received . .	23,139	22,768	21,942
Secondary income paid . . .	−178	−209	−128
Current balance	**−12,314**	**−14,767**	**−22,333**

—continued	2011	2012	2013
Direct investment assets . . .	−12,636	−22,470	−9,968
Direct investment liabilities . .	23,009	17,224	35,188
Portfolio investment assets . .	6,049	−8,611	−1,617
Portfolio investment liabilities .	40,622	81,349	50,360
Financial derivatives and employee stock options (net)	−725	117	−477
Other investment assets . . .	−3,674	−6,274	−27,239
Other investment liabilities . .	−2,461	−10,314	12,535
Net errors and omissions . . .	−9,648	−18,738	−18,672
Reserves and related items .	28,222	17,517	17,778

Source: IMF, *International Financial Statistics*.

External Trade

PRINCIPAL COMMODITIES
(distribution by HS, US $ million)

Imports f.o.b.	2011	2012	2013
Vegetables and vegetable products	11,097.1	11,610.2	10,292.5
Mineral products	36,660.2	34,959.9	34,266.8
Mineral fuels and products . .	34,266.8	33,342.6	32,909.5
Petroleum oils other than crude.	7,872.4	27,229.5	25,329.9
Chemicals and related products	27,325.4	28,761.0	29,348.2
Organic chemicals	9,594.6	9,797.1	10,030.6
Plastics, rubber, and articles thereof	24,050.1	26,156.0	27,093.8
Plastics and articles thereof . .	18,486.5	19,835.8	20,809.7
Iron and steel; other base metals and articles thereof .	29,417.1	32,217.7	30,544.3
Machinery and mechanical appliances; electrical equipment; parts and accessories	129,688.1	138,365.9	146,146.6
Mechanical appliances, boilers, parts	53,836.2	60,758.3	62,450.0
Machinery and electrical equipment	75,851.9	77,607.6	83,696.7
Electrical apparatus for line telephony or line telegraphy .	15,971.8	17,186.3	17,975.6
Insulated electric conductors .	8,021.1	8,851.7	10,161.1
Vehicles, aircraft, vessels and associated transport equipment	30,102.2	34,222.0	34,894.6
Road vehicles and parts . . .	28,571.0	32,427.0	33,393.8
Parts and accessories of vehicles	16,801.3	19,046.0	20,521.9
Optical, photographic, measuring, precision and medical apparatus; clocks and watches; musical instruments	11,630.8	12,207.7	12,864.8
Optical and medical instruments .	11,174.5	11,744.2	12,406.5
Total (incl. others)	350,842.9	370,751.6	381,210.2

Exports f.o.b.	2011	2012	2013
Prepared foodstuffs; beverages, spirits, vinegar; tobacco and articles thereof .	9,519.9	9,390.5	10,642.3
Mineral products	59,799.3	57,154.0	53,534.7
Mineral fuels and products . .	55,701.0	52,164.4	48,691.4
Crude oils	49,380.6	46,852.4	42,723.2
Chemicals and related products	10,268.9	11,379.7	11,413.3
Plastics, rubber, and articles thereof	8,780.0	9,939.1	10,513.8
Pearls, precious stones and metals and articles thereof .	13,313.8	13,217.4	9,817.1
Iron and steel; other base metals and articles thereof .	16,831.8	16,577.0	16,791.8
Machinery and mechanical appliances; electrical equipment; parts and accessories	118,955.4	128,649.0	131,789.1
Mechanical appliances, boilers, parts	48,310.7	53,774.5	53,952.5
Machines for processing data .	16,501.6	18,438.7	17,401.3
Machinery and electrical equipment	70,644.8	74,874.5	77,836.5
Electrical apparatus for line telephony or line telegraphy .	15,971.8	17,186.3	17,975.6
Televisions	18,789.7	17,767.6	16,688.9
Vehicles, aircraft, vessels and associated transport equipment	65,063.1	73,099.6	80,740.0
Road vehicles and parts . . .	62,900.8	70,272.8	77,193.0
Automobiles for tourism . .	26,844.1	29,169.3	32,389.4
Goods vehicles	12,466.3	14,800.0	17,560.5
Parts and accessories of vehicles	16,801.3	19,046.0	20,521.9
Optical, photographic, measuring, precision and medical apparatus; clocks and watches; musical instruments	11,077.8	11,921.9	13,004.3
Optical and medical instruments .	10,882.3	11,731.7	12,807.9
Total (incl. others)	349,433.4	370,769.9	380,026.6

Note: The *maquila* sector is responsible for a large percentage of both merchandise imports and exports, but official figures on the value of the sector were last published in 2006, when imports were valued at US $86,527.3m. (equivalent to some 34% of total imports) and exports were valued at $111,823.8m. (almost 45% of total exports).

PRINCIPAL TRADING PARTNERS*
(US $ million)

Imports c.i.f.	2011	2012	2013
Brazil	4,561.9	4,494.5	4,420.6
Canada	9,645.5	9,889.9	9,847.0
China, People's Republic . .	52,248.0	56,936.1	61,321.4
France	3,359.6	3,466.7	3,685.9
Germany	12,862.6	13,507.8	13,461.0
Italy	4,982.7	5,462.4	5,620.8
Japan	16,493.5	17,655.2	17,076.1
Korea, Republic	13,690.4	13,350.1	13,507.4
Malaysia	5,609.9	4,735.6	5,379.0
Spain	3,843.2	4,081.1	4,311.1
Taiwan	5,769.9	6,183.0	6,689.0
Thailand	3,088.8	3,805.7	4,322.0
USA	174,356.0	185,109.8	187,261.9
Total (incl. others)	350,842.9	370,751.6	381,210.2

Exports f.o.b.	2011	2012	2013
Brazil	4,891.2	5,657.5	5,386.4
Canada	10,694.6	10,937.6	10,452.7
China, People's Republic . .	5,964.2	5,720.7	6,470.0
Colombia	5,632.6	5,592.3	4,735.2
Germany	4,343.0	4,494.6	3,797.2
Spain	4,904.8	7,075.1	7,137.6
USA	274,426.5	287,842.2	299,439.5
Total (incl. others)	349,433.4	370,769.9	380,026.6

* Imports by country of origin; exports by country of destination.

Transport

RAILWAYS
(traffic)

	2010	2011	2012
Passengers carried ('000)* . .	40,399	41,922	43,830
Passenger-km (million) . .	843	891	970
Freight carried ('000 tons) . .	104,564	108,433	111,607
Freight ton-km (million) . . .	78,770	79,728	79,353

* Including passengers carried on Linea 1 of the Ferrocarril Suburbano de la Zona Metropolitana del Valle de México.

Source: Dirección General de Planeación, Secretaría de Comunicaciones y Transportes.

ROAD TRAFFIC
('000 vehicles in use at 31 December, estimates)

	2008	2009	2010
Passenger cars	19,248	20,524	21,640
Lorries and vans . . .	8,453	8,843	9,183
Buses and coaches	334	337	359
Motorcycles and mopeds . . .	1,079	1,201	1,157

Source: IRF, *World Road Statistics*.

SHIPPING

Flag Registered Fleet
(at 31 December)

	2011	2012	2013
Number of vessels	608	628	673
Total displacement ('000 grt) . .	1,585.5	1,650.7	1,804.0

Source: Lloyd's List Intelligence (www.lloydslistintelligence.com).

Seaborne Shipping
(domestic and international freight traffic, '000 metric tons)

	2011	2012	2013
Goods loaded	164,067	160,575	169,816
Goods unloaded	118,836	122,887	118,880

Source: Coordinación General de Puertos y Marina Mercante.

CIVIL AVIATION
(traffic on scheduled services)

	2011	2012	2013
Passengers carried ('000) . .	50,764	55,153	60,007
Freight carried ('000 tons) . .	562	559	582

Source: Dirección General de Planeación, Secretaría de Comunicaciones y Transportes.

Tourism

VISITOR ARRIVALS BY COUNTRY OF ORIGIN
(including cross-border visitors)

	2010	2011	2012
Argentina	170,467	200,687	251,221
Brazil	117,658	196,266	248,899
Canada	1,460,418	1,563,146	1,571,543
Chile	67,661	76,379	88,148
Colombia	102,177	125,882	163,725
France	170,250	186,778	202,855
Germany	163,266	165,133	172,841
Guatemala	50,274	44,422	59,091
Italy	133,292	150,690	156,532
Japan	66,164	72,339	85,687
Korea, Republic	34,965	40,303	47,615
Netherlands	68,964	67,821	63,159
Spain	287,163	279,530	278,812
United Kingdom	295,831	330,071	363,142
USA	17,871,635	18,554,616	18,658,170
Venezuela	84,868	88,804	129,331
Total (incl. others)	23,289,749	23,403,263	23,402,545

Total tourist arrivals ('000): 23,734 in 2013 (provisional).

Tourism receipts (excluding excursionists, US $ million): 11,869 in 2011; 12,739 in 2012; 13,819 in 2013 (provisional).

Source: mainly World Tourism Organization.

Communications Media

	2011	2012	2013
Telephones ('000 main lines in use)	19,731.4	20,587.8	20,590.4
Mobile cellular telephones ('000 subscribers)	94,583.2	100,727.2	105,005.7
Internet subscribers ('000)* . .	11,992.1	n.a.	n.a.
Broadband subscribers ('000) . .	11,868.4	12,717.1	13,626.6

* Preliminary.

Source: International Telecommunication Union.

Education

(2011/12)

	Institutions	Teachers	Students ('000)
Pre-primary	91,253	224,146	4,705.5
Primary	99,378	573,849	14,909.4
Secondary (incl. technical) . .	36,563	388,769	6,167.4
Intermediate: professional/ technical	1,369	27,660	383.5
Intermediate: Baccalaureate . .	14,058	258,314	3,950.1
Higher	6,114	326,022	3,027.4

Pupil-teacher ratio (primary education, UNESCO estimate): 28.1 in 2010/11 (Source: UNESCO Institute for Statistics).

Adult literacy rate (UNESCO estimates): 94.2% (males 95.4%; females 93.2%) in 2012 (Source: UNESCO Institute for Statistics).

Directory

The Constitution

The present Mexican Constitution was proclaimed on 5 February 1917, at the end of the Revolution, which began in 1910, against the regime of Porfirio Díaz. Its provisions regarding religion, education, and the ownership and exploitation of mineral wealth reflect the long revolutionary struggle against the concentration of power in the hands of the Roman Catholic Church and the large landowners, and the struggle that culminated, in the 1930s, in the expropriation of the properties of the foreign petroleum companies. It has been amended from time to time.

GOVERNMENT

The President and Congress

The President of the Republic, in agreement with the Cabinet and with the approval of the Congreso de la Unión (Congress) or of the Permanent Committee when the Congress is not in session, may suspend constitutional guarantees in case of foreign invasion, serious disturbance, or any other emergency endangering the people.

The exercise of supreme executive authority is vested in the President, who is elected for six years and enters office on 1 December of the year of election. The presidential powers include the right to appoint and remove members of the Cabinet and the Attorney-General and to appoint, with the approval of the Senado (Senate), diplomatic officials, the higher officers of the army, and ministers of the supreme and higher courts of justice. The President is also empowered to dispose of the Armed Forces for the internal and external security of the federation.

The Congress is composed of the Cámara Federal de Diputados (Federal Chamber of Deputies), elected every three years, and the Senate, whose members hold office for six years. There is one deputy for every 250,000 people and for every fraction of over 125,000 people. The Senate is composed of 128 members, representing four members for each state and the Distrito Federal (Federal District), three to be elected by majority vote, and one by proportional representation. Regular sessions of the Congress begin on 1 September and may not continue beyond 31 December of the same year. Extraordinary sessions may be convened by the Permanent Committee.

The powers of the Congress include the right to: pass laws and regulations; impose taxes; specify the criteria on which the Executive may negotiate loans; declare war; raise, maintain and regulate the organization of the Armed Forces; establish and maintain schools of various types throughout the country; approve or reject the budget; sanction appointments submitted by the President of the Supreme Court and magistrates of the superior court of the Federal District; approve or reject treaties and conventions made with foreign powers; and ratify diplomatic appointments.

The Permanent Committee, consisting of 29 members of the Congress (15 of whom are deputies and 14 senators), officiates when the Congress is in recess, and is responsible for the convening of extraordinary sessions of the Congress.

The States

Governors are elected by popular vote in a general election every six years. The local legislature is formed by deputies, who are changed every three years. The judicature is specially appointed under the Constitution by the competent authority (it is never subject to the popular vote).

Each state is a separate unit, with the right to levy taxes and to legislate in certain matters. The states are not allowed to levy inter-state customs duties.

The Federal District

The Federal District consists of Mexico City and several neighbouring small towns and villages. The first direct elections for the Head of Government of the Federal District were held in 1997; hitherto, a Regent had been appointed by the President.

EDUCATION

According to the Constitution, the provision of educational facilities is the joint responsibility of the federation, the states and the municipalities. Education shall be democratic, and shall be directed to developing all the faculties of the individual students, while imbuing them with love of their country and a consciousness of international solidarity and justice. Religious bodies may not provide education, except training for the priesthood. Private educational institutions must conform to the requirements of the Constitution with regard to the nature of the teaching given. The education provided by the states shall be free of charge.

RELIGION

Religious bodies of whatever denomination shall not have the capacity to possess or administer real estate or capital invested therein. Churches are the property of the nation; the headquarters of bishops, seminaries, convents and other property used for the propagation of a religious creed shall pass into the hands of the state, to be dedicated to the public service of the federation or of the respective state. Institutions of charity, provided they are not connected with a religious body, may hold real property. The establishment of monastic orders is prohibited. Ministers of religion must be Mexican; they may not criticize the fundamental laws of the country in a public or private meeting; they may not vote or form associations for political purposes. Political meetings may not be held in places of worship.

A reform proposal, whereby constitutional restrictions on the Catholic Church were formally ended, was promulgated as law in January 1992.

LAND AND MINERAL OWNERSHIP

Article 27 of the Constitution vests direct ownership of minerals and other products of the subsoil, including petroleum and water, in the nation, and reserves to the Federal Government alone the right to grant concessions in accordance with the laws to individuals and

companies, on the condition that they establish regular work for the exploitation of the materials. At the same time, the right to acquire ownership of lands and waters belonging to the nation, or concessions for their exploitation, is limited to Mexican individuals and companies, although the state may concede similar rights to foreigners who agree not to invoke the protection of their governments to enforce such rights.

The same article declares null all alienations of lands, waters and forests belonging to towns or communities made by political chiefs or other local authorities in violation of the provisions of the law of 25 June 1856*, and all concessions or sales of communally held lands, waters and forests made by the federal authorities after 1 December 1876. The population settlements that lack *ejidos* (state-owned smallholdings), or cannot obtain restitution of lands previously held, shall be granted lands in proportion to the needs of the population. The area of land granted to the individual may not be less than 10 hectares of irrigated or watered land, or the equivalent in other kinds of land.

The owners affected by decisions to divide and redistribute land (with the exception of the owners of farming or cattle-rearing properties) shall not have any right of redress, nor may they invoke the right of *amparo†* in protection of their interests. They may, however, apply to the Government for indemnification. Small properties, the areas of which are defined in the Constitution, will not be subject to expropriation. The Constitution leaves to the Congress the duty of determining the maximum size of rural properties.

In March 1992 an agrarian reform amendment, whereby the programme of land distribution established by the 1917 Constitution was abolished and the terms of the *ejido* system of tenant farmers were relaxed, was formally adopted.

Monopolies and measures to restrict competition in industry, commerce or public services are prohibited.

A section of the Constitution deals with work and social security.

POLITICAL ORGANIZATIONS AND ELECTORAL PROCEDURE

In December 1977 a Federal Law on Political Organizations and Electoral Procedure was promulgated. It includes the following provisions:

The Federal Chamber of Deputies shall comprise 300 deputies elected by majority vote within single-member electoral districts and up to 100 deputies (increased to 200 from July 1988) elected by a system of proportional representation from regional lists within multi-member constituencies. The Senate is elected by majority vote.

Executive power is exercised by the President of the Republic of the United Mexican States, elected by majority vote.

Ordinary elections will be held every three years for the federal deputies and every six years for the senators and the President of the Republic on the first Sunday of July of the year in question. When a vacancy occurs among members of the Congress elected by majority vote, the house in question shall call extraordinary elections, and when a vacancy occurs among members of the Chamber elected by proportional representation it shall be filled by the candidate of the same party who received the next highest number of votes at the last ordinary election.

Voting is the right and duty of every citizen, male or female, over the age of 18 years.

A political party shall be registered if it has at least 3,000 members in each one of at least half the states in Mexico or at least 300 members in each one of at least half of the single-member constituencies. In either case, the total number of members must be no fewer than 65,000. A party can also obtain conditional registration if it has been active for at least four years. Registration is confirmed if the party obtains at least 1.5% of the popular vote. All political parties shall have free access to the media.

* The Lerdo Law against ecclesiastical privilege, which became the basis of the Liberal Constitution of 1857.

† The Constitution provides for the procedure known as *judicio de amparo*, a wider form of habeas corpus, which the individual may invoke in protection of his constitutional rights.

The Government

HEAD OF STATE

President: ENRIQUE PEÑA NIETO (took office 1 December 2012).

CABINET
(September 2014)

The Government is formed by the Partido Revolucionario Institucional (PRI).

Secretary of the Interior: MIGUEL ANGEL OSORIO CHONG.

Secretary of Foreign Affairs: JOSÉ ANTONIO MEADE KURIBREÑA.

Secretary of Finance and Public Credit: LUIS VIDEGARAY CASO.

Secretary of National Defence: Gen. SALVADOR CIENFUEGOS ZEPEDA.

Secretary of the Navy: Adm. VIDAL FRANCISCO SOBERÓN SANZ.

Secretary of the Economy: ILDEFONSO GUAJARDO VILLARREAL.

Secretary of Social Development: ROSARIO ROBLES BERLANGA.

Secretary of Communications and Transport: GERARDO RUIZ ESPARZA.

Secretary of Labour and Social Welfare: ALFONSO NAVARRETE PRIDA.

Secretary of the Environment and Natural Resources: JUAN JOSÉ GUERRA ABUD.

Secretary of Energy: PEDRO JOAQUÍN COLDWELL.

Secretary of Agriculture, Livestock, Rural Development, Fisheries and Food: ENRIQUE MARTÍNEZ Y MARTÍNEZ.

Secretary of Public Education: EMILIO CHUAYFFET CHEMOR.

Secretary of Health: MERCEDES JUAN LÓPEZ.

Secretary of Tourism: CLAUDIA RUIZ MASSIEU SALINAS.

Secretary of Territorial, Urban and Agrarian Development: JORGE CARLOS RAMÍREZ MARÍN.

Under-Secretary for Administrative and Procurement Responsibilities (Public Function): JULIÁN ALFONSO OLIVAS UGALDE.

Attorney-General: JESÚS MURILLO KARAM.

Legal Counsel to the President: HUMBERTO CASTILLEJOS CERVANTES.

Chief of Staff in the Office of the President: AURELIO NUÑO MAYER.

SECRETARIATS OF STATE

Office of the President: Los Pinos, Col. San Miguel Chapultepec, 11850 México, DF; tel. (55) 5093-5300; fax (55) 5277-2376; e-mail enrique.penanieto@presidencia.gob.mx; internet www.presidencia.gob.mx.

Secretariat of State for Agriculture, Livestock, Rural Development, Fisheries and Food: Avda Municipio Libre 377, Col. Santa Cruz Atoyac, Del. Benito Juárez, 03310 México, DF; tel. (55) 3871-1000; fax (55) 9183-1018; e-mail contacto@sagarpa.gob.mx; internet www.sagarpa.gob.mx.

Secretariat of State for Communications and Transport: Avda Xola, esq. con Ejercito Central, Col. Narvarte, Del. Benito Juárez, 03020 México, DF; tel. (55) 5723-9300; fax (55) 5530-0093; e-mail webmaster@sct.gob.mx; internet www.sct.gob.mx.

Secretariat of State for the Economy: Alfonso Reyes 30, Col. Hipódromo Condesa, Del. Cuauhtémoc, 06140 México, DF; tel. (55) 5729-9100; fax (55) 5729-9320; e-mail primercontacto@economia.gob.mx; internet www.economia.gob.mx.

Secretariat of State for Energy: Insurgentes Sur 890, 17°, Col. del Valle, Del. Benito Juárez, 03100 México, DF; tel. (55) 5000-6000; fax (55) 5000-6222; e-mail calidad@energia.gob.mx; internet www.energia.gob.mx.

Secretariat of State for the Environment and Natural Resources: Blvd Adolfo Ruíz Cortines 4209, Col. Jardines en la Montaña, Del. Tlalpan, 14210 México, DF; tel. (55) 5490-0900; fax (55) 5628-0643; e-mail contactodgeia@semarnat.gob.mx; internet www.semarnat.gob.mx.

Secretariat of State for Finance and Public Credit: Palacio Nacional, Plaza de la Constitución, Col. Centro, Del. Cuauhtémoc, 06000 México, DF; tel. (55) 9158-2000; fax (55) 9158-1142; e-mail secretario@hacienda.gob.mx; internet www.hacienda.gob.mx.

Secretariat of State for Foreign Affairs: Plaza Juárez 20, Col. Centro, Del. Cuauhtémoc, 06010 México, DF; tel. (55) 3686-5100; fax (55) 3686-5582; e-mail atencionciudadanasre@sre.gob.mx; internet www.sre.gob.mx.

Secretariat of State for Health: Lieja 7, 1°, Col. Juárez, Del. Cuauhtémoc, 06600 México, DF; tel. (55) 5286-2383; fax (55) 5553-7917; e-mail portalesweb@salud.gob.mx; internet www.salud.gob.mx.

Secretariat of State for the Interior: Abraham González 48, Col. Juárez, Del. Cuauhtémoc, 06600 México, DF; tel. (55) 5728-7400; fax (55) 5728-7300; e-mail contacto@segob.gob.mx; internet www.gobernacion.gob.mx; includes the Commission of Public Security.

Secretariat of State for Labour and Social Welfare: Periférico Sur 4271, Col. Fuentes del Pedregal, Del. Tlalpan, 14149 México, DF; tel. (55) 3000-2100; fax (55) 5645-5594; e-mail webmaster1@stps.gob.mx; internet www.stps.gob.mx.

Secretariat of State for National Defence: Blvd Manuel Avila Camacho, esq. Avda Industria Militar, 3°, Col. Lomas de Sotelo, Del. Miguel Hidalgo, 11640 México, DF; tel. (55) 2122-8800; fax (55) 5395-2935; e-mail ggalvang@mail.sedena.gob.mx; internet www.sedena.gob.mx.

Secretariat of State for the Navy: Eje 2 oriente, Tramo Heroica, Escuela Naval Militar 861, Col. Los Cipreses, Del. Coyoacán, 04830 México, DF; tel. (55) 5624-6500; e-mail srio@semar.gob.mx; internet www.semar.gob.mx.

Secretariat of State for Public Education: Argentina 28, Col. Centro Histórico, Del. Cuauhtémoc, 06029 México, DF; tel. (55) 3601-1000; fax (55) 5329-6873; e-mail educa@sep.gob.mx; internet www.sep.gob.mx.

Secretariat of State for Public Function: Insurgentes Sur 1735, 10°, Col. Guadalupe Inn, Del. Alvaro Obregón, 01020 México, DF; tel. (55) 2000-3000; e-mail contactociudadano@funcionpublica.gob.mx; internet www.funcionpublica.gob.mx.

Secretariat of State for Social Development: Avda Paseo de la Reforma 116, Col. Juárez, Del. Cuauhtémoc, 06600 México, DF; tel. (55) 5328-5000; e-mail demandasocial@sedesol.gob.mx; internet www.sedesol.gob.mx.

Secretariat of State for Territorial, Urban and Agrarian Development: Avda Heroica Escuela Naval Militar 669, Col. Presidentes Ejidales, 2 Sección, Del. Coyoacán, 04470 México, DF; tel. (55) 5624-0000; fax (55) 5695-6368; e-mail uenlace@sra.gob.mx; internet www.sedatu.gob.mx.

Secretariat of State for Tourism: Avda Presidente Masaryk 172, Col. Bosques de Chapultepec, Del. Miguel Hidalgo, 11580 México, DF; tel. (55) 3002-6300; fax (55) 1036-0789; e-mail atencion@sectur.gob.mx; internet www.sectur.gob.mx.

Office of the Attorney-General: Avda Paseo de la Reforma 211–213, Col. Cuauhtémoc, Del. Cuauhtémoc, 06500 México, DF; tel. (55) 5346-0000; fax (55) 5346-0908; e-mail ofproc@pgr.gob.mx; internet www.pgr.gob.mx.

President and Legislature

PRESIDENT

Election, 1 July 2012

Candidate	Number of valid votes	% of valid votes
Enrique Peña Nieto (PRI–PVEM) . .	19,226,784	39.19
Andrés Manuel López Obrador (Movimiento Progresista*) . . .	15,896,999	32.40
Josefina Eugenia Vázquez Mota (PAN) .	12,786,647	26.06
Gabriel Ricardo Quadri de la Torre (NA) .	1,150,662	2.35
Total valid votes†	49,061,092	100.00

* An alliance of the PRD, the PT and Movimiento Ciudadano.
† In addition, there were 1,241,154 invalid votes and 20,907 votes for unregistered candidates.

CONGRESS OF THE UNION
(Congreso de la Unión)

Senate
(Senado)

Senate: Avda Paseo de la Reforma 135, esq. Insurgentes Centro, Col. Tabacalera, Del. Cuauhtémoc, 06030 México, DF; tel. (55) 5130-2200; internet www.senado.gob.mx.

President: ERNESTO JAVIER CORDERO ARROYO (PAN).

Election, 1 July 2012

Party	Seats
Partido Revolucionario Institucional (PRI) . .	54
Partido Acción Nacional (PAN)	38
Partido de la Revolución Democrática (PRD) . .	22
Partido Verde Ecologista de México (PVEM) . .	7
Partido del Trabajo (PT)	5
Nueva Alianza (NA)	1
Movimiento Ciudadano (MC)	1
Total	**128**

Federal Chamber of Deputies
(Cámara Federal de Diputados)

Federal Chamber of Deputies: Avda Congreso de la Unión 66, Col. El Parque, Del. Venustiano Carranza, 15969 México, DF; tel. (55) 5628-1300; internet www.diputados.gob.mx.

President: FRANCISCO AGUSTÍN ARROYO VIEYRA (PRI).

Election, 1 July 2012

Party	Seats
Partido Revolucionario Institucional (PRI) . .	213
Partido Acción Nacional (PAN)	114
Partido de la Revolución Democrática (PRD) . .	104
Partido Verde Ecologista de México (PVEM) . .	28
Movimiento Ciudadano (MC)	16
Partido del Trabajo (PT)	15
Nueva Alianza (NA)	10
Total	**500**

State Governors

(September 2014)

Aguascalientes: CARLOS LOZANO DE LA TORRE (PRI).

Baja California: FRANCISCO VEGA DE LA MADRID (PAN).

Baja California Sur: MARCOS COVARRUBIAS VILLASEÑOR (PAN).

Campeche: FERNANDO EUTIMIO ORTEGA BERNÉS (PRI).

Chiapas: MANUEL VELASCO COELLO (PVEM).

Chihuahua: CÉSAR HORATIO DUARTE JÁQUEZ (PRI).

Coahuila (de Zaragoza): RUBÉN IGNACIO MOREIRA VALDÉZ (PRI).

Colima: MARIO ANGUIANO MORENO (PRI).

Durango: JORGE HERRERA CALDERA (PRI).

Guanajuato: MIGUEL MÁRQUEZ MÁRQUEZ (PAN).

Guerrero: ANGEL HELADIO AGUIRRE RIVERO (PRD).

Hidalgo: JOSÉ FRANCISCO OLVERA RUIZ (PRI).

Jalisco: JORGE ARISTÓTELES SANDOVAL DÍAZ (PRI).

México: ERUVIEL AVILA VILLEGAS (PRI).

Michoacán (de Ocampo): SALVADOR JARA GUERRERO (acting—Ind.).

Morelos: GRACO LUIS RAMÍREZ GARRIDO ABREU (PRD).

Nayarit: ROBERTO SANDOVAL CASTAÑEDA (PRI).

Nuevo León: RODRIGO MEDINA DE LA CRUZ (PRI).

Oaxaca: GABINO CUÉ MONTEAGUDO (Convergencia).

Puebla: RAFAEL MORENO VALLE ROSAS (PAN).

Querétaro (de Arteaga): JOSÉ CALZADA ROVIROSA (PRI).

Quintana Roo: ROBERTO BORGE ANGULO (PRI).

San Luis Potosí: FERNANDO TORANZO FERNÁNDEZ (PRI).

Sinaloa: MARIO LÓPEZ VALDEZ (PAN).

Sonora: GUILLERMO PADRÉS ELÍAS (PAN).

Tabasco: ARTURO NÚÑEZ JIMÉNEZ (PRD).

Tamaulipas: EGIDIO TORRE CANTÚ (PRI).

Tlaxcala: MARIANO GONZÁLEZ ZARUR (PRI).

Veracruz-Llave: JAVIER DUARTE DE OCHOA (PRI).

Yucatán: ROLANDO RODRIGO ZAPATA BELLO (PRI).

Zacatecas: MIGUEL ALEJANDRO ALONSO REYES (PRI).

Head of Government of the Federal District: MIGUEL ANGEL MANCERA ESPINOSA (PRD).

Election Commission

Instituto Nacional Electoral (INE): Viaducto Tlalpan 100, Col. Arenal Tepepan, Del. Tlalpan, 14610 México, DF; e-mail info@ine .mx; internet www.ine.mx; f. 1990 as Instituto Federal Electoral, reconstituted as above in 2014; independent; Pres. LORENZO CÓRDOVA VIANELLO.

Political Organizations

Movimiento Ciudadano (MC): Louisiana 113, esq. Nueva York, Col. Nápoles, Del. Benito Juárez, 03810 México, DF; tel. (55) 1167-6767; e-mail gestionsocial@convergencia.org.mx; internet www .movimientociudadano.org.mx; f. 1999 as Convergencia por la Democracia; changed name to Convergencia in 2002; restructured and adopted present name in 2011; contested the 2012 elections as part of the Movimiento Progresista; Co-ordinator DANTE ALFONSO DELGADO RANNAURO; Sec. MARÍA ELENA ORANTES LÓPEZ.

Movimiento Regeneración Nacional (Morena): San Luis Potosí 64, esq. Córdoba, Col. Roma, Del. Cuauhtémoc, 06700 México, DF;

tel. (55) 4212-4758; internet www.amlo.org.mx; f. 2012; created by dissidents from the Partido de la Revolución Democrática (PRD); left-wing; Leader ANDRÉS MANUEL LÓPEZ OBRADOR.

Nueva Alianza (NA): Durango 199, Col. Roma, Del. Cuauhtémoc, 06700 México, DF; tel. (55) 3685-8485; fax (55) 3685-8455; e-mail monica.arriola@nueva-alianza.org.mx; internet www .nueva-alianza.org.mx; f. 2005 by dissident faction of the PRI; includes mems of the Sindicato Nacional de Trabajadores de la Educación and supporters of Elba Esther Gordillo Morales; Pres. LUIS CASTRO OBREGÓN; Sec.-Gen. MÓNICA ARRIOLA GORDILLO.

Partido Acción Nacional (PAN): Avda Coyoacán 1546, Col. del Valle, Del. Benito Juárez, 03100 México, DF; tel. (55) 5200-4000; e-mail correo@cen.pan.org.mx; internet www.pan.org.mx; f. 1939; democratic party; 150,000 mems; Pres. GUSTAVO ENRIQUE MADERO MUÑOZ; Sec.-Gen. RICARDO ANAYA CORTÉS.

Partido Popular Socialista (PPS): Avda Alvaro Obregón 185, Col. Roma, Del. Cuauhtémoc, 06797 México, DF; tel. (55) 5208-5063; fax (55) 2454-6593; e-mail info@ppsm.org.mx; internet www.ppsm.org .mx; f. 1948 as Partido Popular; Marxist-Leninist; Sec.-Gen. CUAUHTÉMOC AMEZCUA DROMUNDO.

Partido de la Revolución Democrática (PRD): Avda Benjamín Franklin 84, Col. Escandón, Del. Miguel Hidalgo, 11800 México, DF; tel. (55) 1085-8000; fax (55) 1085-8144; e-mail comunicacion@prd.org .mx; internet www.prd.org.mx; f. 1989; centre-left; contested the 2012 elections as part of the Movimiento Progresista; Pres. JESÚS ZAMBRANO GRIJALVA; Sec.-Gen. ALEJANDRO SÁNCHEZ CAMACHO.

Partido Revolucionario Institucional (PRI): Edif. 2, Insurgentes Norte 59, Col. Buenavista, Del. Cuauhtémoc, 06359 México, DF; tel. (55) 5729-9600; internet www.pri.org.mx; f. 1929 as the Partido Nacional Revolucionario; regarded as the natural successor to the victorious parties of the revolutionary period; broadly based and centrist; Pres. Dr CÉSAR CAMACHO QUIROZ; Sec.-Gen. IVONNE ORTEGA PACHECO; groups within the PRI include: the Corriente Crítica Progresista, the Corriente Crítica del Partido, the Corriente Constitucionalista Democratizadora, Corriente Nuevo PRI XIV Asamblea, Democracia 2000, México Nuevo and Galileo.

Partido del Trabajo (PT): Avda Cuauhtémoc 47, Col. Roma Norte, Del. Miguel Hidalgo, 06700 México, DF; tel. and fax (55) 5525-2727; internet www.partidodeltrabajo.org.mx; f. 1990; labour party; contested the 2012 elections as part of the Movimiento Progresista; Leader ALBERTO ANAYA GUTIÉRREZ.

Partido Verde Ecologista de México (PVEM): Loma Bonita 18, Col. Lomas Altas, Del. Miguel Hidalgo, 11950 México, DF; tel. and fax (55) 5257-0188; internet www.partidoverde.org.mx; f. 1987; ecologist party; Spokesman ARTURO ESCOBAR Y VEGA.

The following parties are not officially registered but continue to be politically active:

Fuerza Ciudadana: Rochester 94, Col. Nápoles, 03810 México, DF; tel. (55) 5534-4628; e-mail info@fuerzaciudadana.org.mx; internet www.fuerzaciudadana.org.mx; f. 2002; citizens' asscn; Pres. JORGE ALCOCER VILLANUEVA; Sec. ALBERTO CONSEJO VARGAS.

Partido Democrático Popular Revolucionario: internet pdpr-epr.blogspot.in; f. 1996; political grouping representing the causes of 14 armed peasant orgs, including the EPR and the PROCUP; Commdr-Gen. FLORENCIA ELODIA CANSECO RUÍZ.

Partido Socialdemócrata (PSD): Tejocotes 164, Col. Tlacoquemécatl del Valle, Del. Benito Juárez, 03200 México, DF; tel. (55) 5488-1520; fax (55) 5488-1598; internet psdmexico.blogspot.in; f. 2005 as Partido Alternativa Socialdemócrata y Campesina; adopted current name 2008; progressive and peasants' rights; lost political registration following 2009 mid-term elections; Pres. JORGE CARLOS DÍAZ CUERVO.

Illegal organizations active in Mexico include the following:

Ejército Revolucionario Popular Insurgente (ERPI): internet www.enlace-erpi.org; f. 1996; left-wing guerrilla group active in Guerrero, Morelos and Oaxaca; Leader ANTONIO .

Ejército Zapatista de Liberación Nacional (EZLN): e-mail laotra@ezln.org.mx; internet www.ezln.org.mx; f. 1993; left-wing guerrilla group active in the Chiapas region; Leader Subcomandante MOISÉS.

Diplomatic Representation

EMBASSIES IN MEXICO

Algeria: Sierra Madre 540, Col. Lomas de Chapultepec, Del. Miguel Hidalgo, 11000 México, DF; tel. (55) 5520-6950; fax (55) 5540-7579; e-mail embajadadeargelia@yahoo.com.mx; Chargé d'affaires a.i. S. S. SAID BOUDAOUD.

Angola: Gaspar de Zúñiga 226, Col. Lomas de Chapultepec, Sección Virreyes, Del. Miguel Hidalgo, 11000 México, DF; tel. (55) 5540-5982;

fax (55) 5540-5928; e-mail info@embangolamex.org; Ambassador LEOVIGILDO DA COSTA E SILVA.

Argentina: Avda Palmas 1670, Col. Lomas de Chapultepec, Del. Miguel Hidalgo, 11000 México, DF; tel. (55) 5520-9430; fax (55) 5540-5011; e-mail embajadaargentina@prodigy.net.mx; internet www .embajadaargentina.mx; Ambassador PATRICIA VACA NARVAJA.

Australia: Rubén Darío 55, Col. Polanco, Del. Miguel Hidalgo, 11580 México, DF; tel. (55) 1101-2200; fax (55) 1101-2201; e-mail embaustmex@yahoo.com.mx; internet www.mexico.embassy.gov .au; Ambassador TIM GEORGE.

Austria: Sierra Tarahumara 420, Col. Lomas de Chapultepec, Del. Miguel Hidalgo, 11000 México, DF; tel. (55) 5251-0806; fax (55) 5245-0198; e-mail mexiko-ob@bmaa.gv.at; internet www .embajadadeaustria.com.mx; Ambassador EVA HAGER.

Azerbaijan: Avda Virreyes 1015, Col. Lomas de Chapultepec, Del. Miguel Hidalgo, 11000 México, DF; tel. (55) 5540-4109; fax (55) 5540-1366; e-mail oficina@azembassy.mx; internet www.azembassy.mx; Ambassador ILGAR MUKHTAROV.

Belgium: Alfredo Musset 41, Col. Polanco, Del. Miguel Hidalgo, 11550 México, DF; tel. (55) 5280-0758; fax (55) 5280-0208; e-mail mexico@diplobel.org; internet www.diplomatie.be/mexico; Ambassador HANS CHRISTIAN KINT.

Belize: Bernardo de Gálvez 215, Col. Lomas de Chapultepec, Del. Miguel Hidalgo, 11000 México, DF; tel. (55) 5520-1274; fax (55) 5520-6089; e-mail embelize@prodigy.net.mx; Ambassador OLIVER DEL CID.

Bolivia: Goethe 104, Col. Anzures, Del. Miguel Hidalgo, 11590 México, DF; tel. and fax (55) 5255-3620; e-mail embajada@embol .org.mx; internet www.embol.org.mx; Ambassador MARCOS DOMIC RUÍZ.

Brazil: Lope de Armendáriz 130, Col. Lomas Virreyes, Del. Miguel Hidalgo, 11000 México, DF; tel. (55) 5201-4531; fax (55) 5520-6480; e-mail brasemb.mexico@itamaraty.gov.br; internet mexico .itamaraty.gov.br; Ambassador MARCOS LEAL RAPOSO LOPES.

Bulgaria: Paseo de la Reforma 1990, Col. Lomas de Chapultepec, Del. Miguel Hidalgo, 11000 México, DF; tel. (55) 5596-3295; fax (55) 5596-3283; e-mail Embassy.Mexico@mfa.bg; internet www.mfa.bg/ embassies/mexico; Ambassador HRISTO GEORGIEV GUDJEV.

Canada: Schiller 529, Col. Polanco, Del. Miguel Hidalgo, 11560 México, DF; tel. (55) 5724-7900; fax (55) 5724-7980; e-mail mxico@ international.gc.ca; internet www.canadainternational.gc.ca/ mexico-mexique; Ambassador SARA HRADECKY.

Chile: Andrés Bello 10, 18°, Col. Polanco, Del. Miguel Hidalgo, 11560 México, DF; tel. (55) 5280-9681; fax (55) 5280-9703; e-mail echilmex@ prodigy.net.mx; internet chileabroad.gov.cl/mexico; Ambassador RICARDO NUÑEZ MUÑOZ.

China, People's Republic: Avda San Jerónimo 217B, Del. Alvaro Obregón, 01090 México, DF; tel. (55) 5616-0609; fax (55) 5616-5849; e-mail chinaemb_mx_admin@mfa.gov.cn; internet www .embajadachina.org.mx; Ambassador QIU XIAOQI.

Colombia: Paseo de la Reforma 379, 1° y 5°–6°, Col. Cuauhtémoc, Del. Cuauhtémoc, 06500 México, DF; tel. (55) 5525-0277; fax (55) 5208-2876; e-mail emexico@cancilleria.gov.co; internet mexico .embajada.gov.co; Ambassador JOSÉ GABRIEL ORTIZ ROBLEDO.

Costa Rica: Río Po 113, Col. Cuauhtémoc, Del. Cuauhtémoc, 06500 México, DF; tel. (55) 5525-7764; fax (55) 5511-9240; e-mail embajada@embajada.decostaricaenmexico.org; internet www .embajada.decostaricaenmexico.org; Ambassador GABRIELA JIMÉNEZ CRUZ.

Côte d'Ivoire: Tennyson 67, Col. Polanco, Del. Miguel Hidalgo, 11560 México, DF; tel. (55) 5280-8573; fax (55) 5282-2954; e-mail ambacimex@cotedivoiremx.org; internet cotedivoiremx.org; Ambassador OBOU MARCELLIN ABIE.

Cuba: Presidente Masaryk 554, Col. Polanco, Del. Miguel Hidalgo, 11560 México, DF; tel. (55) 5280-8039; fax (55) 5280-0839; e-mail embajada@embacuba.com.mx; internet www.cubadiplomatica.cu/ mexico; Ambassador DAGOBERTO RODRÍGUEZ BARRERA.

Cyprus: Sierra Gorda 370, Col. Lomas de Chapultepec, Del. Miguel Hidalgo, 11000 México, DF; tel. (55) 5202-7600; fax (55) 5520-2693; e-mail limassol@prodigy.net.mx; internet www.mfa.gov.cy/ embassymexico; Ambassador EVAGORAS VRYONIDES.

Czech Republic: Cuvier 22, esq. Kepler, Col. Nueva Anzures, Del. Miguel Hidalgo, 11590 México, DF; tel. (55) 5531-2777; fax (55) 5531-1837; e-mail mexico@embassy.mzv.cz; internet www.mzv.cz/mexico; Chargé d'affaires a.i. IRENA VALKYOVA.

Denmark: Tres Picos 43, Col. Chapultepec Morales, Del. Miguel Hidalgo, 11580 México, DF; tel. (55) 5255-3405; fax (55) 5545-5797; e-mail mexamb@um.dk; internet www.ambmexicocity.um.dk; Ambassador SUSANNE RUMOHR HÆKKERUP.

Dominican Republic: Prado Sur 755 (entre Monte Blanco y Monte Everest), Col. Lomas de Chapultepec, Del. Miguel Hidalgo, 11000 México, DF; tel. (55) 5540-3841; fax (55) 5520-0779; e-mail embajada@embadom.org.mx; internet www.embadom.org.mx; Ambassador FERNANDO ANTONIO PÉREZ MEMÉN.

Ecuador: Tennyson 217, Col. Polanco, Del. Miguel Hidalgo, 11560 México, DF; tel. (55) 5545-3141; fax (55) 5254-2442; e-mail mecuamex@prodigy.net.mx; Ambassador PATRICIO ALFONSO LÓPEZ ARAUJO.

Egypt: Alejandro Dumas 131, Col. Polanco, Del. Miguel Hidalgo, 11560 México, DF; tel. (55) 5281-0823; fax (55) 5282-1294; e-mail embassy.mexicocity@mfa.gov.eg; internet www.mfa.gov.eg/ Mexico_Emb; Ambassador YASSER MOHAMED AHMED SHABAN.

El Salvador: Temístocles 88, Col. Polanco, Del. Miguel Hidalgo, 11560 México, DF; tel. (55) 5281-5725; fax (55) 5280-0657; e-mail embesmex@webtelmex.net.mx; Ambassador CARLOS ANTONIO ASCENCIO GIRÓN.

Finland: Monte Pelvoux 111, 4°, Col. Lomas de Chapultepec, Del. Miguel Hidalgo, 11000 México, DF; tel. (55) 5540-6036; fax (55) 5540-0114; e-mail finmex@prodigy.net.mx; internet www.finlandia.org .mx; Ambassador ANNE LAMMILA.

France: Campos Elíseos 339, Col. Polanco, Del. Miguel Hidalgo, 11560 México, DF; tel. (55) 9171-9700; fax (55) 9171-9893; e-mail prensa@ambafrance-mx.org; internet www.ambafrance-mx.org; Ambassador ELISABETH BETON DELÈGUE.

Georgia: Blvd de Los Virreyes 610, Col. Lomas de Virreyes, Del. Miguel Hidalgo, CP 11000 México, DF; tel. (55) 5520-0118; fax (55) 5520-0897; e-mail mexico.emb@mfa.gov.ge; Ambassador MALKHAZ MIKELADZE.

Germany: Horacio 1506, Col. Los Morales, Del. Miguel Hidalgo, 11530 México, DF; tel. (55) 5283-2200; fax (55) 5281-2588; e-mail info@mexi.diplo.de; internet www.mexiko.diplo.de; Ambassador EDMUND DUCKWITZ.

Greece: Monte Ararat 615, Col. Lomas de Chapultepec, Del. Miguel Hidalgo, 11010 México, DF; tel. (55) 5520-2070; fax (55) 5520-0948; e-mail grem.mex@mfa.gr; Ambassador POLYXENI STEFANIDOU.

Guatemala: Explanada 1025, Col. Lomas de Chapultepec, Del. Miguel Hidalgo, 11000 México, DF; tel. (55) 5540-7520; fax (55) 5202-1142; e-mail embaguatemx@minex.gob.gt; Ambassador FERNANDO ANDRADE DÍAZ-DURÁN.

Haiti: Sierra Vertientes 840, Col. Lomas de Chapultepec, Del. Miguel Hidalgo, 11000 México, DF; tel. (55) 5557-2065; fax (55) 5395-1654; e-mail ambadh@mail.internet.com.mx; Ambassador MARIE JOSEPH GUY LAMOTHE.

Holy See: Juan Pablo II 118, Col. Guadalupe Inn, Del. Alvaro Obregón, 01020 México, DF; tel. (55) 5663-3999; fax (55) 5663-5308; Apostolic Nuncio Most Rev. CHRISTOPHE PIERRE (Titular Archbishop of Gunela).

Honduras: Alfonso Reyes 220, Col. Condesa, Del. Cuauhtémoc, 06170 México, DF; tel. (55) 5211-5747; fax (55) 5211-5425; e-mail emhonmex@prodigy.net.mx; Ambassador JOSÉ MARIANO CASTILLO MERCADO.

Hungary: Paseo de las Palmas 2005, Col. Lomas de Chapultepec, Del. Miguel Hidalgo, 11000 México, DF; tel. (55) 5596-0523; fax (55) 5596-2378; internet www.mfa.gov.hu/kulkepviselet/MX/hu; Chargé d'affaires a.i. TIBOR ISTVAN KUN.

India: Musset 325, Col. Polanco, Del. Miguel Hidalgo, 11550 México, DF; tel. (55) 5531-1050; fax (55) 5254-2349; e-mail indembmx@ prodigy.net.mx; internet www.indembassy.org; Ambassador SUJAN R. CHINOY.

Indonesia: Julio Verne 27, Col. Polanco, Del. Miguel Hidalgo, 11560 México, DF; tel. (55) 5280-6363; fax (55) 5280-7062; e-mail kbrimex@ prodigy.net.mx; internet mexicocity.kemlu.go.id; Ambassador HAMDANI DJAFAR.

Iran: Paseo de la Reforma 2350, Col. Lomas Altas, Del. Miguel Hidalgo, 11950 México, DF; tel. (55) 9172-2691; fax (55) 9172-2694; e-mail iranembmex@hotmail.com; internet mexicocity.mfa.ir; Ambassador JALAL KALANTARI.

Iraq: Paseo de la Reforma 1875, Col. Lomas de Chapultepec, Del. Miguel Hidalgo, 11000 México, DF; tel. (55) 5596-0933; fax (55) 5596-0254; e-mail mxcemb@iraqfamail.com; Ambassador ALI YASSIN MOHAMMED.

Ireland: Cerrada Blvd Manuel Avila Camacho 76, 3°, Col. Lomas de Chapultepec, Del. Miguel Hidalgo, 11000 México, DF; tel. (55) 5520-5803; fax (55) 5520-5892; e-mail emexicoembassy@dfa.ie; internet www.irishembassy.com.mx; Ambassador SONJA HYLAND.

Israel: Sierra Madre 215, Col. Lomas de Chapultepec, Del. Miguel Hidalgo, 11000 México, DF; tel. (55) 5201-1500; fax (55) 5201-1555; e-mail ambassadorsec@mexico.mfa.gov.il; internet mexico-city.mfa .gov.il; Ambassador RODICA RADIAN-GORDON.

Italy: Paseo de las Palmas 1994, Col. Lomas de Chapultepec, Del. Miguel Hidalgo, 11000 México, DF; tel. (55) 5596-3655; fax (55) 5596-2472; e-mail segreteria.messico@esteri.it; internet www .ambcittadelmessico.esteri.it; Ambassador ALESSANDRO BUSACCA.

Jamaica: Avda Paseo de las Palmas 1340, Col. Lomas de Chapultepec, 11000 México, DF; tel. (55) 5250-6804; fax (55) 5250-6160; e-mail embajadadejamaica@prodigy.net.mx; Ambassador SANDRA GRANT GRIFFITHS.

Japan: Paseo de la Reforma 395, Apdo 5-101, Col. Cuauhtémoc, Del. Cuauhtémoc, 06500 México, DF; tel. (55) 5211-0028; fax (55) 5207-7743; e-mail embjapmx@mail.internet.com.mx; internet www.mx.emb-japan.go.jp; Ambassador SHUICHIRO MEGATA.

Korea, Democratic People's Republic: Calle Halley 12, Col. Anzures, Del. Miguel Hidalgo, 11590 México, DF; tel. (55) 5250-0263; fax (55) 5545-8775; e-mail dpkoreaemb@prodigy.net.mx; Ambassador AN KUN SONG.

Korea, Republic: Lope de Armendáriz 110, Col. Lomas Virreyes, Del. Miguel Hidalgo, 11000 México, DF; tel. (55) 5202-9866; fax (55) 5540-7446; e-mail embcoreamx@mofat.go.kr; internet mex.mofat.go.kr; Ambassador HONG SEONG-HOA.

Kuwait: Paseo de los Tamarindos 98, Col. Bosques de las Lomas, Del. Cuajimalpa, 05120 México, DF; tel. (55) 9177-8400; fax (55) 9177-8412; e-mail embajadakuwaitmx@gmail.com; Ambassador SAMEEH ESSA JOHAR HAYAT.

Lebanon: Julio Verne 8, Col. Polanco, Del. Miguel Hidalgo, 11560 México, DF; tel. (55) 5280-5614; fax (55) 5280-8870; e-mail embalibano@embajadadelibano.org.mx; internet www.embajadadelibano.org.mx; Ambassador HICHAM HAMDAN.

Libya: Horacio 1003, Col. Polanco, Del. Miguel Hidalgo, 11550 México, DF; tel. (55) 5545-5725; fax (55) 5545-5677; e-mail libia.mexico@yahoo.com; Ambassador MUFTAH ALTAYAR.

Malaysia: Sierra Nevada 435, Col. Lomas de Chapultepec, Del. Miguel Hidalgo, 11000 México, DF; tel. (55) 5282-5166; fax (55) 5282-4910; e-mail mwmexico@prodigy.net.mx; Ambassador Dato' JAMAIYAH MOHAMED YUSOF.

Morocco: Paseo de las Palmas 2020, Col. Lomas de Chapultepec, Del. Miguel Hidalgo, 11000 México, DF; tel. (55) 5245-1786; fax (55) 5245-1791; e-mail sifamex@infosel.net.mx; internet www.marruecos.org.mx; Ambassador ABDERRAHMAN LEIBEK.

Netherlands: Edif. Calakmul, 7°, Avda Vasco de Quiroga 3000, Col. Santa Fe, Del. Alvaro Obregón, 01210 México, DF; tel. (55) 1105-6550; fax (55) 5258-8138; e-mail mex-info@minbuza.nl; internet mexico.nlembajada.org; Ambassador COENRAAD HENDRIK ADOLPH HOGEWONING.

New Zealand: Edif. Corporativo Polanco, 4°, Jaime Balmes 8, Col. Los Morales Polanco, Del. Miguel Hidalgo, 11510 México, DF; tel. (55) 5283-9460; fax (55) 5283-9480; e-mail kiwimexico@prodigy.net.mx; internet www.nzembassy.com/mexico; Ambassador CLARE KELLY.

Nicaragua: Fernando Alencastre 136, Col. Lomas de Chapultepec, Del. Miguel Hidalgo, 11000 México, DF; tel. (55) 5540-5625; fax (55) 5520-2270; e-mail embanic@prodigy.net.mx; Ambassador TAMARA HAWKINS DE BRENES.

Nigeria: Diego Fernández de Córdova 125, Col. Lomas Virreyes, Del. Miguel Hidalgo, 11000 México, DF; tel. (55) 5245-1487; fax (55) 5245-0105; e-mail nigembmx@att.net.mx; internet www.embassyofnigeria.com.mx; Ambassador ZHIRI JAMES GANA.

Norway: Avda de los Virreyes 1460, Col. Lomas Virreyes, Del. Miguel Hidalgo, 11000 México, DF; tel. (55) 5540-3486; fax (55) 5202-3019; e-mail emb.mexico@mfa.no; internet www.noruega.org.mx; Ambassador MERETHE NERGAARD.

Pakistan: Hegel 512, Col. Chapultepec Morales, Del. Miguel Hidalgo, 11570 México, DF; tel. (55) 5203-3636; fax (55) 5203-9907; e-mail parepmex@hotmail.com; Ambassador AITZAZ AHMED.

Panama: Sócrates 339, Col. Polanco, Del. Miguel Hidalgo, 11560 México, DF; tel. (55) 5280-7857; fax (55) 5280-7586; e-mail informes@embpanamamexico.com; Ambassador MANUEL RICARDO PÉREZ.

Paraguay: Homero 415, 1°, esq. Hegel, Col. Polanco, Del. Miguel Hidalgo, 11570 México, DF; tel. (55) 5545-0405; fax (55) 5531-9905; e-mail embapar@prodigy.net.mx; Ambassador CARLOS HERIBERTO RIVEROS SALCEDO.

Peru: Paseo de la Reforma 2601, Col. Lomas Reforma, Del. Miguel Hidalgo, 11000 México, DF; tel. (55) 1105-2270; fax (55) 1105-2279; e-mail embaperu@prodigy.net.mx; Ambassador JAVIER EDUARDO LEÓN OLAVARRÍA.

Philippines: Río Rhin 56, Cuauhtémoc, Del. Cuauhtémoc, 06500 México, DF; tel. (55) 5202-8456; fax (55) 5202-8403; e-mail mexico.pi@dfa.gov.ph; Ambassador CATALINO DILEM, Jr.

Poland: Cracovia 40, Col. San Angel, Del. Alvaro Obregón, 01000 México, DF; tel. (55) 5481-2050; fax (55) 5616-7314; e-mail embajadadepolonia@prodigy.net.mx; internet www.meksyk.polemb.net; Ambassador BEATA WOJNA.

Portugal: Avda Alpes 1370, Lomas de Chapultepec, Del. Miguel Hidalgo, 11000 México, DF; tel. (55) 5520-7897; fax (55) 5520-4688; e-mail embpomex@gmail.com; internet embpomex.wordpress.com; Ambassador JOÃO JOSÉ GOMES CAETANO DA SILVA.

Romania: Sófocles 311, Col. Polanco, Del. Miguel Hidalgo, 11560 México, DF; tel. (55) 5280-0197; fax (55) 5280-0343; e-mail secretariat@rumania.org.mx; internet mexico.mae.ro; Ambassador ANA VOICU.

Russia: José Vasconcelos 204, Col. Hipódromo Condesa, Del. Cuauhtémoc, 06140 México, DF; tel. (55) 5273-1305; fax (55) 5273-1545; e-mail embrumex@yandex.ru; internet www.embrumex.org; Ambassador EDUARD MALAYÁN.

Saudi Arabia: Paseo de las Palmas 2075, Col. Lomas de Chapultepec, Del. Miguel Hidalgo, 11000 México, DF; tel. (55) 5596-0173; fax (55) 5020-3160; e-mail saudiemb@prodigy.net.mx; Ambassador HUSSEIN MOHAMMAD ABDULFATAH AL-ASSIRI.

Serbia: Montañas Rocallosas Oeste 515, Col. Lomas de Chapultepec, Del. Miguel Hidalgo, 11000 México, DF; tel. (55) 5520-0524; fax (55) 5520-9927; e-mail embajadaserbia@alestra.net.mx; Ambassador GORAN MESIĆ.

Slovakia: Julio Verne 35, Col. Polanco, Del. Miguel Hidalgo, 11560 México, DF; tel. (55) 5280-6669; fax (55) 5280-6294; e-mail emb.mexico@mzv.sk; internet www.mzv.sk/mexico; Ambassador JAROSLAV BLAŠKO.

South Africa: Edif. Forum, 9°, Andrés Bello 10, Col. Polanco, Del. Miguel Hidalgo, 11560 México, DF; tel. (55) 1100-4970; fax (55) 5282-9259; e-mail safrica@prodigy.net.mx; Ambassador SANDILE NOGXINA.

Spain: Galileo 114, esq. Horacio, Col. Polanco, Del. Miguel Hidalgo, 11550 México, DF; tel. (55) 5282-2271; fax (55) 5282-1520; e-mail emb.mexico@maec.es; internet www.maec.es/embajadas/mexico; Ambassador LUIS FERNÁNDEZ CID DE LAS ALAS PUMARIÑO.

Sweden: Paseo de las Palmas 1375, Col. Lomas de Chapultepec, Del. Miguel Hidalgo, 11000 México, DF; tel. (55) 9178-5010; fax (55) 5540-3253; e-mail suecia@prodigy.net.mx; internet www.suecia.com.mx; Ambassador JÖRGEN HANS PERSSON.

Switzerland: Paseo de las Palmas 405, 11°, Torre Óptima, Col. Lomas de Chapultepec, Del. Miguel Hidalgo, 11000 México, DF; tel. (55) 9178-4370; fax (55) 5520-8685; e-mail vertretung@mex.rep.admin.ch; internet www.eda.admin.ch/mexico; Chargé d'affaires a.i. MIRKO GIULIETTI KNOBLAUCH.

Thailand: Paseo de las Palmas 1610, Col. Lomas de Chapultepec, Del. Miguel Hidalgo, 11000 México, DF; tel. (55) 5540-4551; fax (55) 5540-4817; e-mail thaimex@prodigy.net.mx; internet www.thaiembmexico.co.nr; Ambassador CHIRACHAI PUNKRASIN.

Turkey: Monte Líbano 885, Col. Lomas de Chapultepec, Del. Miguel Hidalgo, 11000 México, DF; tel. (55) 5282-4277; fax (55) 5282-4894; e-mail embajada.mexico@mfa.gov.tr; internet mexico.emb.mfa.gov.tr; Ambassador OGUZ DEMIRALP.

Ukraine: Paseo de la Reforma 730, Col. Lomas de Chapultepec, Del. Miguel Hidalgo, 11000 México, DF; tel. (55) 5282-4085; fax (55) 5282-4768; e-mail emb_mx@mfa.gov.ua; internet www.mfa.gov.ua/mexico; Ambassador RUSLAN SPIRIN.

United Arab Emirates: Paseo de La Reforma 505, Col. Lomas de Chapultepec, Del. Miguel Hidalgo, 11000 México, DF; tel. (55) 5207-0025; fax (55) 5282-4387; e-mail mexico@mofa.gov.ae; Ambassador SAEED RASHAD OBAID SAIF ALZAABI.

United Kingdom: Río Lerma 71, Col. Cuauhtémoc, Del. Cuauhtémoc, 06500 México, DF; tel. (55) 1670-3204; fax (55) 5242-8517; e-mail ukinmex@att.net.mx; internet www.embajadabritanica.com.mx; Ambassador DUNCAN TAYLOR.

USA: Paseo de la Reforma 305, Del. Cuauhtémoc, 06500 México, DF; tel. (55) 5080-2000; fax (55) 5080-2005; internet mexico.usembassy.gov; Ambassador EARL ANTHONY WAYNE.

Uruguay: Hegel 149, 1°, Col. Chapultepec Morales, Del. Miguel Hidalgo, 11560 México, DF; tel. (55) 5531-0880; fax (55) 5545-3342; e-mail uruguaymex@prodigy.net.mx; Ambassador JORGE ALBERTO FERNÁNDEZ.

Venezuela: Schiller 326, Col. Chapultepec Morales, Del. Miguel Hidalgo, 11570 México, DF; tel. (55) 5203-4233; fax (55) 5254-1457; e-mail venezmex@prodigy.net.mx; Ambassador HUGO JOSÉ GARCÍA HERNÁNDEZ.

Viet Nam: Sierra Ventana 255, Col. Lomas de Chapultepec, Del. Miguel Hidalgo, 11000 México, DF; tel. (55) 5540-1632; fax (55) 5540-1612; e-mail vietnam.mx@mofa.gov.vn; internet www.vietnamembassy-mexico.org/vi; Ambassador TUNG LE THANH.

Judicial System

The judicial system is divided into federal and local. The federal judicial system has both ordinary and constitutional jurisdiction, and judicial power is exercised by the Supreme Court of Justice, the Electoral Court, Collegiate and Unitary Circuit Courts and District Courts. The Supreme Court comprises two separate chambers: Civil and Criminal Affairs, and Administrative and Labour Affairs. The Federal Judicature Council is responsible for the administration, surveillance and discipline of the federal judiciary, except for the Supreme Court.

Mexico is divided into 29 judicial circuits. The Circuit Courts may be collegiate, when dealing with the *derecho de amparo* (protection of constitutional rights of an individual), or unitary, when dealing with appeal cases. The Collegiate Circuit Courts comprise three magistrates with residence in 38 cities around the country. The Unitary Circuit Courts comprise one magistrate with residence mostly in the same cities.

Suprema Corte de Justicia de la Nación: Pino Suárez 2, Col. Centro, Del. Cuauhtémoc, 06065 México, DF; tel. (55) 4113-1000; fax (55) 4195-0913; e-mail scjn_presidencia@scjn.gob.mx; internet www .scjn.gob.mx; Pres. and Chief Justice JUAN NEPOMUCENO SILVA MEZA.

President of the First Chamber—Civil and Criminal Affairs: JORGE MARIO PARDO REBOLLEDO.

President of the Second Chamber—Administrative and Labour Affairs: SERGIO ARMANDO VALLS HERNÁNDEZ.

Tribunal Electoral del Poder Judicial de la Federación (TEPJF): Carlota Amero 5000, Col. Culhuacán, Del. Coyoacán, 04480 México, DF; tel. (55) 5728-2300; fax (55) 5728-2400; e-mail contactoweb@te.gob.mx; internet www.te.gob.mx; Pres. JOSÉ ALEJANDRO LUNA RAMOS.

Attorney-General: JESÚS MURILLO KARAM.

Religion

CHRISTIANITY

The Roman Catholic Church

The prevailing religion is Roman Catholicism, but the Church, disestablished in 1857, was for many years, under the Constitution of 1917, subject to state control. For ecclesiastical purposes, Mexico comprises 18 archdioceses, 69 dioceses, five territorial prelatures and two eparchies (both directly subject to the Holy See). According to the 2010 census, some 83% of the population are Roman Catholics.

Bishops' Conference: Conferencia del Episcopado Mexicano (CEM), Edif. S. S. Juan Pablo II, Prolongación Ministerios 26, Col. Tepeyac Insurgentes, Apdo 118-055, 07020 México, DF; tel. (55) 5781-8462; fax (55) 5577-5489; e-mail comunicacion@cem.org.mx; internet www.cem.org.mx; Pres. JOSÉ FRANCISCO ROBLES ORTEGA (Archbishop of Guadalajara); Sec.-Gen. EUGENIO ANDRÉS LIRA RUGARCÍA.

Archbishop of Acapulco: CARLOS GARFIAS MERLOS, Arzobispado, Quebrada 16, Apdo 201, Centro, 39300 Acapulco, Gro; tel. and fax (744) 482-0763; e-mail parroquiasoledadacapulco@hotmail.com; internet arquiaca.org.

Archbishop of Antequera, Oaxaca: JOSÉ LUIS CHÁVEZ BOTELLO, Leona Vicario 109, Plazuela del Carme Alto, Col. Centro, 68000 Oaxaca, Oax.; tel. (951) 516-4822; fax (951) 514-1348; e-mail comunica@arquioax.org; internet arquioax.org.

Archbishop of Chihuahua: CONSTANCIO MIRANDA WECKMANN, Arzobispado, Avda Cuauhtémoc 1828, Apdo 7, Col. Cuauhtémoc, 31020 Chihuahua, Chih.; tel. (614) 410-3202; fax (614) 410-5621; e-mail arzobispado@arquidiocesischihuahua.com.mx; internet arquidiocesischihuahua.com.mx.

Archbishop of Durango: HÉCTOR GONZÁLEZ MARTÍNEZ, Arzobispado, Avda 20 de Noviembre 306, Poniente Centro, Apdo 116, 34000 Durango, Dgo; tel. (618) 811-4242; fax (618) 812-8881; e-mail prensaarquidiocesisdgo@gmail.com; internet arquidiocesisdgo.org.

Archbishop of Guadalajara: Cardinal JOSÉ FRANCISCO ROBLES ORTEGA, Arzobispado, Alfredo R. Plascencia 995, Apdo 61-33, Col. Chapultepec, 44620 Guadalajara, Jal.; tel. (33) 3614-5504; fax (33) 3658-2300; e-mail arzgdl@arquidiocesisgdl.org; internet www .arquidiocesisgdl.org.

Archbishop of Hermosillo: JOSÉ ULISES MACÍAS SALCEDO, Arzobispado, Calle Dr Paliza y Ocampo, Ala Sur de la Catedral, Col. Centenario, 83260 Hermosillo, Son.; tel. (662) 213-2138; fax (662) 213-1327; e-mail arzohmo2@gmail.com; internet arquidiocesishermosillo.org.

Archbishop of Jalapa: HIPÓLITO REYES LARIOS, Arzobispado, Avda Manuel Avila Camacho 73, Apdo 359, Col. Centro, 91000 Jalapa, Ver.; tel. (228) 812-0579; fax (228) 817-5578; e-mail contacto@ arquidiocesisdexalapa.com; internet www.arquidiocesisdexalapa .com.

Archbishop of León: JOSÉ GUADALUPE MARTÍN RÁBAGO, Arzobispado, Pedro Moreno 312, Apdo 108, 37000 León, Gto; tel. (477) 713-2527; fax (477) 713-1286; e-mail episcopo@arquidiocesisdeleon.org; internet arquideleon.org.

Archbishop of Mexico City: Cardinal NORBERTO RIVERA CARRERA, Curia del Arzobispado de México, Durango 90, 5°, Col. Roma, Apdo 24433, 06700 México, DF; tel. (55) 5208-3200; fax (55) 5208-5350;

e-mail arzobisp@arquidiocesismexico.org.mx; internet www .arquidiocesismexico.org.mx.

Archbishop of Monterrey: Cardinal ROGELIO CABRERA LÓPEZ, Zuazua 1100 Sur con Ocampo Centro, Apdo 7, 64000 Monterrey, NL; tel. (81) 1158-2450; fax (81) 1158-2488; e-mail cancilleria@ arquidiocesismty.org; internet www.arquidiocesismty.org.

Archbishop of Morelia: ALBERTO SUÁREZ INDA, Arzobispado, Costado Catedral, Frente Avda Madero, Apdo 17, 58000 Morelia, Mich.; tel. (443) 313-2493; fax (443) 312-0919; e-mail asuarezi@cem.org.mx; internet arquidiocesismorelia.mx.

Archbishop of Puebla de los Angeles: VÍCTOR SÁNCHEZ ESPINOSA, Avda 16 de Septiembre 901, Col. Centro Histórico, 72000 Puebla, Pue.; tel. (222) 232-4591; fax (222) 246-2277; e-mail redessociales@ arquidiocesisdepuebla.mx; internet www.arquidiocesisdepuebla .mx.

Archbishop of San Luis Potosí: JESÚS CARLOS CABRERO ROMERO, Arzobispado, Francisco Madero 300, Apdo 1, Col. Centro, 78000 San Luis Potosí, SLP; tel. (444) 812-4555; fax (444) 812-7979; e-mail arquinet@iglesiapotosina.org; internet www.iglesiapotosina.org.

Archbishop of Tijuana: RAFAEL ROMO MUÑOZ, Arzobispado, Calle Décima y Avda Ocampo 8525, Apdo 226, 22000 Tijuana, BC; tel. (664) 684-8411; fax (664) 684-7683; e-mail obispado@iglesiatijuana.org; internet www.iglesiatijuana.org.

Archbishop of Tlalnepantla: CARLOS AGUIAR RETES, Arzobispado, Avda Juárez 42, Apdo 268, Col. Centro, 54000 Tlalnepantla, Méx.; tel. (55) 5565-3944; fax (55) 5565-2751; e-mail presidente@celam.org; internet www.tierradeenmedio.org.mx.

Archbishop of Tulancingo: DOMINGO DÍAZ MARTÍNEZ, Arzobispado, Plaza de la Constitución, Apdo 14, 43600 Tulancingo, Hgo; tel. (775) 753-1010; e-mail sgamitra@netpac.net.mx; internet arquidiocesisdetulancingo.org.

Archbishop of Tuxtla Gutiérrez: FABIO MARTÍNEZ CASTILLA, Uruguay 500A, Col. El Retiro, Apdo 365, 29040 Tuxtla Gutiérrez, Chis; tel. (961) 604-0644; fax (961) 614-3297; e-mail aguileracruz@ yahoo.com.mx; internet www.arquidiocesisdetuxtla.org.mx.

Archbishop of Yucatán: EMILIO CARLOS BERLIE BELAUNZARÁN, Arzobispado, Calle 58 501, Col. Centro, 97000 Mérida, Yuc.; tel. (999) 924-7777; fax (999) 923-7983; e-mail aryu@prodigy.net.mx; internet www.arquidiocesisdeyucatan.com.mx.

The Anglican Communion

Mexico is divided into five dioceses, which form the Province of the Anglican Church in Mexico, established in 1995.

Bishop of Cuernavaca: JAMES OTTLEY, Minerva 1, Col. Delicias, 62431 Cuernavaca, Mor.; tel. and fax (777) 315-2870; e-mail diocesisdecuernavaca@hotmail.com.

Bishop of Mexico City and Primate of the Anglican Church in Mexico: CARLOS TOUCHÉ PORTER, La Otra Banda 40, Avda San Jerónimo 117, Col. San Ángel, 01000 México, DF; tel. and fax (55) 5616-2205; e-mail diomex@axtel.net; internet www .iglesiaanglicanademexico.org.

Bishop of Northern Mexico: FRANCISCO MANUEL MORENO, Acatlán 102 Oueste, Col. Mitras Centro, 64460 Monterrey, NL; tel. (81) 8333-0922; fax (81) 8348-7362; e-mail diocesisdelnorte@prodigy.net.mx.

Bishop of South-Eastern Mexico: BENITO JUÁREZ MARTÍNEZ, Avda de las Américas 73, Col. Aguacatl, 91130 Jalapa, Ver.; tel. and fax (228) 814-6951; e-mail diocesisdelsureste@prodigy.net.mx.

Bishop of Western Mexico: LINO RODRÍGUEZ-AMARO, Francisco Javier Gamboa 255, Col. Barrera, 45150 Guadalajara, Jal.; tel. (33) 3615-5070; fax (33) 3615-4413; e-mail iamoccidente@prodigy.net.mx.

Other Christian Churches

According to the 2010 census, some 7% of the population are Pentecostal or Evangelical Christians.

Church of Jesus Christ of Latter-Day Saints (Mormons): Mexico City Temple, Avda 510, No 90, Col. San Juan de Aragón, 07950 México, DF; tel. (55) 5003-3734; internet www.lds.org; 314,932 mems (2010).

Iglesia Evangélica Luterana de México: Mina 5808 Poniente, Nuevo Laredo, Tamaulipas; Pres. ENCARNACIÓN ESTRADA; 3,000 mems (2010).

Iglesia Luterana Mexicana: POB 1-034, 44101 Guadalajara, Jal.; tel. (33) 3639-7253; e-mail dtrejocoria@gmail.com; f. 1951; Pres. DANIEL TREJO CORIA; 1,500 mems.

Iglesia Metodista de México, Asociación Religiosa: Miravelle 209, Col. Albert, 03570 México, DF; tel. (55) 5539-3674; e-mail prenapro@iglesia-metodista.org.mx; internet www .iglesia-metodista.org.mx; f. 1873; 55,000 mems; Pres. Rev. RAÚL GARCÍA DE OCHOA; 700 congregations, 25,370 mems (2010); comprises six episcopal areas.

National Baptist Convention of Mexico: Tlalpan 1025A, Col. Américas Unidas, 03610 México, DF; tel. (55) 5539-7720; fax (55) 5539-2302; e-mail comunicacion@cnbm.org.mx; internet www.cnbm .org.mx; f. 1903; Pres. Rev. JOSÉ TRINIDAD BONILLA MORALES; 252,874 mems (2010).

Testigos de Jehová (Jehovah's Witnesses): Avda Jardín 10, Fraccionamiento El Tejocote, 56239 Texcoco, Méx.; tel. (55) 5133-3000; 1.6m. mems (2010).

BAHÁ'Í FAITH

National Spiritual Assembly of the Bahá'ís of Mexico: Emerson 421, Col. Bosque de Chapultpec, 11580 México, DF; tel. (55) 5545-2155; fax (55) 5255-5972; e-mail secretariado@bahai.mx; internet www.bahai.mx; f. 1959; Sec.-Gen. DARYOUSH YALDAEI; mems resident in 1,069 localities.

JUDAISM

According to the 2010 census, the Jewish community numbers 67,476 (less than 1% of the population).

Comité Central de la Comunidad Judía de México: Cofre de Perote 115, Lomas Barrilaco, 11010 México, DF; tel. (55) 5520-9393; fax (55) 5540-3050; e-mail comitecentral@prodigy.net.mx; internet www.tribuna.org.mx; f. 1938; Pres. RAFAEL ZAGA.

The Press

DAILY NEWSPAPERS

México, DF

La Afición: Ignacio Mariscal 23, Apdo 64 bis, Col. Tabacalera, 06030 México, DF; tel. (55) 5140-4900; fax (55) 5546-5852; internet laaficion .milenio.com; f. 1930; sport; Pres. FRANCISCO A. GONZÁLEZ; Exec. Editor CARLOS MARÍN; circ. 85,000.

La Crónica de Hoy: Londres 38, Col. Juárez, 06600 México, DF; tel. and fax (52) 1084-5800; e-mail cronica@cronica.com.mx; internet www.cronica.com.mx; Pres. JORGE KAHWAGI GASTINE; Editorial Dir FRANCISCO BAEZ RODRÍGUEZ.

Diario de México: Chimalpopoca 38, Col. Obrera, Del. Cuauhtémoc, 06800 México, DF; tel. (55) 5442-6526; fax (55) 5442-6520; e-mail info@diariodemexico.com.mx; internet www.diariodemexico .com.mx; f. 1949; morning; Dir-Gen. FEDERICO BRACAMONTES BAZ; Editorial Dir DANIELA NUÑO; circ. 76,000.

Diario Oficial de la Federación: Río Amazonas 62, Col. Cuauhtémoc, 06500 México, DF; tel. (55) 5093-3200; e-mail dof@segob.gob .mx; internet www.dof.gob.mx; f. 1867; govt gazette; Dir-Gen. ALEJANDRO LÓPEZ GONZÁLEZ.

El Economista: Avda Coyoacán 515, Col. del Valle, 03100 México, DF; tel. (55) 5237-0766; fax (55) 5687-3821; e-mail internet@ eleconomista.com.mx; internet eleconomista.com.mx; f. 1988; financial; Pres. JORGE NACER GOBERA; Editor-in-Chief LUIS MIGUEL GONZÁLEZ; circ. 37,448.

Esto: Guillermo Prieto 7, 1°, Col. San Rafael, Del. Cuauhtémoc, 06470 México, DF; tel. and fax (55) 5566-1511; fax (55) 5591-0866; e-mail salvador@esto.com.mx; internet www.oem.com.mx/esto; f. 1941; publ. by Organización Editorial Mexicana; morning; sport; Dir SALVADOR AGUILERA GONZÁLEZ; Editor-in-Chief CARLOS GABINO CU UC; circ. 400,000, Mon. 450,000.

Excélsior: Bucareli 1, Apdo 120 bis, Col. Centro, 06600 México, DF; tel. (55) 5128-3000; fax (55) 5566-0223; e-mail foro@excelsior.com .mx; internet www.excelsior.com.mx; f. 1917; morning; ind; Pres. OLEGARIO VÁZQUEX RAÑA; Editorial Dir PASCAL BELTRÁN DEL RÍO; circ. 200,000.

El Financiero: Lago Bolsena 176, Col. Anáhuac (Pensil), entre Lago Peypus y Lago Onega, 11320 México, DF; tel. (55) 5227-7600; fax (55) 5254-6427; e-mail contacto@elfinanciero.com.mx; internet www .elfinanciero.com.mx; f. 1981; financial; Dir-Gen. MARÍA DEL PILAR ESTANDÍA GONZÁLEZ LUNA; Editor-Gen. ENRIQUE QUINTANA; circ. 119,000.

La Jornada: Avda Cuauhtémoc 1236, Col. Santa Cruz Atoyac, Del. Benito Juárez, 03310 México, DF; tel. (55) 9183-0300; internet www .jornada.unam.mx; f. 1984; morning; Dir-Gen. CARMEN LIRA SAADE; Gen. Man. JORGE MARTÍNEZ JIMÉNEZ; circ. 86,275.

Milenio Diario: México, DF; tel. (55) 5140-4900; internet www .milenio.com; publishes Mexico City and regional edns, and a weekly news magazine, *Milenio Semanal*; Pres. FRANCISCO A. GONZÁLEZ; Dir-Gen. FRANCISCO D. GONZÁLEZ A.

Ovaciones: Lago Zirahuén 279, 20°, Col. Anáhuac, 11320 México, DF; tel. (55) 5328-0700; fax (55) 5260-2219; e-mail bjonofre@ova.com .mx; internet www.ovaciones.com; f. 1947; morning and evening editions; Pres. and Dir-Gen. MAURICIO VÁZQUEZ RAMOS; circ. 130,000; evening circ. 100,000.

La Prensa: Basilio Vadillo 40, Col. Tabacalera, 06030 México, DF; tel. (55) 5228-9977; fax (55) 5521-8209; e-mail oemenlinea@oem.com .mx; internet www.oem.com.mx/laprensa; f. 1928; publ. by Organización Editorial Mexicana; morning; Dir-Gen. MAURICIO ORTEGA CAMBEROS; Editor-in-Chief JESÚS SÁNCHEZ RAMÍREZ; circ. 270,000.

Reforma: Avda México Coyoacán 40, Col. Santa Cruz Atoyac, 03310 México, DF; tel. (55) 5628-7100; fax (55) 5628-7188; internet www .reforma.com; f. 1993; morning; Pres. and Dir-Gen. ALEJANDRO JUNCO DE LA VEGA ELIZONDO; Editorial Dir LÁZARO RÍOS; circ. 94,000.

El Sol de México: Guillermo Prieto 7, 20°, Col. San Rafael, 06470 México, DF; tel. (55) 5566-1511; fax (55) 5535-5560; e-mail enlinea@ elsoldemexico.com.mx; internet www.oem.com.mx/elsoldemexico; f. 1965; publ. by Organización Editorial Mexicana; morning and midday; Dir-Gen. RUBÉN PÉREZ GARCÍA; circ. 76,000.

El Universal: Bucareli 8, Apdo 909, Col. Centro, Del. Cuauhtémoc, 06040 México, DF; tel. (55) 5709-1313; fax (55) 5510-1269; e-mail rdirgral@eluniversal.com.mx; internet www.eluniversal.com.mx; f. 1916; morning; ind.; centre-left; Pres. JUAN FRANCISCO EALY ORTIZ; Editorial Dir ROBERTO ROCK; circ. 165,629, Sun. 181,615.

Unomásuno: Gabino Barreda 86, Col. San Rafael, México, DF; tel. (55) 1055-5500; fax (55) 5598-8821; e-mail cduran@servidor.unam .mx; internet www.unomasuno.com.mx; f. 1977; morning; left-wing; Pres. NAIM LIBIEN KAUI; circ. 40,000.

PROVINCIAL DAILY NEWSPAPERS

Baja California

El Sol de Tijuana: Rufino Tamayo 4, Zona del Río, 22320 Tijuana, BC; tel. (664) 634-3232; fax (664) 634-2234; e-mail jesparza@ elsoldetijuana.com.mx; internet www.oem.com.mx/elsoldetijuana; f. 1989; publ. by Organización Editorial Mexicana; morning; Dir-Gen. ENRIQUE SÁNCHEZ DÍAZ; Editor-in-Chief JOSUÉ SANTIAGO EVES ZAMARRIPA; circ. 50,000.

La Voz de la Frontera: Avda Francisco I. Madero 1545, Col. Nueva, Apdo 946, 21100 Mexicali, BC; tel. (686) 533-4545; fax (686) 552-4243; e-mail ramondiaz@lavozdelafrontera.com.mx; internet www .oem.com.mx/lavozdelafrontera; f. 1964; morning; publ. by Organización Editorial Mexicana; Dir-Gen. FRANCISCO EDGARDO LEAL CORRALES; Dir JUAN GREGORIO AVILÉS TARÍN; circ. 65,000.

Chihuahua

El Diario: Publicaciones Paso del Norte, Avda Paseo Triunfo de la República 3505, Zona Pronaf, 32310 Ciudad Juárez, Chih.; tel. (656) 629-6900; e-mail rgallegos@redaccion.diario.com.mx; internet www .diario.com.mx; f. 1976; Pres. OSVALDO RODRÍGUEZ BORUNDA; Editor ROCÍO GALLEGOS.

El Heraldo de Chihuahua: Avda Universidad 2507, Apdo 1515, 31240 Chihuahua, Chih.; tel. (614) 432-3800; fax (614) 413-9339; e-mail heraldo@elheraldodechihuahua.com.mx; internet www.oem .com.mx/elheraldodechihuahua; f. 1927; publ. by Organización Editorial Mexicana; morning; Dir Dr JAVIER H. CONTRERAS OROZCO; Editor ROBERTO ALVARADO GATES; circ. 27,520, Sun. 31,223.

El Mexicano: Ramón Corona y Galeana 301, 32000 Ciudad Juárez, Chih.; e-mail publicidad@periodicoelmexicano.com.mx; internet www.oem.com.mx/elmexicano; f. 1959; publ. by Organización Editorial Mexicana; morning; Dir RAFAEL NAVARRO BARRÓN; Editor-in-Chief JAIME SALVADOR NÚÑEZ ANGEL; circ. 80,000.

Coahuila

El Siglo de Torreón: Avda Matamoros 1056 Poniente, Col. Centro, 27000 Torreón, Coah.; tel. (871) 759-1200; e-mail cartas@ elsiglodetorreon.com.mx; internet www.elsiglodetorreon.com.mx; f. 1922; morning; Editor JAVIER GARZA RAMOS; circ. 38,611, Sun. 38,526.

Vanguardia: Blvd Venustiano Carranza 1918, esq. con Chiapas, República Oriente, 25280 Saltillo, Coah.; tel. (844) 450-1000; e-mail hola@vanguardia.com.mx; internet www.vanguardia.com.mx; Editorial Dir ARMANDO CASTILLA GALINDO.

Colima

Diario de Colima: Avda 20 de Noviembre 580, 28060 Colima, Col.; tel. (312) 312-5688; internet www.diariodecolima.com; f. 1953; Dir-Gen. HÉCTOR SÁNCHEZ DE LA MADRID; Editorial Dir GLENDA LIBIER MADRIGAL TRUJILLO.

Guanajuato

Correo de Guanajuato: Carreterra Guanajuato–Juventino Rosas Km 9.5, Col. Carbonera, Apdo 32, 36250 Guanajuato, Gto; tel. (477) 733-1253; fax (477) 733-0057; e-mail correo@correo-gto.com.mx; internet www.periodicocorreo.com.mx; Dir-Gen. PABLO VILLANUEVA MARTÍNEZ; Editorial Dir MARTHA CELIA CAMACHO LEDESMA.

El Sol de Salamanca: Faja de Oro 800, 36700 Salamanca, Gto; tel. (464) 647-0144; e-mail publicidad@elsoldesalamanca.com.mx; internet www.oem.com.mx/elsoldesalamanca; publ. by Organización Editorial Mexicana; Dir-Gen. ALEJANDRO HERRERA SÁNCHEZ; Editor-in-Chief JORGE CAUDILLO ELÍAS.

Guerrero

Novedades de Acapulco: Avda Costera Miguel Aléman 258, Fraccionamiento Hornos, 39355 Acapulco, Gro; tel. (744) 485-1155; e-mail informa@aca-novenet.com.mx; internet www.novedadesacapulco.mx; f. 1969; daily; Editorial Dir MARIO BUSTOS GARCÍA.

Jalisco

El Informador: Independencia 300, Apdo 3 bis, 44100 Guadalajara, Jal.; tel. (33) 3678-7700; e-mail sistemas@informador.com.mx; internet www.informador.com.mx; f. 1917; morning; Editor CARLOS ALVAREZ DEL CASTILLO; circ. 50,000.

El Occidental: Calzada Independencia Sur 324, Apdo 1-699, 44100 Guadalajara, Jal.; tel. (33) 3613-0690; fax (33) 3613-6796; e-mail publicidad@eloccidental.com.mx; internet www.oem.com.mx/eloccidental; f. 1942; publ. by Organización Editorial Mexicana; morning; Dir JAVIER VALLE CHÁVEZ; Editor ANSELMO EDUARDO VÁZQUEZ M.; circ. 49,400.

México

ABC: Avda Hidalgo Oriente 1337, Centro Comercial, Col. Ferrocarriles Nacionales, 50070 Toluca, Méx.; tel. (722) 217-9800; fax (722) 217-8402; e-mail redaccion@abctoluca.com.mx; internet www.miled.com; f. 1984; morning; Pres. and Editor MILED LIBIEN KAUI; circ. 65,000.

El Heraldo de Toluca: Salvador Díaz Mirón 700, Col. Sánchez Colín, 50150 Toluca, Méx.; tel. (722) 217-4913; fax (722) 212-3542; e-mail redaccion@heraldotoluca.com.mx; internet www.heraldotoluca.com.mx; f. 1955; morning; Editor JORGE MENA GARCÍA; circ. 90,000.

Portal–Diario de Toluca: Sebastián Lerdo de Tejada Poniente 864, esq. Agustín Millán, Col. Electricistas Locales, 50040 Toluca, Méx.; tel. (722) 214-5477; fax (722) 214-5463; e-mail portal@portaldigital.com.mx; internet diarioportal.com; f. 1980; morning; Dir-Gen. ESTEBAN RIVERA RIVERA; Editorial Dir FELIPE GONZÁLEZ LÓPEZ; circ. 22,200.

El Sol de Toluca: Santos Degollado 105, Apdo 54, Col. Centro, 50050 Toluca, Méx.; tel. (722) 214-7077; fax (722) 215-2564; e-mail publicidad@elsoldetoluca.com.mx; internet www.oem.com.mx/elsoldetoluca; f. 1947; publ. by Organización Editorial Mexicana; morning; Dir ALEJANDRA CORDERO CASAS; Editor-in-Chief RODRIGO MIRANDA TORRES; circ. 42,000.

Michoacán

La Voz de Michoacán: Blvd del Periodismo 1270, Col. Arriaga Rivera, Apdo 121, 58190 Morelia, Mich.; tel. (443) 327-5600; fax (443) 327-3728; e-mail redaccilavoz@voznet.com.mx; internet www.vozdemichoacan.com.mx; f. 1948; morning; Dir-Gen. MIGUEL MEDINA ROBLES; circ. 50,000.

Morelos

El Diario de Morelos: Avda Morelos Sur 132, Col. Las Palmas, 62050 Cuernavaca, Mor.; tel. (777) 362-0220; fax (777) 362-0225; e-mail redaccion@diariodemorelos.com; internet www.diariodemorelos.com; f. 1978; morning; Propr Grupo BRACA de Comunicación; Pres. MIGUEL ANGEL BRACAMONTES BAZ; Editor-in-Chief MIRIAM ESTRADA DORANTES; circ. 35,000.

Nayarit

Meridiano de Nayarit: Independencia 335, Fracc. Las Aves, Tepic, Nay.; tel. (311) 210-3211; e-mail ventas@meridiano.com.mx; internet meridiano.nnc.mx; f. 1942; morning; Dir EMMANUEL NUÑEZ GARCÍA; circ. 60,000.

Nuevo León

ABC: Platón Sánchez Sur 411, 64000 Monterrey, NL; tel. (81) 8344-2510; fax (81) 8344-2666; e-mail ventas@periodicoabc.mx; internet www.periodicoabc.mx; f. 1985; morning; Dir-Gen. GONZALO ESTRADO TORRES; Editorial Dir REYNALDO MÁRQUEZ; circ. 40,000, Sun. 45,000.

El Norte: Washington 629 Oeste, Apdo 186, 64000 Monterrey, NL; tel. (81) 8150-8100; fax (81) 8343-2476; internet www.elnorte.com; f. 1938; morning; Man. Dir ALEJANDRO JUNCO DE LA VEGA; Editorial Dir MARTHA ALICIA TREVIÑO; circ. 133,872, Sun. 154,951.

El Porvenir: Galeana Sur 344, entre Washington y 5 de Mayo, Col. Centro, Apdo 218, 64000 Monterrey, NL; tel. (81) 8345-4080; fax (81) 8345-7795; e-mail editorial.elporvenir@prodigy.net.mx; internet www.elporvenir.com.mx; f. 1919; morning; Dir-Gen. JOSÉ GERARDO CANTÚ ESCALANTE; Editorial Dir JOSÉ MANUEL RODRÍGUEZ ARROYO; circ. 75,000.

Oaxaca

El Imparcial: Armenta y López 312, Apdo 322, 68000 Oaxaca, Oax.; tel. (951) 516-2812; fax (951) 514-7020; e-mail subdireccion@imparcialenlinea.com; internet www.imparcialenlinea.com; f. 1951; morning; Dir-Gen. BENJAMÍN FERNÁNDEZ PICHARDO; circ. 17,000, Sun. 20,000.

Puebla

La Opinión: 3 Oriente 1207, Barrio del Analco, 238 Puebla, Pue.; tel. (222) 246-4358; fax (222) 232-7772; e-mail director@opinion.com.mx; internet www.opinion.com.mx; f. 1924; morning; Dir-Gen. OSCAR LÓPEZ MORALES; Editor-in-Chief HUGO SÁNCHEZ IZQUIERDO; circ. 40,000.

El Sol de Puebla: Avda 3 Oriente 201, Col. Centro, 72000 Puebla, Pue.; tel. (222) 514-3300; fax (222) 246-0869; e-mail elsoldepuebla@elsoldepuebla.com.mx; internet www.oem.com.mx/elsoldepuebla; f. 1944; publ. by Organización Editorial Mexicana; morning; Dir SERAFÍN SALAZAR ARELLANO; Editor RAMÓN DOMÍNGUEZ SÁNCHEZ; circ. 67,000.

San Luis Potosí

El Heraldo: Villerías 305, 78000 San Luis Potosí, SLP; tel. (444) 812-3312; fax (444) 812-2081; e-mail redaccion@elheraldoslp.com.mx; internet www.elheraldoslp.com.mx; f. 1954; morning; Dir-Gen. ALEJANDRO VILLASANA MENA; Editor AURELIO VENTURA FLORENCIO; circ. 60,620.

Pulso: Galeana 485, Centro Histórico, 78000 San Luis Potosí, SLP; tel. (444) 812-7575; fax (444) 812-3525; internet www.pulsoslp.com.mx; f. 1988; morning; Dir-Gen. PABLO VALLADARES GARCÍA; circ. 60,000.

El Sol de San Luis: Avda Universidad 565, Apdo 342, 78000 San Luis Potosí, SLP; tel. and fax (444) 812-4412; internet www.oem.com.mx/elsoldesanluis; f. 1952; publ. by Organización Editorial Mexicana; morning; Dir JOSÉ ANGEL MARTÍNEZ LIMÓN; Editor-in-Chief RAFAEL RUIZ RANGEL; circ. 60,000.

Sinaloa

El Debate de Culiacán: Madero 556 Poniente, 80000 Culiacán, Sin.; tel. (667) 716-6353; fax (667) 715-7131; e-mail andrea.miranda@debate.com.mx; internet www.debate.com.mx; f. 1972; morning; Dir ROSARIO I. OROPEZA; Editor ANDREA MIRANDA; circ. 23,603, Sun. 23,838.

Noroeste Culiacán: Grupo Periódicos Noroeste, Angel Flores 282 Oeste, Apdo 90, 80000 Culiacán, Sin.; tel. (667) 759-8100; fax (667) 712-8006; e-mail direccion@noroeste.com.mx; internet www.noroeste.com.mx; f. 1973; morning; Dir-Gen. ADRIÁN LÓPEZ ORTIZ; Editor GUILLERMINA GARCÍA NEVARES; circ. 35,000.

El Sol de Sinaloa: Blvd Gabriel Leyva Lozano y Corona 320, Apdo 412, 80000 Culiacán, Sin.; tel. (667) 713-1621; fax (667) 713-1800; e-mail publicidad@elsoldesinaloa.com.mx; internet www.elsoldesinaloa.com.mx; f. 1956; publ. by Organización Editorial Mexicana; morning; Dir JAVIER LÓPEZ LÓPEZ; Editor-in-Chief ARNOLDO ORTEGA MOLINA; circ. 30,000.

Sonora

Expreso: Blvd Abelardo L. Rodríguez 16, Col. San Benito, 83190 Hermosillo, Son.; tel. (662) 108-3000; fax (662) 108-3006; e-mail romandia@expreso.com.mx; internet www.expreso.com.mx; f. 2005; Dir-Gen. LUIS FELIPE ROMANDÍA CACHO; Editor CONRADO QUEZADA RODRÍGUEZ; circ. 17,000, Sun. 18,000.

El Imparcial: Sufragio Efectivo y Mina 71, Col. Centro, Apdo 66, 83000 Hermosillo, Son.; tel. (662) 259-4700; fax (662) 217-4483; e-mail lector@elimparcial.com; internet www.elimparcial.com; f. 1937; morning; Pres. and Dir-Gen. JUAN F. HEALY; Editor LOURDES LUGO; circ. 32,083, Sun. 32,444.

Tabasco

Tabasco Hoy: Avda de los Ríos 206, Col. Tabasco 2000, 86035 Villahermosa, Tab.; tel. (993) 316-2135; internet www.tabascohoy.com.mx; f. 1987; morning; Dir-Gen. MIGUEL CANTÓN ZETINA; Editorial Dir HÉCTOR TAPIA MARTÍNEZ DE ESCOBAR; circ. 50,000.

Tamaulipas

El Bravo: Morelos y Primera 129, Apdo 483, 87300 Matamoros, Tamps; tel. (871) 816-0100; fax (871) 816-2007; e-mail ventas@elbravo.com.mx; internet www.elbravo.com.mx; f. 1951; morning; Dir-Gen. JOSÉ CARRETERO BALBOA; Editorial Dir JESÚS CRUZ MEDRANO; circ. 60,000.

El Diario de Nuevo Laredo: González 2409, Apdo 101, 88000 Nuevo Laredo, Tamps; tel. (867) 712-8444; fax (867) 712-8221; e-mail publicidad@diario.net; internet www.diario.net; f. 1948; morning; Dir-Gen. RUPERTO VILLARREAL MONTEMAYOR; Editor MARCO GUILLERMO VILLARREAL MARROQUÍN; circ. 68,130, Sun. 73,495.

El Mañana de Nuevo Laredo: Juárez y Perú, Col. Juárez, Nuevo Laredo, Tamps; tel. (867) 711-9900; fax (867) 715-0405; e-mail daniel.rosas@elmanana.com.mx; internet www.elmanana.com.mx; f. 1932; morning; Pres. RAMÓN CANTÚ DEÁNDAR; Editor NINFA CANTÚ DEÁNDAR; circ. 16,473, Sun. 20,957.

El Mañana de Reynosa: Calle Matías Canales 504, Apdo 14, Col. Ribereña, 88620 Ciudad Reynosa, Tamps; tel. (899) 921-9950; fax (899) 924-9348; internet www.elmanana.com; f. 1949; morning; Dir JAVIER RAMÍREZ NAVA; Editor ERASMO SALINAS PÉREZ; circ. 52,000.

Prensa de Reynosa: Calle Matamoros y González Ortega, Zona Centro, 88500 Reynosa, Tamps; tel. (899) 922-0299; fax (899) 922-2412; e-mail prensa_88500@yahoo.com; internet laprensa.mx; f. 1963; morning; Dir-Gen. and Editor FÉLIX GARZA ELIZONDO; circ. 60,000.

El Sol de Tampico: Altamira 311 Poniente, Apdo 434, 89000 Tampico, Tamps; tel. (833) 212-1067; fax (833) 212-6821; e-mail publicidad@elsoldetampico.com.mx; internet www.oem.com.mx/elsoldetampico; f. 1950; publ. by Organización Editorial Mexicana; morning; Dir-Gen. AGUSTÍN F. JIMÉNEZ HERNÁNDEZ; Editor-in-Chief MARIO ALBERTO FERNÁNDEZ AVALOS; circ. 77,000.

Veracruz

Diario del Istmo: Avda Hidalgo 1115, Col. Centro, 96400 Coatzacoalcos, Ver.; tel. (921) 211-8000; e-mail info@istmo.com.mx; internet www.diariodelistmo.com; f. 1979; morning; Dir-Gen. HÉCTOR ROBLES BARAJAS; Editor MIGUEL EDUARDO JIMÉNEZ; circ. 64,600.

El Dictamen: Avda Arista 285, esq. 16 de Septiembre, Fracc. Faros, 91709 Veracruz, Ver.; tel. (229) 931-1745; fax (229) 931-5804; e-mail owar@eldictamen.org; internet www.eldictamen.mx; f. 1898; morning; Pres. BERTHA ROSALIA MALPICA DE AHUED; circ. 25,000, Sun. 28,000.

La Opinión: Poza Rica de Hidalgo, Ver.; e-mail publicidad@laopinion.com.mx; internet www.laopinion.com.mx; Dir RAÚL GIBB.

Yucatán

Por Esto!: Calle 60, No 576 entre 73 y 71, 97000 Mérida, Yuc.; tel. (999) 24-7613; fax (999) 28-6514; e-mail redaccion@poresto.net; internet www.poresto.net; f. 1991; morning; Dir-Gen. MARIO RENATO MENÉNDEZ RODRÍGUEZ; circ. 26,985, Sun. 28,727.

Zacatecas

Imagen: Calzada Revolución 24, Col. Tierra y Libertad, 98615 Guadalupe, Zac.; tel. and fax (492) 923-8898; e-mail buzon@imagenzac.com.mx; internet www.imagenzac.com.mx; Dir-Gen. LUIS ENRIQUE MERCADO SÁNCHEZ; Editorial Dir MARÍA DEL CARMEN SALAZAR.

SELECTED WEEKLY NEWSPAPERS

El Heraldo del Bajío: Hermanos Aldama 222, Apdo 299, Zona Centro, 37000 León, Gto; tel. (477) 719-8800; e-mail heraldo@el-heraldo-bajio.com.mx; internet heraldodelbajio.com; f. 1957; Pres. and Dir-Gen. LEÓN MAURICIO BERCÚN LÓPEZ; circ. 85,000.

Zeta: Avda las Américas 4633, Fraccionamiento El Paraíso, La Mesa, 22440 Tijuana, BC; tel. (664) 681-6913; fax (664) 621-0065; e-mail asistente@zetatijuana.com; internet www.zetatijuana.com; f. 1980; news magazine; Editor ROSARIO MOSSO CASTRO.

SELECTED PERIODICALS

Boletín Industrial: Luis Khune 55-B, Col. Las Águilas, 01710 México, DF; tel. (55) 5337-2200; fax (55) 5337-2222; e-mail ventas@boletinindustrial.com; internet www.boletinindustrial.com; f. 1983; publ. by Editorial Nova SA de CV; monthly; Pres. and Editor HUMBERTO VALADÉS DÍAZ; circ. 37,100.

Casas y Gente: Tapachula 31, Col. Roma, 06700 México, DF; tel. (55) 5286-7794; fax (55) 5211-7112; e-mail informac@casasgente.com; internet www.casasgente.com; 10 a year; interior design; Dir-Gen. ANNE SÁNCHEZ OSORIO; Editor DONATELLA LOCKHART.

Contenido: Darwin 101, Col. Anzures, 11590 México, DF; tel. (55) 5531-3162; fax (55) 5545-7478; e-mail contenido@contenido.com.mx; internet www.contenido.com.mx; f. 1963; monthly; popular appeal; Editor-in-Chief JOSÉ ANTONIO OLVERA; circ. 124,190.

Cosmopolitan México: Vasco de Quiroga 2000, Col. Santa Fe, Del. Alvaro Obregón, 01210 México, DF; tel. (55) 5261-2600; fax (55) 5261-2704; internet www.cosmoenespanol.com; f. 1973; fortnightly; women's magazine; Publr KATY GARCÍA LAU; Editor ANA VICTORIA TACHÉ BATRES; circ. 300,000.

Expansión: Avda Constituyentes 956, Col. Lomas Altas, 11950 México, DF; tel. and fax (55) 9177-4100; e-mail adortega@expansion.com.mx; internet www.expansion.com.mx; fortnightly; business and financial; Editor ADOLFO ORTEGA; circ. 54,000.

Fama: Avda Eugenio Garza Sada 2245 Sur, Col. Roma, Apdo 3128, 64700 Monterrey, NL; tel. (81) 8359-2525; internet www.famaweb.com; fortnightly; show business; Pres. JESÚS D. GONZÁLEZ; Dir-Gen. RAÚL MARTÍNEZ GONZÁLEZ; circ. 350,000.

Forbes (Mexico): Montes Urales 754, Reforma Lomas, 11000 México, DF; tel. (55) 5520-0044; e-mail contacto@forbes.com.mx; internet www.forbes.com.mx; Editor VIRIDIANA MENDOZA ESCAMILLA.

Fortuna: Avda Río Churubusco 590, Col. del Carmen, Del. Coyoacán, 04100 México, DF; tel. (55) 5554-9194; e-mail info@revistafortuna.com.mx; internet www.revistafortuna.com.mx; business; monthly; Dir CLAUDIA VILLEGAS.

Gaceta Médica de México: Academia Nacional de Medicina, Unidad de Congresos del Centro Médico Nacional Siglo XXI, Bloque B, Avda Cuauhtémoc 330, Col. Doctores, 06725 México, DF; tel. (55) 5578-2044; fax (55) 5578-4271; e-mail medigraphic@medigraphic.com; internet www.medigraphic.com; f. 1864; every 2 months; journal of the Academia Nacional de Medicina de México; Editor ALFREDO ULLOA AGUIRRE; circ. 20,000.

Kena Mensual: Río Balsas 101, Col. Cuauhtémoc, 06500 México, DF; tel. (55) 5442-9600; e-mail ginaum@grupoarmonia.com.mx; internet kena.com; f. 1977; fortnightly; women's interest; Editor GINA URETA; circ. 80,000.

Manufactura: Avda Chapultepec 230, esq. Córdoba, Col. Roma Norte, Del. Cuauhtemoc, México, DF; tel. (55) 9177-4369; e-mail mramo@expansion.com.mx; internet www.manufactura.mx; f. 1994; monthly; industrial; Editor-Gen. MILDRED RAMO; circ. 30,000.

Marie Claire: Editorial Televisa, SA de CV, Avda Vasco de Quiroga 2000, Edif. E, 3°, Col. Santa Fe, 01210 México, DF; tel. (55) 5261-2706; fax (55) 5261-2733; e-mail gagrantb@televisa.com.mx; internet www.marieclaire.com; f. 1990; monthly; women's interest; Editor ARIADNE GRANT; circ. 145,000.

Men's Health: Avda Vasco de Quiroga 2000, Col. Santa Fe, Del. Alvaro Obregón, 01210 México, DF; tel. (55) 5265-0990; fax (55) 5261-2733; internet www.menshealthlatam.com; f. 1994; monthly; health; Editor JUAN ANTONIO SEMPERE; circ. 130,000.

Muy Interesante: Vasco de Quiroga 2000, Col. Santa Fe, Del. Alvaro Obregón, 01210 México, DF; tel. (55) 5261-2600; fax (55) 5261-2707; e-mail muyinteresante@televisa.com.mx; internet www.muyinteresante.com.mx; f. 1984; monthly; publ. by Editorial Televisa; scientific devt; Dir FRANCISCO VILLASEÑOR; circ. 250,000.

Negocios y Bancos: Insurgentes Sur 1442, Apdo 2, Col. Actpan, Del. Benito Juárez, 03230 México, DF; tel. (55) 5524-0871; fax (55) 5512-9411; e-mail negociosybancos@yahoo.com.mx; internet www.revistanegociosybancos.com; f. 1951; fortnightly; business, economics; Dir SALVADOR MÁRQUEZ SANDÍN; circ. 10,000.

Nexos: Mazatlán 119, Col. Condesa, Del. Cuauhtémoc, 06140 México, DF; tel. (55) 5241-2510; fax (55) 5241-6930; e-mail bortigoza@nexos.com.mx; internet www.nexos.com.mx; f. 1978; current affairs; monthly; Dir HÉCTOR AGUILAR CAMÍN.

Proceso: Fresas 13, Col. del Valle, 03100 México, DF; tel. (55) 5636-2028; e-mail buzon@proceso.com.mx; internet www.proceso.com.mx; f. 1976; weekly; news analysis; Dir RAFAEL RODRÍGUEZ CASTAÑEDA; circ. 98,784.

Quién: Avda Constituyentes 956, Col. Lomas Altas, CP 11950, México, DF; tel. (55) 9177-4342; e-mail quien.com@expansion.com.mx; internet www.quien.com; fortnightly; celebrity news, TV, radio, films; Publr ADRIÁN VILLALBA; Editor LUIS NEREO BUENO.

La Revista Peninsular: Calle 35, 489 x 52 y 54, Zona Centro, Mérida, Yuc.; tel. and fax (999) 926-3014; e-mail direccion@larevista.com.mx; internet www.larevista.com.mx; f. 1988; weekly; news and politics; Dir-Gen. RODRIGO MENÉNDEZ CÁMARA; Editor HUMBERTO ACEVEDO MANZANILLA.

Selecciones del Reader's Digest: Avda Lomas de Sotelo 1102, Col. Loma Hermosa, Del. Miguel Hidalgo, 11200 México, DF; tel. (55) 5351-2500; fax (55) 5395-6691; e-mail servicio.clientes@rd.com; internet mx.selecciones.com; f. 1940; monthly; Editor AUDÓN CORIA; circ. 611,660.

Siempre: Vallarta 20, Col. Tabacalera, 06030 México, DF; tel. and fax (55) 5566-9355; e-mail suscripciones@siempre.com.mx; internet www.siempre.com.mx; f. 1953; weekly; left of centre; Dir BEATRIZ PAGÉS REBOLLAR DE NIETO; Editor ENRIQUE MONTES GARCÍA; circ. 100,000.

Tiempo Libre: Holbein 75 bis, Col. Nochebuena Mixcoac, Del. Benito Juárez, 03720 México, DF; tel. (55) 5611-2884; fax (55) 5611-3982; e-mail buzon@tiempolibre.com.mx; internet www.tiempolibre.com.mx; f. 1980; weekly; entertainment guide; Dir JUAN ALBERTO BECERRA; Editor ALICIA LABRA GÓMEZ; circ. 95,000.

Tú: Vasco de Quiroga 2000, Col. Santa Fe, Del. Alvaro Obregón, 01210 México, DF; tel. (55) 5261-2600; fax (55) 5261-2730; e-mail tu@editorial.televisa.com.mx; internet www.tuenlinea.com; f. 1980; monthly; teenage; Editor MARÍA ANTONIETA SALAMANCA; circ. 250,000.

TV y Novelas: Vasco de Quiroga 2000, Col. Santa Fe, Del. Alvaro Obregón, 01210 México, DF; tel. (55) 5261-2600; fax (55) 5261-2704; internet www.tvynovelas.com; f. 1982; weekly; television guide and short stories; Editor ARMANDO GALLEGOS; circ. 460,000.

Vanidades: Vasco de Quiroga 2000, Col. Santa Fe, Del. Alvaro Obregón, 01210 México, DF; tel. (55) 5261-2600; fax (55) 5261-2704; e-mail vanidades@editorialtelevisa.com; internet www.vanidades.com; f. 1961; fortnightly; women's magazine; Dir JAQUELINE BLANCO; circ. 290,000.

Vogue (México): Condé Nast México, Montes Urales 415, 4°, Col. Lomas de Chapultepec, 11000 México, DF; tel. (55) 5062-3736; fax (55) 5540-5639; e-mail vogue.contacto@condenast.com.mx; internet www.vogue.mx; f. 1999; monthly; women's fashion; Editorial Dir KELLY TALAMAS; circ. 208,180.

ASSOCIATIONS

Federación de Asociaciones de Periodistas Mexicanos (Fapermex): Humboldt 5, Col. Centro, 06030 México, DF; tel. (55) 5510-2679; e-mail boletin@fapermex.mx; internet www.fapermex.com.mx; Pres. TEODORO RAÚL RENTERÍA VILLA; Sec.-Gen. CONSUELO EGUÍA TONELLA; 88 mem. asscns; c. 9,000 mems.

Federación Latinoamericana de Periodistas (FELAP): Nuevo Leon 144, 1°, Col. Hipódromo Condesa, 06170 México, DF; tel. (55) 5286-6055; fax (55) 5286-6085; e-mail webmaster@felap.org; internet www.felap.org; f. 1976; Pres. JUAN CARLOS CAMAÑO; Sec.-Gen. JOSÉ ANTONIO CALCÁNEO.

Fraternidad de Reporteros de México, AC (FREMAC): Avda Juárez 88, Col. Centro, Del. Cuauhtémoc, México, DF; e-mail fraternidadreporteros3000@gmail.com; internet fraternidadreporteros3000.blogspot.com; f. 1995; Pres. RAÚL CORREA ENGUILO; Sec.-Gen. JUAN BAUTISTA AGUILAR.

NEWS AGENCIES

Agencia de Información Integral Periodística (AIIP): Tabasco 263, Col. Roma, Del. Cuauhtémoc, 06700 México, DF; tel. and fax (55) 5514-7389; e-mail aiipmx@aiip.com.mx; internet www.aiip.com.mx; f. 1987; Dir-Gen. MIGUEL HERRERA LÓPEZ.

Agencia Mexicana de Información (AMI): Avda Cuauhtémoc 16, Col. Doctores, 06720 México, DF; tel. (55) 5761-9933; e-mail info@red-ami.com; internet www.ami.com.mx; f. 1971; Dir-Gen. JOSÉ LUIS BECERRA LÓPEZ; Gen. Man. EVA VÁZQUEZ LÓPEZ.

Notimex, SA de CV: Morena 110, 3°, Col. del Valle, 03100 México, DF; tel. (55) 5420-1163; fax (55) 5420-1188; e-mail ventas@notimex.com.mx; internet www.notimex.com.mx; f. 1968; services to press, radio and television in Mexico and throughout the world; Dir-Gen. HÉCTOR VILLARREAL.

Publishers

Alfaomega Grupo Editor, SA de CV: Pitágoras 1139, Col. Del Valle, Del. Benito Juárez, 03100 México, DF; tel. (55) 5575-5022; fax (55) 5575-2420; e-mail atencionalcliente@alfaomega.com.mx; internet www.alfaomega.com.mx; engineering, management, technology and computing; Dir ALBERTO UMAÑA CARRIZOSA.

Artes de México y del Mundo, SA de CV: Córdoba 69, Col. Roma, 06700 México, DF; tel. (55) 5525-5905; fax (55) 5525-5925; e-mail artesdemexico@artesdemexico.com; internet www.artesdemexico.com; f. 1988; art, design, poetry; Dir-Gen. ALBERTO RUY SÁNCHEZ LACY.

Cengage Learning Editores, SA de CV: Avda Santa Fe 505, 12°, Col. Cruz Manca, Del. Cuajimalpa, 05349 México, DF; tel. (55) 1500-6000; fax (55) 1500-6019; e-mail clientes.ca@cengage.com; internet www.cengage.com.mx; educational; Country Man. PEDRO TURBAY GARRIDO.

Cidcli, SC (Centro de Información y Desarrollo de la Comunicación y la Literatura Infantiles): Avda México 145-601, Col. Coyoacán, 04100 México, DF; tel. (55) 5659-7524; fax (55) 5659-3186; e-mail marissa@cidcli.com.mx; internet www.cidcli.com.mx; f. 1980; children's literature; Dir PATRICIA VAN RHIJN ARMIDA.

Círculo Editorial Azteca, SA: Calle de la Luna 225–227, Col. Guerrero, 06300 México, DF; tel. (55) 5526-1157; fax (55) 5526-2557; e-mail info@circuloeditorialazteca.com.mx; internet www.circuloeditorialazteca.com.mx; f. 1956; part of Grupo Salinas; religion, literature and technical; Man. Dir JOSEFINA LARRAGOITI.

Ediciones B México, SA de CV: Bradley 52, Anzures, Del. Miguel Hidalgo, 11590 México, DF; tel. (55) 1101-0660; fax (55) 5254-0569; e-mail info@edicionesb.com; internet www.edicionesb.com.mx; general fiction; Dir CARLOS GRAEF SÁNCHEZ.

Ediciones Era, SA de CV: Calle del Trabajo 31, Col. La Fama, Tlalpan, 14269 México, DF; tel. (55) 5528-1221; fax (55) 5606-2904; e-mail info@edicionesera.com.mx; internet www.edicionesera.com.mx; f. 1960; general and social science, art and literature; Gen. Man. NIEVES ESPRESATE XIRAU.

Ediciones Larousse, SA de CV: Londres 247, Col. Juárez, Del. Cuauhtémoc, 06600 México, DF; tel. (55) 1102-1300; fax (55) 5208-6225; e-mail larousse@larousse.com.mx; internet www.larousse.com.mx; f. 1965; Dir-Gen. GERARDO GUILLERMO GUERRERO IBARRA.

Editorial Avante, SA de CV: Luis G. Obregón 9, 1°, Apdo 45-796, Col. Centro, 06020 México, DF; tel. (55) 5510-8804; fax (55) 5521-5245; e-mail didactips@editorialavante.com.mx; internet www.editorialavante.com.mx; f. 1948; educational, drama, linguistics; Man. Dir Lic. MARIO ALBERTO HINOJOSA SÁENZ.

Editorial Everest Mexicana, SA: Calzada Ermita Iztapalapa 1681, Col. Barrio San Miguel del Iztapalapa, Apdo 55-570, 09360 México, DF; tel. (55) 5685-3704; fax (55) 5685-3433; e-mail editevem@prodigy.net.mx; f. 1980; general textbooks; Dir JOSÉ LUIS HUIDOBRO LEÓN.

Editorial Gustavo Gili de México, SA: Valle de Bravo 21, Naucalpan, 53050 Méx.; tel. (55) 5560-6011; fax (55) 5360-1453; e-mail info@ggili.com.mx; internet www.ggili.com.mx; f. 1902 in Spain; architecture, design, fashion, art and photography; Dir CARLOS LERMA.

Editorial Herder: Tehuantepec 50, esq. con Ures, Col. Roma Sur, Del. Cuauhtémoc, 06760 México, DF; tel. (55) 5523-0105; fax (55) 5669-2387; e-mail herder@herder.com.mx; internet www.herder.com.mx; social sciences; Dir JAN-CORNELIUS SCHULZ SAWADE.

Editorial Iztaccíhuatl, SA de CV: Miguel E. Schultz, No 21 y 25, Col. San Rafael, 06470 México, DF; tel. (55) 5705-0938; fax (55) 5535-2321; e-mail iztagerencia@editorializtaccihuatl.com.mx; internet www.editorializtaccihuatl.com.mx; Dir NORA MARÍA VIEYRA SICILIA.

Editorial Jus, SA de CV: Donceles 66, Centro Histórico, México, DF; tel. (55) 9150-1400; fax (55) 5529-0951; e-mail aramos@jus.com.mx; internet www.jus.com.mx; f. 1938; history of Mexico, law, philosophy, economics, religion; Dir FELIPE GARRIDO.

Editorial Lectorum, SA de CV: Calle Centeno 79A, Col. Granjas Esmeralda, México, DF; tel. (55) 5581-3202; fax (55) 5646-6892; e-mail direccion@lectorum.com.mx; internet www.lectorum.com.mx; humanities, literature and sciences; Dir-Gen. PORFIRIO LIZARRAGA.

Editorial Limusa, SA de CV: Balderas 95, 1°, Col. Centro, Del. Cuauhtémoc, 06040 México, DF; tel. (55) 5130-0700; fax (55) 5510-9415; e-mail limusa@noriegaeditores.com; internet www.noriega.com.mx; f. 1962; part of Grupo Noriega Editores; science, technical, textbooks; Dir-Gen. CARLOS BERNARDO NORIEGA ARIAS.

Editorial Orión: Calle Sierra Mojada 325, Lomas de Chapultepec, 11000 México, DF; tel. (55) 5520-0224; f. 1942; archaeology, philosophy, psychology, literature, fiction; Man. Dir SILVIA HERNÁNDEZ BALTAZAR.

Editorial Planeta Mexicana, SA de CV: Avda Presidente Masarik 111, 2°, Col. Chapultepec Morales, Del. Miguel Hidalgo, 11570 México, DF; tel. (55) 3000-6200; fax (55) 3000-6257; e-mail rrodriguez@planeta.com.mx; internet www.editorialplaneta.com.mx; general literature, non-fiction; part of Grupo Planeta (Spain); Grupo Planeta incorporates Destino, Editorial Diana, Editorial Joaquín Mortiz, Emecé, Espasa Calpe, Lunwerg Editores, Martínez Roca, Seix Barral, Temas de Hoy and Timun Mas; Man. Dir JOSÉ CALAFELL.

Editorial Porrúa Hnos, SA: Argentina 15, 5°, Col. Centro, 06020 México, DF; tel. (55) 5704-7500; fax (55) 5704-7502; e-mail editorial@porrua.com; internet www.porrua.com; f. 1944; general literature; Dir JOSÉ ANTONIO PÉREZ-PORRÚA SUÁREZ.

Editorial Progreso, SA de CV: Sabino 275, Col. Santa María la Ribera, Del. Cuauhtémoc, 06400 México, DF; tel. (55) 1946-0620; fax (55) 1946-0649; e-mail dirgeneral@editorialprogreso.com.mx; internet www.editorialprogreso.com.mx; f. 1899; educational; Dir JOAQUÍN FLORES SEGURA.

Editorial Serpentina, SA de CV: Santa Margarita 430, Col. Del Valle, 03100 Mexico, DF; tel. (55) 5559-8338; fax (55) 5575-8362; e-mail editorial@editorialserpentina.com; internet www.editorialserpentina.com; f. 2004; cultural, adolescent and children's literature; Dir ALEJANDRA CANALES UCHA.

Editorial Trillas, SA: Avda Río Churubusco 385 Pte, Col. Xoco, Apdo 10534, 03330 México, DF; tel. (55) 5688-4233; fax (55) 5604-1364; e-mail fernando@etrillas.com.mx; internet www.etrillas.com.mx; f. 1954; science, technical, textbooks, children's books; Man. Dir FERNANDO TRILLAS SALAZAR.

Fernández Editores, SA de CV: Eje 1 Pte México-Coyoacán 321, Col. Xoco, 03330 México, DF; tel. (55) 5090-7700; fax (55) 5688-9173;

e-mail sfernandez@feduca.com.mx; internet www .fernandezeditores.com.mx; f. 1943; children's literature, textbooks, educational toys; Man. Dir SOFÍA FERNÁNDEZ PEÑA.

Fondo de Cultura Económica: Carretera Picacho-Ajusco 227, Col. Bosques del Pedregal, Tlalpan, 14200 México, DF; tel. (55) 5227-4672; fax (55) 5227-4659; e-mail director.general@ fondodeculturaeconomica.com; internet www .fondodeculturaeconomica.com; f. 1934; economics, history, philosophy, children's books, science, politics, psychology, sociology, literature; state-owned; CEO JOAQUÍN DÍEZ-CANEDO.

Grupo Editorial Patria, SA de CV: Renacimiento 180, Col. San Juan Tlihuaca, Del. Azcapotzalco, 02400 México, DF; tel. (55) 5354-9100; fax (55) 5354-9109; e-mail info@editorialpatria.com.mx; internet www.editorialpatria.com.mx; f. 1933; fiction, general trade, children's books; Pres. CARLOS FRIGOLET LERMA.

McGraw-Hill Interamericana de México, SA de CV: Torre A, 17°, Paseo de la Reforma 1015, Col. Santa Fé, 01376 México, DF; tel. (55) 1500-5000; fax (55) 1500-5159; e-mail adriana_velazquez@ mcgraw-hill.com; internet www.mcgraw-hill.com.mx; education, business, science; Man. Dir ANDRÉS RODRÍGUEZ.

Medios Publicitarios Mexicanos, SA de CV: Eugenia 811, Eje 5 Sur, Col. del Valle, 03100 México, DF; tel. (55) 5523-3342; fax (55) 5523-3379; e-mail editorial@mpm.com.mx; internet www.mpm.com .mx; f. 1958; advertising media rates and data; Gen. Man. FERNANDO VILLAMIL ÁVILA.

Ocean Sur Editorial México, SA de CV: 2a Cerrada de Corola 17, Col. El Reloj, Del. Coyoacán, 04640 México, DF; tel. (55) 5421-4165; fax (55) 5553-5512; e-mail mexico@oceansur.com; internet www .oceansur.com; Ibero-American cultural literature; Dir MIGUEL ÁNGEL ÁGUILAR.

Pearson Educación de México, SA de CV: Atlacomulco 500, 4°, Industrial Atoto, Naucalpan de Juárez, 53519 Méx.; tel. (55) 5387-0700; fax (55) 5358-0808; e-mail alma.vallejo@pearsoned.com; internet www.pearsoneducacion.net; f. 1984; educational books under the imprints Addison-Wesley, Prentice Hall, Allyn & Bacon, Longman and Scott Foresman; Pres. STEVE MARBAN; Dir JAIME ANDRÉS EDUARDO VALENZUELA SOLAR.

Penguin Random House Group Editorial, SA de CV: Miguel de Cervantes Saavedra 301, 1°, Col. Granada, 11520, México, DF; tel. (55) 3067-8400; e-mail www.megustaleermex@ penguinrandomhouse.com; internet www.megustaleer.com.mx; f. 1954 as Mondadori, present name adopted 2013 following merger between Bertelsmann and Pearson; general fiction, history, sciences, philosophy, children's books; CEO ROBERTO BANCHIK.

Petra Ediciones, SA de CV: Calle El Carmen 268, Col. Camino Real, 45040 México, DF; tel. (55) 3629-0832; fax (55) 3629-3376; e-mail petra@petraediciones.com; internet www.petraediciones .com; art, literature, photography and theatre; Dir MARÍA ESPERANZA ESPINOSA BARRAGÁN.

Penguin Random House Group Editorial, SA de CV: Miguel de Cervantes Saavedra 301, 1°, Col. Granada, 11520, México, DF; tel. (55) 3067-8400; e-mail www.megustaleermex@ penguinrandomhouse.com; internet www.megustaleer.com.mx; f. 1954 as Mondadori, present name adopted 2013 following merger between Bertelsmann and Pearson; general fiction, history, sciences, philosophy, children's books; CEO ROBERTO BANCHIK.

Reverté Ediciones, SA de CV: Río Pánuco 141A, Col. Cuauhtémoc, 06500 México, DF; tel. (55) 5533-5658; fax (55) 5514-6799; e-mail reverte@reverte.com.mx; internet www.reverte.com; f. 1955; science, technical, architecture; Man. RAMÓN REVERTÉ MASCÓ.

Siglo XXI Editores, SA de CV: Avda Cerro del Agua 248, Col. Romero de Terreros, Del. Coyoacán, 04310 México, DF; tel. (55) 5658-7999; fax (55) 5658-7588; e-mail informes@sigloxxieditores.com.mx; internet www.sigloxxieditores.com.mx; f. 1966; art, economics, education, history, social sciences, literature, philology and linguistics, philosophy and political science; Dir-Gen. Dr JAIME LABASTIDA OCHOA; Gen. Man. JOSÉ MARÍA CASTRO MUSSOT.

Universidad Nacional Autónoma de México: Dirección General de Publicaciones y Fomento Editorial, Avda del Imán 5, Ciudad Universitaria, 04510 México, DF; tel. (55) 5622-6572; e-mail corbolgg@libros.unam.mx; internet www.unam.mx; f. 1935; publications in all fields; Dir-Gen. JULIA TAGÜEÑA PARGA.

ASSOCIATIONS

Cámara Nacional de la Industria Editorial Mexicana: Holanda 13, Col. San Diego Churubusco, Del. Coyoacán, 04120 México, DF; tel. (55) 5688-2011; fax (55) 5604-3147; e-mail contacto@caniem.com; internet www.caniem.com; f. 1964; Pres. VÍCTORICO ALBORES SANTIAGO; Dir-Gen. CARLOS M. ESPINO GAYTÁN.

Centro Mexicano de Protección y Fomento de los Derechos de Autor, SGC: Avda Cuauhtémoc 1486, Despacho 601A, Col. Santa Cruz Atoyac, Del. Benito Juárez, 03310 México, DF; tel. (55) 5601-3528; fax (55) 5604-9856; e-mail info@cempro.com.mx; internet www

.cempro.com.mx; f. 1998; manages intellectual property rights of authors and publrs; Pres. JULIO SANZ; Dir-Gen. VALERIA LEILANI SÁNCHEZ AGUIÑAGA.

Broadcasting and Communications
TELECOMMUNICATIONS

Legislation allowing for the reform of the telecommunication sector was approved by the Congress in July 2014.

Alestra: Optima II, Paseo de las Palmas 275, 8°, Col. Lomas de Chapultepec, 11000 México, DF; tel. (55) 8503-5000; internet www .alestra.com.mx; 49% owned by AT&T; Chair. ARMANDO GARZA SADA; Dir-Gen. ROLANDO ZUBIRÁN SHETLER.

América Móvil, SA de CV: Edif. Telcel 2, Lago Alberto 366, Col. Anáhuac, 11320 México, DF; tel. (55) 2581-4449; fax (55) 2581-3948; e-mail daniela.lacuna@americamovil.com; internet www .americamovil.com; f. 2000 as a spin off from Telmex; subsidiaries operate mobile telephone services in 18 countries in the Americas; Chair. PATRICK SLIM DOMIT; CEO DANIEL HAJJ ABOUMRAD.

> **Telcel:** tel. (55) 2581-3333; internet www.telcel.com; f. 1978, present name adopted 1989; subsidiary of above, providing mobile services in Mexico; COO PATRICIA RAQUEL HEVIA COTO.

> **Teléfonos de México, SA de CV (Telmex):** Parque Vía 190, Col. Cuauhtémoc, 06599 México, DF; tel. (55) 5222-1212; fax (55) 5545-5500; e-mail ri@telmex.com; internet www.telmex.com.mx; majority-owned by América Móvil since 2010; Pres. CARLOS SLIM DOMIT; Dir-Gen. HÉCTOR SLIM SEADE.

AT&T México: Montes Urales 470, Col. Lomas de Chapultepec, 11000 México, DF; internet www.att.com; Pres. (México) JEFFREY MCELFRESH.

Axtel: Blvd Díaz Ordáz Km 3.33, Zona Industrial, 66215 San Pedro Garza García, NL; tel. (81) 8114-0000; e-mail contacto@axtel.com .mx; internet www.axtel.com.mx; f. 1993; fixed-line operator; Chair. and CEO TOMÁS MILMO SANTOS.

Comunicaciones Nextel de México, SA de CV: Paseo de los Tamarindos 90, 29°, Col. Bosques de las Lomas, Del. Cuajimalpa, CP 05120, México, DF; tel. (55) 1018-4000; internet www.nextel.com .mx; f. 1998; fourth largest mobile telephone operator in Mexico; owned by NII Holdings, Inc (USA); Pres. PETER FOYO.

Iusacell, SA de CV: Montes Urales No 460, Col. Lomas de Chapultepec, Del. Miguel Hidalgo, 11000 México, DF; tel. (55) 5109-4400; e-mail ateclientes@iusacell.com.mx; internet www.iusacell.com.mx; f. 1992; operates third largest mobile cellular telephone network in Mexico; 74% owned by Móvil Access; Pres. RICARDO BENJAMÍN SALINAS PLIEGO.

Maxcom Telecomunicaciones, SAB de CV: Guillermo González Camarena 2000, Col. Centro Ciudad Santa Fe, Del. Álvaro Obregón, 01210 México, DF; tel. (55) 5147-1111; internet www.maxcom.com; f. 1996; fixed-line operator; Chair. and Exec. Pres. JACQUES GILKSBERG; CEO SALVADOR ALVAREZ.

Telecomunicaciones de México (TELECOMM): Torre Central de Telecomunicaciones, Eje Central Lázaro Cárdenas 567, 11°, Ala Norte, Col. Narvarte, Del. Benito Juárez, 03020 México, DF; tel. (55) 5090-1166; fax (55) 1035-2408; e-mail muycerca@telecomm.net.mx; internet www.telecomm.net.mx; govt-owned; Dir-Gen. JORGE A. JURAIDINI RUMILLA.

Telefónica México (Movistar México): Prolongación Paseo de la Reforma 1200, Lote B-2, Col. Santa Fe, Col. Cruz Manca, Del. Cuajimalpa de Morelos, 05348 México, DF; tel. (55) 1616-5000; e-mail francisco.caballero@telefonica.com; internet www.telefonica .com.mx; f. 1924 (in Spain); owned by Telefónica, SA (Spain); fixed line, mobile and broadband services; operates telephone service Telefónica Móviles México (movistar), call centre co Atento, and research and devt co Telefónica I+D; Pres. FRANCISCO GIL DÍAZ.

Unefon: Periférico Sur 4119, Col. Fuentes del Pedregal, 14141 México, DF; tel. (55) 8582-5000; e-mail ainfante@unefon.com.mx; internet www.unefon.com.mx; mobile operator; Pres. RICARDO SALINAS.

Regulatory Authorities

Dirección General de Política de Telecomunicaciones y de Radiodifusión: Centro Nacional SCT, Cuerpo C, 1°, Avda Xola y Universidad s/n, Col. Narvarte, Del. Benito Juárez, 03020 México, DF; tel. (55) 5723-9369; fax (55) 5723-9300; e-mail adelacru@sct.gob .mx; internet dgpt.sct.gob.mx; part of Secretariat of State for Communications and Transport; Dir-Gen. ANDRÉS DE LA CRUZ VIELMA.

Instituto Federal de Telecomunicaciones (IFT): Insurgentes Sur 1143, Col. Noche Buena, Del. Benito Juárez, 03720 México, DF; tel. and fax (55) 5015-4000; e-mail quejas@ift.org.mx; internet www .ift.org.mx; fmrly Comisión Federal de Telecomunicaciones—COFE-

TEL; reformed and renamed as above in 2013; Pres. GABRIEL OSWALDO CONTRERAS SALDIVAR; Dirs-Gen. LUIS FERNANDO PELAEZ ESPINOSA, LUIS ALDO SÁNCHEZ ORTEGA.

BROADCASTING

Radio

ABC Radio (XEABC): Basilio Badillo 29, Col. Tabacalera, Del. Cuauhtémoc, 06030 México, DF; tel. (55) 3640-5210; fax (55) 3640-5277; e-mail rita@abcradio.com.mx; internet www.abcradio.com.mx; Pres. JAVIER MEDINA; Gen. Man. JOSÉ ANTONIO MARTÍNEZ RAMÍREZ.

Corporación Mexicana de Radiodifusión (CMR): Calle Tetitla 23, esq. Calle Coapa, Col. Toriello Guerra, Del. Tlalpan, 14050 México, DF; tel. (55) 5424-6380; fax (55) 5666-5422; e-mail comentarios@cmr.com.mx; internet www.cmr.com.mx; f. 1962; Pres. ENRIQUE BERNAL SERVÍN; Dir-Gen. OSCAR BELTRÁN MARTÍNEZ DE CASTRO.

Firme, SA (Funcionamiento Íntegro de Radiodifusoras Mexicanas Enlazadas, SA): Ejército Nacional 552, Col. Polanco Reforma, 11550 México, DF; tel. (55) 5250-7788; fax (55) 5250-7906; e-mail radiodifusion@firmesa.com.mx; internet www.firmesa.com.mx; f. 1972; Dir-Gen. LUIS IGNACIO SANTIBÁÑEZ FLORES.

Grupo Acir, SA: Monte Pirineos 770, Col. Lomas de Chapultepec, Del. Miguel Hidalgo, 11000 México, DF; tel. (55) 5201-1700; fax (55) 5201-1771; e-mail servicio@grupoacir.com.mx; internet www.grupoacir.com.mx; f. 1965; comprises 140 stations; Exec. Pres. FRANCISCO IBARRA LÓPEZ.

Grupo Imagen Radio: Mariano Escobedo 700, Col. Anzures, 11590 México, DF; tel. (55) 5089-9000; fax (55) 5089-9139; e-mail rfml@imagen.com.mx; internet www.imagen.com.mx; Dir-Gen. ERNESTO RIVERA AGUILAR.

Grupo Radio Capital: Montes Urales 425, Col. Lomas de Chapultepec, 1000 México, DF; tel. (55) 3099-3000; fax (55) 5202-3370; e-mail hckaram@gmail.com; internet gruporadiocapital.com.mx; f. 1968; operates 12 radio stations; Dir-Gen. LUÍS MACCISE URIBE.

Grupo Radio Centro, SA de CV: Constituyentes 1154, Col. Lomas Atlas, Del. Miguel Hidalgo, 11950 México, DF; tel. (55) 5728-4800; fax (55) 5728-4900; e-mail rcentro@grc.com.mx; internet radiocentro .com.mx; f. 1965; comprises 100 radio stations; Pres. FRANCISCO AGUIRRE GÓMEZ; Dir-Gen. CARLOS AGUIRRE GÓMEZ.

Grupo Radio Digital del Sureste: Avda Chapultepec 473, 7°, Col. Juárez, Del. Cuahutémoc, 06600 México, DF; tel. (55) 5211-1734; fax (55) 5211-7534; e-mail info@gruporadiodigital.com.mx; internet www.gruporadiodigital.com.mx; f. 1946; operates 8 radio stations in 4 provinces; Dir-Gen. SIMÓN VALANCI BUZALI.

Grupo Siete Comunicación: Montecito 38, 31°, Of. 33, Col. Nápoles, Del. Benito Juárez, 03810 México, DF; tel. (55) 9000-0787; fax (55) 9000-0747; e-mail info@gruposiete.com.mx; internet www.gruposiete.com.mx; f. 1997; Pres. Lic. FRANCISCO JAVIER SÁNCHEZ CAMPUZANO; Dir-Gen. PEDRO MOGOYÁN SOLANO.

Instituto Mexicano de la Radio (IMER): Mayorazgo 83, 2°, Col. Xoco, Del. Benito Juárez, 03330 México, DF; tel. (55) 5628-1704; fax (55) 5628-1738; e-mail email@imer.com.mx; internet www.imer .com.mx; f. 1983; Dir-Gen. CARLOS LARA SUMANO.

MVS Radio: Copérnico 183, Col. Anzures, 11590 México, DF; tel. (55) 5263-2156; fax (55) 5263-2189; e-mail eahumada@mvs.com; internet www.mvsradio.com.mx; f. 1968; operates 4 stations, EXA FM, La Mejor FM, FM Globo and Noticias MVS; Pres. JOAQUÍN VARGAS.

Núcleo Radio Mil (NRM): Prolongación Paseo de la Reforma 115, Col. Paseo de las Lomas, Santa Fe, 01330 México, DF; tel. (55) 5258-1200; e-mail radiomil@nrm.com.mx; internet www.nrm.com.mx; f. 1942; comprises 7 radio stations; Pres. and Dir-Gen. EDILBERTO HUESCA PERROTÍN.

Radio Cadena Nacional, SA (RCN): Lago Victoria 78, Col. Granada, 11520 México, DF; tel. (55) 5250-0324; fax (55) 2624-0052; e-mail rcnmex@prodigy.net.mx; internet www.rcn.com.mx; f. 1948; Pres. SERGIO FAJARDO ORTIZ; Gen. Man. GUADALUPE CAMPUZANO.

Radio Educación: Angel Urraza 622, Col. del Valle, 03100 México, DF; tel. (55) 4155-1050; e-mail direccion@radioeducacion.edu.mx; internet www.radioeducacion.edu.mx; f. 1968; Dir-Gen. CARLOS ANTONIO TENORIO MUÑOZ COTA.

Radio Fórmula, SA: Privada de Horacio 10, Col. Polanco, 11560 México, DF; tel. (55) 5282-1016; e-mail jcoello@grupoformula.com .mx; internet www.radioformula.com.mx; f. 1968 as Radio Distrito Federal; Pres. ROGERIO AZCÁRRAGA MADERO.

Radio Universidad Nacional Autónoma de México: Adolfo Prieto 133, Col. del Valle, Del. Benito Juárez, 03100 México, DF; tel. (55) 5536-8989; fax (55) 5687-3989; e-mail contacto@radiounam .unam.mx; internet www.radiounam.unam.mx; Dir-Gen. FERNANDO CHAMIZO GUERRERO.

Radiodifusoras Asociadas, SA de CV (RASA): Durango 341, 2°, Col. Roma, 06700 México, DF; tel. (55) 5286-1222; fax (55) 5211-6159;

e-mail rasa@rasa.com.mx; internet www.rasa.com.mx; f. 1956; Exec. Pres. JOSÉ LARIS RODRÍGUEZ; Dir-Gen. SARA LARIS RODRÍGUEZ.

Radiópolis, SA de CV: Tlalpan 3000, Col. Espartaco, Del. Coyoacán, 04870 México, DF; tel. (55) 5327-2000; fax (55) 5679-9710; e-mail rrodriguezg@televisa.com.mx; owned by Televisa, SA de CV and Grupo Prisa; owns 5 radio stations; affiliated to Radiorama, SA de CV (q.v.) in 2004; Dir-Gen. RAÚL RODRÍGUEZ GONZÁLEZ.

Radiorama, SA de CV: Reforma 2620, 2°, Col. Lomas Altas, Del. Miguel Hidalgo, 11950 México, DF; tel. (55) 1105-0000; fax (55) 1105-0002; e-mail grupo@radiorama.com.mx; internet www.radiorama .com.mx; Pres. JAVIER PÉREZ DE ANDA.

Sociedad Mexicana de Radio, SA de CV (SOMER): Paseo de la Reforma 115, 4°, Col. Lomas, Santa Fé, 01330 México, DF; tel. (55) 9177-6660; fax (55) 9177-6677; e-mail somer@somer.com.mx; internet www.somer.com.mx; Dir-Gen. HUMBERTO HUESCA BUSTAMENTE.

El Universal Radio: Bucareli 8, Col. Centro, Del. Cuauhtémoc, 06040 México, DF; tel. (55) 5709-1313; e-mail radio@eluniversal.com .mx; internet www.eluniversalradio.com.mx; Man. ROGELIO ARIAS DÍAZ DE LEÓN.

Television

Canal 22: Edif. Pedro Infante, Atletas 2, Col. Country Club, Del. Coyoacán, 04220 México, DF; tel. (55) 2122-9680; fax (55) 5549-1647; e-mail correo@canal22.org.mx; internet www.canal22.org.mx; f. 1993; part of Consejo Nacional para la Cultura y las Artes of the Govt; Dir-Gen. RAÚL CREMOUX.

MVS (Multivisión): Blvd Manuel Ávila Camacho 147, Col. Chapultepec Morales, 11510 México, DF; tel. (55) 5283-4300; fax (55) 5283-4314; e-mail jvargas@mvs.com; internet www.mvs.com; subscriber-funded; Pres. JOAQUÍN VARGAS GUAJARDO; Vice-Pres. ERNESTO VARGAS.

Once TV: Carpio 475, Col. Casco de Santo Tomás, 11340 México, DF; tel. (55) 5166-4000; fax (55) 5396-8001; e-mail info@oncetvmexico.ipn .mx; internet www.oncetv.ipn.mx; f. 1959; Dir-Gen. MARÍA ENRIQUETA CABRERA CUARÓN.

Televisa, SA de CV: Edif. Televicentro, 8°, Avda Chapultepec 28, Col. Doctores, 06724 México, DF; tel. (55) 5709-3333; fax (55) 5709-3021; e-mail imagencorporativa2@televisa.com.mx; internet www .televisa.com; f. 1973; commercial; 406 affiliated stations; Chair. and CEO EMILIO AZCÁRRAGA JEAN.

Televisión Azteca, SA de CV: Anillo Periférico Sur 4121, Col. Fuentes del Pedregal, 14141 México, DF; tel. (55) 5447-8844; fax (55) 5645-4258; e-mail contacto@tvazteca.com; internet www.tvazteca .com; f. 1992; assumed responsibility for fmr state-owned channels 7 and 13; Pres. RICARDO B. SALINAS PLIEGO; Dir-Gen. MARIO SAN ROMÁN.

Regulatory Authority

Dirección General de Radio, Televisión y Cinematografía (RTC): Roma 41, Col. Juaréz, Del. Cuauhtémoc, 06600 México, DF; tel. (55) 5140-8000; fax (55) 5530-4315; e-mail buzonrtc@segob .gob.mx; internet www.rtc.gob.mx; f. 1977; Dir-Gen. JOSÉ IGNACIO JUÁREZ SÁNCHEZ.

Association

Cámara Nacional de la Industria de Radio y Televisión (CIRT): Avda Horacio 1013, Col. Polanco Reforma, Del. Miguel Hidalgo, 11550 México, DF; tel. (55) 5726-9909; fax (55) 5545-6767; e-mail cirt@cirt.com.mx; internet www.cirt.com.mx; f. 1942; Pres. TRISTÁN CANALES NAJJAR; Dir-Gen. MIGUEL OROZCO GÓMEZ.

Finance

(cap. = capital; res = reserves; dep. = deposits; m. = million;
brs = branches; amounts in new pesos)

BANKING

Banking activity is regulated by the federal Government. Commercial banking institutions are constituted as *Sociedades Anónimas*, with wholly private social capital. Development banking institutions exist as *Sociedades Nacionales de Crédito*; participation in their capital is exclusive to the federal Government, notwithstanding the possibility of accepting limited amounts of private capital.

Supervisory Authority

Comisión Nacional Bancaria y de Valores (CNBV) (National Banking and Securities Commission): Avda Insurgentes Sur 1971, Torre Norte, Sur y III, Col. Guadalupe Inn, Del. Alvaro Obregón, 01020 México, DF; tel. and fax (55) 1454-6000; e-mail info@cnbv.gob .mx; internet www.cnbv.gob.mx; f. 1924; govt commission controlling all credit institutions in Mexico; Pres. JAIME GONZÁLEZ AGUADÉ.

Central Bank

Banco de México (BANXICO): Avda 5 de Mayo 2, Col. Centro, Del. Cuauhtémoc, 06059 México, DF; tel. (55) 5237-2000; fax (55) 5237-2070; e-mail comsoc@banxico.org.mx; internet www.banxico.org.mx; f. 1925; currency issuing authority; autonomous since April 1994; cap. 7.1m., res –66,040m., dep. 878,727m. (Dec. 2009); Gov. AGUSTÍN GUILLERMO CARSTENS CARSTENS; 6 brs.

Commercial Banks

Banco del Bajío, SA: Avda Manuel J. Clouthier 508, Col. Jardines del Campestre, 37128 León, Gto; tel. (477) 710-4649; fax (477) 710-4693; e-mail internacional@bancobajio.com.mx; internet www.bb.com.mx; f. 1994; cap. 2,513.1m., res 7,788.1m., dep. 69,231.1m. (Dec. 2013); Pres. SALVADOR OÑATE ASCENCIO.

Banco Nacional de México, SA (Banamex): Avda Isabel la Católica 44, 06089 México, DF; tel. (55) 5225-5882; fax (55) 5920-7323; e-mail prensa@banamex.com; internet www.banamex.com; f. 1884; transferred to private ownership in 1991; merged with Citibank México, SA in 2001; cap. 35,397m., res 87,469m., dep. 516,258m. (Dec. 2013); CEO MANUEL MEDINA MORA; 1,260 brs.

Banco Santander (Mexico), SA: Mod 401, 4°, Prolongación Paseo de la Reforma 500, Col. Lomas de Santa Fe, Del. Alvaro Obregon, 01219 México, DF; tel. (55) 5261-1543; fax (55) 5261-5549; internet www.santander.com.mx; f. 1864 as Banco Serfin; acquired by Banco Santander Central Hispano (Spain) in Dec. 2000; adopted current name 2008; cap. 11,348m., res 33,715m., dep. 362,470m. (Dec. 2012); Exec. Pres. and Dir-Gen. MARCOS MARTÍNEZ GAVICA; 554 brs.

BANORTE, SA (Grupo Financiero BANORTE): Avda Revolución 3000, Col. Primavera, 64830 Monterrey, NL; tel. (81) 8319-7200; fax (81) 8319-5216; internet www.banorte.com; f. 1899; merged with Banco Regional del Norte in 1985; cap. 15,577m., res 17,933m., dep. 440,145m. (Dec. 2013); Pres. GUILLERMO ORTIZ MARTÍNEZ; CEO ALEJANDRO VALENZUELA DEL RÍO; 1146 brs.

BBVA Bancomer, SA: Centro Bancomer, Avda Universidad 1200, Col. Xoco, 03339 México, DF; tel. (55) 5621-3434; fax (55) 5621-3230; internet www.bancomer.com.mx; f. 2000 by merger of Bancomer (f. 1864) and Mexican operations of Banco Bilbao Vizcaya Argentaria (Spain); privatized in 2002; cap. 9,799m., res 83,466m., dep. 614,634m. (Dec. 2012); Pres. IGNACIO DESCHAMPS GONZÁLEZ; 1,658 brs.

HSBC México: Paseo de la Reforma 347, Col. Cuauhtémoc, Del. Cuauhtémoc, 06500 México, DF; tel. (55) 5721-2222; fax (55) 5721-2393; e-mail contacto@hsbc.com.mx; internet www.hsbc.com.mx; f. 1941; bought by HSBC (United Kingdom) in 2002; name changed from Banco Internacional, SA (BITAL) in 2004; cap. 5,261m., res 33,729m., dep. 291,629m. (Dec. 2012); Chair. LUIS JAVIER PEÑA KEGEL; 1,400 brs.

Scotiabank Inverlat, SA (Canada): Blvd Miguel Avila Camacho 1, 5°, Col. Lomas de Chapultepec, Del. Miguel Hidalgo, 11009 México, DF; tel. (55) 5728-1000; fax (55) 5229-2019; internet www.scotiabankinverlat.com; f. 1977 as Multibanco Comermex, SA; changed name to Banco Inverlat, SA in 1995; 55% holding acquired by Scotiabank Group (Canada) and adopted current name 2001; cap. 7,451m., res 3,871m., dep. 147,133m. (Dec. 2013); Pres. NICOLE REICH DE POLIGNAC; 476 brs.

Development Banks

Banco Nacional de Comercio Exterior, SNC (BANCOMEXT): Periférico Sur 4333, Col. Jardines en la Montaña, Del. Tlalpan, 14210 México, DF; tel. (55) 5449-9100; fax (55) 5652-9408; e-mail bancomext@bancomext.gob.mx; internet www.bancomext.com; f. 1937; cap. 14,959m., res 2,601m., dep. 46,757m. (Dec. 2012); CEO MARIO LABORÍN GÓMEZ; 6 brs.

Banco Nacional del Ejército, Fuerza Aérea y Armada, SNC (BANJERCITO): Avda Industria Militar 1055, 1°, Col. Lomas de Sotelo, Del. Miguel Hidalgo, 11200 México, DF; tel. and fax (55) 5626-0500; e-mail info@banjercito.com.mx; internet www.banjercito.com.mx; f. 1947; cap. 4,853m., res 2,748m., dep. 22,096m. (Dec. 2013); Pres. ERNESTO JOSÉ CORDERO ARROYO.

Banco Nacional de Obras y Servicios Públicos, SNC (BANOBRAS): Avda Javier Barros Sierra 515, Col. Lomas de Santa Fe, Del. Álvaro Obregón, 01219 México, DF; tel. (55) 5270-1200; fax (55) 5270-1564; internet www.banobras.gob.mx; f. 1933; govt-owned; cap. 11,765m., res 3,350m., dep. 245,896m. (Dec. 2009); Dir-Gen. GEORGINA KESSEL MARTÍNEZ.

Compartamos, SAB de CV: Insurgentes Sur 552, Col. Escandón, 11800 México, DF; tel. (55) 5276-7250; fax (55) 5276-7299; e-mail contacto@compartamos.com; internet www.compartamos.com; f. 1990; Dir-Gen. ALVARO RODRÍGUEZ ARREGUI.

Financiera Rural: Agrarismo 227, Col. Escandón, Del. Miguel Hidalgo, CP 11800, México, DF; tel. (55) 5230-1600; internet www.financierarural.gob.mx; f. 2004; state-run devt bank, concerned with agricultural, forestry and fishing sectors; Dir-Gen. JUAN CARLOS CORTÉS.

Nacional Financiera, SNC (NAFIN): Avda Insurgentes Sur 1971, Torre IV, 13°, Col. Guadalupe Inn, 01020 México, DF; tel. (55) 5325-6700; fax (55) 5325-6000; e-mail info@nafin.gob.mx; internet www.nafin.com; f. 1934; cap. 8,805m., res 12,723m., dep. 101,857m. (Dec. 2012); CEO HÉCTOR ALEJANDRO DOMENE; 32 brs.

BANKERS' ASSOCIATION

Asociación de Bancos de México: 16 de Setiembre 27, 3°, Col. Centro Histórico, 06000 México, DF; tel. (55) 5722-4300; internet www.abm.org.mx; f. 1928; Pres. JAVIER ARRIGUNAGA CAMPO; 52 mems.

STOCK EXCHANGE

Bolsa Mexicana de Valores, SA de CV: Paseo de la Reforma 255, Col. Cuauhtémoc, 06500 México, DF; tel. (55) 5726-6000; fax (55) 5726-6836; e-mail cinforma@bmv.com.mx; internet www.bmv.com.mx; f. 1894; Pres. and CEO LUIS TÉLLEZ KUENZLER.

INSURANCE

Supervisory Authority

Comisión Nacional de Seguros y Fianzas: Avda Insurgentes Sur 1971, Torre I Sur, 2°, Col. Guadalupe Inn, Del. Álvaro Obregón, CP 01020, México, DF; tel. (55) 5724-7489; e-mail cdiaz@cnsf.gob.mx; internet www.cnsf.gob.mx; Pres. MANUEL SERGIO AGUILERA VERDUZCO.

Principal Companies

ACE Seguros: Bosques de Alisos, 47A, 1°, Col. Bosques de las Lomas, Del. Cuajimalpa, 05120 México, DF; tel. (55) 5258-5800; fax (55) 5258-5899; e-mail info@acelatinamerica.com; internet www.acelatinamerica.com/ACELatinAmericaRoot/Mexico; f. 1990; fmrly Seguros Cigna; Pres. ROBERTO FLORES.

Aseguradora Cuauhtémoc, SA: Manuel Avila Camacho 164, 11570 México, DF; tel. (55) 5250-9800; fax (55) 5540-3204; f. 1944; general; Exec. Pres. JUAN B. RIVEROLL; Dir-Gen. JAVIER COMPEÁN AMEZCUA.

Aseguradora Interacciones: Paseo de la Reforma 383, México, DF; tel. (55) 5326-8600; e-mail on-line@interacciones.com; internet www.interacciones.com; f. 1966; general; 43% owned by Commercial Union (United Kingdom); Dir-Gen. CARLOS GONZÁLEZ.

BBVA Bancomer Seguros: Centro Bancomer, Avda Universidad 1200, Col. Xoco, 03339 México, DF; e-mail servicioaclientes@segurosbancomer.com.mx; internet www.segurosbancomer.com.mx; Dir-Gen. JUAN PABLO ÁVILA PALAFOX.

Grupo Nacional Provincial, SAB: Avda Cerro de las Torres 395, Col. Campestre Churubusco, Del. Coyoacán, 04200 México, DF; tel. (55) 5227-9000; internet www.gnp.com.mx; f. 1936; mem. of Grupo BAL; general; Chair. ALBERTO BAILLÈRES; CEO ALEJANDRO BAILLÈRES.

MetLife: Blvd Manuel Avila Camacho 32, SKY 14–20 y PH, Col. Lomas de Chapultepec, Del. Miguel Hidalgo, 11000 México, DF; tel. (55) 5328-9000; e-mail contacto@metlife.com.mx; internet www.metlife.com.mx; f. 1931 as Aseguradora Hidalgo, acquired by MetLife Inc in 2002; life; CEO SOFÍA BELMAR.

Quálitas, Cía de seguros: José María Castorena 426, Col. San José de los Cedros, Cuajimalpa, CP 05200, México, DF; e-mail qualitas@qualitas.com.mx; internet www.qualitas.com.mx; Pres. JOAQUÍN BROCKMAN LOZANO.

Royal & SunAlliance Mexico: Blvd Adolfo López Mateos 2448, Col. Altavista, 01060 México, DF; tel. (55) 5723-7999; fax (55) 5723-7941; e-mail direccion.general@mx.rsagroup.com; internet www.royalsun.com.mx; f. 1941; acquired Seguros BBV-Probursa in 2001; general, except life; Chair. JOHN NAPIER.

Seguros Azteca, SA: Insurgentes Sur 3579, Tlalpan La Joya, 14000 México, DF; tel. (55) 1720-9854; e-mail infoseguros@segurosazteca.com.mx; internet www.segurosazteca.com.mx; f. 1933, renamed as above in 2003; general, incl. life; Dir-Gen. ALFREDO HONSBERG.

Seguros Banorte Generali: Presidente Mazaryk 8, Col. Bosques de Chapultepec, Del. Miguel Hidalgo, CP 11588, México DF; tel. (55) 5141-1414; e-mail privacidad.sbg@banorte.com; internet www.segurosbanorte.com.mx; Dir-Gen. FERNANDO SOLÍS SOBERÓN.

Seguros Banamex, SA: Venustiano Carranza 63, Col. Centro Histórico, Del. Cuauhtémoc, 06000 México, DF; tel. (55) 1226-8100; e-mail sbainternet@banamex.com; internet www.segurosbanamex.com.mx; f. 1994; life, accident and health; Dir-Gen. DANIEL GARDUÑO GUTIÉRREZ.

Seguros Monterrey New York Life: Presidente Mazaryk 8, Bosques de Chapultepec, Del. Miguel Hidalgo, México, DF; tel. (55) 5326-9000; fax (55) 5536-9610; e-mail clientes@

monterrey-newyorklife.com.mx; internet www .monterrey-newyorklife.com.mx; f. 1940 as Monterrey Cía de Seguros; acquired by New York Life in 2000; casualty, life, etc.; Dir-Gen. MARIO VELA BERRONDO.

Skandia Vida: Bosque de Ciruelos 162, 1°, Col. Bosques de las Lomas, 11700, México, DF; tel. (55) 5093-0220; e-mail servicio@ skandia.com.mx; internet www.skandia.com.mx; CEO JULIO MÉN-DEZ.

Insurance Association

Asociación Mexicana de Instituciones de Seguros, AC (AMIS): Francisco I Madero 21, Col. Tlacopac, San Angel, 01040 México, DF; tel. (55) 5480-0646; fax (55) 5662-8036; e-mail amis@ mail.internet.com.mx; internet www.amis.com.mx; f. 1946; all insurance cos operating in Mexico are mems; Chair. SOFÍA BELMAR BERUMEN; Pres. MARIO VELA BERRONDO.

Trade and Industry

GOVERNMENT AGENCIES

Comisión Federal de Protección Contra Riesgos Sanitarios (COFEPRIS): Monterrey 33, esq. Oaxaca, Col. Roma, Del. Cuauhtémoc, 06700 México, DF; tel. (55) 5080-5200; fax (55) 5207-5521; e-mail mdiosdado@salud.gob.mx; internet www.cofepris.gob.mx; f. 2003; pharmaceutical regulatory authority; Sec.-Gen. ERWIN ROENIGER SERVÍN.

Comisión Nacional Forestal (CONAFOR): Carretera a Nogales s/n, esq. Periférico Poniente 5360, 5°, San Juan de Ocotán, 45019 Zapopan, Jal.; tel. (33) 3777-7000; fax (33) 3777-7012; e-mail conafor@conafor.gob.mx; internet www.conafor.gob.mx; f. 2001; Dir-Gen. JUAN MANUEL TORRES ROJO.

Comisión Nacional de Hidrocarburos (CNH): Vito Alessio Robles 174, Col. Florida, Del Alvaro Obregón, CP 01030, México, DF; tel. (55) 1454-8500; internet www.cnh.gob.mx; f. 2009; oversees the hydrocarbons sector; Pres. JUAN CARLOS ZEPEDA MOLINA.

Comisión Nacional de Inversiones Extranjeras (CNIE): Dirección General de Inversión Extranjera, Insurgentes Sur 1940, 8°, Col. Florida, 01030 México, DF; tel. (55) 5229-6100; fax (55) 5229-6507; e-mail gcanales@economia.gob.mx; f. 1973; govt commission to co-ordinate foreign investment; Pres. BRUNO FRANCISCO FERRARI GARCÍA DE ALBA.

Comisión Nacional de los Salarios Mínimos (CNSM): Avda Cuauhtémoc 14, 2°, Col. Doctores, Del. Cuauhtémoc, 06720 México 7, DF; tel. (55) 5998-3800; fax (55) 5578-5775; e-mail cnsm1@conasami .gob.mx; internet www.conasami.gob.mx; f. 1962, in accordance with Section VI of Article 123 of the Constitution; national commission on minimum salaries; Pres. Lic. BASILIO GONZÁLEZ NÚÑEZ.

Instituto Nacional de Investigaciones Nucleares (ININ): Centro Nuclear de México, Carretera México–Toluca Km 36.5, La Marquesa, 52750 Ocoyoacac, Méx.; tel. (55) 5329-7200; fax (55) 5329-7296; e-mail hernan.rico@inin.gob.mx; internet www.inin .gob.mx; f. 1979 to plan research and devt of nuclear science and technology; 2 nuclear reactors, each with a generating capacity of 654 MW; Dir-Gen. JOSÉ RAÚL ORTÍZ MAGAÑA.

Instituto Nacional de Pesca (INAPESCA) (National Fishery Institute): Pitágoras 1320, Col. Santa Cruz Atoyac, Del. Benito Juárez, 03310 México, DF; tel. (55) 3871-9517; fax (55) 5604-9169; e-mail gerardo.garcia@inapesca.sagarpa.gob.mx; internet www .inapesca.gob.mx; f. 1962; Dir-in-Chief RAÚL ADÁN ROMO TRUJILLO.

Procuraduría Federal del Consumidor (Profeco): Avda José Vasconcelos 208, Col. Condesa, Del. Cuauhtémoc, 06140 México, DF; tel. (55) 5625-6700; internet www.profeco.gob.mx; f. 1975; consumer protection; Procurator BERNARDO ALTAMIRANO RODRÍGUEZ.

Servicio Geológico Mexicano (SGM): Blvd Felipe Angeles, Carretera México–Pachuca, Km 93.50-4, Col. Venta Prieta, 42080 Pachuca de Soto, Hgo; tel. (771) 711-4266; fax (771) 711-4204; e-mail gintproc@sgm.gob.mx; internet www.sgm.gob.mx; f. 1957; govt agency for the devt of mineral resources; Dir-Gen. RAFAEL ALEXANDRI RIONDA.

DEVELOPMENT ORGANIZATIONS

Centro de Investigación para el Desarollo, AC (CIDAC) (Centre of Research for Development): Jaime Balmes 11, Edif. D, 2°, Col. Los Morales Polanco, 11510 México, DF; tel. (55) 5985-1010; fax (55) 5985-1030; e-mail info@cidac.org.mx; internet www.cidac .org; f. 1984; researches economic and political devt; Dir-Gen. VERÓNICA BAZ.

Comisión Nacional de las Zonas Aridas (CONAZA): Blvd Isidro López Zertuche 2513, Col. Los Maestros, 25260 Saltillo, Coah.; tel. and fax (844) 450-5200; e-mail contacto@conaza.gob.mx; internet

www.conaza.gob.mx; f. 1970; commission to co-ordinate the devt and use of arid areas; Dir-Gen. LUIS CARLOS FIERRO GARCÍA.

Fideicomiso de Fomento Mineiro (FIFOMI): Puente de Tecamachalco 26, 2°, Col. Lomas de Chapultepec, Del. Miguel Hidalgo, 11000 México, DF; tel. (55) 5249-9500; e-mail pguerra@fifomi.gob .mx; internet www.fifomi.gob.mx; trust for the devt of the mineral industries; Dir-Gen. ALBERTO ORTIZ TRILLO.

Fideicomisos Instituídos en Relación con la Agricultura (FIRA): Km 8, Antigua Carretera Pátzcuaro 8555, 58341 Morelia, Mich.; tel. (443) 322-2399; fax (443) 327-6338; e-mail webmaster@ correo.fira.gob.mx; internet www.fira.gob.mx; a group of devt funds to aid agricultural financing, under the Banco de México, comprising Fondo de Garantía y Fomento para la Agricultura, Ganadería y Avicultura (FOGAGA); Fondo Especial para Financiamientos Agropecuarios (FEFA); Fondo Especial de Asistencia Técnica y Garantía para Créditos Agropecuarios (FEGA); Fondo de Garantía y Fomento para las Actividades Pesqueras (FOPESCA); Dir RODRIGO SÁNCHEZ MÚJICA.

Fondo de Operación y Financiamiento Bancario a la Vivienda (FOVI): Ejército Nacional 180, Col. Anzures, 11590 México, DF; tel. (55) 5263-4500; fax (55) 5263-4541; e-mail jmartinez@fovi.gob.mx; internet www.fovi.gob.mx; f. 1963 to promote the construction of low-cost housing through savings and credit schemes; devt fund under the Banco de México; Dir-Gen. MANUEL ZEPEDA PAYERAS.

Instituto Mexicano del Petróleo (IMP): Eje Central Lázaro Cárdenas 152, Col. San Bartolo Atepehuacan, Del. Gustavo A. Madero, 07730 México, DF; tel. (55) 9175-6000; fax (55) 9175-8000; e-mail gdgarcia@imp.mx; internet www.imp.mx; f. 1965 to foster devt of the petroleum, chemical and petrochemical industries; Dir-Gen. VINICIO SURO PÉREZ.

CHAMBERS OF COMMERCE

American Chamber of Commerce of Mexico (Amcham): Lucerna 78, Col. Juárez, 06600 México, DF; tel. (55) 5141-3800; fax (55) 5141-3833; e-mail amchammx@amcham.com.mx; internet www.amcham.com.mx; f. 1917; brs in Guadalajara and Monterrey; Pres. ERNESTO M. HERNÁNDEZ.

Cámara de Comercio, Servicios y Turismo Ciudad de México (CANACO) (Chamber of Commerce, Services and Tourism of Mexico City): Paseo de la Reforma 42, 3°, Col. Centro, Apdo 32005, Del. Cuauhtémoc, 06048 México, DF; tel. (55) 3685-2269; fax (55) 5592-2279; e-mail sos@ccmexico.com.mx; internet www .camaradecomerciodemexico.com.mx; f. 1874; 50,000 mems; Pres. RICARDO NAVARRO BENÍTEZ.

Cámara Nacional de la Industria de Transformación (CANACINTRA): Avda San Antonio 256, Col. Ampliación Nápoles, Del. Benito Juárez, 06849 México, DF; tel. (55) 5482-3000; fax (55) 5598-8044; e-mail direciongeneral@canacintra.org.mx; internet www .canacintra.org.mx; represents majority of smaller manufacturing businesses; Pres. SERGIO ENRIQUE CERVANTES RODILES; Dir-Gen. LINO LANDEROS SANTOS.

Confederación de Cámaras Nacionales de Comercio, Servicios y Turismo (CONCANACO-SERVYTUR) (Confederation of National Chambers of Commerce, Services and Tourism): Balderas 144, 3°, Col. Centro, 06070 México, DF; tel. (55) 5722-9300; e-mail comentarios@concanacored.com; internet www.concanaco.com.mx; f. 1917; Pres. JORGE E. DÁVILA FLORES; Dir-Gen. EDUARDO GARCÍA VILLASEÑOR; comprises 283 regional chambers.

CHAMBERS OF INDUSTRY

Central Confederation

Confederación de Cámaras Industriales de los Estados Unidos Mexicanos (CONCAMIN) (Confed. of Industrial Chambers): Manuel María Contreras 133, 4°, Col. Cuauhtémoc, Del. Cuauhtémoc, 06500 México, DF; tel. (55) 5140-7800; fax (55) 5140-7831; e-mail webmaster@concamin.org.mx; internet www.concamin.org .mx; f. 1918; represents and promotes the activities of the entire industrial sector; Pres. FRANCISCO JAVIER FUNTANET MANGE; 108 mem. orgs.

INDUSTRIAL AND TRADE ASSOCIATIONS

Asociación Nacional de Importadores y Exportadores de la República Mexicana (ANIERM) (National Association of Importers and Exporters): Monterrey 130, Col. Roma, Del. Cuauhtémoc, 06700 México, DF; tel. (55) 5584-9522; fax (55) 5584-5317; e-mail anierm@anierm.org.mx; internet www.anierm.org.mx; f. 1944; Pres. FERNANDO TAMEZ MURGUÍA; Exec. Vice-Pres. LUIS ENRIQUE ZAVALA GALLEGOS.

Asociación Nacional de la Industria Química (ANIQ): Angel Urraza 505, Col. del Valle, 03100 México, DF; tel. (55) 5230-5100; internet www.aniq.org.mx; f. 1959; chemicals asscn; Dir-Gen. MIGUEL BENEDETTO; c. 200 mem. cos.

Comisión Nacional de Seguridad Nuclear y Salvaguardias (CNSNS): Dr José María Barragán 779, Col. Narvarte, Del. Benito Juárez, 03020 México, DF; tel. (55) 5095-3200; fax (55) 5095-3295; e-mail je@cnsns.gob.mx; internet www.cnsns.gob.mx; f. 1979; nuclear regulatory authority; Dir-Gen. JUAN EIBENSCHUTZ HARTMAN.

Consejo Empresarial Mexicano de Comercio Exterior, Inversión y Tecnología (COMCE): Lancaster 15, 2° y 3°, Col. Juárez, 06600 México, DF; tel. (52) 5231-7100; fax (55) 5321-7109; e-mail direccion@comce.org.mx; internet www.comce.org.mx; f. 1999 to promote international trade; Pres. VALENTÍN DIEZ MORODO; Dir-Gen. LORENZO YSASI MARTÍNEZ.

Consejo Mexicano de Asuntos Internacionales (COMEXI): Of. 502, Torre Magnum, Sierra Mojada 620, Col. Lomas de Chapultepec, 11000 México, DF; tel. (55) 5202-3776; e-mail info@consejomexicano .org; internet www.consejomexicano.org; Pres. JAIME ZABLUDOVSKY; Dir-Gen. CLAUDIA CALVIN.

Consejo Nacional de la Industria Maquiladora y Manufacturera de Exportación (INDEX): Ejército Nacional 418, 12°, Of. 1204, Col. Chapultepec Morales, Del. Miguel Hidalgo, 11570 México, DF; tel. (55) 2282-9900; fax (55) 2282-9902; e-mail dirgral@index.org .mx; internet www.index.org.mx; f. 1973; Pres. LUIS AGUIRRE; Dir-Gen. CARLOS PALENCIA.

Instituto Nacional de Investigaciones Forestales, Agrícolas y Pecuarias (INIFAP) (National Research Institute for Forestry, Agriculture and Livestock): Avda Progreso No 5, Col. Barrio de Santa Catarina, Del. Coyoacán, 04010 México, DF; tel. (55) 3871-8700; fax (55) 3626-8639; e-mail brajcich.pedro@inifap.gob.mx; internet www .inifap.gob.mx; f. 1985; forestry conservation and management; plant and animal genetics and management; Dir-Gen. PEDRO BRAJCICH GALLEGOS.

EMPLOYERS' ORGANIZATION

Consejo Coordinador Empresarial (CCE): Lancaster 15, Col. Juárez, 06600 México, DF; tel. (55) 5229-1100; fax (55) 5592-3857; e-mail sistemas@cce.org.mx; internet www.cce.org.mx; f. 1976; co-ordinating body of private sector; Pres. GERARDO GUTIÉRREZ CANDIANI; Dir-Gen. LUIS MIGUEL PANDO LEYVA.

STATE HYDROCARBONS COMPANY

Petróleos Mexicanos (PEMEX): Avda Marina Nacional 329, Col. Petróleos Mexicanos, 11311 México, DF; tel. (55) 1944-2500; fax (55) 5531-6354; e-mail petroleosmexicanos@pemex.com; internet www .pemex.com; f. 1938; govt agency for the exploitation of Mexico's petroleum and natural gas resources; Dir-Gen. EMILIO LOZOYA AUSTIN; 131,000 employees.

MAJOR COMPANIES

Mining and Metals

Altos Hornos de México, SA: Prolongación Juárez s/n, Edif. GAN Modulo II, Col. La Loma, Monclova, 25770 Coah.; tel. (866) 633-2261; fax (866) 633-2390; e-mail servicio@ahmsa.com; internet www .ahmsa.com.mx; f. 1942; fmr state-owned iron and steel foundry and rolling mill; privatized in the early 1990s; subsidiary of Grupo Imsa; Pres. ALONSO ANCIRA ELIZONDO; Dir-Gen. LUIS ZAMUDIO MIECHIELSEN; 17,000 employees (incl. subsidiaries).

Carso Infraestructura y Construcción (CICSA): Edif. Frisco, Plaza Carso, 2°, Lago Zúrich 245, Col. Granada Ampliación, 11529 México, DF; tel. (55) 328-5800; e-mail arco@ccicsa.com.mx; internet www.ccicsa.com.mx; f. 1980; civil engineering, mining, services and infrastructure for petrochemical industry; part of Grupo Carso, SA de CV; Chair. CARLOS SLIM HELÚ; CEO ANTONIO GÓMEZ GARCÍA.

Grupo Industrial Saltillo, SA de CV: Blvd Isidro López Zertuche 1495, Zona Centro, 25000 Saltillo, Coah.; tel. (844) 2421-200; fax (844) 4111-034; e-mail jorge.verastegui@gis.com.mx; internet www .gis.com.mx; f. 1966; ceramics, iron, autoparts, water heaters; Chair. ALFONSO GONZÁLEZ MIGOYA; 10,928 employees (2007).

Grupo México, SA de CV: Campos Eliseos 400, Col. Lomas de Chapultepec, Del. Miguel Hidalgo, 11000 México, DF; tel. (55) 1103-5000; fax (55) 5574-7677; internet www.gmexico.com; f. 1901; began operations in Mexico as Asarco (USA); holding co with interests in extraction and processing of metallic ores, and transportation; Chair. and CEO GERMAN LARREA MOTA-VELASCO; 21,110 employees (2005).

Industrias Cobre, SA de CV (Nacobre): Poniente 134, No 719, Col. Industria Vallejo, 02300 México, DF; tel. (55) 5728-5300; fax (55) 5728-5391; internet www.nacobre.com.mx; f. 1951; copper, brass, aluminium, plastics producers; part of Grupo Carso, SA de CV; Gen. Man. ALEJANDRO OCHOA ABARCA; 6,500 employees.

Industrias Peñoles, SA de CV: Moliere 222, Col. Los Morales Sección Palmas, 11540 México, DF; tel. (55) 5279-3000; fax (55) 5279-3514; internet www.penoles.com.mx; f. 1969; silver, gold, lead, zinc mining; sodium sulphate plant; part of Grupo BAL; Chair. ALBERTO

BAILLÈRES GONZÁLEZ; CEO SERGIO FERNANDO ALANÍS ORTEGA; 9,081 employees.

Oceanografía: Insurgentes Sur 300, 1406 México, DF; tel. 5584-5220; fax 5264-7986; internet www.oceanografia.com.mx; f. 1968; Gen. Dir AMADO OMAR YÁÑEZ OSUNA; CEO AMADO YÁÑEZ CORREA.

TenarisTamsa (Tubos de Acero de México, SA): Km 433, Carretera Veracruz Via Xalapa, México, DF; tel. (55) 9989-1100; fax (55) 5282-9966; e-mail elenah@tamsa.com.mx; internet www.tenaristamsa .com; f. 1952; mfrs of seamless steel tubes and fittings, services for petroleum industry; Chair. and CEO PAOLO ROCCA; Area Man. (North America) GERMÁN CURÁ; 2,500 employees.

Ternium, SA: Avda Guerrero 151, Col. Cuauhtémoc, San Nicolás de los Garza, NL; tel. (81) 8865-2828; fax (55) 8329-8507; internet www .ternium.com.mx; in 2007 Ternium obtained full control of Grupo Imsa; steel; f. 1936; Exec. Pres. MAXIMO VEDOYA; 16,000 employees (2006).

Tubacero, SA de CV: Avda Guerrero 3729 Norte, Col. del Norte, 64500 Monterrey, Nuevo León; tel. (81) 8305-5511; fax (81) 8305-5510; e-mail amarquez@tubacero.com; internet www.tubacero.com; f. 1943; mfrs of piping; CEO TEODORO GONZALEZ.

Motor Vehicles

BMW de México, SA: Paseo de los Tamarindos 100, 5°, Of. 501, Col. Bosque de las Lomas, 05120 México, DF; tel. (55) 9140-8700; fax (55) 9140-8777; e-mail crm@bmw.com.mx; internet www.bmw.com.mx; f. 1994; subsidiary of BMW AG of Germany; motor vehicles and parts; Man. Dir GERD DRESSLER.

Chrysler de México, SA (DCM): Paseo de la Reforma 1240, Col. Santa Fe, Cuajimalpa, 05109 México, DF; tel. (55) 5081-3000; fax (55) 5729-7568; internet www.chrysler.com.mx; f. 1972; subsidiary of the Chrysler Corpn, USA; automobile assembly; CEO BRUNO CATTORI; 9,000 employees.

DACOMSA, SA de CV: Calzada San Bartolo Naucalpan 136, Col. Argentina Poniente, Del. Miguel Hidalgo, 11230 México, DF; tel. (55) 5726-8203; fax (55) 5726-8511; e-mail servicio.clientes@kuoafmkt .com; internet www.dacomsa.com.mx; makers of motor vehicle components; Dir BENJAMÍN CENTURIÓN DÍAZ.

Ford Motor Company, SA de CV: Guillermo González Camarena 1500, 6°, Col. Centro de Ciudad Santa Fe, 01210 México, DF; tel. (55) 5899-7594; internet www.ford.mx; f. 1925 in Mexico; subsidiary of Ford Motor Co, USA; mfrs of motor vehicle, truck and tractor parts; CEO MARK FIELDS; 7,765 employees.

General Motors de México, SA de CV: Avda Ejército Nacional 843, Col. Granada, 11520 México, DF; tel. (55) 5329-0800; fax (55) 5625-3335; internet www.gm.com.mx; f. 1931 in Mexico; subsidiary of General Motors Corpn of the USA; automobile assembly; Pres. and Dir-Gen. ERNESTO HERNÁNDEZ; 11,250 employees.

Nissan Mexicana, SA de CV: Avda Insurgentes Sur 1958, Col. Florida, 01030 México, DF; tel. (55) 5628-2648; fax (55) 5628-2696; e-mail comunicacioncorporativa@nissan.com.mx; internet www .nissan.com.mx; f. 1961 in Mexico; subsidiary of Nissan Motors Co Ltd, Japan; automobile assembly plant; Pres. and Dir-Gen. AIRTON COUSSEAU; 9,000 employees.

Volkswagen de Mexico, SA de CV: Autopista México–Puebla Km 116, San Lorenzo Almecatla, 72008 Cuautlancingo, Pue.; tel. (222) 308-111; fax (222) 230-8959; e-mail contacto@vw.com.mx; internet www.vw.com.mx; f. 1964; subsidiary of Volkswagen AG of Germany; mfrs of motor vehicles; Pres. ANDREAS HINRICHS; CEO OTTO LINDNER; 16,000 employees.

Food and Drink, etc.

Arca Continental, SAB de CV: Avda San Jerónimo 813, 64640 Monterrey, Nuevo León; tel. (81) 8151-1400; e-mail info@e-arca.com .mx; internet www.arcacontal.com; f. 2001; bottling plant; Pres. MANUEL L. BARRAGÁN MORALES; Dir-Gen. FRANCISCO GARZA EGLOFF.

FEMSA, SA de CV (Fomento Económico Mexicano, SA de CV—FEMSA): General Anaya 601 Pte, Col. Bella Vista, 64410 Monterrey, NL; tel. (81) 8328-6000; fax (81) 8328-6080; e-mail comunicacion@ femsa.com; internet www.femsa.com; f. 1890; convenience stores, beer and soft drink producers; Pres. JOSÉ ANTONIO FERNÁNDEZ CARBAJAL; Dir-Gen. CARLOS SALZAR LOMELÍN; 180,000 employees (2012).

Coca-Cola Femsa, SA de CV: Guillermo González Camarena 600, Centro de Cuidad Santa Fe, Delegación Alvaro Obregón, 01210 México, DF; tel. (55) 5081-5100; fax (55) 5292-3474; e-mail krelations@kof.com.mx; internet www.coca-colafemsa.com; f. 1991; subsidiary of Coca-Cola Export Co, USA, and FEMSA, SA de CV; soft drink mfr; bought Grupo Tampico (bottling plant) in 2011; CEO JOHN ANTHONY SANTAMARÍA OTAZUA.

Gruma, SA: Rio de la Plata, 407 Oeste, Col. Calzada del Valle, 66220 San Pedro Garza García, Nueva León; tel. (81) 8399-3349; fax (81) 8399-3359; e-mail ir@gruma.com; internet www.gruma.com; f. 1949;

tortilla and cornflour products mfrs and distributors; Pres. and CEO JUAN GONZÁLEZ MORENO; 17,000 employees (2006).

Grupo Bimbo, SA: Paseo de la Reforma 1000, Col. Peña Blanca, Santa Fe, Del. Alvaro Obregón, 01210 México, DF; tel. (55) 5268-6585; fax (55) 5258-6697; e-mail prensa@grupobimbo.com; internet www.grupobimbo.com; f. 1945; bread, confectionery and canned food mfrs; CEO DANIEL SERVITJE MONTULL; 9,000 employees (2008).

Grupo Modelo, SA de CV: Avda Javier Barros Sierra 555, Col. Zedec Santa Fe, 01210 México, DF; tel. (55) 2266-0000; fax (55) 5280-6718; e-mail atencion.modelo@gmodelo.com.mx; internet www.gmodelo.com.mx; f. 1925; beer producers; Chair. CLAUS WERNER VON WOBESER HOEPFNER; Pres. and CEO CARLOS FERNÁNDEZ GONZÁLEZ; 38,402 employees (2008).

Grupo Sanborns: Calvario 106, Col. Tlalpan, 14000 México, DF; tel. (55) 5325-9900; fax (55) 5523-9974; e-mail sanborns@sanborns.com.mx; internet www.sanborns.com.mx; operates a chain of restaurants, department stores, pharmacies; operates in retail, music promotion; part of Grupo Carso, SA de CV; Chair. CARLOS SLIM DOMIT; Gen. Dir PATRICK SLIM DOMIT; 18,500 employees (2008).

Molinos Azteca y Juper, SA de CV: Calle 7, No 1057, Zona Industrial, 44940 Guadalajara, Jal.; tel. (33) 3645-6980; fax (33) 3645-6205; e-mail informacion@molinosazteca.com; internet www.molinosazteca.com; f. 1950; agro-industrial subsidiary of Gruma, SA; Gen. Man. JAVIER ORTIZ RADILLO; 250 employees.

Savia, SA de CV: Río Sena 500, Col. del Valle Oriente, 66220 San Pedro Garza García, NL; tel. (81) 8173-5500; fax (81) 8173-5509; e-mail rherrera@savia.com.mx; internet www.savia.com.mx; produces and markets seeds for fruit and vegetables through its Seminis and Bionova subsidiaries; develops real estate projects through Desarrollo Inmobiliario Omega; Chair. and CEO ALFONSO ROMO GARZA; 8,000 employees.

Electrical Goods

Grupo Condumex, SA de CV: Miguel de Cervantes Saavedra 255, Col. Ampliación Granada, 11520 México, DF; tel. (55) 5328-5800; fax (55) 5250-2078; e-mail arco@condumex.com.mx; internet www.grupocondumex.com.mx; f. 1954; automotive parts, cables, electronics, mining; part of Grupo Carso, SA de CV; Pres. and Dir-Gen. OLVERA ZUBIZARRETA; 20,000 employees.

IBM de México, SA de CV: Alfonso Napoles Gandara 3111, Parque Corporativo de Peña Blanca, Col. Santa Fe, 01210 México, DF; tel. (55) 5270-3000; internet www.ibm.com.mx; f. 1927; mfrs of computers and office equipment; Pres. and Dir-Gen. SALVADOR MARTÍNEZ VIDAL; 2,100 employees.

Teleindustria Ericsson, SA de CV: Prolongación Paseo de la Reforma 1015, 7°, Col. Santa Fe, Del. Alvaro Obregón, 01210 México, DF; tel. (55) 1103-0104; fax (55) 5726-2333; internet www.ericsson.com.mx; f. 1904; subsidiary of Telefonaktiebolaget L. M. Ericsson of Sweden; makers of telecommunications equipment; Man. Dir JOSÉ LUIS SERRATO; 3,565 employees.

Cement and Construction

CEMEX México, SA de CV: Avda Constitución 444, Zona Centro, Monterrey, NL; tel. (81) 8328-3000; fax (81) 8328-3822; internet www.cemexmexico.com; f. 1906; mfrs and distributors of cement, concrete and building materials; Pres. (Mexico) JUAN ROMERO TORRES; 64,585 employees (2008).

Concretos Cruz Azul: Torres Bringer 517, Del. Benito Juárez, 03300 México, DF; tel. (55) 5980-1123; fax (55) 5980-1197; e-mail atencion.clientes@concretoscruzazul.com.mx; internet www.concretoscruzazul.com; f. 1881; co-operative, mfrs of cement; part of Grupo Cruz Azul; Dir-Gen. GUILLERMO ALVAREZ CUEVAS.

Corporación GEO, SA de CV: Margaritas 433, Col. Guadalupe Chimalistac, 01050 México, DF; tel. (55) 5480-5000; fax (55) 5554-6064; e-mail comunicacionsocial@casasgeo.com; internet www.casasgeo.com; f. 1973; construction and real estate; Pres. and Dir-Gen. LUIS ORVAÑANOS LASCURAIN; 4,906 employees (2005).

Empresas ICA Sociedad Controladora, SA: Blvd Manuel Ávila Camacho 36, Col. Lomas de Chapultepec, Del. Miguel Hidalgo, 11000 México, DF; tel. (55) 5272-9991; fax (55) 5271-1607; e-mail comunicacioncorporativa@ica.com.mx; internet www.ica.com.mx; f. 1947; holding co with interests in the construction industry; Pres. BERNARDO QUINTANA ISSAC; Dir-Gen. ALONSO QUINTANA KAWAGE; 17,902 employees (2007).

Holcim Apasco, SA de CV: Campos Eliseos 345, Col. Polanco Chapultepec, Del. Miguel Hidalgo, 11560 México, DF; tel. (55) 5724-0000; fax (55) 5724-0299; internet www.holcim.com.mx; f. 1963; manufacture and distribution of construction materials; part of Holcim Group, Switzerland; Dir EDUARDO KRETSCHMER; 4,500 employees.

Pharmaceutical

Bayer de México, SA de CV: Blvd Miguel de Cervantes Saavedra 259, Col. Ampliación Granada, 11520 México, DF; tel. (55) 5728-3000; fax (55) 5728-3111; internet www.bayer.com.mx; f. 1921; Pres. KURT SOLAND; 2,500 employees.

Boehringer Ingelheim Promeco, SA de CV: Maíz 49, Barrio Xaltocan, Xochimilco, 16090 México, DF; tel. (55) 5629-8300; e-mail contacto.mex@boehringer-ingelheim.com; internet www.boehringer-ingelheim.com.mx; f. 1971; subsidiary of Boehringer Ingelheim Pharmaceuticals, Germany; Pres. MIGUEL ALBERTO SALÁZAR HERNÁNDEZ.

Bristol-Myers Squibb México: Avda Revolución 1267, Col. Tlacopac, 01040 México, DF; tel. (55) 5337-2800; fax (55) 5651-2092; internet www.bms.com.mx; f. 1947; Chair. JAMES M. CORNELIUS.

Eli Lilly de México, SA de CV: Barranca del Muerto 329, Col. San José Insurgentes, 03900 México, DF; tel. (55) 1719-4500; e-mail infomed@lilly.com; internet www.lilly.com.mx; f. 1943; Pres. and Dir-Gen. CARLOS BAÑOS.

Grupo Casa Saba, SA de CV: Paseo de la Reforma 215, Col. Lomas de Chapultepec, Del. Miguel Hidalgo, 11000 México, DF; tel. (55) 5284-6600; e-mail info@casasaba.com; internet www.casasaba.com; f. 1944; name changed from Grupo Casa Autrey in 2000; pharmaceutical co; Pres. ISAAC SABA RAFFOUL; Dir-Gen. MANUEL SABA ADES; 5,700 employees.

Grupo Roche Syntex de México, SA de CV: Cerrada de Bezares 9, Col. Lomas de Bezares, 11910 México, DF; tel. (55) 5258-5000; fax (55) 5258-5472; e-mail mexico.comunicacion@roche.com; internet www.roche.com.mx; Dir-Gen. VÍCTOR MANUEL MIGUELEZ.

Laboratorios Liomont: Adolfo López Mateos 68, Del. Cuajimalpa, 05000 México, DF; tel. (55) 5814-1200; fax (55) 5812-1074; e-mail direccioncomercial@liomont.com.mx; internet www.liomont.com; f. 1938; Dir-Gen. ALFREDO RIOMOCH; 1,500 employees (2009).

Laboratorios Sanfer: Blvd Adolfo Lópaz Mateos, 1°A, Col. Tlacopac, Del. Alvaro Obregón, 01049 México, DF; tel. (55) 5639-5400; fax (55) 5639-5519; internet www.sanfer.com.mx; f. 1941; Commercial Dir LUIS SERRANO.

Merck Sharp & Dohme—MSD, SA de CV: Avda San Jerónimo 369, 8°, Col. Tizapán San Angel, 01090 México, DF; tel. (55) 5481-9600; fax (55) 5618-1361; e-mail contacto@email.msd.com.mx; internet www.msd.com.mx; f. 1932; prescription medications and vaccinations; Pres. TIMOTHY DAVELER.

Pisa Farmaceutica Mexicana: Avda España 1840, Col. Moderna, 44190 Guadalajara, Jal.; tel. (33) 3678-1600; fax (33) 3810-1609; e-mail saq@pisa.com.mx; internet www.pisafarmaceutica.com.mx; f. 1945; Pres. CARLOS ALVAREZ BERMEJILLO.

Sanofi-aventis México: Avda Universidad 1738, Col. Coyoacán, 04000 México, DF; tel. (55) 5484-4400; fax (55) 5872-0433; internet www.sanofi-aventis.com.mx; Pres. and Dir-Gen. CHRISTOPHER VIEHBACHER.

Teva Mexico: Pasaje Interlomas 16, 5°, Col. San Fernando la Herradura, 52784 Huixquilucan, Méx.; tel. (55) 5950-0200; fax (55) 5950-0201; e-mail servicio.cliente@tevamexico.com; internet www.tevamexico.com; part of Teva Pharmaceutical Industries Ltd; Dir-Gen. ENRIQUE VILLAREAL.

Retail

Controladora Comercial Mexicana, SA de CV (CCM): Avda Revolución 780, Modulo 2, Col. San Juan, 03730 Mexico, DF; tel. (55) 5270-9312; fax (55) 5371-9302; e-mail comercial.mexicana@centrodecontacto.com.mx; internet www.comerci.com.mx; f. 1944; retail traders; Chair. GUILLERMO GONZÁLEZ NOVA; CEO CARLOS GONZÁLEZ ZABALEGUI; 39,191 employees (2009).

Far-Ben, SA de CV (Farmacias Benavides): Avda Fundadores 935, Col. Valle del Mirador, 64750 Monterrey, NL; tel. and fax (81) 8389-9900; e-mail gperez@benavides.com.mx; internet www.benavides.com.mx; f. 1917; retail chemists (pharmacies); Chair. JAIME M. BENAVIDES POMPA; CEO FERNANDO BENAVIDES SAUCEDA; 5,036 employees.

Grupo Corvi: Pico de Tolima 29, Jardines en la Montaña, 14210 México, DF; tel. (55) 5628-5100; fax (55) 5645-1581; e-mail bvillasenor@infosel.net.mx; internet www.grupocorvi.com; retail distribution and confectionery; Pres. BENJAMÍN VILLASEÑOR COSTA.

Grupo Elektra, SA de CV: Avda Insurgentes Sur 3579, Col. Tlalpan La Joya, 14000 México, DF; tel. (55) 1720-7000; fax (55) 1720-7822; e-mail jrangelk@elektra.com.mx; internet www.grupoelektra.com.mx; f. 1950; retail and consumer finance; Chair. RICARDO B. SALINAS PLIEGO; CEO MARIO GORDILLO RINCÓN; 28,510 employees.

Grupo Gigante, SA de CV: Ejército Nacional 769A, Col. Nueva Granada, Del. Miguel Hidalgo, 11520 México, DF; tel. (55) 5269-8000; fax (55) 5269-8308; e-mail buzongigante@gigante.com.mx; internet www.gigante.com.mx; f. 1962; retail traders; Chair. and Dir-

Gen. ANGEL LOSADA MORENO; CEO ANGEL ALVERDE LOSADA; 33,215 employees (2005).

Organización Soriana, SA de CV: Alejandro de Rodas 3102A, Col. Las Cumbres, 8 Sector, 64610 Monterrey, NL; tel. (81) 8329-9000; fax (81) 8329-9003; e-mail comunicacion@soriana.com.mx; internet www.soriana.com.mx; f. 1968; holding co with interests in the grocery, general merchandise and clothing trade; Pres. FRANCISCO JAVIER MARTÍN BRINGAS; CEO RICARDO MARTÍN BRINGAS; 83,000 employees (2008).

El Puerto de Liverpool, SA de CV: Mario Pani 200, Col. Santa Fe, Del. Cuajimalpa de Morelos, 05109 México, DF; tel. (55) 5262-9999; fax (55) 5254-5688; e-mail ventasd@liverpool.com.mx; internet www .liverpool.com.mx; f. 1847; retail traders; Chair. MAX DAVID; CEO JOSÉ CALDERÓN MUÑOZ DE COTE; 24,156 employees (2005).

Sears Roebuck de México, SA de CV: Edif. Presa Falcón, Lago Zurich 25, Del. Miguel Hidalgo, México, DF; tel. (55) 5552-5793; fax (55) 5584-6848; e-mail sears.internet@sears.com.mx; internet www .sears.com.mx; f. 1947; part of Grupo Carso, SA de CV; department stores; Pres. CARLOS HAJJ; CEO CARLOS HAJJ ABOUMRAD; 50,100 employees.

Wal-Mart de México, SA de CV: Blvd Manuel Avila Camacho 647, Col. Periodistas, Del. Miguel Hidalgo, 11220 México, DF; tel. (55) 5328-3500; fax (55) 5328-3557; e-mail miopinion@wal-mart.com; internet www.walmartmexico.com.mx; subsidiary of Walmart Inc of the USA; retail traders; Pres. SCOT RANK; Exec. Vice-Pres. RAFAEL MATUTE; 124,295 employees.

Miscellaneous

Alfa, SA de CV: Avda Gómez Morín 1111 Sur, Col. Carrizalejo, 66254 San Pedro Garza García, NL; tel. (81) 8748-1111; fax (81) 8748-2552; internet www.alfa.com.mx; holding co with interests in steel, petrochemicals, food products and telecommunications; Chair. ARMANDO GARZA SADA; Pres. ALVARO FERNÁNDEZ GARZA; 50,992 employees (2008).

Berol, SA de CV: Vía Dr Gustavo Baz 309, Col. La Loma, 54060 Tlalnepantia, Méx.; tel. (55) 5729-3400; fax (55) 5729-3433; internet www.berol.com.mx; f. 1970; stationery mfrs; part of Sandford Group; Pres. CARLOS MORENO RIVAS; 600 employees.

Comex: Blvd Manuel Avila Camacho 138, Col. Lomas de Chapultepec, CP 11650, Mexico, DF; tel. (55) 5284-1600; internet www.comex .com.mx; PPG acquired Comex in June 2014; manufactures, markets and distributes decorative paints, textures, waterproofing products for wood care, industrial coatings, drywall and accessories; CEO MARCOS ACHAR LEVY.

CYDSA, SAB de CV y Subsidarias: Avda Ricardo Margáin Zozaya 565-B, Parque Corporativo Santa Engracia, 66267 San Pedro Garza García, NL; tel. (81) 8152-4500; fax (81) 8152-4813; e-mail informeanual@cydsa.com; internet www.cydsa.com; f. 1945; mfrs of textiles, chemicals and plastic products; Pres. and Dir-Gen. TOMÁS GONZÁLEZ SADA; 2,513 employees.

Empaques Ponderosa, SA de CV: José Santos Chocano 970, Col. Anahuác, 66220 San Nicolás de los Garza, NL; tel. (81) 8158-1702; fax (81) 8158-1706; e-mail info@ponderosa.com.mx; f. 1989; cardboard mfrs; Chair. MARIO VÁZQUEZ RAÑA; 858 employees.

Grupo Carso, SA de CV: Lago Zurich 245, Edif. Frisco, 6°, Col. Granada Ampliación, México, DF; tel. (55) 5202-8838; fax (55) 5238-0601; internet www.gcarso.com.mx; f. 1980; holding co with interests in retail, food, mining, electricals, tobacco; Pres. CARLOS SLIM DOMIT; CEO JOSÉ HUMBRETO ZUBIZARRETA; 30,840 employees.

Grupo Celanese, SA de CV: Ocotlán Km 787½, Carretera Guadalajara, La Barca Cuitzeo, Municipio de Poncitlán Jalisco, México, DF; tel. (55) 5480-9100; fax (55) 5480-9145; e-mail atencion_ciudadana@celanese.com.mx; internet www.celanese.com .mx; f. 1944; subsidiary of Celanese Corpn of USA; holding co with interests in production of speciality materials and chemicals; Dir JOSÉ MIGUEL GALINDO DIEZ; 800 employees.

Grupo Kuo, SA de CV (KUO): Paseo de los Tamarindos 400B, 31°, Col. Bosque de las Lomas, 05120 México, DF; tel. (55) 5261-8000; fax (55) 5261-8361; e-mail ir@kuo.com.mx; internet www.kuo.com.mx; f. 1973; adopted current name 2007; holding co with interests in auto parts, food, chemicals and real estate; Chair. FERNANDO SENDEROS MESTRE; Pres. and CEO JUAN MARCO GUTIÉRREZ WANLESS; 13,168 employees (2005).

Industrias John Deere de México, SA de CV: Blvd Díaz Ordáz 500, San Pedro Garza García, NL; tel. (81) 8288-1212; internet www .deere.com/es_MX; f. 1955; subsidiary of Deere and Co of the USA; farming machinery and equipment makers; Pres. SAMUEL ALLEN; 1,215 employees.

Internacional de Cerámica, SA de CV: Avda Carlos Pacheco 7200, 31060 Chihuahua, Chih.; tel. (614) 429-1111; fax (614) 4429-1166; internet www.interceramic.com/mx/main.asp; f. 1978; makers of floor tiles; Chair. VÍCTOR DAVID ALMEIDA GARCÍA; 2,900 employees.

Kimberly-Clark de México, SA de CV: Avda Jaime Balmes 8, 9°, Los Mora, 11510 México, DF; tel. (55) 5282-7300; fax (55) 5282-7272; e-mail kcm.informacion@kcc.com; internet www.kimberly-clark .com.mx; f. 1955; subsidiary of Kimberly Clark Corpn of the USA; paper mfrs; Chair. CLAUDIO XAVIER GONZÁLEZ LAPORTE; CEO PABLO GONZÁLEZ GUAJARDO; 7,700 employees.

Nadro, SA de CV: Vasco de Quiroga 3100, Col. Centro de Ciudad Santa Fe, Del. Alvaro Obregón, 01210 México, DF; tel. (52) 5292-4343; fax (52) 5292-4343; internet www.nadro.com.mx; f. 1943 as Nacional de Drogas; distribution of pharmaceuticals and beauty products; Chair. and CEO PABLO ESCANDÓN CUSI.

Mexichem, SAB de CV: Río San Javier 10, Fracc. Viveros del Río, 54060 Tlalnepantla, Méx.; tel. (55) 5366-4000; fax (55) 5397-8836; internet www.mexichem.com; petrochemicals; Chair. JUAN PABLO DEL VALLE PEROCHENA; CEO ANTONIO CARILLO.

Química Magna: Blvd Jesús Valdez Sánchez 130, La Aurora, Saltillo, Coah.; tel. (844) 431-1127; fax (844) 135-2697; e-mail quimicamagna@prodigy.net.mx; internet www.quimicamagna.com; f. 1986; industrial cleaning products; Gen. Man. JORGE VARELA PINALES.

Vitro, SA de CV: Avda Ricardo Margain Zozaya 400, Col. Calle del Campestre, San Pedro Garza García, NL 66265; tel. (81) 8863-1200; fax (81) 8335-7799; e-mail rriva@vitro.com; internet www.vitro.com; f. 1909; mfrs of glass, glass bottles and containers; Chair. ADRIÁN SADA GONZÁLEZ; CEO ADRIÁN SADA CUEVA; 24,637 employees (2005).

UTILITIES

Regulatory Authorities

Comisión Nacional del Agua (CONAGUA): Avda Insurgentes Sur 2416, Col. Copilco el Bajo, Del. Coyoacán, 04340 México, DF; tel. (55) 5174-4000; fax (55) 5550-6721; e-mail direccion@cna.gob.mx; internet www.cna.gob.mx; commission to administer national water resources; Dir-Gen. DAVID KORENFELD FEDERMAN.

Comisión Reguladora de Energía (CRE): Avda Horacio 1750, Col. Los Morales Polanco, Del. Miguel Hidalgo, 11510 México, DF; tel. (55) 5283-1500; e-mail calidad@cre.gob.mx; internet www.cre .gob.mx; f. 1994; commission to control energy policy and planning; Pres. FRANCISCO XAVIER SALAZAR DIEZ DE SOLLANO; Exec. Sec. LUIS ALONSO GONZÁLEZ DE ALBA.

Secretariat of State for Energy: see section on The Government (Secretariats of State).

Electricity

Comisión Federal de Electricidad (CFE): Avda Reforma 64, Col. Juárez México, México, DF; tel. (55) 5229-4400; fax (55) 5553-5321; e-mail servicioalcliente@cfe.gob.mx; internet www.cfe.gob.mx; state-owned power utility; Dir-Gen. ENRIQUE OCHOA REZA.

Gas

Gas Natural México (GNM): Jaime Blames 8-703, Col. Los Morales Polanco, 11510 México, DF; e-mail sugerencias@gnm.com.mx; internet www.gasnaturalmexico.com.mx; f. 1994 in Mexico; distributes natural gas in the states of Tamaulipas, Aguascalientes, Coahuila, San Luis Potosí, Guanajuato, Nuevo León and México and in the Distrito Federal; subsidiary of Gas Natural (Spain); Pres. ANGEL LARRAGA.

Petróleos Mexicanos (PEMEX): see State Hydrocarbons Company; distributes natural gas.

TRADE UNIONS

Confederación Regional Obrera Mexicana (CROM) (Regional Confederation of Mexican Workers): República de Cuba 60, México, DF; f. 1918; Sec.-Gen. LEONARDO CONTRERAS CISNEROS; 120,000 mems, 900 affiliated syndicates.

Confederación Revolucionaria de Obreros y Campesinos de México (CROC) (Revolutionary Confederation of Workers and Farmers): Hamburgo 250, Col. Juárez, Del. Cuauhtémoc, 06600 México, DF; tel. (55) 5208-5444; e-mail crocmodel@hotmail.com; internet www.croc.org.mx; f. 1952; Sec.-Gen. ISIAS GONZÁLEZ CUEVAS; 4.5m. mems in 32 state federations and 17 national unions.

Confederación de Trabajadores de México (CTM) (Confederation of Mexican Workers): Vallarta 8, Col. Tabacalera, Del. Cuauhtémoc, 06030 México, DF; tel. (55) 5141-1730; e-mail ctmorganizacion@prodigy.net.mx; internet ctmorganizacion.org .mx; f. 1936; admitted to ICFTU; Sec.-Gen. JOAQUÍN GAMBOA; 5.5m. mems.

Congreso del Trabajo (CT): Avda Ricardo Flores Magón 44, Col. Guerrero, 06300 México 37, DF; tel. (55) 5583-3817; internet www .congresodeltrabajo.org.mx; f. 1966; trade union congress comprising trade union federations, confederations, etc.; Pres. ANTONINO BAXZI MATA.

Federación Nacional de Sindicatos Independientes (National Federation of Independent Trade Unions): Isaac Garza 311 Oeste, 64000 Monterrey, NL; tel. (81) 8375-6677; e-mail fnsi@prodigy.net .mx; internet www.fnsi.org.mx/esp; f. 1936; Sec.-Gen. JACINTO PADILLA VALDEZ; 230,000 mems.

Federación Obrera de Organizaciones Femeniles (FOOF) (Workers' Federation of Women's Organizations): Vallarta 8, México, DF; tel. (55) 5592-6636; e-mail anderson89@hotmail.com; internet ctmorganizacion.org.mx/femenil.htm; f. 1950; women workers' union within CTM; Sec.-Gen. HILDA ANDERSON NEVÁREZ; 400,000 mems.

Federación de Sindicatos de Trabajadores al Servicio del Estado (FSTSE) (Federation of Unions of Government Workers): Gómez Farías 40, Col. San Rafael, 06470 México, DF; tel. (33) 5128-1600; e-mail contacto@fstse.com; internet www.fstse.com; f. 1938; Sec.-Gen. JOEL AYALA ALMEIDA; 2.5m. mems; 80 unions.

Unión General de Obreros y Campesinos de México, Jacinto López (UGOCM-JL) (General Union of Workers and Farmers of Mexico, Jacinto López): Avda Emiliano Zapata 103, Col. Portales, Del. Benito Juárez, 03300 México, DF; tel. (55) 5672-9730; e-mail contacto@ugocm-jl.mx; internet www.ugocm-jl.mx; f. 1949; admitted to WFTU/CSTAL; Sec.-Gen. JOSÉ LUIS GONZÁLEZ AGUILERA; 7,500 mems, over 2,500 syndicates.

Unión Nacional de Trabajadores (UNT) (National Union of Workers): Villalongen 50, Col. Cuauhtémoc, México, DF; tel. (55) 5140-1425; fax (55) 5703-2583; e-mail secretariageneral@strm.org .mx; internet www.unt.org.mx; f. 1998; Sec.-Gen. FRANCISCO HERNÁNDEZ JUÁREZ.

A number of major unions are non-affiliated, including:

Federación Democrática de Sindicatos de Servidores Públicos (Fedessp) (Democratic Federation of Public Servants): Vallarta 321, frente al Hotel Corinto, Col. Tabacalera, 06030 México, DF; tel. (55) 5546-2755; e-mail ser60gluz@hotmail.com; internet www .fedessp.org; f. 2005; Nat. Sec. JUAN MANUEL ESPINOZA ZAVALA.

Frente Auténtico de los Trabajadores (FAT): Godard 20, Col. Guadalupe Victoria, México, DF; tel. (55) 5556-9314; fax (55) 5556-9316; e-mail contactanos@fat.org.mx; internet www.fatmexico.org.

Sindicato Independiente de Trabajadores de la Educación de México (SITEM): México, DF; tel. (55) 1012-8459; e-mail contacto@ sitemnacional.org.mx; internet www.sitemnacional.org.mx; f. 2011; teachers' union; Sec.-Gen. JUAN CARLOS VILLANUEVA.

Sindicato Nacional de Trabajadores de la Educación (SNTE) (Education Workers): Venezuela 44, Col. Centro, México, DF; tel. (55) 5702-0005; fax (55) 5702-6303; e-mail info@snte.org.mx; internet www.snte.org.mx; f. 1943; Pres. JUAN DIAZ DE LA TORRE; 1.4m. mems.

> **Coordinadora Nacional de Trabajadores de la Educación (CNTE):** cn.trabajadoreseducacion@gmail.com; internet cntrabajadoresdelaeducacion.blogspot.com.au; dissident faction; Leader TEODORO PALOMINO.

Sindicato Nacional de Trabajadores Mineros, Metalúrgicos y Similares de la República Mexicana (SNTMM) (Mine, Metallurgical and Related Workers): Avda Dr Vertiz 668, Col. Narvarte, 03020 México, DF; tel. (55) 5519-5690; e-mail contacto@ sindicatominero.org.mx; internet www.sindicatominero.org.mx; f. 1933; Sec.-Gen. NAPOLEÓN GÓMEZ URRUTIA; 86,000 mems.

Sindicatos Nacionales de la Industria de la Construcción y el Transporte: Cerro del Agua 7, Col. Romero de Terreros, Del. Coyoacán, CP 04310, México, DF; tel. (55) 5339-6255; e-mail info@ ctm.org.mx; internet www.ctm.org.mx; Sec.-Gen. JESÚS RAMÍREZ IRETA.

Sindicato de Trabajadores Ferrocarrileros de la República Mexicana (STFRM) (Railway Workers): Avda Ricardo Flores Magón 206, Col. Guerrero, México 3, DF; tel. (55) 5597-1133; fax (55) 5583-7065; e-mail secretarianacional@stfrm.org; internet www .stfrm.org.mx; f. 1933; Nat. Sec. VÍCTOR F. FLORES MORALES; 100,000 mems.

Sindicato de Trabajadores Petroleros de la República Mexicana (STPRM) (Union of Workers): Zaragoza 15, Col. Guerrero, 06300 México, DF; tel. (55) 5546-0912; e-mail contacto@stprmsec40 .org; internet stprmsec40.org; close links with PEMEX; Sec.-Gen. ANGEL MENDOZA FLORES; 110,000 mems.

Sindicato Unico de Trabajadores Electricistas de la República Mexicana (SUTERM) (Electricity Workers): Río Guadalquivir 106, Col. Cuauhtémoc, 06500 México, DF; tel. (55) 5207-0578; internet www.suterm.org.mx; Sec.-Gen. LEONARDO RODRÍGUEZ ALCAINE.

Sindicato Unico de Trabajadores de la Industria Nuclear (SUTIN) (Nuclear Industry Workers): Viaducto Río Becerra 139, Col. Nápoles, 03810 México, DF; tel. (55) 5523-8048; fax (55) 5687-6353; e-mail exterior@sutin.org.mx; internet www.sutin.org.mx; Sec.-Gen. MANUEL GARCÍA BARAJAS.

The major agricultural unions are:

Confederación Nacional Campesina (CNC) (National Peasant Confederation): Mariano Azuela 121, Col. Santa María de la Ribera, México, DF; tel. (55) 5547-8042; internet www.cnc.org.mx; Pres. GERARDO SÁNCHEZ GARCÍA.

Confederación Nacional de Organizaciones Ganaderas (National Confederation of Stockbreeding Organizations): Calzada Mariano Escobedo 714, Col. Anzures, México, DF; tel. (55) 5254-3118; e-mail teresa.hernandez@cnog.com.mx; internet www.cnog.com.mx; Pres. OSWALDO CHÁZARO MONTALVO; 300,000 mems.

Transport

Secretariat of State for Communications and Transport: see section on The Government (Secretariats of State).

Caminos y Puentes Federales (CAPUFE): Calzada de los Reyes 24, Col. Tetela del Monte, 62130 Cuernavaca, Mor.; tel. (55) 5200-2000; e-mail contacto@capufe.gob.mx; internet www.capufe.gob.mx; Dir-Gen. GUILLERMO CASTILLO CABALLERO.

RAILWAYS

In 2010 there were 26,717 km of main line track. A 300-km railway link across the isthmus of Tehuantepec connects the Caribbean port of Coatzacoalcos with the Pacific port of Salina Cruz. In 2013 the federal Government announced a project, at a cost of an estimated US $18,000m., to build a cross-country railway line linking major Mayan historical sites.

Ferrocarril Mexicano, SA de CV (Ferromex): Bosque de Ciruelos 99, Col. Bosques de las Lomas, 11700 México, DF; tel. (55) 5246-3700; e-mail info@ferromex.com.mx; internet www.ferromex.com .mx; 50-year concession awarded to Grupo Ferroviario Mexicano, SA, (GFM) commencing in 1998; owned by Grupo México, SA de CV; 8,500 km of track and Mexico's largest rail fleet; links from Mexico City to Guadalajara, Hermosillo, Monterrey, Chihuahua and Pacific ports; Exec. Pres. ALFREDO CASAR PÉREZ; Dir-Gen. ROGELIO VÉLEZ LÓPEZ DE LA CERDA.

Ferrocarril del Sureste (Ferrosur): Bosque de Ciruelos 180, 1°, Col. Bosques de las Lomas, 11700 México, DF; tel. (55) 5387-6500; e-mail magarcia@ferrosur.com.mx; internet www.ferrosur.com.mx; 50-year concession awarded to Grupo Tribasa in 1998; 66.7% sold to Empresas Frisco, SA de CV, in 1999, owned by Grupos Carso, SA de CV; Dir-Gen. HUGO GÓMEZ DÍAZ.

Kansas City Southern de México (KCSM): Avda Manuel L. Barragán 4850, Col. Hidalgo, 64420 Monterrey, NL; tel. (81) 8305-7800; fax (81) 8305-7766; e-mail werdman@kcsouthern.com; internet www.kcsouthern.com; fmrly Ferrocarril del Noreste; 4,242 km of line, linking Mexico City with the ports of Lázaro Cárdenas, Veracruz, Tampico/Altamira and north-east Mexico; Chair. MICHAEL R. HAVERTY; Pres. and CEO DAVID L. STARLING.

Servicio de Transportes Eléctricos del Distrito Federal (STE): Avda Municipio Libre 402, 3°, Col. San Andrés Tetepilco, Del. Iztapalapa, 09440 México, DF; tel. (55) 2595-0000; fax (55) 5672-4758; e-mail sugiere@ste.df.gob.mx; internet www.ste.df.gob.mx; suburban tram route with 17 stops upgraded to light rail standard to act as a feeder to the metro; also operates bus and trolleybus networks; Pres. MIGUEL ANGEL MANCERA ESPINOSA (Head of Govt of the Distrito Federal); Dir-Gen. RUFINO H. LEÓN TOVAR.

Sistema de Transporte Colectivo (Metro) (STC): Delicias 67, 06070 México, DF; tel. (55) 5709-1133; fax (55) 5512-3601; internet www.metro.df.gob.mx; f. 1967; the first stage of a combined underground and surface railway system in Mexico City was opened in 1969; 12 lines, covering 226 km, were operating in 2014, a further 5 lines planned by 2017; the system is wholly state-owned and the fares are partially subsidized; Dir-Gen. JOEL ORTEGA CUEVAS.

ROADS

Road transport accounts for about 98% of all public passenger traffic and for about 80% of freight traffic. Mexico's terrain is difficult for overland travel. In 2010 there were 371,936 km of roads, of which 36.4% were paved. Long-distance buses form one of the principal methods of transport in Mexico, and there are some 600 lines operating services throughout the country. In 2010 the Inter-American Development Bank (IDB) approved an amount of US $2.6m. for the Pacific Corridor project (Corredor Pacífico), a highway system connecting Mexico with Panama.

Dirección General de Autotransporte Federal: Calzada de las Bombas 411, Col. Los Girasoles, Del. Coyoacán, 04920 México, DF; tel. (55) 5011-9202; e-mail elizalde@sct.gob.mx; internet dgaf.sct.gob .mx; Dir Dr MIGUEL HERBERTO ELIZALDE LIZARRAGA.

Metrobús: Avda Cuauhtémoc 16, 5°, Col. Doctores, CP 06720, México, DF; tel. (55) 5761-6858; e-mail oip@metrobus.df.gob.mx; internet www.metrobus.df.gob.mx; bus transport system in Federal District; Dir-Gen. GUILLERMO CALDERÓN AGUILERA.

SHIPPING

Mexico has 140 seaports, 29 river docks and a further 29 lake shelters. More than 85% of Mexico's foreign trade is conducted through maritime transport. At the end of 2013 the flag registered fleet comprised 673 vessels, totalling 1,803,991 grt. The Government operates the facilities of seaports.

Coordinación General de Puertos y Marina Mercante (CGPMM): Avda Nuevo León 210, Col. Hipódromo, 06100 México, DF; tel. (55) 5723-9300; fax (55) 5265-3108; e-mail egarciai@sct.gob .mx; internet cgpmm.sct.gob.mx; Co-ordinator ALEJANDRO CHACÓN DOMÍNGUEZ; Dir-Gen. de Puertos ALEJANDRO HERNÁNDEZ CERVANTES; Dir-Gen. de Marina Mercante MARCO ANTONIO VINAZA MARTÍNEZ.

Port of Acapulco: Administración Portuaria Integral Acapulco, Avda Costera Miguel Alemán s/n, Malecón Fiscal s/n, Col. Centro, CP 39300 Acapulco, Gro; tel. (744) 434-1710; fax (744) 483-1648; e-mail marketing@apiacapulco.com; internet www.apiacapulcoport.com; f. 1996; Dir-Gen. OCTAVIO GONZÁLEZ FLORES; Harbour Master Capt. ALEJANDRO MARCHENA.

Port of Coatzacoalcos: Administración Portuaria Integral de Coatzacoalcos, SA de CV, Interior Recinto Portuario s/n, Col. Centro, 96400 Coatzacoalcos, Ver.; tel. (921) 211-0270; fax (921) 211-0272; e-mail dirgral@puertocoatzacoalcos.com.mx; internet www .puertocoatzacoalcos.com.mx; CEO GILBERTO RIOS RUÍZ; Harbour Master Capt. GASPAR CIME ESCOBEDO.

Port of Dos Bocas: Administración Portuaria Integral de Dos Bocas, SA de CV, Carretera Federal Puerto Ceiba–Paraíso 414, Col. Quintín Arzuz, 86600 Paraíso, Tab.; tel. (933) 333-2744; e-mail ventanilla@puertodosbocas.com.mx; internet www .puertodosbocas.com.mx; Dir-Gen. ROBERTO DE LA GARZA LICÓN; Harbour Master Capt. RAFAEL DURÁN LÓPEZ.

Port of Manzanillo: Administración Portuaria Integral de Manzanillo, SA de CV, Avda Teniente Azueta 9, Col. Burócrata, 28250 Manzanillo, Col.; tel. and fax (314) 331-1400; e-mail gcomercial@ puertomanzanillo.com.mx; internet www.puertomanzanillo.com .mx; Dir-Gen. FLOR DE MARÍA CAÑAVERAL PEDRERO; Harbour Master Capt. JORGE ARTURO CASTAÑEDA USCANGA.

Port of Tampico: Administración Portuaria Integral de Tampico, SA de CV, Edif. API de Tampico, Zona Centro, 89000 Tampico, Tamps; tel. (833) 241-1400; fax (833) 212-5744; e-mail contacto@ puertodetampico.com.mx; internet www.puertodetampico.com.mx; Gen. Dir MANUEL FLORES GUERRA; Harbour Master Capt. MANUEL ACEITUNO RODRÍGUEZ.

Port of Veracruz: Administración Portuaria Integral de Veracruz, SA de CV, Avda Marina Mercante 210, 7°, Col. Centro, 91700 Veracruz, Ver.; tel. (229) 932-2170; fax (229) 932-3040; e-mail mespinosa@puertodeveracruz.com; internet www.puertodeveracruz .com.mx; privatized in 1994; Dir-Gen. JUAN IGNACIO FERNÁNDEZ CARBAJAL; Harbour Master Capt. ENRIQUE CASARRUBIAS GARCÍA.

Transportación Marítima Mexicana, SA de CV (TMM): Avda de la Cúspide 4755, Col. Parque del Pedregal, Del. Tlalpan, 14010 México, DF; tel. (55) 5629-8866; fax (55) 5629-8899; e-mail grupotmm@tmm.com.mx; internet www.tmm.com.mx; f. 1955; cargo services to Europe, the Mediterranean, Scandinavia, the USA, South and Central America, the Caribbean and the Far East; Pres. JOSÉ F. SERRANO SEGOVIA; Sec. IGNACIO RODRÍGUEZ PULLEN.

CIVIL AVIATION

There were 62 international airports in Mexico in 2012. Of these, México, Cancún, Guadalajara, Monterrey and Tijuana registered the highest number of operations. In September 2014 the Government announced plans to construct a new airport in the capital, at a cost of US $9,160m.

Aeropuertos y Servicios Auxiliares (ASA): Edif. B, Avda 602 161, Col. San Juan de Aragón, Del. Venustiano Carranza, 15620 México, DF; tel. (55) 5133-1000; fax (55) 5133-2985; e-mail quejasydenuncias@asa.gob.mx; internet www.asa.gob.mx; f. 1965; oversees airport management and devt; Gen. Man. GILBERTO LÓPEZ MEYER.

Dirección General de Aeronáutica Civil (DGAC): Avda Providencia No 807, 6°, Col. Del Valle, 03100 México, DF; tel. (55) 5523-6642; fax (55) 5523-7207; e-mail hgonzalw@sct.gob.mx; internet dgac .sct.gob.mx; subdivision of Secretariat of State for Communications and Transport; regulates civil aviation; Dir-Gen. HÉCTOR GONZÁLEZ WEEKS.

Aeromar, Transportes Aeromar: Hotel María Isabel Sheraton, Paseo de la Reforma 325, Local 10, México, DF; tel. (55) 5514-2248; e-mail web.aeromar@aeromar.com.mx; internet www.aeromar.com .mx; f. 1987; scheduled domestic passenger and cargo services; Dir-Gen. AMI LINDENBERG.

Aeroméxico Cargo: Avda Texococo s/n, esq. Avda Tahel, Col. Peñón de los Baños, 15520 México, DF; tel. (55) 5133-0203; internet www .aeromexicocargo.com.mx; owned by state holding co Consorcio Aeroméxico, SA; cargo airline; Dir-Gen. MAURICIO NIETO.

Aerovías de México (Aeroméxico): Paseo de la Reforma 445, 3°, Torre B, Col. Cuauhtémoc, 06500 México, DF; tel. (55) 5133-4000; fax (55) 5133-4619; internet www.aeromexico.com; f. 1934 as Aeronaves de México, nationalized 1959; sold by state holding co Consorcio Aeroméxico, SA to private investors in 2007; services between most principal cities of Mexico and the USA, Chile, Brazil, Peru, France and Spain; Pres. JOSÉ LUIS BARRAZA; Dir-Gen. ANDRÉS CONESA LABASTIDA.

Aviacsa: Aeropuerto Internacional, Zona C, Hangar 1, Col. Aviación General, 15520 México, DF; tel. (55) 5716-9005; fax (55) 5758-3823; internet www.aviacsa.com; f. 1990; operates internal flights, and flights to the USA; Dir-Gen. ANDRÉS FABRE.

Interjet (ABC Aerolíneas, SA de CV): Aeropuerto Internacional de Toluca, Toluca, Méx.; tel. (55) 1102-5555; e-mail atencionaclientes@ interjet.com.mx; internet www.interjet.com.mx; f. 2005; budget airline operating internal flights; Pres. JOSÉ LUIS GARZA.

Magnicharters (Grupo Aereo Monterrey SA de CV): Calle Donato Guerra No 9, Col. Juárez, México, DF; tel. (55) 5141-1351; internet magnicharters.com.mx; f. 1994; domestic charter flights; Dir-Gen. GABRIEL BOJÓRQUEZ.

VivaAerobus: Aeropuerto de Monterrey, Terminal C, Zona de Carga, Carretera Miguel Alemán Km. 24, Apodaca, 66600 Nuevo León; tel. (81) 8215-0150; e-mail publicidad@vivaaerobus.com; internet www.vivaaerobus.com; f. 2006; low-cost domestic airline; Dir-Gen JUAN CARLOS ZUAZUA COSÍO.

Volaris: Aeropuerto Internacional de la Ciudad de Toluca, 50500 Toluca, Méx.; tel. (55) 1102-8000; e-mail comentarios@volaris.com .mx; internet www.volaris.com.mx; f. 2006; operated by Vuela Compañía de Aviación; budget airline operating internal flights; Pres. GILBERTO PÉREZALONSO CIFUENTES; Dir-Gen. ENRIQUE BELTRANENA.

Tourism

Tourism remains one of Mexico's principal sources of foreign exchange. Mexico received a provisional 23.7m. foreign visitors in 2013, and receipts from tourism in that year were US $13,819m. More than 90% of visitors come from the USA and Canada. The relics of the Mayan and Aztec civilizations and of Spanish Colonial Mexico are of historic and artistic interest. Zihuatanejo, on the Pacific coast, and Cancún, on the Caribbean, have been developed as tourist resorts.

Secretariat of State for Tourism: see section on The Government (Secretariats of State).

Asociación Mexicana de Agencias de Viajes (AMAV): Guanajuato 128, Col. Roma, Del. Cuauhtémoc, 06700 México, DF; tel. (55) 5584-9300; fax (55) 5584-9933; e-mail contacto@amavnacional.com; internet www.ofertasdeviajesmexico.com; f. 1945; asscn of travel agencies; Pres. JORGE HERNÁNDEZ DELGADO; Exec. Vice-Pres. JOSÉ LUIS MONTERO HERNÁNDEZ.

Fondo Nacional de Fomento al Turismo (FONATUR): Tecoyotitla 100, Col. Florida, 01030 México, DF; tel. (55) 5090-4200; fax (55) 5090-4469; e-mail fonatur-dg@fonatur.gob.mx; internet www .fonatur.gob.mx; f. 1956 to finance and promote the devt of tourism; Dir-Gen. ENRIQUE CARRILLO LAVAT.

Defence

As assessed at November 2013, Mexico's regular armed forces numbered 270,250: army 200,000, navy 58,500 (including naval air force, 1,250; marines, 21,500) and air force 11,750. There were also 87,350 reserves. Paramilitary forces numbered 59,500, comprising a federal preventive police force of 37,000, a federal ministerial police force of 4,500 and a rural defence militia numbering 18,000. Military service, on a part-time basis, is by lottery and lasts for one year.

Defence Budget: 75,700m. new pesos in 2013.

Chief of Staff of National Defence: Brig.-Gen. ROBLE ARTURO GRANADOS GALLARDO.

Superintendent and Comptroller of the Army and Air Force: Gen. GILBERTO HERNÁNDEZ ANDREU.

Commander of the Air Force: Gen. CARLOS ANTONIO RODRÍGUEZ MUNGUÍA.

Chief of Staff of the Navy: Vice-Adm. JOAQUÍN ZETINA ANGULO.

Education

State education in Mexico is free and compulsory at primary and secondary level. Primary education lasts for six years between the ages of six and 11. Secondary education lasts for up to six years. In 2011 enrolment at primary schools included 96% of pupils in the relevant age-group, while in 2011 enrolment at secondary schools included 67% of pupils in the relevant age-group. In 2011/12 there were 91,253 nursery schools and 99,378 primary schools. There were 36,563 secondary schools in the same year, attended by 6.2m. pupils. In spite of the existence of more than 80 indigenous languages in Mexico, there were few bilingual secondary schools. In 2011/12 there were an estimated 6,114 institutes of higher education, attended by some 3.0m. students. The 2013 federal budget allocated a preliminary 578,978m. new pesos to education, equivalent to 17.4% of total recurrent expenditure.

Bibliography

Ashbee, E., Balslev Clausen, H., and Pedersen, C. (Eds). *The Politics, Economics, and Culture of Mexican-U.S. Migration: Both Sides of the Border*. Basingstoke, Palgrave Macmillan, 2007.

Bortz, J., and Haber, S. (Eds). *The Mexican Economy, 1870–1930*. Stanford, CA, Stanford University Press, 2002.

Cameron, M. A., and Tomlin, B. W. *The Making of NAFTA*. Ithaca, NY, Cornell University Press, 2002.

Camp, R. A. *The Metamorphosis of Leadership in a Democratic Mexico*. New York, Oxford University Press, 2010.

  Politics in Mexico: Democratic Consolidation or Decline?. New York, Oxford University Press, 2013.

Chappell Lawson, J. *Building the Fourth Estate: Democratization and the Rise of a Free Press in Mexico*. Berkeley, CA, University of California Press, 2002.

Cypher, J. M. *Mexico's Economic Dilemma: The Developmental Failure of Neoliberalism*. Lanham, MD, Rowman & Littlefield Publrs, 2010.

Diez, J. *Political Change and Environmental Policymaking in Mexico*. Abingdon, Routledge, 2006.

Domínguez, J. I., de Castro, R. F. *United States and Mexico: Between Partnership and Conflict*. 2nd edn, Abingdon, Routledge, 2009.

Eisenstadt, T. A. *Courting Democracy in Mexico: Party Strategies and Electoral Institutions*. Cambridge, Cambridge University Press, 2007.

  Politics, Identity, and Mexico's Indigenous Rights Movements. Cambridge, Cambridge University Press, 2011.

Greene, K. F. *Why Dominant Parties Lose: Mexico's Democratization in Comparative Perspective*. Cambridge, Cambridge University Press, 2007.

Hernández Chávez, A. *Mexico: A Brief History*. Berkeley, CA, University of California Press, 2006.

Jung, C. *The Moral Force of Indigenous Politics: Critical Liberalism and the Zapatistas*. Cambridge, Cambridge University Press, 2008.

Kenny, P., Serrano, M., and Sotomayor, A. C. (Eds). *Mexico's Security Failure: Collapse into Criminal Violence*. London, Routledge, 2011.

Kusnetsov, Y., and Dahlman, C. J. (Eds). *Mexico's Transition to a Knowledge-based Economy: Challenges and Opportunities*. Washington, DC, World Bank Publications, 2007.

Levy, D. C., Bruhn, K., and Zebadúa, E. *Mexico: The Struggle for Democratic Development*. Berkeley, CA, University of California Press, 2006.

Longmire, M. *Cartel: The Coming Invasion of Mexico's Drug Wars*. Basingstoke, Palgrave Macmillan, 2011.

Medrano, E. R. *Mexico's Indigenous Communities: Their Lands and Histories, 1500–2010*. Boulder, CO, University Press of Colorado, 2010.

Mentinis, M. *Zapatistas: The Chiapas Revolt and What it Meant for Radical Politics*. London, Pluto Press, 2006.

Morton, A. *Revolution and State in Modern Mexico: The Political Economy of Uneven Development*. Lanham, MD, Rowman & Littlefield Publrs, 2011.

Navarro, A. W. *Political Intelligence and the Creation of Modern Mexico, 1938–1954*. University Park, PA, Pennsylvania State University Press, 2010.

Nevins, J. *Operation Gatekeeper and Beyond: The War on 'Illegals' and the Remaking of the US–Mexico Boundary*. 2nd edn, Abingdon, Routledge, 2010.

O'Toole, G. *The Reinvention of Mexico: National Ideology in a Neoliberal Era*. Liverpool, Liverpool University Press, 2010.

Preston, J., and Dillon, S. *Opening Mexico: The Making of a Democracy*. New York, Farrar, Straus and Giroux, 2004.

Russell, P. *The History of Mexico: From Pre-Conquest to Present*. Abingdon, Routledge, 2010.

Schatz, S. *Murder and Politics in Mexico: Political Killings in the Partido de la Revolución Democrática and its Consequences*. Columbus, OH, Springer, 2011.

Schlefer, J. *Palace Politics: How the Ruling Party Brought Crisis to Mexico*. Austin, TX, University of Texas Press, 2008.

Selee, A., and Peschard, J. (Eds). *Mexico's Democratic Challenges: Politics, Government, and Society*. Washington, DC, Woodrow Wilson Press, 2010.

Selee, A., and Smith, P. *Mexico and the United States: The Politics of Partnership*. Boulder, CO, Lynne Rienner Publrs, 2013.

Serna de la Garza, J. M. *The Constitution of Mexico: A Contextual Analysis*. Oxford, Hart Publishing, 2013.

Suchlicki, J. *Mexico: From Montezuma to the Rise of the PAN*. 3rd revised edn, Dulles, VA, Potomac Books Inc, 2007.

Terry, E. D., Fallaw, B., Joseph, G. M., and Moseley, E. H. (Eds). *Peripheral Visions: Politics, Society and the Challenges of Modernity in Yucatan*. Tuscaloosa, AL, University of Alabama Press, 2010.

Uildriks, N. *Mexico's Unrule of Law: Implementing Human Rights in Police and Judicial Reform under Democratization*. Lanham, MD, Lexington Books, 2010.

Vincent, T. G. *The Legacy of Vincente Guerrero, Mexico's First Black Indian President*. Gainesville, FL, University Press of Florida, 2002.

Weintraub, S. *Unequal Partners: The United States and Mexico*. Pittsburgh, PA, University of Pittsburgh Press, 2010.

MONTSERRAT

Geography

PHYSICAL FEATURES

The devastated island of Montserrat is a United Kingdom Overseas Territory located in the Leeward Islands, in the eastern Caribbean. The nearest other polity to the colony is Antigua and Barbuda, with Antigua island some 43 km (27 miles) to the north-east, although its uninhabited outpost of Redonda is only 24 km to the north-west. Beyond Redonda lies Nevis, the smaller unit of the federation of Saint Christopher (St Kitts) and Nevis. The main islands of the French department of Guadeloupe lie 64 km to the south-east, where the arc of the Lesser Antilles continues. Montserrat is 102 sq km (39.5 sq miles) in extent, only slightly larger than Anguilla (but much more mountainous). Volcanic activity has increased its area somewhat since the mid-1990s.

Montserrat is a roughly pear-shaped island about 19 km long (north–south) and 11 km wide, with a mountainous terrain provided by three groups of highlands, steadily rising towards the south: Silver Hill in the far north; the Centre Hills; and the great Soufrière Hills, which dominate the south. This last range reaches its height at Chance's Peak (914 m—3,000 ft) and now also dominates the island because of the renewed volcanic activity centred here. Previously distinguished by verdant, forest-clad heights, occasionally scarred by areas of sulphurous springs (soufrières), the Soufrière Hills resumed a more active volcanic state for the first time in over 350 years on 18 July 1995. The series of eruptions resulted in the removal of government from the capital, Plymouth (on the south-western coast), and the evacuation of other towns (including the airport, across the island from Plymouth) from an Exclusion Zone covering over one-half of the island by April 1996. People remain generally forbidden to visit this Zone, although a Daytime Entry Zone (volcanic conditions permitting) now moderates this, operating in the west, as far as just to the north of the site of Plymouth.

Eruptions in the Soufrière Hills steadily increased in seriousness up to September 1996, but the deadly pyroclastic flows took their worst toll in June 1997 (19 people died in the Exclusion Zone despite official warnings, and the air and sea ports were finally closed) and, thereafter, the flows destroyed the centre of the abandoned capital. Pyroclastic flows are a particularly fast-moving and deadly form of volcanic emission, making the Exclusion Zone a fundamental safety feature during eruptions. Dome collapses fuel the most devastating flows. The largest dome collapse of the eruption was in July 2000, but most of the flow was down the Tar River in the east of the Zone. Another major conduit is the valley of the White River, the delta of which is also expanding the south of the island, on the south-west coast. A further significant eruption in July 2003 prompted an extension of the Exclusion Zone to embrace the Salem region—formerly on the periphery of the 'safe zone'—which had suffered severe damage from the resultant pyroclastic outflows. A subsequent extension to the Exclusion Zone, since re-designated the Unsafe Area, was necessitated following outflow incursions into safe zones in the south in May 2006. Close monitoring of continuing volcanic activity at the site enabled the authorities more accurately to predict future eruption threats and instigate measures to prevent a repeat of the human tragedy of 1997. The south of Montserrat is now dominated by seven active volcanoes, which have devastated the landscape, emptying it of life and rendering it uninhabitable for at least one decade more. Additionally, three Maritime Exclusion Zones identified as liable to volcanic activity exist to the south and east of the Territory.

Prior to the eruption of the Soufrière Hills, the richest land was in the south, and most people lived in the south-west. The greenery on the hills and coasts had confirmed the sobriquet of the 'Emerald Isle of the Caribbean', earned by Montserrat's Irish heritage. Its forestland sheltered a rich bird and animal life, including the unique black and gold Montserrat oriole and

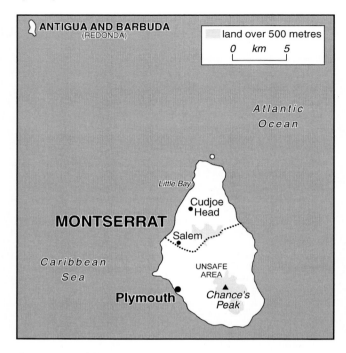

the terrestrial frog ('mountain chicken'), the latter being only otherwise found in Dominica, where it is known as the crapaud. It is as yet uncertain quite how devastating or prolonged the effect of the eruptions has been on Montserrat's natural environment, but, as about one-third of the island has been rendered into a bleak and desolate rockscape, it is severe. The central and northern highlands retain their vegetation, but the north was always drier than the south and woodland less extensive. The mountainous nature of the island has contributed to a rugged coastline, particularly on the Atlantic or weather coast, and there are no natural harbours, although the more sheltered western coast offers some anchorages.

CLIMATE

The climate is subtropical, tempered by the trade winds and by altitude. There is little seasonal variation in temperature, with average monthly maximums ranging between 24°C and 31°C (76°F and 88°F). Rainfall averages some 1,530 mm (60 ins) per year, or more with altitude, and most occurs in November–January. Humidity is low, but the island lies in the hurricane belt.

POPULATION

The population is now predominantly black or of mixed race, but Montserrat was originally noted as the only centre of Roman-Catholic Irish settlement in the West Indies (in the 17th century). Other white families joined the Irish ones, but the main addition to the population was African slaves, whose descendants now preserve the legacy of Irish names and phrases (English is the official language). There is still a large Roman Catholic community in Montserrat, although the Anglican Church is also well represented and there are many other Christian denominations in a traditionally religious society.

According to the census of May 2011 the population was 4,922. Government buildings have been established at Brades, the temporary capital, in the Carr's Bay area, in the north-west. This is on the coastal lowlands, just south of the new port facilities at Little Bay, and to the north of Cudjoe Head Village on the heights above. Cudjoe Head and Salem were the original two settlements of any size in the north of the island, in the area now outside the Unsafe Area. Salem is just north of the boundary, also on hills near the west coast. Montserrat was originally divided into three parishes, but virtually the entire Parish of St Anthony (in the south and south-west) is now in the Unsafe Area, as is most of the eastern Parish of St George. This leaves only the northern, hillier (and originally more sparsely populated) parts of St George's and the Parish of St Peter in the north and north-west.

History

MARK WILSON

Montserrat is a United Kingdom Overseas Territory. A Governor, who is the representative of the British monarch, has important reserve powers, including responsibility for national security and defence, the civil service, the judiciary and certain financial matters. According to a new Constitution, which entered into force in late September 2011, a Premier (hitherto Chief Minister) is responsible to the Legislative Assembly (previously the Legislative Council), similar in function to a parliament, which contains a majority of elected members. The Governor presides over the Executive Cabinet (formerly an Executive Council), which includes the Premier and the other ministers.

Few traces remain of the original Amerindian inhabitants, who knew the island as Alliougana, or land of the prickly bush. Christopher Columbus sighted the island in 1493, and named it after the Spanish monastery of St Ignatius of Loyola. The first British settlers arrived in 1632, most of them Irish Catholics, resettling from Saint Christopher (St Kitts) or from the North American colony of Virginia. To this day Montserrat is sometimes known as the 'Emerald Isle of the Caribbean', and has received some limited reconstruction assistance from the Irish Government. For most of its colonial history small slave plantations grew sugar and other crops, Montserrat being most famous for its limes and its cotton; however, the island was never an economic powerhouse.

From 1871 to 1956 Montserrat formed part of the Leeward Islands Federation. Unlike the larger islands of the eastern Caribbean, it did not join the short-lived Federation of the West Indies in 1958–62, and did not progress to associated statehood, retaining instead its status as a United Kingdom Dependent Territory, at first under an Administrator and then under a Governor.

In the first universal suffrage elections, held in 1952, all the seats were won by the Montserrat Labour Party, linked to the Montserrat Trades and Labour Union. This pattern was repeated in 1955, but broken in 1958. Since then, party allegiances in this small community have been fluid, overridden on most occasions by personal loyalties. The People's Liberation Movement, led by John Osborne, won all seven elected seats in a 1978 election, and remained the majority party with five seats in 1983 and four in 1987, when Osborne sought a fresh mandate during a dispute with the British authorities. Osborne's relations with the United Kingdom and with the Governor had deteriorated sharply as the result of a dispute over the management of the island's offshore financial sector. Several hundred offshore banks had been allowed to operate with no physical presence on the island and no effective supervision; most of these were later closed down, one of them run by Allen Stanford, who later played a prominent role in the affairs of neighbouring Antigua (see separate chapter). There was also some concern over Osborne's proposal to introduce casino gambling. In response, the British Government proposed a revised constitution, with increased powers of control over the financial sector for the Governor.

While this dispute was in progress, the island was devastated in September 1989 by Hurricane Hugo. Most of the housing stock was severely damaged, many public buildings were destroyed, and telephone and overhead electricity distribution systems had to be completely reconstructed. The disaster underlined the advantages of a continuing link with the United Kingdom, and somewhat weakened Osborne's internal political position. Along with his three ministers, British police detectives questioned him in June in connection with a fraud investigation. He lost his majority in September 1991, and the National Progressive Party (NPP), whose leader, Reuben Meade, became Chief Minister, won elections on 8 October.

The Soufrière Hills volcano, which had been inactive since before the time of European settlement, came to life in July 1995. The southern part of the island was temporarily evacuated in August and December of that year, and what turned out to be a permanent evacuation was ordered on 1–3 April 1996. Twenty-three emergency shelters were established in the north of the island, initially housing 1,381; the last residents moved out of emergency accommodation only in 2001. By the time of the April 1996 evacuation, around 3,000 residents had left the island; soon afterwards, the British Government agreed Montserratians would be granted two years' stay in the United Kingdom, with the right to work or to obtain income support and housing benefits; however, no assistance with travel was offered to low-income islanders.

A general election was held in November 1996, despite the volcanic emergency. With a low turnout, the NPP held one seat, with two each for the People's Progressive Alliance and the Movement for National Reconstruction, and two for independent candidates. Bertrand Osborne formed a coalition Government, and, in contrast to some of Montserrat's previous Chief Ministers, enjoyed consistently good relations with the United Kingdom.

In March and April 1997 the pace of volcanic activity quickened. There were flows of hot ash from the volcano, and ash clouds extended up to 12.5 km into the atmosphere. The remaining inhabitants of the southern part of the island, including the former capital, Plymouth, were forced to leave their homes. Most of the south has since been covered by a thick layer of volcanic ash, while volcanic deposits have in one location extended the coastline out to sea by 1.5 km. However, not everyone complied with instructions to stay out of the danger area at all times, and 19 people were killed on 25 June, some of whom were visiting closed areas to tend crops or livestock. The port was destroyed, while the airport lay within the danger zone. Some emergency accommodation was provided in the north, but two-thirds of the population left the island altogether, moving either to the United Kingdom, to Antigua and Barbuda or to other Caribbean islands.

There was considerable public disquiet both locally and in the United Kingdom at what was seen as a lack of assistance from the British Government. After public protests over conditions in emergency accommodation, Osborne resigned in August 1997, and was replaced as Chief Minister by the more vociferous David Brandt, who had been a key member of John Osborne's Government during the offshore banking crisis. Brandt immediately entered into a bitter dispute with the British authorities, which escalated after remarks perceived as insensitive were made by the British Secretary of State for International Development, Clare Short, about Montserratian demands for 'golden elephants'.

Since the entire population now lived in the north of the island, the old constituency system was no longer relevant. Brandt's Government lost its majority in February 2001, and elections were held in April under a new 'at-large' voting system, without constituencies. John Osborne returned to office as Chief Minister, as leader of the New People's Liberation Movement (NPLM), which won seven of the nine elective seats, with the NPP taking the remaining two seats. In contrast to his earlier period in office, Osborne in general enjoyed a harmonious relationship with the British Government and its local representatives.

In February 2002 the Organisation of Eastern Caribbean States (OECS) countries, including Montserrat, agreed, in principle, to allow nationals of member states to travel freely within the OECS area and to remain in a foreign territory within the area for up to six months. It was also planned to introduce a common OECS passport. In May the British Overseas Territories Act, having received royal assent in the United Kingdom in February, came into force and granted British citizenship to the people of its Overseas Territories, including Montserrat. Under the new law, Montserratians were able to hold British passports and work in the United Kingdom and elsewhere in the European Union.

The level of volcanic activity increased again from September 2002, and a small area containing 300 houses was taken out of the 'safe zone'. Most of those affected were wealthy expatriates with winter homes; however, 80 Montserratians were placed in emergency accommodation. A further massive eruption, reported to be the largest since 1995, occurred in July 2003, causing damage to the supply of water and electricity, and the destruction of numerous buildings in the Salem area, which is on the periphery of the 'safe zone'. In July 2004 the USA informed the 200 Montserratians granted emergency residence during the volcanic emergency that they should plan to return home. However, the volcano was far from quiet, with renewed activity occurring in May 2006. Construction work on housing for the 48 people remaining in evacuation shelters began in that same month and it was intended that all shelters should close by the end of that year. However, a further phase of lava dome growth commenced in later months, continuing into early 2007, which prompted the USA in November 2006 to consider an extension to its programme of Temporary Protected Status for Montserratians imperilled by the renewed volcanic threat. Although the authorities remained on moderately high alert in 2007, by mid-April volcanic activity had reportedly abated and plans for further evacuations were suspended. Intermittent volcanic activity has continued since that date, but from 2009 to mid-2014 at a fairly low level. However, the Montserrat Volcano Observatory notes that the volcano remains 'capable of renewed activity'.

At a general election in May 2006, allegations of corruption and mismanagement were made against candidates from both Government and opposition. As no party won a clear majority, Lowell Lewis, the sole elected member for the Montserrat Democratic Party, formed a coalition Government with the three members elected from the NPLM (including former Chief Minister John Osborne) and Brandt, who was elected as an independent. The Movement for Change and Prosperity (MCAP), the largest single party represented, with four seats, formed the opposition. The new Government lasted until 21 February 2008, when Lewis announced an alliance with the MCAP, three of whose members took ministerial portfolios. John Osborne became a government backbencher, along with

the fourth elected member of the MCAP. Two former NPLM cabinet ministers formed the opposition, along with Brandt, and in mid-2008 stated their intention to form a new party. In order to avoid a vote of no confidence by Brandt, in November Lewis handed the economic development portfolio to Reuben Meade, who, in addition to his experience as a former chief minister, has also worked with the Caribbean Development Bank. However, Lewis retained responsibility for finance, and in March presented the annual budget for 2009. Tensions within the coalition increased during 2009, and Lewis called a fresh poll for 8 September, with two years of the current term still to run. The MCAP took six of the nine seats under the at-large voting system, led by Reuben Meade, who became Chief Minister. Lewis retained his seat and sits as one of three independents who form the opposition.

Following preliminary consultations, draft proposals for a new constitution were discussed with representatives from the United Kingdom in May 2010. After an additional round of discussions, the new Constitution was approved by the British Government in October, following a division in the Legislative Council of Montserrat, in which two opposition representatives voted against it. The new Constitution came into force from 27 September 2011. The post of Premier replaced that of Chief Minister, and a Legislative Assembly, with nine members elected for five years, replaced the Legislative Council. The Governor, however, retained responsibility for external affairs, defence, regulation of international financial services, the police and internal security, and some aspects of the public service, but these might also be discussed in an Advisory Council, which included the opposition leader as well as senior government figures. The Constitution contained an extensive section on fundamental rights and freedoms, with provision for periods of public emergency. There was increased provision for transparency and accountability, with guaranteed independence for the office of the Auditor-General. A United Kingdom White Paper published in June 2012 set out a strategy of greater British involvement in the governance of the remaining 14 British Overseas Territories, and stated that the present was not a suitable time to initiate further constitutional reform. In the same month Meade asked the UN Special Committee of 24 on Decolonization to remove Montserrat from its list of non-self-governing countries. The opposition leader, Donaldson Romeo, subsequently filed a motion of no confidence, indicating his dissent, which was defeated in the Assembly.

A general election was held on 11 September 2014. Opposition leader Romeo formed his own party, the People's Democratic Movement (PDM), in advance of the election, while Lowell Lewis was contesting the ballot as part of the Alliance of Independent Candidates coalition. The PDM performed well in the election, winning seven of the nine legislative seats and 50.1% of the valid ballot. The MCAP secured the remaining two seats and 35.3% of the valid votes. Romeo was sworn in as Premier the following day.

Economy

MARK WILSON

Montserrat is an Overseas Territory of the United Kingdom in the eastern Caribbean, with an area of 102 sq km (39.5 sq miles) and a population of 4,922 at the May 2011 census; this figure is much lower than the total of 11,581 in 1994, just before the volcano became active, but considerably more than the low point of 2,850 reached in 1998. A proportion of the increased population were migrant workers, however (and some of the money earned by them was therefore sent abroad in the form of remittances). In spite of the volcanic emergency, the island is reasonably prosperous, with a per-head gross domestic product (GDP) of some EC $31,981 in 2011, and an economy supported by substantial grant aid from the United Kingdom. GDP has been variable: the economy contracted by a cumulative 32% in 2009 and 2010, as public sector construction activity slowed

and the island was affected by Hurricane Earl, then grew by 5.5% in 2011 and by 3.6% in 2012, but contracted by 0.9% in 2013. Construction was estimated to contribute some 6.9% of GDP in 2013, down from 15.4% in 2002.

Montserrat is a member of the Caribbean Community and Common Market, whose members formed a single market in 2006. It is also a member of the Organisation of Eastern Caribbean States, which links nine of the smaller Caribbean territories, while the Eastern Caribbean Central Bank, headquartered in Saint Christopher (St Kitts) and Nevis, supervises its financial affairs. The Territory also uses the services of the regional stock exchange, the Eastern Caribbean Securities Exchange (also based in Saint Christopher and Nevis).

The southern two-thirds of the island form an Unsafe Area around the Soufrière Hills volcano, which has been active since July 1995. Before the recent volcanic devastation, there was a small manufacturing sector, including a rice mill and an electronics assembly plant. These, as well as most tourist accommodation and much of the transport, utilities and infrastructure, were in what is now the Unsafe Area. Since 1997 there has been no significant manufacturing or commercial agriculture. There is a small offshore financial sector; there are six offshore banks, none with a physical presence in Montserrat. The Caribbean Financial Action Task Force completed an evaluation in 2010; however, the IMF has called for stricter financial sector supervision. A Memorandum of Understanding signed in 2013 provides the basis for registering small ships and pleasure vessels as part of the United Kingdom-based Red Ensign group. In the domestic financial sector, a substantial risk to the economy has been exposure of EC $76m. (equivalent to 48% of GDP) to two Trinidad-based insurance companies whose parent, CL Financial, collapsed in 2009. In 2005 the first major export was made since the volcanic eruption: a quantity of aggregate from a quarry in Little Bay was shipped to Antigua. Since then, shipments of volcanic ash have been exported to the Virgin Islands, the islands of the former Netherlands Antilles and Anguilla for use in construction, generating employment of approximately 100, adding royalties to government revenue. The port of Plymouth was in use for ash exports from 2012. Thus, the economy has been able to capitalize on by-products from volcanic activity.

Economic activity has centred since 1997 on the construction of new facilities in the north of the island, supported largely by British development grants, and Montserrat in 2013 agreed a Sustainable Growth and Development Package with the United Kingdom. Although the British Government intended to move its emphasis from support of the recurrent budget towards capital investment programmes, local revenue was to cover 45% of the recurrent budget, with the remainder met by British and other grants, as the local tax base was extremely limited. The development budget of EC $78.5m. was to be funded 80% by the United Kingdom's Department for International Development, 15% by the European Union (EU), and 5% from local and other sources. The budget for 2014/15 proposed expenditure of EC $160.8m., to be funded by EC $44.4m. in local revenue; grants of EC $64.1m. for the recurrent budget; with the development budget funded mainly by the United Kingdom and the EU. Public debt in 2014 was EC $6.6m, or 4% of GDP, composed mainly of borrowing by the Port Authority of Montserrat from the Caribbean Development Bank (CDB). Goals outlined in a Sustainable Development Plan for 2008–10 included a diversified economy, sustained economic growth and graduation from British budgetary support by 2017, with a population of 9,000 by that date. The plan proposed private sector-led growth with improved infrastructure and transport facilities, renewed expansion in tourism, and development of geothermal energy, quarrying and food production. Problems noted included a shortage of entrepreneurial talent, with costly telecommunications services and physical access. The IMF in 2011 noted enormous progress in recovery resulting from donor support, but that the Government still accounted for more than one-half of employment.

The new capital is Brades, formerly a small village with few services. The Montserrat Development Corporation oversees construction of new facilities at Little Bay, scheduled to assume the role of capital by 2020. Already completed in the north are a small port, a housing development, fuel storage facilities, a power plant, a water supply system, schools, a small hospital, a police headquarters, a fire station, sheltered housing for the elderly and a new building for the volcanic observatory. A further EC $100m. port development was planned for Carr's Bay, with designs to be completed in mid-2014. The John A. Osborne Airport at Gerald's with a 600-m runway was completed in 2005, funded by the EU and the United Kingdom; two airlines were providing services with small aircraft in 2014; one of these, Fly Montserrat, was grounded in 2012 following a number of accidents. Privately funded projects have included a small shopping centre and a 700-seat cultural centre, funded by the British record producer Sir George Martin. A new power station building was completed in 2005, while the Department for International Development and the CDB in 2011 announced plans to provide EC $30m. of finance for new and more efficient generating equipment with peak demand at 2 MW. For the longer term, the Iceland Drilling Company was contracted in 2012 to develop geothermal electricity. Results from test wells were expected from mid-2014 to allow detailed design of a power plant; meanwhile an additional thermal power plant was under construction, for completion by May 2015. A Cable & Wireless telecommunications monopoly expired in 2007, and the Government passed legislation in 2009 in preparation for liberalization of the sector. By 2014 Cable & Wireless, operating as LIME, was still the only operator. A small cigarette manufacturer was established in 2013 to serve local and export markets, with employment of 25.

A number of interesting proposals were made with the intention of revitalizing the island's economy, but not all have been followed through. There is a small and specialized tourism industry based on the volcano itself, with facilities for visiting scientists, students and the merely curious, including an interpretation centre at Little Bay. A number of visitors make day trips while staying in Antigua and Barbuda or on other islands; there were 1,519 excursionist visitors in 2013; however, the short air connection is expensive, and this was down from 5,083 in 2004, when a regular ferry service was in operation. For stop-over visitors, there were 60 rooms in hotels and guest houses in 2006; there were 7,201 stop-over tourist arrivals in 2013, a fall from the 2004 peak of 10,110. There were also 1,377 yachting visitors. Receipts from tourism totalled some EC $18.3m. in 2013. Further hotel and scuba-diving developments were under discussion, with a yachting marina and cruise ship facilities also proposed for Carr's Bay; at present, most cruise ships pause offshore, allowing passengers a distant view, while fly-over air tours are based in Antigua and provide no benefit to the local economy. Another early proposal was a graduate school of disaster studies, which was to be operated in collaboration with British and US universities. Besides volcanic activity and hurricanes, the island is at some risk from earthquakes, landslides and tsunamis.

Statistical Survey

Sources (unless otherwise stated): Government Information Service, Media Centre, Chief Minister's Office, Old Towne; tel. 491-2702; fax 491-2711; Eastern Caribbean Central Bank, POB 89, Basseterre, Saint Christopher; internet www.eccb-centralbank.org; OECS Economic Affairs Secretariat, *Statistical Digest*.

AREA AND POPULATION

Area: 102 sq km (39.5 sq miles).

Population: 4,491 at census of 12 May 2001; 4,922 (males 2,546, females 2,376) at census of 12 May 2011.

Population by Age and Sex (at 2011 census): *0–14 years:* 971 (males 490, females 481); *15–64 years:* 3,260 (males 1,709, females 1,551); *65 years and over:* 691 (males 347, females 344); *Total* 4,922 (males 2,546, females 2,376).

Density (at 2011 census): 48.3 per sq km.

Principal Town: Plymouth, the former capital, was abandoned in 1997. Brades is the interim capital, with a population of 465 at mid-2014, according to UN estimates (Source: UN, *World Urbanization Prospects: The 2014 Revision*).

Births and Deaths (1999): 45 live births (birth rate 9.4 per 1,000); 59 deaths (death rate 12.4 per 1,000) (Source: UN, *Population and Vital Statistics Report*). *2013:* Crude birth rate 11.4 per 1,000; Crude death rate 6.6 per 1,000 (Source: Pan American Health Organization).

Life Expectancy (years at birth, estimates): 73.7 (males 75.3; females 71.9) in 2013. Source: Pan American Health Organization.

Economically Active Population (FAO estimate): Total labour force 2,000. Source: FAO.

HEALTH AND WELFARE

Physicians (per 1,000 head, 2011): 0.98.

Hospital Beds (per 1,000 head, 2011): 5.8.

Health Expenditure (public, % of GDP, 2011): 10.0.

Health Expenditure (public, % of total, 1995): 67.0.

Source: Pan American Health Organization.

For sources and definitions, see explanatory note on p. vi.

AGRICULTURE, ETC.

Principal Crops (metric tons, 2012, FAO estimates): Vegetables 793 (incl. melons); Fruit (excl. melons) 930.

Livestock ('000 head, 2012, FAO estimates): Cattle 10.0; Sheep 4.8; Goats 7.1; Pigs 1.2.

Livestock Products ('000 metric tons, 2012, FAO estimates): Cattle meat 0.7; Cows' milk 1.9.

Fishing (metric tons, live weight, 2012, FAO estimate): Total catch 41 (all marine fishes).

Source: FAO.

INDUSTRY

Electric Energy (million kWh): 11.6 in 2007; 11.7 in 2008; 11.8 in 2009.

FINANCE

Currency and Exchange Rates: 100 cents = 1 East Caribbean dollar (EC $). *Sterling, US Dollar and Euro Equivalents* (30 May 2014): £1 sterling = EC $4.542; US $1 = EC $2.700; €1 = EC $3.675; EC $100 = £22.02 = US $37.04 = €27.21. *Exchange Rate*: Fixed at US $1 = EC $2.70 since July 1976.

Budget (EC $ million, 2013): *Revenue:* Revenue from taxation 35.7 (Taxes on income and profits 15.0, Taxes on property 1.0, Taxes on domestic goods and services 3.7, Taxes on international trade and transactions 16.0); Non-tax revenue 6.0; Total 41.7 (excl. grants 112.2). *Expenditure:* Current expenditure 107.7 (Personal emoluments 41.8, Goods and services 26.2, Transfers and subsidies 39.7); Capital expenditure 73.5; Total 181.2.

International Reserves (US $ million at 31 December 2013): Foreign exchange 40.51. Source: IMF, *International Financial Statistics*.

Money Supply (EC $ million at 31 December 2013): Currency outside depository corporations 18.39; Transferable deposits 50.29; Other deposits 166.60; *Broad money* 235.27. Source: IMF, *International Financial Statistics*.

Cost of Living (Consumer Price Index; base: April 1984 = 100): All items 253.7 in 2011; 265.7 in 2012; 268.0 in 2013.

Gross Domestic Product (EC $ million at constant 2006 prices, estimates): 153.34 in 2011; 158.90 in 2012; 157.51 in 2013.

Expenditure on the Gross Domestic Product (EC $ million at current prices, 2013, estimates): Government final consumption expenditure 81.67; Private final consumption expenditure 167.79; Gross fixed capital formation 38.81; *Total domestic expenditure* 288.27; Export of goods and services 37.10; *Less* Imports of goods and services 147.71; *GDP at market prices* 177.67.

Gross Domestic Product by Economic Activity (EC $ million at current prices, 2013, estimates): Agriculture, forestry and fishing 2.44; Mining and quarrying 0.96; Manufacturing 2.73; Electricity and water 4.87; Construction 11.21; Wholesale and retail trade 10.60; Restaurants and hotels 3.61; Transport 5.40; Communications 5.27; Banks and insurance 20.67; Real estate and housing 20.42; Government services 54.01; Other services 20.62; *Sub-total* 162.82; *Less* Financial intermediation services indirectly measured 1.64; *Gross value added at basic prices* 161.17; Taxes, less subsidies, on products 16.50; *GDP at market prices* 177.67.

Balance of Payments (EC $ million, 2013, estimates): Goods (net) −79.17; Services (net) −12.86; *Balance on goods and services* −92.03; Income (net) −8.05 *Balance on goods, services and income* −100.08; Current transfers (net) 25.93; *Current balance* −74.15; Capital account (net) 78.96; Direct investment (net) 6.03; Portfolio investment (net) 0.31; Public sector long-term investment −0.50; Commercial banks 31.54; Other investment assets −16.44; Other investment liabilities −0.69; Net errors and omissions −2.31; *Overall balance* 22.75.

EXTERNAL TRADE

Principal Commodities (distribution by SITC, EC $ million, 2013, estimates): *Imports c.i.f.:* Food and live animals 14.04; Beverages and tobacco 4.39; Mineral fuels and related materials 33.19; Chemicals and related products 6.27; Manufactured goods 15.91; Machinery and transport equipment 23.85; Miscellaneous manufactured articles 7.19; Total (incl. others) 107.84. *Exports (incl. re-exports) f.o.b.:* Crude materials, inedible (except fuels) 3.03; Manufactured goods 4.58; Machinery and transport equipment 7.65; Miscellaneous manufactured articles 0.74; Total (incl. others) 16.10.

Principal Trading Partners (US $ '000, 2009): *Imports c.i.f.:* Barbados 128; Canada 415; China, People's Repub. 237; Dominican Republic 237; Jamaica 654; Japan 1,520; Netherlands 309; St Vincent and the Grenadines 295; Trinidad and Tobago 1,803; United Kingdom 1,666; USA 20,272; Total (incl. others) 29,605. *Exports f.o.b.:* Anguilla 480; Antigua and Barbuda 77; British Virgin Islands 208; Dominica 381; France (incl. Monaco) 133; Netherlands Antilles 211; New Zealand 247; St Christopher and Nevis 366; Trinidad and Tobago 481; United Kingdom 153; USA 384; Total (incl. others) 3,148. *2013* (EC $ million, estimates): Total imports 107.84; Total exports 16.10 (re-exports 10.06).

TOURISM

Tourist Arrivals (2013): Stay-over arrivals 7,201 (USA 1,775, Canada 516, United Kingdom 1,821, Caribbean 2,591, Others 498); Excursionists 1,519; Total visitor arrivals (incl. others) 10,461.

Tourism Receipts (EC $ million, estimates): 14.0 in 2011; 19.0 in 2012; 18.3 in 2013.

COMMUNICATIONS MEDIA

Telephones (2013): 3,000 main lines in use.

Mobile Cellular Telephones (2013): 4,500 subscribers.

Broadband Subscribers: 1,200 in 2013.

Source: International Telecommunication Union.

EDUCATION

Pre-primary: 11 schools (1999); 14 teachers (2008/09); 128 pupils (2008/09).

Primary: 2 schools (1999); 37 teachers (2008/09); 485 pupils (2008/09).

Secondary: 1 school (1999); 27 teachers (2008/09); 358 pupils (2008/09).

Pupil-teacher Ratio (primary education, UNESCO estimate): 13.1 in 2008/09.

Sources: UNESCO, *Statistical Yearbook*; UNESCO Institute for Statistics.

Directory

The Constitution

The Constitution came into force on 27 September 2011 and replaced the 1989 charter that was very similar to the constitutional order established in 1960. The Constitution guarantees the fundamental rights and freedoms of the individual, with provision for periods of public emergency, and grants the Territory the right of self-determination. Montserrat is governed by a Governor. The Constitution made provision for a Deputy Governor, who must be Montserratian. The Deputy Governor is appointed by the Governor, but with the prior approval of a Secretary of State. The Governor retains responsibility for external affairs, defence, regulation of international financial services, the police and internal security, and some aspects of the public service, but these may also be discussed in an Advisory Council, which includes the Leader of the Opposition, as well as senior government figures. The new Constitution replaced the island's Executive and Legislative Councils with an Executive Cabinet and a Legislative Assembly. The Executive Cabinet consists of the Governor as President, the Premier and three other Ministers, the Attorney-General and the Financial Secretary. The Legislative Assembly consists of nine members, elected for five years, and two ex officio members, namely the Attorney-General and the Financial Secretary. There was increased provision for transparency and accountability, with guaranteed independence for the office of the Auditor-General.

The Government

HEAD OF STATE

Queen: HM Queen Elizabeth II.

Governor: Adrian Derek Davis (took office 8 April 2011).

Deputy Governor: Alric Taylor.

EXECUTIVE CABINET
(September 2014)

Following the success of the People's Democratic Movement in the general election of 11 September 2014, the party's leader, Donaldson Romeo, was sworn in as Premier and was to appoint a new Executive Cabinet.

President: Adrian Derek Davis (The Governor).

Attorney-General: (vacant).

Financial Secretary: John Skerritt.

Premier: Donaldson Romeo.

Minister of Education, Health, Community and Social Services, Youth Affairs and Sports: Colin Riley.

Permanent Secretary to the Office of the Premier: Beverley Mendes.

Cabinet Secretary: Angela Greenaway.

Clerk to the Executive Cabinet: Judith Jeffers.

MINISTRIES

Office of the Governor: Unit 8, Farara Plaza, Brades; tel. 491-2688; fax 491-8867; e-mail govoffice.montserrat@fco.gov.uk; internet ukinmontserrat.fco.gov.uk.

Office of the Deputy Governor: No. 3, Farara Plaza, Brades; tel. 491-6524; fax 491-9751; e-mail odg@gov.ms; internet odg.gov.ms.

Office of the Attorney-General: POB 129, Valley View; tel. 491-4686; fax 491-4687; e-mail legal@gov.ms; internet agc.gov.ms.

Office of the Premier: Govt HQ, POB 292, Brades; tel. 491-3378; fax 491-6780; e-mail ocm@gov.ms; internet ocm.gov.ms.

Ministry of Agriculture, Lands, Housing, Environment and Ecclesiastical Affairs: Govt HQ, POB 272, Brades; tel. 491-2546; fax 491-9275; e-mail malhe@gov.ms; internet www.malhe.gov.ms.

Ministry of Communications, Works and Labour: Woodlands; tel. 491-2521; fax 491-3475; e-mail comworks@gov.ms.

Ministry of Education, Health, Community and Social Services, Youth Affairs and Sports: Govt HQ, POB 103, Brades; tel. 491-2541; fax 491-6941.

Ministry of Finance and Economic Management: Govt HQ, POB 292, Brades; tel. 491-2777; fax 491-2367; e-mail minfin@gov.ms; internet www.finance.gov.ms.

LEGISLATIVE ASSEMBLY

Speaker: Teresina Bodkin.

Clerk: Judith Bakers.

Election, 11 September 2014, preliminary results

Party	Seats
People's Democratic Movement	7
Movement for Change and Prosperity	2
Total	**9**

There are also two ex officio members (the Attorney-General and the Financial Secretary).

Political Organizations

Montserrat Democratic Party (MDP): c/o Kelsick & Kelsick, Woodlands Main Rd, POB 185, Brades; tel. 491-2379; e-mail lowell@mdp.ms; internet www.mdp.ms; f. 2006; contested the 2014 election as part of the Alliance of Independent Candidates coalition; Leader Dr Lowell Lewis.

Montserrat Labour Party (MLP): Brades; f. 2009 by fmr mems of the NPLM (q.v.); Leaders Margaret Dyer-Howe, Idabelle Meade.

Montserrat Reformation Party (MRP): Brades; f. 2009; Leaders Adelina Tuitt, Alric Taylor.

Movement for Change and Prosperity (MCAP): POB 419, Brades; e-mail mail@mcap.ms; internet www.mcap.ms; f. 2005 by fmr mems of the National Progressive Party (NPP); Leader Reuben T. Meade; Chair. Randolph Riley.

New People's Liberation Movement (NPLM): f. 1997 as successor party to People's Progressive Alliance and the Movement for National Reconstruction (MNR); opposition party; Leader David Osborne.

People's Democratic Movement (PDM): Brades; e-mail peoplepowermni@gmail.com; f. 2014; Leader Donaldson Romeo; Deputy Leader Delmaude Ryan.

Judicial System

Justice is administered by the Eastern Caribbean Supreme Court (based in Saint Lucia—comprised of the Court of Appeal and the High Court), the Court of Summary Jurisdiction and the Magistrate's Court. A revised edition of the Laws of Montserrat came into force in 2005.

Registrar: Amila Daley.

Magistrate's Office: Govt HQ, Brades; tel. 491-4056; fax 491-8866; e-mail magoff@gov.ms; Magistrate Clifton Warner.

Attorney-General: (vacant).

Religion

CHRISTIANITY

The Montserrat Christian Council: St Peter's Main Rd, POB 227, St Peter's; tel. 491-4864; fax 491-2139; Rep. Rev. Joan Delsol Meade.

The Anglican Communion

Anglicans are adherents of the Church in the Province of the West Indies, comprising eight dioceses. Montserrat forms part of the diocese of the North Eastern Caribbean and Aruba. The Bishop is resident in St John's, Antigua and Barbuda.

The Roman Catholic Church

Montserrat forms part of the diocese of St John's-Basseterre, suffragan to the archdiocese of Castries (Saint Lucia). The Bishop is resident in St John's, Antigua and Barbuda.

Other Christian Churches

There are Baptist, Methodist, Pentecostal and Seventh-day Adventist churches and other places of worship on the island.

The Press

Montserrat Newsletter: Farara Plaza, Unit 8, Brades; tel. 491-2688; fax 491-8867; e-mail richard.aspin@fco.gov.uk; f. 1998; 4 a year; govt information publ; Publicity Officer RICHARD ASPIN.

The Montserrat Reporter: POB 306, Davy Hill; tel. 491-4715; fax 491-2430; e-mail editor@themontserratreporter.com; internet www.themontserratreporter.com; f. 1984; weekly on Fri.; Editor BENNETTE ROACH; circ. 2,000.

Broadcasting and Communications

TELECOMMUNICATIONS

LIME: POB 219, Sweeney's; internet www.time4lime.com/ms; fmrly known as Cable & Wireless (West Indies) Ltd; CEO TONY RICE; Regional CEO GERARD BORELY.

BROADCASTING

Radio

Radio Antilles: POB 35/930, Plymouth; tel. 491-2755; fax 491-2724; f. 1963; in 1989 the Govt of Montserrat, on behalf of the Org. of Eastern Caribbean States, acquired the station; has one of the most powerful transmitters in the region; commercial; regional; broadcasts in English and French; Chair. Dr H. FELLHAUER; Man. Dir KRISTIAN KNAACK; Gen. Man. KEITH GREAVES.

Radio Montserrat (ZJB): POB 51, Sweeney's; tel. 491-2885; fax 491-9250; e-mail zjb@gov.ms; internet www.zjb.gov.ms; f. 1952; govt station; Man. HERMAN SARGEANT.

Television

Television services can also be obtained from Saint Christopher and Nevis, Puerto Rico and from Antigua and Barbuda.

Cable Television of Montserrat Ltd: POB 447, Olveston; tel. 491-2507; fax 491-3081; Man. SYLVIA WHITE.

People's Television (PTV): Manjack; tel. 491-5110; e-mail deedge@candw.ms; internet www.ptvmontserrat.com; Man. DENZIL EDGECOMBE.

Finance

The Eastern Caribbean Central Bank, based in Saint Christopher and Nevis, is the central issuing and monetary authority for Montserrat.

Eastern Caribbean Central Bank—Montserrat Office: 2 Farara Plaza, POB 484, Brades; tel. 491-6877; fax 491-6878; e-mail eccbmni@candw.ms; internet www.eccb-centralbank.org; Resident Rep. CLAUDETTE WEEKES.

Financial Services Commission: Phoenix House, POB 188, Brades; tel. 491-6887; fax 491-9888; e-mail fscmrat@candw.ms; internet www.fscmontserrat.org; f. 2001; the Commission consists of the Commissioner and 4 other mems appointed by the Governor; Head DULCIE JAMES.

BANKING

Bank of Montserrat Ltd: POB 10, Brades; tel. 491-3843; fax 491-3163; e-mail bom@candw.ms; internet www.bankofmontserrat.ms; Gen. Man. MICHAEL JOSEPH.

Montserrat Building Society: POB 101, Brades Main Rd, Brades; tel. 491-2391; fax 491-6127; e-mail mbsl@candw.ms; internet www.mbs.ms; Man. JENNIFER MEADE.

St Patrick's Co-operative Credit Union Ltd: Credit Union House, POB 337, Brades; tel. 491-3666; fax 491-6566; internet www.stpatrickscreditunion.cbt.cc/index.html; Accounting Man. KAREN WEST.

STOCK EXCHANGE

Eastern Caribbean Securities Exchange: based in Bird Rock, Basseterre, Saint Christopher and Nevis; tel. (869) 466-7192; fax (869) 465-3798; e-mail info@ecseonline.com; internet www.ecseonline.com; f. 2001; regional securities market designed to facilitate the buying and selling of financial products for the 8 mem. territories—Anguilla, Antigua and Barbuda, Dominica, Grenada, Montserrat, Saint Christopher and Nevis, Saint Lucia and Saint Vincent and the Grenadines; Chair. Sir K. DWIGHT VENNER; Gen. Man. TREVOR E. BLAKE.

Insurance

INSURANCE

Insurance Services (Montserrat) Ltd: POB 185, Brades; tel. 491-2103; fax 491-9704; e-mail ismcall@candw.ag; Gen. Man. STEPHEN FRANCOIS.

NAGICO: Ryan Investments Ltd, POB 496, Brades; tel. 491-3403; fax 491-7307; e-mail info@ryaninvestments.ms; internet www.nagico.com.

United Insurance Co Ltd: Jacquie Ryan Enterprises Ltd, POB 425, Brades; tel. 491-2055; fax 491-3257; e-mail united_ms@msn.com; internet unitedinsure.com; CEO JACQUIE RYAN.

Trade and Industry

GOVERNMENT AGENCY

Montserrat Economic Development Unit: Govt HQ, POB 292, Brades; tel. 491-2066; fax 491-4632; e-mail devunit@gov.ms; internet www.devunit.gov.ms.

CHAMBER OF COMMERCE

Montserrat Chamber of Commerce and Industry (MCCI): Ryan's Court, POB 384, Olveston; tel. 491-3640; fax 491-6602; e-mail chamber@candw.ms; refounded 1971; 31 company mems, 26 individual mems; Pres. FLORENCE GRIFFITH JOSEPH; Vice-Pres. GRACELYN CASSELL.

UTILITIES

Electricity and Water

Montserrat Utilities Ltd (MUL): POB 324, Davy Hill; tel. 491-2538; fax 491-4904; e-mail mul@mul.ms; internet www.mul.ms; f. 2008 by merger of Montserrat Electricity Services Ltd and Montserrat Water Authority; domestic electricity generation and supply; domestic water supply; Man. Dir PETER WHITE; Man. of Water and Sewerage EMILE DUBERRY.

Gas

Grant Enterprises and Trading: POB 350, Brades; tel. 491-9654; fax 491-4854; e-mail granten@candw.ms; domestic gas supplies.

TRADE UNIONS

Montserrat Allied Workers' Union (MAWU): POB 245, Brades; tel. 491-5049; fax 491-6145; e-mail hylroylb@yahoo.com; f. 1973; private sector employees; Gen. Sec. HYLROY BRAMBLE; 1,000 mems.

Montserrat Civil Service Association: POB 468, Brades; tel. 491-6797; fax 491-5655; e-mail lewisp@gov.ms; Pres. PAUL LEWIS.

Montserrat Union of Teachers: POB 460, Brades; tel. 495-1666; fax 491-5779; e-mail hyacbram@hotmail.com; f. 1978; Pres. INGRID OSBORNE; Gen. Sec. DONELTA WEEKES; 46 mems.

Transport

ROADS

Prior to the 1997 volcanic eruption Montserrat had an extensive and well-constructed road network. There were 203 km (126 miles) of good surfaced main roads, 24 km of secondary unsurfaced roads and 42 km of rough tracks. The 2007 budget allocated funds of over EC $5m. for continued road and infrastructure improvements, particularly in areas to become more densely populated through resettlement. In 2008 a $5.9m. road reinstatement project from Salem to St John funded by the British Department for International Development was begun, although funding for the project was suspended in May 2013 until management of construction was improved.

SHIPPING

Following the destruction of the principal port at Plymouth in 1997, an emergency jetty was constructed at Little Bay in the north of the island. Construction of a new ferry terminal at Little Bay, funded by the European Union, was completed in December 2013. There is a daily ferry service to and from Antigua.

Port Authority of Montserrat: Little Bay, POB 383, Plymouth; tel. 491-2791; fax 491-8063; e-mail monpa@candw.ms; Man. SHAWN O'GARRO.

Montserrat Shipping Services: POB 46, Brades; tel. 491-3614; fax 491-3617; e-mail customerservice@monship.org.

CIVIL AVIATION

The John A. Osborne Airport at Gerald's with a 600-m runway was completed in 2005. The new airport was financed at a cost of

EC \$51.95m. by the European Union and the British Department for International Development. The previous airport, Blackburne at Trants, was destroyed by the volcanic activity of 1997. In the longer term, the Government intended to construct a permanent international airport at Thatch Valley. Two airlines were providing services with small aircraft in 2014; one of these, Fly Montserrat, was grounded in 2012 following a number of accidents. Montserrat is also linked to Antigua by a helicopter service, which operates three times a day. The island is also a shareholder in the regional airline, LIAT (based in Antigua and Barbuda).

FlyMontserrat: John A. Osborne Airport, POB 225, Gerald's; tel. 491-3434; e-mail info@flymontserrat.com; internet www .flymontserrat.com; f. 2009; trading name of Montserrat Airways Ltd; flights between Montserrat, Antigua and Saint Christopher and Nevis; Chair. and Man. Dir Capt. NIGEL HARRIS.

Tourism

Since the 1997 volcanic activity, Montserrat has been marketed as an eco-tourism destination. Known as the 'Emerald Isle of the Caribbean', Montserrat is noted for its Irish connections, and for its range of flora and fauna. In 2013 there were 7,201 stop-over tourist arrivals, 36% of whom were from Caribbean countries, 25% from the United Kingdom and 25% from the USA. In addition, there were 1,519 excursionists. A large proportion of visitors are estimated to be Montserrat nationals residing overseas. Tourism earnings totalled an estimated EC \$18.3m. in 2013.

Montserrat Development Corporation (MDC): Public Market, Little Bay, POB 7, Brades; tel. 491-2230; fax 491-7430; e-mail info@ montserrattourism.ms; internet www.visitmontserrat.com; f. 1993 as Montserrat Tourist Board; merged with MDC in June 2014; CEO IVAN BROWNE; Dir of Tourism ERNESTINE CASSELL.

Defence

The United Kingdom is responsible for the defence of Montserrat.

Education

Education is compulsory between the ages of five and 14 years. Secondary education begins at 12 years of age, and comprises a first cycle of five years and a second, two-year cycle. In 2008 enrolment in primary education included an estimated 92% of children in the relevant age-group, while enrolment in secondary education was an estimated 96% in 2007. Enrolment in tertiary education in 2008 was equivalent to 17%. In 2011 there were four primary schools, including two government schools and one government secondary school. There was a Community College and a Technical College, which provided vocational and technical training. There was also an extramural department of the University of the West Indies in Plymouth and two offshore medical schools. The Ministry of Education was allocated a total of EC \$8.1m. in the 2014 budget.

NICARAGUA

Geography

PHYSICAL FEATURES

The Republic of Nicaragua spans the Central American isthmus and is the largest country lying between Mexico and Colombia. Nicaragua tapers westwards from its long eastern coast on the Caribbean, to a south-west-facing Pacific coast, but also southwards from the long, north-western border (922 km) with Honduras, to the shorter, more east–west border (309 km) with Costa Rica (on the latter frontier, the question of Costa Rican navigation rights on the San Juan River is vexatious). In the far north-west Nicaragua looks across the mouth of the Gulf of Fonseca at El Salvador. Nicaragua has challenged Honduras and Colombia over some 50,000 sq km (19,300 sq miles) of maritime territory in the Caribbean, owing to the Colombian possession of a number of islands and cays lying to the east of the Nicaraguan coast (San Andrés lies 180 km off shore, included administratively with Providencia and a number of other satellites). Nicaraguan territory also includes some islands and islets, notably the Corn Islands, some 70 km off the Caribbean coast near Bluefields, and the Miskito Cays further north. The total area of the country is 130,373 sq km (50,337 sq miles), including 10,034 sq km of inland waters.

Nicaragua is about 440 km from north to south and 450 km, at its widest, from east to west. Like most of the Central American countries, it consists of a central highlands divide between a Pacific coastal region and a wider Caribbean (Atlantic) coastal region. Nicaragua is dominated by the great lake that bears its name in the south-west of the country, where the Pacific lowlands are rather more involved topographically. Rising immediately above the narrow plains along the shore are the Coastal or Diriamba Highlands, which are volcanic and, mainly in the north, still active. These heights subside into the Rivas isthmus as they head south, separating Lake Nicaragua from the ocean. Between this line and the central mountain uplands lies the Great Rift, fertile central lowlands dominated by two great lakes—Managua, on the south-western shores of which is the eponymous national capital, and, to the south of it, the 8,157-sq-km Nicaragua, one of the largest freshwater lakes in the world. The Pacific lowlands broaden southwards around the lakes, following the Rift, sufficient to allow Lake Nicaragua actually to empty into the Caribbean (along the San Juan). This is possible because the central mountain region tapers southwards, as the main thrust of the Continental Divide becomes more diffuse. The highlands, therefore, mainly rise in the north-centre of the country, the highly dissected region contrasting forested ranges with fertile basins and valleys. The highest point is Mogotón (2,438 m—8,002 ft), in the north-west. Finally, the eastern or Caribbean region is dominated by the Mosquito Coast (Costa de Mosquitos—an erroneous adaptation of the name of the local Amerindians, the Miskitos) and its hinterland. This involves the lower slopes of the central uplands merging into an extensive, alluvial plain with gentle valleys, giving way to an often marshy coast of shallow bays, lagoons and salt marshes. The eastern lowlands tend to be savannah, but the coast is dominated by dense rainforest. In fact, about 27% of Nicaragua is forested, and 46% is classified as pastureland. This terrain is well watered, not just by copious rainfall in most places, but by many rivers—the longest is the 780-km Coco, which forms much of the eastern part of the Honduran border. The varied ecosystems common to the countries of Central America (owing to the contrasting topography and its position as the land bridge between two continents) shelter in Nicaragua the usual array of wildlife, but the country's wide maritime shelf also allows it to boast the richest marine fauna in the Caribbean.

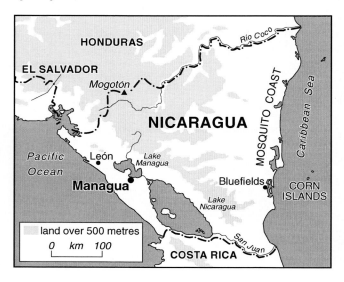

CLIMATE

The climate is tropical in the lowlands and cooler in the highlands. Nicaragua is very susceptible to hurricanes, with volcanoes and earthquakes adding to nature's destructive potential, so the country is particularly prone to landslides. This is not helped by deforestation and the consequent soil erosion. Generally, it is slightly cooler and much wetter in the east than in the Pacific west. The rainy season is May–January, and average annual rainfall in Managua, located in the western lowlands, is 1,140 mm (44 ins). This figure can be more than doubled in the east. The average temperatures in Managua range from 20°C (68°F) to 34°C (93°F) over the year.

POPULATION

Most Nicaraguans (77%) are of mixed race, but there are fairly substantial white (10%) and black (9%) communities, with the balance consisting of indigenous Amerindians (who may be underenumerated). The black population, which is concentrated in the east, mainly along the Caribbean coast, is generally of Jamaican or 'Black Carib' descent (escaped African slaves who married into a Carib Amerindian population, preserving a Carib or Garifuna language, but who were deported from St Vincent island—now in Saint Vincent and the Grenadines—in 1797 to an island off the Honduran coast). Most of the population use Spanish, the official language, but, as well as Garifuna, a Creole dialect and English are also used in the east (apart from those descended from an anglophone background, there are traces of the time when the United Kingdom claimed a protectorate over the Mosquito Coast). The indigenous languages of the country are mainly of the Miskito, Sumo and Rama groups, in the east, with others spoken by the small numbers of Amerindians in the west, the Monimbo and Subtiaba. The majority of the population are Roman Catholic and the remainder mostly Evangelical Protestant.

According to official estimates, in mid-2013 the total population numbered 6.1m. Most people live in the Pacific lowlands and in the adjacent high country. In mid-2012 the capital, Managua, had an estimated population of 1.0m., with the second city, León, to the north-west, totalling 201,100 inhabitants. The country is divided into 15 departments, with the Mosquito Coast consisting of two autonomous regions (Atlántico Norte and Atlántico Sur).

History

DANIEL SACHS

Nicaragua, Central America's largest republic, can roughly be divided into three zones. The Pacific region, with its rich volcanic soils, has always been the most populated part of the country and forms its economic and administrative centre. The Atlantic region is the largest, but also the most sparsely populated and isolated, part of Nicaragua. It is also culturally distinctive, having important minorities from a variety of indigenous groups and a black/creole population. These two regions are separated by the Central Highlands, which are important for coffee cultivation and historically have been major zones of political and military conflict. Nicaragua did not emerge as a fully independent nation state until 1838. During the colonial period the area had been a relatively isolated part of the Guatemalan Audiencia and, following independence from Spain in 1821, was briefly annexed by the Iturbidean Mexican Empire (1821–23) before forming part of the short-lived United Provinces of Central America (1823–38). The country's boundaries have undergone a number of alterations since independence: Guanacaste was ceded to Costa Rica in 1858; in a treaty signed in 1928 the islands of San Andrés, Providencia and Santa Catalina (the San Andrés archipelago) were ceded to Colombia; and a large piece of territory in north-eastern Nicaragua was granted to Honduras by the International Court of Justice (ICJ) in the 1960s.

NICARAGUA, 1838–1936

The first decades of Nicaraguan independence are known as the 'Age of Anarchy', owing to successive civil wars between the Liberal élites of León and the Conservatives of Granada. With these two cities acting like autonomous states, the emergence of a national state apparatus was severely impeded. In 1854 Leonese Liberals recruited a group of North American mercenaries, led by William Walker, to fight their Granadan rivals. After defeating the Conservatives, Walker turned on his Liberal patrons, declared himself President, reintroduced slavery and established English as the official language of the republic. However, his ambitions of regional domination united the rest of Central America against him, and he was eventually removed from office. The Liberals, weakened by their association with Walker, compromised with Conservative Presidents over the next 30 years. The stability that this brought saw the first coherent nation-building project of Nicaragua's history as the country's infrastructure began to be developed and the judicial and institutional basis of the state was enhanced.

While the foundations of the modern Nicaraguan state were laid in the 30 years of Conservative hegemony, it was the Liberal regime of José Santos Zelaya (1893–1909) that marked the definitive insertion of the Nicaraguan economy into the international division of labour as a supplier of primary commodities (mainly coffee, but also bananas, gold and timber). Zelaya introduced a Constitution separating the Church from the state, modernized the army, gained control of the Atlantic Coast from the United Kingdom and encouraged overseas capital investment. However, the courting of European and Japanese capital for the construction of an inter-oceanic canal in southern Nicaragua provoked a US-supported rebellion by Nicaragua's Conservatives, which forced Zelaya into exile in 1909 and ushered in 25 years of intermittent US occupation. US marines were stationed in Nicaragua in 1912–25 and again in 1926–33 in order to protect a series of Conservative Presidents from Liberal rebellions. During this period Nicaragua virtually became a colony of the USA. The incipient Nicaraguan state became enmeshed within a financial system where profligate loans were guaranteed by turning over Nicaragua's customs revenues, the national railroads and the national bank to US interests. Meanwhile, the Bryan-Chamorro Treaty of 1916 granted the USA exclusive rights to the construction of any canal within Nicaraguan territory (thereby safeguarding the Panamanian canal from any rival Nicaraguan project).

The second period of occupation saw the USA modify its support for the Conservatives in a bid to allow the USA to continue to dominate Nicaragua without the constant need to have troops on the ground. In 1927 an agreement between the Liberals and the Conservatives included provisions for US-supervised elections to be held in that year, while allowing the continued presence of US troops in Nicaragua until a new 'non-partisan' National Guard could be trained. Only one Liberal lieutenant, Augusto César Sandino, rejected these measures and, with a 300-strong 'Defending Army of National Sovereignty', continued to fight a sustained guerrilla war against the US forces, their Conservative puppets and the Liberal leadership. Sandino and his followers quickly developed very successful guerrilla tactics and the US forces became embroiled in a protracted conflict.

The US marines eventually left following the election of the Liberal Juan Bautista Sacasa in 1932, leaving the National Guard to carry on the struggle against Sandino. In February 1933, however, Sandino signed a peace accord with the Sacasa Government, which guaranteed that US troops would not return, granted an amnesty to Sandino's followers and created a new department in the north of the country, which they would settle in and police themselves. The Sandinistas, however, continued to be harassed by an uncontrollable National Guard, and in February 1934 Sandino was murdered on the orders of the Guard's director, Anastasio Somoza García. Somoza overthrew Sacasa in May 1936. A highly dubious presidential election was held in December, and on 1 January 1937 Somoza was installed as President of Nicaragua. He and his sons were to stay in control of Nicaragua until 1979.

THE SOMOZA DYNASTY

Somoza García proved to be a skilful manipulator of successive US Administrations. He utilized clever political manoeuvring, strategies of accommodation with the traditional oligarchy and his control of the National Guard to sustain his position within Nicaragua. Following his assassination in 1956 by the poet Rigoberto López Pérez, Somoza was succeeded as President by his son, Luis Somoza Debayle, while his youngest son, Anastasio 'Tachito' Somoza Debayle, became Commander-in-Chief of the National Guard. Luis pursued a much lower profile and more humanitarian style of leadership, opening up the political system, at least ostensibly, and instigating a range of social programmes under the US-sponsored Alliance for Progress. On the death of Luis in 1967, Tachito assumed the presidency and, in spite of lacking the political skill of his father, operated a more repressive form of dictatorship.

Under the Somozas, the Nicaraguan economy expanded considerably as they facilitated the successive evolution of a series of further agro-export crops (including beef, sugar and especially cotton, although coffee continued to be important) and a certain level of industrial development. However, their control of the National Guard, their close ties with the US Administration, as well as rampant nepotism and cronyism enabled the Somozas to ensure that the state essentially acted to service their own business interests (and those of their closest allies), rather than national economic and social development. It is estimated that by 1979 the Somozas owned around 40% of Nicaragua's economy.

The regime finally began to fragment in the 1970s as the brutality, corruption and political weakness of Tachito Somoza grew increasingly apparent. Somoza's abuse of humanitarian aid, following an earthquake that destroyed Managua in 1972, and the assassination of the Conservative opposition leader, Pedro Joaquín Chamorro, in 1978 helped to unite internal opposition to the regime (see below). Moreover, the dictator's excesses also prompted international condemnation and, most importantly, the partial withdrawal of support from the Administration of US President Jimmy Carter (1977–81). Facing international isolation, a growing popular insurrection and a disintegrating National Guard, Somoza resigned the presidency in July 1979. He fled to Paraguay, where he was assassinated in September 1980.

THE SANDINISTA NATIONAL LIBERATION FRONT

The overthrow of the Somoza dictatorship represented one of the most broadly based and popular insurrections in Latin America's history. Its origins lay in 1961 when, inspired by the Cuban revolution, a group of students from the University of León (together with surviving members of Sandino's Defending Army) formed the Frente Sandinista de Liberación Nacional (FSLN—Sandinista National Liberation Front). Despite the fact that many of its founders were Marxists, the FSLN rapidly broadened its ideological base, and its politics represented a mix of nationalism, radical Christianity and a brand of socialism that owed more to cultural practices peculiar to Latin America than to the USSR. By the end of the 1970s the FSLN had become the hegemonic group within an extremely broad revolutionary alliance (which also included the non-Somocista business élite, sections of the Roman Catholic Church, left-wing activists and intellectuals) and had succeeded in mobilizing large numbers of the urban poor and the rural peasantry.

The Somoza regime, however, inflicted serious losses on the FSLN in the late 1960s and early 1970s. By 1974 most of the FSLN's founders were dead or imprisoned, many of its underground networks had been destroyed, and the organization was internally divided. However, the dictator's increasingly brutal and arbitrary repression over the ensuing years contributed to growing public unrest, which enabled the FSLN to attract increasing numbers of new recruits. The murder of Chamorro in January 1978 provoked mass demonstrations against Somoza and was followed by a national strike and a series of uprisings in the major cities in September. Following the Government's brutal suppression of these demonstrations, the FSLN launched a final offensive in mid-1979. By late July Somoza had been removed and Nicaragua was ruled by a Government of National Reconstruction dominated by the FSLN.

THE SANDINISTA GOVERNMENT, 1979–90

The guiding principles of the new regime were the pursuit of political pluralism, a mixed economy, popular participation, and a non-aligned foreign policy. The state was to function according to the 'logic of the majority', with priority given to the interests of the poor, and wide-ranging agricultural, health and educational reforms were subsequently introduced. The five-member governing junta consisted of two members of the anti-Somoza bourgeoisie and three Sandinistas, among them the General Secretary of the FSLN, José Daniel Ortega Saavedra, who became de facto President of Nicaragua. The 1974 Constitution was abrogated, the bicameral Congreso Nacional (National Congress) was dissolved and the National Guard was replaced with the Sandinista People's Army. In May 1980 a 47-seat Council of State was convened (increased to 51 seats in May 1981) to act as a legislative body. The new assembly consisted of representatives of various mass organizations active within civil society. Although the Sandinistas enjoyed an institutionalized parliamentary majority, the non-Sandinista business sectors and constitutional opposition parties were also represented. The new Constitution guaranteed a range of civil liberties common to liberal democracies, abolished the death penalty and established an independent judiciary.

Elections to the presidency and to a new 96-seat Asamblea Nacional (National Assembly) were held on 4 November 1984. The FSLN presidential candidate, Ortega, received 67% of the votes cast, and the FSLN won 61 seats in the National Assembly. Most national and international observers endorsed the legitimacy of the elections (with the significant exception of the USA).

Under the Sandinista Government, Nicaragua was characterized by a series of popular consultations and legislative debates, which led to the promulgation of a new Constitution on 9 January 1987. Prominent among its provisions was the granting of autonomy to the indigenous population of the Atlantic coast. Initially, the Sandinistas had promoted innovative forms of governance across the country, organized at a local community level, but the management demands of the intensifying military conflict against the Contras (counter-revolutionary forces) gradually led to more authoritarian tendencies from the mid-1980s.

For the first few years of the Sandinista regime the economy performed relatively well, especially given the debt crisis experienced by the whole continent. By 1988, however, the effects of the US trade embargo, imposed in 1985, and the ongoing conflict with the Contras had severely undermined the original economic model of the Sandinista regime, which had pursued a number of redistributive policies, including a wide-ranging agrarian reform programme. Production levels and earnings from the agricultural export sector collapsed, leading to unsustainable increases in the national debt. The combination of this worsening external situation with rapidly expanding budget deficits caused by the escalating costs of defence (over one-half of the national budget was spent on defence by 1985) gradually developed into a severe economic crisis. Despite the implementation of an economic adjustment plan, together with the initiation of peace negotiations, which resulted in significant reductions in military expenditure, the parlous state of the economy remained a key problem in the run-up to the elections in early 1990.

OPPOSITION AND THE WAR

The period of relative political stability following the FSLN's insurrection was shortlived. Ronald Reagan's inauguration as US President in 1981 marked the beginning of a US campaign to destabilize the revolution. The US Government claimed that the Sandinistas were totalitarian communists who directly threatened US security interests and other countries in the region, as well as the liberties of the Nicaraguan people. Reagan adopted an active policy of resourcing, arming and training the Contras, which by 1985 had recruited up to 10,000 members, including a significant number of peasants disaffected by the Sandinistas' agrarian reform programme.

With the support of the Honduran army and financial aid from the USA (as well as the direct involvement of US personnel in some operations), the Contras were able to organize numerous incursions into Nicaragua from the early 1980s. It was estimated that nearly 45,000 Nicaraguans were killed, wounded or abducted in the war and about 250,000 people displaced. In 1986 increasing US congressional opposition to the funding of the Contras and growing international censure provoked elements of the Reagan Administration to become involved in the illegal transfer to the Contras of the proceeds of clandestine sales of military equipment to Iran. The eventual exposure of these actions contributed to the strengthening of a congressional ban on aid to the Contras.

Despite their destructive impact on the Sandinista economic project, the failure of the Contras to achieve a decisive military victory, combined with the end of US aid, prompted them to enter into peace negotiations. The first in a series of agreements, known as the Esquipulas Peace Accords, was signed in 1987. These accords laid the foundations for a general disarmament process, with international observation by the Organization of American States (OAS). Subsequent accords (Esquipulas II and III) led to further disarmament and provided the framework for the 1990 elections.

THE 1990 ELECTIONS

The presidential, legislative and municipal elections of February 1990 produced an unexpected victory for the Unión Nacional Opositora (UNO—National Opposition Union), a coalition of 14 anti-Sandinista parties. The UNO's presidential candidate, Violeta Barrios de Chamorro, widow of the assassinated Pedro Joaquín Chamorro, won 55% of the votes cast, compared with Ortega's 41%. The opposition alliance also gained an absolute majority in the National Assembly and control of 101 of 132 municipal councils.

Violeta Chamorro was seen as a figure of national reconciliation. On assuming the presidency she avoided confrontation with the FSLN by reappointing Sandinista Gen. Humberto Ortega as Commander-in-Chief of the Armed Forces, and by agreeing to uphold the 1987 Constitution. However, Chamorro's actions prompted tensions with more extremist factions within the UNO, and infighting led to the collapse of the UNO as a coherent political force in early 1993. A new consensus subsequently was reached between a number of former UNO deputies, the FSLN, the Partido Conservador (PC—Conservative Party), and the President.

The architect of government policy was the Minister to the Presidency, Antonio Lacayo Oyanguren, the son-in-law of Chamorro. Lacayo sought pragmatically to implement a range of market-orientated economic reforms, while recognizing the continued influence of the FSLN. However, Chamorro's conciliatory stance towards the Sandinistas led to the suspension of US aid, while economic measures demanded by the IMF provoked industrial action. By mid-1991 Lacayo's strategic policy of market-led modernization had been replaced by short-term crisis management.

THE FSLN IN OPPOSITION

Despite its electoral defeat, the FSLN remained the largest single party in the National Assembly, and continued to exert considerable influence over the police and the army, both of which were led by prominent Sandinistas, as well as over the trade unions and civil associations. However, the party's popularity among the wider population suffered considerably from what became known as 'la piñata', a process whereby large amounts of state and government property were transferred to the leadership of the FSLN during the two-month transition period between the FSLN and UNO Governments.

In 1994 internal divisions within the FSLN over its co-operation with the Chamorro Government led to the formation of two factions. The Izquierda Democrática Sandinista (Sandinista Democratic Left), led by Daniel Ortega, which advocated a more orthodox revolutionary outlook and was supported by mass organizations, the trade unions and the urban and rural poor, was opposed by the more socio-democratic, 'renewalist' faction, led by former Vice-President Sergio Ramírez Mercado. The Ortega faction emerged successful from the ensuing political struggle, and in January 1995 Ramírez left the FSLN to form the Movimiento de Renovación Sandinista (MRS—Sandinista Renewal Movement). The majority of the Sandinista deputies moved to the MRS, leaving the FSLN with just eight deputies. However, the overwhelming majority of the grassroots membership remained loyal to the FSLN.

OPPOSITION TO THE CHAMORRO GOVERNMENT

As well as constitutional opposition, the Chamorro presidency was challenged by an increasing number of armed groups. Following the 1990 elections, the OAS supervised a progressive demobilization of Contra forces, and the Nicaraguan army was reduced from 90,000 to 15,000 troops. The resettlement into civilian life of both former Contras and former Sandinista soldiers proved problematic, however, and promises guaranteed in the Esquipulas Accords to provide land, social services and credit to facilitate this process were not fulfilled.

As a result, the Government faced its first major military crisis in July 1993, following the occupation of the town of Estelí by a pro-Sandinista armed group. The security forces recaptured the town by force, resulting in 22 deaths. In August a rearmed group of former Contras, Frente Norte 3-80 (FN—Northern Front 3-80), kidnapped a number of deputies who had gone to the northern town of Quilalí to negotiate its disarmament. The FN demanded the resignations of Gen. Humberto Ortega and Antonio Lacayo. In response, former Sandinista soldiers kidnapped a group of right-wing deputies in Managua, including Vice-President Virgilio Godoy Reyes. A peaceful resolution was negotiated by the OAS and a general amnesty was granted. In late 1993 Gen. Ortega was replaced as Commander-in-Chief of the Armed Forces by Gen. Joaquín Cuadra Lacayo, also a Sandinista. Nevertheless, rearmed groups continued to be a serious problem in parts of northern Nicaragua until as late as 2001.

A further source of tension for the UNO Government arose from the political question of how to address the unconsolidated legal status of the buildings and land that had been nationalized or redistributed during the revolutionary years. Many owners who had fled to the USA following the revolution

had returned to Nicaragua since the 1990 elections and were demanding the return of their property. The Government sought to respond to these sometimes violent demands without invalidating the redistribution processes of the 1980s, which would have precipitated a descent into further social and political instability. Eventually, following mediation from former US President Carter, a compromise law of property stability was adopted. Despite the legal protection that this gave to those who had benefited from redistribution, the lack of access of the poorest sectors to legal assistance contributed to a gradual reconcentration of property ownership in the country.

THE 1996 ELECTIONS

Presidential and legislative elections were held on 20 October 1996. Owing to a constitutional amendment adopted in the previous year that prohibited close relatives of a serving President from contesting a presidential election, Lacayo was unable to stand. In the absence of a prominent UNO nominee, the anti-Sandinista platform was filled by the Alianza Liberal (AL—Liberal Alliance). This coalition, under the candidacy of Arnoldo Alemán Lacayo, mayor of Managua, brought together a range of liberal parties, including Somoza's former Partido Liberal Nacionalista (PLN—Nationalist Liberal Party) and Alemán's Partido Liberal Constitucionalista (PLC—Constitutional Liberal Party), although the PLC would eventually come to dominate the coalition. The FSLN and several other parties claimed the provisional results of the presidential contest, which indicated a victory for Alemán, were fraudulent, although international observers declared the ballot to have been generally free and fair. Many of the provisional results were subsequently revised, but the Consejo Supremo Electoral (CSE—Supreme Electoral Council) declared that these anomalies had not affected the overall result. Alemán was declared the winner, with 51% of the valid votes cast, compared with 38% for the FSLN candidate, former President Ortega. The AL also gained a majority of seats in the National Assembly and control of 92 municipalities.

THE ALEMÁN ADMINISTRATION

In contrast to Violeta Chamorro, Arnoldo Alemán had an openly anti-Sandinista agenda. The eviction of families occupying land granted to them by the Sandinistas, as part of the new Government's desire to return land to its former owners, prompted the FSLN to organize national protests in April 1997. The issue was eventually settled via direct negotiations between the FSLN and the Government, resulting in the adoption in November of the definitive law of urban and rural reformed property.

Alemán, together with members of his family, was the subject of a number of investigations by the Comptroller-General's office. In February 1999 a report published by the office revealed that Alemán's personal wealth had increased by some 900% during his terms of office as mayor of Managua and as President. Alemán was widely perceived to have obstructed efforts to investigate such allegations, and in November 1999 the Comptroller-General was briefly imprisoned on charges of illegal use of state funds to employ an investigative journalist to examine Alemán's finances.

The weakness of Nicaragua's public institutions was amply illustrated following Hurricane Mitch in October 1998. The hurricane devastated the north-western parts of the country, killing almost 3,000 people and causing massive infrastructural damage. International donors adopted a strategy of delivering humanitarian aid directly to non-governmental organizations (NGOs), owing to concerns over the possible misappropriation of funds by the Government. Growing accusations of corruption and incompetence in the allocation of reconstruction funds, as well as attacks on the Comptroller-General's office, led some donors to suspend a number of aid programmes in 1999.

THE PLC–FSLN PACT

The FSLN's apparent lack of a long-term strategy led to renewed divisions within the party. Although Ortega was re-elected Secretary-General of the FSLN in May 1998, opposition to his leadership intensified when he subsequently entered into negotiations on political co-operation with the PLC. These negotiations, concluded in October 1999, centred on changes to the Constitution and the electoral system. It was agreed that the PLC and FSLN would appoint their own members to institutions such as the CSE and the Supreme Court, and that elaborate procedures for the granting of legal status to political parties would be established to make it more difficult for smaller parties to function, thereby institutionalizing a two-party system. The principal changes to the electoral laws included the following provisions: each party must obtain 75,000 signatures in order to gain legal recognition; each party must gain 4% of the popular vote in order to retain legal status after an election; and all parties must have a presence in all 150 municipalities. Moreover, the threshold for a first-round victory in the presidential election was reduced from 45% to 35%, albeit on the condition that the victor should have a 5% lead over the second-placed candidate, and all former Presidents were granted a life seat in the National Assembly (and, with it, comprehensive parliamentary immunity). Other reforms transformed the Comptroller-General's office into a collegiate body of five Comptrollers, chosen by the PLC and FSLN.

The PLC-FSLN pact was initiated in the context of a growing crisis within both parties. In March 1998 Daniel Ortega's stepdaughter, Zoilamérica Narváez Murillo, accused him of having abused her as a child. Ortega's decision to avoid a trial by invoking his parliamentary immunity deepened the divisions in the FSLN. Also in early 2000 Alemán was implicated in the 'narcojet scandal', a complex affair involving a stolen plane, drugs-trafficking and the falsification of government documents. He similarly refused to respond to these accusations.

The impact of the constitutional changes was first explicitly felt in the municipal elections of November 2000, when the CSE caused outrage by denying legal status to all political parties except for the FSLN, the PLC, the PC and three smaller groupings. The FSLN won in 11 of the 17 departmental capitals, while the PLC secured control of more municipalities (97, compared with the FSLN's 49).

THE 2001 ELECTIONS

The PLC was again victorious in the presidential and legislative elections of 4 November 2001. In the presidential ballot, former Vice-President Enrique Bolaños Geyer secured 56.3% of votes cast, compared with the 42.3% polled by the FSLN candidate, Daniel Ortega. The PLC won 47 seats in the National Assembly, the FSLN 42 seats, and the PC one seat. A higher than expected turnout (some 92% of the electorate) and the decisive margin of the PLC's victory helped the legitimacy of the electoral process, despite the adverse impacts of the constitutional changes. In accordance with the electoral reforms resulting from the PLC-FSLN pact, Alemán and Ortega, as outgoing President and second-placed presidential candidate, were both given seats in the National Assembly.

THE BOLAÑOS PRESIDENCY

Bolaños' Government faced a considerable number of challenges after taking office in January 2002, the first being Alemán, who was elected to the presidency of the National Assembly as soon as Bolaños took office and seemingly intended to dominate the Government through his former Vice-President. Nevertheless, from the outset, Bolaños resolutely pursued his own political agenda. Key to this agenda was a sustained effort to combat corruption. The first step in this direction was the appointment of a Cabinet composed of party members with few direct links to the Alemán faction of the PLC.

Bolaños' campaign to distance himself from his predecessor intensified in March 2002 when the Attorney-General issued charges against Alemán in connection with fraud involving the state television company and, in May, in connection with the state telecommunications company. Bolaños successfully removed Alemán's parliamentary immunity in December, and the former President was placed under house arrest. The pro-Alemán legislative bloc of the PLC broke definitively with the Government in March 2003. In December of that year

Alemán was sentenced to 20 years' imprisonment on charges of money-laundering, fraud and theft of state property. In December 2004, however, a court of appeal overturned Alemán's conviction on fraud charges in connection with the state television corporation, allowing him to serve his sentence for money-laundering under house arrest.

The central difficulty of Bolaños' presidency was his need, despite urging from the US Administration to adopt a more hardline, anti-Sandinista stance, to reach some sort of rapprochement with the FSLN if he was to have any hope of delivering effective government. As a result, in April 2004 Ortega and Bolaños announced that they had reached a new understanding. Bolaños agreed to the restructuring of the directorate of the Asamblea, from which the FSLN had initially been excluded. The President also made attempts to mould a new political alternative to the PLC and the FSLN, launching an electoral alliance, the Alianza por la República (APRE—Alliance for the Republic), in May. Meanwhile, some of the worst elements of the constitutional changes resulting from the PLC-FSLN pact were reversed. For example, in January 2003 the CSE recognized that the removal of the legal status of most political parties under the 2000 electoral law had been unconstitutional.

In March 2004 the President, the Vice-President, José Rizo Castellón, and 31 other senior members of the PLC were accused of illegal campaign financing during the 2001 presidential election. Seven PLC members were arrested, including the party's President, Jorge Castillo Quant. In October 2004 the Comptroller-General requested that Bolaños be removed from power and fined two months' wages for withholding information regarding the financing of his electoral campaign. Supporters of the President claimed the request was politically motivated, as the office of the Comptroller-General was controlled by the FSLN and the PLC. In the same month the National Assembly approved the creation of an independent judicial council to appoint judges.

The FSLN won a decisive victory in the local elections of 7 November 2004, securing control of 84 of the 151 municipalities, including Managua, while the PLC won power in 57 municipalities and the APRE obtained control of six local councils. On the following day a two-thirds' majority in the National Assembly voted in support of constitutional amendments limiting presidential powers and increasing legislative ones. The reforms would require the President to seek legislative ratification of key appointments, including ministers, and would also enable the Asamblea to remove officials deemed to be incompetent. Furthermore, later that month the PLC and the FSLN approved a law to transfer control of the state energy, water and telecommunications services from the President to one regulatory body, the Superintendencia de Servicios Públicos (Sisep). President Bolaños appealed to the Supreme Court in December, contending that the proposed reforms were unconstitutional and that such an attempt to redefine the powers of the executive and legislative branches of government exceeded the remit of the National Assembly. Nevertheless, in January 2005 the National Assembly ratified the amendments. Bolaños agreed to promulgate the reforms in return for a pledge from the opposition that it would work towards a consensus with the executive on such matters as the budget and social security reform. At the end of March the Supreme Court ruled that the reforms were valid, despite the Central American Court of Justice (CCJ) declaring that they were illegal and could only be approved by a specially convened constituent assembly.

Internal divisions within the FSLN arose in early 2005, ahead of the presidential and legislative elections that were scheduled for November 2006. In January 2005 the FSLN ruled that any prospective presidential nominees must have been party members for at least 10 years. The rule was intended to prevent Herty Lewites, the popular former mayor of Managua, from challenging Ortega in the party's primary election. Lewites and a number of his supporters were expelled from the party in February, and in March the FSLN's national congress duly selected Ortega as its presidential candidate.

Political tensions were heightened in June 2005 when Bolaños issued a presidential decree compelling the police to comply with the CCJ ruling that invalidated the transfer of control of the public utilities from the President to the newly created Sisep. In response to the decree, the Comptroller-General once more demanded that President Bolaños be impeached. In late June an OAS mission arrived in Managua to facilitate dialogue between the President and the National Assembly. However, Bolaños refused to engage in direct discussions with the PLC and the FSLN.

In July 2005 a court released Alemán on probation on the grounds of ill health, but he was returned to house arrest three days later, on the orders of a court of appeal. This decision angered the pro-Alemán faction of the PLC, which threatened to refuse to approve the Dominican Republic-Central American Free Trade Agreement (CAFTA-DR, between Nicaragua, Costa Rica, the Dominican Republic, El Salvador, Guatemala, Honduras and the USA) and to support the removal of Bolaños' immunity from prosecution to allow him to be charged in connection with alleged illegal campaign financing during the 2001 presidential election. In August 2005, however, the Supreme Court overturned the court of appeal's ruling, ordering Alemán's release from house arrest. The Supreme Court also ratified the constitutional reforms adopted by the National Assembly in January.

In October 2005 the political conflict between the President and the legislature was largely resolved, following mediatory efforts by the OAS and the intervention of the USA, which had condemned the PLC-FSLN pact and threatened to exclude Nicaragua from CAFTA-DR unless the National Assembly swiftly approved the agreement. CAFTA-DR was adopted by the National Assembly in that month, after the FSLN withdrew its opposition to the agreement, and Ortega and Bolaños had agreed to delay the implementation of the constitutional reforms until the end of the latter's term of office in January 2007; legislation providing for their postponement was subsequently adopted. Furthermore, the National Assembly rejected a proposal to remove Bolaños' immunity from prosecution. Meanwhile, in October the US Administration decided to resume military aid to Nicaragua after a seven-month suspension imposed as a result of US dissatisfaction with a lack of progress in the destruction of Nicaragua's remaining 1,051 surface-to-air missiles (around 1,000 had been destroyed in 2004).

THE 2006 ELECTIONS

In early April 2006 the PLC formally selected former Vice-President Rizo, a close ally of Alemán, as its presidential candidate; Rizo had resigned as Vice-President in September 2005 in order to seek the party's nomination, and subsequently sought to distance himself from Alemán in response to criticism of the PLC's continued allegiance to the former President. José Antonio Alvarado was elected to contest the presidency for the APRE at the end of April 2006, but decided to accept an offer from Rizo in May to stand as his vice-presidential candidate, prompting the APRE to declare its support for Eduardo Montealegre Rivas, representing a right-wing coalition of the Alianza Liberal Nicaragüense (ALN—Nicaraguan Liberal Alliance) and the PC. In May the formation was announced of a broad-based coalition led by the FSLN, the Unidad Nicaragua Triunfa, which included Yatama and several small conservative parties. In June the historically anti-Sandinista PLN announced that it would support the FSLN in the forthcoming elections. Following the death of Herty Lewites, who had been due to stand for the MRS, from a heart attack in July, the party nominated his running mate, Edmundo Jarquín Calderón, an economist and son-in-law of former President Chamorro, as its candidate.

With the right wing still divided, Ortega was elected President on 5 November 2006, winning 38.0% of the votes cast. His nearest rivals, Montealegre and Rizo, secured 28.3% and 27.1%, respectively. Benefiting from the changes to the electoral law introduced under the PLC-FSLN pact (see above), which reduced the share of votes required for an outright victory from 45% to 35%, Ortega avoided the need to contest a second round of voting. The poorer than expected performance of Jarquín, who received only 6.3% of the votes cast, indicated that significant numbers of hitherto dissident Sandinistas had opted to support Ortega. In the concurrent elections to the

National Assembly the FSLN won 38 seats, while the PLC took 25 (compared with 47 in the 2001 elections), the ALN 22 and the MRS five. Bolaños and Montealegre were also allocated seats in the Asamblea. An estimated 69% of the electorate participated in the polls.

Both during the electoral campaign and following his victory, Ortega sought to reassure voters and business leaders that he had renounced the more radical policies of his previous period in office, vowing to respect private property rights and free enterprise, to maintain economic stability, to encourage foreign investment, to co-operate with the IMF and to support the implementation of CAFTA-DR. The eradication of poverty was identified as a priority of the new administration, as was the promotion of national reconciliation. This message of reconciliation was perhaps best exemplified by the choice of Jaime Morales Carazo, a former Contra leader and PLC deputy, as Ortega's vice-presidential candidate.

ORTEGA'S RETURN TO POWER

Ortega was inaugurated as President on 10 January 2007. His new Cabinet was dominated by Sandinista allies, including Samuel Santos López, mayor of Managua during the 1980s, as Minister of Foreign Affairs and Ortega's wife, Rosario Murillo Zambrana, as Co-ordinator of the Communication and Citizenship Council. Later that month the National Assembly adopted 'urgent' reforms, proposed by Ortega and supported by the PLC, which increased the President's control over the police force and the military and allowed the President to create 'Citizen Power Councils' by decree. Opposition parties expressed concern regarding the potential power of these Councils, which were to make proposals on government policy and monitor the performance of the authorities, while co-ordinating the work of NGOs and public institutions at a departmental level. In addition, despite opposition from the PLC, the National Assembly approved the further postponement of the controversial constitutional amendments limiting presidential powers that had been due to take effect that month. This measure was proposed by the ALN, which advocated a more thorough revision of the Constitution. In February the four parties represented in the legislature appointed a seven-member commission to draft constitutional amendments.

Alemán was granted complete freedom of movement within Nicaragua in March 2007, having been hitherto confined to Managua since his release on probation in mid-2005. Although the decision was ostensibly made by the national prison service, observers speculated that Ortega had ordered the restrictions on Alemán to be eased in an attempt to maintain the FSLN's influence over the PLC, citing continued co-operation over judicial appointments as evidence that the controversial power-sharing pact between the two parties had been renewed. (In December 2007 the Managua Appeals Court ordered Alemán's return to house arrest, but this ruling was later overturned, and in January 2009 he was definitively absolved from his conviction by the Supreme Court.)

In May 2007 the Government launched a 'zero hunger' programme aimed at lifting 75,000 families out of poverty by 2012 by granting them each agricultural aid valued at US $2,000. It was envisaged that 20% of the aid received would eventually be returned by the beneficiaries for the establishment of a rural credit bank to guarantee the continuity of the programme.

The establishment of the controversial Citizen Power Councils, which were central to Ortega's plan to introduce a new political system of 'direct democracy', was postponed from July 2007 until September. In early September, however, the President suffered a reverse when the ALN, the PLC and the MRS united in the National Assembly to adopt legislation stipulating that the Councils could not form part of the executive branch of government, nor implement government programmes. The opposition parties feared that the FSLN intended to consolidate its power by controlling the Councils. Ortega subsequently vetoed the legislation and delayed the inauguration of the Councils further, until November, ostensibly owing to the need to focus on addressing the destruction recently caused by Hurricane Felix, which had killed more than 100 people in the north of the country. In late November the votes of the ALN, PLC and MRS deputies ensured the rejection of the presidential veto by the National Assembly. However, in response to an appeal by several proposed members of the Councils, the Managua Appeals Court (dominated by FSLN-affiliated magistrates) ordered the National Assembly not to publish the legislation in the official gazette (which was required to render it valid), a ruling with which the President of the Asamblea, the FSLN's René Núñez Téllez, complied. Ortega proceeded to create the Citizen Power Councils by decree at the end of the month, prompting condemnation from opposition parties and civil society organizations, which accused the President of violating institutional procedure. Also established by decree was a National Cabinet of Citizen Power, comprising 272 representatives from the departments and autonomous regions, of which Ortega was to serve as President and Murillo as General Co-ordinator. In addition, Murillo was appointed as Executive Secretary of the Consejo Nacional de Planificación Económica y Social (National Council of Economic and Social Planning), which was reformed, again by presidential decree, with the stated aim of further increasing popular participation in the formulation of policy. In early December the Supreme Court upheld the validity of the presidential veto, prompting the ALN, the MRS, the PLC and the newly established Bancada por la Unidad to form the Bloque Contra la Dictadura (Bloc Against the Dictatorship). Meanwhile, constitutional reforms being mooted by the FSLN and the PLC in late 2007, which would introduce a parliamentary system of government and create a new post of Prime Minister, were strongly opposed by the ALN, the APRE, the PC and some members of the PLC itself.

In January 2008 the Supreme Court annulled the legislation postponing the implementation of the constitutional amendments curtailing presidential powers that were adopted in 2005 (see above), which duly entered into force, but declared the law establishing Sisep to be invalid. In the same month the ALN and the PLC announced the formation of a coalition to contest the forthcoming municipal elections, naming Montealegre as their joint mayoral candidate for Managua. However, the CSE ousted Montealegre from the leadership of the ALN and barred him from standing as the party's candidate for mayor of Managua; Montealegre's predecessor as party President, Eliseo Núñez Hernández, was reinstated to the position. The FSLN-controlled CSE cited irregularities during Montealegre's election to the position in 2006 to justify its ruling, but there was speculation that it had in fact been motivated by Montealegre's apparent refusal to enter into a new pact with Ortega to replace that between Ortega and Alemán. In March 2008, having received the support of 17 of the ALN's deputies, Montealegre announced the formation of a new liberal alliance between his personal political movement, Vamos con Eduardo (VCE), and the PLC to contest the municipal elections in November. The CSE provoked further controversy in mid-June by removing the legal status of the MRS and the PC, claiming that the former had failed to submit certain party documentation, while the latter had failed to comply with a requirement to field candidates in at least 80% of the country's municipalities for the November elections; both parties rejected the charges against them. Civil rights groups and opposition parties criticized the decision, as did a number of foreign diplomats.

The FSLN won 105 of the 146 contested mayoralties, including Managua, in the municipal elections held in November 2008, while the PLC secured 37 mayoralties and the ALN four. Allegations of widespread electoral fraud led to a recount in Managua, although demands for monitoring by independent observers were rejected; the FSLN candidate, Alexis Argüello, a former professional boxer, was subsequently confirmed as winner, ahead of Montealegre of the PLC-VCE alliance. Riots and demonstrations across the country ensued, but a PLC-proposed bill to annul the elections failed to generate sufficient support in the National Assembly. In late November the National Assembly was suspended by its President, René Núñez Téllez, in response to the election crisis. When the National Assembly reconvened in January 2009 Núñez was re-elected as its President. PLC candidates elected in the municipal elections refused to attend their inauguration ceremonies

in an attempt to avoid legitimizing the results. The final report by the election observation group Ética y Transparencia (EyT) issued in March indicated that fraud took place in at least 40 of the 146 municipalities. Although the Government had refused to accredit the EyT, some 30,000 volunteers had been sent by the group to observe the elections.

In January 2009, meanwhile, municipal elections were held in the North Atlantic Autonomous Region. At the elections, which had been postponed ostensibly owing to the damage caused by Hurricane Felix, the FSLN retained Bonanza and won control of Bilwi, Waspam and Rosita, leaving Yawata with just one municipality and the PLC with two.

The apparent suicide of Argüello in July 2009, just six months into his post as Mayor of Managua, led to criticism of the way in which his duties had been reorganized while he had been out of the country, amid speculation that he had felt humiliated by the changes. In August Núñez Hernández was replaced as President of the ALN by Alejandro Mejía Ferreti.

At celebrations held in Managua in July 2009 to mark the 30th anniversary of the Sandinista revolution President Ortega confirmed his desire to amend the Constitution to end the ban on consecutive presidential terms. Unable to secure the two-thirds' legislative majority required to effect constitutional change, Ortega turned to the judiciary for support. In October, responding to a petition submitted by Ortega and a group of more than 100 mayors, the constitutional panel of the Supreme Court ruled that the constitutional provision prohibiting presidential re-election was 'unenforceable'. The CSE swiftly endorsed this ruling, which was condemned by opposition parties as being illegal, on the grounds that only the National Assembly could approve amendments to the Constitution, and also criticized by civil society and business groups and by the US Department of State. Well-attended pro- and anti-Government demonstrations took place in Managua in the following month.

Ortega provoked further controversy in January 2010 when he issued a decree indefinitely extending the terms of incumbent electoral and judicial officials in defiance of the Constitution, according to which the National Assembly is responsible for appointments to these posts. The President insisted that the decree was necessary in order to ensure 'institutional stability', owing to the legislature's failure to agree on successors. Opposition parties boycotted the National Assembly in protest against the decree.

Elections to the Atlantic Coast Regional Councils on 7 March 2010 were marked by a high rate of abstention and a lack of independent observers. The FSLN remained the largest party in the North Atlantic Regional Council, as did the PLC in the southern assembly, although neither managed to secure a majority of seats.

Political tensions escalated in April 2010 after two FSLN-aligned Supreme Court judges refused to leave their posts following the expiry of their terms. Violence broke out as government supporters forcibly prevented opposition legislators from convening in an attempt to overturn the decree, prompting expressions of concern from the US Department of State and the OAS. The dismissal of several mayors (belonging to both the FSLN and opposition parties) during May and June appeared to be linked to their hostility to Ortega's bid for re-election. A congress of the PLC held in July nominated Alemán as the party's candidate in the presidential election due in late 2011. The FSLN's dominance of the Supreme Court was reinforced in August 2010, following the replacement of seven PLC-affiliated judges who had refused to participate in court sessions in protest against the continuance in office of the two FSLN judges whose terms had expired: five of the substitute judges were aligned with the ruling party and only two with the opposition.

In September 2010 the Supreme Court upheld both the decree issued by Ortega in January extending the mandates of electoral and judicial officials and the ruling by its constitutional panel in October 2009 that revoked the constitutional provision prohibiting consecutive presidential re-election. (In February 2011 Ortega was officially designated as the FSLN's candidate for the forthcoming presidential election scheduled to take place on 6 November, concurrently with legislative polls.) Opposition deputies disputed the validity of both rulings on the grounds that the Court's judges had not been appointed by the National Assembly. However, a new version of the Constitution, incorporating Ortega's January 2010 decree, was published that month in *La Gaceta*, the Government's official publication; the National Assembly voted to endorse the publication of the amended Constitution in October.

In April 2011 the CSE rejected a challenge by the Partido Liberal Independiente (PLI—Independent Liberal Party) to the legitimacy of Ortega's candidacy. Further controversy arose later that month, when Ortega, in a move allegedly aimed at improving the FSLN's electoral prospects, issued a decree transferring three municipalities from the South Atlantic Autonomous Region (where support for the party was weak) to the Chontales department.

A THIRD TERM FOR ORTEGA

At the presidential election held on 6 November 2011 Ortega was re-elected to serve a third term in office, winning 62.5% of the votes cast, compared with 31.0% for former PLC member Fabio Gadea Mantilla, representing the Unidad Nicaragüense por la Esperanza (Nicaraguan Unity for Hope), an alliance of various opposition parties and movements, including VCE, the MRS and the Partido Liberal Independiente (PLI—Independent Liberal Party). Ortega also substantially strengthened his position in the National Assembly following concurrent legislative elections in which the FSLN secured 63 out of the 92 seats.

Further to the controversy regarding Ortega's circumvention of the Constitution to secure re-election to a third consecutive term in office, the elections were also widely viewed as fraudulent. Opposition party members were denied voter identity cards, independent observation was severely restricted, and the ruling party consistently used state resources for its campaign, in violation of election law. In the final count, according to EyT, the ruling party 'stole' more than 150,000 votes, and between eight and 12 seats in the National Assembly. European Union (EU) election monitors also sharply criticized the conduct of the polls, stating that it 'indicates a serious backwards slide in the quality of democracy in Nicaraguan elections'. Nevertheless, Ortega would probably have won in any event. Broad macroeconomic stability and a pragmatic eschewing of conflict with the powerful private sector, combined with populist rhetoric and pre-election measures, contributed to his victory. Other factors behind Ortega's re-election included the country's relatively benign security environment and the weak and fragmented opposition. He was inaugurated as President on 10 January 2012.

In June 2012 the FSLN-controlled legislature adopted a bill that sought to triple the number of local councillors across the country's 153 municipalities from 2,178 to 6,534. According to the Government, the legislation was designed to increase 'popular democracy'. However, the reform increased concerns that the Government was attempting to strengthen executive control at the local level ahead of municipal elections in November. Civil society groups claimed that—in common with the controversial Citizen Power Councils—the bill represented an attempt to expand the FSLN party structure at the grassroots level. More broadly, the bill underlined the erosion of democracy and the rule of law under Ortega.

At the municipal elections held on 4 November 2012, the FSLN won 75% of the vote, securing 134 of the 153 municipalities. The PLI and the PLC were placed a distant second and third, securing just 16.1% and 6.4% of the ballot, respectively. Daysi Torres, the incumbent FSLN mayor of Managua, was re-elected with just over 83% of the vote. However, the elections were marred by widespread fraud allegations, and widespread reports of opposition supporters having been prevented from voting. The CSE's lack of independence, as well as electoral reforms aimed at expanding the influence of the FSLN, meant that the polls were likely to have been blighted by many of the fraudulent practices that marred the 2011 presidential poll and the 2008 municipal elections.

Continued high opinion poll ratings for Ortega, of 66% at May 2014, largely reflected the strength of the economy in recent years, which appeared to be of greater concern to voters than the state of democracy under his leadership. Ortega also

benefited from a reduction in social unrest, as well as the weak state of the opposition; according to opinion polls, only 3% of those surveyed identified themselves as a member of the leading opposition party, the PLI. Another factor that fuelled his high approval ratings was a sustained reduction in perceived citizen insecurity in recent years. The extent of support for Ortega and the weakness of the opposition was further reflected in the March 2014 regional elections, in which the FSLN won a majority in both the North Atlantic Autonomous Region and the South Atlantic Autonomous Region. The FSLN's victory changed the balance of power in the Atlantic Autonomous regions. For the first time, the party held an absolute majority in both 45-seat Regional Councils, with 28 seats in the North Atlantic region and 30 in the South Atlantic region. In the latter, the FSLN gained control from the opposition PLC, hitherto the predominant political power, which now held just six seats. However, it was thought that the fragile nature of economic stability could yet undermine public confidence in Ortega. The economy remained vulnerable to fluctuations in commodity prices. Moreover, fears that Venezuelan aid flows to Nicaragua might be jeopardized by recent internal developments in the former country (notably, the death—in March 2013—of President Hugo Chávez) prompted concerns that the FSLN's generous subsidies for the working classes might be negatively affected, thereby eliminating a key support factor for the Government. (For further details, see Foreign Relations under Ortega.) The erosion of democracy under Ortega was also increasingly becoming a concern for both local residents and foreign investors. The politicization of state institutions was expected to unsettle investors, the powerful business community and the wider population, and concerns were escalating over the growing reach of the executive, including the politicization of the judiciary, the police, the CSE and the central bank. While Ortega was able to continue to bring about economic and security gains voters put less emphasis on democracy in the country.

There is growing evidence that Ortega will contest the 2016 presidential election. Ortega introduced a number of constitutional reforms which entered into effect in mid-February 2014, after being approved by the National Assembly in late January. The measures notably allow the President to seek re-election, removing successive presidential term limits, through a reform to Article 147, which previously stipulated that anyone who had exercised the full powers of the presidency during the period when the election for the following term was held, or who had exercised them for two presidential terms, could not seek the presidential office. The 2014 amendment omitted these provisions, thus eliminating the two-term limit for the President, as well as the ban on consecutive re-election.

A further term for Ortega increases the likelihood of political continuity. This, in turn, ensures policy continuity for investors in the short to medium term as Ortega consolidates his hold on power. Political stability over the next three to six months is all but assured, given Ortega's overwhelming support among the electorate and the fractured nature of the political opposition.

FOREIGN RELATIONS UNDER ORTEGA

Following Ortega's election as President in November 2006, he initially adopted a conciliatory approach towards the USA, stating his intention to develop a 'respectful' bilateral relationship. However, the first confirmation of expectations that relations would be strained came in February 2007, when Ortega declared his continued opposition to the destruction of Nicaragua's remaining surface-to-air missiles, an issue that had led to the suspension of US military aid to Nicaragua during April–October 2005 (see above). Moreover, in May 2007 Ortega accused the USA of encouraging and funding domestic opposition efforts to unite against his Government. Meanwhile, US-Nicaraguan relations were also jeopardized by Ortega's apparent determination to forge strong ties with regimes of which the US Administration disapproved. In July 2007 Ortega proposed the destruction of 651 of Nicaragua's 1,051 remaining surface-to-air missiles in exchange for the provision of medical equipment and medicines by the USA;

however, no agreement to this end had been reached by mid-2013. In September 2010 the USA included Nicaragua for the first time on its list of major illicit drugs-transit or drugs-producing countries.

Ortega's controversial re-election in November 2011 led to a marked deterioration in relations between the USA and Nicaragua. Although the USA was initially reluctant to criticize publicly the conduct of the presidential election despite widespread accusations of electoral fraud, in part because it continued to require Ortega's co-operation in regional drug interdiction efforts, by June 2012 the USA's official position had notably hardened. The US Department of State's annual *Human Rights Practices* report, which was published in May, strongly criticized the 'increasingly authoritarian' Nicaraguan Government and highlighted US concerns over the weakening of democracy under Ortega. The USA also expressed concern that property rights abuses had increased during Ortega's time in office. Although the USA refrained from directly accusing the Nicaraguan Government of responsibility for a wave of recent property confiscations and land invasions, the development was closely linked to the overall erosion of the rule of law under Ortega, which was undermining state institutions and creating the space for corrupt practices to flourish.

These growing concerns, as well as wider fears regarding Nicaragua's failure to adhere to recognized democratic standards, prompted the USA in June 2012 to cancel the annual 'transparency waiver'. Under US law, the waiver was a prerequisite for the provision of aid to countries maintaining opaque budgets, and its cancellation would undermine the investment environment in Nicaragua. The move also highlighted US reservations regarding the Nicaraguan Government's lack of fiscal transparency, in particular the opaque, and apparently arbitrary, manner in which aid was distributed to Nicaragua by Venezuela. The majority of the funding, which amounted to US $609m. in 2011, is classified under vague titles, while Ortega was believed to have spent much of the aid disbursed in 2012 on campaigning and on financing populist pre-election measures, such as the provision of free housing and raising public sector salaries. Although the direct impact of the waiver's cancellation would be limited, its potential effect on the position of multilateral lending institutions towards Nicaragua was likely to be a source of concern for the Government. In 2011 lending institutions provided $333m. for the public sector and $158m. for the private sector.

Ortega also sought to strengthen his already close links with other Latin American left-wing leaders. Having been flanked by the Presidents of Bolivia and Venezuela at his inauguration, on 10 January 2007, on the following day Ortega confirmed Nicaragua's participation in what became known as the Bolivarian Alliance for the Peoples of our America-People's Trade Treaty (Alianza Bolivariana para los Pueblos de Nuestra América-Tratado de Comercio de los Pueblos—ALBA-TCP), which had been devised by Venezuela as an alternative model to the US-promoted Free Trade Area of the Americas and was also supported by Bolivia and Cuba. Venezuelan President Chávez offered significant financial assistance to Nicaragua, signing a series of bilateral economic agreements with Ortega, most of which focused particularly on the energy sector, with Venezuela proposing the construction of a petroleum refinery in Nicaragua, capable of processing 100,000–150,000 barrels of oil per day (b/d), and pledging to supply Nicaragua with 10,000 b/d of petroleum at preferential rates and a number of electricity generators. Nicaraguan opposition parties criticized the Government for a lack of transparency over the details of these agreements with Venezuela. This criticism was renewed in May 2010, following Ortega's announcement, some two weeks after a visit to Managua by Chávez, that ALBA funds would be used to finance the provision of monthly bonuses of US $25 for some 120,000 (later increased to 147,500) public sector workers and gas and fuel subsidies for 22,000 transport workers. In April 2011, following pressure from the IMF, the central bank published a report on foreign funds received by Nicaragua.

Venezuela has substantially increased its bilateral aid to Nicaragua in recent years, fuelling concerns about Nicaragua's over-reliance on that country. There were fears that Chávez's death in March 2013, as well as the worsening economic situation in Venezuela, could jeopardize aid flows to Nicaragua, and thus the wider health of the Nicaraguan economy. Moreover, Nicaragua relied on heavily subsidized oil imports from Venezuela to prevent possible social unrest. The growth in Venezuelan aid heightened suspicions that much of this money was being used discretionally by the Government for political rather than development purposes. Venezuelan financial assistance was primarily provided in accordance with the terms of an oil agreement, under which Nicaragua imported all of its oil, worth around US $1,000m., from Venezuela, which returned $500m. in the form of soft long-term loans to Albanisa, a private company jointly managed by the two Governments. A portion of these funds was used to finance social programmes, including affordable housing and transport subsidies. Albanisa was also involved in a number of high-profile infrastructure projects, particularly in the renewable energy sector.

Meanwhile, Costa Rica and Nicaragua remained engaged in several long-running border disputes. An 1858 treaty had fixed the boundary between the two countries on the southern bank of the San Juan river, and subsequent arbitration had validated this accord. A 2009 ICJ decision also accepted the river's southern bank as the boundary, but granted Costa Rica unrestricted navigation rights for commercial purposes (though not the right to use the river for police patrols, except in emergencies). However, tensions have increased since November 2010, when Costa Rica dispatched police reinforcements to the border in response to an alleged Nicaraguan military incursion into its territory. Costa Rica claimed that the Nicaraguan troop presence amounted to an 'invasion' and that Nicaragua was causing environmental damage by constructing a channel that would impede the flow of water into one of its own rivers. Costa Rican President Laura Chinchilla appealed for a 'rapid response' from the international community and referred the incident to the ICJ. In March 2011 the Court ordered Nicaragua and Costa Rica to withdraw virtually all of their military and civilian personnel from the disputed area. The announcement in June 2013 that the Ortega Government had awarded a concession to build an inter-oceanic canal across Nicaragua to a Chinese consortium, at a cost of approximately US $40,000m., was likely to exacerbate tensions between Nicaragua and Costa Rica, particularly should the project or its construction encroach upon the bilateral border. Costa Rica was also expected to be particularly sensitive to any environmental implications during development of the canal. (For further details on the proposed canal project, see Economy.) President Chinchilla in August temporarily recalled her ambassador from Managua for 'consultations'. The move was in response to comments made by Ortega earlier in August, when he raised the possibility of reclaiming the Costa Rican border province of Guanacaste (which was part of Nicaraguan territory prior to its independence from Spain but was annexed to Costa Rica in 1824). The recall exacerbated traditionally tense bilateral relations. Chinchilla, who explicitly stated that 'Nicaragua has no rights to Guanacaste', sent a formal complaint to Ortega, as well as bringing the matter before the OAS and the UN.

The proposed Grand Interoceanic project has proven somewhat controversial domestically as well. More than 30 private businesses, opposition parties and civil rights groups launched a number of appeals against the constitutionality of the Grand Interoceanic Canal and the associated Law 800, which was approved by the National Assembly in 2013. The claimants argued that the Law was unconstitutional, since it had been adopted by a government-dominated legislature, ignoring the requirements for debate over it. In December, however, the Supreme Court dismissed the appeals, ruling that the Grand Interoceanic Canal and Law 800 were not unconstitutional. It is unclear what the justification of the Court was, although it had been unlikely to accept the appeals, given its domination by the ruling party as well as the potentially enormous financial rewards for Nicaragua associated with the development of the Canal.

In October 2007 the ICJ ruled on a long-standing territorial dispute between Nicaragua and its other neighbour, Honduras, demarcating a new maritime border approximately midway between the two countries; both Governments accepted the judgment.

In March 2008 Nicaragua followed Venezuela's lead in briefly suspending diplomatic relations with Colombia in protest against an incursion into Ecuador by Colombian forces targeting rebels of the Fuerzas Armadas Revolucionarias de Colombia—Ejército del Pueblo (FARC). Ortega also joined his Venezuelan counterpart, Chávez, in strongly condemning a Colombian-US agreement signed in October 2009 granting the USA access to military bases in Colombia.

A bilateral dispute between Colombia and Nicaragua was formalized in 2001, when Nicaragua presented a territorial demand to the ICJ concerning the two countries' maritime border, as well as sovereignty of the Caribbean islands of San Andrés and Providencia and the tiny Roncador, Serrana and Quitasueno islands. Nicaragua claimed that these islands had been improperly ceded to Colombia under the terms of a 1928 treaty, signed during a period in which Nicaragua was under US military occupation. In December 2007 the ICJ issued an interim decision that granted sovereignty of the San Andrés archipelago to Colombia, but urged both parties to work towards a mutually satisfactory resolution regarding the surrounding waters. The Court was to continue deliberating the sovereignty of the other contested islands, as well as the general delimitation of their maritime border.

The dispute was complicated by ongoing plans by both Nicaragua and Colombia to prospect for petroleum near the islands, which periodically raised tensions. Nevertheless, the territorial disagreement was highly unlikely to move beyond the rhetorical and legal spheres, and there were indications that both countries were increasingly taking a more moderate approach. Colombia announced in 2011 that it would suspend oil and gas exploration in the area, supposedly to 'protect the islands' environment, society and culture', though the move was largely seen as an attempt to defuse tensions after Ortega had warned in July 2010 that Nicaragua would take military action if Colombia granted hydrocarbons concessions in the area. Nicaragua had also lodged a further protest with the ICJ over territory included in a Colombian oil-licensing round in the previous month, with some prospects located in disputed areas of the Caribbean.

Following a ruling issued by the ICJ in mid-November 2012 that upheld Colombia's claim to sovereignty over the San Andrés archipelago but redrew the maritime border between Colombia and Nicaragua in favour of the latter, Colombian President Juan Manuel Santos stated that his Government 'emphatically' rejected moves to redraw the maritime border. Although the Colombian Government had previously publicly committed itself to respecting the ICJ's ruling, public outrage in that country forced Santos to take a firm stance and in late November he announced that Colombia was to withdraw from the American Treaty on Pacific Settlement (also known as the Pact of Bogotá)—one of the treaties that confer jurisdiction on the ICJ. Although the decision that was likely further to exacerbate already strained bilateral tensions, the situation was not expected to escalate into a significant security issue or outright conflict. While Colombian naval forces were maintaining a presence along the former maritime boundary—the 82nd parallel, ostensibly to protect local fishermen, and despite

Ortega instructing the Nicaraguan naval forces in mid-November 2012 to commence patrols of the area, as of mid-2014 there had been no reports of incidents involving the two fleets. Colombia's decision to withdraw from the Pact of Bogotá would not affect the legal validity of the ICJ's ruling on the maritime border; however, the move could deter attempts by Nicaragua to expand its application to the Court in search of more far-reaching rulings concerning sovereignty over the continental shelf. In November 2013 Colombia recalled its ambassador to Nicaragua, following the decision by Ortega earlier that month to file a new case against Colombia at the ICJ in The Hague. The new lawsuit and the ambassador's withdrawal were likely to exacerbate the already strained bilateral relations between Nicaragua and Colombia.

The controversy regarding the results of the November 2008 elections strained relations with the USA and the EU. Both the USA and the EU temporarily suspended budgetary assistance to Nicaragua as a result of the Government's inability to resolve the dispute. In June 2009 the US Government's Millennium Challenge Corporation announced the 'definitive' cancellation of US $62m. (of a total $175m.) of funds to Nicaragua. Ortega criticized the decision and declared that the shortfall would in part be compensated by assistance from ALBA.

Nicaragua has shared increasingly warm relations with Iran in recent years, largely driven by a joint rejection of 'establishment powers' (particularly the USA) and a Nicaraguan desire to secure access to Iranian credit and oil. In 2007 Ortega announced that the Iranian Government would study the possibility of constructing a US $344m. deep-water port on Nicaragua's Caribbean coast as part of a series of agreements valued at over $1,180m. Iran also pledged to support Nicaraguan efforts to build power plants with a combined capacity of 616 MW. Iran's Vice-President for International Affairs, Sayed Ali Saidloo, announced during a visit to Managua in May 2012 that the Iranian Government would remit $161m. of Nicaraguan debt.

However, aside from the debt remittance, Nicaragua's growing diplomatic relationship with Iran appeared to have provided few tangible benefits. Despite the signing of a number of high-profile bilateral agreements since 2007, by mid-2014 there was no evidence to suggest that any major infrastructure projects were under way. In September 2012 Israeli media reports claimed that Iran and Lebanese Shi'a movement Hezbollah had established a training camp in Nicaragua. A report in the English-language online newspaper *Times of Israel*, quoting Israeli public broadcaster Israel Radio, had stated that the training facility was located close to Nicaragua's border with Honduras. The claims remained unsubstantiated, and, although Ortega had declared his support for Iran's controversial nuclear programme and often employed strident anti-US rhetoric to appeal to his core Sandinista support base, it appeared highly unlikely—given Nicaragua's dependence on its trading relationship with the USA—that the President would knowingly have allowed a Hezbollah training camp to be established on Nicaraguan soil.

Economy

DANIEL SACHS

Nicaragua experienced a period of gradual economic recovery from the mid-1990s, despite the huge setback of the devastation caused by Hurricane Mitch in 1998. However, few Nicaraguans shared in the fruits of that recovery. Real gross domestic product (GDP) increased by 2.8% in 2008, contracted by 1.5% in 2009, amid a global downturn, with the most substantial decreases recorded in the construction and mining sectors, before returning to growth, of 4.5%, in 2010, when mining GDP recovered strongly. GDP grew by 4.7% in 2011 and 5.2% in 2012, again driven by strong commodity prices and increased levels of investment from Venezuela, the country's

major source of foreign aid. Partly as a result of a slowdown in the extractives sectors, the rate of growth of GDP decelerated to an estimated 4.6% in 2013. The average annual rate of inflation in 2003–12 was 9.1%, according to the International Labour Organization. Consumer prices increased by annual averages of 8.0% in 2011, 6.6% in 2012 and an estimated 7.4% in 2013. Exports rose from US $866.0m. in 2005 to $1,475.3m. in 2008. Export revenues declined to $1,393.8m. in 2009, as external demand weakened in line with the global economic slowdown, but have subsequently risen strongly, reaching $4,278.0m. in 2013, primarily fuelled by recent economic recovery in the USA. Foreign direct investment (FDI) amounted to $968m. in 2011, compared with $508m. in the previous year, a 90.5% increase; in 2012 inflows increased to $1,280m., representing a 33% year-on-year increase, and grew by a further 16.8% to reach $1,495m. in 2013. Venezuelan aid, which rose from $76m. in 2010 to $609.1m. in 2012 and accounted for some 8% of Nicaragua's GDP, was likely to have been the main factor behind this resurgence in investment and was, along with IMF lending, one of the major driving forces behind the country's recent macroeconomic stability.

Nicaragua's recovery in the latter half of the 1990s followed one of the most extended and profound economic crises ever witnessed in Latin America. Between the late 1970s and the early 1990s the Nicaraguan economy was beset by a prolonged civil war, the international depression of the early 1980s, the imposition of economic sanctions by the USA and government mismanagement. By 1994 economic output was more than 60% below what it had been in 1977.

All these factors served to accentuate a traditional dependence on imports and external financing (after 1990 the flows of international aid into Nicaragua expanded markedly), and, productively, economic performance remained excessively reliant on the country's narrow range of traditional agricultural commodity exports, the most important of which were bananas, coffee, cotton, meat and sugar. By 1994, according to the World Bank, GDP per head in Nicaragua was just US $638, measured at constant 2000 prices, making the country the second poorest in the Western hemisphere, after Haiti. By 2013 GDP per caput still remained low by regional standards, amounting to an estimated $4,500 (on an international purchasing-power parity basis).

AGRICULTURE

Nicaragua's agricultural sector was, along with the rest of the economy, deeply depressed in the 1980s and early 1990s. In addition to all of the normal variables affecting agricultural production in Central America (weather, labour shortages, fluctuating world commodity prices and crop disease), Nicaragua had the additional burden of the impact of war, the effects of which lasted long beyond the cessation of hostilities. Immediately after the revolution of 1979 the state took over more than 1m. ha of land, of which some 70% was converted into state farms, with the remainder transferred to peasant co-operatives. Large areas of underutilized and idle land were then expropriated during the second stage of the Government's land reform programme in mid-1981. From 1986 the emphasis was increasingly placed upon production from co-operatives, or individual smallholders, with the Government continuing to exercise considerable control of the sector through its monopoly purchases of export crops.

The Government of President Violeta Barrios de Chamorro (1990–97) adopted a pragmatic approach, privatizing a number of large state farms, but declining to reverse the Sandinista land reforms. The administration of President Arnoldo Alemán Lacayo (1997–2002) endorsed this flexibility, reaching an agreement with the Sandinista opposition, which sanctioned the land and property distribution to legitimize beneficiaries of the Sandinista reforms. At the same time, the new Government reinforced an arbitration mechanism to adjudicate the claims of many larger property owners who insisted that they had been victims of asset seizures by senior Sandinistas. Instead of returning properties to these claimants, both the Chamorro and Alemán Governments generously compensated those who had been expropriated. The payments (totalling some US $900m. between 1990 and 2003) had a massive impact upon the country's internal debt, representing more than one-half of total internal debt in 2003. The property question continued to be a major political and economic issue in Nicaragua, and some saw it as a major disincentive to significant private investment in agriculture. Although the Sandinistas were returned to power in the elections of November 2006, President Daniel Ortega sought to distance himself from the more extreme policies of the 1980s, pledging to respect free enterprise, to protect private property and to encourage investment.

With the exception of the obvious impact of Hurricane Mitch on the sector in 1998 and 1999, agricultural production showed a modest recovery from the mid-1990s, although it was impeded by a scarcity of inputs and credit and continuing political instability in many rural areas. The recovery became more consistent after 1999. According to FAO, total agricultural production levels in 2012 were 81.7% higher than in 1999. In terms of individual agricultural commodities, over the same period the output of rice grew by 119.8% and milk by 52.6%. The agricultural sector (including hunting, forestry and fishing) remained the mainstay of the economy in 2013, accounting for an estimated 17.1% of GDP.

The output and exchange earnings of export crops have been variable. Production of the country's major export crop, coffee, oscillated in the 2000s. According to FAO, output rose from 78,700 metric tons in 2010, to 103,700 tons in 2011 and further to an estimated 107,000 tons in 2012. Significant increases in coffee export earnings in the early 2010s (reaching US $521.8m. in 2012) reflected the increased price of coffee globally. However, as a result of falling prices and productivity (combined with the outbreak of a coffee fungus), export revenue from coffee fell sharply to $349.4m. in 2013.

The cotton industry, which provided Nicaragua's second highest export earnings in the 1980s, had virtually ceased to exist by 1998, leaving many of the communities in the regions around León and Chinandega (areas harshly affected by Hurricane Mitch) with considerable economic problems. In 1991 revenue from cotton had been as high as US $44.4m., representing the production of 30,000 metric tons of cotton lint. By 2000 earnings from cotton stood at less than $100,000, and production levels did not increase thereafter. In 2006 just 1,050 tons were produced, according to FAO estimates.

The other major traditional agricultural exports were sugar and bananas (and beef, see below). According to FAO estimates, a record sugar cane crop of 7.5m. metric tons was harvested in 2012, compared with 5.9m. in 2011. Despite a relatively stable level of output since the 1990s, the volatility of international prices has produced a fluctuating pattern of sugar export earnings. Revenue reached a record US $194.9m. in 2012, before declining to $175.9m., according to the central bank, in 2013.

The performance of Nicaragua's banana exports has vacillated in a similar fashion. Banana export receipts increased from US $9.6m. in 2008 to reach $11.7m. in 2009, mainly owing to rising international prices, but declined sharply in 2010, to only $6.6m., despite prices remaining high. Despite a 12.5% rise in output to 39,600 metric tons, according to FAO, banana export earnings reached a low of $2.4m. in 2011, increasing only marginally, to $2.5m., in 2012 (when output reached an estimated 42,000 tons) before declining again, to $2.3m., in 2013.

The increasing export of less traditional products has been one of the success stories of the Nicaraguan economy in recent years. Sesame seed exports have become an important source of foreign exchange earnings, contributing US $6.3m. in 2011, $8.6m. in 2012 and $9.0m. in 2013. Similarly, the export of beans, for many years seen as merely a staple of the peasant sector, has expanded rapidly. Earnings from bean exports increased from $13.0m. in 2001 to a record $79.8m. in 2008 (when prices were particularly high). However, export earnings subsequently moderated in line with falling prices, declining from $51.8m. in 2012 to $44.8m. in 2013. The lower prices are currently preventing much-needed investment in critical machinery that would increase exports.

In the early 21st century the livestock industry, like other sectors, has yet to recover fully from the shortage of foreign exchange for new machinery and other essential products that it suffered during the Contra war, and it seems unlikely to recover its former position in terms of export importance. Some sub-sectors have, none the less, gradually shown some improvement. From 1998 beef and veal export earnings increased annually, with earnings reaching US $230.6m. in 2009 and $307.6m. in the following year. Furthermore, the export of meat products has been complemented in recent years by the expanded export of cattle to neighbouring countries, which, according to the central bank, generated earnings of around $39.2m. in 2013, compared with $18.6m. in 2012.

Nicaragua possesses substantial supplies of timber, including considerable reserves of hardwoods such as mahogany, cedar, rosewood, caoba and oak. According to FAO, in 2010–12 roundwood production averaged about 6.3m. cu m annually, an increase on the 4m. cu m averaged in the 1990s. Concern about overexploitation in the mid-1990s led the National Assembly to ban further logging concessions in 1996, although many environmental organizations remained seriously concerned about illegal logging. In 2013, according to the central bank, revenue from forestry exports totalled US $13.0m.

The development of the fishing industry was a major priority around the turn of the 21st century. Three fish-processing plants were rehabilitated and commercial fishing of crab, crayfish, shrimp, lobster and tuna was encouraged. Although total lobster production peaked at 6,534 metric tons in 2000, generally declining thereafter, the total shrimp catch has steadily increased. According to FAO, output of lobster totalled 4,200 tons in 2012, compared with 4,000 tons in 2011, while output of shrimp reached 25,400 tons in 2012, compared with 18,100 tons in 2011. Export earnings from lobster and shrimp increased from US $108.1m. in 2011, to $111.4m. in 2012 and further to $130.2m. in 2013, according to the central bank. According to the Economic Commission for Latin America and the Caribbean (ECLAC), Nicaragua is currently the largest producer of seafood in Central America. Seafood production is expected to increase even further over the coming years, particularly as a result of the ruling by the International Court of Justice in November 2012 to award Nicaragua the offshore platform in the Caribbean that had been contested by Colombia (thereby doubling Nicaragua's maritime exclusive economic zone in the Caribbean).

MINING AND POWER

The mining sector was completely nationalized in 1979. However, following the end of the Sandinista regime in 1990, successive governments ceded the rights of exploitation to private companies under long-term lease agreements. This policy met with some success: an estimated US $70m. of private investment was directed into the sector in the 1990s, while mining's contribution to overall GDP increased from 0.6% in 1994 to an estimated 3.1% in 2013. Mining GDP contracted by 6.2% in 2008 and 8.9% in 2009, as a result of the global downturn and lower demand for raw materials, but recovered strongly in 2010 and 2011, when growth reached 36.9% and 23.1%, respectively; however, the rate of expansion decelerated, to 8.2%, in 2012 on the back of lower demand from the eurozone. The sector encompasses salt, marble and quarried stone, but the real export value lies in Nicaragua's gold and silver mines. Mining exports totalled US $447.9m in 2013; of this total, according to the central bank, gold contributed $431.5m. and silver $10.9m.

Dependence on imported energy sources, particularly petroleum, has proved a major problem for successive Nicaraguan governments. In the early 2000s much of Nicaragua's petroleum needs were met by Venezuela and Mexico, under the concessionary terms of the 1980 San José Agreement. In March 2007 the new Government of President Daniel Ortega signed several co-operation agreements with the Venezuelan Government of Hugo Chávez Frías. Venezuela agreed to supply discounted oil to Nicaragua under its PetroCaribe initiative, as well as to build a refinery in the country. Despite ambitious diversification efforts, in particular the inauguration of the Momotombo geothermal plant in 1984 and the Asturias hydroelectric scheme five years later, imports of petroleum, mineral fuels and lubricants remained crucial in the early 21st century. The cost of petroleum and fuel imports was US $1,186.3m. (equivalent to 23% of total imports) in 2013. In 2013 hydroelectricity provided 8.3% of Nicaragua's total production of electrical energy.

The dilapidated state of the power distribution system in Nicaragua was responsible for the loss of up to 25% of all power generated during the 1990s, when supply covered just one-half of consumer demand. Since becoming a signatory to a number of co-operation agreements with Venezuela the energy sector has benefited from the import of discounted petroleum, additional financing and the provision of capital goods. In late 2008

the state power company, Empresa Nicaragüense de Electricidad (ENEL), announced that, thanks to assistance primarily from Venezuela and Cuba, and the recent installation of an additional 120 MW generating capacity, prolonged power cuts in Nicaragua would be prevented. Plans were announced to expand generating capacity by an additional 40 MW. In recent years Nicaragua has sought to promote investment in the renewable energy sector owing to growing concerns over the country's over-reliance on Venezuelan oil imports. These concerns have increased following Venezuelan President Chavez's death, in March 2013, and the deteriorating economic situation in that country. Nicaragua's rich natural resources mean that the country has a potential electrical generating capacity of more than 4,500 MW. By 2011 the Nicaraguan energy system had a total installed capacity of approximately 1,000 MW and an average demand of 550 MW.

In recent years the Ortega Government has also supported attempts to expand the country's huge hydroelectric potential. The 253-MW Tumarín hydroelectric project in the South Atlantic Autonomous Region is to be undertaken by Centrales Hidroeléctricas de Nicaragua at an estimated cost of some US $1,000m. and, on completion, will be one of Central America's largest hydroelectric dams. The dam, the construction of which was scheduled to commence in 2014 and be completed in 2019, was expected to generate an average of 1,184 GWh of energy per year, using the waters of the Rio Grande de Matagalpa. The Nicaraguan Government planned drastically to cut the cost of energy imports by generating 90% of the country's energy requirements from renewable sources by 2017.

MANUFACTURING AND INDUSTRY

In 2013 manufacturing accounted for an estimated 17.5% of GDP. Traditionally, manufacturing activity in Nicaragua centred on the processing and packing of local agricultural produce, although some heavy industries, such as chemical and cement production, also existed. The end of the Contra war, a sharp reduction in import tariffs and renewed access to the US market provided new opportunities in manufacturing, with many Nicaraguan exiles returning to take advantage of them. However, new export opportunities could not counteract continued contraction in the domestic market, particularly in production sectors such as beverages, processed foods and cigarettes. Manufacturing GDP grew steadily during 2000–08, but contracted by 1.5% in 2009, before returning to strong annual growth averaging some 6.0% in 2010–12; according to the central bank, sectoral growth was 5.6% in 2013. Average annual growth in manufacturing GDP was 4.5% in 2000–10. A glance at the experiences of particular sub-sectors, however, suggested a more complex picture. In 2000–04 certain foodstuffs (meat, biscuits, milk), beer, leather goods, construction materials and certain plastics underwent a considerable expansion. Some of these improvements reflected the acceleration of existing trends, but in other cases they followed prior decreases. Other industries, however, contracted over the same period (examples included rum, some canned goods and most paper goods). The varied performance reflected a major restructuring of the Nicaraguan manufacturing sector, following economic liberalization efforts. An importation tariff reform brought cheap imports and, unable to compete, some traditional manufacturing businesses closed, diversified or formed joint ventures with foreign firms or returning exiles attracted into the country by a more favourable foreign investment environment. The significant textile, clothing and leather goods sub-sector notably suffered in 2009, its GDP contracting by 6.0% in that year, although it recovered strongly in 2010, expanding by 18.0% and accounting for 30.9% of total manufacturing value added.

The most sustained expansion in the sector has been seen in the *maquila*, or offshore assembly, sector. Free trade zone exports increased steadily from US $37.3m. in 1994 to $1,088.0m. in 2007. After declining slightly in 2008 and 2009, owing to reduced demand resulting from the global economic downturn, free trade zone exports recovered strongly thereafter, rising to $1,277.2m. in 2010, $1,740.1m. in 2011 and $1,903.8m. in 2012. The growth of exports has largely been attributed to higher demand in the USA on the back of recovery there. The principal markets for free zone exports remained the USA and Mexico, accounting for 68.7% and 21.8%, respectively, in 2012. Although the principal product was clothing assembled from US-imported textiles, plants also produced car chassis, footwear, aluminium frames and jewellery, with companies from Hong Kong and Taiwan augmenting those from the USA. The number of jobs in the free trade zones expanded from 3,938 (at 14 companies) in 1994 to an estimated 77,035 (at 132 companies) in 2010, having peaked at 84,408 in 2007. The attraction of more of these enterprises formed the key component of the Government's national economic development plan, with an assumption that more US companies would be drawn to Nicaragua following the implementation of the Dominican Republic-Central American Free Trade Agreement (CAFTA-DR) in April 2006. Analysts remained divided as to the probability of sustained growth in this area and the ability of the sector to generate sufficient employment to offset the likely agricultural losses that CAFTA-DR would produce. The main concern was that any economic growth that free trade would promote would disproportionately benefit a very small group of people.

Much of the investment in the construction sector during the 1980s was strategic. By the end of the decade, however, the industry contracted as external assistance ended. The Chamorro Government's reconstruction programme reversed the decline in the early 1990s, although sectoral growth fluctuated in the rest of the decade. The assistance given to the sector by reconstruction efforts in the wake of Hurricane Mitch, combined with several large-scale projects in the tourism and transport sectors, resulted in an expansion of 36.8% in the GDP of the construction sector in 1999, when it accounted for 8.6% of GDP. Sectoral GDP contracted in 2006–10, with the global economic downturn contributing to declines of 15.0% in 2009 and an estimated 14.5% in 2010; however, the sector recorded positive growth of an estimated 21.1% in 2011 and 32.0% in 2012. In 2012 and 2013 construction contributed an estimated 5.3% of GDP. In 2013 sectoral growth decelerated to 17.2%, owing to a slowdown in the residential construction market.

PUBLIC FINANCE AND PAYMENTS

The Governments of Presidents Violeta Chamorro and Arnoldo Alemán Lacayo had some success in controlling what had become one of the most chronic current account budget deficits of any state. Access to external funds from the USA and multilateral lending agencies, a dramatic decrease in inflation, severe reductions in public spending, as well as privatization of state enterprises, improved tax collection and the retirement or renegotiation of some of the country's massive foreign debt, combined to help reduce the budget deficit from the average 25% of GDP that it had reached in the 1980s. By 1998 the budget deficit (before grants) had declined to the equivalent of 4.8% of GDP. However, by 2001 it had reached around 19.0%, as election year spending and the consequences of Hurricane Mitch took a particularly heavy toll. In 2002 and 2003 the budget deficit was dramatically reduced to 4.1% and 2.3% of GDP, respectively, as a result of the severe fiscal measures that the administration of Enrique Bolaños Geyer (2002–07) was forced to impose in order to be eligible for access to the World Bank and IMF's heavily indebted poor countries (HIPC) initiative. In 2012 the budget deficit was equivalent to only 0.6% of GDP, compared with 2.3% in 2009, 1.0% in 2010 and 3.4% in 2011.

In the early 21st century public sector salaries expanded beyond private sector wages. The number of central government employees increased under the Ortega administration that took office in January 2007, reaching 90,200 (equivalent to 4.3% of the employed labour force) in 2009, compared with 69,600 (3.4% of the employed labour force) in 2006.

During the 1980s the growing budget deficits produced by the war effort and growing balance of payments deficits had forced the Sandinista Government to increase its foreign borrowing. Following initial rescheduling, a moratorium on public sector debt service payments had, by September 1982, become inevitable. Unable to pay either interest or principal on its debt, in 1983 Nicaragua entered a state of 'passive default'. However, in 1988–89 the Sandinista Government implemented many of the measures traditionally demanded by the IMF as part of its own austerity programme.

These measures prepared the way for the implementation of the new policies of the Chamorro Government, which was able to take advantage of much more favourable circumstances. Thus, in 1992, with the USA agreeing to waive payment of US $259.5m. in bilateral debt and the 'Paris Club' of Western creditor nations reducing an $830m. debt to $207m., the new Government was able to pay arrears to the World Bank and the Inter-American Development Bank (IDB). This, in turn, opened a series of loan opportunities. The IMF ended its 12-year boycott of Nicaragua by approving a $55.7m. stand-by loan and the IDB approved a loan to support adjustment programmes in the trade and financial sectors. Restructuring of debt payments with various major bilateral creditors such as Mexico, Russia (as the principal successor state of the USSR) and several European countries followed in 1992. However, in 1993 Nicaragua again defaulted on repayment.

In 1994 the Government reached agreement with the IMF on an enhanced structural adjustment loan and redoubled its efforts to secure debt renegotiation and cancellation. The following year the Government secured the purchase of more than 80% of its commercial debt at eight cents in the dollar, effectively paying US $112m. to cancel $1,400m. in debt. This followed the restructuring of debts owed to the Paris Club. In 1998 the Club agreed to a further two-year postponement of $201m. in debt service payments. In April 1996 Nicaragua finally reached agreement with Russia over its $3,500m. debt to the former USSR, with 95% of the outstanding amount being forgiven. Later that year Mexico followed suit, agreeing to waive 91% of the $1,100m. that it was owed. Agreement was also reached with the IMF in 1998 on a second enhanced structural adjustment loan. In November a number of countries pardoned or softened terms on bilateral debt they were owed, in the wake of Hurricane Mitch. Cuba, Austria and France, in particular, waived a total of $157m. in bilateral debt. France then waived a further $90m. in outstanding debt in February 2000. In March 2001 Spain assumed most of Nicaragua's $500m. debt to Guatemala, writing off some $399m. of the total in the process. In April 2003 France, Germany and Spain cancelled a further $263m. in bilateral debt. Iran announced in May 2012 that it would remit Nicaragua's $164m. debt.

In September 1999 Nicaragua was declared eligible for inclusion in the HIPC debt relief initiative, which would eventually make the cancellation of 80%–90% of the country's foreign debt possible. In December 2000 the IMF and World Bank declared that the country had fulfilled the necessary conditions to enter the initiative. In 2002 debt service waivers reached US $206m., almost double the amount of the previous year, following the implementation of a severe fiscal programme by the Bolaños Government, while in 2003 the total relief was $214m. In January 2004, after the fulfilment of all obligations, Nicaragua finally attained HIPC status, which included the forgiveness of 80% of the country's public external debt (totalling $6,400m. in 2003). In addition, the country only had to pay 10% of the total servicing of all World Bank loans contracted between 2001 and 2003, and would also receive a debt release of some $106m. on servicing IMF loans entered into between 2002 and 2009. In June 2005 Nicaragua was among 18 countries to be granted 100% debt relief on multilateral debt agreed by the Group of Eight (G8) leading industrialized nations. This cancellation was approved by the IMF in December, under the Multilateral Debt Relief Initiative. The relief totalled some $201m. and became available from January 2006. In October 2007 a further agreement was finalized with the IMF, ensuring the release of some $111.3m. to the Ortega Government over three years. (The provision of an additional $10m. was approved by the IMF in September 2008 in view of the adverse effects of Hurricane Felix in 2007.) However, the Fund raised concerns over the Government's burgeoning relationship with Venezuela (which had cancelled $32.5m. of Nicaragua's outstanding debt in 2007). From late 2006 onwards Venezuela had made significant contributions to the Ortega administration. However, ongoing questions over the propriety and transparency of these transactions had the effect of undermining the Government during 2007–10. In May 2010 the IMF expressed concerns regarding the potential impact on inflation of recently announced bonuses for public sector workers and gas and fuel subsidies for transport workers (to be funded by Venezuela). None the less, in November the Fund agreed to an extension of the three-year arrangement approved in October 2007 until December 2011. In April, under pressure from the IMF, the central bank released a detailed report on funds received from Venezuela and other foreign donors; the sum provided by Venezuela in 2011 rose to $609m. (from $76m. in 2010).

FOREIGN TRADE

Until the early 1990s Nicaragua's export trade remained dominated by agricultural commodities, mainly coffee, cotton, sugar, beef, bananas and, increasingly, seafood. Import trade was (and continued to be) dominated by petroleum, other raw materials, non-durable consumer goods and machinery. The enormous cost of the war, increased purchases of petroleum and reduced income from exports (chiefly owing to low prices for coffee, sugar and cotton and the loss of the US market because of the embargo) resulted in an increasingly bleak trade deficit by the end of the 1980s. From the early 1990s, however, there was substantial improvement, although the damage caused to export crops by Hurricane Mitch resulted in a decline in merchandise export revenues (f.o.b.), to an estimated US $546.1m. in 1999. Export earnings generally increased steadily thereafter, reaching $2,264.0m. in 2011 and $2,677.4m. in 2012, before declining to $2,400.6m. in 2013, according to the central bank.

At the beginning of the 21st century there was a significant transformation in the relative composition of export trade. In 2000 traditional exports (coffee, cotton, sugar, bananas, meat, etc.) represented 63.5% of total earnings; by 2008 these products represented only 36.9% (of which cotton made no contribution), although their contribution increased to 42.3% in 2010 as a result of particularly high international prices. Non-traditional exports, led by industrial production in the *maquila* zones and non-traditional agricultural exports such as groundnuts and beans, increased dramatically in importance over the same period.

Imports increased in the 1990s, fuelled at the end of that decade by the reconstruction and repair needs resulting from Hurricane Mitch. Merchandise imports (c.i.f) stood at US $1,805.5m. in 2000. The imports bill remained static in 2001 and 2002, but registered a generally upward trend thereafter, reaching $4,863.5m. in 2011, $5,418.1m. in 2012 and $6,401.9m. in 2013, according to the central bank. These levels of importation, coupled with the relative lack of dynamism in the export sector, produced a burgeoning overall trade deficit. In 2009 the deficit narrowed to $1,539.5m., as import costs declined much more sharply than export revenues, before widening again to reach $2,068.4m. in 2011, $2,161.0m. in 2012 and $2,270.4m. in 2013.

The only major new sources of income that helped to offset the generally growing trade deficit were income from tourism and remittances from Nicaraguan citizens living abroad, mainly in the USA and Costa Rica. The tourism sector remained robust in 2009–10, despite the global economic downturn, with arrivals rising to 931,904 in 2009 and to 1,011,251 in 2010, with a 16.9% increase in arrivals by land compensating for a 44.2% decrease in arrivals by sea (and a 0.7% decline in arrivals by air). According to the World Tourism Organization, the number of arrivals increased to 1,060,031 in 2011 and further to 1,179,581 in 2012. Tourism income rose to US $334m. in 2009, but decreased to $309m. in 2010 as a result of the global economic downturn, before increasing again in 2011 to $378m. and further to $422m. in 2012 aided by the onset of the economic recovery in the USA. With the continued US recovery, tourism receipts remained strong, at an estimated $417m., in 2013.

There was a massive increase in remittances in the early 21st century. Remittances totalled US $818m. in 2008; a decline of 6.1%, to $768m. (equivalent to 12.4% of GDP) was recorded in 2009, although this contraction was less severe than that experienced by most other countries in the region,

and remittances recovered and grew thereafter, reaching $911.6m. in 2011, $1,014m. in 2012 and $1,077m. in 2013, mainly as a result of the large Nicaraguan community in the USA benefiting from improved economic conditions therein.

Fighting in the border regions disrupted Nicaragua's trade with neighbouring Central American countries during the 1980s. Non-traditional exports to the Central American Common Market (CACM) suffered most. The irregular availability of foreign exchange was the principal problem, although economic recession throughout the region also had an impact. Trade with Argentina and Brazil increased, owing to the extension of trade credits for Nicaragua's prime agricultural exports. In 2013 exports to the USA represented 25.2% of total exports, while the value of goods from the USA was equivalent to 15.0% of total imports. Venezuela's total trade (imports plus exports) with Nicaragua in 2013 was on a par with that of the USA; in that year Venezuela took 16.0% of export goods, while also providing 18.9% of Nicaragua's imports. Previously, in 2005, the member countries of the CACM had made substantial progress in the harmonization of common external tariffs. In that year some 5,861 tariffs were harmonized, representing 94.6% of total tariffs. Central America represented 20.6% of total Nicaraguan exports in 2013.

President Ortega announced in June 2013 that the Government had awarded a concession to build an inter-oceanic canal across Nicaragua to a Chinese consortium, later named as HK Nicaragua Canal Development Investment Co Ltd, at an estimated cost of around US $40,000m. Several possible routes were under consideration, all of which would cross Lake Nicaragua and exit to the Pacific at Brito, and all of which would involve construction of a canal and a rail line. Commercial enterprises in East Asia, North America and Europe were likely to welcome any prospective challenge to the monopoly in Atlantic–Pacific ship canals held by the Panama canal for 100 years. Construction of a competing canal in Nicaragua would lower shipping costs, thereby creating wider cost savings and boosting competitiveness on key global trade routes. The head of the country's canal authority, Manuel Coronel Kautz, stated in January 2014 that work on the project would probably not commence until 2015, to give sufficient time to carry out feasibility studies and to reach a final decision on the route.

CONCLUSION

In 2014 Nicaragua remained the second poorest country in Latin America (after Haiti) and was heavily dependent on international aid, particularly from Venezuela (which accounted for some 8% of GDP). Under Daniel Ortega, who was inaugurated for a third term in office in early 2012, advances have been made in reducing maternal mortality rates, increasing school enrolment (and literacy rates) and improving access to safe water. Small-scale farmers were offered microcredits as part of an initiative to stimulate agricultural productivity, and the minimum wage was raised. However, donor support was threatened in 2008 by the legislative impasse that followed disputed municipal elections in November (see History), with the USA cancelling some US $62m. in development aid in 2009, and the European Union also suspending budgetary assistance. Although Ortega pledged to further reconciliation with the USA, this endeavour was undermined by allegations of corruption within his administration, together with his pursuit of closer relations with Iran and Venezuela. Rising concerns in the USA over the Nicaraguan Government's lack of transparency, as well as wider fears over the erosion of democracy and the rule of law following the allegedly fraudulent nature of the November 2011 elections, threatened to lead to the cancellation of US financial assistance. Within Nicaragua itself, there were growing fears that the death of Venezuelan President Chávez in March 2013 and increasing political and economic instability in that country could jeopardize aid flows.

Amid improving international conditions, the Nicaraguan economy returned to growth in 2010 following a short recession. In 2013 GDP increased by an estimated 4.6%, slightly down on the previous year but still high compared to average GDP growth in Central America (not including Panama) of 3.1% in 2013. However, the rate of inflation remained high, at an estimated 7.4% in 2013, and inflationary pressures resulting from high commodity prices were a continuing concern. The economy also remained vulnerable to external shocks, notably to natural disasters and fluctuations in the international price of commodities (especially petroleum). On a more positive note, if the plans come to fruition, the proposed inter-oceanic canal project would provide great potential short- and long-term economic benefits to the Nicaraguan economy.

Statistical Survey

Sources (unless otherwise stated): Banco Central de Nicaragua, Carretera Sur, Km 7, Apdos 2252/3, Zona 5, Managua; tel. 265-0500; fax 265-2272; e-mail bcn@cabcn.gob.ni; internet www.bcn.gob.ni; Instituto Nacional de Información de Desarrollo, Los Arcos, Frente Hospital Fonseca, Managua; tel. 266-6178; e-mail webmaster@inide.gob.ni; internet www.inide.gob.ni.

Area and Population

AREA, POPULATION AND DENSITY

Area (sq km)	
Land	120,340
Inland water	10,034
Total	130,373*
Population (census results)	
25 April 1995	4,357,099
28 May–11 June 2005	
Males	2,534,491
Females	2,607,607
Total	5,142,098
Population (official estimates at mid-year)	
2011	5,888,946
2012	6,071,045
2013	6,134,270
Density (per sq km) at mid-2013	51.0†

* 50,337 sq miles.
† Land area only.

POPULATION BY AGE AND SEX
(official estimates at mid-2013)

	Males	Females	Total
0–14 years	1,032,913	992,975	2,025,888
15–64 years	1,867,801	1,961,249	3,829,050
65 years and over	129,276	150,056	279,332
Total	3,029,990	3,104,280	6,134,270

ADMINISTRATIVE DIVISIONS
(land area only, population estimates at mid-2012)

	Area (sq km)	Population	Density (per sq km)	Capital
Departments:				
Chinandega . .	4,822.4	423,062	87.7	Chinandega
León	5,138.0	404,471	78.7	León
Managua . .	3,465.1	1,448,271	418.0	Managua
Masaya . .	610.8	348,254	570.2	Masaya
Carazo . .	1,081.4	186,898	172.8	Jinotepe
Granada . .	1,039.7	200,991	193.3	Granada
Rivas . .	2,161.8	174,589	80.8	Rivas
Estelí . .	2,229.7	220,703	99.0	Estelí
Madriz . .	1,708.2	158,020	92.5	Somoto
Nueva Segovia . .	3,491.3	243,014	69.6	Ocotal
Jinotega . .	9,222.4	417,372	45.3	Jinotega
Matagalpa . .	6,803.9	542,419	79.7	Matagalpa
Boaco . .	4,176.7	174,682	41.8	Boaco
Chontales . .	6,481.3	182,838	28.2	Juigalpa
Río San Juan . .	7,540.9	122,666	16.3	San Carlos
Autonomous Regions:				
Atlántico Norte (RAAN) . .	32,819.7	453,541	13.8	Bilwi
Atlántico Sur (RAAS) . .	27,546.3	369,254	13.4	Bluefields
Total . .	120,339.5	6,071,045	50.4	—

PRINCIPAL TOWNS
(population estimates at mid-2012)

Managua (capital) .	1,028,808	Chinandega . .	133,361
León	201,100	Tipitapa	130,627
Masaya . . .	166,588	Granada . .	123,697
Matagalpa . .	150,643	Estelí	122,924

Mid-2014 (incl. suburbs, UN estimate): Managua 950,736 (Source: UN, *World Urbanization Prospects: The 2014 Revision*).

BIRTHS, MARRIAGES AND DEATHS
(annual averages, UN estimates)

	1995–2000	2000–05	2005–10
Birth rate (per 1,000)	30.1	26.3	24.8
Death rate (per 1,000)	5.6	5.0	4.7

Source: UN, *World Population Prospects: The 2012 Revision*.

2007: Registered live births 128,171; Registered marriages 20,918; Registered deaths 17,288. Note: Registration believed to be incomplete.

Life expectancy (years at birth): 74.5 (males 71.5; females 77.6) in 2012 (Source: World Bank, World Development Indicators database).

ECONOMICALLY ACTIVE POPULATION
('000, population aged 10 years and over)

	2009	2010	2011
Agriculture, forestry and fishing .	600.8	834.2	900.1
Mining and quarrying	5.7	10.9	19.7
Manufacturing	274.6	299.2	326.3
Electricity, gas and water . . .	10.9	13.8	13.4
Construction	99.4	103.0	169.3
Trade, restaurants and hotels .	485.9	638.9	700.7
Transport and communications .	86.6	97.7	104.2
Financial services	82.7	80.8	95.0
Public administration . . .	90.2	—	—
Social and personal services . .	359.6	513.3	530.2
Total employed	2,096.5	2,591.7	2,858.9
Unemployed	186.2	220.1	180.2
Total labour force	2,282.7	2,811.8	3,039.2

2012: Total employed 2,986.4; Unemployed 187.7; Total labour force 3,174.1.

Health and Welfare

KEY INDICATORS

Total fertility rate (children per woman, 2012)	2.5
Under-5 mortality rate (per 1,000 live births, 2012)	24
HIV/AIDS (% of persons aged 15–49, 2012)	0.3
Physicians (per 1,000 head, 2003)	0.4
Hospital beds (per 1,000 head, 2010)	0.8
Health expenditure (2011): US $ per head (PPP)	292
Health expenditure (2011): % of GDP	7.6
Health expenditure (2011): public (% of total)	54.3
Access to water (% of persons, 2012)	85
Access to sanitation (% of persons, 2012)	52
Total carbon emissions ('000 metric tons, 2010)	4,547.1
Carbon dioxide emissions per head (metric tons, 2010)	0.8
Human Development Index (2013): ranking	132
Human Development Index (2013): value	0.614

For sources and definitions, see explanatory note on p. vi.

Agriculture

PRINCIPAL CROPS
('000 metric tons)

	2010	2011	2012
Rice, paddy	454.0	488.0*	440.0*
Maize	457.0	523.0*	471.0*
Sorghum	58.8	91.0	58.0*
Cassava (Manioc)	73.8	75.1†	78.0†
Sugar cane	4,893.9	5,937.5	7,500.0†
Beans, dry	150.8	234.2	140.0†
Groundnuts, in shell*	180.3	184.3	200.0
Oil palm fruit†	86.7	86.7	80.0
Bananas	35.2	39.6	42.0†
Plantains†	57.3	64.4	66.0
Oranges†	84.4	95.1	100.0
Pineapples†	50.5	56.8	60.0
Coffee, green	78.7	103.7	107.0†

* Unofficial figure(s).
† FAO estimate(s).

Aggregate production ('000 metric tons, may include official, semi-official or estimated data): Total cereals 970 in 2010, 1,102 in 2011, 969 in 2012; Total roots and tubers 114 in 2010, 115 in 2011, 1,201 in 2012; Total vegetables (incl. melons) 37 in 2010, 39 in 2011, 42 in 2012; Total fruits (excl. melons) 242 in 2010, 272 in 2011, 285 in 2012.

Source: FAO.

LIVESTOCK
('000 head, year ending September, FAO estimates)

	2010	2011	2012
Cattle	3,700	3,750	3,750
Pigs	480	495	495
Goats	7	8	8
Horses	268	268	269
Asses	9	9	9
Mules	48	48	48
Poultry	19,000	19,800	19,800

Source: FAO.

LIVESTOCK PRODUCTS
('000 metric tons)

	2010	2011*	2012*
Cattle meat	121.0	146.0	134.0
Pig meat	7.7	7.9	8.0
Horse meat*	2.5	2.6	2.7
Chicken meat	102.3	105.0	109.6
Cows' milk	753.3	760.0	765.0
Hen eggs	24.5	26.3	27.8

* FAO estimates.
Source: FAO.

Forestry

ROUNDWOOD REMOVALS
('000 cubic metres, excl. bark, FAO estimates)

	2010	2011	2012
Sawlogs, veneer logs and logs for sleepers	202	118	118
Fuel wood	6,097	6,110	6,125
Total	6,299	6,228	6,243

Source: FAO.

SAWNWOOD PRODUCTION
('000 cubic metres, incl. railway sleepers, FAO estimates)

	2009	2010	2011
Coniferous	12	29	29
Broadleaved	40	77	33
Total	52	106	62

2012: Figures assumed to be unchanged from 2011 (FAO estimates).
Source: FAO.

Fishing

('000 metric tons, live weight)

	2010	2011	2012
Capture	38.1	33.6	33.9
Snooks	0.9	0.8	0.7
Snappers	1.3	1.5	1.9
Yellowfin tuna	10.7	8.9	8.2
Skipjack tuna	4.2	3.9	4.0
Common dolphinfish	0.2	0.3	0.5
Caribbean spiny lobsters	3.7	4.0	4.2
Penaeus shrimp	2.6	2.4	1.1
Aquaculture	17.0	15.8	24.4
Whiteleg shrimp	16.6	15.7	24.3
Total catch	55.0	49.3	58.2

Source: FAO.

Mining

	2010	2011	2012
Gold (kg)	4,900	6,395	6,981
Silver (kg)	6,995	7,927	10,207
Gypsum and anhydrite (metric tons)	20,330	29,710	34,890

Source: US Geological Survey.

Industry

SELECTED PRODUCTS
('000 barrels unless otherwise indicated)

	2011	2012*	2013*
Liquid gas	192	101	127
Motor spirit	828	584	830
Kerosene	275	200	225
Diesel	1,657	1,129	1,556
Fuel oil	2,361	1,558	2,004
Bitumen (asphalt)	74	36	52
Electric energy (million kWh)	3,824.2	3,956.0	4,158.6

* Preliminary figures.

Cement ('000 metric tons, estimates): 530 in 2010; 600 in 2011–12 (Source: US Geological Survey).

Finance

CURRENCY AND EXCHANGE RATES

Monetary Units
100 centavos = 1 córdoba.

Sterling, Dollar and Euro Equivalents (30 April 2014)
£1 sterling = 43.300 córdobas;
US $1 = 25.741 córdobas;
€1 = 35.652 córdobas;
1,000 córdobas = £23.09 = $38.85 = €28.05.

Average Exchange Rate (córdobas per US dollar)
2011   22.424
2012   23.547
2013   24.723

Note: In February 1988 a new córdoba, equivalent to 1,000 of the former units, was introduced, and a uniform exchange rate of US $1 = 10 new córdobas was established. Subsequently, the exchange rate was frequently adjusted. A new currency, the córdoba 'oro' ('gold' córdoba), was introduced as a unit of account in May 1990 and began to be circulated in August. The value of the 'gold' córdoba was initially fixed at par with the US dollar, but in March 1991 the exchange rate was revised to $1 = 25,000,000 new córdobas (or 5 'gold' córdobas). On 30 April 1991 the 'gold' córdoba became the sole legal tender. Since January 1993 a 'crawling peg' system of daily official exchange rate adjustments in the value of the córdoba against the US dollar has been pursued by the central bank.

CENTRAL GOVERNMENT BUDGET
(million córdobas)

Revenue and grants	2011	2012*	2013*
Taxation	31,824.6	37,221.7	40,785.0
Income tax	11,143.7	13,107.4	14,520.8
Property tax	191.2	239.1	311.4
Taxes on goods and services .	18,945.8	22,035.4	23,989.8
Value-added tax . . .	12,876.0	15,151.5	16,736.0
Excise tax	6,069.9	6,884.0	7,253.7
Other taxes	22.0	23.5	77.3
International trade and transactions taxes . . .	1,521.8	1,816.4	1,885.7
Other revenue	2,720.0	3,500.5	3,248.6
Total	34,544.6	40,722.2	44,033.6

Expenditure	2011	2012*	2013*
Compensation of employees . .	11,957.1	13,629.7	15,203.8
Goods and services . . .	5,537.6	6,099.2	6,349.5
Interest payments	2,261.9	2,466.3	2,519.6
Domestic	1,552.8	1,686.7	1,564.7
External	709.1	779.5	954.9
Current and capital transfers .	10,339.6	11,620.1	12,847.8
Social security contributions . .	822.0	1,079.5	963.9
Other expenditure	1,904.4	2,871.7	3,091.2
Total	32,822.7	37,766.2	40,975.7

* Preliminary figures.

2013 (consolidated accounts of central government and public sector, million córdobas): *Revenue* Tax revenues 42,796.7; Social contributions 12,805.5; Other revenue 11,808.2; Total 67,410.4 (excl. grants 2,757.6). *Expenditure* Compensation of employees 18,600.8; Goods and services 14,945.2; Interest payments 2,731.3; Current and capital transfers 12,924.5; Social benefits 8,900.3; Other expenditures 3,475.6; Total 61,577.7 (excl. net acquisition of non-financial assets 11,454.1).

INTERNATIONAL RESERVES
(excluding gold, US $ million at 31 December)

	2011	2012	2013
IMF special drawing rights . .	175.77	163.09	146.86
Foreign exchange	1,716.48	1,724.13	1,846.10
Total	1,892.25	1,887.21	1,992.96

Source: IMF, *International Financial Statistics*.

MONEY SUPPLY
(million córdobas at 31 December)

	2011	2012	2013
Currency outside depository corporations	9,686.4	10,874.4	11,523.1
Transferable deposits . . .	17,622.2	22,001.9	27,819.1
Other deposits	44,754.4	50,279.9	59,047.6
Broad money	72,062.9	83,156.2	98,389.8

Source: IMF, *International Financial Statistics*.

COST OF LIVING
(Consumer Price Index; base: 2006 = 100)

	2011	2012	2013
Food	168.8	183.3	200.5
Clothing	141.7	154.7	163.7
Rent, fuel and light . . .	142.1	148.4	155.9
All items (incl. others) . . .	150.3	161.1	172.5

NATIONAL ACCOUNTS
(million córdobas at current prices)

Expenditure on the Gross Domestic Product

	2011*	2012*	2013†
Final consumption expenditure .	204,898.0	229,796.4	253,673.6
Gross capital formation . . .	51,957.0	58,361.2	56,905.0
Total domestic expenditure .	256,873.0	288,157.6	310,578.6
Exports of goods and services .	88,923.7	107,879.5	112,748.3
Less Imports of goods and services	123,810.1	145,383.8	145,056.8
GDP in purchasers' values .	221,968.6	250,653.4	278,270.2
GDP at constant 2006 prices .	137,085.8	143,876.3	150,503.7

Gross Domestic Product by Economic Activity

	2011*	2012*	2013†
Agriculture, hunting, forestry and fishing	38,593.0	41,477.1	42,611.5
Mining and quarrying . . .	5,975.4	7,636.9	7,817.5
Manufacturing	37,845.4	40,846.3	48,685.8
Electricity, gas and water . .	5,640.6	5,785.2	6,564.1
Construction	8,399.0	12,067.7	14,690.1
Wholesale and retail trade . .	28,238.1	31,646.1	34,973.1
Transport and communications .	13,027.0	15,523.5	16,318.0
Finance, insurance and business services	7,582.3	8,603.2	10,287.4
General government services .	18,786.6	21,385.2	24,890.9
Other services	37,027.4	41,330.5	45,048.1
Sub-total	201,114.8	226,301.7	251,886.5
Net taxes on products . . .	20,853.8	24,351.6	26,383.6
GDP in purchasers' values .	221,968.6	250,653.4	278,270.2

* Preliminary figures.
† Estimates.

BALANCE OF PAYMENTS
(US $ million)

	2010	2011	2012
Exports of goods	2,744.1	3,666.2	4,145.7
Imports of goods	−4,494.6	−5,844.0	−6,441.7
Balance on goods	−1,750.5	−2,177.8	−2,296.0
Exports of services	693.4	772.5	847.0
Imports of services	−739.2	−858.1	−940.4
Balance on goods and services	−1,796.3	−2,263.4	−2,389.4
Primary income received . . .	17.8	21.1	24.8
Primary income paid	−256.6	−271.1	−326.0
Balance on goods, services and primary income	−2,035.1	−2,513.4	−2,690.6
Secondary income (net) . . .	1,160.6	1,229.6	1,309.8
Current balance	−874.5	−1,283.8	−1,380.8

—continued	2010	2011	2012
Capital account (net) . . .	263.5	247.3	225.4
Direct investment assets . . .	−17.5	−6.8	−43.9
Direct investment liabilities . .	508.0	967.9	804.6
Portfolio investment assets . .	−71.1	−207.5	70.4
Portfolio investment liabilities . .	−20.0	−12.9	−6.4
Other investment assets . . .	−350.5	307.1	132.2
Other investment liabilities . .	588.5	717.9	768.4
Net errors and omissions . . .	175.6	−656.6	−572.5
Reserves and related items .	201.9	72.6	−2.5

Source: IMF, *International Financial Statistics.*

External Trade

PRINCIPAL COMMODITIES
(US $ million, preliminary)

Imports c.i.f.	2011	2012	2013
Consumer goods	1,654.8	1,813.1	1,813.4
Non-durable consumer goods .	1,339.3	1,450.2	1,462.2
Durable consumer goods . .	315.5	362.9	351.2
Petroleum, mineral fuels and lubricants	1,256.4	1,286.6	1,186.3
Crude petroleum	615.6	441.8	509.2
Mineral fuels and lubricants .	639.3	844.9	677.1
Intermediate goods	1,337.4	1,522.6	1,520.4
Primary materials and intermediate goods for agriculture and fishing . .	271.9	320.4	312.6
Primary materials and intermediate goods for industry	799.7	887.8	888.7
Construction materials . . .	265.8	314.4	319.1
Capital goods	947.2	1,220.4	1,094.5
For agriculture and fishing . .	64.7	77.8	69.8
For industry	532.1	708.8	577.0
For transport	350.4	433.8	447.7
Miscellaneous	8.0	8.5	9.4
Total	5,203.7	5,851.3	5,624.1

Exports f.o.b.	2011	2012	2013
Cattle on hoof	18.6	18.6	39.2
Fresh fish	16.3	16.8	17.9
Lobster	45.9	43.9	44.5
Shrimp	62.2	67.5	67.8
Coffee	429.3	521.8	349.5
Groundnuts	96.1	132.5	102.9
Beans	30.2	51.8	44.8
Bananas	2.4	2.5	2.3
Tobacco (leaf)	6.3	8.4	4.7
Meat and meat products . . .	427.0	451.4	383.8
Refined sugars, etc. . . .	156.3	194.9	176.0
Cheese	81.4	94.7	94.7
Refined petroleum	15.2	49.8	18.7
Wood products	13.3	11.8	13.0
Chemical products	27.9	35.4	33.4
Gold	352.3	422.8	431.6
Porcelain products	8.3	8.2	8.5
Total (incl. others)	2,264.0	2,677.4	2,400.7

PRINCIPAL TRADING PARTNERS
(US $ million, preliminary)

Imports c.i.f.	2011	2012	2013
Costa Rica	438.2	462.4	477.4
Ecuador	10.0	8.2	8.7
El Salvador	234.0	320.6	278.6
Germany	65.0	68.4	73.4
Guatemala	347.8	350.6	359.3
Honduras	169.7	164.2	209.4
Japan	145.0	174.4	146.5
Korea, Republic	90.8	81.7	82.7
Mexico	406.3	443.2	464.6
Russia	67.9	78.9	66.9
Spain	54.7	107.0	81.8
USA	905.4	1,075.8	842.9
Venezuela	1,139.8	1,176.8	1,064.4
Total (incl. others)	5,203.7	5,851.3	5,624.1

Exports f.o.b.	2011	2012	2013
Belgium	34.1	66.0	21.4
Canada	273.4	317.6	313.6
Costa Rica	98.8	115.4	119.3
El Salvador	206.6	245.3	213.4
France	25.9	30.9	47.0
Germany	32.9	29.1	30.1
Guatemala	71.0	76.4	84.4
Honduras	59.4	66.5	79.3
Italy	33.4	35.5	28.7
Japan	23.3	24.4	20.7
Mexico	82.8	70.1	47.7
Puerto Rico	45.3	35.5	27.7
Spain	36.4	32.7	30.6
Taiwan	38.4	10.7	65.5
United Kingdom	38.5	44.6	40.1
USA	648.8	765.3	605.8
Venezuela	302.6	444.0	384.0
Total (incl. others)	2,264.0	2,677.4	2,400.7

Transport

ROAD TRAFFIC
(motor vehicles in use)

	2007	2009*	2010
Passenger cars	95,498	101,021	96,021
Buses and coaches	38,602	38,665	36,291
Lorries and vans	183,671	192,544	196,700
Motorcycles and mopeds . . .	56,525	87,247	112,632

* Data for 2008 were not available.

Source: IRF, *World Road Statistics.*

SHIPPING

Flag Registered fleet
(at 31 December)

	2011	2012	2013
Number of vessels	8	7	7
Total displacement (grt) . . .	4,814	3,949	4,427

Source: Lloyd's List Intelligence (www.lloydslistintelligence.com).

International Seaborne Freight Traffic
('000 metric tons)

	2011	2012*	2013*
Imports	2,781.3	2,883.3	2,751.6
Exports	654.8	772.3	870.0
Total international cargo movements	3,436.1	3,655.6	3,621.6

* Estimates.

CIVIL AVIATION
(traffic at Augusto César Sandino airport)

	2011	2012*	2013*
Passengers carried ('000) . . .	1,116.2	1,197.2	1,206.3
Freight carried (metric tons) . .	21,835	22,885	22,219

*Estimates.

Tourism

TOURIST ARRIVALS BY COUNTRY OF ORIGIN

	2010	2011	2012
Canada	23,597	25,676	30,710
Costa Rica	125,811	136,466	160,108
El Salvador	135,455	138,120	152,741
Guatemala	76,695	83,408	92,877
Honduras	214,776	230,965	251,804
Panama	20,174	22,451	24,517
USA	210,479	213,986	240,846
Total (incl. others)	1,011,251	1,060,031	1,179,581

Total tourist arrivals ('000): 1,230 in 2013 (provisional).

Tourism receipts (US $ million, excl. passenger transport): 378 in 2011; 422 in 2012; 417 in 2013 (provisional).

Source: World Tourism Organization.

Communications Media

	2011	2012	2013
Telephones ('000 main lines in use)	287.6	299.1	325.0
Mobile cellular telephones ('000 subscribers)	4,823.5	5,851.7	6,808.9
Broadband subscribers ('000) . .	85.1	101.3	131.7

Source: International Telecommunication Union.

Education

(2009/10 unless otherwise indicated)

			Students		
	Institutions*	Teachers	Males	Females	Total
Pre-primary .	5,980	10,289	109,836	108,226	218,062
Primary . . .	8,251	30,571	475,981	447,764	923,745
Secondary: general . .	1,249	15,089	221,894	236,427	458,321
Tertiary: university level	35	3,630†	47,683‡	51,222‡	98,905‡
Tertiary: other higher . . .	73	210†	1,902‡	2,770‡	4,672‡

*2002/03 figures.
† 2001/02 figure.
‡ 2003/04 figure.

Sources: UNESCO, *Statistical Yearbook*; Ministry of Education.

Pupil-teacher ratio (primary education, UNESCO estimate): 30.2 in 2009/10 (Source: UNESCO Institute for Statistics).

Adult literacy rate (UNESCO estimates): 80.5% (males 79.7%; females 81.4%) in 2007 (Source: UNESCO Institute for Statistics).

Directory

The Constitution

Shortly after taking office on 20 July 1979, the Government of National Reconstruction abrogated the 1974 Constitution. On 22 August 1979 the revolutionary junta issued a 'Statute on Rights and Guarantees for the Citizens of Nicaragua', providing for the basic freedoms of the individual, religious freedom and freedom of the press and abolishing the death penalty. The intention of the Statute was formally to re-establish rights that had been violated under the deposed Somoza regime. A fundamental Statute took effect from 20 July 1980 and remained in force until the Council of State drafted a political constitution and proposed an electoral law. A new Constitution was approved by the National Constituent Assembly on 19 November 1986 and promulgated on 9 January 1987. Amendments to the Constitution were approved by the Asamblea Nacional (National Assembly) in July 1995, January 2000 and January 2014. The following are some of the main points of the Constitution.

Nicaragua is an independent, free, sovereign and indivisible state. All Nicaraguans who have reached 16 years of age are full citizens.

POLITICAL RIGHTS

There shall be absolute equality between men and women. It is the obligation of the state to remove obstacles that impede effective participation of Nicaraguans in the political, economic and social life of the country. Citizens have the right to vote, to be elected at elections and to offer themselves for public office. Citizens may organize or affiliate with political parties, with the objective of participating in, exercising or vying for power. The supremacy of civilian authority is enshrined in the Constitution.

SOCIAL RIGHTS

The Nicaraguan people have the right to work, to education and to culture. They have the right to decent, comfortable and safe housing, and to seek accurate information. This right comprises the freedom to seek, receive and disseminate information and ideas, both spoken and written, in graphic or any other form. The mass media are at the service of national interests. No Nicaraguan citizen may disobey the law or prevent others from exercising their rights and fulfilling their duties by invoking religious beliefs or inclinations.

LABOUR RIGHTS

All have a right to work, and to participate in the management of their enterprises. Equal pay shall be given for equal work. The state shall strive for full and productive employment under conditions that guarantee the fundamental rights of the individual. There shall be an eight-hour working day, weekly rest, vacations, remuneration for national holidays and a bonus payment equivalent to one month's salary, in conformity with the law.

EDUCATION

Education is an obligatory function of the state. Planning, direction and organization of the secular education system is the responsibility of the state. All Nicaraguans have free and equal access to education. Private education centres may function at all levels.

LEGISLATIVE POWER

The National Assembly exercises Legislative Power through representative popular mandate. The National Assembly is composed of 90 representatives elected by direct secret vote by means of a system of proportional representation, of which 70 are elected at regional level and 20 at national level. The number of representatives may be increased in accordance with the general census of the population, in conformity with the law. Representatives shall be elected for a period of five years. The functions of the National Assembly are to draft and approve laws and decrees; to decree amnesties and pardons; to consider, discuss and approve the General Budget of the Republic; to elect judges to the Supreme Court of Justice and the Supreme Electoral Council; to fill permanent vacancies for the Presidency or Vice-Presidency; and to determine the political and administrative division of the country.

EXECUTIVE POWER

The Executive Power is exercised by the President of the Republic (assisted by the Vice-President), who is the Head of State, Head of

Government and Commander-in-Chief of the Defence and Security Forces of the Nation. The election of the President (and Vice-President) is by equal, direct and free universal suffrage in a secret ballot. Should a single candidate in a presidential election fail to secure the necessary relative majority to win outright in the first round, a second ballot shall be held. Close relatives of a serving President are prohibited from contesting a presidential election. The President shall serve for a period of five years and may stand for re-election. All outgoing Presidents are granted a seat in the National Assembly.

JUDICIAL POWER

The Judiciary consists of the Supreme Court of Justice, Courts of Appeal and other courts of the Republic. The Supreme Court is composed of at least seven judges, elected by the National Assembly, who shall serve for a term of six years. The functions of the Supreme Court are to organize and direct the administration of justice. There are 12 Supreme Court justices, appointed for a period of seven years.

LOCAL ADMINISTRATION

The country is divided into regions, departments and municipalities for administrative purposes. The municipal governments shall be elected by universal suffrage in a secret ballot and will serve a six-year term. The communities of the Atlantic Coast have the right to live and develop in accordance with a social organization that corresponds to their historical and cultural traditions. The state shall implement, by legal means, autonomous governments in the regions inhabited by the communities of the Atlantic Coast, in order that the communities may exercise their rights.

The Government

HEAD OF STATE

President: JOSÉ DANIEL ORTEGA SAAVEDRA (elected 5 November 2006; re-elected 6 November 2011).

Vice-President: MOISES OMAR HALLESLEVENS ACEVEDO.

CABINET
(September 2014)

The Government is formed by the Frente Sandinista de Liberación Nacional.

Minister of Foreign Affairs: SAMUEL SANTOS LÓPEZ.

Minister of the Interior: ANA ISABEL MORALES MAZÚN.

Minister of Defence: Dr MARTHA RUIZ SEVILLA.

Minister of Finance and Public Credit: IVÁN ACOSTA.

Minister of Development, Industry and Trade: Dr ORLANDO SOLÓRZANO DELGADILLO.

Minister of Labour: ALBA LUZ TORRES BRIONES.

Minister of the Environment and Natural Resources: JUANITA ARGEÑAL SANDOVAL.

Minister of Transport and Infrastructure: PABLO FERNANDO MARTÍNEZ ESPINOZA.

Minister of Agriculture and Forestry: ARIEL BUCARDO ROCHA.

Minister of Health: Dr SONIA CASTRO GONZÁLEZ.

Minister of Education: MIRIAM RÁUDEZ.

Minister of the Family, Adolescence and Childhood: MARCIA RAMÍREZ MERCADO.

Minister of Energy and Mines: EMILIO RAPPACCIOLI BALTODANO.

Secretary to the Presidency: PAUL OQUIST.

Co-ordinator of the Communication and Citizenship Council: ROSARIO MURILLO ZAMBRANA.

MINISTRIES

Office of the President: Casa Presidencial, Managua; fax 2266-3102; e-mail daniel@presidencia.gob.ni; internet www.presidencia.gob.ni.

Ministry of Agriculture and Forestry: Km 8½, Carretera a Masaya, Managua; tel. 2276-0512; fax 2276-0204; e-mail ministro@magfor.gob.ni; internet www.magfor.gob.ni.

Ministry of Defence: De los semáforos el Redentor, 4 c. arriba, donde fue la casa 'Ricardo Morales Aviles', Managua; tel. 2222-2201; fax 2222-5439; e-mail prensa.midef@midef.gob.ni; internet www.midef.gob.ni.

Ministry of Development, Industry and Trade: Edif. Central, Km 6, Carretera a Masaya, Apdo 8, frente a camino de oriente, Managua; tel. 2248-9300; fax 2270-095; e-mail acastilb@mific.gob.ni; internet www.mific.gob.ni.

Ministry of Education: Centro Cívico, Módulo K, Planta Alta, Apdo 505, Managua; tel. 2265-0046; fax 2265-0081; e-mail webmaster@mined.gob.ni; internet www.mined.gob.ni.

Ministry of Energy and Mines: Hospital Bautista, 1 c. al oeste, 1 c. al norte, Managua; tel. 2280-9500; fax 2280-9516; e-mail despacho@mem.gob.ni; internet www.mem.gob.ni.

Ministry of the Environment and Natural Resources: Km 12½, Carretera Norte, Apdo 5123, Managua; tel. 2233-1111; fax 2263-1274; e-mail jargenal@marena.gob.ni; internet www.marena.gob.ni.

Ministry of the Family, Adolescence and Childhood: De donde fue ENEL Central, 100 m al sur, Managua; tel. 2278-1620; e-mail mramirez@mifamilia.gob.ni; internet www.mifamilia.gob.ni.

Ministry of Finance and Public Credit: Frente a la Asamblea Nacional, Apdo 2170, Managua; tel. 2222-6530; fax 2222-6430; e-mail webmaster@mhcp.gob.ni; internet www.hacienda.gob.ni.

Ministry of Foreign Affairs: Del Antiguo Cine González, 1 c. al sur, sobre Avda Bolívar, Managua; tel. 2244-8000; fax 2228-5102; e-mail despacho.ministro@cancilleria.gob.ni; internet www.cancilleria.gob.ni.

Ministry of Health: Complejo Nacional de Salud 'Dra Concepción Palacios', costado oeste Colonia Primero de Mayo, Apdo 107, Managua; tel. 2289-7164; e-mail webmaster@minsa.gob.ni; internet www.minsa.gob.ni.

Ministry of the Interior: Edif. Silvio Mayorga, Costado oeste de la DGI Sajonia, Apdo 68, Managua; tel. 2222-7538; fax 2222-2789; e-mail relacionespublicas@migob.gob.ni; internet www.migob.gob.ni.

Ministry of Labour: Estadio Nacional, 400 m al norte, Apdo 487, Managua; tel. 2222-2115; fax 2228-2103; e-mail info@mitrab.gob.ni; internet www.mitrab.gob.ni.

Ministry of Transport and Infrastructure: Frente al Estadio Nacional Denis Martínez, Apdo 26, Managua; tel. 2222-5952; fax 2222-5111; e-mail webmaster@mti.gob.ni; internet www.mti.gob.ni.

President and Legislature

PRESIDENT

Election, 6 November 2011

Candidate	Votes	% of total
José Daniel Ortega Saavedra (FSLN)	1,569,287	62.46
Fabio Gadea Mantilla (PLI-UNE)	778,889	31.00
Arnoldo Alemán Lacayo (PLC)	148,507	5.91
Enrique Quiñónez (ALN)	10,003	0.40
Roger Guevara (APRE)	5,898	0.23
Total	**2,512,584**	**100.00**

NATIONAL ASSEMBLY
(Asamblea Nacional)

National Assembly: Complejo Legislativo Carlos Nuñez, Avda Peatonal Gen. Augusto C. Sandino, Apdo 4659, Managua; tel. 2276-8488; e-mail info@asamblea.gob.ni; internet www.asamblea.gob.ni.

President: RENÉ NÚÑEZ TÉLLEZ.

Election, 6 November 2011

Party	Valid votes cast	% of valid votes	Seats
Frente Sandinista de Liberación Nacional (FSLN)	3,178,669	60.75	62
Partido Liberal Independiente (PLI)*	1,646,203	31.45	26
Partido Liberal Constitucionalista (PLC)	340,945	6.51	2
Alianza Liberal Nicaragüense (ALN)	44,528	0.86	—
Alianza por la República (APRE)	22,380	0.43	—
Total	**5,232,725†**	**100.00**	**92‡**

* Supported by the Unidad Nicaragüense por la Esperanza (UNE).

† Each elector had two votes: one for representatives at regional level (for which there were 70 seats) and one for representatives at national level (20 seats). The total number of votes cast at regional level was 2,630,889, while at national level 2,601,836 votes were cast.

‡ Under the Constitution, one seat is reserved for the President of the Republic. Furthermore, another seat is given to the second-placed candidate in the presidential election. Thus, the FSLN's total number of seats increased to 63, while the PLI's representation increased to 27.

Election Commission

Consejo Supremo Electoral (CSE): Iglesia Las Palmas, 1 c. al sur, Apdo 2241, Managua; tel. 2268-7948; e-mail info@cse.gob.ni; internet www.cse.gob.ni; Pres. ROBERTO JOSÉ RIVAS REYES.

Political Organizations

Alianza Liberal Nicaragüense (ALN): del Hotel Mansión Teodolinda, 3c abajo, Managua; e-mail hebertaln@hotmail.com; fmrly Movimiento de Salvación Liberal; adopted current name in 2006; Pres. EDUARDO MONTEALEGRE; Sec.-Gen. CARLOS GARCÍA.

Alianza por la República (APRE): Busto José Martí, 4 c. arriba, 3 y ½ c. al lago, Managua; tel. 2264-2446; e-mail partido.apre@gmail .com; f. 2004 by supporters of Pres. Enrique Bolaños Geyer; Pres. CARLOS CANALES.

Partido Social Cristiano Nicaragüense (PSC): Ciudad Jardín, Pizza María, 1 c. al lago, Managua; tel. 2249-3460; e-mail pscnicaragua@hotmail.com; f. 1957; 42,000 mems; Pres. ABEL REYES TÉLLEZ; Sec.-Gen. ANTONIO BENITO GÓMEZ.

Camino Cristiano Nicaragüense (CCN): Costado, 1 c. al sur, 1 c. arriba, Calle 27 de Mayo, Managua; tel. 2254-5411; fax 2254-5405; e-mail info@caminocristianonicaraguense.org; internet www .caminocristianonicaraguense.org; Pres. GUILLERMO ANTONIO OSORNO MOLINA; Sec. OSWALDO BONILLA.

Frente Sandinista de Liberación Nacional (FSLN): Costado oeste Parque El Carmen, Managua; tel. and fax 2266-8173; f. 1960; Gen. Sec. JOSÉ DANIEL ORTEGA SAAVEDRA.

Movimiento Renovador Sandinista (MRS): De los semáforos del Ministerio de Gobernación, ½ c. al norte, Managua; tel. 2250-9461; fax 2278-0268; e-mail info@partidomrs.com; internet www .partidomrs.com; f. 1995; fmr faction of Frente Sandinista de Liberación Nacional (q.v.); contested the 2011 elections in alliance with the Unidad Nicaragüense por la Esperanza (q.v.); Pres. ANA MARGARITA VIJIL.

Movimiento de Unidad Cristiana (MUC): Del Portón del Cementerio Periférico, 1 c. al norte, Avda América 505, Managua; tel. 2249-5672; e-mail paritdomuc@hotmail.com; Pres. Pastor DANIEL ORTEGA REYES.

Partido Conservador (PC): Colegio Centroamérica, 500 m al sur, Managua; tel. 2278-8430; fax 2270-6820; e-mail partidoconservador1@hotmail.com; f. 1992 following merger between Partido Conservador Demócrata and Partido Socialconservadurismo; legal status annulled by the Consejo Supremo Electoral in 2008; Pres. ALFREDO CÉSAR AGUIRRE.

Partido Indígena Multiétnico (PIM): Residencial Los Robles, de Farmacentro 1 c. al este, 80 varas al sur, Managua; Pres. RAYFIELD HODGSON.

Partido Liberal Constitucionalista (PLC): Semáforos Country Club 100 m al este, Apdo 4569, Managua; tel. 2278-8705; fax 2278-1800; f. 1967; formed an alliance in 2014 with the Partido Liberal Independiente (q.v.) to contest the 2016 elections; Pres. MARÍA HAYDÉE OSUNA; Nat. Sec. MIGUEL ROSALES ORTEGA.

Partido Liberal Independiente (PLI): Ciudad Jardín, H-4, Calle Principal, Managua; tel. 2249-5547; internet partidoliberalindependiente.org; f. 1944; formed an alliance with the Partido Liberal Constitucionalista (PLC) in 2014 to contest the 2016 elections; Pres. EDUARDO MONTEALEGRE.

Partido Liberal Nacionalista (PLN): Managua; f. 1913; Pres. CONSTANTINO VELÁSQUEZ ZEPEDA.

Partido Movimiento de Unidad Costeña (PAMUC): Bilwi Puerto Cabeza; Pres. KENNETH SERAPIO HUNTER.

Partido Resistencia Nicaragüense (PRN): Edif. VINSA, frente a Autonica, Carretera Sur, Managua; tel. and fax 2270-6508; e-mail salvata@ibw.com.ni; f. 1993; nationalist; Pres. JULIO CÉSAR BLANDÓN SÁNCHEZ (KALIMÁN).

Partido Unionista Centroamericano (PUCA): Cine Cabrera, 1 c. al este, 20 m al norte, Managua; f. 1904; legal status suspended in April 2013; Pres. BLANCA ROJAS ECHAVERRY.

Unidad Nicaragüense por la Esperanza (UNE): Managua; f. 2010; contested the 2011 elections in alliance with the Partido Liberal Independiente (q.v.).

Unión Demócrata Cristiana (UDC): De Iglesia Santa Ana, 2 c. abajo, Barrio Santa Ana, Apdo 3089, Managua; tel. 2266-2576; f. 1976 as Partido Popular Social Cristiano; present name adopted in 1993; legal status suspended in April 2013; Pres. AGUSTÍN JARQUÍN ANAYA.

Yatama (Yapti Tasba Masraka Nanih Aslatakanka): Of. de Odacan, Busto José Martí, 1 c. al este y ½ c. al norte, Managua; tel. 2228-1494; Atlantic coast Miskito org.; Leader BROOKLYN RIVERA BRYAN.

Diplomatic Representation

EMBASSIES IN NICARAGUA

Argentina: Reparto Las Colinas, Calle Prado Ecuestre 235B (intersección con Calle los Mangos), Apdo 703, Managua; tel. 2255-0062; fax 2276–2654; e-mail enica@mrecic.gov.ar; internet www.enica.mrecic .gov.ar; Ambassador MARCELO FELIPE VALLE FONROUGE.

Brazil: Km 7¾, Carretera Sur, Quinta los Pinos, Apdo 264, Managua; tel. 2265-0035; fax 2265-2206; e-mail ebrasil@ibw.com.ni; Ambassador LUIZ FELIPE MENDOÇA FILHO.

Chile: Entrada principal los Robles, Semáforos Hotel Milton Princess, 1 c. abajo, 1 c. al sur, Apdo 1289, Managua; tel. 2278-0619; fax 2270-4073; e-mail echileni@amnet.com.ni; internet chileabroad.gov .cl/nicaragua; Ambassador HERNÁN JAVIER ALEJANDRO MENA TABOADA.

Colombia: De la Entrada 1, 1 c. al sur, 1 c. al este, 40m al sur, Casa 53, Santo Domingo, Altos del Mirador, Managua; tel. 2255-1742; fax 2276-1549; e-mail enicaragua@cancilleria.gov.co; internet nicaragua.embajada.gov.co; Ambassador LUZ STELLA JARA PORTILLA.

Costa Rica: Reparto Las Colinas, Calle La Floresta 185, Managua; tel. 2276-0314; fax 2276-6399; e-mail infembcr@cablenet.com.ni; Ambassador JAVIER SANCHO BONILLA.

Cuba: 3a Entrada a Las Colinas, 400 varas arriba, 75 al sur, Managua; tel. 2276-0742; fax 2276-0166; e-mail embacuba@ embacuba.net.ni; internet www.cubadiplomatica.cu/nicaragua; Ambassador EDUARDO MARTÍNEZ BORBONET.

Dominican Republic: Reparto Las Colinas, Prado Ecuestre 100, con Curva de los Gallos, Apdo 614, Managua; tel. 2276-2029; fax 2276-0654; e-mail embdom@cablenet.com.ni; Ambassador LUIS JOSÉ GONZÁLEZ SÁNCHEZ.

Ecuador: Barrio Bolonia, Sede Central Los Pipitos, 1½ c. al oeste, Managua; tel. 2268-1098; fax 2266-8081; e-mail ecuador@ibw.com .ni; Ambassador ANTONIO EUTIMIO PRECIADO BEDOYA.

El Salvador: Reparto Las Colinas, Avda del Campo y Pasaje, Los Cerros 142, Apdo 149, Managua; tel. 2276-0712; fax 2276-0711; e-mail embajadanicaragua@rree.gob.sv; internet embajadanicaragua.rree.gob.sv; Ambassador JUAN JOSÉ FIGUEROA TENAS.

France: Iglesia el Carmen 1½ c. abajo, Apdo 1227, Managua; tel. 2264-8970; fax 2264-8991; e-mail info@ambafrance-ni.org; internet www.ambafrance-ni.org; Ambassador ANTOINE JOLY.

Germany: Bolonia, de la Rotonda El Güegüense, 1½ c. al lago, contiguo a Optica Nicaragüense, Apdo 29, Managua; tel. 2266-3917; fax 2266-7667; e-mail alemania@cablenet.com.ni; internet www .managua.diplo.de; Ambassador KARL-OTTO KÖNIG.

Guatemala: Km 11½, Carretera a Masaya, Apdo E-1, Managua; tel. 2279-9609; fax 2279-9610; e-mail embnic@minex.gob.gt; Ambassador HÉCTOR DARÍO GULARTE ESTRADA.

Holy See: Apostolic Nunciature, Km 10.8, Carretera Sur, Apdo 506, Managua; tel. 2265-8657; fax 2265-7416; e-mail nuntius@cablenet .com.ni; Apostolic Nuncio Most Rev. FORTUNATUS NWACHUKWU (Titular Archbishop of Aquaviva).

Honduras: Residencial Las Colinas, 2da entrada, Prado Ecuestre 298, Managua; tel. 2276-2406; fax 2276-1998; e-mail hondurasnic@ yahoo.com; Ambassador LEDIN ORLANDO TORRES.

Iran: De ECAMI 150 mts al oeste, Casa 8-1, Altos de Santo Domingo, Managua; tel. 2276-1010; e-mail embirannic@cablenet.com.ni; Ambassador MORTEZA KHALAJ.

Italy: Residencial Bolonia, Rotonda El Güegüense, 1 c. al norte, ½ c. al oeste, Apdo 2092, Managua 4; tel. 2266-2961; fax 2266-3987; e-mail ambasciata.managua@esteri.it; internet www.ambmanagua.esteri .it; Ambassador RENATO MARIA RICCI.

Japan: Plaza España, 1 c. abajo y 1 c. al lago, Bolonia, Apdo 1789, Managua; tel. 2266-8668; fax 2266-8566; e-mail embjpnic@ibw.com .ni; internet www.ni.emb-japan.go.jp; Ambassador MASAHARU SATO.

Korea, Republic: De la Rotonda El Güegüense 3. al oeste, ½ c. al sur, casa A-45, Apdo LV101, Managua; tel. 2254-8107; fax 2254-8131; e-mail nicaragua@mofat.go.kr; internet nic.mofat.go.kr; Ambassador DOO SIK KIM.

Libya: Bolonia de donde fue la Mansión Teodolinda, 1 c. al sur, Apdo 867, Managua; tel. 2266-8540; fax 2266-8542; e-mail ofilibia@ hotmail.com; Chargé d'affaires a.i. MOHAMED I. A. ISSA.

Luxembourg: Residencial Bolonia del Hospital Militar, 1 c. al lago y 1 ½ abajo, Contiguo al Hotel Maracas Inn, Apdo 969, Managua; tel. 2268-1881; fax 2266-7965; e-mail secretariat.managua@mae.etat.lu; Chargé d'affaires a.i. THIERRY RENÉ LIIPPERT.

Mexico: Contiguo a Optica Matamoros, Km 4½, Carretera a Masaya, 25 varas Arriba, Altamira, Apdo 834, Managua; tel. 2278-4919; fax 2278-2886; e-mail embamex@turbonett.com.ni; internet embamex.sre.gob.mx/nicaragua; Ambassador JUAN RODRIGO LABARDINI FLORES.

Panama: Casa 93, Reparto Mántica, del Cuartel General de Bomberos 1 c. abajo, Apdo 1, Managua; tel. 2277-0501; fax 2278-4083; e-mail embdpma@enitel.com.ni; Ambassador EDDY RODRÍGUEZ.

Peru: Del Hospital Militar, 1 c. al norte, 2 c. hacia oeste, casa 325, Apdo 211, Managua; tel. 2266-8678; fax 2266-8679; e-mail embajada@peruennicaragua.com.ni; internet www.peruennicaragua.com.ni; Ambassador RUDECINDO VEGA CARREAZO.

Russia: Reparto Las Colinas, Calle Vista Alegre 214, Apdo 249, Managua; tel. 2276-0374; fax 2276-0179; e-mail rossia@cablenet.com.ni; internet www.nicaragua.mid.ru; Ambassador NIKOLAY M. VLADIMIR.

Spain: Avda Central 13, Las Colinas, Apdo 284, Managua; tel. 2276-0966; fax 2276-0937; e-mail emb.managua@maec.es; internet www.maec.es/embajadas/managua; Ambassador RAFAEL GARRANZO GARCÍA.

Taiwan (Republic of China): Optica Matamoros, 2 c. abajo, $\frac{1}{2}$ c. al lago, Carretera a Masaya, Planes de Altamira, Apdo 4653, Managua; tel. 2277-1333; fax 2267-4025; e-mail nic@mofa.gov.tw; Ambassador YING-WHEI HSING.

USA: Km 5$\frac{1}{2}$, Carretera Sur, Apdo 327, Managua; tel. 2252-7100; fax 2252-7304; e-mail managuaconsulariv@state.gov; internet nicaragua.usembassy.gov; Ambassador PHYLLIS MARIE POWERS.

Venezuela: Costado norte de la Iglesia Santo Domingo, Las Sierritas, Casa 27, Apdo 406, Managua; tel. 2272-0267; fax 2272-2265; e-mail embaveznica@cablenet.com.ni; Ambassador JOSÉ FRANCISCO ARRÚE DE PABLO.

Judicial System

The Supreme Court deals with both civil and criminal cases, acts as a Court of Cassation, appoints Judges of First Instance, and generally supervises the legal administration of the country.

Corte Suprema de Justicia: Km 7$\frac{1}{2}$ Carretera Norte, Managua; tel. 2233-2128; fax 2233-0004; e-mail webmaster@csj.gob.ni; internet www.poderjudicial.gob.ni; Pres. Dr ALBA LUZ RAMOS VANEGAS.

Attorney-General: Dr JOAQUÍN HERNÁN ESTRADA SANTAMARÍA.

Religion

All religions are tolerated. Almost all of Nicaragua's inhabitants profess Christianity, and the majority belong to the Roman Catholic Church. The Moravian Church predominates on the Caribbean coast.

CHRISTIANITY

The Roman Catholic Church

Nicaragua comprises one archdiocese, six dioceses and the Apostolic Vicariate of Bluefields. According to the latest available census figures (2005), some 58% of the population aged five years and above are Roman Catholics.

Bishops' Conference: Conferencia Episcopal de Nicaragua, Ferretería Lang 1 c. al este, Zona 3, Las Piedrecitas, Apdo 2407, Managua; tel. 2266-6292; fax 2266-8069; e-mail cen@tmx.com.ni; internet www.cen-nicaragua.org; f. 1975; statute approved 1987; Pres. SÓCRATES RENÉ SÁNDIGO JIRÓN (Bishop of Juigalpa).

Archbishop of Managua: Cardinal LEOPOLDO JOSÉ BRENES SOLÓRZANO, Arzobispado, Apdo C-68, Managua; tel. 2255-1019; fax 2276-0130; e-mail prensa@curiamanagua.org; internet www.curiamanagua.org.

The Anglican Communion

Nicaragua comprises one of the five dioceses of the Iglesia Anglicana de la Región Central de América.

Bishop of Nicaragua: Rt Rev. STURDIE W. DOWNS, Apdo 1207, Managua; tel. 2222-5174; fax 2222-6701; e-mail episcnic@tmx.com.ni.

Protestant Churches

Some 22% of the population aged five years and above are members of evangelical churches, according to the last census (2005).

Baptist Convention of Nicaragua: Apdo 2593, Managua; e-mail cbnsgeneral@stbnica.org; f. 1917; 135 churches, 20,000 mems (2006); Pres. Rev. FÉLIX PEDRO RUIZ RIVERA; Sec. Rev. GUADALUPE ANTONIO GÓMEZ RÍOS.

The Moravian Church in Nicaragua: Iglesia Morava, Puerto Cabezas; tel. and fax 2792-2222; e-mail gonzalomoravo@gmail.com; 199 churches, 83,000 mems; Leader Rt Rev. JOHN WILSON.

The Nicaraguan Lutheran Church of Faith and Hope: Apdo 151, Managua; tel. 2266-4467; fax 2268-2401; e-mail luterana@iluterana.org; f. 1994; 7,050 mems (2010); Pres. Rev. VICTORIA CORTEZ RODRÍGUEZ.

The Press

NEWSPAPERS AND PERIODICALS

Bolsa de Noticias: Col. Centroamérica, Grupo L 852, Apdo VF-90, Managua; tel. 2270-0546; fax 2277-4931; e-mail diseno@bolsadenoticias.com.ni; internet www.bolsadenoticias.com.ni; f. 1974; daily; Dir MARÍA ELSA SUÁREZ GARCÍA; Editor-in-Chief MARÍA ELENA PALACIOS.

Confidencial: De Pharoahs Casino, 2 c. abajo, 2 c. al sur, Managua; tel. 2277-5134; fax 2270-7017; e-mail info@confidencial.com.ni; internet www.confidencial.com.ni; weekly; political analysis; Dir CARLOS F. CHAMORRO; Editors IVÁN OLIVARES, CARLOS SALINAS MALDONADO.

La Gaceta, Diario Oficial: De la Rotonda de Plaza Inter, 1 c. arriba, 2 c. al lago, Managua; tel. 2228-3791; fax 2228-4001; e-mail lagaceta@presidencia.gob.ni; internet www.lagaceta.gob.ni; f. 1912; morning; daily; official; Dir Dr LEOPOLDO CASTRILLO.

Hoy: Km 4$\frac{1}{2}$, Carretera Norte, Apdo 192, Managua; tel. 2255-6767; fax 2255-6780; e-mail mario.mairena@hoy.com.ni; internet www.hoy.com.ni; Editor MARIO MAIRENA.

La Jornada: Entrada Principal de Villa Progreso, 3c al norte, Casa A-350, Managua; tel. 2251-8277; e-mail info@lajornadanet.com; internet www.lajornadanet.com; f. 1986; Dir and Editor RAÚL ARÉVALO ALEMÁN.

Nuevo Diario: Pista P. Joaquín Chamorro, Km 4, Carretera Norte, Apdo 4591, Managua; tel. 2249-0499; fax 2249-0700; e-mail info@elnuevodiario.com.ni; internet www.elnuevodiario.com.ni; f. 1980; morning; daily; independent; Editor-in-Chief ROBERTO COLLADO; circ. 45,000.

El Observador Económico: De Pricesmart, 2 c. al lago, Apdo 2074, Managua; tel. 2266-8708; fax 2266-8711; e-mail info@elobservadoreconomico.com; internet www.elobservadoreconomico.com; Dir-Gen. ALEJANDRO MARTÍNEZ CUENCA.

La Prensa: Km 4$\frac{1}{2}$, Carretera Norte, Apdo 192, Managua; tel. 2255-6767; fax 2255-6780; e-mail info@laprensa.com.ni; internet www.laprensa.com.ni; f. 1926; morning; daily; independent; Pres. JAIME CHAMORRO CARDENAL; Editor-in-Chief EDUARDO ENRÍQUEZ; circ. 30,000.

Revista Encuentro: Universidad Centroamericana, Apdo 69, Managua; tel. 2278-3923; fax 2267-0106; e-mail dirinv@ns.uca.edu.ni; internet encuentro.uca.edu.ni; f. 1968; termly; academic publ. of the Universidad Centroamericana; Dir JORGE ALBERTO HUETE PÉREZ; Editor WENDY BELLANGER.

Revista Envío: Edif. Nitlapán, 2°, Campus Universidad Centroamericana, Apdo A-194, Managua; tel. 2278-2557; fax 2278-1402; e-mail info@envio.org.ni; internet www.envio.org.ni; f. 1981; 11 a year; political, economic and social analysis; edns in Spanish, English and Italian; Dir GREGORIO VÁSQUEZ; Editor MARÍA LÓPEZ VIGIL.

Revista Revelaciones: esq. suroeste del Colegio San Francisco, $\frac{1}{2}$ c al oeste, Estelí; tel. 2713-7578; e-mail info@revistarevelaciones.com; internet revistarevelaciones.com; monthly; Dir GEMA HERNÁNDEZ; Editor BRENDA ESTRADA.

Trinchera de la Noticia: Semáforos de la Tenderi, 1 c abajo, 10 vrs abajo, Ciudad Jardín, Managua; tel. 2240-0114; e-mail info@trinchera.com.ni; internet www.trinchera.com.ni; daily; Dir XAVIER REYES ALBA; Man. EMILIO NÚÑEZ TENORIO.

Visión Sandinista: Costado este, Parque El Carmen, Managua; tel. and fax 2268-1565; e-mail vision@ibw.com.ni; internet www.visionsandinista.com; f. 1997; weekly; official publ. of the Frente Sandinista de Liberación Nacional; Dir MAYRA REYES SANDOVAL.

Association

Unión de Periodistas de Nicaragua (UPN): Apdo 4006, Managua; tel. 2271-2436; e-mail uperiodistasnic@yahoo.com; internet www.aquinicaragua.com/periodistas2.html; Pres. CÁNDIDA DÍAZ.

Publishers

Academia Nicaragüense de la Lengua: Avda del Campo, 42 Las Colinas, Apdo 2711, Managua; fax 2249-5389; e-mail pavsa@munditel.com.ni; f. 1928; languages; Dir JORGE EDUARDO ARELLANO SANDINO.

Ediciones Océano, SA: Km 7$\frac{1}{2}$, Carretera a Masaya, Contiguo a Nitalsa, Managua; tel. 2276-1372; fax 2276-1443; e-mail edocanic@ibw.com.ni; internet www.oceano.com; Spanish culture and language; Dir-Gen. ELVIN CANO.

Editora de Arte SA: Etapa 53, Col. Los Robles III, Managua; tel. 2278-5854; e-mail editarte@editarte.com.ni; internet www.editarte.com.ni.

Editorial Nueva Nicaragua: Paseo Salvador Allende, Km $3\frac{1}{2}$, Carretera Sur, Apdo 073, Managua; fax 266-6520; f. 1981; Pres. Dr SERGIO RAMÍREZ MERCADO; Dir-Gen. ROBERTO DÍAZ CASTILLO.

Editorial Unión: Altagracia Rest Los Ranchos, $4\frac{1}{2}$ c. al sur, Managua; tel. 2266-0019; travel.

Librería Hispanoamericana (HISPAMER): Costado este de la UCA, Apdo A-221, Managua; tel. 2278-1210; fax 2278-0825; e-mail hispamer@hispamer.com.ni; internet hispamer.com.ni; f. 1991; Man. JESÚS DE SANTIAGO.

UCA Publicaciónes: Avda Universitaria, Rotonda Rubén Darío 150 m al oeste, Apdo 69, Managua; tel. 2278-5951; fax 2278-5951; e-mail comsj@ns.uca.edu.ni; internet www.uca.edu.ni; academic publishing dept of the Universidad Centroamericana; Publ. Dir GUNTER GADEA BARBERENA.

Universidad Nacional Agraria: Km $12\frac{1}{2}$ Carretera Norte, Apdo 453, Managua; tel. 233-1950; e-mail info@una.edu.ni; internet www.una.edu.ni; sciences.

Broadcasting and Communications

TELECOMMUNICATIONS

Claro: Villafontana, 2°, Apdo 232, Managua; tel. 2277-3057; fax 2270-2128; e-mail cliente@claro.com.ni; internet www.claro.com.ni; f. 2006 by merger of ALÓ PCS (f. 2002) and Empresa Nicaragüense de Telecomunicaciones (Enitel, f. 1925); subsidiary of América Móvil, SA de CV (Mexico); Chair. PATRICIO SLIM DOMIT; Gen. Man. ROBERTO SANSÓN.

Telefónica Celular de Nicaragua, SA (Movistar Nicaragua—TCN): Edif. Movistar, Km $6\frac{1}{2}$, Carretera a Masaya, Managua; tel. 2277-0731; fax 2268-0389; e-mail gerardo.mena@telefonica.com.ni; internet www.movistar.com.ni; Gen. Man. JUAN MANUEL ARGÜELLO.

Regulatory Body

Instituto Nicaragüense de Telecomunicaciones y Correos (Telcor): Edif. Telcor, Avda Bolívar diagonal a Cancillería, Apdo 2264, Managua; tel. 2222-7350; fax 2222-7554; e-mail mgutierrez@telcor.gob.ni; internet www.telcor.gob.ni; Exec. Pres. ORLANDO CASTILLO.

BROADCASTING

Radio

La Nueva Radio YA: Pista de la Resistencia, Frente a la Universidad Centroamericana, Managua; tel. 2278-8336; fax 2278-8334; e-mail info@nuevaya.com.ni; internet nuevaya.com.ni; f. 1990 as Radio Ya; restyled as above in 1999; operated by Entretenimiento Digital, SA; Dir-Gen. DENNIS SCHWARTZ.

Radio Católica: Altamira D'Este 621, 3°, Apdo 2183, Managua; tel. 2278-0836; fax 2278-2544; e-mail oramos@radiocatolica.org; internet www.radiocatolica.org; f. 1961; controlled by Conferencia Episcopal de Nicaragua; Dir Fr ROLANDO ÁLVAREZ; Gen. Man. ALBERTO CARBALLO MADRIGAL.

Radio Corporación, Gadea y Cía: Avda Ponciano Lombillo, Ciudad Jardín Q-20, Apdo 24242, Managua; tel. 2249-1619; fax 2244-3824; e-mail rc540@radio-corporacion.com; internet www.radio-corporacion.com; f. 1995; Gen. Man. FABIO GADEA MANTILLA; Asst Man. CARLOS GADEA MANTILLA.

Radio Estrella: Sierritas de Santo Domingo, frente al Cementerio, Apdo UNICA 104, Managua; tel. 2276-0241; fax 2276-0062; e-mail radiosm@radioestrelladelmar.com; internet www.radioestrelladelmar.org; f. 1997; Catholic; Dir FRANCISCO VELÁSQUEZ.

Radio Nicaragua: Villa Fontana, Contiguo a Enitel, Apdo 4665, Managua; tel. 2227-2330; fax 2267-1448; e-mail director@radionicaragua.com.ni; internet www.radionicaragua.com.ni; f. 1960; govt station; Dir-Gen. ALBERTO CARBALLO MADRIGAL.

Radio Ondas de Luz: Costado Sur del Hospital Bautista, Apdo 607, Managua; tel. and fax 2249-7058; internet www.miradioondasdeluz.com; f. 1959; religious and cultural station; Pres. GUILLERMO OSORNO MOLINA.

Radio Sandino: Paseo Tiscapa Este, Contiguo al Restaurante Mirador, Apdo 4776, Managua; tel. 2228-1330; fax 2262-4052; internet www.radiosandino.com; f. 1977; station controlled by the Frente Sandinista de Liberación Nacional; Pres. RAFAEL ORTEGA MURILLO; Gen. Man. WILLIAM BURGOS.

Radio Segovia: Ocotal, Nueva Segovia; tel. 2732-2870; fax 2732-2271; e-mail info@radiosegovia.net; internet www.radiosegovia.net; f. 1980; commercial; Dir RÓGER SOLÍS COREA.

Radio Tiempo: Barrio San Judas, Supermercado Pali, 2 c. al Sur, Apdo 3337, Managua; tel. 8821-0258; e-mail radionuevotiempofm@yahoo.com; internet www.nuevotiempofm.com; f. 1976; Dir DAVID MURILLO.

Radio Universidad: Avda Card, 3 c. abajo, Apdo 2883, Managua; tel. 2278-4743; fax 2277-5057; internet radiouniversidadnica.com; f. 1984; Dir LUIS LÓPEZ RUIZ.

There are some 50 other radio stations.

Television

Canal 4: Montoya, 1 c. al sur, 2 c. arriba, Managua; tel. 2228-1310; fax 2222-4067; internet www.multinoticiastv4.com.

Canal 15: Lomas de Tiscapa, Frente al Hospital Militar, Managua; tel. 2266-9086; fax 2266-0318; internet www.canal15.com.ni; f. 1995; Dir VERÓNICA CHÁVEZ.

Nicavisión, Canal 12: Bolonia Dual Card, 1 c. abajo, $\frac{1}{2}$ c. al sur, Apdo 2766, Managua; tel. 2266-0691; fax 2266-1424; f. 1993; Dir MARIANO VALLE PETERS.

Televicentro de Nicaragua, SA, Canal 2: Casa del Obrero, $6\frac{1}{2}$ c. al sur, Apdo 688, Managua; tel. 2268-2222; fax 2266-3688; e-mail tvnoticias@canal2.com.ni; internet www.canal2.com.ni; f. 1965; Pres. OCTAVIO SACASA RASKOSKY; Gen. Man. ALEJANDRO SACASA PASOS.

Televisora Nicaragüense, SA (Telenica 8): De la Mansión Teodolinda, 1 c. al sur, $\frac{1}{2}$ c. abajo, Bolonia, Apdo 3611, Managua; tel. 2266-5021; fax 2266-5024; e-mail webmaster@tn8.tv; internet www.tn8.tv; f. 1989; sold to private buyer in 2010; Gen. Man. JOSÉ MOJICA MEJÍA.

TV Red, Canal 11: Hotel Mansión, Teodolinda, 2 c. abajo, Managua; tel. 2222-7788; e-mail veronica.rocha@tvred.com.ni; internet www.tvredcanal11.com.ni; Gen. Man. VERÓNICA ROCHA.

Finance

(cap. = capital; res = reserves; dep. = deposits; m. = million; amounts in córdobas)

BANKING

Supervisory Authority

Superintendencia de Bancos y de Otras Instituciones Financieras: Edif. SIBOIF, Km 7, Carretera Sur, Apdo 788, Managua; tel. 2265-1555; fax 2265-0965; e-mail correo@siboif.gob.ni; internet www.siboif.gob.ni; f. 1991; Supt Dr VICTOR M. URCUYO VIDAURRE.

Central Bank

Banco Central de Nicaragua: Carretera Sur, Km 7, Apdos 2252/3, Zona 5, Managua; tel. 2255-7171; fax 2265-0495; e-mail info@bcn.gob.ni; internet www.bcn.gob.ni; f. 1960; bank of issue and govt fiscal agent; cap. and res 4,941m., dep. 42,721m. (Dec. 2009); Pres. ALBERTO JOSÉ GUEVARA OBREGÓN.

Private Banks

Banco de América Central (BAC): Km $4\frac{1}{2}$, Carretera a Masaya, Managua; tel. 2274-4444; fax 2274-4441; e-mail serviciocliente@bac.com.ni; internet www.bac.net/nicaragua; f. 1991; total assets 10,516m. (1999); Gen. Man. JUAN CARLOS SANSÓN CALDERA; 66 brs.

Banco Citibank de Nicaragua: Plaza España, Rotonda el Güegüense 25 m al oeste, Managua; tel. 2280-9360; fax 2266-8796; e-mail info@bancouno.com.ni; internet www.citi.com.ni; Gen. Man. AMALIA BARRIOS VELÁSQUEZ.

Banco Lafise Bancentro (BANCENTRO): Edif. BANCENTRO, Km $5\frac{1}{2}$ Carretera a Masaya, Managua; tel. 2278-2777; fax 2278-6001; e-mail info@bancolafise.com.ni; internet www.lafise.com; f. 1991; fmrly Banco de Crédito Centroamericano; name changed as above in 2010; cap. 1,344.4m., res 557.9m., dep. 24,826.7m. (Dec. 2012); Pres. ROBERTO JOSÉ ZAMORA LLANES; Gen. Man. CARLOS ALBERTO BRICEÑO RÍOS; 72 brs.

STOCK EXCHANGE

Bolsa de Valores de Nicaragua: Edif. Oscar Pérez Cassar, Centro BANIC, Km $5\frac{1}{2}$, Carretera Masaya, Apdo 121, Managua; tel. 2278-3830; fax 2278-3836; e-mail informacionbvn@bolsanic.com; internet bolsanic.com; f. 1993; Pres. Dr RAÚL A. LACAYO SOLÓRZANO.

INSURANCE

State Company

Instituto Nicaragüense de Seguros y Reaseguros (INISER): Centro Comercial Camino de Oriente, Km 4.5, Carretera a Masaya, Apdo 1147, Managua; tel. 2255-7575; e-mail iniser@iniser.com.ni; internet www.iniser.com.ni; f. 1979 to assume the activities of all the pre-revolution national private insurance cos; Exec. Pres. EDUARDO HALLESLEVENS; Vice-Pres JUAN JOSÉ UBEDA.

Private Companies

ASSA Cía de Seguros, SA: Rotonda El Periodista, 400m al Norte, Edif. El Centro, MR-67, Managua, Nicaragua; tel. 2276-9000; internet www.assanet.com.ni; Pres. Dr LEONEL ARGÜELLO RAMÍREZ; Gen. Man. GIANCARLO BRACCIO.

Mapfre Nicaragua, SA: Edif. Invercasa, 1°, Managua; tel. 2276-8890; fax 2278-6358; e-mail rfong@mapfre.com.ni; internet www .mapfre.com.ni; fmrly Aseguradora Mundial; changed name as above in 2010; Pres. JOSÉ RAMÓN TOMÁS FORÉS; Gen. Man. RYDDER FONG.

Seguros América, SA: Centro Pellas, Km 4½ Carretera a Masaya, Managua; tel. 2274-4200; fax 2274-4202; e-mail info@ segurosamerica.com.ni; internet www.segurosamerica.com.ni; f. 1996; Pres. ADOLFO BENARD; Man. DANILO MANZANARES ENRÍQUEZ.

Seguros Lafise, SA: Centro Financiero Lafise, Km 5½, Carretera a Masaya, Managua; tel. 2278-2777; fax 2278-0888; e-mail seguros@ seguroslafise.com.ni; internet www.seguroslafise.com.ni; fmrly Seguros Centroamericanos (Segurossa); Pres. ROBERTO ZAMORA LLANES; Gen. Man. CLAUDIO TABOADA RODRÍGUEZ.

Trade and Industry

GOVERNMENT AGENCIES

Empresa Nicaragüense de Alimentos Básicos (ENABAS): Salida a Carretera Norte, Apdo 1041, Managua; tel. 2248-1640; e-mail direccion.administrativa@enabas.gob.ni; internet www .enabas.gob.ni; f. 1979; controls trading in basic foodstuffs; Exec. Dir HERMINIO ESCOTO GARCÍA.

Instituto de Desarrollo Rural (IDR) (Institute of Rural Development): B3, Camino de Oriente, Apdo 3593, Managua; tel. 2255-8777; e-mail divulgacion@idr.gob.ni; internet www.idr.gob.ni; f. 1995; Exec. Dir PEDRO HASLAM MENDOZA.

Instituto Nicaragüense de Apoyo a la Pequeña y Mediana Empresa (INPYME): De la Shell Plaza el Sol, 1 c. al sur, 300 m abajo, Apdo 449, Managua; tel. 2278-7836; e-mail bcantillo@inpyme .gob.ni; internet www.inpyme.gob.ni; supports small and medium-sized enterprises; Exec. Dir MARTHA LORENA BRIONES.

Instituto Nicaragüense de Tecnología Agropecuaria (INTA): Col. Centroamérica, contiguo al Distrito 5, Apdo 1247, Managua; tel. 2227-2290; fax 2278-0373; e-mail bayserfe@inta.gob.ni; internet www.inta.gob.ni; f. 1993; Dir-Gen. MARÍA ISABEL MARTÍNEZ.

Instituto de la Vivienda Urbana y Rural (INVUR): Km 4½, Carretera Sur, contiguo a INISER, Managua; tel. 2226-6112; e-mail gmartinez@invur.gob.ni; internet www.invur.gob.ni; housing devt; Pres. JUDITH SILVA; Gen. Man. MARÍA EMILIA RIZO.

DEVELOPMENT ORGANIZATIONS

Asociación de Productores y Exportadores de Nicaragua (APEN): Del Hotel Intercontinental, 2 c. al sur y 2 c. abajo, Bolonia, Managua; tel. 2268-6053; fax 2266-5160; internet www.apen.org.ni; Pres. ENRIQUE ZAMORA LLANES; Gen. Man. AZUCENA CASTILLO.

Cámara de Industrias de Nicaragua: Rotonda el Güegüense, Plaza España 300 m al sur, Apdo 1436, Managua; tel. 2266-8847; fax 2266-1891; e-mail cadin@cadin.org.ni; internet www.cadin.org.ni; f. 1964; Pres. RODRIGO CALDERA; Vice-Pres. MARIO AMADOR.

Cámara Nicaragüense de la Construcción (CNC): Bolonia de Aval Card, 2 c. abajo, 50 varas al sur, Managua; tel. 2226-3363; fax 2266-3327; e-mail info@construccion.org.ni; internet www .construccion.org.ni; f. 1961; construction industry; Pres. BENJAMÍN LANZAS SOMARRIBA; Gen. Man. BRUNO VIDAURRE.

Instituto Nicaragüense de Fomento Municipal (INIFOM): Edif. Central, Carretera a la Refinería, entrada principal residencial Los Arcos, Apdo 3097, Managua; tel. and fax 2266-6050; e-mail eduardo.centeno@inifom.gob.ni; internet www.inifom.gob.ni; Pres. EDUARDO CENTENO GADEA.

PRONicaragua: Edif. PRONicaragua, Restaurante TipTop, 1 c. al oeste, Km 4½, Carretera a Masaya, Managua; tel. 2270-6400; fax 2277-3299; e-mail info@pronicaragua.org; internet www .pronicaragua.org; f. 2002; investment and export promotion agency; br. in Washington, DC (USA); Exec. Dir JAVIER CHAMORRO RUBIALES.

CHAMBERS OF COMMERCE

Cámara de Comercio Americana de Nicaragua: Plaza España, Rotonda el Güegüense, 400 m al sur, 75 m al este, detrás de American Airlines, Managua; tel. and fax 2266-2758; e-mail avil.ramirez@ amcham.org.ni; internet www.amcham.org.ni; f. 1974; Pres. YALI MOLINA PALACIOS.

Cámara de Comercio de Nicaragua (CACONIC): Rotonda el Güegüense 400 m al sur, 20 m al oeste, Managua; tel. 2268-3505; fax 2268-3600; e-mail comercio@caconic.org.ni; internet www.caconic .org.ni; f. 1892; 904 mems; Pres. MARIO GONZÁLES LACAYO; Exec. Dir EDUARDO FONSECA.

Cámara Oficial Española de Comercio de Nicaragua: Restaurante la Marseilleisa, ½ c. arriba, Los Robles, Apdo 4103, Managua; tel. 2278-9047; fax 2278-9088; e-mail camacoesnic@cablenet.com.ni; internet www.camacoesnic.com.ni; Pres. JOSÉ DE LA JARA AHLERS; Sec.-Gen. MARÍA AUXILIADORA MIRANDA DE GUERRERO.

EMPLOYERS' ORGANIZATIONS

Asociación de Café Especiales de Nicaragua (ACEN): Oficentro Norte, Km 5, Carretera Panamericana Norte, Managua; tel. 2249-0180; fax 2249-0182; internet www.acen.org.ni; coffee producers and exporters; Pres. JUAN CARLOS MUNGUÍA; Exec. Dir EDWIN RUÍZ.

Consejo Superior de la Empresa Privada (COSEP): De Telcor Zacarías Guerra, 1 c. abajo, Apdo 5430, Managua; tel. 2276-3333; fax 2276-1666; e-mail cosep@cablenet.com.ni; internet www.cosep.org .ni; f. 1972; private businesses; consists of Cámara de Industrias de Nicaragua (CADIN), Unión de Productores Agropecuarios de Nicaragua (UPANIC), Cámara de Comercio, Cámara de la Construcción, Confederación Nacional de Profesionales (CONAPRO), Instituto Nicaragüense de Desarrollo (INDE); mem. of Coordinadora Democrática Nicaragüense; Pres. Dr JOSÉ ADÁN AGUERRI CHAMORRO; Exec. Dir MARÍA GERMANIA CARRIÓN SOTO.

Instituto Nicaragüense de Desarrollo (INDE): Col. Los Robles, del Hotel Colón 1 c. al sur, 1 c. abajo, mano izquierda, frente a Funeraria Reñazco, Managua; tel. 2252-5800; fax 2270-9866; e-mail inde@inde.org.ni; internet www.inde.org.ni; f. 1963; private business org.; 650 mems; Pres. SERGIO ARGÜELLO; Vice-Pres. EDUARDO CALDERA.

Unión Nacional de Agricultores y Ganaderos (UNAG): Managua; tel. 2268-7429; fax 2266-1675; e-mail unag@unag.org.ni; internet www.unag.org.ni; f. 1981; Pres. ALVARO FIALLOS OYANGUREN; Sec. DOUGLAS ALEMÁN.

Unión de Productores Agropecuarios de Nicaragua (UPANIC): Edif. Jorge Salazar, Reparto Serrano, DGI Central, 1 c. al norte ½ c. al este, Apdo 2351, Managua; tel. 2251-0340; fax 2251-0307; e-mail upanic@ibw.com.ni; internet www.upanic.org.ni; private agriculturalists' asscn; Pres. MANUEL ALVAREZ SOLÓRZANO; Sec. FERNANDO MANSELL VILLANUEVA.

MAJOR COMPANIES

AMANCO Tubosistemas de Nicaragua, SA (Mexichem—Amanco): Km 3½, Carretera Sur, desvío a Batahola, Apdo 2964-1069, Managua; tel. 2266-1551; fax 2266-4074; e-mail info .nicaragua@mexichem.com; internet www.amanco.com; f. 1967 as NICALIT; fmrly AMANCO; subsidiary of Mexichem, SAB de CV (Mexico); producers of asbestos products, pvc pipes and resin; CEO ANTONIO CARRILLO; Dir-Gen. FRANCISCO SILVA LAZO; 300 employees.

British American Tobacco: Km 7½, Carretera Norte, Apdo 1049, Managua; tel. 2263-1900; fax 2263-1642; e-mail gerencia_nicaragua@bat.com; internet www.batca.com; f. 1934; cigarette mfrs; Gen. Man. HUGO ABELLO; 1,100 employees.

Café Soluble, SA (CSSA): Km 8½, Carretera Norte, Apdo 429, Managua; tel. 2233-1122; fax 2233-1110; e-mail info@cafesoluble .com; internet www.cafesoluble.com; f. 1959; instant coffee mfrs; Pres. JOSÉ ANTONIO BALTODANO; Gen. Man. GERARDO BALTODANO; 200 employees.

Camarones de Nicaragua, SA (CAMANICA): Km 130, Carretera León, Chinandega; tel. 2342-9000; fax 2342-9028; e-mail info@ camanica.com.ni; internet www.camanica.com.ni; f. 2000; acquired by Grupo Pescanova (Spain) in 2007; Gen. Man. LARRY DRAZBA.

Cía Cervecera de Nicaragua, SA: Km 6½, Carretera Norte, de Cruz Lorena 600 m al Lago, Managua; tel. 2255-7700; fax 2255-7811; e-mail webmaster@victoria.com.ni; internet www.ccn.com.ni; brewery; f. 1926; Gen. Man. JAIME ROSALES; 1,200 employees.

Cía Licorera de Nicaragua, SA: Centro BAC, 8°, Carretera a Masaya, Km 4½, Managua; tel. 2274-4040; fax 2274-4041; e-mail sales@clnsa.com; internet www.clnsa.com; f. 1890; subsidiary of Grupo Pellas; producers of rum; Chair. CARLOS PELLAS; Gen. Man. RICARDO SELVA.

Embotelladora Nacional, SA (ENSA): Km 7½, Carretera Norte, Apdo 471, Managua; tel. 2255-4500; fax 2255-4504; e-mail sac@ pepsicentroamerica.com; f. 1944; bottlers of Pepsi brand carbonated beverages; Pres. MILTON CALDERA; 700 employees.

Evoluciones Metal Mecánica, SA (EVOMENSA): Enabas 200 m al sur, 1c al oeste, Managua; tel. 2250-9521; fax 2222-3902; internet www.evomensa.com.ni; steel and zinc products; Man. Dir MARIO GÓMEZ GUTIÉRREZ.

Excel Automotriz: Plaza Julio Martinez, de la Rotonda, 300 m al este, Managua; tel. 2260-1120; fax 2260-0088; internet www .excelautomotriz.com; known as Poma Automotriz until 2010; part of the Grupo DIDEA; distributor of cars and car parts; Gen. Man. CARLOS GÓCHEZ.

Grupo Coen: Hospital Militar 75 al oeste, Bolonia, Managua; tel. 2253-8750; e-mail info@grupocoen.com; internet www.grupocoen .com; f. 1960; agri-business, financial services and real estate; Chair. PIERO COEN MONTEALEGRE; CEO and Pres. PIERO P. COEN.

Grupo Industrial Agrosa: Portón Cementerio General, Calle 2 al este, Managua; tel. 2268-1002; internet www.agrosa.com.ni; f. 1978; cleaning and food products; includes the subsidiaries Agrosa, Harinisa and Indegrasa; Gen. Man. PEDRO LACAYO.

Industrial Comercial San Martin, SA: Bolonia de Los Pipitos, 1c al oeste, 1c. al norte y $\frac{1}{2}$c al oeste, Managua; tel. 2248-4356; fax 2254-5077; e-mail ventasnic@sanmartin.com.ni; internet www.sanmartin .com.ni; f. 1975; meat products; Man. JUAN CARLOS SALINAS.

Industrias Farmacéuticas Ceguel, SA: Pista Juan Pablo II, Edif. César Guerrero, Apdo P-188, Managua; tel. 2265-1217; fax 2265-2025; e-mail ceguel@ceguel.com.ni; internet www.ceguel.com.ni; pharmaceuticals; Exec. Pres. EUGENIO GUERRERO LUGO.

Mangos, SA (Mangosa): Km 14 oeste, Las Mojarras, Jicaral, León; internet www.mangosa.com; f. 1978; agro-industrial concern; produces mangoes, asparagus and papaya; Pres. and Chair. FERNANDO PAIZ; Gen. Man. ERNESTO VARGAS MANTICA.

Metales y Estructuras, SA (METASA): Km 28, Carretera Norte, Tipitapa, Managua; tel. 2221-1124; f. 1958; production of metals; Gen. Man. RAFAEL AMADOR CANTARERO; 498 employees.

Molinos de Nicaragua, SA (MONISA): Km 13.2, Carretera Managua, Masaya; tel. 2279-6250; fax 2279-9941; e-mail info@monisa .com; internet www.monisa.com; f. 1964; flour producers, animal food; Exec. Dir ALAN CHAMORRO.

Monte Rosa: Km 148$\frac{1}{2}$, Carretra El Viejo-Potosí, El Viejo, Chinandega; tel. 2342-9040; fax 2342-9043; e-mail fbaltodano@pantaleon .com; internet www.pantaleon.com; f. 1998; sugar production; owned by Pantaleon, Guatemala; Gen. Man. BERNARDO CHAMORRO.

Nicaragua Sugar Estate Ltd: Del Portón de Chichigalpa, 5 Km al sur, Chichigalpa; tel. 2342-9120; fax 8966-8200; e-mail rrhh@ nicaraguasugar.com.ni; internet www.nicaraguasugar.com; f. 1890; sugar refinery; part of Pellas Group; Pres. CARLOS PELLAS CHAMORRO; Exec. Dir XAVIER ARGÜELLO BARILLAS; 3,500 employees.

Plásticos de Nicaragua, SA (PLASTINIC): Km 44$\frac{1}{2}$, Carretera Sur, Dolores, Carazo; tel. 2532-2575; fax 2532-3473; e-mail servicliente@plastinic.com; f. 1963; plastic bag mfrs; Gen. Man. MIRIAM LACAYO; 245 employees.

PriceWaterhouseCoopers: Km 6$\frac{1}{2}$, Carretera a Masaya, Edif. Cobirsa II, 3°, Apdo 2697, Managua; tel. 2270-9950; fax 2270-9540; e-mail david.urcuyo@ni.pwc.com; internet www.pwc.com/ni/es/ index.jhtml; accountants and management consultants; Partners FRANCISCO CASTRO MATUS, ALVARO ARTILES.

Sacos Macen (MACEN): Contiguo Edif. Rosalinda, Matagalpa; tel. 2772-0114; fax 2772-6576; e-mail kspencer@sacnic.com.ni; f. 1957; producers of sacking, string, linings and hammocks; Mans LUISA FERNANDO, KIMBERLY SPENCER; 200 employees.

Siemens, SA: Carreterra Norte Km 6, Apdo 7, Managua; tel. 2249-1111; fax 2248-1540; e-mail daniela.arce@siemens.com; internet www.siemens.com; manufacturer of electrical equipment and machinery; subsidiary of Siemens AG, Germany; CEO (Central America) RUDOLF OTTO.

Vegetales y Frutas Procesadas, SA (VEGYFRUT): Km 19.9, Carretera a Masaya, El Raizón; tel. 8688-0038; fax 2279-5141; e-mail info@vegyfrut.com.ni; internet www.vegyfrut.com.ni; Gen. Man. CARLOS SOLÓRZANO.

UTILITIES

Regulatory Bodies

Comisión Nacional de Energía y Minas (CNEM): Hospital Bautista, 1 c. al oeste, 1 c. al norte, Managua; f. 2010; Pres. EMILIO RAPPACCIOLI BALTODANO (Minister of Energy and Mines).

Instituto Nicaragüense de Acueductos y Alcantarillados (INAA): De la Mansión Teodolinda, 3 c. al sur, Bolonia, Apdo 1084, Managua; tel. 2266-7882; fax 2266-7917; e-mail inaa@inaa .gob.ni; internet www.inaa.gob.ni; f. 1979; water regulator; Exec. Pres. CARLOS SCHUTZE SUGRAÑES.

Instituto Nicaragüense de Energía (INE): Edif. Petronic, 4°, Managua; tel. 2277-5317; fax 2228-3104; e-mail dac@ine.gob.ni; internet www.ine.gob.ni; Pres. JOSÉ DAVID CASTILLO SÁNCHEZ; Exec. Sec. MARIELA DEL CARMEN CERRATO VÁSQUEZ.

Electricity

Empresa Nicaragüense de Electricidad (ENEL): Ofs Centrales, Pista Juan Pablo II y Avda Bolívar, Managua; tel. 2277-4160; fax 2267-2683; e-mail relapub@ibw.com.ni; internet www.enel.gob.ni; responsible for planning, organization, management, administration, research and development of energy resources; Pres. EMILIO RAPPACCIOLI BALTODANO (Minister of Energy and Mines); Sec. RAÚL CASTRO CASCO.

Empresa Nacional de Transmisión Eléctrica, SA (ENATREL): Intersección Avda Bolívar y Pista Juan Pablo II, Apdo 283, Managua; tel. 2277-4159; fax 2267-4379; internet www .enatrel.gob.ni; operates the electricity transmission network; Exec. Pres. SALVADOR MANSELL CASTRILLO.

ORMAT Momotombo Power Co: Momotombo; internet www .ormat.com; f. 1999 on acquisition of 15-year concession to rehabilitate and operate Momotombo power plant; 30 MW capacity geothermal plant; subsidiary of ORMAT International, Inc; CEO YEHUDIT (DITA) BRONICKI; Gen. Man. RÓGER ARCIA LACAYO.

Unión Fenosa DISSUR y DISNORTE: Managua; tel. 2274-4700; e-mail comunicacion@ni.unionfenosa.com; internet www .disnorte-dissur.com.ni; electricity distribution co; privatized in 2000; distributes some 1,460 GWh (DISSUR 658 GWh, DISNORTE 802 GWh); Country Man. CARLOS HERNÁNDEZ.

Water

Empresa Nicaragüense de Acueductos y Alcantarillados Sanitarios (ENACAL): Km 5, Carretera sur 505, Asososca; tel. 2266-7875; e-mail ccomunicacion@enacal.com.ni; internet www .enacal.com.ni; Exec. Pres. EVERT ALEMÁN LARA.

TRADE UNIONS

Asociación de Trabajadores del Campo (ATC) (Association of Rural Workers): Rotonda Metrocentro, 120 m al oeste, Complejo el CIPRES, Apdo A-244, Managua; tel. 2278-4576; fax 2278-4575; e-mail atcnic@ibw.com.ni; internet www.movimientos.org/cloc/ atc-ni; f. 1979; Gen. Sec. EDGARDO GARCÍA; 59,000 mems.

Central Sandinista de Trabajadores (CST): Iglesia del Carmen, 1 c. al este, $\frac{1}{2}$ c. al sur, Managua; tel. 2265-1096; fax 2240-1285; Sec.-Gen. ROBERTO GONZÁLEZ GAITÁN; 40,000 mems.

Central de Trabajadores de Nicaragua (CTN) (Nicaraguan Workers' Congress): De la Iglesia del Carmen, 1 c. al sur, $\frac{1}{2}$ c. arriba y 75 varas al sur, Managua; tel. 2268-3061; fax 2265-2056; f. 1962; mem. of Coordinadora Democrática Nicaragüense; Sec.-Gen. ANTONIO JARQUÍN.

Confederación General de Trabajadores de la Educación de Nicaragua (CGTEN-ANDEN): Costado Norte Parque Las Madres, Managua; tel. 2266-1471; fax 2266-2871; e-mail anden@cablenet .com.ni; internet www.cgten-anden.org.ni; affiliated to FNT; Sec.-Gen. JOSÉ ANTONIO ZEPEDA LÓPEZ; 19 affiliates, 15,000 mems.

Confederación General de Trabajadores Independientes (CGT-i) (Independent General Confederation of Labour): Centro Comercial Nejapa, 1 c. arriba y 3 c. al lago, Managua; tel. 2222-5195; fax 2228-7505; e-mail salasara@yahoo.es; f. 1953; Sec.-Gen. NILO M. SALAZAR AGUILAR; 4,843 mems (est.) from 6 federations with 40 local unions, and 6 non-federated local unions.

Confederación de Unificación Sindical (CUS) (Confederation of United Trade Unions): Casa Q3, del Colegio la Tenderi 2$\frac{1}{2}$ c. arriba, Ciudad Jardín, Managua; tel. 8895-7221; e-mail cusorganizacion@ yahoo.com; internet cusnicaragua.org; f. 1972; affiliated to the Inter-American Regional Organization of Workers; mem. of Coordinadora Democrática Nicaragüense; Sec.-Gen. JOSÉ ESPINOZA NAVAS.

Federación de Trabajadores de la Salud (FETSALUD) (Federation of Health Workers): Optica Nicaragüense, 2 c. arriba, $\frac{1}{2}$ c. al sur, Apdo 1402, Managua; tel. and fax 2266-3065; e-mail fntsid@ibw .com.ni; Sec.-Gen. GUSTAVO PORRAS; 25,000 mems.

Federación de Transportistas de Carga de Nicaragua (FETRACANIC) (Cargo Transport Workers' Federation of Nicaragua): Avda del Ejército del Arbolito, 2$\frac{1}{2}$ c. al sur, Casa 410, Managua; tel. 2266-5255; fax 2254-7381; e-mail fetracanic@ hotmail.com; internet www.fetracanic.com; f. 1986; part of Consejo Centroamericano del Transporte (CONCETRANS); Pres. ENRIQUE GARAY.

Frente Nacional de los Trabajadores (FNT) (National Workers' Front): Residencial Bolonia, de la Optica Nicaragüense, 2 c. arriba, 20 varas al sur, Managua; tel. 2266-3065; fax 2266-7457; e-mail prensa@fnt.org.ni; internet www.fnt.org.ni; f. 1979; affiliated to Frente Sandinista de Liberación Nacional; Sec.-Gen. Dr GUSTAVO PORRAS CORTÉS.

Unión Nacional de Empleados (UNE): Managua; e-mail cocentrafemenino@xerox.com.ni; f. 1978; public sector workers' union; Sec.-Gen. DOMINGO PÉREZ; 18,000 mems.

Transport

RAILWAYS

There are no functioning railways in Nicaragua. The state-owned rail operator, Ferrocarril de Nicaragua, ceased operations in 1994, and the only remaining private line closed in 2001.

ROADS

In 2010 there were an estimated 22,111 km of roads, of which 6,018 km were highways and 2,045 km were secondary roads. In 2010 the Inter-American Development Bank approved a US $20m. loan for road improvements. The Pan-American Highway runs for 384 km in Nicaragua and links Managua with the Honduran and Costa Rican frontiers and the Atlantic and Pacific Highways, connecting Managua with the coastal regions.

Fondo de Mantenimiento Vial (FOMAV): 50 m al sur, Iglesia El Carmen, Managua; tel. 2268-6836; fax 2268-6831; internet www .fomav.gob.ni; devt and maintenance of the national road network; Pres. AMADEO SANTANA RODRÍGUEZ; Exec. Dir KAREN DEYANIRA MOLINA VALLE.

SHIPPING

Corinto, Puerto Sandino, San Juan del Sur and Potosí, on the Pacific, and Puerto Cabezas, El Bluff (Bluefields) and El Rama, on the Caribbean, are the principal ports. Corinto deals with about 60% of trade. In addition to sea ports, there are small ports on two inland lakes. At 31 December 2013 the flag registered fleet comprised seven vessels, totalling 4,427 grt.

Empresa Portuaria Nacional (EPN): Residencial Bolonia, de la Optica Nicaragüense 1 c. abajo, Managua; tel. 2266-3039; fax 2266-3488; e-mail epn_puertos@epn.com.ni; internet www.epn.com.ni; Pres. VIRGILIO SILVA MUNGÜIA.

CIVIL AVIATION

The principal airport is the Augusto C. Sandino International Airport in Managua. There are some 185 additional airports in Nicaragua.

Empresa Administradora de Aeropuertos Internacionales (EAAI): Km 11, Carretera Norte, POB 5179, Managua; tel. 2233-1624; fax 2263-1072; e-mail czamora@eaai.com.ni; internet www .eaai.com.ni; autonomous govt entity; operates Managua International Airport and 3 national airports: Bluefields, Puerto Cabezas and Corn Island; Pres. DANILO LACAYO RAPPACIOLI; Gen. Man. ORLANDO CASTILLO GUERRERO.

La Costeña: Augusto C. Sandino International Airport, Km 11, Carretera Norte, Managua; tel. 2263-2142; fax 2263-1281; e-mail info@lacostena.com.ni; internet www.lacostena.com.ni; Gen. Man. ALFREDO CABALLERO.

Tourism

Nicaragua attracts tourists for its landscapes, the twin volcanoes, Maderas and Concepción, and the lake Cocibolca. Other destinations of interest are the colonial cities of León and Granada, the Corn Islands, and ecological reserves such as the Indio Maíz Biological Reserve. In 2013 tourist arrivals totalled a provisional 1.23m. and receipts from tourism US $417m.

Asociación Nicaragüense de Agencias de Viajes y Turismo (ANAVYT): Edif. Policlínica Nicaragüense, Reparto Bolonia, Apdo 1045, Managua; tel. 2266-9742; fax 2266-4474; e-mail aeromund@ cablenet.com.ni; f. 1966; Pres. ANA MARÍA ROCHA C.

Cámara Nacional de Turismo (CANATUR): Edif. de la Camara Española Nicaragüense, Restaurante la Marseillaise, 50 m al este, Managua; tel. 2270-2587; fax 2278-9971; e-mail direccion@ canaturnicaragua.org; internet www.canatur-nicaragua.org; f. 1976; Pres. SYLVIA DE LEVY; Exec. Dir ZENAYDA LAGUNA.

Instituto Nicaragüense de Turismo (INTUR): Del Hotel Crowne Plaza, 1 c. al sur, 1 c. al oeste, Apdo 5088, Managua; tel. 2254-5191; fax 2222-6610; e-mail promocion@intur.gob.ni; internet www.intur .gob.ni; f. 1998; Exec. Pres. MARÍO SALINAS PASOS; Sec.-Gen. ELVIA ESTRADA ROSALES.

Defence

As assessed at November 2013, Nicaragua's professional armed forces numbered an estimated 12,000: army 10,000, navy 800 and air force 1,200. A constitutional amendment in 2014 allowed for the establishment of military reserves. There is a voluntary military service which lasts 18–36 months.

Defence Budget: an estimated 2,100m. córdobas in 2013.

Commander-in-Chief: Gen. JULIO CÉSAR AVILÉS CASTILLO.

Chief of Staff of the Army: Brig.-Gen. OSCAR SALVADOR MOJICA OBREGÓN.

Education

Primary and secondary education in Nicaragua is provided free of charge. Primary education, which is officially compulsory, begins at seven years of age and lasts for six years. Secondary education, beginning at the age of 13, lasts for up to five years, comprising a first cycle of three years and a second of two years. In 2010 enrolment at primary schools included 92% of children in the relevant age-group. Secondary enrolment in that year included 46% of children in the relevant age-group, according to UNESCO estimates. Some 923,745 pupils attended primary schools and 458,321 students attended secondary schools in 2009/10. There are nine universities, of which four are state-run, and many commercial schools. In 2011 budgetary expenditure on education was projected at US $3.8m, representing 23.0% of total government expenditure.

Bibliography

For works on Central America generally, see Select Bibliography (Books)

Baracco, L. (Ed.). *National Integration and Contested Autonomy: The Caribbean Coast of Nicaragua*. New York, Algora Publishing, 2011.

Bickham Mendez, J. *From the Revolution to the Maquiladoras: Gender, Labor, and Globalization in Nicaragua*. Durham, NC, Duke University Press, 2005.

Binational Study: The State of Migration Flows Between Costa Rica and Nicaragua—An Analysis of Economic and Social Implications for Both Countries. Geneva, Intergovernmental Committee for Migration, 2003.

Blakemore, S. *Voices against the State: Nicaraguan Opposition to the FSLN*. Boulder, CO, Lynne Rienner Publrs, 2006.

Charlip, J. A. *Cultivating Coffee*. Columbus, OH, Ohio University Press, 2002.

Close, D. *Nicaragua: The Chamorro Years*. Boulder, CO, Lynne Rienner Publrs, 1998.

Undoing Democracy: The Politics of Electoral Caudillismo. Lanham, MD, Lexington Books, 2004.

Cruz, C. *Political Culture and Institutional Development in Costa Rica and Nicaragua: World-Making in the Tropics*. Cambridge, Cambridge University Press, 2005.

Diederich, B., and Burt, A. *Somoza and the Legacy of U.S. Involvement in Central America*. Princeton, NJ, Markus Wiener, 2007.

Farell, N. *Nicaragua Before Now: Factory Work, Farming, and Fishing in a Low-wage Global Economy*. Albuquerque, NM, University of New Mexico Press, 2010.

Gambone, M. D. *Eisenhower, Somoza and the Cold War in Nicaragua*. New York, Praeger Publrs, 1997.

Gobat, M. D. *Confronting the American Dream: Nicaragua Under U.S. Imperial Rule*. Durham, NC, Duke University Press, 2005.

Gonzalez-Rivera, V. *Before the Revolution: Women's Rights and Right-Wing Politics in Nicaragua, 1821–1979*. University Park, PA, Pennsylvania State University Press, 2011.

Hendrix, S. E. *The New Nicaragua: Lessons in Development, Democracy, and Nation-Building for the United States*. Westport, CT, Praeger Publrs, 2009.

Kodrich, K. *Tradition and Change in the Nicaraguan Press: Newspapers and Journalists in a New Democratic Era*. Lanham, MD, University Press of America, 2002.

Marti i Puig, S. *The Origins of the Peasant-Contra Rebellion in Nicaragua, 1979–87*. London, Institute of Latin American Studies, 2001.

Moltaván Belliz, C. A. *Hurricane Mitch and the Impact of the NGOs on Indigenous Miskito Communities in Río Coco, North Atlantic Autonomous Region, Nicaragua*. Managua, Universidad de las Regiones Autónomas de la Costa Caribe Nicaragüense, 2002.

Morley, M. H. *Washington, Somoza and the Sandinistas*. Cambridge, Cambridge University Press, 2002.

Morris, K. E. *Unfinished Revolution: Daniel Ortega and Nicaragua's Struggle for Revolution*. Chicago, IL, Chicago Review Press, 2010.

Murphy, J. W. *Uriel Molina and the Sandinista Popular Movement in Nicaragua*. Jefferson, NC, McFarland & Co, 2006.

Orzoco, M. *International Norms and Mobilization of Democracy: Nicaragua in the World*. Burlington, VA, Ashgate, 2002.

Prevost, G., and Vanden, H. E. (Eds). *The Undermining of the Sandinista Revolution*. New York, Palgrave Macmillan, 1999.

Sánchez, M. V., and Vos, R. *DR-CAFTA: ¿Panacea o fatalidad para el desarrollo económico y social en Nicaragua?* New York, United Nations Publications, 2007.

Walker, T. W. (Ed.). *Nicaragua: Living in the Shadow of the Eagle*. 5th Edn, Boulder, CO, Westview Press, 2011.

Weber, C. M. *Visions of Solidarity: U.S. Peace Activists in Nicaragua from War to Women's Activism and Globalization*. Lanham, MD, Lexington Books, 2006.

PANAMA

Geography

PHYSICAL FEATURES

The Republic of Panama is often not included with Central America, its early history being related to Colombia rather than to the countries of the isthmus, but, geographically, it does occupy the narrowest part of the great land bridge connecting South and North America. In shape, Panama is a sinuous east–west land corridor, with the Caribbean to the north and the Pacific to the south. To the east is the South American country of Colombia, from which Panama was hewn in 1903, and to the west Costa Rica. The Costa Rican border is about 330 km (205 miles) in length and the Colombian border 225 km, but the country has an even more extensive coastline, of 2,490 km. From 1903 the USA held 'sovereign rights' over 1,432 sq km (553 sq miles) of Panamanian territory, the Canal Zone that flanked the route of the transisthmian waterway for 8 km (5 miles) on either side. However, the lease was negotiated to an early end on 31 December 1999, when Panama resumed full sovereignty over all of its national territory. The country covers 75,517 sq km (29,157 sq miles), making it larger than El Salvador, Belize or Costa Rica, and a little smaller than Scotland (United Kingdom).

The shape of Panama contributes to its irregular coast, dotted with many islands and islets off shore. In the east, a northward loop encloses the Gulf of Panama, while the southward loop defines the Mosquito Gulf in the Caribbean. On the south coast, a great promontory of land jutting further into the Pacific from the southernmost part of the arc is split into the semi-arid Azuero peninsula and the much smaller Las Palmas peninsula to the west, forming the eastern arm of the Gulf of Chiriquí. The largest Pacific islands are Coiba (used as a prison island), just south-west of the Las Palmas peninsula, and Isla del Rey in the Archipiélago de las Perlas (Pearl Islands), in the Gulf of Panama. The San Blas chain of coral atolls in the northeast, parallel to the coast, are the abode of the indigenous Kuna (Kuna Yala). The bulk of the country consists of a discontinuous spine of steep, rugged mountains, interspersed with upland plains and rolling hills, flanked by coastal plains of varying width. From west to east the country measures about 650 km, but it narrows to as little as 48 km from north to south, at roughly the point where the Canal crosses. There are 2,210 sq km of inland waters, many of them artificially restrained, including the Bayono lake on Chepo river and Gatún lake, one of the largest artificial reservoirs in the world, built as part of the Canal. The Canal, built between 1904 and 1914 by the USA, is about 82 km in length, raising and lowering vessels 26 m by means of six pairs of locks. It crosses a low seat of land, situated in a gap between the western and eastern mountain ranges that form the backbone of the country. This region is known as the central isthmus or the transit zone, and consists of coastal plains and a highland interior. About one-half of the population, 90% of Panama's industry and all the transisthmian links are situated here.

To the east of the transit zone is the sparsely populated and barely developed territory of Darién, covering one-third of Panama with the largest area of rainforest in the Americas outside the Amazon basin. The central mountains here continue nearer the north coast of the isthmus, as the Serranía de San Blas and the Serranía del Darién, with more mountains to the south. Densely wooded and containing the Tuira river, the longest in Panama, Darién is the home of the Choco and other Amerindians. The region contributes the bulk of the country's woodland (most of the northern coast of Panama is also densely forested), which in all accounts for about 44% of the nation's total area. Despite problems of deforestation (immediate concerns with this are focused on soil erosion and the consequent threat of silting in the Canal) and of mining, Panama is still home to a considerable variety of flora and fauna, with more than 2,000 species of tropical plants, numerous native and migratory birds, and many animals common to both South and

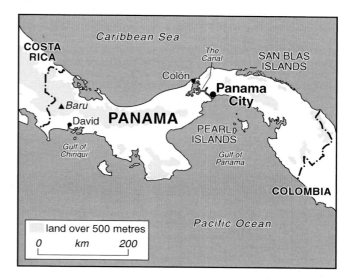

Central America, as well as some unique species (such as the golden tree frog or the giant tree sloth). Biodiversity is less rich west of the Canal and south of the mountains, much of this area having long been cleared for arable farming or ranching. The Continental Divide here forms higher mountains than in the east, where the Cordillera Central reaches its heights in the Serranía de Tabasará, and the highest peak in Panama, here and not in Darién, is the Baru volcano of Chiriquí (3,475 m or 11,405 ft), in the west. Such volcanoes, none now active in the country, have produced the fertile soil that is so widely cultivated in the west of the country. Agriculture dominates Chiriquí—generally the area south of the mountains and extending onto the rolling hills of Las Palmas. Between here and the Canal, along the north-western shores of the Gulf of Panama and in the lowlands west of the transit zone, is the old, settled heartland of central Panama. The final topographical area is the forested north-west, the Atlantic region, between the mountains and the north coast. This region, centred on Bocas del Toro, is the indigenous home of the Guaymí (Ngöbe-Buglé) and of the mainly black descendants of West Indian immigrants, who came to work the banana plantations that once flourished along the Caribbean.

CLIMATE

Panama has a tropical maritime climate, making it hot, humid and cloudy, with a prolonged rainy season (May–January) over the summer and autumn. Prevailing winds are off the Atlantic for most of the year, but change to south-westerlies during the autumn. The Caribbean side of the country is wetter, with Azuero the driest part. The northern mountain slopes receive average rainfall of 2,970 mm (117 ins) per year, with the drier Pacific coast generally on about 1,650 mm annually. The average temperatures in Colón, at the northern, Caribbean end of the Canal, range from the lowest minimum of 20°C to the highest maximum of 32°C (68°F–90°F). At greater altitudes the average temperature can be about 19°C (66°F). Panama falls outside either the Atlantic hurricane belt or the Eastern Pacific one.

POPULATION

The people of Panama (Panameños) are mainly of mixed Spanish and Amerindian race; they constitute some 63% of the population. There are also large communities of predominantly black descent (14%) and Spanish descent (10%), mixed-black descent (5%) and Amerindian peoples (5%). There are also some of Middle Eastern and Asian descent. The official language, and the one in general use, is Spanish, but, after long years of US rule along the Canal and immigration from North America and the West Indies, English is widely spoken (being the main language for up to 14% of the population), and many Panamanians are reckoned to be bilingual. There is also an English-based Creole still used, while a French-based Creole (San Miguel Creole) is virtually extinct. Some indigenous Amerindian languages are also spoken, by the Choco and Chibchan groups. The vast majority of people are still Roman Catholic, but in recent years membership of Protestant groups has increased, while the largest non-Christian community is Muslim. There are also some Jews. Traditional, indigenous belief systems have usually syncretized with Roman Catholic practice.

According to official mid-year estimates, the total population numbered 3.9m. in 2014. Most of these people live in the region of the Canal, in the transit zone of the central isthmus. The largest city and the national capital is Panama City (Panamá), the greater metropolitan area of which had a population of around 1.6m. in mid-2014. Panamá lies at the southern end of the Canal, on the Gulf that bears its name, and was an early viceregal capital for the Spanish (until replaced by Bogotá, Colombia) in the Americas. The second city of the country, Colón, with its own collection of suburbs, lies at the northern end of the Canal and constitutes the world's second largest free zone for trade and industry. David, the capital of the agricultural, western province of Chiriquí, located on the Pacific coastal plains, is the most populous city outside the central isthmus. The country is divided into 10 provinces, and a further three territories constituted for various Amerindian groups.

History

DANIEL SACHS

Geographically, Panama is part of Central America, but, as a result of Spanish colonial divisions and the construction of the Panama Canal through its territory, its history was very different from that of its northern neighbours. The question of the Canal has dominated the country's history. The Spanish arrived in Panama in 1502, and made it the centre of viceregal government over an area stretching as far south as Peru from 1533 to 1751, when the seat of government was moved to Santafé de Bogotá (Colombia, now Bogotá). In 1821, along with the rest of Central America, Panama declared independence from Spain, but instead of joining the Central American Federation (1823–38), it opted for incorporation into the Federation of Gran (Greater) Colombia, which also included Venezuela and Ecuador, both of which seceded in 1830, while Panama, despite a number of revolts, continued under Colombian rule for a further 70 years.

CONSTRUCTION OF THE CANAL

The idea of constructing a transisthmian route was originated by the Spanish, who hoped to build a trading passage for Peruvian silver. The idea gained renewed prominence in the 1840s as a result of the California gold-rush, and led to the construction of the Panama railway in 1850–55 by a US company. The USA directly intervened in the country's internal politics on five occasions between 1860 and 1902, to protect the railway under the terms of a US-Colombian treaty of 1846. The original contract to build a canal was held by the French Panama Canal Co, but the work begun in 1879 proved so much more complex and costly, in terms of human lives, than anticipated that it was suspended in 1888. The Canal was finished by US interests and finally opened in 1914.

INDEPENDENCE

In 1903 Panama achieved independence from Colombia, largely at the instigation of the USA. Earlier in that year the US Government had negotiated a treaty with Colombia, gaining the canal concession for the sum of US $10m., together with a 100-year lease on a 1,432-sq km strip of Panamanian territory (known as the Canal Zone), extending for 8 km on either side of the Panama Canal route. The Colombian Congress raised objections to the treaty, causing a revolt in Panama, which then received US assistance in declaring independence in November. The USA concluded a similar treaty with the new Panamanian Government, according Panama sovereignty and the USA 'sovereign rights', creating an ambiguity that was to cause considerable disagreement between the two countries in the following years. The USA retained the right to military intervention to protect the Canal, and, within the Zone, it had its own military bases, police force, laws, currency and postal service; it also maintained a direct

role in Panama's internal political life until 1918. After more than two decades of relative stability in Panama, constitutional government was disrupted in the 1940s with a progression of bloodless coups and disputed elections. Adolfo de la Guardia (President in 1941 and in 1949–50) pursued a series of right-wing policies, and was impeached and banned from public life in 1950. Antonio Remón was elected President in 1952 and enacted a programme of moderate reforms until his assassination in 1955.

THE TORRIJOS ERA, 1968–81

After 12 years of uninterrupted elected government, political turbulence erupted again in 1968. Dr Arnulfo Arias Madrid won the presidential election, but after 11 days in office he was deposed in a military coup led by the National Guard under the command of Col (later Gen.) Omar Torrijos Herrera. (The National Guard functioned as a defence force, since the formation of an army had been proscribed in the 1904 Constitution.) Freedoms of the press, speech and assembly were suspended for one year, and party political activity was banned from February 1969 until October 1978. The National Guard retained power, first with military, and subsequently with civilian, appointees. Torrijos took the executive title of Chief of Government in 1972, and legislative power was vested in a 505-member Asamblea Nacional de Representantes de Corregimientos (National Assembly of Community Representatives), elected in August on a non-party basis. Under Torrijos, Panama enjoyed a greater degree of internal stability. His Government's most important achievement was the negotiation of a new Canal Treaty with the USA.

The Revision of the Canal Treaty

The 1903 Treaty continued to be a focus for anti-US sentiment. After repeated pressure from Panama and a number of other Latin American countries, negotiations on a new treaty began in 1973. Two draft treaties were signed in September 1977, in which the USA agreed to cede the Canal to the Government of Panama at noon on 31 December 1999. Prior to that, there would be a phased withdrawal of US troops, with Panama eventually taking control of all US military bases in the Canal Zone. The Zone was to be abolished and renamed the Canal Area. The Panama Canal Co would be replaced by a nine-member Panama Canal Commission, a non-profit US government agency with a board of Panamanian and US directors approved by the US Senate, on which the USA was to retain majority representation until 1989. In addition, Panama and the USA were to be jointly responsible for guaranteeing the Canal's permanent neutrality. The treaties were approved by a national referendum in Panama in October 1977, but opposition within the US Congress delayed their ratification in the USA until October 1979.

In 1978 Gen. Torrijos announced plans to return Panama to elected government. He resigned as Chief of Government in October (retaining the post of National Guard Commander), when a newly elected Asamblea Nacional (National Assembly) endorsed his nominee, Dr Arístides Royo Sánchez, as President for a six-year term. However, Gen. Torrijos maintained his hold on power when, at elections in August to the 19-seat Consejo Nacional de Legislación (National Legislative Council—an upper house that also contained 38 members nominated by the National Assembly), his Partido Revolucionario Democrático (PRD) won 10 seats. The elections were boycotted by Arias Madrid's Partido Panameñista Auténtico (PPA). In July 1981 Gen. Torrijos was killed in an aeroplane crash.

THE RISE AND FALL OF NORIEGA

After the death of Gen. Torrijos, relations between the presidency and the National Guard deteriorated, especially after the appointment as Commander, in March 1982, of Gen. Rubén Darío Paredes, a much keener advocate of pro-US foreign policy than President Royo. In July Gen. Paredes forced Royo from office, and the First Vice-President, Ricardo de la Espriella, became President. In the following year Paredes withdrew from the National Guard in order to contest the 1984 presidential election and was replaced by Gen. Manuel Antonio Noriega Morena. Dr Jorge Illueca, who took over as President in February 1984, was also highly critical of the USA and its alleged violations of the new Canal Treaties.

Constitutional amendments introduced in 1983 provided for the direct election of the President and National Legislative Council, replaced the 505-member National Assembly of Community Representatives with a 67-seat Asamblea Legislativa (Legislative Assembly), reduced the presidential term of office to five years, and prevented members of the National Defence Forces (as the National Guard was renamed) from standing as political candidates. In the May 1984 elections the PRD, in coalition with five other parties, won a majority in the Legislative Assembly, and its candidate, Nicolás Ardito Barletta, was elected President. Ardito resigned the presidency in September 1985, however, amid rumours that the National Defence Forces had assisted his election; it was then alleged that Gen. Noriega had removed him in order to disrupt an investigation into the murder, in the same month, of a leading politician, Hugo Spadafora, in which the armed forces' command was implicated. Ardito was succeeded by the First Vice-President, Eric Arturo Delvalle, whose main problems were the growing power of Gen. Noriega and Panamanian claims that the USA was trying to renege on its commitment to withdraw from the Canal Area and also failing to hand over Panama's rightful share of profits.

In February 1988 President Delvalle attempted to dismiss Noriega, following his indictment in the USA on drugs-trafficking charges. Instead, Noriega deposed Delvalle and replaced him with Manuel Solís Palma. Delvalle went into hiding, but continued to be recognized as head of state by the opposition and the US Administration. The May 1989 elections were contested entirely on the issue of Noriega's continuance in power, between two hastily formed coalitions: the government Coalición de Liberación Nacional (COLINA) and the Alianza Democrática de Oposición Civilista (ADOC). There were reports of substantial fraud on the part of COLINA, and, when the ADOC presidential candidate, Guillermo Endara Galimany, claimed victory, the counting was suspended and the whole election annulled. As ADOC refused to accept the annulment, COLINA formed a provisional Government.

US Military Intervention

In December 1989 Gen. Noriega was declared Head of Government. He announced that Panama was at war with the USA, and on 20 December US forces intervened to overthrow him. Endara was installed as President, US economic sanctions (in force since 1987) were ended and full diplomatic relations restored. Although Noriega himself had few allies abroad, the US action was condemned by most Latin American countries, and by the UN General Assembly, as a violation of Panamanian sovereignty. According to US government estimates, 314 Panamanian troops and about 200 civilians were killed, in addition to 23 US troops; the economic cost to Panama was estimated to be at least US $2,000m.

Noriega eventually gave himself up in return for an assurance that he would receive a fair trial and would not face the death penalty. He was flown to the USA, found guilty on charges relating to drugs-trafficking and money-laundering, and in July 1992 was sentenced to 40 years' imprisonment (later reduced to 30 years, after an appeal by his lawyers that he had given years of service to the USA as an 'asset' of the US Central Intelligence Agency). By August 2001 he had received prison sentences in Panama totalling 98 years, on charges that included murder, corruption and drugs-trafficking. Noriega completed his prison term early, in September 2007, having had his sentence reduced on the grounds of good behaviour, but he remained in custody in the USA pending consideration of an extradition request from France. In April 2009 the US federal Court of Appeal ruled that Noriega could be extradited to France, where he had been convicted *in absentia* in 1999 on money-laundering charges, and this was effected in April 2010. In July, following a retrial, a French court sentenced Noriega to seven years' imprisonment and ordered the seizure of €2.3m. of his assets. A French appeals court in November 2011 granted a request by Panama to extradite Noriega. The return of Noriega to Panama in December failed to have any major political impact.

RESTORATION OF THE DEMOCRATIC PROCESS

In order to regain the confidence of the international community, a new Legislative Assembly was formed in February 1990, based on the results of the May 1989 elections. The National Defence Forces were dissolved and a new Public Force created, consisting of the National Police, the National Air Service and the National Maritime Service. However, President Endara's Government lacked domestic confidence.

The PRD returned to power after the May 1994 elections, although it failed to secure an outright majority in legislative polls. In the enlarged 72-seat legislature, the PRD reached an agreement with minority parties to command just 36 seats. The party's presidential candidate, Ernesto Pérez Balladares, won 33% of the votes cast, ahead of Mireya Moscoso de Gruber (widow of former President Arias Madrid) of the Partido Arnulfista (PA—the leading member of the ADOC coalition) with 29%. President Pérez's social and economic policies were highly controversial. The unions opposed the Government's attempts to liberalize the labour market and to implement a privatization programme, and the President's apparent endorsement of a system of political favours damaged public confidence in the administration.

TRANSFER OF THE CANAL TO PANAMANIAN SOVEREIGNTY

The Canal was formally transferred to Panamanian sovereignty on 31 December 1999, becoming a fully commercial operation; under US control it had been run on a non-profit basis. The administration of the Canal was assumed by an 11-member Autoridad del Canal de Panamá (ACP—Panama Canal Authority). In early 2000 a five-year canal modernization project was announced, including the development of technology to raise capacity, a general improvement of facilities, the construction of a second bridge, the widening of the narrowest section, at Culebra Cut, and work to deepen certain sections.

THE MOSCOSO PRESIDENCY, 1999–2004

At the presidential election of May 1999, Mireya Moscoso de Gruber, standing for the PA-led Unión por Panamá (UPP) alliance, defeated PRD nominee Martín Torrijos Espino, son of Gen. Torrijos, the candidate of its Nueva Nación (NN) grouping. Her unexpected victory was perceived as an endorsement of her more populist style and greater emphasis on social justice. Moscoso formed a new 'Government of national unity', comprising members of the Partido Solidaridad (PS), the Partido Liberal Nacional (PLN), the Partido Demócrata Cristiano (PDC) and the Partido Renovación Civilista (PRC). An economic downturn in 2000–01 prompted a series of civilian protests amid a climate of increasing public discontent.

THE TORRIJOS PRESIDENCY, 2004–09

The presidential election of May 2004 resulted in a decisive victory for Martín Torrijos Espino of the PRD, son of the former leader Gen. Omar Torrijos. The PRD also performed well in concurrent elections to the enlarged Legislative Assembly, securing 42 of the 78 seats, while the PA won 16 seats and the PS nine seats.

Torrijos succeeded in securing legislative approval for various constitutional reforms even before assuming the presidency on 1 September 2004. The amendments, adopted in July, included a reduction in the number of seats in the legislature (which was reconstituted as the National Assembly) to 71 from 2009, the abolition of parliamentary immunity from prosecution, and the creation of a constitutional assembly to consider future changes to the Constitution.

In October 2004 some 5,000 people participated in a march organized by the newly created Frente Nacional por la Defensa de la Seguridad Social (FRENADESSO) to protest against the mooted privatization of the social security fund, the Caja de Seguro Social (CSS). In May 2005 the Government presented its plans to address the CSS's financial difficulties. The proposals, which included raising the retirement age and increasing pension contributions, prompted a series of demonstrations, led by FRENADESSO, which claimed that the Government had failed to consult the trade unions about the reforms. Despite ongoing protests, the reforms to the CSS were approved by the National Assembly. However, in late June Torrijos agreed to suspend the pension reform law pending negotiations with representatives of FRENADESSO, industrial organizations and the Roman Catholic Church. In December the National Assembly approved revised legislation, which extended the minimum period required to contribute to a pension from 15 years to 20 years (instead of the 25 years initially envisaged), but maintained the existing retirement age.

Amid concerns over rapidly rising consumer prices, the Frente Nacional por la Defensa de los Derechos Económicos y Sociales (FRENADESO, as FRENADESSO had been renamed after expanding its focus) organized a protest march in November 2007, urging the Government to respond to its demands for a freeze on prices of basic goods and services and an increase in the minimum wage. FRENADESO organized a further day of mass demonstrations in August 2008 in protest against both the rising cost of living and the Government's intention to implement controversial reforms to the security forces by decree. The reforms, which were enacted later that month (under extraordinary powers granted to the President by the National Assembly in June), created several new security bodies, including a National Aero-Naval Service (by merger of the Air and Maritime Services) and a National Intelligence and Security Service.

Expansion of the Canal

In April 2006 the ACP's detailed plans for the expansion of the Panama Canal were announced by President Torrijos. The proposed project, which would involve the construction of a new set of three-chamber locks at either end of the Canal by the end of 2015, at a cost of US $5,250m., was to be financed through increased toll charges, rather than taxation, according to Torrijos, and was to be subject to a referendum, following a national debate. The new locks would allow the Canal to accommodate vessels with container capacities of up to 12,000 20-ft equivalent units (TEUs) rather than the current maximum limit of 5,000 TEUs. However, although the country relied heavily on the revenue from the Canal, environmental groups expressed concern regarding the impact of its enlargement and the accompanying relocation of communities required. Other critics, including former President Endara, claimed that the project was an unnecessary expense, while the Partido Panameñista (PP, as the PA had been renamed in 2005) opposed the ACP's proposals on both environmental and financial grounds. Draft legislation on the expansion of the Canal was approved by the National Assembly in July 2006. At the referendum in October, 78.3% of those who voted were in

favour of the plan to widen the Canal. This clear endorsement was to some extent regarded as a victory for Torrijos, who had strongly advocated the expansion. None the less, the turnout, at 43.3% of the electorate, was much lower than predicted. The expansion project was officially launched at a ceremony held in September 2007.

A contractual dispute between the ACP and Grupo Unidos por el Canal (GUPC), the international consortium constructing the new locks for the Canal, subsequently presented further potential disruption and delay to the project that was beset by spiralling costs amounting to some US $1,600m. The ACP has refused to compensate GUPC for the excessive costs, and GUPC has repeatedly threaten to halt work. Despite the seemingly intransigent positions adopted by GUPC and the ACP, however, a cancellation of the contract was not expected. While the Government has suggested that it could enforce performance-related guarantees, the ACP would be likely to face protracted litigation (not to mention higher costs), if it sought to replace GUPC. Furthermore, doing so would be complicated—despite President Martinelli's assertions to the contrary—and would lead to further delays and increased costs, as well as damage the country's reputation as a proficient proprietor of the canal. At mid-2014 the project appeared on course for completion by the end of 2015.

THE MARTINELLI PRESIDENCY, 2009–14

Three candidates contested the presidential election of 3 May 2009. Ricardo Martinelli Berrocal, a successful retail businessman and the President of Cambio Democrático (CD), secured a comfortable victory with 60.0% of the valid votes cast; contributing to his success was the decision of Juan Carlos Varela Rodríguez of the PP, who had previously intended to contest the election in his own right, to ally his party with Martinelli's campaign and stand as his vice-presidential candidate. The PRD's candidate, former Minister of Housing Balbina del Carmen Herrera Araúz (whose campaign had been tainted by allegations that it had received US $3m. from a convicted Colombian fraudster, David Murcia Guzmán), secured 37.7% of the votes, while former President Endara, in his second consecutive failed bid for the presidency, took just 2.3%. Turnout of 74.0% was recorded. Martinelli's Alianza por el Cambio also won a majority in the National Assembly, securing a total of 42 of the 71 seats (reduced from 78), compared with 27 seats for Herrera's PRD-led alliance, Un País para Todos. The leadership of the PRD resigned in October in an effort to renew the party following its electoral defeat; Francisco Sánchez Cárdenas and Mitchell Constantino Doens were elected to succeed Herrera and Torrijos as PRD President and Secretary-General, respectively.

President Martinelli was sworn in on 1 July 2009. On taking office, he announced immediate plans to effect three of his major campaign pledges: a US $100 monthly salary increase for police officers, monthly payments to the elderly, and the establishment of a government agency to oversee construction of a metro system in Panama City. Martinelli's administration also sought to demonstrate its commitment to addressing government corruption. A judicial investigation into allegations that the Moscoso Government had bribed PRD deputies in December 2001 was reopened in July 2009, and two former PRD Ministers of Education in the Torrijos Government, Belgis Castro and Salvador Rodríguez, were arrested on charges of embezzlement in September and December. In January 2010, moreover, former President Pérez Balladares was placed under house arrest after being charged with money-laundering (although he was acquitted of this charge in April 2011). However, Martinelli's appointment of two close allies to fill vacant positions in the Supreme Court of Justice in December 2009 provoked criticism, particularly from civil society groups, as did his suspected involvement in the following month in the Court's decision to suspend the PRD-appointed Ana Matilde Gómez from the post of Procurator-General pending an investigation into her alleged abuse of office. Gómez was dismissed in August 2010, after being found guilty by the Supreme Court of failing to seek its approval before authorizing the interception of conversations involving a prosecutor being investigated for corruption. Her claim that the verdict was politically motivated was widely endorsed at the time by the media and civil society groups (and was further strengthened by allegations made the following year regarding a plot against her—see below). Allegations that the office of the Procurator-General had been infiltrated by organized criminals, following the release from custody in November of four suspected drugs-traffickers, led to the resignation of Gómez's replacement, Guiseppe Bonissi, in December.

However, by 2014 it had become clear that, despite a promising start, Martinelli had made only limited progress in addressing corruption. Moreover, allegations against Martinelli and other members of his administration not only damaged his personal image but also suggested the pervasiveness of corruption at all levels of government. In April 2013 former Italian presidential aide Valter Lavitola was arrested on charges of blackmailing former Italian Prime Minister Silvio Berlusconi and of bribing Martinelli. The Italian authorities named Martinelli as the beneficiary of bribes relating to prison procurement in Panama. Martinelli admitted knowing Lavitola but denied that either he or any member of his Government had received a bribe from him. However, his emphatic denial of any wrongdoing did little to dampen the ensuing media frenzy, which served to focus attention on the issue of official corruption in Panama. Transparency International ranked Panama 102nd out of 177 countries in its 2013 Corruption Perceptions Index, where the first-placed country is that perceived as least corrupt. In December 2012 Martinelli was forced to deny allegations that he had links with Financial Pacific, a brokerage house under investigation for 'insider' trading. The allegations were made by a former employee of Financial Pacific, who stated in court that Martinelli was the owner of High Spirit, a 'secret account' at the brokerage house that he used for insider trading in shares of a Canadian mining company, Petaquilla Minerals.

Meanwhile, in March 2010, in one of the largest displays of public discontent since Martinelli took office, some 10,000 people participated in protests organized by FRENADESO against recently approved tax reforms, most notably an increase in the rate of value-added tax from 5% to 7%. In April a new Ministry of Public Security, which was to be responsible for the police force, border security and migration was created. José Raúl Mulino, then Minister of the Interior and Justice, became the new Minister of Public Security, while Roxana Méndez, the Deputy Mayor of Panama City, joined the Government as Minister of the Interior. The restructuring formed part of wider government efforts to reduce crime. In May Vice-President Varela issued an official state apology for crimes committed by the military dictatorships in 1968–89 during a ceremony held to commemorate those who 'disappeared' or were murdered during that period.

Swiftly approved legislation, reforming regulations on civil aviation, the environment, the police and labour, *inter alia*, provoked controversy in June 2010. Environmental activists expressed concern regarding the abolishment of the requirement for environmental impact studies for projects declared to be 'in the social interest', while trade unions criticized an amendment to the labour code permitting the dismissal of strikers. After three people were killed, and more than 100 injured, in violent clashes between protesters and the police in the province of Bocas del Toro, the labour reforms were suspended in July for a three-month period. Following discussions with trade unions, President Martinelli agreed to repeal the law entirely in October in favour of proposing separate bills addressing each of the various areas individually. The contentious provisions regarding labour rights and environmental protection were excluded from new legislation approved by the National Assembly later that month. However, the reforms relating to the police, which were enacted in November, retained a controversial article preventing police officers accused of committing crimes on duty from being suspended or held in custody until they had been convicted; trade union officials claimed that the legislation contradicted agreements reached during the negotiations with the Government. Martinelli suffered a second major set-back in the pursuit of his legislative agenda in March 2011, when he was forced to revoke a law that would have allowed investment by foreign governments in the mining sector. Adopted the previous month, the

legislation had provoked widespread protests by environmentalists and civil society groups, as well as by indigenous communities fearing the exploitation of mineral reserves within their territories.

Issues relating to the mining sector proved very difficult for the Martinelli administration. In March 2012 legislation was approved prohibiting mining in the Ngöbe-Buglé region (a designated area where indigenous groups have exclusive land rights and a high level of administrative autonomy), which covers the entire Cerro Colorado. Importantly, the new law not only banned future mining on Ngöbe-Buglé land, but also required the cancellation of all current mining concessions, as well as 25 pending requests. The approval of the legislation was preceded by a prolonged dispute between the residents of the Ngöbe-Buglé, civil society groups and the Government over mining development in the region. In April legislation was passed that reinstated the country's mineral resources code as part of Martinelli's policy agenda to facilitate foreign investment in the mining sector. However, in the face of opposition from civil society groups, Martinelli bowed to pressure and repealed the law a month later.

In January 2011 the constitutional committee of the National Assembly rejected a bill proposed by a deputy from CD to amend the Constitution to permit the President to seek a second consecutive term in office. None the less, President Martinelli announced his intention to seek the approval of other constitutional reforms, including a reduction in the interval that a former President must leave before contesting the presidency again from 10 to five years, and in March a government committee was established to consider possible constitutional changes. The head of the committee, Italo Antinori, resigned shortly afterwards, however, after being accused of involvement in orchestrating Gómez's removal as Procurator-General in 2010. In April 2011 José Abel Almengor, one of the two judges controversially appointed by Martinelli to the Supreme Court of Justice in December 2009, also resigned from his post in connection with the alleged plot against Gómez.

Tensions between CD and its principal coalition partner, the PP, which had emerged over the former's abandoned proposal to allow consecutive presidential re-election, were exacerbated in May 2011 by disagreement regarding CD's desire to introduce a second round in presidential elections if no candidate managed to secure a majority in the first round. The legislative representation of CD (which had absorbed Unión Patriótica, a fellow constituent party of the Alianza por el Cambio, in March) had increased substantially since the May 2009 elections, to 29 seats (from 14), mainly as a result of defections from other parties, while the strength of the PP had declined to 20 seats (from 22). In June 2011, moreover, it emerged that CD had commenced the process of selecting a candidate for the 2014 presidential election, in contravention of the arrangement under which the PP had supported Martinelli's candidacy in the 2009 election. Meanwhile, FRENADESO was seeking registration as a political party, the Frente Amplio por la Democracia.

Escalating tensions between Martinelli and the PP culminated in the collapse of the governing coalition in August 2011, after Martinelli dismissed Varela as Minister of Foreign Affairs. The development laid bare the long-standing divisions between Martinelli's conservative CD and Vice-President Juan Carlos Varela's centre-right PP. In June 2012 the opposition formed a new alliance, the Frente por la Democracia, comprising the PP, the PRD and the Partido Popular. The coalition was broadly formed as a response to Martinelli's alleged 'centralizing' approach, and, more specifically, to his introduction of legislation urging a restructuring of telecoms operator Cable & Wireless Panama. The development also provoked fresh concerns over Martinelli's ambitions regarding the 2014 presidential election. Despite stating in February 2012 that he would not seek re-election, opposition parties claimed that the bill was intended to generate revenue for a fresh presidential campaign. It was claimed, moreover, that attempts to introduce a constitutional chamber in the Supreme Court were aimed at removing legal obstacles to Martinelli's re-election.

As well as prompting the formation of the opposition coalition, the introduction of the bill represented the first major victory for the opposition alliance. Martinelli was forced in June 2012 to withdraw the telecommunications proposals, as well as the planned reforms to the Supreme Court. The announcement followed opposition-led protests in Panama City which resulted in 47 arrests, and a brawl between deputies from the ruling party and the opposition that caused a session of the National Assembly to be suspended.

THE 2014 ELECTIONS

The Electoral Tribunal on 4 May 2014 declared Vice-President and former Minister of Foreign Affairs Juan Carlos Varela of the opposition El Pueblo Primero alliance, comprising the broad-based PP and the Partido Popular, as winner of the presidential election with 39.1% of the votes cast. Varela's election was unlikely to herald a shift in government policy that would significantly affect the investment environment. Varela has pledged to maintain high levels of economic growth by promoting large-scale infrastructure projects—notably the continued expansion of the Panama Canal. Populist aspects of his political agenda, including pledges to address official corruption and high levels of poverty, are not expected to have direct operational implications for foreign companies.

The composition of the National Assembly will require Valera to negotiate with opposition parties in order to secure the approval of legislation. This will be difficult since Martinelli's ruling CD, with which Varela has extremely fractious relations, remains the dominant party, holding 30 seats, while the centre-left PRD has 25. The PP holds just 12 seats in the 71-member Assembly.

Varela's victory in part reflected his success in taking credit for successful policies enacted by the administration of President Martinelli, including the completion of the Panama City metro, while distancing himself from the corruption scandals that had damaged it. His victory was also facilitated by mistakes made by Martinelli and the CD candidate, José Domingo Arias, during the election campaign, including: the selection of the former's wife, Marta Linares, as the running mate of Arias, which was widely denounced as a poorly disguised attempt by Martinelli to retain significant influence of government affairs after his term in office had finished; a highly criticized campaign of denigration directed against Varela; the alleged misuse of government funds during the campaign; and an unseemly public dispute with the Electoral Tribunal. According to official results, Arias and PRD candidate Juan Carlos Navarro secured 31.4% and 28.1% of the vote, respectively.

Varela had withdrawn from the June 2009 presidential election and served as Martinelli's running mate, on the proviso that the latter would support his election campaign in 2014. Martinelli subsequent reneging on this promise caused the highly publicized rift between the two that had culminated in Varela's dismissal as Minister of Foreign Affairs in August 2011 and the collapse of the alliance between the CD and the PP (see above). Varela formally took office on 1 July 2014.

INTERNATIONAL RELATIONS

Political wrangling over the US military presence in Panama shaped the country's relations with the USA in the 1990s, which were further complicated by developments in Panama's relationship with Colombia. One legacy of the Central American civil wars of the 1980s was a vast surplus of arms and ammunition in the region, and Panama became a point of passage for arms-trafficking to Colombia and drugs-trafficking to the USA. The presence of left-wing Colombian guerrillas just inside the Panamanian border, in the province of Darién, had been tacitly accepted since 1993, although under President Pérez, Panama appeared to offer more assistance to Colombia's right-wing paramilitary groups. In September 1999 there was a sharp increase in activity by these groups, which some Panamanians alleged were part of an orchestrated scheme to strengthen the case for a continued US military presence. Cross-border incursions continued, and there were death threats against the local population. Colombian efforts to contain the guerrillas and the drugs trade tended to increase the number of refugees fleeing to Panama. Nevertheless, the two countries continued to co-operate on matters of security in the Darién province. During a joint operation in April 2012 two camps belonging to the leftist guerrilla group the Fuerzas Armadas Revolucionarias de Colombia (FARC—Revolutionary Armed Forces of Colombia) were destroyed in eastern Darién province, which represented a significant success for the 2011 Bi-national Border Security Plan between Panama and Colombia. Under the plan, Panamanian border forces were to receive training from Colombia's security personnel, as well as benefiting from shared aerial intelligence.

Although plans were announced to turn a number of former US bases in Panama into tourist developments, some of these were affected by the presence of discarded US chemical and biological weapons and munitions. US forces had tested chemical and biological weapons in Panama during 1930–68, including napalm and 'Agent Orange' (the defoliant used by the USA during the Viet Nam War). In 2000 the USA maintained that there were insufficient technological resources available to them at that time to ensure the safe removal of the weapons. The Panamanian Government declared its intention to pursue the matter through the Chemical Weapons Convention, to which both countries were signatories.

Although the USA remained the Canal's principal customer, Panama sought to strengthen trading links with the rest of Latin America and with Europe, while moderating its relations with Asia. Like other Central American countries, Panama accorded diplomatic recognition to Taiwan, receiving considerable investment in return; however, the country also extended links to the People's Republic of China, which was the third greatest user of the Canal, and actively encouraged Panama to end its recognition of Taiwan. None the less, President Moscoso and the Taiwanese President, Chen Shuibian, signed a bilateral free trade agreement in 2003, and subsequent administrations maintained diplomatic relations with Taiwan.

President Torrijos made clear his intention to enhance Panama's trading relations within Latin America, and in 2004 Panama was invited to join the Group of Three, comprising Colombia, Mexico and Venezuela, which sought to abolish trade barriers between its members. Furthermore, in 2005 Panama was officially invited to become an associate member of the Mercado Común del Sur (Mercosur—Southern Common Market). A free trade agreement with El Salvador entered into force in 2003, while similar accords with Chile, Costa Rica, Honduras, Guatemala and Nicaragua took effect successively in 2008–09. Negotiations towards a free trade agreement between Panama and Colombia commenced in 2010, and Panama signed a free trade accord with Peru in 2011.

Protracted negotiations on a free trade agreement with the USA resulted in the signing of an accord in June 2007. However, the agreement was subject to ratification by the US legislature, and further negotiations on labour laws were also to be held. After taking office in July 2009, President Martinelli declared that securing US congressional approval of the free trade accord was a priority for his administration. The US Congress finally passed the free trade agreement with Panama in October 2011 following efforts by Martinelli's administration to address the US Government's concerns about financial transparency and Panama's status as a tax haven. (The accord was enacted in October 2012.) Despite this development, there was some expression of concern from the US authorities regarding Martinelli's ongoing efforts to centralize power. Moreover, Martinelli needed to strike a difficult balance between his desire for co-operation with the USA and widespread anti-US sentiment in Panama. In May 2010, meanwhile, Panama was party to a Central American association agreement concluded with the European Union (it entered into effect in 2012) and signed a free trade agreement with Canada, the latter accord being ratified by Panama's legislature in October.

Panama's foreign relations were adversely affected by a reputation for political corruption, money-laundering and providing shelter to allegedly corrupt or ruthless foreign politicians. There was also particular concern in the USA over the apparent use of Panama as a conduit for illegal drugs and immigrants bound for North America. Moreover, it was widely suspected that the practice of allowing foreign vessels to sail under the Panamanian 'flag of convenience' was used as a cover for illegal activity; Panama had the largest shipping registry in the world. In 2004 the Panamanian authorities agreed to permit US officials to board any ships sailing under the Panamanian flag that they suspected of carrying weapons of mass destruction. In 2009 the Organisation for Economic Co-operation and Development (OECD) included Panama on its 'grey list' of territories that had yet substantially to improve the transparency of its financial sector. By October 2010 President Martinelli had concluded enough bilateral agreements in order to secure Panama's removal from the list, and in the following month Panama and the USA signed a tax information exchange agreement that complied with OECD requirements.

In late 2009 Panama unilaterally withdrew from the Central American Parliament (Parlacen), a regional political forum with its headquarters in Guatemala, fulfilling a pre-election pledge made by President Martinelli, who claimed that membership of the body had been of no benefit to Panama. However, in March 2010 the President of Parlacen announced that Panama required the consent of the Presidents of the other member states to withdraw from Parlacen, and that the country owed the organization some US $1.1m. in outstanding dues. A ruling by the Central American Court of Justice in October, confirming that Panama's departure from Parlacen did indeed require the approval of the remaining Parlacen members, was rejected by the Panamanian Government, which declared Panama's formal withdrawal from the Parliament in the following month.

Economy

DANIEL SACHS

Panama's geographic location enabled it to develop as one of the most important shipping crossroads and entrepôts in the world. The country's most famous asset is the 82-km-long Panama Canal, which traverses the Darién isthmus, thus linking the Pacific Ocean with the Caribbean Sea and enabling shipping to avoid the lengthy Cape Horn route around the South American landmass. The Canal diminished in importance with the advent of supertankers and freighters, as the largest of the modern oil and bulk-cargo tankers could not use it. However, with the completion of the widening of the narrowest part of the Canal in 2001 and the rapid growth in cruise ship traffic in both the Caribbean and the Pacific, the Panama Canal regained prominence in terms of income and strategic importance; moreover, a major expansion of the Canal's capacity, scheduled for completion by the end of 2015, will permit the transit of significantly larger vessels. Panama's continued role as a 'land bridge' was also reinforced with the opening, in 1982, of a transisthmian pipeline to carry petroleum deemed economically impractical for transit in the usual way.

For a relatively small country, Panama possesses abundant natural resources, including high-quality fishing grounds, mineral deposits, forests and, above all, a topography and climate that are ideal for the development of hydroelectric and thermoelectric power. Substantial reserves of gold, copper and coal remain underexploited and, apart from some manufacturing in the Colón Free Zone (CFZ, a corridor of land running between Panama City and Colón—roughly following the line of the Canal, which was the second largest free trade zone in the world, after Hong Kong), the primary and secondary sectors of the productive economy are also grossly underdeveloped. Panama is thus traditionally a services-based economy, reliant on revenues from the Canal, ship registration, free trade zone transactions and contributions from offshore banking activities. In 2013 services accounted for an estimated 70.4% of gross domestic product (GDP); among the largest individual sub-sectors are transport, storage and communications, and renting. In the same year agriculture (including hunting, forestry and fishing) accounted for 3.7% of GDP and industry (including manufacturing) 17.9%.

Panama's currency is, effectively, the US dollar, although a nominal local currency, the balboa, exists at par with the dollar. The country's banknote supply is thus determined exclusively by trading relations and capital flows. Balance of payment surpluses automatically increase the money supply, while deficits cause it to dwindle. The country's central bank, the Banco Nacional de Panamá, can influence only the credit-creation constituent of the money supply (although it can issue local coinage), and the Government is unable to use currency devaluation or revaluation as an instrument of economic management.

Import substitution in industry and agriculture was considered an important means of closing the gap between an over-regulated domestic economy and an under-regulated inter-national services sector. To this end, Panama joined the World Trade Organization in September 1997 and began to dismantle its protective import tariff regime. With revenues from the Panama Canal by no means guaranteed, and the credibility of the offshore banking sector damaged by its perceived association with drugs-traffickers, it seemed clear that the Panamanian economic base had to adapt to avoid a steady decline. From the mid-1980s the contribution of the services sector to the Panamanian economy remained fairly steady; however, there was considerable diversification within the sector itself, with tourism a particularly robust growth area.

Economic policies originating in the 1980s were designed to curb the budget deficit by reducing subsidies, rationalizing employment in the public sector and stimulating export growth, particularly in agriculture, by eliminating bureaucracy and offering better incentives. The initial implementation of such policies, however, produced a high level of political instability in Panama. This led to the resignation of President Nicolás Ardito Barletta in 1985 and the ousting of his successor, Eric Arturo Delvalle, by the then Commander of the National Defence Forces, Gen. Manuel Antonio Noriega Morena, in 1988. There is little doubt that the economic situation, worsened immeasurably by the US economic boycott of 1988–89, also played a crucial role in the downfall of Noriega himself, who was ousted by US troops during a brief but devastating invasion of the country in December 1989.

Panama withstood the general global recession of the early 1980s fairly well. However, US economic sanctions provoked a precipitous 15.6% decline in 1988, and there was a further contraction, of 0.4%, in 1989, before the lifting of US sanctions and a more realistic economic policy in 1990–91 stimulated economic growth and steady progress was maintained until 2000. However, the growth rate decelerated in 2001, as elsewhere in the region, to just 0.6%, before recovering during the early 2000s. According to official figures, the economy grew by 12.1% and 10.1% in 2007 and 2008, respectively. GDP growth slowed substantially in 2009, to some 3.2%, as a result of the impact of the global economic downturn, before accelerating to an estimated 7.5% in 2010, owing to improved international conditions, increased investment and renewed domestic demand. Panama's booming transportation and logistics services sectors, along with aggressive infrastructure development projects, led to GDP growth of 10.8% in 2011 and 10.7% in 2012. However, in 2013 the rate of growth moderated to 7.5% as investments in large-scale infrastructure projects, including the US $5,250m. expansion of the Panama Canal, draw to a close.

The rate of increase in consumer prices was low in the first half of the 2000s: annual inflation was just 0.4% in 2004. Consumer prices rose during the latter half of the decade to reach a high of 8.7% in 2008, largely owing to steep rises in the prices of electricity, oil and food, before decreasing to 2.4% in 2009. Inflation remained fairly low in 2010, at 3.5%, despite rising inflationary pressures resulting from increasing domestic demand and global commodity prices, but the annual rate reached an estimated 5.9% in 2011, mainly owing to higher petroleum and food prices. This trend continued in 2012, when inflation increased to 6.1%, before falling back down to an estimated 4.1% in 2013.

Panama has one of the highest foreign debts per head of population in the world (partly because it needs to borrow the money that it cannot print). High real interest rates significantly increased the debt-service ratio (annual amortization and interest, expressed as a proportion of foreign exchange earnings on goods and non-factor services) on Panama's external debt during the 1980s, and in 1988 the country suspended all debt-service payments. Despite a series of financial reforms in 1991–92, total arrears to the IMF, the World Bank and the Inter-American Development Bank (IDB) were estimated at US $3,000m. in early 1994, before the Government intensified its efforts to reach an agreement with commercial and multilateral creditors.

In May 1995 a debt-restructuring agreement was announced, whereby Panama exchanged debt for new bonds with virtually all its commercial creditors, thus reducing the country's debt by more than US $400m. and facilitating fresh credit. In 1997 the country further reduced its debt by renegotiating more than $300m. in petroleum-supply debts incurred with Mexico and Venezuela under the San José Agreement of 1980. This restructuring gave Panama access to concessionary finance from the IMF, the World Bank and the IDB and allowed the country access to international capital markets. Panama took full advantage of this and since March 1999, when it sold $500m. worth of 30-year global bonds, using 40% of the receipts to buy back more foreign debt, has raised money to cancel debt. In January 2011, in its first such sale in the Asian market, the Government issued 41,500m. yen (some $500m.) worth of 10-year bonds. At the end of 2011 total external debt was $12,583m., of which $10,890m. was public and publicly guaranteed debt. In that year, the cost of debt-servicing long-term public and publicly guaranteed debt and repayments to the IMF was equivalent to 3.6% of the value of exports of goods, services and income (excluding workers' remittances). By 2012 public debt was equivalent to 41.0% of GDP, falling slightly to an estimated 39.8% in 2013.

AGRICULTURE, FORESTRY AND FISHING

Agriculture and fishing are vitally important to the success of the economic diversification effort in Panama. In 2013 some 16.4% of the employed labour force were engaged in agriculture, hunting, forestry and fishing. In that year the sector grew by 1.8%. In 2008 about 9.3% of Panama's 7.4m. ha of land was cultivated on a permanent basis, while another 20.6% was permanent pasture land and 44.0% was forest.

Melons, bananas and pineapples are the principal export crops. Melon cultivation increased substantially in the early 21st century. In 2001 melons overtook sugar as the second highest-earning export crop, and in 2005 the fruit became the leading export crop. However, melon exports have fallen substantially in recent years, largely as a result of agro-exporters relying on their own financing, as well as European customs regulations. Melon export earnings fell from US $37.1m. in 2010, to $16.6m. in 2011 and further to $15.8m. in 2012. Panama's exports of bananas, formerly the country's leading export commodity, earned $86.3m. in 2011, $85.9m. in 2012 and $90.4m. in 2013 (the highest annual revenue since 2008). Pineapple exports also performed well in 2013, reaching $44.1m. in that year, compared with $37.1m. in 2012.

The relative importance of banana exports had been in decline since the 1990s; in 1992 bananas accounted for 44.2% of total export earnings, but in 2010 they represented just 9.0% (although rising slightly to 11.0% and 10.5% in 2011 and 2012, respectively). The decline was variously attributed to falling international prices, industrial action in the sector, the adverse effects of the El Niño weather phenomenon (the warm current that periodically appears in the Pacific Ocean, altering normal weather patterns) and, perhaps most crucially, the quotas imposed by the European Union (EU) on banana exports from Latin America. However, from 2006 the

EU quota system was replaced by an increase in import tariffs from €75 per metric ton to €176 per ton. Representatives of the industry claimed that the new tariffs would destabilize the economy and substantially increase unemployment. In December 2009, following a protracted dispute with several Latin American countries (including Panama), the EU agreed to reduce import tariffs on bananas from €176 per metric ton to €114 per ton by 2017.

Export revenue from sugar fluctuated substantially during the 2000s, declining to US $13.4m. in 2009, before increasing to $19.2m. (2.6% of total earnings) in 2010. In 2011 export earnings from sugar almost doubled to reach $37.2m. (4.7% of total export revenue) before decreasing moderately, to $34.5m. (4.2%) in 2012. Total sugar exports in terms of tonnage increased by 5.2% in 2012 and by 8.8% in 2013. However, a reduction in global prices for sugar meant that the actual value of exports fell by 30.5% in the first 11 months of 2013, compared with the same period in the previous year. According to FAO, coffee production increased from 12,500 metric tons in 2010, to 13,100 tons in 2011 and further to an estimated 14,000 tons in 2012. Earnings fluctuated owing to international price movements. Coffee exports earned some $7.1m. in 2012, compared with $9.4m. in the previous year, and decreased further, to $6.1m. in 2013.

Successive governments recognized the urgent need to increase agricultural production in their agreements with the IMF and the World Bank. A five-year agricultural development plan announced in 1985 prioritized the diversification of both crops and markets. However, the need to boost production was undermined by the move to abolish the high import tariffs that had protected Panamanian farmers for many years, causing many of those who catered for domestic consumption to be forced out of business from the mid-1980s. Growth did, however, increase thereafter, but average annual expansion of 4.3% in 2000–08 masked some fundamental structural changes in favour of export-driven production. According to official figures, the sector's GDP recorded annual declines in 2009–11, but grew by 4.9% in 2012 and by 1.8% in 2013.

Exports of shellfish more than doubled in the 1990s, but fluctuated considerably in subsequent years. Revenue from shellfish exports increased from US $35.4m. in 2010 (4.9% of total export earnings), to $37.7m., in 2011 (4.8%) and $40.5m. in 2012 (4.9%). Meanwhile, exports of fresh and frozen fish and fillets reached $275.1m. in 2008 (24.0% of exports), but declined sharply thereafter, reaching $119.8m. in 2010 and just $50.4m. in 2011 (6.4% of exports), owing to unfavourable climatic conditions, an increase in operating costs resulting from higher fuel costs, and the impact of restrictions and measures introduced to protect aquatic resources. Overall fishing revenue declined by 21.9% in 2011. Industrial fishing remained weak in 2012; however, fishing revenue increased by 2.5% in that year owing primarily to a 20.2% increase in shrimp export earnings and a concomitant increase in artisanal fishing. Fisheries continued to perform strongly in 2013 when the sector's GDP grew by 15.2% to total $141.3m.

Meanwhile, the livestock sector, the epitome of the new export-driven policy, underwent particularly rapid expansion, averaging 4.0% annual growth in the late 1980s and early 1990s. Following a dramatic fall in the sector's export earnings in the mid-1990s as a result of credit problems and export restrictions, meat exports subsequently recovered. Export revenue from cattle meat rose from US $14.8m. in 2010 to $18.2m. in 2011 and further to $24.7m. in 2012 (in which year the GDP of the cattle industry expanded by an estimated 7.3%).

MINING AND ENERGY

Despite valuable mineral deposits, which include gold, silver, copper and coal, mineral extraction has traditionally been limited to clay, limestone and salt for local consumption. Mining contributed only 1.9% of GDP in 2012, and engaged a mere 0.3% of the employed labour force in 2013. Protests by environmentalists, civil society groups and indigenous communities prompted the President in March 2011 to revoke recently adopted legislation that would have allowed investment in the mining sector by foreign governments.

The GDP of the mining sector grew by 18.4% in 2011, by 30.0% in 2012 and by 31.4% in 2013, largely as a result of increased demand for stones and sand, required by the fast-growing construction sector. The substantial rise in sectoral growth was also as a result of increased gold exports.

Gold-mining in Panama has traditionally tended to be small scale, but gold-mining concessions have proved attractive to foreign investors owing to the lower capital costs. Following an initial investment of US $25m. in 1995, the Santa Rosa mine in Veraguas province yielded some 57,000 troy oz in 1997, producing $20m. in export revenue. However, output fell steadily thereafter, with export earnings put at just $12m. in 2000, and work at the mine was subsequently abandoned. Commercial production at the Molejón Gold Project in Donoso, operated by Canada's Petaquilla Minerals Ltd, commenced in 2010; measured and indicated resources were estimated at 756,586 troy oz. In 2014 Canada's Pershimco Resources, Inc, was developing the Cerro Quema gold concession, where measured and indicated resources of gold had been estimated at 451,400 troy oz.

In 2013 Canada's First Quantum Minerals Ltd assumed control of the operations of the country's largest mine, the Cobre copper/gold/silver project in Colón province in 2013. First Quantum planned to spend US $600m. on the project in 2014. The project aimed to achieve annual output of 320,000 metric tons of copper, 100,000 troy oz of gold and 1.8m. troy oz of silver.

Panama has enormous hydroelectric and thermoelectric potential and aims eventually to eliminate petroleum-powered electricity generation, and thus to reduce imports of petroleum products; in 2010 fuels and lubricants accounted for some 19.3% of total import expenditure. In 2003 the Estí hydroelectric project increased installed capacity by 120 MW, while the thermoelectric Pedregal power installation added a further 53.4 MW of generating capacity. The Changuinola 75 hydroelectric power station, in the Bocas del Toro province, became operational in 2011 and had a projected capacity of 223 MW. The hydroelectric sector was to be further augmented by the expansion of the La Estrella and Los Valles facilities. In 2011 hydroelectric power accounted for 53% of Panama's net electricity generation (of 7,640m. kWh), while oil-fired generation accounted for 46%. Generation from biomass sources made up the remaining portion of less than 1%. To meet domestic demand for electricity, Panama has collaborated with its neighbours in constructing shared transmission lines. For example, a 300-MW power line was erected stretching roughly 613 km between Panama and Colombia, and a 300-MW transmission line spanning 1,790 km between Panama and Guatemala. Although Panama does not itself produce crude oil, natural gas or coal, it serves as an energy transit point through its control of the Panama Canal and the Trans-Panama pipeline.

MANUFACTURING AND CONSTRUCTION

Manufacturing accounted for an estimated 4.9% of GDP in 2012, and engaged 7.7% of the country's employed labour force in 2013. The sector is based on agricultural-processing and light manufacturing, particularly food and beverages, clothing, household goods, and construction materials. Growth in the sector has fluctuated considerably over the years, successively depressed by a stagnant internal market, political instability and foreign competition, and then buoyed by the removal or neutralization of such impediments. In 2003–12, according to the World Bank, manufacturing GDP increased at an average annual rate of 3.4%. In 2013 the manufacturing sector grew by 2.7%, with particular growth in the production of cement and non-alcoholic bottled beverages.

Industrial activity is concentrated in the CFZ, which is by far the most important manufacturing area in Panama, covering 400 ha and accommodating some 2,500 companies. In the late 1990s competition from other free trade zones and the increasing removal of trade barriers within the region, combined with the severe financial crises that crippled Latin America and Asia, threatened the long-term competitiveness of the CFZ, which responded by emphasizing its geographical location and seeking to reposition itself in the free trade zone market as a transshipment hub. Commercial activities within the CFZ

have steadily increased, with the value of total trade reaching some US $30,800m. in 2012, up from $29,100m. and $21,600m. in 2011 and 2010, respectively. Most of the imports are from the Far East, destined for markets in South and Central America.

The GDP of the construction sector increased at an average annual rate of 17.8% during 2003–12. Construction growth was notably impressive in 2012 and 2013, at 29.1% and 29.8%, respectively, largely attributable to increased public works projects, including the enlargement of the Canal, as well as by the construction of a metro system in Panama City (work on which commenced in 2011 and the first phase of which commenced operations in April 2014). The construction sector contributed an estimated 8.6% of GDP in 2012, and engaged some 11.2% of the employed labour force in 2013.

TRANSPORT AND TOURISM

Although Panama's shipping registry remains the largest in the world, by 2009 the number of vessels registered, including tankers, had fallen to 8,100, from 12,149 in 1990, owing to fierce competition from other countries. Earnings from ship-registration fees had also declined. However, according to Lloyd's List Intelligence, the number of vessels in the Panamanian flag registered fleet totalled 9,290 vessels at the end of 2013. Most shipping remains foreign-owned, reflecting the preferential tax treatment available to shipping companies in Panama. Cristóbal and Balboa, ports in the Canal Area, can accommodate ocean-going freighters and passenger ships. The Manzanillo International Terminal, Colón Container Terminal, Cristóbal and Balboa are among the largest ports in Latin America. Panama's first cruise ship terminals were opened in 2000, at both ends of the Canal.

In 2010, according to preliminary figures, the road network totalled 15,137 km, of which some 42% was paved; in 2009 442,532 vehicles were in use. The Pan-American Highway runs for 545 km in Panama, from the Costa Rican border through Panama City, to Chepo (and is expected to be extended towards Colombia). Three railways serve the banana plantations and other agricultural areas in the western parts of Bocas del Toro and Chiriquí, which borders Costa Rica. On ratification of the 1977 Canal Treaties, Panama also acquired control of the Panama Railroad, which connects Panama City and Colón. The 83-km railway reopened in 2001, operating daily passenger and cargo container services. It is operated by Ferrocarril de Panamá, a subsidiary of Kansas City Southern Railway (USA). The Tocumen (formerly Omar Torrijos) International Airport was officially opened in 1978; a project to expand the airport's facilities at a cost of US $20m. was completed in 2006.

Two long, varied coastlines with good beaches and 800 tropical islands offer vast tourism potential. The southern (Pacific) coast of Panama provides some of the best deep-sea fishing in the world. Other tourist attractions include the mountains and volcanic scenery, the ruins of the original Panama City, and the Panama Canal. Tourist arrivals rose at an average annual rate of 4.8% during 1995–2005. The sector experienced more rapid expansion in 2005–10, increasing by an average of 15.1% per year. Arrivals increased from a total of 1,310,292 in 2011 to 1,478,282 in 2012 and further to an estimated 1,658,000 in 2013. Over the same period, tourism receipts rose from US $2,605m., to $3,067m. and then to an estimated $3,316m. This expansion was largely as a result of the investment in hotels in recent years, a rise in cruise ship arrivals (by 9% in 2013) and generally improving global economic conditions. In 2013 the travel and tourism sector accounted for 13.9% of total GDP and 13.5% of total employment (234,000 jobs, including those indirectly supported by the sector).

The GDP of the services sector overall grew at an average annual rate of 15.9% in 2003–12, according to the World Bank. Strong growth in the sector was attributed primarily to the transport industry and to the rapidly growing tourism sector. According to preliminary figures, the services sector grew by 9.1% in 2012 and by 6.1% in 2013.

THE CANAL AREA

The Canal Area (known as the Canal Zone until 1979) is a strip of land, 16 km wide, between the Pacific and Caribbean coasts, running north-west to south-east. The Canal itself is 82 km long, and raises or lowers ships through 26 m by means of six pairs of locks. An average passage takes about nine hours. The Canal can accommodate ships with a maximum draught of 12.0 m and beams of 32.3 m. Improvements to the Canal in the early 21st century increased the transit capacity to 43 vessels per day.

Under the Canal Treaties of 1977, which came into force in October 1979, the neutrality of the Canal Area is guaranteed, so as to ensure the continuous and clear transit of traffic. Panama has administered the Canal since January 2000, although the USA reserves the right to protect the Canal by military force if necessary. Almost 70% of all cargo transported through the Canal either originates from, or is destined for, the USA. The People's Republic of China was the second most regular user of the Canal in 2009/10, followed by Chile and Japan.

The vessels that use the Canal are predominantly bulk cargo carriers carrying grain, petroleum and related products. The number of transits and the cargo figures remained virtually static from 1995. However, revenue from the Canal rose, owing to increases in transit charges that were introduced in 1995 and 2003. The Autoridad del Canal de Panamá (ACP—Panama Canal Authority) again increased toll charges on the Canal in 2007, despite criticism from shipping companies that the new prices were excessive. The new charges represented an increase of 47% on the previous tariff for large containers and of 20%–30% for other vessels. In 2009/10 canal transit fees earned Panama some US $1,802m. (compared with $460m. in 1995), derived from some 14,230 commercial transits of 204.8m. long tons. The Canal earned revenue of $2,411.3m. in the first nine months of 2013, the largest level of income since its construction.

The US $1,000m. Culebra Cut widening project—the expansion of the narrowest part of the Canal from 152 m to 192 m—which had been initiated in 1996 and was financed entirely from the Canal's revenue, was completed in 2001. The project allowed two vessels to pass at the same time and increased the capacity of the Canal by some 20%. A further expansion project, which would involve the construction of two new sets of locks at either end of the Canal, at a cost of $5,250m., was approved by the National Assembly in 2006 and then by the public via a referendum in 2011. The expansion project could represent a lifeline for the Panama Canal. Since the turn of the century it has become increasingly clear that the Canal has been losing its competitive edge. A fundamental lack of capacity and an outdated structure, along with an inability to divert traffic to alternative routes, lies at the root of the Canal's growing lack of competitiveness, which has seen it lose market share to other trade routes such as the Suez Canal. The number of commercial transits fell from 14,585 in 2010/11 to 13,548 in 2012/13. Through a mixture of deepening and widening of the Canal entrances and navigation channels, the construction of larger locks and the acquisition of more robust tug boats, the ACP hopes that the latest expansion will double the capacity of the Panama Canal by the time the project comes online, initially scheduled to take place in 2014, but now—largely as a result of spiralling cost overruns (amounting to some $1,600m. at mid-2014) and a contractual dispute between the ACP and the Grupo Unidos por el Canal—not expected until December 2015. It is hoped that the expansion will increase capacity to 42 vessels per day, decrease bottlenecks, reduce average transit times and allow for transit of Post-Panamax vessels, equivalent to up to 12,000 20-foot equivalent units (TEU). Currently, the Canal is incapable of accommodating vessels larger than Panamax class ships, equivalent to approximately 4,000 TEU. The ability to handle Post-Panamax vessels is critical given that such ships now account for nearly 40% of the global fleet of container ships. It is estimated that widening the Canal will increase its market share in the Northern trade route from Asia to the US East Coast from 38% to 41%, compared with a projected decline, to just 23%, if it were to continue with its current infrastructure.

Nevertheless, a number of industry experts question whether the expansion project will truly turn around the Canal's ailing fortunes, arguing that, while the new locks will accommodate Post-Panamax vessels, major shipping lines are already looking at constructing ships much larger than this—'Super Post-Panamax' vessels, which will each be capable of carrying 18,000 TEU. Some parties therefore believe that the Canal will be rendered out of date almost as soon as the expansion is complete.

However, this argument is likely to prove overblown. There are relatively few orders for Super Post-Panamax ships. Moreover, only a handful of ports in the world have sufficient draught and crane capacity to accommodate such vessels. For the Canal to remain competitive in the long term, the authorities will have to continue to seek innovative solutions to meet ever-changing capacity demands. However, Post-Panamax capabilities are likely to be sufficient for a number of years yet.

EXTERNAL TRADE AND FINANCE

Panama regularly incurs a large deficit on its merchandise trade account as a result of its heavy dependence on imported fuel and 'invisibles' (banking, ship registration, Canal fees and re-exports). This is, however, partially offset by a surplus on transactions in services. According to the IMF, the trade deficit narrowed from US $7,207.1m. in 2011 to $6,525.8m. in 2012, before rising again, to $6,743.3m., in 2013. The principal imports in 2013 were machinery and apparatus, and mineral products.

Panama tends to be heavily dependent on capital inflows, such as IMF assistance. This is partly because the country's unusually liberal economic system makes it particularly vulnerable to lower world-trading activity during periods of recession. Furthermore, because of its use of the US dollar, Panama is unable to resort to currency devaluation in order to correct trading imbalances. The debt-service ratio (debt-servicing compared with the total value of exports of goods and services) fluctuated between 43% and 55% between 1981 and 1986, but declined steadily thereafter following renegotiation and rescheduling. Nearly a decade of debt-restructuring, including debt forgiveness, repurchasing and exchanging commercial bank debt for bonds, beginning with a Brady bond deal in 1995, enabled the country to reduce its liabilities steadily. With access to concessionary loans and international capital markets, the Panamanian Government was able to issue bonds worth more than $1,500m. to buy back debt in 1998–2003.

Panama has traditionally encouraged foreign investment, a policy that was intensified after 1990, as part of efforts to improve the economy and counterbalance the legacy of sanctions and the US invasion. The privatization programme of the Government of Guillermo Endara Galimany included the lifting of many restrictions on foreign investment. Panama exercises no exchange controls, and transfers of funds are never prevented. There are no restrictions on the transfer of profits, dividends, interest, royalties or fees, nor on the repatriation of capital nor the repayment of principal. A 10% withholding tax is levied on dividends from operations in Panama (excluding the CFZ), but Panama does not levy tax on income earned in offshore financial dealings. In 1997–98 foreign capital inflows increased to an annual average of more than US $1,200m. Although this figure was somewhat distorted by the purchase of a 49% stake in the state telecommunications monopoly, Instituto Nacional de Telecomunicaciones (INTEL), by Cable & Wireless (United Kingdom) for $652m., the incidence of such major investments was increasing. However, the completion of a number of major investment projects caused a decline in foreign direct investment (FDI) from $755.6m. in 1999 to just $98.6m. in 2002. FDI subsequently recovered, reaching $2,547.3m. in 2006, largely owing to the purchase of the Primer Banco del Istmo, which was sold for an estimated $1,700m. to HSBC Bank. A decrease to $1,772.8m. in 2009 (compared with $2,196.2m. in the previous year) was attributed to the effects of the global economic downturn, and investment recovered in 2010, to $2,362.5m. FDI in 2013 was reported to have reached a record $4,651m., representing a 61.1% increase on the previous year's total of $2,887.4m. The large increase was based mainly on higher earnings for foreign companies operating in Panama as well as greater investment in the CFZ.

From the late 1960s onwards Panama developed its potential as an international finance centre, based on the full transferability of its currency, its favourable tax laws and the absence of state controls. The offshore business, foreign exchange, money and reinsurance markets expanded in the early 1980s, and in 2001 the sector accounted for an estimated 11% of GDP. However, the offshore banking sector experienced difficulties caused by political and economic instability and radical changes in business in the late 20th century. Following the onset of the banking crisis the financial services sector in Panama saw its real GDP contract by 7.3% year on year in the third quarter of 2008. In response to the crisis, the Government created a banking fund worth some US $1,100m. in order to protect capitalization of the Panamanian banking sector, which withstood the crisis relatively well. In 2010 the financial services sector accounted for an estimated 8.6% of GDP. In 2011 some 31.5% of all FDI was in the financial services sector. The financial services sector grew by 10.2% in 2012 and by 9.6% in 2013, largely attributable to growth in the banking sector.

By 2011 the net consolidated assets of the banking sector were estimated to be US $81,670m., representing a substantial increase from the $35,651m. recorded in 2003. In 2011 the number of banks registered was 81, significantly fewer than the 118 registered in 1982. As general financial liberalization eroded Panama's competitiveness in the 1990s, competitors in Latin America and the Caribbean were establishing themselves. The relaxation of financial restrictions globally meant that many banks in the USA and Europe began to deal direct with clients in Latin America, denying Panama's banks one of their principal roles. In 2000 the Organisation for Economic Co-operation and Development (OECD) identified Panama as a tax haven. Furthermore, in the same month the Financial Action Task Force on Money Laundering (FATF) included the country on a list of those jurisdictions considered to be 'non-co-operative' in international efforts to prevent money-laundering and the financing of terrorist organizations. Panama protested against its inclusion on both lists and made subsequent efforts to introduce greater legal and administrative transparency in the financial sector. In 2001 the country was removed from the FATF list, and in 2002 Panama met OECD criteria in committing to improve the transparency of its tax and regulatory regime. In 2009, however, OECD included Panama on its 'grey list' of territories that had committed to improving financial transparency but had yet substantially to implement reform. In an effort to be removed from the list, the Government of Panama subsequently began concluding bilateral agreements on the avoidance of double taxation with certain countries. As a result of such efforts, OECD removed Panama from its 'grey list' of tax havens in 2011. However, sizeable concerns remained regarding the wider taxation system, and the Government still needed to address its persistent reputation for being relatively lax on tax transparency, particularly by improving accounting standards. In addition, ongoing high levels of tax evasion, estimated to amount to as much as $700m. per year, have led to serious deficits in the past.

From 1983 Panama's fiscal policies required IMF approval. Satisfaction with the Government's efforts at economic restructuring was signalled by the resumption of lending to the country by the World Bank in 1986. However, in 1987 the Government began to withhold payments to bilateral creditors, and by the end of 1988 accumulated interest and principal arrears on public sector debt were estimated at US $1,400m. In 1991 the Endara Government rescheduled US $520m. in bilateral debts with the 'Paris Club' of Western creditor nations and Panama became eligible for further credits. The trend was consolidated in 1995 when Panama signed a debt-rescheduling agreement based on the Brady Plan. The accord covered $2,000m. in principal arrears and $1,500m. in interest arrears, offering creditors a variety of options with the IMF, the World Bank and the IDB, which were all actively supporting the agreement. Thereafter, Panama repurchased or exchanged $1,220m. of this Brady bond debt for its own 30-year government bonds. In December 1997 the IMF approved a credit of $162m., under the Extended Fund Facility.

Free trade agreements with El Salvador, Taiwan and Chile entered into force in 2003, 2004 and 2008, respectively, while similar accords with Costa Rica, Honduras, Guatemala and Nicaragua took effect successively between November 2008 and November 2009. In June 2007 Panama signed a bilateral free trade agreement with the USA; the accord was ratified by the National Assembly in July, but was not ratified by the US Congress until October 2011. The agreement was expected to improve the operating environment in Panama for foreign companies, to aid economic diversification and have positive implications for medium- to long-term economic stability. Meanwhile, in 2010 Panama signed a free trade agreement with Canada, and was party to a Central American association agreement concluded with the EU. Panama signed a free trade accord with Peru in June 2011. Panama's signature of a free trade agreement with Mexico in April 2014 was one of the prerequisites for Panama eventually joining the Pacific Alliance (Alianza Pacífica) trade group, which currently comprises Mexico, Colombia, Chile and Peru.

CONCLUSION

Panama's exceptional economic performance in 2006–08, when successive growth rates of 8.5%, 12.1% and 10.1% were recorded, was driven by foreign investment and by the expansion of the construction sector, which was stimulated by a number of real estate and infrastructure developments, most notably the project to expand the Canal. Once enlarged, the Canal was expected to increase GDP growth by 1%–2% per year until 2025. Although growth slowed substantially in 2009, to 3.2%, as a result of the impact of the global economic downturn, Panama's economic performance remained relatively strong compared with that of other countries within the region, and the fiscal deficit was contained at 1.1% of GDP. In March 2010 President Martinelli enacted taxation reforms intended to increase annual revenue by US $200m.; notably, value-added tax was raised from 5% to 7% from July. The growth rate accelerated throughout 2010, amounting to 7.5% for the year overall, as external conditions improved, domestic demand recovered and infrastructure projects, such as the expansion of the Canal, stimulated a sharp rise in investment. These favourable conditions continued to fuel high growth rates, with GDP growth exceeding 10% in both 2011 and 2012 and reaching 7.5% in 2013. However, the fiscal deficit widened to 4.4% of GDP in 2013, largely owing to increased expenditure on the development of infrastructure, including the construction of a metro system in Panama City.

Economic prospects remained very good at mid-2014, with the ratification by the US Congress several years earlier of the free trade agreement with the USA, having removed trade tariffs and offering a more positive outlook for the trade deficit. Panama was on course to complete the Canal expansion by the end of 2015; this development, once in operation, was expected to have a substantial positive effect on the national economy. First and foremost, greater capacity will generate higher toll revenues, since tolls are charged on a per tonnage basis and apply to all vessels that transit the Canal. The ACP forecast that toll revenues will reach some US $6,000m. per year by 2020. Such an income would pay for the expansion project in its entirety and generate further revenue for the economy. Second, in addition to reinforcing the Canal's title as the largest transshipment centre in the Americas, the expansion project could also open up other areas of the economy. In particular, increased cargo traffic is likely to benefit the logistics sector. In anticipation of this, Panama has already begun to develop the Panama Pacific Special Economic Area (PPSEA); the business park hosts more than 150 national and international companies and employs some 5,500 people. Nevertheless, the country's ability to take full advantage of this promising sector will require significant improvements to be made in terms of developing technical expertise as well as English-language skills.

Nevertheless, significant infrastructure projects have greatly added to Panama's debt burden. Despite driving high growth rates and offering real opportunities for the country in the longer term, projects including the Panama Canal expansion and the US $1,800m. construction of a metro system increased the country's debt levels from \$10,800m. in 2009 to \$15,683m. by 2013. Furthermore, once the major infrastructure projects have been completed in the coming years economic growth is likely to slow markedly. Linked to this are unemployment concerns; the Panama Canal expansion employs 10,000 people alone. Mounting inflationary pressures, resulting from rising global commodity prices as well as rapid growth rates, are also of some concern, with annual inflation recorded at 5.7% in 2012 and 4.0% in 2013.

However, the country's economic prospects in general remained good (with the IMF forecasting GDP growth of 7.2% in 2014), and new projects coming online in the near future could offset the negative effects of the completion of existing infrastructure projects. The maritime sector remained one of the key industries of future growth and is likely to receive important foreign investment over the next decade. The new Government of Juan Carlos Varela, which came to power in May 2014, will benefit from the recent creation of a wealth fund that will receive contributions from net profits and percentages of tolls from the ACP, which will likely increase each year following the completion of the expansion project in 2015, and would be a source of financing for future projects. Growth prospects will also be facilitated by the Cobre copper mine, construction of which was scheduled to commence in 2014 and which was expected to become operational in 2016, thereby creating an additional source of tax revenues for the state.

The election of Varela in 2014 was not expected to lead to a significant shift in economic policy. Varela has pledged to maintain high levels of economic growth by championing the ongoing large-scale infrastructure projects. Populist aspects of the new President's political agenda, including pledges to address official corruption and high levels of poverty, are unlikely to have direct operational implications for foreign companies in Panama.

Statistical Survey

Sources (unless otherwise stated): Instituto Nacional de Estadística y Censo, Contraloría General de la República, Avda Balboa y Federico Boyd, Apdo 5213, Panamá 5; tel. 210-4800; fax 210-4801; e-mail cgrdec@contraloria.gob.pa; internet www.contraloria.gob.pa/inec; Ministry of the Economy and Finance, Edif. Ogawa, Vía España, Apdo 5245, Panamá 5; e-mail webmaster@mef.gob.pa; internet www.mef.gob.pa.

Area and Population

AREA, POPULATION AND DENSITY

Area (sq km)	75,517*
Population (census results)	
14 May 2000	2,839,177
16 May 2010	
Males	1,712,584
Females	1,693,229
Total	3,405,813
Population (official estimates at mid-year)	
2012	3,787,511
2013	3,850,735
2014	3,913,275
Density (per sq km) at mid-2014	51.8

* 29,157 sq miles.

POPULATION BY AGE AND SEX
(official population estimates at mid-2014)

	Males	Females	Total
0–14 years	555,292	532,365	1,087,657
15–64 years	1,273,925	1,261,340	2,535,265
65 years and over	135,870	154,483	290,353
Total	1,965,087	1,948,188	3,913,275

ADMINISTRATIVE DIVISIONS
(population at 2010 census)

Province	Population	Capital (and population)*
Bocas del Toro	125,461	Bocas del Toro (16,135)
Chiriquí	416,873	David (144,858)
Coclé	233,708	Penonomé (85,737)
Colón	241,928	Colón (206,553)
Comarca Emberá	10,001	—
Comarca Kuna Yala	33,109	—
Comarca Ngöbe-Buglé	156,747	—
Darién	48,378	Chepigana (30,110)
Herrera	109,955	Chitré (50,684)
Los Santos	89,592	Las Tablas (27,146)
Panamá	1,713,070	Panamá (880,691)
Veraguas	226,991	Santiago (88,997)
Total	3,405,813	—

* Population of district in which capital is located.

Note: A new province, Panamá Oeste, with its capital at La Chorrera, was created in October 2013 from five districts previously part of Panamá province.

PRINCIPAL TOWNS
(population at 2010 census)

Panamá (Panama City, capital)	430,299	Puerto Armuelles	55,775
San Miguelito	315,019	Pacora	52,494
Santiago	88,997	Pedregal	51,641
David	82,907	Nuevo Arraiján	41,041
Tocumen	74,952	Colón	34,655
La Chorrera	62,803	Changuinola	31,223

Mid-2014 (incl. suburbs, UN estimate): Panama City 1,637,870 (Source: UN, *World Urbanization Prospects: The 2014 Revision*).

BIRTHS, MARRIAGES AND DEATHS

	Registered live births		Registered marriages*		Registered deaths	
	Number	Rate (per 1,000)†	Number	Rate (per 1,000)†	Number	Rate (per 1,000)†
2005 . .	63,645	19.7	10,512	3.3	14,180	4.4
2006 . .	65,764	20.0	10,747	3.3	14,358	4.4
2007 . .	67,364	20.2	11,516	3.4	14,775	4.4
2008 . .	68,759	20.3	11,508	3.4	15,115	4.5
2009 . .	68,364	19.8	12,273	3.6	15,498	4.5
2010 . .	67,955	19.4	12,981	3.7	16,542	4.7
2011 . .	73,292	19.7	15,135	4.1	16,367	4.4
2012 . .	75,486	19.9	14,201	3.7	17,350	4.6

* Excludes tribal Indian population.
† Based on official mid-year population estimates.

Life expectancy (years at birth): 77.4 (males 74.6, females 80.3) in 2012 (Source: World Bank, World Development Indicators database).

ECONOMICALLY ACTIVE POPULATION
(labour force survey at August, '000 persons aged 15 years and over)

	2011	2012	2013
Agriculture, hunting, forestry and fishing	254.5	270.2	273.5
Mining and quarrying . . .	3.1	3.7	5.0
Manufacturing	107.2	111.1	128.9
Electricity, gas and water supply .	15.9	12.5	16.4
Construction	162.0	167.8	186.5
Wholesale and retail trade; repair of motor vehicles, motorcycles and personal and household goods	276.5	294.9	295.2
Hotels and restaurants . .	77.3	79.9	85.9
Transport, storage and communications	124.9	134.9	141.3
Financial intermediation . .	38.4	39.1	42.1
Real estate, renting and business activities	101.6	107.6	102.5
Public administration and defence; compulsory social service . .	105.1	104.9	106.5
Education	83.8	87.0	90.1
Health and social work . .	57.8	59.1	58.5
Other community, social and personal service activities . .	56.7	66.3	64.5
Private households with employed persons	71.5	76.1	74.3
Extraterritorial organizations and bodies	1.6	2.1	1.2
Total employed	1,538.1	1,617.2	1,672.4
Unemployed	72.2	68.3	71.5
Total labour force	1,610.4	1,685.5	1,743.8
Males	992.1	1020.0	1,052.0
Females	618.1	665.5	691.8

Health and Welfare

KEY INDICATORS

Total fertility rate (children per woman, 2012)	2.5
Under-5 mortality rate (per 1,000 live births, 2012) . . .	19
HIV/AIDS (% of persons aged 15–49, 2012)	0.7
Physicians (per 1,000 head, 2011)	1.6
Hospital beds (per 1,000 head, 2009)	2.2
Health expenditure (2011): US $ per head (PPP) . . .	1,181
Health expenditure (2011): % of GDP	7.9
Health expenditure (2011): public (% of total)	68.2
Access to water (% of persons, 2012)	94
Access to sanitation (% of persons, 2012)	73
Total carbon dioxide emissions ('000 metric tons, 2010) . .	9,633.2
Carbon dioxide emissions per head (metric tons, 2010) . .	2.6
Human Development Index (2013): ranking	65
Human Development Index (2013): value	0.765

For sources and definitions, see explanatory note on p. vi.

Agriculture

PRINCIPAL CROPS
('000 metric tons)

	2010	2011	2012
Rice, paddy	274.0	269.9	250.0*
Maize	87.6	77.3	82.0†
Sugar cane	2,095.0	2,263.9	2,300.0
Watermelons	54.9	31.2	35.0*
Cantaloupes and other melons .	13.6	5.3	5.5*
Bananas	338.3	328.4	335.0*
Plantains	95.2	74.3	78.5*
Oranges	50.7	52.4	55.0*
Coffee, green	12.5	13.1	14.0*
Tobacco, unmanufactured* . .	2.4	3.0	3.0

* FAO estimate(s).
† Unofficial figure.

Aggregate production ('000 metric tons, may include official, semi-official or estimated data): Total cereals 366.3 in 2010, 350.8 in 2011, 337.0 in 2012; Total roots and tubers 77.0 in 2010, 72.8 in 2011, 77.6 in 2012; Total vegetables (incl. melons) 178.7 in 2010, 154.3 in 2011, 162.7 in 2012; Total fruits (excl. melons) 618.1 in 2010, 582.2 in 2011, 599.3 in 2012.

Source: FAO.

LIVESTOCK
('000 head, year ending September)

	2010	2011	2012
Horses	120*	114	115*
Mules	3*	2	2*
Cattle	1,641	1,729	1,723
Pigs	276	322	361
Goats	8*	8	8*
Chickens	17,263	18,719	20,460
Ducks	100*	103	105*
Turkeys	19*	18	18*

* FAO estimate.
Source: FAO.

LIVESTOCK PRODUCTS
('000 metric tons)

	2010	2011	2012*
Cattle meat	79.4	86.3	88.0
Pig meat	29.5	32.3	34.0
Chicken meat	125.8	135.7	138.0
Cows' milk	198.0	194.9	200.0
Hen eggs	24.6	25.3	26.0

* FAO estimates.
Source: FAO.

Forestry

ROUNDWOOD REMOVALS
('000 cubic metres, excluding bark)

	2010	2011	2012
Sawlogs, veneer logs and logs for sleepers .	86	97	100
Other industrial wood* . . .	—	1	1
Fuel wood*	1,128	1,112	1,096
Pulp wood*	90	90	90
Total*	1,304	1,300	1,287

* FAO estimates.
Source: FAO.

SAWNWOOD PRODUCTION
('000 cubic metres, incl. railway sleepers, unofficial figures)

	2010	2011	2012
Total (all broadleaved) . . .	40	45	26

Source: FAO.

Fishing

('000 metric tons, live weight)

	2010	2011	2012
Capture	181.1	168.3	146.9
Snappers and jobfishes . . .	6.3	3.9	1.8
Pacific thread herring . . .	35.4	27.3	20.5
Pacific anchoveta	19.4	31.1	42.1
Skipjack tuna	31.5	44.0	37.3
Yellowfin tuna	40.1	25.8	23.3
Bigeye tuna	11.2	10.1	7.0
Marine fishes	10.3	6.6	7.6
Aquaculture	6.4*	7.4*	7.5
Whiteleg shrimp	5.5	6.2	6.7
Total catch	187.5*	175.7*	154.4

* FAO estimate.

Note: Figures exclude crocodiles. The number of spectacled caimans caught was: 3,556 in 2010; 300 in 2011; 600 in 2012.

Source: FAO.

Industry

SELECTED PRODUCTS
('000 metric tons, unless otherwise indicated)

	2010	2011	2012*
Salt	28	17	16
Sugar	146	170	173
Beer (million litres)	235	247	261
Wines and spirits (million litres) .	13	15	14
Evaporated, condensed and powdered milk	19	19	20
Fish oil	3	4	6
Electricity (million kWh, net) .	7,121	7,530	8,373

* Preliminary.

Finance

CURRENCY AND EXCHANGE RATES

Monetary Units
100 centésimos = 1 balboa (B).

Sterling, Dollar and Euro Equivalents (30 May 2014)
£1 sterling = 1.682 balboas;
US $1 = 1.000 balboas;
€1 = 1.361 balboas;
100 balboas = £59.45 = $100.00 = €73.47.

Exchange Rate: The balboa's value is fixed at par with that of the US dollar.

BUDGET
(consolidated general government budget, '000 balboas)

Revenue	2010	2011	2012*
Central government revenue . .	6,323,571	7,305,161	9,170,484
Current revenue	5,212,028	5,579,941	6,346,649
Tax revenue	3,101,841	3,536,601	4,428,776
Direct taxes	1,588,067	1,644,367	2,316,643
Income tax . . .	1,346,839	1,385,987	2,026,218
Taxes on property and inheritance	182,384	193,204	220,035
Educational insurance .	58,844	65,177	70,391
Indirect taxes . .	1,513,773	1,892,234	2,112,133
Non-tax revenue . . .	1,602,106	1,833,643	1,804,134
Panama Canal	n.a.	n.a.	n.a.
Transfers from balance of public sector	5,010	5,539	6,535
Other current revenue . .	169,874	80,717	32,588
Surplus on cash account . .	286,626	84,323	18,745
Capital revenue	1,111,544	1,725,220	2,823,835
Decentralized institutional revenue	3,798,000	4,221,700	5,103,800
State enterprises	2,936,300	3,121,100	3,319,100
Non-financial	953,700	997,300	1,054,500
Financial	1,982,600	2,123,800	2,264,700
Municipalities	161,500	150,800	n.a.
Total revenue	13,219,400	14,798,800	17,593,400

Expenditure	2011	2012*
Central government expenditure	7,302,093	9,137,650
Current expenditure	4,564,107	5,704,420
National Assembly	60,327	70,838
State treasury	70,400	64,214
Ministry of the Presidency	75,194	96,489
Ministry of the Interior and Justice . .	n.a.	n.a.
Ministry of Foreign Affairs	41,332	47,048
Ministry of Social Development . .	25,841	29,649
Ministry of the Economy and Finance .	380,758	436,925
Ministry of Education	867,444	965,076
Ministry of Commerce and Industry .	42,595	46,280
Ministry of Public Works . . .	29,962	33,237
Ministry of Agricultural Development .	52,533	62,426
Ministry of Public Health . . .	829,900	930,912
Ministry of Labour and Social Welfare .	16,922	14,126
Ministry of Housing	40,003	34,197
Judiciary	64,154	72,726
Ombudsman	—	—
Electoral tribunal	50,049	68,209
Other institutions	—	—
Other expenditures of administration .	13,374	13,795
Debt-servicing	1,322,975	1,979,738
Education fund	60,943	65,756
Ministerial development expenditure . .	2,737,986	3,433,230
Decentralized institutional expenditure . .	3,610,600	4,210,900
State enterprises	3,049,200	3,155,000
Municipalities	148,300	n.a.
Total	14,110,200	16,503,500

* Preliminary figures.

2013 (central government budget only, preliminary): *Revenue:* Current revenue 7,517,445 (Tax revenue 4,859,269, Non-tax revenue 1,863,239, Other current revenue 794,937); Capital revenue 2,111,296; Total 9,628,742. *Expenditure:* Current expenditure 5,287,203; Ministerial development expenditure 4,341,534; Total 9,628,737.

Note: Totals may not be equal to the sum of components, as some figures have been rounded.

INTERNATIONAL RESERVES
(excl. gold, US $ million at 31 December)

	2011	2012	2013
IMF special drawing rights . .	262.4	262.6	263.1
Reserve position in IMF . . .	18.2	18.2	18.3
Foreign exchange	2,023.1	2,185.4	2,566.6
Total	2,303.7	2,466.2	2,848.0

Note: US treasury notes and coins form the bulk of the currency in circulation in Panama.

Source: IMF, *International Financial Statistics*.

MONEY SUPPLY
(million balboas at 31 December)

	2011	2012	2013
Transferable deposits . . .	6,229.3	7,069.2	6,346.5
Other deposits	20,020.2	22,072.0	19,397.2
Securities other than shares . .	27.0	78.6	64.3
Broad money	26,276.5	29,219.9	25,808.0

Source: IMF, *International Financial Statistics*.

COST OF LIVING
(Consumer Price Index, base: October 2002 = 100)

	2011	2012	2013
Food and beverages	151.8	164.1	173.6
Clothing and footwear	103.8	107.5	111.1
Housing, water, electricity and gas	120.2	124.2	129.3
All items (incl. others) . . .	134.7	142.4	148.1

NATIONAL ACCOUNTS
(million balboas at current prices)

National Income and Product

	2010	2011	2012*
Compensation of employees . .	8,260.4	9,505.0	10,897.7
Operating surplus	11,432.8	13,251.1	15,203.5
Net mixed income	3,560.6	4,094.1	4,625.5
Domestic factor incomes . .	23,253.8	26,850.2	30,726.7
Consumption of fixed capital . .	1,518.0	1,708.8	1,913.4
Gross domestic product (GDP) at factor cost	24,771.8	28,559.0	32,640.1
Indirect taxes	2,592.4	3,065.5	3,604.7
Less Subsidies	311.2	304.3	306.6
GDP in purchasers' values .	27,053.0	31,320.2	35,938.2
Less Net factor income paid to the rest of the world	2,226.6	2,401.3	3,016.2
Gross national product . .	24,826.4	28,918.9	32,922.0
Less Consumption of fixed capital	1,518.0	1,708.8	1,913.4
National income in market prices	23,308.4	27,210.1	31,008.6
Other current transfers from abroad (net)	33.3	81.3	−30.0
National disposable income .	23,341.7	27,291.4	30,978.6

*Preliminary figures.

Expenditure on the Gross Domestic Product

	2010	2011	2012*
Government final consumption expenditure	3,545.9	3,780.2	4,173.2
Private final consumption expenditure	16,176.0	20,054.0	20,960.6
Increase in stocks	267.5	339.5	405.4
Gross fixed capital formation .	6,639.3	8,179.5	9,883.2
Total domestic expenditure .	26,628.7	32,353.2	35,422.4
Exports of goods and services .	20,337.0	27,226.7	30,087.9
Less Imports of goods and services	19,912.7	28,259.7	29,572.1
GDP in purchasers' values .	27,053.0	31,320.2	35,938.2
GDP at constant 2007 prices .	25,372.8	28,105.5	30,985.5

*Preliminary figures.

2013 (preliminary): GDP at constant 2007 prices 33,573.5.

Gross Domestic Product by Economic Activity

	2010	2011	2012*
Agriculture, hunting, forestry and fishing	1,043.8	1,078.6	1,267.8
Mining and quarrying	384.9	472.2	639.8
Manufacturing	1,430.1	1,528.6	1,669.8
Electricity, gas and water . .	624.5	710.7	774.0
Construction	1,765.3	2,183.5	2,917.0
Wholesale and retail trade, repair of vehicles, motorcycles and other household goods . . .	3,980.8	5,016.1	5,736.9
Hotels and restaurants . . .	774.6	929.7	1,087.4
Transport, storage and communications	4,742.1	5,616.7	6,280.1
Financial intermediation . . .	2,115.2	2,423.5	2,778.9
Renting, real estate and business services	5,254.4	5,709.8	6,322.1
General government services .	2,387.2	2,634.9	2,875.0
Social services and private education and health . . .	451.0	485.5	533.5
Other community, social and personal services	745.3	838.3	916.9
Private households with employed persons	174.5	192.9	209.0
Sub-total	25,873.7	29,821.0	34,008.2
Less Financial intermediation services indirectly measured .	657.5	796.0	853.2
Gross value added in basic prices	25,216.2	29,025.0	33,155.0
Import duties and other taxes, less subsidies	1,836.8	2,295.2	2,783.2
GDP in market prices . . .	27,053.0	31,320.2	35,938.2

* Preliminary figures.

BALANCE OF PAYMENTS
(US $ million)*

	2011	2012	2013
Exports of goods	16,931.6	18,877.8	17,501.8
Imports of goods	−24,138.7	−25,403.6	−24,245.1
Balance on goods	−7,207.1	−6,525.8	−6,743.3
Exports of services	8,050.8	9,321.6	9,748.5
Imports of services	−4,128.0	−4,172.0	−4,704.8
Balance on goods and services	−3,284.3	−1,376.2	−1,699.6
Primary income received . . .	1,816.1	1,735.9	2,282.7
Primary income paid	−3,727.5	−4,270.1	−5,363.6
Balance on goods, services and primary income . . .	−5,195.7	−3,910.4	−4,780.5
Secondary income received . .	831.9	850.7	820.8
Secondary income paid . . .	−629.5	−756.7	−846.2
Current balance	−4,993.3	−3,816.4	−4,805.9
Capital account (net)	8.9	—	23.4
Direct investment assets . . .	−1,419.1	−88.9	−680.5
Direct investment liabilities . .	4,375.3	3,250.6	5,051.0
Portfolio investment assets . .	−704.9	261.6	−1,206.0
Portfolio investment liabilities .	1,657.6	501.9	1,177.2
Financial derivatives and employee stock options (net)	1.5	64.4	−23.5
Other investment assets . . .	−3,948.7	−3,447.0	−2,123.3
Other investment liabilities . .	4,588.3	3,176.2	3,530.9
Net errors and omissions . . .	207.1	122.5	−321.5
Reserves and related items .	−227.3	24.9	621.8

* Including the transactions of enterprises operating in the Colón Free Zone.

Source: IMF, *International Financial Statistics*.

External Trade

PRINCIPAL COMMODITIES
('000 balboas)

Imports c.i.f.	2010	2011	2012
Food and live animals	1,079,822	1,301,311	1,414,562
Mineral products	1,765,594	2,525,134	2,765,504
Chemicals and chemical products .	856,853	966,123	1,077,954
Plastics, rubber and articles thereof	399,098	478,584	505,375
Textiles and articles thereof . .	418,023	498,914	605,012
Metals and manufactures of metal	712,176	827,548	959,552
Machinery and apparatus . . .	1,805,031	2,135,812	2,350,323
Transport materials	901,393	1,169,711	1,214,168
Total (incl. others)	9,136,517	11,339,727	12,494,341

Exports f.o.b.*	2010	2011	2012
Meat of bovine animals (fresh, chilled or frozen)	14,846	18,240	24,718
Fresh or chilled salmon (excl. livers and roes)	80,287	30,376	26,687
Shellfish	35,384	37,708	40,490
Bananas	65,198	86,339	85,940
Melons	37,062	16,564	15,849
Pineapples	32,064	31,629	37,132
Coffee	13,711	9,390	7,106
Sugar	19,193	37,157	34,490
Waste and scrap of cast iron or steel	29,597	40,748	38,657
Gold (incl. gold plate with platinum unwrought forms)	70,345	116,766	115,784
Total (incl. others)	727,644	784,971	821,626

* Including re-exports.

PRINCIPAL TRADING PARTNERS*
('000 balboas)

Imports c.i.f.†	2010	2011	2012
Argentina	47,886	124,813	150,733
Brazil	244,914	217,386	173,921
China, People's Republic . .	489,541	689,700	810,274
Colombia	298,780	477,558	430,566
Costa Rica	444,698	509,774	571,386
Germany	141,999	166,066	173,889
Guatemala	170,585	196,521	212,228
Japan	289,067	292,057	290,218
Korea, Republic	292,788	303,798	355,723
Mexico	394,548	445,066	561,913
Netherlands	43,758	51,737	153,474
Spain	162,962	294,403	318,471
Thailand	94,147	105,319	125,103
Turkey	48,605	73,197	141,775
USA	2,517,437	2,817,598	2,981,241
Total (incl. others)	9,136,517	11,339,727	12,494,341

Exports f.o.b.	2010	2011	2012
Canada	75,725	121,049	119,797
Chile	6,086	9,182	7,252
China, People's Republic . .	36,079	38,651	33,848
Colombia	9,706	9,264	8,426
Costa Rica	49,364	52,343	54,271
Dominican Republic . . .	8,273	4,497	5,626
El Salvador	8,610	7,614	10,653
Honduras	16,905	16,327	12,971
India	7,305	19,063	21,851
Italy	14,421	20,028	33,183
Korea, Republic	5,032	18,613	24,887
Netherlands	50,563	34,484	48,178

Exports f.o.b.—*continued*	2010	2011	2012
Nicaragua	14,781	18,991	14,120
Portugal	4,323	9,102	1,762
Spain	19,918	16,172	16,129
Suriname	5,398	5,100	9,491
Sweden	49,974	55,010	39,095
Taiwan	36,595	34,841	33,239
United Kingdom	8,419	10,010	17,557
USA	211,582	163,337	160,970
Viet Nam	5,763	8,675	7,035
Total (incl. others)	727,644	784,971	821,626

* Including trade with the Colón Free Zone (CFZ) ('000 balboas): *Imports:* 1,029,975 in 2010; 1,174,976 in 2011; 1,362,163 in 2012. *Exports:* 19,759 in 2010; 28,922 in 2011; 29,301 in 2012.
† Including imports from the Petroleum Free Zone ('000 balboas): 1,489,054 in 2010; 2,259,561 in 2011; 2,473,312 in 2012.

Transport

RAILWAYS
(traffic)

	2002*	2003	2004
Passenger-km (million) . . .	35,693	52,324	53,377
Freight ton-km (million) . . .	20,665	41,863	52,946

* Panama Railway only.

Source: UN, *Statistical Yearbook*.

ROAD TRAFFIC
(motor vehicles in use)

	2010
Passenger cars	359,266
Buses and coaches	19,661
Lorries and vans	104,774
Motorcycles and mopeds	20,133*

* Figure for 2007.

Source: IRF, *World Road Statistics*.

SHIPPING
Flag Registered Fleet
(at 31 December)

	2011	2012	2013
Number of vessels	9,369	9,326	9,290
Total displacement (grt) . . .	222,739.6	228,548.2	228,816.8

Source: Lloyd's List Intelligence (www.lloydslistintelligence.com).

International Seaborne Freight Traffic
(national ports authority, '000 metric tons)

	2010	2011	2012*
Goods handled	57,002	64,831	76,580
Container goods	37,683	45,883	—

* Preliminary.

Panama Canal Traffic

	2010/11	2011/12	2012/13
Transits	14,585	14,448	13,548
Cargo ('000 long tons)	222,358.9	218,053.5	209,878.3

Source: Panama Canal Authority.

CIVIL AVIATION
(traffic on scheduled services)

	2009	2010	2011
Kilometres flown (million) . .	94	118	155
Passengers carried ('000) . . .	6,348	3,614	4,138
Passenger-km (million) . . .	8,414	11,635	13,795
Total ton-km (million)	894	1,219	1,428

Source: UN, *Statistical Yearbook*.

Passengers carried ('000): 7,518 in 2012; 8,626 in 2013 (Source: World Bank, World Development Indicators database).

Tourism

VISITOR ARRIVALS BY COUNTRY OF ORIGIN
(arrivals at Tocumen International Airport)

	2010	2011	2012
Argentina	47,216	62,357	66,623
Brazil	31,520	47,890	59,687
Canada	48,029	52,731	62,792
Colombia	219,250	218,962	244,890
Costa Rica	39,524	40,524	42,978
Ecuador	30,861	43,975	59,782
Guatemala	32,780	27,107	27,913
Mexico	48,132	51,422	57,803
Peru	15,431	22,382	30,824
Spain	30,845	32,560	39,928
USA	252,837	279,742	303,843
Venezuela	131,608	168,184	187,351
Total (incl. others)	1,162,713	1,310,292	1,478,282

Total tourist arrivals ('000): 1,658 in 2013 (provisional).

Tourism receipts (US $ million, excl. passenger transport): 2,605 in 2011; 3,067 in 2012; 3,316 in 2013 (provisional).

Source: World Tourism Organization.

Communications Media

	2011	2012	2013
Telephones ('000 main lines in use)	560.2	569.9	586.3
Mobile cellular telephones ('000 subscribers)	6,735.4	6,213.6	6,297.6
Internet subscribers ('000) . .	289.6	n.a.	n.a.
Broadband subscribers ('000) . .	282.8	294.7	297.8

Source: International Telecommunication Union.

Education

(2011/12 unless otherwise indicated, provisional)

			Students		
	Institutions	Teachers	Males	Females	Total
Pre-primary .	1,662*	5,504	49,109	47,156	96,265
Primary . .	3,116*	19,340	189,781†	174,135†	363,916†
Secondary .	442*	24,631	173,479	175,906	349,385
General .	n.a.	20,671	148,121	152,306	300,427
Vocational .	n.a.	3,960	25,358	23,600	48,958
Tertiary . .	24‡	13,424§	53,366§	80,131§	133,497§

* 2001/02 figure.
† 2012/13, preliminary.
‡ 2009/10.
§ 2010/11.

Sources: Ministry of Education; UNESCO, *Statistical Yearbook*; UNESCO Institute for Statistics.

Pupil-teacher ratio (primary education, UNESCO estimate): 22.6 in 2011/12 (Source: UNESCO Institute for Statistics).

Adult literacy rate (UNESCO estimates): 94.1% (males 94.7%; females 93.5%) in 2010 (Source: UNESCO Institute for Statistics).

Directory

The Constitution

Under the terms of the amendments to the 1972 Constitution, implemented by the adoption of Reform Acts No. 1 and No. 2 in October 1978, and by the approval by referendum of the Constitutional Act in April 1983, the 67 (later 71) members of the unicameral legislature are elected by popular vote every five years. Executive power is exercised by the President of the Republic, who is also elected by popular vote for a term of five years. A Vice-President is elected by popular vote to assist the President. The President appoints the Cabinet. The armed forces are barred from participating in elections. In 2004 further amendments to the Constitution were adopted, including an increase in the number of members of the legislature (which was also renamed the Asamblea Nacional—National Assembly) from 2009 and the abolition of parliamentary immunity from prosecution.

The Government

HEAD OF STATE

President: JUAN CARLOS VARELA RODRÍGUEZ (took office 1 July 2014).
Vice-President: ISABEL SAINT MALO DE ALVARADO.

THE CABINET
(September 2014)

The Government is formed by the Partido Panameñista (PP) and Independents (Ind.).

Minister of Foreign Affairs: ISABEL SAINT MALO DE ALVARADO (Ind.).
Minister of Public Security: RODOLFO AGUILERA FRANSCECHI.
Minister of the Interior: MILTON HENRÍQUEZ (PP).

Minister of Public Works: RAMÓN L. AROSEMENA CRESPO.
Minister of the Economy and Finance: DULCIDIO DE LA GUARDIA (PP).
Minister of Agricultural Development: JORGE ARANGO ARIAS (Ind.).
Minister of Commerce and Industry: MELITÓN ARROCHA RUIZ (PP).
Minister of Health: Dr FRANCISCO JAVIER TERRIENTES.
Minister of Labour and Social Welfare: LUIS ERNESTO CARLES (PP).
Minister of Education: MARCELA PAREDES DE VÁSQUEZ (Ind.).
Minister of Housing and Land Management: MARIO ETCHELECU.
Minister of the Presidency: ALVARO ALEMÁN (PP).
Minister of Social Development: ALCIBÍADES VÁSQUEZ VELÁZQUES (PP).
Minister of Canal Affairs: ROBERTO ROY (Ind.).

MINISTRIES

Office of the President: Palacio de Las Garzas, Corregimiento de San Felipe, Panamá 1; tel. 527-9600; fax 527-9034; e-mail prensa@presidencia.gob.pa; internet www.presidencia.gob.pa.
Ministry of Agricultural Development: Edif. 576, Calle Manuel E. Melo, Altos de Curundú, Apdo 0816-01611, Panamá 5; tel. 507-0600; e-mail infomida@mida.gob.pa; internet www.mida.gob.pa.
Ministry of Canal Affairs: see Transport—Autoridad del Canal de Panamá.
Ministry of Commerce and Industry: Plaza Edison, Sector El Paical, 2° y 3°, Apdo 0815-0111, Panamá 4; tel. 560-0600; fax 261-1942; e-mail contactenos@mici.gob.pa; internet www.mici.gob.pa.
Ministry of the Economy and Finance: (Economy) Edif. Ogawa, Vía España y Calle 52 Este, Calle del Santuario Nacional, Apdo 5245,

Panamá 5; (Finance) Antiguo Edif. de Hacienda y Tesoro, Calle 34 y 35, Avda Perú, Calidonia, Panamá; tel. (Economy) 507-7000; tel. (Finance) 507-7600; e-mail prensa@mef.gob.pa; internet www.mef.gob.pa.

Ministry of Education: Villa Cárdenas, Ancón, Apdo 0816-04049, Panamá 3; tel. 511-4400; fax 511-4440; e-mail meduca@meduca.gob.pa; internet www.meduca.gob.pa.

Ministry of Foreign Affairs: Edif. 26, Palacio Bolívar, Calle 3, San Felipe, Panamá 4; tel. 511-4100; fax 511-4022; e-mail prensa@mire.gob.pa; internet www.mire.gob.pa.

Ministry of Health: Apdo 2048, Panamá 1; tel. and fax 512-9202; e-mail saludaldia@minsa.gob.pa; internet www.minsa.gob.pa.

Ministry of Housing and Land Management: Edif. Plaza Edison, 4°, Avda Ricardo J. Alfaro y Calle El Paical, Corregimiento de Bethania, Apdo 5228, Panamá 5; tel. 579-9200; fax 579-9651; e-mail info@miviot.gob.pa; internet www.miviot.gob.pa.

Ministry of the Interior: Avda 7 y Calle 3, Central San Felipe, Apdo 1628, Panamá 1; tel. 512-7600; fax 512-2126; e-mail despachosuperior@mingob.gob.pa; internet www.mingob.gob.pa.

Ministry of Labour and Social Welfare: Plaza Edison, 5°, Avda Ricardo J. Alfaro (Tumba Muerto) Betania, Apdo 2441, Panamá 3; tel. 560-1100; fax 560-1117; e-mail mitradel@mitradel.gob.pa; internet www.mitradel.gob.pa.

Ministry of the Presidency: Palacio de Las Garzas, Corregimiento de San Felipe, Apdo 2189, Panamá 1; tel. 527-9600; e-mail ofasin@presidencia.gob.pa; internet www.presidencia.gob.pa.

Ministry of Public Security: Avda 7 y Calle 3, Central San Felipe, Apdo 1628, Panamá 1; tel. 512-2000; fax 512-2174; e-mail prensa@minseg.gob.pa; internet www.minseg.gob.pa.

Ministry of Public Works: Edif. Principal 1019, Curundú, Zona 1, Apdo 1632, Panamá 1; tel. 507-9400; fax 507-9561; e-mail info@mop.gob.pa; internet www.mop.gob.pa.

Ministry of Social Development: Plaza Edison, 4°, Avda Ricardo J. Alfaro, Apdo 680-50, El Dorado, Panamá; tel. 500-6001; fax 500-6020; e-mail mides@mides.gob.pa; internet www.mides.gob.pa.

President and Legislature

PRESIDENT

Election, 4 May 2014

Candidate	Votes	% of valid votes
Juan Carlos Varela Rodríguez (El Pueblo Primero*)	724,762	39.09
José Domingo Arias (Unidos por Más Cambios†)	581,828	31.38
Juan Carlos Navarro (Partido Revolucionario Democrático)	521,842	28.14
Genaro López Rodríguez (Frente Amplio por la Democracia)	11,127	0.59
Juan Jované de Puy (Independent)	10,805	0.60
Others	3,838	0.21
Total valid votes‡	1,854,202	100.00

* Electoral alliance comprising the Partido Panameñista and the Partido Popular.
† Electoral alliance comprising the Cambio Democrático and the Movimiento Liberal Republicano Nacionalista.
‡ In addition, there were 14,944 blank and 17,162 invalid ballots.

NATIONAL ASSEMBLY
(Asamblea Nacional)

President: ADOLFO (BEBY) VALDERRAMA RODRÍGUEZ (PP).

Election, 4 May 2014

Party	Seats
Unidos por Más Cambios	32
Cambio Democrático (CD)	30
Movimiento Liberal Republicano Nacionalista (MOLIRENA)	2
Partido Revolucionario Democrático (PRD)	25
El Pueblo Primero	13
Partido Panameñista (PP)	12
Partido Popular	1
Independent	1
Total	71

Election Commission

Tribunal Electoral: Edif. del Tribunal, Avda Omar Torrijos, Corregimiento de Ancón, Apdo 0816-01504, Panamá 5; tel. 507-8000; e-mail secretaria-general@tribunal-electoral.gob.pa; internet www.tribunal-electoral.gob.pa; f. 1956; independent, comprised of three magistrates, one each appointed by the legislature, the executive and the judiciary; Pres. ERASMO PINILLA CASTILLERO; Exec. Dir YARA IVETTE CAMPO B.

Political Organizations

Cambio Democrático (CD): Parque Lefevre, Plaza Carolina, arriba de la Juguetería del Super 99, Panamá; tel. 217-2643; fax 217-2645; e-mail cambio.democratico@hotmail.com; internet www.cambiodemocratico.org.pa; formally registered 1998; merged with the Unión Patriótica in 2011; contested the 2014 elections as part of the Unidos por Más Cambios alliance with MOLIRENA; Pres. RICARDO A. MARTINELLI BERROCAL; Sec.-Gen. RÓMULO ROUX.

Frente Amplio por la Democracia (FAD): Panamá; tel. 203-8147; internet www.partido-fad.com; f. 2011 by Frente Nacional por la Defensa de los Derechos Económicos y Sociales (FRENADESO); left-wing; Pres. FERNANDO CEBAMANOS; Sec. SILVESTRE DÍAZ.

Movimiento Liberal Republicano Nacionalista (MOLIRENA): Calle 66 (Calle Belén), Casa Duplex 46-A, Corregimiento de San Francisco, Panamá; tel. 399-5280; fax 399-5288; f. 1982; conservative; contested the 2014 elections as part of the Unidos por Más Cambios alliance with the Cambio Democrático (alliance ended in July 2014); Pres. SERGIO GONZÁLEZ RUIZ; Sec.-Gen. ARTURO GONZÁLEZ BASO.

Partido Liberal: Edif. Torre Universal, 11°, Avda Federico Boyd, Panamá; tel. 209-2574; fax 209-2575; e-mail partidoliberal@elveloz.com; f. 2005; Pres. JOAQUÍN F. FRANCO, III.

Partido Panameñista (PP): Avda Perú y Calle 37, No 37–41, al lado de Casa la Esperanza, Apdo 9610, Panamá 4; tel. 227-0028; fax 227-0951; e-mail partidopanamenista@hotmail.com; internet partidopanamenista.com; f. 1990 by Arnulfista faction of the Partido Panameñista Auténtico as Partido Arnulfista (PA); name changed as above in 2005; contested the 2014 elections as part of El Pueblo Primero alliance with the Partido Popular; Pres. JUAN CARLOS VARELA RODRÍGUEZ; Sec.-Gen. ALCIBÍADES VÁSQUEZ.

Partido Popular: Avda Perú, frente al Parque Porras, Apdo 6322, Panamá 5; tel. 225-2381; fax 227-3944; e-mail comunicacion@partidopopular.org.pa; internet www.panamaprimermundo.org; f. 1960 as Partido Demócrata Cristiano; name changed as above in 2001; contested the 2014 elections as part of El Pueblo Primero alliance with the Partido Panameñista; Pres. MILTON COHEN-HENRÍQUEZ; Sec.-Gen. JOSÉ RAMOS REYES.

Partido Revolucionario Democrático (PRD): Edif. Policentro, Avda México, entre Calle 26 y 27, Panamá 3; tel. 225-8462; fax 225-8476; e-mail info@prd.org.pa; internet www.prd.org.pa; f. 1979; supports policies of late Gen. Omar Torrijos Herrera; combination of Marxists, Christian Democrats and some business interests; Pres. BENICIO ROBINSON; Sec.-Gen. (vacant).

Diplomatic Representation

EMBASSIES IN PANAMA

Argentina: PH Torre Global, 24°, Calle 50, Apdo 832-0458, Panamá 1; tel. 302-0003; fax 302-0004; e-mail epnma@mrecic.gov.ar; internet www.epnma.mrecic.gov.ar; Ambassador ANA CRISTINA BERTA DE ALBERTO.

Belgium: Ambabel Panama Credicorp, Of. 31-A, 31°, Plaza Calle 50, Apdo 0833-00081, Panamá; tel. 301-1438; e-mail panama@diplobel.fed.be; internet diplomatie.belgium.be/panama/; Ambassador KOENRAAD LENAERTS.

Bolivia: Calle G, Casa 3, El Cangrejo, Apdo 0823-05603, Panamá; tel. 269-0274; fax 264-3868; e-mail emb_bol_pan@cwpanama.net; internet embolivia-panama.com.pa; Ambassador LANDELINO RAFAEL BANDEIRA ARZE.

Brazil: Edif. El Dorado 24, 1°, Calle Elvira Méndez y Avda Ricardo Arango, Urb. Campo Alegre, Apdo 4287, Panamá 5; tel. 263-5322; fax 269-6316; e-mail brasemb.panama@itamaraty.gov.br; internet panama.itamaraty.gov.br/pt-br; Ambassador ADALNIO SENNA GANEM.

Canada: Edif. World Trade Center, Torres de las Américas, Torre A, 11°, Punta Pacífica, Apdo 0832-2446, Panamá; tel. 294-2500; fax 294-2514; e-mail panam@international.gc.ca; internet www.canadainternational.gc.ca/panama; Ambassador SYLVIA CESARATTO.

Chile: Torres de las Américas, 7°, Punta Pacífica, Apdo 7341, Panamá 5; tel. 203-1890; fax 203-1894; e-mail echilepa@cableonda.net; internet chileabroad.gov.cl/panama; Ambassador FLAVIO TARSETTI QUEZADA.

Colombia: Edif. Oceanía, Torre 2000, 17°, Of. 17C, Punta Pacífica, Panamá; tel. 264-9513; fax 223-2811; e-mail epanama@cancilleria.gov.co; internet panama.embajada.gov.co; Ambassador ANGELA MARÍA BENEDETTI VILLANEDA.

Costa Rica: Edif. Plaza Omega, 3°, Calle Samuel Lewis, Apdo 0816-02038, Panamá; tel. 264-2980; fax 264-4057; e-mail embajadacr@cwpanama.net; Ambassador RODRIGO ALBERTO RIVERA FOURNIER.

Cuba: Avda Cuba y Ecuador 33, Apdo 6-2291, Bellavista, Panamá; tel. 227-0359; fax 225-6681; e-mail segundojefemision@pa.embacuba.cu; internet www.cubadiplomatica.cu/panama; Ambassador REINALDO CARLOS CALVIAC LAFERTÉ.

Dominican Republic: Torre Delta, 16°, Calle Elvira Méndez, Área Bancaria, Apdo 6250, Panamá 5; tel. 394-7813; fax 394-7816; e-mail embajadadompa.zlg@cableonda.net; Ambassador OCTAVIO ALFREDO LEÓN LISTER HENRÍQUEZ.

Ecuador: Edif. Torre 2000, 6°, Calle 50, Marbella, Bellavista, Panamá; tel. 264-2654; fax 223-0159; e-mail ecuador@ibw.com.ni; Ambassador (vacant).

Egypt: Calle 55, No 15, El Cangrejo, Apdo 7080, Panamá 5; tel. 263-5020; fax 264-8406; e-mail egempma@hotmail.com; internet www.mfa.gov.eg/PanamaCity_Emb; Ambassador AHMED MOHAMED TAHA DAWOUD.

El Salvador: Edif. ADR, 8°, Avda Samuel Lewis y Calle 58, Apdo 0823-05432, Panamá; tel. 223-3020; fax 264-6148; e-mail embasalva@cwpanama.net; internet embajadapanama.rree.gob.sv; Ambassador EFRÉN ARNOLDO BERNAL CHÉVEZ.

France: Plaza de Francia 1, Las Bovedas, San Felipe, Apdo 0816-07945, Panamá 1; tel. 211-6200; fax 211-6201; e-mail cad.panama-amba@diplomatie.gouv.fr; internet www.ambafrance-pa.org; Ambassador HUGUES GOISBAULT.

Germany: Edif. World Trade Center, 20°, Calle 53E, Marbella, Apdo 0832-0536, Panamá 5; tel. 263-7733; fax 223-6664; e-mail germpanama@cwp.net.pa; internet www.panama.diplo.de; Ambassador HERMANN-JOSEF SAUSEN.

Guatemala: Edif. World Trade Center, 2°, Of. 203, Calle 53, Urb. Marbella, Panamá 9; tel. 269-3475; fax 223-1922; e-mail embpanama@minex.gob.gt; Ambassador ANAMARÍA DIÉGUEZ ARÉVALO.

Haiti: Edif. de Lesseps, 6°, Calle Manuel María, Apto 1, Panamá; tel. 269-3443; fax 223-1767; e-mail embhaitipan@cableonda.net; Ambassador MARIE-PHILIPPE ARCHER.

Holy See: Punta Paitilla, Avda Balboa y Vía Italia, Apdo 0816-00457, Panamá 5 (Apostolic Nunciature); tel. 269-2102; fax 264-2116; e-mail secretarionunciatura@cableonda.net; Apostolic Nuncio Most Rev. ANDRÉS CARRASCOSA COSO (Titular Archbishop of Elo).

Honduras: Edif. Bay Mall, 1°, Avda Balboa 112, Apdo 0816-03427, Panamá 5; tel. 264-5513; fax 264-4628; e-mail info@embajadadehonduras.com.pa; internet www.embajadadehonduras.com.pa; Ambassador NERY M. FÚNES PADILLA.

India: Avda Federico Boyd y Calle 51, Bella Vista, Apdo 0823-05815, Panamá 7; tel. 264-3043; fax 209-6649; e-mail ambassador@indempan.org; internet www.indempan.org; Ambassador YOGESHWAR VARMA.

Indonesia: Oceania Business Plaza, Torre 2000, Módulo 21A, Punta Pacífica, Panamá; tel. 223-2100; fax 223-9626; e-mail embajaindonesiapanama@gmail.com; internet www.kemlu.go.id/panama; Ambassador DWI AYU ARIMAMI.

Israel: Edif. Torre Banco General, 17°, Calle Aquilino de la Guardia, Urb. Marbella, Panamá; tel. 208-4700; fax 208-4755; e-mail info@panama.mfa.gov.il; internet panama.mfa.gov.il; Ambassador ALEXANDER GALILEE.

Italy: Torre Banco Exterior, 25°, Avda Balboa, Apdo 0816-04453, Panamá 9; tel. 225-8950; fax 227-4906; e-mail ambpana.mail@esteri.it; internet www.ambpanama.esteri.it; Ambassador GIANCARLO MARIA CURCIO.

Japan: Calle 50 y 60E, Urb. Obarrio, Apdo 0816-06807, Panamá 1; tel. 263-6155; fax 263-6019; e-mail taiship2@cwpanama.net; internet www.panama.emb-japan.go.jp; Ambassador HIROAKI ISOBE.

Korea, Republic: Torre Global Bank, 30°, Of. 3002, Calle 50, Urb. Obarrio, Apdo 0823-05514, Panamá 7; tel. 264-8203; fax 264-8825; e-mail panama@mofat.go.kr; internet pan.mofat.go.kr; Ambassador CHO BYOUNG-LIP.

Libya: Avda Balboa y Calle 32 (frente al Edif. Atalaya), Apdo 6-894, El Dorado, Panamá; tel. 227-3342; fax 227-3886; Ambassador SENUSSI MOHAMED EL-BIGOU.

Mexico: Edif. Torre ADR, 10°, Avda Samuel Lewis y Calle 54, Urb. Obarrio, Corregimiento de Bella Vista, Apdo 0823-05788, Panamá; tel. 263-4900; fax 263-5446; e-mail embamexpan@cwpanama.net; internet www.sre.gob.mx/panama; Ambassador ALEJANDRA MARÍA GABRIELA BOLOGNA ZUBIKARAI.

Netherlands: Oceania Business Plaza, Torre 1000, 23°, Local 23A, Calle Hanono Missrie, Punta Pacífica, Panamá; tel. 280-6650; fax 280-6699; e-mail pan@minbuza.nl; internet panama.nlambassade.org; Ambassador WIEBE DE BOER.

Nicaragua: Calle 63G Oeste, Casa 61B, Urb. La Alameda, Panamá; tel. 264-3080; fax 264-5425; e-mail embapana@sinfo.net; Ambassador ANTENOR ALBERTO FERREY PERNUDI.

Paraguay: Calle Las Acacias 60, Marbella, Panamá; tel. 263-4782; fax 269-4247; e-mail embaparpanama@mre.gov.py; internet embaparpanama.org; Ambassador CÁNDIDO AGUILERA FERNÁNDEZ.

Peru: Edif. World Trade Center, 12°, Of. 1203, Calle 53, Urb. Marbella, Apdo 4516, Panamá 5; tel. 263-8901; fax 269-6707; e-mail embaperu@cableonda.net; Ambassador GUILLERMO JOSÉ MIGUEL RUSSO CHECA.

Russia: Torre IBC, 10°, Avda Manuel Espinosa Batista, Apdo 6-4697, El Dorado, Panamá; tel. 264-1408; fax 264-1588; e-mail emruspan@sinfo.net; internet www.panama.mid.ru; Ambassador ALEXEI A. ERMAKOV.

Spain: Plaza de Belisario Porras, entre Avda Perú y Calle 33A, Apdo 0816-06600, Panamá 1; tel. 207-1500; fax 227-6284; e-mail emb.panama@maec.es; internet www.exteriores.gob.es/Embajadas/Panama; Ambassador JESÚS SILVA FERNÁNDEZ.

Taiwan (Republic of China): Edif. Torre Hong Kong Bank, 10°, Avda Samuel Lewis, Apdo 7492, Panamá 5; tel. 269-1347; fax 264-9118; e-mail panama@mail.gio.gov.tw; internet www.taiwanembassy.org/pa; Ambassador DIEGO-LIN CHOU.

United Kingdom: MMG Tower, 4°, Calle 53, Urb. Marbella, Apdo 0816-07946, Panamá 1; tel. 297-6550; fax 297-6588; internet ukinpanama.fco.gov.uk; Ambassador Dr IAN FRANK COLLARD.

USA: Edif. 783, Avda Demetrio Basilio Lakas, Apdo 0816-02561, Clayton, Panamá 5; tel. 317-5000; fax 317-5568; e-mail panamaweb@state.gov; internet panama.usembassy.gov; Ambassador JONATHAN DON FARRAR.

Uruguay: Edif. Los Delfines, Of. 8, Avda Balboa, Calle 50E Este, Apdo 0816-03616, Panamá 5; tel. 264-2838; fax 264-8908; e-mail urupanam@cwpanama.net; internet www.urupana.org; Ambassador FRANCISCO HEBER PURIFICATTI GAMARRA.

Venezuela: Torre HSBC, 5°, Avda Samuel Lewis, Apdo 661, Panamá 1; tel. 269-1244; fax 269-1916; e-mail embve.papnm@mppre.gob.ve; internet panama.embajada.gob.ve; Ambassador ALICIA ELENA SALCEDO PENNYROYAL.

Viet Nam: Edif. St George Bank, Local 1, Calle 50 y 53, Urb. Obarrio, Panamá; tel. 264-2551; fax 265-6056; e-mail convietnam@cwpanama.net; Ambassador NGUYEN DUY AN.

Judicial System

The judiciary in Panama comprises the Supreme Court of Justice, with nine judges appointed for a 10-year term and 10 High Courts. There are four judicial districts and seven High Courts of Appeal. There are, in addition, two special High Courts of Appeal: the first hears maritime, labour, family and infancy cases and the second deals with anti-trust cases and consumer affairs.

Corte Suprema de Justicia: Edif. 236, Calle Culebra, Ancón, Apdo 1770, Panamá 1; tel. 212-7300; e-mail informatica@organojudicial.gob.pa; internet www.organojudicial.gob.pa; Pres. ALEJANDRO MONCADA LUNA.

Attorney-General: ANA ISABEL BELFÓN VEJAS.

Religion

The Constitution recognizes freedom of worship and the Roman Catholic Church as the religion of the majority of the population.

CHRISTIANITY

The Roman Catholic Church

For ecclesiastical purposes, Panama comprises one archdiocese, five dioceses, the territorial prelature of Bocas del Toro and the Apostolic Vicariate of Darién. Some 83% of the population are Roman Catholics.

Bishops' Conference: Conferencia Episcopal de Panamá, Secretariado General, Apdo 870933, Panamá 7; tel. 223-0075; fax 223-0042; internet www.iglesia.org.pa; f. 1958; statutes approved 1986; Pres. Rt Rev. JOSÉ DOMINGO ULLOA MENDIENTA (Archbishop of Panama).

Archbishop of Panamá: Most Rev. JOSÉ DOMINGO ULLOA MENDIENTA, Arzobispado Metropolitano, Calle 1a Sur Carrasquilla, Apdo 6386, Panamá 5; tel. 261-0002; fax 261-0820; e-mail comunicacion@arquidiocesisdepanama.org; internet www.arquidiocesisdepanama.org.

The Anglican Communion

Panama comprises one of the five dioceses of the Iglesia Anglicana de la Región Central de América.

Bishop of Panama: Rt Rev. JULIO MURRAY, Edif. 331A, Calle Culebra, Apdo R, Balboa, Panamá; tel. 212-0062; fax 262-2097.

Other Christian Churches

Baptist Convention of Panama (Convención Bautista de Panamá): Cáceres de Arraiján, Carretera Interamericana, Frente a la Estación Delta, Apdo 0816-01761, Panamá 5; tel. and fax 259-5485; e-mail convencionbautistadepanama@hotmail.com; internet www.cbpanama.org; f. 1959; Pres. FRANCISCO MEDINA; Sec. ESMERALDA DE TUY; 7,573 mems.

Church of Jesus Christ of Latter-Day Saints (Mormons): Calle Rufina 3172, Ancón, Cárdenas, Panamá; tel. 317-6900; internet www.lds.org; 48,669 mems.

BAHÁ'Í FAITH

National Spiritual Assembly of the Bahá'ís: Apdo 850-625, Las Cumbres, Panamá 15; tel. 231-1191; fax 231-6909; e-mail panbahai@cwpanama.net; internet panamabahai.net; mems resident in 529 localities; Nat. Sec. YOLANDA RODRÍGUEZ VILLAREAL.

The Press
DAILIES

Crítica Libre: Vía Fernández de Córdoba, Apdo B-4, Panamá 9A; tel. 261-0575; fax 230-0132; e-mail esotop@epasa.com; internet www.critica.com.pa; f. 1958; morning; Pres. RICARDO CHANIS CORREA; Dir JUAN PRITSIOLAS; circ. 40,000.

DIA a DIA: Vía Ricardo J. Alfaro, al lado de la USMA, Apdo B-4, Panamá 9A; tel. 230-7777; fax 230-2279; e-mail editor.diaadia@epasa.com; internet www.diaadia.com.pa; Gen. Man. ELIZABETH M. DE LAO.

La Estrella de Panamá: Calle Alejandro Duque, Vía Transístmica y Frangipani, Panamá; tel. 204-0000; fax 227-2394; e-mail laestre@estrelladepanama.com; internet www.estrelladepanama.com; f. 1853; morning; Dir GERARDO BERROA; circ. 10,000.

El Panamá América: Vía Ricardo J. Alfaro, al lado de la USMA, Apdo 0834-02787, Panamá 9A; tel. 230-7777; fax 230-7773; e-mail director@epasa.com; internet panamaamerica.com.pa; f. 1925; morning; independent; affiliated to Interamerican Press Asscn; Dir DUSTIN GUERRA; Editor JULIO RUILOBA; circ. 25,000.

La Prensa: Avda 12 de Octubre y Calle C, Hato Pintado, Pueblo Nuevo, Apdo 0819-05620, Panamá; tel. 222-1222; fax 221-7328; e-mail editor@prensa.com; internet www.prensa.com; f. 1980; morning; independent; Dir LOURDES DE OBALDÍA; Editor FERNÁN MOLINOS DELASWSKY; circ. 38,000.

El Siglo: Calle Alejandro Duque y Avda Frangipani, Apdo 0515-00662, Panamá; tel. 204-0982; fax 204-0974; e-mail digital@elsiglo.com; internet www.elsiglo.com; f. 1985; morning; Pres. EDUARDO ANTONIO QUIRÓS; Editor MAGALY MONTILLA; circ. 30,000.

PERIODICALS

FOB Colón Free Zone: Apdo 0819-06908, El Dorado, Panamá; tel. 225-6638; fax 225-0466; e-mail info@colonfreezone.com; internet www.colonfreezone.com; f. 1971; annual; bilingual trade directory; publ. by Focus Publications (Int.), SA; Editor ISRAEL ARGUEDAS; circ. 60,000.

Focus Panama: 742 Calle 2A, Perejil, Panamá; tel. 225-6638; fax 225-0466; e-mail focusint@cableonda.net; internet www.focuspublicationsint.com; f. 1970; 2 a year; publ. by Focus Publications; visitors' guide; separate English and Spanish edns; Dir KENNETH J. JONES; circ. 100,000.

Instituto Nacional de Estadística y Censo: Avda Balboa y Federico Boyd, Apdo 0816-01521, Panamá 5; tel. 510-4800; fax 510-4801; e-mail cie_dec@contraloria.gob.pa; internet www.contraloria.gob.pa/inec; f. 1941; publ. by the Contraloría General de la República; statistical survey in series according to subjects; Controller-Gen. GIOCONDA TORRES DE BIANCHINI; Dir of Statistics and Census DANIS P. CEDEÑO H.

Mi Diario, La Voz de Panamá: Avda 12 de Octubre y Calle C, Hato Pintado, Pueblo Nuevo, Apdo 0819-05620, Panamá; tel. 222-9000; fax 222-9090; e-mail midiario@midiario.com; internet www.midiario.com; f. 2003 by La Prensa (q.v.); Dir LORENZO ABREGO.

Revista Mujer: Avda Ricardo J. Alfaro, Apdo B4, Zona 9A, Panama; tel. 230-7777; fax 230-7773; e-mail luz.bonadies@epasa.com; internet mujer.com.pa; Editor LUZ MARIE BONADIES LECARO.

Revista SIETE: Vía Ricardo J. Alfaro, al lado de la USMA, Apdo B-4, Panamá 9A; tel. 230-7777; fax 230-1033; e-mail revista.siete@epasa.com; internet siete.panamaamerica.com.pa; weekly; Editor NAYLA G. MONTENEGRO.

El Visitante/ The Visitor: Calle 2, Perejil 742, Apdo 0819-06908, El Dorado, Panama; tel. 225-6638; fax 225-0466; e-mail focusint@cableonda.net; internet www.thevisitorpanama.com; weekly; bilingual; Editor KENNETH JONES.

PRESS ASSOCIATION

Sindicato de Periodistas de Panamá (SPP): Edif. 287, Avda Gorgas, Panamá; tel. 214-0163; fax 214-0164; e-mail sindiperpana@yahoo.com; internet sindicatodeperiodistasdepanama.org; f. 1949; Sec.-Gen. FILEMÓN MEDINA RAMOS.

Publishers

Editora Géminis, SA: Edif. Don Tomás, Planta Baja, Calle 7, Vista Hermosa, Apdo 0819-04188, El Dorado, Panamá; tel. 229-2972; fax 229-1010; e-mail info@editagerminis.com; internet www.editorageminis.com; f. 1985; dictionaries, general fiction, school texts; Dir-Gen. RAÚL ESQUIVEL.

Editora Panamá América, SA (EPASA): Avda Ricardo J. Alfaro, al lado de la USMA, Apdo 0834-02787, Panamá R; tel. 230-7777; fax 230-7773; e-mail gerente.general@epasa.com; internet www.epasa.com; Pres. RICARDO CHANIS CORREA; Gen. Man. LUIS STANZIOLA S.

Exedra Books: esq. de Vía España y Vía Brasil, diagonal a Galerias Obarrio, Apdo 0831-00125, Paitilla, Panamá; tel. 264-4252; fax 264-4266; e-mail info@exedrabooks.com; internet www.exedrabooks.com; general fiction and non-fiction; Dir-Gen. SHEILA DE TERÁN.

Focus Publications: Calle 2A 742, Perejil, Apdo 0819-06908, El Dorado, Panamá; tel. 225-6638; fax 225-0466; e-mail focusint@sinfo.net; internet www.focuspublicationsint.com; f. 1970; guides, trade directories, yearbooks and maps; Pres. KENNETH J. JONES.

Piggy Press, SA: Apdo 0413-00110, Boquete, Chiriquí; tel. 720-1072; e-mail info@piggypress.com; internet www.piggypress.com; f. 2001; multilingual children's literature; Pres. PAT ALVARADO.

Ruth Casa Editorial: Edif. Los Cristales, Of. 6, Calle 38 y Avda Cuba, Apdo 2235, Zona 9A, Panamá; e-mail ruthcasaeditorial@yahoo.com; internet www.ruthcasaeditorial.org; Pres. FRANÇOIS HOUTART.

Serapis Bey Editores, SA: Parque Lefevre, Calle W-2, Casa 46-B-21, Apdo 0834-01726, Panamá; tel. 302-0213; fax 302-0214; e-mail jorgecarrizo@serapisbey.com; internet www.serapisbey.com; f. 1989; spiritual literature; Gen. Man. JORGE A. CARRIZO.

SIJUSA (Sistemas Juridicos, SA): Edif. Bank Boston, 2°, Vía España y Calle Elvira Méndez, Panamá; tel. 223-2764; fax 223-2766; e-mail servicioalcliente@sijusa.com; internet www.sijusa.com; f. 1989; law and politics; Dir-Gen. JOSÉ ALEJANDRO ESPINO.

Susaeta Ediciones Panamá, SA: Apdo. 0819-08750, Panamá; tel. 220-0833; fax 220-4561; e-mail susaeta@susaetapanama.com; internet www.susaetapanama.net; f. 1982; children's literature; includes the imprints Ediesco, Nacho and Susaeta; Dir-Gen. MIRNA DE DÍAZ.

GOVERNMENT PUBLISHING HOUSE

Editorial Mariano Arosemena: Instituto Nacional de Cultura, Apdo 662, Panamá 1; tel. 501-4000; fax 211-4016; e-mail secretariageneral@inac.gob.pa; internet www.inac.gob.pa; f. 1974; division of National Institute of Culture; literature, history, social sciences, archaeology; Dir-Gen. MARIA EUGENIA HERRERA DE VICTORIA.

ASSOCIATION

Cámara Panameña del Libro: Edif. Tula, Of. 6C, Vía España, entrada de Vía Argentina, arriba del Blockbuster, Apdo 0823-04289, Panamá; tel. 390-4738; fax 390-4739; e-mail info@capali.com.pa; internet www.capali.com.pa; f. 1997; organizes international book fairs; 28 active mems, 3 honorary mems, 2 associate mems; Pres. RENÉE AVILA; Sec. MIRNA DE DÍAZ.

Broadcasting and Communications
REGULATORY AUTHORITY

Autoridad Nacional de los Servicios Públicos (ASEP): Edif. Office Park, Vía España, Apdo 0816-01235, Panamá 5; tel. 508-4500; fax 508-4600; e-mail adminweb@asep.gob.pa; internet www.asep

.gob.pa; f. 1996 as Ente Regulador de los Servicios Públicos; name changed as above in 2006; state regulator with responsibility for television, radio, telecommunications, water and electricity; Administrator-Gen. ZELMAR RODRÍGUEZ CRESPO; Exec. Dir ANTONIO TERCERO GONZÁLEZ.

TELECOMMUNICATIONS

Cable & Wireless Panamá, SA: Edif. Condominio, Torre B, Plaza Internacional, Vía España, Apdo 0834-00659, Panamá; e-mail cwp@cwpanama.com; internet www.cwpanama.com.pa; f. 1997; 49% govt-owned, 49% owned by Cable & Wireless Communications (CWC); Exec. Pres. and Gen. Man. JORGE NICOLAU; Pres. (CWC) PHIL BENTLEY.

Digicel: Edif. Digicel, Vía Transístimica, Panamá; tel. 306-0600; fax 300-0469; e-mail servicioalcliente.pa@digicelgroup.com; internet www.digicelpanama.com; f. 2001; Gen. Man. COLM DELVES; 11m. subscribers.

Galaxy Communications Corpn (ClaroCOM): Edif. Alegre, 4°, Calle 49B Oeste El Cangrejo, Bella Vista, Apdo 0832-2657, Panamá; tel. 200-5555; fax 263-3403; e-mail info@clarocom.com; internet www.clarocom.com; f. 2001; Chair. SETH REDLICH; CEO PEDRO CORDOVEZ.

Movistar: Edif. Magna, Area Bancaria, Calle 51 Este y Manuel M. Icaza, Panamá; tel. 265-0955; internet www.movistar.com.pa; f. 1996 as BellSouth Panamá, SA; acquired by Telefónica Móviles, SA (Spain) in 2004; name changed as above in 2005; mobile telephone services; Gen. Man. CLAUDIO HIDALGO.

BROADCASTING

Radio

La Mega 98.3 FM: Casa 35, Calle 50 y 77 San Francisco, Panamá; tel. 270-3242; fax 226-1021; e-mail ventas@lamegapanama.com; internet www.lamegapanama.com; f. 2000.

Omega Stereo: Calle G, El Cangrejo 3, Panamá; e-mail omegaste@omegastereo.com; internet www.omegastereo.com; f. 1981; Pres. GUILLERMO ANTONIO ADAMES.

RPC Radio: Avda 12 de Octubre, Apdo 0827-00116, Panamá; tel. 390-6700; e-mail mtalessandria@medcom.com.pa; internet www.rpcradio.com; f. 1949; broadcasts news, sports and commentary; Man. MARÍA TERESA ALESSANDRÍA.

SuperQ: Edif. Dominó, 1°, Of. 9, Vía España, Apdo 0816-03034, Panamá; tel. 263-5298; fax 263-0362; e-mail info@superqpanama.com; internet www.superqpanama.net; f. 1984; Pres. G. ARIS DE ICAZA.

WAO 97.5: Edif. Plaza 50, 2°, Calle 50 y Vía Brasil, Panamá; tel. 223-8348; fax 223-8351; e-mail info@wao975.fm; internet www.wao975.fm; Gen. Man. ROGELIO CAMPOS.

Television

Fundación para la Educación en la Televisión—FETV (Canal 5): Vía Ricardo J. Alfaro, Apdo 6-7295, El Dorado, Panamá; tel. 230-8000; fax 230-1955; e-mail comentarios@fetv.org; internet www.fetv.org; f. 1992; Pres. FÁTIMA CUPAS DE MORENO; Gen. Man. FERNANDO TOVAR.

Medcom Panamá, SA (RPC): Avda 12 de Octubre, Hato Pintado, Apdo 0827-00116, Panamá 8; tel. 390-6700; fax 390-6895; e-mail murrutia@medcom.com.pa; internet www.rpctv.com; f. 1998 by merger of RPC Televisión (Canal 4) and Telemetro (Canal 13); commercial; also owns Cable Onda 90 and RPC Radio; CEO NICOLÁS GONZÁLEZ-REVILLA.

Sistema Estatal de Radio y Televisión (Canal 11) (SERTV): Curundu, diagonal al Ministerio de Obras Públicas, Apdo 0843-0256, Panamá; tel. 507-1500; e-mail aportal@sertv.gob.pa; internet www.sertv.gob.pa; f. 1978 as Radio y Televisión Educativa; restructured and assumed present name in 2005; educational and cultural; Dir-Gen. LEO ALVARADO.

Televisora Nacional—TVN (Canal 2): Edif. TVN-TV–MAX, Avda Ricardo J. Alfaro, Apdo 0819-07129, Panamá; tel. 294-6400; fax 236-2987; e-mail tvn@tvn-2.com; internet www.tvn-2.com; f. 1962; Dir JAIME ALBERTO ARIAS.

Broadcasting Association

Asociación Panameña de Radiodifusión: Apdo 7387, Estafeta de Paitilla, Panamá; tel. 263-5252; fax 226-4396; Pres. PEDRO SOLIS.

Finance

(cap. = capital; res = reserves; dep. = deposits; m. = million; br.(s) = branch(es); amounts in balboas, unless otherwise stated)

BANKING

Superintendencia de Bancos (Banking Superintendency): Torre HSBC, 18°, Avda Samuel Lewis, Apdo 0832-2397, Panamá 1; tel. 506-7800; fax 506-7706; e-mail superbancos@superbancos.gob.pa; internet www.superbancos.gob.pa; f. 1970 as Comisión Bancaria Nacional; superseded by Superintendencia de Bancos in 1998 with enhanced powers; licenses and controls banking activities within and from Panamanian territory; Sec.-Gen. GUSTAVO ADOLFO VILLA; Supt YANELA YANISSELLY R (acting).

National Bank

Banco Nacional de Panamá: Vía España y Calle 55, Apdo 5220, Panamá 5; tel. 505-2000; fax 505-0211; e-mail atencionclientes@banconal.com.pa; internet www.banconal.com.pa; f. 1904; govt-owned; cap. 500m., res 11.8m., dep. 5,461.3m. (Dec. 2009); Pres. CARLOS RICARDO HENRÍQUEZ LÓPEZ; Gen. Man. ROLANDO DE LEÓN; 66 brs.

Savings Bank

Caja de Ahorros: Vía España y Calle Thays de Pons, Apdo 1740, Panamá 1; tel. 205-1000; fax 269-3674; e-mail atencionalcliente@cajadeahorros.com.pa; internet www.cajadeahorros.com.pa; f. 1934; govt-owned; cap. 150.7m., res 47.9m., dep. 170.9m. (Dec. 2006); Pres. RICCARDO FRANCOLINI AROSEMENA; Gen. Man. MARIO ROJAS; 42 brs.

Domestic Private Banks

Banco General, SA: Calle Aquilino de la Guardia, Apdo 0816-00843, Panamá 5; tel. 227-3200; fax 265-0210; e-mail info@bgeneral.com; internet www.bgeneral.com; f. 1955; purchased Banco Comercial de Panamá (BANCOMER) in 2000; cap. 550m., res 44.7m., dep. 7,227m. (Dec. 2011); Chair. and CEO FEDERICO HUMBERT; Exec. Vice-Pres. and Gen. Man. RAÚL ALEMÁN Z.; 63 brs.

Banco Panameño de la Vivienda (BANVIVIENDA): Edif. Grupo Mundial, Avda La Rotonda y Blvd Costa del Este, Bella Vista, Apdo 0816-03366, Panamá 5; tel. 300-4700; fax 300-7000; e-mail bpvger@pty.com; internet www.banvivienda.com; f. 1981; cap. 60.2m., res 56m., dep. 853.7m. (Dec. 2012); Pres. FERNANDO LEWIS NAVARRO; Gen. Man. JUAN RICARDO DE DIANOUS; 3 brs.

Banco Pichincha Panamá: Edif. Parque Urraca, entre Avda Federico Boyd y Avda Balboa, Apdo 0832-01382, Panamá; tel. 297-4500; fax 264-6129; e-mail banco@pichinchapanama.com; internet www.pichinchapanama.com; f. 2006; Pres. FIDEL DARIO EGAS GRIJALVA; Man. JUAN CARLOS CORDOVEZ.

Banco Universal: Torre Banco Universal, Calle B Norte y Avda 1, Apdo 0426-00564, David, Chiriquí; tel. 777-9400; fax 777-9432; e-mail cosorio@bancouniversal.com; internet www.bancouniversal.com; f. 1970; present name adopted 1994; cap. 15m., res 2.4m., dep. 390.5m. (Dec. 2013); Pres. JOSÉ ISAAC VIRZI LÓPEZ; Gen. Man. CARLOS RAÚL BARRIOS ICAZA; 10 brs.

Global Bank Corporation: Torre Global Bank, Calle 50, Apdo 0831-01843, Paitilla, Panamá; tel. 206-2000; fax 206-2007; e-mail global@pan.gbm.net; internet www.globalbank.com.pa; f. 1994; cap. 78.2m., res 41.9m., dep 2,886.6m. (June 2013); Pres. LAWRENCE MADURO; Gen. Man. JORGE VALLARINO STRUNZ; 31 brs.

Multibank: Edif. Prosperidad, planta baja, Vía España 127, Apdo 8210, Panamá 7; tel. 294-3500; fax 264-4014; e-mail banco@grupomulticredit.com; internet www.multibank.com.pa; f. 1990 as Multi Credit Bank; current name adopted 2008; cap. 240.4m., res −40.3m., dep. 2,009.6m. (Dec. 2013); Pres. ALBERTO S. BTESH; CEO ISAAC BTESH; 29 brs.

Towerbank International Inc: Edif. Tower Plaza, Calle 50 y Beatriz M. de Cabal, Apdo 0819-06769, Panamá; tel. 269-6900; fax 269-6800; e-mail towerbank@towerbank.com; internet www.towerbank.com; f. 1971; cap. 78.9m., res −2.4m., dep. 770.9m. (Dec. 2013); Pres. FRED KARDONSKI; Gen. Man. JOSÉ CAMPA; 4 brs.

Development Banks

Banco de Desarrollo Agropecuario: Avda de Los Mártires, Calle L, Panamá; tel. 512-9000; e-mail credito@bda.gob.pa; internet www.bda.gob.pa; f. 1941 as Banco Agropecuario e Industrial, present name adopted 1973; rural devt bank, state-run.

Banco Hipotecario Nacional: Panamá; tel. 502-0001; e-mail acliente@bhn.gob.pa; internet www.bhn.gob.pa; f. 1973; state-run; Gen. Man. RAMÓN HERNÁNDEZ (designate); 12 brs.

Foreign Banks

Principal Foreign Banks with General Licence

Balboa Bank & Trust Corpn: Torre Generali, 19°, Avda Samuel Lewis y Calle 50 y Calle Beatriz María Cabal, Urb. Obarrio, Panamá; tel. 208-7300; fax 263-4165; e-mail customerservice@ balboabanktrust.com; internet www.balboabanktrust.com; f. 2003 as Stanford Bank (Panamá), SA; cap. 36.6m., res −2.9m., dep. 393.2m. (Dec. 2013); taken over by the Superintendencia de Bancos de Panamá in 2009; renamed in 2010; Pres. RAMÓN FERNÁNDEZ QUIJANO.

Banco Aliado, SA: Calle 50 y 56, Urb. Obarrio, 0831-02109 Paitilla, Panamá; tel. 302-1555; fax 302-1556; e-mail bkaliado@bancoaliado .com; internet www.bancoaliado.com; f. 1992; cap. 100m., res −0.4m., dep. 1,468.6m. (June 2013); Pres. MOISÉS CHREIM; Gen. Man. ALEXIS A. ARJONA.

Banco BAC de Panamá, SA (Spain): Torre BBVA, Avda Balboa, Calles 42 y 43, Apdo 8673, Panamá 5; tel. 227-2282; fax 227-3663; e-mail informacion@pa.bac.net; internet www.bbvapanama.com; f. 1982 as Banco Bilbao Vizcaya Argentaria (Panama), name changed 2013; owned by Leasing Bogota, SA, Panamá; cap. 28.7m., res 88.5m., dep. 1,633.3m. (Dec. 2012); Chair. ERNESTO CASTEGNARO; Gen. Man. RODOLFO TABASH; 19 brs.

Banco Davivienda (Panamá), SA (Colombia): Avda Manuel María Icaza y Calle 52E, No 18, Campo Alegre, Apdo 0834-00384, Panamá 9A; tel. 366-6500; fax 263-6115; e-mail info@davivienda.com .pa; internet www.davivienda.com.pa; f. 1966 as Banco Cafetero; name changed as Bancafe in 1995; present name adopted in 2012; cap. 29.1m., res 0.9m., dep. 1,055.7m. (Dec. 2013); Pres. EFRAÍN FORERO FONSECO; Gen. Man. FRANCISCO GÓNZALEZ RODRÍGUEZ; 2 brs.

Banco Delta, SA (BMF): Edif. Torre Delta, planta baja, Vía España 122 y Calle Elvira Méndez, Apdo 0816-07831, Panamá; tel. 340-0000; fax 340-0076; e-mail mguerra@bandelta.com; internet www .bandelta.com; f. 2006; cap. 18.6m., res −0.1m., dep. 125m. (June 2013); Pres. ARTURO MÜLLER; Gen. Man. GINA DE SÁENZ; 4 brs.

Banco Internacional de Costa Rica, SA: Casa Matriz, Calle Manuel M. Icaza 25, Apdo 0816-07810, Panamá 1; tel. 208-9500; fax 208-9581; e-mail rmonge@bicsa.com; internet www.bicsapan .com; f. 1976; cap. 100.3m., res 0.2m., dep. 804m. (Dec. 2011); Gen. Man. FEDERICO CARRILLO ZURCHER.

Banco Latinoamericano de Comercio Exterior SA (BLADEX) (Multinational): Torre V, Business Park, Avda La Rotonda, Urb. Costa del Este, Panamá; tel. 210-8500; fax 269-6333; e-mail webmaster@bladex.com; internet www.blx.com; f. 1979 as Banco Latinoamericano de Exportaciones; name changed as above in 2009; groups together 254 Latin American commercial and central banks, 22 international banks and some 3,000 New York Stock Exchange shareholders; cap. US $279.9m., res $119.2m., dep. $2,361.3m. (Dec. 2013); CEO RUBENS V. AMARAL, Jr.

Banistmo, SA: Plaza HSBC, Calle Aquilino de la Guardia, Urb. Marbella, Panamá; tel. 263-5855; fax 263-6009; e-mail panama_contacto@banistmo.com; internet www.banistmo.com; cap. US $1,293.7m., dep. $11,137.7m. (Dec. 2009); acquired the Panama operations of Chase Manhattan Bank in 2000 and Primer Banco del Istmo (Banistmo) in 2006; bought by Bancolombia in 2013; CEO AIMEE SENTMAT DE GRIMALDO; 62 brs.

Citibank Panamá (USA): Edif. Banco Cuscatlán, Calle Aquilino de la Guardia, Apdo 555, Panamá 9A; tel. 208-8600; fax 263-5200; internet www.citibank.com.pa; f. 1904; cap. 124.7m., res 0.2m., dep. 529.9m. (Dec. 2013); Gen. Man. MARCELO GORRINI; 14 brs.

Credicorp Bank, SA: Edif. Plaza Credicorp Bank, Nicanor de Obarrio, Calle 50, Apdo 833-0125, Panamá; tel. 210-1111; fax 210-0071; internet www.credicorpbank.com; f. 1992; cap. 44m., res 6.3m., dep. 1,087.2m. (June 2013); Pres. RAYMOND HARARI; Gen. Man. MAX J. HARARI; 26 brs.

Helm Bank (Panama), SA: Edif. World Trade Center, 19°, Calle 53, Urb. Marbella, Apdo 0819-07070, Panamá; tel. 265-2820; fax 214-9715; e-mail servicioalcliente@helmpanama.com; internet www .helmpanama.com; f. as Banco de Crédito (Panamá) SA, renamed in 2002 as Banco de Crédito Helm Financial Sevices (Panama), and as above in 2009; owned by Helm Bank SA (Colombia); cap. US $65.9m., res US $0.7m., dep. US $937.5m. (Dec. 2013); Gen. Man. CARLOS HUMBERTO ROJAS M.

Scotiabank (Canada): Avda Federico Boyd, esq. Calle 51, Apdo 0816-01999, Panamá 5; tel. 208-7700; fax 208-7702; e-mail paasesorenlineapanama@pa.scotiabank.com; internet www .scotiabank.com/pa; f. 1974; Vice-Pres. and Gen. Man. ROBERT WILLIAMS; 12 brs.

Principal Foreign Banks with International Licence

Austrobank Overseas (Panamá), SA: Edif. MMG, planta baja, Calle 53, Este Marbella, Apdo 0819-07030, El Dorado, Panamá 6; tel. 223-5105; fax 264-6918; e-mail gerencia@austrobank.com; internet www.austrobank.com; f. 1995; Gen. Man. JOSÉ ENRIQUE CÓRDOVA.

Banco de la Nación Argentina: Edif. World Trade Center 501, Calle 53, Urb. Marbella, Panamá; tel. 269-4666; fax 269-6719; e-mail bnapanama@bna.com.pa; internet www.bna.com.ar; f. 1977; Pres. JUAN CARLOS FABREGA; Gen. Man. RUBÉN DARÍO NOCERA.

Banco de Occidente (Panama), SA: Edif. American International, Calle 50 y Aquilino de la Guardia, Apdo 6-7430, El Dorado, Panamá; tel. 263-8144; fax 269-3261; internet www.bancoccidente .com.pa; f. 1982; cap. US $11.8m., res $12.2m., dep. $751.5m. (Dec. 2012); Pres. EFRAÍN OTERO ALVAREZ; Gen. Man. OSCAR LUNA GORDILLO.

Banco del Pacífico (Panama), SA: Calle Aquilino de la Guardia y Calle 52, esq. Edif. Banco del Pacifico, Apdo 0819-07070, El Dorado, Panamá; tel. 263-5373; fax 263-7481; e-mail bpacificopanama@ pacifico.fin.ec; internet www.bancodelpacifico.com.pa; f. 1980; cap. 11.3m., res −0.2m., dep. 150.4m. (Dec. 2010); Pres. JULIO C. CONTRERAS, III.

Bancolombia (Panama), SA: Edif. Bancolombia, Plaza Marbella, Calle Aquilino de la Guardia y Calle 47, Apdo 0816-03320, Panamá; tel. 263-6955; fax 269-1138; e-mail bancolombiapanama@allus.com; internet www.bancolombiapanama.com; f. 1973; current name adopted in 1999; cap. 14m., res 638.8m., dep. 6,263m. (Dec. 2013); Pres. CARLOS RAÚL YEPES JIMÉNEZ; Gen. Man. JUAN GUILLERMO CASTRILLON SIERRA.

FPB Bank Inc: Edif. Banco Continental, Torre C, 16°, Of. A, Calle 50 y Aquilino de la Guardia, Panamá; tel. 210-6600; fax 210-6649; internet www.fpbbank.com; f. 2005; Pres. EDUARDO ROSA PINHEIRO; Gen. Man. JOSÉ APARECIDO PAULUCCI.

Popular Bank Ltd Inc: Edif. Torre Banco General, Calle 47E y Avda Aquilini de la Guardia, Marbella, Apdo 0816-00265, Panamá; tel. 269-4166; fax 269-1309; e-mail contactenos@popularbank.com .pa; internet www.popularbank.com.pa; f. 1983 as Banco Popular Dominicano (Panama), SA; current name adopted in 2003; cap. 42.4m., res 1.3m., dep. 751.2m. (Dec. 2013); Pres. ALEJANDRO E. SANTELISES; Gen. Man. GIANNI VERSARI.

Banking Association

Asociación Bancaria de Panamá (ABP): Torre Hong Kong Bank, 15°, Avda Samuel Lewis, Apdo 4554, Panamá 5; tel. 263-7044; fax 223-5800; e-mail abp@orbi.net; internet www.asociacionbancaria .com; f. 1962; 79 mems; Pres. MOISÉS D. COHEN; Exec. Vice-Pres. MARIO DE DIEGO, Jr.

STOCK EXCHANGE

Bolsa de Valores de Panamá: Edif. Bolsa de Valores de Panamá, Avda Federico Boyd y Calle 49, Apdo 823-00963, Panamá; tel. 269-1966; fax 269-2457; e-mail bvp@panabolsa.com; internet www .panabolsa.com; f. 1960; Pres. FELIPE E. CHAPMAN; Gen. Man. ROBERTO BRENES PÉREZ.

INSURANCE

Acerta, Cía de Seguros: Avda Ricardo Arango y Calle Santa Ana, Urb. Obarrio, Apdo 0823-04175, Panamá; tel. 307-3000; fax 307-3001; e-mail info@acertaseguros.com; internet www.acertaseguros .com; Pres. JUAN CARLOS FÁBREGA.

Arca Internacional de Reaseguros, SA: Edif. Bolsa de Valores, 1°, Avda Federico Boyd, Frente al Restaurante Rinos, Panamá; tel. 300-2858; fax 300-2859; f. 1996; Gen. Man. CARLOS G. DE LA LASTRA.

Aseguradora Ancón, SA: Avda Samuel Lewis y Calle 54, Urb. Obarrio, Panamá; tel. 210-8700; fax 210-8790; e-mail info@ asegurancon.com; internet www.asegurancon.com; f. 1992; Pres. TOBIAS CARRERO NACAR; Exec. Vice-Pres. WILSON ESPINOZA.

ASSA Cía de Seguros, SA: Edif. ASSA, Avda Nicanor de Obarrio (Calle 50), Apdo 0816-01622, Panamá 5; tel. 300-2772; fax 300-2729; e-mail servicioalcliente@assanet.com; internet www.assanet.com; f. 1973; Pres. STANLEY MOTTA; Gen. Man. EDUARDO FÁBREGA ALEMÁN.

Assicurazioni Generali, Spa: Torre Generali, Avda Samuel Lewis y Calle 54, Urb. Obarrio, Apdo 0816-02206, 507 Panamá; tel. 360-0500; fax 360-0548; e-mail mercadeo@generali.com.pa; internet www.generali.com.pa; f. 1977; Gen. Man. GABRIEL R. DE OBARRIO, III.

Cía Interoceánica de Seguros, SA: Plaza Marbella, Frente Banco HSBC, Calle Aquilino de la Guardia, Panamá; tel. 205-0700; fax 264-7668; e-mail info@interoceanica.com; internet www.interoceanica .com; f. 1978; Gen. Man. SALVADOR MORALES BACA.

Empresa General de Seguros, SA: Edif. Plaza 2000, Calles 50 y 53, 1° y 2°, Panamá; tel. 303-2222; fax 303-2223; e-mail scliente-gseguros@egs.com.pa; internet www.asecomer.com; f. 1987; Pres. FEDERICO HUMBERT, Jr.

Internacional de Seguros, SA: Edif. Plaza Credicorp Bank, 17°, Avda Nicanor de Obarrio, Calle 50, Panamá; tel. 227-4000; fax 210-

9100; e-mail conase@conase.net; internet www.iseguros.com; f. 1910; Pres. ROY ICAZA.

Mitsui Sumitomo Insurance Co Ltd: Of. 701, 7°, Plaza Credicorp Bank Panamá, Panamá; tel. 210-0133; fax 210-0122; internet www .msilm.com; f. 1979; Chair. TOSHIAKI EGASHIRA.

Panama Mapfré: Edif. MAPFRE, 1°, Costa del Este, Panamá; tel. 378-5900; fax 378-5916; e-mail info@mapfre.com.pa; internet www .mapfre.com.pa; f. 1937; general; Gen. Man. DINO MON.

Provincial Re Panamá, SA: P.H. Office, 13°, Calle 58 y Calle 50, Obarrio Corregimiento de Bella Vista, Panamá; tel. 397-6940; fax 260-5055; internet www.provincialre.com; f. 1984; Pres. HERNÁN REBOLLEDO C.

QBE del Istmo Cía de Reaseguros, Inc: Costa del Este, Avda Paseo del Mar y Calle Vista del Pacífico, Apdo 51, Panamá; tel. 306-2200; fax 306-2270; internet www.istmore.com; f. 1979; Pres. and CEO RAMÓN E. FERNÁNDEZ.

La Seguridad de Panamá, Cía de Seguros, SA: Edif. American International, Calle 50, esq. Aquilino de la Guardia, Apdo 5306, Panamá 5; tel. 263-6700; f. 1986; Gen. Man. MARIELA OSORIO.

Seguros Sura: Calle Aquilino De La Guardia, entre calle 47 y 48, Plaza Marbella, Apdo 0831-0784, Paitilla, Panamá; tel. 205-0700; e-mail atencionalasegurado@sura.com.pa; internet www.sura.com .pa; Pres. DAVID BOJANINI GARCÍA.

Trade and Industry

Colón Free Zone (CFZ): Avda Roosevelt, Apdo 1118, Colón; tel. 445-1033; fax 445-2165; e-mail zonalibre@zolicol.org; internet www .zolicol.gob.pa; f. 1948 to manufacture, import, handle and re-export all types of merchandise; some 2,500 companies active in 2012, employing 27,347 people; the total area of the CFZ was 450 ha; Gen. Man. SURSE PIERPOINT (designate).

GOVERNMENT AGENCIES

Agencia Panamá-Pacífico (APP): Edif. 2, Blvd Panamá Pacífico con Avda Suliber, Veracruz, Arraiján; tel. 504-2500; fax 504-2566; internet www.app.gob.pa; f. 2004; promotes business in Panama's Pacific Special Economic Area; Administrator LEO GONZÁLEZ (designate).

Autoridad de la Micro, Pequeña y Mediana Empresa: Calle Maritza Alabarca, Edif. 1005 y 1010, Clayton, Panamá; tel. 500-5602; e-mail atencionalcliente@ampyme.gob.pa; internet www.ampyme .gob.pa; f. 2000; promotes the devt of micro-, small and medium-sized enterprises; Dir-Gen. ADA ROMERO.

Autoridad Nacional del Ambiente: Calle Miguel Mejía Dutary, Panamá; tel. 500-0898; e-mail mheras@anam.gob.pa; internet www .anam.gob.pa; environmental agency; Gen. Man. MIREI ENDARA DE HERAS.

CHAMBERS OF COMMERCE

American Chamber of Commerce and Industry of Panama: POB 0843-00152, Panamá; tel. 301-3881; fax 301-3882; e-mail amcham@panamcham.com; internet www.panamcham.com; Pres. DAVID CARIUS; Exec. Dir MAURICE BELANGER.

Cámara de Comercio, Industrias y Agricultura de Panamá: Avda Cuba y Ecuador 33A, Apdo 74, Panamá 1; tel. 207-3440; fax 207-3422; e-mail infocciap@cciap.com; internet www.panacamara.com; f. 1915; Pres. FEDERICO HUMBERT ARIAS; Exec. Dir RAFAEL ZUÑIGA BRID; 1,300 mems.

Cámara Oficial Española de Comercio: Avda Balboa, Edif. Banco BBVA, Torre Menor, 7°, Apdo 1857, Panamá 1; tel. 225-1487; fax 225-6608; e-mail caespan@cwpanama.net; internet www .caespan.com.pa; Pres. ALEJANDRO PÉREZ RODRÍGUEZ; Exec. Dir MARÍA JESÚS ALONSO ROS.

INDUSTRIAL AND TRADE ASSOCIATIONS

Asociación Panameña de Exportadores (APEX): Edif. Ricardo Galindo Quelquejeu, Avda Ricardo J. Alfaro, Urb. Sara Sotillo, Panamá; tel. 230-0169; e-mail apex@cableonda.net; internet www .apexpanama.org; f. 1971; export asscn; Pres. JUAN PLANELLS; Sec. JAIME ORTIZ.

Cámara Panameña de la Construcción: Calle Aquilino de la Guardia y Calle 52, Área Bancaria, diagonal al Hotel Ejecutivo, Apdo 0816-02350, Panamá 5; tel. 265-2500; fax 265-2571; e-mail informacion@capac.org; internet www.capac.org; represents interests of construction sector; Pres. RODERICK MCGOWEN.

Sindicato de Industriales de Panamá: Vía Ricardo J. Alfaro, Entrada Urb. Sara Sotillo, Apdo 6-4798, Estafeta El Dorado, Panamá; tel. 230-0169; fax 230-0805; e-mail sip@cableonda.net; internet www.industriales.org; f. 1945; represents and promotes activities of industrial sector; Pres. JUAN F. KIENER; Sec.-Gen. MÁXIMO GALLARDO.

EMPLOYERS' ORGANIZATIONS

Asociación Panameña de Ejecutivos de Empresas (APEDE): Avda Justo Arosemena, Calle 31, frente a la Piscina Adán Gordón, Apdo 0816-06785, Panamá; tel. 204-1500; fax 204-1510; e-mail apede@apede.org; internet www.apede.org; f. 1958; Pres. FERNANDO ARAMBURÚ PORRAS.

Consejo Nacional de la Empresa Privada (CONEP): Avda Morgan, Balboa, Ancón, Casa 302A–B, Zona 1, Apdo 0816-07197, Panamá 1; tel. 211-2672; fax 211-2694; e-mail conep1@cwpanama .net; internet www.conep.org.pa; Pres. ELISA SUÁREZA DE GÓMEZ.

MAJOR COMPANIES

Beverages and Tobacco

Cervecería Nacional, SA: Costa del Este, Business Park, Torre Oeste, 2°, El Dorado, Apdo 6-1393, Panamá 1; tel. 279-5800; fax 279-5861; e-mail cerveceria.nacional@pa.sabmiller.com; internet www .cerveceria-nacional.com; f. 1909; subsidiary of Grupo SABMiller; production and distribution of beverages, incl. beer and soft drinks; Pres. CHRIS RITCHIE; 400 employees.

Coca-Cola FEMSA, SA: Parque Industrial San Cristóbal, Calle Santa Rosa, Panamá 9A; tel. 236-0700; fax 260-3504; e-mail krelations@kof.com.mx; internet www.coca-colafemsa.com; f. 1913; 53.7% owned by Fomento Económico Mexicano, SA de CV (FEMSA), 31.6% by The Coca-Cola Company, and 14.7% by the public; bottlers of soft drinks; CEO JOHN ANTHONY SANTAMARÍA OTAZUA; 500 employees.

Philip Morris Panama: Edif. Fabrica, Vía José Agustín Arango, Calle 117 Oeste, Panamá; tel. 217-9400; fax 217-9446; e-mail haydee .mudarra@pmintl.com; internet www.pmi.com; f. 1955 as Tabacalera Nacional; bought by Philip Morris in 1992 and adopted current name in 2007; manufacture of cigarettes; Pres., Latin America and Canada Region JAMES R. MORTENSEN; CEO ANDRÉ CALANTZOPOULOS; 33 employees.

Varela Hermanos, SA: Vía Tocumen La Pulida, Calle La Cantera, Apdo 0819-07757, Panamá; tel. 377-4000; fax 377-4069; e-mail varela@varehelahermanos.com; internet www.varelahermanos .com; f. 1950; distillation and bottling of liquors; Dir JOSÉ LUIS VARELA; Gen. Man. MANUEL SOSSA; 300 employees.

Food Products

Cía Agrícola Industrial, SA (CAISA): Calle 7a Final, Nuevo Arraiján, Panamá; tel. 257-1615; fax 257-0403; internet www.caisa .com.pa; f. 1954; pork producers; Owner AGUSTÍN ARANGO NAVARRO.

Cía Azucarera La Estrella, SA: Apdo 0201-000-49, Aguadulce, Prov. de Coclé; tel. 236-1150; fax 236-1079; e-mail info@grupocalesa .com; internet www.grupocalesa.com; f. 1949; sugar mill and refinery; part of Grupo Calesa; Pres. BERTA GARCÍA DE PAREDES CHIARI; Gen. Man. HANS H. HAMMERSCHLAG; 1,069 employees.

Grupo Calesa (Cía Azucarera de la Estrella, SA): Apdo 0201-000-49, Aguadulce, Coclé; tel. 236-1150; fax 236-1079; e-mail info@ grupocalesa.com; internet www.calesa.com.pa; f. 1918; sugar producer; Exec. Vice-Pres. HANS H. HAMMERSCHLAG; 3,200 employees.

Industrias Lácteas, SA: Vía Simón Bolívar, Panamá 4362, Panamá 5; tel. 304-4700; fax 304-4866; e-mail info@estrellaazul.com.pa; internet www.estrellaazul.net; f. 1956; dairy products; Gen. Man. FRANK TEDMAN; 1,300 employees.

Nestlé Panamá, SA: Calle 69, 74D, Urb. La Loma, Apdo 0834-00368, Panamá 9A; tel. 229-1333; fax 229-1982; e-mail servicios .consumidor@pa.nestle.com; internet www.nestle-centroamerica .com; f. 1937; subsidiary of Nestlé Co, SA (Switzerland); manufacture and wholesale of food products; Pres. (Nestlé Central America) LEO LEIMAN; 760 employees.

Productos Alimenticios Pascual, SA: Avda José Agustín Arango, Apdo 8422, Panamá 7; tel. 217-2133; fax 233-2971; e-mail ventaspascual@epa.com.pa; internet www.pascual.com.pa; f. 1946; acquired by Casa Luker de Colombia in 2004; food and food-processing; Pres. JUAN CARLOS JARAMILLO; Dir CAMILO RESTREPO ROMERO; 1800 employees.

Textile Manufactures

Promedias, SA: 111 Pueblo Nuevo, Apdo 6-2841, Panamá; tel. 261-3649; fax 261-5548; e-mail ventas@promedias.com.pa; internet www .promedias.com.pa; mfrs of socks and tights.

Tejidos y Confecciones, SA: Edif. Durex Carrasquilla, Calle 2A, Apdo 0834-02775, Panamá; tel. 209-8888; fax 209-8889; e-mail sales@teyco.com; internet www.teyco.com; f. 1964; part of Attie Group; mfrs of men's and children's clothing; Pres. RAMY ATTIE; 500 employees.

Miscellaneous

Aceti-Oxigeno, SA: Boca La Caja, Avda Principal, Paitilla, Panamá; tel. 270-1977; fax 226-4789; e-mail gerencia@acetioxigeno.com.pa; internet acetioxigeno.com.pa; producer and importer of clinical and industrial gases; Man. ROGELIO SALADO ALBA.

BASF Construction Systems Panamá: Edif. TCC 2, Antigua Base Howard, Avda Perimetral Norte, Panama Pacífico, Panamá; tel. 301-0970; e-mail marbella.escobar@basf.com; internet www.centroamerica.basf-cc.com; owned by BASF, AG (Germany); chemicals; Man. MARBELLA ESCOBAR.

Cemento Panamá, SA: Edif. Cemento Panamá, Calle Jorge Zarak Las Sabanas 2, Apdo 1755, Panamá 1; tel. 366-1690; fax 366-1682; e-mail contactenos@cementopanama.com; internet www.cementopanama.com; f. 1943; mfrs of portland cement; acquired by Holcim (Switzerland) and Argos (Colombia); Gen. Man. ENRIQUE TOMÁS OLARTE; 400 employees.

Cía Atlas, SA: Edif. 40, Calle 16½, Apdo 6-1092, El Dorado, Panamá; tel. 236-0066; fax 236-0044; e-mail info@ciatlas.com; internet www.atlastore.com; f. 1949; holding co with interests in the wholesale manufacture, import and distribution of stationery; Gen. Man. ROBERTO C. HENRÍQUEZ; 110 employees.

Deloitte & Touche (Deloitte LATCO): Edif. Torre Banco Panamá, 10–12°, Avda Boulevard y La Rotonda, Apdo 0816-01558, Panamá; tel. 303-4100; fax 269-2386; e-mail infopanama@deloitte.com; internet www.deloitte.com; accountancy and management consultancy; Chair. CÉSAR CHENG VARGAS; Man. Dir FERNANDO ESPINO.

Excel Automotriz: Sucursal Transístmica, Calle Harry Eno, Panamá; tel. 366-6800; internet www.excelautomotriz.com/pa; known as Poma Automotriz until 2010; part of the Grupo DIDEA; distributor of cars and car parts; Country Man. RICARDO CUELLAR.

Grupo Corcione: Avda Principal, Green Plaza-Planta Baja, Costa el Este, Panamá; tel. 215-0011; fax 269-6057; e-mail ventas@grupocorcione.com; internet www.grupocorcione.com; f. 1992; construction contractors; Pres. NICOLÁS CORCIONE.

KPMG: Torre KPMG, Calle 50, No 54, Apdo 0816-01089, Panamá 5; tel. 208-0700; fax 215-7624; e-mail pa-fminformation@kpmg.com.pa; internet www.kpmg.com.pa; f. 1958; accountancy and management consultancy; CEO CARLOS KARAMAÑITES.

Lindo y Maduro, SA: Apdo 0816-01083, Panamá 5; tel. 301-0100; fax 301-0099; e-mail linduro@linduro.com; mfrs and distributors of non-durable goods and perfumery; Dir JUAN CARLOS; Man. KARINA JAÉN; 60 employees.

Melo y Cía, SA: Apdo 333, Panamá 1; tel. 323-6900; fax 224-2311; e-mail grupomelo@grupomelo.com; internet www.grupomelo.com.pa; vendors of veterinary, agricultural and agrochemical products, building materials, and household goods; Pres. ARTURO DONALDO MELO S.; Gen. Man. FEDERICO MELO K.; 400 employees.

Petroterminal de Panamá, SA: World Trade Center Bldg, 9°, Marbella, Apdo 0832-0920, Panamá; tel. 263-7777; fax 263-9949; e-mail info@petroterminal.com; internet www.petroterminal.com; f. 1977; petroleum and gasfield services and petroleum storage facilities; Dir-Gen. LUIS ROQUEBERT; 80 employees.

H. Tzanetatos Inc: Casa Matriz, Vía Tocumen; tel. 220-1977; fax 220-5122; e-mail grupotza@tzanetatos.com; internet www.htzanetatos.com; f. 1954; general wholesaler; Gen. Man. ALBERTO PAZ RODRÍGUEZ; 400 employees.

UTILITIES

Regulatory Authority

Autoridad Nacional de los Servicios Públicos: see Broadcasting and Communications—Regulatory Authority.

Electricity

AES Panamá: Torre Banco Continental, 25°, Calle 50 y Aquilino de la Guardia, CP 0816-01990, Panamá; tel. 206-2600; fax 206-2645; e-mail aespanama@aes.com; internet www.aespanama.com; f. 1998 upon acquisition by AES Corpn of 49% interest in Empresa de Generación Electrica Bayano and Empresa de Generación Electrica Chiriquí; operates three hydroelectric facilities in Bayano (248 MW), Estí (120 MW) and Chiriquí (90 MW) and one 43-MW thermal facility; Pres. JAIME TUPPER; Gen. Man. JAIME COOPER.

Empresa de Transmisión Eléctrica, SA (ETESA): Plaza Sun Tower, 3°, Avda Ricardo J. Alfaro, El Dorado, Panamá; tel. 501-3800; fax 501-3506; e-mail gerinfo@etesa.com.pa; internet www.etesa.com.pa; f. 1998; state-owned transmission co; Pres. FRANK DE LIMA; Gen. Man. FERNANDO A. MARCISCANO R.

ENSA, SA: Costa del Este, Business Park-Torre Oeste, 3°, Panamá; tel. 340-4600; internet www.ensa.com.pa; f. 1998; fmrly known as Elektra Noreste, SA; electricity distribution; Gen. Man. JAVIER PARIENTE.

Natural Gas Fenosa: Albrook, Edif. 812, Avda Diógenes de la Rosa, Balboa, Ancón, Panamá; tel. 315-7600; e-mail edemet-edechi@ufpanama.com; internet www.ufpanama.com; f. 1998 by acquisition of Empresa de Distribución Eléctrica Metro Oeste (EDEMET) and Empresa de Distribución Eléctrica Chiriquí (EDECHI) by Unión FENOSA, Spain; electricity distributor; includes 2 subsidiaries: Ufinet and ESEPSA; Pres. RICARDO BARRANCO.

Water

Instituto de Acueductos y Alcantarillados Nacionales (IDAAN) (National Waterworks and Sewage Systems Institute): Apdo 5234, Panamá; tel. 523-8567; e-mail relaciones.publicas@idaan.gob.pa; internet www.idaan.gob.pa; state-run; Pres. JOSÉ ANTONIO DÍAZ.

TRADE UNIONS

Central General Autónoma de Trabajadores de Panamá (CGTP): Edif. CGTP, Calle 3a Perejil, detrás del Colegio Javier, Panamá; tel. 269-9741; fax 223-5287; e-mail cgtpan@cwpanama.net; internet www.cgtp.org.pa; fmrly Central Istmeña de Trabajadores; Sec.-Gen. MARIANO E. MENA.

Confederación Nacional de Unidad Sindical Independiente (CONUSI): 0421B Calle Venado, Ancón, Apdo 830344, Zona 3, Panamá; tel. 212-3865; fax 212-2565; e-mail conusipanama@hotmail.com; Sec.-Gen. GENARO LÓPEZ.

Sindicato Unico Nacional de Trabajadores de la Industria de la Construcción y Similares (SUNTRACS): 40,000 mems; part of CONUSI; Gen. Sec. SAÚL MÉNDEZ.

Confederación de Trabajadores de la República de Panamá (CTRP) (Confederation of Workers of the Republic of Panama): Calle 31, entre Avdas México y Justo Arosemena 3-50, Apdo 0816-03647, Panamá 5; tel. 225-0293; fax 225-0259; e-mail ctrp@hotmail.es; internet www.ctrppanama.org; f. 1956; admitted to ITUC/ORIT; Sec.-Gen. GUILLERMO PUGA; 62,000 mems from 26 affiliated groups.

Consejo Nacional de Trabajadores Organizados (CONATO) (National Council of Organized Labour): Edif. 777, 2°, Balboa-Ancón, Panamá; tel. and fax 228-0224; e-mail conato@cwpanama.net; Leader RAFAEL CHAVARRÍA; 150,000 mems.

Convergencia Sindical: Casa 2490, Balboa-Ancón, Calle Bomparte Wise, Apdo 0815-00863, Panamá 4; tel. and fax 314-1615; e-mail conversind@cwpanama.net; f. 1995; Sec.-Gen. MIGUEL ANGEL EDWARDS.

Federación Nacional de Servidores Públicos (FENASEP) (National Federation of Public Employees): Galerías Alvear, 2°, Of. 301, Vía Argentina, Apdo 66-48, Zona 5, Panamá; tel. and fax 269-1316; e-mail fenasep@sinfo.net; internet fenasep.blogspot.com.au; f. 1984; Pres. MIGUEL GARCÍA.

Frente Nacional de Educadores Independientes (Frenei): Panamá; teachers' union; Sec.-Gen. LUIS LÓPEZ.

Sindicato de Industriales de Panamá: Apdo 6-4798, El Dorado, Panamá; tel. 230-0169; e-mail sip@cableonda.net; internet www.industriales.org; f. 1945; Pres. JUAN F. KIENER.

Transport

RAILWAYS

In 1998 there was an estimated 485 km of track in Panama. In 2001 the 83-km Trans-Isthmian railway, originally founded in 1855, reopened. The construction of a metro system in Panama City began in 2011. The first phase of the project, funded by the Corporación Andina de Fomento (CAF) with US $400m., was construction of Consorcio Línea 1. Operations were expected to begin in 2014 and the Government was expected to launch a tender for the second subway line in the same year. Four such lines were planned, one of which was to run above the canal.

Panama Canal Railway Company: Edif. T-376, Corozal Oeste, Apdo 2669, Balboa Ancón, Panamá; tel. 317-6070; fax 317-6061; e-mail info@panarail.com; internet www.panarail.com; private investment under 50-year govt concession; 83 km linking Panama City and Colón, running parallel to Panama Canal; operation on concession by Kansas City Southern (KS, USA) and Mi-Jack Products (IL, USA); modernization programme completed in 2001; operates daily passenger and cargo service; Dir-Gen. THOMAS KENNA.

ROADS

In 2010, according to preliminary figures, there were 15,137 km of roads, of which some 42% were paved. The Pan-American Highway to Mexico City runs for 545 km in Panama and is expected to be extended towards Colombia. The Trans-Isthmian Highway runs from Panama City to Colón. There is also a highway to San José, Costa Rica. The Coastal Beltway, or Cinta Costera, road development project aimed to reduce congestion in Panama City. The first phase of the project was completed in 2009 at a cost of US $189.1m. In the same year, the Government approved $52m. for the second phase, and in 2010 the final phase, expected to cost $776.9m., was approved.

Autoridad del Tránsito y Transporte Terrestre (ATTT): Panamá; tel. 502-0547; internet www.transito.gob.pa; f. 1999; regulatory authority; Dir-Gen. JULIO GONZÁLEZ (designate).

MiBus: Panamá; internet www.mibus.com.pa; f. 2009; operates the Metro bus system in Panamá; Man. IVÁN POSADA.

SHIPPING

Some 5% of all the world's sea-borne trade passes through the Panama Canal. It is 82 km long, and ships take an average of nine hours to complete a transit. In 2011/12 some 14,544 transits were recorded. The widening of the narrowest section of the Canal, the Culebra Cut, was completed in 2005. Plans were also announced to construct a 203-ha international cargo-handling platform at the Atlantic end of the Canal, including terminals, a railway and an international airport. Terminal ports are Balboa, on the Pacific Ocean, and Cristóbal, on the Caribbean Sea. Further expansion of the Canal's capacity to allow the passage of larger commercial container vessels, by constructing a third set of locks at either end of the waterway, was expected to be completed by late 2015.

The Panamanian flag registered fleet was the second largest in the world in December 2013, comprising 9,290 vessels, totalling 228.8m. gross registered tons.

Autoridad del Canal de Panamá (ACP): Administration Bldg, Balboa, Ancón, Panamá; tel. 272-7602; fax 272-7693; e-mail info@pancanal.com; internet www.pancanal.com; f. 1997; manages, operates and maintains the Panama Canal; succeeded the Panama Canal Commission, a US govt agency, on 31 December 1999, when the waterway was ceded to the Govt of Panama; the ACP is the autonomous agency of the Govt of Panama; there is a Board of 11 mems; Pres. of the Bd and Minister of Canal Affairs ROBERTO ROY.

Autoridad Marítima de Panamá: Edif. PanCanal Albrook, Diablo Heights, Balboa, Ancón, Apdo 0843-0533, Panamá 7; tel. 501-5196; fax 501-5406; e-mail ampadmin@amp.gob.pa; internet www.amp.gob.pa; f. 1998 to unite and optimize the function of all state institutions with involvement in the maritime sector; Administrator JORGE BARAKAT (designate).

Panama City Port Authority and Foreign Trade Zone 65: Apdo 15095, Panamá; FL 32406, USA; tel. 767-3220; e-mail wstubbs@portpanamacityusa.com; internet www.portpanamacityusa.com; Chair. GEORGE NORRIS; Exec. Dir WAYNE STUBBS.

CIVIL AVIATION

Tocumen (formerly Omar Torrijos) International Airport, situated 19 km (12 miles) outside Panamá (Panama City), is the country's principal airport and is served by many international airlines. The France Airport in Colón and the Rio Hato Airport in Coclé province have both been declared international airports. There are also 11 smaller airports in the country.

Autoridad de Aeronáutica Civil: Edif. 805, Albrook, Panamá; tel. 501-9000; fax 501-9305; e-mail rpublicas@aeronautica.gob.pa; internet www.aeronautica.gob.pa; f. 1932 as Comisión Nacional de Aviación; civil aviation authority; Dir-Gen. ALFREDO FONSECA MORA.

Air Panama: Marcos A. Gelabert Airport, Albrook, Panamá; tel. 316-9000; e-mail info@flyairpanama.com; internet www.flyairpanama.com; operates flights throughout Panama and to Costa Rica; Gen. Man. EDUARDO STAGG.

Copa Airlines: Avda Justo Arosemena 230 y Calle 39, Apdo 1572, Panamá 1; tel. 227-2522; fax 227-1952; e-mail proquebert@mail.copa.com.pa; internet www.copaair.com; f. 1947 as Compañía Panameña de Aviación; present name adopted 1999; subsidiary of Copa Holdings; scheduled passenger and cargo services from Panamá (Panama City) to Central America, South America, the Caribbean and the USA; Chair. STANLEY MOTTA; CEO PEDRO O. HEILBRON.

Tourism

Panama's attractions include Panamá (Panama City), the ruins of Portobelo and 800 sandy tropical islands, including the resort of Contadora, one of the Pearl Islands in the Gulf of Panama, and the San Blas Islands, lying off the Atlantic coast. In 2013 the number of visitor arrivals stood at an estimated 1,658,000 and income from tourism was a provisional US $3,316m.

Asociación Panameña de Agencias de Viajes y Turismo (APAVIT): Edif. Balmoral, Vía Argentina, diagonal a la Universidad de Panamá, Panamá; tel. 263-9104; fax 263-8937; e-mail info@apavit.org; internet www.apavit.org; f. 1957; Pres. ERNESTO REINA.

Autoridad de Turismo Panamá (IPAT): Edif. Central, 1°, Avda Samuel Lewis y calle Gerardo Ortega, Panamá 5; tel. 526-7000; fax 526-7100; e-mail gerencia@atp.gob.pa; internet www.atp.gob.pa; f. 1960; Administrator JESÚS SIERRA.

Defence

As assessed at November 2013, the Public Force numbered an estimated 12,000, comprising the National Police (11,000) and the National Aeronaval Service (1,000).

Security Expenditure: budgeted at an estimated US $637m. in 2013.

Director of National Civil Protection System: ARTURO ALVARADO DE ICAZA.

Director of National Police: JULIO MOLTÓ.

Director of National Aero-Naval Service: BELSIO GIOLIS GONZALEZ SÁNCHEZ.

Education

The education system in Panama is divided into elementary, secondary and university schooling, each of six years' duration. Education is free up to university level and is officially compulsory between six and 15 years of age. Primary education begins at the age of six and secondary education, which comprises two three-year cycles, at the age of 12. In 2012 enrolment at primary schools included 91% of children in the relevant age-group, while secondary enrolment included 76% of children in the relevant age-group. In 2013 there were 17 universities operating with official accreditation, of which four are public institutions. In 2011 a plan to improve educational standards in indigenous schools was announced, to be financed by a US $30m. loan from the Inter-American Development Bank. Budgetary expenditure on education by the central Government in 2012 amounted to a preliminary 965.1m. balboas, equivalent to 5.8% of consolidated general government expenditure.

Bibliography

For works on Central America generally, see Select Bibliography (Books)

Bolitno, C. *Progress in Panama: Politics, Economics, and Free Trade with the United States.* New York, Nova Science Publrs, 2013.

Coniff, M. L. *Panama and the United States.* Atlanta, GA, University of Georgia Press, 2001.

Diaz Espino, O. *How Wall Street Created a Nation: J. P. Morgan, Teddy Roosevelt and the Panama Canal.* New York, Four Walls Eight Windows, 2001.

Dinges, J. *Our Man in Panama: How General Noriega Fooled the United States and Made Millions in Drugs and Arms.* New York, Random House, 1990.

Dudley Gold, S. *The Panama Canal Transfer: Controversy at the Crossroads.* Austin, TX, Raintree/Steck Vaughn, 1999.

Greene, J. *The Canal Builders: Making America's Empire of the Panama Canal.* London, Penguin Books, 2010.

Guevara Mann, C. *Panamanian Militarism: A Historical Interpretation.* Athens, OH, Ohio University Press, 1996.

Harding, II, R. C. *Military Foundations of Panamanian Politics.* Piscataway, NJ, Transaction Publrs, 2001.

Hensel, H. M., and Michaud, N. *Global Media Perspectives on the Crisis in Panama.* Surrey, Ashgate Publishing, 2011.

Johnsen, V. D. (Ed.) *US-Panama Free Trade Agreement.* Hauppauge, NY, Nova Science Publrs, 2011.

Kempe, F. *Divorcing the Dictator: America's Bungled Affair with Noriega.* New York, G. P. Putnam's Sons, 1990.

Langstaff, E. *Panama.* Oxford, ABC Clio, 2000.

McCullough, D. *Path Between the Seas: Creation of the Panama Canal, 1870–1914*. New York, Simon and Schuster, 1999.

Major, J. *Prize Possession: The United States and the Panama Canal, 1903–1979*. Cambridge, Cambridge University Press, 1993.

Mann, C. G. *Political Careers, Corruption, and Impunity: Panama's Assembly, 1984-2009*. Notre Dame, IN, University of Notre Dame Press, 2011.

Maurer, N. and Yu, C. *The Big Ditch: How America Took, Built, Ran, and Ultimately Gave Away the Panama Canal*. Princeton, NJ, Princeton University Press, 2010.

O'Reggio, T. *Between Alienation and Citizenship: The Evolution of Black West Indian Society in Panama, 1914-1964*. Lanham, MD, University Press of America, 2006.

Pearcy, T. L. *We Answer Only to God: Politics and the Military in Panama, 1903–1947*. Albuquerque, NM, University of New Mexico Press, 1998.

Pérez, O. J. *Post-Invasion Panama*. Lexington, MA, Lexington Books, 2000.

Political Culture in Panama: Democracy after Invasion. Basingstoke, Palgrave Macmillan, 2010.

Rodríguez, J. C. *The Panama Canal: Its History, Its Political Aspects, and Financial Difficulties*. Honolulu, HI, University Press of the Pacific, 2002.

Rudolf, G. *Panama's Poor: Victims, Agents and Historymakers*. Gainesville, FL, University Press of Florida, 1999.

Sanchez, P. *Panama Lost?: U.S. Hegemony, Democracy, and the Canal*. Gainesville, FL, University Press of Florida, 2007.

Sandoval Forero, E. A., and Salazar Pérez, R. *Lectura Crítica del Plan Puebla Panama*. Buenos Aires, Libros en Red, 2002.

Singh Gill Díaz, G. *La Evolución Jurídica del Poder Constituyente en el Istmo de Panamá*. Panamá, Instituto de Estudios Políticos e Internacionales, 2005.

Snapp, J. S. *Destiny by Design: The Construction of the Panama Canal*. Lopez Island, WA, Pacific Heritage Press, 2000.

Sosa, J. B. *In Defiance: The Battle Against Gen. Noriega Fought from Panama's Embassy in Washington*. Washington, DC, The Francis Press, 1999.

Taw, J. M. *Operation Just Cause: Lessons for Operations Other than War*. Skokie, IL, Rand McNally, 1996.

USA Ibp. *Doing Business and Investing in Panama*. Milton Keynes, Lightning Source UK Ltd, 2005.

Panama Canal Handbook: Organization and Business Activity. Milton Keynes, Lightning Source UK Ltd, 2005.

Ward, C. *Imperial Panama: Commerce and Conflict in Isthmian America, 1550–1800*. Albuquerque, NM, University of New Mexico Press, 1993.

PARAGUAY

Geography

PHYSICAL FEATURES

The Republic of Paraguay is one of only two landlocked countries in South America—although, unlike Bolivia, it has never had a coastline. The country did, however, suffer immense loss from war in the 1860s, although in the 1930s it secured control over much of the Chaco after war with Bolivia. Paraguay is located in the south-central part of the continent, with Bolivia to the north-west, beyond a 750-km (466-mile) border. Argentina lies to the south-west, behind a 1,880-km frontier which abuts its neighbour in south-eastern Paraguay, while Brazil (1,290 km) is to the north-east. Paraguay is about the same size as the US state of California, covering an area of 406,752 sq km (157,048 sq miles).

Paraguay consists of two rough rectangles of territory on either side of the north–south river of the same name. The slightly larger block (with the south-west corner sliced off), covering about 60% of the territory, is to the west of the river. Offset slightly to the south is the smaller, original block of territory (a block with a much smaller block removed from the north-east corner), east of the Paraguay river. The two regions, known as Paraguay Occidental and Paraguay Oriental or Paraguay proper, have very different landscapes. The west is dominated by the Gran Chaco, an infertile alluvial plain extending through Paraguay and into Bolivia and Argentina. The region receives little rain, but is poorly drained and prone to flooding, so the rough prairie of dry grass and shadeless trees is patched with reedy marshes or thorny scrub. To the south and east, in the Oriental region, are some grassy plains, although broad, fertile valleys and rolling, wooded hills predominate. The Paraná plateau thrusts down from the north, to create a highland of between 300 m (985 ft) and 600 m, its sharp crest running down the centre of Paraguay proper, highest in the west, but dropping abruptly to the fertile grassy foothills that roll down to the Paraguay river, while descending more gently in the east towards the River Paraná. The Paraná forms the entire eastern (much of it through the reservoir behind the Itaipú dam) and southern border of Paraguay Oriental. Its tributary, the Paraguay, joins the Paraná only after cutting across the country and then forming a west-facing border with Argentina. The confluence of the Paraguay and the Paraná, at 46 m above sea level, is the lowest point in Paraguay. The highest point is in the centre of south-eastern Paraguay. It is Cerro Pero (or Cerro Tres Kandu), at 842 m. The terrain is not favourable to many of the larger mammals, although there are jaguars, tapirs, armadillos and anteaters, for instance, but exotically plumaged birds are common (parrots, toucans, black ducks, etc.), and the grasslands are the natural habitat of the rhea or American ostrich.

CLIMATE

Paraguay is bisected by the Tropic of Capricorn, and about two-thirds of the country experiences a mild, subtropical climate. On the Chaco plains of the Occidental region it is hotter, more humid and drier; temperatures can often reach 38°C (100°F). The far north and west is semi-arid. Rainfall on the plains averages about 815 mm (32 ins) per year, falling heavily in the summer (November–May) and virtually not at all in winter. By contrast, the eastern forests receive about 1,525 mm annually, with Asunción, the national capital, on the Paraguay river, getting 1,120 mm. The average temperatures range from 17°C (63°F) in July to 27°C (81°F) in January. The prevailing summer wind is the hot, north-eastern *sirocco*, while in winter it is the cold *pampero* from the south.

POPULATION

Paraguay has one of the more homogenous populations of South America, 95% of the people being of mixed race. Otherwise, there are some unassimilated Amerindians (notably Guaraní of the eastern forests), and some small groups originating from Spain, Japan, Italy, Portugal, Canada and Germany (the last comprising mainly the Mennonite religious minority). Spanish is joined by Guaraní as an official language, as the latter is commonly spoken by about 90% of the population. Spanish is spoken by about three-quarters of the population, with almost one-half of Paraguayans being completely bilingual. Guaraní was the official language for many of the early years of independence. The majority of people remain at least nominally Roman Catholic. There are other Christians, with the Evangelical Protestants active here as elsewhere in South America, but the largest Protestant minority is that of the Mennonites (based near Filadelfia, in the heart of the Chaco plains).

The total population, according to official estimates at mid-2014, was 6.9m. Two-thirds of the population are urban and most live in western Paraguay proper. The east is very sparsely populated. The capital and largest city is Asunción, a port on the Paraguay, located where the river flows out of the north, having bisected the country that bears its name, and continues south, forming the border with Argentina. Asunción, which had an estimated population of 515,587 in mid-2012, is in a capital district, which, together with 17 departments, forms the local administration of the country. The next largest city is Ciudad del Este (formerly Puerto Presidente Stroessner), on the Paraná, near the Itaipú Dam.

History

Prof. PETER CALVERT

Revised for this edition by the editorial staff

Paraguay was already well populated when the Spanish first arrived in 1524. In 1537 the Spanish founded Asunción. The city enjoyed a brief period of importance until the foundation of Buenos Aires, in what is now Argentina, in 1580, when the seat of regional government was moved to the new port city. In the absence of important resources that were of interest to the Spanish, Paraguay remained economically undeveloped throughout the colonial period, and was politically and economically dependent on Buenos Aires. The indigenous Indians (Amerindians) established good relations with the Spanish and many intermarried; however, they retained their own language, Guaraní.

Jesuit missionaries soon arrived in the country. Indians converted to Christianity were resettled in missions, each farming the surrounding land. They built churches and created a unique, theocratic society. In 1767 the Jesuits were expelled and, for the first time, the Indians were directly exposed to Spanish rule. In 1810 Buenos Aires declared self-government, and on 14 May 1811 Paraguay became the first Spanish territory in the Americas to achieve independence.

The newly independent country was governed by Dr José Gaspar Rodríguez de Francia. Dr Francia, known as 'El Supremo', closed Paraguay's borders to the outside world, thus ensuring Paraguayan sovereignty, despite Argentine plans for annexation. He proclaimed Guaraní the sole language and ruled alone until his death in 1840. His successor, Carlos Antonio López (President, 1842–62), reopened Paraguay's borders. No less a dictator than his predecessor, López encouraged trade, built Paraguay's first railway and abolished slavery. He also gave Paraguay the institution that was to dominate its politics from then on, the army. López's son, Francisco Solano López, succeeded him as President-for-life, and during his rule Paraguay was defeated in the War of the Triple Alliance (1865–70) by the combined forces of Argentina, Brazil and Uruguay. The war, which became known in Paraguay as the 'National Epic' (*Epopeya Nacional*), resulted in the loss of 90% of the country's male population and left the economy devastated. Marshal López himself perished and was buried on the battlefield of Cerro Cora.

International rivalry for control of a defeated Paraguay began with the emergence of national political parties; Anglo-Argentine capital supported the Partido Liberal (Liberal Party), while Brazilian interests supported the Partido Colorado (Red Party), forerunner of the present Asociación Nacional Republicana—Partido Colorado (National Republican Association—Colorado Party). The conservative Colorados remained in power between 1870 and 1904. The 1883 Law of Sale of Public Land enclosed land that had previously been accessible to all and turned it into vast private estates. Peasants were either forced to leave or to work for a pittance. In 1904 a revolution brought the Liberals to power, but achieved little else. The period from 1870 to 1940 was marked by a tumultuous series of coups and counter-coups, as rival groups within each party vied for political control of the riches to be gained from widespread foreign ownership of the national territory.

Of the 45 Presidents who governed between 1870 and 1979, all achieved power by force or by fraud and most were ousted by violence or the threat of it. Factionalism, an inability to compromise and the relative weakness of the parties in government left the army as the central institution in Paraguayan politics. Paraguay's historic need to defend its borders justified the role of the armed forces and led to one of the highest ratios in the world of military and police to population.

THE CHACO WAR AND ITS AFTERMATH

Paraguay gradually extended its control west of the River Paraguay, into the arid Chaco region. In response, Bolivia, which also claimed possession of the region, sent troops into the disputed territory. In the ensuing Chaco War (1932–35), Paraguay defeated Bolivia and, under the terms of a 1938 peace treaty, brokered by Argentina, was awarded three-quarters of the disputed territory.

Dissatisfaction with the Liberal war effort, however, led to the overthrow, by a military coup, of the Government of Eusebio Ayala in February 1936. The coup, led by Col Rafael Franco and supported by war veterans, brought to power the reformist Government of the Partido Revolucionario Febrerista (PRF—February Revolution Party). Although the Government managed to seize and redistribute some land, its tenure was short-lived and the Febreristas, as Franco's followers soon became known, were overthrown in 1937 by army officers loyal to the Liberals.

Following a two-year interim presidency, Marshal José Félix Estigarribia (the Liberal leader in the Chaco War) became President. Estigarribia was a reformist nationalist, popular with both the military and peasants. Nevertheless, his restoration of political freedoms was met with generalized unrest, including strikes, attacks by the press and conspiracies by some military cliques, among which the Febrerista movement survived. Estigarribia therefore declared himself a temporary dictator, repressed opposition and announced a developmentalist land programme which included land expropriation. A new corporatist Constitution, which came into force in August 1940, strengthened executive powers and permitted the President to serve a second term. Estigarribia did not benefit from these constitutional changes, however, as both he and his wife were killed in an aeroplane crash only three weeks after the Constitution was approved.

Former Minister of War, Gen. Higinio Morínigo, assumed power following Estigarribia's death. Initially, Morínigo was regarded as a reasonably benevolent autocrat who had the unenviable task of balancing opposing political forces to retain control of the nation. However, he soon assumed absolute powers, banning all political parties, repressing the activities of the trade union movement and dissolving the legislature. Eminent Liberals were forced into exile and Febrerista uprisings were suppressed.

The Allied victory in the Second World War, however, gave rise to a military movement in 1946, which was directed against the Axis sympathizers behind Morínigo. Exiles were allowed to return, and some conservative Colorados—as well as young, developmentalist Febrerista officers—were invited to join a Colorado-PRF coalition Government, under Morínigo's nominal control. From 1946 there was an increase in public unrest. Threatened by a growth in popular political activity and the emergence of a strong left-wing movement, Morínigo excluded the PRF from the Government and openly supported the Colorados. An attempted coup late in 1946 was followed by the disintegration of the coalition Government. Declaring a state of siege, Morínigo formed a new military cabinet in 1947; on the rebel side, Liberals and Communists joined Febrerista forces, led by Col Rafael Franco, in a civil war that erupted in March 1947 and divided the armed forces, with some four-fifths of officers defecting to the rebels. The Colorados triumphed, partly owing to support from the Argentine Government of Gen. Juan Domingo Perón Sosa.

The defeat of the rebels gave the Colorados control of the army and thus of the country. A number of coups followed, the first of which, in 1948, removed Morínigo from power. A presidential election was held in the same year, but the only candidate was a Colorado, Juan Natalicio González. President González was supported by an all-Colorado legislature; thus Paraguay had become a one-party state. Although Morínigo went into exile, factional infighting continued, with uprisings by Colorado officers against the González Government. Eventually, González also fled abroad. Another Colorado faction, led by Dr Federico Chávez, assumed power.

In October 1951 President Chávez appointed Gen. Alfredo Stroessner Mattiauda, a veteran of the Chaco War, as Commander-in-Chief of the Armed Forces. Paraguay's economy began to deteriorate, however, and as inflation rose, so did political opposition. On 4 May 1954 Stroessner deposed Chávez in a military coup and in the July presidential election Stroessner, a Colorado candidate, was elected unopposed to complete Chávez's term of office.

THE RULE OF GENERAL STROESSNER

Gen. Stroessner immediately established a personal dictatorship. Restrictions were placed on all political activities and the Febrerista and Liberal opposition groups were ruthlessly suppressed. In 1956 Stroessner forced his principal rival within the Partido Colorado, Epifanio Méndez Fleitas, into exile. A state of siege was imposed. For over 30 years, until 1987, this state of siege was renewed every 60 days to comply with constitutional requirements. The unaccustomed sense of order that existed during Stroessner's dictatorship was advantageous to both domestic and foreign companies, and his commitment to IMF austerity measures contributed to the stabilization of the national currency, the guaraní, by 1957. In 1958 Stroessner, as the sole candidate of the only permitted party, was re-elected President and continued to be re-elected in this way every five years until 1988. Opposition continued, but it originated mostly from outside Paraguay; attacks from Argentina by exiles were repelled in 1959 and 1960.

Stroessner's command of the armed forces and of the economy contributed to the strength of his position. Increasing confidence in the economy in the 1960s led to the encouragement of some limited political activity. Stroessner encouraged the pretence of democracy by allowing a dissident wing of the Partido Liberal, the Renovación (Renovation) wing, to participate in controlled legislative elections, in which it received one-third of the seats in the legislature. This did not in any way diminish the President's personal dominance of Paraguayan politics, since he controlled the ruling Partido Colorado, which held the remaining two-thirds of the parliament. In 1959 some 400 Colorado politicians who opposed Stroessner had been imprisoned or had fled into exile, where they formed the Movimiento Popular Colorado (MOPOCO—Colorado Popular Movement), under the leadership of Méndez Fleitas. The President reorganized the purged Partido Colorado to facilitate the entrenchment of an authoritarian style of government. By 1967 the Partido Colorado constituted only members loyal to Stroessner. In that year the President changed the Constitution of 1940 to permit his legal re-election to a fourth term of office.

In the late 1960s the overtly autocratic nature of Stroessner's regime encouraged criticism from the Roman Catholic Church in Paraguay, which, in turn, resulted in popular unrest. However, the upturn in the economy experienced in the 1970s contained much of the opposition. The majority of opposition parties boycotted the presidential and legislative elections of February 1983, enabling Stroessner to obtain more than 90% of the votes cast in the presidential poll, and in August he formally took office for a seventh five-year term. In the mid-1980s the question of who would succeed Stroessner became increasingly important; his son was considered a likely candidate. In 1987 the President ended the state of siege, since extraordinary security powers were no longer necessary to maintain peace. His decision to seek re-election in 1988, for an eighth consecutive term as President, precipitated the final crisis of Stroessner's regime. Although it was announced that he had received 89% of the votes cast, opposition leaders complained of electoral malpractice, and denounced his re-election as fraudulent. On 3 February 1989 Stroessner was overthrown in a coup, led by his son-in-law, Gen. Andrés Rodríguez, the second-in-command of the armed forces. (In 2004 arrest warrants were issued for Stroessner and some 30 retired military personnel, including former Chief of Staff Alejandro Fretes Davalos. The warrants related to three Paraguayan nationals who 'disappeared' in Argentina, allegedly as a result of Plan Condor—an intelligence operation to eliminate opponents of the Latin American military dictatorships in the 1970s. However, Stroessner died in 2006.)

DEMOCRATIZATION

Gen. Rodríguez was elected President in May 1989, as the official candidate of the Partido Colorado, with 74% of the votes cast. The Partido Colorado, having won 73% of the votes in the congressional elections, automatically took two-thirds of the seats in both the lower house of the legislature, the Cámara de Diputados (Chamber of Deputies), and the Senado (Senate). However, the process of democratization continued. The Government's liberalizing austerity programme accelerated the formation of both new trade union and peasant movements, which carried out a series of illegal land occupations. On 20 June 1992 a new Constitution was promulgated.

Luis María Argaña Ferraro, leader of the conservative Movimiento de Reconciliación Colorado (MRC—Movement of Colorado Reconciliation) faction, was nominated in December 1992 as the Partido Colorado's candidate for the 1993 presidential election. His nomination, however, was reversed following pressure from President Rodríguez and from the Commander of the First Corps, Gen. Lino César Oviedo Silva, who had political ambitions of his own. On 9 May 1993, however, the new official candidate, Juan Carlos Wasmosy, a former business associate of President Rodríguez but a political novice, won the presidential election with 40% of the votes cast. International observers agreed that the election was generally fair, despite the partisanship of Gen. Oviedo, and Wasmosy thus became the first civilian President of Paraguay for 39 years.

THE GOVERNMENT OF PRESIDENT WASMOSY

There was widespread concern over the composition of Wasmosy's first Council of Ministers in August 1993, many of whom had served in the administrations of Rodríguez and Stroessner. Despite the new President's apparent desire to restrict the influence of the military, the appointment of Gen. Oviedo as Commander of the Army provoked further criticism. As a result, the Partido Liberal Radical Auténtico (PLRA—Authentic Radical Liberal Party) refused to co-operate with the Colorados and there were violent demonstrations outside the Congreso Nacional (Congress) building. In September 1994 Wasmosy carried out a reshuffle of the command of the armed forces, strengthening the position of Gen. Oviedo, but tensions remained high between the two men and, on 22 April 1996, the President finally requested that Oviedo resign. Oviedo had begun to campaign for the leadership of the Partido Colorado and hoped to succeed Wasmosy as President in 1998. Oviedo refused to step down and, with the support of some 5,000 troops, in turn demanded the resignation of the President, who sought asylum in the US embassy. On 24 April the President agreed to a compromise by which Oviedo would retire from active service in exchange for the offer of the post of defence minister. The Congress, however, refused to ratify Oviedo's appointment, which was retracted. The new Commander of the Army, Gen. Oscar Díaz Delmas, did not intervene, and three days later Argaña was again elected President of the Partido Colorado.

A purge of senior military commanders followed. In June 1996 Oviedo was arrested on a charge of sedition, but was subsequently cleared by the Courts of Appeal and in September he narrowly defeated Argaña to become the Partido Colorado's presidential candidate. The President attempted to exclude him from the presidential contest, and in October an arrest order was issued against Oviedo on charges of making inflammatory public statements. Nevertheless, the general eluded capture until mid-December, when he surrendered.

In 1998 the Special Military Tribunal convened by President Wasmosy found Oviedo guilty of rebellion, sentencing him to 10 years' imprisonment and dishonourable discharge, and in the following month his presidential candidacy was annulled by the Supreme Electoral Tribunal. The nomination of the Partido Colorado was assumed by Raúl Cubas Grau, a wealthy engineer, with Argaña as the new candidate for the vice-presidency. Despite public protests, the election was held as planned in May. Cubas Grau obtained 55% of the votes cast, ahead of the candidate of the Alianza Democrática (Democratic Alliance), Domingo Laíno, who received 44%.

DEMOCRATIZATION FALTERS

Cubas Grau assumed office on 15 August 1998 and appointed a new Council of Ministers, including two pro-Oviedo generals. On 18 August the President issued a decree commuting Oviedo's prison sentence to time already served. The new Congress immediately voted to condemn the decree and to initiate proceedings to impeach the President for unconstitutional behaviour. In December the Supreme Court ruled the decree unconstitutional; shortly afterwards the central apparatus of the Colorados (controlled by the Argaña faction) expelled Oviedo from the party. While the Congress was unable to muster the two-thirds' majority support necessary to impeach President Cubas Grau, the country remained in effective political deadlock, a situation exacerbated by the fact that the economy had been in recession since 1997.

The political impasse ended dramatically on 23 March 1999 when Vice-President Argaña was assassinated in the capital, Asunción, by three men in military uniform. The 66-year-old Vice-President and his supporters had just succeeded in regaining control of the Colorado headquarters, from which they had been expelled on 14 March by supporters of Oviedo and President Cubas Grau, who were immediately accused by supporters of Argaña of being at least the 'moral instigators' of the assassination. Large crowds took to the streets to demand the President's resignation, and the situation was further inflamed when six protesters, demonstrating outside the Congress building on 25 March, were killed, apparently by an official at the finance ministry who was filmed firing at the crowds from a building near the Congress.

On 28 March 1999, hours before the Congress was due to vote on his impeachment, President Cubas Grau resigned and fled to Brazil, where he was granted political asylum. (In February 2002 Cubas Grau surrendered to the Paraguayan authorities to face trial for the killings of the protesters.) At the same time, Oviedo was granted asylum in Argentina. The President of the Congress, pro-Argaña Colorado senator Luis González Macchi, became Head of State for the remainder of Cubas Grau's presidential term (which was scheduled to end in 2003). Hoping to overcome the disagreements existing within the Partido Colorado and between the Government and opposition in the legislature, he announced the composition of a multi-party Government of National Unity. In July Oviedo was officially expelled from the Partido Colorado. His arrest was ordered three days later, but the Argentine authorities twice refused to extradite him, and in December he left Argentina to avoid being extradited by the new Government of Fernando de la Rúa.

On 18 May 2000 rebellious soldiers thought to be sympathetic to Oviedo seized the First Cavalry Division barracks and other strategic points. The coup was swiftly suppressed by the Government, which declared a 30-day nation-wide state of emergency, assuming extraordinary powers which resulted in the arrest of more than 70 people, mostly members of the security forces. (The subsequent trial of 18 military officials accused of involvement in the attempted coup collapsed, in judicially controversial circumstances, in May 2003.) However, in June Oviedo was arrested in Foz do Iguaçu, Brazil. In March 2001 the Brazilian chief prosecutor ruled that Oviedo could be extradited; however, in December Brazil's Supreme Court rejected the ruling, stating that Oviedo was a victim of political persecution, and released him.

The PLRA withdrew from the governing coalition in February 2000 when it became clear that, contrary to the national unity agreement, the Partido Colorado would contest the election for a new Vice-President. In April the Colorados nominated Félix Argaña, son of the late Vice-President, to be their party's candidate. However, at the election, in August, the 53-year Colorado monopoly on power was ended when Argaña was narrowly defeated by the PLRA candidate, Julio César Franco.

The Government was further undermined by tensions between the President and the Vice-President in 2001; in February Franco, as the most senior elected government official, demanded the resignation of President González Macchi in the interest of democratic legitimacy. In May the President of the Central Bank of Paraguay, Washington Ashwell, was forced to resign over his alleged involvement in the fraudulent transfer of US $16m. to a US bank account. In response to allegations that the President had been a beneficiary of the misappropriated funds, opposition parties launched a bid to impeach him, but were forced to abandon the charges when the PLRA failed to secure the necessary two-thirds' majority in the Congress. In June 2006 González Macchi was convicted of charges of false testimony and embezzlement and sentenced to eight years' imprisonment. Three other officials were each sentenced to terms of 10 years.

In January 2002 the credibility of the Government was further undermined after two leaders of the left-wing party Movimiento Patria Libre (MPL—Free Homeland Movement) alleged that they had been illegally detained for 13 days and tortured by the police, with the knowledge of government ministers, as part of an investigation into a kidnapping case. In response to the allegations, the head of the national police force and his deputy, as well as the head of the judicial investigations department, were dismissed. Following sustained public and political pressure, the Minister of the Interior, Julio César Fanego, and the Minister of Justice and Labour, Silvio Ferreira Fernández, resigned, although both protested their innocence. In addition, the national intelligence agency, the Secretaría Nacional de Informaciones, was disbanded. The Chamber of Deputies issued a statement assigning some responsibility for the detention of the MPL leaders to the President and the Attorney-General, and describing the event as 'state terrorism'.

During the first half of 2002 an alliance of farmers, trade unions and left-wing organizations staged mass protests throughout the country, demanding an end to the Government's free market economic policies. The protests succeeded in reversing some of the Government's policies; most notably, the planned privatization of the telecommunications company Corporación Paraguaya de Comunicaciones (COPACO). Nevertheless, the protests continued, and in July González Macchi declared a state of emergency, after two people died in clashes between anti-Government protesters and the security forces. A further mass demonstration took place in September, organized by opposition parties, including Oviedo's Unión Nacional de Ciudadanos Éticos (UNACE—National Union of Ethical Citizens) grouping.

In December 2002 the Chamber of Deputies approved a proposal to impeach President González Macchi on five charges of corruption and failure to fulfil the duties of the presidency. Supported by the pro-Oviedo faction of the Partido Colorado and by the opposition PLRA, this was the third such proposal since July. González Macchi found his position as President ever more tenuous ahead of the presidential election scheduled for April 2003. In an attempt to avoid proceedings against him, Macchi offered to leave office early; however, the Senate voted against approving the charges against him in February.

THE GOVERNMENT OF PRESIDENT DUARTE

The legislative and presidential elections of 27 April 2003 passed off without incident. The Partido Colorado extended its unbroken 56-year hold on power as its candidate, Oscar Nicanor Duarte Frutos, won 37% of the votes cast in the presidential ballot. The PLRA candidate and former Vice-President, Julio César Franco Gómez, secured 24% and Pedro Nicolás Fadul, of the Patria Querida (Beloved Fatherland) movement, came third, with 21%. Concurrent elections to the 80-seat Chamber of Deputies gave the Colorados 37 seats, the PLRA 21 seats, the Patria Querida 10 seats, UNACE 10 seats and the Partido País Solidario (Party for a Country of Solidarity) two seats. The Colorados also won the largest number of seats in the 45-seat Senate.

The new President, who took office on 15 August 2003, advocated free market policies and pledged to address corruption, renegotiate Paraguay's external debt and restore the country's credibility internationally. The IMF initially remained reluctant to revive its lending programme to Paraguay, in view of the Congress's record of hostility towards reform measures. Duarte quickly demonstrated his apparent determination to address the problem of corruption, announcing his intention to reform the judiciary. This stance was somewhat undermined in October, however, when the Minister of the Interior, Roberto Eudez González Segovia, a close ally of the President, was forced to resign after being accused of corrupt practices. As a result of the new Government's policies, in December the World Bank granted the country a structural adjustment loan worth US $30m. to fund the proposed reforms, and in the same month the IMF approved a stand-by loan of $73m. on condition that structural reform continue. In March 2004 reform of the Supreme Court was achieved with the replacement of two-thirds of its nine justices (observers noted that the new appointments were simply distributed between the three main political parties).

In June 2004 Oviedo returned from exile in Brazil, apparently hoping both to avoid conviction for the various charges he faced, including sedition against the Wasmosy administration, and to relaunch his political career. Instead, he was arrested at the airport and taken to a military prison to begin a 10-year sentence.

A spate of kidnappings in 2004 led to the replacement of the Minister of the Interior, Orlando Fiorotto Sánchez, with Nelson Mora, hitherto the Attorney-General, following the kidnap and murder in October of the 11-year-old son of a businessman. The head of the national police was also dismissed. Previously, in September Cecilia Cubas, the 32-year-old daughter of former President Cubas Grau, was abducted in a paramilitary-style operation, apparently by a large criminal syndicate. Despite the alleged payment of a ransom, in February 2005 her body was found in a house near Asunción. Six people subsequently arrested in connection with the kidnap and murder were alleged to have connections to the MPL and to the Fuerzas Armadas Revolucionarias de Colombia—Ejército del Pueblo (FARC), which was believed to be using Paraguay as a transshipment centre for drugs-trafficking. Allegations of serious investigative shortcomings by the authorities prompted the dismissal of Nelson Mora, who was replaced by the popular Rogelio Benítez, a former mayor of Encarnación. A total of 32 senior police officials were also dismissed amid criticism of the deteriorating security situation. In March Colombia and Paraguay signed an agreement to co-operate on security and drugs-trafficking issues, in support of the new three-year security plan for Paraguay announced by Duarte in February. The plan met with vociferous and occasionally violent protests by peasants' groups, owing primarily to fears that a greater military presence in rural areas would lead to increased repression of their campaign for agrarian reform, which had involved illegal land occupations since 2003. By the late 2000s kidnapping remained a significant problem, especially in the Triple Border region, where drugs-trafficking and smuggling were rife. In May 2007 Duarte met his Brazilian counterpart, Luiz Inácio Lula da Silva, in Asunción and agreed to increase legitimate trade and strengthen cross-border co-operation to reduce smuggling. They also signed an agreement to build another bridge across the River Paraná, which separates the two countries.

Meanwhile, amid considerable controversy, in February 2006 President Duarte was elected leader of the Partido Colorado. However, the Electoral Court ruled that the President of the Republic could not hold an additional office, although this was overturned by the Supreme Court and, consequently, Duarte assumed the leadership of his party in March. On the same day he announced a proposed referendum to seek approval for amendments to the Constitution to allow presidential re-election. Opposition to Duarte's leadership of the Colorados continued unabated, with the opposition initiating impeachment proceedings against the President and five Supreme Court justices. Confronted with such resistance, Duarte relinquished the party presidency and José Alderete Rodríguez, hitherto Minister of Public Works and Communications, assumed the post.

THE GOVERNMENT OF PRESIDENT LUGO

In February 2007 more than 30 social and labour groups joined opposition parties in signing an accord to form the Concertación Nacional, subsequently restyled the Alianza Patriótica para el Cambio (APC—Patriotic Alliance for Change), in the hope of defeating the Partido Colorado in the forthcoming elections. During 2007, moreover, a new candidate emerged

who seemed capable of winning the presidency in April 2008, namely Fernando Lugo Méndez, a former Roman Catholic bishop of San Pedro, who had resigned from the priesthood in late 2006 in order to become more actively involved in politics. The Partido Colorado unsuccessfully attempted to disqualify Lugo from standing as a presidential candidate, on the grounds that his resignation had not at that stage been accepted by the Vatican, which regarded entry to the priesthood as a lifelong commitment.

On the other hand, even though President Duarte was forced to abandon his attempt to secure re-election, the Colorados remained divided over their choice of presidential nominee: Duarte favoured the Minister of Education and Culture, Blanca Margarita Ovelar de Duarte, but in June 2007 Vice-President Luis Castiglioni Soria and Partido Colorado President José Alderete Rodríguez also announced their intention to contest the party primaries and later in the year retired Gen. Oviedo was acquitted by the Supreme Court of involvement in the 1996 coup, opening the way for his candidature. Hence at the party primaries in December 2007 Ovelar only narrowly defeated Castiglioni, and, although in late January 2008 the state election commission confirmed Ovelar as the winner (with 45.0% of the votes cast, compared with the 44.5% obtained by Castiglioni), the defeated candidate refused to accept its decision.

Partly as a result of these divisions within the Partido Colorado, at the presidential election on 20 April 2008, Fernando Lugo, standing for the APC, ended 60 years of Colorado rule, securing 41% of the votes cast, followed by Ovelar, with 31%, and Oviedo, representing UNACE, with 22%. In the concurrent legislative elections, however, the Partido Colorado remained the largest party in both congressional chambers. Lugo, who was sworn in on 15 August, advocated agrarian reform, increased support for the indigenous population, and negotiations to secure more revenue from the Itaipú Dam, the joint hydroelectric project with Brazil from which, to date, Brazil had been by far the main beneficiary.

Lugo's support base had included those on both the left and the right, and, notably, the traditional opposition PLRA. However, in Lugo's first year in office at least, the entrenched position of the Partido Colorado was itself enough to enable it successfully to frustrate the hopes of his supporters for real change. His opponents in the Congress were also able to stall the admission of Venezuela to MERCOSUR (Mercado Común del Sur—Southern Common Market) as a full member. Allegations of improper conduct helped to destabilize the President, and Lugo was also diagnosed with lymphatic cancer. It was not until January 2012 that he was confirmed to have made a full recovery. In the meantime, his political opponents in the Partido Colorado had consolidated in the legislature to prevent the approval of the reform programme that he had promised.

Politically the biggest problem arose within the area of agrarian reform, not least because records showed that titles had been granted to some 125% of the national territory. Brazil's armed forces were deployed to the border area between the two countries on 20 October 2008, ostensibly for drug interdiction, but the operation followed more than 80 land occupations and evictions in the first 100 days of the new administration, one resulting in the death of Bienvenido Melgarejo, a member of the Farmers' Association in Alto Paraná. Many of those advocating land invasions objected to the settlement of Brazilians in Paraguayan territory. Although the actual number of invasions was reported to be relatively low, they were symbolic of resentment at the overwhelming influence of absentee landlords.

In late April 2010 some 1,000 additional troops and police officers were sent to the border area to combat a small rural guerrilla movement, the Ejército del Pueblo Paraguayo (EPP—Paraguay People's Army), which was reported to have links to the FARC. The Congress granted special powers to the authorities in the troubled area, which was also a haven for drugs-smugglers. In early May President Lugo met his Brazilian counterpart, Luiz Inácio Lula da Silva. After protracted negotiations, in 2009 President da Silva had finally agreed to make some concessions regarding the cost of electricity from the Itaipú Dam. The attainment of these concessions, which allowed for a considerable increase in payments and enabled Paraguay to sell power directly to Brazilian companies, represented a significant political victory for Lugo; however, the additional funds received remained under the tight control of his political opponents, who further reduced the presidential budget for his promised welfare measures. In 2011 a new problem arose, as continued drought affected nearly one-third of the country and threatened the important soybean crop, and in mid-January 2012 a 90-day food emergency was declared. Three weeks of record rainfall in the Chaco region in April, which threatened the livelihood of more than 40,000 of its indigenous inhabitants, caused the state of food emergency to be extended.

On 12 June 2012 a police operation to evict 150 landless farmers, known as *carperos*, and their families from disputed land in Curuguaty in the north-east of the country resulted in the deaths of 11 farmers and six police officers. The President responded by dismissing his Minister of the Interior, Carlos Filizzola, and the head of the country's police force, but the sackings were not enough to satisfy Lugo's opponents: on 21 June the Senate approved the impeachment of Lugo for 'poor performance'. The Vice-President, Francisco Franco Gómez, a Liberal, assumed power in his place. Both MERCO-SUR and the Union of South American Nations (UNASUR) refused to accept what they regarded as an 'institutional coup', suspending Paraguay's membership of both organizations and withdrawing their ambassadors to Paraguay in protest. Although the legitimacy of the new administration remained questionable within the region and the international community, Paraguay's Supreme Court upheld the impeachment in September, rejecting a complaint filed by Lugo that the process had been unconstitutional.

In early December 2012 Vidal Vega, the leader of the landless farmers' movement was shot dead at his home. Vega, who was the most senior member of the *carpero* movement not to have been killed in the violence in Curuguaty in June 2012, had been assisting police with their investigation of the incident and was expected to give evidence in a trial due to commence in mid-December. A total of 12 landless farmers had been detained without charge since the incident in Curuguaty, accused of involvement in the violence that had led to 17 deaths. No members of the security forces were charged with offences relating to the violence. A demonstration by some 1,000 people took place in Asunción in mid-December protesting at Franco's management of the affair. Many commentators were highly critical of Franco's failure to resolve the issue since taking office, particularly as Lugo's alleged mishandling of the affair had been the supposed cause of his impeachment.

THE GOVERNMENT OF HORACIO CARTES

Campaigning for the elections scheduled for April intensified in early 2013. The death of Gen. Oviedo, presidential candidate for UNACE, in a helicopter accident in February led to much uncertainty about the future of the party, as the identity of the organization had been so closely bound to its leader. His nephew, Lino César Oviedo Sánchez, was subsequently selected to replace him in the forthcoming election.

At the presidential election on 21 April 2013 Horacio Cartes of the Partido Colorado won a convincing victory with 45.8% of the total vote. Cartes was a newcomer to Paraguayan politics, claiming to have registered to vote for the first time in 2008, and was well known in the country as a successful businessman, owning more than 20 companies. He was also the subject of some controversy. In the late 1980s he was imprisoned over allegations of fraud (although charges were subsequently dropped), in 2000 a plane containing large consignments of cocaine and marijuana, which he claimed had made an emergency landing, was found at his ranch, and in 2010 the Wikileaks organization (which published leaked classified information) gave details of an official investigation into Cartes's affairs on suspicion of money-laundering at Banco Amambay, part of his business portfolio. Moreover, Cartes attracted controversy for appointing Francisco Cuadra, a former member of Gen. Augusto Pinochet's Government in Chile, as one of his advisers. His closest rival in the election, the PLRA's Efraín Alegre, secured 36.9% of the votes. At legislative elections held concurrently the Partido Colorado secured 44 seats in the 80-seat Chamber of Deputies, while the PLRA won 27. The Partido Colorado similarly won the largest representation in the 45-seat Senate with 19 seats, compared with 12 for the PLRA.

Former Costa Rican President Oscar Arias, who had overseen the elections as head of an OAS observer mission, declared them to have been 'exemplary'. The statement was shortly followed by an invitation from MERCOSUR to rejoin the organization. Cartes was inaugurated as President on 15 August 2013. A new Council of Ministers was sworn in the same day, including Eladio Loizaga as Minister of Foreign Affairs and Germán Rojas at the Ministry of Finance. Among the heads of state at the inauguration in Asunción were the Presidents of Brazil, Argentina and Uruguay, Paraguay's fellow MERCOSUR co-founders, signalling a rapprochement in regional relations. Cartes announced that his priorities included economic development, reducing poverty and improving Paraguay's relations with neighbouring countries. The absence of agrarian reform, arguably Paraguay's most important issue, from his list of stated priorities was notable.

Cartes's assumption of the presidency precipitated the re-establishment of diplomatic relations with most of Paraguay's neighbours and the country's readmission to UNASUR. However, rejoining MERCOSUR proved to be more challenging, owing to an ongoing dispute over the legitimacy of Venezuela's membership of the organization, which had been controversially approved during Paraguay's suspension, much to the chagrin of the Franco administration. (Conservative Paraguayan politicians, particularly those in the Colorado-dominated Congress, had long opposed and obstructed Venezuelan membership owing to political differences with Venezuela's left-wing Government and concerns about democratic standards in that country.) Nevertheless, the Paraguayan and Venezuelan ministers responsible for foreign affairs met for discussions in October 2013, and this engagement resulted in the restoration of diplomatic ties. Moreover, in December, in a major concession, the Congress finally ratified Venezuela's accession to MERCOSUR, which had been pending since 2006. The formal approval of Venezuela's membership effectively marked an end to the dispute and to Paraguay's regional isolation. Paraguay was officially reintegrated into MERCOSUR at the organization's July 2014 summit meeting.

Fears of increased criminal activity and violence in the border area were heightened in late May 2013, following the killing of a prominent landowner by the EPP (see above). An investigation into the activities of the group revealed that it had attempted to assassinate the departmental police chief of Concepción during the elections of 21 April 2013. Evidence of a plot to assassinate Horacio Cartes on the day of the elections was also discovered. The EPP was believed to be responsible for an increase in kidnappings, extortion and the illegal drugs trade in the area. Shortly after taking office, Cartes (using controversial new powers accorded to him by the Congress) ordered the military to commence anti-EPP operations in Amambay, Concepción and San Pedro, and in October the Government announced that the military presence in the region was to be made permanent. Nevertheless, the EPP remained active during 2013–14, staging a number of deadly attacks against the security forces and other targets.

Demonstrations and strikes were organized by trade unions, student associations and rural groups in late 2013 and 2014 to protest against, *inter alia*, the Cartes administration's neoliberal economic policies. The resumption of land occupations and an upsurge in rural unrest in early 2014 was another concerning development for the new Government.

In an attempt to strengthen the Partido Colorado's legislative position, Cartes had concluded a governability pact with the PLRA, UNACE, Avanza País (AP) and the Partido Encuentro Nacional (PEN) prior to his inauguration. However, in April 2014 seven PLRA deputies opposed to the pact with the Partido Colorado established a separate bloc in the Chamber of Deputies. This opposition front was subsequently expanded to include legislators from AP, the PEN and Lugo's Frente Guasú (FG). In the following month AP, the PEN, the FG and the Partido Democrático Progresista created a left-wing opposition grouping in the Senate, Bloque 11.

Economy

Prof. PETER CALVERT

Revised for this edition by the editorial staff

Increased demand and high prices for its key exports led Paraguay to record its highest ever rate of growth in 2010, of 13.1%, following the recession of 2009. However, a variety of factors meant economic growth was a more modest 4.3% in 2011, and the effects of a serious drought, together with the suspension of meat exports, owing to an outbreak of foot-and-mouth disease, resulted in a contraction of 1.2% in 2012. Nevertheless, the agricultural sector staged a strong recovery in 2013, and real gross domestic product (GDP) rose by a preliminary 13.6% in that year. Paraguay is an agricultural country but its economy is determined to a large extent by its geographical position, which enables a relatively large informal sector to benefit from smuggling, and renders it very vulnerable to economic crises in neighbouring states, especially in Argentina. This informal sector is reputed to be as large as the formal sector. The country has a land area of 406,752 sq km (157,048 sq miles) and is one of the smaller republics of South America. Together with Bolivia, it is one of the continent's two landlocked countries, with Brazil to the north and east, Argentina to the south and Bolivia to the west. According to mid-2014 estimates, the country had a population of 6,893,727 and, therefore, a population density of approximately 17 persons per sq km, making it one of the least densely populated countries in the world. It is also comparatively rural, with only 63% of the population residing in urban areas in 2013.

The country is divided into two distinct geographical regions by the River Paraguay, which joins the River Paraná at an altitude of 46 m above sea level. The majority of the population lives within 160 km of the capital, Asunción, to the east of the river. This region consists of grassy plains and low hills and has a temperate climate. It is divided into two zones by a ridge of hills, to the east of which lies the Paraná plateau, which ranges from 600 m to 2,300 m in height. West of the ridge lie gently rolling hills. To the west of the Paraguay river lies the Chaco region, an arid, marshy plain extending to the foothills of the Andes and to the country's border with Bolivia. The Chaco accounts for 61% of Paraguay's land area but is inhabited by less than 2% of the population.

In 2012 the birth rate was reported by the World Bank to be 23.9 births per 1,000 inhabitants and the death rate 5.7 deaths per 1,000. The under-five mortality rate per 1,000 live births was 22 in that year, compared with 24 in 2004, but estimates of life expectancy at birth had improved steadily in recent years to 72.2 years in 2012. Public sanitation was generally good, although water pollution presented a health risk for many urban residents. Some 14% of the population, mainly in rural areas, had no access to an improved water source as recently as 2008.

Owing to the fertility of eastern Paraguay, economic activity was widespread but unevenly distributed. Historically, the main concentration of activity was around Asunción, with a secondary, more recent, economic zone based in the industrial park, Parque Industrial Oriente, 23 km from Ciudad del Este. The Chaco region accounted for less than 3% of economic activity. Spending on social welfare in the Stroessner era (1954–89) was very low, resulting in a poorly funded education system, inadequate health care and limited sanitation that persisted in the 2000s. The literacy rate, however, was relatively impressive among both men and women and was estimated at 94% in 2011. Most Paraguayans are bilingual in Spanish and the indigenous official language, Guaraní, and legislation was planned to ensure that all Paraguayans were bilingual.

In 2013 the World Bank estimated gross national income (GNI) at US $27,499m. and GNI per head at $4,040 ($7,640 by purchasing power parity—PPP), ranking Paraguay 134th in the world by PPP, and among the World Bank's lower middle-income countries. In the UN Development Programme's Human Development Index 2014, Paraguay ranked 111th in the world, a fall of 16 places since 2007.

AGRICULTURE

Agriculture (including hunting, forestry and fishing) was fundamental to the Paraguayan economy, accounting for 21.7% of GDP in 2013 and the majority of export earnings. Agricultural GDP increased at an average annual rate of 2.4% in 2003–12. Real agricultural GDP grew by 9.3% in 2011, but contracted by 16.0% in the following year, owing to disease and further adverse weather conditions, before expanding again in 2013, by 42.9%. In 2013 the sector still engaged 23.4% of the employed labour force. According to FAO, in 2011 some 3.9m. ha of land were classified as arable (9.8% of the total land area). The ownership of land remained one of the most unequal in Latin America. There was a large subsistence sector, including more than 200,000 families. Land reform was a key electoral promise of President Fernando Lugo Méndez, elected in 2008. However, conservative forces in the Partido Colorado stifled reform, and growing unrest led to widespread land occupations, especially in the eastern region bordering Brazil. Lugo's management of an occupation by landless farmers in 2012 resulted in his removal from office. Although a new President, Horacio Cartes, was elected in April 2013, his administration had made little progress on the land reform question by early 2014, and renewed rural unrest, including further land occupations, was reported.

Paraguay is largely self-sufficient in basic foodstuffs and has expanded production in export crops. Maize, cassava (manioc) and wheat are the main food crops. According to FAO, 3.3m. ha of oil crops were harvested in 2013 and production totalled 1.8m. metric tons. In the same year 1.7m. ha of cereal crops were harvested, yielding a total of 6.3m. tons. In 2013 wheat accounted for 1.4m. tons and maize 4.1m. tons. Some 175,000 ha of cassava were harvested in 2013; production reached 2.8m. tons in that year. The main products grown for export were soybeans, oilseeds, cotton and sugar cane. Production of soya and cotton increased dramatically with the colonization of the eastern border region in the 1970s, and the area planted continued to expand up to the beginning of the 21st century. According to FAO, Paraguay was the world's sixth largest producer of soybeans in 2013, with output of 9.1m. tons, up from 4.3m. tons in the previous year, when a severe drought had adversely affected the harvest. The value of soya seeds exports rose from US $59m. in 2002 to an estimated $2,295m. in 2011, before declining to $1,582m. in 2012, equivalent to 21.7% of the total export value. In order to increase productivity and the pest- and drought-resistance of their crops, Paraguayan farmers agreed in 2005 to pay royalties to a US-based corporation, Monsanto, for its genetically modified (GM) soybeans. All these developments, and the generally harmful impact of soybean cultivation on the countryside and ecosystems, were strongly opposed by the supporters of agrarian reform.

Paraguay is one of the world's largest producers of sesame seeds, growing 30,000 metric tons in 2013 on 50,000 ha of land. Government aid to sesame farmers was extended in 2009. Production of seed cotton lint decreased dramatically in the late 2000s, from 330,000 metric tons in 2004 to just 15,054 tons in 2010. According to FAO estimates, in 2013 sugar cane covered 116,000 ha and production totalled 5.5m. tons. Among tree crops, three were of particular note: in 2013 some 35,980 tons of tung nuts were grown on 8,995 ha of land; in 2012 400 tons of green coffee were produced on 300 ha of land; and, also in 2012, 18,299 ha of land yielded, mostly for domestic consumption, some 85,490 tons of maté (sometimes known as Paraguayan tea, although Paraguay is now only the world's third largest producer).

The gently undulating plains of eastern Paraguay are good ranching country and beef exports make up the largest remaining part of the formal sector. Beef, pork, eggs and milk are produced for domestic consumption. Stocks recorded by FAO in 2012 included 12.6m. head of cattle, 415,000 sheep, 138,000 goats and 23.5m. chickens. The stock of pigs rose again to 1.3m. in 2012, while there were some 300,000 horses. As with land ownership, possession of livestock in Paraguay was unevenly distributed, with 58% of cattle owned by 1% of the producers. Cattle ranching used to be the most important sector of the Paraguayan economy, but Paraguay's exclusion from the European Union (EU)'s Common Agricultural Policy and the Cotonou Agreement meant that all meat-packing plants closed. Exports of beef were adversely affected by outbreaks of foot-and-mouth disease and totalled US $796m. in 2012, compared with $919m. in 2010.

River fishing forms a significant part of the domestic diet. The fishing catch in 2012 totalled an estimated 22,400 metric tons, according to FAO estimates.

Paraguay's once abundant forest resources continue to be severely depleted by competitive logging for export, particularly in eastern Paraguay. Transport costs acted as a deterrent in the Chaco region, where some 10.5m. ha of primary forest cover remained. Given the continued illegal logging trade and the absence of a systematic reforestation programme, it was not surprising that, between 1990 and 2005, Paraguay lost 12.7% of its forest cover, or around 2.7m. ha, and in the latter year forest cover was officially given as 18.5m. ha. FAO forestry statistics showed that in 2012 the country produced 4.0m. cu m of industrial roundwood and an estimated 6.8m. cu m of fuel wood, including charcoal, for domestic consumption. Exports of wood and wood products totalled a preliminary US $88.9m. in 2012, equivalent to 1.2% of total export earnings.

MINING AND ENERGY

Paraguay has few proven mineral resources. Gypsum, limestone and clays found near the Paraguay river are used locally for building purposes. Limestone is mined for the manufacture of Portland cement by the state-owned Industria Nacional de Cemento at Vallemí, in the department of Concepción. Deposits of bauxite, copper, iron ore and manganese are known to exist but have been utilized only on a small scale. In 2010 a significant ilmenite deposit was discovered, while uranium has been found in both the east and west of the country.

Total electricity consumption in 2011 was estimated by the US Energy Information Administration at 7,497m. kWh. In that year some 57,050m. kWh were generated, of which 46,120m. kWh were exported, primarily to Brazil. Paraguay, bordered by two of the great rivers of South America (the Paraguay and Paraná), has abundant potential hydroelectric generating capacity, which has been developed to create substantial revenue. Installed electric generating capacity in 2011 was 8,816 MW, of which hydroelectric accounted for the vast majority. The most important source of power was the Paraguayan-Brazilian Itaipú project on the River Paraná, now the second largest in the world (after the Three Gorges in the People's Republic of China), with an installed generating capacity of 14,000 MW. Under the terms of the agreement, Paraguay and Brazil were each to receive one-half of the energy generated; any that they could not consume was then to be offered to the other country at a preferential rate, and Paraguay is now the largest net exporter in the world. However, under an outdated agreement Brazil only paid Paraguay US $2.70 per MWh for electricity against an international market price of nearly $60 per MWh in 2009. One of the principal successes of the Lugo administration was the conclusion of an agreement that almost tripled the price paid per unit. Repayment of the debt for the costs of the project's construction was a source of tension between the two countries, and in April 2013 the Government of Paraguay requested that the IMF evaluate the country's financial obligations to Brazil, claiming that it had already met its commitments because of the high interest rates levied by the Brazilian Government. Work was carried out in 2012 to improve internal transmission to Asunción.

During 2013 Paraguay consumed 27,200 barrels per day (b/d) of petroleum, all of which were imported. The Petróleos Paraguayos (PETROPAR) refinery at Villa Elisa had a capacity of only 7,500 b/d. In November 2012 the Government announced the discovery of 'abundant' oil deposits in the Chaco region near the border with Argentina. Exploratory drilling was ongoing in mid-2014.

MANUFACTURING

During 2003–12 the manufacturing sector increased by an average of 2.8% per year. Industry as a whole accounted for 27.9% of GDP in 2013 and manufacturing for 11.5%. Manufacturing (including mining and quarrying) employed 10.0% of the economically active population, while total industry, including energy and construction, employed 17.3% in 2013. Industry was dominated by the processing of agricultural inputs, including sugar and wood products. There were also many small companies engaged in import substitution for the domestic market, particularly in the cement, textiles and beverages sub-sectors. The country's membership of the Mercado Común del Sur (MERCOSUR) brought significant export advantages, but also increased competition from Argentine and Brazilian imports.

Paraguay has two steel mills, and 44,000 metric tons of crude steel was produced in 2012. There was some production of metal goods and machinery.

COMMERCE

Paraguay, taking advantage of its geographical position, was able to establish itself as an entrepôt for intra-regional trade. A busy commercial sector was well established, engaged in the import of consumer goods from the USA, Japan and other Asian countries for re-export to neighbouring countries. The services sector accounted for 50.4% of GDP in 2013 and employed 59.3% of the economically active population. Commerce was, however, impeded by excessive bureaucracy. In 2012, moreover, drought limited the movement of food along canals and the important Paraguay river, and made commercial shipping effectively impossible.

Paraguay's informal economy was believed to be as extensive as its formal one. Vastly improved road links with Brazil contributed to Paraguay becoming a major centre for contraband activities. Much of the informal economy consisted of profit from the smuggling of genuine and counterfeit clothing, valuable electronic goods and luxury items such as watches, perfume, spirits and tobacco into Argentina and Brazil. Paraguay was also a major illicit producer of marijuana (cannabis) for the international market, and in recent years played an increasingly significant role in the transshipment of cocaine from Colombia to the USA and Europe. The largest consignment of cocaine in the entire region of South America in 2012 was seized in Paraguay.

Consumer prices have been high in the last decade, rising at an average annual rate of 6.4% in 2003–13. Nevertheless, according to the IMF, the inflation rate declined to 4.9% in 2011, 4.0% in 2012 and an estimated 3.7% in 2013. Paraguay has operated a 'managed float' of its currency since 1998, which is primarily affected by the success of its agriculture. At the end of May 2014 the exchange rate to the US dollar was 4,423 guaraníes.

TRANSPORT AND COMMUNICATIONS

Historically, waterways provided the main mode of transport for foreign trade in Paraguay, although from the 1980s road transport became more important and by 1999 the leading point of exit for exports of cereals and vegetables was Ciudad del Este. The country has some 3,100 km of waterways, with ports at Asunción, Villeta, San Antonio and Encarnación, but low river levels in 2011–12 hampered trade. At the end of 2013 the merchant fleet consisted of 158 vessels, with a total displacement of some 155,900 grt. The country had free port facilities at Nueva Palmira in Uruguay, although services on the Paraguay–Paraná network were both irregular and expensive.

Paraguay's principal road network was a triangle linking Asunción, Encarnación and Ciudad del Este. The Trans-Chaco Highway linked Asunción to the Bolivian border and there were links with Argentina and Brazil via the international bridge over the River Paraná at Ciudad del Este. Of the estimated 29,500 km of roads, 14,986 km were paved; however, most roads have only two lanes and were interrupted by tolls and police checks. Excessive reliance on road-hauled container traffic continued to cause congestion on the bridge at Ciudad del Este, despite the opening of a new container port at Hernandarias on the banks of Lake Itaipú.

The state-owned railway, Ferrocarriles del Paraguay, SA, has closed most of the 374-km line (the Ferrocarril Presidente Carlos Antonio López) formerly linking Asunción with Encarnación, on the Argentine border, and services operated only as far as Ypacaraí, 36 km from Asunción.

There were some 800 airports in the country, 15 of which had paved runways, and of these three had runways of more than 3,047 m. The main international airport, Aeropuerto Internacional Silvio Pettirossi, is situated 15 km from Asunción. The national airline, Transportes Aéreos del MERCOSUR, was 80% owned by TAM Linhas Aéreas of Brazil.

The state-owned telephone service, the Corporación Paraguaya de Comunicaciones (COPACO), had a long history of overstaffing and low productivity, although the telephone system was modernized in the mid-1990s. By 2013, however, the network, covering 402,600 subscribers, was still inadequate, but in the mean time users of mobile cellular telephones had rapidly expanded to reach an estimated 7.1m. subscribers.

GOVERNMENT FINANCE AND INVESTMENT

In 2013 total government expenditure was 23,839,000m. guaraníes, with total revenue amounting to 21,454,000 m. guaraníes. Unlike many lower middle-income countries, Paraguay was not heavily indebted. According to IMF estimates, consolidated public debt totalled 20.9% of GDP in 2013, compared with 15.9% in 2012. Total international reserves were an estimated US $5,889m. in 2013, equivalent to 4.9 months' of import cover.

FOREIGN TRADE AND BALANCE OF PAYMENTS

Paraguay's most important trading partner has traditionally been Brazil, and it has benefited considerably from its membership of MERCOSUR. However, there were substantial differences both between exports and imports and from one year to the next. The main exports in 2012 were soya beans, cereals, animal feed, cotton, meat, edible oils, flour, electricity, and wood and leather. The main destinations for exports in 2012, according to preliminary figures, were Brazil (39.1%),

Russia (9.7%) and Argentina (8.3%). Paraguay imported road vehicles, consumer goods, tobacco (much of which was illegally re-exported), fuels, chemical products, electrical machinery, tractors and vehicle parts. The main sources of imports in 2012, according to preliminary figures, were China (27.7%), Brazil (23.7%) and Argentina (16.4%).

The current account on the balance of payments transitioned from a deficit of US $65.8m. in 2010 to a surplus of $288.8m. in 2011, although this positive balance had narrowed to $115.6m. by 2012. Fluctuations in the trade balance from 2005 impacted on the other MERCOSUR countries, and in 2009 Argentina unilaterally imposed tariffs on a variety of goods including shoes, appliances, farm machinery, processed food, steel, iron and textiles. As a result, Paraguay announced that in order to protect its economy it would have to levy increased tariffs on goods from both Argentina and Brazil. A 'Buy Paraguayan' campaign was also launched.

CONCLUSION

Paraguay's geographical position places its economy at a competitive disadvantage, while also offering opportunities, which the informal sector has been quick to seize. The country's chief economic problems remain the extent of its informal sector, a lack of confidence among investors, the vagaries of climate, a dependency on agriculture and the low intrinsic value of the country's principal agricultural exports. Successive governments attempted to resolve at least some of these problems and Paraguay benefited substantially from its incorporation into MERCOSUR.

In late 2008 the country began to suffer from a prolonged drought, and in October the impact of the world banking crisis forced the Lugo administration to reduce interest rates and ease economic policy. Owing to a sudden collapse in export demand for meat and soybeans, Paraguay was the first country in the region to be affected by the combined effects of the downturn. From 2009 political infighting prevented the Congress from enacting radical legislation. The economy recovered strongly in 2010, expanding by 13.1%, but in 2011–12 it suffered badly as a result of climatic factors, particularly drought, and disease among its livestock. Nevertheless, as conditions normalized in 2013, there was an upsurge in agricultural activity and the economy expanded by an estimated 13.6% in that year—one of the highest growth rates in the world. The financial position, meanwhile, appeared to be sound, bolstered by the approval of a new fiscal responsibility law in October, introduced by the new Cartes administration. The IMF expected that the agricultural sector would continue to expand in 2014 and projected real GDP growth of 4.8% in that year.

Statistical Survey

Sources (unless otherwise stated): Dirección General de Estadística, Encuestas y Censos, Naciones Unidas, esq. Saavedra, Fernando de la Mora, Zona Norte; tel. (21) 51-1016; fax (21) 50-8493; internet www.dgeec.gov.py; Banco Central del Paraguay, Avda Federación Rusa y Marecos, Casilla 861, Barrio Santo Domingo, Asunción; tel. (21) 61-0088; fax (21) 60-8149; e-mail ccs@bcp.gov.py; internet www.bcp.gov.py; Secretaría Técnica de Planificación, Presidencia de la República, Iturbe y Eligio Ayala, Asunción.

Area and Population

AREA, POPULATION AND DENSITY

Area (sq km)	406,752*
Population (census results)	
26 August 1992	4,152,588
28 August 2002	
Males	2,627,831
Females	2,555,249
Total	5,183,080
Population (official estimates at mid-year)	
2012	6,672,631
2013	6,783,374
2014	6,893,727
Density (per sq km) at mid-2014	16.9

* 157,048 sq miles.

POPULATION BY AGE AND SEX
('000, official estimates at mid-2014)

	Males	Females	Total
0–14 years	1,117.2	1,076.4	2,193.6
15–64 years	2,182.1	2,136.6	4,318.7
65 years and over	182.3	199.1	381.4
Total	**3,481.6**	**3,412.1**	**6,893.7**

DEPARTMENTS
(official population estimates at mid-2012)

	Area (sq km)	Population	Density (per sq km)	Capital
Alto Paraguay (incl. Chaco) .	82,349	11,151	0.1	Fuerte Olimpo
Alto Paraná .	14,895	785,747	52.8	Ciudad del Este
Amambay . .	12,933	125,611	9.7	Pedro Juan Caballero
Asunción . .	117	515,587	4,406.7	—
Boquerón (incl. Nueva Asunción) .	91,669	61,107	0.7	Doctor Pedro P. Peña
Caaguazú . .	11,474	483,048	42.1	Coronel Oviedo
Caazapá . . .	9,496	151,415	15.9	Caazapá
Canindeyú . .	14,667	191,447	13.1	Salto del Guairá
Central . . .	2,465	2,221,180	901.1	Asunción
Concepción . .	18,051	189,929	10.5	Concepción
Cordillera . .	4,948	282,981	57.2	Caacupé
Guairá . . .	3,846	198,032	51.5	Villarrica
Itapúa . . .	16,525	545,924	33.0	Encarnación
Misiones . .	9,556	118,798	12.4	San Juan Bautista
Ñeembucú . .	12,147	84,123	6.9	Pilar
Paraguarí . .	8,705	239,633	27.5	Paraguarí
Presidente Hayes	72,907	106,826	1.5	Pozo Colorado
San Pedro . .	20,002	360,094	18.0	San Pedro
Total . . .	**406,752**	**6,672,631**	**16.4**	—

PRINCIPAL TOWNS
(incl. rural environs, population at 2002 census)

Asunción (capital) .	510,910	Lambaré . . .	119,830
Ciudad del Este* .	222,109	Fernando de la Mora	113,990
San Lorenzo . .	203,150	Caaguazú . . .	100,132
Luque	185,670	Encarnación . .	97,000
		Pedro Juan	
Capiatá	154,520	Caballero . . .	88,530

* Formerly Puerto Presidente Stroessner.

Mid-2014 ('000, incl. suburbs, UN estimate): Asunción 2,307 (Source: UN, *World Urbanization Prospects: The 2014 Revision*).

BIRTHS AND DEATHS
(annual averages, UN estimates)

	1995–2000	2000–05	2005–10
Birth rate (per 1,000)	29.3	26.9	24.8
Death rate (per 1,000)	6.0	5.6	5.6

Source: UN, *World Population Prospects: The 2012 Revision*.

2011: Registered live births 60,197; Registered marriages 19,491; Registered deaths 22,648. Note: Registration believed to be incomplete; number of live births includes registered births occurring in year of registration only.

Life expectancy (years at birth): 72.2 (males 70.0; females 74.5) in 2012 (Source: World Bank, World Development Indicators database).

ECONOMICALLY ACTIVE POPULATION
(household survey, '000 persons aged 10 years and over, October-December)

	2011	2012	2013
Agriculture, hunting, forestry and fishing	801,914	882,788	767,233
Manufacturing, mining and quarrying	318,996	341,989	328,262
Electricity, gas and water . . .	14,065	18,988	22,743
Construction	198,979	179,877	214,167
Trade, restaurants and hotels .	768,920	827,679	843,082
Transport, storage and communications	126,420	136,170	135,980
Financing, insurance, real estate and business services . . .	137,763	155,754	166,275
Community, social and personal services	662,788	703,411	795,149
Sub-total	**3,029,845**	**3,246,656**	**3,272,891**
Activities not adequately described	4,926	248	1,928
Total employed	**3,034,771**	**3,246,904**	**3,274,819**
Unemployed	180,739	165,539	171,901
Total labour force	**3,215,510**	**3,412,443**	**3,446,720**

Health and Welfare

KEY INDICATORS

Total fertility rate (children per woman, 2012)	2.9
Under-5 mortality rate (per 1,000 live births, 2012) . . .	22
HIV/AIDS (% of persons aged 15–49, 2012)	0.3
Physicians (per 1,000 head, 2002)	1.1
Hospital beds (per 1,000 head, 2010)	1.3
Health expenditure (2011): US $ per head (PPP)	550
Health expenditure (2011): % of GDP	8.9
Health expenditure (2011): public (% of total)	38.6
Access to water (% of persons, 2012)	94
Access to sanitation (% of persons, 2012)	80
Total carbon dioxide emissions ('000 metric tons, 2010) . .	5,075.1
Carbon dioxide emissions per head (metric tons, 2010) . .	0.8
Human Development Index (2013): ranking	111
Human Development Index (2013): value	0.676

For sources and definitions, see explanatory note on p. vi.

Agriculture

PRINCIPAL CROPS

('000 metric tons)

	2010	2011	2012
Wheat	1,402	1,464	1,400*
Rice, paddy	315	408	380†
Maize	3,109	3,346	3,079*
Sorghum	150	150	145*
Sweet potatoes	43	45	50†
Cassava (Manioc)	2,624	2,454	2,560†
Sugar cane	5,131	5,339	5,450†
Beans, dry	49	53	56†
Soybeans (Soya beans) . . .	7,460	8,310	8,350*
Oil palm fruit†	152	152	152
Sunflower seed	262	109	125†
Tomatoes	58	45	47†
Onions, dry†	35	28	30
Carrots and turnips	12	12	13†
Watermelons†	130	103	110
Cantaloupes and other melons† .	38	30	32
Bananas	80	60	65†
Oranges	230	230	235†
Tangerines, mandarins, clementines and satsumas . .	44	44	46†
Grapefruit and pomelos . . .	42	42	43†
Guavas, mangoes and mangosteens†	32	30	33
Pineapples	59	59	62†
Maté	86	86	86†

* Unofficial figure.
† FAO estimate(s).

Aggregate production ('000 metric tons, may include official, semi-official or estimated data): Total cereals 4,976 in 2010, 5,368 in 2011, 5,004 in 2012; Total roots and tubers 2,668 in 2010, 2,503 in 2011, 2,614 in 2012; Total vegetables (incl. melons) 323 in 2010, 257 in 2011, 272 in 2012; Total fruits (excl. melons) 568 in 2010, 542 in 2011, 562 in 2012.

Source: FAO.

LIVESTOCK

('000 head, year ending September)

	2010	2011	2012
Cattle	12,305	12,437	12,550*
Horses*	290	295	300
Pigs	1,182	1,241	1,275*
Sheep*	400	410	415
Goats*	135	137	138
Chickens*	20,000	22,000	23,500
Ducks*	1,100	1,200	1,250
Geese and guinea fowls* . . .	115	115	115
Turkeys*	190	195	200

* FAO estimate(s).

Source: FAO.

LIVESTOCK PRODUCTS

('000 metric tons, FAO estimates)

	2010	2011	2012
Cattle meat	347	352	355
Pig meat	160	164	126
Chicken meat	37	38	39
Cows' milk	490	512	515
Hen eggs	128	128	130

Source: FAO.

Forestry

ROUNDWOOD REMOVALS

('000 cubic metres, excluding bark, FAO estimates)

	2010	2011	2012
Sawlogs, veneer logs and logs for sleepers	3,515	3,515	3,515
Other industrial wood	529	529	529
Fuel wood	6,576	6,684	6,793
Total	10,620	10,728	10,837

Source: FAO.

SAWNWOOD PRODUCTION

('000 cubic metres, including railway sleepers, FAO estimates)

	2010	2011	2012
Total (all broadleaved) . . .	550	550	550

Note: Annual production assumed to be unchanged from 1997.
Source: FAO.

Fishing

('000 metric tons, live weight, FAO estimates)

	2010	2011	2012
Capture	17.8	17.0	17.0
Characins	6.3	6.0	6.0
Freshwater siluroids . . .	8.4	8.0	8.0
Other freshwater fishes . . .	3.1	3.0	3.0
Aquaculture	3.0	4.9	5.4
Total catch	20.8	21.9	22.4

Source: FAO.

Industry

SELECTED PRODUCTS
('000 metric tons)

	2010	2011	2012
Soya bean oil*†	336	374	208
Hydraulic cement‡	650	650	650

* Unofficial figures.
† Data from FAO.
‡ Data from US Geological Survey.

Finance

CURRENCY AND EXCHANGE RATES

Monetary Units
100 céntimos = 1 guaraní (G).

Sterling, Dollar and Euro Equivalents (30 May 2014)
£1 sterling = 7,441.1 guaraníes;
US $1 = 4,423.4 guaraníes;
€1 = 6,020.7 guaraníes;
100,000 guaraníes = £13.44 = $22.60 = €16.61.

Average Exchange Rate (guaraníes per US dollar)
2011   4,191.4
2012   4,424.9
2013   4,320.7

BUDGET
(central government operations, '000 million guaraníes)

Revenue	2012	2013	2014*
Taxation	13,871	14,790	16,881
Corporate taxes	2,903	3,098	3,301
Value-added tax	7,079	7,884	8,672
Import duties	1,642	1,632	2,206
Non-tax revenue and grants . .	6,288	6,451	10,416
Capital revenues	480	213	600
Total	20,640	21,454	27,896

Expenditure	2012	2013	2014*
Current expenditure	17,395	18,852	23,263
Personal	10,436	11,677	12,410
Other	6,959	7,175	10,853
Capital expenditure	5,231	4,987	7,585
Total	22,626	23,839	30,848

* Budget figures.
Source: Ministry of Finance, Asunción.

INTERNATIONAL RESERVES
(excl. gold, US $ million at 31 December)

	2011	2012	2013
IMF special drawing rights . .	169.76	170.00	170.38
Reserve position in IMF . .	32.97	33.01	33.07
Foreign exchange	4,747.33	4,353.60	5,352.13
Total	4,950.06	4,556.61	5,555.58

Source: IMF, *International Financial Statistics*.

MONEY SUPPLY
('000 million guaraníes at 31 December)

	2011	2012	2013
Currency outside depository corporations	5,761.73	6,429.01	7,127.66
Transferable deposits	15,364.78	16,998.88	20,717.12
Other deposits	11,908.53	12,948.70	15,780.24
Securities other than shares . .	11,843.76	13,779.20	17,031.99
Broad money	44,878.79	50,155.80	60,657.00

Source: IMF, *International Financial Statistics*.

COST OF LIVING
(Consumer Price Index for Asunción; base: December 2007 = 100)

	2011	2012	2013
Food (incl. non-alcoholic beverages)	132.5	130.0	134.2
Clothing (incl. footwear) . .	109.8	114.4	117.6
Housing and energy . . .	121.2	132.9	139.5
All items (incl. others) . .	122.2	126.7	130.1

NATIONAL ACCOUNTS
('000 million guaraníes at current prices, preliminary)

Expenditure on the Gross Domestic Product

	2011	2012	2013
Final consumption expenditure .	84,895.7	91,101.7	103,210.1
Households*	73,739.5	77,332.6	87,783.5
General government . . .	11,156.2	13,769.0	15,426.5
Gross capital formation . .	17,632.7	16,408.8	19,826.4
Gross fixed capital formation .	17,231.6	16,484.1	19,709.7
Changes in inventories† . .	401.1	−75.3	116.7
Total domestic expenditure .	102,528.4	107,510.5	123,036.5
Exports of goods and services . .	55,377.9	54,330.7	61,648.9
Less Imports of goods and services	52,703.1	53,008.8	55,789.0
GDP in purchasers' values .	105,203.2	108,832.3	128,896.4
GDP at constant 1994 prices .	23,933.9	23,637.3	26,840.6

* Including non-profit institutions serving households.
† Including acquisitions, less disposals, of valuables.

Gross Domestic Product by Economic Activity

	2011	2012	2013
Agriculture, hunting, forestry and fishing	21,143.9	17,770.0	25,389.0
Mining and quarrying . . .	136.0	149.8	162.6
Manufacturing	11,535.7	11,941.0	13,438.9
Construction	7,096.0	7,678.0	8,950.1
Electricity and water	9,070.5	10,044.1	10,010.7
Trade	15,951.7	15,367.9	18,812.4
Transport and communications .	5,737.0	6,351.1	7,613.1
Financial intermediation . .	4,345.9	5,212.2	5,865.9
Government services . . .	10,363.5	13,381.2	15,274.9
Real estate, renting and business activities	3,257.0	3,493.7	4,017.8
Hotels and restaurants . . .	1,050.5	1,120.2	1,251.2
Other services	5,230.7	5,627.3	5,980.5
Gross value added in basic prices	94,918.4	98,136.4	116,767.2
Net taxes on products . . .	10,284.9	10,695.8	12,129.1
GDP in market prices . . .	105,203.2	108,832.3	128,896.4

BALANCE OF PAYMENTS
(US $ million)

	2010	2011	2012
Exports of goods	10,366.6	12,520.4	11,903.9
Imports of goods	−9,544.6	−11,684.7	−11,056.1
Balance on goods	822.0	835.7	847.7
Exports of services	722.7	814.5	778.7
Imports of services	−755.3	−903.7	−868.5
Balance on goods and services	789.4	746.6	757.9
Primary income received . . .	45.4	35.9	42.1
Primary income paid . . .	−1,458.0	−1,207.2	−1,443.1
Balance on goods, services and primary income	−623.3	−424.7	−643.1
Secondary income received . .	558.9	715.0	760.1
Secondary income paid . . .	−1.4	−1.4	−1.4
Current balance	−65.8	288.8	115.6
Capital account (net) . . .	40.0	40.0	51.0
Direct investment assets . .	−128.2	111.3	−92.3
Direct investment liabilities . .	355.9	134.4	363.1
Portfolio investment liabilities .	—	—	600.0
Other investment assets . .	−23.3	193.5	−280.8
Other investment liabilities . .	−36.0	−477.9	−192.6
Net errors and omissions . .	176.9	494.2	−588.5
Reserves and related items .	319.4	784.3	−24.5

Source: IMF, *International Financial Statistics*.

External Trade

PRINCIPAL COMMODITIES
(US $ million)

Imports f.o.b.	2010	2011	2012*
Food and live animals	361.9	455.8	461.7
Beverages and tobacco . . .	309.7	350.1	351.5
Mineral fuels	1,072.8	1,506.5	1,693.6
Chemical products	682.1	944.1	898.2
Road vehicles	314.7	444.4	427.9
Transport equipment and accessories	677.2	903.1	778.7
Electrical appliances . . .	344.4	366.0	323.6
Motors, general industrial machinery equipment and parts	2,851.7	3,094.2	2,651.4
Total (incl. others)	9,399.8	11,549.0	10,756.4

Exports f.o.b.	2010	2011	2012*
Meat	919.4	751.2	795.6
Cereals	547.9	603.1	1,042.0
Soya seeds	1,590.8	2,294.6	1,582.3
Soybean oil	222.8	275.4	138.7
Wood and wooden products . .	101.6	96.6	88.9
Cotton fibres	24.4	17.0	44.0
Electrical energy	1,985.7	2,267.4	2,232.2
Total (incl. others)	6,516.6	7,776.4	7,283.9

* Preliminary figures.

PRINCIPAL TRADING PARTNERS
(US $ million)

Imports f.o.b.	2010	2011	2012*
Argentina	1,460.8	1,625.6	1,762.5
Brazil	2,280.7	3,072.3	2,550.6
Chile	116.5	144.0	137.7
China, People's Republic . . .	3,255.6	3,439.2	2,979.5
Germany	147.1	207.4	191.0
Japan	320.9	359.1	287.0
Korea, Republic	139.0	199.7	254.6
Mexico	87.8	179.9	157.0
Russia	7.0	13.9	150.0
Uruguay	141.3	180.7	155.2
USA	404.9	607.7	857.9
Venezuela	208.6	361.6	122.5
Total (incl. others)	9,399.8	11,549.0	10,756.4

Exports f.o.b.	2010	2011	2012*
Argentina	555.3	692.1	604.1
Bolivia	34.7	55.7	89.1
Brazil	2,194.8	2,500.1	2,850.3
Chile	604.2	541.4	187.3
France	52.6	95.9	10.1
Germany	221.3	575.0	433.0
India	72.0	43.9	20.6
Israel	99.0	145.8	142.2
Italy	277.5	330.9	235.2
Korea, Republic	2.4	106.7	31.6
Mexico	59.8	90.7	89.4
Netherlands	256.8	92.2	38.5
Peru	203.9	215.4	161.7
Russia	428.0	405.3	704.3
Spain	192.5	242.8	181.3
Turkey	199.0	206.7	100.3
Uruguay	67.9	84.0	99.6
USA	63.0	109.7	143.0
Venezuela	113.1	107.8	60.5
Total (incl. others)	6,516.6	7,776.4	7,283.9

* Preliminary figures.

Transport

ROAD TRAFFIC
(vehicles in use)

	2010	2011	2012
Passenger cars	200,147	219,022	241,734
Buses and coaches	12,378	12,876	13,151
Vans and lorries	162,901	165,325	168,906
Motorcycles and mopeds . . .	194,817	237,436	270,009

SHIPPING

Flag Registered Fleet
(at 31 December)

	2011	2012	2013
Number of vessels	151	155	158
Total displacement ('000 grt) . .	148.7	157.1	155.9

Source: Lloyd's List Intelligence (www.lloydslistintelligence.com).

CIVIL AVIATION
(traffic)

	2010	2011	2012
Passengers carried ('000) . . .	699.3	792.5	830.7
Freight carried ('000 metric tons) .	19.0	23.1	22.9

Tourism

ARRIVALS BY NATIONALITY

	2010	2011	2012
Argentina	218,418	222,901	254,328
Bolivia	11,646	23,256	18,202
Brazil	159,280	176,440	171,925
Chile	9,829	11,706	11,780
Germany	7,173	9,057	11,486
Spain	4,929	8,364	11,801
Uruguay	11,216	14,154	15,448
USA	10,142	11,285	17,280
Total (incl. others)	465,264	523,740	579,305

Tourism receipts (US $ million, excl. passenger transport): 241 in 2011; 265 in 2012; 273 in 2013 (provisional) (Source: World Tourism Organization).

Communications Media

	2011	2012	2013
Telephones ('000 main lines in use)	368.8	411.0	402.6
Mobile cellular telephones ('000 subscribers)	6,529.1	6,793.7	7,053.3
Broadband subscribers ('000) . .	61.8	79.6	107.8

2010 ('000): Internet subscribers 105.7.

Source: International Telecommunication Union.

Education

(2011 unless otherwise indicated)

	Institutions	Teachers	Students
Pre-primary schools . .	5,799	6,304.5*	153,189
Primary	7,170	32,998.2*	814,651
Secondary	4,423	34,340.7*	334,172
Tertiary: university level .	111†	1,844‡	242,228

* 2007/08.
† 1999.
‡ 1999/2000.

Sources: Ministry of Education and Culture, Asunción; UNESCO Institute for Statistics.

Pupil-teacher ratio (primary education, UNESCO estimate): 21.7 in 2010/11 (Source: UNESCO Institute for Statistics).

Adult literacy rate (UNESCO estimates): 93.9% (males 94.8%; females 92.9%) in 2010 (Source: UNESCO Institute for Statistics).

Directory

The Constitution

A new Constitution for the Republic of Paraguay came into force on 22 June 1992, replacing the Constitution of 25 August 1967.

FUNDAMENTAL RIGHTS, DUTIES AND FREEDOMS

Paraguay is an independent republic whose form of government is representative democracy. The powers accorded to the legislature, executive and judiciary are exercised in a system of independence, equilibrium, co-ordination and reciprocal control. Sovereignty resides in the people, who exercise it through universal, free, direct, equal and secret vote. All citizens over 18 years of age and resident in the national territory are entitled to vote.

All citizens are equal before the law and have freedom of conscience, travel, residence, expression, and the right to privacy. The freedom of the press is guaranteed. The freedom of religion and ideology is guaranteed. Relations between the State and the Catholic Church are based on independence, co-operation and autonomy. All citizens have the right to assemble and demonstrate peacefully. All public and private sector workers, with the exception of the Armed Forces and the police, have the right to form a trade union and to strike. All citizens have the right to associate freely in political parties or movements.

The rights of the indigenous peoples to preserve and develop their ethnic identity in their respective habitat are guaranteed.

LEGISLATURE

The Congreso Nacional (National Congress) comprises the Senado (Senate) and the Cámara de Diputados (Chamber of Deputies). The Senate is composed of 45 members, the Chamber of 80 members, elected directly by the people. Legislation concerning national defence and international agreements may be initiated in the Senate. Departmental and municipal legislation may be initiated in the Chamber of Deputies. Both chambers of the Congress are elected for a period of five years.

GOVERNMENT

Executive power is exercised by the President of the Republic. The President and the Vice-President are elected jointly and directly by the people, by a simple majority of votes, for a period of five years. They may not be elected for a second term. The President and the Vice-President govern with the assistance of an appointed Council of Ministers. The President participates in the formulation of legislation and enacts it. The President is empowered to veto legislation sanctioned by the Congress, to nominate or remove ministers, to direct the foreign relations of the Republic, and to convene extraordinary sessions of the Congress. The President is Commander-in-Chief of the Armed Forces.

JUDICIARY

Judicial power is exercised by the Supreme Court of Justice and by the tribunals. The Supreme Court is composed of nine members who are appointed on the proposal of the Consejo de la Magistratura (Council of the Magistracy), and has the power to declare legislation unconstitutional.

The Government

HEAD OF STATE

President: HORACIO MANUEL CARTES JARA (took office 15 August 2013).

Vice-President: JUAN AFARA.

COUNCIL OF MINISTERS
(September 2014)

The Government comprises members of the Asociación Nacional Republicana (Partido Colorado).

Minister of the Interior: FRANCISCO JOSÉ DE VARGAS.

Minister of Foreign Affairs: ELADIO LOIZAGA.

Minister of Finance: GERMÁN HUGO ROJAS IRIGOYEN.

Minister of Industry and Commerce: GUSTAVO LEITE.

Minister of Public Works and Communications: RAMÓN GIMÉNEZ GAONA.

Minister of National Defence: Gen. BERNARDINO SOTO ESTIGARRIBIA.

Minister of Public Health and Social Welfare: ANTONIO BARRIOS.

Minister of Justice: SHEILA ABED DUARTE.

Minister of Agriculture and Livestock: JORGE GATTINO.

Minister of Education and Culture: MARTA LAFUENTE.

Minister of Labour, Employment and Social Security: GUILLERMO SOSA.

Minister for Women: ANA MARÍA BAIARDI.

Secretary-General to the Presidency: JUAN CARLOS LÓPEZ MOREIRA BORGOGNON.

MINISTRIES

Office of the President: Palacio de los López, Asunción; tel. (21) 414-0200; internet www.presidencia.gov.py.

Ministry of Agriculture and Livestock: Edif. San Rafael, Yegros, entre 25 de Mayo y Cerro Corá 437, Apdo 825, Asunción; tel. (21) 45-0937; fax (21) 49-7965; e-mail prensa@mag.gov.py; internet www.mag.gov.py.

Ministry of Education and Culture: Edif. La Consolidada, Chile 719, Casi Eduardo V. Haedo, Asunción; tel. (21) 45-0014; fax (21) 45-0015; e-mail comunicacion@mec.gov.py; internet www.mec.gov.py.

Ministry of Finance: Chile 252, entre Palma y Presidente Franco, Asunción; tel. (21) 44-0010; fax (21) 44-8283; e-mail info@hacienda.gov.py; internet www.hacienda.gov.py.

Ministry of Foreign Affairs: Edif. Benigno López, Palma y 14 de Mayo, Asunción; tel. (21) 49-3928; fax (21) 49-3910; e-mail sistemas@mre.gov.py; internet www.mre.gov.py.

Ministry of Industry and Commerce: Avda Mariscal López 3333, esq. Dr Wiss, Villa Morra, Casilla 2151, Asunción; tel. (21) 616-3012; fax (21) 616-3118; e-mail sprivada@mic.gov.py; internet www.mic.gov.py.

Ministry of the Interior: Chile 1002, esq. Manduvira, Asunción; tel. (21) 415-2000; fax (21) 44-6448; e-mail ministro@mdi.gov.py; internet www.mdi.gov.py.

Ministry of Justice: Avda Dr José Gaspar Rodríguez de Francia, esq. Estados Unidos, Asunción; tel. (21) 49-3209; fax (21) 20-8469; e-mail info@mjt.gov.py; internet www.mjt.gov.py.

Ministry of Labour, Employment and Social Security: Asunción.

Ministry of National Defence: Avda Mariscal López, esq. Vicepresidente Sánchez y 22 de Septiembre, Asunción; tel. (21) 21-0052; fax (21) 21-1815; e-mail ministro@mdn.gov.py; internet www.mdn.gov.py.

Ministry of Public Health and Social Welfare: Avda Pettirossi, esq. Brasil, Asunción; tel. (21) 20-4601; fax (21) 20-6700; internet www.mspbs.gov.py.

Ministry of Public Works and Communications: Oliva y Alberdi 411, Casilla 1221, Asunción; tel. (21) 414-9000; fax (21) 44-4421; e-mail comunicaciones@mopc.gov.py; internet www.mopc.gov.py.

Ministry for Women: Edif. Ayfra, 13°, entre Bloque B y Planta Baja, Avda Presidente Franco, esq. Ayolas, Asunción; tel. (21) 45-0036; fax (21) 45-0041; e-mail info@mujer.gov.py; internet www.mujer.gov.py.

President and Legislature

PRESIDENT

Election, 21 April 2013

Candidate	Votes	% of votes
Horacio Manuel Cartes Jara (ANR)	1,095,469	45.80
Pedro Efraín Alegre Sasiain (PLRA)	883,630	36.94
Mario Aníbal Ferreiro Sanabría (Avanza País)	140,622	5.88
Aníbal Enrique Carrillo Iramain (FG)	79,327	3.32
Miguel Carrizosa Galiano (PPQ)	27,036	1.13
Lino César Oviedo Sánchez (UNACE)	19,124	0.80
Others	15,777	0.66
Total votes	2,391,790*	100.00

* Including 71,388 blank and 59,417 invalid ballots.

NATIONAL CONGRESS

President of the Senate and the National Congress: BLAS LLANO (PLRA).

Senate
(Senado)

Senate: Calle 14 de Mayo, esq. Avda de la República, 1°, Asuncíon; tel. (21) 414-5198; e-mail informes@senado.gov.py; internet www.senado.gov.py.

General Election, 21 April 2013

Party	Seats
Asociación Nacional Republicana (Partido Colorado)	19
Partido Liberal Radical Auténtico	13
Frente Guasú	5
Partido Democrático Progresista	3
Avanza País	2
Unión Nacional de Ciudadanos Eticos	2
Partido Encuentro Nacional	1
Total	45

Chamber of Deputies
(Cámara de Diputados)

Chamber of Deputies: Avda República y 15 de Agosto, Asunción; tel. (21) 414-4000; e-mail dircom@diputados.gov.py; internet www.diputados.gov.py.

President of the Chamber of Deputies: JUAN BARTOLOMÉ RAMÍREZ BRIZUELA (PLRA).

General Election, 21 April 2013

Party	Seats
Asociación Nacional Republicana (Partido Colorado)	44
Partido Liberal Radical Auténtico	28
Unión Nacional de Ciudadanos Eticos	2
Avanza País	2
Partido Encuentro Nacional	2
Partido Patria Querida	1
Frente Guasú	1
Total	80

Election Commission

Tribunal Superior de Justicia Electoral (TSJE): Avda Eusebio Ayala 2759 y Santa Cruz de la Sierra, Casilla 1209, Asunción; tel. and fax (21) 618-0111; e-mail protocolo@tsje.gov.py; internet www.tsje.gov.py; f. 1995; Pres. ALBERTO RAMÍREZ ZAMBONINI.

Political Organizations

Asociación Nacional Republicana (ANR) (Partido Colorado): Casa de los Colorados, 25 de Mayo 842, Asunción; tel. (21) 45-2543; fax (21) 45-4136; e-mail contacto@anr.gov.py; internet www.anr.org.py; f. 19th century; Pres. LILIAN SAMANIEGO.

Avanza País: Eligio Ayala 1728, casi República Francesa, Asunción; tel. (21) 20-4392; e-mail info@avanzapais.com; internet avanzapais.com; f. 2012 by breakaway mems of the Frente Guasú; Leader MARIO FERREIRO.

Convergencia Popular Socialista (CPS): Caballero 766, Asunción; tel. (21) 44-3705; e-mail prensapcps@gmail.com; internet partidoconvergencia.wordpress.com; f. 2002; Sec.-Gen. RAMÓN MEDINA VELAZCO.

Frente Guasú (FG): Teniente Bauza 4121, con Cerro Corá, Asunción; tel. (21) 20-1494; e-mail frenteguasu@frenteguasu.org.py; internet frenteguasu.org.py; f. 2010; a coalition of political orgs and social movts supportive of Fernando Lugo Méndez, incl. the constituent parties of the APC; Sec.-Gen. RICARDO CANESE.

Movimiento 20 de Abril: Colón 262, entre Avda Presidente Franco y Avda Palma, Asunción; tel. (21) 49-0991; e-mail movimiento20deabril2012@gmail.com; internet movimiento20deabril.blogspot.com; f. 2010 by supporters of Fernando Lugo Méndez; Leader MIGUEL ANGEL LÓPEZ PERITO; Sec.-Gen. LIZ TORRES.

Partido Comunista Paraguayo (PCP): Brasil 228, Asunción; internet www.pcparaguay.org; f. 1928; banned 1928–46, 1947–89; Sec.-Gen. DERLYS VILLAGRA.

Partido Demócrata Cristiano (PDC): Dupuis 962, entre Montevideo y Colón, Asunción; tel. (21) 42-0434; e-mail info@pdc.org.py; internet www.pdc.org.py; f. 1960; 20,500 mems; Pres. ALBA ESPINOLA DE CRISTALDO; Sec.-Gen. ANÍBAL RODAS.

Partido Democrático Progresista (PDP): Avda 25 de Mayo, entre Constitución y Brasil, Asunción; tel. (21) 22-5354; e-mail info@pdp.org.py; internet www.pdp.org.py; f. 2007; democratic socialist; Pres. DESIRÉE MASI.

Partido Encuentro Nacional (PEN): Avda Mariscal López, con General Aquino 834, Asunción; tel. (21) 21-0229; fax (21) 21-4716; e-mail prensa.pen@gmail.com; internet www.encuentronacional.org.py; f. 1991 as Movimiento Encuentro Nacional; Pres. FERNANDO CAMACHO PAREDES.

Partido Frente Amplio: Antequera 764, esq. Fulgencio R. Moreno, Asunción; tel. (21) 44-1389; e-mail arevalovicente@hotmail.com; Leader PEDRO ALMADA.

Partido Humanista Paraguayo: San Francisco 1318, San Antonio, Barrio Jara, Asunción; tel. (21) 23-3085; e-mail phfernandodelamora@hotmail.com; f. 1985; legally recognized 1989; campaigns for the protection of human rights and environmental issues; Pres. ROBERTO CARLOS FERREIRA FRANCO.

Partido Liberal Radical Auténtico (PLRA): Iturbe 936, entre Manuel Domínguez y Teniente Fariña, Asunción; tel. (21) 49-8442; fax (21) 49-8443; e-mail prensa@plra.org.py; internet www.plra.org.py; f. 1978; centre; 806,000 mems; Pres. BLAS ANTONIO LLANO RAMOS; Sec.-Gen. AMANDA ROSALIA NUÑEZ DE FIGUEREDO.

Partido del Movimiento al Socialismo (PMAS): Jejui y 15 de agosto 582, Asunción; tel. (21) 45-5977; e-mail prensa@pmas.org.py; internet p-mas.org; f. 2006; Pres. CAMILO SOARES; Sec.-Gen. RODRIGO BUONGERMINI.

Partido País Solidario: Avda 5, esq. Méjico, Asunción; tel. (21) 39-1271; e-mail presidencia@paissolidario.org.py; internet www.paissolidario.org.py; f. 2000; mem. of Socialist International; Pres. Dr CARLOS FILIZZOLA PALLARÉS; Exec. Sec. MARÍA TERESA FERREIRA.

Partido Patria Querida (PPQ): Padre Cardozo 469, Asunción; tel. 21-3300; e-mail comunicaciones@patriaquerida.org; internet www.patriaquerida.org; f. 2002; legally recognized 2004; Pres. SEBASTIÁN ACHA; Sec.-Gen. ARSENIO OCAMPOS VELÁZQUEZ.

Partido Popular Tekojojá: Carios, esq. Médicos del Chaco, Asunción; tel. and fax (21) 55-4104; e-mail tekojoja@tekojoja.org.py; internet www.tekojoja.org; f. 2006; left-wing, mainly comprising social and indigenous groups; Pres. STILBER VALDES; Sec. SANDRA GALLARDO.

Partido Revolucionario Febrerista (PRF): Casa del Pueblo, Mandivira 522, entre 14 de Mayo y 15 de Agosto, Asunción; tel. (21) 49-4041; e-mail partyce@mixmail.com; internet www.prf.org.py; f. 1951; social democratic; mem. of Socialist International; Pres. HILDA JOSEFINA DUARTE BENÍTEZ; Sec.-Gen. OSVALDO SEGOVIA.

Partido Social Demócrata (PSD): 25 de Mayo, esq. Tacuarí, Asunción; tel. (21) 45-3293; e-mail partidosocialdemocrata.paraguay@gmail.com; f. 2007; Pres. MANUEL DOLDÁN DEL PUERTO.

Partido de los Trabajadores (PT): Hernandarias y Piribebuy 890, Asunción; tel. (21) 44-5009; e-mail info@ptparaguay.org; internet www.ptparaguay.org; f. 1989; Socialist; Pres. JULIO LÓPEZ.

Partido de la Unidad Popular (PUP): Palma 571, entre 14 de Mayo y 15 de Agosto, Planta Alta, Asunción; tel. (21) 21-5059; fax (21) 49-8018; e-mail p.unidadpopular@gmail.com; legally recognized 2004; Pres. JUAN DE DIOS ACOSTA MENA.

Unión Nacional de Ciudadanos Eticos (UNACE): Avda Mariscal López, Saturio Ríos, Asunción; tel. (21) 59-1900; e-mail loviedo@unace.org.py; internet www.unace.org.py; f. 1996 as Unión Nacional de Colorados Eticos, a faction of the Partido Colorado, current name adopted 2002; left-wing; Exec. Sec. HERMINIO CHENA VALDEZ.

Diplomatic Representation

EMBASSIES IN PARAGUAY

Argentina: Avda España, esq. Avda Perú, Casilla 757, Asunción; tel. (21) 21-2320; fax (21) 21-1029; e-mail contacto_epara@cancilleria.gov.ar; internet www.embajada-argentina.org.py; Ambassador ANA MARÍA CORRADI.

Bolivia: Calle Israel 309, esq. Río de Janeiro, Asunción; tel. (21) 21-1430; fax (21) 21-1217; e-mail emboliviapy@tigo.com.py; Chargé d'affaires a.i. ZANDRA ELIZABETH RODRÍGUEZ CAMPOY.

Brazil: Coronel Irrazábal, esq. Eligio Ayala, Casilla 22, Asunción; tel. (21) 248-4000; fax (21) 21-2693; e-mail parbrem@embajadabrasil.org.py; internet assuncao.itamaraty.gov.br; Ambassador JOSÉ EDUARDO MARTINS FELICIO.

Chile: Capital Emilio Nudelman 351, esq. Campos Cervera, Asunción; tel. (21) 61-3855; fax (21) 66-2755; e-mail echilepy@tigo.com.py; Ambassador ALEJANDRO BAHAMONDES.

Colombia: Coronel Francisco Brizuela 3089, esq. Ciudad del Vaticano, Asunción; tel. (21) 22-9888; fax (21) 22-9703; e-mail easuncio@cancilleria.gov.co; internet paraguay.embajada.gov.co/; Ambassador JUAN EDGAR AUGUSTO CELY NÚÑEZ.

Costa Rica: Cerro Cora 2454, casi General Santos, Barrio Ciudad Nueva, Asunción; tel. and fax (21) 22-7559; fax (21) 62-4909; e-mail embcr.py@gmail.com; Ambassador MARCO AURELIO PERAZA SALAZAR.

Cuba: Luis Morales 766, esq. Luis de León y Luis de Granada, Barrio Jara, Asunción; tel. (21) 22-2763; fax (21) 20-4276; e-mail embajada@py.embacuba.cu; internet www.cubadiplomatica.cu/paraguay; Ambassador JUAN DOMINGO ASTIASARÁN CEBALLO.

Dominican Republic: Edif. Maria Antonia 1, 3°, Residenta 1440, Asunción; tel. (21) 21-3143; e-mail embajadadominicanapy@hotmail.com; Ambassador MARINO BERIGÜETE.

Ecuador: Dr Bestard 861, esq. Juan XXIII, Barrio Manorá, Casilla 13162, Asunción; tel. (21) 61-4814; fax (21) 61-4813; e-mail eecuparaguay@mmree.gov.ec; internet www.ecuador.com.py; Ambassador JOSÉ ENRIQUE NÚÑEZ TAMAYO.

France: Avda España 893, esq. Padre Pucheu, Casilla 97, Asunción; tel. (21) 21-2449; fax (21) 21-1690; e-mail chancellerie@ambafran.gov.py; internet www.ambafrance-py.org; Ambassador OLIVIER POUPARD.

Germany: Avda Venezuela 241, Casilla 471, Asunción; tel. (21) 21-4009; fax (21) 21-2863; e-mail info@asuncion.diplo.de; internet www.asuncion.diplo.de; Ambassador Dr CLAUDE ROBERT ELLNER.

Holy See: Ciudad del Vaticano 350, casi con 25 de Mayo, Casilla 83, Asunción (Apostolic Nunciature); tel. (21) 21-5139; fax (21) 21-2590; e-mail nunciatura.paraguay@gmail.com; Apostolic Nuncio Most Rev. ELISEO ANTONIO ARIOTTI (Titular Archbishop of Vibiana).

Italy: Quesada 5871 con Bélgica, Asunción; tel. (21) 61-5620; fax (21) 61-5622; e-mail amb.assunzione@cert.esteri.it; internet www.ambassunzione.esteri.it; Ambassador ANTONELLA CAVALLARI.

Japan: Avda Mariscal López 2364, Casilla 1957, Asunción; tel. (21) 60-4616; fax (21) 60-6901; e-mail embajaponpy@rieder.net.py; internet www.py.emb-japan.go.jp; Ambassador YOSHIHISA UEDA.

Korea, Republic: Avda Rep. Argentina Norte 678, esq. Pacheco, Casilla 1303, Asunción; tel. (21) 60-5606; fax (21) 60-1376; e-mail paraguay@mofat.go.kr; internet pry.mofat.go.kr; Ambassador HAHN MYUNG-JAE.

Lebanon: San Francisco 629, esq. República Siria y Juan de Salazar, Asunción; tel. (21) 22-9375; fax (21) 23-2012; e-mail embajadadelibano@tigo.com.py; Ambassador ZEIN EL MOUSSAWI.

Mexico: Avda España 1428, casi San Rafael, Casilla 1184, Asunción; tel. (21) 618-2000; fax (21) 618-2500; e-mail embamex@embamex.com.py; internet embamex.sre.gob.mx/paraguay; Ambassador CARLOS PUJALTE PIÑEIRO.

Panama: Carmen Soler 3912, esq. Radio Operadores del Chaco, Barrio Seminario, Asunción; tel. and fax (21) 21-1091; e-mail embpanamaparaguay@mire.gov.pa; Ambassador SABRINA DEL CARMEN GARCÍA BARRERA.

Peru: Edif. Santa Teresa, Dept 8B, Avda Santa Teresa 2415, Aviadores del Chaco, Casilla 433, Asunción; tel. (21) 60-0226; fax (21) 60-0901; e-mail embperu@embperu.com.py; internet www.embperu.org.py; Ambassador JORGE ANTONIO LÁZARO GELDRES.

Russia: Avda Dr Felipe Molas López 689, casi San Martín, Asunción; tel. (21) 62-3733; fax (21) 62-3735; e-mail embruspar@ya.ru; internet www.paraguay.mid.ru; Ambassador GRIGÓRY MASHKÓV.

Spain: Edif. S. Rafael, 5° y 6°, Yegros 437, Asunción; tel. (21) 49-0686; fax (21) 44-5394; e-mail emb.asuncion@maec.es; internet www.maec.es/embajadas/asuncion; Ambassador DIEGO BERMEJO ROMERO DE TERREROS.

Switzerland: Edif. Parapití, 4°, Ofs 419–423, Juan E. O'Leary 409, esq. Estrella, Casilla 552, Asunción; tel. (21) 44-8022; fax (21) 44-5853; e-mail asu.vertretung@eda.admin.ch; internet www.eda.admin.ch/asuncion; Ambassador ALAIN-DENIS HENCHOZ.

Taiwan (Republic of China): Avda Mariscal López 1133 y Vicepresidente Sánchez, Casilla 503, Asunción; tel. (21) 21-3362; fax (21) 21-2373; e-mail embroc01@rieder.net.py; internet www.taiwanembassy.org/py; Ambassador JOSÉ MARÍA LIU.

United Kingdom: Edif. Citicenter, 5°, Avda Mariscal López 3794 y Cruz del Chaco, Asunción; tel. (21) 328-5507; fax (21) 325-5507; e-mail be-asuncion.enquiries@fco.gov.uk; internet www.gov.uk/government/world/paraguay; Ambassador Dr JEREMY HOBBS.

USA: Avda Mariscal López 1776, Casilla 402, Asunción; tel. (21) 21-3715; fax (21) 21-3728; e-mail paraguayusembassy@state.gov; internet paraguay.usembassy.gov; Ambassador JAMES H. THESSIN.

Uruguay: Edif. Maria Luisa, 3°, Avda Boggiani 5832, esq. Alas Paraguayas, Asunción; tel. (21) 66-4244; fax (21) 60-1335; e-mail uruasun@embajadauruguay.com.py; internet www.embajadauruguay.com.py; Ambassador FEDERICO PERAZZA.

Venezuela: Soldado Desconocido 348, Avda España, Barrio Manorá, Asunción; tel. (21) 66-4682; fax (21) 66-4683; e-mail despacho2@embaven.org.py; internet paraguay.embajada.gob.ve; Ambassador ALFREDO MURGA RIVAS.

Judicial System

The Supreme Court of Justice is composed of nine judges appointed on the recommendation of the Council of the Magistracy.

Corte Suprema de Justicia: Palacio de Justicia, 10º, Torre Norte, entre Avdas Alonso y Testanova, Asunción; tel. (21) 439-4000; internet www.pj.gov.py; Pres. Dr José Raúl Torres Kirmser.

Attorney-General: Javier Díaz Verón.

Religion

The Roman Catholic Church is the established religion, although all sects are tolerated.

CHRISTIANITY

The Roman Catholic Church

For ecclesiastical purposes, Paraguay comprises one archdiocese, 11 dioceses and two Apostolic Vicariates. According to the latest available (2002) census figures, some 68% of the population are Roman Catholics.

Bishops' Conference: Conferencia Episcopal Paraguaya, Calle Alberdi 782, Casilla 1436, 1209 Asunción; tel. (21) 49-0920; fax (21) 49-5115; e-mail sgeneral@episcopal.org.py; internet www.episcopal.org.py; f. 1977, statutes approved 2000; Pres. Most Rev. Claudio Gimenez (Bishop of Caacupé).

Archbishop of Asunción: Most Rev. Eustaquio Pastor Cuquejo Verga, Arzobispado, Avda Mariscal López 130 esq. Independencia Nacional, Casilla 654, Asunción; tel. (21) 44-5551; fax (21) 44-4150; e-mail comunicacioncuriapastoral@yahoo.es; internet www.arzobispado.org.py.

The Anglican Communion

Paraguay constitutes a single diocese of the Iglesia Anglicana del Cono Sur de América (Anglican Church of the Southern Cone of America). The Presiding Bishop of the Church is the Bishop of Northern Argentina.

Bishop of Paraguay: Rt Rev. Peter John Henry Bartlett, Iglesia Anglicana, Avda España casi Santos, Casilla 1124, Asunción; tel. (21) 20-0933; fax (21) 21-4328; e-mail peterparaguay@gmail.com.

Other Christian Churches

Baptist Evangelical Convention of Paraguay: Pettirossi 593, Calle República Francesa, Casilla 1194, Asunción; tel. (21) 22-7110; fax (21) 21-0588; e-mail cebp@sce.cnc.una.py; internet ubla.net/paises/paraguay.htm; Pres. Jorge Rochaix.

Church of Jesus Christ of Latter-Day Saints (Mormons): Esq. Brasilia y España 1441, Asunción; internet www.lds.org; 84,806 mems.

Evangelical Lutheran Church of Paraguay: Hohenau II, Itapua; e-mail ielpar@gmail.com; internet www.iglesialuterana.org.py; f. 1937; 4,009 mems (2011); Pres. Rev. Norberto Gerke.

BAHÁ'Í FAITH

National Spiritual Assembly of the Bahá'ís of Paraguay: Eligio Ayala 1456, Apdo 742, Asunción; tel. (21) 22-5747; e-mail bahai@highway.com.py; internet www.bahai.org.py; Sec. Mirna Llamosas de Riquelme.

The Press

DAILIES

5 Días: Avda España 1755, entre Dominicana y Pitiantuta, Asunción; tel. (21) 20-4114; internet www.5dias.com.py; business; Dir Víctor Raúl Benítez González; circ. 10,500.

ABC Color: Yegros 745, Apdo 1421, Asunción; tel. (21) 49-1160; fax (21) 49-3059; e-mail diarioabc@abc.com.py; internet www.abc.com.py; f. 1967; independent; Dir Eleno Martínez; Editor Julio Benítez; circ. 45,000.

ADN Paraguayo: Calle Tebicuary y Aguaray, Area 5, Poniente Franco, Alto Paraná; tel. (61) 55-0333; e-mail redaccion@adndigital.com.py; internet www.adndigital.com.py; Dir Héctor Ignacio Guerín Gómez.

Crónica: Avda Zavala Cué, entre 2da y 3ra, Fernando de la Mora, Zona Sur, Asunción; tel. (21) 51-2520; e-mail digital@cronica.com.py; internet www.cronica.com.py; sports; Dir Alejandro Domínguez.

La Jornada: Avda 11 de Septiembre 400, Calle Alejo García, Ciudad del Este; tel. (61) 50-5479; e-mail director@diariolajornada.com.py; internet www.diariolajornada.com.py; Dir José Espínola.

La Nación: Avda Zavala Cué entre 2da y 3ra, Fernando de la Mora, Zona Sur, Asunción; tel. (21) 51-2520; fax (21) 51-2535; e-mail redaccion@lanacion.com.py; internet www.lanacion.com.py; f. 1995; Dir Alejandro Domínguez Wilson-Smith; Editor Néstor Insaurralde; circ. 10,000.

Popular: Avda Mariscal López 2948, Casi McArthur, Asunción; tel. and fax (21) 60-3400; e-mail redaccion@mm.com.py; internet www.hoy.com.py; owned by Grupo Multimedia; Dir Amanda Pedrozo; Editor Carlos Sosa; circ. 28,000.

Ultima Hora: Benjamín Constant 658, Asunción; tel. (21) 49-6261; fax (21) 44-7071; e-mail ultimahora@uhora.com.py; internet www.ultimahora.com; f. 1973; independent; Dir Oscar Ayala Bogarín; Editor Estela Ruiz; circ. 30,000.

Vanguardia: Avda San Blas, Kilometro 8, Acaray, Ciudad del Este; tel. (61) 57-5530; fax (61) 57-5534; e-mail contacto@diariovanguardia.com.py; internet www.vanguardia.com.py; Dir Nelson Zapata.

PERIODICALS

Acción: CEPAG, Vicepresidente Sánchez 612, casi Azara, Asunción; tel. (21) 23-3541; e-mail revistaaccion@cepag.org.py; internet www.cepag.org.py/accion.php; f. 1923; monthly; published by the Centro de Estudios Paraguayos Antonio Guasch (CEPAG—Jesuit org.); Sec. Nuridia Molinas.

High Class: Benjamin Constant 658, esq. 15 de Agosto, Asunción; tel. (21) 49-6261; e-mail suscripciones@highclass.com.py; internet www.highclass.com.py; lifestyle magazine; fortnightly; Dir Gabriela Murdoch; Editor Raquel Allegretti García de Zúniga.

Revista Cartelera: Tobatí 3455, Barrio San Pablo, Asunción; tel. (21) 50-5005; e-mail info@revistacartelera.com.py; internet www.revistacartelera.com; Dir Olavo Heikel.

Revista PLUS: Avda España 1755, casi Pitiantuta, Asunción; tel. (21) 20-1724; e-mail info@revistaplus.com.py; internet www.revistaplus.com.py; f. 2006; business; monthly; Editor Silvia Nuñez; circ. 2,500.

Revista Zeta: Infante Rivarola 554, entre Lillo y Moises Bertoni, Villa Morra, Asunción; tel. (21) 60-5918; e-mail contacto@revistazeta.com; internet www.revistazeta.com; f. 2000; monthly; general interest; Dir Zuni Castiñeira.

TVO: Santa Margarita de Youville 250, Santa María, Asunción; tel. (21) 67-2079; fax (21) 21-1236; e-mail sugerencias@teveo.com.py; internet www.teveo.com.py; f. 1992; fmrly *TeVeo*; weekly; news and society; Editor Lorena Fernández.

NEWS AGENCY

Agencia de Información Paraguay (IP Paraguay): Ayolas 451, entre Estrella y Oliva, Asunción; tel. (21) 44-9111; e-mail ip@sicom.gov.py; internet www.ipparaguay.com.py; f. 2009; attached to the Office of the President; Dir Carlos Troya.

Publishers

Arandurã Editorial: Tte Fariña, Calle 884, entre Brasil y Estados Unidos, Asunción; tel. (21) 21-4295; fax (21) 22-0272; e-mail arandura@hotmail.com; internet www.arandura.pyglobal.com; f. 1991; poetry, literature, social history; Man. Cayetano Quattrocchi.

Ediciones Fotosíntesis: Teniente Oddone 1869, Calle Juan XXIII, Asunción; tel. (21) 61-3588; fax (21) 62-2631; e-mail info@fotosintesis.biz; internet www.fotosintesis.biz; art, culture and history; Dir Fernando Allen.

Ediciones Librería El Foro, SA: Avda Chile 862, Calle Humaitá, Asunción; tel. (21) 49-0249; fax (21) 45-2911; e-mail venta@elforo.com.py; internet www.elforo.com.py; general non-fiction; Pres. Vicente R. Simbrón.

Editorial Servilibro: 25 de Mayo y México, Plaza Uruguaya, Asunción; tel. (21) 44-4770; fax (21) 41-5615; e-mail servilibro@gmail.com; internet www.servilibro.com.py; Dir-Gen. Vidalia Sánchez.

Editorial Tiempo de Historia: Rodó 120, esq. Avda Mariscal López, Asunción; tel. (21) 21-2062; fax (21) 22-2580; e-mail info@tiempodehistoria.org; internet tiempodehistoria.org; historical documents; Dir Martín Romano.

Editorial Vazpi: San Francisco 843, entre Patria y Libertad, Barrio Jara, Asunción; tel. (21) 22-6945; e-mail vazpi@conexion.com.py; internet vazpipy.com; f. 1994; education, general interest and science; Dir-Gen. Lillia Piatti.

Fausto Cultural: Eligio Ayala 1060, entre Estados Unidos y Brasil, Asunción; tel. (21) 22-1996; fax (21) 22-4988; f. 1992; children's literature; Dir Nilda Díaz de García.

Librería Intercontinental: Caballero 270, Calle Mariscal, Estigarribia, Asunción; tel. (21) 49-6991; fax (21) 44-8721; e-mail agatti@ libreriaintercontinental.com.py; internet libreriaintercontinental .com.py; f. 1987; political science, law, literature, poetry; Dir ALEJANDRO GATTI VAN HUMBEECK.

Libros Aguila: Avda Eusebio Ayala 1067, Calle Rodó, Asunción; tel. (21) 21-4613; e-mail ventas@librosaguila.com.py; internet www .librosaguila.com.py; academic; Gen. Man. RAMÓN TORRES.

Santillana: Avda Venezuela 276, Asunción; fax (21) 20-2942; e-mail cls@santillana.com.py; internet www.santillana.com.py; educational books; Dir-Gen. JAVIER BARRETO CURTINA.

ASSOCIATION

Cámara Paraguaya del Libro (CAPEL): Ayolas 129, esq. Benjamin Constant, Asunción; tel. (21) 49-7352; fax (21) 44-7053; internet camaraparaguayadellibro.com.py; f. 1993; Pres. MARTA VÁZQUEZ PIATTI.

Broadcasting and Communications

REGULATORY AUTHORITY

Comisión Nacional de Telecomunicaciones (CONATEL): Presidente Franco 780, esq. Ayolas, Asunción; tel. (21) 44-0020; fax (21) 49-8982; e-mail info@conatel.gov.py; internet www.conatel.gov.py; Pres. CARLOS LEOPOLDO GÓMEZ ZELADA.

TELECOMMUNICATIONS

Claro (AMX Paraguay, SA): Avda Mariscal López 1730, Asunción; tel. (21) 249-9000; fax (21) 249-9099; e-mail empresaspy@claro.com .py; internet www.claro.com.py; subsidiary of América Móvil, SA de CV (Mexico); fmrly CTI Móvil; mobile cellular telephone services; Gen. Man. LUCIANO MAURONI.

Corporación Paraguaya de Comunicaciones, SA (COPACO): Edif. Morotí, 1°–2°, esq. Gen. Bruguez y Teodoro S. Mongelos, Casilla 2042, Asunción; tel. (21) 20-3800; fax (21) 20-3888; e-mail infoweb@ copaco.com.py; internet www.copaco.com.py; fmrly Administración Nacional de Telecomunicaciones (ANTELCO); adopted current name in 2001; state-owned; Pres. FRANCISCO JAVIER GALIANO.

Personal Paraguay (Núcleo, SA): Avda España 224, casi Máximo Lira, Asunción; tel. (21) 217-7000; internet www.personal.com.py; f. 1998; subsidiary of Telecom Argentina; Gen. Man. JUAN CARLOS PEPE.

Tigo Paraguay: Edif. Casa Central Tigo, Avda Mariscal López 4050, esq. Avda República Argentina, Asunción; tel. (21) 618-9000; internet www.tigo.com.py; fmrly Telefónica Celular del Paraguay; relaunched in 2004 as Tigo; largest mobile operator with 2.8m. subscribers; subsidiary of Grupo Millicom International Cellular, Luxembourg; Gen. Man. TOM GUTJAHR.

BROADCASTING

Radio

FM Popular 103.1: Avda Mariscal López 2948, casi McArthur, Asunción; tel. (21) 60-3400; e-mail redaccion@mm.com.py; internet www.fmpopular.com; owned by Grupo Multimedia; Man. DAHIANA BRESANOVICH.

Radio Arapysandú: Avda Mariscal López y Capitán del Puerto San Ignacio, Misiones; tel. (82) 2374; fax (82) 2206; e-mail arapysanduam@gmail.com; internet arapysanduam.blogspot.com; f. 1982; AM; Dir HECTOR BOTTINO.

Radio Asunción: Avda Artígas y Capitán Lombardo 174, Asunción; tel. and fax (21) 28-2662; fax (21) 28-2661; e-mail radioasuncion@ cmm.com.py; internet www.radioasuncion.comyr.com; AM; Propr MIGUEL GERÓNIMO FERNÁNDEZ; Dir-Gen. BIBIANA LANDO MEYER.

Radio Cardinal: Comendador Nicolás Bó 1334 y Guaraníes, Casilla 2532, Lambaré, Asunción; tel. (21) 31-0555; fax (21) 30-3089; e-mail info@cardinal.com.py; internet www.cardinal.com.py; f. 1991; AM and FM; Pres. ALFREDO CHENA; Man. Dir ANDREA BITTAR.

Radio Cáritas: Avda Kubitschek 661 y Azara, Asunción; tel. (21) 21-3570; fax (21) 20-4161; e-mail caritas@caritas.com.py; internet www .caritas.com.py; f. 1936; station of the Archdiocese of Asunción and the Universidad Católica Nuestra Señora de la Asunción; AM; Dir-Gen. JORGE BAZÁN.

Radio Guairá: Presidente Franco 788 y Alejo García, Villarica; tel. (541) 42130; fax (541) 42385; e-mail fmguaira@gmail.com; internet www.fmguaira.com; f. 1950; AM and FM; Dir ENRIQUE TRAVERSI.

Radio Itapiru SRL: Avda San Blás, esq. Coronel Julián Sánchez, Ciudad del Este; tel. (61) 57-2207; fax (61) 57-2210; internet www .radioitapiru.com; f. 1969; AM and FM; Dir-Gen. RICHARD ARANDA.

Radio Nacional del Paraguay: Blas Garay 241, esq. Iturbe y Yegros, Asunción; tel. (21) 39-0374; fax (21) 39-0375; e-mail direccion@radionacionaldelparaguay.com.py; internet www .radionacionaldelparaguay.com.py; f. 1957; AM and FM; Dir JUDITH MARÍA VERA DE BIRBAUMER.

Radio Ñandutí: Choferes del Chaco y Carmen Soler, Asunción; tel. (21) 60-4308; fax (21) 60-6074; e-mail prensaam@holdingderadio .com.py; internet www.nanduti.com.py; f. 1962; FM; Dir HUMBERTO LEÓN RUBÍN.

Radio Primero de Marzo: Avda Gen. Perón y Concepción Prieto Yegros, Casilla 1456, Asunción; tel. (21) 30-0380; fax (21) 33-3427; e-mail prensa@780am.com.py; internet www.780am.com.py; AM and FM; Dir-Gen. ANGEL R. GUERREÑOS.

Radio Uno: Avda Mariscal López 2948, Asunción; tel. (21) 61-2151; fax prensa650@mm.com.py; internet www.radiouno.com.py; f. 1968 as Radio Chaco Boreal; AM; Dir JAVIER MARÍA PIROVANO SILVA.

Radio Venus: Avda República Argentina y Souza, Asunción; tel. (21) 61-0151; fax (21) 60-6484; e-mail info@venus.com.py; internet www.venus.com.py; f. 1987; FM; Dir ANGEL AGUILERA.

Radio Ysapy: Independencia Nacional 1260, 1°, Asunción; tel. (21) 44-4037; e-mail info@radioysapy.com.py; internet www.radioysapy .com.py; FM; Dir JOSÉ TOMÁS CABRIZA SALVIONI.

Television

Paravision: Bélgica 4498, casi Mariscal López, Asunción; tel. (21) 66-4380; e-mail francisco.gomez@paravision.com.py; internet www .paravision.com.py; Exec. Dir MARIAN ALONSO; Gen. Man. FRANCISCO GÓMEZ.

Red Guaraní (Canal 2): Complejo Textilia, Gen. Santos 1024, casi Concordia, Asunción; tel. (21) 20-5444; e-mail oescobar@redguarani .com.py; internet www.redguarani.com.py; Exec. Dir FLAVIO FLORENTÍN; Gen. Man. OSCAR ESCOBAR.

Sistema Nacional de Televisión Cerro Corá—Canal 9 (SNT): Avda Carlos Antonio López 572, entre Colón y Santiago Leguizamón, Asunción; tel. (21) 42-4222; e-mail info@snt.com.py; internet www .snt.com.py; f. 1965; commercial; Dir MARCELO FLEITAS.

La Tele-Canal 11 (Hispanoamérica TV del Paraguay): Avda Eusebio Ayala 2995, esq. Pasaje Tembetary, Asunción; tel. (21) 415-7400; e-mail prensa@latele.com.py; internet www.latele.com.py; Dir LEONARDO SALOMÓN.

Teledifusora Paraguaya—Canal 13: Comendador Nicolás Bó y Guaraníes, Lambaré, Asunción; tel. (21) 33-2823; fax (21) 33-2826; e-mail info@canal13.com.py; internet www.rpc.com.py; f. 1981; Pres. ANDREA VITTAR DE BENÍTEZ; Dir-Gen. GUSTAVO CUBILLA.

Telefuturo-Canal 4 (TV Acción, SA): Andrade 1499 y O'Higgins, Asunción; tel. (21) 618-4000; fax (21) 618-4166; e-mail telefuturo@ telefuturo.com.py; internet www.telefuturo.com.py; Gen. Man. MARCOS GALANTI.

TV Pública Paraguay-Canal 14: Avda Alberdi 633, casi Gen. Díaz, Asunción; tel. (21) 49-4000; fax (21) 49-4050; e-mail programacion@ tvpublica.com.py; internet www.tvpublica.com.py; Dir SERGIO MARCOS GUSTAFSON.

Finance

(cap. = capital; res = reserves; dep. = deposits; m. = million; brs = branches; amounts in guaraníes)

BANKING

Central Bank

Banco Central del Paraguay: Avda Federación Rusa y Cabo 1° Marecos, Casilla 861, Barrio Santo Domingo, Asunción; tel. (21) 60-8011; fax (21) 61-1118; e-mail informaciones@bcp.gov.py; internet www.bcp.gov.py; f. 1952; cap. 683,092.0m., res −1,577,631.0m., dep. 11,942,860.0m. (Dec. 2009); Pres. CARLOS GUSTAVO VALDOVINOS; Gen. Man. CARLOS DANIEL VIEIRA (acting); Supt of Banking HERNÁN COLMAN.

Development Banks

Banco Nacional de Fomento: Independencia Nacional, entre Cerro Cora y 25 de Mayo, Asunción; tel. (21) 44-4440; fax (21) 44-6056; e-mail correo@bnf.gov.py; internet www.bnf.gov.py; f. 1961 to take over the deposit and private banking activities of the Banco del Paraguay; cap. 307,689.3m., res 160,858.2m., dep. 2,691,110.2m. (Dec. 2012); Pres. CARLOS ALBERTO PEREIRA OLMEDO; Sec.-Gen. CÉSAR LEONARDO FURIASSE ROLÓN; 52 brs.

Crédito Agrícola de Habilitación (CAH): Caríos 362 y William Richardson, Asunción; tel. (21) 569-0100; fax (21) 55-4956; e-mail info@cah.gov.py; internet www.cah.gov.py; f. 1943; Pres. AMANDA LEÓN.

Fondo Ganadero: Avda Mariscal López 1669 esq. República Dominicana, Asunción; tel. (21) 22-7288; fax (21) 22-7378; e-mail info@fondogan.gov.py; internet www.fondogan.gov.py; f. 1969; govt-owned; Pres. MARTÍN ADALBERTO BARRETO.

Commercial Banks

Banco Amambay, SA: Avda Aviadores del Chaco, entre San Martín y Pablo Alborno, Asunción; tel. (21) 618-7000; fax (21) 618-7333; e-mail bcoama@bancoamambay.com.py; internet www .bancoamambay.com.py; f. 1992; cap. 156,870m., res 62,577.5m., dep. 1,380,994.3m. (Dec. 2012); Pres. and Gen. Man. EDUARDO CÉSAR CAMPOS MARIN; 6 brs.

Banco Atlas, SA: Avda Mariscal López, entre Dr Weiss y Bulnes, Asunción; tel. (21) 217-5000; fax (21) 217-5142; e-mail consultas@ atlas.com.py; internet www.bancoatlas.com.py; f. 1989 as Cristal Financiera, SA; changed name as above in 2010; cap. 147,414m., res 26,288.8m., dep. 1,738,101.3m. (Dec. 2010); Pres. MIGUEL A. ZALDÍVAR SILVERA; Gen. Man. JUAN CARLOS MARTÍN.

Banco Bilbao Vizcaya Argentaria Paraguay, SA: Yegros 435, esq. 25 de Mayo, Casilla 824, Asunción; tel. (21) 49-2072; fax (21) 44-8103; e-mail info@bbva.com.py; internet www.bbva.com.py; f. 1961 as Banco Exterior de España, SA; present name adopted in 2000; cap. 325,000m., res 201,566m., dep. 6,637,354.8m. (Dec. 2013); Pres. VICENTE LUIS BOGLIOLO DEL RÍO; 5 brs.

Banco Continental, SAECA: Estrella 621, Calle 15 de Agosto, Asunción; tel. (21) 44-2002; fax (21) 44-2001; e-mail contil@connexion .com.py; internet www.bancontinental.com.py; f. 1980; cap. 299,027.0m. (Dec. 2010), res 701,524.5m., dep. 9,554,295.6m. (Dec. 2012); Pres. GUILLERMO GROSS BROWN; 28 brs.

Banco Itaú Paraguay: Oliva 349, esq. Chile y Alberdi, Asunción; tel. (21) 617-1000; fax (21) 417-1372; e-mail sac@itau.com.py; internet www.itau.com.py; f. 1978; known as Interbanco until 2009; cap. 500,000m., res 614,607.7m., dep. 7,747,528.7m. (Dec. 2012); Pres. VIVIANA VARAS; 35 brs.

Sudameris Bank, SAECA: Independencia Nacional y Cerro Corá, Casilla 1433, Asunción; tel. (21) 416-6000; fax (21) 44-8670; e-mail gerencia@sudameris.com.py; internet www.sudamerisbank.com.py; f. 1961; savings and commercial bank; cap. 198,776.5m., res 116,090.9m., dep. 2,545,766.6m. (Dec. 2012); Chair. CONOR MCENROY; Gen. Man. GUSTAVO CARTES ARAUJO; 23 brs.

Banking Association

Asociación de Bancos del Paraguay: Aca Caraya 397, esq. Leandro Prieto, Asunción; tel. (21) 22-3571; fax (21) 21-0356; e-mail asoban@asoban.org.py; internet asoban.org.py; mems: Paraguayan banks and foreign banks with brs in Asunción; Pres. PEDRO JERÓNIMO NASSER.

STOCK EXCHANGE

Bolsa de Valores y Productos de Asunción, SA: 15 de Agosto 640, esq. General Díaz y Víctor Haedo, Asunción; tel. (21) 44-2445; fax (21) 44-2446; e-mail rodrigo.callizo@bvpasa.com.py; internet www.bvpasa.com.py; f. 1977; Pres. RODRIGO CALLIZO LÓPEZ MOREIRA.

INSURANCE

Supervisory Authority

Superintendencia de Seguros: Edif. Banco Central del Paraguay, 1°, Federación Rusa y Sargento Marecos, Asunción; tel. (21) 619-2380; fax (21) 619-2637; e-mail dmarti@bcp.gov.py; internet www .bcp.gov.py; part of the Banco Central de Paraguay; Supt BERNARDO NAVARRO AMARILLA.

Principal Companies

La Agrícola SA de Seguros Generales: Mariscal López 5377 y Concejal Vargas, Asunción; tel. (21) 60-9509; fax (21) 60-9606; e-mail sagricola@tigo.com.py; internet www.seguroslaagricola.com.py; f. 1982; general; Pres. CARLOS ALBERTO LEVI SOSA.

ALFA SA de Seguros y Reaseguros: Yegros 944 esq. Tte Fariña, Asunción; tel. (21) 44-9992; fax (21) 44-9991; e-mail alfa.seg@ conexion.com.py; internet www.alfaseguros.com.py; Pres. NICOLÁS SARUBBI ZAYAS.

Aseguradora del Este SA de Seguros: Avda República Argentina 778, entre Pacheco y Souza, Asunción; tel. (21) 60-5015; e-mail ngoiris@aesaseguros.com.py; internet www.aesaseguros.com.py; Pres. VÍCTOR ANDRÉS RIBEIRO ESPÍNOLA.

Aseguradora Paraguaya, SA (ASEPASA): Avda Guido Boggiani 5848, Asunción; tel. (21) 61-2870; fax (21) 22-2217; e-mail asepasa@ asepasa.com.py; internet www.asepasa.com.py; f. 1976; Pres. and Gen. Man. GERARDO TORCIDA CONEJERO.

Aseguradora Yacyretá SA de Seguros: Avda del Chaco 1690 y Pintor Pablo Alborno, Asunción; tel. (21) 617-8000; fax (21) 617-8125; e-mail sac@yacyreta.com.py; internet www.yacyreta.com.py; f. 1980; Pres. OSCAR HARRISON JACQUET; Vice-Pres. NORMAN HARRISON PALEARI; Gen. Man. EDUARDO BARRIOS PERINI.

Atalaya SA de Seguros Generales: Independencia Nacional 565, 1°, esq. Azara y Cerro Corá, Asunción; tel. (21) 49-2811; fax (21) 49-6966; e-mail ataseg@telesurf.com.py; internet www.atalayaseguros .com; f. 1964; general; Pres. KARIN M. DOLL.

Cenit, SA: Ayolas 1082, Calle Jejui, Asunción; tel. (21) 49-4972; fax (21) 44-9502; e-mail cenit@cenit.com.py; internet www.cenit.com.py; Pres. Dr FELIPE OSCAR ARMELE BONZI.

Central SA de Seguros: Edif. Betón I, 1° y 2°, Eduardo Víctor Haedo 179, Independencia Nacional, Casilla 1802, Asunción; tel. (21) 49-4653; fax (21) 49-4655; e-mail centralseguros@centralseguros .com.py; internet www.centralseguros.com.py; f. 1977; Pres. MIGUEL JACOBO VILLASANTI; Gen. Man. ALBERTO AYALA.

El Comercio Paraguayo SA Cía de Seguros Generales: Alberdi 453 y Oliva, Asunción; tel. (21) 49-2324; fax (21) 49-3562; e-mail elcomercioparaguayo@elcomercioparaguayo.com.py; internet www .elcomercioparaguayo.com.py; f. 1947; Dir VICTORIA MARTÍNEZ DE ELIZECHE.

La Consolidada SA de Seguros y Reaseguros: Edif. AYMAC, 7°, Avda Aviadores del Chaco 1669, San Martín, Asunción; tel. (21) 619-1000; fax (21) 44-5795; e-mail info@consolidada.com.py; internet www.consolidada.com.py; f. 1961; Pres. JUAN CARLOS DELGADILLO ECHAGÜE.

Fénix SA de Seguros y Reaseguros: Iturbe 823 y Fulgencio R. Moreno, Asunción; tel. (21) 49-4909; fax (21) 44-5643; e-mail fenixsa@fenixseguros.com.py; internet www.fenixseguros.com.py; Pres. JAIME LAUFER.

Garantía SA de Seguros y Reaseguros: Edif. Garantía, 1°, 25 de Mayo 640, Asunción; tel. (21) 44-5452; fax (21) 49-0678; e-mail administracion@migarantia.com.py; internet www.migarantia.com .py; Gen. Man. NELSON MURDOCH GUIRLAND.

Grupo General de Seguros: Avda España 2210, Asunción; tel. (21) 20-7071; fax (21) 23-4200; e-mail casa_matriz@ggeneral.com.py; internet www.ggeneral.com.py; Pres. HUGO FERNANDO CAMPERCHIOLI.

La Independencia de Seguros y Reaseguros, SA: Edif. Parapatí, 1°, Juan E. O'Leary 409, esq. Estrella, Casilla 980, Asunción; tel. (21) 44-7021; fax (21) 44-8996; e-mail liseguros@laindependencia.com.py; internet www.laindependencia.com.py; f. 1965; Pres. EDMUNDO EMILIO RICHER BÉCKER.

Intercontinental SA de Seguros y Reaseguros: Iturbe 1047 con Teniente Fariña, Altos, Asunción; tel. (21) 49-2348; fax (21) 49-1227; e-mail info@intercontinentaldeseguros.com.py; internet www .intercontinentaldeseguros.com.py; f. 1978; Pres. Dr JUAN MÓDICA LUCENTE; Gen. Man. MARIO VICENTE MÓDICA LUCENTE.

Mapfre Paraguay, SA: Avda Mariscal López 910 y General Aquino, Asunción; tel. (21) 217-6000; fax (21) 217-6107; e-mail sac@mapfre .com.py; internet www.mapfre.com.py; Pres. ZAIDA GABAS DE REQUENA.

La Meridional Paraguaya SA de Seguros: Iturbe 1046, Teniente Fariña, Asunción; tel. (21) 44-0713; fax (21) 49-8826; e-mail f .mujica@meridional.com.py; internet www.meridional.com.py; f. 1991; Gen. Man. FEDERICO EDUARDO MUJICA VALINOTTI.

La Paraguaya SA de Seguros: Estrella 675, 7°, Asunción; tel. (21) 49-1367; fax (21) 44-8235; e-mail lps@laparaguaya.com.py; internet www.laparaguaya.com.py; f. 1905; Pres. JUAN BOSCH BEYNEN.

Patria SA de Seguros y Reaseguros: General Santos 715 esq. Siria, Asunción; tel. (21) 22-5250; fax (21) 21-4001; e-mail segurospatria@segurospatria.com.py; internet www.segurospatria .com.py; f. 1967; general; Pres. Dr PABLO PARRA GARCÍA.

El Productor SA de Seguros y Reaseguros: Ind. Nacional 811 esq. Fulgencio R. Moreno, 8°, Asunción; tel. (21) 44-8620; fax (21) 49-1599; e-mail info@elproductor.com.py; internet www.elproductor .com.py; Pres. REINALDO PAVÍA MALDONADO.

Rumbos SA de Seguros: Estrella 851, Ayolas, Casilla 1017, Asunción; tel. (21) 44-9488; fax (21) 44-9492; e-mail rumbos@rumbos.com .py; internet www.rumbos.com.py; f. 1960; Pres. MIGUEL A. LARREINEGABE LESME; Man. Dir MIGUEL LARREINEGABE BENZA.

La Rural SA de Seguros: Argentina 940, casi MacMahon, Asunción; tel. (21) 617-4000; fax (21) 617-4200; e-mail larural@larural .com.py; internet www.larural.com.py; f. 1920; Pres. MARIA CRISTINA MATSUMIYA DE TANAKA; Gen. Man. JUAN FRANCISCO PÉREZ SALDÍVAR.

Seguros Chaco SA de Seguros y Reaseguros: Mariscal Estigarribia 982, Casilla 3248, Asunción; tel. (21) 44-7118; fax (21) 44-9551; e-mail seguroschaco@pla.net.py; f. 1977; general; Pres. EMILIO VELILLA LACONICH.

Seguros Generales, SA (SEGESA): Edif. SEGESA, 1°, Oliva 393 esq. Alberdi, Casilla 802, Asunción; tel. (21) 49-1362; fax (21) 49-

1360; e-mail segesa@segesa.com.py; internet segesa.com.py; f. 1956; Man. Dir NICOLÁS RIBÓN G.

El Sol del Paraguay, Cía de Seguros y Reaseguros, SA: Cerro Corá 1031, Asunción; tel. (21) 49-1110; fax (21) 21-0604; e-mail elsol@elsol.com.py; internet www.elsol.com.py; f. 1978; Pres. CAROLINA VEGA CAMERONI.

Insurance Association

Asociación Paraguaya de Cías de Seguros: 15 de Agosto, esq. Lugano, Casilla 1435, Asunción; tel. (21) 44-6474; fax (21) 44-4343; e-mail apcs@consultronic.com.py; internet www.apcs.org.py; f. 1963; Pres. ANTONIO VACCARO PAVIA.

Trade and Industry

GOVERNMENT AGENCIES

Instituto Nacional de Desarrollo Rural y de la Tierra (INDERT): Tacuary 276, esq. Mariscal Estigarribia, Asunción; tel. and fax (21) 44-3161; e-mail presidencia@indert.gov.py; internet www.indert.gov.py; f. 2003; land reform institute; Pres. JUAN CARLOS RAMÍREZ MONTALBETTI; Gen. Man. JORGE GALEANO.

Instituto Nacional de Tecnología, Normalización y Metrología (INTN): Avda General Artigas 3973 y General Roa, Casilla 967, Asunción; tel. (21) 29-0160; fax (21) 29-0873; e-mail intn@intn.gov.py; internet www.intn.gov.py; national standards institute; Dir-Gen. MARIO GUSTAVO LEIVA ENRIQUE.

Instituto de Previsión Social: Edif. de la Caja Central, Constitución y Luis Alberto de Herrera, Casilla 437, Asunción; tel. (21) 22-3141; fax (21) 22-3654; e-mail secretaria_general@ips.gov.py; internet www.ips.gov.py; f. 1943; responsible for employees' welfare and health insurance scheme; Pres. LUIS ALBERTO LÓPEZ GONZÁLEZ.

DEVELOPMENT ORGANIZATIONS

Alter Vida (Centro de Estudios y Formación para el Ecodesarrollo): Itapúa 1372, esq. Primer Presidente y Río Monday, Barrio Trinidad, Asunción; tel. (21) 29-8842; fax (21) 29-8845; e-mail info@altervida.org.py; internet www.altervida.org.py; f. 1985; ecological devt; Exec. Dir VÍCTOR BENÍTEZ INSFRÁN.

Centro de Cooperación Empresarial y Desarrollo Industrial (CEDIAL): Edif. UIP, 2°, Cerro Corá 1038, esq. Estados Unidos y Brasil, Asunción; tel. and fax (21) 23-0047; e-mail cedial@cedial.org.py; internet www.cedial.org.py; f. 1991; promotes commerce and industrial devt; Gen. Man. HERNÁN RAMÍREZ.

Centro de Información y Recursos para el Desarrollo (CIRD): Avda Mariscal López 2029, esq. Acá Carayá, Casilla 1580, Asunción; tel. (21) 22-6071; fax (21) 21-2540; e-mail cird@cird.org.py; internet www.cird.org.py; f. 1988; information and resources for devt orgs; Exec. Pres. AGUSTÍN CARRIZOSA.

Instituto de Biotecnología Agrícola (INBIO): Avda Brasilia 939, Calle Ciancio, Asunción; tel. (21) 23-3892; e-mail info@inbio.org.py; internet www.inbio.org.py; bio-technological research for agricultural devt; Pres. RICARDO WOLLMEISTER; Sec. LUIS MARÍA CORVALÁN.

Instituto Paraguayo de Artesanía (IPA): Teófilo del Puerto, entre Capt. Pedro Villamayor y Dr Prieto, Barrio Villa Aurelia, Asunción; tel. (21) 52-6533; fax (21) 60-0035; e-mail ipa@artesania.gov.py; internet www.artesania.gov.py; f. 2004; promotes handicraft industries; Pres. CLAUDIA ALDANA DÍAZ CORTAZAR.

Instituto Paraguayo del Indígena (INDI): Don Bosco 745, entre Haedo y Humaita, Asunción; tel. (21) 49-7317; fax (21) 44-0046; e-mail informes@indi.gov.py; internet www.indi.gov.py; f. 1981; responsible for welfare of Indian population; Pres. RUBÉN QUESNEL.

Red de Inversiones y Exportaciones (REDIEX): Avda Mariscal López 3333, CP 1892, Asunción; tel. (21) 616-3028; fax (21) 616-3034; e-mail info@rediex.gov.py; internet www.rediex.gov.py; replaced ProParaguay in 2007; responsible for promoting investment in Paraguay and the export of national products; Dir OSCAR STARK ROBLEDO.

Red Rural de Organizaciones Privadas de Desarrollo (Red Rural): Paraguari 1162, Calle Gaspar Rodríguez de Francia, Asunción; tel. (21) 44-3022; e-mail redrural@redrural.org.py; internet www.redrural.org.py; f. 1989; co-ordinating body for rural devt orgs; Gen. Co-ordinator HERMES GARCÍA; Sec. JOSÉ LARROZA.

Secretaría Técnica de Planificación: Estrella 505, esq. 14 de Mayo, Asunción; tel. (21) 45-0422; fax (21) 49-6510; e-mail comunicacion@stp.gov.py; internet www.stp.gov.py; govt body responsible for overall economic and social planning; Minister RICHARD WILLIAM KENT FERREIRA.

CHAMBERS OF COMMERCE

Cámara de Comercio e Industria Paraguayo-Alemana: Avda República Argentina 1616, Calle Alfredo Seiferheld, Casilla 1887, Asunción; tel. (21) 61-5848; fax (21) 61-5844; e-mail wloewen@ahkasu.com.py; internet www.ahkparaguay.com; f. 1956; Pres. WILFRIDO FERNÁNDEZ; Man. JOHN-WESLEY LÖWEN.

Cámara de Comercio Paraguayo-Americana: 25 de Mayo 2090, esq. Mayor Bullo, Asunción; tel. (21) 22-2160; fax (21) 22-1926; e-mail kcoronel@pamcham.com.py; internet www.pamcham.com.py; f. 1981; Pres. ALEJANDRO CONTI; Exec. Dir KAREN CORONEL; c. 300 mem. cos.

Cámara de Comercio Paraguayo-Argentina: Banco de la Nación Argentina, entre Palma y Alberdi (al lado del Consulado Argentino), Asunción; tel. (21) 49-7804; fax (21) 49-7805; e-mail administracion@campyarg.org.py; internet www.campyarg.org.py; f. 1991; Pres. ERNESTO GÓMEZ ESPECHE; Man. MARCELA ESCOBAR.

Cámara de Comercio Paraguayo-Británica: Edif. Internacional Faro, 2°, Avda Gen. Díaz 521, Asunción; tel. (21) 49-8274; e-mail britcham@conexion.com.py; internet www.britchampy.com; Pres. GUILLERMO ALONSO.

Cámara de Comercio Paraguayo-Francesa (CCPF): Yegros 837, 1°, Of. 12, CP 3009, Asunción; tel. (21) 49-7852; fax (21) 44-6324; e-mail info@ccpf.com.py; internet www.ccpf.com.py; Pres. ANTONIO LUIS PECCI MILTOS; Man. IRIS FELIU DE FLEITAS.

Cámara Nacional de Comercio y Servicios de Paraguay: Estrella 540, esq. 14 de Mayo y 15 de Agosto, Asunción; tel. (21) 49-3321; fax (21) 44-0817; e-mail info@ccparaguay.com.py; internet www.ccparaguay.com.py; f. 1898; fmrly Cámara y Bolsa de Comercio; adopted current name 2002; Pres. BELTRÁN MACCHI SALIN; Gen. Man. MIGUEL RIQUELME OLAZAR.

AGRICULTURAL, INDUSTRIAL AND EMPLOYERS' ORGANIZATIONS

Asociación de Empresas Financieras del Paraguay (ADEFI): Edif. Ahorros Paraguayos, Torre II, 6°, Of. 05, General Díaz 471, Asunción; tel. (21) 44-8298; fax (21) 49-8071; e-mail adefi@adefi.org.py; internet www.adefi.org.py; f. 1975; grouping of financial cos; Pres. JULIO ALBERTO SQUEF; Sec. FELIPE BURRÓ GUSTALE.

Asociación Paraguaya de la Calidad: Eduardo Víctor Haedo 680, O'Leary, Asunción; tel. (21) 44-7348; fax (21) 45-0705; e-mail apc@apc.org.py; internet www.apc.org.py; f. 1988; grouping of cos to promote quality of goods and services; Pres. JORGE MIGUEL BRUNOTTE; Sec. SANTIAGO LLANO CAVINA.

Asociación de Productores de Soja, Oleaginosas y Cereales del Paraguay (APS): Edif. Maynumby, 1°, Of. 11, Avda Mariscal López, Ciudad del Este, Alto Paraná; tel. (61) 570-115; e-mail aps_central@aps.org.py; internet www.aps.org.py; soya and grain producers' asscn; Pres. KARSTEN FRIEDRICHSEN; Sec. CLAUDIA AVEIRO.

Asociación Rural del Paraguay (ARP): Ruta Transchaco, Km 14, Mariano Roque Alonso; tel. (21) 75-4412; e-mail ania@arp.org.py; internet www.arp.org.py; grouping of agricultural cos and farmers; Pres. GERMÁN RUIZ; Exec. Dir VÍCTOR PERSANO.

Cámara Paraguaya de Exportadores y Comercializadores de Cereales y Oleaginosas (CAPECO): Avda Brasilia 840, Asunción; tel. (21) 20-8855; fax (21) 21-3971; e-mail capeco@capeco.org.py; internet www.capeco.org.py; f. 1980; grain exporters' asscn; Pres. JOSÉ BEREA; Gen. Man. IGNACIO SANTIVIAGO.

Centro de Importadores del Paraguay (CIP): Avda Brasilia 1947, casi Artigas, Casillas 2609, Asunción; tel. (21) 29-9800; e-mail cip@cip.org.py; internet www.cip.org.py; f. 1939; importers' asscn; Pres. MAX HABER NEUMANN; Man. JULIO SÁNCHEZ LASPINA.

Federación de Cooperativas de Producción Ltda (FECO-PROD): Sacramento 2279, Calle Teniente Silverio Molinas, Asunción; tel. (21) 29-7050; fax (21) 29-4727; e-mail info@fecoprod.com.py; internet www.fecoprod.com.py; f. 1975; agricultural producers' org.; Pres. EUGENIO SCHÖLLER; Sec. SIEGHARD DÜCK.

Federación de la Producción, Industria y Comercio (FEPRINCO): Edif. Union Club, Palma 751, 3°, esq. O'Leary y Ayolas, Asunción; tel. (21) 44-4963; fax (21) 44-6638; e-mail feprinco@quanta.com.py; internet www.feprinco.com.py; org. of private sector business execs; Pres. MAX HABER.

Unión de Gremios de la Producción (UGP): Avda Brasilia 939 y Calle Ciancio, Asunción; tel. (21) 22-4232; internet www.ugp.org.py; f. 2005; agricultural producers' org.; Pres. RAMÓN SÁNCHEZ VEGA.

Unión Industrial Paraguaya (UIP): Avda Sacramento 945, Calle Profesor Chávez, Asunción; tel. (21) 60-6988; fax (21) 21-3360; e-mail uip@uip.org.py; internet www.uip.org.py; f. 1936; org. of business entrepreneurs; Pres. EDUARDO FELIPPO; Sec. RAÚL HOECKLE.

MAJOR COMPANIES

Azucarera Paraguaya, SA (AZPA): Avda General Artigas 552, Casi San Jose, Casilla 43, CP 1404, Asunción; tel. (21) 21-3778; fax (21) 21-3150; e-mail informes@azpa.com.py; internet www.azpa.com.py; f. 1905; refining and wholesale distribution of cane sugar, alcohol and carbon dioxide; Pres. CARLOS CONRADO HOECKLE; Dir-Gen. JAN MARC BOSCH; 700 employees.

Botica Magistral, SA: Avda Mariscal López, esq. República Argentina, Paseo Los Lapachos, Local 3, Asunción; tel. (21) 66-4050; e-mail atencionalcliente@botica.com.py; internet www.botica.com.py; f. 1994; biotechnology and pharmaceuticals; Pres. SANDRO LUIS DA SILVA.

British American Tobacco Productora de Cigarrillos, SA (PROBAT): Avda Brasilia 767, casi Enrique Solano López, Barrio Jara, Asunción; tel. (21) 20-1145; fax (21) 22-3339; e-mail fernando_torres@bat.com; internet www.bat.com.py; f. 1994; Gen. Man. FERNANDO TORRES; 200 employees.

Cañas Paraguayas, SA (CAPASA): Palma, esq. Garibaldi, Asunción; tel. (21) 44-5783; fax (21) 44-3229; e-mail ventas@capasa.com.py; internet www.capasa.com.py; f. 1941 as Corporación Paraguaya de Alcoholes (COPAL); name changed to CAPASA in 1993; Pres. IVAN OJEDA.

Coca-Cola Paresa Paraguay: Acceso Sur, Km 3.5, Casilla 1403, San Lorenzo; tel. (21) 959-1000; fax (21) 959-1215; internet www.koandina.com; f. 1965; owned by Embotelladora Andina, SA; bottling co for Coca-Cola.

Consorcio de Ingeniería Electromecanica, SA (CIE): Avda General Artigas 3443, Casilla 2078, Asunción; tel. (21) 64-2850; fax (21) 64-4130; e-mail ventas@cie.com.py; internet www.cie.com.py; f. 1978; manufacture of sheet metal work; Pres. HUGO ARANDA NÚÑEZ; Gen. Man. CARLOS RODIÑO; 800 employees.

Empresa Distribuidora Especializada, SA (EDESA): Prof. Conradi 1690, esq. Avda Eusebio Ayala, Asunción; tel. (21) 50-1652; fax (21) 50-8549; e-mail edesa@edesa.com.py; internet www.edesa.com.py; f. 1981; wholesale distribution of durable goods; Pres. RAÚL ALBERTO DÍAZ DE ESPADA; Gen. Man. ALFREDO SCHIAPPACASSEE; 450 employees.

Grandes Tiendas La Riojana, SA: Avda Mariscal Estigarribia 171, esq. Yegros, Asunción; tel. (21) 49-2211; fax (21) 44-6698; e-mail info@lariojana.com.py; internet www.lariojana.com.py; department stores; Chair LÁZARO MORGA LACALLE; 480 employees.

Grupo A. J. Vierci: Edif. Oliva, Avda Oliva 845, entre Calle Montevideo y Ayolas, Asunción; tel. (21) 414-1101; fax (21) 414-1116; e-mail contacto@aj.com.py; internet www.grupovierci.com; f. 1967; multiple interests incl. import, retail, media and real estate; Pres. ANTONIO J. VIERCI.

Grupo Luminotecnia: Avda Eusebio Ayala 2288, Calle Juan del Castillo, Asunción; tel. (21) 55-1075; fax (21) 55-1212; e-mail info@luminotecnia.com; internet www.luminotecnia.com.py; manufacturers of electronic products; Pres. RUBÉN MUJICA.

Industria Nacional de Cemento (INC): Teniente Alcorta, esq. Avda Fernando de la Mora, Asunción; tel. (21) 55-7417; e-mail gerencia_general@inc.gov.py; internet www.inc.gov.py; f. 1969 following collapse of private co Vallemi, SA; state-owned; cement manufacturers; Pres. JORGE MÉNDEZ CUEVAS.

IRIS, SAIC: Gobernador Irala 1952, Barrio Sajonia, Asunción; tel. (21) 238-1709; fax (21) 22-0520; e-mail iris@iris.com.py; internet www.iris.com.py; f. 1936; manufacture and marketing of cleaning and insecticide products; 50% owned by Chemopharma SA (Chile); Pres. FRANCISCO COSP; Gen. Man. CARMEN COSP.

La Mercantil Guaraní, SA: Avda República Argentina, esq. Carios, Asunción; tel. and fax (21) 55-2600; e-mail buzon@mguarani.com.py; internet www.mguarani.com.py; f. 1957; imports alcoholic beverages and food; CEO OMAR DAHAR.

Louis Dreyfus Commodities, Paraguay: 8 de Junio 3457, casi Teniente Espinola Bo Santisima Trinidad, Asunción; tel. (21) 29-4782; fax (21) 29-4792; internet www.ldc.com.ar/ldc_paraguay; f. 2004; export of oil and cereals.

Petróleos Paraguayos, SA (PETROPAR): Edif. Oga Rape, 9°, Avda Chile 753, Casi Eduardo V. Haedo, Asunción; tel. (21) 44-8503; fax (21) 45-2306; e-mail contactenos@petropar.gov.py; internet www.petropar.gov.py; f. 1986; govt-owned; petroleum refining; Pres. FLEMING RAÚL DUARTE RAMOS; 400 employees.

Scavone Hermanos, SA: Santa Ana 431 y Avda España, Asunción; tel. (21) 60-8171; fax (21) 66-1480; e-mail preshsa@scavonehnos.com.py; internet www.scavonehnos.com.py; f. 1905; manufacture and retail distribution of pharmaceuticals; Pres. FELIPE C. RESCK B.; Gen. Man. CARLOS SÍRTORI; 530 employees.

Tecno Electric, SA: Teniente Primero Demetrio Araujo Miño, Calle Sacramento, Asunción; tel. (21) 29-0080; fax (21) 29-2863; e-mail tesa@tecnoelectric.com.py; internet www.tecnoelectric.com.py;

f. 1962; manufacture of electrical equipment and construction of electric installations; 200 employees.

Vargas Peña Apezteguia y Compañía, SAIC: ADe Gaulle 219, Calle Quesada, Villa Morra, Casilla 1176, Asunción; tel. (21) 60-2841; fax (21) 60-0262; e-mail administracionvm3@vargaspena.com.py; internet www.vargaspena.com.py; f. 1977; production of cotton and edible oils; Pres. JOSÉ MARÍA HERNAN VARGAS PEÑA APEZTEGUIA; 600 employees.

UTILITIES

Electricity

Administración Nacional de Electricidad (ANDE): Avda España 1268, casi Padre Cardozo, Asunción; tel. (21) 21-1001; fax (21) 21-2371; e-mail luis_rojas@ande.gov.py; internet www.ande.gov.py; f. 1949; national electricity board; Pres. CARLOS DIONISIO HEISELE SOSA; Sec.-Gen. LUIS RAMÓN ROJAS IBARRA.

Entidad Binacional Yacyretá: General Díaz 831 esq. Ayolas y Montevideo, Edif. Héroes de Marzo, Asunción; tel. and fax (21) 44-5611; internet www.eby.gov.py; owned jtly by Paraguay and Argentina; operates the hydroelectric dam at Yacyretá on the Paraná river, completed in 1998; installed capacity of 3,200 MW; 14,673 GWh of electricity produced in 2007; Dir (Paraguay) GUILLERMO LÓPEZ FLORES.

Itaipu Binacional: Centro Administrativo, Ruta Internacional Km 3.5, Avda Monseñor Rodríguez 150, Ciudad del Este, Depto Alto Paraná; tel. (61) 599-8989; fax (61) 599-8045; e-mail itaipu@itaipu.gov.br; internet www.itaipu.gov.py; f. 1974; jtly owned by Paraguay and Brazil; hydroelectric power station on Brazilian–Paraguayan border; 98,630 GWh of electricity produced in 2013; Dir-Gen. (Paraguay) JAMES EDWARD CLIFTON SPALDING HELLMERS.

Water

Empresa de Servicios Sanitarios del Paraguay, SA (ESSAP): José Berges 516, entre Brasil y San José, Asunción; tel. (21) 21-0330; fax (21) 21-2624; e-mail secretaria@essap.com.py; internet www.essap.com.py; f. 1954 as Corporación de Obras Sanitarias (CORPOSANA); responsible for public water supply, sewage disposal and drainage; Pres. ANDRÉS RIVAROLA CASACCIA.

TRADE UNIONS

Central Nacional de Trabajadores (CNT): Piribebuy 1078, Asunción; tel. (21) 44-4084; fax (21) 49-2154; e-mail cnt@cnt.org.py; internet www.cnt.org.py; Sec.-Gen. MIGUEL ZAYAS; 120,840 mems (2007).

Central Sindical de Trabajadores del Estado Paraguayo (Cesitep): Brasil y Fulgencio Moreno, Asunción; tel. (21) 21-0339; fax (21) 22-8244; e-mail vf_fases@hotmail.com; public sector workers; Pres. REINALDO BARRETO MEDINA.

Central Unitaria de Trabajadores Autentica (CUT-A): R. Moreno 566, esq. Paraguari y México, Asunción; tel. (21) 45-1212; e-mail cutautentica@hotmail.com; internet cutautentica.org.py; Pres. BERNARDO ROJAS DACOSTA; Sec.-Gen. VÍCTOR PEDRO FERREIRA.

Confederación Paraguaya de Trabajadores (CPT): Yegros 1333, esq. Simón Bolívar, Asunción; tel. 981878479 (mobile); e-mail conpartra@gmail.com; f. 1951; Sec.-Gen. FRANCISCO BRITEZ RUIZ; 43,500 mems from 189 affiliated groups.

Coordinadora Agrícola del Paraguay (CAP): Juan B. Flores y Tacuary, Hernandarias; tel. (983) 52-7003; e-mail bhjca@tigo.com.py; farmers' org.; Pres. HÉCTOR CRISTALDO; Sec.-Gen. ALBERTO ESTECHE.

Coordinadora Nacional de Camioneros: Asunción; represents lorry drivers' interests; Sec. VICTORIANO ROMERO.

Federación Nacional Campesina (FNC): Nangariry 1196, esq. Cacique Cará Cará, Asunción; tel. (21) 51-2384; internet fncmarandu.blogspot.com; grouping of peasants' orgs; Sec. ADRIÁN VÁZQUEZ.

Organización de Trabajadores de Educación del Paraguay (OTEP): Avda del Pueblo 845 con Ybyra Pyta, Barrio Santa Lucía, Lambaré; tel. and fax (21) 55-5525; e-mail otepsn@gmail.com; internet otepsn.blogspot.com; Sec. BLANCA AVALOS.

La Unión Nacional de Educadores–Sindicato Nacional (UNE–SN): Sicilia 630, esq. 15 de Agosto y O'Leary, Asunción; tel. and fax (21) 44-6777; e-mail info@une.com.py; internet www.unesn.org.py; f. 1992; Leader ELADIO BENÍTEZ.

Transport

RAILWAYS

Ferrocarriles del Paraguay, SA (FEPASA): México 145, Casilla 453, Asunción; tel. (21) 44-6789; fax (21) 44-3273; e-mail informaciones@ferrocarriles.com.py; internet www.ferrocarriles

.com.py; f. 1854; state-owned since 1961; scheduled for privatization; 376 km of track; Pres. MARCELO WAGNER.

ROADS

In 2010 there were an estimated 32,059 km of roads, of which 15.2% were paved. The Pan-American Highway runs for over 700 km in Paraguay and the Trans-Chaco Highway extends from Asunción to Bolivia. In 2011 the Government announced a US $170m. plan to improve some 5,150 km of roads and 189 bridges in the country's eastern region, under its national rural roads programme.

Centro de Empresarios del Transporte del Area Metropolitana (Cetrapam): Asunción; public transport provider asscn; Pres. CÉSAR RUIZ DÍAZ.

SHIPPING

The rivers Paraguay and Paraná constitute the principal waterways for cargo transportation in the country. There are 3,100 km of navigable waterways. The country has six ports, of which the port of Asunción is the most important. At December 2013 the flag registered fleet comprised 158 vessels, totalling 155,933 grt.

Administración Nacional de Navegación y Puertos (ANNP) (National Shipping and Ports Administration): Colón y El Paraguayo Independiente, Asunción; tel. (21) 49-2883; fax (21) 49-7485; e-mail gciacomercial@annp.gov.py; internet www.annp.gov.py; f. 1965; responsible for ports services and maintaining navigable channels in rivers and for improving navigation on the Paraguay and Paraná rivers; Pres. VIDAL FRANCIA ZARACHO.

Compañía Paraguaya de Navegación de Ultramar, SA (Copanu): Avda General Artigas 4145, Calle General Delgado, Asunción; tel. (21) 28-3665; fax (21) 28-1224; e-mail info@copanu .com.py; internet www.copanu.com.py; f. 1963; 10 vessels; Exec. Pres. IAN BOSCH.

Navemar, SA: Avda República Argentina 1412, Casilla 273, Asunción; tel. (21) 61-2527; fax (21) 61-2526; e-mail navemar@navemar .com.py; internet www.navemar.com.py; f. 1969; shipping agency, stowage, fleet operations and management; 5 vessels; Dir RICARDO DOS SANTOS.

Transporte Fluvial Paraguayo SACI: Edif. de la Encarnación, 13°, 14 de Mayo 563, Asunción; tel. (21) 49-3411; fax (21) 49-8218; e-mail tfpsaci@tm.com.py; Pres. MARCELO TOYOTOSHI; Man. EINAR DOMÍNGUEZ; 1 vessel.

CIVIL AVIATION

There are two major international airports: Aeropuerto Internacional Silvio Pettirossi, situated 15 km from Asunción; and Aeropuerto Internacional Guaraní, 30 km from Ciudad del Este.

Transportes Aéreos del Mercosur (TAM Mercosur): Aeropuerto Internacional Silvio Pettirossi, Hangar TAM/ARPA, Luque, Asunción; tel. (21) 49-1039; fax (21) 64-5146; e-mail tammercosur@ uninet.com.py; internet www.tam.com.py; f. 1963 as Líneas Aéreas Paraguayas (LAP); name changed as above in 1997; services to destinations within South America; 80% owned by TAM Linhas Aéreas (Brazil); Pres. LÍBANO MIRANDA BARROSO.

Tourism

Tourism is undeveloped, but, with recent improvements in infrastructure, efforts were being made to promote the sector. Tourist arrivals in Paraguay in 2012 totalled 579,305. In 2013 tourism receipts were a provisional US $273m. (excluding passenger transport).

Secretaría Nacional de Turismo: Palma 468, Calle 14 de Mayo, Asunción; tel. (21) 49-4110; fax (21) 49-1230; e-mail infosenatur@ senatur.gov.py; internet www.senatur.gov.py; f. 1998; Exec. Sec. MARCELA BACIGALUPO.

Defence

As assessed at November 2013, Paraguay's armed forces numbered 10,650, of which 2,550 were conscripts. There was an army of 7,600 and an air force of 1,100. The navy, which is largely river-based, had 1,950 members, including 900 marines and a naval air force of 100. There is also a 14,800-strong paramilitary police force, including 4,000 conscripts. Military service, which is compulsory, lasts for 12 months in the army and for two years in the navy.

Defence Budget: 1,540,000m. guaraníes in 2013.

Commander-in-Chief of the Armed Forces: President of the Republic.

Commander of the Armed Forces: Gen. JORGE FRANCISCO RAMÍREZ GÓMEZ.

Commander of the Army: Gen. LUIS GONZAGA GARCETE ESPÍNOLA.

Commander of the Air Force: Gen. LUIS NOCEDA.

Commander of the Navy: Adm. PABLO RICARDO OSORIO FLEITAS.

Education

Education is, where possible, compulsory for six years, to be undertaken between six and 12 years of age. Primary education begins at the age of six and lasts for six years. Secondary education, beginning at 12 years of age, lasts for a further six years. In 2011 enrolment at primary schools included 92% of children in the relevant age-group, while enrolment at secondary schools included 63% of those in the relevant age-group. There are 12 universities in Paraguay. The 2013 budget allocated an estimated 111,000m. guaraníes to the Ministry of Education and Culture.

Bibliography

For works on South America generally, see Select Bibliography (Books)

Alexander, R. *A History of Organized Labor in Uruguay and Paraguay.* Westport, CT, Praeger Publrs, Inc, 2005.

Cooney, J. W., and Mora, F. O. *Paraguay and the United States: Distant Allies.* Athens, GA, University of Georgia Press, 2007.

Duckworth, C. *Land and Dignity in Paraguay.* London, Continuum Books, 2011.

Franks, J. *Paraguay, Corruption, Reform, and the Financial System.* Washington, DC, IMF Publications, 2005.

Gaska, H. *Constructing Ava Guaraní Ethnic Identity: The Emergence of Indian Organization in Paraguay.* Saarbrücken, VDM Verlag Dr. Müller, 2010.

Hetherington, K. *Guerrilla Auditors: The Politics of Transparency in Neoliberal Paraguay.* Durham, NC, Duke University Press, 2011.

Horst, R. H. *The Stroessner Regime and Indigenous Resistance in Paraguay.* Gainesville, FL, University Press of Florida, 2010.

Kolinsky, C., and Nickson, R. A. *Historical Dictionary of Paraguay.* Lanham, MD, Rowman & Littlefield Publrs, 2000.

Kraay, H., and Whigham, T. *I Die with My Country: Perspectives on the Paraguayan War, 1864–1870.* Lincoln, NE, University of Nebraska Press, 2005.

Leuchars, C. *To the Bitter End: Paraguay and the War of the Triple Alliance.* Westport, CT, Greenwood Publishing Group, 2002.

Lewis, P. H. *Political Parties and Generations in Paraguay's Liberal Era, 1869–1940.* Chapel Hill, NC, University of North Carolina Press, 2009.

The Politics of Exile: Paraguay's Febrerista Party. Chapel Hill, NC, University of North Carolina Press, 2012.

O'Shaughnessy, H. *The Priest of Paraguay: Fernando Lugo and the Making of a Nation.* London, Zed Books, 2009.

Santos, A. (Ed.). *Paraguay: Addressing the Stagnation and Instability Trap.* Washington, DC, International Monetary Fund, 2010.

PERU

Geography

PHYSICAL FEATURES

The Republic of Peru is the third largest country in South America and is located on the west coast of the continent, astride the Andes and descending into the Amazonian plains. The country's longest border is with Brazil (1,560 km or 969 miles), which lies to the east of central Peru. Colombia (1,496 km of border) lies to the north-east, and Ecuador (1,420 km) to the north. Peru has 2,414 km of Pacific coastline, which includes the westernmost bulge of the South American continent, but then runs generally south-eastwards. In the south-east, there is a short southern border with Chile (160 km) and a much longer eastern border with Bolivia (900 km). Only in the late 1990s did Peru settle its outstanding border disputes with Ecuador and Chile, although the maritime boundary with the latter remains unresolved. Slightly smaller than the US state of Alaska, in total Peru covers 1,285,216 sq km (496,225 sq miles), including 5,130 sq km of inland waters.

Apart from some offshore islands, Peru consists of the Costa (the Pacific littoral and the foothills of the Continental Divide), the Sierra of the high Andes and the north-eastern Montaña or Selvas (the wooded lower slopes of the mountains, the high Selvas, and the rainforests of the Amazonian plains, the low Selvas). The coastal plains and lowlands stretch the length of the country, some 65 km–160 km in width, accounting for some 10% of the country. There are few natural harbours, while inland are dry, flat plains and sand dunes near the Sechura Desert, rising to the foothills. This country is an extension of the extremely arid Atacama Desert of Chile, and is so dry that only 10 of the 52 rivers that leave the Andes for the Pacific have sufficient flow to make it to the sea. Dotted along its length are about 40 'oases' suitable for farming. Parallel to the coast, and covering about 30% of the country, is the broad Sierra region. The Andes here consist of three ranges, the main one being the one closest to the sea, the Cordillera Occidental. The mountain ranges, which narrow in width from about 400 km in the south to 240 km in the north, are interspersed with lofty plateaux and deep valleys and gorges. The average height of the region is 3,660 m (about 1,180 ft), but in the mountains north of Lima, the coastal capital of Peru, Nevada de Huascarán reaches 6,768 m (22,213 ft). In the south-east, the interior plateau is broad enough to contain Lake Titicaca, the highest navigable lake in the world, which is shared with Bolivia. Directly west of here, but rather closer to the Pacific seashore to the south-west, is the source of the Amazon (which drains into the Atlantic, far to the east, 6,516 km later), which is usually cited as Lake McIntyre. Those rivers that do not drain into the Amazon or directly into the Pacific drain into Lake Titicaca, which drains through Desaguadero into Lake Poopó in Bolivia. On the rainier eastern slopes of the Andes the rivers have carved deep valleys and sharp crests, and it is this that forms the main barrier between the highlands and the Amazon basin. These forested slopes of the high Selvas in the north-east broaden into the flat, tropical jungle of the Amazon basin, the region (60% of the country's land area) collectively being known as the Montaña. The Montaña, the eastern strip of foothills and the north-east, is largely unexplored and reaches a maximum width of 965 km in the north, where the rainforest continues into Brazil. About one-half of the country is wooded and one-fifth is pasture, the dense rainforest dominating the east, but with more varied tropical vegetation in the centre and west (and still greater variety at altitude). There is some volcanic activity in the mountains, which are prone to earthquakes and landslides, with tsunamis and flooding occurring at lower levels.

CLIMATE

The climate is tropical in the lowlands, but it can be arctic on the highest mountains—there is permanent snow and ice on

heights over 5,000 m. Agriculture is possible up to 4,400 m, with the country able to grow a great range of crops and vegetation types at different altitudes. The Costa has an equable climate (temperatures averaging about 20°C—68°F—all year round), cooled by a major offshore sea current, but little rainfall gets past the mountains. For much of the coastal region average rainfall can be only about 50 mm (2 ins) per year, with slightly more in the north and less in the south. The grasslands of the foothills or the western slopes of the Andes survive, when there is no rain, in the mists of the clouds that often cloak the heights. The interior and eastern parts of the Sierra, however, can receive heavy rainfall in October–April. The south-east Sierra, in Cusco (Cuzco), for instance, gets average annual rainfall of 815 mm, but it is the exposed eastern slopes that get most (more than 2,500 mm in places). Minimum and maximum temperatures, on average, range seasonally between –7°C and 21°C (20°F–70°F). Although it is much hotter than the other two major regions of Peru, as is to be expected for a region concentrated in the north and east, it is the Montaña that gets most rainfall (mainly November–April). Here, it is very hot, particularly lower down, and very humid. Total rainfall where the land is beginning to rise can be as much as 3,800 mm per year, although much of the water drains back into the lower Montaña from which it was originally evaporated by the prevailing north-easterlies. Normal patterns can, of course, be disrupted, notably during that periodic feature of the climate known as El Niño. This weather phenomenon can have severe repercussions for Peru, as it brings the heavy rainfall normally delivered to the western Pacific to the east, to a region unsuited to such conditions, which can result in widespread destruction.

POPULATION

There are pronounced class and ethnic divisions, originating in the colonial period, that persist to this day, with the white, urban élite dominating the largely Amerindian and Mestizo countryside. Most indigenous people are descendants of the imperial Incas, who were based in the Peruvian highlands.

About 45% of the population are Amerindian, mainly Quechua-speaking, with some Aymará in the south and about 100 other, isolated groups in the east. A further 37% are of mixed Amerindian and white (mainly Spanish) ancestry. About 15% are of white descent, mainly living in Lima and elsewhere along the Costa, with the rest being black, mixed-black or of Arab, Japanese or Chinese ancestry. Spanish, the principal language of 70% of the population, was the sole official language until 1975, when it was joined by Quechua (of which 28 dialects are spoken in Peru), followed by Aymará. According to the latest census, 81% of Peruvians are Roman Catholic, which was the established religion of the state for much of the 20th century.

About 12% belong to the Evangelical Church, with a number of other religious or non-faith minorities.

According to official estimates, the total population at mid-2014 was 30.8m. About three-quarters of these people are urbanized, the largest city by far being the national capital, Lima (with an estimated 9.7m. inhabitants in mid-2014), which is on the central coast. Other important centres include Callao, the port of Lima, and the larger cities of Arequipa (the country's second city, but with less than one-10th the population of Lima), to the south and inland from the coast, and Trujillo, to the north. High in the Sierra, to the north of Arequipa, is the ancient Inca city of Cusco (Cuzco). The country is divided into 24 regions and one province (Callao).

History

Dr JOHN CRABTREE

INTRODUCTION

Until the Spanish invasion in the 16th century, the lands that were to become modern Peru were inhabited by a succession of cultures which culminated in the Inca empire in the 15th century. Archaeological remains attest to the strength and sophistication of these cultures, especially in fields such as architecture, textiles and jewellery. At its height, the Inca empire spread out from its centre in Cusco (Cuzco) over a huge area from what is now northern Argentina to the south, to southern Colombia in the north. The social structure of the empire was highly hierarchical, with the figure of the Inca at its zenith. The political power of the empire had been weakened prior to the arrival of the Spanish by a civil war between two rival contenders, Huascar and Atahualpa.

COLONIAL AND REPUBLICAN PERU

The arrival of the Spanish and the defeat of Atahualpa at the hands of conquistador Francisco Pizarro led to the rapid consolidation of Spanish power in this part of the Americas. With Lima as its capital, Spain rapidly took control of South America, except for Brazil which was colonized by Portugal. The conquest led to a rapid process of depopulation, largely as a result of diseases for which indigenous people had no immunity. The economy of colonial Peru was dominated by mining, and particularly the extraction of silver from the mines of Potosí (in today's Bolivia) and its shipment to the coast at Lima and from there by boat to Spain. A new, but often mestizo, élite replaced that of the Incas. The unwieldy nature of the Spanish empire led to its fracture in the 18th century, with other urban centres (notably Buenos Aires, Bogotá and Caracas) challenging the primacy of Lima. The empire also suffered from indigenous revolts, of which the rebellion of José Gabriel Condorcanqui (otherwise known as Túpac Amaru II) in the 1780s was the most notable.

Republican Peru was officially born in 1821, one of the last vestiges of the Spanish empire to remain loyal. However it took the battles of Junín and Ayacucho in 1824, led by non-Peruvians Simón Bolívar and José Antonio de Sucre, to finally end Spanish rule in South America. The first few decades of independence brought constant strife between regional caudillos struggling for power. With the guano boom of the 1840s, the Peruvian state recovered a modicum of stability under President Ramón Castilla. Economic decline thereafter led to the country's bankruptcy in the 1870s. The War of the Pacific (1879 to 1883) was a disaster for Peru, leading to the loss of nitrate-rich territories in what today is northern Chile. But global economic expansion brought demand for new commodity exports, such as sugar, cotton and rubber, at the end of the 19th century, and with it the emergence of new élites within what became known as the 'Aristocratic Republic'.

PERU IN THE EARLY 20TH CENTURY

Social changes and the emergence of new sectors into the political life of Peru brought new challenges to the old élite, particularly with new influences from abroad. New parties, based on middle and working class support, emerged. They included the Alianza Popular Revolucionaria Americana (APRA) led by Víctor Raúl Haya de la Torre, founded in exile in 1924, and the Socialist Party (which became the Communist Party) founded in 1930 and led by José Carlos Mariátegui. Relative economic stability, which coincided with the 11-year dictatorship (*oncenio*) of Augusto Leguía, ended with the crash of 1929. In the economic chaos that followed, Leguía was ousted.

In elections held in 1931, APRA claimed it had been robbed of victory. This gave way to a period in which political élites sought to prevent APRA taking office. In 1932, following an Aprista revolt in Trujillo, the conservative Sánchez Cerro Government killed some 1,000 party militants in a massacre in the ruins of Chan Chan, near the northern city. A succession of military or military-backed Governments ensued until the late 1940s, when APRA emerged to participate in the post-World War II liberal Bustamante y Rivero Government. However, in 1948 this too was toppled by a conservative military regime led by General Manuel Odría, who ruled Peru for most of the 1950s. For its part, the Communist Party, following Mariátegui's early death in 1930, remained a small grouping with strength only in sectors of the organized working class.

CHALLENGES TO THE OLD ORDER

By the late 1950s, some new reformist parties had emerged. They included Acción Popular (AP), a party established in 1956 by Fernando Belaúnde Terry, and the Peruvian Christian Democrat Party (PDC). By the early 1960s, Belaúnde had emerged as a strong contender for power. He vied with APRA in the 1963 elections (which were cancelled and led to a short-lived military government) and then won a convincing victory in 1964. The Belaúnde administration sought to introduce a number of moderate social reforms, notably an agrarian reform to challenge the old quasi-feudal system of landholding. He was supported, to a certain extent, by the US Alliance for Progress. However, Washington did little to prevent a military coup in 1968, perpetrated by General Juan Velasco Alvarado.

Unlike military governments elsewhere at the time, the Velasco regime (1968-75) was unusual in that it represented a left-wing, nationalist position. It began by nationalizing the US-owned International Petroleum Corporation (IPC), leading to the establishment of Petroperú. It subsequently nationalized a number of other US-owned assets, including Cerro de Pasco (copper mining) and Marcona (iron ore) in the mining sector. It greatly accelerated the process of agrarian reform initiated by Belaúnde, and initiated schemes of worker participation modelled on the Yugoslav experience. In economic policy, it sought to pursue policies of import-substitutive industrialization. In foreign affairs, Peru under Velasco gave strong support to the Non-aligned Movement, and switched purchases of military equipment from the USA to the USSR.

However, by 1975, the Velasco Government was encountering growing balance of payments difficulties. Also by 1975, Velasco himself was ailing physically. A putsch led by more conservative officers led to Velasco's removal and his replacement by his former economy minister General Francisco Morales Bermúdez. Morales Bermúdez put Velasco's reform agenda on hold, and sought urgent accommodation with the IMF. He faced strong resistance from organized sectors of the peasantry and working class, strengthened politically under Velasco. A series of general strikes in 1977 and 1978 revealed the lack of public support for the regime. In 1978, in a bid to build consensus, the military Government agreed to a process of democratization. The first step in this direction was elections that year to a constituent assembly to rewrite the Constitution. With the APRA leader Haya de la Torre presiding over the *constituyente* (the nearest he ever came to power), a new Constitution was ratified in 1979. Presidential elections were scheduled for 1980.

CIVILIAN GOVERNMENT RESTORED

The 1980 elections led to the return of Fernando Belaúnde to the presidency after 12 years of military rule. His AP party entered into a congressional coalition with the right-wing Partido Popular Cristiano (PPC), a conservative offshoot from the PDC. The 1980s also brought other significant changes to the world of politics. Following Haya's death in 1979, the leadership of APRA jumped a generation and was eventually clinched by a young Haya protégé, Alan García Pérez. García sought to renovate his party and to give it a social democratic gloss. At the same time, Peru's various Marxist parties, which had gained ground during the Velasco Government within the organized labour movement, came together to form the Izquierda Unida (IU) coalition. The 1993 municipal elections saw the victory of IU candidate Alfonso Barrantes in metropolitan Lima.

The liberalizing agenda of Belaúnde's economic team, spearheaded by Prime Minister Manuel Ulloa, quickly aroused public hostility. This only increased as the economy, which contracted a full 12.5% in 1983, failed to respond to the attempt to attract foreign investment. Between 1983 and 1985, with the economy in the doldrums, the initiative passed to Belaúnde's opponents in both APRA and the left. Barrantes' electoral victory in Lima in 1983 betokened the collapse of AP in the 1985 elections. With considerable personal charisma, García took full advantage of Belaúnde's lacklustre record in government to beat the left into second place and seize the presidency for APRA.

APRA AND THE FAILURE OF HETERODOXY

García's victory in 1985 brought with it a retreat from the liberalizing economic orthodoxy of the Belaúnde years and an attempt to restore Peru's economic fortunes through the use of heterodox policies. In particular, Garcia challenged the international banking community by announcing that he would limit debt servicing to the equivalent of 10% of exports, a policy promise that he never managed to fulfil. Reacting against IMF policy prescriptions, García presided over two years of rapid growth. But the record turned sour after 1987 when Peru entered severe balance of payments difficulties and failed to secure help from the IMF and creditor banks.

Having started his administration with aplomb, García also ran into increased domestic political opposition, particularly as the economy faltered. His attempted nationalization of the domestic banking system in 1987 proved a particularly costly political mistake. It gave rise to renewed opposition on the right, particularly with Peru's famed novelist Mario Vargas Llosa seizing the initiative and building an opposition coalition with both AP and the PPC. As the economy entered into deep recession in 1998 and 1999, accompanied by accelerating inflation, García's popularity quickly evaporated. The left, associated with the same sort of policies that sullied García's reputation, found itself unable to take advantage of the situation.

The 1990 elections were fought against the background of a deep political vacuum. While Vargas Llosa seemed to have the advantage for much of the campaign, it was an outsider, Alberto Fujimori, who emerged triumphant. Fujimori took advantage of Vargas Llosa's promises of a liberalizing shock to galvanise support. He also enjoyed tactical support from García who saw him as the only way to prevent a Vargas Llosa victory. For both APRA and the left, the 1990 elections were a sharp rebuff, demonstrating a widespread public rejection of political parties and the constituted party system.

SENDERO LUMINOSO

The politics of the 1980s were deeply affected by the emergence and spread of a Maoist-inspired insurrection, Sendero Luminoso (Shining Path). Sendero's origins went back to the Sino-Soviet split of the 1960s. Peru was one of the few countries in Latin America where Maoist parties enjoyed some strong support. Sendero was a dissident faction of Peru's mainstream Maoist Communist Party, Patria Roja. Its origins were located in Ayacucho, where its founder, leader and ideologue, Abimael Guzmán, was a university professor. Sendero launched its 'popular war' against the Peruvian state at the time of the 1980 elections with an attack on a rural Ayacuchan polling station.

Taking advantage of the weak presence of the Peruvian state in Ayacucho and neighbouring departments and the ill-conceived campaign of repression launched by the Peruvian police and army, its influence quickly spread. By 1985, Sendero and its allies were involved in armed attacks over much of central and southern Peru. Its incursion into coca- and cocaine-producing areas, and the support it was able to give to farmers fighting coca eradication, gave it access to arms and cash. As a result of the killing, both by the armed forces and by Sendero, some 67,000 people are estimated to have been killed, the vast majority being innocent peasants caught in the cross-fire. By the late 1980s, Sendero had begun to launch armed attacks in urban areas, notably in Lima. The insurgency appeared to be advancing inexorably, while the García Government seemed unable to contain it. As well as the imploding economy on state institutions, these seemed inoperative in mounting a credible response. In 1985, a second, smaller guerrilla group, the Movimiento Revolucionario Túpac Amaru (MRTA) entered the fray, compounding such doubts.

THE FUJIMORI DECADE

Fujimori's election victory in 1990 thus took place against a backdrop of deep economic and political malaise. On the economic front, Fujimori quickly reneged on campaign promises and sought an accommodation with the IMF and the World Bank on terms for an economic rescue. The 'Fujishock' of December 1990 was as drastic as anything contemplated by Vargas Llosa. It was accompanied by a raft of policies to liberalize and deregulate the Peruvian economy, including a radical programme of privatization of public companies. With regard to politics, in April 1992 Fujimori staged an autogolpe (self-coup) by which he closed Congress, suspended the Supreme Court, and ordered the election of a new assembly to rewrite the Constitution. Six months later, the police authorities captured Abimael Guzmán in a house in Lima, a spectacular political coup. The reduction of inflation, the closure of Congress and the capture of Guzmán did wonders for Fujimori's personal popularity.

Behind the scenes, new institutional alliances were forming, with power shifting to a troika composed of Fujimori, his security 'expert' and factotum, Vladimiro Montesinos, and the head of the army, General Nicolás Hermoza Ríos. The 1993 Constitution, approved narrowly in a referendum, greatly increased their room for manoeuvre by removing a number of checks and balances. In particular, it removed the constitutional bar on Fujimori's re-election, allowing him to stand for re-election in 1995 for a further five-year term. With his popularity in the ascendant and given the poor standing enjoyed by Peru's political parties, Fujimori's re-election seemed assured. Indeed, he won the 1995 elections (amid some accusations of fraud) in the first round with more than 50% of the vote.

Fujimori's second term in office proved much less successful than his first. As the gloss from his successes against inflation and Sendero receded, he found it harder to maintain his public support. At the same time, opposition started to build up, particularly over the vexed issue as to whether Fujimori could constitutionally stand again in 2000, under the argument that this would be his first re-election under the 1993 Constitution. As judicial manipulations to this end became increasingly blatant, even those that had supported him in 1995 began to have doubts. These surfaced with force in 1999 when Fujimori officially announced his candidacy. The build-up to the elections saw widespread protests on the street, in particular the so-called 'Marcha de los Cuatro Suyos' (a reference to the four districts, or 'suyu', in which the Incan empire was divided) a co-ordinated protest march from the provinces on Lima. The 2000 elections, which Fujimori officially won, were plagued with irregularities, and evidence of official corruption behind these—principally involving Montesinos and his Servicio de Inteligencia Nacional (National Intelligence Service—SIN)—eventually made Fujimori's situation unsustainable. Videos screened on television in which Montesinos was seen distributing wads of money to influential opinion formers proved the last straw. In November, only months after taking office for the third time, Fujimori announced by fax from Tokyo that he was resigning the presidency.

RETURN TO DEMOCRACY

Fujimori was replaced as President by Valentín Paniagua on an interim basis (2000–01), pending legislative changes to reduce the more egregiously authoritarian laws of the Fujimori era and the holding of fresh presidential elections in 2001. Since these there have been three administrations, all democratically elected: that of Alejandro Toledo (2001–06), Alan García (2006–11) and, since 2011, that of Ollanta Humala, whose term is due to expire in 2016.

Alejandro Toledo, 2001–06

Toledo emerged as the victor in the 2001 elections on the basis of a second-round contest with Alan García. He had emerged as one of the key opponents of Fujimori, particularly during the Marcha de los Cuatro Suyos. Toledo started off in alliance with the centre-left, but his administration shifted ground towards the centre-right as time went on. His initial popularity proved short-lived, and for most of his period in office his ratings seldom reached double figures. This was partly because of political errors and an unconvincing style of leadership, but also due to unrelenting opposition from APRA and from the pro-Fujimori camp which retained an important presence in the Congress.

His economic policies were broadly liberal and pro-business, and followed on from those of the Fujimori era. His Government benefited from the restoration of growth, based in large part on strong foreign investment inflows, but this failed to translate into support for his Government or its policies. Programmes to reform the army, the police and the judiciary failed to make much of a mark, while legislation to buttress the party system signally failed to fulfil its intentions. The Toledo Government made some progress on decentralizing the public administration, but its agenda was knocked off course when referendums to create macro-regions failed to win public sympathy.

Toledo's Government faced a number of protest movements, particularly towards the development of mining operations in the highlands. These were opposed, frequently with resort to violence, by local communities on account of the negative social and environmental impacts of mining.

Alan García, 2006–11

In the 2006 elections, in which Toledo was constitutionally barred and his party all but disappeared as a force in Congress, García emerged triumphant, beating Ollanta Humala in the second round. Humala had made his mark previously as the perpetrator of a coup attempt against Fujimori in 2000, and had rallied the votes of the discontented against an increasingly conservative Alan García. Lacking a majority in Congress, García was dependent on an informal alliance with the supporters of Fujimori. His second Government proved very different from his first, with strident support for liberal economic policies designed to attract foreign investment. The rhythm of rapid growth that had begun under Toledo continued under García, spurred on by high world prices for most of Peru's commodity exports, particularly minerals, and by strong capital inflows from abroad. García, indeed, made attracting investment the leitmotiv of his administration, relegating distributive policies to the sidelines. The strongest statement he made on this subject came with an article he wrote for the conservative daily *El Comercio* in 2008, in which he accused environmental and social movements of seeking to sabotage the country's progress, citing Aesop's fable about the dog in the manger who would neither eat nor let others do so.

In his attempt to encourage investment in hydrocarbons, García sought to introduce legislation that made it easier for foreign companies to initiate exploration in the Amazon jungle region. Protests by indigenous tribes produced a major confrontation with police in the northern town of Bagua in 2009, in which 33 people were killed. Other protests multiplied in the highlands where peasant communities continued to resist inroads by mining companies. The García Government saw a notable expansion in the area of the country given in concession to mining and hydrocarbon companies. It also had to contend with protests by coca farmers against crop eradication policies and by informal mining operations which resisted government attempts to bring them within the formal sector of the economy. Also, García had to contend with periodic attacks launched on the security forces in those parts of the country—chiefly the Upper Huallaga valley to the north-east of Lima and the river valleys of the Apurímac and Ene to the south-east—where Sendero Luminoso retained a presence.

García's initial popularity declined sharply after his election, albeit not plumbing quite the same depths as Toledo. His Government was widely criticized for favouring the interests of foreign companies without taking effective steps to spread the benefits of growth during these years. It was largely this critique that fuelled the electoral campaign of Ollanta Humala in 2011, bringing him in from rank outsider to the centre of the political fray. With García unable to contest the presidency, APRA found itself reduced to a rump of only four congressmen in the 2011 elections.

Ollanta Humala, 2011–

As in 2006, Humala's support in the 2011 campaign was concentrated in provincial Peru where voters felt they had not received their fair share of the benefits of growth under García. Humala's radical discourse distinguished him from the rest of the presidential candidates in 2011, most of whom came from positions in the centre and centre-right. In the end, he managed narrowly to prevail over Fujimori's daughter, Keiko, on the second round, confounding political pundits who had previously classified him as a 'no hope' candidate.

Once in office and under heavy pressure from the business community, Humala rapidly shifted his political position, adopting a far more conciliatory posture towards foreign investors. By the same token, during his first six months in office he sacked most of those on the left who had won office in return for the support they had given him in the campaign. In December 2011, in response to violent local protests against Conga, a large mining venture that would have expanded Yanacocha's gold mining operations in Cajamarca, he dismissed his conciliatory prime minister, Salomon Lerner, appointing instead a hard-liner with strong links to the pro-Fujimori members of Congress and to the military, Oscar Valdés. But Valdés' tough approach proved no more effective in dealing with social protest, and he himself was replaced by the more conciliatory Juan Jiménez within six months. Jiménez was dismissed as prime minister in October 2013 following a fall in the Government's approval ratings, and was, in turn, replaced by César Villanueva.

Humala's popularity did not dissipate quite as quickly as that of his two predecessors. Even so, in 2014, nearly three years into his five-year term, it had shrunk to around 25%. Consistently more popular than the President was his wife, Nadine Heredia, who, as first lady, played a highly conspicuous role on the political stage, associating herself with the Government's expansive social policies. Despite her denials, Heredia was routinely viewed in the media as harbouring presidential ambitions of her own once her husband stepped down in 2016. Ambitious and telegenic, she provided a counterpoint to Humala's dour political demeanour. However, she faced legal obstacles to running for President in the form of a law, passed by Fujimori and designed to prevent his wife from running against him in 2000, which prevents relatives or spouses of presidential incumbents from contesting the top office. Her putative candidacy was routinely criticized by by Alan García, who also made no secret of his desire to return to the presidency for a third term. Humala, seen as vacillating between right and left, was criticized for allowing Heredia to exercise excessive influence over government decisions; she was widely seen as being responsible for the departure from government of César Villanueva in February 2014; he was replaced as prime minister by René Cornejo Díaz, hitherto housing minister. The ensuing cabinet reshuffle only received congressional approval after Cornejo gave assurances that there would be no 'interference' in government matters from Heredia. Nevertheless, Cornejo's tenure lasted only until July, when he was implicated in an attempt to discredit an opposition deputy. He resigned and was replaced by Ana Jara, hitherto Minister of Labour and Employment, although again, congressional approval for her appointment was difficult to secure.

Humala's economic policies remained similar to those of his two predecessors, but with more emphasis placed on achieving a better distribution of the fruits of growth. His Government has expanded on previously existing social programmes, including a number of targeted Conditional Cash Transfer (CCT) schemes designed to reduce poverty levels. Its model, in this regard, was the social policies implemented by the Brazilian Government under Lula da Silva and Dilma Rousseff. Peru's success in negotiating an agreement with Chile over the two countries' maritime border that extended Peruvian sovereignty in the Pacific helped provide a temporary fillip to Humala's standing in early 2014.

In the security sphere, Humala continued to be challenged by the remnants of Sendero Luminoso, entrenched in the remote but strategically important valleys of the Apurímac, Ene and Mantaro, the so-called VRAEM (Valle de los Ríos Apurímac, Ene y Mantaro). Sendero Luminoso threatened inroads into the jungle region of Cusco, the country's main source of natural gas. The capture of several Sendero leaders in 2012 and 2013 showed that the organization was vulnerable to counter-insurgency operations. At the same time, Humala faced frequent bouts of opposition to the expansion of extractive industries, principally mining. Apart from the Conga gold-mining project in Cajamarca, there were numerous other mining investment schemes that met with frequently violent protests from local peasant communities.

CONCLUSION AND PROSPECTS

The next presidential and legislative elections in Peru were scheduled to be held in April 2016. Humala is constitutionally barred from seeking re-election, and doubts as to whether his wife, Nadine Heredia, would be a candidate opened the way to other possible contenders. These included former heads of state García and Toledo, as well as former presidential contenders Pedro Pablo Kuczynski and Keiko Fujimori. As of July 2014, with two years of Humala's mandate to run, campaigning to succeed him was well under way. Humala's dwindling political standing appeared difficult to reverse. He was criticized by both the left and the right and under constant attack from the likely candidates in 2016. Ultimately, Humala's reputation would depend on his ability to ensure a better distribution of the fruits of economic growth on the basis of increased social spending among the poorer sectors of the population, especially in the highlands and the jungle. Moreover, lower growth rates in 2014 and 2015 threatened to undermine his capacity to use public spending to achieve these social objectives.

Economy

Dr JOHN CRABTREE

OVERALL POLICY DIRECTION

Peru has since the 1990s distinguished itself in having adopted and adhered to a broadly liberalizing economic agenda. There has been a strong degree of continuity in economic policy-making under four successive administrations: those of Alberto Fujimori (1990–2000), Alejandro Toledo (2001–06), Alan García (2006–11) and most recently Ollanta Humala (2011–). Most of Peru's public companies were privatized under Fujimori, and although tougher regulation has since been introduced, this has not been reversed. In its foreign trade, Peru has negotiated free trade agreements with its main trade partners (the USA, China and the European Union—EU), and has adopted policies designed to attract foreign investment, particularly in the all-important mining sector. Under the García presidency, there was a significant increase in the number of concessions granted to mining and hydrocarbons firms for exploratory operations in Peru.

The public sector represents a significantly smaller proportion of the economy than it did 25 years ago. Debt as a proportion of gross domestic product (GDP) has consistently fallen in recent years: at the end of 2013 the public external debt ratio stood at 8.6%. With foreign reserves far exceeding the country's overseas debt, Peru's credit rating has improved substantially.

The election of Humala to the presidency in 2011 brought fears that Peru would resort to more interventionist policies, but this has not been the case. On taking office, Humala swiftly changed his stance, partly in response to the strength of the business lobbies, most of which had supported his opponents in the election. The overall approach adopted by the Humala administration has been to focus on policies designed to perpetuate growth while addressing the country's skewed pattern of distribution. In particular, Humala has placed greater emphasis than did his predecessors on social policies designed to tackle poverty. In so doing, he has been able to make use of significant increases in tax receipts in recent years. He has also sought to assuage fears that the state is unable to manage the conflicts arising from rapid investment in extractives, principally mining and hydrocarbons.

ECONOMIC GROWTH

Largely because of the scale of investment, the expansion of traditional industries and sustained high prices for most of Peru's commodity exports in recent years, GDP has undergone rapid expansion. Indeed, it has been one of Latin America's star performers in the last decade, with an average annual growth rate since 2003 of 6.4%. GDP per head has risen as a result. This stood at US $6,796 at the end of 2012, compared with $4,493 at the end of 2009, according to the World Bank. In recent years domestic consumption has taken over from exports as the prime motor of growth, with particularly rapid expansion in sectors such as construction and services. Growth in construction did slow in 2013, but, at 8.5%, this was still well in excess of the overall GDP expansion of 5.0%.

The results of growth are particularly evident along Peru's coastal strip, especially in the main cities there such as Lima, Arequipa, Trujillo, Ica and Piura. This has given rise to charges that governments have failed to distribute the results of growth equitably between different parts of the country and between different social classes. However, policies to boost public investment in the interior—in the Andean highlands and the Amazon jungle—seem to have had some impact in correcting this imbalance. As a result of the large amounts of revenues available from extractive industries, traditionally poor parts of the country like Cusco (Cuzco) have been among the fastest growing regional economies.

INFLATION

Largely as a result of prudent macroeconomic policies, in recent years Peru has had one of the lowest inflation rates in Latin America. In 2013 the annual rate of inflation was 2.8%, only slightly up on 2.6% the previous year. The country has managed to avoid incurring large fiscal deficits—indeed, it has generated surpluses in recent years—and has maintained a relatively stable monetary policy aided by low rates of inflation. Domestic prices have also been kept in check by a tendency for the new sol/dollar exchange rate to appreciate, although this trend was partly reversed in 2013. Given the country's history of inflation—it experienced hyperinflation at the end of the 1980s—there is a broad political consensus on the importance of avoiding rising rates.

FOREIGN TRADE

Foreign trade has grown rapidly in recent years, although it tailed off in 2013 because of lower international prices for the country's export commodities. Exports totalled US $42,177m. in 2013, compared with $9,090m. 10 years earlier. This rate of expansion reflects both an important increase in productive capacity and relatively buoyant prices for most of the country's key exports. Imports, too, have grown rapidly, to $42,217m. in 2013—up from $8,200m. in 2003. This increase has been in response to high domestic growth rates and rising consumption levels, as well as increased investment and associated imports of capital goods. It also reflects trade liberalization and the lowering of import tariffs as a result of a succession of free trade agreements. Peru has run a trade surplus for several years; in 2013, however, there was a small deficit, of $40m.

Minerals constitute the most important export sector, accounting for just over 55% of total exports in 2013. Peru is among the world's principal producers of copper, zinc, silver and gold. Copper exports led the way in 2013, at US $9,813m. (down from $10,731m. in 2012 because of lower international prices), followed by gold exports worth $8,061m. Until recently a net importer of hydrocarbons, Peru started exporting natural gas from the Camisea production area in Cusco in 2008. Gas exports were worth $1,372m. in 2013. There has been a significant increase in exports in the agricultural sector, led by coffee. Peru is also an important exporter of fish and fishmeal, with sales in 2013 earning $1,707m. The People's Republic of China has taken over from the USA as Peru's single most important trading partner, taking exports worth US $7,330m. in 2013, according to official figures. Peru has taken advantage of China's seemingly insatiable demand for minerals, although export earnings in 2013 declined slightly on those of the previous year. Imports of manufactures from China have become increasingly technically sophisticated. Subdued growth conditions in 2013 in the USA and the EU, both of which have free trade agreements with Peru, led to a relative decline in trade patterns.

BALANCE OF PAYMENTS

Given strong export performance and large inflows of foreign investment, Peru's balance of payments has gone from strength to strength in recent years. Foreign reserves stood at a record US $65,700m. at the end of 2013, equivalent to almost 19 months of imports. The current account deficit increased in 2013 to $9,126m., equivalent to 4.5% of GDP. This was substantially higher than in 2012, largely because of the elimination of the trade surplus. However, the current account deficit was more than offset on the capital account by foreign investment inflows of a roughly similar amount.

Peru's debt situation has also continued to improve. At the end of 2013 the total public debt stood at 19.2% of GDP, down from 21.2% at the end of 2011 and 23.3% at the end of 2010. The external public debt was 8.6% of GDP, compared with 11.2% at the end of 2011 and 12.9% at the end of 2010. Domestic borrowing as a percentage of GDP has also continued to decline.

FISCAL SITUATION

Rapid economic growth has led to increased tax revenues generated by both direct (income and profits) taxes and indirect taxation on consumption. This has helped successive governments to balance the fiscal accounts. In 2013 the public sector (non-financial) surplus stood at 0.8% of GDP. At 16% of GDP, however, Peru's tax take is not high by comparative Latin American standards, and it is believed that tax evasion remains at high levels. Government spending, both current and capital, has risen in real terms over the last five years, with substantial amounts directed towards public investment on infrastructure. The canon system of decentralized finance means that sub-national governments have larger amounts at their disposal.

ECONOMIC SECTORS

Mining

From colonial times to the present, Peru has been integrated into the global economy primarily through its mining industry. It was from Callao that boats set sail for metropolitan Spain laden with silver. In the 19th and 20th centuries copper took over from silver as the country's principal mineral export, although the mid-19th century also brought a short-run boom in guano (for use in Europe as a natural fertilizer). The industry remained primarily in the hands of foreign, mainly US, companies until the 1970s, when under the Velasco administration key mining ventures were taken over by the Peruvian state. The most important of these was the Cerro de Pasco Corporation, in the central highlands, which was renamed Centromin. Through Mineroperú, the state also took over responsibility for trading minerals. The main exception to the tide of nationalization was Southern Peru Copper Corporation (SPCC), with its main mining centre at Toquepala in Tacna department in the extreme south. SPCC indeed expanded its activities under military rule with the development of Cuajone in neighbouring Moquegua.

The mining industry returned to private hands under the Fujimori Government in the 1990s with the privatization of Centromin, Mineroperú and Hierroperú (the state-owned iron ore mining concern). As part of his economic restructuring programme, Fujimori radically changed the country's mining code in order to make it more appealing to foreign investors. He also introduced tax stability agreements whereby investors were shielded from subsequent changes to the tax codes. Given its untapped mineral wealth, technological changes in mining and processing, and the attractive conditions on offer to mining investment, world-scale mining companies were attracted to Peru. This was particularly the case when, from 2000 onwards, the rise in mineral prices on international markets made mining a highly profitable business. Investors in Peru included Newmont Mining, which teamed up with local company Buenaventura to create Yanacocha, a large gold mining operation in Cajamarca. BHP-Billiton entered Peru and won the concession to develop Antamina, in the north-central highlands in Ancash. BHP-Billiton also took control of the formerly state-run Tintaya mine, in Cusco, although it later sold its stake to Xstrata. Anglo American won a contract to develop Quellaveco, in Moquegua.

By the 2000s there were other new entrants into the Peruvian mining industry, particularly from China. Major Chinese interests in Peru included Toromocho (Chinalco), Galeno (Jiangxi Copper and China Minmetal) and Rio Blanco (Zijin). Shougang of China also bought up Marcona (previously Hierroperú) when this major iron ore deposit was privatized. In 2014 Minmetal bought the Las Bambas copper project from Xstrata for a reported US $5,820m. Other big players in Peru include Rio Tinto, Anglo American, Barrack Gold and Xstrata. Improvements in efficiency in existing mining operations, together with the discovery of new mining resources, have led to a significant increase in output since the end of the 1990s. Much of the Peruvian highlands is now under concession to

Peruvian or foreign mining enterprises, many of them 'juniors', focusing their activities primarily on exploration.

However, this sudden expansion in mining activity has also led to multiple conflicts involving companies with neighbouring communities, many of them concerned about the negative environmental and social impacts brought about by mining activity. On some occasions—Tambogrande in Piura, and Cerro Quilish in Cajamarca, for example—opposition caused mining plans to be scrapped. In other instances—as in Yanacocha's Conga project, in Cajamarca—community opposition has led to projects being suspended. Social conflicts over mining frequently become violent. At the beginning of 2013 the Humala Government outlined proposals for improved policing in mining areas. As a consequence of their often remote location, state authorities are virtually absent in many such areas. Informal mining activities—small, often lawless enterprises, encouraged by high prices to engage in mining activity—have also had major negative environmental impacts. This is particularly the case with alluvial gold mining in the Amazon jungle region. In 2014 the Humala administration introduced measures designed to 'formalize' informal mining operations.

Hydrocarbons

Oil extraction in Peru dates originally from the 1920s, primarily in and around the district of Talara, in Piura on the northern coast. Until the late 1960s the main investor was Standard Oil of New Jersey. In 1968 the International Petroleum Corporation (IPC), owned by Standard Oil, was nationalized by the Velasco Government following a protracted wrangle over tax payments. The company that emerged, Petroperú, remains Peru's state oil company, although its remit was severely curtailed by President Fujimori in the 1990s. The discovery of oil in the northern Amazon in the 1960s never met initially optimistic expectations, and by the 1980s Peru had become a net importer of oil.

Major efforts have been made in recent years to reverse this situation, with concessions being offered to many foreign oil companies in the jungle, off shore in the Pacific, and even in parts of the highlands. No new major discoveries of crude have been made hitherto. As with metals, however, measures to make it easier for companies to move in to explore for oil have led to conflicts with local communities. The biggest of these was in 2009 near the town of Bagua, in the Amazonas region, when police clashed with indigenous peoples who were protesting against government efforts to encourage further exploration.

The single most important discovery of the last 20 years was that of the Camisea gas deposits in the jungles of northern Cusco region. Because of Camisea, Peru is now using natural gas for industrial and household consumption, as well as for transport. Gas is transported from Cusco to the coast via a pipeline linking Camisea with Pisco, south of Lima. The discovery of gas in more than just one field in Cusco has allowed the export of liquefied natural gas (LNG). Peru's main foreign markets for LNG are Mexico and Spain. Total proven gas reserves exceed 3,590m. cu m at the beginning of 2013, according to official estimates. At the end of 2012, after lengthy prevarication, the Humala Government finally agreed to the construction of a pipeline linking Camisea with towns and cities in the south of Peru, including Cusco and Arequipa. Advocates of the scheme say that this will give an important fillip to the regional economy, including the possibility of developing petrochemicals and fertilizer industries.

Agriculture

Agriculture in Peru has traditionally been concentrated in the highlands and in the coastal valleys, where water is available for irrigation. Until the agrarian reforms of the 1960s and 1970s, highland agriculture was based around the quasi-feudal hacienda and around subsistence farming by peasant communities. In the coastal valleys, capital-intensive agriculture prevailed, producing export crops like cotton and sugar. Agrarian reform changed the structure of landholding, eliminating large private estates. However, it had a negative impact on agricultural production overall. The restructuring of private landownership since the 1990s has brought about a revival in cash crop agriculture, mainly on the coast. Massively expensive irrigation schemes have also contributed, with

water being brought from the other side of the Andes to irrigate the desert.

Migration from the highlands to the Amazon has also led to the development of agriculture in the jungle regions of the country, particularly in the jungle fringe (ceja de selva). Coffee has become an important export commodity, and new crops such as palm oil are being developed and used for ethanol production. Coca, too, is an important crop (see below). Peru has also had considerable success in developing certain 'niche' crops, such as asparagus and paprika, primarily for export. None the less, agricultural output is dependent on adequate rainfall, and the periodic climatic phenomenon known as 'El Niño' can have devastating effects, especially for peasant agriculture.

The structure of agriculture remains dualistic: highly mechanized, privately owned cash crop production, mainly on the coast and in parts of the Amazon; and a labour-intensive, low-productivity peasant sector, mainly in the highlands. Policy priorities tend to be equally split, but the issue of how to raise output, as well as improve living standards and reduce poverty in the highlands remains on the agenda.

Coca

Coca has been produced in Peru from time immemorial—coca leaves having a symbolic and religious importance, as well as being an aid to counteract fatigue. However, production has increased rapidly since the 1970s, as use of coca leaves in the manufacture of cocaine increased (with the latter gaining popularity in Europe and the USA as a recreational drug). The main areas of production are in the valleys of the Ene, Apurímac and Mantaro rivers (known as the VRAEM—Valle de los Ríos Apurímac, Ene y Mantaro) and the districts of Lares and La Convención in Cusco. Of these, the last two tend to produce for the domestic, non-cocaine market.

Since the 1980s, and encouraged by the USA, successive governments have sought to suppress coca cultivation by means of manual eradication and the encouragement of substitute crops. This has not been a conspicuous success. Relatively high prices for coca, compared with those for other crops, mean that peasant producers have a powerful incentive to continue growing coca. Although Colombia overtook Peru as the world's largest coca producer in the 1990s, this distinction returned to Peru in 2012, according to the UN Office on Drugs and Crime (UNODC). Peru maintained this position in 2013, according to UNODC, with 60,400 ha under production, compared to Colombia's 49,800 ha. However, estimating coca output is fraught with difficulty, and annual crop surveys by UNODC and by the USA serve, at best, as rough guides.

Eradication efforts in major production areas have tended to lead to the development of others, usually in remote areas far from centres of political control. However, Peru has had some success in achieving lasting reductions in coca output in the Upper Huallaga valley, previously a major production area. In part, this is linked to the defeat of Sendero Luminoso there; but it is also a consequence of the development of the palm oil industry, which has provided a source of alternative employment. The activities of Sendero in the Upper Huallaga and in the VRAEM have served to provide protection for coca farmers from the activities of crop eradicators. The relative success of the Colombian authorities in suppressing coca growing and cocaine have led drugs-traffickers to move their operations south into Peru and Bolivia. Violent conflict between drugs gangs has increased in recent years—especially in port cities such as Trujillo and Chimbote, through which cocaine is traded.

Manufacturing

Despite being primarily a mining country, Peru has developed a fairly large manufacturing sector, directed mainly towards the domestic market. Much of what is officially classified as manufacturing consists of the processing of raw materials, usually adding little by way of added value. Many manufacturing concerns, encouraged by import-substitutive industrialization in the 1970s, failed to survive the more internationally competitive conditions brought about by trade liberalization. Among the more important industrial sectors are food production, textiles and clothing, and pharmaceuticals. Of these, the most important export-orientated sector is that of textiles, which accounted for earnings of US $1,926m. in 2013 (slightly down on the previous year). Textile manufacturers have found it hard, if not impossible, to compete with Chinese imports—both in the domestic and foreign markets. An overvalued exchange rate has not helped. One of the objectives of various free trade agreements has been to promote sales by Peruvian manufacturers in foreign markets.

Transport

Peru's geography has always represented an obstacle to the development of land communications, with the Andes dividing the country into three separate zones: the coast, highlands and the Amazon jungle. The best transport communications link the main towns of the coast, along the Pan-American highway that runs from the Ecuadorean border in the north to that with Chile in the south. Road connections between the coast and the towns of the highlands have improved greatly in the last 25 years, with links to Cajamarca, Huaraz, Huancayo, Ayacucho, Cusco and Puno. Air links have also improved in frequency and reliability, although prices are high and competition lacking on most routes. Given Peru's importance as a tourist destination, and the need otherwise to undertake lengthy bus journeys between destinations, there is high demand for air travel. Railways, built in the 19th century, are used mainly for the transport of bulk goods such as minerals, although some routes have been opened up for tourist travel.

Tourism

Given its historical, cultural and geographic attractions, Peru has become one of Latin America's most important travel destinations. In particular, sites like Machu Picchu in Cusco, along with the Sacred Valley of the Incas and the city of Cusco itself, have become world-class tourist destinations. However, tourist services have been slow to match growing demand, and transport facilities have until recently been poor. Large-scale investment in tourism in the last 10–15 years has radically altered the nature of the industry, with some destinations (including Cusco and Machu Picchu) becoming threatened by excessive influxes of tourists. A project to build a new international airport near to Cusco will increase tourist flows. While for many years Peru tended to attract young, low-budget travellers, luxury travel facilities are now available in many parts of the country. The Government has also made major efforts to publicize Peru's tourist appeal internationally.

CONCLUSION AND PROSPECTS

Peru's growth prospects remain good, particularly while strong Asian demand for its mineral products is sustained. The economy would, however, be hard hit if the recent decline in international commodity prices was to turn into a sharp and prolonged downturn, given its dependence on commodities for foreign exchange. The strength of the balance of payments and foreign reserves stocks provide the country with an important cushion against global macroeconomic instability over the short-to-medium term. The overall policy direction seems likely to remain business-friendly during what remains of Humala's presidency, and probably beyond, although concessions will need to be made to accommodate dissident groups. A key challenge for the incumbent Government is to try to spread the fruits of growth more widely, particularly among the poor and indigenous of the interior. Given the shortcomings of public administration in Peru, this is by no means an easy task—particularly as it involves building state capacities in areas where these are very weak, or do not exist.

Statistical Survey

Sources (unless otherwise stated): Banco Central de Reserva del Perú, Jirón Antonio Miró Quesada 441–445, Lima 1; tel. (1) 6132000; fax (1) 4273091; e-mail webmaster@bcrp.gob.pe; internet www.bcrp.gob.pe; Instituto Nacional de Estadística e Informática, Avda General Garzón 658, Jesús María, Lima; tel. (1) 6520000; fax (1) 4333591; e-mail infoinei@inei.gob.pe; internet www.inei.gob.pe.

Area and Population

AREA, POPULATION AND DENSITY
(excluding Indian jungle population)

Area (sq km)	
Land	1,280,086
Inland water	5,130
Total	1,285,216*
Population (census results)†‡	
11 July 1993	22,048,356
21 October 2007	
Males	13,622,640
Females	13,789,517
Total	27,412,157
Population (official estimates at mid-year)	
2012	30,135,875
2013	30,475,144
2014	30,814,175
Density (per sq km) at mid-2014 . .	24.1

* 496,225 sq miles.
† Excluding adjustment for underenumeration, estimated at 2.35% in 1993.
‡ An additional census was compiled, according to different methodology, during 18 July–20 August 2005. The total population was recorded at 27,219,264 in that year, including adjustment for an estimated 3.92% underenumeration (when the enumerated total was 26,152,265).

POPULATION BY AGE AND SEX
(official estimates at mid-2014)

	Males	Females	Total
0–14 years	4,447,212	4,280,238	8,727,450
15–64 years	10,087,586	10,025,699	20,113,285
65 years and over . . .	904,089	1,069,351	1,973,440
Total	**15,438,887**	**15,375,288**	**30,814,175**

REGIONS
(official estimates at mid-2014)

	Area (sq km)	Population	Density (per sq km)	Capital
Amazonas . .	39,249	421,122	10.7	Chachapoyas
Ancash . .	35,915	1,142,409	31.8	Huaraz
Apurímac . .	20,896	456,652	21.9	Abancay
Arequipa . .	63,345	1,273,180	20.1	Arequipa
Ayacucho . .	43,815	681,149	15.5	Ayacucho
Cajamarca . .	33,318	1,525,064	45.8	Cajamarca
Callao* . . .	147	996,455	6,778.6	Callao
Cusco . . .	71,987	1,308,806	18.2	Cusco (Cuzco)
Huancavelica .	22,131	491,278	22.2	Huancavelica
Huánuco . .	36,849	854,234	23.2	Huánuco
Ica . . .	21,328	779,372	36.5	Ica
Junín . . .	44,197	1,341,064	30.3	Huancayo
La Libertad .	25,500	1,836,960	72.0	Trujillo
Lambayeque .	14,231	1,250,349	87.9	Chiclayo
Lima . . .	34,802	9,689,011	278.4	Lima
Loreto . . .	368,852	1,028,968	2.8	Iquitos

—continued	Area (sq km)	Population	Density (per sq km)	Capital
Madre de Dios .	85,301	134,105	1.6	Puerto Maldonado
Moquegua . .	15,734	178,612	11.4	Moquegua
Pasco . .	25,320	301,988	11.9	Cerro de Pasco
Piura . .	35,892	1,829,496	51.0	Piura
Puno . . .	71,999	1,402,496	19.5	Puno
San Martín .	51,253	829,520	16.2	Moyabamba
Tacna . . .	16,076	337,583	21.0	Tacna
Tumbes . .	4,669	234,638	50.3	Tumbes
Ucayali . . .	102,411	489,664	4.8	Pucallpa
Total . .	1,285,216	30,814,175	24.0	—

* Province.

PRINCIPAL TOWNS
(population of towns and urban environs at 21 October 2007)

Lima (capital) . .	8,472,935*	Iquitos . . .	370,962
Arequipa . . .	749,291	Cusco (Cuzco) . .	348,935
Trujillo . . .	682,834	Chimbote . .	334,568
Chiclayo . . .	524,442	Huancayo . . .	323,054
Callao . . .	515,200†	Tacna . . .	242,451
Piura . . .	377,496	Ica	219,856

* Metropolitan area (Gran Lima) only.
† Estimated population of town, excluding urban environs, at mid-1985.
Mid-2014 (incl. suburbs, official estimates): Lima (capital) 9,735,587.

BIRTHS, MARRIAGES AND DEATHS

	Registered live births		Registered marriages		Registered deaths	
	Number	Rate (per 1,000)	Number	Rate (per 1,000)	Number	Rate (per 1,000)
2005 . .	611,459	22.0	82,277	3.0	103,207	3.7
2006 . .	637,974	22.7	89,162	3.2	105,074	3.7
2007 . .	663,056	23.3	90,883	3.2	107,249	3.8
2008 . .	679,122	23.6	94,971	3.3	108,100	3.8
2009 . .	660,716	22.7	87,561	3.0	110,811	3.8
2010 . .	640,291	21.8	82,043	2.8	108,178	3.7
2011 . .	794,040	26.6	97,693	3.3	118,456	4.0
2012 . .	698,954	23.2	107,380	3.6	119,652	4.0

Life expectancy (years at birth): 74.5 (males 71.9; females 77.3) in 2012 (Source: World Bank, World Development Indicators database).

ECONOMICALLY ACTIVE POPULATION
(national household survey, '000 persons)

	2010	2011	2012
Agriculture, hunting and forestry .	3,795.8	3,854.4	3,755.6
Fishing	80.8	87.3	77.9
Mining and quarrying . . .	175.6	200.9	205.4
Manufacturing	1,588.3	1,548.2	1,626.5
Construction	843.1	866.2	917.6
Wholesale and retail trade; repair of motor vehicles, motorcycles and personal and household goods	2,792.2	2,789.4	2,938.8
Hotels and restaurants . .	999.3	996.0	1,012.4
Transport, storage and communications	1,196.6	1,226.0	1,190.3
Real estate, renting and business activities	623.3	685.4	693.9
Public administration and defence; compulsory social security . .	648.0	638.4	711.1
Education	797.2	875.5	894.2
Other services	1,549.8	1,539.7	1,517.9
Total employed	15,089.9	15,307.3	15,541.5
Unemployed	645.8	641.8	600.6
Total labour force	15,735.7	15,949.1	16,142.1
Males	8,741.6	8,885.2	9,005.4
Females	6,994.1	7,063.9	7,136.8

Health and Welfare

KEY INDICATORS

Total fertility rate (children per woman, 2012)	2.4
Under-5 mortality rate (per 1,000 live births, 2012) . .	18
HIV/AIDS (% of persons aged 15–49, 2012)	0.4
Physicians (per 1,000 head, 2012)	1.1
Hospital beds (per 1,000 head, 2010)	1.3
Health expenditure (2011): US $ per head (PPP) . . .	483
Health expenditure (2011): % of GDP	4.7
Health expenditure (2011): public (% of total) . . .	56.9
Access to water (% of persons, 2012)	82
Access to sanitation (% of persons, 2012)	73
Total carbon dioxide emissions ('000 metric tons, 2010) .	57,579.2
Carbon dioxide emissions per head (metric tons, 2010) . .	2.0
Human Development Index (2013): ranking	82
Human Development Index (2013): value	0.737

For sources and definitions, see explanatory note on p. vi.

Agriculture

PRINCIPAL CROPS
('000 metric tons)

	2010	2011	2012
Wheat	219.5	214.1	226.1
Rice, paddy	2,831.4	2,624.5	3,019.3
Barley	216.2	201.2	213.9
Maize	1,541.2	1,514.4	1,679.3
Potatoes	3,814.4	4,072.5	4,473.5
Sweet potatoes	263.5	299.1	304.0
Cassava (Manioc) . . .	1,240.1	1,115.6	1,119.6
Sugar cane	9,660.9	9,884.9	10,368.9
Beans, dry	92.8	87.9	91.6
Oil palm fruit	291.8	359.8	515.5
Cabbages	37.0	37.1	40.1
Asparagus	335.2	392.3	376.6
Tomatoes	224.9	186.0	229.3
Pumpkins, squash and gourds .	179.5	199.0	221.5
Chillies and peppers, green* . .	11.4	11.5	12.5
Onions, dry	724.0	727.0	775.5
Garlic	63.0	88.5	82.1
Peas, green	102.3	100.8	117.6
Broad beans, dry	67.1	64.6	73.4
Carrots and turnips . . .	182.4	183.9	178.9
Maize, green	408.2	368.0	361.6
Plantains	2,007.3	1,967.9	2,000.0*
Oranges	394.6	418.6	425.0
Tangerines, mandarins, clementines and satsumas .	221.3	236.3	281.0
Lemons and limes . . .	233.0	224.7	234.1
Apples	143.9	149.5	147.1
Grapes	280.5	296.9	365.1
Watermelons	91.7	87.0	94.8
Guavas, mangoes and mangosteens . . .	457.8	355.4	355.4*
Avocados	184.4	212.9	215.0*
Pineapples	310.6	400.4	415.0*
Papayas	186.8	125.8	123.7
Coffee, green	264.6	331.5	303.3

* FAO estimate(s).

Aggregate production ('000 metric tons, may include official, semi-official or estimated data): Total cereals 4,868.1 in 2010, 4,617.2 in 2011, 5,204.3 in 2012; Total roots and tubers 5,604.4 in 2010, 5,774.0 in 2011, 6,182.1 in 2012; Total vegetables (incl. melons) 2,846.6 in 2010, 2,886.6 in 2011, 2,992.4 in 2012; Total fruits (excl. melons) 4,813.8 in 2010, 4,812.0 in 2011, 5,002.4 in 2012.

Source: FAO.

LIVESTOCK
('000 head, year ending September)

	2010	2011	2012
Horses*	735	740	742
Asses*	640	640	640
Mules*	305	305	307
Cattle	5,520	5,689	5,661
Pigs	3,254	3,263	2,991
Sheep	14,160	14,050	12,184
Goats	1,968	1,946	1,949
Chickens	130,779	128,943	137,669

* FAO estimates.

Source: FAO.

LIVESTOCK PRODUCTS
('000 metric tons)

	2010	2011	2012
Cattle meat	171.9	177.2	183.8
Sheep meat	33.7	35.3	36.3
Pig meat	115.7	117.4	121.2
Chicken meat	1,020.0	1,084.8	1,171.5
Cows' milk	1,678.4	1,745.5	1,798.9
Hen eggs	285.1	317.7	314.0
Wool, greasy	10.2	10.3	11.0*

* FAO estimate.

Source: FAO.

Forestry

ROUNDWOOD REMOVALS
('000 cubic metres, excluding bark)

	2010	2011	2012
Sawlogs, veneer logs and logs for sleepers	1,212	1,373	1,372
Other industrial wood	140	123	120
Fuel wood	7,338	7,425	7,308
Total	8,690	8,921	8,800

Source: FAO.

SAWNWOOD PRODUCTION
('000 cubic metres, including railway sleepers)

	2010	2011	2012
Coniferous (softwood)	2	9	8
Broadleaved (hardwood)	626	702	697
Total	628	711	705

Source: FAO.

Fishing

('000 metric tons, live weight)

	2010	2011	2012
Capture	4,216.1	8,248.5	4,841.5
Chilean jack mackerel	17.6	257.2	185.0
Anchoveta (Peruvian anchovy)	3,450.6	7,125.2	3,776.9
Jumbo flying squid	369.8	404.7	497.5
Aquaculture	89.0	92.2	72.1
Total catch	4,305.1	8,340.7	4,913.7

Note: Figures exclude aquatic plants ('000 metric tons, all capture): 4.4 in 2010; 5.8 in 2011; 3.6 in 2012.

Source: FAO.

Mining

('000 metric tons unless otherwise indicated)*

	2010	2011	2012
Crude petroleum ('000 barrels)	57,363.0	55,741.2	55,991.3
Natural gas (million cu ft)	255,609.2	401,169.4	418,794.8
Copper	1,024.0	1,024.8	1,120.7
Lead	241.2	211.9	228.9
Molybdenum	16.3	18.4	16.1
Tin	29.4	25.1	22.7
Zinc	1,258.4	1,075.2	1,096.3
Iron ore	6,139.3	7,123.1	6,791.5
Gold ('000 kg)	159.4	161.4	156.7
Silver ('000 kg)	3,422.6	3,214.3	3,270.9

* Figures for metallic minerals refer to metal content only.

2013: Crude petroleum ('000 barrels) 61,143.1; Natural gas (million cu ft) 393,765.7.

Industry

SELECTED PRODUCTS
('000 metric tons, unless otherwise indicated)

	2010	2011	2012
Canned fish	77.8	118.7	64.0
Wheat flour	1,214	1,249	1,255
Raw sugar	1,039.2	1,076.2	1,097.8
Beer ('000 hl)	12,303	13,054	13,643
Motor spirit (petrol, '000 barrels)*.	15,185†	14,037	n.a.
Kerosene ('000 barrels)*	80†	64	n.a.
Distillate fuel oils ('000 barrels)*	24,606†	30,979	n.a.
Residual fuel oils ('000 barrels)*	10,124†	9,207	n.a.
Portland cement	6,941	7,026	8,038
Crude steel*	750	750‡	n.a.
Copper (refined)	111.5	110.6	86.0
Electric energy (million kWh)	35,500.3	38,701.4	40,985.2

* Source: US Geological Survey.
† Preliminary figure.
‡ Estimate.

Finance

CURRENCY AND EXCHANGE RATES

Monetary Units
100 céntimos = 1 nuevo sol (new sol).

Sterling, Dollar and Euro Equivalents (30 April 2014)
£1 sterling = 4.723 new soles;
US $1 = 2.808 new soles;
€1 = 3.889 new soles;
100 new soles = £21.71= $35.61 = €25.71.

Average Exchange Rate (new soles per US $)
2011   2.7541
2012   2.6376
2013   2.7019

Note: On 1 February 1985 Peru replaced its former currency, the sol, with the inti, valued at 1,000 soles. A new currency, the nuevo sol (equivalent to 1m. intis), was introduced in July 1991.

CENTRAL GOVERNMENT BUDGET
(million new soles, preliminary figures)

Revenue	2011	2012	2013
Taxation	75,541	84,079	89,319
Taxes on income, profits, etc.	33,628	37,278	36,512
Taxes on imports (excl. VAT)	1,380	1,526	1,706
Value-added tax	40,424	44,042	47,817
Domestic	22,029	24,543	27,164
Imports	18,395	19,499	20,653
Excises	4,718	4,918	5,480
Fuel duty	2,231	2,149	2,487
Other taxes	5,098	6,902	9,075
Less Refunds	9,707	10,587	11,272
Other current revenue	12,685	13,208	13,963
Capital revenue	295	344	772
Total	88,521	97,631	104,054

Expenditure	2011	2012	2013
Current expenditure	63,372	90,992	102,041
Compensation of employees	17,642	19,898	23,236
Goods and non-labour services	17,048	19,843	22,067
Transfers	23,644	23,543	24,948
Interest payments	5,039	5,233	5,729
Internal	2,430	2,524	2,710
External	2,789	2,709	3,018
Capital expenditure	20,413	22,474	26,062
Gross capital formation	13,848	14,756	16,626
Total	83,785	113,467	128,103

General Budget (million new soles, preliminary figures): *2011:* Total revenue 102,443 (Current 102,134, Capital 310); Total expenditure 92,969 (Current non-interest 63,191, Capital 24,350, Interest payments 5,428). *2012:* Total revenue 113,794 (Current 113,528, Capital 267); Total expenditure 103,357 (Current non-interest 68,948, Capital 28,951, Interest payments 5,458). *2013:* Total revenue 121,966 (Current 121,065, Capital 901); Total expenditure 117,871 (Current non-interest 78,398, Capital 33,515, Interest payments 5,958).

INTERNATIONAL RESERVES
(US $ million at 31 December)

	2011	2012	2013
Gold	1,722.3	1,866.5	1,339.0
IMF special drawing rights	805.0	808.9	817.9
Foreign exchange	46,096.5	61,167.8	63,247.3
Total	48,623.8	63,843.2	65,404.2

Source: IMF, *International Financial Statistics.*

MONEY SUPPLY
(million new soles at 31 December)

	2011	2012	2013
Currency outside banks	27,643	32,677	35,705
Demand deposits at commercial and development banks	38,079	46,066	50,263
Total money (incl. others)	68,349	83,164	91,077

Source: IMF, *International Financial Statistics.*

COST OF LIVING
(Consumer Price Index, Lima metropolitan area; base: 2000 = 100)

	2010	2011	2012
Food (incl. beverages)	131.8	138.2	146.0
All items (incl. others)	126.3	130.6	135.4

Source: ILO.

All items (Consumer price Index, Lima metropolitan area; base: 2009 = 100): 105.0 in 2011; 108.8 in 2012; 111.8 in 2013.

NATIONAL ACCOUNTS
(million new soles at current prices, preliminary)

Expenditure on the Gross Domestic Product

	2011	2012	2013
Government final consumption expenditure	48,111	55,002	61,210
Private final consumption expenditure	281,718	310,040	335,904
Gross capital formation	117,133	131,889	147,261
Total domestic expenditure	446,962	496,931	544,375
Exports of goods and services	145,227	140,036	133,141
Less Imports of goods and services	120,531	128,425	135,400
GDP in purchasers' values	471,658	508,542	542,116
GDP at constant 2007 prices	407,052	431,273	456,103

Gross Domestic Product by Economic Activity

	2011	2012	2013
Agriculture, hunting and forestry	30,053	32,197	32,533
Fishing	3,953	2,707	3,679
Mining and quarrying	69,177	67,083	63,506
Manufacturing	73,225	74,482	78,258
Electricity and water	7,986	8,703	9,470
Construction	28,205	33,105	37,053
Wholesale and retail trade	49,398	54,802	59,527
Restaurants and hotels	15,924	18,461	20,752
Transport and communications	34,394	39,641	42,975
Government services	21,547	23,984	26,648
Other services	100,399	110,435	120,927
Gross value added at basic prices	434,261	465,600	495,328
Import duties	1,254	1,430	1,636
Taxes on products	36,143	41,512	45,152
GDP in purchasers' values	471,658	508,542	542,116

BALANCE OF PAYMENTS
(US $ million)

	2010	2011	2012
Exports of goods	35,565	46,269	45,933
Imports of goods	−28,390	−36,264	−40,374
Balance on goods	7,175	10,005	5,559
Exports of services	3,273	3,666	4,396
Imports of services	−6,044	−6,501	−7,392
Balance on goods and services	4,404	7,169	2,563
Primary income received	1,149	1,111	1,180
Primary income paid	−12,361	−14,821	−13,881
Balance on goods, services and primary income	−6,808	−6,540	−10,138
Secondary income received	3,033	3,210	3,304
Secondary income paid	−7	−11	−7
Current balance	−3,782	−3,341	−6,842

—continued	2010	2011	2012
Capital account (net) . . .	−115	−109	−106
Direct investment assets . .	−266	−113	57
Direct investment liabilities .	8,455	8,233	12,244
Portfolio investment assets .	−1,145	−1,472	−3,015
Portfolio investment liabilities	6,358	921	4,883
Other investment assets . .	−1,949	−1,343	353
Other investment liabilities .	1,938	2,919	5,624
Net errors and omissions . .	1,476	−1,011	1,968
Reserves and related items .	10,970	4,684	15,167

Source: IMF, *International Financial Statistics*.

External Trade

PRINCIPAL COMMODITIES
(distribution by HS, US $ million)

Imports c.i.f.	2010	2011	2012
Vegetables and vegetable products	1,305.5	1,775.2	1,783.3
Cereals and cereal preparations .	980.5	1,406.6	1,368.8
Prepared foodstuffs; beverages, spirits, vinegars; tobacco and articles thereof .	1,091.7	1,280.0	1,626.7
Mineral products	4,462.7	6,161.6	6,291.2
Mineral fuels, oils and distillation products	4,257.3	5,936.4	6,086.9
Crude petroleum oils . . .	2,689.5	3,642.5	3,675.7
Non-crude petroleum oils . .	1,421.9	2,172.0	2,291.4
Chemicals and related products	3,026.7	3,745.6	4,066.1
Plastics, rubber, and articles thereof	2,138.4	2,647.3	2,821.6
Plastics and articles thereof . .	1,063.6	1,950.5	2,024.9
Textiles and textile articles .	1,254.4	1,663.6	1,735.3
Iron and steel; other base metals and articles of base metal . . .	2,817.6	3,365.9	3,705.7
Iron and steel	1,486.1	1,552.2	1,674.7
Articles of iron or steel . . .	828.7	1,175.5	1,272.0
Machinery and mechanical appliances; electrical equipment; parts thereof .	7,203.3	9,275.8	10,518.0
Machinery, boilers, etc. . . .	4,446.7	5,758.7	6,479.6
Electrical, electronic equipment .	2,756.6	3,517.1	4,038.4
Vehicles, aircraft, vessels and associated transport equipment .	3,310.4	3,826.8	5,079.8
Vehicles other than railway, tramway	3,162.7	3,732.0	4,926.5
Cars (incl. station wagons) . .	1,103.0	1,229.0	1,771.2
Trucks and vehicles for transport of goods	980.4	1,156.8	1,548.0
Total (incl. others)	30,030.4	37,747.1	42,274.3

Exports f.o.b.	2010	2011	2012
Vegetables and vegetable products	2,155.6	3,252.9	2,894.0
Coffee, tea, mate and spices . .	993.4	1,721.2	1,140.1
Coffee	888.3	1,580.8	1,020.7
Prepared foodstuffs; beverages, spirits, vinegars; tobacco and articles thereof .	2,663.8	3,167.8	3,210.4
Mineral products	13,703.2	18,473.1	19,260.9
Ores, slag and ash . . .	10,259.5	13,159.6	13,395.3
Copper ores and concentrates .	6,156.8	7,796.7	8,426.4
Lead ores and concentrates .	1,277.3	1,783.1	1,996.1
Zinc ores and concentrates . .	1,478.2	1,182.9	1,041.1
Mineral fuels, oils and distillation products	3,345.3	5,019.2	5,364.3
Non-crude petroleum oils . .	2,300.7	2,933.9	3,305.2
Petroleum gases	521.7	1,486.9	1,436.6

Exports f.o.b.—*continued*	2010	2011	2012
Textiles and textile articles .	1,573.2	2,017.6	2,191.5
Articles of apparel and accessories	1,070.7	1,357.8	1,430.5
Pearls, precious or semi-precious stones, precious metals, and articles thereof .	7,971.0	10,257.1	10,177.5
Gold, unwrought or in semi-manufactured forms . . .	7,725.5	9,930.8	9,673.5
Iron and steel; other base metals and articles of base metals .	4,108.4	4,511.7	3,973.2
Copper and articles thereof . .	3,110.5	3,396.4	2,772.0
Refined copper and copper alloys	2,527.2	2,745.3	1,967.3
Total (incl. others)	35,205.1	45,636.1	45,946.2

Source: Trade Map-Trade Competitiveness Map, International Trade Centre, www.intracen.org/marketanalysis.

2013 (US $ million): *Imports c.i.f.:* Consumer goods 8,827.6; Intermediate goods 19,503.1; Capital goods 13,649.5; Total imports (incl. others) 42,190.8; *Exports f.o.b.:* Agricultural goods 3,400.4; Mineral products 23,029.8; Textiles 1,919.3; Chemicals 1,495.2; Total exports (incl. others) 41,826.2.

PRINCIPAL TRADING PARTNERS
(US $ million)

Imports c.i.f.	2010	2011	2012
Angola	227.5	700.2	418.2
Argentina	1,110.2	1,834.8	1,951.3
Bolivia	310.4	288.1	503.7
Brazil	2,185.7	2,433.3	2,581.0
Canada	544.6	584.1	589.1
Chile	1,049.0	1,333.4	1,244.0
China, People's Republic . .	5,144.5	6,321.0	7,807.5
Colombia	1,331.1	1,462.0	1,567.0
Ecuador	1,423.3	1,870.6	2,012.4
Germany	895.5	1,119.5	1,367.9
India	499.8	587.6	742.4
Italy	415.7	590.3	696.4
Japan	1,376.8	1,309.3	1,503.2
Korea, Republic . . .	1,043.8	1,491.5	1,648.4
Mexico	1,127.3	1,377.9	1,675.1
Nigeria	649.8	336.3	922.7
Russia	183.4	513.2	334.3
Spain	406.8	562.9	802.3
Sweden	266.4	389.4	369.9
Taiwan	328.4	439.7	461.8
Thailand	374.9	443.6	453.7
USA	5,854.0	7,430.7	8,020.5
Total (incl. others)	30,030.4	37,747.1	42,274.3

Exports f.o.b.	2010	2011	2012
Belgium	581.8	777.6	704.9
Bolivia	382.8	452.2	560.1
Brazil	947.9	1,266.9	1,402.9
Bulgaria	358.0	466.9	315.3
Canada	3,329.0	4,176.3	3,445.3
Chile	1,370.1	1,976.6	2,028.3
China, People's Republic . .	5,434.0	6,961.4	7,849.0
Colombia	795.9	1,042.3	918.2
Ecuador	814.9	833.9	926.6
Germany	1,514.6	1,900.2	1,866.2
Italy	939.1	1,297.1	1,021.2
Japan	1,790.5	2,174.6	2,575.3
Korea, Republic . . .	895.9	1,694.9	1,545.4
Netherlands	645.9	845.3	681.9
Panama	254.1	332.5	496.3
Spain	1,168.5	1,666.2	1,842.8
Switzerland-Liechtenstein . .	3,845.3	5,887.1	5,074.5
United Kingdom . . .	244.8	263.8	461.5
USA	5,826.3	6,083.9	6,516.6
Venezuela	513.5	921.5	1,210.6
Total (incl. others)	35,205.1	45,636.1	45,946.2

Source: Trade Map-Trade Competitiveness Map, International Trade Centre, www.intracen.org/marketanalysis.

2013 (US $ million): Total imports 42,190.8; Total exports 41,826.2.

Transport

RAILWAYS
(traffic)

	2010	2011	2012
Number of passengers ('000) . .	1,379	1,760	2,031
Passenger-km (million) . . .	74	95	117
Freight ('000 metric tons) . . .	8,137	7,906	7,618
Freight ton-km (million) . . .	1,110	1,038	1,045

ROAD TRAFFIC
(motor vehicles in use)

	2010	2011	2012
Passenger cars	1,275,821	1,495,722	1,691,279
Buses and coaches	68,096	82,747	93,860
Lorries and vans	790,518	978,437	1,145,147
Trailers and semi-trailers . .	48,843	59,731	68,937
Motorcycles	122,868	152,822	170,220
Total	**2,306,146**	**2,769,459**	**3,169,443**

SHIPPING

Flag Registered Fleet
(at 31 December)

	2011	2012	2013
Number of vessels	200	206	215
Total displacement ('000 grt) . .	443.6	448.1	453.8

Source: Lloyd's List Intelligence (www.lloydslistintelligence.com).

International Seaborne Freight Traffic
('000 metric tons)

	2012	2013
Goods loaded	13,056	14,073
Goods unloaded	21,876	23,756

Source: UN, *Monthly Bulletin of Statistics.*

CIVIL AVIATION
(traffic on scheduled services)

	2010	2011
Kilometres flown (million)	110	134
Passengers carried ('000)	7,106	8,610
Passenger-km (million)	9,031	13,313
Total ton-km (million)	1,049	1,603

Source: UN, *Statistical Yearbook.*

Passengers carried ('000): 10,074.9 in 2012, 10,977.3 in 2013 (Source: World Bank, World Development Indicators database).

Tourism

ARRIVALS BY NATIONALITY

	2010	2011	2012
Argentina	127,062	147,403	158,950
Bolivia	86,181	88,042	101,546
Brazil	87,674	117,537	126,085
Canada	52,955	57,454	61,362
Chile	595,944	741,717	806,929
Colombia	98,642	112,816	133,975
Ecuador	152,445	160,841	176,071
France	66,985	72,900	81,851
Germany	53,201	56,197	62,051
Spain	96,666	105,231	111,041
United Kingdom	54,182	55,415	56,386
USA	417,232	411,935	447,218
Total (incl. others)	**2,291,871**	**2,589,587**	**2,836,756**

Source: World Tourism Organization.

Tourism receipts (US $ million, excl. passenger transport): 2,008 in 2010; 2,360 in 2011; 2,657 in 2012.

Communications Media

	2011	2012	2013
Telephones ('000 main lines in use)	3,250.4	3,415.5	3,420.2
Mobile cellular telephones ('000 subscribers)	32,461.4	29,388.1	29,793.4
Internet subscribers ('000) . .	1,197.2	n.a.	n.a.
Broadband subscribers ('000) . .	1,190.3	1,422.8	1,574.2

Source: International Telecommunication Union.

Education

(2013 unless otherwise indicated)

	Institutions	Teachers	Pupils
Nursery	48,444	78,541	1,585,121
Primary	37,753	200,983	3,504,168
Secondary	13,414	179,983	2,501,788
Higher: universities* . . .	78	33,177	435,637
Higher: other tertiary . . .	1,002	24,164	89,926
Special	469	3,344	18,485
Vocational	1,853	10,953	257,798

* Figures for 2000.

Source: Ministerio de Educación del Perú.

Pupil-teacher ratio (primary education, UNESCO estimate): 19.3 in 2011/12 (Source: UNESCO Institute for Statistics).

Adult literacy rate (UNESCO estimates): 93.8% (males 97.0%; females 90.7%) in 2012 (Source: UNESCO Institute for Statistics).

Directory

The Constitution

In 1993 the Congreso Constituyente Democrático (CCD) began drafting a new constitution to replace the 1979 Constitution. The CCD approved the final document in September 1993, and the Constitution was endorsed by a popular national referendum that was conducted on 31 October. The Constitution was promulgated on 29 December 1993.

EXECUTIVE POWER

Executive power is vested in the President, who is elected for a five-year term of office by universal adult suffrage; this mandate is renewable once. The successful presidential candidate must obtain at least 50% of the votes cast, and a second round of voting is held if necessary. Two Vice-Presidents are elected in simultaneous rounds of voting. The President is competent to initiate and submit draft bills, to review laws drafted by the Congreso (Congress) and, if delegated by the Congress, to enact laws. The President is empowered to appoint ambassadors and senior military officials without congressional ratification, and retains the right to dissolve parliament if two or more ministers have been censured or have received a vote of no confidence from the Congress. In certain circumstances the President may, in accordance with the Council of Ministers, declare a state of emergency for a period of 60 days, during which individual constitutional rights are suspended and the armed forces may assume control of civil order. The President appoints the Council of Ministers.

LEGISLATIVE POWER

Legislative power is vested in a single-chamber Congress (removing the distinction in the 1979 Constitution of an upper and lower house) consisting of 130 members. The members of the Congress are elected for a five-year term by universal adult suffrage. The Congress is responsible for approving the budget, for endorsing loans and international treaties, and for drafting and approving bills. It may conduct investigations into matters of public concern, and question and censure the Council of Ministers and its individual members. Members of the Congress elect a Standing Committee, to consist of not more than 25% of the total number of members (representation being proportional to the different political groupings in the legislature), which is empowered to make certain official appointments, approve credit loans and transfers relating to the budget during a parliamentary recess, and conduct other business as delegated by parliament.

ELECTORAL SYSTEM

All citizens aged 18 years and above, including illiterate persons, are eligible to vote. Voting in elections is compulsory for all citizens aged 18–70, and is optional thereafter.

JUDICIAL POWER

Judicial power is vested in the Supreme Court of Justice and other tribunals. The Constitution provides for the establishment of a National Council of the Judiciary, consisting of nine independently elected members, which is empowered to appoint judges to the Supreme Court. An independent Constitutional Court, comprising seven members elected by the Congress for a five-year term, may interpret the Constitution and declare legislation and acts of government to be unconstitutional.

The death penalty may be applied by the judiciary in cases of terrorism or of treason (the latter in times of war).

Under the Constitution, a People's Counsel is elected by the Congress with a five-year mandate, which authorizes the Counsel to defend the constitutional and fundamental rights of the individual. The Counsel may draft laws and present evidence to the legislature.

According to the Constitution, the state promotes economic and social development, particularly in the areas of employment, health, education, security, public services and infrastructure. The state recognizes a plurality of economic ownership and activity, supports free competition, and promotes the growth of small businesses. Private initiative is permitted within the framework of a social market economy. The state also guarantees the free exchange of foreign currency.

The Government

HEAD OF STATE

President: Lt-Col (retd) OLLANTA MOISÉS HUMALA TASSO (took office 28 July 2011).
First Vice-President: MARISOL ESPINOZA CRUZ.

COUNCIL OF MINISTERS
(September 2014)

The Government was formed by a coalition led by the Partido Nacionalista Peruano.

President of the Council of Ministers: ANA JARA VELÁSQUEZ.
Minister of Foreign Affairs: GONZALO GUTIÉRREZ REINEL.
Minister of Defence: PEDRO ALVARO CATERIANO BELLIDO.
Minister of Economy and Finance: ALONSO SEGURA.
Minister of the Interior: DANIEL URRESTI.
Minister of Justice and Human Rights: DANIEL FIGALLO.
Minister of Education: JAIME SAAVEDRA CHANDUVI.
Minister of Health: MIDORI MUSME DE HABICH ROSPIGLIOSI.
Minister of Agriculture and Irrigation: JUAN MANUEL BENITES RAMOS.
Minister of Labour and Employment: FREDY ROLANDO OTAROLA PEÑARANDA.
Minister of International Trade and Tourism: BLANCA MAGALI SILVA VELARDE.
Minister of Transport and Communications: JOSÉ GALLARDO KU.

Minister of Housing, Construction and Sanitation: MILTON MARTÍN VON HESSE LA SERNA.
Minister of Energy and Mines: ELEODORO MAYORGA ALBA.
Minister of Production: PIERO GHEZZI.
Minister of Culture: DIANA ALVAREZ CALDERÓN.
Minister of Women and Vulnerable Populations: CARMEN OMONTE.
Minister of the Environment: MANUEL PULGAR-VIDAL.
Minister of Development and Social Inclusion: PAOLA BUSTAMANTE SUÁREZ.

MINISTRIES

Office of the President of the Council of Ministers: Jirón Carabaya, cuadra 1 s/n, Anexo 1105-1107, Lima; tel. (1) 2197000; fax (1) 4449168; e-mail atencionciudadana@pcm.gob.pe; internet www.pcm.gob.pe.

Ministry of Agriculture and Irrigation: Avda La Universidad 200, La Molina, Lima; tel. (1) 2098625; e-mail portal@minag.gob.pe; internet www.minag.gob.pe.

Ministry of Culture: Avda Javier Prado Este 2465, San Borja, Lima 41; tel. (1) 6189393; e-mail comunicaciones@mcultura.gob.pe; internet www.mcultura.gob.pe.

Ministry of Defence: Edif. Quiñones, Avda de la Peruanidad s/n, Jesús María, Lima 1; tel. (1) 2098530; e-mail despacho@mindef.gob.pe; internet www.mindef.gob.pe.

Ministry of Development and Social Inclusion: Avda Paseo de la República 3101, San Isidro, Lima; tel. (1) 2098000; e-mail fosorio@midis.gob.pe; internet www.midis.gob.pe.

Ministry of Economy and Finance: Jirón Junín 319, 4°, Circado de Lima, Lima 1; tel. (1) 3115930; e-mail postmaster@mef.gob.pe; internet www.mef.gob.pe.

Ministry of Education: Biblioteca Nacional del Perú, Avda de la Poesía 160, San Borja, Lima 41; tel. (1) 6155800; fax (1) 4370471; e-mail webmaster@minedu.gob.pe; internet www.minedu.gob.pe.

Ministry of Energy and Mines: Avda Las Artes Sur 260, San Borja, Lima 41; tel. (1) 4111100; e-mail webmaster@minem.gob.pe; internet www.minem.gob.pe.

Ministry of the Environment: Avda Javier Prado Oeste 1440, San Isidro, Lima; tel. (1) 6116000; fax (1) 2255369; e-mail minam@minam.gob.pe; internet www.minam.gob.pe.

Ministry of Foreign Affairs: Jirón Lampa 535, Lima 1; tel. (1) 2042400; e-mail informes@rree.gob.pe; internet www.rree.gob.pe.

Ministry of Health: Avda Salaverry 801, Jesús María, Lima 11; tel. (1) 3156600; fax (1) 6271600; e-mail webmaster@minsa.gob.pe; internet www.minsa.gob.pe.

Ministry of Housing, Construction and Sanitation: Edif. de Petroperú, Avda Paseo de la República 3361, San Isidro, Lima; tel. (1) 2117930; e-mail webmaster@vivienda.gob.pe; internet www.vivienda.gob.pe.

Ministry of the Interior: Plaza 30 de Agosto s/n, Urb. Córpac, San Isidro, Lima 27; tel. (1) 5180000; fax (1) 2242405; e-mail dm@mininter.gob.pe; internet www.mininter.gob.pe.

Ministry of International Trade and Tourism: Calle Uno Oeste 50, Urb. Córpac, San Isidro, Lima 27; tel. (1) 5136100; fax (1) 2243362; e-mail webmaster@mincetur.gob.pe; internet www.mincetur.gob.pe.

Ministry of Justice and Human Rights: Scipión Llona 350, Miraflores, Lima 18; tel. (1) 2048020; fax (1) 4223577; e-mail webmaster@minjus.gob.pe; internet www.minjus.gob.pe.

Ministry of Labour and Employment: Avda Salaverry 655, cuadra 8, Jesús María, Lima 11; tel. (1) 6306000; fax (1) 6306060; e-mail informes@trabajo.gob.pe; internet www.mintra.gob.pe.

Ministry of the Presidency: Jirón de la Unión s/n, Cuadra 1, Lima 1; tel. (1) 3113900; fax (1) 3114300; internet www.presidencia.gob.pe.

Ministry of Production: Calle Uno Oeste 60, Urb. Córpac, San Isidro, Lima 27; tel. (1) 6162222; e-mail portal@produce.gob.pe; internet www.produce.gob.pe.

Ministry of Transport and Communications: Jirón Zorritos 1203, Lima 1; tel. (1) 6157800; e-mail atencionalciudadano@mtc.gob.pe; internet www.mtc.gob.pe.

Ministry of Women and Vulnerable Populations: Jirón Camaná 616, Lima 1; tel. (1) 4165200; fax (1) 4261665; e-mail postmaster@mimp.gob.pe; internet www.mimp.gob.pe.

President and Legislature

PRESIDENT

Election, first round, 10 April 2011

Candidate	Valid votes cast	% of votes
Lt-Col (retd) Ollanta Moisés Humala Tasso (Gana Perú*)	4,643,064	31.70
Keiko Sofía Fujimori Higuchi (Fuerza 2011)	3,449,562	23.56
Pedro Pablo Kuczynski Godard (Alianza por el Gran Cambio)	2,711,332	18.51
Alejandro Toledo Manrique (Perú Posible)	2,289,540	15.63
Luis Castañeda Lossio (Solidaridad Nacional)	1,440,242	9.83
Others	113,423	0.78
Total valid votes†	14,647,163	100.00

*An alliance led by the Partido Nacionalista Peruano.
† In addition, there were 1,477,696 blank votes and 574,875 invalid votes cast.

Election, second round, 5 June 2011

Candidate	Valid votes cast	% of votes
Lt-Col (retd) Ollanta Moisés Humala Tasso (Gana Perú)	7,937,704	51.45
Keiko Sofía Fujimori Higuchi (Fuerza 2011)	7,490,647	48.55
Total*	15,428,351	100.00

*In addition, there were 116,335 blank votes and 921,711 invalid votes cast.

CONGRESS

President: Ana María Solórzano.
General Election, 10 April 2011

Parties	% of valid votes	Seats
Gana Perú*	25.43	47
Fuerza 2011	22.91	37
Perú Posible (PP)	14.82	21
Alianza por el Gran Cambio	14.35	12
Solidaridad Nacional (SN)	10.19	9
Partido Aprista Peruano (PAP)	6.46	4
Cambio Radical	2.68	—
Asociación Nacional de Fonavistas de los Pueblos del Perú (ANFPP)	1.33	—
Others	1.83	—
Total†	100.00	130

*An alliance led by the Partido Nacionalista Peruano.
† Excluding blank votes and spoiled votes.

Regional Presidents

(September 2014)

Amazonas: José Berley Arista Arbildo.
Ancash: Zenón Ayala López (acting).
Apurímac: Efraín Ambía Vivanco.
Arequipa: Juan Manuel Guillén Benavides.
Ayacucho: Wilfredo Oscorima Núñez.
Cajamarca: Gregorio Santos Guerrero.
Callao: Félix Moreno Caballero (took leave of absence to campaign for re-election in Oct. 2014), Ana Victoria Bejarano Preciado (acting).
Cusco: René Concha Lezama.
Huancavelica: Alejandro Maciste Díaz Abad.
Huánuco: Luis Raúl Picón Quedo (took leave of absence to campaign for re-election in Oct. 2014), Jhony Julián Miraval Venturo (acting).
Ica: Alonso Alberto Navarro Cabanillas.
Junín: Vladimir Roy Cerrón Rojas.
La Libertad: José Humberto Murgia Zannier.
Lambayeque: Humberto Acuña Peralta.
Lima (Provincias): Javier Alvarado Gonzáles del Valle.

Loreto: Yván Enrique Vásquez Valera.
Madre de Dios: Jorge Aldazábal Soto.
Moquegua: Martín Alberto Vizcarra Cornejo.
Pasco: Dionisio Salcedo Meza (acting).
Piura: Javier Miguel Atkins Lerggios.
Puno: Mauricio Rodríguez Rodríguez.
San Martín: Javier Ocampo Ruiz.
Tacna: Tito Guillermo Chocano Olivera.
Tumbes: Orlando La Chira Pasache (acting).
Ucayali: Jorge Velásquez Portocarrero.

Election Commissions

Jurado Nacional de Elecciones (JNE): Avda Nicolás de Piérola 1070, Lima 1; tel. (11) 3111700; e-mail consultas@jne.gob.pe; internet www.jne.gob.pe; f. 1931; autonomous electoral body; 5-mem. council; Pres. Francisco Artemio Távara Córdova.

Oficina Nacional de Procesos Electorales (ONPE): Jirón Washington 1894, Lima 1; tel. (1) 4170630; e-mail informes@onpe.gob.pe; internet www.onpe.gob.pe; f. 1995; independent; Nat. Dir Mariano Cucho Espinoza.

Political Organizations

Acción Popular (AP): Paseo Colón 218, Lima 1; tel. and fax (1) 3321965; e-mail webmaster@accionpopular.pe; internet accionpopular.com.pe; f. 1956; 1.2m. mems; liberal; contested the 2011 elections as part of the Perú Posible alliance; Pres. Javier Alva Orlandini; Sec.-Gen. Allen Helmunt Kessel del Río.

Alianza por el Gran Cambio: Avda Salaverry 2007, Lima; tel. (1) 4710985; e-mail contacto@ppk.pe; internet www.ppk.pe; f. 2010; right-wing coalition formed to contest the 2011 elections; Presidential candidate Pedro Pablo Kuczynski; comprises the following parties:

> **Alianza para el Progreso:** Avda de la Policía 643, entre Cuadra 8 y 9 de Gregorio Escobedo, Jesús María, Lima; tel. (1) 4613197; e-mail informes@app-peru.org.pe; internet www.app-peru.org.pe; f. 2001; Founder and Pres. César Acuña Peralta; Nat. Exec. Sec. Luis Carlos Antonio Iberico Nuñez.

> **Partido Humanista Peruano (PHP):** Canaval y Moreyra 680, San Isidro, Lima; tel. (1) 2241243; e-mail contactenos@partidohumanista.org.pe; internet www.partidohumanista.org.pe; Pres. Yehudé Simón Munaro; Sec.-Gen. Marco Cardoso Montoya.

> **Partido Popular Cristiano (PPC):** Avda Alfonso Ugarte 1484, Breña, Lima; tel. (1) 4238722; fax (1) 4238721; e-mail estflores@terra.com.pe; internet www.ppc.pe; f. 1967; 250,000 mems; Pres. Raúl Castro Stagnaro; Sec.-Gen. Rafael Yamashiro Oré.

> **Restauración Nacional:** Calle Chacarilla 240, San Isidro, Lima; tel. (1) 3117546; f. 2005; evangelical Christian party; Pres. Humberto Lay Sun; Sec.-Gen. Rubén Gavino Sánchez.

APRA: see entry for PAP.

Democracia Directa: Jirón Caylloma 824, Of. 102, Lima; tel. (1) 4242913; e-mail informes@fonavistas.com; internet www.fonavistas.com; political party of the Asociación Nacional de Fonavistas de los Pueblos del Perú; Pres. Andrés Avelino Alcantara Paredes.

Despertar Nacional: Avda Benavides 2470, Miraflores, Lima 18; tel. (1) 3583657; e-mail comunicaciones@despertarnacional.com; internet www.despertarnacional.com; f. 1999; Leader Ricardo Noriega Salaverry.

El Frente Amplio por Justicia, Vida y Libertad: Avda Petit Thouars 1306, Lima; Co-ordinator-Gen. Pedro Francke Ballve.

Fuerza Popular: Paseo Colón 422, Cercado de Lima, Lima; tel. 999383300 (mobile); e-mail contacto@fuerza2011.com; internet www.fuerzapopular.pe; contested the 2011 elections as Fuerza 2011; Pres. Keiko Sofía Fujimori Higuchi; Sec.-Gen. Clemente Jaime Yoshiyama Tanaka.

Partido Aprista Peruano (PAP): Avda Alfonso Ugarte 1012, Breña, Lima 5; tel. (1) 4250218; e-mail ofisistemapap@apra.pe; internet www.apra.pe; f. in Mexico 1924, in Peru 1930; legalized 1945; democratic left-wing party; although legally known as PAP, the party is commonly known as APRA; Pres. Alan Gabriel Ludwig García Pérez; Secs-Gen. Carlos Arana Vivar, Omar Quezada Martínez; 700,000 mems.

Partido Descentralista Fuerza Social: Jíron Cápac Yupanqui 1076, Jesús María, Lima; tel. (1) 4717895; e-mail central@fuerzasocial.pe; internet fuerzasocial.pe; f. 2007; Pres. Gustavo Guerra-García; Nat. Co-ordinator Rocío Peñafiel.

Partido Nacionalista Peruano (PNP): Avda Arequipa 3410, Lima 27; tel. (1) 4223592; internet www .partidonacionalistaperuano.net; f. 2005; contested the 2011 elections as part of the Gana Perú alliance; Pres. NADINE HEREDIA ALARCÓN DE HUMALA.

Partido Político Adelante: Jirón Ricardo Palma 120, San Isidro, Lima; tel. (1) 2212563; e-mail 2004adelante@gmail.com; internet www.adelante.org.pe; f. 2004; Sec.-Gen. RAFAEL BELAUNDE AUBRY.

Perú Patria Segura: Avda Jorge Aprile 312, San Borja, Lima; f. 2013 by fmr mems of Cambio 90; centre-right; Pres. OSCAR REGGIARDO SAYÁN; Sec.-Gen. RENZO REGGIARDO BARRETO.

Perú Posible (PP): Avda Faustino Sánchez Carrión 601, Jesús María, Lima 11; tel. (1) 4602493; fax (1) 2612418; e-mail sgpp@ mixmail.com; internet www.peruposible.org.pe; f. 1994; contested the 2011 elections in alliance with Acción Popular and Somos Perú; Leader ALEJANDRO TOLEDO MANRIQUE; Sec.-Gen. LUIS ALBERTO THAIS DÍAZ.

Renovación Nacional: Avda Camino Real 1206, 2°, San Isidro, Lima; tel. (1) 5673798; f. 1992; contested the 2011 elections in alliance with Fuerza 2011 (now Fuerza Popular); Pres. RAFAEL REY; Sec.-Gen. WILDER RUÍZ SILVA.

Siempre Unidos: Avda Angélica Gamarra 647, Urb. El Trebol, Lima; tel. (1) 6505254; internet siempreunidos.org.pe; f. 2012; Sec.-Gen. LUIS FELIPE CASTILLO OLIVA.

Solidaridad Nacional (SN): Amador Merino Reyna 140, San Isidro, Lima 27; tel. (1) 4213348; e-mail fsandoval@psn.org.pe; internet www.psn.org.pe; f. 1999; centre-left; Pres. LUIS CASTAÑEDA LOSSIO; Sec.-Gen. JOSÉ LEÓN LUNA GLAVEZ.

Somos Perú (Partido Democrático Somos Perú): Mariscal Las Heras 393, Lince, Lima 14; tel. (1) 4714484; e-mail postmaster@somosperu .org.pe; internet www.somosperu.org.pe; f. 1998; contested the 2011 elections as part of the Perú Posible alliance; Pres. FERNANDO ANDRADE CARMONA; Sec.-Gen. VÍCTOR YURI VILELA SEMINARIO.

Todos por el Perú: Las Moreras 293, San Isidro, Lima; Sec.-Gen. RAQUEL LOZADA VALENTÍN.

Unión por el Perú (UPP): Avda Cuba 543, Jesús María, Lima; tel. (1) 4271941; e-mail ivega@partidoupp.org; internet www .partidopoliticoupp.org; f. 1994; ind. movt; Sec.-Gen. JOSÉ VEGA ANTONIO.

Vamos Perú: Avda Paseo Colón 301, Lima; f. ; Pres. JUAN RABASA LAVARELLO; Sec.-Gen. OSCAR JAVIER ZEGARRA GUZMÁN.

ILLEGAL GROUPS

Movimiento Nacionalista Peruano (MNP) (Movimiento Etnocacerista): Pasaje Velarde 188, Of. 204, Lima; tel. (1) 4338781; e-mail eletnocacerista@yahoo.com; internet eletnocacerista.galeon.com; ultra-nationalist paramilitary group; Pres. Dr ISAAC HUMALA NÚÑEZ; Leader of paramilitary wing Maj. (retd) ANTAURO IGOR HUMALA TASSO (arrested Jan. 2005 following an armed uprising in Andahuaylas).

Movimiento Por Amnistía y Derechos Fundamentales (Movadef): Jirón Pasco 3679, San Martín de Porres; e-mail movadefperu@ hotmail.com; internet movamnsitiayderfundamentales.blogspot.co .uk; f. 1990; political wing of Sendero Luminoso (Shining Path) f. 1970 by Abimael Guzmán Gonzalo (alias Chairman Gonzalo); began armed struggle 1980; splinter group of Partido Comunista Peruano; active in the Apurímac-Ene and Upper Huallaga valleys; advocated the policies of Mao Zedong in the People's Republic of China; from the mid-2000s it became increasingly involved in the illegal drugs trade; Sec.-Gen. MANUEL FAJARDO CAVERO.

Diplomatic Representation

EMBASSIES IN PERU

Algeria: Avda El Rosario 380, San Isidro, Lima; tel. (1) 4217582; fax (1) 4217580; e-mail embarg@embajadadeargelia.com; internet www .argelia-pe.org; Ambassador MUHAMMAD BENSABRI.

Argentina: Avda Las Flores 326, San Isidro, Lima 1; tel. (1) 4414444; fax (1) 4224304; e-mail contacto_eperu@mrecic.gov.ar; internet eperu.mrecic.gov.ar; Ambassador DARÍO PEDRO ALESSANDRO.

Australia: Avda La Paz 1049, 10°, Miraflores, Lima 18; tel. (1) 6300500; fax (1) 6300520; e-mail consular.lima@dfat.gov.au; internet www.peru.embassy.gov.au; Ambassador JOHN M. L. WOODS.

Austria: Edif. de las Naciones, Avda República de Colombia 643, 5°, San Isidro, Lima 27; tel. (1) 4420503; fax (1) 4428851; e-mail lima-ob@ bmeia.gv.at; internet www.aussenministerium.at/lima; Ambassador ANDREAS A. RENDL.

Belgium: Avda Angamos Oeste 380, Miraflores, Lima 18; tel. (1) 2417566; fax (1) 2416379; e-mail lima@diplobel.fed.be; internet www .diplomatie.be/lima; Ambassador MICHEL DEWEZ.

Bolivia: Los Castaños 235, San Isidro, Lima 27; tel. (1) 4402095; fax (1) 4402298; e-mail embajada@boliviaenperu.com; Ambassador JORGE LEDEZMA CORNEJO.

Brazil: Avda José Pardo 850, Miraflores, Lima; tel. (1) 5120830; fax (1) 4452421; e-mail embajada@embajadabrasil.org.pe; internet lima .itamaraty.gov.br; Ambassador CARLOS LAZARY TEIXEIRA.

Canada: Calle Bolognesi 228, Miraflores, Casilla 18-1126, Lima; tel. (1) 3193200; fax (1) 4464912; e-mail lima@international.gc.ca; internet www.canadainternational.gc.ca/peru-perou; Ambassador PATRICIA FORTIER.

Chile: Avda Javier Prado Oeste 790, San Isidro, Lima; tel. (1) 7102211; fax (1) 7102223; e-mail contacto@chileabroad.gov.cl; internet chileabroad.gov.cl/peru; Ambassador ROBERTO IBARRA GARCÍA.

China, People's Republic: Jirón José Granda 150, San Isidro, Apdo 375, Lima 27; tel. (1) 4429458; fax (1) 4429467; e-mail chinaemb_pe@mfa.gov.cn; internet www.embajadachina.org.pe; Ambassador HUANG MINHUI.

Colombia: Avda J. Basadre 1580, San Isidro, Lima 27; tel. (1) 4410954; fax (1) 4419806; e-mail elima@cancilleria.gov.co; Ambassador MARÍA ELVIRA POMBO HOLGUÍN.

Costa Rica: Baltazar La Torre 828, San Isidro, Lima; tel. (1) 2642999; fax (1) 2642711; e-mail embcr.peru@gmail.com; Ambassador MELVIN ALFREDO SÁENZ BIOLLEY.

Cuba: Coronel Portillo 110, San Isidro, Lima; tel. (1) 5123400; fax (1) 2644525; e-mail embacuba@pe.embacuba.cu; internet www .cubadiplomatica.cu/peru; Ambassador JUANA MARTÍNEZ GONZÁLEZ.

Czech Republic: Baltazar La Torre 398, San Isidro, Lima 27; tel. (1) 2643374; fax (1) 2641708; e-mail lima@embassy.mzv.cz; internet www.mfa.cz/lima; Ambassador VLADIMIR EISENBRUK.

Dominican Republic: Calle Baltazar La Torre 832, San Isidro, Lima 27; tel. (1) 2642874; fax (1) 2642947; e-mail embdomperu@ speedy.com.pe; internet www.embajadadominicanaperu.org; Ambassador RAFAEL JULIÁN CEDANO.

Ecuador: Las Palmeras 356 y Javier Prado Oeste, San Isidro, Lima 27; tel. (1) 2124171; fax (1) 4215907; e-mail embajada@ mecuadorperu.org.pe; internet www.mecuadorperu.org.pe; Ambassador JOSÉ RAMIRO SANDOVAL ZAMBRANO.

Egypt: Avda Jorge Basadre 1470, San Isidro, Lima 27; tel. (1) 4222531; fax (1) 4402547; e-mail egipto@sspeedy.com.pe; internet embajadadeegipto.webs.com; Ambassador AHMAD SALAMA.

El Salvador: Avda Dos de Mayo 843, San Isidro, Lima 27; tel. (1) 4403500; fax (1) 2212561; e-mail embajadasv@terra.com.pe; Ambassador IDALIA GERTRUDIZ MENJIVAR CAMPOS.

Finland: Edif. Real Tres, Of. 502, 5°, Avda Víctor Andrés Belaúnde 147, San Isidro, Lima; tel. (1) 2224466; fax (1) 2224463; e-mail sanomat.lim@formin.fi; internet www.finlandia.org.pe; Ambassador JUHA VIRTANEN.

France: Avda Arequipa 3415, Lima 27; tel. (1) 2158400; fax (1) 2158441; e-mail france.chancellerie@ambafrance-pe.org; internet www.ambafrance-pe.org; Ambassador JEAN-JACQUES BEAUSSOU.

Germany: Edif. Caral Alto, 7°, Avda Dionisio Derteano 144, San Isidro, Lima 18; tel. (1) 2125016; fax (1) 4226475; e-mail info@lima .diplo.de; internet www.lima.diplo.de; Ambassador JOACHIM CHRISTOPH SCHMILLEN.

Greece: Avda Principal 190, Urb. Santa Catalina, La Victoria, Lima 13; tel. (1) 4761548; fax (1) 2232486; e-mail gremb.lim@mfa.gr; internet www.mfa.gr/lima; Ambassador DIMITRIS HATZOPOULOS.

Guatemala: Inca Ripac 309, Jesús María, Lima 11; tel. (1) 4602078; fax (1) 4635885; e-mail embperu@minex.gob.gt; internet www .embajadadeguatemalaenperu.org; Ambassador GABRIEL AGUILERA PERALTA.

Holy See: Avda Salaverry, 6a cuadra, Lima 11 (Apostolic Nunciature); tel. (1) 7174897; fax (1) 7174896; e-mail nunciaturaperu@inbox .com; Apostolic Nuncio Most Rev. JAMES PATRICK GREEN (Titular Archbishop of Altinum).

Honduras: Calle Juan Dellepiani 231, 2°, San Isidro, Lima 27; tel. (1) 2644600; fax (1) 2640008; e-mail info@embhonpe.org; internet www .embhonpe.org; Ambassador HUMBERTO LÓPEZ VILLAMIL OCHOA.

India: Avda Salaverry 3006, San Isidro, Lima 27; tel. (1) 4602289; fax (1) 4610374; e-mail hoc@indembassy.org.pe; internet www .indembassy.org.pe; Ambassador MANPREET VOHRA.

Indonesia: Calle Las Flores 334-336, San Isidro, Lima; tel. (1) 2220308; fax (1) 2222684; e-mail kbrilima@indonesia-peru.org.pe; internet www.indonesia-peru.org.pe; f. 2002; Ambassador MOENIR ARI SOENANDA.

Israel: Centro Empresarial Platinum Plaza II, 13°, Avda Andres Reyes 437, San Isidro, Lima; tel. (1) 4180500; fax (1) 4180555; e-mail info@lima.mfa.gov.il; internet lima.mfa.gov.il; Ambassador MODI EPHRAIM.

Italy: Avda Giuseppe Garibaldi 298, Apdo 0490, Lima 11; tel. (1) 4632727; fax (1) 4635317; e-mail ambasciata.lima@esteri.it; internet www.amblima.esteri.it; Ambassador GUGLIELMO ARDIZZONE.

Japan: Avda San Felipe 356, Apdo 3708, Jesús María, Lima 11; tel. (1) 2199500; fax (1) 4630302; e-mail cultjapon@embajadajapon.org .pe; internet www.pe.emb-japan.go.jp; Ambassador MASAJIRO FUJU-KAWA.

Korea, Democratic People's Republic: Los Nogales 227, San Isidro, Lima; tel. (1) 4411120; fax (1) 4409877; e-mail embcorea@ hotmail.com; Ambassador KIM HAK CHOL.

Korea, Republic: Calle Guillermo Marconi 165, San Isidro, Lima; tel. (1) 4760815; fax (1) 4760950; e-mail per@mofat.go.kr; internet per.mofat.go.kr; Ambassador PARK HEE-KWON.

Malaysia: Avda Daniel Hernández 350, San Isidro, Lima 27; tel. (1) 4220297; fax (1) 2210786; e-mail mallima@kln.gov.my; internet www .kln.gov.my/perwakilan/lima; Ambassador AYAUF BACHI.

Mexico: Avda Jorge Basadre 710, esq. Los Ficus, San Isidro, Lima; tel. (1) 6121600; fax (1) 6121627; e-mail info@mexico.org.pe; internet embamex.sre.gob.mx/peru; Ambassador MANUEL RODRÍGUEZ ARRIAGA.

Morocco: Calle Los Virreyes 123, Urb. Pancho Fierro, Santiago de Surco, Lima; tel. (1) 2040830; fax (1) 2790242; e-mail sifa@ embajadamarruecoslima.com; internet www .embajadamarruecoslima.com; Ambassador OUMAMA AOUAD LAH-RECH.

Netherlands: Torre Parque Mar, 13°, Avda José Larco 1301, Miraflores, Lima; tel. (1) 2139800; fax (1) 2139805; e-mail info@ nlgovlim.com; internet www.nlgovlim.com; Ambassador JOHAN LAMMERT CHRISTIAAN VAN DER WERFF.

Nicaragua: Paul de Beaudiez 471, San Isidro, Lima 27; tel. (1) 4223892; fax (1) 4223895; e-mail embanic@telefonica.net.pe; Ambassador MARCELA MARTHA PERÉZ SILVA.

Panama: Avda Trinidad Morán 1426, Lince, Lima; tel. (1) 4228084; fax (1) 4227871; e-mail secretaria@panaembaperu.com.pe; internet www.panaembaperu.com.pe; Ambassador CARLOS LUIS LINARES BRIN.

Paraguay: Alcanfores 1286, Miraflores, Lima; tel. (1) 4474762; fax (1) 4453539; e-mail embaparpe@infonegocio.net.pe; Chargé d'affaires a.i. FELIPE SANTIAGO JARA AGUERO.

Poland: Avda Salaverry 1978, Jesús María, Lima 11; tel. (1) 4713920; fax (1) 4714813; e-mail lima.amb.sekretariat@msz.gov.pl; internet www.lima.polemb.net; Ambassador IZABELA MATUSZ.

Portugal: Avda Felipe Pardo y Aliaga 640, 16°, San Isidro, POB 3692, Lima 100; tel. (1) 6287164; fax (1) 4429655; e-mail limaportugal@hotmail.com; Ambassador HELENA MARGARIDA REZENDE DE ALMEIDA COUTINHO.

Qatar: Avda Santa Cruz 1136, Miraflores, Lima; tel. (1) 6373500; fax (1) 6384574; e-mail lima@mofa.gov.ga; Ambassador JAMAL NASSER AL-BADER.

Romania: Avda Jorge Basadre 690, San Isidro, Lima; tel. (1) 4224587; fax (1) 4210609; e-mail ambrom@terra.com.pe; Chargé d'affaires a.i. ȘTEFAN NICOLAE.

Russia: Avda Salaverry 3424, San Isidro, Lima 27; tel. (1) 2640036; fax (1) 2640130; e-mail embrusa@infonegocio.net.pe; internet www .embajada-rusa.org; Ambassador NIKOLAY V. SOFINSKIY.

South Africa: Edif. Real Tres, Avda Víctor Andrés Belaúnde 147, Of. 801, Lima 27; tel. (1) 6124848; fax (1) 4223881; e-mail general .peru@dirco.gov.za; Ambassador ELSA DRY.

Spain: Jorge Basadre 498, San Isidro, Lima 27; tel. (1) 2125155; fax (1) 4402020; e-mail emb.lima@maec.es; internet www.maec.es/ embajadas/lima; Ambassador JUAN CARLOS SÁNCHEZ ALONSO.

Switzerland: Avda Salaverry 3240, San Isidro, Lima 27; tel. (1) 2640305; fax (1) 2641319; e-mail lim.vertretung@eda.admin.ch; internet www.eda.admin.ch/lima; Ambassador HANS-RUEDI BORTIS.

Thailand: Avda Coronel Portillo 678, San Isidro, Lima 27; tel. (1) 6375620; fax (1) 6384073; e-mail thailim@mfa.go.th; internet www .thaiembassyperu.org; Ambassador RUENGDEJ MAHASARANOND.

Turkey: Calle Miguel de Cervantes 504-510, San Isidro, Lima 27; tel. (1) 2047000; fax (1) 4216304; e-mail embajada.lima@mfa.gov.tr; Ambassador FERDA ACKKERMAN.

Ukraine: José Dellepiani 470, San Isidro, Lima; tel. (1) 2642884; fax (1) 2642892; e-mail emb_pe@mfa.gov.ua; internet www.mfa.gov.ua/ peru; Ambassador OLEKSANDR MYKHALCHUK.

United Kingdom: Torre Parque Mar, 22°, Avda José Larco 1301, Miraflores, Lima; tel. (1) 6173000; fax (1) 6173100; e-mail belima@fco .gov.uk; internet www.ukinperu.fco.gov.uk; Ambassador ANWAR CHOUDHURY.

USA: Avda La Encalada 17, Surco, Lima 33; tel. (1) 6182000; fax (1) 6182397; internet lima.usembassy.gov; Ambassador BRIAN A. NICHOLS.

Uruguay: José D. Anchorena 84, San Isidro, Lima 27; tel. (1) 7192550; fax (1) 7192865; e-mail uruinca@americatelnet.com.pe; Ambassador JUAN JOSÉ ARTEAGA SÁENZ DE ZUMARÁN.

Venezuela: Avda Arequipa 298, Urb. Santa Beatriz, Lima; tel. (1) 4334511; fax (1) 4331191; e-mail consulve@millicom.com.pe; Ambassador ALEXANDER YAÑEZ DELEUZE.

Judicial System

The Supreme Court consists of a President and 17 members. There are also Higher Courts and Courts of First Instance in provincial capitals.

Corte Suprema de Justicia: Palacio de Justicia, 2°, Avda Paseo de la República, Cercado, Lima 1; tel. (1) 4284457; fax (1) 4269437; internet www.pj.gob.pe; f. 1971; Pres. Dr ENRIQUE JAVIER MENDOZA RAMÍREZ.

Attorney-General: CARLOS RAMOS HEREDIA.

Religion

CHRISTIANITY

The Roman Catholic Church

For ecclesiastical purposes, Peru comprises seven archdioceses, 19 dioceses, 10 territorial prelatures and eight Apostolic Vicariates. According to the latest census (2007), some 81% of the population are Roman Catholics.

Bishops' Conference: Conferencia Episcopal Peruana, Jirón Estados Unidos 838, Apdo 310, Lima 100; tel. (1) 4631010; fax (1) 2618572; e-mail prensa@iglesiacatolica.org.pe; internet www.iglesiacatolica .org.pe; f. 1981; Pres. SALVADOR PIÑEIRO GARCÍA-CALDERÓN (Archbishop of Ayacucho).

Archbishop of Arequipa: JAVIER AUGUSTO DEL RIO ALBA, Arzobispado, Moral San Francisco 118, Apdo 149, Arequipa; tel. (54) 234094; fax (54) 242721; e-mail info@arzobispadoarequipa.org.pe; internet www.arzobispadoarequipa.org.pe.

Archbishop of Ayacucho or Huamanga: SALVADOR PIÑEIRO GARCÍA-CALDERÓN, Arzobispado, Jirón 28 de Julio 148, Apdo 30, Ayacucho; tel. and fax (64) 812367; e-mail arzaya@speedy.com.pe; internet www.arquidiocesisdeayacucho.org.

Archbishop of Cusco: JUAN ANTONIO UGARTE PÉREZ, Arzobispado, Herrajes, Hatun Rumiyoc s/n, Apdo 148, Cusco; tel. (84) 225211; fax (84) 222781; e-mail riial@arzobispadodelcusco.org; internet www .arzobispadodelcusco.org.

Archbishop of Huancayo: PEDRO RICARDO BARRETO JIMENO, Arzobispado, Jirón Puno 430, Apdo 245, Huancayo; tel. (64) 234952; fax (64) 239189; e-mail info@arzhuancayoperu.org; internet www .arzhuancayoperu.org.

Archbishop of Lima: Cardinal JUAN LUIS CIPRIANI THORNE, Arzobispado, Jirón Chancay 282, Lima 100; tel. (1) 2037700; fax (1) 3330015; e-mail prensa@arzobispadodelima.org; internet www .arzobispadodelima.org.

Archbishop of Piura: JOSÉ ANTONIO EGUREN ANSELMI, Arzobispado, Libertad 1105, Apdo 197, Piura; tel. and fax (74) 327561; e-mail ocordova@upiura.edu.pe; internet www.arzobispadodepiura.org.

Archbishop of Trujillo: HÉCTOR MIGUEL CABREJOS VIDARTE, Arzobispado, Jirón Mariscal de Orbegozo 451, Apdo 42, Trujillo; tel. (44) 256812; fax (44) 231473; e-mail prensa@arzobispadodetrujillo.org; internet www.arzobispadodetrujillo.org.

The Anglican Communion

The Iglesia Anglicana del Cono Sur de América (Anglican Church of the Southern Cone of America) comprises seven dioceses, including Peru. The Presiding Bishop of the Church is the Bishop of Northern Argentina.

Bishop of Peru: Rt Rev. HAROLD WILLIAM GODFREY, Apdo 18-1032, Miraflores, Lima 18; tel. and fax (1) 4229160; e-mail diocesisperu@ anglicanperu.org; internet www.peru.anglican.org.

Other Christian Churches

Among the most popular are the Iglesia Evangélica del Perú (accounting for some 12% of the population at the 2007 census), the Asamblea de Dios, the Iglesia del Nazareno, the Alianza Cristiana y Misionera and the Iglesia de Dios del Perú.

Church of Jesus Christ of Latter-Day Saints (Mormons): Avda Javier Prado Este 6420, La Molina, Lima 12; tel. (1) 6127200; internet www.lds.org; 527,759 mems.

Iglesia Metodista del Perú: Baylones 186, Lima 5; Apdo 1386, Lima 100; tel. (1) 4245970; fax (1) 4318995; e-mail informes@

iglesiametodista.org.pe; internet www.iglesiametodista.org.pe; Pres. Rev. JORGE BRAZO CABALLERO; 4,200 mems.

BAHÁ'Í FAITH

National Spiritual Assembly of the Bahá'ís of Peru: Horacio Urteaga 827, Jesús María, Apdo 11-0209, Lima 11; tel. (1) 4333005; e-mail secretaria@bahai.org.pe; internet www.bahai.org.pe; Sec. ROSANNA RIVERA; mems resident in 220 localities.

The Press

DAILIES

Lima

El Bocón: Jirón Jorge Salazar Araoz 171, Urb. Santa Catalina, Apdo 152, Lima 1; tel. (1) 6908090; fax (1) 6908127; e-mail web@grupoepensa.pe; internet elbocon.pe; f. 1994; football; Editorial Dir JORGE ESTÉVES ALFARO; circ. 90,000.

El Comercio: Jirón Antonio Miró Quesada 300, Lima; tel. (1) 3116310; fax (1) 4260810; e-mail editorweb@comercio.com.pe; internet elcomercio.pe; f. 1839; morning; Dir-Gen. FRITZ DU BOIS FREUND; Editor FABRICIO TORRES DEL AGUILA; circ. 150,000 weekdays, 220,000 Sun.

Expreso: Jorge Basadre 592, Of. 601, San Isidro, Lima; tel. (1) 6124000; fax (1) 6124024; e-mail sugerencias@expreso.com.pe; internet www.expreso.com.pe; f. 1961; morning; conservative; Dir LUIS GARCÍA MIRÓ; circ. 100,000.

Extra: Jirón Libertad 117, Miraflores, Lima; tel. (1) 4447088; fax (1) 4447117; e-mail extra@expreso.com.pe; f. 1964; evening edition of Expreso; Dir ANTONIO RAMÍREZ PANDO; circ. 80,000.

Gestión: Jíron Miró Quesada 247, 8°, Lima 1; tel. (1) 3116370; fax (1) 3116500; e-mail gestion2@diariogestion.com.pe; internet www.gestion.pe; f. 1990; Dir JULIO LIRA SEGURA; Editor MANUEL BURGOS; circ. 131,200.

Ojo: Jirón Jorge Salazar Araoz 171, Urb. Santa Catalina, Apdo 152, Lima; tel. (1) 6311111; fax (1) 6311100; e-mail redaccion@grupoepensa.pe; internet www.ojo.com.pe; f. 1968; morning; Dir VÍCTOR RAMÍREZ CANALES; circ. 100,000.

Perú 21: Jirón Miró Quesada 247, 6°, Lima; tel. (1) 3116500; fax (1) 3116391; e-mail mtumi@peru21.com; internet peru21.pe; independent; Dir JUAN JOSÉ GARRIDO; Editor MANUEL TUMI.

El Peruano (Diario Oficial): Avda Alfonso Ugarte 873, Lima 1; tel. (1) 3150400; fax (1) 4245023; e-mail gbarraza@editoraperu.com.pe; internet www.elperuano.com.pe; f. 1825; morning; official State Gazette; Dir JOSÉ LUIS BRAVO RUSSO; circ. 27,000.

La República: Jirón Camaná 320, Lima 1; tel. (1) 7116000; fax (1) 2511029; e-mail otxoa@larepublica.com.pe; internet www.larepublica.pe; f. 1982; left-wing; Dir GUSTAVO MOHME SEMINARIO; circ. 50,000.

Arequipa

Noticias: Calle Consuelo 404-A, Arequipa; tel. (54) 281026; fax (54) 280784; e-mail contacto@diarionoticias.pe; internet www.diarionoticias.pe; morning; Dir JAVIER ARISTA VALDIVIA; Editor NERY Alemán Puma.

El Pueblo: Sucre 213, Arequipa; tel. and fax (54) 205086; internet www.elpueblo.com.pe; f. 1905; morning; independent; Pres. DANIEL MACEDO GUTIÉRREZ; Dir CARLOS MENESES CORNEJO; circ. 70,000.

Chiclayo

La Industria: Jirón Tacna 610, Chiclayo; tel. (74) 237952; fax (74) 227678; internet laindustriadechiclayo.pe; f. 1952; Dir AUGUSTO RUBIO ACOSTA; circ. 20,000.

Cusco

El Diario del Cusco: Centro Comercial Ollanta, Avda El Sol 346, Cusco; tel. (84) 229898; fax (84) 229822; e-mail diariocusco@gmail.com; internet www.diariodelcusco.com; morning; independent; Exec. Pres. WASHINGTON ALOSILLA PORTILLO; Gen. Man. JOSÉ FERNANDEZ NÚÑEZ.

Huacho

El Imparcial: Avda Grau 203, Huacho; tel. (34) 2392187; e-mail elimparcial1891@hotmail.com; f. 1891; evening; Dir ADÁN MANRIQUE ROMERO; circ. 5,000.

Huancayo

Primicia: Calle Real 455, Interior 1, Huancayo; tel. (64) 201309; fax (64) 216594; e-mail criverab@diarioprimicia.pe; internet www.diarioprimicia.pe; f. 1997; Dir ABEL EGOÁVIL SORIANO.

Ica

La Opinión: Avda Los Maestros 801, Apdo 186, Ica; tel. (56) 235571; f. 1922; evening; independent; Dir GONZALO TUEROS RAMÍREZ.

La Voz de Ica: Castrovirreyna 191–193, Ica; tel. (56) 218717; fax (56) 232112; tel. and fax (56) 232112; e-mail info@lavozdeica.com; internet www.lavozdeica.com; f. 1918; Dir ATILIO NIERI BOGGIANO; Man. MARIELLA NIERI DE MACEDO; circ. 4,500.

Pacasmayo

Diario Ultimas Noticias: Jirón 2 de Mayo 33, Pacasmayo, La Libertad; tel. (44) 528319; fax (44) 523022; e-mail escribanos@ultimasnoticiasdiario.com; internet www.ultimasnoticiasdiario.com; f. 1973; morning; independent; Editor MARÍA DEL CARMEN BALLENA RAZURI; circ. 3,000.

Piura

El Tiempo: Jirón Ayacucho 751, Piura; tel. (74) 325141; fax (74) 327478; e-mail rlaban@eltiempo.com.pe; internet www.eltiempo.com.pe; f. 1916; morning; independent; Dir ROSARIO ARÁMBULO; Editor ROSA LABÁN; circ. 18,000.

Trujillo

La Industria: Jirón Gamarra 443, Trujillo; tel. (44) 295757; fax (44) 290901; e-mail redaccion@laindustria.com; internet laindustria.pe; f. 1895; morning; independent; Dir JOSÉ BRINGAS; circ. 8,000.

PERIODICALS

Business: Avda La Molina 1110, Of. 203, La Molina, Lima 12; tel. (1) 2500596; fax (1) 2500597; e-mail info@businessperu.com.pe; internet www.businessperu.com.pe; f. 1994; monthly; Dir DANIEL VALERA LOZA.

Caretas: Jirón Huallaya 122, Portal de Botoneros, Plaza de Armas, Lima 1; Apdo 737, Lima 100; tel. (1) 4289490; fax (1) 4262524; e-mail info@caretas.com.pe; internet www.caretas.com.pe; weekly; current affairs; Dir MARCO ZILERI DOUGALL; Editor JAIME BEDOYA; circ. 90,000.

Cosas: Calle Alcanfores 1262, Miraflores, Lima 18; tel. (1) 2023000; fax (1) 4473776; e-mail contacto@cosas.pe; internet www.cosas.pe; f. 1992; weekly; society; Dir ELIZABETH DULANTO DE MIRÓ QUESADA; Editor ISABEL DE MIRÓ QUESADA.

Debate Agrario: Avda Salaverry 818, Lima 11; tel. (1) 4336610; fax (1) 4331744; e-mail fegurenl@cepes.org.pe; internet www.cepes.org.pe/debate/debate.htm; f. 1987 by Centro Peruano de Estudios Sociales; annual; rural issues; Dir FERNANDO EGUREN L.

Gente Peru: Calle Piura 731, Miraflores, Lima 14; tel. (1) 2422930; fax (1) 4413646; e-mail correo@revista-gente.com; internet www.revista-gente.com; f. 1958; monthly; circ. 25,000; Dir ENRIQUE ESCARDÓ.

Industria Peruana: Los Laureles 365, San Isidro, Apdo 632, Lima 27; tel. (1) 6164444; fax (1) 6164412; e-mail industriaperuana@sni.org.pe; internet www.sni.org.pe/page_id=465; f. 1932; monthly publication of the Sociedad Nacional de Industrias; Editor-Gen. ENZO CHAPARRO MORALES.

Orbita: Parque Rochdale 129, Lima; tel. (1) 4610676; e-mail redaccion@orbitamagazine.com; internet www.orbitamagazine.com; monthly; music; f. 1970; Dir ALBERTO SÁNCHEZ; Editor FERNANDO FUENTES.

Perú Económico: Apdo 671, Lima 100; tel. (1) 2425656; fax (1) 4455946; internet perueconomico.com; f. 1978; monthly; Editor SANDRA BELAUNDE.

The Peruvian Times: Paseo de la República 291, Of. 702, Lima 1; tel. (1) 4676609; e-mail egriffis@peruviantimes.com; internet www.peruviantimes.com; f. 1940, successor to *West Coast Leader* (f. 1912); refounded 2007 as an online publ; general news, analysis and features; English; daily; Publr ELEANOR GRIFFIS; Editor RICK VECCHIO.

QueHacer: León de la Fuente 110, Magdalena, Lima 17; tel. (1) 6138300; fax (1) 6138308; e-mail monica@desco.org.pe; internet www.desco.org.pe/ediciones; f. 1979; 6 a year; supported by Desco research and devt agency; Dir ABELARDO SÁNCHEZ-LEÓN; circ. 5,000.

Revista Agraria: Avda Salaverry 818, Lima 11; tel. (1) 4336610; fax (1) 4331744; e-mail agraria@cepes.org.pe; internet www.larevistaagraria.org; f. 1987 by Centro Peruano de Estudios Sociales; monthly review of rural problems; Dir FERNANDO EGUREN; circ. 100,000.

Semana Económica: Avda 28 de Julio 1370, Miraflores, Lima 18; tel. (1) 2130600; fax (1) 4445240; e-mail redaccion@se.pe; internet semanaeconomica.com; f. 1985; weekly; Exec. Dir GONZALO ZEGARRA MULANOVICH; Editor ANDREA STIGLICH WATSON.

NEWS AGENCY

Andina—Agencia de Noticias Peruana: Avda Alfonso Ugarte 873, Lima 1; tel. (1) 3150400; fax (1) 4312849; e-mail andina@editoraperu.com.pe; internet www.andina.com.pe; f. 1981; state-owned; Pres. HUGO COYA HONORES; Dir JOSÉ LUIS BRAVO RUSSO.

PRESS ASSOCIATIONS

Asociación Nacional de Periodistas del Perú: Jirón Huanca-vélica 320, Of. 501, Apdo 2079, Lima 1; tel. (1) 4270687; fax (1) 4278493; internet www.anp.org.pe; f. 1928; 8,800 mems; Pres. ROBERTO MARCOS MEJÍA ALARCÓN; Sec.-Gen. ZULIANA LAINEZ OTERO.

Federación de Periodistas del Perú (FPP): Avda Abancay 173, 3°, Lima; tel. (1) 4261806; e-mail fpp@omco.org; internet www.fpp.org.pe; f. 1950; Pres. ANGEL SÁNCHEZ DUEÑAS; Sec.-Gen. OLGGER SEVERO PODESTÁ.

Publishers

Asociación Editorial Bruño: Avda Arica 751, Breña, Lima 5; tel. (1) 4237890; fax (1) 4240424; e-mail federico@brunoeditorial.com.pe; internet www.brunoeditorial.com.pe; f. 1950; educational; Man. FEDERICO DÍAZ TINEO.

Biblioteca Nacional del Perú: Avda de la Poesia 160, San Borja, Lima 41; tel. (1) 5136900; fax (1) 5137060; e-mail contactobnp@bnp.gob.pe; internet www.bnp.gob.pe; f. 1821; general non-fiction, directories; Dir RAMÓN ELÍAS MUJICA PINILLA.

Borrador Editores: Avda Fray Luis de León 39, San Borja; tel. (1) 2710192; e-mail borradoreditores@gmail.com; internet www.borradoreditores.blogspot.com; Man. PEDRO VILLA GAMARRA.

Ediciones del Hipocampo: Avda Alfredo Franco 195, Urb. Chama, Lima 33; tel. (1) 3586783; fax (1) 3586783; e-mail editor@hipocampo.com.pe; internet www.hipocampo.com.pe; f. 2000; travel literature; Gen. Man. JOSÉ MIGUEL HELFER ARGUEDAS.

Ediciones PEISA: Avda 2 de Mayo 1285, San Isidro, Lima; tel. and fax (1) 2215988; e-mail peisa@terra.com.pe; internet www.peisa.com.pe; f. 1968; fiction and scholarly; Dir GERMÁN CORONADO.

Ediciones SM: Calle Micaela Bastidas 125, San Isidro, Lima; tel. (1) 6148900; fax (1) 6148914; e-mail contacto@ediciones-sm.com.pe; internet www.ediciones-sm.com.pe; textbooks, education, children's literature; Gen. Man. SIMÓN BERNILLA CARRILLO.

Edigraber Editora Gráfica: Avda Tacna 685, 5°, Of. 54, Lima; tel. and fax (1) 4287073; e-mail info@edigraberperu.com; internet www.edigraberperu.com; Gen. Man. SIMÓN BERNILLA CARRILLO.

Editora Normas Legales, SA: Angamos Oeste 526, Miraflores, Lima; tel. and fax (1) 4861410; e-mail ventas@normaslegales.com; internet www.normaslegales.com; law textbooks; Man. JAVIER SANTA MARÍA SILVE.

Editorial Arkabas: Jirón Miraflores 291, Barranco, Lima; tel. (1) 6525350; internet www.arkabas.com; Gen. Man. DANIEL ZÚÑIGA-RIVERA.

Editorial Salesiana: Avda Brasil 218, Apdo 0071, Lima 5; tel. (1) 4235225; internet www.libreriasalesiana.com; f. 1918; religious and general textbooks; Man. Dir Dr FRANCESCO VACARELLO.

Editorial San Marcos: Jirón Dávalos Lissón 135, Lima; tel. (1) 3311535; fax (1) 3302405; e-mail informes@editorialsanmarcos.com; internet www.editorialsanmarcos.com; educational, academic, legal; Gen. Man. ANÍBAL JESÚS PAREDES GALVÁN.

Editorial Santillana: Avda Primavera 2160, Santiago de Surco, Lima; tel. (1) 3134000; fax (1) 3134001; e-mail santillana@santillana.com.pe; internet www.gruposantillana.com.pe; literature, scholarly and reference; Man. ANA CECILIA HALLO.

Grijley: Jirón Lampa 1221, Lima; tel. (1) 4273147; e-mail info@grijley.com; internet www.grijley.com; law.

Grupo Editorial Mesa Redonda: Pasaje José Payán 141, Miraflores, Lima; tel. (1) 2212957; e-mail editoramesaredonda@gmail.com; internet www.editorialmesaredonda.com; f. 2003; literature, humanities; imprints incl. Mesa Redonda and Calcomanía; Dir JUAN MIGUEL MARTHANS.

Palestra Editores: Jirón Ica 435, Of. 201, Lima 1; tel. (1) 4261363; fax (1) 4271025; e-mail palestra@palestraeditores.com; internet www.palestraeditores.com; law; Gen. Man. PEDRO GRANDEZ CASTRO.

Pontificia Universidad Católica del Perú, Fondo Editorial: Avda Universitaria 1801, San Miguel, Lima 32; tel. (1) 6262650; fax (1) 6262913; e-mail feditor@pucp.edu.pe; internet www.pucp.edu.pe; Dir-Gen. ANA PATRICIA ARÉVALO MAJLUF.

Sociedad Bíblica Peruana, AC: Avda Petit Thouars 991, Apdo 14-0295, Lima 100; tel. (1) 4336608; fax (1) 4336389; internet www.casadelabiblia.org; f. 1821; Christian literature and bibles; Gen. Sec. PEDRO ARANA-QUIROZ.

Universidad Nacional Mayor de San Marcos: Of. General de Editorial, Avda República de Chile 295, 5°, Of. 508, Lima; tel. (1) 4319689; internet www.unmsm.edu.pe; f. 1850; textbooks, education; Man. Dir JORGE CAMPOS REY DE CASTRO.

PUBLISHING ASSOCIATIONS

Alianza Peruana de Editores (ALPE): Lima; tel. (1) 2759081; e-mail alianzaeditores@gmail.com; internet alpe.wordpress.com; f. 2007; independent publrs' asscn; Pres. GERMÁN CORONADO.

Cámara Peruana del Libro: Avda Cuba 427, esq. Jesús María, Apdo 10253, Lima 11; tel. (1) 4729516; fax (1) 2650735; e-mail cp-libro@amauta.rep.net.pe; internet www.cpl.org.pe; f. 1946; 102 mems; Pres. CARLOS A. BENVIDES AGULJE; Exec. Dir LOYDA MORÁN BUSTAMANTE.

Vida y Espiritualidad: Avda Pedro de Osma 434, Barranco, Lima; tel. (1) 4672548; fax (1) 4617153; e-mail consultas@vidayespiritualidad.com; internet vidayespiritualidad.com; f. 1984; Dir KLAUS BERCKHOLTZ BENAVIDES.

Broadcasting and Communications

TELECOMMUNICATIONS

Claro Perú: Avda Nicolás Arriola 480, Urb. Santa Catalina, Lima; tel. (1) 6131000; e-mail prensa@claro.com.pe; internet www.claro.com.pe; f. 2005; owned by América Móvil, SA de SV (Mexico); mobile cellular telecommunications services; Exec. Dir JUAN JOSÉ RIVADE-NEYRA SÁNCHEZ.

Nextel del Perú: Avda República de Colombia 791, 14°, esq. Cuadra 34, Paseo D, San Isidro, Lima; tel. (1) 6117777; fax (1) 6111111; internet www.nextel.com.pe; f. 1998; subsidiary of NII Holdings, USA; Gen. Man. MIGUEL EDUARDO RIVERA AGUIRRE.

Telefónica del Perú, SA: Avda Arequipa 1155, Santa Beatriz, Lima 1; tel. (1) 2101013; internet www.telefonica.com.pe; tv and internet services operated under the Movistar brand; Pres. JAVIER MANZA-NARES GUTIÉRREZ.

Regulatory Authorities

Dirección General de Regulación y Asuntos Internacionales de Telecomunicaciones: Avda Jirón Zorritos 1203, Lima 1; tel. (1) 6157800; Dir-Gen. PATRICIA CARREÑO FERRÉ.

Instituto Nacional de Investigación y Capacitación de Tele-comunicaciones (INICTEL): Avda San Luis 1771, esq. Bailetti, San Borja, Lima 41; tel. (1) 6261400; fax (1) 6261402; e-mail informes@inictel-uni.edu.pe; internet www.inictel-uni.edu.pe; Pres. MANUEL ADRIANZEN.

Organismo Supervisor de Inversión Privada en Telecomuni-caciones (OSIPTEL): Calle de la Prosa 136, San Borja, Lima 41; tel. (1) 2251313; fax (1) 4751816; e-mail jgutierrez@osiptel.gob.pe; internet www.osiptel.gob.pe; f. 1993; established by the Peruvian Telecommunications Act to oversee competition and tariffs, to monitor the quality of services and to settle disputes in the sector; Pres. GONZALO MARTÍN RUIZ DÍAZ.

BROADCASTING

Instituto Nacional de Radio y Televisión Peruana (IRTP): Avda José Galvez 1040, Lima 1; tel. (1) 6190707; fax (1) 6190723; e-mail comercial@irtp.com.pe; internet www.irtp.com.pe; f. 1996; state-run, part of the Ministry of Culture from 2010; Exec. Pres. MARÍA LUISA MÁLAGA SILVA; Gen. Man. Dr LUIGINO PILOTTO CARREÑO; runs the following stations:

Radio Nacional del Perú: Avda Petit Thouars 447, Lima 1; tel. (1) 6190660; e-mail lllontop@irtp.com.pe; internet www.radionacional.com.pe; f. 1925; state broadcaster; Gen. Man. LUIS ENRIQUE LLONTOP SAMILLAN.

Televisión Nacional del Perú (TV Perú): Avda José Gálvez 1040, Santa Beatriz, Lima; tel. (1) 6190704; e-mail adelgado@irtp.com.pe; internet www.tvperu.gob.pe; f. 1958 as Radio y Televisión Peruana; state broadcaster; 22 stations; Gen. Man. ANGELA DELGADO POPOLIZIO.

Radio

Radio Agricultura del Perú, SA—La Peruanísima: Casilla 625, Lima 11; tel. (1) 4246677; e-mail radioagriculturadelperu@yahoo.com; internet www.laperuanisima.com; f. 1963; Gen. Man. LUZ ISABEL DEXTRE NÚÑEZ.

Radio América: Montero Rosas 1099, Santa Beatriz, Lima 1; tel. (1) 2653841; fax (1) 2653844; f. 1943; Dir-Gen. KAREN CROUSILLAT.

Radio Cutivalú, La Voz del Desierto: Jirón Ignacio de Loyola 300, Urb. Miraflores, Castilla, Piura; tel. (73) 343370; e-mail cutivalu630am@hotmail.com; internet www.radiocutivalu.org; f. 1986; Pres. FRANCISCO MUGUIRO IBARRA; Dir RODOLFO AQUINO RUIZ.

Emisoras Cruz del Perú: Jirón Victorino Laynes 1402, Urb. Elio, Lima 1; tel. (1) 3190240; fax (1) 3190244; e-mail info@emisorascruz .com.pe; internet www.emisorascruz.com.pe; Pres. FERNANDO CRUZ MENDOZA; Gen. Man. MARCO CRUZ MENDOZA.

Radio Panamericana: Paseo Parodi 340, San Isidro, Lima 27; tel. (1) 4226787; fax (1) 4221182; internet www.radiopanamericana.com; f. 1953.

Radio Programas del Perú (RPP): Avda Paseo de la República 3866, San Isidro, Lima; tel. (1) 2150200; fax (1) 2150269; internet www.rpp.com.pe; radio and television station; broadcasts RPP Noticias, Radio Capital, Studio 92, Radio Oxígeno, La Zona, Radio Corazón, Radio Felicidad; Pres. HUGO DELGADO NACHTIGAL; Dir of News RAÚL VARGAS VEGA.

Television

América Televisión, Canal 4: Jirón Montero Rosas 1099, Santa Beatriz, Lima; tel. (1) 4194000; fax (1) 2656979; e-mail web@ americatv.com.pe; internet www.americatv.com.pe; CEO and Gen. Man. ERIC JURGENSEN.

ATV, Canal 9: Avda Arequipa 3570, San Isidro, Lima 27; tel. (1) 2118800; fax (1) 4427636; e-mail webmaster@atv.com.pe; internet www.tuteve.tv; f. 1983; Gen. Man. MARCELLO CÚNEO LOBIANO.

Frecuencia Latina, Canal 2: Avda San Felipe 968, Jesús María, Lima; tel. (1) 2191000; fax (1) 2656660; internet www .frecuencialatina.com.pe; Pres. BARUCH IVCHER.

Panamericana Televisión SA: Avda Arequipa 1110, Santa Beatriz, Lima 1; tel. (1) 4113200; internet www.24horas.com.pe.

RBC Televisión, Canal 11: Avda Manco Cápac 333, La Victoria, Lima; tel. (1) 6132929; fax (1) 4331237; internet www.rbctelevision .com; f. 1966; Pres. FERNANDO GONZÁLEZ DEL CAMPO; Gen. Man. JUAN SÁENZ MARÓN.

RPP Televisión: see Radio—Radio Programas del Perú.

Uranio, Canal 15: Avda Arequipa 3570, 6°, San Isidro, Lima; e-mail agamarra@atv.com.pe; Gen. Man. ADELA GAMARRA VÁSQUEZ.

Regulatory Authority

Coordinadora Nacional de Radio: Edif. J. F. Kennedy, Of. 706, Avda República de Chile 295, Santa Beatriz; tel. and fax (1) 4242748; e-mail prensa@cnr.org.pe; internet www.cnr.org.pe; f. 1978; Exec. Dir RODOLFO AQUINO RUIZ.

Association

Asociación Peruana de Radio y Televisión (APERTV): Avda Manco Capac 333, La Victoria, Lima 13; tel. (1) 3321656; internet www.apertv.org; Pres. RICARDO BELMONT CASSINELLI.

Finance

BANKING

(cap. = capital; res = reserves; dep. = deposits; m. = million; brs = branches; amounts in new soles)

Superintendencia de Banca y Seguros: Los Laureles 214, San Isidro, Lima 27; tel. (1) 6309000; fax (1) 6309239; e-mail mostos@sbs .gob.pe; internet www.sbs.gob.pe; f. 1931; Supt DANIEL SCHYDLOWSKY ROSENBERG; Sec.-Gen. MARCO OJEDA PACHECO.

Central Bank

Banco Central de Reserva del Perú: Jirón Antonio Miró Quesada 441-445, Lima 1; tel. (1) 6132000; fax (1) 6132524; e-mail webmaster@bcrp.gob.pe; internet www.bcrp.gob.pe; f. 1922; refounded 1931; cap. 591.3m., res 1,385m., dep. 54,458.4m. (Dec. 2009); Chair. JULIO VELARDE FLORES; Gen. Man. RENZO ROSSINI MIÑÁN; 7 brs.

Other Government Banks

Banco de la Nación: Avda República de Panamá 3664, San Isidro, Lima 1; tel. (1) 5192164; fax (1) 2214793; e-mail dep_ccorporativa@bn .com.pe; internet www.bn.com.pe; f. 1966; cap. 1,000m., res 210.6m., dep. 24,661.7m. (Dec. 2013); conducts all commercial banking operations of official govt agencies; Exec. Pres. CARLOS MANUEL DÍAZ MARIÑOS; Gen. Man. JUAN GALFRÉ GARCÍA; 444 brs.

Corporación Financiera de Desarrollo (COFIDE): Augusto Tamayo 160, San Isidro, Lima 27; tel. (1) 4422795; fax (1) 4423319; e-mail postmaster@cofide.com.pe; internet www.cofide .com.pe; f. 1971; also owners of Banco Latino; Pres. ALFONSO ZÁRATE; 11 brs.

Commercial Banks

Banco de Comercio: Avda Canaval y Moreyra 452-454, San Isidro, Lima; tel. (1) 5136000; fax (1) 5137032; e-mail postmaster@ bancomercio.com.pe; internet www.bancomercio.com; f. 1967; fmrly Banco Peruano de Comercio y Construcción; cap. 146.2m., res 10.4m., dep. 1,369.3m. (Dec. 2013); Pres. JOSÉ RICARDO STOK CAPELLA; Gen. Man. JUAN MANUEL ARELLANO; 23 brs.

Banco de Crédito del Perú: Calle Centenario 156, Urb. Las Laderas de Melgarejo, Apdo 12-067, Lima 12; tel. (1) 3132000; fax (1) 3132238; internet www.viabcp.com; f. 1889; cap. 3,752.6m., res 2,794.9m., dep. 66,141.8m. (Dec. 2013); Pres. and Chair. DIONISIO ROMERO PAOLETTI; Gen. Man. WALTER BAYLY; 349 brs.

Banco Interamericano de Finanzas, SA: Avda Rivera Navarrete 600, San Isidro, Lima 27; tel. (1) 6133000; fax (1) 2212489; e-mail gchang@bif.com.pe; internet www.bif.com.pe; f. 1991; cap. 433.7m., res 124.1m., dep. 5,411.9m. (Dec. 2013); Chair. SANDRO ACURIO; 37 brs.

BBVA Banco Continental: Avda República de Panamá 3055, San Isidro, Lima 27; tel. (1) 2111000; fax (1) 2111788; internet www .bbvabancocontinental.com; f. 1951; merged with BBVA of Spain in 1995; 92.01% owned by Holding Continental, SA; cap. 2,724.7m., res 861.4m., dep. 37,419.5m. (Dec. 2013); Pres. and Chair. ALEX BRESCIA; Gen. Man. EDUARDO TORRES-LLOSA VILLACORTA; 297 brs.

INTERBANK (Banco Internacional del Perú): Carlos Villarán 140, Urb. Santa Catalina, Lima 13; tel. (1) 2192347; fax (1) 2192118; e-mail krubin@intercorp.com.pe; internet www.interbank.com.pe; f. 1897; commercial bank; cap. 1,423.5m., res 380.4m., dep. 14,649.2m. (Dec. 2012); Chair. and Pres. CARLOS RODRÍGUEZ-PASTOR; Gen. Man. LUIS FELIPE CASTELLANOS LÓPEZ-TORRES; 232 brs.

Scotiabank Perú (Canada): Avda Dionisio Derteano 102, San Isidro, Apdo 1235, Lima; tel. (1) 2116060; fax (1) 2116000; e-mail scotiaenlinea@scotiabank.com.pe; internet www.scotiabank.com.pe; f. 2006 by merger of Banco Sudamericano (owned by Scotiabank, Canada) and Banco Wiese Sudameris; cap. 2,299.3m., res 804.2m., dep. 20,117.6m. (Dec. 2011); CEO CARLOS GONZÁLEZ-TABOADA.

Banking Association

Asociación de Bancos del Perú: Calle 41, No 975, Urb. Córpac, San Isidro, Lima 27; tel. (1) 6123333; fax (1) 6123316; e-mail estudioseconomicos@asbanc.com.pe; internet www.asbanc.com.pe; f. 1929; refounded 1967; Pres. OSCAR JOSÉ RIVERA; Gen. Man. ADRIÁN REVILLA.

STOCK EXCHANGE

Bolsa de Valores de Lima: Pasaje Acuña 106, Lima 1; tel. (1) 6193333; fax (1) 6193354; internet www.bvl.com.pe; f. 1860; Pres. CHRISTIAN LAUB BENAVIDES; Gen. Man. FRANCIS STENNING DE LAVALLE.

Regulatory Authority

Superintendencia del Mercado de Valores: Santa Cruz 315, Miraflores, Lima; tel. (1) 6106300; fax (1) 6106325; e-mail webmaster@smv.gob.pe; internet www.smv.gob.pe; f. 1968; regulates the securities and commodities markets; responsible to Ministry of Economy and Finance; Supt LILIAN ROCCA CARBAJAL.

INSURANCE

ACE Seguros, SA: Calle Amador Merino Reyna 267, Of. 402, San Isidro, Lima; tel. (1) 4175000; fax (1) 2212943; internet www .acelatinamerica.com; Pres. JUAN CARLOS PUYÓ.

CARDIF del Perú Cía de Seguros y Reaseguros: Avda Canaval y Moreyra 380, 1101°, San Isidro, Lima; tel. (1) 6151700; fax (1) 6151721; e-mail servicioalcliente@cardif.com.pe; internet www .bnpparibascardif.com.pe; Chair. PIERRE DE VILLENEUVE; Gen. Man. DANIEL WEIS CILLERO.

Interseguro Cía de Seguros, SA: Avda Pardo y Aliaga 640, 2°, San Isidro, Lima; tel. (1) 6119230; fax (1) 6114720; e-mail gonzalo .basadre@interseguro.com.pe; internet www.interseguro.com.pe; f. 1998; life and non-life, annuities; owned by Intergroup Financial Services; Chair. FELIPE MORRIS GUERINONI; CEO GONZALO BASADRE BRAZZINI.

Invita Seguros de Vida, SA: Torre Wiese, Canaval y Moreyra 532, San Isidro, Lima; tel. (1) 2222222; fax (1) 2211683; e-mail servicioalcliente@invita.com.pe; internet www.invita.com.pe; f. 2000; life; fmrly Wiese Aetna, SA; Chair. CARIDAD DE LA PUENTE WIESE; Gen. Man. MARIO VENTURA VERME.

Mapfre Perú Cía de Seguros: Avda 28 de Julio 873, Miraflores, Apdo 323, Lima 100; tel. (1) 2137373; fax (1) 2139148; e-mail contacto@mapfre.com.pe; internet www.mapfreperu.com; f. 1994; general; fmrly Seguros El Sol, SA; CEO RENZO CALDA GIURATO.

Pacífico, Cía de Seguros y Reaseguros: Avda Juan de Arona 830, San Isidro, Lima 27; tel. (1) 5184000; fax (1) 5184295; e-mail arodrigo@pps.com.pe; internet www.pacificoseguros.com; f. 1943; general; Pres. DIONISIO ROMERO SEMINARIO; CEO ALVARO CORREA MALACHOWSKI.

La Positiva Cía de Seguros y Reaseguros, SA: Esq. Javier Prado Este y Francisco Masías 370, San Isidro, Lima; tel. (511) 2110000; fax (511) 2110011; e-mail lineapositiva@lapositiva.com.pe; internet www.lapositiva.com.pe; f. 1947; Pres. JUAN MANUEL PEÑA ROCA; Gen. Man. GUSTAVO CERDEÑA RODRÍGUEZ.

Rimac Seguros: Las Begonias 475, 3°, San Isidro, Lima; tel. (1) 4111111; fax (1) 4210570; e-mail jortecho@rimac.com.pe; internet www.rimac.com.pe; f. 1896; acquired Seguros Fénix in 2004; Gen. Man. RAFAEL VENEGAS.

SECREX: Avda Angamos Oeste 1234, Apdo 0511, Miraflores, Lima; tel. (1) 4424033; fax (1) 4423890; e-mail ciaseg@secrex.com.pe; internet www.secrex.com.pe; f. 1980; mem. of Grupo CESCE.

Insurance Association

Asociación Peruana de Empresas de Seguros (APESEG): Calle Amador Merino Reyna 267, Of. 402, San Isidro, Lima; tel. (1) 4175000; fax (1) 2213313; e-mail seguros@apeseg.org.pe; internet www.apeseg.org.pe; f. 1904; Pres. FELIPE MORRIS GUERINONI.

Trade and Industry

GOVERNMENT AGENCIES

Agencia de Promoción de la Inversión Privada (ProInversión): Avda Enrique Canaval Moreyra 150, 9°, San Isidro, Lima 27; tel. (1) 2001200; fax (1) 2212941; e-mail contact@proinversion.gob.pe; internet www.proinversion.gob.pe; f. 2002 to promote economic investment; Exec. Dir JAVIER ILLESCAS; Sec.-Gen. GUSTAVO VILLEGAS DEL SOLAR.

Empresa Nacional de la Coca, SA (ENACO): Avda Arequipa 4528, Miraflores, Lima; tel. (1) 4442292; fax (1) 4471667; e-mail jjara@enaco.com.pe; internet www.enaco.com.pe; f. 1949; agency with exclusive responsibility for the purchase and resale of legally produced coca and the promotion of its derivatives; Pres. JULIO BALTAZAR JARA LADRÓN DE GUEVARA; Gen. Man. JUAN CARLOS GALDOS TEJADA.

Fondo Nacional de Cooperación para el Desarrollo Social (FONCODES): Avda Paseo de la República 3101, San Isidro, Lima; tel. (1) 4212102; fax (1) 4214128; e-mail cacurio@foncodes.mimdes.gob.pe; internet www.foncodes.gob.pe; f. 1991; responsible for social devt and eradicating poverty; Exec. Dir CÉSAR AURELIO ACURIO ZAVALA.

Instituto de Investigaciones de la Amazonía Peruana (IIAP): Avda Abelardo Quiñones Km 2.5, Apdo 784, Loreto; tel. (65) 265516; fax (65) 2265527; e-mail info@iiap.org.pe; internet www.iiap.org.pe; promotes sustainable devt of Amazon region; Pres. LUIS CAMPOS BACA.

Perúpetro, SA: Luis Aldana 320, San Borja, Lima; tel. (1) 6171800; fax (1) 6171801; e-mail asistemas@perupetro.com.pe; internet www.perupetro.com.pe; f. 1993; responsible for promoting investment in hydrocarbon exploration and exploitation; Chair. AURELIO ERNESTO OCHOA ALENCASTRE; CEO ISABEL TAFUR MARÍN.

DEVELOPMENT ORGANIZATIONS

Asociación de Exportadores (ADEX): Avda Javier Prado Este 2875, San Borja, Lima 41; Apdo 1806, Lima 1; tel. (1) 6183333; fax (1) 6183355; e-mail prensa@adexperu.org.pe; internet www.adexperu.org.pe; f. 1973; exporters' asscn; Pres. JUAN MANUEL VARILIAS VELÁSQUEZ; Gen. Man. JUAN C. LEÓN SILES; 600 mems.

Asociación Kallpa para la Promoción Integral de la Salud y el Desarrollo: Pasaje Capri 140, Urb. Palomar Norte, La Victoria, Lima 13; tel. (1) 2243344; fax (1) 2429693; e-mail peru@kallpa.org.pe; internet www.kallpa.org.pe; health devt for youths; Pres. AUREA BOLAÑOS HIDALGO; Sec. MARIE SPRUAGLI.

Asociación Nacional de Centros de Investigación, Promoción Social y Desarrollo: Belisario Flores, Lince, Lima 14; tel. (1) 4728888; fax (1) 4728962; e-mail anc@anc.org.pe; internet www.anc.org.pe; umbrella grouping of devt orgs; Pres. JULIA CUADROS FALLA; Exec. Sec. JOSEFINA HUAMÁN V.

Asociación para la Naturaleza y Desarrollo Sostenible (ANDES): Calle Ruinas 451, Casilla 567, Cusco; tel. (8) 4245021; fax (8) 4232603; e-mail tammy@andes.org.pe; internet www.andes.org.pe; f. 2007; poverty alleviation, biodiversity management, recognition and strengthening of traditional community rights; Exec. Dir CÉSAR ARGUMEDO.

Grupo ACP: Avda Domingo Orue 165, 5°, Surquillo, Lima 34; tel. (1) 4181930; fax (1) 2224166; e-mail grupoacp@grupoacp.com.pe; internet www.grupoacp.com.pe; f. 1969; fmrly Acción Comunitaria

del Perú; promotes economic, social and cultural devt; Chair. MARIANA RODRÍGUEZ RISCO.

Sociedad Nacional de Industrias (SNI) (National Industrial Association): Los Laureles 365, San Isidro, Apdo 632, Lima 27; tel. (1) 6164444; fax (1) 6164433; e-mail sni@sni.org.pe; internet www.sni.org.pe; f. 1896; comprises permanent commissions covering various aspects of industry including labour, integration, fairs and exhibitions, industrial promotion; its Small Industry Cttee groups over 2,000 small enterprises; Pres. LUIS SALAZAR; Gen. Man. ROSA ASCA; 90 dirs (reps of firms); 2,500 mems; 60 sectorial cttees.

Centro de Desarrollo Industrial (CDI): Los Laureles 365, San Isidro, Lima; tel. (1) 2158888; fax (1) 2158877; e-mail cdi@sni.org.pe; internet www.cdi.org.pe; f. 1986; Exec. Dir LUIS TENORIO PUENTES.

CHAMBERS OF COMMERCE

Cámara de Comercio de Lima (Lima Chamber of Commerce): Avda Giuseppe Garibaldi 396, Jesús María, Lima 11; tel. (1) 4633434; fax (1) 2191674; e-mail sereceex@camaralima.org.pe; internet www.camaralima.org.pe; f. 1888; Pres. CARLOS DURAND CHAHUD; Gen. Man. JOSÉ ROSAS BERNEDO; 5,500 mems.

Cámara Nacional de Comercio, Producción y Servicios (PERUCAMARAS): Giuseppe Garibaldi 396, 6°, Jesús María, Lima 11; tel. (1) 2191580; fax (1) 2191586; e-mail cnadministracion@perucam.com; internet www.perucam.com; Pres. SAMUEL GLEISER KATZ; Gen. Man. RUBÉN RONDINELLI ZAGA.

EMPLOYERS' ORGANIZATIONS

Asociación Automotriz del Perú: Avda Javier Prado Oeste 278, Apdo 1248, San Isidro, Lima 27; tel. (1) 6403636; fax (1) 4428865; e-mail aap@aap.org.pe; internet www.aap.org.pe; f. 1926; asscn of importers of motor cars and accessories; 360 mems; Pres. EDWIN DERTEANO DYER; Gen. Man. ENRIQUE PRADO REY.

Asociación de Ganaderos Lecheros del Perú (Agalep) (Association of Stock Farmers of Peru): Pumacahua 877, 3°, Jesús María, Lima; f. 1915; Gen. Man. JAVIER VALERA.

Confederación Nacional de Instituciones Empresariales Privadas (CONFIEP): Edif. Real Tres, Of. 401, Avda Víctor Andrés Belaúnde 147, San Isidro, Lima; tel. (1) 4223311; e-mail postmaster@confiep.org.pe; internet www.confiep.org.pe; f. 1984; fed. of 20 employers' orgs; Pres. HUMBERTO SPEZIANI; Gen. Man. GABRIEL AMARO ALZAMORA.

Junta Nacional del Café (JNC): Jirón Ramón Dagnino 369, Jesús María, Lima; tel. (1) 4331477; fax (1) 3327914; e-mail jnc@juntadelcafe.org.pe; internet www.juntadelcafe.org.pe; reps of govt and industrial coffee growers; Pres. CÉSAR RIVAS PEÑA; Gen. Man. LORENZO CASTILLO.

Sociedad Nacional de Minería y Petróleo: Francisco Graña 671, Magdalena del Mar, Lima 17; tel. (1) 2159250; fax (1) 4601616; e-mail postmaster@snmpe.org.pe; internet www.snmpe.org.pe; f. 1940; asscn of cos involved in mining, petroleum and energy; Pres. PEDRO MARTÍNEZ CARLEVARINO; Gen. Man. CATERINA PODESTÁ MEVIUS.

Sociedad Nacional de Pesquería (SNP): Avda República de Panamá 3591, 9°, San Isidro, Lima 27; tel. (1) 422-8844; fax (1) 422-8589; e-mail snpnet@snp.org.pe; internet www.snp.org.pe; f. 1952; private sector fishing interests; Pres. ELENA CONTERNO MARTINELLI; Gen. Man. JORGE RISI MUSSIO.

STATE HYDROCARBONS COMPANY

Petroperú (Petróleos del Perú, SA): Avda Enrique Canaval Moreyra 150, Lima 27; tel. (1) 2117800; fax (1) 6145000; internet www.petroperu.com; f. 1969; state-owned petroleum-refining co, 49% scheduled to be sold off in 2014; Pres. HÉCTOR REYES CRUZ; Gen. Man. PEDRO MÉNDEZ MILLA.

MAJOR COMPANIES

Metals, Mining and Petroleum

Compañía Barrick Misquichilca, SA: Avda Manuel Olguín 375, 11°, Santiago de Surco, Lima 33; tel. (1) 612-4100; e-mail informacion@barrick.com; internet www.barrickperu.com; runs Lagunas Norte and Pierina gold mines; Regional Pres. GUILLERMO CALÓ.

Compañía de Minas Buenaventura, SA: Avda Carlos Villarán 790, Santa Catalina, La Victoria, Lima 13; tel. (1) 4192500; fax (1) 4717349; e-mail recursos@buenaventura.com.pe; internet www.buenaventura.com; f. 1953; mining of silver ores; sales of US $819m. (2009); Chair. and CEO ROQUE BENAVIDES GENOZA; 1,400 employees.

Compañía Minera Antamina, SA: Avda el Derby 55, Santiago de Surco, Lima; tel. (1) 2173000; fax (1) 2173093; e-mail ascorp@antamina.com; internet www.antamina.com; mine produces copper, lead, zinc and molybdenum; owned by Xstrata (33.75%), BHP Biliton

PLC (33.75%), Teck-Cominco Ltd (22.5%), Mitsubishi Corpn (10%); Pres. and CEO ABRAHAM CHAHUÁN; 1,850 employees (2012).

Compañía Minera San Juan (Perú), SA (Nyrstar Coricancha): Baltazar La Torre 915, San Isidro, Lima 27; tel. (1) 2190500; fax (1) 2642942; internet www.nyrstar.com/operations/Pages/mining.aspx; f. 1912; 85% owned by Nyrstar (Belgium); lead-, zinc- and arsenic-mining; Chair. JULIEN DE WILDE; CEO ROLAND JUNCK; 597 employees (Coricancha).

Compañía Rex, SA (Ladrillos Rex): Avda Alfreo Mendiola 1879, San Martín de Porres, Lima 31; tel. (1) 5342143; fax (1) 5342295; e-mail informes@ladrillosrex.com; internet www.ladrillosrex.com; f. 1958; brick production; Gen. Man. HUMBERTO ROSALES; 341 employees.

Corporación Aceros Arequipa, SA: Avda Enrique Meiggs 297, Parque Internacional de la Industria y Comercio, Callao, Lima; tel. (1) 5171800; fax (1) 4520059; internet www.acerosarequipa.com; f. 1966; iron and steel mfr; fmrly ACERSA; Exec. Pres. RICARDO CILLÓNIZ CHAMPIN; 792 employees.

Doe Run Peru: Torre Real 3, 9°, Avda Víctor Andrés Belaúnde 147, Centro Camino Real, Lima 27; tel. (1) 2151200; internet www.doerun .com.pe; f. 1997 in Peru, after Doe Run Co bought Complejo Metalúrgico de La Oroya; subsidiary of Renco Holding Co (USA); Gen. Man. AYAR LÓPEZ CANO.

Empresa Siderúrgica del Perú (SIDERPERU): Avda Los Rosales 245, Santa Anita, Lima; tel. (1) 6186868; fax (1) 6186873; e-mail marketing@sider.com.pe; internet www.sider.com.pe; f. 1971; part of Gerdau Group; processing of steel; Gen. Man. JUAN PABLO GARCÍA BAYCE; 4,195 employees.

Grupo Milpo, SA: San Borja Norte 523, Lima 41; tel. (1) 7105500; fax (1) 7105511; e-mail comunicaciones@milpo.com; internet www .milpo.com; f. 1946; lead-, silver- and zinc-mining; operates 5 mining units; sales of US $211.2m. (2008); Pres. IVO UCOVICH DORSNER; Gen. Man. VÍCTOR GOBITZ COLCHADO; 314 employees.

Pan American Silver Corporation: Avda La Floresta 497, Of. 301, Charcarilla del Estanque, San Borja, Lima; tel. (1) 6189700; fax (1) 6189729; e-mail info@panamericansilver.com; internet www .panamericansilver.com; f. 1994; silver- and zinc-mining; exploits Quiruvilca, Huarón and Morococha mines and the silver-rich stockpiles of Cerro de Pasco owned by Volcán Compañía Minera, SA (q.v.); CEO GEOFFREY BURNS; Country Man. JORGE UGARTE.

Perú LNG: Torre 12, Of. 101, Avda Víctor Andrés Belaúnde 147, Vía Real 185, San Isidro, Lima; tel. (1) 7072100; e-mail perulnginfo@ perulng.com; internet www.perulng.com; f. 2010; operated by a consortium incl. Hunt Oil Co (USA), Repsol YPF (Spain), Pluspetrol, SA (Argentina) and SK Group (South Korea); liquid natural gas export plant, at Melchorita; CEO JUAN IGOR SALAZAR ZANELLI.

Pluspetrol Norte, SA: Avda República de Panamá 3055, 8°, San Isidro, Lima; tel. (1) 4117100; fax (1) 4117120; e-mail rrhh-cv-peru@ pluspetrol.net; internet www.pluspetrolnorte.com.pe; f. 1996 as Pluspetrol Perú Corpn; name changed as above 2002; oil and gas exploration and production; 55% shares held by Pluspetrol Resources Corpn and 45% by China National Petroleum Corpn (CNPC); CEO STEVE CROWELL; Deputy Gen. Man. ENYONG ZHU.

SAVIA Perú: Avda Rivera Navarrete 501, 11°, San Isidro, Lima; tel. (1) 5137500; fax (1) 4414217; e-mail ptp@petro-tech.com.pe; internet www.saviaperu.com; fmrly Petro-tech Peruana; renamed as above in 2009, following acquisition by Korean National Oil Corpn (Knoc) and Ecopetrol (Colombia); petroleum exploration and production; f. 1993, in Peru; CEO JIN-HYUN SONG; Exec. Pres. JORGE DUARTE.

Shougang Hierro Perú, SA: Avda República de Chile 262, Jesús María, Lima 1; tel. (1) 7145200; fax (1) 3305136; e-mail comercial@ shp.com.pe; internet www.shougang.com.pe; f. 1993; owned by Shougang Corpn, People's Republic of China; mining, processing and shipment of iron ore; Chair. ZHONGYI TAO; CEO AIMIN KONG; 1,988 employees.

Southern Peru Copper Corporation (SPCC): Avda Caminos del Inca 171, Urb. Chacarilla del Estanque, Santiago de Surco, Lima 33; tel. (1) 5120440; fax (1) 5120492; internet www.southernperu.com; f. 1952; copper-mining; owned by Grupo México (54.1%), Cerro Trading Co, and Phelps Dodge; Dir J. EDUARDO GONZÁLEZ FÉLIX; Chair. and CEO GERMÁN LARREA MOTA-VELASCO; 3,554 employees.

Volcán Compañía Minera, SA: Avda Giuseppe Garibaldi 710, Jésus María, Lima; tel. (1) 2194000; fax (1) 2619716; e-mail info@ volcan.com.pe; internet www.volcan.com.pe; f. 1943; lead-, zinc- and silver-mining; owns 495 mining concessions; Chair. JOSÉ PICASSO SALINAS; CEO JUAN IGNACIO GÓMEZ DE LA TORRE; 3,000 employees.

Food and Drink

Alicorp, SA: Avda Argentina 4793, Lima; tel. (1) 3150800; fax (1) 315 0850; e-mail web@alicorp.com.pe; internet www.alicorp.com.pe; f. 1946; mfrs of edible oils, lard and soaps; fmrly Compañía Oleaginosa del Perú, SA; part of Grupo Romero; Pres. DIONISIO ROMERO; CEO PAOLO SACCHI GIURATO; 3,304 employees.

Alimentos Procesados, SA (Alprosa): Avda Pérez Aranibar, Variante de Uchumayo Km 1.5, Sachaca, Arequipa; tel. (54) 449473; fax (54) 449498; e-mail aqp@alprosa.com.pe; internet www.alprosa.com .pe; f. 1988; part of Corporación Cervesur; production and exportation of processed foods; Gen. Man. CARLOS PAREDES RODRÍGUEZ.

Corporación Cervesur: Edif. Parque Plaza, 13°, Calle Amador Merino Reyna 267, San Isidro, Lima; tel. (1) 6184000; fax (1) 4210373; e-mail postmaster@cercorp.com.pe; internet www .corporacioncervesur.com.pe; f. 1898; agro-industrial products, foods, real estate, services, textiles, tourism, transport; Pres. ANDRÉS VON WEDEMEYER KNIGGE; 3,838 employees.

Nestlé Perú, SA (Perulac): Avda Los Castillos, cuadra 3, Urb. Ind. Santa Rosa, Apdo 1457, Lima 1; tel. (1) 4364040; fax (1) 4361414; e-mail sentirsebien@pe.nestle.com; internet www.nestle.com.pe; wholly owned subsidiary of Nestlé Corpn (Switzerland); various foodstuffs; Chair. PETER BRABECK-LEMATHE; Zone Dir. CHRIS JOHNSON.

Unión de Cervecerías Peruanas Backus y Johnston, SA (Backus): Avda Asturias 588, Ate Vitarte, Lima; tel. (1) 3512190; fax (1) 3113166; e-mail comunicaciones.externas@backus.sabmiller .com; internet www.backus.com.pe; f. 1879 as The Backus & Johnson Brewery Ltd; beverages and bottling corpn; subsidiary of SABMiller PLC (United Kingdom); Pres. ALEJANDRO SANTO DOMINGO DÁVILA; Gen. Man. ROBERT DAMIAN PRIDAY WOODWORTH; 1,457 employees.

Rubber and Cement

Lima Caucho, SA: Carretera Central 345–349, Km 1, Zona Industrial de Santa Anita, Lima 3; tel. (1) 3170500; fax (1) 3624069; e-mail spalomino@limacaucho.com.pe; internet www.limacaucho.com.pe; f. 1955; mfrs of tyres and industrial rubber products; Dir CARLOS URIBE; 300 employees.

Unión Andina de Cementos, SA (UNACEM): Avda Atocongo 2440, Villa María del Triunfo, Lima; tel. (1) 2170200; fax (1) 2171496; e-mail postmaster@unacem.com.pe; internet www.unacem.com.pe; f. 1967; cement producers; Pres. JAIME RIZO PATRÓN REMY; Gen. Man. CARLOS UGAS DELGADO; 500 employees.

Textiles and Clothing

Compañía Industrial Nuevo Mundo, SA: Jirón José Celendón 750, Lima; tel. (1) 4154000; fax (1) 3368193; e-mail ventas@ nuevomundosa.com; internet www.nuevomundosa.com; f. 1949; mfrs of corduroy, denim and industrial fabrics; Pres. NISSIM MAYO; Gen. Man. JACQUES MAYO; 870 employees.

Creditex: Calle Los Hornos 185, Ate Vitarte, Urb. Vulcano, Casilla 2652, Lima 3; tel. (1) 7157500; fax (1) 3480488; e-mail postmaster@ creditex.com.pe; internet www.creditex.com.pe; formed by merger of Hilanderías Pimafine, Textil Trujillo-Trutex, Credisa and Textil El Progreso; part of Corporación Cervesur; 8 textile production plants; Gen. Man. JOSÉ IGNACIO LLOSA.

Michell y Compañía, SA: Avda Juan de la Torre 101, San Lázaro, Arequipa; tel. (54) 202525; fax (54) 202626; e-mail michell@michell .com.pe; internet www.michell.com.pe; f. 1931; yarn mills; Exec. Pres. MICHAEL MICHELL STAFFORD; Gen. Man. MAURICIO CHIRINOS; 419 employees.

Universal Textil, SA: Avda Venezuela 2505, Apdo 554, Lima 1; tel. (1) 3375260; fax (1) 3375270; e-mail postmaster@unitex.com.pe; internet www.universaltextil.com.pe; f. 1952; mfrs of synthetic fabrics for outerwear; part of Romero group; Chair. DIONISIO ROMERO PAOLETTI; Gen. Man. FRANCISCO JAVIER SEMINARIO DE LA FUENTE; 850 employees.

Miscellaneous

Aggreko Peru: Urb. Bocanegra, Callao, Lima; tel. (1) 2012900; internet www.aggreko.com.pe; owned by Aggreko (United Kingdom); temperature control equipment; Country Man. GUILHERME MARINHO.

Bayer, SA: Avda Paseo de la República 3074, 10°, San Isidro, Lima; tel. (1) 2113800; fax (1) 4213381; internet www.bayerandina.com; f. 1969; chemicals, plastics and pharmaceuticals mfr; Pres. DOMINIQUE DORISON; Gen. Man. CARLOS ENRIQUE CORNEJO DE LA PIEDRA; 150 employees.

British American Tobacco Perú: Pasaje Santa Rosa 256, Lima; tel. (1) 3151060; fax (1) 3151067; internet www.batperu.com; f. 1964 as Tabacalera Nacional, SA; acquired by British American Tobacco Peru Holdings Ltd in 2003; cigarette mfrs; Dir LUIZ HEEREN; 580 employees.

Indeco, SA: Avda Universitaria 583, Lima 1; tel. (1) 2054800; fax (1) 2054802; e-mail ventas.peru@nexans.com; internet www.indeco .com.pe; f. 1952; mfrs of electrical cables; Pres. ERNESTO BAERTL MONTORI; Gen. Man. JUAN ENRIQUE RIVERA DE LA BARRA; 247 employees.

Industrias Eletro Químicas, SA (IEQSA): Avda Elmer Faucett 1920, Callao, Lima; tel. (1) 6144300; fax (1) 5720118; e-mail export@ieqsa.com.pe; internet www.ieqsa.com.pe; f. 1963; zinc production; Gen. Man. Raúl Musso Vento; Pres. Carlos Gliksman Latowicka; 400 employees.

Ingenieros Constratistas Cosapi, SA: Avda República de Colombia 791, San Isidro, Lima; tel. (1) 2113500; fax (1) 2248665; e-mail postmaster@cosapi.com.pe; internet www.cosapi.com.pe; f. 1967; engineering and construction; Dir-Gen. Walter Piazza Tangüis; 4,350 employees.

Louis Dreyfus Commodities Peru: Avda Republica de Panamá 3591, 14°, San Isidro, Lima; tel. (1) 6145600; internet www.ldc.com.ar/ldc_peru; Exec. Chair. Serge Schoen.

Nissan Motors del Perú, SA: Avda Camino Real 290, San Isidro, Lima; tel. (1) 5342248; fax (1) 6145555; e-mail webmaster@maquinarias.com.pe; internet www.nissan.com.pe; f. 1957 as Maquinarias, SA; subsidiary of Nissan Motors (Japan); automobile assembly plant; Man. Carlos Chiappori Samengo; 435 employees.

Procesos Agroindustriales, SA (Proagro): Avda Rivera Navarrete 525, 2°, Lima 27; tel. (1) 2218282; fax (1) 2213233; internet www.proagro.com.pe; f. 1990; part of Corporación Cervesur; agro-industrial mfrs; Gen. Man. Andrés Juan Jochamowitz Stafford.

Quimpac, SA: Avda Nestor Gambetta 8585, Km 8.5 Carretera Ventanilla, Apdo 3741, Callao; tel. (1) 6142000; fax (1) 6142020; e-mail quimpac@quimpac.com.pe; internet www.quimpac.com.pe; f. 1964 as Química del Pacífico, SA; acquired in 1994 by Quimpac; salt production, chemical products; Gen. Man. Fernando Carranza; 3,000 employees.

Unilever Andina Perú: Francisco Graña 155, Urb. Santa Catalina, La Victoria, Lima 13; tel. (1) 4111600; fax (1) 4111846; e-mail renzo.muente@unilever.com; internet www.unilever.com.pe; f. 1971; mfrs of detergents, soaps, fats and vegetable oils; subsidiary of Unilever (United Kingdom/Netherlands); Gen. Man. Hans Eugenio Eben Ivanschitz; 675 employees.

UTILITIES

Electricity

Distriluz: Edif. Torre el Pilar, 13°, Avda Camino Real 348, San Isidro, Lima 27; tel. (1) 2115500; e-mail central@distriluz.com.pe; internet www.distriluz.com.pe; generation and distribution of electricity; operates 4 energy distribution cos: Electronoroeste, Electronorte, Hidrandina and Electrocentro; Pres. Genaro Vélez Castro.

Edegel (Empresa de Generación Eléctrica de Lima): Lima; e-mail comunicacion@edegel.com; internet www.edegel.com; privatized in 1995; generates electricity; Pres. Blanco Fernández; Gen. Man. Carlos Alberto Luna Cabrera.

Electroperú: Prolongación Pedro Miotta 421, San Juan de Miraflores, Lima 29; tel. (1) 2170000; fax (1) 2170621; internet www.electroperu.com.pe; state-owned; Pres. David Abraham Grández Gómez; Gen. Man. César Raúl Tengan Matsutahara.

EnerSur: Avda República de Panamá 3490, San Isidro, Lima 27; tel. (1) 6167979; fax (1) 6167878; e-mail contacto@enersur.com.pe; internet www.enersur.com.pe; f. 1996; part of Grupo GDF SUEZ; electricity generation and transmission; Gen. Man. Patrick Eeckelers.

Water

Autoridad Nacional del Agua: Calle Diecisiete 355, Urb. El Palomar, San Isidro, Lima; tel. and fax (1) 2243298; e-mail comunicaciones@ana.gob.pe; internet www.ana.gob.pe; f. 2008; Dir Hugo Eduardo Jara Facundo.

TRADE UNIONS

Central Unitaria de Trabajadores del Perú (CUT-PERU): Alejandro Tirado 780, Santa Beatriz, Lima 1; tel. (1) 4723691; e-mail juliocesarbazan@gmail.com; internet www.cutperu.org.pe; f. 1993; Pres. Julio César Bazán Figueroa; includes:

Confederación General de Trabajadores del Perú (CGTP): Plaza 2 de Mayo 4, Lima 1; tel. (1) 4242357; e-mail cgtp@cgtp.org.pe; internet www.cgtp.org.pe; f. 1968; Pres. Carmela Sifuentes Inostroza; Sec.-Gen. Mario Huamán Rivera.

Confederación Intersectorial de Trabajadores Estatales (CITE) (Union of Public Sector Workers): Pasaje García Calderón 170, Lima; tel. (1) 4238474; e-mail cite_peru2005_3@hotmail.com; f. 1978; Sec.-Gen. Luis Aguilar; Asst Sec. Omar Campos; 600,000 mems.

Confederación Nacional de Productores Agropecuarios de las Cuencas Cocaleras del Perú (CONPACCP): Lima; coca-growers' confederation; Sec.-Gen. Serafín Andrés Luján.

Confederación Nacional de Trabajadores (CNT): Avda Iquitos 1198, Lima; tel. (1) 4711385; e-mail david.quintana@cnt.pe; affiliated to the PPC; c. 12,000 mems; Sec.-Gen. David Quintana.

Confederación de Trabajadores del Perú (CTP): Jirón Ayacucho 173, CP 3616, Lima 1; tel. (1) 4261310; e-mail ctp7319@hotmail.com; affiliated to PAP; Sec.-Gen. Elías Grijalva.

Federación Nacional de Trabajadores Mineros, Metalúrgicos y Siderúrgicos (FNTMMS) (Federation of Peruvian Mineworkers): Avda Guzmán Blanco 240, Of. 501, Lima; tel. (1) 4234549; e-mail fntmmsp@hotmail.com; internet www.fntmmsp.org; f. 1969; Sec.-Gen. Luis Pablo Castillo Carlos; 70,000 mems.

Sindicato Unitario de los Trabajadores en la Educación del Perú (SUTEP) (Union of Peruvian Teachers): Camaná 550, Lima; tel. (1) 4276677; fax (1) 4268692; e-mail suteperu@yahoo.es; internet www.sutep.org.pe; f. 1972; Sec.-Gen. Renee Ramírez Puerta.

Transport

RAILWAYS

In 2010 there were some 2,020 km of track.

Consorcio Ferrocarriles del Perú: in 1999, following the privatization of the state railway company, Empresa Nacional de Ferrocarriles (ENAFER), the above consortium won a 30-year concession to operate the following lines:

Ferrocarril Tacna–Arica: Avda Aldarracín 484, Tacna; 62 km open; Administrator Orlando Angulo Blanco.

Ferrocarril Transandino, SA (Southern Railway): Avdas Tacna y Arica 200, Arequipa; tel. (54) 215350; fax (54) 231603; internet www.ferrocarriltransandino.com; 915 km open; operates Ferrocarril del Sur y Oriente; also operates steamship service on Lake Titicaca; Gen. Man. Alberto Valdez Galdós.

Ferrovías Central Andina, SA: Avda José Galvez Barrenechea 566, 5°, San Isidro, Lima; tel. (1) 2266363; e-mail reservas@fcca.com.pe; internet www.ferroviasperu.com.pe; f. 1999; operates Ferrocarril del Centro del Perú; Gen. Man. Jaime Fernando Blanco Ravina.

ROADS

There are 125,045 km of roads in Peru as estimated in 2010, of which approximately 23,596 km are highways and national roads. The most important highways are: the Pan-American Highway (3,008 km), which runs from the Ecuadorean border along the coast to Lima; Camino del Inca Highway (3,193 km) from Piura to Puno; Marginal de la Selva (1,688 km) from Cajamarca to Madre de Dios; and the Trans-Andean Highway (834 km), which runs from Lima to Pucallpa. In 2010 plans were announced for the Línea Amarilla toll road in Lima, funded by the Inter-American Development Bank. The estimated total cost of the project was US \$600m.

SHIPPING

Most trade is through the port of Callao, but there are 13 deep-water ports. There are river ports at Iquitos, Pucallpa and Yurimaguas, aimed at improving communications between Lima and Iquitos. At December 2013 the flag registered fleet comprised 215 vessels, totalling 453,779 grt.

Agencia Naviera Maynas, SA: Avda San Borja Norte 761, San Borja, Lima 41; tel. (1) 4752033; fax (1) 4759680; e-mail lima@navieramaynas.com.pe; internet www.peruvianamazonline.com.pe; f. 1970; owned by the Naviera Yacu Puma, SA; liner services to and from Amazon river ports and Gulf of Mexico; Pres. Luis Vargas V.; Gen. Man. Roberto Melgar Barabino.

Asociación Marítima del Perú: Avda Camino Real 479, Of. 701, San Isidro, Apdo 3520, Lima 27; tel. and fax (1) 4214939; fax (1) 2215856; internet www.asmarpe.org.pe; f. 1957; asscn of 14 int. and Peruvian shipping cos; Pres. Guillermo Acosta Rodríguez.

Consorcio Naviero Peruano, SA: Avda República de Colombia 643, 7° y 8°, San Isidro, Lima 27; tel. (1) 4116500; fax (1) 4116599; e-mail cnp@cnpsa.com; internet www.cnpsa.com; f. 1959; Gen. Man. Alejandro José Pedraza MacLean.

Empresa Nacional de Puertos, SA (Enapu): Avda Manco Capac 255, Callao; tel. (1) 6517828; fax (1) 4691010; e-mail enapu@inconet.net.pe; internet www.enapu.com.pe; f. 1970; govt agency administering all coastal and river ports; Pres. Jaime Thorne; Gen. Man. Juan Arrisueño Gómez de la Torre.

Naviera Humboldt, SA: Edif. Pacífico–Washington, 9°, Natalio Sánchez 125, Apdo 3639, Lima 1; tel. (1) 4334005; fax (1) 4330503; e-mail info@humboldt.com.pe; internet www.humboldt.com.pe; f. 1970; cargo services; Pres. Augusto Bedoya Camere; Gen. Man. Ernesto Ferraro Amico.

Naviera Transoceánica, SA (PETRANSO): Edif. Macros, 12°, Manuel Olguín 501, Lima 33; tel. (1) 5139300; fax (1) 5139321; e-mail comercial@navitranso.com; internet www.navitranso.com; f. 1956 as Petrolera Transoceánica; privatized in 1993; CEO LUIS RAFAEL MEDINA ZAMBRANO; Gen. Man. ALVARO VALDEZ.

CIVIL AVIATION

Of Peru's 294 airports and airfields, the major international airport is Jorge Chávez Airport near Lima. Other important international airports are Coronel Francisco Secada Vignetta Airport, near Iquitos, Velasco Astete Airport, near Cusco, and Rodríguez Ballón Airport, near Arequipa.

Corporación Peruana de Aeropuertos y Aviación Comercial: Aeropuerto Internacional Jorge Chávez, Avda Elmer Faucett, Callao; tel. (1) 6301000; fax (1) 5745578; e-mail sugerencias@corpac.gob.pe; internet www.corpac.gob.pe; f. 1943; Pres. WALTER HUGO TELLO CASTILLO; Gen. Man. JUAN CARLOS CROVETTO LUNA.

Domestic Airlines

Aero Cóndor: Juan de Arona 781, San Isidro, Lima; tel. (1) 4425215; fax (1) 2215783; domestic services; Pres. CARLOS PALACÍN FERNÁNDEZ; Exec. Dir LUIS EDUARDO PALACÍN.

LAN Perú, SA: Centro Comercial Real Plaza, Avda Garcilazo de la Vega 1337, Tienda 1001, Lima; tel. (1) 2138200; internet www.lan.com; f. 1999; CEO JORGE VILCHEZ; Gen. Man. NICOLÁS GOLDSTEIN.

StarPerú: Avda Comandante Espinar 331, Miraflores, Lima 18; tel. (1) 7059000; fax (1) 3324789; e-mail atencionalcliente@starperu.com; internet www.starperu.com; f. 1997; operates services to 8 domestic destinations; Gen. Man. ROMÁN KASIANOV.

Tourism

Tourism is centred on Lima, with its Spanish colonial architecture, and Cusco, with its pre-Inca and Inca civilization, notably the 'lost city' of Machu Picchu. Lake Titicaca, lying at an altitude of 3,850 m above sea level, and the Amazon jungle region to the north-east are also popular destinations. In 2012 Peru received 2,836,756 visitors. Receipts from tourism generated US $2,657m. (excluding passenger transport) in that year.

Cámara Nacional de Turismo del Perú (CANATUR): Avda Paseo de la República No 6348, Miraflores, Lima; tel. (1) 2057500; fax (1) 2427555; e-mail secretaria@canaturperu.org; internet www.canaturperu.org; f. 1971; Pres. CARLOS CANALES ANCHORENA; Exec. Dir CÉSAR ALCORTA SUERO.

Comisión de Promoción del Perú (PromPerú): Edif. Mitinci, Calle Uno Oeste, 13°, Urb. Corpac, San Isidro, Lima 27; tel. (1) 2243279; fax (1) 2243323; e-mail postmaster@promperu.gob.pe; internet www.peru.info; f. 1993; Dir of Tourism MARÍA DEL CARMEN DE REAPARAZ.

Defence

As assessed at November 2013, Peru's armed forces numbered 115,000: army 74,000, navy 24,000, air force 17,000. Paramilitary police forces numbered 77,000. There were 188,000 army reserves. Compulsory military service was reintroduced in 2013.

Defence Budget: an estimated 7,440m. new soles for defence and domestic security in 2013.

Chief of the Joint Command of the Armed Forces: Gen. LEONEL CABRERA PINO.

Joint Chief of the Armed Forces: Vice-Adm. VICTOR POMAR CALDERÓN.

Commander-General of the Army: Gen. RONALD HURTADO JIMÉNEZ.

Commander-General of the Air Force: Gen. JAIME MARIN FIGUEROA OLIVOS.

Commander-General of the Navy: Adm. CARLOS ROBERTO TEJADA MERA.

Education

The educational system in Peru is divided into three levels: the first level is for children up to six years of age in either nurseries or kindergartens. Basic education is provided at the second level. It is free and, where possible, compulsory between six and 15 years of age. Primary education lasts for six years. Secondary education, beginning at the age of 12, is divided into two stages, of two and three years, respectively. In 2012 enrolment at primary schools included 89% of pupils in the relevant age-group, while secondary enrolment included 73% of students in the relevant age-group. Higher education includes the pre-university and university levels. There were 25 national universities and 10 private universities in 2007. The 2012 budget allocated some 95,535m. new soles to education.

Bibliography

For works on South America generally, see Select Bibliography (Books)

Alcade, M. C. *The Woman in the Violence: Gender, Violence, Poverty, and Resistance in Peru.* Nashville, TN, Vanderbilt University Press, 2010.

Burt, J. M. *Political Violence and the Authoritarian State in Peru: Silencing Civil Society.* Basingstoke, Palgrave Macmillan, 2008.

Carrion, J. *The Fujimori Legacy: The Rise of Electoral Authoritarianism in Peru.* University Park, PA, 2006.

Conaghan, C. *Fujimori's Peru: Deception in the Public Sphere.* Pittsburgh, PA, University of Pittsburgh Press, 2005.

Crabtree, J. (Ed.). *Fractured Politics: Peruvian Democracy Past and Present.* London, Institute for the Study of the Americas, 2011.

Degregori, C. I. *How Difficult It Is to Be God: Shining Path's Politics of War in Peru, 1980–1999.* Madison, WI, University of Wisconsin Press, 2012.

Ewig, C. *Second-Wave Neoliberalism: Gender, Race, and Health Sector Reform in Peru.* University Park, PA, Pennsylvania State University Press, 2010.

Gagliano, J. A. *Coca Prohibition in Peru: The Historical Debates.* Tucson, AZ, University of Arizona Press, 2010.

McClintock, C., and Vallas, F. *The United States and Peru.* London, Routledge, 2002.

McNulty, S. *Voice and Vote: Decentralization and Participation in Post-Fujimori Peru.* Palo Alto, CA, Stanford University Press, 2011.

Prescott, W. H. *History of the Conquest of Peru.* London, Phoenix Press, Revised edn, 2005.

Skuban, W. E. *Lines in the Sand: Nationalism and Identity on the Peruvian-Chilean Frontier.* Albuquerque, NM, University of New Mexico Press, 2007.

St John, R. B. *Toledo's Peru: Vision and Reality.* Gainesville, FL, University Press of Florida, 2010.

Starn, O., Degregori, C., and Kirk, R. *The Peru Reader: History, Culture, Politics.* Durham, NC, Duke University Press, Revised edn, 2005.

Thorp, R., and Paredes, M. *Ethnicity and the Persistence of Inequality: The Case of Peru.* Basingstoke, Palgrave Macmillan, 2010.

Walter, R. J. *Peru and the United States, 1960-1975: How Their Ambassadors Managed Foreign Relations in a Turbulent Era.* University Park, PA, Pennsylvania State University Press, 2010.

PUERTO RICO

Geography

PHYSICAL FEATURES

The Commonwealth (Estado Libre Asociado) of Puerto Rico is a US territory based on the smallest and easternmost island of the Greater Antilles. Puerto Rico and its offshore islands comprise a Commonwealth Territory in voluntary association with the USA since 1952, but a colonial possession of the North American country since its military victory against Spain in 1898. Puerto Rico was also known as Borinquén by the Spanish, after the Amerindian name for the island, Boriquén or Boriken. To the east is more US territory, the island of St Thomas in the Virgin Islands being 64 km from the main island of Puerto Rico, although the Isla de Culebra and its own offshore islands lie mid-way between the two. About 15 km to the south-west of Culebra is Vieques, which itself lies only 11 km off the south-eastern coast of Puerto Rico island. In the west, Puerto Rico lies on the strategic Mona Passage, which separates it from the Dominican Republic on the island of Hispaniola. The two islands are only 120 km apart at the narrowest part of this sea lane from the Atlantic into the Caribbean. Their territories come closer only owing to Puerto Rico possessing the small, now uninhabited island of Mona (80 km west of the port of Mayagüez). Puerto Rico, which has 501 km of coastline and a number of fine, natural harbours, has an area of 8,959 sq km (3,459 sq miles), including about 145 sq km of inland waters.

The island of Puerto Rico is roughly rectangular in shape, with a missing south-eastern corner. It is almost 180 km in length (east–west) and nearly 60 km wide, an island of high, central peaks, surrounded by coastal lowlands, except in the west, where the mountains are sheer to the sea. The rugged mountain range, running from east to west, is known as the Cordillera Central and reaches 1,338 m (4,391 ft) at Cerro de Punta, north of the city of Ponce. Parts of the mountains are densely vegetated and there are fairly extensive protected woodland areas; for instance, there is the unique dry-forest vegetation at Guánica (700 plant species, of which 48 are endangered and 16 exist only there), or the main reserve on the island, the El Yunque tropical rainforest, which is a bird sanctuary and the home of the few remaining Puerto Rican Amazons, a critically endangered species of parrot. In the 1930s about 90% of Puerto Rico was devoted to agriculture but, as a result of post-war industrialization, the rural population migrated and forest coverage grew from 10% in the 1940s to more than 40% at the turn of the 21st century; urban areas occupied 14% of the island. To the north of the Cordillera Central is a coastal belt, where the limestone has been formed into karst country of conical hills and holes by water erosion, very different to the ancient volcanic peaks. There are also many rock caverns, with the Camuy underground river system, the third largest such in the world. Rain-catching highlands, from which many small rivers spring (falling steeply to the sea, as waterfalls over cliffs in the more rugged terrain), ensure that the island is well watered.

The largest offshore island of Puerto Rico, and the first leading east into the chain of the Lesser Antilles, is Vieques. It is about 34 km long and 6 km wide, and in the past has also been called Graciosa and then Crab Island. Two-thirds of the hilly island was owned until May 2003 by the US Navy; upon the withdrawal of naval personnel, the land was ceded to the US Department of the Interior. To the north of the eastern end of Vieques, and directly east of north-eastern Puerto Rico, is

Culebra and its cluster of smaller satellites, much of which is a nature reserve. Culebra, which bears a closer resemblance to the Virgin Islands, is some 11 km long and 5 km wide.

CLIMATE

The climate is a mild, subtropical marine one. The south of the island is often in the rain shadow of the central highlands, making it drier. Average annual rainfall is good, being about 2,300 mm (90 ins) on the north coast, and about one-half that on the south coast. Rain falls regularly from May, but mostly in July–October, which also coincides with the hurricane season—the word hurricane is derived from the name of the local Amerindian weather god, Juracan. There is little seasonal variation in temperature. Atlantic trade winds moderate the heat of the higher summer (July–August) averages of up to 30°C (86°F), while in winter the thermometer readings drop to a range of 21°C–26°C (70°F–79°F).

POPULATION

According to the 2010 census, 99% of the population identified as Hispanic/Latino, while 15% of the population were black or African American alone or in combination with another race. Another sign of the island's Spanish past is that Roman Catholics make up almost three-quarters of the total population, and there are few non-Christian religions on the island. Over one century of rule by the USA, however, has had a significant impact on the culture, not least that English has joined Spanish as an official language.

The total population of 3.6m. at mid-2014 (US Census Bureau estimate) was about 99% urbanized. The capital, San Juan (with a population of 395,326 at the 2010 census), has one of the best natural harbours in the Caribbean. It is located in the north-east of Puerto Rico, about one-third of the way along the northern coast. Traditionally, the second city is Ponce (named for Juan Ponce de León, the Spanish nobleman who led the colonization of the island and who sought the mythical fountain of eternal youth here), on the south coast, and the third city is Mayagüez, on the west coast. The territory is divided into 78 municipalities for local administration.

History

Prof. ROBERT E. LOONEY

Based on an earlier article by Prof. PETER CALVERT

INTRODUCTION

Puerto Rico was discovered by a Spanish expedition, led by the navigator Christopher Columbus, in 1493, and named by him San Juan Bautista. Known to its indigenous Taino inhabitants as Boriquén, the island takes its modern name from the name given in 1509 to its capital, Puerto Rico, now known as San Juan. The excellence of its harbour and its strategic position commanding the Mona Passage made it an important Spanish military outpost. However, the island tended to be neglected by Spain in favour of richer possessions, and it was only after trade had been opened up by royal decree in 1815 that a significant coffee and sugar plantation economy developed. The slave trade was ended in 1835, but slavery on the island was not abolished until 1873. A movement for autonomy emerged slowly after the change of government in Spain in 1868, but it was not until 1897 that Spain granted its colony a Carta Autonómica (Autonomy Charter). However, Puerto Rico's new-found autonomy abruptly ended just a year later when, following its capture by US forces during the Spanish–American War, the Caribbean possession was ceded to the USA by the Treaty of Paris.

In 1900 the island was reorganized as a US Territory and a civil government replaced the military government that had ruled since 1898. As a Territory, Puerto Rico became subject to most laws of the US Congress, and the US President appointed the Governor and members of the island's Executive Council, which functioned as an upper house of the legislative branch, the lower house being elected by popular vote. In 1917 Congress extended US citizenship to the island's inhabitants over the objections of the island's lower house, and provided for the popular election of the members of an upper house or Senate. The island's Governor, however, continued to be appointed by the US President.

Further internal self-government was achieved under President Harry S Truman in 1947, when Congress approved a law giving the people of Puerto Rico the right to elect their own Governor; a year later they chose as their first elected Governor the charismatic Luis Muñoz Marín. Now recognized as the 'father of modern Puerto Rico', it was he who persuaded the US Government to approve and in large measure to fund Operation Bootstrap (see Economy), a programme to industrialize Puerto Rico and raise its standard of living. In 1950, in yet another move towards greater internal autonomy, Congress approved Public Law 600, allowing Puerto Rico to draft its own constitution, although this was subject to congressional review. This process culminated in 1952, when, in a special referendum, the people of Puerto Rico approved the island's first Constitution under US rule. Puerto Rico was given the status of a Commonwealth (in Spanish Estado Libre Asociado, or associated free state) in its relation to the USA, and the following year, 1953, the island became self-governing. Although Puerto Rico gained wide powers of organization over its internal affairs, it has remained US sovereign territory and most federal laws have continued to apply to it, with the important exception of taxation. Critics maintain that Commonwealth status, although more liberal than earlier forms of US rule, affords fewer powers of self-government than Puerto Rico enjoyed under Spain's Carta Autonómica.

DOMESTIC POLITICS

Since 1898 Puerto Ricans have been divided on the question of the island's political relationship with the USA. The island's two dominant parties both favour continued strong links with the USA. The Partido Popular Democrático (PPD—Popular Democratic Party) supports the existing Commonwealth status with 'enhancements', such as greater autonomy, while the Partido Nuevo Progresista (PNP—New Progressive Party) favours Puerto Rico's inclusion as a US state. The island's

third party, the smaller Partido Independentista Puertorriqueño (PIP—Puerto Rican Independence Party) campaigns for independence, which in recent years has commanded the support of only some 3% of the population.

Historically, various clandestine, pro-independence forces have operated in Puerto Rico outside the electoral process. During the 1940s and 1950s the most influential of these groups was the Partido Nacionalista (Nationalist Party), led by the charismatic Pedro Albizu Campos. The Partido Nacionalista was responsible for an uprising in Puerto Rico in 1950, involving an armed attack on La Fortaleza, and a simultaneous, but unsuccessful attempt on the life of President Truman in Washington, DC, USA. It also launched an armed attack during a session of the US House of Representatives on 1 March 1954. In the 1970s another pro-independence group, the Partido Socialista Puertorriqueño (PSP—Puerto Rican Socialist Party) succeeded in raising the question of Puerto Rico's status before the UN's Decolonization Committee and the Conference of Non-Aligned Nations. With the active participation of Cuba, the Decolonization Committee approved a resolution recognizing Puerto Rico's inalienable right to self-determination and independence. However, the USA was able to prevent the UN General Assembly from returning Puerto Rico to the list of political dependencies from which it had been removed in 1953, following the approval of the Commonwealth Constitution. In the early 1980s the most important clandestine pro-independence group was the Ejército Popular Boricua (Puerto Rican Popular Army), known as 'Los Macheteros'. This group claimed responsibility for armed attacks in the USA and Puerto Rico against military targets. However, in 1985 the group fragmented, following a series of raids by the US Federal Bureau of Investigation (FBI), in both Puerto Rico and the USA. Seventeen members of Los Macheteros, including most of its leadership, were arrested and imprisoned. Its most important leader, Filiberto Ojeda Ríos, escaped, but was killed by FBI agents in an exchange of gunfire in September 2005, although his group had not been active recently. Other insurgent and dissident groups active from time to time have included the Armed Forces for National Liberation (FALN), the Armed Forces of Popular Resistance, and the Volunteers of the Puerto Rican Revolution.

The PPD, under the leadership of Muñoz Marín, dominated Puerto Rican electoral politics from 1940 to 1968; he voluntarily retired from the leadership of the party in 1964, after serving four terms as Governor. He nominated his successor, Roberto Sánchez Vilella, who was elected Governor in 1964. A division in the PPD allowed the gubernatorial candidate of the newly formed PNP, Luis A. Ferré, to win the governorship in 1968. In the 1972 gubernatorial election the PPD returned to power under the leadership of Senate President Rafael Hernández Colón. He was defeated in 1976 by the PNP Mayor of San Juan, Carlos Romero Barceló, who won again in 1980. The PPD, however, secured a majority in both the House of Representatives and the Senate, thus preventing Romero Barceló from holding a referendum to determine whether people favoured US statehood for Puerto Rico.

During 1981 dissatisfaction with Romero Barceló's leadership developed. The murder of two independence activists, allegedly by Puerto Rican police, brought into question the role of Governor Romero Barceló in the affair. He faced additional problems from his own party when the Mayor of San Juan, Hernán Padilla Ramírez, left the PNP over the issue of internal party democracy and formed a new political grouping, the Partido de Renovación Puertorriqueño (PRP—Puerto Rican Renewal Party). Padilla entered the 1984 gubernatorial election as the PRP candidate and received about 4% of the total votes cast. The division in the PNP was enough to ensure the election of former Governor Hernández Colón, the PPD candidate.

The Mayor of San Juan, Baltasar Corrada del Río, assumed control of the PNP following Romero Barceló's electoral defeat in 1984. He was the party's candidate in the 1988 election, but was defeated by Hernández Colón. For the first time in 20 years the PNP lost its traditional bastion of power, the island's capital city of San Juan, to the PPD candidate, Héctor Luis Acevedo. At his third gubernatorial inauguration, Hernández Colón announced that he would seek congressional approval for a status referendum to be held in mid-1991; subsequently, the leaders of the island's three political parties formally petitioned the US Congress to approve legislation to authorize and implement such a referendum. In late 1989, after the US House of Representatives had approved a non-binding status plebiscite bill for Puerto Rico, the US Senate's Energy and Natural Resources Committee, which had jurisdiction in the Senate over territorial matters, defeated the proposed legislation in a dramatic tied vote, thus ending the decolonization initiative. In Puerto Rico the defeat of the plebiscite measure was attributed to the reluctance of the US Congress to approve legislation that could lead to statehood for Puerto Rico.

Following the defeat of the status legislation in the US Congress, Hernández Colón's administration, which held a majority in both legislative chambers, introduced legislation establishing a charter of 'democratic rights'. The charter included guarantees of US citizenship regardless of future changes in the island's constitutional status, and made Spanish the only official language of Puerto Rico, abrogating a 1902 law that had established both Spanish and English as the island's official languages—by this time one-fifth of the inhabitants had English as their first language. The PPD also approved legislation, opposed by the PNP, to hold a plebiscite to amend the island's Constitution by adding six 'principles of self-determination'. The electorate rejected the proposed amendment with 54% voting against. The referendum represented a major defeat for Governor Hernández Colón, and a victory for the new PNP leader, Dr Pedro J. Rosselló. On 8 January 1992, one year before his gubernatorial term expired, Hernández Colón resigned as leader of the PPD, a position that he had occupied almost continuously since 1969. He was succeeded by Victoria Muñoz Mendoza, the daughter of former Governor Luis Muñoz Marín.

In the 1992 election campaign the pro-statehood PNP candidate, Rosselló, pledged to hold a referendum on the three traditional status options: statehood, enhanced Commonwealth or independence. Rosselló secured 50% of the votes cast in the November ballot, and the PNP won control of both the Senate and the House of Representatives, as well as 58 of the island's 78 municipalities.

THE STATUS ISSUE

Upon taking office in January 1993, the first bill adopted by the PNP-dominated legislature restored English as an official language. Rosselló strove to fulfil his promise to reduce crime by mobilizing the National Guard in several low-income residential areas of San Juan with high crime rates. He also moved to privatize the island's public health system by subsidizing private health insurance for the poor and selling or renting out the Government's health care facilities. Legislation presented by Rosselló to enable a status plebiscite to be held was overwhelmingly endorsed in the island legislature: on 14 November, 48.6% of the electorate voted for the retention of Commonwealth status, 46.3% supported statehood and 4% advocated independence; some 73% of registered voters participated. The results were disappointing for the governing PNP, which had hoped to win a mandate to urge the US Congress to grant the island statehood. Those in favour of continued Commonwealth status, which included the PPD, were equally disappointed that their formula had not received a clear majority and shocked to see their share of the vote, approximately 60% in the 1967 plebiscite, decline to less than 50%. In the 1996 election Rosselló was re-elected by an even greater margin than in 1992, with 51% of the votes cast, compared with 44% for the PPD's Héctor Acevedo. The PNP retained control of both houses of the island legislature and won 54 of the 78 island municipalities.

In November 1994 the Republicans won control of both the US House of Representatives and the Senate. In the following year a bill was introduced that required Puerto Rico to hold periodic plebiscites until the issue of the island's status was resolved. The legislation was withdrawn in 1996 at the insistence of the Resident Commissioner, Romero Barceló, after it had been amended to make English the sole official language of a future US state of Puerto Rico. It was revived in 1997, but was opposed by the PPD, owing to the bill's categorization of the Commonwealth as a territory of the USA. The PPD argued that when the Commonwealth was established in 1952, Puerto Rico ceased to be a colonial dependency of the USA, an interpretation that has been continually challenged by both the PNP and the PIP. In 1998, however, the US House of Representatives adopted the bill by one vote. The law authorized a plebiscite to be held that year to allow Puerto Rico to choose between Commonwealth status, independence and statehood. In the event of the electorate voting for the Commonwealth formula, a plebiscite was to be held every 10 years until the island chose either independence or statehood. However, the US Senate leadership opposed the plebiscite and the bill was not voted on in the upper house. Subsequently, Governor Rosselló held another Puerto Rican-sponsored plebiscite in December, which allowed a choice between five options: maintaining the existing Commonwealth status, defined as territorial; independence; statehood; free association with the USA (whereby the USA would yield sovereignty over Puerto Rico); or 'none of the above'. The PPD campaigned for the last of the five options, 'none of the above', which won the plebiscite with 50.2% of the vote, compared with 46.5% in favour of statehood, 2.5% in favour of independence, and less than 1% supporting free association or the existing Commonwealth status.

In June 2000, at the insistence of Rosselló, US President Bill Clinton (1993–2001) met with representatives of the island's three major political parties to discuss a new formula for resolving the status issue. However, the Republican congressional leadership boycotted the meeting. In November Sila María Calderón Serra of the PPD became the first woman to be elected Governor of Puerto Rico. Aníbal Acevedo Vilá, also of the PPD, was elected to the post of Resident Commissioner. The PPD also gained control of the Senate, the House of Representatives and 46 of the island's 78 municipalities. The simultaneous election of the Republican President George W. Bush and a Republican majority in both houses of the US Congress blocked further moves on the status issue. In July 2002 Governor Calderón announced the creation of a 'status committee' to resolve the issue; the committee was to consist of representatives of the PPD, PNP and PIP, including former Governors Hernández Colón and Romero Barceló. However, the PNP leadership rejected the proposal and the status issue continued to divide local politicians.

THE STATUS ISSUE REVIVES

In the gubernatorial election of November 2004, the PPD's candidate was Aníbal Acevedo Vilá, the island's delegate to the US Congress, while the PNP's nominee was former Governor Rosselló. The result was as close as the election of 1980. It led to a recount and a court challenge, but on 2 January 2005 Acevedo Vilá was officially declared the winner, taking office the same day. However, in the ballot to elect Puerto Rico's non-voting delegate in the US Congress, the pro-statehood PNP candidate, Luis G. Fortuño Burset, won. Rosselló's PNP also took control of the legislature from the PPD in the Senate. Rosselló himself won a seat in the Senate.

The new Governor initially promised to co-operate with opposition leaders. Then, in mid-March 2005, he presented budget proposals for 2006 that included a spending reduction of US $370m. and the elimination of some 23,000 government jobs. The proposals were rejected by the House of Representatives. After some delay, an alternative budget was proposed by the legislature, but was vetoed by Acevedo Vilá in August, the first time that this had happened in the history of the Commonwealth. Consequently, by April 2006 the Governor had to announce that there were insufficient funds to continue the business of government. When the House rejected his request to raise a temporary loan of $500m. in May, Acevedo

Vilá closed schools and government agencies, leading to popular protest. Within two weeks a temporary agreement was negotiated with legislative leaders. However, the ongoing confrontation, which had led to the Commonwealth's debt being downgraded, had done nothing to resolve the dilemma faced by successive governments of a stagnant economy where most residents were directly or indirectly dependent on the Government (see Economy).

Acevedo Vilá had promised to summon a constitutional assembly to discuss Puerto Rico's status in 2005. He favoured maintaining the Commonwealth system with changes to allow for greater autonomy, particularly in economic development. Following the 2004 election members of the island's main political parties agreed a tripartite status bill. The proposed legislation scheduled a referendum for 10 July 2005, when Puerto Rican voters would vote for or against a petition urging the US Congress and President to provide Puerto Rico with 'non-colonial and non-territorial' status options and to pledge that the results would be honoured. Although the legislation was approved by both chambers, Acevedo Vilá refused to sign it. A hastily prepared substitute bill included an amendment stating that the US Congress was fully committed to legislation that would allow the Puerto Rican electorate to choose a mechanism to determine status, either by means of a constituent assembly or through a request for a direct congressionally binding referendum, in the event that the US Government did not commit itself to a process of free self-determination before the end of 2006. Although it was unanimously approved by the Puerto Rican congress on 10 April, that legislation was also vetoed by Acevedo Vilá as 'deceptive', because it did not guarantee that the method favoured by the Governor would be adopted.

In December 2005 a US presidential task force urged the US Congress to authorize a binding referendum on the status of Puerto Rico. At the time, this proposal was not accepted and in March 2006 Congress also rejected an appeal to allow the island's inhabitants to vote in US presidential elections. However, following the 2006 elections, the US House of Representatives again took up the status issue. Sponsored by José Serrano, a New York Democratic representative, and Luis Fortuño, the Republican Resident Commissioner for Puerto Rico, the proposed Puerto Rico Democracy Act of 2007 would establish a two-stage plebiscite process. Islanders would choose first between maintaining their current Commonwealth status or assuming a 'permanent non-territorial status' and, in a second vote, between statehood and some form of independence. Ratification of Acevedo Vilá's preferred option, a permanent, 'enhanced Commonwealth' status, was considered improbable, since it would allow Puerto Ricans to enter into trade and tax agreements with third party countries and even waive certain federal laws. The Puerto Rico Self-Determination Act of 2007, that would empower Puerto Ricans from both the territory and diaspora to formulate their own system for determining Puerto Rico's future status, was submitted for consideration by the US Congress simultaneously with the Puerto Rico Democracy Act.

In February 2008 Acevedo Vilá endorsed Barack Obama as Democratic candidate for the US presidency, giving the candidate key support from one of the island's 'superdelegates' in a close fight for the Democratic presidential nomination. Obama had already promised to respect Puerto Ricans' decisions about their own future and accepted Commonwealth status, statehood and independence as valid options.

FORTUÑO IN OFFICE

In March 2008 the Governor and 12 associates were accused of improper financial dealings and tax fraud, following an FBI investigation. Acevedo Vilá denied the 19 criminal charges brought against him, which related to electoral campaigns during 1999–2004, and reiterated his plan to seek re-election in November. However, the charges were still outstanding at the time of the gubernatorial election in November 2008, in which Luis Fortuño (PNP) became the first Republican to be elected Governor since 1969, with 1,025,945 (52.8%) votes against only 801,053 (41.3%) for the incumbent. The post of Resident Commissioner in Washington, DC, was won in the concur-

rently held general election by Pedro Pierluisi, also of the PNP. In March 2009 a federal jury found former Governor Acevedo Vilá not guilty on nine counts of conspiracy, giving false statements and wire fraud.

When Fortuño took office in January 2009 the budget shortfall for that year was estimated at 46%, equivalent to US $3,490m. The new Governor presented his first budget in April, in which he proposed to address the Commonwealth's growing financial crisis by cutting $1,800m. from the $9,480m. of government spending in the current fiscal year. During the course of the year the recession in the USA abated, and in 2011 Puerto Rico benefited from increased revenues against an enlarged budget gap in 2010. This was because the loss of more than 12,000 jobs would be somewhat offset by tax cuts for both individuals and businesses that became effective in 2010, although these, in turn, were offset by an increased property tax and a new tax on students attending public universities in the territory. By May 2011 Fortuño had cut 17,000 jobs and some 20% of the Commonwealth budget since taking office. However, there was severe student unrest at the increase of college fees by some 50%.

As a sign of the times, between 2000 and 2010 there was net emigration of 288,000 people to the US mainland. The pace of emigration has accelerated in the past few years as the economic situation has worsened, with a net loss of some 54,000 migrants annually in 2011 and 2012, on an island of just over 3.6m. people. Preliminary figures for 2013 suggest the outflow is still strong. The pace of Puerto Rico's population loss is expected to increase over the remainder of the decade, but to decline by some 8% overall by 2020, according to official government projections.

In May 2009 Pierluisi introduced a bill in the US Congress, which became known as the Puerto Rico Democracy Act of 2010, to authorize a 'fair, impartial and democratic process of self-determination' for the island. It would provide for a referendum asking islanders if they wanted to change their political status. If the answer was no, eight years would elapse before the same question would be asked again. However, if the answer was yes, a second referendum would be held, offering a choice between statehood, independence, or 'sovereignty in association with the United States'. In April 2010 the bill was adopted by the US House of Representatives; however, the proposal was not approved by the Senate and lapsed at the end of the session.

In March 2011 the President's Task Force on Puerto Rico's Status reiterated in its third report that no relationship, mutually agreed, could override the right of a future US Congress to change it. The Task Force recommended a two-stage plebiscite: the first vote would offer the electorate a choice between independence or some sort of association with the USA; the second vote would ask the electorate to choose from the available status options, as determined by the outcome of the first vote. In November the Puerto Rican legislature agreed to hold a referendum on the issue concurrently with the legislative and gubernatorial elections of 6 November 2012. Any change to the status quo would require the approval of the President and the US Congress.

On 19 August 2012, in a separate constitutional referendum, the electorate voted against proposals to reduce the size of the Legislative Assembly and to restrict bail rights. In both cases, the 'no' vote represented approximately 55% of the ballot, although the rate of voter participation was just 35.5%.

During 2012 several members of the Caribbean Community and Common Market (CARICOM) threatened to file a complaint with the World Trade Organization owing to concerns about the USA's 'cover over' programme, which redistributed 98% of rum excise duties collected in the USA to Puerto Rico and the US Virgin Islands. CARICOM argued that the programme was effectively an illegal subsidization scheme and that it was distorting the regional rum market, leaving its members at a disadvantage. In spite of this criticism, in January 2013 the US Congress approved the extension of the 'cover over' programme for a further two years.

Puerto Rico has been approached by Venezuela to join Petrocaribe, an alliance that many Caribbean states have with Venezuela to receive oil on preferential terms. Heads of state of Petrocaribe nations have discussed promoting a regional economic bloc to increase the flow of food and services between member nations. However, likely opposition from the US Department of State means that despite affording it potentially huge savings on oil import expenditure, Petrocaribe is not a viable option for Puerto Rico.

2012 ELECTION AND REFERENDUM

PPD President Alejandro García Padilla won 47.9% of the ballot in the November 2012 gubernatorial election, narrowly defeating Fortuño, who garnered 47.0%. In the legislative polls, the PPD secured control of 28 of the 51 seats in the House of Representatives and 18 of the 27 Senate seats. The remaining seats were secured by the PNP, with the exception of one Senate seat won by the PIP. Pierluisi was re-elected as Resident Commissioner in Washington, DC. In the concurrent status referendum, 54.0% of voters declared themselves to be dissatisfied with the territory's existing relationship with the USA, with 61.2% of those who answered the follow-up question supporting a transition to statehood, 33.3% voting in favour of sovereign free association and 5.5% endorsing independence. (However, when including blank votes, the statehood option only accounted for 45% of the ballot.) Turnout (in the elections and the referendum) was 78.2%.

As the referendum results were non-binding, President Obama reiterated the view that unless there was a clear and strong majority in favour of a change in status, Congress would be unlikely to act on the matter in the short term.

One thing lacking in the debate over statehood versus the Commonwealth status quo was some sense of the economic costs and benefits of each alternative. In April 2014 the US Government Accountability Office (GAO) issued a report addressing these issues. Both sides of the debate have claimed the report's findings support their position.

Those advocating statehood point to the report's assertion that Puerto Rico would receive an additional US $5,000,000m. annually to the funds currently earmarked for the Commonwealth under various federal-transfer programmes, including Medicare, Medicaid, Social Security and the Nutritional Assistance Program.

However, the report documented how these benefits entailed costs. Those in support of the status quo refer to the report's claim that there would be a sharp increase in taxes with statehood. According to the GAO, residents in Puerto Rico would pay in aggregate between US $2,200,000m. and $2,300,000m. in federal taxes, as opposed to the $20m. paid under the current commonwealth status.

Corporations, in contrast, would pay a total in federal taxes of anything from zero to US $3,400,000m. Clearly the wide range of outcomes stems from uncertainty as to how many US corporations currently on the island for tax reasons would choose to relocate. The potential exodus of US firms from the island could mean the loss of about 80,000 jobs. However, statehood could make Puerto Rico a more attractive destination for other US investors, thereby helping the island's economy.

The report did not make any recommendations with regard to political status. Given that neither side's position received a clear victory, and the fact that the US Congress is reluctant to act, the issue is not likely to be revisited for some years.

RECENT DEVELOPMENTS

In mid-2014 the Puerto Rican economy continued to suffer one of its most protracted crises. The situation may intensify as the full effects of the Government's austerity measures are felt. With rapidly falling popularity, Governor García Padilla may find that further austerity measures have an adverse impact on his public standing.

The Government's attempts at stabilizing its finances have been met with opposition from various sources. García Padilla presented a pension reform proposal to the island's legislature under pressure from credit rating agencies in February 2014. The legislature quickly approved the plan, known as Law 160, but this was promptly challenged by teachers' organizations, who mounted a challenge in the Commonwealth's Supreme Court. On 14 April the Supreme Court rejected the legislation. As it stands, the teachers' pension plan faces an actuarial deficit of more than US $10,000,000m. The court's decision will force the Governor to start looking for new ways to reform the pension plan, which only has sufficient assets to remain solvent until 2020.

Economy

Prof. ROBERT E. LOONEY

Based on an earlier article by Prof. PETER CALVERT

INTRODUCTION

Until the 1950s Puerto Rico's economy was based on agriculture; in the 19th and early 20th centuries its principal cash crops were coffee, sugar and tobacco. However, following the Second World War the Government planned to encourage economic growth through industrialization. The governing Partido Popular Democrático (PPD—Popular Democratic Party) decided to seek external capital, mainly from the USA, to spur economic growth. US capital was encouraged to invest in manufacturing facilities on the island through a unique combination of low wages supported by massive local and federal tax exemptions. The strategy was dubbed Operation Bootstrap, the results of which were immediate, and astonishing, and soon became known throughout the world. Real gross national product (GNP) increased by 68% in the 1950s and by 90% in the 1960s. By 1970 manufacturing constituted approximately 40% of the island's gross domestic product (GDP) and unemployment declined to 10% of the labour force—astonishing progress given the island's traditional agricultural economy with its massive seasonal unemployment and widespread underemployment.

The extraordinary growth produced by Operation Bootstrap ended following the world petroleum crisis of 1973. The dramatic increases in world oil prices imposed by the Organization of the Petroleum Exporting Countries (OPEC) severely impeded Puerto Rico's capacity to sustain high economic growth, dependent as it was on imported oil and gas to meet all but a tiny fraction of its energy needs. At the same time, wage increases and reduced US tariffs on foreign products hampered Puerto Rico's ability to attract US capital, compared with other low-wage economies.

Governor Rafael Hernández Colón, during his first term in office (1973–77), attempted to combat the economic slowdown through aggressive government intervention in the economy. Under his leadership, the Government purchased the Puerto Rico Telephone Company, the two major shipping lines serving Puerto Rico and US ports, and most of the island's sugar mills. Nevertheless, these efforts did not slow the relative economic decline and Puerto Rico's growth rate dropped to an annual average of 1.8% between 1974 and 1984. Economic disaster was avoided only by a massive increase in federal (US Government) funds, which offset the decline in the productive sectors.

Governor Hernández Colón won his second term in office in 1984 on the strength of his pledge to make job creation his main priority. His new term of office coincided with the recovery of the USA from the 1981 recession, which was accompanied by a fall in world petroleum prices. Nevertheless, he was faced with a serious challenge from the US Administration of President

Ronald Reagan (1981–89), which sought to eliminate the special federal tax incentives for US investment in Puerto Rico. In response, Hernández Colón proposed an ambitious 'twin-plant' programme to promote industrial development in the Caribbean. His idea was to use the capital generated by the operations of US companies in Puerto Rico to invest in secondary Caribbean plants that would feed the companies' Puerto Rico operations. His programme won the approval of the Reagan Administration, which was deeply committed to assisting the Caribbean region under the Caribbean Basin Initiative, and efforts to eliminate the federal tax incentives for Puerto Rico were subsequently postponed.

In 1993 the incoming administration of Governor Pedro J. Rosselló (1993–2001) structured a new economic development programme in which the private sector was to be the primary vehicle for economic development. In 1996–2004 Puerto Rico's GDP grew, in real terms, by an average of 3.7% per year, as the island mirrored the general success of the US economy over the same period. However, in 1996, in a major reversal for the island, the US Congress approved legislation ending the island's tax credit (see below), the same federal tax incentive—used to attract manufacturing investment from US corporations to Puerto Rico—that the Reagan Administration had tried to eliminate in the 1980s.

The results of the tax change were disastrous. The informal economy began growing until it accounted for around one-quarter of the economy. This forced legal companies to assume additional tax burdens. The domestic tax code set high rates, but was full of exemptions, enabling many companies to avoid them altogether. The domestic deficit and external debt expanded rapidly and the economy entered a lengthy period of recession beginning in 2006.

The unemployment rate rose sharply from 10.5% in 2006 to 16.0% in 2011, in part reflecting the impact of the global economic downturn on, *inter alia*, the construction and housing markets. The financial crisis prevented the Government from resorting to the usual remedy of increasing the size of the state sector. Instead, the administration of Luis Fortuño (2008–13) eliminated some 20,000 government jobs, reducing the Territory's fiscal deficit by some 90%.

Since assuming office in January 2013, the García Padilla administration finds itself in a much more difficult situation than its predecessors because of the severe limitations in terms of new debt that could be issued. In order to address the situation, it has had to accept fiscal restructuring, including sharp increases in taxes.

AGRICULTURE

Only 6.8% of the land area of the country was regarded by FAO as arable in 2011, with 4.5% under permanent crops and 10.1% permanent pasture. However, the sector remained a major contributor to the economy. In 1914 agriculture accounted for approximately 70% of the island's GDP. By 2013 this figure had declined to 0.7%. Similarly employment in the sector declined from a high of 263,577 in 1930 to 19,000 by 2013. Traditional crops such as sugar have disappeared completely. The decline of coffee has been almost as spectacular. Having enjoyed world renowned status in the late 19th century, when it accounted for nearly 80% of the island's exports, it now meets just 25% of domestic demand.

The composition of production has changed slightly in recent years with coffee contracting from 5.5% of farm income in 2004 to 4.3% in 2012. Livestock, however, has maintained its share of approximately 50% of farm income. Other major crops contributing to farm income in 2012 included fruit (3.2%) and starchy vegetables (10.8%). Currently Puerto Rico imports about 80% of its food, representing expenditure of between US $3,500m. and $4,000m. annually, at wholesale value.

MANUFACTURING

The growth of manufacturing in Puerto Rico has been almost entirely the result of special tax benefits from both the US and Puerto Rican Governments. Under US law (Section 936 of the US Tax Code), the income of a subsidiary of a US corporation operating a manufacturing facility in Puerto Rico was eligible to receive a federal tax credit, which practically exempted the corporation from the payment of US income taxes on its Puerto Rican earnings. The Puerto Rican Government in 1948 matched the federal possessions tax credit with its own equally generous tax incentive programme. The combined incentives created a powerful lure to attract US corporate investment to Puerto Rico. In the early years of Operation Bootstrap the island attracted the labour-intensive textiles and apparel industries. Over the years, and as the federal incentive grew more generous, Puerto Rico manufacturing became more capital intensive and diversified, marked by substantial investment in sectors such as pharmaceuticals and medical products, scientific instruments, computers, microprocessors, and electrical goods.

Puerto Rico's industrialization programme began to decline from 1996, when the US Congress repealed Section 936. Nevertheless, the full impact of the credit's elimination came only in December 2005, at the scheduled end of the 10-year 'grace' period, granted to companies operating in Puerto Rico at the time of the repeal of the tax credit. Growth in the manufacturing sector in the late 1990s resulted mainly from the expansion of those US companies (largely from the pharmaceutical sector) that were converting their legal structures to become Controlled Foreign Corporations (CFCs). Under US tax law, a CFC does not have to pay federal taxes on income earned in a foreign jurisdiction as long as the money remains outside the USA. For the purpose of US tax law, Puerto Rico is considered a foreign tax jurisdiction, so CFCs pay only royalties to their parent companies plus 10% in local taxes. This provision has been particularly attractive to pharmaceutical companies and other large corporations with global manufacturing and distribution networks. Since 1996 some 57 large manufacturing firms operating in Puerto Rico have reincorporated as CFCs; the majority engaged, however, not in manufacturing but in services (31.4%), information technology (25.9%) and the distribution and transportation of goods (21.7%).

The manufacturing sector has increased its share of GDP in recent years, expanding from 42.7% in 2004 to 46.5% in 2013. The sector is still dominated by chemicals, largely pharmaceuticals, although this is changing. In 2004 chemicals accounted for 72.3% of total manufacturing, but declined to 64.9% in 2013. On the other hand computers and electronics increased from 11.2% to 21.9% over the same period. The food industry also declined, with its share falling from 2.9% in 2004 to 1.7% in 2013.

The decline in Puerto Rico's pharmaceutical industry reflects the global decline of branded pharmaceuticals, which are in the middle of a major period of patent-expiration. As patents of branded medicines expire, they are quickly replaced by generic drugs made around the world. About 50 patented drugs, worth more than US $1,000m. in sales, will expire by 2018, including about 10 manufactured in Puerto Rico. The expiry of the US Internal Revenue Service Section 936 in 2006 also contributed to the decline.

The sector is also likely to be seriously affected by the island's government obligation bonds degraded to junk status in early 2014. Specifically, firms will find it harder to get capital to establish operations on the island, while manufacturers already operating in Puerto Rico could face higher electrical and water rates owing to the downgrade, since these public corporations will be forced to increase rates because the commonwealth will be unable to support these utilities.

Currently the Government is focused on attracting South American pharmaceutical companies to Puerto Rico so that they can become established and familiar with the procedures for US Food and Drug Administration compliance needed to gain entry to US markets. The Government is also promoting Puerto Rico's advantages as a place to make generic drugs in facilities previously devoted to drugs whose patents have expired.

These initiatives may bring major benefits to the island. In a November 2012 study Estudios Técnicos Inc. found that Puerto Rico's pharmaceutical industry generated nearly 18,000 direct and 68,000 indirect jobs. The study found at the time that the payroll for the industry was more than US $1,100m., and the average salary was $62,000. The pharmaceutical industry also paid $3,000m. in taxes to local governments, and provided 57.4% of all local manufacturing jobs.

The Government's other strategy towards manufacturing is to diversify by growing and deepening the island's other manufacturing clusters, of which seven are targeted: electronics, information technology, aerospace, biotechnology, medical devices, agroindustry and textiles (the latter primarily for military uniforms). The Government is also hoping to attract firms that are bringing some of their operations back to the USA from East Asia—a process known as reshoring.

COMMERCE

Wholesale and retail trade played a significant role in Puerto Rico's economy, although the sector has been growing at a slower rate than the overall economy in recent years. In 2004 commerce accounted for 8.8% (3.2% for wholesale trade, 5.6% for retail trade) of GDP, but by 2013 this had fallen to 7.7% (2.9% for wholesale trade, 4.8% for retail trade). Nevertheless, the sector is the second largest employer on the island, accounting for approximately 25% of all jobs.

The sector has taken the brunt of the island's post-2006 recession, but was showing signs of recovery in early 2014 with upcoming developments, such as the Mall of San Juan shopping centre scheme, due to open in March 2015, and a Grupo Sambil project in Guaynabo, expected to be completed in the same year. The island's bond downgrades in early 2014 are likely to have some of their greatest effects on shopping centres with consumers more cautious and mall renters likely to attempt to renegotiate lower rental agreements.

Another problem facing the sector stems from the fact that retail giants Wal-Mart and Target have had second thoughts about their plans to do business in Puerto Rico, with Wal-Mart reconsidering its intention to open more stores on the island for the foreseeable future, while Target has called off a long-intended entry into the local market, according to industry sources. Reasons given by both chains centre on uncertainty over the tax situation they are likely to encounter, as well as pending legislation that aims to protect small and medium-size businesses (pymes by its Spanish acronym) by imposing additional requirements for the establishment of so-called 'megastores'.

FINANCE

Finance and insurance, together with real estate and rental employ 3%–4% of the island's workforce, and their contribution to GDP has increased from 18.3% in 2004 to 20.4% in 2013. However, the two sectors have had considerably different patterns of growth in recent years with banking and insurance contracting from 7.5% of GDP in 2004 to 5.6% in 2013, while real estate and rentals expanded from 10.8% in 2004 to 14.8% in 2013. The financial sector is represented by a broad spectrum of services, from large commercial banks and investment brokerage houses, to small loan companies and money transfer outlets.

The Commonwealth's prolonged post-2006 economic slump has taken a heavy toll on the financial sector. In May 2010 a massive intervention by the US Federal Deposit Insurance Corporation (FDIC) was needed to stave off the collapse of the Commonwealth's banking sector. The FDIC seized the assets of three local depository institutions—Eurobank, RG Premier Bank and Westernbank—with a view to recapitalization by sale. This followed the closure at the end of April of all branches of Westernbank, Puerto Rico's oldest and second largest bank, and the transfer of its business to Banco Popular de Puerto Rico, the island's largest firm. Through an FDIC silent auction, Oriental Bank and Trust took over the assets of Eurobank, while Scotiabank de Puerto Rico acquired those of RG Premier Bank.

Unfortunately, the sector's problems did not end with the 2010 consolidation. While down from their 2009 peak of US $9,500m. (15.9% of total loans), delinquency levels remained high in 2013, at $5,200m. (11.6% of total loans), especially among residential mortgages, at $2,800m., representing 16% of total delinquent loans, a level more than twice the US average.

In mid-2014 the banks were still facing a number of threats to their profitability and even survival. The island's economic situation has eroded residential prices, on top of a housing-inventory surplus linked to foreclosures, that since 2008 have increased continuously each year, reaching 10.3% in 2013.

In May 2014 credit rating agencies Moody's and Fitch warned that weak economic fundamentals in Puerto Rico and ongoing budgetary challenges for the island's Government were likely to weigh on the operating performance and credit profiles of local banks. According to Fitch, economic conditions in Puerto Rico have kept the non-performing assets (NPA) of banks on the island very high relative to US mid-tier and community banks. Combined, the NPA rate of Fitch-rated Puerto Rican banks was 11.9% at the end of 2013, compared with 2.5% for similar sized mainland lending institutions.

TOURISM

Puerto Rico is a major vacation destination because of its fine year-round climate and air and sea transportation links. The island's tourist infrastructure is well developed with many hotels, guest houses and condominium developments located along its coastline. In the 1990s there was a boom in hotel construction, as a result of tax incentives and other financial assistance from the island's Government.

Tourism accounts for approximately 2% of the island's GDP, while employing a similar percentage of the workforce. In recent years the island has also become an attractive destination for many cruise ships. Cruise ship arrivals increased by 16% in 2013/14, and were thus one of the few local economic activities that have experienced healthy growth in recent years.

TRANSPORTATION

Transportation is another sector that has grown more slowly than the economy as a whole in recent years. As a result, its share of GDP declined from 1.1% in 2004 to 0.9% in 2013. The sector's employment has also declined from 2.1% of the workforce in 2004 to 1.7% in 2013.

The island's transport facilities are excellent. The Luis Muñoz Marín International Airport, in San Juan, was served by approximately 45 US and international airlines. In 2011/12 the airport served over 8.4m. passengers. The airport offered daily direct air services between San Juan and more than seven US cities, and regular scheduled services to other Caribbean islands and major Latin American and European cities. There are 26,186 km of roads, 94% of which are paved, 96 km of narrow-gauge railway and 10 major ports apart from San Juan itself, regarded by many as the finest in the Caribbean. In recent years, however, the Government's increasingly constrained budgets have prevented any major new transport projects or upgrades to the current system.

THE PUBLIC SECTOR

The Government plays a critical role in the island's economy, both in terms of its employment, but also its level of expenditures. In 2013 the public sector accounted for 217,000 jobs or 21.1% of the employed labour force, making it the Commonwealth's third largest employer after services (348,000) and trade (229,000). On the expenditure side, government purchases, while still significant, have also been declining in importance in recent years. Government consumption fell from 17.6% in 2004 to 15.1% in 2013. On the other hand public investment fell at a more rapid rate, declining from 8.3% in 2004 to 4.8% by 2013. Clearly the decline in the public sector stems from the Government's fiscal constraints. In turn, the public sector's retrenchment has reinforced the country's ongoing recession.

In the 1990s the Puerto Rican Government privatized several state-run businesses, notably hotels, food-processing facilities, telecommunications and transportation companies, and hospitals. In recent years, in addition to transferring the management of the Luis Muñoz Marín International Airport to the private sector, budgetary pressures have forced the Government to attempt various reforms to make its remaining enterprises capable of operating without budgetary subsidies or deficit financing.

ENERGY

Puerto Rico has few natural sources of energy and must import most of its needs; the Commonwealth is the largest importer of energy in the Caribbean. The island generates about 55% of its energy from oil, while natural gas accounts for about 28% and coal 16% of energy production. Renewable energy accounts for a mere 1%.

The cost of electricity for Puerto Rico residents averaged 26.78 cents per kilowatt-hour (kWh) during 2012, more than twice the US average of 12 cents per kWh, and many business and finance experts believe that expensive electricity is the biggest obstacle to attracting offshore investment and operating a business on the island. The Government is attempting to reduce power rates and has initiated a series of reforms. Those aimed at the Puerto Rico Electric Power Authority (commonly known as PREPA) include the creation of a regulatory board, rate reductions by as much as 20% by the end of 2014 and a plan for cutting energy costs by 50% in 12 years. PREPA's plan is to carry out investments on a scale large enough to expand gas usage and reduce oil dependence to as low as 2% by 2017. However, PREPA's credit rating has been downgraded to 'junk' level and consequently the company will be hard pressed to undertake the required infrastructure projects critical to implementing its plans.

TRADE

Although Puerto Rico for import/export purposes is a distinct entity, the Commonwealth lies within the customs barrier of the USA. Consequently, exports and imports are dominated by that country. Puerto Rico is the ninth largest exporter in the western hemisphere in terms of the total value of its exports, ahead of such larger countries as Peru, Ecuador and Bolivia.

The island's export relationship with the USA has weakened somewhat in recent years. In 2004 82.5% of Puerto Rico's exports were destined for the US market. However by 2013 this figure had dropped to 71.6%. On the other hand, the island's imports form the USA remained at around 45% for both years.

Puerto Rico normally runs a large trade balance with the USA and a deficit with the rest of the world. The net result has been consistently large trade surpluses. The Commonwealth's trade balance was US $16,182.6m. in 2004, increasing slightly to $17,358.2m. in 2013.

As Puerto Rico's exports became more diversified by destination, they have become more concentrated in recent years. In both 2004 and 2013 the country's top three exports were pharmaceuticals, food and medical supplies, with the share of pharmaceuticals increasing from 65.7% to 70.3%, medical supplies from 5.7% to 7.6% and food from 4.8% to 6.5%. Patterns are more mixed on the import side. Between 2004 and 2013 the share of pharmaceuticals declined from 39.1% to 29.8%, while basic chemicals also declined from 8.4% to 7.4%. On the other hand food imports increased from 5.3% to 7.4%.

The Government's efforts to increase trade have focused on five target areas: Florida and the east coast of the USA; the US Hispanic/Latino market; Mexico (a NAFTA trading partner); the Dominican Republic, the island's fourth largest trading partner; and the Greater Caribbean area. The island Government believed that it was competitive internationally in food and beverage production, contract manufacturing, technology, construction and associated services (particularly engineering and architecture), environmental engineering and finance. Puerto Rico intended to strengthen bilateral relations with other important economies, including Costa Rica, Panama, Chile and the European Union, and to become more active in regional economic organizations.

PUBLIC FINANCE

Puerto Rico is constitutionally required to operate within a balanced budget. The island's Constitution provided for a limitation on the amount of general debt that could be issued, equal to 15% of the average annual revenues raised over the previous two years. Historically, Puerto Rico kept within its constitutional bounds; as late as mid-2002 the Commonwealth had a 6.7% borrowing margin, well within its 15% limit. However, the impact of the economic downturn in the USA led to a budget crisis in the island in May 2008, when the Government ran out of money two months before the end of the fiscal year. The contraction of the Puerto Rican economy beginning in 2006, the global recession beginning in 2008 and the large out migration of Puerto Ricans to the USA has resulted in a series of chronic deficits, financed by spiralling debt.

Governor García Padilla's first year in office saw the introduction of a number of new taxes, designed to eliminate the Government's fiscal deficit as quickly as possible. A cornerstone of the new taxes was the patente nacional, or additional tax on gross income (more commonly known as the gross receipts tax). The patente nacional, was expected to raise roughly US $500m., or more than one-third of the projected new tax revenue for 2013/14. This is a tax based on revenue from businesses with at least $1m. in revenue, regardless of profits. There has been an outcry from the business community that that tax will force a number of firms into bankruptcy. There is some credibility to this position. Tax revenues in the first 10 months of the fiscal year ending April 2014 were $442m. below expectations. One suggested explanation was that many businesses were unable to raise the cash to comply with the new patente.

The inability to produce a balanced budget for fiscal 2014 forced the Government to enact an emergency fiscal law in late June 2014. The legislation is intended to allow the administration to make the spending cuts necessary for a balanced budget. The emergency law will be in place for three years but could be extended if three conditions are not met: the previous fiscal year must end with a balanced budget; a Wall Street credit rating agency must peg Puerto Rico's general obligation bonds at investment grade; and the economic growth forecast for the upcoming fiscal year must be at least 1.5%. A Senate amendment would allow agencies to unfreeze collective bargaining accords if their fiscal conditions improve before then.

The fiscal emergency measure was presented along with the Governor's US $9,640m. spending plan for 2014/15, which called for more than $1,400m. in cuts and adjustments by consolidating 25 government agencies and imposing an average 8% spending reduction for most agencies. The budget included $775m. to pay off debt—$525m. more than in the previous year's budget. At least 100 underutilized public schools were to be closed.

Statistical Survey

Source (unless otherwise stated): Puerto Rico Planning Board, POB 41119, San Juan, 00940-1119; tel. (787) 723-6200; internet www.jp.gobierno.pr.

Area and Population

AREA, POPULATION AND DENSITY

Area (sq km)	8,959*
Population (census results)	
1 April 2000	3,808,610
1 April 2010	3,725,789
Males	1,785,171
Females	1,940,618
Population (estimates at mid-year)†	
2012	3,672,561
2013	3,645,648
2014	3,620,897
Density (per sq km) at mid-2014	404.2

* 3,459 sq miles.
† Source: Population Division, US Census Bureau.

POPULATION BY AGE AND SEX
(population estimates at mid-2014)

	Males	Females	Total
0–14 years	335,142	319,765	654,907
15–64 years	1,129,944	1,222,038	2,351,982
65 years and over	265,674	348,334	614,008
Total	1,730,760	1,890,137	3,620,897

Source: Population Division, US Census Bureau.

PRINCIPAL TOWNS
(population at 2010 census)

San Juan (capital) .	395,326	Caguas	142,893
Bayamón . . .	208,116	Guaynabo . . .	97,924
Carolina	176,762	Arecibo	96,440
Ponce	166,327		

Source: Population Division, US Census Bureau.

BIRTHS, MARRIAGES AND DEATHS

	Registered live births		Registered marriages		Registered deaths	
	Number	Rate (per 1,000)*	Number	Rate (per 1,000)*	Number	Rate (per 1,000)*
2003	50,803	13.3	25,236	6.6	28,843	7.5
2004	51,239	13.4	23,650	6.2	29,601	7.7
2005	50,687	13.3	23,511	6.2	29,977	7.8
2006	48,744	12.8	23,219	6.1	28,589	7.5
2007	46,738	12.4	21,635	5.7	29,320	7.8
2008	45,683	12.1	18,626	5.0	29,096	7.7
2009	44,836	12.0	18,407	4.9	29,184	7.8
2010	42,203	11.3	17,786	4.8	29,290	7.9

* Rates calculated using mid-year population estimates from Population Division, US Census Bureau.

Sources: Department of Health, Commonwealth of Puerto Rico; Population Division, US Census Bureau.

Life expectancy (years at birth): 78.5 (males 74.9; females 82.4) in 2012 (Source: World Bank, World Development Indicators database).

ECONOMICALLY ACTIVE POPULATION
('000 persons aged 16 years and over)

	2010/11	2011/12	2012/13
Agriculture, forestry and fishing .	17	17	17
Manufacturing	97	95	95
Construction	48	50	47
Trade	234	231	229
Transportation, communication and other public utilities . .	48	40	47
Finance, insurance and real estate	39	34	29
Services	333	342	348
Government	230	225	217
Total employed	1,047	1,035	1,030
Unemployed	202	185	167
Total labour force	1,249	1,221	1,197

Note: Totals may not be equal to the sum of components, owing to rounding.

Health and Welfare

KEY INDICATORS

Total fertility rate (children per woman, 2013)	1.6
Under-5 mortality rate (per 1,000 live births, 2011) . . .	8.8
Physicians (per 1,000 head, c. 2007)	2.2
Hospital beds (per 1,000 head, 2012)	3.4
Health expenditure (public, 2004): % of GDP	3.5

Source: mainly Pan American Health Organization.

For other sources and definitions see explanatory note on p. vi.

Agriculture

PRINCIPAL CROPS
('000 metric tons, FAO estimates)

	2010	2011	2012
Tomatoes	17.0	20.2	22.0
Pumpkins, squash and gourds .	11.6	11.6	12.0
Bananas	62.2	68.2	70.0
Plantains	81.1	90.5	92.0
Oranges	15.4	12.8	13.5
Guavas, mangoes and mangosteens	13.8	12.7	13.0
Pineapples	24.9	32.5	33.0
Coffee, green	5.0	5.2	5.8

Aggregate production (may include official, semi-official or estimated data): Total fruits (excl. melons) 218.0 in 2010, 237.4 in 2011, 242.6 in 2012; Total roots and tubers 13.0 in 2010, 12.7 in 2011, 13.0 in 2012; Total vegetables (incl. melons) 40.7 in 2010, 46.1 in 2011, 49.0 in 2012.

Source: FAO.

LIVESTOCK
('000 head, year ending September, FAO estimates)

	2010	2011	2012
Asses	2	2	2
Cattle	380.0	380.0	380.0
Sheep	6.3	6.3	6.3
Goats	3.3	3.3	3.3
Pigs	50.0	50.0	50.0
Horses	6.6	6.6	6.6
Chickens	14,000	14,500	14,600

Source: FAO.

LIVESTOCK PRODUCTS
('000 metric tons, FAO estimates)

	2010	2011	2012
Cattle meat	10.3	10.3	10.3
Pig meat	11.9	12.0	12.5
Chicken meat	55.0	58.0	58.0
Cows' milk	378.6	380.0	382.0
Hen eggs	11.7	11.7	11.7

Source: FAO.

Fishing

(metric tons, live weight)

	2010	2011	2012
Capture	1,898	1,461	1,268
Groupers	10	6	3
Snappers and jobfishes . . .	29	21	66
Caribbean spiny lobster . . .	148	109	72
Stromboid conchs	915	741	793
Aquaculture*	17	20	20
Tilapias*	3	5	5
Total catch*	1,915	1,481	1,288

* FAO estimates.

Source: FAO.

Industry

PRODUCTION

	2006	2007	2008
Cement ('000 metric tons) . . .	1,550	1,390	1,300

Source: US Geological Survey.

Electric energy (million kWh): 22,631.1 in 2010/11; 22,191.5 in 2011/12; 21,954.6 in 2012/13.

Finance

CURRENCY AND EXCHANGE RATES

Monetary Units
United States currency: 100 cents = 1 US dollar (US $).

Sterling and Euro Equivalents (30 May 2014)
£1 sterling = US $1.682;
€1 = US $1.361;
US $100 = £59.45 = €73.47.

BUDGET
(US $ '000, general government operations, year ending 30 June)

Revenue*	2010/11	2011/12	2012/13
Income tax	4,749,942	4,068,802	4,229,193
Excise tax	2,106,784	2,695,543	2,870,741
Sales and use tax	555,990	543,266	543,170
Other taxes	83,589	90,514	81,449
Charges for services	632,005	624,069	698,373
Intergovernmental transfers . .	6,002,950	6,634,415	6,502,506
Interest	22,138	18,200	16,249
Other revenue	597,455	369,848	284,491
Total	14,750,853	15,044,657	15,226,172

Expenditure	2010/11	2011/12	2012/13
General government services . .	1,145,340	1,935,622	894,282
Public safety	2,044,398	2,315,808	2,186,195
Health	2,928,477	2,942,970	3,220,682
Public housing and welfare . .	3,734,850	3,399,071	3,627,405
Education	4,450,805	4,596,366	4,831,777
Economic development . . .	460,878	578,374	794,859
Intergovernmental transfers . .	429,702	376,767	470,135
Capital outlays	227,003	131,488	205,755
Principal on debt servicing . .	658,752	1,087,775	154,353
Interest	312,462	201,394	187,535
Debt issuance costs	—	4,876	—
Total	16,392,667	17,570,511	16,572,978

* Excluding net financing (US $ '000): 1,938,050 in 2010/11; 1,669,688 in 2011/12; 503,975 in 2012/13.

Source: Department of the Treasury, Commonwealth of Puerto Rico.

COST OF LIVING
(Consumer Price Index; base: 2006 = 100)

	2011	2012	2013*
Food (incl. non-alcoholic beverages)	117.8	120.2	122.0
Housing	113.3	114.3	115.0
Clothing	95.7	95.1	94.2
All items (incl. others) . . .	113.7	115.2	116.4

* Preliminary.

NATIONAL ACCOUNTS
(US $ million at current prices, year ending 30 June)

Expenditure on the Gross Domestic Product

	2010/11	2011/12	2012/13*
Government final consumption expenditure	10,506.6	10,784.7	10,716.0
Private final consumption expenditure	58,154.8	60,966.3	62,511.1
Gross domestic investment .	10,105.1	10,537.8	9,982.9
Net sales to the rest of the world	−13,045.8	−13,591.2	−12,469.7
Gross national product . .	65,720.7	68,697.6	70,740.3
Exports of goods and services .			
Less Imports of goods and services	34,631.0	32,383.1	32,394.5
GDP in purchasers' values .	100,351.7	101,080.7	103,134.8
GDP at constant 1954 prices	10,597.3	10,394.6	10,417.3

* Preliminary.

Gross Domestic Product by Economic Activity

	2010/11	2011/12	2012/13*
Agriculture	795.0	717.3	712.6
Mining†	28.4	32.5	31.7
Manufacturing	46,760.0	45,914.7	47,996.8
Utilities	1,867.5	2,081.4	1,752.1
Construction	1,303.9	1,390.7	1,381.2
Transportation, storage and communications	3,508.0	3,543.5	3,484.4
Trade	7,696.3	7,821.4	7,943.4
Hotels and restaurants . . .	1,779.8	1,839.5	1,904.7
Finance, insurance, real estate and business activities . . .	23,291.1	24,822.0	24,671.5
Government services	8,215.9	8,276.7	8,242.3
Education	683.9	737.5	764.4
Health and social work . . .	3,394.0	3,538.3	3,641.0
Other services	469.1	486.7	509.0
Sub-total	99,792.9	101,202.2	103,035.1
Statistical discrepancy . . .	558.8	−121.5	99.7
Total	100,351.7	101,080.7	103,134.8

* Preliminary.
† Mining includes only quarries.

BALANCE OF PAYMENTS
(US $ million, year ending 30 June)

	2010/11	2011/12	2012/13*
Merchandise exports	69,891.8	67,998.1	68,269.1
Merchandise imports	−48,910.0	−49,996.2	−49,569.5
Trade balance	20,981.8	18,001.9	18,699.6
Exports of services	5,756.6	5,995.5	6,133.0
Imports of services	−4,001.5	−4,005.0	−3,702.9
Balance on goods and services	22,736.9	19,992.4	21,129.7
Other income received . . .	570.1	482.1	423.9
Other income paid	−36,352.8	−34,065.6	−34,023.3
Balance on goods, services and income	−13,045.8	−13,591.2	−12,469.7
Net government interest . . .	−250.1	−335.9	−203.7
Private remittances	287.5	300.3	313.0
Federal government transfers .	17,851.0	16,598.5	16,055.2
US state government transfers .	20.2	15.9	26.2
Other non-resident transfers . .	710.3	854.9	1,020.7
Current balance	5,573.1	3,842.6	4,741.7
Net capital movements . . .	7,650.6	−2,425.2	−4,808.4
Overall balance	13,223.7	1,417.3	−66.7

* Preliminary.

External Trade

PRINCIPAL COMMODITIES
(US $ million, year ending 30 June)

Imports	2010/11	2011/12	2012/13*
Mining products	424.1	604.8	801.7
Manufacturing products . .	42,250.6	44,284.8	42,356.3
Food	3,178.5	3,385.2	3,317.1
Products of petroleum and coal .	5,738.8	6,603.4	5,872.6
Chemical products . . .	20,022.9	20,573.5	19,496.2
Basic chemicals . . .	4,428.5	3,917.7	3,469.9
Pharmaceuticals and medicines	14,476.8	15,503.0	13,409.4
Machinery, except electrical .	1,048.6	1,183.5	1,150.5
Computer and electronic products	2,398.4	2,415.4	2,350.8
Transport equipment . .	2,002.6	2,271.7	2,490.9
Motor vehicles	1,713.3	1,965.3	1,996.8
Miscellaneous manufacturing .	1,650.2	1,696.3	1,644.7
Total (incl. others)	44,670.6	46,574.6	45,038.7

Exports	2010/11	2011/12	2012/13*
Manufacturing products . .	62,875.2	58,164.6	61,674.2
Food	3,980.4	3,670.4	4,080.8
Chemicals	48,763.7	44,488.3	47,967.4
Pharmaceuticals and medicines	43,224.0	40,848.0	43,887.0
Computer and electronic products	2,005.4	1,575.1	1,481.4
Computers and peripheral equipment	815.0	440.5	433.2
Electrical equipment, appliances and components .	872.2	1,023.9	1,064.4
Miscellaneous manufacturing .	4,574.2	4,517.4	4,793.1
Medical equipment and supplies	4,539.9	4,481.6	4,758.7
Total (incl. others)	64,876.0	58,914.1	62,396.9

* Preliminary.

PRINCIPAL TRADING PARTNERS
(US $ million, year ending 30 June)

Imports	2010/11	2011/12	2012/13
Brazil	406.3	1,210.5	1,198.9
Canada	687.4	651.0	872.7
China, People's Republic . . .	807.2	827.8	855.0
Dominican Republic	505.1	568.8	514.7
Germany	569.1	612.2	416.8
Ireland	8,011.8	8,433.4	6,792.4
Italy	481.7	337.5	433.6
Japan	2,101.1	1,792.8	1,876.0
Lithuania	349.7	401.5	961.3
Mexico	378.9	404.9	466.6
Netherlands	356.8	324.8	645.5
Singapore	2,839.4	3,922.7	3,861.6
United Kingdom	508.3	680.9	639.6
USA	20,579.1	19,837.1	20,454.9
US Virgin Islands	2,015.0	1,775.1	8.8
Total (incl. others)	44,670.6	46,574.6	45,038.7

Transport

ROAD TRAFFIC
(motor vehicles registered at 31 December)

	2004	2006*	2007
Passenger cars	2,210,998	2,341,820	2,421,055
Buses and coaches	3,308	3,503	3,698
Lorries (trucks) and vans . . .	36,063†	100,841	106,446
Motorcycles	31,770	91,082	115,865

* Data for 2005 were not available.
† Privately owned vehicles only.

Source: Federal Highway Administration, US Department of Transportation, *Highway Statistics*.

2010 (motor vehicles in use at 31 December): Passenger cars 2,311,686; Buses and coaches 13,226; Motorcycles and mopeds 122,351 (Source: IRF, *World Road Statistics*).

SHIPPING
(Port of San Juan, year ending 30 June)

	2007/08	2008/09	2009/10
Cruise passenger movements . .	1,496,853	1,236,121	1,185,780
Cruise ship calls	581	470	466
Cargo movements ('000 short tons)	9,395.9	8,272.9	7,949.0

Source: Puerto Rico Ports Authority.

CIVIL AVIATION
(year ending 30 June)

	2007/08	2008/09	2009/10
Luis Muñoz Marín International Airport			
Passenger movements ('000) .	n.a.	8,352.5	8,523.4
Freight (million lbs)	n.a.	445.9	413.9
Regional airports			
Passenger movements ('000) .	1,294.7	1,093.1	1,149.0
Freight (million lbs)	243.2	199.1	203.0

Source: Puerto Rico Ports Authority.

Tourism

(year ending 30 June)

	2010/11	2011/12	2012/13*
Total visitors ('000)	3,047.9	3,069.1	3,199.7
From USA	2,586.6	2,581.0	2,730.4
From US Virgin Islands . .	7.2	6.9	8.2
From elsewhere	454.1	481.1	461.1
Excursionists (incl. cruise passengers)	1,165.8	1,127.8	1,038.0
Expenditure (US $ million) . .	3,142.8	3,192.9	3,333.5

* Preliminary figures.

Communications Media

	2011	2012	2013
Telephones ('000 main lines in use)	826.1	706.3	660.8
Mobile cellular telephones ('000 subscribers)	3,108.4	3,049.7	3,085.1
Internet subscribers ('000) . .	568.1	n.a.	n.a.
Broadband subscribers ('000) . .	558.1	573.0	600.0

Source: International Telecommunication Union.

Education

(public education at late 2011 unless otherwise indicated)

	Institutes	Teachers	Enrolment
Elementary and secondary . .	1,511*	33,079	452,740
Post-secondary†	17‡	13,874§	62,579

* 2008/09.

† Excluding adult and vocational education.

‡ 2009/10.

§ Four-year full-time equivalent teaching staff.

Adult and vocational education: 80 institutes (private only); 33,463 students enrolled (public only) in 2008.

Source: National Center for Education Statistics, US Department of Education.

Private education (accredited private institutions, 2012/13 unless otherwise indicated): Institutes 145 (2003/04); Pre-primary enrolment 21,722; Elementary and secondary enrolment 132,095; Post-secondary enrolment 28,137 (Source: Consejo General de Educacíon, San Juan).

Pupil-teacher Ratio (primary education, UNESCO estimate): 12.1 in 2010/11 (Source: UNESCO Institute for Statistics).

Adult literacy rate (UNESCO estimates): 90.3% (males 89.7%; females 90.9%) in 2011 (Source: UNESCO Institute for Statistics).

Directory

The Constitution

RELATIONSHIP WITH THE USA

On 3 July 1950 the Congress of the United States of America adopted Public Law No. 600, which was to allow 'the people of Puerto Rico to organize a government pursuant to a constitution of their own adoption'. This Law was submitted to the voters of Puerto Rico in a referendum and was accepted in the summer of 1951. A new Constitution was drafted in which Puerto Rico was styled as a Commonwealth, or Estado Libre Asociado, 'a state which is free of superior authority in the management of its own local affairs', though it remained in association with the USA. This Constitution, with its amendments and resolutions, was ratified by the people of Puerto Rico on 3 March 1952, and by the Congress of the USA on 3 July 1952; and the Commonwealth of Puerto Rico was established on 25 July 1952.

Under the terms of the political and economic union between the USA and Puerto Rico, US citizens in Puerto Rico enjoy the same privileges and immunities as if Puerto Rico were a member state of the Union. Puerto Rican citizens are citizens of the USA and may freely enter and leave that country.

The Congress of the USA has no control of, and may not intervene in, the internal affairs of Puerto Rico.

Puerto Rico is exempted from the tax laws of the USA, although most other federal legislation does apply to the island. Puerto Rico is represented in the US House of Representatives by a non-voting delegate, the Resident Commissioner, who is directly elected for a four-year term. The island has no representation in the US Senate.

There are no customs duties between the USA and Puerto Rico. Foreign products entering Puerto Rico—with the single exception of coffee, which is subject to customs duty in Puerto Rico, but not in the USA—incur the same customs duties as would be paid on their entry into the USA.

The US social security system is extended to Puerto Rico, except for unemployment insurance provisions. Laws providing for economic co-operation between the Federal Government and the States of the Union for the construction of roads, schools, public health services and similar purposes are extended to Puerto Rico. Such joint programmes are administered by the Commonwealth Government.

Amendments to the Constitution are not subject to approval by the US Congress, provided that they are consistent with the US federal Constitution, the Federal Relations Act defining federal relations with Puerto Rico and Public Law No. 600. Subject to these limitations, the Constitution may be amended by a two-thirds' vote of the Puerto Rican Legislature and by the subsequent majority approval of the electorate.

BILL OF RIGHTS

No discrimination shall be made on account of race, colour, sex, birth, social origin or condition, or political or religious ideas. Suffrage shall be direct, equal and universal for all over the age of 18. Public property and funds shall not be used to support schools other than state schools. The death penalty shall not exist. The rights of the individual, of the family and of property are guaranteed. The Constitution establishes trial by jury in all cases of felony, as well as the right of habeas corpus. Every person is to receive free elementary and secondary education. Social protection is to be afforded to the old, the disabled, the sick and the unemployed.

THE LEGISLATURE

The Legislative Assembly consists of two chambers, the members of which are elected by direct vote for a four-year term. The Senate is composed of 27 members, who must be over 30 years of age. The House of Representatives is composed of 51 members, of whom 40 are elected on a constituency basis, and a further 11 are at large members, elected by proportional representation. Representatives must be over 25 years of age. The Constitution guarantees the minority parties additional representation in the Senate and the House of Representatives, which may fluctuate from one-quarter to one-third of the seats in each House.

The Senate elects a President and the House of Representatives a Speaker from their respective members. The sessions of each house are public. A majority of the total number of members of each house constitutes a quorum. Either house can initiate legislation, although bills for raising revenue must originate in the House of Representatives. Once passed by both Houses, a bill is submitted to the Governor, who can either sign it into law or return it, with his reasons for refusal, within 10 days. If it is returned, the Houses may pass it again by a two-thirds' majority, in which case the Governor must accept it.

The House of Representatives, or the Senate, can impeach one of its members for treason, bribery, other felonies and 'misdemeanours involving moral turpitude'. A two-thirds' majority is necessary before an indictment may be brought. The cases are tried by the Senate. If a Representative or Senator is declared guilty, he is deprived of his office and becomes punishable by law.

THE EXECUTIVE

The Governor, who must be at least 35 years of age, is elected by direct suffrage and serves for four years. Responsible for the execution of laws, the Governor is Commander-in-Chief of the militia and has the power to proclaim martial law. At the beginning of every regular session of the Assembly, in January, the Governor presents a report on the state of the treasury, and on proposed expenditure. The Governor chooses the Secretaries of Departments, subject to the approval of the Legislative Assembly. These are led by the Secretary of State, who replaces the Governor at need.

LOCAL GOVERNMENT

The island is divided into 78 municipal districts for the purposes of local administration. The municipalities comprise both urban areas and the surrounding neighbourhood. They are governed by a mayor and a municipal assembly, both elected for a four-year term.

The Government

HEAD OF STATE

President: BARACK HUSSEIN OBAMA (took office 20 January 2009, re-elected 6 November 2012).

EXECUTIVE

(September 2014)

The Government is formed by the Partido Popular Democrático.

Governor: ALEJANDRO GARCÍA PADILLA (took office on 2 January 2013).

Secretary of State: DAVID BERNIER.

Secretary of Justice: CÉSAR R. MIRANDA RODRÍGUEZ.

Secretary of the Treasury: MELBA ACOSTA.

Secretary of Education: RAFAEL ROMÁN MELÉNDEZ.

Secretary of the Family: IDALIA COLÓN RONDÓN.

Secretary of Labour and Human Resources: VANCE THOMAS.

Secretary of Transportation and Public Works: MIGUEL TORRES DÍAZ.

Secretary of Health: ANA RÍUS ARMENDÁRIZ.

Secretary of Agriculture: MYRNA COMAS PAGÁN.

Secretary of Housing: RUBÉN RÍOS PAGÁN.

Secretary of Natural and Environmental Resources: CARMEN GUERRERO PÉREZ.

Secretary of Recreation and Sports: RAMÓN ORTA.

Secretary of Economic Development and Commerce: ALBERTO BACO BAGUÉ.

Secretary of Correction and Rehabilitation: JOSÉ NEGRÓN FERNÁNDEZ.

Attorney-General: OBDULIO MELÉNDEZ.

Resident Commissioner in Washington: PEDRO PIERLUISI URRUTIA.

Officials with Cabinet Rank

Secretary of the Interior: INGRID VILA BIAGGI.

Director of the Office of Management and Budget: CARLOS D. RIVAS QUIÑONES.

GOVERNMENT OFFICES

Office of the Governor: La Fortaleza, POB 9020082, PR 00902-0082; tel. (787) 721-7000; fax (787) 724-1472; internet www.fortaleza .pr.gobierno.pr.

Department of Agriculture: Avda Fernández Juncos 1309, 2°, Parada 19 1/2, PR 00908-1163; POB 10163, Santurce, PR 00909; tel. (787) 721-2120; fax (787) 723-8512; e-mail enegron@da.gobierno.pr; internet www.agricultura.gobierno.pr.

Department of Consumer Affairs: Edif. Norte, 4°, Avda José de Diego, Parada 22, Centro Gubernamental Minillas, San Juan, PR 00940-1059; POB 41059, Minillas Station, Santurce, PR 00940; tel. (787) 722-7555; fax (787) 726-5707; e-mail confidencia@daco .gobierno.pr; internet www.daco.gobierno.pr.

Department of Correction and Rehabilitation: Avda Teniente César González, esq. Calle Juan Calaf 34, Urb. Industrial Tres Monjitas, San Juan, PR 00917; POB 71308, Río Piedras, PR 00936; tel. (787) 273-6464; fax (787) 792-7677; internet www.ac .gobierno.pr.

Department of Economic Development and Commerce: Avda Roosevelt 355, Suite 401, San Juan, PR 00936-2350; POB 362350, Hato Rey, PR 00918; tel. (787) 758-4747; fax (787) 753-6874; internet www.ddec.gobierno.pr.

Department of Education: Avda Teniente César González, esq. Calaf, Urb. Industrial Tres Monjitas, Hato Rey, PR 00919-0759; POB 190759, San Juan, PR 00917; tel. (787) 759-2000; fax (787) 250-0275; internet www.de.gobierno.pr.

Department of the Family: POB 11398, Santurce, San Juan, PR 00910-1398; tel. (787) 294-4900; fax (787) 294-0732; internet www .familia.gobierno.pr.

Department of Health: Edif. A, Antiguo Hospital de Psiquiatría, Area Centro Médico, Río Piedras, San Juan, PR 00936-0184; POB 70184, Río Piedras, PR 00936; tel. (787) 274-7676; fax (787) 250-6547; e-mail webmaster@salud.gov.pr; internet www.salud.gov.pr.

Department of Housing: Edif. Juan C. Cordero, Avda Barbosa 606, Río Piedras, PR 00928-1365; Apdo 21365, San Juan, PR 00928-1365; tel. (787) 274-2527; fax (787) 758-9263; e-mail mcardona@vivienda .gobierno.pr; internet www.vivienda.gobierno.pr.

Department of Justice: Edif. Principal del Depto de Justicia, 11°, Calle Olimpo, esq. Axtmayer, Parada 11, No 601, Miramar, San Juan, PR 00902-0192; POB 9020192, San Juan, PR 00907; tel. (787) 721-2900; fax (787) 724-4770; e-mail aalamo@justicia.gobierno.pr; internet www.justicia.gobierno.pr; incl. the Office of the Attorney-General.

Department of Labour and Human Resources: Edif. Prudencio Rivera Martínez, Avda Muñoz Rivera 505, Hato Rey, PR 00918; POB 191020, San Juan, PR 00919-1020; tel. (787) 754-5353; fax (787) 756-1149; e-mail webmaster@dtrh.gobierno.pr; internet www.dtrh .gobierno.pr.

Department of Natural and Environmental Resources: Carretera 8838, Km 6.3, Sector El Cinco, Río Piedras, PR 00906-6600; POB 366147, San Juan, PR 00936; tel. (787) 999-2200; fax (787) 999-2303; e-mail webmaster@drna.gobierno.pr; internet www.drna .gobierno.pr.

Department of Recreation and Sports: Parque de Santurce, Calle Los Ángeles, San Juan, PR 00902-3207; POB 9023207, Santurce, PR 00909; tel. (787) 721-2800; fax (787) 728-0313; e-mail mraffaele@drd.gobierno.pr; internet www.drd.gobierno.pr.

Department of State: Calle San José, esq. San Francisco, San Juan, PR 00902-3271; Apdo 9023271, San Juan, PR 00901; tel. (787) 722-2121; fax (787) 725-7303; e-mail estado@gobierno.pr; internet www.estado.gobierno.pr.

Department of Transportation and Public Works: Edif. Sur, 17°, Avda de Diego, Santurce, PR 00940-1269; POB 41269, Minillas Station, Santurce, PR 00940; tel. (787) 722-2929; fax (787) 725-1620; e-mail servciud@act.dtop.gov.pr; internet www.dtop.gov.pr.

Department of the Treasury: Edif. Intendente Ramírez, Parada 1, Paseo Covandonga 10, San Juan, PR 00902-4140; POB 9024140, San Juan, PR 00902; tel. (787) 722-0216; fax (787) 723-6213; e-mail infoserv@hacienda.gobierno.pr; internet www.hacienda.gobierno .pr.

Office of Management and Budget: POB 9023228, San Juan, PR 00902-3228; tel. (787) 725-9420; fax (787) 722-0299; internet www2 .pr.gov/agencias/OMB.

Office of the Resident Commissioner in Washington: POB 9023958, San Juan, PR 00901; tel. (787) 723-6333; fax (787) 729-7738; internet www.pierluisi.house.gov.

Gubernatorial Election, 6 November 2012

Candidate			Votes	%
Alejandro García Padilla (PPD)	.	.	873,072	47.85
Luis G. Fortuño Burset (PNP)	.	.	858,361	47.04
Juan Dalmau Ramírez (PIP)	.	.	46,112	2.53
Rafael Bernabe (PPT)	.	.	17,545	0.96
Arturo Hernández (MUS)	.	.	10,154	0.56
Rogelio Figueroa García (PPR)	.	.	6,346	0.35
Total (incl. others)*	.	.	1,824,764	100.00

* Including 1,373 votes for write-in candidates, 4,291 blank votes and 7,510 invalid votes.

Legislature

LEGISLATIVE ASSEMBLY

Senate

President of the Senate: EDUARDO BHATIA GAUTIER.

Election, 6 November 2012

Party	Seats
Partido Popular Democrático	18
Partido Nuevo Progresista	8
Partido Independentista Puertorriqueño	1
Total	27

House of Representatives

Speaker of the House: JAIME R. PERELLÓ BORRAS.
Election, 6 November 2012

Party								Seats
Partido Popular Democrático	.	.	.	.	.	.	.	28
Partido Nuevo Progresista	.	.	.	.	.	.	.	23
Total	.	.	.	.	.	.	.	51

Election Commission

Comisión Estatal de Elecciones de Puerto Rico (CEE): Edif. Administrativo, Avda Arterial B 550, Hato Rey, San Juan, PR 00940-5552; POB 19555, San Juan, PR 00919; tel. (787) 777-8682; fax (787) 296-0173; e-mail presidencia@cee.gobierno.pr; internet www.ceepur.org; f. 1977; independent; Pres. ANGEL GONZÁLEZ-ROMÁN; Vice-Pres. LIZA GARCÍA-VÉLEZ.

Political Organizations

Frente Socialista: Buzón 69, POB 71325, San Juan, PR 00936; tel. (787) 617-7105; e-mail fs@frentesocialistapr.org; f. 1990; mem. orgs incl. Los Macheteros and Movimiento Socialista de Trabajadores.

Movimiento Socialista de Trabajadores (MST): POB 123, Río Piedras, PR 00123; e-mail info@bandera.org; internet www.bandera.org; f. 1982 by merger of the Movimiento Socialista Popular and Partido Socialista Revolucionario; pro-independence.

Movimiento Independentista Nacional Hostosiano (MINH): Of. Central, Calle 25 NE 339, San Juan, PR 00920; tel. (787) 774-8585; e-mail minhpuertorico@minhpuertorico.com.ar; internet minhpuertorico.com.ar; f. 2004 by merger of the Congreso Nacional Hostosiano and Nuevo Movimiento Independentista (fmr mems of the Partido Socialista Puertorriqueño); pro-independence; Co-Pres JOSÉ RIVERA SANTANA, HÉCTOR PESQUERA SEVILLANO.

Movimiento Unión Soberanista (MUS): POB 9023323, San Juan, PR 00902-3323; tel. (787) 294-9142; fax (787) 294-9143; e-mail info@muspr.org; internet muspr.org; f. 2012; pro-sovereignty; Pres MARÍA DE LOURDES GUZMÁN; Co Vice-Pres ARTURO HERNÁNDEZ, ROSA BELL BAYRON.

Partido Comunista de Puerto Rico: POB 13362, San Juan, PR 00908-3362; internet partidocomunistapr.org; f. 2001 as Refundación Comunista Puerto Rico, present name adopted 2010; Marxist-Leninist; pro-independence.

Partido Independentista Puertorriqueño (PIP): Avda Roosevelt 963, San Juan, PR 00920-2901; tel. (787) 782-1430; fax (787) 782-2000; e-mail correopip@independencia.net; internet www.independencia.net; f. 1946; advocates full independence for Puerto Rico as a socialist democratic republic; Leader RUBÉN BERRÍOS MARTÍNEZ; Sec.-Gen. JUAN DALMAU RAMÍREZ; c. 6,000 mems.

Partido Nuevo Progresista (PNP): POB 1992, Fernández Zuncos Station, San Juan 00910-1992; tel. (787) 289-2000; internet www.pnppr.com; f. 1967; pro-statehood; Pres. LUIS G. FORTUÑO BURSET; c. 225,000 mems.

Partido Popular Democrático (PPD): Avda Constitución 403, San Juan, PR 00906; POB 9065788, San Juan, PR 00906-5788; tel. (787) 725-7001; e-mail info@ppdpr.net; internet ppdpr.net; f. 1938; supports continuation and improvement of the present Commonwealth status of Puerto Rico; Pres. ALEJANDRO GARCÍA PADILLA; Vice-Pres. BRENDA LÓPEZ DE ARRARÁS; c. 950,000 mems.

Partido del Pueblo Trabajador (PPT): POB 21042, San Juan, PR 00928; tel. (787) 374-8061; e-mail rescatapuertorico@gmail.com; internet www.pueblotrabajador.org; f. 2010; Pres. ANNELIESSE SÁNCHEZ.

Partido Puertorriqueños por Puerto Rico (PPR): Avda Ponce de León 611, Hato Rey; tel. (787) 340-4476; e-mail contacto@porpuertorico.com; internet www.porpuertorico.com; f. 2003, formally registered as political party in 2007; promotes citizen participation, sustainable devt and quality of life; Pres. ROGELIO FIGUEROA GARCÍA.

Puerto Rican Republican Party: Suite 203, Avda Piñero 1629, San Juan, PR 00920; tel. (787) 462-7474; internet www.goppr.org; Pres. CARLOS MÉNDEZ MARTÍNEZ; Exec. Dir RICARDO APONTE.

Puerto Rico Democratic Party: American Airlines Bldg, 1509 Lopez Landrón, 10th Floor, POB 19328, San Juan, PR 00910-3939; tel. (787) 721-6010; fax (787) 759-9075; internet www.democrats.org; Chair. ROBERTO PRATS.

Judicial System

The judiciary is vested in the Supreme Court and other courts as may be established by law. The Supreme Court comprises a Chief Justice and up to nine Associate Justices, appointed by the Governor with the consent of the Senate. The lower judiciary consists of Superior and District Courts and Municipal Justices equally appointed.

There is also a US Federal District Court, the judges of which are appointed by the President of the USA. Judges of the US Territorial District Court are appointed by the Governor.

Supreme Court of Puerto Rico: POB 2392, Puerta de Tierra, San Juan, PR 00902-2392; tel. (787) 724-3551; fax (787) 725-4910; e-mail buzon@tribunales.gobierno.pr; internet www.ramajudicial.pr; Chief Justice LIANA FIOL MATTA.

US District Court for the District of Puerto Rico: Clemente Ruiz-Nazario US Courthouse and Federico Degetau Federal Bldg, Avda Carlos Chardón 150, Hato Rey, PR 00918; tel. (787) 772-3011; fax (787) 766-5693; internet www.prd.uscourts.gov; Chief Judge AIDA M. DELGADO-COLÓN.

Religion

CHRISTIANITY

The Roman Catholic Church

Puerto Rico comprises one archdiocese and five dioceses. About 73% of the population are Roman Catholics.

Bishops' Conference of Puerto Rico: POB 40682, San Juan, PR 00940-0682; tel. (787) 728-1650; fax (787) 728-1654; e-mail ceppr@coqui.net; f. 1960; Pres. Mgr ROBERTO OCTAVIO GONZÁLEZ NIEVES (Archbishop of San Juan de Puerto Rico).

Archbishop of San Juan de Puerto Rico: Mgr ROBERTO OCTAVIO GONZÁLEZ NIEVES, Arzobispado, Calle San Jorge 201, Santurce, POB 00902-1967; tel. (787) 727-7373; fax (787) 726-8280; e-mail cancilleria@arqsj.org; internet www.arqsj.org.

Other Christian Churches

The churches active in Puerto Rico include the Episcopalian, Baptist, Presbyterian, Methodist, Mormon, Seventh-day Adventist, Lutheran, Mennonite, Salvation Army and Christian Science.

Episcopal Church of Puerto Rico: POB 902, St Just, PR 00978; tel. (787) 761-9800; fax (787) 761-0320; e-mail obispoalvarez@episcopalpr.org; internet www.episcopalpr.org; f. 1872; diocese of the Episcopal Church in the USA, part of the Anglican Communion; Leader Bishop Rt Rev. DAVID ANDRÉS ALVAREZ; 42,000 baptized mems.

Puerto Rico Council of Churches: Calle El Roble 54, Apdo 21343, Río Piedras, San Juan, PR 00928; tel. (787) 765-6030; fax (787) 765-5977; f. 1954 as the Evangelical Council of Puerto Rico; Pres. Rev. HÉCTOR SOTO; Exec. Sec. Rev. ANGEL L. RIVERA-AGOSTO; 8 mem. churches.

BAHÁ'Í FAITH

Spiritual Assembly of the Bahá'ís of Puerto Rico: POB 11603, San Juan, PR 00910-2703; tel. (787) 763-0982; fax (787) 753-4449; e-mail bahaipr@prtc.net; internet www.bahaipr.org; f. 1972.

JUDAISM

There is a small Jewish community numbering around 2,500 adherents (less than 1% of the population).

Sha'are Zedek Synagogue-Community Center: Avda Ponce de León 903, Santurce, San Juan, PR 00907; tel. (809) 724-4157; fax (809) 722-4157; f. 1942; conservative congregation with 250 families; Rabbi GABRIEL FRYDMAN; Pres. JOEL BENDER.

The Press

Puerto Rico has high readership figures for its few newspapers and magazines, as well as for mainland US periodicals. Several newspapers have a large additional readership among the immigrant communities in New York.

DAILIES

(m = morning; s = Sunday)

El Nuevo Día: Parque Industrial Amelia, Carretera 165, Guaynabo; POB 9067512, San Juan, PR 00906-7512; tel. (787) 641-8000; fax (787) 641-3924; e-mail opinion@elnuevodia.com; internet www.elnuevodia.com; f. 1970; Dir LUIS ALBERTO FERRÉ RANGEL; circ. 202,212 (m), 254,769 (s).

Primera Hora: Calle Génova A16, Extensión Villa Caparra, Guaynabo, PR 00965; POB 2009, Cataño, PR 00963-2009; tel. (787) 641-5454; fax (787) 641-4472; e-mail correo@primerahora.com; internet www.primerahora.com; Pres. and Editor MARÍA LUISA FERRÉ RANGEL; circ. 133,483 (m), 92,584 (Sat.).

The San Juan Star: POB 364187, San Juan, PR 00936-4187; tel. (787) 782-4200; fax (787) 783-5788; internet www.thesanjuanstar .com; f. 1959; English; Pres. and Publr GERRY ANGULO; Gen. Man. SALVADOR HASBÚN; circ. 50,000.

El Vocero de Puerto Rico: Avda Constitución 206, San Juan, PR 00901; tel. (787) 721-2300; fax (787) 722-0131; e-mail opinion@vocero .com; internet www.vocero.com; f. 1974; Dir and Editor EDWARD ZAYAS; circ. 143,150 (m), 123,869 (Sat.).

PERIODICALS

BuenaVIDA: Avda Fernández Juncos 1700, San Juan, PR 00909; tel. (787) 728-3000; fax (787) 268-1001; e-mail buenavidaedit@ casiano.com; internet buenavida.pr; f. 1990 as *Buena Salud*; monthly; health and fitness; Editor ELENA MENÉNDEZ; circ. 61,000.

Caribbean Business: Avda Fernández Juncos 1700, San Juan, PR 00909-2938; POB 12130, San Juan, PR 00914-0130; tel. (787) 728-9300; fax (787) 726-1626; e-mail cbeditor@caribbeanbusinesspr.com; internet www.cb.pr; f. 1973; weekly; business and finance; Man. Editor PHILIPE SCHOENE; circ. 45,000.

Diálogo: Universidad de Puerto Rico, Jardín Botánico Sur 1187, Calle Flamboyán, San Juan, PR 00926-1117; tel. (787) 763-1399; fax (787) 250-8729; e-mail dialogo.digital@upr.edu; internet dialogodigital.upr.edu; publ. by the University of Puerto Rico; Editor ODALYS RIVERA.

La Estrella de Puerto Rico: Edif. Roosevelt 140, Avda F. D. Roosevelt, Hato Rey, PR 00917; tel. (787) 754-4440; fax (787) 754-4457; e-mail editor@periodicolaestrella.com; internet www .periodicolaestrella.com; f. 1983; weekly; Spanish and English; Editor-in-Chief FRANK GAUD; circ. 123,500.

Imagen: Avda Fernández Juncos 1700, Stop 25, San Juan, PR 00909-2999; tel. (787) 728-2350; fax (787) 728-7325; e-mail online@ imagen.pr; internet www.casiano.com/imagen.php; f. 1986; monthly; women's interest; Editor ANNETTE OLIVERAS; circ. 80,000.

¡Qué Pasa!: Loiza St Station, POB 6338, San Juan, PR 00914; tel. (787) 728-3000; fax (787) 728-1075; e-mail manoly@casiano.com; internet www.casiano.com/quepasa.php; f. 1948; every other month; English; publ. by Puerto Rico Tourism Co; official tourist guide; Editor RONALD FLORES; circ. 120,000.

Revista Ego: Avda Palmas 1108, Suite 2-2, San Juan, PR 00907-5214; tel. (787) 661-7770; e-mail info@egomoda.com; internet egomoda.com; f. 2005; fashion and lifestyle; Dir FRANCISCO PARRA.

Revista del Instituto de Cultura Puertorriqueña: Oficina de Publicaciones, Ventas y Mercadeo, POB 9024184, San Juan, PR 00902-4184; tel. (787) 721-0901; e-mail revista@icp.gobierno.pr; internet www.icp.gobierno.pr; f. 1958; 2 a year; Spanish; arts, literature, history, theatre, Puerto Rican culture; Editor GLORIA TAPIA; circ. 3,000.

La Semana: Calle Cristóbal Colón, esq. Ponce de León, Casilla 6537, Caguas 00726-6537; tel. (787) 743-5606; fax (787) 743-5500; e-mail editorial@periodicolasemana.net; internet www.lasemana.com; weekly; f. 1963; Spanish; regional interest; Gen. Man. MARJORIE M. RIVERA.

El Visitante: POB 41305, San Juan, PR 00940-1305; tel. (787) 728-3710; fax (787) 268-1748; e-mail director@elvisitante.biz; internet www.elvisitante.net; f. 1975; weekly; Roman Catholic; Dir JAIME TORRES TORRES; Editor Rev. EFRAÍN ZABALA; circ. 59,000.

Publishers

Ediciones Huracán Inc: 874 Baldorioty de Castro, San Juan, PR 00925; tel. (787) 763-7407; fax (787) 753-1486; e-mail edhucan@ caribe.net; f. 1975; textbooks, literature, social studies, history; Pres. CARMEN RIVERA-IZCOA.

Editorial Cordillera Inc: Of. 1A, Calle México 17, Hato Rey, PR 00917; tel. (787) 767-6188; fax (787) 767-8646; e-mail info@ editorialcordillera.com; internet www.editorialcordillera.com; f. 1962; Puerto Rican history, culture and literature, educational, trade; Pres. PATRICIA GUTIÉRREZ; Man. ADOLFO R. LÓPEZ.

Editorial Cultural Inc: POB 21056, Río Piedras, San Juan, PR 00928; tel. and fax (787) 765-9767; e-mail ventas@editorialculturalpr .com; internet editorialculturalpr.com; f. 1949; general literature and political science; Dir FRANCISCO M. VÁZQUEZ.

Instituto de Cultura Puertorriqueña: Oficina de Publicaciones, Ventas y Mercadeo, POB 9024184, San Juan, PR 00902-4184; tel. (787) 724-4295; fax (787) 723-0168; e-mail tiendaicp@gmail.com;

internet www.icp.gobierno.pr; f. 1955; literature, history, poetry, music, textbooks, arts and crafts; Dir GLORIA TAPIA RIOS.

University of Puerto Rico Press (EDUPR): POB 23322, UPR Station, Río Piedras, San Juan, PR 00931-3322; tel. (787) 250-0550; fax (787) 753-9116; e-mail info@laeditorialupr.com; internet www .laeditorialupr.com; f. 1947; general literature, children's literature, Caribbean studies, law, philosophy, science, educational; Exec. Dir JOSEPH R. ORTIZ-VALLADARES.

Broadcasting and Communications

TELECOMMUNICATIONS

Puerto Rico Telephone Co (PRTC): Avda Juan Ponce de León 562, Hato Rey; POB 360998, San Juan, PR 00936-0998; tel. (787) 782-8282; fax (787) 774-0037; internet www.telefonicapr.com; provides all telecommunications services in Puerto Rico; fmrly state-owned; acquired by America Móvil in 2007; Pres. and CEO ENRIQUE ORTIZ DE MONTELLANO RANGEL.

WorldNet: Centro Internacional de Mercadeo, 90 Carretera 165, Guaynabo, PR 00968-8059; tel. (787) 705-0505; fax (787) 277-0788; e-mail ventas@worldnetpr.com; internet www.worldnetpr.com; internet service provider; Pres. and CEO DAVID BOGATY.

Regulatory Authority

Junta Reglamentadora de Telecomunicaciones de Puerto Rico: Avda Roberto H. Todd 500, Parada 18, Santurce, San Juan, PR 00907-3981; tel. (787) 756-0804; fax (787) 756-0814; e-mail correspondencia@jrtpr.gobierno.pr; internet www.jrtpr.gobierno.pr; telecommunications regulator; Pres. JAVIER J. RÚA JOVET.

BROADCASTING

The only non-commercial stations are the radio station and the two television stations operated by the Puerto Rico Department of Education. The US Armed Forces also operate a radio station and three television channels.

Asociación de Radiodifusores de Puerto Rico (Puerto Rican Radio Broadcasters' Asscn): POB 11208, San Juan, PR 00922; tel. (787) 783-8810; fax (787) 781-7647; e-mail radiodifusorespr@gmail .com; internet www.radiodifusorespr.com; f. 1947; Pres. ALAN CORALES VALLE; Exec. Dir JOSÉ A. RIBAS DOMINICCI; 102 mems.

WAPA TV: POB 362050, San Juan, PR 00936-2050; tel. (787) 792-4444; e-mail annie.berrios@wapa-tv.com; internet www.wapa.tv; owned by Intermedia Español; largest TV network in Puerto Rico; merger with WAPA Americas and Cinelatino (both based in the USA) announced in early 2013; Pres. and Gen. Man. JOE E. RAMOS.

Finance

(cap. = capital; res = reserves; dep. = deposits; brs = branches; m. = million; amounts in US dollars)

BANKING

Government Bank

Banco Gubernamental de Fomento para Puerto Rico (BGF): Roberto Sánchez Vilella Government Centre, Avda de Diego, Stop 22, Santurce, PR 00907; POB 42001, San Juan, PR 00940-2001; tel. (787) 722-2525; fax (787) 721-1443; e-mail gdbpr@bgf.gobierno.pr; internet www.gdb-pur.com; f. 1942; independent govt agency; acts as fiscal (borrowing) agent to the Commonwealth Govt and its public corpns and provides long- and medium-term loans to private businesses; equity 2,450.6m., dep. 11,420.8m. (June 2009); Pres. JOSÉ V. PAGÁN-BEAUCHAMP (acting); Chair. DAVID H. CHAFEY, Jr

Autoridad para el Financiamiento de la Vivienda de Puerto Rico: Edif. Juan C. Cordero, Avda Barbosa 606, Río Piedras, PR 00919-0345; POB 71361, San Juan, PR 00936-8461; tel. (787) 765-7577; fax (787) 620-3521; f. 1961; fmrly Banco y Agencia de Financiamiento de la Vivienda de Puerto Rico; present name adopted in 2001; subsidiary of the Government Development Bank for Puerto Rico; finance agency; helps low-income families to purchase houses; Exec. Dir JOSÉ A. SIERRA MORALES.

Commercial Banks

Banco Popular de Puerto Rico: POB 362708, San Juan, PR 00936-2708; tel. (787) 724-3659; fax (787) 758-2714; e-mail internet@bppr.com; internet www.popular.com; f. 1893; cap. 7.0m., res 1,070m., dep. 20,772m. (Dec. 2013); Chair. and CEO RICHARD L. CARRIÓN; 183 brs.

Banco Santander Puerto Rico: Avda Ponce de León 207, Hato Rey, PR 00919; POB 362589, San Juan, PR 00936-0062; tel. (787) 777-4193; fax (787) 767-7913; e-mail bspr@santanderpr.com;

internet www.santanderpr.com; f. 1976; cap. 183.7m., res 386.6m., dep. 5,723.3m. (Dec. 2013); Pres. and CEO JAVIER HIDALGO; Chair. GONZALO DE LAS HERAS; 53 brs.

Citibank NA: Avda Muñoz Rivera 270, 6°, Hato Rey, PR 00918; tel. (787) 282-2201; internet www.latam.citibank.com/puertorico; Country Officer RAYMOND GATCLIFFE; 14 brs.

Doral Bank: Avda Franklin D. Roosevelt 1451, San Juan, PR 00920; tel. (787) 725-6060; fax (787) 764-4646; e-mail dbcw@doralbank.com; internet www.doralbank.com; cap. 20.0m., dep. 6,866.1m., assets 7,797.0m. (Dec. 2012); 90% investor-owned, through Doral Holdings Delaware, LLC; subsidiary of local bank holding co, Doral Financial Corpn, which completed buyout negotiations with financial group led by Bear Stearn Cos Inc (USA) in 2007; Pres. and CEO JOSÉ G. VIGOREAUX; 37 brs.

FirstBank Puerto Rico: First Federal Bldg, Avda Ponce de León 1519, POB 9146, Santurce, PR 00908-0146; tel. (787) 760-8100; fax (787) 725-8339; internet www.firstbankpr.com; f. 1948, adopted current name in 1998; part of First BanCorp; cap. 487.6m., res 1,066m., dep. 9,920.9m. (Dec. 2013); Pres. AURELIO ALEMÁN; 45 brs.

Scotiabank de Puerto Rico (Canada): Edif. Scotia, Avda Jesus T. Piñero, San Juan, PR 00918; tel. (787) 758-8989; fax (787) 766-7879; internet www.scotiabankpr.com; f. 1910; cap. 227.3m., res 304.1m., dep. 3,605.5m. (Dec. 2013); Pres. and CEO PETER C. BESSEY; 46 brs.

Savings Bank

Oriental Bank: Professional Office Park 997, Calle San Roberto, San Juan, PR 00926; tel. (787) 771-6800; fax (787) 850-8280; e-mail ofg@anreder.com; internet www.orientalonline.com; cap. 7.9m., res 692.9m., dep. 5,386.6m. (Dec. 2013); Pres. and CEO JOSÉ ENRIQUE FERNÁNDEZ; Chair. JOSÉ J. GIL DE LAMADRID.

Banking Organization

Puerto Rico Bankers' Association: Avda Ponce de León 208, Suite 1014, San Juan, PR 00918-1002; tel. (787) 753-8630; fax (787) 754-6022; e-mail info@abpr.com; internet www.abpr.com; Pres. AURELIO ALEMÁN; Vice-Pres. JOSÉ RAFAEL FERNÁNDEZ.

INSURANCE

Oficina del Comisionado de Seguros: B5 Calle Tabonuco, Suite 216, POB 356, Guaynabo, PR 00968 3029; tel. (787) 304-8686; fax (787) 273-6082; e-mail webmaster@ocs.gobierno.pr; internet www .ocs.gobierno.pr; regulatory authority for insurance sector; Commr RAMÓN L. CRUZ COLÓN.

Asociación de Compañías de Seguros de Puerto Rico: POB 363395, San Juan, PR 00936-3395; tel. (787) 793-4430; fax (787) 793-4447; internet www.acodese.com; Pres. JACQUELINE DÁVILA; Sec. HERIBERTO COLÓN.

Atlantic Southern Insurance Co: POB 362889, San Juan, PR 00936-2889; tel. (787) 767-9750; fax (787) 764-4707; e-mail executive@atlanticsouthern.com; internet www.atlanticsouthern .com; f. 1945; Pres. and CEO ALEXIS GONZÁLEZ.

Caribbean American Life Assurance Co: Scotiabank Plaza, Avda Ponce de León 273, Suite 1300, Scotiabank Plaza, San Juan, PR 00917; tel. (787) 250-6470; fax (787) 250-7680; e-mail customerservicepr@assurant.com; internet www.calac.com; owned by Assurant Solutions; Group Pres. and CEO S. CRAIG LEMASTERS; Pres. CHRISTIAN FORMBY.

Cooperativa de Seguros Multiples de Puerto Rico: POB 363846, San Juan, PR 00936-3846; internet www .segurosmultiples.coop; general insurance; Pres. JUAN GONZÁLEZ FELICIANO.

FirstBank Insurance Agency, Inc: Avda Muñoz Rivera 1130, POB 9146, San Juan, PR 00908-0146; tel. (787) 760-8100; e-mail seguros@firstbankpr.com; internet www.firstbankpr.com; f. 2003; owned by First BanCorp; Pres. VÍCTOR SANTIAGO.

MAPFRE Puerto Rico: Urb. Tres Monjitas Industrial, Avda Carlos Chardón 297, San Juan, PR 00918-1410; tel. (787) 250-5214; fax (787) 772-8409; e-mail telemapfre@mapfrepr.com; internet www .mapfrelife.com; f. 1920 as the Puerto Rican and American Insurance Co; comprises 4 insurance cos: MAPFRE PRAICO, MAPFRE Preferred Risk, MAPFRE Pan American, and MAPFRE Life; Chair. and CEO ANTONIO HUERTAS MEJÍAS; 28 brs.

Multinational Insurance Co: Torre Multinational, 510 Avda Muñoz Rivera, San Juan, PR 00918; tel. (787) 758-0909; fax (787) 543-9227; e-mail suscripcion@multinationalpr.com; internet www .multinationalinsurance.com; f. 1961; subsidiary of National Financial Group; Chair., Pres. and CEO CARLOS M. BENÍTEZ, Jr.

Pan American Life Insurance Co: POB 364865, San Juan, PR 00936-4865; tel. (787) 620-1414; fax (787) 999-1250; e-mail CRMCPuertoRico@panamericanlife.com; internet www.palig.com; Man. JOSÉ LUIS VARGAS.

Triple-S Salud: POB 363628, San Juan, PR 00936-3628; tel. (787) 774-6060; fax (787) 706-2833; e-mail servicioalcliente@ssspr.com; internet www.ssspr.com; bought Cruz Azul de Puerto Rico in 2009; health insurance provider; Pres. JESÚS R. SÁNCHEZ COLÓN.

Universal Insurance Group: Calle 1, Lote 10, 3°, Metro Office Park, Guaynabo; POB 2145, San Juan, PR 00922-2145; tel. (787) 793-7202; fax (787) 782-0692; internet www.universalpr.com; f. 1972; comprises Universal Insurance Co, Eastern America Insurance Agency and Caribbean Alliance Insurance Co; Pres. MONIQUE MIRANDA MERLE.

Trade and Industry
DEVELOPMENT ORGANIZATION

Puerto Rico Industrial Development Co (PRIDCO): POB 362350, San Juan, PR 00936-2350; Avda Roosevelt 355, Hato Rey, San Juan, PR 00918; tel. (787) 758-4747; fax (787) 764-1415; internet www.pridco.com; public agency responsible for the govt-sponsored industrial devt programme; Exec. Dir ANTONIO MEDINA.

CHAMBERS OF COMMERCE

Chamber of Commerce of Puerto Rico: 100 Calle Tetuán, Viejo San Juan, PR 00901; POB 9024033, San Juan, PR 00902-4033; tel. (787) 721-6060; fax (787) 723-1891; e-mail camarapr@camarapr.net; internet www.camarapr.org; f. 1913; Pres. SALVADOR CALAF LEGRAND; Exec. Vice-Pres. EDGARDO BIGAS VALLADARES; 1,800 mems.

Chamber of Commerce of the South of Puerto Rico: 65 Calle Isabel, POB 7455, Ponce, PR 00732-7455; tel. (787) 844-4400; fax (787) 844-4705; e-mail camarasur@prtc.net; f. 1885; Exec. Dir HÉCTOR E. LÓPEZ PALERMO; 550 mems.

Chamber of Commerce of the West of Puerto Rico, Inc: Edif. Doral Bank, Of. 905, 101 Calle Méndez Vigo Oeste, POB 9, Mayagüez, PR 00680; tel. (787) 832-3749; fax (787) 832-4287; e-mail info@ ccopr.com; internet www.ccopr.com; f. 1962; Pres. JOSÉ A. JUSTINIANO; 300 mems.

INDUSTRIAL AND TRADE ASSOCIATIONS

Asociación de Constructores de Hogares de Puerto Rico (ACH) (Home Builders' Association of Puerto Rico): Avda Ponce de León 1605, Condominium San Martín, Santurce, San Juan, PR 00909; tel. (787) 723-0279; internet www.constructorespr.com; Pres. ALEJANDRO BRITO; 150 mems.

Centro Unido de Detallistas de Puerto Rico (CUD) (Puerto Rico United Retailers' Association): 501 Avda Muñoz Rivera, Hato Rey; tel. (787) 641-8405; fax (787) 641-8406; e-mail info@centrounido.com; internet www.centrounido.com; f. 1891; represents small and medium-sized businesses; Pres. RUBEN PIÑERO; 20,000 mems.

Compañía de Comercio y Exportación de Puerto Rico (CCE): Avda Chardón, POB 195009, San Juan, PR 00918; tel. (787) 294-0101; fax (787) 878-4630; internet www.comercioyexportacion.com; Dir FRANCISCO CHÉVERE.

Pharmaceutical Industry Association of Puerto Rico (PIA-PR): City View Plaza, Suite 407, Guaynabo, PR 00968; tel. (787) 622-0500; fax (787) 622-0503; e-mail contact@piapr.com; internet www .piapr.com; Man. Dir Dr ELSA SAAVEDRA-GARAY; Chair. CAMILO GÓMEZ; 19 mem. cos.

Puerto Rico Farm Bureau: Avda Ponce de León 1605, Suite 403, Condominium San Martín, San Juan, PR 00909-1895; tel. (787) 721-5970; fax (787) 724-6932; f. 1925; Pres. RAMÓN GONZÁLEZ; over 1,500 mems.

Puerto Rico Manufacturers' Association (PRMA) (Industriales Puerto Rico): Centro Internacional de Mercadeo, Torre II, Suite 702m, Carretera 165, Guaynabo, PR 00968; POB 195477, San Juan, PR 00919-5477; tel. (787) 759-9445; fax (787) 756-7670; e-mail prma_info@prma.com; internet www.prma.com; Pres. PEDRO WATLINGTON; Exec. Vice-Pres. WILLIAM RIEFKOHL.

MAJOR COMPANIES
Construction

Aireko General Construction: Avda Las Casas, Lot 20, Bairoa Industrial Park, Caguas, PR 00725; POB 2128, San Juan, PR 00922-2128; tel. (787) 653-6300; fax (787) 653-0121; e-mail anazario@aireko .com; internet www.aireko.com; f. 1963; principal co of Aireko Enterprises (group of cos), Puerto Rico; management and construction of commercial, industrial and institutional buildings; sales of US $105.5m. (2003); Pres. PAULINO LÓPEZ; 1,000 employees.

Bermúdez, Longo, Díaz-Massó S.E.: Rd 845, Km 0.5, Cupey Bajo Ward, San Juan, PR 00926; POB 191213, San Juan, PR 00919-1213; tel. (787) 761-3030; fax (787) 760-0855; e-mail lfeliciano@ bermudez-longo.com; internet www.bldmpr.com; f. 1962; electrical and mechanical contractors; sales of US $108.3m. (2004); Pres. FRANCISCO DÍAZ-MASSÓ; 1,300 employees.

Cemex Puerto Rico: POB 364487, San Juan, PR 00936-4487; tel. (787) 783-3000; fax (787) 781-8850; internet www.cemexpuertorico .com; f. 2002; cement hydraulics; subsidiary of Cemex, SA, Mexico; fmrly Puerto Rican Cement Co, Inc; Pres. ALEJANDRO RAMÍREZ CANTU; Dir JOSÉ MANUEL FRATICELLI LUGO; 1,060 employees.

F. & R. Construction Group, Inc: Urb. University Gardens, 1010 Harvard, San Juan, PR 00927; POB 9932 San Juan, PR 00908-9932; tel. (787) 753-7010; fax (787) 763-0269; e-mail ito@frcg.net; internet www.frcg.net; f. 1972; sales of US $230m. (2006); Pres. ANGEL ANTONIO FULLANA OLIVENCIA; 1,072 employees.

Electronics and Computers

Hewlett-Packard Puerto Rico Co: Torre Chardón, Suite 801, Avda Chardón 350, esq. Calle Teniente César Gonzales, San Juan, PR 00918; tel. (787) 474-8900; fax (787) 474-8925; internet welcome .hp.com/country/pr/es; f. 1980; subsidiary of Hewlett-Packard Co, USA; mfrs of computer hardware; Gen. Man. MARTIN CASTILLO; 1,700 employees.

Microsoft Puerto Rico, SA: City View Plaza II, Suite 107, 48 State Rd 165, Km 1.2, Guaynabo, PR 00968; tel. (787) 273-3600; fax (787) 273-3634; internet www.microsoft.com/puertorico; f. 1990; subsidiary of Microsoft Corpn, USA; mfrs of computer software; Pres. RODOLFO ACEVEDO; 100 employees.

Food and Beverages

Bacardi Caribbean Corpn: Carretera 165, Km 2.6, Cataño, PR 00962; tel. (787) 788-1500; fax (787) 788-0340; internet www.bacardi .com; f. 1992; distillers and distributors of rum; Pres. JOAQUINE E. BACARDI, III; 1,200 employees.

Ballester Hermanos, Inc: Carretera 869, Parque Industrial Westgate, Barrio Palmas, Cataño, PR; tel. (787) 788-4110; fax (787) 788-6460; e-mail info@bhipr.com; internet www.ballesterhermanos.com; f. 1914; food and beverage distributors; sales of US $156.5m. (2004); Chair., and CEO ALFONSO F. BALLESTER; 200 employees.

> **La Enoteca:** Carretera 869, Parque Industrial Westgate, Barrio Palmas, Cataño, PR; tel. (787) 275-6670; fax (787) 788-6460; e-mail laenoteca@ballesterhermanos.com; internet www.laenotecapr .com; wholly owned subsidiary of Ballester Hermanos, Inc; wine distributors; Gen. Man. JOSEPH MAGRUDER.

Destilería Serrallés, Inc: 1 Calle La Esperanza, POB 198, Mercedita, PR 00715; tel. (787) 840-1000; fax (787) 840-1155; e-mail webmaster@donq.com; internet www.destileriaserralles.com; f. 1949; mfrs of distilled alcoholic beverages; sales of US $118.9m. (2004); Pres. and CEO FÉLIX J. SERRALLÉS; 376 employees.

B. Fernández & Hermanos Group: Carretera 5, 305 Urb. Industrial Luchetti, Bayamón, PR 00961; tel. (787) 288-7272; fax (787) 288-7291; e-mail info@bfernandez.com; internet www.bfernandez.com; f. 1888; holding co; food and beverage manufacture and distribution; real estate; sales of US $300m. (2008); Pres. and CEO JOSÉ TEIXIDOR; Gen. Man. ANGEL VÁZQUEZ; 240 employees.

Goya Foods of Puerto Rico, Inc: Carretera 28, esq. Carretera 5, Urb. Industrial Luchetti, Bayamón, PR 00961; POB 601467 Bayamón, PR 00960-6067; tel. (787) 740-4900; fax (787) 740-5040; e-mail nramos@goyapr.com; internet www.goyapr.com; f. 1949; mfrs of canned fruit and vegetables; subsidiary of Goya Foods, USA; sales of US $105m. (2004); Pres. BOB UNANUE; 500 employees.

Holsum de Puerto Rico, Inc: Carretera 2, Km 20.1, Barrio Candelaria, Toa Baja, PR 00949; tel. (787) 798-8282; e-mail contacto@holsumpr.com; internet www.holsumpr.com; f. 1958; sales of US $107.5m. (2004); mfrs and distributors of bakery products; Pres RAMÓN CALDERÓN RIVERA; 840 employees.

José Santiago, Inc: Marginal Carretera 5, Km 4.4, Urb. Industrial Luchetti, Bayamón; POB 191795, San Juan, PR 00919-1795; tel. (787) 288-8835; fax (787) 288-8809; internet www.josesantiago.com; f. 1902; food and beverage distributors; Pres. JOSÉ E. SANTIAGO; 300 employees.

Méndez & Co, Inc: Carretera 20, Km 2.4, Guaynabo, PR 00969; tel. (787) 793-8888; fax (787) 783-4085; e-mail mdz@mendezcopr.com; internet www.mendezcopr.com; f. 1912; food and beverage distributors; sales of US $246.0m. (2004). Chair. SALUSTIANO 'TITO' ALVAREZ MÉNDEZ; Pres. and CEO JOSÉ ARTURO ALVAREZ; 503 employees.

Northwestern Selecta, Inc: 599 Calle 15, NW, San Juan, PR 00920; POB 10718, San Juan, PR 00922-0718; tel. (787) 781-1950; fax (787) 781-1125; e-mail peteynunez@northwesternselecta.com; internet www.northwesternselecta.com; f. 1980; meat and fish processors and distributors; affiliate of Northwestern Meat, Inc, USA; Pres. ELPIDIO NUÑEZ, Jr; 300 employees.

Plaza Provision Co: Carretera 165, esq. Carretera 28, Avda El Caño, Guyanabo, PR 00965; POB 363328, San Juan, PR 00936-3328; tel. (787) 781-2070; fax (787) 781-2210; internet www.plazaprovision

.com; f. 1907; food and beverage distributors; Chair. JAMES N. CIMINO; CEO ROBERT CIMINO; 410 employees.

Puerto Rico Supplies Co, Inc: Lot 22–23, Luchetti Industrial Park, Bayamón, PR 00959-4390; POB 11908, San Juan, PR 00922-1908; tel. (787) 780-4043; fax (787) 622-4465; e-mail oficina@ prsupplies.com; internet www.prsupplies.com; f. 1945; tobacco and food distributors; sales of US $183.2m. (2004); Chair. and CEO STANLEY PASARELL; Pres. EDWIN PÉREZ; 715 employees.

V. Suárez & Co, Inc: El Horreo de V. Suárez, Highway 165 and Buchanan, Guaynabo, PR 00968; POB 364588, San Juan, PR 00936; tel. (787) 792-1212; fax (787) 792-0735; e-mail jorge.rivera@vsuarez .com; internet www.vsuarez.com; f. 1943; investment management; food and beverage distribution; real estate; sales of US $600m. (2012); Chair. DIEGO SUÁREZ SÁNCHEZ; Pres. and CEO DIEGO SUÁREZ, Jr; 525 employees.

> **Packers Provision Co of Puerto Rico:** Mercado Central, Edif. C, Zona Portuaria, Puerto Nuevo, PR 00920; tel. (787) 783-0011; fax (787) 782-7134; e-mail packers@packersprovision.com; f. 1974; acquired by V. Suárez & Co, Inc in 2004; meat packers, distributors of frozen and refrigerated products; Pres. GUILLERMO S. GARCÍA; c. 600 employees.

Pharmaceuticals, Biotechnology and Medical Supplies

Abbott (Puerto Rico), Inc: Montehiedra Office Centre, Suite 700, 9615 Avda Los Romeros, San Juan, PR 00926-7038; tel. (787) 622-5454; fax (787) 276-3016; internet www.abbott.com; f. 1968; subsidiary of Abbott Laboratories, USA; mfrs of pharmaceuticals; sales of US $500m. (2008); Chair. and CEO MILES WHITE; Exec. Vice-Pres. THOMAS FREYMAN; 2,400 employees.

Amgen Manufacturing, Ltd: Carretera 865, Km 24.4, POB 4060, Juncos, PR 00777; tel. (787) 656-2000; fax (787) 734-6161; internet www.amgen.com; mfrs of biotechnology and pharmaceuticals; subsidiary of Amgen, Inc, USA; Pres. EMILIO RIVERA; Vice-Pres. and Gen. Man. ROBERT MARONEY; c. 1,000 employees at 2 locations.

IPR Pharmaceuticals, Inc: South Main St, Sabana Gardens Industrial Park, POB 1967, Carolina, PR 00984-1967; tel. (787) 750-5353; fax (787) 750-5332; internet www.astrazeneca.com; subsidiary of AstraZeneca, United Kingdom; Pres. and Gen. Man. RUBÉN FREIRE; 2 locations.

Johnson & Johnson: c/o Ethicon LLC, Carretera 183, Km 8.3, POB 982, San Lorenzo, PR 00754; tel. (787) 783-7070; fax (787) 273-6838; e-mail cdiaz4@psgapr.jnj.com; comprises 14 subsidiaries of Johnson & Johnson, USA; mfrs of pharmaceuticals, biotechnology and medical supplies; Gen. Man. EUGENIA VALDES.

Lilly del Caribe, Inc: 65th Infantry Rd, Carretera 3, Km 12.6, POB 1198, Carolina, PR 00986-1198; tel. (787) 257-6240; fax (787) 251-5555; f. 1985; subsidiary of Eli Lilly & Co, USA; mfrs of pharmaceuticals; inaugurated new biotech facility on the island in 2006, creating 550 new jobs; sales of US $850m. (2008); 14,900 employees in 3 locations (2008).

Medtronic Puerto Rico Operations Co (MPROC): Carretera 149, Km 56, Calle 3, POB 6001, Villalba, PR 00766; tel. (787) 847-3500; fax (787) 847-3545; f. 1974; subsidiary of Medtronic, Inc, USA; medical supplies mfrs, particularly electrodes for use in pacemakers; operates 3 plants on the island; 2,250 employees in 6 locations.

Merck Sharp & Dohme (I.A) Corpn (Merck Sharp & Dohme Química de Puerto Rico): Puerto Rico Industrial Park, 65th Infantry Rd, Km 12.6, Carolina, PR 00985; POB 3689, Carolina, PR 00984-3689; tel. (787) 474-8094; internet www.msd.com.pr; f. 1953; subsidiary of Merck & Co, Inc, USA; mfrs of pharmaceuticals; Chair., Pres. and CEO KENNETH C. FRAZIER; Man. Dir (Caribbean) CESAR SIMICH; over 2,000 employees in 4 locations.

Patheon, Inc: State Rd 670, Km 2.7, Manatí, PR 00674; tel. (787) 621-2500; fax (787) 621-2525; internet www.patheon.com; f. 2004 following the purchase of MOVA Pharmaceutical Corpn (f. 1986) by Patheon, Canada; mfrs and distributors of pharmaceuticals; CEO JAMES C. MULLEN; c. 1,600 employees at 3 sites.

Pfizer Global Manufacturing: Carretera 689, Km 1.9, Barrio Carmelita, Vega Baja, PR 00693; POB 786, Vega Baja, PR 00694; tel. (787) 858-2323; fax (787) 855-447; subsidiary of Pfizer, Inc, USA; Vice-Pres. and Gen. Man. IVÁN DEL RÍO ROMÁN; over 5,500 employees in 5 locations.

Miscellaneous

AKM Sheet Metal, Inc: Urb. Industrial Mario Julia, 418 Carretera A, Suite 1, San Juan, PR 00920-2012; tel. (787) 620-4950; fax (787) 620-4956; e-mail amarcano@akmmfg.com; internet www.akmmfg .com; f. 1997; subsidiary of AKM Corpn; mfrs of sheet metal parts and electrical products; Vice-Pres. PEDRO A. ARVESÚ; Gen. Man. ANGEL L. MARCANO.

Bella Group Corpn: POB 190816, San Juan, PR 00918-0816; tel. (787) 620-7010; fax (787) 783-5265; internet www.bellainternational

.com; f. 1963; sales of US \$212.9m. (2004); motor vehicle distributors; Pres. and CEO CARLOS A. LÓPÉZ-LAY; 421 employees.

Cardinal Health Puerto Rico: Centro Internacional de Distribución, Edif. 10, Carretera 869, Km 4.2, Guaynabo, PR 00962; POB 366211, San Juan, PR 00936-6211; tel. (787) 625-4100; fax (787) 625-4395; e-mail infopr@cardinalhealth.com; internet www.cardinalhealth.pr; f. 1951; pharmaceutical product and medical supplies distributors; owned by Cardinal Health (USA); fmrly known as Borschow Hospital & Medical Supplies; sales US \$410.6m. (2006); Gen. Man. DEBBIE WEITZMAN; 320 employees.

Colgate-Palmolive (Puerto Rico), Inc: Puente de Jobos, POB 540, Guayama, PR 00784; tel. (787) 723-5625; fax (787) 864-5053; f. 1988; subsidiary of Colgate-Palmolive Co, USA; mfrs of toiletries and cleaning products; Vice-Pres. and Gen. Man. (Caribbean) SABORIO BERNAL; 90 employees.

Empresas Cordero Badillo, Inc: Avda Ponce de León 56, Barrio Amelia, Guaynabo, PR 00962; POB 458, Cataño, PR 00963-0458; tel. (787) 749-1400; fax (787) 749-1500; f. 1967; supermarkets; sales of US \$365.0m. (2004); Chair., Pres. and CEO ATILANO CORDERO BADILLO; 2,100 employees.

Empresas Fonalledas, Inc: POB 71450, San Juan, PR 00936-8550; tel. (787) 474-7474; f. 1890; retail and property devt, owns Plaza Las Americas shopping mall in San Juan; sales of US \$300.0m. (2006); Pres. and CEO JAIME FONALLEDAS, Jr.

Hilton International of Puerto Rico (Caribe Hilton International Hotel): Calle San Geronimo, San Juan, PR 00901; tel. and fax (787) 721-0303; fax (787) 725-8849; e-mail sjnhi_sales@hilton.com; internet hiltoncaribbean.com/sanjuan; f. 1981; hotel management; Gen. Man. JOSÉ CAMPO; 875 employees.

NYPRO Puerto Rico, Inc: Avda Industrial 15, Km 25.4, POB 8000, Cayey, PR 00737-8000; tel. (787) 738-4211; e-mail rey.encarnacion@nypropr.com; internet www.nypro.com; f. 1973; mfrs of plastics and associated products; bought by Jabil Circuit Inc in 2013; Pres. and CEO TED LAPRES.

Supermercados Mr Special, Inc: Carretera 114, Km 0.3, Avda Santa Teresa Jornet, POB 3389, Mayagüez, PR 00681; tel. (787) 834-2695; fax (787) 833-9843; f. 1966; supermarket chain; sales of US \$245.1m. (2006); Pres. SANTOS ALONSO MALDONADO; 1,082 employees.

UTILITIES

Regulatory Body

Oficina Estatal de Política Pública Energética (State Energy Public Policy Office): San Juan; f. 2014; regulatory body, responsible for developing and updating Puerto Rico's energy policies, as well as overseeing the electricity sector.

Electricity

Autoridad de Energía Eléctrica (AEE): POB 364267, San Juan, PR 00936-4267; tel. (787) 521-3434; fax (787) 521-4120; e-mail prensa@prepa.com; internet www.prepa.com; f. 1941 as Puerto Rico Water Resources Authority, name changed to Puerto Rico Electric Power Authority (PREPA) in 1979; govt-owned electricity corpn; monopoly on power transmission and distribution ended in 2009; installed capacity of 4,404 MW; Exec. Dir JUAN F. ALICEA FLORES.

TRADE UNIONS

American Federation of Labor–Congress of Industrial Organizations (AFL–CIO): POB 19689, San Juan, PR; tel. (787) 728-0300; fax (787) 728-0470; internet www.afl-cio.org; c. 60,000 mems.

Central Puertorriqueña de Trabajadores (CPT): POB 364084, San Juan, PR 00936-4084; tel. (787) 781-6649; fax (787) 277-9290; f. 1982; Leader VÍCTOR VILLALBA.

Federación de Maestros de Puerto Rico (FMPR): Urb. El Caribe 1572, Avda Ponce de León, San Juan, PR 00926-2710; tel. (787) 766-1818; e-mail info@fmprlucha.org; internet www.fmprlucha.org; teachers' union; Chair. MARÍA ELENA LARA FONTÁNEZ.

Federación de Trabajadores de Puerto Rico (FTPR-AFL/CIO): Avda Ponce de León 1704, POB S-1648, San Juan, PR 00903; tel. (787) 728-0300; fax (787) 728-0470; e-mail ftpr@coqui.net; internet ftpr-aflcio.org; f. 1952; Pres. JOSÉ RODRÍGUEZ BÁEZ; Sec.-Treas. NÉSTOR SOTO LÓPEZ; 200,000 mems.

Unión General de Trabajadores de Puerto Rico: Calle Niza 611, Esq. Verona, Urb. Villa Capri, Río Piedras, PR 00924; tel. (787) 760-5050; fax (787) 761-5830; e-mail info@ugtpr.org; internet www.ugtpr.org; f. 1965; Pres. MANUEL PERFECTO TORRES.

Unión de Trabajadores de la Industría Eléctrica y Riego de Puerto Rico (UTIER): POB 13068, Santurce, San Juan, PR 00908; tel. (787) 721-1700; fax (787) 724-4696; e-mail utier@coqui.net; internet www.utier.org; Pres. ANGEL FIGUEROA JARAMILLO; 6,000 mems.

Transport

In August 2014 the Governor announced plans to merge all the transport regulatory agencies into one integrated tranport authority.

RAILWAYS

In 2004 a 17-km urban railway (Tren Urbano), capable of carrying some 300,000 passengers per day, was inaugurated in greater San Juan. The railway took eight years to build and cost some US \$2,150m. In 2007 plans were announced for a light-rail line to connect the urban area of Caguas with the Tren Urbano system, at a cost of \$450m. Work on the project was expected to begin by November 2013.

Alternativa de Transporte Integrado (ATI): San Juan; internet www.ati.gobierno.pr; govt agency; operates the Tren Urbano railway system.

ROADS

The road network totalled 26,856 km (16,687 miles) in 2010, of which 21,216 km were secondary roads, while 5,102 km were national roads. A modern highway system links all cities and towns along the coast and cross-country.

Autoridad de Carreteras: Centro Gobierno Roberto Sánchez Vilella, Edif. Sur Avda de Diego 328, POB 42007, Santurce, San Juan, PR 00940-2007; tel. (787) 721-8787; fax (787) 727-5456; internet www.dtop.gov.pr/carretera; f. 1965; regulatory authority; Exec. Dir RUBEN HERNÁNDEZ GREGORAT.

Autoridad Metropolitana de Autobuses (AMA-Metrobus): POB 195349, San Juan, PR; tel. (787) 294-0500; f. 1959; govt agency.

SHIPPING

There are 11 major ports on the island, the principal ones being San Juan, Ponce and Mayagüez. Other ports include Guayama, Guayanilla, Guánica, Yabucoa, Aguirre, Aguadilla, Fajardo, Arecibo, Humacao and Arroyo. San Juan, one of the finest and longest all-weather natural harbours in the Caribbean, is the main port of entry for foodstuffs and raw materials and for shipping finished industrial products. In 2009/10 it handled 7.9m. short tons of cargo. Under US cabotage laws all maritime freight traffic between the USA and Puerto Rico must be conducted using US-registered vessels. Passenger traffic is limited to tourist cruise vessels. Work on the US \$84.4m. Port of the Americas megaport at Ponce was ongoing in 2013. In December 2013 Puerto Rico's flag registered fleet comprised 13 vessels, with an aggregate displacement of some 8,149 grt.

Autoridad de los Puertos: Calle Lindbergh, 64 Antigua Base Naval Miramar, San Juan, PR 00907; POB 362829, San Juan, PR 00936-2829; tel. (787) 723-2260; fax (787) 722-7867; e-mail webmaster@prpa.gobierno.pr; internet www.prpa.gobierno.pr; f. 1942 as the Autoridad de Transporte de Puerto Rico; present name adopted in 1955; manages and administers all ports and airports; Exec. Dir VÍCTOR SUÁREZ.

CIVIL AVIATION

There are two international airports on the island (Luis Muñoz Marín at Carolina, San Juan, and Rafael Hernández at Aguadilla) and nine regional airports. There are also six heliports. In 2014 plans to transfer the management of Luis Muñoz Marín airport to the private sector were under way. Southwest Airlines of the USA commenced direct flights to San Juan in 2013.

Air Sunshine: POB 37698, San Juan, PR 00937; tel. (888) 879-8900; e-mail email@airsunshine.com; internet www.airsunshine.com; f. 1982; private charters, and scheduled passenger and cargo services to other Caribbean destinations.

Seaborne Airlines: 268 Avda Muñoz Rivera, 9°, Hato Rey, PR 00918; tel. (787) 946-7800; fax (787) 773-8798; internet www.seaborneairlines.com; f. 1992 in the US Virgin Islands; moved HQ to Puerto Rico in 2014; CEO and Pres. GARY FOSS.

Tourism

An estimated 3.2m. tourists visited Puerto Rico in 2012/13. In addition, there were an estimated 1.0m. excursionists. Some 85% of all tourist visitors were from the US mainland. Tourism revenue was estimated at US \$3,334m. in 2012/13. In 2010 there were approximately 12,000 guest rooms.

Compañía de Turismo: Edif. La Princesa, 2 Paseo La Princesa, POB 9023960, San Juan, PR 00902-3960; tel. (787) 721-2400; fax (787) 722-6238; e-mail drodriguez2@prtourism.com; internet www.seepuertorico.com; f. 1970; Exec. Dir INGRID RIVERA ROCAFORT.

Puerto Rico Hotel & Tourism Association (PRHTA): Doral Bank Plaza, Calle Resolución 33, Suite 701-B, San Juan, PR 00920; tel. (787) 758-8001; fax (787) 758-8091; e-mail mtosses@prhta.org;

internet www.prhta.org; more than 550 corporate mems; Chair. Ismael Vega; Pres. and CEO Clarisa Jiménez.

Defence

The USA is responsible for the defence of Puerto Rico. In 2003 the US Navy withdrew from Puerto Rico closing its bases at Roosevelt Roads and on the island of Vieques. Puerto Rico has a paramilitary National Guard of some 11,000 men, which is funded mainly by the US Department of Defense.

Education

The public education system is centrally administered by the Department of Education. Education is compulsory for children between six and 16 years of age. The 12-year curriculum, beginning at five years of age, is subdivided into six grades of elementary school, three years at junior high school and three years at senior high school. Vocational schools at the high-school level and kindergartens also form part of the public education system. Instruction is conducted in Spanish, but English is a required subject at all levels. In 2010 there were 894 elementary schools, attended by 299,746 pupils. There were 380 secondary schools in the same year, attended by 146,819 pupils. The state university system consists of three principal campuses and six regional colleges. In 2011 the number of students enrolled in public higher education was 62,579. Some 28,137 students were enrolled in private post-secondary institutions in 2012/13 and 29,631 students were attending adult education courses in 2012. In 2012/13 US $4,831.8m. of general government expenditure was allocated to education (29.2% of total expenditure).

Bibliography

For works on the Caribbean generally, see Select Bibliography (Books)

Ayala, Cesar J., and Bernabe, Rafael. *Puerto Rico in the American Century: A History since 1898*. Chapel Hill, NC, University of North Carolina Press, 2009.

Barreto, A. A. *Vieques, the Navy and Puerto Rican Politics*. Gainesville, FL, University Press of Florida, 2002.

Bosque-Pérez, R., and Colón Morera, J. (Eds). *Puerto Rico Under Colonial Rule: Political Persecution and the Quest for Human Rights*. Albany, NY, State University of New York Press, 2006.

Briggs, L. *Reproducing Empire: Race, Sex, Science and U.S. Imperialism in Puerto Rico*. Berkeley, CA, and London, University of California Press, 2002.

Caban, P. A. *Constructing a Colonial People: Puerto Rico and the United States, 1898–1932*. Boulder, CO, Westview Press, 1999.

Carrasquillo, R. E. *Our Landless Patria: Marginal Citizenship and Race in Caguas, Puerto Rico, 1880–1910*. Lincoln, NE, University of Nebraska Press, 2006.

Chinea, J. L. *Race and Labor in the Hispanic Caribbean: the West Indian Immigrant Worker Experience in Puerto Rico, 1800–1850*. Gainesville, FL, University Press of Florida, 2005.

Curet Cuevas, E. *Economía Política de Puerto Rico: 1950–2000*. San Juan, Ediciones M.A.C., 2003.

Dietz, J. L. *Puerto Rico: Negotiating Development and Change*. Boulder, CO, Lynne Rienner Publrs, 2003.

Duany, J. *The Puerto Rican Nation on the Move*. Chapel Hill, NC, University of North Carolina Press, 2002.

Duffy Burnett, C., and Marshall, B. (Eds). *Foreign in a Domestic Sense: Puerto Rico, American Expansion, and the Constitution*. American Encounters/Global Interactions, Durham, NC, Duke University Press, 2001.

Figueroa, L. A. *Sugar, Slavery, and Freedom in Nineteenth-century Puerto Rico*. Chapel Hill, NC, University of North Carolina Press, 2005.

Garcia-Colon, I. *Land Reform in Puerto Rico: Modernizing the Colonial State, 1941-1969*. Gainesville, FL, University Press of Florida, 2009.

Grosfoguel, R. *Colonial Subjects: Puerto Ricans in a Global Perspective*. Berkeley, CA, University of California Press, 2003.

Lewis, G. K. *Puerto Rico: Freedom and Power in the Caribbean*. Oxford, James Currey Publrs, and Kingston, Ian Randle Publrs, 2004.

McCaffrey, K. T. *Military Power and Popular Protest: the U.S. Navy in Vieques, Puerto Rico*. New Brunswick, NJ, and London, Rutgers University Press, 2002.

Malavet, P. A. *America's Colony: The Political and Cultural Conflict Between the United States and Puerto Rico*. New York, New York University Press, 2004.

Negrón-Muntaner, F. *Boricua Pop: Puerto Ricans and the Latinization of American Culture*. New York, and London, New York University Press, 2004.

    None of the Above: Puerto Ricans in the Global Era. New York, Palgrave Macmillan, 2007.

Pedreira, A. S. (translated by Rivera Serrano, A.). *Insularismo*. New York, Ausubo Press, 2005.

Picó, F. *A General History of Puerto Rico*. Princeton, NJ, Markus Wiener Publrs, 2005.

Rivero, Y. M. *Tuning Out Blackness: Race and Nation in the History of Puerto Rican Television*. Durham, NC, Duke University Press, 2005.

Romberg, R. *Witchcraft and Welfare: Spiritual Capital and the Business of Magic in Modern Puerto Rico*. Austin, TX, University of Texas Press, 2003.

Schmidt-Nowara, C. *Empire and Antislavery: Spain, Cuba and Puerto Rico, 1833–1874*. Pittsburgh, PA, University of Pittsburgh Press, 1999.

Schmidt-Nowara, C., and Nieto-Phillips, J. M. (Eds). *Interpreting Spanish Colonialism: Empires, Nations, and Legends*. Albuquerque, NM, University of New Mexico Press, 2005.

Villaronga, G. *Toward a Discourse of Consent: Mass Mobilization and Colonial Politics in Puerto Rico, 1932–1948*. Westport, CT, Praeger Publrs, 2004.

Whalen, C. T., and Vazquez-Hernandez, V. (Eds). *The Puerto Rican Diaspora: Historical Perspectives*. Philadelphia, PA, Temple University Press, 2005.

Zilkia, J. *Puerto Rican Nation-building Literature: Impossible Romance*. Gainesville, FL, University Press of Florida, 2005.

SABA

The small, volcanic island of Saba lies in the north-eastern Caribbean Sea, about 27 km (17 miles) north-west of Sint (St) Eustatius. With Sint (St) Maarten, 45 km (28 miles) north of Saba, these three islands comprise the Bovenwindse Eilands, or Windward Islands, although actually in the Leeward group of the Lesser Antilles. Saba is 13 sq km (5 sq miles) in area. The climate is tropical, moderated by the sea, with an average annual temperature of 27.5°C (81°F) and little rainfall. English is the official and principal language, although Dutch is also spoken. Almost all of the inhabitants, of which there were 1,846 in January 2014, profess Christianity, predominantly Roman Catholicism. The population density of the territory was 142 inhabitants per sq km in January 2014. The state flag (proportions 2 by 3) is divided into four triangles, two red at the top, two blue at the bottom. In the centre of the flag is a white diamond, with a yellow five-pointed star in the centre. The capital is The Bottom.

The Dutch captured Saba, once settled by Carib Indians, in 1640. After frequent changes in possession, the islands were finally confirmed as Dutch territory in 1816, administered by the Dutch West Indian Company. Owing to its difficult terrain, Saba remained sparsely populated. In 1845 Saba was ceded to the Dutch Crown and administered as Curaçao and Dependencies, comprising the Windward Islands and the three territories of the Leeward Islands—Aruba, Bonaire and Curaçao. During the Second World War Queen Wilhelmina of the Netherlands promised independence, and in 1954 a Charter gave the federation of six islands full autonomy in domestic affairs, and declared the Netherlands Antilles to be an integral part of the Kingdom of the Netherlands.

Despite the 1954 Charter, there were demands for further self-government from elements within the federation for most of the latter half of the 20th century. A referendum on the status issue was held on Saba in October 1994; 91% of voters opted for continued membership of the Antillean federation. Nevertheless, similar plebiscites in the other constituent members of the Netherlands Antilles produced differing results and in October 2004 the Jesurun Commission, established by the Dutch and Antillean Governments and headed by Edsel Jesurun (a former Governor of the Netherlands Antilles), recommended the dissolution of the federation. The Commission proposed that Saba (as well as Bonaire and St Eustatius) should be directly administered by the Dutch Government. In November, in another official referendum, a majority of voters (86%) on Saba again voted in favour of becoming part of the Netherlands. On 3 December 2005 a preliminary agreement with the Dutch Government that the extant federation be dissolved by 1 July 2007 was duly signed in Curaçao. Under the new structure, Saba was to become a koninkrijseilande, or kingdom island, with direct ties to the Netherlands, a status equivalent to that of a Dutch province. The future status of Saba was subsequently refined to that of a bijzondere gemeete, or special nuinicipality, similar in most ways to other metropolitan Dutch municipalities, although with separate social security and currency arrangements.

An agreement confirming Saba's impending accession to special municipality status was signed in The Hague, Netherlands, on 12 October 2006, and included provisions for citizens of the island to participate in Dutch national and local elections and in the election of candidates to the European Parliament. A further transition accord was signed by the Netherlands Antilles central Government, the Island Council, and the Netherlands on 12 February 2007, envisaging the island's complete secession from the federation. Under the terms of this covenant, the Netherlands was to pledge over NA Fl. 1,000m. to facilitate the process of disintegration. The metropolitan administration also agreed to write off almost three-quarters of the Antilles' debt. A meeting was held in Curaçao on 15 December 2008 at which the Dutch Prime Minister, Jan Peter Balkenende, and the Antillean premier, Emily de Jongh-Elhage, signed an agreement confirming the new status of the island.

The Antilles Government's announcement in August 2009 that a general election would be held in January 2010, despite plans for the dissolution of the Netherlands Antilles to take place later that year, prompted the Executive Council of Saba to declare its intention to become independent from the Netherlands Antilles. The Island Council argued that the central Government lacked the political will to complete the transition process. However, it was generally agreed that Saba's secession from the federation at this stage would not be legally feasible. In September 2009 it was agreed that the target date for dissolution of the Netherlands Antilles would be 10 October 2010, at which date Saba would become a special municipality of the Netherlands. The US dollar was formally adopted as the island's currency from 1 January 2011, replacing the Netherlands Antilles guilder; the Island Council had opposed the introduction of the euro, the currency of the Netherlands.

Elections to Saba's Island Council were held on 2 March 2011. The Windward Islands People's Movement won four of the five available seats, while the Saba Labour Party secured the remaining seat. The new Council was sworn into office on 11 March.

Owing to Saba's change in administrative status, the island's residents were henceforth entitled to vote in Dutch polls. The islanders' first opportunity to exercise this right came on 12 September 2012, when elections to the Tweede Kamer (Second Chamber—the lower house of the Dutch parliament) were conducted. Democraten 66 (D66) received 54.5% of the valid votes cast in Saba, while the Partij van de Arbeid garnered 19.8% and the Socialistische Partij (SP) 9.0%. The rate of participation by the electorate was just 28.4% (compared with 74.6% nationwide). Commentators attributed this very low turnout to a lack of campaigning on the island.

Elections to the European Parliament took place in Saba on 22 May 2014. D66 secured 47.8% of the local ballot and the SP obtained 23.0%. Turnout, however, was just 14.2%.

As Saba is a dormant volcano with rocky shores and only one rocky beach, tourism was slow to develop. However, the island has become known for its eco-tourism opportunities, such as scuba diving, rock climbing, and hiking, and tourism has been steadily increasing in recent years, becoming the largest contributor to the economy. According to the Caribbean Tourism Organization, air arrivals rose from 7,061 in 2008 to 7,675 in 2009 and 8,056 in 2010, while the number of tourists arriving by sea was recorded at 4,982 in 2008, 4,282 in 2009 and 4,271 in 2010. The largest number of tourists came from the Netherlands in 2010, but the USA and Canada were also significant markets. Same-day visitors, mainly arriving from St Maarten, totalled 10,178 in 2010, down from 11,693 in the previous year. Approximately 11,000 air passenger arrivals were recorded in 2012, with the majority travelling from the Netherlands and the USA. Around 150 people are directly employed in the hotel and restaurant sector on the island. The Saba University School of Medicine has grown in importance, educating about 350 medical students. The institution created about 200 jobs (directly and indirectly) and contributed some US $4.8m. to the economy in 2011. Agriculture remains an important sector, primarily livestock and vegetables, especially potatoes. Saba lace continues to be sold on the island. The unemployment rate in 2012 was recorded at 3.9%. Electricity production in that year totalled 8.9m. kWh. In 2012 the inflation rate was 3.7%, although this declined to 1.2% in 2013, owing predominantly to lower electricity prices. As a special municipality, Saba must maintain a balanced budget, supervised by the financial supervision authority, the College Financieel Toezicht. Any future economic development of the island depended on, in particular, growth in tourism and the medical school remaining one of island's economic pillars.

Lieutenant-Governor: JONATHAN JOHNSON, 1 Power St, The Bottom; tel. 416-3311; fax 416-3274; e-mail governor@sabagov.nl; internet www.sabagovernment.com.

Island Council: ROLANDO RICARDO WILSON, CARL ALBERT BUNCAMPER, ISHMAEL LEVENSTONE, EVITON HEYLIGER.

Island Secretary: (vacant).

Executive Council: BRUCE PETER ZAGERS, CHRIS JOHNSON.

National Office for the Caribbean Netherlands Saba (Rijksdienst Caribisch Nederland Saba): Captain Mathew Levenstone St, Old Antique Inn, The Bottom; tel. 416-3934; e-mail info@rijksdienstcn.com; internet www.rijksdienstcn.com; Kingdom Rep. (resident in Bonaire) GILBERT ISABELLA.

SAINT-BARTHÉLEMY

Saint-Barthélemy is one of the Leeward Islands in the Lesser Antilles. The volcanic island lies in the Caribbean Sea, 230 km north-west of Guadeloupe and 20 km south-east of Saint-Martin. Saint-Barthélemy occupies only 21 sq km, but has green-clad volcanic hillsides, as well as white beaches and surrounding reefs and islets. The climate is tropical, moderated by the sea, with an annual average temperature of 27.5°C (81°F) and a more humid and wet season between May and November. The island normally receives about 1,100 mm (43 ins) of rain annually. According to official estimates, at 1 January 2011 Saint-Barthélemy had a permanent population of 9,035 predominantly white inhabitants of Breton, Norman and Poitevin descent. There are fewer descendants of the Swedish inhabitants, who ruled Saint-Barthélemy for almost one century (until a referendum in 1878). French is the official language, but English and two Creole patois are widely spoken. A Norman dialect of French is also still sometimes in use. The majority of the population professes Christianity and belongs to the Roman Catholic Church. The principal town is Gustavia, its main port, in the south-west.

On 7 December 2003 the Guadeloupean dependency of Saint-Barthélemy participated in a department-wide referendum on Guadeloupe's future constitutional relationship with France. Although the proposal to streamline administrative and political processes was defeated, an overwhelming majority of those participating in Saint-Barthélemy, 95.5%, voted in favour of secession from Guadeloupe to form a separate Collectivité d'Outre-mer (Overseas Collectivity). The reorganization was subsequently approved by the French Sénat (Senate) on 6 February 2007 and by the Assemblée Nationale (National Assembly) the following day. On 21 February the island was formally designated an Overseas Collectivity.

Legislative elections to form a 19-member legislative assembly, the Conseil Territorial (Territorial Council), were held in July 2007. At the first round of elections the Saint-Barth d'abord/Union pour un Mouvement Populaire (UMP) list, headed by Bruno Magras, won a clear majority of 72.2% of the total votes cast, thereby obviating the need for a second round. The election was also contested by three other groupings: the Tous unis pour St-Barthélemy list, lead by Karine Miot-Richard, the Action Equilibre et Transparence list headed by Maxime Desouches—each of which secured 9.9% of the ballot—and Benoît Chauvin's Ensemble pour St-Barthélemy, which attracted the remaining 7.9% of the votes cast. Some 70.6% of the electorate participated in the election. The Saint-Barth d'abord/UMP list obtained 16 of the 19 legislative seats, while the three other contenders were allocated one seat each. On 15 July Magras assumed the presidency of the Territorial Council and Saint-Barthélemy was officially installed as an Overseas Collectivity.

At an election held on 21 September 2008 Michel Magras of the UMP was elected as the territory's representative in the French Senate. In December 2011 Philippe Chopin replaced Jacques Simonnet as Prefect-Delegate. In elections to the Territorial Council on 18 March 2012, Magras's party, Saint-Barth d'abord, won 73.8% of the ballot and retained its 16 seats. The list led by Tous pour Saint Barth increased its representation to two seats while the remaining seat was secured by Saint Barth en Mouvement.

The first round of the French presidential election was conducted on 21 April 2012 (one day earlier than in mainland France). Nicolas Sarkozy, representing the UMP, attracted 43.6% of the votes in Saint-Barthélemy and Saint-Martin, compared with 26.8% for François Hollande of the Parti socialiste. A second round run-off election was held two weeks later, at which Sarkozy secured 59.4% of the ballot, defeating Hollande, who won 40.6%. Nevertheless, Hollande triumphed nationally and was sworn in as President in mid-May. In an election to the National Assembly in June Daniel Gibbes of the UMP was chosen to represent the territory (and Saint-Martin).

Legislation to address the problem of inflated prices in Saint-Barthélemy and other French Overseas Possessions was approved by the French Parliament in November 2012. Most notably, the legislation provided for the imposition of price controls on a range of staple goods and the introduction of measures to encourage competition.

An election to Saint-Barthélemy's seat in the French Senate was scheduled to be held on 28 September 2014. The incumbent, Michel Magras, was seeking re-election.

Prefect-Delegate: PHILIPPE CHOPIN.

Territorial Council

Hôtel de la Collectivité, BP 133, Gustavia; e-mail contact@comstbarth.fr; internet www.comstbarth.fr.

President: BRUNO MAGRAS (Saint-Barth d'abord/UMP).

Election, 18 March 2012

	Seats
Saint-Barth d'abord	16
Tous pour Saint Barth	2
Saint Barth en Mouvement	1
Total	**19**

Deputy to the French National Assembly: DANIEL GIBBES (UMP).

Representative to the French Senate: MICHEL MAGRAS (UMP).

SAINT CHRISTOPHER* AND NEVIS

Geography

PHYSICAL FEATURES

Saint Christopher and Nevis, a federation of two of the Leeward Islands, is in the Lesser Antilles. The larger island, St Christopher (usually known as St Kitts), is separated from Nevis to the south-east by a 3-km (2-mile) channel called The Narrows. Rather more distance (20 km) separates Saint Christopher from the next island in the chain, St Eustatius (Netherlands), to the north-west. South-east of Nevis, about 40 km away, is Redonda, a small and uninhabited island dependency of Antigua and Barbuda (the main islands of which are to the east), and 24 km beyond that is Montserrat. All of these islands lie in the Caribbean Sea. Saint Christopher covers 176.1 sq km (68 sq miles) and Nevis 93.3 sq km, giving a total area of 269.4 sq km, the smallest for any sovereign state in the Americas.

Saint Christopher is 37 km (23 miles) long and tapers south-eastwards, forming a low-lying peninsula (which widens at the end and is dotted with salt ponds) pointing towards the more globular island of Nevis. Both islands are of volcanic origin, with mountainous interiors. The main landmass of Saint Christopher is dominated by mountains grouped in three ranges, highest in the north-west, where Mt Liamuiga (formerly Mt Misery, but now renamed with the old Carib name for the island) reaches 1,156 m (3,794 ft). A narrow, sea-flanked ridge connects the main part of the island to the flat lands around the Great Salt Pond. Nevis is also lofty, and cone-shaped, with its central Nevis Peak rising to 985 m. Both islands are fertile and green, although much of the original forest has long since disappeared, except on the higher slopes. Native wildlife suffered not only from the intensive cultivation of sugar cane, but also from the introduction of the mongoose, which has had a serious effect in several Caribbean islands. Other immigrants include green vervet monkeys, originally imported by the French from West Africa (also found in Barbados), and some deer on Saint Christopher. Monkeys are said to outnumber Kittitians, and donkeys Nevisians. Fauna as well as flora is expected to benefit from the recent expansion in woodland, as agriculture contractors and the authorities make efforts to enhance the environment.

CLIMATE

The climate is subtropical marine and falls within the hurricane belt. The average annual temperature is 26°C (79°F), with sea breezes keeping the islands relatively cool, particularly during the driest months of December–March. Temperatures rarely exceed 33°C (91°F) or fall below 17°C (63°F), even in the cooler heights—or on Nevis (despite its name, derived from the Spanish for snow). The hurricane season is in July–October. There is relatively little humidity. Average annual rainfall on Saint Christopher is about 1,400 mm (55 ins) and on Nevis some 1,220 mm (48 ins).

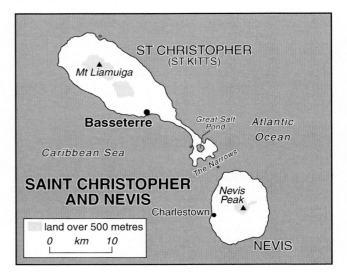

POPULATION

Saint Christopher and Nevis is important in the history of the old British West Indies, with Saint Christopher the 'mother' colony and Nevis long one of the wealthiest. There are still some traces of the French influence on Saint Christopher (the island was at one time partitioned), notably military ruins built in an age of great-power competition—and to protect against the doomed struggle of the native Caribs resisting European encroachment. However, the cultural legacy on both islands is predominantly British, although most of the population (more than 90%) is now black, descended from the African slaves brought to work the plantations. The official language is English and the leading Christian denomination is Anglican. Roman Catholics and Nonconformist Protestants (Methodists established themselves in the islands early) are also represented, and there is a small contingent of Orthodox Christians, as well as some Rastafarians.

The total population of Saint Christopher and Nevis was estimated to be 54,338 in mid-2013. About five-sixths of the inhabitants live on Saint Christopher, and almost one-third of these in or around the capital city, Basseterre, in the south-west of the island. The chief town of Nevis, located on the central western coast, is the old settlement of Charlestown (even so, it was preceded as the capital by Jamestown, to the north, which was completely destroyed in 1690 by an earthquake and tidal wave). The country is split into 14 parishes for administrative purposes.

---

*While this island is officially called Saint Christopher as part of the state, the name is usually abbreviated to St Kitts.

History

MARK WILSON

Saint Christopher (also known as St Kitts) and Nevis is a constitutional monarchy within the Commonwealth. Queen Elizabeth II is Head of State, and is represented in Saint Christopher and Nevis by a Governor-General. There is a bicameral legislature with an elected chamber representing both islands, to which the federal Government is responsible. Nevis has a five-member Assembly, and an administration, headed by a Premier, which manages the island's affairs; Saint Christopher, on the other hand, is managed directly by the federal Government.

Few traces remain of the islands' original Amerindian inhabitants. The islands were visited and named by Christopher Columbus in 1493 as San Cristóbal and Nieves. British settlement on Saint Christopher dates from 1623, making the island the first British possession in the Caribbean; Nevis was settled five years later. However, the larger island was later partitioned, with France taking the centre, and Great Britain the extreme north and south, an arrangement that came to an end with the Treaty of Utrecht in 1713. The islands were administered together with Anguilla and the British Virgin Islands from 1816 until 1871, and then as part of the Leeward Islands Federation.

Poverty among the rural working class was extreme in the first part of the 20th century, and in 1935 resulted in a bitter sugar workers' strike; several strikers were killed by police. Political life on the island of Saint Christopher was dominated in the 1950s, 1960s and 1970s by Robert Llewellyn Bradshaw, leader of the St Kitts-Nevis Labour Party (SKNLP), which, in spite of its name, has never had a substantial following outside the larger island. Bradshaw's most solid political support was among the sugar workers of Saint Christopher, who benefited under his leadership from increased wages and improved education and welfare services. However, his relations with the urban middle class and with the populations of Nevis and Anguilla were in general very poor.

With the Leeward Islands Federation disbanded in 1957, Saint Christopher-Nevis-Anguilla joined the Federation of the West Indies in 1958, along with nine other British colonies. When Jamaica and Trinidad and Tobago left in 1962 the Federation collapsed, and an attempt to unite the remaining colonies as the 'little eight' was unsuccessful. Along with its neighbours, Saint Christopher-Nevis-Anguilla became a British Associated State in 1967, responsible for its internal affairs, with the United Kingdom retaining control of external affairs and defence. However, this arrangement was fiercely resisted by Anguilla, which feared domination by its larger neighbour, and broke forcibly away from the three-island grouping in 1967; a British commissioner administered that island separately from 1969.

The Bradshaw Government's poor relations with the island of Nevis led to the smaller island delaying the move to full independence, originally scheduled for 1980. In an election held that year, the SKNLP lost its overall majority, and a new Government was formed by a coalition of the People's Action Movement on Saint Christopher (PAM) and the Nevis Reformation Party (NRP), which took the three Nevis seats. Together, they agreed an arrangement which granted a high degree of autonomy to Nevis, while Saint Christopher, where the SKNLP retained a local majority, remained under the direct control of a federal Government. On this basis, the islands moved to independence on 19 September 1983.

The PAM remained in office for 15 years. However, the latter part of this period was overshadowed by widespread reports that the Government had failed to control major cocaine-traffickers, who had established powerful positions in local politics and business.

On Nevis, the leading position of the NRP came under challenge from the Concerned Citizens Movement (CCM), led by Vance Amory, which won island Assembly elections in 1992. The CCM has in general favoured independence for Nevis, but has not pushed actively for separation in recent years.

In a general election in November 1993 the SKNLP, led by Dr Denzil Douglas, gained four of the eight seats on the main island, with the remainder taken by the PAM. On Nevis, one seat was taken by the NRP while the CCM, which was not willing to form an alliance with either of the Saint Christopher parties, won two seats. The leader of the PAM, Dr Kennedy A. Simmonds, remained in office with a minority Government, an arrangement that was fiercely opposed by SKNLP supporters on Saint Christopher. There was rioting in the capital, Basseterre, in December, which was countered by a state of emergency and a curfew, but was controlled after intervention by the Barbados-based Regional Security System. In November 1994 the two parties agreed that fresh elections should be held within a year.

Elections were held in July 1995 and resulted in a clear victory for the SKNLP; the Nevis seats remained as they had been the previous year. The SKNLP, still led by Douglas, was returned for a second term in March 2000.

On Nevis, the CCM won a second term of office in 1997. A proposal to secede from the federation received unanimous support in the Nevis assembly, although the NRP later changed its position. The island administration exercised its constitutional option to call a referendum on secession, which was held on 10 August 1998. On a 58% voter turnout, the proposal received 62% of the votes cast, fewer than the required two-thirds' majority. The federal Government has also proposed constitutional reforms, including replacement of the Queen as Head of State with a President, and a separate assembly and island administration for Saint Christopher. However, any change would require a two-thirds' majority on each island, a difficult target in view of the strongly partisan nature of political debate in both Saint Christopher and Nevis. In 2003 a parliamentary select committee on constitutional reform was asked to undertake further consultations. In April Amory announced that the CCM would seek to hold a second referendum on the issue of separation.

In elections to the Nevis Island Assembly in September 2001 the CCM, still led by Amory, strengthened its control of the legislature, gaining a total of four elective seats. The NRP, under the leadership of Joseph Parry, took the remaining seat. The island assembly voted in June 2003 to hold another secession referendum; this initiative was opposed, however, both by the Caribbean Community and Common Market (CARICOM) and the USA, and no further progress was made before the CCM lost office in July 2006 (see below).

At a general election in October 2004 the SKNLP won seven of the eight seats on Saint Christopher; the PAM took the remaining seat. On Nevis the CCM again secured two of the three seats in the National Assembly; the remaining seat was won by the NRP. Commonwealth and CARICOM observer teams made several criticisms of the electoral process. The Government subsequently promised reforms, and in February 2007 a consultative committee reported its findings. In 2008 some reforms were implemented, including a full revision of the electoral list that eliminated the names of 15,000 dead or absent voters and added 3,500 new electors, thus reducing the overall total to 26,542 from 38,865 in 2004. A commission was appointed in September 2008 to propose new constituency boundaries. The PAM, however, had not participated in the reforms and remained sharply critical of the electoral process.

Douglas won a fourth successive parliamentary term for the SKNLP at a general election on 25 January 2010, taking six of the eight seats on Saint Christopher (with 47% of the popular vote), while two seats were secured by the PAM (with 32%). The three Nevis seats in the federal Parliament remained as before, with two being held by the CCM (with 11% of the overall vote), and one by the NRP (with 10%). The CCM's Mark Brantley remained as leader of the federal opposition. The NRP, however, remained in control of the island administration. Election observers from the Commonwealth and the Organization of American States (OAS) again noted the need for reforms, including the creation of more equal constituencies and introduction of equal access to state media, a preliminary count at the polling station to increase transparency, and moves to ensure confidence in the independence of election officials.

At an election to the Nevis Island Assembly on 11 July 2011, the NRP was returned to office, securing three of the five elective seats. The CCM won the remaining two seats. The NRP's leader, Joseph Parry, began a second term as Nevis Island Premier. The CCM contested the results; an election petition relating to one seat was upheld by the courts in March 2012. The Supervisor of Elections resigned in response to a ruling that he was 'guilty of malfeasance in public office'. Rather than call a by-election, Parry asked the Governor-General to dissolve the Island Assembly; at a fresh election in January 2013, the CCM was returned to office with three of the five seats and 54% of the popular vote.

In September 2012 Shawn Richards replaced Lindsay Grant as leader of the PAM. Soon afterwards an inter-faction fight within the SKNLP developed into an open split, with the Deputy Prime Minister Sam Condor and the agriculture minister Timothy Harris opposing a proposal to sell state lands to reduce government debt. With two CCM members and two from PAM joining them in a Team Unity partnership led by Harris, this left the remaining supporters of Douglas as a minority of the elected members in the National Assembly. In December the opposition filed a motion of no confidence in the Douglas Government, but the Prime Minister avoided debate initially by failing to convene parliament for its usual monthly meetings and then, in response to legal action on the part of the opposition, by arguing that no debate could take place while procedural matters were before the courts. A second no confidence motion tabled in July 2013 also failed to reach the floor for debate; this led to an opposition boycott of the National Assembly. Condor and Harris in June 2013 formed a new party, the People's Labour Party. The high court ruled in February 2014 that there were no legal reasons why parliament could not debate the motion; however, the Speaker in July won the right to appeal against this ruling, and obtained a stay which removed the requirement to call a debate until the appeal had been heard. In spite of a further appeal by the opposition, there appeared in mid-2014 to be little chance that the no confidence motion would be debated before the next election, which must be held by May 2015 at the latest. A further complication is an attempt by the Government to revise existing constituency boundaries, on which the population of the smallest constituency on Saint Christopher was only 43% of that of the largest. However, the opposition took legal action to prevent a revision of constituency boundaries which, it held, would operate to the advantage of the Government, and in September 2013 obtained an interim injunction in its favour.

Saint Christopher and Nevis, along with its CARICOM partners Saint Lucia, Saint Vincent and the Grenadines and Belize, remains one of the few countries to recognize Taiwan, and has received significant Taiwanese aid. In common with many of its neighbours in the Organisation of Eastern Caribbean States, Saint Christopher and Nevis has repeatedly supported Japanese proposals for renewed commercial whaling, receiving substantial Japanese assistance; the Nevis administration announced in August 2013, a project to build a US $12m. Japanese-funded fisheries complex on the island, although construction was delayed by a lack of federal agreement on its site. St Kitts and Nevis also participates actively in the Venezuelan Petrocaribe initiative, under which refined petroleum products are supplied on advantageous terms. In January 2014 St Christopher and Nevis applied to join the Venezuelan-led Bolivarian Alliance for the Peoples of our America-People's Trade Treaty (Alianza Bolivariana para los Pueblos de Nuestra América-Tratado de Comercio de los Pueblos—ALBA-TCP) grouping, alongside fellow CARICOM members Dominica, Saint Vincent and the Grenadines, Antigua and Barbuda and Saint Lucia. In an unexplained but seemingly unconnected incident, the Venezuelan embassy in Basseterre was burnt down in the same month, while the office of the OAS was damaged in an apparent arson attack; the Nevis Treasury building was also burnt down in a similar attack also in January 2014.

Narcotics-trafficking and violent crime remained serious concerns for the SKNLP Government, with local gangs working closely with resident representatives of South American criminal groups. The US Department of State reported in 2008 that the Royal Saint Christopher and Nevis Police Force Drug Unit had been largely ineffective, with insufficient political will and a lack of complete operational independence. Cocaine trafficking through the eastern Caribbean is reported to have increased sharply in 2013. There are no drugs rehabilitation centres on the islands; the prison on Saint Christopher has capacity for 182 inmates, but held 334 in 2013. The US Department of State lists Saint Christopher and Nevis as a 'country of concern' for money-laundering. A contribution of US $250,000 to the Government's Sugar Industry Diversification Foundation is sufficient to secure citizenship, through the country's longstanding Citizenship by Investment Programme, although Iranians were, in principle, excluded from December 2011 and Afghans from 2013; however, a man of Iranian origin attempted to travel to Canada in November 2013 on a Saint Christopher and Nevis diplomatic passport issued earlier that year. The Financial Crimes Enforcement Network of the US Department of State warned in May 2014 that the passport programme was subject to abuse owing to 'lax' controls. In response, the Government announced that an advisory board to address problems with the programme would be formed. Others with a Saint Christopher and Nevis passport include Teodoro Nguema Obiang Mangue, the son of President Teodoro Obiang Nguema Mbasogo of Equatorial Guinea. There was no indication of how many have taken advantage of this programme, or how the estimated EC $100m. per year raised by the programme have been used, although it was announced in 2012 that participation could be via purchase of US $400,000 shares in a proposed Park Hyatt hotel (which was under construction in mid-2014). The US Government maintained that the islands were at major risk from corruption and money-laundering, and called for sufficient resources and training to create an effective control regime.

The number of murders stood at 21 in 2013, down from 34 in 2011. There was a per-head murder rate of 38 in 2012, the second highest in the English-speaking Caribbean, and approximately 12 times that of the USA; 10 murders were on Nevis, giving the smaller island a per-head murder rate of 88 per 100,000 inhabitants. The role of St Kitts and Nevis in international drugs-transshipment was clearly a contributing factor to the crime rate. There was also concern over crime affecting foreign residents and tourists. Douglas took direct responsibility for the police and the small defence force from September 2011, creating a special anti-crime unit in the Office of the Prime Minister, with a new police commissioner, Celvin Walwyn, appointed, and anti-gang legislation approved by parliament. There have been repeated allegations of political interference in the police and in the judiciary.

Economy

MARK WILSON

Saint Christopher and Nevis is the smallest country in the western hemisphere in terms of both area and population, with an area of 269.4 sq km and an estimated 54,338 inhabitants in mid-2013, with 11,108 on Nevis at the time of the 2001 census. The islands have developed a prosperous middle-income economy, with an estimated per head gross domestic product (GDP), at market prices, of US $12,804 in 2012, according to IMF estimates. GDP contracted by a cumulative 5.1% in 2000–03, but growth picked up to an annual average of 5.3% in 2004–08. However, the effects of the international recession on investment, construction and tourism were felt in 2009 and 2010 as the economy contracted by a cumulative 8.6% over the two years. Growth of a mere 1.7% in 2011 was all but wiped out by a further contraction of 1.2% in 2012; there was an incipient recovery with estimated growth of 2.0% in 2013. Saint Kitts and Nevis ranked 73rd out of 187 countries in the UN Development Programme's Human Development Index in 2014, the seventh ranking in the English-speaking Caribbean.

There has been concern over the overall fiscal deficit, which at its peak was equivalent to 16.6% of GDP in 2002, and over the level of external debt service payments, which reached 26% of goods and services exports in 2004. Total government and government-guaranteed debt, including borrowing by Nevis, was estimated by the IMF at 195% of GDP at the end of 2004. The Government brought the overall fiscal deficit down to 4.1% of GDP by 2005, achieving a small surplus of 0.7% in 2009 with the assistance of grant inflows equivalent to 5% of GDP. There was improved revenue collection, fuel pricing reform and higher electricity charges; losses from the Government's electricity department had previously reached 2.5% of GDP. A property tax reform was instigated in 2007; the Government also introduced a value-added tax in 2010. Other measures announced in the aftermath of the 2010 election included expenditure cuts and a freeze on public sector salaries and recruitment, as well as increased charges by the state-run Electricity Department, which was responsible for the generation and distribution of power, and was given autonomous status as the St Kitts Electricity Company in 2011. Debt remained extremely high, nevertheless, and was estimated by the IMF at 164% of GDP in 2010. Debt-servicing remained a heavy burden and was equivalent to 61% of total fiscal revenue and grants in 2012, and exceeded the combined total of health and education spending. The IMF in 2011 agreed a stand-by arrangement, with support of SDR 52.3m. (US $84m.) over three years. The Government in 2012 also restructured its debt through a debt exchange agreed by creditors, reducing its estimated value by one-third to less than 100% of GDP, and tightened financial management. There was political controversy over a proposal to transfer 5 sq km of government-owned land on St Kitts as a swap for debt into a special purpose company with a mandate to sell to investors. Domestic debt made up more than two-thirds of government borrowing, leaving the local financial sector heavily exposed and increasing the risks attendant on any moves to reduce interest costs. The Nevis island administration announced in September 2012 that it was in severe financial difficulties, with debt of EC $344m. in 2012; in 2013 a new administration succeeded in restructuring debt owed to its three main domestic creditors, but defaulted on some treasury bill interest payments. The island administration in 2012 proposed its own land-for-debt swap; after a change of administration in 2013, the new team in May 2014 was reluctantly forced to accept the arrangement in order to pay public service salaries.

In a final review of its 2011 stand-by arrangement in May 2014, the IMF noted renewed growth, low inflation, a recovery in tourism, and strong inflows from sale of citizenship. Fiscal performance was in line with IMF targets with a surplus of 12.25% of GDP, and there was progress with structural reforms. With significant restructuring and completion of the St Kitts debt-for-land swap, debt was 104% of GDP at the end of 2013, down from 164% in 2010, and on track to reach 60% by 2020. St Kitts Nevis made an early repayment of US $17m. to the IMF in June 2014.

Saint Christopher and Nevis is a member of the Caribbean Community and Common Market, whose members formed a single market in 2006. It is also a member of the Organisation of Eastern Caribbean States, which links nine of the smaller Caribbean territories. The Eastern Caribbean Central Bank, which has its headquarters just outside the capital, Basseterre, supervises its financial affairs. In 2006 Saint Christopher and Nevis joined Venezuela's Petrocaribe initiative, which offered Venezuelan petroleum products on preferential terms to its members.

The natural beauty, beaches and climate of both islands provide the basis for a prosperous tourism industry. On both islands, there are large modern resorts, but several former plantation houses have also been converted to small luxury hotels, while historic sites such as the Brimstone Hill Fortress National Park are important tourist attractions. A 900-room hotel with a casino and golf course opened in 2003 and was followed by several other large tourism projects. The number of stop-over visitors reached a peak of 140,504 in 2005, with visitor spending reaching EC $355.4m. in 2006. However, totals declined after 2006, falling to 93,081 in 2009, but recovering to 106,904 in 2013, with spending down to an estimated EC $256.4m. in 2012. Cruise ship passenger numbers continued to increase until 2011, reaching 605,407. Cruise passengers totalled 575,434 in 2013, but because of low per-head spending, they have a much lower contribution to the economy, equivalent in 2006 to only 6% of total tourist expenditure. Of tourist arrivals in 2013, 64.9% were from the USA, 6.7% from Canada and 9.7% from Europe. Hotels and restaurants accounted for 6.5% of GDP in 2013. With tourism as the principal industry, there is a continuing need for infrastructural improvement within the country; to this end a US $14m. expansion of the international airport, funded by the Export-Import Bank of the Republic of China in Taiwan, was completed in 2006. A second cruise ship pier for the port of Basseterre in St Kitts was proposed in 2014, while a 10 sq km Christophe Harbour second home and marina development was agreed for the south-east peninsula of St Kitts.

Agriculture made up only 1.3% of GDP in 2013, down from 5.5% in 1997, and the fishing industry for a further 0.5%. The sugar industry, which dominated the economy of Saint Christopher until the 1960s, closed in 2005. In spite of a guaranteed European Union sugar price, which in the years before the closure had been at least three times world market levels, the sugar industry survived only as a result of government subsidies, with accumulated debts equal to 30% of GDP. Large areas formerly used for sugar were redesignated for tourism, and the Government made provision for the retraining of the 1,400 sugar industry employees, who in the main were able to find other employment.

Manufacturing comprised 11.2% of GDP in 2013, up from 7.0% in 2008. Industries such as brewing produce mainly for the local market, while others, including the assembly of electronic components, are orientated entirely to exports; employment is predominantly female. The telecommunications sector has been liberalized; the Government viewed call centres and telemarketing as important growth areas for the economy. The construction sector made up 12.5% of GDP in 2013, down from 24.3% in 2001, with private sector investments on hold because of the economic downturn.

There is an offshore financial sector on both St Kitts and on Nevis. The Nevis Island administration announced plans in 2010 to contract a Lebanese concern, the United Trading Investment Company, to manage its international companies registry on a 20-year contract, in return for a payment equivalent to 20% of fees collected and reimbursement of expenses; however, this proposal was placed on hold after trenchant criticism from the then opposition. The division of regulatory powers between the island administration on Nevis and the federal Government has at times been unclear. Partly for this reason, Saint Christopher and Nevis was, in 2000, listed as a 'non-co-operative jurisdiction' by the Financial Action Task Force on Money Laundering (FATF, based in Paris, France); the country was removed from this list in 2002 after instituting stricter regulatory controls, and is now listed by the US Department of State as a 'country of concern' for money-laundering, an intermediate category. In 2003 a report indicated that the islands' offshore banking operations had been halved as a result of the FATF action and the subsequent financial reforms. However, in 2006 Nevis was implicated in reports identifying the use of offshore accounts by international criminals, most notoriously paedophiles. A sufficient number of Tax Information Exchange Agreements were signed by 2010 for the Organization for Economic Co-operation and Development to remove Saint Christopher and Nevis from its 'grey list' of jurisdictions that did not meet international reporting standards. Like its neighbours, St Kitts and Nevis suffered in 2009 and afterwards from the collapse of a Trinidad-based insurance conglomerate, CL Financial, which posed risks to financial stability throughout the Eastern Caribbean, with an important subsidiary, the British American Insurance Company, being declared insolvent. The IMF estimated the total Eastern Caribbean exposure to the CL group at EC $2,100m., or 17% of the sub-regional GDP. Weakening the domestic financial sector, the non-performing loan ratio rose to 10.6% in March 2013. Income is also derived from the sale of citizenship, with close to 700 applicants in 2012 and earnings equivalent to 4.6% of GDP. The programme has received considerable criticism, both locally and internationally, not least for its lack of transparency.

There are seven medical, veterinary and nursing schools, of which the best-known is the Ross University School of Veterinary Medicine, with a total of approximately 2,000 overseas students and an annual economic contribution estimated by some sources at US $50m. However, net earnings from services are not sufficient to cover the deficit on merchandise trade, and the current account balance of payments deficit stood at 8.5% of GDP in 2013 (down from 27.4% in 2009). This was covered by a capital account surplus, stemming mainly from foreign direct investment inflows.

The islands lie in the heart of the hurricane belt, and have been damaged by several storms in recent years. The IMF in 2009 approved US $3.4m. in Emergency Natural Disaster Assistance for Saint Christopher and Nevis. There is also a risk of earthquakes, although Mt Liamuiga (on St Kitts) and Nevis Peak are not presently active. Development of a 10-MW geothermal power station was proposed for development on Nevis in 2007; however, the island Government in 2012 ended its relationship with a proposed developer, West Indies Power, and was in talks with another potential partner in 2014. A geothermal plant has also been proposed for St Kitts. A wind power plant on Nevis came into operation in 2010.

Statistical Survey

Source (unless otherwise stated): St Kitts and Nevis Information Service, Government Headquarters, Church St, POB 186, Basseterre; tel. 465-2521; fax 466-4504; e-mail skninfo@caribsurf.com; internet www.stkittsnevis.net.

AREA AND POPULATION

Area (sq km): 269.4 (Saint Christopher 176.1, Nevis 93.3).

Population: 40,618 at census of 12 May 1991; 45,841 (males 22,784, females 23,057) at census of 14 May 2001. *Mid-2013* (UN estimate): 54,338. Sources: UN, *Population and Vital Statistics Report* and *World Population Prospects: The 2010 Revision*.

Density (mid-2013): 201.7 per sq km.

Population by Age and Sex (at mid-2000): *0–14 years:* 12,390 (males 6,390, females 6,000); *15–64 years:* 24,450 (males 12,340, females 12,110); *65 years and over:* 3,570 (males 1,670, females 1,900); *Total* 40,410 (males 20,400, females 20,010). (Source: UN, *Demographic Yearbook*).

Principal Town (estimated population incl. suburbs, mid-2014): Basseterre (capital) 14,149. Source: UN, *World Urbanization Prospects: The 2014 Revision*.

Births and Deaths (2001): Registered live births 803 (birth rate 17.4 per 1,000); Registered deaths 352 (death rate 7.6 per 1,000). *2013:* Crude birth rate 13.8 per 1,000; Crude death rate 7.1 per 1,000 (Source: Pan American Health Organization).

Life Expectancy (years at birth): 75.1 (males 72.7; females 77.5) in 2013. Source: Pan American Health Organization.

Employment (labour force survey, 1994): Sugar cane production/manufacturing 1,525; Non-sugar agriculture 914; Mining and quarrying 29; Manufacturing (excl. sugar) 1,290; Electricity, gas and water 416; Construction 1,745; Trade (except tourism) 1,249; Tourism 2,118; Transport and communications 534; Business and general services 3,708; Government services 2,738; Other statutory bodies 342; *Total* 16,608 (Saint Christopher 12,516, Nevis 4,092). Source: IMF, *St Kitts and Nevis: Recent Economic Developments* (August 1997).

HEALTH AND WELFARE

Key Indicators

Total Fertility Rate (children per woman, 2012): 1.8.

Under-5 Mortality Rate (per 1,000 live births, 2012): 9.

Physicians (per 1,000 head, 2001): 1.2.

Hospital Beds (per 1,000 head, 2010): 4.8.

Health Expenditure (2011): US $ per head (PPP): 1,046.

Health Expenditure (2011): % of GDP: 5.8.

Health Expenditure (2011): public (% of total): 37.9.

Access to Water (% of persons, 2012): 98.

Access to Sanitation (% of persons, 2011): 100.

Total Carbon Dioxide Emissions ('000 metric tons, 2010): 249.4.

Carbon Dioxide Emissions Per Head (metric tons, 2010): 4.8.

Human Development Index (2013): ranking: 73.

Human Development Index (2013): value: 0.750.

Source: partly Pan American Health Organization; for other sources and definitions, see explanatory note on p. vi.

AGRICULTURE, ETC.

Principal Crops ('000 metric tons, 2012, unless otherwise indicated): Sugar cane 110.0 (2009) (FAO estimate); Coconuts 1.1 (FAO estimate). *Aggregate Production* ('000 metric tons, may include official, semi-official or estimated data): Roots and tubers 1.0; Vegetables (incl. melons) 1.1; Fruits (excl. melons) 2.1.

Livestock ('000 head, 2012, FAO estimates): Cattle 3.5; Sheep 7.0; Goats 9.0; Pigs 7.1.

Livestock Products ('000 metric tons, 2012, FAO estimates): Chicken meat 0.2; Hen eggs 0.3.

Fishing (metric tons, live weight, 2012): Groupers 5; Snappers 11; Grunts, Sweetlips 12; Parrotfishes 17; Surgeonfishes 7; European pilchard 4,044; European anchovy 3,165; Sardinellas 6,384; Caribbean spiny lobster 21; Stromboid conchs 1,770; *Total catch* (incl. others) 21,802.

Source: FAO.

INDUSTRY

Production: Raw sugar 10,700 metric tons in 2005; Electric energy 228.4 million kWh in 2010 (provisional). Sources: IMF, *St Kitts and Nevis: Statistical Appendix* (April 2008) and Eastern Caribbean Central Bank.

FINANCE

Currency and Exchange Rates: 100 cents = 1 Eastern Caribbean dollar (EC $). *Sterling, US Dollar and Euro Equivalents* (30 May 2014): £1 sterling = EC $4.542; US $1 = EC $2.700; €1 = EC $3.675; EC $100 = £22.02 = US $37.04 = €27.21. *Exchange Rate*: Fixed at US $1 = EC $2.70 since July 1976.

Budget (EC $ million, 2013): *Revenue:* Revenue from taxation 428.6 (Taxes on income 85.4, Taxes on property 14.9, Taxes on domestic goods and services 218.0, Taxes on international trade and transactions 110.3); Other current revenue 359.2; Capital revenue 25.2; Foreign grants 109.9; Total 922.9. *Expenditure:* Current expenditure 538.1 (Personal emoluments and wages 237.8, Goods and services 135.6, Interest payments 81.9, Transfers and subsidies 82.7); Capital expenditure and net lending 93.6; Total 631.7. Source: Eastern Caribbean Central Bank.

International Reserves (US $ million at 31 December 2013): Reserve position in IMF 0.13; IMF special drawing rights 10.53; Foreign exchange 291.30; *Total* 301.95. Source: IMF, *International Financial Statistics.*

Money Supply (EC $ million at 31 December 2013): Currency outside depository corporations 133.10; Transferable deposits 1,067.98; Other deposits 2,035.36; *Broad money* 3,236.44. Source: IMF, *International Financial Statistics.*

Cost of Living (Consumer Price Index; base: 2010 = 100): All items 107.1 in 2011; 108.6 in 2012; 109.4 in 2013. Source: IMF, *International Financial Statistics.*

Gross Domestic Product (EC $ million at constant 2006 prices): 1,679.98 in 2010; 1,708.46 in 2011; 1,687.51 in 2012. Source: Eastern Caribbean Central Bank.

Expenditure on the Gross Domestic Product (EC $ million at current prices, 2012): Government final consumption expenditure 379.37; Private final consumption expenditure 1,312.82; Gross capital formation 524.51; *Total domestic expenditure* 2,216.70; Exports of goods and services 697.26; *Less* Imports of goods and services 937.77; *GDP at market prices* 1,976.18. Source: Eastern Caribbean Central Bank.

Gross Domestic Product by Economic Activity (EC $ million at current prices, 2012): Agriculture, hunting, forestry and fishing 27.16; Mining and quarrying 1.44; Manufacturing 213.46; Electricity and water 30.09; Construction 195.81; Wholesale and retail trade 142.89; Restaurants and hotels 105.72; Transport, storage and communications 224.09; Finance and insurance 113.82; Real estate and housing 283.80; Government services 166.25; Other community, social and personal services 188.49; *Sub-total* 1,693.03; *Less* Financial intermediation services indirectly measured 16.02; *Total in basic prices* 1,677.02; Taxes, less subsidies, on products 299.17; *GDP at market prices* 1,976.18. Source: Eastern Caribbean Central Bank.

Balance of Payments (EC $ million, 2013): Exports of goods 156.94; Imports of goods −678.39; *Trade balance* −521.45; Services (net) 297.12; *Balance on goods and services* −224.33; Other income received (net) −39.48; *Balance on goods, services and income* −263.81; Current transfers received (net) 94.50; *Current balance* −169.31; Capital account (net) 359.57; Direct investment (net) 299.13; Portfolio investment (net) 0.00; Other investment (net) −454.41; Net errors and omissions 72.07; *Overall balance* 107.07. Source: Eastern Caribbean Central Bank.

EXTERNAL TRADE

Principal Commodities (EC $ million, 2013): *Imports c.i.f.:* Food and live animals 125.7; Chemicals 52.9; Basic manufactures 124.4; Machinery and transport equipment 190.5; Miscellaneous manufactured articles 128.8; Total (incl. others) 672.0. *Exports f.o.b.* (incl. re-exports): Beverages and tobacco 9.6; Machinery and transport equip-

ment 123.4; Miscellaneous manufactures 114.2; Total (incl. others) 153.6. Source: Eastern Caribbean Central Bank.

Principal Trading Partners (US $ million, 2011): *Imports:* Barbados 2.6; Canada 5.5; China, People's Rep. 6.2; Dominican Republic 2.7; Jamaica 3.9; Japan 5.2; former Netherlands Antilles 2.8; Trinidad and Tobago 15.5; United Kingdom 10.1; USA 166.1; Total (incl. others) 246.7. *Exports* (excl. re-exports): Antigua and Barbuda 1.4; Dominica 1.0; France 0.6; Grenada 0.5; former Netherlands Antilles 0.5; Saint Lucia 1.1; Trinidad and Tobago 1.2; USA 36.7; Total (incl. others) 44.9. Source: Trade Map-Trade Competitiveness Map, International Trade Centre, www.intracen.org/marketanalysis.

TRANSPORT

Shipping: *Flag Registered Fleet* (at 31 December 2013): Number 366; Total displacement 1,560,083 grt. Source: Lloyd's List Intelligence (www.lloydslistintelligence.com).

TOURISM

Visitor Arrivals (estimates): 715,250 (101,701 stop-over visitors, 3,682 excursionists, 4,460 yacht passengers, 605,407 cruise ship passengers) in 2011; 635,426 (104,240 stop-over visitors, 3,230 excursionists, 1,651 yacht passengers, 526,305 cruise ship passengers) in 2012; 690,340 (106,906 stop-over visitors, 3,831 excursionists, 4,069 yacht passengers, 575,534 cruise ship passengers) in 2013. *Stop-over Visitors by Origin* (2013): Canada 7,138; Caribbean 17,667; United Kingdom 8,444; USA 68,534; Other 5,123; Total 106,906.

Tourism Receipts (EC $ million, estimates): 254.06 in 2011; 256.51 in 2012; 272.82 in 2013.

Source: Eastern Caribbean Central Bank.

COMMUNICATIONS MEDIA

Telephones ('000 main lines in use, 2013): 19.2.

Mobile Cellular Telephones (subscribers, 2013): 77,000.

Internet Users (2009): 17,000.

Broadband Subscribers (2013): 13,300.

Source: International Telecommunication Union.

EDUCATION

Pre-primary (2010/11 unless otherwise indicated): 77 schools (2003/04); 89 teachers; 1,796 pupils.

Primary (2011/12 unless otherwise indicated): 23 schools (2003/04); 355 teachers; 5,812 pupils.

Secondary (2011/12 unless otherwise indicated): 7 schools (2003/04); 448 teachers; 3,673 pupils.

Tertiary (2007/08 unless otherwise indicated): 1 institution; 79 teachers (2003/04); 859 students.

Pupil-teacher Ratio (primary education, UNESCO estimate): 16.4 in 2011/12.

Adult Literacy Rate: 97.8% in 2004 (Source: UN Development Programme, *Human Development Report*).

Source: mostly UNESCO Institute for Statistics.

Directory

The Constitution

The Constitution of the Federation of Saint Christopher and Nevis took effect from 19 September 1983, when the territory achieved independence. Its main provisions are summarized below:

FUNDAMENTAL RIGHTS AND FREEDOMS

Regardless of race, place of origin, political opinion, colour, creed or sex, but subject to respect for the rights and freedoms of others and for the public interest, every person in Saint Christopher and Nevis is entitled to the rights of life, liberty, security of person, equality before the law and the protection of the law. Freedom of conscience, of expression, of assembly and of association is guaranteed, and the inviolability of personal privacy, family life and property is maintained. Protection is afforded from slavery, forced labour, torture and inhuman treatment.

THE GOVERNOR-GENERAL

The Governor-General is appointed by the British monarch, whom the Governor-General represents locally. The Governor-General must be a citizen of Saint Christopher and Nevis, and must appoint a Deputy Governor-General, in accordance with the wishes of the Premier of Nevis, to represent the Governor-General on that island.

PARLIAMENT

Parliament consists of the British monarch, represented by the Governor-General, and the National Assembly, which includes a Speaker, three (or, if a nominated member is Attorney-General, four) nominated members (Senators) and 11 elected members (Representatives). Senators are appointed by the Governor-General: one on the advice of the Leader of the Opposition, and the other two in accordance with the wishes of the Prime Minister. The Representatives are elected by universal suffrage, one from each of the 11 single-member constituencies.

Every citizen over the age of 18 years is eligible to vote. Parliament may alter any of the provisions of the Constitution.

THE EXECUTIVE

Executive authority is vested in the British monarch, as Head of State, and is exercised on the monarch's behalf by the Governor-General, either directly or through subordinate officers. The Governor-General appoints as Prime Minister that Representative who, in the Governor-General's opinion, appears to be best able to command the support of the majority of the Representatives. Other ministerial appointments are made by the Governor-General, in consultation with the Prime Minister, from among the members of the National Assembly. The Governor-General may remove the Prime Minister from office if a resolution of no confidence in the Government is passed by the National Assembly and if the Prime Minister does not resign within three days or advise the Governor-General to dissolve Parliament.

The Cabinet consists of the Prime Minister and other Ministers. When the office of Attorney-General is a public office, the Attorney-General shall, by virtue of holding that office, be a member of the Cabinet in addition to the other Ministers. The Governor-General appoints as Leader of the Opposition in the National Assembly that Representative who, in the Governor-General's opinion, appears to be best able to command the support of the majority of the Representatives who do not support the Government.

CITIZENSHIP

All persons born in Saint Christopher and Nevis before independence who, immediately before independence, were citizens of the United Kingdom and Colonies automatically become citizens of Saint Christopher and Nevis. All persons born in Saint Christopher and Nevis after independence automatically acquire citizenship, as do those born outside Saint Christopher and Nevis after independence to a parent possessing citizenship. There are provisions for the acquisition of citizenship by those to whom it is not automatically granted.

THE ISLAND OF NEVIS

There is a legislature for the island of Nevis, which consists of the British monarch, represented by the Governor-General, and the Nevis Island Assembly. The Assembly consists of three nominated members (one appointed by the Governor-General in accordance with the advice of the Leader of the Opposition in the Assembly, and two appointed by the Governor-General in accordance with the advice of the Premier) and such number of elected members as corresponds directly with the number of electoral districts on the island.

There is a Nevis Island Administration, consisting of a premier and two other members who are appointed by the Governor-General. The Governor-General appoints the Premier as the person who, in the Governor-General's opinion, is best able to command the support of the majority of the elected members of the Assembly. The other members of the Administration are appointed by the Governor-General, acting in accordance with the wishes of the Premier. The Administration has exclusive responsibility for administration within the island of Nevis, in accordance with the provisions of any relevant laws.

The Nevis Island legislature may provide that the island of Nevis is to cease to belong to the Federation of Saint Christopher and Nevis, in which case this Constitution would cease to have effect in the island of Nevis. Provisions for the possible secession of the island contain the following requirements: that the island must give full and detailed proposals for the future Constitution of the island of Nevis, which must be laid before the Assembly for a period of at least six months prior to the proposed date of secession; and that a two-thirds' majority has been gained in a referendum, which is to be held after the Assembly has approved the motion.

The Government

HEAD OF STATE

Queen: HM Queen ELIZABETH II.

Governor-General: Sir EDMUND LAWRENCE (took office 1 January 2013).

CABINET
(September 2014)

The Cabinet consists of members of the St Kitts-Nevis Labour Party and one member of the Nevis Reformation Party.

Prime Minister and Minister of Finance and Sustainable Development: Dr DENZIL LLEWELLYN DOUGLAS.

Deputy Prime Minister and Minister of Housing, Public Works, Energy and Public Utilities: Dr EARL ASIM MARTIN.

Minister of Justice and Legal Affairs and of Foreign Affairs, Homeland Security, Immigration and Labour: PATRICE NISBETT (NRP).

Minister of Health and of Social and Community Development and Gender Affairs: MARCELLA A. LIBURD.

Minister of Youth Empowerment and Sports and of Information Technology, Telecommunications and Posts: GLENN F. PHILLIP.

Minister of Education and Information and of Agriculture, Marine Resource and Co-operatives: NIGEL ALEXIS CARTY.

Minister of International Trade, Industry, Commerce and Consumer Affairs and of Tourism and International Transport: RICHARD OLIVER SKERRITT.

MINISTRIES

Office of the Governor-General: Government House, Basseterre; tel. 465-2315.

Government Headquarters: Church St, POB 186, Basseterre; tel. 465-2521; fax 466-4505; e-mail infocom@sisterisles.kn; internet www.gov.kn.

Prime Minister's Office: Government Headquarters, Church St, POB 186, Basseterre; tel. 465-0299; fax 465-1001; e-mail sknpmpresssec@cuopm.com; internet www.cuopm.org.

All ministries are located at Government Headquarters.

NEVIS ISLAND ADMINISTRATION

Premier: VANCE WINKWORTH AMORY.

There are also two appointed members.

Administrative Centre: Main St, POB 689, Charlestown, Nevis; tel. 469-1469; fax 469-0039; e-mail info@niagov.com; internet www.nia.gov.kn.

Legislature

NATIONAL ASSEMBLY

Speaker: CURTIS MARTIN.

Elected members: 11. Nominated members: 3. Ex officio members: 1.

Election, 25 January 2010

Party						Seats
St Kitts-Nevis Labour Party (SKNLP)	.	.	.			6
Concerned Citizens' Movement (CCM)	.	.	.			2
People's Action Movement (PAM)	.	.	.	.		2
Nevis Reformation Party (NRP)	.	.	.	.		1
Total	.	.	.	.	.	**11**

NEVIS ISLAND ASSEMBLY

President: FARREL SMITHEN.

Elected members: 5. Nominated members: 3.

Elections to the Nevis Island Assembly took place on 22 January 2013. The Concerned Citizens' Movement took three seats and the Nevis Reformation Party secured the remaining two seats.

Election Commission

Office of the Supervisor of Elections: Basseterre; Supervisor of Elections RAPHAEL ARCHIBALD.

Political Organizations

Concerned Citizens' Movement (CCM): Charlestown, Nevis; tel. 469-3519; e-mail admin@myccmparty.com; internet myccmparty.com; f. 1986; mem. of Team Unity, formed to contest the 2015 elections; Leader VANCE W. AMORY; Chair. STEDMOND TROSS.

National Integrity Party (NIP): Basseterre; f. 2013; Leader GLENROY BLANCHETTE.

Nevis Reformation Party (NRP): Government Rd, POB 480, Charlestown, Nevis; tel. 469-0630; e-mail info@nrpnevis.com; internet nrpnevis.com; f. 1970; Pres. JOSEPH W. PARRY; Gen. Sec. LLEWELYN PARRIS.

People's Action Movement (PAM): Lockhart St, POB 1294, Basseterre; tel. 662-2073; fax 466-3854; e-mail pam.publicrelations@gmail.com; internet pamforchange.com; f. 1965;

mem. of Team Unity, formed to contest the 2015 elections; Leader SHAWN RICHARDS.

People's Labour Party (PLP): Basseterre; f. 2013 by fmr mems of the SKNLP; mem. of Team Unity, formed to contest the 2015 elections; Leader Dr TIMOTHY HARRIS; Deputy Leader SAM CONDOR.

St Kitts-Nevis Labour Party (SKNLP): Masses House, Church St, POB 239, Basseterre; tel. 465-5347; fax 465-8328; e-mail wanda .connor@sknlabourparty.com; internet www.sknlabourparty.com; f. 1932; socialist party; Chair. MARCELLA LIBURD; Leader Dr DENZIL LLEWELLYN DOUGLAS.

Diplomatic Representation

EMBASSIES IN SAINT CHRISTOPHER AND NEVIS

Brazil: St Kitts Marriott, Suite 17-206, 858 Frigate Bay Rd, Frigate Bay, Basseterre; tel. 465-1054; fax 465-2015; e-mail info@brazilskn .org; internet www.brazilskn.org; Ambassador ANTONIO JOSÉ REZENDE DE CASTRO.

Cuba: 34 Bladen Housing Devt, POB 600, Basseterre; tel. 466-3374; fax 465-8072; e-mail embacubask@sisterisles.kn; internet www .cubadiplomatica.cu/saintkittsnevis; Ambassador HUGO RUIZ CABRERA.

Taiwan (Republic of China): Taylor's Range, POB 119, Basseterre; tel. 465-2421; fax 465-7921; e-mail rocemb@caribsurf.com; internet www.taiwanembassy.org/kn; Ambassador MIGUEL TSAO.

Venezuela: Wigley Ave, Fortlands, Basseterre; tel. 465-2073; fax 465-5452; e-mail embve.knbas@mppre.gob.ve; Ambassador RÓMULO CAMILO HENRÍQUEZ GONZÁLEZ.

Diplomatic relations with other countries are maintained at consular level, or with ambassadors and high commissioners resident in other countries of the region, or directly with the other country.

Judicial System

Justice is administered by the Eastern Caribbean Supreme Court (ECSC), based in Saint Lucia and consisting of a Court of Appeal and a High Court. Two judges of the High Court are responsible for Saint Christopher and Nevis and preside over the Court of Summary Jurisdiction. One of two ECSC Masters, chiefly responsible for procedural and interlocutory matters, is also resident in St Kitts. The Magistrates' Courts deal with summary offences and civil offences involving sums of not more than EC $5,000.

High Court Judges: IANTHEA LEIGERTWOOD-OCTAVE (acting), DARSHAN RAMDHANI (acting).

Master: PEARLETTA LANNS.

Registrar: JANINE HARRIS.

Magistrates' Office: Losack Rd, Basseterre; tel. 465-2170; fax 465-2482; Chief Magistrate JOSEPHINE MALLALIEU.

Attorney-General: JASON AKIL HAMILTON.

Religion

CHRISTIANITY

St Kitts Christian Council: Victoria Rd, POB 55, Basseterre; tel. 465-2167; e-mail stgeorgesk@yahoo.com; Chair. Archdeacon VALENTINE HODGE.

The Anglican Communion

Anglicans in Saint Christopher and Nevis are adherents of the Church in the Province of the West Indies. The islands form part of the diocese of the North Eastern Caribbean and Aruba. The Bishop is resident in St John's, Antigua and Barbuda.

The Roman Catholic Church

The diocese of Saint John's-Basseterre, suffragan to the archdiocese of Castries (Saint Lucia), includes Anguilla, Antigua and Barbuda, the British Virgin Islands, Montserrat and Saint Christopher and Nevis. The Bishop participates in the Antilles Episcopal Conference (currently based in Port of Spain, Trinidad and Tobago).

Bishop of Saint John's-Basseterre: Mgr KENNETH DAVID OSWIN RICHARDS, POB 836, St John's, Antigua; e-mail diocesesjb@gmail .com.

Other Churches

There are also communities of Methodists, Moravians, Seventh-day Adventists, Baptists, Pilgrim Holiness, the Church of God, Apostolic Faith and Plymouth Brethren.

The Press

The Democrat: Cayon St and Walwyn Ave, POB 30, Basseterre; tel. 466-2091; fax 465-0857; e-mail info@skndemocrat.com; internet www.skndemocrat.com; f. 1948; weekly (Sat.); Man. Editor DENIECE ALLEYNE; circ. 3,000.

The Labour Spokesman: Masses House, Church St, POB 239, Basseterre; tel. 465-2229; fax 466-9866; e-mail sknunion@sisterisles .kn; internet www.labourspokesman.com; f. 1957; Wed. and Sat.; organ of St Kitts-Nevis Trades and Labour Union; Man. Editor DAWUD ST LLOYD BYRON; circ. 6,000.

The Leewards Times: Pinneys Industrial Site, POB 146, Nevis; tel. 469-1049; fax 469-0662; e-mail hbramble@caribsurf.com; internet www.leewardstimes.net; weekly (Fri.); Gen. Man. PAMELA MARTIN.

The St Kitts and Nevis Observer: Cayon St, POB 657, Basseterre; tel. 469-5907; fax 469-5891; e-mail contact@thestkittsnevisobserver .com; internet www.thestkittsnevisobserver.com; weekly (Fri.); independent; Publr and Editor-in-Chief KENNETH A. WILLIAMS.

Publishers

Caribbean Publishing Co (St Kitts-Nevis) Ltd: Dr William Herbert Complex, Frigate Bay Rd, POB 745, Basseterre; tel. 465-5178; fax 466-0307; e-mail sbrisban@caribpub.com; internet stkittsyp.com.

MacPennies Publishing Co: 10A Cayon St East, POB 318, Basseterre; tel. 465-2274; fax 465-8668; e-mail mcpenltd@macpennies .com; internet www.macpennies.com; f. 1969; publr of magazines, books, tel. directories and cable TV guides.

St Kitts-Nevis Publishing Association Ltd: 1 Observer Plaza, Observer Dr., POB 510, Charlestown, Nevis; tel. 469-5907; fax 469-5891; e-mail observnv@sisterisles.kn; internet www .thestkittsnevisobserver.com; f. 1994; Publr and Editor-in-Chief KENNETH A. WILLIAMS.

Broadcasting and Communications

TELECOMMUNICATIONS

Caribbean Cable Communications (CCC): Charlestown, Nevis; tel. 469-5601; e-mail customersupport@caribcable.com; internet ccc2 .caribcable.com; provides internet and cable television services to Nevis; nationalized by Nevis Island Assembly in 2009 and ownership transferred to Nevis Cable Communications Corpn.

Digicel St Kitts and Nevis: Wireless Ventures (Saint Kitts and Nevis) Ltd, Bldg 16, Of. 4, POB 1033, Basseterre; tel. 762-4000; fax 466-4194; e-mail customercarestkittsandnevis@digicelgroup.com; internet www.digicelstkittsandnevis.com; acquired Cingular Wireless' Caribbean operations and licences in 2005; owned by an Irish consortium; Group CEO KEVIN WHITE; Gen. Man. (St Kitts and Nevis) SEAN LATTY.

LIME (St Kitts and Nevis): Cayon St, POB 86, Basseterre; tel. 465-1000; fax 465-1106; e-mail customerservice@lime.com; internet www .lime.com; f. 1985 as St Kitts and Nevis Telecommunications Co Ltd (SKANTEL); fmrly Cable & Wireless St Kitts and Nevis; name changed as above 2008; CEO TONY RICE; CEO (Barbados and Eastern Caribbean) GERARD BORELY.

Regulatory Authority

National Telecommunications Regulatory Commission (NTRC): Fortlands, POB 1958, Basseterre; tel. 466-6872; fax 466-6817; e-mail ntrcskn@ectel.int; internet ntrc.kn; f. 2000; regulates the sector in conjunction with the Eastern Caribbean Telecommunications Authority (based in Saint Lucia); Chair CHRISTOPHER MCMAHON; Dir ERVIN WILLIAMS.

BROADCASTING

Radio

Radio One (SKNBC): Bakers Corner, POB 1773, Basseterre; tel. 466-0941; fax 465-1141; e-mail radio1941fm@yahoo.com; internet www.radioone941fm.com; owned by St Kitts & Nevis Broadcasting Corpn; music and commentary.

Radio Paradise: Bath Plains, POB 508, Charlestown, Nevis; tel. 469-1994; fax 469-1642; e-mail info@radioparadiseonline.com; internet www.radioparadiseonline.com; owned by Trinity Broadcasting Network (USA); Christian; Gen. Man. ANDRE GILBERT.

SKN Choice Times (Choice Radio): POB 146, Pinney's Industrial Site, Nevis; tel. 469-5300; fax 469-1049; e-mail choicefm1053@gmail .com; internet www.skncIt.com.

Sugar City Roc FM: Greenlands, Basseterre; tel. 466-1113; e-mail sugarcityroc903fm@hotmail.com; Gen. Man. VAL THOMAS.

Voice of Nevis (VON) Radio 895 AM: Bath Plains, POB 195, Charlestown, Nevis; tel. 469-1616; fax 469-5329; e-mail gmanager@vonradio.com; internet www.vonradio.com; f. 1988; owned by Nevis Broadcasting Co Ltd; Gen. Man. MERRIT HERBERT.

WINN FM: Unit C24, The Sands, Newtown Bay Rd, Basseterre; tel. 466-9586; fax 466-7904; e-mail info@winnfm.com; internet www.winnfm.com; owned by Federation Media Group; Man. Dir CLIVE BACCHUS.

ZIZ Radio and Television: Springfield, POB 331, Basseterre; tel. 465-2622; fax 466-2159; e-mail info@zizonline.com; internet www.zizonline.com; f. 1961; television from 1972; Music and News; Government Corporation; Gen. Man. CLEMENT O'GARRO.

Television

ZIZ Radio and Television: see Radio.

Finance

(cap. = capital; res = reserves; dep. = deposits; brs = branches; amounts in EC dollars)

REGULATORY AUTHORITY

Financial Services Regulatory Commission: Liverpool Row, POB 898, Basseterre; tel. 466-5048; fax 466-5317; e-mail skanfsd@sisterisles.kn; internet www.skbfinancialservices.com; regulatory authority for banks and insurance companies; Dir FIDELA CLARKE.

BANKING

Central Bank

Eastern Caribbean Central Bank (ECCB): Headquarters Bldg, Bird Rock, POB 89, Basseterre; tel. 465-2537; fax 465-9562; e-mail info@eccb-centralbank.org; internet www.eccb-centralbank.org; f. 1965 as East Caribbean Currency Authority; expanded responsibilities and changed name 1983; responsible for issue of currency in Anguilla, Antigua and Barbuda, Dominica, Grenada, Montserrat, Saint Christopher and Nevis, Saint Lucia and Saint Vincent and the Grenadines; res 248.3m., dep. 1,302.5m., total assets 2,383.0m. (March 2009); Gov. and Chair. Sir K. DWIGHT VENNER; Man. Dir JENNIFER NERO.

Other Banks

Bank of Nevis Ltd: Main St, POB 450, Charlestown, Nevis; tel. 469-5564; fax 469-5798; e-mail info@thebankofnevis.com; internet www.thebankofnevis.com; cap. 9.3m., res 26.3m., dep. 391.3m., total assets 455.7m. (June 2013); Chair. RAWLINSON ISAAC; Gen. Man. L. EVERETTE MARTIN.

CIBC FirstCaribbean International Bank: The Circus, POB 42, Basseterre; tel. 465-2449; fax 465-1041; internet www.cibcfcib.com; f. 2002 following merger of Caribbean operations of Barclays Bank PLC and CIBC; Barclays relinquished its stake to CIBC in 2006, adopted present name in 2011; CEO RIK PARKHILL; 2 brs.

RBTT Bank (SKN) Ltd: Chappel St, POB 673, Charlestown, Nevis; tel. 469-5277; fax 469-1493; internet www.rbtt.com; f. 1955 as Nevis Co-operative Banking Co Ltd; acquired by Royal Bank of Trinidad and Tobago (later known as RBTT) in 1996; Group CEO SURESH SOOKOO.

Scotiabank St Kitts and Nevis (Canada): Fort St, POB 433, Basseterre; tel. 465-4141; fax 465-8600; e-mail bns.stkitts@scotiabank.com; internet www.scotiabank.com/kn/en; f. 1982; Country Man. MARCIA GAUDET; 3 brs.

St Kitts-Nevis-Anguilla National Bank Ltd: Central St, POB 343, Basseterre; tel. 465-2204; fax 465-1060; e-mail webmaster@sknanb.com; internet www.sknanb.com; f. 1971; Govt of St Kitts and Nevis owns 51%; cap. 135.0m., res 295.1m., dep. 2,053.8m. (June 2013); Chair. LINKON MAYNARD; Man. Dir EDMUND LAWRENCE; 5 brs.

Development Bank

Development Bank of St Kitts and Nevis: Church St, POB 249, Basseterre; tel. 465-2288; fax 465-4016; e-mail info@skndb.com; internet www.skndb.com; f. 1981; cap. 10.8m., res 8.9m., dep. 33.5m. (Dec. 2010); Chair. ELVIS NEWTON; Gen. Man. LENWORTH HARRIS.

STOCK EXCHANGE

Eastern Caribbean Securities Exchange: Bird Rock, POB 94, Basseterre; tel. 466-7192; fax 465-3798; e-mail info@ecseonline.com; internet www.ecseonline.com; f. 2001; regional securities market designed to facilitate the buying and selling of financial products for the 8 mem. territories—Anguilla, Antigua and Barbuda, Dominica, Grenada, Montserrat, Saint Christopher and Nevis, Saint Lucia, and Saint Vincent and the Grenadines; Chair. Sir K. DWIGHT VENNER; Gen. Man. TREVOR E. BLAKE.

INSURANCE

National Caribbean Insurance Co Ltd: Church St, POB 374, Basseterre; tel. 465-2694; fax 465-3659; e-mail ncic@sknanb.com; internet www.nci-biz.com; f. 1973; subsidiary of St Kitts-Nevis-Anguilla National Bank Ltd; Gen. Man. JUDITH ATTONG.

Pan-American Life Insurance Co of the Eastern Caribbean: Quinlan, Walwyn and Assocs, Quincott House, 23 Cayon St West, Basseterre; tel. 465–2681; fax 466-2681; internet www.palig.com; f. 2012; part of Pan-American Life Insurance Group (USA); CEO and Man. Dir (Caribbean) WILLIAM R. SCHULZ, Jr.

St Kitts-Nevis Insurance Co Ltd (SNIC): Central St, POB 142, Basseterre; tel. 465-2845; fax 465-5410; e-mail snic@tdcltd.com; subsidiary of St Kitts-Nevis-Anguilla Trading & Devt Co Ltd (TDC); Chair. EARLE KELLY; Gen. Man. CARL THOMPSON.

Several foreign companies also have offices in Saint Christopher and Nevis.

Trade and Industry

GOVERNMENT AGENCY

St Kitts Investment Promotion Agency (SKIPA): POB 1433, Basseterre; tel. 465-1153; fax 465-1154; e-mail info@stkittsipa.org; internet www.stkittsipa.org; f. 2007; CEO ROSALYN HAZELLE.

DEVELOPMENT ORGANIZATION

Foundation for National Development (St Kitts and Nevis) Ltd: Box 507, Bladen Commercial Development, Basseterre; tel. 465-2576; fax 465-9187; e-mail fndskbnev@thecable.net; internet www.carib-hotels.com/stkitts/fndskn; f. 1988; non-profit, non-governmental agency providing loans and technical assistance to small businesses; br. in Nevis.

CHAMBER OF COMMERCE

St Kitts-Nevis Chamber of Industry and Commerce: Horsford Rd, Fortlands, POB 332, Basseterre; tel. 465-2980; fax 465-4490; e-mail sknchamber@sisterisles.kn; internet www.stkittsnevischamber.org; f. 1949; Pres. DAMION HOBSON; Exec. Dir CALVIN CABLE.

UTILITIES

Nevis Electricity Company Ltd (NEVLEC): ValuMart Business Complex, Long Point Rd, POB 852, Charlestown, Nevis; tel. 469-7245; fax 469-7249; e-mail info@nevlec.com; internet www.nevlec.com; f. 2000; owned by the Nevis Island Administration; Pres. MCLEVON (MACKIE) TROSS; Gen. Man. JERVAN SWANSTON (acting).

St Kitts Electricity Co Ltd (SKELEC): Central St, POB 245, Basseterre; tel. 465-2000; fax 466-7308; internet www.skelec.kn; f. 2011 under present name, fmrly state-run Electricity Dept; govt-run autonomous co; generation and distribution of electricity; CEO CARTWRIGHT FARRELL.

West Indies Power (Nevis) Ltd (WIPN): POB 368, Charlestown, Nevis; tel. 662-4032; fax 469-0792; subsidiary of West Indies Power Holdings; devt of geothermal energy; CEO KERRY MCDONALD; Man. (Nevis) RAWLINSON A. ISAAC.

TRADE UNIONS

Nevis Teachers' Union: POB 559, Charlestown, Nevis; tel. 469-8465; fax 469-5663; e-mail nevteach@caribsurf.com; Pres. ERMILITA ELLIOT; Gen. Sec. ORNETTE WEBBE.

St Kitts-Nevis Trades and Labour Union (SKTLU): Masses House, Church St, POB 239, Basseterre; tel. 465-2229; fax 466-9866; e-mail sknunion@caribsurf.com; f. 1940; affiliated to Caribbean Maritime and Aviation Council, Caribbean Congress of Labour, International Federation of Plantation, Agricultural and Allied Workers, and International Trade Union Confederation; associated with St Kitts-Nevis Labour Party; Pres. CLIFFORD THOMAS; Gen. Sec. BATUMBA TAK; c. 3,000 mems.

St Kitts Teachers' Union: Green Tree Housing Devt, POB 545, Basseterre; tel. 465-1921; e-mail stkittsteachersunion@yahoo.com; Pres. RON COLLINS.

Transport

RAILWAYS

There are 58 km (36 miles) of narrow-gauge light railway on Saint Christopher, serving the sugar plantations and tourist routes.

St Kitts Scenic Railway: Sands Unit A6, Bay Rd, POB 191, Basseterre; tel. 465-7263; fax 466-4815; e-mail reservations@stkittsscenicrailway.com; internet www.stkittsscenicrailway.com; f. 2002; Pres. STEVE HITES; Exec. Vice-Pres. and Gen. Man. THOMAS A. WILLIAMS.

ROADS

There were 320 km (199 miles) of road in Saint Christopher and Nevis in 2000, of which approximately 136 km (84 miles) were paved. In 2012 the Caribbean Development Bank approved a loan of US $6.3m. for further expansion of the West Basseterre Bypass Road.

SHIPPING

The Government maintains a commercial motorboat service between the islands, and numerous regional and international shipping lines call at the islands. There is also a deep-water port, Port Zante, at Basseterre, as well as a ferry dock. A second cruise ship pier was planned at Port Zante, to be completed by 2015, at a cost of US $31m. There are three ports in Nevis, at Charlestown, Long Point Port and New Castle. A ferry service operates between Charlestown and Basseterre. In December 2013 the flag registered fleet comprised 366 vessels, with an aggregate displacement of some 1,560,083 grt.

Nevis Air and Sea Ports Authority: Nisbett Bldg, Main St, POB 741, Charlestown; tel. 469-2001; fax 469-2004; e-mail nevports@sisterisles.kn; internet www.nevisports.com; f. 1995; Chair. LAURIE LAWRENCE; Gen. Man. SPENCER HANLEY; Airport Man. STEPHEN HANLEY; Sea Port Man. EVERETTE MASON.

St Christopher Air and Sea Ports Authority: Bird Rock, POB 963, Basseterre; tel. 465-8121; fax 465-8124; e-mail info@scaspa.com; internet www.scaspa.com; f. 1993 to combine St Kitts Port Authority and Airports Authority; Chair. CAROL EVELYN; CEO and Gen. Man. JONATHAN BASS; Airport Man. ELSWORTH WARNER (acting); Sea Port Man. LOUI HENDRICKSON.

Shipping Companies

Delisle Walwyn and Co Ltd: Liverpool Row, POB 44, Basseterre; tel. 465-2631; fax 465-1125; e-mail info@delislewalwyn.com; internet www.delislewalwyn.com; f. 1951; shipping agents; represents Tropical Shipping; Chair. KISHU CHANDIRAMANI; Man. Dir CLAYTON PERKINS.

Hobson Enterprises Ltd: POB 105, Basseterre; tel. 465-8753; fax 465-6154; e-mail contact@hobsonenterprises.com; internet www.hobsonenterprises.com; f. 1987; shipping agent, freight forwarders; CEO DAMION HOBSON.

Woodsrite Enterprises: Bird Rock Industrial Park, POB 92, Basseterre; tel. 465-2532; fax 465-3230; e-mail contact@woodsrite.com; internet www.woodsrite.com; f. 1975; shipping agent, freight forwarders; Man. Dir CUTHBERT WOODS.

CIVIL AVIATION

Robert Llewellyn Bradshaw (formerly Golden Rock) International Airport, 4 km from Basseterre, is equipped to handle jet aircraft and is served by scheduled links with most Caribbean destinations, the United Kingdom, the USA and Canada. A US $17m. expansion and development project at the airport, financed by Taiwan and the St Kitts-Nevis-Anguilla National Bank Ltd, was completed in 2006. St Kitts and Nevis is a shareholder in the regional airline LIAT (see Antigua and Barbuda). Vance W. Amory International Airport (formerly Newcastle Airfield), 11 km from Charlestown, Nevis, has regular scheduled services to St Kitts and other islands in the region.

Nevis Air and Sea Ports Authority: see Shipping.

St Christopher Air and Sea Ports Authority: see Shipping.

LIAT Airlines: Robert Llewellyn Bradshaw International Airport; tel. 465-5491; fax 465-7042; e-mail customerrelations@liatairline.com; internet www.liatairline.com; f. 1956 as Leeward Islands Air Transport Services; privatized in 1995; shares are held by the Govts of Antigua and Barbuda, Montserrat, Grenada, Barbados, Trinidad and Tobago, Jamaica, Guyana, Dominica, Saint Lucia, Saint Vincent and the Grenadines, and Saint Christopher and Nevis (30.8%), Caribbean Airlines (29.2%), LIAT employees (13.3%) and private investors (26.7%); acquired Caribbean Star Airlines in March 2007; scheduled passenger and cargo services to 19 destinations in the Caribbean; charter flights are also undertaken; Chair. JEAN HOLDER; CEO DAVID EVANS.

Tourism

The introduction of regular air services to the US cities of Miami and New York has opened up the islands as a tourist destination. Visitors are attracted by the excellent beaches and the historical Brimstone Hill Fortress National Park on Saint Christopher, the spectacular mountain scenery of Nevis and the islands' associations with Lord Nelson and Alexander Hamilton. In 2013 there were 575,534 cruise ship passengers and 106,906 stop-over visitors. Receipts from tourism were EC $272.8m. in that year. It was hoped that construction of a second cruise ship pier at Port Zante would increase cruise ship arrivals from 2015.

Nevis Tourism Authority: Main St, POB 184, Charlestown, Nevis; tel. 469-7550; fax 469-7551; e-mail info@nevisisland.com; internet www.nevisisland.com; f. 2001; Chair. GARY COLT (acting); CEO GREG PHILLIP.

St Kitts-Nevis Hotel and Tourism Association: Unit C9, Sands Complex, POB 438, Basseterre; tel. 465-5304; fax 465-7746; e-mail info@stkittsnevishta.org; internet www.stkittsnevishta.org; f. 1972; Pres. NICOLAS MENON; Exec. Dir KALOMA O'MARDE-HAMILTON.

St Kitts Tourism Authority: Pelican Mall, Bay Rd, POB 132, Basseterre; tel. 465-4040; fax 465-8794; e-mail ceo@stkittstourism.kn; internet www.stkittstourism.kn; CEO CAROLYN JAMES (acting).

Defence

The small army was disbanded by the Government in 1981, and its duties were absorbed by the St Kitts and Nevis Defence Force and a special tactical unit of the police. Saint Christopher and Nevis participates in the US-sponsored Regional Security System, comprising police, coastguards and army units.

Commander of the St Kitts and Nevis Defence Force: PATRICK WALLACE.

Education

Education is compulsory for 12 years between five and 17 years of age. Primary education begins at the age of five, and lasts for seven years. Secondary education, from the age of 12, generally comprises a first cycle of four years, followed by a second cycle of two years. In 2012 enrolment at primary schools included 81% of children in the relevant age-group, according to UNESCO estimates, while comparable enrolment at secondary schools included 70% of pupils. There are 30 state, eight private and five denominational schools. There is also a technical college. The Ross University School of Veterinary Medicine and the International University of Nursing operated on Saint Christopher and there was a privately financed offshore medical college, the Medical University of the Americas, in Nevis. The 2013 budget allocated the Ministry of Education and Information EC $56.7m., equivalent to 13.9% of recurrent expenditure.

SAINT LUCIA

Geography

PHYSICAL FEATURES

Saint Lucia is the second largest of the Windward Islands, and is located in the eastern Caribbean, between the French department of Martinique and the fellow Commonwealth state of Saint Vincent and the Grenadines. Martinique lies 34 km away, north of the Saint Lucia Channel (a sea lane from the Atlantic into the Caribbean), while the main island of Saint Vincent lies 42 km to the south, across the Saint Vincent Passage. The total area of the country is 616.3 sq km (238 sq miles), most of which consists of the main island itself, although there are a few small islands offshore, such as the uninhabited Maria Islands in the south-east.

The island of Saint Lucia is rugged and volcanic, bulked around a great barrier range of mountains along the backbone of the island, the Barre de l'Isle. The highlands are loftiest towards the south, reaching their highest point at Morne Gimie (950 m or 3,118 ft) in the south-west, although the peaks considered most emblematic of the island lie still further to the south-west. Here twin mountain horns rear above the spa town of Soufrière, jungle-clad volcanic plugs known as the Pitons (Petit Piton and, to its south, Gros Piton), steep cones plunging straight into the sea. Elsewhere on the island there are places where the highland terrain gives way to broad, fertile valleys, while the rich soil generally makes for a verdant landscape. The native rainforest has suffered since European colonization, particularly in the later 20th century, but is now protected and is still home to a rich variety of flora and fauna (deforestation was also affecting water supply). Like other islands in the Windwards, Saint Lucia is home to animals such as the iguana, the fer de lance (the only poisonous snake on the island), the manicou, the rarely seen agouti and the historically introduced mongoose. There are some endemic species, such as nine types of flamboyant tree, the pygmy gecko, the Saint Lucia tree lizard and, on the protected Maria Islands, a ground lizard and a grass snake. Bird species include the Saint Lucia parrot, the endangered Saint Lucia oriole and Saint Lucia black finch, and the Semper's warbler, which may now be extinct. On the rougher Atlantic coast turtles lay their eggs and other birds nest.

CLIMATE

The climate is subtropical marine, moderated by the eastern and north-eastern trade winds. The island lies within the hurricane belt, and storms can cause flooding and mudslides in the steep terrain. Most rain falls between May and November, with annual averages varying considerably in different parts of the island, mainly owing to altitude. The range is between 1,540 mm and 3,540 mm (60 ins–138 ins). Temperatures are fairly constant at around 27°C (80°F), though are sometimes slightly lower in the drier months or in the highlands.

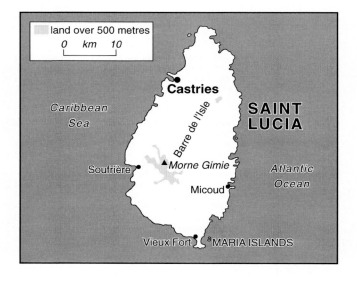

POPULATION

The long years of alternating French and British rule have left a rich cultural legacy. About 90% of the population are black, and use English as their official language, but a French patois or Creole (known as Kweyol locally) is widespread. About 61% of the population are Roman Catholics, according to the 2010 census. About 11% of the population are Seventh-day Adventists, 9% are Pentecostalists, 2% are Evangelical Christians, 2% are Baptists and 2% are Anglicans. The island has produced some of the Caribbean's foremost writers, artists and thinkers—the country has the highest per head rate of Nobel laureates (Sir Arthur Lewis, Economics, 1979, and Derek Walcott, Literature, 1992).

UN estimates put the total population of Saint Lucia at 183,599 in mid-2014. About two-fifths of this total live in and around the island's capital, Castries, which is sited on the north-western coast. Other important towns include Micoud, on the south-eastern coast, across the island from Soufrière, and Vieux Fort, the main industrial centre, by the airport, near the southern tip of the island. Gros Islet is north of Castries, towards the end of the island, and Dennery is north of Micoud, where the road across the Barre de l'Isle reaches the east coast. For administrative purposes the island is divided into quarters, although, confusingly, there are 11 of these.

History

MARK WILSON

Saint Lucia is a constitutional monarchy within the Commonwealth. Queen Elizabeth II is Head of State, and is represented in Saint Lucia by a Governor-General. There is a bicameral legislature with an elected chamber.

A small number of Saint Lucians trace their ancestry to the island's original Amerindian inhabitants, who knew the island as Hiwanarau or Hewanorra. There is no mention of Saint Lucia in Christopher Columbus's logbook, although a local tradition holds that he discovered and named the island on 13 December 1502, St Lucy's day. The first successful European settlement was French. The island changed hands on 14 occasions before passing to British rule in 1814, but extended periods of French rule in the 17th and 18th centuries established a French Creole as the main spoken language, and the Roman Catholic religion as the faith of the majority of the population. The island's hybrid legal code also contains elements of the pre-Revolutionary French legal tradition.

As in the United Kingdom's other Caribbean colonies, slavery was abolished in 1834. After this date, some former slaves established small peasant farms. Saint Lucia received significant numbers of Indian indentured labourers in the 19th century; their descendants form a significant minority in some parts of the island.

During the Second World War the USA built an important airbase at Vieux Fort in the south of the island, part of which was later developed as Hewanorra International Airport. After the war the introduction of banana cultivation brought a modest increase in rural living standards. The Saint Lucia Labour Party (SLP) was formed in 1949, won the first universal suffrage election in 1951, and remained in office until its 1964 defeat at the hands of the United Workers' Party (UWP), which then retained power until 1979, with John (later Sir John) Compton as Prime Minister.

Saint Lucia joined the Federation of the West Indies in 1958, along with nine other British colonies. When Jamaica and Trinidad and Tobago left in 1962, the Federation collapsed, and an attempt to unite the remaining colonies as the 'little eight' was unsuccessful. Along with its neighbours, Saint Lucia became a British Associated State in 1967, responsible for its internal affairs, with the United Kingdom retaining control of external affairs and defence. Independence was granted on 22 February 1979.

The SLP won a general election in July 1979, but the new Government was torn apart by fierce factional rivalries between the Prime Minister, Allan Louisy, and a populist faction led by George Odlum. The Government was further damaged by allegations of mismanagement. After a Government defeat in Parliament, Winston Cenac replaced Louisy as Prime Minister. However, factional struggles continued; a series of protests, including an organized short-term closure of private sector businesses in 1982, led to the formation of an interim Government led by Michael Pilgrim, which presided over fresh elections in that year. The UWP regained power with a convincing majority; Odlum fought the election as leader of the newly formed Progressive Labour Party, but was beaten into third place by the mainstream SLP.

Compton's majority was reduced to a single seat in the 1987 elections. Another election held immediately afterwards produced exactly the same result; however, the Government's position was strengthened when an SLP member crossed the floor.

After a total of 29 years in office, Compton resigned as Prime Minister in March 1996, in preparation for retirement. He was succeeded by Vaughan Lewis, a former Director-General of the Organisation of Eastern Caribbean States. The SLP at the same time chose a new leader, Kenny Anthony, a lawyer with an academic post in the University of the West Indies. An election in May 1997 resulted in an overwhelming victory for the SLP, which took 16 of the House of Assembly's 17 seats. A disunited UWP did not perform well in opposition, and was not strengthened by the return of Compton from retirement, nor the formation of an alliance with Odlum, who had, for the

second time in his career, broken with an SLP Government. In spite of the continuing troubles of the banana industry and in a poor year for tourism, the SLP won a second comfortable election victory in December 2001, winning 14 of the 17 parliamentary seats; the UWP increased its strength to three seats.

The removal of the Minister of Home Affairs and Gender Relations, Sarah Flood-Beaubrun, in January 2004 over her vehement opposition to a liberalization of abortion law—and her subsequent move to the opposition benches as an independent—had little initial impact on the Government. However, the disruption provoked a further split in the opposition in April, when UWP leader Arsene James was replaced by Marcus Nicholas, his former deputy. Nicholas enjoyed the support of Flood-Beaubrun and Wilson, but not of the UWP itself, leaving the former party of government with James as its sole loyal supporter in the legislature. Concerned by the deteriorating position of the UWP, Sir John Compton once again emerged from retirement in 2005, now aged 79 years, to replace his chosen successor, Dr Vaughn Lewis, as party leader; like Lewis, however, he did not hold a parliamentary seat.

At a general election held in December 2006 the UWP took 11 of the 17 seats, some by a very narrow margin. The SLP retained only six seats, which, although surprising to most observers, appeared to reflect the view of many voters that the party had become arrogant and élitist in its approach.

The Minister of Foreign Affairs, Rufus Bousquet, announced in April 2007 that Saint Lucia would resume diplomatic relations with Taiwan. There were, however, deep divisions on the issue within the Cabinet, with Prime Minister Compton reportedly among those expressing grave doubts. Saint Lucia had entered into diplomatic relations with Taiwan soon after independence, but switched to the People's Republic of China following the election of the SLP Government in 1997; in return, China had funded the construction of an 8,000-seat stadium and designated a free trade zone, with further plans announced for a national cultural complex and the construction of a US $10m. psychiatric hospital, work on which began in 2007. Compton had held discussions on behalf of his party with a Taiwanese representative in Saint Vincent before the 2006 election, but was believed to favour a restoration of trade and technical relations, rather than full recognition. Taiwan offered to complete projects initiated by China, but with construction in progress, a change in sponsor was not straightforward. Following the establishment of relations with Taiwan, China suspended diplomatic relations with Saint Lucia and closed its embassy in Castries.

Compton suffered a series of strokes in April 2007. Stephenson King, the Minister of Health and UWP Chairman, was appointed acting Prime Minister. Compton died in early September at the age of 82. On 9 September King was sworn in as Prime Minister, having won the support, after some intra-party manoeuvring, of nine of the UWP's remaining 10 representatives in the House of Assembly. This was a bare majority of the 16 sitting members of the House, with Compton's seat at that point vacant. In a by-election in November Compton's daughter Jeannine Compton-Rambally was elected, restoring the UWP's strength in the House to 11. Divisions within the governing party persisted, however, and Compton-Rambally's by-election opponents included two dissident members of the UWP.

King's Government remained deeply divided, with continuing disputes between party factions. In June 2007, while King was acting premier, Rufus Bousquet was removed from his ministerial post. Bousquet repeatedly questioned the circumstances of his removal, and pressed strongly for readmission to the Cabinet. He abstained on the budget vote in April 2008, and wrote formally to the Governor-General in May to withdraw his support for King as Prime Minister, as did the Deputy Speaker, Marcus Nicholas. In response to this pressure, Bousquet was in June, after a year on the back benches, reappointed to the Cabinet, as Minister for External Affairs, International Trade and Investment.

The Minister for Physical Development, Housing, Urban Renewal, Local Government and the Environment, Richard Frederick, in July 2007 was questioned over alleged under-invoicing of vehicles imported for his private use. The matter was referred to the Director of Public Prosecutions. However, in May 2008 the Prime Minister made a controversial request to the customs department to treat it on an administrative rather than criminal basis; Frederick then initiated legal action contesting the seizure of his vehicles. Indicating that concern over his alleged misconduct extended beyond Saint Lucia, the USA in September 2011 revoked his diplomatic and other visas, after which he resigned from the Cabinet, still maintaining that he had done nothing wrong.

Ausbert d'Auvergne, an appointed government Senator, resigned in May 2008 as Minister of Economic Affairs, Economic Planning, Investment and National Development, under strong pressure from party colleagues, particularly Bousquet and Frederick, who complained that he had excessive influence. D'Auvergne had been strongly criticized in 1999 in the report of a commission of inquiry by a British Queen's Counsel, Louis Blom-Cooper. The report noted serious conflicts of interest in his role as Permanent Secretary in the Ministry of Planning, Development and the Environment in the early 1990s during the sale of a valuable parcel of state land to a company of which he was Chairman and Managing Director.

A commission of inquiry was appointed in February 2009 under the Guyanese attorney Fenton Ramsahoye into allegations of corruption under the Anthony Government. The commission examined a road development project, which cost close to three times the original estimate, the affairs of the National Conservation Authority, and a government debt guarantee for a company linked to the construction of a Hyatt Hotel. The report, made public in October, indicated serious mismanagement of public funds, but not corruption. Accusations of corruption, meanwhile, continued to be levelled against the current administration by its political opponents, while a June 2010 judgment of the Eastern Caribbean Court of Appeal was sharply critical of duty concessions granted to a cabinet minister in connection with a resort development.

In 2006 the outgoing SLP Government recruited 10 former British police officers on two-year contracts as part of a drive to reform the police force. Soon after his appointment as Minister of Home Affairs and National Security, Keith Mondesir ordered Deputy Police Commissioner Hermangild Francis to take mandatory leave from January 2007, while the Police Commissioner, Ausbert Regis, together with two other senior officers, was sent on leave from June. A former British police officer, John Broughton, was appointed acting Police Commissioner, but he developed a difficult relationship with many of his colleagues. In May 2008 the Police Welfare Association (PWA) organized a march by police officers to demand his dismissal, claiming that the security of the country had been compromised. Tensions between the PWA and Broughton subsequently subsided to some extent, but by the end of May three of the 10 British officers had tendered their resignation. Broughton's contract ended in October, with his remaining British colleagues leaving at around the same time, after which Regis resumed his post as Commissioner. However, Regis was unexpectedly removed from the post in May 2010, appointed Special Adviser to the Prime Minister on national security, and replaced as police commissioner by Vernon Francois. Regis subsequently launched a legal challenge to his reassignment, with a ruling in his favour in November 2011; however, after reaching an agreement with the SLP Government elected in the same month (see below), he agreed in March 2012 to take up

the disputed post in the Prime Minister's office. US agencies have expressed concern over the personnel changes, which were seen as disrupting anti-drugs enforcement efforts. Francois was, in 2013, barred from travel to the USA to participate in training programmes; this was believed to be a US response to the previous year's spate of police killings under the so-called Leahy Law, which blocks assistance to security forces believed responsible for human rights violations.

Janine Compton-Antoine, the daughter of the former Prime Minister Sir John Compton, resigned from the UWP in February 2011, reducing the party's parliamentary strength to 10 of the 17 seats. King called a general election for 28 November 2011, slightly ahead of the constitutional deadline. After a troubled five years, the UWP lost to the SLP, which took just 51.0% of the popular vote and 11 of the 17 seats, to 47.0% and six seats for the UWP. In five seats, the winning margin was fewer than 100 votes, with the SLP winning one of them by just two of the 5,892 votes cast, and another by seven out of 10,475. Kenny Anthony was again sworn in as Prime Minister. The former tourism minister, Allen Chastenet, in July 2013 replaced King as leader of the UWP. As Chastenet had no seat in parliament, he was unable to take the constitutional position of Leader of the Opposition. This was retained initially by his rival, King, who was, however, ousted in January 2014 by Gale Rigobert.

Although his previous Government had enjoyed good relations with China, Anthony announced in September 2012 that his new administration would continue to recognize Taiwan. In March 2013 the SLP Government asked the Eastern Caribbean Court of Appeal to rule on the constitutional procedure required to replace the Privy Council sitting in the United Kingdom with the Caribbean Court of Justice in Trinidad and Tobago, as the final court of appeal for Saint Lucia. The Court ruled in May that the change could be made by legislation and without the need for a referendum; however there was no further progress on the matter by mid-2014. In August 2013 Saint Lucia joined Venezuela's Petrocaribe initiative, in which petroleum products are supplied on favourable terms of credit. In the same year the country also became a member of the Venezuelan-led Bolivarian Alliance for the Peoples of our America-People's Trade Treaty (Alianza Bolivariana para los Pueblos de Nuestra América-Tratado de Comercio de los Pueblos—ALBA-TCP).

Drugs transshipment and violent crime remained serious concerns. Marijuana is imported from Saint Vincent for local use, and is also grown within Saint Lucia. Cocaine is transshipped from Venezuela; according to the US Department of State, around 40% of the shipment moves on to the French Overseas Departments, 25% to the United Kingdom, and 25% to the USA or Canada; most of the local marijuana market is supplied from Saint Vincent and the Grenadines. Cocaine transshipment through the eastern Caribbean increased sharply from 2013. There were 39 murders in 2012, with a per head murder rate of 22 per 100,000 inhabitants, which was high by international standards and more than five times that of the USA. The US Department of State reported 12 killings of criminal suspects by the police in 2011–12, but only one in January–November 2013, along with one suspicious death in custody. The prison has capacity for 500 inmates but held 587 in 2013, of whom 57% were in pre-trial detention, which can last up to 10 years. The murders of British tourists in 2006, 2011 and 2014, and of a British hotelier also in 2014, with resulting adverse publicity in the British media, underlined the potential threat to tourism. Murders of witnesses in gang-related cases have prompted calls for a regional witness protection programme. The US Department of State lists Saint Lucia as a 'country of concern' for money-laundering.

Economy

MARK WILSON

With a population of 166,526 inhabitants on 616.3 sq km (238 sq miles) at the May 2010 census, Saint Lucia has a larger population than its neighbours in the Organisation of Eastern Caribbean States (OECS); however, the census recorded a total 4.1% below the expected number, and showed an average yearly increase of only 0.7% since 2000. With a per head gross domestic product (GDP) at market prices of US $7,276 in 2012, Saint Lucia was a reasonably prosperous middle-income economy. Growth averaged an annual 4.1% from 2003 to 2008, with tourism performing well, and in spite of continuing problems with the banana industry. However, the economy has been generally stagnant since the onset of the international recession, and contracted by a cumulative 1.2% over the period 2009–13. Since 2010 the IMF has noted an increase in non-performing loans and regulatory weaknesses in the non-bank financial sector, a consequence of an earlier credit boom. Like its neighbours, Saint Lucia suffered in 2009 and afterwards from the collapse of a Trinidad-based insurance conglomerate, CL Financial, which posed risks to financial stability throughout the eastern Caribbean, with an important subsidiary, the British American Insurance Company, declared insolvent. The IMF estimated the total eastern Caribbean exposure to the CL group at EC $2,100m., or 17% of the sub-regional GDP. In 2014 Saint Lucia ranked 97th out of 187 countries in the UN Development Programme's Human Development Index, the second-lowest ranking in the English-speaking Caribbean.

The fiscal position deteriorated from 1999, with the fiscal deficit reaching more than 6% of GDP in 2006; there was a recovery to a more sustainable 1.1% in 2008. In 2009 the IMF approved a US $10.7m. disbursement under the rapid-access component of the Exogenous Shocks Facility. The Government at that time proposed introduction of a value-added tax (VAT) in 2010, property tax reform and strict control of spending. The deficit averaged 5.9% of GDP in 2009–13, and rose to 9.2% for the fiscal year ending in March 2013, as the economy suffered from the international recession, while public sector salary costs increased by 69% in the 10 years to 2014, when they reached 53% of total expenditure. These problems were compounded by the effects of Hurricane Tomas in late 2010. Introduction of VAT was rescheduled for October 2012. In spite of this new revenue source and other attempts to address the fiscal imbalance, the budget was at 5.7% of GDP for the year to March 2014, financed in part by Taiwanese and European Union (EU) grants. Meanwhile, the unemployment rate was 24.9% in late 2013, up from 16.8% in 2008, with the construction and tourism sectors suffering a downturn. Total public debt was estimated at 75% of GDP at the end of 2013, an increase from 59% in 2006, with interest payments doubling in the nine years to 2013; none the less, the ratio was still below levels recorded in some neighbouring islands, and Prime Minister Kenny Anthony in July 2012 rejected proposals to seek IMF assistance, but instead pursued a strict fiscal path, with most public sector trade unions accepting a salary freeze for 2010–13. Anthony in June 2014 outlined options for reducing the unfinanced portion of the fiscal deficit, which included salary reductions of 5% for all but the lowest paid, with a further three-year salaries freeze until 2016, and pay increases beyond that date dependent on positive macroeconomic indicators, including a GDP growth rate exceeding 2.5%. These proposals met strong trade union opposition.

Saint Lucia is a member of the Caribbean Community and Common Market (CARICOM), whose members formed the Caribbean Single Market and Economy (CSME) in 2006. The CSME was intended to enshrine the free movement of goods, services and labour throughout the CARICOM region. Saint Lucia also houses the secretariat of the OECS, which links nine of the smaller Caribbean territories, while the Eastern Caribbean Central Bank, based in Saint Christopher and Nevis, supervises its financial affairs.

Agriculture comprised only 2.4% of GDP in 2013, down from 14.7% in 1990; however, the sector still employed some 12.2% of the working population in 2007. Banana exports to the United Kingdom under protected market access arrangements were an economic mainstay from the 1950s, but the industry suffered a steep decline from the 1990s as the trade privileges of Caribbean producers in the European market were eroded. In 1992 income from banana exports was equivalent to 53.6% of merchandise exports. After a decrease in export values in the mid-2000s, by 2009 banana exports recovered to US $28.9m., equivalent to 13.7% of merchandise exports, but from that year an outbreak of Black Sigatoka disease compounded the industry's troubles, covering around 70% of the crop area by 2012. In 2011 export values were US $6.3m., equivalent to 12.4% of the total value; however, there was a partial recovery by 2013 with 12,202 tons exported, generating US $7.8m. in earnings. Significant grant aid from the EU was available for irrigation and technical support, as well as for economic diversification and social support. Small farmers produced a wide variety of fruits, vegetables and livestock products for the local market, with some produce being exported to neighbouring islands.

Saint Lucia's natural attractions and direct air links to North America and the United Kingdom have encouraged the development of tourism, which is the principal source of foreign exchange. Tourism receipts increased from EC $415.3m. in 1990 to EC $1,030.5m. in 2005, slipping back, however, to an average of EC $832.1m. for the next six years, before a partial recovery to EC $955.4m. in 2013. In that year the island attracted some 318,626 stop-over tourists, 0.2% more than the previous peak year of 2005, and more than any of its OECS neighbours. There were also some 594,118 cruise ship passengers in 2013, 15.0% fewer than in 2009, but 65.2% higher than in 2006, although cruise passengers had much lower per head spending than stop-over tourists. The US-Norwegian company Royal Caribbean International collaborated with the Government on waterfront development in the capital, Castries, with proposed expansion of more lucrative home port activity. In 2013 some 51.6% of tourist arrivals were from North America and 27.8% were from Europe, mainly the United Kingdom. Tourism in Saint Lucia is reliant to a great extent on all-inclusive properties, where meals and other facilities are pre-paid; the Sandals Jamaican all-inclusive group had three properties in operation in 2014, and its strong marketing effort was, in part, responsible for the recent resilience of the industry. These and other hotel and residential development investments provided strong support to the construction industry, despite several major hotel and resort investments being placed on hold in 2008, in some cases in mid-construction, as credit conditions tightened and the second-home market stagnated. Yachting is an important sub-sector of tourism, with 7,793 yacht calls in 2013. The Jazz Festival in May is also a significant attraction, as is the annual Carnival, now held in July in place of its traditional pre-Lenten date. However, the high rate of violent crime, much of it drugs-related, was a potential threat to tourism; the per head murder rate of 20 per 100,000 inhabitants in 2013 was high by world standards and more than four times that of the USA.

Manufacturing comprised 3.4% of GDP in 2013, down from 8.2% in 1990. A brewery exports some of its products to the regional market. A transshipment facility operated by the US-based Hess Corporation at Cul de Sac, south of Castries, was offered for sale in 2012; an agreement for sale to Buckeye Partners was announced in October 2013. Saint Lucia houses the headquarters of the Eastern Caribbean Telecommunications Authority; the telecommunications sector has been liberalized, and the Government regarded telemarketing and informatics as areas with great potential for economic growth.

The offshore financial services sector was only established in 2000 and was in some ways better regulated than those of most other OECS members. Saint Lucia, in contrast to several of its neighbours, was not listed in 2000 by the Financial Action Task Force on Money Laundering (based in Paris, France) as 'non-co-operative' in the control of money-laundering, but is classed by the US Department of State as a 'country of concern', an intermediate category. In 2010 Saint Lucia was removed from the Organization for Economic Co-operation and Development's 'grey list' of jurisdictions which did not meet international reporting standards, after signing Tax Information Exchange Agreements with the United Kingdom, France and other partners.

The island is at some risk from hurricanes, as well as from less powerful tropical storms, which can cause serious damage to the banana industry. Along with its neighbours, Saint Lucia suffered flooding and severe damage outside the hurricane season from a December 2013 weather system, which brought exceptionally heavy rain of 150 mm in 24 hours, with at least six deaths and widespread infrastructural and other damage. There is a volcanic centre at Soufrière in the south of the island, which has no recent history of threatening activity and has some importance as a tourist attraction, but could become

active at any time. The development of geothermal power was being promoted in order to reduce the country's dependency on oil, and a 30-year development agreement was signed in 2010 for development by a Canadian company, Qualibou Energy, which stated that there are proven reserves capable of generating 30 MW of power and potential reserves for an additional 140 MW. However, no substantial progress had been made by mid-2014. The generating capacity of St Lucia Electricity Services Ltd (LUCELEC), majority-owned by Emera Inc of Canada, was 76 MW in 2011. A waste-to-energy generation plant and a wind farm were also proposed, along with a 8–10 MW photovoltaic power plant. The Government has declared the ambitious goal of generating 35% of energy from renewable sources by 2020, with the removal of LUCELEC's monopoly on power generation.

Statistical Survey

Source (unless otherwise indicated): St Lucian Government Statistics Department, Block A, Government Bldgs, Waterfront, Castries; tel. 452-7670; fax 451-8254; e-mail statsdept@candw.lc; internet www.stats.gov.lc.

AREA AND POPULATION

Area: 616.3 sq km (238 sq miles).

Population: 162,982 at census of 22 May 2001 (including estimate for underenumeration); 165,595 (males 82,194, females 83,401) at census of 10 May 2010 (preliminary). *By District* (population at 2010 census, preliminary): Castries 65,656; Anse La Raye 6,247; Canaries 2,044; Soufrière 8,472; Choiseul 6,098; Laborie 6,701; Vieux Fort 16,284; Micoud 16,284; Dennery 12,599; Gros Islet 25,210. *Mid-2014* (UN estimate): 183,599 (Source: UN, *World Population Prospects: The 2012 Revision*).

Density (at mid-2014): 297.9 per sq km.

Population by Age and Sex (UN estimates at mid-2014): *0–14 years:* 43,158 (males 21,791, females 21,367); *15–64 years:* 124,112 (males 61,015, females 63,097); *65 years and over:* 16,329 (males 7,304, females 9,025); *Total:* 183,599 (males 90,110, females 93,489) (Source: UN, *World Population Prospects: The 2012 Revision*).

Principal Town (incl. suburbs, population at 2010 census, preliminary): Castries (capital) 22,111. *Mid-2014* (incl. suburbs, UN estimate): Castries (capital) 22,186 (Source: UN, *World Urbanization Prospects: The 2014 Revision*).

Births, Marriages and Deaths (2011, unless otherwise indicated): Registered live births 2,009 (birth rate 12.0 per 1,000); Registered marriages 591 (2005, preliminary); Registered deaths 983 (death rate 5.9 per 1,000). *2013:* Crude birth rate 14.2 per 1,000; Crude death rate 7.2 per 1,000 (Source: Pan American Health Organization).

Life Expectancy (years at birth): 77.2 (males 74.5, females 80.1) in 2013. Source: Pan American Health Organization.

Economically Active Population (persons aged 15 years and over, labour survey for October–December 2007): Agriculture, hunting and forestry 7,670; Fishing 600; Manufacturing 4,160; Electricity, gas and water 420; Construction 8,940; Wholesale and retail trade, repair of motor vehicles, motorcycles and personal and household goods 11,210; Hotels and restaurants 8,870; Transport, storage and communications 4,370; Financial intermediation 1,090; Real estate, renting and business activities 2,950; Public administration and compulsory social security 12,200; Education 890; Health and social work 280; Other community, social and personal service activities 2,080; Private households with employed persons 2,280; *Subtotal* 68,010; Activities not adequately defined 420; Not reported 4,350; *Total employed* 72,780; Unemployed 12,480; *Total labour force* 85,260 (males 45,510, females 39,750). *2013* (labour survey, January–March 2013): Total employed 72,189 (males 37,883, females 34,306); Unemployed 21,113 (males 10,627, females 10,486); Total labour force 93,302 (males 48,510, females 44,792).

HEALTH AND WELFARE

Key Indicators

Total Fertility Rate (children per woman, 2012): 1.9.

Under-5 Mortality Rate (per 1,000 live births, 2012): 18.

Physicians (per 1,000 head, 2012): 1.3.

Hospital Beds (per 1,000 head, 2012): 1.6.

Health Expenditure (2011): US $ per head (PPP): 860.

Health Expenditure (2011): % of GDP: 7.6.

Health Expenditure (2011): public (% of total): 46.6.

Access to Water (% of persons, 2012): 94.

Access to Sanitation (% of persons, 2011): 65.

Total Carbon Dioxide Emissions ('000 metric tons, 2010): 403.4.

Carbon Dioxide Emissions Per Head (metric tons, 2010): 2.3.

Human Development Index (2013): ranking: 97.

Human Development Index (2013): value: 0.714.

Source: partly Pan American Health Organization; for other sources and definitions, see explanatory note on p. vi.

AGRICULTURE, ETC.

Principal Crops ('000 metric tons, 2012, FAO estimates): Cassava 1.3; Yams 0.5; Coconuts 14.9; Bananas 25.0; Plantains 1.7; Citrus fruits 1.9. *Aggregate Production* ('000 metric tons, may include official, semi-official or estimated data): Roots and tubers 4.7; Vegetables (incl. melons) 3.2; Fruits (excl. melons) 35.8.

Livestock ('000 head, 2012, FAO estimates): Cattle 11.0; Sheep 10.0; Goats 9.5; Pigs 20.0; Horses 1.1; Poultry 450.

Livestock Products ('000 metric tons, 2012, FAO estimates): Pig meat 1.4; Chicken meat 1.6; Cows' milk 1.2; Hen eggs 1.2.

Fishing (metric tons, live weight, 2012): Capture 2,205 (Wahoo 151; Skipjack tuna 109; Blackfin tuna 192; Yellowfin tuna 98; Common dolphinfish 504; Stromboid conchs 473); Aquaculture 13; *Total catch* 2,218. Note: Figures exclude aquatic plants.

Source: FAO.

INDUSTRY

Production (2007 unless otherwise indicated): Electric energy 380.9 million kWh (2010, preliminary); Copra 1,094 metric tons (2004); Coconut oil (unrefined) 0.1m. litres; Coconut oil (refined) 118,100 litres; Coconut meal 389,500 kg; Rum 115,100 proof gallons (Source: partly Eastern Caribbean Central Bank).

FINANCE

Currency and Exchange Rates: 100 cents = 1 Eastern Caribbean dollar (EC $). *Sterling, US Dollar and Euro Equivalents* (30 May 2014): £1 sterling = EC $4.542; US $1 = EC $2.700; €1 = EC $3.675; EC $100 = £22.02 = US $37.04 = €27.21. *Exchange Rate:* Fixed at US $1 = EC $2.70 since July 1976.

Budget (EC $ million, 2013): *Revenue:* Tax revenue 813.6 (Taxes on income and profits 223.1, Taxes on property 8.3, Taxes on domestic goods and services 362.4, Taxes on international trade and transactions 219.8); Other current revenue 49.4; Capital revenue 0.4; Total 863.4 (excl. grants 17.3). *Expenditure:* Current expenditure 841.0 (Personal emoluments 371.0, Goods and services 163.2, Interest payments 134.8, Transfers and subsidies 172.0); Capital expenditure and net lending 268.4; Total 1,109.4. Source: Eastern Caribbean Central Bank.

International Reserves (US $ million at 31 December 2013): IMF special drawing rights 23.75; Reserve position in IMF 0.01; Foreign exchange 168.46; *Total* 192.22. Source: IMF, *International Financial Statistics*.

Money Supply (EC $ million at 31 December 2013): Currency outside depository corporations 159.97; Transferable deposits 738.49; Other deposits 2,401.72; *Broad money* 3,300.17. Source: IMF, *International Financial Statistics.*

Cost of Living (Consumer Price Index; base: 2010 = 100): All items 102.8 in 2011; 107.1 in 2012; 108.6 in 2013. Source: IMF, *International Financial Statistics.*

Gross Domestic Product (EC $ million at constant 2006 prices): 2,996.6 in 2010; 3,039.2 in 2011; 3,000.0 in 2012. Source: Eastern Caribbean Central Bank.

Expenditure on the Gross Domestic Product (EC $ million at current prices, 2012): Government final consumption expenditure 512.94; Private final consumption expenditure 2,489.37; Gross capital formation 937.52; *Total domestic expenditure* 3,939.83; Exports of goods and services 1,583.80; *Less* Imports of goods and services 1,964.11; *GDP at market prices* 3,559.52. Source: Eastern Caribbean Central Bank.

Gross Domestic Product by Economic Activity (EC $ million in current prices, 2012): Agriculture, hunting, forestry and fishing 92.90; Mining and quarrying 7.18; Manufacturing 109.63; Electricity and water 117.02; Construction 228.74; Wholesale and retail trade 259.22; Restaurants and hotels 479.18; Transport 398.97; Communications 180.58; Banking and insurance 178.10; Real estate and housing 538.84; Public administration, defence and social security 211.96; Education 130.86; Health and social work 63.59; Other services 155.36; *Sub-total* 3,152.14; *Less* Imputed bank service charge 62.52; *Total in basic prices* 3,089.62; Taxes, less subsidies, on products 469.91; *GDP at market prices* 3,559.52. Source: Eastern Caribbean Central Bank.

Balance of Payments (EC $ million, 2013): Exports of goods 554.38; Imports of goods –1,340.98; *Trade balance* –786.60; Services (net) 598.20; *Balance on goods and services* –188.40; Other income received (net) –102.10; *Balance on goods, services and income* –290.50; Current transfers received (net) 19.62; *Current balance* –270.88; Capital account (net) 76.23; Direct investment (net) 225.49; Portfolio investment (net) 253.97; Other investment –326.82; Net errors and omissions –65.36; *Overall balance* –107.37. Source: Eastern Caribbean Central Bank.

EXTERNAL TRADE

Principal Commodities (EC $ million, 2013, estimates): *Imports c.i.f.:* Food and live animals 364.08; Beverages and tobacco 71.1; Mineral fuels, lubricants, etc. 221.6; Chemicals 135.9; Basic manufactures 234.2; Machinery and transport equipment 289.9; Miscellaneous manufactured articles 148.1; Total (incl. others) 1,523.9. *Exports f.o.b.* (incl. re-exports): Food and live animals 47.4; Beverages and tobacco 87.6; Mineral fuels, lubricants, etc. 128.9; Chemicals 25.0; Basic manufactures 31.1; Machinery and transport equipment 75.1; Miscellaneous manufactured articles 57.8; Total (incl. others) 469.3. Source: Eastern Caribbean Central Bank.

Principal Trading Partners (US $ million, 2008): *Imports c.i.f.:* Barbados 23.1; Canada 11.9; China, People's Repub. 7.1; Finland 0.4; France (incl. Monaco) 8.4; Germany 5.9; Japan 28.2; Netherlands 7.0; Panama 8.8; Saint Vincent and the Grenadines 5.4; Thailand 11.4; Trinidad and Tobago 156.0; United Kingdom 26.8; USA 279.1; Total (incl. others) 655.7. *Exports f.o.b.* (excl. re-exports): Antigua and Barbuda 3.7; Barbados 13.9; Dominica 4.6; France (incl. Monaco) 1.9; Grenada 3.0; Saint Vincent and the Grenadines 4.9; Trinidad and Tobago 38.1; United Kingdom 24.8; USA 55.8; Total (incl. others) 164.0. Source: UN, *International Trade Statistics Yearbook.*

TRANSPORT

Road Traffic (registered motor vehicles at 31 December 2007): Passenger cars 34,126; Buses and motor coaches 3,690; Motorcycles and mopeds 830. Source: IRF, *World Road Statistics.*

Shipping: *Arrivals* (2006): 1,557 vessels. *Flag Registered Fleet* (at 31 December 2013): 2 vessels (total displacement 639 grt) (Source: Lloyd's List Intelligence—www.lloydslistintelligence.com). *International Seaborne Freight Traffic* (at Castries and Vieux Fort, metric tons, 2012): Goods loaded 113,578; Goods unloaded 475,538 (Source: Saint Lucia Air and Sea Ports Authority).

Civil Aviation (traffic at George F. L. Charles and Hewanorra International airports, 2012): Aircraft movements 36,658; Passenger departures 384,138; Passenger arrivals 399,004; Cargo loaded (metric tons) 1,470.2; Cargo unloaded (metric tons) 1,647.1. Source: Saint Lucia Air and Sea Ports Authority.

TOURISM

Visitor Arrivals: 994,961 (312,404 stop-over visitors, 10,523 excursionists, 41,730 yacht passengers, 630,304 cruise ship passengers) in 2011; 931,222 (306,801 stop-over visitors, 10,354 excursionists, 42,173 yacht passengers, 571,894 cruise ship passengers) in 2012; 960,617 (318,626 stop-over visitors, 8,227 excursionists, 39,646 yacht passengers, 594,118 cruise ship passengers) in 2013. *Stop-over Visitors by Origin* (2013): Canada 35,985; Caribbean 60,521; United Kingdom 70,868; USA 128,331; Other 22,921; Total 318,626.

Tourism Receipts (EC $ million): 865.5 in 2011; 910.7 in 2012; 955.9 in 2013.

Source: Eastern Caribbean Central Bank.

COMMUNICATIONS MEDIA

Telephones ('000 main lines in use, 2013): 33.5.

Mobile Cellular Telephones ('000 subscribers, 2013): 212.0.

Internet Subscribers ('000 subscribers, 2011): 21.7.

Broadband Subscribers ('000 subscribers, 2013): 25.0.

Source: International Telecommunication Union.

EDUCATION

Pre-primary (2011/12 unless otherwise indicated): 148 schools (2005/06); 340 teachers; 3,483 pupils.

Primary (2011/12 unless otherwise indicated): 75 schools (2007/08); 1,054 teachers; 18,172 pupils.

General Secondary (2011/12 unless otherwise indicated): 23 schools (2007/08); 1,009 teachers; 14,565 pupils.

Technical/Vocational Secondary (2011/12): 18 teachers; 156 pupils.

Special Education (state institutions only, 2007/08): 4 schools; 47 teachers; 227 students.

Adult Education (state institutions only, 2006/07 unless otherwise indicated): 13 centres; 70 facilitators; 1,395 learners.

Tertiary (2011/12): 242 teachers; 1,683 students.

Sources: Caribbean Development Bank, *Social and Economic Indicators*; UNESCO Institute for Statistics.

Pupil-teacher Ratio (primary education, UNESCO estimate): 17.2 in 2011/12. Source: UNESCO Institute for Statistics.

Adult Literacy Rate (UNESCO estimate): 94.8% in 2004. Source: UN Development Programme, *Human Development Report.*

Directory

The Constitution

The Constitution came into force at the independence of Saint Lucia on 22 February 1979. Its main provisions are summarized below:

FUNDAMENTAL RIGHTS AND FREEDOMS

Regardless of race, place of origin, political opinion, colour, creed or sex but subject to respect for the rights and freedoms of others and for the public interest, every person in Saint Lucia is entitled to the rights of life, liberty, security of the person, equality before the law and the protection of the law. Freedom of conscience, of expression, of assembly and of association is guaranteed, and the inviolability of personal privacy, family life and property is maintained. Protection is afforded from slavery, forced labour, torture and inhuman treatment.

THE GOVERNOR-GENERAL

The British monarch, as Head of State, is represented in Saint Lucia by the Governor-General.

PARLIAMENT

Parliament consists of the British monarch, represented by the Governor-General, the 11-member Senate and the House of Assembly, composed of 17 elected Representatives. Senators are appointed by the Governor-General: six on the advice of the Prime Minister, three on the advice of the Leader of the Opposition and two acting on his own deliberate judgement. The life of Parliament is five years.

Each constituency returns one Representative to the House who is directly elected in accordance with the Constitution.

At a time when the office of Attorney-General is a public office, the Attorney-General is an ex officio member of the House.

Every citizen over the age of 21 is eligible to vote.

Parliament may alter any of the provisions of the Constitution.

THE EXECUTIVE

Executive authority is vested in the British monarch and exercisable by the Governor-General. The Governor-General appoints as Prime Minister that member of the House who, in the Governor-General's view, is best able to command the support of the majority of the members of the House, and other Ministers on the advice of the Prime Minister. The Governor-General may remove the Prime Minister from office if the House approves a resolution expressing no confidence in the Government, and if the Prime Minister does not resign within three days or advise the Governor-General to dissolve Parliament.

The Cabinet consists of the Prime Minister and other Ministers, and the Attorney-General as an ex officio member at a time when the office of Attorney-General is a public office.

The Leader of the Opposition is appointed by the Governor-General as that member of the House who, in the Governor-General's view, is best able to command the support of a majority of members of the house who do not support the Government.

CITIZENSHIP

All persons born in Saint Lucia before independence who immediately prior to independence were citizens of the United Kingdom and Colonies automatically become citizens of Saint Lucia. All persons born in Saint Lucia after independence automatically acquire Saint Lucian citizenship, as do those born outside Saint Lucia after independence to a parent possessing Saint Lucian citizenship. Provision is made for the acquisition of citizenship by those to whom it is not automatically granted.

The Government

HEAD OF STATE

Queen: HM Queen ELIZABETH II.

Governor-General: Dame PEARLETTE LOUISY (took office 17 September 1997).

CABINET
(September 2014)

The Government is formed by the Saint Lucia Labour Party.

Prime Minister and Minister of Finance and Economic Affairs: Dr KENNY DAVIS ANTHONY.

Deputy Prime Minister and Minister of Infrastructure, Port Services and Transport: PHILIP J. PIERRE.

Minister of External Affairs, International Trade and Civil Aviation: ALVA BAPTISTE.

Minister of Education, Human Resource Development and Labour: Dr ROBERT K. LEWIS.

Minister of Health, Wellness, Human Services and Gender Relations: ALVINA REYNOLDS.

Minister of Agriculture, Food Production, Fisheries, Co-operatives and Rural Development: MOSES JEAN BAPTISTE.

Minister of Social Transformation, Local Government and Community Empowerment: HAROLD DALSON.

Minister of Commerce, Business Development, Investment and Consumer Affairs: EMMA HIPPOLYTE.

Minister of Legal Affairs and of Home Affairs and National Security: VICTOR PHILIP LA CORBINIERE.

Minister of Tourism, Heritage and the Creative Industries: LORNE THEOPHILUS.

Minister of Youth Development and Sports: SHAWN EDWARD.

Minister of Public Service, Information and Broadcasting and of Sustainable Development, Energy, Science and Technology: Dr JAMES LOUIS FLETCHER.

Minister of Physical Development, Housing and Urban Renewal: STANLEY FELIX.

MINISTRIES

Office of the Prime Minister: Greaham Louisy Administrative Bldg, 5th Floor, Waterfront, Castries; tel. 468-2111; fax 453-7352; internet opm.govt.lc.

Ministry of Agriculture, Food Production, Fisheries, Co-operatives and Rural Development: Sir Stanislaus James Bldg, 5th Floor, Waterfront, Castries; tel. 453-6314; fax 452-2526; e-mail info@agriculture.govt.lc; internet agriculture.govt.lc.

Ministry of Commerce, Business Development, Investment and Consumer Affairs: Ives Heraldine Rock Bldg, 4th Floor, Block B, Waterfront, Castries; tel. 468-4218; fax 453-7347; e-mail mincommerce@govt.lc; internet commerce.govt.lc.

Ministry of Education, Human Resource Development and Labour: Francis Compton Bldg, 4th Floor, Waterfront, Castries; tel. 468-5202; fax 453-2299; e-mail pssecretaryed@gov.lc; internet education.govt.lc.

Ministry of External Affairs, International Trade and Civil Aviation: Level 5, Baywalk, Gros Islet; tel. 468-4519; fax 452-7427; e-mail external@govt.lc; internet externalaffairs.govt.lc.

Ministry of Finance and Economic Affairs: Financial Centre, 3rd Floor, Bridge St, Castries; tel. 468-5580; fax 451-9231; e-mail info@finance.govt.lc; internet finance.govt.lc.

Ministry of Health, Wellness, Human Services and Gender Relations: Sir Stanislaus James Bldg, 2nd Floor, Castries; tel. 468-5300; fax 452-5655; e-mail ministryofhealth@govt.lc; internet health.govt.lc.

Ministry of Home Affairs and National Security: Sir Stanislaus James Bldg, 1st Floor, Waterfront, Castries; tel. 468-3600; fax 468-3617; e-mail homeaffairs@gosl.gov.lc; internet homeaffairs.govt.lc.

Ministry of Infrastructure, Port Services and Transport: Union Office Complex, Castries; tel. 468-4300; fax 453-2769; e-mail min_com@gosl.gov.lc; internet infrastructure.govt.lc.

Ministry of Legal Affairs: Sir Stanislaus James Bldg, 1st Floor, Waterfront, Castries; tel. 468-3600; fax 456-0228; e-mail legalaffairs@gosl.gov.lc; internet legalaffairs.govt.lc.

Ministry of Physical Development, Housing and Urban Renewal: Greaham Louisy Administrative Bldg, 3rd Floor, Waterfront, Castries; tel. 468-4410; fax 452-2506; e-mail mpde@gosl.gov.lc; internet physicaldevelopment.govt.lc.

Ministry of Public Service, Information and Broadcasting: Greaham Louisy Administrative Bldg, 2nd Floor, Waterfront, Castries; tel. 468-2234; fax 453-1305; e-mail minpet@candw.lc; internet publicservice.govt.lc.

Ministry of Social Transformation, Local Government and Community Empowerment: Greaham Louisy Administrative Bldg, 4th Floor, Waterfront, Castries; tel. 468-5108; fax 453-7921; e-mail most@gosl.gov.lc; internet socialtransformation.govt.lc.

Ministry of Sustainable Development, Energy, Science and Technology: Hewanorra House, Point Seraphine, Castries; tel. 468-5842; fax 456-6049; internet sustainabledevelopment.govt.lc.

Ministry of Tourism, Heritage and the Creative Industries: Sir Stanislaus James Bldg, 3rd Floor, Waterfront, Castries; tel. 468-4629; fax 451-7414; e-mail psmot@gosl.gov.lc; internet tourism.govt.lc.

Ministry of Youth Development and Sports: Sir Stanislaus James Bldg, 2nd Floor, Castries; tel. 468-5300; fax 452-5655; internet sports.govt.lc.

Legislature

PARLIAMENT

Senate

The Senate has nine nominated members and two independent members.

President: CLAUDIUS JAMES FRANCIS.

House of Assembly

Speaker: PETER I. FOSTER.

Election, 28 November 2011

Party	Seats
Saint Lucia Labour Party (SLP)	11
United Workers' Party (UWP)	6
Total	**17**

Election Commission

Saint Lucia Electoral Dept: 23 High St, POB 1074, Castries; tel. 452-3725; fax 451-6513; e-mail admin@electoral.gov.lc; internet www.electoral.gov.lc; Chief Elections Officer CARSON RAGGIE.

Political Organizations

Lucian People's Movement: Marie Therese St, Gros Islet, Castries; tel. 287-6814; internet www.lpmstlucia.com; f. 2010; Leader THEROLD PRUDENT.

Organization for National Empowerment (ONE): POB 1496, Castries; tel. 484-9424; fax 452-9574; e-mail aziea99@yahoo.com; f. 2004; Leader PETER ALEXANDER; Chair. ROSEMUND CLERY.

Saint Lucia Labour Party (SLP): Tom Walcott Bldg, 2nd Floor, Jeremie St, POB 427, Castries; tel. and fax 453-1470; internet www .voteslp.com; f. 1946; socialist party; Leader Dr KENNY DAVIS ANTHONY; Deputy Leader PHILIP J. PIERRE.

United Workers' Party (UWP): Alfiona Plaza, Rodney Bay, Gros Islet; tel. 572-4949; e-mail info@uwpstlucia.org; internet www .uwpstlucia.org; f. 1964; right-wing; Chair. EZEKIEL JOSEPH; Leader ALLEN CHASTANET.

Diplomatic Representation

EMBASSIES AND HIGH COMMISSION IN SAINT LUCIA

Brazil: 1 Bella Rosa Rd, 3rd Floor, POB 6136, Gros Islet; tel. 450-1671; fax 450-4733; e-mail brasemb.castries@itamaraty.gov.br; Ambassador JOAQUIM A. WHITAKER SALLES.

Cuba: Rodney Heights, Gros Islet, POB 2150, Castries; tel. 458-4665; fax 458-4666; e-mail embacubasantalucia@candw.lc; internet www.cubadiplomatica.cu/santalucia; Ambassador LYDIA GONZÁLEZ NAVARRO.

France: French Embassy to the OECS, GPO Private Box 937, Vigie, Castries; tel. 455-6060; fax 455-6056; e-mail frenchembassy@candw .lc; internet www.ambafrance-lc.org; Ambassador ERIC DE LA MOUSSAYE.

Mexico: Nelson Mandela Dr., POB 6096, Vigie, Castries; tel. 453-1250; fax 451-4252; e-mail mexicanembassy@candw.lc; internet embamex.sre.gob.mx/santalucia; Ambassador LUIS MANUEL LÓPEZ MORENO.

Taiwan (Republic of China): Reduit Beach Ave, Rodney Bay; tel. 452-8105; fax 452-0441; e-mail luciaemb@gmail.com; internet www .taiwanembassy.org/lc; Ambassador JAMES CHANG.

United Kingdom: Francis Compton Bldg, Waterfront, POB 227, Castries; tel. 452-2484; fax 453-1543; e-mail postmaster.castries@fco .gov.uk; internet www.gov.uk/government/world/st-lucia; High Commissioner VICTORIA GLYNIS DEAN (resident in Barbados).

Venezuela: Casa Santa Lucía, POB 494, Castries; tel. 452-4033; fax 453-6747; e-mail vembassy@candw.lc; Ambassador LEIFF ESCALONA.

Judicial System

Eastern Caribbean Supreme Court: Heraldine Rock Bldg, Block B, Waterfront, POB 1093, Castries; tel. 457-3600; fax 457-3601; e-mail offices@eccourts.org; internet www.eccourts.org; the West Indies Associated States Supreme Court was established in 1967 and was known as the Supreme Court of Grenada and the West Indies Associated States from 1974 until 1979, when it became the Eastern Caribbean Supreme Court. Its jurisdiction extends to Anguilla, Antigua and Barbuda, the British Virgin Islands, Dominica, Grenada, Montserrat, Saint Christopher and Nevis, Saint Lucia and Saint Vincent and the Grenadines. It is composed of the High Court of Justice and the Court of Appeal. The High Court is composed of the Chief Justice, who is head of the judiciary, and 16 High Court Judges, three of whom are resident in Saint Lucia. The Court of Appeal is itinerant and presided over by the Chief Justice and three other Justices of Appeal. Additionally, there are two Masters whose principal responsibilities extend to procedural and interlocutory matters. Jurisdiction of the High Court includes fundamental rights and freedoms, membership of the parliaments, and matters concerning the interpretation of constitutions; Chief Justice JANICE MESADIS PEREIRA; Chief Registrar KIMBERLEY CENAC PHULGENCE.

Attorney-General: VICTOR PHILIP LA CORBINIERE.

Religion

CHRISTIANITY

The Roman Catholic Church

Saint Lucia forms a single archdiocese. The Archbishop participates in the Antilles Episcopal Conference (currently based in Port of Spain, Trinidad and Tobago). According to the 2010 census, some 61% of the population are Roman Catholics.

Archbishop of Castries: ROBERT RIVAS, Archbishop's House, Nelson Mandela Dr., POB 267, Castries; tel. 452-2416; fax 452-3697; e-mail sarchbishopslu@gmail.com; internet www.aocslu.org.

The Anglican Communion

Anglicans in Saint Lucia are adherents of the Church in the Province of the West Indies, comprising eight dioceses. The Archbishop of the West Indies currently is the Bishop of Barbados. Saint Lucia forms part of the diocese of the Windward Islands (the Bishop is resident in Kingstown, Saint Vincent). Some 2% of the population are Anglicans, according to the 2010 census.

Other Christian Churches

According to the 2010 census, 11% of the population are Seventh-day Adventists, 9% are Pentecostalists, 2% are Evangelical Christians and 2% are Baptists. Other churches include Church of God, Jehovah's Witnesses, Methodists and Lutherans.

Seventh-day Adventist Church: St Louis St, POB GM 912, Castries; tel. 451-8657; e-mail info@stluciaadventist.org; internet www.stluciaadventist.org; Pres. JOHNSON FREDERICK.

Trinity Evangelical Lutheran Church: Gablewoods Mall, POB 858, Castries; tel. 458-4638; e-mail trinitylutheranstlucia@gmail .com; internet www.islandlutherans.com; Pastor Rev. TOM SPIEGELBERG.

OTHER RELIGIONS

According to the 2010 census, about 2% of the population were Rastafarian.

The Press

The Catholic Chronicle: POB 778, Castries; f. 1957; monthly; Editor Rev. PATRICK A. B. ANTHONY; circ. 3,000.

She Caribbean: Rodney Bay Industrial Estate, Massade, Gros Islet, POB 1146, Castries; tel. 450-7827; fax 450-8694; e-mail shanna.h@ stluciastar.com; internet www.shecaribbean.com; f. 1998; quarterly; Publr and Editor-in-Chief MAE WAYNE.

The Star: Rodney Bay Industrial Estate, Gros Islet, POB 1146, Castries; tel. 450-7827; fax 450-8690; e-mail mae.w@stluciastar.com; internet www.stluciastar.com; f. 1987; 3 a week (Wed. and weekend edns); circ. 8,000; Man. Dir MAE WAYNE; Editor TONI NICHOLAS.

Tropical Traveller: Rodney Bay Industrial Estate, Massade, Gros Islet, POB 1146, Castries; tel. 450-7827; fax 450-8694; e-mail infostar@stluciastar.com; internet www.tropicaltraveller.com; f. 1989; monthly; Editorial Dir MAE WAYNE; Man. Editor NANCY ATKINSON.

Visions of St Lucia Island Guide: 7 Maurice Mason Ave, Sans Soucis, POB 947, Castries; tel. 453-0427; fax 452-1522; e-mail visions@candw.lc; internet visionsofstlucia.com; f. 1989; official tourist guide; publ. by Island Visions Ltd; annual; Publr ANTHONY NEIL AUSTIN; Editor CAROLINE POPOVIC; circ. 120,000.

The Voice: Odessa Bldg, Darling Rd, POB 104, Castries; tel. 452-2590; fax 453-1453; internet www.thevoiceslu.com; f. 1953; Man. Dir GEORGE RUDDOCK.

Publishers

Caribbean Publishing Co Ltd: American Drywall Bldg, Vide Bouteille Hwy, POB 104, Castries; tel. 452-3188; fax 452-3181; e-mail publish@candw.lc; internet stluciayp.com; publr of telephone directories and magazines; Chair. RANDY FRENCH.

Island Visions Ltd: 7 Maurice Mason Ave, Sans Soucis, POB 947, Castries; tel. 453-0472; fax 452-1522; e-mail visions@candw.lc; internet www.visionsofstlucia.com; f. 1989; Chair. and Man. Dir ANTHONY NEIL AUSTIN.

Mirror Publishing Co Ltd: Bisee Industrial Estate, POB 1782, Castries; tel. 451-6181; fax 451-6503; e-mail mirror@candw.lc; internet www.stluciamirroronline.org; f. 1994; Man. Editor GUY MAYERS.

Star Publishing Co: Rodney Bay Industrial Estate, Massade, Gros Islet, POB 1146, Castries; tel. 450-7827; fax 450-8694; e-mail infostar@stluciastar.com; internet www.stluciastar.com; f. 1987; Propr, Publr and CEO RICK WAYNE.

The Voice Publishing Co. Ltd: Odessa Bldg, Darling Rd, Castries; tel. 452-2590; fax 453-1453; e-mail voice@candw.lc; internet thevoiceslu.com; f. 1953; publr of *The Voice* newspaper and *Yo* magazine.

Broadcasting and Communications

TELECOMMUNICATIONS

Digicel St Lucia: Rodney Bay, Gros Islet, POB GM 791, Castries; tel. 728-3400; fax 450-3872; e-mail customercare.stlucia@digicelgroup.com; internet www.digicelstlucia.com; f. 2003; owned by an Irish consortium; acquired operations of Cingular Wireless in Saint Lucia in 2006; Chair. DENIS O'BRIEN; Country Man. HOLLY HUGHES.

Karib Cable: William Peter Blvd, Castries; tel. 572-5151; fax 572-5150; e-mail mykaribcable@karibcable.com; internet www.karibcable.com; internet service provider; Man. Dir KELLY GLASS.

LIME: Bridge St, POB 111, Castries; tel. 453-9720; fax 453-9700; internet www.lime.com; fmrly Cable & Wireless St Lucia; name changed as above 2008; provides fixed-line, mobile, internet and cable television services; Group CEO TONY RICE; CEO (Caribbean) MARTIN JOOS (acting).

Regulatory Authorities

Eastern Caribbean Telecommunications Authority (ECTEL): Vide Bouteille, POB 1886, Castries; tel. 458-1701; fax 458-1698; e-mail ectel@ectel.int; internet www.ectel.int; f. 2000 to regulate telecommunications in Saint Lucia, Dominica, Grenada, Saint Christopher and Nevis and Saint Vincent and the Grenadines; Chair. DENNIS CLARKE; Man. Dir EMBERT CHARLES.

National Telecommunications Regulatory Commission (NTRC): Rajana Group of Cos Bldg, Bois D'Orange, POB GM 690, Castries; tel. 458-2035; fax 453-2558; e-mail ntrc_slu@candw.lc; internet www.ntrc.org.lc; f. 2000; regulates the sector in conjunction with ECTEL; Chair. JEROME JULES.

BROADCASTING

Radio

Radio Caribbean International: 11 Mongiraud St, POB 121, Castries; tel. 452-2636; fax 452-2637; e-mail rci@candw.lc; internet www.rcistlucia.com/now/listen.aspx; operates Radio Caraïbes; English and Creole services; broadcasts 24 hrs; Station Mans PETER EPHRAIM, PET GIBSON.

Radio Saint Lucia Co Ltd (RSL97): Morne Fortune, POB 660, Castries; tel. 452-2337; fax 453-1568; e-mail info@rslonline.com; internet www.rslonline.com; f. 1972; govt-owned; English and Creole services; Man. Dir CLAUDE EMMANUEL.

Television

National Television Network (NTN): Greaham Louisy Administrative Bldg, Waterfront, Castries; tel. 468-2116; fax 453-1614; f. 2001; operated by the Government Information Service; provides information on the operations of the public sector.

Finance

(cap. = capital; res = reserves; dep. = deposits; m. = million; brs = branches)

REGULATORY AUTHORITY

Financial Sector Supervision Unit: Financial Centre, 3rd Floor, Bridge St, Castries; tel. 468-5590; fax 451-7655; e-mail cleon@gosl.gov.lc; Dir JOHN CALIXTE LEON.

BANKING

The Eastern Caribbean Central Bank, based in Saint Christopher, is the central issuing and monetary authority for Saint Lucia.

Eastern Caribbean Central Bank—Saint Lucia Office: Colony House, Unit 5, John Compton Hwy, POB 295, Castries; tel. 452-7449; fax 453-6022; e-mail eccbslu@candw.lc; internet www.eccb-centralbank.org; Country Dir ISAAC ANTHONY; Rep. GREGOR FRANKLYN.

Commercial Banks

1st National Bank Saint Lucia Ltd: 21 Bridge St, POB 168, Castries; tel. 455-7000; fax 453-1630; e-mail manager@1stnationalbankslu.com; internet www.1stnationalbankonline.com;

inc. 1937 as Saint Lucia Co-operative Bank Ltd; name changed as above Jan. 2005; commercial bank; cap. EC $7.9m., res EC $13.5m., dep. EC $365.3m. (Dec. 2009); Chair. and Pres. CHARMAINE GARDNER; Man. Dir ANDY DELMAR; 4 brs.

Bank of Saint Lucia Ltd: Financial Centre, 5th Floor, 1 Bridge St, POB 1860, Castries; tel. 456-6000; fax 456-6720; e-mail info@bankofsaintlucia.com; internet www.bankofsaintlucia.com; f. 2001 by merger of National Commercial Bank of St Lucia Ltd and Saint Lucia Devt Bank; cap. EC $197.7m., res EC $89.2m., dep. EC $1,391.6m. (Dec. 2010); 35% state-owned; parent co is East Caribbean Financial Holding Co Ltd; Chair. HILDRETH ALEXANDER; Gen. Man. HADYN GITTENS; 7 brs.

CIBC FirstCaribbean International Bank: Bridge St, POB 335, Castries; tel. 456-2422; fax 452-3735; internet www.firstcaribbeanbank.com; f. 2002 following merger of Caribbean operations of Barclays Bank PLC and CIBC; CIBC acquired Barclays' 43.7% stake in 2006, present name adopted in 2011; CEO RIK PARKHILL; 4 brs.

RBTT Bank Caribbean Ltd: 22 Micoud St, POB 1531, Castries; tel. 452-2265; fax 452-1668; e-mail rbttslu.isd@candw.lc; internet www.rbtt.com; f. 1985 as Caribbean Banking Corpn Ltd, name changed as above in March 2002; owned by R and M Holdings Ltd; Chair. JIM WESTLAKE; CEO SURESH SOOKOO; 4 brs.

Scotiabank St Lucia (Canada): 6 William Peter Blvd, POB 301, Castries; tel. 456-2100; fax 456-2130; e-mail bns.stlucia@scotiabank.com; internet www.scotiabank.com/lc/en; f. 1964; Country Head PHILLIP CROSS; 3 brs.

STOCK EXCHANGE

Eastern Caribbean Securities Exchange: based in Basseterre, Saint Christopher and Nevis; tel. 466-7192; fax 465-3798; e-mail info@ecseonline.com; internet www.ecseonline.com; f. 2001; regional securities market designed to facilitate the buying and selling of financial products for the 8 mem. territories—Anguilla, Antigua and Barbuda, Dominica, Grenada, Montserrat, Saint Christopher and Nevis, Saint Lucia and Saint Vincent and the Grenadines; Chair. Sir K. DWIGHT VENNER; Gen. Man. TREVOR E. BLAKE.

INSURANCE

Demerara Mutual Life Assurance Ltd: 37 Chisel St, Castries; tel. 452-3979; fax 451-7729; e-mail dmllucia@demeraramutual.com; internet www.demeraramutual.net; f. 1919 in Saint Lucia; headquarters in Guyana; Country Man. FIDUCIA EMMANUEL.

Eastern Caribbean Insurance Ltd: Laborie St, POB 290, Castries; tel. 452-2410; fax 452-3393; e-mail cgi.ltd@candw.lc.

EC Global Insurance Company Ltd: ECFH Financial Centre Bldg, 1st Floor, Bridge St, Castries; tel. 451-3244; fax 458-1222; e-mail ecglobal@ecfh.com; internet www.ecglobalinsurance.com; Man. Dir ANDREW LEVY.

First Citizens Investment Services: 9–11 Brazil St, 1st Floor, Castries; tel. 450-2662; fax 451-7984; e-mail invest@firstcitizensslu.com; internet www.firstcitizensinvestment.com; Group CEO LARRY NATH; Gen. Man. JASON JULIEN.

GTM Saint Lucia (Guyana and Trinidad Mutual Group of Insurance Companies): Cnr Chaussee Rd and Brazil St, Castries; tel. 452-2871; internet www.gtm-gy.com/stlucia; f. 1954; headquarters in Guyana; Country Man. CLINTON CHARLERY; 3 brs.

Pan-American Life Insurance Co of the Eastern Caribbean: Mardini Bldg, 3rd Floor, Rodney Bay, Gros Islet; tel. 457-6500; fax 456–0628; internet www.palig.com; f. 2012; part of Pan-American Life Insurance Group (USA); CEO and Man. Dir (Caribbean) WILLIAM R. SCHULZ, Jr; Operations Man. MILTON HARIPAUL.

Saint Lucia Insurances Ltd: 48 Micoud St, POB 1084, Castries; tel. 452-3240; fax 452-2240; e-mail info@stluciainsurances.com; internet www.stluciainsurances.com; principal agents of Caribbean Alliance Insurance Co Ltd.

Saint Lucia Motor and General Insurance Co Ltd: 38 Micoud St, POB 767, Castries; tel. 452-3323; fax 452-6072.

Trade and Industry

DEVELOPMENT ORGANIZATIONS

Invest Saint Lucia: Heraldine Rock Bldg, 1st Floor, The Waterfront, POB 495, Castries; tel. 452-3400; fax 452-1841; e-mail info@investstlucia.com; internet www.investstlucia.com; f. 1971 to stimulate, facilitate and promote investment opportunities for foreign and local investors and to promote the economic devt of Saint Lucia; owns and manages 7 industrial estates; br. in Miami, FL, USA; Chair. COSTELLO MICHEL; CEO MCHALE ANDREW.

Small Enterprise Development Unit (SEDU): Heraldine Rock Bldg, 4th Floor, Waterfront, Castries; tel. 468-4202; fax 453-7347; e-mail barbara.innocent-charles@govt.lc; e-mail www.commerce .gov.lc/departments/view/1; f. 1994; technical assistance and training for the devt of the micro- and small business sectors; part of the Ministry of Commerce, Business Development, Investment and Consumer Affairs; Dir BARBARA INNOCENT-CHARLES.

CHAMBER OF COMMERCE

Saint Lucia Chamber of Commerce, Industry and Agriculture: American Drywall Bldg, 2nd Floor, Vide Bouteille, POB 482, Castries; tel. 452-3165; fax 453-6907; e-mail info@stluciachamber .org; internet www.stluciachamber.org; f. 1884; Pres. GORDON CHARLES; Exec. Dir BRIAN LOUISY; 150 mems.

EMPLOYERS' ASSOCIATIONS

Saint Lucia Coconut Growers' Association Ltd: Palmiste Rd, POB 269, Soufrière; tel. 459-7227; fax 459-7216; f. 1939; Gen. Man. GERALD MORRIS.

Saint Lucia Employers' Federation: c/o The Morgan Bldg, L'Anse Rd, POB 160, Castries; tel. 452-2190; fax 452-7335; e-mail slefslu@candw.lc; internet www.slef-slu.org; Pres. CALLISTUS VERN GILL.

Saint Lucia Fish Marketing Corpn (SLFMC): POB 891, Sans Souci, Castries; tel. 452-1341; fax 451-7073; e-mail slfmc@candw.lc; Gen. Man. VAUGHAN CHARLES.

Saint Lucia Industrial and Small Business Association: POB 585, La Panse, Castries; tel. 452-1608; fax 453-1023; e-mail slisbaslu@gmail.com; internet www.slisbastlucia.com; Pres. FLAVIA CHERRY.

WINFRESH: Agricultural Marketing Complex, Odsan, POB 115, Castries; tel. 457-8600; fax 453-1638; e-mail info@winfresh.net; internet www.winfresh.net; f. 1994 in succession to the Windward Islands Banana Growers' Asscn (WINBAN), fmrly known as WIBDECO (Windward Islands Banana Devt and Exporting Co), adopted present name in 2007 and restructured; regional org. dealing with crop diversification and agro devt and investment in Windward Islands; jtly owned by govts of St Lucia, St Vincent and the Grenadines, Dominica and Grenada; Chair. MONTGOMERY DANIEL; CEO BERNARD CORNIBERT.

UTILITIES

Electricity

Caribbean Electric Utility Services Corpn (CARILEC): Desir Ave, Sans Soucis, POB 5907, Castries; tel. 452-0140; fax 452-0142; e-mail info@carilec.org; internet www.carilec.org; f. 1989; Exec. Dir ALLISON JEAN.

St Lucia Electricity Services Ltd (LUCELEC): Sans Soucis, POB 230, Castries; tel. 457-4400; fax 457-4409; internet www.lucelec .com; f. 1964; Chair. TREVOR A. BYER; Man. Dir TREVOR M. LOUISY.

Water

Water and Sewerage Company (WASCO): L'Anse Rd, POB 1481, Castries; tel. 452-5344; fax 452-6844; e-mail wasco@candw.lc; f. 1999 as the Water and Sewerage Authority (WASA); planned privatization under review; Chair. EGBERT LOUIS; Man. Dir JOHN C. JOSEPH.

TRADE UNIONS

National Workers' Union (NWU): Bour Bon St, POB 713, Castries; tel. 452-3664; fax 453-2896; e-mail natwork3@hotmail.com; internet www.nationalworkersunion.org; f. 1973; represents daily paid workers; affiliated to World Federation of Trade Unions; Pres.-Gen. TYRONE MAYNARD; Sec.-Gen. GEORGE GODDARD, Jr; 3,200 mems (2005).

Saint Lucia Civil Service Association: Sans Soucis, POB 244, Castries; tel. 452-3903; fax 453-6061; e-mail csa@candw.lc; internet www.csastlucia.org; f. 1951; Pres. MARY ISAAC; Sec. PATRICK MATHURIN; 2,381 mems.

Saint Lucia Medical and Dental Association: POB GM691, Castries; tel. 451-8441; fax 458-1147; e-mail slmdaoffice@gmail .com; internet www.slmda.org; f. 1969; Pres. Dr R. G. SWAMY; Sec. Dr ANTHEA EMMANUEL.

Saint Lucia Nurses' Association: Victoria Hospital, Nurses' Home, 2nd Floor, POB 819, Castries; tel. 452-1403; fax 456-0121; e-mail slna1970@gmail.com; internet www.stlucianursesassociation .org; f. 1947; Pres. LYDIA LEONCE; Gen. Sec. LYDIA LABADEE-BISCETTE.

Saint Lucia Seamen, Waterfront and General Workers' Trade Union: L'Anse Rd, POB 166, Castries; tel. 452-1669; fax 452-5452; e-mail seamen@candw.lc; f. 1945; affiliated to Int. Trade Union Confed., Int. Transport Fed. and Caribbean Congress of Labour; Pres. ESTHER ST MARIE (acting); Sec. CELICA ADOLPH; 1,000 mems.

Saint Lucia Teachers' Union: La Clery, POB 821, Castries; tel. 452-4469; fax 453-6668; e-mail sltu@candw.lc; f. 1934; Pres. JULIAN MONROSE; Gen. Sec. WAYNE CUMBERBATCH.

Saint Lucia Trade Union Federation: c/o Saint Lucia Teachers' Union, La Clery, POB 821, Castries; tel. 452-4469; fax 453-6668; e-mail cumbatch42@gmail.com; f. 2005; comprises 9 trade unions of Saint Lucia, including the Saint Lucia Civil Service Asscn, Saint Lucia Teachers' Union, Saint Lucia Medical and Dental Asscn, Saint Lucia Nurses' Asscn, Saint Lucia Seamen and Waterfront General Workers' Union, National Farmers' Asscn, Police Welfare Asscn, Saint Lucia Fire Service Asscn and Vieux Fort General and Dock Workers' Union; Pres. JULIAN MONROSE; Gen. Sec. WAYNE CUMBERBATCH.

Vieux Fort General and Dock Workers' Union: New Dock Rd, POB 224, Vieux Fort; tel. 454-5128; e-mail dockworkersunion@ hotmail.com; f. 1954.

Transport

RAILWAYS

There are no railways in Saint Lucia.

ROADS

There was an estimated total road network of 910 km, of which 150 km were main roads and 127 km were secondary roads. The main highway passes through every town and village on the island. There is also a coastal highway linking Castries with Cul de Sac Bay. The estimated budget for the Ministry of Infrastructure, Port Services and Transport in the 2012/13 financial year was $125.4m. In November 2013 the Government announced that construction of a new Bois d'Orange bridge would begin before the end of the year, following destruction of the previous bridge by Hurricane Tomas in 2010.

SHIPPING

The ports at Castries and Vieux Fort have been fully mechanized. Castries has six berths with a total length of 2,470 ft (753 m). The port of Soufrière has a deep-water anchorage, but no alongside berth for ocean-going vessels. The Rodney Bay marina was upgraded in 2009. There is a petroleum transshipment terminal at Cul de Sac Bay. In 2012 some 571,894 cruise ship passengers called at Saint Lucia. Regular services are provided by a number of shipping lines, including ferry services to neighbouring islands. There were plans to develop the waterfront area at Castries in order for it to become a dedicated cruise ship port; the port at Vieux Fort was also to be expanded in order to handle all commercial cargo.

Saint Lucia Air and Sea Ports Authority (SLASPA): Manoel St, POB 651, Castries; tel. 452-2893; fax 452-2062; e-mail info@slaspa .com; internet www.slaspa.com; f. 1983; Chair. ISAAC ANTHONY; Gen. Man. SEAN MATTHEW; Dir of Airports PETER FERGUSON JEAN; Dir of Sea Ports ADRIAN HILAIRE.

Saint Lucia Marine Terminals Ltd (SLMTL): POB VF 355, Vieux Fort; tel. 454-8738; fax 454-8745; e-mail info@slmtl.com; internet www.slmtl.com; f. 1995; wholly owned subsidiary of the Saint Lucia Air and Sea Ports Authority; private port management co; manages Port Vieux Fort; Chair MARTIN JAMES; Gen. Man. LENIUS LENDOR.

CIVIL AVIATION

There are two airports: Hewanorra International (formerly Beane Field near Vieux Fort), 64 km from Castries, which is equipped to handle large jet aircraft, and George F. L. Charles Airport, which is at Vigie, in Castries, and which is capable of handling medium-range jets. In mid-2014 the Government announced a major redevelopment of Hewanorra International. Saint Lucia is served by scheduled flights to the USA, Canada, Europe and most destinations in the Caribbean. The country is a shareholder in the regional airline LIAT (see Antigua and Barbuda).

Saint Lucia Air and Sea Ports Authority: see Shipping.

LIAT Airlines: Brazil St, POB 416, Castries; tel. 452-3051; fax 453-6563; e-mail slu@liatairline.com; internet www.liatairline.com; Man. JOSSE MESMIN; Chair. Dr JEAN HOLDER; CEO DAVID EVANS.

Tourism

Saint Lucia possesses spectacular mountain scenery, a tropical climate and sandy beaches. Historical sites, rich birdlife and the sulphur baths at Soufrière are other attractions. Visitor arrivals totalled 960,617 in 2013. Tourism receipts in that year were EC $955.9m. The USA is the principal market (40% of total stopover visitors in 2013), followed by the United Kingdom (with 22%).

Saint Lucia Hotel and Tourism Association (SLHTA): 2 Alfiona Plaza, Rodney Heights, POB 545, Gros Islet; tel. 453-1811; fax 452-7967; e-mail slhta@candw.lc; internet www.slhta.com; f. 1963; Pres. KAROLIN TROUBETZKOY.

Saint Lucia Tourist Board: Sureline Bldg, Top Floor, Vide Bouteille, POB 221, Castries; tel. 452-4094; fax 453-1121; e-mail slutour@candw.lc; internet www.stlucia.org; f. 1981; 5 brs overseas; Chair. MATTHEW BEAUBRUN; Dir LOUIS LEWIS.

Defence

The Royal Saint Lucia Police Force, which numbers about 300 officers, includes a 100-strong Special Service Unit for purposes of defence. Saint Lucia participates in the US-sponsored Regional Security System, comprising police, coastguards and army units, which was established by independent East Caribbean states in 1982. There are also two patrol vessels for coastguard duties. Some EC \$113.7m. (equivalent to 7.8%) of the total expenditure was allocated to the Ministry of Home Affairs and National Security in the 2012/13 budget.

Education

Education is compulsory for 10 years between five and 15 years of age. Primary education begins at the age of five and lasts for seven years. Secondary education, beginning at 12 years of age, lasts for five years, comprising a first cycle of three years and a second cycle of two years. Enrolment at primary schools in 2012 included 82% of children in the relevant age-group, while comparable enrolment in secondary level education, according to UNESCO estimates, was equivalent to 82% of pupils. Facilities for industrial, technical and teacher-training are available at the Sir Arthur Lewis Community College at Morne Fortune, which also houses an extra-mural branch of the University of the West Indies. Some EC \$211.6m. was allocated to the Ministry of Education, Human Resource Development and Labour in the 2012/13 budget (equivalent to 14.5% of total planned recurrent expenditure).

SAINT-MARTIN

The Collectivité d'Outre-mer (French Overseas Collectivity) of Saint-Martin forms the northern half of the island of Saint Martin (the remainder, Sint Maarten, being part of the Kingdom of the Netherlands). The small volcanic island lies among the Leeward group of the Lesser Antilles in the Caribbean Sea, 8 km south of the British Overseas Territory of Anguilla and 265 km north-west of the French Overseas Department of Guadeloupe, of which Saint-Martin was formerly a dependency. The 10.2-km border between the French and the Dutch territories of the island is the only land frontier in the Lesser Antilles. Saint-Martin occupies about 60% of the island (51 sq km or 20 sq miles). The climate is tropical and moderated by the sea. Saint-Martin normally receives about 1,000 mm (43 ins) of rain annually. According to official estimates, at 1 January 2011 Saint-Martin had a population of 36,286. French is the official language, but a Creole patois is widely spoken, as well as English, Dutch and Spanish. The majority of the population professes Christianity and belongs to the Roman Catholic Church. The principal town is Marigot, in the south-west of the territory, on the north coast of the island, between the sea and the Simpson Bay Lagoon.

On 7 December 2003 the Guadeloupean dependency of Saint-Martin participated in a department-wide referendum on Guadeloupe's future constitutional relationship with France. Although the proposal to streamline administrative and political processes was defeated, a majority of those participating in Saint-Martin, 76.2%, elected to secede from Guadeloupe to form a separate Overseas Collectivity. The reorganization was subsequently approved by the French Sénat (Senate) on 6 February 2007 and by the Assemblée Nationale (National Assembly) the following day. On 21 February the territory of Saint-Martin was formally designated an Overseas Collectivity.

Legislative elections to form a 23-member legislative assembly to be known as the Conseil Territorial (Territorial Council) were held in July 2007. At the first round ballot, held on 1 July, the Union pour le Progrès/Union pour un Mouvement Populaire (UPP/UMP) list, headed by Louis-Constant Fleming, won 40.4% of the total votes cast, while the Rassemblement, responsabilité et réussite (RRR) list, led by Alain Richardson, secured 31.9%, and Jean-Luc Hamlet's Réussir Saint-Martin obtained 10.9%. As no list emerged with an absolute majority, a further round of voting was contested by the three parties that had secured more than 10% of the vote. At this second round, held on 8 July, the UPP/UMP list won 49.0% of the vote and obtained 16 of the 23 legislative seats, the RRR received 42.2% of the vote (six seats), and Réussir Saint-Martin 8.9% (one seat). Voter participation was slightly higher, at 50.8%. Fleming assumed the presidency of the Territorial Council on 15 July, and Saint-Martin was officially installed as an Overseas Collectivity. However, in July 2008 Fleming was forced to resign the presidency after the French Council of State disqualified him from his seat on the Territorial Council for one year, owing to irregularities in his financial accounts for the 2007 election campaign. In August the Territorial Council elected Frantz Gumbs as its new President; however, in April 2009 the Council of State annulled the election of Gumbs due to voting irregularities. First Vice-President Daniel Gibbes was installed as interim President pending a re-run of the election, which was to be held within 30 days. On 5 May Gumbs was re-elected as President with 16 votes, defeating Alain Richardson, who received six votes, and Marthe Ogoundélé, who gained one vote.

Meanwhile, at an election held on 21 September 2008 Fleming, representing the UMP, was elected as Saint-Martin's representative to the French Senate. In December 2011 Philippe Chopin replaced Jacques Simonnet as Prefect-Delegate. First round elections to the 16-member Territorial Council took place on 18 March 2012. The RRR won the largest percentage of valid votes (34.1%, or 3,077 votes), just ahead of the list headed by Daniel Gibbes (Team Daniel Gibbes 2012), which secured 32.0% (2,889 votes). The UPP attracted 13.3% of the ballot. The RRR consolidated its success at a second round of voting, held on 25 March; the party secured 56.9% of the ballot (5,451 votes), compared to Team Daniel Gibbes 2012, which attracted 43.1% (4,134 votes). Alain Richardson was sworn in as President of the Territorial Council on 1 April. However, Gibbes was chosen to represent the territory (and Saint-Barthélemy) in elections to the National Assembly in June.

The first round of the French presidential election was conducted on 21 April 2012 (one day earlier than in mainland France). Nicolas Sarkozy of the UMP attracted 43.6% of the votes in Saint-Martin and Saint-Barthélemy, compared with 26.8% for François Hollande of the Parti socialiste. A second round run-off election was held two weeks later, at which Sarkozy secured 59.4% of the ballot, defeating Hollande, who won 40.6%. Nevertheless, Hollande triumphed nationally and was sworn in as President in mid-May.

Legislation to address the problem of inflated prices in Saint-Martin and other French Overseas Possessions was approved by the French Parliament in November 2012. Most notably, the bill provided for the imposition of price controls on a range of staple goods and the introduction of measures to encourage competition.

The Council of State ordered Richardson to relinquish the presidency of the Territorial Council in April 2013 after it was determined that he had breached campaign finance regulations. Aline Hanson was installed as his replacement later that month. Meanwhile, in December Fleming resigned as the territory's senator. An election to determine his successor was not due to be conducted until 28 September 2014, however, leaving Saint-Martin without senatorial representation in the interim.

Prefect-Delegate: PHILIPPE CHOPIN.

Territorial Council

rue de l'Hôtel de la Collectivité, BP 374, Marigot; tel. 5-90-87-50-04; fax 5-90-87-88-53; internet www.com-saint-martin.fr.

President: ALINE HANSON.

Election, 18 and 25 March 2012

	% of first round votes	% of second round votes
Rassemblement, responsabilité et réussite (RRR)	34.1	56.9
Team Daniel Gibbes 2012	32.0	43.1
Union pour le Progrès (UPP)	13.3	—
Saint Martin pour Tous	9.4	—
Movement for the Advancement of the People (MAP)	7.4	—
Génération Solidaire	3.7	—
Total	**100.0**	**100.0**

Deputy to the French National Assembly: DANIEL GIBBES (UMP).

Representative to the French Senate: (vacant).

SAINT VINCENT AND THE GRENADINES

Geography

PHYSICAL FEATURES

Saint Vincent and the Grenadines is in the Windward Islands and consists of the main island of Saint Vincent itself and 32 other islands and cays to its south. The country is surrounded by other Commonwealth states on the Antillean chain that separates the Caribbean Sea, to the west, from the Atlantic Ocean, to the east. The Lesser Antilles here begin to arc more towards the south-west as they head towards the South American mainland. Saint Lucia lies 47 km (29 miles) to the north, and a little east, while yet another Commonwealth country, Grenada, is southwards along the chain. The large islands of Saint Vincent and Grenada, which are about 100 km apart, are connected by the many smaller islands of the Grenadines, which are split between the two countries. Only a narrow channel separates Petit St Vincent from Petit Martinique, the northernmost island of Grenada. About 160 km to the east, beyond the main arc of the Lesser Antilles, lies Barbados. Saint Vincent and the Grenadines is the third smallest independent state in the Western hemisphere, with an area of 389.3 sq km (150.3 sq miles), 88% of which is accounted for by the main island of Saint Vincent itself.

The main island of Saint Vincent is 29 km from north to south and almost 18 km at its widest. Like the rest of the Windwards, Saint Vincent has rugged eastern Atlantic coasts and gentler western and south-western shores. The interior, however, is generally mountainous and steep, formed on the largely sunken volcanic ridge that runs north from Grenada and through the connecting archipelago. The Grenadines are largely coralline, although the larger ones are hilly, while the main island is steep and lofty. Saint Vincent is dominated by the central mass of the precipitous Morne Garu range, which runs from south to north and thrusts side spurs to the east and west coasts, but the highest point is to the north, in the Waterloo mountains, where the Soufrière volcano reaches 1,234 m (4,050 ft). This is an active volcano, which last erupted in April 1979, but without the loss of life that accompanied the eruptions of 1902 or 1812. Apart from land in the immediate vicinity of the volcano, the island is fertile and productive, the central mountains being covered in rainforest and the lower hillsides and few flatter areas planted with crops, notably bananas and arrowroot (the island is the world's leading producer of the latter, while economic dependence on the fluctuating prices of the former has led to the alternative, but illicit, cultivation of marijuana). The woodland areas are home to a number of plant, animal and bird species, most notable among the last being the protected Saint Vincent parrot and the whistling warbler, both of which are unique to the island. Marine life is especially rich among the reefs and islands of the Grenadines.

The largest of the Grenadines, and the closest to Saint Vincent itself (14 km), is Bequia, which covers about 18 sq km, its hills wooded with fruit and nut trees. There are a number of smaller islands to the south, such as Isle à Quatre, while to the east of them are Baliceaux and the smaller Battowia, which stand at the end of the main chain of the Grenadines running south-west from here towards Union Island. The main islands in this chain are Mustique (5 km in length and over 2 km wide), then, beyond some smaller islands and an unusually wide sea channel, Canouan (almost 8 sq km in area, and 40 km south of Saint Vincent), followed by Mayreau and the Tobago Cays, and Union Island (the main island of the south, 64 km from Saint Vincent—5 km in length and almost 2 km in width, or just over 8 sq km). Union Island has hills that reach 305 m. To the east, and a little south, the Vincentian Grenadines end at Petit St Vincent, a resort island.

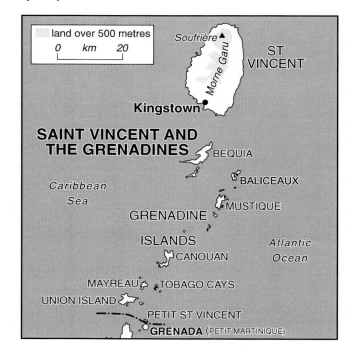

CLIMATE

The climate is subtropical, and the country is on the edge of the hurricane belt, although swell from storms passing to the north can still cause damage on the coasts. The hurricane season coincides with the rainy season (roughly July–October), which contributes substantially to the high annual rainfall, averaging some 2,050 mm (80 ins) on the coast, but up to 3,850 mm in the hilly interior of the main island. The Grenadines, being lower and less forested than Saint Vincent, receive slightly less rainfall than the main island (around 1,500 mm). Average temperatures range between about 25°C and 27°C (77°F–81°F).

POPULATION

The population is a heterogeneous mix, but of predominantly black African descent. Some 73% are counted as black, 20% as mixed race (mainly black-white), 4% as Carib, 1% as 'East' Indian and 1% as white. The main religion is Christianity, with the Church in the Province of the West Indies being the largest single denomination (Anglicans comprised 18% of the population, according to 2001 census figures, as did Pentecostalists), followed by Methodists (11%) and Seventh-day Adventists (10%). Roman Catholics accounted for 7% of the population. The city of Kingstown is the seat of both the Anglican and Roman Catholic bishops. There are also a number of adherents of non-Christian traditions. A local blend of African and Christian traditions produced a faith the observers of which were known as Spiritual Baptists. These 'Shakers' (not to be confused with the millenarian sect founded in the United Kingdom in the 18th century), like the 'Shouters' of Trinidad (Trinidad and Tobago), emerged in the 1830s in the aftermath of emancipation, but were banned between 1912 and 1965. English is both the official and the spoken tongue, although a French patois or Creole is used in some areas.

In mid-2014 the total population of Saint Vincent and the Grenadines was 109,370, according to UN estimates. Just over 25% (30,863 in mid-2011) of the population live in and around Kingstown, the capital on the south-western coast. Some 8% of the population lives on the Grenadines. The main towns of the smaller islands are Port Elizabeth on Bequia, Charlestown on Canouan and Ashton (and, to a lesser extent, Clifton) on Union Island. The Grenadines are described as dependencies, while Saint Vincent itself is divided into six administrative parishes.

History

MARK WILSON

Saint Vincent and the Grenadines is a constitutional monarchy within the Commonwealth. Queen Elizabeth II is Head of State, and is represented by a Governor-General. There is a bicameral legislature with an elected chamber.

Saint Vincent's Amerindian inhabitants knew the island as Hairoun. It was given its present name by Christopher Columbus in 1498, although fierce Amerindian resistance delayed European settlement. In 1675 a Dutch ship carrying African slaves was shipwrecked to the south of the island. The human cargo reached land, where they intermarried with the local population, producing a mixed-race Black Carib community. There was fierce resistance to European colonization and when settlements were established, the island changed hands on several occasions between the United Kingdom and France, finally passing to the United Kingdom in 1783. A rebellion by the Black Caribs in 1795–96 succeeded in gaining control of most of the island, but was eventually suppressed. Most of the Black Caribs were deported in 1797 to the island of Roatan, off the coast of Honduras. Their descendants now form the Garifuna community of Belize. Smaller groups of Black Caribs remain in Saint Vincent, and are concentrated in the north-east of the island. As in the rest of the British Caribbean, slavery was abolished in 1834. Poverty remained extreme, and there was some immigration of indentured Portuguese and Indian labourers after emancipation.

The first universal suffrage elections were in 1951, and were won by the loosely organized Workers', Peasants' and Rate-payers' Union. After the elections Ebenezer Joshua founded the People's Political Party (PPP), while Milton Cato formed the Saint Vincent Labour Party (SVLP) in 1954. The SVLP won a general election in 1967, holding office with Cato as Prime Minister until 1972, and again during 1974–84. In the 1972 election, each of the main parties won six seats on the main island. James Mitchell took the Grenadines seat as an independent, and persuaded the PPP to join a Government in which he was Prime Minister, an arrangement which lasted for two years. However, in 1974 the PPP and SVLP joined forces to bring down the Government. In the election that followed, Mitchell again won a single seat, but Cato became Prime Minister, with Joshua as Minister of Finance. Joshua's wife, Ivy, sat on the opposition benches, and she, rather than Mitchell, was appointed Leader of the Opposition.

Saint Vincent and the Grenadines joined the Federation of the West Indies in 1958, along with nine other British colonies. When Jamaica and Trinidad and Tobago left in 1962, the Federation collapsed, and an attempt to unite the remaining colonies as the 'little eight' was unsuccessful. In 1969, two years later than its neighbours, Saint Vincent and the Grenadines became a British Associated State, responsible for its internal affairs, with the United Kingdom retaining control of external affairs and defence, before moving to full independence on 27 October 1979.

James (Sir James from 1995) Mitchell, won a general election in 1984 as leader of the National Democratic Party (NDP), defeating Cato's SVLP which was by then widely perceived to be tainted by corruption. The NDP Government won all 15 seats in the 1989 election, and 12 in 1994, with an alliance of the opposition Labour Party and Movement for National Unity taking three. By 1998 the opposition parties had merged to form the Unity Labour Party (ULP) and were able to mount a strong challenge to the NDP Government, which was itself by now widely accused of corruption, and was further damaged by the serious problems facing the banana industry. Although the ULP attracted more votes in the election in June, the NDP held onto eight of the 15 legislative seats, some with very narrow minorities and amid accusations of electoral malpractice.

The political climate became confrontational thereafter and a serious controversy developed over a move in April 2000 to increase the pensions paid to retired politicians. In May the Caribbean Community and Common Market brokered an agreement under which fresh elections were to be held by March 2001, giving Mitchell time to retire as Prime Minister in October 2000 at the age of 69; in August his party chose Arnhim Eustace as his successor. At a general election of March 2001 the ULP took 12 of the 15 legislative seats; its leader, Dr Ralph Gonsalves, thus became Prime Minister.

In June 2001 Gonsalves announced his intention to establish a commission to review the Constitution. A 25-member body was appointed in December 2002; a referendum was expected to be held on any proposed reforms. The commission submitted its report, to be used as a basis for further discussion, in February 2005. Its proposals included replacing the Queen as Head of State with an indirectly elected President; the establishment of a non-legislative National Advisory Council of Elders; and the introduction of a revamped single-chamber National Assembly, to include three appointed senators and seven civil society representatives.

At a general election held on 7 December 2005, the ULP again won 12 of the 15 seats, although its share of the popular vote was marginally reduced, to 55%, compared with 57% in the 2001 election. Observers noted the need to revise the electoral list by removing voters who had died or migrated, as it contained 91,000 names, equivalent to 87% of the all-age population.

Tensions between the Government and opposition parties intensified during 2007, as reciprocal controversies developed that challenged the political integrity of each. An inquiry into the failed Ottley Hall marina and dockyard development project, financially underwritten by the former NDP Government, had been launched in 2003, but remained uncompleted in 2014 after repeated procedural challenges; the losses incurred under the scheme, according to sources, accounted for more than one-quarter of Saint Vincent's total external debt. The NDP, meanwhile, attempted to increase its popularity by protesting against government plans to increase taxation by the introduction of a value-added tax. Eustace further argued that the Government had failed adequately to enforce penal law in the islands, resulting in the escalation of violent and drugs-related crime. Moreover, the discovery of a ballot box containing voting papers from the 2005 general election further reinforced the opposition's argument for the removal of the ULP from power before the expiry (in 2010) of its term in office.

The referendum on constitutional reform in Saint Vincent and the Grenadines was held on 25 November 2009. In addition to removing the Queen as Head of State, the proposals included replacing the Privy Council in the United Kingdom with the Caribbean Court of Justice in Trinidad as final court of appeal, and the establishment of an Integrity Commission to investigate and control corruption in public life, as well as an ombudsman to look into apparent administrative abuse. In order to gain popular and church support, there was also a proposal to define marriage as between a man and a woman, reinforcing a legal code under which homosexual relations remain subject to imprisonment. The results of the plebiscite showed that 55.6%

of those voting were against the proposals and 43.1% were in favour.

In March 2010 the ULP used its parliamentary majority to approve an increase in the number of electoral seats in the House of Assembly from 15 to 17 in time for the anticipated December election. The move was opposed by the NDP, which launched a constitutional challenge, although the increase in seats was not implemented for the 2010 general election.

Defeat in the constitutional referendum of 2009, together with the continuing high crime rate (see below) and economic difficulties, weakened the standing of the Gonsalves Government. A general election was held on 13 December 2010; in the months preceding the ballot the opposition accused the Government of corruption and links to criminal elements, while the Government claimed credit for public sector and social welfare projects, and for progress in the construction of an international airport at Argyle. The incumbent ULP lost four of the 15 legislative seats to the NDP, but retained eight seats, and therefore a narrow parliamentary majority, with 51.6% of the popular vote. Gonsalves reshuffled his Cabinet in February 2012, and again in September 2013 when his son Camilo Gonsalves was appointed foreign minister. Gonsalves appeared to be firmly in control of his party in 2014; a new election must be called for April 2016 at the latest, but was expected to be held sooner.

There was continuing concern in Saint Vincent and the Grenadines over violent crime. Long periods of pre-trial detention and poor prison conditions were serious issues; the two prisons held 410 inmates in 2013. The murder rate of 36 per 100,000 inhabitants in 2007 was second only to Jamaica's within the English-speaking Caribbean; the murder rate fell back to 28 per 100,000 in 2013, although at this level it remained higher than any year before 2007 and six times that of the USA. Saint Vincent is a centre for cocaine transshipment and is also the main marijuana producer in the eastern Caribbean, with 145 ha under cultivation in the north of the island, and an estimated 50% of exports going to other Caribbean markets, almost 25% to Europe, 15% to the USA and 10% to Canada. Cocaine transshipment through the eastern Caribbean increased in 2013, with Barbados, Dominica, and Grenada all reporting increased drugs-trafficking from Saint Vincent, as well as difficulties in effective co-ordination of counter-narcotics operations with the country. The trade with Trinidad and Tobago involves the exchange of marijuana for guns, cocaine and stolen goods. The US Department of State lists Saint Vincent as a 'country of concern' for money-laundering, and advocates stricter supervision and regulation of the offshore financial sector, although money-laundering legislation was strengthened in 2013. Gonsalves called in 2013 for a discussion within the Caribbean Community and Common Market (CARICOM) on the possible decriminalization of marijuana.

Saint Vincent has been a member of the Petrocaribe initiative since its inception in 2005, under which Venezuela supplies oil products to Caribbean neighbours on preferential terms. In 2009 the country formally joined the Venezuelan-led Bolivarian Alliance for the Peoples of our America-People's Trade Treaty (Alianza Bolivariana para los Pueblos de Nuestra América-Tratado de Comercio de los Pueblos—ALBA-TCP) grouping to encourage regional unity and open the way to additional financial assistance. The Gonsalves Government has also maintained close relations with a variety of countries, including Cuba, Libya, Iran and Taiwan, many of them useful sources of development assistance for the international airport under construction in 2014, and other projects; however, relations with Libya were placed on hold in 2011, following the collapse of the regime of Muammar al-Qaddafi. Saint Vincent supports Argentina in its dispute with the United Kingdom over the Falkland Islands. Saint Vincent has been enthusiastic in lobbying for reparations for slavery and for the forced deportation of the Garifuna people to Belize.

A potential embarrassment for the Government arose in 2006, after Japan pledged to provide US $7m. for the construction of a fisheries complex at Owia. It was claimed that, in return for Japanese financial aid, Saint Vincent and the Grenadines would support the pro-whaling bloc at meetings of the International Whaling Commission (IWC); Gonsalves denied the allegation. However, at an IWC meeting in June 2006, the island, in accordance with several other members of the Organisation of Eastern Caribbean States, endorsed Japan's proposal to end the moratorium on whaling, invoking the criticism of prominent international trading partners and raising a potential threat to the region's crucial tourism economy. Saint Vincent maintained its support for commercial whaling, retaining its own quota until 2018.

Economy

MARK WILSON

Saint Vincent and the Grenadines is the third smallest country in the western hemisphere in terms of area, with 389.3 sq km (150.3 miles), and had an estimated 109,370 inhabitants in mid-2014, a slight increase from the 2001 census total of 106,253. Most of the population live on the main island. Of the Grenadine islands to the south, the most significant are Bequia, Mustique and Union Island. The islands have developed a modest middle-income economy, with a per head gross domestic product (GDP) of US $6,489 at market prices in 2012 (according to IMF estimates). GDP grew by an annual average of 4.4% in 2002–08. GDP contracted by a cumulative 5.8% in 2009–11, according to the Eastern Caribbean Central Bank (ECCB), as the tourism, construction and banana production industries declined; however, migrant remittances were only moderately affected by the international economic recession, remaining close to 7% of GDP. The economy remained weak, with growth of 1.6% and 2.8% recorded in 2012 and 2013, respectively. In 2014 the country ranked 91st out of 187 countries in the UN Development Programme's Human Development Index, the seventh ranking in the English-speaking Caribbean.

The current account deficit on the balance of payments widened from 9.2% of GDP in 2000 to 30.3% in 2012, while public sector debt increased from the equivalent of 43.3% of GDP in 1996 to an estimated 69% of GDP in 2011. With the Government adopting a policy of counter-cyclical spending, the overall fiscal balance moved from a surplus of 0.1% of GDP in 2000 to a deficit averaging 3.5% in 2006–07. The capital budget was financed in part by grants from the European Union (EU), Taiwan, and Trinidad and Tobago, and from external and domestic borrowing. A value-added tax was implemented in 2007, with the income tax threshold raised in partial compensation. Fuel prices were also increased, as existing subsidies had risen to unsustainable levels. With these measures in place, the overall fiscal deficit declined by an estimated 0.8% of GDP in 2008, rose again to 5.7% in 2010 as a result of the economic difficulties experienced from 2009, and was at 6.3% of GDP in 2013, in part because of a 7.2% decline in government revenues in that year. The IMF repeatedly proposed a tightening of fiscal policy. Along with other donor agencies, it urged the Government strictly to restrain current expenditure and to widen the tax base with the aim of protecting its capital investment programme; however, the Government maintained its counter-cyclical stance with a continuing high level of spending, and 'soft' loans from Venezuela through the Petrocaribe scheme (under which countries could buy cheap oil) and other friendly donors. Indicating increased pressures within the domestic economy, the non-performing loans ratio increased from 3.9% at the end of 2008 to 7.4% in mid-2011; difficulties were most acute for the state-owned National

Commercial Bank, of which a 51% stake was sold in 2010 to the East Caribbean Financial Holding Company, based in Saint Lucia, with the remaining 49% earmarked for sale to local investors. The collapse of the Trinidad-based CL Financial conglomerate in 2009 posed risks to financial stability throughout the eastern Caribbean, with an important subsidiary, the British American Insurance Company, declared insolvent. The IMF estimated the exposure of Saint Vincent and Grenadines to the CL group at EC $384.8m., or 21% of GDP. The credit rating agency Moody's in October 2012 downgraded its rating for St Vincent and the Grenadines to B2 from B1 owing to poor growth prospects for tourism and a weak fiscal outlook.

Saint Vincent and the Grenadines is a member of the Caribbean Community and Common Market (CARICOM), whose members formed a single market in 2006. It is also a member of the Organisation of Eastern Caribbean States (OECS), which links nine of the smaller Caribbean territories, while the ECCB, based in Saint Christopher and Nevis, supervises its financial affairs.

Agriculture comprised some 6.7% of GDP in 2013, down from 21.2% in 1990. Banana exports to the United Kingdom under protected market access arrangements were an economic mainstay from the 1950s, but the industry suffered a steep decline in the 1990s as the trade privileges of Caribbean producers in the European market were eroded. In 1990 income from banana exports was US $45.5m., equivalent to 52.2% of merchandise exports. By 2009 exports had diminished to an estimated US $7.8m., equivalent to 16% of merchandise exports, and export volumes totalled 18,053 tons, from 33,243 tons in 2001, with further problems stemming from Black Sigatoka disease. There was significant additional damage in 2010 caused by Hurricane Tomas, which affected production in 2011; exports declined to $1.2m in that year and remained at that level in 2012. However, significant grant aid from the EU was available for irrigation and technical support, as well as for economic diversification and social assistance, and there were some remaining hopes that the industry would survive in some form. Small farmers produce a wide variety of fruits, vegetables and livestock products for the local market, and significant quantities are exported to Trinidad and Tobago, and Barbados. Illegal cultivation of marijuana for export to other islands plays a significant role in the parallel economy.

The E. T. Joshua Airport on Saint Vincent cannot accommodate intercontinental flights, and inbound passengers must transfer by short-haul flight from Barbados or Saint Lucia. This lack of direct air connections impeded the growth of tourism, and in 2005 the Government proposed an international airport at Argyle, in south-eastern Saint Vincent. In mid-2014 with the passenger terminal complete, the Government remained hopeful for a planned opening date by the end of the year; opposition sources raised concerns over timing, cost, design and construction standards. The cost of the project was put at EC $700m. (equivalent to 36% of GDP in 2013), with financial assistance from Taiwan, Venezuela, Cuba, Trinidad and Tobago, and others. The IMF has raised concerns over a funding gap, which the Government intended to compensate for with land sales. The runway of the airport on Canouan island, which serves a major hotel development, was extended in 2008 from 550 m to 1,800 m, allowing direct flights from North America. The main island has few white sand beaches, and most tourism development has taken place on the Grenadines, where a dry climate, clear water and fine beaches have proved powerful attractions for luxury development, and difficulty of public access has been turned into an asset for those who seek seclusion. Two major employers on the Grenadines—the Mustique company and the Canouan resort—each employ around 1,000 staff from a national labour force of approximately 35,000. Yachting is an important sub-sector, but yacht passenger arrivals fell from 93,638 in 2006 to 42,277 in the following year, and have since remained at around this level, with 45,548 arrivals in 2013. A failed marina project at Ottley Hall on the main island was responsible for up to 25% of government debt (EC $156m.); an official inquiry into this project began in 2003 and remained in progress in 2014 after extended procedural challenges and delays. The Government in 2007 succeeded in a write-off and restructuring of the debt incurred by the previous administration for this project, which

had been equivalent to 11.5% of GDP in 2005. An additional source of foreign exchange are three offshore medical schools, with a total of 400 students in 2014; a fourth was expected to open in that year.

Tourism receipts increased from EC $111m. in 1992 to a peak value of EC $306m. in 2006, but fell back to EC $249m. by 2013. In that year the islands attracted 71,725 stop-over tourists, 26.4% below the 2006 peak, a result of continuing fallout from the global economic downturn. There were also 82,974 cruise ship passengers in 2013, 44.5% fewer than in 2009; this group had much lower per head spending than stop-over tourists. In 2013 some 28% of stop-over tourists were from the USA, with 10% from Canada and 27% from Europe, principally the United Kingdom.

Manufacturing comprised some 4.9% of GDP in 2013. The most important facility is a mill, which produces flour, milled rice and animal feed for the local and Eastern Caribbean markets. Milling products (mainly flour) totalled some US $11.7m. in 2012 and comprised 27.2% of total merchandise exports. The flour trade was protected from non-OECS imports even after the commencement of the CARICOM single market, but Antigua and other importers obtained permission in 2008 to seek lower-cost imports from other regional sources. Other enterprises include a brewery, and 'enclave' industries producing electronic components for export.

Saint Vincent and the Grenadines is a member of the Eastern Caribbean Telecommunications Authority (based in Saint Lucia) and has liberalized its telecommunications regime. The Government saw telemarketing and informatics as a potentially important source of employment, although call centres opened from 2001 were not as successful as had originally been anticipated.

There is a small offshore financial services sector. Saint Vincent and the Grenadines was in 2000 listed as a 'non-co-operative jurisdiction' by the Financial Action Task Force on Money Laundering (FATF, based in Paris, France). Following some regulatory and legislative reforms, including the establishment of a Financial Intelligence Unit, Saint Vincent and the Grenadines was delisted by the FATF in 2003, and is currently classed by the US Department of State as a 'country of concern', an intermediate category; the US Government has called for a registry of beneficial owners, immobilization of bearer shares, and proper supervision and regulation of the offshore sector. In 2009 the Organisation for Economic Co-operation and Development included Saint Vincent and the Grenadines on a 'grey list' of countries with inadequate provision for tax information exchange; however, enough treaties had been signed to allow the country to be removed from this list in 2010. As an indication of continuing problems within the sector, the Swiss-owned and Saint Vincent-based Millennium Bank was placed in receivership in 2009 following US allegations that it was running a US $68m. fraudulent investment (Ponzi) scheme. The IMF in 2010 and the Caribbean Financial Action Task Force in 2012 recommended further tightening of the anti money-laundering regime.

Saint Vincent and the Grenadines lies on the southern fringe of the hurricane belt, and is frequently affected by hurricanes, most recently by Hurricane Tomas in 2010 (for which the IMF agreed to a disbursement of US $3.3m. from its rapid credit facility, with damage estimated at 5% of GDP). Along with its neighbours, Saint Vincent and the Grenadines suffered flooding and severe damage outside the hurricane season from a December 2013 weather system, which brought exceptionally heavy rain of more than 300 mm to some districts in 24 hours, with at least nine deaths and widespread infrastructural, housing and other damage, valued at 17% of GDP. In August 2014 the IMF approved disbursement of $6.4m. to aid recovery. The Soufrière volcano in the north of the island erupted in 1902 and 1979, causing several thousand deaths on the first occasion. There are other volcanic centres in the Grenadines, and there is some long-term risk from the underwater volcano of Kick'em Jenny, just north of Grenada; in common with several other Eastern Caribbean governments, the country was actively considering the development of geothermal power in partnership with overseas investors, with the target of a 10 MW plant by 2017. There is also a risk of earthquakes.

Statistical Survey

Source (unless otherwise stated): Statistical Office, Ministry of Finance and Economic Planning, Administrative Centre, Bay St, Kingstown; tel. 457-2921; e-mail statssvg@vincysurf.com; internet www.stats.gov.vc.

AREA AND POPULATION

Area: 389.3 sq km (150.3 sq miles). The island of Saint Vincent covers 344 sq km (133 sq miles).

Population: 109,022 at census of 12 June 2001; 109,991 (males 56,419, females 53,572) at census of 12 June 2012 (preliminary). *Mid-2014* (UN estimate): 109,370. Source: UN, *World Population Prospects: The 2012 Revision.*

Density (at mid-2014): 317.9 per sq km.

Population by Age and Sex (UN estimates at mid-2014): *0–14 years:* 27,239 (males 13,768, females 13,471); *15–64 years:* 74,346 (males 37,859, females 36,487); *65 years and over:* 7,785 (males 3,565, females 4,220); *Total* 109,370 (males 55,192, females 54,178) (Source: UN, *World Population Prospects: The 2012 Revision*).

Principal Town: Kingstown (capital) population 12,712 at 2012 census (preliminary). *Mid-2014* (population incl. suburbs, UN estimate): Kingstown 27,314. Source: UN, *World Urbanization Prospects: The 2014 Revision.*

Births, Marriages and Deaths (registrations, 2009): Live births 1,905 (birth rate 18.9 per 1,000); Marriages 573 (marriage rate 5.7 per 1,000); Deaths 765 (death rate 7.6 per 1,000). Source: UN, *Demographic Yearbook.*

Life Expectancy (years at birth): 74.6 (males 72.7; females 76.6) in 2013. Source: Pan American Health Organization.

Economically Active Population (persons aged 15 years and over, 2001 census): Agriculture, hunting, forestry and fishing 5,303; Mining and quarrying 104; Manufacturing 2,444; Electricity, gas and water 596; Construction 3,659; Trade, restaurants and hotels 8,271; Transport, storage and communications 2,594; Financing, insurance, real estate and business services 1,905; Public administration and defence 2,151; Education 2,500; Health and social work 743; Community, social and personal services 4,251; *Total employed* 34,521 (males 21,274, females 13,247); Unemployed 9,258 (males 6,229, females 3,029); *Total labour force* 43,779 (males 27,503, females 16,276).

HEALTH AND WELFARE

Key Indicators

Total Fertility Rate (children per woman, 2012): 2.0.

Under-5 Mortality Rate (per 1,000 live births, 2012): 23.

Physicians (per 1,000 head, 2009): 0.6.

Hospital Beds (per 1,000 head, 2010): 2.6.

Health Expenditure (2011): US $ per head (PPP): 519.

Health Expenditure (2011): % of GDP: 4.9.

Health Expenditure (2011): public (% of total): 81.7.

Access to Water (% of persons, 2012): 95.

Total Carbon Dioxide Emissions ('000 metric tons, 2010): 209.0.

Carbon Dioxide Emissions Per Head (metric tons, 2010): 1.9.

Human Development Index (2013): ranking: 91.

Human Development Index (2013): value: 0.719.

Source: partly Pan American Health Organization; for other sources and definitions, see explanatory note on p. vi.

AGRICULTURE, ETC.

Principal Crops ('000 metric tons, 2012 unless otherwise indicated): Maize 0.9; Cassava 0.6; Sweet potatoes 2.5; Yams 2.4; Sugar cane 18.0 (FAO estimate); Coconuts 2.0 (FAO estimate); Plantains 2.2; Oranges 1.4; Lemons and limes 1.0; Apples 1.2; Mangoes 1.7. *Aggregate Production* ('000 metric tons, may include official, semi-official or estimated data): Roots and tubers 17.2; Vegetables (incl. melons) 5.9; Fruits (excl. melons) 75.1.

Livestock ('000 head, year ending September 2012, FAO estimates): Cattle 4.8; Sheep 11.0; Goats 9.7; Pigs 5.0; Chickens 270.

Livestock Products ('000 metric tons, 2012, FAO estimates): Pig meat 0.3; Chicken meat 0.5; Cows' milk 1.4; Hen eggs 0.6.

Fishing (metric tons, live weight of capture, 2012): Albacore 397; Skipjack tuna 34; Wahoo 29; Yellowfin tuna 551; Other tuna-like fishes 19; Other marine fishes 641 (FAO estimate); Total catch (incl. others) 10,364 (FAO estimate).

Source: FAO.

INDUSTRY

Selected Products ('000 metric tons, 2005 unless otherwise stated): Copra 2 (FAO estimate); Raw sugar 1.6 (2002); Rum 9,000 hl (2003); Electric energy 127.2 million kWh (2010, provisional). Sources: FAO, Eastern Caribbean Central Bank and UN Industrial Commodity Statistics Database.

FINANCE

Currency and Exchange Rates: 100 cents = 1 Eastern Caribbean dollar (EC $). *Sterling, US Dollar and Euro Equivalents* (30 May 2014): £1 sterling = EC $4.542; US $1 = EC $2.700; €1 = EC $3.675; EC $100 = £22.02 = US $37.04 = €27.21. *Exchange Rate:* Fixed at US $1 = EC $2.70 since July 1976.

Budget (EC $ million, 2013): *Revenue:* Revenue from taxation 417.0 (Taxes on income 113.5, Taxes on goods and services 219.4, Taxes on property 4.0, Taxes on international trade and transactions 80.1); Other current revenue 39.1; Capital revenue 29.0; Foreign grants 17.4; Total 502.5. *Expenditure:* Current expenditure 501.0 (Personal emoluments 250.8, Other goods and services 65.2, Interest payments 47.3, Transfers and subsidies 137.6); Capital expenditure and net lending 123.9; Total 624.9. Source: Eastern Caribbean Central Bank.

International Reserves (US $ million at 31 December 2013): IMF special drawing rights 1.21; Reserve position in IMF 0.77; Foreign exchange 133.12; *Total* 135.10. Source: IMF, *International Financial Statistics.*

Money Supply (EC $ million at 31 December 2012): Currency outside depository corporations 43.87; Transferable deposits 375.96; Other deposits 900.30; *Broad money* 1,320.13. Source: IMF, *International Financial Statistics.*

Cost of Living (Consumer Price Index; base: January 2010 = 100): All items 1103.9 in 2011; 106.6 in 2012; 107.5 in 2013.

Gross Domestic Product (EC $ million at constant 2006 prices): 1,639.16 in 2010; 1,632.49 in 2011; 1,658.45 in 2012. Source: Eastern Caribbean Central Bank.

Expenditure on the Gross Domestic Product (EC $ million at current prices, 2012): Government final consumption expenditure 337.18; Private final consumption expenditure 1,671.81; Gross capital formation 443.11; *Total domestic expenditure* 2,452.10; Exports of goods and services 508.58; *Less* Imports of goods and services 1,085.68; *GDP at market prices* 1,875.00.

Gross Domestic Product by Economic Activity (EC $ million at current prices, 2012): Agriculture, hunting, forestry and fishing 114.96; Mining and quarrying 2.29; Manufacturing 79.83; Electricity and water 72.91; Construction 134.59; Wholesale and retail trade 228.61; Restaurants and hotels 37.56; Transport 146.78; Communications 72.98; Banking and insurance 105.76; Real estate, renting and business activities 244.64; Public administration and defence 187.28; Other services 188.63; *Sub-total* 1,616.82; *Less* Financial intermediation services indirectly measured 20.21; *Total in basic prices* 1,596.61; Taxes, less subsidies, on products 278.39; *GDP at market prices* 1,875.00. Source: Eastern Caribbean Central Bank.

Balance of Payments (EC $ million, 2013): Exports of goods 144.08; Imports of goods −900.35; *Trade balance* −756.28; Services (net) 133.13; *Balance on goods and services* −623.14; Other income received (net) −10.05; *Balance on goods, services and income* −633.19; Current transfers (net) 65.45; *Current balance* −567.75; Capital account (net) 34.67; Direct investment (net) 342.18; Portfolio investment (net) 39.75; Other investment (net) 185.87; Net errors and omissions 30.04; *Overall balance* 64.76. Source: Eastern Caribbean Central Bank.

EXTERNAL TRADE

Principal Commodities (US $ million, 2012): *Imports c.i.f.:* Live animals and animal products 24.3 (Meat and edible offal 14.9); Vegetable products 28.5 (Cereals 21.0); Prepared foodstuffs, beverages and tobacco 43.5; Mineral products 123.1 (Mineral fuels, oils, distillation products, etc. 115.0); Chemicals and related products 24.3; Plastic, rubber and articles thereof 13.6; Iron and steel, base metals and articles thereof 24.9; Machinery and mechanical appliances 45.0 (Machinery, boilers, etc. 25.0, Electrical, electronic equipment 20.0); Vehicles, aircraft, vessels and associated transport equipment 16.5 (Vehicles other than railway, tramway 14.3); Total (incl. others) 403.2. *Exports f.o.b.:* Vegetable products 23.6 (Edible vegetables and certain roots and tubers 5.0; Edible fruit, nuts, peel of citrus fruit, melons 1.9; Cereals 4.4; Milling products, malt, starches, inulin, wheat gluten 11.7; Prepared foodstuffs, beverages and tobacco 8.3 (Beverages, spirits and vinegar 4.4; Residues, wastes of food industry, animal fodder 3.7); Paper and paperboard 1.8 (Paper and paperboard, articles of pulp, paper and board 1.7); Iron and steel, base metals and articles thereof 3.9 (Iron and steel 2.4); Machinery and mechanical appliances 2.1; Total (incl. others) 43.0. Source: Trade Map-Trade Competitiveness Map, International Trade Centre, www.intracen.org/marketanalysis.

Principal Trading Partners (US $ million, 2012): *Imports c.i.f.:* Antigua and Barbuda 9.2; Barbados 8.8; Brazil 4.1; Canada 6.2; China, People's Rep. 13.1; Colombia 4.9; Guyana 4.3; Italy 7.4; Jamaica 5.1; Japan 5.2; Trinidad and Tobago 108.2; United Kingdom 19.3; USA 143.4; Venezuela 22.5; Total (incl. others) 403.2. *Exports f.o.b.:* Antigua and Barbuda 5.3; Barbados 6.2; British Virgin Islands 0.4; Dominica 3.3; Grenada 1.5; Guyana 0.5; Jamaica 0.7; Saint Christopher and Nevis 2.7; Saint Lucia 11.0; Suriname 0.8; Trinidad and Tobago 6.8; United Kingdom 0.8; USA 1.4; Total (incl. others) 43.0. Source: Trade Map-Trade Competitiveness Map, International Trade Centre, www.intracen.org/marketanalysis.

TRANSPORT

Road Traffic (motor vehicles in use, 2008): Private cars 9,247; Buses and coaches 122; Lorries and vans 12,897; Motorcycles 1,217. Source: IRF, *World Road Statistics*.

Shipping: *Flag Registered Fleet* (at 31 December 2013): Number of vessels 1,589; Total displacement 4,034,887 grt. Source: Lloyd's List Intelligence (www.lloydslistintelligence.com).

Civil Aviation (visitor arrivals): 99,657 in 2004; 104,432 in 2005; 106,466 in 2006 (estimate). Source: IMF, *St Vincent and the Grenadines: Statistical Appendix* (April 2009).

TOURISM

Visitor Arrivals: 207,997 (73,866 stop-over visitors, 3,941 excursionists, 41,266 yacht passengers, 88,924 cruise ship passengers) in 2011; 199,840 (74,364 stop-over visitors, 3,051 excursionists, 45,246 yacht passengers, 77,179 cruise ship passengers) in 2012; 200,121 (71,725 stop-over visitors, 2,663 excursionists, 45,548 yacht passengers, 80,185 cruise ship passengers) in 2013. *Stop-over Visitors by Origin* (2013): Canada 7,146; Caribbean 21,745; United Kingdom 15,183; USA 20,106; Other 7,545; Total 71,725.

Tourism Receipts (EC $ million, estimates): 247.6 in 2011; 254.2 in 2012; 249.3 in 2013.

Source: Eastern Caribbean Central Bank.

COMMUNICATIONS MEDIA

Telephones ('000 main lines in use, 2013): 19.1.

Mobile Cellular Telephones (subscribers, 2013): 125,378.

Fixed Internet Subscribers ('000, 2010): 14.2.

Broadband Subscribers ('000, 2013): 14.6.

Source: International Telecommunication Union.

EDUCATION

Pre-primary (2008/09 unless otherwise indicated): 97 schools (1993/94); 378 teachers; 2,925 pupils.

Primary (2011/12 unless otherwise indicated): 60 schools (2000); 877 teachers; 13,811 pupils.

Secondary (2011/12): 26 schools; 680 teachers; 10,419 pupils.

Teacher Training (2000): 1 institution; 10 teachers; 107 students.

Technical College (2000): 1 institution; 19 teachers; 187 students.

Community College (2000): 1 institution; 13 teachers; 550 students.

Nursing College (2000): 1 institution; 6 teachers; 60 students.

Pupil-teacher Ratio (primary education, UNESCO estimate): 15.7 in 2011/12.

Sources: partly Caribbean Development Bank, *Social and Economic Indicators*, and UNESCO Institute for Statistics.

Adult Literacy Rate: 88.1% in 2004. Source: UN Development Programme, *Human Development Report*.

Directory

The Constitution

The Constitution came into force at the independence of Saint Vincent and the Grenadines on 27 October 1979. The following is a summary of its main provisions.

FUNDAMENTAL RIGHTS AND FREEDOMS

Regardless of race, place of origin, political opinion, colour, creed or sex, but subject to respect for the rights and freedoms of others and for the public interest, every person in Saint Vincent and the Grenadines is entitled to the rights of life, liberty, security of the person and the protection of the law. Freedom of conscience, of expression, of assembly and of association is guaranteed, and the inviolability of a person's home and other property is maintained. Protection is afforded from slavery, forced labour, torture and inhuman treatment.

THE GOVERNOR-GENERAL

The British monarch is represented in Saint Vincent and the Grenadines by the Governor-General.

PARLIAMENT

Parliament consists of the British monarch, represented by the Governor-General, and the House of Assembly, comprising 15 elected Representatives (increased from 13 under the provisions of an amendment approved in 1986) and six Senators. Senators are appointed by the Governor-General—four on the advice of the Prime Minister and two on the advice of the Leader of the Opposition. The life of Parliament is five years. Each constituency returns one Representative to the House who is directly elected in accordance with the Constitution. The Attorney-General is an ex officio member of the House. Every citizen over the age of 18 is eligible to vote. Parliament may alter any of the provisions of the Constitution.

THE EXECUTIVE

Executive authority is vested in the British monarch and is exercisable by the Governor-General. The Governor-General appoints as Prime Minister that member of the House who, in the Governor-General's view, is the best able to command the support of the majority of the members of the House, and selects other ministers on the advice of the Prime Minister. The Governor-General may remove the Prime Minister from office if a resolution of no confidence in the Government is adopted by the House and the Prime Minister does not either resign within three days or advise the Governor-General to dissolve Parliament.

The Cabinet consists of the Prime Minister and other ministers and the Attorney-General as an ex officio member. The Leader of the Opposition is appointed by the Governor-General as that member of the House who, in the Governor-General's view, is best able to command the support of a majority of members of the House who do not support the Government.

CITIZENSHIP

All persons born in Saint Vincent and the Grenadines before independence who, immediately prior to independence, were citizens of the United Kingdom and Colonies automatically become citizens of Saint Vincent and the Grenadines. All persons born outside the country after independence to a parent possessing citizenship of Saint Vincent and the Grenadines automatically acquire citizenship, as do those born in the country after independence. Citizenship can be acquired by those to whom it would not automatically be granted.

The Government

HEAD OF STATE

Queen: HM Queen ELIZABETH II.

Governor-General: Sir FREDERICK NATHANIEL BALLANTYNE (took office 2 September 2002).

CABINET
(September 2014)

The Government was formed by the Unity Labour Party.

Prime Minister and Minister of Finance and Economic Planning, National Security, Airport and Seaport Development, Grenadines Affairs, Legal Affairs and of Transport, Works, Urban Development and Local Government: Dr RALPH E. GONSALVES.

Deputy Prime Minister and Minister of Education: GIRLYN MIGUEL.

Minister of Foreign Affairs, Foreign Trade and Consumer Affairs: CAMILO GONSALVES.

Minister of Housing, Informal Human Settlements, Physical Planning, and Lands and Surveys: MONTGOMERY DANIEL.

Minister of Agriculture, Rural Transformation, Forestry, Fisheries and Industry: SABOTO CAESAR.

Minister of Tourism, Sports and Culture: CECIL McKIE.

Minister of National Reconciliation, Public Service, Information, Labour and Ecclesiastical Affairs: MAXWELL CHARLES.

Minister of Health, Wellness and the Environment: CLAYTON BURGIN.

Minister of National Mobilization, Social Development, Family, Gender Affairs, Persons with Disabilities, and Youth: FREDERICK A. STEPHENSON.

Minister of State in the Ministry of Transport, Works, Urban Development and Local Government: JULIAN FRANCIS.

Attorney-General: JUDITH S. JONES-MORGAN.

MINISTRIES

Office of the Governor-General: Government House, Kingstown; tel. 456-1401; fax 457-9701.

Office of the Prime Minister: Administrative Bldg, 4th Floor, Bay St, Kingstown; tel. 456-1703; fax 457-2152; e-mail pmosvg@vincysurf .com.

Office of the Attorney-General and Ministry of Legal Affairs: Methodist Church Bldg, 3rd Floor, Granby St, Kingstown; tel. 457-2807; fax 457-2898; e-mail ag.gov.vc@gmail.com; internet www.legal .gov.vc.

Ministry of Agriculture, Rural Transformation, Forestry, Fisheries and Industry: Richmond Hill, Kingstown; tel. 456-1410; fax 457-1688; e-mail agriculture@gov.vc; internet www .agriculture.gov.vc.

Ministry of Education: Halifax St, Kingstown; tel. 457-1104; fax 457-1114; e-mail office.education@mail.gov.vc; internet www .education.gov.vc.

Ministry of Finance and Economic Planning: Halifax St, Kingstown; tel. 457-1343; fax 457-2943; e-mail office.finance@mail.gov.vc.

Ministry of Foreign Affairs, Foreign Trade and Consumer Affairs: Administrative Bldg, 3rd Floor, Bay St, Kingstown; tel. 456-2060; fax 456-2610; e-mail office.foreignaffairs@mail.gov.vc; internet www.foreign.gov.vc.

Ministry of Health, Wellness and the Environment: Ministerial Bldg, 1st Floor, Bay St, Kingstown; tel. 457-2586; fax 457-2684; e-mail office.health@mail.gov.vc; internet www.health.gov.vc.

Ministry of Housing, Informal Human Settlements, Physical Planning, and Lands and Surveys: Methodist Church Bldg, Granby St, Kingstown; tel. 456-1111; fax 451-2479; e-mail office .housing@mail.gov.vc; internet www.housing.gov.vc.

Ministry of National Mobilization, Social Development, Family, Gender Affairs, Persons with Disabilities, and Youth: DMG Bldg, 2nd and 3rd Floors, Halifax St, Kingstown; tel. 450-0395; fax 457-2476; e-mail office.socialdevelopment@mail.gov.vc; internet www.mobilization.gov.vc.

Ministry of National Reconciliation, Public Service, Information, Labour and Ecclesiastical Affairs: Ministerial Bldg, 2nd Floor, Halifax St, Kingstown; tel. 451-2707; fax 451-2820; e-mail office.reconciliation@gov.vc; internet www.reconciliation.gov.vc.

Ministry of National Security, Airport and Seaport Development: Ministerial Bldg, 2nd Floor, Halifax St, Kingstown; tel. 456-1111; fax 457-2152; e-mail office.natsec@mail.gov.vc; internet www .security.gov.vc.

Ministry of Tourism, Sports and Culture: NIS Bldg, 2nd Floor, Upper Bay St, POB 834, Kingstown; tel. 457-1502; fax 451-2425; e-mail tourism@vincysurf.com; internet www.tourism.gov.vc.

Ministry of Transport, Works, Urban Development and Local Government: Halifax St, Kingstown; tel. 457-2031; fax 457-1289; e-mail office.mtw@gov.vc; internet www.transport.gov.vc.

Legislature

HOUSE OF ASSEMBLY

Senators: 6.

Elected Members: 15.

Speaker: HENDRICK ALEXANDER.

Election, 13 December 2010

Party	Valid votes	% of votes	Seats
Unity Labour Party (ULP) .	32,099	51.11	8
New Democratic Party (NDP) .	30,568	48.67	7
Saint Vincent and the Grenadines Green Party	138	0.22	—
Total	62,805	100.00	15

Election Commission

Electoral Office: Glenville St, Kingstown; tel. 457-1762; e-mail electoraloffice@gov.vc; Supervisor of Elections SYLVIA FINDLAY SCRUBB.

Political Organizations

Democratic Republican Party (DRP): Kingstown; f. 2012; Leader ANESIA BAPTISTE.

New Democratic Party (NDP): Democrat House, Murray Rd, POB 1300, Kingstown; tel. 451-2845; fax 457-2647; e-mail info@ndpsvg .org; internet www.ndpsvg.org; f. 1975; democratic party supporting political unity in the Caribbean, social devt and free enterprise; Chair. LINTON LEWIS; Leader ARNHIM ULRIC EUSTACE; Gen. Sec. ALLAN CRUICKSHANK; 7,000 mems.

Saint Vincent and the Grenadines Green Party: POB 1707, Kingstown; tel. and fax 456-9579; e-mail mail@svggreenparty.org; internet www.svggreenparty.org; f. 2005; Leader IVAN O'NEAL; Gen. Sec. ORDAN O. GRAHAM.

Unity Labour Party (ULP): Tennis Court Cnr, Murrays Rd, POB 1651, Kingstown; tel. 457-2761; fax 457-1292; e-mail info@voteulp .com; internet voteulp.com; f. 1994 by merger of Movement for National Unity and the Saint Vincent Labour Party; moderate, social democratic party; Chair. EDWIN SNAGG; Political Leader Dr RALPH E. GONSALVES; Gen. Sec. JULIAN FRANCIS.

Diplomatic Representation

EMBASSIES IN SAINT VINCENT AND THE GRENADINES

Brazil: Villa, POB 2222, Kingstown; tel. and fax 457-4565; fax 457-4021; Ambassador RENATO XAVIER.

Cuba: Ratho Mill, Kingstown; tel. 458-5844; fax 456-9344; e-mail embajador@vc.embacuba.cu; internet www.cubadiplomatica.cu/ sanvicentegranadinas; Ambassador PABLO ANTONIO RODRÍGUEZ VIDAL.

Taiwan (Republic of China): Murray Rd, POB 878, Kingstown; tel. 456-2431; fax 456-2913; e-mail rocemsvg@caribsurf.com; internet www.taiwanembassy.org/VC; Ambassador WEBER SHIH.

Venezuela: Baynes Bros Bldg, Granby St, POB 852, Kingstown; tel. 456-1374; fax 457-1934; e-mail embavenezsanvicente@vincysurf .com; Ambassador YOEL PÉREZ MARCANO.

Judicial System

Justice is administered by the Eastern Caribbean Supreme Court, based in Saint Lucia and consisting of a Court of Appeal and a High Court. Three High Court Judges are resident in Saint Vincent and the Grenadines. There are five magistrates, including the Registrar of the Supreme Court, who acts as an additional magistrate.

High Court Judges: FREDERICK VICTOR BRUCE-LYLE, GERTEL THOM.

Registrar: (vacant).

Attorney-General: JUDITH S. JONES-MORGAN.

Religion

CHRISTIANITY

Saint Vincent Christian Council: Melville St, POB 445, Kingstown; tel. 456-1408; f. 1969; 4 mem. churches; Chair. Rt Rev. CALVERT LEOPOLD FRIDAY.

The Anglican Communion

Anglicans in Saint Vincent and the Grenadines are adherents of the Church in the Province of the West Indies, comprising eight dioceses. The Archbishop of the West Indies is currently the Bishop of Barbados. The diocese of the Windward Islands includes Grenada, Saint Lucia and Saint Vincent and the Grenadines. Some 18% of the population were Anglican, according to the latest available census (2001).

Bishop of the Windward Islands: Rt Rev. CALVERT LEOPOLD FRIDAY, Bishop's Court, POB 502, Kingstown; tel. 456-1895; fax 456-2591; e-mail diocesewi@vincysurf.com; internet www.anglicandiocesewi.org.

The Roman Catholic Church

Saint Vincent and the Grenadines comprises a single diocese, which is suffragan to the archdiocese of Port of Spain (Trinidad and Tobago). The Bishop participates in the Antilles Episcopal Conference, currently based in Port of Spain. Some 7% of the population are Roman Catholics.

Bishop of Kingstown: CHARLES JASON GORDON, Bishop's Office, POB 862, Edinboro, Kingstown; tel. 457-2363; fax 457-1903; e-mail catholicsvg@gmail.com.

Other Christian Churches

Pentecostal, Methodists, Seventh-day Adventists, Spiritual Baptists and other denominations also have places of worship.

BAHÁ'Í FAITH

National Spiritual Assembly: POB 1043, Kingstown; tel. 456-4717.

The Press

SELECTED WEEKLIES

Searchlight: Interactive Media Ltd, POB 152, Kingstown; tel. 456-1558; fax 457-2250; e-mail editor@searchlight.vc; internet searchlight.vc; weekly on Fri.; Chair. CORLETHA OLLIVERRE; Editor CLARE KEIZER.

The Vincentian: St George's Pl., POB 592, Kingstown; tel. 456-1123; fax 457-2821; e-mail vinpub@thevincentian.com; internet thevincentianonline.com; f. 1899; weekly on Fri.; owned by the Vincentian Publishing Co; CEO DESIREE RICHARDS; Editor-in-Chief CYPRIAN NEEHALL; circ. 6,000.

The Westindian Crusader: Kingstown; tel. and fax 458-0073; e-mail crusader@caribsurf.com; weekly; Editor ESLEE CARBERRY; Man. Editor LINA CLARKE.

SELECTED PERIODICALS

Caribbean Compass: Compass Publishing Ltd, POB 175, Bequia; tel. 457-3409; fax 457-3410; e-mail sally@caribbeancompass.com; internet www.caribbeancompass.com; f. 1995; marine news; monthly; free distribution in the Caribbean; online; circ. 11,000; Man. Dir TOM HOPMAN; Editor SALLY ERDLE.

Government Gazette: Govt Printery, Campden Park St, POB 12, Kingstown; tel. 457-1840; fax 453-3240; e-mail govprint@vincysurf.com; f. 1844; Govt Printer OTHNIEL WHITE; circ. 492.

Ins & Outs of St Vincent & the Grenadines: POB 2125, Kingstown; e-mail chrisw@millerpublising.net; internet www.insandoutsofsvg.com; f. 2001; official publ. of the St Vincent and the Grenadines Hotel and Tourism Asscn; annual; Editor CHRISTINE WILKIE.

Publishers

Interactive Media Ltd: Lower Kingstown Park, POB 152, Kingstown; tel. 456-1558; fax 457-2250; e-mail search@vincysurf.com; internet searchlight.vc; f. 1995; Chair. CORLETHA OLLIVIERRE; CEO CLARE KEIZER (acting).

SVG Publishers Inc: Campden Park Industrial Estate, POB 1609, Kingstown; tel. 453-3166; fax 453-3538; e-mail info@svgpublishers .com; internet www.svgpublishers.com; f. 2005; Dir CLARE KEIZER; Gen. Man. CARL JAMES.

The Vincentian Publishing Co Ltd: St George's Pl., Kingstown; tel. 456-1123; fax 457-2821; e-mail info@thevincentian.com; internet www.thevincentian.com; Man. Dir EGERTON M. RICHARDS; CEO DESIREE RICHARDS.

Broadcasting and Communications

TELECOMMUNICATIONS

Digicel: Suite KO59, cnr Granby and Sharpe Sts, Kingstown; tel. 453-3000; fax 453-3010; e-mail customercaresvg@digicelgroup.com; internet www.digicelsvg.com; f. 2003; mobile cellular phone operator; owned by an Irish consortium; Group CEO and Dir COLM DELVES; Gen. Man. SEAN LATTY.

KaribCable: Frenches Gate, POB 1684, Kingstown; tel. 570-1600; fax 570-1666; e-mail info@karibcable.com; internet www.karibcable .com/vc; internet service provider; Man. Dir KELLY GLASS.

LIME: Halifax St, POB 103, Kingstown; tel. 457-1901; fax 457-2777; internet www.lime.com; fmrly Cable & Wireless (St Vincent and the Grenadines) Ltd; name changed as above 2008; CEO TONY RICE; CEO, Eastern Caribbean GERARD BORELY.

Regulatory Authorities

Eastern Caribbean Telecommunications Authority (ECTEL): based in Castries, Saint Lucia; f. 2000 to regulate telecommunications in Saint Vincent and the Grenadines, Dominica, Grenada, Saint Christopher and Nevis, and Saint Lucia.

National Telecom Regulatory Commission (NTRC): NIS Bldg, 2nd Floor, Upper Bay St, Kingstown; tel. 457-2279; fax 457-2834; e-mail ntrc@ntrc.vc; internet www.ntrc.vc; f. 2001 by the Telecommunications Act to regulate the sector in collaboration with ECTEL; Chair S. MARSHALL.

BROADCASTING

National Broadcasting Corporation of Saint Vincent and the Grenadines (NBC): Richmond Hill, POB 705, Kingstown; tel. 457-1111; fax 456-2749; e-mail nbcsvgadmin@nbcsvg.com; internet www .nbcsvg.com; govt-owned; Chair. ELSON CRICK; Gen. Man. CORLITA OLLIVERRE.

Radio

NBC Radio: National Broadcasting Corpn, Richmond Hill, POB 705, Kingstown; tel. 457-1111; fax 456-2749; e-mail nbcsvgadmin@ nbcsvg.com; internet www.nbcsvg.com; commercial; broadcasts BBC World Service (United Kingdom) and local programmes.

Nice Radio FM: BDS Company Ltd, Dorsetshire Hill, POB 324, Kingstown; tel. 458-1013; fax 456-5556; e-mail bdsnice@caribsurf .com; internet www.niceradio.org; Man. Dir DOUGLAS DE FREITAS.

Television

National Broadcasting Corporation of Saint Vincent and the Grenadines: see above.

SVG Television (SVGTV): Dorsetshire Hill, POB 617, Kingstown; tel. 456-1078; fax 456-1015; e-mail svgbc@vincysurf.com; internet www.svgbc.com/svgtv.htm; f. 1980; broadcasts local, regional and international programmes; Man. Dir R. PAUL MACLEISH.

Television services from Barbados can be received in parts of the islands.

Finance

(cap. = capital; res = reserves; dep. = deposits; m. = million; br. = branch)

BANKING

The Eastern Caribbean Central Bank, based in Saint Christopher, is the central issuing and monetary authority for Saint Vincent and the Grenadines.

Eastern Caribbean Central Bank—Saint Vincent and the Grenadines Office: Frenches House, POB 839, Frenches; tel. 456-1413; fax 456-1412; e-mail eccbnetwork@vincysurf.com; Country Dir ELRITHA DICK.

Local Banks

Bank of St Vincent and the Grenadines Ltd: Granby St, POB 880, Kingstown; tel. 457-1844; fax 456-2612; e-mail natbank@ caribsurf.com; internet www.bosvg.com; f. 1977 as National Commercial Bank (SVG) Ltd, present name adopted 2010; govt-owned until 2010 when 51% stake sold to East Caribbean Financial Holding Ltd (Saint Lucia); cap. EC $14.8m., res EC $16.4m., dep. EC $631.9m. (Dec. 2013); Man. Dir DERRY WILLIAMS; Chair. ERROL ALLEN.

CIBC FirstCaribbean International Bank: Halifax St, POB 604, Kingstown; tel. 457-1706; fax 457-2985; e-mail earl.crichton@ firstcaribbeanbank.com; internet www.firstcaribbeanbank.com; f. 2002 following merger of Caribbean operations of Barclays Bank PLC and CIBC; CIBC acquired Barclays' 43.7% stake in 2006, present name adopted 2011; CEO RIK PARKHILL; 1 br.

RBTT Bank Caribbean Ltd: 81 South River Rd, POB 81, Kingstown; tel. 456-1501; fax 456-2141; internet www.rbtt.com; f. 1985 as Caribbean Banking Corpn Ltd, name changed as above in 2002; Group CEO SURESH SOOKOO.

Scotiabank (Canada): 76 Halifax St, POB 237, Kingstown; tel. 457-1601; fax 457-2623; e-mail bruce.sali@scotiabank.com; internet www .scotiabank.com/vc/en; f. 1977; Country Man. BASIL ALEXANDER.

REGULATORY AUTHORITY

Financial Services Authority (FSA): Upper Bay St, POB 356, Kingstown; tel. 456-2577; fax 457-2568; e-mail info@svgfsa.com; internet www.svgfsa.com; f. 1996 as International Financial Services Authority; Chair. LEON SNAGG; Exec. Dir SHARDA SINANAN-BOLLERS.

> **Financial Intelligence Unit (FIU):** Bonadie's Bldg, 3rd Floor, POB 1826, Kingstown; tel. 451-2070; fax 457-2014; e-mail svgfiu@ vincysurf.com; internet www.svgfiu.com; f. 2002; Dir GRENVILLE WILLIAMS.

OFFSHORE FINANCIAL SECTOR

In 2013 the offshore financial sector included 7,728 International Business Companies, 130 trusts and five banks.

Offshore Banks

B2B Bank Ltd: St Clair Investments, Arnos Vale Bldg, 2nd Floor, Suite A, POB 2043, Arnos Vale; tel. and fax 482-9656; e-mail w .clarke@b2b-bank.com; Contact WALT CLARKE.

Euro Pacific Bank Ltd: 111 Euro House, Financial Services Centre, Stoney Ground, Kingstown; tel. 453-2086; fax 453-2085; internet www.europacbank.com; Pres. GORDON MCBEAN; CEO PETER SCHIFF.

European Commerce Bank: The Financial Services Centre, Paul's Ave, POB 1822, Kingstown; tel. 456-1460; fax 456-1455; e-mail ecb@vincysurf.com; Contact MARCUS BALLANTYNE.

Loyal Bank Ltd: Cedar Hill Crest, POB 1825, Kingstown; tel. 485-6705; fax 451-2757; e-mail ceo@loyalbank.com; internet www .loyalbank.com; f. 1997; owned by Ost West Stiftung; cap. 5.0m., dep. EC $211.2m. (Dec. 2012); CEO ADRIAN BARON.

STOCK EXCHANGE

Eastern Caribbean Securities Exchange: based in Basseterre, Saint Christopher and Nevis; tel. (869) 466-7192; fax (869) 465-3798; e-mail info@ecseonline.com; internet www.ecseonline.com; f. 2001; regional securities market designed to facilitate the buying and selling of financial products for the 8 mem. territories—Anguilla, Antigua and Barbuda, Dominica, Grenada, Montserrat, Saint Christopher and Nevis, Saint Lucia, and Saint Vincent and the Grenadines; Chair. Sir K. DWIGHT VENNER; Gen. Man. TREVOR E. BLAKE.

INSURANCE

There were 13 domestic general insurance companies and nine domestic life insurance companies in operation in 2013. A number of foreign insurance companies also have offices in Kingstown.

Demerara Mutual Life Assurance Society Ltd: 65 Grenville St, Kingstown; tel. 457-1897; fax 456-2686; e-mail dmlvincent@ demeraramutual.com; internet www.demeraramutual.net; f. 1891 in Guyana; Country Man. FREDERICK RICHARDS.

GTM Saint Vincent (Guyana and Trinidad Mutual Group of Insurance Companies): MTM Bldg, Halifax St, Kingstown; tel. 456-1537; e-mail gtmgroup@gtm-gy.com; internet www.gtm-gy .com/stvincent; f. 1952; headquarters in Guyana; Man. COLLIN D. CAMBRIDGE.

Haydock Insurances Ltd: Granby St, POB 1179, Kingstown; tel. 457-2903; fax 456-2952; e-mail haydock@vincysurf.com; internet www.caribbeanalliance.com.

Metrocint General Insurance Co Ltd: Paul's Ave, POB 692, Kingstown; tel. 456-1821; fax 457-2821; e-mail metrocint@vincysurf .com; internet metrocintsvg.com.

Pan-American Life Insurance Co of the Eastern Caribbean: MetroLife Agency Inc, Paul's Ave, POB 692, Kingstown; tel. 456-1821; fax 457–2821; internet www.palig.com; f. 2012; part of Pan-

American Life Insurance Group (USA); CEO and Man. Dir (Caribbean) WILLIAM R. SCHULZ, Jr.

Saint Vincent Insurances Ltd: Lot 69, Grenville St, POB 210, Kingstown; tel. 456-1733; fax 456-2225; e-mail admin@ stvincentinsurances.com; internet www.stvincentinsurances.com.

Trade and Industry

DEVELOPMENT ORGANIZATION

Invest SVG: Reigate Bldg, 2nd Floor, Granby St, POB 2442, Kingstown; tel. 457-2159; fax 456-2688; e-mail info@investsvg.com; internet www.investsvg.com; f. 2003 as National Investment Promotions Inc; assumed DEVCO's responsibilities for investment promotion and foreign direct investment; reports to the Office of the Prime Minister; board mems appointed from both public and private sectors by the Cabinet; Chair. EDMOND A. JACKSON; Exec. Dir CLEO HUGGINS (acting).

CHAMBER OF COMMERCE

Saint Vincent and the Grenadines Chamber of Industry and Commerce (Inc): Unit 27, Cruise Ship Terminal, POB 134, Kingstown; tel. 457-1464; fax 456-2944; e-mail svgchamber@svg-cic.org; internet svg-cic.org; f. 1925; Pres. CHRISTINE DA SILVA.

EMPLOYERS' ORGANIZATIONS

Saint Vincent Employers' Federation: Corea's Bldg, 3rd Floor, Middle St, POB 348, Kingstown; tel. 456-1269; fax 457-2777; e-mail svef@caribsurf.com; Pres. NOEL DICKSON; Exec. Dir PHYLLIS JOHN-PRIMUS.

Windward Islands Farmers' Association (WINFA): Paul's Ave, POB 817, Kingstown; tel. 456-2704; fax 456-1383; e-mail winfa@ winfacaribbean.org; internet www.winfacaribbean.org; f. 1982; Chair. JULIUS POLIUS; Co-ordinator RENWICK ROSE.

UTILITIES

Electricity

Saint Vincent Electricity Services Ltd (VINLEC): Paul's Ave, POB 865, Kingstown; tel. 456-17011.0; fax 456-2436; e-mail vinlec@ vinlec.com; internet www.vinlec.com; f. 1931; 100% state-owned; country's sole electricity supplier; Chair. DOUGLAS COLE; CEO THORNLEY O. A. O. MYERS; 280 employees.

Water

Central Water and Sewerage Authority (CWSA): New Montrose, POB 363, Kingstown; tel. 456-2946; fax 456-2552; e-mail cwsa@vincysurf.com; internet www.cwsasvg.com; f. 1970; Chair. MICHAEL BROWNE; Gen. Man. GARTH SAUNDERS.

TRADE UNIONS

Commercial, Technical and Allied Workers' Union (CTAWU): Lower Middle St, POB 245, Kingstown; tel. 456-1525; fax 457-1676; e-mail ctawu@vincysurf.com; f. 1962; affiliated to CCL, ICFTU and other international workers' orgs; Pres. CHERYL BACCHUS; Gen. Sec. LLOYD SMALL; 2,500 mems.

National Labour Congress: POB 875, Kingstown; tel. 457-1062; fax 457-1705; e-mail svgtu@vincysurf.com; 5 affiliated unions; Pres. NOEL JACKSON.

National Workers' Movement: Burkes Bldg, Grenville St, POB 1290, Kingstown; tel. 457-1950; fax 456-2858; e-mail natwok@ karicable.com; Gen. Sec. NOEL C. JACKSON.

Public Services Union of Saint Vincent and the Grenadines: McKie's Hill, POB 875, Kingstown; tel. 457-1801; fax 457-1705; e-mail psuofsvg@caribsurf.com; f. 1943; Chair GARETH CLARKE; Pres. COOLS VANLOO; Gen. Sec. ELROY BOUCHER; 738 mems.

Saint Vincent and the Grenadines Teachers' Union: McKies Hill, POB 304, Kingstown; tel. 457-1062; fax 456-1098; e-mail svgtu@ caribsurf.com; f. 1952; Pres. OSWALD ROBINSON; Gen. Sec. JOY MATTHEWS; 1,250 mems.

Transport

RAILWAYS

There are no railways in the islands.

ROADS

In 2009 there was an estimated total road network of 1,033 km, of which 70% were paved. Extension of the Windward Highway was completed in 2010 and in June 2014 a EC $40m. project to upgrade the South Leeward Highway was to begin.

SHIPPING

The deep-water harbour at Kingstown can accommodate two ocean-going vessels and about five motor vessels. In addition, a cruise terminal allows two cruise ships to berth at the same time. There are regular motor-vessel services between the Grenadines and Saint Vincent and in 2014 the Government announced a US $100,000 loan from Petrocaribe to support the ferry industry. Numerous shipping lines call at Kingstown harbour. In December 2013 Saint Vincent and the Grenadines' flag registered fleet comprised 1,589 vessels, with an aggregate displacement of some 4,034,887 grt.

Saint Vincent and the Grenadines Port Authority: Upper Bay St, POB 1237, Kingstown; tel. 456-1830; fax 456-2732; e-mail bjohn@svgpa.com; internet www.svgpa.com; CEO and Port Man. BISHEN JOHN.

CIVIL AVIATION

There is a civilian airport, E. T. Joshua Airport, at Arnos Vale, situated about 3 km (2 miles) south-east of Kingstown, that does not accommodate long-haul jet aircraft. An international airport at Argyle, 13 miles east of Kingstown, was under construction in 2014 and was expected to be operational from mid-2015. The new airport would be able to accommodate international jet services and would have facilities for 1.4m. passengers per year, more than five times the capacity at the existing airport. The project was estimated to cost EC $750m. The island of Canouan has a small airport with a runway and passenger terminal; construction of a jet airport was completed in 2008. In 2009 LIAT (in which Saint Vincent and the Grenadines is a shareholder) began scheduled flights from Grenada and Barbados to Canouan. Other airports include the J. F. Mitchell Airport in Bequia, Union Island Airport and one in Mustique island, which has a landing strip for light aircraft only.

LIAT Airlines: tel. 456-6333; fax 456-6111; e-mail pattersond@liatairline.com; internet www.liatairline.com; f. 2009; Chair. JEAN HOLDER; CEO DAVID EVANS.

Mustique Airways: POB 1232, E. T. Joshua Airport, Arnos Vale; tel. 458-4380; fax 456-4586; e-mail info@mustique.com; internet www.mustique.com; f. 1979; charter and scheduled flights; Chair. JONATHAN PALMER.

Saint Vincent and the Grenadines Air Ltd (SVG Air): POB 39, Arnos Vale; tel. 457-5124; fax 457-5077; e-mail info@svgair.com; internet www.svgair.com; f. 1990; charter and scheduled flights; CEO MARTIN BARNARD.

Tourism

The island chain of the Grenadines is the country's main tourism asset. There are superior yachting facilities, but the lack of major air links with countries outside the region has resulted in a relatively slow development for tourism. In 2013 Saint Vincent and the Grenadines received 80,185 cruise ship passengers and 71,725 stop-over tourists. Tourism receipts totalled EC $249.3m. in that year.

Saint Vincent and the Grenadines Hotel and Tourism Association (SVGHTA): Tourism Bureau, Cruise Ship Terminal, POB 2125, Kingstown; tel. 458-4379; fax 456-4456; e-mail svghotels@gmail.com; internet www.svghotels.com; f. 1968 as Saint Vincent Hotel Asscn; renamed as above in 1999; non-profit org.; mem. of the Caribbean Hotels Asscn; Pres. KIM HAILBICH; 75 mems.

St Vincent and the Grenadines Tourism Authority (SVGTA): NIS Bldg, Upper Bay St, POB 834, Kingstown; tel. 456-6222; fax 485-6020; e-mail svgta@discoversvg.com; internet www.discoversvg.com; f. 2009; CEO GLEN BEACHE.

Defence

Saint Vincent and the Grenadines participates in the US-sponsored Regional Security System, comprising police, coastguards and army units, which was established by independent Eastern Caribbean states in 1982. The budget for 2012 allocated some EC $28.56m. to the police force and a further $3.8m. to the Coast Guard.

Education

Free primary education, beginning at five years of age and lasting for seven years, is available to all children in government schools, although it is not compulsory and attendance is low. There are 61 government, and five private, primary schools. Secondary education, beginning at 12 years of age, comprises a first cycle of five years and a second, two-year cycle. However, government facilities at this level are limited, and much secondary education is provided in schools administered by religious organizations, with government assistance. There are also a number of junior secondary schools. Enrolment at primary schools during 2012 included 95% of children in the relevant age-group, while comparable enrolment in secondary schools in 2010 included 85% of pupils. There are teacher training, technical, nursing and community colleges. Recurrent budgetary expenditure on education by the Government was a projected EC $120.7m. in 2013 (19.4% of the recurrent expenditure).

SINT EUSTATIUS

Sint (St) Eustatius (also known as Statia—from the original Spanish name St Anastasia) is a volcanic island, some 21 sq km (8 sq miles) in area, in the north-eastern Caribbean Sea, about 20 km north-east of Saint Christopher (St Kitts) and Nevis. Together with Saba and Sint (St) Maarten, St Eustatius comprises the Bovenwindse Eilands or Windward Islands (although actually in the Leeward group of the Lesser Antilles). The climate is tropical, moderated by the sea, with an average annual temperature of 27.5°C (81°F) and little rainfall. English is the official and principal language, although Dutch is also spoken. There were 4,020 inhabitants of St Eustatius in January 2014, giving a population density of 191.4 people per sq km. Almost all of the inhabitants profess Christianity, predominantly Protestantism. The state flag (proportions 2 by 3) is divided into four five-sided blue squares with red borders. In the centre of the flag is a white diamond, in which an outline of the island appears. At the top of the diamond is a five-pointed gold star. The capital is Oranjestad.

The Dutch settled the Windward Islands, once settled by Carib Indians, in the mid-17th century. St Eustatius came under Dutch control in 1635. After frequent changes in possession, the islands were finally confirmed as Dutch territory in 1816. Together with the Leeward Islands (comprising Aruba, Bonaire and Curaçao), the Windward islands were administered as Curaçao and Dependencies between 1845 and 1948. In the early 18th century St Eustatius prospered as a trading centre and transshipment centre for African slaves. During the Second World War Queen Wilhelmina of the Netherlands promised independence, and in 1954 a Charter gave the federation of six islands full autonomy in domestic affairs, and declared it to be an integral part of the Kingdom of the Netherlands.

Political allegiance within the federation was traditionally along island, rather than party lines. These divisions increased following Aruba's secession from the federation in 1986. Demands for further autonomy increased in Curaçao and St Maarten, although the population of St Eustatius remained broadly in favour of maintaining the status quo. In a referendum on status held in October 1994 some 86% of voters opted for continued membership of the Antillean federation. Nevertheless, plebiscites in the other constituent parts of the federation produced differing results, and in the 1990s and early 2000s movements to obtain autonomy in Curaçao and St Maarten increased. In October 2004 the Jesurun Commission, established by the Dutch and Antillean Governments and headed by Edsel Jesurun (a former Governor of the Netherlands Antilles), recommended the dissolution of the federation; support for the continued union had, it was argued, virtually disintegrated on most of the islands. The Commission proposed that Curaçao and St Maarten should become autonomous states within the Netherlands (i.e. have *status aparte*), while Saba, Bonaire and St Eustatius should be directly administered by the Dutch Government. A further referendum on the constitutional futures of St Eustatius took place on 8 April 2005: from a voter turnout of 55%, 76% of the electorate favoured remaining part of the Netherlands Antilles, while 20% voted for closer ties with the Netherlands and 1% preferred to seek complete independence for the tiny island. On 3 December 2005 a preliminary agreement with the Dutch Government that the extant federation be dissolved by 1 July 2007 was duly signed in Curaçao. Under the new structure, St Eustatius was to become a koninkrijseilande, or kingdom island, with direct ties to the Netherlands, a status equivalent to that of a Dutch province. The future status of St Eustatius was subsequently refined to that of a bijzondere gemeete, or special municipality, similar in most ways to other metropolitan Dutch municipalities, although with separate social security and currency arrangements.

An agreement confirming St Eustatius's impending accession to special municipality status was signed in The Hague, Netherlands, on 12 October 2006, and included provisions for citizens of the island to participate in Dutch national and local elections and in the election of candidates to the European Parliament. A further transition accord was signed by the Netherlands Antilles central Government, the Island Council of St Eustatius, and the Netherlands on 12 February 2007, envisaging the island's complete secession from the federation. Under the terms of this covenant, the Netherlands was to pledge over NA Fl. 1,000m. to facilitate the process of disintegration, with St Eustatius, Saba and Bonaire receiving individual allocations. The metropolitan administration also agreed to write off almost three-quarters of the Antilles' debt.

On 15 December 2008 the Dutch Prime Minister, Jan Peter Balkenende, and the Antillean premier, Emily de Jongh-Elhage, signed an agreement confirming the new status of the island. In September 2009, at a meeting of the Dutch State Secretary for the Interior and Kingdom Relations, Ank Bijleveld-Schouten, and representatives of the Netherlands Antilles, it was agreed that the target date for dissolution of the federation would be 10 October 2010, at which date St Eustatius would become a special municipality of the Netherlands. The US dollar was formally adopted as the island's currency from 1 January 2011, replacing the Netherlands Antilles guilder; the Island Council had opposed the introduction of the euro, the currency of the Netherlands.

In elections to the new five-member Island Council held on 2 March 2011, the Democratic Party of St Eustatius (DP) won two seats, while the Progressive Labour Party, the United People's Coalition (UPC) and the St Eustatius Empowerment Party each won one seat. The new members of the Council were sworn into office on 11 March.

Owing to St Eustatius's change in administrative status, the island's residents were henceforth entitled to vote in Dutch polls. The islanders' first opportunity to exercise this right came on 12 September 2012, when elections to the Tweede Kamer (Second Chamber—the lower house of the Dutch parliament) were conducted. The Partij van de Arbeid received 28.2% of the valid votes cast in St Eustatius, while Democraten 66 (D66) garnered 27.9% and the Socialistische Partij 21.8%. The rate of participation by the electorate was just 15.6% (compared with 74.6% nationwide). Commentators attributed this very low turnout to a lack of campaigning on the island.

Executive Council Commissioner Nicolaas Sneek of the DP was forced to stand down from his post in July 2013 after being defeated in a confidence motion in the Island Council. Sneek, who was succeeded by the UPC's Reginald Zaandam, had been accused of nepotism. Meanwhile, on several occasions during 2013 the island authorities expressed an interest in organizing another referendum on St Eustatius's constitutional relationship with the Netherlands. Although the local Government had intended to stage the plebiscite in 2014, no firm plans had been announced by the middle of that year.

Elections to the European Parliament took place in St Eustatius on 22 May 2014. D66 secured 38.5% of the local ballot, compared with 15.4% for the 'ikkiesvooreerlijk.eu' list and 11.5% for GroenLinks. Turnout, however, was just 7.4%.

The economy of St Eustatius is primarily based on oil transshipment, tourism, commerce and harbour activities, the medical school, and the public sector. The most important private company is Statia Oil Terminal, which is operated and owned by the US company NuStar. The terminal, which employs about 140 people, has 67 tanks with a total storage capacity of over 13m. barrels. The terminal has no harbour: tankers anchor off shore and are connected to the terminal by pipelines. Tankers with a capacity of up to 520,000 dwt can be handled at the terminal. NuStar planned to expand its operations on the island.

Another important employer is the University of Sint Eustatius School of Medicine, with about 30 employees and 120 students. Tourism is relatively under-developed. Approximately 19,000 air passenger arrivals were recorded in 2012, with the majority travelling from other Caribbean islands and the Netherlands. The agricultural and fishery sectors are not well developed and St Eustatius imported a substantial proportion of its food. Electricity production in 2012 totalled 13.7m. kWh. As a result of the constitutional changes, in 2010–12 public investments and consumption increased. The unemployment rate in 2012 was recorded at 3.2%. The average annual inflation rate was 9.9% in 2011, declining to 5.3% in 2012 and 2.3% in 2013. As a special municipality, St Eustatius must maintain a balanced budget, supervised by the financial supervision authority, the College Financieel Toezicht. The economic prospects of the island depended on NuStar's plans for the terminal, and efforts to develop the tourism sector.

Lieutenant-Governor: GERALD BERKEL, Govt Bldg, Oranjestad; tel. 318-2552; fax 318-2324; e-mail lt.governor@statiagovernment .com; internet www.statiagovernment.com.

Island Council: REUBEN MERKMAN, MILLICENT LIJFROCK-MARSDIN, ELVIN HENRIQUEZ, FRANKLIN BROWN, ADELKA SPANNER.

Island Secretary: MILITZA C. CONNELL-MADURO; tel. 318-3395; fax 318-3394; e-mail sec.islandcouncil@statiagov.com.

Executive Council: REGINALD C. ZAANDAM, C. TEARR.

National Office for the Caribbean Netherlands Sint Eustatius (Rijksdienst Caribisch Nederland Sint-Eustatius): Mazinga Complex A and B, Fort Oranjestraat, POB 26, Oranjestad; tel. 318-3370; e-mail info@rijksvertegenwoordiger.nl; internet www.rijksdienstcn .com; Kingdom Rep. (resident in Bonaire) GILBERT ISABELLA.

SINT MAARTEN

Geography

PHYSICAL FEATURES

Sint (St) Maarten is part of the quadripartite Kingdom of the Netherlands. Lying in the north-eastern Caribbean, the dependency forms the Dutch (southern) half of the island of Saint Martin. The French Overseas Collectivity of Saint-Martin constitutes the northern part of the island. Until October 2010 St Maarten formed part of the Netherlands Antilles, a five-member federation that also included the island territories of Curaçao, Bonaire, St Eustatius (Statia—from the original Spanish name, St Anastasia) and Saba. Following formal dissolution of the so-called Antilles of the Five on 10 October 2010, St Maarten was redesignated an autonomous country within the Kingdom of the Netherlands, along with Curaçao and (since 1986) Aruba. St Maarten is grouped in the Bovenwindse Eilands (Windward Islands—the Dutch adopted this terminology from the Spanish, at variance with the anglophone tradition, which terms the surrounding islands in the north-eastern Caribbean as the Leeward Islands). The Bovenwindse Eilands are sometimes known as the 'three Ss' (St Maarten, Saba and St Eustatius). St Maarten lies 56 km to the north of St Eustatius and 45 km from Saba. On St Maarten is the only land border (10.2 km) in the Lesser Antilles. The British overseas territory of Anguilla lies just to the north of the Franco-Dutch island, with the Virgin Islands some distance to the west. The territory covers an area of 34 sq km (13.1 sq miles).

The island of St Martin (Sint Maarten or Saint-Martin) is of volcanic origin, but is fairly flat and comprised primarily of a coralline limestone base. The dry, often scrubby landscape is dotted with salt ponds and other inland waters, notably the great Simpson's Bay Lagoon, which dominates the low-lying, west-pointing peninsula that extends the island in the south-west. The highest point is in the centre of the hillier, eastern bulk of the island, at Pic du Paradis (424 m), and lies in the French sector. At 87 sq km, Saint Martin is the smallest island in the world to be divided between two nations. (The 34 sq km area of the Dutch territory was finally agreed in the 1839 revision of the original 1648 Franco-Dutch Treaty of Mount Concordia). St Maarten has a slightly larger population than Saint-Martin and is heavily developed.

CLIMATE

St Maarten has a subtropical climate. The dependency lies firmly in the hurricane belt, and the average annual rainfall is

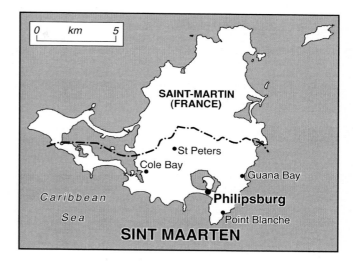

about 1,100 mm, with February and March being the driest months and August and September the wettest. Minimum and maximum temperatures, on average, range seasonally from 24°C to 28°C (76°F–88°F).

POPULATION

The majority of the population are of mixed black descent (85%), including some claiming descent from the original Amerindians. About 82% of the population are Christians, according to the 2011 census, with Roman Catholicism the largest denomination (33% of the population). English tends to be the first language for many, although Dutch is also spoken and is the official language of the territory.

The total population was estimated at 33,609 at the census of 9 April 2011. The capital is Philipsburg, in the south of the island, between an inland lake and the Great Bay on the southern coast. Its population at the 2011 census was 1,327.

History

CHARLES ARTHUR

Revised for this edition by the editorial staff

The island of Saint Martin in the north-eastern Caribbean, which is divided into two, French and Dutch, territories known, respectively, as Saint-Martin and Sint (St) Maarten, was originally inhabited by Arawak Amerindians. In 1493 Christopher Columbus, on his second voyage to the Caribbean, sailed around the island without landing and named it Isla de San Martín. Although Spain claimed the island, it made little effort to colonize it. In 1631 the Dutch founded a settlement and the Dutch East India Company began salt-mining operations. In time, French and British settlements were also established on the island. Spain seized control of the island in 1633 but abandoned it 1648. The Dutch and the French re-established their settlements, and in 1648 the two countries signed the

Treaty of Mount Concordia, which divided the island in two, with the northern part administered by the French and the southern part by the Dutch. Between 1648 and 1816 conflicts changed the border 16 times before finally, in 1817, the current partition line was established, with Dutch St Maarten comprising approximately 40% of the island's total area of 87 sq km. From this time, St Maarten, together with the Netherlands' five other Caribbean island colonies, was administered as Curaçao and Dependencies, a single administrative colony within the Kingdom of the Netherlands.

In the aftermath of the Second World War (1939–45), elements within the colony became vocal in demanding independence from the Netherlands. However, greater autonomy was not granted until 1954 when the Dutch Government agreed to allow self-government except in relation to foreign affairs, defence, security and migration. The status of St Maarten and the five other Dutch islands was promoted from that of a colonial territory to part of the Kingdom of the Netherlands, as an associated state within a federation. Willemstad in Curaçao became the seat of government of the Netherlands Antilles federation. In 1986 Aruba seceded from the Netherlands Antilles, paving the way for a series of plebiscites among the remaining islands on the future of the federation.

Referendums asking the population for their preferred option were held in the 1990s and produced a conclusive vote in favour of maintaining the federation. However, subsequent ballots held between 2000 and 2005 produced markedly different results, beginning in June 2000 when 69% of voters in St Maarten expressed a preference for obtaining *status aparte* within the Kingdom of the Netherlands. In October 2004 a commission established by the Dutch and Antillean Governments recommended the dissolution of the federation on the grounds that public support for it had more or less evaporated. An inter-island constitutional conference held in April 2005 recommended the abolition of the federation by July 2007. Curaçao and St Maarten were to be granted *status aparte*, and the other three islands, Bonaire, St Eustatius and Saba, would come under more direct control of the Netherlands.

Negotiations concerning the details of the transition were marred by controversy, with opposition leaders, in particular in Curaçao, accusing the Dutch authorities of acting in bad faith. Despite the best efforts of the Dutch and federation authorities to further the transition process, including the creation of a specially convened financial supervision body, the College Financieel Toezicht (CFT), the break-up of the federation of the Netherlands Antilles was repeatedly delayed. The main problems concerned the cancellation of the debt owed by the Netherlands Antilles to the Netherlands; the establishment of sound financial management; and responsibility for law and order. The CFT began supervising the finances of the respective island councils of St Maarten and Curaçao at the end of 2008, and some progress was made in resolving outstanding issues during 2009. A new deadline for the dissolution of the federation was agreed for October 2010.

On 10 October 2010 the federation of the Netherlands Antilles was officially dissolved. St Maarten became an independent nation within the Kingdom of the Netherlands, making it a constitutional equal partner with Aruba, Curaçao, and the Netherlands itself. St Maarten was to maintain close relations with the Kingdom of the Netherlands, which would remain responsible for its foreign policy, defence, and guarantees of freedom, legal rights and good governance. The new country's first Government was a coalition between the Democratic Party (Democratische Partij—DP) and the newly formed United People's Party (UP). In elections, held just weeks before the dissolution, the National Alliance (NA) had emerged as the largest party, gaining seven of the 15 seats in the new parliament. However, with the NA one seat short of the majority needed to form a single-party government, the UP and DP seized the opportunity and formed a coalition. The DP leader, Sarah Wescot-Williams, became the country's first Prime Minister. Eugene Holiday was nominated by the Kingdom Government as the country's first Governor.

The first Government of St Maarten faced many challenges, in particular those associated with the high costs of running the new country and a deteriorating security situation. In April 2012 the UP-DP coalition collapsed owing to, *inter alia*, a dispute over the handling of redundant employees at the bankrupt Pelican timeshare resort. An agreement on the formation of a new administration was signed by the NA, the DP and three independents on 11 May. The new coalition Government, which was again headed by Wescot-Williams, took office on 21 May. However, in May 2013 this administration also collapsed after several members of the coalition withdrew their support for the Government. The UP and the DP, together with an independent deputy, agreed to form another coalition administration, which was duly inaugurated on 14 June. Wescot-Williams returned as Prime Minister.

Elections to the European Parliament took place in St Maarten on 22 May 2014. Democraten 66 won the majority of the local ballot, although the rate of participation by the electorate was very low. Meanwhile, during the first half of 2014 St Maarten was granted associate membership of the Association of Caribbean States and the UN Economic Commission for Latin America and the Caribbean.

A general election was held on 29 August 2014. The UP won the largest proportion of the ballot, equivalent to 42.5% of the valid votes cast, and gained seven parliamentary seats. The NA won four seats (and 27.7% of the valid votes), while the DP and the newly formed United St Maarten Party (US Party), led by Frans Richardson, each won two seats. Following negotiations overseen by the Governor, in early September the NA, the DP and the US Party reached an agreement on the formation of a new coalition Government, most likely to be headed by NA leader William Marlin.

Economy

ROLAND VAN DEN BERGH

Based on an earlier article by CHARLES ARTHUR and subsequently revised by the editorial staff

In the 17th, 18th and 19th centuries Spanish, Dutch and French colonists developed an economy based on plantations, on which cotton, tobacco and sugar were cultivated. Large numbers of slaves from Africa were imported to work on the plantations on the island of Sint (St) Maarten/Saint-Martin, and in a short time the slave population grew larger than that of the land owners. Following the abolition of slavery, in 1848 on the French part of the island, and in 1863 on the Dutch side, the economy stagnated. For the next 100 years the only industry of any note was the production of salt, dried in the sun and collected from salt ponds. It was not until the 1950s, when St Maarten began to focus on the development of a tourism industry, that the economy began to expand. The construction of some hotels catered for tourists from the USA. Central to the development of the tourism industry was the existence of an airport. In 1943 a military runway, constructed by the USA after it entered the Second World War, was converted into a civilian airport and was named after Princess Juliana of the Netherlands. The airport was remodelled and relocated in 1964. Tourism in St Maarten further prospered when Caribbean cruise ship holidays grew in popularity in the 1970s, and cruise ship operators began to include the deep-water port at the capital, Philipsburg, in their itineraries. Since then, St Maarten has become one of the Caribbean's leading ports for visits by cruise ships. During 1972–92 the population of St Maarten increased from 7,807 to 33,331. In 2014 the population stood at 37,224, on an area of 34 sq km. No border controls exist between the Dutch and French sides of the island: all goods and persons have freedom of movement.

During the 1980s and early 1990s there was a tourism boom in St Maarten (and in the French Saint-Martin). As a consequence of the flourishing economy, there was large-scale immigration from neighbouring islands, in particular from Haiti, the Dominican Republic, Jamaica and Guyana, as well as from Aruba and the other islands of the Netherlands Antilles. A series of devastating hurricanes in the late 1990s, however, seriously damaged the tourism infrastructure. Despite these setbacks, the economy made a strong recovery and hotel capacity was significantly expanded in the early years of the 21st century.

Tourism generates 85% of foreign exchange, according to the IMF. Tourism receipts totalled an estimated NA Fl. 1,571m. in 2013. The sector is quite diversified and comprises hotel tourists, timeshare owners, second home owners of villas and condominiums, and yachting and cruise tourists. Although more than one-half of the tourists are American, other markets in Europe and Canada are gaining in importance. Tourism development was facilitated by the construction of a new terminal and facilities at Princess Juliana Airport, which was completed in 2007, increasing capacity by 50%. The airport is an important passenger hub to the other smaller Caribbean islands. Stay-over tourist arrivals decreased by 7.4% in 2009, stabilized in 2010 (with a rise of 0.7%) and declined in 2011 by 4.2%, to 424,300 tourists, mainly as a result of the closure of a large timeshare resort, Pelican. The number of stay-over tourists rose to 456,700 in 2012 and 467,000 in 2013. The hotel room capacity on the island has remained at around 3,600 since 2007. An increasing number of regular hotel rooms were transformed into timeshare units. The occupancy rate for timeshare units was 72% in 2011, compared with a rate of 61% for hotel rooms in the same year.

The pier facilities at the port of Philipsburg were also expanded; the port can accommodate up to six cruise liners. There is also a large cargo facility. After a gradual decline in cruise tourism from the 2005 peak of 1.5m., to 1.2m. in 2009, cruise passenger arrivals increased in 2010 and 2011 (by 24.5% and 9.5%, respectively), reaching nearly 1.7m. arrivals. The number of cruise passenger arrivals rose by a further 5.9% in 2012 and by 1.5% in 2013, to almost 1.8m. The hotel and restaurant sector alone contributed 24.3% of gross domestic product (GDP) in 2012.

The marine and yachting industry has become an important sector of the economy in the last decade. An extensive yachting service and maintenance sector has developed on the island, servicing all types of vessels, including yachts and 'mega yachts'. During the 2011/12 season the sector suffered a decline of approximately 15%–20%, mainly caused by the recession in the charter business, as well as by increased competition from other destinations such as Antigua, Puerto Rico, the Dominican Republic and Saint Lucia.

The construction industry is important for St Maarten. The sector contributed 6.7% of GDP in 2012. However, activity within the sector was slow during 2009–12, forcing many small construction companies out of business. Nevertheless, the commencement of various new private and public investment initiatives during 2013–14, including several major infrastructural development projects, transformed the outlook for the industry from poor to positive. The construction sector was consequently expected to be a key driver of economic growth in the near term.

Water and electricity output increased by an average of 5% per year until 2011, when the production of electricity decreased by 4.6% and that of water rose by only 2.1%. This was attributed to efforts by companies and domestic households to save on utilities. Electricity and water production increased, respectively, by 2.4% and 1.5% in 2012 and by 0.9% and 5.5% in 2013. Utilities contributed 3.3% of GDP in 2012.

St Maarten's economy was, like the other Caribbean tourism-orientated islands, adversely affected by the global economic recession from 2008. St Maarten's economic performance follows in particular that of the USA, although the impact is normally felt six months later. In 2009–11 real GDP declined, and growth rates of just 1.5% and 1.1% were reported in 2012 and 2013, respectively. Consequently, the unemployment rate, at an estimated 11% in 2013, remained very high.

Private consumption increased substantially during 2005–08 as a result of developments in tourism and tourism-dependent and -related sectors. In 2009, however, the trend was reversed when the volume of imports decreased and government revenue from sales tax declined. Private investment also suffered a decline in 2009, of 11.2%. The share of net foreign direct investment as a percentage of GDP decreased from 8.8% in 2008 to 3.5% in 2011. There was a trade deficit of NA Fl. 1,342m. in 2013, which was to a large extent offset by a positive trade-in-services balance.

St Maarten's transition to an autonomous country within the Kingdom of the Netherlands in October 2010 had an impact on the fiscal situation, with the need for the island to establish and develop institutions to provide a range of services previously provided by the Netherlands Antilles. St Maarten's debt, including the island's debt and its share of the Netherlands Antilles' debt, was reduced to NA Fl. 302m., equivalent to 28.3% of GDP. This debt is financed by the Dutch Ministry of Finance and enjoys low interest rates. The new fiscal framework prohibits current budget deficits, limits interest payments to 5% of the fiscal revenues, and requires medium-term budgeting. A common fiscal supervision agency was established to oversee this, the Council for Financial Supervision (College Financieel Toezicht). Borrowing is only allowed for capital expenditures. Initially, the 2011 budget deficit was estimated at about 5% of GDP. However, the Government delayed major planned infrastructure spending, resulting in a surplus of 2.7% of GDP for 2011. The budget surplus narrowed slightly, to 1.8% of GDP, in 2012. The percentage share of revenue in GDP for St Maarten is still relatively low, according to IMF estimates, at 27.9% in 2011, compared with, for example, that of Curaçao, at 31%, or Barbados, at 38%. St Maarten's percentage share of revenue in GDP was 24.2% in 2012, according to the central bank.

Since October 2010 St Maarten and Curaçao have maintained a monetary union; both have the Netherlands Antilles guilder or florin as their legal tender, which is pegged to the US dollar at a rate of NA Fl. 1.79. A monetary union required a synchronized monetary policy, and sound and uniform financial legislation, which was lacking. The huge current account deficit recorded by Curaçao and the credit restriction that it introduced in order to counteract this did not benefit St Maarten's economy. As a result of this, and the fact that most of its transactions were in US dollars, St Maarten was considering the replacement of the guilder with the dollar. However, any introduction of a new currency was not expected in the near term.

With the gradual recovery of the US economy, St Maarten's economy returned to growth, albeit at a modest pace, in 2012. Although real GDP growth slowed in 2013, compared with other Caribbean islands St Maarten's economy was in better shape in terms of its debt-to-GDP ratio, inflation rate and current account deficit. The economy was well placed for further expansion and was more able to absorb shocks than its neighbours. The Department of Economic Affairs, Transportation and Telecommunication projected economic growth of 1.4% in 2014, predicated on an expected upturn in visitor numbers, increased activity in the construction sector and a continued recovery in the global economy.

Statistical Survey

Note: The Netherlands Antilles was officially dissolved on 10 October 2010. The figures in this Statistical Survey refer to Sint Maarten only, unless otherwise indicated.

Sources (unless otherwise stated): Department of Statistics (STAT), Ministry of Tourism, Economic Affairs, Traffic & Telecommunications (TEZVT), Juancho Yrausquin Blvd 6, Units 7/8, Philipsburg; tel. 542-2151; fax 542-9907; internet www.sintmaartengov.org; Centrale Bank van Curaçao en Sint Maarten, Walter Nisbeth Rd 25, Philipsburg; tel. 542-3529; fax 542-4307; e-mail info@centralbank.an; internet www .centralbank.cw.

AREA AND POPULATION

Area: 34 sq km (13.1 sq miles).

Population (resident population at census of 9 April 2011): 33,609 (males 15,868, females 17,741).

Density (at 2011 census): 988.5 per sq km.

Population by Age and Sex (resident population at 2011 census): *0–14 years:* 7,405 (males 3,543, females 3,862); *15–64 years:* 24,275 (males 11,415, females 12,860); *65 years and over:* 1,929 (males 910, females 1,019); *Total* 33,609 (males 15,868, females 17,741).

Births, Marriages and Deaths (2010 unless otherwise indicated): Births 496; Registered marriages 232 (marriage rate 5.7 per 1,000, 2008); Deaths 160.

Life Expectancy (years at birth, 2013): 77.6 (males 75.3; females 80.0). Source Pan American Health Organization.

Immigration and Emigration (2009): *Immigration:* Dominican Republic 160; Guadeloupe 79; Guyana 128; India 84; Netherlands 297; Total (incl. others) 2,170. *Emigration:* Aruba 40; Netherlands 365; USA 10; Total (incl. others) 827. *2010:* Total immigration 859; Total emigration 873.

Economically Active Population (labour force survey at June, persons aged 15 years and over, 2009): Agriculture, fishing and mining 163; Manufacturing 646; Electricity, gas and water 325; Construction 2,307; Wholesale and retail trade, repairs 4,146; Hotels and restaurants 2,729; Transport, storage and communications 2,031; Financial intermediation 692; Real estate, renting and business activities 2,520; Public administration, defence and social security 1,600; Education 723; Health and social work 633; Other community, social and personal services 1,910; Private households with employed persons 648; Extraterritorial organizations and bodies 305; *Total employed* 21,378; Unemployed 2,966; *Total labour force* 24,344 (males 12,545, females 11,799). Source: Netherlands Antilles Central Bureau of Statistics.

FISHING

Fishing (all capture, metric tons, live weight, 2012, FAO estimate): Marine fishes 180; Total catch (incl. others) 181 (Source: FAO).

FINANCE

Currency and Exchange Rates: 100 cents = 1 Netherlands Antilles gulden (guilder) or florin (NA Fl.). *Sterling, Dollar and Euro Equivalents* (30 May 2014): £1 sterling = NA Fl. 3.011; US $1 = NA Fl. 1.790; €1 = NA Fl. 2.436; NA Fl. 100 = £33.21 = $55.87 = €41.04. *Exchange Rate:* In December 1971 the Netherlands Antilles' central bank's mid-point rate was fixed at US $1 = NA Fl. 1.80. In 1989 this was adjusted to $1 = NA Fl. 1.79. In December 2009 it was announced that the US dollar would replace the Netherlands Antilles guilder and florin in Bonaire, St Eustatius and Saba from 1 January 2011, following the dissolution of the previous federation of the Netherlands Antilles in October 2010. In Curaçao and St Maarten, the Netherlands Antilles guilder was expected to be replaced with a newly created Caribbean guilder, but negotiations on the introduction of the new currency appeared to have stalled by mid-2014.

Budget (NA Fl. million, 2012): *Revenue:* Tax revenue 344.6 (Taxes on income and profits 148.1, Taxes on goods and services 182.0, Taxes on property 14.5); Non-tax revenue 71.5; Social contributions 19.7; Total 435.8. *Expenditure:* Total 407.9.

Cost of Living (Consumer Price Index; base: October 2006 = 100): All items 116.3 in 2011; 121.0 in 2012; 124.0 in 2013.

Gross Domestic Product (million NA Fl. at current prices): 1,597.2 in 2010; 1,667.7 in 2011; 1,760.2 in 2012.

Gross Domestic Product by Economic Activity (million NA Fl. at current prices, 2012): Agriculture, fishing and mining 2.8; Electricity, gas and water 54.1; Manufacturing 28.9; Construction 108.6; Trade, restaurants and hotels 392.8; Transport, storage and communications 201.7; Real estate, renting and business activities 394.4; Health and social welfare 47.1; Other community, social and personal services 73.0; Financial corporations 163.2; Government 151.4; *Sub-total* 1,618.1; Net of indirect taxes 142.2; *GDP in purchasers' values* 1,760.2.

Balance of Payments (NA Fl. million, 2013): Exports of goods f.o.b. 316.2; Imports of goods f.o.b. –1,658.2; *Trade balance* –1,342.0; Services (net) 1,432.1; *Balance on goods and services* 90.1; Income (net) –40.7; *Balance on goods, services and income* 49.4; Current transfers (net) –24.1; *Current balance* 25.3; Capital account (net) 15.4; Direct investment (net) 54.5; Portfolio investment (net) –94.5; Other investment (net) –135.8; Net errors and omissions 122.6; *Overall balance* –12.5.

EXTERNAL TRADE

Principal Commodities (distribution by SITC, NA Fl. million, 2008): *Imports:* Food and live animals 92.4; Beverages and tobacco 38.3; Mineral fuels, lubricants, etc. 165.6; Manufactured goods classified chiefly by material 116.1; Machinery and transport equipment 86.5; Miscellaneous manufactured articles 277.0; Total (incl. others) 813.2. *Exports f.o.b.:* Food and live animals 15.8; Beverages and tobacco 33.3; Manufactured goods classified chiefly by material 7.1; Machinery and transport equipment 9.3; Miscellaneous manufactured articles 46.0; Total (incl. others) 116.1. *Imports* 1,736 in 2011; 1,838 in 2012; 1,904 in 2013 (estimate). *Exports:* 1,842 in 2011; 2,095 in 2012; 2,171 in 2013 (estimate).

TRANSPORT

Road Traffic (motor vehicles registered as 31 December 2008, excl. government-owned vehicles): Passenger cars 17,882; Lorries 2,950; Buses 135; Taxis 249; Rental cars 2,496; Motorcycles and mopeds 828.

Shipping (cruise ship arrivals): 596 in 2011; 622 in 2012; 629 in 2013.

Civil Aviation (Princess Juliana International Airport traffic, 2008, unless otherwise indicated): Commercial landings 62,757; Passenger movements 1,644,323 (2012).

TOURISM

Tourist Arrivals: *Stop-overs:* 424,340 (Canada 33,256; Netherlands 16,607; USA 219,204) in 2011; 456,720 (Canada 40,426; Netherlands 16,414; USA 238,538) in 2012; 466,955 (Canada 46,300; Netherlands 16,019; USA 246,188) in 2013. *Cruise ship passengers:* 1,656,159 in 2011; 1,753,215 in 2012; 1,779,384 in 2013.

COMMUNICATIONS MEDIA

Telephones (2008): 12,779 main lines in use.

Mobile Cellular Telephones (2008): 68,749 subscribers.

EDUCATION

University of Sint Maarten (2006/07): 217 students (males 64, females 153).

Directory

Constitution

The Constitution of Sint (St) Maarten was adopted by the Island Council of St Maarten by a majority vote on 21 July 2010. Following the dissolution of the Netherlands Antilles on 10 October 2010, the new Constitution entered into force.

The form of government for St Maarten is embodied in the Charter of the Kingdom of the Netherlands, which came into force on 20 December 1954. The Charter designated the Netherlands Antilles (comprising St Maarten, Curaçao, Bonaire, Saba and St Eustatius from 1986) as a separate territory forming the Kingdom of the Netherlands with the Netherlands. An amendment to the Charter of the Kingdom of the Netherlands to reflect the dissolution of the Netherlands Antilles was signed off at a Round-table conference in The Hague on 9 September 2010.

As a constituent country of the Kingdom of the Netherlands, St Maarten enjoys full autonomy in domestic and internal affairs. The Government of the Netherlands is responsible for foreign affairs and defence. The monarch of the the Netherlands is represented in St Maarten by the Governor, appointed by the Dutch Crown for a term of six years. The central Government of St Maarten appoints a Minister Plenipotentiary to represent the island in the Government of the Kingdom.

Executive power in internal affairs is vested in the nominated Council of Ministers, responsible to the legislature, the Staten (States). The States consists of 15 members elected by universal adult suffrage for four years (subject to dissolution).

The Government

HEAD OF STATE

King of the Netherlands: HM King WILLEM-ALEXANDER.

Governor: EUGENE HOLIDAY.

COUNCIL OF MINISTERS
(September 2014)

Following the general election of 29 August 2014 the National Alliance (NA), the Democratic Party and the United St Maarten Party agreed to form a coalition Government by 24 September. William Marlin, leader of the NA, was appointed *formateur* of the new administration.

Prime Minister and Minister of General Affairs: SARAH A. WESCOT-WILLIAMS.

Deputy Prime Minister and Minister of Justice: DENNIS L. RICHARDSON.

Minister of Finance: MARTINUS J. HASSINK.

Minister of Housing, Spatial Planning, Environment and Infrastructure: MAURICE A. LAKE.

Minister of Education, Culture, Youth and Sports: PATRICIA D. LOURENS-PHILIP.

Minister of Health Care, Social Development and Labour: VAN HUGH CORNELIUS DE WEEVER.

Minister of Tourism, Economic Affairs, Transport and Tele-communication: THADEUS RICHARDSON.

Minister Plenipotentiary of Sint Maarten in the Netherlands: MATHIAS S. VOGES.

MINISTRIES

Office of the Governor: 3 Falcon Dr., Harbour View, Philipsburg; tel. 542-1160; fax 542-1187; e-mail kabinet@kabgsxm.com; internet www.kabgsxm.com.

Office of the Prime Minister: Clem Labega Sq., POB 943, Philipsburg; tel. 542-2233; fax 542-4300; internet www.sintmaartengov.org. All government offices are located in Philipsburg.

Legislature

STATES
(Staten)

President: GRACITA R. ARRINDELL.
General Election, 29 August 2014, preliminary results

Party	Valid votes	% of valid votes	Seats
United People's Party (UP) . .	6,156	42.46	7
National Alliance (NA) . . .	4,011	27.66	4
Democratic Party (DP) . . .	2,398	16.54	2
United St Maarten Party (US Party)	1,636	11.28	2
One St Maarten People Party (OSPP)	168	1.16	—
Social Reform Party (SRP) . .	131	0.90	—
Total*	14,500	100.00	15

* In addition, there were 79 blank and 303 invalid votes cast.

Political Organizations

Democratic Party (DP) (Democratische Partij): Tamarind Tree Dr. 4, Union Rd, Cole Bay; tel. 543-1166; fax 542-4296; Leader SARAH A. WESCOT-WILLIAMS.

National Alliance (NA): Philipsburg; comprises the Sint Maarten Patriotic Alliance and the National Progressive Party; Leader WILLIAM MARLIN.

One St Maarten People Party (OSPP): Philipsburg; e-mail onestmaartenpeopleparty@gmail.com; internet www.facebook.com/OSPPSXM; f. 2013; Leader LENNY F. PRIEST.

Social Reform Party (SRP): Philipsburg; f. 2013; Pres. JACINTO MOCK; Vice-Pres. ALEJANDRO ALVAREZ.

United People's Party (UP): Philipsburg; f. 2010; Leader THEO HEYLIGER.

United St Maarten Party (US Party): Philipsburg; e-mail unitedstmaartenparty@gmail.com; internet www.facebook.com/sxmusp; f. 2013; Pres. CECILE NICOLAS; Leader FRANS RICHARDSON.

Judicial System

Legal authority is exercised by the Joint Court of Justice of Aruba, Curaçao and St Maarten and of Bonaire, St Eustatius and Saba. Its headquarters are in Curaçao. The Joint Court hears civil, criminal and administrative cases in the first instance and on appeal. The Supreme Court of the Netherlands (based in The Hague) is the court of Final Instance for any appeal.

Joint Court of Justice: The Courthouse, Front St 58, Philipsburg; tel. 542-3205; fax 542-5451; e-mail sintmaarten@caribjustitia.org; internet www.gemhofvanjustitie.org; Chief Justice LISBETH HOEF-DRAAD.

Constitutional Court: Philipsburg; Judges JACOB (BOB) WIT (Pres.), JAN DE BOER, BEN VERMEULEN; Registrar MARITZA JAMES-CHRISTINA.

Court of First Instance: The Courthouse, Front St 58, Philipsburg; tel. 542-3205; fax 542-5451; Chief Judge KOEN LUIJKS.

Attorney-General: GUUS SCHRAM.

Religion

The majority of Sint (St) Maarten's population profess Christianity (82% at the 2011 census). Roman Catholicism forms the largest single group on St Maarten, with 33% claiming adherence. St Maarten and the other former constituent territories of the former Netherlands Antilles, as well as Aruba, together form the diocese of Willemstad, suffragan to the archdiocese of Port of Spain (Trinidad and Tobago). The Bishop participates in the Antilles Episcopal Conference, currently based in Trinidad and Tobago. Other churches include Pentecostalist (15%), Methodist (10%), Adventist (7%) and Baptist (5%). Within the Anglican Communion (3% of the population), St Maarten forms part of the diocese of the North Eastern Caribbean and Aruba, within the Church in the Province of the West Indies. The Bishop is resident in St John's, Antigua and Barbuda. Some 5% of the population are Hindu.

The Press

Daily Herald: Bush Rd 22, POB 828, Philipsburg; tel. 542-5253; fax 542-5913; e-mail editorial@thedailyherald.com; internet www.thedailyherald.com; daily; English.

Teen Times: Bush Rd 22, POB 828, Philipsburg; tel. 542-5597; e-mail info@teentimes.com; for teenagers by teenagers; sponsored by the *Daily Herald*; English; Editor-in-Chief MICHAEL GRANGER.

Publisher

House of Nehesi Publishers (HNP): POB 460, Philipsburg; tel. 554-7089; e-mail nehesi@sintmaarten.net; internet www.houseofnehesipublish.com; f. 1986; fiction and non-fiction; Pres. JACQUELINE SAMPLE.

Broadcasting and Communications

TELECOMMUNICATIONS

Caribserve (New Technologies Group, NV): Harbor View Corporate Park, Brooks Tower, Suite 5A/B, Philipsburg; tel. 542-4233; fax 542-4229; e-mail info@caribserve.net; internet www.caribserve.net; internet service provider; subsidiary of UTS, NV; Gen. Man. ROY RICHARDSON.

Scarlet, BV: Three Palms Plaza, 60 Welfare Rd, Colebay; tel. 544-5529; fax 544-2336; e-mail info@scarlet-sxm.com; internet www.scarlet-sxm.com.

TelEm Group (St Maarten Telecommunications Group): Soualiga Blvd 5, Philipsburg; tel. 546-0200; fax 543-0101; e-mail info@telemgroup.an; internet www.telemgroup.an; f. 1975; comprises TelEm (providing local services), TelCell NV (digital mobile services), TelNet Communications NV (internet services) and SMIT-COMS NV (international services); 15,000 subscribers (TelEm); Chair. RAFAEL BOASMAN; CEO (vacant).

UTS St Maarten: Codville Webster Rd 2, Philipsburg; tel. 542-0101; fax 542-4922; e-mail info@uts.sx; internet www.sxm.uts.an; CEO GLEN CARTY; Man. CHRISTINA SPROCK.

Regulatory Authority

Bureau Telecommunications and Post St Maarten (BTP): Sparrow Rd 1-D, Harbour View, Philipsburg; tel. 542-4699; fax 542-4817; e-mail info@sxmregulator.sx; internet www.sxmregulator.sx; f. 2010; regulatory authority; Chair. BRENDA BROOKS; CEO PEGGY ANN BRANDON.

BROADCASTING

Radio

Philipsburg Broadcasting: 106 A. T. Illidge Rd, Philipsburg; tel. 543-2200; fax 543-2229; owns and operates 3 radio stations; Man. Dir FRANCIS CARTY.

   Laser 101 FM: e-mail master@laser101.com; internet www.laser101.fm; 24 hours a day; music; English and Papiamento.

   Oasis 96.3 FM: tel. 543-7963; internet www.oasis963.fm.

   Tropixx 105.5FM: tel. 543-7960; internet www.tropixx.fm.

Voice of St Maarten (PJD2 Radio): 187 Back St, POB 366, Philipsburg; tel. 542-2580; fax 542-2356; internet www.pjd2radio.com; f. 1959; also operates PJD3 on FM (24 hrs); commercial; programmes in English; Gen. Man. DONALD R. HUGHES.

Television

Leeward Broadcasting Corporation—Television: POB 375, Philipsburg; tel. 525-3491; transmissions for approx. 10 hours daily.

TV 15 (Sint Maarten Cable TV Channel 15): 4 Johan Vermeer St, POB 515, Madame Estate; tel. 542-4361; fax 542-5284; e-mail info@sxmtv15.com; internet www.sxmtv15.com; local programming; Station Man. DAVEY WOODS.

WTN TV (Channel 10): Obersi Bldg, Sparrow Rd 1B, Harbour View, Philipsburg; tel. 542-2785; e-mail info@wtntv.com; internet www.wtntv.com; f. 2010; subsidiary of Obersi Group of Cos; CEO ALVIN OBERSI; Gen. Man. ROBERTO GIBBS.

Relay stations provide St Maarten with programmes from Puerto Rico.

Finance

(cap. = capital; res = reserves; dep. = deposits; m. = million; brs = branches)

BANKING

Regulatory Authority

College Financieel Toezicht (CFT): Convent Bldg, 26 Front St, Philipsburg; tel. 543-0331; fax 543-0379; e-mail info@cft.an; internet www.cft.an; f. 2008; board of financial supervision; office on Curaçao (q.v.); Chair. AGE BAKKER; Mem. (St Maarten) RICHARD GIBSON.

Central Bank

Centrale Bank van Curaçao en Sint Maarten: 25 W. J. A. Nisbeth Rd, Pondfill, Philipsburg; tel. 542-3520; fax 542-4307; e-mail info@centralbank.cw; internet centralbank.cw; Br. Man. L. HASSELL.

Commercial Banks

CIBC FirstCaribbean International Bank: 38 Back St, Philipsburg; tel. 542-3511; fax 542-4531; internet www.firstcaribbeanbank.com; f. 2002 following merger of Caribbean operations of Barclays Bank PLC and CIBC; Barclays relinquished its stake to CIBC in 2006, present name adopted in 2011; CEO RIK PARKHILL; Man. Dir (Dutch Caribbean) PIM VAN DER BURG; 2 brs.

Scotiabank St Maarten (Canada): 62 Back St, Philipsburg; tel. 542-2262; fax 542–2435; e-mail bns.stmaarten@scotiabank.com; internet www.scotiabank/ansma/en; f. 1969; Country Man. RAYMOND GREEN; 3 brs.

Windward Islands Bank Ltd: Clem Labega Sq. 7, POB 220, Philipsburg; tel. 546-2942; fax 542-4761; e-mail info@wib-bank.net; internet www.wib-bank.net; affiliated to Maduro & Curiel's Bank NV; f. 1960; cap. and res 53.2m. NA Fl., dep. 662.2m. NA Fl. (Dec. 2006); Chair. LEONEL CAPRILES, III; Man. Dir JAN J. BEAUJON.

Banking Association

St Maarten Bankers' Association: Clem Labega Sq. 7, Philipsburg; tel. 542-2313; fax 542-6355; Pres. J. BEAUJON.

INSURANCE

Pan-American Life Insurance Company of Curaçao and St Maarten, NV: Professional Office Park, Osprey Dr. 4, Bldg 2, Unit 1B, Yuancho Yrausquin Blvd, Philipsburg; tel. 542-3195; fax 542-5001; internet www.palig.com; f. 2012; part of Pan-American Life Insurance Group (USA); CEO and Man. Dir (Caribbean) WILLIAM R. SCHULZ, Jr; Gen. Man. VALERY SINOT.

Trade and Industry

CHAMBER OF COMMERCE

St Maarten Chamber of Commerce and Industry: Cannegieter St 11, POB 454, Philipsburg; tel. 542-3590; fax 542-3512; e-mail info@sxmcoci.org; internet www.sxmcoci.org; f. 1979; Pres. TAMARA LEONARD; Exec. Dir CLARET CONNOR.

INDUSTRIAL AND TRADE ASSOCIATION

St Maarten Hospitality and Trade Association: W. J. A. Nisbeth Rd 33A, POB 486, Philipsburg; tel. 542-0108; fax 542-0107; e-mail info@shta.com; internet www.shta.com; Pres. EMIL LEE; Exec. Dir ROBERT DUIBOURCQ (acting).

UTILITY

GEBE St Maarten: W. J. A. Nisbeth Rd 35, Pondfill, POB 123, Philipsburg; tel. 542-2213; fax 542-4810; e-mail gebesxm@nvgebe.com; internet www.nvgebe.com; f. 1961; generates and distributes electricity via island network; operates island water supply system on St Maarten and St Eustatius; Chair. JULIUS LAMBERT; Dir PAUL MARSHALL (acting).

TRADE UNION

Windward Islands Chamber of Labour Unions (WIFOL): W. J. A. Nisbeth Rd 89, POB 1097, Pondfill, Philipsburg; tel. 542-2797; fax 542-6631; e-mail wifol@sintmaarten.net; comprises 6 unions: Windward Islands Federation of Labour (WIFOL); Windward Islands Civil Servants Union/Private Sector Union (WICSU/PSU); Windward Islands Teachers' Union (WITU); St Maarten Communications Union; Windward Islands Health Care Union Asscn (WIHCUA); and the Asscn of Staff Employees of GEBE; Pres. THEOPHILUS THOMPSON.

Transport

SHIPPING

St Maarten is one of the Caribbean's leading ports for visits by cruise ships. Pier facilities can accommodate up to six cruise ships.

Intermar, SA: 1 Intermar Dr., 2 Groundove Rd, POB 497, Philipsburg; tel. 542-4734; fax 542-5895; e-mail bvdmark@intermar-sxm.com; internet www.intermar-sxm.com; Gen. Man. BOB VAN DER MARK.

SEL Maduro & Sons (WWI) Inc.: 1 Emmaplein Bldg, POB 63, Philipsburg; tel. 542-3407; fax 542-2958; e-mail madops@maduro.org; internet www.maduro-sxm.com; f. 1837; Man. Dir H. L. CHANCE.

St Maarten Ports Authority (SMPA): J. Yrausquin Blvd, POB 146, Philipsburg; tel. 542-2307; fax 542-5048; e-mail comments@portofstmaarten.com; internet www.portofstmaarten.com; f. 1989; Chair. JOSEPH RICHARDSON; Man. Dir MARK MINGO.

CIVIL AVIATION

Princess Juliana International Airport is located 16 km from Philipsburg. A new terminal was completed in 2006, enhancing the airport's annual passenger-handling capacity by 2.5m.

Windward Express Airways: Princess Juliana International Airport; tel. 545-2001; fax 545-2224; e-mail reservations@windwardexpress.com; internet www.windwardexpress.com; f. 2000; domestic and limited Caribbean island charter flights, incl. destinations with restricted access; passenger and cargo flights; Pres. JEAN HALLEY.

Windward Islands Airways International (WIA—Winair) NV: POB 2088, Princess Juliana International Airport; tel. 545-4237; fax 545-2002; e-mail info@fly-winair.com; internet www.fly-winair.com; f. 1961; govt-owned since 1974; scheduled and charter flights throughout north-eastern Caribbean; Man. Dir EDWIN HODGE.

Tourism

The island is famous for its diving and snorkelling locations, and hiking trails to Mount Concordia and to the cliffs of Cupecoy. The annual Heineken Regatta and the St Maarten Carnival also attract visitors. There were 466,955 stop-over arrivals and 1,779,384 cruise ship passengers in 2013, while tourism receipts were estimated at US $719m. in 2011.

St Maarten Tourism Bureau: Krippa Bldg, Unit 10, Juancho Yrausquin Blvd 6, Philipsburg; tel. 542-2337; fax 542-2734; e-mail info@e-stmaarten.com; internet www.vacationstmaarten.com; Dir EDWARD DEST (acting).

Defence

The Netherlands is responsible for the defence of St Maarten. Military service is compulsory. The Governor is Commander-in-Chief of the armed forces in the territory. A Coast Guard Force operates from St Maarten.

Education

Education was made compulsory in 1992. The education system is the same as that of the Netherlands, and is generally of a high standard. English is the official language of instruction. Primary education begins at six years of age and lasts for six years. Secondary education lasts for a further five years.

SOUTH GEORGIA AND THE SOUTH SANDWICH ISLANDS

South Georgia, an island of 3,592 sq km (1,387 sq miles), lies in the South Atlantic Ocean, about 1,300 km (800 miles) east-south-east of the Falkland Islands. The South Sandwich Islands, which have an area of 311 sq km, lie about 750 km south-east of South Georgia.

The United Kingdom annexed South Georgia and the South Sandwich Islands in 1775. Together with a segment of the Antarctic mainland and other nearby islands (now the British Antarctic Territory), they were constituted as the Falkland Islands Dependencies in 1908. Argentina made formal claim to South Georgia in 1927, and to the South Sandwich Islands in 1948. In 1955 the United Kingdom unilaterally submitted the dispute over sovereignty to the International Court of Justice (based in the Netherlands), which decided not to hear the application in view of Argentina's refusal to submit to the Court's jurisdiction. South Georgia was the site of a British Antarctic Survey base (staffed by 22 scientists and support personnel) until it was invaded in April 1982 by Argentine forces, who occupied the island until its recapture by British forces three weeks later. The South Sandwich Islands were uninhabited until the occupation of Southern Thule in December 1976 by about 50 Argentines, reported to be scientists. Argentine personnel remained until removed by British forces in June 1982.

Under the provisions of the South Georgia and South Sandwich Islands Order of 1985, the islands ceased to be governed as dependencies of the Falkland Islands on 3 October 1985. The Governor of the Falkland Islands is, ex officio, Commissioner for the territory.

In 1993, in response to the Argentine Government's decision to commence the sale of fishing licences for the region's waters, the British Government announced an extension, from 12 to 200 nautical miles, of its territorial jurisdiction in the waters surrounding the islands, in order to conserve crucial fishing stocks.

In 1998 the British Government announced that it would withdraw its military detachment from South Georgia in 2000, while it would increase its scientific presence on the island with the installation of a permanent team from the British Antarctic Survey to investigate the fisheries around the island for possible exploitation. The small military detachment finally withdrew in March 2001. The British garrison stationed in the Falkland Islands would remain responsible for the security of South Georgia and the South Sandwich Islands.

Increased volcanic activity on Montagu Island, in the South Sandwich Islands, previously thought to be dormant, had been monitored closely by the British Antarctic Survey since 2001. In late 2005 Mount Belinda erupted, adding some 50 acres to the island's land area in just one month. The island is largely ice-covered and the eruption allowed scientists the rare opportunity to make direct observations of volcanic activity under ice sheets.

Budget revenue for 2012 amounted to £5.4m., while expenditure (including special expenditure) totalled £5.5m. The main sources of revenue are the sale of fishing licences (£3.7m.), incomes from visitor landing charges (£0.7m.), philatelic and commemorative coin sales, heritage funding and customs and harbour duties. The largest expenditure item in 2012 was fisheries patrol costs (£2.8m.). A reduction in the toothfish fishing quota in 2011, from 3,500 metric tons to 1,900 tons, led to a decline in government revenue; however, an increase in the quota in 2013, to 2,100 tons, was expected to boost income from fishing licences.

At the close of the 2012/13 cruise ship season, South Georgia had recorded a total of 51 ship calls and 5,792 passengers to the island. Greater numbers of visitors to this inhospitable territory—coupled with a growing recognition of the climate change phenomenon—prompted the Government to review its existing biosecurity policy. In May 2011 Commissioner Nigel Haywood ratified the Wildlife and Protected Areas Ordinance, which outlined new measures to protect the territory's delicate ecosystem and to prevent the introduction of potentially destructive species of flora and fauna. Furthermore, in an effort to conserve maritime biodiversity, legislation was adopted in February 2012 that designated South Georgia and the South Sandwich Islands' territorial waters a Marine Protected Area. In June 2013 a revised Marine Protected Area Order came into force which included additional measures to protect marine diversity.

A reindeer eradication programme was begun in early 2013; a total of 3,455 reindeer were killed. A further 3,140 reindeer were killed during the second phase of the programme in 2014. The South Georgia Heritage Trust continued its rat eradication project in 2013.

Colin Roberts succeeded Haywood as Commissioner in April 2014.

The British Antarctic Survey maintains two research stations on South Georgia, at King Edward Point (usually 12 winter personnel, 22 summer personnel) and Bird Island (four winter personnel, 10 summer personnel).

Commissioner: COLIN ROBERTS (took office 29 April 2014).

Chief Executive Officer and Director of Fisheries: Dr MARTIN COLLINS (Stanley, Falkland Islands).

SURINAME

Geography

PHYSICAL FEATURES

The Republic of Suriname is on the north coast of South America and is the smallest country on the continent. Until independence in 1975 Suriname (usually rendered Surinam in English) was known as Dutch or Netherlands Guiana, and it is flanked by the smaller territory of French Guiana (part of France) on the east and Guyana (formerly British Guiana) on the west. Brazil lies beyond a 597-km (371-mile) border in the south. The Atlantic coast is 386 km in extent, while the border with French Guiana is 510 km and that with Guyana is 600 km. However, Suriname disputes the current course of the western and eastern borders and maintains territorial claims on its neighbours on the Guianese coast. Suriname claims part of south-western French Guiana, between the Itany (Litani—the current border) and the Marowijne (Marouini) rivers. In the west, the country claims territory in south-eastern Guyana as far as the New River and not along the current upper reach of the Corantijn (Corentyne) that is used as a border (Koetari or Kutari). The country covers an area of 163,820 sq km (63,251 sq miles).

The north of Suriname consists of a typically Guianan coastal strip, with rich, alluvial soil made usable and habitable by extensive dykes and irrigation systems. These plains can be as much as 2 m below sea level, so, where not protected or reclaimed, the coastlands tend to be swampy mangrove country. The Atlantic littoral, up to 80 km in width, accounts for about 16% of the country, and is where most of the population lives. Between the plains and the densely forested interior is an intermediate plateau with a landscape alternating tracts of savannah with dunes or woodland. This gives way to a more solid forest cover, a region that accounts for about three-quarters of the country, as rolling hills climb into more mountainous terrain. The highlands of the forest region rear relatively abruptly once away from the coastal belt and its immediate hinterland, so that the country's highest point, at Juliana Top (1,230 m or 4,037 ft) is located near the centre of Suriname. The mountain is just beyond the north end of the Eilerts de Haan Gebergste (a ridge thrusting up from the south and marking off the south-west) and to the west of the Wilhelmina Gebergste; the main range of the south-east is the Oranje Gebergste. Much of this territory is dense tropical rainforest, which hosts a considerable diversity of flora and fauna (although deforestation and the pollution from small-scale mining threaten the environment—the country's timber and mineral reserves, notably bauxite, are the most lucrative natural resources). The discovery of 24 previously undocumented species of fauna in 2007, highlighted the importance of Suriname as a rare example of untouched tropical rainforest. The international scientific community strenuously promotes the protection of such regions. Finally, in the far south-west, there is a region of high savannah. This entire landscape is laced with numerous rivers, some feeding large reservoirs. Inland waters cover 1,800 sq km of the country's territory. The main rivers, apart from the Corantijn (700 km in length—most of it marking the border with Guyana) and the Marowijne (720 km—also defining much of a border, but with French Guiana, and including its upper reaches, such as the Lawa and its tributaries), are the Suriname, the Coppename and the Saramacca.

CLIMATE

Suriname experiences high rainfall, humidity and temperatures, although its tropical climate is tempered by the Atlantic trade winds. There are two wet seasons, April–August and November–February, although neither wet nor dry seasons are absolute. The average annual precipitation in Paramaribo, the capital, which is on the coast, is over 2,200 mm (86 ins).

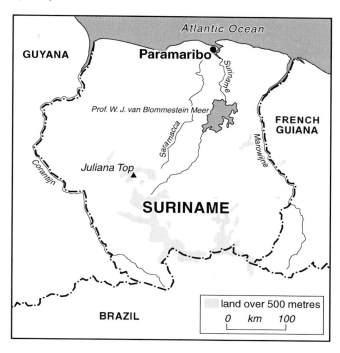

Inland, rainfall is more like 1,500 mm per year. Average temperatures range between 23°C and 32°C (73°F–90°F), but there is little seasonal variation.

POPULATION

Suriname is one of the most racially diverse countries in the Americas or, indeed, in the world. According to the 2012 census, some 27% of the population were Hindustani (descendants of indentured workers brought from the Indian subcontinent in the 19th century, generally referred to as 'East' Indians in the Caribbean), 22% identified themselves as Maroons (descendants of slaves who escaped into freedom in the mountainous interior in the 17th and 18th centuries), 16% were Creole and 14% described themselves as Javanese. Dutch is the official language, but many others are also still spoken—not only a Hindi dialect (known as Hindustani—Sarnami Hindi) and Javanese, but also some English-based Creoles, the main dialect being known as Sranan Tongo or Taki-Taki (Djukka and Saramaccan are others); English itself is widely known in the cities or among the better educated. The cosmopolitan nature of Surinamese society is also seen in the country's variety of religious affiliations—just under one-half the people were Christian (the largest denominations were the Roman Catholics, with 22% of the population, and Pentecostalists and the Moravian Brethren, each with 11%), 22% were Hindu and 14% Muslim. Others practise native or adapted African tribal beliefs, although these are often not considered incompatible with more orthodox faiths.

Most of the population live on the coast and about 65% are classed as urban, with somewhere between one-third and one-half in or around the capital city. Over recent decades many people have emigrated to the Netherlands. The total population in mid-2014 was 543,927, according to UN estimates. Paramaribo, the country's only major urban area, its main seaport and the national capital, is east of centre on the coast, in the north of Suriname. There are 10 districts.

History

MARK WILSON

Based on an earlier article by JAMES MCDONOUGH

In the 15th century the only inhabitants of Suriname were Carib, Arawak and Awarao Indians (Amerindians). Another tribe, the Surinas, who inhabited the country at an earlier time, is considered the source of the name Suriname. In 1499 Alonso de Ojeada, a Spanish lieutenant serving the Italian navigator Amerigo Vespucci, landed on the north-eastern coast of South America, which was called Guiana by the Amerindians. The Spanish claimed possession of the coast, but no actual settlement was attempted. During the next century the Dutch began establishing trading posts along the Commewijne and Corentyne (Corantijn) rivers (now in Suriname), and later along the Essequibo and Berbice (now in Guyana). However, it was the English who founded the first successful colony in Suriname, as the result of an expedition financed by Lord Francis Willoughby, the colonial Governor of the flourishing but overcrowded English sugar island of Barbados. The group of English planters and their slaves established a large settlement on the Suriname River, near what is now Paramaribo. The British Crown ceded its Suriname colony to the Netherlands in the Treaty of Breda (1667), in exchange for the colony of Nieuw Amsterdam (now New York, USA). The colony remained under Dutch rule for the next 300 years, except for two brief periods of British control in 1799–1802 and 1804–14, during the Napoleonic wars.

The territory became known as Dutch Guiana, and was flanked to the west by British Guiana (now Guyana) and to the east by French Guiana. The colony was administered by a Governor, with the assistance of the Political Council, the members of which were appointed by the Governor, following nomination by the colonial planter class. In 1828 the administration of all Dutch West Indies colonies was centralized under a Governor-General, stationed in Suriname, who reported directly to the Colonial Office in the Netherlands. During this early period the colony flourished on the basis of large, Dutch-owned sugar plantations, worked by African slave labour. Between 1650 and 1820 some 300,000 West African slaves were brought into Suriname. Nevertheless, the plantations suffered a continual labour drain owing to escaping slaves, who would seek refuge from the authorities in the vast and underdeveloped interior of the country. By 1728 these runaway slaves, known as Maroons, had established a number of settlements based on African tribal customs and were warring with the white plantation owners and the colonial authorities. Expeditions were sent into the jungle to subdue them, but without success. Finally, in 1761 the Dutch signed a treaty with the Maroons, guaranteeing their liberty and supplying them with yearly shipments of arms. In return, they promised to return all future runaway slaves and never to appear in Paramaribo in armed groups of more than six persons.

The abolition of slavery in neighbouring British Guiana in 1834 and in French Guiana in 1848 produced a period of unrest in Suriname, leading to the abolition of slavery in 1863. The Dutch instead turned to overseas contract or indentured labour. Between 1873 and 1917 some 37,000 indentured labourers were brought to Suriname from India. A similar influx of contract labourers, numbering about 33,000, were brought from the Dutch East Indies (now Indonesia) between 1893 and 1939. Furthermore, the Dutch encouraged the immigration of Chinese, Portuguese and, later, Lebanese workers. Suriname's ethnic and racial make-up reflect the plantation colony's historic need for cheap labour. It is the most ethnically fragmented country in the Latin American and Caribbean region and among the 20 most fragmented countries in the world. This ethnic fragmentation also exists in the political arena, where the majority of political parties are organized along ethnic lines.

INDEPENDENCE AND POLITICAL DEVELOPMENT

In 1866 the Koloniale Staten (Colonial Assembly, also known as the Staten van Suriname) was established. A representative body with limited local power, its members were elected from a small group of colonial planters, who were extended the franchise on the basis of a poll tax. While ultimate power continued to reside in the Netherlands, the Colonial Assembly remained the principal administrative body in Suriname until the colony gained independence. In the 20th century the exploitation of Suriname's large bauxite reserves and the cultivation of rice replaced sugar as the principal foreign exchange earner, although the Dutch Government found it necessary to subsidize an ever-increasing share of the colony's budget. In 1950 the Dutch Government granted Suriname internal self-government. Then in 1954 Suriname became an overseas territory of the Dutch 'Tripartite Kingdom', composed of the Netherlands, the now dissolved Netherlands Antilles and Suriname. Full and complete independence was granted to Suriname by the Dutch on 25 November 1975.

Local political parties began forming during the Second World War (1939–45), at the time of the promise of local autonomy. Further political participation was stimulated by the introduction of universal suffrage for the general election of 1949. The Nationale Partij Suriname (NPS—Suriname National Party), representing the Afro-Surinamese population, won the majority of the seats in the Koloniale Staten, under the leadership of Johan Pengel. During the 1950s the Verenigde Hindostaanse Partij (VHP—United Hindustani Party, renamed the Vooruitstrevende Hervormings Partij, or Progressive Reform Party, in 1973), representing the Hindustani population, gained prominence under the leadership of Jaggernath Lachmon. The NPS and VHP formed an alliance during the 1960s, which gave Suriname a long period of stability. In the 1973 general election the NPS formed the Nationale Partij Kombinatie (NPK—Combined National Party) alliance with three other parties and won 22 of 39 seats in the Koloniale Staten. Henck Arron, who had replaced Pengel as party leader upon the latter's death in 1970, was named Prime Minister and was in power when the country gained independence in 1975.

Dutch aid, worth 3,500m. guilders, gave considerable support to the economy of the new republic. However, the international economic recession of the mid-1970s, brought on by the petroleum crisis and a decrease in the world price of bauxite, caused growing concern that Suriname would be unable to promote economic development, despite the country's large natural resources and relatively small population. Moreover, more than 40,000 persons, mostly the well-educated and well-trained, emigrated to the Netherlands on the eve of independence, in order to qualify for Dutch citizenship. A series of strikes underlined the growing dissatisfaction of the people, while corruption scandals involving cabinet ministers undermined the Government. Nevertheless, the NPK again won the general election of 1977.

MILITARY TAKEOVER, 1980–87

On 25 February 1980 the armed forces took control of government in a coup; the immediate cause of this action was the civilian Government's refusal to recognize demands of members of the military to form a trade union. The takeover was led by a junior army officer, Sgt-Maj. (later Lt-Col) Desiré (Desi) Bouterse, who seized power in alliance with the left-wing Partij Nationalistiche Republiek (PNR—Nationalist Republican Party). Dr Henk Chin-A-Sen, a PNR leader, was chosen as Prime Minister, presiding over a PNR-assembled Government and the eight-member Nationale Militaire Raad (NMR—National Military Council) named by Bouterse. In August 1980, following a disagreement over policy, Bouterse strengthened his control over the Government by dissolving the legislature and declaring a state of emergency. In March 1981 Sgt-Maj. Wilfred Hawker led an unsuccessful coup against Bouterse. In December Bouterse launched the Revolutionaire Volksfront (Revolutionary People's Front) and in February 1982 Chin-A-Sen, who had earlier been named President, was dismissed along with his civilian Government. In March a second coup attempt by Sgt-Maj. Hawker failed, resulting in his execution.

As a result of the coup attempt, Bouterse declared a state of siege and imposed martial law. However, to prevent the Netherlands from suspending aid under the terms of the independence treaty, the military regime appointed a 12-member Council of Ministers with a civilian majority, and Henry Neyhorst, a moderate economist, was appointed Prime Minister. The failure to solve Suriname's economic difficulties lost Bouterse the support of the left-wing groups and the trade unions, and soon the country was plagued by demonstrations. Bouterse promised to hold elections for a constituent assembly to draft a new constitution. On 8 December 1982 members of the armed forces burned down Paramaribo offices of those opposed to Bouterse. In the ensuing disturbances some 15 leading politicians, trade unionists, lawyers, journalists and academics were arrested and shot dead within the historic army headquarters, Fort Zeelandia, in what became known as the December Murders.

In response to the December Murders, the Dutch Government suspended its 3,500m. guilder aid programme to the country. The USA and the European Union (EU—then known as the European Community) immediately followed suit and the Council of Ministers resigned. Bouterse purged the 3,000-man military by dismissing two-thirds of the officer corps. In February 1983 he formed a new civilian-military Council of Ministers, with Errol Alibux (a former Minister of Social Affairs) as Prime Minister. The new Government was composed of two left-wing parties, the Progressieve Arbeiders en Landbouwers Unie (PALU—Progressive Workers' and Farmers' Union) and the Revolutionaire Volkspartij (Revolutionary People's Party).

In foreign affairs, the Bouterse Government established close relations with Cuba and Libya, in place of the historically close links with the USA and the Netherlands. These moves alarmed both the French and the US authorities. The French saw potential danger to its Kourou space centre, the launching site for the European Ariane rocket, which was located close to the Surinamese border in French Guiana. The USA, determined to stop the spread of 'Communist' governments in the western hemisphere, was very wary of Suriname's growing ties with Cuba and the large presence of Cuban advisers in the country. George Schultz, former US Secretary of State under President Ronald Reagan (1981–89), revealed in a 1993 memoir that the US Administration had been ready to intervene militarily as a result of the 1982 December Murders; however, US plans for the military overthrow of the Bouterse regime were abandoned. Some sources in both the Netherlands and Suriname allege that the Netherlands supported plans for an invasion, in alliance with the USA, in both 1982 and 1986.

CIVILIAN RESTORATION

The state of emergency imposed in 1982 was lifted in August 1984, as the military Government began to move the country towards civilian rule. In December plans were announced for the formation of a supreme deliberating council, the Topberaad, comprising representatives of the trade unions, the business sector and Stanvaste, a new movement Bouterse had established in November 1983 as a political power base. The Topberaad met in January 1985, with the main task of drafting a new constitution. In March 1987 a draft document consisting of some 186 articles was completed. The Constitution was approved by referendum in September of that year, and a general election was held in November, for the first time in eight years.

In July 1987 Standvaste was reconstituted as the Nationale Democratische Partij (NDP—National Democratic Party), under the leadership of Jules Wijdenbosch, Prime Minister in the last Bouterse-appointed Cabinet of Ministers prior to the November election. In August the three major opposition parties, the Afro-Surinamese NPS, the Indo-Surinamese VHP and the ethnic Javanese Kaum-Tani Persuatan Indonesia (KTPI—Javanese Indonesian Farmers' Union, since renamed the Kerukanan Tulodo Pranatan Ingit, the Party for National Unity and Solidarity), formed an electoral alliance, the Front voor Demokratie en Ontwikkeling (FDO—Front for Democracy and Development). With the restoration of electoral politics Suriname's ethnic parties, which had dominated the political scene prior to the 1980 military coup, returned to prominence. At the November 1987 election the FDO won a decisive victory, taking 40 seats in the new 51-seat National Assembly, with PALU, the Progressieve Bosneger Partij (PBP—Progressive Bosneger Party) and the NDP sharing out the remaining seats. The National Assembly took over political control in January 1988 and unanimously elected Ramsewak Shankar of the VHP to the presidency. Henck Arron of the NPS was elected Vice-President and Prime Minister.

ANTI-GOVERNMENT REVOLT

The return to constitutional rule did not end Suriname's internal conflicts, and the army, in practice, remained a dominant force. From 1986 the military was fighting against an anti-Government insurgency in the interior of the country, led by Ronnie Brunswijk, who had formerly been a member of Bouterse's personal bodyguard. Brunswijk claimed that government plans to control the interior of the country violated the autonomy of tribal society, which had been guaranteed by the 1761 treaty and subsequent agreements. In 1987 Brunswijk's Surinamese Liberation Army (SLA—popularly known as the Jungle Commando) attacked economic targets, causing severe disruption, including the closure of the main bauxite smelting and refining plants.

Bouterse retaliated against the insurgency with raids into the interior; rebel claims that the army massacred civilians in the settlement of Moiwana and elsewhere were later supported by the Inter-American Court of Human Rights (see below). The military also moved to arm about 1,000 Amerindians, leading to armed clashes. As a result of the fighting, the French reinforced the border with Suriname with paratroopers and legionnaires, refusing to let the Suriname military pursue the insurgents across the Marowijne river, which forms the border.

In June 1988 negotiations began between the Government and representatives of the SLA, and both sides signed a peace accord at Kourou, French Guiana, in July 1989. The provisions of the Kourou Accord included a general amnesty for those involved in the conflict, the ending of the state of emergency established in December 1986, the incorporation of members of the SLA into the national police and measures to provide for the safe return of the Surinamese refugees in French Guiana. However, the Accord failed when Bouterse vetoed the clause demanding the integration of Brunswijk's fighting force into the national police, and the Amerindians refused to abide by its terms. In addition, many refugees refused to move back to Suriname from French Guiana, fearing reprisals by either the army or the Amerindians.

The Kourou Accord included proposals for a Consultative Council for the Development of the Interior. Much of the interior's infrastructure had been destroyed and development suspended during the insurgency. The Council was finally appointed in 1995. However, the Government failed to consult indigenous representatives about the granting of gold and timber concessions on their land. These communities were concerned about the impact of mining activity on their way of life and, in particular, about the damaging effects on the food chain by the gold miners' widespread use of mercury.

THE MILITARY INTERREGNUM

In 1990 the US Department of State noted that the Surinamese military had 're-established itself as the dominant political force in the country'. Only a few of the 120 new laws required to implement the Constitution had been passed by the Assembly, and the Constitutional Court, which was to interpret the Constitution and rule on human rights issues, had not been established. Moreover, the Government had not taken steps to divest the military of such powers as the investigation and detention of civilians, the issue of visas and the supervision of customs and immigration at airports and harbours. Of particular concern to the USA was the growing military involvement in the international trafficking of illicit drugs. Western intelligence sources reported that Suriname had become a major centre of the illegal drugs trade, serving as a transshipment point for increasing quantities of cocaine intended for Europe and the USA. The country also served as a transshipment point for the sale of illegal arms to the Colombian drugs cartels. Sources in the USA and in Suriname alleged that Bouterse and the army were behind the illegal trade in drugs and arms.

In 1990 President Shankar's Government renewed contacts with the SLA, following the failure of the Kourou Accord. With a presidential guarantee of safety, Ronnie Brunswijk travelled to Paramaribo to negotiate. However, Bouterse violated the guarantee and arrested Brunswijk. Although Brunswijk was later released on the insistence of President Shankar, the action of the military revealed the weakness of the civilian Government and ultimately led to its downfall. On 24 December the military overthrew the Shankar Government and installed leaders of the NDP in the executive. Jules Wijdenbosch held the posts of Vice-President, Prime Minister and Minister of Finance until the elections of May 1991. In August 1992 the new administration signed an accord with the SLA, finally ending the insurgency. The former rebels recognized the Government's authority over the entire country, while the Government promised to honour the rights of the descendants of former slaves, including their right to engage in gold prospecting and forestry, and to join the army. Nevertheless, there were continuing protests (for example in 2005 and 2007) over the Government's perceived failure to implement the provisions agreed under the 1992 accord.

THE FIRST VENETIAAN GOVERNMENT

The general election of May 1991 was monitored by a delegation from the Organization of American States (OAS). The Nieuw Front coalition (NF—New Front, formerly the FDO), comprising the dominant NPS, the VHP, the KTPI and the Surinaamse Partij van de Arbeid (SPA—Suriname Labour Party), won a majority of seats in parliament. The NPS leader, Runaldo Ronald Venetiaan, was elected President and Jules Adjodhia, Prime Minister.

In March 1992 the Government requested that the National Assembly remove references in the Constitution that allowed the army to act in a way that contravened the proper democratic functioning of the State. The action to curb the military was taken as a measure designed in part to improve relations with the Netherlands, Suriname's main international benefactor. With the restoration of democracy in 1987, the Dutch Government had renewed aid to Suriname, but under more restrictive conditions than those imposed at the time of independence. In 1990 some US $700m., which had accumulated over the period of outright military control, had yet to be disbursed by the Netherlands. In 1992 the Netherlands agreed to renew economic assistance, but required the Surinamese Government to implement the IMF's stringent structural adjustment programme, which involved reduced public spending, increased taxes and the removal of food and fuel subsidies. The programme, implemented in 1994, proved highly successful, although the economic reforms caused widespread hardship and the Government became increasingly unpopular.

THE WIJDENBOSCH GOVERNMENT

The results of the elections to the National Assembly in May 1996 represented a reverse for the ruling NF, winning, as it did, fewer seats than in 1991, while Bouterse's NDP increased its legislative representation. The poll was also significant for the fact that Amerindians were elected to the Assembly for the first time. In an attempt to secure broader support, the NDP chose Jules Wijdenbosch, rather than Bouterse, as its candidate to contest the presidency. In the National Assembly's first vote to select the new President, Venetiaan gained more support than Wijdenbosch, but not the two-thirds' majority necessary to win the election outright. Responsibility for electing the President

then passed to the United People's Assembly (Verenigde Volksvergadering), a body comprising national, regional and local representatives. With only a simple majority required, Wijdenbosch was elected President. The NF alliance disintegrated, with a faction of the VHP and the KTPI joining an NDP-led coalition, on condition that Bouterse should not hold office in the new administration. The new coalition Government comprised representatives of four different political groupings.

The Wijdenbosch Government soon became characterized by internal political crisis and increasing pressure from diverse opposition groups. In August 1997 the dismissal of the Minister of Finance, Motilal Mungra, following his outspoken criticism of the President's extravagant use of public funds prompted Mungra's Beweging voor Vernieuwing en Democratie (BVD—Movement for Renewal and Democracy) and two other small parties to withdraw from the governing coalition. Wijdenbosch managed to secure sufficient support to maintain a narrow parliamentary majority, but frequently failed to secure the quorum needed for the National Assembly to meet. The President also drew accusations of political corruption, for example a committee appointed to investigate past human rights abuses, in particular the 1982 December Murders, was led by a former lawyer of Bouterse. Moreover, the Government's mismanagement of the economy caused a rapid rise in inflation and a depreciation in the currency.

THE RE-ELECTION OF VENETIAAN

In early 1999 the economic situation became extremely grave, with spiralling inflation caused by an ever-widening budget deficit and a decline in the international price of bauxite, by far Suriname's most important source of foreign exchange earnings. Furthermore, the Dutch Government had suspended aid in 1998. Under pressure from the Netherlands, in April 1999 President Wijdenbosch dismissed Bouterse from the advisory Council of State, then dismissed his entire Cabinet of Ministers in the following month in an attempt to avoid demands for his own resignation. On 31 May some 30,000 protesters gathered in Paramaribo to demand President Wijdenbosch's removal, while a general strike paralysed the country. On 1 June the National Assembly passed a vote of no confidence in the Government, although the vote fell short of the two-thirds' majority needed to remove the President from office. Wijdenbosch refused to resign, but did agree to hold new elections in May 2000, one year earlier than was constitutionally required.

In the elections of 25 May 2000 the NF, led by Venetiaan, secured a majority of seats in the National Assembly. Bouterse, as an NDP candidate, won a seat in the legislature, even as a Dutch appeals court upheld an earlier drugs-trafficking conviction (see below). As the NF narrowly failed to win the two-thirds' majority to appoint a new President directly, it immediately began coalition negotiations with smaller parties, winning the support of an ethnic Javanese party, the Pertjajah Luhur (Full Confidence Party), led by Paul Somohardjo, who had fled to the Netherlands after narrowly escaping the December 1982 murders. Venetiaan was elected to the presidency in August. The new administration instituted a series of economic reforms aimed at reversing the failed economic policies of the Wijdenbosch Government, and subsequently made progress in stabilizing the economy.

DECEMBER MURDERS INVESTIGATION

Following the election of Venetiaan, there were calls for the new Government to investigate the December Murders, before the 18-year time limit under the statute of limitations expired in December 2000. In October the country's highest court, the Court of Justice, began hearings on the murders in response to a request by relatives of the victims. Following an order from the Court, an examining magistrate instigated a full investigation into the incident, including the alleged involvement of 36 individuals. In late 2002 the Court ordered the exhumation of the remains of 15 of the murder victims. In December 2004, following a four-year investigation, a military court indicted Bouterse and 25 other suspects for the murders.

Requests from the opposition NDP that, in the interest of national unity, an amnesty be offered in respect of the December Murders were formally submitted for consideration by

History

parliament in April 2007. However, discussions on the matter appeared to have closed in June when a local court ruled that 10 of the 26 defendants who had been pursuing appeals to be exempted from trial would face prosecution together with the remaining suspects, now numbering 15 since the acquittal of former Minister of Justice Ivan Graanoogst during the same proceedings. At the military tribunal in July 2008, Bouterse's lawyer challenged the impartiality of the judge, as a result of which the trial was temporarily suspended. Bouterse's lawyer unsuccessfully sought a court order to prohibit further media coverage of the trial, claiming that there existed a 'deep animosity' between the media and his client.

Meanwhile, in August 2005 the OAS's Inter-American Court of Human Rights instructed the Government to investigate a massacre that occurred in the Maroon village of Moiwana in 1986, during Bouterse's presidency, to pay US $13,000 in compensation to the 130 survivors and to establish a $1.2m. development fund for the district. President Venetiaan formally apologized for the massacre at a ceremony in Moengo in July 2006.

THE 2005 ELECTIONS

In the general election held on 25 May 2005 the NF, which enjoyed the support of the governments of the Netherlands and the USA, retained its position as the largest party in the National Assembly, securing 23 of the 51 seats. However, this was 10 seats fewer than in the previous legislature. The NDP won 15 seats, while the Volksalliantie Voor Vooruitgang (VVV)—an alliance forged by the Democratisch Nationaal Platform 2000 (DNP 2000—National Democratic Platform 2000, headed by former President Wijdenbosch)—secured just five seats. A-Combinatie, a coalition including the Algemene Bevrijdings- en Ontwikkelingspartij (General Liberation and Development Party), led by former guerrilla leader Ronnie Brunswijk, who, like Bouterse, had been convicted *in absentia* in the Netherlands for cocaine-trafficking, also secured five seats, while the A1 alliance obtained the remaining three seats.

The major parties subsequently entered into negotiations to form alliances with smaller groupings in an attempt to garner the two-thirds' parliamentary majority needed directly to appoint a presidential nominee. The NF formed a 'Nieuw Front Plus' alliance with the A-Combinatie and Democratisch Alternatief '91 (a single-seat component of the A1 alliance) and in July nominated Venetiaan as its candidate for the forthcoming presidential election. A few days later Bouterse, who had originally been the NDP's preferred candidate for the presidency, withdrew in favour of the party's vice-presidential candidate, Rabin Parmessar. However, neither candidate was able to secure the required two-thirds' majority in the National Assembly, despite two rounds of voting. Responsibility for electing the new head of state therefore passed to the 891-member United People's Assembly. With only a simple majority required, Venetiaan secured the presidency and was inaugurated for a third term in office.

VENETIAAN'S THIRD TERM IN OFFICE

The steep increases in petroleum prices, and, consequently, in transport costs, led to civil unrest in the latter half of 2005 and early 2006. Power shortages in the west of the country in February prompted further protests. Nevertheless, the third Venetiaan Government presided over a period of gradual economic recovery, but was viewed as largely uninspiring by the majority of younger voters. There was some jockeying for power between its ethnic components, which intensified as the 2010 elections approached and the question of succession came to the fore.

Venetiaan's Cabinet of Ministers underwent a number of changes during 2006 and 2007, precipitated by a number of incidents of corruption and misconduct that threatened to undermine the Government's integrity. In January 2006 the Minister of Trade and Industry, Siegfried Gilds, resigned following accusations of money-laundering and membership of a criminal organization. In March 2007 the Minister of Transport, Communications and Tourism, Alice Amafo, stood down from her post following allegations of financial misconduct. Meanwhile, in August 2005 Bouterse's son Dino was sentenced to eight years in prison for smuggling offences (he was released in 2008), and in November Bouterse's half-brother Eric was sentenced to nine years in prison on drugs-related charges.

There was further evidence of civil unrest in late 2007 and early 2008 when workers from four different sectors staged strikes, causing disruption and drawing attention to their poor working conditions. Teachers, air traffic controllers, banana plant workers and bauxite workers all undertook industrial action in support of demands for salary increases.

Violent clashes between local residents and Brazilian mine operators (*garimpeiros*) in the town of Albina in December 2009 highlighted the issue of ethnic tensions and general lawlessness in the interior gold fields. An initial minor incident that resulted in the murder of a Surinamese national by a Brazilian worker led to a night of rioting during which a number of people were injured and buildings and local businesses were set alight, leaving up to 100 people homeless (most of whom were Brazilian or Chinese). To regulate cross-border travel, the Governments of Brazil and Suriname agreed upon an immigration accord in December 2010.

BOUTERSE'S RETURN TO POWER

A total of 20 parties, mostly grouped into coalitions, contested the general election on 25 May 2010. Former President Desi Bouterse formed the Megacombinatie (an alliance that included the NDP—which had earlier merged with the DNP 2000 of Jules Wijdenbosch—as well as Nieuw Suriname, PALU and the KTPI) to challenge the ruling NF alliance. A powerful public speaker, Bouterse won considerable support among younger voters. At the election the Megacombinatie secured 23 of the 51 legislative seats and 40.2% of the votes, while the NF alliance obtained only 14 seats and 31.7% of the ballot. Two former components of the NF Plus alliance contested the poll separately, outside the alliance; the A-Combinatie (headed by former rebel leader Ronnie Brunswijk) won seven seats and the Volksalliantie (a grouping of Javanese parties led by Paul Somohardjo of the Pertjajah Luhur) took six. As no single group had secured even a simple majority in the National Assembly, a short period of intense negotiations followed. The Megacombinatie quickly won the backing of the A-Combinatie and the Volksalliantie, each of which was led by a former bitter enemy of Bouterse. This meant that the Megacombinatie had sufficient support to achieve a two-thirds' majority, and on 19 July Bouterse was elected President with the votes of 36 of the 51 members of the National Assembly. His election was greeted with dismay by his opponents and by many international commentators. Bouterse, who at the time of his election remained on trial for his role in the December Murders, was believed to be the first convicted drugs-trafficker to be elected to the presidency of any country in the region. The Dutch Government issued a statement to say that the former dictator would not be welcome in the Netherlands unless he had travelled there to serve his 11-year prison sentence (a penalty he had received *in absentia* following his conviction for drugs-trafficking in the latter country in 1999—see International Relations).

The A-Combinatie was rewarded with six cabinet posts in the new Government, including the justice and the police portfolio. The Volksalliantie was granted three government positions; most notably, Soewarto Moestadja was appointed as the new Minister of Home Affairs. The remaining portfolios were secured by Megacombinatie members, with Winston Lackin becoming Minister of Foreign Affairs and the non-party Winnie Boedhoe given responsibility for finance; Alice Amafo of the A-Combinatie was sworn in as Minister of Social Affairs and Housing, provoking some controversy due to her alleged involvement in a corruption scandal in 2007. In another controversial move, in early 2011 Bouterse declared 25 February a national holiday, in remembrance of the coup of 25 February 1980.

A number of changes were made to the governing coalition, but its main lines remained consistent. Boedhoe resigned as Minister of Finance in June 2011 and was replaced by Adelien Wijnerman, also a member of the NDP. It was reported that

Boedhoe, who had promoted austerity measures to strengthen the country's fiscal position, disapproved of the President's expansionary spending plans. Nieuw Suriname, which had two members in the National Assembly, withdrew from the ruling coalition in March, forming an independent parliamentary group. Relations between the constituent parties of the A-Combinatie proved difficult, leading to the loss of two parliamentarians from one of its components, Broederschap en Eenheid in de Politiek (Brotherhood and Unity in Politics). Following a cabinet reorganization in April 2012, the parliamentary strength of the Megacombinatie was reduced from its original 36 seats to 32, which, although still a comfortable majority in the 51-seat chamber, was not enough to pass constitutional amendments. Accordingly, little progress was expected to be achieved by a commission established by Bouterse in July 2011 to review the Constitution and to investigate the proposed change to a fully presidential system of government (from the mixed parliamentary-presidential structure currently in force).

The trial of Bouterse and 24 other defendants before a military court, for the December 1982 murders, was interrupted in mid-2012, at a point when the hearings were making progress and a verdict within a reasonable period of time seemed possible. On 4 April the National Assembly extended an existing amnesty law to cover the period 1980–85 and to include any offences 'in the context of the defence of the state'; previously, only robbery, rape, arson, assault and manslaughter had been covered. With some remaining uncertainty over the legal standing of the amnesty in relation to a trial already in progress, court hearings were adjourned on 11 May. The amendment to the amnesty law was opposed by trade unions, opposition parties and human rights organisations, who were expected to initiate a legal challenge before the Inter-American Commission on Human Rights and the Inter-American Court of Human Rights. The Netherlands imposed a travel ban on the 25 accused, and froze its small remaining aid programme, while the EU attempted, without success, to change the location of a meeting of the Joint Parliamentary Assembly of the European Union and Africa, Caribbean and Pacific countries, held in Paramaribo in November. However, the OAS, whose Assistant Secretary-General at the time, Albert Ramdin, was Surinamese, offered technical assistance for a Truth and Reconciliation Commission established as part of the amendments to the legislation. In December the military court referred the status of the trial to a constitutional court, a body provided for in principle by Article 144 of the 1987 Constitution but not yet established by the National Assembly. Following a cabinet reorganization in May and June 2013 the Ministers of Public Works, Physical Planning, Land and Forestry Management, and Education and Community Development were replaced. Pertjajah Luhur, the main Javanese party and the leading component of the Volksalliantie, was expelled from the coalition in April 2014, with its leader Paul Salam Somohardjo accused by Bouterse of practising 'blackmail politics'; this left the Government with support from 27 of the 51 national assembly members. Pertjajah Luhur then formed an alliance with six other opposition parties, most of them members of the former Nieuw Front Government. With less than a year to the scheduled May 2015 general election, Bouterse's political position meanwhile remained fairly strong in mid-2014, with the economy performing reasonably well; however, neither he nor the opposition appeared likely to win the two-thirds' majority needed to elect a President in the National Assembly.

INTERNATIONAL RELATIONS

Relations with the Government of the Netherlands have generally been poor during periods when Bouterse and his allies have been in office, and more positive when the NF has headed the Surinamese administration. From 1995 relations deteriorated rapidly under President Wijdenbosch, principally owing to his Government's continued links with Bouterse, and worsened further in 1997 when the President appointed Bouterse to the cabinet-level position of an adviser to the Government of Suriname (Counsellor of State), despite an ongoing investigation by the Dutch Government into drugs-trafficking allegations against the former dictator. In March

1999 the Dutch authorities began legal proceedings against Bouterse, and in July a Dutch court convicted Bouterse *in absentia* of leading a Surinamese cartel that had attempted to smuggle about two metric tons of cocaine seized at Dutch and Belgian ports and airports in 1989–97. Bouterse received a sentence of 16 years' imprisonment (later reduced to 11 years) and a US $2.2m. fine. The Dutch Government secured a warrant from the International Criminal Police Commission (Interpol) for Bouterse's arrest on drugs-trafficking charges with hopes of detaining him in a third country, since the Surinamese Constitution barred extradition of its nationals. The Attorney-General of the Netherlands filed further charges (this time for torture resulting in death) against Bouterse in January 2000. The new suit concerned the December Murders in 1982 and arose because of a complaint filed by relatives of the victims.

Relations improved dramatically with the change of administration in 2000, partly as a result of the efforts made by Venetiaan's Government to investigate the December Murders, and in October the Dutch Government agreed to resume aid to Suriname, which had been suspended since 1998. A Dutch loan guarantee fund allowed the Government to renegotiate the crippling debt portfolio inherited from the Wijdenbosch administration, while the Netherlands agreed to begin spending the remaining 600m. guilders of the independence aid package.

In February 2001 President Venetiaan announced his intention to seek the amendment of an article in the Constitution that banned the extradition of Surinamese citizens to other countries for trial. However, this proposal was not followed through, and there was continuing intermittent friction between the Netherlands and Suriname over issues such as the Dutch practice of subjecting passengers arriving from Suriname to a full body search.

Successive governments of all leanings have made formal moves against illegal drugs-trafficking, in part to appease both their European and US allies. In 1997 President Wijdenbosch installed a commission to monitor the drugs trade. In 1998 the Government signed the Anti-Drugs Strategy for the Western Hemisphere, which had been prepared by the OAS. New legislation was passed in 1999 providing for heavier sentences for drugs-trafficking. In 2004 the Dutch and Surinamese Governments agreed to co-operate on intelligence-gathering and to increase security on both passenger and cargo flights from Suriname. Notwithstanding these and other measures, the Government has been unable effectively to stem the tide of drugs-trafficking; according to some official estimates, roughly 26,000 kg of cocaine, with a street value of slightly over US $1,000m., are shipped to Europe each year, mainly in container cargo and some transshipped through Africa. However, despite the high level of drugs-trafficking, the rate of violent crime in Suriname remains relatively low; the reported murder rate in 2012 of five persons per 100,000 was close to that of the USA. The US Department of State classes Suriname as a 'country of concern' for money-laundering. Indicating continuing US concerns over high-level criminal connections, Desi Bouterse's son Dino was arrested in Panama in August 2013, and deported to the USA where he was charged with drugs-trafficking and terrorist offences, after offering Surinamese passports and training facilities to US agents purporting to represent militant Lebanese organization Hezbollah, and agreeing to send weekly 20-kg consignments of cocaine to Florida, USA. In spite of his 2005 smuggling conviction, he had in 2010 been appointed to lead Suriname's counterterrorism operations. Embarrassingly, the arrest came immediately before the opening in Paramaribo of a summit of the Union of South American Nations (UNASUR); however, Bouterse assumed the chair of the organisation, and was chosen along with Colombia to lead its ministerial council on defence.

In 2008 Suriname acceded to the Inter-American Convention Against Illicit Manufacturing of and Trafficking in Firearms, Ammunition, Explosives and Similar Devices; it was hoped the measure would facilitate the delivery of an enhanced security programme for Suriname through regional co-operation and intelligence-sharing. Suriname and Guyana declared their joint commitment to reducing the movement of criminals, and trafficking of drugs and firearms across the countries' border in May 2008, when they signed the Nieuw-Nickerie Declaration.

Relations with France were difficult at the time of the interior war in the 1980s when a large number of refugees fled to French Guiana, but are now generally amicable. France has considered using Paramaribo as a hub for the shipment of goods to French Guiana, where the ports are subject to severe silting, with French finance to improve the road connection from the Surinamese capital to the border town of Albina. There was a minor dispute between the two countries in 2007 when the French Government designated a 20,000 sq km region along the disputed border with French Guiana, encompassing land between the Marowijne (Marouini) and Itany (Litani) rivers, as a national park. Under its new protected status, the traditional hunting and fishing practices of the indigenous Surinamese communities were strictly prohibited in the park. In response, the Organisatie van Inheemsen in Suriname (Organization of Indigenous People in Suriname) submitted a petition to the French authorities, expressing its rejection of the newly instituted park and averring that the development contravened the native groups' human rights.

Since 1976 Suriname has maintained diplomatic relations with the People's Republic of China, and the relationship between the two countries has increased greatly in significance over recent years. China is a significant aid donor, and has financed major road-surfacing projects since the 1990s. There was substantial Chinese migration to Suriname in the 19th century, while a new wave of migrants from the 1980s has become active in retailing and the restaurant business. President Bouterse visited China in June 2013, chartering the only Airbus of the national airline, Surinaamse Luchtvaart Maatschappij, thus avoiding any legal difficulties in transit that might have complicated the use of scheduled flights. Bouterse has also cultivated cordial relations with President Obiang Nguema Mbasogo of Equatorial Guinea, and visited that country in 2012, using Mbasogo's private jet.

Border Disputes with Guyana

Immediately prior to its departure from office, the Wijdenbosch administration initiated a conflict with Guyana over the maritime border shared by Suriname and Guyana. This followed an extended period of dispute over both the land and the marine boundary between the two countries. The present border between Guyana and Suriname was established by the United Kingdom and the Netherlands after the Napoleonic wars, on the left bank of the Corentyne river. A draft treaty between the two colonial powers, which was agreed in 1939 but never ratified, demarcated the southern part of this boundary along the river known to the British as the Upper Corentyne, but to the Dutch as the Koetari, terminating in an agreed triple junction with Brazil. However, in 1962 the Netherlands questioned Guyana's sovereignty over a largely uninhabited triangular area of land (the New River triangle) between the Koetari/Upper Corentyne and a western branch of the river's headwaters known to the British and Guyanese as the New

River, but to the Dutch as the Boven Corantijn. The Dutch proposed a modification of the 1939 treaty, favouring a boundary that followed the central thalweg, instead of the left bank of the Corantijn (as a concession to what was then British Guiana), but with the New River triangle awarded to Suriname. However, the British Government refused to reopen discussions on the issue. A small Surinamese contingent attempted in 1975 to establish a presence at Post Tigri on the New River; they were ejected by the Guyanese, who have since occupied the site as a military base, Camp Jaguar.

A later and more economically significant border dispute related to the maritime boundary between Guyana and Suriname, which begins at an agreed demarcation point on the left bank of the Corantyne estuary. According to the Guyanese, the line followed a compass bearing 15° E, while, according to Suriname, it ran along the bearing 5° E. In 1998 Guyana granted the Canadian-based CGX Energy Inc a concession to explore for petroleum and gas along the continental shelf off its coastline, up to the 15° E bearing and including a triangular area that lay within waters claimed by Suriname. The Surinamese Government made a formal protest against the CGX concession in 2000, claiming it violated Suriname's sovereignty and territorial integrity. The Guyanese Government maintained that the exploration activities were being conducted in Guyanese territory, but indicated its willingness to attend talks. In June a gunboat of the Suriname navy forced CGX to remove the drilling rig from the disputed waters. Later that month representatives from the two countries, meeting in Trinidad and Tobago, agreed that a Joint Technical Committee be established to resolve the dispute, but both sides remained at an impasse. With an agreement between Suriname and Guyana appearing unlikely, CGX withdrew from the area later in the month.

After several years of intermittent negotiations, in 2004 Guyana referred the maritime boundary dispute to arbitration under the provisions of Article 287 of the UN Convention on the Law of the Sea. In September 2007 the International Tribunal for the Law of the Sea ruled largely in favour of Guyana, with a boundary mainly following the median line, and granting that country sovereignty over 33,152 sq km (12,800 sq miles) of coastal waters, including the most promising areas for petroleum exploration; Suriname was awarded 17,891 sq km (6,900 sq miles). With the maritime dispute definitively settled, CGX resumed exploration in the area in 2008, but an exploration well drilled in 2012 proved disappointing. Relations between Suriname and Guyana have been generally positive since 2007. Two rounds of constructive talks were held in 2010, during which both sides agreed to focus on security and economic co-operation rather than the border dispute. In 2011 Suriname proposed the construction of a bridge over the Corantijn river (without direct Guyanese involvement in the main structure, as the river lies entirely within Surinamese territory).

Economy

MARK WILSON

Suriname occupies 163,820 sq km (63,251 sq miles) on the north coast of South America, lying between Guyana to the west and French Guiana to the east, and had a population of 534,189 at the census of August 2012. Suriname's economy is based on gold-mining, bauxite, petroleum and, to a lesser extent, agriculture. In 2012 gold alone accounted for 67% of goods exports, alumina for 15% and petroleum 14%. Gold produced 13% of government revenue in the same year, and oil a further 25%, but bauxite and alumina only 2%. Suriname has enjoyed macroeconomic stability with low inflation and a stable currency since 2000, and in more recent years steady growth, a positive trade balance and healthy public finances, largely because of strong gold and petroleum prices and

expanding production. The informal and 'parallel' economy, including illegal drugs transshipments, is also of some significance. However, the performance of the agricultural sector has been weak, there are concerns over the development of bauxite deposits, and Suriname's economy remains susceptible to 'boom and bust' cycles caused by variations in the international price of gold, petroleum and alumina. The tax receipts that Suriname receives from the export of these three commodities provides the revenue to support the large public sector, which employed some 49,700 of the working population of about 100,000 in 2010. The cost of the public sector increased significantly following a salary restructuring in 2010 which raised the public sector salary bill from 12% of gross domestic product

(GDP) to 19.6%. Another concern is weak financial sector governance and supervision; the non-performing loan ratio rose to 8% in 2010, although this fell back to 6.2% in 2012, and new banking legislation was passed in 2011. In 2000–12, according to the World Bank, the economy grew at an average annual rate of 4.5%, with growth of an estimated 5.3% in 2011, 3.9% in 2012 and 4.4% in 2013. GDP per head was reasonably high, at US $9,010 in 2012. However, there are significant problems with social deprivation. It was estimated that some 70% of the population were living in poverty. Suriname ranked 105th out of 186 countries on the UN Development Programme's Human Development index for 2013; within the Caribbean Community and Common Market only Guyana, in 118th place, ranked lower.

AGRICULTURE

In the 18th century Suriname's economy was based on the sugar industry, but by the 19th century coffee, cocoa and cotton were the country's main commodities. With the decline of large-scale plantation agriculture in the 20th century the former contract labourers from India and Indonesia were induced to remain in Suriname by the offer of free land. The Government distributed small plots of land for the growing of rice along the country's rich coastal plain. Since the 1990s rice has been the country's principal agricultural export, followed by bananas. The coastal polders (land that had been drained) remain the country's focus of agricultural activity and settlement. At least 70% of Suriname's population live on the estuarine lands of the Suriname river, within 25 km of the capital, Paramaribo, while a further 15% live along the rest of the coastal plain.

The majority of Suriname's 58,000 ha of cultivated land, which represents only 0.4% of the country's total land area, is on the coastal plain. One-half of the cultivated area is in the polders close to Paramaribo, between the Commewijne and Saramacca estuaries. The country's agricultural potential is far from being realized, partly because of economic and environmental difficulties, and partly because of the pattern of land tenure. In 2002–11 the sector grew by an average of 3.4% per year. According to the Central Bank, sectoral growth was 4.6% in 2011 and 13.9% in 2012, but the sector contracted by 1.9% in 2013. In the latter year agriculture (including hunting and forestry) contributed 7.9% of GDP. The sector employed an estimated 11.2% of the working population in 2010. The state-owned oil company Staatsolie in 2013 announced a US $300m. proposal for sugar and ethanol production at Wageningen, in western Suriname.

In the early 21st century rice remained the crop of greatest commercial value in Suriname. About 50% of all cultivated land is devoted to rice, chiefly in the western polders of the Nickerie district. Much of the rice is produced by Indo-Surinamese and Javanese on plots of less than 1 ha, located on the more mature polders. On the new polders, land holdings are typically of 80 ha or more and cultivation is mechanized. The total cultivated land area dedicated to rice stood at 45,563 ha in 2005, and the Government planned to increase this to 150,000 ha by 2020. Rice production reached a low of 157,100 metric tons in 2002, but had recovered to 235,500 tons by 2011 following a US $3.4m. grant from the Inter-American Development Bank and a further $15m. from the European Union (EU), intended to aid the restructuring of the drainage and irrigation system. Rice exports totalled 49,258 tons in 2011, contributing $33.7m., or 1.4% of total export revenues. Rice exports increased to a reported 76,762 tons in 2012.

Bananas are grown on plantations in the Paramaribo region and in western Suriname, which have been owned since January 2014 by a Belgian company, Univeg, operating locally as Food and Agriculture Industries NV, with a 10% minority state holding. In 2002 the Government closed its banana plantation company, Surland, which had been responsible for all commercial production. Surland was subsequently restructured as the Stichting Behoud Banansector Suriname (SBBS) with European financial aid, and exports resumed in 2004. Banana production recovered strongly; by 2012 output was 85,668 tons, a 24% increase over the previous year, with exports of US $34.1m., or 1.4% of total export

revenues. Since the 1990s the banana industry has suffered from the loss of protection against lower-cost Latin American producers in the traditional European market, but prospects were improved from December 2011 as EU proposals for assistance to traditional banana suppliers were finalized, and exports in recent years have exceeded those of previous decades in both volume and value. The 2014 privatization had been planned for some years, and Katopé Agrisol (France), now a Univeg subsidiary, held a management contract from 2006.

Livestock receives little attention and the output of livestock products is insufficient for local needs. The few cattle that are reared by small-scale farmers are not of high quality and are used more as draught animals than for the production of either beef or milk. In 2011, according to FAO estimates, there were some 55,000 head of cattle and beef production totalled 2,000 metric tons. Fishing plays a small, though significant, role in the economy. There is a modern fishing industry, operating mainly from Paramaribo, which contributed 2.3% of GDP in 2013. This industry is dominated by Japanese and Korean companies, which export most of their catch to the USA and Canada. Shrimps are the most important single fisheries export, although their contribution to export earnings has fallen in recent years. In 2011 shrimps and fish contributed US $33.5m. in export revenues, equivalent to 1.4% of total earnings. In 2011, according to FAO, the total catch measured 34,500 metric tons.

According to FAO, 95% of Suriname's land area was covered by forest in 2011, making it one of the most densely forested countries in the world. Large areas remain unexploited, but timber exports were valued at US $8.9m. in 2011, equivalent to 0.4% of total export revenues.

MINING

Mining, dominated by the extraction of gold, petroleum and bauxite, is the single most important economic activity in Suriname. In 2010 mining employed 3.0% of the working population and in 2013, according to the Central Bank, mining and quarrying and utilities contributed 6.4% of GDP. However, the manufacturing sector, which was mainly concerned with mineral processing, accounted for a further 20.2% of GDP in 2013.

Suriname is the world's 10th most important bauxite producer, accounting for about 1.3% of total global bauxite production and 2.1% of total bauxite reserves in 2013. All locally produced bauxite is refined as alumina then exported to aluminium smelters overseas; Suriname accounted for 1.6% of total global alumina production in 2011. Bauxite has been mined from deposits found along the northern edge of the central plateau in eastern Suriname. However, these deposits were close to depletion by 2014, and the future of the industry depended on the development of new reserves. Mining operations were commenced in 1915, by Suralco, a wholly owned subsidiary of the Aluminum Company of America (Alcoa), then the world's largest producer of aluminium. The Brokopondo-Afobaka dam on the Suriname river, 100 km from its mouth, was completed by Suralco in 1964 at a cost of US $150m., creating a 1,560 sq km lake, one of the largest artificial lakes in the world, and is operated under an agreement which runs to 2033. It provides power, initially used for an alumina refinery at Paranam. In 1939 Billiton Maatschappij Suriname (BMS), then a subsidiary of the Royal Dutch Shell-owned Billiton Company, initiated bauxite mining operations in Suriname's Para district, some 35 km south of Paramaribo. A close relationship between the two companies developed in 1983 when BMS bought a 46% interest in Suralco's Paranam refinery, and Suralco purchased 24% of BMS's bauxite-mining operations. A project completed in 2005 increased alumina refining capacity by 250,000 metric tons, to 2.2m. tons per year. In 2001 BMS merged with the Australian Broken Hill Proprietary Company (BHP) to become BHP Billiton, but withdrew from Suriname in 2009 as the country's existing bauxite reserves approached depletion, selling its stake in the Paranam refinery. By contrast, Suralco signed an agreement with the Government in 2012 to develop new gold and bauxite reserves in the Nassau Range, to the south-east, in partnership with a US company, Newmont Mining Corporation, for completion in 2018 or later.

However, Alcoa informed the Government in May 2014 that it would from that year reduce production by two-thirds in order to maintain some output and keep the Paranam refinery in operation during the intervening period. Alcoa also stated that bauxite and alumina production would not be viable without a subsidized price for fuel supplied by the state-owned oil company Staatsolie. The most promising reserves, totalling 90m.–160m. tons, are located in the Bakhuys Range of western Suriname. Negotiations in the years after 2000 with BHP and Suralco for their development did not come to a satisfactory conclusion; a state-owned company, Alamsur, has since been established to develop these reserves, and has attempted to identify an international mining company as a partner; however, no clear progress had been made towards this objective by mid-2014.

The bauxite industry was heavily taxed and accounted for 25% of the Government's revenue as recently as 2005. However, with falling production and profitability, this had declined to US $19.4m. or 1.6% of government revenue, by 2013, and was exceeded by the $53.2m. paid by the state-owned electricity company for power generated at the Afobaka dam. Suriname's traditional markets for alumina are the USA, Canada and Norway. Suriname's annual bauxite output remained fairly constant in the mid-2000s, at just over 4.0m. metric tons, but production decreased from 2009 as reserves approached depletion, and in 2012 totalled 2.87m. tons, a 11.4% decrease compared with the previous year. Suriname's annual alumina production also declined from 2009 (falling to 1.2m. tons in 2012, 45% below the 2007 peak). Alumina has been displaced by gold as Suriname's main export, slipping from 51.9% of goods exports in 2007 to 19.9% in 2011, with a value of $491m.

There are two broad divisions to the gold mining industry in Suriname. For many years, gold and diamonds have been extracted in small quantities from the river beds by around 25,000 small-scale miners, many of them Brazilian garimpeiros (prospectors) or Guyanese 'pork-knockers', who operate concessions granted to Bosnegers and other Surinamese. The Government has little control over the small-scale mining sector of the interior, and only a limited proportion of output is formally declared and taxed. However, since 2010 the Government has been attempting to increase its control over the sector and raise the level of tax revenue; as a result, there have been intermittent clashes with small-scale miners. At the other end of the scale are large international investors. A Canadian company, Cambior, began development of the Rosebel gold mine in 2002 and commercial production commenced in 2004. In 2006 the mine was sold to another Canadian company, IAMGOLD, with a continuing 5% stake being held by the Government. The Rosebel mine was expanded in 2005 and 2009, increasing annual capacity to 11m. metric tons of ore. Gold production at Rosebel reached a record 416,000 troy oz in 2010; however, production decreased to 354,000 troy oz in 2013, in part because of weaker gold prices, with cumulative production to that date of 3.8m. troy oz. The proven and probable reserves of the Rosebel mine area at the end of 2012 were estimated at 7.7m. troy oz of gold. Payments by IAMGOLD made up 8.9% of government revenue in 2013, and the company in May 2013 signed a provisional agreement with the Government for expansion of the mine, with the state to take a 30% equity stake. US company Newmont and Suralco in 2012 signed an agreement with the Government for gold and bauxite mining in the Nassau Range, with a 25% government equity stake. Government investment in both projects (if finalized) was expected to reach US $400m., with a $500m. bond issue to fund these and other public sector investments. Two other Canadian mining companies, Canarc and Golden Star, have reported gold discoveries and proposed large-scale developments. With the development of the Rosebel mine and strong international prices, exports of gold increased dramatically in the early 2000s, from 218,900 troy oz in 2001 to 997,900 troy oz in 2011. As a result, gold displaced bauxite as Suriname's main export, contributing 61.4% of total export revenues, $1,513.6m., in 2011, compared with $140.3m., or 25.1%, in 2003. Total gold production in 2012 was 11.1m. troy oz, a 4.9% increase compared with 2011, with gold representing some 67% of total export revenue. Gold prices at mid-2014 were strong by historic standards, but below the high levels recorded between 2011 and mid-2013, creating some uncertainty for major investment plans, exports and government finances.

Petroleum was discovered in the Saramacca district in 1981 by the Gulf Oil Corporation of the USA. As a result, the Suriname State Oil Company (Staatsolie) was formed to exploit the reserves. Taxes and dividends from Staatsolie totalling US $284m. contributed one-quarter (23.7%) of government revenue in 2012, while crude petroleum constituted 13.7% of total exports in 2012. Output in 2013 was 16,400 barrels per day (b/d). It is estimated that there are onshore reserves totalling 75m. barrels in the Tambaredjo and Calcutta oilfields, equivalent to 12.5 years at current output levels, but regional geology suggests more significant additional potential offshore. A total of 10 international companies were involved in offshore exploration by 2014, although no significant finds have yet been announced. Staatsolie has a small oil refinery at Tout Lui Faut, just south of Paramaribo, and began work in 2012 on a $700m. project to increase the refinery's capacity to 15,000 b/d, which was scheduled for completion in 2014; the company in 2014 borrowed $275m. towards the financing of its $1,845m. investment programme.

MANUFACTURING

The industrial sector is dominated by the production of alumina and oil refining. However, the country also manufactures some foodstuffs (flour, margarine, cattle fodder), tobacco products, beverages, construction materials, clothing and furniture, using some local raw materials, but mainly imported machinery. Manufacturing (excluding bauxite processing) employed an estimated 6.8% of the working population in 2010.

TRANSPORT AND COMMUNICATIONS INFRASTRUCTURE

Infrastructure remains only minimally developed in Suriname. In 2003 there were an estimated 4,304 km of roads, mainly in the north of the country. Two ferry links between Suriname and Guyana, across the Corantijn river, operate, as does one between Suriname and French Guiana, across the Marowijne river. The People's Republic of China has financed extensive road resurfacing projects, and in 2007 agreed to finance the resurfacing of the Afobakka road, a key route linking the southern district of Brokopondo with the capital Paramaribo. The road network has been ugraded since the 1990s largely by a Chinese company Dalien; on completion of current contracts approximately 2,500 km will have been paved, including the connections to Brokopondo in the interior and Albina on the border with French Guiana. The port at Paramaribo has been upgraded, and there are proposals for it to service French Guiana as well as Suriname. The state-owned telecommunications company, Telecommunication Corporation Suriname (Telesur), is now in competition in the mobile telephone market with Digicel, an Irish-owned company headquartered in Jamaica, and with Uniqa, a joint venture between local and Dutch interests (which was offered for sale in July 2014). Mobile telephone penetration was high at 127 subscriptions per 100 inhabitants in 2013, as many people have connections with more than one company; 37% of the population were regular internet users in 2013, and 6.9% had broadband connections.

FOREIGN TRADE AND BALANCE OF PAYMENTS

Exports are dominated by gold, alumina and crude petroleum, which together accounted for over 95% of Suriname's total export earnings in 2012. Other exports include rice, bananas, shrimps and timber products. Imports consist largely of consumer goods, machinery and transport equipment, as well as manufactured goods, and mineral fuels and lubricants. Owing to an increase in mineral commodity prices (notably gold), and an expansion in the volume of exports, the trade balance was in surplus from 2003, with a deficit in most years on trade in services. The trade surplus stood at US $701.3m. in 2012, but fell to $220.6m in 2013, partly because of lower gold prices; in that year there was a deficit of $197.8m. on the current account of the balance of payments. As a percentage of GDP, total government external debt was 14.9% of GDP in 2012, one of the lowest figures in the Caribbean, while total government debt was equivalent to 30.5% of GDP. Meanwhile, the country's international reserves rose from $127.4m. in 2000 to $1,008.4m. at the end of 2012, equivalent to 5.1 months of import cover; however, reserves fell to $775.4m. at the end of 2013, with a deterioration in the balance of payments. In 2011 the principal destinations for Suriname's exports were the United Arab Emirates (26.1%), Canada (18.6%), the USA (11.2%) and Belgium (10.2%). In the same year imports came chiefly from the USA (28.6%), Trinidad and Tobago (24.7%) and the Netherlands (15.6%).

Suriname was one of 13 Caribbean countries to approve an Economic Partnership Agreement (EPA) with the EU in 2008. The accord eased restrictions on Caribbean exports of goods and services, and gave European businesses greater freedom to expand into the region. The EPA was intended to stimulate trade and investment in the Caribbean, although critics believed it was more beneficial to EU producers.

INVESTMENT AND FINANCE

Suriname's economy declined in the 1980s after the military regime came to power. Official capital imports came to a virtual halt in 1982, when the Netherlands suspended its development co-operation because of the December Murders. A reduction in foreign capital investment and in exports, owing to the weakness of the world market for alumina and aluminium products, was reflected in a 20% fall in government revenues. Nevertheless, the military Government increased expenditure excessively, doubling the level of spending during the 1980s. The number of public employees grew by one-fifth. By contrast, spending on development projects collapsed. Over 50% of total government expenditure in the early 1990s was allocated to wages, with a mere 2% devoted to development projects.

Suriname's budget deficit increased from the equivalent of barely 5% of gross national product in 1980 to over 25% in 1992. The Government financed its expenditures first with international reserves and then by printing money, which by 1994 had precipitated a 'hyperinflationary' crisis, with the annual rate of inflation at 368.5%. Subsequently, the implementation of a stringent austerity programme and an increase in revenues caused by a rise in the world price of bauxite derivatives brought about a dramatic improvement in the country's economic situation. By 1996 the depreciation of the Surinamese guilder had been halted, international reserves had reached almost US $100m. and the country was experiencing deflation. However, in the late 1990s a decline in revenues from exports of alumina and aluminium, along with increased government spending and a relaxation of fiscal controls by the Wijdenbosch administration, combined to recreate the conditions of an economic crisis and rapid inflation. In 1998 the budget deficit increased to the equivalent of 11.1% of GDP, financed mainly through domestic borrowing. The deficit was eradicated in the early 2000s, however, and by 2007 the budget surplus increased to 5.7% of GDP, largely owing to a rise in export revenues and commodity prices. However, following substantial public sector pay awards, the overall fiscal balance again moved into deficit from 2009, with the shortfall rising to 2.8% of GDP in 2012. In the early months of 2013 the Government was having some difficulty in promptly meeting commitments, while planning extensive mining sector and other productive investments; accordingly, a $500m. bond issue was planned, to take advantage of Suriname's greatly improved international credit rating. However, declining gold prices in 2013 threat-

ened both the success of the bond issue and the outlook for the planned mining investments. In order to broaden the tax base, a value-added tax (VAT) was to be introduced in 2014.

Inflation increased to 98.9% in 1999. This figure fell to 59.3% in 2000 and continued to decrease, owing to the new Government's imposition of limits on borrowing from the Central Bank. Inflation declined to 9.1% in 2004, remaining between around that level in 2005–07, but rose sharply in 2008, to 14.6%. Consumer prices remained virtually constant in 2009, before increasing by an estimated 6.9% in 2010. There was another steep rise in inflation, to 17.7% in 2011, as a result of currency devaluation and increased fuel taxes, but it fell back to 5.0% in 2012.

The Surinamese guilder depreciated rapidly on the parallel market, with a 43% devaluation of the official exchange rate at the beginning of 1999. The differential between the official and parallel exchange rate, which had all but been eliminated with the devaluation, reached an average of 82% in 1999–2000. In an attempt to halt the economic decline, the second Venetiaan administration again devalued the official exchange rate, this time by 89%. As well as ending government borrowing from the Central Bank, the Government also eliminated subsidies on petroleum products, substantially increased electricity and water rates, rationalized the list of price controls on 12 basic food items, and raised the tax on cigarettes, alcohol and soft drinks. A new banking supervisory act was passed in 2003, which aimed to strengthen the powers of the Central Bank. Providing a psychological break with a history of currency devaluation and inflation, in January 2005 the Government replaced the Surinamese guilder with a new currency, the Surinamese dollar, with a rate of one Surinamese dollar to 1,000 former guilders, giving an initial exchange rate of 2.8 Surinamese dollars to the US dollar. There was a 20% devaluation in the official exchange rate in 2011, after which the exchange rate stabilized once more, at 3.3 Surinamese dollars to the US dollar, with no significant parallel market.

OUTLOOK

Although the economy was over-reliant on minerals exports, it stood up well to the global economic recession from mid-2008, with growth slowing only moderately to 3.0% in 2009 and recovering to an average of 4.5% in 2011–13. Although earlier Governments supported by the current President, Desi Bouterse, had overseen periods of economic instability and inflation, IMF reports since 2011 have broadly commended the policies of the current administration, while the World Bank in 2012 reactivated relations after a 30-year gap. However, the country remained vulnerable to economic shocks. Much of Staatsolie's windfall profit has been saved and the Government in 2013 proposed legislation to establish a sovereign wealth fund; however, this long-planned proposal came at a point when gold prices were in decline and had not been implemented by mid-2014, while the fiscal balance had also fallen back into deficit from 2012. The IMF in 2012 noted a number of challenges, including the decline in gold prices from recent peaks and a deteriorating fiscal balance. To address these challenges adequately would involve moderating increases in public sector salaries, strengthening the revenue base with implementation of a VAT, improving state regulation of small-scale gold-mining, restraining expenditure to below the rate of growth in nominal GDP, improving the implementation capacity of the Ministry of Public Works and dealing with a complex series of water and electricity supply subsidies.

Statistical Survey

Sources (unless otherwise stated): Algemeen Bureau voor de Statistiek, Klipstenenstraat 5, POB 244, Paramaribo; tel. 474861; fax 425004; e-mail info@statistics-suriname.org; internet www.statistics-suriname.org; Centrale Bank van Suriname, Waterkant 20, Paramaribo; tel. 473741; fax 476444; internet www.cbvs.sr; Ministry of Trade and Industry, Havenlaan 3, POB 9354, Paramaribo; tel. 402080; fax 402602.

AREA AND POPULATION

Area: 163,820 sq km (63,251 sq miles).

Population: 492,829 at census of 2 August 2004; 541,638 (males 270,629, females 271,009) at census of 13 August 2012. *Mid-2014* (estimate): 543,927 (Source: UN, *World Population Prospects: The 2012 Revision*).

Density (at mid-2014): 3.3 per sq km.

Population by Age and Sex (UN estimates at mid-2014): *0–14 years:* 146,343 (males 75,029, females 71,314); *15–64 years:* 361,026 (males 181,930, females 179,096); *65 years and over:* 36,558 (males 15,540, females 21,018); *Total* 543,927 (males 272,499, females 271,428) (Source: UN, *World Population Prospects: The 2012 Revision*).

Population by Ethnic Group (2012 census): Maroon 117,567; Hindustani 148,443; Creole 84,933; Javanese 73,975; Mixed 72,340; Other and undeclared 44,380; *Total* 541,638. Note: Classification of ethnicity reflects national census methodology.

Administrative Districts (population at census of 13 August 2012): Paramaribo 240,924; Wanica 118,222; Nickerie 34,233; Coronie 3,391; Saramacca 17,480; Commewijne 31,420; Marowijne 18,294; Para 24,700; Brokopondo 15,909; Sipaliwini 37,065; *Total* 541,638.

Principal Town (incl. suburbs, UN estimate at mid-2014): Paramaribo (capital) 234,483. Source: UN, *World Urbanization Prospects: The 2014 Revision*.

Births, Marriages and Deaths (2009 unless otherwise indicated): Registered live births 9,792 (birth rate 18.7 per 1,000); Marriages (2007) 2,161 (4.2 per 1,000); Registered deaths 3,293 (death rate 6.3 per 1,000). *2013:* Birth rate 17.7 per 1,000; Death rate 7.3 per 1,000. Sources: UN, *Demographic Yearbook*; Pan American Health Organization.

Life Expectancy (years at birth): 71.0 (males 67.9; females 74.3) in 2013. Source: Pan American Health Organization.

Economically Active Population (persons aged 15–64 years, census of 2004): Agriculture, hunting, forestry and fishing 12,593; Mining and quarrying 9,308; Manufacturing 10,971; Utilities 1,659; Construction 14,031; Trade 25,012; Hotels, restaurants and bars 4,833; Transport, storage and communication 8,711; Financial intermediation 2,723; Real estate, renting and business activities 6,350; Public administration and defence 27,995; Education 8,355; Health and social work 6,797; Other community, social and personal service activities 9,911; *Sub-total* 149,249; Unknown 7,456; *Total employed* 156,705 (males 101,919, females 54,768, unknown 18); Unemployed 16,425; *Total labour force* 173,130. *2012:* Employed 188,229; Unemployed 21,512; Total labour force 209,741.

HEALTH AND WELFARE

Key Indicators

Total Fertility Rate (children per woman, 2013): 2.3.

Under-5 Mortality Rate (per 1,000 live births, 2012): 21.

HIV/AIDS (% of persons aged 15–49, 2012): 1.1.

Physicians (per 1,000 head, 2012): 1.0.

Hospital Beds (per 1,000 head, 2010): 3.1.

Health Expenditure (2011): US $ per head (PPP): 504.

Health Expenditure (2011): % of GDP: 6.0.

Health Expenditure (2011): public (% of total): 49.8.

Access to Water (% of persons, 2012): 95.

Access to Sanitation (% of persons, 2012): 80.

Total Carbon Dioxide Emissions ('000 metric tons, 2010): 2,383.6.

Carbon Dioxide Emissions Per Head (metric tons, 2010): 4.5.

Human Development Index (2013): ranking: 100.

Human Development Index (2013): value: 0.705.

Source: partly Pan American Health Organization; for other sources and definitions, see explanatory note on p. vi.

AGRICULTURE, ETC.

Principal Crops ('000 metric tons, 2012, FAO estimates): Rice, paddy 220; Roots and tubers 4; Sugar cane 120; Coconuts 4; Vegetables 17; Bananas 86; Plantains 13; Oranges 17; Other citrus fruit 2.

Livestock ('000 head, 2012, FAO estimates): Cattle 57; Sheep 8; Goats 6; Pigs 36; Chickens 7,000.

Livestock Products ('000 metric tons, 2012, FAO estimates): Cattle meat 2; Pig meat 2; Chicken meat 10; Cows' milk 7; Hen eggs 1.

Forestry ('000 cu m, 2012): *Roundwood Removals:* Sawlogs, veneer logs and logs for sleepers 432; Other industrial wood 3; Fuel wood 49 (FAO estimate); Total 484 (FAO estimate). *Sawnwood Production:* Total (incl. railway sleepers) 138.

Fishing ('000 metric tons, 2012, FAO estimates): Capture 36.6 (Marine fishes 24.6; Penaeus shrimps 0.5; Atlantic seabob 7.6); Aquaculture 0.1; *Total catch* 36.7.

Source: FAO.

MINING

Selected Products (2011): Crude petroleum ('000 barrels) 5,840; Bauxite 3,236 ('000 metric tons); Gold (Au content, kg) 21,000 (estimate). Sources: US Geological Survey.

INDUSTRY

Selected Products ('000 metric tons, 2010, unless otherwise indicated): Gold-bearing ores 16,500 (kg, 2009); Gravel and crushed stone 85 (2002); Distillate fuel oil 56; Residual fuel oils 779; Cement 65 (2004); Alumina 1,536 (2009); Beer of barley 30 (2012, FAO estimate); Coconut oil 0.40 (2012, FAO estimate); Palm oil 0.24 (2012, FAO estimate); Cigarettes 483 (million, 1996); Plywood 3 (2011, '000 cubic metres); Electricity 1,634 (million kWh). Sources: mainly UN Industrial Commodity Statistics Database and FAO.

FINANCE

Currency and Exchange Rates: 100 cents = 1 Surinamese dollar. *Sterling, Dollar and Euro Equivalents* (30 May 2014): £1 sterling = 5.551 Surinamese dollars; US $1 = 3.300 Surinamese dollars; €1 = 4.492 Surinamese dollars; 100 Surinamese dollars = £18.01 = US $30.30 = €22.26. *Average Exchange Rate* (Surinamese dollars per US $): 3.268 in 2011; 3.300 in 2012; 3.300 in 2013. *Note:* Between 1971 and 1993 the official market rate was US $1 = Surinamese 1.785 guilders. A new free market rate was introduced in June 1993, and a unified, market-determined rate took effect in July 1994. A mid-point rate of US $1 = 401.0 guilders was in effect between September 1996 and January 1999. A new currency, the Surinamese dollar, was introduced on 1 January 2004, and was equivalent to 1,000 old guilders.

Budget (million Surinamese dollars, 2013, preliminary): *Revenue:* Direct taxation 1,686.6; Indirect taxation 1,447.1; Non-tax revenue 826.6; Total 3,960.2. *Expenditure:* Wages and salaries 1,565.9; Subsidies and transfers 1,038.6; Goods and services 1,135.7; Interest payments 232.2; Capital 756.0; Total 4,728.4.

International Reserves (US $ million at 31 December 2013): Gold (national valuation) 40.35; IMF special drawing rights 125.17; Reserve position in IMF 9.43; Foreign exchange 600.46; *Total* 775.41. Source: IMF, *International Financial Statistics*.

Money Supply ('000 Surinamese dollars at 31 December 2013): Currency outside depository corporations 865,815; Transferable deposits 3,582,577; Other deposits 4,519,430; Securities other than shares 42,225; *Broad money* 9,010,047. Source: IMF, *International Financial Statistics*.

Cost of Living (Consumer Price Index for Paramaribo area; base: April–June 2009 = 100): 127.5 in 2011; 133.9 in 2012; 136.5 in 2013.

Gross Domestic Product (million Surinamese dollars at constant 2007 prices, preliminary): 9,490 in 2011; 9,858 in 2012; 10,296 in 2013.

Expenditure on the Gross Domestic Product (million Surinamese dollars at current prices, 2012): Government final consumption expenditure 2,053; Private final consumption expenditure 6,954; Gross capital formation 6,586; Changes in inventories –234; *Total domestic expenditure* 15,360; Exports of goods and non-factor services 9,051; *Less* Imports of goods and non-factor services 6,668; Statistical discrepancy –1,204; *GDP in purchasers' values* 16,540. Source: UN National Accounts Main Aggregates Database.

Gross Domestic Product by Economic Activity (million Surinamese dollars at current prices, 2013, preliminary): Agriculture, hunting, forestry and fishing 1,613; Mining and quarrying 1,014; Manufacturing 3,187; Electricity, gas and water supply 356; Construction 1,081; Wholesale and retail trade 3,420; Hotels and restaurants 481; Transport, storage and communications 1,227; Financial intermediation 991; Real estate, renting and business activities 518; Education 12; Health and social work 93; Other services 1,814; *Sub-total* 15,807; Net of indirect taxes 1,455; *GDP in purchasers' values* 17,262.

Balance of Payments (US $ million, 2013): Exports of goods 2,394.8; Imports of goods –2,125.6; *Balance on goods* 269.2; Exports of services 172.2; Imports of services –583.7; *Balance on goods and services* –142.4; Primary income received 27.1; Primary income paid –149.2; *Balance on goods, services and primary income* –264.4; Secondary income received 153.2; Secondary income paid –86.6; *Current balance* –197.9; Capital account (net) 0.1; Direct investment assets 0.8; Direct investment liabilities 112.0; Portfolio investment assets –1.2; Other investment assets 43.9; Other investment liabilities 206.7; Net errors and omissions –315.5; *Reserves and related items* –151.0. Source: IMF, *International Financial Statistics*.

EXTERNAL TRADE

Principal Commodities (distribution by HS, US $ million, 2011): *Imports c.i.f.:* Prepared foodstuff, beverages and tobacco 137.8; Mineral fuels, lubricants, etc. 420.9; Chemicals 200.5; Plastic, rubber and their article 87.0; Iron and steel, base metals and their articles 113.3; Machinery and mechanical appliances 298.7; Transport and transport equipment 113.3; Total (incl. others) 1,637.8. *Exports f.o.b.:* Vegetable products 37.6; Prepared foodstuff, beverages and tobacco 48.7; Mineral fuels, lubricants, etc. 221.0; Machinery and mechanical appliances 50.1; Total (incl. others) 2,466.9. Source: Trade Map-Trade Competitiveness Map, International Trade Centre, www.intracen.org/marketanalysis.

Principal Trading Partners (US $ million, 2011): *Imports c.i.f.:* Antigua and Barbuda 19.6; Brazil 52.9; China, People's Republic 106.6; Colombia 22.2; Dominican Republic 17.3; Japan 42.0; Netherlands Antilles 17.5; Netherlands 262.5; Panama 21.4; Trinidad and Tobago 416.1; USA 437.1; Total (incl. others) 1,637.8. *Exports f.o.b.:* Barbados 97.8; Belgium 250.7; Canada 458.2; France (incl. Monaco) 37.8; Guyana 137.5; Jamaica 40.5; Netherlands 37.9; Norway 85.0; Switzerland-Liechtenstein 231.1; Trinidad and Tobago 58.6; United Arab Emirates 643.0; USA 276.2; Total (incl. others) 2,466.9. Source: Trade Map-Trade Competitiveness Map, International Trade Centre, www.intracen.org/marketanalysis.

TRANSPORT

Road Traffic (registered motor vehicles, 2010): Passenger cars 119,270; Buses and coaches 3,022; Lorries and vans 30,117; Motorcycles and mopeds 45,013 (Source: IRF, *World Road Statistics*).

Shipping: *Flag Registered Fleet* (at 31 December 2013): Number of vessels 10; Total displacement 4,866 grt. Source: (Lloyd's List Intelligence (www.lloydslistintelligence.com).

Civil Aviation (traffic on scheduled services, 2011): Kilometres flown (million) 5; Passengers carried ('000) 204; Passenger-km (million) 1,000; Total ton-km (million) 114. *2013:* Passengers carried 259,070. Sources: UN, *Statistical Yearbook*; World Bank, World Development Indicators database.

TOURISM

Tourist Arrivals (number of non-resident arrivals at national borders, '000): 220.0 in 2011; 240.0 in 2012; 249.0 in 2013 (provisional).

Tourism Receipts (US $ million, excl. passenger transport): 61 in 2011; 71 in 2012; 84 in 2013 (provisional).

Source: World Tourism Organization.

COMMUNICATIONS MEDIA

Telephones (2013): 84,941 main lines in use.

Mobile Cellular Telephones (2013): 686,600 subscribers.

Internet Subscribers (2011, preliminary): 24,200.

Broadband Subscribers (2013): 37,095.

Source: International Telecommunication Union.

EDUCATION

Pre-primary (2010/11): 722 teachers; 17,910 pupils.

Primary (2010/11 unless otherwise stated, incl. special education): 308 schools (2001/02); 4,697 teachers; 71,606 pupils.

Secondary (2010/11 unless otherwise stated, incl. teacher-training): 141 schools (2001/02); 4,334 teachers; 55,431 pupils.

University (2001/02): 1 institution; 350 teachers; 3,250 students.

Other Higher (2001/02): 3 institutions; 200 teachers; 1,936 students.

Pupil-teacher Ratio (primary education, UNESCO estimate): 15.2 in 2010/11.

Adult Literacy Rate (UNESCO estimates): 94.7% (males 95.4%; females 94.0%) in 2010.

Source: mainly UNESCO Institute for Statistics.

Directory

The Constitution

The 1987 Constitution was approved by the National Assembly on 31 March and by 93% of voters in a national referendum in September.

THE LEGISLATURE

Legislative power is exercised jointly by the National Assembly and the Government. The National Assembly comprises 51 members, elected for a five-year term by universal adult suffrage. The Assembly elects a President and a Vice-President and has the right of amendment in any proposal of law by the Government. The approval of a majority of at least two-thirds of the number of members of the National Assembly is required for the amendment of the Constitution, the election of the President or the Vice-President, the decision to organize a plebiscite and a People's Congress and for the amendment of electoral law. If it is unable to obtain a two-thirds' majority following two rounds of voting, the Assembly may convene a United People's Assembly (Verenigde Volksvergadering) and supplement its numbers with members of local councils. The approval by a simple majority is sufficient in the United People's Assembly.

THE EXECUTIVE

Executive authority is vested in the President, who is elected for a term of five years as Head of State, Head of Government, Head of the Armed Forces, Chairman of the Council of State, the Cabinet of Ministers and the Security Council.

The Government comprises the President, the Vice-President and the Cabinet of Ministers. The Cabinet of Ministers is appointed by the President from among the members of the National Assembly. The Vice-President is the Prime Minister and leader of the Cabinet, and is responsible to the President.

In the event of war, a state of siege, or exceptional circumstances to be determined by law, a Security Council assumes all government functions.

THE COUNCIL OF STATE

The Council of State comprises the President (its Chairman) and 14 additional members, composed of two representatives of the combined trade unions, one representative of the associations of employers, one representative of the National Army and 10 representatives of the political parties in the National Assembly. Its duties are to advise the President and the legislature and to supervise the correct execution by the Government of the decisions of the National Assembly. The Council may present proposals of law or of general administrative measures to the Government. The Council has the authority to suspend any legislation approved by the National Assembly which, in the opinion of the Council, is in violation of the Constitution. In this event, the President must decide within one month whether or not to ratify the Council's decision.

The Government

HEAD OF STATE

President: DESIRÉ (DESI) DELANO BOUTERSE (took office 12 August 2010).

Council of State: Chair. DESIRÉ (DESI) DELANO BOUTERSE (President of the Republic); 14 mems; 10 to represent the political parties in the National Assembly, one for the National Army, two for the trade unions and one for employers.

CABINET OF MINISTERS
(September 2014)

The Government is formed by members of the Megacombinatie (MC), A-Combinatie (AC) and Volksalliantie (VA) alliances, and Independents.

Vice-President: ROBERT AMEERALI (Ind.).

Minister of Foreign Affairs: WINSTON LACKIN (MC).

Minister of Finance: ANDOJO (ANDY) RUSLAND (MC).

Minister of Defence: LAMURÉ LATOUR (MC).

Minister of Home Affairs: EDMUND LEILIS.

Minister of Sport and Youth Affairs: ISMANTO ADNA (MC).

Minister of Agriculture, Animal Husbandry and Fisheries: SOERESH ALGOE.

Minister of Transport, Communications and Tourism: FALISIE PINAS (AC).

Minister of Public Works: RABINDRE T. PARMESSAR (Ind.).

Minister of Social Affairs and Housing: ALICE AMAFO (AC).

Minister of Trade and Industry: DON SOEJIT TOSENDJOJO.

Minister of Regional Development: STANLEY BETTERSON (AC).

Minister of Education and Community Development: ASHWIN ADHIN (Ind.).

Minister of Health: MICHAEL BLOKLAND (MC).

Minister of Labour, Technological Development and the Environment: MICHAEL MISKIN (MC).

Minister of Natural Resources: JIM HOK (MC).

Minister of Physical Planning, Land and Forestry Management: STEVEN RELYVELD (MC).

Minister of Justice and the Police: EDWARD BELFORT (AC).

MINISTRIES

Office of the President: Kleine Combêweg 2–4, Centrum, Paramaribo; tel. 472841; fax 475266; e-mail secretariaat@president.gov .sr; internet www.kabinet.sr.org.

Office of the Vice-President: Dr Sophie Redmondstraat 118, Frank Essed Gebouw, Paramaribo; tel. 474805; fax 472917; e-mail kabinet@vicepresident.gov.sr; internet www.gov.sr/sr/ kabinet-van-de-vice-president.aspx.

Ministry of Agriculture, Animal Husbandry and Fisheries: Letitia Vriesdelaan 8–10, Paramaribo; tel. 479112; fax 470301; e-mail minlvvv@sr.net; internet www.gov.sr/sr/ministerie-van-lvv .aspx.

Ministry of Defence: Kwattaweg 29, Paramaribo; tel. 471511; fax 420055; e-mail defensie@sr.net; internet www.gov.sr/sr/ ministerie-van-defensie.aspx.

Ministry of Education and Community Development: Dr Samuel Kafiluddistraat 117–123, Paramaribo; tel. 498383; fax 495083; e-mail minond@sr.net; internet www.gov.sr/sr/ ministerie-van-onderwijs-en-volksontwikkeling.aspx.

Ministry of Finance: Tamarindelaan 3, Paramaribo; tel. 472610; fax 476314; e-mail secmin@finance.gov.sr; internet www.gov.sr/sr/ ministerie-van-financien.aspx.

Ministry of Foreign Affairs: Henck Aaronstraat 8, Paramaribo; tel. 471209; fax 410411; e-mail sec.minister@foreignaffairs.gov.sr; internet www.gov.sr/sr/ministerie-van-buza/contact.aspx.

Ministry of Health: Henck Arronstraat 64, POB 201, Paramaribo; tel. 474941; fax 410702; e-mail vogez@sr.net; internet www.gov.sr/sr/ ministerie-van-volksgezondheid.aspx.

Ministry of Home Affairs: Wilhelminastraat 3, Paramaribo; tel. 473141; fax 421170; e-mail minbiza@sr.net; internet www.gov.sr/sr/ ministerie-van-biza.aspx.

Ministry of Justice and the Police: Henck Arronstraat 1, Paramaribo; tel. 427197; fax 412109; e-mail min.jus-pol@sr.net; internet www.gov.sr/sr/ministerie-van-juspol.aspx.

Ministry of Labour, Technological Development and the Environment: Wageswegstraat 22, POB 911, Paramaribo; tel. 475241; fax 410465; e-mail voorlichting@atm.sr.org; internet www .atm.sr.org.

Ministry of Natural Resources: Dr J. C. de Mirandastraat 13–15, Paramaribo; tel. 474666; fax 472911; e-mail minnh@sr.net; internet www.gov.sr/sr/ministerie-van-nh.aspx.

Ministry of Physical Planning, Land and Forestry Management: Cornelis Jongbawstraat 10–12, Paramaribo; tel. 470700; fax

470876; e-mail mpjong@datsunsuriname.com; internet www.gov.sr/ sr/ministerie-van-rgb.aspx.

Ministry of Public Works: Verlengde Jagernath Lachmonstraat 167, Paramaribo; tel. 490666; fax 464901; e-mail voorlichting@ publicworks.gov.sr; internet www.gov.sr/sr/ ministerie-van-openbare-werken.aspx.

Ministry of Regional Development: Van Rooseveltkade 2, Paramaribo; tel. 471574; fax 424517; e-mail regon@sr.net; internet www .gov.sr/sr/ministerie-van-ro.aspx.

Ministry of Social Affairs and Housing: Waterkant 30, Paramaribo; tel. 472340; fax 470516; e-mail soza@sr.net; internet www .gov.sr/sr/ministerie-van-sozavo.aspx.

Ministry of Sport and Youth Affairs: Directorate of Sports, Dr Samuel Kaffiludistraat 117, Paramaribo; tel. 499021; fax 498662; Directorate of Youth Affairs, Prince Hendrikstraat 11, Paramaribo; tel. 473411; fax 477827; e-mail dir-jeugdzaken@sr.netinternet www .gov.sr/sr/ministerie-van-sport-en-jeugdzaken.aspx.

Ministry of Trade and Industry: Havenlaan 3, POB 9354, Paramaribo; tel. 402080; fax 402602; e-mail hi.voorlichting@minhi.gov .sr; internet www.gov.sr/sr/ministerie-van-hi.aspx.

Ministry of Transport, Communications and Tourism: Prins Hendrikstraat 26–28, Paramaribo; tel. 420905; fax 420100; e-mail secretariaatdirecteur@tct.gov.sr; internet www.tct.gov.sr.

Legislature
NATIONAL ASSEMBLY

Chairman: JENNIFER SIMONS.
General Election, 25 May 2010

Party	% of votes cast	Seats
Megacombinatie (MC)*	40.22	23
Nieuw Front (NF)†	31.65	14
A-Combinatie (AC)‡	4.70	7
Volksalliantie§	12.98	6
Partij voor Demokratie en Ontwikkeling in Eenheid (DOE)	5.09	1
Basispartij voor Vernieuwing en Democratie/ Politieke Vleugel van de FAL (BVD/PVF)	5.07	—
Other parties	0.29	—
Total	100.00	51

* An alliance of the Kerukunan Tulodo Pranatan Inggil (KTPI), the Nationale Democratische Partij (NDP), the Nieuw Suriname (NS) and the Progressieve Arbeiders en Landbouwers Unie (PALU).

† An alliance of the Nationale Partij Suriname (NPS), the Surinaamse Partij van de Arbeid (SPA) and the Vooruitstrevende Hervormings Partij (VHP).

‡ Including candidates of the Algemene Bevrijdings- en Ontwikkelingspartij (ABOP) and the Broederschap en Eenheid in Politiek (BEP).

§ An alliance of the Democraten van de 21, Pertijajah Luhur (PL), the Progressieve Surinaamse Volkspartij (PSV) and the Unie van Progressieve Surinamers (UPS).

Election Commission

Centraal Hoofdstembureau (CHS) (Central Polling Authority): Wilhelminastraat 3, Paramaribo; tel. 410362; independent; Chair. (vacant).

Political Organizations

A-Combinatie (AC): Paramaribo; alliance including:

Algemene Bevrijdings- en Ontwikkelingspartij (ABOP) (General Liberation and Development Party): Jaguarstraat 15, Paramaribo; tel. 486886; e-mail webmaster@abop-suriname.net; internet www.abop-suriname.net; f. 1990; Pres. RONNIE BRUNSWIJK; Sec. CARLO ADA.

Seeka: Paramaribo; Chair. PAUL ABENA.

Basispartij voor Vernieuwing en Democratie (BVD) (Base Party for Renewal and Democracy): Hoogestraat 28–30, Paramaribo; tel. 422231; e-mail info@bvdsuriname.org; contested the 2010 election in coalition with the Politiek Vleugel van de FAL (PVF); new faction De Nieuwe Leeuw (DNL) created after split in 2012, led by Dharm Mungra; Chair. DHARMVIR KARAMCHAND MUNGRA; Sec. ANUSHKA GOPALRAJ.

Broederschap en Eenheid in Politiek (BEP): Theodorusstraat 55, Land van Dijk, Paramaribo; tel. 402509; fax 422996; e-mail info@bep.sr; internet beppartij.org; f. 1957 as Maroon Party Suriname (MPS); name changed as above in 1987; contested the 2010 elections as part of the A-Combinatie alliance; left the alliance in 2012; Chair. CELSIUS WATERBERG; Sec. WENSLEY MISIEDJAN.

Megacombinatie (MC) (Mega Combination): Paramaribo; Leader DESIRÉ (DESI) DELANO BOUTERSE; alliance formed to contest the 2010 election, comprising:.**Kerukunan Tulodo Pranatan Ingit (KTPI)** (Party for National Unity and Solidarity): Bonistraat 64, Geyersvlijt, Paramaribo; tel. 456116; f. 1949 as the Kaum Tani Persatuan Indonesia; largely Indonesian; Leader WILLY SOEMITA; Sec. ROBBY DRAGMAN.

Nationale Democratische Partij (NDP) (National Democratic Party): Dr H. D. Benjaminstraat 38, Paramaribo; tel. 499183; fax 432174; e-mail ndpsur@sr.net; internet www.ndp.sr; f. 1987 by Standvaste (the 25 February Movt); army-supported; Chair. DESIRÉ (DESI) DELANO BOUTERSE; Sec. CAROLINE HEILBRON.

Progressieve Arbeiders en Landbouwers Unie (PALU) (Progressive Workers' and Farmers' Union): Dr S. Kafiluddistraat 27, Paramaribo; tel. 400115; e-mail palu.suriname@gmail.com; internet www.palu-suriname.org; f. 1977; socialist party; Chair. JIM K. HOK; Vice-Chair. HENK R. RAMNANDANLAL.

Nationale Unie (NU): Postbus 5193, Paramaribo; tel. 499675; fax 499678; e-mail info@nationaleunie.net; internet www.nationaleunie.net; f. 1991; Leader MAHIN JANKIE; Chair. SOENIEL DEWKALI (acting).

Nieuw Front (NF) (New Front): Paramaribo; f. 1987 as Front voor Demokratie en Ontwikkeling (FDO—Front for Democracy and Devt); name changed as above in 1991; Pres. RUNALDO R. VENETIAAN; an alliance comprising:

Democratisch Alternatief 1991 (DA '91) (Democratic Alternative 1991): Gladiolenstraat 17, POB 91, Paramaribo; tel. 432342; fax 493121; e-mail info@da91.sr; f. 1991 as the Alternatief Forum (AF); social democratic; Chair. WINSTON JESSURUN; Sec. WILFRIED MEYER.

Nationale Partij Suriname (NPS) (Suriname National Party): Grun Dyari, Johan Adolf Pengelstraat 77, Paramaribo; tel. 477302; fax 475796; e-mail nps@sr.net; internet www.nps.sr; f. 1946; predominantly Creole; Pres. Dr GREGORY RUSLAND; Sec. S. OEMRAWSINGH.

Surinaamse Partij van de Arbeid (SPA) (Suriname Labour Party): Rust en Vredestraat 64, Paramaribo; tel. 425912; fax 420394; f. 1987; affiliated with C-47 trade union; social democratic party; joined NF in 1991; Chair. GUNO CASTELEN; Sec.-Gen. ROY ADEMA.

Vooruitstrevende Hervormings Partij (VHP) (Progressive Reform Party): De Olifant, Jagernath Lachmonstraat, Paramaribo; tel. 494497; fax 434158; e-mail Info@vhp.sr; internet www.vhp.sr; f. 1949 as Verenigde Hindostaanse Partij; name changed as above in 1973; leading left-wing party; predominantly Indian; Leader CHANDRIKAPERSAD SANTOKHI; Sec. GANESHKOEMAR KANDHAI.

Nieuw Suriname (NS) (New Suriname): Paramaribo; f. 2003; fmr mem. of the Megacombinatie, left the alliance in 2012; Pres. JOHN NASIBDAR; Sec. SAFIEK JAHANGIER.

Partij voor Demokratie en Ontwikkeling in Eenheid (DOE) (Party for Democracy and Development in Unity): Prinsenstraat 47, Hoek Waaldijkstraat, Paramaribo; tel. 491701; e-mail info@doepartij.org; internet www.doepartij.org; f. 1999; Chair. CARL BREEVELD; Sec. PAUL BRANDON.

Pendawa Lima: Bonistraat 115, Geyersvlij, Paramaribo; tel. 551802; f. 1977; predominantly Indonesian; Chair. RAYMOND SAPOEN; Sec. RANDY KROMODIHARDJO.

Permanente Voorspoed Republiek Suriname (PVRS) (Lasting Prosperity Party of Suriname): Engelslootstraat 8, Projectsloot, Paramaribo; tel. 493928; e-mail info@nieuwpvrs.com; internet www.nieuwpvrs.com; Chair. CHAS MIJNALS.

Politieke Vleugel van de FAL (PVF): Keizerstraat 150, Paramaribo; f. 1995; political wing of farmers' org. Federatie van Agrariërs en Landarbeiders; contested the 2010 election in coalition with the Basispartij voor Vernieuwing en Democratie (BVD); Chair. SOEDESCHAND JAIRAM; Sec. RADJOE BIKHARIE.

Volksalliantie (People's Alliance): Paramaribo; alliance formed to contest the 2010 election; Leader PAUL SALAM SOMOHARDJO; comprising:

Democraten van de 21 (D21) (Democrats of the 21st Century): Goudstraat 22, Paramaribo; f. 1996; Chair. SOEWARTO MOESTADJA; Sec. KANIMAN PASIRAN.

Pertjajah Luhur (PL) (Full Confidence Party): Hoek Gemenlandsweg-Daniel Coutinhostraat, Paramaribo; tel.

401087; fax 420394; internet www.pertijajahluhur.org; f. 1998; withdrew its support for the governing coalition in 2014; Pres. PAUL SALAM SOMOHARDJO.

Progressieve Surinaamse Volkspartij (PSV) (Suriname Progressive People's Party): Keizerstraat 122, Paramaribo; tel. 472979; internet www.psv.sr; f. 1947; resumed political activities 1987; Christian democratic party; Chair. JOHN COURTAR.

Unie van Progressieve Surinamers (UPS): Keizerstraat 122, Paramaribo; tel. 472979; f. 2004; Chair. HENRI ORI.

Diplomatic Representation

EMBASSIES IN SURINAME

Brazil: Maratakkastraat 2, Zorg en Hoop, POB 925, Paramaribo; tel. 400200; fax 400205; e-mail brasemb.paramaribo@itamaraty.gov.br; internet paramaribo.itamaraty.gov.br; Ambassador MARCELO BAUMBACH.

China, People's Republic: Anton Dragtenweg 154, POB 3042, Paramaribo; tel. 451570; fax 452540; e-mail chinaemb_sr@mfa.gov.cn; internet sr.chineseembassy.org; Ambassador YANG ZIGANG.

Cuba: Brokopondolaan 4, Paramaribo; tel. 434917; fax 432626; e-mail embajadacubasuriname@gmail.com; internet www.cubadiplomatica.cu/suriname; Ambassador JULIO ARMANDO SOLÍS FERREIRO.

France: Dr J. F. Nassylaan 23, POB 2648, Paramaribo; tel. 475222; fax 427301; e-mail ambafrance.paramaribo@diplomatie.gouv.fr; internet www.ambafrance-sr.org; Ambassador MICHEL PROM.

Guyana: Henckarronstraat 82, POB 785, Paramaribo; tel. 477895; fax 472679; e-mail guyembassy@sr.net; Ambassador KEITH GEORGE.

India: Dr Sophie Redmondstraat 239, POB 1329, Paramaribo; tel. 498344; fax 491106; e-mail india@sr.net; internet www.indembassysuriname.com; Ambassador M. SUBASHINI.

Indonesia: Van Brussellaan 3, Uitvlugt, POB 157, Paramaribo; tel. 431230; fax 498234; e-mail indonemb@sr.net; internet paramaribo.kemlu.go.id; Ambassador NUR SYAHRIR RAHARDJO.

Netherlands: Van Roseveltkade 5, POB 1877, Paramaribo; tel. 477211; fax 477792; e-mail prm@minbuza.nl; internet www.nederlandseambassade.sr; Chargé d'affaires a.i. ERNST NOORMAN.

USA: Dr Sophie Redmondstraat 129, POB 1821, Paramaribo; tel. 472900; fax 472900; e-mail embuscen@sr.net; internet suriname.usembassy.gov; Ambassador JAY NICHOLAS ANANIA.

Venezuela: Henck Arronstraat 23–25, POB 3001, Paramaribo; tel. 475401; fax 475602; e-mail embve.srprm@mppre.gob.ve; internet suriname.embajada.gob.ve; Ambassador OLGA DÍAZ MARTÍNEZ.

Judicial System

The administration of justice is entrusted to a Court of Justice, the six members of which are nominated for life, and three Cantonal Courts. Suriname recognizes the Caribbean Court of Justice (CCJ) on matters of original jurisdiction pertaining to international trade. The CCJ was inaugurated in Trinidad and Tobago in April 2005.

President of the Court of Justice: CYNTHIA VALSTEIN-MONTNOR.

Attorney-General: SUBHAS PUNWASI.

Religion

CHRISTIANITY

According to the 2012 census, Christians represent approximately 48% of the population.

Committee of Christian Churches: Paramaribo; tel. 476306; Chair. (vacant).

The Roman Catholic Church

For ecclesiastical purposes, Suriname comprises the single diocese of Paramaribo, suffragan to the archdiocese of Port of Spain (Trinidad and Tobago). The Bishop participates in the Antilles Episcopal Conference (currently based in Port of Spain, Trinidad and Tobago). Some 22% of the population are Roman Catholics, according to the 2012 census.

Bishop of Paramaribo: (vacant), Bisschopshuis, Henck Arronstraat 12, POB 1230, Paramaribo; tel. 426092; fax 471602; e-mail s.tjonpoengie@bisdomparamaribo.org; internet www.bisdomparamaribo.org.

The Anglican Communion

Within the Church in the Province of the West Indies, Suriname forms part of the diocese of Guyana. The Bishop is resident in Georgetown, Guyana. The Episcopal Church is also represented.

Protestant Churches

Evangelisch Lutherse Kerk in Suriname: Waterkant 102, POB 585, Paramaribo; tel. and fax 476782; e-mail marymolgo@hotmail .com; f. 1741; Pres. MARYAN MOLGO; 4,000 mems.

Moravian Church in Suriname (Evangelische Broeder Gemeente): Maagdenstraat 50, POB 1811, Paramaribo; tel. 473073; fax 475794; e-mail ebgs@sr.net; internet www .moravianchurch.sr; f. 1735; Bishop JOHN KENT; 40,000 mems (2004).

Adherents to the Moravian Church and Pentecostalist Churches each constitute some 11% of the population. Also represented are the Christian Reformed Church, the Dutch Reformed Church, the Baptist Church, the Evangelical Methodist Church, Pentecostal Missions, the Seventh-day Adventists and the Wesleyan Methodist Congregation.

HINDUISM

According to the 2012 census, around 22% of the population are Hindus.

Arya Dewaker: Johan Adolf Pengelstraat 210, Paramaribo; tel. 400706; e-mail aryadewaker@sr.net; members preach the Vedic Dharma; disciples of Maha Rishi Swami Dayanand Sarswati, the founder of the Arya Samaj in India; f. 1929; Chair. INDERDATH TILAKDHARIE.

Sanatan Dharm: Commissaris Roblesweg 1299, Paramaribo; tel. 450264; e-mail info@ssdp-sr.org; internet www.ssdp-sr.org; f. 1930; Sec. A. V. SOEKNANDAN; over 150,000 mems.

Shri Krishna Mandir Sanatan Dharam: Jagernath Lachmanstraat 44, Paramaribo; tel. 499484; fax 491622; e-mail krishna@sr .net; internet www.krishnadham.com; f. 1979; Chair. Pandit KRISHNA SHARMA MATHOERAPERSAD.

ISLAM

Some 14% of the population are Muslims, according to the 2012 census.

Federatie Islamitische Gemeenten in Suriname: Paramaribo; Indonesian Islamic org.; Chair. K. KAAIMAN.

Stichting der Islamitische Gemeenten Suriname: Verlengde Mahonielaan 39, Paramaribo; Indonesian Islamic org.

Surinaamse Islamitische Organisatie (SIO): Watermolenstraat 10, POB 278, Paramaribo; tel. 475220; fax 472075; e-mail ijamaludin@hotmail.com; f. 1978; Pres. Dr I. JAMALUDIN; Sec. Dr K. M. MOENNE; 6 brs.

Surinaamse Islamitische Vereniging (SIV): Keizerstraat 88, Paramaribo; tel. 473849; e-mail sivsr.org@gmail.com; internet www.sivsr.org; f. 1929.

Surinaamse Moeslim Associatie: Kankantriestraat 32–40, Paramaribo; tel. and fax 406467; internet www.sma.sr; Javanese Islamic org.

JUDAISM

The Dutch Jewish Congregation and the Dutch Portuguese-Jewish Congregation are represented in Suriname.

Jewish Community: The Synagogue Neve Shalom, Keizerstraat, POB 1834, Paramaribo; tel. 400236; fax 402380; e-mail rene-fernandes@cq-link.sr; internet ujcl.org; f. 1854; mem. of Union of Jewish Congregations of Latin America and the Caribbean; Officiant JACQUES VAN NIEL; 300 mems (2005).

The Press

DAILIES

Dagblad Suriname: Zwartenhovenbrugstraat 154, POB 975, Paramaribo; tel. 426336; fax 471718; e-mail general@dbsuriname.com; internet www.dbsuriname.com; f. 2002; Dir FARIED PIERKHAN; Editor JAMES LALMOHAMED.

De Ware Tijd: Malebatrumstraat 9–11, POB 1200, Paramaribo; tel. 472823; fax 411169; e-mail dwt@dwt.net; internet www.dwtonline .com; f. 1957; morning; Dutch; independent/liberal; Asst Dir FABIENNE SPONG; Editor-in-Chief MEREDITH HELSTONE.

De West: Dr J. C. de Mirandastraat 2–6, POB 176, Paramaribo; tel. 471249; fax 470322; e-mail dewest@sr.net; internet www .dewest-online.com; f. 1909; midday; Dutch; liberal; Editor GEORGE D. C. FINDLAY; circ. 15,000–18,000.

PERIODICAL

Kerkbode: Burenstraat 17–19, POB 219, Paramaribo; tel. 473079; fax 475635; e-mail stadje@sr.net; f. 1906; weekly; religious; CEO CONSTAN LANDVREUGD; circ. 1,200.

Publishers

Afaka International NV: Residastraat 23, Paramaribo; tel. and fax 530640; e-mail info@afaka.biz; internet www.afaka.net; f. 1996; Dir GERRIT BARRON.

IMWO, Universiteit van Suriname: Universiteitscomplex, Leysweg 86, POB 9212, Paramaribo; tel. 462003; fax 439100; e-mail imwo@sr.net; internet www.uvs.edu; f. 1987; Dir Dr EDGAR AKRUM.

Okopipi Publ. (Publishing Services Suriname): Van Idsingastraat 133, Paramaribo; tel. 472746; e-mail pssmoniz@sr.net; fmrly I. Krishnadath.

Papaya Media Counseling: Hendrikstraat 2, POB 8304, Paramaribo; tel. and fax 432041; e-mail roy_bhikharie@sr.net; f. 2002; Man. Dir ROY BHIKHARIE.

Stichting Wetenschappelijke Informatie (Foundation for Information and Development): Prins Hendrikstraat 38, Paramaribo; tel. 475232; fax 422195; e-mail swin@sr.net; internet www.swi77.org; f. 1977; Chair. JACK MENKE.

VACO, NV: Domineestraat 26, POB 1841, Paramaribo; tel. 472545; fax 410563; internet www.vaco.sr; f. 1952; Dir EDUARD HOGENBOOM.

Broadcasting and Communications

TELECOMMUNICATIONS

Digicel Suriname: Henck Arronstraat 27–29, POB 1848, Paramaribo; tel. 462626; fax 475502; e-mail customer.caresuriname@ digicelgroup.com; internet www.digicelsuriname.com; f. 2007; Chair. DENIS O'BRIEN; CEO (Suriname) HANS LUTE.

Telesur (Telecommunication Corporation Suriname): Heiligenweg 14, POB 1839, Paramaribo; tel. 473944; fax 421919; internet www .telesur.sr; liberalization of the telecommunications sector ended Telesur's monopoly in 2007; supervisory function of Telesur assumed by Telecommunications Authority Suriname; Chair. ADOLFINA CAIRO; Man. Dir DIRK CURRIE.

Uniqa (IntelSur/UTS): Bonistraat 114, Paramaribo; tel. 459802; fax 459801; e-mail info@uniqa.sr; internet www.uniqa.sr; f. 2007; jt venture between UTS, NV and Intelsur, NV; CEO RUSSEL BERNADINA.

Regulatory Authority

Telecommunications Authority Suriname (TAS): Lalla Rookhweg 228, POB 3013, Paramaribo; tel. 532523; fax 497411; e-mail dsecretariaat@tas.sr; internet www.tas.sr; f. 2007; Dir G. GADDEN-AMELO (acting).

BROADCASTING

Radio

ABC Radio (Ampie's Broadcasting Corporation): Maystraat 57, Paramaribo; tel. 464609; fax 464680; e-mail info@abcsuriname .com; internet www.abcsuriname.com; f. 1975; reopened in 1993; commercial; Dutch and some local languages; Man. JOHNNY KAMPERVEEN.

Radika Radio & TV: Indira Gandhiweg 165, Paramaribo; tel. 482800; fax 482910; e-mail radika@sr.net; internet www.radikartv .com; f. 1962; re-opened in 1989; Dutch and Hindi; Dir ROSHNI RADHAKISHUN.

Radio Apintie: Verlengde Gemenelandsweg 37, POB 595, Paramaribo; tel. 400500; fax 400684; e-mail apintie@sr.net; internet www .apintie.sr; f. 1958; commercial; Dutch and some local languages; Dir CHARLES VERVUURT.

Radio Bersama: Bonnistraat 115, Paramaribo; tel. 551802; fax 551803; internet www.radio-bersama.com; f. 1997; Gen. Man. AJOEB MOENTARI.

Radio Boskopu: Roseveltkade 1, Paramaribo; tel. 410300; govt-owned; Sranang Tongo and Dutch; Head LEO VAN VARSSEVELD.

Radio Nickerie (RANI): Waterloostraat 3, Nieuw Nickerie; tel. 231462; commercial; Hindi and Dutch.

Radio Paramaribo (Rapar): Verlengde Jagernath Lachmonstraat 34, POB 975, Paramaribo; tel. 499995; fax 493121; e-mail rapar@sr .net; f. 1957; commercial; Dutch and some local languages; Dir FARIED PIERKHAN.

Radio Sangeet Mala: Indira Gandhiweg 40, Paramaribo; tel. 485893; e-mail info@sgmsuriname.com; internet www .sgmsuriname.com; f. 1998; Dutch and Hindi; Dirs RADJEN SOEKHRADJ, SOEDESH RAMSARAN.

Radio SRS (Stichting Radio Omroep Suriname): Jacques van Eerstraat 20, POB 271, Paramaribo; tel. 498115; fax 498116; e-mail adm@radiosrs.com; internet www.radiosrs.com; f. 1965; commercial; govt-owned; Dutch and some local languages; Dir ROSELINE A. DAAN.

Radio & Televisie Garuda: Goudstraat 14–16, Paramaribo; tel. 456869; f. 2001; Dir TOMMY RADJI.

Radio Ten: Stadionlaan 3, POB 110, Paramaribo; tel. 410881; fax 422294; e-mail info@radio10.sr; internet www.radio10.sr; Dir WERNER DUTTENHOFER.

Television

ABC Televisie (Ampie's Broadcasting Corporation): Maystraat 57, Paramaribo; tel. 464555; fax 464680; e-mail info@abcsuriname.com; internet www.abcsuriname.com; f. 1975, re-opened 1993; Channel 4.

Algemene Televisie Verzorging (ATV): van het Hogerhuysstraat 58–60; tel. 404611; fax 402660; e-mail info@atv.sr; internet www.atv .sr; f. 1985; govt-owned; commercial; Dutch, English, Portuguese, Spanish and some local languages; Channel 12; Man. GUNO COOMAN.

Radio & Televisie Garuda: see Radio section.

Radika Radio & TV: see Radio section; Hindi entertainment TV channel.

STVS (Surinaamse Televisie Stichting): Letitia Vriesdelaan 5, POB 535, Paramaribo; tel. 473032; fax 477216; e-mail info@stvs.sr; internet www.stvs.sr; f. 1965; govt-owned; commercial; local languages, Dutch and English; Channels 6, 8, 11 and 13; Dir SHURLY LACKIN.

Finance

(cap. = capital; res = reserves; dep. = deposits; m. = million; brs = branches; amounts in Surinamese dollars)

BANKING

Central Bank

Centrale Bank van Suriname: Waterkant 20, POB 1801, Paramaribo; tel. 473741; fax 476444; e-mail info@cbvs.sr; internet www .cbvs.sr; f. 1957; cap. and res. 210.7m., dep. 858.2m. (Dec. 2009); Gov. GILMORE HOEFDRAAD; Exec. Dir O. EZECHIËLS.

Commercial Banks

Finabank NV: Dr Sophie Redmondstraat 59–61, Paramaribo; tel. 472266; fax 422672; e-mail executive@finabanknv.com; internet www.finabanknv.com; f. 1991; cap. 1m., res. 10.1m., dep. 275.4m. (Dec. 2011); Chair. CORNELIS DILWEG; CEO EBLEIN FRANGIE.

Handels-Krediet- en Industriebank (Hakrinbank NV): Dr Sophie Redmondstraat 11–13, POB 1813, Paramaribo; tel. 477722; fax 472066; e-mail hakrindp@sr.net; internet www.hakrinbank.com; f. 1936; cap. 0.7m., res 141m., dep. 886.7m. (Dec. 2013); Pres. and Chair. A. K. R. SHYAMNARAIN; CEO J. D. BOUSAID; 7 brs.

Landbouwbank NV: FHR Lim A Postraat 30, POB 929, Paramaribo; tel. 475945; fax 411965; e-mail lbbank@sr.net; f. 1972; govt-owned; agricultural bank; Chair. D. FERRIER; 5 brs.

RBC Royal Bank (Suriname) NV: Kerkplein 1, Paramaribo; tel. 471555; fax 411325; e-mail tt-info@rbc.com; internet www.rbtt.com/ sr/personal; fmrly Amsterdam Rotterdam Bank NV; present name adopted in 2012; Man. Dir PATRICIA BORGER; CEO, Caribbean SURESH SOOKOO.

Stichting Surinaamse Volkscredietbank (VCB): Waterkant 104, POB 1804, Paramaribo; tel. 472616; fax 473257; e-mail info@ vcbbank.sr; internet www.vcbbank.sr; f. 1949; Man. Dir P. CLENEM; 3 brs.

Surichange Bank NV: Dr Sophie Redmondstraat 71, Paramaribo; tel. 471151; fax 474554; e-mail info@surichange.sr; internet www .scbbank.sr; cap. 4.5m., res. 8.2m., dep. 200.3m. (Dec. 2011); Exec. Dirs STANLEY MATHURA, RAJINDREKOEMAR MERHAI.

De Surinaamsche Bank NV: Henck Arronstraat 26–30, POB 1806, Paramaribo; tel. 471100; fax 411750; e-mail info@dsbbank.sr; internet www.dsbbank.sr; f. 1865; cap. 0.8m., res 209.3m., dep. 3,224.1m. (Dec. 2013); Chair. S. SMIT; CEO SIGMUND L. J. PROEVE; 11 brs.

INSURANCE

Assuria NV: Grote Combeweg 37, POB 1501, Paramaribo; tel. 477955; fax 472390; e-mail assurialeven@assuria.sr; internet www

.assuria.sr; f. 1961; life and indemnity insurance; Man. Dir Dr S. SMIT.

Assuria Schadeverzekering NV: Henck Arronstraat 5–7, POB 1030, Paramaribo; tel. 473400; fax 476669; e-mail customer.service@ assuria.sr; internet www.assuria.sr; Chair. A. K. ACHAIBERSING; Man. Dir Dr S. SMIT.

Fatum Levensverzekering NV: Noorderkerkstraat 5–7, Paramaribo; tel. 471541; fax 410067; e-mail fatum@sr.net; internet www.fatum-suriname.com; Chair. C. A. CALOR; Exec. Dir N. W. LALBIHARIE.

Parsasco NV: Henck Arronstraat 119, Paramaribo; tel. 421212; fax 421325; e-mail parsasco@sr.net; internet www.parsasco.com; f. 1995; Man. Dir AMAR RANDJITSING.

Self Reliance: Heerenstraat 48–50 en Henck Arronstraat 69–71, Paramaribo; tel. 472582; fax 475588; e-mail self-reliance@sr.net; internet www.self-reliance.sr; f. 1980; general and life insurance; Pres. MAURICE L. ROEMER.

Trade and Industry

DEVELOPMENT ORGANIZATIONS

Stichting Planbureau Suriname (National Planning Office of Suriname): Dr Sophie Redmondstraat 118, POB 172, Paramaribo; tel. 447408; fax 475001; e-mail dirsps@sr.net; f. 1951; responsible for regional socio-economic planning; Man. Dir HESDY ORMSKIRK.

Suriname Business Development Centre (SBC): Hendrikstraat 69, 1st Floor, Paramaribo; tel. 499010; fax 499011; e-mail info@sbc .sr; internet www.sbc.sr; f. 2008; devt of private sector industries; Gen. Man. GILBERT VAN DIJK.

CHAMBERS OF COMMERCE

Kamer van Koophandel en Fabrieken (Chamber of Commerce and Industry): Dr J. C. de Mirandastraat 10, POB 149, Paramaribo; tel. 530311; fax 437971; e-mail chamber@sr.net; internet www .surinamechamber.com; f. 1910; Pres. ROBERT AMEERALI; 16,109 mems.

Surinaams–Nederlandse Kamer voor Handel en Industrie (Suriname–Netherlands Chamber of Commerce and Industry): Jagernath Lachmonstraat 158, Paramaribo; tel. and fax 476909; e-mail nedcar@xs4all.nl; internet nederlandscaribischekamer.com; f. 1976; Sec.-Gen. RONALD SCHERMEL; Dir LEON FERRIER.

INDUSTRIAL AND TRADE ASSOCIATIONS

Associatie van Surinaamse Fabrikanten (ASFA) (Suriname Manufacturers' Asscn): Jaggernath Lachmonstraat 187, POB 3046, Paramaribo; tel. 434014; fax 439798; e-mail info@asfasuriname.com; internet www.asfasuriname.com; f. 1980; Chair. RAHID DOEKHIE; 317 mems.

Vereniging Surinaams Bedrijfsleven (Suriname Trade and Industry Association): Prins Hendrikstraat 18, POB 111, Paramaribo; tel. 475286; fax 475287; e-mail info@vsbstia.org; internet www .vsbstia.org; f. 1950; Pres. FERDINAND WELZIJN; 245 mems.

MAJOR COMPANIES

Bruynzeel Suriname Houtmaatschappij NV: Slangenhoutstraat 1, POB 1831, Paramaribo; tel. 403811; fax 402304; e-mail bruynzeel@sr.net; internet bruynzee.sr.net; subsidiary of House Factory International (Romania); timber merchants; producers of sawnwood, plywood and precut and prefabricated houses; Dir P. PENEUX.

CHM Suriname NV: Dr Sophie Redmondstraat 2–14, POB 1819, Paramaribo; tel. 471166; fax 471534; e-mail chmsur@gmail.com; internet www.chmsuriname.com; f. 1888; subsidiary of Handelen Industrie Mij Ceteco NV (Netherlands); electrical appliances, televisions and radios; importer of Toyota automobiles; Gen. Man. EDMUND KASIMBEG; 160 employees.

NV Consolidated Industries Corporation: Industrieweg-zuid 34, POB 635, Paramaribo; tel. 482050; fax 481431; e-mail info@cicsur .com; internet www.cicsur.com; f. 1967; mfrs of detergents and disinfectants, packaging materials and cosmetics and toiletries; Chair. J. HEALY; Man. Dir WOUTER VAN MEEGDENBURG; 220 employees.

Fernandes Concern Beheer NV (The Fernandes Group): Klipstenenstraat 2–10, POB 1834, Paramaribo; tel. 471313; fax 471154; e-mail postmaster@fernandesconcern.com; internet fernandesconcern.com; holding co; Chair. MICHEL BRAHIM; 800 employees.

Fernandes Autohandel NV (Fernandes Automotive Ltd): Keizerstraat 105–117, Paramaribo; tel. 475046; fax 473891; e-mail automotive@fernandesautomotive.com; f. 1963; sole importer and distributor for Honda, Isuzu cars; also agricultural equipment, bicycles, fire extinguishers, auto paints; Gen. Man. MAURICE BRAHIM; 105 employees.

Fernandes Bakkerij NV (Fernandes Bakery Ltd): Kernkampweg 82–84, POB 1834, Paramaribo; tel. 463232; fax 492177; e-mail consumerresponse@fernandesbakery.com; internet www .fernandesbakkerij.com; f. 1918; bread, pastry, biscuits; rice, potato and corn snacks; Gen. Man. OSCAR TJON KIE SIM; 1,100 employees.

Fernandes Bottling Company NV: Indira Gandhiweg 12, Ephraïmzegen, POB 1834, Paramaribo; tel. 482121; fax 483091; e-mail postmaster@fernandesbottling.com; internet www .fernandesbottling.com; f. 1939; franchise for Coca-Cola; Gen. Man. BRYAN RENTEN; 175 employees.

Fernandes Handelmaatschappij NV (Fernandes Trading Co, Ltd): Klipstenenstraat 2–10, POB 1834, Paramaribo; tel. 471313; fax 474306; f. 1957; incl. aluminium doors and windows, household, hardware and building materials, wholesale and distribution; Gen. Man. ERNIE DE VRIES.

Fernandes Ice Cream NV: Kernkampweg 82–84, Paramaribo; tel. 439711; fax 49718; e-mail ifsice@sr.net; f. 1999; Gen. Man. GEORGE CHENG; 40 employees.

Food and Agriculture Industries, NV (FAI, NV): Lakatanweg, Jarikaba, BR 173, Saramacca; tel. 328170; f. 2004; banana producers and exporters; 2,000 ha of banana production area; known as Surland until closure in 2002, restructured and reopened as state-run Stichting Behoud Bananensector Suriname in 2004, 90% sold to Univeg (Belgium) in 2014 and present name adopted; CEO (Univeg) FRANCIS KINT.

Jong A. Kiem NV: Jagernath Lachmonstraat 203, POB 272, Paramaribo; tel. 491600; fax 491855; e-mail info@jongakiem.com; internet www.jongakiem.com; mfr of pharmaceutical products; owned by AstraZeneca PLC (UK).

C. Kersten en Co NV (CKC): Domineestraat 36–38, Paramaribo; tel. 471150; fax 478524; e-mail holding@kersten.sr; internet www .kersten.sr; f. 1768; holding co for distributors of durable goods; operates 14 cos; CEO SHIRLEY SOWMA-SUMTER; Chair. DAVID VOÛTE; 500 employees.

Kirpalani's Kleding Industrie NV: Domineestraat 52–56, POB 251 and 1917, Paramaribo; tel. 471400; fax 410527; e-mail kirpa@ kirpalani.com; internet www.kirpalani.com; textile and clothing producers; Gen. Man. JHAMATMAL T. KIRPALANI; 636 employees.

Kuldipsingh Group: Anamoestraat, POB 8089, Paramaribo; tel. 551204; fax 550669; e-mail hkanamoe@kuldipsingh.net; internet www.kuldipsingh.net; f. 1979; consists of 8 cos; manufactures and distributes metal and building products; Man. Dir SWITRANG KULDIPSINGH; Man. RANDJIET KULDIPSINGH; 600 employees.

Nationale Metaal & Constructie Maatschappij NV (Nameco): Industrial Park Behesda, Hallen 5–6, POB 1560, Paramaribo; tel. 482014; f. 1975; construction and civil engineering projects.

Rosebel Gold Mines NV: Heerenstraat 8, Paramaribo; tel. 422741; fax 478447; 95% owned by IAMGOLD (Canada), 5% state-owned; agreement reached in 2013 for expansion of mine, to Sarafina NV's mine; Pres. and CEO (IAMGOLD) STEPHEN LETWIN.

Shell Suriname Verkoopmaatschappij NV: POB 849, Paramaribo; tel. 482027; fax 482569; f. 1975; producers of fuel oil and lubricants; CEO PETER VOSER; 190 employees.

Suralco L.L.C (Suralco) (Suriname Aluminium Company): van 't Hogerhuysstraat 13, POB 1810, Paramaribo; tel. 323281; fax 323314; internet www.alcoa.com/suriname; subsidiary of Alcoa, USA; bauxite mining and refining, alumina production; bought bauxite and alumina refining interests of BHP Billiton Maatschappij Suriname in 2009; Man. Dir RUBEN H. HALFHUID; Gen. Man. PETER DE WIT.

Surinaams-Amerikaanse Industrie Maatschappij NV (SAIL): Cornelis Jongbawstraat 48, POB 3045, Paramaribo; tel. 474014; fax 473521; e-mail sail@sr.net; f. 1955; processors and exporters of marine and farm-raised shrimps and fish; Dir ERROL MANNES; 137 employees.

Varossieau Suriname NV: Mastanaweg 4, POB 995, Paramaribo; tel. 484447; fax 483590; e-mail info@varossieau-paints.com; internet www.varossieau-paints.com; f. 1959; mfrs of industrial paints and enamels; Chair. R. POPPELAARS; Man. Dir R. G. DWARKASING; 58 employees (2011).

H. J. de Vries Beheersmaatschappij NV: Waterkant 92–96, POB 1849–1850, Paramaribo; tel. 471222; fax 475718; e-mail devries@ hj-devries.com; internet www.hj-devries.com; f. 1903; holding co: import, wholesale, retail and distribution of food and durable goods and mfr of paints, household chemicals and claybricks; CEO KWOK KEUNG CHOY; over 250 employees.

Chemco NV: Indira Gandhiweg, Paramaribo; tel. 481661; fax 481880; e-mail chemco@hj-devries.com; f. 1982; import, wholesale, retail and distribution of chlorine and bleach.

Esuverfa NV (Eerste Surinaamse Verffabriek NV): Indira Gandhiweg, Paramaribo; tel. 483084; fax 483082; e-mail esuverfa@ hj-devries.com; f. 1979; paint mfr; 19 employees.

H. J. de Vries Agro NV: Indira Gandhiweg 9, Paramaribo; tel. 482733; fax 480731; e-mail agro@hj-devries.com; importer of pesticides and agricultural products; Supervisor MARJORIE BRANDON.

H. J. de Vries Engros NV: Indira Gandhiweg, Paramaribo; tel. 482733; fax 480731; e-mail engros@hj-devries.com; f. 1903; wholesale and distribution of quality food and non-food products, alcoholic and non-alcoholic beverages and tobacco products.

H. J. de Vries Motors NV: Slangenhoustraat 46–48, Paramaribo; tel. 402169; fax 401533; e-mail motors@hj-devries.com; official dealer for Suzuki, Mazda, Kia cars.

H. J. de Vries Nickerie NV: G. G. Maynardstraat 25, Nieuw Nickerie; tel. 231832; fax 231220; e-mail nickerie@hj-devries.com; internet www.nickerie.com; chemicals and machinery for the rice sector.

H. J. de Vries Retail NV: Waterkant 92–96, Paramaribo; tel. 471222; fax 475718; e-mail retail@hj-devries.com; operates retail outlets in Paramaribo, Lelydorp, Tamanredjo and Nickerie.

Keram: Indira Gandhiweg 26, Paramaribo; tel. 352015; fax 475718; e-mail keram@hj-devries.com; brick mfr.

UTILITIES

Electricity

NV Energie Bedrijven Suriname (EBS): Noorderkerkstraat 2–14, POB 1825, Paramaribo; tel. 471045; fax 474866; e-mail g.lau@ nvebs.com; internet www.nvebs.com; f. 1932 as Nederlands-Indische Gas Maatschappij; present name adopted in 1968; electricity and gas distribution; owns and operates Electricity Co of Paramaribo (EPAR) and Ogane Paramaribo (OPAR); Dir GERARD LAU.

Staatsolie Maatschappij Suriname NV: Dr Ir H. S. Adhinstraat 21, POB 4069, Paramaribo; tel. 499649; fax 491105; e-mail mailstaatsolie@staatsolie.com; internet www.staatsolie.com; f. 1980; state petroleum exploration and exploitation co; electricity and steam generation and supplies; aims to produce 16,000 barrels per day of Saramacca Crude oil by 2013; Man. Dir MARC C. H. WAALDIJK; 810 employees (2011).

Paradise Oil Company: Dr Ir H. S. Adhinstraat 21, POB 4069, Paramaribo; tel. and fax 499649; e-mail poc@staatsolie.com; internet www.paradise-oil.com; f. 2005; 100% owned by Staatsolie Maatschappij Suriname NV; oil exploration co; Operations Man. PATRICK BRUNINGS.

Water

NV Surinaamsche Waterleiding Maatschappij (SWM): Henck Arronstraat 9–11, POB 1818, Paramaribo; tel. 471414; fax 476343; e-mail swmsecretariaat@swm.sr; internet www.swm.sr; f. 1932; govt-owned; Dir SVEN SJAUW KOEN FA; 578 employees (2012).

TRADE UNIONS

Council of the Surinamese Federation of Trade Unions (RAVAKSUR) (Raad van Vakcentrales Suriname): f. 1987; Pres. ROBBY BERENSTEIN; includes:

Algemeen Verbond van Vakverenigingen in Suriname 'De Moederbond' (AVVS) (General Confederation of Trade Unions): Verlengde Jagernath Lachmonstraat 134, POB 2951, Paramaribo; tel. 465118; fax 463116; e-mail avvsmoederbond51@hotmail.com; right-wing; Pres. ERROLL G. SNIJDERS; Gen. Sec. ALESSANDRO SPRONG; 15,000 mems.

Organisatie van Samenwerkende Autonome Vakbonden (OSAV): Miguelitastraat 18, Paramaribo; tel. and fax 431429; fax 431429; e-mail sovas46@hotmail.com; f. 1986; Pres. SONNY D. CHOTKAN.

Progressieve Werknemers Organisatie (PWO) (Progressive Workers' Organization): Limesgracht 80, POB 406, Paramaribo; tel. 475840; fax 477814; f. 1948; covers the commercial, hotel and banking sectors; Pres. ANDRE KOORNAAR; 4,000 mems.

Progressive Trade Union Federation (C-47): Johan Adolf Pengelstraat 230, Paramaribo; tel. 401120; fax 401149; e-mail c47@sr.net; Pres. ROBBY BERENSTEIN; Gen. Sec. CLAUDETTE ETNEL.

Federation of Farmers and Agrarians (FAL): Keizerstraat 150, Paramaribo; tel. 420833; fax 474517; Pres. JIWAN SITAL; Gen. Sec. ANAND DWARKA.

Transport

RAILWAYS

There are no public railways operating in Suriname.

ROADS

In 2003 Suriname had an estimated 4,304 km (2,674 miles) of roads, of which 26.3% were paved. The principal east–west road, 390 km in length, links Albina, on the eastern border, with Nieuw Nickerie, in the west. Modernization of the Martin Luther King Highway was expected to begin in mid-2013. The US $250m. project was funded by the China Investment Bank.

SHIPPING

Suriname is served by many shipping companies and has about 1,500 km (930 miles) of navigable rivers and canals. There are two ferry services linking Suriname with Guyana, across the Corantijn (Corentyne) river, and one with French Guiana, across the Marowijne (Marouini) river. In 2012 Suriname and Guyana asked the Inter-American Development Bank to fund a feasibility study looking into the construction of a bridge across the Corantijn river. At December 2013 the flag registered fleet comprised 10 vessels, totalling 4,866 grt.

Continental Shipping Agencies NV (CSA): Abattoirstraat 8, Paramaribo; tel. 401801; fax 401805; e-mail nfo@csasr.com; internet www.csa.sr; f. 1988; shipping agents and stevedores; Man. DINO IROKARSO.

Maritieme Autoriteit Suriname (Maritime Authority Suriname): Cornelis Jongbawstraat 2, POB 888, Paramaribo; tel. 476733; fax 472940; e-mail info@mas.sr; internet www.mas.sr; fmrly Dienst voor de Scheepvaart; govt authority supervising and controlling shipping in Surinamese waters; Dir and Harbour Master M. AMAFO.

Scheepvaart Maatschappij Suriname NV (SMS) (Suriname Shipping Line Ltd): Waterkant 44, POB 1824, Paramaribo; tel. 472447; fax 474814; e-mail surinam_line@sr.net; f. 1936; state-owned; passenger services in the interior; Dir J. ROZENHOUT.

Suriname Coast Traders NV: Flocislaan 4, Duisburglaan, POB 9216, Paramaribo; tel. 463040; fax 463831; internet www.pasonsgroup.com; f. 1981; subsidiary of Pasons Group.

NV VSH Verenigde Surinaamse Holdingmij (United Suriname Shipping Company): van 't Hogerhuysstraat 9–11, POB 1860, Paramaribo; tel. 402558; fax 403515; e-mail info@vshunited.com; internet www.vshunited.com/shipping.html; shipping agents and freight carriers; operates NV VSH Scheepvaartmij, NV VSH Transportmij and NV Uniblue Shipping; Man. Dirs JAMES J. HEALY, Jr, PATRICK HEALY.

CIVIL AVIATION

The main airport is Johan Adolf Pengel International Airport, 45 km from Paramaribo. Domestic flights operate from Zorg-en-Hoop Airport, located in a suburb of Paramaribo. There are some 35 airstrips throughout the country.

Blue Wing Airlines (BWA): Doekhieweg 3, Zorg-en-Hoop Airport, POB 13007, Paramaribo; tel. 434393; fax 433909; e-mail sales@bluewingairlines.com; internet www.bluewingairlines.com; f. 2002; privately owned; chartered and scheduled flights; services the domestic and Caribbean region; Chair. F. PENGEL; Gen. Man. A. JHAUW.

Civil Aviation Department of Suriname (CAD): Paramaribo; e-mail cad.dca@tct.gov.sr; internet www.cadsur.sr; govt. regulatory authority; Dir STANLEY BETTERSON (acting).

Gum Air NV: Doekhieweg 3, Zorg-en-Hoop Airfield, Paramaribo; tel. 498760; fax 491740; e-mail info@gumair.com; internet www.gumair.com; f. 1974; privately owned; unscheduled domestic and regional flights; Man. DEAN GUMMELS.

Surinaamse Luchtvaart Maatschappij NV (SLM) (Suriname Airways): Mr Jagernath Lachmonstraat 136, POB 2029, Paramaribo; tel. 465700; fax 491213; e-mail publicrelations@slm.firm.sr; internet www.flyslm.com; f. 1962; services to Amsterdam (Netherlands) and to destinations in North America, South America and the Caribbean; Vice-Pres. CLYDE CAIRO.

Tourism

Tourist attractions include the varied cultural activities, a number of historical sites and an unspoiled interior with many species of plants, birds and animals. There are 13 nature reserves and one nature park. There were an estimated 249,000 stop-over arrivals in 2013, most of whom came from the Netherlands. In 2013 tourism receipts totalled a provisional US $84m.

Suriname Tourism Foundation: Dr J. F. Nassylaan 2, POB 656, Paramaribo; tel. 424878; fax 477786; e-mail secretariat@surinametourism.sr; internet www.surinametourism.sr; f. 1996; Exec. Dir FARIDY LILA.

Defence

The army numbered an estimated 1,840 men and women, as assessed at November 2013. There was an army of 1,400, a navy of 240 and an air force of some 200.

Defence Budget: an estimated 134m. Surinamese dollars in 2012.

Commander of the Army: Col HEDWIG GILAARD.

Education

Education is compulsory for children between the ages of seven and 12. Primary education lasts for six years, and is followed by a further seven years of secondary education, comprising a junior secondary cycle of four years followed by a senior cycle of three years. All education in government and denominational schools is provided free of charge. In 2011 enrolment in primary education included 92% of children in the relevant age-group, while enrolment in secondary education included 57% of children in the relevant age-group. Higher education is provided by three technical and vocational schools and by the University of Suriname at Paramaribo. In 2003 the Inter-American Development Bank (IDB) approved a US $12.5m. loan to fund the reform of the basic education system. In 2012 the IDB approved a further grant of $13.7m. towards a second Basic Education Improvement Program for developing the curriculum framework, improving learning outcomes, and increasing enrolment rates.

Bibliography

For works on the region generally, see Select Bibliography (Books)

Carlin, E. *In the Shadow of the Tiger: The Amerindians of Suriname*. Amsterdam, KIT Publrs, 2010.

Carlin, E., and Arends, J. (Eds). *Atlas of the Languages of Suriname*. Kingston, Jamaica, Ian Randle Publrs, 2003.

Dew, E. M. *The Trouble in Suriname, 1975–1993*. New York, Praeger Publrs, 1995.

Hoefte, R., and Meel, P. (Eds). *Twentieth Century Suriname: Continuities and Discontinuities in a New World Society*. Kingston, Jamaica, Ian Randle Publrs, 2001.

Kambel, E.-R., and MacKay, F. *The Rights of Indigenous Peoples and Maroons in Suriname*. Copenhagen, International Work Group for Indigenous Affairs, 2000.

Mangré, B. *Suriname: An Example of the Reverse Fortune Hypothesis*. Saarbrücken, Lambert Academic Publishing, 2010.

Meel, P. *Tussen autonomie en onafhankelijkheid: Nederlands-Surinaamse betrekkingen 1954–1961*. Leiden, KITLV Uitgeverij, 1999.

Norton, A. *U da sembe fa aki (we are people of this place): Place-attachment and belonging. A Saramaka response to globalization*. Ann Arbor, MI, ProQuest, 2006.

Thoden van Velzen, H. U. E., and van Wetering, W. *In the Shadow of the Oracle: Religion as Politics in a Suriname Maroon Society*. Prospect Heights, IL, Waveland Press Inc, 2004.

USA Ibp. *Suriname Central Bank and Financial Policy Handbook*. Milton Keynes, Lightning Source UK Ltd, 2005.

TRINIDAD AND TOBAGO

Geography

PHYSICAL FEATURES

Trinidad and Tobago lies in the West Indies, its constituent parts being considered the southernmost islands of the Caribbean, although, geologically, they are extensions of the South American continent. Venezuela (specifically, the Paria peninsula) lies only 11 km (seven miles) from the island of Trinidad, the two countries embracing the Gulf of Paria. The Gulf is entered by sea channels known as the Bocas, in the north by the Dragon's Mouths and in the south by the slightly broader Serpent's Mouth, which joins the eastward-widening Columbus Channel between the southern coast of Trinidad and the delta lands of the Orinoco in Venezuela. Some 145 km (90 miles) to the north of Trinidad is Grenada, the next nearest neighbour. Tobago, which accounts for only 300 sq km (116 sq miles) of the country's total area of 5,128 sq km, lies some 32 km to the north-east of Trinidad island.

Trinidad (80 km by 60 km in extent) is an anvil-shaped island, with tapering extensions in both the south-west and the north-west that reach further westward towards the coast of Venezuela and help enclose the Gulf of Paria. This provides a vast sheltered anchorage in the lee of Trinidad island, and it is on this shore that the capital, Port of Spain, is located. West of here, near the tip of the north-western peninsula, is the only natural harbour, Chaguaramas: the northern coast is rocky, the eastern coast exposed to heavy seas directly off the Atlantic and the southern coast steep. Three ranges of highlands cross the island from east to west, the highest being in the north, where El Cerro del Aripo reaches 940 m (3,085 ft), amid the densely forested slopes of the Northern Range. There are also the Central Range and the Trinity Hills in the south-east. Midway along the northern coast of the south-western peninsula is the 47 ha (116 acre) Pitch Lake near La Brea, the largest natural asphalt reservoir in the world, which testifies to the country's hydrocarbons wealth, while another geographical oddity, mud volcanoes, indicates the volcanic origins of the island. Plains dominate the rest of the south and the land along the Caroni river between the Central and Northern Ranges. Here the landscape is predominantly agricultural, giving way to wetlands near the coast, such as the Caroni Swamp in the west and the Nariva Swamp on the east coast. Still-extensive natural habitats such as these, as well as the dense northern rainforest, are widely protected, as both Trinidad and Tobago, once attached separately to the continental landmass, host probably the greatest ecological diversity in the insular Caribbean.

Tobago, the summit of a single mountain mass rising from the sea floor, is aligned from south-west to north-east, its northerly shores, facing the Caribbean, bearing the leeward beaches protected from the Atlantic weather. The island is about 42 km in length and up to 14 km wide, with plains of a coralline origin in the south rising towards the backbone of a central 29-km Main Ridge range, rising towards the north-east and reaching its highest point at Pigeon Peak (594 m). At this end of the island the peaks are cloaked with the oldest protected rainforest region in the Americas (since 1764). Tobago boasts an even greater variety of bird and animal life than the more developed Trinidad. The marine environment is also flourishing, encouraged by the confluence of Atlantic currents with the warmer Caribbean and the rich discharge of the Orinoco.

CLIMATE

The climate is tropical, with a rainy season from June to November and a slightly cooler season between December and April. The islands are not in the hurricane belt, but fairly constant breezes off the Atlantic keep the temperatures from becoming too hot. The average maximum temperature is 32°C (89°F), although Tobago is slightly cooler, owing to its more

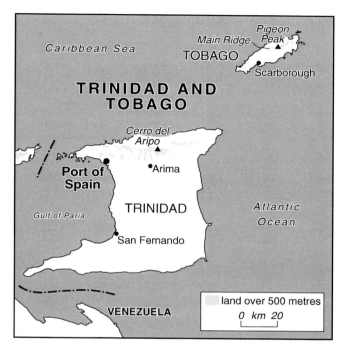

constant exposure to the trade winds. Average annual rainfall is about 2,050 mm (80 ins) over most of the country, being higher in the mountains.

POPULATION

The population is one of the most varied in the Caribbean, a complex colonial history of competing Spanish, French and, finally, British rule, augmented by the immigration of Africans (originally as slaves), Indians (mainly from north India as indentured labour) and many others. The largest single ethnic group is now 'East' Indian, followed closely by those of African descent (each constituting about 35% of the population), with 23% of mixed heritage. Culturally, there are two folk traditions in the country, the Creole and the East Indian, the latter including Hindus and Muslims. Christianity remains the main religion, with Roman Catholicism the leading denomination (22%), but Hindus represent 18% of the population, and Pentecostalists/Evangelicals make up 12%. Other Protestant groups include Baptists (7%) and Seventh-day Adventists (4%), while Anglicans claim the adherence of 6%. Muslims account for 5% of the population. This diversity is reflected in the variety of languages spoken by the populace, with a French Creole patois surviving in some areas, Hindi being widely spoken among East Indians, and others using Chinese or Spanish. However, the most widely spoken tongue and the official language of the country is English.

The 2011 census put total population at 1,328,019, with only some 4.5% living on Tobago. The population in mid-2013 was provisionally estimated at 1,340,557. The capital, Port of Spain (including its suburbs), had a population of some 37,074 in 2011, while San Fernando, at the southern end of the west coast, is a major population centre (48,838 in 2011), followed by Arima (33,606), inland to the east of Port of Spain. The chief town of Tobago is Scarborough, on the southern coast at the south-western end of the island. The other important towns are Plymouth, across on the north coast from Scarborough, and Roxborough, towards the northern end of the south-facing coast.

History

MARK WILSON

The two islands that constitute the modern state of Trinidad and Tobago were both first settled by Carib and other Amerindian populations from the South American mainland. Contact with Europe and North America dates from the third voyage of the Spanish navigator Christopher Columbus, in 1498. Small Spanish settlements were established from 1592, which formed an insignificant part of the Viceroyalty of New Granada, based in Bogotá, Colombia.

Larger-scale settlement began from 1776, when Spain began to encourage settlers from Grenada and other former French possessions that had passed to British rule. Later, settlers came from Martinique and Guadeloupe, where slavery had been temporarily abolished as a result of the French Revolution. A Spanish cedula of 1783 established a system of land grants for French planters, with additional allocations for those who brought slaves. Coffee, cocoa and sugar plantations were established, and there was considerable growth in trade. Until the late 19th century French creole remained the main spoken vernacular. In the early 21st century Roman Catholicism remained the largest Christian denomination.

Trinidad was captured by the United Kingdom in 1797, and was formally ceded to that country by Spain in 1802. Tobago was colonized by the Dutch in 1628, but then claimed by a succession of European countries until the British took possession in 1762, following 100 years of French occupation; France ceded the island to the United Kingdom in the following year. However, it was not until 1814 that the British gained the island in perpetuity. Throughout the 19th century in Trinidad there remained a latent conflict between the British administration and a mainly French planter and commercial class. For this reason, Trinidad, unlike most West Indian colonies, had no elected Assembly.

The abolition of slavery in 1834 was followed by four years in which slaves were forced to remain on the plantations under a system of indentureship. From 1838 many former slaves moved to Port of Spain or established peasant farms on unoccupied land; as did a large number of immigrants from other West Indian colonies. With a labour shortage developing on the plantations, from 1845 the Government encouraged the immigration of indentured labourers, mainly Indian, but also Chinese and Madeiran. On the expiry of a 10-year period, of which the first five were contracted to a single employer, the workers received either their passage home or title to a small plot of land. This form of immigration continued until 1917, and the majority of the rural population in modern Trinidad was descended from Indian indentured labourers. Tobago's sugar industry performed badly after emancipation, and was close to collapse by the 1880s. For this reason, the smaller colony was attached to Trinidad from 1889.

Agitation for increased political rights began in Trinidad from the 1880s, earlier than in most other West Indian colonies. From 1896 the Trinidad Workingmen's Association played an important role in political life. Against this background, in 1899 the colonial authorities unwisely abolished the elected Borough Council in Port of Spain. In 1914 the Council was re-established and, from 1925, there were elected members on the Legislative Council, although the electoral roll was limited by property qualifications.

THE MOVE TO INDEPENDENCE

Disturbances resulting from the depressed economic situation of the 1930s provided propitious conditions for the foundation of the labour movements. These, in turn, evolved into political movements, particularly after the introduction of universal adult suffrage in 1946. The People's National Movement (PNM), founded in 1956 by Dr Eric Williams, won 39% of the votes cast in legislative elections held in 1956, and gained control of the Legislative Council (securing 13 of the 24 elected seats), under the provision of the new constitutional arrangements that provided for self-government. Williams became Trinidad and Tobago's Chief Minister.

Along with most other British Caribbean colonies, Trinidad and Tobago joined the Federation of the West Indies in 1958. However, when Jamaica left the grouping in 1961 in order to seek independence individually, Trinidad and Tobago also withdrew, reluctant to take financial responsibility for the other, and, at that time, poorer, islands, in the north of the region, and the Federation collapsed. Internal self-government for Trinidad and Tobago in 1961 was followed by independence on 31 August 1962.

THE PNM AND PARTY POLITICS

Elective politics in Trinidad and Tobago mostly ran along racial lines, although all parties attempted to win at least token support from other groups. The PNM was mainly urban and Afro-Trinidadian, with some backing from Muslim and Christian Indians (mainly Presbyterian). Its early opponent, the Democratic Labour Party (DLP), led by Rudranath Capildeo, was based in the Hindu section of the Indian-origin community. Although Indo- and Afro-Trinidadians were roughly equal numerically, support from minority, Muslim and mixed-race voters, together with the pattern of constituency boundaries, was enough to give the PNM a secure parliamentary majority over the DLP and its ethnically based successor parties until 1986. Williams remained Prime Minister until his death in 1981.

The PNM's strongest challenge in this period came from the 'Black Power' movement, which came to prominence on the islands in 1970. Influenced to some extent by African-American radicalism, support for the movement stemmed mainly from a well-established perception that, eight years after independence, there was significant discrimination against Afro-Trinidadians in private sector employment, and that insufficient respect was given to black people and their culture. A series of demonstrations in 1970 was accompanied by some violence, and a state of emergency was declared. Unrest extended to junior army officers, who unsuccessfully attempted to overthrow the Government. The leaders of the Black Power movement were imprisoned without trial, and marches were banned. Nevertheless, many of their aims were achieved in the 1970s, when there were broader economic opportunities and more attention to cultural development.

Political difficulties persisted for some time, however, and there was an opposition boycott of the 1971 elections. In September 1973 Williams announced his resignation, but was persuaded to rescind it. A new Constitution came into effect on 1 August 1976, making Trinidad and Tobago a republic within the Commonwealth. In elections to the House of Representatives in the following month, the PNM won 24 of the 36 seats, while an alliance of petroleum and sugar workers within the newly formed United Labour Front (ULF), a mainly Indian party with trade union support led by Basdeo Panday, secured 10 seats. The two Tobago seats were won by the Democratic Action Congress (DAC), led by Arthur N. R. Robinson, a former PNM cabinet minister. The former Governor-General, Ellis Clarke, was sworn in as the islands' first President in December.

At this time, the PNM was presiding over a buoyant economy, following steep rises in the world price of petroleum in 1973 and 1974 that transformed Trinidad and Tobago's relatively small reserves of petroleum into a major financial and political asset. Petroleum prices remained high until 1981, by which time the PNM's dominance of national politics was such that, at the time of his death in March of that year, Williams was without serious rivals.

THE RISE OF THE NATIONAL ALLIANCE FOR RECONSTRUCTION

Williams was succeeded as Prime Minister by George Chambers, a deputy leader of the PNM. Chambers was seen as moderate and generally fair, but failed to command enthusiastic support. He presided over another election victory for the PNM in November 1981, winning 26 seats in the Parliament. The DAC and the ULF, as well as an intellectual pressure group, the Tapia House Movement, formed the National Alliance and took the two Tobago seats and eight, mainly Indian, rural seats, gaining 21% of the votes cast. The conservative Organization for National Reconstruction (ONR), led by another former PNM minister, Karl Hudson-Phillips, won 22% of the ballot but took no seats, because its mainly middle-class support was evenly spread across a large number of constituencies.

In August 1983 the four opposition parties formed an alliance to contest local elections and won 66 of the 120 local council seats. A united opposition party, the National Alliance for Reconstruction (NAR), was formed a year later. The NAR aimed to offer a credible alternative to the Government, at a time when stagnant and then decreasing petroleum prices were severely reducing government revenues and highlighting the defects of the policies pursued during the increase in prices of the previous decade. In the November 1984 elections to the Tobago House of Assembly, which had been formed in 1980, the DAC (part of the NAR) reduced the PNM's share of the 12 elective seats from four to one. Prime Minister Chambers was increasingly losing political respect, and his position was not strengthened by his failure to support the US-led military intervention in Grenada in October 1983. A 33% devaluation of the currency in December 1985 was deeply unpopular, and was seen as further eroding purchasing power in what was still an import-dependent economy.

Accusations of government economic mismanagement and corruption increased in the months preceding the December 1986 general election, intensified by the Government's failure to publish an official report on drugs-trafficking. The NAR, led by Robinson, won an overwhelming victory, winning 33 of the 36 seats in the House of Representatives. The PNM's parliamentary representation was reduced to just three seats. Robinson was appointed Prime Minister.

THE GOVERNMENT OF A. N. R. ROBINSON

The NAR Government was an unwieldy coalition of the ULF, the ONR, the DAC and the Tapia House Movement. Divisions emerged almost immediately over the allocation of cabinet portfolios and positions on state boards, and extended to policy matters, as the Government was forced to implement unpopular measures in response to a deepening economic crisis. There were also accusations that Indo-Trinidadians, who formed a majority of NAR voters, were being excluded from positions of real power.

The small Tapia House Movement left the NAR in June 1987. The Minister of External Affairs and International Trade and former ULF leader, Basdeo Panday, was dismissed in February 1988, along with one cabinet colleague and a junior minister. All three accused the NAR leadership of racism and were expelled from the party in October. In April 1989 Panday announced the formation of a new party, the United National Congress (UNC), which became the official opposition in September 1990, by virtue of holding six seats to the PNM's three. The UNC at this time was widely perceived to be a rural, Indo-Trinidadian party with strong links to the sugar workers' trade union.

The Government's unpopularity increased as it was forced to take further austerity measures. A compensatory financing agreement with the IMF was followed by stand-by agreements in 1989 and 1990. There was a further 15% currency devaluation in August 1988, which increased retail-price levels.

In July 1990 a group of insurgents from the Jamaat al Muslimeen, a sect of mainly Afro-Trinidadian Muslim converts led by Yasin Abu Bakr, a former policeman, stormed the parliament building during a session of the House of Representatives, taking 46 hostages including the Prime Minister and most of the Cabinet. At the same time, they blew up the police headquarters building and took over the sole television station, using it to broadcast their demands that the Prime Minister should resign, and his deputy lead an interim government into elections within 90 days. Widespread looting and fires began almost immediately in the capital and some sub-urban centres. The siege lasted for five days, during which time 23 people were killed and 500 wounded, most of them looters shot by the police. The Prime Minister was shot in the leg by the rebels after refusing to sign a letter of resignation. However, the acting President was induced to sign an amnesty for the rebels, which was delivered to them in the parliament building. An official inquiry into the events surrounding the attempted coup was in progress in 2013, led by a former Chief Justice and Attorney-General of Barbados, Sir David Simmons.

Following the surrender of the Jamaat al Muslimeen, the Government announced that the amnesty agreement had been made under duress and was therefore invalid. Abu Bakr and 113 others were charged with murder and treason. The Judicial Committee of the Privy Council (the country's final court of appeal, based in London, United Kingdom) ruled, in November 1991, that the validity of the presidential amnesty should be determined before the case came to trial. In June 1992 the High Court ruled that the pardon was valid, and ordered the release of the accused. In October 1993 the Government lost an appeal against the ruling, but a year later the Privy Council ruled that the Jamaat al Muslimeen had invalidated the pardon by failing to surrender as soon as it was agreed, instead continuing the siege in an attempt to win further concessions. However, it was also ruled that it would be an abuse of process for the accused to be rearrested and tried. In January 2000 the Jamaat al Muslimeen was ordered to pay TT $20m. for damage incurred during the insurrection. In May 2001, however, the High Court awarded TT $625,000 in compensation to the group for damage done to its headquarters, in addition to an earlier payment of TT $1.5m. After a preliminary magistrates' court hearing in July 2004, Abu Bakr was committed to stand trial for conspiracy to murder a former member of the Jamaat al Muslimeen, who had been shot dead in mid-2003. The trial jury was unable in March 2005 to agree a verdict, and a retrial was expected. In 2004 another leading figure of the Jamaat al Muslimeen was extradited to the USA to face arms-smuggling charges. In July–October 2005 a series of five bombs exploded in Port of Spain. Following the fourth explosion in mid-October, five people, including Abu Bakr, were arrested, but were subsequently released without charge. The Jamaat al Muslimeen denied responsibility for the attacks. In November Abu Bakr was rearrested and charged with seditious speech, incitement and terrorism, after allegedly preaching a sermon that appealed for a war on affluent Muslims who refused to pay *zakat*, a tithe for the poor, to his organization; a trial on this charge ended in a hung jury in August 2012. The presiding judge ordered a retrial, although this had not yet happened by mid-2014. In February 2006 the Attorney-General sought high court authorization for the state to confiscate 12 properties from members of the Jamaat al Muslimeen in compensation for damage caused during the attempted coup in 1990.

THE RETURN OF THE PNM

In the general election of December 1991, the NAR secured a mere 24% of the valid votes cast and only the two seats on Robinson's home island, Tobago. The PNM won 21 legislative seats and 45% of the popular vote, while the UNC took 29% of the ballot and 13 seats.

The new PNM Government, led by Patrick Manning, contained few members of previous PNM administrations. Economic policies reversed many aspects of the party's previous policies, focusing on financial and trade liberalization, divestment of state enterprises, and foreign investment, particularly in heavy industries based on offshore natural gas resources. The economy moved back into steady growth from 1994.

A state of emergency was briefly declared in August 1995, in order to allow the Government to remove from office the Speaker of the House of Representatives, Occah Seapaul, who was the subject of damaging financial allegations. This, in turn, led to the defection from the Government of her brother, Ralph Maraj, the Minister of Public Utilities (and former Minister of Foreign Affairs). With only a narrow majority now remaining, the Prime Minister responded by announcing that an early general election was to be held on 6 November.

THE ELECTION OF THE UNC

In the election, although the PNM increased its share of the votes to 49%, its support was concentrated heavily in its urban strongholds. The UNC received enthusiastic backing from some important members of the business community, and raised its share of the ballot to 46%. The UNC secured control of three marginal constituencies, which left each party with 17 of the 34 Trinidad seats. The NAR's remaining support in Trinidad had collapsed, but with the support of the two Tobago members, the UNC was able to form a Government and Basdeo Panday became Prime Minister. In spite of the electoral defeat, Manning resisted continuing demands from within the PNM for his resignation as party leader, winning a further five-year term in the post in 1996. However, he lost the support of important sections of the PNM, which weakened his ability to organize an effective opposition to Panday's Government.

The new administration continued most of the economic policies of its predecessor. In February 1997 the Government's parliamentary position was strengthened by the defection of two PNM members, who subsequently sat as independents. The Government presided over a period of strong economic growth, but there were persistent and widespread reports of corruption and mismanagement. On 14 February an electoral college of both houses of Parliament elected Robinson as President. He immediately relinquished his parliamentary and cabinet seats, as well as the leadership of the NAR. The PNM was opposed to a head of state who had, until his nomination, played a active role in party politics, and for the first time a presidential election was contested, although Robinson won a definitive victory. The NAR retained President Robinson's former seat at a by-election in May. However, in April the representative of the other Tobago seat, Pamela Nicholson, resigned from the Government and from the NAR to sit as an independent. As a result of these changes, from mid-1997 the Government could command the support of 20 members of the House of Representatives.

A serious dispute between the Government and the Chief Justice, Michael de la Bastide, began in September 1999, when he claimed that the independence of the judiciary was threatened by an attempt by the Attorney-General, Ramesh Lawrence Maharaj, to tighten administrative and financial controls. The Government responded in December by announcing that a former British Lord Chancellor, Lord Mackay of Clashfern, would lead a three-member Commission of Inquiry into the administration of justice on the islands. President Robinson, clearly unhappy with this decision, did not appoint the Commission until February 2000, signalling an unprecedented breach between the largely ceremonial head of state and the Cabinet. The Commission announced its findings and recommendations in October, clearing the Attorney-General of seeking to undermine the independence of the judiciary, but apparently failing to settle the fundamental disagreement between de la Bastide and Maharaj.

In January 2000 Hansraj Sumairsingh, a member of the UNC and leader of one of Trinidad's nine regional corporations, was found murdered. It was subsequently reported that Sumairsingh had written to the Prime Minister several times regarding threats made to him by the Minister of Local Government, Dhanraj Singh, following Sumairsingh's revelation of alleged corruption in the unemployment relief programme administered by Singh's ministry. A full investigation was initiated and in October Singh was dismissed from his government post. Singh was charged with corruption in the unemployment relief programme in January 2001 and, in February, with the murder of Sumairsingh. Singh was acquitted in October 2003.

THE RE-ELECTION OF THE UNC

The general election of 11 December 2000 was won by the UNC with 52% of the votes cast, compared with 46% for the PNM. The UNC gained two marginal seats on Trinidad, bringing its total in the 36-seat House of Representatives to 19, while the PNM won 16 seats and the NAR held one of the two Tobago seats. Panday was appointed Prime Minister for the second time.

At elections to the Tobago House of Assembly, held on 29 January 2001, the PNM took control of the Assembly for the first time, winning eight of the 12 seats. The NAR secured the remaining four seats.

The 2000 general election was marred by allegations of fraud. Opposition charges that the electoral list had been manipulated were highlighted by police investigations of prominent government supporters, and arrests were made following attempted manipulation of the electoral register. In January 2001 Panday announced his Cabinet and his nominations to the Senate. However, President Robinson at first refused to approve the senate nominations of seven UNC members, declaring them to be unconstitutional, as they had been defeated as candidates in the congressional election. His refusal was widely felt to be outside the President's discretionary powers under the Constitution.

Despite its election victory and the continuing growth of the economy, the UNC Government continued to be dogged by allegations of corruption in early 2001, including alleged fraud within the North West Regional Health Authority and irregularities at the state-owned Petroleum Company of Trinidad and Tobago Ltd (Petrotrin).

Relations between Panday and UNC deputy leader (and Attorney-General) Maharaj began to deteriorate in 2001. Panday pointedly failed to appoint Maharaj to act as Prime Minister when he travelled overseas. During the September budget debate, Maharaj and two cabinet colleagues, Ralph Maraj and Trevor Sudama, were sharply critical of the Government on corruption and other issues. Although the three dissidents did vote in favour of the budget proposals, Maharaj resigned as Attorney-General on 1 October, and his two supporters subsequently resigned their posts. They formed a temporary alliance with the PNM, proposing to form a new Government; however, President Robinson instead agreed to a request by Panday on 10 October to dissolve Parliament and hold a general election on 10 December. Maharaj and his majority on the UNC executive were unable to establish their right to the party's name and symbol, and fought the election as a new grouping, Team Unity.

A HUNG PARLIAMENT

Panday's fiercely loyal ethnic Indian support was barely diminished in the legislative elections of 10 December 2001, despite the divisions within the UNC and the allegations of corruption. The UNC retained 50% of the popular vote, with 46% for the PNM. However, the PNM narrowly gained a marginal seat in Trinidad from the UNC, as well as the NAR's remaining Tobago seat. This left each main party with 18 legislative seats.

As a result, on 16 December 2001 the UNC and PNM leaders signed the so-called 'Crowne Plaza Accord' in a Port of Spain hotel, which, if implemented, would have allowed Parliament to function. They agreed on the choice of Speaker for the House of Representatives and to accept the choice of President Robinson for Prime Minister. Following several days' deliberation, the President announced that Manning should be Prime Minister. Panday immediately declared the choice illegal and unconstitutional, and maintained that the candidate for Speaker previously agreed in the Crowne Plaza Accord was closely linked to the PNM. With no Speaker, Parliament could not function, nor could an electoral college be convened to choose a successor for President Robinson, whose term in office was due to expire on 19 March 2002.

In spite of deep political polarization, society continued to function more or less as normal. The budget adopted in September 2001 provided a financial basis for administration to continue. Robinson agreed to remain in office for up to one year, or until an electoral college could be convened. In line with normal practice in Trinidad and Tobago, the PNM replaced UNC appointees with its own supporters in key positions in the state sector; but with both parties agreeing on most points of economic and social policy, there were few other changes. According to the Constitution, a six-month interval was allowed between meetings of Parliament. Close to this deadline, on 5 April 2002, an attempt was made to convene the House of Representatives. The UNC voted against the PNM's nominees for Speaker, further complicating the issue by nominating several thousand nominees of its own, while at the same time voting against them, in case any were acceptable to the Government. After two days Parliament was prorogued.

The new Government appointed Commissions of Inquiry to investigate some of the allegations of corruption made against the UNC Government. In March 2002 Brian Kuei Tung, Panday's Minister of Finance in 1995–2000, and five associates were charged with corruption, conspiracy and misbehaviour in public office. The charges were brought in connection with contracts for a new airport terminal, and carried a maximum sentence of 10 years' imprisonment. Further charges were laid in May 2004 against Kuei Tung, former UNC Minister of Works, Sadiq Baksh, and 11 others. Panday himself was charged in September 2002 with failure to note large deposits made to a bank account in the United Kingdom in his statutory declaration of financial assets. However, defence lawyers in these and other cases raised a series of procedural issues, delaying the progress of the cases. Furthermore, a magistrate's ruling on whether the airport terminal charges should be heard in the High Court was subject to protracted procedural disputes. Hearings in the High Court and the Court of Appeal had taken place by mid-2014, although a final verdict in this case still awaited the outcome of a forthcoming hearing in the Privy Council.

THE SECOND MANNING ADMINISTRATION

Government was able to continue to function on the basis of the 2001 budget until the end of October 2002, but not beyond. The parliamentary impasse over the appointment of a Speaker eventually forced Prime Minister Manning to announce that a further general election would be held on 7 October—the third in 22 months. At this election the PNM gained 20 seats, compared with 16 seats for the UNC. In February 2003 the PNM's majority enabled an electoral college of the members of both houses of Parliament to elect George Maxwell Richards, a former principal of the local campus of the University of the West Indies, as President, allowing Robinson to retire.

In an election to the Tobago House of Assembly in January 2005, the PNM increased its legislative strength from eight to 11 of the 12 seats; the remaining seat was taken by the Democratic Action Congress, a group formed by a former NAR Chairman of the island assembly, Hochoy Charles.

The UNC's parliamentary presence was reduced to 14 in April 2005, when two members of Parliament, Fuad Khan and Gillian Lucky, realigned themselves as independents in protest against Panday's handling of an incident in which a UNC member of Parliament, Chandresh Sharma, alleged that the Minister of Housing, Keith Rowley, had thrown a teacup at him in September 2004. Sharma was suspended from the House in May 2005 for failing to apologize for his allegations. In the same month further corruption charges were filed against Panday, his wife Oma, his former Minister of Works and Transport, Carlos John, and a business associate. Tensions between Panday's hardline supporters and the UNC's moderate wing increased, and elections were held for a new party leadership in October. Panday remained Chairman, but stood aside as political leader in favour of the moderate Winston Dookeran, who had been a member of the 1986–91 NAR Government, and subsequently Governor of the Central Bank. However, Panday supporters took most party executive positions, and Dookeran was effectively marginalized from decision-making.

In April 2006 Panday was sentenced to two years' imprisonment, in addition to a fine of TT $60,000 and a forfeiture of TT $1.6m., for failing to declare monies held in a bank account in London. He was released on bail pending an appeal, but under the terms of the Constitution was suspended as member of Parliament, and removed as constitutional Leader of the Opposition. He was replaced as opposition leader, not by Dookeran but by Kamla Persad-Bissessar, a former Attorney-General, Minister of Legal Affairs and Minister of Education in the 1995–2001 Panday Government. Dookeran and four other members of Parliament left the UNC in September 2006 to form the Congress of the People (COP). With one other former UNC legislator remaining as an independent, and Panday's seat declared vacant in October, this reduced the UNC's parliamentary presence to nine.

An appeal by Panday against his conviction was upheld in March 2007, on the basis that the Chief Magistrate who heard the case had failed to make public his concerns over alleged improper interference in the case by the Chief Justice, and over a suspicious cheque received from a company owned by one of Panday's defence witnesses. The Court of Appeal ordered a retrial to be held 'expeditiously'; this was delayed by further procedural appeals from the defence, but was concluded in June 2012, with a magistrate's ruling that the Integrity Commission (a body established under the 1976 Constitution and subsequent legislation to promote integrity in public life) had failed to establish a tribunal before bringing criminal charges in 2002. Magistrates' court hearings on unrelated corruption charges against Panday, his wife, John and a businessman began in June 2007, but hearings were also subject to repeated procedural delays, and were unlikely ever to reach a verdict even at high court level. Panday was reinstated as UNC leader in April, but Persad-Bissessar remained parliamentary Leader of the Opposition.

Meanwhile, in June 2005 Parliament agreed to proposed electoral boundary changes: the changes enlarged the number of constituencies from 36 to 41, thereby preventing the recurrence of a hung parliament and increasing the number of marginal seats, while reducing the influence of the two Tobago members.

A general election was held on 5 November 2007. The PNM took 26 of the 41 seats, with 46% of the popular vote, while the UNC secured 15 seats and 30% of the vote. The COP won 23% of the votes cast, but no seats. The PNM's share of the vote was down from 2002, in part because of concerns over violent crime and apparent mismanagement in certain policy areas. The UNC, along with four very small groups, contested the election as the UNC-Alliance, led by Panday, who resumed the position of Leader of the Opposition after the poll.

Maxwell Richards was elected to a second five-year presidential term in February 2008. In elections to the Tobago House of Assembly, held on 19 January 2009, the PNM lost ground to a newly formed opposition coalition, the Tobago Organisation of the People (TOP), which took four of the 12 seats; the TOP did not include the UNC, which had no significant presence in Tobago.

From the early part of 2003 political attention was focused on the rate of murders and kidnappings, which had accelerated since 2001. The number of murders rose from an average of 108 per year in 1991–99 to a peak of 547 in 2008, with a per head murder rate of 42 per 100,000, an extremely high figure by international standards but lower than that of some other Caribbean countries, including Jamaica. Much of the violence stemmed from feuding between rival drugs gangs in lower-income districts within the urbanized east–west corridor running through Port of Spain. There was also a sharp increase in kidnappings for ransom, with a high proportion apparently also drugs-related. The authorities viewed the control of drugs-transshipment as an essential element of the control of crime. Installation of a new coastal radar system was completed in 2005, and the Government also planned to double the strength of the Defence Force and coast guard and purchase new patrol and interception vessels. Companies in the United Kingdom and Australia were commissioned to deliver offshore patrol vessels; six Austal craft were delivered in 2009. A Special Anti-Crime Unit (SAUTT) established in 2003 included former members of the police, Defence Force and other services. Kidnapping was sharply reduced from 56 cases in 2005 to 12 in 2007, owing to improved surveillance and to legislation under which alleged members of dismantled kidnapping gangs were refused bail. Police training programmes were upgraded and modernized, and former police officers from the United Kingdom brought in to train local officers. These and other measures were expected to have a medium- and long-term effect, rather than an immediate impact, on gang violence. There was no clear explanation for the increase in violent crime, although contributory factors included the import and distribution of illegal guns by narcotics traffickers, the growth of youth gangs in low-income areas, the continuing ineffectiveness of police methods and delays in judicial hearings, which, in turn, facilitated the killing or intimidation of witnesses. There were widespread allegations that the Government allowed criminal gangs to infiltrate urban job-creation schemes. Opinion polls demonstrated that crime was the primary issue of concern for the general public, and the polls also indicated low public confidence in the ability of the police, Government and other institutions to bring criminality under control.

Corruption allegations against the PNM persisted from 2005. In April the UNC raised allegations against the Minister of Works and Transport, Franklyn Khan, and the Minister of Energy and Energy Industries, Eric Williams (no relative of former premier Dr Eric Williams). Khan submitted his resignation in May and was formally charged on six counts of corruption in November. In December Khan also tendered his resignation from his post as Chairman of the PNM. Williams was charged with accepting bribes from a potential contractor and resigned from office in January 2006. A magistrates' court ruled in December 2007 that the evidence against Williams did not merit a high court trial; the prosecution abandoned its case against Khan in September 2011 on the basis that there was insufficient evidence. Neither stood as a candidate in the 2007 general election, but Khan was elected PNM Chairman in March 2011, re-entering the political arena. A more serious dispute surfaced in 2008. Dr Keith Rowley, a fiercely outspoken senior member of the Cabinet, was removed from his post as Minister of Trade and Industry in April after forcefully objecting to what he saw as a lack of transparency or accountability in the management of the Urban Development Corporation of Trinidad and Tobago (UDECOTT), a state-owned company responsible for the management of several large government construction projects. The leading private sector organizations joined Rowley in appealing for a public inquiry into the affairs of UDECOTT. A Commission of Inquiry was established in July, under the leadership of a British lawyer and civil engineer, Prof. John Uff, sitting with three local members, and published its report in March 2010, despite attempts by UDECOTT and others to derail the proceedings through legal actions alleging bias by the commissioners. The so-called Uff Commission identified several apparent instances of mismanagement or corruption on the part of UDECOTT, and noted that procedures and accountability were not clearly defined. Among a long list of serious concerns, it was noted that the construction (managed by UDECOTT) of a stadium intended for use in the 2007 Cricket World Cup remained unfinished; it was still unfinished in 2013, by which time its estimated cost had increased from TT $272m. to more than TT $1,100m. Furthermore, a TT $368m. contract for the construction of an office building had been awarded to a company led by the Malaysian brother-in-law of UDECOTT Chairman Calder Hart, which did not appear to meet the formal terms to qualify as a bidder. Hart, a Canadian by origin but granted citizenship of Trinidad and Tobago in 2004, resigned from his post in March 2010, and left Trinidad soon afterwards for Florida, USA, while a criminal inquiry into issues raised by the Commission was in progress.

Meanwhile, concerns over the scale of corruption were heightened in February 2009, when the members of the Integrity Commission resigned over judicial findings that an investigation into Rowley had been conducted in bad faith. A new Commission was appointed in April, but immediately collapsed after the majority of its members were deemed ineligible or were suspected of personal corruption; a replacement Commission was not announced until March 2010.

In addition to more general allegations of corruption and incompetence in the public sector, there was also widespread disquiet over perceived extravagance in government spending—for example, in the construction of a TT $175m. diplomatic centre and Prime Minister's residence, and in the priority given to government offices and cultural centres within the Government's capital spending plans. Moreover, provisions suggested in 2008 for a new constitution were seen as proposing too much power for a newly envisaged position of Executive President.

New divisions within the UNC emerged in 2008, with three high-profile members of Parliament appealing for elections to choose a new party leadership. This faction comprised former Attorney-General Ramesh Lawrence Maharaj, Jack Warner, a Vice-President of Fédération Internationale de Football Asso-

ciation (FIFA), and the prominent calypsonian musician Winston 'Gypsy' Peters. In the leadership ballot, held in January 2010, Kamla Persad-Bissessar, hitherto a loyal ally of Panday, stood against him, and, with the support of Warner, Peters and others, won by a convincing margin, becoming the first female opposition leader in Trinidad and Tobago's history.

THE PERSAD-BISSESSAR PREMIERSHIP

On 8 April 2010 Prime Minister Manning advised President Maxwell Richards to dissolve Parliament, and called an election for 24 May. No official reason was offered for the decision. Manning retained a clear majority, and there was no constitutional requirement to call an election before March 2013. Possible concerns he may have had included a motion of no confidence due to have been debated, which would have allowed damaging allegations to be reported under parliamentary privilege. With the election called, Persad-Bissessar swiftly formed an alliance with the COP, the TOP and two minor parties, and fought a vigorous campaign, under the banner of the People's Partnership, in which she pledged to combat crime, corruption and mismanagement, also opposing a proposed increase in property tax, and promising to raise state pensions and other spending commitments. The People's Partnership coalition won a convincing victory at the polls on 24 May, securing 29 of the 41 seats with 60.0% of the popular vote, and taking many seats hitherto regarded as PNM strongholds as well as both seats in Tobago; turnout was recorded at 69.4% of the registered electorate. Persad-Bissessar was inaugurated as Prime Minister on 26 May. Dookeran was appointed Minister of Finance, while Jack Warner was awarded the influential works and transport portfolio, and a former Chief of Defence Staff, Brig. John Sandy, a widely respected non-partisan figure, was appointed Minister of National Security. Manning was swiftly replaced as PNM leader after the election by his rival, Keith Rowley, who won a clear victory in a leadership challenge held in May 2014, by which time he appeared to have successfully rallied the party's traditional base to his support.

The People's Partnership was troubled by a number of corruption allegations and other controversies in its first year in office, although these initial scandals were minor in comparison to those that had marred the final stages of the Panday and Manning Governments. The Minister of Planning, Economic and Social Restructuring and Gender Affairs, Mary King, was removed from her post in May 2011, after reports that a software contract had been awarded to a company controlled by her immediate family. There were also some tensions both within and between the coalition parties. Dookeran resigned as Leader of the COP; in a strenuously contested internal election, the Minister of Legal Affairs, Prakash Ramadhar, was chosen as his replacement. More seriously, Warner was involved in controversies surrounding a presidential election campaign at FIFA; he had reportedly facilitated a meeting of the Caribbean Football Union in May, during which participants were each offered US $40,000 in cash on behalf of one of the candidates, Mohamed bin Hammam. Warner in June resigned from his positions as Vice-President of FIFA and President of the Confederation of North, Central American and Caribbean Association Football (CONCACAF) and the Caribbean Football Union; as a consequence, proceedings against him in FIFA's ethics committee were closed. Although there were at this point no major domestic political repercussions from this incident, the Ministry of Works and Transport was divided, and in a cabinet reorganization at the end of the month, Devant Maharaj was appointed Minister of Transport, with Warner, in an apparent demotion, retaining only the works portfolio. Verna St Rose-Greaves, an opponent of the death penalty, became Minister of Gender, Youth and Child Development; Bhoendradatt Tewarie had earlier been awarded the planning, economic and social restructuring portfolio. Dr Fuad Khan was appointed Minister of Health.

The number of murders, which had peaked in 2008, fell by 7.1% in 2009 and 7.3% in 2010, with a murder rate in that year of 36 per 100,000, the fourth highest in the English-speaking Caribbean. As with the earlier rapid escalation in killings, the precise reasons for this relative improvement were not clear.

At the same time, increased attention was given in 2011 to killings by the police, which totalled 265 in the years between 2000 and 2011; although thorough investigations were promised by Gillian Lucky, the director of the Police Complaints Authority, a forceful lawyer and a former member of Parliament. Six police officers were in July 2013 committed to stand trial for the murder two years earlier of two women and a man from the southern village of Moruga; however, the trial had not started by mid-2014. In order to reduce backlogs of up to 10 years in the criminal courts, the Chief Justice, Ivor Archie, in September 2013 proposed the abolition of preliminary inquiries in the magistrates' courts and of jury trials, as well as the increased use of plea bargaining and decriminalization of the possession of small quantities of marijuana.

In September 2010, with the fiscal outlook now believed to be more dismal than initially anticipated, the Government cancelled the planned purchase of three offshore patrol vessels, at a combined cost of £150m., from the major British aerospace and defence manufacturer BAE Systems. The SAUTT (see above) was also disbanded. A much-derided airship, 'the Blimp', used by SAUTT for surveillance purposes was decommissioned. Six Austal patrol vessels purchased by the PNM Government were reported to be out of action by early 2014, along with 12 interceptor craft, leaving the coastguard with very limited capability to prevent the flow of drugs and guns from Venezuela. The Government intended to buy three long-range patrol vessels, but these were not expected to be ready for several years. There was concern in late 2010 and early 2011 over revelations that the Security Intelligence Agency (SIA) had under the PNM administration 'tapped' the telecommunications of a wide range of individuals, from the President, members of Parliament and Chief Justice to journalists, academics, lawyers and business people. Without a clear legal basis, the agency had, according to some reports, been active since the 1990s, and appeared to have been singularly ineffective in stemming the activities of narcotics traffickers, corrupt officials or criminal gangs. Legislation providing a formal basis for interception of communications was adopted in December 2010, and it was announced that the SIA was to be merged with the Strategic Services Agency, a separate entity that had been created by Parliament in 1995.

Voters who had blamed the former PNM administration for the upsurge in violent crime since 2000 were disappointed that there was no immediate or dramatic reduction in the murder rate under the Partnership Government. Concerned that drugs gang conflicts were initiating a further deterioration, the Government on 21 August 2011 declared a state of emergency. A strictly enforced night-time curfew was imposed in most urban areas until 7 October, and the police and army were given additional powers; 436 suspects were arrested under new anti-gang legislation, but were released without charge. Murders averaged 3.3 per week during the state of emergency, down from 7.7 in September–November 2010. There was a similar impact on police reports of wounding, shooting, robbery and car theft. An average of 12.5 illegal guns were seized each week, up from a weekly 6.8 in January–August. The emergency state was allowed to lapse on 5 December and the murder rate swiftly returned to earlier levels; 382 murders were reported in 2012, and 406 in 2013, a rate of 30 per 100,000. There were 213 murders in the first half of 2014; these included the assassination on 4 May of Dana Seetahal, a prominent lawyer and former independent senator. Dwayne Gibbs, a Canadian who had been appointed Commissioner of Police in 2010, resigned in July 2012.

Warner's position was strengthened in March 2012, when he was elected as UNC Chairman. As part of a far-reaching cabinet reorganization in June, Warner replaced Sandy as Minister of National Security, a move that was viewed with concern in some circles as legal issues surrounding his former role at FIFA had not been resolved. Claims by players that financial commitments made by Warner for the 2006 football World Cup had not been honoured were still before the local courts. At the same time, Dookeran became Minister of Foreign Affairs, a fairly prestigious post but outside of the central policy-making circle; he was replaced as Minister of Finance by Larry Howai, the former Chief Executive of state-owned First

Citizens Bank. Of 33 ministers in an enlarged Cabinet, only 12 retained their posts from the previous configuration.

The Government suffered political damage in August 2012, when Section 34 of the Administration of Justice (Indictable Proceedings) Act 2011 entered into force. This allowed the accused to apply for a case to be discharged if proceedings had not advanced beyond the magistrate's court to a full trial within seven years. Among those who appeared likely to benefit from this legislation were Panday, along with former government ministers and others charged with corruption-related offences in connection with the construction of an airport terminal during the Panday administration. After a public outcry, Section 34 was swiftly repealed; a challenge to the repeal failed in the local appeal court in June 2014. As a result of the debacle, in September 2012 Minister of Justice Herbert Volney was replaced by Christlyn Moore, a member of the TOP.

The Government's morale was damaged in 2013 by the loss of electoral contests for the Tobago House of Assembly in January, for the parliamentary seat of Chaguanas West in July, for local government bodies in Trinidad in October, and for the St Joseph parliamentary seat in November. The Tobago election was held on 21 January 2013; the PNM won 61.4% of votes cast and all 12 seats, up from eight seats in 2009. This created an expectation that the party was likely to gain the two Tobago parliamentary seats from the TOP in the forthcoming general election.

Maxwell Richards' term of office as President ended in February 2013. Parliament, with all-party agreement, elected a high court judge, Anthony Carmona, to succeed him. Signalling his independent role as head of state, Carmona opened the new parliamentary session on 1 August with a speech that called for new rules on the financing of political campaigns, investigation by the tax authorities of politicians whose assets did not match their declared income, improved conduct of parliamentary debate, as well as a secret conscience vote in Parliament or referendum on replacement of the Privy Council by the Caribbean Court of Justice. On the previous day the new President had also broken with tradition by revoking the appointment of four of the independent senators previously appointed by Richards, appointing two lawyers, an energy expert and an economist in their stead.

In April 2013 an inquiry led by former Barbados Chief Justice Sir David Simmons reported to CONCACAF on allegations relating to Warner's former role at the Confederation. It found that the balance of probabilities suggested that Warner had committed fraud and misappropriated funds. On 20 April Warner resigned as Minister of National Security, and on the following day he stepped down as UNC Chairman. At a public rally on 24 April, Warner also resigned as the member of Parliament for Chaguanas West, although he immediately announced that he would seek vindication from the electorate by standing in the resulting by-election. However, after failing to win the UNC nomination, Warner formed a new grouping, the Independent Liberal Party (ILP). Warner took 69% of the by-election vote, held on 29 July 2013, compared with 30% for the UNC and 1% for the PNM. This defeat by an Afro-Trinidadian candidate in the party's Indo-Trinidadian heartland represented a severe setback for the People's Partnership coalition; this was compounded by an initially enthusiastic response to Warner's victory from three cabinet ministers.

However, the success of the ILP proved limited in scope. In local government elections in Trinidad held on 21 October 2013, the party won 23% of the popular vote after an expensive, high-profile campaign, but only three of the 136 seats, two of them in Warner's Chaguanas stronghold. The PNM won control of eight of the 14 councils with 42% of votes cast, up from 33% in 2010, while the UNC took five seats with 27% of the votes, down from 51%, with its strength concentrated in its rural south Trinidad heartlands. There was a three-way split and no overall control in Chaguanas, while the COP lost heavily to the PNM in the mainly urban and suburban seats it contested, taking only four seats and 7% of the national vote, down from 16% in 2010. For the first time, councils included aldermen elected by proportional representation; because of the particular system chosen, this did not result in significant minority representation. The local election result created an expectation that neither the COP nor the ILP would fare well in the general election.

Meanwhile, in September 2013 Volney declared that he no longer supported the UNC. Under Trinidad and Tobago parliamentary rules on crossing the floor, he had to fight a by-election for his St Joseph seat, which was held on 4 November. Although Volney declared his support for the ILP, the party chose as its candidate a lawyer, Om Lalla, who took just 14% of votes cast, compared with 45% for the PNM. The UNC took 39%, down from 58% at the 2010 general election. If repeated nationally, this swing would be sufficient to give the PNM 23 of the 41 parliamentary seats.

A further round of cabinet changes appeared to indicate a level of government weakness. In a reshuffle announced in September 2013, Emmanuel George, who had taken over from Warner as the Minister of National Security in April, was in turn replaced by Gary Griffith, the fourth minister to hold that post in 16 months. George replaced Christlyn Moore as Minister of Justice. The Minister of Tourism, Chandresh Sharma, and Minister of Social Development, Glenn Ramadharsingh, resigned in March 2014 over allegations of improper personal conduct. The Minister of Sport, Anil Roberts, also resigned, in July, over the apparent infiltration of the TT $114m. Life Sport job creation programme by criminal elements.

In August 2014 Parliament approved amendments to the Constitution that included the introduction of a two-term limit for the Prime Minister, the right to recall members of Parliament, and the need for a run-off election if a parliamentary candidate receives less than 50% of the votes in any ballot.

INTERNATIONAL RELATIONS

In April 2000 Trinidad and Tobago received widespread international condemnation following an announcement that the country was to withdraw from the first optional protocol to the International Covenant on Civil and Political Rights, owing to its continued support of capital punishment. The Government stated that the withdrawal was intended to prevent condemned murderers from addressing lengthy appeals. Both major parties, while in office, pressed for the use of capital punishment, but, in most cases, were unsuccessful. In January 2011 the People's Partnership Government attempted to amend the Constitution to remove obstacles to use of the death penalty; this would have required a three-quarters' majority, and hence opposition support. However, the PNM voted against the proposal, on the basis that it was insufficiently far-reaching in its attempt to restore the death penalty.

Talks were held from 1995 to demarcate the maritime boundary between Trinidad and Tobago and Barbados and to revise a 1991 agreement granting Barbados limited fishing rights. Although fishing issues were prominently reported, oil and gas-bearing geological structures close to the probable boundary line were believed to be of greater interest to both sides. Differences escalated sharply from January 2004; in February Barbados imposed limited licensing requirements on some imports from Trinidad and Tobago, and then referred the maritime dispute for arbitration under the UN Law of the Sea.

A tribunal ruled in April 2006 on an Exclusive Economic Zone boundary that followed the line of equidistance for most of its length. This allocated a large area to the north-east of Tobago, thought to have some deep-water oil and gas potential, to Barbados. Trinidad and Tobago retained an area of similar size to the north of Tobago, where Barbados had claimed fishing rights, but was instructed to negotiate a fisheries agreement; no tangible progress had been made on this issue by mid-2014. Meanwhile, a maritime boundary agreement with Grenada was signed in April 2010.

Barbados and Trinidad and Tobago were the only Caribbean Community and Common Market (CARICOM) members to remain outside Venezuela's 2005 Petrocaribe initiative, which offered oil concessions and favourable financing terms to Caribbean nations. This was expected to threaten the regional market of the state-owned oil company, Petrotrin. However, in April 2006 Trinidad and Tobago agreed to the waiver of CARICOM rules, allowing Petrocaribe to proceed. Progress was subsequently reported in negotiations with Venezuela for the use of cross-border oil and gas reserves, with a framework agreement signed in March 2007 providing a basis for detailed proposals. However, there had been little further progress by mid-2014, and the Venezuelan Government was not thought to favour an agreement. Trinidad and Tobago, meanwhile, appeared less ready under the People's Partnership to offer financial assistance to other CARICOM members or to pursue ambitious regional unity initiatives, not least because its own fiscal position was more restricted than it had been in 2007–08.

In April 2005 the Caribbean Court of Justice was officially inaugurated. The regional Court, based in Port of Spain, was to replace the Privy Council in the United Kingdom as the final court of appeal, and was also to adjudicate on disputes relating to the implementation of CARICOM agreements. An agreement to establish the Court had been signed by the leaders of 11 Caribbean states in February 2001, at a CARICOM summit in Barbados. However, by mid-2014 only Barbados, Belize and Guyana had adopted the appellate jurisdiction of the Court. Dominica had passed legislation to adopt the CCJ, and was expected to complete formal procedures; however, other member states were at this point using it only to settle CARICOM matters. The Manning administration had been in favour of the Court; however, while in opposition, the UNC had stated that it would not support the Court, reversing the position that it adopted while in office prior to 2001. With a further change of position, in April 2012 Persad-Bissessar announced that she would introduce a constitutional amendment for Trinidad and Tobago to adopt the jurisdiction of the court in criminal, but not civil, matters, a proposal that left many dissatisfied on both sides of the debate. Legislation to effect the change would require a three-quarters' parliamentary majority and would (if limited to criminal matters) have to be accepted by the Court itself. Along with most of its CARICOM associates, Trinidad and Tobago remained a strong supporter of the International Criminal Court, established in 2002, and refused to sign an agreement exempting US military personnel from its proceedings.

Economy

MARK WILSON

At the beginning of the 21st century the economy of Trinidad and Tobago contrasted sharply with those of its Caribbean neighbours. Although no longer dependent on the extraction and refining of petroleum, it remained underpinned by the energy sector, with the extraction of natural gas and crude oil providing the basis for processing and manufacturing industries. Energy industries accounted for 43% of GDP, 50% of government revenue and 85% of exports in 2013. Tourism, 'offshore' finance, and agriculture, by contrast, were less well developed. In 2013 Trinidad and Tobago ranked 67th out of 186 countries in the UN Development Programme's Human Development Index, the fourth ranking country in the English-speaking Caribbean.

A phase of rapid economic development began when petroleum prices rose from US $1.30 per barrel in 1970 to $33.50 in 1982. This led to rapid growth in gross domestic product (GDP) in this period, with strong positive effects on foreign exchange earnings and on government revenue. The Government attempted to spread the benefits of the increase in petroleum prices through spending on infrastructure, investment in state-owned, heavy industries and other capital projects. Imports were restricted in an effort to encourage local manufacturing, while protection also extended to services such as insurance.

World oil prices fell sharply in the 1980s, adversely affecting domestic petroleum production, while new facilities for crude petroleum imports to the USA had already prompted the removal of that country's strategically motivated tax incentives for petroleum products refined in the Caribbean. Production levels also declined. However, there were also some important discoveries at the end of the century. Production rose to 144,500 barrels per day (b/d) in 2005, with newly developed reserves coming on-stream, but fell back to 81,140 b/d in 2013, mainly because of reserve depletion, but also in part owing to operational difficulties. Proven oil reserves were 990m. barrels in 2004 (the most recent publicly available audit), with 324m. barrels of probable reserves and 2,000m. barrels of possible reserves. BP estimated proven reserves at 800m. barrels in 2013.

Owing to an economic recession, in 1986 the Government adopted a structural adjustment programme and negotiated two successive stand-by agreements with the IMF. This was followed in 1990 by debt-rescheduling agreements with lending agencies and a loan agreement with the Inter-American Development Bank (IDB). These measures, along with enhanced use of natural gas resources, overseas investment in energy industries and increased activity in other manufacturing industries and the financial sector, contributed to a general economic recovery in the 1990s. According to the Central Bank of Trinidad and Tobago, GDP grew at an average annual rate of 3.9% in 1996–2001 and exceeded 5% each year from 2001, slipping back to a still brisk growth rate of 4.6% in 2007, and then to 2.3% in 2008; however, there was a reversal in 2009, with the economy contracting by 4.4% in that year, barely stagnating in 2010 and contracting by a further 2.6% in 2011, as energy prices fell and the effects of the global economic downturn took hold. Overall growth was put at 1.2% in 2012, picking up slightly to 1.6% in 2013, with a weak recovery in the non-energy sector. Official unemployment remained low, and in part because of government job-creation schemes was recorded at just 3.7% in March 2013, in spite of the economic downturn, although the underlying rate was believed to be significantly higher.

From mid-1999 to mid-2008 a strong upward trend in international energy prices had a positive effect on government revenues. Chemicals and steel prices as well as those of oil and gas recovered from declines in the late 1990s. However, the economy came under some pressure from the second half of 2008 as the global economic downturn affected energy commodity prices and, as a result, the economy moved from rapid growth to a cumulative contraction of 6.8% in 2009–11. The average West Texas Intermediate oil price in 2009 was 38% lower than that in 2008, at US $61.7 per barrel; ammonia prices declined to US $228 per metric ton from $732 per ton in 2008, while methanol prices fell to US $241 per ton (from an average of $729 in the first quarter of 2008). Export prices of liquefied natural gas (LNG) also declined substantially, with the Henry Hub (the pricing point for natural gas futures contracts traded on the New York Mercantile Exchange) gas price averaging below US $3.00 at the beginning of 2012, compared with an average of US $8.64 in 2005, although this was partially offset by higher LNG prices in Europe and Asia. Although there was some recovery in energy prices in 2010 and 2011, they remained generally constant from that point, and were still below pre-2008 levels. These price trends placed considerable pressure on government finances, as energy sector revenue fell from 20.0% of GDP in the financial year to October 2008, to 14.3% for 2008/09, with a partial recovery to 17.4% in 2012/13. Major private sector energy investment projects were placed on hold, and the construction sector contracted by a cumulative 40.6% in 2009–12, after working at or above full capacity for several years, with 3.0% growth indicating a weak recovery in 2013. The index of retail sales revealed a 7.6% decline in 2009, in sharp contrast to consumer spending growth of 20.1% in 2007 and 13.7% in 2008; retail sales remained flat in cash terms in 2010, with inflation at 10.5%, indicating a substantial reduction in the volume of goods sold and a significant cut in real incomes. Sales recovered by 8.4% in 2011 and 2.5% in 2012, with inflation at 5.3% and 7.2%, but still indicating a weak trend in demand. Reflecting the swings in consumer confidence, sales of building materials and hardware declined by 31.4% in 2008–10 and remained flat in 2011 and 2012, while those of motor vehicles and parts fell by 28.6% in 2009, but recovered by 14.3% in the next two years.

The population totalled an estimated 1,328,019 at the 2011 census, with a population density of 259 per sq km. Approximately one-half of the population lived in an urbanized 'east–west corridor', stretching from Diego Martin in the west, through Port of Spain to Arima in the east. One-sixth of the population lived in other urban areas, principally the San Fernando conurbation in southern Trinidad and Chaguanas in the centre of the country, with 54,084 in the smaller island of Tobago. The average annual population growth rate was 0.5% in 2000–11.

AGRICULTURE

The strength of the energy-based economy led to the relative neglect of agriculture from the 1950s, while agricultural wage rates could not compete with other areas of employment. As a result, in 2013 the sector contributed only 0.6% of GDP (down from 6.9% in 1972), but employed 3.5% of the employed labour force.

The principal commercial crop until 2007 was sugar. Until mid-2003 the main producer was a state-owned company, Caroni (1975) Ltd, which operated two sugar factories. The Government wrote off the company's accumulated debts of TT $2,400m. in 1994; however, by 2002 continuing losses had increased the debt again, to TT $2,300m., and in July 2003 the Government closed the company down. One of Caroni's successors, the state-owned Sugar Manufacturing Company, operated the remaining sugar factory at Sainte Madeleine until 2007, but did not grow sugar cane, buying the crop from independent farmers. Exports, which went mainly to Europe at the preferential price agreed under the European Union's (EU) Cotonou Agreement, totalled 60,900 metric tons in 2002, but fell to 26,600 tons in 2007. With the EU about to phase out its preferential sugar prices, the closure of the Sainte Madeleine factory was announced in 2007. Sugar used on the local market from 2008 was imported from Guyana, Belize and other suppliers.

Premium-quality cocoa was a traditional export, but production fell from 7,542 metric tons in 1972 to just 381 tons in 2013. Low-grade robusta coffee was grown: production was

4,586 tons in 1968, but had fallen to just two tons in 2012. A wide variety of vegetables and fruits was grown mainly for the local market, as well as some rice. In 2001–08 commercial citrus production ranged from 167 tons to 7,495 tons (standing at 355 tons in 2012). Local producers supplied virtually the entire domestic market with eggs and broiler chicken (some 25.1m. birds in 2012), using mainly imported feed.

Teak was produced in small quantities, and was used in the yacht repair industry. However, most lumber requirements were imported. The fishing sector was also small in scale, employing approximately 3,140 people in 2000; most of the catch was used locally, but frozen shrimps were exported. Trinidad was also used as a base by Asian vessels for deep-sea fishing in the Caribbean and mid-Atlantic.

PETROLEUM AND GAS

Energy-based industries were of central importance to the Trinidad and Tobago economy. Commercial petroleum production started in 1908, although the first oil well was sunk as early as 1857. Refining of local and imported petroleum was well established by the 1930s, and the sector accounted for 29.2% of GDP by 1955, in which year offshore petroleum production began; most petroleum and gas was produced on the east coast continental shelf. The energy sector's contribution to GDP increased to 42.8% in 1980, owing to higher petroleum prices, but fell to 21.8% in 1986. After a long and powerful recovery, by 2008 the petroleum sector (including mining, refining and petrochemicals) accounted for 50.8% of GDP, assisted by record-high petroleum prices. The sector's contribution to GDP fell back to 34.6% in 2009, as a result of markedly lower energy prices, but rose again, to 42.9%, in 2013. However, the sector's contribution to employment was much lower, at only 3.4% of the working population in 2013.

A wide range of international companies were involved in petroleum and gas exploration and production in Trinidad and Tobago's offshore areas. The state-owned Petroleum Company of Trinidad and Tobago Ltd (Petrotrin) and the National Gas Company of Trinidad and Tobago Ltd (NGC), as well as small, local, privately owned producers, operated both onshore and offshore. The leading producer was BP Trinidad and Tobago (BPTT—70% owned by BP and 30% by Repsol-YPF of Spain). The Australian company BHP Billiton, with its Angostura field, was a significant producer. In 2010 public sector producers were responsible for 43% of oil production, BP for 35%, Repsol for 25% and BHP for 17%. There was just one refinery, at Pointe-à-Pierre, owned by Petrotrin, which refined local and imported crude petroleum. A US $1,880m. redevelopment of the plant was close to completion in 2014, albeit six years behind schedule and with costs more than four times the original budget. Most of BP's local crude petroleum was refined overseas, although some was processed by Petrotrin.

Natural gas use increased at an average annual rate of 19% in 1997–2006, but by an average annual rate of only 1.8% in 2007–10, with just one major new petrochemicals plant commencing operations during that period. Natural gas use then contracted by a cumulative 4.5% in 2011–12, in part because of maintenance shutdowns, with a partial recovery by 0.8% in 2013. BPTT accounted for 51%, BG Group for 24%, EOG Resources for 13%, and BHP for 10% of natural gas production in 2012. A major LNG plant, the Atlantic LNG Company of Trinidad and Tobago, came on-stream in 1999, initially purchasing 450m. cu ft per day of natural gas directly from BP, equivalent to some 30% of total national gas production. The plant was owned by a consortium of BP, BG Trinidad and Tobago Ltd, Shell, Summer Soca LNG Liquefaction (a subsidiary of China Investment Corporation), and the NGC, which had a 10% shareholding. The capital cost of the first-phase project was US $950m. An expansion project completed in 2003 increased gas consumption to approximately 1,400m. cu ft per day, with 62.5% of gas used by the LNG plant supplied by BP and 37.5% by BG and its partners, using a new pipeline that allowed Trinidad's north coast gas fields to be exploited for the first time. A further US $1,160m. expansion was completed in 2005 by BP, BG, Repsol and the NGC, making Trinidad a leading LNG producer, with additional daily gas usage for LNG of 800m. cu ft (bringing the total for the plant to 2,350m.

cu ft) and annual output of 15m. metric tons. After presenting a tough stance on project benefits in negotiations, the Government projected an annual revenue of TT $58,000m. over 20 years from the latest expansion, assuming a natural gas price in the USA of US $5 per million British thermal units (Btu). Markets have shifted dramatically owing to the growth of US shale gas production and gas shortages in Europe, Asia and South America; the proportion sold to the USA fell from 99% in 2004 to 14% in the seven months to April 2013 (with a further 7% taken by Puerto Rico), while the proportion sold to Chile, Argentina and Brazil rose to 45%, with Spain receiving a further 15%. Proposals for a fifth LNG train were mooted after 2005; however, such proposals were unlikely to come to fruition unless any significant new gas discoveries were made.

The exploitation of shale gas in the USA and elsewhere was a source of concern, as it provided a low-cost onshore source of supply, which has displaced imports, reduced gas prices, and can allow the establishment or reopening of gas-based petrochemicals plants within the USA and other major markets, making the development of high-cost offshore gas fields in Trinidad and Tobago waters increasingly unattractive. Some new discoveries were made in recent years and the potential for new deep-water finds was thought to be good. Proven reserves were 13,106,000 m. cu ft at the end of 2012, an amount that would be exhausted in 8.8 years from that date at 2013 usage rates. However, there was a further 12,111,000 m. cu ft in probable and possible reserves, which would be sufficient for a further 8.0 years at 2013 usage rates. Moreover, industry estimates suggest exploration potential of 31,616,000m. cu ft, which, if confirmed, would bring the total to a level that would comfortably accommodate the proposed level of production. However, the proven reserves total includes cross-border resources, and the exploitation of these requires an agreement with Venezuela, on which there had been no significant progress by mid-2014, despite many years of intermittent talks. There was some optimism in Trinidad and Tobago that Venezuela would agree to the processing of its own otherwise inaccessible gas reserves in Trinidad, but the Venezuelan Government had by mid-2014 offered no indication that this was likely.

In 2013 some 43% of the natural gas used in Trinidad and Tobago was purchased by the NGC, which supplied the needs of all end-users except the LNG plant. Natural gas production averaged 4,144m. cu ft per day in 2013, according to the Central Bank (of which 3,854 was used productively). In that year some 57% of gas use was in the manufacture of LNG, 29% for petrochemicals, and 8% in electric power generation, with most of the remainder used in the iron and steel industry and cement manufacturing. Efforts to increase the local content of energy sector projects resulted in eight locally constructed oil-drilling platform being completed by 2011; however there has been a dearth of new orders since then. There was continuing use of local service companies in engineering, fabrication or instrumentation, some of which have developed overseas operations.

MANUFACTURING

The manufacturing sector, excluding petroleum, contributed 6.1% of GDP in 2013 and employed 8.2% of the employed labour force in 2012. Energy-based manufacturing expanded rapidly to 2008. Trinidad and Tobago became the world's largest methanol exporter in 2000, and in 2010 accounted for an estimated 8% of world production. The first methanol plant was established in 1984, under state ownership, and was sold in 1997 to Methanol Holdings (Trinidad) Ltd. There were seven methanol plants in total, with a total capacity of 6.5m. metric tons, including the M5000 plant at Point Lisas.

Trinidad and Tobago was also the world's principal exporter of ammonia; production started in 1959, and in 2010 it was the world's fifth largest producer, after the People's Republic of China, India, Russia and the USA, with 4% of global production. Several major petrochemicals projects were placed on hold from 2008, as international credit markets tightened and energy and chemicals prices fell sharply. However, in 2009 Methanol Holdings commissioned a major component of a

US \$1,700m. ammonia-urea ammonium nitrate-melamine (AUM) complex, which began production of melamine in 2011.

The state-owned Iron and Steel Company of Trinidad and Tobago made large losses until the commencement of a lease arrangement with the local subsidiary of an Indian company, Ispat, in 1989. Caribbean Ispat Ltd subsequently acquired the plant in 1994; and is now part of Arcelor Mittal.

Low-cost natural gas assisted the development of other manufacturing industries. Trinidad Cement Ltd used locally quarried limestone in gas-fired kilns; between 2009 and 2012 cement production declined by almost 25% to 654,100 metric tons, of which 31% was exported to regional markets. Carib Glassworks was another manufacturing concern to benefit from cheap energy, producing bottles for national and export markets, while low-cost electricity from gas-powered generating stations allowed local soft-drink manufacturers to operate competitively for export to the wider Caribbean and beyond. There was also a wide range of consumer goods, food and other industries.

TRANSPORT AND COMMUNICATIONS

There were 8,320 km (5,169 miles) of roads in Trinidad and Tobago. Major routes were covered by four-lane highways, which, however, suffered from heavy congestion, with an estimated 471,479 vehicles in use by 2008.

The main international ports were at Port of Spain (container, cargo and cruise ships), run by the Port Authority of Trinidad and Tobago; and Point Lisas (private sector, handling mainly specialized bulk cargo piers, but also container cargo). The smaller port of Scarborough in Tobago handled general cargo, ferry services and cruise ships. There were also specialized port facilities at Point Fortin (LNG), Pointe-à-Pierre (crude petroleum and refinery products), and Claxton Bay (cement). Further specialized port facilities were under proposal or development. Port of Spain was unable to accommodate Panamax vessels, still less the Post-Panamax vessels to be used when the Panama Canal expansion was completed in 2015, and much of its container cargo was therefore transshipped through Kingston in Jamaica or another regional hub.

Trinidad's airport at Piarco offered direct connections to North America, Europe, most other Caribbean islands, Guyana, Suriname and Venezuela. In 2010 some 1.62m. international passengers used the airport. There was a frequent service to ANR Robinson airport in Tobago, carrying some 630,000 passengers in 2010; Tobago was also served by direct connections to Europe, North America and some neighbouring Caribbean islands. These services carried 70,000 passengers in 2010. The national airline, Caribbean Airlines, opened in 2007 as the successor to BWIA International Airways. Caribbean Airlines completed the purchase of Air Jamaica in 2011, but was making heavy losses by 2014 in spite of a generous fuel subsidy.

Trinidad and Tobago benefited from good telecommunication links. The landline telecommunications sector was a monopoly until 2008, controlled by Telecommunication Services of Trinidad and Tobago (TSTT) Ltd, 51% of which was owned by the Government and 49% by a British company, Cable & Wireless. A competing cellular telephone operator, Digicel, launched operations in 2006, gaining an estimated market share of 52% by 2010. In 2013 there were an estimated 22 landline and 146 cellular subscribers per 100 population (with many people having more than one mobile connection). The monopoly cable television company, Columbus Communications, launched landline services in competition with TSTT from 2008. There were 17 fixed broadband subscriptions per 100 population in 2013 and it was estimated that 63.8% of the population had access to the internet.

TOURISM

For many years the tourism potential of Trinidad and Tobago was not fully developed. From the early 1980s, however, successive governments placed greater emphasis on the sector, providing new facilities, including a cruise ship terminal in Port of Spain, and conducting more effective promotional campaigns. There were 454,683 air arrivals in 2012. In 2010 47% of stop-over visitors were from the USA, 12% from Canada and 13% from Europe, with most of the remainder from the Caribbean. The industry remained significantly less developed than that of other Caribbean islands: in 2011 49% of tourist spending was by visiting friends and relatives, 19% by business visitors and 27% by other hotel tourists. Net earnings from tourism contributed US \$362m., equivalent to 4.0% of merchandise imports, in 2012. There were 49,275 cruise passenger arrivals in 2012, of whom 64% went to Tobago; the islands were south of the main cruise routes, but some ships were attracted by low-cost fuel.

The number of hotel rooms stood at 3,728 in 2008, of which some 42.4% were on Tobago. On Trinidad the main hotels catered principally for business visitors, although the annual pre-Lenten Carnival was a major attraction. There was an important yacht- and powerboat-service industry based at marinas on the north-west peninsula of the island. For insurance purposes, Trinidad lies outside the hurricane belt. This factor, as well as a combination of competitive wage rates and engineering skills, has produced an attractive environment for repair services, which at its peak generated an estimated US \$24m. per year. Yacht arrivals increased from 637 in 1990 to 3,249 in 2000, but declined to 1,471 by 2012.

PUBLIC FINANCE

In response to a sharp deterioration in government finances in the 1980s, successive governments implemented austerity and emergency budgets, reducing expenditure and increasing taxation, and made use of IMF compensatory financing and stand-by credit. Value-added tax was introduced at the rate of 15% in 1990, leading to a further stand-by agreement with the IMF, while the IDB provided funds over four years for housing, infrastructure development and major energy investments, including an upgrade of the Pointe-à-Pierre petroleum refinery. The IDB's conditions emphasized relaxation of import and foreign exchange controls, reduced tariffs, currency liberalization and privatization of state-owned industries.

The fiscal balance oscillated between modest deficit and surplus from the mid-1990s, influenced primarily by energy price fluctuations, before moving firmly into positive territory—there was an overall surplus of 5.2% of GDP by 2004/05, which increased further to 6.9% in 2005/06, with strong energy prices and rising production. The overall surplus declined to 1.8% of GDP in 2006/07, but recovered to 7.8% in 2007/08 as a rise in energy revenue more than compensated for increased capital spending. However, the fiscal balance moved sharply into a deficit of 5.0% of GDP in 2008/09 as energy prices fell significantly below budget forecasts. The fiscal accounts were broadly in balance for the next two years, but the deficit increased again to reach 1.4% of GDP in 2011/12 and 2.6% in 2012/13. There had been concerns over the use of extra-budgetary expenditure by state-owned implementation companies to fund capital programmes. There was apparent consensus on the need for increased transparency and efficiency in the award of public sector contracts; however, views differed greatly with regard to the means by which these sometimes contradictory objectives could be achieved, with widespread criticism of the operations of state-owned companies used for project implementation, particularly the Urban Development Corporation of Trinidad and Tobago (UDECOTT). In 2010 a Commission of Inquiry into UDECOTT was severely critical of the company and more generally of state management of the construction sector (see History). New public procurement legislation had been submitted to Parliament by mid-2014. Meanwhile, an interim Revenue Stabilization Fund was established in 2000, before being placed on a firm statutory footing in 2007 as the Heritage and Stabilization Fund; in July 2014 the Fund held US \$5,500m., close to 20% of GDP.

The inflation increased from 2004 to reach a high of 15.4% in October 2008, at which point food price inflation reached 33.4%. With tighter monetary policy and a stabilization of international commodity prices, inflation declined to 1.3% in December 2009. However, inflationary pressures subsequently returned, with inflation rising to 16.2% for the year to August 2010, driven predominantly by steep increases in the price of foods. Annual inflation was 5.1% in 2011, 9.2% in 2012 and 5.2% in 2013, at which point there had been a five-year cumulative price increase of 97% for food and 43% for all items.

FINANCIAL SERVICES

Trinidad and Tobago had a large domestic banking sector. Of the four main commercial banks Republic Bank Ltd was in local private sector ownership; RBC Royal Bank Trinidad and Tobago Ltd was the successor to locally owned RBTT Ltd, which had been purchased in 2008 by Royal Bank of Canada; Scotiabank Trinidad and Tobago Ltd was the local subsidiary of the Canadian Scotiabank; First Citizens Bank Ltd was state-owned, but with a public offering of 20% of its share capital in August 2013; in addition, Citibank (Trinidad and Tobago) Ltd and the local operation of First Caribbean International Bank specialized in services for corporate clients.

Trinidad and Tobago was a regional centre for some financial services. Royal Bank of Canada moved its regional centre of operations to Trinidad and Tobago, while Republic Bank had subsidiaries in Grenada, Guyana and Barbados, and in 2013 acquired a 32% stake in a Ghanaian bank, HFC (with a bid for full control in 2014). In 2007 financial institutions based in Trinidad and Tobago led 37 bond issues with a total value of TT $2,592m. in local currency and US $357m. in US currency for the local and regional private and public sectors; however, as the international financial crisis took hold the emphasis shifted, with issues in 2013 of TT $6,942m. for the local public and private sectors, and TT $3,059m. for the Government. Some losses had, meanwhile, been incurred from increased exposure to country risk in Caribbean markets.

At mid-2014 the Trinidad and Tobago Stock Exchange listed 24 local and four other Caribbean companies. Between July 2008 and June 2009 the index declined by 32%, as the local economy experienced difficulties, but had advanced by 86% by July 2014. As part of its move to diversify the economy away from the energy sector, from 2008 the former People's National Movement Government promoted proposals for an international financial services centre. However, with increased international financial instability and the ensuing regulatory pressure on Caribbean offshore centres, this project was unlikely to come to fruition. The Financial Intelligence Unit was admitted to the international Egmont Group in June 2013.

CL Financial conglomerate grew out of the Colonial Life Insurance Company, and by 2008 held a majority shareholding in Republic Bank and interests in property, supermarkets, media, rum, foods and methanol and ammonia plants, claiming assets equivalent to 74% of GDP in 2007. Its operations had expanded rapidly as a result of very high leveraging, with unregulated deposits taken from the public at extremely high interest rates of up to 11%, and extensive related-party lending; by early 2009 the group was in severe financial difficulties resulting, in part, from a tighter credit environment and falling methanol prices. The Trinidad and Tobago operation of Colonial Life, which held 55% of the country's insurance sector assets, along with several financial sector subsidiaries, was taken into public sector control in January, with the Government subsequently taking majority board representation to control the parent company. After a rescue operation with an estimated net cost of TT $22,000m., or 13% of GDP, the Government in November 2012 compensated holders of large unregulated deposits with interest-free bonds payable over an extended period, representing a significant loss from the face value of their assets, but redeemable in exchange for shares in a mutual fund, which held shares in CL Financial assets. A commission of enquiry by a senior British judge, Anthony Colman, into the failure of CL Financial (and also a large credit union) was appointed in 2010, but had not delivered its full report by mid-2014.

FOREIGN TRADE, DEBT AND BALANCE OF PAYMENTS

The trade balance moved strongly into surplus at the turn of the century, rising from US $63.6m. in 1999 to US $969m. in 2000 and, buoyed by record-high energy prices, to US $9,064m. in 2008; the current account surplus in 2008 stood at US $8,519m., equivalent to 32.6% of GDP. However, there was a deterioration in the trade balance in 2009. Exports declined by 50%, with a sharp fall in energy prices; although imports also decreased, by 27%. However, the surplus on merchandise trade remained comfortable at US $2,241m. or 11.6% of GDP. By 2013 exports had recovered to US $12,770, or 32% below their 2008 peak, with a trade surplus of US $3,899m., or 15.1% of GDP. There was a positive services balance of US $662m. in 2013, sufficient to cover 7.5% of merchandise imports. Income flows were a strong outflow item in 2013, equivalent to 15.8% of merchandise exports, largely owing to remittances of energy company profits. The current account balance in 2013 was US $2,571m., or 10.0% of GDP. In 2011 the principal merchandise exports were fuels (oil and LNG), which accounted for 56% of the total, and chemicals (28%). Crude oil for local refining comprised 38.8% of merchandise imports in 2011, with capital goods comprising a further 23.5%.

As a result of amortization, external debt was reduced from US $2,510m. in 1990 to US $1,281m. at the end of 2009, equivalent to 6.0% of GDP. Borrowing for capital projects in 1998–2001 increased total domestic and foreign public debt to 59.3% of GDP at the end of 2002; however, with GDP expanding steadily, this figure decreased to 29.0% at the end of 2009. By 2008 the external debt service ratio had declined to 1.0% (from 49% in 1993), while interest payments made up 9.4% of current government expenditure in 2009. However, new borrowing to stimulate the economy from the IDB and other sources, as well as borrowing to cover the liabilities of the CL Financial group, raised total public debt (excluding open market operations of the Central Bank, but including contingent liabilities) to 57% of GDP by December 2013.

The capital and financial account on the balance of payments was in deficit by US $1,785m. in 2013, equivalent to 6.9% of GDP, leaving the overall balance of payments in surplus by US $786m., or 3.1% of GDP. There were net short-term private sector capital outflows of US $2,725m., reflecting a lack of attractive local non-energy investment opportunities, and net direct investment inflows of US $971m. Exports and foreign direct investment inflows increased gross official reserves to US $9,987m. by the end of 2013, equivalent to 12 months of goods and services import cover.

CONCLUSION

High energy prices from 1999 to 2008 greatly improved Trinidad and Tobago's fiscal position, allowing an increase in both current and capital spending. From late 2008 continuing weakness in energy and chemicals prices placed government spending under pressure, while further difficulties stemmed from the collapse of the CL Financial conglomerate. However, the overall economy remained stable, and a recovery in energy prices maintained stability, allowing slow growth to resume from 2012. In the longer term, the major questions relate to the sustainability of projected levels of natural gas use, given the fairly limited local resource base, to the increased availability of shale gas within the USA, which reduced the attractiveness of Trinidad and Tobago as an exporter, and to increased supplies of LNG from Qatar and other producers; at mid-2014 major new investments in LNG, petrochemicals or metals were unlikely unless significant new discoveries were made. Government efforts to diversify the economy into sectors such as financial services, information and communications technology, and tourism have hitherto met with only limited success.

Statistical Survey

Sources (unless otherwise stated): Central Statistical Office, National Statistics Bldg, 80 Independence Sq., POB 98, Port of Spain; tel. 623-6495; fax 625-3802; e-mail info@cso.gov.tt; internet www.cso.planning.gov.tt; Central Bank of Trinidad and Tobago, POB 1250, Port of Spain; tel. 625-4835; fax 627-4696; e-mail info@central-bank.org.tt; internet www.central-bank.org.tt.

Area and Population

AREA, POPULATION AND DENSITY

Area (sq km)	5,128*
Population (census results)	
15 May 2000	1,262,366
9 January 2011	
Males	666,305
Females	661,714
Total	1,328,019
Population (official estimates at mid-year)†	
2012	1,335,194
2013	1,340,557
Density (per sq km) at mid-2013	261.4

* 1,980 sq miles. Of the total area, Trinidad is 4,828 sq km (1,864 sq miles) and Tobago 300 sq km (116 sq miles).
† Provisional figures.

POPULATION BY AGE AND SEX
(at 2011 census)

	Males	Females	Total
0–14 years	139,179	134,236	273,415
15–64 years	472,664	462,915	935,579
65 years and over . . .	54,462	64,563	119,025
Total	**666,305**	**661,714**	**1,328,019**

POPULATION BY ETHNIC GROUP
(at 2011 census)*

	Males	Females	Total	%
'East' Indian	236,823	231,701	468,524	35.43
African	228,068	224,469	452,537	34.22
Mixed	146,850	155,016	301,866	22.82
White	4,174	3,657	7,831	0.59
Other	4,918	4,624	9,542	0.72
Not stated	41,517	40,729	82,246	6.22
Total	**662,350**	**660,196**	**1,322,546**	**100.00**

*Excludes some institutional population and members of unenumerated households.

Note: Classification of ethnicity reflects national census methodology.

ADMINISTRATIVE DIVISIONS
(population at 2011 census)

	Population ('000)	Capital
Trinidad	1,267.1	Port of Spain
Arima (borough) . . .	33.6	Arima
Chaguanas (borough) . .	83.5	Chaguanas
Couva/Tabaquite/Talparo . .	178.4	Couva
Diego Martin	103.0	Petit Valley
Mayaro/Rio Claro . . .	35.7	Rio Claro
Penal/Debe	89.4	Penal
Point Fortin (borough) . .	20.2	Point Fortin
Port of Spain (city, capital) . .	37.1	—
Princes Town	102.4	Princes Town
San Fernando (city) . . .	48.8	—
San Juan/Laventille . . .	157.3	Laventille
Sangre Grande . . .	75.8	Sangre Grande
Siparia	86.9	Siparia
Tunapuna/Piarco . . .	215.1	Tunapuna
Tobago	60.9	Scarborough
Total	**1,328.0**	—

BIRTHS AND DEATHS
(annual averages, UN estimates)

	1995–2000	2000–05	2005–10
Birth rate (per 1,000) . . .	15.1	14.9	15.3
Death rate (per 1,000) . . .	7.8	8.3	8.9

Source: UN, *World Population Prospects: The 2012 Revision.*

Birth rate (per 1,000): 15.1 in 2011; 14.8 in 2012; 14.0 in 2013.
Death rate (per 1,000): 7.1 in 2011; 7.2 in 2012; 7.7 in 2013.
Life expectancy (years at birth): 69.8 (males 66.3, females 73.5) in 2012 (Source: World Bank, World Development Indicators database).

ECONOMICALLY ACTIVE POPULATION
('000 persons aged 15 years and over, April—June)

	2011	2012
Agriculture, forestry, hunting and fishing . .	20.5	19.5
Mining and quarrying	18.6	20.9
Petroleum and gas	17.6	20.0
Manufacturing	46.1	46.3
Electricity, gas and water	6.0	8.5
Construction	86.8	92.1
Wholesale and retail trade, restaurants and hotels	107.2	107.9
Transport, storage and communication . . .	42.0	44.1
Finance, insurance, real estate and business services	52.9	52.6
Community, social and personal services . .	200.1	202.5
Sub-total	**580.2**	**594.4**
Activities not adequately defined	1.5	2.4
Total employed	**581.9**	**596.8**
Unemployed	35.9	30.5
Total labour force	**617.8**	**627.3**

Health and Welfare

KEY INDICATORS

Total fertility rate (children per woman, 2012)	1.8
Under-5 mortality rate (per 1,000 live births, 2012) . . .	21
HIV/AIDS (% of persons, aged 15–49, 2011)	1.5
Physicians (per 1,000 head, 2007)	1.2
Hospital beds (per 1,000 head, 2009)	2.6
Health expenditure (2011): US $ per head (PPP) . . .	1,370
Health expenditure (2011): % of GDP	5.3
Health expenditure (2011): public (% of total) . . .	49.2
Access to water (% of persons, 2011)	94
Access to sanitation (% of persons, 2012)	92
Total carbon dioxide emissions ('000 metric tons, 2010) . .	50,681.6
Carbon dioxide emissions per head (metric tons, 2010) . .	38.2
Human Development Index (2013): ranking	64
Human Development Index (2013): value	0.766

For sources and definitions, see explanatory note on p. vi.

Agriculture

PRINCIPAL CROPS
('000 metric tons)

	2010	2011	2012
Rice, paddy	2.3	2.7	2.1
Maize	3.2*	3.4*	3.5†
Taro (Cocoyam)	5.7*	2.7	2.8
Pigeon peas	0.9	1.0	1.5
Coconuts†	16.6	16.3	16.3
Cabbages	0.3	0.8	1.2
Lettuce	1.4	2.0	2.2
Tomatoes	2.2	1.6	1.5
Pumpkins, squash and gourds	1.8	4.8	2.6
Cucumbers and gherkins	1.3	1.2	1.4
Aubergines	0.9	1.6	1.3
Watermelons	0.7†	0.9	0.8
Bananas*	3.5	3.5	3.6
Plantains*	4.0	5.0	5.3
Oranges*	3.6	3.5	4.0
Lemons and limes*	2.2	2.3	2.3
Grapefruit and pomelo*	2.4	1.9	2.0
Pineapples*	6.2	8.0	8.3
Cocoa beans†	0.7	0.4	0.5

* FAO estimate(s).
† Unofficial figure(s).

Sugar cane: 810.0 in 2009 (FAO estimate).

Aggregate production ('000 metric tons, may include official, semi-official or estimated data): Total cereals 5.4 in 2010, 6.1 in 2011; 5.6 in 2012; Total roots and tubers 13.2 in 2010, 10.4 in 2011, 10.0 in 2012; Total vegetables (incl. melons) 16.0 in 2010, 20.6 in 2011, 19.1 in 2012; Total fruits (excl. melons) 76.6 in 2010, 76.3 in 2011, 78.6 in 2012.

Source: FAO.

LIVESTOCK
('000 head year ending September)

	2010	2011	2012
Horses*	1.4	1.4	1.4
Asses*	2.3	2.3	2.3
Mules*	2.0	2.0	2.0
Cattle*	32.5	33.0	34.0
Buffaloes*	5.9	5.9	6.0
Pigs	34.8	35.4	34.1
Chickens*	33,000	34,000	34,500
Sheep	17.3	8.2	11.1
Goats	7.1	5.0	8.7

* FAO estimates.

Source: FAO.

LIVESTOCK PRODUCTS
('000 metric tons)

	2010	2011	2012
Cattle meat*	1.2	1.0	1.0
Pig meat	3.3	3.3	3.5
Chicken meat	65.3	64.3	65.9
Cows' milk	4.3	5.6	4.2
Hen eggs*	5.3	3.6	3.5

* FAO estimates.

Source: FAO.

Forestry

ROUNDWOOD REMOVALS
('000 cubic metres, excl. bark, FAO estimates)

	2010	2011	2012
Sawlogs, veneer logs and logs for sleepers	47.0	47.0	47.0
Fuel wood	32.8	32.5	32.2
Total	79.8	79.5	79.2

Source: FAO.

SAWNWOOD PRODUCTION
('000 cubic metres, incl. railway sleepers, unofficial figures)

	2007	2008	2009
Total (all broadleaved)	41	30	31

2010–12: Production assumed to be unchanged from 2009 (unofficial figures).

Source: FAO.

Fishing

('000 metric tons, live weight of capture)

	2010	2011	2012
Capture	13.9	13.2	12.0
King mackerel	0.8	0.7	0.5
Serra Spanish mackerel	1.2	0.9	0.6
Yellowfin tuna	0.8	0.8	0.9
Other marine fishes	7.3	6.2	5.9
Demersal percomorphs	2.4	2.1	2.0
Penaeus shrimps	0.9	0.9	0.9
Aquaculture	0.0	0.0	0.0
Total catch	13.9	13.2	12.0

Source: FAO.

Mining

('000 barrels, unless otherwise indicated)

	2011	2012	2013
Crude petroleum	33,550	29,915	29,617
Natural gas (million cu m)*†	42,883	38,025	n.a.
Motor gasoline	8,590	4,830	9,200
Diesel oil	10,300	6,870	9,460
Fuel oil	16,400	15,300	19,300
Kerosene	5,430	3,380	5,050
Natural gas liquids	16,043	12,890	11,550

* Figures refer to the gross volume of output.
† Source: US Geological Survey.

Industry

SELECTED PRODUCTS
('000 metric tons unless otherwise indicated)

	2011	2012	2013
Fertilizers	5,715	5,453	4,644
Methanol	5,904	5,491	5,161
Cement	827	654	802
Iron (direct reduced)	1,706	1,684	1,750
Steel:			
billets	603	624	616
wire rods	427	394	297

2009: Sugar 31; Beer ('000 litres) 50,377; Electric energy (million kWh) 7,873.3.

Finance

CURRENCY AND EXCHANGE RATES

Monetary Units
100 cents = 1 Trinidad and Tobago dollar (TT $).

Sterling, US Dollar and Euro Equivalents (30 May 2014)
£1 sterling = TT $10.777;
US $1 = TT $6.406;
€1 = TT $8.719;
TT $100 = £9.28 = US $15.61 = €11.47. .

Average Exchange Rate (TT $ per US $)
2011   6.4093
2012   6.4296
2013   6.4426

CENTRAL GOVERNMENT BUDGET
(TT $ million)

Revenue	2010/11	2011/12	2012/13*
Current revenue	47,213.6	49,234.5	52,497.3
Tax revenue	42,017.3	43,568.8	45,150.6
Taxes on income and profit	33,245.1	33,078.3	34,108.9
Taxes on property	32.0	31.3	39.6
Taxes on goods and services	6,387.7	7,925.6	8,261.1
Taxes on international trade	2,167.8	2,319.4	2,496.9
Other taxes	184.7	214.2	244.1
Non-tax revenue	5,196.3	5,665.7	7,346.7
Royalties on petroleum	2,416.7	2,449.7	2,098.4
Profits	1,695.1	2,090.5	2,785.6
Non-financial enterprises	1,213.8	1,593.1	2,219.2
Financial enterprises	481.3	497.4	566.4
Interest	50.0	21.0	20.5
Capital revenue and grants	287.0	43.4	487.5
Total	47,500.6	49,277.9	52,984.8

Expenditure	2010/11	2011/12	2012/13*
Current expenditure	43,914.9	45,068.9	50,467.1
Wages and salaries	7,179.7	7,282.3	9,618.8
Goods and services	6,504.3	7,061.6	7,969.3
Interest payments	2,866.4	2,937.1	3,063.7
Domestic	2,486.9	2,547.9	2,512.1
External	379.5	389.2	551.6
Transfers and subsidies	27,364.5	27,787.9	29,815.3
Capital expenditure and net lending	7,577.5	7,738.0	9,003.1
Total	51,492.4	52,806.9	59,470.2

* Provisional figures.

2013/14 (projected figures): Total revenue 56,041.0 (Petroleum revenue 23,374.0, Non-petroleum revenue 32,667.0); Total expenditure 61,398.0.
Source: Ministry of Finance, Trinidad and Tobago.

INTERNATIONAL RESERVES
(US $ million at 31 December)

	2011	2012	2013
Gold (national valuation)	97.4	102.9	74.1
IMF special drawing rights	423.2	423.7	424.6
Reserve position in IMF	160.2	170.0	188.9
Foreign exchange	9,822.7	9,200.6	9,987.0
Total	10,503.5	9,897.2	10,674.6

Source: IMF, *International Financial Statistics*.

MONEY SUPPLY
(TT $ million at 31 December)

	2012	2013
Currency outside depository corporations	5,315.0	5,978.6
Transferable deposits	37,374.4	37,315.1
Other deposits	49,896.1	52,261.4
Broad money	92,585.6	95,555.2

Source: IMF, *International Financial Statistics*.

COST OF LIVING
(Retail Price Index; base: January 2003 = 100)

	2011	2012	2013
Food (incl. non-alcoholic beverages)	416.3	495.8	539.1
Clothing	95.0	97.7	98.2
Housing and utilities	127.3	130.3	130.5
All items (incl. others)	183.8	200.8	211.3

NATIONAL ACCOUNTS
(TT $ million at current prices)

Expenditure on the Gross Domestic Product

	2010	2011	2012
Government final consumption expenditure	18,188.2	19,435.0	20,125.1
Private final consumption expenditure	61,484.4	71,668.0	72,711.2
Gross capital formation	18,249.2	20,987.8	20,771.2
Total domestic expenditure	97,921.9	112,090.9	113,607.5
Exports of goods and services	77,173.6	102,298.6	90,775.3
Less Imports of goods and services	43,897.5	63,503.0	55,054.0
Statistical discrepancy	—	—	-2.1
GDP in purchasers' values	131,198.0	150,886.5	149,326.6

Source: UN National Accounts Main Aggregates Database.

Gross Domestic Product by Economic Activity

	2011	2012	2013*
Agriculture, hunting, forestry and fishing	902.8	880.7	927.8
Mining and hydrocarbons	70,313.7	62,140.3	64,887.5
Manufacturing	8,566.2	9,131.0	9,615.8
Electricity and water	2,000.1	1,930.2	2,053.5
Construction	8,772.3	8,778.5	9,352.3
Transport, storage and communication	8,290.6	8,744.5	8,889.3
Distribution	19,449.2	21,180.2	22,281.6
Finance, insurance and real estate	16,229.5	18,118.8	19,298.7
Government	11,219.8	11,272.5	12,130.6
Education and cultural services	3,691.6	4,176.9	4,571.5
Other services	2,255.5	2,426.0	2,567.5
Sub-total	151,691.3	148,779.6	156,576.1
Less Financial intermediation services indirectly measured	5,721.8	5,950.6	5,828.3
Value-added tax	4,917.0	6,497.6	6,670.0
GDP in purchaser's values	150,886.5	149,326.6	157,417.8

* Provisional figures.

BALANCE OF PAYMENTS
(US $ million)

	2009	2010	2011
Exports of goods	9,221.4	11,238.9	14,943.9
Imports of goods	−6,980.2	−6,503.5	−9,510.9
Balance on goods . . .	2,241.2	4,735.4	5,433.0
Exports of services . . .	764.8	874.2	5,802.9
Imports of services . . .	−383.1	−386.6	−5,296.5
Balance on goods and services	2,622.9	5,223.0	5,939.4
Primary income received . . .	297.6	299.7	445.5
Primary income paid	−1,314.7	−1,379.2	−3,519.4
Balance on goods, services and primary income	1,605.8	4,143.5	2,865.5
Secondary income received . .	137.3	108.8	145.2
Secondary income paid . .	−110.3	−80.0	−112.1
Current balance	1,632.8	4,172.3	2,898.5
Direct investment (net) . .	709.1	549.4	770.6
Other investment (net) . .	−3,145.5	−4,562.3	−1,543.4
Net errors and omissions . .	91.0	259.0	−1,373.2
Reserves and related items .	−712.6	418.4	752.5

2012 (provisional figures): Exports of goods 12,983.4; Imports of goods −9,065.0; *Balance on goods* 3,918.4; Services (net) 369.2; *Balance on goods and services* 4,287.6; Primary income (net) −3,387.3; *Balance on goods, services and primary income* 900.3; Secondary income (net) 39.3; *Current balance* 939.7; Direct investment (net) 772.1; Other investment (net) −2,942.1; Net errors and omissions 608.2; *Reserves and related items* −622.1.

2013 (provisional figures): Exports of goods 12,769.6; Imports of goods −8,870.8; *Balance on goods* 3,898.8; Services (net) 662.0; *Balance on goods and services* 4,560.8; Primary income (net) −2,015.3; *Balance on goods, services and primary income* 2,545.5; Secondary income (net) 26.1; *Current balance* 2,571.5; Direct investment (net) 970.7; Other investment (net) 1,407.5; Net errors and omissions −4,163.4; *Reserves and related items* 786.3.

External Trade

PRINCIPAL COMMODITIES
(TT $ million)

Imports c.i.f.	2009	2010	2011
Food and live animals	3,813.7	3,968.0	4,719.4
Beverages and tobacco . . .	340.3	348.0	414.4
Crude materials except fuels .	1,353.3	2,084.4	3,187.0
Mineral fuels and lubricants . .	14,482.5	13,755.4	23,641.0
Animal and vegetable oils and fats	207.4	230.6	343.8
Chemicals	3,444.3	3,157.9	3,930.9
Manufactured goods . . .	5,749.4	4,740.1	5,119.1
Machinery and transport equipment	12,139.5	10,705.2	16,942.3
Miscellaneous manufactured articles	2,385.8	2,261.5	2,524.6
Total (incl. others)	43,973.3	41,283.4	60,864.9

Exports f.o.b.*	2009	2010	2011
Food and live animals	965.0	927.7	1,232.4
Beverages and tobacco . . .	881.2	739.7	1,258.4
Crude materials except fuels . .	1,750.8	3,668.4	4,475.7
Mineral fuels and lubricants . .	44,128.5	43,725.7	53,387.4
Animal and vegetable oils and fats	16.2	12.1	16.3
Chemicals	5,542.3	15,405.1	27,230.5
Manufactured goods . . .	2,702.2	4,195.6	6,288.1
Machinery and transport equipment	1,661.1	2,259.0	1,280.1
Miscellaneous manufactured articles	441.9	408.1	457.6
Miscellaneous transactions and commodities	2.7	3.3	7.4
Total	58,092.0	71,344.7	95,633.9

* Including ships' stores and bunkers.

PRINCIPAL TRADING PARTNERS
(TT $ million)

Imports c.i.f.	2009	2010	2011
Barbados	190.0	242.5	326.6
Canada	941.7	1,172.9	2,061.2
Central and South America* . .	8,758.7	8,570.2	12,826.3
Brazil	2,221.2	2,973.9	3,910.0
Venezuela	412.5	78.9	71.8
China, People's Rep.	2,231.6	2,379.5	2,832.5
European Free Trade Association (EFTA)	181.0	190.7	233.1
European Union (EU)† . . .	3,786.8	2,854.6	3,404.3
Guyana	163.1	160.6	198.1
Jamaica	139.2	69.0	109.1
Japan	887.4	1,030.5	1,070.8
Russia	3,436.7	1,400.7	5,129.3
Thailand	458.1	585.3	621.8
United Kingdom	1,211.0	872.9	916.6
USA	13,557.9	11,426.5	16,196.1
Total (incl. others)	43,973.3	41,284.0	60,864.9

Exports f.o.b.‡	2009	2010	2011
Barbados	1,739.9	2,381.7	2,498.7
Canada	418.8	1,203.6	1,366.7
Central and South America* . .	3,472.9	8,003.7	11,412.8
European Free Trade Association (EFTA)	20.3	475.5	39.8
European Union (EU)† . . .	5,570.9	4,179.0	11,351.4
Guyana	1,074.3	1,712.9	1,843.0
Jamaica	3,012.2	4,536.6	4,007.8
Puerto Rico and US Virgin Islands	736.1	593.9	1,063.8
United Kingdom	2,562.1	1,417.7	2,238.0
USA	30,732.2	33,517.5	45,695.0
Total (incl. others)	58,092.0	71,344.7	95,633.8

* Excluding Belize, French Guiana, Guyana and Suriname.
† Excluding the United Kingdom, listed separately.
‡ Excluding ships' stores and bunkers.

Transport

ROAD TRAFFIC
(registered vehicles)

	2006	2007	2008
Total	441,541	468,255	471,749

SHIPPING

Flag Registered Fleet
(at 31 December)

	2011	2012	2013
Number of vessels	81	82	84
Total displacement (grt) . . .	38,835	39,085	51,586

Source: Lloyd's List Intelligence (www.lloydslistintelligence.com).

CIVIL AVIATION
(traffic on scheduled services)

	2010	2011
Kilometres flown (million)	37	52
Passengers carried ('000)	1,842	2,625
Passenger-km (million)	3,009	4,463
Total ton-km (million)	288	419

Source: UN, *Statistical Yearbook*.

Passengers carried ('000): 2,625.1 in 2012; 2,648.8 in 2013 (Source: World Bank, World Development Indicators database).

Tourism

FOREIGN TOURIST ARRIVALS

Country of origin	2008	2009	2010
Barbados	19,350	15,672	13,576
Canada	54,205	49,514	46,390
Germany	4,876	4,895	4,657
Grenada	9,162	7,339	7,269
Guyana	25,097	20,679	18,339
Saint Lucia	5,071	4,429	4,187
Saint Vincent and Grenadines	8,064	7,421	6,726
United Kingdom	42,924	38,400	34,179
USA	189,553	195,438	183,171
Venezuela	12,252	11,521	9,543
Total (incl. others)	437,279	418,864	385,510

Tourism receipts (US $ million, excl. passenger transport): 450 in 2010; 472 in 2011.

Source: World Tourism Organization.

Communications Media

	2011	2012	2013
Telephones ('000 main lines in use)	292.0	286.6	291.3
Mobile cellular telephones ('000 subscribers)	1,826.2	1,883.7	1,943.9
Internet subscribers ('000)	157.2	n.a.	n.a.
Broadband subscribers ('000)	155.0	184.0	195.2

Source: International Telecommunication Union.

Education

(2009/10 unless otherwise indicated)

	Institutions	Teachers	Students Males	Students Females	Total
Pre-primary	50*	2,186†	15,021†	14,564†	29,585†
Primary	480‡	7,447	67,698	63,652	131,350
Secondary	101‡	7,045§	46,613§	48,662§	95,275§
Tertiary	3‖	1,800¶	7,515¶	9,405¶	16,920¶

* Government schools and assisted schools only, in 1992/93.
† 2006/07.
‡ 2001/02.
§ 2007/08.
‖ 2003/04; university and equivalent institutions.
¶ 2004/05.

Source: UNESCO Institute for Statistics.

Pupil-teacher ratio (primary education, UNESCO estimate): 17.6 in 2009/10 (Source: UNESCO Institute for Statistics).

Adult literacy rate (UNESCO estimates): 98.8% (males 99.2%, females 98.5%) in 2011 (Source: UNESCO Institute for Statistics).

Directory

The Constitution

Trinidad and Tobago became a republic, within the Commonwealth, under a new Constitution on 1 August 1976. The Constitution provides for a President and a bicameral Parliament comprising a Senate and a House of Representatives. The President is elected by an Electoral College of members of both the Senate and the House of Representatives. The Senate consists of 31 members appointed by the President: 16 on the advice of the Prime Minister, six on the advice of the Leader of the Opposition and nine at the President's own discretion from among outstanding persons from economic, social or community organizations. The House of Representatives consists of 41 members who are elected by universal adult suffrage. The duration of a Parliament is five years. The Cabinet, presided over by the Prime Minister, is responsible for the general direction and control of the Government. It is collectively responsible to Parliament. Amendments to the Constitution approved by Parliament in August 2014 included the introduction of a two-term limit on the Prime Minister and the right to recall members of Parliament and the need for a run-off ballot if any parliamentary candidate receives less than 50% of a ballot.

The Government

HEAD OF STATE

President: ANTHONY THOMAS AQUINAS CARMONA (took office 18 March 2013).

THE CABINET
(September 2014)

The Government is formed by the People's Partnership coalition, comprising the United National Congress, the Congress of the People and the Tobago Organisation of the People.

Prime Minister and Minister of the People and Social Development: KAMLA PERSAD-BISSESSAR.

Minister of Finance and the Economy: LARRY HOWAI.

Minister of National Security: GARY GRIFFITH.

Minister of Foreign Affairs: WINSTON DOOKERAN.

Minister of Public Administration: CAROLYN SEEPERSAD-BACHAN.

Minister of Energy and Energy Affairs: KEVIN RAMNARINE.

Minister of Tertiary Education and Skills Training: FAZAL KARIM.

Minister of Health: Dr FUAD KHAN.

Minister of Public Utilities: NIZAM BAKSH.

Minister of Food Production: DEVANT MAHARAJ.

Minister of Planning and Sustainable Development: Dr BHOENDRADATT TEWARIE.

Minister of Local Government: MARLENE COUDRAY.

Minister of Works and Infrastructure: Dr SURUJRATTAN RAMBACHAN.

Minister of Housing and Urban Development: Dr ROODAL MOONILAL.

Minister of Communications and of Trade, Industry and Investment: VASANT BHARATH.

Minister of Tourism: GERALD HADEED.

Minister of Justice: EMMANUEL GEORGE.

Minister of Education: Dr TIM GOPEESINGH.

Minister of Community Development: WINSTON PETERS.

Minister of Legal Affairs: PRAKASH RAMADHAR.

Minister of Labour and Small and Micro Enterprise Development: ERROL MCLEOD.

Minister of Tobago Development: Dr DELMON BAKER.

Minister of the Arts and Multiculturalism: Dr LINCOLN DOUGLAS.

Minister of Gender, Youth and Child Development: CLIFTON DE COTEAU.

Minister of Transport: STEPHEN CADIZ.

Minister of Science and Technology and Acting Minister of Sport: Dr RUBERT GRIFFITH.

Minister of Environment and Water Resources: GANGA SINGH.

Minister of National Diversity and Social Integration: RODGER SAMUEL.

Minister of Land and Marine Resources: JAIRAM SEEMUNGAL.

Minister in the Ministry of National Diversity and Social Integration: EMBAU MOHENI.

Minister in the Ministry of Gender, Youth and Child Development: RAZIAH AHMED.

Minister in the Ministry of the People and Social Development: VERNELLA ALLEYNE-TOPPIN.

Minister in the Ministry of Works and Infrastructure: STACY ROOPNARINE.

Minister of State in the Ministry of Finance and the Economy: RUDRANATH INDARSINGH.

Minister of State in the Office of the Prime Minister: RODGER SAMUEL.

Attorney-General: ANAND RAMLOGAN.

MINISTRIES

Office of the President: President's House, Circular Rd, St Ann's, Port of Spain; tel. 624-1261; fax 625-7950; e-mail info@thepresident .tt; internet www.thepresident.tt.

Office of the Prime Minister: Whitehall, 13–15 St Clair Ave, St Clair, Port of Spain; tel. 622-1625; fax 622-0055; e-mail permsec@ opm.gov.tt; internet www.opm.gov.tt.

Ministry of the Arts and Multiculturalism: JOBCO Bldg, 51–55 Frederick St, Port of Spain; tel. 625-8519; fax 627-4991; e-mail culturedivision.tt@gmail.com; internet www.culture.gov.tt.

Ministry of the Attorney-General: Cabildo Chambers, 23–27 St Vincent St, Port of Spain; tel. 623-7010; fax 625-0470; e-mail communication@ag.gov.tt; internet www.ag.gov.tt.

Ministry of Communications: Level 5, Nicholas Tower, 63–65 Independence Sq., Port of Spain; tel. 627-2664; fax 623-4731.

Ministry of Community Development: ALGICO Bldg, cnr Jerningham Ave and Queens Park East, Belmont, Port of Spain; tel. 625-3012; fax 625-5954; e-mail communications@community.gov.tt; internet www.community.gov.tt.

Ministry of Education: 18 Alexandra St, St Clair, Port of Spain; tel. 622-2181; fax 622-4892; e-mail mined@tstt.net.tt; internet www.moe .gov.tt.

Ministry of Energy and Energy Affairs: Energy Tower, Levels 15 and 22–26, International Waterfront Centre, 1 Wrightson Rd, Port of Spain; tel. 623-6708; fax 625-6878; e-mail info@energy.gov.tt; internet www.energy.gov.tt.

Ministry of Environment and Water Resources: c/o Water and Sewerage Authority, Farm Rd, St Joseph; tel. 663-2762.

Ministry of Finance and the Economy: Eric Williams Finance Bldg, Level 18, Independence Sq., Port of Spain; tel. 627-9700; fax 627-5882; e-mail comm.finance@gov.tt; internet www.finance.gov.tt.

Ministry of Food Production: St Clair Circle, St Clair, Port of Spain; tel. 662-1221; fax 622-8202; e-mail info@fplma.gov.tt; internet agriculture.gov.tt.

Ministry of Foreign Affairs: Tower C, Levels 10–14, Waterfront Complex, 1 Wrightson Rd, Port of Spain; tel. 623-6894; fax 623-5853; e-mail website@foreign.gov.tt; internet www.foreign.gov.tt.

Ministry of Gender, Youth and Child Development: Level 21, Tower D, International Waterfront Complex, 1 Wrightson Rd, Port of Spain; tel. 627-1163.

Ministry of Health: 63 Park St, Port of Spain; tel. 627-0010; fax 623-9528; e-mail suggestions@health.gov.tt; internet www.health.gov.tt.

Ministry of Housing and Urban Development: NHA Bldg, 44–46 South Quay, Port of Spain; tel. 623-4663; fax 625-2793; e-mail info@housing.gov.tt; internet www.mphe.gov.tt.

Ministry of Justice: Tower C, Level 19–21, International Waterfront Complex, 1 Wrightson Rd, Port of Spain; tel. 625-5878; fax 623-5596; internet www.moj.gov.tt.

Ministry of Labour and Small and Micro Enterprise Development: Levels 5 and 6, Tower C, International Waterfront Centre, 1 Wrightson Rd, Port of Spain; tel. 625-8478; fax 624-9126; e-mail communicationsmolsmed@gov.tt; internet www.molsmed.gov.tt.

Ministry of Land and Marine Resources: Port of Spain.

Ministry of Legal Affairs: Registration House, Huggins Bldg, 72–74 South Quay, Port of Spain; tel. 624-9971; fax 625-9803; e-mail info@legalaffairs.gov.tt; internet www.legalaffairs.gov.tt.

Ministry of Local Government: Kent House, Long Circular Rd, Maraval, Port of Spain; tel. 622-1669; fax 628-7283; e-mail localgovminister@gov.tt; internet www.localgov.gov.tt.

Ministry of National Diversity and Social Integration: JOBCO Bldg, Level 2, 51–55 Frederick St, Port of Spain; tel. 623-9311.

Ministry of National Security: Temple Court, 31–33 Abercromby St, Port of Spain; tel. 623-2441; fax 627-8044; e-mail info@mns.gov.tt; internet www.nationalsecurity.gov.tt.

Ministry of the People and Social Development: ANSA Bldg, cnr Independence Sq. and Abercromby St, Port of Spain; tel. 625-9221; fax 627-4853; e-mail people@mpsd.gov.tt; internet www2 .mpsd.gov.tt.

Ministry of Planning and Sustainable Development: Eric Williams Financial Complex, Level 14, Independence Sq., Port of Spain; tel. 627-9700; fax 623-8123; e-mail mpesrga@phe.gov.tt; internet pesrga.gov.tt.

Ministry of Public Administration: National Library Bldg, Level 7, cnr Hart and Abercromby Sts, Port of Spain; tel. 625-6724; fax 623-6027; e-mail communicationsdivision@mpa.gov.tt; internet www .mpa.gov.tt.

Ministry of Public Utilities: 2 Elizabeth St, St Clair, Port of Spain; tel. 628-0749; fax 628-6067; e-mail cgeorge@mpu.gov.tt; internet www.mpu.gov.tt.

Ministry of Science and Technology: International Water Front Center, Level 19, Tower D, 1A Wrightson Rd, Port of Spain; tel. 625-5776; fax 627-1720; e-mail communicationstte@gov.tt.

Ministry of Sport: 12 Abercromby St, Port of Spain; tel. 625-5622; fax 623-0174; internet www.msya.gov.tt.

Ministry of Tertiary Education and Skills Training: International Water Front Center, Level 16-18, Tower C, 1A Wrightson Rd, Port of Spain; tel. 623-9922; e-mail mtestcommunications@gov .tt; internet www.stte.gov.tt.

Ministry of Tobago Development: Jerningham St, Scarborough, Tobago; tel. 639-2652; fax 639-2655.

Ministry of Tourism: Levels 8 and 9, Tower C, International Waterfront Complex, 1 Wrightson Rd, Port of Spain; tel. 624-1403; fax 625-3894; e-mail mintourism@tourism.gov.tt; internet www .tourism.gov.tt.

Ministry of Trade, Industry and Investment: Nicholas Tower, Levels 11–17, 63–65 Independence Sq., Port of Spain; tel. 623-2931; fax 627-8488; e-mail mti-info@gov.tt; internet www.tradeind.gov.tt.

Ministry of Transport: Level 23, Tower D, International Waterfront Complex, 1 Wrightson Rd, Port of Spain; tel. 625-4701; fax 623-8261.

Ministry of Works and Infrastructure: Main Administrative Bldg, cnr Richmond and London Sts, Port of Spain; tel. 625-1225; fax 625-8070; internet www.mowt.gov.tt.

Legislature

PARLIAMENT

Senate

President: TIMOTHY HAMEL-SMITH.

The Senate consists of 31 members appointed by the President of the Republic.

House of Representatives

Speaker: WADE MARK.
Election, 24 May 2010

Party	Valid votes	% of valid votes cast	Seats
People's Partnership* . . .	432,026	60.03	29
People's National Movement .	285,354	39.65	12
Others	2,347	0.32	—
Total†	719,727	100.00	41

* An electoral alliance comprising the United National Congress, the Congress of the People, the Tobago Organisation of the People, the National Joint Action Committee and the Movement for Social Justice.
† In addition, there were 2,595 invalid votes.

TOBAGO HOUSE OF ASSEMBLY

The House is elected for a four-year term of office and consists of 12 elected members and three members selected by the majority party.

Chief Secretary: ORVILLE LONDON.

Election, 21 January 2013

Party	% of valid votes cast	Seats
People's National Movement	61.42	12
Tobago Organisation of the People	36.50	—
Tobago Platform of the People	2.08	—
Total	100.00	12

Election Commission

Elections and Boundaries Commission (EBC): Scott House, 134–138 Frederick St, Port of Spain; tel. 623-4622; fax 627-7881; e-mail ebc.research@gmail.com; internet www.ebctt.com; Chair. Dr NORBERT J. MASSON; Chief Election Officer RAMESH NANAN.

Political Organizations

Congress of the People (COP): 2 Broome St, Woodbrook, cnr Tragarete Rd, Port of Spain; tel. 622-5817; e-mail secretariat@coptnt.com; internet www.coptnt.com; f. 2006; contested the 2010 general election as a mem. of the People's Partnership coalition; Leader PRAKASH RAMADHAR; Chair. CAROLYN SEEPERSAD-BACHAN.

Independent Liberal Party (ILP): Port of Spain; f. 2013; Leader LYNDIRA OUDIT.

Movement for Social Justice: Bay Rd Junction, 74 Southern Main Rd, Marabella, Port of Spain; tel. 762-0133; e-mail msjtnt@gmail.com; internet msjtnt.org; contested the 2010 election as a mem. of the People's Partnership, left coalition in 2012; Leader DAVID ABDULLAH; Chair. VINCENT CABRERA.

National Joint Action Committee (NJAC): 40 Duke St, Port of Spain; tel. 623-5470; e-mail njaccommunications@gmail.com; internet www.njactt.org; f. 1969; contested the 2010 general election as a mem. of the People's Partnership coalition; Leader MAKANDAL DAAGA; Pres. AIYEGORO OME.

National Transformation Movement (NTM): Port of Spain; f. 2006; Leader LLOYD ELCOCK.

New National Vision (NNV): Freedom House, 30 Victoria Sq., Port of Spain; tel. 221-0807; f. 1994; Leader FUAD ABU BAKR.

People's National Movement (PNM): Balisier House, 1 Tranquility St, Port of Spain; tel. 625-1533; fax 627-3311; e-mail info@pnmtt.org; internet www.pnm.org.tt; f. 1956; moderate nationalist party; Leader Dr KEITH ROWLEY; Chair. FRANKLIN KHAN.

The Platform of Truth: Breeze Hall, Scarborough, Tobago; tel. 639-5135; e-mail tpttobago@gmail.com; internet www.tpttobago.com; f. 2011; Leader HOCHOY CHARLES.

Tobago Organisation of the People (TOP): 2 Picton St, Scarborough, Tobago; tel. 635-1003; e-mail toptobago@gmail.com; internet www.top.org.tt; f. 2007; active only in Tobago; contested the 2010 election as a mem. of the People's Partnership coalition; Leader ASHWORTH JACK.

Tobago Forwards: Scarborough, Tobago; f. 2014 by dissident mems of the Tobago Organisation of the People (q.v.); active only in Tobago; Chair. ANSLEM RICHARDS.

United National Congress (UNC): Rienzi Complex, 78–81 Southern Main Rd, Couva; tel. 636-8145; e-mail info@unc.org.tt; internet unctt.org; f. 1988; contested the 2010 general election as a mem. of the People's Partnership coalition; social democratic; Leader KAMLA PERSAD-BISSESSAR; Gen. Sec. DAVE TANCOO.

Diplomatic Representation

EMBASSIES AND HIGH COMMISSIONS IN TRINIDAD AND TOBAGO

Argentina: TATIL Bldg, 4th Floor, 11 Maraval Rd, POB 162, Port of Spain; tel. 628-7557; fax 628-7544; e-mail etrin@mrecic.gov.ar; internet www.etrin.mrecic.gov.ar; Ambassador MARCELO ALDO SALVIOLO.

Australia: 18 Herbert St, St Clair, Port of Spain; tel. and fax 822-5450; fax 822-5490; e-mail australianhighcommission.pos@gmail.com; internet www.trinidadandtobago.embassy.gov.au; High Commissioner ROSS TYSOE.

Brazil: 18 Sweet Briar Rd, St Clair, POB 382, Port of Spain; tel. 622-5779; fax 622-4323; e-mail brasil@tstt.net.tt; internet portofspain.itamaraty.gov.br; Ambassador PAULO SERGIO TRABALLI BOZZI.

Canada: Maple House, 3–3A Sweet Briar Rd, St Clair, POB 1246, Port of Spain; tel. 622-6232; fax 628-1830; e-mail pspan@international.gc.ca; internet www.canadainternational.gc.ca/trinidad_and_tobago-trinite_et_tobago; High Commissioner GÉRARD LATULIPPE.

Chile: 4 Alexandra St, St Clair, POB 5099, Port of Spain; tel. 628-0540; fax 622-9894; e-mail echile@tstt.net.tt; internet chileabroad.gov.cl/trinidad-y-tobago; Ambassador FERNANDO SCHMIDT ARIZTÍA.

China, People's Republic: 39 Alexandra St, St Clair, Port of Spain; tel. 622-1832; fax 622-7613; e-mail chinaemb_tt@mfa.gov.cn; internet tt.china-embassy.org; Ambassador HUANG XINGYUAN.

Colombia: Newtown Centre, 4th Floor, 30–36 Maraval Rd, Port of Spain; tel. 628-5656; fax 628-5522; e-mail etrinidadytobago@cancilleria.gov.co; internet trinidadytobago.embajada.gov.co; Ambassador (vacant).

Costa Rica: 38 Carlos St, Woodbrook, Port of Spain; tel. 628-9201; fax 628-9203; e-mail embrctt1@tstt.net.tt; Ambassador EDGAR GARCÍA MIRANDA.

Cuba: 14 Coblentz Garden, St Ann's, POB 1779, Port of Spain; tel. 621-1622; fax 621-3573; e-mail embacubatrinidad@tstt.net.tt; internet www.cubadiplomatica.cu/trinidadtobago; Ambassador GUILLERMO VÁZQUEZ MORENO.

Dominican Republic: Suite 101, 10B Queen's Park West, Port of Spain; tel. 624-7930; fax 623-7779; e-mail embdomtrinidadytobago@serex.gov.do; Ambassador JOSÉ A. SERULLE RAMIA.

El Salvador: 29 Long Circular Rd, St James, Port of Spain; tel. 628-4454; fax 622-8314; e-mail elsalvadortt@gmail.com; Ambassador RAYMUNDO ERNESTO RODRÍGUEZ DÍAZ.

France: TATIL Bldg, 6th Floor, 11 Maraval Rd, POB 1242, Port of Spain; tel. 622-7447; fax 628-2632; e-mail cad.port-d-espagne-amba@diplomatie.gouv.fr; internet www.ambafrance-tt.org; Ambassador JACQUES STURM.

Germany: 19 St Clair Ave, St Clair, POB 828, Port of Spain; tel. 628-1630; fax 628-5278; e-mail info@ports.diplo.de; internet www.port-of-spain.diplo.de; Ambassador STEFAN SCHLÜTER.

Guatemala: Regents Towers, Apt 701, Westmoorings-by-the-Sea, Westmoorings; tel. and fax 632-7629; e-mail embtrintobago@minex.gob.gt; Ambassador GIOVANNI RENE CASTILLO POLANCO.

Holy See: 11 Mary St, St Clair, POB 854, Port of Spain; tel. 622-5009; fax 222-9814; e-mail apnuntt@googlemail.com; Apostolic Nuncio NICOLAS GIRASOLI.

India: 6 Victoria Ave, POB 530, Port of Spain; tel. 627-7480; fax 627-6985; e-mail hc@hcipos.org; internet www.hcipos.org; High Commissioner GAURI SHANKAR GUPTA.

Jamaica: 2 Newbold St, St Clair, Port of Spain; tel. 622-4995; fax 628-9043; e-mail jhctnt@tstt.net.tt; High Commissioner SHARON SAUNDERS.

Japan: 5 Hayes St, St Clair, POB 1039, Port of Spain; tel. 628-5991; fax 622-0858; e-mail embassyofjapan@tstt.net.tt; internet www.tt.emb-japan.go.jp; Ambassador YOSHIMASA TEZUKA.

Korea, Republic: 36 Elizabeth St, St Clair, Port of Spain; tel. 622-9081; fax 628-8745; e-mail koremb.tt@gmail.com; internet tto.mofat.go.kr; Ambassador WONKUN HWANG.

Mexico: 12 Hayes St, St Clair, Port of Spain; tel. 622-1422; fax 628-8488; e-mail info@mexico.tt; internet www.mexico.tt; Ambassador MARIO ARREOLA WOOG.

Netherlands: 69–71 Edward St, POB 870, Port of Spain; tel. 625-1210; fax 625-1704; e-mail por@minbuza.nl; internet tt.nlembassy.org; Ambassador LUCITA MOENIRALAM.

Nigeria: 3 Maxwell-Phillip St, St Clair, POB 140, Newtown, Port of Spain; tel. 622-4002; fax 622-7162; e-mail contact@nigerianhighcommission-tt.org; internet www.nigerianhighcommission-tt.org; High Commissioner MUSA JOHN JEN.

Panama: 25 De Verteuil St, Wookbrook, Port of Spain; tel. 628-9957; fax 622-8992; e-mail embapatt@flowtrinidad.com; Ambassador ARLINE GONZÁLEZ COSTA.

South Africa: 4 Scott St, St Clair, POB 7111, Port of Spain; tel. 622-9869; fax 622-7089; e-mail betsie.erasmus@southafrica.org.tt; High Commissioner MAUREEN ISABELLA MODISELLE.

Spain: TATIL Bldg, 7th Floor, 11 Maraval Rd, Port of Spain; tel. 625-7938; fax 624-4983; e-mail emb.trinidad@mae.es; Ambassador JOSÉ MARÍA FERNÁNDEZ LÓPEZ DE TURISO.

Suriname: TATIL Bldg, 5th Floor, 11 Maraval Rd, Port of Spain; tel. 628-0704; fax 628-0086; e-mail surinameembassy@tstt.net.tt; Ambassador FIDELIA GRAAND-GALON.

United Kingdom: 19 St Clair Ave, St Clair, POB 778, Port of Spain; tel. 350-0444; fax 350-0425; e-mail generalenquiries.ptofs@fco.gov.uk; internet ukintt.fco.gov.uk; High Commissioner ARTHUR SNELL.

USA: 15 Queen's Park West, POB 752, Port of Spain; tel. 622-6371; fax 822-5905; e-mail ircpos@state.gov; internet trinidad.usembassy.gov; Chargé d'affaires a.i. MARGARET DIOP.

Venezuela: 16 Victoria Ave, POB 1300, Port of Spain; tel. 627-9821; fax 624-2508; e-mail embaveneztt@tstt.net.tt; Ambassador COROMOTO GODOY.

Judicial System

The Chief Justice, who has overall responsibility for the administration of justice in Trinidad and Tobago, is appointed by the President after consultation with the Prime Minister and the Leader of the Opposition. The President appoints and promotes judges on the advice of the Judicial and Legal Service Commission. The Judicial and Legal Service Commission, which comprises the Chief Justice as chairman, the chairman of the Public Service Commission, two former judges and a senior member of the bar, appoints all judicial and legal officers. The Judiciary comprises the Supreme Court and the Magistracy. The Supreme Court consists of the High Court of Justice and the Court of Appeal. The Court of Appeal hears appeals against decisions of the Magistracy and the High Court. Further appeals are directed to the Judicial Committee of the Privy Council of the United Kingdom. The Court of Appeal consists of the Chief Justice, who is President, and six other Justices.

The Magistracy and the High Court exercise original jurisdiction in civil and criminal matters. The High Court hears indictable criminal matters, family matters where the parties are married, and civil matters involving sums over the petty civil court limit. High Court judges are referred to as either Judges of the High Court or Puisne Judges. The Masters of the High Court, of which there are four, have the jurisdiction of judges in civil chamber courts. The Magistracy exercises summary jurisdiction in criminal matters and hears preliminary inquiries in indictable matters.

In 2005 Parliament voted to accept the authority of the Caribbean Court of Justice to settle international trade disputes. The Court was formally inaugurated in Port of Spain in April of that year.

Chief Justice: IVOR ARCHIE.

Supreme Court of Judicature: Hall of Justice, Knox St, Port of Spain; tel. 628-8529; fax 627-5477; e-mail cpiu@ttlawcourts.org; internet www.ttlawcourts.org; consists of the High Court of Justice and the Court of Appeal. Three locations: Port of Spain, San Fernando and Tobago. There are 23 Supreme Court Puisne Judges who sit in criminal, civil, and matrimonial divisions; Registrar MARISSA ROBERTSON.

Magistracy: St Vincent St, Port of Spain; tel. 625-2781; divided into 13 districts; consists of a Chief Magistrate, a Deputy Chief Magistrate, 13 Senior Magistrates and 29 Magistrates; Chief Magistrate MARCIA AYERS-CAESAR.

Attorney-General: ANAND RAMLOGAN.

Religion

CHRISTIANITY

Caribbean Conference of Churches: POB 876, Curepe; tel. 662-2979; fax 662-1303; e-mail trinidad-headoffice@ccc-caribe.org; internet www.ccc-caribe.org; f. 1973; 33 mem. churches; Pres. Rev. Dr LESLEY G. ANDERSON; Gen. Sec. GERARD A. J. GRANADO.

Christian Council of Trinidad and Tobago: Hayes Court, 21 Maraval Rd, Port of Spain; tel. 637-9329; f. 1967; church unity org. formed by the Roman Catholic, Anglican, Presbyterian, Methodist, African Methodist, Spiritual Baptist and Moravian Churches, the Church of Scotland and the Salvation Army, with the Ethiopian Orthodox Church and the Baptist Union as observers; Pres. ADRIANA NOEL (acting); Sec. GRACE STEELE.

The Anglican Communion

Anglicans are adherents of the Church in the Province of the West Indies, comprising eight dioceses. The Archbishop of the West Indies is the Bishop of Barbados. According to figures from the 2011 census, some 6% of the population were Anglicans.

Bishop of Trinidad and Tobago: CLAUDE BERKLEY, Hayes Court, 21 Maraval Rd, Port of Spain; tel. 622-7387; fax 628-1319; e-mail diocesett@tstt.net.tt; internet www.trinidad.anglican.org.

Protestant Churches

According to the 2011 census, 12% of the population were Pentecostalists/Evangelicals, 7% were Baptists and 4% were Seventh-day Adventists, 3% were Presbyterian or Congregational, almost 2% were Jehovah's Witnesses and 1% were Methodist.

Association of Jehovah's Witnesses of Trinidad and Tobago: Lower Rapsey St and Laxmi Lane, Curepe; tel. 663-3392; internet www.jw.org/en/jehovahs-witnesses/offices/trinidad-and-tobago.

Baptist Union of Trinidad and Tobago: 104 High St, Princes Town; tel. 655-2291; e-mail baptuni@tstt.net.tt; f. 1816; Pres. Rev. FRANCIS IVAN BAPTISTE; Gen. Sec. Rev. ANSLEM WARRICK; 24 churches, 3,600 mems.

Presbyterian Church of Trinidad and Tobago: POB 187, Paradise Hill, San Fernando; tel. and fax 652-4829; e-mail pctt@tstt.net.tt; internet www.presbyterianchurchtt.org; f. 1868; Moderator Rt Rev. BRENDA BULLOCK; Gen. Sec. APHZAL SELWYN ACKBARALI; 40,000 mems.

South Caribbean Conference (Seventh-day Adventist Church in Trinidad): Port of Spain; tel. 662-7024; fax 645-3551; e-mail info@trinidadadventist.org; internet www.southcaribadventists.org; Pres. Pastor WAYNE ANDREWS.

United Pentecostalist Church of Trinidad and Tobago: Port of Spain; internet upctt.org.

The Roman Catholic Church

For ecclesiastical purposes, Trinidad and Tobago comprises the single archdiocese of Port of Spain. According to the 2011 census, 22% of the population were Roman Catholics.

Antilles Episcopal Conference: 9A Gray St, Port of Spain; tel. 622-2932; fax 628-3688; e-mail secretariat@aec.org; internet www.aecrc.org; f. 1975; 21 mems from the Caribbean and Central American regions; Pres. Most Rev. PATRICK PINDER (Archbishop of Nassau in Bahamas).

Archbishop of Port of Spain: JOSEPH EVERARD HARRIS, 27 Maraval Rd, Port of Spain; tel. 622-1103; fax 622-1165; e-mail abishop@carib-link.net.

HINDUISM

Hindu immigrants from India first arrived in Trinidad and Tobago in 1845. The vast majority of migrants, who were generally from Uttar Pradesh, were Vishnavite Hindus, who belonged to sects such as the Ramanandi, the Kabir and the Sieunaraini. The majority of Hindus currently subscribe to the doctrine of Sanathan Dharma, which evolved from Ramanandi teaching. According to the 2011 census, 18% of the population were Hindus.

Arya Pratinidhi Sabha of Trinidad (Arya Samaj): Seereeram Memorial Vedic School, Old Southern Main Rd, Montrose Village, Chaguanas; tel. 663-1721; e-mail president@trinidadaryasamaj.org; Sr Vice-Pres. BALRAM RAMDIAL; Sec. MANGAROO RAMPHAL.

Sanathan Dharma Maha Sabha of Trinidad and Tobago Inc: Maha Sabha Headquarters, Eastern Main Rd, St Augustine; tel. 645-3240; e-mail mahasabha@ttemail.com; f. 1952; Hindu pressure group and public org.; organizes the provision of Hindu education; Pres. Dr D. OMAH MAHARAJH; Sec.-Gen. SATNARAYAN MAHARAJ.

ISLAM

According to the 2011 census, 5% of the population were Muslims.

The Press

DAILIES

Newsday: 23A Chacon St, Port of Spain; tel. 623-2459; fax 625-8362; e-mail newsday@newsday.co.tt; internet www.newsday.co.tt; f. 1993; Editor-in-Chief JONES P. MADEIRA; circ. 2,200,000.

Trinidad Guardian: 22 St Vincent St, POB 122, Port of Spain; tel. 623-8871; fax 625-5702; e-mail letters@ttol.co.tt; internet guardian.co.tt; f. 1917; morning; independent; Editor-in-Chief JUDY RAYMOND; circ. 52,617.

Trinidad and Tobago Express: 35 Independence Sq., Port of Spain; tel. 623-1711; fax 627-1451; e-mail express@trinidadexpress.com; internet www.trinidadexpress.com; f. 1967; morning; Editor-in-Chief OMATIE LYDER; circ. 55,000.

PERIODICALS

The Boca: 27A Saddle Rd, Maraval; tel. 634-2055; fax 622-6580; e-mail boca@boatersenterprise.com; internet www.boatersenterprise.com; 6 a year; magazine of the sailing and boating community; Editor TIFFANY LUCAS.

The Bomb: Southern Main Rd, Curepe; tel. 645-2744; weekly; Publr SAT MAHARAJ.

Caribbean Beat Magazine: MEP Publishers, 6 Prospect Ave, Maraval, Port of Spain; tel. 622-3821; fax 628-0639; e-mail caribbean-beat@meppublishers.com; internet www.caribbean-beat

.com; f. 1992; 6 a year; inflight magazine of Caribbean Airlines; Publr JEREMY TAYLOR; Editor NICHOLAS LAUGHLIN.

Catholic News: 31 Independence Sq., Port of Spain; tel. 623-6093; fax 623-9468; e-mail mail@catholicnews-tt.net; internet www .catholicnews-tt.net; f. 1892; weekly; Editor KATHLEEN MAHARAJ; circ. 18,000.

Energy Caribbean: 6 Prospect Ave, Maraval, Port of Spain; tel. 622-3821; fax 628-0639; e-mail yuri@meppublishers.com; internet www.meppublishers.com; f. 2002; fortnightly; Editor DAVID RENWICK.

Sunday Guardian: 22 St Vincent St, POB 122, Port of Spain; tel. 623-8870; fax 625-7211; e-mail esunday@ttol.co.tt; internet www .guardian.co.tt; f. 1917; independent; morning; Editor-in-Chief JUDY RAYMOND; Editor IRVING WARD; circ. 48,324.

Tobago News: 18 eTeck Mall, Sangster's Hill, Scarborough; tel. 660-7107; fax 639-5565; e-mail ccngroupc@tstt.net.tt; internet www .thetobagonews.com; f. 1985; 2 a month; Editor CORDELL MCCLURE.

Trinidad and Tobago Gazette: 22–24 Victoria Ave, Port of Spain; tel. 625-4139; fax 625-5973; internet www.news.gov.tt; weekly; official govt paper; Dir MICHAEL LALBIHARIE; circ. 3,300.

Trinidad and Tobago Mirror: 35 Rapsey St, Curepe; tel. 645-3364; e-mail news@tntmirror.com; internet www.tntmirror.com; f. 1981; 2 a week; bought by Integrated Media Co Ltd in 2011; Publr MAXIE CUFFIE; circ. 35,000.

ASSOCIATION

Media Association of Trinidad and Tobago (MATT): Port of Spain; e-mail mattexecutive@gmail.com; f. 1986; Pres. CURTIS WILLIAMS; Sec. AKASH SAMAROO.

Publishers

Caribbean Children's Press: 7 Coronation St, St James; tel. and fax 628-4248; f. 1987; educational publishers for primary schools.

Caribbean Educational Publishers: Gulf View Link Rd, La Romaine; tel. 657-9613; fax 652-5620; e-mail mbscep@tstt.net.tt; Pres. TEDDY MOHAMMED.

Charran Publishing House Ltd: Wrightson Road, POB 126, Port of Spain; tel. 638-9205; fax 674-0817; e-mail siras@ charranpublishers.com; internet www.charranpublishers.com; Man. Dir REGINALD CHARRAN.

Lexicon Trinidad Ltd: Lot 87, Frederick Settlement Industrial Estate, Caroni; tel. 662-1863; fax 663-0081; e-mail lexiconadmin@ gmail.com; Dir KEN JAIKARANSINGH.

Morton Publishing: 97 Saddle Rd, Maraval; tel. 348-3777; fax 762-9923; e-mail morton@morton-pub.com; internet www.morton-pub .com; f. 1977; educational books; Pres. DOUG MORTON; Dir JULIE MORTON.

Paria Publishing Co Ltd: Third Ave, Cascade; tel. 624-4187; e-mail pariapublishing@gmail.com; internet www.pariapublishing .com; f. 1981; Dir DOMINIC BESSON.

Royards Publishing Co: 7A Macoya Industrial Estate, Macoya; tel. 663-6002; fax 663-3616; e-mail royards@aol.com; internet www .royards.com; f. 1984; educational publishers; Dirs CLIFFORD NARINESINGH, DWIGHT NARINESINGH.

Toute Bagai Publishing: 26 Kelly Kenny St, Woodbrook, Port of Spain; tel. 622-0519; fax 628-6909; e-mail info@macomag.com; internet www.macomag.com; f. 1999; magazines; publ. *MACO Caribbean Living*; Man. Dir NEYSHA SOODEEN.

Trinidad Publishing Co Ltd: 22–24 St Vincent St, Port of Spain; tel. 623-8870; fax 625-7211; e-mail business@ttol.co.tt; internet guardian.co.tt; f. 1917; Man. Dir GRENFELL KISSOON; Gen. Man. DOUGLAS WILSON.

ASSOCIATION

Trinidad and Tobago Publishers and Broadcasters Association (TTPBA): c/o i95.5FM, 47 Tragarete Rd, Newtown, Port Of Spain; tel. 622-9292; fax 628-7024; e-mail fazilettem@ttpba.org.tt; internet www.ttpba.org.tt; f. 1991; Pres. DAREN LEE SING.

Broadcasting and Communications
REGULATORY BODY

Telecommunications Authority of Trinidad and Tobago (TATT): 5 Eighth Ave Ext., off 12th St, Barataria; tel. 675-8288; fax 674-1055; e-mail info@tatt.org.tt; internet www.tatt.org.tt; f. 2001 to oversee the liberalization of the telecommunications

sector; regulates the telecommunications and broadcasting sectors; Chair. SELBY WILSON; CEO CRIS SEECHERAN.

TELECOMMUNICATIONS

Columbus Communications Trinidad Ltd (Flow): 29 Victoria Sq., Port of Spain; tel. 223-3569; fax 624-9584; e-mail mediainquiries@columbustrinidad.com; internet discoverflow.co/ trinidad; f. 2005; digital cable television, internet and local telephone service providers; mobile cellular telephone licence granted in 2006; Man. Dir BRIAN COLLINS; 250 employees (2007).

Digicel Trinidad and Tobago: Ansa Centre, 11C Maraval Rd, Port of Spain; tel. 628-7000; fax 628-9540; e-mail tt.customer.care@ digicelgroup.com; internet www.digiceltrinidadandtobago.com; owned by an Irish consortium; f. 2001; mobile cellular telephone licence granted in 2005; Chair. DENIS O'BRIEN; CEO JOHN DELVES.

One Caribbean Media Ltd (OCM): 35 Independence Sq., Port of Spain; tel. 623-1711; fax 627-4886; e-mail john.lumyoung@ocmnews .com; internet www.onecaribbeanmedia.net; f. 2006 by merger of Caribbean Communications Network (CCN) and The Nation Corpn (Barbados); Chair. Sir FRED GOLLOP; CEO DAWN THOMAS.

Open Telecom Ltd: 88 Edward St, Port of Spain; tel. 627-6559; e-mail sales@opentelecomtt.com; internet www.opentelecomtt.com; f. 1992; Chair. PETER GILLETTE; Chief Operations Man. NICHOLAS LOOK HONG.

Telecommunication Services of Trinidad and Tobago (TSTT) Ltd: 1 Edward St, POB 3, Port of Spain; tel. 625-4431; fax 627-0856; e-mail tsttceo@tstt.net.tt; internet www.tstt.co.tt; 51% state-owned, 49% by Cable & Wireless (UK); 51% privatization pending; CEO GEORGE HILL (acting).

> **blink Broadband:** TSTT Broadband Marketing, 12 Richmond St, Port of Spain; tel. 824-8788; fax 623-6501; e-mail support@tstt.net .tt; internet www.blinkbroadband.tt; f. 2007; internet service provider; Exec. Vice-Pres. DIANNA DE SOUSA.

> **bmobile:** 52 Jerningham Ave, Belmont; fax 627-1534; e-mail service@tstt.co.tt; internet www.bmobile.co.tt; f. 1991 as TSTT Cellnet; name changed as above 2006; mobile cellular telephone operator; Exec. Vice-Pres. RONALD WALCOTT (acting).

BROADCASTING
Radio

The Caribbean New Media Group (CNMG): 11A Maraval, Port of Spain; tel. 622-4141; fax 622-0344; e-mail webmaster@ctntworld .com; internet www.ctntworld.com; state-owned; operates three radio stations: Talk City 91.1 FM, Next 99.1 FM and Sweet 100.1 FM; and three television channels: 6 (cable), 9 and 13; CEO INGRID ISAAC.

i95.5 FM: 47 Tragarete Rd, Newtown, Port of Spain; tel. 628-4955; fax 628-0251; e-mail info@i955fm.com; internet www.i955fm.com; Exec. Chair. and CEO LOUIS LEE SING.

I.S.A.A.C. 98.1 FM: 115A Woodford St, Newtown, Port of Spain; tel. 628-0904; fax 628-3108; e-mail info@isaac981.com; internet www .isaac981.com; f. 2002; 24-hour Christian radio station; CEO MARGARET ELCOCK.

Power 102 FM: Radio Vision Ltd, 88–90 Abercromby St, Port of Spain; tel. 627-6937; fax 627-9320; e-mail power102fm@gmail.com; internet www.power102fm.com; f. 1997; CEO PETER PENA; Man. SHARON PITT.

Radio Jaagriti 102.7 FM: cnr Pasea Main Rd Ext. and Churchill Roosevelt Hwy, Tunapuna; tel. 645-0613; fax 663-8961; e-mail comments@jaagriti.com; internet www.jaagriti.com; f. 2007; Hindu broadcasting network; Man. Dir SAT MAHARAJ; CEO DEVANT MAHARAJ.

Radio Tambrin 92.7: 3 Picton St, Scarborough, Tobago; tel. 639-3437; fax 660-7351; e-mail tambrin@tstt.net.tt; internet www .tambrintobago.com; f. 1998; CEO GEORGE LEACOCK.

Red 96.7: 47 Tragarete Rd, New Town, Port of Spain; tel. 628-4967; fax 628-0251; e-mail info@citadel.co.tt; internet www.red967fm.com; f. 2005; Exec. Chair. and CEO LOUIS LEE SING.

Soca 91.9 FM (Trini Bashment): 56A Maraval Rd, Port of Spain; tel. 628-3460; fax 622-7674; e-mail info@soca919.com; internet www .919socafm.com; Man. Dir ANTHONY DEVON GEORGE.

Telemedia Ltd: Long Circular Mall, 4th Floor, Long Circular Rd, St James; tel. 622-4124; fax 622-6693; operates three commercial radio stations: Music Radio 97 FM (www.musicradio97.com), Ebony Radio 104 FM (www.ebony104.com) and Heartbeat 103.5 FM (www.heartbeatradiott.com); Gen. Man. KIRAN MAHARAJ.

Trinidad Broadcasting Co Ltd: Guardian Bldg, 2nd Floor, 22–24 St Vincent St, Port of Spain; tel. 623-9202; fax 623-8972; e-mail tbcnews@ttol.co.tt; operates five radio stations: Inspirational Radio 730 AM, Mix 95.1 FM, Vibe CT 105 FM, Sangeet 106 FM and Aakash Vani 106.5 FM; Gen. Man. BRANDON KHAN.

Trinidad and Tobago Radio Network: 153 Tragarete Rd, Port of Spain; tel. 628-6937; internet www.1077musicforlife.com; operates two stations: 96.1 WEFM and 107.7 FM.

Wack Radio 90.1 FM: 129c Coffee St, San Fernando; tel. 652-9774; fax 657-1888; e-mail contact@wackradio901fm.com; internet www.wackradio901fm.com; CEO KENNY PHILLIPS; Man. Dir DIANNE PHILLIPS.

WMJX 100.5 FM: 9 Long Circular Rd, St James; tel. 628-9516; fax 622-2756; e-mail comments@wmjxfm.com; internet www.wmjxfm.com; Gen. Man. KEITH CADET.

Television

Columbus Communications Trinidad Ltd: cable television provider—see above.

ieTV Channel 1: 76 Tragarete Rd, Port of Spain; tel. 622-3541; fax 622-3097; e-mail ietv@tstt.net.tt; internet www.ietv1.com; owned by CL Communications Group; Indian entertainment-programming; CEO ANTHONY MAHARAJ.

TV6: 35 Independence Sq., Port of Spain; tel. 627-8806; fax 623-0785; e-mail enquiries@tv6tnt.com; internet www.tv6tnt.com; f. 1991; operates channels 6 and 18; owned by One Caribbean Media Ltd (OCM); Chair. Sir FRED GOLLOP; Gen. Man. SHIDA BOLAI.

Association

Trinidad and Tobago Publishers and Broadcasters Association: C/o I95.5 FM, 47 Tragarete Rd, Newtown, Port Of Spain; tel. 688-7412; fax 628-7024; e-mail fazilettem@ttpba.org.tt; internet www.ttpba.org.tt; Pres. DARREN MARK LEE SING.

Finance

(cap. = capital; res = reserves; dep. = deposits; m. = million;
brs = branches; amounts in TT $)

BANKING

Central Bank

Central Bank of Trinidad and Tobago: Eric Williams Plaza, Brian Lara Promenade, POB 1250, Port of Spain; tel. 625-4835; fax 627-4696; e-mail info@central-bank.org.tt; internet www.central-bank.org.tt; f. 1964; cap. 800.0m., res 534.8m., dep. 53.5m. (Sept. 2009); Gov. JWALA RAMBARRAN.

Commercial Banks

CIBC FirstCaribbean International Bank: 74 Long Circular Rd, Maraval; tel. 628-4685; fax 628-8906; internet www.firstcaribbeanbank.com; adopted present name in 2002 following merger of Caribbean operations of CIBC and Barclays Bank PLC; Barclays relinquished its stake in 2006, present name adopted in 2011; CEO RIK PARKHILL; Man. Dir (Trinidad) DUANE HINKSON; 1 br.

Citibank (Trinidad and Tobago) Ltd: 12 Queen's Park East, POB 1249, Port of Spain; tel. 625-1046; fax 624-8131; internet www.citibank.com/trinidad; f. 1983; fmrly The United Bank of Trinidad and Tobago Ltd; name changed as above 1989; owned by Citicorp Merchant Bank Ltd; cap. 157.8m., res 94.4m., dep. 3,727.6m. (Dec. 2010); Chair. SURESH MAHARAJ; Country Man. CATALINA HERRERA ROCA; 1 br.

Citicorp Merchant Bank Ltd: 12 Queen's Park East, POB 1249, Port of Spain; tel. 623-3344; fax 624-8131; cap. 57.1m., res 151.8m., dep. 3,796.7m. (Dec. 2010); owned by Citibank Overseas Investment Corpn; Man. Dir KAREN DARBASIE.

First Citizens Bank Ltd: 9 Queen's Park East, Port of Spain; tel. 624-3178; fax 624-5981; e-mail info@firstcitizenstt.com; internet www.firstcitizenstt.com; f. 1993 following merger of National Commercial Bank of Trinidad and Tobago Ltd, Trinidad Co-operative Bank Ltd and Workers' Bank of Trinidad and Tobago; state-owned; 20% of shares offered for sale in 2013; cap. 643.5m., res 1,866.6m., dep. 21,500.3m. (Sept. 2013); Chair. NYREE D. ALFONSO; CEO LARRY NATH; 25 brs.

RBC Royal Bank Trinidad and Tobago Ltd: 7-9 St Clair Pl., Clair Ave, POB 287, Port of Spain; tel. 625-7288; fax 623-2081; e-mail tt-info@rbc.com; internet www.rbtt.com/tt/personal; f. 1972 as Royal Bank of Trinidad and Tobago to take over local brs of Royal Bank of Canada; changed name to RBTT Bank Ltd in 2002, present name adopted 2011; bought by Royal Bank of Canada in 2008; cap. 404m., res 540m., dep. 17,511.4m. (Oct. 2011); CEO, Caribbean SURESH SOOKOO; 21 brs.

Republic Bank Ltd: 9-17 Park St, POB 1153, Port of Spain; tel. 623-1056; fax 624-1323; e-mail email@republictt.com; internet www.republictt.com; f. 1837 as Colonial Bank; became Barclays Bank in 1972; name changed as above in 1981; merged with Bank of Commerce Trinidad and Tobago Ltd in 1997; cap. 649.9m., res

2,120.8m., dep. 42,098.3m. (Sept. 2013); Chair. RONALD F. HARFORD; Man. Dir DAVID DULAL-WHITEWAY; 34 brs.

Republic Finance & Merchant Bank Ltd: 9–17 Park St, POB 1153, Port of Spain; tel. 625-4411; fax 624-1296; e-mail email@republictt.com; internet www.republictt.com; f. 1965; owned by Republic Bank Ltd; Man. Dir CHERYL F. GREAVES.

Scotiabank Trinidad and Tobago Ltd (Canada): 56–58 Richmond St, POB 621, Port of Spain; tel. 625-3566; fax 627-5278; e-mail scotiamain@tstt.net.tt; internet www.scotiabanktt.com; f. 1954; cap. 267.6m., res 454.4m., dep. 13,003m. (Oct. 2012); Chair. SYLVIA D. CHROMINSKA; Man. Dir ANYA M. SCHNOOR; 24 brs.

Development Banks

Agricultural Development Bank of Trinidad and Tobago: 87 Henry St, POB 154, Port of Spain; tel. 623-6261; fax 625-0341; e-mail northbranch@adbtt.com; internet www.adbtt.com; f. 1968; provides long-, medium- and short-term loans to farmers and the agri-business sector; Chair. YASID GILBERT; CEO SHEIVAN RAMNATH.

Development Finance Ltd: 10 Cipriani Blvd, POB 187, Port of Spain; tel. 623-4665; fax 624-3563; e-mail info@dfltt.com; internet www.dfltt.com; provides commercial loans, merchant banking facilities and foreign exchange services; total assets 433m. (Dec. 2013); Chair. ANDREW FERGUSON; Gen. Man. SIEW PALTOO.

Credit Union

Co-operative Credit Union League of Trinidad and Tobago Ltd: 3 cnr John and De Verteuil Sts, Montrose, Chaguanas; tel. 671-4711; fax 672-0165; e-mail culeague@tstt.net.tt; internet www.ccultt.org; Pres. JOSEPH REMY; 400,000 mems.

STOCK EXCHANGES

Trinidad and Tobago Securities and Exchange Commission (TTSEC): 57–59 Dundonald St, Port of Spain; tel. 624-3017; fax 624-8232; e-mail ttsec@ttsec.org.tt; internet www.ttsec.org.tt; f. 1997; Chair. Prof. PATRICK WATSON; CEO C. WAINWRIGHT ITON.

Trinidad and Tobago Stock Exchange Ltd: Nicholas Tower, 10th Floor, 63–65 Independence Sq., Port of Spain; tel. 625-5107; fax 623-0089; e-mail ttstockx@stockex.co.tt; internet www.stockex.co.tt; f. 1981; 31 cos listed (2014); electronic depository system came into operation in 2003; Chair. PETER CLARKE; CEO MICHELLE PERSAD.

INSURANCE

Atrius Life Insurance Co Ltd: Level 15, Eric Williams Financial Complex, Independence Sq., Port of Spain; f. 2013 as successor co to CLICO (dissolved 2009); govt-owned; Chair. SHUBHASH GOSINE; Sec. and Dir SHIREEN AZIZ.

Bankers Insurance Co of Trinidad and Tobago Ltd: 5 Mulchan Seuchan Rd, Chaguanas; tel. 672-1057; fax 672-2808; e-mail admin@bankerstt.com; internet www.bankerstt.com; CEO VANCE GABRIEL.

Beacon Insurance Co Ltd: 13 Stanmore Ave, POB 837, Port of Spain; tel. 623-2266; fax 623-9900; e-mail info@beacon.co.tt; internet www.beacon.co.tt; f. 1996; Chair. GERALD S. HADEED; CEO ROBERT MOWSER.

CUNA Caribbean Insurance Society Ltd: 7 Gray St, St Clair, Port of Spain; tel. 628-2862; fax 628-3506; e-mail cunains@trinidad.net; internet www.cunacaribbean.com; f. 1991; marine aviation and transport; motor vehicle, personal accident, property; Man. Dir and CEO ANDRE GOINDOO; 3 brs.

Furness Anchorage General Insurance Ltd: 11–13 Milling Ave, Sea Lots, POB 283, Port of Spain; tel. 625-1746; fax 625-1243; e-mail furness@tstt.net.tt; internet www.furnessgroup.com; f. 1979; general; Chair. IGNATIUS SEVEIRANO FERREIRA; Exec. Chair. WILLIAM A. FERREIRA.

Guardian General Insurance Ltd: Newtown Centre, 30–36 Maraval Rd, Port of Spain; tel. 625-4445; fax 622-9994; e-mail guardian.general@ggil.biz; internet www.ggil.biz; founded by merger of NEMWIL and Caribbean Home; CEO RICHARD ESPINET; Vice-Pres. (Trinidad Operations) JOAN MITCHELL.

Guardian Life of the Caribbean: 1 Guardian Dr., West Moorings, Port of Spain; tel. 625-5433; fax 632-5695; e-mail guardian@gloc.biz; internet www.gloc.biz; f. 1980; Group Pres. RAVI TEWARI.

Gulf Insurance Ltd: 1 Gray St, St Clair, Port of Spain; tel. 622-5878; fax 628-0272; e-mail info@gulfinsuranceltd.com; internet www.gulfinsuranceltd.com; f. 1974; general; Chair. STEPHEN SMITH.

Maritime Financial Group: Maritime Centre, 10th Ave, POB 710, Barataria; tel. 674-0130; fax 638-6663; e-mail email@maritimefinancial.com; internet www.maritimefinancial.com; f. 1978; property and casualty; CEO ANDREW S. FERGUSON.

New India Assurance Co (T & T) Ltd: Guardian Bldg, 3rd Floor, 22–24 St Vincent St, POB 884, Port of Spain; tel. 623-1326; fax 625-

0670; e-mail hoffice@newindiatt.com; tel. www.newindiatt.com; f. 1919; Man. Dir G. SRINIVASAN.

Pan-American Life Insurance Company of Trinidad and Tobago Ltd: Pan-American Life Plaza, 91–93 St Vincent St, POB 943, Port of Spain; tel. 625-4426; fax 623-4923; internet www.palig .com; f. 1977; (part of Pan-American Life Insurance Group (USA); fmrly known as ALGICO Trinidad and Tobago; CEO and Man. Dir (Caribbean) WILLIAM R. SCHULZ, Jr; Man. Dir MIGUEL SIERRA.

Sagicor Life Inc: Sagicor Financial Centre, 16 Queen's Park West, Port of Spain; tel. 628-1636; fax 628-1639; e-mail comments@sagicor .com; internet www.sagicorlife.com; f. 1840 as Barbados Mutual Life Assurance Society, name changed as above in 2002; Gen. Man. (Trinidad and Tobago) ROBERT TRESTRAIL.

Trinidad and Tobago Insurance Ltd (TATIL): 11A Maraval Rd, POB 1004, Port of Spain; tel. 628-2845; fax 628-0035; e-mail info@ tatil.co.tt; internet www.tatil.co.tt; acquired by ANSA McAL in 2004; Man. Dir MUSA IBRAHIM (TATIL General); Man. Dir RONALD LAI FANG (TATIL Life).

United Insurance Co (Trinidad): 18–20 London St, Port of Spain; tel. 627-7530; fax 627-3674; e-mail trinidad@unitedinsure.com; internet unitedinsure.com; 95.0% owned by Barbados Shipping and Trading Co; Gen. Man. DENNIS BENISAR.

INSURANCE ORGANIZATIONS

Association of Trinidad and Tobago Insurance Companies: 9A Stanmore Ave, POB 208, Port of Spain; tel. 624-2817; fax 625-5132; e-mail mail@attic.org.tt; internet www.attic.org.tt; Chair. DOUGLAS CAMACHO; Pres. WILLARD P. HARRIS.

National Insurance Board: NIB House, Cipriani Pl., 2A Cipriani Blvd, Port of Spain; tel. 625-2171; fax 627-1787; e-mail info@nibtt .net; internet www.nibtt.net; f. 1971; statutory corpn; Chair. ADRIAN BHARATH; Exec. Dir KAREN GOPAUL.

Trade and Industry

GOVERNMENT AGENCIES

Cocoa and Coffee Industry Board: 27 Frederick St, POB 1, Port of Spain; tel. 625-0298; fax 627-4172; e-mail ccib@tstt.net.tt; f. 1962; marketing of coffee and cocoa beans, regulation of cocoa and coffee industry; Man. BARRY JOEFIELD.

Export-Import Bank of Trinidad and Tobago Ltd (EXIM-BANK): 30 Queen's Park West, Port of Spain; tel. 628-2762; fax 622-3545; e-mail eximbank@wow.net; internet www.eximbanktt .com; Chair. CLARRY BENN; CEO BRIAN AWANG.

Trinidad and Tobago Forest Products Ltd (TANTEAK): Connector Rd, Carlsen Field, Chaguanas; tel. 665-0078; fax 665-6645; f. 1975; harvesting, processing and marketing of state plantation-grown teak and pine; privatization pending; Chair. RUSKIN PUNCH; Man. Dir CLARENCE BACCHUS.

DEVELOPMENT ORGANIZATIONS

Housing Development Corporation: 44–46 South Quay, POB 555, Port of Spain; tel. 623-4663; fax 627-6940; e-mail info@housing .gov.tt; internet www.mphe.gov.tt/agenciesdivisions/hdc.html; f. 1962 as Nat. Housing Authority; adopted present name 2005; Chair. HENCKLE LALL; Man. Dir JEARLEAN JOHN.

National Energy Corporation of Trinidad and Tobago Ltd: PLIPDECO House, Orinoco Dr., POB 191, Point Lisas, Couva; tel. 636-4662; fax 679-2384; e-mail infocent@carib-link.net; internet www.ngc.co.tt; owned by the Nat. Gas Co of Trinidad and Tobago Ltd; f. 1979; Chair. ROOP CHAN CHADEESINGH; Pres. INDAR MAHARAJ.

Point Lisas Industrial Port Development Corporation Ltd (PLIPDECO): PLIPDECO House, Orinoco Dr., POB 191, Point Lisas, Couva; tel. 636-2201; fax 636-4008; e-mail plipdeco@plipdeco .com; internet www.plipdeco.com; f. 1966; privatized in the late 1990s; deep-water port handling general cargo, liquid and dry bulk, to serve adjacent industrial estate, which now includes iron and steel complex, methanol, ammonia, urea and related downstream industries; Chair. IAN ATHERLY; Pres. ERNEST ASHLEY TAYLOR.

Urban Development Corporation of Trinidad and Tobago (UDeCOTT): 38–40 Sackville St, Port of Spain; tel. 627-0083; fax 623-5358; e-mail contact@udecott.com; internet www.udecott.com; f. 1994; Chair. JEARLEAN JOHN.

CHAMBERS OF COMMERCE

The Energy Chamber of Trinidad and Tobago: Suite B2.03, Atlantic Plaza, Atlantic Ave, Point Lisas; tel. 636-3749; fax 679-4242; e-mail execoffice@energy.tt; internet www.energy.tt; f. 1956; Chair. ROGER PACKER; CEO Dr THACKWRAY DRIVER.

Trinidad and Tobago Chamber of Industry and Commerce: Chamber Bldg, Columbus Circle, Westmoorings, POB 499, Port of Spain; tel. 637-6966; fax 637-7425; e-mail chamber@chamber.org.tt; internet www.chamber.org.tt; f. 1891; Pres. MOONILAL LALCHAN; CEO CATHERINE KUMAR; 600 mems.

INDUSTRIAL AND TRADE ASSOCIATIONS

Agricultural Society of Trinidad and Tobago: 52 Penco St, Penco Court, Lange Park, Chaguanas; e-mail agrisocietytt@gmail .com; f. 1839; represents farmers' interests; Pres. NAWAS KARIM.

Co-operative Citrus Growers' Association of Trinidad and Tobago Ltd: Eastern Main Rd, POB 174, Laventille, Port of Spain; tel. 623-5127; fax 623-2487; e-mail ccga@wow.net; f. 1932; Gen. Man. GARY PRENTICE; 437 mems.

Pan Trinbago Inc: Victoria Park Suites, 14–17 Park St, Port of Spain; tel. 623-4486; fax 625-6715; e-mail panadmin@pantrinbago.co .tt; internet www.pantrinbago.co.tt; f. 1971; official body for Trinidad and Tobago steelbands; Pres. KEITH DIAZ; Sec. RICHARD FORTEAU.

Sugar Association of the Caribbean: Brechin Castle, Couva; tel. 636-2449; fax 636-2847; f. 1942; promotes and protects sugar industry in the Caribbean; Chair. KARL JAMES; 6 mem. asscns.

Trinidad and Tobago Contractors' Association: The Professional Centre, Unit B 203, 11–13 Fitzblackman Dr., Wrightson Rd Extension, Port of Spain; tel. 627-1266; fax 623-2949; e-mail ttcaservice@rave-tt.net; internet www.ttca.com; f. 1968; represents contractors, manufacturers and suppliers to the sector; Pres. MIKEY JOSEPH.

Trinidad and Tobago Manufacturers' Association: TTMA Bldg, 42 10th Ave, Barataria; tel. 675-8862; fax 675-9000; e-mail info@ttma.com; internet www.ttma.com; f. 1956; Pres. NICHOLAS LOK JAK; CEO MAHINDRA RAMDEEN; 337 mems.

EMPLOYERS' ORGANIZATION

Employers' Consultative Association of Trinidad and Tobago (ECA): 17 Samaroo Rd, Aranguez Roundabout North, Aranguez; tel. 675-9388; fax 675-4866; e-mail ecatt@tstt.net.tt; internet www.ecatt .org; f. 1959; Chair. KESTON NANCOO; Exec. Dir LINDA BESSON; 700 mems.

STATE HYDROCARBONS COMPANIES

National Gas Co of Trinidad and Tobago Ltd (NGC): Orinoco Dr., Point Lisas Industrial Estate, POB 1127, Port of Spain; tel. 636-4662; fax 679-2384; e-mail info@ngc.co.tt; internet www.ngc.co.tt; f. 1975; purchases, sells, compresses, transmits and distributes natural gas to consumers; Chair. ROOP CHAN CHADEESINGH; Pres. INDAR MAHARAJ.

Petroleum Co of Trinidad and Tobago Ltd (Petrotrin): Petrotrin Administration Bldg, Southern Main Rd, Pointe-à-Pierre; tel. 658-3336; fax 658-2513; e-mail ken.allum@petrotrin.com; internet www.petrotrin.com; f. 1993 following merger between Trinidad and Tobago Oil Co Ltd (Trintoc) and Trinidad and Tobago Petroleum Co Ltd (Trintopec); govt-owned; petroleum and gas exploration and production; operates refineries and a manufacturing complex, producing a variety of petroleum and petrochemical products; Chair. LINDSAY GILLETTE; Pres. KHALID HASSANALI.

MAJOR COMPANIES

Food and Beverages

Angostura Holdings Ltd: cnr Eastern Main Rd and Trinity Ave, Laventille; tel. 623-1841; fax 623-1847; e-mail glarondew@angostura .com; internet www.angostura.com; f. 1921; manufacturers of rum, Angostura aromatic bitters and other alcoholic beverages; gross sales of TT $6.96m. (2011); Chair. GERALD YETMING; CEO ROBERT WONG; 35 employees.

Bermudez Biscuit Co Ltd: 6 Maloney St, POB 885, Mount Lambert; tel. 675-3615; fax 674-2167; e-mail bgladmin@ bermudezgroupltd.com; f. 1950; producers of biscuits and other food products; Gen. Man. IAN MITCHELL; 367 employees.

S.M. Jaleel and Co Ltd (SMJ): Otaheite Industrial Estate, South Oropouche, Fyzabad; tel. 677-7520; e-mail hrsmj@chubbysd.com; internet www.smjaleel.net; f. 1924; mfrs of non-alcoholic drinks; Chair. ALEEM MOHAMMED.

Kiss Baking Co Ltd: 12–14 Gaston St, POB 776, Lange Park, Chaguanas; tel. 671-5675; fax 672-3840; e-mail kissbaking@ cariblink.net; f. 1975; bakery; Gen. Man. PETER MCCARTHY; 2,890 employees.

National Flour Mills Ltd: 27–29 Wrightson Rd, POB 1154, Port of Spain; tel. 625-2416; fax 625-4389; e-mail nfm@nfm.co.tt; internet www.nfm.co.tt; f. 1966; milling of flour and grains; mfrs and distributors of rice, edible oils, other food items and animal feed; 51% owned by National Enterprises Ltd; sales of TT $439.3m. (2010); CEO DARREN GOSINE; 384 employees.

Nestlé Trinidad and Tobago Ltd: Churchill Roosevelt Highway, Valsayn, POB 172, Port of Spain; tel. and fax 663-6832; fax 663-6840; internet www.nestle-caribbean.com; manufacture and distribution of dairy products, canned vegetables, fruit juices, pasta products; subsidiary of Nestlé SA (Switzerland).

Metals

ArcelorMittal Point Lisas Ltd: Mediterranean Dr., Point Lisas Industrial Estate, POB 476, Couva; tel. 636-2211; fax 636-5696; internet www.arcelormittal.com; f. 2005; owned by ArcelorMittal, Luxembourg; fmrly Iron and Steel Co of Trinidad and Tobago Ltd; name changed to Caribbean Ispat Ltd in 1998; name changed to Mittal Steel Point Lisas Ltd in 2005 and as above in 2006; acquired International Steel Group (USA) in April 2005; production of iron and steel wire and rods; Chair. and CEO LAKSHMI MITTAL; 732 employees.

Bhagwansingh's Hardware and Steel Industries Ltd: 1 Development Circular Rd, Sea Lots, Port of Spain; tel. 627-8335; fax 623-0804; e-mail bhsil@bhsil.com; f. 1974; mfrs of aluminium products; wholesale of steel and electrical products; Man. Dir HELEN BHAGWANSINGH; 310 employees.

> **Central Trinidad Steel Ltd (CENTRIN):** Mediterranean Dr., Point Lisas Industrial Estate, Point Lisas; tel. 679-2996; fax 679-3073; e-mail centrin@tstt.net.tt; internet www.centrintt.com; f. 1983; owned by Bhagwansingh's Hardware and Steel Industries Ltd; mfrs of steel and bldg materials; Man. Dir HELEN BHAGWANSINGH.

Petroleum, Natural Gas and Asphalt
(see also State Hydrocarbons Companies)

Atlantic LNG Co of Trinidad and Tobago: Princes Court, 5°, Corner Keate and Pembroke St, Port of Spain; tel. 624-2916; fax 624-8057; e-mail atlanticinfo@atlanticlng.com; internet www.atlanticlng.com; f. 1995; operates 4 natural gas trains; production of liquefied natural gas; owned by consortium of BP, BG Trinidad and Tobago Ltd, Repsol-YPF, Summer Soca LNG Liquefaction (a subsidiary of China Investment Corpn) and the NGC; CEO NIGEL DARLOW.

BG Trinidad and Tobago Ltd (BG T&T): BG House, 5 St Clair Ave, Port of Spain; tel. 628-0888; fax 622-2424; internet www.bg-group.com; f. 1989; extraction of natural gas; Chair. ANDREW GOULD; Exec.Chair. ANDREW GOULD.

BHP Billiton Trinidad and Tobago: Invaders Bay Tower, Invaders Bay, off Audrey Jeffers Hwy, Port of Spain; tel. 821-5100; fax 627-1277; internet www.bhpbilliton.com; oil and gas production, operates the Angostura field; Chair. JAC NASEER; Country Man. VINCENT PEREIRA.

BP Trinidad and Tobago (BPTT): 5–5A Queen's Park West, POB 714, Port of Spain; tel. 623-2862; fax 628-5058; e-mail bptt@bp.com; internet www.bp.com; f. 1961; 70% owned by BP and 30% by Repsol (Spain); exploration and extraction of natural gas and petroleum; Regional Pres. NORMAN CHRISTIE; 900 employees.

Eastern Caribbean Gas Pipeline Co Ltd (ECGPC): Cove Eco Business and Industrial Park, Cove Estate, Scarborough; f. 2013; proposed 959 km natural gas pipeline from Tobago to other eastern Caribbean islands; the 300 km first phase connects Tobago to Barbados, scheduled to begin in 2014; the second phase expected to expand to St Lucia, Dominica, Martinique, and Guadeloupe; shares jtly owned by the US cos Beowulf Energy and First Reserve Energy International Fund (60%) and Trinidad and Tobago companies: Guardian Holdings, Unit Trust Corprn, and the National Gas Co (40%); CEO GREG RICH.

EOG Resources Trinidad Ltd: Briar Pl., 10–12 Sweet Briar Rd, St Clair, Port of Spain; tel. 622-8653; fax 628-4218; internet www.eogresources.com; subsidiary of EOG Resources (USA); natural gas and petroleum production; Man. Dir SAMMY G. PICKERING.

Lake Asphalt of Trinidad and Tobago (1978) Ltd: Brighton, La Brea; tel. 648-7556; fax 648-7433; e-mail dsarabjit@trinidadlakeasphalt.com; internet www.trinidadlakeasphalt.com; state-owned; mfrs of asphalt; CEO LEARY A. HOSEIN; Chair. ERNEST ASHLEY TAYLOR.

Mora Ven Holdings Ltd (MORA VEN): Suite 405, Level 4, Long Circular Mall, St James; tel. 622-0427; fax 628-3708; e-mail mail@moraven.com; f. 1994 as Mora Oil Ventures; oil production; Exec. Chair. GEORGE NICHOLAS, III.

Petrochemicals

EthylChem: Lot A11-6, Amazon Dr., POB 1150, Point Lisas Industrial Estate, Couva; tel. 636-2458; fax 679-2267; e-mail admin@ethylchem.com; internet www.ethylchem.com; ethanol dehydration plant; Denham (USA) is major shareholder; Man. Dir NAMDEO MAHARAJ.

Methanex: Maracaibo Dr., Point Lisas, POB 723, Couva; tel. 679-4400; fax 679-2400; e-mail mxtrinidad@methanex.com; internet www.methanex.com; operates Trinidad and Tobago's largest methanol plant; Chair. THOMAS HAMILTON; Pres. and CEO JOHN FLOREN.

Methanol Holdings (Trinidad) Ltd: Atlantic Ave, POB 457, Point Lisas Industrial Estate, Couva; tel. 636-2906; fax 636-4501; e-mail mhtlweb@ttmethanol.com; internet www.ttmethanol.com; f. 1999 to manage Trinidad and Tobago Methanol Co Ltd (TTMC), Caribbean Methanol Co Ltd (CMC) and Methanol IV Co Ltd (MIV); methanol production; new complex opened in 2010 to produce urea ammonium nitrate and melamine; Chair. JAGDEESH SIEWRATTAN; CEO DENNIS PATRICK (acting); 300 employees.

PCS (Potash Corpn of Saskatchewan) Nitrogen Ltd: Mediterranean Dr., POB 201, Point Lisas, Couva; tel. 636-2205; e-mail iewelch@pcsnitrogen.co.tt; internet www.potashcorp.com; f. 1977; fmrly state-owned Fertilizers of Trinidad and Tobago (Fertrin) Ltd, bought by Arcadian Partners (USA) in 1993; Arcadian Partners bought by PCS in 1997; mfrs of fertilizers; CEO CHRISTOPHER M. BURLEY.

Pt Lisas Nitrogen Ltd: North Caspian Dr., PO Bag 38, Point Lisas, Couva; tel. 679-3625; fax 636-3768; e-mail media@plnl.co.tt; fmrly Farmland MissChem; renamed as above in 2002; 50% owned by Koch Minerals; ammonia production; Pres. ROBERTO MANTELLINI.

Miscellaneous

Agostini's Ltd: 18 Victoria Ave, POB 191, Port of Spain; tel. 623-4871; fax 623-1966; e-mail marketing@agostini-mktg.com; internet www.agostini-mktg.com; f. 1925; importers and wholesale distributors of construction materials, foodstuffs and pharmaceuticals; sales of TT $385m. (2006); Chair. JOSEPH P. ESAU; Man. Dir ANTHONY J. AGOSTINI; 650 employees.

ANSA McAL: Edif. Tatil, 9–11°, 11 Maraval Rd, Port of Spain; tel. 625-3670; fax 624-8753; internet www.ansamcal.com; activities include glass making, construction, finance, media; owns Caribbean Devt Co brewery; Group Chair. and CEO A. NORMAN SABGA.

Automotive Components Ltd: O'Meara Industrial Estate, Lots 10 and 11, O'Meara Rd, POB 1298, Arima; tel. 642-4236; fax 642-7807; e-mail info@massygroup.com; internet www.acl-tt.com; f. 1964; mfrs of automobile batteries; owned by Massy (q.v.); Exec. Chair. DAVID O'BRIEN; CEO ALOYSIUS BEREAUX.

Berger Paints Trinidad Ltd: 11 Concessions Rd, Sea Lots, POB 546, Port of Spain; tel. 623-2231; fax 623-1682; e-mail berger@tstt.net.tt; internet www.bergeronline.com; f. 1760; mfrs of paint, wood stains, wood preservatives, auto refinishes; Gen. Man OMWATIE BIRBAL; 100 employees.

A. S. Bryden and Sons (Trinidad) Ltd: 1 Ibis Ave, San Juan; tel. 674-9191; fax 674-0781; e-mail info@brydenstt.com; internet www.brydenstt.com; f. 1923; importers and distributors of alcoholic beverages, food products, household goods and pharmaceuticals; Chair. IAN FITZWILLIAM; Man. Dir DAVID FRANCO; 225 employees.

Carib Glassworks Ltd: Eastern Main Rd, POB 1287, Champs Fleurs, Port of Spain; tel. 662-2231; fax 663-1779; e-mail marketing@caribglass.com; internet www.caribglass.com; f. 1948; part of ANSA McAL Group; glass mfrs; Man. Dir ROGER MEW; 420 employees.

CGA Ltd (Coconut Growers' Asscn): Eastern Main Rd, POB 229, Laventille, Port of Spain; tel. 623-5207; fax 623-2359; internet cgacaribbean.com; f. 1936; soaps, edible products, oils and fats.

Fujitsu Transaction Solutions (Trinidad) Ltd: 6th Ave South Ext. and Ibis Ave, Barataria; tel. 223-2826; fax 675-1956; internet www.fujitsu.com/caribbean; subsidiary of Fujitsu Ltd (Japan); mfrs of computers and telecommunications equipment; Pres. and CEO MERVYN EYRE.

Massy: 63 Park St, POB 544, Port of Spain; tel. 625-3426; fax 627-9061; e-mail info@massygroup.com; internet www.massygroup.com; f. 1923 as Neal & Massy Group, present name adopted 2014; industrial, trading and financial group involved in metals, engineering and automobile assembly; CEO and Pres. GERVASE WARNER; 6,500 employees.

Thomas Peake and Co Ltd: 177 Western Main Rd, Cocorite, Port of Spain; tel. 622-7325; fax 622-7288; e-mail peake@peakeco.net; internet www.peakeco.net; f. 1949; mfrs and repairers of air conditioning equipment; Dir PAUL PEAKE; 500 employees.

Trinidad Cement Ltd (TCL): Southern Main Rd, Claxton Bay; tel. 659-2381; fax 659-2420; e-mail tclmktg@tclgroup.com; internet www.tclgroup.com; f. 1951; manufacture and sale of Portland, sulphate-resisting and oil-well cement and paper sacks and bags; owned by TCL Group; Chair. ANDY J. BHAJAN; Group CEO Dr ROLLIN BERTRAND; 400 employees.

Trinidad and Tobago National Petroleum Marketing Co Ltd: National Dr., POB 666, Sea Lots, Port of Spain; tel. 625-1364; fax 627-4028; e-mail customer_service@np.co.tt; internet www.np.co.tt; f. 1972; marketing of petroleum products; state-owned; Chair. NEIL GOSINE.

Unilever Caribbean Ltd: Eastern Main Rd, POB 295, Champ Fleurs, Port of Spain; tel. 663-1787; fax 662-1780; internet www .unilevercaribbean.com; f. 1964 as Lever Brothers (West Indies) Ltd; name changed as above 2004; subsidiary of Unilever PLC (United Kingdom); mfrs of soaps, detergents, cosmetic products and foods; Chair. MICHAEL TRESCHOW; CEO PAUL POLMAN; 600 employees.

West Indian Tobacco Co Ltd (WITCO): Eastern Main Rd, POB 177, Champ Fleurs, Port of Spain; tel. 662-2271; fax 663-5451; internet www.westindiantobacco.com; f. 1904; subsidiary of British-American Tobacco Co Ltd (United Kingdom); cigarette mfrs; Chair. ANTHONY PHILLIP; Man. Dir JEAN-PIERRE S. DU COUDRAY; 200 employees.

L. J. Williams Ltd: JSAC Compound, El Socorro Extension South, San Juan; tel. 674-1500; fax 675-9831; e-mail info@ljw.co.tt; f. 1925; mfrs of glues and sealants; distribution of groceries and beverages; ships and insurance agent; 4 subsidiaries; Chair. J. G. FURNESS-SMITH; Man. Dir P. J. WILLIAMS; 500 employees.

UTILITIES

Regulatory Authority

Regulated Industries Commission: Furness House, cnr Wrightson Rd & Independence Sq., Port of Spain; tel. 625-5384; fax 624-2027; e-mail complaints@ric.org.tt; internet www.ric.org.tt; f. 2000; Chair. ANNE-MARIE MOHAMMED; Exec. Dir HARJINDER S. ATWAL.

Electricity

Power Generation Co of Trinidad and Tobago (PowerGen): 6A Queen's Park West, Port of Spain; tel. 624-0383; fax 624-0983; e-mail pgcinfo@powergen.co.tt; internet www.powergen.co.tt; f. 1994; 51% owned by The Trinidad and Tobago Electricity Commission (T&TEC); operates 3 generation plants in Point Lisas, Port of Spain and Penal; Gen. Man. GARTH CHATOOR.

Trinidad and Tobago Electricity Commission (T&TEC): 63 Frederick St, Port of Spain; tel. 623-2611; fax 623-3759; e-mail comments@ttec.co.tt; internet www.ttec.co.tt; state-owned transmission and distribution co; Chair. SUSILLA RAMKISSOON-MARK; Gen. Man. KELVIN RAMSOOK.

Trinity Power Ltd: Railway Rd, Dow Village, Couva; tel. 679-4542; fax 679-4463; e-mail gthompson@trinitypm.com; f. 1999; fmrly Inncogen Ltd; owned by York Research Corpn; Gen. Man. JACQUELINE LOOK LOY.

Gas

National Gas Co of Trinidad and Tobago Ltd: see State Hydrocarbons Companies.

Water

Water and Sewerage Authority (WASA): Farm Rd, St Joseph; tel. 662-2302; e-mail contact@wasa.gov.tt; internet www.wasa.gov.tt; f. 1965; Chair. INDAR MAHARAJ; CEO GANGA SINGH.

TRADE UNIONS

Federation of Independent Trade Unions and NGOs (FITUN): Paramount Bldg, 99A Circular Rd, San Fernando; tel. 652-2701; fax 652-7170; e-mail fitun_tt@yahoo.com; f. 2003; Pres. DAVID ABDULLAH; Gen. Sec. MICHAEL DEFREITAS.

National Trade Union Centre (NATUC): 16 New St, Port of Spain; tel. 625-3023; fax 627-7588; e-mail natuc@carib-link.net; f. 1991 as umbrella org. unifying entire trade union movt, incl. fmr Trinidad and Tobago Labour Congress and Council of Progressive Trade Unions; Pres. MICHAEL ANNISETTE; Gen. Sec. JACQUELINE JACK.

Principal Affiliates

All-Trinidad General Workers' Trade Union (ATGWTU): Rienzi Complex, Exchange Village, 79–81 Southern Main Rd, Couva; tel. 636-2354; fax 636-3372; e-mail atsgwtu@tstt.net.tt; f. 1937; Pres. NIRVAN MAHARAJ; Gen. Sec. ANAND TIWARI; 2,000 mems.

Amalgamated Workers' Union: 16 New St, Port of Spain; tel. 627-6717; fax 627-8993; f. 1953; Pres.-Gen. CLYDE DE FREITAS; Asst Gen. Sec. HAROLD SCOTT; c. 7,000 mems.

Banking, Insurance and General Workers' Union: 85 Eight St, Barataria, Port of Spain; tel. 675-2426; fax 675-8648; e-mail union@ bigwu.org; internet www.bigwu.org; f. 1974 as Bank and General Workers' Union; name changed as above following merger with Bank Employees' Union in 2003; Pres. VINCENT CABRERA; Gen. Sec. TREVOR JOHNSON.

Communication, Transport and General Workers' Trade Union: Aero Services Credit Union Bldg, Orange Grove Rd, Tacarigua; tel. and fax 640-8785; e-mail cattu@tstt.net.tt; Pres. JAGDEO JAGROOP; Gen. Sec. RAYMOND SMALL.

Communication Workers' Union: 146 Henry St, Port of Spain; tel. 623-5588; fax 625-3308; e-mail cwutdad@tstt.net.tt; f. 1953; Pres. JOSEPH REMY; Gen. Sec. JOHN JULIEN; c. 2,100 mems.

Contractors and General Workers' Trade Union (CAGWTU): 37 Rushworth St, San Fernando; tel. 657-8072; fax 657-6834; e-mail cgtwunion@gmail.com; Pres.-Gen. AYNSLEY MATTHEWS; Vice-Pres. JOSEPH PHILLIP.

Customs and Excise Extra Guard Association: Nicholas Court, Abercromby St, Port of Spain; tel. 625-3311; Pres. ANDRE CABARR; Gen. Sec. NATHAN HERBERT.

National Union of Domestic Employees (NUDE): 53 Wattley Circular Rd, Mount Pleasant Rd, Arima; tel. 667-5247; fax 664-0546; e-mail domestic@tstt.net.tt; internet www.ttdomesticworkers .blogspot.com; f. 1982; Gen. Sec. IDA LE BLANC.

National Union of Government and Federated Workers: 145–147 Henry St, Port of Spain; tel. 623-4591; fax 625-7756; e-mail headoffice@nugfw.org.tt; internet nugfw.org.tt; f. 1937; Pres.-Gen. JAMES LAMBERT; Gen. Sec. JACQUELINE JACK; c. 20,000 mems.

National Workers Union: 43 Fifth St, Barataria; tel. 223-4698; fax 223-4697; e-mail headoffice@workersunion.org.tt; internet www .workersunion.org.tt; f. 2004; Pres. FRANK SEARS; Gen. Sec. DAVE SMITH.

Oilfield Workers' Trade Union (OWTU): Paramount Bldg, 99A Circular Rd, San Fernando; tel. 652-2701; fax 652-7170; e-mail owtu@owtu.org; internet www.owtu.org; f. 1937; Pres. ANCEL ROGET; Gen. Sec. DAVID ABDULAH; 9,000 mems.

Public Services Association: 89–91 Abercromby St, POB 353, Port of Spain; tel. 623-7987; fax 627-2980; e-mail psa@tstt.net.tt; f. 1938; Pres. WATSON DUKE; Sec. NIXON CALLENDER; c. 15,000 mems.

Seamen and Waterfront Workers' Trade Union: 1D Wrightson Rd, Port of Spain; tel. 625-1351; fax 625-1182; e-mail swwtu@tstt.net .tt; f. 1937; Pres.-Gen. MICHAEL ANNISETTE; Sec.-Gen. ROSS ALEXANDER; c. 3,000 mems.

Steel Workers' Union of Trinidad and Tobago: 115 Southern Main Rd, California, Port of Spain; tel. 679-4666; fax 679-4175; e-mail swutt@tstt.net.tt; f. 1980; Pres. CHRISTOPHER HENRY; Gen. Sec. LANCELOT SMART.

Transport and Industrial Workers' Union: 114 Eastern Main Rd, Laventille, Port of Spain; tel. 623-4943; fax 623-2361; e-mail tiwu@tstt.net.tt; f. 1962; Pres. ROLAND SUTHERLAND; Gen. Sec. JUDY CHARLES; c. 5,000 mems.

Trinidad and Tobago Airline Pilots' Association (TTALPA): 35A Brunton Rd, St James; tel. 628-6556; fax 628-2418; e-mail info@ ttalpa.org; internet www.ttalpa.org; Chair. JOHN O'BRIEN; Man. CHRISTINE DAVIS.

Trinidad and Tobago Fire Service Association (Second Division) (FSA): 127 Edward St, Port of Spain; tel. 627-6700; fax 627-6701; e-mail fsa2@tstt.net.tt; internet www.ttfsa.org; Pres. CHARLES RAMSARROP; Sec. SHARON NICHOLSON-CHARLES.

Trinidad and Tobago Postal Workers' Union: c/o General Post Office, Wrightson Rd, POB 692, Port of Spain; tel. 625-2121; fax 642-4303; Pres. (vacant); Gen. Sec. REGINALD CRICHLOW.

Trinidad and Tobago Unified Teachers' Association: cnr Fowler and Southern Main Rd, Curepe; tel. 645-2134; fax 662-1813; e-mail generalsecretary@ttuta.org; internet www.ttuta.org; Pres. CLYDE PERMELL; Gen. Sec. DAVID LEWIS.

Union of Commercial and Industrial Workers: TIWU Bldg, 114 Eastern Main Rd, POB 460, Port of Spain; tel. and fax 626-2285; f. 1951; Pres. KELVIN GONZALES; Gen. Sec. ROSALIE FRASER; c. 1,500 mems.

Transport

RAILWAYS

The Government in 2005 announced plans to reintroduce a railway service, which had been discontinued in 1968. The design phase of the project began in 2008 and construction was expected to take 10–15 years, costing an estimated TT $15,000m.

ROADS

There were 8,320 km (5,170 miles) of roads in Trinidad and Tobago in 2001, of which 51.1% were paved.

Public Transport Service Corporation: 60 Railway Bldg, South Quay, POB 391, Port of Spain; tel. 623-2341; fax 625-6502; e-mail ptscpos@ptsc.co.tt; internet www.ptsc.co.tt; f. 1965; national bus services, operates a fleet of buses; Chair. Dr VINCENT LASSE; Gen. Man. SELWYN SYLVESTER.

SHIPPING

The chief ports are Port of Spain, Pointe-à-Pierre and Point Lisas in Trinidad, and Scarborough in Tobago. Port of Spain handles 85% of all container traffic, and all international cruise arrivals. Port of Spain possesses a dedicated container terminal, with two large overhead cranes. At December 2013 the flag registered fleet comprised 84 vessels, totalling 51,586 grt.

Point Lisas Industrial Port Development Corporation Ltd (PLIPDECO): see Trade and Industry—Development Organizations.

Port Authority of Trinidad and Tobago: Dock Rd, POB 549, Port of Spain; tel. 623-2901; fax 627-2666; e-mail vilmal@patnt.com; internet www.patnt.com; f. 1962; Chair. JOSEPH TONEY; CEO COLIN LUCAS.

Shipping Association of Trinidad and Tobago: 15 Scott Bushe St, Port of Spain; tel. 623-3355; fax 623-8570; e-mail satt@wow.net; internet shipping.co.tt; f. 1938; Pres. RHETT CHEE PING; Gen. Man. E. JOANNE EDWARDS-ALLEYNE.

CIVIL AVIATION

Piarco International Airport is situated 25.7 km (16 miles) south-east of Port of Spain. There is also A. N. R. International Airport at Crown Point, 13 km from Scarborough. There is a domestic service between Trinidad and Tobago. The regional airline LIAT (based in Antigua and Barbuda, and in which Trinidad and Tobago is a shareholder) operates scheduled flights connecting it with other islands in the Eastern Caribbean.

Airports Authority of Trinidad and Tobago (AATT): Airport Administration Centre, Piarco Int. Airport, South Terminal, Golden Grove Rd, Piarco; tel. 669-5311; fax 669-2319; e-mail aatt@tntairports.com; internet www.tntairports.com; administers Piarco and Crown Point International Airports; Chair. GERALD HADEED; Gen. Man. DAYANAND BIRJU (acting).

Caribbean Airlines Ltd (CAL): Sunjet House, 30 Edward St, Port of Spain; tel. 625-7200; e-mail mail@caribbean-airlines.com; internet www.caribbean-airlines.com; f. 2007 as successor to BWIA (f. 1940); services within the Caribbean and to South America, North America and Europe; Chair. PHILIP MARSHALL; CEO MICHAEL DiLOLLO.

Tourism

The climate and coastline attract visitors to Trinidad and Tobago. The latter island is generally believed to be the more beautiful and is less developed. The annual pre-Lenten carnival is a major attraction. Total tourist arrivals numbered an estimated 385,510 in 2010. Tourism receipts were estimated at US $472m in 2011. There were 3,815 hotel rooms in Trinidad and Tobago in 2008, of which 57.5% were on Tobago.

Tobago Department of Tourism: 12 Sangster Hill, Scarborough; tel. 639-2125; fax 639-3566; internet www.visittobago.gov.tt; Administrator ETHEL HECTOR-BERKLEY SYLVESTER.

Tourism Development Co of Trinidad and Tobago (TDC): Maritime Centre, Level 1, 29 10th Ave, Barataria; tel. 675-7034; fax 675-7722; e-mail info@tdc.co.tt; internet www.tdc.co.tt; f. 1993 as Tourism and Industrial Devt Co of Trinidad and Tobago; restructured and renamed as above in 2005; govt-owned; Chair. BRIAN FRONTIN; CEO KEITH CHIN.

Trinidad Hotels, Restaurants and Tourism Association (THRTA): c/o Trinidad & Tobago Hospitality and Tourism Institute, Airway Rd, Chaguaramas; tel. 634-1174; fax 634-1176; e-mail info@tnthotels.com; internet www.tnthotels.com; Exec. Dir LOUANNA CHAI-ALVES.

> **Tobago Hotel and Tourism Association (THTA):** Apt 1, Lambeau Credit Union Bldg, Auchenskeoch Rd, Carnbee; POB 295, Scarborough; tel. and fax 639-9543; e-mail thta@tstt.net.tt; internet www.tobagohoteltourism.com; Pres. CHRISTOPHER JAMES.

Defence

As assessed at November 2013, the Trinidad and Tobago Defence Force consisted of an army of an estimated 3,000 men and a coastguard of 1,050. Included in the coastguard was an air wing of 50.

Defence Budget: TT $2,550m. (US $400m.) in 2013.

Chief of Defence Staff: Brig-Gen. KENRICK MAHARAJ.

Education

Primary and secondary education is provided free of charge. Attendance at school is officially compulsory for children between five and 12 years of age. Primary education begins at the age of five and lasts for seven years. In 2010 some 95% of children in this age-group were enrolled at primary schools. Secondary education, beginning at 12 years of age, lasts for up to five years, comprising a first cycle of three years and a second of two years. The ratio for secondary enrolment in 2008 was 74% of those in the relevant age-group, according to UNESCO estimates.

Free tertiary tuition was introduced in 2006. As well as the University of Trinidad and Tobago, the University of the West Indies has a campus at St Augustine. Budgeted expenditure on education and training by the central Government in 2013 was projected at TT $9,149.1m.

Bibliography

For works on the Caribbean generally, see Select Bibliography (Books)

Anthony, M. *Historical Dictionary of Trinidad and Tobago.* Lanham, MD, Scarecrow Press, 1997.

Figueira, D. *The Politics of Racist Hegemony in Trinidad and Tobago.* Bloomington, IN, iUniverse Inc, 2010.

Hintzen, P. C., and Campbell, E. Q. (Eds). *Costs of Regime Survival: Racial Mobilization, Elite Domination and Control of the State in Guyana and Trinidad.* Cambridge, Cambridge University Press, 2007.

Ishmael, B. *International Competitiveness: The case of a small developing country as Trinidad and Tobago.* Saarbrücken, Lambert Academic Publishing, 2010.

Khan, A. *Callaloo Nation: Metaphors of Race and Religious Identity among South Asians in Trinidad.* Durham, NC, Duke University Press, 2004.

Meighoo, K. P. *Politics in a Half Made Society: Trinidad and Tobago, 1925–2002.* New York, Markus Wiener Publrs, 2003.

Munasinghe, V. *Callaloo or Tossed Salad? East Indians and the Cultural Politics of Identity in Trinidad.* Ithaca, NY, Cornell University Press, 2001.

Palmer, C. A. A. *Eric Williams and the Making of the Modern Caribbean.* Chapel Hill, NC, University of North Carolina Press, 2006.

Senauth, F. *The Making of Trinidad and Tobago.* Bloomington, IN, AuthorHouse, 2010.

THE TURKS AND CAICOS ISLANDS

Geography

PHYSICAL FEATURES

The Turks and Caicos Islands is an Overseas Territory of the United Kingdom, a former British Crown Colony, and once a dependency of Jamaica, until the latter's independence in 1962. The two groups of islands, the Caicos to the west and the Turks to the east, form the south-eastern extremity of the Atlantic archipelago dominated by the Bahamas. The territory continues the main chain some 63 km (39 miles) to the south-east of Mayaguana, although it lies directly east from the two more isolated Inagua islands. There is only about 45 km between West Caicos and Little Inagua. The Turks and Caicos Islands lies 145 km north of the island of Hispaniola. Some 40 islands, islets and cays, with a total coastline of 389 km, cover 948 sq km (366 sq miles) of territory (this figure includes area at low water level for all islands, but excludes area to high water mark).

The two groups of islands are separated by the Columbus or Turks Island Passage (35 km long and reaching a depth of some 7,000 ft—over 2,130 m) between the Atlantic and the Caribbean. The islands are low and coralline, with thin, poor soil on limestone bases, but this dry and semi-barren surface (particularly in the east) belies the submarine luxuriance of the third largest coral reef system in the world. Moreover, the flat terrain, prone to marshiness and mangrove swamps, and dotted with salt pans and salinas, is attractive to birds and hardy wildlife. Although the rocky interiors, generally covered in scrub, cacti and thorny acacias, remain bleak, the creeks, flats, marshlands and sand flats have delicate and unique ecosystems, teeming with attractions for resident and migratory birds. As a result, the natural and historical environment of the islands and their reefs is protected by over 30 reserves (including wildlife such as the endemic rock iguana or the pygmy boa). All the islands tend to higher terrain, with limestone cliffs and sand dunes, on the northern or north-eastern weather sides. The highest point on the islands is unclear, but is about 49 m (161 ft), be it the peak of the Ridge on Grand Turk or the only recently named Blue Hills on Providenciales. Flamingo Hill (48 m), on East Caicos, is also sometimes quoted as the highest point in the territory.

The Turks Islands (named for the fez-like Turks Head cactus) define the south-eastern edge of the territory, forming an arc of mainly small islands heading from the south-west and culminating in the northward-pointing, and much larger, Grand Turk. Although only 18 sq km in area, the island is the second largest population centre and the site of the capital, Cockburn Town. The only other one of the Turks of any size or population is Salt Cay, a designated UNESCO World Heritage Site, 11 km southwards from Grand Turk.

South Caicos (sometimes known as East Harbour or the Rock) is 35 km west of Grand Turk. It is the easternmost bulge of the Caicos Islands (named for the Lucayan—Taino—word for a chain of islands), which box in the infamous Caicos Banks, where the sea depth goes from some 2,000 m to less than 10 m in under 1 km. The main land masses define the northern edge, while South Caicos and a line of cays (such as the Ambergris and Seal Cays) facing the Turks form the eastern edge. There are more islands and cays to the west, but only treacherous reefs mark the south, with dry land rarely breaching the sea surface. The main islands are East Caicos, Middle Caicos and North Caicos, stretching north-westwards, before another chain of islets heads south-westwards to the hooked island of Providenciales ('Provo'). The more isolated and uninhabited West Caicos is just south-west of Providenciales. East Caicos

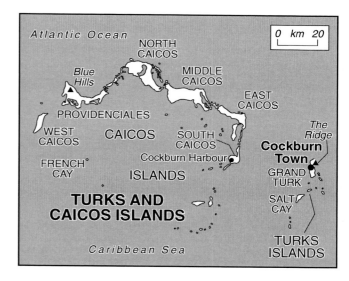

covers about 47 sq km, with a northern ridge protecting wetlands of creeks, mudflats and mangrove swamp. Middle or Grand Caicos is the largest island in the territory (124 sq km), with more dry land and dramatic coasts than most. North Caicos, at the north-western apex of the territory, has relatively good tree cover and good rainfall and it is known as a sanctuary for flamingos and the West Indian whistling duck. Providenciales, about 40 km in length and 5 km wide, has grown to be the leading population centre only since tourism development began in the late 1960s.

CLIMATE

The climate is subtropical marine, relatively dry and sunny, and exposed to the trade winds off the Atlantic. There are frequently hurricanes. The average annual temperature is 27°C (81°F), with little seasonal variation. Rainfall annually averages about 530 mm (21 ins) in the Turks and eastern Caicos, but reaches almost 1,000 mm in the west.

POPULATION

Almost all of the native population (known as 'belongers') is black and Christian. The official language is English, although there is also a local Creole in use. Most belongers are Protestants, while many of the recent immigrants are Roman Catholics, having come from Haiti or the Dominican Republic. According to the 2001 census, some 36% of the total population are Baptists, 12% belong to the Church of God, 11% are Roman Catholics, 10% are Anglicans, 9% are Methodists and 6% are Seventh-day Adventists.

The population was 31,458, according to preliminary results from the 2012 census, giving a population density of 33.2 per sq km. Six islands are permanently inhabited: Grand Turk and Salt Cay, and South Caicos, Middle Caicos, North Caicos and the tourist-dominated Providenciales. There are also resorts on Parrot Cay and Pine Cay. The main towns are Cockburn Town, which only has a population of about 2,500, and Cockburn Harbour on South Caicos.

History

The Turks and Caicos Islands constitute a United Kingdom Overseas Territory and the British monarch is represented locally by a Governor who presides over the Executive Council. From February 1998 the British Dependent Territories were referred to as the Overseas Territories, following the announcement of the interim findings of a British Government review of the United Kingdom's relations with its remaining imperial possessions.

The islands, which had been a Jamaican dependency from 1874 until 1959, became a separate colony in 1962, following the dissolution of the West Indian Federation and Jamaican independence. They were accorded their own resident Governor in the early 1970s. At the 1976 elections the pro-independence People's Democratic Movement (PDM) won a majority of seats in the Legislative Council, and the party leader, J. A. G. S. McCartney, became Chief Minister. In 1980 the PDM reached an agreement with the United Kingdom that, if it won the next election, the islands would be granted independence. However, the election was won by the opposition Progressive National Party (PNP), which is committed to continued dependent status. In the 1984 election the PNP, led by Norman Saunders, maintained its lead.

In March 1985 Saunders was arrested in Miami, FL, USA on charges involving illicit drugs and accepting a bribe. He resigned as Chief Minister and was replaced by Nathaniel Francis. In 1986 an official report on the destruction of a government building by fire in 1985 forced the resignation of Francis and two other ministers and discredited the Government amid allegations of unconstitutional behaviour and ministerial malpractice. The Governor proceeded to dissolve the Government and an Order-in-Council authorized him to replace the Executive Council with an interim Advisory Council. In March 1987 the British Government announced that it had accepted a constitutional commission's central recommendations and a general election was held in March 1988, after which there was a return to ministerial government.

The PDM won 11 of the 13 seats on the Legislative Council in the 1988 elections and Oswald Skippings, the leader of the PDM, was appointed Chief Minister. In the April 1991 general election the PNP secured eight seats and Washington Misick, the PNP leader, replaced Skippings as Chief Minister. In January 1995 the PDM, now led by Derek Taylor, gained eight seats. The PDM increased its representation in the Legislative Council to nine seats in the March 1999 elections. In the same month the British Government published draft legislation on its future relationship with its overseas dependencies. The Government announced that in future citizens of Overseas Territories would have the right to reside in the United Kingdom, provided they meet international standards in the areas of human rights and the regulation of the financial services sector.

In May 2002 the British Overseas Territories Act, having received royal assent in the United Kingdom in February, came into force and granted British citizenship rights to the people of the Overseas Territories, including the Turks and Caicos Islands. Under the new law Turks and Caicos Islanders were able to hold British passports and work in the United Kingdom and anywhere else in the European Union. In October capital punishment for treason and piracy, the only remaining capital crimes in the United Kingdom Overseas Territories, was abolished in the Turks and Caicos Islands.

At a general election held on 24 April 2003 the PDM won seven of the 13 seats in the Legislative Council. The PNP took the remaining six seats, but challenged the results in two constituencies. The election was largely fought over Chief Minister Taylor's claims of economic progress, which Michael Misick, leader of the PNP, argued had benefited expatriates rather than Turks and Caicos 'belongers'.

In June 2003 the Supreme Court ruled in favour of the defeated PNP candidates in the two disputed constituencies; Chief Justice Richard Ground found evidence of bribery by supporters of the PDM in one constituency and irregularities in voter registration lists in the other. Following the judicial ruling, by-elections, in which the PNP secured victory and

therefore wrested overall control of the Legislative Council from the PDM, were held in the two constituencies on 7 August. Taylor resigned as Chief Minister on 15 August and Misick was sworn in as his replacement on the same day.

In April 2006 a consultation process took place over a draft constitution for the islands, following the achievement of agreement between local and United Kingdom representatives in the previous October, allowing for greater self-government. The draft constitution was endorsed by the Legislative Council on 28 June, before final submission to the British Foreign and Commonwealth Office (FCO). An Order in Council adopted the new Constitution on 19 July and it came into force on 9 August, which was declared a public holiday. On the same day Chief Minister Misick and Deputy Chief Minister Floyd Hall were sworn in as Premier and Deputy Premier, respectively. Mahala Wynns, hitherto the Chief Secretary, was also inaugurated as the territory's first Deputy Governor as part of the new administrative structure; according to the new Constitution, this office was to be fulfilled by a 'belonger'. A unicameral system of parliament was to be instituted, comprising a 21-member House of Assembly, replacing and enlarging upon the former Legislative Council, and a nine-member Cabinet (formerly the Executive Council) over which the Governor would preside. The legislature also approved the enactment of the Electoral District Boundaries 2006 Bill, under constitutional statute, that sanctioned the creation of two new constituencies—to reflect the two additional elected members of the House of Assembly—and which was ratified by the House of Assembly on 8 January 2007.

The PNP was returned to power for a second term at the 9 February 2007 general election, securing 13 of the 15 elected seats in the House of Assembly; the remaining two seats went to the PDM. Misick was reappointed Premier.

In December 2008 Misick avoided a debate on a motion of no confidence submitted by the PDM, as a result of a dispute over parliamentary procedure. Parliament was subsequently prorogued by the Governor, Gordon Wetherell, to be reconvened in April 2009. Later in that month Lillian Boyce, Minister of Health and Human Services, and eight other PNP members, drafted a letter to the Governor requesting that Misick resign, citing a loss of confidence from legislators. Boyce was dismissed by Misick in January of that year and replaced by Royal Robinson.

Hall resigned in February 2009, citing the legislative stalemate caused by the ongoing suspension of Parliament. Galmore 'Galmo' Williams, the Minister for Home Affairs, had resigned the previous day. Following the resignations Misick reorganized his Cabinet; Boyce notably returned to office as Deputy Premier and Minister for Home Affairs only a month after her dismissal. Misick also announced that he would resign as Premier by the end of March, and that he would not be seeking re-election as leader of the PNP. At a special PNP convention held on 28 February, Williams was elected to succeed Misick. Misick stood down on 23 March, at which point Williams was sworn in as Premier. Williams promptly announced the formation of a new Cabinet.

The United Kingdom's House of Commons Foreign Affairs Committee (FAC) published a report in July 2008 regarding the administration of its Overseas Territories, in which it detailed claims of corruption and intimidation made by residents of the Turks and Caicos Islands. The allegations of corruption referred to the sale of Crown land for unsustainable developments or for the personal gain of government members; nepotism in the distribution of development contracts and irregularities in the purchase of property for government use; the granting of 'belonger' status to individuals who were ineligible under the current law; and the misuse of public funds. The report criticized the Governor, who had failed to investigate the allegations of corrupt practice. The Premier denied the allegations and drew attention to anti-corruption legislation that had been introduced by his Government. However, the Committee's recommendation of the establishment of a Commission of Inquiry was heeded by the Governor and the body began its investigations later that month. The publication of the report led to a truculent dialogue between the two main parties as Misick blamed opposition opponents for the inception of the allegations; in response, the PDM accused Misick of trying to intimidate members of the public to prevent them from revealing further information to the Commission. In February 2009 Sir Robin Auld issued the Commission of Inquiry's interim report, which referred to a 'high probability of systemic corruption and serious dishonesty', 'political amorality and general incompetence' and contained 24 recommendations, including the partial or full suspension of the Constitution and direct rule of the islands by the United Kingdom, acting through the Governor, with the advice of an Advisory Council. The report also recommended that criminal investigations be instigated against Misick and four of his former cabinet ministers. The Commission's final report, which was submitted to the Governor at the end of May, confirmed the findings and recommendations of the interim document. Following a delay in the implementation of these recommendations, owing to an ultimately unsuccessful legal challenge, on 14 August the British Government announced the imposition of direct rule from the United Kingdom, the partial suspension of the Constitution and the removal of the Premier and Cabinet. The House of Assembly was also dissolved. The FCO announced its intention to hold elections in the territory no later than July 2011 and stated that its aim was to establish a lasting basis for good governance, sound financial management and sustainable development.

The Advisory Council immediately instituted a Stabilization Plan to reduce expenditure, increase revenue and lower the national debt. In late August 2009 12 'belongers' were appointed as members of a Consultative Forum, which was to make recommendations on proposed legislation and policies referred to it by the Governor. A Special Prosecutor, Helen Garlick, was also appointed to examine possible criminal charges against the former PNP Government arising from the Commission of Inquiry's report. Former Premier Williams denounced the imposition of direct rule as a *coup d'état*. The decision by Governor Wetherell not to appoint a successor to Mahala Wynns following her retirement as Deputy Governor at the end of September further inflamed tensions between the Advisory Council and the former administration. The Constitution stated that the post must be held by a 'belonger' and the fact that it remained vacant was perceived as an insult to the islanders. Continued political discontent over the imposition of direct rule was evident in March 2010, when the PNP and the PDM held a joint protest march.

At the end of March 2010 the FAC issued a report describing the FCO's plan to hold elections in July 2011 as 'unrealistic', citing the slow pace of political reform, inadequate funding arrangements for the work of the Special Investigation and Prosecution Team, and a consequent lack of progress in the investigation of those suspected of corruption. Auld had earlier raised similar concerns in a letter to the British Foreign Secretary. In April Special Prosecutor Garlick announced that criminal investigations into between six and 10 people had been initiated and could take up to 18 months to complete, and that campaign financing to both the PNP and the PDM was also to be probed. In September 2010 the FAC announced that the 2011 elections would be postponed, citing a lack of progress on both the territory's reform programme and the investigation into alleged government corruption. Leaders of the PNP and the PDM, as well as the Caribbean Community and Common Market, expressed their opposition to the postponement of the ballot, and demonstrations were held during that month in protest against the delay. Further small-scale protest action was conducted in March 2011, and Providenciales airport was temporarily blockaded by demonstrators. It was expected that new elections would be held in 2012, although this was contingent upon eight 'milestones' being reached, including constitutional, governmental, electoral and financial reform, a return to fiscal stability, and progress in the investigation into alleged government corruption.

The process of constitutional reform continued in 2011. A draft constitution was published in March, with consultation of the document lasting until the end of May. The proposed charter was similar to the existing Constitution, but incorporated the findings of the 2008 Commission of Inquiry. The document proposed, *inter alia*, increased financial and political transparency and accountability, granting greater powers to the Governor, allowing a non-'belonger' to be appointed Deputy Governor, reform of the electoral system, and an end to the right to trial by jury. The PDM rejected the draft constitution outright, accusing the British Government of attempting to 'colonize' the Turks and Caicos. Following all-party negotiations in mid-June, held in London, United Kingdom, with representatives of the FCO, alterations were made to the draft charter, including dropping a proposal to introduce proportional representation and retaining the stipulation that the Deputy Governor be a 'belonger', although the phrase 'belonger' was to be replaced by 'Turks and Caicos Islander'.

Governor Wetherell was succeeded by Damian Roderic (Ric) Todd in September 2011. Former Chief Minister Derek Taylor was elected as PDM leader in November.

Following progress in the government corruption investigation, Floyd Hall and three other former ministers, along with several of their family members and associates, were detained in late 2011. They were accused of involvement in a fraudulent scheme whereby Crown land had allegedly been sold at vastly reduced rates to favoured PNP associates. According to the British Government, total losses resulting from the scandal amounted to as much as US $5,000m. In February 2012 Clayton Greene, the leader of the PNP, was also charged in connection with the illicit land sales. Furthermore, charges were filed against Misick's brother, Chalmers, for money-laundering, and against former PNP minister McAllister Hanchell for receiving bribes. In March a new Crown Land Ordinance (one of the eight 'milestones') entered into force. Also in that month, former Premier Misick, who had reportedly fled to the Dominican Republic, was subjected to an international arrest warrant, following the imposition of an assets freeze in June 2011. Also in March 2012, the interim territorial authorities commenced legal action against the PNP: it was alleged that the party's headquarters had been illegally built on Crown land and hence should be seized. (In July 2013 the Supreme Court ruled against the PNP, awarding the disputed land and property to the Government.) In mid-2012 Oswald Skippings and Rufus Ewing became leaders of the PDM and the PNP, respectively.

In June 2012 the British Secretary of State for Foreign and Commonwealth Affairs, William Hague, announced that, with the exception of achieving a fiscal surplus (which was realized in 2012/13), all the 'milestones' had now been reached. New ordinances governing, *inter alia*, elections, party-funding, government transparency and public finances had been introduced, while significant progress on the draft constitution and the corruption investigation had been made. Consequently, Hague declared that elections would be held in the territory on 9 November. The new Constitution entered into force on 15 October, although the PNP and the PDM remained opposed to the expansion of the Governor's powers.

The general election took place as scheduled on 9 November 2012. Although the PNP lost the popular vote, the party won eight of the 15 seats in the House of Assembly, compared with seven seats for the PDM. The rate of voter participation was recorded at 84%. On 13 November Ewing was sworn in as Premier, and he subsequently announced a new administration, which included former Premier Misick's brother, Charles, as the minister responsible for finance, while his cousin, Amanda, received the health portfolio. In December Skippings, who had lost his seat in the election, was succeeded as PDM leader by Sharlene Cartwright-Robinson. In February 2013 the Supreme Court, in response to a PDM petition, annulled Amanda Misick's electoral victory on procedural grounds. None the less, on 22 March Misick emerged triumphant in the consequent by-election, and she was named as the new Minister of Environment, Home Affairs and Agriculture shortly thereafter. Peter Beckingham replaced Todd as Governor in October. Later that month Huw Shepheard tendered his resignation as Attorney-General. According to the opposition, the Ewing administration had pressured Shepheard to step down owing to the extensive support that he had provided to the government corruption inquiry and to the legal case that had resulted in the seizure of the PNP's headquarters. Shepheard, who was subsequently replaced as Attorney-General by Rhondalee Braithwaite-Knowles, claimed that he had been defamed by Ewing and other PNP members and initiated legal action against the Government.

Meanwhile, in December 2012 erstwhile Premier Misick was arrested in Brazil, where he had been residing since late 2011. Misick's application for political asylum was denied by the Brazilian authorities, which instead, in October 2013,

approved his extradition to the Turks and Caicos Islands. Misick was transferred to the territory in January 2014, whereupon he was charged with corruption and granted bail. Misick and the other accused members of his administration were due to stand trial in October. The presiding judge announced in June that the trial would be conducted without a jury owing to concerns about media influence and the expected complexity of the legal proceedings.

Economy

Agriculture is not practised on any significant scale in the Turks Islands or on South Caicos (the most populous island of the territory). The other islands of the Caicos group grow some beans, maize and a few fruits and vegetables. There is some livestock-rearing, but the islands' principal natural resource is fisheries, which account for almost all commodity exports, the principal species caught being the spiny lobster (200 metric tons in 2012) and the conch (3,570 tons in that year). Conchs are now being developed commercially (on the largest conch farm in the world), and there is potential for larger-scale fishing. Exports of lobster and conch earned an estimated US $4.3m. in 2009. However, agricultural possibilities were limited and most foodstuffs were imported. Industrial activity consists mainly of construction (especially for the tourism industry) and fish-processing. Construction of both tourism resorts and residential housing led to large-scale growth in the sector in the mid-2000s, bringing consequent beneficial effects for employment and import levels. In 2000–09 the construction sector grew at an average annual rate of 5.6%, although the 2008–09 global financial crisis had a negative impact on construction activity. In 2012 the sector's contribution to gross domestic product (GDP) stood at 6.6%.

The principal economic sector is the service industry, which contributed 86.4% of GDP in 2012. This is dominated by the expanding tourism sector, which is concentrated on the island of Providenciales. The market is for wealthier visitors, most of whom come from the USA. Stop-over tourist arrivals reached 290,587 in 2013. Visitor expenditure totalled US $355.1m. in 2005. The majority of stop-over visitors were from the USA (79.7% in 2013). As a result of the growth in tourism throughout the last decade many new hotels and resorts have been developed. However, concern has been expressed that the islands are in danger of becoming overdeveloped, thereby damaging their reputation as an unspoiled tourist location. In 2006 a new $40m. cruise ship terminal, constructed by Carnival Cruise Lines (USA), was opened on Grand Turk, enabling, for the first time, large passenger liners to stop in the territory. The number of cruise ship passengers visiting the islands rose from just 17,052 in 2004 to 778,920 in 2013. The tourism industry suffered in 2008 and 2009 as a result of the global financial crisis and subsequent economic downturn, which particularly affected the USA.

New regulatory legislation to develop an offshore financial sector was ratified in 1989. In 2012/13 there were 13,296 companies active in the islands. In 2000 the Turks and Caicos Islands were included in the list of so-called 'unco-operative tax havens' compiled by the Organisation for Economic Co-operation and Development (OECD). OECD urged the jurisdictions included on the list to improve their legal and administrative transparency to prevent companies using the jurisdictions' tax systems in an attempt to launder money or avoid paying income tax. The Turks and Caicos Islands were removed from the list in 2002, after OECD deemed the territory had made sufficient commitments to improve transparency in the sector. However, in 2009 the territory was included in OECD's so-called 'grey list' of jurisdictions that had yet substantially to improve transparency in the financial sector, although the islands succeeded in securing their removal from the list after concluding international tax information sharing agreements with 12 other nations. Nevertheless, concerns about transparency persisted, and in May 2013 the Turks and Caicos Islands reached agreement with the United

Kingdom to share information about bank accounts held in the territory; an accord formalizing this arrangement was signed in November. (A similar agreement had been concluded with the USA in September.) Meanwhile, in June delegations from several United Kingdom Overseas Territories, including the Turks and Caicos Islands, met with British Prime Minister David Cameron in London, United Kingdom, to discuss the further reform of their respective offshore financial industries. Following the meeting, Cameron announced that the Turks and Caicos Islands (along with the other territories) would become a signatory to OECD's Multilateral Convention on Mutual Administrative Assistance in Tax Matters and would maintain a company ownership register. The Turks and Caicos Islands duly acceded to the OECD Convention in August, and the instrument entered into force in December. The financial intermediation sector contributed 13.1% of GDP in 2009. There is no direct taxation in the country. The main sources of government revenue are derived from import duties (26.9% of recurrent revenue in 2012/13) and hotel and restaurant tax (18.9%), as well as stamp duty on land transactions, the offshore sector (business licence fees), and immigrant workers' permits and residence fees.

During 2000–09 the islands' GDP increased, in real terms, by 11.2% per year. Real GDP grew by 8.3% in 2008, but contracted by 19.6% in 2009 as a result of the global economic downturn, before rising by 1.0% in 2010 and 4.1% in 2011. The economy contracted again in 2012, by 0.7%, owing to decreased tourism and construction activity, although the Government reported that these sectors had recovered by 2013, driving renewed economic growth of 3.4% in that year. In 2008 the unemployment rate increased to 8.3% (from 5.4% in 2007). Newly created jobs were often taken by low-wage migrant workers or by highly skilled expatriate workers, and the rate of immigration was likely to become a significant issue for the islands. In addition, the islands' growth is highly dependent on external factors, and the pressure exerted by OECD, Europe and the USA on the offshore financial services sector is therefore of particular concern. Total revenue increased to US $216.8m. in 2012/13; total expenditure was $169.2m. There was an overall budget surplus of $47.6m. in that year.

Following the imposition of direct rule from the United Kingdom in August 2009 (see History), the Advisory Council that replaced the Cabinet identified the containment and rescheduling of the national debt (estimated at £135m.) and fiscal stabilization as its main economic priorities. Government revenue had declined in 2009 owing to the destruction caused by Hurricane Ike in the previous year, as well as the adverse effects of the global economic downturn, notably on the tourism and construction sectors. A large proportion of the territory's debt was rescheduled in February 2011, after the British Government agreed to act as guarantor on a low-interest US $260m. loan (replaced by a bond issue in April); nevertheless, public arrears increased further during that year. Measures were also implemented to lower the budget deficit—by rationalizing the civil service, reducing public sector salaries and reforming the tax system. The 2011/12 budget introduced several new taxes and increased the rates of other duties. By late 2011 these revenue-raising measures had reinforced the territory's fiscal position, although government spending in 2011/12 was higher than anticipated owing to the discovery of further unpaid debts. In an attempt to boost revenues further, another round of tax and duty increases was effected in mid-

2013, but plans to levy a value-added tax had been abandoned earlier that year. Budget surpluses were recorded in 2012/13 and 2013/14. Economic growth in the islands—driven more by inward investment than by domestic production—remained highly dependent on external factors, and it remained to be seen whether the territory's economic reform programme and the restoration of self-government would deter or encourage potential investors.

Statistical Survey

Source: Department of Economic Planning and Statistics, Ministry of Finance, South Base, Grand Turk; tel. 946-2801; fax 946-2557; e-mail info@depstc.org; internet www.depstc.org.

AREA AND POPULATION

Area: 948 sq km (366 sq miles). Note: Area includes low water level for all islands, but excludes area to high water mark.

Population: 19,886 at census of 20 August 2001; 31,458 (males 16,037, females 15,421) at census of 25 January 2012 (preliminary). *By Island* (at 2012 census, preliminary): Grand Turk 4,831; South Caicos 1,139; Middle Caicos 168; North Caicos 1,312; Salt Cay 108; Parrot Cay 131; Providenciales 23,769.

Density (at 2012 census): 33.2 per sq km.

Population by Age and Sex (at 2001 census): *0–14 years:* 5,693 (males 2,736, females 2,957); *15–64 years:* 13,436 (males 6,826, females 6,610); *65 years and over:* 758 (males 335, females 423); *Total* 19,886 (males 9,897, females 9,989) (Source: UN, *Demographic Yearbook*).

Principal Towns: Cockburn Town (capital, on Grand Turk), population 2,500 (1987 estimate). *Mid-2014* (UN estimate, incl. suburbs): Grand Turk 5,055 (Source: UN, *World Urbanization Prospects: The 2014 Revision*).

Births, Marriages and Deaths (2008): Live births 453 (birth rate 12.4 per 1,000); Marriages 486; Deaths 65 (death rate 1.8 per 1,000). *2013:* Crude birth rate 17.1; Crude death rate 3.1 (Source: Pan American Health Organization).

Life Expectancy (years at birth, 2013): 79.4 (males 76.7; females 82.3). Source: Pan American Health Organization.

Economically Active Population (2008): Agriculture and fishing 259; Mining and quarrying 18; Manufacturing 290; Utilities 183; Construction 4,468; Wholesale and retail trade 1,841; Hotels and restaurants 4,098; Transport, storage and communications 1,053; Financial intermediation 610; Real estate, renting and business services 2,920; Public administration 2,432; Education, health and social work 944; Other community, social and personal services 1,491; Private household employment 526; *Sub-total* 21,133; Activities not adequately defined 360; *Total employed* 21,493; Unemployed 1,945; *Total labour force* 23,438.

HEALTH AND WELFARE

Total Fertility Rate (children per woman, 2013): 1.7.

Under-5 Mortality Rate (per 1,000 live births, 1997): 22.0.

Hospital Beds (per 1,000 head, 2012): 0.9.

Physicians (per 1,000 head, 2001): 7.3.

Health Expenditure (public, % of total, 2007): 8.8.

Health Expenditure (US $ per head, 2004): 741.2.

Access to Water (% of persons, 2010): 99.

Access to Sanitation (% of persons, 2010): 98.

Source: partly Pan American Health Organization.

For other sources and definitions see explanatory note on p. vi.

AGRICULTURE, ETC.

Fishing (metric tons, live weight of capture, 2012, FAO estimates): Caribbean spiny lobster 200; Stromboid conchs 3,570; Total catch (incl. others) 3,780.

Source: FAO.

INDUSTRY

Electric Energy (production, million kWh): 182 in 2007; 198 in 2008; 209 in 2009. Source: UN Industrial Commodity Statistics Database.

FINANCE

Currency and Exchange Rate: United States currency is used: 100 cents = 1 US dollar ($). *Sterling and Euro Equivalents* (30 May 2014): £1 sterling = US $1.682; €1 = US $1.361; $100 = £59.45 = €73.47.

Budget (US $ million, fiscal year ending 31 March 2012): Total revenue 175.0 (Recurrent 170.9, Other 4.2); Total operating expenditure 201.5 (Employee costs 67.6, Non-salary, non-interest recurrent expenditure 99.4, Other cost items 28.9, Development expenditure 5.6). *2012/13:* Total revenue 216.8; Total expenditure 169.2.

Gross Domestic Product (US $ million at constant 2005 prices): 633.9 in 2010; 659.9 in 2011; 655.5 in 2012. Source: UN, National Accounts Main Aggregates Database.

Expenditure on the Gross Domestic Product (US $ million, 2012): Government final consumption expenditure 165.8; Private final consumption expenditure 185.7; Gross capital formation 157.6; *Total domestic expenditure* 509.1; Exports of goods and services 616.8; *Less* Imports of goods and services 398.0; *GDP in market prices* 727.9. Source: UN, National Accounts Main Aggregates Database.

Gross Domestic Product by Economic Activity (US $ million, 2012): Agriculture and fishing 4.7; Mining and utilities 34.5; Manufacturing 10.0; Construction 46.1; Wholesale and retail trade, hotels and restaurants 266.6; Transport, storage and communications 52.3; Other services 288.2; *Gross value added in basic prices* 702.4; Net of taxes on products 25.5 (figure obtained as residual) *GDP in market prices* 727.9. Source: UN, National Accounts Main Aggregates Database.

Balance of Payments (US $ million, 2002): Exports of goods f.o.b. 7.7; Imports of goods f.o.b. −177.5; *Trade balance* −169.8; Exports of services 163.1; Imports of services −81.8; *Balance on goods and services* −88.5. Source: Caribbean Development Bank, *Social and Economic Indicators*.

EXTERNAL TRADE

Principal Commodities (US $ million, 2009, provisional): *Imports:* Food and live animals 62.2; Beverages and tobacco 15.3; Crude materials (inedible) except fuels 9.9; Mineral fuels, lubricants, etc. 42.3 (Petroleum and petroleum products 40.9); Chemicals and related products 21.9; Basic manufactures 68.4; Machinery and transport equipment 75.8 (Road vehicles 16.4); Miscellaneous manufactured articles 78.2; Total (incl. others) 375.4. *Exports:* Food and live animals 4.4 (Conchs 3.2; Lobsters 1.1); Machinery and transport equipment 11.4; Total exports (incl. others) 19.4. Note: Figures for exports exclude re-exports valued at 1.4.

Principal Trading Partners (US $ million, 2009, provisional): *Imports c.i.f.:* Bahamas 3.2; USA 370.4; Total (incl. others) 375.4. *Exports f.o.b.:* USA 20.7; Total (incl. others) 20.8. Note: Figures for exports include re-exports valued at 1.4.

TOURISM

Tourist Arrivals ('000): 968.4 in 2012 (cruise ship passengers 676.6, stay-over visitors 291.7); 1,069.5 in 2013 (cruise ship passengers 778.9, stay-over visitors 290.6).

Stay-over Visitors by Place of Origin ('000, 2013): Canada 31.8; USA 231.7; Total (incl. others) 290.6.

Tourism Receipts (US $ million, estimates): 275.6 in 2003; 317.9 in 2004; 355.1 in 2005.

Sources: World Tourism Organization; Turks and Caicos Islands Tourist Board; Caribbean Development Bank, *Social and Economic Indicators*.

COMMUNICATIONS MEDIA

Telephones (2013): 4,000 main lines in use.

Mobile Cellular Telephones (2008): 25,100 subscribers.

Internet Subscribers (2008): 3,000.

Source: International Telecommunication Union.

EDUCATION

Pre-primary (2008/09 unless otherwise indicated): 9 schools (2005/06); 87 teachers (2004/05, estimate); 1,174 pupils.

Primary (2008/09 unless otherwise indicated): 14 schools (2005/06); 126 teachers (state schools only, 2005/06); 2,891 pupils.

General Secondary (2008/09 unless otherwise indicated): 8 schools (2005/06); 135 teachers (state schools only, 2005/06); 2,095 pupils.

Note: In addition, 6 further private schools offered both primary and secondary education to 674 pupils in 2005/06.

Tertiary Education (2005/06): 2 schools; 257 pupils.

Special Education (2005/06): 2 schools; 99 pupils.

Pupil-teacher Ratio (primary education, UNESCO estimate): 15.0 in 2004/05. Source: UNESCO Institute for Statistics.

Adult Literacy Rate (UNESCO estimates): 99% (males 99%; females 98%) in 1998.

Sources: partly UNESCO Institute for Statistics; Caribbean Development Bank, *Social and Economic Indicators*.

Directory

The Constitution

On 15 October 2012 a new Constitutional Order (Constitutional Order 2011) took effect in the Turks and Caicos following three years of direct rule by the United Kingdom. The imposition of direct rule followed publication of the findings of a commission of inquiry into allegations of widespread and systemic corruption and mismanagement in the governance of the territory. Parts of the 2006 Constitution were suspended and government of the territory was taken over by the United Kingdom acting through the Governor and assisted by an Advisory Council. The 2012 Constitution was effected following reform to improve transparency and accountability in government. A new Cabinet and House of Assembly were sworn in following elections on 9 November 2012.

Executive authority is vested in the British monarch and is exercised by the Governor (the monarch's appointed representative), who also holds responsibility for external affairs, internal security, including the police force, the regulation of international financial services, defence, the appointment of any person to any public office, the suspension and termination of appointment of any public officer, and the taking of disciplinary action against any public officer. The Deputy Governor is appointed by the Governor and must be a Turks and Caicos Islander.

The Constitution provides for a Cabinet and a House of Assembly. The Cabinet comprises: the Governor; the Premier (appointed by the Governor); not more than six other ministers from among the elected or nominated members of the House of Assembly, appointed by the Governor on the advice of the Premier; and the Deputy Governor and Attorney-General. The Cabinet is presided over by the Governor and shall meet at least once a fortnight.

The House of Assembly consists of the Speaker, 15 members elected by residents aged 18 and over, four nominated members (appointed by the Governor, two on the advice of the Premier and two at the Governor's discretion), and the Attorney-General. The Attorney-General does not have voting rights in the House of Assembly. No legislation shall become law until it has received the assent of the British monarch, acting through the Governor. The Governor also has reserve powers to enact legislation without the agreement of the Cabinet in certain circumstances, including in order to comply with an international obligation and to ensure compliance with the Statement of Governance Principles. A general election shall be held no more than three months, but no less than 35 days, after the dissolution of the House of Assembly.

A Public Service Commission shall comprise a Chairman, appointed by the Governor, and four members, appointed by the Governor after consultation with the Premier, the Leader of the Opposition and the Civil Servants' Association. The Commission's purpose is to uphold the principles of merit, neutrality and integrity in the public service. In order further to promote good governance, the following bodies or posts shall be established: an Auditor-General and a National Audit Office; a Complaints Commissioner; a Director of Public Prosecutions; a Human Rights Commission; an Integrity Commission; and a Supervisor of Elections. The Government shall, after public consultation, formulate a framework document stating its principles of public financial management. This document is subject to the approval of the legislature.

The Government

HEAD OF STATE

Queen: HM Queen ELIZABETH II.

Governor: PETER BECKINGHAM (took office 9 October 2013).

Deputy Governor: ANYA WILLIAMS.

THE CABINET
(September 2014)

The Cabinet is formed by the Progressive National Party

Premier and Minister of Tourism: Dr RUFUS WASHINGTON EWING.

Deputy Premier and Minister of Education, Youth, Sports and Culture: AKIERRA MARY DEANNE MISSICK.

Minister of Finance with responsibility for Investment and Trade, Airport Authority and Government Computer Services: CHARLES WASHINGTON MISICK.

Minister of Health and Human Services (Gender Affairs, Social Services): PORSHA MONIQUE STUBBS-SMITH.

Minister of Environment, Home Affairs and Agriculture: AMANDA ANISHA MISICK.

Minister of Border Control and Labour: RICARDO DON-HUE GARDINER.

Minister of Government Support Services: GEORGE ALEXANDER LIGHTBOURNE.

Attorney-General*: RHONDALEE BRAITHWAITE-KNOWLES.

Chief Financial Officer*: STEPHEN TURNBULL.

* Appointed by the Governor.

GOVERNMENT OFFICES

Office of the Governor: Govt House, Waterloo, Grand Turk; tel. 946-2308; fax 946-2903; e-mail governorgt@fco.gov.uk.

Office of the Premier: N. J. S. Francis Bldg, Govt Sq., Grand Turk; tel. 946-2801; fax 946-2777; e-mail premier@gov.tc.

Office of the Deputy Governor: South Base, Grand Turk; tel. 946-2702; fax 946-2886; e-mail cso@gov.tc.

Attorney-General's Chambers: South Base, Grand Turk; tel. 946-2096; fax 946-2588; e-mail attorneygeneral@tciway.tc; internet www.lawsconsolidated.tc.

All ministries are based on Grand Turk.

Legislature

HOUSE OF ASSEMBLY

Speaker: ROBERT HALL.

Election, 9 November 2012

Party	Seats
Progressive National Party (PNP)	8
People's Democratic Movement (PDM) . . .	7
Total	**15**

In addition to the 15 directly elected members, two members are appointed by the Governor, and one each by the Premier and the Leader of the Opposition. The Attorney-General is also a non-voting member of the legislature.

Election Commission

Office of the Supervisor of Elections: Providenciales; Supervisor DUDLEY LEWIS.

Political Organizations

People's Democratic Movement (PDM): POB 309, Providenciales; tel. 231-6898; f. 1975; favours internal self-govt and eventual independence; Chair. LYNDEN HALL; Leader SHARLENE CARTWRIGHT-ROBINSON; Sec.-Gen. CYNCLAIR MUSGROVE.

Progressive National Party (PNP): Progress House, Airport Rd, Providenciales; tel. 442-5050; fax 946-8206; e-mail pnptci@me.com; internet www.pnp.tc; supports full internal self-govt; Chair. TREVOR COOKE; Leader RUFUS W. EWING; Sec.-Gen. SHARON SIMMONS.

People's Progressive Party (PPP): Providenciales; f. 2012; Leader HAROLD CHARLES; Treas. EDWARD SMITH.

Judicial System

Justice is administered by the Supreme Court of the islands, presided over by the Chief Justice. There is a Chief Magistrate resident on Grand Turk, who also acts as Judge of the Supreme Court. There are also three Deputy Magistrates.

The Court of Appeal comprises a President and two Justices of Appeal. In certain cases, appeals are made to the Judicial Committee of the Privy Council in the United Kingdom.

Judicial Department: Grand Turk; tel. 946-2114; fax 946-2720; Chief Justice EDWIN GOLDSBOROUGH (until late 2014), MARGARET RAMSAY-HALE (designate); Chief Magistrate CLIFTON WARNER (Providenciales).

President of the Court of Appeal: EDWARD ZACCA.

Religion

CHRISTIANITY

The Anglican Communion

Within the Church in the Province of the West Indies, the territory forms part of the diocese of the Bahamas and the Turks and Caicos Islands. The Bishop is resident in Nassau. According to the latest census (2001), around 10% of the population are Anglicans.

Diocese of the Bahamas and the Turks and Caicos Islands: St Mary's Church, Front St, Grand Turk; tel. 946-2289; e-mail media@bahamasanglicans.org; internet bahamasanglicans.org; Bishop Rt Rev. LAISH Z. BOYD (resident in the Bahamas).

The Roman Catholic Church

The Bishop of Nassau, Bahamas (suffragan to the archdiocese of Kingston in Jamaica), has jurisdiction in the Turks and Caicos Islands as Superior of the Mission to the Territory (founded in 1984). According to the 2001 census, around 11% of the population are Roman Catholics.

Roman Catholic Mission: Leeward Hwy, POB 340, Providenciales; tel. and fax 941-5136; e-mail rcmission@catholic.tc; internet www.catholic.tc; churches on Grand Turk, South and North Caicos, and on Providenciales; 132 adherents in 1990 (according to census results); Chancellor Fr PETER BALDACCHINO.

Other Christian Churches

According to the 2001 census, some 36% of the population are Baptists, 12% belong to the Church of God, 9% are Methodists, 6% are Seventh-day Adventists and 2% are Jehovah's Witnesses.

Baptist Union of the Turks and Caicos Islands: South Caicos; tel. 946-3220; Gen. Sec. Rev. GOLDSTONE WILLIAMS.

Jehovah's Witnesses: Kingdom Hall, Intersection 21 Bridge Rd, Turtle Cove, POB 400, Providenciales; tel. 941-5583; fax 941-3496; e-mail englishprovo@yahoo.com.

New Testament Church of God: POB N-30, Grand Turk; tel. 946-4318; fax 364-0140; e-mail chofgodbtci@yahoo.com; internet www.churchofgodbtci.org.

Seventh-day Adventist Church: Shop No 8, Southern Shore Complex, Leeward Hwy, POB 803, Providenciales; tel. 941-8735; e-mail info@turksandcaicosmission.org; internet turksandcaicosmission.org; f. 1945; 2,000 mems in 8 churches; Pres. Pastor MICHAEL A. SMITH; Sec. and Treas. HOPTON BANSIE.

The Press

Times of the Islands: Lucille Lightbourne Bldg 7, POB 234, Providenciales; tel. and fax 946-4788; e-mail timespub@tciway.tc; internet www.timespub.tc; f. 1988; quarterly; circ. 10,000; Man. Editor KATHY BORSUK.

Turks and Caicos Free Press: Market Pl., POB 179, Providenciales; tel. 332-5615; fax 941-3402; e-mail info@fptci.com; internet tcfreepress.com; f. 1991; publ. by Vox-Global Télématique; weekly; circ. 3,000; Editor Dr GILBERT MORRIS.

Turks & Caicos Islands Real Estate Association Real Estate Magazine: Lucille Lightbourne Bldg, POB 234, Providenciales; tel. and fax 946-4788; e-mail timespub@tciway.tc; internet www.tcrea.com; publ. by Times Publ. Ltd; 2 a year; circ. 15,000; Man. Editor KATHY BORSUK.

Turks and Caicos Sun: Airport Plaza, Suite 5, POB 439, Providenciales; tel. 946-8542; fax 941-3281; e-mail sun@suntci.com; internet www.suntci.com; f. 2005; publ. by Island Publishing Co Ltd; weekly; Publr and Editor-in-Chief HAYDEN BOYCE.

Turks and Caicos Weekly News: Cheshire House, Leeward Hwy, POB 52, Providenciales; tel. 946-4664; fax 946-4661; e-mail tcnews@tciway.tc; internet www.tcweeklynews.com; f. 1982; Editor BLYTHE DUNCANSON.

Where, When, How: Ad Vantage Ltd, J105 Regent Village, Grace Bay, Providenciales; tel. 946-4815; fax 941-3497; e-mail info@wwhtci.com; internet www.wherewhenhow.com; f. 1994; 5 a year; travel magazine; Co-Editors CHARLES ZDENEK, BRENDA ZDENEK; circ. 70,000 a year.

Publisher

Ad Vantage Ltd: J105 Regent Village, Grace Bay, Providenciales; tel. 946-4815; fax 941-3497; e-mail info@wwhtci.com; internet www.wherewhenhow.com; f. 1994; publr of *Where When How* magazine and *Providenciales Dining Guide*; Co-Editors CHARLES ZDENEK, BRENDA ZDENEK.

Broadcasting and Communications

TELECOMMUNICATIONS

Andrew's Communications Ltd: Stubbs Diamond Plaza, The Bight, Providenciales; tel. 941-8006; fax 941-7879; e-mail admin@acltci.tc; internet www.acltci.com; f. 2008; wireless broadband and cable TV services; CEO PETER A. STUBBS.

Digicel: Graceway House, Unit 207, Leeward Hwy, Providenciales; tel. 941-7600; fax 941-7601; e-mail tcicustomercare@digicelgroup.com; internet www.digiceltci.com; owned by an Irish consortium; granted licence in 2006 to provide mobile telecommunications services in Turks and Caicos; Group CEO and Dir COLM DELVES; Country Man. E. JAY SAUNDERS.

LIME: Cable & Wireless (TCI) Ltd, Leeward Hwy, POB 78, Providenciales; tel. 946-2200; fax 941-3051; internet www.lime.com; f. 1973; monopoly ended in Jan. 2006; fmrly Cable & Wireless; name changed as above 2008; telecommunications and internet services provider; CEO TONY RICE; CEO (Caribbean) MARTIN JOOS (acting).

Regulatory Authority

Telecommunication Commission: Business Solutions Bldg, Leeward Hwy, POB 203, Providenciales; tel. 946-1900; fax 946-1119; e-mail johnwilliams@tcitelecommission.tc; internet www.tcitelecom.com; f. 2004; Telecommunications Officer JOHN WILLIAMS.

BROADCASTING

Radio

Radio Turks and Caicos (RTC): POB 69, Grand Turk; tel. 946-2010; fax 946-1600; e-mail rtcdirector@rtc107fm.com; internet www.rtc107fm.com; f. 1972; govt-owned; commercial; broadcasts 105 hrs weekly; Dir CHRISTOPHER JARRETT.

Radio Visión Cristiana Internacional: North End, South Caicos; tel. and fax 946-6847; fax 946-3724; e-mail wns_72@hotmail.com; internet www.radiovision.net; commercial; Man. WENDELL SEYMOUR.

Television

People's Television Ltd: Stubb's Diamond Plaza, The Bight, Providenciales; tel. 941-8006; fax 941-7879; internet www.ptv8tci.com; f. 2008; owned by Andrew's Communications Ltd; cable television; CEO PETER A. STUBBS.

WIV Cable TV: Tower Raza, Leeward Hwy, POB 679, Providenciales; tel. 946-4866; fax 946-4790; e-mail info@wivgroup.com; internet wivtc.com; Chair. G. ROBERT BLANCHARD, Jr.

Finance

(cap. = capital; res = reserves; dep. = deposits; br(s). = branch(es);
amounts in US $ unless otherwise indicated)

BANKING

Bordier Bank (TCI) Ltd: Caribbean Pl., Leeward Hwy, POB 5, Providenciales; tel. 946-4335; fax 946-4540; e-mail enquiries@bibt .com; internet www.bibt.com; Chair. FRANÇOIS BOHN; Man. ELISE HARTSHORN (acting).

British Caribbean Bank: Governors Rd, POB 270, Providenciales; tel. 941-5028; fax 941-5029; e-mail info@bcbtci.com; internet www .bcbtci.com; fmrly Belize Bank, Turks & Caicos; Man. Dir ANDREW ASHCROFT.

CIBC FirstCaribbean International Bank: Leeward Hwy, POB 698, Providenciales; tel. 946-4007; fax 946-4573; internet www .cibcfcib.com; f. 2002 following merger of Caribbean operations of Barclays Bank PLC and CIBC, present name adopted 2011; Barclays relinquished its stake to CIBC in 2006; CEO RIK PARKHILL; Man. Dir (Bahamas, Turks and Caicos) MARIE RODLAND-ALLEN; 4 brs.

Scotiabank Turks and Caicos (CanadaCanada): 88 Cherokee Rd, POB 15, Providenciales; tel. 339-7100; fax 946-4755; e-mail bns .turkscaicos@scotiabank.com; internet turksandcaicos.scotiabank .com; f. 1982; Man. Dir CECIL ARNOLD; 3 brs.

Turks and Caicos Banking Co Ltd (TCBC): Duke St, POB 123, Cockburn Town, Grand Turk; tel. 946-2368; fax 946-2365; e-mail services@tcbc.tc; internet www.turksandcaicosbanking.tc; f. 1980; dep. 71m., total assets 81.4m. (Dec. 2011); Pres. ANTON J. B. FAESSLER; CEO DAVID J. BEE.

REGULATORY AUTHORITY

Financial Services Commission (FSC): Harry E. Francis Bldg, Pond St, POB 173, Grand Turk; tel. 946-2791; fax 946-2821; e-mail fsc@tciway.tc; internet www.tcifsc.tc; f. 2002; regulates local and offshore financial services sector; Chair. ERROL ALLEN; Man. Dir J. KEVIN HIGGINS.

TRUST COMPANIES

Berkshire Trust Co Ltd: Caribbean Pl., POB 657, Providenciales; tel. 946-4324; fax 946-4354; e-mail berkshire.trust@tciway.tc; internet www.berkshire.tc; Dir GORDON WILLIAMSON.

Chartered Trust Co: Town Centre Mall, Mezzanine Floor, Butterfield Sq., POB 125, Providenciales; tel. 946-4881; fax 946-4041; e-mail reception@chartered-tci.com; internet www.chartered-tci .com; Man. Dir PETER A. SAVORY.

M & S Trust Co Ltd: Butterfield Sq., POB 260, Providenciales; tel. 946-4650; fax 946-4663; e-mail sr@mslaw.tc; internet www.mslaw .tc/Trust; Man. Partner TIMOTHY P. O'SULLIVAN; Man. STEVEN ROSS.

Meridian Trust Co Ltd: Caribbean Pl., Leeward Hwy, POB 599, Providenciales; tel. 941-3082; fax 941-3223; e-mail mtcl@tciway.tc; internet www.meridiantrust.tc; Man. Dir KEITH BURANT.

Temple Trust Co Ltd: 1143 Leeward Hwy, Providenciales; tel. 946-5740; fax 946-5739; e-mail info@temple-group.com; internet www .templefinancialgroup.com; f. 1985; CEO DAVID C. KNIPE.

INSURANCE

Colonial Insurance Brokers Ltd: Suite 2G, Courtyard Plaza, Leeward Hwy, POB 355, Providenciales; tel. 941-3195; fax 941-3197; internet turksandcaicos.cgigroup.com; owned by Colonial Group International (Bermuda).

Turks and Caicos Islands National Insurance Board: Waterloo Plaza, POB 250, Grand Turk; tel. 946-1048; fax 946-1362; internet www.tcinib.tc; f. 1992; Chair. LILLIAN MISICK; Dir COLIN HEARTWELL; 4 brs.

Association

Turks and Caicos Association of Insurance Managers (TC-AIM): Southwinds Pl., Unit 6, Leeward Hwy, Providenciales; tel. 946-4987; fax 946-4621; internet turksandcaicos.tc/aim; f. 2000 as Asscn of Insurance Managers; name changed as above in 2003 when registered as a non-profit asscn; protects interests of domestic and offshore insurance cos in the islands; Pres. ADRIAN CORR; Treas. ROSS BLUMENTRITT.

Trade and Industry

In 2014 plans were proceeding to create a national chamber of commerce incorporating existing local chambers as chapters.

CHAMBERS OF COMMERCE

Grand Turk Chamber of Commerce: POB 148, Grand Turk; tel. 946-2324; fax 946-2504; e-mail gtchamberofcomm@tciway.tc; internet tcimall.tc/grandturkchamber; f. 1974; 57 mem. cos; Pres. and Exec. Dir GLENN CLARKE.

Providenciales Chamber of Commerce: POB 361, Providenciales; tel. 332-6418; e-mail provochambertci@gmail.com; internet www.provochamber.com; f. 1991; 131 mems (2006); Pres. TINA FENIMORE; Vice-Pres. E. JAY SAUNDERS.

UTILITIES
Electricity and Gas

Fortis TCI Ltd (FTCI): 1030 Leeward Hwy, POB 132, Providenciales; tel. 946-4313; fax 946-4532; internet www.fortistci.com; Fortis Energy (Bermuda) completed its acquisition of co in 2006; acquired Turks and Caicos Utilities Ltd in Aug. 2012; subsidiary of Fortis Inc (Canada); sole provider of electricity in South Caicos; Pres. and CEO EDDINTON POWELL; Dir, Grand Turk Operations ALDEN SMITH.

Water

Provo Water Co Ltd: 197A, Grace Bay Rd, Providenciales; tel. 946-5202; fax 946-5204; internet www.habgroup.com/water/; owned by the HAB Group; water distribution; CEO ROBERT C. HALL.

Turks and Caicos Water Co: Provo Golf Clubhouse, Grace Bay Rd, POB 124, Providenciales; tel. 946-5659; fax 946-5830; e-mail jared@ habgroup.com; internet www.habgroup.com/water/; owned by the HAB Group; production of desalinated water.

TRADE UNION

Civil Servants Association: Providenciales; internet www.tcicsa .org; f. 1973, relaunched 2011; Pres. RUFUS EWING; Sec.-Gen. SAMANTHA GLINTON.

Transport

ROADS

There are 121 km (75 miles) of roads in the islands, of which 24 km, on Grand Turk, South Caicos and Providenciales, are surfaced with tarmac. A causeway linking the North and Middle Caicos islands was completed in 2007.

SHIPPING

There are regular freight services from Miami, FL, USA. The main sea ports are Grand Turk, Providenciales, Salt Cay and Cockburn Harbour on South Caicos. A new US $40m. cruise ship terminal in Grand Turk, with capacity for large passenger liners, opened in 2006.

AL Services Ltd (AlServ): SDR Commercial Centre, 176 South Dock Rd, POB 253, Providenciales; tel. 941-3267; fax 941-3269; e-mail piper@tciway.tc; internet www.al-services.tc; freight forwarders; Man. Dir MCALLISTER (PIPER) HANCHELL.

Cargo Express Shipping Service Ltd: South Dock Rd, Bldg 70, Providenciales; tel. 941-5006; fax 941-5062; e-mail cargoexp@ express.tc; represents Tropical Shipping.

Seacair Ltd: 1 Churchill Bldg, Front St, POB 170, Grand Turk; tel. 946-2591; fax 946-2226; e-mail seacairltd@tciway.tc; represents G & G Shipping; cargo and freight services; Gen. Man. ERIC SMITH.

CIVIL AVIATION

There are international airfields on Grand Turk, South Caicos, North Caicos and Providenciales, the last being the most important; there are also landing strips on Middle Caicos, Pine Cay, Parrot Cay and Salt Cay. An expansion project at Providenciales airport that included a new terminal building and the lengthening of the runway to accommodate transatlantic flights was expected to be completed by the end of 2014.

Civil Aviation Authority: POB 168, Grand Turk; tel. 946-2137; fax 946-1185; e-mail info@tcicaa.org; internet tcicaa.org; Chair. BRIAN LIGHTBOURNE; Man. Dir THOMAS SWANN.

Caicos Express Airways: Southern Shores Bldg, Leeward Hwy, POB 18, Providenciales; tel. 941-5730; fax 946-8131; e-mail info@ caicosexpressairways.com; internet www.caicosexpressairways .com; chartered flights; Man. Dir RICHARDSON ARTHUR.

Cairsea Services Ltd: 29 Old Airport Rd, POB 138, Providenciales; tel. 946-4205; fax 946-4504; e-mail shipping@cairsea.com; internet www.cairsea.com; Man. Dir RODNEY THOMPSON.

Global Airways Ltd: POB 359, Providenciales; tel. 941-3222; fax 946-7290; e-mail global@tciway.tc; internet www.globalairways.tc; operates inter-island connections and Caribbean charter flights; Man. Dir LINDSEY GARDINER.

InterCaribbean Airways Ltd: 1 Interisland Plaza, Old Airport Rd, POB 191, Providenciales; tel. 946-4181; fax 946-4040; e-mail info@flyairtc.com; internet www.airturksandcaicos.com; fmrly Air Turks and Caicos, name changed to above in Nov. 2013; also operates SkyKing Ltd; Chair. LYNDON R. GARDINER.

Turks and Caicos Islands Airport Authority (TCIAA): Providenciales International Airport, Providenciales; tel. 946-4420; fax 941-5996; e-mail info@tciairports.com; internet www.tciairports.com/web; CEO JOHN T. SMITH.

Tourism

The islands' main tourist attractions are the numerous unspoilt beaches, and the opportunities for diving. Salt Cay has been designated a World Heritage site by UNESCO. Hotel accommodation is available on Grand Turk, Salt Cay, South Caicos, Parrot Cay, Pine Cay and Providenciales. In 2013 there were some 1,069,497 tourist arrivals, of whom 290,587 were stop-over visitors and 778,920 were cruise ship passengers. The majority of stop-overs (79.7% in 2013) were from the USA. Revenue from the sector in 2005 totalled an estimated US $355.1m.

Turks and Caicos Hotel and Tourism Association: POB 251, Ports of Call, Providenciales; tel. 941-5787; fax 946-4001; e-mail manager@turksandcaicoshta.com; internet www.turksandcaicoshta.com; fmrly Turks and Caicos Hotel Asscn; over 90 mem. orgs; Pres. MICHEL NEUTELINGS; CEO STACY COX.

Turks and Caicos Islands Tourist Board: Front St, POB 128, Grand Turk; tel. 946-2321; fax 946-2733; e-mail info@turksandcaicostourism.com; internet www.turksandcaicostourism.com; f. 1970; br. in Providenciales; Dir RALPH HIGGS.

Defence

The United Kingdom is responsible for the defence of the Turks and Caicos Islands.

Education

Primary education, beginning at seven years of age and lasting seven years, is compulsory, and is provided free of charge in government schools. Secondary education, from the age of 14, lasts for five years, and is also free. In 2005, according to UNESCO estimates, 78% of children in the relevant age-group were enrolled in primary education, while the comparable ratio for secondary education was 70%. In 2005/06 there were 14 government primary schools and eight government secondary schools. According to the 2013/14 government budget communication, $25.5m. was allocated to education (accounting for 12.8% of government spending).

THE UNITED STATES VIRGIN ISLANDS

Geography

PHYSICAL FEATURES

The United States Virgin Islands is an unincorporated territory of the USA, a Caribbean colony formerly known as the Danish West Indies (purchased in 1917). The Virgin Islands are the first main group of the Lesser Antilles and are divided between two sovereignties, that of the USA and of the United Kingdom. The main island of the British Virgin Islands, Tortola, lies across a narrow sea channel, to the north-east of St John. About 64 km (40 miles) to the west is the mainland of the US commonwealth territory of Puerto Rico (its offshore island of Culebra lying about mid-way between it and St Thomas). St Thomas is about 8 km to the west of St John, while the third main island of the US Virgins, St Croix, is some distance to the south (64 km from St Thomas and 56 km from St John), making it, geographically, not truly part of the Virgin Islands. St Croix is also the largest of the islands, covering 215 sq km (83 sq miles), out of a total area for the territory of 347 sq km (including about 3 sq km of inland waters).

There are 68 islands in all, but only the main islands are permanently inhabited. All the main islands are mountainous, fertile and of volcanic origin, but much territory has been added by reef action, and there are numerous coralline islands, islets and cays (keys). St Croix (Santa Cruz to the Spanish, but first decisively settled by the Knights of St John of Malta for the French—there were also Dutch and British attempts at colonization) is the largest island, with a less indented coast than the other islands and rolling green hills. St Croix is rockier and more arid in the east, but with wetter, wooded heights in the west. St Thomas (80 sq km) is dominated by an east–west central ridge running the length of the island and towards the west reaching the highest point in the territory, Crown Mountain (474 m or 1,556 ft). Numerous smaller islands surround St Thomas, the largest being Water Island, to the south of the central coast, which is the other inhabited island of the territory and sometimes called the 'fourth Virgin Island'. East of St Thomas is St John, similarly steep and island- and reef-fringed, but covering only 52 sq km. Two-thirds of the island is national park, forming the main part of the wide-ranging protected areas in the islands. Marine ecology is generally of the highest priority in the US Virgin Islands (the area is important for leatherback turtles, for instance, and has extensive reefs), as development has long since damaged the land environment. Thus, as happened in several other islands of the West Indies, the introduction of the mongoose (supposedly to deal with rats—although rats are usually nocturnal and the mongoose is not), which is partial to eggs, severely affected many parrot and snake species, although iguanas have survived in places.

CLIMATE

The climate is subtropical marine, as the heat and humidity is tempered by the Atlantic trade winds. There is little seasonal variation in temperature, with the cooler 'winter' months (December–March) averaging about 25°C (77°F), rising to 28°C (82°F) in summer. There is a rainy season from May to November, the average annual precipitation being 1,030 mm (40 ins). The islands can suffer from hurricanes and the afflictions of both drought and flood.

POPULATION

Ethnically, the local population is 80% black and 15% white. By place of birth, 78% are West Indian (49% born in the Virgin

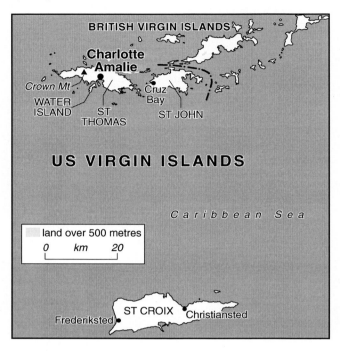

Islands, the remaining 29% from elsewhere in the West Indies), 13% are from the US mainland and 5% are from Puerto Rico. The high level of immigration is illustrated on St Croix, where the population is described as either native Crucian or North American 'Continentals'. In terms of religion, most people are Christian, with 42% claiming to be Baptist, 28% Roman Catholic and 17% Episcopalian (Anglican Communion). The longest established denomination is the Dutch Reformed Church (17th century), and there are also groups of Lutherans and other Protestants. The Jewish congregation is also venerable, having been established in the late 18th century. The cosmopolitan history and nature of the islands is visually apparent, particularly the long period of Danish rule, but, culturally, US rule has proved decisive. The official language is English, which is generally spoken, although there are some Spanish-speakers (some on St Croix and Hispanic immigrants) and a local patois—St Croix Creole or Crucian—has survived.

The total population was 106,794 in mid-2014, according to UN estimates. The most populous island was St Thomas (51,634 at the 2010 census), closely followed by St Croix (50,601). St John had only 4,170 inhabitants in that year. However, the islands also host some 2m. visitors annually, with the territorial capital, Charlotte Amalie, the most-visited port in the Caribbean. The town, with 10,354 residents in 2010, is located on the central south coast of St Thomas and was originally named for the consort of the then Danish king. The main towns of St Croix are Christiansted, the island headquarters (on the north coast, where the island begins to narrow towards the east), and Frederiksted (on the west coast). Cruz Bay, at the western end of St John, is the centre of activity on that island.

History

The Virgin Islands constitute a US External Territory. Executive power is vested in the popularly elected Governor and there is a legislature of 15 Senators; the islands send a non-voting delegate to the US House of Representatives.

Originally inhabited by Carib and Arawak Indians (Amerindians), the islands eventually came under Danish control. In 1917 they were sold by Denmark to the USA for US $25m. The islands were granted a measure of self-government in 1954, but subsequent attempts to give them greater autonomy were all rejected by popular referendum. The Democratic Party held a majority in the legislature for many years, although a member of the Independent Citizens' Movement (which split from the Democratic Party), Cyril E. King, was elected Governor in 1974. On King's death in 1978, Juan Luis became Governor, being elected in his own right in 1982. The governorship returned to the Democratic Party with the election of Alexander Farrelly in 1986; he was re-elected in 1990. A further referendum on the islands' status took place in 1993; however, the result was invalidated by the low turnout. In 1994 an independent, Dr Roy Schneider, was elected to succeed Farrelly as Governor. The governorship was regained by a Democrat, Charles Turnbull, in the 1998 elections; he was re-elected to the post in 2002. At legislative elections in November of that year, the Democratic Party won an overall majority of seats in the Senate. The Democratic Party retained its senate majority in the legislative elections of November 2004, winning 10 of the 15 seats; however, later in that month three Democratic senators defected from the party to form a narrow majority with the three Independent Citizens' Movement senators and two independent senators.

Following the presentation of legislation to create a constitutional convention of the US Virgin Islands Senate, in May 2000 a committee of the US House of Representatives was considering a range of measures to enlarge the scope of local self-government in the territory. In November 2004 Governor Turnbull approved legislation allowing the creation of a further constituent assembly to redraft the Constitution.

In February 2005 a 7,000-signature petition was submitted to the US Congress by residents of St Croix, in support of making the island a separate US External Territory from St Thomas and St John. Organizers of the petition claimed that such a move would generate more federal funding for the island, which was affected by a higher unemployment rate than the other two islands, despite being the location for one of the world's largest petroleum refineries. In May the territorial Government brought a court case against the owners of the Hovensa LLC oil refinery and the defunct St Croix Alumina plant for contaminating the sole groundwater supply on St Croix. Both companies had reached an agreement with the US Environmental Protection Agency (EPA) in 2001 to clean up petroleum spillages; according to the EPA some 2m. gallons of petroleum leaked into the local aquifer between 1978 and 1991.

An inconclusive outcome in the election of a new Governor of the US Virgin Islands' Senate on 7 November 2006 necessitated a run-off election between the two leading candidates, John deJongh of the Democratic Party and independent Kenneth Mapp on 21 November; deJongh defeated Mapp and was sworn into office on 1 January 2007.

Combating crime was a stated objective of Governor deJongh's administration. An anti-crime initiative was announced in February 2007; measures included an increase in the size of the police force and establishment of a forensic facility. The murder rate rose to 66 in 2010, although it decreased to 48 in 2011, before increasing again, to 59, in 2012. There were 38 murders recorded in 2013.

Advances towards formulating a new constitution for the territory accelerated in 2007 when a Special Election was held on 12 June to enact the US Virgin Islands' Fifth Constitutional Convention; four previous such Conventions had been appointed in 1964, 1971, 1977 and 1980, but had failed to generate proposals regarded as suitable for adoption. The election was intended to determine the composition of a 30-member constitutional development committee, formed of delegates representing the territory's four constituent islands: 13 were to be elected from St Croix district, 13 from St Thomas-St John, with four at-large representatives (two each from the former electoral districts), as elected by the entire eligible Virgin Islands electorate, completing the committee. However, turnout was very low, provoking concerns that voting on the new constitution might fall short of the minimum 50% plus one required to guarantee its passage. The Fifth Constitutional Convention was assembled on 29 October 2007 to commence work upon the drafting of a new constitution. A final draft document would require the approval of two-thirds of all delegates. Assuming such an endorsement, the document would then have to be approved by the Governor of the US Virgin Islands, the President of the USA and US Congress before being put to a public referendum in the territory. The Convention submitted a proposed constitution in June 2009, although this version was rejected by the Governor for apparently not complying with local and federal laws. Governor deJongh asserted that any proposed constitution must recognize the US Constitution as the supreme law of the land or adhere to its basic rights and protections. It had been hoped that the constitutional development process would facilitate the US Virgin Islands' transition from a US Constitution- and Organic Act-governed state to one enjoying greater autonomy, and that a greater distinction between the legislative, executive and judicial branches of government might be achieved. Despite deJongh's objections, the constitution was forwarded to the US Congress; the document was returned to the territory in June 2010 for further consultation and amendment. In particular, provisions giving enhanced rights to 'native' Virgin Islanders were to be re-examined. The Fifth Constitutional Convention duly revised the charter in October 2012, although some commentators argued that the correct procedures had not been followed. A date for the referendum had not been established by mid-2014.

Governor deJongh was re-elected in an election held on 2 November 2010, attracting 56.3% of the votes cast. Kenneth Mapp, an independent, was once again deJongh's rival, receiving 43.6% of the ballot. Governor deJongh was inaugurated on 6 January 2011; he reiterated his commitment to addressing crime and boosting economic activity on the islands.

On 6 November 2012 Donna Christensen was re-elected as the territory's Delegate to the US Congress for an eighth consecutive term. In concurrent elections to the territorial Senate, the Democratic Party secured 10 seats, independent candidates gained four and the remaining seat was won by the Independent Citizens' Movement. A gubernatorial election was due to be held on 4 November 2014. As DeJongh was constitutionally prohibited from contesting the poll, the Democratic Party organized a primary election in early August to select its gubernatorial candidate. Christensen emerged victorious from this process and was regarded as the favourite to win the gubernatorial poll later that year.

Economy

The islands are heavily dependent on links to the US mainland; more than 90% of trade is conducted with Puerto Rico and the USA. Until its closure in early 2012, St Croix had the world's second largest petroleum refinery, Hovensa LLC (a joint venture between the US oil company Amerada Hess and Petróleos de Venezuela, SA), which was the territory's largest private sector employer. In 2011 exports of refined petroleum products to the USA were worth US $10,486m. Following serious losses as a result of the global economic downturn, in 2011 Hovensa LLC reduced its capacity from 500,000 barrels per day (b/d) to 350,000 b/d. However, with demand continuing to decline, it became evident that the refinery was no longer economically viable, and operations consequently ceased in February 2012. In July 2013 Governor John deJongh sought senatorial approval of an agreement between the Government and Hovensa that would facilitate the sale of the plant and thus potentially lead to the recommencement of refining activities. However, in August the agreement was rejected by the Senate, which regarded the terms of the arrangement as overly favourable to Hovensa. The legislature finally granted its approval in November, but no firm offers to purchase the facility had been reported by mid-2014.

Rum is an important product; in 2011 a distillery for Diageo on St Croix was inaugurated. The new plant was to produce 20m. proof gallons annually for its Captain Morgan brand from 2012. The project was part of an agreement reached between the Government and Diageo in 2009: the US Virgin Islands authorities agreed to finance construction of the plant in return for receiving an estimated US $3,000m. in additional excise revenue over the 30-year duration of the contract. The agreement prompted protests from Puerto Rico where Diageo's operations had previously been located. In 2009 the Government also agreed to fund expansion of the existing Cruzan Rum distillery in exchange for a guarantee that the rum producer would maintain a presence in the territory for 30 years. Federal excise taxes collected on rum exports to the USA (the so-called cover over programme) returned $193.2m. of revenue in 2012. During that year several members of the Caribbean Community and Common Market (CARICOM) threatened to appeal to the World Trade Organization owing to their concerns about the cover over programme, which, they asserted, effectively operated as an illegal subsidization scheme. CARICOM argued that the programme was distorting the regional rum market, leaving its members at a disadvantage. Notwithstanding this opposition, the US Congress continued to renew the cover over programme, authorizing its extension most recently in April 2014.

According to official figures, just 0.1% of the economically active population was engaged in agriculture, forestry and fishing in 2010. Some fruit and food crops (notably sorghum) are grown for local consumption, but the land is unsuitable for large-scale cultivation. Industry (including mining, transportation and warehouses) provided 10.7% of the waged and salaried jobs in 2012, while public administration accounted for 27.1%.

Tourism is a major source of income and employment, with the emphasis on the visiting cruise ship business and the sale of duty-free products to visitors from the US mainland. According to the World Travel and Tourism Council, in 2013 the sector accounted for 31.8% of gross domestic product (GDP) and 28.4% of total employment. In that year visitor arrivals totalled 2.7m.; in 2010 visitor expenditures amounted to US $1,012.5m.

In spite of the approval of legislation in July 2011 to reduce public sector salaries, as well as the introduction of a voluntary retirement scheme, a budget deficit of US $43.4m. was recorded in 2011/12 owing to the decline in tax receipts following the closure of the Hovensa refinery. The Senate rejected a further wage reduction bill in December 2011, forcing the Government to implement a civil service retrenchment plan. Although further austerity measures were introduced during 2012–14, a smaller deficit (of $13.7m.) was registered in 2012/13 and a considerably larger deficit, of $70.5m., was estimated for 2013/14. A deficit of $85.2m. was forecast for 2014/15. In mid-2013 the islands' general obligation debt amounted to $782.5m. The islands were expected to continue to receive grants and other remittances from the US Government, although greater efforts towards achieving improved financial accountability were demanded.

Owing to the islands' heavy reliance on imported goods, local prices and inflation are higher than on the mainland. The level of inflation increased to 9.0% in 2011, before moderating to 3.1% in 2012. In 2012 the territory recorded a trade deficit of US $703.5m. In that year the USA provided 58.0% of imports and took 60.9% of exports. Of total exports in 2011, 78.8% were refined petroleum products; crude petroleum accounted for 74.0% of the islands' total imports in that year. These proportions decreased sharply in 2012, however, owing to the closure of the Hovensa refinery.

In 2009 the economy, particularly the tourism and construction sectors, was adversely affected by the global economic downturn. Real GDP contracted by 5.5% in that year, while lower tax receipts put government finances under strain. The economy expanded by 1.7% in 2010, driven predominantly by the oil-refining sector, but declined by a further 6.6% in 2011; tourist arrivals increased in both years. Over 2,000 jobs were lost as a result of the Hovensa plant's closure in February 2012, and the unemployment rate consequently rose to 11.7% in that year and to an estimated 13.4% in 2013, up from 8.9% in 2011. The cessation of refining activities led to an economic contraction of 13.2% in 2012, although the economy expanded by an estimated 0.5% in 2013.

Statistical Survey

Sources (unless otherwise stated): Office of Public Relations, Office of the Governor, Charlotte Amalie, VI 00802; tel. (340) 774-0294; fax (340) 774-4988; Bureau of Economic Research, Dept of Economic Development and Agriculture, 1050 Norre Gade No. 5, Suite 301, Charlotte Amalie, VI 00802; POB 6400, Charlotte Amalie, VI 00804; tel. (340) 714-1700; fax (340) 776-7953; e-mail dhazell@usviber.org; internet www.usviber.org.

AREA AND POPULATION

Area: 347.1 sq km (134 sq miles): St Croix 215 sq km (83 sq miles); St Thomas 80.3 sq km (31 sq miles); St John 51.8 sq km (20 sq miles).

Population: 108,612 (males 51,864, females 56,748) at census of 1 April 2000; 106,405 at census of 1 April 2010. *By Island* (2010 census): St Croix 50,601, St Thomas 51,634, St John 4,170 (Source: US Census Bureau). *Mid-2014* (UN estimate): 106,794 (Source: UN, *World Population Prospects: The 2012 Revision*).

Density (at mid-2014): 307.7 per sq km.

Population by Age and Sex (UN estimates at mid-2014): *0–14 years:* 22,174 (males 11,298, females 10,876); *15–64 years:* 66,685 (males 31,537, females 35,148); *65 years and over:* 17,935 (males 8,092, females 9,843); *Total* 106,794 (males 50,927, females 55,867) (Source: UN, *World Population Prospects: The 2012 Revision*).

Principal Towns (population at 2010 census): Charlotte Amalie (capital) 10,354; Christiansted 2,433; Frederiksted 859. Source: US Census Bureau.

Births and Deaths (2012 unless otherwise indicated): Registered live births 1,415 (birth rate 13.4 per 1,000); Registered deaths 715 (death rate 6.7 per 1,000, 2010) (Source: US National Center for Health Statistics). *2013:* Birth rate 10.7 per 1,000; Death rate 8.0 per 1,000 (Source: Pan American Health Organization).

Life Expectancy (years at birth, estimates): 79.6 (males 76.6; females 82.8) in 2013. Source: Pan American Health Organization.

Employment (persons aged 16 years and over, 2000 census): Agriculture, forestry, fishing, hunting and mining 324; Manufacturing 2,754; Construction 4,900; Wholesale trade 912; Retail trade 6,476; Transportation, warehousing and utilities 3,321; Information 931; Finance, insurance, real estate, rental and leasing 2,330; Professional, scientific, management, administrative and waste management services 3,058; Educational, health, and social services 6,742; Arts, entertainment, recreation, accommodation and food services 7,351; Public administration 4,931; Other services 2,535; *Total employed* 46,565 (Source: US Bureau of the Census). *2012* (number of waged and salaried jobs, official figures): Construction and mining 1,756; Manufacturing 1,271; Transportation, warehouses and utilities 1,487; Wholesale and retail trade 6,820; Financial activities 2,279; Leisure and hospitality 7,237; Information 807; Other services 9,163; Federal government 946; Territorial government 10,530; Total 42,296. *Economically Active Population* (civilians only, annual averages, 2012): Total employed 44,659, Unemployed 5,918; Total labour force 50,577.

HEALTH AND WELFARE

Total Fertility Rate (children per woman, 2013): 1.8.

Under-5 Mortality Rate (per 1,000 live births, 2010): 9.8.

Physicians (per 1,000 head, 2003): 1.47.

Hospital Beds (per 1,000 head, 1996): 18.7.

Source: Pan American Health Organization.

For definitions, see explanatory note on p. vi.

AGRICULTURE, ETC.

Livestock (2012, FAO estimates): Cattle 8,200; Sheep 3,250; Pigs 2,650; Goats 4,100; Chickens 40,000.

Fishing (metric tons, live weight, 2012): Total catch (all capture) 515 (Groupers 32; Snappers, jobfishes, etc. 54; Grunts, sweetlips, etc. 18; Parrotfishes 61; Triggerfishes, durgons, etc. 30; Caribbean spiny lobster 76; Stromboid conchs 126).

Source: FAO.

INDUSTRY

Production ('000 metric tons, unless otherwise indicated, 2002, estimates): Jet fuels 1,745; Motor spirit (petrol) 2,654; Kerosene 91; Gas-diesel (distillate fuel) oil 5,725; Residual fuel oils 3,550; Liquefied petroleum gas 164; Electric energy (2010) 958 million kWh. Source: UN, *Industrial Commodity Statistics Yearbook* and Database.

FINANCE

Currency and Exchange Rates: 100 cents = 1 United States dollar (US $). *Sterling and Euro Equivalents* (30 May 2014): £1 sterling = US $1.682; €1 = US $1.361; US $100 = £59.45= €73.47.

Budget (budget proposals, US $ million, year ending 30 September 2015): Total revenues 765.3 (Taxes 589.1); Total expenditure 850.5 (Education 165.9; Health and Human Services 136.2; Debt service 146.8).

Cost of Living (Consumer Price Index; base: 2009 = 100): All items 104.0 in 2010; 113.4 in 2011; 116.9 in 2012.

Gross Domestic Product (US $ million at current prices): 4,356 in 2011; 4,233 in 2012; 4,253 in 2013 (estimate) (Source: Bureau of Economic Analysis, US Department of Commerce).

EXTERNAL TRADE

Total Trade (US $ million): *Imports:* 12,153.9 in 2010; 13,972.7 in 2011; 2,966.7 in 2012. *Exports:* 11,929.5 in 2010; 13,313.5 in 2011; 2,263.2 in 2012. Note: The main import is crude petroleum (660.3m. in 2012), while the principal exports are refined petroleum products (932.4m. in 2012).

Trade with the USA (US $ million): *Imports:* 1,548.9 in 2010; 1,767.6 in 2011; 1,719.4 in 2012. *Exports:* 9,992.5 in 2010; 10,994.8 in 2011; 1,377.7 in 2012.

TRANSPORT

Road Traffic (registered motor vehicles, 2011): 75,585.

Shipping: *Cruise Ship Arrivals:* 698 in 2011; 667 in 2012; 626 in 2013. *Passenger Arrivals:* 2,008,991 in 2011; 1,904,468 in 2012; 1,998,579 in 2013.

Civil Aviation (visitor arrivals): 678,961 in 2011; 737,681 in 2012; 702,963 in 2013.

TOURISM

Visitor Arrivals ('000): 2,686.1 in 2011 (arrivals by air 677.1, cruise ship passengers 2,009.0); 2,642.1 in 2012 (arrivals by air 737.6, cruise ship passengers 1,904.5); 2,701.6 in 2013 (arrivals by air 703.0, cruise ship passengers 1,998.6).

Visitor Receipts (US $ million, 2010): Total receipts 1,012.5 (tourists 678.2, excursionists 334.3).

COMMUNICATIONS MEDIA

Telephones (2013): 76,000 main lines in use.

Mobile Cellular Telephones (2009): 80,300 subscribers.

Internet Users (2009): 30,000.

Broadband Subscribers (2013): 9,100.

Source: International Telecommunication Union.

EDUCATION

Pre-primary (1992/93, unless otherwise indicated): 62 schools; 121 teachers; 4,714 students (2000).

Elementary (1992/93, unless otherwise indicated): 62 schools; 790 teachers (public schools only); 11,728 students (2005).

Secondary: 541 teachers (public schools only, 1990); 5,022 students (2005).

Higher Education: 266 teachers (2003/04); 2,610 students (2004).

2012: Total student enrolment (all levels) 20,310; University graduates 359.

Sources: UNESCO, *Statistical Yearbook*; US Bureau of the Census.

Directory

The Constitution

The Government of the US Virgin Islands is organized under the provisions of the Organic Act of the Virgin Islands, passed by the Congress of the United States in 1936 and revised in 1954 and 1984. Subsequent amendments provided for the popular election of the Governor and Lieutenant-Governor of the Virgin Islands in 1970 and, since 1973, for representation in the US House of Representatives by a popularly elected delegate. The delegate has voting powers only in committees of the House. Executive power is vested in the Governor, who is elected for a term of four years by universal adult suffrage and who appoints, with the advice and consent of the legislature, the heads of the executive departments. The Governor may also appoint administrative assistants as his representatives on St John and St Croix. Legislative power is vested in the legislature of the Virgin Islands, a unicameral body comprising 15 senators, elected for a two-year term by popular vote. Legislation is subject to the approval of the Governor, whose veto can be overridden by a two-thirds vote of the legislature. All residents of the islands who are citizens of the USA and at least 18 years of age have the right to vote in local elections, but not in national elections. In 1976 the Virgin Islands were granted the right to draft their own constitution, subject to the approval of the US President and Congress. A constitution permitting a degree of autonomy was drawn up in 1978 and gained the necessary approval, but was then rejected by the people of the Virgin Islands in a referendum in 1979. A fourth draft, providing for greater autonomy than the 1978 draft, was rejected in a referendum in 1981. At a further attempt, in 1993, the referendum was invalidated by the insufficient turn-out of registered voters. In November 2004 legislation was approved to allow the creation of a constituent assembly to redraft the Constitution. A constitutional convention, composed of 30 publicly elected delegates, was convened in October 2007 to draft a new constitution. The subsequent proposed charter, however, was rejected by the US Congress in June 2010 on the grounds that certain provisions were in contravention of the US Constitution and federal law. A Fifth Constitutional Convention duly revised the charter in October 2012, although a referendum on the Constitution had yet to take place.

The Government

HEAD OF STATE

President: BARACK HUSSEIN OBAMA (took office 20 January 2009, re-elected 6 November 2012).

EXECUTIVE
(September 2014)

The Government is formed by the Democratic Party of the Virgin Islands.

Governor: JOHN deJONGH, Jr (took office 1 January 2007, re-elected 2 November 2010).

Lieutenant-Governor: GREGORY R. FRANCIS.

Commissioner of Agriculture: LOUIS E. PETERSON, Jr.

Commissioner of Education: DONNA FRETT-GREGORY.

Commissioner of Finance: ANGEL DAWSON, Jr.

Commissioner of Health: DARICE PLASKETT.

Commissioner of Human Services: CHRISTOPHER FINCH.

Commissioner of Labor: ALBERT BRYAN, Jr.

Commissioner of Licensing and Consumer Affairs: WAYNE L. BIGGS, Jr.

Commissioner of Planning and Natural Resources: ALICIA BARNES.

Commissioner of Police: RODNEY F. QUERRARD, Sr.

Commissioner of Property and Procurement: LYNN A. MILLIN MADURO.

Commissioner of Public Works: DARRYL SMALLS.

Commissioner of Sports, Parks and Recreation: ST CLAIRE N. WILLIAMS.

Commissioner of Tourism: BEVERLY NICHOLSON-DOTY.

Attorney-General: VINCENT FRAZER.

US Virgin Islands Delegate to the US Congress: DONNA M. CHRISTENSEN.

GOVERNMENT OFFICES

Office of the Governor: Government House, 21–22 Kongens Gade, Charlotte Amalie, VI 00802; tel. (340) 774-0001; fax (340) 693-4309; e-mail contact@governordejongh.com; internet www.governordejongh.com.

Office of the Lieutenant-Governor: Government Hill, 18 Kongens Gade, Charlotte Amalie, VI 00802; tel. (340) 774-2991; fax (340) 774-6953; internet www.ltg.gov.vi.

Department of Agriculture: Estate Lower Love, Kingshill, St Croix, VI 00850; tel. (340) 778-0997; fax (340) 778-7977; e-mail lpeters@uvi.edu; internet www.vifresh.com/.

Department of Education: 1834 Kongens Gade, Charlotte Amalie, VI 00802-6746; tel. (340) 774-0100; fax (340) 779-7153; e-mail ideas@doe.vi; internet www.doe.vi.

Department of Finance: GERS Bldg, 2nd Floor, 76 Kronprindsens Gade, Charlotte Amalie, VI 00802; tel. (340) 774-4750; fax (340) 776-4028; e-mail aedawson@dof.gov.vi; internet www.usvifinance.info.

Department of Health: 1303 Hospital Ground Suite 10, Charlotte Amalie, St Thomas, VI 00802; tel. (340) 774-9000; fax (340) 777-4001; e-mail julia.sheen@usvi-doh.org; internet www.healthvi.org.

Department of Human Services: Knud Hansen Complex, Bldg A, 1303 Hospital Ground, Charlotte Amalie, VI 00802; tel. (340) 774-0930; fax (340) 774-3466; internet www.dhs.gov.vi.

Department of Justice: GERS Bldg, 2nd Floor, 34–38 Kronprindsens Gade, Charlotte Amalie, VI 00802; tel. (340) 774-5666; fax (340) 774-9710; e-mail vfrazer@doj.vi.gov; internet doj.vi.gov.

Department of Labor: 53A–54AB Kronprindsens Gade, St Thomas, VI 00803-2608; tel. (340) 776-3700; fax (340) 774-5908; e-mail customersupport@vidol.gov; internet www.vidol.gov.

Department of Licensing and Consumer Affairs: Property & Procurement Bldg, 1 Sub Base, Rm 205, Charlotte Amalie, St Thomas, VI 00802; tel. (340) 774-3130; fax (340) 776-0675; e-mail dlcacommissioner@dlca.gov.vi; internet www.dlca.gov.vi.

Department of Planning and Natural Resources: Cyril E. King Airport, Terminal Bldg, 2nd Floor, Suite 6, 8100 Lindberg Bay, St

Thomas, VI 00802; tel. (340) 774-3320; fax (340) 775-5706; e-mail robertmathes@dpnr.gov.vi; internet www.dpnr.gov.vi.

Department of Police: Alexander Farrelly Criminal Justice Center, Charlotte Amalie, St Thomas, VI 00802; tel. (340) 774-2211; fax (340) 715-5517; e-mail police.commissioner@vipd.gov.vi; internet www.vipd.gov.vi.

Department of Property and Procurement: Property & Procurement Bldg No. 1, 3rd Floor, Sub Base, Charlotte Amalie, VI 00802; tel. (340) 774-0828; fax (340) 774-9704; e-mail lmillin@pnpvi.org.

Department of Public Works: Bldg No. 8, Sub Base, Charlotte Amalie, VI 00802; tel. (340) 776-4844; fax (340) 774-5869; e-mail darryl.smalls@dpw.vi.gov.

Department of Sports, Parks and Recreation: Property & Procurement Bldg No. 1, Sub Base, 2nd Floor, Rm 206, Charlotte Amalie, VI 00802; tel. (340) 774-0255; fax (340) 774-4600; e-mail info@dspr.vi; internet www.dspr.vi.

Department of Tourism: POB 6400, St Thomas, VI 00804; tel. (340) 774-8784; fax (340) 774-4390; e-mail info@usvitourism.vi; internet www.visitusvi.com.

Legislature

LEGISLATIVE ASSEMBLY
Senate

President of the Senate: SHAWN-MICHAEL MALONE.
Election, 6 November 2012

Party	Seats
Democratic Party	10
Independent Citizens' Movement	1
Independent	4
Total	**15**

Election Commission

Election Board: Election Systems of the Virgin Islands, POB 1499, Kingshill, St Croix, VI 00851-1499; tel. (340) 773-1021; fax (340) 773-4523; e-mail electionsys@unitedstates.vi; internet www.vivote.gov; Supervisor of Elections CAROLINE F. FAWKES; brs on St Thomas and St John.

Political Organizations

Democratic Party of the Virgin Islands: POB 8507, St Thomas, VI 00801; tel. (340) 775-9675; internet www.democrats.org; affiliated to the Democratic Party of the USA; Chair. EMMETT HANSEN, III.

Independent Citizens' Movement (The ICM Party, VI): POB 305188, St Thomas, VI 00803-5188; tel. (340) 772-9524; f. 1968; Chair. Sen. TERRENCE NELSON.

Republican Party of the Virgin Islands: 6067 Questa Verde, Christiansted, St Croix, VI 00820-4485; tel. (340) 332-2579; e-mail info@virepublicanwomen.com; internet www.vigop.com; f. 1948; affiliated to the Republican Party of the USA since 1952; Chair. HERBERT SCHOENBOHM; Exec. Dir WARREN COLE.

Judicial System

Supreme Court of the Virgin Islands: No. 161B, Crown Bay, St Thomas, VI 00802; tel. (340) 774-2237; fax (340) 774-2258; e-mail administrative.services@visupremecourt.org; internet www.visupremecourt.org; f. 2007; assumed jurisdiction for all appeals formerly administered by the Superior Court; highest local appellate body, established to administer justice independently of the US federal justice system; judges are appointed by the Governor; Chief Justice RHYS S. HODGE.

Superior Court of the Virgin Islands: Alexander A. Farrelly Justice Center, 5400 Veteran's Dr., St Thomas, VI 00802; tel. (340) 774-6680; fax (340) 776-9889; e-mail court.administrator@visuperiorcourt.org; internet www.visuperiorcourt.org; f. 1976 as the Territorial Court of the Virgin Islands; name officially changed in 2004; jurisdiction over all local civil actions and criminal matters; court in St Croix also; judges are appointed by the Governor; Presiding Judge MICHAEL C. DUNSTON.

US Federal District Court of the Virgin Islands: Division of St Thomas/St John: 5500 Veteran's Dr., Charlotte Amalie, St Thomas, VI 00802-6424; Division of St Croix: 3013 Estate Golden Rock, Christiansted, St Croix, VI 00820-4355; tel. (340) 774-0640; fax (340) 774-1293; internet www.vid.uscourts.gov; jurisdiction in civil, criminal and federal actions; judges are appointed by the President of the USA with the advice and consent of the Senate; Chief Judge WILMA A. LEWIS.

Religion

The population is mainly Christian. The main churches with followings in the islands are Baptist, Roman Catholic, Episcopalian, Lutheran, Methodist, Moravian and Seventh-day Adventist. There is also a small Jewish community, numbering around 900 adherents.

CHRISTIANITY

The Roman Catholic Church

The US Virgin Islands comprises a single diocese, suffragan to the archdiocese of Washington, DC, USA. Some 28% of the population are Roman Catholics.

Bishop of St Thomas: Most Rev. HERBERT A. BEVARD, Bishop's Residence, 29A Princesse Gade, POB 301825, Charlotte Amalie, VI 00803-1825; tel. (340) 774-3166; fax (340) 774-5816; e-mail chancery@islands.vi; internet www.catholicvi.com.

The Anglican Communion

The US and British Virgin Islands form a single, missionary diocese of the Episcopal Church of the United States of America.

Bishop of the Diocese of the Virgin Islands: Rt Rev. E. AMBROSE GUMBS, POB 7488, St Thomas, VI 00801; tel. (340) 776-1797; fax (340) 777-8485; e-mail bpambrosegumbs@yahoo.com; internet www.episcopalvi.org.

The Press

St Croix This Week: POB 11199, St Thomas, VI 00801-4199; tel. (340) 774-2500; fax (340) 776-1466; e-mail stcroixthisweek@gmail.com; internet www.stcroixthisweek.com; monthly; comprises the *St Thomas/St John This Week* and *St Thomas This Week Cruise Edn*; Publr FRANCES NEWBOLD; Man. Editor SUSAN WALL.

St John Tradewinds: The Marketplace, Office Suites II, Office 104, POB 1500, Cruz Bay, St John, VI 00831; tel. (340) 776-6496; fax (340) 693-8885; e-mail info@tradewinds.vi; internet www.stjohntradewindsnews.com; f. 1972; weekly; Publr MALINDA NELSON; circ. 2,500.

Virgin Islands Daily News: 9155 Estate Thomas, VI 00802; tel. (340) 774-8772; fax (340) 776-0740; e-mail letters@dailynews.vi; internet www.virginislandsdailynews.com; f. 1930; acquired from Innovative Communication Corpn by Times-Shamrock Communications, USA in 2008; morning; Publr JASON ROBBINS; Exec. Editor GERRY YANDEL; circ. 15,000.

Virgin Islands Source: St Thomas; tel. (340) 777-8144; fax (340) 777-8136; e-mail visource@gmail.com; internet www.visource.com; f. 1998; comprises the *St Thomas Source*, *St Croix Source* and *St John Source*; daily; digital; Publr SHAUN A. PENNINGTON.

Broadcasting and Communications

TELECOMMUNICATIONS

Broadband VI: POB 26304, Christiansted, VI 00824; tel. 719-2943; e-mail office@broadband.VI; internet www.broadband.vi; internet service provider.

Innovative Telephone: Bjerget House, POB 1730, St Croix, VI 00821; tel. (340) 779-9999; fax (340) 777-7701; e-mail webmaster@iccvi.com; internet www.innovativetelephone.com; f. 1959 as Virgin Islands Telephone Corpn (Vitelco); acquired by Innovative Communication Corpn in 1987; present name adopted in 2001; provides telephone services throughout the islands; launched internet service, Innovative PowerNet, in 1999; Vice-Pres. JENNIFER MATAR-ANGAS-KING.

Innovative Wireless: 4006 Estate Diamond, Christiansted, St Croix, VI 00820; fax (340) 778-6011; internet www.vitelcellular.com; f. 1989 as VitelCellular; subsidiary of Innovative Communication Corpn; mobile cellular telecommunications; Man. Dir BEULAH JONIS.

Radio

WDHP 1620 AM, WRRA 1290 AM, WAXJ 103.5 FM: 79A Castle Coakley, Christiansted, St Croix, VI 00820; tel. (340) 719-1620; fax (340) 778-1686; e-mail wrra@islands.vi; internet www.reefbroadcasting.com; operated by Reef Broadcasting, Inc; commercial; broadcasts to the US and British Virgin Islands, Puerto Rico and the Eastern Caribbean; Owner and Gen. Man. HUGH PEMBERTON.

WEVI (Power 101.7 WeVi-FM): 2C Hogensborg, Frederiksted, St Croix, VI 00840; POB 892, Christiansted, VI 00821; tel. (340) 719-9384; e-mail aw@frontlinemissions.org; internet www.wevifm.net; operated by FrontLine Missions International, Inc; non-commercial; Christian programming; English, Spanish and Creole/Patois.

WGOD (97.9 FM): 22A, Estate Dorothea, POB 305012, Charlotte Amalie, St Thomas, VI 00803; tel. (340) 774-4498; fax (340) 777-9978; internet wgodvi.org; part of Three Angels Broadcasting Network (3ABN); Christian religious programming; Pres. Rev. REYNALD CHARLES; Business Mans MARIE RHYMER-MARTIN, VEEDA CHARLES.

WIUJ: POB 2477, St Thomas, VI 00803; e-mail information@wiuj.com; internet www.wiuj.com; operated by V. I. Youth Development Radio, Inc; non-commercial; educational and public service programmes; Gen. Man. LEO MORON.

WJKC (Isle 95-FM), WMNG (Mongoose), WVIQ (Sunny): 5020 Anchor Way, POB 25680, Christiansted, St Croix, VI 00824; tel. (340) 773-0995; fax (340) 770-9093; e-mail jkc@viradio.com; f. 1982; commercial; Gen. Man. JONATHAN K. COHEN.

WSTA (Lucky 13): 121 Sub Base, POB 1340, St Thomas, VI 00804; tel. (340) 774-4500; fax (340) 776-1316; e-mail nfo@wsta.com; internet www.wsta.com; f. 1950; acquired by Ottley Communications Corpn in 1984; commercial; Owner and Gen. Man. ATHNIEL C. OTTLEY.

WVGN: 8000 Nisky Centre, Suite 714, St Thomas, VI 00802; tel. (800) 275-6437; e-mail info@wvgn.org; internet www.wvgn.org; f. 2002; operated by Caribbean Community Broadcasting Co; non-commercial; news and public affairs programming; affiliated to NBC, USA; Gen. Man. KEITH BASS.

WVWI (Radio One), WVJZ (Jamz), WWKS (Kiss), WIVI (Hitz) (Ackley Media Group Stations): POB 302179, St Thomas, VI 00803-2179; tel. (340) 776-1000; fax (340) 776-5357; e-mail info@amg.vi; internet www.amg.vi; f. 1962; acquired from Knight Quality Stations by Ackley Media Group in 2006; commercial; Pres. and CEO GORDON P. ACKLEY.

WZIN FM (The Buzz): Nisky Mall Center, PMB 696, St Thomas, VI 00802; tel. (340) 776-1043; e-mail cristy@buzzrocks.com; operated by Pan Caribbean Broadcasting, Inc; commercial; Gen. Man. ALAN FRIEDMAN.

Television

Innovative Cable Television (St Croix, St Thomas, St John): 4006 Estate Diamond, Christiansted, St Croix, VI 00820; POB 6100, St Thomas, VI 00804; fax (340) 778-6011; e-mail info@iccvi.com; internet www.innovativecable.com; f. 1997 following acquisition of St Croix Cable TV (f. 1981); subsidiary of Innovative Communication Corpn; acquired Caribbean Communication Corpn in 1998; comprises TV2 (f. 2000); broadcasts to 7 Caribbean islands and France; Vice-Pres. JENNIFER MATARANGAS-KING.

WSVI-TV8 (Channel 8): Sunny Isle Shopping Center, POB 6000, Christiansted, St Croix, VI 00823; tel. (340) 778-5008; fax (340) 778-5011; e-mail channel8@wsvitv.com; internet www.wsvi.tv; f. 1965; operated by Alpha Broadcasting Corpn; affiliated to ABC, USA; 1 satellite channel and 1 analogue translator.

WTJX-TV (Public Television Service): POB 808, St Croix, VI 00820; tel. (340) 773-3337; fax (340) 773-4555; e-mail pphipps@wtjxtv.org; internet www.wtjxtv.org; f. 1968; educational and public service programmes; affiliated to PBS, USA; broadcasts on 1 terrestrial and 4 digital (cable) channels; broadcasts to the US and British Virgin Islands and Puerto Rico; Chair. RAÚL CARRILLO; Exec. Dir OSBERT POTTER.

Finance

(cap. = capital; res = reserves; dep. = deposits; br.(s) = branch(es); amounts in US dollars)

BANKING

Banco Popular of the Virgin Islands: 5 Orange Grove, Christiansted, VI 00820; tel. (340) 693-2966; fax (340) 693-2782; e-mail internet@bppr.com; internet www.bancopopular.com; Pres. and CEO RICHARD L. CARRIÓN; 8 brs.

Bank of St Croix: 5025 Anchor Way, Gallows Bay, Christiansted, St Croix 00820; tel. (340) 773-8500; fax (340) 773-8508; e-mail info@

bankofstcroix.com; internet www.bankofstcroix.com; f. 1994; cap. 2.6m., res. 1.9m, dep. 109.3m. (Dec. 2013); CEO JAMES BRISBOIS; 1 br.

FirstBank VI: POB 309600, St Thomas, VI 00803; tel. (866) 695-2511; fax (340) 776-1313; internet www.firstbankvi.com; acquired First Virgin Islands Federal Savings Bank in 2000 and Virgin Islands Community Bank in 2008; Regional Pres. and CEO AURELIO ALEMÁN-BERMÚDEZ; 2 brs.

Scotiabank (Canada): 214C Altona and Welgunst, POB 420, Charlotte Amalie, VI 00804; tel. (340) 774-0037; fax (340) 693-5994; e-mail lawrence.aqui@scotiabank.com; internet www.scotiabank.com/vi/en; f. 1963; Vice-Pres. and Country Man. LAWRENCE AQUI; 5 brs.

INSURANCE

A number of mainland US companies have agencies in the Virgin Islands.

Trade and Industry

GOVERNMENT AGENCY

US Virgin Islands Economic Development Authority: Government Development Bank Bldg, 5055 Norre Gade No. 5, POB 305038, St Thomas, VI 00803; tel. (340) 714-1700; internet www.usvieda.org; semi-autonomous body comprising Government Devt Bank, Economic Devt Commission, Industrial Park Devt Corpn, Small Business Devt Agency and the Enterprise Zone programme; offices in St Thomas and St Croix; Chair. ALBERT BRYAN, Jr; CEO PERCIVAL CLOUDEN.

CHAMBERS OF COMMERCE

St Croix Chamber of Commerce: 3009 Orange Grove, Suite 12, Christiansted, St Croix, VI 00820; tel. (340) 718-1435; fax (340) 773-8172; e-mail info@stxchamber.org; internet www.stxchamber.org; f. 1924; Chair. MARK ECKARD; 300 mems.

St Thomas-St John Chamber of Commerce: 6–7 Dronningens Gade, POB 324, Charlotte Amalie, VI 00804; tel. (340) 776-0100; fax (340) 776-0588; e-mail chamber.vi@gmail.com; internet www .chamber.vi; f. 1927; Pres. SEBASTIANO PAIEWONSKY CASSINELLI; Exec. Dir JOSEPH S. AUBAIN; c. 700 mems.

UTILITIES

Regulatory Authority

Virgin Islands Energy Office: 4101 Estate Mars Hill, Frederiksted, St Croix, VI 00840; tel. (340) 713-8436; fax (340) 772-0063; e-mail don.buchanan@eo.vi.gov; internet www.vienergy.org; f. 1974; Dir KARL KNIGHT.

Electricity and Water

Virgin Islands Water and Power Authority (WAPA): POB 1450, Charlotte Amalie, VI 00804-1450; e-mail communications@viwapa .vi; internet www.viwapa.vi; f. 1964; public corpn; manufactures and distributes electric power and desalinated sea water; CEO HUGO V. HODGE, Jr; c. 55,000 customers.

Transport

ROADS

The islands' road network totals approximately 855.5 km (531.6 miles).

SHIPPING

The US Virgin Islands are a popular port of call for cruise ships. The bulk of cargo traffic is handled at a container port on St Croix. A passenger and freight ferry service provides frequent daily connections between St Thomas and St John and between St Thomas and Tortola (British Virgin Islands). A US $150m. marina restoration project on St Thomas, completed in 2006, included provision for 'mega-yacht' docking facilities in addition to conventional moorings.

Virgin Islands Port Authority: Administrative Bldg 8074, Lindberg Bay, POB 301707, St Thomas, VI 00803-1707; tel. (340) 774-1629; fax (340) 774-0025; e-mail info@viport.com; internet www .viport.com; f. 1968; semi-autonomous govt agency; maintains, operates and develops marine and airport facilities; Chair. BEVERLY NICHOLSON-DOTY; Exec. Dir KENN HOBSON.

CIVIL AVIATION

There are airports on St Thomas and St Croix, and an airfield on St John. Seaplane services link the three islands. The runways at Cyril E. King Airport, St Thomas, and Henry E. Rohlsen Airport, St Croix, can accommodate intercontinental flights. In 2011 Air Canada and JetBlue began weekly non-stop flights to St Thomas and St Croix.

Tourism

The islands have a well-developed tourism infrastructure, offering excellent facilities for fishing, yachting and other aquatic sports. A National Park covers about two-thirds of St John. In 2013 there were some 2.7m. visitors to the islands, of whom 703,000 were stop-over tourists, mainly from the USA, and 2.0m. were cruise ship passengers. Visitor expenditure amounted to US $1,012.5m. in 2010.

St Croix Hotel and Tourism Association: POB 24238, Christiansted, St Croix, VI 00824; tel. (340) 773-7117; fax (340) 773-5883; e-mail info@stcroixhotelandtourism.com; internet www .stcroixhotelandtourism.com; Pres. JULIE PRINTY.

US Virgin Islands Department of Tourism: c/o Office of Film Promotion, POB 6400, St Thomas, VI 00804; tel. (340) 774-8784; fax (340) 774-4390; internet www.visitusvi.com; Commr BEVERLY NICHOLSON-DOTY.

US Virgin Islands Hotel and Tourism Association: POB 2300, Charlotte Amalie, VI 00803; tel. (340) 774-6835; fax (340) 774-4993; e-mail info@virgin-islands-hotels.com; internet usvihta .com; Chair. TRUDIE PRIOR; Pres. LISA HAMILTON.

Defence

The USA is responsible for the defence of the United States Virgin Islands.

Education

The public education system in the US Virgin Islands comprises a State Education Agency and two Local Education Agencies, serving the St Thomas/St John District and the St Croix District. Education is compulsory up to the age of 16 years. It generally comprises eight years at primary school and four years at secondary school. There are two high schools, three middle schools and 13 elementary schools in St Thomas/St John District, while the district of St Croix has two high schools, three middle schools, 10 elementary schools and an alternative and a vocational school. In 2012 there were 20,310 students enrolled at all levels of education. The University of the Virgin Islands has campuses on St Thomas and St Croix. The proposed budget for 2013/14 allocated US $38.6m. in federal funds and $162.5m. from the General Fund to the Department of Education.

URUGUAY

Geography

PHYSICAL FEATURES

The Eastern Republic of Uruguay is in south-eastern South America, on the east bank of the River Uruguay (hence described as Eastern). On the other side of the Uruguay is Argentina, which also faces the country across the great estuary of the Río de la Plata (River Plate) to the south. Originally the east-bank (Banda Oriental) territory of the Argentine possessions of Spain, it proclaimed independence in 1825 and was recognized in 1828. There remains only a dispute, unresolved but uncontested, over some river islands along the border with Brazil to the north-east (which stretches for about 1,000 km—620 miles; the Argentine border is almost 60% this length). Uruguay is the second smallest country in South America (after Suriname), with an area of 176,215 sq km (68,037 sq miles). There are 1,199 sq km of inland waters, mainly from coastal lagoons and lakes and the great reservoirs along the Río Negro.

Uruguay sits on the Plate, the estuary formed where the Uruguay and the Paraná rivers enter the Atlantic, although it also has a stretch of south-east-facing coastline running up into Brazil. The country has 660 km of seashore and 813 km of river boundaries (435 km along the Uruguay alone). It is roughly triangular in shape, extending for over 560 km north–south and 480 km east–west. Although the defining feature of Uruguay is the river from which it takes its name, the central feature is its tributary, the Negro, which traverses the middle of the country from east to west, ending in the south-west. Its basin lies between two low ranges, the Cuchilla Grande, to the south, and the Cuchilla de Haedo, striking down from the north to bisect the northern part of the country. These ranges rise from plateau uplands of rolling hills, which occupy most of the country. The coastal plains, which only account for 15% of Uruguay's territory, lie along a shore of lagoons, and sandy beaches and dunes that can extend inland for up to 8 km. Beyond this sandy coast the land is very fertile, supporting the vast pasturelands of tall, bluish-tinted prairie grass (which gives way to shorter, scrubbier grasses on the ridges). Pastureland, most of it ideal for ranching, accounts for three-quarters of the country, while woodland can only be found on about 3% (the lowest proportion in South America). In the eastern third of the country the uplands mount into a gentle arc of low mountains (Serranas) and the Cuchilla Grande forms a watershed between the narrow river valleys that drain into the Uruguay and the shorter, steeper valleys heading directly for the Atlantic. In this region is the country's highest point, Cerro Catedral (only 514 m or 1,687 ft). The highlands of the north and east are continuations of the basaltic plateau underlying the Brazilian highlands, while the plains begin the landscape of the Argentine Pampas. Once the plains, hills and coasts were rich with wildlife, but subsequent to European colonization wildlife has become scarcer, although there are deer, rheas, alligators, seals, armadillos, wild pigs and many birds.

CLIMATE

Uruguay is the only country in Latin America to lie completely outside the tropics. The maritime influence also ensures warm summers and mild winters, although the flatness of the country makes flooding likely during the heavy rains to which a country without significant mountains can be exposed. Droughts are also not uncommon. In winter (June–September) there can be cold wind currents, pamperos, blowing from the south-west, but there is seldom frost. The summer features the hot zonda wind from the north. While the climate overall is temperate, average figures can obscure the experience of actual day- and night-time temperatures, and the interior

has more of these extremes. The average temperature for the mid-summer months of January and February is 22°C (72°F), and for the coldest month, June, it is 10°C (50°F). It is hotter in the north-west, where it is also wetter. It is slightly less wet in the south. Generally, rainfall is well distributed and totals about 1,000 mm (about 40 ins) per year.

POPULATION

Unlike in most Latin American countries, most of the population of Uruguay is white, some 91% according to the 2011 census. About 8% of the population were black or of African descent in 2011, while 5% were indigenous. A large number of people are foreign-born. Most originate from Argentina, Brazil and Spain. About 46% of Uruguayans were Roman Catholic in 2006, and a further 10% belonged to other Christian churches. Just over 1% belonged to other religions, and 16% were non-believers. The official and most widely spoken language is Spanish, although there are some speakers of a Spanish–Portuguese patois, Brazilero, near the eastern borders. English and French are the most popular second languages.

The population was 3.4m., according to official projected estimates in mid-2014. Despite the importance of agriculture to the economy, the population is very urbanized—only 8% live in the countryside (most of whom are very poor). Uruguayans are well educated, and the country is one of the few territories in the western hemisphere where all education is free. Most people live near the coast and almost one-half in Greater Montevideo alone. By far the largest city, port and economic centre, Montevideo is the national capital. It is located on the south coast near the mouth of the Plate. The next largest cities are both on the River Uruguay, Salto and Paysandú. The main city on the Brazilian border is Rivera, mid-way along the frontier, in the north of Uruguay. The country is divided into 19 departments.

History

DR FRANCISCO PANIZZA

During the early 20th century Uruguay acquired a reputation as 'the Switzerland of South America'—one of the most stable, prosperous and democratic countries in the region. That image, albeit tarnished by a period of military rule in 1973–85, was at variance with the country's early history. From the 16th century to the early 19th century the Banda Oriental, the territory of the east bank of the Uruguay, changed hands between the Spanish and Portuguese several times. In 1776 it became part of the newly created Spanish Viceroyalty of Río de la Plata, but when in 1814 under the leadership of José Artigas it rebelled against the dominance of Buenos Aires it was soon conquered by the Portuguese. Uruguay's independence from both Brazil and Argentina, proclaimed in 1825 and recognized in 1828, was supported by the British Government to provide a buffer state. Both countries continued to influence domestic affairs through their support of rival military rulers (*caudillos*). The first 50 years of nationhood was a period of anarchy, as the rival bands of Blancos (Whites) and Colorados (Reds), the respective forerunners of the modern conservative and liberal political groupings, struggled for land and power.

The transition from anarchy to stability began in the 1870s, with the creation of the apparatus of a modern state. As world demand for wool and hides increased, Uruguayan landowners sought protection from the damage to livestock caused by persistently warring factions. Trading interests, strong in the capital, Montevideo, because of the port's natural advantages in the River Plate region, also sought peace. The replacement of weak civilian government by a military regime (1876–86) and the introduction of modern armaments, railways and telegraph services secured the dominance of central authority in Montevideo over regional *caudillos*. Public utilities received substantial British capital investment, and foreign trade expanded. Ironically, the modernization of the rural export economy displaced much of the labour force, many of whom were to form the armies of the Blanco rebels and the Colorado Government, which fought each other in Uruguay's last civil war, in 1904.

THE RULE AND INFLUENCE OF JOSÉ BATLLE Y ORDÓÑEZ

The Colorados' victory confirmed the authority of José Batlle y Ordóñez, twice President (1903–07 and 1911–15) and the dominant figure in Uruguayan politics until his death in 1929. Under his leadership, Uruguay became South America's first welfare state. Women were given the vote, the Church was disestablished and the death penalty was abolished. The country's social structure was transformed by immigrants from the Mediterranean countries of Europe, and its economic prosperity was founded on export growth. Batlle y Ordóñez tried to limit the power of British capital in the country by encouraging domestic investment in manufacturing and cultivating closer relations with the USA as a counter-weight.

Although Batlle y Ordóñez's radicalism drew support from the middle and working classes, it antagonized foreign and domestic investors and alarmed his own Partido Colorado (Colorado Party). His proposals for constitutional reform, which, in modified form, were embodied in the 1919 Constitution, led to the emergence of the Batllistas and other factions in the party. The Constitution, which divided the executive branch of government between a President and eight other members of a National Council of Government based on the Swiss model, remained in force until the overthrow of the Government by a coup, led by Gabriel Terra, in 1933. Terra claimed he was acting against the inadequacies of the Council, but the coup was more probably a reflection of the anxiety of landowners to maintain access to the British market for their beef exports.

Terra attempted to follow the policies of Benito Mussolini, the Fascist leader of Italy. For most of the Second World War (1939–45) Uruguay was formally neutral, although its political sympathies (and commercial advantage) lay with the Allies, led by the USA and the United Kingdom. In 1942 political and constitutional change led to the restoration to power of the Batllistas, who represented the interests of the urban economy, rather than those of rural exporters. As in the First World War (1914–18), Uruguay found easy markets for its exports, and commercial relations were strengthened with the USA. After the Second World War the United Kingdom regained its importance as an export market, although the special relationship between the two countries declined with the sale of the mainly British-built railways to the Uruguayan Government in 1948.

THE DEMISE OF TWO-PARTY DOMINANCE

The manufacturing sector expanded rapidly in the decade following the Second World War, although export earnings did not keep pace with industrial growth, and from 1956 until the early 1970s the country experienced economic stagnation. Political parties proved to be adept at staying in power by distributing rewards to their political clientele, and the traditional parties' dominance was maintained by the use of the unique Uruguayan voting system of 'lemas' (otherwise known as the 'double simultaneous vote'). The votes of all the factions were given to the party (lema) to which they belonged, and the presidency went to the candidate of the sub-lema that received the most votes within the winning party. Thus, even if a given ticket garnered more votes than any other running for election, it could not win unless its party also won.

In 1951 the collegiate executive was reintroduced (whereby the presidency was rotated annually among the members of the National Council of Government), rendering decision-making even more tortuous. In 1959, however, the Partido Nacional (National Party, the Blancos) defeated the increasingly divided Colorados, and by securing a majority in the National Council took power for the first time in the 20th century. Although the Government adopted an IMF-sponsored austerity programme, economic decline continued. Political and social frustration intensified in the 1960s, and the political left, small in electoral terms but strong in the trade union movement, became more militant.

A new Constitution in 1966 reintroduced the presidential system of government. The presidential election was won by Gen. (retd) Oscar Daniel Gestido of the Colorados, who took office in March 1967 but died in December. His successor, Vice-President Jorge Pacheco Areco, a former pugilist and newspaper editor, lacked both Gestido's charisma and his political skills. He used emergency powers to confront students and organized labour to reduce the influence of professional politicians. With political life radicalized, an urban guerrilla movement, the Movimiento de Liberación Nacional (MLN—National Liberation Movement, known popularly as the Tupamaros), turned to violence, beginning a series of kidnappings and other spectacular operations. The movement peaked in 1970–71 with the arrest and torture of its leader, Raúl Sendic, and the Government's use of 'death squads', but remained active until the armed forces took control of internal security in 1972.

MILITARY DICTATORSHIP, 1973–85

In the 1971 presidential election, Juan María Bordaberry Arocena, a Colorado candidate, was declared victorious, even though Wilson Ferreira Aldunate of the Blancos was the most popular individual candidate. Bordaberry took office in March 1972, but was little more than a figurehead President: in February 1973 he accepted the armed forces' demand for military participation in political affairs. In June both chambers of the elected Congreso (Congress) were dissolved, and in December Bordaberry appointed a new legislature, the Council of State, comprising 25 (later 35) nominated members. Left-wing groups were banned and political activity was suspended. With an estimated 6,000 political prisoners detained by 1976, the military-backed regime came to be regarded as one of the most repressive in South America. In June Bordaberry was deposed by the army because of his refusal to consider any return to constitutional rule. The newly formed Council of the Nation, comprising the Council of State and the 21-member Joint Council of the Armed Forces, chose Dr Aparicio Méndez Manfredini (a former Minister of Health) as the new President. Under military rule, economic growth resumed, but real wages declined sharply and some 10% of the population emigrated, for economic or political reasons. Close political and commercial links developed with Brazil and Argentina, but relations with the USA became strained during US President Jimmy Carter's Administration (1977–81), as a result of his criticism of the Uruguayan regime's flagrant violations of human rights.

In November 1980 the military leadership submitted a draft constitution to a referendum. Large sections of the Colorado and Blanco parties campaigned against the military's proposals, on the grounds that they institutionalized the army's role in security matters. When the proposed document was rejected, by 57.8% of those voting, the military leadership was forced to consult with leaders of the recognized parties on the constitutional future of the country.

THE RETURN TO CIVILIAN RULE

The Joint Council of the Armed Forces appointed Lt-Gen. Gregorio Alvarez Armellino to the presidency in September 1981. Restrictions on political activity were eased, and in June 1982 the Partido Colorado, the Partido Nacional and the smaller Unión Cívica (Civic Union) were allowed to operate, although left-wing parties remained banned, and censorship increased. Constitutional negotiations foundered in 1983 over attempts by the military leaders to preserve their authority in future governments, and in August the authorities suspended all political activity. Distinctions between the two main parties, the liberal Colorados and the more conservative Blancos, gradually eroded, and pro- and anti-military tendencies developed within each of them. Two national days of protest were organized by the opposition in November, two months after the Plenario Intersindical de Trabajadores—Convención Nacional de Trabajadores (PIT—CNT, Intersyndical Plenary of Workers—National Convention of Workers), the country's main trade union federation, had organized the first industrial action in the country for 10 years. The PIT—CNT was banned in January 1984, following a 24-hour strike protesting against continued political repression and a 28% increase in prices.

Negotiations between the Government and the Partido Colorado, the still-proscribed Frente Amplio (FA, Broad Front, a left-wing coalition) and the Unión Cívica resumed in July 1984. The Partido Nacional refused to participate while its leader, Ferreira Aldunate, was detained (he had been arrested in June, on returning from an 11-year exile). In August the Government withdrew its suspension of political activity and began to release some political prisoners, but Ferreira Aldunate and Gen. Líber Seregni Mosquera, the FA leader, were banned from political activity. In November the presidential election was won by Dr Julio María Sanguinetti Cairolo of the Colorado's Unidad y Reforma (Unity and Reform) faction. In the legislative elections, however, the Partido Colorado did not gain an absolute majority in either congressional chamber. In preparation for the full restoration of civilian rule, most remaining political prisoners, including Ferreira Aldunate, were released in November, and the Tupamaro leader, Raúl Sendic, was freed in March 1985. In December the MLN formally agreed to become a political party and voted to join the FA.

THE AMNESTY LAW

President Sanguinetti was inaugurated in March 1985, and formed a Council of Ministers including two members of the Partido Nacional and one of the Unión Cívica. The Partido Comunista (Communist Party) and other previously outlawed organizations were legalized, and remaining restrictions on press freedom were lifted.

The most controversial issue for the Sanguinetti administration was the introduction in August 1986 of a draft amnesty law, protecting all members of the security forces from prosecution for alleged violations of human rights during the period of military rule. After considerable debate, a revised version of the original proposals was approved by both congressional chambers in December, despite violent outbursts in the streets of Montevideo and within the Cámara de Representantes (Chamber of Representatives) itself. The Ley de Caducidad de la Pretensión Punitiva del Estado (Law of Expiry of the Punitive Powers of the State) ended ongoing military trials and made President Sanguinetti responsible for any further investigations into the whereabouts of the 'disappeared'. By this time it was known that under military rule more than 170 Uruguayan citizens had been seized and subsequently murdered by the military; 33 had 'disappeared' within Uruguay, 132 in Argentina and the remainder in Paraguay and Chile. Public opposition to the legislation increased, and during 1988 a sufficient number of signatures (a minimum of 25% of the electorate) was gathered to force a referendum, which was held in April 1989. For the first time in a national referendum, voting was declared compulsory, and the law was confirmed by a vote of 57% in favour.

ECONOMIC LIBERALIZATION

With the resolution of the amnesty question, economic policy again became the Government's chief concern. Trade unions criticized the Government for adhering to the dictates of international financial agencies at the expense of the domestic workforce, and organized general strikes in late 1987 and mid-1988. The Government's economic performance cost the Colorados the elections, held in November 1989 (the first fully free elections since 1971), even though there was little material difference between the economic manifestos of the two leading presidential candidates. Luis Alberto Lacalle de Herrera of the Blancos won 37% of the votes cast, compared with 30% for Jorge Batlle Ibáñez of the Colorados; Líber Seregni of the FA secured 21% of the votes.

The Partido Nacional could form only a minority Government, and Lacalle reached a power-sharing agreement with the Colorados, although disagreement over economic policy, particularly a proposed privatization programme, led to divisions within the coalition. Lacking reliable political support, Lacalle's Government became more sympathetic to the armed forces: legislation extending military powers was prepared, and the Government appeared reluctant to pursue investigations into past violent incidents implicating members of the military.

ELECTORAL REFORM

The presidential and legislative elections of November 1994 marked an end to traditional two-party politics. The vote was almost evenly split between the Partido Colorado, the Partido Nacional and a predominantly left-wing electoral alliance, the Encuentro Progresista (EP—Progressive Congress)—FA. Sanguinetti, the leading Colorado presidential candidate, was re-elected President, and was obliged to form a coalition administration with the Partido Nacional, leaving the EP—FA as the main opposition force. The principal member of this alliance, the FA, reportedly gave an undertaking to co-operate with the new administration in return for government consideration of its views when determining social policy.

The new Government immediately tackled the existing electoral system that had been criticized both for promoting factionalism and for yielding an unclear result. Under the proposed reform, each party would present a single candidate and, in the event of no candidate securing an absolute majority, a second round of voting would take place. FA members claimed that the change was a deliberate attempt to deny any left-wing group the chance to win the presidency. The amendment was approved by Congress, and narrowly (by 50.5%) in a plebiscite in late 1996.

In March 1995 President Sanguinetti commenced restructuring the social-security system, his fifth attempt at such a reform (see also Economy). The fiscal burden of the pension system was growing to such an extent that on this occasion the proposed reform received support from the two larger parties, and within a year of its introduction nearly one-third of the workforce had subscribed.

In May 1996 the Colorados and the Blancos strengthened their 'governability pact'. The attempt to establish a common political agenda was the first such occurrence in 160 years and underlined the shift away from the traditional two-party rivalry. However, divisions began to emerge within the FA, much of which was prompted by in-fighting concerning privatization. In April 1997 FA senator Felipe Michelini, whose father was among the 'disappeared', demanded an investigation into allegations that 32 of the victims of the dictatorship had been interred in the grounds of military property and covertly removed from the burial sites in the mid-1980s. A judicial ruling in the same month promised to facilitate such an inquiry, and in May 20,000 people attended a rally in Montevideo to demand that the Government and the armed forces acquiesce. However, in June a court of appeal overturned the ruling on the grounds that it contravened the Ley de Caducidad. The human rights issue continued to be prominent. In May 1998 the country's principal religious and human rights groups published a National Reconciliation Declaration, making explicit their opposition to the amnesty law. In July a former intelligence chief, Rear-Adm. (retd) Eladio Moll, caused a diplomatic crisis when he alleged that US military officers had instructed the Uruguayan security forces on the detention and torture of Tupamaro suspects. He even claimed that Uruguayan officers had resisted US demands that the suspects be killed after interrogation.

BATLLE IBÁÑEZ VERSUS TABARÉ VÁZQUEZ

In accordance with the electoral reforms, a presidential primary election was held in April 1999 at which the Partido Colorado nomination was won by Jorge Batlle Ibáñez and the EP—FA leader, Tabaré Vázquez, was selected as the coalition's candidate. The Partido Nacional's campaign for the primary election was seriously divisive. During the campaign the Blanco candidate, former President Lacalle, had been accused of corruption, and in the months preceding the poll it became clear that the presidential election would be, in effect, a contest between Batlle and Vázquez. The Colorados and Blancos attempted to portray Vázquez (an eminent oncologist) as a Marxist firebrand, claiming that he would destroy the country's economy. His main manifesto promises were government-led job creation, and the rather less popular introduction of an income-tax system.

In presidential and legislative elections held in October 1999 the EP—FA won the largest number of seats in both the Chamber of Representatives and the Cámara de Senadores (Chamber of Senators), followed by the Partido Colorado. In the presidential ballot, Vázquez won 38.5% of the vote, ahead of Batlle (31.3%) and Lacalle (21.3%). Under the new electoral law a second round of voting was required, and this took place in November. Most of the Blanco support was transferred to the Colorado candidate, and Batlle won with 51.6% of the votes cast.

Batlle's inauguration speech in March 2000 included undertakings to reduce public spending, address the farming crisis, investigate the fate of the 'disappeared' and institutionalize the Southern Common Market (Mercado Común del Sur—MERCOSUR, see Economy). His new cabinet comprised eight Colorados and five Blancos. In April he dismissed Gen. Manuel Fernández, a senior army official who had sought to justify the military repression of the 1970s and a six-member Commission for Peace was formed to investigate 'disappearances' during the military dictatorship. In May 2001 the bodies of two Uruguayan exiles were found in Argentine soil. The Commission released its first report in October 2002, detailing instances of collusion between Argentine and Uruguayan armed forces. It was reported that many of Uruguay's 'disappeared' had been killed in Argentina by members of that country's armed forces.

ECONOMIC CRISIS

The new Government inherited a prolonged economic crisis, which continued to provoke unrest over public spending reductions and privatization proposals. In January 2002 the problems escalated with the impact of the Argentine financial crisis. In May Argentine withdrawals from deposits held in Uruguay increased sharply, prompting a 'run' on Uruguayan banks by Uruguayan nationals, and the Government introduced highly unpopular austerity measures. The competence of the Government inevitably became the dominant issue for the left-wing opposition and the trade unions. In July the Minister of Economy and Finance, Alberto Bensión, resigned and the Government temporarily closed the banks (see Economy), amid fears that the country might be obliged to default on the national debt. However, a bridging loan from the US Government, followed by assistance from the IMF averted further drastic measures.

The economic crisis deepened the rift between the two governing parties. The Blancos became increasingly critical of government policy, objecting to what they termed the 'high social cost' of financing the national debt. All five Blanco ministers resigned from the Council of Ministers in November. In early 2003 the opposition was more conciliatory and did not obstruct the Government's negotiations with the IMF and its efforts to restructure debt payments.

The advent of presidential and legislative elections in October 2004 brought the Batlle administration under further pressure, and broad support for the IMF programme began to wane. In December 2003, following a campaign by the FA, a referendum had been held regarding controversial legislation enacted in 2001 allowing private sector involvement in the petroleum, cement and alcohol monopoly, the Administración Nacional de Combustibles, Alcohol y Portland (ANCAP); 62% voted to repeal the law.

Traditionally, Uruguay had enjoyed relative prosperity, more equal distribution of income, a lower rate of poverty, and well-funded education, social security and health systems compared with other South American countries. It also had a reputation for more liberal legislation on social issues, and Batlle advocated a measured decriminalization of certain illegal drugs. An opinion poll conducted in 2001 indicated that support for the principle of democratic governance ran at one of the highest levels on the continent, despite criticism of the incumbent Government. By 2002, however, an increasing number of citizens were unable to meet the cost of health insurance and, in common with other countries in the region, there was a marked rise in street violence and organized crime. Although Uruguay retained the lowest incidence of poverty in Latin America, living standards were in decline even before the 2002 crisis. The poverty index rose from 9.4% in 1999 to 11.4% in 2001, while the extreme poverty index increased from 1.8% to 2.4% in that year and emigration accelerated markedly.

THE 2004 ELECTIONS

In the presidential primary election in mid-2004, the EP—FA joined forces with another party, Nuevo Espacio, and adopted the name EP—FA—Nueva Mayoría (NM), and Vázquez was confirmed as its candidate. In the Blanco party, Jorge Larrañaga secured the party's nomination, while the Colorado party chose former interior minister Guillermo Stirling as its candidate.

Vázquez was elected to the presidency in the first round of voting on 31 October 2004, narrowly securing an absolute majority, with 50.7% of the votes cast. His nearest rival, Larrañaga, won 34.1% of the vote, while Stirling received 10.3%, the worst ever result for the Partido Colorado. Vázquez's victory brought an end to more than 170 years of rule by the Blancos and Colorados. The left-wing coalition was also successful in concurrent legislative elections, winning an absolute majority in both chambers.

Also on 31 October 2004 a constitutional reform guaranteeing that the supply of water and sanitation services would remain under state control was approved by 64.5% of voters in a referendum. The proposal was supported by the leaders of the winning coalition and the Partido Nacional, but opposed by the Colorados.

THE VÁZQUEZ PRESIDENCY, 2005–10

Vázquez took office in March 2005 as the country's first left-wing President. His new Council of Ministers largely comprised members of the various factions of the EP—FA—NM, although two independents received posts, including Jorge

Lepra, a former executive of a US energy company, who became Minister of Industry, Energy and Mining. Reforming ANCAP, the privatization of which the EP—FA—NM had opposed, was expected to be a priority for Lepra.

Investigations into the fate of those who 'disappeared' during the military dictatorship began shortly after Vázquez's inauguration, and in August 2005 the President received a report from the heads of Uruguay's armed forces admitting the kidnap, torture and murder of political detainees. In November information from the report led to the exhumation of the bodies of two dissidents murdered by members of the air force, and in the following month 35 unidentified corpses were exhumed from a cemetery near the border with Brazil. Also in November the Government presented draft legislation to Congress, 'interpreting' the Ley de Caducidad (see above). The bill would enable the judiciary to commence investigating a case until it became apparent whether it was covered by the amnesty, and allow for the trial of former senior officers for crimes committed before and after the dictatorship ('disappearances' could be considered as crimes continuing beyond 1985). In order to reduce tensions between the Government and the armed forces, Vázquez made it clear that there were no plans to repeal the Ley de Caducidad.

In March 2005 Vázquez announced the introduction of the Plan de Atención Nacional de Emergencia Social, a two-year social welfare programme aimed at reducing poverty, in which the Government was expected to invest some US $200m. over two years. However, the President was criticized by the Movimiento de Participación Popular (MPP, a component of the EP—FA—NM) for commitments made to the IMF on the fiscal balance and external debt, who claimed that financial stability was being prioritized at the expense of the social welfare programme in order to satisfy the Fund.

Despite the damage done to the economy in 2005–06 by Argentine protests against plans to construct two pulp mills near Fray Bentos (see Economy), good rates of growth were achieved thereafter, and in 2007 per head income returned to pre-crisis levels. In November the Chamber of Senators adopted a bill on reproductive rights that would decriminalize abortions carried out within the first 12 weeks of pregnancy, in certain circumstances. Although the bill was subsequently approved by the Chamber of Representatives, it was vetoed by President Vázquez on ethical grounds. His action was strongly criticized by his party, the Partido Socialista del Uruguay, prompting his resignation from the party shortly afterwards. A law allowing same-sex couples living together to formalize their union came into effect on 1 January 2008; the first ceremony under the new law, unprecedented in Latin America, took place in April.

Preparations for the presidential and legislative elections began in early 2009, ahead of the primary elections to determine the candidates who would contest the presidency in October. In late 2008 the ruling coalition nominated José Mujica (an outspoken senator and erstwhile Tupamaro) of the MPP as its official candidate in the forthcoming presidential elections, although Vázquez openly favoured the more orthodox Danilo Astori, former Minister of Economy and Finance, as his successor. The selection procedure proved divisive within the FA. Meanwhile, Lacalle reversed the outcome of the 2004 primary election by defeating Larrañaga to secure the nomination of the Partido Nacional, and Pedro Bordaberry Herrán won the support of the Partido Colorado. The main candidates in the presidential election ran largely negative campaigns with few specific policy proposals. Mujica sought to reassure his doubters by stressing that his government would offer significant continuity with that of President Vázquez and underlining that Astori would be in charge of economic policy. Lacalle, the main opposition candidate, failed to impress the electorate during a lacklustre and error-prone campaign in which he focused on criticizing Mujica's character. Lacalle also emphasized that Mujica's political sympathies lay further to the left than those of President Vázquez. In the first round of the presidential election on 25 October 2009, Mujica narrowly failed to win an overall majority, securing 48.0% of the votes compared with the 29.1% won by Lacalle. Nevertheless, Mujica won the consequent run-off election in November with 52.4% of the votes. In the legislative elections, held

concurrently with the first round of the presidential ballot, the FA secured a narrow but vital majority in both chambers of Congress. A referendum to consider whether to repeal the Ley de Caducidad was also held simultaneously with the national elections, but failed to achieve the required majority of over 50%; an additional plebiscite on whether to allow Uruguayan emigrants to vote in elections from 2014 was also unsuccessful (some 600,000 Uruguayans were estimated to live abroad, of whom the majority were believed to be FA supporters).

THE MUJICA PRESIDENCY, 2010–

José Mujica was sworn in as President on 1 March 2010. As promised in the electoral campaign, Mujica appointed Fernando Lorenzo, a close ally of Vice-President Astori, as Minister of Economy and Finance. Mujica's conciliatory inaugural speech set the tone for the first 100 days of his administration. The new President reaffirmed the continuity of his administration with that of President Vázquez, stressing that education was to be his Government's main priority, with immediate attention also to be given to the reform of the state and an emergency social housing programme. In February, before taking office, Mujica met domestic and Argentine entrepreneurs to promote further investment in the country and to reiterate that there would be no tax increases or unexpected changes to the business environment under his administration. While Uruguay's crime rate remains among the lowest in Latin America, violent crime has been rising in recent years and has become one of the main concerns of the population. In response to a succession of particularly shocking crime headlines, the Government announced a package of security initiatives in June 2012. Among the proposals was the legalization of the production and sale of marijuana. Mujica argued that traditional approaches to combating the trafficking of the drug had failed, leading to a rise in drug-related violence, and that marijuana inflicted less harm on the country than did the black market. A law legalizing the cultivation, distribution and sale of marijuana, with effect from April 2014, was approved by the Chamber of Senators in December 2013, making Uruguay the first country in the world to legalize the production, sale and consumption of the drug. The legalization of marijuana was one of a number of liberal social initiatives promoted by the FA Government. In October 2012 the Chamber of Senators narrowly approved legislation legalizing abortion in the first 12 weeks of pregnancy, and in April 2013 it voted to legalize gay marriage, making Uruguay the third country in the Americas to do so. The abortion law was particularly divisive, as anti-abortion campaigners sought to promote a referendum to repeal the law, although they failed to garner sufficient votes in a ballot to force the referendum.

One of the main bones of contention within the governing party has been the continuation of attempts to repeal the Ley de Caducidad. In July 2011 a presidential decree sanctioned the investigation and prosecution of an estimated 80 cases of human rights violations committed between 1973 and 1985. The decree invalidated the clauses of the 1986 Ley de Caducidad (which had been approved after Uruguay returned to democratic rule) that gave the Executive the final say over which cases of human rights violations could be investigated. In most instances in the past, Presidents had used this power to close cases, effectively allowing individuals responsible for crimes to evade justice. In October 2011 Congress approved a law repealing a statute of limitations that would have prevented victims from filing criminal complaints as of 1 November 2011. However, in February 2013 Uruguay's Supreme Court ruled that, being retroactive, much of the 2011 law was itself unconstitutional. The Court's decision created tensions with the Government and with the ruling FA, some members of which demanded the impeachment of the Court's judges. The legal verdict was also condemned by international human rights organizations and by the Inter-American Court of Human Rights and the UN's High Commissioner for Human Rights. In June some 300 demonstrators stormed the Court's building in Montevideo in protest at the decision.

Approaching the last year of its five-year mandate the Government was faced with a mixed picture. While the economy continued to show relatively strong growth, President Mujica was coming under increasing criticism from the opposition for the failure of his administration to reform the ailing education system, improve public security and reform the bloated and inefficient state system. The proximity of elections scheduled for October 2014 was likely to make it difficult for the Government to enact further substantive reforms. The Government was also afflicted by internal divisions. In spite of a substantial increase in funding during the administration of President Vázquez and in the first two years of Mujica's Government, there was a general consensus that there had been no significant improvement in educational standards. While Uruguay has historically had one of the best-educated populations in Latin America, international indicators reveal that the country is at risk of falling behind other developing nations in educational standards. According to the Organisation for Economic Co-operation and Development (OECD)'s Programme for International Student Assessment (PISA) 2012 survey, Uruguay's cumulative expenditure by educational institutions per student aged between six and 15 years was one of the lowest among PISA-participating countries. Uruguay's 15-year-old students' mean score in maths placed them 54th out of 64 participating countries and their mean score in problem-solving performance ranked Uruguay 40th out of 42 participating countries.

In December 2013 Minister of Economy and Finance Lorenzo resigned amid allegations that he had been involved in the irregular sale of seven aircraft belonging to the dissolved national flag carrier PLUNA (Primeras Líneas Uruguayas de Navegación Aérea), in October 2012. In April 2014 Lorenzo, together with the President of the state bank Banco de la República Oriental del Uruguay (BROU), Fernando Calloia, was criminally charged with abuse of power in connection with the illegal granting of a loan guarantee by the BROU to a newly established Spanish airline, Cosmo Líneas Aéreas, for the purchase of the aircraft. Lorenzo was replaced as Minister of Economy and Finance by Mario Esteban Bergara Duque, hitherto President of Banco Central del Uruguay.

Presidential candidates for the October 2014 election were chosen in open primary elections in June. As expected, former President Vázquez secured the nomination for the ruling FA. Luis Lacalle Pou unexpectedly beat the frontrunner Jorge Larrañaga to secure the nomination of the Partido Nacional (PN, also known as the Blancos). Lacalle Pou, the son of former President Luis Alberto Lacalle, and, at 40, the youngest of the presidential candidates, presented himself as a new face in Uruguayan politics and was running on a campaign of 'positive politics'. Senator Pedro Bordaberry, the son of former dictator Juan María Bordaberry, was elected as the candidate of the Partido Colorado; his main campaign proposal was the lowering of the age of criminal responsibility from 18 to 16 years. Opinion polls at mid-2014 indicated that Vázquez was the frontrunner but suggested that the FA was unlikely to retain its parliamentary majority.

FOREIGN RELATIONS

The administration of President Vázquez emphasized the importance of strengthening relations with other Latin American countries, particularly within MERCOSUR. On the day after his inauguration, Vázquez signed agreements on trade and the supply of energy with his Venezuelan counterpart, President Hugo Chávez, and an accord on human rights with Argentina's President Néstor Carlos Kirchner, which was aimed at facilitating the exchange of information on abuses stemming from both countries' military dictatorships. Vázquez's first foreign visit was to Brazil in April 2005, when he signed six agreements on co-operation with Brazilian President Luiz Inácio Lula da Silva. In one of his first official acts, in March, Vázquez had restored full diplomatic ties with Cuba (which had been severed in 2002).

President Vázquez, however, became increasingly disenchanted with MERCOSUR, which he regarded as being dominated by the interests of Brazil and Argentina, and sought to strengthen relations with the USA to counterbalance the power of Uruguay's largest neighbours. A bilateral investment treaty with the USA, first signed by outgoing President Batlle in December 2004, was renegotiated by the Vázquez administration and approved in December 2005, despite criticism from members of the ruling FA. In May 2006 Vázquez visited the USA, and, following a meeting with President George W. Bush, confirmed his desire to forge closer bilateral trade relations. President Bush's visit to Montevideo in March 2007 attracted protests in Brazil, and some 5,000 protesters gathered in Uruguay for the visit, while Venezuelan President Chávez, conducting his alternative tour of the region, addressed 40,000 anti-Bush protesters in Argentina, across the River Plate. Bush's visit, however, appeared to seal the surprisingly cordial relations between the right-wing US President and his left-wing Uruguayan counterpart.

President Mujica renewed the Vázquez administration's original priority to strengthen MERCOSUR and other Latin American integration initiatives. During the first months of his presidency he visited Chile, Bolivia and Venezuela, and aligned the country closely to Brazil's regional leadership. However, his Government also intended to seek closer economic ties with the USA and other economies outside the region. In May 2014 Mujica made a six-day official visit to the USA, during which he met with US President Barack Obama, Vice-President John Kerry and Secretary of Agriculture Thomas Vilsack, and addressed the World Bank and a number of think tanks. The Obama Administration stated that the visit highlighted the close bilateral partnership and the US Government's strong support for the Mujica administration's leadership on human rights, social inclusion and global peace and security. The visit followed the Uruguayan Government's announcement that it had agreed to a US government request to host a number of prisoners currently detained at the US naval base at Guantánamo Bay.

The administration of President Mujica made a concerted effort to increase trade and economic relations with Asia. As part of a tour of South American nations, the Premier of the People's Republic of China, Wen Jiabao, visited Uruguay in June 2012, during which the two sides signed a number of co-operation agreements in the fields of economy, technology and agriculture. Wen's visit, the first by a Chinese Premier, underlined the growing economic importance of Uruguay's trade with China, which in 2012 became Uruguay's second largest trading partner after Brazil. In May 2013 Mujica reciprocated with a visit to China, during which he discussed China's investment in a deep water port on the Atlantic coast and in the recovery of the rail cargo network. Mujica also sought to interest China in the dredging of one of the two River Plate navigation channels that run parallel to the Uruguayan coast and in investing in alternative energy resources.

Relations with Argentina continue to be strained. Although bilateral relations improved during the first months of the Mujica administration, Argentina's protectionist measures against Uruguayan exports and an ongoing dispute over the joint management of the River Plate navigation channels revived political tensions between the two countries. Bilateral relations further deteriorated in June 2014 when the Uruguayan Government announced that it had authorized a pulp mill built on the banks of the River Uruguay, which acts as a natural border between the two countries, to increase production. The pulp mill, owned by the Finnish firm UPM-Kymmene Corporation, has been the subject of a bitter conflict between the two countries for almost a decade. Argentina has alleged that the mill pollutes the river waters and that Uruguay's decision, in 2003, to allow its construction was in violation of the bilateral Statute of the River Uruguay, which regulates the joint management of the river. In 2010 the International Court of Justice (ICJ) had ruled that Uruguay had violated the treaty but that there was no evidence that the mill contaminated the river, as alleged by Argentina. Following the decision of the Mujica administration to authorize the increase in production, Argentina's Minister of Foreign Affairs, International Trade and Worship Héctor Marcos Timerman, stated that his country was in the process of reassessing 'all policies referred to bilateral relations with Uruguay' and announced that Argentina would again be referring the dispute to the ICJ.

Economy

DR FRANCISCO PANIZZA

Uruguay is a relatively small country, with an area of 176,215 sq km (68,037 sq miles) and an estimated population of 3.40m. at mid-2014. Average annual population growth of 0.1% in 2000–10 was the lowest in Latin America. The proportion of people resident in urban areas in 2013 was 92% of the total, the highest in the region, with 39.2% of the population living in the capital, Montevideo. In 2013 Uruguay had one of the highest gross domestic products (GDP) per caput in Latin America, estimated at US $16,600 measured on an international purchasing-power parity basis. Owing principally to the 2001–02 economic crisis in Argentina, poverty grew dramatically in 2002–04, affecting almost 40% of the population in 2003, but declined to 11.5% by 2013, according to the Instituto Nacional de Estadística (INE—National Institute of Statistics). In a region characterized by very high levels of inequality, Uruguay was in 2013 the most equal society in Latin America, according to the Economic Commission for Latin America and the Caribbean (ECLAC).

Uruguay is an interesting test case, a country that developed a modern economy with a strong social security system on an almost exclusively agricultural base. From the late 19th century Uruguay developed as an agricultural export economy by selling wool, beef and hides, mainly to European countries. With favourable natural conditions and a low population density, export values per head were high, and under the leadership of José Batlle y Ordóñez Uruguay was transformed into a stable democratic welfare state. Government policy encouraged domestic manufacturing, and protection was intensified in the 1930s and after the Second World War. However, the rate of growth of exports was low, and the small size of the domestic market meant that the strategy of industrialization by import substitution was exhausted by the mid-1950s. A period of economic stagnation followed and continued into the early 1970s, when the prevailing social unrest led to the army assuming power (see History). The economic policies of the military regime after 1973, based on a reduction of the public sector and incentives to non-traditional exports, helped to stimulate GDP growth. However, attempts to control inflation and the general effects of the world recession halted economic expansion.

Although the economy was always closely linked to the economies of neighbouring countries, the establishment in 1995 of the Southern Common Market (Mercado Común del Sur—MERCOSUR, or, in Portuguese, Mercado Comum do Sul—MERCOSUL) accentuated the influence of markets in Brazil and Argentina. GDP growth resumed in the 1990s, but the economy then entered a decline towards the end of the decade, owing to a devaluation of the Brazilian currency, the recession in Argentina and persistently low prices for agricultural exports. In 2001 production was drastically affected by an outbreak of foot-and-mouth disease. In 2002 the country experienced a major economic crisis caused by Argentina's debt default. In 2002–03 the economy contracted by 11.2%, unemployment reached almost 20% and the gross public sector debt-to-GDP ratio increased to over 100%. External debt restructuring and international financial assistance led to a swift recovery, with growth of 2.4% in 2003. Effective macroeconomic policies, a favourable environment for investment, rising real wages and the international boom in agricultural prices contributed to average annual growth in GDP per head of about 6% in 2006–11.

While not immune to the impact of the 2008–09 global financial crisis, the Uruguayan economy proved to be remarkably resilient, posting overall GDP growth of 2.9% in 2009, 8.9% in 2010 and 5.7% in 2011. Growth slowed to a still-respectable 3.9% in 2012—mainly reflecting the sharp fall in economic growth in Brazil and Argentina, on which the Uruguayan economy is heavily dependent for exports, investment and tourism—and jumped to 4.4% in 2013. In 2014 economic growth was expected to slow to around 3%, mainly owing to the further deterioration of the Argentinean economy and poor economic prospects in Brazil.

AGRICULTURE

Agriculture has traditionally formed the basis of the Uruguayan economy, and still accounts (directly or indirectly) for almost all commodity export earnings. Some 11% of the working population were employed in the sector in 2011, compared with 20% in 1965. The sector performed strongly in the 2000s, largely reflecting substantial investment in infrastructure and new technology. Agricultural GDP increased at an average annual rate of 1.2% in 2005–12, according to the World Bank. In 2013 agriculture (including forestry) accounted for 9.1% of GDP. The strong recovery in international agricultural prices since 2003 has led to a marked increase in linked investment and record prices for land. Uruguay's two main export products have historically been meat (especially beef) and wool. During the 2000s, however, external demand led to an expansion in arable crops and a consequent decline in cattle- and sheep-raising, and there was also a significant increase in the production of dairy and dairy products and of timber and timber products. In 2013 some 70.8% of the national territory was devoted to the rearing of sheep and cattle (down from 85% in 2005), with an estimated 12.7% used for arable land (compared with 7.8% in 2005) and 7.8% for forestry, according to official data. In the same year cattle and sheep production accounted for 47.4% of agricultural GDP, while arable crops accounted for 46.3% and forestry for 6.3%.

Meat is an important item of the national diet, with beef consumption rising from 48 kg per head in 2004 to 60 kg per head in 2012. In 2012 the cattle herd was estimated at 12.0m. head, and cattle meat production totalled 500,000 metric tons, according to unofficial FAO figures. Beef exports have risen steadily since 2003, prompted by high prices and international demand. The value of beef exports reached an estimated US $1,403.8m. in 2012. The main market for Uruguayan beef in that year was Russia, followed by the European Union (EU). The dairy sector, centred in the south-western and southern departments of the country, was also a significant source of export revenues. In 2012 Uruguay produced a record 2,177m. litres of fresh milk. Sheep stocks declined from 9.7m. head in 2005 to 7.3m. head in 2012. Exports of sheep's meat provided revenue of $74m. in 2012. The principal purchasers were the EU and Brazil. Revenue from wool exports in 2012 totalled $228,900m. The principal market was the People's Republic of China.

After growing by 4.2% in 2011, gross agricultural production declined by 1.3% in 2012, owing to adverse economic conditions. However, the sector rebounded strongly in the first quarter of 2013 with a 5.7% increase in output, according to the Banco Central del Uruguay (BCU), reflecting a record soybean harvest and strong international prices, together with good climatic conditions. Over the past decade Uruguay has experienced a huge expansion in the production of arable crops. Land under cultivation has grown from 600,000 ha in 2005/06 to just under 1.8m. ha in 2012/13. Traditionally, beef has been the country's main export product; however, it now accounts for just 16.5% of total exports, compared with 30% for cereal exports, while dairy products account for 9%. The main crops by output in 2012/13 were soybeans, wheat, rice, barley, maize, sugar cane and potatoes, with cereal production based in the west of the country and rice in the east. Citrus fruit is grown mainly in the department of Salto, while other fruits in production include grapes, apples, pears, peaches and nectarines. In 2012 some 140,000 metric tons of oranges and 130,000 tons of grapes were produced. Flowers and vines are cultivated around Montevideo and Canelones to the north. The wine industry in Uruguay has developed considerably in recent years; in 2012 an estimated 67.0 metric tons of wine were produced. Brazil is the principal market for Uruguayan wine, followed by Russia and the EU.

Successive governments have attempted to increase timber production, with a view to making forestry one of Uruguay's main economic sectors. In 2005 plans to construct a pulp mill near Fray Bentos on the banks of the River Uruguay, which forms the boundary between Argentina and Uruguay, proved controversial. The construction of the plant was opposed by the Argentine Government, which claimed that it would contaminate the river and was therefore contrary to the binational Statute of the River Uruguay. These allegations were refuted by the Uruguayan authorities, but popular protests continued until the International Court of Justice ruled in 2010 that the plant, which had commenced production in 2007, was not polluting the river waters. A second plant constructed on the banks of the River Plate, commenced production in 2014. At an estimated cost of around US $2,000m., the plant, co-owned by the Chilean firm Celulosa Arauco y Constitución and the Swedish-Finnish firm Stora Enso, constituted the single largest foreign direct investment (FDI) in Uruguay. When fully operational the plant was expected to produce around 1.3m. metric tons of cellulose per year. Exports of cellulose, timber and related products increased from $206m. in 2005 to $535m. in 2012. Timber production rose from 3.0m. cu m in 2001 to 11.9m. cu m in 2010, falling slightly to 10.2m. cu m in 2012.

Although small in scale, the fishing industry grew rapidly from the late 1970s before stabilizing in the mid-2000s. However, with the opening of the South Atlantic to factory fishing, stocks began to decline. According to FAO estimates, the total catch fell from 81,500 metric tons in 2009 to 76,300 tons in 2012. Concern over dwindling fishery reserves prompted attempts at diversification, including the production of beluga caviar. Approximately 4 tons of caviar are produced per year.

MINING AND MANUFACTURING

Manufacturing output accounted for 12.2% of GDP in 2013. The most important branches of manufacturing are food products (mainly processed meat for export and dairy products), beverages and tobacco, cellulose and timber products, chemicals, metal products, machinery and equipment, textiles, clothing and leather products. By 2000 the number of people working in industry was only one-half the level of 1988, reflecting both greater productivity (with a consequent loss of jobs) and a major expansion of the service sector. Manufacturing GDP increased at an average annual rate of 3.3% between 2005 and 2013, according to the World Bank; however, output has stagnated since, with a 0.7% increase in 2012 and a 0.4% decline in 2013, according to the BCU. Industrial production was adversely affected by the high value of the peso, high domestic costs and import restrictions, as well as lower prices of goods from Argentina and subdued growth in Brazil. In recent years the textile industry has also been badly affected by competition from China and other Asian manufacturers, and the sector has become dependent on government subsidies. Since the opening in 2007 of a paper mill on the River Uruguay, cellulose and other timber products have become an important part of the country's industrial base. Almost all basic resources have to be imported. Apart from quarrying for marble, sand, clay, gravel and other construction materials, raw materials for ceramics and glass manufacture, and the limited extraction of semi-precious stones, there is little mining activity. The GDP of the mining sector decreased 26.0% in 2013. Mining and quarrying (and fishing) accounted for only 0.6% of GDP in 2013, and employed just 0.2% of the economically active population in 2011 (excluding fishing). The British-based company Minera Aratirí, part of the multinational Zamin Ferrous group, has expressed interest in developing a major iron ore open pit mining project in the region of Valentines, approximately 250 km from Montevideo. According to company figures, annual production could be around 18m. metric tons of iron ore and could generate an annual return of US $400m. for Uruguay, with the creation of 1,500 direct jobs. However, the proposed project is strongly opposed by environmental organizations and some local residents. Although the Senate has approved the project, President José Mujica has requested evidence of Zamin's ability to finance the project first. In 2014 the company was in the process of producing a revised environmental impact assessment study, following objections to the original study by Uruguay's National Environment Department. Negotiations between the Government and Zamin continued in 2014 and, although the Government has expressed

optimism about reaching an agreement, work on the ground was not expected to start before 2015 at the earliest.

ENERGY

The absence of any commercially viable deposits of petroleum, natural gas or coal makes Uruguay heavily dependent on imports of crude petroleum, which accounts for some two-thirds of its energy requirements. In 2009 Uruguay began to explore the possibilities of searching for oil and gas in its territorial waters by launching its first round of licensing for the exploration and exploitation of hydrocarbons in offshore areas. It subsequently awarded two concessions to a consortium comprising Yacimientos Petrolíferos Fiscales (YPF, Argentina), Petrobras (Brazil) and Galp Energia (Portugal). A second round of licensing was launched in 2011. In 2013 oil imports amounted to 13,880,000 barrels. The figure was 4% lower than in 2012 but above the 10-year average, according to data from the Ministry of Industry, Energy and Mining. Uruguay imported 59m. cu m of natural gas in 2013, which was around one-half the 2007 peak. A natural gas pipeline between Uruguay and Argentina, the Gasoducto Cruz del Sur (GCDS), with a capacity of 180m. cu ft per day, was completed in 2002, as part of a greater scheme to link the gas network of the MERCOSUR countries. The project held a concession for a possible extension of the GCDS to Porto Alegre, Brazil. However, Argentina's declining gas production meant that exports to Uruguay and utilization of the pipeline stopped. In May 2013 Uruguay awarded the French company GDF Suez a contract to build a liquefied natural gas (LNG) regasification plant, at an estimated cost of US $1,120m. Uruguay was to pay GDF Suez $14m. per month during the 20-year concession. The terminal was to have a storage capacity of 267m. cu m. In order to cover the costs of the investment, Uruguay was planning to increase domestic gas consumption by promoting the use of LNG to power vehicles, and to export part of the output to Argentina.

In an attempt to reduce the dependence on imported petroleum, successive governments have promoted the use of hydroelectricity, which accounted for 60% of total electricity production in 2013. Exploitation of hydroelectric resources began in the 1930s, but there was substantial development in the 1970s, as a result of major investments in the 1,800-MW Salto Grande project with Argentina, and in the 300-MW Palmar installation. The output from these two plants and two others on the River Negro, which runs through the middle of the country, made Uruguay a net exporter of electric energy by the 1980s. However, the risk of over-dependency on hydroelectric power became apparent when drought drastically reduced output from the hydroelectric plants and forced the state generating company, Administración Nacional de Usinas y Transmisiones Eléctricas (UTE), to utilize its expensive oil-fuelled plants in 2008, in 2010 and again in 2012.

In order to reduce overdependence on hydroelectric generation and the use of oil-fuelled plants, Uruguay is investing heavily in alternative energy sources. In 2013 13% of energy production was generated by biomass. Wind generated just 1% of energy output in 2013, but heavy investment in wind farms was expected to increase this to one-third of total energy supply by 2016, according to the Ministry of Industry, Energy and Mining. This would place Uruguay as the world leader in terms of the share of wind-generated energy in total energy output. In addition, Uruguay is building a new connection line with Brazil; collectively, these measures should ensure energy supply for the next decade.

Both energy generation and consumption have been increasing in recent years. In 2013 Uruguay generated 11,451m. kWh of electric energy, while consumption totalled 9,850m. kWh.— the first time in over 20 years that Uruguay did not have to import energy to satisfy demand; this was largely because good climatic conditions allowed the full-capacity use of the country's hydroelectric plants.

TRANSPORT, INFRASTRUCTURE AND COMMUNICATIONS

The transport, storage and communications sector contributed 7.3% of GDP in 2013, and was one of the fastest growing economic sectors, expanding by 8.9% in that year. Montevideo is the focal point of all Uruguay's transport systems, and the city's port is the principal gateway for foreign trade. The railway system is relatively extensive, with 3,002 km of track radiating from Montevideo, and links to the Argentine and Brazilian networks. Uruguay's roads, like the railways, link interior cities with the capital, rather than with each other. In 2008 Uruguay had an estimated 8,696 km of motorways (forming the densest motorway network in South America).

Uruguay enjoys the highest rate of broadband penetration and the second highest fixed-line density (after Costa Rica) in Latin America, and one of the highest mobile phone penetration rates in the world. According to a report by BuddeComm, an independent telecommunications research and consultancy organization, in 2012 there were 1.8m. internet users in Uruguay out of a total population of 3.3m., giving an internet penetration rate of 55.9%. Figures from the World Bank show that in the same year Uruguay had 147 mobile cellular subscriptions per 100 people. Three players compete in the Uruguayan mobile market: Administración Nacional de Telecomunicaciones (Antel—the state telecommunications company), Telefónica Móviles de Uruguay (operating under the brand name Movistar Uruguay) and Claro (owned by Mexico's América Móvil). Antel is the mobile market leader, followed by Movistar. Antel has plans to connect every Uruguayan home to the internet, offering basic ADSL (asymmetric digital subscriber line) access via a fixed line.

In 2012 the Government announced that it planned to build the country's first deep water port, on the coast of Rocha department near the border with Brazil, with an initial investment of more than US $700m. Funding has not yet been secured, although China has emerged as a potential partner. Initially, the port's main activity was expected to be the export of iron ore from the proposed Valentines mining project (see Mining and Manufacturing); however, delays in the authorization of that project could undermine the viability of the port scheme.

PRIVATIZATION

The process of privatization has been much slower than in other South American countries—in part because Uruguay's state sector had been more efficient, and also because of more effective political opposition to the policy. Government attempts to introduce a major privatization programme in the early 1990s met with resistance from the Frente Amplio (FA) and the trade unions, which successfully blocked plans by demanding a referendum on each individual sale. The Government was forced to adopt instead a more gradual approach that encouraged competition and the use of private capital in state concerns. The state monopolies on insurance and the financing of new homes were ended in 1993 and 1996, respectively, and the now-bankrupt national airline, PLUNA (Primeras Líneas Uruguayas de Navegación Aérea), was privatized in 1995. The Administración Nacional de Combustibles, Alcoholes y Portland (ANCAP) lost its monopoly over the manufacture of alcohol and cement in 1996, and in 1997 the Government ended the state monopoly on the generation of electricity and introduced legislation allowing the use of private capital in electricity distribution. Cellular telephone services, road maintenance and port and airport administration were also opened to private sector participation in the 1990s.

The restructuring of the social security system was undertaken under the second presidency of Julio María Sanguinetti (1995–2000). (Sanguinetti had made four earlier attempts at such a reform.) A key factor was the pressing need to alleviate the fiscal pressure exerted by pensions. The new legislation, approved in 1996, increased the period of contribution, raised the retirement age, and established a mixed capitalization and distribution system. The first pension fund administration company was inaugurated in that year, and by 2000 some 85% of the workforce had joined a new private pension scheme.

A cautious liberalization policy was continued under President Jorge Batlle Ibáñez (2000–05), involving the introduction of competition rather than the dismantling of state concerns, although the FA and the trade unions maintained their opposition. Further efforts were made to deregulate

telecommunications, and ANCAP was enabled to use private sector partners to develop its refining capacity. The privatization programme gained impetus in 2002 when the Government sought IMF assistance to counter the effects of the Argentine default. The Government undertook to end the remaining state monopolies in the energy and telecommunications sectors, eliminate the pension fund deficit, and allow private companies into the administration of roads and airports. In 2003, however, legislation to allow private sector involvement in ANCAP was rejected in a referendum. The FA administration of President Tabaré Vázquez (2005–10) renationalized two water companies, but otherwise did not reverse earlier privatizations.

In 2011 the Government of President Mujica passed a law that established the regulatory framework for public-private partnerships (PPPs). The initiative was aimed at attracting much-needed private investment; however, very few contracts were signed in the first two years of the new regime owing largely to over-regulation and concerns about low returns of capital.

INVESTMENT

Legislation adopted in 1987 allowed for the establishment of free trade zones for various industries. In the mid-1990s the opening up of the public sector to private capital and joint venture schemes encouraged significant levels of FDI. A new investment law in 1998 promised further opportunities for private finance. Since the recovery from the 2002 financial crisis, Uruguay has been attracting increasing levels of FDI and in the mid-2010s was one of the main recipients of FDI in Latin America in relation to the size of its economy. According to ECLAC, Uruguayan FDI has risen from an average of US $551m. annually during 2000–06 to a record $2,796m. in 2013 (the latter representing a 4% increase from 2012 and around 5% of GDP in 2013). In 2013 capital contributions made up nearly 62% of inflows, 30% were reinvested earnings and the remainder consisted of intra-company loans. Although the sectoral distribution is not yet available for 2013, the 2012 data show the start of a surge in investment in utilities, which jumped from a medium-term average of $16m. to $117m. that year. This is consistent with the Government's efforts to promote wind energy and the strong inflows of investment into that sector. FDI's contribution to GDP gross capital formation reached a record 22% in 2012. FDI has been particularly high in the areas of forestation and cellulose production, agriculture, real estate in the exclusive coastal resort of Punta del Este and, more recently, renewable energy generation. Among the main projects announced in 2012 were a $120m. wind power project; a $120m. cement plant to supply southern Brazil; and a $100m. development project in Punta del Este. Discussions continued in 2014 between the Government and the Zamin Ferrous group concerning the $3,500m. plan for the major iron ore open pit mining project in the region of Valentines (see above), which, if realized, would constitute Uruguay's largest ever FDI project.

PUBLIC FINANCES

The Uruguayan economy experienced serious difficulties following the 2002 Argentine default. Citizens of Argentina had long sought to insure against the chronic financial instability of their own country by holding substantial assets in Uruguayan banks. In May the Argentine Government drastically restricted monthly withdrawals from Argentine banks, precipitating a run on Uruguay's banking sector. In July the Uruguayan Government floated the peso, increasing pressure on the banks, and 10 days later it closed all banks for four days and suspended four of them; in that month international reserves had declined to US $655m., from $3,000m. in January. The banks reopened with the assistance of an emergency loan of $1,500m. from the USA, which also facilitated the disbursement of IMF and other international funds. The effective devaluation of the peso in 2002 dramatically affected the Government's economic targets, particularly regarding the national debt. Before the flotation the exchange rate had been US $1 = 17 pesos, and the rate decreased to $1 = 35 pesos before stabilizing at around $1 = 28 pesos in late 2002; at mid-2014 the rate stood at $1 = 23 pesos.

A new plan, agreed with the IMF in February 2003, included a commitment to implement banking reforms and restructure at least part of the debt. In March, in compliance with IMF demands, a new state-owned bank (Nuevo Banco Comercial—NBC) was created from the merger of three of the suspended banks. (The NBC was privatized in 2006.) The economy generally began to recover faster than anticipated, prompting the IMF upwardly to revise its forecasts following an assessment in mid-2003. In 2004 the fiscal deficit stood at 2.9% of GDP, following the impressive economic growth.

The assumption of office of the left-wing FA in 2005 raised concerns about possible deviation from IMF targets. However, the Vázquez administration committed to honouring the IMF agreements and to fiscal prudence. In 2005–09 the annual fiscal deficit remained below 2% of GDP. During its first two years in office the Mujica administration maintained fiscal discipline, with a deficit of 1.2% of GDP in 2010 and of just 0.8% of GDP in 2011. The deficit rose to the equivalent of 2.8% of GDP in 2012 but fell again to 2.3% of GDP in 2013. Revenue for the non-financial public sector amounted to 30.7% of GDP in 2013, a year-on-year rise of 2.2% of GDP, while primary public spending rose by 1.6% of GDP over the same period, according to figures from the Ministry of Economy and Finance.

PUBLIC DEBT AND FOREIGN RESERVES

Uruguay's total foreign debt rose from US $2,156m. in 1981 to $4,279m. by the end of 1987; nearly 90% of this was publicly held. A series of agreements with creditors reduced interest payments, and by 1990 the total debt had been reduced to $3,707m. By 1997 the country's debt profile had improved sufficiently for it to be accorded an investment-grade rating, but the picture changed drastically in 2002. The investment-grade rating was lost, and the currency flotation had the effect of increasing the debt from $8,500m. in July to $10,000m. in August. The debt rose from the equivalent of 38% of GDP in 1998 to some 90% in both 2002 and 2003. In the latter year the Government reached a debt exchange agreement on about one-half of the debt. In 2004 the total debt reached $12,376m. Although the external debt increased in nominal terms in 2005, in relation to GDP it declined, primarily as a result of robust economic growth and a stronger currency. In 2006–07 all debt to the IMF was replaced by longer-tenured capital market debt, and additional debt swaps were made to take advantage of market conditions.

The administrations of Presidents Vázquez and Mujica have actively sought to reduce the country's debt vulnerabilities. The average maturity of the total public debt rose from 7.4 years in 2004 to 11.9 years in March 2014, rendering Uruguay part of a shrinking group of countries with a debt maturity in excess of 10 years. At mid-2014 annual principal payments over the coming three to five years were of the order of 2% of GDP, according to the credit rating agency Moody's Investor Service. A successful debt exchange at the end of 2011 contributed to a rise in the peso-denominated debt as a share of total public sector debt to 58% in 2013 (from only around 5% in 2005), thus reducing exchange rate risk. At 42.9% of GDP in 2013, the gross public debt remained relatively high, but Uruguay's good credit ratings and the spread of maturities meant that the country had no problems in raising the necessary funds to cover its international obligations. Reflecting the improvement in basic economic indicators and the Government's good debt management, in 2012 the credit rating agency Standard & Poor's restored the investment grade to Uruguay's public debt. In May 2014 Moody's upgraded Uruguay's public debt to Baa2 from Baa3 and assigned a stable outlook to the rating. Taking advantage of the upgrade, in June 2014 the economic authorities announced a global offering of US $2,000m. in bonds due to mature in 2050.

The 2002 financial crisis almost completely drained the country's foreign reserves, placing Uruguay on the verge of insolvency. However, by the end of 2005 total international reserves were estimated at US $3,078m., compared with just $772m. at the end of 2002. Reserves continued to grow, as economic expansion attracted high levels of foreign invest-

ment. By mid-June 2014 the foreign currency reserves of the BCU amounted to a record $18,600m., equivalent to just over 30% of GDP and 18 months' worth of goods and services exports.

INFLATION

During the 1990s successive governments made considerable efforts to counter inflation, which had risen as high as 112.5% in 1990. The rate was brought down to 44.7% in 1994, mainly through the use of exchange controls and public sector wage restraints. Inflation continued to decline, to 4.4% in 2001, assisted by the recession in Brazil and Argentina. In the wake of the financial crisis, consumer prices again rose rapidly, averaging 19.4% in 2003. However, during 2004–09 they increased at a more moderate average annual rate of 7.4%. Inflation started to creep up again during the Mujica administration, increasing from 6.9% in 2010 to 7.7% in 2012 and further to 9.1% in the 12 months to May 2014—well above the targeted range of 4%–7% and prompting concerns about a possible overheating of the economy. High public and private consumption and the indexation of salaries have been the main drivers of inflation. The Minister of Economy and Finance has stated that bringing inflation back within target is his ministry's main priority; however, the proximity of presidential and legislative elections, due to be held in October 2014, is likely to delay any necessary adjustments.

FOREIGN TRADE AND BALANCE OF PAYMENTS

Exports of goods (free on board) in 2013 amounted to a record US $10,000m., an increase of 4.8% from 2012, according to the BCU. Agriculture dominates Uruguay's exports. Traditional exports are meat, wool and other unprocessed animal products, which, until the mid-1970s, together provided about 80% of the country's total export earnings. By 2012 that proportion had contracted to around 28%. The principal exports were soya beans and cereals, beef, dairy products and cellulose. The main export partners in 2013 were China (accounting for 21% of the total), Brazil (19.1%), Argentina (5.2%), Venezuela (4.9%) and Germany (4.0%). Exports to China, mainly of soya beans and other agricultural products, grew by 45.2% in 2013, helping China to overtake Brazil as Uruguay's largest export market. Imports (cost, insurance and freight) were worth an estimated $11,500m. in 2013. The principal goods imported were oil and oil products, cars, telecommunications, machinery and transport equipment, and chemicals and related products. The main import partners were China, Brazil, Argentina and Venezuela.

Following eight consecutive years of the trade balance being in deficit, in 2000 the trade deficit widened to US $927m., but there was a major change with the recession of 2002: a sharp reduction in imports resulted in a visible trade surplus of $48.3m. In 2005–09 exports of goods and services increased by an average of just over 8% per year, and imports by 8.7% per year. The higher growth of imports was a result of the demand for capital goods, strong domestic consumption and rising oil prices. Although the visible trade balance was in deficit in 2006–12, this was offset by surpluses in the services balance. In 2013, however, the services balance turned negative, thereby increasing the current account deficit (see below).

In 2002 the current account of the balance of payments recorded its first surplus (of US $322.2m.) since 1992, equivalent to 2.1% of GDP. This surplus was reduced to $3.1m. in 2004 and rose to $24.3m., in 2005. However, owing to the sharp deterioration in the trade balance, a current account deficit of $369.2m. was recorded in 2006; the deficit narrowed to $220m. in 2007, but widened again in 2008 to a record $1,510m. In 2009 the current account deficit fell to $449m., and in 2010 it grew to $863m. as imports soared by almost 25%. The current account deficit rose substantially in 2011–13, reaching some $3,100m. (equivalent to 5.6% of GDP) in 2013, according to the BCU. Current account deficits have been offset by surpluses on the capital account largely owing to FDI levels, resulting in a net increase in foreign reserves between 2012 and 2013, from $13,605m. to $16,280m.

MERCOSUR

Uruguay generally recorded a trade deficit within MERCO-SUR, and closer ties increased its vulnerability to economic events in the other member countries—notably the Argentine economic crises in 1995 and 2001–02, austerity measures in Brazil in 1996, and the Brazilian devaluation in 1999. However, membership of the common market did bring economic advantages through the presence of the MERCOSUR secretariat in Uruguay, a reduction in tariffs, and interest in investment from a number of multinational companies. By the end of the 1990s most duties between the member countries had been eliminated, and a common external tariff had been established for trade outside MERCOSUR. In 2010 the countries of MERCOSUR agreed on a common customs code, with the aim of reducing transaction costs between the member countries and progressing towards the elimination of double taxation on common external levies. While the administration of President Mujica has made MERCOSUR one of its main foreign policy priorities, trade relations between the member countries continue to be hampered by unilateral protectionist measures (particularly on the part of Argentina), such as import licences and other non-tariff restrictions that contravene the rules of the market. In an attempt to circumvent the protectionism of its neighbours and access new markets, Uruguay has sought greater flexibility to draw up bilateral trade agreements with countries outside MERCOSUR. Uruguay has also supported MERCOSUR's negotiations on a free trade agreement with the EU, which were formally launched in May 2010 and remained ongoing at mid-2014.

At a meeting of the Uruguay-US Joint Commission of Trade and Investment in October 2006, it was agreed to start negotiations towards a bilateral agreement to strengthen trading relations. A Trade and Investment Framework Agreement (TIFA) established a Uruguay-US Council on Trade and Investment in 2007. Two bilateral TIFA protocols were signed in 2008 to further trade facilitation.

TOURISM

Tourism and financial services had become the major contributors to the country's balance of payments by the mid-1990s, with tourism revenues outstripping receipts from exports of wool and meat. Uruguay's principal attractions for tourists are the fashionable resort of Punta del Este and the chain of beaches between it and Montevideo. The recession in Argentina (which accounted for the majority of total arrivals in Uruguay) and Brazil severely affected tourism receipts from 1999; in January 2002 the number of Argentine tourists in Punta del Este was estimated at only 10% of its usual level, and this downward trend continued. The total number of visitors declined steadily, from 2.3m. in 1998 to 1.4m. in 2002. Thereafter, however, a recovery in tourist numbers was experienced, with 1.9m. visitors in 2004. Receipts from tourism also began to increase, from US $409m. in 2002 to $494m. in 2004.

In the 2005/06 summer season the number of visitors from Argentina was estimated to have declined by 12%, primarily as a result of the bridge blockades by Argentines protesting against the construction of the new pulp mills (see above). However, the strength of the real meant that arrivals from Brazil rose considerably in 2003–06, and in 2006 receipts from tourism were valued at US $711m. A Social Tourism Plan was announced in 2006, with the aim of encouraging domestic tourism; agreements were also signed with Argentina and Brazil to promote tourism within the region. Also in 2006 Uruguay was granted Approved Destination Status by China. Total arrivals rose to 2.4m. in 2010, an increase of 14.7% from 2009. In 2012–13 the economic crisis in Argentina and foreign currency restrictions to travellers, together with the overvaluation of the Uruguayan currency, affected the influx of tourists from the neighbouring country, and this was only partially offset by a rise in visitors from Brazil, the USA, Europe and elsewhere, leading to a decline in total arrivals. Uruguay received 2.8m. visitors in 2012, compared with almost 3m. in 2011, and the figure was estimated to have been significantly lower in 2013; a 2.4% fall in the number of visitors and a 12.4% fall in tourism earnings were recorded in the first quarter of the year (the peak of the tourism season), according

to the Ministry of Tourism and Sport. Receipts for tourism reached $2,076m. in 2012.

THE ENVIRONMENT

By the mid-1990s certain recreational areas in Montevideo had been severely damaged by industrial pollution from meat-processing and tannery plants in the Miguelete river. In 2003 Uruguay, Brazil, Argentina and Paraguay began work on an agreement covering the future usage and protection of the Guaraní aquifer. Concern that effluent from the proposed pulp mills on the River Uruguay would pollute both the river and the River Plate estuary was a major factor in Argentine hostility to the development, although subsequent studies indicated that no significant damage had been caused.

In 2007 the Government announced the creation of seven 'protected areas' (with additional areas to follow) under the Sistema Nacional de Areas Protegidas (National System of Protected Areas) to safeguard biological diversity and natural resources in the country. These would include the sparsely populated Cabo Polonio in Rocha, well known for its sand dunes and sea lion colonies.

As a small agricultural country, Uruguay is vulnerable to abnormal weather conditions. Like other countries of the region, it suffered from the impact of El Niño in 1997–98, with severe flooding in the west of the country and considerable damage to the rice crop. In August 2005 an unpredicted wind and rain storm struck the southern and eastern parts of Uruguay, where some 70% of the population live, destroying infrastructure. In May 2007, in the worst flooding for half a century, some 12,000 people in and around Durazno and Mercedes in central Uruguay were driven from their homes by heavy rains and overflowing rivers. Most schools in seven of the country's 19 departments were closed; electricity and telephone lines were disrupted; and some 30,000 people were left without access to clean drinking water. In 2008–09 and again in 2009 and 2010 a prolonged drought led to severe losses in the agricultural sector, and the decline in water volumes in the River Uruguay and River Negro resulted in a drastic reduction in output from the hydroelectric plants that provided most of the country's power.

CONCLUSION

In the second half of the 20th century Uruguay was among the slowest growing economies in the Western hemisphere. In 2002 the country suffered one of the worst economic downturns in its modern history, largely as a ramification of the crisis in Argentina. Since 2004, however, Uruguay has been among the fastest growing economies in Latin America, and by 2013 it had experienced 11 years of uninterrupted economic growth. The economy was expected to continue growing in 2014, albeit at a slower pace.

Although in 2005 international financial markets reacted with caution to the inauguration of the new left-wing Encuentro Progresista—Frente Amplio—Nueva Mayoría administration led by Tabaré Vázquez, the appointment of the economist Danilo Astori as Minister of Economy and Finance, and commitments to structural reform, low inflation and fiscal orthodoxy, proved reassuring. Prudent fiscal policies, a proactive management of the external debt that led to a significant reduction in the debt-to-GDP ratio, improvements in bank regulation and high international reserves all contributed to economic confidence. The Government of President Mujica, which took office in March 2010, largely continued the orthodox economic policies of the previous administration. Mujica identified a technologically advanced agricultural sector, tourism and regional logistics as the country's strategic development sectors, with infrastructure (particularly railways, ports and telecommunications), energy and social housing as the main investment priorities. Political and economic stability have attracted large inflows of FDI, particularly in the construction and agricultural sectors, which have led to significant increases in productivity. The country has also benefited from high commodity prices, low international interest rates and the strong economic growth of its neighbouring countries, particularly Brazil. Rising employment and real wages have fostered domestic demand, which, together with exports and investment, has been the engine of economic growth.

Although the FA's candidate, Tabaré Vázquez, was the frontrunner to win the presidential contest scheduled to be held, concurrently with legislative elections, in October 2014, the result was far from certain. It is a measure of the political consensus on Uruguay's economic model that the economy has not become the main point of contention in the electoral campaign, which has been dominated by issues such as crime and education. Vázquez has stated that, were he to become President, Astori would again be his Minister of Economy and Finance, a development that, were it to come to pass, would be widely welcomed by the business community. However, regardless of the electoral outcome, there was likely to be a significant degree of continuity with current economic policies.

While the economic outlook at mid-2014 was largely positive, there were a number of concerns. The economy remained vulnerable to fluctuations in the price of commodities, and also to the misfortunes of neighbouring countries—as exemplified by the impact on Uruguay of the economic crises in Brazil in 1999 and in Argentina in 2002 and again in 2013–14. The appreciation of the local currency against the US dollar was also worrying (particularly for tourism and exporters of

industrial goods), as was the low value-added of Uruguay's exports. Domestically, high levels of industrial conflict and rigid wage settlements have negatively affected the business climate. Low unemployment levels were resulting in shortages of skilled labour. Economic growth was placing increasing pressure on the country's infrastructure, which remained in urgent need of investment. The Government planned to use PPPs to supplement chronically low public investment. Although the Governments of Presidents Vázquez and Mujica significantly increased investment in education, there were indications that this input has not improved quality, and that Uruguay's traditionally high educational standards were starting to lag behind those of other Latin American countries. In the short term, the main concern was the deterioration in the global economic outlook and the prospect of economic instability in Argentina. To ensure the attainment of a more sustainable path, the Government must restrain increases in public spending and wage settlements, improve infrastructure and address failings in the education and training of the workforce. If these issues are dealt with successfully, Uruguay should be able to sustain its remarkable turnaround in economic performance in the years to come.

Statistical Survey

Sources (unless otherwise stated): Instituto Nacional de Estadística, Río Negro 1520, 11100 Montevideo; tel. 2902 7303; internet www.ine.gub.uy; Banco Central del Uruguay, Avda Juan P. Fabini, esq. Florida 777, Casilla 1467, 11100 Montevideo; tel. 2908 5629; fax 2902 1634; e-mail info@bcu.gub.uy; internet www.bcu .gub.uy; Cámara Nacional de Comercio y Servicios del Uruguay, Edif. Bolsa de Comercio, Rincón 454, 2°, Casilla 1000, 11000 Montevideo; tel. 2916 1277; fax 2916 1243; e-mail info@cncs.com.uy; internet www.cncs.com.uy.

Area and Population

AREA, POPULATION AND DENSITY

Area (sq km)	
Land area	175,016
Inland water	1,199
Total	176,215*
Population (census results)	
May–July 2004†	3,241,003
1–30 September 2011‡	
Males	1,577,416
Females	1,708,461
Total	3,285,877
Population (official projected estimates at mid-year)§	
2012	3,380,544
2013	3,392,407
2014	3,404,189
Density (per sq km) at mid-2014	19.5

* 68,037 sq miles.
† Excluding adjustment for underenumeration.
‡ Excluding 437 persons classified as homeless.
§ Estimates not adjusted to take account of results of 2011 census.

POPULATION BY AGE AND SEX
(official projected estimates at mid-2014)

	Males	Females	Total
0–14 years	372,043	355,343	727,386
15–64 years	1,089,397	1,117,961	2,207,358
65 years and over	184,572	284,873	469,445
Total	1,646,012	1,758,177	3,404,189

Note: Estimates not adjusted to take account of results of 2011 census.

DEPARTMENTS
(official projected estimates at mid-2014)*

	Area (sq km)	Population	Density (per sq km)	Capital
Artigas . . .	11,928	79,286	6.6	Artigas
Canelones . .	4,536	549,091	121.1	Canelones
Cerro Largo . .	13,648	92,988	6.8	Melo
Colonia . . .	6,106	121,060	19.8	Colonia del Sacramento
Durazno . . .	11,643	63,906	5.5	Durazno
Flores . . .	5,144	25,857	5.0	Trinidad
Florida . . .	10,417	72,042	6.9	Florida
Lavalleja . . .	10,016	62,212	6.2	Minas
Maldonado . .	4,793	159,614	33.3	Maldonado
Montevideo . .	530	1,330,840	2,511.0	Montevideo
Paysandú . .	13,922	117,521	8.4	Paysandú
Río Negro . .	9,282	57,707	6.2	Fray Bentos
Rivera . . .	9,370	116,041	12.4	Rivera
Rocha . . .	10,551	70,067	6.6	Rocha
Salto	14,163	131,593	9.3	Salto
San José . . .	4,992	114,887	23.0	San José de Mayo
Soriano . . .	9,008	90,436	10.0	Mercedes
Tacuarembó . .	15,438	99,863	6.5	Tacuarembó
Treinta y Tres .	9,529	49,187	5.2	Treinta y Tres
Total . . .	175,016†	3,404,189	19.5	

* Estimates not adjusted to take account of results of 2011 census.
† Land area only.

PRINCIPAL TOWNS
(population at 2011 census)

Montevideo (capital)	1,318,755	Maldonado . . .	62,590
Salto	104,011	Tacuarembó . .	54,755
Paysandú . . .	76,412	Melo	51,830
Las Piedras . . .	71,258	Mercedes . . .	41,974
Rivera	64,465		

BIRTHS, MARRIAGES AND DEATHS*

	Registered live births Number	Rate (per 1,000)	Registered marriages Number	Rate (per 1,000)	Registered deaths Number	Rate (per 1,000)
2005 . . .	46,944†	14.2†	13,075	4.0	32,319†	9.8†
2006 . . .	47,410†	14.2†	12,415	3.7	31,056†	9.4†
2007 . . .	47,373	14.3	12,771	3.8	33,706†	10.3†
2008 . . .	47,484	14.2	12,180	3.7	31,363	9.4
2009 . . .	47,152	14.1	11,080	3.3	32,179	9.6
2010 . . .	47,420	14.1	10,629	3.2	33,474	10.0
2011 . . .	46,699	14.2	9,604	2.9	32,807	n.a.
2012 . . .	48,200	n.a.	9,631	n.a.	33,002	n.a.

* Data are tabulated by year of registration rather than by year of occurrence and have not been adjusted to take account of the most recent census.
† Preliminary.

Life expectancy (years at birth): 76.9 (males 73.5; females 80.4) in 2012 (Source: World Bank, World Development Indicators database).

ECONOMICALLY ACTIVE POPULATION
(annual averages, '000 persons aged 14 years and over)

	2009	2010	2011
Agriculture, hunting, forestry and fishing . .	169.2	181.0	175.1
Mining and quarrying . . .	2.2	2.6	3.7
Manufacturing	202.4	203.9	212.7
Electricity, gas and water supply .	13.9	14.0	14.3
Construction	104.7	114.0	120.3
Wholesale and retail trade, repair of motor vehicles, motorcycles and personal and household goods	289.1	289.1	302.5
Hotels and restaurants . . .	46.9	46.2	49.4
Transport, storage and communications	87.6	84.0	95.6
Financing, insurance, real estate and business services . . .	128.6	131.4	143.2
Public administration and defence, compulsory social security . .	93.3	92.4	95.7
Education	86.2	87.3	99.4
Health and social work . . .	107.6	108.7	122.5
Community, social and personal services	75.7	72.7	77.9
Private households with employed persons	133.8	134.0	129.9
Extraterritorial organizations .	1.4	1.1	1.9
Total employed . . .	**1,542.5**	**1,562.3**	**1,644.1**
Males	876.8	865.5	911.8
Females	665.7	696.9	732.3
Unemployed	121.5	114.1	110.9
Total labour force	**1,664.0**	**1,676.4**	**1,755.0**

2012: Total employed 1,616.1; Unemployed 111.3; Total labour force 1,727.4.
Source: ILO.

Mid-2014 ('000, estimates): Agriculture, etc. 183; Total labour force 1,700 (Source: FAO).

Health and Welfare

KEY INDICATORS

Total fertility rate (children per woman, 2012)	2.1
Under-5 mortality rate (per 1,000 live births, 2012) . . .	7
HIV/AIDS (% of persons aged 15–49, 2012)	0.7
Physicians (per 1,000 head, 2008)	3.7
Hospital beds (per 1,000 head, 2010)	1.2
Health expenditure (2011): US $ per head (PPP) . . .	1,294
Health expenditure (2011): % of GDP	8.6
Health expenditure (2011): public (% of total)	69.5
Total carbon dioxide emissions ('000 metric tons, 2010) . .	6,644.6
Carbon dioxide emissions per head (metric tons, 2010) . .	2.0
Human Development Index (2013): ranking	50
Human Development Index (2013): value	0.790

For sources and definitions, see explanatory note on p. vi.

Agriculture

PRINCIPAL CROPS
('000 metric tons)

	2010	2011	2012
Wheat . . . . . . † . .	1,300.7	2,016.3	1,000.0*
Rice, paddy	1,148.7	1,643.0	1,423.9
Barley	186.4	326.9	235.0*
Maize	529.1	286.2	550.0†
Oats*	42.9	48.5	50.0
Sorghum	138.0	123.4	105.0†
Potatoes	114.7	90.2	95.0*
Sweet potatoes*	72.5	74.0	75.5
Sugar cane	313.3	314.0*	320.0*
Sunflower seed	9.1	3.9	4.0*
Tomatoes	31.6	30.6*	32.0*
Onions, dry	17.5	17.3*	17.9*
Carrots and turnips . . .	18.3	19.6*	20.5*
Soybeans (Soya beans)† . .	2,000.0	1,830.0	3,000.0
Oranges	154.2	135.2	140.0*
Tangerines, mandarins, clementines and satsumas . .	121.5	93.4	101.0*
Lemons and limes	37.7	38.2	40.0*
Apples	52.2	73.4	80.0*
Pears	18.7	14.8	16.0*
Peaches and nectarines . .	23.0	22.6*	24.0*
Grapes	110.3	126.2	130.0*

* FAO estimate(s).
† Unofficial figure(s).

Aggregate production ('000 metric tons, may include official, semi-official or estimated data): Total cereals 3,348.9 in 2010, 4,447.7 in 2011, 3,367.5 in 2012; Total fruits (excl. melons) 532.2 in 2010, 522.8 in 2011, 550.7 in 2012; Total vegetables (incl. melons) 148.1 in 2010, 153.0 in 2011; 158.9 in 2012.
Source: FAO.

LIVESTOCK
('000 head, year ending September)

	2010	2011	2012
Cattle	11,800*	11,808*	12,000†
Sheep	7,710	7,474	7,350
Pigs	210	220	222†
Horses	399	405†	407†
Chickens†	16,500	17,500	18,000

* Unofficial figure.
† FAO estimate(s).
Source: FAO.

LIVESTOCK PRODUCTS
('000 metric tons)

	2010	2011	2012†
Cattle meat	524.0	479.0*	500.0
Sheep meat	31.6*	32.0†	32.5
Pig meat	18.4	20.9	22.5
Chicken meat†	69.2	85.3	88.0
Cows' milk	1,820.8	2,057.0	2,100.0
Hen eggs	52.5	53.5†	54.0
Wool, greasy	34.7*	34.7†	36.0

* Unofficial figure.
† FAO estimate(s).
Source: FAO.

Forestry

ROUNDWOOD REMOVALS
('000 cubic metres, excl. bark)

	2010	2011	2012
Sawlogs and veneer logs . . .	1,547	1,779	1,716
Pulpwood	7,841	6,207	6,207
Other industrial wood* . . .	14	14	14
Fuel wood	2,430	2,430	2,400
Total*	11,832	10,430	10,157

* FAO estimates.

Source: FAO.

SAWNWOOD PRODUCTION
('000 cubic metres, incl. railway sleepers)

	2009	2010	2011
Coniferous (softwood)	102	131	128
Broadleaved (hardwood) . . .	162	215	248
Total	264	346	376

2012: Figures assumed to be unchanged from 2011.

Source: FAO.

Fishing

('000 metric tons, live weight)

	2010	2011	2012
Capture	74.1	89.2*	76.1
Argentine hake	33.9	36.7	25.5
Striped weakfish	5.5	7.1	6.6
Whitemouth croaker . .	15.4	24.8	24.2
Castaneta	0.6	2.3	0.2
Rays, stingrays and mantas .	1.1	1.5	1.0
Argentine shortfin squid . .	2.4	1.5	1.4
Aquaculture	0.1	0.1	0.1
Total catch*	74.2	89.3	76.3

* FAO estimate(s).

Note: Figures exclude aquatic mammals, recorded by number rather than by weight. The number of South American fur seals and sea lions caught was: 80 in 2010; 53 in 2011; 55 in 2012.

Source: FAO.

Mining

('000 metric tons unless otherwise indicated)

	2008	2009	2010*
Gold (kg)	2,182	1,690	1,736
Gypsum*	1,150	1,150	1,150
Feldspar (metric tons)	2,500	2,500	2,500

* Estimates.

Gold (kg): 1,736 in 2011; 1,725 in 2012.

Source: US Geological Survey.

Industry

SELECTED PRODUCTS
('000 metric tons unless otherwise indicated)

	2008	2009	2010
Raw sugar	7	10	15
Wine	79.9	61.8	65.0*
Motor spirit (petrol, '000 barrels)†	1,850	1,850	1,850
Kerosene ('000 barrels)† . . .	100	100	100
Distillate fuel oils ('000 barrels)† .	8,500	8,500	8,500
Residual fuel oils ('000 barrels)† .	3,650	3,650	3,650
Cement (hydraulic)†	620	620	620
Electric energy (million kWh) .	8,769	8,838	10,659

* FAO estimate.
† US Geological Survey estimates.

Wine (FAO estimate): 66.5 in 2011; 67.0 in 2012.

Cement: 620 in 2011–12.

Sources: FAO; US Geological Survey; UN Industrial Commodity Statistics Database.

Finance

CURRENCY AND EXCHANGE RATES

Monetary Units
100 centésimos = 1 peso uruguayo.

Sterling, Dollar and Euro Equivalents (30 May 2014)
£1 sterling = 38.546 pesos;
US $1 = 22.914 pesos;
€1 = 31.188 pesos;
1,000 pesos uruguayos = £25.94 = $43.64 = €32.06.

Average Exchange Rate (pesos per US $)
2011   19.314
2012   20.311
2013   20.482

Note: On 1 March 1993 a new currency, the peso uruguayo (equivalent to 1,000 former new pesos), was introduced.

CENTRAL GOVERNMENT BUDGET*
(million pesos uruguayos)

Revenue	2010	2011	2012
Tax revenue	165,536	189,838	213,480
Taxes on income, profits, etc. .	41,162	46,845	53,276
Individual taxes	18,930	—	—
Corporate taxes	948	—	—
Taxes on property	11,361	12,724	14,025
Domestic taxes on goods and services	100,751	115,412	129,103
General sales, take-over or value-added tax	83,341	—	—
Taxes on international trade and transactions	5,338	6,754	7,817
Taxes on leisure activities . .	71	78	83
Other taxes and rates	6,853	7,210	8,260
Non-tax revenue	10,898	13,091	14,015
Transfers	6,470	6,011	4,290
Other income	2,464	2,689	2,932
Total	185,368	211,629	234,718

Expenditure	2004	2005	2006
General public services . . .	23,204	25,519	28,230
Government administration .	13,444	15,058	16,290
Defence	4,376	4,660	5,187
Public order and safety . .	5,385	5,801	6,753
Special and community services .	37,148	38,747	58,271
Education	11,873	12,573	14,392
Health	6,521	7,135	8,654
Social security and welfare . .	16,817	17,109	32,375
Housing and community amenities	1,259	1,371	2,029
Recreational, cultural and religious affairs . . .	679	559	821
Economic affairs and services .	3,353	5,931	6,435
Fuel and energy	186	179	194
Agriculture, fishing, forestry and hunting	1,421	2,033	1,584
Mining and mineral resources .	253	273	275
Transport and communications .	2,530	2,728	3,725
Other economic services . .	964	718	657
Debt-servicing and governmental transfers	22,805	20,322	24,289
Total	**88,510**	**90,519**	**117,225**

* Figures represent the consolidated accounts of the central Government, which include social security revenue and expenditure.

2010: Current expenditure 179,445; Capital expenditure 17,152; Total 196,597.

2011: Current expenditure 204,069; Capital expenditure 18,564; Total expenditure 222,633.

2012: Current expenditure 236,359; Capital expenditure 18,704; Total expenditure 255,063.

General government finances (consolidated accounts of general government, million pesos uruguayos, cash basis): *Revenue:* Total 250,377 in 2011; 280,092 in 2012 (preliminary). *Expenditure:* 255,520 in 2011; 301,115 in 2012 (preliminary).

INTERNATIONAL RESERVES
(US $ million at 31 December)

	2011	2012	2013
Gold	13	14	10
IMF special drawing rights . .	377	378	378
Reserve position in the IMF . .	146	155	171
Foreign exchange	9,765	13,058	15,721
Total	**10,301**	**13,605**	**16,280**

Source: IMF, *International Financial Statistics*.

MONEY SUPPLY
(million pesos uruguayos at 31 December)

	2011	2012	2013
Currency outside depository corporations	35,034.1	39,486.5	45,075.4
Transferable deposits	151,576.9	163,838.9	196,575.6
Other deposits	213,244.3	231,589.7	280,441.0
Securities other than shares . .	2,501.1	4,650.3	5,211.0
Broad money	**402,356.4**	**439,565.4**	**527,303.0**

Source: IMF, *International Financial Statistics*.

COST OF LIVING
(Consumer Price Index for Montevideo; base: December 2010 = 100)

	2011	2012	2013
Food and beverages	106.2	115.5	127.7
Housing	106.9	117.6	130.7
Clothing and footwear . . .	101.4	104.9	110.6
All items (incl. others) . . .	**105.4**	**114.2**	**124.1**

NATIONAL ACCOUNTS
('000 million pesos uruguayos at current prices, preliminary figures)

Expenditure on the Gross Domestic Product

	2011	2012	2013
Government final consumption expenditure	118,207.3	138,293.7	157,987.0
Private final consumption expenditure	605,892.3	672,474.6	751,198.5
Increase in stocks	16,371.7	9,290.7	7,698.4
Gross fixed capital formation . .	176,378.8	230,113.6	261,420.9
Total domestic expenditure .	**916,850.1**	**1,050,172.6**	**1,178,304.8**
Exports of goods and services . .	245,131.5	270,763.9	273,880.7
Less Imports of goods and services	249,641.9	305,339.8	311,196.6
GDP in market prices . .	**912,339.7**	**1,015,596.6**	**1,140,988.8**
GDP at constant 2005 prices .	**601,692.8**	**623,813.2**	**651,239.7**

Gross Domestic Product by Economic Activity

	2011	2012	2013
Agriculture, hunting and forestry .	83,303.2	85,868.2	93,709.7
Fishing and mining	4,006.1	4,774.1	5,787.0
Manufacturing	113,798.3	122,371.7	126,045.7
Electricity, gas and water . . .	17,752.4	10,776.5	25,977.9
Construction	65,941.6	85,770.4	101,785.3
Trade, restaurants and hotels .	125,408.4	139,788.9	149,742.7
Transport, storage and communications	62,942.8	68,714.2	75,714.0
Finance and insurance . . .	39,296.9	45,637.6	51,373.9
Real estate and business services .	136,356.0	157,926.8	180,865.3
Public administration and defence; compulsory social security . .	46,916.7	52,430.9	59,164.7
Other community, social and personal services	122,129.6	140,521.6	160,453.6
Sub-total	**817,851.9**	**914,581.0**	**1,030,620.0**
Less Financial intermediation services indirectly measured .	23,645.5	28,551.5	31,276.2
Gross value added in basic prices	**794,206.4**	**886,029.5**	**999,343.8**
Taxes, less subsidies, on products .	118,133.4	129,567.1	141,645.1
GDP in market prices . . .	**912,339.7**	**1,015,596.6**	**1,140,988.8**

BALANCE OF PAYMENTS
(US $ million)

	2010	2011	2012
Exports of goods	8,030.7	9,274.0	9,906.6
Imports of goods	−8,557.7	−10,705.1	−12,217.0
Balance on goods	**−527.0**	**−1,431.1**	**−2,310.4**
Exports of services	2,688.2	3,587.6	3,383.1
Imports of services	−1,530.9	−2,039.8	−2,323.6
Balance on goods and services	**630.2**	**116.7**	**−1,251.0**
Primary income received . . .	454.6	504.8	354.1
Primary income paid	−1,955.5	−2,117.1	−1,819.3
Balance on goods, services and primary income	**−870.7**	**−1,495.7**	**−2,716.2**
Secondary income received . .	175.0	179.1	167.8
Secondary income paid . . .	−57.0	−50.6	−77.1
Current balance	**−752.7**	**−1,367.2**	**−2,625.5**
Capital account (net)	—	—	40.0
Direct investment assets . . .	157.7	−179.2	−188.2
Direct investment liabilities . .	2,191.1	2,722.9	2,906.6
Portfolio investment assets . .	−1,340.6	1,156.8	−391.9
Portfolio investment liabilities .	686.5	819.5	2,036.2
Other investment assets . . .	352.3	894.0	−2,591.1
Other investment liabilities . .	−961.8	−1,180.1	2,200.7
Net errors and omissions . . .	−694.0	−302.5	1,900.3
Reserves and related items .	**−361.5**	**2,564.3**	**3,287.2**

Source: IMF, *International Financial Statistics*.

External Trade

PRINCIPAL COMMODITIES
(US $ million, provisional)

Imports c.i.f.	2010	2011	2012
Crops and vegetable products	195.9	334.7	260.6
Food industry products; beverages, tobacco, alcohol and vinegars	472.9	639.3	646.9
Mineral products	1,745.2	2,263.6	3,157.8
Mineral fuels, petroleum and petroleum products	1,699.7	2,214.0	3,102.6
Chemicals and related products	1,148.1	1,392.7	1,501.4
Fertilizers	249.5	358.6	353.1
Plastics and plastic products; rubber and manufactures thereof	641.0	768.1	765.1
Plastics and plastic products	456.0	560.0	562.6
Textiles and textile manufactures	373.0	496.3	471.8
Base metals and metal manufactures	383.6	492.1	493.8
Machinery and appliances, electrical materials, audio-visual recording and reproducing apparatus	1,636.7	1,887.0	1,902.5
Boilers, etc., machinery and apparatus	963.9	1,107.8	1,119.9
Transport equipment	1,026.4	1,196.4	1,128.7
Automobiles, tractors, cycles, parts and accessories	957.4	1,185.2	1,115.4
Total (incl. others)	8,621.8	10,726.4	11,614.3

Exports f.o.b.	2010	2011	2012
Live animals and animal products	2,157.3	2,650.1	2,724.5
Chilled beef products	263.4	320.0	384.7
Frozen beef products	833.5	971.3	1,019.1
Dairy products and birds' eggs	541.2	733.5	797.6
Crops and vegetable products	1,717.6	1,918.4	2,782.5
Rice	386.0	472.1	560.3
Cereals	353.9	309.7	515.5
Food industry products; beverages, tobacco, alcohol and vinegars	201.2	250.4	221.4
Mineral products	227.7	87.1	105.7
Chemicals and related products	339.1	413.8	487.0
Plastics and plastic products; rubber and manufactures thereof	346.2	439.2	444.9
Pelts, skins, hides and products thereof	235.5	275.3	285.6
Hides and leathers	211.4	246.4	264.6
Wood, charcoal, cork, etc. and products thereof	473.3	520.8	471.4
Textiles and textile manufactures	301.8	377.3	324.2
Total (incl. others)	6,724.2	7,911.8	8,743.1

PRINCIPAL TRADING PARTNERS
(US $ million)

Imports c.i.f.	2010	2011	2012
Argentina	1,468.9	2,003.8	1,741.4
Brazil	1,578.1	2,082.4	2,091.1
Chile	117.2	135.1	142.8
China, People's Republic	1,123.8	1,438.8	1,662.5
Denmark	61.2	119.4	91.9
France (incl. Monaco)	136.7	186.7	189.1
Germany	198.0	257.8	247.7
India	68.6	115.7	146.9
Italy	160.9	148.4	152.8
Japan	94.6	96.0	101.7
Korea, Republic	100.2	204.1	177.1
Mexico	173.3	243.8	292.8
Netherlands	32.6	125.4	99.5
Nigeria	160.6	129.8	342.6
Russia	272.2	137.8	589.2
South Africa	97.3	253.0	12.2
Spain	151.4	154.6	151.5
Taiwan	99.2	110.8	123.4
United Kingdom	71.5	125.2	97.7
USA	855.2	1,100.6	866.2
Venezuela	660.1	398.9	826.8
Total (incl. others)	8,621.8	10,726.4	11,614.3

Exports f.o.b.	2010	2011	2012
Argentina	574.6	588.3	504.6
Brazil	1,419.3	1,625.1	1,688.8
Chile	120.4	139.1	208.1
China, People's Republic	363.8	526.1	801.7
Germany	237.8	301.8	258.6
Israel	78.0	118.0	176.6
Italy	144.2	158.4	129.7
Mexico	124.0	163.0	147.5
Netherlands	126.0	147.7	128.4
Paraguay	159.8	191.7	146.2
Peru	66.3	102.4	140.5
Portugal	75.6	94.1	57.3
Russia	351.6	394.9	393.5
Spain	178.7	200.2	127.6
Switzerland	87.5	109.5	136.5
Turkey	125.6	154.2	64.7
United Kingdom	108.6	121.8	118.4
USA	194.5	243.7	324.2
Venezuela	246.7	314.3	417.1
Total (incl. others)	6,724.2	7,911.8	8,743.1

Transport

RAILWAYS
(traffic)

	2010	2011	2012
Passenger-km (million)	20	19	11
Net ton-km (million)	226	195	205

ROAD TRAFFIC
(motor vehicles in use)

	2010	2011	2012
Passenger cars	618,545	655,783	693,155
Buses and coaches	8,218	8,639	9,030
Trailers and semi-trailers	34,057	27,891	30,016
Trucks and tractors	64,640	67,982	67,907
Motorcycles and mopeds	746,415	844,169	747,432

SHIPPING

Flag Registered Fleet
(at 31 December)

	2011	2012	2013
Number of vessels	91	90	100
Total displacement ('000 grt) . .	97.5	102.3	143.4

Source: Lloyd's List Intelligence (www.lloydslistintelligence.com).

CIVIL AVIATION
(traffic)

	2007	2008	2009
Kilometres flown (million) . .	8	9	8
Passengers carried ('000) . . .	524	613	564
Passenger-km (million) . . .	926	1,047	982
Total ton-km (million) . . .	83	99	93

Source: UN, *Statistical Yearbook*.

Passengers carried ('000): 744 in 2010 (Source: World Bank, World Development Indicators database).

Tourism

ARRIVALS BY NATIONALITY*

	2010	2011	2012
Argentina	1,261,516	1,723,005	1,763,518
Brazil	376,894	426,315	396,828
Chile	53,194	57,283	53,385
Germany	19,102	20,267	18,017
Italy	16,603	17,518	15,423
Mexico	14,370	16,327	13,771
Paraguay	36,672	42,980	39,321
Peru	13,673	15,623	39,321
Spain	31,531	32,307	21,184
United Kingdom	15,737	17,420	13,755
USA	62,428	60,576	57,552
Total (incl. others)	2,407,676	2,960,155	2,845,989

*Figures refer to arrivals at frontiers of visitors from abroad, including Uruguayan nationals permanently resident elsewhere.

Total arrivals: 2,684,000 in 2013 (provisional).

Tourism receipts (US $ million, excl. passenger transport): 2,203 in 2011; 2,076 in 2012; 1,920 in 2013 (provisional).

Source: World Tourism Organization.

Communications Media

	2011	2012	2013
Telephones ('000 main lines in use)	964.9	1,011.0	1,048.4
Mobile cellular telephones ('000 subscribers)	4,757.4	4,995.5	5,267.9
Internet subscribers ('000) . .	455.2	n.a.	n.a.
Broadband subscribers ('000) . .	455.2	563.1	720.0

Source: International Telecommunication Union.

Education

(2012 unless otherwise indicated)

	Institutions	Teachers	Students
Pre-primary	1,430	4,377	108,808
Primary	2,421	18,439	319,238
Secondary: general*	586	25,168†	227,858
Secondary: vocational	123	n.a.	79,895
University and equivalent institutions*‡	6	7,723	72,100

* Public education only, including both day shifts and night shifts.
† 2003.
‡ 2005.

Pupil-teacher ratio (primary education, UNESCO estimate): 13.8 in 2010/11 (Source: UNESCO Institute for Statistics).

Adult literacy rate (UNESCO estimates): 98.4% (males 98.1%; females 98.7%) in 2012 (Source: UNESCO Institute for Statistics).

Directory

The Constitution

The Constitution of Uruguay was ratified by plebiscite, on 27 November 1966, when the country voted to return to the presidential form of government after 15 years of 'collegiate' government. The main points of the Constitution, as amended in January 1997, are as follows:

GENERAL PROVISIONS

Uruguay shall have a democratic republican form of government, sovereignty being exercised directly by the electoral body in cases of election, by initiative or by referendum, and indirectly by representative powers established by the Constitution, according to the rules set out therein.

There shall be freedom of religion; there is no state religion; property shall be inviolable; there shall be freedom of thought. Anyone may enter Uruguay. There are two forms of citizenship: natural, being persons born in Uruguay or of Uruguayan parents, and legal, being people established in Uruguay with at least three years' residence in the case of those with family, and five years' for those without family. Every citizen has the right and obligation to vote.

LEGISLATURE

Legislative power is vested in the Congreso (Congress), comprising two houses, which may act separately or together according to the dispositions of the Constitution. It elects in joint session the members of the Supreme Court of Justice, of the Electoral Court, Tribunals, Administrative Litigation and the Accounts Tribunal.

Elections for both houses, the President and the Vice-President shall take place every five years on the last Sunday in October; sessions of the Congress begin on 1 March each year and last until 15 December (15 September in election years, in which case the new Congress takes office on 15 February). Extraordinary sessions can be convened only in case of extreme urgency.

CHAMBER OF REPRESENTATIVES

The Chamber of Representatives has 99 members elected by direct suffrage according to the system of proportional representation, with at least two representatives for each Department. The number of representatives can be altered by law by a two-thirds' majority in both houses. Their term of office is five years and they must be over 25 years of age and be natural citizens or legal citizens with five years' exercise of their citizenship. Representatives have the right to bring accusations against any member of the Government or judiciary for violation of the Constitution or any other serious offence.

SENATE

The Senate comprises 31 members, including the Vice-President, who sits as President of the Senate, and 30 members elected directly by proportional representation on the same lists as the representatives, for a term of five years. They must be natural citizens or legal citizens with seven years' exercise of their rights, and be over 30 years of age. The Senate is responsible for hearing cases brought by the representatives and can deprive a guilty person of a post by a two-thirds' majority.

THE EXECUTIVE

Executive power is exercised by the President and the Council of Ministers. There is a Vice-President, who is also President of the Congress and of the Senate. The President and Vice-President are directly elected by absolute majority, and remain in office for five years. They must be over 35 years of age and be natural citizens. The Council of Ministers comprises the office holders in the ministries or their deputies, and is responsible for all acts of government and administration. It is presided over by the President of the Republic, who has a vote.

THE JUDICIARY

Judicial power is exercised by the five-member Supreme Court of Justice and by Tribunals and local courts; members of the Supreme Court must be over 40 years of age and be natural citizens, or legal citizens with 10 years' exercise and 25 years' residence, and must be lawyers of 10 years' standing, eight of them in public or fiscal ministry or judicature. Members serve for 10 years and can be re-elected after a break of five years. The Court nominates all other judges and judicial officials.

The Government

HEAD OF STATE

President: José Alberto Mujica Cordano (took office on 1 March 2010).

Vice-President: Danilo Astori (AU).

COUNCIL OF MINISTERS
(September 2014)

The Government is composed of members of the Frente Amplio coalition.

Minister of the Interior: Eduardo Bonomi Varela (MPP).

Minister of Foreign Affairs: Luis Leonardo Almagro Lemes (MPP).

Minister of National Defence: Eleuterio Fernández Huidobro (CAP-L).

Minister of Social Development: Daniel Olesker (PS).

Minister of Economy and Finance: Mario Esteban Bergara Duque (Ind.).

Minister of Industry, Energy and Mining: Roberto Kreimerman (PS).

Minister of Livestock, Agriculture and Fishing: Tabaré Aguerre (Ind.).

Minister of Tourism and Sport: Liliam Kechichián (AP).

Minister of Transport and Public Works: Enrique Pintado (AU).

Minister of Labour and Social Security: José Bayardi (VA).

Minister of Education and Culture: Ricardo Ehrlich (FA).

Minister of Public Health: Susana Muñiz (PCU).

Minister of Housing, Territorial Regulation and the Environment: Francisco Beltrame (MPP).

Director of the Planning and Budget Office: Gabriel Frugoni (MPP).

Secretary to the Presidency: Homero Guerrero.

Assistant Secretary to the Presidency: Diego Cánepa.

MINISTRIES

Office of the President: Casa de Gobierno, Plaza Independencia 710, Torre Ejecutiva, 1° y 2°, 11000 Montevideo; tel. 2150 2647; fax 2917 1121; e-mail sci@presidencia.gub.uy; internet www .presidencia.gub.uy.

Ministry of Economy and Finance: Colonia 1089, 3°, 11100 Montevideo; tel. 2712 2910; fax 2712 2919; e-mail seprimef@mef .gub.uy; internet www.mef.gub.uy.

Ministry of Education and Culture: Reconquista 535, 9°, 11000 Montevideo; tel. 2916 1174; fax 2916 1048; e-mail centrodeinformacion@mec.gub.uy; internet www.mec.gub.uy.

Ministry of Foreign Affairs: Edif. Nuevo Colonia 1206, Palacio Santos, Avda 18 de Julio 1205, 11100 Montevideo; tel. 2902 1010; fax 2902 1349; e-mail webmaster@mrree.gub.uy; internet www.mrree .gub.uy.

Ministry of Housing, Territorial Regulation and the Environment: Zabala 1432, esq. 25 de Mayo, 11000 Montevideo; tel. 2917 0710; fax 2916 3914; e-mail ministro@mvotma.gub.uy; internet www .mvotma.gub.uy.

Ministry of Industry, Energy and Mining: Paysandú s/n, esq. Avda Libertador Brig. Gral Lavalleja, 4°, Montevideo; tel. 2900 0231; fax 2900 0291; e-mail ministro@miem.gub.uy; internet www.miem .gub.uy.

Ministry of the Interior: Mercedes 993, 11100 Montevideo; tel. 2152 4000; fax 2902 3142; e-mail unicom@minterior.gub.uy; internet www.minterior.gub.uy.

Ministry of Labour and Social Security: Juncal 1511, 4°, Planta Baja, 11000 Montevideo; tel. 2916 2681; fax 2916 2966; e-mail consultas@mtss.gub.uy; internet www.mtss.gub.uy.

Ministry of Livestock, Agriculture and Fishing: Avda Constituyente 1476, 1°, 11200 Montevideo; tel. 2412 6326; fax 2418 4051; e-mail ministro@mgap.gub.uy; internet www.mgap.gub.uy.

Ministry of National Defence: Edif. General Artigas, Avda 8 de Octubre 2628, Montevideo; tel. 2487 2828; fax 2481 4833; e-mail rrpp .secretaria@mdn.gub.uy; internet www.mdn.gub.uy.

Ministry of Public Health: Avda 18 de Julio 1892, 11100 Montevideo; tel. 2400 0101; fax 2408 5360; e-mail comunicaciones@msp .gub.uy; internet www.msp.gub.uy.

Ministry of Social Development: Avda 18 de Julio 1453, esq. Dr Javier Barrios Amorín, 2°, 11200 Montevideo; tel. and fax 2400 0302; e-mail ministra@mides.gub.uy; internet www.mides.gub.uy.

Ministry of Tourism and Sport: Rambla 25 de Agosto 1825, esq. Yacaré s/n, 11000 Montevideo; tel. 2188 5100; fax 2916 2487; e-mail webmaster@mintur.gub.uy; internet www.mintur.gub.uy.

Ministry of Transport and Public Works: Rincón 561, 11000 Montevideo; tel. 2915 8333; fax 2916 2883; e-mail difusion@mtop.gub .uy; internet www.mtop.gub.uy.

Planning and Budget Office: Plaza Independencia 710, Torre Ejecutivo, 11000 Montevideo; tel. 2150 3581; fax 2209 9730; e-mail direccion@opp.gub.uy; internet www.opp.gub.uy.

President and Legislature

PRESIDENT

Election, 25 October and 29 November 2009

Candidate	First round % of vote	Second round % of vote
José Alberto Mujica Cordano (Frente Amplio)	47.96	52.39
Luis Alberto Lacalle de Herrera (Partido Nacional)	29.07	43.51
Pedro Bordaberry Herrán (Partido Colorado)	17.02	—
Pablo Mieres Gómez (Partido Independiente)	2.49	—
Raúl Rodríguez da Silva (Asamblea Popular)	0.67	—
Invalid votes	2.79	4.10
Total	100.00	100.00

CONGRESS

Senate
(Cámara de Senadores)

President: Vice-Pres. Danilo Astori.

Election, 25 October 2009

Party	Seats
Frente Amplio	16
Partido Nacional	9
Partido Colorado	5
Total*	30

* An additional seat is reserved for the Vice-President, who sits as President of the Senate.

Chamber of Representatives
(Cámara de Representantes)

President: GERMÁN CARDOSO.
Election, 25 October 2009

Party	Seats
Frente Amplio	50
Partido Nacional	30
Partido Colorado	17
Partido Independiente	2
Total	**99**

Election Commission

Corte Electoral: Ituzaingó 1467, Montevideo; tel. 2915 8950; fax 2916 5088; e-mail corelect@adinet.com.uy; internet www.corteelectoral.gub.uy; f. 1967; Pres. Dr JOSÉ AROCENA.

Political Organizations

Asamblea Popular: Avda Daniel Fernández Crespo 1910 bis, esq. La Paz, Montevideo; tel. 2929 0861; e-mail prensaasambleapopular@gmail.com; internet www.asambleapopular.webcindario.com; f. 2008; extreme left-wing; mems include:

Movimiento de Defensa de los Jubilados: Leader HÉCTOR MORALES.

Movimiento 26 de Marzo: Durazno 1118, 11200 Montevideo; tel. 2902 3903; e-mail siempre26m@gmail.com; internet m26demarzo.blogspot.in; f. 1971; socialist; Pres. EDUARDO RUBIO; Sec.-Gen. FERNANDO VÁZQUEZ.

Partido Comunista Revolucionario: tel. 099962411 (mobile); e-mail pcruruguay@yahoo.com; internet www.pcr.org.uy; Sec.-Gen. RICARDO COHEN.

Partido Humanista: Durazno 1602, entre Lorenzo Carnelli y Minas, Montevideo; tel. 098001969 (mobile); e-mail partidohumanistauy@gmail.com; internet partidohumanistauy.jimdo.com; f. 1984; Leader DANIEL ROCCA.

Frente Amplio (FA): Colonia 1367, 2°, 11100 Montevideo; tel. 2902 6666; e-mail comunicacion@frenteamplio.org.uy; internet www.frenteamplio.org.uy; f. 1971; left-wing grouping; Pres. MÓNICA XAVIER; mems include:

Alianza Progresista 738 (AP): Colonia 1831, Montevideo; tel. and fax 2401 6365; e-mail a738@adinet.com.uy; internet alianza738.com.uy; f. 1998; left-wing; Leader RODOLFO NIN NOVOA.

Asamblea Uruguay (AU): Carlos Quijano 1273, Montevideo; tel. 2903 2121; fax 2924 1147; e-mail info@2121.org.uy; internet www.2121.org.uy; f. 1994; left; Leader DANILO ASTORI.

Corriente de Acción y Pensamiento-Libertad (CAP-L): Batoví 2169, esq. Nicaragua, Montevideo; tel. 2929 1740; e-mail 7373@caplibertad.org.uy; internet www.caplibertad.org.uy; f. 2007; Leader ELEUTERIO FERNÁNDEZ HUIDOBRO.

Frente Izquierda de Liberación (FIDEL): Mercedes 1244, Montevideo; tel. 2908 7530; e-mail contacto@fidel.com.uy; internet www.fidel.com.uy; f. 1962; socialist; Sec.-Gen. DOREEN IBARRA.

Movimiento de Liberación Nacional (MLN)—Tupamaros: Tristán Narvaja 1578, 11200 Montevideo; tel. 2409 2298; fax 2409 9957; e-mail mln@chasque.apc.org; internet www.chasque.net/mlnweb; f. 1962; radical socialist; during 1962–73 the MLN, operating under its popular name of the Tupamaros, conducted a campaign of urban guerrilla warfare until it was defeated by the military in 1973; following the return to civilian rule, in 1985, the MLN announced its decision to abandon its armed struggle; legally recognized in 1989; part of the MPP; Sec.-Gen. JULIO MARENALES.

Movimiento de Participación Popular (MPP): Mercedes 1368, 11200 Montevideo; tel. 2908 8900; fax 2903 2248; e-mail info@mppuruguay.org.uy; internet www.mpp.org.uy; f. 1989; grouping of left-wing parties incl. MLN—Tupamaros; Leader LUCÍA TOPOLANSKY.

Nuevo Espacio: Eduardo Acevedo 1615, 11200 Montevideo; tel. 2402 6990; fax 2402 6989; e-mail internacionales@nuevoespacio.org.uy; internet www.nuevoespacio.org.uy; f. 1994; social-democratic; allied to the FA since Dec. 2002; moderate left-wing; Leader RAFAEL MICHELINI; Sec. EDGARDO CARVALHO.

Partido Comunista de Uruguay (PCU): Fernández Crespo 2098, 11100 Montevideo; tel. 2924 2697; fax 2901 1050; e-mail partidocomunista@adinet.com.uy; internet www.pcu.org.uy; f. 1920; Sec.-Gen. EDUARDO LORIER; c. 42,000 mems.

Partido Demócrata Cristiano (PDC): Aquiles Lanza 1318 bis, 11100 Montevideo; tel. 2903 0704; fax 2902 1044; e-mail pdc@chasque.net; internet www.pdcuruguay.uy; f. 1962; fmrly Unión Cívica del Uruguay; allied to the Alianza Progresista 738; Pres. Dr JORGE RODRÍGUEZ MELÉNDEZ; Sec.-Gen. MATÍAS RODRÍGUEZ.

Partido Socialista del Uruguay (PS): Casa del Pueblo, Soriano 1218, 11100 Montevideo; tel. 2901 3344; fax 2908 2548; e-mail info@ps.org.uy; internet www.ps.org.uy; f. 1910; Pres. REINALDO GARGANO; Sec.-Gen. YERÚ PARDIÑAS.

Partido por la Victoria del Pueblo (PVP): Mercedes 1469, esq. Tacuarembó, Montevideo; tel. 2402 0370; e-mail info@pvp.org.uy; internet www.pvp.org.uy; f. 1975 in Buenos Aires, Argentina; left-wing; Sec.-Gen. PABLO ANZALONE; Spokesperson ANGEL VERA.

Vertiente Artiguista (VA): San José 1191, 11200 Montevideo; tel. 2900 0177; e-mail vertiente@vertiente.org.uy; internet www.vertiente.org.uy; f. 1989; left-wing; Leader Dr DAOIZ URIARTE.

Partido Colorado: Andrés Martínez Trueba 1271, 11100 Montevideo; tel. 2409 0180; e-mail info@partidocolorado.com.uy; internet www.partidocolorado.com.uy; f. 1836; Pres. MAX SAPOLINSKY; factions include:

Foro Batllista: Col. 1243, 11100 Montevideo; tel. 2903 0154; e-mail info@forobatllista.com.uy; internet www.forobatllista.com.uy; Leader Dr JULIO MARÍA SANGUINETTI CAIROLO.

Vanguardia Batllista: Casa de Vanguardia, Paysandú 1333, entre Ejido y Curiales, Montevideo; tel. 2902 7779; e-mail albertoscavarelli@yahoo.com; internet www.scavarelli.com; f. 1999.

Partido Independiente: Avda 18 de Julio 2015, Montevideo; tel. 2402 0120; e-mail info@partidoindependiente.org.uy; internet www.partidoindependiente.org.uy; Leader PABLO MIERES GÓMEZ.

Partido Nacional (Blanco): Juan Carlos Gómez 1384, Montevideo; tel. 2916 3831; fax 2916 3758; e-mail partidonacional@partidonacional.com.uy; internet www.partidonacional.com.uy; f. 1836; Exec. Pres. LUIS ALBERTO HEBER FONTANA; factions within the party include:

Alianza Nacional: Avda de las Leyes, Montevideo; tel. 2402 2020; fax 2209 7898; e-mail info@alianzanacional.com.uy; internet alianzanacional.com.uy; Leader JORGE LARRAÑAGA.

Concordia Nacional 747: Avda 18 de Julio 2139, esq. Juan Paullier, Montevideo; tel. 2401 4320; internet www.concordianacional.com.uy.

Consejo Nacional Herrerista: internet www.herrerismo.com.uy; Leader LUIS ALBERTO LACALLE DE HERRERA.

Desafío Nacional: Leader JUAN ANDRÉS RAMÍREZ.

Unión Cívica: Montevideo; tel. 2900 5535; e-mail info@unioncivica.org; internet unioncivica.org.uy; f. 1912; recognized Christian Democrat faction, split from the Partido Demócrata Cristiano in 1980; Leader ALDO LAMORTE.

Diplomatic Representation

EMBASSIES IN URUGUAY

Argentina: Cuareim 1470, 11800 Montevideo; tel. 2902 8166; fax 2900 8408; e-mail eurug@mrecic.gov.ar; internet www.eurug.mrecic.gov.ar; Ambassador MIGUEL DANTE DOVENA.

Bolivia: Dr Prudencio de Peña 2469, entre Campbell y Ponce, Casilla 11600, 11300 Montevideo; tel. 2708 3573; fax 2708 0066; e-mail embouy@adinet.com; Ambassador JUAN CARLOS BLANCO FERRI.

Brazil: Blvd Artigas 1328, 11300 Montevideo; tel. 2707 2119; fax 2707 2086; e-mail montevideu@brasemb.org.uy; internet www.brasil.org.uy; Ambassador JOÃO CARLOS DE SOUZA-GOMES.

Canada: Plaza Independencia 749, Of. 102, 11100 Montevideo; tel. 2902 2030; fax 2902 2029; e-mail mvdeo@international.gc.ca; internet www.canadainternational.gc.ca/uruguay; Ambassador CLAIRE POULIN.

Chile: 25 de Mayo 575, entre Juan Carlos Gómez e Ituzaingo, Montevideo; tel. 2916 4090; fax 2916 4083; e-mail echileuy@netgate.com.uy; internet chileabroad.gov.cl/uruguay; Ambassador EDUARDO CONTRERAS.

China, People's Republic: Miraflores 1508, esq. Pedro Blanes Viale, Carrasco, Casilla 18966, Montevideo; tel. 2606 2958; fax 2604 2637; e-mail embchina@adinet.com.uy; internet uy.china-embassy.org; Ambassador YAN BANGHUA.

Colombia: Calle Dr José Scosería 2815, Montevideo; tel. 2711 5424; fax 2711 5424; e-mail euruguay@cancilleria.gov.co; internet uruguay.embajada.gov.co/; Ambassador ALEJANDRO BORDA ROJAS.

Costa Rica: Roque Graseras 740, entre Solano Antuña y Juan María Pérez, Casilla 12242, Montevideo; tel. 2711 6408; fax 2712 0872; e-mail embarica@adinet.com.uy; Ambassador JOSÉ MARÍA TIJERINO PACHECO.

Cuba: Feliciano Rodríguez 2690, entre Francisco Soca y General Espartero, Parque Batlle, Montevideo; tel. 2709 0035; fax 2708 2133; e-mail emcuburu@adinet.com.uy; internet embacu.cubaminrex.cu/uruguay; Ambassador MERCEDES VICENTE SOTOLONGO.

Dominican Republic: Tomás de Tezanos 1186, entre Arturo Prat y Miguel Grau, 11300 Montevideo; tel. 2628 7766; fax 2628 9655; e-mail embajadomuruguay@adinet.com.uy; Ambassador DANIEL GUERRERO TAVERAS.

Ecuador: Juan María Pérez 2810, Montevideo; tel. 2711 0448; fax 2710 2492; e-mail embajadaecuador@netgate.com.uy; Ambassador EMILIO IZQUIERDO MIÑO.

Egypt: Avda Brasil 2663, 11300 Montevideo; tel. 2709 6412; fax 2708 0977; e-mail embassy.montevideo@mfa.gov.eg; Ambassador SAMI MAHMOUD ALI SALEM.

El Salvador: Arq. Raúl Lerena Acevedo 1453, Punta Gorda, 11300 Montevideo; tel. 2613 4143; fax 2619 9473; e-mail embasauy@dedicado.net.uy; Ambassador CARLOS ABARCA GÓMEZ.

France: Avda Uruguay 853, Casilla 290, 11100 Montevideo; tel. 2705 0000; fax 2705 0110; e-mail ambafranceuruguay@gmail.com; internet www.ambafranceuruguay.org; Ambassador SYLVAIN ITTE.

Germany: La Cumparsita 1435, Plaza Alemania, Casilla 20014, 11200 Montevideo; tel. 2902 5222; fax 2902 3422; e-mail info@montevideo.diplo.de; internet www.montevideo.diplo.de; Ambassador Dr HEINZ PETERS.

Greece: Blvd José G. Artigas 1231, 11600 Montevideo; tel. 2706 9092; fax 2709 8959; e-mail gremb.mvd@mfa.gr; internet www.mfa.gr/montevideo; Ambassador LOUIS-ALKIVIADIS ABATÍS.

Guatemala: Costa Rica 1538, Carrasco, Montevideo; tel. and fax 2601 2225; fax 2601 4057; e-mail embaguate-uruguay@minex.gob.gt; Ambassador ROBERTO LEVA RAPELA.

Holy See: Blvd Artigas 1330, Casilla 1503, 11300 Montevideo (Apostolic Nunciature); tel. 2707 2016; fax 2707 2209; e-mail nuntius@adinet.com.uy; Apostolic Nuncio Rev. GEORGE PANIKULAM.

Iran: Blvd Artigas 531, Montevideo; tel. 2711 6657; fax 2711 6659; e-mail embajada.iran@adinet.com.uy; Ambassador ESLAMIAN KOUPEI SAFAR ALÍ.

Israel: Blvd Artigas 1585, 11200 Montevideo; tel. 2400 4164; fax 2409 5821; e-mail info@montevideo.mfa.gov.il; internet montevideo.mfa.gov.il; Ambassador DORI GOREN.

Italy: José Benito Lamas 2857, Casilla 268, 11300 Montevideo; tel. 2708 4916; fax 2708 4148; e-mail ambasciata.montevideo@esteri.it; internet www.ambmontevideo.esteri.it; Ambassador VINCENZO PALLADINO.

Japan: Blvd Artigas 953, 11300 Montevideo; tel. 2418 7645; fax 2418 7980; e-mail embjapon@adinet.com.uy; internet www.uy.emb-japan.go.jp; Ambassador KAZUAKI OBE.

Korea, Republic: Edif. World Trade Center, Avda Luis Alberto de Herrera 1248, Torre 2, 10°, Montevideo; tel. 2628 9374; fax 2628 9376; e-mail koemur@gmail.com; internet ury.mofat.go.kr; Ambassador CHOI YEON-CHOONG.

Lebanon: Avda General Rivera 2278, Montevideo; tel. 2408 6640; fax 2408 6365; e-mail embliban@adinet.com.uy; Chargé d'affaires a.i. JIMMY ZAKHIA DOUAIHY.

Mexico: Radisson Victoria Plaza Hotel, 7°, Torre Vieja, Plaza Independencia 753, 11100 Montevideo; tel. 2900 7345; fax 2908 7452; e-mail embajada-mexico@embamex.com.uy; internet embamex.sre.gob.mx/uruguay; Ambassador FELIPE ENRÍQUEZ HERNÁNDEZ.

Nicaragua: Calle Sarandí 669, Montevideo; tel. 2916 2175; e-mail embanic.uy@gmail.com; Ambassador MAURIZIO GELLI.

Panama: Juan Benito Blanco 3388, Montevideo; tel. 2623 0301; fax 2623 0300; e-mail empanuru@netgate.com.uy; Ambassador ANSELMO CASTRO STRUNZ.

Paraguay: García Cortina 2365, Montevideo; tel. 2710 6774; fax 2711 8326; e-mail embapur@gmail.com; Ambassador LUÍS ENRIQUE CHASE PLATE.

Peru: Obligado 1384, 11300 Montevideo; tel. 2707 6862; fax 2707 7793; e-mail embamontevideo@embaperu.org.uy; Ambassador AIDA DEL CARMEN JESÚS NARANJO MORALES.

Portugal: Avda Dr Francisco Soca 1128, Apto 701, 11300 Montevideo; tel. 2708 4061; fax 2709 6456; e-mail embport@montevideu.dgaccp.pt; internet www.embajadadeportugalmontevideo.com; Chargé d'affaires a.i. ANTÓNIO JOSÉ ALVES DE CARVALHO.

Qatar: Gral Santander 1698, Montevideo; tel. 2902 0111; fax 2902 0131; e-mail Montevideo@mofa.gov.qa; Ambassador MOHAMMED HASSEN AL-JABIR.

Romania: Echevarriarza 3452, Casilla 12040, 11000 Montevideo; tel. 2622 0135; fax 2622 0685; e-mail ambromvd@adinet.com.uy; Ambassador VALENTIN FLOREA.

Russia: Blvd España 2741, 11300 Montevideo; tel. 2708 1884; fax 2708 6597; e-mail embaru@montevideo.com.uy; internet www.uruguay.mid.ru; Ambassador ALEXEY K. LABETSKIY.

South Africa: Dr Gabriel Otero 6337, Carrasco, 11300 Montevideo; tel. 2601 7591; fax 2600 3165; e-mail montevideo.general@foreign.gov.za; Chargé d'affaires a.i. ELLEN MOSOLWA HAJIE.

Spain: Avda Libertad 2738, 11300 Montevideo; tel. 2708 6010; fax 2707 9551; e-mail emb.montevideo@maec.es; internet www.exteriores.gob.es/embajadas/montevideo; Ambassador ROBERTO VARELA FARIÑA.

Switzerland: Ing. Federico Abadie 2936/40, 11°, Casilla 12261, 11300 Montevideo; tel. 4311 6491; fax 2711 5031; e-mail mtv.vertretung@eda.admin.ch; internet www.eda.admin.ch/montevideo; Ambassador DIDIER PFIRTER.

United Kingdom: Marco Bruto 1073, Casilla 16024, 11300 Montevideo; tel. 2622 3630; fax 2622 3650; e-mail ukinuruguay@gmail.com; internet ukinuruguay.fco.gov.uk; Ambassador BEN LYSTER-BINNS.

USA: Lauro Muller 1776, 11200 Montevideo; tel. 1770 2162; fax 1770 2128; e-mail webmastermvd@state.gov; internet uruguay.usembassy.gov; Ambassador JULISSA REYNOSO.

Venezuela: Rincón 745, Esq. Ciudadela, Ciudad Vieja, Montevideo; tel. 2900 2444; fax 2901 7642; e-mail embve.uymtv@mppre.gob.ve; internet www.embvenezuelauy.org; Ambassador JULIO RAMÓN CHIRINO RODRÍGUEZ.

Judicial System

The Supreme Court of Justice comprises five members for a period of five years. It has original jurisdiction in constitutional, international and admiralty cases, and hears appeals from the appellate courts, of which there are seven, each with three judges.

Cases involving the functioning of the state administration are heard in the ordinary Administrative Courts and in the Supreme Administrative Court, which consists of five members appointed in the same way as members of the Supreme Court of Justice.

In Montevideo there are 19 civil courts, 10 criminal and correctional courts, 19 courts presided over by justices of the peace, three juvenile courts, three labour courts and courts for government and other cases. Each departmental capital, and some other cities, have a departmental court; each of the 224 judicial divisions has a justice of the peace.

Suprema Corte de Justicia: Pasaje de los Derechos Humanos 1310, Montevideo; tel. 2900 1041; fax 2902 3500; e-mail secruibal@poderjudicial.gub.uy; internet www.poderjudicial.gub.uy; Pres. JORGE RUIBAL PINO.

Tribunal de lo Contencioso Administrativo (Supreme Administrative Court): Mercedes 961, 11100 Montevideo; tel. 2901 5205; fax 2908 0539; e-mail epineyrua@tca.gub.uy; internet www.tca.gub.uy; Pres. Dr JUAN PEDRO TOBÍA FERNÁNDEZ.

Religion

Under the Constitution, the Church and the State are declared separate and toleration for all forms of worship was proclaimed. Roman Catholicism predominates.

CHRISTIANITY

Federación de Iglesias Evangélicas del Uruguay: Avda 8 de Octubre 3324, 11600 Montevideo; tel. and fax 2487 5907; e-mail fieul@adinet.com.uy; internet www.chasque.net/obra/skontakt.htm; f. 1956; eight mem. churches; Pres. OSCAR BOLIOLI; Sec. OBED BODYAJIAN.

The Roman Catholic Church

Uruguay comprises one archdiocese and nine dioceses. Some 46% of the population are Roman Catholics.

Bishops' Conference: Conferencia Episcopal Uruguaya, Avda Uruguay 1319, 11100 Montevideo; tel. 2900 2642; fax 2901 1802; e-mail ceudecos@adinet.com.uy; internet www.iglesiacatolica.org.uy; f. 1972; Pres. Rt Rev. RODOLFO COLLAZZI WIRZ (Bishop of Maldonado-Punta del Este).

Archbishop of Montevideo: Mgr DANIEL FERNANDO STURLA BERHOUET, Arzobispado, Treinta y Tres 1368, Casilla 356, 11000 Montevideo; tel. 2915 8127; fax 2915 8926; e-mail info@arquidiocesis.net; internet www.arquidiocesis.net.

The Anglican Communion

Uruguay constitutes a diocese in the Province of the Southern Cone of America. The presiding Bishop of the Iglesia Anglicana del Cono Sur de América is the Bishop of Northern Argentina.

Bishop of Uruguay: Rt Rev. MICHELE FRANK POLLESEL, Centro Diocesano, Reconquista 522, Casilla 6108, 11000 Montevideo; tel. 2915 9627; fax 2916 2519; e-mail mtamayo@netgate.com.uy; internet www.uruguay.anglican.org.

Other Churches

Church of Jesus Christ of Latter-Day Saints (Mormons): Bolonia 1722, Carrasco, 11500 Montevideo; tel. 2604 2212; internet www.lds.org; 99,758 mems.

Iglesia Adventista del Séptimo Día (Seventh Day Adventist Church): Mateo Vidal 3211, 11600 Montevideo; tel. 2481 0173; e-mail contact@adventistas.org.uy; internet www.adventistas.org.uy; f. 1893; Pres. CARLOS SÁNCHEZ; 4,000 mems.

Iglesia Evangélica Valdense (Waldensian Evangelical Church): Avda 8 de Octubre 3039, 11600 Montevideo; tel. and fax 2487 9406; e-mail ievm@internet.com.uy; f. 1952; 13,000 mems; Pastor HUGO ARMAND PILÓN.

Iglesia Metodista en el Uruguay (Methodist Church in Uruguay): Javier Barrios Amorín 1310, 11200 Montevideo; tel. 2413 6552; fax 2413 6554; e-mail informes@imu.org.uy; internet www.imu.org.uy; f. 1878; 1,193 mems (1997); Pres. Rev. OSCAR BOLIOLI.

Iglesia Pentecostal Unida Internacional en Uruguay (United Pentecostal Church International in Uruguay): Avda 8 de Octubre 2816, 12200 Montevideo; tel. 2487 8195; e-mail secretario@ipuruguay.org; internet ipuruguay.org; Pres. DARRY CROSSLEY.

Primera Iglesia Evangélica Bautista (First Evangelical Baptist Church): Avda Daniel Fernández Crespo 1741, Casilla 5051, 11200 Montevideo; tel. 2409 8744; fax 2409 4356; e-mail piebu@adinet.com.uy; internet www.piebu.org; f. 1911; 314 mems; Pastor LEMUEL J. LARROSA.

Other denominations active in Uruguay include the Iglesia Evangélica del Río de la Plata and the Iglesia Evangélica Menonita (Evangelical Mennonite Church).

BAHÁ'Í FAITH

National Spiritual Assembly of the Bahá'ís: Blvd Artigas 2440, 11600 Montevideo; tel. 2487 5890; fax 2480 2165; e-mail bahai@multi.com.uy; f. 1938; mems resident in 140 localities.

The Press

DAILIES

Montevideo

El Diario Español: Cerrito 551–555, Casilla 899, 11000 Montevideo; tel. 2915 9481; fax 2915 7389; e-mail marcelo.reinante@eldiarioespanol.com.uy; f. 1905; morning (except Monday); newspaper of the Spanish community; Editor MARCELO REINANTE; circ. 20,000.

Diario Oficial: Avda 18 de Julio 1373, Montevideo; tel. 2908 5042; fax 2902 3098; e-mail impo@impo.com.uy; internet www.impo.com.uy; f. 1905; bi-weekly; publishes laws, official decrees, parliamentary debates, judicial decisions and legal transactions; Dir-Gen. GONZALO REBOLEDO.

El Observador: Cuareim 2052, 11800 Montevideo; tel. 2924 7000; fax 2924 8698; e-mail usuarios@elobservador.com.uy; internet www.elobservador.com.uy; f. 1991; morning; Dir RICARDO PEIRANO; Chief Editor GABRIEL PEREYRA; circ. 26,000.

El País: Zelmar Michelini 1287, 5°, 11100 Montevideo; tel. 2902 0115; fax 2902 0464; e-mail comunidad@elpais.com.uy; internet www.elpais.com.uy; f. 1918; morning; supports the Partido Nacional; Editor MARTÍN AGUIRRE REGULES; circ. 106,000.

La República: Avda Gral Garibaldi 2579, 11600 Montevideo; tel. 2487 3565; fax 2487 3824; e-mail web.la.republica@gmail.com; internet www.republica.com.uy; f. 1988; morning; Editor GUSTAVO CARABAJAL; Gen. Man. VALENTÍN ACOSTA; circ. 25,000.

Ultimas Noticias: Paysandú 1179, 11100 Montevideo; tel. 2902 0452; fax 2902 4669; e-mail redaccion@unoticias.com.uy; internet www.unoticias.com.uy; f. 1981; evening (except Sat.); owned by Impresora Polo; Dir ÁLVARO GIZ; circ. 25,000.

Florida

El Heraldo: Independencia 824, 94000 Florida; tel. 4352 2229; fax 4352 4546; e-mail elheraldo@elheraldo.com.uy; internet www.diarioelheraldo.com.uy; f. 1919; morning; independent; Dir ALVARO RIVA REY; circ. 20,000.

Maldonado

Correo de Punta del Este: Edif. del Virrey, Casi 33 Sarandí, 20000 Maldonado; tel. and fax 4223 5633; e-mail info@correodepuntadeleste.com; internet correodepuntadeleste.com; f. 1993; morning; Editor MARCELO GALLARDO; circ. 2,500.

Paysandú

El Telégrafo: Avda 18 de Julio 1027, 60000 Paysandú; tel. 4722 3141; fax 4722 7999; e-mail correo@eltelegrafo.com; internet www.eltelegrafo.com; f. 1910; morning; independent; Dir ALBERTO BACCARO; circ. 9,000.

Salto

El Pueblo: Avda 18 de Julio 151, entre Artigas y Rivera, Salto; tel. 4733 4133; e-mail dipueblo@adinet.com.uy; internet www.diarioelpueblo.com.uy; f. 1959; morning; Dir ADRIANA MARTÍNEZ.

PERIODICALS

Brecha: Avda Uruguay 844, 11100 Montevideo; tel. 2902 5042; fax 2902 0388; e-mail brecha@brecha.com.uy; internet brecha.com.uy; f. 1985; weekly; politics, current affairs; Dir and Editor DANIEL EROSA; circ. 8,500.

Búsqueda: Mercedes 1131, 11100 Montevideo; tel. 2902 1300; fax 2902 2036; e-mail busqueda@busqueda.com.uy; internet semanario.busqueda.com.uy; f. 1972; weekly (Thurs.); independent; politics and economics; Dir CLAUDIO PAOLILLO; Editor ANDRÉS DANZA; circ. 25,000.

Charoná: Avda General Garibaldi 2579, Montevideo; tel. 2487 3565; e-mail administracion@charona.com; internet www.charona.com.uy; f. 1968; fortnightly; children's; Dir SERGIO BOFFANO; circ. 25,000.

Crónicas Económicas: Avda Libertador Brig.-Gen. Lavalleja 1532, Montevideo; tel. 2900 4790; fax 2902 0759; e-mail cronicas@netgate.com.uy; internet www.cronicas.com.uy; f. 1981; weekly; independent; business and economics; Dirs JULIO ARIEL FRANCO, WALTER HUGO PAGÉS, JORGE ESTELLANO.

El Derecho Digital: Montevideo; tel. 2409 9643; e-mail administracion@elderechodigital.com.uy; internet www.elderechodigital.com.uy; legal; Dir LUIS FERNANDO IGLESIAS; Editor FERNANDO VARGAS.

El Diario Medico: Avda 18 de Julio 1485, 2°, Montevideo; tel. and fax 2408 3797; e-mail eldiariomedico@eldiariomedico.com.uy; internet www.eldiariomedico.com.uy; f. 1997; health; Dir ELBIO D. ALVAREZ.

Guambia: Rimac 1576, 11400 Montevideo; tel. and fax 2613 2703; e-mail info@guambia.com.uy; internet www.guambia.com.uy; f. 1983; monthly; satirical; Dir and Editor ANTONIO DABEZIES.

La Justicia Uruguaya: Avda 25 de Mayo 555, Apto 404, 11000 Montevideo; tel. 2915 7587; fax 2915 9721; e-mail lajusticiauruguaya@lju.com.uy; internet www.lajusticiauruguaya.com.uy; f. 1940; bimonthly; jurisprudence; Dirs EDUARDO ALBANELL MARTINO, ADOLFO ALBANELL MARTINO (Editor); circ. 3,000.

Marketing Directo: Guaná 2237 bis, 11200 Montevideo; tel. 9961 6758; fax 2408 7221; e-mail cieccweb@adinet.com.uy; internet www.coaching.edu.uy; f. 1988; monthly; Dir EDGARDO MARTÍNEZ ZIMARIOFF; circ. 9,500.

Opinar: Río Negro 1192/60, Montevideo; tel. 099686125 (mobile); e-mail cgarcia@opinar.com; internet www.opinar.com.uy; communist; Dir TABARÉ VIERA DUARTE; Editor CÉSAR GARCÍA ACOSTA.

Patria: Montevideo; e-mail redaccion@patria.com.uy; internet www.patria.com.uy; weekly; organ of the Partido Nacional; right-wing; Dir LUIS A. HEBER; Editor Dr JOSÉ LUIS BELLANI.

Propiedades: Yaguarón 1407, Of. 1203, Montevideo; tel. 2711 8384; fax 2712 1674; e-mail redaccion@revistapropiedades.com.uy; internet www.revistapropiedades.com.uy; f. 1987; construction and real estate; Dir JULIO C. VILLAMIDE.

Uruguay Natural: Ibiray 2293, 11300 Montevideo; tel. 2711 4900; fax 2712 3421; e-mail info@uruguaynatural.com.uy; internet www.uruguaynatural.com.uy; tourism; Pres. JAVIER SANTOMÉ SOSA DIAS; Dir FERNANDO ROJO SANTANA.

Voces: Chaná 2389, Montevideo; tel. 2401 8298; e-mail voces@voces.com.uy; internet www.voces.com.uy; political, social, economic and cultural; Editor ALFREDO GARCÍA.

PRESS ASSOCIATIONS

Asociación de Diarios y Periódicos del Uruguay (ADYPU): Río Negro 1308, 6°, 11100 Montevideo; f. 1922; Pres. GUILLERMO SCHECK.

Asociación de la Prensa Uruguaya: San José 1330, Montevideo; tel. and fax 2901 3695; e-mail apu@adinet.com.uy; internet www.apu.org.uy; f. 1944; Pres. RÚBEN HERNÁNDEZ; Sec.-Gen. LUIS CURBELO.

Publishers

Cemar Editorial: Martin C. Maritinez 1664, 11200 Montevideo; tel. 2401 9137; fax 2409 7261; e-mail info@cemar.com.uy; internet www .cemar.com.uy; general non-fiction; Dir MERCEDES RIPOLL.

CENCI—Uruguay (Centro de Estadísticas Nacionales y Comercio Internacional): Juncal 1327D, Of. 1603, Casilla 1510, 11000 Montevideo; tel. 2915 2930; fax 2915 4578; e-mail cenci@cenci.com.uy; internet www.cenci.com.uy; f. 1956; economics, statistics; Dir KENNETH BRUNNER.

Ediciones de la Banda Oriental: Gaboto 1582, 11200 Montevideo; tel. 2408 3206; fax 2409 8138; e-mail info@bandaoriental.com.uy; internet www.bandaoriental.com.uy; f. 1961; general literature; Man. Dir ALCIDES ABELLA.

Ediciones HUM (Casa Editorial Hum): Jackson 1111, 11200 Montevideo; tel. and fax 2410 3936; e-mail info@casaeditorialhum.com; internet www.casaeditorialhum.com; f. 2005; Dir MARTÍN FERNÁNDEZ.

Ediciones Trilce: Durazno 1888, 11200 Montevideo; tel. 2412 7662; fax 2412 7722; e-mail trilce@trilce.com.uy; internet www.trilce.com .uy; f. 1985; science, politics, history; Dir PABLO HARARI.

Ediciones Urano: Uruguay 1579, 11200 Montevideo; tel. 2402 8469; fax 2408 5293; e-mail infour@edicionesurano.com; internet www.edicionesurano.com; subsidiary of Ediciones Uranos, Spain; alternative medicine, health and lifestyle; Dir REINALDO RODRÍGUEZ.

Editorial Agropecuaria Hemisferio Sur: Buenos Aires 335, Casilla 1755, 11000 Montevideo; tel. 2916 4515; fax 2916 4520; e-mail editorial@hemisferiosur.com; internet www.hemisferiosur .com; f. 1951; agronomy and veterinary science; Dir MARGARITA PERI.

Editorial Arca: Maldonado 1343, esq. Ejido, Montevideo; tel. 2900 6478; fax 2900 6478; e-mail arcaeditorial@adinet.com.uy; internet www.arcaeditorial.com; f. 1963; general literature, social science and history; Man. Dir GABRIELA MÁRQUEZ.

Editorial Océano del Uruguay, SA: Salvador Ferrer Serra 1966, 11200 Montevideo; tel. and fax 2403 6090; e-mail gbosca@ oceanouruguay.com; internet www.oceanouruguay.com; subsidiary of Grupo Océano, Spain; Dir-Gen. GUSTAVO BOSCA.

Editorial Sudamericana Uruguaya, SA (Random House Mondadori): Yaguarón 1568, 11100 Montevideo; tel. 2901 3668; e-mail ventas@rhm.com.uy; internet www.rhm.com.uy; general fiction and non-fiction; Dir LUIS SICA.

Fundación de Cultura Universitaria: 25 de Mayo 568, Casilla 1155, 11000 Montevideo; tel. 2916 1152; fax 2915 1103; e-mail administrador@fcu.com.uy; internet www.fcu.com.uy; f. 1968; law and social sciences; Pres. Dr MARCELO VIGO.

Granica Ediciones: Scoseria 2639, 11300 Montevideo; tel. 2712 4857; fax 2712 4858; e-mail granica.uy@granicaeditor.com; internet www.granicaeditor.com; general non-fiction; Dir DIEGO SIMÓN.

Librería Linardi y Risso: Juan Carlos Gómez 1435, 11000 Montevideo; tel. 2915 7129; fax 2915 7431; e-mail libros@linardiyrisso .com.uy; internet www.linardiyrisso.com.uy; f. 1944; general; Man. Dirs ALVARO RISSO, ANDRÉS LINARDI.

A. Monteverde & Cía, SA (Editorial Monteverde): Treinta y Tres 1475, Casilla 371, 11000 Montevideo; tel. 2915 2939; fax 2915 2012; e-mail monteverde@monteverde.com.uy; internet www.monteverde .com.uy; f. 1879; educational; Man. Dir TERESITA MUSSINI.

Mosca Hermanos SA: Avda 18 de Julio 1578, 11300 Montevideo; tel. 2409 3141; fax 2408 8059; e-mail mosca@mosca.com.uy; internet www.mosca.com.uy; f. 1888 as Librería La Popular; changed name as above in 1947; general; Pres. SILVIA HERNÁNDEZ.

Psicolibros Waslala: Mercedes 1673, Montevideo; tel. 2400 3808; fax 2403 0332; e-mail lperez@psicolibroswaslala.com; internet www .psicolibroswaslala.com; f. 1997; psychology; Dir LOURDES PÉREZ.

Vintén Editor: Hocquart 1771, 11804 Montevideo; tel. 2209 0223; internet vinten-uy.com; f. 1980; poetry, theatre, history, art, literature.

PUBLISHERS' ASSOCIATION

Cámara Uruguaya del Libro: Colón 1476, Casilla 102, 11000 Montevideo; tel. 2916 7628; fax 2916 9374; e-mail gerencia@ camaradellibro.com.uy; internet www.camaradellibro.com.uy; f. 1944; Pres. ALVARO RISSO; Man. CRISTINA APPRATTO.

Broadcasting and Communications

REGULATORY AUTHORITY

Unidad Reguladora de Servicios de Comunicaciones (URSEC): Uruguay 988, 11100, Montevideo; tel. 2902 8082; fax 2900 5708; e-mail webmaster@ursec.gub.uy; internet www.ursec .gub.uy; regulates broadcasting, telecommunications and postal sectors; Pres. GABRIEL LOMBIDE; Gen. Man. GONZALO BALSEIRO GIGLIO.

TELECOMMUNICATIONS

Administración Nacional de Telecomunicaciones (Antel): Complejo Torre de las Telecomunicaciones, Guatemala 1075, Montevideo; tel. 2928 0000; e-mail antel@antel.com.uy; internet www .antel.com.uy; f. 1974; state-owned; Pres. CAROLINA COSSE; Gen. Man. HORACIO ANDRÉS TOLOSA.

Claro: Avda General San Martin 2460, Montevideo; tel. 2201 1500; e-mail webmaster@claro.com.uy; internet www.claro.com.uy; owned by América Móvil, SA de CV (Mexico); fmrly CTI Móvil; name changed as above in 2008; mobile telephone services; Gen. Man. HORACIO ALVARELLOS.

Dedicado, SA: Plaza Independencia 755, 10°, Torre Radisson Victoria Plaza, Montevideo; tel. 2901 1010; fax 2900 9923; e-mail info@dedicado.com.uy; internet www.dedicado.com.uy; internet services provider; CEO ARTURO VARGAS.

Movistar Uruguay (Telefónica Móviles de Uruguay): Avda Francisco Soca 1444, 11200 Montevideo; tel. 9570 2611; fax 2402 2395; internet www.movistar.com.uy; f. 2005; owned by Telefónica Móviles, SA (Spain); mobile telephone services; Pres. PABLO DE SALTERAIN.

BROADCASTING

Radio

El Espectador: Río Branco 1481, 11100 Montevideo; tel. 2902 3531; fax 2908 3192; e-mail ventas@espectador.com; internet www .espectador.com; f. 1923; commercial; Gen. Man. ESTELA BARTOLIC.

FM del Sol: Plaza Independencia 753, Of. 201, 2°, Montevideo; tel. 2903 2225; e-mail marketing@fmdelsol.com; internet www.fmdelsol .com.

Radio Carve: Mercedes 973, 11100 Montevideo; tel. 2902 6162; fax 2902 0126; e-mail carve@sadrep.com.uy; internet www.carve850 .com.uy; f. 1928; commercial; Dir HÉCTOR CARLOS VERA.

Radio Montecarlo: Avda 18 de Julio 1224, 1°, 11100 Montevideo; tel. 2901 4433; fax 2901 7762; e-mail cx20@radiomontecarlo.com.uy; internet www.radiomontecarlo.com.uy; f. 1924; commercial; Dir DANIEL ROMAY.

Radio Sarandí: Enriqueta Compte y Riqué 1250, 11800 Montevideo; tel. 2208 2612; fax 2203 6906; e-mail direccion@sarandi690 .com.uy; internet www.radiosarandi.com.uy; f. 1931; commercial; Pres. RAMIRO RODRÍGUEZ VALLAMIL RIVIERE.

Radio Universal: Avda 18 de Julio 1220, 3°, 11100 Montevideo; tel. 2903 2222; fax 2902 6050; e-mail info@22universal.com; internet www.22universal.com; f. 1929; commercial; Pres. OSCAR IMPERIO.

Radiodifusión Nacional SODRE: Sarandí 430, 11000 Montevideo; tel. 2916 1933; fax 2916 1934; e-mail dirradio@sodre.gub.uy; internet www.sodre.gub.uy; f. 1929; state-owned; operates Radio Clásica 650 AM, Radio Uruguay 1050 AM, Emisora del Sur 94.7 FM and Babel 97.1 FM; Dir SERGIO SACOMANI.

Television

The Uruguayan Government holds a 10% stake in the regional television channel Telesur, which began operations in 2005 and is based in Caracas, Venezuela.

Canal 4 Monte Carlo: Paraguay 2253, 11800 Montevideo; tel. 2924 4444; fax 2924 7929; e-mail webmontecarlotv@montecarlotv.com.uy; internet www.canal4.com.uy; f. 1961; Dir HUGO ROMAY SALVO.

SAETA TV—Canal 10: Dr Lorenzo Carnelli 1234, 11200 Montevideo; tel. 2410 2120; fax 2400 9771; internet www.canal10.com.uy; f. 1956; Pres. JORGE DE FEO.

SODRE (Servicio Oficial de Difusión Radiotelevisión y Espectáculos): Blvd Artigas 2552, 11600 Montevideo; tel. 2480 6448; fax 2480 8515; e-mail direccion@tveo.com.uy; internet www.sodre.gub.uy; f. 1963; Pres. FERNANDO BUTAZZONI.

Teledoce Televisora Color—Canal 12: Enriqueta Compte y Riqué 1276, 11800 Montevideo; tel. 2208 3555; fax 2203 7623; e-mail latele@teledoce.com; internet www.teledoce.com; f. 1962; Gen. Man. (vacant).

Tevé Ciudad: Javier Barrios Amorín 1460, Montevideo; tel. 2400 1908; fax 2402 9369; e-mail griselda.diaz@imm.gub.uy; internet www.teveciudad.com; f. 1996; state-owned; Gen. Dir GRISELDA DÍAZ LARREA.

Association

Asociación Nacional de Broadcasters Uruguayos (ANDEBU): Carlos Quijano 1264, 11100 Montevideo; tel. 2902 1525; fax 2908 0037; e-mail info@andebu.org; internet www.andebu.org; f. 1933; represents private radio and television broadcasters; 101 mems; Pres. RAFAEL INCHAUSTI; Sec. GABRIEL SILVA.

Finance

BANKING

(cap. = capital; res = reserves; dep. = deposits; m. = million; brs = branches; amounts in pesos uruguayos, unless otherwise indicated)

State Banks

Banco Central del Uruguay: Avda Juan P. Fabini 777, Casilla 1467, 11100 Montevideo; tel. 2908 5629; fax 2902 1634; e-mail info@bcu.gub.uy; internet www.bcu.gub.uy; f. 1967; note-issuing bank, also controls private banking; cap. 10,027.0m., res 4,529.0m., dep. 193,431.0m. (Dec. 2009); Pres. ALBERTO GRAÑA; Dir WASHINGTON RIBEIRO; Vice-Pres. JORGE GAMARRA.

Banco Hipotecario del Uruguay (BHU): Avda Daniel Fernández Crespo 1508, Montevideo; tel. 2409 0000; fax 2409 0782; e-mail info@bhu.net; internet www.bhu.net; f. 1892; state mortgage bank; in 1977 assumed responsibility for housing projects in Uruguay; cap. 28,700m., res 15,494.9m., dep. 12,670.7m. (Dec. 2012); Pres. ANA SALVERAGLIO.

Banco de la República Oriental del Uruguay (BROU): Cerrito y Zabala 351, 11000 Montevideo; tel. 2915 0157; fax 2916 2064; e-mail broupte@adinet.com.uy; internet www.brounet.com.uy; f. 1896; cap. 18,029.5m., res −218.5m., dep. 205,967.5m. (Dec. 2011); Pres. JULIO CÉSAR PORTEIRO; Gen. Man. DANIEL GARCÍA AZPIROZ; 117 brs.

Principal Commercial Banks

Banco Bilbao Vizcaya Argentaria Uruguay SA (BBVA): 25 de Mayo 401, esq. Zabala, 11000 Montevideo; tel. 2916 1444; fax 2916 2821; internet www.bbva.com.uy; f. 1968; fmrly Unión de Bancos del Uruguay, and later Banesto Banco Uruguay, SA and Banco Francés Uruguay, SA; adopted current name in 2000 following merger with Banco Exterior de América, SA; bought Crédit Uruguay Banco SA in April 2011; cap. 3,766.3m., res −281.5m., dep. 47,566.7m. (Dec. 2012); Pres. RAFAEL GONZÁLEZ MOYA; 9 brs.

Banco Santander, SA: Julio Herrera y Obes 1365, Casilla 888, 11100 Montevideo; tel. 2903 1073; fax 2902 5011; internet www.santander.com.uy; f. 1952 as ABN AMRO Bank Uruguay; bought by Grupo Santander (Spain) in 2008; cap. 7,265.8m., res 1,021m., dep. 77,160.1m. (Dec. 2012); Pres. JORGE JOURDAN; 38 brs.

Banque Heritage (Uruguay): Rincón 530, 11000 Montevideo; tel. 2916 0177; fax 2916 5256; e-mail banqueheritage@heritage.com.uy; internet www.heritage.com.uy; f. 1981 as Surinvest Casa Bancaria; name changed to Banco Surinvest in 1991; present name adopted 2011; owned by Banque Heritage (Switzerland); cap. 368.1m., res 60.4m., dep. 2,448m. (Dec. 2011); Dir MARCOS ESTEVES.

Discount Bank (Latin America), SA: Rincón 390, 11000 Montevideo; tel. 2916 4848; fax 2916 0890; e-mail mensajes@discbank.com.uy; internet www.discbank.com.uy; f. 1978; owned by Israel Discount Bank of New York (USA); cap. 546m., res 401.8m., dep. 23,928.5m. (Dec. 2013); Pres. and Chair. EHUD ARNON; Dir and Gen. Man. JORGE LEONEL PÉREZ FERNÁNDEZ; 14 brs.

HSBC Bank (Uruguay), SA: Zabala 1403, 11000 Montevideo; tel. 2915 3395; fax 2916 0125; e-mail contacto@hsbc.com.uy; internet www.hsbc.com.uy; f. 1995; owned by HSBC Bank PLC (United Kingdom); cap. 1,264.8m., res 46.8m., dep. 20,421.1m. (Dec. 2012); CEO VIRGINIA SUÁREZ.

Nuevo Banco Comercial, SA (NBC): Misiones 1399, 11000 Montevideo; tel. 2140 1300; fax 2140 1185; e-mail servicioalcliente@nbc.com.uy; internet www.nbc.com.uy; f. 2003 by merger of Banco Comercial, Banco La Caja Obrera and Banco de Montevideo; fmrly state-owned, privatized in 2006; cap. 2,398m., res 742m., dep. 30,863.1m. (Dec. 2012); Pres. CARLOS GONZÁLEZ TABOADA; Gen. Man. HORACIO ENRIQUE CORREGE; 40 brs.

Development Bank

Banco Bandes Uruguay: Sarandí 402, 111000, Montevideo; tel. 2916 0100; fax 2916 0031; internet www.bandes.com.uy; owned by Banco de Desarrollo Económico y Social (BANDES) of Venezuela; cap. 1,015m., res −733.2m., dep. 5,333.8m. (Dec. 2012); Gen. Man. REINIER JOSÉ PARRA.

Credit Co-operative

Federación Uruguaya de Cooperativas de Ahorro y Crédito (FUCAC): Blvd Artigas 1472, Montevideo; tel. and fax 2708 8888; e-mail info@fucac.com.uy; internet www.fucac.com.uy; f. 1972; Pres. MARÍA TERESA GOYENOLA; Gen. Man. JAVIER HUMBERTO PI LEÓN.

Bankers' Association

Asociación de Bancarios del Uruguay (Bankers' Association of Uruguay—AEBU): Camacuá 575, Montevideo; tel. 2916 1060; e-mail secprensa@aebu.org.uy; internet www.aebu.org.uy; f. 1945; 7 mem. banks; Pres. GUSTAVO PÉREZ.

STOCK EXCHANGE

Bolsa de Valores de Montevideo: Edif. Bolsa de Comercio, Misiones 1400, 11000 Montevideo; tel. 2916 5051; fax 2916 1900; e-mail info@bvm.com.uy; internet www.bvm.com.uy; f. 1867; 75 mems; Pres. PABLO SITJAR PIZZORNO.

INSURANCE

Banco de Seguros del Estado: Avda Libertador 1465, Montevideo; tel. 2908 9303; fax 2901 7030; e-mail info@bse.com.uy; internet www.bse.com.uy; f. 1912; state insurance org.; all risks; Pres. MARIO CASTRO; Gen. Man. RAÚL ONETTO.

Chartis Uruguay: Colonia 999, 1°, Montevideo; tel. 2900 0330; fax 2908 4552; e-mail chartis.uruguay@chartisinsurance.com; internet www.aig.com.uy; f. 1996; all classes; Gen. Man. JORGE FERRANTE.

Compañía de Seguros Aliança da Bahia Uruguay, SA (Brazil): Río Negro 1394, Of. 702, 11100 Montevideo; tel. 2902 1086; fax 2902 1087; e-mail alianca@aliancadabahia.com; internet www.aliancadabahia.com; f. 1905transport.

HDI Seguros Uruguay: Misiones 1549, 11000, Montevideo; tel. 2916 0850; fax 2916 0847; e-mail hdi@hdi.com.uy; internet www.hdi.com.uy; f. 1897 as L'Union IARD, known as L'Union de Paris Cía Uruguaya de Seguros, SA in 2004–11; present name adopted 2011; part of HDI Seguros group; general.

Mapfre Uruguay (Spain): Juncal 1385, esq. Plaza Independencia, Montevideo; tel. 2915 5555; fax 2915 7305; e-mail vida@mapfre.com.uy; internet www.mapfre.com.uy; f. 1995; general.

MetLife Seguros de Vida, SA (USA): Avda 18 de Julio 1738, Montevideo; tel. 2403 3939; fax 2403 3938; e-mail atencion.clientes@metlife.com.uy; internet www.metlife.com.uy; f. 1996 as Alico Cía de Seguros de Vida; bought by MetLife in 2010; life.

Porto Seguro, Seguros del Uruguay SA (Brazil): Avda Américo Ricaldoni 2750 esq. Brito del Pino, Montevideo; tel. 2402 8000; fax 2402 7355; e-mail admin@portoseguro.com.uy; internet www.portoseguro.com.uy; f. 1995; car and property; Dir-Gen. LUIS POMAROLE.

RSA Uruguay (United Kingdom): Edif. RSA, Peatonal Sarandí 620, Montevideo; tel. 2917 0505; fax 2917 5115; internet www.royalsun.com.ar/rsauy_site; f. 1997; fmrly known as Royal & SunAlliance; life and property; Gen. Man. ESTEBAN PIGNANELLI.

Surco Seguros: Blvd Artigas 1388, Montevideo; tel. 2709 0089; fax 2707 7313; e-mail surco@surco.com.uy; internet www.surco.com.uy; f. 1995; insurance co-operative; all classes; Pres. SERGIO FUENTES; Gen. Man. ANDRÉS ELOLA.

INSURANCE ASSOCIATION

Asociación Uruguaya de Empresas Aseguradoras (AUDEA): Edif. Torre del Congreso, Of. 1501, Avda 8 de Octubre 2355, Montevideo; tel. 2402 9896; fax 2916 5991; e-mail audea@adinet.org.uy; internet www.audea.org.uy; Pres. ANDRÉS ELOLA; Gen. Man. MAURICIO CASTELLANOS.

Trade and Industry

GOVERNMENT AGENCIES

Administración Nacional de Combustibles, Alcohol y Portland (ANCAP): Payasandú y Avda del Libertador Brig.-Gen. Lavalleja, 11100 Montevideo; tel. 2902 0608; fax 2902 1136; e-mail webmaster@ancap.com.uy; internet www.ancap.com.uy; f. 1931; deals with transport, refining and sale of petroleum products, and the manufacture of alcohol, spirits and cement; tanker services, also river transport; Pres. JOSÉ COYA; Sec.-Gen. MIGUEL A. TATO.

Oficina de Planeamiento y Presupuesto de la Presidencia de la República: Plaza Independencia 710, 11000 Montevideo; tel. 2487 2110; fax 2209 9730; e-mail direccion@opp.gub.uy; internet www.opp.gub.uy; f. 1967; responsible for the implementation of devt plans; co-ordinates the policies of the various ministries; advises on the preparation of the budget of public enterprises; Dir GABRIEL FRUGONI.

Uruguay XXI (Instituto de Promoción de Inversiones y Exportaciones de Bienes y Servicios): Rincón 518/528, 11100 Montevideo; tel. 2915 3838; fax 2916 3059; e-mail info@uruguayxxi.gub.uy; internet www.uruguayxxi.gub.uy; f. 1996; govt agency to promote economic investment and export; Exec. Dir ROBERTO VILLAMIL; Gen. Man. ALVARO INCHAUSPE.

DEVELOPMENT ORGANIZATIONS

Asociación Nacional de Micro y Pequeños Empresarios (ANMYPE): Miguelete 1584, Montevideo; tel. 2924 1010; e-mail info@anmype.org.uy; internet www.anmype.org.uy; promotes small businesses; f. 1988; Pres. JULIO DURANTE; Sec. GUILLERMO SABELLA.

Asociación Nacional de Organizaciones No Gubernamentales Orientadas al Desarrollo: Avda del Libertador 1985, esq. 202, Montevideo; tel. and fax 2924 0812; e-mail anong@anong.com.uy; internet www.anong.org.uy; f. 1992; umbrella grouping of devt NGOs; Pres. MARÍA TERESA MIRA; Sec. EMILIO CAPUTI.

Centro Interdisciplinario de Estudios sobre el Desarrollo, Uruguay (CIEDUR): Avda 18 de Julio 1645-1647, 11200 Montevideo; tel. and fax 2408 4520; e-mail ciedur@ciedur.org.uy; internet www.ciedur.org.uy; f. 1977; devt studies and training; Pres. SOLEDAD SALVADOR; Exec. Sec. ALMA ESPINA.

Corporación Nacional para el Desarrollo (CND): Rincón 528, 7°, Casilla 977, 11000 Montevideo; tel. 2916 2800; fax 2915 9662; e-mail cnd@cnd.org.uy; internet www.cnd.org.uy; f. 1985; national devt corpn; mixed-capital org.; obtains 60% of funding from state; Pres. PEDRO BUONOMO; Vice-Pres. PABLO GUTIÉRREZ.

Fundación Uruguaya de Cooperación y Desarrollo Solidario (FUNDASOL) (Uruguayan Foundation for Supportive Co-operation and Development): Blvd Artigas 1165, esq. Maldonado, 11200 Montevideo; tel. 2400 2020; fax 2408 1485; e-mail consultas@fundasol.org.uy; internet www.fundasol.org.uy; f. 1979; Pres. MARIO BUZZALINO; Gen. Man. JORGE NAYA.

CHAMBERS OF COMMERCE

Cámara de Industrias del Uruguay (Chamber of Industries): Avda Italia 6101, 11500 Montevideo; tel. 2604 0464; fax 2604 0501; e-mail ciu@ciu.com.uy; internet www.ciu.com.uy; f. 1898; Pres. JAVIER CARRAU; Sec. JUAN CARLOS DE LEÓN.

Cámara Mercantil de Productos del País (Chamber of Commerce for Local Products): Avda General Rondeau 1908, 1°, 11800 Montevideo; tel. 2924 0644; fax 2924 4701; e-mail info@camaramercantil.com.uy; internet www.camaramercantil.com.uy; f. 1891; 180 mems; Pres. PEDRO OTEGUI; Gen. Man. GONZALO GONZÁLEZ PIEDRAS.

Cámara Nacional de Comercio y Servicios del Uruguay (National Chamber of Commerce): Edif. Bolsa de Comercio, Rincón 454, 2°, Casilla 1000, 11000 Montevideo; tel. 2916 1277; fax 2916 1243; e-mail info@cncs.com.uy; internet www.cncs.com.uy; f. 1867; 1,500 mems; Pres. ALFONSO VARELA.

EMPLOYERS' ORGANIZATIONS

Asociación de Importadores Mayoristas de Almacén (Wholesale Importers' Asscn): Edif. Bolsa de Comercio, Of. 317/319, Rincón 454, 11000 Montevideo; tel. 2915 6103; fax 2916 0796; e-mail fmelissari@nidera.com.uy; f. 1926; 52 mems; Pres. FERNANDO MELISSARI.

Asociación Rural del Uruguay (ARU): Avda Uruguay 864, 11100 Montevideo; tel. 2902 0484; fax 2902 0489; e-mail aru@netgate.com.uy; internet www.aru.com.uy; f. 1871; 1,800 mems; Pres. RUBÉN ECHEVERRÍA NÚÑEZ; Gen. Man. Dr GONZALO ARROYO FACELLO.

Federación Rural: Avda 18 de Julio 965, 1°, 11100 Montevideo; tel. 2900 4791; fax 2900 5583; e-mail fedrural@gmail.com; internet www.federacionrural.org.uy; f. 1915; 2,000 mems; Pres. MIGUEL SANGUINETTI.

Unión de Exportadores del Uruguay (Uruguayan Exporters' Asscn): Avda Uruguay 917, 1°, esq. Convención, 11100 Montevideo; tel. 2901 0105; fax 2916 5967; e-mail info@uniondeexportadores.com; internet www.uniondeexportadores.com; Pres. ALVARO QUEIJO; Exec. Sec. TERESA AISHEMBERG.

MAJOR COMPANIES

Acindar Uruguay: Edif. World Trade Center, Avda Luis A. de Herrera 1248, Of. 321, 11300 Montevideo; tel. and fax 2622 8273; e-mail sac@acindar.com.ar; internet www.acindar.com.ar; part of Grupo ArcelorMittal; production of iron and steel; Gen. Man. GABRIEL DATTILO.

Azucarera del Litoral, SA (AZUCARLITO): 25 de Mayo 444, 5°, 11000 Montevideo; tel. 2916 0868; fax 2916 1192; e-mail azupay@azucarlito.com; f. 1943; processors of raw cane sugar; CEO MIGUEL FASCHINI; Gen. Man. RAÚL CONCELO; 495 employees.

Chery Automobile: Barra de Carrasco, Montevideo; e-mail helpdesk@mychery.com; internet cheryinternational.com; f. 2007; jtly owned by Chery Automobile (People's Republic of China, 51%) and Socma (Argentina, 49%); car assembly plant.

Compañía Industrial de Tabacos Monte Paz, SA: San Ramón 716, Montevideo; tel. 2200 8821; fax 2203 7890; e-mail info@montepaz.com.uy; internet www.montepaz.com.uy; f. 1930; tobacco and cigarette mfrs; Pres. JORGE LUIS MAILHOS; 425 employees.

Compañía Sudamericana de Empresas Eléctricas, Mecánicas y Obras Públicas (SACEEM): Brecha 572, 11000 Montevideo; tel. 2915 9103; fax 2916 3939; e-mail saceem@saceem.com.uy; internet www.saceem.com.uy; f. 1951; construction of industrial buildings and warehouses; Pres. Dr ASSIS DE SOUZA; Dir ALEJANDRO RUIBAL; 800 employees.

Compañía Uruguaya de Transportes Colectivos, SA (CUTCSA): Avda Garzón y Plaza Vidiella 1163, Montevideo; tel. 2915 5933; fax 2203 2037; e-mail cac@cutcsa.com.uy; internet www.cutcsa.com.uy; f. 1937; passenger transport services; Pres. JUAN ANTONIO SALGADO VILA; Gen. Man. FERNANDO BARCIA; 4,866 employees.

Cooperativa Nacional de Productores de Leche, SA (CONAPROLE): Nueva York 1648, 1°, 11800 Montevideo; tel. 2924 6733; fax 2924 6712; e-mail jfernandez@conaprole.com.uy; internet www.conaprole.com.uy; f. 1936; mfrs and wholesalers of milk and dairy products; Pres. ALVARO AMBROIS; Gen. Man. RUBÉN R. NÚÑEZ HERNÁNDEZ; 2,200 employees.

Fábrica Nacional de Papel, SA (FANAPEL): Rincón 477, 6°, 11000 Montevideo; tel. 2915 0917; fax 2916 3096; e-mail secretaria.comercial@fanapel.com.uy; internet www.fanapel.com.uy; f. 1898; pulp and paper mill; Pres. DOUGLAS LEE ALBRECHT; Gen. Man. LIBERATO TURINELLI DUCASSOU; 1,120 employees.

Fábrica Uruguaya de Neumáticos, SA (FUNSA): Corrales 3076, Casilla 15175, Montevideo; tel. 2508 3141; fax 2507 0611; e-mail funsa@ciu.com.uy; internet www.funsa.com.uy; f. 1935; mfrs of rubber tyres, gloves, shoes and insulated electrical cables; workers' co-operative since 2005; Pres. ENRIQUE ROMERO; 210 employees (2007).

FNC, SA (Fábricas Nacionales de Cerveza): Entre Ríos 1060, Montevideo; tel. and fax 2200 1681; e-mail fnc@multi.com.uy; internet www.fnc.com.uy; f. 1932; bought by Anheuser-Busch InBev (Belgium) in 2003; brewery; Pres. (Latin America South) MARCIO FROES; 500 employees.

FRIPUR, SA: Avda General Rondeau 2260, Montevideo; tel. 2924 5821; fax 2924 3149; e-mail informes@fripur.com.uy; internet www.fripur.com.uy; f. 1976; foodstuffs and fish processing; Pres. ALBERTO FERNÁNDEZ; 1,185 employees.

Industrias Philips del Uruguay, SA: Rambla O'Higgins 5303, 11400 Montevideo; tel. 2619 6666; fax 2619 7777; e-mail martin.spinelli@philips.com; internet www.philips.com.uy; f. 1957; subsidiary of NV Philips (Netherlands); mfrs of lighting and other electrical goods; Gen. Man. LUIS PENNA; Contact MARTÍN RICARDO SPINELLI; 300 employees.

Montevideo Refrescos, SA: Camino Carrasco 6173, 12100 Montevideo; tel. 2600 8401; fax 2604 2541; f. 1946; owned by Coca-Cola Corpn of the USA; producers of carbonated beverages; CEO ANDRY McCUBIN; 560 employees.

Motociclo, SA: Avda Sayago 1385, Montevideo; tel. 2354 2184; fax 2902 1702; e-mail ventas@motociclo.com.uy; internet www.motociclo.com.uy; f. 1931; bicycle and motorcycle mfrs; annual capacity of 370,000 units; Pres. LEONARDO ROZENBLUM TROSMAN; 450 employees.

Paysandú Industrias del Cuero, SA (PAYCUEROS): Cerro 777, 11100 Montevideo; tel. 2902 0139; fax 2902 1321; e-mail omar.tkacz@sadesa.com; internet www.sadesa.com; f. 1946; tannery, mfr of handbags and other leather products; owned by SADESA (Argentina); Contact OMAR TKACZ; 700 employees.

Sociedad Anónima Arroceros Nacionales (SAMAN): Rambla Baltasar Brum 2772, Montevideo; tel. 2208 1421; fax 2203 7007; e-mail info@saman.com.uy; internet www.saman.com.uy; f. 1942; rice mills; Gen. Man. LEOMAR GOLDONI; 538 employees.

Supermercados Disco del Uruguay: Jaime Zudáñez 2627, Montevideo; tel. 2710 7421; fax 2711 7903; internet www.disco.com.uy; f. 1960; Uruguayan subsidiary of Disco, SA (Argentina); Gen. Man. LUIS EDUARDO CORDUZO.

UPM: Edif. Blue, 2°, Avda Italy 7519, Art Carrasco Business, Montevideo; tel. (4) 2604-6660; fax (4) 2604-5406; internet www.upmuruguay.com.uy; f. 2005; operates pulp mill in Fray Bentos; bought 91% of mill from Botnia in 2010; also operates Forestal Oriental forestry co; Group Chair. FRANCISCO CENTURIÓN; Gen. Man. MAGDALENA IBÁÑEZ; 21,000 employees.

UTILITIES

Electricity

Administración Nacional de Usinas y Transmisiones Eléctricas (UTE): Palacio de la Luz, Paraguay 2431, 10°, 11100 Montevideo; tel. 2200 3424; fax 2203 7082; e-mail ute@ute.com.uy; internet www.ute.com.uy; f. 1912; autonomous state body; sole purveyor of electricity until 1997; Pres. GONZALO CASARAVILLA; Gen. Man. CARLOS POMBO.

Gas

Conecta: Avda Giannattasio, Km 20, 800 Ciudad de la Costa, Canelones, Montevideo; tel. 2682 6817; fax 2600 6732; internet www.conecta.com.uy; gas distribution.

MontevideoGas: Plaza Independencia 831, 10°, 11000 Montevideo; tel. 2901 7454; e-mail mlcoitino@montevideogas.com.uy; internet www.montevideogas.com.uy; f. 2007; owned by Petrobras (Brazil); gas producers; Pres. (Petrobras Uruguay) CLOVIS CORREA; Pres. CARLOS DA COSTA.

Water

Aguas de la Costa: Calle 1 y 20, La Barra, Maldonado; tel. 4277 1930; fax 4277 1932; e-mail adlcosta@adinet.com.uy; internet www .aguasdelacosta.com.uy; subsidiary of Aguas de Barcelona (Spain); management of water supply in Maldonado Dept; Pres. MILTON MACHADO; Gen. Man. GERMÁN ALVAREZ.

Obras Sanitarias del Estado (OSE): Carlos Roxlo 1275, 11200 Montevideo; tel. 2400 1151; fax 2408 8069; e-mail info@ose.com.uy; internet www.ose.com.uy; f. 1952; processing and distribution of drinking water, sinking wells, supplying industrial zones of the country; Pres. MILTON EDUARDO MACHADO LENS.

TRADE UNIONS

Assocacion de Bancarios del Uruguay: Camacuá 575, Montevideo; tel. 2916 1060; e-mail secprensa@aebu.org.uy; internet www .aebu.org.uy; Sec.-Gen. FERNANDO GAMBERA.

Plenario Intersindical de Trabajadores—Convención Nacional de Trabajadores (PIT—CNT): Jackson 1283, 11200 Montevideo; tel. 2409 6680; fax 2400 4160; e-mail pitcnt@adinet.com.uy; internet www.pitcnt.org.uy; f. 1966; org. comprising 83 trade unions, 17 labour federations; 320,000 mems; Exec. Sec. JUAN CASTILLO.

Federación de Trabajadores de la Industria Láctea (FTIL): Avda Joaquín Suárez 2878, Montevideo; tel. 2209 7244; fax 2200 7513; f. 1950; represents dairy farmers; Pres. ROBERT ROMASO.

Sindicato Médico del Uruguay: Blvd Artigas 1565, 11200 Montevideo; tel. 2401 4701; fax 2409 1603; e-mail secretaria@smu.org.uy; internet www.smu.org.uy; Pres. MARTÍN REBELLA.

Sindicato de Policias del Uruguay: Sede Social Minas 1581 entre Mercedes y Uruguay, Montevideo; tel. 2400 7666; e-mail contacto@ sinpolur.com; internet www.sinpolur.com; Pres. OTILIO FERREIRA.

Sindicato Único de Telecomunicaciones: Miguelete 2332, Montevideo; tel. 2402 2332; e-mail secretaria@sutel.org.uy; internet www .sutel.org.uy; Pres. GABRIEL MOLINA.

Transport

Dirección Nacional de Transporte: Rincón 575, 5°, 11000 Montevideo; tel. and fax 2915 7933; e-mail infodnt@dnt.gub.uy; internet www.dnt.gub.uy; co-ordinates national and international transport services; Gen. Man. FELIPE MARTÍN.

RAILWAYS

Administración de los Ferrocarriles del Estado (AFE): Avda Rondeau 1921, esq. Lima, Montevideo; tel. 2924 3924; e-mail secretariogeneral@afe.com.uy; internet www.afe.com.uy; f. 1952; state org.; 3,002 km of track connecting all parts of the country; connections with the Argentine and Brazilian networks; Pres. ALEJANDRO ORELLANO; Gen. Man. JOSÉ NUNES.

ROADS

In 2008 Uruguay had an estimated 8,696 km of motorways (forming the densest motorway network in South America), connecting Montevideo with the main towns of the interior and the Argentine and Brazilian frontiers. There was also a network of approximately 40,000 km of paved roads.

Corporación Vial del Uruguay, SA: Rincón 528, 5°, 11000 Montevideo; tel. 2916 2680; fax 2917 0114; e-mail cvu@cnd.org.uy; internet www.cvu.com.uy; road construction agency; owned by Corporación Nacional para el Desarrollo; Pres. ADRIANA RODRÍGUEZ; Gen. Man. RICHARD SERVAN.

INLAND WATERWAYS

There are about 1,600 km of navigable waterways, which provide an important means of transport.

Nobleza Naviera, SA: Avda General Rondeau 2257, Montevideo; tel. 2924 3222; fax 2924 3769; e-mail nobleza@deambrosi.com.uy; internet www.noblezanaviera.com; cargo services; Pres. TABARÉ VÁZQUEZ; Gen. Man. JORGE RAZQUÍN.

SHIPPING

There are 13 sea ports in the country. At December 2013 the flag registered fleet comprised 100 vessels, totalling 143,398 grt.

Administración Nacional de Puertos (ANP): Rambla 25 de Agosto de 1825, No 160, Montevideo; tel. 2915 1441; fax 2916 1704; e-mail presidencia@anp.com.uy; internet www.anp.com.uy; f. 1916; national ports admin; Pres. ALBERTO DÍAZ; Gen. Mans OSVALDO TABACCHI, SCHUBERT MÉNDEZ.

Grupo Christophersen, SA: Rincón 550, Puerta Baja, Casilla 295, 11000 Montevideo; tel. 2916 0109; fax 2916 9243; e-mail chris@ christophersen.com.uy; internet www.christophersen.com.uy; f. 1892; owns Transportes Fluviales Fray Bentos, Tramaco, Magrausa and Newlar; Pres. JORGE FERNÁNDEZ BAUBETA.

Mediterranean Shipping Co (MSC Uruguay): 1365 Andes, 13°, 11100 Montevideo; tel. 2902 2935; fax 2902 9155; e-mail distribution@mscuy.mscgva.ch; internet www.mscuruguay.com; f. 1999; Man. Dir ROBERTO GONZÁLEZ FACAL.

Navegación Atlántica Uruguay: Rambla 25 de Agosto de 1825, No 508, 5°, 11100 Montevideo; tel. 2917 2005; e-mail navemvd@nave .com.uy; freight services; Man. JUAN TABORELLI.

Prefectura Nacional Naval: Edif. Comando General de la Armada, 4°, Rambla 25 de Agosto de 1825 s/n, esq. Maciel, Montevideo; tel. 2915 2210; fax 2916 0022; e-mail premo_imdg@armada.mil .uy; internet mercanciaspeligrosas.com.uy; f. 1829; supervisory body; Sec.-Gen. Rear-Adm. OSCAR DEBALI DE PALLEJA.

CIVIL AVIATION

Civil aviation is controlled by the Dirección General de Aviación Civil and the Dirección General de Infraestructura Aeronáutica. The main airport is at Carrasco, 21 km from Montevideo, and there are also airports at Paysandú, Rivera, Salto, Melo, Artigas, Punta del Este and Durazno. The state-owned airline PLUNA was dissolved in 2012.

Aeromás, SA (MaxAir, SA): Avda de las Américas 5120, Montevideo; tel. 2604 6359; e-mail aeromas@aeromas.com; internet www .aeromas.com; f. 1983; private hire, cargo, and air ambulance flights; Dir DANIEL DALMÁS.

Tourism

The sandy beaches and woodlands on the coast and the grasslands of the interior, with their variety of fauna and flora, provide the main tourist attractions. About 62% of tourists came from Argentina and 14% from Brazil in 2012. Uruguay received an estimated 2.7m. visitors in 2013, while tourism receipts totalled a provisional US $1,920m. in that year.

Asociación Uruguaya de Agencias de Viajes (AUDAVI): Río Branco 1407, Of. 205, 11100 Montevideo; tel. 2901 2326; fax 2902 1972; e-mail audavi@netgate.com.uy; internet www.audavi.com.uy; f. 1951; 100 mems; Pres. SERGIO BAÑALES.

Cámara Uruguaya de Turismo: San José 942, 2°, Of. 4, 11200 Montevideo; tel. and fax 2900 0453; internet camtur.com.uy; f. 1993; Pres. LUIS BORSARI.

Uruguay Natural: Rambla 25 de Agosto de 1825, esq. Yacaré, Montevideo; tel. 2188 5100; e-mail webmaster@mintur.gub.uy; internet www.uruguaynatural.com; f. 2003; state-run tourism promotion agency; Dir-Gen. BENJAMÍN LIBEROFF.

Defence

As assessed at November 2013, Uruguay's Armed Forces consisted of 24,650 volunteers between the ages of 18 and 45, who contract for one or two years of service. There was an army of 16,250, a navy of 5,400 and an air force of 3,000. There were also paramilitary forces numbering 800.

Defence Budget: an estimated 9,750m. pesos uruguayos in 2014.

Commander-in-Chief of the Army: Gen. JUAN A. VILLAGRÁN.

Commander-in-Chief of the Navy: Adm. RICARDO GIAMBRUNO.

Commander-in-Chief of the Air Force: Brig.-Gen. WASHINGTON R. MARTÍNEZ.

Education

All education, including university tuition, is provided free of charge. Education is officially compulsory between six and 14 years of age. Primary education begins at the age of six and lasts for six years. Secondary education, beginning at 12 years of age, lasts for a further six years, comprising two cycles of three years each. In 2009 primary enrolment included 99% of children in the relevant age-group, while the equivalent ratio for secondary enrolment was 90% in 2010. The programmes of instruction are the same in both public and private schools and private schools are subject to certain state controls. There are four universities in Uruguay, including the state Universidad de la República. In 2013 a total of 35,629m. pesos uruguayos of general government expenditure was allocated to the Administración Nacional de Educación Pública.

Bibliography

For works on South America generally, see Select Bibliography (Books)

Andrews, G. R. *Blackness in the White Nation: A History of Afro-Uruguay*. Chapel Hill, NC, University of North Carolina Press, 2010.

Gregory, S. *Intellectuals and Left Politics in Uruguay, 1958–2006*. Eastbourne, Sussex Academic Press, 2009.

Lavin, A. *Women, Feminism and Social Change in Argentina, Chile and Uruguay, 1840–1940*. Lincoln, NE, University of Nebraska, 1998.

Markarian, V. *Left in Transformation: Uruguayan Exiles and the Latin American Human Rights Network, 1967–1984*. Abingdon, Routledge, 2005.

Nuñéz, R. C. *The Politics of Social Policy Change in Chile and Uruguay: Retrenchment versus Maintenance, 1973–1998*. London, Routledge, 2005.

Palermo, V., and Reboratti, C. *Del otro lado del río. Ambientalismo y política entre uruguayos y argentinos*. Buenos Aires, Edhasa, 2007.

Roniger, L., and Sznajder, M. *The Legacy of Human-Rights Violations in the Southern Cone: Argentina, Chile and Uruguay*. Oxford, Oxford University Press, 1999.

Vanger, M. I. *Uruguay's José Batlle y Ordóñez: The Determined Visionary, 1915–1917*. Boulder, CO, Lynne Rienner Publrs, 2009.

Weschler, L. *A Miracle, a Universe: Settling Accounts with Torturers*. Chicago, IL, University of Chicago Press, 1998.

VENEZUELA

Geography

PHYSICAL FEATURES

The Bolivarian Republic of Venezuela is on the northern coast of South America. Colombia lies to the west of the country, pushing into it in the south-west. This border (2,050 km or 1,273 miles) is only a little shorter than that with Brazil (2,200 km), which lies to the south. To the east is Guyana—beyond a 743-km frontier, which Venezuela claims should be further east still, along the Essequibo river. There is also a dispute over maritime boundaries in the Gulf of Venezuela with Colombia, and several Caribbean nations object to Venezuelan possession of the isolated Isla de Aves (Island of Birds), 565 km north of the mainland, on a similar latitude to northern Dominica (over 200 km to the east). There are islands that are not Venezuelan territory much closer to the mainland: northern Trinidad (Trinidad and Tobago) is 11 km off shore, to the east of the Paria peninsula and dropping south above the Orinoco delta; at the other end of the country, in the west, the Dutch island of Aruba is 25 km north of the Paraguaná peninsula (at the mouth of the Gulf of Venezuela); while a little further east is Curaçao (55 km off shore), and then Bonaire (80 km), although Bonaire is further from the mainland than it is from the Venezuelan dependencies in the Lesser Antilles (specifically, the Islas Las Aves—not to be confused with the single, northerly Aves island mentioned above). Aves is the most northerly of the 72 Caribbean islands, islets or cays included within the territory of Venezuela, which totals 916,445 sq km (353,841 sq miles).

Venezuela stretches along a mainly north-facing coast, the west penetrating less deeply inland than the east, but with a southern extension in the centre of the country thrusting towards the Amazon basin to include the headwaters of the Orinoco. More than 2,700 km of coast is mainly along the Caribbean; it is narrow, steep and deeply indented, owing to the mountains coming so close to the sea. Only in the far east is it low and marshy, around the delta through which the Orinoco debouches into the Atlantic. Just north of this delta is the Gulf of Paria, between Venezuela and the island of Trinidad, and most of the shore runs west from here to the Gulf of Venezuela, near the Colombian border. Parallel to this coast are most of Venezuela's Caribbean islands, the largest being Isla de Margarita. The Gulf of Venezuela is between two peninsulas, that of Paraguaná and that of Guajira, the latter on the west, its head being Colombian territory. Leading south from the Gulf is a channel of 8 km–15 km in width (dredged to a depth of 11 m—36 ft—in 1956, to make it navigable for larger vessels) into Lake Maracaibo, the largest lake in South America (210 km by 120 km). In all, Venezuela has about 30,000 sq km of inland waters. The country can be divided into four topographical regions: the Maracaibo lowlands; the Andean highlands of the north-west and the Caribbean coast; the vast plains (Los Llanos) of the centre-north; and the Guianan highlands, which dominate the east and south.

The lowlands around Lake Maracaibo, surrounded by heights and giving on to coastal lowlands along the Gulf of Venezuela, constitute the smallest natural region of the country (about 15% of its territory). The fairly brackish lake is in the far north-west, and the original stilt-supported villages of the local Amerindians along its shores inspired the Spanish name for the country ('little Venice'). Maracaibo is famous for its petroleum wealth, although it also has a diverse natural environment—semi-arid brush cloaks the dry north, with wooded savannah intervening before the tropical forest and swampy lagoons of the south. Forests continue up the flanks of the mountains, as Maracaibo is cupped between two Andean ranges. The Andes of Colombia's Cordillera Oriental split just before they enter western Venezuela, the crest of the more westerly Sierra de Perijá heading northwards to form much of the border between the two countries. Some of the Perijá peaks reach over 3,400 m, but the higher range, the Cordillera de

Mérida, runs in a north-easterly direction, towards the Caribbean. Here is the highest point in Venezuela, the Pico Bolívar, or La Columna, at 5,007 m (16,433 ft). Before hitting the Caribbean coast, the general alignment of the heavily forested mountains turns east, and the main range runs between the sea and the Orinoco plains, to peter out and then briefly rear up again before descending into the flat, marshy Orinoco delta. The south-eastern half of western Venezuela is occupied by the uplands of the broad Llanos, tropical grasslands that lap the foothills of the Cordillera de Mérida and the coastal range. The Llanos, which covers about one-third of the country, seldom itself exceeds 215 m above sea level and slopes steadily towards the Orinoco delta. All this area, indeed four-fifths of the country, is drained by the Orinoco, which forms some of the western border of Venezuela's southern extension, before heading east and a little north, between the coastal and Guianan highlands, towards the sea. The plains stretch a considerable distance to the north and west of the main river, and vast tracts are flood prone in May–November, yet are parched in summer. The lower reaches remain wetter and there are permanent wetlands and mangroves in the delta. A further one-third of the country comprises the Guianan highlands of the south-east. The centre of the country is dominated by the rugged, hilly plateau that marks the start of the highlands that stretch eastwards to divide the Guiana coast from the Amazon basin. In Venezuela the central heights push south to cup the westward-opening basin of the Orinoco headwaters, and east to fall steeply into the Orinoco valley to the north. The landscape alternates between open grasslands and dense forests. Some of the mountains exceed 2,700 m, and the precipitous terrain allows for some dramatic scenery, such as the Angel Falls, the highest waterfall in the world. Deforestation and irresponsible mining threaten this environment, with industrial pollution more of an issue in the west, but over one-half of the country is still wooded, and one-fifth is classed as pastureland. The type of vegetation is determined more by elevation than latitude, with plants common to a temperate zone established above 900 m, tropical forests in the lower country, mangroves in the Orinoco delta and long prairie grass on the Llanos.

CLIMATE

The country lies entirely in the Tropic of Cancer, and its climate is tropical on the Llanos and on the coast, but temperate in the mountains. Altitude is very important, with hot, temperate and cold climates distinguished locally. There is a wet season in May–November, with more rain falling on the southern slopes than the northern, annual averages ranging from about 1,400 mm (55 ins) in the Andes to 280 mm on the coast. Caracas, the national capital in the mountains immediately above the Caribbean coast, has an average daily temperature range of 59°F–78°F (15°C–26°C) in January and 63°F–80°F (17°C–26°C) in July. Lowland Maracaibo has ranges of 73°F–90°F (23°C–32°C) and 76°F–94°F (24°C–34°C), respectively.

POPULATION

The population is predominantly of mixed ancestry (67%), with 21% as largely of European descent (predominantly Spanish). Most of the rest of the population are black, and 3% are Amerindian. There are at least 40 indigenous groups, mainly in the Amazon basin, the more isolated ones retaining principal use of their native languages, rather than the more widely used official language, Spanish. The country is overwhelmingly Roman Catholic (some 85%), with about 2% Protestant, and some of the Jewish and other faiths (including native, animist faiths).

The population was 30.2m. in 2014, according to official mid-year estimates. Most people live in the coastal highlands, and 87% are urbanized. Society is also divided between extremes of rich and poor. Caracas, the federal capital (with a population of 2.9m. at mid-2014), is in the central coastal highlands, its port being La Guaira. The second city of the country is Maracaibo (2.2m. in 2011), in the west, on the north-western shore of the lake that shares its name. Another important city is the manufacturing centre of Valencia (1.8m.), mid-way between Caracas and Barquisimeto, a transport hub situated at the northern end of the main Cordillera de Mérida and the western end of the coastal range. The country is a federal republic constituted of 23 states, a Capital District (Caracas) and 11 federally controlled Caribbean island groups (totalling 72 islands), described as Federal Dependencies.

History

Dr JULIA BUXTON

With additional content by PABLO NAVARRETE

Europeans first discovered Venezuela in 1498, during the navigator Christopher Columbus's third Spanish expedition to the New World. Following the re-establishment of Nueva Granada as a Viceroyalty in 1739, the Spanish administered Venezuela from Lima, in modern-day Peru. In 1777 Venezuela became a Spanish Captaincy-General, with an enhanced degree of administrative autonomy from Bogotá, the capital of Nueva Granada.

INDEPENDENCE

In 1724 a company of Basque merchants, the Caracas Company, obtained a monopoly of foreign trade out of Venezuelan territory and developed new markets in Europe and the Caribbean for local produce, including cocoa and coffee. The export market fostered a small élite of native European planters, the so-called Marqueses de Chocolate, and it was a member of this class, Simón Bolívar, who led the successful campaign for independence of the Andean region from the Spanish. Venezuela gained independence in 1819, and joined Colombia, Ecuador and Panama to form the 'Gran Colombia' federation. Bolívar viewed regional integration as a defensive counter to the emerging power of the USA, but this was undermined by infighting between Venezuelan and Colombian élites. The federation was dissolved in 1830, and Venezuela became a separate republic. For the next 80 years military oligarchs (*caudillos*) fought each other for control of the country. It was only after one of these *caudillos*, Juan Vicente Gómez, seized power that centralization of the national territory progressed and a semblance of stability emerged. The repressive Gómez dictatorship (1908–35) coincided with the discovery and exploitation of petroleum reserves, which fuelled rapid economic growth. This in turn accelerated social change and pressure for democratic reform. A fledgling opposition student movement emerged in the 1930s. This was led by Rómulo Betancourt and Dr Rafael Caldera Rodríguez, who went on to form Venezuela's first mass parties, the social democratic Acción Democrática (AD—Democratic Action) and the Christian democrat Comité de Organización Política Electoral Independiente (COPEI—Committee of Independent Electoral Political Organization). After the death of Gómez, his military successors, Eleízar López Contreras (1935–41) and Isaías Medina Angarita (1941–45), were unable to contain pressures for democratic reform.

Collaboration between AD and progressive elements of the military led to a coup in 1945 that brought democratic elections and propelled AD to power for three years. However, the reformist AD Government was weakened by partisan conflict and unrest in the military, which led to a military coup in 1948 and the seizure of power by Gen. Marcos Pérez Jiménez. Pérez Jiménez occupied the presidency for 10 years. His regime was notable for its nation-building projects, but also for corruption and political oppression. A military rebellion and general strike forced the dictator to flee to Spain in 1958. Prior to the co-ordinated uprising against Pérez Jiménez, AD, COPEI and representatives of the private sector, the union movement and the Roman Catholic Church had signed the Pact of Punto Fijo in 1957. This established a political alliance and centrist policy consensus between the two parties. Such institutional engineering aimed to ensure political stability and avoid further military intrusions into national politics. The Pact committed AD and COPEI to share appointments to the state administration and to balance the interests of business and labour. Petroleum export revenues facilitated the consolidation of the new democratic system that was established following elections in 1959, which brought Betancourt to the presidency. The distribution of petroleum revenues through the network of clientelist interests affiliated to AD and COPEI, as well as to potentially destabilizing actors such as the military and the Roman Catholic Church, created strong support for the Punto Fijo system and the two parties that had created it. The revenues ensured that the demands of the majority of organized and sectoral interests could be met, enabling Venezuela to avoid class-based conflicts.

THE DEVELOPMENT OF PETROLEUM RESOURCES

Venezuela was the world's third largest producer of coffee in the 19th century, after Brazil and Java (the latter now part of Indonesia). Following the discovery of petroleum reserves at the end of that century, oil overtook coffee as the country's primary export commodity. Venezuela's importance as a petroleum exporter was enhanced by the nationalization of Mexico's oil industry in 1938, and by the outbreak of the Second World War in Europe in 1939. As Venezuelan dependence on revenue from petroleum grew, and the country's role in global supply became more important, Venezuelan oil policy became increasingly nationalistic. In 1943 reforms to national oil legislation revised earlier profit-sharing agreements between the private sector and the Governments of Gómez and López Contreras, ensuring that the Venezuelan state received a 50% share of oil production and export profits. This 'oil nationalism' led Venezuela to defend oil producer interests through co-operation efforts with producer countries in the Middle East from 1949 onwards. This culminated in the formation of the Organization of the Petroleum Exporting Countries (OPEC) in September 1960.

Venezuela's petroleum industry was nationalized in 1976, following the expiry of private sector concessions. In the early 1990s the Governments of Carlos Andrés Pérez and Rafael Caldera pursued an *apertura*, or opening, of the national oil sector to private investors through joint venture agreements with the state petroleum company Petróleos de Venezuela, SA (PDVSA). This prompted a powerful nationalist backlash from left-wing political organizations such as La Causa Radical (La Causa R—Radical Cause), which argued that the contracts had not been subject to congressional scrutiny and went against the Constitution, which reserved hydrocarbon exploitation to the state. Under the agreements, PDVSA paid a fixed amount for the oil extracted by private sector partners. This meant that when the price of oil declined on international markets towards the end of the 1990s, PDVSA was producing at a loss. La Causa R's oil specialist, Alí Rodríguez Araque, who subsequently assumed various senior positions during the presidency of Lt-Col (retd) Hugo Chávez Frías, including President of PDVSA, argued that PDVSA was operating as a 'state within a state', outside the jurisdiction of the energy ministry.

The Chávez administration, which took office in 1999, reversed the opening and reasserted oil 'sovereignty' through the 1999 Constitution and the hydrocarbons law in 2001, which required PDVSA to have a majority share in all new production and exploration activities. PDVSA's strategy of 'internationalizing' operations was reversed, and the 32 operating service agreements negotiated with foreign private oil companies in 1996 were revised to increase taxes and royalties paid to the Venezuelan state. The Chávez Government pursued a strongly nationalistic oil policy, assuming an uncompromising position in OPEC through alliances with other members, such as Iran, in order to secure production cuts and increase international oil prices. The strategy was met with strong resistance domestically from PDVSA managers, who engaged in a protracted strike at the end of 2002 that terminated output and forced the Government to declare *force majeure* on oil contracts. When the stoppage collapsed, the Government dismissed more than 18,000 PDVSA workers and replaced them with government sympathizers.

After 2004 the rise in international petroleum prices increased the revenues available to the Government for social investment. PDVSA allocated more than US $13,700m. to social development in 2006, a share that rose to $14,733m. in 2008. Critics maintained that the profits should be invested in production facilities, and that the country was becoming overdependent on its oil export earnings. When the price of oil fell in 2009, Venezuela's exports declined, forcing a steep reduction in social investment, to $3,514m. For the first three-quarters of 2010 export earnings from oil rose, and so too did PDVSA's allocation to social development, to $3,807m. (a 353% rise compared with the same period in 2009). There was a sharp rise in PDVSA social spending, to $17,300m., in the presidential election year of 2012, which reduced PDVSA profits to $4,300m. In 2013 PDVSA reported an improvement in profits to $15,800m. as a result of currency devaluation, the sale of assets and a $4,000m. reduction in its contribution to social projects.

Under the Chávez Government, Venezuela's oil wealth was used as a tool for promoting regional integration and insulating the Chávez Government from US pressure through initiatives such as Petrocaribe, under which PDVSA supplied oil at discounted cost to 18 oil-importing Central American and Caribbean countries. In 2007 heavy shale sand reserves in the Orinoco Belt, which had been opened to private sector exploration and drilling, were classified as conventional

reserves, rendering Venezuela the country with the world's largest oil reserves. The Government subsequently renegotiated the original exploration contracts, thereby assigning to PDVSA a majority stake in the Orinoco projects. In 2014 contracts were awarded to national oil companies from the People's Republic of China and Russia for the development of the Junín 1 and Junín 10 blocks in the Orinoco. An additional US $4,000m. in financing until 2022 was secured from Spain's Repsol SA to increase oil production in established fields.

THE ADMINISTRATION OF CARLOS PÉREZ RODRÍGUEZ

Venezuela's democracy was seen to be rapidly consolidated following the overthrow of the Pérez Jiménez dictatorship in 1958. Major social progress was made in the 1960s and 1970s, as successive AD and COPEI governments channelled earnings from petroleum exports into state subsidies and social investment. A welfare state system was established, and a programme of land distribution implemented. After the presidential elections of 1973, which brought the AD candidate, Carlos Andrés Pérez Rodríguez, to power, Venezuela experienced a dramatic change in economic fortunes, as the Middle East oil embargo led to a sharp rise in international petroleum prices. This coincided with the nationalization of the Venezuelan petroleum industry, resulting in a 10-fold increase in central government revenues. However, the oil 'boom' laid the foundations of a subsequent economic crisis that ultimately delegitimized the Punto Fijo model. The extraordinary levels of revenue accruing to the state exacerbated corruption, and led the national administration to become excessively bureaucratic and inefficient. The Government borrowed from international creditors in order to sustain state investment projects when the price of petroleum began to decline. During the administration of Luis Herrera Campins (1979–84), the Government used the investment fund of PDVSA to stabilize the economy after a devaluation of the currency in 1983. The move was unsuccessfully resisted by the company's managers, who subsequently began to protect PDVSA's revenues from what they considered to be an increasingly incompetent state. This led to a strategy of 'transfer pricing' and 'internationalization', whereby PDVSA moved its profits abroad and invested in refineries outside Venezuela.

There was mounting popular disaffection with AD and COPEI in the 1980s, as the economy went into recession. Despite the increasingly negative evaluation of their performance, their institutionalized control of the state and election administration meant that AD and COPEI remained the dominant political forces.

Pérez was re-elected to the presidency in 1988, amid critical economic conditions but popular expectations of a return to the 'boom years'. These expectations were crushed, as an orthodox programme of liberal economic policies was swiftly introduced. The strict austerity measures increased fuel and transport prices, and reduced state subsidies, provoking serious civil disturbances in early 1989. These were violently suppressed by government security services, resulting in the death of 276 people, according to official figures, although other sources put the number of people killed at as many as 2,000. This event, known as the 'Caracazo', galvanized junior ranks in the armed forces to the overthrow of the Punto Fijo system.

President Pérez rapidly lost the support of his own party and of the pro-AD Confederación de Trabajadores de Venezuela (CTV), which organized the first general strike since democratization in 1958. A series of reforms, including administrative and political decentralization and changes to the electoral system were introduced in 1989. This enabled minor parties of the centre-left to win control of a number of state and municipal governments, but it failed to relegitimize the Punto Fijo system.

FAILED MILITARY COUP

In February 1992 there was an attempted *coup d'état* by a nationalist faction of junior officers known as the Movimiento Bolivariano Revolucionario-200 (MBR-200—Bolivarian Revolutionary Movement 200), formed by Hugo Chávez and three colleagues 10 years earlier. MBR-200 proposed a 'Bolivarian' alternative to the Punto Fijo model, which addressed the needs of the poor and which would realize the ambitions of a united continent held by the Liberator, Simón Bolívar. Although the coup attempt failed, it transformed Chávez into a popular hero, despite his subsequent imprisonment. A second coup attempt, in November, by forces indirectly linked to MBR-200 seriously weakened President Pérez. He was suspended from office by the AD-controlled Congreso Nacional (National Congress) in May 1993, following allegations of misappropriation of public funds. In May 1996 he was found guilty and sentenced to two years and four months under house arrest.

THE ADMINISTRATION OF RAFAEL CALDERA RODRÍGUEZ

Following Pérez's suspension, in June 1993 the Congress elected Ramón José Velásquez, an independent senator, as interim President until fresh elections were held in December. The octogenarian Rafael Caldera Rodríguez, standing as an independent candidate following his expulsion from COPEI in June, won the presidency on an anti-party, anti-liberalization platform. He was supported by a 17-party electoral alliance, Convergencia Nacional (CN), that included representatives of the traditional left. On taking office, Caldera released the coup plotters of 1992, including Chávez. Chávez subsequently formed the Movimiento Quinta República (MVR) political party, which began mobilizing support for a presidential bid.

Although Caldera promised to overhaul the 1961 Constitution and address rising poverty, little was achieved. The banking sector collapsed within months of his taking office, precipitating a major economic crisis that forced the administration to renege on electoral promises and sign a US $1,400m. stand-by agreement with the IMF in 1996. The resulting structural adjustment measures exacerbated popular discontent and fractured Caldera's CN alliance, forcing the President to become increasingly reliant on the AD and COPEI parties in the Congress to advance his legislative agenda.

A rise in the oil price afforded the Government fiscal leeway in 1997, and structural reforms were postponed. However, the oil price fell in 1998, an election year, forcing the Government to reduce spending by US $6,000m. Underscoring the profound popular hostility towards the established political parties, all the leading presidential candidates contested the election as independents. The two front-running candidates, Henrique Salas Römer and Irene Sáez, both ran on neo-liberal platforms, but saw their popularity collapse after they accepted the endorsement of AD and COPEI. This benefited Hugo Chávez. Chávez was supported by a multi-party alliance, the Polo Patriótico (PP), comprising his MVR party and smaller leftist organizations. The Chávez manifesto promised a 'Bolivarian revolution' that would rewrite the Constitution, restructure state institutions, address corruption and terminate the internationalization strategy of PDVSA. Chávez's emphasized a moderate 'third way' model of capitalism, in which the state only intervened when the market failed. His nationalist rhetoric and identification with politically and economically marginalized groups, particularly the indigenous and black communities, gave Chávez—of mixed race and modest background—a strong connection with the popular sectors.

Despite attempts by COPEI and AD to forestall a victory by Chávez by revising the election schedule, Chávez won a majority of votes (56%) in the December 1998 presidential election. In the legislative elections, held a month earlier, AD secured the most congressional seats. The PP also performed strongly.

THE ADMINISTRATION OF HUGO CHÁVEZ FRÍAS

President Chávez used his inauguration in February 1999 to launch his Bolivarian revolution. He decreed a national referendum on the convening of a constituent assembly to draft a new constitution. In the plebiscite, held in April, 88% of voters endorsed his proposals. AD, COPEI and interests affiliated to those parties (such as the CTV and leading business groups) adopted a strategy of withdrawal from the formal political process in order to delegitimize the new Government and its reform programme.

In the July 1999 election to the Constituent Assembly, supporters of Chávez won 125 of the 131 seats. The Constituent Assembly completed its work in November. The new Constitution was approved by 71% of voters at a referendum in December. The Bolivarian Constitution introduced radical institutional changes, including a renewable six-year term for the President (replacing the traditional non-renewable five-year term); the establishment of a post of Vice-President; the replacement of the bicameral legislature with a unicameral, 165-seat Asamblea Nacional (National Assembly); and the abolition of the Supreme Court, which was to be superseded by the Tribunal Suprema de Justicia (TSJ—Supreme Court of Justice). Two new state powers were created: the Consejo Moral Republicano, with responsibility to uphold the Constitution, and the Consejo Nacional Electoral (CNE—National Electoral Council). Serving military officers were given the right to vote; military promotions were reassigned from the legislature to the President; and the army, navy and air force were merged into a single unified command. The Constitution changed the official name of the country to the Bolivarian Republic of Venezuela. There was a strong emphasis throughout the document on the state's role in the economy and in the provision of welfare. Citizen participation was also institutionalized through a variety of mechanisms, including recall referendums and participation by civil society groups in state appointments.

Following the promulgation of the new Constitution, the Constituent Assembly appointed an unelected, 21-member congresillo (mini-congress) pending fresh national elections scheduled for May 2000. In a move that fuelled opposition claims of authoritarianism, the congresillo began filling the new posts created by the Constitution with individuals closely identified with the PP, on the grounds that the country was in a 'transitional phase'. Opposition criticism regarding Chávez's democratic credentials increased following the appointment of military officers to a number of senior cabinet and administrative positions. Chávez viewed the military as an integral actor in his project for national reconstruction, and this was reflected in the Government's first social policy initiative, the 'Plan Bolívar 2000', launched in February 1999. This was intended to rehabilitate public property and land, and led to the deployment of the armed forces in local communities to build schools and hospitals. Viewed as a means of bypassing the ineffective state administration, the Plan was nevertheless repudiated by influential senior and retired military officers, who linked up with Chávez's party political opponents.

Throughout 1999 opposition to President Chávez was fierce among the former beneficiaries of the Punto Fijo model in the business, union and media sectors. In February 2000, on the eighth anniversary of the 1992 military coup attempt, Francisco Arias Cárdenas, a former colleague of Chávez, and five other prominent figures within MBR-200 issued the Declaration of Maracay, arguing that Chávez had betrayed the democratic ideals of MBR-200. Arias subsequently announced his intention to contest the presidency.

The 2000 Elections

The elections scheduled for May 2000 were the largest and most complex in Venezuela's history. They were intended to relegitimize all publicly elected officials, including the President. More than 6,000 posts were to be contested, in polls administered by a new and inexperienced CNE. Arias was the only significant challenger to Chávez for the presidency, following the decision by AD and COPEI not to present presidential candidates. Three days before the elections were due to be held, the TSJ ruled in favour of an injunction against the elections introduced by civil society organizations, on the grounds that the CNE was not technically competent to administer the process. Voting was postponed, with the presidential, legislative and gubernatorial elections rescheduled for July 2000. Chávez received 60% of the vote, and Arias 38%. At elections to the new National Assembly, the MVR-led PP alliance won 104 of the 165 seats, more than the three-fifths' majority required to make appointments to the positions of Fiscal- and Comptroller-General and to the judiciary. AD emerged as the largest opposition party, winning 32 seats, while COPEI secured just five seats. The National Assembly in

November granted 'enabling powers' to the executive for one year, allowing Chávez to legislate by decree in a range of areas.

Political polarization deepened as the Chávez administration pressed ahead with its Bolivarian project of radical transformation. In October 2000 Chávez decreed a referendum on measures to reform the trade union movement through the introduction of direct internal elections. The CTV leadership, which viewed this as an attack by the Government, convoked a series of stoppages, including a costly four-day strike by workers in the oil industry. The referendum on trade union reform proceeded in December, and the proposals were supported by 63% of voters. However, with an abstention rate of 78%, the legitimacy of the Government's reforms was questioned.

CTV protests gained momentum in 2001, drawing support from diverse interests affected by government policy. These included the Roman Catholic Church (which opposed changes to education funding), Fedecámaras (the leading private sector lobby group), landowners and the senior management within PDVSA. Opposition to the Government became more unified following the introduction of 49 new pieces of legislation in November of that year, affecting areas including tourism, fishing and banking. Particularly contentious were the Hydrocarbons Law and the Agricultural Development Land Reform Law. The Hydrocarbons Law and gas laws reserved resource ownership to the state, reversing the opening to the private sector that had been introduced by President Caldera in the mid-1990s. The Land Reform Law allowed for the expropriation in the national interest of privately held land deemed 'idle'. Lobby groups and sectoral interests, some of which received financial support from US quasi-governmental organizations such as the National Endowment for Democracy (NED), substituted the weak and disorganized opposition political parties. The economic élite used its control of the private sector media to criticize the Government and mobilize support against Chávez. There was a second general strike in January 2002, along with appeals by government opponents for the military to remove Chávez from power.

The April 2002 Coup

Bolstered by positive signals from the US authorities, the opposition maintained street-based protests and civil disturbance into 2002. In one protest, on 11 April, at least 19 people were killed, and more than 100 injured, as pro- and anti-Government demonstrators clashed near the presidential palace. Amid claims in the private media that Chávez had ordered his supporters to fire on opposition demonstrators, senior military officers, including the Commander-in-Chief of the Armed Forces, announced that Chávez had resigned and was under arrest. Chávez was subsequently transferred to a military base on a nearby Caribbean island. Senior cabinet figures were detained, and an interim junta was installed under the President of Fedecámaras, Pedro Carmona. The break with the constitutional order was condemned by regional organizations such as the Organization of American States (OAS), but not by the US, British or Spanish Governments. The military and trade unions withdrew their support from the junta, and the USA revised its position when Carmona appointed a cabinet composed of right-wing economists, dissolved the democratically elected legislature and regional assemblies and suspended the Constitution. The junta collapsed on 13 April, following a revolt by junior military ranks and mass popular demonstrations to demand the reinstatement of Chávez, who was returned to office the following day.

The 2004 Recall Referendum

In the immediate aftermath of the coup, the Government dismissed the senior military command and 18,000 of the 33,000 full-time workers at PDVSA. Restaffing followed a pattern of appointment based on political support for the Bolivarian revolution that was also seen in other 'disloyal' institutions, such as the judiciary, after the opposition-dominated senior judges dismissed charges of military rebellion against the coup leaders. The President of Fedecámaras was later arrested and charged with crimes including treason, although he fled to Colombia; and the CTV President, Carlos Ortega, unsuccessfully sought political asylum in Costa Rica and was arrested in 2006. The Government convened a series of

dialogue committees to engage with the opposition; however, polarization and political tension persisted in the context of perceived government politicization of state institutions. The opposition created the Coordinadora Democrática (CD—Democratic Co-ordinator) as an umbrella organization for anti-Chávez groups, and in December 2002 initiated an indefinite general strike concentrated in strategic sectors of the economy, most significantly the oil industry. The stoppage lasted until February 2003, with a resulting collapse in petroleum production. The Government was deprived of US $17,000m. in oil export revenue, technical installations were sabotaged, and PDVSA was obliged to import petroleum and declare *force majeure* on existing contracts. Owing to the repercussions of the strike, which heightened unemployment and shortages over the Christmas period, support for the opposition was eroded.

In May 2003 the Government and the opposition signed an accord committing all parties to a constitutional resolution to the crisis. The opposition strategy subsequently shifted from stoppages and protests to electoral methods of replacing President Chávez. A possible such channel was the recall referendum, a mechanism introduced by the 1999 Constitution.

In order for a recall referendum on the executive to be convened, 20% of the electorate (more than 2.4m. voters) were constitutionally required to sign a petition. The non-governmental organization Sumate, headed by María Corina Machado and funded by the US NED, mobilized a signature campaign. In June 2004 the CNE ruled that the opposition had succeeded in gathering the requisite number of signatures, and the recall referendum was scheduled for 15 August, on the basis that if a greater proportion of the electorate voted against Chávez than had supported him at the 2000 election (59.7% of voters), fresh elections were to be convened within 30 days of the recall result. The opposition went into the recall campaign with alliance factions vying for the CD candidacy in the event of a presidential election, and lacking a clear proposal for government. By contrast, Chávez approached the referendum with a solid organizational base of grass-roots organizations. Higher than expected oil prices in 2004 further strengthened the position of the Government, which used the resultant revenues to fund social programmes, called misiones, in areas such as health, education and work training.

Chávez won the recall referendum, with 59% voting in favour of his presidency. Participation in the referendum was high, at 70%. In the aftermath of his victory, Chávez instituted a deepening of the Bolivarian revolution: land distribution programmes were accelerated; the oil-financed misiones were expanded; and more than 8,500 integrated health care clinics were built in areas previously lacking access to medical services. The clinics were staffed by some 30,000 Cuban doctors, under oil exchange programmes negotiated by the Venezuelan and Cuban Governments in 2000 and 2005. Although the health provision was popular with Chávez's support base among the poor, it brought protests from the Venezuelan medical association, as well as opposition claims of Cuban infiltration.

In response to persistent lock-outs co-ordinated by the opposition, the Government created subsidized food-distribution schemes, such as 6,000 Mercal supermarkets, which were maintained in the aftermath of opposition protests. Financial support was also provided by the Government to workers who took over industries shut down by private sector owners. Social production companies based on co-operative practices received Government subsidies and were expanded across the country. The administration thus emerged strengthened and more committed to its revolutionary goals following four years of political turmoil. Pro-Chávez candidates won control of 21 of the country's 23 state governments in regional elections convened in October 2004. President Chávez announced that Venezuela was striving to achieve a model of '21st century socialism'.

The capacity of the CD alliance to agitate against the Government was restricted in December, when the Government introduced a 'media responsibility law'. This followed the assassination of public prosecutor Danilo Anderson, who had been investigating the events surrounding the coup attempt of April 2002. The legislation made defamation of a public official, incitement to violence and the distribution of inaccurate reports offences punishable by imprisonment.

A Third Term for Chávez

The political ascendancy of the governing alliance was demonstrated in the elections to the National Assembly in December 2005, which were boycotted by the opposition on the grounds that a fair and free election could not be guaranteed, despite reassurance from the OAS and international election observer groups.

The opposition was divided going into the presidential election contest of December 2006, finally agreeing on the candidacy of Manuel Rosales, Governor of Zulia state. However, the Rosales campaign lacked clarity over policy and the future composition of an eventual administration, resulting in a heavy defeat for the CD. Chávez was re-elected, winning 63% of the total vote.

The third Chávez term was launched with a flurry of activity, as the President announced plans to accelerate his '21st century socialism'. In January 2007 Chávez successfully petitioned the National Assembly for enabling powers, allowing the executive the right to decree policy in an extensive range of areas for an 18-month period. Enabling powers formed one of the 'five motors' of the revolution, intended to reshape Venezuelan politics and institutions: the other four embraced an expansion of communal power, a new geometry of power, constitutional reform, and the promotion of moral and educational values. Taken together, these changes prefigured a redesign of institutions to reflect a redistribution of power down to grass-roots community councils. Measures were decreed that expanded the role of the state in the economy, by nationalizing strategic areas such as telecommunications, electricity and hydrocarbons; and in 2008 a unified Partido Socialista Unido de Venezuela (PSUV—United Socialist Party of Venezuela) was created out of the multi-party pro-Government alliance. There was particular controversy over plans to revise the Constitution, as presented by Chávez in August 2007. These included the removal of the limit on renewal of the presidential mandate, the institution of executive control over international reserves, and the introduction of a six-hour working day. The Government subsequently experienced its first electoral defeat, in a referendum on the proposals held in December, amid a high rate of abstention. Although the measures were rejected, Chávez used enabling powers to introduce some of his planned changes on a case-by-case basis. Ahead of the expiry of enabling authority at the beginning of August 2008, 23 measures was introduced, including laws against financial speculation and hoarding (which became punishable by imprisonment) and the creation of a civil militia intended to improve security at community level. In February 2009 the Government convened a referendum on whether term limits for all publicly elected officials should be abolished. Some 55% of voters approved the constitutional amendment, effectively allowing Chávez to run for re-election indefinitely.

Throughout 2009 and 2010 the Government's popularity was compromised by economic issues including high inflation, scarcity of basic goods and a nationwide power shortage (which led to electricity rationing in 2009). At the September 2010 elections to the National Assembly, the political opposition to the Government, largely unified under the Mesa de la Unidad Democrática (MUD—Table for Democratic Unity), won 47% of the popular vote and 65 seats. The PSUV, with 98 seats, retained an overall majority, although this fell short of the two-thirds' majority required to appoint state officials and pass enabling legislation. Divisions within the PSUV, and disaffection with the performance of individual PSUV officials in national and regional politics, pointed to increased reliance on the unifying figure of Chávez.

The 2012 Presidential Election

Anticipation of the presidential election scheduled for 7 October 2012 was dominated by the issue of Chávez's health. In July 2011 it was announced that the 57-year-old Chávez would receive treatment in Cuba for an unspecified cancer diagnosis. In contrast to his ubiquitous presence in Venezuelan public life throughout his presidency, Chávez's appearances were greatly reduced, and speculation as to who would succeed him in the event of his death intensified. While the PSUV was faced with serious internal challenges, the opposition was strengthened by enhanced unity within the MUD, and by the decision to determine the MUD presidential candidate through a primary process conducted in February 2012. Opinion polls forecast that the winner of the primary, Henrique Capriles Radonski (the Governor of Miranda state), would defeat any PSUV candidate other than Hugo Chávez. This increased the pressure on the ailing President to remain in the contest, despite gruelling rounds of chemotherapy. Chávez's campaign was buoyed by high levels of public spending, and popular sympathy for the largely absent President, who retained the presidency with 55.1% of the vote; Capriles won 44.3%. Chávez returned to Cuba in early December for a further round of treatment, announcing before his departure that he wished the foreign minister, Nicolás Maduro, to succeed him. The President was not seen in public for three months. Amid mounting uncertainty over Chávez's ability to attend his scheduled inauguration in early February 2013, the MUD pushed for Chávez to be declared constitutionally incapable of returning to office, necessitating fresh elections within a 30-day period. This was resisted by the PSUV, which secured judicial support for a delay to the inauguration. Chávez returned to Venezuela in mid-February but remained out of public view, with the exception the release of a photograph of an evidently weak President with two of his daughters. The announcement of his death, on 5 March, led to a public outpouring of grief for Chávez; his funeral took place three days later. The CNE scheduled a presidential election for 14 April, and Capriles announced his intention to contest the presidency once again.

Chávez's designation of Maduro as his successor was not openly challenged within the PSUV, although it generated internal tensions that pitted Maduro's trade union base and Marxist grouping within the PSUV against the nationalist-oriented military faction, represented by the President of the Asemblea Nacional, former Vice-President Diosdado Cabello.

THE ADMINISTRATION OF NICOLÁS MADURO

Although Maduro's election campaign drew heavily on the image of Chávez, expectations of a sympathy vote were not realized, and Maduro lost more than 600,000 of the votes that had been cast for Chávez just six months earlier. The narrowness of Maduro's victory over Capriles, just 1.8%, galvanized MUD street protests to demand a recount. Eight people, including two children, were killed in post-election violence.

Although Venezuela's regional allies acknowledged Maduro's victory, the USA supported the MUD in its demands for a full audit of the election result. This was duly conducted by the CNE. Despite no irregularities being determined, the USA continued to withhold recognition of the Maduro administration. Maduro set out to govern from a broad base, appointing a large cabinet made up of diverse interests within the PSUV. He prioritized addressing crime, corruption and the macroeconomic imbalances that had been highlighted by Chávez as priorities for his fourth term. While limited progress was made in respect of corruption and economic imbalances, initiatives such as the Plan Patria Segura, which targeted areas of high crime and violence with military deployments, helped to stabilize support for Maduro among a disaffected Chavista grass roots. Maduro worked to connect with Chávez loyalists, including through the convening of more than 1,000 street meetings (gobierno de calle) at which senior officials could hear community grievances. In December 2013 the governing PSUV and its allies in the Gran Polo Patriótico won 49% of the vote in municipal elections and secured control of three-quarters (255) of mayoral offices. The results consolidated Maduro's authority within the PSUV, and the elections were followed by a series of cabinet changes that consolidated policy influence within a narrow circle of advisers close to the President.

In January 2014 Maduro sought to initiate a dialogue with MUD leader Capriles on crime and murder, following the murder in that month of a former Miss Venezuela, and an increase in the murder rate to 79 per 100,000 persons in 2013. The latter represented a quadrupling of the murder rate during the course of the Chávez presidency, and placed Venezuela's among the five highest worldwide. An opposition dialogue with the Government was rejected by the Voluntad Popular (VP) party, led by Leopoldo López and María Corina Machado, which broke with the MUD and mobilized with students from private sector universities in street protests to force *la salida* (the exit) of Maduro. Launched in February, the protracted demonstrations resulted in the deaths of more than 40 people from the pro- and anti-Government sides as well as the security forces, but they failed in their objective of removing Maduro from the presidency. Efforts at dialogue under the auspices of the Vatican and the Union of South American Nations (Unión de Naciones Suramericanas—UNASUR) collapsed in May, amid ongoing resistance to negotiations on the part of the VP and the Government's refusal to meet the opposition's preliminary conditions for talks, including the release from detention of opposition figures detained during the protests. While the mass protests were destabilizing for the Government, internal divisions were a more significant preoccupation—most notably after the removal of Jorge Giordani, a key adviser to Chávez, from his post as Minister of Planning. Disputes in the aftermath of Giordani's dismissal revealed ongoing tensions within the regime over the direction of the Bolivarian revolution and the construction of '21st century socialism' in the post-Chávez era.

INTERNATIONAL RELATIONS

Venezuela's international relations under Hugo Chávez were guided by four central concepts under the rubric of the Government's 'Bolivarian' approach: multipolarism; regional integration; state sovereignty; and close ties with other oil-producing nations. These principles had informed Venezuela's foreign policy throughout the post-1958 democratic period, but they were proactively pursued by the Chávez administration, which dedicated significant energy and resources to the achievement of its foreign policy objectives. The 2000s presented an important enabling environment for the Government's external agenda, with factors including the strong rise in the international oil prices, the spread of left-of-centre governments across Latin America, growing sentiment against US foreign policy, resource nationalism in countries such as Russia, and the emergence of China as an important trading partner. The diversification of Venezuela's oil markets away from the USA, along with Chávez's vocal opposition to US initiatives such as the Free Trade Area of the Americas (FTAA) and the 'war on terror' under President George W. Bush contributed to a chronic deterioration in relations between Venezuela and the USA. Chávez's successor, Nicolás Maduro, emphasized his commitment to maintaining this direction of foreign policy, to which he had contributed in his previous role as Minister of Foreign Affairs.

Bolivarianism is named after South America's 19th-century independence leader, Simón Bolívar. Drawing on Bolívar's vision of an integrated Latin America as a counter to the emerging USA, the Chávez Government pursued regional integration based on principles of social justice. An outspoken opponent of the planned, US-promoted FTAA, Chávez posited a Bolivarian Alliance for the Peoples of our America (Alianza Bolivariana para los Pueblos de Nuestra América—ALBA) as a counter-model that excluded the USA and Canada. Launched by Venezuela and Cuba in 2004, ALBA counted nine members by mid-2012, including Bolivia, Nicaragua and Ecuador, and launched its own virtual trading currency, the sucre, in 2010. Venezuela forged strong links with Brazil, Argentina and Uruguay, and a number of economic and cultural integration projects based on ALBA principles of social justice and exploitation of comparative advantages were launched, including the broadcasting initiative Telesur and the Banco del Sur (intended as a regional alternative to the World Bank). Regional energy integration strategies were pursued, as exemplified by projects such as the regional oil company PetroSur.

At the beginning of 2006 Venezuela withdrew from the Comunidad Andina de Naciones (CAN—Andean Community of Nations, comprising Bolivia, Colombia, Ecuador and Peru) on the grounds that CAN membership and bilateral trade deals between the USA and individual CAN members were incompatible. Venezuela was admitted to full membership of the Southern Common Market (Mercado Común del Sur—MER-

COSUR) in July of that year after nearly a decade of entry negotiations, although its membership was subject to ratification by all existing members—a process that was only completed at the end of June 2012, after Paraguay, whose Congress had refused to ratify Venezuela's full membership, was expelled from MERCOSUR following the controversial impeachment of President Fernando Lugo by the Paraguayan Congress. Venezuela participated in the founding conference of UNASUR, established by 12 South American countries in May 2008 (with Mexico and Panama holding observer status). UNASUR advanced its agenda of creating closer ties between its member states, and created the South American Defense Council, which held its first meeting in March. Venezuela was also a key advocate for the formation of the Comunidad de Estados de América Latina y el Caribe (CELAC—Community of Latin American and Caribbean States), a regional organization including all countries of the Americas except the USA and Canada, and was widely seen as a challenge to the OAS and to US influence within that organization. The establishment of CELAC was formalized at an inaugural summit of heads of state of its 33 members in Caracas in December 2011.

Relations between Venezuela and Cuba strengthened significantly under President Chávez. More than 875 reciprocal agreements in areas such as economic and social investment, trade and energy were signed by Chávez and Cuban Presidents Dr Fidel Castro Ruz and Raúl Castro Ruz. Venezuela remained opposed to the US embargo on Cuba, and the reinforcement of bilateral ties between Caracas and Havana aggravated US–Venezuelan tensions.

As part of his anti-imperialist Bolivarian vision, Chávez sought to reduce Venezuela's trade dependence on the USA, and to loosen the close economic and political relationship that had existed between the two countries throughout the 20th century. The Chávez administration condemned the US-led invasions of Afghanistan and Iraq in 2001 and 2003, respectively. Relations between the two countries were further strained amid allegations by Chávez that the Administration of George W. Bush was working with the opposition alliance in Venezuela to remove him from power. The USA channelled extensive financial resources to the Venezuelan opposition through NED, and also sought to isolate Venezuela at the regional level. In 2005 the USA imposed an arms export embargo on Venezuela, and after 2006 Venezuela was annually 'decertified' for non-compliance in the USA's counter-narcotics policy, despite an increase in interdiction and enforcement activities and good co-operative relations between Venezuela and other countries on anti-drugs issues.

Tensions were exacerbated by the failure of US authorities to extradite a self-acknowledged terrorist and former employee of the US Central Intelligence Agency (CIA), Luis Posada Carriles, to Venezuela on charges relating to the bombing of a Cuban aircraft in 1976, in which 73 people died. Relations between Venezuela and the USA reached an all-time low in September 2008, when the Chávez administration expelled the US ambassador to Venezuela in 'solidarity' with the Morales Government in Bolivia, which had expelled the US ambassador for allegedly colluding with Bolivian opposition groups. The USA responded by expelling Venezuela's ambassador. Hopes were raised of an improvement in US-Venezuelan relations following Barack Obama's inauguration as US President in January 2009. Diplomatic representation was briefly restored, but relations were swiftly set back as a result of US support for the regime that ousted President Zelaya of Honduras in June, along with a controversial agreement, signed in October, allowing the USA to use Colombian military bases, which was interpreted by the Chávez Government as hostile towards Venezuela. In May 2011 the USA imposed sanctions on Venezuela's state-owned PDVSA, as part of a new round of sanctions on entities that were alleged to be aiding Iran's energy sector. The USA's decision not to recognize the outcome of the April 2013 presidential election result in Venezuela placed relations between the Obama Administration and the incoming President Maduro on a difficult footing, and financial support for the Venezuelan opposition continued to be channelled through NED. In May 2014 the US House of Representatives and Senate both voted in favour of sanctions targeted at senior Venezuelan officials alleged to have committed human rights abuses. However, the US State Department rejected the imposition of sanctions, on the grounds that this would impede efforts to encourage the Venezuelan Government and opposition to engage in dialogue.

Antagonism between the USA and Venezuela was particularly pronounced in relation to petroleum. The Chávez Government pursued close relations with other oil-producing nations, including Iraq, Libya, Iran and Russia. In 2000 President Chávez undertook a tour of the Middle East, during which he visited Iraq and Libya and met the Iraqi leader Saddam Hussain. The USA condemned the meeting, and was critical of the Caracas Energy Accord of 2000, which extended to Cuba the preferential terms for oil offered by Venezuela and Mexico to other countries in the region. In 2005 Chávez publicly stated his commitment to co-operating with the Iranian Government in the peaceful use of nuclear energy, and bilateral agreements between the two countries were signed in areas including agriculture, manufacturing, culture and economic development. In improving the traditionally poor relations between Venezuela and other OPEC member countries, and seeking close co-operation within the cartel to achieve high and stable oil prices, Venezuela went against the energy security interests of the USA.

These US interests were seen to be most conspicuously threatened by the forging of amicable links with China. In 2001 a China-Venezuela High-Level Joint Commission was established to develop strategic relations between the two countries, resulting in more than 300 agreements and joint ventures on technology, infrastructure, housing, agriculture and oil over the following decade. These agreements were underpinned by US $7,000m. in Chinese loans and investment in Venezuela, and by Venezuela's agreement to increase its oil exports to China from less than 100,000 b/d in 2005 to 1m. b/d by 2012. In February 2012 Chinese finance totalling $40,000m. was made available to fund a range of industrial and infrastructure projects in Venezuela, and in 2013 two separate agreements, for $14, 000m. and $28,000m., were negotiated between PDVSA and the national Chinese companies China Petrochemical Corporation (Sinopec) and China National Petroleum Corporation (CNPC) for the development of oil fields in the Orinoco belt. Notwithstanding the antagonistic rhetoric between Venezuela and the USA, the volume of trade between the two countries increased, and commercial ties remained vibrant. Venezuela remained one of the top four suppliers of oil to the USA, and one of the largest Latin American investors in the USA, while the USA was Venezuela's most important trading partner.

Relations between Venezuela and Colombia swung between strained and amicable under President Chávez. The Venezuelan President supported a peaceful resolution of Colombia's civil conflict, and sought to facilitate dialogue between the Colombian Government of President Andrés Pastrana Arango (1998–2002) and the left-wing guerrilla group Fuerzas Armadas Revolucionarias de Colombia—Ejército del Pueblo (FARC). Colombian President Alvaro Uribe Vélez, who was first elected in May 2002, adopted a military solution to the conflict, which was supported by the Bush Administration in the USA and thereafter conceived as a 'war on terror'. This definition was rejected by the Venezuelan Government, which accused right-wing Colombian paramilitary 'terrorists' of colluding with the Venezuelan opposition. Relations between the two countries deteriorated in December 2004 when a senior figure in the FARC, Rodrigo Granda Escobar, was abducted in Venezuela by Venezuelan security officials paid by Colombian authorities. In mid-2007 Chávez was invited by his Colombian counterpart to facilitate a release of hostages held by the FARC. However, bilateral ties came under severe strain when Uribe accused Chávez of violating the terms of the mediation by contacting the head of the Colombian armed forces. In March 2008 Venezuela mobilized troops to its border with Colombia, after an incursion into Ecuadorean territory by Colombian troops led to the death of the FARC's second-in-command, Raúl Reyes. Colombia and the USA alleged that

Venezuela was providing financial support to the FARC, citing evidence allegedly found on two computers belonging to Reyes that were seized during the raid. However, no direct evidence to substantiate the claims was presented by Colombian authorities. The subsequent restoration of amicable relations between President Chávez and his Colombian counterpart, despite their profoundly different ideologies, exemplified the perennial capacity for pragmatism on the part of Chávez. Hostilities resumed in mid-2009 following accusations by Colombia that Venezuela was supplying weapons to the FARC. In response to this, and to an expansion of US military activity in Colombia, Chávez ordered the withdrawal of the Venezuelan ambassador from Colombia. Under Colombia's new President, Juan Manuel Santos, who took office in August 2010, relations between the two countries improved dramatically. A new pragmatism, based on the extensive economic ties between the two countries, took precedence over ideological differences between their Governments, and Santos saw co-operation with Venezuela on border security as essential to the peace-building process in Colombia. Reflecting this spirit of co-operation, by May 2011 Venezuela had handed over eight high-profile alleged FARC activists. In a further sign of improved relations between Colombia and Venezuela, in that month Presidents Santos and Chávez brokered an agreement on the return of deposed President Manuel Zelaya to Honduras. In March 2012 Santos and Chávez met in Cuba to conclude six new agreements aimed at enhancing bilateral trade and integration. Venezuela played an important role in supporting and facilitating peace negotiations between the Santos Government and the FARC, which were convened in Cuba and Norway in 2013. Colombia became an important source of emergency food and energy imports for Venezuela during periods of scarcity in 2013–14. President Maduro maintained the amicable ties with the Santos administration that had been forged during his period as Minister of Foreign Affairs, and Venezuela remained proactively engaged in Colombia's peace process.

Venezuela's historically strained relations with neighbouring Guyana, arising from territorial and border disputes, improved under the Chávez's leadership. Venezuela had historical claims to all territory west of the gas-rich Essequibo river area in Guyana, and in November 1989 a UN mediator was appointed to resolve this territorial dispute. Limited progress was made, and relations deteriorated in July 2000 when Venezuela protested strongly against the decision by the Government of Guyana to lease land to a US company in the disputed Essequibo delta for the purpose of developing a satellite launch facility. In March 2004 President Chávez met with his Guyanese counterpart, Bharrat Jagdeo, and the Venezuelan Government modified its position with regard to the area under dispute, no longer opposing Guyana's initiative to grant mineral exploration concessions in the Essequibo region. In mid-2005 Guyana signed the Petrocaribe energy accord with Venezuela, granting Guyana preferential terms for purchasing Venezuelan oil. In July 2008 Venezuela, Guyana and Suriname began negotiations to construct a US $1,100m. natural gas pipeline to facilitate regional energy integration within the framework of UNASUR. In July 2010, despite the historical land disputes, Chávez and Jagdeo signed four agreements promoting co-operation in the areas of agriculture, energy and chemical industries. Although President Maduro sought to consolidate improved bilateral relations—including through a visit to Guyana in August 2013 to participate in a joint declaration of co-operation with his Guyanese counterpart, Donald Ramotar—events including, in October, Venezuela's detention of a US survey ship operating under a Guyanese licence, and the arrest of its crew, briefly set back progress. At the end of 2013 the UN Secretary-General's Personal Representative on the Border Controversy between Guyana and Venezuela, Norman Girvan, reported on productive meetings with the foreign ministers of Venezuela and Guyana over the status of the Essequibo region.

Economy

Dr JULIA BUXTON

Venezuela has the largest proven crude oil reserves in the world, at 298,350m. barrels in 2013. Petroleum has been the mainstay of the economy since the discovery of deposits at the end of the 19th century, and successive governments relied on oil as the driving force of economic modernization. This reliance on petroleum-related taxes and export revenues rendered the country vulnerable to fluctuations in international oil prices, with the performance of the domestic economy characterized by 'boom and bust' cycles. High petroleum prices led to expansionary spending policies, which in turn led to severe fiscal problems when the petroleum price dropped. Venezuela remained trapped in a development dilemma common to many commodity-dependent countries. Strong petroleum prices have traditionally inflated the value of the domestic currency, the bolívar, making non-oil imports cheap and Venezuela's own non-oil exports uncompetitive. This rendered Venezuela import-dependent, and without food sovereignty. Declines in the oil price on international markets, combined with the devaluation of the currency, have prompted attempts to stimulate non-oil sectors over the short term, but this strategy has been repeatedly abandoned when the oil price resumed an upward trend. Such efforts included agricultural reform programmes in the 1960s, state-led heavy industrialization projects in the 1970s, and a neo-liberal-inspired programme in the 1990s that looked to the private sector as the driver of non-oil export growth. The Government under President Hugo Chávez rejected orthodox economic strategies and looked to widen the economic base through state promotion of small and medium-sized industries, co-operatives, and diversification into 'downstream' and agricultural activities. These programmes were implemented ineffectively. They were weakened by corruption and bureaucracy, and they failed to break the country's dependence on oil export revenue. After re-election in 2006, the Chávez administration sought to exploit the benefits of high international petroleum prices, with the oil sector serving as the economic motor of the 'Bolivarian revolution'—which supported high levels of social spending and state intervention. This reinforced Venezuela's dependence on revenue from petroleum exports, and led to contradictions in the Government's development policy, for example by undercutting-state sponsored initiatives in the manufacturing and agricultural sectors.

The strong rise in international oil prices between 2003 and 2008 boosted economic performance, allowing the Government to increase public sector spending and investment. The Government's expansionary fiscal policy contributed to growth over this period, with the non-oil sector and private economic activity also showing strong improvement. However, the economy contracted by 3.2% in 2009 and by 1.5% in 2010, reflecting the fall in oil prices with the global economic downturn and an associated sharp reduction in domestic public sector investment. As a result of a pro-cyclical economic policy, Venezuela experienced strong recovery in 2011, with GDP growth of 4.2%. This continued into 2012, with economic growth of 5.6%—of which 58.2% was from the private sector. However, a threefold increase in public spending which coincided with President Chávez's 2012 re-election bid, together with uncertainty generated by the elections, and bottlenecks in the economy, led to slower growth in 2013, of 1.4%. Chávez's successor as President, Nicolás Maduro, inherited a state as dependent on petroleum revenues as it had been before the Bolivarian revolution of 1999.

As a result of a high birth rate in proportion to the death rate, and significant immigration, the Venezuelan population increased rapidly from 1958; it was estimated to total some 28.5m. in 2014. In that year the labour force was an estimated 14.01m., of whom 39.7% were employed in the informal sector.

The structure of employment and the distribution of the population in the early 2010s were markedly different from the 1960s, when agriculture generated one-third of total employment. By 2013 agriculture accounted for less than 7.3% of employment, despite government efforts to repopulate rural areas through land distribution and infrastructure investment schemes. Services sector employment accounted for an estimated 70.9% of the labour force, with the remainder (some 22%) engaged in industry. The public sector continued to be an important source of employment, occupying 2.9m. people, equivalent to 18.4% of the total labour force in 2012. In April 2014 the unemployment rate was 7.1%. Unemployment averaged 11.1% in 1999–2014, reaching a high of 20.7% in 2003 and a record low of 5.6% in December 2013.

Rates of poverty and inequality in Venezuela have historically been among the highest in the region. When President Chávez took office in 1999, some 43.9% of households lived below the poverty line and the Gini index was 0.5%. Economic growth, sustained increases in social expenditure and a commitment to redistributive measures led the UN Economic Commission for Latin America and the Caribbean (ECLAC) to report that Venezuela had achieved the highest rate of poverty reduction on the continent, with rates of extreme poverty falling from 29.5% in 2011 to 23.9% in 2012. According to the UN Development Programme (UNDP), Venezuela had the lowest recorded Gini coefficient in Latin America, with a decrease from 0.4865 in 1998 to 0.3940 in 2012.

The Chávez administration disbanded the tripartite committees that had set minimum wage levels. These were now determined by the central Government, which prioritized boosting minimum salary rates as part of its anti-poverty drive. In April 2008 the monthly minimum wage rose by 30%, to US $371.6, and—despite economic recession—it increased by a further 10% in April 2009. Two upward adjustments were made to minimum wage levels in 2010: of 10% in May, and a further 15% in September. In April 2011 the minimum wage was increased by 26.5%. In April 2012 the Government announced that the minimum wage, already the highest in Latin America, would increase by 32.3%, with a 15% increase in May and September, lifting the minimum wage to $476 per month. Along with monthly food tickets valued at $223, the gross minimum income of formal sector employees was increased to a total of $700. The incoming Government of President Maduro continued with staggered increases in May and September 2013, which raised the minimum wage by 59% overall in that year. Further increases of 10% and 30% followed in January and May 2014, resulting in a minimum wage of $520 (4,252 bolívares fuertes). The pensions of 2.7m. retirees were adjusted to the new minimum salary.

AGRICULTURE

Agriculture has played a marginal role in the economy, and accounted for less than 4% of GDP in 2013. The sector went into steep decline with the exploitation of petroleum from the beginning of the 20th century. Oil-led economic growth and rapid urbanization reduced pressure for reform of the tenure system, which was characterized by large *latifundio* landholdings concentrated among a small number of families. During the early democratic period there were attempts to reverse high levels of rural poverty and underdevelopment. The Agrarian Reform Law of 1960 redistributed public and some underused privately held land through the Instituto Nacional Agrario (INA—National Agrarian Institute). Efforts to support smallholders, including through infrastructure schemes, were offset by state protection of large agricultural oligopolies and élite resistance to the redistribution process. Competition and dynamism in the sector remained weak, driving up the cost of staple goods. Venezuela failed to achieve self-sufficiency in agricultural production, and overvaluation of the domestic currency artificially cheapened agricultural imports. By the 1990s Venezuela was not sovereign in food production, and the structure of landownership remained concentrated—with the largest 3% of farms accounting for 80% of arable land, and less than 3% of 92m. ha under cultivation.

In 2001 the Chávez Government introduced the Land Law, intended to address food import dependency, rural underdevelopment and inequalities in landholdings. Under Misión Zamora, the law transferred, under certain conditions, idle public and privately held land to peasants, with technical, credit and marketing support provided by the Government through the Instituto Nacional de Tierras (INTI—National Land Institute). The legislation was resisted by those land-owners who were unable to demonstrate legal ownership as required under the new law, and peasants added to rural tensions by occupying privately held land. More than 300 peasant leaders and activists were reported to have been assassinated by landholding interests. In April 2012 INTI announced that some 7.7m. ha of land had been redistributed since the introduction of the 2001 law, of which 1.1m. ha had gone to rural labourers involved in state agricultural co-operatives. In 2009 the Government stated that almost 1m. ha (or 90%) of redistributed land was producing food for domestic consumption, including through supplies to dis-counted Mercal supermarkets located in poor neighbourhoods. Nevertheless, the land distribution programme failed to gen-erate growth of agricultural output, and reliance on imports increased. Food shortages, which fuelled inflation, were driven by price controls that disincentivized private sector food pro-duction and encouraged imports of cheaper products from the USA, Brazil and Colombia, as well as hoarding by private producers and significant increases in food consumption, espe-cially among poorer sectors. In order to guarantee access to essential foods, state-controlled dairy and milk production facilities were introduced in 2007–08 and in 2010. The Gov-ernment nationalized a major flour producer and dairy facil-ities, granted low-interest credits to small and medium-sized producers, sanctioned price speculators and hoarders, and announced reforms of the Land Law. In January 2011 President Chávez launched Misión Agro Venezuela. In the first eight months of the programme, according to Government figures, some 775,000 ha of land had been put to use for cultivating a range of crops.

A number of factors accounted for the setback to government plans for the agricultural sector. Amid uncertainty over gov-ernment policy, large private landholders continued to keep approximately one-half of their land uncultivated, while the land transferred to co-operatives was not transformed into productive farms. President Maduro inherited a burgeoning food security crisis, with Venezuela reliant on imports for more than 70% of agricultural needs. However, exchange controls and dollar shortages reduced agricultural import capacity, while price controls on meat, cereals and dairy products gen-erated a thriving black market and cross-border trade in subsidized goods. Maduro was forced to request two emergency food shipments from Colombia, and in May 2014 the Govern-ment introduced the Secure Food Supply card (Tarjeta de Abastecimiento Seguro), which was to track and limit pur-chases in order to prevent reselling of subsidized food supplies. Maduro remained committed to the goals of land redistribution and food sovereignty set out by his predecessor, and at the end of 2013 announced plans to increase public investment in state co-operatives and to increase the number of urban food gardens (organopónicos) from 24,000 to 80,000 within a year.

MINING AND POWER

Metallic Minerals

Venezuela possesses vast metallic mineral wealth, including an estimated 4,000m. metric tons of iron ore reserves; 5.2m. tons of bauxite; deposits of zinc, copper, lead, phos-phorus, nickel, diamond, silver, uranium; and gold reserves estimated at 10,000 tons.

Successive governments have sought to exploit the country's minerals in order to reduce dependence on petroleum. During the neo-liberal *apertura* (opening) of the 1990s, a number of mining interests were sold to foreign, predominantly North American, investors. This strategy was reversed under the presidency of Hugo Chávez. The sector was designated an essential element of plans for integrated industrial develop-ment, under the direction of the Ministry of Basic Industry and Mining. Contracts in the sector were brought into line with the constitutional requirement that the state had a majority share in strategic ventures. This generated investor uncertainty, and

led to a series of legal claims against the Government as it rescinded earlier agreements and signed new public-private partnerships with foreign-owned state and private companies from Russia and the People's Republic of China.

China positioned itself as a leading player in Venezuela's mining sector during the Chávez administration, framed by investment agreements signed under the 2001 China-Venezuela High-Level Joint Commission. In July 2010 Vene-zuela's state-owned mining holding company, CVG, made a deal to supply 40m. metric tons of iron ore over the next seven years to China's third largest steel and iron company, WISCO; and in 2013 an agreement was signed with the Chinese state-owned company CITIC Group for prospecting and mapping the Venezuela's mining reserves. CITIC additionally acquired the rights to develop the Las Cristinas gold mine—one of the world's largest gold deposits, with 20m. oz in confirmed and potential reserves valued at $32,000m. This followed the nationalization of the gold industry in 2011. Ongoing uncer-tainty in the sector led to a 21.1% contraction of mining activity in 2013.

Coal

Venezuela has estimated coal reserves of 479m. short tons with 2013 production of 2,328m. tons. The bulk of reserves are located in the Guasare Basin, near the border with Colombia. Poor transport links in this region of the country and under-investment by Carbozulia, a subsidiary of the state-owned Petróleos de Venezuela (PDVSA) limited the development of the sector. At the end of the 1980s, however, a strategy of outsourcing mining activities to predominantly German and South African commercial partners led to an increase in coal production, which rose from 46m. short tons in 1980 to 2,413m. tons a decade later. Coal production fell by 25.2% in 2013, to 1.7m. short tons, from 2.3m. tons in 2012.

Coal exports peaked at 8,741m. short tons in 2000 and 8,365m. tons in 2006, but declined steeply thereafter, to just 2,283m. tons in 2011. The reversal of the sector's performance was due to regulatory and contractual uncertainty during the presidency of Hugo Chávez. In 2008 the Government announced plans to create state-managed 'socialist' enter-prises, in line with trends in heavy industry. The Zulia state development agency, Corpozulia, acquired a 51% share in the biggest coal-mining operation in the Zulia region, Carbones de la Guajira. Disputes between investors and the Government in relation to rescinded contracts, together with a lack of infra-structure development, continued to impede the expansion of the sector, while state-led investment plans were met with resistance from the indigenous Yukpa people, whose leader, Sabino Romero, was assassinated in March 2013.

Electricity

The electricity sector has experienced acute crisis, manifested in national blackouts and government-imposed rationing in 2007, 2010, April and September 2013, and May 2014. Total installed generation capacity in the country is around 23,600 MW, but total effective capacity is around 17,600 MW. An estimated 85,054 residential and industrial customers are on the electricity grid. However, of the total installed generation, only 18,350 MW are available for con-sumption, while peak demand can reach 19,300 MW. In 2007 the Government reversed the privatization of the largest electricity company, Electricidad de Caracas, which had been implemented in 2000. This followed payment of US $740m to AES Corp, with the national oil company PDVSA acquiring a 93% holding. Despite state investment of some $7,650m. in the generation and distribution system, supply has not kept up with an annual 6% increase in demand. Venezuela is the second biggest user of electricity in Latin America, with demand driven by the freezing of electricity tariffs and the requirements of large-scale housing projects.

Poor planning, wasteful investment and a high turnover of senior managers undermined the performance of the sector, while water shortages and drought exacerbated the sector's structural vulnerability. More than 80% of Venezuela's elec-tricity is generated by the Raúl Leoni hydroelectric complex (or Guri dam), on the Caroní river. This feeds 20 turbines and three major hydroelectric plants. Water levels in the dam have fallen as low as 248 m above sea level. A drop below 240 m would force eight turbines to close, representing the loss of 5,000 MW of capacity. The Maduro administration maintained that the blackouts and shortages experienced in 2013 and 2014 were the result of opposition sabotage. Under Misión Eléctrica Venezuela, launched in April 2013, the military was deployed to guard facilities, and the Government undertook to add 1,000 MW to the system over a 100-day period. However, this commitment had not been fulfilled by mid-2014.

Petroleum and Natural Gas

Heavy shale sand reserves in the Orinoco Belt, which had been opened to private sector exploration and drilling, were classified as conventional reserves in 2007, rendering Venezuela the country with the world's largest petroleum reserves with 298,350m. barrels in 2013, according to the Organization of the Petroleum Exporting Countries (OPEC).

The petroleum industry is the mainstay of the economy, providing some 40% of government revenue, 95% of export revenues and 12% of GDP. The Government extracted oil rents from PDVSA through taxes, royalties and special dividend payments. Successive governments and management teams at PDVSA have differed over how the country should best exploit and manage its oil wealth. In the 1990s a strategy was pursued of maximizing output, breaking production quotas set by OPEC and incorporating the private sector into production, exploration and refining projects. At the same time, PDVSA executives pursued a strategy of 'internationalizing' the company's assets in order to prevent the Government from drawing on its profits to fund fiscal spending and debt payments, as it had done in the first half of the 1980s. The Chávez administration reversed this approach. The 1999 Constitution enshrined state ownership of PDVSA; and the 2001 Hydrocarbons Law mandated a majority PDVSA share in all production and exploration ventures, and increased royalty rates on oil production from 17% to 30%. This provoked conflict with the PDVSA management, and caused the near-paralysis of production after a general strike in the industry in December 2002. The defeat of the strike enabled the Government to remove more than 18,000 PDVSA staff and thereafter pursue an oil strategy in accordance with the 2001 legislation. The Government's 2005–30 Plan Siembra Petrolera (PSP) integrated PDVSA and the oil economy into the national development strategy. Operations within PDVSA were restructured into regional divisions, with management control transferred from a traditionally independent PDVSA to the Ministry of Energy and Petroleum.

In 2005 the Ministry of Energy and Petroleum undertook a review of the entire framework of contracts between PDVSA and the private sector. The 32 operating service agreements signed with foreign companies were redrafted as joint ventures. PDVSA's share in these new joint ventures was increased to 70%, and the income tax rate was adjusted upwards, to 50%. PDVSA acquired the shares of two private companies, ExxonMobil and ConocoPhillips, which rejected the new contract terms. This led to a protracted legal dispute with ExxonMobil, and eventual arbitration by the International Centre for Settlement of Investment Disputes, which found in favour of ExxonMobil and ordered Venezuela to pay US $900m. in compensation. From 2008 the Government changed its position regarding private sector involvement in the industry. In February 2010 private companies from Japan, India, Malaysia, Spain, the USA and Venezuela won the rights to explore and exploit the Carabobo I Block of Venezuela's Orinoco oil belt, after the first major bidding process since the initial *apertura* of the 1990s.

Significant energy agreements were signed with a range of private and public sector partners in countries including Brazil, Japan, Iran, Colombia, Russia and Argentina, but Venezuela focused on Asia as the main source of investment in future heavy oil developments, in addition to oil services. In 2001 China agreed US $36,000m. in loans and investment to PDVSA, as part of an agreement to increase Venezuelan exports of crude and oil products to China from less than 100,000 barrels of oil equivalent per day (boe/d) in 2005 to 1m. boe/d by 2012. In 2005 new joint ventures in oil services, including for the supply of 13 rigs, were signed at the fourth meeting of the China-Venezuela High-Level Joint Commis-

sion, and PDVSA opened its first office in China. In 2008 PDVSA Services and China National Petroleum Corporation (CNPC) established a joint-venture service company for the manufacture of tankers, drilling equipment and rigs. Between 2008 and 2013 Venezuela received an additional $40,000m. in lending from China in exchange for future oil deliveries of up to 550,000 boe/d. China's imports of Venezuelan crude rose by 8.9% in 2013, while imports of refined products such as fuel oil fell by 8.3%. Overall, its oil imports from Venezuela totalled 369,000 boe/d, up 4.5% from 2012. India emerged as the most significant destination for Venezuela's crude market in Asia, with 403,000 b/d imported in 2013 (a 10% increase from 2012). This followed the signing in 2012 of a 15-year oil export deal between PDVSA and the Indian energy group Reliance Industries Ltd. Total exports of crude to Asia averaged 726,000 b/d in 2013, while the export of products increased by 9.8%, to 289,000 b/d. Conversely, Venezuelan oil exports to the USA, traditionally its largest market, fell to a 28-year low of 792,000 b/d.

Production of crude petroleum, mostly from the Maracaibo, Apure-Barinas and eastern Venezuela basins, declined from a peak annual average of 3.7m. b/d in 1970 to 1.6m. b/d in 1985. Under President Rafael Caldera Rodríguez (1994–99), a strategy was pursued of maximizing output beyond OPEC quotas. Venezuela's oil production then peaked in 1997 at 3.38m. b/d. The steep decline in petroleum prices in 1998 forced Venezuela to embrace OPEC-negotiated production decreases in an effort to stabilize prices. Under President Chávez, the Government pursued high and stable prices through the reduction of production levels and co-operation with OPEC and non-OPEC countries. Production collapsed during the 2002 PDVSA strike. Venezuela was forced to import oil to cover its domestic needs, and PDVSA declared *force majeure*. Oil production fell to 2.84m. b/d in 2010 and to 2.77m. b/d in 2011. There was a further decline in output in 2012, to 2.65m b/d, with a further 0.8% contraction in 2013, to 2.62m b/d. Venezuela's total worldwide crude exports dropped by 6.1% in 2013, to 1.935m. b/d, while exports of petroleum products fell by 3.5%, to 490,000 b/d. Under its strategic investment plan, PDVSA aimed to increase production to 6m. b/d by 2019.

Petroleum export revenue fluctuated in line with levels of production and prices. In 2008 earnings from oil exports surged to US $91,500m., as the price per barrel increased to an annual average of $86.50 (from $65.20 in the previous year). In 2009 the price per barrel fell to an annual average of $57.02, with oil export earnings also declining, to $54,201m. In 2010 the price per barrel rose significantly, to average $72.43 for the year. Venezuela's oil export earnings reached an estimated $60,000m. in 2011, with a rise in the annual average oil price to $101.06 per barrel; and increased further, to $88,130m., in 2012, as the price per barrel rose to $103.42. The average price in 2013 dipped to $99.49 per barrel, but the value of Venezuela's exports, as reported by OPEC, increased to $97,340m.

As part of the Government's plans to create an oil industry at the service of national development, PDVSA makes significant contributions to government finances, mainly through social programmes. In 2008 PDVSA's spending on social programmes rose to more than $14,700m. This figure fell dramatically in 2009, to $3,514m., as oil export earnings declined. However, the rise in the 2012 international oil price lifted PDVSA revenues to $124,500m., of which $17,300m. was spent on social programmes. Critics maintained that this social spending was at the cost of necessary investment in oil production and refining facilities, an assessment that was increasingly shared by PDVSA executives as the company looked to an increase in production. In 2013 PDVSA reduced its contribution to social spending to $13,000m. Combined with currency devaluation and the sale of assets, this lifted PDVSA's net profits for the year more than threefold, to $15,835m., from $4,335m. in 2012. In 2014 the Government was considering adjustments to the costly subsidy on domestic fuel sales, which had been fixed for 17 years at $US 0.015 per litre and which rendered Venezuelan prices the cheapest in the world (and below the equivalent price of bottled water).

Venezuela uses its oil reserves as a tool of regional diplomacy. Building on the San José Agreement, whereby Venezuela and Mexico sell oil on preferential financial terms to 11

Caribbean and Central American countries, Venezuela was instrumental in developing the Caribbean regional oil initiative, Petrocaribe, which was launched in 2005. Petrocaribe offers discounted oil totalling approximately 400,000 b/d to 18 oil-importing countries in Central America and the Caribbean. Under the agreement, covering 40% of regional energy needs, recipient countries pay 40% of the oil invoice value within the first 90 days, with the remainder being financed at a 1% interest rate over 25 years. In separate agreements with Cuba signed in 2000 and 2005, Venezuela provides 53,000 b/d—roughly 60% of Cuba's energy needs—in exchange for medical technology and services from 30,000 Cuban staff.

Limited progress was made in raising petrochemical production, despite the early ambitions of the Chávez Government. Petrochemical production is concentrated in four sites: CIAMCA, on the west coast, José in the east of the country, El Palito and Morón

In 2005 the Chávez Government restructured the state-owned petrochemical corporation Pequiven and made it independent of PDVSA, within the portfolio of the Ministry of Energy and Petroleum. In 2007 a five-year strategy for investment in petrochemical plants and new technologies was begun. Venezuela looked to Iran, Russia and Brazil for around US $65,000m. in two phases of investment, which were expected to generate 700,000 new jobs over a 15-year period. However, planned projects were delayed, beset by operational problems or cancelled, requiring Venezuela to import basic petrochemicals including polymer, ethylene and derivatives.

The exploitation of the country's massive natural gas reserves has been a central element of the Government's diversification programme. With an estimated 5,600,000m. cu m of proven gas reserves at the end of 2013, Venezuela had the second largest proven gas reserves in the western hemisphere, after the USA. An estimated 90% of natural gas reserves are associated, meaning they are located in the same place as oil reserves. These resources are underdeveloped, despite the aim of the 1999 Gas Hydrocarbons Law to increase development of non-associated natural gas and expand the role of natural gas in the energy sector. In 2012 Venezuela produced an estimated 29,500m. cu m of natural gas, of which some 70% was consumed by the petroleum industry. Production contracted by 3.2% in 2013, to 28,400m. cu m.

Exploitation and production of natural gas is undertaken by PDV Servicios, a subsidiary of PDVSA. The price of natural gas is fixed at artificially low levels, making it an attractive energy source. Development of the sector gained a new sense of urgency in 2007, after PDVSA acquired a majority stake in the Orinoco Belt oil projects, which required gas injection for pumping, and as the Chávez Government advanced plans for regional energy integration—including through the US $25,000m. Gasoducto del Sur project to develop a major export pipeline to Brazil and Argentina. Work on Phase 1, connecting the gasfields of Mariscal Sucre to Porto de Sauipe near Recife in Brazil, began in 2007. In 2006 construction began on a 225-km natural gas pipeline supplying 150m. cu ft of natural gas per day from the Ballenas oilfield in Colombia to western Venezuela. The project was intended as part of a wider Andean gas distribution network, and its first phase was opened in October 2007. In the same year Chávez launched the Organización de Países Productores y Exportadores de Gas de América del Sur (Opegasur), an OPEC-style organization for South American gas producers. Venezuela increased its co-operation with Argentina in gas production, and in 2009 PDVSA and Argentina's gas company Galileo initiated a feasibility study on the creation of a binational company to produce natural gas compressors, transport natural gas and construct fuel stations for natural gas-powered vehicles. In 2012 the Venezuelan Government announced that Venezuela and Ecuador would investigate a gas pipeline project to connect both countries through Colombia. International companies including Repsol, ENI, Total, Statoil and Chevron were awarded offshore exploration blocks that yielded some of the largest natural gas discoveries in the country's history in the Gulf of Venezuela.

FINANCE

Historically, there has been distrust of the banking sector in Venezuela, after a series of collapses and corruption scandals. Legislation to improve supervision of the sector and create universal banks was introduced in 1996. Many of the largest banks were privatized, increasing the foreign presence in the sector and resulting in an estimated 40,000 job losses. The trend of financial sector liberalization went into reverse in July 2008, when the Government announced plans to nationalize the country's third largest privately held bank, Banco de Venezuela, a subsidiary of the Spanish bank Santander with assets of US $11,000m. In May 2009 the Government announced the purchase of Banco de Venezuela from Santander Group for $1,050m. At the end of that year the Government opened national investigations into eight private banks, one state-owned bank and several stock brokerage firms in connection with alleged fraud. Two of the banks were liquidated, two were rehabilitated, and four were merged into a new state-owned bank, Bicentenario Banco Universal. Reforms were approved to the General Law on Banks and Other Financial Institutions, raising the bank deposit guarantee from 10,000 bolívares ($4,650) to 30,000 bolívares ($13,950) per depositor, and increasing banks' mandatory contributions to the public deposit insurance fund. In 2012 10 of the 25 banking institutions operating in the country belonged to the state; of these, six were development banks.

The Chávez Government sought to expand credit facilities to those sectors of the population who had traditionally been excluded from formal lending. The special banks played an important role in developing the 'social economy' by lending to targeted sectors including small and medium-sized industries, indigenous groups and women. Pressure on the privately owned banks to increase access to credit caused tensions between the financial sector and the Chávez administration. Interest rate increases became an important element of the Government's efforts to counter rising inflation, encourage saving and reduce consumption.

Interest in the stock exchange, the Bolsa de Valores de Caracas (IBVC), grew rapidly from 2003, when investors realized that equities could be exchanged for US currency, circumventing the Government's exchange rate restrictions. In 2007 the Government's nationalization strategy resulted in the index contracting by 20%. By the end of 2009 the market capitalization of the Caracas stock exchange fell to US $10,100m., from $12,700m. a year earlier. There were 60 listed companies in 2012. From 1993 until 2013 the IBVC averaged 49871 Index points, reaching a record low of 761 Index points in April of 1993 and an all-time high of 987565 Index points in June 2013. Financial services recorded growth of 33.5% in 2012, and of 20% in 2013, as exchange controls kept domestic liquidity locked into the domestic financial system through the purchase of bonds and stocks. The Caracas stock market generated one of the world's highest returns in 2013, with a rise of 452%. At the beginning of 2014 the IBVC announced a 1000: 1 index split.

TELECOMMUNICATIONS

Following the introduction of a model telecommunications law in 2000, the sector experienced a decade of strong growth, including in periods of national economic recession. This was primarily driven by CANTV (Compañía Anónima Nacional de Teléfonos de Venezuela), founded in 1930. In 2007 the Chávez Government reversed the 1991 privatization of CANTV, in view of the strategic significance of the sector to the national economy and as a result of dissatisfaction with the company's monopoly on fixed-line services—which had led to a surge in mobile cellular telephone use: at 104 per 100 persons in March 2012, Venezuela had one of the highest mobile penetration rates in South America. Smartphone penetration is also one of the highest in the region, in part because of high rates of use of social media such as Twitter and Facebook. Venezuela had the third highest Twitter penetration rate in the world, and was the largest market for BlackBerry in South America. The state-owned CANTV subsidiary, Movilnet, and private operator Movistar dominated the cellular market, generating 74.1% of total revenue in 2012 (roughly 37% each), with Movistar growth projected to increase to 44% of total telecom services revenue by 2018. Conversely, the CANTV-Movilnet revenue share was predicted to decline as a result of discounted services to low-income consumers. In 2009 the Government launched a mobile phone made by state-owned telecommunications company Vetelca at a price approximately 25% below the next cheapest mobile. By 2012 Vetelca and state-owned company Orinoquia had produced more than 2m. affordable mobile phones. In 2012 additional spectrum was opened up in the 1800 MHz and 1900 MHz bands to service providers to support (third-generation) 3G networks and Long-Term Evolution (LTE).

Exchange controls, currency devaluation and economic uncertainty all had a negative impact on infrastructure investment, network expansion and the launch of new technologies in 2013. This reduced the ability of providers to meet demand for new services and device availability. In January 2014 the Government announced that currency for imported telecoms equipment and software would be assigned by the parallel exchange system, making imports of these goods more expensive.

In 2013 Venezuela had 14.95m. internet users and 3.7m. broadband subscriptions. The Government, supported by UNDP, launched a project to provide Wi-Fi wireless local area networking technology to expand internet access nationwide. Growth continued in the fixed-line market meanwhile, with 7.86m. subscriptions (a 2.8% increase from 2012).

Growth of cable subscription television was strong, with an estimated 4,609,000 subscribers and a penetration rate of 62.6% in 2012. Digital services were subscribed to by 53% of users, with 41% subscribed to satellite services. In 2005 the Government launched Televisora del Sur (Telesur—Television of the South), a media venture in partnership with the governments of Cuba, Argentina and Uruguay. The initiative was intended to promote a regional news agenda, to challenge US foreign policy and to extend Spanish-language media influence in the region. Private media groups continued to dominate terrestrial broadcasting, despite the increase in public broadcasting and government financial support for community-based initiatives. State television channels had an estimated audience share of 6%, compared with the 60% registered by privately owned television channels including Corporación Venezolana de Televisión (Venevisión).

MANUFACTURING

The manufacturing sector in Venezuela historically has been weak and heavily protected, with growth correlating with government spending levels and the international oil price. Small and medium-sized industries in the private sector concentrated on production of consumer goods for the domestic market, while the major capital-intensive industries were state-owned and located in the Ciudad Guayana development region, in the east of the country. The strong improvement recorded in manufacturing in 2004–07 was based on economic growth in the wider economy, expansionist economic policies and a strong rise in consumer demand. However, the manufacturing sector shrank by 3.4% in 2010, with a 1.5% decrease in the country's overall GDP. Manufacturing rebounded in 2011, registering growth of 3.8%, but was negatively impacted by currency controls and dollar shortages, which restricted imports of parts and materials. More modest growth, of 1.8%, was recorded in 2012, and the sector contracted 0.3% in 2013.

CONSTRUCTION

Growth in Venezuela's construction industry has followed trends in the petroleum economy. Periods of high oil prices on international markets have led to increased levels of public spending and growth of the sector, while falling prices have resulted in pronounced contractions. Growth rates of 4.8% and 16.8% were registered in 2011 and 2012 respectively, reflecting economic recovery and high levels of public investment in housing construction. The latter was under a government initiative to build 2m. homes over a seven-year period under the Gran Misión Vivienda, launched in 2011. In 2013, however, economic uncertainty and currency restrictions meant that the

operating environment turned sharply negative, and contributing to a 2.3% contraction in the construction sector.

TRANSPORT

Venezuela is internally connected by road and air. Owing to the heavily discounted cost of petroleum, roads are the preferred transport option. Historically high levels of public investment in the transport infrastructure allowed for the development of an extensive highway network totalling 96,200 km, and, at 32,300 km, the highest extent of paved highways in Latin America. A decline in public spending led to a deterioration of the road network, which the Government sought to address through the introduction of tolls on major arteries in the 1990s. However, this was deemed politically unpalatable and was abandoned. The administration of President Hugo Chávez planned to construct a strategic highway corridor connecting Venezuela to Guyana and Suriname, as part of the Integration of Regional Infrastructure in South America (IIRSA) strategy. By mid-2012 US $300m. had been committed to the project.

Venezuela looked heavily to China for investment in its transport infrastructure, including in the small and underdeveloped railway network of 584 km, one-half of which was privately owned. In 2008 the Government announced a series of regional rail network projects, including a connection to Colombia and a trilateral regional airline and train network with Argentina and Brazil. By mid-2014 these had not materialized, and projects planned with China Railway Corporation, among them the US $7,500m. rail construction project to connect the cities of Tinaco and Anaco, were subject to heavy delays, as was a line linking Puerto Cabello and La Encrucijada, in the centre of the country.

There are 11 international airports, with 90% of international flights handled by Simón Bolívar International Airport in Caracas. A national state airline, Consorcio Venezolano de Industrias Aeronáutica y Servicios Aéreos (CONVIASA), was established by the Chávez Government in 2004, with an investment of US $16m. By 2012 CONVIASA was flying on Latin American routes and to global destinations, which initially included Syria and Iran. In April of that year the European Union added the airline to the list of carriers banned from its airspace, citing safety considerations. Venezuela denounced this action as disproportionate, and contrary to the conclusions of the International Civil Aviation Organization (ICAO) regarding CONVIASA's safety performance. Having been refused requests to inspect security measures at Venezuela's airports, the US Transportation Security Administration (TSA) commenced public notification of safety concerns in 2008 for passengers departing for Venezuelan from US airports. There was a dramatic fall in international flights to Venezuela in the first half of 2014, as a result of ongoing disputes between airline operators and the Venezuelan Government over pricing, repatriation of revenue from ticket sales and the payment of debts to international carriers amounting to some US $4,000m. In May of that year agreement was reached on debt payments with six airlines and the Venezuelan Government announced plans to peg ticket prices to the new Sistema Cambiario Alternativo de Divisas (SICAD II) exchange rate, which traded at approximately five times the rate previously used to calculate US dollar exchange. This had the effect of raising the already excessive cost of international travel to and from Venezuela, and dampened the trend of Venezuelans taking foreign trips in order to obtain dollars from overseas banks.

Venezuela has 13 major ports and harbours. La Guaira, Puerto Cabello and Maracaibo handle 80% of bulk trade. The Orinoco river is navigable for about 1,120 km. Investment has been prioritized in waterways and ports, particularly those related to export routes to China and countries of the Southern Common Market (Mercado Común del Sur—MERCOSUR). In 2013 Venezuela negotiated a US $480m. loan for the construction of a petrochemical wharf at the port of Morón by the China Harbour Engineering Company (CHEC). The transport sector recorded growth of 6.6% in 2012, but contracted by 3.3% in 2013.

TOURISM

Despite a vast array of potential tourist attractions, including the world's highest waterfall (Angel Falls), a 2,718-km Caribbean coastline and an Andean mountain range extending from the south-west to the north-east of the country, Venezuela's tourism industry remains underdeveloped, with the exception of Margarita Island, which was visited by more than one-half of all tourists to Venezuela. Political instability, a lack of facilities, uncompetitive costs, currency controls and problems of personal security impeded growth in the sector. The World Economic Forum's 2013 *Travel and Tourism Competitiveness Report* ranked Venezuela second to last (of 140 countries) in terms of its welcome to foreign visitors. The Ministry of Tourism's vigorous promotion of the sector, under the National Tourism Development Plan (2007–12), contributed to growth. Foreign tourist arrivals increased by 25% in 2012, compared with the previous year, to approximately 800,000; of these, 428,211 came from other South American countries, 198,922 from Europe and 76,663 from North America. Despite continued political instability into 2013, there were an estimated 1,084,776 international tourist visits to Venezuela in 2013: 269,030 from Europe, 102,556 from North America, and 566,539 from South America. Total tourist expenditure in 2013 was $1,544m. Tourism was negatively impacted by disputes between international airlines and the Venezuelan Government in 2014, which reduced services and increased the cost of flights to the country. In an effort to support the sector, the central bank announced preferential low interest rates, at a maximum of 9.7%, on all loans for investment in tourism. The number of Venezuelans travelling abroad increased from 1,734,078 in 2012 to 1,931,397 in 2013, with the USA, Spain, Colombia and Argentina being the leading destination countries.

PUBLIC FINANCE

High public spending led to increases in the fiscal deficit in the early 2000s. A deficit equivalent to an estimated 1.9% of GDP was recorded In 2004, despite a substantial increase in international oil prices and a strong improvement in non-oil tax collection, as the Government accelerated its public spending plans. However, a fiscal surplus equivalent to 1.6% of GDP was achieved in 2005. The 2006 budget provided for a 30% increase in expenditure, and central government spending rose by an estimated 48% in that year, ahead of the December presidential election. This was none the less offset by a 90% increase in non-oil taxes and a 36% increase in oil tax revenue, leading to fiscal parity. In 2007, driven by record oil revenues, the Government recorded a fiscal surplus of 3% of GDP. However, in 2009, partly reflecting the global economic downturn, a fiscal deficit of around 6% of GDP was registered. According to government figures, US $883,000m. in national revenue was accumulated during the period 1998–2012, of which about 62% ($552,000m.) was put towards social spending. Approximately 40% of the 2012 budget, equivalent to some $27,000m. or 12% of GDP, was allocated to social spending. This contributed to a widening of Venezuela's fiscal gap to the equivalent of 15.6% of GDP in that year. Despite the devaluation of the currency in 2013, the gap between government income and social expenditures remained wide, with a fiscal deficit of 11.5% of GDP being recorded.

COST OF LIVING

In 2013 Venezuela had the highest inflation rate in Latin America, and one of the highest in the world, at 56.2%. Inflation has been a long-term problem, reaching an historic peak of 103.2% in 1996. This followed two devaluations of the bolívar and the liberalization of the exchange rate. The introduction of a 'crawling peg' banded exchange rate succeeded in reducing the annual rate of inflation, to 12.3% in 2001, but at the cost of an increasingly overvalued domestic currency. In 2002 the crawling peg was abandoned, with the devaluation of the currency leading to an acceleration of price increases, and annual inflation rose to 31.2%. A new exchange rate regime in 2003 contained escalating prices. The exchange rate was fixed at 2,150 bolívares to US $1 in 2007, but this was still an estimated 48% overvaluation relative to the US dollar. The bolívar was revalued in March 2007 at a ratio of 1:1,000, and relaunched on 1 January 2008 as the bolívar fuerte, at a rate of $1 = 2.147 bolívares fuertes. A two-tier exchange rate devaluation was announced in January 2010: to $1 = 2.6 bolívares fuertes for imports of essential goods and services; and $1 = 4.3 bolívares fuertes for manufacturing imports. In that year the annual inflation rate was 27.2%. In January 2011 the exchange rate for priority goods was devalued to $1 = 4.3 bolívares fuertes, and a new round of price controls followed. At 27.6% in 2011, inflation remained at a similar rate to that in 2010. Inflation fell to 21.1% in 2012. The currency was devalued for the fifth time in nine years in February 2013, to $1 = 6.3 bolívares fuertes and to $1 = 11.3 bolívares fuertes on the second-tier exchange, but it rapidly lost value on the black market with the heightened political uncertainty caused by the death of President Chávez in March. Amid unmet demand for dollars, the parallel rate escalated sharply, reaching $1 = 70 bolívares fuertes by the end of the year. Shortages of food and electrical items fuelled inflationary pressures, which the Government sought to address through further price controls, policed by civic brigades, and a military-enforced presidential order at the end of 2013 that required retailers to reduce the price of electrical goods. Following widespread national protests, in part fanned by dollar shortages, in March 2014 the Government introduced a third, free-floating foreign exchange rate through SICAD II. This resurrected the market-based swap system open to private bank operators, which had been closed down by Chávez in 2010 in a drive against currency speculation. The SICAD II rate accounted for 8% of dollar sales, and was trading at a rate of approximately $1 = 49 bolívares fuertes as of August 2014.

Central bank reserves dropped to US $21,478m. in 2013, compared with $29,887m. in 2012, $29,889m. in 2011 and $29,500m. in 2010. Gold accounted for approximately 72% of holdings, with the 30% fall in international gold prices eroding Venezuela's reserve position. This did not include funds held in joint development schemes such as the China-Venezuela development fund, with an estimated $16,000m. in an off-budget account, or the Government's social development fund Fondo de Desarrollo Nacional (Fonden). Since 2005 reserves estimated at an average of $16,000m. per year have been transferred from the central bank to Fonden. Opposition groups were critical of the creation of Fonden, which, they argued, reduced transparency in government accounts. In 2013 Fonden was estimated to have funds of around $9,500m., compared with $17,100m. in the previous year. At the beginning of 2014 the Government instructed the state oil company PDVSA to transfer $7,900m. to Fonden, and an additional $3,700m. contribution came from the central bank.

FOREIGN DEBT

Venezuela began to acquire foreign debt, rather than reduce state expenditures, when the international oil price dipped in the 1980s. After the collapse of the domestic banking sector in 1994, Venezuela fell behind on repayment of its obligations to the 'Paris Club' of Western official creditors. A structural adjustment programme was introduced in 1996, and a rise in petroleum export revenues enabled the Government to repay the bulk of the debt that had been accumulated during the previous three years. Despite market concerns that the Chávez Government would renege on its external debt obligations, the administration prioritized paying off the foreign debt. Venezuela's access to foreign borrowing was initially restricted because of the heightened perceptions of risk that surrounded the country. Sentiment changed after 2003, however, as the country's international reserves rose and international oil prices increased, allowing for a series of highly successful debt issues. Venezuela's external debt averaged US $23,098m. between 1996 and June 2014. Debt stocks reached an historic high, of $218,900m., in September 2013, but had fallen to $68,000m. by April 2014. The ratio of foreign public debt to GDP was 20.4% in 2013 and averaged 25.4% of GDP in 2003–13. The Government relied increasingly on domestic debt paid in local currency for deficit financing. This led to a strong increase in levels of domestic internal public debt, which increased by 60% between December 2011 and September 2012 to reach $57,400m. The total stock of Venezuela's debt in 2013 was equivalent to 45.9% of GDP. In May 2014 the Maduro administration suspended payment of domestic commercial debt amounting to $14,000m. This included obligations to airlines and importers of cars and auto parts, and the suspension resulted in a reduction in international airline services to the country, as well as a sharp decline in domestic vehicle manufacture.

Foreign direct investment (FDI) net inflows to Venezuela represented roughly 1.7% of Venezuela's GDP in 2011, down from a peak of 7.2% in 1997 (the year before Hugo Chávez was elected President). In 2012 FDI contracted by 15%, to $3,216m., of which 56% was accounted for by the oil sector. Outward FDI totalled $2,460m., largely accounted for by the state oil company PDVSA. ECLAC reported a 44% growth in FDI in the first half of 2013, the second fastest for the region. Venezuela received $2,736m. in January–June 2013, compared with $1,897m. over the same period in 2012. Fixed investment declined by 9% in 2013, with a sharp contraction, of 16.6%, in the fourth quarter.

BALANCE OF PAYMENTS AND TRADE

Venezuela's external trade is dominated by petroleum. The performance of the non-oil sector is weak and this increased reliance on petroleum revenues, which remained volatile and generated a high level of import dependence. In 2004, 2005 and 2006 strong growth in exports, owing primarily to high oil prices, led to a doubling of the surplus on the current account, which represented 14.4% of GDP in 2006. A new record on the current account was posted in 2008, with a surplus of US $39,200m., but this narrowed sharply in 2009 and 2010 before recovering to $27,140m., or 7.7% of GDP, in 2011. In 2012 the current account surplus contracted to 2.8% of GDP, as economic recovery drove an increase in imports, and an explosion at the Amuay refinery necessitated an 88% increase in oil imports. Export volumes fell by 6.2% in 2013, with particularly sharp year-on-year contractions of 9.7% and 6.8%, respectively, recorded in the third and fourth quarters. The reduced availability of US dollars led to a 9.7% fall in imports in 2013, which, like the export sector, showed particularly sharp drops in the third and fourth quarters, of 13.8% and 20.3%.

The USA remained Venezuela's most important trading partner, although with a declining share of the country's commerce. According to the Venezuelan Instituto Nacional de Estadística (INE—National Institute of Statistics), the USA was the destination for US $550.14m. of Venezuelan exports in 2013, followed by China ($254.07m.), Colombia ($236.36m.) and Brazil ($172.98m.). Venezuela was the USA's 19th largest goods trading partner, with $45,000m. in total goods trade in 2013. Venezuela was the USA's 24th largest export market in 2013, with goods exports mainly comprised of mineral fuels, machinery, organic chemicals, electrical machinery and cereals totalling $13,200m., a fall of 24.5% from 2012.

Oil dominates US imports from Venezuela, which is one of the top four external suppliers of oil to the USA. US imports from Venezuela totalled US $32,000m. in 2013, a 17.4% decrease from 2012, and the USA ran a goods trade deficit with Venezuela of $19,000m. in 2013. Mineral fuel and crude oil accounted for $30,900m. of US imports from Venezuela. Other import categories included organic chemicals, iron and steel, and precious stones. In 2011 the USA imposed sanctions on the Venezuelan state oil company PDVSA for delivering a blending component for gasoline to Iran. The sanctions blocked lending from the Export-Import Bank of the United States, and prevented PDVSA from competing for US government contracts.

Venezuela has traditionally run a deficit on its trade with neighbouring Colombia. Commercial relations were set back by the political antagonism between President Chávez and Colombian President Alvaro Uribe. Bilateral exchange between the two countries fell from US $7,290m. to $1,680m. during the diplomatic tensions of 2008–10. Under the new Colombian President, Juan Manuel Santos, bilateral relations improved dramatically from the latter part of 2010. Illustrating this new tone, 13 new bilateral trade agreements had been signed by the end of 2012. Trade between Venezuela and Colombia increased by 40% in 2012, compared with the previous year, from $2,340m. to $3,280m. However, commercial relations were set back by instability and currency controls in Venezuela. Between January and November 2013 Colombian exports to Venezuela amounted to $2,100m., equivalent to 4% of Colombia's total exports of $53,500m. and an 8% fall on the same period in 2012. Imports from China dipped slightly, to $7,645m., from $7,793m. in the same period in 2012, but still strongly above the $4,132m. recorded in 2011. After falling back to $1,765m. in 2012, imports from Russia resumed an upward trend in 2013, at $2,540m.

The Chávez Government withdrew Venezuela from both the Comunidad Andina de Naciones (CAN—Andean Community of Nations) and, the 'Group of Three' organization in 2006, in protest against the decision of other member states to negotiate bilateral trade agreements with the USA. In December 2005 Venezuela received the rights of full membership of MERCOSUR, prior to its formal integration. Membership was subject to ratification by all the group's existing members, a process that was only completed at the end of June 2012 after Paraguay, whose legislature had refused to ratify Venezuela's full membership, was expelled from MERCOSUR. Venezuela looked to expand its trading relations with other MERCOSUR countries, while developing the Bolivarian Alliance for the Peoples of our America-People's Trade Treaty (Alianza Bolivariana para los Pueblos de Nuestra América-Tratado de Comercio de los Pueblos—ALBA-TCP). Launched by Venezuela and Cuba in 2004 as a socially orientated regional integration mechanism, ALBA-TCP counted nine members by mid-2012, including Bolivia, Nicaragua and Ecuador. Venezuela was also a member of the Union of South American Nations (Unión de Naciones Suramericanas—UNASUR), which was formally established in 2008 as an intergovernmental union between MERCOSUR and the CAN. Venezuela was a founder member of the 33-country Comunidad de Estados de América Latina y el Caribe (CELAC—Community of Latin American and Caribbean States), which was launched in 2011.

CONCLUSION

When Hugo Chávez came to power in 1999, he inherited a dire economic situation. Growing poverty, informality and unemployment were the main trends after two decades of political and economic turmoil. The objectives of regaining state sovereignty in strategic sectors of the economy, improving distribution to the most deprived sectors of society, strengthening the international oil price and promoting regional integration shaped economic policy under his administration. Strategies to overcome the profound inequalities that characterized Venezuelan society, including land reform and improved tax collection, were negatively received by the wealthiest sectors, which protested against the changes. After 2004 the strong rise in international oil prices enhanced the Government's position, both domestically and internationally, and allowed Chávez to advance his programme of revolutionary change, regional integration and diversification of international commercial partners. However, this deepened the country's dependence on petroleum export revenue, casting into doubt the sustainability of the Government's long-term development strategy of diversifying the economy away from oil. Measures introduced during the period of early political turmoil included price and exchange controls. These were initially effective in arresting capital flight and hoarding, but their deepening during President Chávez's third term (2006–11) heightened distortions and bottlenecks in the economy. Venezuela suffered a period of recession from 2008–10, but emerged with the strongest GDP growth in Latin American in 2012, driven by elevated public spending and private sector growth. Following Chávez's death, the incoming administration of President Nicolás Maduro, from 2013, was committed to maintaining the economic policies of his predecessor. Amid a large fiscal deficit, overvalued exchange rate and ongoing inflationary pressures, critics maintained that the Maduro Government urgently needed to liberalize and restructure the economy. Mass protests in early 2014, fuelled by shortages and a lack of access to US dollars, pushed the Government towards an increasingly pragmatic economic line, although this was countered by pressure from the grass roots of the *Chavista* movement, which pressed for accelerated state intervention in line with ambitions to build a model of '21st century socialism'.

Venezuela's comparatively low debt levels, access to international credit lines, significant international reserves, and control over its foreign exchange, monetary and fiscal policies gave it significant leverage to manage its significant economic challenges and attract non-traditional investors.

Statistical Survey

Sources (unless otherwise stated): Instituto Nacional de Estadística (formerly Oficina Central de Estadística e Informática), Edif. Fundación La Salle, Avda Boyacá, Caracas 1050; tel. (212) 782-1133; fax (212) 782-2243; e-mail ocei@platino.gov.ve; internet www.ine.gov.ve; Banco Central de Venezuela, Avda Urdaneta, esq. de las Carmelitas, Caracas 1010; tel. (212) 801-5111; fax (212) 861-0048; e-mail mbatista@bcv.org.ve; internet www.bcv.org.ve.

Area and Population

AREA, POPULATION AND DENSITY

Area (sq km)	916,445*
Population (census results)	
30 October 2001†	23,054,210
1 September 2011	
Males	13,549,752
Females	13,678,178
Total	27,227,930
Population (official estimates at mid-year)	
2012	29,365,451
2013	29,786,263
2014	30,206,307
Density (per sq km) at mid-2014	33.0

* 353,841 sq miles.
† Excluding Indian jungle population, enumerated at 183,143 in a separate census of indigenous communities in 2001. Also excluding adjustment for underenumeration, estimated at 6.7%.

POPULATION BY AGE AND SEX
(population at 2011 census)

	Males	Females	Total
0–14 years	3,788,616	3,568,158	7,356,774
15–64 years	9,034,671	9,215,986	18,250,657
65 years and over	726,465	894,034	1,620,499
Total	13,549,752	13,678,178	27,227,930

Population by Sex (official estimates at mid-2014): Males 15,144,744; Females 15,061,563; *Total* 30,206,307.

ADMINISTRATIVE DIVISIONS
(official population estimates at mid-2014)

	Area (sq km)	Population	Density (per sq km)	Capital
Amazonas . . .	177,617	173,144	1.0	Puerto Ayacucho
Anzoátegui . .	43,300	1,634,549	37.7	Barcelona
Apure	76,500	556,478	7.3	San Fernando
Aragua . . .	7,014	1,787,297	254.8	Maracay
Barinas . . .	35,200	865,038	24.6	Barinas
Bolívar . . .	240,528	1,723,361	7.2	Ciudad Bolívar
Capital District .	433	2,079,994	4,803.7	Caracas
Carabobo . . .	4,650	2,415,506	519.5	Valencia
Cojedes . . .	14,800	339,568	22.9	San Carlos
Delta Amacuro .	40,200	184,208	4.6	Tucupita
Falcón	24,800	999,600	40.3	Coro
Federal Dependencies .	120	2,182	18.2	—
Guárico . . .	64,986	850,951	13.1	San Juan de los Morros
Lara	19,800	1,954,433	98.7	Barquisimeto
Mérida	11,300	954,582	84.5	Mérida
Miranda . . .	7,950	3,122,374	392.8	Los Teques

—*continued*	Area (sq km)	Population	Density (per sq km)	Capital
Monagas . . .	28,900	955,109	33.0	Maturín
Nueva Esparta .	1,150	539,398	469.0	La Asunción
Portuguesa . .	15,200	977,050	64.3	Guanare
Sucre	11,800	1,011,671	85.7	Cumaná
Táchira . . .	11,100	1,229,430	110.8	San Cristóbal
Trujillo . . .	7,400	799,406	108.0	Trujillo
Vargas . . .	1,497	678,853	453.5	La Guaira
Yaracuy . . .	7,100	4,023,467	566.7	San Felipe
Zulia	63,100	348,658	5.5	Maracaibo
Total	916,445	30,206,307	33.0	—

PRINCIPAL TOWNS
(urban agglomerations, UN estimates at mid-2010)

Caracas (capital) .	2,900,895	Guarenas . . .	351,389
Maracaibo . . .	2,037,473	Cabimas . . .	315,650
Valencia	1,621,381	Cumana	311,170
Maracay . . .	1,067,988	Merida	304,930
		El Tigre-San José de	
Barquisimeto . .	1,015,534	Guanipa . . .	300,671
Ciudad Guayana .	666,804	Barinas	290,246
Barcelona-Puerto La			
Cruz	647,246	Lagunillas . . .	283,998
Maturin	469,486	Acarigua-Aruare .	280,484
Ciudad Bolívar . .	354,340	Punto Fijo . . .	279,479
San Cristóbal . .	353,246		

Mid-2014: Caracas (capital) 2,912,070.

Source: UN, *World Urbanization Prospects: The 2014 Revision.*

BIRTHS, MARRIAGES AND DEATHS*

	Registered live births		Registered marriages		Registered deaths	
	Number	Rate (per 1,000)	Number	Rate (per 1,000)	Number	Rate (per 1,000)
2005 . .	665,997	22.0	86,093	3.2	110,301	5.0
2006 . .	646,225	21.8	89,772	3.2	115,348	5.1
2007 . .	615,371	21.5	93,003	3.4	118,594	5.1
2008 . .	581,480	21.3	93,741	3.4	124,062	4.4
2009 . .	593,845	20.9	94,870	3.3	123,530	4.4
2010 . .	591,303	20.6	94,977	3.3	130,597	4.3
2011 . .	615,132	21.0	103,004	3.5	136,803	4.7
2012 . .	619,530	21.1	102,077	3.5	142,988	4.9

* Figures for numbers of births and deaths exclude adjustment for underenumeration. Rates are calculated using adjusted data.

Life expectancy (years at birth): 74.5 (males 71.6, females 77.5) in 2012 (Source: World Bank, World Development Indicators database).

ECONOMICALLY ACTIVE POPULATION

(labour force survey at July–December, '000 persons aged 15 years and over)*

	2011	2012	2013
Agriculture, hunting, forestry and fishing	980	963	962
Mining and quarrying	133	160	168
Manufacturing	1,399	1,355	1,462
Electricity, gas and water	58	60	56
Construction	1,118	1,086	1,069
Wholesale and retail trade, restaurants and hotels	2,962	3,080	3,172
Transport, storage and communications	1,148	1,135	1,202
Financing, insurance, real estate business services	689	697	756
Community, social and personal services	3,868	3,993	4,071
Sub-total	12,355	12,529	12,918
Activities not adequately defined	33	42	31
Total employed	12,388	12,571	12,948
Unemployed	1,054	1,006	1,047
Total labour force	13,443	13,577	13,995
Males	8,130	8,204	8,431
Females	5,313	5,373	5,564

* Figures exclude members of the armed forces.

2014: (labour force sample survey, April, '000 persons aged 15 years and over): Total employed 13,074 (males 7,880, females 5,194); Unemployed 998 (males 558, females 440); Total labour force 14,072 (males 8,438, females 5,634).

Note: Totals may not be equal to the sum of components owing to rounding.

Health and Welfare

KEY INDICATORS

Total fertility rate (children per woman, 2012)	2.4
Under-5 mortality rate (per 1,000 live births, 2012)	15
HIV/AIDS (% of persons aged 15–49, 2012)	0.6
Physicians (per 1,000 head, 2001)	1.94
Hospital beds (per 1,000 head, 2009)	1.1
Health expenditure (2011): US $ per head (PPP)	575
Health expenditure (2011): % of GDP	4.5
Health expenditure (2011): public (% of total)	36.6
Access to water (% of persons, 2010)	92
Access to sanitation (% of persons, 2010)	91
Total carbon dioxide emissions ('000 metric tons, 2010)	201,747.3
Carbon dioxide emissions per head (metric tons, 2010)	6.9
Human Development Index (2013): ranking	67
Human Development Index (2013): value	0.764

For sources and definitions, see explanatory note on p. vi.

Agriculture

PRINCIPAL CROPS

('000 metric tons, FAO estimates unless otherwise indicated)

	2010	2011	2012
Rice, paddy	1,250.0	1,422.6	1,330.0
Maize	2,145.0	2,118.0*	3,000.0*
Sorghum	451.8	491.0*	500.0*
Potatoes	511.0	525.0	535.0
Cassava (Manioc)	496.6	505.3	520.0
Yautia (Cocoyam)	84.9	90.3	95.0
Yams	115.3	102.1	104.0
Sugar cane	9,000.0	9,200.0	9,350.0
Coconuts	157.0*	153.6	165.0
Oil palm fruit	325.0	325.0	330.0
Cabbages and other brassicas	109.2	115.5	116.5
Tomatoes	202.0	195.9	205.0
Chillies and peppers, green	110.0	100.5	102.0
Onions, dry	300.3	298.2	300.0
Carrots and turnips	203.4	218.2	225.0
Watermelons	172.0	174.9	185.0

—continued	2010	2011	2012
Cantaloupes and other melons	200.0	199.7	205.0
Bananas	413.2	415.7	450.0
Plantains	477.6	488.9	500.0
Oranges	390.1	410.4	420.0
Tangerines, mandarins, etc.	75.4	71.3	73.5
Lemons and limes	51.6	56.9	60.0
Guavas, mangoes and mangosteens	74.2	77.3	80.0
Avocados	73.1	81.6	83.0
Pineapples	378.7	419.8	425.0
Papayas	133.4	125.6	130.0
Coffee, green	71.8	69.1	70.0

* Unofficial figure.

Aggregate production ('000 metric tons, may include official, semi-official or estimated data): Total cereals 3,847 in 2010, 4,032 in 2011, 4,830 in 2012; Total roots and tubers 1,262 in 2010, 1,275 in 2011, 1,309 in 2012; Total vegetables (incl. melons) 1,522 in 2010, 1,537 in 2011, 1,585 in 2012; Total fruits (excl. melons) 2,295 in 2010, 2,377 in 2011, 2,460 in 2012.

Source: FAO.

LIVESTOCK

('000 head, year ending September, FAO estimates)

	2010	2011	2012
Horses	515	518	520
Asses	440	440	440
Mules	72	72	72
Cattle	17,250	17,350	17,400
Pigs	3,385	3,450	3,500
Sheep	575	580	585
Goats	1,450	1,480	1,500
Chickens	117,000	118,000	120,000

Source: FAO.

LIVESTOCK PRODUCTS

('000 metric tons)

	2010	2011	2012
Cattle meat	492.0	494.5	500.0
Pig meat	168.0	172.0	175.0
Chicken meat	819.0	827.0	831.0
Cows' milk	2,300.0	2,380.0	2,400.0
Hen eggs	159.8	160.0	162.0

Source: FAO.

Forestry

ROUNDWOOD REMOVALS

('000 cubic metres, excl. bark)

	2010	2011	2012
Sawlogs, veneer logs and logs for sleepers	445	336	336*
Pulpwood*	920	920	920
Fuel wood*	4,055	4,089	4,125
Total*	5,420	5,345	5,381

* FAO estimate(s).

Source: FAO.

SAWNWOOD PRODUCTION
('000 cubic metres, incl. railway sleepers)

	2006	2007	2008*
Coniferous (softwood)	538	598	670
Broadleaved (hardwood) . . .	300	250	280
Total	838	848	950

* Unofficial figures.

2009–12: Production assumed to be unchanged from 2008 (unofficial figures).

Source: FAO.

Fishing

('000 metric tons, live weight)

	2010	2011	2012
Capture	218.5*	201.8	213.1
Freshwater fishes	8.2*	6.8	4.8
Sea catfishes	1.3*	2.3	2.6
Round sardinella	41.9	34.8	41.9
Skipjack tuna	10.8	27.6	21.8
Yellowfin tuna	33.9	24.8	29.5
Marine crabs	0.1*	—	—
Ark clams	40.0*	19.8	12.7
Aquaculture	18.2*	24.0	26.1*
Whiteleg shrimp	13.4	18.1	19.6
Total catch	236.7*	225.7	239.2*

* FAO estimate.

Note: Figures exclude crocodiles, recorded by number rather than by weight. The number of spectacled caimans caught was: 13,652 in 2010; 27,797 in 2011; 26,130 in 2012.

Source: FAO.

Mining

('000 metric tons unless otherwise indicated)

	2010	2011	2012
Hard coal	8,793	8,792*	n.a.
Crude petroleum†	145,700	141,500	136,620
Natural gas (million cu m)‡ . .	31,000	31,300	33,800
Iron ore: gross weight* . . .	22,200	27,000	14,900
Iron ore: metal content* . . .	14,000	17,000	17,000
Nickel ore (metric tons)*§ . . .	10,400	10,400	10,400
Bauxite	2,500	2,455	2,000*
Gold (kg)§	12,000	12,000*	12,000*
Phosphate rock	400	400*	n.a.
Salt (evaporated)*	350	350	n.a.
Diamonds (carats): Gem* . . .	6,000	6,000	6,000
Diamonds (carats): Industrial* .	9,000	9,000	9,000

* Estimated production.
† Source: BP, *Statistical Review of World Energy.*
‡ Figures refer to the gross volume of output: estimated marketed production (in million cu m) was: 24,900 in 2010–12.
§ Figures refer to the metal content of ores and concentrates.

2013: Crude petroleum 135,100.

Source (unless otherwise indicated): US Geological Survey.

Industry

PETROLEUM PRODUCTS
('000 barrels)

	2010	2011	2012*
Motor spirit (petrol)	89,300	87,880	87,900
Kerosene	126	124	124
Jet fuel	33,600	33,084	33,100
Distillate fuel oils	115,000	112,692	113,000
Residual fuel oils	94,600	93,048	93,000

* Estimated figures.

Source: US Geological Survey.

SELECTED OTHER PRODUCTS
('000 metric tons unless otherwise indicated)

	2010	2011	2012
Raw sugar*	550	n.a.	n.a.
Cement†‡	8,000	7,700	7,700
Crude steel†	2,207	3,070‡	2,555
Aluminium†	335	380‡	380‡
Electric energy (million kWh)* .	118,272	n.a.	n.a.

* Source: UN Industrial Commodity Statistics Database.
† Data from US Geological Survey.
‡ Estimate(s).

Finance

CURRENCY AND EXCHANGE RATES

Monetary Units
100 céntimos = 1 bolívar fuerte.

Sterling, Dollar and Euro Equivalents (30 May 2014)
£1 sterling = 10.571 bolívares fuertes;
US $1 = 6.284 bolívares fuertes;
€1 = 8.553 bolívares fuertes;
10 bolívares fuertes = £0.95 = $1.59 = €1.17.

Average Exchange Rate: From 1 March 2005 to 8 January 2010 the national currency was pegged to the US dollar at a fixed rate of US $1 = 2.147 bolívares fuertes. From 8 January 2010, when the currency was devalued, a dual fixed rate of US $1 = 2.6 bolívares fuertes for some essential goods (including foods and medicines), and US $1 = 4.3 bolívares fuertes for others, was established. A further devaluation of the currency's official exchange rates, to US $1 = 6.3 bolívares fuertes, was announced in February 2013. Note: Venezuela adopted a new currency, the bolívar fuerte, equivalent to 1,000 of the former currency, on 1 January 2008; this became the sole legal tender from the end of June of the same year.

CENTRAL GOVERNMENT BUDGET
(million bolívares fuertes, preliminary figures)

Revenue	2010	2011	2012
Tax revenue	113,191.4	169,602.8	216,517.9
Petroleum revenue . . .	8,705.1	16,509.6	22,879.5
Non-petroleum revenue . .	104,486.3	153,093.2	193,638.4
Non-tax revenue	83,290.2	135,197.2	168,019.6
Petroleum revenue . . .	71,675.4	110,105.0	137,910.7
Non-petroleum revenue . . .	11,614.8	25,092.2	30,108.9
Total revenue	196,481.6	304,800.1	384,537.5

Expenditure*	2010	2011	2012
Current expenditure	192,707.2	294,549.7	385,741.3
Wages and salaries	50,491.8	71,017.7	94,890.4
Purchase of goods and services	4,950.9	13,053.0	15,240.5
Interest payments	15,053.2	29,040.5	43,919.2
Transfers	122,211.3	181,438.6	230,912.5
Other operating expenditure	—	—	778.8
Capital expenditure	29,014.6	42,191.3	77,954.1
Transfers	28,235.3	39,488.1	75,706.8
Extra-budgetary expenditure	2,159.0	327.0	11.8
Total expenditure	223,880.8	337,068.0	463,707.2

* Excluding net lending (million bolívares fuertes): 9,280.0 in 2010; 21,808.2 in 2011; 305.9 in 2012.

General Government Budget (consolidated accounts of central government, Petróleos de Venezuela S.A., non-financial public enterprises, Venezuelan social security institute and deposit and guarantee fund, million bolívares fuertes, preliminary figures): *Total revenue:* 173,870.0 in 2009; 215,722.5 in 2010; 378,474.7 in 2011. *Total expenditure and net lending:* 235,302.5 in 2009; 321,105.4 in 2010; 535,833.6 in 2011.

CENTRAL BANK RESERVES
(US $ million at 31 December)

	2011	2012	2013
Gold (national valuation) . . .	19,959	19,987	15,440
IMF special drawing rights . .	3,438	3,441	3,478
Reserve position in IMF . . .	494	495	496
Foreign exchange	5,998	5,964	2,064
Total	29,889	29,887	21,478

Source: IMF, *International Financial Statistics.*

MONEY SUPPLY
(million bolívares fuertes at 31 December)

	2010	2011	2012
Currency outside banks . . .	36,409	46,193	71,702
Demand deposits at commercial banks	262,094	417,043	679,544
Total (incl. others)	305,158	475,087	760,999

2013: Currency outside depository corporations 117,006; Transferable deposits 1,141,064; Other deposits 19,796; Securities other than shares 942; *Broad money* 1,278,808.

Source: IMF, *International Financial Statistics.*

COST OF LIVING
(Consumer Price Index; base: December 2007 = 100)

	2011	2012	2013
Food and non-alcoholic beverages .	265.7	331.6	511.1
Clothing and footwear	177.6	200.0	271.4
Housing	151.8	166.8	187.0
Fuel and utilities	122.5	133.5	147.4
All items (incl. others) . . .	238.5	288.8	406.2

NATIONAL ACCOUNTS
('000 million bolívares at constant 1997 prices, preliminary)

Expenditure on the Gross Domestic Product

	2010	2011	2012
Final consumption expenditure .	48,984.6	51,145.5	54,656.6
Households			
Non-profit institutions serving households	38,974.0	40,542.3	43,389.9
General government . . .	10,010.5	10,603.2	11,266.7
Gross capital formation . . .	20,348.1	23,439.6	29,079.2
Gross fixed capital formation .			
Acquisitions, *less* disposals, of valuables	16,925.9	17,665.5	21,783.0
Changes in inventories* . .	3,422.2	5,774.1	7,296.2
Total domestic expenditure .	69,332.7	74,585.1	83,735.8
Exports of goods and services .	7,825.8	8,190.9	8,321.4
Less Imports of goods and services	21,351.0	24,637.6	30,648.1
GDP in market prices . .	55,807.5	58,138.3	61,409.1

* Including statistical discrepancy.

Gross Domestic Product by Economic Activity

	2010	2011	2012
Petroleum-related activities .	6,554.3	6,593.1	6,682.7
Non-petroleum activities . .	45,639.3	47,905.2	51,522.3
Mining and quarrying . .	265.0	278.5	261.2
Manufacturing	8,095.5	8,405.2	8,555.5
Electricity and water . . .	1,258.9	1,322.1	1,372.6
Construction	4,018.5	4,209.4	4,907.1
Wholesale and retail trade; repair of motor vehicles, motorcycles and personal and household goods . .	5,243.2	5,585.1	6,096.1
Transport and storage . .	1,940.9	2,052.5	2,187.8
Communications . . .	3,560.8	3,820.2	4,086.5
Financial intermediation and insurance	2,269.8	2,541.5	3,392.8
Real estate, renting and business activities . .	5,485.3	5,678.9	5,917.7
Community, social and personal services . .	3,243.6	3,430.3	3,684.3
Government services . .	6,798.4	7,171.5	7,543.4
Others*	3,459.6	3,410.0	3,517.3
Sub-total	52,193.6	54,498.3	58,205.0
Less Financial intermediation services indirectly measured .	2,512.4	2,849.8	3,873.9
Gross value added in basic prices	49,681.3	51,648.5	54,331.1
Taxes on products . . . *Less* Subsidies on products . .	6,126.3	6,489.6	7,078.0
GDP in market prices . .	55,807.5	58,138.3	61,409.1

* Including agriculture and hotels and restaurants.

BALANCE OF PAYMENTS
(US $ million)

	2010	2011	2012
Exports of goods	65,741	92,807	97,336
Imports of goods	−38,507	−46,781	−59,305
Balance on goods	27,234	46,026	38,031
Exports of services	1,862	1,997	2,209
Imports of services	−13,087	−15,722	−18,198
Balance on goods and services	16,009	32,301	22,042
Primary income received . . .	1,981	2,238	1,998
Primary income paid	−8,285	−9,362	−12,046
Balance on goods, services and primary income	9,705	25,177	11,994
Secondary income received . .	164	160	140
Secondary income paid . . .	−1,059	−950	−1,118
Current balance	8,810	24,387	11,016

—continued	2010	2011	2012
Capital account (net)	−211	—	—
Direct investment assets . . .	−1,830	1,030	−1,443
Direct investment liabilities . .	1,903	3,889	2,199
Portfolio investment assets . .	474	−723	28
Portfolio investment liabilities .	2,702	2,730	3,974
Other investment assets . . .	−27,135	−39,841	−14,389
Other investment liabilities . .	10,301	8,160	952
Net errors and omissions . .	−2,955	−3,645	−3,183
Reserves and related items .	−7,941	−4,013	−846

Source: IMF, *International Financial Statistics*.

External Trade

PRINCIPAL COMMODITIES
(US $ million)

Imports f.o.b.	2011	2012	2013
Live animals and animal products	2,474.8	3,559.0	4,014.0
Vegetables and vegetable products	1,820.9	2,308.1	2,627.3
Prepared foodstuffs; beverages, spirits, vinegars; tobacco and articles thereof .	2,347.1	2,341.3	2,662.8
Chemicals and related products	8,196.8	9,173.1	7,502.1
Organic chemicals	2,055.3	2,132.3	1,392.0
Pharmaceuticals	2,968.5	3,410.7	3,207.0
Plastics, rubber, and articles thereof	2,047.3	2,424.9	2,095.1
Textiles and textile articles .	1,677.9	1,924.2	1,337.1
Iron and steel; other base metals and articles of base metal	2,635.3	4,042.6	4,311.3
Articles of iron or steel . . .	1,261.5	2,184.8	2,681.3
Machinery and mechanical appliances; electrical equipment; parts thereof .	13,395.9	17,106.6	12,405.9
Boilers, machinery and mechanical appliances, parts of these machines or appliances . . .	8,708.8	11,517.5	8,350.5
Machinery and electrical equipment and parts thereof; recording or sound reproducing apparatus for recording or reproducing sound and images on television, and parts and accessories thereof . . .	4,687.1	5,589.1	4,055.5
Vehicles, aircraft, vessels and associated transport equipment	2,530.4	2,306.7	1,214.5
Motor vehicles, tractors, cycles and other land vehicles, and parts and accessories	1,196.8	2,027.1	955.8
Ships, boats and floating structures	1,227.8	132.6	120.7
Optical, medical apparatus, etc.; clocks and watches; musical instruments; parts thereof	2,432.1	1,930.1	1,320.8
Instruments and optical, photographic, cinematographic, measuring, checking, precision, medical or surgical instruments and apparatus parts and accessories thereof	2,343.3	1,812.8	1,257.0
Total (incl. others)	46,009.6	54,766.7	45,151.1

Exports f.o.b.	2008	2009	2010
Mineral fuels, lubricants and related materials	78,199.5	54,232.2	62,541.1
Petroleum, petroleum products and related materials	77,882.2	54,201.8	62,330.3
Crude petroleum	61,005.6	35,844.0	44,156.6
Basic manufactures	2,874.6	1,445.9	1,951.0
Iron and steel	1,703.6	904.8	1,085.1
Total (incl. others)	83,477.8	56,583.1	66,962.7

2012: *Non-petroleum exports:* Mineral products 653.2; Chemicals and related products 1,074.7; Iron and steel, other base metals and articles of base metal 921.9; Total (incl. others) 3,020.0.

2013: *Non-petroleum exports:* Mineral products 331.6; Chemicals and related products 996.3; Iron and steel, other base metals and articles of base metal 448.6; Total (incl. others) 2,100.1.

Source: partly UN, *International Trade Statistics Yearbook*.

PRINCIPAL TRADING PARTNERS
(US $ million)

Imports f.o.b.	2011	2012	2013
Argentina	1,640.5	2,077.6	2,003.8
Brazil	4,290.4	4,951.9	4,602.8
Canada	802.2	607.7	684.9
Chile	1,500.4	744.3	607.1
China, People's Republic . .	6,147.8	9,173.1	7,637.0
Colombia	1,575.3	2,489.8	2,119.1
Ecuador	861.3	1,233.5	936.6
France (incl. Monaco) . . .	549.6	581.7	561.5
Germany	1,165.7	1,324.1	1,294.7
Italy	1,065.0	1,339.3	1,141.2
Japan	771.4	676.6	442.3
Korea, Republic	551.1	562.9	295.6
Mexico	1,685.9	2,260.6	2,337.8
Panama	1,715.6	1,761.1	905.5
Peru	928.8	1,329.2	613.0
Spain	1,671.2	1,533.1	1,019.8
United Kingdom	476.3	498.8	493.0
USA	12,046.6	13,841.9	10,539.8
Total (incl. others)	46,009.6	54,766.7	45,151.1

Exports f.o.b.	2008	2009	2010
Brazil	1,808.3	112.7	272.5
Canada	141.6	35.6	84.2
Chile	1,167.4	26.4	61.1
China, People's Republic . .	270.3	304.0	719.4
Colombia	929.6	424.3	591.4
Germany	1,452.6	57.9	74.1
Netherlands	1,193.1	108.2	196.5
Netherlands Antilles . . .	13,198.1	17.0	30.1
Spain	1,603.4	41.0	115.6
United Kingdom	1,190.4	3.1	26.3
USA	26,750.5	491.1	970.9
Total (incl. others)	83,477.8	56,583.1	66,962.7

2012: *Non-petroleum exports:* Belgium 82; Brazil 207; Chile 131; China, People's Republic 428; Colombia 236; Ecuador 67; Egypt 62; France 58; Italy 97; Mexico 87; Netherlands 158; Spain 74; Trinidad and Tobago 42; USA 733; Total (incl. others) 3,020.

2013: *Non-petroleum exports:* Argentina 34; Belgium 80; Brazil 173; Chile 56; China, People's Republic 254; Colombia 236; Italy 35; Mexico 42; Netherlands 196; Spain 38; Trinidad and Tobago 62; Turkey 33; USA 550; Total (incl. others) 2,100.

Source: partly UN, *International Trade Statistics Yearbook*.

Transport

ROAD TRAFFIC
(motor vehicles in use at 31 December)

	2007
Passenger cars	2,952,129
Commercial vehicles	40,440

Source: IRF, *World Road Statistics*.

SHIPPING

Flag Registered Fleet
(at 31 December)

	2011	2012	2013
Number of vessels	283	297	328
Total displacement ('000 grt)	1,191.7	1,472.4	1,706.4

Source: Lloyd's List Intelligence (www.lloydslistintelligence.com).

CIVIL AVIATION
(traffic on scheduled services)

	2009	2010
Kilometres flown (million)	52	49
Passengers carried ('000)	6,428	7,728
Passenger-km (million)	4,385	4,965
Total ton-km (million)	436	498

Source: UN, *Statistical Yearbook*.

Passengers carried ('000): 7,728 in 2011; 7,739 in 2012; 7,621 in 2013 (Source: World Bank, World Development Indicators database).

Tourism

ARRIVALS BY NATIONALITY

	2010	2011	2012
Argentina	24,585	35,286	32,243
Brazil	48,099	58,550	54,088
Canada	21,151	24,712	13,196
Chile	10,656	10,645	10,761
Colombia	52,599	74,989	270,691
Ecuador	10,319	12,707	15,104
France	22,600	22,645	13,068
Germany	21,985	18,488	9,408
Italy	37,382	36,384	31,057
Mexico	12,934	13,636	11,553
Netherlands	10,889	14,269	11,888
Peru	19,545	18,413	18,862
Portugal	13,906	13,347	13,660
Spain	47,840	44,991	37,074
Trinidad and Tobago	19,379	21,302	17,825
United Kingdom	11,481	11,831	6,762
USA	63,164	67,849	50,479
Total (incl. others)	526,255	594,681	709,585

Tourism receipts (US $ million, excl. passenger transport): 740 in 2010; 739 in 2011; 844 in 2012.

Source: World Tourism Organization.

Communications Media

	2011	2012	2013
Telephones ('000 main lines in use)	7,332.1	7,648.8	7,773.8
Mobile cellular telephones ('000 subscribers)	28,782.0	30,569.1	30,896.1
Internet subscribers ('000)	2,038.5	n.a.	n.a.
Broadband subscribers ('000)	1,781.9	2,007.5	2,222.8

Source: International Telecommunication Union.

Education

(enrolment, 2011/12 unless otherwise indicated)

	Students		
	Males	Females	Total
Pre-primary	644,715	625,503	1,270,218
Primary	1,799,161	1,687,204	3,486,365
Secondary	1,148,598	1,205,814	2,354,412
Tertiary*	798,887	1,310,444	2,109,331

* 2007/08.

Sources: UNESCO Institute for Statistics.

2012/13: *Institutions:* Total 27,460. *Teachers:* Pre-school 115,621; Basic education 287,728; Further education 321,893 (General education 274,325, Technical education 47,568). *Students:* Pre-school 1,605,391; Basic education (grades 1–6) 3,473,886.

Pupil-teacher ratio (primary education, UNESCO estimate): 12.1 in 2009/10 (Source: UNESCO Institute for Statistics).

Adult literacy rate (UNESCO estimates): 95.5% (males 95.7%; females 95.4%) in 2009 (Source: UNESCO Institute for Statistics).

Directory

The Constitution

The Bolivarian Constitution of Venezuela was promulgated on 30 December 1999.

The Bolivarian Republic of Venezuela is divided into states, a Capital District and Federal Dependencies. The states are autonomous but must comply with the laws and Constitution of the Republic.

LEGISLATURE

Legislative power is exercised by the unicameral National Assembly (Asamblea Nacional). This replaced the bicameral Congreso Nacional (National Congress) following the introduction of the 1999 Constitution.

Deputies are elected by direct universal and secret suffrage, the number representing each state being determined by population size on a proportional basis. A deputy must be of Venezuelan nationality and be over 21 years of age. Indigenous minorities have the right to select three representatives. Ordinary sessions of the National Assembly begin on the fifth day of January of each year and continue until the 15th day of the following August; thereafter, sessions are renewed from the 15th day of September to the 15th day of December, both dates inclusive. The National Assembly is empowered to initiate legislation. The National Assembly also elects a Comptroller-General to preside over the Audit Office (Contraloría General de la República), which investigates Treasury income and expenditure, and the finances of the autonomous institutes.

GOVERNMENT

Executive power is vested in a President of the Republic, elected by universal suffrage for a term of six years. (In February 2009 a constitutional amendment removed any limit on the number of terms a President may serve.) The President is empowered to discharge the Constitution and the laws, to nominate or remove ministers, to take supreme command of the Armed Forces, to direct foreign relations of the state, to declare a state of emergency and withdraw the civil guarantees laid down in the Constitution, to convene extraordinary sessions of the National Assembly and to administer national finance.

JUDICIARY

Judicial power is exercised by the Supreme Tribunal of Justice (Tribunal Supremo de Justicia) and by the other tribunals. The Supreme Tribunal forms the highest court of the Republic and the Magistrates of the Supreme Tribunal are appointed by the National Assembly following recommendations from the Committee for Judicial Postulations, which consults with civil society groups. Magistrates serve a maximum of 12 years.

The 1999 Constitution created two new elements of power. The Moral Republican Council (Consejo Moral Republicano) is comprised of the Comptroller-General, the Attorney-General and the Peoples' Defender (or ombudsman). Its principal duty is to uphold the Constitution. The National Electoral Council (Consejo Nacional Electoral) administers and supervises elections.

The Government

HEAD OF STATE

President of the Republic: NICOLÁS MADURO MOROS (took office 19 April 2013).
Executive Vice-President: JORGE ALBERTO ARREAZA MONTSERRAT.

COUNCIL OF MINISTERS
(September 2014)

The Government is formed by the Partido Socialista Unido de Venezuela (PSUV).

Vice-President of Economy and Finance and Minister of Finance and Public Banking: Brig.-Gen. RODOLFO MARCO TORRES.
Vice-President of Planning and Knowledge and Minister of Planning: RICARDO JOSÉ MENÉNDEZ PRIETO.
Vice-President of Social Development and the Missions and Minister of Education: HÉCTOR RODRÍGUEZ CASTRO.
Vice-President of Development and Territorial Socialism and Minister of Communes and Social Protection: ELÍAS JAUA MILANO.
Vice-President of Food Security and Sovereignty: YVÁN GIL.
Minister of Foreign Affairs: RAFAEL DARÍO RAMÍREZ CARREÑO.
Minister of the Interior Relations and Justice: Gen. MIGUEL RODRÍGUEZ TORRES.
Minister of Agriculture and Lands: JOSÉ LUÍS BERROTERÁN.

Minister of Health: FRANCISCO ARMADA.
Minister of Science, Technology and University Education: MANUEL FERNÁNDEZ.
Minister of Energy and Petroleum: ASDRÚBAL CHÁVEZ.
Minister of Electric Energy: JESSE CHACÓN ESCAMILLO.
Minister of Defence: Adm. CARMEN TERESA MELÉNDEZ.
Minister of Commerce: ISABEL DELGADO.
Minister of Labour: JESÚS MARTÍNEZ.
Minister of Food: Col IVÁN JOSÉ BELLO.
Minister of Tourism: ANDRÉS IZARRA.
Minister of Housing, Habitat and EcoSocialism: RICARDO MOLINA PEÑALOZA.
Minister of Communication and Information: DELCY ELOYNA RODRÍGUEZ GÓMEZ.
Minister of Youth and Sport: ANTONIO (POTRO) ALVAREZ.
Minister of Culture: REINALDO ITURRIZA.
Minister of Indigenous Peoples: ALOA NÚÑEZ.
Minister of Women's Affairs and Gender Equality: ANDREÍNA TARAZÓN.
Minister of Land Transport: HAIMAN EL TROUDI.
Minister of Industries: JOSÉ DAVID CABELLO.
Minister of the Penitentiary System: IRIS VARELA.
Minister of Air and Water Transport: Gen. GIUSEPPE GIOFFREDA.
Minister of the Office of the Presidency and Government Management: CARLOS OSORIO.

MINISTRIES

Ministry of Agriculture and Lands: Avda Urdaneta, entre esq. Platanal a Candilito, a media cuadra de la Plaza la Candelaria, Parroquia la Candelaria, Caracas; tel. (212) 509-0347; e-mail pda2007@mat.gob.ve; internet www.mat.gob.ve.
Ministry of Air and Water Transport: Avda Francisco de Miranda, Torre Pequiven, 12°, Municipio Chacao, Caracas 1010; tel. (212) 274-5458; fax (212) 263-2570; e-mail ccmpptaa@gmail.com; internet www.mpptaa.gob.ve.
Ministry of Commerce: Torre Oeste de Parque Central, entrada por el Nivel Lecuna, Avda Lecuna, Caracas 1010; tel. (212) 509-6861; fax (212) 574-2432; e-mail ministro@milco.gob.ve; internet www.mincomercio.gob.ve.
Ministry of Communes and Social Protection: Edif. INCE, Avda Nueva Granada, Apdo 10340, Caracas 1040; tel. (212) 603-2396; internet www.mpcomunas.gob.ve.
Ministry of Communication and Information: Torre Ministerial, 9° y 10°, Avda Universidad, esq. el Chorro, Caracas 1010; tel. (212) 505-3322; e-mail contactenos@minci.gob.ve; internet www.minci.gob.ve.
Ministry of Culture: Edif. Archivo General de la Nación, Avda Panteón Foro Libertador, Caracas; tel. (212) 509-5681; e-mail mppc@mincultura.gob.ve; internet www.mincultura.gob.ve.
Ministry of Defence: Edif. 17 de Diciembre, planta baja, Base Aérea Francisco de Miranda, La Carlota, Caracas; tel. (212) 908-1264; fax (212) 237-4974; e-mail noiralith.gil@mindefensa.gov.ve; internet www.mindefensa.gob.ve.
Ministry of Education: Edif. Sede del MPPE, Mezzanina, esq. de Salas a Caja de Agua, Parroquia Altagracia, Caracas 1010; tel. (212) 596-4111; e-mail atencionsocial@me.gob.ve; internet www.me.gob.ve.
Ministry of Electric Energy: Avda Vollmer, Urb. San Bernardino, Municipio Libertador, Caracas 1010; tel. (212) 502-2650; internet www.mppee.gob.ve.
Ministry of Energy and Petroleum: Edif. Petróleos de Venezuela, Torre Oeste, Avda Libertador con Avda Empalme, La Campiña, Porroquia El Recreo, Caracas; tel. (212) 708-7581; fax (212) 708-7598; e-mail atencionalpublico@menpet.gob.ve; internet www.menpet.gob.ve.
Ministry of Finance and Public Banking: Edif. Ministerio de Finanzas, esq. Carmelitas, Avda Urdaneta, Caracas 1010; tel. (212) 802-1000; internet www.mppef.gob.ve.
Ministry of Food: Edif. Las Fundaciones, Avda Andrés Bello, Caracas; tel. (212) 395-7474; e-mail oirp@minpal.gob.ve; internet www.minpal.gob.ve.
Ministry of Foreign Affairs: Torre MRE, al lado del Correo de Carmelitas, Avda Urdaneta, Caracas 1010; tel. (212) 806-4400; fax (212) 861-2505; e-mail web.master@mre.gov.ve; internet www.mre.gov.ve.

Ministry of Health: Edif. Sur, 8°, Avda Baralt, Centro Simón Bolívar, El Silencio, Caracas 1010; tel. (212) 408-0033; fax 483-2560; e-mail mpps@mpps.gob.ve; internet www.mpps.gob.ve.

Ministry of Housing, Habitat and EcoSocialism: Avda Francisco de Miranda, antigua sede de INAVI, Municipio Chacao, Caracas 1010; tel. (212) 266-8625; fax (212) 265-4644; internet www.mvh.gob.ve.

Ministry of Indigenous Peoples: Antiguo Edif. Sudeban, Avda Universidad, esq. Traposos, 8°, Caracas 1010; tel. (212) 543-1599; fax (212) 543-3100; e-mail atencionlindigena@minpi.gob.ve; internet www.minpi.gob.ve.

Ministry of Industries: Caracas.

Ministry of Interior Relations and Justice: Edif. Ministerio, esq. de Platanal, Avda Urdaneta, Caracas 1010; tel. (212) 506-1101; fax (212) 506-1559; e-mail webmaster@mij.gov.ve; internet www.mpprij.gob.ve.

Ministry of Labour: Torre Sur, 5°, Centro Simón Bolívar, Caracas 1010; tel. (212) 481-1368; fax (212) 483-8914; internet www.mintra.gov.ve.

Ministry of Land Transport: Torre MTT, Avda Francisco de Miranda, Municipio Chacao, Caracas; tel. (212) 201-5515; internet www.mtc.gob.ve.

Ministry of the Office of the Presidency and Government Management: Palacio de Miraflores, final Avda Urdaneta, esq. de Bolero, Caracas; tel. (212) 806-3111; fax (212) 806-3229; e-mail dggcomunicacional@presidencia.gob.ve; internet www.presidencia.gob.ve.

Ministry of the Penitentiary System: Caracas; internet www.mppsp.gob.ve.

Ministry of Planning and Finance: Edif. Ministerio de Finanzas, esq. Carmelitas, Avda Urdaneta, Caracas 1010; tel. (212) 802-1000; internet www.mppef.gob.ve.

Ministry of Science, Technology and University Education: Torre Ministerial, Avda Universidad, esq. El Chorro, La Hoyada, Caracas; tel. (212) 555-7410; fax (212) 555-7504; e-mail mcti@mcti.gob.ve; internet www.mct.gob.ve.

Ministry of Tourism: Edif. Mintur, Avda Francisco de Miranda con Avda Principal de la Floresta, Municipio Chacao, Caracas; tel. (212) 208-4651; e-mail auditoria@mintur.gob.ve; internet www.mintur.gob.ve.

Ministry of Women's Affairs and Gender Equality: Torre Este, 4°, Parque Central, Avda Lecuna, Caracas; e-mail minmujer@minmujer.gob.ve; internet www.minmujer.gob.ve.

Ministry of Youth and Sport: Sede Principal, Avda Teheran, Urb. Montalbán, La Vega, Caracas 1020; tel. (212) 443-2682; fax (212) 443-3224; e-mail nororiente@mindeporte.gob.ve; internet www.mindeporte.gob.ve.

State Agencies

Autoridad Única Nacional en Trámites y Permisología: Caracas; f. 2014; aims to reduce bureaucracy and state inefficiency; Sec. DANTE RIVAS QUIJADA.

Contraloría General de la República (CGR): Edif. Contraloría, Avda Andrés Bello, Guaicaipuro, Caracas 1050; tel. (212) 508-3656; e-mail dict@cgr.gob.ve; internet www.cgr.gob.ve; national audit office; Comptroller-Gen. ADELINA GONZÁLEZ.

Defensoría del Pueblo: Edif. Defensoría del Pueblo, 8°, Avda México, Plaza Morelos, Los Caobos, Caracas; tel. (212) 575-4703; fax (212) 575-4467; e-mail prensadefensoria@hotmail.com; internet www.defensoria.gob.ve; investigates complaints between citizens and the authorities; Ombudsman GABRIELA DEL MAR RAMÍREZ.

Procuraduría General de la República: Paseo Los Ilustres con Avda Lazo Martí, Santa Mónica, Caracas; tel. (212) 597-3300; e-mail webmaster@pgr.gov.ve; internet www.pgr.gob.ve; Procurator-Gen. MANUEL ENRIQUE GALINDO BALLESTEROS.

President

Election, 14 April 2013

Candidates	Votes	% of total
Nicolás Maduro Moros (Partido Socialista Unido de Venezuela)	7,575,506	50.78
Henrique Capriles Radonski (Mesa de Unidad Democrática)	7,302,641	48.95
Others	38,910	0.26
Total valid votes*	14,917,057	100.00

* In addition, there were 66,691 blank or spoiled votes.

Legislature

NATIONAL ASSEMBLY
(Asamblea Nacional)

President: DIOSDADO CABELLO RONDÓN.

General Election, 26 September 2010

Party	Seats
Partido Socialista Unido de Venezuela (PSUV)	98
Mesa de Unidad Democrática (MUD)	65
Patria para Todos (PPT)	2
Total	165

Governors

STATES
(September 2014)

Amazonas: LIBORIO GUARULLA.
Anzoátegui: ARISTÓBULO ISTÚRIZ.
Apure: RAMÓN CARRIZALEZ.
Aragua: TARECK EL AISSAMI.
Barinas: ADÁN CHÁVEZ FRÍAS.
Bolívar: FRANCISCO JOSÉ RANGEL GÓMEZ.
Carabobo: FRANCISCO AMELIACH ORTA.
Cojedes: ERIKA FARÍAS.
Delta Amacuro: LIZETA HERNÁNDEZ.
Falcón: STELLA LUGO DE MONTILLA.
Guárico: RAMÓN RODRÍGUEZ CHACÍN.
Lara: HENRI FALCÓN FUENTES.
Mérida: ALEXIS RAMÍREZ.
Miranda: HENRIQUE CAPRILES RADONSKI.
Monagas: YELITZE SANTAELLA.
Nueva Esparta: CARLOS MATA FIGUEROA.
Portuguesa: WILMAR CASTRO SOTELDO.
Sucre: LUIS ACUÑA.
Táchira: JOSÉ GREGORIO VIELMA MORA.
Trujillo: HENRY RANGEL SILVA.
Vargas: JORGE LUIS GARCÍA CARNEIRO.
Yaracuy: JULIO LEÓN HEREDIA.
Zulia: FRANCISCO ARIAS CÁRDENAS.

FEDERAL DISTRICT

Caracas: ANTONIO LEDEZMA.

Election Commission

Consejo Nacional Electoral (CNE): Edif. Sede del Consejo Nacional Electoral, Centro Simón Bolívar, Frente a la Plaza Caracas, Caracas; tel. (212) 408-5200; fax (212) 576-5603; internet www.cne.gov.ve; f. 2002; Pres. TIBISAY LUCENA RAMÍREZ.

Political Organizations

Mesa de Unidad Democrática (MUD): Caracas; internet www.unidadvenezuela.org; f. 2008; opposition coalition; Sec.-Gen. (vacant); comprises the following parties.

Acción Democrática (AD): Casa Nacional Acción Democrática, Calle Los Cedros, La Florida, Caracas 1050; tel. (212) 731-4742; e-mail hramosallup@gmail.com; internet www.acciondemocratica.org.ve; f. 1936 as Partido Democrático Nacional; adopted present name and obtained legal recognition in 1941; social democratic; Pres. ISABEL CARMONA DE SERRA; Sec.-Gen. HENRY RAMOS ALLUP.

Alianza Bravo Pueblo: Caracas; e-mail alianzabravopueblo@gmail.com; internet www.alianzabravopueblo.com; merged with Visión Emergente in 2010; Pres. ANTONIO LEDEZMA; Sec.-Gen. EDWIN LUZARDO.

Avanzada Progresista: Caracas; internet www.avanzadaprogresista.org; f. 2012; Pres. HENRI FALCÓN; Sec.-Gen. JUAN JOSÉ MOLINA.

959

La Causa Radical (La Causa R): Santa Teresa a Cipreses, Residencias Santa Teresa, 2°, Ofs 21 y 22, Caracas; tel. (212) 545-7002; e-mail lacausarbolivar@gmail.com; internet lacausarbolivar .com; f. 1971; Leader ANDRÉS VELÁSQUEZ; Sec.-Gen. DANIEL SANTOLO.

Movimiento Progresista de Venezuela: Caracas; f. 2012; Sec.-Gen. SIMÓN CALZADILLA.

Movimiento al Socialismo (MAS): Quinta Alemar, Avda Valencia, Las Palmas, Caracas 1050; tel. (212) 793-7800; fax (212) 761-9297; e-mail asamblea07@cantv.net; internet www.masvenezuela .com.ve; f. 1971 by PCV dissidents; opposition democratic socialist party; Pres. NICOLÁS SOSA; Sec.-Gen. FELIPE MUJICA.

Partido Social-Cristiano (Comité de Organización Política Electoral Independiente) (COPEI): El Bosque, Avda Principal El Bosque, cruce con Avda Gloria Quinta Cujicito, Chacao, Caracas; tel. (212) 731-4746; fax (212) 731-4953; e-mail info@copeivenezuela.com; internet www.copeivenezuela.com; f. 1946; Pres. ROBERTO ENRÍQUEZ; Sec.-Gen. JESÚS ALBERTO BARRIOS.

Primero Justicia: Edif. Primero Justicia, 3ra Transversal, entre Avda 4 y Avda Luis Guillermo Villegas Blanco, Urb. Los Palos Grandes, Caracas; tel. (212) 285-8391; e-mail pjelhaltillo@cantv .net; internet www.primerojusticia.org.ve; f. 2000; Nat. Co-ordinator JULIO ANDRÉS BORGES; Nat. Sec. TOMÁS GUANIPA.

Un Nuevo Tiempo (UNT): Edif. Montral, Avda Principal de Las Palmas, Municipio Libertador, Caracas; tel. (212) 425-1239; e-mail prensa@partidounnuevotiempo.org; internet www .partidounnuevotiempo.org; f. 2005; Exec. Chair. OMAR BARBOZA; Exec. Sec. LUIS EMILIO RONDÓN.

Voluntad Popular: Edif. Menegrande, 5°, Of. 51, Avda Francisco de Miranda, Urb. Los Palos Grandes, Miranda, Caracas 1060; tel. (212) 740-7442; e-mail administracion@voluntadpopular@gmail .com; internet www.voluntadpopular.com; f. 2004; registered as a political party in 2011; Nat. Co-ordinator LEOPOLDO LÓPEZ; Nat. Leader LUIS FLORIDO.

Movimiento Demócrata Liberal (MDL): Quinta El Encuentro, 1°, Avda de Santa Eduvigis, entre 5a y 6a Transversal, Caracas; tel. (212) 442-3956; fax (212) 471-3856; e-mail info@democrataliberales .org; internet www.democrataliberales.org; right wing; f. 2007; Political Dir EBER FLORES.

Movimiento Electoral del Pueblo (MEP): Calle Buenos Aires, Urb. Los Caobos, Parroquia El Recreo Municipio Libertador, Caracas 1050; tel. (212) 793-4135; internet www.mep.com.ve/nosotros.html; f. 1967 by left-wing AD dissidents; 100,000 mems; Pres. ANDRÉS LUCIANO LARA OJEDA; Sec.-Gen. WILMER JOSÉ NOLASCO.

Movimiento Independiente Ganamos Todos (MIGATO): Caracas; f. 1997; fmr supporter of the PSUV, now dissident.

Movimiento Republicano (MR): Edif. Yetesa, Of. 1, Avda Libertador, con Avda Principal Las Palmas, Caracas; tel. (212) 693-2937; e-mail elrepublicano.ve@gmail.com; f. 1997; Pres. CARLOS PADILLA; Sec.-Gen. JULIO ALBARRÁN.

Movimiento Tupamaro (Tendencia Unificada para Alcanzar el Movimiento de Acción Revolucionario): Caracas; internet www .tupamaro.org.ve; Sec.-Gen. JOSÉ TOMÁS PINTO.

Organización Renovadora Auténtica: Caracas; internet oraporvenezuela.org; f. 1987; Pres. LUIS REYES CASTILLO.

Partido Comunista de Venezuela (PCV): Edif. Cantaclaro, Calle Jesús Faría, esq. de San Pedro a San Francisquito, Parroquia San Juan, Caracas; tel. (212) 484-0061; fax (212) 481-9737; internet www .pcv-venezuela.org; f. 1931; Pres. PEDRO EUSSE; Sec. OSCAR FIGUERA.

Partido Socialista Unido de Venezuela (PSUV): Calle Lima, cruce con Avda Libertador, Los Caobos, Caracas; tel. (212) 782-3808; fax (212) 782-9720; e-mail contacto@psuv.org.ve; internet www.psuv .org.ve; f. 2007; successor party to the Movimiento V República; promotes Bolivarian revolution; Pres. NICOLÁS MADURO MOROS.

Patria Para Todos (PPT): Calle Montevideo, Quinta Plaza, Calle Maripérez, Plaza Venezuela, Caracas; tel. (212) 578-3098; fax (212) 577-4545; e-mail partidoppt@gmail.com; internet www .patriaparatodos.com.ve; f. 1997; breakaway faction of La Causa Radical; revolutionary humanist party; Nat. Sec.-Gen. RAFAEL UZCÁTEGUI.

Por la Democracia Social (PODEMOS): Caracas; f. 2001 by dissident mems of MAS (q.v.); Leader DIDALCO BOLÍVAR.

Proyecto Venezuela (PRVZL): Edif. El Nacional, 2°, De Puente Nuevo a Puerto Escondido, El Silencio, Caracas; f. 1998; humanist party; supported the MUD in the 2012 presidential election; Leader HENRIQUE SALAS RÖMER; Sec.-Gen. CARLOS BERRIZBEITIA.

OTHER ORGANIZATIONS

Comité de Familiares Víctimas de los Sucesos de Febrero y Marzo de 1989 (COFAVIC): Edif. El Candil, 1°, Of. 1-A, Avda Urdaneta, Esq. El Candilito, Apdo 16150, Caracas; tel. (212) 572-9631; fax (212) 572-9908; e-mail cofavic@cofavic.org; internet www

.cofavic.org; f. 1989; promotes human rights and democracy; Exec. Dir LILIANA ORTEGA.

Súmate: Torre A, 5°, Avda Francisco de Miranda, Centro Plaza, Urb. Los Palos Grandes, Caracas; tel. (212) 285-4562; e-mail prensa@sumate.org; internet www.sumate.org; f. 2002; citizens' rights; Co-ordinator CAROLINA REYES.

Diplomatic Representation

EMBASSIES IN VENEZUELA

Algeria: 8a Transversal con 3ra Avda, Quinta Azahar, Urb. Altamira, Caracas 1062; tel. (212) 263-2092; fax (212) 261-4254; e-mail ambalgcar@cantv.net; Ambassador RACHID BLADEHANE.

Argentina: Edif. Fedecámaras, 3°, Avda El Empalme, El Bosque, Apdo 569, Caracas; tel. (212) 731-3311; fax (212) 731-2659; e-mail evene@mrecic.gov.ar; internet evene.mrecic.gov.ar; Ambassador CARLOS ALBERTO CHEPPI.

Austria: Edif. Torre D&D, Piso PT, Of. PTN, Avda Orinoco, entre Mucuchíes y Perijá, Urb. Las Mercedes, Apdo 61381, Caracas 1060-A; tel. (212) 999-1211; fax (212) 993-2753; e-mail caracas-ob@bmeia .gv.at; internet www.aussenministerium.at/caracas; Ambassador GERHARD MAYER.

Barbados: Edif. Los Frailes, 5°, Of. 501, Avda Principal de Chuao, Chuao, Apdo 68829, Caracas 1060; tel. (212) 992-0545; fax (212) 991-0333; e-mail caracas@foreign.gov.bb; Ambassador SANDRA PHILLIPS.

Belarus: Quinta Campanera, 3ra Transversal (Calle Aveledo) con Avda 7, Urb. Los Chorros, Sucre, Caracas 1071; tel. (212) 239-2760; fax (212) 239-0419; e-mail venezuela@belembassy.org; internet venezuela.mfa.gov.by; Ambassador OLEG PAFEROV.

Bolivia: Edif. Los Llanos, 1°, Avda Francisco Zolano, esq. San Gerónimo, Zabana Grande, Caracas; tel. (212) 267-0136; fax (212) 261-3386; e-mail embaboliviaven@hotmail.com; internet www .embajada-boliviana-venezuela.com; Ambassador LUIS ADOLFO TRIGO ANTELO.

Brazil: Avda Mohedano con Calle Los Chaguaramos, Centro Gerencial Mohedano, 6°, La Castellana, Caracas 1060; tel. (212) 918-6000; fax (212) 261-9601; e-mail brasembcaracas@cantv.net; internet caracas.itamaraty.gov.br; Ambassador RUY CARLOS PEREIRA.

Canada: Edif. Embajada de Canadá, Avda Francisco de Miranda con Avda Sur, Altamira, Apdo 62302, Caracas 1060-A; tel. (212) 600-3000; fax (212) 261-8741; e-mail crcas@international.gc.ca; internet www.canadainternational.gc.ca/venezuela; Ambassador BEN ROWSWELL.

Chile: Edif. Torre La Noria, 10°, Of. 10A, Paseo Enrique Eraso, Urb. Las Mercedes, Caracas; tel. (212) 992-3378; fax (212) 992-0614; e-mail echileve@cantv.net; internet chileabroad.gov.cl/venezuela; Ambassador MAURICIO UGALDE BILBAO.

China, People's Republic: Avda Orinoco con Calle Monterrey, Urb. Las Mercedes, Baruta, Caracas; tel. (212) 993-1171; fax (212) 993-5685; e-mail chinaemb_ve@mfa.gov.cn; internet ve .china-embassy.org; Ambassador ZHAO RONGXIAN.

Colombia: Torre Credival, 11°, 2A Calle de Campo Alegre con Avda Francisco de Miranda, Apdo 60887, Caracas; tel. (212) 216-9596; fax (212) 261-1358; e-mail ecaracas@minrelext.gov.co; internet www .embajadaenvenezuela.gov.co; Ambassador LUIS ELADIO PÉREZ.

Costa Rica: Edif. For You, 11°, Avda San Juan Bosco, entre 1a y 2a Transversal, Urb. Altamira, Chacao, Apdo 62239, Caracas; tel. (212) 267-1104; fax (212) 265-4660; e-mail embaricavene@yahoo.com.mx; Ambassador NAZARETH AVENDAÑO SOLANO.

Cuba: Calle Roraima, entre Río de Janeiro y Choroní, Chuao, Caracas 1060; tel. (212) 991-6661; fax (212) 993-5695; e-mail ministroconsejero@embajadacuba.com.ve; internet www .cubadiplomatica.cu/venezuela; Ambassador ROGELIO POLANCO FUENTES.

Dominican Republic: Edif. Argentum, Ofs 1 y 2, 2a Transversal, entre 1a Avda y Avda Andrés Bello, Los Palos Grandes, Caracas 1060; tel. (212) 283-3709; fax (212) 283-3965; e-mail embajada_dominicana@hotmail.com; Ambassador ADONAIDA MEDINA.

Ecuador: Edif. Bancaracas, 8°, Of. 8-01, Avda Principal de la Castellana con 2da Transversal, Apdo 62124, Caracas 1060; tel. (212) 265-0801; fax (212) 264-6917; e-mail embve.ecuador@mppre .gob.ve; internet venezuela.embajada.gob.ec; Ambassador MARÍA AUGUSTA CALLE.

Egypt: Calle Caucagua con Calle Guaicaipuro, Quinta Maribel, Urb. San Román, Baruta, Apdo 49007, Caracas 1042-A; tel. (212) 992-6259; fax (212) 993-1555; e-mail embassy.caracas@mfa.gov.eg; internet www.mfa.gov.eg/Caracas_Emb; Ambassador AYMAN TOMOUM.

El Salvador: Avda Nicólas Copérnico, Quinta Cuscatlán, Urb. Valle Arriba, Sector Los Naranjos, Baruta, Miranda, Caracas; tel. (212) 991-4472; fax (212) 959-3920; e-mail embasalve@cantv.net; internet embajadavenezuela.rree.gob.sv; Ambassador ROMÁN ANTONIO MOYORGA QUIROZ.

France: Calle Madrid con Avda Trinidad, Las Mercedes, Apdo 60385, Caracas 1060; tel. (212) 909-6500; fax (212) 909-6630; e-mail infos@francia.org.ve; internet www.ambafrance-ve.org; Ambassador FREDERIC DESAGNEAUX.

The Gambia: 4a Avda con 8a Transversal, Quinta La Paz, Urb. Los Palos Grandes, Chacao, Caracas; tel. (212) 285-2554; fax (212) 285-6250; Ambassador BALA GARBA JAHUMPA.

Germany: Torre La Castellana, 10°, Avda Eugenio Mendoza, cruce con Avda José Angel Lamas, La Castellana, Apdo 2078, Caracas 1010-A; tel. (212) 219-2500; fax (212) 261-0641; e-mail info@caracas.diplo.de; internet www.caracas.diplo.de; Ambassador WALTER LINDNER.

Greece: Quinta Maryland, Avda Principal del Avila, Alta Florida, Caracas 1050; tel. (212) 730-3833; fax (212) 731-0429; e-mail gremb.car@mfa.gr; Ambassador ANASTASSIOS PETROVAS.

Grenada: Centro Plaza, Torre B, 10°, Avda Francisco de Miranda, Los Palos Grande, Chacao, Caracas; tel. (212) 285-2639; fax (212) 286-4114; e-mail egrenada@cantv.net; Ambassador HASSAN HADEED.

Guatemala: Avda de Francisco de Miranda, Torre Dozsa, 1°, Urb. El Rosal, Caracas; tel. (212) 952-5247; fax (212) 954-0051; e-mail embaguat@cantv.net; Ambassador ERICK ROBERTO MOLINA SANDOVAL.

Guyana: Quinta Los Tutis, 2a Avda entre 9a y 10a Transversal Urb. Altamira, Chacao, Caracas 1050; tel. (212) 267-7095; fax (212) 976-3765; e-mail embaguy@cantv.net; Ambassador GEOFFREY DA SILVA.

Haiti: Quinta Flor 59, Avda Las Rosas, La Florida, Caracas; tel. (212) 730-7220; fax (212) 730-4605; Ambassador LESLY DAVID.

Holy See: Avda La Salle, Los Caobos, Apdo 29, Caracas 1010-A (Apostolic Nunciature); tel. (212) 781-8939; fax (212) 793-2403; e-mail nunapos@cantv.net; Apostolic Nuncio Mgr ALDO GIORDANO (Titular Archbishop of Tamada).

Honduras: Edif. Banco de Lara, 8°, Of. B2, Avda Principal de la Castellana con 1a Transversal de Altamira, La Castellana, Apdo 68259, Caracas; tel. (212) 263-3184; fax (212) 263-4379; e-mail honduven@cantv.net; Ambassador GERMAN ESPINAL ZUÑIGA.

India: Quinta Tagore, No. 12, Avda San Carlos, La Floresta, Apdo 61585, Caracas; tel. (212) 285-7887; fax (212) 286-5131; e-mail info@embindia.org; internet www.embindia.org; Ambassador SMITA PURUSHOTTAM.

Indonesia: Quinta 'Indonesia', Avda El Paseo, con Calle Maracaibo, Prados del Este, Apdo 80807, Caracas 1080; tel. (212) 976-2725; fax (212) 976-0550; e-mail kbricaracas1@yahoo1.com; internet www.kemlu.go.id/caracas; Ambassador PRIANTI GAGARIN DJATMIKO SINGGIH.

Iran: Quinta Ommat, Calle Kemal Atatürk, Urb. Valle Arriba, Apdo 68460, Caracas; tel. (212) 992-3575; fax (212) 992-9989; e-mail embairanve@cantv.net; Ambassador HOJATTOLAH SOLTANI.

Iraq: Quinta Babilonia, Avda Nicolás Copérnico con Calle Los Malabares, Urb. Valle Arriba, Caracas; tel. (212) 993-3446; fax (212) 993-0819; e-mail crcemb@iraqmfamail.com; Ambassador FAKHRI HASSAN MEHDI AL-ISSA.

Italy: Edif. Atrium PH, Calle Sorocaima, entre Avdas Tamanaco y Venezuela, El Rosal, Apdo 3995, Caracas 1060; tel. (212) 952-7311; fax (212) 952-4960; e-mail ambcaracas@esteri.it; internet www.ambcaracas.esteri.it; Ambassador PAOLO SERPI.

Jamaica: Edif. Los Frailes, 5°, Calle La Guairita, Urb. Chuao, Caracas 1062; tel. (212) 916-9055; fax (212) 991-5708; e-mail embjaven@cantv.net; Ambassador SHARON WEBER.

Japan: Torre Digitel, 9°, Avda Don Eugenio Mendoza con Esq. Calle Miranda, La Castellana, Caracas; tel. (212) 262-3435; fax (212) 262-3484; e-mail ajapon@genesisbci.net; internet www.ve.emb-japan.go.jp; Ambassador TETSUSABURO HAYASHI.

Korea, Republic: Avda Francisco de Miranda, Centro Lido, Torre B, 9°, Ofs 91-B y 92-B, El Rosal, Caracas; tel. (212) 954-1270; fax (212) 954-0619; e-mail venezuela@mofat.go.kr; internet ven.mofat.go.kr; Ambassador KIM JOO-TECK.

Kuwait: Quinta El-Kuwait, Avda Las Magnolias con Calle Los Olivos, Los Chorros, Caracas; tel. (212) 235-3864; fax (212) 238-1752; e-mail caracas@mofa.gov.kw; Ambassador MARZOUK AL SHABO.

Lebanon: Edif. Embajada del Líbano, Prolongación Avda Parima, Colinas de Bello Monte, Calle Motatán, Caracas 1041; tel. (212) 751-6165; fax (212) 753-0726; e-mail emblibano@cantv.net; internet www.lebanonembassy.org.ve; Ambassador ELÍAS LEBBOS.

Malaysia: Centro Profesional Eurobuilding, 6°, Ofs 6D-G, Calle La Guairita, Apdo 65107, Chuao, Caracas 1060; tel. (212) 992-1011; fax (212) 992-1277; e-mail malcaracas@kln.gov.my; internet www.kln.gov.my/perwakilan/caracas; Ambassador MAHINDER SINGH.

Mexico: Edif. Forum, Calle Guaicaipuro con Principal de las Mercedes, 5°, El Rosal, Chacao, Apdo 61371, Caracas; tel. (212) 952-2729; fax (212) 952-2408; e-mail embvenezuela@sre.gob.mx; internet embamex.sre.gob.mx/venezuela; Ambassador LEANDRO ARELLANO RESENDIZ.

Netherlands: Edif. San Juan, 9°, Avda San Juan Bosco con 2a Transversal de Altamira, Caracas; tel. (212) 276-9300; fax (212) 276-9311; e-mail car@minbuza.nl; internet venezuela.nlambassade.org; Ambassador ONNO KERVERS.

Nicaragua: Avda El Paseo, Quinta Doña Dilia, Prados del Este, Caracas; tel. (212) 977-3289; fax (212) 977-3973; e-mail spoveda@cancilleria.gob.ni; Ambassador RAMÓN ENRIQUE LEETS CASTILLO.

Nigeria: Calle Chivacoa cruce con Calle Taría, Quinta Leticia, Urb. San Román, Apdo 62062, Chacao, Caracas 1060-A; tel. (212) 993-1520; fax (212) 993-7648; e-mail embnig@cantv.net; Ambassador S. A. A. ADENIRAN.

Panama: Edif. Los Frailes, 6°, Calle La Guairita, Chuao, Apdo 1989, Caracas; tel. (212) 992-9093; fax (212) 992-8107; e-mail empanve@cantv.net; Ambassador (vacant).

Paraguay: Quinta Helechales, 4a Avda, entre 7a y 8a Transversal, Urb. Altamira, Chacao, Caracas; tel. (212) 263-2559; fax (212) 267-5543; e-mail venezuelaembaparsc@mre.gov.py; Ambassador ENRIQUE JARA OCAMPOS.

Peru: Edif. San Juan, 5°, Avda San Juan Bosco con 2a Transversal, Altamira, Caracas; tel. (212) 264-1483; fax (212) 265-7592; e-mail leprucaracas@cantv.net; Ambassador MARIO JUVENAL LÓPEZ CHÁVARRI.

Philippines: 5a Transversal de Altamira, Quinta Filipinas, Altamira, Chacao, Caracas 1060; tel. (212) 267-8873; fax (212) 266-6443; e-mail caracas@embassyph.com; Ambassador JOCELYN BATOON-GARCÍA.

Poland: Quinta Ambar, Calle Nicolás Copérnico, Sector Los Naranjos, Valle Arriba, Apdo 62293, Chacao, Caracas; tel. (212) 991-6167; fax (212) 992-2164; e-mail ambcarac@cantv.net; internet www.caracas.msz.gov.pl; Ambassador PIOTR KASZUBA.

Portugal: Torre La Castellana, 3°, Avda Eugénio Mendoza, cruce con Calle José Angel Lamas, Urb. La Castellana, Caracas 1062; tel. (212) 263-2529; fax (212) 267-9766; e-mail caracas@mne.pt; Ambassador MÁRIO ALBERTO LINO DA SILVA.

Qatar: Avda Principal Lomas El Mirador, Quinta Alto Claro, Baruta, Caracas; tel. (212) 993-7925; fax (212) 993-2917; e-mail qatarven@cantv.net; Ambassador BATAL MOJAB BATAL ALDOSARI.

Romania: Avda 6a de Altamira, entre 8a y 9a Transversales, Quinta Guardatinajas 49-19, Chacao, Caracas; tel. (212) 261-9480; fax (212) 263-5697; e-mail secretariat.amb@gmail.com; internet www.caracas.mae.ro; Chargé d'affaires a.i. EMIL GHIȚULESCU.

Russia: Quinta Soyuz, Calle Las Lomas, Las Mercedes, Apdo 60313, Caracas; tel. (212) 993-4395; fax (212) 993-6526; e-mail rusemb@cantv.net; internet www.venezuela.mid.ru; Ambassador VLADIMIR F. ZAEMSKY.

Saudi Arabia: Calle Andrés Pietri, Quinta Makkah, Los Chorros, Caracas 1071; tel. (212) 239-0290; fax (212) 239-6494; e-mail veemb@mofa.gov.sa; internet embassies.mofa.gov.sa/sites/venezuela; Ambassador ABDELRAHMAN BIN ABDULAZIZ BIN SULAIMAN ABANAMY.

South Africa: Edif. Atrium, PH-1A, Sorocaima con Avda Venezuela, Urb. El Rosal, Chacao, Apdo 2613, Caracas 1064; tel. (212) 952-0026; fax (212) 952-0277; e-mail embajador.caracas@foreign.gov.za; Ambassador T. SHOPE LINNEY.

Spain: Avda Mohedano entre 1a y 2a Transversal, La Castellana, Apdo 62297, Caracas; tel. (212) 263-2855; fax (212) 261-0892; e-mail emb.caracas@maec.es; internet www.maec.es/embajadas/caracas; Ambassador ANTONIO PÉREZ-HERNÁNDEZ.

Sudan: Caracas; Ambassador SIDDIQ MOHAMED ABDALLA.

Suriname: 4a Avda entre 7a y 8a Transversal, Quinta 41, Altamira, Caracas; Apdo 61140, Chacao, Caracas; tel. (212) 261-2724; fax (212) 263-9006; e-mail emsurl@cantv.net; Ambassador SAMUEL PAWIRONADI.

Switzerland: Centro Letonia, Torre Ing-Bank, 15°, Avda Eugenio Mendoza y San Felipe, La Castellana, Apdo 62555, Chacao, Caracas 1060-A; tel. (212) 267-9585; fax (212) 267-7745; e-mail car.vertretung@eda.admin.ch; internet www.eda.admin.ch/caracas; Ambassador SABINE ULMANN SHABAN.

Syria: Avda Casiquiare, Quinta Damasco, Colinas de Bello Monte, Caracas; tel. (212) 753-5375; fax (212) 751-6146; Ambassador GHASSAN SULEIMAN ABBAS.

Trinidad and Tobago: 22-12 Quinta Poshika, 3ra Avda entre 6a y 7a Transversales, Altamira, Chacao, Caracas; tel. (212) 261-5796; fax (212) 261-9801; e-mail embassytt@cantv.net; Ambassador ANTHONY DAVID EDGHILL.

Turkey: Calle Kemal Atatürk, Quinta Turquesa 6, Valle Arriba, Apdo 62078, Caracas 1060-A; tel. (212) 991-0075; fax (212) 992-0442; e-mail embajada.caracas@mfa.gov.tr; internet caracas.emb.mfa.gov.tr; Ambassador SULE ÖZTUNÇ.

United Kingdom: Torre La Castellana, 11°, Avda Principal La Castellana, Caracas 1061; tel. (212) 319-5800; fax (212) 267-1275; e-mail britishembassy@internet.ve; internet ukinvenezuela.fco.gov.uk; Ambassador JOHN SAVILLE (from Oct. 2014).

USA: Calle Suapure con Calle F, Urb. Colinas de Valle Arriba, Caracas 1080; tel. (212) 975-6411; fax (212) 975-6710; e-mail embajada@state.gov; internet caracas.usembassy.gov; Chargé d'affaires a.i. LEE MCCLENNY.

Uruguay: Torre Seguros Altamira, 4°, Of. D y E, 4a Avda de los Palos Grandes, Apdo 60366, Caracas 1060-A; tel. (212) 285-3549; fax (212) 286-6777; e-mail uruvene@cantv.net; internet www.uruvene.com; Ambassador OSCAR MILTON RAMOS FERNÁNDEZ.

Viet Nam: 9a Transversal, entre 6a y 7a Avdas, Quinta Las Mercedes, Urb. Altamira, Chacao 1060-025, Caracas; tel. (212) 635-7402; fax (212) 264-7324; e-mail embavive@yahoo.com.vn; internet www.vietnamembassy-venezuela.org; Ambassador NGO TIEN DUNG.

Judicial System

The judicature is headed by the Supreme Tribunal of Justice, which replaced the Supreme Court of Justice after the promulgation of the December 1999 Constitution. The judiciary is divided into penal, civil and mercantile judges; there are military, juvenile, labour, administrative litigation, finance and agrarian tribunals. In each state there is a superior court and several secondary courts which act on civil and criminal cases. A number of reforms to the judicial system were introduced under the Organic Criminal Trial Code of 1998. The Code replaced the inquisitorial system, based on the Napoleonic code, with an adversarial system in 1999.

SUPREME TRIBUNAL OF JUSTICE

The Supreme Tribunal comprises 32 judges appointed by the National Assembly for 12 years. It is divided into six courts, each with three judges: political-administrative, civil, constitutional, electoral, social and criminal. When these act together the court is in full session. It has the power to abrogate any laws, regulations or other acts of the executive or legislative branches conflicting with the Constitution. It hears accusations against members of the Government and high public officials, cases involving diplomatic representatives and certain civil actions arising between the state and individuals.

Supreme Tribunal of Justice: Final Avda Baralt, esq. Dos Pilitas, Foro Libertador, Caracas 1010; tel. (212) 801-9178; fax (212) 564-8596; e-mail cperez@tsj.gov.ve; internet www.tsj.gov.ve; Pres. GLADYS GUTIÉRREZ ALVARADO.

President of the Constitutional Court: GLADYS GUTIÉRREZ ALVARADO.

President of the Court of Civil Cassation: YRIS ARMENIA PEÑA DE ANDUEZA.

President of the Court of Penal Cassation: DEYANIRA NIEVES BASTIDAS.

President of the Court of Social Cassation: LUIS EDUARDO FRANCESCHI GUTIÉRREZ.

President of the Electoral Court: FERNANDO VEGAS TORREALBA.

President of the Political-Administrative Court: EMIRO ROSAS GARCÍA.

Prosecutor-General: LUISA ORTEGA DÍAZ.

Religion

Roman Catholicism is the religion of the majority of the population, but there is complete freedom of worship.

CHRISTIANITY

The Roman Catholic Church

For ecclesiastical purposes, Venezuela comprises nine archdioceses, 24 dioceses and three Apostolic Vicariates. There are also apostolic exarchates for the Melkite and Syrian Rites. Some 85% of the population are Roman Catholics.

Latin Rite

Bishops' Conference: Conferencia Episcopal de Venezuela, Prolongación Avda Páez, Montalbán, Apdo 4897, Caracas 1010; tel. (212) 471-6593; fax (212) 442-0128; e-mail vmorales395@cantv.net;

internet www.cev.org.ve; f. 1985; statutes approved in 2000; Pres. Most Rev. DIEGO PADRÓN SÁNCHEZ (Archbishop of Cumaná).

Archbishop of Barquisimeto: Most Rev. ANTONIO JOSÉ LÓPEZ CASTILLO, Arzobispado, Avda Libertador, Centro Pastoral (Mons. Críspulo Benítez), Barquisimeto; tel. (251) 420-0100; fax (251) 231-3724; e-mail arbarquisimeto@gmail.com; internet www.arquidiocesisdebarquisimeto.org.ve.

Archbishop of Calabozo: MANUEL FELIPE DÍAZ SÁNCHEZ, Arzobispado, Calle 4, No 11–82, Apdo 954, Calabozo 2312; tel. (246) 205-5888; fax (246) 871-2097; e-mail el.real@telcel.net.ve.

Archbishop of Caracas (Santiago de Venezuela): Cardinal JORGE LIBERATO UROSA SAVINO, Arzobispado, Apdo 954, Caracas 1010-A; tel. (212) 542-1611; fax (212) 542-0297; e-mail arzobispado@cantv.net; internet www.arquidiocesisdecaracas.com.

Archbishop of Ciudad Bolívar: Most Rev. ULISES ANTONIO GUTIÉRREZ REYES, Arzobispado, Avda Andrés Eloy Blanco con Calle Naiguatá, Apdo 43, Ciudad Bolívar 8001; tel. (285) 654-4960; fax (285) 654-0821; e-mail arzcb@cantv.net.ve.

Archbishop of Coro: Most Rev. ROBERTO LÜCKERT LEÓN, Arzobispado, Calle Federación con Palmasola, Apdo 7342, Coro 4101-A; tel. (268) 251-7024; fax (268) 251-1636; e-mail dioceco@reaccium.ve.

Archbishop of Cumaná: Most Rev. DIEGO RAFAEL PADRÓN SÁNCHEZ, Arzobispado, Calle Bolívar 34 con Catedral, Apdo 134, Cumaná 6101-A; tel. (293) 431-4131; fax (293) 433-3413; e-mail dipa@cantv.net.

Archbishop of Maracaibo: Most Rev. UBALDO RAMÓN SANTANA SEQUERA, Arzobispado, Calle 95, entre Avdas 2 y 3, Apdo 439, Maracaibo; tel. (261) 722-5351; fax (261) 721-0805; e-mail ubrasan@hotmail.com.

Archbishop of Mérida: Most Rev. BALTAZAR ENRIQUE PORRAS CARDOZO, Arzobispado, Avda 4, Plaza Bolívar, Apdo 26, Mérida 5101-A; tel. (274) 252-5786; fax (274) 252-1238; e-mail administracion99@cantv.net; internet www.arquidiocesisdemerida.org.ve.

Archbishop of Valencia: Most Rev. CARLOS OSORO SIERRA, Arzobispado, Avda Urdaneta 100-54, Apdo 32, Valencia 2001-A; tel. (241) 858-5865; fax (241) 857-8061; e-mail arqui_valencia@cantv.net; internet www.archivalencia.org.

Melkite Rite

Apostolic Exarch: Rt Rev. GEORGES KAHHALÉ ZOUHAÏRATY, Catedral San Jorge, Final Avda 3, Urb. Montalbán II, Apdo 20120, Caracas; tel. (212) 443-3019; fax (212) 443-0131; e-mail georgeskahhale@catedralsanjorge.org.ve; internet www.catedralsanjorge.org.ve.

Syrian Rite

Apostolic Exarch: HIKMAT BEYLOUNI, Parroquia Nuestra Señora de la Asunción, 1A Calle San Jacinto, Apdo 11, Maracay; tel. (243) 235-0821; fax (243) 235-7213.

The Anglican Communion

Anglicans in Venezuela are adherents of the Episcopal Church in the USA, in which the country forms a single, extra-provincial diocese attached to Province IX.

Bishop of Venezuela: Rt Rev. ORLANDO DE JESÚS GUERRERO, Avda Caroní 100, Apdo 49-143, Colinas de Bello Monte, Caracas 1042-A; tel. (212) 753-0723; fax (212) 751-3180; e-mail mons.guerrero@hotmail.com.

Other Christian Churches

Church of Jesus Christ of Latter-Day Saints (Mormons): Avda C con Calle C-1, Urb. Caurimare, Caracas 1062-A; internet www.lds.org; 157,795 mems.

Convención Nacional Bautista de Venezuela: Avda Santiago de Chile 12–14, Urb. Los Caobos, Caracas 1050; Apdo 61152, Chacao, Caracas 1060-A; tel. (212) 782-2308; fax (212) 781-9043; e-mail convencionbautista@cantv.net; internet www.cnbv.org.ve; f. 1951; Pres. Rev. NATHAN VELÁSQUEZ MARTÍNEZ; Dir-Gen. Rev. ALEXANDER MONTERO.

Iglesia Evangélica Luterana en Venezuela: Apdo 68738, Caracas 1062-A; tel. and fax (212) 264-1868; e-mail ielv.venezuela@gmail.com; internet ielv.tripod.com; Pres. GUILLERMINA CHAPARRO; 1,950 mems.

JUDAISM

Confederación de Asociaciones Israelitas de Venezuela: Avda Washington, al lado del Hotel Avila, San Bernardino, Caracas; tel. (212) 551-0368; fax (212) 551-0377; e-mail caiv.org@gmail.com; internet www.caiv.org; f. 1966; federation of 5 Jewish orgs; Pres. DAVID BITTAN OBADIA; Exec. Dir JACQUELINE FLUGELMAN.

ISLAM

Mezquita Sheikh Ibrahim bin-Abdulaziz bin-Ibrahim: Calle Real de Quebrada Honda, Los Caobos, Caracas; tel. (212) 577-7382; f. 1994; Leader OMAR KADWA.

BAHÁ'Í FAITH

National Spiritual Assembly of the Bahá'ís: Avda Tuy con Avda Chama, Bello Monte, Caracas 1050; tel. and fax (212) 751-7669; e-mail aenbaven@telcel.net.ve; internet bahai.org.ve; f. 1961; Sec. CARLOS CHIRINOS; mems resident in 954 localities.

The Press

PRINCIPAL DAILIES

Caracas

Diario 2001: Edif. Bloque DeArmas, 2°, final Avda San Martín cruce con Avda La Paz, Caracas; tel. (212) 406-4111; fax (212) 443-4961; e-mail contacto@dearmas.com; internet www.2001.com.ve; f. 1973; Dir LUZ MELY REYES ZAMBRANO; Editor-in-Chief JUAN PÁEZ-PUMAR.

Meridiano: Edif. Bloque DeArmas, final Avda San Martín cruce con Avda La Paz, Caracas 1010; tel. (212) 406-4040; fax (212) 442-5836; e-mail opina@dearmas.com; internet www.meridiano.com.ve; f. 1969; morning; sport; Dir RAMÓN NAVARRO; Editor-in-Chief HUMBERTO GALARZA.

El Mundo: Edif. Cadena Capriles, 2°, Final Avda Rómulo Gallegos con calle 4 de La Urbina, Apdo 1073, Caracas; tel. (212) 240-9911; fax (212) 240-9478; e-mail olugo@cadena-capriles.com; internet www.elmundo.com.ve; f. 1958; morning; ind; economics and business; Pres. RICARDO CASTELLANOS; Dir ERYS ALVARADO.

El Nacional: Avda Principal de Los Cortijos de Lourdes con 3a Transversal, Caracas 1071-A; tel. (212) 203-3243; fax (212) 203-3158; e-mail contactenos@el-nacional.com; internet www.el-nacional.com; f. 1943; morning; right-wing; ind; Pres. and Editor MIGUEL HENRIQUE OTERO.

TalCual: Edif. Menegrande, 5°, Of. 51, Avda Francisco de Miranda, Caracas; tel. (212) 286-7446; fax (212) 232-7446; e-mail tpetkoff@talcualdigital.com; internet www.talcualdigital.com; f. 2000; evening; right-wing; Dir and Editor TEODORO PETKOFF.

Ultimas Noticias: Edif. Torre de la Prensa, 3°, Plaza del Panteón, Parroquia Altagracia, Apdo 1192, Caracas; tel. (212) 596-1911; fax (212) 596-1433; e-mail edrangel@cadena-capriles.com; internet www.ultimasnoticias.com.ve; f. 1941; morning; ind; Dir ELEAZAR DÍAZ RANGEL; Editor-in-Chief ERYS WILFREDO ALVARADO.

El Universal: Edif. El Universal, Avda Urdaneta, esq. de Animas, Apdo 1909, Caracas; tel. (212) 505-2314; fax (212) 505-3710; e-mail consejoeditorial@eluniversal.com; internet www.eluniversal.com; f. 1909; morning; Dir ANDRÉS MATA OSORIO; Chief Editor ELIDES ROJAS.

Vea: Edif. San Martín, Sótano Uno, Parque Central, Caracas 1010; tel. (212) 578-3639; fax (212) 578-3031; e-mail webmaster@diariovea.com.ve; internet www.diariovea.com.ve; f. 2003; morning; left-wing; Dir SERVANDO GARCÍA PONCE; Editor-in-Chief ANGELIO PÉREZ.

Barcelona

El Norte: Avda Intercomunal Jorge Rodríguez, Sector Las Garzas, Grupo UP, entre el Banco Exterior y el BOD, Barcelona; tel. (281) 286-2484; e-mail fmartinez@elnorte.com.ve; internet www.elnorte.com.ve; f. 1989; morning; Exec. Dir FERNANDO MARTÍNEZ; Editor MEURY MANZANO.

Barquisimeto

El Impulso: Edif. El Impulso, Calle Juan Carmona, Urb. El Parque, Apdo 2 y 602, Barquisimeto; tel. (251) 256-1111; fax (251) 256-1129; e-mail reaccion@elimpulso.com; internet www.elimpulso.com; f. 1904; morning; ind; Dir JUAN M. CARMONA P.; Editor-in-Chief JOSÉ A. OCANTO.

El Informador: Edif. El Informador, Carrera 21, esq. Calle 23, Barquisimeto; tel. (251) 231-1811; fax (251) 231-0624; e-mail informatica@elinformador.com.ve; internet www.elinformador.com.ve; f. 1968; morning; Dir-Gen. MAURICIO GÓMEZ SIGALA.

Ciudad Bolívar

El Expreso: Edif. El Expreso, Paseo Gáspari con Calle Democracia, Ciudad Bolívar 8001; tel. and fax (285) 632-3246; e-mail info@diarioelexpreso.com.ve; internet www.diarioelexpreso.com.ve; f. 1969; morning; ind; Dir and Editor LUIS ALBERTO GUZMÁN ALFONZO.

Maracaibo

Panorama: Avda 15, No 95-60, Apdo 425, Maracaibo; tel. (261) 725-6888; fax (261) 725-6911; e-mail panorama@panorama.com.ve; internet www.panorama.com.ve; f. 1914; morning; ind; Pres. PATRICIA PINEDA; Editorial Dir MARÍA INÉS DELGADO.

Maracay

El Aragüeño: Calle 3a Oeste con Avda 1 Oeste, Urb. Ind. San Jacinto, Maracay; tel. (243) 235-9018; fax (243) 235-7866; e-mail diarioelaragueno@gesindoni.com.ve; internet www.elaragueno.com.ve; f. 1972; morning; Pres. GIUSEPPE SINDONI; Editor ROSELYS PEÑA.

El Periodiquito: Calle Páez Este 178, Maracay; tel. (243) 237-7776; fax (243) 233-6987; e-mail redaccion@elperiodiquito.com; internet www.elperiodiquito.com; f. 1986; Dir JORGE ALBORNOZ; Editor RAFAEL RODRÍGUEZ RONDÓN.

El Siglo: Edif. El Siglo, Avda Bolívar Oeste 244, La Romana, Maracay; tel. (243) 554-9265; fax (243) 554-5154; e-mail informaciones@elsiglo.com.ve; internet www.elsiglo.com.ve; f. 1973; morning; ind; Pres. TULIO CAPRILES MENDOZA.

Puerto la Cruz

El Tiempo: Edif. Diario El Tiempo, Avda Municipal 153, Puerto La Cruz; tel. (281) 260-0600; fax (281) 260-0660; e-mail ediaz@eltiempo.com.ve; internet www.eltiempo.com.ve; f. 1958; ind; Dir GIOCONDA DE MÁRQUEZ; Editor EDDER DÍAZ.

San Cristóbal

Diario La Nación: Edif. La Nación, Calle 4 con Carrera 6 bis, La Concordia, Apdo 651, San Cristóbal; tel. (276) 346-4263; fax (276) 346-5051; e-mail lanacion@lanacion.com.ve; internet www.lanacion.com.ve; f. 1968; morning; ind; Editor JOSÉ RAFAEL CORTEZ.

El Tigre

Antorcha: Edif. Antorcha, Avda Francisco de Miranda, El Tigre; tel. (283) 235-2383; fax (283) 235-3923; e-mail webmaster@diarioantorcha.com; internet www.diarioantorcha.com; f. 1954; morning; ind; Pres. and Editor ANTONIO BRICEÑO AMPARÁN.

Valencia

El Carabobeño: Edif. El Carabobeño, Avda Universidad, Urb. La Granja, Naguanagua, Valencia; tel. (241) 867-2918; fax (241) 867-3450; e-mail redaccion@el-carabobeno.com; internet www.el-carabobeno.com; f. 1933; morning; Dir EDUARDO ALEMÁN PÉREZ; Editor-in-Chief CAROLINA GONZÁLEZ.

Notitarde: Avda Boyacá, entre Navas Spínola y Flores, Apdo 1958, Valencia; tel. (241) 850-1666; fax (241) 850-1534; e-mail redaccion@notitarde.com; internet www.notitarde.com; f. 1976; evening; Dir LAURENTZI ODRIOZOLA ECHEGARAY; Editor-in-Chief HUMBERTO TORRES.

SELECTED PERIODICALS

Automóvil de Venezuela: Avda Caurimare, Quinta Expo, Colinas de Bello Monte, Caracas 1050; tel. (212) 751-1355; fax (212) 751-1122; e-mail ortizauto@gmail.com; internet www.automovildevenezuela.com; f. 1961; monthly; automotive trade; Editor MARÍA A. ORTIZ; circ. 6,000.

Business Venezuela: Torre Credival, Avda de Campo Alegre, Apdo 5181, Caracas 1010-A; tel. (212) 263-0833; fax (212) 263-2060; e-mail yrojas@venamcham.org; internet www.bvonline.com.ve; every 2 months; business and economics journal in English; published by the Venezuelan-American Chamber of Commerce and Industry; Dir YUSMERRY ROJAS; Editor-in-Chief CARLOS TEJERA.

ComputerWorld Venezuela: Apdo 76276, Caracas 1071; tel. (212) 976-7423; fax (212) 416-9144; e-mail cwv@computerworld.net.ve; internet www.cwv.com.ve; Dir and Editor CLELIA SANTAMBROGIO.

Dinero: Torre Sur, 1°, Centro Comercial El Recreo, Avda Casanova, Sabana Grande, Caracas 1050; tel. (212) 750-5011; fax (212) 750-5005; e-mail lectores@dinero.com.ve; internet www.dinero.com.ve; monthly; business and finance; Dir SALVATORE LOMONACO.

Nueva Sociedad: Edif. IASA, 6°, Of. 606, Plaza La Castellana, Apdo 61712, Caracas; tel. (212) 265-9975; fax (212) 267-3397; e-mail info@nuso.org; internet www.nuso.org; f. 1972; Latin American affairs; Dir SVENJA BLANKE; Editor PABLO STEFANONI.

Producto: Torre Sur, 8°, Ofs 8-1 y 8-2, Centro Comercial El Recreo, Avda Venezuela, Caracas 1050; tel. (212) 750-5011; fax (212) 750-5005; e-mail mcastillo@producto.com.ve; internet www.producto.com.ve; f. 1983; monthly; business; Editor ERNESTO LOTITTO; circ. 18,000.

Quinto Día: Avda Principal de Los Ruíces con Avda Romúlo Gallegos, Residencia Los Almendros, Nivel Mezzanina, Of. 5, Los Ruíces, Caracas; tel. (212) 237-9809; fax (212) 239-2955; e-mail acarrera@quintodia.com; internet www.quintodia.net; weekly; current affairs; Dir CARLOS CROES.

La Razón: Edif. Valores, Sótano A, Avda Urdaneta, esq. de Urapal, Apdo 16362, La Candelaria, Caracas; tel. (212) 578-3143; fax (212) 578-2397; e-mail larazon@internet.ve; internet www.larazon.net; weekly, Sun.; ind; Dir PABLO LÓPEZ ULACIO.

La Red: Urb. Vista Alegre, Calle 7, Quinta Luisa Amelia, Caracas; tel. (212) 472-0703; fax (212) 471-7749; e-mail info@lared.com.ve; internet www.lared.com.ve; f. 1996; information technology; Editor LUIS MANUEL DÁVILA.

Ronda: Edif. Bloque DeArmas, final Avda San Martín cruce con Avda La Paz, Caracas 1020; tel. (212) 406-4018; fax (212) 406-4158; e-mail jmiranda@dearmas.com; internet www.bloquedearmas.com/ronda; fortnightly; celebrities and entertainment; Dir JENNIFER MIRANDA; Editor-in-Chief MARTHA COTORET.

Sic: Edif. Centro de Valores, esq. de Luneta, Centro Gumilla, Caracas; tel. (212) 564-9803; fax (212) 564-7557; e-mail sic@gumilla.org; internet www.gumilla.org; f. 1938; owned by Compañía de Jesús; monthly; liberal Jesuit publ; Dir WILFREDO GONZÁLEZ.

Tendencia: Torre Tendencia, 5°, Of. 5A, Avda El Milagro 2, Sector Gonzaga, Maracaibo; tel. (261) 743-7674; fax (261) 742-0960; e-mail info@tendencia.com; internet www.tendencia.com; every 2 months; lifestyle; Dir ROSANNA BERNARDONI; Editor ANA BRACHO.

Variedades: Edif. Bloque DeArmas, 6°, final Avda San Martín cruce con Avda La Paz, Caracas 1020; tel. (212) 406-4111; fax (212) 406-4112; e-mail mrodriguez@dearmas.com; internet www.bloquedearmas.com/variedades; f. 1963; monthly; women's interest; Dir LAVINIA MUÑOZ; Editor GABRIELA TORO; circ. 35,000.

VenEconomía: Edif. Gran Sabana, 1°, Avda Abraham Lincoln 174, Blvr de Sabana Grande, Caracas 1050; tel. (212) 761-9121; fax (212) 762-8160; e-mail editor@veneconomia.com; internet www.veneconomia.com; f. 1982; weekly and monthly edns; Spanish and English; business, economic and political issues; Editor ROBERT BOTTOME.

PRESS ASSOCIATIONS

Bloque de Prensa Venezolano (BEV): Edif. El Universal, 5°, Of. C, Avda Urdaneta, Caracas; tel. (212) 561-7704; fax (212) 561-9409; e-mail contacto@bloquedeprensavenezolano.com; asscn of newspaper owners; Pres. Dr DAVID NATERA FEBRES; Sec.-Gen. LUISA CHIOSSONE.

Colegio Nacional de Periodistas (CNP): Casa Nacional del Periodista, 3°, Avda Andrés Bello, Caracas; tel. and fax (212) 781-7601; e-mail colegiodeperiodistasjdn@yahoo.com; internet www.cnpven.org; journalists' asscn; Pres. TINEDO GUÍA; Sec.-Gen. DELVALLE CANELÓN.

Instituto Prensa y Sociedad Venezuela (IPYS): Caracas; tel. (212) 421-2327; e-mail venezuela@ipys.org; internet www.ipys.org.ve; f. 2002; promotes press freedom.

NEWS AGENCY

Agencia Venezolana de Noticias (AVN): Torre Lincoln, 7°, Sabana Grande, Caracas; tel. (212) 572-6543; fax (212) 781-2711; internet www.avn.info.ve; Pres. FREDDY FERNÁNDEZ.

Publishers

Armitano Editores, CA: Edif. Centro Industrial Boleita Sur, 4a Transversal de Boleita, Apdo 50853, Caracas 1070; tel. (212) 234-2565; fax (212) 234-1647; e-mail armiedit@telcel.net.ve; internet www.armitano.com; art, architecture, ecology, botany, anthropology, history, geography; Pres. ERNESTO ARMITANO.

Colegial Bolivariana, CA (Ediciones Co-Bo): Edif. COBO, 1°, Avda Diego Cisneros (Principal), Los Ruices, Apdo 70324, Caracas 1071-A; tel. (212) 239-1433; fax (212) 239-6502; e-mail ventas@co-bo.com; internet www.co-bo.com.ve; f. 1961; general, educational; Dir FABRICIO ACERO.

Ediciones Ekaré: Edif. Banco del Libro, Avda Luis Roche, Altamira Sur, Caracas 1062; tel. (212) 264-7615; fax (212) 263-3291; e-mail editorial@ekare.com.ve; internet www.ekare.com; f. 1978; children's literature; Pres. CARMEN DIANA DEARDEN; Exec. Dir MARÍA FRANCISCA MAYOBRE.

Ediciones IESA: Edif. IESA, 3°, final Avda IESA, San Bernardino, Apdo 1640, Caracas 1010-A; tel. (212) 555-4504; e-mail comunicacionesiesa@iesa.edu.ve; internet www.iesa.edu.ve/publicaciones/ediciones/; f. 1984; economics, business; Pres. FRANCISCO SANÁNEZ.

Ediciones Universitarias Venezolanas, SA (EDUVEN): Edif. Atenev, 1°, Calle Segundaria, Urb. Lebrun, Petare; tel. and fax (212) 256-7237; e-mail eduvensa@cantv.net; internet www.eduven.com

.ve; f. 1989; Pres. JOSÉ ANTONIO NAVARRO GISBERT; Gen. Man. CARMEN TERESA ALDANA D'SANTIAGO.

Editorial Biosfera: Avda Chama, Quinta Coral, Colinas de Bello Monte, Apdo 50634, Caracas 1050; tel. (212) 751-9119; fax (212) 751-9320; e-mail julio@editorialbiosfera.com; internet www.editorialbiosfera.com; f. 1978; academic and cultural; Pres. SERAFIN MAZPARROTE.

Editorial Medica Panamericana: Edif. Polar, Of. 6-C, 6°, Torre Oeste, Plaza, Caracas; tel. (212) 793-2857; fax (212) 793-5885; e-mail info@medicapanamericana.com.ve; internet www.medicapanamericana.com.ve; health and medicine; Gen. Man. MARÍA ROSALES.

Editorial Océano de Venezuela y Ocelibros: Edif. El Candor, Calle 8, entre calles 4 y 5, Zona Industrial La Urbina, Caracas; tel. (212) 242-0508; fax (212) 242-0516; e-mail info@oceano.com.ve; internet www.oceano.com.ve; Dir-Gen. JOSÉ FARRES.

Editorial Romor: Avda El Cortijo, Quinta El León 21, Urb. Los Rosales, Caracas; tel. (212) 633-0933; fax (212) 632-6355; e-mail mercadeo.caracas@editorialromor.com.ve; internet www.editorialromor.com.ve; Gen. Man. CARLOS CASTILLO.

Fundación Biblioteca Ayacucho: Centro Financiero Latino, 12°, Ofs 1, 2 y 3, Avda Urdaneta, Animas a Plaza España, Apdo 14413, Caracas 1010; tel. (212) 561-6691; fax (212) 564-5643; e-mail biblioayacucho@cantv.net; internet www.bibliotecayacucho.gob.ve/fba; f. 1974; indigenous literature; Pres. HUMBERTO MATA; Exec. Dir LUIS EDGAR PÁEZ.

Fundación Editorial Salesiana: Avda Andrés Bello, Paradero a Salesianos 6, La Candelaria, Apdo 369, Caracas; tel. (212) 571-6109; fax (212) 574-9451; e-mail gerenciales@cantv.net; internet www.salesiana.com.ve; f. 1960; education; Pres. LUCIANO STÉFANI; Gen. Man. JAIME GARCÍA.

Magenta Ediciones: Edif. Rupi, 2°, Of. 21, Calle El Recreo con Avda Casanova, El Recreo, Caracas 1050; tel. (212) 762-5420; fax (212) 832-3171; e-mail magenta@magentaediciones.com; internet www.magentaediciones.com; f. 2006; general; Editorial Dir BLANCA STREPPONI.

Monte Avila Editores Latinoamericana, CA: Centro Simón Bolívar, La Torre Norte, 22°, El Silencio, Caracas; tel. (212) 482-2850; fax (212) 482-0472; e-mail editorial@monteavila.gob.ve; internet www.monteavila.gob.ve; f. 1968; general; Pres. CARLOS NOGUERA; Exec. Dir NELCI MARIN.

Vadell Hermanos Editores, CA: Edif. Golden, Avda Sur 15, esq. Peligro a Pele el Ojo, Sótano, La Candelaria, Caracas; tel. (212) 572-3108; fax (212) 572-5243; e-mail edvadell1@gmail.com; internet www.vadellhermanos.com; f. 1973; science, social sciences; Gen. Man. MANUEL VADELL GRATEROL.

PUBLISHERS' ASSOCIATION

Cámara Venezolana del Libro: Centro Andrés Bello, Torre Oeste, 11°, Of. 112-O, Avda Andrés Bello, Caracas 1050-A; tel. (212) 793-1347; fax (212) 793-1368; e-mail direccion_ejecutiva@cavelibro.org; internet www.cavelibro.org; f. 1969; Pres. YOLANDA DE FERNÁNDEZ; Exec. Dir DALILA DA SILVA.

Broadcasting and Communications

TELECOMMUNICATIONS

AT&T Venezuela: Edif. Centro Banaven, Avda La Estancia A, Chuao, Caracas 1060; internet www.att.com.

Compañía Anónima Nacional Teléfonos de Venezuela (CANTV): Edif. NEA, 20, Avda Libertador, Caracas 1010-A; tel. (212) 500-3016; fax (212) 500-3512; e-mail amora@cantv.com.ve; internet www.cantv.com.ve; privatized in 1991; renationalized in 2007; Pres. MANUEL FERNÁNDEZ.

Movilnet: Edif. NEA, 20, Avda Libertador, Caracas 1010-A; tel. (202) 705-7901; e-mail info@movilnet.com.ve; internet www.movilnet.com.ve; f. 1992; mobile cellular telephone operator; owned by CANTV; 6.3m. subscribers (June 2006); Pres. MANUEL FERNÁNDEZ.

Digitel TIM: Caracas; tel. (212) 280-5902; fax (212) 280-5943; e-mail 0412empres@digitel.com.ve; internet www.digitel.com.ve; f. 2000; mobile cellular telephone operator; owned by Telecom Italia, Italy; 2.4m. subscribers (June 2006); Pres. OSWALDO CISNEROS.

Inter: Urb. Chuao, Centro Ciudad Comercial Tamanaco (CCCT), Nivel C2, Caracas; internet www.inter.com.ve; f. 1996 as Intercable; changed name as above in 2007; cable, internet and telecommunications services; CEO EDUARDO STIGOL.

Movistar: Edif. Parque Cristal, Torre Oeste, Avda Francisco Miranda, 14°, Los Palos Grandes, Caracas 1062; tel. (582) 201-8200;

internet www.movistar.com.ve; f. 2005; subsidiary of Telefónica Móviles (Spain); 6.5m. subscribers (June 2006); Pres. PEDRO CORTEZ.

NetUno: Edif. Insenica II, planta baja, Calle 7, La Urbina, Caracas; tel. (212) 710-0404; e-mail atccaracas@netuno.net; internet www .netuno.net; f. 1995; voice, data and video transmission services; Pres. GILBERT MINIONIS.

Telecom Venezuela: Torre Fondo Común, 5°, Avda Andrés Bello, Caracas; tel. (212) 393-2931; e-mail eauverana@cvgtelecom.com.ve; internet www.telecom.gob.ve; f. 2004 as CVG Telecomunicaciones, CA; present name adopted Aug. 2007; state-owned telecommunications co; Pres. KAI CHEN; Man. EVELYN RANGEL.

Telecomunicaciones Gran Caribe: Caracas; f. 2007; owned by Telecom Venezuela (60%) and Transbit of Cuba (40%); construction and operation of 1,550 km fibre-optic cable connecting La Guaira (Venezuela) and Siboney (Cuba); Pres. WILFREDO MORALES.

Regulatory Authority

Comisión Nacional de Telecomunicaciones (CONATEL): Avda Veracruz con Cali, Edif. Conatel, 6°, Las Mercedes, Municipio Baruta, Caracas 1060; tel. (212) 909-0493; fax (212) 993-6122; e-mail conatel@conatel.gob.ve; internet www.conatel.gob.ve; regulatory body for telecommunications; Dir-Gen. PEDRO ROLANDO MALDONADO MARÍN.

BROADCASTING

Radio

Radio Nacional de Venezuela (RNV): Final Calle Las Marías, entre Chapellín y Country Club, La Florida, Caracas 1050; tel. (212) 730-6022; fax (212) 731-1457; e-mail infornv@rnv.gob.ve; internet www.rnv.gov.ve; f. 1936; state broadcasting org.; 15 stations; Pres. DESIRÉ SANTOS AMARAL.

Television

Government Stations

Telesur (Televisora del Sur): Edif. Telesur, Calle Vargas con Calle Santa Clara, Urb. Boleíta Norte, Caracas; tel. (212) 600-0202; e-mail contactenos@telesurtv.net; internet www.telesurtv.net; f. 2005; jtly owned by Govts of Venezuela (51%), Argentina (20%), Cuba (19%) and Uruguay (10%); regional current affairs and general interest; Pres. Lt (retd) ANDRÉS IZARRA; Vice-Pres. ARAM AHARONIAN.

Televisora Venezolana Social—Canal 2 (TVes): Quinta Thaizza, Avda Principal Augusto César Sandino con 10a Transversal, Maripérez, Municipio Libertador, Caracas; tel. (212) 781-8069; e-mail info@tves.com.ve; internet tvestv.blogspot.com; f. May 2007 to replace private channel RCTV (q.v.); govt-owned; Pres. LIL RODRÍGUEZ.

Venezolana de Televisión (VTV)—Canal 8: Edif. VTV, Avda Principal Los Ruices, Caracas; tel. (212) 207-1220; fax (212) 239-8102; e-mail web@vtv.gob.ve; internet www.vtv.gob.ve; f. 1964; 26 relay stations; Vice-Pres. VANESSA DAVIES.

ViVe TV (Visión Venezuela): Edif. Biblioteca Nacional, AP-4, final Avda Panteón, Foro Libertador, Altagracia, Caracas; tel. (212) 505-1611; e-mail webmaster@vive.gob.ve; internet www.vive.gob.ve; f. 2003; govt-run cultural channel; Pres. RICARDO MÁRQUEZ.

Private Stations

Corporación Venezolana de Televisión (Venevisión)—Canal 4: Edif. Venevisión, final Avda La Salle, Colinas de los Caobos, Apdo 6674, Caracas; tel. (212) 708-9224; fax (212) 708-9535; e-mail mponce@venevision.com.ve; internet www.venevision.net; f. 1961; privately owned; Pres. GUSTAVO CISNEROS.

Globovisión—Canal 33: Quinta Globovisión, Avda Los Pinos, Urb. Alta Florida, Caracas; tel. (212) 730-2290; fax (212) 731-4380; e-mail info@globovision.com; internet www.globovision.com; f. 1994; 24-hour news and current affairs channel; Pres. GUILLERMO ZULOAGA; Dir-Gen. (vacant).

Meridiano Televisión: Caracas; e-mail opina@dearmas.com; internet www.meridiano.com.ve; f. 1997; sports programming; Pres. MARTÍN DE ARMAS; Dir-Gen. JUAN ANDRÉS DAZA.

Radio Caracas Televisión (RCTV): Edif. RCTV, Dolores a Puente Soublette, Quinta Crespo, Caracas; tel. (212) 401-2222; fax (212) 401-2647; e-mail marriaga@rctv.net; internet www.rctv.net; f. 1953; fmrly broadcast on terrestrial channel as Radio Caracas Televisión—Canal 2; ceased broadcasting in May 2007; subsidiary RCTV International (based in Miami, FL, USA) recommenced broadcasting in Venezuela via cable in July 2007; Pres. MARCEL GRANIER.

Televén—Canal 10 (Televisión de Venezuela): Edif. Televén, 4a Transversal con Avda Rómulo Gallegos, Urb. Horizonte, Apdo 1070, Caracas; tel. (212) 280-0011; fax (212) 280-0204; e-mail aferro@televen.com; internet www.televen.com; f. 1988; privately owned; Pres. OMAR CAMERO ZAMORA.

Televisora Andina de Mérida (TAM)—Canal 6: Edif. Imperador, Entrada Independiente, Avda 6 y 7, Calle 23, Mérida 5101; tel. and fax (274) 251-0660; f. 1982; regional channel; Pres. Most Rev. BALTAZAR ENRIQUE PORRAS CARDOZO.

VALE TV (Valores Educativos Televisión)—Canal 5: Quinta VALE TV, final Avda La Salle, Colinas de los Caobos, Caracas 1050; tel. (212) 793-9215; fax (212) 708-9743; e-mail info@valetv.com; internet www.valetv.com; f. 1998; Pres. JORGE CARDENAL L. UROSA SAVINO.

Zuliana de Televisión—Canal 30: Edif. 95.5 América, Avda 11 (Veritas), Maracaibo; tel. (265) 641-0355; fax (265) 641-0565; e-mail elregionalredac@iamnet.com; Pres. GILBERTO URDANETA FIDOL.

Zuvisión: Maracaibo; f. 2007; regional channel for the state of Zulia; Pres. RAFAEL URDANETA.

Regulatory Authorities

Cámara Venezolana de la Industria de Radiodifusión: Avda Antonio José Istúriz Transversal 3, Urb. La Castellana, Caracas 1060; tel. (212) 261-1651; fax (212) 261-4783; e-mail camradio@camradio.org.ve; internet www.camradio.org; Pres. ENZA CARBONE; Exec. Dir JESÚS R. SARCOS.

Cámara Venezolana de Televisión por Suscripción: Edif. Banco Venezolano de Crédito, Avda Londres con Avda Principal de Las Mercedes, Caracas; tel. and fax (212) 993-7553; e-mail cavetesu@gmail.com; internet www.cavetesu.org.ve; f. 1995; regulatory body for private stations; Pres. ALEXANDER ELORRIAGA.

Finance

(cap. = capital; res = reserves; dep. = deposits; m. = million; brs = branches; amounts in bolívares fuertes unless otherwise indicated)

BANKING

Regulatory Authority

Superintendencia de las Instituciones del Sector Bancario (SUDEBAN): Edif. Centro Empresarial Parque del Este, Avda Francisco de Miranda, Urb. La Carlota, Municipio Sucre del Estado Miranda, Apdo 6761, Caracas; tel. (212) 280-6933; fax (212) 238-2516; e-mail sudeban@sudeban.gob.ve; internet www.sudeban.gob .ve; regulates banking sector; Supt MARY ESPINOZA DE ROBLES.

Central Bank

Banco Central de Venezuela: Avda Urdaneta, esq. de Carmelitas, Caracas 1010; tel. (212) 801-5111; fax (212) 861-0048; e-mail info@bcv.org.ve; internet www.bcv.org.ve; f. 1940; bank of issue and clearing house for commercial banks; granted autonomy 1992; controls international reserves, interest rates and exchange rates; res 18,892.0m., dep. 83,303.7m. (Dec. 2009); Pres. and Chair. NELSON JOSÉ MERENTES DÍAZ; 2 brs.

Commercial Banks

Banco del Caribe, CA: Centro Empresarial Galipán, Torre A, Avda Francisco de Miranda, Chacao, Caracas 1060; tel. (212) 505-5103; fax (212) 562-0460; e-mail producto@bancaribe.com.ve; internet www .bancaribe.com.ve; f. 1954; cap. 281m., res 1,410.2m., dep. 66,492.2m. (Dec. 2013); Pres. ARTURO GANTEAUME; Exec. Pres. JUAN CARLOS DAO; 109 brs.

Banco Caroní: Edif. Multicentro Banco Caroní, Vía Venezuela, Puerto Ordaz, Estado Bolívar; tel. (286) 920-5456; fax (286) 920-0995; e-mail contactenos.caroni@bancocaroni.com.ve; internet www .bancocaroni.com.ve; cap. 526.8m., res 441.3m., dep. 8,803.2m. (Dec. 2011); Pres. ARÍSTIDES MAZA TIRADO.

Banco Exterior, CA—Banco Universal: Edif. Banco Exterior, 1°, Avda Urdaneta, esq. Urapal a Río, Candelaria, Apdo 14278, Caracas 1011-A; tel. (212) 501-0211; fax (212) 501-0745; e-mail lperez@bancoexterior.com; internet www.bancoexterior.com; f. 1958; cap. 223.3m., res 636m., dep. 35,980.1m. (Dec. 2012); Chair. LUIS ENRIQUE FRANCESCHI; Exec. Pres. RAÚL BALTAR ESTÉVEZ; 101 brs.

Banco Guayana, CA: Edif. Los Bancos, Avda Guayana con Calle Caura, Puerto Ordaz, Bolívar; e-mail bguayana06@cantv.net; f. 1955; state-owned; cap. 158m., res 27.5m., dep. 2,476m. (Dec. 2011); Pres. OSCAR EUSEBIO JIMÉNEZ AYESA; Exec. Pres. BERNARDO KABCHE.

Banco Industrial de Venezuela, CA: Torre Financiera BIV, Avda Las Delicias de Sabana Grande, cruce con Avda Francisco Solano López, Caracas 1010; tel. (212) 952-4051; fax (212) 952-6282; e-mail webmaster@biv.com.ve; internet www.biv.com.ve; f. 1937; 98% state-owned; took over Banco de Inversión Industrial de Venezuela in Sept. 2011; cap. 9,840m., res 278,645m., dep. 8,600,674m. (Dec. 2006); Pres. RODOLFO PORRO ALETTI; 60 brs.

Banco Occidental de Descuento Banco Universal, CA: Calle 77, esq. Avda 17, Maracaibo 4001, Apdo 695, Zulia; tel. (261) 759-3011; fax (261) 750-2274; e-mail atclient@bodinternet.com; internet www.bod.com.ve; f. 1957; transferred to private ownership in 1991; took over Corp Banca in 2013; cap. 629.7m., res 381.3m., dep. 15,233.8m. (Dec. 2010); Pres. VÍCTOR J. VARGAS IRAUSQUIN; Exec. Pres. TOMÁS NIEMBRO CONCHA; 17 brs.

Banco de Venezuela, SA: Torre Banco de Venezuela, 18°, Avda Universidad, esq. Sociedad a Traposos, Apdo 6268, Caracas 1010-A; tel. (212) 501-3333; fax (212) 501-2570; e-mail bancodevenezuela@banvenez.com; internet www.bancodevenezuela.com; f. 1890; nationalized in July 2009; cap. 364.7m., res 1,361m., dep. 47,861.6m. (Dec. 2010); Pres. RODOLFO C. MARCO TORRES; 422 brs.

Banesco Banco Universal, CA: Edif. Banesco, 4°, Avda Guaicaipura con Avda Principal de Las Mercedes, Caracas; tel. (212) 501-7111; fax (212) 952-7124; e-mail atclient@banesco.com; internet www.banesco.com; cap. 1,250m., res 1,916.3m., dep. 198,990.2m. (Dec. 2013); Chair. JUAN CARLOS ESCOTET RODRÍGUEZ; Exec. Pres. MIGUEL ANGEL MARCANO CARTEA; 466 brs.

BBVA Banco Provincial, SA: Centro Financiero Provincial, 27°, Avda Vollmer con Avda Este O, San Bernadino, Apdo 1269, Caracas 1011; tel. (212) 504-5098; fax (212) 574-9408; e-mail calidad@provincial.com; internet www.provincial.com; f. 1952; 55.14% owned by Banco Bilbao Vizcaya Argentaria, 26.27% owned by Grupo Polar; cap. 1,078.3m., res 3,163.9m., dep. 168,159.5m. (Dec. 2013); Chair. LEÓN HENRIQUE COTTIN; Exec. Pres. PEDRO RODRÍGUEZ SERRANO.

Bicentenario Banco Universal: Edif. Banco Bicentenario, Avda Venezuela, El Rosal, Chacao, Miranda; tel. (212) 958-5113; fax (212) 901-6920; e-mail irene.mora@bicentenariobu.com; internet www.bicentenariobu.com; f. 2009 by merger of Banco Bolívar, Banco Confederado, Banfoandes and Banco Central; BaNorte incorporated in 2010; state-owned; Pres. DARÍO ENRIQUE BAUTE DELGADO; 455 brs.

Mercantil CA Banco Universal: Edif. Mercantil, 35°, Avda Andrés Bello 1, San Bernardino, Apdo 789, Caracas 1010-A; tel. (212) 503-1111; fax (212) 503-1075; e-mail mercan24@bancomercantil.com; internet www.bancomercantil.com; f. 1925; cap. 6,093.2m., res 4,112.7m., dep. 91,519m. (Dec. 2012); Pres. Dr GUSTAVO J. VOLLMER; 273 brs.

Venezolano de Crédito, SA—Banco Universal: Edif. Banco Venezolano de Crédito, Avda Alameda, San Bernadino, Caracas 1011; tel. (212) 806-6111; fax (212) 550-2173; e-mail info@venezolano.com; internet www.venezolano.com; f. 1925 as Banco Venezolano de Crédito, SACA; name changed as above in 2001; cap. 330.6m., res 429.7m., dep. 17,716.4m. (Dec. 2013); Pres. Dr OSCAR GARCÍA MENDOZA; 95 brs in Venezuela and abroad.

Development Banks

Banco Agrícola de Venezuela (BAV): Edif. Cavendes, 17°, Avda Francisco de Miranda, Los Palos Grandes, Caracas; tel. (212) 208-8788; internet www.bav.com.ve; state-run agricultural devt bank; Pres. YVÁN GIL.

Banco de Comercio Exterior (Bancoex): Central Gerencial Mohedano, 1°, Calle Los Chaguaramos, La Castellana, Caracas 1060; tel. (212) 277-4611; fax (212) 265-6533; e-mail exporte@bancoex.gob.ve; internet www.bancoex.gob.ve; f. 1997 principally to promote non-traditional exports; state-owned; cap. 825.4m., res 206.7m. (Dec. 2010); Pres. RAMÓN ANTONIO GORDILS MONTES.

Banco de Desarrollo Económico y Social de Venezuela (BANDES): Torre Bandes, Avda Universidad, Traposos a Colón, Caracas 1010; tel. (212) 505-8010; fax (212) 505-8126; e-mail apublicos@bandes.gov.ve; internet www.bandes.gov.ve; state-owned; Pres. GUSTAVO HERNÁNDEZ JIMÉNEZ.

Banco del Pueblo Soberano, CA: Edif. El Gallo de Oro, Gradillas a San Jacinto Parroquia Catedral, Caracas; tel. (212) 505-2800; fax (212) 505-2995; e-mail abarrera@bancodelpueblo.gob.ve; internet www.bancodelpueblo.gob.ve; f. 1999; microfinance; Pres. RICARDO FONG.

Banco del Sur: Edif. Bancaracas, 6°, Chacao, Caracas; e-mail atencionalcliente@delsur.com.ve; internet www.delsur.com.ve; f. 2007 by Govts of Argentina, Bolivia, Brazil, Ecuador, Paraguay, Uruguay and Venezuela; regional devt bank; brs in Buenos Aires (Argentina) and La Paz (Bolivia); cap. 116.4m., res 34.9m., dep. 1,619.4m. (Dec. 2009); Pres. CÉSAR NAVARRETE.

Fondo de Desarrollo Microfinanciero (FONDEMI): Edif. Sudameris, 2°, Avda Urdaneta con Fuerzas Armadas, esq. Plaza España, Caracas 1030; tel. (212) 287-7611; fax (212) 287-7658; e-mail fondemi@fondemi.gob.ve; internet www.fondemi.gob.ve; f. 2001; microfinancing devt fund; Pres. WILLY CASANOVA; Gen. Man. DANY MACAYO.

Banking Association

Asociación Bancaria de Venezuela: Torre Asociación Bancaria de Venezuela, 1°, Avda Venezuela, El Rosal, Caracas; tel. (212) 951-4711; fax (212) 951-2534; e-mail abvinfo@asobanca.com.ve; internet www.asobanca.com.ve; f. 1959; 49 mems; Pres. ARÍSTIDES MAZA TIRADO; Dir JORGE NOGUEROLES.

STOCK EXCHANGE

Bolsa de Valores de Caracas, CA: Edif. Atrium, Nivel C-1, Calle Sorocaima entre Avdas Tamanaco y Venezuela, Urb. El Rosal, Apdo 62724-A, Caracas 1060-A; tel. (212) 905-5511; fax (212) 952-2640; e-mail bvc@bolsadecaracas.com; internet www.bolsadecaracas.com; f. 1947; 63 mems; Pres. MANUEL ALONSO REBAREDA; Gen. Man. JUAN CARLOS DA SILVA.

INSURANCE

Supervisory Board

Superintendencia de Seguros: Edif. Torre del Desarrollo, P. H., Avda Venezuela, El Rosal, Chacao, Caracas 1060; tel. (212) 905-1611; fax (212) 953-8615; e-mail sudeseg@sudeseg.gob.ve; internet www.sudeseg.gob.ve; Supt YOSMER ARELLÁN ZURITA.

Principal Insurance Companies

Adriática, CA de Seguros: Edif. Adriática de Seguros, Avda Andrés Bello, esq. de Salesianos, Caracas; tel. (212) 571-5702; fax (212) 508-0770; e-mail adriatica@adriatica.com.ve; internet www.adriatica.com.ve; f. 1952; Pres. BARTOLOMÉ RUGGIERO IMBRIACO.

Avila, CA de Seguros: Edif. Torre Británica de Seguros, P. H., Avda José Felix Sosa, Urb. El Dorado, Altamira, Chacao, Caracas; tel. (212) 610-1600; fax (212) 239-9743; internet www.segurosavila.com; f. 1936; Pres. RAMÓN RODRÍGUEZ; Gen. Man. WILLIAM CARRILLO.

Bolivariana de Seguros: Torre La Previsora, Ala Norte, 15°, Avda Abraham Lincoln, Caracas; tel. (212) 339-4647; e-mail atencionalcliente@bsr.gob.ve; internet www.bsr.gob.ve; f. 2010; state-owned; Pres. OMAR ARIAS ZURITA.

Carabobo, CA de Seguros: Edif. Mene Grande, 7°, Avda Francisco de Miranda, Urb. Los Palos Grandes, Caracas; tel. (212) 286-9229; fax (212) 620-7320; e-mail info@seguroscarabobo.com; internet www.seguroscarabobo.com; f. 1955; Chair. JESÚS QUINTERO YAMÍN; CEO MANUEL RODRÍGUEZ COSTA.

Mapfre La Seguridad, CA de Seguros: Calle 3A, frente a La Torre Express, La Urbina Sur, Apdo 473, Caracas 1010; tel. (212) 213-8000; fax (212) 204-8751; e-mail tucontactomapfre@mapfre.com.ve; internet www.mapfre.com.ve; f. 1943; owned by Seguros Mapfre (Spain); Pres. MIGUEL MARÍA MUÑOZ MEDINA.

La Occidental, CA de Seguros: Edif. Seguros Occidental, Avda 4 (Bella Vista) esq. con Calle 71, No 10126, Maracaibo, Zulia; tel. (261) 200-2222; fax (261) 200-2292; e-mail clientes@laoccidental.com; internet www.laoccidental.com; f. 1956; Pres. JOSÉ OMAR GUEVARA; Dir CARLOS SILVA ALCALÁ.

La Oriental, CA de Seguros: Torre Oriental de Seguros, Avda Venezuela, entre Calle Sojo y Avda Sorocaima, Urb. El Rosal, Chacao, Caracas 1060; tel. (212) 905-9999; fax (212) 905-9652; internet www.laoriental.com; f. 1975; Chair. GONZALO LAURÍA ALCALÁ.

Seguros Los Andes, CA: Avda Ernesto Blonh, Centro Comercial Ciudad Tamanaco, Chacao, Caracas; tel. (212) 211-5060; fax (212) 211-5064; internet www.seguroslosandes.com; Pres. NICOLÁS MANGIERI.

Seguros Caracas de Liberty Mutual, CAV: Torre Seguros Caracas C-4, Centro Comercial El Parque, Avda Francisco de Miranda, Los Palos Grandes, Caracas; tel. (212) 209-9111; fax (212) 209-9556; e-mail informatica@seguroscaracas.com; internet www.seguroscaracas.com; f. 1943; Pres. GUSTAVO LUENGO DECARLI.

Seguros Catatumbo, CA: Edif. Seguros Catatumbo, Avda 4 (Bella Vista), No 77–55, Apdo 1083, Maracaibo; tel. (261) 700-5555; fax (261) 216-0037; e-mail mercado@seguroscatatumbo.com; internet www.seguroscatatumbo.com; f. 1957; cap. 9,300m. (2003); Pres. ERNESTO PINEDA HERNÁNDEZ; Dir-Gen. RAFAEL ARRAGA HUERTA.

Seguros Constitución: Torre Constitución, Avda Venezuela, entre Avda Lazo Martí y Calle Mohedano, El Rosal, Caracas; tel. (212) 957-9800; internet www.segurosconstitucion.com; Pres. OMAR JESÚS FARÍAS LUCES.

Seguros Horizante: Avda Francisco de Miranda, Torre la Primera, Chacao, Miranda; tel. (212) 750-9080; e-mail marian.guevara@seguroshorizonte.com; internet www.seguroshorizonte.gob.ve; f. 1956; Pres. JIMMY LENÍN GUZMÁN PINTO.

Seguros Mercantil, CA: Edif. Seguros Mercantil, Avda Libertador con calle Andrés Galarraga, Chacao, Caracas; tel. (212) 276-2000; fax (212) 276-2001; e-mail cat@segurosmercantil.com; internet www.segurosmercantil.com; f. 1988; acquired Seguros Orinoco in 2002; Pres. ALBERTO BENSHIMOL; CEO MARÍA SILVIA RODRÍGUEZ FEO.

Seguros Nuevo Mundo, SA: Torre Nuevo Mundo, Avda Luis Roche con 3a Transversal, Urb. Altamira, Apdo 2062, Caracas; tel. (212

201-1111; fax (212) 201-1428; e-mail jesus.heredia@nuevomundo .com.ve; internet www.nuevomundo.com.ve; f. 1856; cap. 100m. (2003); Pres. RAFAEL PEÑA ALVAREZ.

Seguros La Previsora, CNA: Torre La Previsora, Avda Abraham Lincoln, Sábana Grande, Caracas; tel. (212) 709-1555; fax (212) 709-1976; internet www.previsora.com; f. 1914; nationalized in 2009; Pres. LUIS RODRÍGUEZ GUEVARA.

Seguros Venezuela, CA: Edif. Seguros Venezuela, 8° y 9°, Avda Francisco de Miranda, Urb. Campo Alegre, Caracas; tel. (212) 901-7111; fax (212) 901-7400; e-mail servicio@segurosvenezuela .com; internet www.segurosvenezuela.com; f. 1948; part of American International group; Exec. Pres. ENRIQUE BANCHIERI ORTIZ; Gen. Man. ENZO D'ANGELO.

Universitas de Seguros, CA: Edif. Centro Empresarial El Rosal, 9–10°, Avda Tamanaco del Rosal, Caracas; tel. (212) 655-6100; fax (212) 901-7506; e-mail tbarrera@universitasdeseguros.com; internet www.segurosuniversitas.com; cap. 6,500m; Man. MARISELA GUEDEZ.

Insurance Association

Cámara de Aseguradores de Venezuela: Torre Taeca, 2°, Avda Guaicaipuro, Urb. El Rosal, Apdo 3460, Caracas 1010-A; tel. (212) 952-4411; fax (212) 951-3268; e-mail rrpp@camaraseg.org; internet www.camaraseg.org; f. 1951; 42 mems; Pres. OMAR GUEVARA; Exec. Pres. ALESIA RODRÍGUEZ PARDO.

Trade and Industry

GOVERNMENT AGENCIES

Corporación Venezolana de Guayana (CVG): Edif. General, 2°, Avda La Estancia, Apdo 7000, Chuao, Caracas; tel. (212) 992-1813; fax (212) 993-4306; e-mail presidenciaccs@cvg.com; internet www .cvg.com; f. 1960 to organize devt of Guayana area, particularly its metal ore and hydroelectric resources; 15 subsidiaries; 18,000 employees.

Instituto Nacional de Tierras (INTI): Quinta La Barranca, Calle San Carlos, Urb. Vista Alegre, Caracas; tel. (212) 471-0222; fax (212) 576-2201; internet www.inti.gob.ve; f. 1945 as Instituto Agrario Nacional; present name adopted in 2001; authorized to expropriate and redistribute idle or unproductive lands; Pres. JUAN CARLOS LOYO.

Instituto Nacional de la Vivienda: Torre Inavi, Avda Francisco de Miranda, Chacao, Caracas; tel. (212) 206-9279; e-mail comunica@ inavi.gov.ve; internet www.inavi.gob.ve; f. 1928 as Instituto Autónomo Banco Obrero, adopted current name in 1975; administers govt housing projects; part of the Ministry of Housing and Habitat; Pres. NELSON RODRÍGUEZ.

DEVELOPMENT ORGANIZATIONS

Fonden (Fondo de Desarrollo Nacional): Edif. Sede Ministerio del Poder Popular para las Finanzas, 1°, Avda Urdaneta, Esq. de Carmelitas, Caracas; tel. (212) 802-1213; e-mail fondensa@mppf .gob.ve; internet www.fonden.gob.ve; f. 2005; govt investment agency; Pres. Minister of Finance ; Exec. Sec. CLAUDIA DÍAZ GUILLÉN.

FONDAS (Fondo para el Desarrollo Agrario Socialista): Edif. FONDAFA, Avda Fuerzas Armadas, esq. Salvador de León a Socarras, La Hoyada, Caracas; tel. (212) 543-2066; internet www.fondas.gob.ve; f. 1974; devt of agriculture, fishing and forestry; Pres. RICARDO JAVIER SÁNCHEZ NIÑO.

Instituto de Desarrollo de la Pequeña y Mediana Industria (INAPYMI): Torre Británica, 14°, 15°, 16° y planta baja, Avda José Felix Sosa, Altamira Sur, Caracas; tel. (212) 276-9511; e-mail zcarrillo@inapymi.gob.ve; internet www.inapymi.gob.ve; f. 2001; govt agency; promotes the devt of small and medium-sized industries; Pres. RAFAEL ERNESTO CONTRERAS.

CHAMBERS OF COMMERCE AND INDUSTRY

Consejo Nacional del Comercio y los Servicios (CONSECO-MERCIO): Edif. Polar Torre Este, 8°, Ofs 8A y 8B, Avda Lima con Paseo Colón, Sector Plaza Venezuela, Caracas; tel. (212) 576-9254; fax (212) 571-1021; e-mail info@consecomercio.org; internet conscomercio.org.ve; f. 1971; non-profit org. fostering devt of the trade and services sector; Pres. MAURICIO TANCREDI PLAZA.

Federación de Artesanos, Micros, Pequeños y Medianos Industriales y Empresarios de Venezuela (Fedeindustria): Edif. Catuche, Of. 20M-09 y 20M-10, Avda Lecuna, Parque Central, Caracas; tel. (212) 574-5113; e-mail atencionalafiloado@ fedeindustria.org; internet www.fedeindustria.org; Pres. MIGUEL PÉREZ ABAD.

Federación Venezolana de Cámaras y Asociaciones de Comercio y Producción (Fedecámaras): Edif. Fedecámaras, Avda El Empalme, Urb. El Bosque, Apdo 2568, Caracas; tel. (212) 731-1711; fax (212) 730-2097; e-mail presidencia@fedecamaras.org

.ve; internet www.fedecamaras.org.ve; f. 1944; 307 mems; Pres. JORGE ROIG.

Cámara de Comercio, Industria y Servicios de Caracas: Edif. Cámara de Comercio de Caracas, 8°, Avda Andrés Eloy Blanco 215, Los Caobos, Caracas; tel. (212) 571-3222; fax (212) 571-0050; e-mail servicios@lacamaradecaracas.org.ve; internet www .lacamaradecaracas.org.ve; f. 1893; 650 mems; Pres. FERNANDO ESEVERRI; Exec. Dir VÍCTOR MALDONADO.

Cámara Venezolano-Americana de Industria y Comercio (Venamcham): Torre Credival, 10°, Of. A, 2a Avda Campo Alegre, Apdo 5181, Caracas 1010-A; tel. (212) 263-0833; fax (212) 266-3437; e-mail venam@venamcham.org; internet www.venamcham.org; f. 1950; Gen. Man. CARLOS TEJERA.

EMPLOYERS' ORGANIZATIONS

Asociación Nacional de Cultivadores Agrícolas (ANCA) (National Agricultural Growers' Association): Edif. Anca, 1°, Of. 1, Avda Los Pioneros, Sector San Vicente, Areure, Portuguesa; tel. (255) 600-1800; fax (255) 621-4368; e-mail anca@asoanca.com; f. 1945.

Asociación Nacional de Industriales Metalúrgicos y de Minería de Venezuela (AIMM): Centro Empresarial Senderos, 3°, Ofs 302 y 303A, Avda Principal Los Cortijos de Lourdes, 2a Transversal, Sucre, Caracas 1071; tel. and fax (212) 237-5169; e-mail aimmv@cantv.net; internet www.aimm-ven.org; metallurgy and mining; Pres. JORGE ROIG; Exec. Dir MARÍA GRACIELA FERREIRA.

Asociación Venezolana de Exportadores (AVEX): Centro Comercial Concresa, Of. 435, 2°, Avda Río Caura, Prados del Este, Baruta, Caracas; tel. (212) 979-0824; fax (212) 979-4542; e-mail asistentedepresidencia@avex.com.ve; internet www.avex.com.ve; Pres. RAMÓN GOYO U.; Gen. Man. MARÍA ISABEL SÁEZ.

Cámara Petrolera de Venezuela: Torre Domus, 3°, Of. 3A, Avda Abraham Lincoln con Calle Olimpo, Sábana Grande, Caracas; tel. (212) 794-1222; fax (212) 794-0068; e-mail informacion.web@ camarapetrolera.org; internet www.camarapetrolera.org; f. 1978; asscn of petroleum sector cos; Pres. ALBERTO HELD.

Confederación de Asociaciones de Productores Agropecuarios (FEDEAGRO): Edif. Casa de Italia, Planta Baja, Avda La Industria, San Bernardino, Caracas 1010; tel. (212) 571-4035; fax (212) 573-4423; e-mail fedeagro@fedeagro.org; internet www .fedeagro.org; f. 1960; agricultural producers; 133 affiliated asscns; Pres. ANTONIO PESTANO; Exec. Dir PEDRO VICENTE PÉREZ.

Confederación Venezolana de Industriales (CONINDUS-TRIA): Edif. CIEMI, Avda Principal de Chuao, Caracas 1061; tel. (212) 991-2116; fax (212) 991-7737; e-mail conindustria@ conindustria.org; internet www.conindustria.org; asscn of industrialists; Pres. EDUARDO GARMENDIA.

Federación Nacional de Ganaderos de Venezuela (FEDE-NAGA): Avda Urdaneta, Centro Financiero Latino, 18°, Ofs 18-2 y 18-4, La Candelaria, Caracas; tel. (212) 563-2153; fax (212) 564-7273; e-mail fedenagat@cantv.net; internet www.fedenaga.org; f. 1962; cattle owners; Pres. RUBÉN DARÍO BARBOSA.

STATE HYDROCARBONS COMPANIES

PDVSA Petróleo SA: Edif. Petróleos de Venezuela, Torre Este, Avda Libertador, La Campiña, Apdo 169, Caracas 1010-A; tel. (212) 708-4743; fax (212) 708-4661; e-mail saladeprensa@pdvsa.com; internet www.pdvsa.com; f. 1975; responsible for petrochemical sector since 1978 and for devt of coal resources in western Venezuela since 1985; in 1997 the 3 operating brs (Lagoven, SA, Maraven, SA and Corpoven, SA) were reintegrated to form PDVSA Petróleo y Gas; in 2001 gas-related activity passed to PDVSA Gas; state-owned; Pres. EULOGIO DEL PINO; the following are subsidiaries of PDVSA:

Bariven, SA: Edif. PDVSA Los Chaguaramos, 6°, Avda Leonardo Da Vinci, Urb. Los Chaguaramos, Apdo 1889, Caracas 1010-A; tel. (212) 606-4060; fax (212) 606-2741; handles the petroleum, petrochemical and hydrocarbons industries' overseas purchases of equipment and materials.

Corporación Venezolana del Petróleo (CVP): Edif. Pawa, Calle Cali con Avda Veracruz, Las Mercedes, Caracas; f. 1960, reformed 2003; responsible for PDVSA's negotiations with other petroleum cos.

Deltaven, SA: Edif. PDVSA Deltaven, Avda Principal de La Floresta, La Floresta, Caracas 1060; tel. (212) 208-1111; f. 1997; markets PDVSA products and services within Venezuela.

Intevep, SA: Centro de Investigación y Apoyo Tecnológico, Edif. Sede Central, Urb. Santa Rosa, Sector El Tambor, Los Teques, Apdo 76343, Caracas 1070-A; tel. (212) 330-6011; fax (212) 330-6448; f. 1973 as Fundación para la Investigación de Hidrocarburos y Petroquímica; present name adopted in 1979; research and devt br. of PDVSA.

Palmaven: Avda Principal de la Urbina, Torre Olimpia, 7°, Caracas; tel. (212) 204-4511; sustainable devt agency of PDVSA.

PDV Marina: Edif. Petróleos de Venezuela Refinación, Suminstro y Comercio, Torre Oeste, 9°, Avda Libertador, La Campiña, Apdo 2103, Caracas 1010-A; tel. (212) 708-1111; fax (212) 708-2200; f. 1990; responsible for the distribution, by ship, of PDVSA products.

PDVSA Gas: Edif. Sucre, Avda Francisco de Miranda, La Floresta, Caracas; tel. (212) 208-6212; fax (212) 208-6288; e-mail messina@pdvsa.com; f. 1998; gas exploration and extraction.

Pequiven (Corporación Petroquímica de Venezuela, SA—CPV): Zona Industrial Municipal Sur, Avda 73, con Calle 79B, Valencia, Carabobo; tel. (241) 839-4859; e-mail deinterespequiven@pequiven .com; internet www.pequiven.com; f. 1955 as Instituto Venezolano de Petroquímica; became Pequiven, part of PDVSA, in 1977, then restructured as above in 2005 and independent of PDVSA; part of Ministry of Energy and Petroleum; involved in many jt ventures with foreign and private Venezuelan interests for expanding petrochemical industry; Pres. SAÚL AMELIACH.

MAJOR COMPANIES

Metals and Mining

CVG Aluminio del Caroní, SA (ALCASA): Avda Fuerzas Armadas, Zona Industrial Matanzas, Apdo 115, Ciudad Guayana, Bolívar; tel. (286) 980-1567; fax (286) 980-1891; internet www.alcasa .com.ve; f. 1960; state-owned mfr of aluminium products; Pres. ANGEL MARCANO; 1,700 employees.

CVG Bauxilum, CA (Industria Integrado de Aluminio): Edif. Administrativo-CVG Bauxilum, Avda Fuerzas Armadas, Zona Industrial Matanzas, Ciudad Guayana, Bolívar; tel. (286) 950-6271; fax (286) 950-6270; e-mail asuntos.publicos@bauxilum.com .ve; internet www.bauxilum.com; f. 1994; state-owned mfr of aluminium products; Pres. JOSÉ CHINA.

CVG Ferrominera Orinoco, CA: Edif. Administrativo I, Puerto Ordaz, Apdo 399, Vía Caracas, Bolívar 8015; tel. (286) 930-3775; fax (286) 930-3783; e-mail contacto@ferrominera.com; internet www .ferrominera.com; f. 1976; subsidiary of the state-owned Corporación Venezolana de Guayana (see section on Government Agencies); iron ore mining; operates 2 railway lines, San Isidro mine–Puerto Ordaz (316 km) and El Pao–Palua (55 km), for transport of iron ore; Pres. Gen. JESÚS MANUEL ZAMBRANO; 4,100 employees.

Siderúrgica del Orinoco (Alfredo Maneiro), CA (SIDOR): Edif. General de Seguros, 7°, Avda La Estancia, Chuao, Caracas; tel. (212) 600-7696; fax (212) 993-2930; internet www.sidor.com; f. 1964; fmrly state-owned, privatized in 1997; renationalized in 2008; Ternium (Argentina) retains 10% stake; steel-processing; Pres. ANDREA SCHWAB ROMANIUK; 13,000 employees.

Siderúrgica del Turbio, SA (SIDETUR): Avda Intercomunal de Antímano, Zona Industrial La Yaguara, Caracas 1060; tel. (212) 407-0361; fax (212) 407-0372; internet www.sidetur.com.ve; f. 1972; mfrs of steel products including galvanized wire and steel rods; owned by SIVENSA (see below); Gen. Man. NICOLÁS IZQUIERDO; 600 employees.

Siderúrgica Venezolana, SACA (SIVENSA): Edif. Torre América, 11°, Avda Venezuela, Urb. Bello Monte, Caracas 1060; tel. (212) 707-6200; fax (212) 707-6352; e-mail antonio.osorio@sivensa.com; internet www.sivensa.com.ve; f. 1948; mfrs of briquetted iron, steel products, wire and wire products; Pres. OSCAR AUGUSTO MACHADO KOENEKE; 2,906 employees.

UNICON: Avda Beethoven, Torre Financiera, 9°, Collinas de Bello Monte, Caracas 1050; tel. (212) 753-4111; fax (212) 751-1542; e-mail webmaster@unicon.com.ve; internet www.unicon.com.ve; f. 1959 as Conduven; mfrs of welded pipe for use in petroleum industry, fluid conduction, electrical installations; CEO HÉCTOR RODRÍGUEZ.

Rubber and Tobacco

Bigott, SA: Edif. Cigarrera Bigott, Avda Francisco de Miranda, Los Ruices, Caracas 1071; tel. (212) 203-7511; fax (212) 203-7524; e-mail cigarrera_bigott@bat.com; internet www.bigott.com.ve; f. 1921; tobacco products; subsidiary of British American Tobacco (UK); 1,000 employees.

Bridgestone Firestone Venezolana, CA: Carrera Nacional Valencia-Los Guayos, cruce con San Diego, Zona Industrial, Valencia, Apdo 194, Carabobo; tel. (241) 874-7611; fax (241) 832-8254; internet www.bfvz.com; f. 1954; subsidiary of Bridgestone Corpn (USA); rubber tyre producers; Group CEO MASAAKI TSUYA; 1,111 employees.

Tabacalera Nacional, CA: Torre KPMG, 6°, Avda Francisco de Miranda, Campo Alegre, Chacao, Caracas 1060; tel. (212) 276-3401; internet www.philipmorrisinternational.com; f. 1953; subsidiary of Philip Morris Int. (USA); cigarette mfrs; Pres., Latin America and Canada Region JAMES R. MORTENSEN; 174 employees.

Food and Drink

Cervecería Destilo, CA: Hotel Caracas Palace, 3°, Of. OH3, Avda Francisco de Miranda, Caracas; tel. (212) 887-1371; fax (212) 771-2305; e-mail info@cerveceriadestilo.com; internet www .cerveceriadestilo.com; Gen. Man. HÉCTOR SOUCY.

Empresas Polar: Edif. Centro Empresarial Polar, 2a Avda de Los Cortijos de Lourdes, Caracas 1010; internet www.empresas-polar .com; f. 1941 as Cervecería Polar; food and drink mfrs; brands include Cervecería Polar, CA, Alimentos Polar, and Pepsi-Cola Venezuela; Pres. LORENZO MENDOZA.

Parmalat Venezuela (INDULAC): Edif. Parmalat, entre Avda San Francisco y Palmarito, Apdo 1546, Urb. Colinas de la California, Caracas 1010-A; tel. (212) 257-1422; fax (212) 257-7195; internet jperezor@parmalat.com.ve; internet www.parmalat.com.ve; f. 1966; mfrs and distributors of dairy products; owned by Parmalat (Italy); Pres. GIANLUCA PESCI; 2,198 employees.

Chemicals

Clariant (Venezuela), SA: Edif. Clariant, Zona Industrial San Vicente I, Avda Anton Philips, Apdo 34, Maracay 2101; tel. (435) 503-3131; fax (435) 503-3134; e-mail info@chemie.de; internet www .clariant.com.ve; f. 1952; subsidiary of Clariant Int. (Switzerland); mfrs and distributors of chemicals, textiles, leather, paper, paint, adhesives, plastics; Group CEO HARIOLF KOTTMANN; 207 employees.

Corimón, CA: Edif. Corimón, Urb. Los Cortijos de Lourdes, Calle Hans Neumann, Caracas; tel. (212) 400-5530; e-mail info@corimon .com; internet www.corimon.com; f. 1949; holding co. for subsidiaries producing paint, packaging and processed food; Pres. CARLOS GILL; CEO ESTEBAN SZEKELY; 2,655 employees.

DuPont Venezuela, CA: Edif. Los Frailes, 1°, Calle La Guairita, Urb. Chuao, Caracas 1060-A; tel. (212) 300-8420; fax (212) 992-6022; e-mail vanessa.carrasquel@ven.dupont.com; internet www2.dupont .com/Venezuela_Country_Site/es_VE; f. 1956; mfrs of industrial chemicals, plastics, pesticides, resins and films; Chair. and CEO ELLEN J. KULLMAN; Pres., Latin America JUDD O'CONNOR; 350 employees.

Pfizer, SA: Edif. Pfizer, Principal de los Ruices, entre 2a y 3a, Transversal, Caracas 1071; tel. (212) 630-2900; e-mail soporte .ventas.ve@pfizer.com; internet www.pfizer.com.ve; f. 1953; subsidiary of Pfizer Inc (USA); mfrs of pharmaceutical products; Group CEO IAN READ; Pres. ALVARO SALAZAR; 250 employees.

Procter and Gamble de Venezuela, SA: Edif. P&G, Calle Altagracia, Urb. Sorokaima 30, Trinidad, Caracas 1080; tel. (212) 903-7408; fax (212) 206-6364; e-mail robles.c@pg.com; internet www.pg .com/es_LATAM/VE/index.shtml; subsidiary of Procter and Gamble Co (USA); mfrs of soaps, detergents and pharmaceuticals; Pres. MARCIO ANDREAZZI; 380 employees.

Miscellaneous

Cerámica Carabobo, SA: Avda Lisandro Alvarado, Calle de Servicio, Sector C-04, Valencia, Carabobo; tel. (241) 813-4299; fax (241) 813-4194; e-mail infocc@ceramica-carabobo.com; internet www .ceramica-carabobo.com; f. 1956; mfrs of ceramic floor and wall tiles; also owns Cerámica Industrial del Caribe and Pan-American Ceramics; Pres. CARLOS CARLES RODRÍGUEZ; Gen. Man. TULIO HIDALGO; 3,000 employees.

Constructora Camsa, CA: Edif. Maya, Avda 2B 5°, Calle 72, Apdo 637, Maracaibo, Zulia; tel. (261) 763-0000; fax (261) 762-5690; e-mail edward.mendez@camsa.com.ve; internet www.camsa.com.ve; f. 1948 as Constructora Heerema; civil engineering and construction, including services to petroleum and gas sectors; Gen. Man. EDWARD MÉNDEZ; 390 employees.

Ford Motors de Venezuela, SA: Avda Henry Ford, Zona Industrial Sur, Valencia, Carabobo 1041; tel. (241) 874-6253; fax (241) 874-6375; internet www.ford.com.ve; f. 1962; subsidiary of Ford Motor Co (USA); assembly and production of motor vehicles, trucks and farm machinery; Pres. GABRIEL LÓPEZ; 1,500 employees.

General Electric de Venezuela, SA: Edif. Centro Banaven, Torre A, 6°, Avda La Estancia, Caracas; tel. (212) 901-4101; fax (212) 902-5300; e-mail corpcommunicationsvenezuela@ge.com; internet www .ge.com/ve; f. 1927; subsidiary of General Electric Corpn (USA); mfrs of television sets, radio receivers and household electrical appliances; Pres. (Venezuela, Colombia, Suriname and Guyana) FABIOLA SOJET; 2,600 employees.

Promociones Ferroca, SA (CVG FERROCASA): Calle Caicara con Carretera El Miamo, Centro Empresarial Ferrocasa, Torre A, Puerto Ordaz, Bolívar; tel. (286) 923-0319; e-mail jose.ramirez@ cvgferrocasa.com; internet www.cvgferrocasa.com; f. 1987; state-owned construction co involved in devt of Guayana region; Pres. ELIZABETH ALVES DE PRIMO.

UTILITIES
Electricity

Corporación Eléctrica Nacional (CORPOELEC): Edif. Centro Eléctrico Nacional, Avda Sanz, Urb. El Marqués, Sucre, Caracas; tel. (212) 280-8111; internet www.corpoelec.gob.ve; f. 2007; state-owned; generation, transmission, distribution and marketing of electric power and energy; subsidiaries include EDELCA (Electrificación del Caroní), La Nueva Electricidad de Caracas, ENELVEN (Energía Eléctrica de Venezuela), ENELCO (Energía Eléctrica de la Costa Oriental), ENELBAR (Energía Eléctrica de Barquisimeto), CADAFE (Compañía de Administración y Fomento Eléctrico, f. 1958), GENEVAPCA, ELEBOL, ELEVAL, Seneca, ENAGAS, TURBOVEN; Pres. JESSE CHACÓN ESCAMILLO (Minister of Electric Energy).

Gas

ENAGAS (Ente Nacional del Gas): Calle Panamá con Avda Libertador, 8°, Urb. Los Caobos, Caracas; tel. (212) 706-6654; fax (212) 706-6471; e-mail presidencia@enagas.gov.ve; internet www.enagas.gob.ve; f. 1999; subsidiary of CORPOELEC; Pres. JORGE LUIS SÁNCHEZ.

Water

Hidroven: Edif. Hidroven, Avda Augusto César Sandino con 9a Transversal, Maripérez, Caracas; tel. (212) 781-4778; fax (212) 781-6424; e-mail ngamboa@cantv.net; internet www.hidroven.gov.ve; f. 1990; successor co to Instituto Nacional de Obras Sanitarias; national water co; subsidiaries include Hidroandes, Hidrocapital, Hidrocaribe, Hidrocentro, Hidrofalcon, Hidrolago, Hidrollanos, Hidropaez, Hidrosuroeste, Aguas de Monagas, Aguas de Ejido, Hidrolara; Pres. CRISTÓBAL FRANCISCO ORTIZ; Vice-Pres. FRANCISCO DURÁN.

Hidrocapital (Hidrocapital): Edif. Hidrocapital, Avda Augusto César Sandino con 9a Transversal, Maripérez, Caracas; tel. (212) 793-1638; fax (212) 793-6794; internet www.hidrocapital.com.ve; f. 1992; operates water supply in Capital District and states of Miranda and Vargas; Pres. ERNESTO PAIVA.

Hidrocaribe: Prolongación Avda 5 de Julio, Los Ángeles, Local 5 y 22, Frente al Estadio Venezuela, Barcelona, Anzoátegui; tel. (281) 277-2161; internet hidrocaribe.gob.ve; operates in Anzoátegui, Nueva Esparta and Sucre; Pres. ELIO BELLORÍN.

Hidrocentro: Final de la Avda Julio Centeno, Antigua Planta de Tto Díaz Moreno, Urb. Terrazas de los Nisperos, Carabobo; tel. (241) 839-1200; e-mail atencionalciudadano@hidrocentro.gob.ve; internet www.hidrocentro.gob.ve; f. 1990; operates in Aragua, Carabobo and Cojedes; Pres. LUIGINA CERCIO.

Hidrolago: Edif. Empresarial, Planta Baja, OSAC Unión, Calle 84 No 3F-125, Maracaibo, Zulia; tel. (261) 200-7720; internet www.hidrolago.gov.ve; f. 1990; operates in Zulia; Pres. FREDDY RODRÍGUEZ MORALES.

Hidropaez: Final Avda Romulo Gallegos, Diagonal Colegio de Ingenieros, San Juan de los Morros, Guárico; internet hidropaez.gob.ve; f. 1991; operates in Guárico.

TRADE UNIONS

Confederación de Trabajadores de Venezuela (CTV) (Confederation of Venezuelan Workers): Edif. José Vargas, 17°, Avda Este 2, Los Caobos, Caracas; tel. (212) 574-1049; f. 1936; principally active in public sector; Pres. CARLOS ALFONSO ORTEGA CARVAJAL; Sec.-Gen. MANUEL JOSÉ COVA FERMÍN; 26 regional and 57 industrial feds.

Fedepetrol: union of petroleum workers; Pres. RAFAEL ROSALES.

Federación Campesina de Venezuela (FCV): internet www.fcvvenezuela.blogspot.com; peasant union; CTV affiliate; Pres. MIGUEL ULISES MORENO.

Fetrametal: union of metal workers; Pres. ELIS MONTAÑEZ.

Fuerza Bolivariana de Trabajadores (FBT): internet www.fbtvenezuela.com; f. 2000; pro-Govt union.

Unión Nacional de Trabajadores (UNT): f. 2003; pro-Govt federation; Nat. Co-ordinator MARCELA MÁSPERO.

Transport
RAILWAYS

Lines under construction in 2014 included: a link between Puerto Cabello and La Encrucijada in the centre of the country; a 468-km line connecting Anaco and Tinaco; a 252.5-km line connecting San Juan de los Moros and San Fernando de Apure; a 44.3-km line linking Acarigua and Turén; and a 201-km line between Chaguaramas and Cabruta.

CA Metro de Caracas: Multicentro Empresarial del Este, Edif. Miranda, Torre B, 7°, Avda Francisco de Miranda, Calle Los Maristas, Apdo 61036, Caracas; tel. (212) 206-7111; fax (212) 266-3346; e-mail sugerencias@metrodecaracas.com.ve; internet www.metrodecaracas.com.ve; f. 1976 to supervise the construction and use of the underground railway system; services began in 1983; state-owned; Pres. HAIMAN EL TROUDI.

Ferrocarril de CVG Bauxilum—Operadora de Bauxita: Edif. Administrativo, Avda Fuerzas Armadas, Zona Industrial Matanzas, Ciudad Guayana, Bolívar; tel. (286) 950-6271; fax (286) 950-6270; e-mail asuntos.publicos@bauxilum.com.ve; internet www.bauxilum.com; f. 1989; state-owned; operates line linking Los Pijiguaos with river Orinoco port of Gumilla (52 km) for transporting bauxite; Pres. JOSÉ CHINA.

Instituto de Ferrocarriles del Estado (IFE): Edif. Torre Británica de Seguros, 7° y 8°, Avda José Félix Sosa, Urb. Altamira, Chacao, Caracas 1062-A; tel. (212) 201-8736; fax (212) 201-8902; e-mail tlopez@ife.gob.ve; internet www.ife.gob.ve; state co; Pres. FRANKLIN PÉREZ COLINA.

ROADS

In 2006 there were an estimated 96,200 km of roads, of which 32,300 km were paved. Responsibility for road maintenance generally lies with state governments; however, legislation adopted in 2009 allowed the central Government to take control of motorways and major roads, as well as ports and airports.

INLAND WATERWAYS

Instituto Nacional de Canalizaciones: Edif. INC, Calle Caracas, al lado de la Torre Diamen, Chuao, Caracas; tel. (212) 908-5106; fax (212) 959-6906; e-mail atencionalciudadano@incanal.gov.ve; internet www.incanal.gov.ve; f. 1952; semi-autonomous institution; Vice-Pres. NELSON FREDYS MARIÑA MULLER.

SHIPPING

There are 13 major ports, 34 petroleum and mineral ports and five fishing ports. The main ports for imports are La Guaira, the port for Caracas, and Puerto Cabello, which handles raw materials for the industrial region around Valencia. Maracaibo is the chief port for the petroleum industry. Puerto Ordaz, on the Orinoco river, was also developed to deal with the shipments of iron from Cerro Bolívar. At December 2013 the flag registered fleet comprised 328 vessels, totalling 1,706,396 grt, of which five were gas tankers and 32 were fishing vessels.

Consolidada de Ferrys, CA (CONFERRY): Edif. Conferry, Planta Baja, Of. Comercial, Avda Terranova con Llano Adentro, Porlamar, Isla de Margarita; tel. (295) 263-9878; fax (295) 263-8372; internet www.conferry.com; f. 1970; ferry services to Margarita island; Dir ROSSANA GONZÁLEZ.

Instituto Nacional de los Espacios Acuáticos (INEA): Edif. INEA, Avda Orinoco, entre Calles Perijá y Mucuchies, Urb. Las Mercedes, Municipio Baruta, Caracas; tel. (212) 909-1430; fax (212) 909-1431; internet www.inea.gob.ve; f. 2001; supervises marine and related activities; Pres. JORGE MIGUEL SIERRALTA.

PDV Marina: Edif. Sede Administrativa del Centro de Refinación Paraguaná, 2°, Ala 2, Of. 21, Comunidad Cardón, Falcón; tel. (269) 240-9215; fax (269) 240-9112; e-mail angolamd@pdvsa.com; f. 1990; shipping subsidiary of Venezuela's state oil company PDVSA; Pres. FERNANDO CAMEJO ARENAS.

Scat, CA: Edif. Scat, Avda Juan Bautista Arismendi, Isla de Margarita; tel. (295) 274-5882; fax (295) 274-1525; e-mail contacto@scatca.com; internet www.scatca.com; operates in Puerto del Guamache.

Transpapel, CA: Edif. Centro, 11°, Of. 111, Centro Parque Boyaca, Avda Sucre, Los Dos Caminos, Apdo 61316, Caracas 1071; tel. (212) 283-8366; fax (212) 285-7749; e-mail nmaldonado@cantv.net; f. 1985; Man. Dir ERNESTO VILLASMIL.

CIVIL AVIATION

There are two adjacent airports 13 km from Caracas: Maiquetía for domestic and Simón Bolívar for international services. There are 11 international airports.

Regulatory Authority

Instituto Nacional de Aeronáutica Civil: Torre Británica, 2°–8°, Avda José Félix Sosa, Urb. Altamira Sur, Chacao, Caracas 1060; tel. (212) 267-5031; e-mail contacto@inac.gob.ve; internet www.inac.gob.ve; f. 2005; Pres. PEDRO ALBERTO GONZÁLEZ; Dir MERCEDES LOZADA.

National Airlines

Aeropostal (Alas de Venezuela): Torre Polar Oeste, 22°, Avda Paseo Colón, Plaza Venezuela, Los Caobos, Caracas 1051; tel. (212) 708-6211; fax (212) 782-6323; e-mail corporativa@aeropostal.com; internet www.aeropostal.com; f. 1933; privatized in 1996, acquired by Venezuelan/US consortium Corporación Alas de Venezuela; Pres. and CEO LUIS GRATEROL CARABALLO.

Aserca Airlines: Edif. Aserca Airlines, Avda Andrés Eloy Blanco, Calle 137-C, Urb. Prebo I, Valencia; tel. (241) 237-111; fax (241) 220-

210; e-mail rsv@asercaairlines.com; internet www.asercaairlines
.com; f. 1968; domestic services and flights to Caribbean; Pres.
SIMEÓN GARCÍA; Dir-Gen. ROBERTO JORGEZ.

Consorcio Venezolano de Industrias Aeronáutica y Servicios Aéreos, SA (CONVIASA): Aeropuerto Internacional de Maiquetía, Edif. Sector 6.3, Avda Intercomunal, Adyacente a Tránsito Terrestre, Maiquetia; tel. (212) 303-7332; e-mail mercadeo@conviasa.aero; internet www.conviasa.aero; f. 2004; state-owned; CEO (vacant).

LASER (Línea Aérea de Servicio Ejecutivo Regional, CA): Torre Bazar Bolívar, 8°, Avda Francisco de Miranda, El Marqués, Caracas; tel. (212) 202-0100; fax (212) 235-8359; internet www.laser.com.ve; f. 1994; domestic and international services; Pres. INOCENCIO ALVAREZ.

Línea Turística Aereotuy, CA: Edif. Gran Sábana, 5°, Blvd de Sábana Grande, Apdo 2923, Carmelitas, Caracas; tel. (212) 761-6231; fax (212) 762-5254; e-mail tuysales@etheron.net; internet www.tuy.com; f. 1982; operates on domestic and international routes; Pres. JUAN CARLOS MÁRQUEZ.

Santa Barbara Airlines (SBA): Edif. Tokay, 3°, Calle 3-B, La Urbina, Caracas; tel. (212) 204-4400; fax (212) 242-3260; e-mail atc@sbairlines.com; internet www.sbairlines.com; f. 1995; domestic and international services; Pres. ORLAN VILORIA.

Tourism

In 2012 Venezuela received 709,585 tourists. Receipts from tourism in that year amounted to a provisional US $844m. An estimated 90% of tourists visit the island of Margarita, while only 20% of tourists visit the mainland.

Asociación Venezolana de Agencias de Viajes y Turismo (AVAVIT): Avda 6, entre 6 y 7, Transversal, Quinta 17, Altamira, Caracas; tel. (212) 261-1845; fax (212) 261-0821; e-mail turvspecialtours@cantv.net; internet www.avavit.com; Pres. MARÍA LUCILA BELTRÁN.

Instituto Nacional de Turismo (INATUR): Edif. MINTUR, Avda Francisco de Miranda, con Avda Ppal de La Floresta, Municipio Chacao, Caracas; tel. (212) 208-4651; fax (212) 208-4652; e-mail inatur@inatur.gob.ve; internet www.inatur.gob.ve; f. 2001; govt

tourism devt agency; Pres. ALEJANDRO FLEMING; Exec. Dir DAVID RIVAS.

Venezolana de Turismo, SA (VENETUR): Centro Empresarial Centro Plaza, Torre B, 16°, Los Palos Grandes, Caracas; tel. (212) 208-4812; fax (212) 208-8160; e-mail sugurencias@venetur.gob.ve; internet www.venetur.gob.ve; govt tourism promotion agency; Gen. Man. ANTONIO J MORILLO P.

Defence

As assessed at November 2013, the armed forces numbered 115,000 men: an army of 63,000, a navy of 17,500 (including an estimated 7,000 marines), an air force of 11,500 and a National Guard of 23,000. There was also an army reserve numbering 8,000. Military service is selective and the length of service varies by region for all services. The President is Commander-in-Chief of the Armed Forces.

Defence Budget: 32,100m. bolívares in 2013.

Commander-General of the National Guard: Maj.-Gen. JUSTO NOGUERA PIETRI.

Commander-General of the Navy: Adm. GILBERTO PINTO BLANCO.

Commander-General of the Army: Maj.-Gen. ALEXIS LÓPEZ RAMÍREZ.

Commander-General of the Air Force: Maj.-Gen. GIUSEPPE ANGELO YOFFREDA YORIO.

Commander-General of the Bolivarian National Militia: Maj.-Gen. JOSÉ ANTONIO MORENO BRICEÑO.

Education

Primary education in Venezuela is free and compulsory between the ages of six and 15 years. Secondary education begins at the age of 15 years and lasts for a further two years. In 2012 enrolment at primary schools included 92% of children in the relevant age-group, while the equivalent ratio for secondary enrolment was 85% (males 82%; females 89%). In 2012 there were 63 universities. Expenditure by the central Government on education was an estimated 47,913m. bolívares in 2012.

Bibliography

For works on the region generally, see Select Bibliography (Books)

Brewer-Carías, A. R. *Dismantling Democracy in Venezuela: The Chávez Authoritarian Experiment.* New York, Cambridge University Press, 2010.

Buxton, J. 'Venezuela', in Buxton, J., and Phillips, N. *Case Studies in Latin American Political Economy.* Manchester, Manchester University Press, 1999.

   The Failure of Political Reform in Venezuela. Aldershot, Ashgate Publishing Ltd, 2001.

Cannon, B. *Hugo Chávez and the Bolivarian Revolution.* Manchester, Manchester University Press, 2009.

Castro, F., Deutschmann, D. (Ed.), and Salado, J. (Ed.). *Venezuela y Chávez.* Havana, Ocean Press, 2007.

Chávez, H., Deutschmann, D., and Salado, J. *Chávez: Venezuela and the New Latin America.* New York, Consortium, 2004.

Ciccariello-Maher, G. *We Created Chavez: A People's History of the Venezuelan Revolution.* Durham, NC, Duke University Press, 2013.

Clem, R. S., Eguizabal, C. and Manigot, A. P. *Venezuela's Petro-Diplomacy: Hugo Chávez's Foreign Policy.* Gainesville, FL, University Press of Florida, 2011.

Corrales, J. and Penfold, M. *Dragon in the Tropics: Hugo Chávez and the Political Economy of Revolution in Venezuela.* Washington, DC, Brookings Institution Press, 2010.

Ellner, S. *Rethinking Venezuelan Politics: Class, Conflict, and the Chávez Phenomenon.* Boulder, CO, Lynne Rienner Publrs, 2008.

Ellner, S., and Tinker Salas, M. (Eds). *Venezuela: Hugo Chávez and the Decline of an Exceptional Democracy.* Lanham, MD, Rowman and Littlefield Publrs, 2007.

Fernandes, S. *Who Can Stop the Drums?: Urban Social Movements in Chávez's Venezuela.* Durham, NC, Duke University Press, 2010.

Friedman, E. J. *Unfinished Transitions: Women and the Gendered Development of Democracy in Venezuela, 1936–1996.* University Park, PA, Penn State University Press, 2000.

Gates, L. C. *Electing Chávez: The Business of Anti-Neoliberal Politics in Venezuela.* Pittsburgh, PA, University of Pittsburgh Press, 2010.

Goforth, S. *Axis of Unity: Venezuela, Iran & the Threat to America.* Dulles, VA, Potomac Books, 2011.

Guevara, A. *Chávez: Venezuela and the New Latin America—Hugo Chávez Interviewed by Aleida Guevara.* New York, Ocean Press, 2005.

Hawkins, K. A. *Venezuela's Chavismo and Populism in Comparative Perspective.* Cambridge, Cambridge University Press, 2010.

Kozloff, N. *Hugo Chávez: Oil, Politics, and the Challenge to the U.S.* Basingstoke, Palgrave Macmillan, 2006.

Landau, S. *The Chávez Code: Cracking US Intervention in Venezuela.* Redford, MI, Olive Branch Press, 2006.

McBeth, B. S. *Juan Vicente Gómez and the Oil Companies in Venezuela, 1908–1935.* Cambridge, Cambridge University Press, 2002.

McCaughan, M. *The Battle of Venezuela.* London, Latin America Bureau, 2004.

McCoy, J., and Myers, D. J. (Eds) *The Unraveling of Representative Democracy in Venezuela.* Baltimore, MD, Johns Hopkins University Press, 2005.

Nelson, B. A. *The Silence and the Scorpion: The Coup Against Chávez and the Making of Modern Venezuela.* New York, Nation Books, 2009.

Sullivan, M., and Olhero, N. *Venezuela: Political Conditions and U.S. Policy.* Hauppuage, NY, Nova Science Publishers, 2008.

Tarver, H. M. *The Rise And Fall Of Venezuelan President Carlos Andrés Pérez: The Early Years, 1936–1973.* Lewiston, NY, Edwin Mellen Press, 2001.

Wilbert, G. *Changing Venezuela by Taking Power: The History and Policies of the Chávez Government.* London and New York, Verso, 2006.

PART THREE
Regional Information

REGIONAL ORGANIZATIONS

UNITED NATIONS

Address: United Nations, New York, NY 10017, USA.

Telephone: (212) 963-1234; **fax:** (212) 963-4879; **internet:** www.un .org.

The United Nations (UN) was founded on 24 October 1945. The organization, which has 193 member states, aims to maintain international peace and security and to develop international co-operation in addressing economic, social, cultural and humanitarian problems. The principal organs of the UN are the General Assembly, the Security Council, the Economic and Social Council, the International Court of Justice and the Secretariat. The General Assembly, which meets for three months each year, comprises representatives of all UN member states. The Security Council investigates disputes between member countries, and may recommend ways and means of peaceful settlement: it comprises five permanent members (the People's Republic of China, France, Russia, the United Kingdom and the USA) and 10 other members elected by the General Assembly for a two-year period. The Economic and Social Council comprises representatives of 54 member states, elected by the General Assembly for a three-year period: it promotes co-operation on economic, social, cultural and humanitarian matters, acting as a central policy-making body and co-ordinating the activities of the UN's specialized agencies. The International Court of Justice comprises 15 judges of different nationalities, elected for nine-year terms by the General Assembly and the Security Council: it adjudicates in legal disputes between UN member states.

Secretary-General: BAN KI-MOON (Republic of Korea) (2007–16).

MEMBER STATES IN SOUTH AMERICA, CENTRAL AMERICA AND THE CARIBBEAN
(with assessments for percentage contributions to UN budget during 2013–15, and year of admission)

Antigua and Barbuda	0.002	1981
Argentina	0.432	1945
Bahamas	0.017	1973
Barbados	0.008	1966
Belize	0.001	1981
Bolivia	0.009	1945
Brazil	2.984	1945
Chile	0.334	1945
Colombia	0.259	1945
Costa Rica	0.038	1945
Cuba	0.069	1945
Dominica	0.001	1978
Dominican Republic	0.045	1945
Ecuador	0.044	1945
El Salvador	0.016	1945
Grenada	0.001	1974
Guatemala	0.027	1945
Guyana	0.001	1966
Haiti	0.003	1945
Honduras	0.008	1945
Jamaica	0.014	1962
Mexico	1.842	1945
Nicaragua	0.003	1945
Panama	0.026	1945
Paraguay	0.010	1945
Peru	0.117	1945
Saint Christopher and Nevis	0.001	1983
Saint Lucia	0.001	1979
Saint Vincent and the Grenadines	0.001	1980
Suriname	0.004	1975
Trinidad and Tobago	0.044	1962
Uruguay	0.052	1945
Venezuela	0.627	1945

Diplomatic Representation

PERMANENT MISSIONS TO THE UNITED NATIONS
(September 2014)

Antigua and Barbuda: 305 East 47th St, 6th Floor, New York, NY 10017; tel. (212) 541-4117; fax (212) 757-1607; e-mail unmission@ abgov.org; internet www.abgov.org; Permanent Representative Dr JOHN W. ASHE.

Argentina: One United Nations Plaza, 25th Floor, New York, NY 10017; tel. (212) 688-6300; fax (212) 980-8395; e-mail enaun@mrecic .gov.ar; internet enaun.mrecic.gov.ar; Permanent Representative MARÍA CRISTINA PERCEVAL.

Bahamas: 231 East 46th St, New York, NY 10017; tel. (212) 421-6925; fax (212) 759-2135; e-mail mission@bahamasny.com; Permanent Representative ELLISTON RAHMING.

Barbados: 820 Second Ave, 9th Floor, New York, NY 10017; tel. (212) 551-4300; fax (212) 986-1030; e-mail prun@foreign.gov.bb; Permanent Representative JOSEPH E. GODDARD.

Belize: 675 Third Ave, Suite 1911, New York, NY 10017; tel. (212) 986-1240; fax (212) 593-0932; e-mail blzun@aol.com; Permanent Representative LOIS MICHELE YOUNG.

Bolivia: 801 Second Ave, 4th Floor, Suite 402, New York, NY 10017; tel. (212) 682-8132; fax (212) 687-4642; e-mail delgaliviaonu@ hotmail.com; Permanent Representative SACHA SERGIO LLORENTTY SOLÍZ.

Brazil: 747 Third Ave, 9th Floor, New York, NY 10017; tel. (212) 372-2600; fax (212) 371-5716; e-mail delbrasonu@delbrasonu.org; internet www.un.int/brazil; Permanent Representative ANTONIO DE AGUIAR PATRIOTA.

Chile: One Dag Hammarskjöld Plaza, 885 Second Ave, 40th Floor, New York, NY 10017; tel. (917) 322-6800; fax (917) 322-6890; e-mail chile.un@minrel.gov.cl; internet chileabroad.gov.cl/onu/en; Permanent Representative CRISTIÁN BARROS MELET.

Colombia: 140 East 57th St, 5th Floor, New York, NY 10022; tel. (212) 355-7776; fax (212) 371-2813; e-mail colombia@colombiaun .org; internet www.colombia.un.org; Permanent Representative MARIA EMMA MEJÍA VÉLEZ.

Costa Rica: 211 East 43rd St, Rm 903, New York, NY 10017; tel. (212) 986-6373; fax (212) 986-6842; e-mail contact@missioncrun.org; Permanent Representative JUAN CARLOS MENDOZA GARCÍA.

Cuba: 315 Lexington Ave and 38th St, New York, NY 10016; tel. (212) 689-7215; fax (212) 779-1697; e-mail cuba_onu@cubanmission .com; Permanent Representative RODOLFO REYES RODRÍGUEZ.

Dominica: 800 Second Ave, Suite 400H, New York, NY 10017; tel. (212) 949-0853; fax (212) 808-4975; e-mail dominicaun@gmail.com; Permanent Representative VINCE HENDERSON.

Dominican Republic: 144 East 44th St, 4th Floor, New York, NY 10017; tel. (212) 867-0833; fax (212) 986-4694; e-mail drun@un.int; internet www.un.int/dr; Permanent Representative FRANCISCO ANTONIO CORTORREAL.

Ecuador: 866 United Nations Plaza, Rm 516, New York, NY 10017; tel. (212) 935-1680; fax (212) 935-1835; e-mail ecuador@un.int; internet www.ecuadoronu.com; Permanent Representative XAVIER LASSO MENDOZA.

El Salvador: 46 Park Ave, New York, NY 10016; tel. (212) 679-1616; fax (212) 725-3467; e-mail elsalvadormissiontoun@outlook.com; Permanent Representative RUBEN I. ZAMORA.

Grenada: 800 Second Ave, Suite 400K, New York, NY 10017; tel. (212) 599-0301; fax (212) 599-1540; e-mail grenada@un.int; Permanent Representative DENIS G. ANTOINE.

Guatemala: 57 Park Ave, New York, NY 10016; tel. (212) 679-4760; fax (212) 685-8741; e-mail guatemala@un.int; internet www .guatemalaun.org; Permanent Representative GERT ROSENTHAL (outgoing).

Guyana: 801 Second Ave, 5th Floor, New York, NY 10017; tel. (212) 573-5828; fax (212) 573-6225; e-mail guyana@un.int; Permanent Representative GEORGE WILFRIED TALBOT.

Haiti: 815 Second Ave, 6th Floor, New York, NY 10017; tel. (212) 370-4840; fax (212) 661-8698; e-mail mphonu.newyork@diplomatie .ht; Permanent Representative DENIS REGIS.

Honduras: 866 United Nations Plaza, Suite 417, New York, NY 10017; tel. (212) 752-3370; fax (212) 223-0498; e-mail honduras_un@ hotmail.com; internet www.un.int/honduras; Permanent Representative MARY ELIZABETH FLORES FLAKE.

Jamaica: 767 Third Ave, 9th Floor, New York, NY 10017; tel. (212) 935-7509; fax (212) 935-7607; e-mail jamaica@un.int; internet www .un.int/jamaica; Permanent Representative COURTENEY RATTRAY.

Mexico: Two United Nations Plaza, 28th Floor, New York, NY 10017; tel. (212) 752-0220; fax (212) 688-8862; e-mail onuusr1@sre .gob.mx; internet www.sre.gob.mx/onu; Permanent Representative JORGE MARIO MONTAÑO Y MARTÍNEZ.

Nicaragua: 820 Second Ave, 8th Floor, New York, NY 10017; tel. (212) 490-7997; fax (212) 286-0815; e-mail nicaragua@un.int; internet www.un.int/nicaragua; Permanent Representative MARÍA RUBIALES DE CHAMORRO.

Panama: 866 United Nations Plaza, Suite 4030, New York, NY 10017; tel. (212) 421-5420; fax (212) 421-2694; e-mail emb@ panama-un.org; internet www.panama-un.org; Permanent Representative LAURA FLORES HERRERA.

Paraguay: 801 Second Ave, Suite 702, New York, NY 10017; tel. (212) 687-3490; fax (212) 818-1282; e-mail paraguay@un.int; Permanent Representative JOSÉ ANTONIO DOS SANTOS.

Peru: 820 Second Ave, Suite 1600, New York, NY 10017; tel. (212) 687-3336; fax (212) 972-6975; e-mail onuper@unperu.org; internet www.un.int/peru; Permanent Representative GUSTAVO MEZA-CUADRA VELÁSQUEZ.

Saint Christopher and Nevis: 414 East 75th St, 5th Floor, New York, NY 10021; tel. (212) 535-1234; fax (212) 535-6854; e-mail sknmission@aol.com; Permanent Representative DELANO FRANK BART.

Saint Lucia: 800 Second Ave, 9th Floor, New York, NY 10017; tel. (212) 697-9360; fax (212) 697-4993; e-mail info@stluciamission.org; Permanent Representative MENISSA RAMBALLY.

Saint Vincent and the Grenadines: 800 Second Ave, Suite 400G, New York, NY 10017; tel. (212) 599-0950; fax (212) 599-1020; e-mail mission@svg-un.org; Permanent Representative INGA RHONDA KING.

Suriname: 866 United Nations Plaza, Suite 320, New York, NY 10017; tel. (212) 826-0660; fax (212) 980-7029; e-mail suriname@un .int; Permanent Representative HENRY LEONARD MACDONALD.

Trinidad and Tobago: 633 Third Ave, 12th Floor, New York, NY 10017; tel. (212) 697-7620; fax (212) 682-3580; e-mail tto@un.int; internet www.un.int/trinidadandtobago; Permanent Representative RODNEY CHARLES.

Uruguay: 866 United Nations Plaza, Suite 322, New York, NY 10017; tel. (212) 752-8240; fax (212) 593-0935; e-mail uruguay@un .int; internet www.un.int/uruguay; Permanent Representative GONZALO KONCKE PIZZORNO.

Venezuela: 335 East 46th St, New York, NY 10017; tel. (212) 557-2055; fax (212) 557-3528; e-mail missionvene@venezuela.gob.ve; Permanent Representative JORGE SAMUEL MONCADA.

OBSERVERS

Intergovernmental organizations, etc., active in the region that participate in the sessions and the work of the UN General Assembly as Observers, maintaining permanent offices at the UN.

Caribbean Community: 88 Burnett Ave, Maplewood, NJ 07040; tel. (973) 378-9333; fax (973) 327-2671; e-mail caripoun@gmail.com; Permanent Observer NOEL SINCLAIR.

Central American Integration System: 320 West 75th St, Suite 1A, New York, NY 10023; tel. (212) 682-1550; fax (212) 877-9021; e-mail ccampos@sgsica-ny.org; Permanent Observer CARLOS CAMPOS.

Commonwealth Secretariat: 800 Second Ave, 4th Floor, New York, NY 10017; tel. (212) 599-6190; fax (212) 808-4975; e-mail comsec@onecommonwealth.org.

International Development Law Organization: 336 East 45th St, 11th Floor, New York, NY 10017; tel. (212) 867-9707; fax (212) 867-9719; e-mail pcivili@idlo.int; internet www.idlo.int; Permanent Observer PATRIZIO M. CIVILI.

International Institute for Democracy and Electoral Assistance: 336 East 45th St, 14th Floor, New York, NY 10017; tel. (212) 286-1084; fax (212) 286-0260; e-mail unobserver@idea.int; Permanent Observer MASSIMO TOMMASOLI.

International Olympic Committee: 708 Third Ave, 6th Floor, New York, NY 10017; tel. (212) 209-3952; fax (212) 209-7100; e-mail IOC-UNObserver@olympic.org; internet www.olympic.org; Permanent Observer MARIO PESCANTE.

Inter-Parliamentary Union: 336 East 45th St, 10th Floor, New York, NY 10017; tel. (212) 557-5880; fax (212) 557-3954; e-mail ny-office@mail.ipu.org; internet www.ipu.org/Un-e/un-opo.htm; Permanent Observer PATRICIA ANN TORSNEY.

International Union for Conservation of Nature (IUCN): 551 Fifth Ave, Suites 800 A-B, New York, NY 10176; tel. (212) 346-1163; fax (212) 346-1046; e-mail iucn@un.int; internet www.iucn.org; Permanent Observer NARINDER KAKAR (India).

Partners in Population and Development: 336 East 45th St, 14th Floor, New York, NY 10017; tel. (212) 286-1082; fax (212) 286-0260; e-mail nalam@ppdsec.org; internet www.partners-popdev.org; Permanent Observer MOHAMMAD NURUL ALAM.

University for Peace: 551 Fifth Ave, Suites 800 A-B, New York, NY 10176; tel. (212) 346-1163; fax (212) 346-1046; e-mail nyinfo@upeace .org; internet www.upeace.org; Permanent Observer NARINDER KAKAR (India).

The African, Caribbean and Pacific Group of States, Agency for the Prohibition of Nuclear Weapons in Latin America and the Caribbean, Andean Community, Central American Integration System, Inter-American Development Bank, Latin American Economic System, Latin American Integration Association, Latin American Parliament, the Organisation of Eastern Caribbean States, the Organization of American States, and the Union of South American Nations are among a number of intergovernmental organizations that have a standing invitation to participate as Observers, but do not maintain permanent offices at the United Nations.

United Nations Information Centres/Services

Argentina: Junín 1940, 1°, 1113 Buenos Aires; tel. (11) 4803-7671; fax (11) 4804-7545; e-mail unic.buenosaires@unic.org; internet www .unic.org.ar; also covers Uruguay.

Bolivia: Calle 14 esq. Sánchez Bustamante, Ed. Metrobol II, Calacoto, La Paz; tel. (2) 2795544; fax (2) 2795820; e-mail unic.lapaz@unic .org; internet www.nu.org.bo.

Brazil: Palacio Itamaraty, Avda Marechal Floriano 196, 20080-002 Rio de Janeiro; tel. (21) 2253-2211; fax (21) 2233-5753; e-mail unic .brazil@unic.org; internet unicrio.org.br.

Colombia: Calle 100, No. 8A-55, 10°, Edificio World Trade Center, Torre C, Bogotá 2; tel. (1) 257-6044; fax (1) 257-6244; e-mail unic .bogota@unic.org; internet www.nacionesunidas.org.co; also covers Ecuador and Venezuela.

Mexico: Montes Urales 440, 3°, Col. Chapultepec Morales, México 11 000, DF; tel. (55) 4000-9725; fax (55) 5203-8638; e-mail unicmex@un .org.mx; internet www.cinu.mx; also covers Cuba and the Dominican Republic.

Panama: UN House Bldg 128, Ciudad del Saber, Clayton, Panama City; tel. (7) 301-0035; fax (7) 301-0037; e-mail unic.panama@unic .org; internet www.cinup.org.

Paraguay: Casilla de Correo 1107; Edif. Naciones Unidas, Avda Mariscal López, Asunción; tel. (21) 614443; fax (21) 611988; e-mail unic.py@undp.org; internet asuncion.unic.org.

Peru: POB 14-0199, Av. Perez Aranibar 750, Magdalena, Lima 17; tel. (1) 625-9140; fax (1) 625-9100; e-mail unic.lima@unic.org; internet www.uniclima.org.pe.

Trinidad and Tobago: 2nd Floor, Bretton Hall, 16 Victoria Ave, Port of Spain; tel. 623-4813; fax 623-4332; e-mail unic.portofspain@ unic.org; internet portofspain.unic.org; also covers Antigua and Barbuda, Aruba, the Bahamas, Barbados, Belize, Dominica, Grenada, Guyana, Jamaica, the Netherlands Antilles, Saint Christopher and Nevis, Saint Lucia, Saint Vincent and the Grenadines, and Suriname.

Economic Commission for Latin America and the Caribbean—ECLAC

Address: Edif. Naciones Unidas, Avda Dag Hammarskjöld 3477, Vitacura, Casilla 179-D, Santiago, Chile.

Telephone: (2) 2102000; **fax:** (2) 2080252; **e-mail:** dpisantiago@eclac.cl; **internet:** www.eclac.cl.

ECLAC was established (as the UN Economic Commission for Latin America, current name adopted in 1984) in 1948 to co-ordinate policies for the promotion of economic development in the Latin American region.

MEMBERS

Antigua and Barbuda	El Salvador	Paraguay
Argentina	France	Peru
Bahamas	Germany	Portugal
Barbados	Grenada	Saint Christopher
Belize	Guatemala	and Nevis
Bolivia	Guyana	Saint Lucia
Brazil	Haiti	Saint Vincent and
Canada	Honduras	the Grenadines
Chile	Italy	Spain
Colombia	Jamaica	Suriname
Costa Rica	Japan	Trinidad and
Cuba	Korea, Republic	Tobago
Dominica	Mexico	United Kingdom
Dominican	Netherlands	USA
Republic	Nicaragua	Uruguay
Ecuador	Panama	Venezuela

ASSOCIATE MEMBERS

Anguilla	Cayman Islands	Puerto Rico
Aruba	Curaçao	Saint Martin
Bermuda	Guadaloupe	Turks and Caicos
British Virgin	Martinique	United States
Islands	Montserrat	Virgin Islands

Organization

(September 2014)

COMMISSION

The Commission, comprising representatives of every member state, normally meets every two years at ministerial level. It considers matters relating to the economic and social development of the region, reviews activities of the organization, and adopts programmes of work. The 35th session was held in Lima, Peru, in May 2014. Member states may meet between Commission meetings in an ad hoc Committee of the Whole. The Commission has established the following ad hoc and permanent bodies:

Caribbean Development and Co-operation Committee;

Committee of High-level Government Experts;

Committee on Central American Economic Co-operation;

Committee on South-South Co-operation;

Regional Conference on Population and Development;

Regional Conference on Social Development;

Regional Conference on Women;

Regional Council for Planning of ILPES;

Statistical Conference of the Americas.

SECRETARIAT

The Secretariat employs more than 500 staff and is headed by the Offices of the Executive Secretary and of the Secretary of the Commission. ECLAC's work programme is carried out by the following divisions: Economic Development (including a Development Studies Unit); Economic and Social Planning (ILPES); Financing for Development; International Trade and Integration; Natural Resources and Infrastructure (including a Transport Unit); Population (CELADE); Production, Productivity and Management (including an Agricultural Development Unit, a joint ECLAC/UNIDO Industrial and Technological Development Unit and a Unit on Investment and Corporate Strategies); Social Development; Statistics; Programme Planning and Operations; Sustainable Development and Human Settlements; and Gender Affairs. There are also a Development Studies Unit and a Public Information and Web Services Section.

Executive Secretary: ALICIA BÁRCENA IBARRA (Mexico).

SUBREGIONAL OFFICES

Caribbean: 1 Chancery Lane, POB 1113, Port of Spain, Trinidad and Tobago; tel. 224-8000; fax 623-8485; e-mail registry@eclacpos.org; internet www.eclacpos.org; f. 1956; covers non-Spanish-speaking Caribbean countries; functions as the secretariat for the Caribbean Development and Co-operation Committee; Dir DIANE QUARLESS (Jamaica).

Central America and Spanish-speaking Caribbean: Edif. Corporativo MCS, Av. Miguel de Cervantes Saavedra 193, piso 12, Col. Granada. Del. Miguel Hidalgo, CP11520, México, DF; tel. (55) 4170-5600; fax (55) 5531-1151; e-mail registromexico@cepal.org; internet www.cepal.org.mx; f. 1951; covers Central America and Spanish-speaking Caribbean countries; Dir HUGO E. BETETA.

There are also national offices, in Buenos Aires, Argentina; Brasília, Brazil; Bogotá, Colombia; and Montevideo, Uruguay; and a liaison office in Washington, DC, USA.

Activities

ECLAC collaborates with regional governments in the investigation and analysis of regional and national economic problems, and provides guidance in the formulation of development plans. The activities of its different divisions include research, monitoring of trends and policies, and comparative studies; analysis; publication of information; provision of technical assistance; organizing and participating in workshops, seminars and conferences; training courses; and co-operation with national, regional and international organizations, including non-governmental organizations and the private sector. ECLAC's 29th session, held in Brasília, Brazil, in May 2002, adopted the Brasília Resolution, which outlined a strategic agenda to meet the challenges of globalization. Proposed action included the consolidation of democracy, strengthening social protection, the formulation of policies to reduce macroeconomic and financial vulnerability, and the development of sustainable and systemic competitiveness in order to build, gradually, an international social agenda based on rights.

The 34th session of the Commission, convened in August 2012, in San Salvador, El Salvador, proposed the implementation of structural changes to diversify the region's economies and to promote social equality and environmental sustainability, and presented a report entitled *Structural Change for Equality: An Integrated Development View*. In June 2013 a ministerial meeting on Innovation and Structural Change in Latin America, organized by ECLAC in Rio de Janeiro, Brazil, adopted the Rio de Janeiro Declaration on promoting strategies and industrial policies aimed at boosting inclusive regional development. In May 2014 the Commission's 35th session, held in Lima, Peru, established a new Regional Conference on Social Development, with the aim of advancing bilateral, regional and international co-operation towards, and improving national policies on, social development; and, furthermore, examining multidimensional poverty in the region, and improving the measurement of poverty, inequality and structural gaps. The inaugural meeting of the Conference was to take place in the second half of 2015. The 35th session also fostered dialogue on the region's vision of the UN's post-2015 development agenda, and relating to the preparation of new UN system-wide Sustainable Development Goals. The priority areas addressed by ECLAC's work programme for the two-year period 2014–15 were: improving macroeconomic stability, and enhancing policies aimed at reducing vulnerability and mitigating the effects of economic and financial crises; strengthening access to financing for development, and enhancing the financial architecture at all levels; increasing the region's productive potential, with a particular emphasis on innovation and new technologies; advancing—through trade, regional integration and co-operation—the region's position in the global economy; improving social equality, reducing social risks and strengthening gender mainstreaming in public policies; enhancing policies on sustainable development, improving energy efficiency, addressing the impacts of climate change, facilitating implementation of the outcomes of the June 2012 UN Conference on Sustainable Development, and reducing vulnerability in key sectors; reinforcing public management, particularly through progressive fiscal policies; and improving institution-building related to the management of global and transboundary issues, and the provision of public goods at the regional level.

ECLAC works closely with other UN agencies and with other regional and multinational organizations. In January 2010 ECLAC offered its total co-operation in the immediate humanitarian tasks resulting from the earthquake that caused extensive damage and loss of life in Haiti and in any future reconstruction process. In March, following a massive earthquake in Chile, ECLAC established a joint working group, with the UN Development Programme (UNDP), the Office for the Co-ordination of Humanitarian Affairs (OCHA) and the Chilean authorities, to define priority areas for emergency funding.

ECLAC supports member countries in negotiations of bilateral or subregional free trade agreements, in particular with the USA. In January 2002 ECLAC hosted an Interregional Conference on Financing for Development, held in Mexico City, Mexico, which it had organized as part of the negotiating process prior to the World Summit on Financing for Development, held in March. In June senior representatives of ECLAC, UNDP, the World Bank and the Inter-American Development Bank (IADB) agreed to co-ordinate activities in pursuit of the Millennium Development Goals. In July 2004 the 30th session of the Commission approved the establishment of an intergovernmental forum to monitor the implementation of decisions emerging from the World Summit on Sustainable Development, held in Johannesburg, South Africa, in September 2002. In January 2006 ECLAC organized the first Regional Implementation Forum on Sustainable Development, as mandated by the UN Commission on Sustainable Development. In June 2012 the ECLAC Executive Secretary and the President of the People's Republic of China discussed the creation of a new China-Latin America Cooperation Forum, with a view to strengthening inter-regional relations. In July ECLAC, the Latin American Integration Association, and the Corporación Andina de Fomento concluded an inter-agency co-operation agreement on establishing a Latin America/Asia-Pacific Observatory, which was to analyse systematically economic relations between the countries of those regions, with a view to strengthening inter-regional co-operation.

A regional ministerial meeting convened, at the request of the Commission, in June 2005, in Rio de Janeiro, approved a Regional Action Plan—eLAC 2007—to support national and regional projects that incorporate information and communications technology for use in economic and social development in the region. A second plan, eLAC2010, was adopted by ministers in February 2008, to assist countries to attain the global targets identified by the World Summit on the Information Society (WSIS, convened held in two instalments, in December 2003, in Geneva, Switzerland, and in November 2005, in Tunis, Tunisia). The first Follow-up Meeting of eLAC2010 was convened in April 2009. A third Ministerial Conference on the Information Society in Latin America and the Caribbean was held in Lima, Peru, in November 2010, at which a new action plan, eLAC2015, was approved. ECLAC serves as the technical secretariat for a regional dialogue on the costs of international connections, broadband services and digital inclusion, which was inaugurated in August 2010. In May 2011 ECLAC launched a new Regional Broadband Observatory (ORBA), which aims to facilitate public policy decision-making with regard to the provision of broadband services, and in October ECLAC organized its first so-called School for broadband policymakers. In that month, the fourth meeting of the regional dialogue on broadband endorsed ORBA proposals relating to minimum download speeds and connectivity. In April 2013 the fourth Ministerial Conference on the Information Society in Latin America and the Caribbean was convened in Montevideo, Uruguay. Ministers and representatives from 15 countries reaffirmed their commitment to the targets outlined in eLAC2015 and agreed to strengthen regional collaboration to develop further the digital economy.

In November 2003 a Regional Intergovernmental Conference on Ageing was convened, in Santiago, to further the objectives of a World Assembly on Ageing that had been held in Madrid, Spain, in April 2002. A second Regional Intergovernmental Conference on Ageing was held in Brasília, in December 2007, and a third was held in May 2012, in San José, Costa Rica, on the theme 'Ageing, Solidarity and Social Protection: Time to Move Towards Equality'. The 2012 Conference adopted the San José Letter on the rights of the elderly, expressing regional commitment to the eradication of all forms of discrimination, and to establishing networks for the protection of old people. In November 2013 ECLAC organized the seventh Statistical Conference of the Americas (SCA), which is convened every two years to promote the development and improvement of national statistics (in particular their comparability), and to encourage co-operation between national statistical offices and regional and international organizations. ECLAC organizes an annual competition to encourage small-scale innovative social projects in local communities. In July 2009 ECLAC signed an agreement with the UN World Tourism Organization to strengthen co-operation in measuring and analysing tourism statistics and indicators. In January 2010 ECLAC initiated a joint project with the IADB to conduct an economic analysis of the impact of climate change on the region. A database on coastal dynamics in Latin America and the Caribbean, for use in planning on coastal vulnerability and the impact of climate change, was initiated in October 2013 jointly by ECLAC, the Spanish Government and the University of Cantabria (Spain). In January 2012 ECLAC and the Union of Universities of Latin America and the Caribbean signed a five-year co-operation

agreement providing a framework for collaboration between officials and consultants in the shared goal of improving research, debate and training of professionals. ECLAC acts as the secretariat for the Observatory on Gender Equality for Latin America and the Caribbean, which was established in 2008 and is supported by partners including UN Women and the UN Population Fund. In October 2013 the 12th session of ECLAC's Regional Conference on Women adopted the Santo Domingo Consensus on progress towards gender equality, which focused on the linkage between economic autonomy and women's rights, and detailed actions aimed at building a technological, scientific and digital culture geared towards the economic advancement of women and girls. The Consensus also addressed the elimination of violence, female political participation, and sexual and reproductive rights.

In August 2013 ECLAC, with support from the UN Population Fund, hosted the inaugural gathering of the Regional Conference on Population and Development in Latin America and the Caribbean; the meeting adopted the Montevideo Consensus on Population and Development, setting out a series of measures related to eight priority areas for action identified in the regional agenda to follow up the Programme of Action of the International Conference on Population and Development beyond 2014.

In July 2006 Japan became the first Asian nation to be granted full membership of ECLAC. The membership of the Republic of Korea was formally approved in July 2007. A new co-operation agreement between Korea and ECLAC was signed in June 2014.

Latin American and Caribbean Institute for Economic and Social Planning (Instituto Latinoamericano y del Caribe de Planificacion Economica y Social—ILPES): Edif. Naciones Unidas, Avda Dag Hammarskjöld 3477, Vitacura, Casilla 179-D, Santiago, Chile; tel. (2) 2102507; fax (2) 2066104; e-mail ilpes@cepal.org; internet www.eclac.cl/ilpes; f. 1962; supports regional governments through the provision of training, advisory services and research in the field of public planning policy and co-ordination; Dir JORGE MATTAR MÁRQUEZ (Mexico).

Latin American Demographic Centre (Centro Latinoamericano y Caribeno de Demografia—CELADE): Edif. Naciones Unidas, Avda Dag Hammarskjöld 3477, Casilla 179-D, Santiago, Chile; tel. (2) 2102021; fax (2) 2080196; e-mail celade@eclac.cl; internet www.eclac.cl/celade; f. 1957, became an autonomous entity within ECLAC in 1971 and was fully incorporated into ECLAC as its Population Division in 1997; provides technical assistance to governments, universities and research centres in demographic analysis, population policies, integration of population factors in development planning, and data processing; conducts courses on demographic analysis for development and various national and regional seminars; provides demographic estimates and projections, documentation, data processing, computer packages and training; Dir DIRK JASPERS-FAIJER (Netherlands).

Finance

For the two-year period 2014–15 ECLAC's proposed regular budget, an appropriation from the UN, amounted to US $116.7m. In addition, extra-budgetary activities are financed by governments, other organizations, and UN agencies.

Publications

(in English and Spanish)

CEPAL Review (3 a year).

Challenges / Desafios (2–3 a year, with UNICEF).

Demographic Observatory (2 a year).

ECLAC Notes (quarterly).

Economic and Social Panorama of the Community of Latin American and Caribbean States.

Economic Survey of Latin America and the Caribbean (annually).

FAL Bulletin (Trade Facilitation and Transport in Latin America) (monthly, electronic).

Foreign Investment in Latin America and the Caribbean (annually).

Latin America and the Caribbean in the World Economy (annually).

Latin American Economic Outlook (annually).

Macroeconomic Report on Latin America and the Caribbean (annually).

Notas de Población (2 a year).

Preliminary Overview of the Economies of Latin America and the Caribbean (annually).

Statistical Yearbook for Latin America and the Caribbean.

Studies, reports, bibliographical bulletins.

United Nations Development Programme—UNDP

Address: One United Nations Plaza, New York, NY 10017, USA.
Telephone: (212) 906-5300; **fax:** (212) 906-5364; **e-mail:** hq@undp.org; **internet:** www.undp.org.

UNDP was established in 1965 by the UN General Assembly. Its central mission is to help countries to eradicate poverty and achieve a sustainable level of human development, an approach to economic growth that encompasses individual well-being and choice, equitable distribution of the benefits of development, and conservation of the environment. UNDP co-ordinates global and national efforts to achieve the UN Millennium Development Goals, and is contributing to the formulation of a post-2015 UN system-wide development framework.

Organization

(September 2014)

UNDP is responsible to the UN General Assembly, to which it reports through the Economic and Social Council (ECOSOC).

EXECUTIVE BOARD

The Executive Board is responsible for providing intergovernmental support to, and supervision of, the activities of UNDP and the UN Population Fund (UNFPA). It comprises 36 members: eight from Africa, seven from Asia and the Pacific, four from Eastern Europe, five from Latin America and the Caribbean and 12 from Western Europe and other countries. Members serve a three-year term.

SECRETARIAT

Offices and divisions at the Secretariat include an Operations Support Group; Offices of the United Nations Development Group, the Human Development Report, Development Studies, Audit and Performance Review, Evaluation, and Communications; and Bureaux for Crisis Prevention and Recovery; Partnerships; Development Policy; and Management. Five regional bureaux, all headed by an assistant administrator, cover Africa; Asia and the Pacific; the Arab states; Latin America and the Caribbean; and Europe and the Commonwealth of Independent States. UNDP's Administrator (the third most senior UN official, after the Secretary-General and the Deputy Secretary-General) is in charge of strategic policy and overall co-ordination of UN development activities (including the chairing of the UN Development Group), while the Associate Administrator supervises the operations and management of UNDP programmes.

Administrator: HELEN CLARK (New Zealand).

Associate Administrator: MARÍA EUGENIA CASAR (Mexico).

Assistant Administrator and Director, Regional Bureau for Latin America and the Caribbean: JESSICA FAIETA (Ecuador).

COUNTRY OFFICES

In almost every country receiving UNDP assistance there is an office, headed by the UNDP Resident Representative, who usually also serves as the UN Resident Co-ordinator and Humanitarian Co-ordinator, responsible for the co-ordination of all UN technical assistance, humanitarian operations and development activities in that country, so as to ensure the most effective use of UN and international aid resources.

OFFICES OF UN RESIDENT CO-ORDINATORS IN SOUTH AMERICA, CENTRAL AMERICA AND THE CARIBBEAN

Argentina: Esmeralda 130, Piso 13, CPA C1035ABD, Buenos Aires; tel. (1) 4320-8700; fax (1) 4320-8754; e-mail registry.ar@undp.org; internet www.ar.undp.org; Resident Rep. RENÉ MAURICIO VALDÉS.

Barbados: Marine Gardens, Hastings, Christ Church; tel. 467-6000; fax 429-2448; e-mail registry.bb@undp.org; internet www.bb.undp.org; also covers Anguilla, Antigua and Barbuda, British Virgin Islands, Dominica, Grenada, Montserrat, Saint Christopher and Nevis, Saint Lucia, Saint Vincent and the Grenadines; Resident Coordinator STEPHEN O'MALLEY.

Bolivia: Calle 14 Eq. Avda Sánchez Bustamante, Edif. Metrobol II, Calacoto, Casilla 9072, La Paz, Bolivia; tel. (2) 242-6000; fax (2) 279-5820; e-mail registry.bo@undp.org; internet www.bo.undp.org; Resident Rep. KATHERINE GRIGSBY.

Brazil: CP 0285, 70359 Brasília, DF; tel. (61) 3038-9300; e-mail jorge.chediek@undp.org; internet www.pnud.org.br; Resident Co-ordinator JORGE CHEDIEK.

Chile: Avda Dag Hammarskjöld, 3241 Vitacura, 7630412 Santiago; tel. (2) 654-1000; fax (2) 654-1099; e-mail registry.cl@undp.org; internet www.cl.undp.org; Resident Co-ordinator ANTONIO MOLPECERES.

Colombia: Avda 82, 10-62, Piso 3, Bogotá; tel. (1) 488-9000; e-mail fo.col@undp.org; internet www.pnud.org.co; Resident Co-ordinator FABRIZIO HOCHSCHILD.

Costa Rica: Apdo Postal 4540-1000, San José; tel. 22961544; fax 22961545; e-mail registry.cr@undp.org; internet www.cr.undp.org; Resident Co-ordinator YORIKO YASUKAWA.

Cuba: Calle 18 No. 110 (entre 1ra y 3ra), Miramar, Playa, Havana; tel. (7) 204-1513; fax (7) 204-1516; e-mail registry.cu@undp.org; internet www.cu.undp.org; Resident Co-ordinator BARBARA PESCE-MONTEIRO.

Dominican Republic: Casa de las Naciones Unidas, Av. Anacaona 9, Mirador Sur. Apdo 1424, Santo Domingo; tel. 537-0909; fax 537-3507; e-mail registry.do@undp.org; internet www.do.undp.org; Resident Co-ordinator VALERIE JULLIAND.

Ecuador: Avda Amazonas 2889 y la Granja, Quito; tel. (2) 2460-330; fax (2) 2461-960; e-mail registry.ec@undp.org; internet www.pnud.org.ec; Resident Co-ordinator DIEGO ZORRILLA.

El Salvador: Edif. Naciones Unidas, Blvd Orden de Malta Sur, 2B Santa Elena, Antiguo Cuscatlan,San Salvador; tel. 22630066; fax 22093588; e-mail registry.sv@undp.org; internet www.sv.undp.org; Resident Representative ROBERTO VALENT; also covers Belize.

Guatemala: 5A Av. 5-55, Zona 14, Edificio Europlaza, Torre IV, Nivel 10, 01014 Guatemala City; tel. (2) 3843100; fax (2) 3843200; e-mail pnud.gt@undp.org; internet www.gt.undp.org; Resident Co-ordinator VALERIE JULLIAND.

Guyana: 42 Brickdam and Boyle Pl., POB 10960, Georgetown, Guyana; tel. (2) 64040; fax (2) 62942; e-mail registry.gy@undp.org; internet www.gy.undp.org; Resident Co-ordinator KHADIJA MUSA.

Haiti: 18 blvd Toussaint Louverture et Claircine, BP 557, Port-au-Prince; tel. 2244-9350; fax 2244-9366; e-mail registry.ht@undp.org; internet www.ht.undp.org; Resident Co-ordinator PETER DE CLERCQ.

Honduras: Colonia Palmira, Apdo Postal 976, Tegucigalpa DC; tel. 220-1100; fax 239-8010; e-mail webmaster.hn@undp.org; internet www.hn.undp.org; Resident Co-ordinator CONSUELO VIDAL-BRUCE.

Jamaica: 1-3 Lady Musgrave Rd, POB 280, Kingston; tel. 978-2390; fax 946-2163; e-mail registry.jm@undp.org; internet www.jm.undp.org; Resident Co-ordinator Dr ARUN KASHYAP; also covers Bahamas, Cayman Islands, Turks and Caicos Islands.

Mexico: Montes Urales 440, Col. Lomas de Chapultepec, Del. Miguel Hidalgo 11000, México, DF; tel. (55) 4000-9700; fax (55) 5255-0095; e-mail fo.mex@undp.org; internet www.mx.undp.org; Resident Co-ordinator MARCIA DE CASTRO.

Nicaragua: Apdo Postal 3260, Managua; tel. 266-1701; fax 266-6909; e-mail registry.ni@undp.org; internet www.ni.undp.org; Resident Co-ordinator SILVIA RUCKS.

Panama: Apdo 0816-1914, Casa de las Naciones Unidas, Ciudad del Saber, Edif. 129, Panamá; tel. 302-4500; fax 306-4500; e-mail info@undp.org.pa; internet www.pa.undp.org; Resident Co-ordinator MARTÍN SANTIAGO HERRERO.

Paraguay: Avda Mcal. López esq. Saraví, Edificio Naciones Unidas, Asunción; tel. (21) 611980; fax (21) 611981; e-mail registry.py@undp.org; internet www.py.undp.org; Resident Co-ordinator CECILIA UGAZ ESTRADA.

Peru: Complejo Javier Pérez de Cuéllar, Av. Pérez Araníbar 750, Magdalena del Mar, Lima 17; tel. (1) 6259000; fax (1) 6259100; e-mail fo.per@undp.org; internet www.pe.undp.org; Resident Co-ordinator REBECA ARIAS.

Uruguay: J. Barrias Amorín 870, 2°, Montevideo; tel. 2412 3356; fax 2412 3360; e-mail fouru@undp.org; internet www.uy.undp.org; Resident Co-ordinator DENISE COOK.

Venezuela: Avda Francisco de Miranda, Torre Hewlett-Packard, 6°, oficina 6A, Urb. Los Palos Grandes, Caracas; tel. (212) 208-4444; fax (212) 263-8179; e-mail recepcion.ven@undp.org; internet www.ve.undp.org; Resident Co-ordinator NIKY FABIANCIC.

Activities

UNDP works as the UN's global development network, advocating for change and connecting countries to knowledge, experience and resources to help people to build a better life. In 2014 UNDP was active in 177 countries. It provides advisory and support services to governments and UN teams with the aim of advancing sustainable human development and building national development capabilities. Assistance is mostly non-monetary, comprising the provision of experts' services, consultancies, equipment and training for local workers. Developing countries themselves contribute significantly to the total project costs in terms of personnel, facilities, equipment and supplies. UNDP also supports programme countries in attracting aid and utilizing it efficiently.

The UNDP Administrator chairs the UN Development Group (UNDG), which promotes coherent policy at country level through the system of UN Resident Co-ordinators, the Common Country Assessment mechanism (CCA, a process for evaluating national development needs), and the UN Development Assistance Framework (UNDAF, for planning and co-ordination development operations at country level, based on the CCA). UNDP maintains a series of Thematic Trust Funds to channel support to priority programme activities.

UNDP's 2014–17 Strategic Plan, adopted in September 2013, focused the organization's work around the following desired outcomes: inclusive and sustainable development and growth; stronger systems of democratic governance; strengthened delivery of universal basic services; faster progress in reducing gender inequality; enabling member states to reduce the likelihood of conflict and natural disasters; promoting the rapid return to sustainable development pathways in post-conflict and post-natural disaster scenarios; and the prioritization of poverty, inequality and exclusion in development debates and actions at all levels. UNDP's development activities were to place particular emphasis on: people living in poverty (as defined by UNDP's Multidimensional Poverty Index, the global US \$1.25 per day poverty line, and national poverty lines); and groups experiencing the greatest social inequalities and exclusion, especially women, female-headed households and youth. The principal focal areas of work under the Strategic Plan were: how to adopt sustainable development pathways; how to build and/or strengthen inclusive and effective democratic governance; and how to build resilience.

UNDP, jointly with the World Bank, leads an initiative on 'additional financing for the most vulnerable', the first of nine activities that were launched in April 2009 by the UN System Chief Executives Board for Co-ordination (CEB), with the aim of alleviating the impact on poor and vulnerable populations of the developing global economic crisis.

In 2014 UNDP was implementing 1,074 projects in Latin America and the Caribbean, at a cost of US \$390.4m. Of total expenditure in the region in that year, some 45% was allocated to projects related to poverty reduction and MDG achievement, while activities related to promoting democratic governance accounted for 30%, environment and sustainable development 17%, crisis prevention and recovery 7%, and South–South co-operation 6%. The top recipient country offices in the region in 2014 were Argentina (\$512m.), Brazil (\$243m.), Peru (\$237m.), Venezuela (\$106m.), Colombia (\$86m.), and Haiti (\$65m.).

MILLENNIUM DEVELOPMENT GOALS

UNDP, through its leadership of the UNDG and management of the Resident Co-ordinator system, has a co-ordinating function as the focus of UN system-wide efforts to achieve the so-called Millennium Development Goals (MDGs), pledged by UN member governments attending a summit meeting of the UN General Assembly in September 2000. The objectives were to establish a defined agenda to reduce poverty and improve the quality of lives of millions of people and to serve as a framework for measuring development. There are eight MDGs, as follows, for which one or more specific targets have been identified:

i) to eradicate extreme poverty and hunger, with the aim of reducing by 50% (compared with the 1990 figure) the number of people with an income of less than US \$1 a day and those suffering from hunger by 2015, and to achieve full and productive employment and decent work for all, including women and young people;

ii) to achieve universal primary education by 2015;

iii) to promote gender equality and empower women, in particular to eliminate gender disparities in primary and secondary education by 2005 and at all levels by 2015;

iv) to reduce child mortality, with a target reduction of two-thirds in the mortality rate among children under five by 2015 (compared with the 1990 level);

v) to improve maternal health, specifically to reduce by 75% the numbers of women dying in childbirth and to achieve universal access to reproductive health by 2015 (compared with the 1990 level);

vi) to combat HIV/AIDS, malaria and other diseases, with targets to have halted and begun to reverse the incidence of HIV/AIDS, malaria and other major diseases by 2015 and to achieve universal access to treatment for HIV/AIDS for all those who need it by 2010;

vii) to ensure environmental sustainability, including targets to integrate the principles of sustainable development into country policies and programmes, to reduce by 50% (compared with the 1990 level) the number of people without access to safe drinking water by 2015, and to achieve significant improvement in the lives of at least 100m. slum dwellers by 2020;

viii) to develop a global partnership for development, including an open, rule-based, non-discriminatory trading and financial system, and efforts to deal with international debt, to address the needs of least developed countries (LDCs) and landlocked and small island developing states, to provide access to affordable, essential drugs in developing countries, and to make available the benefits of new technologies.

UNDP has played a leading role in efforts to integrate the MDGs into all aspects of UN activities at country level and to ensure that the MDGs are incorporated into national development strategies. UNDP supports efforts by countries, as well as regions and subregions, to report on progress towards achievement of the goals, and on specific social, economic and environmental indicators, through the formulation of MDG reports. These form the basis of an annual global report, issued by the UN Secretary-General. UNDP also works to raise awareness of the MDGs and to support advocacy efforts at all levels. UNDP provides administrative and technical support to the Millennium Project, an independent advisory body established by the UN Secretary-General in 2002 to develop a practical action plan to achieve the MDGs. Financial support of the Project is channelled through a Millennium Trust Fund, administered by UNDP. In January 2005 the Millennium Project presented its report, based on extensive research conducted by teams of experts, which included recommendations for the international system to support country level development efforts and identified a series of 'Quick Wins' to bring conclusive benefit to millions of people in the short-term. International commitment to achieve the MDGs by 2015 was reiterated at a World Summit, convened in September 2005. UNDP and the UN Department of Economic and Social Affairs (UNDESA) are lead agencies in co-ordinating the work of the MDG Gap Task Force, which was established by the UN Secretary-General in May 2007 to track, systematically and at both international and country level, existing international commitments in the areas of official development assistance, market access, debt relief, access to essential medicines and technology. In November the UN, in partnership with two major US companies, launched an online MDG Monitor to track progress and to support organizations working to achieve the goals. In September 2010 UNDP launched the MDGs Acceleration Framework, which aimed to support countries in identifying and overcoming barriers to eradicating extreme poverty and achieving sustainable development. The 2013 edition of the *Millennium Development Goals Report*, issued in July of that year, reported that progress towards achieving the MDGs remained uneven between regions, countries, and also between population groups within countries, with communities living in poverty or in rural areas facing unfair disadvantage.

POST-2015 DEVELOPMENT FRAMEWORK

In January 2012 the UN Secretary-General established a UN System Task Team—led jointly by the UNDP Administrator-General and the UN Under-Secretary-General for Economic and Social Affairs—which supports system-wide consultations in 11 thematic areas, each led by specified UN agencies, on the advancement of the post-2015 global development agenda. In May and July, respectively, the Co-Chairs and membership were announced of a new High-level Panel to Advise on the Global Development Agenda Beyond 2015, and in September 2012 the Panel's Executive Secretary was appointed and the Panel's inaugural meeting was held, on the sidelines of the UN General Assembly. In May 2013 the Panel presented to the UN Secretary-General a draft document entitled *A New Global Partnership: Eradicate Poverty and Transform Economies through Sustainable Development*, which set out a universal agenda to eradicate extreme poverty globally by 2030, and to pursue and deliver sustainable development. The Panel consulted closely with a working group of experts tasked by the UN Conference on Sustainable Development (convened in June 2012) to formulate a series of Sustainable Development Goals. In September 2013 a special event on the MDGs, convened by the UN General Assembly, requested that a summit meeting be held in September 2015 to adopt a set of follow-on Development Goals that would build on and supersede the MDGs. During 2013 the UN organized 88 national dialogues and a series of thematic consultations on the post-2015 agenda, covering: conflict and fragility; education; energy; environmental sustainability; food security and nutrition; governance; growth and employment; health; inequalities; population dynamics; and water. An interactive social media platform (entitled 'World We Want') was also inaugurated. In March 2014 the UNDG announced that a series of Dialogues on Implementation of the Post-2015 Development Agenda were to be initiated in, at first, some 50 countries, with participation by policy makers, and representatives of civil society, local communities and the private sector; the Dialogues were to be supplemented by internet-based public consultations, focused on the World We Want social media platform. The six thematic areas of the Dialogues were: localizing the post-2015 agenda; strengthening capacities and institutions; participatory monitoring, existing and new forms of accountability; partnerships with civil society and other actors; partnerships with the private sector; and culture and development. In August 2014 the UN Secretary-General announced the membership of an Independent Expert Advisory Group on the Data Revolution for Sustainable Development, which was to help to shape an ambitious but achievable vision for the new agenda.

DEMOCRATIC GOVERNANCE

UNDP supports national efforts to ensure efficient and accountable governance, to improve the quality of democratic processes, and to build effective relations between the state, the private sector and civil society, which are essential to achieving sustainable development. As in other practice areas, UNDP assistance includes policy advice and technical support, the capacity building of institutions and individuals, advocacy and public information and communication, the promotion and brokering of dialogue, and knowledge networking and sharing of good practices.

UNDP works to strengthen parliaments and other legislative bodies as institutions of democratic participation. It assists with constitutional reviews and reform, training of parliamentary staff, and capacity building of political parties and civil organizations as part of this objective. In April 2012, jointly with the Inter-Parliamentary Union, UNDP released the *Global Parliamentary Report*, which addressed means of improving strategies to meet public expectations of parliaments. UNDP undertakes missions to help prepare for and ensure the conduct of free and fair elections. It helps to build the long-term capacity of electoral institutions and practices within a country, for example by assisting with voter registration, the establishment of electoral commissions, providing observers to verify that elections are free and fair, projects to educate voters, and training journalists to provide impartial election coverage.

Within its justice sector programme UNDP supports projects to improve access to justice, in particular for the poor and disadvantaged, and to promote judicial independence, legal reform and understanding of the legal system. UNDP also works to promote access to information, the integration of human rights issues into activities concerned with sustainable human development, and support for the international human rights system.

UNDP is mandated to assist developing countries to fight corruption and improve accountability, transparency and integrity (ATI). It has worked to establish national and international partnerships in support of its anti-corruption efforts and used its role as a broker of knowledge and experience to uphold ATI principles at all levels of public financial management and governance. UNDP publishes case studies of its anti-corruption efforts and assists governments to conduct self-assessments of their public financial management systems. UNDP leads the new secretariat of the International Aid Transparency Initiative, which was inaugurated, in collaboration with other members of the multi-stakeholder steering committee, in September 2013.

In March 2002 a UNDP Governance Centre was inaugurated in Oslo, Norway, to enhance the role of UNDP in support of democratic governance and to assist countries to implement democratic reforms in order to achieve the MDGs. The Centre undertakes analysis of governance projects and emerging issues, and provides training programmes and workshops. The Democratic Governance Network allows discussion and the sharing of information. An iKnow Politics Network, supported by UNDP, aims to help women become involved in politics.

POVERTY REDUCTION

UNDP aims to promote sustainable human development by ensuring that national development policies emphasize the needs of the poor and marginalized, and by supporting developing countries in integrating human rights principles and standards into the design and implementation of development policies (on the basis that equal opportunities and freedoms are conducive to the promotion of economic growth with an inclusive impact). Activities aimed at facilitating poverty eradication include support for capacity-building programmes and initiatives to generate sustainable livelihoods, for example by improving access to credit, land and technologies, and the promotion of strategies to improve education and health provision for the poorest elements of populations (especially women and girls). UNDP aims to help governments to reassess their development priorities and to design initiatives for sustainable human development. Following the introduction, in 1999, by the World Bank and IMF of Poverty Reduction Strategy Papers (PRSPs), UNDP has helped governments to draft these documents, and, since 2001, has linked the papers to efforts to achieve and monitor progress towards

the MDGs. In 2004 UNDP inaugurated the International Poverty Centre for Inclusive Growth (IPC-IG), in Brasília, Brazil, which fosters the capacity of countries to formulate and implement poverty reduction strategies and encourages South-South co-operation in all relevant areas of research and decision making. In particular, the Centre aims to assist countries to meet MDGs through research into and implementation of pro-poor policies that encourage social protection and human development, and through the monitoring of poverty and inequality. UNDP's Secretariat hosts the UN Office for South-South Cooperation, which was established, as the Special Unit for South-South Cooperation, by the United Nations General Assembly in 1978.

UNDP country offices support the formulation of national human development reports (NHDRs), which aim to facilitate activities such as policymaking, the allocation of resources, and monitoring progress towards poverty eradication and sustainable development. In addition, the preparation of Advisory Notes and Country Co-operation Frameworks by UNDP officials helps to highlight country-specific aspects of poverty eradication and national strategic priorities. Since 1990 UNDP has published an annual *Human Development Report*, incorporating a Human Development Index, which ranks countries in terms of human development, using three key indicators: life expectancy, adult literacy and basic income required for a decent standard of living. The Report also includes a Human Poverty Index and a Gender-related Development Index, which assesses gender equality on the basis of life expectancy, education and income. The 2014 edition of the Report, *Sustaining Human Progress: Reducing Vulnerabilities and Building Resilience*, was released in late July. UNDP proposed to the June 2012 UNCSD a future 'Sustainable Human Development Index', which would recognize the impact on future generations of contemporary development, and place a high value on factors such as dignity and sustainability, alongside economic development. Jointly with the International Labour Organization (ILO), UNDP operates a Programme on Employment for Poverty Reduction, which undertakes analysis and studies, and supports countries in improving their employment strategies. In March 2012 the first Global Human Development Forum was convened, under UNDP auspices, in İstanbul, Turkey; delegates (comprising experts on development, and representatives of the UN, governments, the private sector and civil society) adopted the İstanbul Declaration, urging that the global development agenda should be redrafted, and calling for concerted global action against social inequities and environmental degradation.

In March 2014 UNDP launched its first ever Youth Strategy ('Empowered Youth, Sustainable Future'), which made recommendations for the engagement of young people and a wide range of partners in addressing youth empowerment issues globally.

UNDP is committed to ensuring that the process of economic and financial globalization, including national and global trade, debt and capital flow policies, incorporates human development concerns. It aimed to ensure that the Doha Development Round of World Trade Organization (WTO) negotiations should achieve an expansion of trade opportunities and economic growth to less developed countries. UNDP is a partner—with the IMF, the International Trade Centre, the UN Conference on Trade and Development (UNCTAD), the World Bank and the WTO—in the Enhanced Integrated Framework (EIF) for trade-related assistance to LDCs, a multi-donor programme which aims to support greater participation by LDCs in the global trading system; EIF funds are channelled through a dedicated EIF Trust Fund.

A *Regional Human Development Report for Latin America and the Caribbean* was published in 2010. The 2012 *Caribbean Human Development Report: Human Development and the Shift to Better Citizen Security*, issued in February of that year, focused on the threat posed by crime to economies and livelihoods in the region, and on recommendations for combating this. National human development reports were published for Argentina and Jamaica (in 2013), and on Panama (in 2014).

UNDP has a leading role in the World Alliance of Cities Against Poverty, which was inaugurated in 1996 as a network of municipal authorities committed to addressing and co-operating on the challenges of urbanization, including poor housing, transport, the management of waste disposal, water supply and sanitation. The eighth global Forum of the Alliance convened in Dublin, Ireland, in February 2013.

UNDP sponsors the International Day for the Eradication of Poverty, held annually on 17 October.

ENVIRONMENT AND ENERGY

UNDP aims to strengthen national capacities to implement effective and sustainable environmental management policies and practices, including addressing the challenges of climate change. Together with the UN Environment Programme (UNEP) and the World Bank, UNDP is an implementing agency of the Global Environment Facility (GEF), which was established in 1991 to finance international co-operation in projects to benefit the environment.

In November 2013 UNDP, with UNEP and the UNFCC, issued a joint publication, *Guidance for NAMA Design: Building on Country Experiences*, which outlined practical means by which governments and organizations might design and implement Nationally Appropriate Mitigation Actions (NAMAs) aimed at mitigating greenhouse gas emissions.

UNDP recognizes that desertification, land degradation and drought (DLDD) are major causes of rural poverty and promotes sustainable land management, drought preparedness and reform of land tenure as means of addressing the problem. It also aims to reduce poverty caused by land degradation through implementation of environmental conventions at national and international level. In June 2009 UNDP and the Secretariat of the UN Convention to Combat Desertification in Those Countries Experiencing Serious Drought and/or Desertification, Particularly in Africa (UNCCD) agreed a pilot strategic working partnership, based on the UNCCD's strategic priorities in combating DLDD and on UNDP's implementation support capabilities at the national level. A formal UNDP/UNCCD programme of co-operation was concluded in March 2012. UNDP is also concerned with sustainable management of forestries, fisheries and agriculture. Since 1992 UNDP has administered a Small Grants Programme, funded by the GEF, to support community-based initiatives concerned with biodiversity conservation, prevention of land degradation and the elimination of persistent organic pollutants. The Equator Initiative, inaugurated in 2002, as a partnership between UNDP and representatives of governments, civil society and businesses, aims to reduce poverty in communities along the equatorial belt by fostering local partnerships, harnessing local knowledge and promoting conservation and sustainable practices. UNDP is a partner agency of the Climate and Clean Air Coalition to Reduce Short Lived Climate Pollutants (SLCPs), which was launched in February 2012 with the aim of combating SLCPs, including methane, black carbon and certain hydrofluorocarbons. UNDP also implements projects funded by the International Climate Initiative (launched in 2008 by the German Government).

In 2012 the MDG Carbon Facility helped to expand the use of 'Turbococina' cooking stoves in El Salvador, with a view to reducing usage of firewood.

UNDP supports efforts to promote international co-operation in the management of chemicals. It was actively involved in the development of a Strategic Approach to International Chemicals Management which was adopted by representatives of 100 governments at an international conference convened in Dubai, United Arab Emirates, in February 2006. UNDP also assists countries to integrate the 'sound management of chemicals' into national development planning.

UNDP works to ensure the effective governance of freshwater and aquatic resources, and promotes co-operation in transboundary water management, ocean and coastal management, efforts to promote safe sanitation and community water supplies. In 1996 UNDP, with the World Bank and the Swedish International Development Agency, established a Global Water Partnership to promote and implement water resources management. UNDP, with the GEF, supports a range of projects which incorporate development and ecological requirements in the sustainable management of international waters. including the Global Mercury Project, a project for improved municipal waste-water management in coastal cities of the African, Caribbean and Pacific states, a Global Ballast Water Management Programme and an International Waters Learning Exchange and Resources Network.

UNDP projects concerned with protecting international waters in South America and the Caribbean include the conservation of biodiversity in the Lake Titicaca Basin, protection of the Rio de la Plata, and management of coastal areas and watersheds in small Caribbean island states.

CRISIS PREVENTION AND RECOVERY

UNDP collaborates with other UN agencies jn to promote relief and development efforts in countries in crisis, in order to secure the foundations for sustainable human development and thereby increase national capabilities to prevent or mitigate future crises. In particular, UNDP is concerned to achieve reconciliation, reintegration and reconstruction in affected countries, as well as to support emergency interventions and management and delivery of programme aid. It aims to facilitate the transition from relief to longer-term recovery and rehabilitation. Special development initiatives in post-conflict countries include the demobilization of former combatants and destruction of illicit small armaments, rehabilitation of communities for the sustainable reintegration of returning populations and the restoration and strengthening of democratic institutions. UNDP established a mine action unit within its Bureau for Crisis Prevention and Recovery in order to strengthen national and local de-mining capabilities including surveying, mapping and clearance of anti-personnel landmines. It also works to increase awareness of the harm done to civilians by cluster munitions, and participated in the negotiations that culminated in the entry into force in August 2010 of the international Convention on Cluster Munitions. UNDP works closely with UNICEF to raise awareness and implement risk reduction education programmes, and manages global partnership projects concerned with training, legislation and the socio-economic impact of anti-personnel devices. UNDP's '8-Point Agenda', adopted in 2005, aims to improve the security of women and girls in conflict situations and promote their participation in post-crisis recovery processes. In late 2006 UNDP began to administer the then newly established UN Peacebuilding Fund of the UN Peacebuilding Support Office. During 2008 UNDP developed a new global programme aimed at strengthening the rule of law in conflict and post-conflict countries; the programme placed particular focus on women's access to justice, institution building and transitional justice.

In 2006 UNDP launched an Immediate Crisis Response programme (known as 'SURGE') aimed at strengthening its capacity to respond quickly and effectively in the recovery phase following a conflict or natural disaster. Under the programme Immediate Crisis Response Advisors—UNDP staff with special expertise in at least one of 12 identified areas, including early recovery, operational support and resource mobilization—are swiftly deployed, in a 'SURGETeam', to UNDP country offices dealing with crises.

UNDP is the focal point within the UN system for strengthening national capacities for natural disaster reduction (prevention, preparedness and mitigation relating to natural, environmental and technological hazards). UNDP's Bureau of Crisis Prevention and Recovery, in conjunction with the Office for the Co-ordination of Humanitarian Affairs and the secretariat of the International Strategy for Disaster Reduction, oversees the system-wide Capacity for Disaster Reduction Initiative (CADRI), which was inaugurated in 2007. UNDP was actively involved in preparations for the second World Conference on Disaster Reduction, which was held in Kobe, Japan, in January 2005. Following the Kobe Conference UNDP initiated a new Global Risk Identification Programme. During 2005 the Inter-Agency Standing Committee, concerned with co-ordinating the international response to humanitarian disasters, developed a concept of providing assistance through a 'Cluster Approach', comprising core areas of activity. UNDP was designated the lead agency for the Early Recovery cluster, linking the immediate needs following a disaster with medium- and long-term recovery efforts. UNDP has participated in a series of consultations on a successor arrangement for the Hyogo Framework for Action that were launched in 2012 by the UN International Strategy for Disaster Reduction (UN/ISDR—the focal point of UN disaster planning); it was envisaged that the post-Hyogo arrangement (expected to be adopted by the third World Conference on Disaster Reduction, to be held in March 2015 in Sendai City, Japan) would specify measurable outcomes of disaster risk reduction planning, in addition to detailing processes, and that, in view of rapidly increasing urbanization globally, it would have a focus on building safer cities. UNDP hosts the Global Risk Identification Programme (GRIP), initiated in 2007 to support activities worldwide aimed at identifying and monitoring disaster risks. Jointly with a German postal and delivery company, UNDP also administers a 'Get Airports Ready for Disaster' programme to train local officials and formulate post-disaster preparedness strategies. In August 2012 the UNDP Administrator, stating that disaster risk management should become central to development planning, announced that UNDP disaster reduction assistance would be doubled over the next five years.

GRIP has helped Tijuana in Mexico, Kathmandu in Nepal and Maputo in Mozambique to carry out Urban Risk Assessments. The Programme has also supported Laos in completing a National Risk Assessment and finalizing a comprehensive National Hazard Risk Profile, which was to be the basis for the formulation of a national Disaster Risk Management Strategy. Meanwhile, UNDP has supported Armenia, Lebanon, Mozambique, Nepal, and Tajikistan to complete a Country Situation Analysis and to undertake National Risk Assessments.

UNDP co-operates with the Coordination Centre for the Prevention of Natural Disasters in Central America (CEPREDENAC) and with the Caribbean Disaster Emergency Management Agency (CDEMA). UNDP supports the long-term recovery under way in Haiti following the severe earthquake that struck that country in January 2010. Projects undertaken by UNDP in Haiti have included cash-for-work initiatives aimed at injecting cash into the fragile local economy, supporting the local population in providing shelter, food and education for their families; and providing labour for rehabilitation work. In March 2011 UNDP and the Haiti Government launched a prevention plan to reduce future vulnerability to seismic threats through improving the resilience of local infrastructure and the quality of housing. By 2014 a joint UNDP-Haitian programme had cleared some 80m. cubic metres of cement and steel debris that had been caused by the earthquake, of which a proportion was to be recycled. An ongoing joint UNDP-UNEP-WFP initiative to reforest part of the Haiti-Dominican Republic border had by that time resulted in more than 300m. ha of land being replanted.

HIV/AIDS

UNDP regards the HIV/AIDS pandemic as a major challenge to development. It advocates making HIV/AIDS a focus of national planning and national poverty reduction strategies; supports decentralized action against HIV/AIDS at the community level; helps to strengthen national capacities at all levels to combat the disease; and aims to link support for prevention activities, education and treatment with broader development planning and responses. UNDP places a particular focus on combating the spread of HIV/AIDS through the promotion of women's rights. UNDP is a co-sponsor, jointly with the World Health Organization (WHO) and other UN bodies, of the Joint UN Programme on HIV/AIDS (UNAIDS), which became operational on 1 January 1996. UNAIDS co-ordinates UNDP's HIV and Development Programme. UNDP works in partnership with the Global Fund to Fight HIV/AIDS, Tuberculosis and Malaria, in particular to support the local principal recipient of grant financing and to help to manage fund projects.

Finance

From 2014–17 UNDP, UNICEF, UNFPA and UN Women were to maintain synchronized strategic planning cycles.

Publications

Annual Report of the Administrator.
Choices (quarterly).
Cooperation South.
Human Development Report (annually).
Poverty Report (annually).
Results-Oriented Annual Report.

Associated Funds and Programmes

UNDP is the central funding, planning and co-ordinating body for technical co-operation within the UN system. A number of associated funds and programmes, financed separately by means of voluntary contributions, provide specific services through the UNDP network. UNDP manages a trust fund to promote economic and technical co-operation among developing countries.

GLOBAL ENVIRONMENT FACILITY (GEF)

The GEF, which is managed jointly by UNDP, the World Bank (which hosts its secretariat) and UNEP, began operations in 1991 and was restructured in 1994. Its aim is to support projects in the six thematic areas of climate change; the conservation of biological diversity; the protection of international waters; reducing the depletion of the ozone layer in the atmosphere; arresting land degradation; and addressing the issue of persistent organic pollutants. Capacity building to allow countries to meet their obligations under international environmental agreements, and adaptation to climate change, are priority cross-cutting components of these projects. The GEF acts as the financial mechanism for the Convention on Biological Diversity and the UN Framework Convention on Climate Change. UNDP is responsible for capacity building, targeted research, pre-investment activities and technical assistance. UNDP also administers the Small Grants Programme of the GEF, which supports community-based activities by local non-governmental organizations, and the Country Dialogue Workshop Programme, which promotes dialogue on national priorities with regard to the GEF; by June 2014 the Small Grants Programme had supported more than 14,500 community-based projects in some 125 countries. In April 2014 donor countries pledged US $4,430m. for the sixth periodic replenishment of GEF funds (GEF-6), covering the period 2015–18.

In 2012 21 countries in Latin America and the Caribbean implemented 65 GEF-financed projects with UNDP support, receiving some US $270m. in grant funding from the Facility.

Chair. and CEO: Dr NAOKO ISHII (Japan).

Executive Co-ordinator of UNDP-GEF Unit: YANNICK GLE-MAREC; 304 East 45th St, 9th Floor, New York, NY 10017, USA; fax (212) 906-6998; e-mail gefinfo@undp.org; internet www.undp.org/gef.

MONTREAL PROTOCOL

Through its Montreal Protocol/Chemicals Unit UNDP collaborates with public and private partners in developing countries to assist them in eliminating the use of ozone-depleting substances (ODS), in accordance with the Montreal Protocol to the Vienna Convention for the Protection of the Ozone Layer, through the design, monitoring and evaluation of ODS phase-out projects and programmes. In particular, UNDP provides technical assistance and training, national capacity building and demonstration projects and technology transfer investment projects.

SUSTAINABLE DEVELOPMENT GOALS ACHIEVEMENT FUND (SDG-F)

The Fund, established in 2014 in accordance with an agreement concluded—on behalf of the UN system—between UNDP and the Spanish Government, is tasked with supporting sustainable development activities through the implementation, through the UN development system at country level, of integrated and multi-dimensional joint programmes. Having superseded the former MDG Achievement Fund (established in 2007), the SDG focuses on the advancement of public-private partnerships, on the Busan Global Partnership for Effective Development Co-operation (endorsed by the Fourth High Level Forum on Aid Effectiveness convened in Busan, Republic of Korea, in November–December 2011), and on the planned Post-2015 Development Agenda. Gender and women's empowerment represents a priority dimension cutting across all areas of the new Fund's work. During 2014 the Fund's first programme proposals, submitted by UN Resident Co-ordinators, were under consideration.

Senior Adviser, SDG-F Secretariat: (vacant); SDG-F Secretariat, c/o UNDP, One United Nations Plaza, New York, NY 10017, USA; tel. (212) 906-6180; fax (212) 906-5364; internet proposals.sdgfund.org.

UNDP DRYLANDS DEVELOPMENT CENTRE (DDC)

The Centre, based in Nairobi, Kenya, was established in February 2002, superseding the former UN Office to Combat Desertification and Drought (UNSO). (UNSO had been established following the conclusion, in October 1994, of the UN Convention to Combat Desertification in Those Countries Experiencing Serious Drought and/or Desertification, Particularly in Africa; in turn, UNSO had replaced the former UN Sudano-Sahelian Office.) The DDC was to focus on the following areas: ensuring that national development planning takes account of the needs of communities based in drylands (arid, semi-arid and dry sub-humid areas, with vulnerable ecosystems), particularly in poverty reduction strategies; helping countries to cope with the effects of climate variability, especially drought, and to prepare for future climate change; and addressing local issues affecting the utilization of resources. The DDC delivers UNDP's Integrated Drylands Development Programme, currently in its second phase focusing on mainstreaming drylands issues and climate change adaptation and mitigation into national policy and development frameworks; building the capacity of drylands communities to address environmental, economic and socio-cultural challenges; and supporting drylands communities through improved local governance, management and utilization of natural resources.

UN Gigiri Compound, United Nations Ave, POB 30552, 00100 Nairobi, Kenya; tel. (20) 7624640; fax (20) 7624648; e-mail ddc@undp.org; internet www.undp.org/drylands.

UNDP-UNEP POVERTY-ENVIRONMENT INITIATIVE (UNPEI)

UNPEI, inaugurated in February 2007, supports countries in developing their capacity to launch and maintain programmes that mainstream poverty-environment linkages into national development planning processes, such as MDG achievement strategies and PRSPs. In May 2007 UNDP and UNEP launched the Poverty-Environment Facility (UNPEF) to co-ordinate, and raise funds in support of, UNPEI. In 2014 UNPEI was supporting programmes in 25 countries, and providing technical advice across all regions.

UN Gigiri Compound, United Nations Ave, POB 30552, 00100 Nairobi, Kenya; e-mail facility.unpei@unpei.org; internet www.unpei.org.

UNITED NATIONS CAPITAL DEVELOPMENT FUND (UNCDF)

The Fund was established in 1966 and became fully operational in 1974. It invests in poor communities in LDCs through local governance projects and microfinance operations, with the aim of increasing such communities' access to essential local infrastructure and services and thereby improving their productive capacities and self-reliance. UNCDF encourages participation by local people and local governments in the planning, implementation and monitoring of projects. The Fund aims to promote the interests of women in community projects and to enhance their earning capacities. UNCDF helps to develop financial services for poor communities and supports UNDP's MicroStart initiative, which assists private sector and community-based initiatives aimed at generating employment opportunities. In November 2008 UNCDF launched MicroLead, a fund (initially amounting to US $26m.) that provides loans to leading microfinance institutions and other financial service providers (MFIs/FSPs) in developing countries; MicroLead was also to focus on the provision of early support to countries in post-conflict situations. In September 2011 UNCDF and the MasterCard Foundation agreed a $23m. six-year expansion of MicroLead with a focus on sub-Saharan Africa. In October 2012 MicroLead was extended into Myanmar, with a $7m. grant from LIFT Myanmar (a multi-donor trust fund).

Executive Secretary: MARC BICHLER (Luxembourg); Two United Nations Plaza, 26th Floor, New York, NY 10017, USA; fax (212) 906-6479; e-mail info@uncdf.org; internet www.uncdf.org.

UNITED NATIONS OFFICE FOR SOUTH-SOUTH COOPERATION

The Office was established as the Special Unit for South-South Cooperation in 1978 by the UN General Assembly and is hosted by UNDP. It was renamed, as above, in 2012 in order to strengthen the work of the body within the UN. The Office aims to co-ordinate and support South-South co-operation in the political, economic, social, environmental and technical areas, and to support 'triangular' collaboration on a UN system-wide and global basis. It organizes the annual UN Day for South-South Cooperation (12 September), and manages the UN Trust Fund for South-South Cooperation (UNFSC) and the Perez-Guerrero Trust Fund for Economic and Technical Co-operation among Developing Countries (PGTF), as well as undertaking programmes financed by UNDP.

Director: YIPING ZHOU (People's Republic of China); 304 East 45th St, 12th Floor, New York, NY 11017, USA; tel. (212) 906-6944; fax (212) 906-6352; e-mail ssc.info@undp.org; internet ssc.undp.org.

UNITED NATIONS VOLUNTEERS (UNV)

The United Nations Volunteers is an important source of middle-level skills for the UN development system supplied at modest cost, particularly in the LDCs. Volunteers expand the scope of UNDP project activities by supplementing the work of international and host country experts and by extending the influence of projects to local community levels. UNV also supports technical co-operation within and among the developing countries by encouraging volunteers from the countries themselves and by forming regional exchange teams comprising such volunteers. UNV is involved in areas such as peacebuilding, elections, human rights, humanitarian relief and community-based environmental programmes, in addition to development activities.

The UN International Short-term Advisory Resources (UNISTAR) Programme, which is the private sector development arm of UNV, has increasingly focused its attention on countries in the process of economic transition. Since 1994 UNV has administered UNDP's Transfer of Knowledge Through Expatriate Nationals (TOKTEN) programme, which was initiated in 1977 to enable specialists and professionals from developing countries to contribute to development efforts in their countries of origin through short-term technical assignments. In March 2000 UNV established an Online Volunteering Service to connect development organizations and volunteers using the internet; in 2013 11,328 online volunteers, working on 17,370 assignments, made their skills available through the Online Volunteering Service.

In December 2011 UNV issued the first *State of the World's Volunteerism Report*, on the theme 'Universal Values for Global Well-being'.

During 2013 some 6,351 national and international UNVs were deployed in 129 countries, on 6,459 assignments; some 10% of UNV assignments were undertaken in Latin America and the Caribbean in 2013.

Executive Co-ordinator: RICHARD DICTUS (Netherlands); POB 260111, 53153 Bonn, Germany; tel. (228) 8152000; fax (228) 8152001; e-mail information@unvolunteers.org; internet www.unv.org.

United Nations Environment Programme—UNEP

Address: POB 30552, Nairobi 00100, Kenya.

Telephone: (20) 621234; **fax:** (20) 623927; **e-mail:** unepinfo@unep.org; **internet:** www.unep.org.

UNEP was established in 1972 by the UN General Assembly, following recommendations of the 1972 UN Conference on the Human Environment, in Stockholm, Sweden, to encourage international co-operation in matters relating to the human environment.

Organization

(September 2014)

UN ENVIRONMENTAL ASSEMBLY

The inaugural meeting of the UN Environmental Assembly (UNEA)—which replaced UNEP's former Governing Council—was convened in late June 2014, in view of a decision made in December 2012 by the UN General Assembly to expand the governance of UNEP from 58 members to universal representation of all UN member states. The UNEA is assisted in its work by a Committee of Permanent Representatives.

SECRETARIAT

The Secretariat of Governing Bodies (SGB) organizes and services all meetings of the UN Environment Assembly and the Committee of Permanent Representatives. Offices and divisions at UNEP headquarters in Nairobi, Kenya, include the Offices of the Executive Director and Deputy Executive Director; the Secretariat for Governing Bodies; Offices for Evaluation and Oversight, Programme Co-ordination and Management, Resource Mobilization, and Global Environment Facility Co-ordination; and Divisions of Communications and Public Information, Early Warning and Assessment, Environmental Policy Implementation, Technology, Industry and Economics, Regional Co-operation, and Environmental Law and Conventions.

Executive Director: ACHIM STEINER (Germany).

Deputy Executive Director: IBRAHIM THIAW (Mauritania).

REGIONAL OFFICES

UNEP maintains six regional offices. These work to initiate and promote UNEP objectives and to ensure that all programme formulation and delivery meets the specific needs of countries and regions. They also provide a focal point for building national, subregional and regional partnerships and enhancing local participation in UNEP initiatives. A co-ordination office has been established at headquarters to promote regional policy integration, to co-ordinate programme planning, and to provide necessary services to the regional offices.

Latin America and the Caribbean: Ciudad del Saber, Edif. 103, Avda Morse, Corregimiento de Ancón, Ciudad de Panamá, Panama; tel. 305-3100; fax 305-3105; e-mail enlace@pnuma.org; internet www.pnuma.org.

UNEP Brasília Office: EQSW 103/104 Lote 1, Bloco C, CEP 70670–350, Setor Sudoeste, Brasília, Brazil; tel. (61) 3038-9233; fax (61) 3038-9239; e-mail pnuma.brasil@unep.org; internet www.pnuma.org.br.

OTHER OFFICES

Basel, Rotterdam and Stockholm Conventions, Secretariat: 11–13 chemin des Anémones, 1219 Châtelaine, Geneva, Switzerland; tel. 229178729; fax 229178098; e-mail brs@brsmeas.org; internet www.basel.int; www.pic.int; www.pops.int; Exec. Sec. Dr ROLPH PAYET (Seychelles) (from 6 Oct. 2014).

Convention on International Trade in Endangered Species of Wild Fauna and Flora (CITES), Secretariat: 15 chemin des Anémones, 1219 Châtelaine, Geneva, Switzerland; tel. 229178139; fax 227973417; e-mail info@cites.org; internet www.cites.org; Sec.-Gen. JOHN SCANLON (Australia).

Global Programme of Action for the Protection of the Marine Environment from Land-based Activities: GPA Co-ordination Unit, UNEP, POB 30552, 00100 Nairobi, Kenya; tel. (20) 7621206; fax (20) 7624249; internet www.gpa.unep.org.

Multilateral Fund for the Implementation of the Montreal Protocol, Secretariat: Suite 4100, 1000 De La Gauchetière St, Montréal, QC H3B 4W5, Canada; tel. (514) 282-1122; fax (514) 282-0068; e-mail secretariat@unmfs.org; internet www.multilateralfund.org; Chief Officer EDUARDO GANEM (Mexico).

Regional Co-ordinating Unit for the Caribbean Environment Programme: 14–20 Port Royal St, Kingston, Jamaica; tel. 922-9267; fax 922-9292; e-mail rcu@cep.unep.org; internet www.cep.unep.org; Co-ordinator NELSON ANDRADE COLMENARES.

UNEP/CMS (Convention on the Conservation of Migratory Species of Wild Animals), Secretariat: Platz der Vereinten Nationen 1, 53113 Bonn, Germany; tel. (228) 8152402; fax (228) 8152449; e-mail secretariat@cms.int; internet www.cms.int; Exec. Sec. BRADNEE CHAMBERS.

UNEP Division of Technology, Industry and Economics: 15 rue de Milan, 75441 Paris, Cedex 09, France; tel. 1-44-37-14-50; fax 1-44-37-14-74; e-mail unep.tie@unep.fr; internet www.unep.org/dtie; Dir TIM KASTEN (USA) (acting).

UNEP International Environmental Technology Centre (IETC): 2–110 Ryokuchi koen, Tsurumi-ku, Osaka 538-0036, Japan; tel. (6) 6915-4581; fax (6) 6915-0304; e-mail ietc@unep.org; internet www.unep.org/ietc; Dir SURENDRA SHRESTHA.

UNEP Ozone Secretariat: POB 30552, Nairobi, Kenya; tel. (20) 762-3851; fax (20) 762-0335; e-mail ozoneinfo@unep.org; internet ozone.unep.org; services both the 1985 Vienna Convention for the Protection of the Ozone Layer and its 1987 Montreal Protocol; Exec. Sec. TINA BIRBILI (Greece).

UNEP Post-Conflict and Disaster Management Branch: 11–15 chemin des Anémones, 1219 Châtelaine, Geneva, Switzerland; tel. 229178530; fax 229178064; e-mail postconflict@unep.org; internet www.unep.org/disastersandconflicts; Chief Officer HENRIK ALEXAN-DER SLOTTE.

UNEP Risoe Centre on Energy, Environment and Sustainable Development: Risoe Campus, Technical University of Denmark, Frederiksborgvej 399, Bldg 142, POB 49, 4000 Roskilde, Denmark; tel. 46-77-51-29; fax 46-32-19-99; e-mail unep@risoe.dtu.dk; internet uneprisoe.org; f. 1990 as the UNEP Collaborating Centre on Energy and Environment; supports UNEP in the planning and implementation of its energy-related policy and activities; provides technical support to governments towards the preparation of national Technology Needs Assessments on climate change adaptation; Head JOHN M. CHRISTENSEN.

UNEP-SCBD (Convention on Biological Diversity, Secretariat): 413 St Jacques St, Suite 800, Montréal, QC, H2Y 1N9, Canada; tel. (514) 288-2220; fax (514) 288-6588; e-mail secretariat@cbd.int; internet www.cbd.int; Exec. Sec. BRAULIO FERREIRA DE SOUZA DIAS (Brazil).

UNEP Secretariat for the UN Scientific Committee on the Effects of Atomic Radiation: Vienna International Centre, Wagramerstr. 5, POB 500, 1400 Vienna, Austria; tel. (1) 26060-4330; fax (1) 26060-5902; e-mail malcolm.crick@unscear.org; internet www.unscear.org; Sec. MALCOLM CRICK.

Activities

UNEP aims to maintain a constant watch on the changing state of the environment; to analyse trends; to assess problems using a wide range of data and techniques; and to undertake or support projects leading to environmentally sound development. It plays a catalytic and co-ordinating role within and beyond the UN system; many UNEP projects are implemented in co-operation with other UN agencies. About 45 intergovernmental organizations outside the UN system and 60 international non-governmental organizations (NGOs) have official observer status on UNEP's Governing Council, and, through the Environment Liaison Centre in Nairobi, Kenya, UNEP is linked to more than 6,000 non-governmental bodies concerned with the environment. UNEP also sponsors international conferences, programmes, plans and agreements regarding all aspects of the environment.

In February 1997 the Governing Council, at its 19th session, adopted a ministerial declaration (the Nairobi Declaration) on UNEP's future role and mandate, which recognized the organization as the principal UN body working in the field of the environment and as the leading global environmental authority, setting and overseeing the international environmental agenda. In June a special session of the UN General Assembly was convened to review the state of the environment and progress achieved in implementing the objectives of the UN Conference on Environment and Development (UNCED—known as the Earth Summit), that had been held in Rio de Janeiro, Brazil, in June 1992. UNCED had adopted Agenda 21 (a programme of activities to promote sustainable development in the 21st century) and the so-called Rio+5 meeting adopted a Programme for Further Implementation of Agenda 21 in order to intensify efforts in areas such as energy, freshwater resources and technology transfer. The meeting confirmed UNEP's essential role in advancing the Programme and as a global authority promoting a coherent legal and political approach to the environmental challenges of sustainable

development. UNEP played a leading role in preparing for the World Summit on Sustainable Development (WSSD), held in August–September 2002 in Johannesburg, South Africa, to assess strategies for strengthening the implementation of Agenda 21. Governments participating in the conference adopted the Johannesburg Declaration and WSSD Plan of Implementation, in which they strongly reaffirmed commitment to the principles underlying Agenda 21 and also pledged support to all internationally agreed development goals, including the UN Millennium Development Goals (MDGs) adopted by governments attending a summit meeting of the UN General Assembly in September 2000. A UN Conference on Sustainable Development (UNCSD—also referred to as Earth Summit 2012 and Rio+20), was convened in June 2012, again in Rio de Janeiro, with participation by more than 100 heads of state and government, and by an estimated 50,000 representatives of international agencies, NGOs, civil society groups, and the private sector. The meeting determined to strengthen the institutional framework and intergovernmental arrangements for sustainable development and to establish a high-level intergovernmental forum to promote system-wide co-ordination and coherence of sustainable development policies and to follow up the implementation of sustainable development objectives. UNCSD determined that UNEP's role should be strengthened as the lead agency in setting the global environmental agenda and co-ordinating UN system-wide implementation of the environmental dimension of sustainable development. It resolved to request the UN General Assembly, during its 67th session (commencing in September 2012), to adopt a resolution that would upgrade UNEP by establishing universal membership of its governing body; ensuring increased financial resources to enable the Programme to fulfil its mandate; strengthening UNEP's participation in the main UN co-ordinating bodies; and empowering UNEP to lead efforts to develop UN system-wide strategies on the environment. The resolution was approved by the General Assembly in December, and, consequently, a new UN Environmental Assembly (UNEA), replacing UNEP's Governing Council, was established in 2014. The participants in UNCSD endorsed an outcome document, entitled *The Future We Want*, which reaffirmed commitment to working towards an economically, socially and environmentally sustainable future, and to the eradication of poverty as an indispensable requirement for sustainable development; and deemed the implementation of green economy policy options, in the context of sustainable development and poverty eradication, to be an important tool for achieving sustainable development. UNCSD approved a set of Sustainable Development Goals (SDGs), setting global targets in sustainable development challenges; it was envisaged that the SDGs would complement the post-2015 UN development agenda. A 10-year framework on sustainable consumption and production was also announced, and the Conference decided to develop a new global wealth indicator that was to incorporate more dimensions than gross national product (the traditional indicator). UNCSD invited all UN agencies and entities to mainstream sustainable development in their mandates, programmes, and strategies. The importance of enhancing the participation of developing countries in international economic decision-making was emphasized. UNEP was to provide the Secretariat with a 10-Year Framework of Programmes (YFP) on Sustainable Consumption and Production that was adopted by the UNCSD participating states. A World Congress on Justice, Governance and Law for Environmental Sustainability, which convened during the Conference, with participation by leading judges, prosecutors and auditor generals, adopted a landmark series of principles to guide the Advancement of Justice, Governance and Law for Environmental Sustainability. During 2012 UNEP established a nine-member International Advisory Council, comprising senior judges, auditors and academics, with a mandate to provide strategic guidance to the international community in improving the legal foundations for achieving international environmental goals. In August 2013 the inaugural session was convened of a UN intergovernmental Committee of Experts on Sustainable Development Financing, comprising 30 experts, which was tasked with preparing a report proposing options on an effective sustainable development financing strategy.

In July 2013 a High-level Political Forum, which had been proposed by UNCSD to build on the work of, and eventually replace, the UN Commission on Sustainable Development, was established. The inaugural meeting of the Forum was held in late September, at the start of the 68th session of the UN General Assembly. It was to be convened annually at ministerial level under the auspices of ECO-SOC, and every four years at the level of heads of state and government.

In May 2000 UNEP initiated an annual Global Ministerial Environment Forum (GMEF), with participation by environment ministers and other senior government delegates. The 2013 session, held in February, at UNEP's Nairobi headquarters, determined to discontinue gatherings of the Forum.

CLIMATE CHANGE

UNEP worked in collaboration with the World Meteorological Organization (WMO) to formulate the 1992 UN Framework Convention on Climate Change (UNFCCC), with the aim of reducing the emission of gases that have a warming effect on the atmosphere (known as greenhouse gases). In 1998 UNEP and WMO established the Intergovernmental Panel on Climate Change (IPCC), as an objective source of scientific information about the warming of the earth's atmosphere.

UNEP's climate change-related activities have a particular focus on strengthening the capabilities of countries (in particular developing countries) to integrate climate change responses into their national development processes, including improving preparedness for participating in UN Reduced Emissions from Deforestation and Forest Degradation (UN-REDD) initiatives; Ecosystem Based Adaptation; and Clean Tech Readiness. UN-REDD, launched in September 2008 as a collaboration between UNEP, the UN Development Programme (UNDP) and FAO, aims to enable donors to pool resources (through a trust fund established for that purpose) to promote a transformation of forest resource use patterns. In August 2011 UN-REDD endorsed a Global Programme Framework covering 2011–15. Leaders from countries in the Amazon, Congo and Borneo-Mekong forest basins participated, in June 2011, in the Summit of Heads of State and Government on Tropical Forest Ecosystems, held in Brazzaville, Republic of the Congo; the meeting issued a declaration recognising the need to protect forests in order to combat climate change, and to conduct future mutual dialogue. In that month UNEP issued a report focusing on the economic benefits of expanding funding for forests.

In September 2012 UNEP and INTERPOL jointly reported that 50%–90% of logging in certain countries of the Amazon basin, Central Africa and South-East Asia was being conducted by organized criminal groups, posing a significant threat to efforts aimed at combating climate change, conserving wildlife, and eradicating poverty. Illegal logging was reported to account at that time for at least 15% of the total global trade in tropical timber products. A related increase in violence against indigenous forest dwellers in affected areas was also reported. During September–November UNEP supported INTERPOL in the implementation of Operation Lead, which united law enforcement agencies in combating forestry crime in 12 countries in Central and South America. Participating national agencies subsequently conducted follow-up investigations, and consequently by July 2013 timber with a value of nearly US $40m. had been confiscated.

UNEP is a founding member of the Climate and Clean Air Coalition to Reduce Short Lived Climate Pollutants (SLCPs), which was launched in February 2012 as an international partnership, with the aim of reducing SLCPs, including methane and black carbon, to counter their negative impact on human health, crop yields and global warming. By September 2014 the partnership comprised 39 governments, the European Union, and 52 institutes and international agencies.

UNEP's Technology Needs Assessment and Technology Action Plan aims to support some 35–45 countries with the implementation of improved national Technology Needs Assessments within the framework of the UNFCCC, involving, *inter alia*, detailed analysis of mitigation and adaptation technologies, and prioritization of these technologies. The UNEP Risoe Centre of Denmark supports governments in the preparation of these Assessments. It was announced in February 2013 that UNEP would lead a consortium, including the UN Industrial Development Organization (UNIDO) and other agencies, as the hosts of a new Climate Technology Centre and Network (CTCN), which was to accelerate the transfer of climate-related technology and expertise to developing nations.

UNEP encourages the development of alternative and renewable sources of energy, as part of its efforts to mitigate climate change. To achieve this, UNEP has created the Global Network on Energy for Sustainable Development, linking 21 centres of excellence in industrialized and developing countries to conduct research and exchange information on environmentally sound energy technology resources. UNEP's Rural Energy Enterprise Development (REED) initiative (operating within Africa as AREED) helps the private sector to develop affordable 'clean' energy technologies, such as solar crop-drying and water-heating, wind-powered water pumps and efficient cooking stoves. UNEP is a member of the Global Bioenergy Partnership initiated by the G8 group of industrialized countries to support the sustainable use of biofuels. Through its Transport Programme UNEP promotes the use of renewable fuels and the integration of environmental factors into transport planning, leading a worldwide Partnership for Clean Fuels and Vehicles, a Global Fuel Economy Initiative, and a Non Motorised Transport 'Share the Road' scheme. Meanwhile, UNDP's Sustainable Buildings and Construction Initiative promotes energy efficiency in the construction industry. In conjunction with UN-Habitat, UNDP, the World Bank and other organizations and institutions, UNEP promotes environmental concerns in urban planning and management through the Sustainable Cities Programme, and projects concerned with waste management, urban pollution and the impact of transportation systems. In June 2012 UNEP and other partners inaugurated a new Global Initiative for Resource-Efficient Cities, which aimed to lower pollution levels, advance efficiency in the utilization of resources (including through the promotion of energy-efficient buildings), and reduce infrastructure costs in urban areas worldwide with populations in excess of 500,000.

During 2007 UNEP (with WMO and the WTO) convened a second International Conference on Climate Change and Tourism, together with two meetings on sustainable tourism development and a conference on global eco-tourism. In June 2009 UNEP and WTO jointly issued a report entitled *Trade and Climate Change*, reviewing the intersections between trade and climate change from the perspectives of the science of climate change; economics; multilateral efforts to combat climate change; and the effects on trade of national climate change policies.

GREEN ECONOMY

In October 2008, in response to the global economic, fuel and food crises that escalated during that year, UNEP launched the 'Green Economy Initiative' (GEI), which aimed to mobilize and refocus the global economy towards investments in clean technologies and the natural infrastructure (for example the infrastructures of forests and soils), with a view to, simultaneously, combating climate change and promoting employment. The UNEP Executive Director stated that the global crises were in part related to a broad market failure that promoted speculation while precipitating escalating losses of natural capital and nature-based assets, compounded by an over-reliance on finite, often subsidized fossil fuels. The three principal dimensions of the GEI were the compilation of the *Green Economy Report*, to provide an analysis of how public policy might support markets in accelerating the transition towards a low-carbon green economy; the Green Jobs Initiative, a partnership launched by UNEP, the International Labour Organization and the International Trade Union Confederation in 2007 (and joined in 2008 by the International Organisation of Employers); and the Economics of Ecosystems and Biodiversity (TEEB) partnership project, focusing on valuation issues. In April 2010 the UN System Chief Executives Board for Co-ordination (CEB) endorsed the GEI as the fourth of nine UN initiatives aimed at alleviating the impact of the global economic crisis on poor and vulnerable populations. UNEP participates in the SEED Initiative, a global partnership for action on sustainable development and the green economy that was launched collaboratively with UNDP and the International Union for the Conservation of Nature at the 2002 WSSD. SEED supports innovative locally driven small-scale businesses that actively work towards providing social and environmental benefits. A Green Economy Coalition was established in 2008 as a loose grouping of UNEP and other UN agencies, research institutes, business interests, trade unions, and NGOs, with the aim of promoting environmental sustainability and social equity.

In February 2013 UNEP, the ILO, UNIDO and the United Nations Institute for Training and Research launched the Partnership for Action on Green Economy (PAGE), which aimed, during the period 2013–20, to support 30 countries in developing national green economy strategies aimed at generating employment and skills, promoting clean technologies, and reducing environmental risks and poverty.

In June 2009 UNEP welcomed the 'Green Growth' declaration of Organisation for Economic Co-operation and Development (OECD), which urged the adoption of targeted policy instruments to promote green investment, and emphasized commitment to the realization of an ambitious and comprehensive post-2012 global climate agreement. In January 2012 UNEP, OECD, the World Bank, and the Global Green Growth Institute (established in June 2010 in Seoul, Republic of Korea—South Korea) launched the Green Growth Knowledge Platform. The Platform, accessible at www.greengrowthknowledge.org, aims to advance efforts to identify and address major knowledge gaps in green growth theory and practice, and to support countries in formulating and implementing policies aimed at developing a green economy.

In January 2011 UNEP and the World Tourism Organization launched the Global Partnership for Sustainable Tourism, also comprising other UN agencies, OECD, 18 governments, and other partners, with the aim of guiding policy and developing projects in the area of sustainable tourism, providing a global platform for discussion, and facilitating progress towards a green economy.

UNEP Finance Initiatives (FI) is a programme encouraging banks, insurance companies and other financial institutions to invest in an environmentally responsible way: an annual FI Global Roundtable meeting is held, together with regional meetings. In April 2007 UNEP hosted the first annual Business for Environment (B4E) meeting, on corporate environmental responsibility, in Singapore; the 2013 meeting was held in April, in New Delhi, India. During 2007 UNEP's Programme on Sustainable Consumption and Production

(SCP) established an International Panel for Sustainable Resource Management (comprising experts whose initial subjects of study were to be the environmental risks of biofuels and of metal recycling), and initiated forums for businesses and NGOs in this field. In May 2011 the International Panel issued a *Decoupling Report* that urged the separation of the global economic growth rate from the rate of natural resource consumption. The report warned that, by 2050, without a change of direction, humanity's consumption of minerals, ores, fossil fuels and biomass were on course to increase three-fold. In 2014 UNEP launched an online Global SCP Clearinghouse, to facilitate access to information and promote new innovations relating to SCP.

In 2009 UNEP organized the fifth regional meeting on sustainable consumption and production in Latin America and the Caribbean, which was held in Cartagena, Colombia, in September.

In 1994 UNEP inaugurated the International Environmental Technology Centre (IETC), based in Osaka, Japan. The Centre promotes and implements environmentally sound technologies for disaster prevention and post-disaster reconstruction; sustainable production and consumption; and water and sanitation (in particular waste-water management and more efficient use of rainwater).

EARLY WARNING AND ASSESSMENT

The Nairobi Declaration resolved that the strengthening of UNEP's information, monitoring and assessment capabilities was a crucial element of the organization's restructuring, in order to help to establish priorities for international, national and regional action, and to ensure the efficient and accurate dissemination of information on emerging environmental trends and emergencies.

UNEP's Division of Early Warning and Assessment analyses the world environment, provides early warning information and assesses global and regional trends. It provides governments with data and helps them to use environmental information for decision-making and planning. Major assessments undertaken by UNEP include the International Assessment of Agricultural Science and Technology for Development; the Solar and Wind Energy Resource Assessment; the Regionally Based Assessment of Persistent Toxic Substances; the Land Degradation Assessment in Drylands; and the Global Methodology for Mapping Human Impacts on the Biosphere (GLOBIO) project.

UNEP's Global Environment Outlook (GEO) process of environmental analysis and assessment, launched in 1995, is supported by an extensive network of collaborating centres. The fifth 'umbrella' report on the GEO process (*GEO-5*) was issued in June 2012, just in advance of the UN Conference on Sustainable Development. The fifth report assessed progress achieved towards the attainment of some 90 environmental challenges, and identified four objectives—the elimination of the production and use of ozone layer-depleting substances; the removal of lead from fuel; access to improved water supplies; and promoting research into reducing pollution of the marine environment—as the areas in which most progress had been made. Little or no progress, however, was found to have been attained in the pursuit of 24 objectives, including managing climate change, desertification and drought; and deterioration was found to have occurred in the state of the world's coral reefs. In recent years regional and national GEO reports have been issued focusing on Africa, the Andean region, the Atlantic and Indian oceans, Brazil, the Caucasus, Latin America and the Caribbean, North America, and the Pacific; and the following thematic GEO reports have been produced: *The Global Deserts Outlook*, and *The Global Outlook for Ice and Snow*.

UNEP's Global International Waters Assessment (GIWA) considers all aspects of the world's water-related issues, in particular problems of shared transboundary waters, and of future sustainable management of water resources. UNEP is also a sponsoring agency of the Joint Group of Experts on the Scientific Aspects of Marine Environmental Pollution and contributes to the preparation of reports on the state of the marine environment and on the impact of land-based activities on that environment. The UNEP-World Conservation Monitoring Centre (UNEP-WCMC), established in June 2000 in Cambridge, United Kingdom, manages and interprets data concerning biodiversity and ecosystems, and makes the results available to governments and businesses. In October 2008 UNEP-WCMC, in partnership with the IUCN, launched the World Database on Protected Areas (WDPA), which details the world's terrestrial and marine protected areas. In 2007 the Centre undertook the 2010 Biodiversity Indicators Programme, with the aim of supporting decision-making by governments so as to reduce the threat of extinction facing vulnerable species. UNEP is a partner in the International Coral Reef Action Network—ICRAN, which was established in 2000 to monitor, manage and protect coral reefs worldwide.

In June 2010 delegates from 85 countries, meeting in Busan, South Korea, at the third conference addressing the creation of a new Intergovernmental Science-Policy Platform on Biodiversity and Ecosystem Services (IPBES), adopted the Busan Outcome Document finalizing details of the establishment of the IPBES; the Outcome Document was subsequently approved by the UN General Assembly. The Platform, inaugurated in April 2012, was to undertake, periodically, assessments, based on current scientific literature, of biodiversity and ecosystem outputs beneficial to humans, including timber, fresh water, fish and climatic stability.

DISASTERS AND CONFLICTS

UNEP aims to minimize environmental causes and consequences of disasters and conflicts, and supports member states in combating environmental degradation and natural resources mismanagement, deeming these to be underlying risk factors for conflicts and natural hazards. UNEP promotes the integration of environmental concerns into risk reduction policy and practices. UNEP undertakes assessments to establish the risks posed by environmental impacts on human health, security and livelihoods, and provides field-based capacity building and technical support, in countries affected by natural disaster and conflict.

An independent report of the Senior Advisory Group to the UN Secretary-General on Civilian Capacity in the Aftermath of Conflict, issued in February 2011, identified natural resources (such as minerals, oil, gas and timber) as a key area of focus. The report designated UNEP as the lead agency for identifying best practices in managing natural resources in support of peacebuilding. In December 2013 a UN report entitled *The Role of Natural Resources in Disarmament, Demobilization and Reintegration—Addressing Risks and Seizing Opportunities*, indicated that the incorporation of a focus on the fair management and distribution of natural resources into plans for post-conflict reintegration and recovery might help mitigate potential future conflicts, such as disputes over territory or water.

ENVIRONMENTAL GOVERNANCE

UNEP promotes international environmental legislation and the development of policy tools and guidelines in order to achieve the sustainable management of the world environment. It helps governments to implement multilateral environmental agreements, and to report on their results. At national level it assists governments to develop and implement appropriate environmental instruments and aims to co-ordinate policy initiatives. Training in various aspects of environmental law and its applications is provided. UNEP supports the development of new legal, economic and other policy instruments to improve the effectiveness of existing environmental agreements. It updates a register of international environmental treaties, and publishes handbooks on negotiating and enforcing environmental law. It acts as the secretariat for a number of regional and global environmental conventions. In June 2011 UNEP launched the Multilateral Environmental Agreements Information and Knowledge Management Initiative, which aimed to expand the sharing of information on more than 12 international agreements relating to the protection of the environment.

UNEP is the principal UN agency for promoting environmentally sustainable water management. It regards the unsustainable use of water as one of the most urgent environmental issues, and estimates that two-thirds of the world's population will suffer chronic water shortages by 2025, owing to growing populations, decreasing quality of water because of pollution, and increasing requirements of industries and agriculture. In 2000 UNEP adopted a new water policy and strategy, comprising assessment, management and co-ordination components. The Global International Waters Assessment is the primary framework for the assessment component. The management component includes the Global Programme of Action (GPA) for the Protection of the Marine Environment from Land-based Activities (adopted in November 1995), which focuses on the effects of pollution on freshwater resources, marine biodiversity and the coastal ecosystems of small island developing states. UNEP promotes international co-operation in the management of river basins and coastal areas and for the development of tools and guidelines to achieve the sustainable management of freshwater and coastal resources. During 2014 UNEP was undertaking preparations for the first International Environment Forum for Basin Organizations, scheduled to be convened in November, in Bangkok, Thailand. UNEP provides scientific, technical and administrative support to facilitate the implementation and co-ordination of 13 regional seas conventions and associated regional plans of action. UNEP's Regional Seas Programme aims to protect marine and coastal ecosystems, particularly by helping governments to put relevant legislation into practice.

UNEP was instrumental in the drafting of a Convention on Biological Diversity (CBD) to preserve the immense variety of plant and animal species, in particular those threatened with extinction. The Convention entered into force at the end of 1993; by September 2014 193 states and the European Union (EU) were parties to the CBD. The CBD's Cartagena Protocol on Biosafety (so called as it had been addressed at an extraordinary session of parties to the CBD convened in Cartagena, Colombia, in February 1999) was adopted at a meeting of parties to the CBD in January 2000, and entered into force in September 2003; by September 2014 the Protocol had been ratified by

167 states parties. The Protocol regulates the transboundary movement and use of living modified organisms resulting from biotechnology, in order to reduce any potential adverse effects on biodiversity and human health. It established an Advanced Informed Agreement procedure to govern the import of such organisms. Prior to the Protocol's entry into force, UNEP undertook a major project aimed at supporting developing countries to assess the potential health and environmental risks and benefits of genetically modified (GM) crops. The sixth Conference of the Parties (COP) to the CBD, held in April 2002, adopted detailed voluntary guidelines concerning access to genetic resources and sharing the benefits attained from such resources with the countries and local communities where they originate; a global work programme on forests; and a set of guiding principles for combating alien invasive species. In October 2010 the 10th COP, meeting in Nagoya, Japan, approved the Nagoya-Kuala Lumpur Supplementary Protocol to the CBD, with a view to establishing an international regime on access and benefit sharing (ABS) of genetic resources, alongside a strategic 10-year Strategic Plan for Biodiversity, comprising targets and timetables to combat loss of the planet's nature-based resources. The Supplementary Protocol was opened for signature in March 2011, and was to enter into force on 12 October 2014. The 12th COP to the CBD, convened in October 2012, in Hyderabad, India, agreed that developed countries should double by 2015 resources dedicated towards biodiversity protection. The conference pledged to focus particular attention towards the sustainable management of marine areas, such as the Sargasso Sea and Tonga archipelago, and determined formally to classify marine areas of ecological or biological significance. The UN Decade on Biodiversity was being celebrated during 2011–20. UNEP supports co-operation for biodiversity assessment and management in selected developing regions and for the development of strategies for the conservation and sustainable exploitation of individual threatened species (e.g. the Global Tiger Action Plan). It also provides assistance for the preparation of individual country studies and strategies to strengthen national biodiversity management and research. UNEP administers the Convention on International Trade in Endangered Species of Wild Flora and Fauna (CITES), which entered into force in 1975 and comprised 180 states parties at September 2014. CITES, whose states parties meet in conference every three years, regulates international trade in nearly 35,000 species of plants and animals, as well as products and derivatives therefrom. The Convention has special programmes on the protection of elephants (including an African Elephant Action Plan, finalized in 2010), falcons, great apes, hawksbill turtles, sturgeons, tropical timber (jointly with the International Tropical Timber Organization), and big leaf mahogany. Meeting in St Petersburg, Russia, in November 2010, at the International Tiger Forum, the heads of the UN Office on Drugs and Crime, CITES, the World Customs Organization, INTERPOL and the World Bank jointly approved the establishment of a new International Consortium on Combating Wildlife Crime (ICCWC), with the aim of combating the poaching of wild animals and illegal trade in wild animals and wild animal products. The 2013 CITES conference, which was held in March, in Bangkok, strengthened the international regime covering trade in precious tropical hardwoods (including rosewoods and ebonies; with special procedures to be implemented for musicians travelling with instruments made therefrom); tortoises and turtles; five species of shark that are harvested for their fins or meat; manta rays (whose gill plates are traded); elephants (including stronger controls on e-commerce, and stricter monitoring of ivory stockpiles); rhinoceros; and big cats (with a focus on trophy leopard hunting). The conference agenda focused on means of combating the over-exploitation of marine and forest reserves, and escalating wildlife crime, determined to consider the use of the GEF as a financial instrument for the Convention, and declared 3 March as annual World Wildlife Day. ICCWC organized the first global meeting of wildlife enforcement networks on the sidelines of the conference. In June 2014 UNEP, with INTERPOL, published a report, *The Environmental Crime Crisis*, which assessed the extent of and impact to sustainable development from the illegal exploitation and trade in wildlife and forest resources.

The Convention on the Conservation of Migratory Species of Wild Animals (CMS, also referred to as the Bonn Convention), concluded under UNEP auspices in 1979, aims to conserve migratory avian, marine and terrestrial species throughout the range of their migration. The secretariat of the CMS is hosted by UNEP. At September 2014 there were 120 states parties to the Convention. A number of agreements and Memoranda of Understanding (MOU) concerning conservation have been concluded under the CMS. An Agreement on the Conservation of Albatrosses and Petrels (ACAP) was concluded, under CMS auspices, in 2001 and entered into force in 2004. It is envisaged that the scope of ACAP, currently covering only the Southern Hemisphere, will be extended to include species from the Northern Hemisphere. MOU have been concluded under the CMS relating to: the Ruddy-headed Goose (of Argentina and Chile), Grassland Birds of Southern South America, and High Andean Flamingoes and their Habitats. In August 2012 the conference of

the parties to the CMS determined to develop a new strategic plan to guide the Convention over the period 2015–23.

In February 2004 the Executive Secretary of the CBD was requested, by the seventh conference of the parties of the CBD, to form the Liaison Group of Biodiversity-related Conventions (BLG), with the aim of enhancing synergies and coherence between the CBD and related conventions. The BLG comprises the heads of the secretariats of the seven biodiversity-related conventions: the CBD, CITES, CMS, the International Treaty on Plant Genetic Resources for Food and Agriculture (Seed Treaty), Ramsar Convention on Wetlands, World Heritage Convention, and the International Plant Protection Convention (admitted to the BLG in August 2014).

ECOSYSTEM MANAGEMENT
The Millennium Ecosystem Assessment, a scientific study of the state of 24 ecosystems, that was commissioned by the UN Secretary-General in 2001, found that 15 of the ecosystems under assessment were being used unsustainably. UNEP's Ecosystem Management Programme aims to develop an adaptive approach that integrates the management of forests, land, freshwater and coastal systems, focusing on sustaining ecosystems to meet future ecological needs, and to enhance human well-being. UNEP places particular emphasis on six ecosystem services deemed to be especially in decline: climate regulation; water regulation; natural hazard regulation; energy; freshwater; nutrient cycling; and recreation and ecotourism. Secondary importance is given to water purification and waste treatment; disease regulation; fisheries; and primary production. UNEP supports national and regional governments to build capacity in order to promote the role of sustainably managed ecosystems in support of social and economic development; to determine which ecosystem services to prioritize; and to incorporate an ecosystem management approach into their national and developmental planning and investment strategies.

In February 2012 UNEP and the Chinese Academy of Sciences (CAS) signed an agreement establishing the International Ecosystem Management Partnership of the United Nations Environment Programme (UNEP-IEMP), a new global centre on ecosystem management, based in Beijing, with a mandate to promote ecosystem management in developing nations.

HARMFUL SUBSTANCES AND HAZARDOUS WASTE
UNEP administers the Basel Convention on the Control of Transboundary Movements of Hazardous Wastes and their Disposal, which entered into force in 1992 with the aim of preventing the uncontrolled movement and disposal of toxic and other hazardous wastes, particularly the illegal dumping of waste in developing countries by companies from industrialized countries. At September 2014 180 countries and the EU were parties to the Convention.

In February 2004 a new international convention on prior informed consent (PIC) for hazardous chemicals and pesticides in international trade entered into force, having been formulated and promoted by UNEP, in collaboration with FAO. The Convention aimed to reduce risks to human health and the environment by restricting the production, export and use of hazardous substances and enhancing information exchange procedures. UNEP played a leading role in formulating a multilateral agreement to reduce and ultimately eliminate the manufacture and use of Persistent Organic Pollutants (POPs), which are considered to be a major global environmental hazard. The Stockholm Convention on POPs, targeting 12 particularly hazardous pollutants, was adopted by 127 countries in May 2001 and entered into force in May 2004. In May 2009 the fourth Conference of the Parties to the Stockholm Convention agreed on a list of nine further POPs; these were incorporated into the Convention in an amendment that entered into force in August 2010.

In January 2013, meeting in Geneva, Switzerland, more than 140 governments finalized the Minamata Convention on Mercury, which provides for controls relating to the usage, release, mining, import and export, and safe storage of mercury, and for the phasing-out by 2020 of the production of several mercury-containing products. The Convention—which had been under negotiation since February 2009—was adopted and opened for signature at a meeting convened in Minamata, Japan, in October 2013. By September 2014 the Convention had been signed by 102 countries and ratified by one (the USA). Pending the entry into force of the Convention, requiring 50 ratifications, a voluntary Global Mercury Partnership addresses activities related to combating mercury pollution. A Global Alliance to Eliminate Lead Paint was endorsed in May 2009 by the second International Conference on Chemicals Management, with the aim of minimizing occupational exposure to, and preventing children's exposure to paints containing lead. The third full meeting of the Global Alliance was convened in September 2014, in New Delhi, India.

UNEP was the principal agency in formulating the 1987 Montreal Protocol to the Vienna Convention for the Protection of the Ozone Layer (1985), which provided for a 50% reduction in the production of chlorofluorocarbons (CFCs) by 2000. An amendment to the Protocol was adopted in 1990, which required complete cessation of the production of CFCs by 2000 in industrialized countries and by 2010 in developing countries. The Copenhagen Amendment, adopted in 1992, stipulated the phasing out of production of hydrochloro-fluorocarbons (HCFCs) by 2030 in developed countries and by 2040 in developing nations. Subsequent amendments aimed to introduce a licensing system for all controlled substances, and imposed stricter controls on the import and export of HCFCs, and on the production and consumption of bromochloromethane (Halon-1011, an industrial solvent and fire extinguisher). In September 2007 the states parties to the Vienna Convention agreed to advance the deadline for the elimination of HCFCs to 2020 in developed countries and to 2030 in developing countries. A Multilateral Fund for the Implementation of the Montreal Protocol was established in June 1990 to promote the use of suitable technologies and the transfer of technologies to developing countries, and support compliance by developing countries with relevant control measures. UNEP, UNDP, the World Bank and UNIDO are the sponsors of the Fund, which by February 2012 had approved financing for more than 6,875 projects and activities in 145 developing countries at a cost of more than US $2,800m. The eighth replenishment of the Fund, covering the period 2012–14, raised $400m. in new contributions from donors. In September 2009 the Montreal Protocol, with 196 states parties, became the first agreement on the global environment to attain universal ratification. UNEP's OzonAction branch promotes information exchange, training and technological awareness, helping governments and industry in developing countries to undertake measures towards the cost-effective phasing-out of ozone-depleting substances.

UNEP encourages governments and the private sector to develop and adopt policies and practices that are cleaner and safer, make efficient use of natural resources, incorporate environmental costs, ensure the environmentally sound management of chemicals, and reduce pollution and risks to human health and the environment. In collaboration with other organizations UNEP works to formulate international guidelines and agreements to address these issues. UNEP also promotes the transfer of appropriate technologies and organizes conferences and training workshops to provide sustainable production practices. Relevant information is disseminated through the International Cleaner Production Information Clearing House. By 2014 more than 50 National Cleaner Production Centres (NCPCs), and, in Latin America, a regional network of cleaner production centres, had been established, under a joint UNEP/UNIDO programme that was launched in 1994 to promote the use and development of environmentally sustainable technologies and to build national capacities in cleaner production. In October 2009 UNIDO and UNEP endorsed the creation of the global network for Resource Efficient and Cleaner Production (RECPnet), with the aim of utilizing the capabilities of NCPCs in developing and transition countries. RECPnet was launched in November 2011. In October 1998 UNEP adopted an International Declaration on Cleaner Production, with a commitment to implement cleaner and more sustainable production methods and to monitor results. UNEP was a co-founder (in 1997) of the Global Reporting Initiative, which, with participation by corporations, business associations and other organizations, develops guidelines for voluntary reporting by companies on their economic, environmental and social performance. In 2002 UNEP, with the Society of Environmental Toxicology and Chemistry, launched the Life Cycle Initiative (currently in its third phase covering 2012–16), which evaluates the impact of products over their entire life cycle (from manufacture to disposal) and aims to assist governments, businesses and other consumers with adopting environmentally sound policies and practice, in view of the upward trend in global consumption patterns.

In accordance with a decision made by UNEP's former Governing Council in February 2002, a Preparatory Committee for the Development of a Strategic Approach to International Chemicals Management was established; the work of the Committee culminated in the first session, held in February 2006, in Dubai, United Arab Emirates, of the International Conference on Chemicals Management (ICCM-1), comprising governments and intergovernmental and non-governmental organizations. ICCM-1 adopted the Strategic Approach to International Chemicals Management (SAICM), a policy framework to promote the sound management of chemicals in support of the objective (determined by the 2002 WSSD) of ensuring that, by 2020, chemicals are produced and used in ways that minimize significant adverse impacts on the environment and human health. ICCM-2, convened in May 2009, in Geneva, reviewed the implementation of the SAICM and adopted 20 indicators to measure its future progress. ICCM-3, held in September 2012, in Nairobi, evaluated data on the 20 indicators. UNEP provides technical support for implementing the Convention on Persistent Organic Pollutants, encouraging the use of alternative pesticides, and monitoring the emission of pollutants through the burning of waste. In September 2012 UNEP published the *Global Chemical Outlook*, highlighting the effect of chemicals on human health and the environment, and assessing the negative impact on emerging and developing economies.

In March 2013 UNEP and WHO issued a joint report entitled *State of the Science of Endocrine Disrupting Chemicals*, which assessed the potential disrupting effects on the human hormone system and the environment of synthetic chemicals found in many household products.

A Pollutant Release and Transfer Register (PRTR), for collecting and disseminating data on toxic emissions, is in effect in Mexico; the so-called *Registro de Emisiones y Transferencia de Contaminantes* was made mandatory in 2004. PRTRs have also been developed for Argentina, Cuba and Ecuador.

GLOBAL ENVIRONMENT FACILITY

UNEP, together with UNDP and the World Bank, is an implementing agency of the Global Environment Facility (GEF), established in 1991 to help developing countries and those undergoing economic transition to meet the costs of projects that benefit the environment in six specific areas: biological diversity; climate change; international waters; depletion of the ozone layer; land degradation; and persistent organic pollutants. Important cross-cutting components of these projects include capacity building to allow countries to meet their obligations under international environmental agreements, and adaptation to climate change. UNEP services the Scientific and Technical Advisory Panel, which provides expert advice on GEF programmes and operational strategies.

COMMUNICATIONS AND PUBLIC INFORMATION

UNEP's public education campaigns and outreach programmes promote community involvement in environmental issues. Further communication of environmental concerns is undertaken through coverage in the press, broadcasting and electronic media, publications, an information centre service and special promotional events, including World Environment Day (celebrated on 5 June; slogan in 2014: 'Small Islands and Climate Change'), the Focus on Your World photography competition, and the awarding of the annual Sasakawa Prize (to recognize distinguished service to the environment by individuals and groups) and of the Champions of the Earth awards (for outstanding environmental leaders from each of UNEP's six regions). An annual Global Civil Society Forum (preceded by regional consultative meetings) is convened by UNEP. A global media round-table was alongside the inaugural session, in June 2014, of the UNEA. UNEP's Tunza programme for children and young people includes conferences, online discussions and publications. The Online Access to Research in the Environment, a UNEP-led initiative, provides access to more than 17,000 peer reviewed scientific journals, online books, and other resources, for use by some 6,000 environmental institutions in 109 low- and middle-income countries. UNEP co-operates with the International Olympic Committee, the Commonwealth Games organizing body and international federations for football, athletics and other sports to encourage 'carbon neutral' sporting events and to use sport as a means of outreach.

Finance

Project budgetary resources approved by the Governing Council for UNEP's activities during 2014–15 totalled US $530.3m. UNEP is allocated a contribution from the regular budget of the United Nations, and derives most of its finances from voluntary contributions to the Environment Fund and to trust funds.

Publications

Annual Report.
CBTF (Capacity Building Task Force on Trade, Environment and Development) Newsletter.
DEWA/GRID Europe Quarterly Bulletin. E+ (Energy, Climate and Sustainable Development).
Emissions Gap Report.
The Environment and Poverty Times.
Global Chemicals Outlook.
Great Apes Survival Project Newsletter.
Green Economy Report.
IETC (International Environmental Technology Centre) Insight.
Life Cycle Initiatives Newsletter.
Our Planet (quarterly).
Planet in Peril: Atlas of Current Threats to People and the Environment.
ROA (Regional Office for Africa) News (2 a year).
Tourism Focus (2 a year).

RRC.AP (Regional Resource Centre for Asia and the Pacific) Newsletter.

Sustainable Consumption Newsletter.

Tunza (quarterly magazine for children and young people).

UNEP Chemicals Newsletter.

UNEP Year Book (annually).

World Atlas of Biodiversity.

World Atlas of Coral Reefs.

World Atlas of Desertification.

Studies, reports (including the *Global Environment Outlook* series), legal texts, technical guidelines, etc.

Associated Bodies

Intergovernmental Panel on Climate Change (IPCC): c/o WMO, 7 bis, ave de la Paix, 1211 Geneva 2, Switzerland; tel. 227308208; fax 227308025; e-mail ipcc-sec@wmo.int; internet www.ipcc.ch; established in 1988 by the World Meteorological Organization (WMO) and UNEP; comprises some 3,000 scientists as well as other experts and representatives of all UN member governments. Approximately every five years the IPCC assesses all available scientific, technical and socio-economic information on anthropogenic climate change. The IPCC provides, on request, scientific, technical and socio-economic advice to the Conference of the Parties to the UN Framework Convention on Climate Change (UNFCCC) and to its subsidiary bodies, and compiles reports on specialized topics, such as *Aviation and the Global Atmosphere*, *Regional Impacts of Climate Change*, and *Managing the Risks of Extreme Events and Disasters to Advance Climate Change Adaptation*. The IPCC informs and guides, but does not prescribe, policy. The IPCC's *Fourth Assessment Report*, the final instalment of which was issued in Nov. 2007, concluded that increases in global average air and ocean temperatures, widespread melting of snow and ice, and the rising global average sea level, demonstrate that the warming of the climate system is unequivocal; that observational evidence from all continents and most oceans indicates that many natural systems are being affected by regional climate changes; that a global assessment of data since 1970 has shown that it is likely that anthropogenic warming has had a discernable influence on many physical and biological systems; and that other effects of regional climate changes are emerging. The *Fourth Assessment Report* was awarded a share of the Nobel Peace Prize for 2007. In Jan. 2010 the IPCC accepted criticism that an assertion in the 2007 *Report*, concerning the rate at which Himalayan glaciers were melting, was exaggerated, and in Feb. 2010 the Panel agreed that the *Report* had overstated the proportion of the Netherlands below sea level. Later in that month it was announced that an independent board of scientists would be appointed to review the work of the IPCC. In May 2011 a meeting of delegates from IPCC member states determined that a 13-member executive committee, under the leadership of the IPCC Chairman, should be established to supervise the day-to-day operations of the Panel and to consider matters requiring urgent action. Publication of the *Fifth Assessment Report* of the IPCC was phased, with three Working Group reports released in Sept. 2013, and in March and April 2014, and a Synthesis Report due in Oct. The Sept. 2013 report presented new research on the physical science basis of climate change, and concluded that it was virtually certain there will be more extremes of temperatures and a continued rise in sea levels. The March 2014 report stated emphatically that the impacts of global warming were likely to be 'severe, pervasive and irreversible'—including on food security, the availability of fresh water, and in terms of increasing occurrence of extreme natural events—and that human adaptation strategies (such as the construction of defences against flooding) would be essential as means of partially mitigating the economic and societal consequences. The report released in April stressed that increasing numbers of policies on arresting climate change had failed to prevent the recent rapid acceleration in the growth of greenhouse gas emissions, but found that, were major institutional and technological changes introduced aimed at reducing emissions from energy production and use, buildings, industry, human settlements, land use, and transport, it would be possible to limit the increase in global mean temperature to the goal of 2° Celsius above pre-industrial levels.

Chairperson: RAJENDRA K. PACHAURI (India).

United Nations Convention to Combat Desertification in Those Countries Experiencing Serious Drought and/or Desertification, Particularly in Africa, Secretariat (UNCCD): Platz der Vereinten Nationen 1, 53113 Bonn, Germany; tel. (228) 815-2800; fax (228) 815-2898; e-mail secretariat@unccd.int; internet www.unccd.int; the UN Conference on Environment and Development, convened in June 1992, in Rio de Janeiro, Brazil, endorsed an integrated approach to addressing the issue of accelerating desertification, with an emphasis on promoting sustainable development at the community level, and requested the UN General Assembly to establish a negotiating committee to draft the Convention; consequently, UNCCD was adopted in June 1994, and came into force in Dec. 1996. In Oct. 1998 a Global Mechanism was established under UNCCD, to provide strategic advisory services to developing countries on means of attracting and increasing investments in sustainable land management, for example by channelling investments from innovative financial sources such as micro-finance and climate change funds. The eighth session of the UNCCD Conference of the Parties (COP), held in Sept. 2007, in Madrid, Spain, adopted The Strategy, a 10-year strategic plan and framework, which aimed to enhance the implementation of the Convention, with a focus on forging global partnerships towards the reversal and prevention of desertification and land degradation, and on establishing a global framework to support the development and implementation of national and regional poverty reduction policies. COP 10, convened in Oct. 2011, in Changwon, Republic of Korea, adopted the Changwon Initiative, to complement activities being undertaken in accordance with The Strategy, including enhancing UNCCD scientific processes; mobilizing additional resources and facilitating partnership arrangements; and supporting a global framework for the promotion of best practice. COP 11 was held in Windhoek, Namibia, in Sept.–Oct. 2013; the meeting agreed to establish a Science Policy Interface to facilitate the communication of scientific findings to policymakers. COP 12 was scheduled to be convened in Turkey, in 2015. By September 2014 UNCCD had been ratified by 194 states and the EU.

Executive Secretary: MONIQUE BARBUT (France).

United Nations Framework Convention on Climate Change, Secretariat (UNFCCC): UN Campus, Platz der Vereinten Nationen 1, 53113 Bonn, Germany; tel. (228) 815-1000; fax (228) 815-1999; e-mail secretariat@unfccc.int; internet unfccc.int; the World Meteorological Organization (WMO) and UNEP worked together to formulate the Convention, in response to the first report of the IPCC, issued in August 1990, which predicted an increase in the concentration of greenhouse gases (i.e. carbon dioxide and other gases that have a warming effect on the atmosphere) owing to human activity. The UNFCCC was signed in May 1992 and formally adopted at the UN Conference on Environment and Development, held in June. It entered into force in March 1994, committing countries to submitting reports on measures being taken to reduce the emission of greenhouse gases and recommended stabilizing these emissions at 1990 levels by 2000; however, this was not legally binding. Following the second session of the Conference of the Parties (COP) of the Convention, held in July 1996, multilateral negotiations ensued to formulate legally binding objectives for emission limitations. At the third COP, held in Kyoto, Japan, in Dec. 1997, 38 industrial nations endorsed mandatory reductions of combined emissions of the six major gases by an average of 5.2% during the five-year period 2008–12, to pre-1990 levels. The so-called Kyoto Protocol was to enter into force on being ratified by at least 55 countries party to the UNFCCC, including industrialized countries with combined emissions of carbon dioxide in 1990 accounting for at least 55% of the total global greenhouse gas emissions by developed nations. The fourth COP, convened in Buenos Aires, Argentina, in Nov. 1998, adopted a plan of action to promote implementation of the UNFCCC and to finalize the operational details of the Kyoto Protocol. These included the Clean Development Mechanism, by which industrialized countries may obtain credits towards achieving their reduction targets by assisting developing countries to implement emission-reducing measures, and a system of trading emission quotas. Agreement on the implementation of the Buenos Aires action plan was not achieved until the second session of the sixth COP, held in Bonn in July 2001. The seventh COP, convened in Marrakesh, Morocco, in Oct.–Nov., formally adopted the decisions reached in July, and elected 15 members to the Executive Board of the Clean Development Mechanism. In March 2002 the USA (the most prolific national producer of harmful gas emissions) announced that it would not ratify the Kyoto Protocol. The Kyoto Protocol eventually entered into force on 16 Feb. 2005, 90 days after its ratification by Russia. Negotiations commenced in May 2007 on establishing a new international arrangement eventually to succeed the Kyoto Protocol. Participants in COP 13, convened in Bali, Indonesia, in Dec. 2007, adopted the Bali Roadmap, detailing a two-year process leading to the planned conclusion of the schedule of negotiations in Dec. 2009. The UN Climate Change Conference (COP 14), convened in Poznań, Poland, in Dec. 2008, finalized the Kyoto Protocol's Adaptation Fund, which was to finance projects and programmes in developing signatory states that were particularly vulnerable to the adverse effects of climate change. Addressing the Conference, the UN Secretary-General urged the advancement of a 'Green New Deal', to address simultaneously the ongoing global climate and economic crises. COP 15 was held, concurrently with the fifth meeting of parties to the Kyoto Protocol, in Copenhagen, Denmark, in Dec. 2009. Heads of state and government and other delegates attending the Conference approved the Copenhagen Accord, which determined that international co-operative action should be taken, in the context of sustainable development, to reduce global greenhouse gas emissions so as to hold the ongoing increase in global temperature below 2°C. It was agreed that enhanced efforts should be undertaken to reduce vulnerability to climate change in developing countries, with special reference to least developed countries, small island states and Africa. Developed countries agreed to pursue the achievement by 2020 of strengthened carbon emissions targets, while developing nations were to implement actions to slow down growth in emissions. A Green Climate Fund was to be established to support climate change mitigation actions in developing countries, and a Technology Mechanism was also to be established, with the aim of accelerating technology development and transfer in support of climate change adaptation and mitigation activities. COP 16, convened, concurrently with the sixth meeting of parties to the Kyoto Protocol, in Cancún, Mexico, in Nov.–Dec. 2010, adopted several decisions, which included mandating the establishment of a Cancún Adaptation Framework and associated Adaptation Committee, and approving a work programme which was to consider approaches to environmental damage linked to unavoidable impacts of climate change in vulnerable countries, as well as addressing forms of adaptation action, such as: strengthening the resilience of ecological systems; undertaking impact, vulnerability and adaptation assessments; engaging the participation of vulnerable communities in ongoing processes; and valuing traditional indigenous knowledge alongside the best available science. UN system-wide activities to address climate change are co-ordinated by an action framework established by the UN Chief Executives Board for Co-ordination under the UN *Delivering as One* commitment. COP 17, held in Durban, South Africa, in Nov.–Dec. 2011 concluded with an agreement on a 'Durban

Platform for Enhanced Action'. The Platform incorporated agreements to extend the Kyoto provisions regarding emissions reductions by industrialized nations for a second phase, to follow on from the expiry at end-2012 of the first commitment phase, and to initiate negotiations on a new, inclusive global emissions arrangement, to be concluded in 2015, that would come into effect in 2020 with 'legal force'. During the conference sufficient funds were committed to enable the inauguration of the Green Climate Fund, and a commitment was concluded to establish the Adaptation Committee. In Dec. 2012 COP 18, convened in Doha, Qatar, approved an amendment of the Kyoto Protocol to initiate a second commitment period of eight years and endorsed the timetable for negotiating a new climate agreement by May 2015 (with a meeting of world heads of state to be convened in Sept. 2014). States parties committed to reducing greenhouse gas emissions by at least 18% below 1990 levels during 2013–20. COP 18 also secured a commitment by developed nations to mobilize US \$100,000m. by 2020 to support climate change adaptation and mitigation initiatives in affected developing countries. It was envisaged that the Green Climate Fund would become fully operational in 2014, based in Sondgo, South Korea. As at Sept. 2014 the Kyoto Protocol had 192 states parties (191 countries and the European Community). The USA has not signed the Protocol. Canada withdrew its participation with effect from Dec. 2012. In Nov. 2013 states participating in COP 19, convened in Warsaw, Poland, agreed to intensify immediate actions to combat climate change and to confirm national commitments to reducing greenhouse gas emissions in advance of the 2015 deadline to conclude a new legally binding treaty.

Executive Secretary: CHRISTIANA FIGUERES (Costa Rica).

United Nations High Commissioner for Refugees—UNHCR

Address: CP 2500, 1211 Geneva 2 dépôt, Switzerland.
Telephone: 227398111; **fax:** 227397312; **e-mail:** unhcr@unhcr.org; **internet:** www.unhcr.org.

The Office of the High Commissioner was established in 1951 to provide international protection for refugees and to seek durable solutions to their problems. In 1981 UNHCR was awarded the Nobel Peace Prize.

Organization

(September 2014)

HIGH COMMISSIONER

The High Commissioner is elected by the United Nations General Assembly on the nomination of the Secretary-General, and is responsible to the General Assembly and to the UN Economic and Social Council (ECOSOC).

High Commissioner: ANTÓNIO MANUEL DE OLIVEIRA GUTERRES (Portugal).

Deputy High Commissioner: THOMAS ALEXANDER ALEINIKOFF (USA).

EXECUTIVE COMMITTEE

The Executive Committee of the High Commissioner's Programme (ExCom), established by ECOSOC, gives the High Commissioner policy directives in respect of material assistance programmes and advice in the field of international protection. In addition, it oversees UNHCR's general policies and use of funds. ExCom, which comprises representatives of 87 states, meets once a year.

ADMINISTRATION

Headquarters, based in Geneva, Switzerland, include the Executive Office, comprising the offices of the High Commissioner, the Deputy High Commissioner and the two Assistant High Commissioners (for Operations and Protection). The Inspector General, the Director of the UNHCR liaison office in New York, and the Director of the Ethics Office report directly to the High Commissioner. The principal administrative Divisions cover International Protection; Programme and Support Management; Emergency Security and Supply; Financial and Administrative Management; Human Resources Management; External Relations; and Information Systems and Telecommunications. A UNHCR Global Service Centre, based in Budapest, Hungary, provides administrative support to the headquarters. There are five regional bureaux covering Africa, Asia and

the Pacific, Europe, the Americas, and North Africa and the Middle East. In 2014 UNHCR employed around 7,140 regular staff, of whom about 85% were working in the field. At that time there were around 450 UNHCR offices in 123 countries.

OFFICES IN SOUTH AND CENTRAL AMERICA AND THE CARIBBEAN

Regional Office for the USA and the Caribbean: 1775 K St, NW, Suite 300, Washington, DC 20006, USA; e-mail usawa@unhcr.ch.

Regional Office for Northern South America: Apdo 69045, Caracas 1062-A, Venezuela; e-mail venca@unhcr.ch.

Regional Office for Southern South America: Cerrito 836, 10°, Buenos Aires 1010, Argentina; e-mail argbu@unhcr.ch.

Activities

The competence of the High Commissioner extends to any person who, owing to well-founded fear of being persecuted for reasons of race, religion, nationality, social group or political opinion, is outside the country of his or her nationality and is unable or, owing to such fear or for reasons other than personal convenience, remains unwilling to accept the protection of that country; or who, not having a nationality and being outside the country of his or her former habitual residence, is unable or, owing to such fear or for reasons other than personal convenience, is unwilling to return to it. This competence may be extended, by resolutions of the UN General Assembly and decisions of ExCom, to cover certain other 'persons of concern'. Although its core mandate relates to refugees, UNHCR also supports people who are threatened with displacement, and those who have been displaced from their homes inside their own country (i.e. with similar needs to those of refugees but who have not crossed an international border); these include—additionally to conflict-affected populations—people displaced by natural disasters, environmental degradation and the detrimental effects of climate change.

In July 2006 UNHCR issued a '10 Point Plan of Action on Refugee Protection and Mixed Migration' (*10 Point Plan*), detailing the following areas in which UNHCR might make an impact in supporting member states with the development of comprehensive migration strategies: co-operation among key players; data collection and analysis; protection-sensitive entry systems; reception arrangements; mechanisms for profiling and referral; differentiated processes and procedures; solutions for refugees; addressing secondary movements; return of non-refugees and alternative migration options; and information strategy. A revised version of the document was published in January 2007. UNHCR aims to address the fundamental causes of refugee flows, and has urged recognition and comprehension of the broad patterns of global displacement and migration, and of the mixed nature of many 21st-century population flows, which often comprise economic migrants, refugees, asylum seekers, and victims of trafficking requiring detection and support.

During 2005 the UN's Inter-Agency Standing Committee (IASC), concerned with co-ordinating the international response to humanitarian disasters, developed a concept of organizing agency assistance to internally displaced persons (IDPs) through the institutionalization of a 'Cluster Approach', currently comprising 11 core areas of activity. UNHCR is the lead agency for the clusters on Camp Co-ordination and Management (in conflict situations; the International Organization for Migration leads that cluster in natural disaster situations), Emergency Shelter, and (jointly with OHCHR and UNICEF) Protection. The IASC maintains a series of *Guidelines on Mental Health and Psychosocial Support in Emergency Settings*.

In 2009 UNHCR launched the first annual Global Needs Assessment (GNA), with the aim of mapping comprehensively the situation and needs of populations of concern falling under the mandate of the Office, to provide a blueprint for planning and decision-making for itself, governments and other partners.

UNHCR's global strategic priorities in 2014–15 were: promoting a favourable protection environment; fair processes and documentation; security from violence and exploitation; basic needs and services; community empowerment and self reliance; and durable solutions.

A Policy Development and Evaluation Service (PDES) reviews systematically UNHCR's operational effectiveness. In 2013 the PDES supported the formulation and implementation of the Office's policy on refugee protection and solutions in urban areas, by undertaking a global survey on the implementation of urban refugee policy; establishing internet-based compilation of effective operational practices in urban areas; and by implementing a review of an urban refugee programme then ongoing in New Delhi, India. It has also recently given consideration to areas including emergency response capabilities; protection and solutions; protracted refugee situations; sexual and gender-based violence; and refugee youth.

At December 2013 the total global population of concern to UNHCR, based on provisional figures, amounted to 42.9m. At that time the refugee population worldwide totalled 11.7m., of whom 8.5m. were being assisted by UNHCR. UNHCR was also concerned with some 414,554 recently returned refugees, 23.9m. IDPs, 1.4m. returned IDPs, 3.5m. stateless persons, and 1.2m. asylum seekers. UNHCR maintains an online statistical population database.

World Refugee Day, sponsored by UNHCR, is held annually on 20 June. The theme in 2014 was 'One family torn apart by war is too many'.

INTERNATIONAL PROTECTION

In the exercise of its mandate UNHCR seeks to ensure that refugees and asylum seekers are protected against *refoulement* (forcible return), that they receive asylum, and that they are treated according to internationally recognized standards. The Office discourages the detention and encampment of refugees and asylum seekers, as this restricts their freedom of movement and opportunities to become self-reliant. UNHCR pursues these objectives by a variety of means that include promoting the conclusion and ratification by states of international instruments for the protection of refugees. The Office supervises the application of, and actively encourages states to accede to, the 1951 United Nations Convention relating to the Status of Refugees (with 145 parties at September 2014) and its 1967 Protocol (which had 146 parties at that time). These define the rights and duties of refugees and contain provisions dealing with a variety of matters that affect their day-to-day lives. Important provisions for the treatment of refugees are also contained in a number of instruments adopted at the regional level, including the 1969 Convention Governing the Specific Aspects of Refugee Problems, the European Agreement on the Abolition of Visas for Refugees, and the 1969 American Convention on Human Rights. In October 2009 African Union (AU) member states adopted the AU Convention for the Protection and Assistance of IDPs in Africa, the first legally binding international treaty providing legal protection and support to internally displaced populations. An increasing number of states have also adopted domestic legislation and/or administrative measures to implement the international instruments, particularly in the field of procedures for the determination of refugee status. UNHCR seeks to ensure swift, fair asylum procedure systems. The Office works in countries of origin and countries of asylum to ensure that policies, laws and practices comply with international standards, and in situations of forced displacement it advocates for the adoption of fair practices ensuring the protection of populations of concern.

UNHCR has sought to address the specific needs of refugee women, children, and elderly refugees, and prioritizes their needs in its programme planning and implementation. The Office actively seeks solutions to support refugees residing in urban areas (who by 2014 represented more than one-half of all refugees). It has attempted to

deal with the problem of military attacks on refugee camps, by adopting and encouraging the acceptance of a set of principles to ensure the refugee safety. The post of Senior Adviser to the High Commissioner on Gender Issues was established in 2004, and in June 2011 UNHCR issued an updated strategy on Action against Sexual and Gender-Based Violence. UNHCR gives consideration to the environmental impact of its assistance programmes.

UNHCR has increasingly placed a focus on statelessness (lack of legal nationality), and promotes new accessions to the 1951 Convention Relating to the Status of Stateless Persons and the 1961 Convention on the Reduction of Statelessness, while maintaining that a significant proportion of the global stateless population has not hitherto been systematically identified. The Office promotes improved procedures for identifying stateless people on their territories, enhancing civil registration systems, and raising awareness of the options available to stateless people. Some US $79m. was allocated by the Office in 2013 to 61 projects on addressing statelessness.

ASSISTANCE ACTIVITIES

The first phase of an assistance operation uses UNHCR's capacity of emergency response. This enables UNHCR to address the immediate needs of refugees at short notice, for example, by employing specially trained emergency teams and maintaining stockpiles of basic equipment, medical aid and materials. A significant proportion of UNHCR expenditure is allocated to the next phase of an operation, providing 'care and maintenance' in stable refugee circumstances. This assistance can take various forms, including the provision of clean water, sanitation, medical care, shelter, and relief items (for example household goods, jerry cans, sleeping mats and blankets). UNHCR organizes, or else supports, refugee registration. Also covered in many instances are basic services, including education, counselling, and assistance with asylum applications. UNHCR is one of the 10 co-sponsors of UNAIDS, and promotes access for displaced populations to HIV/AIDS prevention services, treatment, and care.

As far as possible, assistance is geared towards the identification and implementation of durable solutions to refugee problems—this being the second statutory responsibility of UNHCR. Such solutions generally take one of three forms: voluntary repatriation; local integration; or resettlement onwards to a third country. UNHCR supports the implementation of the Guidance Note on Durable Solutions for Displaced Persons, adopted in 2004 by the UN Development Group.

Where voluntary repatriation, generally the preferred solution, is feasible, the Office assists refugees to overcome obstacles preventing their return to their country of origin. This may be done through negotiations with governments involved, and by arranging transport for and providing basic assistance packages to repatriating refugees, and also by implementing or supporting local integration or reintegration programmes in their home countries, including Quick Impact Projects aimed at income generation and at the restoration of local infrastructures. Some 414,600 refugees repatriated voluntarily to their home countries in 2013. Similarly, UNHCR works to enable local communities support returned IDPs.

When voluntary repatriation is not an option, efforts are made to assist refugees to integrate locally and to become self-supporting in their countries of asylum. This may be done either by granting loans to refugees, or by assisting them, through vocational training or in other ways, to learn a skill and to establish themselves in gainful occupations. One major form of assistance to help refugees re-establish themselves outside camps is the provision of housing.

In cases where resettlement through emigration is the only viable solution to a refugee problem, UNHCR negotiates with governments in an endeavour to obtain suitable resettlement opportunities, to encourage liberalization of admission criteria and to draw up special immigration schemes. During 2013 an estimated 71,600 refugees were resettled under UNHCR auspices. In total, 98,400 refugees were resettled during that year, with the USA receiving around two-thirds of these (66,200).

THE AMERICAS AND THE CARIBBEAN

In December 1994 a meeting was held, in San José, Costa Rica, to commemorate the 10th anniversary of the November 1984 Cartagena Declaration, which had provided a comprehensive framework for refugee protection in the region. The meeting adopted the San José Declaration on Refugees and Displaced Persons, which aimed to harmonize legal criteria and procedures to consolidate actions for durable solutions of voluntary repatriation and local integration in the region. UNHCR's efforts in the region subsequently emphasized legal issues and refugee protection, while assisting governments to formulate national legislation on asylum and refugees. UNHCR's activities in Central and South America are currently guided by the Mexico Plan of Action (MPA), adopted in November 2004 by regional leaders convened in Mexico City to commemorate the 20th anniversary of the Cartagena Declaration. The MPA aims to address ongoing population displacement problems in Latin America, with a particular focus on the humanitarian crisis in Colombia and the border areas of its neighbouring countries, and the increasing numbers of refugees concentrated in urban centres in the region. The Cities of Solidarity pillar of the MPA assists UNHCR with facilitating the local integration and self-sufficiency of people in urban areas who require international protection; the Borders of Solidarity pillar addresses protection at international borders; and the Resettlement in Solidarity pillar promotes co-operation in resettling refugees. During 2004–11 around 1,100 people were resettled under the Resettlement in Solidarity pillar. In November 2010 regional leaders adopted the Brasília Declaration on the Protection of Refugees and Stateless Persons in the Americas, in which they committed to revitalizing the MPA pillars. During 2014 UNHCR and states in the region were devising a new plan of action, to cover the period 2015–24, which was to supersede the MPA.

UNHCR supports the 'Puebla Process', which was launched in March 1996 to promote regional co-operation on migration, and comprises the governments of Belize, Canada, Costa Rica, the Dominican Republic, El Salvador, Guatemala, Honduras, Mexico, Nicaragua, Panama and the USA. A Regional Conference on Refugee Protection and International Migration in the Americas, held in San José, Costa Rica, in November 2009, addressed key protection challenges in the context of an environment characterized by complex mixed migratory population movements.

In 1999 the Colombian Government approved an operational plan proposed by UNHCR to address a massive population displacement that had arisen in that country (escalating significantly from 1997), as a consequence of ongoing long-term internal conflict and alleged human rights abuses committed by paramilitary groups. Although the military capacity of the Colombian security forces improved in the 2000s, leading to the demobilization of significant numbers of militants, insecurity and population displacement persisted, exacerbated by a rise in organized crime and by the emergence of new illegal armed groups. Some 230,000 Colombians were newly displaced in 2012. Indigenous and Afro-Colombian peoples in remote, rural districts, particularly along the Pacific Coast, in central areas, in Antioquia, and in border areas neighbouring Ecuador and Venezuela, have been particularly vulnerable. Intra-urban displacement among 1.7m. Colombian urban IDPs has also caused concern. Gang conflict, sexual and gender-based violence, forced recruitment, forced disappearances, extortion and murder have been prevalent. In 2014 UNHCR aimed to explore possible viable solutions to the displacement situation in the context of an ongoing peace dialogue between the Government and the Fuerzas Armadas Revolucionarias de Colombia (FARC, the largest Colombian rebel group), and of the Law on Victims and Land Restitution, which was adopted in June 2011 to enable victims of forced displacement to claim reparations for and restitution of their holdings. Despite the dialogue, FARC elements and other armed militants continued to destabilize the country and to prompt continuing displacement; some 61 large population displacements were recorded in 2013. Within Colombia UNHCR's protection activities have included ensuring an adequate, functioning legal framework for the protection of IDPs and enabling domestic institutions to supervise compliance with national legislation regarding the rights of IDPs; strengthening representation for IDPs and other vulnerable people; and working with the authorities to promote sustainable solutions, with a focus on self-reliance and local integration (particularly as more than one-half of registered IDPs have assembled in urban areas and are unlikely to return to their native communities). UNHCR has also advised on public policy formulation in the areas of emergency response, IDP registration, health, education, housing, income generation and protection of policy rights; and provided technical assistance to national and local authorities. The Office has co-operated with UNICEF to improve the provision of education to displaced children. UNHCR, jointly with UNDP, has implemented since 2010 a Transitional Solutions Initiative, under which methodologies for sustainable solutions in 17 communities are being developed, with a focus on local integration, relocation and returnee processes. UNHCR works to provide legal protection and educational and medical support to around 500,000 Colombians who have fled to but not sought asylum in neighbouring countries. The Office's strategy for supporting countries receiving displaced Colombians (of whom the majority were not registered as refugees) has included border-monitoring activities, entailing the early warning of potential refugee movements, and provision of detailed country-of-origin data. UNHCR has offered technical assistance in relation to the Colombia-Ecuador Neighborhood Commission, established in 1989 and reactivated, following a period of inactivity, in November 2010. During 2014 UNHCR was to monitor the implementation of recently reformed, more restrictive asylum procedures in Ecuador, where, since 2000, asylum has been requested by some 160,000 people (nearly all Colombians). In 2014 UNHCR aimed to help refugees in that country secure access to education, health care, banking, government programmes, and employment. In that year the Office aimed to support the Venezuelan authorities with enhancing registration and documentation procedures. At the end of 2013 around 5.4m. IDPs within Colombia remained of concern to UNHCR. (In June 2013 Colombia's Consti-

tutional Court determined to revise statistics on displacement upwards to reflect hitherto unrecognized cases caused by violence perpetrated by militia post-demobilization.) At end-2013 Ecuador was sheltering nearly 56,000 Colombian refugees, while at least a further 68,000 Colombians were reported to be in a refugee-like situation in that country but had not sought official protection. It was reported that around 1,000 Colombians were crossing the border into Ecuador every month at the end of 2013, and that mainly they were settling in poorer, fragile districts. Some 200,000 Colombian refugees and persons in a refugee-like situation were sheltering in Venezuela at 31 December 2013. In 2014 UNHCR's presence in Colombia included 11 field offices and a branch office in Bogotá.

In the aftermath of the devastating earthquake that struck Haiti in January 2010, UNHCR provided assistance to the international humanitarian response operation in the areas of camp registration and profiling matters; shelter co-ordination; and supporting OHCHR in its efforts to assist the displaced population outside Port-au-Prince and earthquake survivors living outside registered camps. UNHCR also implemented a number of QIPs, and provided material support to Haitian evacuees in the neighbouring Dominican Republic. In June 2010 UNHCR opened an office in Santo Domingo, Dominican Republic. In July 2011 UNHCR and OHCHR urged governments to suspend all involuntary returns to Haiti, owing to the ongoing fragile protection environment in that country and continuing massive displacement; it was subsequently reported, however, that the request by UNHCR and OHCHR had not been widely heeded. By the end of 2013 some 300,000 individuals displaced by the 2010 earthquake remained in camps, reportedly in slum-like conditions, while others were sheltering in nearby spontaneous settlements. In 2014 UNHCR's activities in Haiti were to focus on the provision of documentation and on the development of the civil registry, with a view to reducing risk of statelessness; and on improving protection for victims of sexual and other gender-based violence, with a particular focus on gay, lesbian, bisexual, transgender and intersex individuals. In the Dominican Republic the Office was to assist with the processing of a backlog of asylum claims, and was to continue to support the basic needs of refugees, while pursuing durable solutions for those of undetermined nationality or at risk of statelessness. It is of concern to UNHCR that a significant number of descendants of migrant Haitians born outside Haiti, as well as children unable to acquire nationality from their mothers under existing legislation governing nationality, are stateless or are at risk of becoming so in the Caribbean region.

In May 2013 UNHCR and the IOM organized a Caribbean regional conference, in Nassau, Bahamas, on promoting co-operation and identification of good practices in the protection of vulnerable persons in mixed migration flows. In 2014 UNHCR was to follow up the conference by supporting several Caribbean states with establishing or enhancing national asylum systems and more protection-sensitive migration management strategies.

CO-OPERATION WITH OTHER ORGANIZATIONS

UNHCR works closely with other UN agencies, intergovernmental organizations and non-governmental organizations (NGOs) to increase the scope and effectiveness of its operations. Within the UN system UNHCR co-operates, principally, with WFP in the distribution of food aid, UNICEF and WHO in the provision of family welfare and child immunization programmes, OCHA in the delivery of emergency humanitarian relief, UNDP in development-related activities and the preparation of guidelines for the continuum of emergency assistance to development programmes, and the Office of the UN High Commissioner for Human Rights. UNHCR also has close working relationships with the International Federation of Red Cross and Red Crescent Societies and the International Organization for Migration. UNHCR planned to engage with 740 NGOs as implementing partners in 2014–15. UNHCR engages private sector businesses in supporting its activities through the provision of (cash and 'in kind') donations, loaned expertise, and marketing related to designated causes. The Office maintains a private sector partnerships unit, in London, United Kingdom.

TRAINING

UNHCR organizes training programmes and workshops to enhance the capabilities of field workers and non-UNHCR staff, in the following areas: the identification and registration of refugees; people-orientated planning; resettlement procedures and policies; emergency response and management; security awareness; stress management; and the dissemination of information through the electronic media.

Finance

The regular budget of the UN finances a proportion of UNHCR's administrative expenditure. The majority of UNHCR's programme expenditure (about 98%) is funded by voluntary contributions, mainly from governments. The Private Sector and Public Affairs Service aims to increase funding from non-governmental donor sources, for example by developing partnerships with foundations and corporations. Following approval of the Unified Annual Programme Budget any subsequently identified requirements are managed in the form of Supplementary Programmes, financed by separate appeals. UNHCR's projected funding requirements for 2014 totalled US $5,307.8m. The proposed field programme budget for that year was projected at $4,460.7m., of which 42.4% was to be allocated to operations in sub-Saharan Africa, 34.3% to the Middle East and North Africa, 13.0% to Asia and the Pacific, 7.7% to Europe, and 2.5% to the Americas.

Publications

Assessing Mental Health and Psychosocial Needs and Resources: Toolkit for Humanitarian Settings.

Global Trends (annually).

Refugees (quarterly, in English, French, German, Italian, Japanese and Spanish).

Refugee Resettlement: An International Handbook to Guide Reception and Integration.

Refugee Survey Quarterly.

Refworld (annually).

Sexual and Gender-based Violence Against Refugees, Returnees and Displaced Persons: Guidelines for Prevention and Response.

The State of the World's Refugees (every 2 years).

Statistical Yearbook (annually).

UNHCR Handbook for Emergencies.

Press releases, reports.

Statistics

PERSONS OF CONCERN TO UNHCR IN LATIN AMERICA AND THE CARIBBEAN

(at 31 December 2013, provisional figures*)

Host Country	Refugees†	Asylum seekers	Returnees	Others
Argentina . . .	3,362	916	—	—
Brazil . . .	5,196	4,634	—	12,320
Chile . . .	1,743	353,421	—	—
Colombia . . .	224	71	17	5,368,150‡
Costa Rica . . .	20,569	616	—	—
Dominican Rep. .	721	824	—	210,000
Ecuador . . .	123,133	12,454	1	—
Mexico	1,831	1,352	—	13
Panama . . .	17,665	630	—	2
Peru	1,162	507	—	—
Venezuela . . .	204,340	1,073	—	—

* Countries with fewer than 1,000 persons of concern to UNHCR are not listed.
† Includes persons in refugee-like situations.
‡ Mainly internally displaced persons.

United Nations Peacekeeping

Address: Department of Peacekeeping Operations, Room S-3727B, United Nations, New York, NY 10017, USA.

Telephone: (212) 963-8077; **fax:** (212) 963-9222; **internet:** www.un.org/Depts/dpko/.

United Nations peacekeeping operations have been conceived as instruments of conflict control. The UN has used these operations in various conflicts, with the consent of the parties involved, to maintain international peace and security, without prejudice to the positions or claims of parties, in order to facilitate the search for political settlements through peaceful means. Each operation is established with a specific mandate, which requires periodic review by the UN Security Council. In 1988 the United Nations Peacekeeping Forces were awarded the Nobel Peace Prize.

United Nations peacekeeping operations fall into two categories: peacekeeping forces and observer missions. Both must at all times maintain complete impartiality and avoid any action that might affect the claims or positions of the parties. Peacekeeping forces are composed of contingents of military and civilian personnel, made available by member states. These forces assist in preventing the recurrence of fighting, restoring and maintaining peace, and promoting a return to normal conditions. To this end, peacekeeping forces are authorized as necessary to undertake negotiations, persuasion, observation and fact-finding. They conduct patrols and interpose physically between the opposing parties. Peacekeeping forces are permitted to use their weapons only in self-defence.

Military observer missions are composed of officers who are made available, on the Secretary-General's request, by member states. A mission's function is to observe and report to the Secretary-General (who, in turn, informs the Security Council) on the maintenance of a ceasefire, to investigate violations and to do what it can to improve the situation.

The UN's peacekeeping forces and observer missions are financed in most cases by assessed contributions from member states. (The exceptions are the UN Peacekeeping Force in Cyprus, which is funded partly by voluntary contributions; and the UN Military Observer Group in India and Pakistan and the UN Truce Supervision Organization, financed from the UN regular budget.) At 30 June 2014 outstanding assessed contributions to the peacekeeping budget amounted to some US $1,110m.

By September 2014 the UN had deployed a total of 69 peacekeeping operations, of which 13 were authorized in the period 1948–88 and 56 since 1988. At 31 July 2014 122 countries were contributing some 96,535 uniformed personnel to the 16 operations that were ongoing at that time, of whom 83,327 were peacekeeping troops, 11,420 police officers and 1,788 military observers.

United Nations Stabilization Mission in Haiti—MINUSTAH

Address: Port-au-Prince, Haiti.

Special Representative of the UN Secretary-General and Head of Mission: SANDRA HONORÉ (Trinidad and Tobago).

Force Commander: Lt-Gen. JOSE LUIZ JABORANDY, Jr (Brazil).

Police Commissioner: LUIS MIGUEL CARRILHO (Portugal).

Establishment and Mandate: In February 2004 the UN Security Council authorized the establishment of a Multinational Interim Force (MIF) to help to secure law and order in Haiti, where political tensions had escalated prior to the resignation of President Jean-Bertrand Aristide. In April the Security Council agreed to establish MINUSTAH, which was to assume authority from the MIF with effect from 1 June. MINUSTAH was mandated to create a stable and secure environment, to support the transitional government in institutional development and organizing and monitoring elections, and to monitor the human rights situation. Among its declared objectives was the improvement of living conditions of the population through security measures, humanitarian actions and economic development.

Activities, 2004–09: During 2004 mission civil support units covering electoral assistance, child protection, gender, civil affairs, human rights, and HIV/AIDS became operational. MINUSTAH forces worked to stabilize the security situation in the country, including by reducing the criminal activities of armed groups in poorer urban areas. In June 2005 the Security Council approved a temporary reinforcement of MINUSTAH to provide increased security in advance of planned local, legislative and presidential elections; the mission also deployed experts to train electoral agents and supervisors. After some delay the presidential and first round of legislative elections were conducted in early February 2006, with MINUSTAH officers providing security during the voting process and maintaining order as the results were being clarified. The mission subsequently pledged to support a post-election process of national dialogue and reconciliation and measures to strengthen the country's police force in order to re-establish law and order in areas of the capital, Port-au-Prince. A second round of voting in the legislative election was conducted in April. In August the UN Security Council determined that the mission should strengthen its role in preventing crime and reducing community violence, in particular kidnappings and other activities by local armed groups. In February 2007 MINUSTAH launched a large-scale operation in the Cité Soleil quarter of Port-au-Prince in order to extend its security presence in the most vulnerable locations and to counter the activities of criminal gangs. At the same time UN personnel helped to rehabilitate education, youth and medical facilities in those areas. In April MINUSTAH provided security and logistical support during the conduct of local municipal and mayoral elections. By November an estimated 9,000 local police officers had graduated from MINUSTAH training institutes. In April 2008 there were violent local demonstrations concerning the rising cost of living, during which several MINUSTAH personnel were attacked and property was damaged. A contingent of the mission subsequently distributed food aid to some 3,000 families in the poorest quarters of the capital. In August–September MINUSTAH personnel undertook emergency relief and rehabilitation activities, including evacuation of local residents and the distribution of humanitarian aid, to assist some of the 800,000 people affected by tropical storms which struck the country consecutively during a period of three weeks. From mid-2008 MINUSTAH strengthened its presence along the country's border with the Dominican Republic to counter illegal drugs-trafficking and improve security in the region. In December the mission undertook its first joint operation with the local police authorities to seize illegal drugs. During 2009 MINUSTAH, as well as implementing projects aimed at reducing violence in the community, provided technical security capacity-building support to the national police.

2010–14: In January 2010 a major earthquake struck Haiti, and destroyed the MINUSTAH headquarters in Port-au-Prince. Subsequently it was confirmed that 102 mission staff had been killed, among them Hédi Annabi, the then Special Representative of the UN Secretary-General, his deputy, and the acting police commissioner for the mission. Later in January the UN Security Council adopted a resolution increasing the strength of the mission, to enable it to support the immediate recovery, reconstruction and stability efforts in Haiti. The temporary deployment of an additional 680 police officers was authorized by the Security Council in June. MINUSTAH extended technical, logistical and administrative assistance to the country's authorities in preparation for presidential and legislative elections, which were conducted in November. MINUSTAH contributed to efforts to restore order and to maintain stability following violent reactions to preliminary election results in December. The mission developed a revised security strategy to ensure a stable environment for the second round of voting in the presidential election, held in March 2011. In January of that year MINUSTAH launched a major initiative, with the national police force, to seize known criminals, as well as to support vulnerable young people in some of the most socially fragile urban areas through the provision of skills training, income-generating activities, and the implementation of psychosocial initiatives. A five-year Haitian National Police Development Plan, finalized in March 2012 jointly by MINUSTAH's police component and the national police service, aimed to strengthen the national police force by 2016 to a minimum of 15,000 serving officers. In October 2012, in response to the onset of Hurricane Sandy, MINUSTAH co-ordinated with other organizations to support local authorities in executing the rapid evacuations of more than 17,000 people from areas at risk of severe flood and wind damage.

From October 2010 MINUSTAH provided logistical support to counter a severe outbreak of cholera, including the construction of temporary treatment centres, public education efforts, transportation of personnel, emergency medicines and supplies, and the distribution of potable water in affected areas. In January 2011 the UN Secretary-General appointed a panel of independent experts to assess the outbreak amid widespread speculation within the country that a contingent of MINUSTAH troops was the source. A claim for compensation was brought against the UN in November on behalf of victims of the cholera outbreak; in February 2013, however, the compensation claim was formally rejected by the UN Secretary-General. In December 2012 the UN Secretary-General appointed a Special Adviser for Community-based Medicine and Lessons from Haiti to support existing national elimination efforts through investment in prevention, treatment, and education, with a focus on the provision of clean drinking water and sanitation systems, and of an oral cholera vaccine. According to Haiti government sources a total of 698,304 people in Haiti were infected with cholera from October 2010–end-January 2014, resulting in 8,562 fatalities. In July 2014 the UN Secretary-General Ban attended the launch of a new 'Total Sanitation Campaign', a World Bank-supported initiative of the Haiti Government that aimed to improve sanitation systems during 2014–19, with a view to protecting Haitians from water-borne diseases and eliminating cholera infections.

In October 2011 the UN Security Council authorized a reduction in the mission's authorized strength by 1,600 personnel, to be completed by mid-2012, in order to redress the mission's post-earthquake expansion. A further reduction in the mission's strength, to 6,270 troops and 2,601 police officers, was authorized by the Council in October 2012; and in October 2013 the Council endorsed another reduction in troop numbers, to 5,021, while maintaining the police component of 2,601 personnel.

During 2012 MINUSTAH and the UN country team in Haiti finalized a new integrated strategic framework covering 2013–16, which was aligned with the Haiti Government's strategic priorities for that period; the framework focused on strengthening Haitian institutions to manage the delivery of basic social services; and the ongoing downsizing of the mission. In April 2013 a MINUSTAH and the Haiti authorities established a joint workshop to monitor the gradual transfer of responsibilities from the mission to the Government. In May, against a background of dissatisfaction from some civil society and politcal stakeholders with the continuing presence of the mission, the Haiti Senate passed a non-binding resolution requesting the progressive withdrawal of the mission.

Meanwhile MINUSTAH continued to monitor the security situation during 2013–mid-2014, conducting joint operations with the national police in the most challenging districts of Port-au-Prince, supporting police development efforts, and implementing initiatives aimed at addressing high levels of youth unemployment, criminal gang activities, and weak security institutions. MINUSTAH military and police components maintained a presence in camps accommodating around 146,000 people who remained homeless in the aftermath of the 2010 earthquake, as well as in fragile urban districts.

Operational Strength: At 31 July 2014 MINUSTAH comprised 4,973 troops and 2,435 police officers; there was also a support team of 135 UN Volunteers and 362 international civilian staff and 1,229 local civilian staff.

Finance: The mission is financed by assessments in respect of a Special Account. The approved budget for the period 1 July 2014–30 June 2015 amounted to US $500.1m.

World Food Programme—WFP

Address: Via Cesare Giulio Viola 68, Parco dei Medici, 00148 Rome, Italy.

Telephone: (06) 65131; **fax:** (06) 6513-2840; **e-mail:** wfpinfo@wfp .org; **internet:** www.wfp.org.

WFP, the principal food assistance organization of the UN, became operational in 1963. It aims to alleviate acute hunger by providing emergency relief following natural or man-made humanitarian disasters, and supplies food assistance in post-disaster situations, and to vulnerable populations in developing countries to improve nutrition and eradicate chronic undernourishment, and to further social advancement through developing assets and promoting the self-reliance of poor families and communities.

Organization

(September 2014)

EXECUTIVE BOARD

The governing body of WFP is the Executive Board, comprising 36 members, 18 of whom are elected by the UN Economic and Social Council (ECOSOC) and 18 by the Council of the Food and Agriculture Organization (FAO). The Board meets four times each year at WFP headquarters, in Rome, Italy.

SECRETARIAT

WFP's Executive Director is appointed jointly by the UN Secretary-General and the Director-General of FAO and is responsible for the management and administration of the Programme. Around 90% of WFP staff members work in the field. WFP administers some 87 country offices, and maintains six regional bureaux, located in Bangkok, Thailand (for Asia), Cairo, Egypt (for the Middle East, Central Asia and Eastern Europe), Panama City, Panama (for Latin America and the Caribbean), Johannesburg, South Africa (for Southern Africa), Kampala, Uganda (for Central and Eastern Africa), and Dakar, Senegal (for West Africa). A Vulnerability Analysis and Mapping (VAM) unit is maintained within the Secretariat.

Executive Director: ERTHARIN COUSIN (USA).

Activities

WFP, which is the frontline UN agency in combating hunger, focuses its efforts on the world's poorest countries, and aims to provide at least 90% of its total assistance to those designated as 'low-income food-deficit'. During 2012 WFP food assistance, distributed through development projects, emergency operations (EMOPs) and protracted relief and recovery operations (PRROs), benefited some 97.2m. people, including 82.1m. women and children, and 6.5m. internally displaced persons (IDPs), in 80 countries. Total food deliveries in 2012 amounted to 3.5m. metric tons. The four principal objectives of WFP's strategic plan governing its activities during 2014–17 were saving lives and protecting livelihoods in emergencies; supporting food security and nutrition and building livelihoods in fragile settings and in the aftermath of emergencies; reducing risk and enabling people, communities and countries to meet their own food and nutrition needs; and reducing undernutrition and breaking the intergenerational cycle of hunger.

Since 2008 WFP has shifted its primary focus from the supply of food towards the provision of food assistance. The implementation, where possible, of targeted cash and voucher schemes as an efficient alternative to food rations, has reduced the Programme's food transportation and storage costs as well as helping to sustain local economies. Vouchers are considered to be relatively easy to monitor, and also may be flexibly increased or reduced depending upon the severity of an emergency situation. There were some 6m. beneficiaries of cash and voucher programmes in 2012. WFP continues to provide basic rations in emergency situations, and special nutrition support where needed. It is WFP policy to buy food as near to where it is needed as possible. In cases where food donations are received, they must meet internationally agreed standards applicable to trade in food products. Basic WFP rations comprise basic food items (staple foods such as wheat flour or rice; pulses such as lentils and chickpeas; vegetable oil fortified with vitamins A and D; sugar; and iodized salt). Where possible basic rations are complemented with special products designed to improve the nutritional intake of beneficiaries. These include fortified blended foods, principally Corn Soya Blend, containing important micronutrients; Super Cereals; ready-to-use foods, principally peanut-based pastes enriched with vitamins and minerals trade-marked as Plumpy'Doz and Plumpy'Sup, which are better suited to meeting the nutritional needs of young and moderately malnourished children; high energy biscuits, distributed in the first phases of emergencies when cooking facilities may be scarce; micronutrient powder ('sprinkles'), which can be used to fortify home cooking; and compressed food bars, given out during disaster relief operations when the distribution and preparation of local food is not possible. Some 9.8m. children were in receipt of special nutrition support in 2012.

WFP aims to address the causes of chronic malnourishment, which it identifies as poverty and lack of opportunity. It emphasizes the role played by women (who are most likely to sow, reap, harvest and cook household food) in combating hunger, and endeavours to address the specific nutritional needs of women, to increase their access to food and development resources, and to promote girls' education. WFP estimates that females represent four-fifths of people engaged in farming in Africa and three-fifths of people engaged in farming in Asia, and that globally women are the sole breadwinners in one-third of households. Increasingly WFP distributes food assistance through women, believing that vulnerable children are more likely to be reached in this way.

With other UN agencies, governments, research institutions, and representatives of civil society and of the private sector, WFP supports the Scaling up Nutrition (SUN) initiative, which was initiated in 2009, under the co-ordination of the UN Secretary-General's Special Representative for Food Security and Nutrition, with the aim of increasing the coverage of interventions that improve nutrition during the first 1,000 days of a child's life (such as exclusive breastfeeding, optimal complementary feeding practices, and provision of essential vitamins and minerals); and ensuring that nutrition plans are implemented at national level, and that government programmes take nutrition into account. In 2013 WFP, FAO, and the International Fund for Agricultural Development (IFAD) participated in global consultations on formulating a post-2015 development framework in the thematic area of food and nutrition.

In September 2012 WFP, FAO, IFAD and UN Women launched 'Accelerating Progress Toward the Economic Empowerment of Rural Women', a five-year initiative that was to be implemented initially in Ethiopia, Guatemala, Kyrgyzstan, Liberia, Nepal, Niger and Rwanda.

The Programme, which is a co-sponsor of the Joint UN Programme on HIV/AIDS (UNAIDS) also focuses resources on supporting the nutrition and food security of households and communities affected by HIV/AIDS, and on promoting food security as a means of mitigating extreme poverty and vulnerability and thereby combating the spread and impact of HIV/AIDS.

WFP is a participant in the High Level Task Force (HLTF) on the Global Food Security Crisis, which was established by the UN Secretary-General in April 2008 with the aim of addressing the global impact of soaring levels of food and commodity prices, and of formulating a comprehensive framework for action. In January 2009 the HLTF determined to establish a Global Partnership for Agriculture, Food Security and Nutrition. The long-standing Committee on World Food Security (CFS), open to member states of WFP, FAO and IFAD, became a central component of the new Global Partnership, tasked with influencing hunger elimination programmes at global, regional and national level, taking into account that food security relates not just to agriculture but also to economic access to food, adequate nutrition, social safety nets and human rights. WFP participated in a World Summit on Food Security, organized by FAO, in Rome, in November 2009, which aimed to secure greater coherence in the global governance of food security and set a 'new world food order'. WFP, with FAO, IFAD and other agencies, contributes to the Agriculture Market Information System, established in 2011 to improve transparency in agricultural markets and contribute to stabilizing food price volatility. WFP, with FAO and IFAD, implements a food security initiative to strengthen feeding programmes and expand support to farmers in developing countries, the second of nine activities that were launched in April 2009 by the UN System Chief Executives Board for Co-ordination (CEB), with the aim of alleviating the impact on poor and vulnerable populations of the global economic crisis. WFP also solely leads an initiative on emergency activities to meet humanitarian needs and promote security, the seventh of the CEB activities launched in April 2009.

In November 2014 WFP, FAO and the World Health Organization (WHO), in co-operation with the HLTF, and other partners, were to organize the Second International Conference on Nutrition (ICN2, the first having been convened in December 1992), at FAO headquarters in Rome. ICN2, with participation by senior policymakers in areas including agriculture and health, representatives of UN and other international agencies, and of civil society, was to review progress achieved since 1992 towards improving nutrition, and to consider future policy options in that area, taking into account advances in science and technology and changes to food systems.

WFP has developed a range of mechanisms to enhance its preparedness for emergency situations (such as conflict, drought and other natural disasters) and to improve its capacity for responding effectively to crises as they arise. Through its Vulnerability Analysis and Mapping (VAM) project, WFP aims to identify potentially vulnerable groups by providing information on food security and the capacity of different groups for coping with shortages, and to enhance emergency contingency-planning and long-term assistance objectives. VAM—co-ordinated from a dedicated unit at the WFP Secretariat in Rome, and also comprising, in 2014, more than 150 analysts worldwide—produces food security analysis reports, guidelines, reference documents and maps. VAM's online Food and Commodity Price Data Store provides data on the most commonly consumed staples in 1,226 markets in 75 countries. The key elements of WFP's emergency response capacity comprises its strategic stores of food and logistics equipment (drawn from 'stocks afloat': ships loaded with WFP food supplies that can be re-routed to assist in crisis situations; development project stocks redesignated as emergency project contingency reserves; and in-country borrowing from national food reserves enabled by bilateral agreements); stand-by arrangements to enable the rapid deployment of personnel, communications and other essential equipment; and the Augmented Logistics Intervention Team for Emergencies (ALITE), which undertakes capacity assessments and contingency-planning. When engaging in a crisis WFP dispatches an emergency preparedness team to quantify the amount and type of food assistance required, and to identify the beneficiaries of and the timescale and logistics (e.g. means of transportation; location of humanitarian corridors, if necessary; and designated food distribution sites, such as refugee camps, other emergency shelters and therapeutic feeding centres) underpinning the ensuing EMOP. Once the EMOP has been drafted, WFP launches an appeal to the international donor community for funds and assistance to enable its implementation. WFP special operations are short-term logistics and infrastructure projects that are undertaken to facilitate the movement of food aid, regardless of whether the food is provided by the Agency itself. Special operations typically complement EMOPs or longer rehabilitation projects.

During 2000 WFP led efforts, undertaken with other UN humanitarian agencies, for the design and application of local UN Joint Logistics Centre facilities, aimed at co-ordinating resources in an emergency situation. In 2001 a UN Humanitarian Response Depot was opened in Brindisi, Italy, under the direction of WFP experts, for the storage of essential rapid response equipment. Since 2003 WFP has been mandated to provide aviation transport services to the wider humanitarian community. During 2005 the UN's Inter-Agency Standing Committee (IASC), concerned with co-ordinating the international response to humanitarian disasters, developed a concept of organizing agency assistance to IDPs through the institutionalization of a 'Cluster Approach', currently comprising 11 core areas of activity. WFP was designated the lead agency for the clusters on Emergency Telecommunications (jointly with the Office for the Co-ordination of Humanitarian Affairs—OCHA—and UNICEF) and Logistics. A new cluster on Food Security, established in 2011, is led jointly by WFP and FAO, and aims to combine expertise in food aid and agricultural assistance in order to boost food security and to improve the resilience of food-insecure disaster-affected communities. WFP manages the UN Humanitarian Air Service (UNHAS), which provides air transportation in emergency response situations.

WFP aims to link its relief and development activities to provide a continuum between short-term relief and longer-term rehabilitation and development. In order to achieve this objective, WFP aims to promote capacity-building elements within relief operations, e.g. training, income-generating activities and environmental protection measures; and to integrate elements that strengthen disaster mitigation into development projects, including soil conservation, reafforestation, irrigation infrastructure, and transport construction and rehabilitation. In all its projects WFP aims to assist the most vulnerable groups (such as nursing mothers and children) and to ensure that beneficiaries have an adequate and balanced diet. Through its development activities, WFP aims to alleviate poverty in developing countries by promoting self-reliant families and communities. No individual country is permitted to receive more than 10% of the Programme's available development resources. WFP's Food-for-Assets development operations pay workers living in poverty with food in return for participation in self-help schemes and labour-intensive projects, with the aim of enabling vulnerable households and communities to focus time and resources on investing in lasting assets with which to raise themselves out of poverty (rather than on day-to-day survival). Food-for-Assets projects provide training in new techniques for achieving improved food security (such as training in new agricultural skills or in the establishment of home gardening businesses); and include, for example, building new irrigation or terracing infrastructures; soil and water conservation activities; and allocating food rations to villagers to enable them to devote time to building schools and clinics. In areas undermined by conflict WFP offers food assistance as an incentive for former combatants to learn new skills and reintegrate into society. In 2012 some 15.1m. people were in receipt of food from WFP as an incentive to build assets, attend training, strengthen resilience to shocks and preserve livelihoods. WFP focuses on providing good nutrition for the first 1,000 days of life, from the womb to two years of age, in order to lay the foundations for a healthy childhood and adulthood. WFP's '1,000 days plus' approach supports children over the age of two through school feeding activities, which aim to expand educational opportunities for poor children (given that it is difficult for children to concentrate on studies without adequate food and nutrition, and that food-insecure households frequently have to choose between educating their children or making them work to help the family to survive), and to improve the quality of the teaching environment. During 2012 school feeding projects benefited 24.7m. children. As an incentive to promote the education of vulnerable children, including orphans and children with HIV/AIDS, and to encourage families to send their daughters to school, WFP also implements 'take-home ration' projects, under which it provides basic food items to certain households, usually including sacks of rice and cans of cooking oil. WFP's Purchase for Progress (P4P) programme, launched in September 2008, expands the Programme's long-term 'local procurement' policy, enabling smallholder and low-income farmers in developing countries to supply food to WFP's global assistance operations. Under P4P farmers are taught techniques and provided with tools to enable them to compete competitively in the market-place. P4P also aims to identify and test specific successful local practices that could be replicated to benefit small-scale farmers on a wider scale. P4P pilot initiatives were undertaken in 20 countries, in Africa, Latin America and Asia during 2008–13, and in 2014 the programme was entering its post-pilot phase; by that time WFP had established links under P4P with some 1,000 farmers' organizations representing more than 1.1m. farmers worldwide.

Since 1999 WFP has been implementing PRROs, where the emphasis is on fostering stability, rehabilitation and long-term development for victims of natural disasters, displaced persons and refugees. PRROs are introduced no later than 18 months after the initial EMOP and last no more than three years. When undertaken in collaboration with UNHCR and other international agencies, WFP has responsibility for mobilizing basic food commodities and for related transport, handling and storage costs.

In 2013 WFP's operational expenditure in Latin America and the Caribbean totalled US $151.7m., representing some 4% of total expenditure in that year. During July 2011–December 2014 WFP was implementing a $13.6m. PRRO aimed at supporting 120,100 Colombian refugees sheltering in Ecuador. A PRRO being implemented within Colombia during the period 2012–14 was providing food aid to 675,000 displaced persons requiring relief assistance and 855,000 beneficiaries requiring recovery support. A country programme being undertaken in Nicaragua during the period 2013–18, at a cost of $19.7m., was focused on providing nutritional support to vulnerable groups, supporting access to education, enhancing community and household resilience, and mitigating the impact of HIV/AIDS. A country programme (costing $12m. and aimed at 177,200 beneficiaries) being undertaken in Bolivia during 2013–17 focused on providing food-based interventions for children aged between two and five years; giving food assistance to primary school children and street children; and offering technical assistance in emergency preparedness and response to government institutions. During 2008–13 WFP's new P4P programme was piloted in El Salvador, Honduras, Guatemala and Nicaragua. A PRRO aimed at restoring food security and livelihood for vulnerable groups affected by recurrent economic shocks in El Salvador, Guatemala, Honduras and Nicaragua, was being implemented during 2014–16, at a total cost to WFP of $70.5m.; the operation was to provide food transfers and cash and vouchers annually to some 428,000 beneficiaries.

In February 2010 WFP hosted a high-level meeting in Rome to launch a global partnership aimed at developing a future food security plan for Haiti, where, even prior to the earthquake that devastated that country in January of that year, one-third of the population was estimated by WFP to be vulnerable to food insecurity, owing to persistent political and civil unrest, successive natural disasters (including hurricanes), high food prices, and poor infrastructure. The impact of further adverse natural events in 2012, including, in October, Hurricane Sandy, resulted in some 1.5m. Haitians being declared 'severely food insecure' by the end of that year. Prolonged drought in 2013 aggravated the food security crisis. WFP, in response, distributed take-home rations, via schools and health centres, to 200,000 Haitians. During April 2014–March 2017 a US $118.6m. PRRO was under way in Haiti that aimed to respond to the needs of more than 2m. affected and at-risk people in the most food insecure and disaster-prone districts, with a focus on saving lives, rebuilding livelihoods and enhancing resilience to shocks. A development operation aimed at supporting the national school meals programme, costing WFP some $70.5m., was under way during 2012–14.

In March 2011 WFP and the Brazilian authorities inaugurated a Centre of Excellence Against Hunger, in Brasília, Brazil, which aimed to utilize techniques used in a long-term Brazilian initiative known as Fome Zero (Zero Hunger) to support other countries in ending malnutrition and hunger. The Centre is a global reference point on school meals, nutrition and food security. In 2014 its activities were focused on 18 countries in Africa and Asia.

Finance

The Programme is funded by voluntary contributions from donor countries, intergovernmental bodies such as the European Commission, and the private sector. Contributions are made in the form of commodities, finance and services (particularly shipping). Commitments to the International Emergency Food Reserve, from which WFP provides the majority of its food supplies, and to the Immediate Response Account of the IEFR, are also made on a voluntary basis by donors. WFP's projected operational requirements for 2014 amounted to some US $5,857m.

Publications

Cost of Hunger in Africa series.
Emergency Food Security Assessment Handbook.
Food and Nutrition Handbook.
State of Food Insecurity in the World (annually, with FAO and IFAD).
World Hunger Series.
Year in Review.

Food and Agriculture Organization of the United Nations—FAO

Address: Viale delle Terme di Caracalla, 00100 Rome, Italy.

Telephone: (06) 5705-1; **fax:** (06) 5705-3152; **e-mail:** fao-hq@fao.org; **internet:** www.fao.org.

FAO, the first specialized agency of the UN to be founded after the Second World War, aims to raise levels of nutrition and achieve food security for all; to eliminate poverty and facilitate economic and social progress for all; and to promote the sustainable management and utilization of natural resources (land, water, air, climate and genetic) for the benefit of present and future generations. FAO serves as a co-ordinating agency for development programmes in the whole range of food and agriculture, including forestry and fisheries. It helps developing countries to promote educational and training facilities and to create appropriate institutions.

Organization

(September 2014)

CONFERENCE

The governing body is the FAO Conference of member nations. It meets every two years, formulates policy, determines the organization's programme and budget on a biennial basis, and elects new members. It also elects the Director-General of the Secretariat and the Independent Chairman of the Council. Regional conferences are also held each year.

COUNCIL

The FAO Council is composed of representatives of 49 member nations, elected by the Conference for rotating three-year terms. It is the interim governing body of FAO between sessions of the Conference, and normally holds at least five sessions in each biennium. There are eight main Governing Committees of the Council: the Finance, Programme, and Constitutional and Legal Matters Committees, and the Committees on Commodity Problems, Fisheries, Agriculture, Forestry, and World Food Security.

HEADQUARTERS

The Office of the Director-General includes the Office of Evaluation; Office of the Inspector-General; Legal Office; Ethics Office; Office for Communication, Partnerships and Advocacy; and Office of Strategy, Planning and Resources Management. There are Departments covering: Agriculture and Consumer Protection; Economic and Social Development; Fisheries and Aquaculture; Forestry; Natural Resources Management and Environment; Corporate Services; Human Resources and Finance; and Technical Co-operation.

Director-General: Dr JOSÉ GRAZIANO DA SILVA (Brazil).

REGIONAL OFFICES

FAO maintains five regional offices, 10 subregional offices, five liaison offices (in Yokohama, Japan; Washington, DC, USA; Geneva, Switzerland, and New York, USA: liaison with the UN; and Brussels, Belgium: liaison with the European Union), and more than 130 country offices.

Latin America and the Caribbean: Avda Dag Hammarskjöld 3241, Casilla 10095, Vitacura, Santiago, Chile; tel. (2) 923-2100; fax (2) 923-2101; e-mail fao-rlc@field.fao.org; internet www.rlc.fao.org; a Regional Conference for Latin America and the Caribbean (LARC) is convened every two years (2014: Santiago, Chile, in May); Regional Rep. RAÚL OSVALDO BENÍTEZ (Argentina).

Subregional Office for the Caribbean: POB 631-C, Bridgetown, Barbados; tel. 426-7110; fax 427-6075; e-mail fao-slac@fao.org; Subregional Co-ordinator for the Caribbean Dr JOHN RONALD DIPCHANDRA (DEEP) FORD.

Subregional Office for Mesoamerica: Edificio 238, Ciudad del Saber, Clayton, Ancon, Panama City; tel. 301-0326; e-mail FAO-SLM@fao.org; Subregional Rep. IGNACIO RIVERA RODRIGUEZ.

Activities

FAO focuses on four priority areas of activity: serving as a knowledge network; sharing policy expertise; providing a neutral forum for nations; and bringing knowledge directly to the field. The Organization pursues the following five strategic objectives: helping to eliminate hunger, food insecurity and malnutrition; making agriculture, forestry and fisheries more productive and sustainable; reducing rural poverty; enabling inclusive and efficient agricultural and food systems; and increasing the resilience of livelihoods to disasters. World Food Day, commemorating the foundation of FAO, is held annually on 16 October.

ECONOMIC AND SOCIAL DEVELOPMENT

The Economic and Social Development Department comprises divisions of Agricultural Development; Economics; Statistics; Trade and Markets; and Gender, Equity and Rural Employment. The Department's priority areas of focus are: the world food situation; investment in agriculture; long-term perspectives in agriculture; gender right to food; and food volatility in agricultural markets.

FAO provides a focal point for economic research and policy analysis relating to food security and sustainable development. FAO's long-term commitment to reducing hunger was in recent years based on the objectives of the Rome Declaration on World Food Security and the World Food Summit Plan of Action adopted by the World Food Summit, convened under FAO auspices in November 1996, and aiming to halve by 2015 the number of people (around 800m.) then afflicted by undernutrition; this objective was subsequently incorporated into a Strategic Framework for the period 2000–15 that was approved by the FAO Conference in November 1999, and also into the UN Millennium Development Goals (MDGs). The commitment was further reaffirmed by World Food Summit: Five Years Later, held in June 2002 to review the 1996 conference. In 2013 FAO, the World Food Programme (WFP), and the International Fund for Agricultural Development (IFAD) participated in global consultations on formulating a post-2015 development framework in the thematic area of food and nutrition. In April 2014 the three agencies identified five future targets, to be achieved through the development of innovative partnerships: promoting access to adequate food all year round for all people; ending malnutrition in all its forms with special attention to stunting; making all food production systems more productive, sustainable, resilient and efficient; securing access for all small food producers, especially women, to adequate inputs, knowledge, productive resources and services; and promoting more efficient post-production food systems that reduce by one-half the global rate of food loss and waste. The 2013 edition of the joint FAO-IFAD-WFP annual *State of Food Insecurity in the World* report, released in October, found that, during 2011–13, some 842m. people globally were suffering from chronic malnutrition, of whom around 826m. resided in developing countries.

With a view to countering an escalation from 2006 in commodity prices, FAO launched, in October 2007, an online Global Forum on Food Security and Nutrition; and inaugurated, in December of that year, an Initiative on Soaring Food Prices, which sought to boost food production in low-income developing countries by improving smallholders' access to agricultural supplies. In April 2008 the UN Secretary-General appointed FAO's Director-General as Vice-Chairman of a High Level Task Force (HLTF) on the Global Food Security Crisis. A High Level Conference on World Food Security and the Challenges of Climate Change and Bioenergy that was hosted in June by FAO adopted a Declaration on Food Security, urging the international donor community to increase investment in rural development, agriculture and agribusiness in developing countries and countries with economies in transition. During 2009 the long-standing Committee on World Food Security (CFS), open to member states of FAO, the WFP and IFAD, underwent reform, becoming a central component of a new Global Partnership for Agriculture, Food Security and Nutrition; thereafter the CFS was tasked with influencing hunger elimination programmes at global, regional and national level, taking into account that food security relates not just to agriculture but also to economic access to food, adequate nutrition, social safety nets and human rights. The CFS appoints the steering committee of the High Level Panel of Experts on Food Security and Nutrition, established in October 2009. In July of that year the FAO Director-General welcomed the Food Security Initiative—with commitments of US $20,000m.—approved in that month by leaders of the Group of Eight (G8) industrialized nations. In November FAO organized a World Summit on Food Security, in Rome, which adopted the Five Rome Principles for Sustainable Global Food Security: (i) investment in country-owned plans aimed at channelling resources to efficient results-based programmes and partnerships; (ii) fostering strategic co-ordination at the national, regional and global level to improve governance, promote better allocation of resources, avoid duplication of efforts and identify response gaps; (iii) striving for a comprehensive twin-track approach to food security comprising direct action to combat hunger in the most vulnerable, and also medium- and long-term sustainable agricultural, food security, nutrition and rural development programmes to eliminate the root causes of hunger and poverty, including through the progressive realization of the right to adequate food; (iv) ensuring a strong role for the multilateral system by sustained improvements in efficiency, responsiveness, co-ordination and effectiveness of multilateral institutions; and (v) ensuring sustained and substantial commitment by all partners to investment in agriculture and food security and nutrition, with provision of necessary resources in a timely and reliable fashion, aimed at multi-year plans and programmes. In November 2014 FAO, WFP and the World Health Organization (WHO), in co-operation with the HLTF, and other partners, were to organize the Second International Conference on Nutrition (ICN2, ICN1 having been convened in December 1992), at FAO headquarters. ICN2, with participation by senior policymakers in areas including agriculture and health, representatives of UN and other international agencies, and of civil society, was to review progress achieved since 1992 towards improving nutrition, and to consider future policy options in that area, taking into account advances in science and technology and changes to food systems.

FAO, with WFP and IFAD, leads an initiative to strengthen feeding programmes and expand support to farmers in developing countries, the second of nine activities that were launched in April 2009 by the UN System Chief Executives Board for Co-ordination (CEB), with the aim of alleviating the impact on poor and vulnerable populations of the developing global economic crisis. In May 2010 FAO launched an online petition entitled the *1billionhungry project*, with the aim of raising awareness of the plight of people worldwide suffering from chronic hunger. In May 2012 the CFS endorsed a set of landmark Voluntary Guidelines on the Responsible Governance of Tenure of Land, Fisheries and Forests in the Context of National Food Security, with the aim of supporting governments in safeguarding the rights of citizens to own or have access to natural resources. The FAO Director-General welcomed a new 'Zero Hunger Challenge' initiative announced by the UN Secretary-General in the following month, which aimed to eliminate malnutrition through measures such as boosting the productivity of smallholders, creating sustainable food systems, and reducing food wastage. In January 2013 FAO and the International Finance Corporation signed a Memorandum of Understanding (MOU) jointly to promote responsible private investment in agribusiness, and to promote the development of economic opportunities for rural communities.

In February 2011 FAO's Food Price Index recorded the highest levels of global food prices since 1990 (reaching 238 points). In June agriculture ministers from G20 countries adopted an action plan aimed at stabilizing food price volatility and agriculture, with a focus on improving international policy co-ordination and agricultural production; promoting targeted emergency humanitarian food reserves; and developing, under FAO auspices, an Agricultural Market Information System (AMIS) to improve market transparency and help to stabilize food price volatility. FAO maintains, additionally to the Food Price Index—which averaged 196.6 points (the lowest level for four years) in August 2014—price indices for cereal, dairy, oils and fats, meat, and sugar.

FAO produces studies and reports on agricultural development, the impact of development programmes and projects, and the world food situation, as well as on commodity prices, trade and medium-term projections. It supports the development of methodologies and guidelines to improve research into food and agriculture and the integration of wider concepts, such as social welfare, environmental factors and nutrition, into research projects. FAO's Statistical Division assembles, analyses and disseminates statistical data on world food and agriculture and aims to ensure the consistency, broad coverage and quality of available data. The Division advises member countries on enhancing their statistical capabilities. It maintains FAOSTAT (accessible at faostat.fao.org) as a core database of statistical information relating to nutrition, fisheries, forestry, food production, land use, population, etc. In 2004 FAO developed a new statistical framework, CountrySTAT, to provide for the organization and integration of statistical data and metadata from sources within a particular country. By 2014 CountrySTAT systems had been established in 25 developing countries. A new Global Land Cover SHARE (GLC-SHARE) database was initiated in March 2014, which was to monitor trends in global land coverage, categorized into: artificial surfaces (accounting for 0.6% of land coverage at that time), bare soils (15.2%), croplands (12.6%), forests (27.7%), grasslands (13%), herbacious vegetation (1.3%), inland water bodies (2.6%), mangroves (0.1%), shrubs (9.5%), snow and glaciers (9.7%), and sparse vegetation (7.7%). GLC-SHARE was also to be utilized in assessing the impact of climate change on food production, and in land-use planning activities. FAO's internet-based interactive World Agricultural Information Centre (WAICENT) offers access to agricultural publications, technical documentation, codes of conduct, data, statistics and multimedia resources. FAO compiles and co-ordinates an extensive range of international databases on agriculture, fisheries, forestry, food and statistics, the most important of these being AGRIS (the International Information System for the

Agricultural Sciences and Technology) and CARIS (the Current Agricultural Research Information System).

In 1999 FAO signed an MOU with UNAIDS on strengthening co-operation to combat the threat posed by the HIV/AIDS epidemic to food security, nutrition and rural livelihoods. FAO is committed to incorporating HIV/AIDS into food security and livelihood projects, to strengthening community care and to highlighting the importance of nutrition in the care of those living with HIV/AIDS.

In September 2012 FAO, IFAD, WFP and UN Women launched 'Accelerating Progress Toward the Economic Empowerment of Rural Women', a five-year initiative that was to be implemented initially in Ethiopia, Guatemala, Kyrgyzstan, Liberia, Nepal, Niger and Rwanda.

FAO's Special Programme for Food Security (SPFS), initiated in 1994, assists low-income countries with a food deficit to increase food production and productivity as rapidly as possible, primarily through the widespread adoption by farmers of improved production technologies, with emphasis on areas of high potential. Under the Programme, which promotes South-South co-operation, some 40 bilateral co-operation agreements are in effect. In 2014 some 62 countries were categorized formally as 'low-income food-deficit'.

FAO's Global Information and Early Warning System (GIEWS), which become operational in 1975, monitors and maintains a database on the crop and food outlook at the global, regional, national and sub-national level in order to detect emerging food supply difficulties and disasters and to ensure rapid intervention in countries experiencing food supply shortages. It publishes regular reports on the weather conditions and crop prospects in sub-Saharan Africa and in the Sahel region, issues special alerts which describe the situation in countries or subregions experiencing food difficulties, and recommends an appropriate international response. The publication *Crop Prospects and Food Situation* reviews the global situation, and provides regional updates and a special focus on countries experiencing food crises and requiring external assistance, on a quarterly basis. *Food Outlook*, issued in June and November, analyses developments in global food and animal feed markets.

AGRICULTURE AND CONSUMER PROTECTION

The Department of Agriculture and Consumer Protection comprises the following divisions: Animal Production and Health; Food Safety and Quality; Plant Production and Protection; Rural Infrastructure and Agro-Industries; and the Joint FAO/IAEA Division of Nuclear Techniques in Food and Agriculture.

FAO is concerned to improve crop and grassland and pasture productivity and to develop sustainable agricultural systems. It provides member countries with technical advice for plant improvement, the application of plant biotechnology, the development of integrated production systems and rational grassland management. There are groups concerned with the main field cereal crops, i.e. rice, maize and wheat, which *inter alia* identify means of enhancing production, collect and analyse relevant data and promote collaboration between research institutions, government bodies and other farm management organizations. FAO's International Rice Commission has endorsed the use of hybrid rice, and it has subsequently assisted member countries to acquire the necessary technology and training to develop hybrid rice production. FAO actively promotes the concept of Conservation Agriculture, which aims to minimize the need for mechanical soil tillage or additional farming resources and to reduce soil degradation and erosion.

FAO is also concerned with the development and diversification of horticultural and industrial crops, for example oil seeds, fibres and medicinal plants. FAO collects and disseminates data regarding crop trials and new technologies. It has developed an information processing site, Ecocrop, to help farmers to identify appropriate crops and environmental requirements.

FAO's plant protection service incorporates a range of programmes concerned with the control of pests and the use of pesticides. Negotiations initiated in 1996 under the auspices of FAO and the UN Environment Programme (UNEP) culminated in September 1998 in the adoption of the Rotterdam Convention on the Prior Informed Consent Procedure for Certain Hazardous Chemicals and Pesticides in International Trade, which required that hazardous chemicals and pesticides banned or severely restricted in at least two countries should not be exported unless explicitly agreed by the importing country. The treaty entered into force in February 2004. In November 2002 FAO launched a revised International Code of Conduct on the Distribution and Use of Pesticides (first adopted in 1985) to reduce the inappropriate distribution and use of pesticides and other toxic compounds, particularly in developing countries. FAO co-operates with UNEP to provide secretariat services for the Convention. FAO has promoted the use of Integrated Pest Management (IPM) initiatives to encourage the use, at the local level, of safer and more effective methods of pest control, such as biological control methods and natural predators.

FAO hosts the secretariat of the International Plant Protection Convention (first adopted in 1951, revised in 1997) which aims to prevent the spread of plant pests and to promote effective control measures. The secretariat helps to define phytosanitary standards, promote the exchange of information and extend technical assistance to contracting parties (181 at September 2014). In mid-August 2014 the Convention became the seventh member of the Liaison Group of Biodiversity-related Conventions; accordingly, states parties were urged to establish contacts with national focal points of the Convention on Biological Diversity, with a view to exploring potential areas of co-operation.

FAO's Animal Production and Health Division is concerned with the control and management of major animal diseases, and, in recent years, with safeguarding humans from livestock diseases. Other programmes are concerned with the contribution of livestock to poverty alleviation, the efficient use of natural resources in livestock production, the management of animal genetic resources, promoting exchange of information, and mapping the global distribution of livestock.

The Emergency Prevention System for Transboundary Animal and Plant Pests and Diseases (EMPRES) was established in 1994 to strengthen FAO's activities in the prevention, early warning, control and, where possible, eradication of pests and highly contagious livestock diseases (which the system categorizes as epidemic diseases of strategic importance, such as rinderpest or foot-and-mouth; diseases requiring tactical attention at international or regional level, e.g. Rift Valley fever; and emerging diseases, e.g. bovine spongiform encephalopathy—BSE). EMPRES has a desert locust component, and has published guidelines on all aspects of desert locust monitoring. A web-based EMPRES Global Animal Disease Information System (EMPRES-i) aims to support veterinary services through the timely release of disease information to enhance early warning and response to transboundary animal diseases, including emergent zoonoses. In November 2004 FAO established a specialized Emergency Centre for Transboundary Animal Disease Operations (ECTAD) to enhance FAO's role in assisting member states to combat animal disease outbreaks and in co-ordinating international efforts to research, monitor and control transboundary disease crises. In May 2004 FAO and the World Organization for Animal Health (OIE) signed an agreement to clarify their respective areas of competence and improve co-operation, in response to an increase in contagious transboundary animal diseases (such as foot-and-mouth disease and avian influenza). The two bodies agreed to establish a global framework on the control of transboundary animal diseases, entailing improved international collaboration and circulation of information. In 2006 FAO, the OIE and WHO launched a Global Early Warning and Response System for Major Animal Diseases, including Zoonoses (GLEWS). In October of that year FAO inaugurated a Crisis Management Centre to co-ordinate (in close co-operation with the OIE) it's response to major emergencies related to animal or food health.

In June 2011 the FAO Conference adopted a resolution declaring global freedom from rinderpest, following long-term efforts by the FAO-led Global Rinderpest Eradication Programme in pursuit of that goal. FAO and the OIE adopted two resolutions during 2011 relating to the destruction/safe storage of remaining stocks of rinderpest virus and on banning the use of the live virus in research. In July 2013, however, FAO and the OIE, having established a set of strict criteria and procedures, lifted the ban on the use of live rinderpest virus for approved research purposes. In June 2012 a conference convened in Bangkok, Thailand, under the auspices of FAO, the OIE and the Thai Government, endorsed a new Global Foot and Mouth Disease Control Strategy.

In September 2004 FAO and WHO declared an ongoing epidemic in certain East Asian countries of the H5N1 strain of highly pathogenic avian influenza (HPAI) to be a 'crisis of global importance': the disease was spreading rapidly through bird populations and was also transmitting to human populations through contact with diseased birds (mainly poultry). In May 2005 FAO, with WHO and the OIE, launched a global strategy for the progressive control of avian influenza. In October 2008, at the sixth international ministerial conference on avian influenza, convened in Sharm el-Sheikh, Egypt, FAO, with WHO, UNICEF, the OIE, the World Bank and the UN System Influenza Co-ordinator, presented a new strategic framework within the concept of a 'One World, One Health' policy focused on caring for the health of animals, humans, and the ecosystems that support them. The framework aimed to advance co-operation with respect to emerging infectious diseases, to strengthen animal and public health surveillance and to enhance response mechanisms. During 2003–14 outbreaks of H5N1 were recorded in 63 countries and territories, and more than 400m. domestic and wild birds consequently died or were culled. FAO warned in January 2013— at which time the virus remained endemic in parts of Asia and the Middle East—that the implementation of global health measures aimed at monitoring and controlling H5N1 and other diseases of animal origin (with particular reference to Peste des Petits Ruminants, affecting goats and sheep) was being put at risk by national budgetary restrictions arising from the ongoing global economic downturn. In 2014 FAO was monitoring, and providing preparedness and response support in relation to, an outbreak that arose in poultry and wild birds in China in early 2013 of the highly pathogenic H7N9 virus. Meanwhile the OFFLU was analysing the genetic sequence of the new virus to determine its characteristics, including its response to antivirals.

In December 2011 the Conference of the Parties to the Convention on Migratory Species (CMS) established a Scientific Task Force on Wildlife and Ecosystem Health, with FAO participation, reflecting the ongoing 'One World, One Health' policy; a Task Force on Avian Influenza and Wild Birds, established under the CMS in August 2005, was to continue as a core focus area within the larger Scientific Task Force.

In December 2013 FAO issued a report entitled *World Livestock 2013: Changing Disease Landscapes*, which stated that in recent years some 70% of new diseases emerging in humans were of animal origin, and frequently related to the increasingly intensive production of and trade in animal-sourced nutrition. The report outlined how agricultural expansion into formerly wild areas, thereby promoting the transfer of pathogens—in both directions—between livestock and wildlife; population growth combined with persisting poverty; and modern globe-spanning food supply chains have affected the emergence of disease, its transference across species boundaries, and its spread. The report recommended a more holistic approach to managing the animal-human-environment interface.

FAO is committed to promoting food quality and safety in all different stages of food production and processing. It supports the development of integrated food control systems by member states, which incorporate aspects of food control management, inspection, risk analysis and quality assurance. The joint FAO/WHO Codex Alimentarius Commission, established in 1962, aims to protect the health of consumers, ensure fair trade practices and promote the co-ordination of food standards activities at an international level. The Commission maintains databases of standards for food additives, and for maximum residue levels of veterinary drugs and pesticides. In July 2001 the Commission agreed the first global principles for assessing the safety of foods derived from biotechnology (i.e. genetically modified—GM—foods), and approved a series of maximum levels of environmental contaminants in food. In June 2004 FAO published guidelines for assessing possible risks posed to plants by living modified organisms. In March 2014 the FAO warned that, as a result of increasing production of GM crops worldwide, and in the absence of an international agreement clarifying mutually accepted standards with regard to the presence of GM organisms (GMOs), rising incidents of low levels of GMOs were being reported in traded shipments of food and animal feed. In 2007 FAO published a *Toolkit* to help countries to develop and implement national systems on biosecurity (i.e. the prevention, control and management of risks to animal, human and plant life and health) and to enhance biosecurity capacity.

FAO aims to assist member states to enhance the efficiency, competitiveness and profitability of their agricultural and food enterprises. FAO extends assistance in training, capacity building and the formulation of agribusiness development strategies. It promotes the development of effective 'value chains', connecting primary producers with consumers, and supports other linkages within the agribusiness industry. Similarly, FAO aims to strengthen marketing systems, links between producers and retailers and training in agricultural marketing, and works to improve the regulatory framework for agricultural marketing. FAO promotes the use of new technologies to increase agricultural production and extends a range of services to support mechanization, including training, maintenance, testing and the promotion of labour-saving technologies. Other programmes are focused on farm management, post-harvest management, food and non-food processing, rural finance, and rural infrastructure. FAO helps to reduce immediate post-harvest losses, through the introduction of improved processing methods and storage systems.

FAO's Joint Division with the International Atomic Energy Agency (IAEA) is concerned with the use of nuclear techniques in food and agriculture. It co-ordinates research projects, provides scientific and technical support to technical co-operation projects and administers training courses. A joint laboratory in Seibersdorf, Austria, is concerned with testing biotechnologies and in developing non-toxic fertilizers (especially those that are locally available) and improved strains of food crops (especially from indigenous varieties). In the area of animal production and health, the Joint Division has developed progesterone-measuring and disease diagnostic kits. Other sub-programmes of the Joint Division are concerned with soil and water, plant breeding and nutrition, insect pest control and food and environmental protection.

NATURAL RESOURCES MANAGEMENT AND ENVIRONMENT

FAO's Natural Resources Management and Environment Department is mandated to provide leadership, knowledge, and technical and policy advice regarding the sustainable use of the planet's land, water, genetic resources and biodiversity; to improve responses to challenges to the global environment that affect food and agriculture, including climate change and land degradation; to address issues related to bioenergy; and to serve as a neutral forum for dialogue on the sustainable use of natural resources. The Department comprises two divisions: Climate, Energy and Tenure, and Land and Water. FAO hosts the secretariat of the Commission on Genetic Resources for Food and Agriculture, established in 1983, with a mandate to address the impact of biodiversity on food and agriculture.

The Climate, Energy and Tenure Division supports member states to develop adaptive capacities in the agriculture, fisheries and forestry sectors to enhance the resilience of agricultural systems to climate change (which increases the risk of crop and livestock failure in fragile ecosystems, causing changing growing conditions and an increase in extreme weather events); and to promote sustainable agricultural practices aimed at reducing the emission of greenhouse gases. The Division serves as the secretariat for FAO interdepartmental working groups on climate change and on bioenergy. Emissions can also be reduced by sustainable agricultural practices. In 2006 FAO established the International Bioenergy Platform to serve as a focal point for research, data collection, capacity building and strategy formulation by local, regional and international bodies concerned with bioenergy. FAO also serves as the secretariat for the Global Bioenergy Partnership, which was inaugurated in May 2006 to facilitate the collaboration between governments, international agencies and representatives of the private sector and civil society in the sustainable development of bioenergy. In 2012 FAO initiated a new Energy-Smart Food for people and climate (ESF) programme, which aims to support states in promoting energy-smart agrifood systems, through the identification, development and implementation of energy, water, food security and climate-smart strategies that promote agricultural growth and rural development. FAO has also developed a Sustainable Bioenergy Support Package, to promote good practices and monitoring of bioenergy development.

FAO aims to enhance the sustainability of land and water systems, and to secure agricultural productivity, through the improved tenure, management, development and conservation of those natural resources. The organization promotes equitable access to land and water resources and supports integrated land and water management, including river basin management and improved irrigation systems. FAO has developed AQUASTAT as a global information system concerned with water and agricultural issues, comprising databases, country and regional profiles, surveys and maps. Aqua-Crop, CropWat and ClimWat are further productivity models and databases which have been developed to help to assess crop requirements and potential yields. Since 2003 FAO has participated in UN Water, an inter-agency initiative to co-ordinate existing approaches to water-related issues. In August 2012 FAO launched an initiative entitled 'Coping with water scarcity: An action framework for agriculture and food security', which aimed to support the improved management of water resources in agricultural production, including through the development of irrigation schemes, the recycling and re-using of waste water, and the implementation of measures to reduce water pollution.

FAO is concerned with the conservation and sustainable use of plant and animal genetic resources. It works with regional and international associations to develop seed networks, to encourage the use of improved seed production systems, to elaborate quality control and certification mechanisms and to co-ordinate seed security activities, in particular in areas prone to natural or man-made disasters. FAO has developed a World Information and Early Warning System (WIEWS) to gather and disseminate information concerning plant genetic resources for food and agriculture and to undertake periodic assessments of the state of those resources. FAO is also developing, as part of the WIEWS, a Seed Information Service to extend information to member states on seeds, planting and new technologies. In November 2001 the FAO Conference adopted the International Treaty on Plant Genetic Resources for Food and Agriculture ('the Seed Treaty'), with the aim of providing a framework to ensure access to plant genetic resources and to related knowledge, technologies, and—through the Treaty's Benefit-sharing Fund (BSF)—funding. The Seed Treaty entered into force in June 2004, and had 131 parties (130 contracting states and the European Union) by September 2014. In 2004 the Treaty became a member of the Liaison Group of Biodiversity Conventions. The BSF assists poor farmers in developing countries with conserving, and also adapting to climate change, their most important food crops. By 2014 around 1,750 gene banks had been established worldwide, storing more than 7m. plant samples, covering both food crops and related wild variants. In January of that year FAO published a series of voluntary standards to guide the activities of the gene banks.

FAO's Agro-Ecological Zoning (AEZ) methodology, developed jointly with the International Institute for Applied Systems Analysis, is the main tool used for land resources assessment, identifying homogenous and contiguous areas possessing similar soil, land and climate characteristics. FAO's database of Global Agro-Ecological Zones (GAEZ) is updated periodically.

FAO is the UN lead agency of an initiative, 'Education for Rural People', which aims to improve the quality of and access to basic education for people living in rural areas and to raise awareness of the issue as an essential element of achieving the MDGs. FAO also hosts the secretariat of the Global Forum on Agricultural Research, which was established in 1996 as a collaboration of research centres, non-governmental and private sector organizations and development agencies. The Forum aims to strengthen research and promote knowledge partnerships concerned with the alleviation of poverty, the increase in food security and the sustainable use of natural resources. Furthermore FAO hosts the secretariat of the Science Council of the Consultative Group on International Agricultural Research (CGIAR), which, specifically, aims to enhance and promote the quality, relevance and impact of science within the network of CGIAR research centres and to mobilize global scientific expertise.

A High-level Meeting on National Drought Policy, organized in March 2013, in Geneva, Switzerland, by FAO, WMO, and the UN Convention to Combat Desertification, issued a declaration that urged governments to develop and implement national drought management policies consistent with their development objectives, and provided supporting scientific and policy guidance.

FISHERIES AND AQUACULTURE

FAO's Fisheries and Aquaculture Department comprises divisions of fisheries and aquaculture policy and economics; and fisheries and aquaculture resources use and conservation. Fish was estimated in 2014 to be the primary source of protein for 17% of the global population, and for about one-quarter of the populations of 'low-income food-deficit' countries. Aquaculture contributes almost one-third of annual global fish landings (predicted to rise to three-fifths by 2030), and accounts for nearly one-half of fish consumed by humans (forecast at two-thirds by 2030). FAO reported record global production, of 160m. metric tons, in 2013 from both wild capture fisheries and aquaculture, with exports of fish totalling an estimated US $136,000m. in that year. In February 2014 FAO, the World Bank and the International Food Policy Research Institute issued a report entitled *Fish to 2030: Prospects for Fisheries and Aquaculture*, which emphasized the predominant directional flow in fish exports from developing to developed countries, and predicted that by 2030 China would account for 38% of global consumption of food fish.

FAO undertakes extensive monitoring, publishing every two years *The State of World Fisheries and Aquaculture*, and collates and maintains relevant databases. It formulates country and regional profiles and has developed a specific information network for the fisheries sector, GLOBEFISH, which gathers and disseminates information regarding market trends, tariffs and other industry issues. FAO aims to extend technical support to member states with regard to the management and conservation of aquatic resources, and other measures to improve the utilization and trade of products, including the reduction of post-harvest losses, preservation marketing and quality assurance. FAO works to ensure that small-scale fishing communities (accounting for around 90% of the sector's work force) reap equitable benefits from the dynamic international trade in fish and fish products, and to explore the development of new markets to ensure that maximum economic and nutritional benefits are derived from by-products, such as fish heads, backbones and viscera.

FAO aims to facilitate and secure the long-term sustainable development of fisheries and aquaculture, in both inland and marine waters, and to promote its contribution to world food security. In February 1999 the FAO Committee on Fisheries adopted new international measures, within the framework of a 1995 Code of Conduct for Responsible Fishing (CCRF), in order to reduce over-exploitation of the world's fish resources, as well as plans of action for the conservation and management of sharks and the reduction in the incidental catch of seabirds in longline fisheries. The voluntary measures were endorsed at a ministerial meeting, held in March, which issued a declaration to promote the implementation of the CCRF and to achieve sustainable management of fisheries and aquaculture. Several international plans of action (IPOA) have been elaborated within the context of the CCRF: the IPOA for Conservation and Management of Sharks (IPOA-Sharks, 1999); the IPOA for the Management of Fishing Capacity (IPOA-Capacity, 1999); the IPOA for Reducing Incidental Catch of Seabirds in Longline Fisheries (IPOA-Seabirds, 1999); and the IPOA to Prevent, Deter and Eliminate Illegal, Unreported and Unregulated Fishing (IPOA-IUU, 2001). FAO has prepared guidelines to support member countries with implementing IPOAs and has encouraged states to develop national plans of action to complement the international plans. FishCode, an inter-regional assistance programme, supports developing countries in implementing the CCRF.

In October 2001 FAO and the Icelandic Government jointly organized the Reykjavík Conference on Responsible Fisheries in the Marine Ecosystem, which adopted a declaration on pursuing responsible and sustainable fishing activities in the context of ecosystem-based fisheries management (EBFM). EBFM involves determining the boundaries of individual marine ecosystems, and maintaining or rebuilding the habitats and biodiversity of each of these so that all species will be supported at levels of maximum production. In March 2005 FAO's Committee on Fisheries adopted voluntary guidelines for the so-called eco-labelling and certification of fish and fish products, i.e. based on information regarding capture management and the sustainable use of resources. In November 2009 an Agreement on Port State Measures to Prevent, Deter and Eliminate Illegal, Unreported and Unregulated Fishing, negotiated by the Committee, and denying port access to fishing vessels involved in IUU activities (estimated to account for up to 30% of total catches in certain fisheries), was endorsed by the FAO Conference. In May 2011 FAO initiated a Technical Consultation on flag state performance, aimed at assessing the performance of flag states, and establishing means of preventing vessels from flying the flags of irresponsible states. Voluntary Guidelines for Flag State Performance were approved by a session of the Technical Consultation that was held in February 2013, and were endorsed by the Committee on Fisheries in June 2014. FAO was committed to supporting countries to implement these effectively.

FAO promotes aquaculture as a valuable source of animal protein and income-generating activity for rural communities. It has undertaken to develop an ecosystem approach to aquaculture and works to integrate aquaculture with agricultural and irrigation systems. In February 2000 FAO and the Network of Aquaculture Centres in Asia and the Pacific (NACA) jointly convened a Conference on Aquaculture in the Third Millennium, which adopted the Bangkok Declaration and Strategy for Aquaculture Beyond 2000. In September 2010 FAO and NACA convened the Global Conference on Aquaculture, in Phuket, Thailand, on the theme 'Farming the Waters for People and Food'; the Global Conference adopted a set of recommendations on further advancing aquaculture. In October 2012 development agencies, governments and research institutions launched a new three-year project 'Aquaculture for Food Security, Poverty Alleviation and Nutrition' (AFSPAN)—under FAO management and with funding by the European Union—with the aim of advancing understanding of the role of aquaculture in maintaining food security in poorer countries, and using that knowledge to develop sustainable policies for improving livelihoods. The establishment of a new Global Aquaculture Advancement Partnership (GAAP), conceptualized by FAO, and comprising governments, UN agencies, non-governmental organizations and private sector interests, was approved by more than 50 states in October 2013; GAAP was tasked with pursuing sustainable solutions to meeting the growing global demand for fish products, over a 10–15-year time period.

In 2014—building on a Blue Economy model that arose from the June 2012 UN Conference on Sustainable Development, and emphasizes sustainable ocean management—FAO was developing a new 'Blue Growth Initiative', through which it was to assist countries with drafting and implementing national Blue Economy and growth agendas.

FORESTRY

FAO's Forestry Department comprises divisions of forest economics, policy and products; and forest assessment, management and conservation.

FAO is committed to the sustainable management of trees, forests and forestry resources. It aims to address the critical balance of ensuring the conservation of forests and forestry resources while maximising their potential to contribute to food security and social and economic development. In March 2009 the Committee on Forestry approved a new 10-year FAO Strategic Plan for Forestry, covering the social, economic and environmental aspects of forestry. The first World Forest Week, sponsored by FAO, was held in March 2009, and the first World Forest Day, sponsored by FAO and the UN Forum on Forests, was observed on 21 March 2013. In May 2013 FAO hosted an International Conference on Forests for Food Security and Nutrition.

FAO assists member countries to formulate, implement and monitor national forestry programmes, and encourages the participation of all stakeholders in developing plans for the sustainable management of tree and forest resources. FAO also helps to implement national assessments of those programmes and of other forestry activities. At a global level FAO undertakes surveillance of the state of the world's forests and publishes a report every two years. A separate *Forest Resources Assessment* is published every five years; the process to compile the 2015 edition was initiated in June 2011. In 2012 FAO issued a report on *The State of the World's Forest Genetic Resources*. FAO maintains the Forestry Information System (FORIS).

In September 2008 FAO, with UNEP and the UN Development Programme, launched the UN Collaborative Programme on Reducing Emissions from Deforestation and Forest Degradation in Developing Countries (UN-REDD), with the aim of enabling donors to pool resources (through a trust fund established for that purpose) to promote a transformation of forest resource use patterns. In August 2011 UN-REDD endorsed a Global Programme Framework covering 2011–15.

FAO is a member of the Collaborative Partnership on Forests, an informal, voluntary arrangement among 14 agencies with significant forestry programmes, which was established in April 2004 on the recommendation of the UN's Economic and Social Council. FAO organizes a World Forestry Congress, generally held every six years; the 14th Congress was to be held in September 2015, in Durban, South Africa.

TECHNICAL CO-OPERATION

The Technical Co-operation Department has responsibility for FAO's operational activities, including policy and programme development assistance to member countries; the mobilization of resources; investment support; field operations; emergency operations and rehabilitation; and the Technical Co-operation Programme.

FAO provides policy advice to support the formulation, implementation and evaluation of agriculture, rural development and food security strategies in member countries. It administers a project to assist developing countries to strengthen their technical negotiating skills, in respect to agricultural trade issues. FAO also aims to co-ordinate and facilitate the mobilization of extra-budgetary funds from donors and governments for particular projects. It administers a range of trust funds, including a Trust Fund for Food Security and Food Safety, established in 2002 to generate resources for projects to combat hunger, and the Government Co-operative Programme. FAO's Investment Centre, established in 1964, aims to promote greater external investment in agriculture and rural development by assisting member countries to formulate effective and sustainable projects and programmes. The Centre collaborates with international financing institutions and bilateral donors in the preparation of projects, and administers cost-sharing arrangements, with, typically, FAO funding 40% of a project. The Centre is a co-chair (with the German Government) of the Global Donor Platform for Rural Development, which was established in 2004, comprising multilateral, donor and international agencies, development banks and research institutions, to improve the co-ordination and effectiveness of rural development assistance.

FAO's Technical Co-operation Programme, which was inaugurated in 1976, provides technical expertise and funding for small-scale projects to address specific issues within a country's agriculture, fisheries or forestry sectors. An Associate Professional Officers programme co-ordinates the sponsorship and placement of young professionals to gain experience working in an aspect of rural or agricultural development.

FAO was designated the lead agency for directing activities under the International Year of Family Farming (2014), which aimed to reposition small-scale family farming at the centre of national agricultural, environmental and social policies.

The Technical Co-operation Division co-ordinates FAO's emergency operations, concerned with all aspects of disaster and risk prevention, mitigation, reduction and emergency relief and rehabilitation, with a particular emphasis on food security and rural populations. FAO works with governments to develop and implement disaster prevention policies and practices. It aims to strengthen the capacity of local institutions to manage and mitigate risk and provides technical assistance to improve access to land for displaced populations in countries following conflict or a natural disaster. Other disaster prevention and reduction efforts include dissemination of information from the various early warning systems and support for adaptation to climate variability and change, for example by the use of drought-resistant crops or the adoption of conservation agriculture techniques. Following an emergency FAO works with governments and other development and humanitarian partners to assess the immediate and longer-term agriculture and food security needs of the affected population. It has developed an Integrated Food Security and Humanitarian Phase Classification Scheme to determine the appropriate response to a disaster situation. Emergency co-ordination units may be established to manage the local response to an emergency and to facilitate and co-ordinate the delivery of inter-agency assistance. In order to rehabilitate agricultural production following a natural or man-made disaster FAO provides emergency seed, tools, other materials and technical and training assistance. Under the UN's cluster approach to co-ordinating the international response to humanitarian disasters with a focus on core areas of activity, FAO and WFP jointly lead the Food Security cluster, which was established in 2011, and aims to combine expertise in agricultural assistance and food aid to improve the resilience of food-insecure disaster-affected communities. FAO also contributes the agricultural relief and rehabilitation component of the UN's Consolidated Appeals Process (CAP), which aims to co-ordinate and enhance the effectiveness of the international community's response to an emergency. In April 2004 FAO established a Special Fund for Emergency and Rehabilitation Activities to enable it to respond promptly to a humanitarian crisis before making an emergency appeal for additional resources.

FAO requested some US $3m. under the 2014 UN CAP to assist 6.3m. people in Haiti who were experiencing food insecurity. In that year FAO's activities in Haiti including supporting small seed growers' associations; the promotion of gardening, composting and recycling activities in urban areas; and training in nutrition, food preservation and marketing.

FAO Statutory Bodies and Associated Entities

(based at the Rome headquarters, unless otherwise indicated)

Agricultural Market Information System (AMIS): AMIS Secretariat, FAO, Viale delle Terme di Caracalla, 00153 Rome, Italy; tel. (6) 5705-2057; fax (6) 5705-3152; e-mail amis-secretariat@fao.org; internet www.amis-outlook.org; f. 2011 to improve transparency in agricultural markets and contribute to stabilizing food price volatility; a partnership of FAO, the International Food Policy Research Institute, IFAD, OECD, UNCTAD, the World Bank, WFP, WTO, and the UN High Level Task Force on the Global Food Security Crisis (f. 2008).

Codex Alimentarius Commission (Joint FAO/WHO Food Standards Programme): e-mail codex@fao.org; internet www.codexalimentarius.org; f. 1962 to make proposals for the co-ordination of all international food standards work and to publish a code of international food standards; Trust Fund to support participation by least developed countries was inaugurated in 2003; there are numerous specialized Codex committees, e.g. contaminants in foods, food additives, food hygiene, food import and export inspection and certification systems, food labelling, nutrition and foods for special dietary uses, pesticide and veterinary drug residues, spices and culinary herbs, and processed fruits and vegetables; intergovernmental task forces may be appointed; had established by mid-2014 212 food standards and 125 guidelines, codes of practice, limits and principles relating to food production and processing; 185 mem. states and the EU; 224 observers.

Commission for Inland Fisheries of Latin America: c/o FAO Regional Office for Latin America and the Caribbean, Avda Dag Hammarskjöld 3241, Casilla 10095, Vitacura, Santiago, Chile; f. 1976 to promote, co-ordinate and assist national and regional fishery and limnological surveys and programmes of research and development leading to the rational utilization of inland fishery resources; 13th session: Dec. 2013, in Buenos Aires, Argentina; 21 mem. states.

Commission on Livestock Development for Latin America and the Caribbean: c/o FAO Regional Office for Latin America and the Caribbean, Avda Dag Hammarskjöld 3241, Casilla 10095, Vitacura, Santiago, Chile; f. 1986; 33rd conference: May 2014, in Santiago, Chile; 24 mem. states.

Emergency Prevention System for Transboundary Animal and Plant Pests and Diseases (EMPRES): e-mail vincent.martin@fao.org; internet www.fao.org/ag/againfo/programmes/en/empres.html; f. 1994 to strengthen FAO's activities in prevention, early warning, control and eradication of pests and highly contagious livestock diseases; maintains an internet-based EMPRES Global Animal Disease Information System (EMPRES-i).

International Rice Commission (IRC): internet www.fao.org/ag/irc; f. 1949 to promote national and international action on production, conservation, distribution and consumption of rice, except matters relating to international trade; supports the International Task Force on Hybrid Rice, the Working Group on Advanced Rice Breeding in Latin America and the Caribbean, the Inter-regional Collaborative Research Network on Rice in the Mediterranean Climate Areas, and the Technical Co-operation Network on Wetland Development and Management/Inland Valley Swamps; in July 2012 27 experts from 22 IRC member countries convened a Global Rice Roundtable, in Le Corum, Montpellier, France, to consider possible future directions of the IRC; 62 mem. states (accounting for around 93% of global rice production).

International Treaty on Plant Genetic Resources for Food and Agriculture (Seed Treaty), Governing Body: c/o FAO, Viale delle Terme di Caracalla 1, 00153 Rome, Italy; e-mail pgrfa-treaty@fao.org; internet www.planttreaty.org; f. 2004 to oversee the implementation of the Seed Treaty; sixth session: Oct. 2015, Rome, Italy; 132 mem. states and the EU.

Latin American and Caribbean Forestry Commission: c/o FAO Regional Office for Latin America and the Caribbean, Avda Dag Hammarskjöld 3241, Casilla 10095, Vitacura, Santiago, Chile; internet www.fao.org/forestry/31106/en; f. 1948 to advise on formulation of forest policy and review and co-ordinate its implementation throughout the region; to exchange information and advise on technical problems; meets every two years; 28th session: Sept. 2013; 35 mem. states.

Western Central Atlantic Fishery Commission: c/o FAO Regional Office for Latin America and the Caribbean, Avda Dag Hammarskjöld 3241, Casilla 10095, Vitacura, Santiago, Chile; f. 1973 to assist international co-operation for the conservation, development and utilization of the living resources, especially shrimps, of the Western Central Atlantic; 15th session: March 2014, in Port-of-Spain, Trinidad and Tobago.

Finance

FAO's Regular Programme, which is financed by contributions from member governments, covers the cost of FAO's Secretariat, its Technical Co-operation Programme (TCP) and part of the cost of several special action programmes. The regular budget for the two-year period 2014–15 totalled US $1,006m. Much of FAO's technical assistance programme and emergency (including rehabilitation) support activities are funded from extra-budgetary sources, predominantly by trust funds that come mainly from donor countries and international financing institutions; voluntary donor contributions to FAO were projected at around $1,400m. in 2014–15.

Publications

Commodity Review and Outlook (annually).

Crop Prospects and Food Situation (5/6 a year).

Desert Locust Bulletin.

Ethical Issues in Food and Agriculture.

FAO Statistical Yearbook (annually).

FAOSTAT Statistical Database (online).

Food Outlook (2 a year).

Food Safety and Quality Update (monthly; electronic bulletin).

Forest Resources Assessment (every 5 years).

The State of Agricultural Commodity Markets (every 2 years).

The State of Food and Agriculture (annually).

The State of Food Insecurity in the World (annually, with IFAD and WFP).

The State of World Fisheries and Aquaculture (every 2 years).

The State of the World's Forests (every 2 years).

Unasylva (quarterly).

Yearbook of Fishery Statistics.

Yearbook of Forest Products.

Commodity reviews, studies, manuals. A complete catalogue of publications is available at www.fao.org/icatalog/inter-e.htm.

International Bank for Reconstruction and Development— IBRD (World Bank)

Address: 1818 H St, NW, Washington, DC 20433, USA.

Telephone: (202) 473-1000; **fax:** (202) 477-6391; **e-mail:** pic@worldbank.org; **internet:** www.worldbank.org.

The IBRD was established in December 1945. Initially, it was concerned with post-war reconstruction in Europe; since then its aim has been to assist the economic development of member nations by making loans where private capital is not available on reasonable terms to finance productive investments. Loans are made either directly to governments, or to private enterprises with the guarantee of their governments. The World Bank, as it is commonly known, comprises the IBRD and the International Development Association (IDA). The affiliated group of institutions, comprising the IBRD,

IDA, the International Finance Corporation (IFC), the Multilateral Investment Guarantee Agency (MIGA) and the International Centre for Settlement of Investment Disputes (ICSID), is referred to as the World Bank Group, and aims to eradicate extreme poverty, and pursue shared prosperity, while promoting environmentally sustainable development.

Organization
(September 2014)

Officers and staff of the IBRD serve concurrently as officers and staff in IDA. The World Bank has offices in New York, Brussels, Paris (for Europe), Frankfurt, London, Geneva and Tokyo, as well as in more than 100 countries of operation. Country Directors are located in some 30 country offices.

BOARD OF GOVERNORS

The Board of Governors consists of one Governor appointed by each member nation. Typically, a Governor is the country's finance minister, central bank governor, or a minister or an official of comparable rank. The Board normally meets once a year.

EXECUTIVE DIRECTORS

The general operations of the Bank are conducted by a Board of 25 Executive Directors. Six Directors are appointed by the six members having the largest number of shares of capital stock, and the rest are elected by the Governors representing the other members. The President of the Bank is Chairman of the Board.

PRINCIPAL OFFICERS

The principal officers of the Bank are the President of the Bank, three Managing Directors, two Senior Vice-Presidents and 25 Vice-Presidents.

President and Chairman of Executive Directors: Dr JIM YONG KIM (USA).

Vice-President, Latin America and the Caribbean: HASAN TULUY (Turkey).

Activities

The World Bank's primary objectives are the achievement of sustainable economic growth and the reduction of poverty in developing countries. In the context of stimulating economic growth the Bank promotes both private sector development and human resource development and has attempted to respond to the growing demands by developing countries for assistance in these areas. In September 2001 the Bank announced that it was to become a full partner in implementing the UN Millennium Development Goals (MDGs), and was to make them central to its development agenda. The objectives, which were approved by governments attending a special session of the UN General Assembly in September 2000, represented a new international consensus to achieve determined poverty reduction targets. The Bank was closely involved in preparations for the International Conference on Financing for Development, which was held in Monterrey, Mexico, in March 2002. The meeting adopted the Monterrey Consensus, which outlined measures to support national development efforts and to achieve the MDGs. During 2002/03 the Bank, with the IMF, undertook to develop a monitoring framework to review progress in the MDG agenda. The first *Global Monitoring Report* was issued by the Bank and the IMF in April 2004 and has since been published annually. In 2013 the Bank, with other agencies, co-led global consultations on formulating a post-2015 development framework in the thematic area of energy.

In October 2007 the Bank's President defined the following six strategic themes as priorities for Bank development activities: the poorest countries; fragile and post-conflict states; middle-income countries; global public goods; the Arab world; and knowledge and learning. In May 2008 the Bank established a Global Food Crisis Response Programme (GFRP) to assist developing countries affected by the escalating cost of food production. In December the Bank resolved to establish a new facility to accelerate the provision of funds, through IDA, for developing countries affected by the global decline in economic and financial market conditions. The Bank participated in the meeting of heads of state and government of the Group of 20 (G20) leading economies, that was held in Washington, DC, USA, in November 2008 to address the global economic situation, and pursued close collaboration with other multinational organizations, in particular the IMF and the Organisation for Economic Co-operation and Development (OECD), to analyse the impact of the ongoing economic instability. During early 2009 the Bank elaborated its operational response to the global economic crisis. Three operational platforms were devised to address the areas identified as priority themes, i.e. protecting the most vulnerable against the effects of the crisis; maintaining long-term infrastructure investment programmes; and sustaining the potential for private sector-led economic growth and employment creation. Consequently, a new Vulnerability Financing Facility was established, incorporating the GFRP and a new Rapid Social Response Programme, to extend immediate assistance to the poorest groups in affected low- and middle-income countries. Infrastructure investment was to be supported through a new Infrastructure Recovery and Assets Platform, which was mandated to release funds to secure existing infrastructure projects and to finance new initiatives in support of longer-term economic development. Private sector support for infrastructure projects, bank recapitalization, microfinance, and trade financing was to be led by IFC.

The Bank's efforts to reduce poverty include the compilation of country-specific assessments and the formulation of country assistance strategies (CASs) to review and guide the Bank's country programmes. In 1998/99 the Bank's Executive Directors endorsed a Comprehensive Development Framework (CDF) to effect a new approach to development assistance based on partnerships and country responsibility, with an emphasis on the interdependence of the social, structural, human, governmental, economic and environmental elements of development. The CDF, which aimed to enhance the overall effectiveness of development assistance, was formulated after a series of consultative meetings organized by the Bank and attended by representatives of governments, donor agencies, financial institutions, non-governmental organizations (NGOs), the private sector and academics. In December 1999 the Bank introduced a new approach to implement the principles of the CDF, as part of its strategy to enhance the debt relief scheme for heavily indebted poor countries (HIPCs, q.v.). Applicant countries were requested to formulate, in consultation with external partners and other stakeholders, a results-oriented national strategy to reduce poverty, to be presented in the form of a Poverty Reduction Strategy Paper (PRSP). In cases where there might be some delay in issuing a full PRSP, it was permissible for a country to submit a less detailed 'interim' PRSP (I-PRSP) in order to secure the preliminary qualification for debt relief. The approach also requires the publication of annual progress reports. In 2001 the Bank introduced a new Poverty Reduction Support Credit to help low-income countries to implement the policy and institutional reforms outlined in their PRSP. Increasingly, PRSPs have been considered by the international community to be the appropriate country-level framework to assess progress towards achieving the MDGs.

The Bank's annual publication *World Development Report* addresses specific aspects of development. The 2014 edition, published in October 2013, focused on the theme 'Managing Risk for Development'.

In September 2011 the Bank introduced a Corporate Scorecard, which uses a framework of performance indicators to monitor the IBRD and IDA's ongoing progress and achievement of development results. In April 2012 an interactive internet-based version of the Corporate Scorecard was initiated.

FINANCIAL OPERATIONS

IBRD capital is derived from members' subscriptions to capital shares, the calculation of which is based on their quotas in the IMF. At 30 June 2013 the total subscribed capital of the IBRD was US $223,181m., of which the paid-in portion was $13,434m. (6.0%); the remainder is subject to call if required. Most of the IBRD's lendable funds come from its borrowing, on commercial terms, in world capital markets, and also from its retained earnings and the flow of repayments on its loans. IBRD loans carry a variable interest rate, rather than a rate fixed at the time of borrowing.

IBRD loans usually have a 'grace period' of five years and are repayable over 15 years or fewer. Loans are made to governments, or must be guaranteed by the government concerned, and are normally made for projects likely to offer a commercially viable rate of return. In 1980 the World Bank introduced structural adjustment lending, which (instead of financing specific projects) supports programmes and changes necessary to modify the structure of an economy so that it can restore or maintain its growth and viability in its balance of payments over the medium term.

The IBRD and IDA together made 276 new lending and investment commitments totalling US $31,547m. during the year ending 30 June 2013. During 2012/13 the IBRD alone approved commitments totalling $15,249m. (compared with $20,582m. in the previous year), of which $4,769m. (31%) was allocated to projects in Latin America and the Caribbean. Total disbursements by the IBRD in the year ending 30 June 2013 amounted to $15,830m.

In September 1996 the World Bank/IMF Development Committee endorsed a joint initiative to assist heavily indebted poor countries (HIPCs) to reduce their debt burden to a sustainable level, in order to make more resources available for poverty reduction and economic growth. A new Trust Fund was established by the World Bank in November to finance the initiative. The Fund, consisting of an initial allocation of US $500m. from the IBRD surplus and other contributions from multilateral creditors, was to be administered by IDA. Of the 41 HIPCs identified by the Bank, 33 were in sub-Saharan Africa. In early 1999 the World Bank and IMF initiated a comprehensive review of the HIPC initiative. By April meetings of the Group of Seven industrialized nations (G7) and of the governing bodies of the Bank and IMF indicated a consensus that the scheme needed to be amended and strengthened, in order to allow more countries to benefit from the initiative, to accelerate the process by which a country may qualify for assistance, and to enhance the effectiveness of debt relief. In June the G7 and Russia (the G8), meeting in Cologne, Germany, agreed to increase contributions to the HIPC Trust Fund and to cancel substantial amounts of outstanding debt, and proposed more flexible terms for eligibility. In September the Bank and IMF reached an agreement on an enhanced HIPC scheme, with further revenue to be generated through the revaluation of a percentage of IMF gold reserves. Under the enhanced initiative it was agreed that, during the initial phase of the process to ensure suitability for debt relief, each applicant country should formulate a PRSP, and should demonstrate prudent financial management in the implementation of the strategy for at least one year, with support from IDA and IMF. At the pivotal 'decision point' of the process, having thus developed and successfully applied the poverty reduction strategy, applicant countries still deemed to have an unsustainable level of debt were to qualify for interim debt relief from the IMF and IDA, as well as relief on highly concessional terms from other official bilateral creditors and multilateral institutions. During the ensuing 'interim period' countries were required successfully to implement further economic and social development reforms, as a final demonstration of suitability for securing full debt relief at the 'completion point' of the scheme. Data produced at the decision point was to form the base for calculating the final debt relief (in contrast to the original initiative, which based its calculations on projections of a country's debt stock at the completion point). In the majority of cases a sustainable level of debt was targeted at 150% of the net present value (NPV) of the debt in relation to total annual exports (compared with 200%–250% under the original initiative). Other countries with a lower debt-to-export ratio were to be eligible for assistance under the scheme, providing that their export earnings were at least 30% of GDP (lowered from 40% under the original initiative) and government revenue at least 15% of GDP (reduced from 20%). In June 2005 finance ministers of the G8 proposed providing additional resources to achieve the full cancellation of debts owed by eligible HIPCs, in order to assist those countries to meet their MDG targets. Countries that had reached their completion point were to qualify for immediate assistance. In July the heads of state and government of G8 countries requested that the Bank ensure the effective delivery of the additional funds and provide a framework for performance measurement. In September the Bank's Development Committee and the International Monetary and Financial Committee of the IMF endorsed the proposal, subsequently referred to as the Multilateral Debt Relief Initiative (MDRI). By mid-2014 35 countries had reached completion point under the enhanced HIPC initiative, including Bolivia ($1,302m. in NPV terms approved in June 2001), Guyana ($1,553m. in April 2003), Nicaragua ($3,308m. in January 2004), Honduras ($556m. in April 2005) and Haiti ($140m. in June 2009). At 31 December 2012 assistance committed under the HIPC initiative amounted to an estimated $76,000m. (in end-2011 NPV terms), of which the World Bank Group had committed $14,800. At that time the estimated costs of the MDRI amounted to $39,900m. in nominal value terms, of which the Bank Group's share amounted to an estimated $24,100m.

In January 2012 the Bank launched the Program for Results (PforR), a new lending instrument that links the disbursement of funds to the delivery of pre-defined results. By April 2014 11 PforR projects had been approved and a further 17 were under consideration.

During 2000/01 the World Bank strengthened its efforts to counter the problem of HIV and AIDS in developing countries. In November 2001 the Bank appointed its first Global HIV/AIDS Adviser. In 2001 a Multi-Country HIV/AIDS Prevention and Control Programme for the Caribbean was launched, with an allocated budget of US $155m. Under this initiative loans and grants have been made available to Barbados, Dominican Republic, Jamaica, Grenada, Guyana, Saint Christopher and Nevis, Trinidad and Tobago and a Pan-Caribbean Partnership against HIV/AIDS. In addition, the Bank has extended some $425m. to an AIDS/sexually transmitted disease control project in Brazil. In July 2009 the Bank published a report, with UNAIDS, concerned with the impact of the global economic crisis on HIV prevention and treatment programmes.

In March 2007 the Board of Executive Directors approved an action plan to develop further its Clean Energy for Development Investment Framework, which had been formulated in response to a request by the G8 heads of state, meeting in Gleneagles, United Kingdom, in July 2005. The action plan focused on efforts to improve

access to clean energy, in particular in sub-Saharan Africa; to accelerate the transition to low carbon emission development; and to support adaptation to climate change. In October 2008 the Bank Group endorsed a new Strategic Framework on Development and Climate Change, which aimed to guide the Bank in supporting the efforts of developing countries to achieving growth and reducing poverty, while recognizing the operational challenges of climate change. In June 2010 the Bank appointed a Special Envoy to lead the Bank's representation in international discussions on climate change. In February 2012 the Bank supported the establishment of a Global Partnership for Oceans.

TECHNICAL ASSISTANCE AND ADVISORY SERVICES

In addition to providing financial services, the Bank also undertakes analytical and advisory services, and supports learning and capacity building, in particular through the World Bank Institute, the Staff Exchange Programme and knowledge-sharing initiatives. The Bank has supported efforts, such as the Global Development Gateway, to disseminate information on development issues and programmes, and, since 1988, has organized the Annual Bank Conference on Development Economics (ABCDE) to provide a forum for the exchange and discussion of development-related ideas and research. The 2014 gathering was held, in June, on the theme 'The Role of Theory in Development Economics'. In September 1995 the Bank initiated the Information for Development Programme (InfoDev) with the aim of fostering partnerships between governments, multilateral institutions and private sector experts in order to promote reform and investment in developing countries through improved access to information technology.

The provision of technical assistance to member countries has become a major component of World Bank activities. The economic and sector work (ESW) undertaken by the Bank is the vehicle for considerable technical assistance and often forms the basis of CASs and other strategic or advisory reports. In addition, project loans and credits may include funds earmarked specifically for feasibility studies, resource surveys, management or planning advice, and training. The World Bank Institute has become one of the most important of the Bank's activities in technical assistance. It provides training in national economic management and project analysis for government officials at the middle and upper levels of responsibility. It also runs overseas courses aiming to build up local training capability, and administers a graduate scholarship programme. Technical assistance (usually reimbursable) is also extended to countries that do not need Bank financial support, e.g. for training and transfer of technology. The Bank encourages the use of local consultants to assist with projects and to strengthen institutional capability.

The Project Preparation Facility (PPF) was established in 1975 to provide cash advances to prepare projects that may be financed by the Bank. In 1992 the Bank established an Institutional Development Fund (IDF), which became operational on 1 July; the purpose of the Fund was to provide rapid, small-scale financial assistance, to a maximum value of US $750,000, for capacity-building proposals. In 2002 the IDF was reoriented to focus on good governance, in particular financial accountability and system reforms.

ECONOMIC RESEARCH AND STUDIES

In the 1990s the World Bank's research, conducted by its own research staff, was increasingly concerned with providing information to reinforce the Bank's expanding advisory role to developing countries and to improve policy in the Bank's borrowing countries. The principal areas of current research focus on issues such as maintaining sustainable growth while protecting the environment and the poorest sectors of society, encouraging the development of the private sector, and reducing and decentralizing government activities.

The Bank chairs the Consultative Group on International Agricultural Research (CGIAR), which was founded in 1971 to raise financial support for international agricultural research work for improving crops and animal production in developing countries; it supports 15 research centres.

CO-OPERATION WITH OTHER ORGANIZATIONS

The World Bank co-operates with other international partners with the aim of improving the impact of development efforts. It collaborates with the IMF in implementing the HIPC scheme and the two agencies work closely to achieve a common approach to development initiatives. The Bank has established strong working relationships with many other UN bodies, in particular through a mutual commitment to poverty reduction objectives. In May 2000 the Bank signed a joint statement of co-operation with OECD. The Bank holds regular consultations with other multilateral development banks and with the EU with respect to development issues. The Bank-NGO Committee provides an annual forum for discussion with NGOs. Strengthening co-operation with external partners was a fundamental element of the Comprehensive Development Framework, which was adopted in 1998/99 (see above). In 2001/02 a Partnership Approval and Tracking System was implemented to provide information on the Bank's regional and global partnerships. In June 2007 the World Bank and the UN Office on Drugs and Crime launched a joint Stolen Asset Recovery (StAR) initiative, as part of the Bank's new Governance and Anti-Corruption (GAC) strategy. In April 2009 the G20 recommended that StAR review and propose mechanisms to strengthen international co-operation relating to asset recovery. The first global forum on stolen asset recovery and development was convened by StAR in June 2010.

The Bank is a partner, with the IMF, the UN Conference on Trade and Development (UNCTAD), UNDP, the World Trade Organization (WTO) and the International Trade Commission, in the Enhanced Integrated Framework (EIF) for trade-related assistance to least developed countries (LDCs), which aims to facilitate greater participation by LDCs in the global trading system; EIF activities are supported by a dedicated EIF Trust Fund. The EIF replaced in 2007, and builds upon, a previous Integrated Framework, established in 1997. In 1997 a Partnerships Group was established to strengthen the Bank's work with development institutions, representatives of civil society and the private sector. The Group established a new Development Grant Facility, which became operational in October, to support partnership initiatives and to co-ordinate all of the Bank's grant-making activities. The Bank establishes and administers trust funds, open to contributions from member countries and multilateral organizations, NGOs, and private sector institutions, in order to support development partnerships. By 30 June 2013 the Bank had a portfolio of 1,030 active trust funds, with assets of some US $28,900m.

In June 1995 the World Bank joined other international donors (including regional development banks, other UN bodies, Canada, France, the Netherlands and the USA) in establishing a Consultative Group to Assist the Poorest (CGAP), with the aim of channelling funds to the most needy through grass-roots agencies. An initial credit of approximately US $200m. was committed by the donors. The Bank manages the CGAP Secretariat, which is responsible for the administration of external funding and for the evaluation and approval of project financing. The CGAP provides technical assistance, training and strategic advice to microfinance institutions and other relevant bodies. As an implementing agency of the Global Environment Facility (GEF) the Bank assists countries to prepare and supervise GEF projects relating to biological diversity, climate change and other environmental protection measures. It is an example of a partnership in action which addresses a global agenda, complementing Bank country assistance activities. Other funds administered by the Bank include the Global Program to Eradicate Poliomyelitis, launched during the financial year 2002/03, the Least Developed Countries Fund for Climate Change, established in September 2002, an Education for All Fast-Track Initiative Catalytic Trust Fund, established in 2003/04, a Carbon Finance Assistance Trust Fund, established in 2004/05, and a Trust Fund for Anti-Money Laundering and Combating Financing of Terrorism for Asia-Pacific and for Central America and the Caribbean, established in 2005/06. In 2006/07 the Bank established a Global Facility for Disaster Reduction and Recovery. In September 2007 the Bank's Executive Directors approved a Carbon Partnership Facility and a Forest Carbon Partnership Facility to support its climate change activities. In December 2010 the Bank inaugurated a Partnership for Market Readiness, with initial pledged contributions of US $20m., to support developing countries to use carbon market and emissions trading mechanisms. In May 2008 the Bank inaugurated the Global Food Crisis Response Programme (GFRP) to provide financial support, with resources of some $1,200m., to help meet the immediate needs of countries affected by the escalating cost of food production and by food shortages. Grants and loans were to be allocated on the basis of rapid needs assessments, conducted by the Bank with the FAO, the WFP and IFAD. As part of the facility a Multi-Donor Trust Fund was established to facilitate co-ordination among donors and to leverage financial support for the rapid delivery of seeds and fertilizer to small-scale farmers. In April 2009 the Bank increased the resources available under the GFRP to $2,000m. By March 2013 $1,560m. had been approved under the GFRP for initiatives in 49 countries, of which some $1,390m. had been disbursed. In April 2010 a new trust fund was established to support a Global Agriculture and Food Security Programme (GAFSP); by March 2014 donors had pledged some $1,350m. in funding to the GAFSP, and resources of $912m. had been allocated to support projects in 25 countries worldwide.

The Bank is a lead organization in providing reconstruction assistance following natural disasters or conflicts, usually in collaboration with other UN agencies or international organizations, and through special trust funds. In May–June 2004 the Bank, jointly with the Inter-American Development Bank, the European Commission and the UN, assisted the Haitian Government to prepare an Interim Co-operation Framework (ICF) as an assessment of the country's technical and financial needs in the next two years. In July the ICF was presented to an International Donor Conference on Haiti, held in Washington, DC. Participants to the conference, which was hosted by the four lead institutions, pledged some US $1,085m. to support Haiti's economic, social and political recovery. In February 2007 the World Bank hosted a donor conference to raise funds for the establishment of a Caribbean Catastrophe Risk Insurance Facility. In June the Bank hosted a Conference on the Caribbean, organized jointly with the Inter-American Development Bank and the Organization of American States, at which some 15 heads of state or government met with policy makers and representatives of the private, academic and social sectors to discuss the growth and development of the Caribbean region and strengthening relations with the USA. In January 2010 the Bank issued $100m. in immediate emergency funding to support recovery efforts in Haiti following an earthquake which caused extensive damage and loss of life. By June the Bank had committed some $479m. in grants to support the reconstruction and rehabilitation of Haiti, of which $240m. had been made available. At the end of May it cancelled the remaining $36m. outstanding debt owed by Haiti. The Bank acts as trustee of a multi-donor Haiti Reconstruction Fund, which was established in March at an international donors' conference.

The Bank has worked with FAO, the World Health Organization (WHO) and the World Organisation of Animal Health (OIE) to develop strategies to monitor, contain and eradicate the spread of highly pathogenic avian influenza. In September 2005 the Bank organized a meeting of leading experts on the issue and in November it co-sponsored, with FAO, WHO and the OIE, an international partners' conference, focusing on control of the disease and preparedness planning for any future related influenza pandemic in humans. In January 2006 the Bank's Board of Directors approved the establishment of a funding programme (the Global Program for Avian Influenza Control and Human Pandemic Preparedness and Response—GPAI), with resources of up to US $500m., to assist countries to combat the disease. Later in that month the Bank co-sponsored, with the European Commission and the People's Republic of China, an International Ministerial Pledging Conference on Avian and Human Pandemic Influenza (AHI), convened in Beijing. Participants pledged some $1,900m. to fund disease control and pandemic preparedness activities at global, regional and country levels. Commitments to the AHI facility amounted to $126m. at January 2009. In June the Bank approved an additional $500m. to expand the GPAI in order to fund emergency operations required to prevent and control outbreaks of the new swine influenza variant pandemic (H1N1).

EVALUATION

The Independent Evaluation Group is an independent unit within the World Bank. It conducts Country Assistance Evaluations to assess the development effectiveness of a Bank country programme, and studies and publishes the results of projects after a loan has been fully disbursed, so as to identify problems and possible improvements in future activities. In addition, the department reviews the Bank's global programmes and produces the *Annual Review of Development Effectiveness*. In 1996 a Quality Assurance Group was established to monitor the effectiveness of the Bank's operations and performance. In March 2009 the Bank published an Action Plan on Aid Effectiveness, based on the Accra Agenda for Action that had been adopted in September 2008 during the Third High Level Forum on Aid Effectiveness, held in Ghana.

In September 1993 the Bank established an independent Inspection Panel, consistent with the Bank's objective of improving project implementation and accountability. The Panel, which began operations in September 1994, was to conduct independent investigations and report on complaints from local people concerning the design, appraisal and implementation of development projects supported by the Bank. By July 2014 the Panel had received 94 formal requests for inspection.

IBRD INSTITUTIONS

World Bank Institute (WBI): founded in March 1999 by merger of the Bank's Learning and Leadership Centre, previously responsible for internal staff training, and the Economic Development Institute (EDI), which had been established in 1955 to train government officials concerned with development programmes and policies. The new Institute aimed to emphasize the Bank's priority areas through the provision of training courses and seminars relating to poverty, crisis response, good governance and anti-corruption strategies. The Institute supports a Global Knowledge Partnership, which was established in 1997 to promote alliances between governments, companies, other agencies and organizations committed to applying information and communication technologies for development purposes. Under the EDI a World Links for Development programme was also initiated to connect schools in developing countries with partner establishments in industrialized nations via the internet. In 1999 the WBI expanded its programmes through distance learning, a Global Development Network, and use of new technologies. A new initiative, Global Development Learning Network (GDLN), aimed to expand access to information and learning opportunities through the internet, video conferences and organized exchanges. The WBI had also established 60 formal partnership arrangements with learning centres and public, private and NGOs to support joint capacity building programmes; many other informal partnerships were also in place. During 2009/10 new South-South and middle-income country (MIC)–OECD Knowledge Exchange facilities were established. In 2014 the WBI was focusing its work on the following areas: climate change; fragile and conflict-affected states; governance; growth and competitiveness; health systems; public-private partnerships in infrastructure; and urban development; Vice-Pres. SANJAY PRADHAN (India); publs *Annual Report, Development Outreach* (quarterly), other books, working papers, case studies.

International Centre for Settlement of Investment Disputes (ICSID): founded in 1966 under the Convention of the Settlement of Investment Disputes between States and Nationals of Other States. The Convention was designed to encourage the growth of private foreign investment for economic development, by creating the possibility, always subject to the consent of both parties, for a Contracting State and a foreign investor who is a national of another Contracting State to settle any legal dispute that might arise out of such an investment by conciliation and/or arbitration before an impartial, international forum. The governing body of the Centre is its Administrative Council, composed of one representative of each Contracting State, all of whom have equal voting power. The President of the World Bank is (ex officio) the non-voting Chairman of the Administrative Council. At late August 2014 some 486 cases had been registered with the Centre, of which 288 had been concluded and 198 were pending consideration. At that time 150 countries had signed and ratified the Convention to become ICSID Contracting States; Sec.-Gen. MEG KINNEAR (Canada).

Publications

African Development Indicators (annually).
Annual Report on Portfolio Performance.
Atlas of Global Development.
Commodity Markets Outlook (quarterly).
Doing Business (annually).
Environment Matters (annually).
Global Development Finance (annually).
Global Economic Prospects (2 a year).
Global Financial Development Report (annually).
Global Monitoring Report (annually).
ICSID Annual Report.
ICSID Review—Foreign Investment Law Journal (2 a year).
Inequality in Focus (quarterly).
International Debt Statistics (annually).
Joint External Debt Hub.
Poverty Reduction and the World Bank (annually).
Research News (quarterly).
Results and Performance of the World Bank Group (annually).
Staff Working Papers.
The World Bank and the Environment (annually).
World Bank Annual Report.
World Bank Economic Review (3 a year).
World Bank Research Observer.
World Development Indicators (annually).
World Development Report (annually).

Statistics

IBRD OPERATIONS APPROVED IN LATIN AMERICA AND THE CARIBBEAN, 1 JULY 2012–30 JUNE 2013
(US $ million)

Country	Purpose	Amount
Antigua and Barbuda	Public and social sector transformation	10.0
Brazil	Tocantins integrated sustainable regional development	300.0
	Third Minas Gerais development partnership development policy loan	450.0
	Fiscal efficiency for quality of public service delivery	300.0
	Sector-wide approach for Paraná multisector development	350.0
	Rio de Janeiro sustainable rural development (additional financing)	100.0
	Development policies for Sergipe State	150.0
	Belo Horizonte urban development	200.0
	Strengthening public sector management	16.2
	São Paulo sustainable transport investment	300.0
	Rio Grande do Norte regional development and governance	360.0
	Pernambuco equity and inclusive growth	550.0
Colombia	Second disaster risk management development policy loan (with a catastrophe deferred drawdown option)	250.0
	Second programmatic fiscal sustainability and growth resilience development policy loan	200.0
	First programmatic productive and sustainable cities development policy loan	150.0
Costa Rica	Higher education improvements	200.0
Guatemala	'Fiscal space for greater opportunities' first programmatic development policy loan	200.0
Mexico	Sustainable rural development (additional financing)	50.0
	Second programmatic fiscal management and efficiency of expenditures development policy	100.0
Panama	Higher education quality improvement	25.0
Peru	First social inclusion development policy loan	45.0
	Social inclusion	10.0
	Basic education	25.0
	Sierra rural development (additional financing)	20.0
Uruguay	National Water Supply and Sanitation Company (OSE) sustainable and efficient specific investment loan	42.0
	Support to Uruguayan public schools	40.0
	Road rehabilitation and maintenance	66.0
	Public sector management and social inclusion development policy loan (with a deferred drawdown option)	260.0

Source: World Bank, *Annual Report 2013.*

International Development Association—IDA

Address: 1818 H Street, NW, Washington, DC 20433, USA.
Telephone: (202) 473-1000; **fax:** (202) 477-6391; **internet:** www .worldbank.org/ida.

IDA began operations in November 1960. Affiliated to the International Band for Reconstruction and Development (IBRD), IDA advances capital to the poorer developing member countries on more flexible terms than those offered by the IBRD.

Organization
(September 2014)

Officers and staff of the IBRD serve concurrently as officers and staff of IDA.
President and Chairman of Executive Directors: Dr JIM YONG KIM (USA).

Activities

IDA assistance is aimed at the poorer developing countries (i.e. those with a 2012 annual gross national income (GNI) per caput of less than US $1,205 qualified for assistance in 2013/14) in order to support their poverty reduction strategies. Under IDA lending conditions, credits can be extended to countries whose balance of payments could not sustain the burden of repayment required for IBRD loans. Terms are more favourable than those provided by the IBRD; since 1 July 2011 the maturity of credits has been 25 or 40 years, with a grace period of five or 10 years. In 2014 82 countries were eligible for IDA assistance, including 13 small island economies with a 2012 GNI per caput greater than $1,205, but which would otherwise have little or no access to Bank funds, and 18 so-called blend borrowers which are entitled to borrow from both IDA and the IBRD.

IDA's total development resources, consisting of members' subscriptions and supplementary resources (additional subscriptions and contributions), are replenished periodically by contributions from the more affluent member countries. The 17th replenishment of IDA funds (IDA17) was agreed at a meeting convened in Moscow, Russia, in December 2013. It amounted to US $52,000m., pledged by 46 donor countries, to cover the period 1 July 2014–30 June 2017. During the replenishment negotiations participants determined that the overarching theme of IDA17 should be maximizing development impact, including leveraging the collective resources of the World Bank Group, and the following areas of focus be 'special themes': climate change; fragile and conflict-affected states; gender; inclusive growth; and regional transformative initiatives.

During the year ending 30 June 2013 new IDA commitments amounted to US $16,298m. for 184 projects, compared with $14,753m. for 160 projects in the previous year. In that financial year some 37% of lending was for infrastructure projects, 26% for social sector projects, and 22% for projects in the area of public administration and law.

In December 2008 the Bank's Board of Executive Directors approved the Financial Crisis Response Fast Track Facility, to accelerate the provision of up to US $2,000m. of IDA15 resources to help the poorest countries to counter the impact of the global economic and financial crisis. In December 2009 the Board of Executive Directors approved a pilot Crisis Response Window to deploy an additional $1,300m. of IDA funds to support the poorest countries affected by the economic crisis until the end of the IDA15 period (30 June 2011), with the aim of assisting those countries to maintain spending on sectors critical to achieving the Millennium Development Goals. Permanent funding for the Crisis Response Window, which additionally was to assist low-income countries to manage the impact of natural disasters, was agreed as part of the IDA16 replenishment accord in December 2010. In December 2011 the World Bank's Board of Executive Directors approved the establishment of an Immediate Response Mechanism in order to accelerate the provision of assistance to IDA-eligible countries following a natural disaster or economic crisis.

IDA administers a Trust Fund, which was established in November 1996 as part of a World Bank/IMF initiative to assist heavily indebted poor countries (HIPCs). In September 2005 the World Bank's Development Committee and the International Monetary and Financial Committee of the IMF endorsed a proposal of the Group of Eight (G8) industrialized nations to cancel the remaining multilateral debt owed by HIPCs that had reached their completion point under the scheme (see IBRD). In December IDA convened a meeting of donor countries to discuss funding to uphold its financial capability upon its contribution to the so-called Multilateral Debt Relief Initiative (MDRI). The scheme was approved by the Board of Executive Directors in March 2006 and entered into effect on 1 July. By September 2014 35 countries had reached completion point, including Bolivia, Guyana, Haiti, Honduras and Nicaragua.

Publication

Annual Report.

Statistics

IDA CREDITS APPROVED IN SOUTH AMERICA AND THE CARIBBEAN, 1 JULY 2012–30 JUNE 2013
(US $ million)

Country/Region	Purpose	Amount
Bolivia	Urban infrastructure (additional financing)	24.0
	Second rural alliances specific investment credit	50.0
Haiti	Rebuilding energy infrastructure and access	90.0
	Infrastructure and institutions emergency recovery grant (additional financing)	35.0
	Improving maternal health and child health through integrated social services	70.0
	Business development and investment	20.0
	Economic reconstruction and growth	20.0
Honduras	Safer municipalities specific investment credit	15.0
	Disaster risk management	30.0
	Rural infrastructure (additional financing)	20.0
	Water and sanitation sector modernization (additional financing)	10.0
Nicaragua	Hurricane Felix emergency recovery grant (additional financing)	5.0
	Rural water supply and sanitation specific investment grant (additional financing)	6.0
	Second land administration specific investment credit	40.0

Source: World Bank, *Annual Report 2013.*

International Finance Corporation—IFC

Address: 2121 Pennsylvania Ave, NW, Washington, DC 20433, USA.

Telephone: (202) 473-3800; **fax:** (202) 974-4384; **e-mail:** information@ifc.org; **internet:** www.ifc.org.

IFC was founded in 1956 as a member of the World Bank Group to stimulate economic growth in developing countries by financing private sector investments, mobilizing capital in international financial markets, and providing technical assistance and advice to governments and businesses.

Organization

(September 2014)

IFC is a separate legal entity in the World Bank Group. Executive Directors of the World Bank also serve as Directors of IFC. The President of the World Bank is ex officio Chairman of the IFC Board of Directors, which has appointed him President of IFC. Subject to his overall supervision, the day-to-day operations of IFC are conducted by its staff under the direction of the Executive Vice-President. The senior management team includes 10 Vice-Presidents responsible for regional and thematic groupings. At the end of June 2013 IFC had 4,015 staff members, of whom 57% were based in field offices in 99 countries.

PRINCIPAL OFFICERS

President: Dr JIM YONG KIM (USA).

Executive Vice-President: JIN-YONG CAI (People's Republic of China).

Vice-President, Sub-Saharan Africa, Latin America and the Caribbean, Western Europe: JEAN PHILIPPE PROSPER (Haiti).

MISSIONS AND OFFICES IN SOUTH AMERICA, CENTRAL AMERICA AND THE CARIBBEAN

Argentina: Bouchard Plaza, Bouchard 557, 11°, 1106 Buenos Aires; tel. (11) 4114-7200; fax (11) 4312-7184; e-mail abrizio@ifc.org; 'hub' for Chile, Paraguay and Uruguay; Country Man. SALEM ROHANA.

Bolivia: Edif. Victor, 8°, Calle Fernando Guachalla 342, La Paz; tel. (2) 211-5400; fax (2) 244-5499; e-mail cgutierrez1@ifc.org; Resident Rep. MANUEL ROSINI.

Brazil (Rio de Janeiro): Rua Redentor 14, Ipanema, 22421-030, Rio de Janeiro; tel. (21) 2525-5850; fax (21) 2525-5879.

Brazil (São Paulo): Edif. Torre Sul, Rua James Jouse 65, Ciudade Monções, São Paulo; tel. (11) 5185-6888; fax (11) 5185-6890; e-mail msouza1@ifc.org; Senior Man. HECTOR GOMEZ ANG.

Colombia: Carrera 7, 71-21, Torre A, 14°, Edif. Fiduagraria, Bogotá, DC; tel. (1) 319-2330; fax (1) 319-2359; e-mail arodriguez6@ifc.org; 'hub' for Bolivia, Ecuador, Peru and Venezuela; Country Man. JUAN GONZALO FLORES (acting).

Dominican Republic: Avda Lope de Vega No. 29, Torre Novo-Centro, Ensanche Naco Santo Domingo; tel. 566-6815; fax 566-7746; e-mail jsantiago@ifc.org; 'hub' for Antigua and Barbuda, Barbados, Belize, Dominica, Grenada, Guyana, Haiti, Jamaica, Saint Christopher and Nevis, Saint Lucia, the Bahamas and Trinidad and Tobago; Country Head ARY NAIM.

El Salvador: Edificio Torre Futura, Nivel 9, Locales 904-905, Calle El Mirador, 87 Avda Norte, Col. Escalon El Salvador; tel. 2526-5900; fax 2526-5903; Senior Operations Officer MAYRA ALFARO DE MORAN.

Guatemala: 13 calle 3-40, Zona 10, Edif. Atlantis Nivel 14, Of. 1402, Guatemala City; tel. 2329-8047; fax 2329-8099; e-mail jgarcia@ifc.org; Investment Officer EDUARDO CUEVAS.

Haiti: 7 rue Oge, Petion-Ville; tel. 2256-4260; fax 2256-0848; e-mail mvictor@ifc.org; Country Head ARY NAIM.

Honduras: Centro Financiero Citi, 4°, blvd San Juan Bosco, Col. Payaqui, Tegucigalpa; tel. 239-4551; fax 239-4555; e-mail nvilchis@ifc.org; Investment Officer JAVIER POSAS.

Jamaica: Island Life Center, 6 St Lucia Ave, Suite 8 South, Kingston 5; tel. 960-0459; fax 960-0463; e-mail asangster@ifc.org; also serves Belize; Resident Rep. RAJEEV GOPAL.

Mexico: Montes Urales 715, Col. Lomas de Chapultepec, 11000 México, DF; tel. (55) 3098-0130; fax (55) 3098-0146; e-mail nvilchis@ifc.org; 'hub' for Costa Rica, El Salvador, Guatemala, Honduras, Nicaragua and Panama; Senior Man. ROBERTO ALBISETTI.

Nicaragua: Plaza Santo Domingo, Km 6 1/2 Carretera a Masaya, Edif. Cobirsa 2, Managua; tel. 270-0000; fax 270-0077; e-mail jgadeavillanueva@ifc.org; Investment Officer CAROLINA CARDENAS.

Panama: Avda Aquilino de la Guardia, Calle 47, Edif. Ocean Business Plaza, Panama City; tel. 831-2032; e-mail nquiroz@ifc.org; Country Head ANGELA MARIA FONSECA.

Peru: Calle Miguel Dasso 104, 5°, San Isidro, Lima; tel. (11) 6112500; fax (11) 6112525; e-mail ppruss@ifc.org; Country Head MARC TRISTANT.

IFC Advisory Services in Latin America and the Caribbean: Avda Miguel Dasso 104, 5°, San Isidro, Lima, Peru; tel. (11) 6112601; fax (11) 6112525; e-mail ralfaro@ifc.org; Senior Man. MARY PORTER PESCHKA.

Activities

IFC aims to promote economic development in developing member countries by assisting the growth of private enterprise and effective capital markets. It finances private sector projects, through loans, the purchase of equity, quasi-equity products, and risk management services, and assists governments to create conditions that stimulate the flow of domestic and foreign private savings and investment. IFC may provide finance for a project that is partly state-owned, provided that there is participation by the private sector and that the project is operated on a commercial basis. IFC also mobilizes additional resources from other financial institutions, in particular through syndicated loans, thus providing access to international capital markets. IFC provides a range of advisory services to help to improve the investment climate in developing countries and offers technical assistance to private enterprises and governments. From late 2008 IFC worked to respond effectively to the difficulties facing member countries affected by the global economic and financial crisis and to maintain a sustainable level of development. In particular it aimed to preserve and create employment opportunities, to support supply chains for local businesses, and to provide credit. During 2014–16 IFC's activities were guided by a roadmap, which identified five strategic 'pillars' as priority areas of activity: strengthening the focus on frontier markets (i.e. the lowest income countries or underdeveloped regions of middle-income countries, and fragile and conflict-affected countries); addressing climate change, and securing environmental and social sustainability; promoting private sector growth in infrastructure, including education, health, water, and the food supply chain; developing local financial markets through institution building, the use of innovative financial products and mobilization, and focusing on micro, small and medium enterprises; and establishing and maintaining long-term client relationships with firms in developing countries, using the full range of IFC's products and services, and assisting their cross-border growth. Gender was a cross-cutting theme, and a special emphasis was placed on job creation.

To be eligible for financing projects must be profitable for investors, as well as financially and economically viable; must benefit the economy of the country concerned; and must comply with IFC's environmental and social guidelines. IFC aims to promote best corporate governance and management methods and sustainable business practices, and encourages partnerships between governments, non-governmental organizations and community groups. In 2001/02 IFC developed a Sustainability Framework to help to assess the longer-term economic, environmental and social impact of projects; following an 18-month consultation process an updated Sustainability Framework came into effect on 1 January 2012. In 2002/03 IFC assisted 10 international banks to draft a voluntary set of guidelines (the Equator Principles), based on IFC's environmental, social and safeguard monitoring policies, to be applied to their global project finance activities. In September 2009 IFC initiated a Performance Standards Review Process to define new standards to be applied within the Equator Principles framework. At September 2014 80 financial institutions had signed up to the Equator Principles.

In November 2004 IFC announced the establishment of a Global Trade Finance Programme (GTFP), with initial funding of some US $500m., which aimed to support small-scale importers and exporters in emerging markets, and to facilitate South–South trade in goods and services, by providing guarantees for trade transactions, as well as extending technical assistance and training to local financial institutions. Additional funding of $500m. was approved in January 2007, and in October 2008. In December, as part of a set of measures to support the global economy, the Board of Directors approved an expansion of the GTFP, doubling its funding to $3,000m. This was increased further to $5,000m. in September 2012. By mid-2014 more than 550 global and regional banks and local financial institutions operating in around 150 countries were participating in the Programme. Other initiatives included the establishment of an

Infrastructure Crisis Facility to provide investment for existing projects affected by a lack of private funding, and a new Bank Capitalization Fund (to be financed, up to $3,000m., with the Japan Bank for International Co-operation) to provide investment and advisory services to banks in emerging markets. In May 2009 IFC established an Asset Management Company, as a wholly owned subsidiary, to administer the Capitalization Fund. In February of that year IFC inaugurated a Microfinance Enhancement Facility, with a German development bank, to extend credit to microfinancing institutions and to support lending to low-income borrowers, with funds of up to $500m. IFC committed $1,000m. in funds to a new Global Trade Liquidity Program (GTLP), which was inaugurated by the World Bank Group in April, with the aim of mobilizing support of up to $50,000m. in trade transactions through financing extended by governments, other development banks and the private sector. In October IFC established a Debt and Asset Recovery Program to help to restore stability and growth by facilitating loan restructuring for businesses and by investing in funds targeting distressed assets and companies. IFC pledged to contribute $1,550m. to the Program over a three-year period, and aimed to mobilize resources through partnerships with other international financial institutions and private sector companies. IFC's first Green Bond was issued in April 2010 (and matured in April 2014). Proceeds from IFC Green Bonds—amounting to $3.5m. by April 2014—have been invested in energy efficient, renewable energy, and other climate-friendly projects. Two $1m. green bonds were issued, in February and November 2013. During 2011/12 IFC launched a Critical Commodities Finance Program, which aimed to expand agricultural-commodity trade finance in developing countries, providing up to $18,000m. in trade over a period of three years.

IFC's authorized capital is US $2,580m. (In July 2010 the Board of Directors recommended a special capital increase of $130m., to raise authorized capital from $2,450m. to the current $2,580m; the increase took effect on 27 June 2012, having received the approval of the Board of Governors.) At 30 September 2013 paid-in capital was $2,403m. The World Bank was originally the principal source of borrowed funds, but IFC also borrows from private capital markets. IFC's net income amounted to $1,018m. (after a $340m. grant transfer to IDA) in 2012/13, compared with $1,328m. in 2011/12 (after a $330m. transfer to IDA). In December 2008 the Board of Directors approved a Sovereign Funds Initiative to enable IFC to raise and manage commercial capital from sovereign funds.

In the year ending 30 June 2013 project financing approved by IFC amounted to US $24,853m. for 612 projects in 113 countries (compared with $20,358m. for 576 projects in the previous year). Of the total approved in 2012/13, $18,349m. was for IFC's own account, while $6,540m. was in the form of loan syndications and parallel loans, underwriting of securities issues and investment funds and funds mobilized by the IFC Asset Management Company. Generally, IFC limits its financing to less than 25% of the total cost of a project, but may take up to a 35% stake in a venture (although never as a majority shareholder). Disbursements for IFC's account amounted to $9,971m. in 2012/13.

IFC has identified the following as priority strategic areas for future activity in Latin America and the Caribbean: to improve the environment to promote and support businesses; to broaden and facilitate access to finance; to increase private sector participation in infrastructure and advise on reforms of the regulatory framework; and to promote sustainability through higher standards for corporate governance and environmental and social performance. In the year ending 30 June 2013 IFC committed its largest ever amount for the region totalling some US $4,822m., compared with $3,680m. in the previous financial year. An additional $1,750m. was mobilized during 2012/13 in the form of loan participation, parallel loans and structured finance. During 2008/09 IFC participated, with other International Financial Institutions, in establishing a Latin American and Caribbean (LAC) Multilateral Crisis Initiative, committing some $7,900m. of the total $90,000m. over a two-year period. IFC pledged $150m. in support of a $950m. Caribbean Joint Action Plan which was signed in May 2010, with the Caribbean Development Bank, the European Investment Bank and three other development institutions.

In 2010 an IFC African, Latin American and Caribbean (ALAC) Fund was inaugurated, to co-invest, with IFC, in equity investments across a wide range of sectors. In 2012/13 the ALAC Fund made investment commitments totalling US $262m.

IFC's Advisory Services are a major part of the organization's involvement with member countries to support the development of private enterprises and efforts to generate funding, as well as to enhance private sector participation in developing infrastructure. Advisory services cover the following five main areas of expertise: the business enabling environment (i.e. improving the investment climate in a country); access to financing (including developing financing institutions, improving financial infrastructure and strengthening regulatory frameworks); infrastructure (mainly encouraging private sector participation); environment and social sustainability; and corporate advice (in particular in support of small and medium-sized enterprises—SMEs). In December 2008 the Board of Directors determined to provide additional funding to IFC advisory services in order to strengthen the capacity of financial institutions and governments to respond to the crisis in the global financial markets. At 30 June 2013 there were more than 660 active Advisory Service projects in 105 countries; some 65% of projects were being implemented in IDA countries, and 18% in fragile and conflict-affected areas. Total expenditure on Advisory Services during that year amounted to US $232m. IFC manages, jointly financed with the World Bank and MIGA, the Foreign Investment Advisory Service (FIAS), which provides technical assistance and advice on promoting foreign investment and strengthening the country's investment framework at the request of governments. Under the Technical Assistance Trust Funds Program (TATF), established in 1988, IFC manages resources contributed by various governments and agencies to provide finance for feasibility studies, project identification studies and other types of technical assistance relating to project preparation. In 2004 a Grassroots Business Initiative was established, with external donor funding, to support businesses that provide economic opportunities for disadvantaged communities in Africa, Latin America, and South and South-East Asia. Since 2002 IFC has administered an online SME Toolkit to enhance the accessibility of business training and advice. By 2014 the service was available in 18 languages.

Since 2004 IFC has presented an annual Client Leadership Award to a chosen corporate client who most represents IFC values in innovation, operational excellence and corporate governance.

Publications

Annual Report.

Doing Business (annually).

Lessons of Experience (series).

Other handbooks, discussion papers, technical documents, policy toolkits, public policy journals.

Multilateral Investment Guarantee Agency—MIGA

Address: 1818 H Street, NW, Washington, DC 20433, USA.

Telephone: (202) 473-6163; **fax:** (202) 522-2630; **internet:** www.miga.org.

MIGA was founded in 1988 as an affiliate of the World Bank. Its mandate is to encourage the flow of foreign direct investment to, and among, developing member countries, through the provision of political risk insurance and investment marketing services to foreign investors and host governments, respectively.

Organization

(September 2014)

MIGA is legally and financially separate from the World Bank. It is supervised by a Council of Governors (comprising one Governor and one Alternate of each member country) and an elected Board of Directors (of no less than 12 members).

President: Dr JIM YONG KIM (USA).

Executive Vice-President: KEIKO HONDA (Japan).

Activities

The convention establishing MIGA took effect in April 1988. Authorized capital was initially set at 100,000 shares, equivalent to US $1,082m. The convention provided for an automatic increase of capital stock upon the admission of new members. In April 1998 the Board of Governors endorsed an increase in MIGA's capital base, amounting to $700m. callable capital and $150m. paid-in capital. A grant of $150 was transferred from the IBRD as part of the General Capital Increase (GCI) package. A subscription period then ensued, covering April 1999–March 2003. By 30 June 2013 some $749.9m. of the GCI had been subscribed (of which $132.3m. was paid-in and $617.5m. callable). At that time MIGA's capital base comprised 186,359 shares, equivalent to $2,016m. (Comoros and São Tomé and Príncipe were granted membership in 2012/13.) At 30 June 2013 total subscriptions to the capital stock amounted to $1,916.3m., of which $365.6m. was paid-in.

MIGA's activities are guided by four strategic priorities: promoting foreign direct investment into the world's poorest countries; complex projects; South–South investments; and assisting conflict-affected and fragile economies. Eligible investments are guaranteed against losses resulting from non-commercial risks, under the following main categories:

(i) transfer risk resulting from host government restrictions on currency conversion and transfer;

(ii) risk of loss resulting from legislative or administrative actions of the host government;

(iii) repudiation by the host government of contracts with investors in cases in which the investor has no access to a competent forum;

(iv) the risk of armed conflict and civil unrest;

(v) risk of a sovereign not honouring a financial obligation or guarantee.

Before guaranteeing any investment, MIGA must ensure that it is commercially viable, contributes to the development process and is not harmful to the environment. The MIGA/IFC Office of the Compliance Advisor/Ombudsman (established in the fiscal year 1998/99) considers the concerns of local communities directly affected by MIGA- or IFC-sponsored projects. In February 1999 the Board of Directors approved an increase in the amount of political risk insurance available for each project, from US $75m. to $200m. During 2003/04 MIGA established a new fund, the Invest-in-Development Facility, to enhance the role of foreign investment in attaining the Millennium Development Goals. In 2005/06 MIGA supported for the first time a project aimed at selling carbon credits gained by reducing greenhouse gas emissions; it provided $2m. in guarantee coverage to the El Salvador-based initiative. In April 2009 the Board of Directors approved modifications to MIGA's policies and operational regulations in order to enhance operational flexibility and efficiency, in particular in the poorest countries and those affected by conflict. In November 2010 the Council of Governors endorsed amendments to MIGA's convention (the first since 1988) to broaden the eligibility for investment projects and to enhance the effectiveness of MIGA's development impact. In April 2013 the Board of Directors approved a new Conflict-Affected and Fragile Economies Facility, with the aim of providing political risk insurance to enable projects to be implemented in challenging environments that might assist with reconstruction, bring in capital, and generate employment.

During the year ending 30 June 2013 MIGA issued 47 investment insurance contracts for 30 projects with a value of US $2,781m. (compared with 66 contracts amounting to $2,657m. in 2011/12). Around three-quarters of guarantees went to projects in IDA countries. Since 1990 the total investment guarantees issued amounted to some $30,000m., through 1,143 contracts in support of 727 projects.

MIGA works with local insurers, export credit agencies, development finance institutions and other organizations to promote insurance in a country, to ensure a level of consistency among insurers and to support capacity building within the insurance industry. MIGA also offers investment marketing services to help to promote foreign direct investment in developing countries and in transitional economies, and to disseminate information on investment opportunities. MIGA's annual flagship report *World Investment and Political Risk*, is the focal point of the Agency's knowledge dissemination of resources on political risk management and insurance. In early 2007 MIGA's technical assistance services were amalgamated into the Foreign Advisory Investment Service (FIAS, see IFC), of which MIGA became a lead partner, along with IFC and the World Bank. During 2000/01 an office was established in Paris, France, to promote and co-ordinate European investment in developing countries, in particular in Africa and Eastern Europe. In 2002, to facilitate foreign investment in sub-Saharan Africa and Asia, MIGA opened offices in Johannesburg, South Africa and in Singapore. The role of Regional Director for Asia and the Pacific was created in August 2010 to head a new Asian Hub, operating from offices in Singapore, Hong Kong SAR and the People's Republic of China.

Publications

Annual Report.

MIGA News (online newsletter; every 2 months).

World Investment and Political Risk (annually).

Other guides, brochures and regional briefs.

International Fund for Agricultural Development—IFAD

Address: Via Paolo di Dono 44, 00142 Rome, Italy.

Telephone: (06) 54591; **fax:** (06) 5043463; **e-mail:** ifad@ifad.org; **internet:** www.ifad.org.

IFAD was established in 1977, following a decision by the 1974 UN World Food Conference, with a mandate to combat hunger and eradicate poverty on a sustainable basis in the low-income, food-deficit regions of the world. Funding operations began in January 1978.

four List B (petroleum-exporting developing donor countries), and six List C (recipient developing countries), divided equally among the three Sub-List C categories (i.e. for Africa, Europe, Asia and the Pacific, and Latin America and the Caribbean).

President and Chairman of Executive Board: Kanayo F. Nwanze (Nigeria).

Organization

(September 2014)

GOVERNING COUNCIL

Each member state is represented in the Governing Council (the Fund's highest authority) by a Governor and an Alternate. Sessions are held annually with special sessions as required. The Governing Council elects the President of the Fund (who also chairs the Executive Board) by a two-thirds' majority for a four-year term. The President is eligible for re-election.

EXECUTIVE BOARD

Consists of 18 members and 18 alternates, elected by the Governing Council, who serve for three years. The Executive Board is responsible for the conduct and general operation of IFAD and approves loans and grants for projects; it holds three regular sessions each year. An independent Office of Evaluation reports directly to the Board.

The governance structure of the Fund is based on the classification of members. Membership of the Executive Board is distributed as follows: eight List A countries (i.e. industrialized donor countries),

Activities

IFAD provides financing primarily for projects designed to improve food production systems in developing member states and to strengthen related policies, services and institutions. In allocating resources IFAD is guided by the need to increase food production in the poorest food-deficit countries; the potential for increasing food production in other developing countries; and the importance of improving the nutrition, health and education of the poorest people in developing countries, i.e. small-scale farmers, artisanal fishermen, nomadic pastoralists, indigenous populations, rural women, and the rural landless. All projects emphasize the participation of beneficiaries in development initiatives, both at the local and national level. Issues relating to gender and household food security are incorporated into all aspects of its activities. IFAD has worked towards achieving the Millennium Development Goals (MDGs), in particular in relation to reducing, by 2015, the proportion of people living in extreme poverty. In 2013 IFAD, FAO and WFP jointly discussed the development of a post-2015 framework in the area of food and nutrition. An IFAD Post-2015 Task Force was established in May 2013 to co-ordinate IFAD's contribution to the development of the new framework.

In May 2011 the Executive Board adopted IFAD's Strategic Framework for 2011–15, in which it reiterated its commitment to improving rural food security and nutrition, and enabling the rural poor to overcome their poverty. The 2011–15 Strategic Framework was underpinned by five strategic objectives: developing a natural resource and economic asset base for poor rural communities, with improved resilience to climate change, environmental degradation and market transformation; facilitating access for the rural poor to services aimed at reducing poverty, improving nutrition, raising incomes and building resilience in a changing environment; supporting the rural poor in managing profitable, sustainable and resilient farm and non-farm enterprises and benefiting from decent employment opportunities; enabling the rural poor to influence policies and institutions that affect their livelihoods; and enabling institutional and policy environments that support agricultural production and the related non-farm activities.

From 2009 IFAD implemented a new business model, with the direct supervision of projects, and maintaining a stable presence in countries of operations, as its two main pillars. Consequently, by 2011 the Fund directly supervised some 93% of the projects it was funding, compared with 18% in 2007.

IFAD has participated in the High Level Task Force (HLTF) on the Global Food Security Crisis, which was established by the UN Secretary-General in April 2008, tasked with addressing the impact of then soaring global levels of food and fuel prices, and with formulating a comprehensive framework for action. In June IFAD participated in the High-Level Conference on World Food Security and the Challenges of Climate Change and Bioenergy, convened by FAO in Rome, Italy. The meeting adopted a Declaration on Food Security, which noted an urgent need to develop the agricultural sectors and expand food production in developing countries and countries with economies in transition, and for increased investment in rural development, agriculture and agribusiness. In January 2009 the HLTF participated in a follow-up high-level meeting convened in Madrid, Spain, which agreed to initiate a consultation process with regard to the establishment of a Global Partnership for Agriculture, Food Security and Nutrition. During 2009 the long-standing Committee on World Food Security (CFS), open to member states of IFAD, FAO, and the World Food Programme (WFP), underwent reform, becoming a central component of the new Global Partnership; thereafter the CFS was tasked with influencing hunger elimination programmes at the global, regional and national level, taking into account that food security relates not just to agriculture but also to economic access to food, adequate nutrition, social safety nets and human rights. IFAD contributes, with FAO, WFP and other agencies, to a new Agricultural Market Information System (AMIS), which was agreed by a meeting of agriculture ministers from G20 countries, held in June 2011 to increase market transparency and to address the stabilization of food price volatility. IFAD welcomed a commitment made, in May 2012, by G8 heads of state and government and leaders of African countries, to supporting a New Alliance for Food Security and Nutrition; the Alliance was to promote sustainable and inclusive agricultural growth over a 10-year period. The 2013 edition of the joint IFAD-FAO-WFP annual *State of Food Insecurity in the World* report, released in October, addressed the multidimensional nature of the determinants and outcomes of food insecurity, and demonstrated the importance of mainstreaming food security and nutrition in public policies and programmes.

IFAD, with FAO and WFP, leads an initiative on ensuring food security by strengthening feeding programmes and expanding support to farmers in developing countries, the second of nine activities that were launched in April 2009 by the UN System Chief Executives Board for Co-ordination (CEB), with the aim of alleviating the impact on poor and vulnerable populations of the developing global economic crisis.

In September 2012 IFAD, FAO, WFP and UN Women launched 'Accelerating Progress Toward the Economic Empowerment of Rural Women', a five-year initiative that was to be implemented initially in Ethiopia, Guatemala, Kyrgyzstan, Liberia, Nepal, Niger and Rwanda.

In March 2010 the Executive Board endorsed a new IFAD Climate Change Strategy, under which the Fund aimed to create a climate-smart portfolio, and to support smallholder farmers increase their resilience to climate change. In October 2012 a new Adaptation for Smallholder Agriculture Programme (ASAP) became operational; under the ASAP finance for climate adaptation initiatives was to be integrated into IFAD-supported investments.

IFAD is a leading repository of knowledge, resources and expertise in the field of rural hunger and poverty alleviation. In 2001 it renewed its commitment to becoming a global knowledge institution for rural poverty-related issues. Through its technical assistance grants, IFAD aims to promote research and capacity building in the agricultural sector, as well as the development of technologies to increase production and alleviate rural poverty. In 1996 IFAD supported the establishment of the Support Group of the Global Forum on Agricultural Research (GFAR), which facilitates dialogue between research centres and institutions, farmers' organizations, non-governmental bodies, the private sector and donors. In recent years IFAD has been increasingly involved in promoting the use of

communication technology to facilitate the exchange of information and experience among rural communities, specialized institutions and organizations, and IFAD-sponsored projects. Within the strategic context of knowledge management, IFAD has supported initiatives to establish regional electronic networks, such as Electronic Networking for Rural Asia/Pacific (ENRAP, conducted over three phases during the period 1998–2010), and FIDAMERICA in Latin America and the Caribbean (conducted over four phases during 1995–2009), as well as to develop other lines of communication between organizations, local agents and the rural poor.

In February 2014 IFAD and the global consumer goods enterprise Unilever concluded a five-year public-private partnership agreement (the first such contract to be signed by IFAD), with the aim of co-operating in improving the livelihoods of smallholder farmers, and consequently food security, globally.

IFAD is empowered to make both loans and grants. Loans are available on highly concessional, hardened, intermediate and ordinary terms. Highly concessionary loans carry no interest but have an annual service charge of 0.75% and a repayment period of 40 years; loans approved on hardened terms carry no interest charge, have an annual service charge of 0.75%, and are repaid over 20 years; intermediate loans are subject to a variable interest charge, equivalent to 50% of the interest rate charged on World Bank loans, and are repaid over 20 years; and ordinary loans carry a variable interest charge equal to that levied by the World Bank, and are repaid over 15–18 years. New Debt Sustainability Framework (DSF) grant financing was introduced in 2007 in place of highly concessional loans for heavily indebted poor countries (HIPCs). In 2013 highly concessionary loans represented some 63% of total lending in that year, DSF grants 19%, ordinary loans 14%, and blend loans 4%. Research and technical assistance grants are awarded to projects focusing on research and training, and for project preparation and development. In order to increase the impact of its lending resources on food production, the Fund seeks as much as possible to attract other external donors and beneficiary governments as cofinanciers of its projects. In 2013 external co-financing accounted for some 26.5% of all project funding, while domestic contributions, i.e. from recipient governments and other local sources, accounted for 34.2%.

The IFAD Indigenous Peoples Assistance Facility was created in 2007 to fund microprojects that aim to build upon the knowledge and natural resources of indigenous communities and organizations. Under IFAD's Policy on Engagement with Indigenous Peoples, adopted by the Executive Board in September 2009, an Indigenous Peoples' Forum was established in February 2011; this was to be hosted by IFAD and to convene every two years. The inaugural session of the Forum was held in February 2013. In September 2010, the Executive Board approved the establishment of a new Spanish Food Security Cofinancing Facility Trust Fund (the 'Spanish Trust Fund'), which is used to provide loans to IFAD borrower nations. On 31 December 2010 the Spanish Government provided, on a loan basis, €285.5m. to the Spanish Trust Fund.

In November 2006 IFAD was granted access to the core resources of the HIPC Trust Fund, administered by the World Bank, to assist in financing the outstanding debt relief on post-completion point countries participating in the HIPC debt relief initiative (see under IBRD). By mid-2014 36 of 39 eligible countries had passed their decision points, thereby qualifying for HIPC debt relief assistance from IFAD; of those countries 35 had reached completion point, thereby qualifying for full and irrevocable debt reduction.

IFAD's development projects usually include a number of components, such as infrastructure (e.g. improvement of water supplies, small-scale irrigation and road construction); input supply (e.g. improved seeds, fertilizers and pesticides); institutional support (e.g. research, training and extension services); and producer incentives (e.g. pricing and marketing improvements). IFAD also attempts to enable the landless to acquire income-generating assets: by increasing the provision of credit for the rural poor, it seeks to free them from dependence on the capital market and to generate productive activities.

In addition to its regular efforts to identify projects and programmes, IFAD organizes special programming missions to selected countries to undertake a comprehensive review of the constraints affecting the rural poor, and to help countries to design strategies for the removal of these constraints. In general, projects based on the recommendations of these missions tend to focus on institutional improvements at the national and local level to direct inputs and services to small farmers and the landless rural poor. Monitoring and evaluation missions are also sent to check the progress of projects and to assess the impact of poverty reduction efforts.

The Fund supports projects that are concerned with environmental conservation, in an effort to alleviate poverty that results from the deterioration of natural resources. In addition, it extends environmental assessment grants to review the environmental consequences of projects under preparation. IFAD administers the Global Mechanism of the 1996 Convention to Combat Desertification in those Countries Experiencing Drought and Desertification, particularly in Africa. The Mechanism mobilizes and channels resources for the implementation of the Convention, and IFAD is its largest financial contributor. IFAD is an executing agency of the Global Environmental Facility, specializing in the area of combating rural poverty and environmental degradation.

In Latin America and the Caribbean IFAD has aimed to formulate and implement projects that integrate the rural poor into the mainstream economy as well as local and centralized decision-making processes, enhance the productivity and market competitiveness of small-scale farmers, promote sustainable production and utilization of natural resources in environmentally fragile areas, and encourage the participation of women in rural development programmes. During 2013 IFAD approved $107.1m. in loans for five projects in the Latin America and the Caribbean region (representing some 28% of total IFAD lending in that year). At the end of 2013 41 programmes and projects were ongoing in 19 countries in the region.

During 1998 the Executive Board endorsed a policy framework for the Fund's provision of assistance in post-conflict situations, with the aim of achieving a continuum from emergency relief to a secure basis from which to pursue sustainable development. In September 2012 a High Level Expert Forum on Food Insecurity in Protracted Crises, convened by IFAD, FAO and WFP within the framework of the CFS, drafted an Agenda for Action. The document recommended utilizing integrated strategies—with a focus on building resilience—to address food insecurity in protracted crises, i.e. integrating food security into peacebuilding and governance initiatives at the national and regional level, and integrating food security into regional and global initiatives aimed at improving governance and addressing vulnerability.

IFAD co-operates with other agencies and partners within the context of the Global Partnership for Effective Development Co-operation, established by the Fourth High Level Forum on Aid Effectiveness, convened in Busan, Republic of Korea, in November–December 2011. Since the late 1990s IFAD has established partnerships within the agribusiness sector, with a view to improving performance at project level, broadening access to capital markets, and encouraging the advancement of new technologies. In October 2001 IFAD became a co-sponsor of the Consultative Group on International Agricultural Research (CGIAR). In November 2009 IFAD and the Islamic Development Bank concluded a US $1,500m. framework co-financing agreement for jointly financing priority projects during 2010–12 in many of the 52 countries that had membership of both organizations.

IFAD has actively supported the UN International Year of Family Farming (2014).

Finance

In accordance with the Articles of Agreement establishing IFAD, the Governing Council periodically undertakes a review of the adequacy of resources available to the Fund and may request members to make additional contributions. In February 2012 a target of US $1,500m. was set for the ninth replenishment of IFAD funds (IFAD9), covering the period 2013–15. IFAD9 became effective on 30 November 2012. (A Fund replenishment becomes effective upon receipt of one-half of the funds pledged; by the end of December 2012 member states had pledged 92% of the ninth replenishment target.) During 2014 a consultation period was under way with regard to IFAD10, which was to cover 2016–18. The provisional regular budget for 2014 amounted to $150.4m.

Publications

Annual Report.
Rural Poverty Report.
Staff Working Papers (series).
State of Food Insecurity in the World (annually, with FAO and WFP).

Statistics

PROJECTS IN LATIN AMERICA AND THE CARIBBEAN APPROVED IN 2013
(amounts in million US dollars)

Country	Purpose	Loan amount	DSF grant amount	ASAP grant amount
Bolivia	Economic inclusion programme for families and rural communities	—	—	10.0
Brazil	Rural sustainable development project in the semi-arid region of Bahia	45.0	—	—
	Policy co-ordination and dialogue for reducing poverty and inequalities in semi-arid northeast Brazil	—	3.0	—
Cuba	Co-operative rural development project in the Oriental region	10.2	0.5	—
Honduras	Competitiveness and sustainable development in the southwestern border region	14.3	—	—
Nicaragua	Adapting to markets and climate change	8.0	8.0	8.0

International Monetary Fund—IMF

Address: 700 19th St, NW, Washington, DC 20431, USA.
Telephone: (202) 623-7000; **fax:** (202) 623-4661; **e-mail:** publicaffairs@imf.org; **internet:** www.imf.org.

The IMF was established at the same time as the World Bank in December 1945, to promote international monetary co-operation, to facilitate the expansion and balanced growth of international trade and to promote stability in foreign exchange.

Organization
(September 2014)

Managing Director: CHRISTINE LAGARDE (France).
First Deputy Managing Director: DAVID LIPTON (USA).
Deputy Managing Directors: NAOYUKI SHINOHARA (Japan), MIN ZHU (People's Republic of China).
Director, Western Hemisphere Department: ALEJANDRO WERNER (Mexico).

BOARD OF GOVERNORS

The highest authority of the Fund is exercised by the Board of Governors, on which each member country is represented by a Governor and an Alternate Governor. The Board normally meets annually. The voting power of each country is related to its quota in the Fund. An International Monetary and Financial Committee (IMFC, formerly the Interim Committee) advises and reports to the Board on matters relating to the management and adaptation of the international monetary and financial system, sudden disturbances that might threaten the system and proposals to amend the Articles of Agreement.

BOARD OF EXECUTIVE DIRECTORS

The 24-member Board of Executive Directors is responsible for the day-to-day operations of the Fund. The USA, United Kingdom, Germany, France and Japan each appoint one Executive Director. There is also one Executive Director from the People's Republic of

China, Russia and Saudi Arabia, while the remainder are elected by groups of the remaining countries.

REGIONAL REPRESENTATION

There is a network of regional offices and Resident Representatives in more than 90 member countries. In addition, special information and liaison offices are located in Tokyo, Japan (for Asia and the Pacific), in New York, USA (for the United Nations), and in Europe (Paris, France; Geneva, Switzerland; Belgium, Brussels; and Warsaw, Poland, for Central Europe and the Baltic states).

Activities

The purposes of the IMF, as defined in the Articles of Agreement, are:

(i) To promote international monetary co-operation through a permanent institution which provides the machinery for consultation and collaboration on monetary problems;

(ii) To facilitate the expansion and balanced growth of international trade, and to contribute thereby to the promotion and maintenance of high levels of employment and real income and to the development of members' productive resources;

(iii) To promote exchange stability, to maintain orderly exchange arrangements among members, and to avoid competitive exchange depreciation;

(iv) To assist in the establishment of a multilateral system of payments in respect of current transactions between members and in the elimination of foreign exchange restrictions which hamper the growth of trade;

(v) To give confidence to members by making the general resources of the Fund temporarily available to them, under adequate safeguards, thus providing them with the opportunity to correct maladjustments in their balance of payments, without resorting to measures destructive of national or international prosperity;

(vi) In accordance with the above, to shorten the duration of and lessen the degree of disequilibrium in the international balances of payments of members.

In joining the Fund, each country agrees to co-operate with the above objectives. In accordance with its objective of facilitating the expansion of international trade, the IMF encourages its members to accept the obligations of Article VIII, Sections two, three and four, of the Articles of Agreement. Members that accept Article VIII undertake to refrain from imposing restrictions on the making of payments and transfers for current international transactions and from engaging in discriminatory currency arrangements or multiple currency practices without IMF approval. By September 2014 some 90% of members had accepted Article VIII status.

In 2000/01 the Fund established an International Capital Markets Department to improve its understanding of financial markets and a separate Consultative Group on capital markets to serve as a forum for regular dialogue between the Fund and representatives of the private sector. In mid-2006 the International Capital Markets Department was merged with the Monetary and Financial Systems Department to create the Monetary and Capital Markets Department, with the intention of strengthening surveillance of global financial transactions and monetary arrangements. In June 2008 the Managing Director presented a new Work Programme, comprising the following four immediate priorities for the Fund: to enable member countries to deal with the current crises of reduced economic growth and escalating food and fuel prices, including efforts by the Fund to strengthen surveillance activities; to review the Fund's lending instruments; to implement new organizational tools and working practices; and to advance further the Fund's governance agenda.

The deceleration of economic growth in the world's major economies in 2007 and 2008 and the sharp decline in global financial market conditions, in particular in the second half of 2008, focused international attention on the adequacy of the governance of the international financial system and of regulatory and supervisory frameworks. The IMF aimed to provide appropriate and rapid financial and technical assistance to low-income and emerging economies most affected by the crisis and to support a co-ordinated, multinational recovery effort. The Fund worked closely with the Group of 20 (G20) leading economies to produce an Action Plan, in November 2008, concerned with strengthening regulation, transparency and integrity in financial markets and reform of the international financial system. In March 2009 the IMF released a study on the 'Impact of the Financial Crisis on Low-income Countries', and in that month convened, with the Government of Tanzania, a high-level conference, held in Dar es Salaam, to con-

sider the effects of the global financial situation on African countries, as well as areas for future partnership and growth. Later in that month the Executive Board approved a series of reforms to enhance the effectiveness of the Fund's lending framework, including new conditionality criteria, a new flexible credit facility and increased access limits.

In April 2009 a meeting of G20 heads of state and government, convened in London, United Kingdom, determined to make available substantial additional resources through the IMF and other multinational development institutions in order to strengthen global financial liquidity and support economic recovery. There was a commitment to extend US $250,000m. to the IMF in immediate bilateral financial contributions (which would be incorporated into an expanded New Arrangements to Borrow facility) and to support a general allocation of special drawing rights (SDRs), amounting to a further $250,000m. It was agreed that additional resources from sales of IMF gold were to be used to provide $6,000m. in concessional financing for the poorest countries over the next two to three years. The G20 meeting also resolved to implement several major reforms to strengthen the regulation and supervision of the international financial system, which envisaged the IMF collaborating closely with a new Financial Stability Board. In September G20 heads of state and government endorsed a Mutual Assessment Programme, which aimed to achieve sustainable and balanced growth, with the IMF providing analysis and technical assistance. In January 2010 the IMF initiated a process to review its mandate and role in the 'post-crisis' global economy. Short-term priorities included advising countries on moving beyond the policies they implemented during the crisis; reviewing the Fund's mandate in surveillance and lending, and investigating ways of improving the stability of the international monetary system; strengthening macro-financial and cross-country analyses, including early warning exercises; and studying ways to make policy frameworks more resilient to crises. In November 2011 G20 heads of state and government, meeting in Cannes, France, agreed to initiate an immediate review of the Fund's resources, with a view to securing global financial stability which had been undermined by high levels of debt in several eurozone countries. In December European Union heads of state and government agreed to allocate to the IMF additional resources of up to $270,000m. in the form of bilateral loans.

During 2012–13 the Executive Board approved the modalities to enable bilateral borrowing from member countries as a means of supplementing both quota resources and the institution's standing borrowing arrangements; by 30 April 2013 25 such bilateral agreements had been signed by the Board, and a further 13 states had committed to providing resources in this way. Furthermore, the Board had signed bilateral borrowing agreements with 14 member states aimed specifically at supporting the Fund's concessional financing. The Fund was, meanwhile, reviewing means of ensuring more sustainable long-term funding of its concessional finanancing.

A joint meeting of the IMFC, G20 ministers responsible for finance and governors of central banks, convened in April 2012 in Washington, DC, welcomed a decision in March by eurozone member states to strengthen European firewalls through broader reform efforts and the availability of central bank swap lines, and determined to enhance IMF resources for crisis prevention and resolution, announcing commitments from G20 member states to increasing, by more than US $430,000m., resources to be made available to the IMF as part of a protective firewall to serve the entire IMF membership. Additional resources pledged by emerging economies (notably by the People's Republic of China, Brazil, India, Mexico and Russia) at a meeting of G20 heads of state and government held in June, in Los Cabos, Baja California Sur, Mexico, raised the universal firewall to $456,000m. Meeting in October, in Tokyo, Japan, the IMFC urged national policymakers to implement policies agreed in recent months aimed at restarting economic growth and promoting job creation. The global economy was reported to have decelerated to a greater extent than had been previously anticipated: a contraction in output in the eurozone was noted, and, additionally, a slowdown in economic activity in many other advanced economies and also in emerging markets and developing economies, reflecting weaker external and domestic demand, and also in some cases the impact of policies aimed at addressing inflationary pressures.

In August 2009 the Fund's Board of Governors approved the new general allocation of SDRs, amounting to SDR 161,200m., which became available to all members, in proportion to their existing quotas, from 28 August. A further SDR 21,400m. (equivalent to US $33,000m.) became available on 9 September under a special allocation provided for by the Fourth Amendment to the Articles of Agreement, which entered into force in the previous month having been ratified by members holding 85% of the total voting power.

QUOTAS
IMF MEMBERSHIP AND QUOTAS IN LATIN AMERICA AND THE CARIBBEAN
(million SDR*)

Country	September 2014
Antigua and Barbuda	13.5
Argentina	2,117.1
The Bahamas	130.3
Barbados	67.5
Belize	18.8
Bolivia	171.5
Brazil	4,250.5
Chile	856.1
Colombia	774.0
Costa Rica	164.1
Dominica	8.2
Dominican Republic	218.9
Ecuador	347.8
El Salvador	171.3
Grenada	11.7
Guatemala	210.2
Guyana	90.9
Haiti	81.9
Honduras	129.5
Jamaica	273.5
Mexico	3,625.7
Nicaragua	130.0
Panama	206.6
Paraguay	99.9
Peru	638.4
Saint Christopher and Nevis	8.9
Saint Lucia	15.3
Saint Vincent and the Grenadines	8.3
Suriname	92.1
Trinidad and Tobago	335.6
Uruguay	306.5
Venezuela	2,659.1

*The Special Drawing Right (SDR) was introduced in 1970 as a substitute for gold in international payments, and was intended eventually to become the principal reserve asset in the international monetary system. Its value (which was US $1.50154 at 8 September 2014 and averaged $1.51973 in 2013) is based on a basket of international currencies comprising the US dollar, Japanese yen, euro and pound sterling. Each member is assigned a quota related to its national income, monetary reserves, trade balance and other economic indicators; the quota approximately determines a member's voting power and the amount of foreign exchange it may purchase from the Fund. A member's subscription is equal to its quota. Quotas are reviewed at intervals of not more than five years, to take into account the state of the world economy and members' different rates of development. In December 2010 the Board of Governors concluded the 14th General Review, with an agreement to increase quotas by 100%, to realign quota shares to ensure greater representation of emerging economies and to preserve the basic votes share of low-income countries. The reforms required approval by member states constituting 85% of total quotas in order to enter into effect. By August 2014 146 members accounting for 77.07% of the Fund's voting power had accepted the amendment. A Quota and Voice Reform agreement, concluded in March 2008 to increase quotas by a total of SDR 20,800m. for 54 member countries, entered into effect in March 2011. As at September 2014 total quotas in the Fund amounted to SDR 238,120.6m.

RESOURCES
Members' subscriptions form the basic resource of the IMF. They are supplemented by borrowing. Under the General Arrangements to Borrow (GAB), established in 1962, the Group of Ten industrialized nations (G10—Belgium, Canada, France, Germany, Italy, Japan, the Netherlands, Sweden, the United Kingdom and the USA) and Switzerland (which became a member of the IMF in May 1992 but which had been a full participant in the GAB from April 1984) undertake to lend the Fund as much as SDR 17,000m. in their own currencies to assist in fulfilling the balance of payments requirements of any member of the group, or in response to requests to the Fund from countries with balance of payments problems that could threaten the stability of the international monetary system. In 1983 the Fund entered into an agreement with Saudi Arabia, in association with the GAB, making available SDR 1,500m., and other borrowing arrangements were completed in 1984 with the Bank for International Settlements, the Saudi Arabian Monetary Agency, Belgium and Japan, making available a further SDR 6,000m. In 1986 another borrowing arrangement with Japan made available

SDR 3,000m. In May 1996 GAB participants concluded an agreement in principle to expand the resources available for borrowing to SDR 34,000m., by securing the support of 25 countries with the financial capacity to support the international monetary system. The so-called New Arrangements to Borrow (NAB) was approved by the Executive Board in January 1997. It was to enter into force, for an initial five-year period, as soon as the five largest potential creditors participating in NAB had approved the initiative and the total credit arrangement of participants endorsing the scheme had reached at least SDR 28,900m. While the GAB credit arrangement was to remain in effect, the NAB was expected to be the first facility to be activated in the event of the Fund's requiring supplementary resources. In July 1998 the GAB was activated for the first time in more than 20 years—and for the last time to date—in order to provide funds of up to US $6,300m. in support of an IMF emergency assistance package for Russia (the first time the GAB had been used for a non-participant). The Fund's long-standing arrangement with Saudi Arabia to make available SDR 1,500m. if required under the GAB was most recently extended to December 2018. The NAB became effective in November 2008, and was called upon for the first time as part of an extensive programme of support for Brazil, which was adopted by the IMF in December. (In March 1999, however, the activation was cancelled.) In November 2008 the Executive Board initiated an assessment of IMF resource requirements and options for supplementing resources in view of an exceptional increase in demand for IMF assistance. In February 2009 the Board approved the terms of a borrowing agreement with the Government of Japan to extend some SDR 67,000m. (some $100,000m.) in supplemental funding, for an initial one-year period. In April G20 heads of state and government resolved to expand the NAB facility, to incorporate all G20 economies, in order to increase its resources by up to SDR 367,500m. ($500,000m.). The G20 summit meeting held in September confirmed that it had contributed the additional resources to the NAB. In April 2010 the IMF's Executive Board approved the expansion and enlargement of NAB borrowing arrangements; these came into effect in March 2011, having completed the ratification process. By 2014 38 members or state institutions were participating in the NAB, and had committed SDR 369,997m. in supplementary resources.

FINANCIAL ASSISTANCE
The Fund makes resources available to eligible members on an essentially short-term and revolving basis to provide members with temporary assistance to contribute to the solution of their payments problems. Before making a purchase, a member must show that its balance of payments or reserve position makes the purchase necessary. Apart from this requirement, reserve tranche purchases (i.e. purchases that do not bring the Fund's holdings of the member's currency to a level above its quota) are permitted unconditionally. Exchange transactions within the Fund take the form of members' purchases (i.e. drawings) from the Fund of the currencies of other members for the equivalent amounts of their own currencies.

With further purchases, however, the Fund's policy of conditionality means that a recipient country must agree to adjust its economic policies, as stipulated by the IMF. All requests other than for use of the reserve tranche are examined by the Executive Board to determine whether the proposed use would be consistent with the Fund's policies, and a member must discuss its proposed adjustment programme (including fiscal, monetary, exchange and trade policies) with IMF staff. New guidelines on conditionality, which, *inter alia*, aimed to promote national ownership of policy reforms and to introduce specific criteria for the implementation of conditions given different states' circumstances, were approved by the Executive Board in September 2002. In March 2009 the Executive Board approved reforms to modernize the Fund's conditionality policy, including greater use of pre-set qualification criteria and monitoring structural policy implementation by programme review (rather than by structural performance criteria).

Purchases outside the reserve tranche are made in four credit tranches, each equivalent to 25% of the member's quota; a member must reverse the transaction by repurchasing its own currency (with SDRs or currencies specified by the Fund) within a specified time. A credit tranche purchase is usually made under a Stand-by Arrangement with the Fund, or under the Extended Fund Facility. A Stand-by Arrangement is normally of one or two years' duration, and the amount is made available in instalments, subject to the member's observance of 'performance criteria'; repurchases must be made within three-and-a-quarter to five years. In March 2012 the Executive Board approved an amendment to the Extended Fund Facility permitting extended arrangements to be approved from the start for up to a maximum of four years (the Facility had hitherto been approved for up to three years, with the possibility of a subsequent one-year extension). The member must submit detailed economic programmes and progress reports for each year; repurchases must be made within four-and-a-half to 10 years. In October 1994 the Executive Board approved an increase in members' access to IMF resources, on the basis of a recommendation by the then Interim Committee. The annual access limit under IMF regular tranche drawings, Stand-by Arrangements and Extended Fund Facility credits was increased from 68% to 100% of a member's quota, with the cumulative access limit set at 300%. In March 2009 the Executive Board agreed to double access limits for non-concessional loans to 200% and 600% of a member's quota for annual and cumulative access respectively. In 2012/13 regular funding arrangements approved (and augmented) amounted to SDR 75,111.6m. (compared with SDR 52,601.2m. in the previous financial year, SDR 129,628m. in 2010/11, and SDR 74,175m. in 2009/10).

In addition, special-purpose arrangements have been introduced, all of which are subject to the member's co-operation with the Fund to find an appropriate solution to its difficulties. In December 1997 the Executive Board established a new Supplemental Reserve Facility (SRF) to provide short-term assistance to members experiencing exceptional balance of payments difficulties resulting from a sudden loss of market confidence. In December 1998 some SDR 9,100m. was extended to Brazil under the SRF as part of a new Stand-by Arrangement. In January 2001 some SDR 2,100m. in SRF resources were approved for Argentina as part of an SDR 5,187m. Stand-by Arrangement augmentation. The SDR 22,821m. Stand-by credit approved for Brazil in September 2002 included some SDR 7,600m. committed under the SRF. In March 2009 the Executive Board decided to terminate the SRF.

In October 2008 the Executive Board approved a new Short-Term Liquidity Facility (SLF) to extend exceptional funds (up to 500% of quotas) to emerging economies affected by the turmoil in international financial markets and economic deceleration in advanced economies. Eligibility for lending under the new Facility was to be based on a country's record of strong macroeconomic policies and having a sustainable level of debt. In March 2009 the Executive Board decided to replace the SLF with a Flexible Credit Line (FCL) facility, which, similarly, was to provide credit to countries with very strong economic foundations, but was also to be primarily considered as precautionary. In addition, it was to have a longer repayment period (of up to five years) and have no access 'cap'. The first arrangement under the FCL was approved in April for Mexico, making available funds of up to SDR 31,528m. for a one-year period. In August 2010 the duration of the FCL, and credit available through it, were increased, and a new Precautionary Credit Line (PCL) was established for member states with sound economic policies that had not yet met the requirements of the FCL. In November 2011 the PCL was replaced by a new, more flexible Precautionary and Liquidity Line (PLL), which was to be made available to countries 'with sound economic fundamentals' and 'sound policies', for use in broader circumstances than the PCL, including as insurance against shocks and as a short-term liquidity window; PLL arrangements may have a duration of either six months or 1–2 years. One FCL arrangement, amounting to SDR 3,870m., was approved in 2011/12, for Colombia, while during the 2012/13 financial year a successor FCL arrangement was approved (in November 2012) for Mexico, totalling SDR 47,292m.

In January 2010 the Fund introduced new concessional facilities for low-income countries as part of broader reforms to enhance flexibility of lending and to focus support closer to specific national requirements. The three new facilities aimed to support country-owned programmes to achieve macroeconomic positions consistent with sustainable poverty reduction and economic growth. They carried zero interest rate, although this was to be reviewed every two years. An Extended Credit Facility (ECF) succeeded the existing PRGF to provide medium-term balance of payments assistance to low-income members. ECF loans were to be repayable over 10 years, with a five-and-a-half-year grace period. A Standby Credit Facility (SCF) replaced the high-access component of a former Exogenous Shocks Facility (operational from January 2006–December 2009) in order to provide short-term balance of payments financial assistance in response to the adverse economic impact of events beyond government control, including on a precautionary basis. SCF loans were to be repayable over eight years, with a grace period of four years. A new Rapid Credit Facility (RCF) was to provide rapid financial assistance to PRGF-eligible members requiring urgent balance of payments assistance, under a range of circumstances. Loans were repayable over 10 years, with a five-and-a-half-year grace period. A Post-Catastrophe Debt Relief (PCDR) Trust was established in June 2010 to enable the Fund—in the event of a catastrophic disaster—to provide debt relief to any vulnerable low-income eligible member state in order to free up resources to meet exceptional balance of payments needs. In November 2011 a new Rapid Financing Instrument (RFI) was launched, for which all member states were to be eligible, and which was to support urgent balance of payments requirements, including those arising from exogenous shocks such as commodity price changes, natural disasters, and post-conflict and other fragile situations. Low-income member states may also make use of a non-financial Policy Support Instrument (PSI), providing access to IMF monitoring and other support aimed at consolidating economic performance.

In August 2014 the Executive Board approved a disbursement of SDR 4.15m. (some US $6.4m.) for St. Vincent and the Grenadines, to be drawn equally from the Rapid Credit Facility and the Rapid Financing Instrument, to assist with rehabilitation and reconstruction efforts resulting from severe flooding in December 2013.

During 2012/13 members' purchases from the general resources account amounted to SDR 10,587m., compared with SDR 32,270m. in the previous year. Outstanding IMF credit at 30 April 2013 totalled SDR 90,182m., compared with SDR 94,182m. in 2011/12. The largest users of IMF credit during the 2012/13 financial year were Greece, Ireland and Portugal.

The arrangement approved in September 2002, in support of the Brazilian Government's efforts to secure economic and financial stability, was the largest ever Stand-by credit agreed by the Fund at that time, amounting to SDR 22,821m. During the financial year 2011/12 a new Stand-by Arrangement was agreed for Saint Christopher and Nevis (concluded in July 2011, and amounting to SDR 52.5m. to be disbursed over three years).

IMF participates in the initiative to provide exceptional assistance to heavily indebted poor countries (HIPCs), in order to help them to achieve a sustainable level of debt management. The initiative was formally approved at the September 1996 meeting of the Interim Committee, having received the support of the 'Paris Club' of official creditors, which agreed to increase the relief on official debt from 67% to 80%. In all 41 HIPCs were identified, of which 33 were in sub-Saharan Africa. Resources for the HIPC initiative were channelled through the PRGF Trust. In early 1999 the IMF and the World Bank initiated a comprehensive review of the HIPC scheme, in order to consider modifications of the initiative and to strengthen the link between debt relief and poverty reduction. A consensus emerged among the financial institutions and leading industrialized nations to enhance the scheme, in order to make it available to more countries, and to accelerate the process of providing debt relief. In September the IMF Board of Governors expressed its commitment to undertaking an off-market transaction of a percentage of the Fund's gold reserves (i.e. a sale, at market prices, to central banks of member countries with repayment obligations to the Fund, which were then to be made in gold), as part of the funding arrangements of the enhanced HIPC scheme; this was undertaken during the period December 1999–April 2000. Under the enhanced initiative it was agreed that countries seeking debt relief should first formulate, and successfully implement for at least one year, a national poverty reduction strategy. In May 2000 Uganda became the first country to qualify for full debt relief under the enhanced scheme. In September 2005 the IMF and the World Bank endorsed a proposal by G8 to achieve the cancellation by the IMF, IDA and the African Development Bank of 100% of debt claims on countries that had reached completion point under the HIPC initiative, in order to help them to achieve their Millennium Development Goals. The debt cancellation was to be undertaken within the framework of a Multilateral Debt Relief Initiative (MDRI). The IMF's Executive Board determined, additionally, to extend MDRI debt relief to all countries with an annual per caput GDP of US $380, to be financed by IMF's own resources. Other financing was to be made from existing bilateral contributions to the PRGF Trust Subsidy Account. In December the Executive Board gave final approval to the first group of countries assessed as eligible for 100% debt relief under the MDRI, including 17 countries that had reached completion point at that time, as well as Cambodia and Tajikistan. The initiative became effective in January 2006 once the final consent of the 43 contributors to the PRGF Trust Subsidy Account had been received. By mid-2014 a total of 37 countries had qualified for MDRI relief. As at September 2014 the IMF had committed some $2,421m. in debt relief under the HIPC initiative, of a total of $74,000m. pledged overall (in end-2012 net present value terms); at that time the cost to the IMF of the MDRI amounted to some $3,537m. In June 2010 the Executive Board approved the establishment of a Post-Catastrophe Debt Relief Trust (PCDR Trust) to provide balance of payments assistance to low-income members following an exceptional natural disaster.

In early September 2014, in the context of the third UN International Conference on Small Island Developing States (SIDS), convened in Apia, Samoa, the IMF pledged to continue to provide financial and technical assistance in support of the sustainable economic development of SIDS, which are deemed to be at increased risk of vulnerability to external shocks, and to have an increased likelihood of low economic growth and national debt. At that time 20 SIDS were eligible for concessional lending from the Fund.

The IMF is a partner in the Enhanced Integrated Framework (EIF) for trade-related assistance to Least Developed Countries (LDCs), a multi-donor programme which aims to support greater participation by LDCs in the global trading system.

SURVEILLANCE

Under its Articles of Agreement, the Fund is mandated to oversee the effective functioning of the international monetary system. Accordingly, the Fund aims to exercise firm surveillance over the exchange rate policies of member states and to assess whether a country's economic situation and policies are consistent with the objectives of sustainable development and domestic and external stability. The Fund's main tools of surveillance are regular, bilateral consultations with member countries conducted in accordance with Article IV of the Articles of Agreement, which cover fiscal and monetary policies, balance of payments and external debt developments, as well as policies that affect the economic performance of a country, such as the labour market, social and environmental issues and good governance, and aspects of the country's capital accounts, and finance and banking sectors. In April 1997 the Executive Board agreed to the voluntary issue of Press Information Notices (PINs) following each member's Article IV consultation, to those member countries wishing to make public the Fund's views. Other background papers providing information on and analysis of economic developments in individual countries continued to be made available. The Executive Board monitors global economic developments and discusses policy implications from a multilateral perspective, based partly on World Economic Outlook reports and Global Financial Stability Reports. In addition, the IMF studies the regional implications of global developments and policies pursued under regional fiscal arrangements. The Fund's medium-term strategy, initiated in 2006, determined to strengthen its surveillance policies to reflect new challenges of globalization for international financial and macroeconomic stability. The IMF, with the UN Department for Economic and Social Affairs, leads an initiative to strengthen monitoring and analysis surveillance, and to implement an effective warning system, one of nine initiatives that were endorsed in April 2009 by the UN System Chief Executives Board for Co-ordination (CEB), with the aim of alleviating the impact of the global crisis on poor and vulnerable populations. In September 2010 the Executive Board decided that regular financial stability assessments, within the Financial Sector Assessment Programme framework, were to be a mandatory exercise for 25 jurisdictions considered to have systemically important financial sectors. In July 2012 the Executive Board adopted a Decision on Bilateral and Multilateral Surveillance (the so-called Integrated Surveillance Decision), which aimed to strengthen the legal framework underpinning surveillance activities. In September the Board endorsed a Financial Surveillance Strategy detailing steps towards further strengthening the financial surveillance framework.

In April 1996 the IMF established the Special Data Dissemination Standard (SDDS), which was intended to improve access to reliable economic statistical information for member countries that have, or are seeking, access to international capital markets. In March 1999 the IMF undertook to strengthen the Standard by the introduction of a new reserves data template. By April 2013 71 countries had subscribed to the Standard. The eurozone also voluntarily issues metadata in SDDS format. The financial crisis in Asia, which became apparent in mid-1997, focused attention on the importance of IMF surveillance of the economies and financial policies of member states and prompted the Fund further to enhance the effectiveness of its surveillance through the development of international standards in order to maintain fiscal transparency. In December 1997 the Executive Board approved a new General Data Dissemination System (GDDS), to encourage all member countries to improve the production and dissemination of core economic data. The operational phase of the GDDS commenced in May 2000. By mid-2014 112 countries were actively participating in the GDDS. The Fund maintains a Dissemination Standards Bulletin Board, which aims to ensure that information on SDDS subscribing countries is widely available.

In April 1998 the then Interim Committee adopted a voluntary Code of Good Practices on Fiscal Transparency: Declaration of Principles, which aimed to increase the quality and promptness of official reports on economic indicators, and in September 1999 it adopted a Code of Good Practices on Transparency in Monetary and Financial Policies: Declaration of Principles. The IMF and World Bank jointly established a Financial Sector Assessment Programme (FSAP) in May 1999, initially as a pilot project, which aimed to promote greater global financial security through the preparation of confidential detailed evaluations of the financial sectors of individual countries. In September 2009 the IMF and World Bank determined to enhance the FSAP's surveillance effectiveness with new features, for example introducing a risk assessment matrix, targeting it more closely to country needs, and improving its cross-country analysis and perspective. As part of the FSAP Fund staff may conclude a Financial System Stability Assessment (FSSA), addressing issues relating to macroeconomic stability and the strength of a country's financial system. A separate component of the FSAP are Reports on the Observance of Standards and Codes (ROSCs), which are compiled after an assessment of a country's implementation and observance of internationally recognized financial standards.

In April 2001 the Executive Board agreed on measures to enhance international efforts to counter money-laundering, in particular through the Fund's ongoing financial supervision activities and its programme of assessment of offshore financial centres (OFCs). In November the IMFC, in response to the terrorist attacks against targets in the USA, which had occurred in September, resolved, *inter*

alia, to strengthen the Fund's focus on surveillance, and, in particular, to extend measures to counter money-laundering to include the funds of terrorist organizations. It determined to accelerate efforts to assess offshore centres and to provide technical support to enable poorer countries to meet international financial standards. In March 2004 the Board of Directors resolved that an anti-money laundering and countering the financing of terrorism (AML/CFT) component be introduced into regular OFC and FSAP assessments conducted by the Fund and the World Bank. In May 2008 the IMF's Executive Board agreed to integrate the OFC programme into the FSAP.

TECHNICAL ASSISTANCE

Technical assistance is provided by special missions or resident representatives who advise members on every aspect of economic management, while more specialized assistance is provided by the IMF's various departments. In 2000/01 the IMFC determined that technical assistance should be central to the IMF's work in crisis prevention and management, in capacity building for low-income countries, and in restoring macroeconomic stability in countries following a financial crisis. Technical assistance activities subsequently underwent a process of review and reorganization to align them more closely with IMF policy priorities and other initiatives.

The IMF delivers some technical assistance, aimed at strengthening local capacity in economic and financial management, through regional centres. A Caribbean Regional Technical Assistance Centre (CARTAC), located in Barbados, began operations in November 2001. A Regional Technical Assistance Centre for Central America, Panama and the Dominican Republic (CAPTAC-DR), was inaugurated in June 2009, in Guatemala City, Guatemala.

In May 2009 the IMF launched the first of a series of Topical Trust Funds (TTFs—providing support to member states towards addressing economic policy challenges), on Anti-Money Laundering and Combating the Financing of Terrorism. In May 2011 two further TTFs were created, on Tax Policy and Administration, and on Managing Natural Resource Wealth.

In May 2012, following the merger of the former IMF Institute (established in 1964) and Office of Technical Assistance Management, a new Institute for Capacity Development was inaugurated, to provide technical assistance and training to support member countries with developing the capacity of national economic and financial institutions. The IMF is a co-sponsor, with the Austrian authorities, the European Bank for Reconstruction and Development, Organisation for Economic Co-operation and Development and the World Trade Organization, of the Joint Vienna Institute, which was opened in the Austrian capital in October 1992 and which trains officials from former centrally planned economies in various aspects of economic management and public administration. In May 1998 an IMF-Singapore Regional Training Institute was inaugurated, in collaboration with the Singaporean Government, in order to provide training for officials from the Asia-Pacific region. In 1999 a Joint Regional Training Programme, administered with the Arab Monetary Fund, was established in the United Arab Emirates, and during 2000/01 a joint training programme for Chinese government officials was established in Dalian, Liaoning Province. A Joint Regional Training Centre for Latin America became operational in Brasília, Brazil, in 2001. In July 2006 a Joint India-IMF Training Programme was inaugurated in Pune, India. In May 2011 a new IMF-Middle East Center for Economics and Finance was inaugurated in Kuwait.

Publications

Annual Report.

Balance of Payments Statistics Yearbook.

Civil Society Newsletter (quarterly).

Direction of Trade Statistics (quarterly and annually).

Emerging Markets Financing (quarterly).

F & D—Finance and Development (quarterly).

Financial Statements of the IMF (quarterly).

Global Financial Stability Report (2 a year).

Global Monitoring Report (annually, with the World Bank).

Government Finance Statistics Yearbook.

Handbook on Securities Statistics (published jointly by IMF, BIS and the European Central Bank).

IMF Commodity Prices (monthly).

IMF Financial Activities (weekly, online).

IMF in Focus (annually).

IMF Research Bulletin (quarterly).

IMF Survey (monthly, and online).

International Financial Statistics (monthly and annually).

Joint BIS-IMF-OECD-World Bank Statistics on External Debt (quarterly).
Quarterly Report on the Assessments of Standards and Codes.
Spillover Report (annually).

Staff Papers (quarterly).
World Economic Outlook (2 a year).
Other country reports, regional economic outlooks, economic and financial surveys, occasional papers, pamphlets, books.

United Nations Educational, Scientific and Cultural Organization—UNESCO

Address: 7 place de Fontenoy, 75352 Paris 07 SP, France.
Telephone: 1-45-68-10-00; **fax:** 1-45-67-16-90; **e-mail:** bpi@unesco.org; **internet:** www.unesco.org.

UNESCO was established in 1946 and aims to contribute, through education, the sciences, culture, communication and information, to the building of peace and the eradication of poverty, and to advancing sustainable development and intercultural dialogue.

Santiago, Chile; Casilla 127, Correo 29, Providencia, Santiago, Chile; tel. (2) 472-4600; fax (2) 655-1046; e-mail santiago@unesco.org; internet www.unesco.org/santiago; f. 1963; Dir JORGE SEQUEIRA.

Regional Bureau for Science for Latin America and the Caribbean: Calle Dr Luis Piera 1992, 2°, Casilla 859, 11000 Montevideo, Uruguay; tel. 2413 2075; fax 2413 2094; e-mail orcyt@unesco.org.uy; internet www.unesco.org.uy; also cluster office for Argentina, Brazil, Chile, Paraguay, Uruguay; Dir JORGE GRANDI.

Organization
(September 2014)

GENERAL CONFERENCE

The supreme governing body of the Organization, the Conference meets in ordinary session once in two years and is composed of representatives of the member states. It determines policies, approves work programmes and budgets and elects members of the Executive Board.

EXECUTIVE BOARD

The Board, comprising 58 members, prepares the programme to be submitted to the Conference and supervises its execution; it meets twice a year.

SECRETARIAT

UNESCO is headed by a Director-General, appointed for a four-year term. Assistant Directors-General are responsible for education; natural sciences; social and human sciences; culture; communication and information; external relations and co-operation; and administration.
Director-General: IRINA BOKOVA (Bulgaria).

CO-OPERATING BODIES

In accordance with UNESCO's constitution, national Commissions have been set up in most member states, which help to integrate work within the member states and the work of UNESCO. Most members also have their own permanent delegations to UNESCO. UNESCO aims to develop partnerships with cities and local authorities.

FIELD CO-ORDINATION

UNESCO maintains a network of offices to support a more decentralized approach to its activities and enhance their implementation at field level. Cluster offices provide the main structure of the field co-ordination network. These cover a group of countries and help to co-ordinate between member states and with other UN and partner agencies operating in the area. In 2014 there were 17 cluster offices covering 113 states. In addition 27 national offices serve a single country, including those in post-conflict situations or economic transition and the nine most highly populated countries. The regional bureaux provide specialized support at the national level.

UNESCO Caribbean Office: The Towers, 3rd Floor, 25 Dominica Drive, Kingston 5, Jamaica; tel. 929-7087; fax 929-8468; e-mail kingston@unesco.org; internet www.unesco.org/new/en/bfc/office-in-kingston; Dir ROBERT PARUA.

REGIONAL BUREAUX

Regional Bureau for Culture in Latin America and the Caribbean (ORCALC): Calzada 551, esq. D, Vedado, Havana 4, Cuba; tel. (7) 833-3438; fax (7) 833-3144; e-mail habana@unesco.org; internet www.unesco.org/new/es/havana; f. 1950; activities include research and programmes of cultural development and cultural tourism; maintains a documentation centre and a library of 14,500 vols; Dir HERMAN VAN HOOFF; publs *Oralidad* (annually), *Boletín Electrónico* (quarterly).

Regional Bureau for Education in Latin America and the Caribbean (OREALC): Calle Enrique Delpiano 2058, Providencia,

Activities

In the implementation of all its activities UNESCO aims to contribute to achieving the UN Millennium Development Goal (MDG) of halving levels of extreme poverty by 2015, as well as other MDGs concerned with education and sustainable development. During October 2012–March 2013 UNESCO, with UNICEF, co-led a series of global consultations on formulating a post-2015 development framework in the thematic area of education.

In November 2013 the General Conference approved a new medium-term strategy for the period 2014–21. The strategy had two overarching objectives: contributing to lasting peace; and contributing to sustainable development and the eradication of poverty, and designated UNESCO's five primary functions, to be implemented at global, regional and national levels, as: serving as a laboratory of ideas and generating innovative proposals and policy advice in its fields of competence; developing and reinforcing the global agenda in its fields of competence through policy analysis, monitoring and bench-marking; setting norms and standards in its fields of competence and supporting and monitoring their implementation; strengthening international and regional co-operation in its fields of competence, and fostering alliances, intellectual co-operation, knowledge sharing and operational partnerships; and providing advice for policy development and implementation, and developing institutional and human capacities. UNESCO's strategic objectives during 2014–21 were defined as:

developing education systems to foster quality lifelong learning opportunities for all;

empowering learners to be creative and responsible global citizens;

shaping the future education agenda;

promoting the interface between science, policy and society and ethical and inclusive policies for sustainable development;

strengthening international science co-operation for peace, sustainability and social inclusion;

supporting inclusive social development and promoting intercultural dialogue and the rapprochement of cultures;

protecting, promoting and transmitting heritage;

fostering creativity and the diversity of cultural expressions;

promoting freedom of expression, media development and universal access to information and knowledge.

The 2014–21 strategy reaffirmed UNESCO's commitment to its global priority areas of activity 'Priority Africa' and 'Priority Gender Equality'; aimed to mainstream specific interventions in relation to youth, most marginalized social groups, least developed countries (LDCs), small island developing states (SIDS); and focused on contributing to building knowledge societies, including through the use of the internet and other information and communication technologies (ICTs). The Organization continued to be committed to responding to post-conflict and post-natural disaster situations.

During 2014–21 UNESCO was implementing a Priority Gender Equality Action Plan, representing a roadmap for the implementation of gender mainstreaming and gender-specific programming across the Organization's activities and programmes.

EDUCATION

UNESCO recognizes education as an essential human right, and is committed under its medium-term strategy for 2014–21 to developing education systems to foster quality lifelong learning opportunities for all; to empowering learners to be creative and responsible global citizens; and shaping the future education agenda.

UNESCO leads and co-ordinates global efforts in support of 'Education for All' (EFA), which was adopted as a guiding principle of UNESCO's contribution to development following a world conference, convened in March 1990. In April 2000 several UN agencies, including UNESCO and UNICEF, and other partners sponsored the World Education Forum, held in Dakar, Senegal, to assess international progress in achieving the goal of Education for All and to adopt a strategy for further action (the 'Dakar Framework'), with the aim of ensuring universal basic education by 2015. An EFA Global Action Plan was formulated in 2006 to reinvigorate efforts to achieve EFA objectives and, in particular, to provide a framework for international co-operation and better definition of the roles of international partners and of UNESCO in leading the initiative. In September 2012 the UN Secretary-General launched 'Education First', a new initiative aimed at increasing access to education, and the quality thereof, worldwide. An EFA Global Monitoring Report is prepared periodically; the 2013/14 edition (released in January 2014), focused on the importance of investing in teachers and educational reforms to promote equitable learning, and stated that some 250m. children worldwide were receiving a poor quality education and therefore failing to acquire basic skills. The focus of many of UNESCO's initiatives are the nine most highly populated developing countries (Bangladesh, Brazil, the People's Republic of China, Egypt, India, Indonesia, Mexico, Nigeria and Pakistan), known collectively as the E-9 (Education-9) countries.

UNESCO advocates 'Literacy for All' as a key component of Education for All, regarding literacy as essential to basic education and to social and human development. A Literacy Initiative for Empowerment (LIFE) was developed as an element of a UN Literacy Decade (2003–12) to accelerate efforts in some 35 countries where illiteracy is a critical challenge to development. UNESCO is the co-ordinating agency for the UN Decade of Education for Sustainable Development (2005–14), through which it aims to establish a global framework for action and strengthen the capacity of education systems to incorporate the concepts of sustainable development into education programmes. In November 2014 UNESCO was to organize, with the Government of Japan, a UNESCO World Conference on Education for Sustainable Development, in Okayama, Japan, to assess the implementation of the UN Decade.

The April 2000 World Education Forum recognized the global HIV/AIDS pandemic to be a significant challenge to the attainment of Education for All. UNESCO, as a co-sponsor of UNAIDS, takes an active role in promoting formal and non-formal preventive health education. Through a Global Initiative on HIV/AIDS and Education (EDUCAIDS) UNESCO aims to develop comprehensive responses to HIV/AIDS rooted in the education sector, with a particular focus on vulnerable children and young people. An initiative covering the 10-year period 2006–15, the Teacher Training Initiative in sub-Saharan Africa, has aimed to address teacher shortages in that region (owing to HIV/AIDS, armed conflict and other causes) and to improve the quality of teaching.

Under the medium-term strategy for 2014–21 UNESCO aimed to promote expanded access to learning opportunities throughout the life cycle and through multiple pathways (formal education, non-formal and informal learning), and was to promote inclusive and rights-based learning systems reflecting the diversity of all learners. During 2014–18 priority was to be given to areas in which UNESCO has a strong comparative advantage: literacy; technical and vocational education and training; and higher education.

A key priority area of UNESCO's education programme is to foster quality education for all, through formal and non-formal educational opportunities. It assists members to improve the quality of education provision through curricula content, school management and teacher training. UNESCO aims to expand access to education at all levels and to work to achieve gender equality. In particular, UNESCO aims to strengthen capacity building and education in natural, social and human sciences and promote the use of new technologies in teaching and learning processes. In May 2010 UNESCO, jointly with the International Telecommunication Union (ITU), established a Broadband Commission for Digital Development, to comprise high level representatives of governments, industry and international agencies concerned with the effective deployment of broadband networks as an essential element of economic and social development objectives. The 2013 edition of the Commission's flagship report, *State of Broadband*, released in September, addressed the expansion of wireless broadband.

The Associated Schools Project (ASPnet—comprising nearly 9,600 institutions in 180 countries in 2014) has, since 1953, promoted the principles of peace, human rights, democracy and international co-operation through education. It provides a forum for dialogue and for promoting best practices. At tertiary level UNESCO chairs a University Twinning and Networking (UNITWIN) initiative, which was established in 1992 to establish links between higher education institutions and to foster research, training and programme development. A complementary initiative, Academics Across Borders, was inaugurated in November 2005 to strengthen communication and the sharing of knowledge and expertise among higher education professionals. In October 2002 UNESCO organized the first Global Forum on International Quality Assurance, Accreditation and the Recognition of Qualifications to establish international standards and promote capacity building for the sustainable development of higher education systems.

NATURAL SCIENCES

UNESCO recognizes the essential role of science (including mathematics, engineering and technology) as a foundation for achieving the eradication of extreme poverty and ensuring environmental sustainability. In June 2012, in advance of the UN Conference on Sustainable Development (Rio+20), which was convened later in that month, UNESCO, with the International Council of Scientific Unions and other partners, participated in a Forum on Science, Technology and Innovation (STI) for Sustainable Development, addressing the role to be played by science and innovation in promoting sustainable development, poverty eradication, and the transition to a green economy. UNESCO hosts a Scientific Advisory Board, comprising 26 eminent scientists, that was inaugurated in January 2014, on the recommendation of the UN Secretary-General, to provide advice to the UN leadership on the use of STI in the advancement of sustainable development.

Under UNESCO's medium-term strategy for 2014–21 the Organization was to continue to provide through its science programmes policy advice on STI, as well as to strengthen member states' STI capacities, and to enhance international scientific co-operation for the advancement of inclusive sustainable development. Furthermore, UNESCO was to exercise leadership in ocean and fresh water issues, and was to develop holistic solutions to climate change adaptation and disaster risk reduction.

In November 1999 the General Conference endorsed a Declaration on Science and the Use of Scientific Knowledge and an agenda for action, which had been adopted at the World Conference on Science, held in June–July 1999, in Budapest, Hungary. By leveraging scientific knowledge, and global, regional and country level science networks, UNESCO aims to support sustainable development and the sound management of natural resources. It also advises governments on approaches to natural resource management, in particular the collection of scientific data, documenting and disseminating good practices and integrating social and cultural aspects into management structures and policies. UNESCO's Man and the Biosphere Programme supports a worldwide network of biosphere reserves (comprising 631 biosphere reserves in 119 countries, including 14 transboundary sites, in 2014), which aim to promote environmental conservation and research, education and training in biodiversity and problems of land use (including the fertility of tropical soils and the cultivation of sacred sites). The third World Congress of Biosphere Reserves, held in Madrid, Spain, in February 2008, adopted the Madrid Action Plan, which aimed to promote biosphere reserves as the main internationally designated areas dedicated to sustainable development. UNESCO also supports a Global Network of National Geoparks (100 in 30 countries in 2014) which was inaugurated in 2004 to promote collaboration among managed areas of geological significance to exchange knowledge and expertise and raise awareness of the benefits of protecting those environments. Member geoparks must have effective management structures that facilitate sustainable development, with a particular emphasis on sustainable tourism. UNESCO organizes regular International Geoparks Conferences; the sixth was held in Stonehammer, Canada, in September 2014.

UNESCO promotes and supports international scientific partnerships to monitor, assess and report on the state of Earth systems. With the World Meteorological Organization and the International Council of Science, UNESCO sponsors the World Climate Research Programme, which was established in 1980 to determine the predictability of climate and the effect of human activity on climate. UNESCO hosts the secretariat of the World Water Assessment Programme, which prepares the periodic *World Water Development Report*. UNESCO is actively involved in the 10-year project, agreed by more than 60 governments in February 2005, to develop a Global Earth Observation System of Systems (GEOSS). The project aims to link existing and planned observation systems in order to provide for greater understanding of the earth's processes and dissemination of detailed data, for example predicting health epidemics or weather phenomena or concerning the management of ecosystems and natural resources. UNESCO's Intergovernmental Oceanographic Commission (UNESCO-IOC) serves as the Secretariat of the Global Ocean Observing System. The International Geoscience Programme, undertaken jointly with the International Union of Geological Sciences (IUGS), facilitates the exchange of knowledge and methodology among scientists concerned with geological processes and aims to raise awareness of the links between geoscience and sustainable socio-economic development.

In March 2013 a Caribbean Tsunami Warning Exercise was conducted under the auspices of UNESCO-IOC, with the aim of testing the tsunami reaction capacity of some 32 countries in the Caribbean and adjacent regions. A similar warning and preparedness exercise was conducted with 39 Pacific Rim countries in May.

UNESCO is committed to contributing to international efforts to enhance disaster preparedness and mitigation. Through education UNESCO aims to reduce the vulnerability of poorer communities to disasters and improve disaster management at local and national levels. It also co-ordinates efforts at an international level to establish monitoring networks and early warning systems to mitigate natural disasters, in particular in developing tsunami early warning systems in Africa, the Caribbean, the South Pacific, the Mediterranean Sea and the North-East Atlantic similar to those already established for the Indian and Pacific oceans. Other regional partnerships and knowledge networks were to be developed to strengthen capacity building and the dissemination of information and good practices relating to risk awareness and mitigation and disaster management. Disaster education and awareness were to be incorporated as key elements in the UN Decade of Education for Sustainable Development. UNESCO is also the lead agency for the International Flood Initiative, which was inaugurated in January 2005 at the World Conference on Disaster Reduction, held in Kobe, Japan. The Initiative aims to promote an integrated approach to flood management in order to minimize the damage and loss of life caused by floods, mainly with a focus on research, training, promoting good governance and providing technical assistance. The sixth International Conference on Flood Management was convened in São Paulo, Brazil, in September 2014.

With the International Council of Scientific Unions and the Third World Academy of Sciences, UNESCO operates a short-term fellowship programme in the basic sciences and an exchange programme of visiting lecturers.

SOCIAL AND HUMAN SCIENCES

UNESCO is mandated to contribute to the worldwide development of the social and human sciences and philosophy, which it regards as of great importance in policymaking and maintaining ethical vigilance. The structure of UNESCO's Social and Human Sciences programme takes into account both an ethical and standard-setting dimension, and research, policymaking, action in the field and future-oriented activities.

A priority area of UNESCO's work programme on Social and Human Sciences has been to promote principles, practices and ethical norms relevant for scientific and technological development. The programme fosters international co-operation and dialogue on emerging issues, as well as raising awareness and promoting the sharing of knowledge at regional and national levels. UNESCO supports the activities of the International Bioethics Committee (IBC—a group of 36 specialists who meet under UNESCO auspices) and the Intergovernmental Bioethics Committee, and hosts the secretariat of the 18-member World Commission on the Ethics of Scientific Knowledge and Technology (COMEST), established in 1999, which aims to serve as a forum for the exchange of information and ideas and to promote dialogue between scientific communities, decision-makers and the public.

The priority Ethics of science and technology element aims to promote intergovernmental discussion and co-operation; to conduct explorative studies on possible UNESCO action on environmental ethics and developing a code of conduct for scientists; to enhance public awareness; to make available teaching expertise and create regional networks of experts; to promote the development of international and national databases on ethical issues; to identify ethical issues related to emerging technologies; to follow up relevant declarations, including the Universal Declaration on the Human Genome and Human Rights; and to support the Global Ethics Observatory, an online worldwide database of information on applied bioethics and other applied science- and technology-related areas (including environmental ethics) that was launched in December 2005 by the IBC.

UNESCO itself provides an interdisciplinary, multicultural and pluralistic forum for reflection on issues relating to the ethical dimension of scientific advances, and promotes the application of international guidelines. In May 1997 the IBC approved a draft version of a Universal Declaration on the Human Genome and Human Rights, in an attempt to provide ethical guidelines for developments in human genetics. The Declaration, which identified some 100,000 hereditary genes as 'common heritage', was adopted by the UNESCO General Conference in November and committed states to promoting the dissemination of relevant scientific knowledge and co-operating in genome research. In October 2003 the General Conference adopted an International Declaration on Human Genetic Data, establishing standards for scientists working in that field, and in October 2005 the General Conference adopted the Universal Declaration on Bioethics and Human Rights. At all levels UNESCO aims to raise awareness and foster debate about the ethical implications of scientific and technological developments and to promote exchange of experiences and knowledge between governments and research bodies.

UNESCO recognizes that globalization has a broad and significant impact on societies. It is committed to strengthening the links between research and policy formulation by national and local authorities, in particular concerning poverty eradication. In that respect, UNESCO promotes the concept that freedom from poverty is a fundamental human right. In 1994 UNESCO initiated an international social science research programme, the Management of Social Transformations (MOST), to promote capacity building in social planning at all levels of decision-making. In 2003 the Executive Board approved a continuation of the programme but with a revised strategic objective of strengthening links between research, policy and practice. UNESCO's medium-term strategy for 2014–21 emphasized the role played by the social sciences in deepening understanding of barriers to equitable participation and inclusion at all career levels.

UNESCO aims to monitor emerging social or ethical issues and, through its associated offices and institutes, formulate preventative action to ensure they have minimal impact on the attainment of UNESCO's objectives. As a specific challenge UNESCO is committed to promoting the International Convention against Doping in Sport, which entered into force in 2007. UNESCO also focuses on the educational and cultural dimensions of physical education and sport and their capacity to preserve and improve health.

Fundamental to UNESCO's mission is the rejection of all forms of discrimination. It disseminates information aimed at combating racial prejudice, works to improve the status of women and their access to education, promotes equality between men and women, and raises awareness of discrimination against people affected by HIV/AIDS, in particular among young people. In 2004 UNESCO inaugurated an initiative to enable city authorities to share experiences and collaborate in efforts to counter racism, discrimination, xenophobia and exclusion. As well as the International Coalition of Cities against Racism, regional coalitions were to be formed with more defined programmes of action. A Latin American and Caribbean coalition was inaugurated in October 2006 and its first General Conference was convened, in Montevideo, Uruguay, in September 2007. An International Youth Clearing House and Information Service (Infoyouth) aims to increase and consolidate the information available on the situation of young people in society, and to heighten awareness of their needs, aspirations and potential among public and private decision-makers. Supporting efforts to facilitate dialogue among different cultures and societies and promoting opportunities for reflection and consideration of philosophy and human rights, for example the celebration of World Philosophy Day, are also among UNESCO's fundamental aims.

CULTURE

In undertaking efforts to preserve the world's cultural and natural heritage UNESCO has attempted to emphasize the link between culture and development. In December 1992 UNESCO established the World Commission on Culture and Development; the first World Conference on Culture and Development was held in June 1999, in Havana, Cuba. In November 2001 the General Conference adopted the UNESCO Universal Declaration on Cultural Diversity, which affirmed the importance of intercultural dialogue in establishing a climate of peace. UNESCO's medium-term strategy for 2014–21 placed a particular focus on addressing challenges in achieving gender equality in cultural life, including difficulties faced by women in attaining senior management positions and decision-making roles; unequal value attributed to the roles of women and men in heritage protection and transmission; unequal opportunities for women to share their creativity with audiences; limitations on freedom of expression based on gender; and unequal access to technical and entrepreneurial training, as well as to financial resources, based on gender.

UNESCO aims to promote cultural diversity through the safeguarding of heritage and enhancement of cultural expressions. In January 2002 UNESCO inaugurated the Global Alliance on Cultural Diversity, to promote partnerships between governments, non-governmental bodies and the private sector with a view to supporting cultural diversity through the strengthening of cultural industries and the prevention of cultural piracy. An International Convention on the Protection of the Diversity of Cultural Expressions, approved by the General Conference in 2005, entered into force in March 2007.

UNESCO's World Heritage Programme, inaugurated in 1978, aims to protect historic sites and natural landmarks of outstanding universal significance, in accordance with the 1972 UNESCO Convention Concerning the Protection of the World Cultural and Natural Heritage, by providing financial aid for restoration, technical assistance, training and management planning. UNESCO recognizes that new global threats may affect natural and cultural heritage, and emphasizes that conservation of sites contributes to social cohesion. States parties compile 'Tentative Lists', detailing sites under consideration for nomination to the formal 'World Heritage List'; at September 2014 some 171 countries had compiled Tentative Lists, comprising some 1,599 prospective sites. During mid-2014–mid-2015 the World Heritage List comprised 1,007 sites globally, of which 779 had cultural significance, 197 were natural landmarks, and 31 were of 'mixed' importance. Examples include the city of Potosí (Bolivia); the Galápagos Islands (Ecuador); the Inca city of Machu Picchu in Peru; the Pitons Management Area in Saint Lucia; Historic Bridgetown and its Garrison in Barbados; the Carioca Landscapes between the Mountain and the Sea, in Rio de Janeiro, Brazil (including Tijuca National Park, Corcovado Mountain and its statue of Christ, and landscapes along Copacabana Bay); the 5,200 km-long Qhapaq Ñan ('Royal Road') Inca road system, covering parts of Peru, Argentina, Bolivia, Chile, Colombia and Ecuador (inscribed in 2014); and numerous other historic sites and nature reserves in the region. UNESCO also maintains a list of World Heritage in Danger. At August 2014 this numbered 46 sites, including the Belize Barrier Reef Reserve System; the Humberstone and Santa Laura saltpeter works in Chile; Los Katíos National Park in Colombia; the Chan Chan Archaeological Zone in Peru; the colonial port town of Coro in Venezuela; the Río Plátano Biosphere Reserve in Honduras; and the Fortifications on the Caribbean Side of Panama: Portobelo-San Lorenzo (exemplifying 17th- and 18th-century Spanish colonial military architecture). In February 2010 UNESCO agreed to form an International Co-ordination Committee in support of Haitian culture, in view of the devastation caused by the earthquake that had struck that country in January, causing 230,000 fatalities and the destruction of local infrastructure and architecture.

UNESCO supports the safeguarding of humanity's non-material 'intangible' heritage, including oral traditions, music, dance and medicine. An Endangered Languages Programme was initiated in 1993. By 2014 the Programme estimated that, of the more than 6,000 languages spoken worldwide, about one-half were endangered. It works to raise awareness of the issue, for example through publication of the *Atlas of the World's Languages in Danger of Disappearing*, to strengthen local and national capacities to safeguard and document languages, and administers a Register of Good Practices in Language Preservation. In October 2003 the UNESCO General Conference adopted a Convention for the Safeguarding of Intangible Cultural Heritage, which provided for the establishment of an intergovernmental committee and for participating states to formulate national inventories of intangible heritage. The Convention entered into force in April 2006 and the intergovernmental committee convened its inaugural session in November. A Representative List of the Intangible Cultural Heritage of Humanity, inaugurated in November 2008, comprised, at mid-2014, 282 elements ('masterpieces of the oral and intangible heritage of humanity') deemed to be of outstanding value; these included Chinese calligraphy; falconry; several dances, such as the tango, which originated in Argentina and Uruguay, and the dances of the Ainu in Japan; Turkish coffee culture and tradition; craftsmanship of Horezu ceramics in Romania; and the Ifa divination system in Nigeria. The related List of Intangible Cultural Heritage in Need of Urgent Safeguarding comprised 31 elements at mid-2014, including the Naqqāli form of story-telling in Iran, the Saman dance in Sumatra, Indonesia; earthenware pottery-making skills in Kgatleng District, Botswana; and the Qiang New Year Festival in Sichuan Province, China. UNESCO's culture programme also aims to safeguard movable cultural heritage and to support and develop museums as a means of preserving heritage and making it accessible to society as a whole.

In November 2001 the General Conference authorized the formulation of a Declaration against the Intentional Destruction of Cultural Heritage. In addition, the Conference adopted the Convention on the Protection of the Underwater Cultural Heritage, covering the protection from commercial exploitation of shipwrecks, submerged historical sites, etc., situated in the territorial waters of signatory states. UNESCO also administers the 1954 Hague Convention on the Protection of Cultural Property in the Event of Armed Conflict and the 1970 Convention on the Means of Prohibiting and Preventing the Illicit Import, Export and Transfer of Ownership of Cultural Property. In 1992 a World Heritage Centre was established to enable rapid mobilization of international technical assistance for the preservation of cultural sites. Through the World Heritage Information Network, a worldwide network of more than 800 information providers, UNESCO promotes global awareness and information exchange.

UNESCO aims to support the development of creative industries and or creative expression. Through a variety of projects UNESCO promotes art education, supports the rights of artists, and encourages crafts, design, digital art and performance arts. In October 2004 UNESCO launched a Creative Cities Network to facilitate public and private sector partnerships, international links, and recognition of a city's unique expertise. In 2014 41 cities were participating in the Network, including Buenos Aires, Argentina (City of Design) and Popayan, Colombia (City of Gastronomy). UNESCO is active in preparing and encouraging the enforcement of international legislation on copyright, raising awareness on the need for copyright protection to uphold cultural diversity, and is contributing to the international debate on digital copyright issues and piracy.

Within its ambition of ensuring cultural diversity, UNESCO recognizes the role of culture as a means of promoting peace and dialogue. Several projects have been formulated within a broader concept of Roads of Dialogue. In Central Asia a project on inter-cultural dialogue follows on from an earlier multidisciplinary study of the ancient Silk Roads trading routes linking Asia and Europe, which illustrated many examples of common heritage. Other projects include a study of the movement of peoples and cultures during the slave trade, a Mediterranean Programme, the Caucasus Project and the Arabia Plan, which aims to promote worldwide knowledge and understanding of Arab culture. UNESCO has overseen an extensive programme of work to formulate histories of humanity and regions, focused on ideas, civilizations and the evolution of societies and cultures. These have included the *General History of Africa, History of Civilizations of Central Asia,* and *History of Humanity*. UNESCO endeavoured to consider and implement the findings of the Alliance of Civilizations, a high-level group convened by the UN Secretary-General that published a report in November 2006. UNESCO signed a Memorandum of Understanding with the Alliance during its first forum, convened in Madrid, Spain, in January 2008.

COMMUNICATION AND INFORMATION

UNESCO regards information, communication and knowledge as being at the core of human progress and well-being. It advocates the concept of inclusive, equitable, open and participatory knowledge societies, based on the principles of freedom of expression (through traditional, contemporary and new forms of media—including the internet), universal access to information and knowledge, respect for cultural and linguistic diversity, and equal access to quality education. UNESCO determined to consolidate and implement this concept, in accordance with the Declaration of Principles and Plan of Action adopted by the second phase of the World Summit on the Information Society (WSIS) in November 2005. UNESCO hosted the WSIS+10 Review meeting, in February 2013 (the first WSIS phase having taken place in December 2003), in Paris, on the theme 'Towards Knowledge Societies for Peace and Sustainable Development'. Under UNESCO's 2014–21 medium-term strategy member states were to be supported in exploiting the use of ICTs, information and data flows, and the Organization was to continue to stimulate debate on the ethical, political and societal challenges to building sustainable knowledge societies.

A key strategic objective of building inclusive knowledge societies is enhancing universal access to communication and information. At the national and global level UNESCO promotes the rights of freedom of expression and of access to information. It promotes the free flow and broad diffusion of information, knowledge, data and best practices, through the development of communications infrastructures, the elimination of impediments to freedom of expression, and the development of independent and pluralistic media, including through the provision of advisory services on media legislation, particularly in post-conflict countries and in countries in transition. UNESCO recognizes that the so-called global digital divide, in addition to other developmental differences between countries, generates exclusion and marginalization, and that increased participation in the democratic process can be attained through strengthening national communication and information capacities. UNESCO promotes policies and mechanisms that enhance provision for marginalized and disadvantaged groups to benefit from information and community opportunities. Activities at local and national level include developing effective 'infostructures', such as libraries and archives and strengthening low-cost community media and information access points, for example through the establishment of Community Multimedia Centres (CMCs). Many of UNESCO's principles and objectives in this area are pursued through the Information for All Programme, which entered into force in 2001. It is administered by an intergovernmental council, the secretariat of which is provided by UNESCO. UNESCO also established, in 1982, the International Programme for the Development of Communication (IPDC), which aims to promote and develop independent and pluralistic media in developing countries, for example by the establishment or modernization of news agencies and newspapers and training media professionals, the promotion of the right to information, and through efforts to harness informatics for development purposes and strengthen member states' capacities in this field. In March 2013 the IPDC approved funding for 63 new media development projects in developing and emerging countries worldwide. In 2011, on the basis of discussions held at the 2010 session of the Internet Governance Forum (established by the second phase of the WSIS to support the implementation of the Summit's mandate) UNESCO published a report entitled *Freedom of Connection-*

Freedom of Expression: the Changing Legal and Regulatory Ecology Shaping the Internet. UNESCO has engaged with the Freedom Online Coalition, launched in December 2011 by the first Freedom Online Conference, held in The Hague, Netherlands, with the objective of facilitating global dialogue regarding the role of governments in furthering freedom on the internet. The second Freedom Online Conference was convened in Nairobi, Kenya, in September 2012, and the third Conference was held in Tunis, Tunisia, in June 2013, by which time the Freedom Online Coalition had 21 member states.

UNESCO supports cultural and linguistic diversity in information sources to reinforce the principle of universal access. It aims to raise awareness of the issue of equitable access and diversity, encourage good practices and develop policies to strengthen cultural diversity in all media. In 2002 UNESCO established Initiative B@bel as a multidisciplinary programme to promote linguistic diversity, with the aim of enhancing access of under-represented groups to information sources as well as protecting underused minority languages. In December 2009 UNESCO and the Internet Corporation for Assigned Names and Numbers (ICANN) signed a joint agreement which aimed to promote the use of multilingual domain names using non-Latin script, with a view to promoting linguistic diversity. UNESCO's Programme for Creative Content supports the development of and access to diverse content in both the electronic and audiovisual media. The Memory of the World project, established in 1992, aims to preserve in digital form, and thereby to promote wide access to, the world's documentary heritage. Documentary material includes stone tablets, celluloid, parchment and audio recordings. By mid-2014 299 inscriptions had been included on the project's register; five inscriptions originated from international organizations, including the Archives of the ICRC's former International Prisoners of War Agency, 1914–23, submitted by the ICRC, and inscribed in 2007; the League of Nations Archives, 1919–46, submitted by the UN Geneva Office, and inscribed in 2009; and documentary heritage of the International Commission for the International Tracing Service (ITS), submitted by the ITS, and inscribed in 2013. In September 2012 UNESCO organized an international conference on the 'Memory of the World in the Digital Age: Digitization and Preservation', in Vancouver, Canada. The conference adopted the Vancouver Declaration, emphasizing that every individual should be guaranteed access to information, including in digital format, and that digital information should be available in the long term. UNESCO also supports other efforts to preserve and disseminate digital archives and, in 2003, adopted a Charter for the Preservation of Digital Heritage. In April 2009 UNESCO launched the internet based World Digital Library, accessible at www.wdl.org, which aims to display primary documents (including texts, charts and illustrations), and authoritative explanations, relating to the accumulated knowledge of a broad spectrum of human cultures.

UNESCO promotes freedom of expression, of the press and independence of the media as fundamental human rights and the basis of democracy. It aims to assist member states to formulate policies and legal frameworks to uphold independent and pluralistic media and infostructures and to enhance the capacities of public service broadcasting institutions. In regions affected by conflict UNESCO supports efforts to establish and maintain an independent media service and to use it as a means of consolidating peace. UNESCO also aims to develop media and information systems to respond to and mitigate the impact of disaster situations, and to integrate these objectives into wider UN peacebuilding or reconstruction initiatives. UNESCO is the co-ordinating agency for 'World Press Freedom Day', which is held annually on 3 May; it also awards an annual World Press Freedom Prize. A conference convened in Tunis, in celebration of the May 2012 World Press Freedom Day—held on the theme 'New Voices: Media Freedom Helping to Transform Societies', with a focus on the transition towards democracy in several countries of North Africa and the Middle East—adopted the Carthage Declaration, urging the creation of free and safe environments for media workers and the promotion of journalistic ethics. The Declaration also requested UNESCO to pursue implementation of the UN Plan of Action on the Safety of Journalists and the Issue of Impunity, which had been drafted with guidance from UNESCO, and endorsed in April by the UN System Chief Executives Board for Co-ordination. UNESCO maintains an Observatory on the Information Society, which provides up-to-date information on the development of new ICTs, analyses major trends, and aims to raise awareness of related ethical, legal and societal issues. UNESCO promotes the upholding of human rights in the use of cyberspace.

UNESCO promotes the application of ICT for sustainable development. In particular it supports efforts to improve teaching and learning processes through electronic media and to develop innovative literacy and education initiatives, such as the ICT-Enhanced Learning (ICTEL) project. UNESCO also aims to enhance understanding and use of new technologies and support training and ongoing learning opportunities for librarians, archivists and other information providers.

Finance

UNESCO's activities are funded through a regular budget provided by contributions from member states and extra-budgetary funds from other sources, particularly the UN Development Programme, the World Bank, regional banks and other bilateral Funds-in-Trust arrangements. UNESCO co-operates with many other UN agencies and international non-governmental organizations.

In response to a decision, in late October 2011, by a majority of member states participating in the UNESCO General Conference to admit Palestine as a new member state, the USA decided to withhold from UNESCO significant annual funding. In the following month UNESCO launched an Emergency Multi-Donor Fund, as a channel for donations made by international donors with the aim of addressing the funding shortfall.

UNESCO's Regular Programme budget for the two-year period 2014–15 was US $507m.

Publications

(mostly in English, French and Spanish editions; Arabic, Chinese and Russian versions are also available in many cases)

Atlas of the World's Languages in Danger (online).

Best Practices of Island and Coastal Biospheres.

CI Newsletter.

Encyclopedia of Life Support Systems (online).

Education for All Global Monitoring Report.

International Review of Education (quarterly).

International Social Science Journal (quarterly).

Memory of the World, The Treasures that Record our History from 1700 BC to the Present Day.

Museum International (quarterly).

Nature and Resources (quarterly).

Prospects (quarterly review on education).

UNESCO Courier (quarterly).

UNESCO Science Report.

UNESCO World Atlas of Gender Equality in Education.

World Heritage Review (quarterly).

World Science Report (every 2 years).

World Trends in Freedom of Expression and Media Development.

Books, databases, video and radio documentaries, statistics, scientific maps and atlases.

Specialized Institutes and Centres

Abdus Salam International Centre for Theoretical Physics: Strada Costiera 11, 34151 Trieste, Italy; tel. (040) 2240111; fax (040) 224163; e-mail sci_info@ictp.it; internet www.ictp.it; f. 1964; promotes and enables advanced study and research in physics and mathematical sciences; organizes and sponsors training opportunities, in particular for scientists from developing countries; aims to provide an international forum for the exchange of information and ideas; operates under a tripartite agreement between UNESCO, IAEA and the Italian Government; Dir FERNANDO QUEVEDO (Guatemala).

International Bureau of Education (IBE): POB 199, 1211 Geneva 20, Switzerland; tel. 229177800; fax 229177801; e-mail doc .centre@ibe.unesco.org; internet www.ibe.unesco.org; f. 1925, became an intergovernmental organization in 1929 and was incorporated into UNESCO in 1969; the Council of the IBE is composed of representatives of 28 member states of UNESCO, designated by the General Conference; the Bureau's fundamental mission is to deal with matters concerning educational content, methods, and teaching/learning strategies; an International Conference on Education is held periodically; Dir CLEMENTINA ACEDO (Venezuela); publs *Prospects* (quarterly review), *Educational Innovation* (newsletter), educational practices series, monographs, other reference works.

UNESCO Institute for Information Technologies in Education: 117292 Moscow, ul. Kedrova 8, Bldg 3, Russia; tel. (499) 129-29-90; fax (499) 129-12-25; e-mail liste.info.iite@unesco.org; internet iite .unesco.org; f. 1988; the Institute aims to formulate policies regarding the development of, and to support and monitor the use of, information and communication technologies in education; it conducts research and organizes training programmes; Dir a.i. DENDEV BADARCH.

UNESCO Institute for Lifelong Learning: Feldbrunnenstr. 58, 20148 Hamburg, Germany; tel. (40) 448-0410; fax (40) 410-7723; e-mail uil@unesco.org; internet www.unesco.org/uil/index.htm; f. 1951, as the Institute for Education; a research, training, information, documentation and publishing centre, with a particular focus on adult basic and further education and adult literacy; Dir ARNE CARLSEN (Denmark).

UNESCO Institute for Statistics: CP 6128, Succursale Centre-Ville, Montréal, QC, H3C 3J7, Canada; tel. (514) 343-6880; fax (514) 343-5740; e-mail uis.information@unesco.org; internet www.uis .unesco.org; f. 2001; collects and analyses national statistics on education, science, technology, culture and communications; Dir HENDRIK VAN DER POL (Netherlands).

UNESCO Institute for Water Education: Westvest 7, 2611 AX Delft, Netherlands; tel. (15) 2151715; fax (15) 2122921; e-mail info@ unesco-ihe.org; internet www.unesco-ihe.org; f. 2003; activities include education, training and research; and co-ordination of a global network of water sector organizations; advisory and policy-making functions; setting international standards for postgraduate education programmes; and professional training in the water sector; Rector Prof. ANDRÁS SZÖLLÖSI-NAGY (Hungary).

UNESCO-UNEVOC International Centre for Technical and Vocational Education and Training: UN Campus, Platz der Vereinten Nationen 1, 53113 Bonn, Germany; tel. (228) 8150-100; fax (228) 8150-199; e-mail unevoc@unesco.org; internet www.unevoc .unesco.org; f. 2002; the centre assists member states to strengthen and upgrade their technical vocational education and training (TVET) systems; promotes high-quality lifelong technical and vocational education, with a particular focus on young people, girls and women, and the disadvantaged; Head SHYAMAL MAJUMDAR (India).

UNESCO International Institute for Educational Planning (IIEP): 7–9 rue Eugène Delacroix, 75116 Paris, France; tel. 1-45-03-77-00; fax 1-40-72-83-66; e-mail info@iiep.unesco.org; internet www .iiep.unesco.org; f. 1963; serves as a world centre for advanced training and research in educational planning; aims to help all member states of UNESCO in their social and economic development efforts, by enlarging the fund of knowledge about educational planning and the supply of competent experts in this field; legally and administratively a part of UNESCO, the Institute is autonomous, and its policies and programme are controlled by its own Governing Board, under special statutes voted by the General Conference of UNESCO; a satellite office of the IIEP is based in Buenos Aires, Argentina; Dir a.i. SUZANNE GRANT LEWIS (USA).

UNESCO International Institute for Higher Education in Latin America and the Caribbean: Avda Los Chorros con Calle Acueducto, Edif. Asovincar, Altos de Sebucán, Apdo 68394, Caracas 1062-A, Venezuela; tel. (212) 286-0555; fax (212) 286-0527; e-mail iesalc@unesco.org.ve; internet www.iesalc.unesco.org.ve; CEO PEDRO HERNÁN HENRÍQUEZ GUAJARDO (Chile).

World Health Organization—WHO

Address: 20 ave Appia, 1211 Geneva 27, Switzerland.
Telephone: 227912111; **fax:** 227913111; **e-mail:** info@who.int; **internet:** www.who.int.
WHO, established in 1948, is the lead agency within the UN system concerned with the protection and improvement of public health.

Organization
(September 2014)

WORLD HEALTH ASSEMBLY

The Assembly meets in Geneva, Switzerland, once a year. It is responsible for policy-making and the biennial budget; appoints the Director-General; admits new members; and reviews budget contributions. The 67th Assembly was convened in May 2014.

EXECUTIVE BOARD

The Board is composed of 34 health experts designated by a member state that has been elected by the World Health Assembly to serve on the Board; each expert serves for three years. The Board meets at least twice a year to review the Director-General's programme, which it forwards to the Assembly with any recommendations that seem necessary. It advises on questions referred to it by the Assembly and is responsible for putting into effect the decisions and policies of the Assembly. It is also empowered to take emergency measures in case of epidemics or disasters. Meeting in November 2011 the Board agreed several proposed organizational reforms aimed at improving health outcomes, achieving greater coherence in global health matters, and promoting efficiency and transparency throughout WHO.

Chairman: Dr MARIYAM SHAKEELA (Maldives).

SECRETARIAT

Director-General: Dr MARGARET CHAN (People's Republic of China).

Deputy Director-General: Dr ANARFI ASAMOA-BAAH (Ghana).

Assistant Directors-General: Dr BRUCE AYLWARD (Canada) (Polio, Emergencies and Country Collaboration), FLAVIA BUSTREO (Italy) (Family, Women's and Children's Health), OLEG CHESTNOV (Russia) (Non-communicable Diseases and Mental Health), KEIJI FUKUDA (USA) (Health Security), MARIE-PAULE KIENY (France) (Health Systems and Innovation), HIROKI NAKATANI (Japan) (HIV/AIDS, TB, Malaria and Neglected Tropical Diseases), HANS TROEDSSON (Sweden) (General Management).

UN System Co-ordinator for Ebola Virus Disease: Dr DAVID NABARRO (United Kingdom).

PRINCIPAL OFFICES

Each of WHO's six geographical regions has its own organization, consisting of a regional committee representing relevant member states and associate members, and a regional office staffed by experts in various fields of health.

International Health Regulations Coordination—WHO Lyon Office: 58 ave Debourg, 69007 Lyon, France; tel. 4-72-71-64-70; fax 4-72-71-64-71; e-mail ihrinfo@who.int; internet www.who.int/ihr/ lyon/en/index.html; supports (with regional offices) countries in strengthening their national surveillance and response systems, with the aim of improving the detection, assessment and notification of events, and responding to public health risks and emergencies of international concern under the International Health Regulations.

WHO Centre for Health Development: I. H. D. Centre Bldg, 9th Floor, 5–1, 1-chome, Wakinohama-Kaigandori, Chuo-ku, Kobe, Japan; tel. (78) 230-3100; fax (78) 230-3178; e-mail wkc@who.int; internet www.who.int/kobe_centre/en/; f. 1995 to address health development issues; Dir ALEX ROSS (USA).

Activities

WHO is the UN system's co-ordinating authority for health (defined as 'a state of complete physical, mental and social well-being and not merely the absence of disease and infirmity'). WHO's objective is stated in its constitution as 'the attainment by all peoples of the highest possible level of health'. In May 2013 the 66th World Health Assembly (WHA) adopted the 12th General Programme of Work, to guide its activities during 2014–19; this was underpinned by six leadership priorities: advancing universal health coverage; addressing unfinished and future challenges (beyond 2015) in respect of the health-related Millennium Development Goals (MDGs); addressing the challenge of non-communicable diseases and mental health, violence and injuries and disabilities; implementing the provisions of the International Health Regulations; increasing access to essential, high-quality and affordable medical products; and addressing the social, economic and environmental determinants of health as a means of reducing health inequities within and between countries. WHO's core functions, emphasized in the 2014–19 programme of work, are to provide leadership on global public health matters, in partnership, where necessary, with other agencies; to help to shape the global health research agenda; to set, and monitor the implementation of, norms and standards; to articulate ethical and evidence-based policy options; to provide technical and policy support to member countries; and to monitor and assess health trends. Aid is provided in emergencies and natural disasters. The 12th General Programme of Work takes into account global challenges to health, including the negative impact on public spending on health of the continuing economic downturn in a number of developed countries; rapid unplanned urbanization, particularly in low- and middle-income countries (simultaneously providing new opportunities for

WHO of health provision and increased risks of social exclusion and inequity); health risks associated with economic migration; the potential health and social impact of a worldwide high level of youth unemployment; and pressure on the global environment, including significant loss of biodiversity, and climate change (potentially affecting fundamental requirements for health, including clean urban air, safe drinking water, a secure and nutritious food supply, and protection from extreme weather events).

WHO has developed a structured system of formulating and disseminating international standards of health issues. Its so-called Family of International Classifications (WHO-FIC) includes the *International Classification of Diseases (ICD)*, providing an etiological framework of health conditions, and currently in its 10th edition (11th revision due in 2017); and the complementary *International Classification of Functioning, Disability and Health (ICF)*, which describes how people live with their conditions. The WHO-FIC Network, comprising WHO collaborating centres that have been designated to work on international classifications, the WHO regional offices, and relevant departments of the Organization's headquarters, meets on an annual basis (in 2014 in Barcelona, Spain, in October), and develops, disseminates and maintains the WHO-FIC. Globally there are more than 800 WHO collaborating centres in more than 80 countries; networks of centres covering specific areas of expertise have been established, including (as well as those designated for developing international classifications) communicable diseases, food safety, nursing and midwifery, nutrition, occupational health, prevention of injuries and violence, radiation, tobacco control, and traditional medicine.

WHO keeps diseases and other health problems under constant surveillance, promotes the exchange of prompt and accurate information and of notification of outbreaks of diseases, and administers the International Health Regulations (which are regularly revised). WHO undertakes to collect and disseminate health data and undertake statistical analyses and comparative studies in such diseases as cancer, heart disease and mental illness; set standards for the quality control of drugs, vaccines and other substances affecting health, and communicate reports or any known adverse reactions to drugs to all member states; formulate health regulations for international travel; and promote improved environmental conditions, including housing, sanitation and working conditions.

WHO has contributed to the pursuit, by 2015, of the UN MDGs, with particular responsibility for the MDGs of reducing child mortality (with a target reduction of two-thirds in the mortality rate among children under the age of five); improving maternal health (with a specific goal of reducing by 75% the numbers of women dying in childbirth); and combating HIV/AIDS, malaria and other diseases. In addition, it has directly supported the following millennium 'targets': halving the proportion of people suffering from malnutrition; halving the proportion of people without sustainable access to safe drinking water and basic sanitation; and providing access, in co-operation with pharmaceutical companies, to affordable, essential drugs in developing countries. In 2013 WHO, with UNICEF, co-led consultations on formulating a post-2015 development framework in the thematic area of health.

During 2005 the UN's Inter-Agency Standing Committee (IASC), concerned with co-ordinating the international response to humanitarian disasters, developed a concept of organizing agency assistance to internally displaced persons through the institutionalization of a 'Cluster Approach', comprising 11 core areas of activity. WHO was designated the lead agency for the Health Cluster. The 65th WHA, convened in May 2012, adopted a resolution endorsing WHO's role as Health Cluster lead and urging international donors to allocate sufficient resources towards health sector activities during humanitarian emergencies.

COMMUNICABLE DISEASES

WHO aims to reduce the burden of infectious and parasitic communicable diseases, HIV/AIDS, tuberculosis (TB), malaria, neglected tropical diseases and vaccine-preventable diseases, identifying these as a major obstacle to social and economic progress, particularly in developing countries, where, in addition to disabilities and loss of productivity and household earnings, they cause nearly one-half of all deaths. Emerging and re-emerging diseases, those likely to cause epidemics, increasing incidence of zoonoses (diseases or infections passed from vertebrate animals to humans by means of parasites, viruses, bacteria or unconventional agents), attributable to factors such as environmental changes and changes in farming practices, outbreaks of unknown etiology, and the undermining of some drug therapies by the spread of antimicrobial resistance, are main areas of concern. In recent years WHO has noted the global spread of communicable diseases through international travel, voluntary human migration and involuntary population displacement.

WHO's Global Alert and Response (GAR) framework aims to provide an effective international system for co-ordinated response to epidemics and other public health emergencies, underpinned by strong national public health systems. In 2000 WHO and several partner institutions in epidemic surveillance established the Global Outbreak Alert and Response Network (GOARN), which maintains constant vigilance regarding outbreaks of disease, and links world-wide expertise—for example through co-ordinated regional and global Emerging and Dangerous Pathogens Laboratory Networks, that cover both the human and animal sectors—to provide an immediate response capability. WHO aims to strengthen biorisk reduction capacity, biosecurity, and readiness for outbreaks of dangerous and emerging pathogens. The Organization assists member states in the development and implementation of domestic capacities for epidemic preparedness and response through strengthening national laboratory capacities and early warning alert and response mechanisms; promoting relevant national and international training programmes; promoting standardized approaches in relation to epidemic-prone infections, such as cholera; influenza; meningitis; plague (in its bubonic, pneumonic and septicemic presentations), which can be carried to humans by infected rodents and domestic cats; Severe Acute Respiratory Syndrome (SARS), viral haemorrhagic fevers (including the Crimean-Congo, Ebola, Lassa and Marburg types), which are spread by direct contact with infected blood, body fluids and tissues, including of wild animals; and yellow fever. In July 2011 WHO launched the Global Infection Prevention and Control (GIPC) Network, which provides technical support to member states through the dissemination of epidemic-prone infection prevention and control policies and guidance; the compilation of relevant indicators; and generic training curricula.

In mid-2014 WHO reported that an outbreak of Ebola Virus Disease (EVD) in West Africa, that had emerged in Guinea in February, and had soon spread to Liberia and eastern Sierra Leone, was the most intensive ever recorded, with the greatest geographic extent and highest case load. At the beginning of August the WHO Director-General and regional presidents, meeting in Conakry, Guinea, adopted a reinforced EVD Outbreak Response Plan in West Africa, and shortly afterwards the World Bank announced an allocation of some US $200m. in emergency assistance to WHO and to the governments of the affected countries, in support of the ongoing efforts to combat EVD. On 8 August the WHO Director-General declared the EVD outbreak to be a Public Health Emergency of International Concern. Soon afterwards the UN Secretary-General appointed a UN System Co-ordinator for EVD. In mid-August a gathering of medical ethicists convened by WHO agreed that unregistered experimental anti-EVD treatments should be used on patients affected by the ongoing emergency. It was envisaged that clinical trials of EVD vaccines would be initiated by a major pharmaceutical company in September 2014, and that an approved vaccine might become publicly available in 2015. In August WHO, the International Civil Aviation Association, and the International Air Transport Association were co-operating in ascertaining the implications for international air connectivity of the EVD outbreak. A roadmap to guide and co-ordinate the international response to the West African EVD outbreak, and to manage and halt onwards transmission of the virus within six–nine months, was issued by WHO on 28 August. The roadmap emphasized the need to address, simultaneously, the broad socioeconomic impact of the outbreak. By 31 August some 3,685 probable and confirmed cases had been reported in the 2014 'widespread and intense' EVD outbreak in Guinea, Liberia and Sierra Leone, resulting in 1,841 fatalities. Furthermore—as a result of international travel from the affected subregion, and onwards infection—21 further cases of EVD and seven fatalities had been reported in Nigeria (both in Lagos, the capital, and Port Harcourt). At the end of August the first EVD case in Senegal was reported. In early September WHO was to host a consultation on the safety and efficacy of possible EVD treatments, with participation by more than 100 medical experts.

Combating the human immunodeficiency virus/acquired immunodeficiency syndrome (HIV/AIDS), TB and malaria are organization-wide priorities and, as such, are supported not only by their own areas of work but also by activities undertaken in other areas. TB is the principal cause of death for people infected with the HIV virus and an estimated one-third of people living with HIV/AIDS globally are co-infected with TB. In July 2000 a meeting of the Group of Seven industrialized nations and Russia, convened in Genoa, Italy, announced the formation of the Global Fund to Fight AIDS, TB and Malaria (as previously proposed by the UN Secretary-General and recommended by the WHA).

Some 95% of those known to be infected with HIV/AIDS live in developing countries, and AIDS-related illnesses are the leading cause of death in sub-Saharan Africa. It is estimated that around 30m. people worldwide died of AIDS during 1981–2011. WHO supports governments to develop effective health sector responses to the HIV/AIDS epidemic through enhancing their planning and managerial capabilities, implementation capacity, and health systems resources. The Joint UN Programme on HIV/AIDS (UNAIDS) became operational on 1 January 1996, sponsored by WHO and other UN agencies; the UNAIDS secretariat is based at WHO headquarters. In May 2000 the WHA adopted a resolution urging WHO member states to improve access to the prevention and treatment of

HIV-related illnesses and to increase the availability and affordability of drugs. A WHO-UNAIDS HIV Vaccine Initiative was launched in that year. In July 2012 WHO published the first report detailing levels of HIV drug resistance in low- and middle-income countries; the overall rate was estimated at that time to be 6.8%. WHO guidelines on the use of antiretroviral therapy (ART) were first released in 2002, and have subsequently been revised, with the most recent update released in June 2013. In the following month UNAIDS initiated the Treatment 2015 framework, aimed at facilitating the provision by 2015 of ART to some 15m. people infected with HIV. At mid-2013 it was reported that around 10m. people requiring ART globally had access to the treatment.

In May 2011 the 64th WHA adopted a new Global Health Sector Strategy on HIV/AIDS, covering 2011–15, which aimed to promote greater innovation in HIV prevention, diagnosis, treatment, and the improvement of care services to facilitate universal access to care for HIV patients. In December 2011 the UN General Assembly adopted a Political Declaration on HIV/AIDS, outlining 10 targets to be attained by 2015: reducing by 50% sexual transmission of HIV; reducing by 50% HIV transmission among people who inject drugs; eliminating new HIV infections among children, and reducing AIDS-related maternal deaths; ensuring that at least 15m. people living with HIV are receiving ART; reducing by 50% TB deaths in people living with HIV; reaching annual global investment of at least US $22,000m. in combating AIDS in low- and medium-resource countries; eliminating gender inequalities and increasing the capacity of women and girls to self-protect from HIV; promoting the adoption of legislation and policies aimed at eliminating stigma and discrimination against people living with HIV; eliminating HIV-related restrictions on travel; strengthening the integration of the AIDS response in global health and development efforts.

At December 2012 some 1.5m. people in Latin America (including around 600,000 people in Brazil) and 250,000 people in the Caribbean were reported to have HIV/AIDS. The Caribbean has the second highest rate of HIV prevalence in the world (1%), after sub-Saharan Africa. In December 2012 it was reported, however, that over the period 2001–11 the rate of new infections in the Caribbean fell by more than 42%. At end-2012 there were estimated prevalence rates of 3.3% in the Bahamas and 2.1% in Haiti.

According to WHO estimates, one-third of the world's population carries the TB bacillus. In 2011 this generated 8.7m. new active cases (13% in people co-infected with HIV), and killed 1.4m. people (430,000 of whom were also HIV-positive). Some 22 countries account for four-fifths of global TB cases. The largest concentration of TB cases is in South-East Asia. WHO provides technical support to all member countries, with special attention given to those with high TB prevalence, to establish effective national tuberculosis control programmes. WHO's strategy for TB control includes the use of the expanded DOTS (direct observation treatment, short-course) regime, involving the following five tenets: sustained political commitment to increase human and financial resources and to make TB control in endemic countries a nationwide activity and an integral part of the national health system; access to quality-assured TB sputum microscopy; standardized short-course chemotherapy for all cases of TB under proper case-management conditions; uninterrupted supply of quality-assured drugs; and maintaining a recording and reporting system to enable outcome assessment. Simultaneously, WHO is encouraging research with the aim of further advancing DOTS, developing new tools for prevention, diagnosis and treatment, and containing new threats (such as the HIV/TB co-epidemic). Inadequate control of DOTS in some areas, leading to partial and inconsistent treatments, has resulted in the development of drug-resistant and, often, incurable strains of TB. The incidence of so-called Multidrug Resistant TB (MDR-TB) strains has risen in recent years; an estimated 3.7% of new TB cases were reported to be MDR in 2011. MDR-TB cases occur most frequently in the People's Republic of China, India, Russia and South Africa; it was reported in 2011 that in Russia around 20% of new cases and 46% of cases presenting for retreatment were MDR. WHO has developed DOTS-Plus, a specialized strategy for controlling the spread of MDR-TB in areas of high prevalence. By the end of 2011 some 84 countries had reported at least one case of Extensive Drug Resistant TB (XDR-TB), defined as MDR-TB plus resistance to any fluoroquinolone, and to any of the three second-line anti-TB drugs. XDR-TB is believed to be most prevalent in Eastern Europe and Asia. TB cases resistant to all drugs have been reported in Europe and in Iran. In 2007 WHO launched the Global MDR/XDR Response Plan, which aimed to expand diagnosis and treatment to cover, by 2015, some 85% of TB patients with MDR-TB.

The 'Stop TB' partnership, launched by WHO in 1999, in partnership with the World Bank, the US Government and a coalition of NGOs, co-ordinates the Global Plan to Stop TB, which represents a roadmap for TB control covering the period 2006–15. The Global Plan aims to facilitate the achievement of the MDG of halting and beginning to reverse by 2015 the incidence of TB by means of access to quality diagnosis and treatment for all; to supply ART to 3m. TB patients co-infected with HIV; to treat nearly 1m. people for MDR-TB

(this target was subsequently altered by the 2007 Global MDR/XDR Response Plan); to develop a new anti-TB drug and a new vaccine; and to develop rapid and inexpensive diagnostic tests at the point of care. A second phase of the Global Plan, launched in late 2010 and covering 2011–15, updated the Plan to take account of actual progress achieved since its instigation in 2006. The Global TB Drug Facility, launched by 'Stop TB' in 2001, aims to increase access to high-quality anti-TB drugs for sufferers in developing countries. In 2007 'Stop TB' endorsed the establishment of a Global Laboratory Initiative with the aim of expanding laboratory capacity.

In October 2013 WHO and partners launched the 'Roadmap for childhood TB: towards zero deaths', recommending 10 actions aimed at eradicating childhood deaths from TB, including incorporating the needs of children and adolescents into TB research, policy development and clinical practices; making use of critical intervention strategies, such as contact tracing and preventive therapy; implementing policies to enable early diagnosis and ensuring an uninterrupted supply of high-quality anti-TB medicines for children; addressing research gaps, and closing all funding gaps relating to childhood TB; and establishing partnerships to study and evaluate the best strategies for preventing, managing and treating childhood TB. Some US $120m. was pledged at that time in new donor funding towards addressing childhood TB (including $40m. allocated to the provision of ARTs for children co-infected with TB and HIV).

In October 1998 WHO, jointly with UNICEF, the World Bank and UNDP, formally launched the Roll Back Malaria (RBM) programme. The disease acutely affects at least 350m.–500m. people, and kills an estimated 1m. people, every year. Some 85% of all malaria cases occur in sub-Saharan Africa. It is estimated that the disease directly causes nearly one-fifth of all child deaths in that region. The Democratic Republic of the Congo and Nigeria have the highest levels of infection in sub-Saharan Africa. The global RBM Partnership, linking governments, development agencies, and other parties, aims to mobilize resources and support for controlling malaria. The RBM Partnership Global Strategic Plan for the period 2005–15, adopted in November 2005, listed steps required to intensify malaria control interventions with a view to a 75% reduction in malaria morbidity and mortality by 2015, over levels at 2005. WHO recommends a number of guidelines for malaria control, focusing on the need for prompt, effective antimalarial treatment, and the issue of drug resistance; vector control, including the use of insecticide-treated bed nets; malaria in pregnancy; malaria epidemics; and monitoring and evaluation activities. WHO, with several private and public sector partners, supports the development of more effective anti-malaria drugs and vaccines through the 'Medicines for Malaria' venture. A draft Global Technical Strategy for Malaria Control and Elimination, to cover the period 2016–25, was under development in 2014. It was envisaged that the first vaccine against malaria would be ready for release in 2016; from July 2014 clinical evidence relating to the vaccine was to be assessed by WHO and the European Medicines Agency.

During 2012–20 WHO was implementing a global strategy for the prevention and control of the mosquito-borne dengue virus, the incidence of which has increased significantly in humans in recent years, with at least 50m. new cases arising annually, resulting in some 20,000 deaths, in more than 100 endemic countries, particularly in the Asia-Pacific region and Latin America. The strategy focuses on improving—through co-ordinated epidemiological and entomological surveillance—outbreak prediction and detection, and on the deployment of locally-adapted vector control measures.

The Special Programme for Research and Training in Tropical Diseases, established in 1975 and sponsored jointly by WHO, UNDP and the World Bank, as well as by contributions from donor countries, involves a worldwide network of some 5,000 scientists working on the development and application of vaccines, new drugs, diagnostic kits and preventive measures, and applied research on practical community issues affecting the target diseases. In May 2013 the 66th WHA adopted a resolution on Neglected Tropical Diseases that urged member states to ensure country ownership of prevention, control, elimination and eradication programmes, urged international partners to supply adequate funding in support of these, and encouraged the development of new technologies aimed at supporting vector control and infection prevention.

From March 2003 WHO began to co-ordinate an international investigation into the global spread of SARS, a previously unknown atypical pneumonia. In 2014 WHO was monitoring the spread of Middle East respiratory syndrome coronavirus (MERS-CoV), a related acute respiratory condition; by mid-June 699 laboratory-confirmed cases of MERS-CoV had been reported to WHO since September 2012, including 209 deaths. The reported cases had arisen in Iran, Jordan, Kuwait, Qatar, Saudi Arabia, the United Arab Emirates (UAE) and Yemen. Laboratory-confirmed cases had also been reported in six European countries, two countries in Asia, and in the USA. From the end of 2003 WHO was monitoring the spread through several Asian countries of the virus H5N1 (a rapidly mutating strain of zoonotic highly pathogenic avian influenza—HPAI) that was transmitting to human populations through contact with diseased birds, mainly poultry. It was then greatly feared that H5N1, which has since become endemic among poultry in parts of Asia and Africa, might mutate into a form transmissable from human to human, although WHO reported in 2014 that, by then, H5N1 still did not appear to transmit easily among people. In March 2005 WHO issued a *Global Influenza Preparedness Plan*, and urged all countries to develop national influenza pandemic preparedness plans and to stockpile antiviral drugs. In May, in co-operation with FAO and the World Organisation for Animal Health (OIE), WHO launched a Global Strategy for the Progressive Control of Highly Pathogenic Avian Influenza. A conference on Avian Influenza and Human Pandemic Influenza that was jointly organized by WHO, FAO, the OIE and the World Bank in November 2005 issued a plan of action identifying a number of responses for disease control, preparedness, response and vaccine research. WHO has continued to report on cases of H5N1 on a monthly basis, and by 27 June 2014 a total of 667 human cases of H5N1 had been laboratory confirmed, in Azerbaijan, Bangladesh, Cambodia, China, Djibouti, Egypt, Indonesia, Iraq, Laos, Myanmar, Nigeria, Pakistan, Thailand, Turkey and Viet Nam, resulting in 393 deaths. Two further general subtypes of avian influenza—H7 and H9—have also been reported in humans. In April 2013 WHO and the Chinese authorities deployed a joint mission to investigate and make recommendations concerning the control of an outbreak of H7N9 in humans that had emerged in February in China. By the end of June 2014 450 cases of H7N9 in humans had been reported to WHO. These were mainly concentrated in two waves, occurring during February–May 2013, and from October of that year onwards, and had resulted in 165 fatalities.

WHO works with animal health sector partners at the human–animal interface at national level to identify and reduce animal health and public health risks, with a strong focus on pigs, as they can become infected with influenza viruses from a variety of different hosts (including birds and humans), and can act as a 'mixing vessel', generating new reassortant viruses that, it is feared, may spread easily among humans. In the context of avian influenza, WHO in August 2013 initiated a so-called 'Four-Way Linking Project' in H5N1-endemic countries to assess health risks arising at the human–animal interface, as a means of supporting effective national disease control measures; it was envisaged that the project might subsequently be adapted to address other priority zoonotic diseases.

In 1988 the WHA launched the Global Polio Eradication Initiative (GPEI), which aimed, initially, to eradicate poliomyelitis by the end of 2000; this target was subsequently extended to the end of 2018. Co-ordinated periods of Supplementary Immunization Activity (SIA, facilitated in conflict zones by the negotiation of so-called days of tranquility), including National Immunization Days (NIDs), Sub-National Immunization Days (SNIDs), mop-up campaigns, VitA campaigns (Vitamin A is administered in order to reduce nutritional deficiencies in children and thereby boost their immunity), and Follow up/Catch up campaigns, have been employed in combating the disease, alongside the strengthening of routine immunization services. Since the inauguration of the GPEI WHO has declared the following regions 'polio-free': the Americas (1994); Western Pacific (2000); and Europe (2002). Furthermore, type 2 wild poliovirus has been eradicated globally (since 1999), although a type 2 circulating vaccine-derived poliovirus (cVDPV) was reported to be active in northern Nigeria during 2006–early 2010. In January 2004 ministers responsible for health of affected countries, and global partners, meeting under the auspices of WHO and UNICEF, adopted the Geneva Declaration on the Eradication of Poliomyelitis, in which they made a commitment to accelerate the drive towards eradication of the disease, by improving the scope of vaccination programmes. In February 2007 the GPEI launched an intensified eradication effort aimed at identifying and addressing the outstanding operational, technical and financial barriers to eradication. The May 2008 WHA adopted a resolution urging all remaining polio-affected member states to achieve the vaccination of every child. In April 2013, acting upon a request made in May 2012 by the 65th WHA, the GPEI issued a new Polio Eradication and Endgame Strategic Plan covering the period 2013–18. Under the Plan countries were urged to ensure the administration of at least one dose of inactivated poliovirus vaccine (IPV), and—with a view to eliminating the risk of vaccine-associated polio outbreaks—to begin the phased removal of oral polio vaccines. In November 2013 the GAVI Alliance determined to add IPV to its routine immunisation programme, in support of the Plan. During 2013 416 polio cases were confirmed worldwide, of which 160 were in the then three polio-endemic countries (Pakistan, 93 cases, Nigeria, 53 cases, and Afghanistan, 14 cases), and 256 cases were recorded in non-endemic countries (Somalia, 194 cases, Syria, 34, Kenya, 14, Ethiopia, nine, and Cameroon, four). (In 1988, by comparison, 35,000 cases had been confirmed in 125 countries, with the actual number of cases estimated at around 350,000.) In March 2014 the WHO South-East Asia region was certified by an independent commission to be polio-free. However, an increase in the spread of wild poliovirus occurred from early 2014, with Cameroon, Equatorial Guinea, Pakistan and Syria all reported to be exporting the virus. Consequently, in May 2014 WHO declared the ongoing spread of wild

poliovirus to be a Public Health Emergency of International Concern. (This decision was extended from 3 August.) The countries that were exporting wild poliovirus were to ensure that all residents and long-term visitors (of over 4 weeks) receive a dose of oral polio vaccine or inactivated poliovirus vaccine prior to international travel, and to provide such travellers with proof of vaccination.

The Onchocerciasis Elimination Programme in the Americas (OEPA), launched in 1992, co-ordinates work to control the disease in six Latin American countries where it is endemic. South American trypanosomiasis ('Chagas disease') is endemic in Central and South America, causing the deaths of some 45,000 people each year and infecting a further 16m.–18m. A regional intergovernmental commission is implementing a programme to eliminate Chagas from the Southern Cone region of Latin America. In July 2007, to combat the expansion of Chagas disease into some European countries, the Western Pacific, and the USA, as well as the re-emergence of the disease in areas such as the Chaco, in Argentina and Bolivia, where it was thought to have been eradicated, WHO established a Global Network for Chagas Disease Elimination.

WHO is committed to the elimination of leprosy. The use of a highly effective combination of three drugs (known as multi drug therapy—MDT) resulted in a reduction in the number of leprosy cases worldwide from 10m.–12m. in 1988 to 181,941 registered cases in January 2012. In 2013 leprosy remained endemic in parts of Brazil, Indonesia, Philippines, Democratic Republic of the Congo, India, Madagascar, Mozambique, Nepal and Tanzania. The Global Alliance for the Elimination of Leprosy was launched in November 1999 by WHO, in collaboration with governments of affected countries and several private partners, to support the eradication of the disease through the provision of free MDT treatment; WHO's Enhanced Global Strategy for Further Reducing the Disease Burden Due to Leprosy was being implemented during 2011–15 through national programmes in the remaining endemic countries, with the aim of reducing the global rate of new leprosy cases with Grade 2 (visible) disabilities per 100,000 of the population by at least 35% by end-2015, compared with the situation in 2010. In 1998 WHO launched the Global Buruli Ulcer Initiative, which aimed to co-ordinate control of and research into Buruli ulcer, another mycobacterial disease. In July of that year the Director-General of WHO and representatives of more than 20 countries, meeting in Yamoussoukro, Côte d'Ivoire, signed a declaration on the control of Buruli ulcer; a further declaration was signed in March 2009 by WHO's Regional Director for Africa, representatives of affected countries, and other stakeholders.

The objective of providing immunization for all children by 1990 was adopted by the WHA in 1977. Six diseases (measles, whooping cough, tetanus, poliomyelitis, tuberculosis and diphtheria) became the target of the Expanded Programme on Immunization (EPI), in which WHO, UNICEF and many other organizations collaborated. As a result of massive international and national efforts, the global immunization coverage increased from 20% in the early 1980s to the targeted rate of 80% by the end of 1990, and stood at 83% at the end of 2011. WHO's Strategic Advisory Group of Experts (SAGE) on Immunization was established in 1999 to guide the Organization on vaccines and immunization for all age groups, including on formulating global policies and strategies relating to technology; research and development; the delivery of immunization; and its linkages with other health interventions. In 2006 WHO, UNICEF and other partners launched the Global Immunization Vision and Strategy (GIVS), a global 10-year framework, covering 2006–15, aimed at increasing national vaccination coverage levels, for all ages, to at least 90% by 2015. In May 2012 the 65th WHA endorsed a Global Vaccine Action Plan (GVAP), building on the GIVS, which aimed to facilitate more equitable access to vaccines by 2020.

In recent years WHO has been concerned with the problem of Antimicrobial Resistance (AMR): the spread of infections caused by micro-organisms (including bacteria, viruses and certain parasites)—'super-pathogens'—that are resistant to conventional treatments (antibiotics, antivirals and antimalarials), such as multidrug-resistant TB, multidrug- and cephalosporin-resistant gonorrhea, and hospital-acquired infections such as methicillin-resistant Staphylococcus Aureus (MRSA). First-line medicines are increasingly failing, with second-line agents proving generally more costly, more toxic, and less effective, causing WHO to warn of the imminent advent of a post-antibiotic era. In 2011 WHO issued a six-point policy package on AMR, and in September 2013 a Strategic and Technical Advisory Group was established, to advise WHO on its co-ordination role in combating AMR, and to help develop a Global Action Plan on AMR; it was envisaged that the Plan would be presented in May 2015 to the 68th WHA for approval. The Plan was to address contributory factors to the spread of AMR, such as over-prescribing (caused by the vested commercial interests of some private providers), the use of antimicrobials in livestock reared for human consumption, weak national drug policies and regulatory agencies in many developing countries, and the commonplace open-market purchase of non-prescribed antimicrobial medicines in some countries. In April 2014 WHO issued a report entitled *Antimicrobial resistance: global report on surveillance*, which focused on antibiotic resistance in seven bacteria responsible for common, serious diseases, including bloodstream infections, diarrhoea, gonorrhoea, pneumonia, and urinary tract infections; the report found evidence of resistance to 'last resort' antibiotics throughout all regions of the world, and of insufficient monitoring systems.

In mid-2012 WHO released a Global Action Plan to Control the Spread and Impact of AMR in Neisseria Gonorrhoeae (gonorrhoea, of which an estimated 106m. new cases emerge annually). The first incidence of an untreatable strain of gonorrhoea, known as H041, was recorded in 2009, in Japan, and that variant was subsequently reported in Australia and Europe.

Joint UN Programme on HIV/AIDS (UNAIDS): 20 ave Appia, 1211 Geneva 27, Switzerland; tel. 227913666; fax 227914187; e-mail communications@unaids.org; internet www.unaids.org; f. 1996 to lead, strengthen and support an expanded response to the global HIV/AIDS pandemic; activities focus on prevention, care and support, reducing vulnerability to infection, and alleviating the socio-economic and human effects of HIV/AIDS; launched the Global Coalition on Women and AIDS in Feb. 2004; guided by UN Security Council Resolution 1308, focusing on the possible impact of AIDS on social instability and emergency situations, and the potential impact of HIV on the health of international peacekeeping personnel; by the MDGs adopted in Sept. 2000; by the Declaration of Commitment on HIV/AIDS agreed in June 2001 by the first Special Session of the UN General Assembly on HIV/AIDS, which acknowledged the AIDS epidemic as a 'global emergency'; and the Political Declaration on HIV/AIDS, adopted by the June 2006 UN General Assembly High Level Meeting on AIDS; in Nov. 2012 UNAIDS appointed Aung San Suu Kyi as Global Advocate for Zero Discrimination; in Dec. 2013 a fourth international replenishment meeting secured funding of US $12,000m. for the three-year period 2014–16; co-sponsors: WHO, UN Women, UNICEF, UNDP, UNFPA, UNODC, the ILO, UNESCO, the World Bank, WFP, UNHCR; Exec. Dir MICHEL SIDIBÉ (Mali).

NON-COMMUNICABLE DISEASES AND MENTAL HEALTH

WHO's activities in the area of non-communicable diseases (NCDs) and mental health aim—through health promotion and risk reduction, prevention, treatment and monitoring of NCDs and their risk factors—to reduce the burden of heart disease, cancer, lung disease, diabetes, mental disorders, disability, and injuries. The surveillance, prevention and management of NCDs, tobacco, and mental health are organization-wide priorities. Tobacco use, unhealthy diet and physical inactivity are regarded as common, preventable risk factors for the four most prominent NCDs, i.e. cardiovascular diseases, cancer, chronic respiratory disease and diabetes. It is estimated that these NCDs are collectively responsible for an estimated 35m. deaths—60% of all deaths—globally each year, and that up to 80% of cases of heart disease, stroke and type 2 diabetes, and more than one-third of cancers, could be prevented by eliminating shared risk factors, the main ones being tobacco use, unhealthy diet, physical inactivity and harmful use of alcohol. WHO aims to monitor the global epidemiological situation of NCDs, to co-ordinate multinational research activities concerned with prevention and care, and to analyse determining factors such as gender and poverty. In May 2013 the 66th WHA endorsed a Global Action Plan for 2013–20 for the Prevention and Control of NCDs, incorporating nine targets for reducing the impact of NCDs, as well as a monitoring framework. In July 2013 the UN Economic and Social Council adopted a resolution requesting the UN Secretary-General to establish an inter-agency UN Task Force on the Prevention and Control of NCDs. The Task Force, convened and led by WHO, held its inaugural meeting in October, and was to support the implementation of the 1999 WHO Framework Convention on Tobacco Control (q.v.) and also to co-ordinate the activities of all UN organizations in implementing the Global Action Plan for 2013–20 for the Prevention and Control of NCDs. In May 2014 the 67th WHA approved a set of nine indicators aimed at measuring progress in implementing the 2013–20 Global Action Plan.

In May 2004 the WHA endorsed a Global Strategy on Diet, Physical Activity and Health; it is estimated that more than 1,000m. adults worldwide are overweight, and of these some 300m. are clinically obese, carrying a raised risk of contracting chronic diseases. WHO has studied obesity-related issues in co-operation with the International Association for the Study of Obesity (IASO). The International Task Force on Obesity, affiliated to the IASO, aims to encourage the development of new policies for managing obesity. In May 2014 the WHO Director-General tasked a newly-established high-level Commission on Ending Childhood Obesity with compiling a report detailing the most effective interventions for combating childhood obesity in various contexts worldwide; this was to be presented to the 68th WHA in May 2015.

In March 2014, with a view to reducing levels of obesity and dental decay, WHO launched a public consultation on a draft update to its most recent (2002) guideline on the intake of sugars. Under the new proposed guideline—which stressed the often hidden presence of sugars in processed foods—monosaccharides (including glucose and fructose), disaccharides (such as sucrose or table sugar), and naturally present sugars (for example in honey and fruit juices) should provide less than 10% of total energy intake per day, while the benefits were emphasized of a reduction to below 5% of daily energy intake.

WHO's programmes for diabetes mellitus, chronic rheumatic diseases and asthma assist with the development of national initiatives, based upon goals and targets for the improvement of early detection, care and reduction of long-term complications. WHO's cardiovascular diseases programme aims to prevent and control the major cardiovascular diseases, which are responsible for more than 14m. deaths each year. It is estimated that one-third of these deaths could have been prevented with existing scientific knowledge.

The Cancer Control is Programme is concerned with the prevention of cancer, improving its early detection and treatment, and ensuring care of all cancer patients in need. In May 2009 WHO and the International Atomic Energy Agency launched a Joint Programme on Cancer Control, aimed at enhancing efforts to fight cancer in the developing world. Inter-agency collaboration on combating cancer was intensified following the Political Declaration on the Prevention and Control of NCDs made in September 2011 by a High-level Meeting of the UN General Assembly. WHO is a co-sponsor of the Global Day Against Pain, which is held annually on 11 October to highlight the need for improved pain management and palliative care for sufferers of diseases such as cancer and AIDS, with a particular focus on patients living in low-income countries with minimal access to opioid analgesics, and to promote recognition of access to pain relief as a basic human right.

In April 2014 WHO issued its first guidelines on the treatment of chronic Hepatitis C infections, with a view to reducing the number of deaths globally (estimated at up to 500,000 annually) from Hepatitis C-related cirrhosis and cancer of the liver.

The WHO Human Genetics Programme manages genetic approaches for the prevention and control of common hereditary diseases and of those with a genetic predisposition representing a major health factor. The Programme also concentrates on the further development of genetic approaches suitable for incorporation into health care systems, as well as developing a network of international collaborating programmes.

WHO's health promotion division promotes decentralized and community-based health programmes and is concerned with developing new approaches to population ageing and encouraging healthy lifestyles and self-care. It also seeks to relieve the negative impact of social changes such as urbanization, migration and changes in family structure upon health. Several health promotion projects have been undertaken, in collaboration between WHO regional and country offices and other relevant organizations, including the Global School Health Initiative, to bridge the sectors of health and education and to promote the health of school-age children; the Global Strategy for Occupational Health, to promote the health of the working population and the control of occupational health risks; Community-based Rehabilitation, aimed at providing a more enabling environment for people with disabilities; and a communication strategy to provide training and support for health communications personnel and initiatives. In 2000 WHO, UNESCO, the World Bank and UNICEF adopted the joint Focusing Resources for Effective School Health (FRESH Start) approach to promoting life skills among adolescents.

WHO supports the UN Convention, and its Optional Protocol, on the Rights of Persons with Disabilities, which came into force in May 2008, and seeks to address challenges that prevent the full participation of people with disabilities in the social, economic and cultural lives of their communities and societies; at that time the WHO Director-General appointed a Taskforce on Disability to ensure that WHO was reflecting the provisions of the Convention in its programme of work. In December 2011 WHO and the World Bank jointly released the first *World Report on Disability*, focusing on the areas of health care, rehabilitation, education, employment and support services, and detailing a number of recommendations for governments aimed at creating environments that would enable people with disabilities to flourish. The WHO Disability Assessment Schedule, introduced in November 2012, measures health and disability across six areas: cognition (understanding and communicating); mobility; self-care (hygiene, dressing, eating and coping alone); interaction with other people; life activities (including domestic responsibilities, leisure, education and work); and participation in community life. In May 2013 the 66th WHA adopted a resolution urging member states to develop national action plans for the implementation of the Convention on the Rights of Persons with Disabilities.

In February 1999 WHO initiated the programme, 'Vision 2020: the Right to Sight', which aimed to eliminate avoidable blindness (estimated to be as much as 80% of all cases) by 2020. Blindness was otherwise predicted to increase by as much as two-fold, owing to the increased longevity of the global population. In May 2013 the 66th WHA endorsed a Global Action Plan, covering 2014–19, that focused on improving eye health, reducing avoidable visual impairment, and securing access to rehabilitation services.

In 2012 WHO estimated that tobacco would lead to more than 8m. deaths annually by 2030 (through lung cancer, heart disease, chronic bronchitis and other effects). The Tobacco or Health Programme aims to reduce the use of tobacco, by educating tobacco-users and preventing young people from adopting the habit. In May 1999 the WHA endorsed the formulation of a Framework Convention on Tobacco Control (FCTC) to help to combat the increase in tobacco use (although a number of tobacco growers expressed concerns about the effect of the convention on their livelihoods). The FCTC entered into force in February 2005. In 2008 WHO published a comprehensive analysis of global tobacco use and control, the *WHO Report on the Global Tobacco Epidemic*, which designated abuse of tobacco as one of the principal global threats to health, and predicted that during the latter part of the 21st century the vast majority of tobacco-related deaths would occur in developing countries. The report identified and condemned a tobacco industry strategy to target young people and adults in the developing world, and detailed six key proven strategies, collectively known as the 'MPOWER package', aimed at combating global tobacco use: monitoring tobacco use and implementing prevention policies; protecting people from tobacco smoke; offering support to people to enable them to give up tobacco use; warning about the dangers of tobacco; enforcing bans on tobacco advertising, promotion and sponsorship; and raising taxes on tobacco. The MPOWER package supports countries in building on their obligations under the FCTC. The FCTC obligates its states parties to require 'health warnings describing the harmful effects of tobacco use' to appear on packs of tobacco and their outside packaging, and recommends the use of warnings that contain pictures. WHO provides technical and other assistance to countries to support them in meeting this obligation through the Tobacco Free Initiative. WHO encourages governments to adopt tobacco health warnings meeting the agreed criteria for maximum effectiveness in convincing consumers not to smoke. In November 2012 the fifth Conference of the Parties to the FCTC adopted a Protocol to Eliminate Illicit Trade in Tobacco Products. This was opened for signature in January 2013 and required ratification by 40 member states to enter into force.

WHO defines mental health as a 'state of well-being in which every individual realizes his or her own potential, can cope with the normal stresses of life, can work productively and fruitfully, and is able to make a contribution to her or his community'. WHO's Mental Health Programme is concerned with mental health problems that include unipolar and bipolar affective disorders, psychosis, epilepsy, dementia, Parkinson's disease, multiple sclerosis, drug and alcohol dependency, and neuropsychiatric disorders such as post-traumatic stress disorder, obsessive compulsive disorder and panic disorder. WHO aims to increase awareness of mental health issues and promote improved mental health services and primary care. In October 2008 WHO launched the so-called mental health Gap Action Programme (mhGAP), which aimed to improve services addressing mental, neurological and substance use disorders, with a special focus on low and middle income countries. A main focus of mhGAP concerns forging strategic partnerships to enhance countries' capacity to combat stigma commonly associated with mental illness, reduce the burden of mental disorders, and promote mental health. In August 2013 WHO extended mhGAP to incorporate new clinical protocols and guidelines aimed at supporting health care workers in treating post-traumatic stress disorder. In May of that year the 66th WHA adopted a Mental Health Action Plan covering the period 2013–20, with the objectives of strengthening effective mental health leadership and governance; providing comprehensive, integrated and responsive mental health and social care services in community-based settings; implementing strategies for mental health prevention and promotion; and strengthening information systems, evidence and research. In December 2013 WHO launched MiNDbank, an online platform consolidating international resources and national legislation, policies, and service standards relating to mental health, substance abuse, disability, human rights, general health and development. WHO is a joint partner in the Global Campaign against Epilepsy: Out of the Shadows, which aims to advance understanding, treatment, services and prevention of epilepsy worldwide.

The Substance Abuse Programme addresses the misuse of all psychoactive substances, irrespective of legal status. WHO provides technical support to assist countries in formulating policies with regard to the prevention and reduction of the health and social effects of psychoactive substance abuse, and undertakes epidemiological surveillance and risk assessment, advocacy and the dissemination of information, strengthening national and regional prevention and health promotion techniques and strategies, the development of cost-effective treatment and rehabilitation approaches, and also encompasses regulatory activities as required under the international drugs-control treaties in force. In May 2010 WHO endorsed a new global strategy to reduce the harmful use of alcohol; this promoted measures including taxation on alcohol, minimizing outlets selling alcohol, raising age limits for those buying alcohol, and the employment of effective measures to deter people from driving while under the influence of alcohol.

PROMOTING HEALTH THROUGH THE LIFE COURSE

WHO's aims to reduce morbidity and mortality and improve health during pregnancy, childbirth, the neonatal period, childhood and adolescence; to improve sexual and reproductive health; and to promote active and healthy ageing. Activities take into consideration the need to address the social and environmental determinants of health (a main priority of WHO), and internationally agreed development goals, in particular the health-related MDGs. In October 2011 WHO convened a global conference on the social determinants of health, in Rio de Janeiro, Brazil; the conference adopted the Rio Political Declaration on Social Determinants of Health, expressing commitment to reducing inequities in health and health care provision. The eighth Global Conference on Health Promotion, convened by WHO and the Finnish Government in June 2013, in Helsinki, Finland, issued the Helsinki Statement on Health in All Policies, aimed at promoting health in all levels of national policymaking.

WHO aims to improve access to sustainable health care for all by strengthening health systems and fostering individual, family and community development. Activities include newborn care; child health, including promoting and protecting the health and development of the child through such approaches as promotion of breastfeeding and use of the mother-baby package, as well as care of the sick child, including diarrhoeal and acute respiratory disease control, and support to women and children in difficult circumstances; the promotion of safe motherhood and maternal health; adolescent health, including the promotion and development of young people and the prevention of specific health problems; women, health and development, including addressing issues of gender, sexual violence, and harmful traditional practices; and human reproduction, including research related to contraceptive technologies and effective methods. In addition, WHO aims to provide technical leadership and co-ordination on reproductive health and to support countries in their efforts to ensure that people: experience healthy sexual development and maturation; have the capacity for healthy, equitable and responsible relationships; can achieve their reproductive intentions safely and healthily; avoid illnesses, diseases and injury related to sexuality and reproduction; and receive appropriate counselling, care and rehabilitation for diseases and conditions related to sexuality and reproduction.

WHO supports the Global Strategy for Women's and Children's Health, launched by heads of state and government participating in the September 2010 UN Summit on the MDGs; some US $40,000m. has been pledged towards women's and child's health and achieving goals (iv) Reducing Child Mortality and (v) Improving Maternal Health. In May 2012 the WHA adopted a resolution on raising awareness of early marriage (entered into by more than 30% of women in developing countries) and adolescent pregnancy, and the consequences thereof for young women and infants.

In September 1997 WHO, in collaboration with UNICEF, formally launched a programme advocating the Integrated Management of Childhood Illness (IMCI). IMCI recognizes that pneumonia, diarrhoea, measles, malaria and malnutrition cause some 70% of the approximately 11m. childhood deaths each year. WHO encourages national programmes aimed at reducing childhood deaths as a result of diarrhoea, particularly through the use of oral rehydration therapy and preventive measures. In November 2009 WHO and UNICEF launched a Global Action Plan for the Prevention and Control of Pneumonia. In April 2013 WHO and UNICEF launched a new Integrated Global Action Plan for the Prevention and Control of Pneumonia and Diarrhoea, focusing on interventions such as improved nutrition and maintaining a clean environment to protect children from contracting both diseases. Accelerated efforts by WHO to promote vaccination against measles through its Measles Initiative (subsequently renamed the Measles and Rubella Initiative), established in 2001, contributed to a three-quarters' reduction in global mortality from that disease during the period 2000–10. In April 2012 WHO and other partners launched a global strategy that aimed to eliminate measles deaths and congenital rubella syndrome.

WHO seeks to monitor the advantages and disadvantages for health, nutrition, environment and development arising from the process of globalization; to integrate the issue of health into poverty reduction programmes; and to promote human rights and equality. WHO collaborates with FAO, WFP, UNICEF and other UN agencies in pursuing its objectives relating to nutrition and food safety. It has been estimated that 780m. people worldwide cannot meet basic needs for energy and protein, more than 2,000m. people lack essential vitamins and minerals, and that 170m. children are malnourished. In December 1992 WHO and FAO hosted an international conference on nutrition, at which a World Declaration and Plan of Action on Nutrition was adopted to make the fight against malnutrition a development priority. WHO aims to support the enhancement of member states' capabilities in dealing with their nutrition situations, and addressing scientific issues related to preventing, managing and monitoring protein-energy malnutrition; micronutrient malnutrition, including iodine deficiency disorders, vitamin A deficiency, and nutritional anaemia; and diet-related conditions and NCDs such as obesity (increasingly affecting children, adolescents and adults, mainly in industrialized countries), cancer and heart disease. In 1990 the WHA resolved to eliminate iodine deficiency (believed to cause mental retardation); a strategy of universal salt iodization was launched in 1993. In collaboration with other international agencies, WHO is implementing a comprehensive strategy for promoting appropriate infant, young child and maternal nutrition, and for dealing effectively with nutritional emergencies in large populations. Areas of emphasis include promoting health care practices that enhance successful breastfeeding; appropriate complementary feeding; refining the use and interpretation of body measurements for assessing nutritional status; relevant information, education and training; and action to give effect to the International Code of Marketing of Breast-milk Substitutes. (WHO reported in July 2013 that only 37 countries worldwide had adopted legislation reflecting all the recommendations of the International Code.) In May 2014 the 67th WHA approved a global monitoring framework on maternal, infant and young child nutrition. The food safety programme aims to protect human health against risks associated with biological and chemical contaminants and additives in food. With FAO, WHO establishes food standards (through the work of the Codex Alimentarius Commission and its subsidiary committees) and evaluates food additives, pesticide residues and other contaminants and their implications for health. The programme provides expert advice on such issues as food-borne diseases and pathogens (e.g. bovine spongiform encephalopathy, campylobacter, escherichia coli, listeria, and salmonella), production methods (e.g. aquaculture) and food biotechnology (e.g. genetic modification). WHO also addresses the methods of producing, processing and preparing foods that contribute to the incidence (especially in parts of East and South-East Asia and Latin America) of foodborne trematode infections (parasitic infections caused by flatworms). WHO's Global Foodborne Infections Network (GNP), established in 2001, and currently guided by a strategic plan covering 2011–15, promotes integrated laboratory-based surveillance and intersectoral collaboration among human health, veterinary and food-related entitities. In July 2001 the Codex Alimentarius Commission adopted the first global principles for assessing the safety of genetically modified (GM) foods. In March 2002 an intergovernmental task force established by the Commission finalized 'principles for the risk analysis of foods derived from biotechnology', which were to provide a framework for assessing the safety of GM foods and plants. A Codex Trust Fund, initiated in 2003, assists the efficient participation of developing countries in the work of the Commission. WHO supports, with other UN agencies, governments, research institutions, and representatives of civil society and of the private sector, the initiative on Scaling up Nutrition (SUN), which was initiated in 2009, under the co-ordination of the UN Secretary-General's Special Representative for Food Security and Nutrition, with the aim of increasing the coverage of interventions that improve nutrition during the first 1,000 days of a child's life (such as exclusive breastfeeding, optimal complementary feeding practices, and provision of essential vitamins and minerals); and ensuring that nutrition plans are implemented at national level, and that government programmes take nutrition into account. The activities of SUN are guided by the Framework for Scaling up Nutrition, which was published in April 2010, and by the SUN Roadmap, finalized in September 2010.

In November 2014 WHO, FAO, WFP, and other partners, were to organize the Second International Conference on Nutrition (ICN2, ICN1 having been convened in December 1992), at FAO headquarters in Rome, Italy. ICN2, with participation by senior policy-makers in areas including agriculture and health, representatives of UN and other international agencies, and of civil society, was to review progress achieved since 1992 towards improving nutrition, and to consider future policy options in that area, taking into account advances in science and technology and changes to food systems.

WHO's programme area on environmental health undertakes a wide range of initiatives to tackle the increasing threats to health and well-being from a changing environment, especially in relation to air pollution, water quality, sanitation, protection against radiation, management of hazardous waste, chemical safety and housing hygiene. In October 2013 WHO's subsidiary International Agency for Research on Cancer formally classified outdoor air pollution as carcinogenic to humans, having concluded that there is sufficient evidence to link exposure to outdoor pollution with lung and also bladder cancer. Particulate matter within outdoor air pollution was evaluated separately and also classified as carcinogenic to humans. In April 2014 WHO reported that in 2012 exposure to air pollution (both outside and indoors) was the cause of some 7m. deaths worldwide, establishing air pollution as the largest single global environmental health risk. In addition to increased risk of cancer, raised susceptibility to cardiovascular diseases was attributed to air pollution. In May 2014 WHO announced findings of its database of ambient urban air pollution (monitoring levels of fine particulate matter in 1,600 cities in 91 countries) that demonstrated that in most cities globally the Organization's safety guidelines on air quality were not being met. WHO supports the Global Alliance against

Chronic Respiratory Diseases, established in March 2006. In 2012 it was estimated that some 783m. people worldwide had no access to clean drinking water, while a further 2,500m. people are denied suitable sanitation systems. WHO helped to launch the Water Supply and Sanitation Council in 1990 and regularly updates its *Guidelines for Drinking Water Quality*. In rural areas the emphasis continues to be on the provision and maintenance of safe and sufficient water supplies and adequate sanitation, the health aspects of rural housing, vector control in water resource management, and the safe use of agrochemicals. In urban areas assistance is provided to identify local environmental health priorities and to improve municipal governments' ability to deal with environmental conditions and health problems in an integrated manner; promotion of the 'Healthy City' approach is a major component of the programme. Other programme activities include environmental health information development and management, human resources development, environmental health planning methods, research and work on problems relating to global environment change, such as UV-radiation. The WHO Global Strategy for Health and Environment provides the framework for programme activities.

In July 2014 WHO, with the World Meteorological Office, established a joint office of climate and health to promote the development and use of climate services to enhance public health, including disease surveillance and emergency preparedness. WHO convened the first global conference on health and climate in late August, which concluded that climate change adversely affected the social and environmental determinants of health, thereby endangering human health, and substantially contributed to escalating health budgets.

WHO forecasts that by 2050 nearly 2,000m. people globally will be aged over 60 years. In June 2010 WHO launched the Global Network of Age-Friendly Cities, as part of a broader response to the ageing of populations worldwide. The Network aims to support cities in creating urban environments that would enable older people to remain active and healthy. The first International Conference on Age-Friendly Cities was convened in September 2011, in Dublin, Ireland; the second was held in Québec, Canada, in September 2013 on the theme 'Living and Aging Together in our Community'.

HEALTH SYSTEMS

WHO supports the strengthening of health systems, with a focus on the development of integrated quality service delivery; robust financing mechanisms; universal health coverage; strengthening well trained human resources for health; reliable health information systems; promoting access to and facilitating transfer of affordable, quality, safe, and efficacious health technologies; ensuring well maintained facilities and logistics to deliver quality medicines and technologies; and promoting health systems research. Through the generation and dissemination of evidence WHO aims to assist policymakers to assess health needs, choose intervention strategies, design policy and monitor performance, and thereby improve the performance of national health systems. International and national dialogue on health policy are also promoted. WHO appoints and administers the secretariat of the Alliance for Health Policy and Systems Research, initiated in 1999 with the aim of improving health and health systems in developing countries. In 2010 the Alliance broadened its core focus from the areas of human resources for health, health financing, and the role of non-state health actors (of particular concern in low-income and fragile states), to launch a project supporting new research and analysis on access to medicines. In May 2013 the WHA determined to establish an open-ended working group to address means of eliminating so-called Sub-standard/Spurious/Falsely-labelled/Falsified/Counterfeit (SSFFC) medical products.

The WHO International Clinical Trials Registry Platform, established in August 2005, links clinical trials worldwide (i.e. all research studies that assign human participants to health-related interventions, with a view to evaluating the health outcomes of these), and aims to ensure complete transparency of clinical research and its accessibility to all those involved in health care decision making.

WHO reports that 2m. children die each year of diseases for which common vaccines exist. A comprehensive survey, *State of the World's Vaccines and Immunization*, was published by WHO, jointly with UNICEF, in 1996; revised editions of the survey were issued in 2003 and 2010. In 1999 WHO, UNICEF, the World Bank and a number of public and private sector partners formed the Global Alliance for Vaccines and Immunization (GAVI), which aimed to expand the provision of existing vaccines and to accelerate the development and introduction of new vaccines and technologies, with the ultimate goal of protecting children of all nations and from all socio-economic backgrounds against vaccine-preventable diseases.

WHO co-ordinates the Health InterNetwork Access to Research Initiative (HINARI), which was launched in July 2001 to enable relevant authorities in developing countries to access biomedical journals through the internet at no or greatly reduced cost, in order to improve the worldwide circulation of scientific information; by 2014 around 13,000 journals and 28,800 e-books were being made available to health institutions in more than 100 countries. A virtual Healthy Academy provides eLearning courses, on topics such as HIV/AIDS; malaria; oral health; and safer food. The WHO e-Library of Evidence for Nutrition Actions (eLENA) provides evidence-informed guidelines and recommendations for nutrition interventions. WHO Patient Safety (launched in 2004 as the World Alliance on Patient Safety, and subsequently renamed) facilitates the development of patient safety policy and practice across all WHO member states. In May 2011 WHO launched a new internet-based Global Health Observatory, a repository of data on health topics, which also provides online access to WHO's annual *World Health Statistics*. In May 2013 the 66th WHA adopted a resolution on e-Health standardization and interoperability, noting the importance of health data in underpinning the efficient functioning of health systems and services, as well as the need to protect the security of such information and the privacy of personal clinical data.

PREPAREDNESS, SURVEILLANCE AND RESPONSE

WHO contributes to human security by working to support the preparedness, surveillance and effective response to disease outbreaks, acute public health emergencies, and the effective management of health-related aspects of humanitarian disasters. Within the UN system, WHO co-ordinates the international response to emergencies and natural disasters in the health field, in close co-operation with other agencies and within the framework set out by the Office for the Co-ordination of Humanitarian Affairs. In this context, WHO provides expert advice on epidemiological surveillance, control of communicable diseases, public health information and health emergency training. Its emergency preparedness activities include co-ordination, policy-making and planning, awareness-building, technical advice, training, publication of standards and guidelines, and research. Its emergency relief activities include organizational support, the provision of emergency drugs and supplies and conducting technical emergency assessment missions. WHO aims to strengthen the national capacity of member states to reduce the adverse health consequences of disasters, including conflict, natural disasters, food insecurity. In responding to emergency situations, WHO always tries to develop projects and activities that will assist the national authorities concerned in rebuilding or strengthening their own capacity to handle the impact of such situations. WHO appeals through the UN's inter-agency Consolidated Appeals Process (CAP) for funding for its emergency humanitarian operations.

Since the major terrorist attacks perpetrated against targets in the USA in September 2001, WHO has focused renewed attention on the potential malevolent use of bacteria (such as bacillus anthracis, which causes anthrax), viruses (for example, the variola virus, causing smallpox) or toxins, or of chemical agents, in acts of biological or chemical terrorism. In September 2001 WHO issued draft guidelines entitled 'Health Aspects of Biological and Chemical Weapons'. In March 2013 the UN Secretary-General announced that a mission comprising UN weapons experts, in co-operation with specialists from WHO and the Organisation for the Prohibition of Chemical Weapons, would initiate an investigation into the alleged misuse of chemical weapons by combatants in the ongoing conflict in Syria. In mid-September the mission issued a report on the alleged use on 21 August of chemical weapons against unarmed civilians in the rebel-held area of Ghouta, Damascus, causing significant injuries and fatalities, in which it found 'clear and convincing evidence' of the use of surface-to-surface rockets containing sarin gas, and that chemical weapons had been used on a relatively large scale generally during the Syrian conflict, including against children.

WHO's work in the promotion of chemical safety is undertaken in collaboration with the ILO and UNEP through the International Programme on Chemical Safety (IPCS), the Central Unit for which is located in WHO. The Programme provides internationally evaluated scientific information on chemicals, promotes the use of such infor-

mation in national programmes, assists member states in establishment of their own chemical safety measures and programmes, and helps them strengthen their capabilities in chemical emergency preparedness and response and in chemical risk reduction. WHO administers the Inter-organization Programme for the Social Management of Chemicals, established in 1995 jointly with UNEP, the ILO, FAO, WHO, the World Bank, the UN Industrial Development Organization (UNIDO) and OECD, in order to strengthen international co-operation in the field of chemical safety.

Through its International EMF Project WHO is compiling a comprehensive assessment of the potential adverse effects on human health deriving from exposure to electromagnetic fields (EMF). In May 2011 the International Agency for Research on Cancer, an agency of WHO, classified radiofrequency EMF as possibly carcinogenic to humans, on the basis of an increased risk of glioma (malignant brain cancer) associated with the use of wireless phones.

In March 2013 WHO and UNEP issued a joint report entitled *State of the Science of Endocrine Disrupting Chemicals*, which assessed the potential disrupting effects on the human hormone system and the environment of synthetic chemicals found in many household products.

Finance

WHO's regular budget is provided by assessment of member states and associate members. An additional fund for specific projects is provided by voluntary contributions from members and other sources, including UNDP and UNFPA.

A total programme budget of US $3,977m. was approved for the two years 2014–15, of which some 4.4%, or $176m., was provisionally allocated to the Americas.

Publications

Bulletin of WHO (monthly).

Eastern Mediterranean Health Journal (annually).

Global Tuberculosis Report.

International Classification of Diseases.

International Classification of Functioning, Disability and Health— ICF.

International Classification of Health Interventions.

International Pharmacopoeia.

International Travel and Health.

Model List of Essential Medicines (every 2 years).

Pan-American Journal of Public Health (annually).

Weekly Epidemiological Record.

Western Pacific Surveillance and Response.

WHO Drug Information (quarterly).

WHO South-East Asia Journal of Public Health.

World Health Statistics.

WHO Model Formulary.

WHO Report on the Global Tobacco Epidemic.

World Health Report (annually).

World Cancer Report (every 5–6 years).

World Malaria Report (annually, with UNICEF).

Technical report series; guidelines; catalogues of specific scientific, technical and medical fields available.

Other UN Organizations Active in the Region

OFFICE FOR THE CO-ORDINATION OF HUMANITARIAN AFFAIRS—OCHA

Address: United Nations Plaza, New York, NY 10017, USA.

Telephone: (212) 963-1234; **fax:** (212) 963-1312; **e-mail:** ochany@un.org; **internet:** unocha.org.

The Office was established in January 1998 as part of the UN Secretariat, with a mandate to co-ordinate international humanitarian assistance and to provide policy and other advice on humanitarian issues. It administers the Humanitarian Early Warning System, as well as Integrated Regional Information Networks

(IRIN), to monitor the situation in some 70 different countries, and a Disaster Response System. A complementary service, Reliefweb monitors crises and publishes information on the internet.

OCHA facilitates the inter-agency Consolidated Appeals Process (CAP), which aims to organize a co-ordinated response to resource mobilization following humanitarian crises. CAP appeals for 2014, seeking an estimated US $12,900m. (the largest ever total amount requested), were issued in December 2013, under OCHA's Overview of Global Humanitarian Response for 2014. They contained action plans relating to complex humanitarian crises affecting some 52m.

people worldwide, and involving more than 500 globally active humanitarian organizations.

Immediately following the earthquake that devastated Haiti in January 2010, with its epicentre just 17 km south of the capital, Port-au-Prince, OCHA launched an emergency appeal, initially for US $562m. (subsequently revised to $577m.). In February OCHA released a revised appeal, covering January–December 2010, which aimed to raise $1,400m. for assistance including providing shelter and sanitation in time for the start of the rainy season, removing rubble, camp management, supporting cash-for-work activities, restoring livelihoods and economic activities, assisting people with earthquake-related disabilities, and addressing protection concerns, with a particular focus on preventing sexual violence in temporary settlements. Subsequently OCHA has supported the national authorities to implement sustainable housing solutions, the provision of basic services and an effective response to a country-wide cholera epidemic. Under the CAP process for 2014 some US $169m. was requested to fund humanitarian operations in Haiti that were to assist 396,000 people.

Under-Secretary-General for Humanitarian Affairs and Emergency Relief Co-ordinator: VALERIE AMOS (United Kingdom).

UNITED NATIONS OFFICE FOR DISASTER RISK REDUCTION—UNISDR

Address: International Environment House II, 7–9 chemin de Balexert, 1219 Châtelaine, Geneva 10, Switzerland.

Telephone: 229178908; **fax:** 229178964; **e-mail:** isdr@un.org; **internet:** www.unisdr.org.

UNISDR was established by the UN General Assembly as the inter-agency secretariat of the International Strategy for Disaster Reduction (ISDR), adopted by UN member states in 2000 as a strategic framework aimed at guiding and co-ordinating international efforts towards achieving substantive reduction in disaster losses, and building resilient communities and nations as the foundation for sustainable development activities. UNISDR promotes information sharing to reduce disaster risk, and serves as the focal point providing guidance for the implementation of the Hyogo Framework for Action (HFA), adopted in 2005 as a 10-year plan of action for protecting lives and livelihoods against disasters. It also organizes the biennial sessions of the Global Platform for Disaster Risk Reduction (fourth session: held in May 2013, in Geneva).

In early 2012 UNISDR initiated consultations on formulating a blueprint on a post-2015 diaster risk reduction framework in advance of the third World Conference on Disaster Reduction that was scheduled to be held in March 2015, in Sendai City, Japan. The first meeting of an intergovernmental preparatory committee on the conference took place in July 2014. In 2013 UNISDR co-led the global consultations on addressing conflict and fragility in the post-2015 development framework.

UNISDR implements a 'Making Cities Resilient' campaign in view in increasing urbanization worldwide.

Special Representative of the UN Secretary-General for Disaster Risk Reduction: MARGARETA WAHLSTRÖM.

UN WOMEN—UNITED NATIONS ENTITY FOR GENDER EQUALITY AND THE EMPOWERMENT OF WOMEN

Address: 304 East 45th St, 15th Floor, New York, NY 10017, USA.
Telephone: (212) 906-6400; **fax:** (212) 906-6705; **internet:** www.unwomen.org.

UN Women was established by the UN General Assembly in July 2010 in order to strengthen the UN's capacity to promote gender equality, the empowerment of women, and the elimination of discrimination against women and girls. It commenced operations on 1 January 2011, incorporating the functions of the Office of the Special Adviser on Gender Issues and Advancement of Women, the Division for the Advancement of Women of the Secretariat, the United Nations Development Fund for Women (UNIFEM) and the International Research and Training Institute for the Advancement of Women (INSTRAW).

A UN Women Civil Society Regional Advisory Group for Latin America and the Caribbean was established in May 2012.

Executive Director: PHUMZILE MLAMBO-NGCUKA (South Africa).

Regional Director for Latin America and the Caribbean: MONI PIZANI.

UNITED NATIONS OFFICE FOR DISARMAMENT AFFAIRS—UNODA

Address: UN Plaza, Rm S-3185, New York, NY 10017, USA.
Fax: (212) 963-4066; **e-mail:** UNODA-web@un.org; **internet:** www.un.org/disarmament.

UNODA—established in 1982 as the UN Department for Disarmament Affairs, with its current name adopted in 2007—works to promote nuclear disarmament and non-proliferation; to strengthen disarmament regimes with regard to biological and chemical weapons and other weapons of mass destruction; and to support disarmament activities relating to conventional weapons, with a particular focus on landmines and small arms. UNODA maintains subsidiary offices in Geneva, Switzerland; Kathmandu, Nepal; Lima, Peru; Lomé, Togo; and Vienna, Austria.

Under-Secretary-General and High Representative for Disarmament Affairs: ANGELA KANE (Germany).

United Nations Regional Centre for Peace, Disarmament and Development in Latin America and the Caribbean: Avda Pérez Araníbar 750, Magdalena del Mar, Lima, Peru; tel. (1) 6259000; e-mail officeofthedirector@unlirec.org.

UNITED NATIONS OFFICE ON DRUGS AND CRIME—UNODC

Address: Vienna International Centre, POB 500, 1400 Vienna, Austria.

Telephone: (1) 26060-0; **fax:** (1) 26060-5866; **e-mail:** unodc@unodc.org; **internet:** www.unodc.org.

The Office was established in November 1997 (as the UN Office of Drug Control and Crime Prevention) to strengthen the UN's integrated approach to issues relating to drug control, crime prevention and international terrorism.

Executive Director: YURI FEDOTOV (Russia).

OFFICE OF THE UNITED NATIONS HIGH COMMISSIONER FOR HUMAN RIGHTS—OHCHR

Address: Palais Wilson, 52 rue de Paquis, 1201 Geneva, Switzerland.

Telephone: 229179290; **fax:** 229179022; **e-mail:** infodesk@ohchr.org; **internet:** www.ohchr.org.

The Office is a body of the UN Secretariat and is the focal point for UN human-rights activities. Since September 1997 it has incorporated the Centre for Human Rights. The High Commissioner is the UN official with principal responsibility for UN human rights activities.

At July 2014 OHCHR was concerned with 37 thematic mandates, and with 14 country mandates, including for Haiti (mandate established in 1995; and most recently extended in 2014).

High Commissioner: Prince ZEID RA'AD ZEID AL-HUSSEIN (Jordan).

UNITED NATIONS HUMAN SETTLEMENTS PROGRAMME—UN-HABITAT

Address: POB 30030, Nairobi, Kenya.

Telephone: (20) 621234; **fax:** (20) 624266; **e-mail:** infohabitat@unhabitat.org; **internet:** www.unhabitat.org.

UN-Habitat was established, as the United Nations Centre for Human Settlements, in October 1978 to service the intergovernmental Commission on Human Settlements. It became a full UN programme on 1 January 2002, serving as the focus for human settlements activities in the UN system.

Executive Director: JOAN CLOS (Spain).

Regional Office for Latin America and the Caribbean: Rua Rumânia 20, Cosme Velho 22240-140, Rio de Janeiro, Brazil; tel. (21) 3235-8550; fax (21) 3235-8566; e-mail rolac@habitat-lac.org; internet www.onuhabitat.org.

UNITED NATIONS CHILDREN'S FUND—UNICEF

Address: 3 United Nations Plaza, New York, NY 10017, USA.

Telephone: (212) 326-7000; **fax:** (212) 888-7465; **e-mail:** info@unicef.org; **internet:** www.unicef.org.

UNICEF was established in 1946 by the UN General Assembly as the UN International Children's Emergency Fund, to meet the emergency needs of children in post-war Europe and China. In 1950 its mandate was changed to emphasize programmes giving long-term benefits to children everywhere, particularly those in developing countries who are in the greatest need.

UNICEF's annual publication *The State of the World's Children* includes social and economic data relevant to the well-being of children.

Executive Director: ANTHONY LAKE (USA).

Regional Office for the Americas and the Caribbean: Apdo 0843-03045, Panamá, Panama; tel. (507) 301-7400; e-mail thahn@unicef.org; internet www.uniceflac.org.

UNITED NATIONS CONFERENCE ON TRADE AND DEVELOPMENT—UNCTAD

Address: Palais des Nations, 1211 Geneva 10, Switzerland.

Telephone: 229171234; **fax:** 229070057; **e-mail:** info@unctad.org; **internet:** www.unctad.org.

UNCTAD was established in 1964. It is the principal organ of the UN General Assembly concerned with trade and development, and is the focal point within the UN system for integrated activities relating to trade, finance, technology, investment and sustainable development. It aims to maximize the trade and development opportunities of developing countries, in particular least-developed countries, and to assist them to adapt to the increasing globalization and liberalization of the world economy. UNCTAD undertakes consensus-building activities, research and policy analysis and technical co-operation.

Secretary-General: MUKHISA KITUYI (Kenya).

UNITED NATIONS POPULATION FUND—UNFPA

Address: 605 Third Ave, New York, NY 10158, USA.

Telephone: (212) 297-5000; **fax:** (212) 370-0201; **e-mail:** hq@unfpa .org; **internet:** www.unfpa.org.

Created in 1967 as the Trust Fund for Population Activities, the UN Fund for Population Activities (UNFPA) was established as a Fund of the UN General Assembly in 1972 and was made a subsidiary organ of the UN General Assembly in 1979, with the UNDP Governing Council (now the Executive Board) designated as its governing body. In 1987 UNFPA's name was changed to the United Nations Population Fund (retaining the same acronym).

Executive Director: BABATUNDE OSOTIMEHIN (Nigeria).

Regional Office for Latin America and the Caribbean: Edif. Clayton 102, Ave Morse, Ciudad del Saber, Panamá, Panama; tel. (507) 301-7366; fax (507) 317-0258; e-mail lacro@unfpa.org; a subregional office, serving the Caribbean, is located in Jamaica.

UN Specialized Agencies

INTERNATIONAL ATOMIC ENERGY AGENCY—IAEA

Address: POB 100, Wagramerstrasse 5, 1400 Vienna, Austria.

Telephone: (1) 26000; **fax:** (1) 26007; **e-mail:** official.mail@iaea.org; **internet:** www.iaea.org.

The Agency was founded in 1957 as an autonomous intergovernmental organization, although it is administratively part of the UN system and reports annually to the UN General Assembly. Its main objectives are to enlarge the contribution of atomic energy to peace, health and prosperity throughout the world, and to ensure that materials and services provided by the Agency are not used to further any military purpose.

Several regional nuclear weapons treaties require their member states to conclude CSAs with the IAEA, including the Treaty for the Prohibition of Nuclear Weapons in Latin America (Tlatelolco Treaty, with 33 states parties at Sept. 2013).

Director-General: YUKIYA AMANO (Japan).

INTERNATIONAL CIVIL AVIATION ORGANIZATION—ICAO

Address: 999 University St, Montréal, QC H3C 5H7, Canada.

Telephone: (514) 954-8219; **fax:** (514) 954-6077; **e-mail:** icaohq@ icao.org; **internet:** www.icao.int.

ICAO was founded in 1947, on the basis of the Convention on International Civil Aviation, signed in Chicago, in 1944, to develop the techniques of international air navigation and to help in the planning and improvement of international air transport.

In August 2014 ICAO, the International Air Transport Association and the World Health Organization (WHO) were co-operating in ascertaining the implications for international air connectivity of an intensive outbreak in Guinea, Liberia and Sierra Leone of Ebola Virus Disease (declared—on 8 August—by WHO to be a Public Health Emergency of International Concern).

Secretary-General: RAYMOND BENJAMIN (France).

North America, Central America and the Caribbean Office: Apdo Postal 5-377, CP 06500, México, DF, Mexico; tel. (55) 5250-3211; fax (55) 5203-2757; e-mail icaonacc@icao.int; internet www .icao.int/NACC.

South American Office: ave Víctor Andrés Belaúnde 147, San Isidro, Lima, Peru; tel. (1) 611-8686; fax (1) 611-8689; e-mail mail@ lima.icao.int; internet www.lima.icao.int.

INTERNATIONAL LABOUR ORGANIZATION—ILO

Address: 4 route des Morillons, 1211 Geneva 22, Switzerland.

Telephone: 227996111; **fax:** 227988685; **e-mail:** ilo@ilo.org; **internet:** www.ilo.org.

ILO was founded in 1919 to work for social justice as a basis for lasting peace. It carries out this mandate by promoting decent living standards, satisfactory conditions of work and pay and adequate employment opportunities. Methods of action include the creation of international labour standards; the provision of technical co-operation services; and training, education, research and publishing activities to advance ILO objectives.

Director-General: GUY RYDER (United Kingdom).

Regional Office for Latin America and the Caribbean: Las Flores 275 San Isidro, Apdo 14-124 Lima, Peru; tel. (1) 6150300; fax (1) 6150400; e-mail oit@oit.org.pe; internet www.ilo.org/americas.

INTERNATIONAL MARITIME ORGANIZATION—IMO

Address: 4 Albert Embankment, London, SE1 7SR, United Kingdom.

Telephone: (20) 7735-7611; **fax:** (20) 7587-3210; **e-mail:** info@imo .org; **internet:** www.imo.org.

The Inter-Governmental Maritime Consultative Organization (IMCO) began operations in 1959, as a specialized agency of the UN to facilitate co-operation among governments on technical matters affecting international shipping. Its main aims are to improve the safety of international shipping, and to control pollution caused by ships. IMCO became IMO in 1982.

Secretary-General: KOJI SEKIMIZU (Japan).

INTERNATIONAL TELECOMMUNICATION UNION—ITU

Address: Place des Nations, 1211 Geneva 20, Switzerland.

Telephone: 227305111; **fax:** 227337256; **e-mail:** itumail@itu.int; **internet:** www.itu.int.

Founded in 1865, ITU became a specialized agency of the UN in 1947. It acts to encourage world co-operation for the improvement and use of telecommunications, to promote technical development, to harmonize national policies in the field, and to promote the extension of telecommunications throughout the world. ITU helped to organize the World Summit on the Information Society, held, in two phases, in 2003 and 2005, and supports follow-up initiatives. ITU has assumed responsibility for issues relating to cybersecurity. In December 2012 a World Conference on International Communications endorsed new International Telecommunication Regulations (ITRs), updating those previously set down in 1988. The new ITRs included provisions to secure freedom of expression, to assist developing countries to enhance their telecommunications infrastructure, to promote accessibility to persons with disabilities, to limit unsolicited bulk electronic communications, and to improve the energy efficiency of telecommunications networks.

In July 2012 a 'Connect Americas' summit was convened, under the auspices of ITU, in Panama City, Panama, to address the promotion of digital inclusion, and means of accelerating secure and affordable access to broadband connectivity across the continent.

Secretary-General: HAMADOUN TOURÉ (Mali).

UNITED NATIONS INDUSTRIAL DEVELOPMENT ORGANIZATION—UNIDO

Address: Vienna International Centre, Wagramerstr. 5, POB 300, 1400 Vienna, Austria.

Telephone: (1) 260260; **fax:** (1) 2692669; **e-mail:** unido@unido.org; **internet:** www.unido.org.

UNIDO began operations in 1967 and became a specialized agency in 1985. Its objectives are to promote sustainable and socially equitable industrial development in developing countries and in countries with economies in transition. It aims to assist such countries to integrate fully into global economic system by mobilizing knowledge, skills, information and technology to promote productive employment, competitive economies and sound environment.

Director-General: LI YONG (People's Republic of China).

UNIVERSAL POSTAL UNION—UPU

Address: CP 13, 3000 Bern 15, Switzerland.

Telephone: 313503111; **fax:** 313503110; **e-mail:** info@upu.int; **internet:** www.upu.int.

The General Postal Union was founded by the Treaty of Berne (1874), beginning operations in July 1875. Three years later its name was changed to the Universal Postal Union. In 1948 UPU became a specialized agency of the UN. It aims to develop and unify the international postal service, to study problems and to provide training.

Director-General: BISHAR ABDIRAHMAN HUSSEIN (Kenya).

WORLD INTELLECTUAL PROPERTY ORGANIZATION—WIPO

Address: 34 chemin des Colombettes, 1211 Geneva 20, Switzerland.

Telephone: 223389111; **fax:** 227335428; **e-mail:** wipo.mail@wipo .int; **internet:** www.wipo.int.

WIPO was established in 1970. It became a specialized agency of the UN in 1974 concerned with the protection of intellectual property (e.g. patents, trademarks, industrial designs and literary copyrights) throughout the world. WIPO formulates and administers treaties embodying international norms and standards of intellectual property, establishes model laws, and facilitates applications for the protection of inventions, trademarks etc. WIPO provides legal and technical assistance to developing countries and countries with economies in transition and advises countries on obligations under the World Trade Organization's agreement on Trade-Related Aspects of Intellectual Property Rights (TRIPS).

Director-General: FRANCIS GURRY (Australia).

WORLD METEOROLOGICAL ORGANIZATION—WMO

Address: 7 bis, ave de la Paix, 1211 Geneva 2, Switzerland.

Telephone: 227308111; **fax:** 227308181; **e-mail:** wmo@wmo.int; **internet:** www.wmo.int.

WMO was established in 1950 and was recognized as a Specialized Agency of the UN in 1951, aiming to improve the exchange of information in the fields of meteorology, climatology, operational hydrology and related fields, as well as their applications. WMO jointly implements, with UNEP, the UN Framework Convention on Climate Change. In June 2011 the 16th World Meteorological Congress endorsed a new Global Framework for Climate Services.

Secretary-General: MICHEL JARRAUD (France).

WORLD TOURISM ORGANIZATION—UNWTO

Address: Capitán Haya 42, 28020 Madrid, Spain.

Telephone: (91) 5678100; **fax:** (91) 5713733; **e-mail:** omt@unwto .org; **internet:** www.world-tourism.org.

The World Tourism Organization was established in 1975 and was recognized as a Specialized Agency of the UN in December 2003. It works to promote and develop sustainable tourism, in particular in support of socio-economic growth in developing countries.

Secretary-General: TALEB RIFAI (Jordan).

SPECIAL HIGH LEVEL APPOINTMENTS OF THE UN SECRETARY-GENERAL

Head of the International Commission against Impunity in Guatemala: IVÁN VELÁSQUEZ GÓMEZ (Colombia).

Personal Envoy for Haiti: BILL (WILLIAM JEFFERSON) CLINTON (USA).

Personal Representative on the Border Controversy between Guyana and Venezuela: (vacant).

Special Envoy for HIV/AIDS in the Caribbean Region: Dr EDWARD GREENE (Guyana).

ANDEAN COMMUNITY OF NATIONS

(COMUNIDAD ANDINA DE NACIONES—CAN)

Address: Paseo de la República 3895, San Isidro, Lima 27; Apdo 18-1177, Lima 18, Peru.

Telephone: (1) 7106400; **fax:** (1) 2213329; **e-mail:** contacto@ comunidadandina.org; **internet:** www.comunidadandina.org.

The Acuerdo de Cartagena (the Cartagena Agreement), also referred to as the Grupo Andino (Andean Group) or the Pacto Andino (Andean Pact), was established in 1969. In March 1996 member countries signed a Reform Protocol of the Cartagena Agreement, in accordance with which the Andean Group was superseded in August 1997 by the Andean Community of Nations (CAN). The Community was to promote greater economic, commercial and political integration within a new Andean Integration System (Sistema Andino de Integración), comprising the organization's bodies and institutions.

MEMBERS

Bolivia	Colombia	Ecuador	Peru

Note: Argentina, Brazil, Chile, Paraguay and Uruguay are associate members. Mexico, Panama and Spain have observer status. Venezuela withdrew from the Community in April 2006.

Organization

(September 2014)

ANDEAN PRESIDENTIAL COUNCIL

The presidential summits, which had been held annually since 1989, were formalized under the 1996 Reform Protocol of the Cartagena Agreement as the Andean Presidential Council. The Council is the highest-level body of the Andean Integration System, and provides the political leadership of the Community.

COMMISSION

The Commission consists of a plenipotentiary representative from each member country, with each country holding the presidency in turn. The Commission is the main policymaking organ of the Andean Community, and is responsible for co-ordinating Andean trade policy.

COUNCIL OF FOREIGN MINISTERS

The Council of Foreign Ministers meets annually or whenever it is considered necessary, to formulate common external policy and to co-ordinate the process of integration.

GENERAL SECRETARIAT

In August 1997 the General Secretariat assumed the functions of the Board of the Cartagena Agreement. The General Secretariat is the body charged with implementation of all guidelines and decisions issued by the bodies listed above. It submits proposals to the Commission for facilitating the fulfilment of the Community's objectives. The Secretary-General is elected by the Council of Foreign Ministers for a five-year term, and has enhanced powers to adjudicate in disputes arising between member states, as well as to manage the sub-regional integration process. There are three Directors-General.

Secretary-General: PABLO GUZMÁN LAUGIER (Bolivia).

PARLIAMENT

Parlamento Andino: Avda Caracas, No. 70A-61, Bogotá, Colombia; tel. (1) 217-3357; fax (1) 348-2805; e-mail carias@parlamentoandino .org; internet www.parlamentoandino.org; f. 1979; comprises five members from each country, elected by direct voting, and meets in each capital city in turn; makes recommendations on regional policy; Pres. (2013–14) PEDRO DE LA CRUZ (Ecuador); Sec.-Gen. Dr RUBÉN VÉLEZ NÚÑEZ.

COURT OF JUSTICE

Tribunal de Justicia de la Comunidad Andina: Juan de Dios Martínez Mera 34-380 y Portugal, Sector Iglesia de Fátima, Quito, Ecuador; tel. (2) 3331417; e-mail tjca@tribunalandino.org.ec; internet www.tribunalandino.org.ec; f. 1979, began operating in 1984; a protocol approved in May 1996 (which came into force in August 1999) modified the Court's functions; its main responsibilities are to resolve disputes among member countries and interpret community legislation; comprises one judge from each member country, appointed for a six-year renewable period; the Presidency is assumed annually by each judge in turn; Pres. Dr LEONOR PERDOMO PERDOMO (Colombia); Sec.-Gen. Dr GUSTAVO GARCÍA BRITO.

Activities

In May 1989 the previous framework for Andean integration, the Grupo Andino (Andean Group), undertook to revitalize the process of Andean integration, by withdrawing measures that obstructed the programme of trade liberalization, and by complying with tariff reductions that had already been agreed upon. In May 1991, in Caracas, Venezuela, a summit meeting of the Group agreed the framework for the establishment of a free trade area on 1 January 1992 (achieved in February 1993) and for an eventual Andean common market.

In March 1996 heads of state, meeting in Trujillo, Peru, signed the Reform Protocol of the Cartagena Agreement, providing for the establishment of the Andean Community of Nations, which was to have greater ambitious economic and political objectives than the Andean Group. Consequently, in August 1997 the Andean Community was inaugurated, and the Group's Junta was replaced by a new General Secretariat, headed by a Secretary-General with enhanced executive and decision making powers. In January 2003 heads of state, convened in Quirama, Colombia, endorsed a strategic direction for the Andean integration process based on developing the Andean common market, common foreign policy and social agenda, physical integration, and sustainable development.

In February 2010 the Council of Foreign Ministers approved a new Andean Strategic Agenda, which was supported by a New Andean Strategic Agenda Implementation Plan, and focused on 12 priority strategic areas: citizen participation; common foreign policy; trade integration and economic complementation, and promotion of production, trade and sustainable consumption; physical integration and border development; social development; environment; tourism; security; culture; co-operation; energy integration and natural resources; and development of the Community's institutions.

In April 2006 the President of Venezuela announced his intention to withdraw that country from the Andean Community, with immediate effect, expressing opposition to the bilateral free trade agreements signed by Colombia and Peru with the USA, on the grounds that they would undermine efforts to achieve regional economic integration. The Community countered that Venezuela's commitment to Andean integration had been placed in doubt by its declared allegiance to other regional groupings, in particular the Mercado Común del Sur (MERCOSUR—Southern Common Market).

In June 2012 Colombia and Peru, together with Chile and Mexico, inaugurated the Pacific Alliance, aimed at furthering economic integration.

ANTI-CORRUPTION AND DEMOCRACY

A subregional workshop to formulate an Andean Plan to Fight Corruption was held in April 2005, organized by the General Secretariat and the European Commission. Heads of state expressed their commitment to the Plan in mid-2007, and in September 2008 Offices of the Controller General and other supervisory bodies in Andean countries agreed its implementation. The Plan aims to promote a region-wide culture of legality, the adoption of common positions in relation to the implementation of international conventions, transparency in public administration, and the strengthening of regional control bodies. The Andean Community General Secretariat monitors elections in member states; in 2014 a mission was sent to observe local elections held in Ecuador in February.

CULTURE

An Andean Council of Education Ministers and Persons Responsible for Cultural Policy was established in July 2004. Common policies and mechanisms for the registration, conservation, surveillance and return of member states' cultural heritage were also adopted in that month. In March 2010 representatives of Andean cultural authorities determined to initiate an Andean Development Plan for Cultural Industries. In March 2012 the inaugural meeting of a new Andean Council of Ministers of Culture launched the Plan, covering 2012–15, with a focus on the areas of cultural information, cultural and artistic training, and the promotion and dissemination of culture. The Community's online cultural portal, CULTURANDE, was to be enhanced. A Permanent Working Network on Andean Cinema was established in February 2010.

DRUGS CONTROL

In June 2001, heads of state adopted an Andean Co-operation Plan for the Control of Illegal Drugs and Related Offences. In July 2005 the Council of Foreign Ministers approved an Andean Alternative Development Strategy, which aimed to support sustainable local development initiatives, including alternatives to the production of illicit crops. In August 2009 the Council approved a financing agreement with the European Union (EU) to implement an anti-illegal drugs programme in the Andean Community. In June 2012 a joint CAN-EU-Pan American Health Organization programme known as

'Familias Fuertes' ('Strong Families') was initiated, with the aim of preventing drugs use and associated risk behaviours among adolescents in the region. In November a High-Level International Conference on Alternative Development, convened at the Community's headquarters, considered a draft Andean Strategy for Jointly Addressing the Global Drug Problem during 2012–19, which was to promote sustainable alternative development in illicit crop cultivation areas.

ENVIRONMENT

In March–April 2005 the first meeting of an Andean Community Council of Ministers of the Environment and Sustainable Development was convened, in Paracas, Peru. Successive Andean Environmental Agendas have aimed to strengthen the capacities of member countries with regard to environmental and sustainable development issues, in particular biodiversity, climate change and water resources. The 2012–16 Agenda—adopted by CAN ministers responsible for the environment and sustainable development in April 2012, alongside an action plan for the implementation of the Andean Strategy for Integrated Management of Water Resources—provides, *inter alia*, for the strengthening of biodiversity management, with a focus on protected areas; the promotion of joint initiatives on biosafety; the strengthening of national processes aimed at protecting traditional knowledge; improving the exchange of information on conservation and biodiversity; the development of joint actions in relation to the implementation of the Nagoya Protocol on Access to Genetic Resources and the Fair and Equitable Sharing of Benefits Arising from their Utilization; the development of an Andean Plan of Action on Climate Change; and promoting responsible and efficient water use, advancing the prevention of water pollution, evaluating the impact of climate variability on Andean water resources, and developing appropriate adaptation measures. In September 2012 CAN launched a new 'One Amazon' campaign, aimed at raising awareness of the environmentally strategic importance of the Amazon ecosystem.

In June 2007 the Secretariat signed an agreement with Finland to develop a regional biodiversity programme in the Amazon region of Andean member countries (BioCAN); the implementation of BioCAN was approved in February 2013 by a meeting of the Council of Foreign Ministers. Pilot projects implemented during 2012–13 included developing an Amazon Regional Information Platform (PIRAA), and formulating norms for wildlife management and guidelines for land zoning and for the sustainable use of Amazonian biodiversity. Also in 2012 BioCAN supported workshops of Andean Community wildlife officials and experts that aimed to address, respectively, proposals for an appropriate subregional co-ordination mechanism to combat illegal trafficking in wild Amazonian flora and fauna; and the management of Amazonian areas, with a special focus on priority species. In October 2007 the Secretariat organized Clima Latino, hosted by two city authorities in Ecuador, comprising conferences, workshops and cultural events at which climate change was addressed. The Community represented member countries at the Conference of the Parties to the UN Framework Convention on Climate Change (UNFCCC), held in Bali, Indonesia, in December, and demanded greater international political commitment and funding to combat the effects of climate change, in particular to monitor and protect the Amazon rainforest. In November 2011, at a special meeting of the Andean Council of Presidents in Bogotá, Colombia, heads of state asserted their intention to work together to reach a common position for the UN Conference on Sustainable Development (Rio+20), which was held in June 2012.

In July 2002 an Andean Committee for Disaster Prevention and Relief (CAPRADE) was established to help to mitigate the risk and impact of natural disasters in the subregion, and to implement the Andean Strategy for Disaster Prevention and Relief, which was approved by the Council of Foreign Ministers in July 2004. A new Strategy for Natural Disaster Prevention and Relief was approved in August 2009, which aimed to link activities for disaster prevention and relief to those related to the environmental agenda, climate change and integrated water management. An Andean University Network in Risk Management and Climate Change promotes information exchange between some 32 institutions.

INDUSTRY AND ENERGY

In May 1987 member countries signed the Quito Protocol, modifying the Cartagena Agreement, to amend the strict rules that had formerly been imposed on foreign investors in the region. In March 1991 the Protocol was amended, with the aim of further liberalizing foreign investment and stimulating an inflow of foreign capital and technology. External and regional investors were to be permitted to repatriate their profits (in accordance with the laws of the country concerned) and there was no stipulation that a majority shareholding must eventually be transferred to local investors. A further directive, adopted in March, covered the formation of multinational enterprises to ensure that at least two member countries have a shareholding of 15% or more of the capital, including the country where the enterprise was to be based. These enterprises were entitled to participate in sectors otherwise reserved for national enterprises, subject to the same conditions as national enterprises in terms of taxation and export regulations, and to gain access to the markets of all member countries. In September 1999 Colombia, Ecuador and Venezuela signed an accord to facilitate the production and sale of vehicles within the region; the agreement became effective in January 2000.

In November 1988 member states established a bank, the Banco Intermunicipal Andino, which was to finance public works. In October 2004 a subregional committee on small and medium-sized enterprises (SMEs) endorsed efforts by the Community Secretariat to establish an Andean System of SME Guarantees to facilitate their access to credit.

During 2003 efforts were undertaken to establish an Andean Energy Alliance, with the aim of fostering the development of integrated electricity and gas markets, as well as developing renewable energy sources, promoting 'energy clusters' and ensuring regional energy security. The first meeting of ministers responsible for energy, electricity, hydrocarbons and mines, convened in Quito, Ecuador, in January 2004, endorsed the Alliance. In August 2011 representatives of Andean electricity regulatory bodies, including that of Chile, agreed upon transitional arrangements to provide for trade in surplus electricity and greater interconnectivity. Andean Community heads of state, meeting in Bogotá, in November, pledged to boost the integration of regional energy. In February 2012 the Community held the first meeting of representatives of mining and environment authorities to discuss issues relating to illegal mining activities, in order to promote co-ordinated efforts against those activities, and to initiate the development of a legal directive to counter illegal mining.

RURAL DEVELOPMENT AND FOOD SECURITY

The 12th Andean presidential summit, held in June 2000, authorized the adoption of an Andean Common Agricultural Policy, which included measures to harmonize trade policy instruments and legislation on animal and plant health. In January 2002, at a special Andean presidential summit, it was agreed that all countries in the bloc would adopt price stabilization mechanisms for agricultural products. In July 2004 Andean ministers responsible for agriculture approved a series of objectives and priority actions to form the framework of a Regional Food Security Policy. Also in July Andean heads of state endorsed the Andean Rural Development and Agricultural Competitiveness Programme to promote subregional efforts in areas such as rural development, food security, production competitiveness, animal health and technological innovation. In October 2005 ministers responsible for trade and for agriculture approved the establishment of the Fund for Rural Development and Agricultural Productivity to finance the Programme. In June 2013 Community agriculture ministers approved a set of common strategic guidelines and objectives that were to guide joint efforts to advance subregional rural and agricultural development. The ministers also established an Andean Rural Territorial Development Committee to advise on the implementation of an Integral Subregional Rural Territorial Development Program.

REGIONAL SECURITY

In June 2002 Community ministers responsible for defence and for foreign affairs approved an Andean Charter for Peace and Security, establishing principles and commitments for the formulation of a policy on subregional security, the establishment of a zone of peace, joint action in efforts to counter terrorism, and the limitation of external defence spending. Other provisions included commitments to eradicate illegal trafficking in firearms, ammunition and explosives, to expand and reinforce confidence-building measures, and to establish verification mechanisms to strengthen dialogue and efforts in those areas. In January 2003 the Community concluded a co-operation agreement with INTERPOL providing for collaboration in combating national and transnational crime, and in June the presidential summit adopted an Andean Plan for the Prevention, Combating and Eradication of Small, Light Weapons. In July 2004 the Council of Foreign Ministers adopted Policy Guidelines on Andean Common External Security.

SOCIAL INTEGRATION

The first Andean Social Summit, organized in April 1994 by the Andean Parliament, adopted a non-binding Andean Social Charter. The second Andean Social Summit was convened in February 1999. Participants in the third Andean Social Summit, organized by the Andean Parliament in May 2012, endorsed an updated Andean Social Charter, incorporating additional provisions covering human mobility and the rights of migrants; Andean ethical and moral values (including protection for modern as well as traditional family configurations); disability; female empowerment; access to decent housing for senior citizens; urban renewal; guaranteed rights to all gender identities and sexual orientations; environmental issues; food security; and corporate social responsibility.

Several formal agreements and institutions have been established within the framework of the Andean Integration System to enhance social development and welfare. In June 2003 ministers responsible for foreign affairs and for foreign trade adopted 16 legal provisions aimed at giving maximum priority to the social dimension of integration within the Community, including a measure providing for mobility of workers between member countries. In July 2004 Community heads of state declared support for a new Andean Council of Social Development Ministers. Other bodies established in 2003/04 included Councils of Ministers of Education and of Ministers responsible for Cultural Policies, and a Consultative Council of Municipal Authorities. An Integral Plan for Social Development, first approved by the Council of Foreign Ministers in September 2004, has remained under development. In August 2009 the Council of Foreign Ministers endorsed the establishment of an Andean Council of Authorities of Women's Affairs as a forum for regional consideration of equal opportunities and gender issues. In September 2012 the Council approved priority actions aimed, *inter alia*, at combating violence against women, promoting women's political participation and economic autonomy, and preventing adolescent pregnancy, within the framework of a new Andean Programme for Gender Equality and Equal Opportunities. In April 2013 six indicators were adopted by the Council with the aim of harmonizing measurements of political participation by women. In July 2011 Andean ministers responsible for social development approved 11 Andean Social Development Objectives, which they pledged to achieve by 2019, and a new Andean Economic and Social Cohesion Strategy to support the accomplishment of those targets. In November 2012 CAN ministers responsible for labour—with a view to facilitating workers' employability in any of the four member states—endorsed the establishment of a new Andean Employment Network (Red ANDE), which was to match labour supply and demand within member states; approved new regulations aimed at ensuring equal labour conditions in the member states; and also determined to promote the regional mutual labour skills certification mechanism (CERTIANDINA). Social and labour policies in the Community are analysed through an Andean Labour Observatory Pilot Plan implemented under the auspices of the Convenio Simón Rodríguez. In that month the Commission determined to expand science and technology programmes in member states, with a view to developing human capital regionally.

An Andean Charter for the Promotion and Protection of Human Rights was adopted by the Presidential Council in July 2002. In June 2007 Community heads of state approved the establishment of a Working Committee on Indigenous People's Rights. A Consultative Council of Indigenous Peoples of the Andean Community was founded in September to promote the participation of representatives of indigenous communities in the Andean integration process. In November 2010 the first Andean Meeting of Racial Equality Bodies was held, and during 2011 national meetings were convened in member countries aimed at enhancing the participation of people of African descent in the activities of the Community. A Working Committee on Peoples of African Descent in the Andean Community was launched in August 2011.

TOURISM

Tourist arrivals in the CAN region rose from around 2.7m. in 2002 to some 6.2m. in 2011. In December 2010 the Andean Committee of Tourism Authorities (comprising representatives of national tourism authorities) approved an Agenda for Tourism Development in the Andean Community, covering the period 2011–15, which aimed to develop the region as a major global tourism destination, by facilitating tourist flows between member states and promoting innovative tourism products. The development of an information system on the Community tourism sector is under way, with the objective of establishing a tourism observatory.

TRADE AND MACROECONOMY

A council for customs affairs met for the first time in January 1982, aiming to harmonize national legislation within the group. In December 1984 the member states launched a common currency, the Andean peso, aiming to reduce dependence on the US dollar and to increase regional trade. The new currency was to be supported by special contributions to the Fondo Andino de Reservas (now the Fondo Latinoamericano de Reservas) amounting to US \$80m., and was to be 'pegged' to the US dollar, taking the form of financial drafts rather than notes and coins.

The Caracas Declaration of May 1991 provided for the establishment of an Andean free trade area (AFTA), which entered into effect (excluding Peru) in February 1993. Heads of state also agreed in May 1991 to create a common external tariff (CET), to standardize member countries' trade barriers in their dealings with the rest of the world, and envisaged the eventual creation of an Andean common market. In November 1994 ministers responsible for trade and integration, meeting in Quito, concluded a final agreement on a four-tier structure of external tariffs (although Bolivia was to retain a two-level system). The CET agreement came into effect on 1 February 1995, covering 90% of the region's imports. In June 1997 an agreement was concluded to provide for Peru's integration into AFTA. The Peruvian Government determined to eliminate customs duties on some 2,500 products with immediate effect. The process of incorporating Peru into AFTA was completed by January 2006.

In May 1999 the 11th presidential summit agreed to establish the Andean Common Market by 2005; the Community adopted a policy on border integration and development to prepare the border regions of member countries for the envisaged free circulation of people, goods, capital and services, while consolidating subregional security. In June 2001 the Community agreed to recognize national identification documents issued by member states as sufficient for tourist travel in the subregion. The so-called Andean passport system entered into effect in December 2005. Community heads of state, meeting in January 2002 at a special Andean presidential summit, agreed to consolidate and improve the free trade zone by mid-2002 and apply a new CET. To facilitate this process a common agricultural policy was to be adopted and macro-economic policies were to be harmonized. In October member governments determined the new tariff levels applicable to 62% of products and agreed the criteria for negotiating levels for the remainder. Although the new CET was to become effective on 1 January 2004, this date was subsequently postponed. In January 2006 ministers responsible trade approved a working programme to define the Community's common tariff policy, which was to incorporate a flexible CET. The value of intra-Community trade totalled some US $9,261m. in 2011, and increased to $10,349m. in 2012.

In November 2012 the Commission adopted a new work plan which detailed several priority areas of trade-related activity, including the promotion of industrial complementarity and production chains between the Andean states; certification of organic products; and macroeconomic co-ordination of the regional response to the global economic downturn.

In May 2011 the Commission approved the establishment of an Andean Committee on Micro, Small and Medium-sized Enterprises (MSMEs), mandated to advise and support the Commission and General Secretariat in efforts to support MSMEs. At the same time the Commission endorsed the establishment of an Andean Observatory on MSMEs as a mechanism for monitoring the development and needs of MSMEs in the subregion, as well as the impact of corporate policy instruments on their competitiveness.

An Andean Business Meeting is convened periodically to promote inter-regional trade.

In November 2008 a meeting was convened, at the request of heads of state, of a Community Council of treasury or finance ministers, heads of central banks and ministers responsible for economic planning, in order to analyse the effects on the region of the severe global economic and financial downturn. The Council met again in February 2009 to consider various technical studies that had been undertaken.

TRANSPORT AND COMMUNICATIONS

The Andean Community has pursued efforts to improve infrastructure throughout the region. An 'open skies' agreement, giving airlines of member states equal rights to airspace and airport facilities within the grouping, was signed in May 1991. In June 1998 the Commission approved the establishment of an Andean Commission of Land Transportation Authorities, to oversee the operation and development of land transportation services. Similarly, an Andean Committee of Water Transportation Authorities was established to ensure compliance with Community regulations regarding ocean transportation activities. The Community aims to facilitate the movement of goods throughout the region by the use of different modes of transport ('multimodal transport') and to guarantee operational standards. It also intends to harmonize Community transport regulations and standards with those of MERCOSUR countries.

In August 1996 a regulatory framework was approved for the development of a commercial Andean satellite system. In December 1997 the General Secretariat approved regulations for granting authorization for the use of the system; the Commission subsequently granted the first Community authorization to an Andean multinational enterprise (Andesat), comprising 48 companies from all five member states. In 1994 the Community initiated efforts to establish digital technology infrastructure throughout the Community: the resulting Andean Digital Corridor comprises ground, underwater and satellite routes providing a series of cross-border interconnections between the member countries. In May 1999 the Andean Committee of Telecommunications Authorities agreed to remove all restrictions to free trade in telecommunications services (excluding sound broadcasting and television) by 1 January 2002. The Committee also intends to formulate provisions on interconnection and the safeguarding of free competition and principles of transparency within the sector. In November 2006 the Andean Community approved a new regulatory framework for the commercial exploitation of the Andean satellite system belonging to member states. In February 2014 the Community concluded an agreement with the Netherlands-based company SES World Skies on the construction of a satellite, which, once launched and operational, was to provide high power satellite capacity to Andean telecommunications operators, broadcasters and service providers, over a 15-year period.

Asociación de Empresas de Telecomunicaciones de la Comunidad Andina (ASETA): Calle La Pradera E7–41 y San Salvador, Casilla 17-1106042, Quito, Ecuador; tel. (2) 256-3812; fax (2) 256-2499; e-mail aseta@aseta.org; internet www.aseta.org; f. 1974; co-ordinates improvements in national telecommunications services, in order to contribute to the further integration of the countries of the Andean Community; Sec.-Gen. Marcelo López Arjona.

EXTERNAL RELATIONS

In 1999 the Council of Foreign Ministers approved guidelines establishing the principles, objectives and mechanisms of a common foreign policy. In July 2004 Andean ministers responsible for foreign affairs approved new guidelines for an Andean common policy on external security. The ministers, meeting in Quito, also adopted a Declaration on the Establishment of an Andean Peace Zone, free from nuclear, chemical or biological weapons. In April 2005 the Community Secretariat signed a Memorandum of Understanding with the Organization for the Prohibition of Chemical Weapons, which aimed to consolidate the Andean Peace Zone, assist countries to implement the Chemical Arms Convention and promote further collaboration between the two groupings.

At the first summit meeting of Latin American and Caribbean (LAC) and EU leaders held in Rio de Janeiro, Brazil, in June 1999, Community-EU discussions were held on strengthening economic, trade and political co-operation and on the possibility of concluding an Association Agreement. Following the second LAC and EU summit meeting, held in May 2002 in Madrid, Spain, a Political Dialogue and Co-operation Agreement was signed in December 2003. In May 2004 a meeting of the two sides held during the third LAC-EU summit, in Guadalajara, Mexico, confirmed that an EU-CAN Association Agreement was a common strategic objective. In January 2005 an ad hoc working group was established in order to undertake a joint appraisal exercise on regional economic integration. The fourth LAC and EU summit meeting, held in Vienna, Austria, in May 2006, approved the establishment of an EU-LAC Parliamentary Assembly; this was inaugurated in November. Negotiations on an Association Agreement were formally inaugurated at the meeting of Andean heads of state held in Tarifa, Bolivia, in June 2007, and the first round of negotiations was held in September. In May 2008 heads of state of the Andean Community confirmed that they would continue to negotiate the agreement as a single group; however, in December the EU announced that it was to commence separate free trade agreement negotiations with Colombia and Peru. Bolivia criticized the decision as undermining the Andean integration process. In March 2010 the EU-CAN Mixed Commission (established in 1993) agreed on a programme of co-operation in 2011–13, with funding commitments of €17.5m. for projects concerned with economic integration, countering illicit drugs production and trafficking, and environmental protection. An EU-CAN summit meeting was held in Madrid in May 2010. In June 2012 Colombia and Peru concluded a Multi-Party Commercial Agreement with the EU; reservations were expressed at that time by the EU concerning progress on human rights and environmental protection in those countries. The Agreement entered into effect, provisionally, with Peru on 1 March 2013 and with Colombia on 1 August; its full entry into force would be achieved following ratification by the legislatures of all the EU member states.

In August 2002 a new US Andean Trade Preference and Drug Eradication Act provided duty free access for more than 6,000 products from the Andean Community with the objective of supporting legal trade transactions in order to help to counter the production and trafficking of illegal narcotic drugs. The Act was initially scheduled to expire in December 2006, but has been periodically extended by the US Congress. In December 2008 the US President suspended Bolivia's eligibility under the Act owing to its failure to meet its counternarcotics requirements.

In March 2000 the Andean Community concluded an agreement to establish a political consultation and co-operation mechanism with the People's Republic of China. At the first ministerial meeting within this framework, which took place in October 2002, it was agreed that consultations would be held thereafter on a biennial basis. The first meeting of the Council of Foreign Ministers with the Chinese Vice-President took place in January 2005.

In April 1998, at the 10th Andean presidential summit, an agreement was signed with Panama establishing a framework for negotiations providing for the conclusion of a free trade accord by the end of 1998 and for Panama's eventual associate membership of the Community. A political dialogue and co-operation agreement, a requirement for Panama's associate membership status, was signed by both sides in September 2007. Mexico was invited to assume observer status in September 2004. In November 2006 Mexico and the Andean Community signed an agreement to establish a mechanism for political dialogue and co-operation in areas of mutual interest. The first meeting of the mechanism was held in New York, USA, in September 2007. In November 2004 the Community signed a framework agreement with the Central American Integration System (SICA) to strengthen dialogue and co-operation between the two blocs of countries. In January 2011 the Secretaries-General of the two organizations, meeting in San Salvador, El Salvador, determined to reactivate the agreement and pursue greater collaboration.

The Community signed a framework agreement with MERCO-SUR on the establishment of a free trade accord in April 1998. Although negotiations between the Community and MERCOSUR were subsequently delayed, bilateral agreements between the countries of the two groupings were extended. In September 2000 leaders of the Community and MERCOSUR, meeting at a summit of Latin American heads of state, determined to relaunch negotiations, with a view to establishing a free trade area. In July 2001 ministers responsible for foreign affairs of the two groupings approved the establishment of a formal mechanism for political dialogue and co-ordination in order to facilitate negotiations and to enhance economic and social integration. In December 2003 MERCOSUR and the Andean Community signed an Economic Complementary Agreement providing for free trade provisions, according to which tariffs on 80% of trade between the two groupings were to be phased out by 2014 and tariffs were to be removed from the remaining 20% of, initially protected, products by 2019. The accord did not enter into force in July 2004, as planned, owing to delays in drafting the tariff reduction schedule. Members of the Latin American Integration Association (Aladi) remaining outside MERCOSUR and the Andean Community—Cuba, Chile and Mexico—were to be permitted to apply to join the envisaged larger free trade zone. In July 2005 the Community granted Argentina, Brazil, Paraguay and Uruguay associate membership of the grouping, as part of efforts to achieve a reciprocal association agreement. Chile was granted observer status in December 2004, and in September 2006 was formally invited to join the Community as an associate member. In December the first meeting of the CAN-Chile Joint Commission was convened in Cochabamba, Bolivia. An agreement on Chile's full participation in all Community bodies and mechanisms was approved in July 2007. In February 2010 ministers responsible for foreign affairs of the Community and MERCOSUR agreed to establish a CAN–MERCO-SUR Mixed Commission to facilitate enhanced co-operation between the countries of the two organizations.

In April 2007, at the first South American Energy Summit, held in Margarita Island, Venezuela, heads of state endorsed the establishment of a Union of South American Nations (UNASUR) to be the lead organization for regional integration; UNASUR was to have political decision-making functions, supported by a small Quito-based permanent secretariat, and was to co-ordinate on economic and trade matters with the Andean Community, MERCOSUR and Aladi. The first informal meeting of the General Secretariat of the Andean Community and UNASUR was held in January 2010, in Lima, Peru. At a special meeting of the Andean Council of Presidents, held in Bogotá, in November 2011, heads of state agreed to strengthen the CAN, and requested that the then acting Secretary-General of the Community identify jointly, with the General Secretariats of both MERCOSUR and UNASUR, common and complementary elements and differences prior to the future convergence of the three processes. In January 2012 the process of listing complementary elements commenced. Meeting in June 2013 Andean Community ministers responsible foreign affairs and of foreign trade established a high-level working group which was mandated to submit a proposal to the Council of Foreign Ministers that was to cover the Community's new vision, strategic guidelines and priority areas of action.

The Community participated in the first and second editions of a new Meeting of Regional and Subregional Integration Mechanisms and Bodies, held, respectively, in August 2012, in Montevideo, Uruguay, and in November, in Santiago, Chile, with the aim of defining and deepening integration in Latin America and the Caribbean. In November it was reported that the UN Economic Commission for Latin America and the Caribbean (ECLAC) was to undertake a study relating to institution building by the Community in the context of ongoing developments in the continental integration process.

Spain was awarded observer status at the Community in August 2011.

INSTITUTIONS

Consejo Consultivo de Pueblos Indígenos de la Comunidad Andina (Consultative Council of Indigenous Peoples of the Andean Community): Paseo de la República 3895, Lima, Peru; tel. (1) 4111400; fax (1) 2213329; f. 2007; comprising an indigenous representative from each mem. country; first meeting held in Sept. 2008; normally meets twice a year; aims to strengthen the participation of indigenous peoples in the subregional integration process.

Consejo Consultivo Empresarial Andino (Andean Business Advisory Council): Asociación Nacional de Industriales, Calle 73, No. 8–13, Bogotá, Colombia; tel. (1) 3268500; fax (1) 3473198; e-mail jnarino@andi.com.co; first meeting held in Nov. 1998; an advisory institution within the framework of the Sistema Andino de Integración; comprises elected representatives of business orgs; advises Community ministers and officials on integration activities affecting the business sector; Chair. LUÍS CARLOS VILLEGAS ECHE-VERRI (Colombia).

Consejo Consultivo Laboral Andino (Andean Labour Advisory Council): Paseo de la República 3832, Of. 502, San Isidro, Lima 27, Peru; tel. (1) 6181701; fax (1) 6100139; e-mail cutperujcb@gmail.com; f. 1998; an advisory institution within the framework of the Sistema Andino de Integración; comprises elected representatives of labour orgs; advises Community ministers and officers on related labour issues; Pres. CÉRVULO BAUTISTA MATOMA (Colombia).

Convenio Andrés Bello (Andrés Bello Agreement): Calle 93B 17-49, Bogotá, Colombia; tel. and fax (1) 644-9292; fax (1) 644-9292; internet www.convenioandresbello.org; f. 1970, modified in 1990; aims to promote integration in the educational, technical and cultural sectors; a new Inter-institutional Co-operation Agreement was signed with the Secretariat of the CAN in Aug. 2003; mems: Bolivia, Chile, Colombia, Cuba, Dominican Republic, Ecuador, Mexico, Panama, Paraguay, Peru, Spain, Venezuela; Exec. Sec. MÓNICA LÓPEZ CASTRO (Colombia).

Convenio Hipólito Unanue (Hipólito Unanue Agreement): Edif. Cartagena, Paseo de la República 3832, 3°, San Isidro, Lima, Peru; tel. (1) 2210074; fax (1) 2222663; e-mail contacto@conhu.org.pe; internet www.orasconhu.org; f. 1971 on the occasion of the first meeting of Andean ministers responsible for health; became part of the institutional structure of the Community in 1998; aims to enhance the devt of health services, and to promote regional co-ordination in areas such as environmental health, disaster preparedness and the prevention and control of drug abuse; Exec. Sec. Dr CAROLINE CHANG CAMPOS (Ecuador).

Convenio Simón Rodríguez (Simón Rodríguez Agreement): Paseo de la República 3895, esq. Aramburú, San Isidro, Lima 27, Peru; tel. (1) 4111400; fax (1) 2213329; promotes a convergence of social and labour conditions throughout the Community, for example, working hours and conditions, employment and social security policies, and promotes the participation of workers and employers in the subregional integration process; Protocol of Modification signed in June 2001, and had by 2014 been ratified by all member states apart from Colombia; analyses Community social and labour policies through the ongoing Andean Labour Observatory Pilot Plan.

Corporación Andina de Fomento (CAF) (Andean Development Corporation): Torre CAF, Avda Luis Roche, Altamira, Apdo 5086, Caracas, Venezuela; tel. (212) 2092111; fax (212) 2092444; e-mail infocaf@caf.com; internet www.caf.com; f. 1968, began operations in 1970; aims to encourage the integration of the Andean countries by specialization and an equitable distribution of investments; conducts research to identify investment opportunities, and prepares the resulting investment projects; gives technical and financial assistance; and attracts internal and external credit; in July 2012 the CAF signed an inter-agency co-operation agreement, with ECLAC and the Latin American Integration Association, establishing the internet-based Latin America/Asia-Pacific Observatory, which aims to deepen knowledge about economic relations between the countries of both regions; participates in an annual meeting, focused on development issues, with the OAS and US-based Inter-American Dialogue (held most recently in Sept. 2014); auth. cap. US $10,000m.; subscribed or underwritten by the governments of mem. countries, or by public, semi-public and private sector institutions authorized by those govts; the Board of Directors comprises representatives of each country at ministerial level; mems: the Andean Community, Argentina, Brazil, Chile, Costa Rica, Jamaica, Mexico, Panama, Paraguay, Spain, Trinidad and Tobago, Uruguay, Venezuela, and 14 private banks in the Andean region; has subsidiary offices in Buenos Aires, Argentina; La Paz, Bolivia; Brasília, Brasil; Bogotá, Colombia; Quito, Ecuador; Lima, Peru; Madrid, Spain; and Montevideo, Uruguay; Exec. Pres. ENRIQUE GARCÍA RODRÍGUEZ (Bolivia).

Fondo Latinoamericano de Reservas (FLAR) (Latin American Reserve Fund): Avda 82 12–18, 7°, POB 241523, Bogotá, Colombia; tel. (1) 634-4360; fax (1) 634-4384; e-mail info@flar.net; internet www .flar.net; f. 1978 as the Fondo Andino de Reservas to support the balance of payments of member countries, provide credit, guarantee loans, and contribute to the harmonization of monetary and financial policies; adopted present name in 1991, in order to allow the admission of other Latin American countries; in 1992 the Fund began extending credit lines to commercial cos for export financing; it is administered by an Assembly of the ministers responsible for finance and economic affairs of the mem. countries, and a Board of Directors comprising the Presidents of the central banks of the mem. states; mems: Bolivia, Colombia, Costa Rica, Ecuador, Peru, Uruguay,

Venezuela; subscribed cap. US $2,343.8m. cap. p.u. $2,034.1m. (31 Dec. 2011); Exec. Pres. ANA MARÍA CARRASQUILLA.

Universidad Andina Simón Bolívar (Simón Bolívar Andean University): Real Audiencia 73, Casilla 545, Sucre, Bolivia; tel. (4) 6460265; fax (4) 6460833; e-mail uasb@uasb.edu.bo; internet www .uasb.edu.bo; f. 1985; institution for postgraduate study and research; promotes co-operation between other universities in the Andean region; branches in Quito (Ecuador), La Paz (Bolivia),

Caracas (Venezuela) and Cali (Colombia); Pres. (Sucre Office) JOSÉ LUIS GUITIÉRREZ SARDÁN; Pres. (Quito Office) ENRIQUE AYALA MORA.

Publications

Reports, working papers, sector documents, council proceedings.

CARIBBEAN COMMUNITY AND COMMON MARKET—CARICOM

Address: POB 10827, Turkeyen, Greater Georgetown, Guyana.

Telephone: (2) 222-0001; **fax:** (2) 222-0171; **e-mail:** registry@ caricom.org; **internet:** www.caricom.org.

CARICOM was formed in 1973 by the Treaty of Chaguaramas, signed in Trinidad, as a movement towards unity in the Caribbean; it replaced the Caribbean Free Trade Association (CARIFTA), founded in 1965. A revision of the Treaty of Chaguaramas (by means of nine separate Protocols), in order to institute greater regional integration and to establish a CARICOM Single Market and Economy (CSME), was instigated in the 1990s and completed in July 2001. The single market component of the CSME was formally inaugurated on 1 January 2006.

MEMBERS

Antigua and Barbuda	Jamaica
Bahamas*	Montserrat
Barbados	Saint Christopher and Nevis
Belize	Saint Lucia
Dominica	Saint Vincent and the
Grenada	Grenadines
Guyana	Suriname
Haiti	Trinidad and Tobago

* The Bahamas is a member of the Community but not the Common Market.

ASSOCIATE MEMBERS

Anguilla	Cayman Islands
Bermuda	Turks and Caicos Islands
British Virgin Islands	

Note: At September 2014 applications for associate membership by French Guiana, Guadeloupe, Martinique, and Curaçao and St. Maarten were under consideration. Colombia, Dominican Republic, Mexico, Puerto Rico, and Venezuela have observer status with the Community.

Organization

(September 2014)

HEADS OF GOVERNMENT CONFERENCE AND BUREAU

The Conference is the final authority of the Community and determines policy. It is responsible for the conclusion of treaties on behalf of the Community and for entering into relationships between the Community and international organizations and states. Decisions of the Conference are generally taken unanimously. Heads of government meet annually, although inter-sessional meetings may be convened.

At a special meeting of the Conference, held in Trinidad and Tobago in October 1992, participants decided to establish a Heads of Government Bureau, with the capacity to initiate proposals, to update consensus and to secure the implementation of CARICOM decisions. The Bureau became operational in December, comprising the Chairman of the Conference, as Chairman, as well as the incoming and outgoing Chairmen of the Conference, and the Secretary-General of the Conference, in the capacity of Chief Executive Officer.

COMMUNITY COUNCIL OF MINISTERS

In October 1992 CARICOM heads of government agreed that a Caribbean Community Council of Ministers should be established to replace the existing Common Market Council of Ministers as the second highest organ of the Community. Protocol I amending the Treaty of Chaguaramas, to restructure the organs and institutions of

the Community, was formally adopted at a meeting of CARICOM heads of government in February 1997 and was signed by all member states in July. The inaugural meeting of the Community Council of Ministers was held in Nassau, Bahamas, in February 1998. The Council consists of ministers responsible for community affairs, as well as other government ministers designated by member states, and is responsible for the development of the Community's strategic planning and co-ordination in the areas of economic integration, functional co-operation and external relations.

COURT OF JUSTICE

Caribbean Court of Justice (CCJ): 134 Henry St, POB 1768, Port of Spain, Trinidad and Tobago; tel. 623-2225; fax 627-1193; e-mail info@caribbeancourtofjustice.org; internet www .caribbeancourtofjustice.org; inaugurated in April 2005; an agreement establishing the Court was formally signed by 10 member countries in February 2001, and by two further states in February 2003; in January 2004 a revised agreement on the establishment of the CCJ, which incorporated provision for a Trust Fund, entered into force; serves as a tribunal to enforce rights and to consider disputes relating to the CARICOM Single Market and Economy; intended to replace the Judicial Committee of the Privy Council as the Court of Final Appeal (effective for Barbados, Belize and Guyana at Sept. 2014); Pres. Sir DENNIS BYRON (Saint Christopher and Nevis).

MINISTERIAL COUNCILS

The principal organs of the Community are assisted in their functions by the following bodies, established under Protocol I amending the Treaty of Chaguaramas: the Council for Trade and Economic Development (COTED); the Council for Foreign and Community Relations (COFCOR); the Council for Human and Social Development (COHSOD); and the Council for Finance and Planning (COFAP). The Councils are responsible for formulating policies, promoting their implementation and supervising co-operation in the relevant areas.

SECRETARIAT

The Secretariat is the main administrative body of the Caribbean Community. The functions of the Secretariat are to service meetings of the Community and of its Committees; to take appropriate follow-up action on decisions made at such meetings; to carry out studies on questions of economic and functional co-operation relating to the region as a whole; to provide services to member states at their request in respect of matters relating to the achievement of the objectives of the Community. The Secretariat incorporates Directorates, each headed by an Assistant Secretary-General, for Trade and Economic Integration; Foreign and Community Relations; Human and Social Development; and CARIFORUM.

Secretary-General: IRWIN LAROCQUE (Dominica).

Activities

In March 2012 heads of government, convened in Paramaribo, Suriname, considered a final report of a review of the organization that was initiated in July 2010: *Turning around CARICOM: Proposals to restructure the Secretariat.* Heads of government subsequently agreed to initiate a reform process to effect change within the Community and its Secretariat. As part of the process, in July 2014, heads of government approved the first Strategic Plan for the Community, to cover the period 2015–19. The Plan, formulated following widespread consultation with stakeholders throughout the region, identified the following as priority areas: Accelerate implementation and use of the CARICOM Single Market and Economy (CSME); Introduce measures for macro-economic stabilization; Build competitiveness and unleash key economic drivers to transition to growth and generate employment; Human capital development; Advance health and wellness; Enhance citizen security and justice; Climate adaptation and mitigation and disaster mitigation and management; Develop the single ICT space; Deepen foreign policy co-ordination (to support the strategic repositioning of CARICOM and desired outcomes); Public education, public information and advocacy; Reform of the CARICOM Secretariat, the organs, bodies, institutions and governance arrangements.

ECONOMIC CO-OPERATION

The Caribbean Community's main field of activity is economic integration, by means of a Caribbean Common Market. The Secretariat and the Caribbean Development Bank undertake research on the best means of tackling economic difficulties, and meetings of the chief executives of commercial banks and of central bank officials are also held with the aim of strengthening regional co-operation. In March 2009 heads of government, meeting in Belize City, Belize, resolved to pursue a regional strategy to counter the effects on the region of the severe global economic and financial downturn. A new Heads of Government Task Force on the Regional Financial and Economic Crisis held its inaugural meeting in August, in Jamaica. The new Strategic Plan for 2015–19 identified 'Building economic resilience' as a core strategic priority for the Community.

In 1989 the Conference of Heads of Government agreed to implement, by July 1993, a series of measures to encourage the creation of a single Caribbean market. These included the establishment of a CARICOM Industrial Programming Scheme; the inauguration of the CARICOM Enterprise Regime; facilitation of travel for CARICOM nationals within the region; full implementation of the rules of origin and the revised scheme for the harmonization of fiscal incentives; free movement of skilled workers; removal of all remaining regional barriers to trade; establishment of a regional system of air and sea transport; and the introduction of a scheme for regional capital movement. In August 1990 CARICOM heads of government mandated the governors of CARICOM members' central banks to begin a study of the means to achieve monetary union within CARICOM; they also institutionalized biannual meetings of CARICOM ministers responsible for finance and senior finance officials.

The initial deadline of 1991 for the establishment of a common external tariff (CET—first agreed in 1984) was not achieved. At a special meeting, held in October 1992, CARICOM heads of government agreed to reduce the maximum level of tariffs from 45% to between 30% and 35%, to be in effect by 30 June 1993 (the level was to be further lowered, to 25%–30% by 1995). The Bahamas, however, was not party to these trading arrangements (since it is a member of the Community but not of the Common Market), and Belize was granted an extension for the implementation of the new tariff levels. At the Heads of Government Conference, held in July 1995 in Guyana, Suriname was admitted as a full member of CARICOM and acceded to the treaty establishing the Common Market. It was granted until 1 January 1996 for implementation of the tariff reductions. The 1995 Conference approved additional measures to promote the single market. The free movement of skilled workers was to be permitted from 1 January 1996. At the same time an agreement on the mutual protection and provision of social security benefits was to enter into force. In July 1996 heads of government agreed to extend the provisions of free movement to sportsmen and women, musicians and others working in the arts and media.

In July 1997 the Conference, meeting in Montego Bay, Jamaica, determined to accelerate economic integration, with the aim of completing a single market by 1999. At the meeting 11 member states signed Protocol II amending the Treaty of Chaguaramas, which constituted a central element of a CARICOM Single Market and Economy (CSME), providing for the right to establish enterprises, the provision of services and the free movement of capital and labour throughout participating countries. In July 1998, at the meeting of heads of government, held in Saint Lucia, an agreement was signed with the Insurance Company of the West Indies to accelerate the establishment of a Caribbean Investment Fund, which was to mobilize foreign currency from extra-regional capital markets for investment in new or existing enterprises in the region. Some 60% of all funds generated were to be used by CARICOM countries and the remainder by non-CARICOM members of the Association of Caribbean States. In February 2001 heads of government agreed to establish a new high-level sub-committee to accelerate the establishment of the CSME and to promote its objectives. The sub-committee was to be supported by a Technical Advisory Council, comprising representatives of the public and private sectors. By June all member states had signed and declared the provisional application of Protocol II.

In October 2001 CARICOM heads of government, convened for a special emergency meeting, considered the impact on the region's economy of the terrorist attacks perpetrated against targets in the USA in the previous month. The meeting resolved to enhance aviation security, implement promotion and marketing campaigns

in support of the tourist industry, and approach international institutions to assist with emergency financing. The economic situation, which had been further adversely affected by the reduced access to the European Union (EU) banana market, the economic downturn in the USA, and the effects on the investment climate of the OECD Harmful Taxation Initiative, was considered at the Heads of Government Conference, held in Guyana, in July 2002.

On 1 January 2006 the single market component of the CSME was formally inaugurated, with Barbados, Belize, Guyana, Jamaica, Suriname and Trinidad and Tobago as active participants. Six more countries (Antigua and Barbuda, Dominica, Grenada, Saint Christopher and Nevis, Saint Lucia, Saint Vincent and the Grenadines) formally joined the single market in July. At the same time CARICOM heads of government approved a contribution formula allowing for the establishment of a regional development fund. The Caribbean Development Fund (CDF), launched in mid-2008, with initial finances of US $60m. commenced full operations in August 2009. In February 2011 heads of government signed an agreement to enable the CDF to grant funds on preferential terms to low-income member countries. In March 2013 a $3.5m. CSME Standby Facility was launched, to be administered by the Caribbean Development Bank.

In February 2007 an inter-sessional meeting of the Conference of Heads of Government, held in Saint Vincent and the Grenadines, approved a timetable for the full implementation of the CSME: phase I (mid-2005–08) for the consolidation of the single market and the initiation of a single economy; phase II (2009–15) for the consolidation and completion of the single economy process, including the harmonization and co-ordination of economic policies in the region and the establishment of new institutions to implement those policies. In July 2007 CARICOM heads of government endorsed the report, *Towards a Single Development Vision and the Role of the Single Economy*, on which the elaboration of the CSME was based. In January 2008 a Caribbean Competition Commission was inaugurated, in Paramaribo, Suriname, to enforce the rules of competition within the CSME. In February Haiti signed the revised Treaty of Chaguaramas.

In December 2007 a special meeting of the Conference of Heads of Government, convened in Georgetown, Guyana, considered issues relating to regional poverty and the rising cost of living in member states. The meeting resolved to establish a technical team to review the CET on essential commodities to determine whether it should be removed or reduced to deter inflationary pressures. The meeting also agreed to review the supply and distribution of food throughout the region, including transportation issues affecting the price of goods and services, and determined to expand agricultural production and agro-processing. Efforts to harness renewable energy sources were to be strengthened to counter rising fuel prices.

In July 2014 a two-year project was initiated that aimed to develop a harmonized framework for establishing and operating businesses within the CSME.

REGIONAL INTEGRATION

In July 1992 a West Indian Commission, established to study regional political and economic integration, recommended that CARICOM should remain a community of sovereign states (rather than a federation), but should strengthen the integration process and expand to include the wider Caribbean region. It recommended the formation of an Association of Caribbean States (ACS), to include all the countries within and surrounding the Caribbean Basin. In November 1997 the Secretaries-General of CARICOM and the ACS signed a Co-operation Agreement to formalize the reciprocal procedures through which the organizations work to enhance and facilitate regional integration. Suriname was admitted to CARICOM in July 1995. In July 1997 the Heads of Government Conference agreed to admit Haiti as a member, although the terms and conditions of its accession to the organization were not finalized until July 1999. In July 2001 the CARICOM Secretary-General formally inaugurated a CARICOM Office in Haiti, which aimed to provide technical assistance in preparation for Haiti's accession to the Community. In January 2002 a CARICOM special mission visited Haiti, following an escalation of the political violence that had started in the previous month. Ministers responsible for foreign affairs emphasized the need for international aid for Haiti when they met their US counterpart in February. Haiti was admitted as the 15th member of CARICOM at the Heads of Government Conference, held in July. It hosted a meeting of CARICOM heads of government for the first time in February 2013.

In July 1998 heads of government expressed concern at the hostility between the Government and opposition groupings in Guyana. The two sides signed an agreement, under CARICOM auspices, and in September a CARICOM mediation mission visited Guyana to promote further dialogue. CARICOM has declared its support for Guyana in its territorial disputes with Venezuela and Suriname. A CARICOM electoral observer mission monitored the conduct of a general election in Guyana in November 2011.

In February 1997 Community heads of government signed a new Charter of Civil Society for the Community, which set out principles in the areas of democracy, government, parliament, freedom of the press and human rights. In July 2002 a conference was held, in Liliendaal, Guyana, attended by representatives of civil society and CARICOM heads of government. The meeting issued a statement of principles on 'Forward Together', recognizing the role of civil society in meeting the challenges to the region. It was agreed to hold regular meetings and to establish a task force to develop a regional strategic framework for pursuing the main recommendations of the conference. In February 2007 an inter-sessional meeting of CARICOM heads of government determined to add security (including crime) as a fourth pillar of regional integration, in addition to those identified: economic integration; co-ordination of foreign policy; and functional co-operation.

CO-ORDINATION OF FOREIGN POLICY

The co-ordination of foreign policies of member states is listed as one of the main objectives of the Community in its founding treaty. Activities include strengthening member states' position in international organizations; joint diplomatic action on issues of particular interest to the Caribbean; joint co-operation arrangements with third countries and organizations; and the negotiation of free trade agreements with third countries and other regional groupings. In April 1997 CARICOM inaugurated a Caribbean Regional Negotiating Machinery (CRNM) body, based in Kingston, Jamaica, to co-ordinate and strengthen the region's presence at external economic negotiations. The main areas of activity were negotiations to establish a Free Trade Area of the Americas (FTAA—now stalled), ACP relations with the EU, and multilateral trade negotiations under the World Trade Organization (WTO). In July 2009 the CRNM was renamed the Office of Trade Negotiations, reporting directly to the Council for Trade and Economic Development; its mandate was expanded to include responsibility for all external trade negotiations on behalf of the Community. Since 2001 CARICOM has conducted regular meetings with representatives of the UN. The sixth meeting, convened in July 2011, agreed to revise the existing Regional Strategic Framework for co-operation and to initiate negotiations towards a more effective mechanism for UN activities in the region.

In July 1993 a joint commission was inaugurated to establish closer ties between CARICOM and Cuba and provide a mechanism for regular dialogue. A Trade and Economic Agreement was signed by the two sides in July 2000, and in February 2001 a CARICOM office was established in Cuba. At the first meeting of heads of state and government in December 2002, convened in Havana, Cuba, it was agreed to commemorate the start of diplomatic relations between the two sides, some 30 years previously, on 8 December each year as Cuba/CARICOM Day. The second summit meeting, held in December 2005 in Bridgetown, Barbados, agreed to strengthen co-operation in education, culture and the environment, access to health care and efforts to counter international terrorism. A second meeting of CARICOM-Cuba ministers responsible for foreign affairs was convened in May 2007 (the first having taken place in July 2004). The third meeting at the level of heads of state and government was held in December 2008 in Santiago de Cuba, Cuba. CARICOM leaders urged the new US administration to reconsider its restrictions on trade with Cuba. A similar appeal was made at the fourth summit meeting, convened in December 2011, in Port of Spain, Trinidad and Tobago. The meeting also focused on collaboration with regard to the illegal trafficking of drugs and small arms. The fifth CARICOM-Cuba summit meeting was scheduled to be convened in Cuba, in December 2014.

In May 1997 a meeting of CARICOM heads of government and the US President established a partnership for prosperity and security, and arrangements were instituted for annual consultations between the ministers responsible for foreign affairs of CARICOM countries and the US Secretary of State. However, the Community failed to secure a commitment by the USA to grant the region's exports 'NAFTA-parity' status, or to guarantee concessions to the region's banana industry. The USA's opposition to a new EU banana policy (which was to terminate the import licensing system, extending import quotas to 'dollar' producers, while maintaining a limited duty-free quota for Caribbean producers) was strongly criticized by CARICOM leaders, meeting in July 1998. In March 1999 the Inter-Sessional meeting of the Conference of Heads of Government issued a statement condemning the imposition by the USA of sanctions against a number of EU imports, in protest at the revised EU banana regime, and the consequences of this action on Caribbean economies, and agreed to review its co-operation with the USA under the partnership for prosperity and security.

In August 1998 CARICOM and the Dominican Republic signed a free trade accord, covering trade in goods and services, technical barriers to trade, government procurement, and sanitary and phytosanitary measures and standards. A protocol to the agreement was signed in April 2000, following the resolution of differences concerning exempted items. The accord was ratified by the Dominican Republic in February 2001 and entered partially into force on 1 December. A Task Force to strengthen bilateral relations was established in 2007 and held its first meeting in November 2008. In November 2001 the CARICOM Secretary-General formally inaugurated a Caribbean Regional Technical Assistance Centre (CARTAC), in Barbados, to provide technical advice and training to officials from member countries and the Dominican Republic in support of the region's development. The Centre's operations are managed by the IMF.

In March 2000 heads of government issued a statement supporting the territorial integrity and security of Belize in that country's ongoing border dispute with Guatemala. CARICOM subsequently urged both countries to implement the provisions of an agreement signed in November and has continued to monitor the situation regularly. CARICOM has expressed support for a new roadmap to strengthen bilateral relations, signed in January 2014 under the auspices of the Organization of American States (OAS).

In February 2002 the first meeting of heads of state and of government of CARICOM and the Central American Integration System (SICA) was convened in Belize City. The meeting aimed to strengthen co-operation between the groupings, in particular in international negotiations, efforts to counter transnational organized crime, and support for the regions' economies. In 2002 a joint CARICOM-Spain commission was inaugurated to foster greater co-operation between the two parties. In August 2012 a new CARICOM-Spain Joint Fund was launched, and, within its framework, a number of regional projects were approved. In March 2004 CARICOM signed a free trade agreement with Costa Rica.

In January 2004 CARICOM heads of government resolved to address the escalating political crisis in Haiti. Following a visit by a high-level delegation to that country early in the month discussions were held with representatives of opposition political parties and civil society groups. At the end of January several CARICOM leaders met with Haiti's President Aristide and members of his Government and announced a Prior Action Plan, incorporating opposition demands for political reform. The Plan, however, was rejected by opposition parties since it permitted Aristide to complete his term-in-office. CARICOM, together with the OAS, continued to pursue diplomatic efforts to secure a peaceful solution to the crisis. On 29 February Aristide resigned and left the country and a provisional president was appointed. In March CARICOM heads of government determined not to allow representatives of the new interim administration to participate in the councils of the Community until constitutional rule had been reinstated. In July heads of government resolved to send a five-member ministerial team to Haiti to discuss developments in that country with the interim authorities. In July 2005 CARICOM heads of government expressed concern at the deterioration of the situation in Haiti, but reiterated their readiness to provide technical assistance for the electoral process, under the auspices of the UN mission. In March 2006 the CARICOM Chairman endorsed the results of the presidential election, conducted in February, and pledged to support Haiti's return to democratic rule. In August 2010 CARICOM sent a joint election observation mission (JEOM), with the OAS, to monitor presidential and legislative elections in Haiti, scheduled for November. Although the JEOM reported several procedural irregularities in the voting process, and expressed concern at allegations by some candidates and their supporters of fraudulence or intimidation at polling stations, it confirmed that the elections were valid. The mission also monitored the second round of voting in the presidential election, held in March 2011, before being terminated in May of that year. In February 2012 a Memorandum of Understanding was concluded between CARICOM and Haiti that identified various areas in which CARICOM might provide future support.

In March 2006 a CARICOM-Mexico Joint Commission signed an agreement to promote future co-operation, in particular in seven priority areas. The first summit-level meeting between heads of state and government of Mexico and CARICOM was held in February 2010, in Riviera Maya, Mexico. A second CARICOM-Mexico summit meeting was held in Bridgetown, Barbados, in May 2012 and a third was convened in Mérida, Mexico, in April 2014. In February 2007 the Secretaries-General of CARICOM and SICA signed a plan of action on future co-operation between the two groupings. A second CARICOM-SICA meeting of heads of state and of government was convened in May, in Belize. The meeting endorsed the plan of action and, in addition, instructed their ministers responsible for foreign affairs and for trade to pursue efforts to negotiate a free trade agreement, to be based on that signed by CARICOM with Costa Rica. Trade negotiations were formally inaugurated in August. The third CARICOM-SICA summit meeting was convened in El Salvador, in August 2011. A joint declaration recognized the need to develop transport and cultural links, and detailed measures to strengthen co-operation in international environmental negotiations, combating transnational crime, disaster management, the prevention of non-communicable diseases, and the management of migratory fish stocks in the Caribbean Sea.

In March 2006 CARICOM ministers responsible for foreign affairs met with the US Secretary of State and agreed to strengthen co-operation and enhance bilateral relations. In June 2007 a major meeting, the 'Conference on the Caribbean: a 20/20 Vision', was held in Washington, DC, USA. A series of meetings was held to consider issues and challenges relating to CARICOM's development and integration efforts and to the strengthening of relations with other countries in the region and with the USA. An Experts' Forum was hosted by the World Bank, a Private Sector Dialogue was held at the headquarters of the Inter-American Development Bank, and a Diaspora Forum was convened at the OAS. A summit meeting of CARICOM heads of government and then US President George W. Bush was held in the context of the Conference, at which issues concerning trade, economic growth and development, security and social investment were discussed. A second Conference on the Caribbean was held in New York, USA, in June 2008. A meeting of CARICOM foreign ministers with the US Secretary of State was held in June 2010, in Barbados, at which a series of commitments was concluded to enhance co-operation on a range of issues including energy security, climate change, health and trade relations.

In November 2013 CARICOM signed a Memorandum of Understanding with UNESCO, providing a framework for future co-operation in areas including assessment of natural hazards; heritage preservation and the development of national cultural policies; promotion of inclusive education; and implementation of the Plan of Action for the Sustainable Development of Small Island Developing States.

In July 2013 CARICOM heads of government determined that, with respect to the pursuit of reparations for historic acts of slavery and native genocide, national reparations committees should be established in every member state, and that the chairperson of each of these should participate in a new CARICOM Reparations Commission. The first CARICOM Regional Reparations Conference was held in September, in St Vincent and the Grenadines. In March 2014 CARICOM heads of state or government endorsed a new Caribbean Reparatory Justice Programme (CRJP) as the basis for future regional discussions on reparations. Priority areas of the CRJP included seeking a full apology from the governments of European countries that were implicated in the transatlantic slave trade; the initiation of an educational programme to address illiteracy; the establishment of Caribbean cultural institutions; and a debt cancellation initiative.

In July 2014 the first meeting of heads of government of CARICOM and Japan took place, in Port-of-Spain, Trinidad and Tobago. Japan's policy towards CARICOM was clarified, based on three pillars: co-operation towards sustainable development, including overcoming vulnerabilities particular to small island states; deepening and expanding bonds founded on exchanges and friendship; co-operation in addressing challenges of the international community.

CARICOM was actively involved in preparations for the Third International Conference on Small Island Developing States, convened in Apia, Samoa, in September 2014. CARICOM, with the UN Economic Commission for Latin America and the Caribbean, organized a sideline event that focused on the specific vulnerabilities of Caribbean small island states.

CRIME AND SECURITY

In December 1996 CARICOM heads of government determined to strengthen comprehensive co-operation and technical assistance to combat illegal drugs-trafficking. The Conference decided to establish a Caribbean Security Task Force to help to formulate a single regional agreement on maritime interdiction, incorporating agreements already concluded by individual members. A Regional Drugs Control Programme at the CARICOM Secretariat aims to co-ordinate regional initiatives with the overall objective of reducing the demand and supply of illegal substances.

In July 2000 the Heads of Government meeting issued a statement strongly opposing the OECD Harmful Tax Initiative, under which punitive measures had been threatened against 35 countries, including CARICOM member states, if they failed to tighten taxation legislation. The meeting also condemned a separate list, issued by OECD's Financial Action Task Force on Money Laundering (FATF), which identified 15 countries, including five Caribbean states, of failing to counter effectively international money-laundering. The statement reaffirmed CARICOM's commitment to fighting financial crimes and support for any necessary reform of supervisory practices or legislation, but insisted that national taxation jurisdictions, and specifically competitive regimes designed to attract offshore business, was not a matter for OECD concern. CARICOM remained actively involved in efforts to counter the scheme, and in April 2001 presented its case to the US President. In September the FATF issued a revised list of 19 'unco-operative jurisdictions', including Dominica, Grenada, Saint Christopher and Nevis, and Saint Vincent and the Grenadines. In early 2002 most Caribbean states concluded a provisional agreement with OECD to work to improve the transparency and supervision of 'offshore' sectors.

In July 2001 heads of government resolved to establish a task force to be responsible for producing recommendations for a forthcoming meeting of national security advisers. In October heads of government convened an emergency meeting in Nassau, Bahamas, to consider the impact of the terrorist attacks against the USA that had occurred in September. The meeting determined to convene immediately the so-called Task Force on Crime and Security in order to implement new policy directives. It was agreed to enhance co-ordination and collaboration of security services throughout the region, in particular in intelligence gathering, analysis and sharing in relation to crime, illicit drugs and terrorism, and to strengthen security at airports, seaports and borders. In July 2002 heads of government agreed on a series of initiatives recommended by the Task Force to counter the escalation in crime and violence. These included strengthening border controls, preparing national anti-crime master plans, establishing broad-based National Commissions on law and order and furthering the exchange of information and intelligence.

In July 2005 CARICOM heads of government endorsed a new Management Framework for Crime and Security, which provided for regular meetings of a Council of Ministers responsible for national security and law enforcement, a Security Policy Advisory Committee, and the establishment of an Implementation Agency for Crime and Security (IMPACS). In July 2007 CARICOM heads of government agreed in principle to extend these security efforts, including the introduction of a voluntary CARICOM Travel Card, CARIPASS, to facilitate the establishment of a single domestic space. An agreement to implement CARIPASS was signed by heads of government meeting in Dominica, in March 2010.

In April 2010 US President Barack Obama announced a Caribbean Basin Security Initiative (CBSI), which was to structure its regional security policy around a bilateral partnership with CARICOM, in particular to advance public safety and security, substantially to reduce the trafficking of illicit substances and to promote social justice. In the following month an inaugural Caribbean-US Security Co-operation Dialogue was held, in Washington, DC, to pursue discussion of the CBSI. The first meeting of a CBSI Commission was convened in Kingston, in November. Also in November, at the second meeting of the CARICOM-US Security Co-operation Dialogue, held in the Bahamas, officials agreed to facilitate region-wide information sharing, and to develop a regional juvenile justice policy.

In September 2011 a delegation from the UN Office on Drugs and Crime met with officials from IMPACS in Trinidad and Tobago. Discussions centred on strengthening regional forensics capacity, the proliferation of illegal guns, human trafficking, smuggling of migrants, and money-laundering. The establishment of an INTERPOL Liaison Office within IMPACS is under consideration.

INDUSTRY, ENERGY AND THE ENVIRONMENT

A protocol relating to the CARICOM Industrial Programming Scheme (CIPS), approved in 1988, is the Community's instrument for promoting the co-operative development of industry in the region. Protocol III amending the Treaty of Chaguaramas, with respect to industrial policy, was opened for signature in July 1998. In 1999 members agreed to establish a new CARICOM Regional Organisation for Standards and Quality (CROSQ), as a successor to the Caribbean Common Market Standards Council. The agreement to establish CROSQ, to be located in Barbados, was signed in February 2002.

The CARICOM Alternative Energy Systems Project provides training, assesses energy needs and conducts energy audits. Implementation of a Caribbean Renewable Energy Development Programme, a project initiated in 1998, commenced in 2004. The Programme aimed to remove barriers to renewable energy development, establish a foundation for a sustainable renewable energy industry, and to create a framework for co-operation among regional and national renewable energy projects. A Caribbean Renewable Energy Fund was established to provide equity and development financing for renewable energy projects. In March 2013 the Council for Trade and Economic Development (COTED) endorsed a new Regional Energy Policy to strengthen energy efficiency and support the adoption of renewable sources of energy throughout the Community.

In January 2001 (COTED) approved the development of a specialized CARICOM agency to co-ordinate the gathering of information and other activities relating to climate change. The Caribbean Community Climate Change Centre became operational in early 2004 and was formally inaugurated, in Belmopan, Belize, in August 2005. It serves as an official clearing house and repository of data relating to climate change in the Caribbean region, provides advice to governments and other expertise for the development of projects to manage and adapt to climate change, and undertakes training. The results of the Centre's Mainstreaming Adaptation to Climate Change (MACC) Project were presented to governments at a Caribbean Climate Change Conference, held in Saint Lucia, in March 2009. In June 2012, during the UN Conference on Sustainable Development, held in Rio de Janeiro, Brazil, the Centre, the Indian Ocean Commission and the Secretariat of the Pacific Regional Environment Programme signed two agreements on co-operation in addressing climate change and promoting sustainable development.

In July 2008 CARICOM heads of government established a Task Force on Climate Change and Development to consider future action in relation to developments in energy and climate change, and in particular food insecurity caused by global rising food and fuel prices. The inaugural meeting of the Task Force was held in November, in Saint Lucia. In March 2012 CARICOM heads of government endorsed an Implementation Plan for the Regional Framework for Achieving Development Resilient to Climate Change, to cover the period 2011–21. 'Environmental resilience' was one of the strategic priorities identified in the Strategic Plan 2015–19.

TRANSPORT, COMMUNICATIONS AND TOURISM

A Multilateral Agreement Concerning the Operations of Air Services within the Caribbean Community entered into force in November 1998, providing a formal framework for the regulation of the air transport industry and enabling CARICOM-owned and -controlled airlines to operate freely within the region. In July 1999 heads of government signed Protocol VI amending the Treaty of Chaguaramas providing for a common transportation policy, with harmonized standards and practices, which was to be an integral component of the development of a single market and economy. In November 2001 representatives of national civil aviation authorities signed a MOU, providing for the establishment of a regional body, the Regional Aviation Safety Oversight System. This was succeeded, in July 2008, by a Caribbean Aviation Safety and Security Oversight System upon the signing of an agreement by Barbados, Guyana, Saint Lucia and Trinidad and Tobago.

In 1989 a Caribbean Telecommunications Union was established to oversee developments in regional telecommunications. In July 2006 the Conference of Heads of Government, convened in Saint Christopher and Nevis, mandated the development of C@ribNET, a project to extend the availability of high-speed internet access throughout the region. In May 2007 the inaugural meeting of a Regional Information Communications and Technology Steering Committee was held, in Georgetown, Guyana, to determine areas of activity for future co-operation in support of the establishment of a Caribbean Information Society. In July 2012 government representatives, potential investors and organizations from nine CARICOM member states participated in a multi-stakeholder meeting on the sidelines of a 'Connect to the Americas Summit', which was convened, under the auspices of the International Telecommunication Union, in Panama City, Panama, to address the promotion of digital inclusion and means of accelerating secure and affordable access to broadband connectivity across the continent. In March 2014 it was announced that a CARICOM Single Information Communication Technology (ICT) Space, and Digital Agenda 2025, would be developed.

In 1997 CARICOM heads of government requested ministers responsible for tourism to meet regularly to develop tourism policies. A regional summit on tourism was held in the Bahamas in December 2001. A new Caribbean passport, introduced in January 2005, is issued by all 12 member countries participating in the CSME. In February 2013 representatives of regional and international tourism agencies met in Managua, Nicaragua, to develop a Regional Agenda for Sustainable Tourism in the Greater Caribbean.

AGRICULTURE AND FISHERIES

The CARICOM Secretariat supports national agricultural programmes with assistance in policy formulation, human resource development and the promotion of research and technology development in the areas of productivity, marketing, agri-business and water resources management. Protocol V amending the Treaty of Chaguaramas, which was concerned with agricultural policy, was opened for signature in July 1998. In July 2002 heads of government approved an initiative to develop a CARIFORUM Special Programme for Food Security. CARICOM Governments have continually aimed to generate awareness of the economic and social importance of the banana industry to the region, in particular within the framework of the WTO multilateral trade negotiations.

In July 2005 CARICOM heads of government issued a statement protesting against proposals by the European Commission, issued in the previous month, to reform the EU sugar regime. Particular concern was expressed at a proposed price reduction in the cost of refined sugar of 39% over a four-year period. The heads of government insisted that, in accordance with the ACP-EU Cotonou Agreement, any review of the Sugar Protocol was required to be undertaken with the agreement of both parties and with regard to safeguarding benefits. In December CARICOM heads of government held a special meeting to discuss the EU sugar and banana regimes, in advance of a ministerial meeting of the WTO, held in Hong Kong that month. The Conference reiterated the potentially devastating effects on regional economies of the sugar price reduction and

proposed new banana tariffs, and expressed the need for greater compensation and for the WTO multilateral negotiations to address fairly issues of preferential access. Negotiations between the ACP Caribbean signatory countries (the so-called CARIFORUM) and the EU on an Economic Partnership Agreement (EPA) to succeed the Cotonou Agreement, which had commenced in April 2004, were concluded in December 2007. In January 2008 CARICOM's Council for Trade and Economic Development resolved to conduct an independent review of the new agreement. The EPA was signed (initially, with the exception of Guyana and Haiti) in October. The first meeting of a new CARIFORUM-EU Trade and Development Committee was convened in July 2011 within the framework of the EPA. The text of a new Joint Caribbean-EU Partnership Strategy was concluded by CARIFORUM and the EU in November 2012, representing a framework for future co-operation in areas such as regional integration, climate change, natural disasters, crime, security, the reconstruction of Haiti, and joint action in multilateral fora. In March 2013 a US $3.5m. EPA Standby Facility was launched, to be administered by the Caribbean Development Bank.

A Caribbean Regional Fisheries Mechanism was established in 2002 to promote the sustainable use of fisheries and aquaculture resources in the region. It incorporates a Caribbean Fisheries Forum, which serves as the main technical and scientific decision-making body of the Mechanism. In March 2010 a Caribbean Agricultural Health and Food Safety Agency (CAHFSA) was inaugurated in Paramaribo.

HEALTH AND SOCIAL POLICY

In July 2001 heads of government, meeting in the Bahamas, issued the Nassau Declaration on Health, advocating greater regional strategic co-ordination and planning in the health sector and institutional reform, as well as increased resources. In that year CARICOM established the Pan-Caribbean Partnership against HIV/AIDS (PANCAP), with the aim of reducing the spread and impact of HIV and AIDS in member countries. In February 2002 PANCAP initiated regional negotiations with pharmaceutical companies to secure reductions in the cost of anti-retroviral drugs. In February 2006 PANCAP and UNAIDS organized a regional consultation on the outcomes of country-based assessments of the HIV/AIDS crisis that had been undertaken in the region, and formulated a Regional Roadmap for Universal Access to HIV and AIDS Prevention, Care, Treatment and Support over the period 2006–10. A special meeting of COHSOD, convened in June 2006, in Trinidad and Tobago, issued the Port of Spain Declaration on the Education Sector Response to HIV and AIDS, which committed member states to supporting the Roadmap through education policy. In July 2008 CARICOM heads of government endorsed a new Caribbean Regional Strategy Framework on HIV and AIDS for the period 2008–12.

In March 2010 Caribbean heads of government approved the establishment of a Caribbean Public Health Agency (CARPHA), which was intended to promote a co-ordinated approach to public health issues, in accordance with the Nassau Declaration. CARPHA was legally established in July 2011, began operations in January 2013, and was officially launched in July of that year. The Agency represents a merger of five former regional bodies: the Caribbean Environmental Health Institute, Caribbean Epidemiology Centre, Caribbean Food and Nutrition Institute, Caribbean Health Research Council, and Caribbean Regional Drug Testing Laboratory.

CARICOM education programmes have included the improvement of reading in schools through assistance for teacher training and ensuring the availability of low-cost educational material throughout the region. In March 2004 CARICOM ministers responsible for education endorsed the establishment of a Caribbean Knowledge and Learning Network (CKLN) to strengthen tertiary education institutions throughout the region and to enhance knowledge sharing. The CKLN was formally inaugurated in July, in co-operation with the OECS, in Grenada. A Caribbean Vocational Qualification was introduced in 2007. In March 2010, during an intersessional meeting of the Heads of Government Conference, convened in Dominica, an Agreement Establishing a Caribbean Knowledge and Learning Network Agency (CKLNA) was opened for signature, providing for the establishment of the Network as a full CARICOM institution. In July 2012, at the 23rd ordinary meeting of the Conference, held in Gros Islet, St Lucia, an Amendment to the Agreement Establishing the CKLNA was adopted, with the aim of establishing a more efficient organizational structure for the planned Agency.

Youth activities supported by the Community have included new programmes for disadvantaged youths, a mechanism for youth exchange and the convening of a Caribbean Youth Parliament. In October 2012 the CARICOM Secretariat, in partnership with the UN Development Programme, convened a subregional meeting on youth gangs and violence, in Guyana; the meeting addressed the first phase of a new CARICOM Social Development and Crime Prevention Plan, which aimed to enhance the capacity of youth and community members to implement programmes aimed at addressing youth gang formation and violence, and to improve livelihood opportunities for marginalized young people. During 2014 a pilot project—financed by the CARICOM-Spain Joint Fund—on Reducing Youth-on-Youth Violence in CARCIOM Member States was being implemented in Antigua and Barbuda, Jamaica, Saint Christopher and Nevis, Saint Lucia, and Trinidad and Tobago. In July CARICOM initiated a new Creativity for Employment and Business (CEBO) programme in Saint Vincent and the Grenadines, with the aim of inspiring entrepreneurial activities and fostering economic resilience among young people aged 15–29.

CARICOM organizes a biennial Caribbean Festival of Arts (CARIFESTA). CARIFESTA XII was to take place in Haiti, in 2015, and CARIFESTA XIII was to be hosted by Barbados in 2017. A CARICOM Regional Sports Academy was inaugurated, in Paramaribo, in March 2012.

EMERGENCY ASSISTANCE

A Caribbean Disaster Emergency Response Agency (CDERA) was established in 1991 to co-ordinate immediate disaster relief, primarily in the event of hurricanes. In January 2005, meeting on the sidelines of the fifth Summit of the Alliance of Small Island States, in Port Louis, Mauritius, the Secretaries-General of CARICOM, the Commonwealth, the Pacific Islands Forum and the Indian Ocean Commission determined to take collective action to strengthen the disaster preparedness and response capabilities of their member countries in the Caribbean, Pacific and Indian Ocean areas. In September 2006 CARICOM, the EU and the Caribbean ACP states signed a Financing Agreement for Institutional Support and Capacity Building for Disaster Management in the Caribbean, which aimed to support CDERA by providing €3.4m. to facilitate the implementation of revised legislation, improved co-ordination between countries in the region and the increased use of information and communications technology in emergency planning. A new Caribbean Catastrophe Risk Insurance Facility (CCRIF), a multi-country initiative enabling participating states to draw funds for responding immediately to adverse natural events, such as earthquakes and hurricanes, became operational in June 2007, with support from international donors, including the Caribbean Development Bank and the World Bank. In September 2009 a new Caribbean Disaster Emergency Management Agency (CDEMA) formally replaced the CDERA, which had 18 participating states. It was announced in June 2014 that CDEMA member states had developed a model flood disaster risk reduction system.

In January 2010 CARICOM provided immediate assistance to Haiti, after a massive earthquake caused extensive damage and loss of life in the country. A Tactical Mission was deployed to assess relief requirements and logistics, in particular in providing health services. A Special Co-ordinator, to be based in Haiti, was appointed to ensure the effectiveness of the Community's assistance, working closely with CDEMA and other international relief efforts. At the International Donors' Conference Towards a New Future for Haiti, held in New York, in March, UN member countries and other international partners pledged US $5,300m. in support of an Action Plan for the National Recovery and Development of the country. CARICOM pledged to support the Haitian Government in working with the international community and to provide all necessary institutional and technical assistance during the rehabilitation process. CARICOM was represented on the Board of the Interim Commission for the Reconstruction of Haiti, inaugurated in June, following a World Summit on the Future of Haiti, held to discuss the effective implementation of the Action Plan.

INSTITUTIONS

The following are among the institutions formally established within the framework of CARICOM:

Assembly of Caribbean Community Parliamentarians: c/o CARICOM Secretariat; an intergovernmental agreement on the establishment of a regional parliament entered into force in August 1994; inaugural meeting held in Barbados in May 1996. Comprises up to four representatives of the parliaments of each member country, and up to two of each associate member. It aims to provide a forum for wider community involvement in the process of integration and for enhanced deliberation on CARICOM affairs; authorized to issue recommendations for the Conference of Heads of Government and to adopt resolutions on any matter arising under the Treaty of Chaguaramas.

Caribbean Agricultural Research and Development Institute (CARDI): UWI Campus, St Augustine, Trinidad and Tobago; tel. 645-1205; fax 645-1208; e-mail infocentre@cardi.org; internet www.cardi.org; f. 1975; aims to contribute to the competitiveness and sustainability of Caribbean agriculture by generating and transferring new and appropriate technologies and by developing effective partnerships with regional and international entities; Exec. Dir Dr ARLINGTON CHESNEY; publs *CARDI Weekly*, *CARDI Review*, technical bulletin series.

Caribbean Association of Professional Statisticians: f. 2013 as a forum addressing statistical issues and developments, and promoting research on statistical methodology and its applications.

Caribbean Centre for Development Administration (CARICAD): Weymouth Corporate Centre, 1st Floor, Roebuck St, St Michael, Barbados; tel. 427-8535; fax 436-1709; e-mail info@caricad.net; internet www.caricad.net; f. 1980; aims to assist governments in the reform of the public sector and to strengthen their managerial capacities for public administration; promotes the involvement of the private sector, NGOs and other bodies in all decision-making processes; Exec. Dir JENNIFER ASTAPHAN.

Caribbean Community Climate Change Centre (5Cs): Lawrence Nicholas Bldg, 2nd Floor, Ring Rd, POB 563, Belmopan, Belize; tel. 822-1094; fax 822-1365; e-mail evalladares@caribbeanclimate.bz; internet www.caribbeanclimate.bz; f. 2005 to co-ordinate the region's response to climate change; Exec. Dir Dr KENRICK LESLIE.

Caribbean Competition Commission: Hendrikstraat 69, Paramaribo, Suriname; tel. 491439; fax 530639; e-mail senioradmin@ccc.sr; internet www.caricomcompetitioncommission.com; f. 2008; mandated to enforce the rules of competition of the CARICOM Single Market and Economy; Chair. Dr KUSHA HARAKSINGH (Trinidad and Tobago).

Caribbean Disaster Emergency Management Agency (CDEMA): Bldg 1, Manor Lodge, Lodge Hill, St Michael, Barbados; tel. 425-0386; fax 425-8854; e-mail cdema@cdema.org; internet www.cdema.org; f. 1991; aims to respond with immediate assistance following a request by a participating state in the event of a natural or man-made disaster; co-ordinates other relief efforts; assists states to establish disaster preparedness and response capabilities; incorporates national disaster orgs, headed by a co-ordinator, in each participating state; Exec. Dir RONALD JACKSON.

Caribbean Examinations Council: The Garrison, St Michael, BB14038, Barbados; tel. 227-1700; fax 429-5421; e-mail cxcezo@cxc.org; internet www.cxc.org; f. 1972; develops syllabuses and conducts examinations for the Caribbean Advanced Proficiency Examination (CAPE), the Caribbean Secondary Education Certificate (CSEC), the Caribbean Certificate of Secondary Level Competence (CCSLC) and the Caribbean Primary Exit Assessment (CPEA); mems: govts of 16 English-speaking countries and territories; Registrar and CEO GLENROY CUMBERBATCH (acting).

Caribbean Meteorological Organization (CMO): 27 O'Connor St, Woodbrook, Port of Spain, Trinidad and Tobago; tel. 622-4711; fax 622-0277; e-mail cmohq@cmo.org.tt; internet www.cmo.org.tt; f. 1973 as successor to the British Caribbean Meteorological Service (founded 1951) to co-ordinate regional activities in meteorology, operational hydrology and allied sciences; became a specialized institution of CARICOM in 1973; comprises a Council of Government Ministers, a Headquarters Unit, the Caribbean Meteorological Foundation and the Caribbean Institute for Meteorology and Hydrology, located in Barbados; mems: govts of 16 countries and territories represented by the National Meteorological and Hydrometeorological Services; Co-ordinating Dir TYRONE W. SUTHERLAND.

Caribbean Public Health Agency (CARPHA): 16–18 Jamaica Blvd, Federation Park, Port of Spain, Trinidad and Tobago; tel. 622-4261; fax 622-2792; e-mail postmaster@carpha.org; internet carpha.org; f. 2011 (began operations in 2013) as a new single public health agency for the region, representing a merger of the fmr Caribbean Environmental Health Institute, Caribbean Epidemiology Centre, Caribbean Food and Nutrition Institute, Caribbean Health Research Council, and Caribbean Regional Drug Testing Laboratory; aims to facilitate emergency responses to natural disasters, such as hurricanes, earthquakes and flooding; to provide surveillance and management of non-communicable conditions prevalent in the region, such as cancer, diabetes, heart disease and obesity; to provide surveillance and management of communicable diseases, including HIV/AIDS and TB; to address surveillance and prevention of injuries, violence and employment-related conditions; and to contribute to global health agreements and compliance with international health regulations; pursues a people-centred and evidence-based approach to address regional public health challenges; provides specialized laboratory services; issues guidelines, handbooks, reports and alerts on regional public health issues; Exec. Dir Dr C. JAMES HOSPEDALES (Trinidad and Tobago).

Caribbean Telecommunications Union (CTU): Victoria Park Suites, 3rd Floor, 14–17 Victoria Sq., Port of Spain, Trinidad and Tobago; tel. 627-0281; fax 623-1523; internet www.ctu.int; f. 1989; aims to co-ordinate the planning and development of telecommunications in the region; encourages the development of regional telecommunications standards, the transfer of technology and the exchange of information among national telecommunications administrations; membership includes mems of CARICOM and other countries in the region, private sector orgs and NGOs; Sec.-Gen. BERNADETTE LEWIS (Trinidad and Tobago).

CARICOM Implementation Agency for Crime and Security (IMPACS): Sagicor Bldg, Ground Floor, 16 Queen's Park West, Port of Spain, Trinidad and Tobago; tel. 622-0245; fax 628-9795; e-mail enquiries@caricomimpacs.org; internet www.caricomimpacs.org; f. 2006 as a permanent institution to co-ordinate activities in the region relating to crime and security; incorporates two sub-agencies: a Joint Regional Communications Centre and a Regional Intelligence Fusion Centre; a Regional Integrated Ballistic Information Network was initiated in 2013; Exec. Dir FRANCIS FORBES (Jamaica).

CARICOM Regional Organisation for Standards and Quality: Baobab Towers, Warrens, St Michael, Barbados; tel. 622-7670; fax 622-7678; e-mail crosq.caricom@crosq.org; internet www.crosq.org; f. 2002; aims to enhance and promote the implementation of standards, infrastructure and quality verification throughout the region and liaise with international standards orgs; CEO WINSTON BENNETT.

Council of Legal Education: c/o Gordon St, St Augustine, Trinidad and Tobago; tel. 662-5860; fax 662-0927; internet www.clecaribbean.com; f. 1971; responsible for the training of members of the legal profession; administers law schools in Jamaica, Trinidad and Tobago, and the Bahamas; mems: govts of 12 countries and territories; Chair. JACQUELINE SAMUELS-BROWN.

ASSOCIATE INSTITUTIONS

Caribbean Development Bank: POB 408, Wildey, St Michael, Barbados; tel. 431-1600; fax 426-7269; e-mail info@caribank.org; internet www.caribank.org; f. 1969 to stimulate regional economic growth through support for agriculture, industry, transport and other infrastructure, tourism, housing and education; in May 2010 the Board of Governors approved an ordinary capital increase of US $1,000m., including a paid-up component of $216m.; in 2013 new loans approved totalled $139m. (compared with $104m. in 2012), while grant approvals amounted to $18.4m.; total assets $1,452.3m. (31 Dec. 2013); mems: 27 mems, incl. 19 regional borrowing mem. states, Colombia, Mexico, Venezuela (non-borrowing regional mems), and Canada, the People's Republic of China, Germany, Italy, United Kingdom (non-regional mems); Pres. Dr WILLIAM WARREN SMITH (Jamaica).

Caribbean Law Institute Centre: Caricom Research Bldg, Faculty of Law, University of the West Indies, Cave Hill Campus, Cave Hill, Barbados; tel. (246) 417-4652; e-mail clic@cavehill.uwi.edu; internet www.cavehill.uwi.edu/clic/clic.asp; f. 1988 to harmonize and modernize commercial laws in the region; Dir Prof. VELMA NEWTON.

Other Associate Institutions of CARICOM, in accordance with its constitution, are the University of Guyana, the University of the West Indies and the Secretariat of the Organisation of Eastern Caribbean States.

Publications

CARICOM Perspective (annually).
CARICOM View (6 a year).

CENTRAL AMERICAN INTEGRATION SYSTEM
(SISTEMA DE LA INTEGRACIÓN CENTROAMERICANA—SICA)

Address: Final Blv. Cancillería, Distrito El Espino, Ciudad Merliot, Antiguo Cuscatlán La Libertad, San Salvador, El Salvador.
Telephone: 2248-8800; **fax:** 2248-8899; **e-mail:** info@sica.int; **internet:** www.sica.int.

Founded in December 1991, when the heads of state of six Central American countries signed the Protocol of Tegucigalpa to the agreement establishing the Organization of Central American States (f. 1951), creating a new framework for regional integration. A General Secretariat of the Sistema de la Integración Centroamericana was inaugurated in February 1993 to co-ordinate the process of political, economic, social cultural and environmental integration and to promote democracy and respect for human rights throughout the region. In September 1997 Central American Common Market (CACM) heads of state, meeting in the Nicaraguan capital, signed the Managua Declaration in support of further regional integration and the establishment of a political union.

MEMBERS

Belize	El Salvador	Nicaragua
Costa Rica	Guatemala	Panama
Dominican Republic	Honduras	

Note: Argentina, Australia, Brazil, Chile, the People's Republic of China, Colombia, Ecuador, the European Union, France, Germany, the Holy See, Italy, Japan, the Republic of Korea, Mexico, Morocco, Peru, Spain, Taiwan, United Kingdom, Uruguay and the USA have observer status with SICA.

Organization
(September 2014)

SUMMIT MEETINGS
The meetings of heads of state of member countries serve as the supreme decision making organ of SICA.

COUNCIL OF MINISTERS
Ministers responsible for foreign affairs of member states meet regularly to provide policy direction for the process of integration.

EXECUTIVE COMMITTEE
Comprises a government representative of each member state tasked with ensuring the implementation of decisions adopted by heads of state or the Council of Ministers, and with overseeing the activities of the General Secretariat.

CONSULTATIVE COMMITTEE
The Committee comprises representatives of business organizations, trade unions, academic institutions and other federations concerned with the process of integration in the region. It is a fundamental element of the integration system and assists the Secretary-General in determining the organization's policies.

GENERAL SECRETARIAT
The General Secretariat of SICA was established in February 1993 to co-ordinate the process of enhanced regional integration. It comprises Directorates-General of Social Integration, Economic Integration, and of Environmental Affairs.
Secretary-General: Dr VICTORIA MARINA VELÁSQUEZ DE AVILÉS (El Salvador).

CORE INSTITUTIONS

Central American Parliament (PARLACEN)
12 Avda 33-04, Zona 5, 01005 Guatemala City, Guatemala; tel. 2424-4600; fax 2424-4610; e-mail guatemala@parlacen.int; internet www.parlacen.org.gt.; officially inaugurated in 1991; comprises 20 elected representatives of the Domincan Republic, El Salvador, Guatemala, Honduras, Nicaragua and Panama, as well as former Presidents and Vice-Presidents of mem. countries; Haiti, Mexico, Puerto Rico, Venezuela and Taiwan have observer status; Pres. PAULA LORENA RODRÍGUEZ (Guatemala); publ. *Foro Parlamentario*.

Central American Court of Justice
Apdo Postal 907, Managua, Nicaragua; tel. 266-6273; fax 266-4604; e-mail cortecen@ccj.org.ni; internet portal.ccj.org.ni.; officially inaugurated in 1994; tribunal authorized to consider disputes relating to treaties agreed within the regional integration system; in February 1998 Central American heads of state agreed to limit the number of magistrats in the Court to one per country; Sec.-Gen. Dr ORLANDO GUERRERO MAYORGA

SPECIALIZED SECRETARIATS
In addition to those listed below, various technical or executive secretariat units support meetings of ministerial Councils, concerned, *inter alia*, with women, housing, health and finance.

Secretaría General de la Coordinación Educativa y Cultural Centroamericana (SG-CECC): 400m este y 25m norte de la Iglesia Santa Teresita en Barrio Escalante, 262-1007 San José, Costa Rica; tel. 2283-7629; fax 2283-7719; e-mail sgcecc@racsa.co.cr; internet www.sica.int/cecc; f. 1982; promotes development of regional programmes in the fields of education and culture; Sec.-Gen. MARÍA EUGENIA PANIAGUA PADILLA.

Secretaría de Integración Económica Centroamericana (SIECA): 4A Avda 10–25, Zona 14, Apdo 1237, 01901 Guatemala City, Guatemala; tel. 2368-2151; fax 2368-1071; e-mail info@sieca .int; internet www.sieca.int; f. 1960 to assist the process of economic integration and the creation of a Central American Common Market (CACM—established by the organization of Central American States under the General Treaty of Central American Economic Integration, signed in December 1960 and ratified by Costa Rica, Guatemala, El Salvador, Honduras and Nicaragua in September 1963); supervises the correct implementation of the legal instruments of economic integration, conducts relevant studies at the request of the CACM, and arranges meetings; comprises departments covering the working of the CACM: negotiations and external trade policy; external co-operation; systems and statistics; finance and administration; also includes a unit for co-operation with the private sector and finance institutions, and a legal consultative committee; Sec.-Gen. CARMEN GISELA VERGERA (Panama); publs *Anuario Estadístico Centroamericano de Comercio Exterior*, *Carta Informativa* (monthly), *Cuadernos de la SIECA* (2 a year), *Estadísticas Macroeconómicas de Centroamérica* (annually), *Series Estadísticas Seleccionadas de Centroamérica* (annually), *Boletín Informativo* (fortnightly).

Secretaría de Integración Turística Centroamericana (SITCA): Final Blv. Cancillería, Distrito El Espino, Ciudad Merliot, Antiguo Cuscatlán La Libertad, El Salvador; tel. 2248-8837; fax 2248-8897; e-mail info.stcct@sica.int; internet www.sica.int/cct; f. 1965 to develop regional tourism activities; provides administrative support to the Central American Tourism Council, comprising national ministers and directors responsible for tourism; Dir SHANTANNY ANASHA CAMPBELL LEWIS (Nicaragua).

Secretaría de la Integración Social Centroamericana (SISCA): Final Blv. Cancillería, Distrito El Espino Ciudad Merliot, Antiguo Cuscatlán La Libertad, El Salvador; tel. 2248-8857; fax 2248-6943; e-mail info.sisca@sica.int; internet www.sica.int/sisca; f. 1995; co-ordinates various intergovernmental secretariats, including regional councils concerned with social security, sport and recreation, and housing and human settlements; Sec. ANA HAZEL ESCRICH CAÑAS (Costa Rica).

Secretaría del Consejo Agropecuario Centroamericano (SCAC): 600m noreste del Cruce de Ipis-Coronado, San Isidro de Coronado, Apdo Postal 55-2200, San José, Costa Rica; tel. 2216-0303; fax 2216-0285; e-mail info.cac@sica.int; internet www.sica.int/cac; f. 1991 to determine and co-ordinate regional policies and programmes relating to agriculture and agroindustry; Exec. Sec. JULIO O. CALDERÓN ARTIEDA.

Secretaría Ejecutiva de la Comisión Centroamericana de Ambiente y Desarrollo (SE-CCAD): Final Blv. Cancillería, Distrito El Espino, Ciudad Merliot, Antiguo Cuscatlán La Libertad, El Salvador; tel. 2248-8843; fax 2248-8899; e-mail info.ccad@sica.int; internet www.sica.int/ccad; f. 1989 to enhance collaboration in the promotion of sustainable development and environmental protection; convened in Sept. 2014 a workshop aimed at developing a 2015–20 Regional Environmental Strategy; Exec. Sec. CHRISTA CASTRO VARELA (Honduras).

Secretaría Ejecutiva del Consejo Monetario Centroamericano (SECMCA) (Central American Monetary Council): 400m suroeste de la Rotonda La Bandera, Barrio Dent, Contiguo al BANHVI, San José, Costa Rica; tel. 2280-9522; fax 2524-1062; e-mail secma@secmca.org; internet www.secmca.org; f. 1964 by the presidents of Central American central banks, to co-ordinate monetary policies; Exec. Sec. ANGEL ALBERTO ARITA ORELLANA; publs *Boletín Estadístico* (annually), *Informe Económico* (annually).

OTHER SPECIALIZED INSTITUTIONS

Agriculture and Fisheries

Organismo Internacional Regional de Sanidad Agropecuaria (OIRSA) (International Regional Organization of Plant Protection and Animal Health): Calle Ramón Belloso, Final Pasaje Isolde, Colonia Escalón, Apdo (01) 61, San Salvador, El Salvador; tel. 2209-9200; fax 2263-1128; e-mail oirsa@oirsa.org; internet www .oirsa.org; f. 1953 for the prevention of the introduction of animal and plant pests and diseases unknown in the region; research, control and eradication programmes of the principal pests present in agriculture; technical assistance and advice to the ministries of agriculture and livestock of member countries; education and qualification of personnel; mems: Belize, Costa Rica, Dominican Republic, El Salvador, Guatemala, Honduras, Mexico, Nicaragua, Panama; Exec. Dir EFRAÍN MEDINA GUERRA (Guatemala).

Unidad Coordinadora de la Organización del Sector Pesquero y Acuícola del Istmo Centroamericano (OSPESCA) (Organization of Fishing and Aquaculture in Central America): Final Blv. Cancillería, Distrito El Espino, Ciudad Merliot, Antiguo Cus-

catlán La Libertad, El Salvador; tel. 2248-8841; fax 2248-8899; e-mail info.ospesca@sica.int; internet www.sica.int/ospesca; f. 1995, incorporated into SICA in 1999; Regional Co-ordinator MARIO GONZÁLEZ RECINOS.

Education, Health and Sport

Consejo Superior Universitario Centroamericano (CSUCA) (Central American University Council): Avda Las Américas 1–03, Zona 14, International Club Los Arcos, 01014 Guatemala City, Guatemala; tel. 2502-7500; fax 2502-7501; e-mail sg@csuca.org; internet www.csuca.org; f. 1948 to guarantee academic, administrative and economic autonomy for universities and to encourage regional integration of higher education; maintains libraries and documentation centres; Council of 32 mems; mems: 18 universities, in Belize, Costa Rica (four), Dominican Republic, El Salvador, Guatemala, Honduras (two), Nicaragua (four) and Panama (four); Sec.-Gen. Dr JUAN ALFONSO FUENTES SORIA; publs *Estudios Sociales Centroamericanos* (quarterly), *Cuadernos de Investigación* (monthly), *Carta Informativa de la Secretaría General* (monthly).

Consejo del Istmo Centroamericano de Deportes y Recreación (CODICADER) (Committee of the Central American Isthmus for Sport and Recreation): Juan Díaz, Vía José Agustín Arango, Instituto Panameño de Deportes, Apartado Postal 00066, Panama; tel. 500-5480; fax 500-5484; e-mail dgeneral@pandeportes.gob.pa; internet www.sica.int/sisca/codicader; f. 1992; Pres. MARTÍN ALEJANDRO MACHÓN.

Instituto de Nutrición de Centro América y Panamá (INCAP) (Institute of Nutrition of Central America and Panama): Calzada Roosevelt 6–25, Zona 11, Apdo Postal 1188-01901, Guatemala City, Guatemala; tel. 2472-3762; fax 2473-6529; e-mail info.incap@sica .int; internet www.sica.int/incap; f. 1949 to promote the development of nutritional sciences and their application and to strengthen the technical capacity of member countries to reach food and nutrition security; provides training and technical assistance for nutrition education and planning; conducts applied research; disseminates information; maintains library (including about 600 periodicals); administered by the Pan American Health Organization and the World Health Organization; mems: CACM mems, Belize and Panama; Dir CAROLINA SIÚ; publ. *Annual Report*.

Energy and the Environment

Secretaría Ejecutiva de la Comisión Regional de Recursos Hidráulicos (SE-CRRH) (Executive Secretariat of the Regional Commission for Water Resources): 500 mts norte, 200 oeste y 25 norte de Super Blvd Pavas, San José, Costa Rica; tel. 2231-5791; fax 2296-0047; e-mail secretaria@recursoshidricos.org; internet www .recursoshidricos.org; f. 1966; mems: Belize, Costa Rica, El Salvador, Guatemala, Honduras, Nicaragua, Panama; Exec. Sec. PATRICIA RAMÍREZ OBANDO.

Secretaría Ejecutiva del Consejo de Electrificación de América Central (CEAC) (Central American Electrification Council): Apdo 0816, 01552 Panamá, Panama; tel. 2211-6175; fax 501-3990; e-mail jfisher@etesa.com.pa; internet www.ceaconline.org; f. 1985; Exec. Sec. JORGE FISHER MILLER.

Finance

Banco Centroamericano de Integración Económica (BCIE) (Central American Bank for Economic Integration): Blv. Suyapa, Contigua a Banco de Honduras, Apdo 772, Tegucigalpa, Honduras; tel. 2240-2243; fax 2240-2231; e-mail hcepeda@bcie.org; internet www.bcie.org; f. 1961 to promote the economic integration and balanced economic development of member countries; finances public and private development projects, particularly those related to industrialization and infrastructure; auth. cap. US $2,000m; regional mems: Costa Rica, El Salvador, Guatemala, Honduras, Nicaragua; non-regional mems: Argentina, Colombia, Dominican Republic, Mexico, Panama, Spain, Taiwan; Exec. Pres. NICK RISCHBIETH GLÖE; publs *Annual Report*, *Revista de la Integración y el Desarrollo de Centroamérica*.

Organización Centroamericana y del Caribe de Entidades Fiscalizadores Superiores (OCCEFS) (Organization of Central American and Caribbean Supreme Audit Institutions): Tribunal Superior de Cuentas de la República de Honduras, Centro Cívico Gubernamental, Col. Las Brisas Comayagüela, Honduras; tel. and fax 234-5210; e-mail info.occefs@sica.int; internet www.sica.int/ occefs; f. 1995 as the Organización Centroamericana de Entidades Fiscalizadores Superiores, within the framework of the Organización Latinoamericana y del Caribe de Entidades Fiscalizadoras Superiores; assumed present name in 1998; aims to promote co-operation among members, facilitate exchange of information, and provide technical assistance.

Public Administration

Centro de Coordinación para la Prevención de Desastres Naturales en América Central (CEPREDENAC) (Co-ordination Center for the Prevention of Natural Disasters in Central America): Avda Hincapié 21–72, Zona 13 Guatemala City, Guatemala; tel. and fax 2390-0200; fax 2390-0202; e-mail info.cepredenac@sica.int; internet www.sica.int/cepredenac; f. 1988, integrated into SICA in 1995; aims to strengthen the capacity of the region to reduce its vulnerability to natural disasters; Exec. Sec. ROY BARBOZA SEQUEIRA.

Instituto Centroamericano de Administración Pública (ICAP) (Central American Institute of Public Administration): Apdo Postal 10025-1000, San José, Costa Rica; tel. 2234-1011; fax 2225-2049; e-mail info@icap.ac.cr; internet www.icap.ac.cr; f. 1954 by the five Central American Republics and the UN, with later participation by Panama; the Institute aims to train the region's public servants, provide technical assistance and carry out research leading to reforms in public administration.

Science and Technology

Comisión para el Desarrollo Científico y Tecnológico de Centroamérica y Panamá (CTCAP) (Committee for the Scientific and Technological Development of Central America and Panama): 3A Avda 13–28, Zona 1, Guatemala City, Guatemala; tel. and fax 2228-6019; fax 2360-2664; e-mail info.ctcap@sica.int; internet www.sica.int/ctcap; f. 1976; Pres. ROSA MARÍA AMAYA FABIÁN DE LÓPEZ.

Security

Comisión Centroamericana Permanente para la Erradicación de la Producción, Tráfico, Consumo y Uso Ilícitos de Estupefacientes y Sustancias Psicotrópicas y Delitos Conexos (CCP): Blv. Suyapa, Colonia Florencia Norte, Edificio Florencia, Oficina 412, Tegucigalpa, Honduras; tel. 235-6349; e-mail ccp@info.com; f. 1993; supports regional efforts to combat the production, trafficking and use of illicit substances, and related crimes; Exec. Sec. OSCAR ROBERTO HERNÁNDEZ HIDALGO.

Transport and Communications

Comisión Centroamericana de Transporte Marítimo (COCATRAM) (Central American Maritime Transport Commission): Frente al costado oeste del Hotel Mansión Teodolinda, Barrio Bolonia, Apdo Postal 2423, Managua, Nicaragua; tel. 2222-3667; fax 2222-2759; e-mail info@cocatram.org.ni; internet www.cocatram.org.ni; f. 1981; Exec. Dir OTTO NOACK SIERRA; publ. *Boletín Informativo*.

Comisión de Telecomunicaciones de Centroamérica (COMTELCA) (Commission for Telecommunications in Central America): Col. Palmira, Edif. Alpha 608, Avda Brasil, Apdo 1793, Tegucigalpa, Honduras; tel. 2220-1011; fax 2220-1197; e-mail sec@comtelca.org; internet www.comtelca.org; f. 1966 to co-ordinate and improve the regional telecommunications network; Dir-Gen. RAFAEL A. MARADIAGA.

Corporación Centroamericana de Servicios de Navegación Aérea (COCESNA) (Central American Air Navigation Services Corporation): Apdo 660, 150 sur de Aeropuerto de Toncontín, Tegucigalpa, Honduras; tel. 2234-3360; fax 2234-2488; e-mail notam@cocesna.org; internet www.cocesna.org; f. 1960; offers radar air traffic control services, aeronautical telecommunications services, flight inspections and radio assistance services for air navigation; provides support in the areas of safety, aeronautical training and aeronautical software; Exec. Pres. BAYARDO PAGOADA FIGUEROA.

Activities

In June 1990 the presidents of Costa Rica, El Salvador, Guatemala, Honduras and Nicaragua signed a declaration appealing for a revitalization of CACM, as a means of promoting lasting peace in the region. In December the presidents committed themselves to the creation of an effective common market. They requested the support of multilateral lending institutions through investment in regional development, and the cancellation or rescheduling of member countries' debts. In December 1991 the heads of state of the five Central American Common Market (CACM) countries and Panama signed the Protocol of Tegucigalpa; in February 1993 the General Secretariat of SICA was inaugurated to co-ordinate the integration process in the region.

In June 2009 SICA ministers responsible for foreign affairs, meeting in Managua, Nicaragua, issued a special declaration condemning the removal, by military force, of the Honduran President Manuel Zelaya and the illegal detention of members of his Government. SICA heads of state subsequently met in an extraordinary session and agreed a series of immediate measures, including the suspension of all meetings with the new Honduran authorities, the suspension—through the Central American Bank for Economic Integration—of all loans and disbursements to Honduras, and support for an Organization of American States (OAS) resolution demanding a reinstatement of the democratically elected government. Costa Rica and Panama recognized the results of a general election, held in November. In July 2010 SICA heads of state (excluding the Nicaraguan President) signed a Special Declaration on Honduras, permitting that country's full participation in the grouping and supporting its readmission into the OAS.

In May 2008 Brazil was invited to become an observer of SICA. In June 2009 the Council of Ministers agreed to admit Japan as an extra-regional observer of the grouping. The agreement was formalized with the Japanese Government in January 2010. The Republic of Korea was approved as an observer at the meeting of heads of state held in July 2011. In June, meanwhile, at the International Conference in Support of the Regional Strategy for Central America and Mexico, the US Secretary of State announced that the USA was to apply for regional observer status with SICA. This was approved at the SICA summit meeting held in December, and granted by the signing of a Memorandum of Understanding in May 2012. At the December 2011 meeting Australia and France became extra-regional observers; Peru was admitted with regional observer status in February 2012. An agreement formally admitting the Holy See as an observer was concluded in January 2013. Applications for observer status by Colombia, Ecuador, Haiti, the United Kingdom and Uruguay were approved by SICA heads of state and government in December 2012. Ecuador and Uruguay were admitted, accordingly, in March 2013, and Colombia in September, as regional observers, and in June the United Kingdom became an extra-regional observer. In April 2014 Morocco was admitted as an extra-regional observer. An application by Qatar to be admitted as an extra-regional observer was under consideration in late 2014.

In December 2011 SICA heads of state and government mandated regional ministers responsible for women's affairs to formulate a Regional Policy on Gender Equality and Equity; this remained under development in 2014.

In September 2014 the SICA Secretary-General met the Executive Secretary of the Trinational Commission of the Trifinio Plan (established in 1997 by El Salvador, Guatemala and Honduras), with the aim of developing synergies between the two bodies.

TRADE AGREEMENTS AND EXTERNAL RELATIONS

In November 1997, at a special summit meeting of CACM heads of state, an agreement was reached with the president of the Dominican Republic to initiate a gradual process of incorporating that country into the process of Central American integration, with the aim of promoting sustainable development throughout the region. A free trade accord with the Dominican Republic was concluded in April 1998, and formally signed in November. At a meeting of heads of state in June 2013, the Dominican Republic became the eighth full member of the grouping.

In April 2001 Costa Rica concluded a free trade accord with Canada; the other four CACM countries commenced negotiations with Canada in November with the aim of reaching a similar agreement. In February 2002 Central American heads of state convened an extraordinary summit meeting in Managua, Nicaragua, at which they resolved to implement measures to further the political and economic integration of the region. The leaders determined to pursue initial proposals for a free trade accord with the USA, a Central American Free Trade Area (CAFTA), during the visit to the region of the then US President, George W. Bush, in the following month, and, more generally, to strengthen trading relations with the European Union (EU). They also pledged to resolve all regional conflicts by peaceful means. Earlier in February the first meeting of heads of state or government of Central American and Caribbean Community and Common Market (CARICOM) countries took place in Belize, with the aim of strengthening political and economic relations between the two groupings. The meeting agreed to work towards concluding common negotiating positions, for example in respect of the World Trade Organization.

Negotiations on CAFTA between the CACM countries and the USA were initiated in January 2003. An agreement was concluded between the USA and El Salvador, Guatemala, Honduras and Nicaragua in December, and with Costa Rica in January 2004. Under the resulting US-Central America Free Trade Agreement some 80% of US exports of consumer and industrial goods and more than 50% of US agricultural exports to CAFTA countries were to become duty-free immediately upon its entry into force, with remaining tariffs to be eliminated over a 10-year period for consumer and industrial goods and over a 15-year period for agricultural exports. Almost all CAFTA exports of consumer and industrial products to the USA were to be duty-free on the Agreement's entry into force. The Agreement was signed by the US Trade Representative and CACM ministers responsible for trade and economy, convened in Washington, DC, USA, in May 2004. It required ratification by all national legislatures before entering into effect. Negotiations on a US-Dominican Republic free trade agreement, to integrate the Dominican Republic into CAFTA, were concluded in March and the agreement was signed in August. The so-called CAFTA-DR accord was formally ratified by the USA in August 2005. Subsequently, the agreement entered into force with El Salvador on 1 March 2006, Honduras and Nicaragua on 1 April, Guatemala on 1 July, the Dominican Republic on 1 March 2007, and Costa Rica on 1 January 2009.

In May 2006 a meeting of EU and Central American heads of state resolved to initiate negotiations to conclude an Association Agreement. The first round of negotiations was concluded in San José, Costa Rica, in October 2007. In April 2009 the seventh round of negotiations, being held in Tegucigalpa, Honduras, was suspended when the delegation from Nicaragua withdrew from the talks. Negotiations to conclude the accord resumed in February 2010; Panama participated in the negotiations as a full member for the first time in March and an agreement was finalized in May. It provided for immediate duty-free access into the EU for some 92% of Central American products into the EU (48% for EU goods entering Central America), with the remainder of tariffs (on all but 4% of products) being phased out over a 15-year period. The accord also incorporated new import quotas for meat, dairy products and rice, and market access agreements for car manufacturers and the service industry. The Association Agreement, which included 'pillars' concerned with political dialogue and co-operation, as well as trade, was initialled in March 2011 and formally signed by both sides in June 2012. On 1 August 2013 trade liberalization measures became operational between the EU and Honduras, Nicaragua and Panama. Guatemala acceded to the trade accord in December. In that month the EU was granted observer status.

In February 2007 the Secretaries-General of SICA and CARICOM signed a plan of action to foster greater co-operation in areas including foreign policy, international trade relations, security and combating crime, and the environment. Meetings of ministers responsible for foreign affairs and for the economy and foreign trade were convened in the same month at which preparations were initiated for trade negotiations between the two groupings. In May the second Central American-CARICOM summit meeting was convened, in Belize City, Belize. Heads of state and of government endorsed the efforts to enhance co-operation between the organizations and approved the elaboration of a free trade agreement, based on the existing bilateral accord signed between CARICOM and Costa Rica. Formal negotiations were inaugurated at a meeting of ministers responsible for trade in August. In December 2010 SICA heads of state, meeting in Belize, resolved to strengthen co-operation with CARICOM and the Association of Caribbean States (ACS). The third meeting of SICA and CARICOM heads of state or government was held in August 2011, in San Salvador, El Salvador. Also in August, the OAS convened a high-level meeting of CEOs and business executives from the two blocs to discuss measures to expand trade and investment in the region following the global economic downturn. In July 2013 SICA's Secretary-General stated that the grouping was to seek agreements with CARICOM and the Union of South American Nations (UNASUR).

A framework agreement with the Andean Community was signed with SICA in November 2004 to strengthen dialogue and co-operation between the two blocs of countries. In January 2011 the Secretaries-General of the two organizations, meeting in San Salvador, determined to reactivate the agreement and pursue greater collaboration.

In May 2008 SICA heads of state and government met their Brazilian counterparts in San Salvador. The summit meeting reaffirmed the willingness of both sides to enhance political and economic co-operation with the grouping of Southern Common Market (MERCOSUR) countries and determined to establish mechanisms, in particular, to promote trade and political dialogue.

ECONOMIC INTEGRATION AND FINANCIAL CO-OPERATION

In March 2002 Central American leaders adopted the San Salvador Plan of Action for Central American Economic Integration, establishing several objectives as the basis for the future creation of a regional customs union, with a single tariff. CACM heads of state, meeting in December in Costa Rica, adopted the Declaration of San José, supporting the planned establishment of the Central American customs union. Negotiations on technical aspects of the proposed union—the development of which was a regional commitment made by SICA under the Association Agreement concluded in 2012 with the EU—were ongoing in 2013–14.

In January 2007 the Treaty on Payment Systems and the Liquidation of Assets in Central America and the Dominican Republic was presented to the Secretary-General of SICA. The treaty aimed to increase greater financial co-operation and further develop the financial markets in the region.

In December 2008 a summit meeting, convened in San Pedro Sula, Honduras, adopted a plan of urgent measures to address the effects of the global economic and financial downturn, including a commitment of greater investment in infrastructure projects and the establishment of a common credit fund. Heads of state ratified an agreement to establish a Central American Statistical Commission (Centroestad) to develop a regional statistics service, provide technical statistical assistance to member countries and harmonize national and regional statistics.

The San Salvador-based Regional Centre for the Promotion of Micro and Small Enterprises—MSMEs is pursuing a strategic plan for the development of MSMEs in Central American states over the period 2014–18.

A Regional Strategy for Developing the Information Society and Knowledge in SICA, and a roadmap for its implementation, were under development in 2014.

INTEGRATED DISASTER RISK MANAGEMENT, ENERGY AND CLIMATE CHANGE

In December 1994 SICA and the USA signed a joint declaration (CONCAUSA), covering co-operation in the following areas: conservation of biodiversity; sound management of energy; environmental legislation; and sustainable economic development. In June 2001 both sides signed a renewed and expanded CONCAUSA, now also covering co-operation in addressing climate change, and in disaster preparedness.

In June 2001 the heads of state and representatives of Belize, Costa, Rica, El Salvador, Guatemala, Honduras, Mexico, Nicaragua and Panama, meeting within the framework of the 'Tuxtla dialogue mechanism' (so-called after an agreement signed in 1991 between Mexico and Central American countries to strengthen co-ordination between the parties) agreed to activate a Puebla-Panamá Plan (PPP) to promote sustainable social and economic development in the region and to reinforce integration efforts among Central America and the southern states of Mexico (referred to as Mesoamerica). In June 2008 the 10th Tuxtla summit meeting, convened in Villahermosa, Mexico, agreed to establish the Mesoamerican Integration and Development Project to supersede the PPP. The new Project was to incorporate ongoing initiatives on highways and infrastructure and implement energy, electricity and information networks.

In 1997 a Mesoamerican Biological Corridor was inaugurated, with the aim of preserving subregional biodiversity, enhancing ecosystems and landscape connectivity, and promoting productive sustainable processes to improve local communities' quality of life.

Representatives of SICA and of Colombia, the Dominican Republic and Mexico adopted the Declaration of Romana in June 2006, wherein they agreed to implement the Mesoamerican Energy Integration Program, aimed at developing regional oil, electricity and natural gas markets, promoting the use of renewable energy, and increasing electricity generation and interconnection capacity across the region. In the following month, SICA member states approved the legal framework for the Central American Electrical Connection System (known as SIEPAC), which was to be co-funded by the Central American Bank for Economic Integration and the Inter-American Development Bank.

In November 2007 SICA heads of state endorsed a Sustainable Energy Strategy for Central America 2020. Its main areas of concern were access to energy by the least advantaged populations; the rational and efficient use of energy; renewable sources of energy; biofuels for the transport sector; and climate change. The SICA Secretary-General participates in the Supervisory Board of the Energy and Environment Partnership with Central America, which was established in 2002, and convenes regional sustainable energy fora (most recently in October 2013, in Panama), with the aim of promoting the use of renewable energy, and contributing to sustainable development and to the mitigation of the impacts of climate change.

SICA heads of state adopted, in December 2010, the Regional Strategy for Climate Change (ERCC), to accelerate efforts to reduce the region's vulnerability to natural disasters and the effects of climate change. At the third SICA-CARICOM meeting, held in San Salvador, El Salvador, in August 2011, heads of state welcomed an initiative by Panama to establish a Regional Humanitarian Logistic Assistance Centre to respond to emergency situations in the region within 24 to 48 hours. The meeting recognized the need to strengthen transport and cultural links and detailed measures to bolster co-operation in international environmental negotiations and disaster management. In December, at the summit meeting of SICA heads of state, environmental preservation and tackling natural disasters were central to the agenda, and members agreed to adopt the constitution of a Central American Fund for the Promotion of Integrated Risk Management to provide technical assistance and resources as needed. In June 2012 SICA heads of state and government approved a plan of action under which regional joint regional initiatives implemented within the framework of the ERCC were to be strengthened and multiplied. In September 2014 a Central Regional Search and Rescue Academy was inaugurated in San José, Costa Rica, with a view to strengthening the capabilities of the Co-ordination Center for the Prevention of Natural Disasters in Central America.

HEALTH, SOCIAL AFFAIRS AND TOURISM

During the SICA-CARICOM heads of state meeting in El Salvador, in August 2011, it was agreed that the two organizations would collaborate on the early detection (and prevention) of non-communicable diseases. In early September 2014 SICA ministers responsible for health held a consultation on the development of a proposed regional health policy.

In 2006 SICA launched a regional programme on food and nutrition security in Central America (known as 'PRESANCA', currently in its second phase), and a regional programme on statistics and indicators in food and nutrition security in Central America ('PRESISAN'). In June 2008 the SICA summit meeting, convened in San Salvador, reiterated concerns regarding then escalating petroleum and food prices, and welcomed several initiatives concerned with strengthening the region's food security. In February 2013 a meeting of the secretaries of SICA national focal points on food security and nutrition was convened, with the aim of consolidating the regional food security framework.

An intersectoral co-ordination meeting on strengthening the youth sector, convened in September 2014, reviewed ongoing regional youth projects, proposed means of intensifying co-operation between relevant agencies in the region, and addressed the proposed establishment of a SICA Platform for Youth.

At the meeting of CACM heads of state in December 2002, the establishment of a Central American Tourism Agency was announced. In July 2011 SICA heads of state declared 2012 to be the Central American Year of Sustainable Tourism. In early 2014 SICA, with other partners including the OAS, the Caribbean Tourism Organization and Sustainable Travel International, a non-governmental organization, launched the Americas Sustainable Destinations (SDAA) initiative, with the aim of strengthening public-private partnerships to protect, and to improve the lives of local people in, destination areas. In September 2014 two SDAA destinations in Central America were announced: Honduras and Nicaragua.

REGIONAL SECURITY

In March 2005 SICA ministers responsible for security, defence and the interior resolved to establish a special regional force to combat crime, drugs and arms trafficking and terrorism. In June 2008 SICA heads of state and government, convened in San Salvador, agreed to establish a peacekeeping operations unit within the secretariat in order to co-ordinate participation in international missions.

In June 2008 the US Congress approved US \$65m. to fund a Central American initiative to counter drugs-trafficking and organized crime, as part of a larger agreement arranged with the Mexican Government (the so-called Mérida Initiative). The scheme was subsequently relaunched as the Central American Regional Security Initiative, with additional approved funds of some \$100m. to provide equipment, training, and technical assistance to build the capacity of Central American institutions to counter crime. In February 2010, at a meeting of the Inter-American Development Bank (IDB), several countries and other multilateral organizations determined to establish a Group of Friends for Central American Security, in order to support the region to counter organized crime. In March 2011 the US President, Barack Obama, announced the establishment of a Central American Citizen Security Partnership to strengthen law enforcement and to provide young people with alternatives to organized crime.

In 2011 an Ad Hoc Regional Expert Task Force was established to help to elaborate a regional security strategy, in advance of an international conference, convened in Guatemala City, Guatemala, in June. At the International Conference in Support of the Regional Security Strategy for Central America and Mexico, the US Secretary of State committed US \$300m. in support of security initiatives, including more specialized police units and a new SICA Regional Crime Observatory. Negotiations to formulate a Central American Security Strategy (Estrategia de Seguridad de Centroamérica—ESCA), based on 22 priority projects identified at the International Conference, recommenced in September. ESCA's main activities were to incorporate combating crime and preventing violence, rehabilitation of offenders, prison management, and institutional strengthening. In February 2012 the IDB hosted a meeting of the SICA Security Commission and the so-called Group of Friends of the Central America Security Strategy to inaugurate an initial eight ESCA projects. A high-level debate on promoting and implementing the Security Strategy was conducted at the UN in New York, USA, in May. In February 2013 the Mexican President attended a meeting of SICA heads of state, convened in San José, to discuss joint efforts to counter organized crime in the region. The summit meeting determined to establish a specialized secretariat to focus on regional security issues. In April 2014 SICA signed a strategic agreement with the UN High Commissioner for Refugees to strengthen co-ordination on issues concerning the protection of forcibly displaced persons, enhancing national legal frameworks and disseminating international refugee legislation.

THE COMMONWEALTH

Address: Commonwealth Secretariat, Marlborough House, Pall Mall, London, SW1Y 5HX, United Kingdom.

Telephone: (20) 7747-6500; **fax:** (20) 7930-0827; **e-mail:** info@commonwealth.int; **internet:** www.thecommonwealth.org.

The Commonwealth is a voluntary association of independent sovereign states, comprising about one-quarter of the world's population. It includes the United Kingdom and most of its former dependencies, and former dependencies of Australia and New Zealand (themselves Commonwealth countries). All Commonwealth countries accept Queen Elizabeth II as the symbol of the free association of the independent member nations and as such the Head of the Commonwealth.

The Commonwealth Secretariat, established in 1965, operates as an intergovernmental organization at the service of all Commonwealth countries.

MEMBERS IN SOUTH AMERICA AND THE CARIBBEAN

Antigua and Barbuda	Saint Vincent and the Grenadines
Bahamas	Trinidad and Tobago
Barbados	UK Overseas Territories:
Belize	Anguilla
Dominica	Bermuda
Grenada	British Virgin Islands
Guyana	Cayman Islands
Jamaica	Falkland Islands
Saint Christopher and Nevis	Montserrat
Saint Lucia	Turks and Caicos Islands

Organization

(September 2014)

The Commonwealth is not a federation: there is no central government nor are there any rigid contractual obligations such as bind members of the UN. In December 2012 Commonwealth heads of government adopted a non-binding Charter of the Commonwealth, and, in March 2013, it was signed by Queen Elizabeth II and launched throughout the Commonwealth.

MEETINGS OF HEADS OF GOVERNMENT

Commonwealth Heads of Government Meetings (CHOGMs) are private and informal and operate by consensus. The emphasis is on consultation and exchange of views for co-operation. A communiqué is issued at the end of every meeting. Meetings are normally held every two years in different capitals in the Commonwealth. The 2013 meeting was held in November, in Colombo, Sri Lanka; the 2015 meeting was to be hosted by Malta.

OTHER CONSULTATIONS

The Commonwealth Ministerial Action Group on the Harare Declaration was formed in 1995 to support democracy in member countries. It comprises a group of nine ministers responsible for foreign affairs, with rotating membership.

Commonwealth ministers responsible for finance meet in the week prior to the annual meetings of the IMF and the World Bank. Ministers responsible for civil society, education, the environment, foreign affairs, gender issues, health, law, tourism and youth also hold regular meetings.

Biennial conferences of representatives of Commonwealth small states are convened.

Senior officials—cabinet secretaries, permanent secretaries to heads of government and others—meet regularly in the year between CHOGMs to provide continuity and to exchange views on various developments.

COMMONWEALTH SECRETARIAT

The Secretariat organizes consultations between governments and runs programmes of co-operation. Meetings of Heads of Government, ministers and senior officials decide these programmes and provide overall direction. A Board of Governors, on which all eligible member governments are represented, meets annually to review the Secretariat's work and approve its budget. The Board is supported by an Executive Committee which convenes four times a year to monitor implementation of the Secretariat's work programme. The Secretariat is led by a Secretary-General, elected by heads of government. The Secretariat has observer status at the UN.

The Secretariat's divisional structure is as follows: Legal and constitutional affairs; Political affairs; Corporate services; Communications and public affairs; Strategic planning and evaluation; Economic affairs; Governance and institutional development; Social transformation programmes; Gender affairs; Youth affairs; and Special advisory services. In addition there are units responsible for human rights; and for technical co-operation and strategic response; and an Office of the Secretary-General.

Secretary-General: KAMALESH SHARMA (India).

Deputy Secretaries-General: MMASEKGOA MASIRE-MWAMBA (Botswana) (Political, Legal and Constitutional and Youth Affairs, and Human Rights), DEODAT MAHARAJ (Trinidad and Tobago) (Economic Affairs, Trade and Debt, Social Development, and Public Sector Governance), GARY DUNN (Australia) (Corporate Affairs).

Activities

In July 2010, in view of a decision of the 2009 Commonwealth Heads of Government Meeting (CHOGM), a Commonwealth Eminent Persons Group was inaugurated, with a mandate to make recommendations on means of strengthening the organization. The summit meeting held in Perth, Australia, in October 2011, agreed that a Charter of the Commonwealth, proposed by the Eminent Persons Group, embodying the principles contained in previous summit declarations, should be drafted, in consultation with member governments and civil society organizations; the new Commonwealth Charter was adopted by heads of government in December 2012, and signed by the Head of the Commonwealth, Queen Elizabeth II, in March 2013.

The November 2013 CHOGM was notable for the representation by only 27 heads of state or government of the 50 member countries that attended, owing to concerns regarding the human rights record of the Sri Lankan authorities hosting the meeting.

STRATEGIC PLAN

A Strategic Plan to guide the Secretariat during 2013/14–2016/17, and aimed at creating a more dynamic contemporary organization, in line with the newly adopted Commonwealth Charter, was endorsed by the Commonwealth Heads of Government Meeting in November 2013. The Plan takes into consideration the following three longer term objectives: strong democracy, rule of law, promotion and protection of human rights, and respect for diversity; inclusive growth and sustainable development; and maintaining a well-connected and networked Commonwealth; and focuses on six strategic outcomes:

i. Democracy: greater adherence to Commonwealth political values and principles;

ii. Public institutions: more effective, efficient and equitable public governance;

iii. Social development: enhanced positive impact of social development;

iv. Youth: enhanced integration of, and appreciation of the value of, youth in political and developmental processes;

v. Development (pan-Commonwealth): more effective frameworks for inclusive economic growth and social and sustainable development;

vi. Development (small states and vulnerable states): strengthened resilience.

The Plan—which is underpinned by a Strategic Results Framework comprising intermediate outcomes and indicators—provides for a reduction in the scope of activities undertaken by the Secretariat; increased use of information and communication technologies; the promotion of strategic partnerships; enhanced collaboration between member states; and, where appropriate, the promotion of external assistance.

PROMOTING PEACE, DEMOCRACY AND CONSENSUS BUILDING

The Commonwealth Secretariat's Political Affairs Division, together with the Office of the Secretary-General, and assisted by the divisions on Legal and Constitutional Affairs, Governance and Institutional Development, and Communications and Public Affairs, as well as the Human Rights Unit, delivers the organization's work in promoting peace, democracy and consensus building. The Commonwealth promotes best practice, issues publications and organizes workshops and conferences aimed at strengthening democratic values, and provides, upon request, technical assistance in member states.

Through his good offices the Commonwealth Secretary-General works at promoting political dialogue in member states, fostering greater democratic space for political and civil actors, and strengthening institutions. The Secretary-General's good offices may involve discreet 'behind the scenes' diplomacy, sometimes conducted by Special Envoys, to prevent or resolve conflict and assist other international efforts to promote political stability. Advisers may be appointed in support of the organization's long-term promotion of democracy.

The Commonwealth, often working alongside observation teams from regional organizations, monitors the preparations for and conduct of parliamentary, presidential or other elections in member countries at the request of national election management bodies or governments. Furthermore, it offers peer support to enhance the functioning of the electoral process, and assists with the strengthening of institutions between elections. In May 2010 a Commonwealth Network of National Election Management Bodies was inaugurated; the Network aims to enhance collaboration among institutions and to promote good practice in election management. Meetings convened under the auspices of the Network during 2011–13 addressed issues including voter education and registration, electoral participation, independence of election management bodies, and campaign financing. A Junior Election Professionals Initiative was launched in June 2013, under the direction of the Network, with a view to strengthening democratic culture in member states and building national electoral administration capacity.

During 2014 Commonwealth Observer Groups were dispatched to monitor parliamentary elections that were held in the Maldives (in March); tripartite elections in Malawi (in May); national and provincial elections in South Africa (also in May); and general elections in Antigua and Barbuda (in June) and in Montserrat (in September).

In November 1995 Commonwealth Heads of Government, convened in New Zealand, formulated and adopted the Millbrook Commonwealth Action Programme on the Harare Declaration, to promote adherence by member countries to the fundamental principles of democracy and human rights (as proclaimed in the Harare Declaration, adopted in October 1991). The Programme incorporated a framework of measures to be pursued in support of democratic processes and institutions, and actions to be taken in response to violations of the Harare Declaration principles, in particular the unlawful removal of a democratically elected government. A Commonwealth Ministerial Action Group on the Harare Declaration (CMAG) was established in December 1995 to implement this process. In March 2002 Commonwealth leaders expanded CMAG's mandate to enable it to consider action against serious violations of the Commonwealth's core values perpetrated by elected administrations as well as by military regimes. In October 2011 the Perth CHOGM agreed a series of reforms aimed at strengthening further the role of CMAG in addressing serious violations of Commonwealth political values; these included clearer guidelines and time frames for engagement when the situation in a country causes concern, with a view to shifting from a reactive to a more proactive role. The unjustified postponement of elections, systematic violation of human rights, abrogation of constitutions, undermining of the rule of law and independence of the judiciary, suppression of media freedoms, and closing of the national political space were specified as events that might cause investigation by CMAG.

In November 2013 Heads of Government reconstituted CMAG's membership to comprise over the next biennium the ministers responsible for foreign affairs of Cyprus, Guyana, India, New Zealand, Pakistan, Sierra Leone, Solomon Islands, Sri Lanka (ex officio as Chair in Office) and Tanzania.

RULE OF LAW

The Commonwealth Secretariat works to strengthen the rule of law underpinning strong and accountable democratic governance in member states. The Legal and Constitutional Affairs Division offers assistance with legislative drafting; with the placement and training of judges and other legal experts; with the training of prosecutors and police; and in the provision of judicial education. The Division also promotes and facilitates co-operation and the exchange of information among member governments on legal matters, and assists in combating corruption and financial and organized crime, in particular transborder criminal activities. The Division organizes the triennial meeting of ministers, Attorneys-General and senior ministry officials concerned with the legal systems in Commonwealth countries. It has also implemented schemes for co-operation on extradition, the protection of material cultural heritage, mutual assistance in criminal matters and the transfer of convicted offenders within the Commonwealth. It liaises with the Commonwealth Magistrates' and Judges' Association, the Commonwealth Legal Education Association, the Commonwealth Lawyers' Association (with which it helps to prepare the triennial Commonwealth Law Conference for the practising profession), the Commonwealth Association of Legislative Counsel, and with other international non-governmental organizations (NGOs). The Division provides in-house legal advice for the Secretariat.

HUMAN RIGHTS

The Commonwealth's human rights programme is managed by the Secretariat's Human Rights Unit. The Unit provides technical assistance towards the establishment and capacity building of national human rights institutions in member states; facilitates the exchange of best practice on human rights matters; and raises awareness and promotes human rights education. It also strengthens the capacities of member states to participate in the UN's Universal Periodic Review (which assesses, cyclically, the human rights situation in all UN member states).

GOVERNANCE AND PUBLIC SECTOR DEVELOPMENT

The Commonwealth Secretariat's Governance and Institutional Development Division provides support to member states in strengthening the so-called political administrative interface between elected politicians and senior public officials. The Secretariat offers advice, training and other expertise in order to build capacity in the national public institutions of member states, and promotes the effective use of information and communication technologies in governance and public sector development. The Secretariat convenes post-election victory retreats, with participation by ministers and senior government officials, aimed at promoting good governance through the promotion of confidential discussions and experience sharing. The Commonwealth promotes the development of local government and fiscal decentralization in member states. A Commonwealth Cybercrime Initiative (CCI), launched by Commonwealth Heads of Government in October 2011, aims to ensure that member countries have appropriate legal frameworks in place to combat cybercrime. In May 2014 Commonwealth ministers responsible for law endorsed CCI mechanisms for delivering technical assistance aimed at combating cybercrime. A Commonwealth Conference on Public Administration in Very Small States was convened in April 2013.

ECONOMIC DEVELOPMENT

The Commonwealth's Economic Development Programme is managed by the Economic Affairs Division and Special Advisory Services Division, with—as a priority focus is the empowerment of women and young people—support from the Gender Affairs Section and the Youth Affairs Division. The Economic Affairs Division organizes and services the annual meetings of Commonwealth ministers responsible for finance and the ministerial group on small states (accounting for 32 of the Commonwealth member states) and assists in servicing the biennial meetings of Heads of Government. It engages in research and analysis on economic issues of interest to member governments and organizes seminars and conferences of government officials and experts.

The Commonwealth has consistently urged improved responsiveness by some international organizations mandated to promote economic stability, and has promoted greater representation for developing countries in international economic decision-making, with particular reference to the IMF and the World Bank. In June 2008 heads of government expressed concern that many Commonwealth countries were failing to meet the Millennium Development Goal (MDG) targets, and resolved to strengthen existing networks of co-operation: in particular, they undertook to take measures to improve the quality of data used in policymaking, and to strengthen the links between research and policymaking. A Commonwealth Partnership Platform Portal was established to provide practical support for sharing ideas and best practices.

The Secretariat advises member states on the development of sound debt management policies and strategies. Through its Debt Recording and Management System (DRMS)—an integrated debt recording, monitoring and analysing tool, which was first used in 1985, and updated in 2002—it aims to assist both member and non-member countries in managing sovereign debt; by 2014 the DRMS had been used by 61 states. The DRMS is complemented by 'Horizon', a software tool that assists member states in undertaking prudent

sovereign debt management; and by the Securities Auctioning System (CS-SAS), which was initiated in 2008 to support institutions involved in securities auctions to manage all phases of that process.

The Economic Affairs Division actively supports developing Commonwealth countries to participate in the multilateral trading system, including in World Trade Organization (WTO) negotiations, and promotes policy discourse on issues related to the WTO's Aid for Trade initiative. In July 2013 it issued a comprehensive review entitled 'Aid For Trade: Effectiveness, Current Issues and Future Directions'. Active engagement within the G20 Development Working Group is also pursued, to promote the concerns of small and vulnerable states. Since 2011 an annual Commonwealth-Organisation Internationale de la Francophonie-G20 meeting has been held (2014: in April). The Economic Affairs Division is assisting the ACP group of countries to negotiate economic partnership agreements with the European Union (EU). It supports developing countries in strengthening their links with international capital markets and foreign investors, and services groups of experts on economic affairs that have been commissioned by governments to report on, among other things, protectionism; obstacles to the North-South negotiating process; reform of the international financial and trading system; the debt crisis; management of technological change; the impact of change on the development process; environmental issues; women and structural adjustment; and youth unemployment.

The Economic Affairs Division addresses the specific needs of, and provides technical assistance to, small states, with a focus on trade, vulnerability, environment, politics and economics. In June 2010 the first Commonwealth Biennial Small States Conference was convened, in London, comprising representatives of small states from the Africa, Asia-Pacific and Caribbean regions. In January 2011 a new Commonwealth Small States Office was inaugurated in Geneva; the Office provides subsidized office space for the Geneva-based diplomatic missions of Commonwealth small states, and business facilities for both diplomatic personnel and visiting delegations from small member states, and has a resident Trade Adviser. The second Commonwealth Biennial Global Small States Conference was held in September 2012, again in London; participating representatives of small states discussed the development of sustainable economies, job creation and improving livelihoods, agreeing that 'green growth' might act as a vehicle for progress. In June 2013 a technical workshop was convened with a focus on strengthening resilience in small states, including developing an index to measure countries' capacities to absorb external shocks caused by adverse global economic conditions, extreme weather events, and natural disasters. The third Biennial Global Small States Conference, convened in March 2014, in St Lucia, focused on building the resilience of small states in the areas of debt, economic development, governance, environmental management, and social cohesion. The Secretariat's Political Affairs Division manages a joint office in New York, USA, to enable small states to maintain a presence at the UN.

In 1998 the Tiona Fund for the Commonwealth Caribbean was inaugurated, under the Commonwealth Private Investment Initiative (CPII); this was subsequently absorbed into the Caribbean Investment Fund (established in 1993 by member states of the Caribbean Community and Common Market—CARICOM).

In November 2005 Commonwealth Heads of Government endorsed a new Commonwealth Action Programme for the Digital Divide and approved the establishment of a special fund to enable implementation of the Programme's objectives to make available to all the benefits of new information technologies. Accordingly, a Commonwealth Connects programme was established in August 2006 to develop partnerships and to help to strengthen the use of and access to information technology in all Commonwealth countries; a Commonwealth Connects web portal was launched at the October 2011 Heads of Government summit.

The Commonwealth Secretariat provides assistance to member states on negotiations relating to the delimitation of maritime boundaries, and on issues related to the law of the sea. It also assists member states in the area of natural resources management, including in the preparation of policy, and legislative and contractual arrangements for the governance of extractive industries development, and the negotiation of investment terms.

The CHOGM held in Perth, Australia, in October 2011, issued the Perth Declaration on Food Security Principles, reaffirming the universal right to safe, sufficient and nutritious food.

ENVIRONMENTALLY SUSTAINABLE DEVELOPMENT

The Commonwealth's Environmentally Sustainable Development Programme is managed by the Economic Affairs Division, working with the Office of the Secretary-General, the Special Advisory Services Division, and the Technical Cooperation and Strategic Response Unit. The Economic Affairs Division undertakes analytical research, partnership building and skill-building activities to assist member states in managing their risk and identifying opportunities for environmentally sustainable growth.

The Commonwealth Climate Change Action Plan, adopted by heads of government in November 2007, acknowledged that climate change posed a serious threat to the very existence of some small island states within the Commonwealth, and to the low-lying coastal areas of others. It offered support for the UN Framework Convention on Climate Change, and recognized the need to overcome technical, economic and policymaking barriers to reducing carbon emissions, to using renewable energy, and to increasing energy efficiency. The Plan undertook to assist developing member states in international negotiations on climate change; to support improved land use management, including the use of forest resources; to investigate the carbon footprint of agricultural exports from member countries; to increase support for the management of natural disasters in member countries; and to provide technical assistance to help least developed members and small states to assess the implications of climate change and adapt accordingly. A Commonwealth expert group on climate finance was established in June 2013, to assess and propose remedies for the challenges faced by small and vulnerable states in accessing and disbursing climate finance. The Secretariat pursues strategic partnerships with regional institutions representing small states—such as the Caribbean Community Climate Change Centre, Indian Ocean Commission and Secretariat of the Pacific Regional Environment Programme—aimed at building institutional capacities in climate financing and sustainable development.

In October 2012 the Commonwealth launched *Integrating Sustainable Development into International Investment Agreements: A Guide for Developing Country Negotiators*, intended as a handbook for developing member states to use in navigating the international investment agreements that support their development needs.

In November 2013 the Heads of Government Meeting adopted the Colombo Declaration on Sustainable, Inclusive and Equitable Development, in which they expressed commitment to developing supportive global policies aimed at addressing climate change mitigation and adaptation, food security, poverty, inequalities in trade, predictable and sufficient finances, investments, knowledge and technology transfers, and processes promoting growth with equity. The CHOGM endorsed the establishment of a Commonwealth Climate Finance Skills Hub and Response Mechanism to facilitate access to climate finance and technical assistance.

In advance of the third Global Conference on the Sustainable Development of Small Island States, convened in September 2014, in Apia, Samoa, a technical working group established by the Commonwealth Secretariat reviewed issues relating to resilience building in small island states, including the effectiveness of national policy frameworks, and of the international financing and capacity agenda. At the Conference the Commonwealth Secretariat launched a new report, entitled *Building the Resilience of Small States: The Revised Framework*.

The Commonwealth Secretariat supports the work of the Iwokrama International Centre for Rainforest Conservation and Development, which it helped to establish in 1996, with the Guyanese authorities, to promote environmentally balanced, sustainable tropical rainforest management.

HUMAN AND SOCIAL DEVELOPMENT

The Commonwealth Secretariat's Social Transformation Programmes Division is primarily responsible for managing activities in the area of human and social development, covering health, education and gender equality. Gender equality is a cross-cutting theme that is integrated across the Secretariat's activities.

Ministerial, technical and expert group meetings and workshops, are convened regularly to foster co-operation on health matters, and to promote the exchange of health information and expertise. Studies are commissioned, and professional and technical advice is provided to member states. The Secretariat supports the work of regional health organizations. The priority areas of focus with regard to health are: e-health; health worker migration; HIV/AIDS; maternal and child health; non-communicable diseases; and mental health. A Commonwealth Advisory Committee on Health advises the Secretariat on public health matters.

The Commonwealth Secretariat works to improve the quality of and access to basic education in member states; to strengthen science, technology and mathematics education; to improve the quality of management in institutions of higher learning and basic education; to enhance—in accordance with the Pan-Commonwealth Framework on Professional Standards for Teachers and School Leaders—the performance of educational staff; to strengthen examination assessment systems; and to promote the movement of students between Commonwealth countries. Advancing inclusive education—focusing on reaching excluded and underperforming groups—is a priority area of activity. Support for education is also offered in difficult circumstances, such as areas affected by conflict or natural disasters, and mitigating the impact of HIV and AIDS on education. Collaboration between governments, the private sector and other NGOs is promoted. A meeting of Commonwealth ministers responsible for education, held at the end of August 2012, in Port

Louis, Mauritius, discussed means of achieving education-related MDGs by 2015 and considered priorities for the Commonwealth's contribution to a post-2015 development framework. The meeting was synchronized with parallel fora for Commonwealth teachers, post-secondary and tertiary education leaders, young people, and stakeholders.

The Commonwealth Plan of Action for Gender Equality, covering the period 2005–15, supports efforts towards achieving the MDGs, and the objectives of gender equality adopted by the 1995 Beijing Declaration and Platform for Action and the follow-up Beijing+5 review conference, held in 2000, and Beijing+10 in 2005. Gender equality, poverty eradication, promotion of human rights, and strengthening democracy are recognized as intrinsically interrelated, and the Plan has a particular focus on the advancement of gender mainstreaming in the following areas: democracy, peace and conflict; human rights and law; poverty eradication and economic empowerment; and HIV/AIDS. Commonwealth Women's Affairs Ministers Meetings (WAMMs) have been held every three years since 1985; the 10th WAMM was convened in Dhaka, Bangladesh, in June 2013, on the theme 'Women's Leadership for Enterprise'.

YOUTH

The Secretariat's Youth Affairs Division administers the Commonwealth Youth Programme (CYP), which was initiated in 1973 to promote the involvement of young people in the economic and social development of their countries. The CYP is funded by dedicated voluntary contributions from governments. The Programme's activities are in three areas: Youth Enterprise and Sustainable Livelihoods; Governance, Development and Youth Networks; and Youth Work Education and Training. Regional centres are located in Zambia (for Africa), India (for Asia), Guyana (for the Caribbean), and Solomon Islands (for the Pacific). The Programme administers a Youth Study Fellowship scheme, a Youth Project Fund, a Youth Exchange Programme (in the Caribbean), and a Youth Development Awards Scheme. It also holds conferences and seminars, carries out research and disseminates information. The CYP Diploma in Youth Development Work is offered by partner institutions in 45 countries, primarily through distance education. The Commonwealth Youth Credit Initiative, initiated in 1995, provides funds and advice for young entrepreneurs setting up small businesses. A Plan of Action for Youth Empowerment, covering the period 2007–15, was approved by the sixth meeting of Commonwealth ministers responsible for youth affairs, held in Nassau, Bahamas, in May 2006. In September 2012 a Commonwealth Pacific Youth Leadership and Integrity Conference was convened in Honiara, Solomon Islands. A new pan-Commonwealth Student Association was launched in August of that year. The first Commonwealth Conference on the Education and Training of Youth Workers was held in Pretoria, South Africa, in March 2013. In September the first Commonwealth Youth Development Index was launched, comprising indicators measuring development and empowerment with respect to young people globally.

In November 2013 heads of government, meeting in Sri Lanka, adopted the Magampura Declaration of Commitment to Young People. The enhanced integration of, and appreciation of the value of, youth in political and developmental processes was the fourth strategic objective stipulated under the Commonwealth's Strategic Plan for 2013/14–2016/17, adopted in November 2013; accordingly, national and pan-Commonwealth frameworks aimed at advancing the social, political and economic empowerment of young people, and the further development of youth-led initiatives, were to be promoted during the term of the Plan. In November the Commonwealth Youth Forum (which since 1997 has been convened alongside CHOGMs) elected the Executive Committee of a new Commonwealth Youth Council (CYC), the constitution of which was approved by heads of government.

Since 2000 Commonwealth Youth Games have been convened at regular (normally four-yearly) intervals; the fifth Games were to be held in September 2015, in Samoa.

TECHNICAL ASSISTANCE

Commonwealth Fund for Technical Co-operation (CFTC): f. 1971 to facilitate the exchange of skills between member countries and to promote economic and social devt; it is administered by the Commonwealth Secretariat and financed by voluntary subscriptions from member governments. The CFTC responds to requests from member governments for technical assistance, such as the provision of experts for short- or medium-term projects, advice on economic or legal matters, and training programmes. Public sector devt, allowing member states to build on their capacities, is the principal element in CFTC activities. This includes assistance for improvement of supervision and combating corruption; improving economic management, for example by advising on exports and investment promotion; strengthening democratic institutions, such as electoral commissions; and improvement of education and health policies. The CFTC also administers the Langkawi awards for the study of environmental issues, which is funded by the Canadian Government; the CFTC's annual budget amounts to £29m., supplemented by external resources through partnerships.

Finance

Member governments meet the costs of the Secretariat through subscriptions on a scale related to income and population.

Publications

Commonwealth News (weekly e-mail newsletter).
Commonwealth Human Rights Law Digest.
Commonwealth Law Bulletin (quarterly).
Global (electronic magazine).
Report of the Commonwealth Secretary-General (every 2 years).
Small States Digest (periodic newsletter).
Numerous reports, studies and papers (catalogue available).

Commonwealth Organizations

(in the United Kingdom, unless otherwise stated)

The two principal intergovernmental organizations established by Commonwealth member states, apart from the Commonwealth Secretariat itself, are the Commonwealth Foundation and the Commonwealth of Learning. In 2014 there were nearly 90 other professional or advocacy organizations bearing the Commonwealth's name and associated with or accredited to the Commonwealth, a selection of which are listed below.

PRINCIPAL INTERGOVERNMENTAL ORGANIZATIONS

Commonwealth Foundation: Marlborough House, Pall Mall, London, SW1Y 5HY; tel. (20) 7930-3783; fax (20) 7839-8157; e-mail foundation@commonwealth.int; internet www.commonwealthfoundation.com; f. 1966; intergovernmental body promoting people-to-people interaction, and collaboration within the non-governmental sector of the Commonwealth; supports non-governmental orgs, professional asscns and Commonwealth arts and culture; funds are provided by Commonwealth govts; Chair. Sir ANAND SATYANAND (New Zealand); Dir VIJAY KRISHNARAYAN (Trinidad and Tobago); publ. *Commonwealth People* (quarterly).

Commonwealth of Learning (COL): 1055 West Hastings St, Suite 1200, Vancouver, BC V6E 2E9, Canada; tel. (604) 775-8200; fax (604) 775-8210; e-mail info@col.org; internet www.col.org; f. 1987 by Commonwealth Heads of Government to promote the devt and sharing of distance education and open learning resources, including materials, expertise and technologies, throughout the Commonwealth and in other countries; implements and assists with national and regional educational programmes; acts as consultant to international agencies and national govts; conducts seminars and studies on specific educational needs; convened the seventh Pan-Commonwealth Forum on Open Learning in Dec. 2013, in Abuja, Nigeria; core financing for COL is provided by Commonwealth govts on a voluntary basis; COL has an annual budget of approx. C $12m; Pres. and CEO Prof. ASHA KANWAR (India); publ. *Connections*.

The following represents a selection of other Commonwealth organizations:

ADMINISTRATION AND PLANNING

Commonwealth Association for Public Administration and Management (CAPAM): 291 Dalhousie St, Suite 202, Ottawa, ON K1N 7E5, Canada; tel. (819) 956-7952; fax (613) 701-4236; e-mail capam@capam.org; internet www.capam.org; f. 1994; aims to promote sound management of the public sector in Commonwealth countries and to assist those countries undergoing political or financial reforms; an international awards programme to reward innovation within the public sector was introduced in 1997, and is awarded every two years; more than 1,200 individual mems and 80 institutional memberships in some 80 countries; Pres. PAUL ZAHRA (Malta); Exec. Dir and CEO GAY HAMILTON (Canada).

Commonwealth Association of Planners: c/o Royal Town Planning Institute in Scotland, 18 Atholl Crescent, Edinburgh, EH3 8HQ; tel. (131) 229-9628; fax (131) 229-9332; e-mail annette.odonnell@rtpi.org.uk; internet www.commonwealth-planners.org; aims to develop urban and regional planning in Commonwealth countries, to meet the challenges of urbanization and the sustainable devt of human

settlements; Pres. CHRISTINE PLATT (South Africa); Sec.-Gen. CLIVE HARRIDGE (United Kingdom).

Commonwealth Local Government Forum: 16A Northumberland Ave, London, WC2N 5AP; tel. (20) 7389-1490; fax (20) 7389-1499; e-mail info@clgf.org.uk; internet www.clgf.org.uk; works to promote democratic local govt in Commonwealth countries, and to encourage good practice through confs, programmes, research and the provision of information; regional offices in Fiji, India and South Africa; Sec.-Gen. CARL WRIGHT.

AGRICULTURE AND FORESTRY

Commonwealth Forestry Association: The Crib, Dinchope, Craven Arms, Shropshire, SY7 9JJ; tel. (1588) 672868; e-mail cfa@cfa-international.org; internet www.cfa-international.org; f. 1921; produces, collects and circulates information relating to world forestry and promotes good management, use and conservation of forests and forest lands throughout the world; mems: 1,200; Chair. JOHN INNES (Canada); Pres. JIM BALL (United Kingdom); publs *International Forestry Review* (quarterly), *Commonwealth Forestry News* (quarterly), *Commonwealth Forestry Handbook* (irregular).

Royal Agricultural Society of the Commonwealth: Royal Highland Centre, Ingleston, Edinburgh, EH28 8NF; tel. (131) 335-6200; fax (131) 335-6229; e-mail info@therasc.com; internet www.therasc.com; f. 1957 to promote devt of agricultural shows and good farming practice, in order to improve incomes and food production in Commonwealth countries; Chair. Lord VESTEY.

Standing Committee on Commonwealth Forestry: Forestry Commission, 231 Corstorphine Rd, Edinburgh, EH12 7AT; tel. (131) 314-6405; fax (131) 316-4344; e-mail commonwealth.standing-committee@forestry.gsi.gov.uk; f. 1923 to provide continuity between Commonwealth Forestry Conferences (usually held every four years), and to provide a forum for discussion on any forestry matters of common interest to mem. govts which may be brought to the Committee's notice by any mem. country or org.; 54 mems; Sec. JONATHAN TAYLOR.

BUSINESS

Commonwealth Business Council: 18 Pall Mall, London, SW1Y 5LU; tel. (20) 7024-8200; fax (20) 7024-8201; e-mail info@cbcglobal.org; internet www.cbcglobal.org; f. 1997 by the Commonwealth Heads of Government Meeting to promote co-operation between govts and the private sector in support of trade, investment and devt; the Council aims to identify and promote investment opportunities, in particular in Commonwealth developing countries, to support countries and local businesses to work within the context of globalization, to promote capacity building and the exchange of skills and knowledge (in particular through its Information Communication Technologies for Development programme), and to encourage co-operation among Commonwealth members; promotes good governance; supports the process of multilateral trade negotiations and other liberalization of trade and services; represents the private sector at govt level; CEO PETER CALLAGHAN.

EDUCATION AND CULTURE

Association of Commonwealth Universities (ACU): Woburn House, 20-24 Tavistock Sq., London, WC1H 9HF; tel. (20) 7380-6700; fax (20) 7387-2655; e-mail info@acu.ac.uk; internet www.acu.ac.uk; f. 1913; promotes international co-operation and understanding; provides assistance with staff and student mobility and devt programmes; researches and disseminates information about universities and relevant policy issues; organizes major meetings of Commonwealth universities and their representatives; acts as a liaison office and information centre; administers scholarship and fellowship schemes; operates a policy research unit; mems: c. 500 universities in 36 Commonwealth countries or regions; Sec.-Gen. Prof. JOHN WOOD; publs include *Yearly Review*, *Commonwealth Universities Yearbook*, *ACU Bulletin* (quarterly), *Who's Who of Executive Heads: Vice-Chancellors, Presidents, Principals and Rectors*, *International Awards*, student information papers (study abroad series).

Commonwealth Association of Museums: 10023 93 St, Edmonton, Alberta T5H 1W6, Canada; tel. and fax (780) 424-2229; e-mail catherinec.cole@telus.net; internet www.maltwood.uvic.ca/cam; f. 1974; professional asscn working for the improvement of museums throughout the Commonwealth; encourages links between museums and assists professional devt and training through distance learning, workshops and seminars; general assembly held every three years; mems in 38 Commonwealth countries; Pres. ROOKSANA OMAR.

Commonwealth Association of Science, Technology and Mathematics Educators (CASTME): 7 Lion Yard, Tremadoc Rd, London, SW4 7NQ; tel. (20) 7819-3936; e-mail admin@castme.org.uk; internet www.castme.org.uk; f. 1974; special emphasis is given to the social significance of education in these subjects;

organizes an Awards Scheme to promote effective teaching and learning in these subjects, and biennial regional seminars; Chair. COLIN MATHESON; publ. *CASTME Journal* (3 a year).

Commonwealth Council for Educational Administration and Management: 86 Ellison Rd, Springwood, NSW 2777, Australia; tel. and fax (2) 4751-7974; e-mail admin@cceam.org; internet www.cceam.org; f. 1970; aims to foster quality in professional devt and links among educational administrators; holds national and regional confs, as well as visits and seminars; mems: 28 affiliated groups representing 3,000 persons; Pres. KEN BRIEN; Exec. Dir JENNY LEWIS; publ. *International Studies in Educational Administration* (2 a year).

Commonwealth Education Trust: New Zealand House, 6th Floor, 80 Haymarket, London, SW1Y 4TE; tel. (20) 7024-9822; fax (20) 7024-9833; e-mail info@commonwealth-institute.org; internet www.commonwealtheducationtrust.org; f. 2007 as the successor trust to the Commonwealth Institute; funds the Centre of Commonwealth Education, established in 2004 as part of Cambridge University; supports the Lifestyle of Our Kids (LOOK) project initiated in 2005 by the Commonwealth Institute (Australia); Chief Exec. JUDY CURRY.

Institute of Commonwealth Studies: South Block, 2nd Floor, Senate House, Malet Street, London, WC1E 7HU; tel. (20) 7862-8844; fax (20) 7862-8813; e-mail ics@sas.ac.uk; internet commonwealth.sas.ac.uk; f. 1949 to promote advanced study of the Commonwealth; provides a library and meeting place for postgraduate students and academic staff engaged in research in this field; offers postgraduate teaching; Dir PHILIP MURPHY; publs *Annual Report, Collected Seminar Papers, Newsletter, Theses in Progress in Commonwealth Studies.*

HEALTH AND WELFARE

Commonwealth Medical Trust (COMMAT): BMA House, Tavistock Sq., London, WC1H 9JP; tel. (20) 7272-8492; e-mail office@commat.org; internet www.commat.org; f. 1962 (as the Commonwealth Medical Association) for the exchange of information; provision of techical co-operation and advice; formulation and maintenance of a code of ethics; promotes the Right to Health; liaison with WHO and other UN agencies on health issues; meetings of its Council are held every three years; mems: medical asscns in Commonwealth countries; Dir MARIANNE HASLEGRAVE.

Commonwealth Nurses and Midwives Federation: c/o Royal College of Nursing, 20 Cavendish Sq., London, W1G 0RN; tel. (20) 7647-3593; e-mail jill@commonwealthnurses.org; internet www.commonwealthnurses.org; f. 1973 to link national nursing and midwifery asscns in Commonwealth countries; aims to influence health policy, develop nursing networks, improve nursing education and standards, and strengthen leadership; 3rd Conference (2016: London, United Kingdom); Exec. Sec. JILL ILIFFE.

Commonwealth Organization for Social Work: Halifax, Canada; tel. (902) 455-5515; e-mail moniqueauffrey@eastlink.ca; promotes communication and collaboration between social workers in Commonwealth countries; provides network for information and sharing of expertise; Sec.-Gen. MONIQUE AUFFREY (Canada).

Commonwealth Pharmacists Association: 1 Lambeth High St, London, SE1 7JN; tel. (20) 7572-2216; fax (20) 7572-2504; e-mail admin@commonwealthpharmacy.org; internet www.commonwealthpharmacy.org; f. 1970 (as the Commonwealth Pharmaceutical Association) to promote the interests of pharmaceutical sciences and the profession of pharmacy in the Commonwealth; to maintain high professional standards, encourage links between members and the creation of nat. asscns; and to facilitate the dissemination of information; holds confs (every four years) and regional meetings; mems: pharmaceutical asscns from over 40 Commonwealth countries; Pres. RAYMOND ANDERSON (United Kingdom); publ. *Quarterly Newsletter.*

Commonwealth Society for the Deaf (Sound Seekers): UCL Ear Institute, 332–336 Gray's Inn Rd, London, WC1X 8EE; tel. (20) 7833-0035; fax (20) 7233-5800; e-mail admin@sound-seekers.org.uk; internet www.sound-seekers.org.uk; f. 1959; undertakes initiatives to establish audiology services in developing Commonwealth countries, including mobile clinics to provide outreach services; aims to educate local communities in aural hygiene and the prevention of ear infection and deafness; provides audiological equipment and organizes the training of audiological maintenance technicians; conducts research into the causes and prevention of deafness; Chief Exec. LUCY CARTER; publ. *Annual Report.*

Royal Commonwealth Ex-Services League: Haig House, 199 Borough High St, London, SE1 1AA; tel. (20) 3207-2413; fax (20) 3207-2115; e-mail mgordon-roe@commonwealthveterans.org.uk; internet www.commonwealthveterans.org.uk; links the former service orgs in the Commonwealth, assists former servicemen of the Crown who are resident abroad; holds confs every four years; 56

mem. orgs in 48 countries; Grand Pres. HRH The Duke of EDINBURGH; publ. *Annual Report.*

Sightsavers (Royal Commonwealth Society for the Blind): Grosvenor Hall, Bolnore Rd, Haywards Heath, West Sussex, RH16 4BX; tel. (1444) 446600; fax (1444) 446688; e-mail info@sightsavers.org; internet www.sightsavers.org; f. 1950 to prevent blindness and restore sight in developing countries, and to provide education and community-based training for incurably blind people; operates in collaboration with local partners in some 30 developing countries, with high priority given to training local staff; Chair. Lord NIGEL CRISP; Chief Exec. Dr CAROLINE HARPER; publ. *Sightsavers News.*

INFORMATION AND THE MEDIA

Commonwealth Broadcasting Association: 17 Fleet St, London, EC4Y 1AA; tel. (20) 7583-5550; fax (20) 7583-5549; e-mail cba@cba.org.uk; internet www.cba.org.uk; f. 1945; general confs are held every two years (2014: Glasgow, United Kingdom, in May); mems: c. 100 in more than 50 countries; Pres. MONEEZA HASHMI; Sec.-Gen. SALLY-ANN WILSON; publs *Commonwealth Broadcaster* (quarterly), *Commonwealth Broadcaster Directory* (annually).

Commonwealth Journalists Association: c/o Canadian Newspaper Association, 890 Yonge St, Suite 200, Toronto, ON M4W 3P4, Canada; tel. (416) 575-5377; fax (416) 923-7206; e-mail pat.perkel@commonwealthjournalists.com; internet www.commonwealthjournalists.com; f. 1978 to promote co-operation between journalists in Commonwealth countries, organize training facilities and confs, and foster understanding among Commonwealth peoples; Exec. Dir PATRICIA PERKEL; publ. *Newsletter* (3 a year).

CPU Media Trust (Association of Commonwealth Newspapers, News Agencies and Periodicals): e-mail webform@cpu.org.uk; internet www.cpu.org.uk; f. 2008 as a 'virtual' org. charged with carrying on the aims of the Commonwealth Press Union (CPU, f. 1950, terminated 2008); promotes the welfare of the Commonwealth press; Chair. GUY BLACK.

LAW

Commonwealth Lawyers Association: c/o Institute of Advanced Legal Studies, 17 Russell Sq., London, WC1B 5DR; tel. (20) 7862-8824; fax (20) 7862-8816; e-mail cla@sas.ac.uk; internet www.commonwealthlawyers.com; f. 1983 (fmrly the Commonwealth Legal Bureau); seeks to maintain and promote the rule of law throughout the Commonwealth, by ensuring that the people of the Commonwealth are served by an independent and efficient legal profession; upholds professional standards and promotes the availability of legal services; organizes events including a Commonwealth Law Conference every two years (2015: Glasgow, United Kingdom); Pres. MARK STEPHENS; publ. *The Commonwealth Lawyer.*

Commonwealth Legal Advisory Service: c/o British Institute of International and Comparative Law, Charles Clore House, 17 Russell Sq., London, WC1B 5DR; tel. (20) 7862-5151; fax (20) 7862-5152; e-mail contact@biicl.org; internet www.biicl.org; f. 1962; financed by the British Institute and by contributions from Commonwealth govts; provides research facilities for Commonwealth govts and law reform commissions; publ. *New Memoranda* series.

Commonwealth Legal Education Association: c/o Legal and Constitutional Affairs Division, Commonwealth Secretariat, Marlborough House, Pall Mall, London, SW1Y 5HX; tel. (20) 7747-6415; fax (20) 7004-3649; e-mail clea@commonwealth.int; internet www.clea-web.com; f. 1971 to promote contacts and exchanges and to provide information regarding legal education; Gen. Secs PATRICIA McKELLAR, MICHAEL BROMBY; publ. *Commonwealth Legal Education Association Newsletter* (2 a year).

Commonwealth Magistrates' and Judges' Association: Uganda House, 58–59 Trafalgar Sq., London, WC2N 5DX; tel. (20) 7976-1007; fax (20) 7976-2394; e-mail info@cmja.org; internet www.cmja.org; f. 1970 to advance the administration of the law by promoting the independence of the judiciary, to further education in law and crime prevention and to disseminate information; confs and study tours; corporate membership for asscns of the judiciary or courts of limited jurisdiction; assoc. membership for individuals; Sec.-Gen. Dr KAREN BREWER; publs *Commonwealth Judicial Journal* (2 a year), *CMJA News.*

PARLIAMENTARY AFFAIRS

Commonwealth Parliamentary Association: Westminster House, Suite 700, 7 Millbank, London, SW1P 3JA; tel. (20) 7799-1460; fax (20) 7222-6073; e-mail hq.sec@cpahq.org; internet www.cpahq.org; f. 1911 to promote understanding and co-operation between Commonwealth parliamentarians; an Executive Committee of 35 MPs is responsible to annual Gen. Assembly; 176 brs in national, state, provincial and territorial parliaments and legislatures throughout the Commonwealth; holds annual Commonwealth

Parliamentary Conferences and seminars; also regional conferencs and seminars; Chair. Sir ALAN HASELHURST; Sec.-Gen. Dr WILLIAM F. SHIJA; publ. *The Parliamentarian* (quarterly).

SCIENCE AND TECHNOLOGY

Commonwealth Association of Architects: POB 1166, Stamford, PE2 2HL; tel. and fax (1780) 238091; e-mail info@comarchitect .org; internet www.comarchitect.org; f. 1964; aims to facilitate the reciprocal recognition of professional qualifications; to provide a clearing house for information on architectural practice; and to encourage collaboration. Plenary confs every three years; regional confs are also held; 38 societies of architects in various Commonwealth countries; Pres. RUKSHAN WIDYALANKARA; Exec. Dir TONY GODWIN; publs *Handbook, Objectives and Procedures: CAA Schools Visiting Boards, Architectural Education in the Commonwealth* (annotated bibliography of research), *CAA Newsnet* (2 a year), a survey and list of schools of architecture.

Commonwealth Engineers' Council: c/o Institution of Civil Engineers, One Great George St, London, SW1P 3AA; tel. (20) 7222-7722; e-mail secretariat@ice.org.uk; internet www.cec.ice.org.uk; f. 1946; links and represents engineering institutions across the Commonwealth, providing them with an opportunity to exchange views on collaboration and mutual support; holds international and regional confs and workshops; mems: 45 institutions in 44 countries; Sec.-Gen. NEIL BAILEY.

Commonwealth Telecommunications Organization: 64-66 Glenthorne Rd, London, W6 0LR; tel. (20) 8600-3800; fax (20) 8600-3819; e-mail info@cto.int; internet www.cto.int; f. 1967 as an international devt partnership between Commonwealth and non-Commonwealth govts, business and civil society orgs; aims to help to bridge the digital divide and to achieve social and economic devt by delivering to developing countries knowledge-sharing programmes in the use of information and communication technologies in the specific areas of telecommunications, broadcasting and the internet; convened in March 2014, in London, jointly with the Commonwealth Secretariat, the first forum of Commonwealth ICT ministers, to discuss recommendations on pan-Commonwealth cyber-governance; Sec.-Gen. Prof. TIM UNWIN; publs *CTO Update* (quarterly), *Annual Report, Research Reports.*

Conference of Commonwealth Meteorologists: c/o International Branch, Meteorological Office, FitzRoy Rd, Exeter, EX1 3PB; tel. (1392) 885680; fax (1392) 885681; e-mail commonwealth@ metoffice.gov.uk; internet www.commonwealthmet.org; links national meteorological and hydrological services in Commonwealth countries.

SPORT AND YOUTH

Commonwealth Games Federation: 138 Piccadilly, 2nd Floor, London, W1J 7NR; tel. (20) 7491-8801; fax (20) 7409-7803; e-mail info@thecgf.com; internet www.thecgf.com; the Games were first held in 1930 and are now held every four years; participation is limited to competitors representing the mem. countries of the Commonwealth; 2014 games: Glasgow, United Kingdom (in July); mems: 72 affiliated bodies; Pres. HRH Prince IMRAN (Malaysia); CEO MICHAEL HOOPER.

Commonwealth Student Association: c/o Youth Affairs Division, Commonwealth Secretariat, Marlborough House, Pall Mall, London, SW1Y 5HX; tel. (20) 7747-6462; e-mail o.said@commonwealth.int; internet cmmnwlthstdnt.tumblr.com/CSA; f. 2012; aims to serve as a forum for student orgs throughout the Commonwealth; a strategic plan was launched in Feb. 2013, which prioritized building the capacity of national student orgs and their leaders to influence education policy; a nine-member steering committee is elected from student leaders across the Commonwealth; Chair. STANLEY NJOROGE.

Commonwealth Youth Exchange Council (CYEC): 7 Lion Yard, Tremadoc Rd, London, SW4 7NQ; tel. (20) 7498-6151; fax (20) 7622-4365; e-mail mail@cyec.org.uk; internet www.cyec.org.uk; f. 1970; promotes contact between groups of young people of the United Kingdom and other Commonwealth countries by means of educational exchange visits; provides host govts with technical assistance for delivery of the Commonwealth Youth Forum, held every two

years; since July 2011 administers the Commonwealth Teacher Exchange Programme (CTEP); mems: 222 orgs, 134 local authorities, 88 voluntary bodies; Dir of Programmes HELEN JONES; publs *Contact* (handbook), *Exchange* (newsletter), *Final Communiqués* (of the Commonwealth Youth Forums), *Safety and Welfare* (guidelines for Commonwealth Youth Exchange groups).

RELATIONS WITHIN THE COMMONWEALTH

Commonwealth Countries League: 37 Priory Ave, Sudbury, HA0 2SB; tel. (19) 2382-1364; e-mail info@ccl-int.org; internet www .ccl-int.org; f. 1925; aims to secure equality of liberties, status and opportunities between women and men and to promote friendship and mutual understanding throughout the Commonwealth; promotes women's political and social education and links together women's orgs in most countries of the Commonwealth; an education sponsorship scheme was established in 1967 to finance the secondary education of bright girls from lower-income backgrounds in their own Commonwealth countries; the CCL Education Fund sponsors 300–400 girls throughout the Commonwealth; in March 2011 the Fund launched the 'A Thousand Schools for a Thousand Girls' initiative, aiming to increase to 1,000 the number of girls sponsored annually; Exec. Chair. MAJORIE RENNIE; publs *News Update* (3 a year), *Annual Report.*

Commonwealth War Graves Commission: 2 Marlow Rd, Maidenhead, SL6 7DX; tel. (1628) 634221; fax (1628) 771208; internet www.cwgc.org; casualty and cemetery enquiries; e-mail casualty .enq@cwgc.org; f. 1917 (as Imperial War Graves Commission); responsible for the commemoration in perpetuity of the 1.7m. members of the Commonwealth Forces who died during the wars of 1914–18 and 1939–45; provides for the marking and maintenance of war graves and memorials at some 23,000 locations in 150 countries; mems: Australia, Canada, India, New Zealand, South Africa, United Kingdom; Pres. HRH The Duke of KENT; Dir-Gen. ALAN PATEMAN-JONES.

Council of Commonwealth Societies: c/o Royal Commonwealth Society, 7 Lion Yard, Tremadoc Rd, London, SW4 7NQ; tel. (20) 7766-9206; fax (20) 7622-4365; e-mail ccs@rcsint.org; internet www.rcsint .org/day; f. 1947; provides a forum for the exchange of information regarding activities of member orgs which promote understanding among countries of the Commonwealth; organizes the observance of and promotes Commonwealth Day (held annually on the second Monday in March; 2015 theme: 'A Young Commonwealth'), produces educational materials relating to the occasion, and co-ordinates the distribution of the Commonwealth Day message by Queen Elizabeth II; seeks to raise the profile of the Commonwealth; mems: 30 official and unofficial Commonwealth orgs; Chair. Lord ALAN WATSON.

Royal Commonwealth Society: Award House, 7–11 St Matthew St, London SW1P 2JT, United Kingdom; tel. (20) 3727-4300; fax (20) 7930-9705; e-mail info@thercs.org; internet www.thercs.org; f. 1868; aims to improve the lives and prospects of Commonwealth citizens across the world; the society is constituted by Royal Charter (most recently amended in 2013) and as a charity; organizes meetings and seminars on topical issues, projects for young people, a youth leadership programme, and cultural and social events; Chair. CLAIRE WHITAKER; Dir MICHAEL LAKE; publs *RCS Exchange* (3 a year), conference reports.

Royal Over-Seas League: Over-Seas House, Park Pl., St James's St, London, SW1A 1LR; tel. (20) 7408-0214; fax (20) 7499-6738; e-mail info@rosl.org.uk; internet www.rosl.org.uk; f. 1910 to promote friendship and understanding in the Commonwealth; club houses in London and Edinburgh; membership is open to all British subjects and Commonwealth citizens; Dir-Gen. Maj.-Gen. RODDY PORTER; publ. *Overseas* (quarterly).

Victoria League for Commonwealth Friendship: 55 Leinster Sq., London, W2 4PW; tel. (20) 7243-2633; fax (20) 7229-2994; e-mail enquiries@victorialeague.co.uk; internet www.victorialeague.co.uk; f. 1901; aims to further personal friendship among Commonwealth peoples and to provide hospitality for visitors; maintains Student House, providing accommodation for students from Commonwealth countries; has branches elsewhere in the UK and abroad; Chair. LYN D. HOPKINS; Gen. Man. DOREEN HENRY; publ. *Annual Report.*

EUROPEAN UNION—EU

Presidency of the Council of the European Union: Italy (July–December 2014); Latvia (January–June 2015); Luxembourg (July–December 2015).

President of the European Council: HERMAN VAN ROMPUY (Belgium).

High Representative of the Union for Foreign Affairs and Security Policy: CATHERINE ASHTON (United Kingdom) (outgoing), FEDERICA MOGHERINI (Italy) (designate, from 1 Dec. 2014).

Latin America

A non-preferential trade agreement was signed with Uruguay in 1974, and economic and commercial co-operation agreements with Mexico in 1975 and with Brazil in 1980. A five-year co-operation agreement with the members of the Central American Common Market and with Panama entered into force in 1987, as did a similar agreement with the member countries (see below) of the Andean Group (now the Andean Community). Co-operation agreements were signed with Argentina and Chile in 1990, and in that year tariff preferences were approved for Bolivia, Colombia, Ecuador and Peru, in support of those countries' efforts to combat drugs-trafficking. In May 1992 an inter-institutional co-operation agreement was signed with the Southern Common Market (Mercado Común del Sur—MERCOSUR); in the following month the European Community (EC) and the members of the Andean Group (Bolivia, Colombia, Ecuador, Peru and Venezuela) initialled a new co-operation agreement, which was to broaden the scope of economic and development co-operation and enhance trade relations, and a new co-operation agreement was signed with Brazil. In July 1993 the EC introduced a tariff regime to limit the import of bananas from Latin America, in order to protect the banana-producing countries of the African, Caribbean and Pacific (ACP) group, then linked to the EC by the Lomé Convention. In December 2009, in resolution to a long dispute over the tariff regime, the EU and Latin American states initialled the EU-Latin America Bananas Agreement, which provided for a gradual reduction in the tariff rate—see African, Caribbean and Pacific Countries.

From 1996 the EU, as the EC became in 1993, forged closer links with Latin America, by means of strengthened political ties, an increase in economic integration and free trade, and co-operation in other areas. In April 1997 the EU extended further trade benefits to the countries of the Andean Community. In September 2009 the Commission adopted 'The European Union and Latin America: Global Players in Partnership', updating an earlier communication, published in 2005, on 'A Stronger Partnership between the European Union and Latin America'.

In July 1997 the EU and Mexico concluded an Economic Partnership, Political Co-ordination and Co-operation Agreement (the Global Agreement) and an interim agreement on trade. The accords were signed in December, and entered into effect in 2000. In November 1999 the EU and Mexico concluded a free trade agreement, which provided for the removal of all tariffs on bilateral trade in industrial products by 2007. The first meeting of the Joint Council established by the Economic Partnership, Political Co-ordination and Co-operation Agreement between the EU and Mexico was held in February 2001; further meetings have since been held on a regular basis. In July 2008, in acknowledgement of the gradual strengthening of EU-Mexico relations, the European Commission proposed the establishment of a Strategic Partnership with Mexico. An EU-Mexico summit meeting was held in Comillas, Spain, in May 2010. In May 2007 the European Commission proposed to launch a Strategic Partnership with Brazil, in recognition of its increasing international prominence and strong bilateral ties with Europe. The first EU-Brazil summit was duly held in Lisbon, Portugal, in July.

In November 2002 the EU and Chile signed an association and free trade agreement, which entered into force in March 2005; it provided for the liberalization of trade within seven years for industrial products and 10 years for agricultural products. The first meeting of the Association Council set up by the agreement took place in Athens, Greece, in March 2003.

In late December 1994 the EU and MERCOSUR signed a joint declaration that aimed to promote trade liberalization and greater political co-operation. In September 1995, at a meeting in Montevideo, Uruguay, a framework agreement on the establishment of a free trade regime between the two organizations was initialled. The agreement was formally signed in December. In July 1998 the European Commission voted to commence negotiations towards an interregional Association Agreement with MERCOSUR, which would strengthen existing co-operation agreements. Negotiations were initiated in April 2000 (focusing on the three pillars of political

dialogue, co-operation, and establishing a free trade area), but were suspended in 2004–10; none the less, political relations were maintained, and notably were extended in May 2008 to include the additional areas of science and technology, infrastructure, and renewable energy.

The first ministerial conference between the EC and the Rio Group of Latin American and Caribbean states took place in April 1991; high-level joint ministerial meetings were held every two years until 2009. The first summit meeting of all EU and Latin American and Caribbean heads of state or government was held in Rio de Janeiro, Brazil, in June 1999, when a strategic partnership was launched. A second EU-Latin America/Caribbean (EU-LAC) summit took place in Madrid, Spain, in May 2002, and covered co-operation in political, economic, social and cultural fields. A political dialogue and co-operation agreement with the Andean Community and its member states was signed in December 2003. At the fourth EU-LAC summit, held in Vienna, Austria, in May 2006, it was decided that negotiations for Association Agreements with Central America and with the Andean Community should be initiated. The summit also endorsed a proposal to establish an EU-Latin America parliamentary assembly. The assembly met for the first time in November. In 2007 the EU concluded negotiations for an Economic Partnership Agreement with the Caribbean Forum (CARIFORUM) grouping of 16 states. In mid-2007 the EU and the Andean Community initiated negotiations on the planned Association Agreement in Tarija, Bolivia. However, negotiations were suspended in June 2008, reportedly owing to divergent views of the aims and scope of the trade provisions. In January 2009 negotiations recommenced between three of the Andean Community countries, Colombia, Ecuador and Peru, with the goal of concluding a multi-party trade agreement; Ecuador provisionally suspended its participation in the negotiations in July. Negotiations were concluded on 1 March 2010, with an agreement on trade between the EU and Colombia and Peru, providing for the liberalization of trade in 65% of industrial products with Colombia, and 80% with Peru. The trade agreement was signed in June 2012, and entered into effect in August 2014. Talks on an Association Agreement between the EU and the countries of Central America (Costa Rica, El Salvador, Guatemala, Honduras, Nicaragua and Panama) commenced in Costa Rica in October 2007, but negotiations were suspended temporarily during 2009 owing to the unstable political situation in Honduras. In May 2010 the EU concluded negotiations on an Association Agreement with Central America, covering three areas: trade; political dialogue; and co-operation. The Association Agreement was signed in Tegucigalpa, Honduras, in June 2012, and approved by the European Parliament in December. In May 2014 a new EU-Central America Political Dialogue and Co-operation Agreement entered into effect, pending ratification of the Association Agreement (the trade element of which had already come into force). In November 2012 the Council had endorsed a Joint Caribbean-EU Partnership Strategy, which was conceived at an EU-CARIFORUM summit held in Madrid in May 2010.

In 2010 the Rio Group merged with Cumbres América Latina y Caribe (CALC—internal LAC Summits), under the framework of the Community of Latin American and Caribbean States (CELAC), which began to represent the region in negotiations with third countries and regional grouping. The first EU-CELAC summit meeting took place in Santiago, Chile, in January 2013. An EU-CELAC action plan for 2013–15 was agreed, focusing on the following principal areas: (i) the development of an EU-LAC Knowledge Area, with co-operation and investment in science, research, innovation and technology; (ii) sustainable development, the environment, climate change, biodiversity and energy; (iii) regional integration; (iv) migration; (v) education and employment; (vi) combating drugs; (vii) tackling gender inequalities; and (viii) investment and entrepreneurship. In June 2013 the EU and the Organisation of Eastern Caribbean States established diplomatic relations, in order to promote co-operation between the two organizations.

Cuba remained the only Latin American country that did not have a formal economic co-operation agreement with the EU. In June 1995 a Commission communication advocated greater economic co-operation with Cuba; this policy was criticized by the US Government, which maintained an economic embargo against Cuba. Later that year the EU agreed to make the extent of economic co-operation with Cuba (a one-party state) contingent on progress towards democracy. An EU legation office opened in the Cuban capital, Havana, in March 2003, and the EU supported a renewed application by Cuba to join the successor to the Lomé Convention, the Cotonou Agreement. However, human rights abuses perpetrated by the Cuban regime in April (the imprisonment of a large number of dissidents) led to the downgrading of diplomatic relations with Cuba by the EU, the instigation of an EU policy of inviting dissidents to embassy receptions in Havana (the so-called cocktail wars) and the indefinite postponement of Cuba's application to join the Cotonou Agreement. In May Cuba withdrew its application for membership, and in July the Cuban President, Fidel Castro, announced that the Government would not accept aid from the EU and would terminate all political contact with the organization. In December 2004 the EU proposed a compromise—namely not to invite any Cubans, whether government ministers or dissidents, to future embassy receptions—but reiterated its demand that Cuba unconditionally release all political prisoners who remained in detention (several dissidents had already been released). Cuba announced in January 2005 that it was restoring diplomatic ties with all EU states. At the end of that month the EU temporarily suspended the diplomatic sanctions imposed on Cuba in mid-2003 and announced its intention to resume a 'constructive dialogue' with the Cuban authorities. The EU extended the temporary suspension of diplomatic sanctions against Cuba for one year in June 2005, and annually thereafter. Sanctions were lifted in June 2008, subject to an annual review. In May 2010 the European Commission adopted a country strategy paper on Cuba, which identified three priority areas for intervention: food security; the environment, and adaptation to climate change; and exchanges of expertise, training and studies. In February 2014 EU ministers responsible for foreign affairs endorsed a mandate to initiate efforts to negotiate a political and co-operation agreement with Cuba; talks commenced in April.

The EU's natural disaster prevention and preparedness programme (Dipecho) has targeted earthquake, flood, hurricane, and volcanic eruption preparedness throughout Latin America and the Caribbean. An earthquake devastated Haiti's infrastructure in January 2010. By March EU humanitarian assistance (including planned pledges), totalled more than €320m. (from member states and the European Commission's Humanitarian Aid Office—ECHO). Emergency relief from ECHO was worth €120m., including €3m. in emergency funding allocated within 24 hours of the earthquake taking place. Following an outbreak of cholera in October, an alert system was put in place, and the Commission approved new funding of some €10m. at the end of December to help to fund the efforts of ECHO to provide support for health staff; to implement preventive strategies, such as the promotion of chlorination and a hygiene-awareness campaign; and to improve the collection and analysis of health-related data. In 2010–13 ECHO contributed a total of €213m. to Haiti.

The EU has adopted the following decentralized programmes to provide economic assistance to Latin America: AL-INVEST (supporting European investment in Latin America-based small and medium-sized enterprises that seek to operate internationally); ALFA (promoting bilateral co-operation in higher education); URB-AL (promoting links between European and Latin American cities); ALBAN (promoting higher education through the provision of scholarships); @LIS (supporting the use of information technologies); OBREAL (aimed at establishing a network of non-profit-making institutions from both regions); and EUROSociAL (inaugurated in May 2004 to assist Latin American countries with developing and implementing social policies aimed at strengthening social cohesion). In May 2010 the Latin American Investment Facility (LAIF) was officially launched with the aim of promoting investment in Latin America by beneficiary governments and public organizations. In April 2011 ECHO launched the South America Disaster Preparedness Plan, which sought to help to reduce the risk of emergencies and to improve disaster preparedness in eight countries. Humanitarian aid allocated in 2013 included €13.5m. to assist those affected by conflict in Colombia. In 2013–14 ECHO allocated €14.5m. to improve resistance to natural disasters and drought in Argentina, Bolivia, Brazil, Chile, Colombia, Ecuador, Paraguay, Peru, Uruguay and Venezuela.

African, Caribbean and Pacific (ACP) Countries

In June 2000, meeting in Cotonou, Benin, heads of state and of government of the EU and African, Caribbean and Pacific (ACP) countries concluded a new 20-year partnership accord between the EU and ACP states. The EU-ACP Partnership Agreement, known as the Cotonou Agreement, entered into force on 1 April 2003 (although many of its provisions had been applicable for a transitional period since August 2000), following ratification by the then 15 EU member states and more than the requisite two-thirds of the ACP countries. Previously, the principal means of co-operation between the European Community (EC) and developing countries were the Lomé Conventions. The First Lomé Convention (Lomé I), which was concluded at Lomé, Togo, in February 1975 and came into force on 1 April 1976, replaced the Yaoundé Conventions and the Arusha Agreement. Lomé I was designed to provide a new framework of co-operation, taking into account the varying needs of developing ACP countries.

The Second Lomé Convention entered into force on 1 January 1981 and the Third Lomé Convention on 1 March 1985 (trade provisions) and 1 May 1986 (aid). The Fourth Lomé Convention, which had a 10-year commitment period, was signed in December 1989: its trade provisions entered into force on 1 March 1990, and the remainder entered into force in September 1991.

The Cotonou Agreement was to cover a 20-year period from 2000 and was subject to revision every five years. A financial protocol was attached to the Agreement, which indicated the funds available to the ACP through the European Development Fund (EDF), the main instrument for Community aid for development co-operation in ACP countries. The ninth EDF, covering the initial five-year period from March 2000, provided a total budget of €13,500m., of which €1,300m. was allocated to regional co-operation and €2,200m. was for the new investment facility for the development of the private sector. In addition, uncommitted balances from previous EDFs amounted to a further €2,500m. The new Agreement envisaged a more participatory approach with more effective political co-operation to encourage good governance and democracy, increased flexibility in the provision of aid to reward performance, and a new framework for economic and trade co-operation. Its objectives were to alleviate poverty, contribute to sustainable development and integrate the ACP economies into the global economy. Negotiations to revise the Cotonou Agreement were concluded in February 2005. The political dimension of the Agreement was broadly strengthened and a reference to co-operation in counter-terrorism and the prevention of the proliferation of weapons of mass destruction was included. The revised Cotonou Agreement was signed on 24 June.

Under the provisions of the new accord, the EU was to finalize free trade arrangements (replacing the previous non-reciprocal trade preferences) with the most developed ACP countries during 2000–08, structured around six regional free trade zones, and be designed to ensure full compatibility with World Trade Organization (WTO) provisions. The agreements would be subject to revision every five years. The first general stage of negotiations for the Economic Partnership Agreements (EPAs), involving discussions with all ACP countries regarding common procedures, began in September 2002. The regional phase of EPA negotiations to establish a new framework for trade and investment commenced in October 2003. Negotiations had been scheduled for completion in mid-2007. However, the negotiation period was subsequently extended, and in 2014 negotiations were ongoing.

In March 2010 negotiations were concluded on the second revision of the Cotonou Agreement, which sought to take into account factors including the increasing importance of enhanced regional co-operation and a more inclusive partnership in ACP countries; the need for security; efforts to meet the Millennium Development Goals; the new trade relationship developed following the expiry of trade preferences at the end of 2007; and the need to ensure the effectiveness and coherence of international aid efforts. The second revised Cotonou Agreement was formally signed in Ouagadougou, Burkina Faso, in June 2010, and entered into effect, on a provisional basis, at the beginning of November.

Meanwhile, the EU had launched an initiative to allow free access to the products of the least developed ACP nations by 2005. Stabex and Sysmin, instruments under the Lomé Conventions designed to stabilize export prices for agricultural and mining commodities, respectively, were replaced by a system called FLEX, introduced in 2000, to compensate ACP countries for short-term fluctuations in export earnings. In February 2001 the EU agreed to phase out trade barriers on imports of everything but military weapons from the world's 48 least developed countries, 39 of which were in the ACP group. Duties on sugar, rice, bananas and some other products were maintained until 2009, and withdrawn from October of that year. In May 2001 the EU announced that it was to cancel all outstanding debts arising from its trade accords with former colonies of member states.

A major new programme set up on behalf of the ACP countries and financed by the EDF was Pro€Invest, which was launched in 2002, with funding of €110m. over a seven-year period. In October 2003 the Commission proposed the incorporation of the EDF into the EU budget (it had previously been a fund outside the EU budget, to which the EU member states made direct voluntary contributions). The cost-sharing formula for the member states would automatically apply, obviating the need for negotiations about contributions for the 10th EDF. The Commission proposal was endorsed by the European Parliament in April 2004. The 10th EDF was agreed in December 2005 by the European Council and provided funds of €22,682m. for 2008–13. The Multi-Annual Financial Framework adopted by the Council in December 2013 provided for overall funding of €26,984m. for the 11th EDF in 2014–20.

On 1 July 1993 the EC introduced a regime to allow the preferential import into the Community of bananas from former French and British colonies in the Caribbean. This was designed to protect the banana industries of ACP countries from the availability of cheaper bananas, produced by countries in Latin America. Latin American and later US producers brought a series of complaints before the

WTO, claiming that the EU banana import regime was in contravention of free trade principles. The WTO upheld their complaints on each occasion leading to adjustments of the complex quota and tariffs systems in place. Following the WTO authorization of punitive US trade sanctions, in April 2001 the EU reached agreement with the USA and Ecuador on a new banana regime. Under the new accord, the EU was granted the so-called Cotonou waiver, which allowed it to maintain preferential access for ACP banana exports, in return for the adoption of a new tariff-only system for bananas from Latin American countries from 1 January 2006. The Latin American producers were guaranteed total market access under the agreement and were permitted to seek arbitration if dissatisfied with the EU's proposed tariff levels. Following the WTO rejection of EU proposals for tariff levels of €230 and €187 per metric ton (in comparison with existing rates of €75 for a quota of 2.2m. tons and €680 thereafter), in November 2005 the EU announced that a tariff of €176, with a duty-free quota of 775,000 tons for ACP producers, would be implemented on 1 January 2006. In late 2006 Ecuador initiated a challenge to the EU's proposals at the WTO. Twelve other countries subsequently initiated third-party challenges to the proposals at the WTO, in support of the challenge by Ecuador. In April 2008 the WTO upheld the challenge by Ecuador, and ordered the EU to align its tariffs with WTO regulations. In December 2009 representatives from the EU and Latin American countries initialled the Geneva Agreement on Trade in Bananas (GATB), which aimed to end the dispute. Under the Agreement, which made no provision for import quotas, the EU was gradually to reduce its import tariff on bananas from Latin American countries, from €176 per ton to €114 per ton by 2017. In March 2010 the EU also approved the implementation of Banana Accompanying Measures, which aimed to mobilize €190m. to support the 10 main ACP banana-exporting countries in adjusting to the anticipated increase in market competition from Latin America during 2010–13. (ACP countries would continue to benefit from duty- and quota-free access to EU markets.) For their part, Latin American banana-producing countries undertook not to demand further tariff reductions; and to withdraw several related cases against the EU that were pending at the WTO. In response to the Agreement, the US authorities determined to settle ongoing parallel complaints lodged with the WTO against the EU relating to bananas. On 8 November 2012, following the certification by the WTO of the reduced banana tariffs agreed under the GATB, the EU and the 10 main banana-producing countries (Brazil, Colombia, Costa Rica, Ecuador, Guatemala, Honduras, Mexico, Nicaragua, Panama, Peru and Venezuela) signed a Mutually Agreed Solution, ending eight pending banana dispute settlement proceedings at the WTO.

Following a WTO ruling at the request of Brazil, Australia and Thailand in 2005 that the EU's subsidized exports of sugar breached legal limits, reform of the EU's sugar regime was required by May 2006. Previously, the EU purchased fixed quotas of sugar from ACP producers at two or three times the world price, the same price that it paid to sugar growers in the EU. In November 2005 the EU agreed to reform the sugar industry through a phased reduction of its prices for white sugar of 36% by 2009 (which was still twice the market price in 2005).

In May 2003 Timor-Leste joined the ACP and the ACP-EC Council of Ministers approved its accession to the ACP-EC Partnership Agreement. Cuba, which had been admitted to the ACP in December 2000, was granted observer status. Cuba withdrew its application to join the Cotonou Agreement in July 2003.

Article 96 of the Cotonou Agreement, which provides for suspension of the Agreement in specific countries in the event of violation of one of its essential elements (respect for human rights, democratic principles and the rule of law), was invoked against Haiti in 2001, and this was extended annually to December 2004. However, relations with Haiti began to be normalized from September of that year.

INTER-AMERICAN DEVELOPMENT BANK—IDB

Address: 1300 New York Ave, NW, Washington, DC 20577, USA.

Telephone: (202) 623-1000; **fax:** (202) 623-3096; **e-mail:** pic@iadb .org; **internet:** www.iadb.org.

The Bank was founded in 1959 to promote the individual and collective development of Latin American and Caribbean countries through the financing of economic and social development projects and the provision of technical assistance. From 1976 membership was extended to include countries outside the region.

MEMBERS

Argentina	Ecuador	Nicaragua
Austria	El Salvador	Norway
Bahamas	Finland	Panama
Barbados	France	Paraguay
Belgium	Germany	Peru
Belize	Guatemala	Portugal
Bolivia	Guyana	Slovenia
Brazil	Haiti	Spain
Canada	Honduras	Suriname
Chile	Israel	Sweden
China, People's Rep.	Italy	Switzerland
Colombia	Jamaica	Trinidad and
Costa Rica	Japan	Tobago
Croatia	Republic of	United Kingdom
Denmark	Korea	USA
Dominican	Mexico	Uruguay
Republic	Netherlands	Venezuela

Organization

(September 2014)

BOARD OF GOVERNORS

All the powers of the Bank are vested in a Board of Governors, consisting of one Governor and one alternate appointed by each member country (usually ministers responsible for finance or presidents of central banks). The Board meets annually, with special meetings when necessary. The 55th annual meeting was convened in Costa do Sauípe, Bahía, Brazil, in March 2014.

BOARD OF EXECUTIVE DIRECTORS

The Board of Executive Directors is responsible for the operations of the Bank. It establishes the Bank's policies, approves loan and technical co-operation proposals that are submitted by the President of the Bank, and authorizes the Bank's borrowings on capital markets.

There are 14 Executive Directors and 14 alternates. Each Director is elected by a group of two or more countries, except the Directors representing Canada and the USA. The USA holds 30% of votes on the Board, in respect of its contribution to the Bank's capital. The Board has five permanent committees, relating to Policy and evaluation; Organization, human resources and board matters; Budget, financial policies and audit; Programming; and a Steering Committee.

ADMINISTRATION

In December 2006 the Board of Executive Directors approved a new structure which aimed to strengthen the Bank's country focus and improve its operational efficiency. Three new positions of Vice-Presidents were created. Accordingly the executive structure comprises the President, Executive Vice-President and Vice-Presidents for Countries (with responsibility for four regional departments); Sectors and Knowledge; Private Sector and Non-sovereign Guaranteed Operations; and Finance and Administration. The principal Offices are of the Auditor-General, Outreach and Partnerships, External Relations, Risk Management, and Strategic Planning and Development Effectiveness. An Independent Consultation and Investigation Mechanism, to monitor compliance with the Bank's environmental and social policies, was established in February 2010. The Bank has country offices in each of its borrowing member states, and special offices in Tokyo, Japan (covering Japan, the People's Republic of China and Republic of Korea), and in Madrid, Spain (covering Europe). There are some 1,800 Bank staff (excluding the Board of Executive Directors and the Evaluation Office), of whom almost 30% are based in country offices. The total Bank group administrative expenses for 2013 amounted to US $837m.

President: LUIS ALBERTO MORENO (Colombia).

Executive Vice-President: JULIE T. KATZMAN (USA).

Activities

Loans are made to governments and to public and private entities for specific economic and social development projects and for sectoral reforms. These loans are repayable in the currencies lent and their terms range from 12 to 40 years. Total lending authorized by the Bank amounted to US $230,414m. by the end of 2013. During 2013 the Bank approved loans and guarantees amounting to $13,811m., of which Ordinary Capital loans totalled $13,290m. (compared with a total of $10,799m. in 2012). Disbursements on Ordinary Capital loans amounted to $10,558m. in 2013, compared with $6,882m. in the previous year. Some 168 projects were approved in 2013, of which 148 were investment projects. In October 2008 the Bank announced measures to help to counter the effects on the region of the downturn in the world's major economies and the restrictions on the availability of credit. It resolved to accelerate lending and establish an emergency liquidity facility, with funds of up to $6,000m., in order to sustain regional economic growth and to support social welfare programmes.

In March 2009 the Board of Governors agreed to initiate a capital review, in recognition of unprecedented demand for Bank resources owing to the sharp contraction of international capital markets. An agreement to increase the Bank's authorized capital by US $70,000m. was concluded in March 2010 and endorsed, as the Ninth General Capital Increase (IDB-9), by the Board of Governors in July. Of the total increase, $1,700m. was expected to be paid in by member countries over a five-year period. Under IDB-9, the Bank is mandated to focus by 2015 some 35% of total lending on small and vulnerable countries, and to target lending at the following sectors: Social Policy for Productivity; Global and Regional Integration; Institutions for Growth and Productivity; and Climate Change and Sustainable Energy. In January 2012 member states approved the resolution authorizing IDB-9, and it entered into effect in the following month. At the end of 2013 the subscribed Ordinary Capital stock, including inter-regional capital, which was merged into it in 1987, totalled $128,781m., of which $4,941m. was paid-in and $123,840m. was callable. The callable capital constitutes, in effect, a guarantee of the securities that the Bank issues in the capital markets in order to increase its resources available for lending.

In 2013 operating income amounted to US $881m. At the end of 2013 total borrowings outstanding amounted to $67,460m., compared with $59,754m. at the end of the previous year.

The Fund for Special Operations (FSO) enables the Bank to make concessional loans for economic and social projects where circumstances call for special treatment, such as lower interest rates and longer repayment terms than those applied to loans from the ordinary resources. Assistance may be provided to countries adversely affected by economic crises or natural disasters through a new Development Sustainability Contingent Credit Line (DSL), which was approved by the Board of Directors in September 2012 to replace the previous emergency lending facility. The DSL is capped at a maximum of US $300m. per country, or 2% of a country's gross domestic product (if less), and was developed to provide an efficient response to the types of crisis that may impact the region. In 2013 22 policy-based loans, totalling $4,000m., and one project, were approved under the DSL. In March 2007 the Board of Governors approved a reform of the Bank's concessional lending (at the same time as endorsing arrangements for participation in the Multilateral Debt Relief Initiative, see below), and resolved that FSO lending may be 'blended' with Ordinary Capital loans by means of a parallel lending mechanism. At 31 December 2013 cumulative FSO lending amounted to $19,622m., and in 2013 FSO lending totalled $251m. The terms and conditions of IDB-9, approved by the Board of Governors in July 2010, incorporated a commitment to replenish FSO resources by $479m.

On 1 January 2012 a new Flexible Financing Facility (FFF) entered into effect, which was, thereafter, to be the only financial product platform for approval of all new Ordinary Capital sovereign guaranteed loans.

In June 2007 a new IDB Grant Facility (GRF) was established, funded by transfers from the FSO, to make available resources for specific projects or countries in specific circumstances. By the end of 2013 resources had only been granted to support reconstruction and development in Haiti. In accordance with IDB-9 the Board of Governors may approve transfers of US $200m. from Ordinary Capital to the GRF annually during 2011–20. Consequently, such transfers were approved by the Board of Governors in March 2011, March 2012, and March 2013. During 2013 the Bank approved grants to Haiti from the GRF totalling $188m. In May 2011 the Board of Governors approved a new Small and Medium-sized Enterprises (SME) Financing Facility, with funds of up to $100m. in order to improve access to finance for SMEs, to promote job creation and stimulate economic growth.

In 1998 the Bank agreed to participate in an initiative of the IMF and the World Bank to assist heavily indebted poor countries (HIPCs) to maintain a sustainable level of debt. Also in 1998,

following projections of reduced resources for the FSO, borrowing member countries agreed to convert about US $2,400m. in local currencies held by the Bank, in order to maintain a convertible concessional Fund for poorer countries, and to help to reduce the debt-servicing payments under the HIPC initiative. In mid-2000 a committee of the Board of Governors endorsed a financial framework for the Bank's participation in an enhanced HIPC initiative, which aimed to broaden the eligibility criteria and accelerate the process of debt reduction. The Bank was to provide $896m. (in net present value), in addition to $204m. committed under the original scheme, of which $307m. was for Bolivia, $65m. for Guyana, $391m. for Nicaragua and $133m. for Honduras. The Bank assisted the preparation of national Poverty Reduction Strategy Papers, a condition of reaching the 'completion point' of the process. In January 2007 the Bank concluded an agreement to participate in the Multilateral Debt Relief Initiative (MDRI), which had been approved by the World Bank and IMF in 2005 as a means of achieving 100% cancellation of debts for eligible HIPCs. The agreement to support the MDRI was endorsed by the Bank's Board of Governors in March 2007. Under the initiative the eligible completion point countries, along with Haiti (which had reached 'decision point' in November 2006), were to receive additional debt relief amounting to some $3,370m. in principal payments and $1,000m. in future interest payments, cancelling loan balances with the FSO (outstanding as of 31 December 2004). Haiti reached 'completion point' under the HIPC initiative in June 2009. Accordingly, FSO delivered debt relief under the enhanced HIPC initiative and the MDRI amounting to some $419m. The general capital increase, approved in 2010, intended to provide for cancellation of all Haiti's outstanding debts to the Bank. In September 2010 the US Government made available an advance contribution of $204m. to the FSO, enabling the Bank to announce the cancellation of Haiti's outstanding debts, amounting to $484m.

In June 2006 the Bank inaugurated a new initiative, Opportunities for the Majority, to improve conditions for low-income communities throughout the region. Under the scheme the Bank was to support the development of partnerships between communities, private sector bodies and non-governmental organizations to generate employment, deliver services and integrate poorer members of society into the productive economy. During 2013 a total of 10 projects were approved under the initiative with a value of US $100m.

In March 2007 the Bank's Board of Governors endorsed the Sustainable Energy and Climate Change Initiative (SECCI), which aimed to expand the development and use of biofuels and other sources of renewable energy, to enhance energy efficiency and to facilitate adaptation to climate change. A Bank fund, with an initial US $20m. in resources, was established to finance feasibility studies and technical co-operation projects. In November 2009 the Bank signed a Memorandum of Understanding with the Asian Development Bank to support projects and programmes that promote sustainable, low-carbon transport in both regions. In accordance with the priorities of the lending agreement approved along with IDB-9 in July 2010, support for climate change adaptation initiatives and other projects concerned with renewable energy and environmental sustainability was expected to reach 25% of total lending by the end of 2015. In March 2013 the Bank launched a Biodiversity and Ecosystems Services Programme, which was to support projects aimed at leveraging the region's natural capital in pursuit of sustainable development.

The Bank supports a range of consultative groups in order to strengthen donor co-operation with countries in the Latin America and Caribbean region, in particular to co-ordinate emergency relief and reconstruction following a natural disaster or to support peace efforts within a country. In November 2001 the Bank hosted the first meeting of a Network for the Prevention and Mitigation of Natural Disasters in Latin America and the Caribbean, which was part of a regional policy dialogue, sponsored by the Bank to promote broad debate on strategic issues. In April 2006 the Bank established the Disaster Prevention Fund, financed through Ordinary Capital funds, to help countries to improve their disaster preparedness and reduce their vulnerability to natural hazards. A separate Multidonor Disaster Prevention Trust Fund was established at the end of 2006 to finance technical assistance and investment in preparedness projects.

In July 2004 the Bank co-hosted an international donor conference, together with the World Bank, the European Union (EU) and the UN, to consider the immediate and medium-term needs for Haiti following a period of political unrest. Some US $1,080m. was pledged at the conference, of which the Bank's contribution was $260m. In April 2009 international donors, meeting under the Bank's auspices, pledged further contributions of $324m. to Haiti's economic and social development. In January 2010 the Bank determined to redirect undisbursed funds of up to $90m. to finance priority emergency assistance and reconstruction efforts in Haiti following a devastating earthquake. In March the Board of Governors agreed to cancel Haiti's outstanding debt and to convert undisbursed loans in order to provide grant assistance amounting to $2,000m. over the coming

10 years. In mid-March the Bank organized a conference of representatives of the private sector in Haiti, in preparation for the International Donors' Conference, which was then held at the end of that month in New York, USA. The Bank also supported the Haitian Government in preparing, jointly with the UN, the World Bank and the European Commission, a Preliminary Damage and Needs Assessment report for presentation at the Conference. During 2013 some $186m. of the $188m. committed by the Bank in grants to Haiti was disbursed, in particular to fund activities in the areas of education, private sector development, energy, agriculture, transportation, and water and sanitation.

An increasing number of donor countries have placed funds under the Bank's administration for assistance to Latin America, outside the framework of the Ordinary Resources and the Bank's Special Operations. These include the Social Progress Trust Fund (set up by the USA in 1961); the Venezuelan Trust Fund (set up in 1975); the Japan Special Fund (1988); and other funds administered on behalf of Austria, Belgium, Canada, Chile, Denmark, Finland, France, Israel, Italy, Japan, the Netherlands, Norway, Portugal, Spain, Sweden, Switzerland, the United Kingdom and the EU. A Program for the Development of Technical Co-operation was established in 1991, which is financed by European countries and the EU.

The Bank provides technical co-operation to help member countries to identify and prepare new projects, to improve loan execution, to strengthen the institutional capacity of public and private agencies, to address extreme conditions of poverty and to promote small- and micro-enterprise development. The Bank has established a special co-operation programme to facilitate the transfer of experience and technology among regional programmes. Technical co-operation operations are mainly financed by income from the FSO and donor trust funds. The Bank supports the efforts of the countries of the region to achieve economic integration and has provided extensive technical support for the formulation of integration strategies in the Andean, Central American and Southern Cone regions. In June 2010 the Bank agreed to collaborate with the Spanish Government, the Bill and Melinda Gates Foundation and the Carlos Slim Health Institute in administering a new 'Salud Mesoamérica 2015' initiative, which aimed to support efforts to achieve the millennium development health objectives in the region over a five-year period. The Bank is a member of the technical co-ordinating committee of the Integration of Regional Infrastructure in South America initiative, which aimed to promote multinational development projects, capacity building and integration in that region. In September 2006 the Bank established a new fund to support the preparation of infrastructure projects, InfraFund, with an initial US $20m. in resources. In 2005 the Bank inaugurated a Trade Finance Facilitation Program (TFFP) to support economic growth in the region by expanding the financing available for international trade activities. The programme was given permanent status in November 2006. In May 2008 the Bank launched a training initiative within the framework of the TFFP. In January 2009 the Bank determined to expand the TFFP to include loans, as well as guarantees, and to increase the programme limit from $400m. to $1,000m. By December 2013 there were more than 90 issuing banks from 21 Latin American and Caribbean countries participating in the programme, and nearly 300 confirming banks worldwide. In September 2009 the Bank supported the establishment, jointly with the Multilateral Investment Fund (MIF), Inter-American Investment Corporation (IIC), the Andean Development Corporation, the US private investment corporation and a Swiss investment management company, of a Microenterprise Growth Facility (MIGROF), which aimed to provide up to $250m. to microfinance institutions in Latin America and the Caribbean.

An Emerging and Sustainable Cities Initiative, initiated by the Bank in 2011, worked in 2013 to support sustainable growth in 26 Latin American cities. The Bank's Biodiversity and Ecosystem Services programme focused in 2013 on the economics of biodiversity systems and means of integrating natural capital in private and public investments. In April 2012 the Bank launched a Citizen Security Initiative, which provides grants for technical co-operation projects aimed at strengthening the effectiveness of public policies in promoting citizen security and justice. A Special Broadband Program, inaugurated in 2013, and supported by US $3.5m. Broadband Fund, promotes increased region-wide adoption of, access to and usage of broadband.

AFFILIATES

Inter-American Investment Corporation (IIC): 1350 New York Ave, NW, Washington, DC 20577, USA; tel. (202) 623-3900; fax (202) 623-2360; e-mail iicmail@iadb.org; internet www.iic.int; f. 1986 as a legally autonomous affiliate of the Inter-American Development Bank, to promote the economic development of the region; commenced operations in 1989; initial capital stock was US $200m., of which 55% was contributed by developing member nations, 25.3% by the USA, and the remainder by non-regional members; in 2001 the Board of Governors of the Bank agreed to increase the IIC's capital to $500m; places emphasis on investment in SMEs without access to other suitable sources of equity or long-term loans; developed FINPYME as an online service to support SMEs and to improve their access to potential sources of financing; in March 2013 launched an $80m. initiative to provide technical assistance aimed at improving the corporate governance of regional SMEs; in 2013 the IIC approved 71 operations with commitments amounting to $415m., with an additional $197m. mobilized from other sources; mems: 45 countries as shareholders; Gen. Man. CARL MUÑANA; publ. *Annual Report* (in English, French, Portuguese and Spanish).

Multilateral Investment Fund (MIF) (Fondo Multilateral de Inversiones (FOMIN): 1300 New York Ave, NW, Washington, DC 20577, USA; tel. (202) 942-8211; fax (202) 942-8100; e-mail mifcontact@iadb.org; internet www.iadb.org/mif; f. 1993 as an autonomous fund administered by the Bank, to promote private sector development in the region; the 21 Bank members who signed the initial draft agreement in 1992 to establish the Fund pledged to contribute US $1,200m.; the Fund's activities are undertaken through three separate facilities concerned with technical co-operation, human resources development and small enterprise development; resources are targeted at the following core areas of activity: small business development; market functioning; and financial and capital markets; the Bank's Social Entrepreneurship Program makes available credit to individuals or groups without access to commercial or development loans; some $10.6m. was awarded under the programme to fund 12 projects in 2013; in July 2013 launched WEVentureScope, an initiative aimed at evaluating business opportunities for women in the countries of Latin America and the Caribbean; in 2012, jointly with the Nordic Development Fund, the Fund launched EcoMiro, a regional programme providing microfinance institutions in Latin American and the Caribbean with technical assistance to develop green financial products; a Microenterprise Forum, 'Foromic', is held annually (Nov. 2014: Guayaquil, Ecuador); in April 2005 38 donor countries agreed to establish MIF II, and replenish the Fund's resources with commitments totalling $502m.; MIF II entered into force in March 2007 and was to expire in 2015; in mid-2010 MIF supported the establishment of an Emergency Liquidity Program for Haiti; during 2013 MIF approved $108m. to finance 68 operations; Gen. Man. NANCY LEE; publ. *MicAméricas*.

INSTITUTIONS

Instituto para la Integración de América Latina y el Caribe (INTAL) (Institute for the Integration of Latin America and the Caribbean): Esmeralda 130, 17°, 1035 Buenos Aires, Argentina; tel. (11) 4323-2350; fax (11) 4320-1865; e-mail intal@iadb.org; internet www.iadb.org/intal; f. 1965 under the auspices of the Inter-American Development Bank; undertakes research on all aspects of regional integration and co-operation and issues related to international trade, hemispheric integration and relations with other regions and countries of the world; activities come under four main headings: regional and national technical co-operation projects on integration; policy fora; integration fora; and journals and information; hosts the secretariat of the Integration of Regional Infrastructure in South America (IIRSA) initiative; maintains an extensive Documentation Center and various statistical databases; Dir GUSTAVO BÉLIZ; publs *Integración y Comercio/Integration and Trade* (2 a year), *INTAL Monthly Newsletter, Informe Andino/Andean Report, CARICOM Report, Informe Centroamericano/Central American Report, Informe MERCOSUR/MERCOSUR Report* (2 a year).

Inter-American Institute for Social Development (INDES): 1350 New York Ave, NW, Washington, DC 20057, USA; fax (202) 623-2008; e-mail bid-indes@iadb.org; internet indes.iadb.org; commenced operations in 1995; aims to support the training of senior officials from public sector institutions and organizations involved with social policies and social services; organizes specialized subregional courses and seminars and national training programmes; produces teaching materials and also serves as a forum for the exchange of ideas on social reform; Head JUAN CRISTOBAL BONNEFOY (Chile).

Publications

Annual Report (in English, French, Portuguese and Spanish).

Development in the Americas (series).

Development Effectiveness Overview (annually).

IDB Edu (quarterly).

Latin American and Caribbean Macroeconomic Report.

Puentes (periodic civil society newsletter).

Revelation of Expectations in Latin America (monthly analysis of market expectations of inflation and growth).

Sustainability Report (annually).

Brochure series, occasional papers, working papers, reports.

Statistics

APPROVALS BY SECTOR, 2013*

Sector	Amount (US $ million)	% of total	Number of projects
Infrastructure and environment	4,702	34	53
Agriculture and rural development	227	2	7
Energy	534	4	9
Environment and natural disasters	178	1	6
Sustainable tourism	185	1	5
Transport	2,804	20	20
Water and sanitation	775	6	6
Institutions for development	4,970	36	73
Financial markets	1,614	12	20
Industry	4	0	1
Private firms and SME development	463	3	15
Reform/modernization of the state	2,319	17	26
Science and technology	24	0	1
Urban development and housing	545	4	10
Integration and trade	1,223	9	22
Social sector	3,004	21	19
Education	726	5	6
Health	751	5	5
Social investment	1,527	11	8
Total	10,558	100	167

* Includes loans, guarantees, and operations financed by the IDB Grant Facility, but excludes lending and projects (one in 2013) approved under the DSL.

YEARLY AND CUMULATIVE LOANS AND GUARANTEES, 1961–2013
(US $ million; after cancellations and exchange adjustments)

Country	Total Amount* 2013	Total Amount* 1961–2013	Ordinary Capital 1961–2013	Fund for Special Operations 1961–2013	Funds in Administration 1961–2013
Argentina	1,260.0	33,897.7	33,203.6	644.9	49.2
Bahamas	—	711.4	709.5	—	2.0
Barbados	—	787.6	726.5	40.9	19.0
Belize	—	182.4	182.4	—	—
Bolivia	396.5	5,322.8	2,515.9	2,278.5	78.4
Brazil	3,386.5	47,004.7	45,315.0	1,555.8	133.9
Chile	441.4	6,876.1	6,606.3	204.9	64.9
Colombia	1,054.0	19,652.1	18,750.3	766.0	135.8
Costa Rica	615.5	4,920.5	4,344.3	363.5	212.7
Dominican Republic	661.0	5,544.5	4,708.0	747.8	88.7
Ecuador	502.0	7,630.6	6,555.1	981.4	94.1
El Salvador	360.0	5,129.7	4,183.9	797.9	147.9
Guatemala	196.0	4,846.9	4,026.9	749.7	70.3
Guyana	17.0	1,313.1	251.1	1,055.1	6.9
Haiti	192.0	2,449.3	7.0	1,146.0	1,296.3
Honduras	275.1	4,154.1	1,545.7	2,542.4	66.0
Jamaica	25.0	3,291.3	2,909.8	171.6	209.9
Mexico	2,095.7	33,679.2	32,900.1	559.0	220.1
Nicaragua	236.6	3,635.3	915.4	2,645.8	74.1
Panama	281.5	4,713.9	4,378.0	294.0	41.9
Paraguay	286.3	3,414.7	2,687.6	709.7	17.4
Peru	195.0	10,653.0	9,994.9	434.5	222.6
Suriname	175.0	555.4	499.0	6.4	50.0
Trinidad and Tobago	159.5	2,062.2	2,006.4	30.6	25.2
Uruguay	781.9	6,929.0	6,738.6	104.4	86.0
Venezuela	—	7,617.8	7,443.5	101.4	72.9
Regional	400.0	4,729.6	4,476.7	239.0	13.9
Total	13,997.5	231,703.8	208,581.5	19,622.1	3,500.1

* Includes non-sovereign guaranteed loans, net of participations, and guarantees, as applicable. Excludes the IDB Grant Facility or lines of credit approved and guarantees issued under the Trade Finance Facilitation Program.

Source: Inter-American Development Bank, *Annual Report 2013*.

LATIN AMERICAN INTEGRATION ASSOCIATION—LAIA
(ASOCIACIÓN LATINOAMERICANA DE INTEGRACIÓN—ALADI)

Address: Cebollatí 1461, Casilla 20.005, 11200 Montevideo, Uruguay.

Telephone: 2410 1121; **fax:** 2419 0649; **e-mail:** sgaladi@aladi.org; **internet:** www.aladi.org.

The Latin American Integration Association was established by the Montevideo Treaty in August 1980 to replace the Latin American Free Trade Association, founded in February 1960.

MEMBERS

Argentina	Cuba	Paraguay
Bolivia	Ecuador	Peru
Brazil	Mexico	Uruguay
Chile	Panama	Venezuela
Colombia		

In August 2011 the Council of Ministers approved the admission of Nicaragua as a full member of the Association; the process of concluding the legal requirements for membership was ongoing in 2014.

Observers: People's Republic of China, Costa Rica, Dominican Republic, El Salvador, Guatemala, Honduras, Italy, Japan, Republic of Korea, Pakistan, Portugal, Romania, Russia, San Marino, Spain, Switzerland and Ukraine; also the UN Economic Commission for Latin America and the Caribbean, the UN Development Programme, the Andean Development Corporation, the European Union, the Ibero-American General Secretariat, the Inter-American Development Bank, the Inter-American Institute for Co-operation on Agriculture, the Latin American Economic System, the Organization of American States, and the Pan American Health Organization/World Health Organization.

Organization
(September 2014)

COUNCIL OF MINISTERS

The Council of Ministers of Foreign Affairs is responsible for the adoption of the Association's policies. It meets when convened by the Committee of Representatives.

CONFERENCE OF EVALUATION AND CONVERGENCE

The Conference, comprising plenipotentiaries of the member governments, assesses the integration process and encourages negotiations between members. It also promotes the convergence of agreements and other actions on economic integration. The Conference meets when convened by the Committee of Representatives.

COMMITTEE OF REPRESENTATIVES

The Committee, the permanent political body of the Association, comprises a permanent and a deputy representative from each member country. The Committee is the main forum for the negotiation of ALADI's initiatives and is responsible for the correct implementation of the Treaty and its supplementary regulations. It is supported by several specialized auxiliary bodies and working groups.

GENERAL SECRETARIAT

The General Secretariat is the technical body of the Association; it submits proposals for action, carries out research and evaluates activities. The Secretary-General is elected for a three-year term, which is renewable. There are two Assistant Secretaries-General.

Secretary-General: CARLOS ALBERTO ('CHACHO') ÁLVAREZ (Argentina).

Activities

A treaty to establish the Latin American Integration Association (Asociación Latinoamericana de Integración—ALADI), as a replacement to the Latin American Free Trade Association (LAFTA), was signed in Montevideo, Uruguay, in 1980, and entered into force in March 1981. ALADI aimed to establish an area of economic preferences, comprising a regional tariff preference for goods originating in member states (in effect from 1 July 1984) and regional and partial scope agreements (on economic complementation, trade promotion, trade in agricultural goods, scientific and technical co-operation, the environment, tourism, and other matters), taking into account the different stages of development of the members, and with no definite timetable for the establishment of a full common market. By 2011 the estimated total of intra-ALADI trade amounted to US $160,000m.

Certain LAFTA institutions were retained and adapted by ALADI, e.g. the Reciprocal Payments and Credits Agreement (1965, modified in 1982) and the Multilateral Credit Agreement to Alleviate Temporary Shortages of Liquidity, known as the Santo Domingo Agreement (1969, extended in 1981 to include mechanisms for counteracting global balance of payments difficulties and for assisting in times of natural disaster).

Agreements concluded under ALADI auspices include a regional tariff preference agreement, whereby members allow imports from other member states to enter with tariffs 20% lower than those imposed on imports from other countries, and a Market Opening Lists agreement in favour of the three least developed member states, which provides for the total elimination of duties and other restrictions on imports of certain products. Other 'partial scope agreements' (in which two or more member states participate), include renegotiation agreements (pertaining to tariff cuts under LAFTA); trade agreements covering particular industrial sectors; the agreements establishing the Southern Common Market (Mercado Común del Sur— MERCOSUR) and the Group of Three (G-3); and agreements covering agriculture, gas supply, tourism, environmental protection, books, transport, sanitation and trade facilitation. A new system of tariff nomenclature, based on the 'harmonized system', was adopted from 1 January 1990 as a basis for common trade negotiations and statistics. General regimes on safeguards and rules of origin entered into force in 1987. The Secretariat convenes meetings of entrepreneurs in various private industrial sectors, to encourage regional trade and co-operation.

ALADI has worked to establish multilateral links or agreements with Latin American non-member countries or integration organizations, and with other developing countries or economic groups outside the continent. In February 1994 the Council of Ministers of Foreign Affairs urged that ALADI should become the co-ordinating body for the various bilateral, multilateral and regional accords (with the Andean Community, MERCOSUR and G-3, etc.), with the aim of eventually forming a region-wide common market. The General Secretariat initiated studies in preparation for a programme to undertake this co-ordination work. At the same meeting in February there was a serious disagreement regarding the proposed adoption of a protocol to the Montevideo Treaty to enable Mexico to participate in the North American Free Trade Agreement, while remaining a member of ALADI. However, in June the first Interpretative Protocol to the Montevideo Treaty was signed by the Ministers of Foreign Affairs: the Protocol allows member states to establish preferential trade agreements with developed nations, with a temporary waiver of the most favoured nation clause, subject to the negotiation of unilateral compensation. In December 2011 the Secretary-General of ALADI welcomed the establishment of the Community of Latin American and Caribbean States as a further means of strengthening regional integration and of formulating a unified regional position in global fora. In March 2012 ALADI hosted a ministerial meeting, attended by high-level representatives of other regional organizations, which discussed current approaches to development in Latin America.

MERCOSUR (comprising Argentina, Brazil, Paraguay and Uruguay) aims to conclude free trade agreements with the other members of ALADI. In March 2001 ALADI signed a co-operation agreement with the Andean Community to facilitate the exchange of information and consolidate regional and sub-regional integration. In December 2003 MERCOSUR and the Andean Community signed an Economic Complementary Agreement, and in April 2004 they concluded a free trade agreement, to come into effect on 1 July 2004 (although later postponed). Those ALADI member states remaining outside MERCOSUR and the Andean Community would be permitted to apply to join the envisaged larger free trade zone.

In May 2012 ALADI member states met to exchange information and views on sustainability and the Green Economy in advance of the UN Conference on Sustainable Development (Rio+20), which was convened in the following month.

In July 2012 ALADI, the UN Economic Commission for Latin America and the Caribbean, and the Corporación Andina de Fomento concluded an inter-agency co-operation agreement establishing the internet-based Latin America/Asia-Pacific Observatory. The Observatory (which, in 2014, covered 19 Latin American and 18 Asia-Pacific economies) aims to deepen knowledge about economic relations between the countries of both regions, with a view to strengthening inter-regional co-operation.

In May 2013 ALADI and the Uruguay Government jointly announced that they were to organize EXPO ALADI, the first ALADI trade and investment meeting; this was to be convened in early October 2014 in Montevideo. Meeting in August 2014 the Council of Ministers determined to pursue a plan of action to promote business opportunities throughout member states.

Publications

Estadísticas y Comercio (quarterly, in Spanish).
Noticias ALADI (monthly, in Spanish).
Reports, studies, brochures, texts of agreements.

NORTH AMERICAN FREE TRADE AGREEMENT—NAFTA

Address: *(Canadian section)* 111 Sussex Drive, 5th Floor, Ottawa, ON K1N 1J1.
Telephone: (613) 992-9388; **fax:** (613) 992-9392; **e-mail:** canada@nafta-sec-alena.org; **internet:** www.nafta-sec-alena.org/canada.
Address: *(Mexican section)* Blvd Adolfo López Mateos 3025, 2°, Col Héroes de Padierna, 10700 México, DF.
Telephone: (55) 5629-9630; **fax:** (55) 5629-9637; **e-mail:** mexico@nafta-sec-alena.org.
Address: *(US section)* 14th St and Constitution Ave, NW, Room 2061, Washington, DC 20230.
Telephone: (202) 482-5438; **fax:** (202) 482-0148; **e-mail:** usa@nafta-sec-alena.org; **internet:** www.nafta-sec-alena.org.

NAFTA developed from the free trade agreement between the USA and Canada that was signed in January 1988 and came into effect on 1 January 1989. Negotiations on the terms of NAFTA, which incorporated Mexico into the free trade area, were concluded in October 1992 and the Agreement was signed in December. It was ratified in November 1993 and entered into force on 1 January 1994. The NAFTA Secretariat is composed of national sections in each member country.

MEMBERS

Canada	Mexico	USA

MAIN PROVISIONS OF THE AGREEMENT

Under NAFTA almost all restrictions on trade and investment between Canada, Mexico and the USA were removed during the period 1 January 1994–1 January 2008. Tariffs on trade between the USA and Mexico in 94% of agricultural products were eliminated immediately, with trade restrictions on further agricultural products eliminated more gradually.

NAFTA also provided for the phasing out by 2004 of tariffs on automobiles and textiles between all three countries, and for Mexico to open its financial sector to US and Canadian investment, with all restrictions removed by 2008. Mexico was to liberalize government procurement, removing preferential treatment for domestic companies over a 10-year period. Barriers to investment were removed in most sectors, with exemptions for petroleum in Mexico, culture in Canada and airlines and radio communications in the USA. In April 1998 the fifth meeting of the three-member ministerial Free Trade Commission, held in Paris, France, agreed to remove, from 1 August, tariffs on some 600 goods, including certain chemicals, pharmaceuticals, steel and wire products, textiles, toys, and watches. As a result of that agreement, a number of tariffs were eliminated as much as 10 years earlier than had been originally planned.

In transport, it was initially planned that heavy goods vehicles would have complete freedom of movement between the three countries by 2000. However, owing to concerns on the part of the US Government relating to the implementation of adequate safety standards by Mexican truck drivers, the deadline for the free circulation of heavy goods vehicles was not met. In February 2001 a five-member NAFTA panel of experts appointed to adjudicate on the dispute ruled that the USA was violating the Agreement. In December the US Senate approved legislation entitling Mexican long-haul trucks to operate anywhere in the USA following compliance with rigorous safety checks to be enforced by US inspectors.

In the case of a sudden influx of goods from one country to another that adversely affects a domestic industry, the Agreement makes provision for the imposition of short-term 'snap-back' tariffs.

Disputes are to be settled in the first instance by intergovernmental consultation. If a dispute is not resolved within 30 to 40 days, a government may call a meeting of the Free Trade Commission. The Commission's Advisory Committee on Private Commercial Disputes and its Advisory Committee on Private Commercial Disputes Regarding Agricultural Goods recommend procedures for the reso-

lution of such complex disputes. If the Commission is unable to settle an issue a panel of experts in the relevant field is appointed to adjudicate.

In June 1996 Canada and Mexico announced their decision to refer the newly enacted US 'Helms-Burton' legislation on trade with Cuba to the Commission. They claimed that the legislation, which provides for punitive measures against foreign companies that engage in trade with Cuba, imposed undue restrictions on Canadian and Mexican companies and was, therefore, in contravention of NAFTA. However, at the beginning of 1997 certain controversial provisions of the Helms-Burton legislation were suspended for a period of six months by the US Administration. The relevant provisions have continued subsequently to be suspended at six-monthly intervals.

In December 1994 NAFTA members issued a formal invitation to Chile to seek membership of the Agreement. Formal discussions on Chile's entry began in June 1995, but were stalled in December when the US Congress failed to approve 'fast-track' negotiating authority for the US Government, which was to have allowed the latter to negotiate a trade agreement with Chile, without risk of incurring a line-by-line veto from the US Congress. In February 1996 Chile began high-level negotiations with Canada on a wide-ranging bilateral free trade agreement. Chile, which already had extensive bilateral trade agreements with Mexico, was regarded as advancing its position with regard to NAFTA membership by means of the proposed accord with Canada. The bilateral agreement, which provided for the extensive elimination of customs duties by 2002, was signed in November 1996 and ratified by Chile in July 1997. However, in November 1997 the US Government was obliged to request the removal of the 'fast-track' proposal from the legislative agenda, owing to insufficient support within Congress.

In April 1998 heads of state of 34 countries, meeting in Santiago, Chile, agreed formally to initiate the negotiating process to establish a Free Trade Area of the Americas (FTAA). The US Government had originally proposed creating the FTAA through the gradual extension of NAFTA trading privileges on a bilateral basis. However, the framework agreed upon by ministers of trade of the 34 countries, meeting in March, provided for countries to negotiate and accept FTAA provisions on an individual basis and as part of a subregional economic bloc. It was envisaged that the FTAA would exist alongside the subregional associations, including NAFTA. At a special summit of the Americas, held in January 2004 in Monterrey, Mexico, the leaders adopted a declaration committing themselves to the eventual establishment of the FTAA; however, they did not specify a completion date for the negotiations. In March the negotiations were suspended, and in 2014 they remained so.

ADDITIONAL AGREEMENTS

During 1993, as a result of domestic pressure, the new US Government negotiated two 'side agreements' with its NAFTA partners, which were to provide safeguards for workers' rights and the environment. A Commission for Labor Cooperation was established under the North American Agreement on Labor Cooperation (NAALC) to monitor implementation of labour accords and to foster co-operation in that area. Panels of experts, with representatives from each country, were established to adjudicate in cases of alleged infringement of workers' rights or environmental damage. The panels were given the power to impose fines and trade sanctions, but only with regard to the USA and Mexico; Canada, which was opposed to such measures, was to enforce compliance with NAFTA by means of its own legal system. The Commission for Environmental Cooperation (CEC), initiated in 1994 under the provisions of the 1993 North American Agreement on Environmental Cooperation (which complements the relevant environmental provisions of NAFTA), addresses regional environmental concerns, assists in the prevention of potential trade and environmental conflicts, advises on the environmental impact of trade issues, encourages private sector investment in environmental trade issues, and promotes the effective enforcement of environmental law. During 1994–September 2014 the CEC adopted numerous resolutions, including on the sound management of chemicals, the environmentally sound management and tracking of hazardous wastes and hazardous recyclable materials, the conservation of butterflies and birds, the availability of pollutant release and transfer data, and on co-operation in the conservation of biodiversity. The CEC-financed North American Fund for Environmental Cooperation (NAFEC), established in 1995, supports community environmental projects.

With regard to the NAALC, National Administration Offices have been established in each of the NAFTA countries in order to monitor labour issues and to address complaints about non-compliance with domestic labour legislation. However, punitive measures in the form of trade sanctions or fines (up to US $20m.) may only be imposed in the specific instances of contravention of national legislation regarding child labour, a minimum wage or health and safety standards.

Border Environmental Cooperation Commission (BECC): POB 221648, El Paso, TX 79913, USA; tel. (877) 277-1703; e-mail becc@cocef.org; internet www.cocef.org; f. 1993; supports the co-ordination of projects for the improvement of infrastructure and monitors the environmental impact of NAFTA on the US–Mexican border area; by 31 Dec. 2013 the BECC had certified at total of 227 projects (120 in Mexico and 107 in the USA), at a cost of US $6,985m., and at that time it was actively implementing 76 certified projects; Gen. Man. MARIA ELENA GINER (USA).

Commission for Environmental Cooperation (CEC): 393 rue St Jacques Ouest, Bureau 200, Montréal, QC H2Y IN9, Canada; tel. (514) 350-4300; fax (514) 350-4314; e-mail info@cec.org; internet www.cec.org; f. 1994; Exec. Dir Dr IRASEMA CORONADO (USA); publs *Annual Report, North American Environmental Atlas, Taking Stock* (annually), industry reports, policy studies.

North American Development Bank (NADB/NADBank): 203 South St Mary's, Suite 300, San Antonio, TX 78205, USA; tel. (210) 231-8000; fax (210) 231-6232; internet www.nadbank.org; f. 1993; mandated to finance environmental and infrastructure projects along the US–Mexican border; at Sept. 2014 the NADB had authorized capital of US $3,000m., subscribed equally by Mexico and the USA, of which $450m. was paid-up; Man. Dir GERÓNIMO GUTIÉRREZ FERNÁNDEZ (Mexico); publs *Annual Report, NADBank News*.

ORGANIZATION OF AMERICAN STATES—OAS

(ORGANIZACIÓN DE LOS ESTADOS AMERICANOS—OEA)

Address: 17th St and Constitution Ave, NW, Washington, DC 20006, USA.

Telephone: (202) 370-5000; **fax:** (202) 458-6319; **e-mail:** websection@oas.org; **internet:** www.oas.org.

The ninth International Conference of American States (held in Bogotá, Colombia, in 1948) adopted the Charter of the Organization of American States, creating a successor to the Commercial Bureau of American Republics, founded in 1890, and the Pan-American Union. The purpose of the OAS is to strengthen the peace and security of the continent; to promote human rights and to promote and consolidate representative democracy, with due respect for the principle of non-intervention; to prevent possible causes of difficulties and to ensure the peaceful settlement of disputes that may arise among the member states; to provide for common action in the event of aggression; to seek the solution of political, juridical and economic problems that may arise among the member states; to promote, by co-operative action, their economic, social and cultural development; to achieve an effective limitation of conventional weapons; to devote the largest amount of resources to the economic and social development of the member states; and to confront shared problems such as poverty, terrorism, the trade in illegal drugs, and corruption. The OAS plays a leading role in implementing mandates established by the hemisphere's leaders through the Summits of the Americas.

MEMBERS

Antigua and Barbuda	Guyana
Argentina	Haiti
Bahamas	Honduras
Barbados	Jamaica
Belize	Mexico
Bolivia	Nicaragua
Brazil	Panama
Canada	Paraguay
Chile	Peru
Colombia	Saint Christopher and Nevis
Costa Rica	Saint Lucia
Cuba*	Saint Vincent and the
Dominica	Grenadines
Dominican Republic	Suriname
Ecuador	Trinidad and Tobago
El Salvador	USA
Grenada	Uruguay
Guatemala	Venezuela

* The Cuban Government was suspended from OAS activities in 1962; the suspension was revoked by the OAS General Assembly in June 2009, although Cuba's participation in the organization was to be subject to further review.

Permanent Observers: Albania, Algeria, Angola, Armenia, Austria, Azerbaijan, Belgium, Benin, Bosnia and Herzegovina, Bulgaria, People's Republic of China, Croatia, Cyprus, Czech Republic, Denmark, Egypt, Equatorial Guinea, Estonia, Finland, France, Georgia, Germany, Ghana, Greece, Holy See, Hungary, Iceland, India, Ireland, Israel, Italy, Japan, Kazakhstan, Republic of Korea, Latvia, Lebanon, Lithuania, Luxembourg, Monaco, Morocco, Netherlands, Nigeria, Norway, Pakistan, Philippines, Poland, Portugal, Qatar, Romania, Russia, Saudi Arabia, Serbia, Slovakia, Slovenia, Spain, Sri Lanka, Sweden, Switzerland, Thailand, Tunisia, Turkey, Ukraine, United Kingdom, Vanuatu, Yemen and the European Union.

Organization

(September 2014)

GENERAL ASSEMBLY

The Assembly meets annually and may also hold special sessions when convoked by the Permanent Council. As the highest decision-making body of the OAS, it decides general action and policy. In March 2013 an Extraordinary General Assembly was convened at the OAS headquarters in Washington, DC, USA, to consider means of strengthening the Inter-American human rights system. The 44th regular session of Assembly was hosted by Asunción, Paraguay, in June 2014. A special session of the Assembly was convened in mid-September 2014, in Washington, DC, with a focus on finalizing a Strategic Vision for the Organization that had been under development by the Permanent Council. A further special session, on the theme 'For a Hemispheric Drug Policy in the Twenty-First Century', was held later in September, in Guatemala City, Guatemala.

MEETINGS OF CONSULTATION OF MINISTERS OF FOREIGN AFFAIRS

Meetings are convened, at the request of any member state, to consider problems of an urgent nature and of common interest to member states, or to serve as an organ of consultation in cases of armed attack or other threats to international peace and security. The Permanent Council determines whether a meeting should be convened and acts as a provisional organ of consultation until ministers are able to assemble.

PERMANENT COUNCIL

The Council meets regularly throughout the year at the OAS headquarters comprising representatives of each member state with the rank of ambassador. The office of Chairman is held in turn by each of the representatives, following alphabetical order according to the names of the countries in Spanish. The Vice-Chairman is determined in the same way, following reverse alphabetical order. Their terms of office are three months.

The Council guides ongoing policies and actions and oversees the maintenance of friendly relations between members. It supervises the work of the OAS and promotes co-operation with a variety of other international bodies including the UN. It comprises a General Committee and Committees on Juridical and Political Affairs, Hemispheric Security, Inter-American Summits Management and Civil Society Participation in OAS Activities, and Administrative and Budgetary Affairs. There are also ad hoc working groups.

In January 2012 the Secretary-General presented to the Permanent Council, for further development, 'A Strategic Vision of the OAS', proposing a refocusing of its core tasks, prioritizing mandates in accordance with the principal strategic objectives, and a rationalization of the use of its financial resources. In September 2014 the Council presented a draft resolution on the Strategic Vision to a special session of the General Assembly, which was to review the proposed organizational reforms in order that they might be reflected in forthcoming OAS budgeting and programming.

GENERAL SECRETARIAT

The Secretariat, the central and permanent organ of the organization, performs the duties entrusted to it by the General Assembly, Meetings of Consultation of Ministers of Foreign Affairs and the Councils. The work of the General Secretariat is undertaken by a Secretariat for Political Affairs; the Executive Secretariat of Integral Development; the Secretariat for Multidimensional Security; the Secretariat for Administration and Finance; the Secretariat for Legal Affairs; and the Secretariat for External Relations. There is an Administrative Tribunal, comprising six elected members, to settle staffing disputes.

Secretary-General: JOSÉ MIGUEL INSULZA (Chile).

Assistant Secretary-General: ALBERT R. RAMDIN (Suriname).

INTER-AMERICAN COUNCIL FOR INTEGRAL DEVELOPMENT (CIDI)

The Council was established in 1996, replacing the Inter-American Economic and Social Council and the Inter-American Council for Education, Science and Culture. Its aim is to promote co-operation among the countries of the region, in order to accelerate economic and social development. An Executive Secretariat for Integral Development provides CIDI with technical and secretarial services and co-ordinates a Special Multilateral Fund of CICI (FEMCIDI), the New Programming Approaches programme, a Hemispheric Integral Development Program, a Universal Civil Identity Program in the Americas, and Migration and Development Innovative Programs. Technical co-operation and training programmes are managed by a subsidiary body of the Council, the Inter-American Agency for Co-operation and Development, which was established in 1999. A meeting of ministers and high-level authorities concerned with science and technology was to be convened, within the framework of the CIDI, in Guatemala City, in March 2015.

Executive Secretary: SHERRY TROSS (USA).

INTER-AMERICAN JURIDICAL COMMITTEE (IAJC)

The Committee's purposes are to serve as an advisory body to the OAS on juridical matters; to promote the progressive development and codification of international law; and to study juridical problems relating to the integration of the developing countries in the hemisphere, and, in so far as may appear desirable, the possibility of attaining uniformity in legislation. It comprises 11 jurists, nationals of different member states, elected for a period of four years, with the possibility of re-election.

Chairperson: JOAO CLEMENTE BAENA SOARES (Brazil); Av. Marechal Floriano 196, 3° andar, Palácio Itamaraty, Centro, 20080-002, Rio de Janeiro, Brazil; tel. (21) 2206-9903; fax (21) 2203-2090; e-mail cjioea.trp@terra.com.br.

INTER-AMERICAN COMMISSION ON HUMAN RIGHTS

The Commission was established in 1960 to promote the observance and protection of human rights in the member states of the OAS. It examines and reports on the human rights situation in member countries and considers individual petitions relating to alleged human rights violations by member states. A Special Rapporteurship on the Rights of People of Afro-Descendants, and against Racial Discrimination was established in 2005. Other rapporteurs analyse and report on the rights of children, women, indigenous peoples, migrant workers, prisoners and displaced persons, and on freedom of expression. An OAS Extraordinary General Assembly, held in March 2013, adopted a resolution that provided for refinements to the operations of the Commission with a view to strengthening the Inter-American human rights system.

Executive Secretary: EMILIO ÁLVAREZ ICAZA LONGORIA (Mexico); 1889F St, NW, Washington, DC 20006, USA; tel. (202) 370-9000; fax (202) 458-3992; e-mail cidhdenuncias@oas.org; internet www.cidh.oas.org.

SUBSIDIARY ORGANS AND AGENCIES

Inter-American Committee Against Terrorism (Comité Interamericano Contra el Terrorismo—CICTE): 1889 F St, NW, Washington, DC 20006, USA; tel. (202) 370-4973; fax (202) 458-3857; e-mail cicte@oas.org; internet www.cicte.oas.org; f. 1999 to enhance the exchange of information via national authorities, formulate proposals to assist mem. states in drafting counter-terrorism legislation in all states, compile bilateral, subregional, regional and multilateral treaties and agreements signed by member states and promote

universal adherence to international counter-terrorism conventions, strengthen border co-operation and travel documentation security measures, and develop activities for training and crisis management; Exec. Sec. NEIL KLOPFENSTEIN (USA).

Inter-American Committee on Ports (Comisión Interamericana de Puertos—CIP): 1889 F St, NW, Washington, DC 20006, USA; tel. (202) 370-9703; fax (202) 458-3517; e-mail cip@oas.org; internet www.oas.org/cip; f. 1998; serves as the permanent inter-American forum to strengthen co-operation on port-related issues among the member states, with the active participation of the private sector; the Committee, comprising 34 mem. states, meets every two years; its Executive Board, which executes policy decisions, meets annually; four technical advisory groups have been established to advise on logistics and competition (formerly port operations), port security, navigation control, and environmental protection.

Inter-American Court of Human Rights (IACHR) (Corte Interamericana de Derechos Humanos): Avda 10, St 45-47 Los Yoses, San Pedro, San José; Postal 6906-1000, San José, Costa Rica; tel. (506) 2527-1600; fax (506) 2234-0584; e-mail corteidh@corteidh.or.cr; internet www.corteidh.or.cr; f. 1979 as an autonomous judicial institution whose purpose is to apply and interpret the American Convention on Human Rights (which entered into force in 1978, and is also known as the Pact of San José); comprises seven jurists from OAS member states; in Sept. 2013 Venezuela withdrew from the American Convention on Human Rights; Pres. HUMBERTO SIERRA PORTO (Colombia); publ. *Annual Report.*

Inter-American Defense Board (Junta Interamericana de Defensa—JID): 2600 16th St, NW, Washington, DC 20441, USA; tel. (202) 939-6041; fax (202) 319-2791; e-mail jid@jid.org; internet www.jid.org; promotes co-operative security interests in the Western Hemisphere; new statutes adopted in 2006 formally designated the Board as an OAS agency; works on issues such as disaster assistance and confidence-building measures directly supporting the hemispheric security goals of the OAS and of regional ministers responsible for defence; also provides a senior-level academic programme in security studies for military, national police and civilian leaders at the Inter-American Defense College; Dir-Gen. Vice-Adm. BENTO COSTA LIMA LEITE DE ALBUQUERQUE, Jr (Brazil).

Inter-American Drug Abuse Control Commission (Comisión Interamericana para el Control del Abuso de Drogas—CICAD): 1889 F St, NW, Washington, DC 20006, USA; tel. (202) 458-3178; fax (202) 458-3658; e-mail oidcicad@oas.org; internet www.cicad.oas.org; f. 1986 by the OAS to promote and facilitate multilateral co-operation in the control and prevention of the trafficking, production and use of illegal drugs, and related crimes; reports regularly, through the Multilateral Evaluation Mechanism, on progress against illegal drugs in each mem. state and region-wide; mems: 34 countries; Exec. Sec. PAUL E. SIMONS; publs *Statistical Survey* (annually), *Directory of Governmental Institutions Charged with the Fight Against the Illicit Production, Trafficking, Use and Abuse of Narcotic Drugs and Psychotropic Substances, Evaluation of Progress in Drug Control, Progress Report on Drug Control—Implementation and Recommendations* (2 a year).

Inter-American Telecommunication Commission (Comisión Interamericana de Telecomunicaciones—CITEL): 1889 F St, NW, Washington, DC 20006, USA; tel. (202) 370-4713; e-mail citel@oas.org; internet www.citel.oas.org; f. 1993 to promote the development and harmonization of telecommunications in the region, in co-operation with governments and the private sector; CITEL has more than 200 associate mems representing private associations or companies, permanent observers, and international organizations; under its Permanent Executive Committee specialized consultative committees focus on telecommunication standardization and radio-communication, including broadcasting; mems: 34 countries; Exec. Sec. CLOVIS JOSÉ BAPTISTA NETO.

Justice Studies Center of the Americas (Centro de Estudios de Justicia de las Américas): Rodó 1950, Providencia, Santiago, Chile; tel. (2) 2742933; fax (2) 3415769; e-mail info@cejamericas.org; internet www.cejamericas.org; f. 1999; aims to support the modernization of justice systems in the region; Exec. Dir JAIME ARELLANO QUINTANA (Chile).

Pan American Development Foundation (PADF) (Fundación Panamericana para el Desarrollo): 1889 F St, NW, Washington, DC 20006, USA; tel. (202) 458-3969; fax (202) 458-6316; e-mail padf-dc@padf.org; internet www.padf.org; f. 1962 to promote and facilitate economic and social development in Latin America and the Caribbean by means of innovative partnerships and integrated involvement of the public and private sectors; provides low-interest credit for small-scale entrepreneurs, vocational training, improved health care, agricultural development and reafforestation, and strengthening local non-governmental orgs; provides emergency disaster relief and reconstruction assistance; Exec. Dir JOHN A. SANBRAILO.

Activities

STRENGTHENING DEMOCRACY

The OAS promotes and supports good governance in its member states through various activities, including electoral observations, crisis-prevention missions, and programmes to strengthen government institutions and to support a regional culture of democracy. In September 2001 the member states adopted the Inter-American Democratic Charter, which details the essential elements of representative democracy, including free and fair elections; respect for human rights and fundamental freedoms; the exercise of power in accordance with the rule of law; a pluralistic political party system; and the separation and independence of the branches of government. Transparency and responsible administration by governments, respect for social rights, freedom of expression and citizen participation are among other elements deemed by the Charter to define democracy. The 41st General Assembly, held in June 2011, in San Salvador, El Salvador, approved a final Declaration on Citizen Security in the Americas, which incorporated a request to ministers to draft a hemispheric plan of action for consideration the following year. Since 2010 the OAS, jointly with the International Institute for Democracy and Electoral Assistance and Mexican partners, has convened an annual Latin American Democracy Forum; the fourth forum was held in November 2013, in Santiago, Chile, on the theme 'Youth engagement in politics'.

The observation of elections is given high priority by the OAS. Depending on the specific situation and the particular needs of each country, missions vary from a few technical experts sent for a limited time to a large country-wide team of monitors dispatched to observe the full electoral process for an extended period commencing with the political parties' campaigns. The missions present their observations to the OAS Permanent Council, along with recommendations for how each country's electoral process might be strengthened. In October 2012 the Permanent Council approved a resolution to designate 4 February as OAS Electoral Observation Day, to commemorate 50 years since the first mission was dispatched. OAS teams were dispatched to monitor two rounds of a presidential election held in El Salvador in February and March 2014; legislative elections held in Colombia in early March; legislative elections held in Costa Rica in February; a presidential election organized in that country in two rounds, in February and April; a presidential election held in Colombia, in May; a parliamentary election held in Panama, also in May; and a general election staged in Antigua and Barbuda, in June. An OAS electoral mission was to observe a general election scheduled to be held in Bolivia in October. In September the OAS and the International Foundation for Electoral Systems concluded a Memorandum of Understanding on strengthening co-operation.

The OAS has responded to numerous political crises in the region. In some cases, at the request of member states, it has sent special missions to provide critical support to the democratic process. During 2005–06 the OAS was particularly active in Nicaragua. In June 2005, responding to issues raised by the Government of President Enrique Bolaños, the OAS General Assembly expressed concern about developments that posed a threat to the separation and independence of branches of government. Citing the Inter-American Democratic Charter and the OAS Charter, the General Assembly authorized an OAS mission to help establish a broad national dialogue in that country; accordingly, the OAS Secretary-General led a high-level mission to Nicaragua to support efforts to find democratic solutions to the situation, and also appointed a special envoy to facilitate dialogue there. In 2006 the OAS Special Mission to Accompany the Democratic and Electoral Process in Nicaragua monitored regional elections, conducted in March, and a general election in November. In a subsequent report to the OAS Permanent Council, the Chief of Mission noted that Nicaragua had made significant steps forward in its democratic development and that its elections were 'increasingly clean and competitive'.

In 2005, following an institutional crisis in Ecuador, the OAS offered support for the establishment of an impartial, independent Supreme Court of Justice. The OAS Secretary-General appointed two distinguished jurists as his special representatives to observe the selection process; members of Ecuador's new Supreme Court were sworn in during November. The OAS also played a role in Bolivia in 2005, following the resignation in June of President Carlos Mesa. The OAS Secretary-General appointed a special representative to facilitate political dialogue and to head the OAS observation mission on the electoral process that resulted in Evo Morales winning the presidency.

In August 2000 the OAS Secretary-General undertook the first of several high-level missions to negotiate with the authorities in Haiti in order to resolve the political crisis resulting from a disputed general election in May. In January 2001, following a meeting with the Haitian Prime Minister, the Assistant Secretary-General recommended that the OAS renew its efforts to establish a dialogue between the Government, opposition parties and representatives of civil society in that country. In May and June the OAS and the Caribbean Community and Common Market (CARICOM) undertook joint missions to Haiti in order to assess and promote prospects for a democratic resolution to the political uncertainties. Following political and social unrest in Haiti in December, the OAS and CARICOM pledged to conduct an independent investigation into the violence, and in March 2002 an agreement to establish a Special OAS Mission for Strengthening Democracy in Haiti was signed in the capital, Port-au-Prince. The independent commission of inquiry reported to the OAS at the beginning of July, and listed a set of recommendations relating to law reform, security and other confidence-building measures to help to secure democracy in Haiti. In January 2004 the OAS Special Mission condemned the escalation of political violence in Haiti and in February took a lead in facilitating the implementation of a CARICOM-brokered action plan to resolve the crisis. In late February the Permanent Council met in special session, and urged the UN to take necessary and appropriate action to address the deteriorating situation in Haiti. On 29 February President Jean-Bertrand Aristide resigned and left the country; amid ongoing civil unrest, a provisional leader was sworn in. The OAS Mission continued to attempt to maintain law and order, in co-operation with a UN-authorized Multinational Interim Force, and facilitated political discussions on the establishment of a transitional government. From March the Special Mission participated in the process to develop an Interim Co-operation Framework, identifying the urgent and medium-term needs of Haiti, which was presented to a meeting of international donors held in July. In June the OAS General Assembly adopted a resolution instructing the Permanent Council to undertake all necessary diplomatic initiatives to foster the restoration of democracy in Haiti, and called upon the Special Mission to work with the new UN Stabilization Mission in Haiti in preparing, organizing and monitoring future elections. During 2005 OAS technical experts, together with UN counterparts, assisted Haiti's Provisional Electoral Council (PEC) with the process of voter registration for legislative and presidential elections, initially scheduled for later in that year, as well as to formulate an electronic vote tabulation system, which was to serve as the basis for a permanent civil registry. In January 2006 the OAS Permanent Council declared its grave concern at a further postponement of the elections. In the following month, however, the Council expressed its satisfaction that polling had taken place in a free and fair manner. The Secretary-General visited Haiti to meet with officials and offer his support for the declared President-elect, Réné Préval. The OAS has continued to extend support to the country and to co-ordinate international assistance, mainly through its Haiti Task Force, chaired by the Assistant Secretary-General. In February 2008 a special mission of the Permanent Council visited Haiti to assess priorities for future support. In July the Assistant Secretary-General announced the establishment of an OAS Haiti Fund to support the organization's mandate and priorities in that country. In September the Assistant Secretary-General, visiting Haiti after it had been struck by a series of tropical cyclones, reiterated OAS commitment to Haiti's socio-economic development and stability. In early 2009 the OAS pledged to support the electoral process in Haiti, and to monitor the forthcoming senate elections.

In February 2004 the Permanent Council authorized the establishment of the OAS Mission to Support the Peace Process in Colombia (MAPP), with a mandate to provide assistance in support of the ongoing process and to advise on, monitor and verify the peacebuilding activities being undertaken by the Colombian authorities; the OAS has undertaken specific projects and measures in support of local initiatives aimed at promoting reconciliation and strengthening democracy.

In June 2009 the OAS Secretary-General and Permanent Council condemned the forced expulsion from power of President José Manuel Zelaya of Honduras by members of that country's armed forces. A special session of the General Assembly was convened, which urged the Secretary-General to pursue diplomatic efforts to restore constitutional order and the rule of law. When this was not achieved within the required 72-hour period, the Assembly, on 4 July, resolved to suspend the membership rights of Honduras to participate in the organization. President Oscar Arias of Costa Rica agreed to lead efforts on behalf of the OAS to mediate with the new authorities in Honduras in order to resolve the crisis. In August the OAS organized a delegation of ministers of foreign affairs to visit Honduras and promote a settlement based on the San José Accord formulated by President Arias, which envisaged Zelaya returning to the country as head of a government of national unity, and the holding of a general election a month earlier than scheduled, in late October. Political amnesty was to be offered to all sides under the proposed agreement. The interim authorities permitted the delegation's visit conditional on the OAS Secretary-General participating only as an observer. The opposing leaders signed an accord in October, although it was soon rejected by Zelaya after he was excluded from an interim national unity government. A special session of the Permanent Council was convened in December to consider the political situation in Honduras following a general election conducted in late November. The Council urged the newly elected leader, Porfirio Lobo, fully to re-establish respect for human rights, to end the 'persecution' of Zelaya, and to establish a national unity government to serve until the original presidential term ended in January 2010. In June the OAS General Assembly determined to establish a high-level commission to assess the political and human rights situation in Honduras. The commission's report, issued in late July, included the following recommendations: the termination of legal proceedings initiated against former President Zelaya; support for Zelaya's application for membership of the Central American Parliament with the status of a former constitutional president; continued investigation into alleged human rights violations; and implementation, by the new government, of further measures to protect activists, journalists, judges and others who had opposed the *coup d'etat*. The suspension of Honduras' OAS membership was removed in June 2011.

In June 2012 the Permanent Council determined to send a fact-finding team to investigate the political situation in Paraguay where the president, Fernando Lugo, had been impeached by that country's congress. The team, led by the OAS Secretary-General, visited Paraguay in July, and concluded that any decisions taken by the OAS on the situation there should have as objectives: promoting the completion of the related ongoing domestic judicial process; strengthening the national democratic system during the transition to elections (held in April 2013), through the promotion of public dialogue and support for legal reforms that might be put in place to avoid further crises; and ensuring that the electoral process should be participatory and transparent, and that no reprisals or exclusions should occur in relation to the July 2012 political crisis, in particular reprisals aimed at Lugo or his supporters. In view of the findings of the mission, the OAS Secretary-General determined in early July to deploy an OAS mission to Paraguay to observe the process leading to the April 2013 elections and to facilitate political dialogue.

In early March 2014 the Permanent Council, meeting in special session, at the request of Panama, to consider ongoing anti-government unrest in Venezuela, issued a Declaration of Solidarity and Support for Democratic institutions, Dialogue, and Peace in Venezuela.

In special situations, when both or all member states involved in a dispute ask for its assistance, the OAS plays a longer-term role in supporting countries to resolve bilateral or multilateral issues. In September 2005 Belize and Guatemala signed an agreement at the OAS establishing a framework for negotiations and confidence-building measures to help to maintain good bilateral relations while they sought a permanent solution to a long-standing territorial dispute. Following a series of negotiations under OAS auspices, both sides signed a Special Agreement to resolve the dispute in December 2008. In April 2006 another OAS-supported effort was concluded successfully when El Salvador and Honduras signed an accord settling differences over the demarcation of their common border. In March 2008 a Meeting of Consultation of OAS ministers responsible for foreign affairs was convened following an escalation of diplomatic tension between Colombia and Ecuador resulting from a violation of Ecuador's borders by Colombian soldiers in pursuit of opposition insurgents. The meeting approved a resolution to establish a Good Offices Mission to restore confidence between the two countries and to negotiate an appropriate settlement to the dispute. A Verification Commission of the Good Offices Mission presented a report in July 2009, which included proposals to strengthen bilateral relations. In November 2010 a special meeting of the Permanent Council was convened, at the request of the Costa Rican government, to consider a border dispute with Nicaragua in the San Juan river area. The Council adopted a resolution in support of recommendations of the OAS Secretary-General, who had recently visited the area, to implement various confidence-building measures, including the resumption of bilateral talks on boundary demarcation, the convening of a Binational Committee and strengthening collaborative mechanisms to counter organized crime and arms- and drugs-trafficking.

The OAS aims to combat corruption in recognition of the undermining effect this has on democratic institutions. In 1996 the OAS member states adopted the Inter-American Convention against Corruption, which by 2014 had been ratified or acceded to by 33 member states. In 2002 the treaty's signatory states initiated a peer review process to examine their compliance with the treaty's key provisions. The Follow-Up Mechanism for the Implementation of the Inter-American Convention against Corruption assesses progress and recommends concrete measures that the states parties can implement to improve compliance. Representatives of civil society organizations are also given the opportunity to meet with experts and present information for their consideration. All participating countries have been assessed at least once and the completed progress reports are available to the public. The OAS has also held seminars and training sessions in the region on such matters as improving transparency in government and drafting model anti-corruption legislation. In May 2010 the Follow-up Mechanism organized a Conference on the Progress and Challenges in Hemispheric

Co-operation against Corruption, held in Lima, Peru. A second conference was convened in Cali, Colombia, in June 2011. In 2014 the Follow-Up Mechanism was conducting a fourth round of member country evaluations.

In recent years, the OAS has expanded its outreach to civil society. More than 200 non-governmental organizations (NGOs) are registered to take part in OAS activities. Civil society groups are encouraged to participate in workshops and round tables in advance of the OAS General Assembly to prepare proposals and recommendations to present to the member states. This is also the case with Summits of the Americas and the periodic ministerial meetings, such as those on education, labour, culture, and science and technology. NGOs contributed ideas to the development of the Inter-American Democratic Charter and have participated in follow-up work on hemispheric treaties against corruption and terrorism.

The OAS has also focused on strengthening ties with the private sector. In 2006 it concluded a co-operation agreement with the business forum Private Sector of the Americas which aimed to promote dialogue and to support public-private alliances with a view to creating jobs, combating poverty and strengthening development. Business leaders from the region develop proposals and recommendations to present to the OAS General Assembly and to the Summits of the Americas.

DEFENDING HUMAN RIGHTS

Under the Democratic Charter a 'respect for human rights and fundamental freedoms' is deemed to be an essential element of a democracy. The Inter-American Commission on Human Rights and the Inter-American Court of Human Rights are the pillars of a system designed to protect individuals in the Americas who have suffered violations of their rights. A key function of the Commission is to consider petitions from individuals who claim that a state has violated a protected right and that they have been unable to find justice. The Commission brings together the petitioner and the state to explore a 'friendly settlement'. If such an outcome is not possible, the Commission may recommend specific measures to be carried out by the state to remedy the violation. If a state does not follow the recommendations the Commission has the option to publish its report or take the case to the Inter-American Court of Human Rights, as long as the state involved has accepted the Court's compulsory jurisdiction. The Commission convenes for six weeks each year. In July 2011 a special working group was established to review the work of the Commission. An OAS Extraordinary General Assembly convened in March 2013 considered the findings of the working group, and adopted a resolution on refining the operations of the Commission with a view to strengthening the functioning of the Inter-American human rights framework.

In addition to hearing cases the Court may exercise its advisory jurisdiction to interpret the human rights treaties in effect in the region. The Commission, for its part, may conduct an on-site visit to a country, at the invitation of its Government, to analyse and report on the human rights situation. The Commission has also created rapporteurships focusing on particular human rights issues. In 2005 it created a rapporteurship on the rights of persons of African descent and against racial discrimination. Other rapporteurs analyse and report on the rights of children, women, indigenous peoples migrant workers, prisoners and displaced persons, and on freedom of expression. The Commission also has a special unit on human rights defenders. The OAS also works beyond the inter-American human rights system to promote the rights of vulnerable groups. The member states are in the process of negotiating the draft American Declaration on the Rights of Indigenous Peoples, which is intended to promote and protect a range of rights covering such areas as family, spirituality, work, culture, health, the environment, and systems of knowledge, language and communication. A special fund was established for voluntary contributions by member states and permanent observers in order to help cover the costs involved in broadening indigenous participation. The OAS also works to promote and protect women's rights. The Inter-American Commission of Women (CIM), established in 1928, has had an impact on shaping laws and policies in many countries. One of its key initiatives led to the adoption of the Inter-American Convention on the Prevention, Punishment and Eradication of Violence against Women, also known as the Convention of Belém do Pará, which was adopted in 1994 by the OAS General Assembly. Since 2005 parties to the Belém do Pará Convention have participated in a follow-up mechanism designed to determine how the countries are complying with the treaty and progress achieved in preventing and punishing violence against women. In 2006 the CIM also initiated an examination of strategies for reversing the spread of HIV/AIDS among women in the region. The Commission has urged greater efforts to integrate a gender perspective into every aspect of the OAS agenda. In April 2011 and July 2012 the Commission hosted hemispheric fora aiming to promote equal participation of women in the democracies of the Americas. An Inter-American Year of Women was inaugurated in February 2010.

SOCIAL AND ECONOMIC DEVELOPMENT

Combating poverty and promoting social equity and economic development are priority concerns of the OAS, and the OAS pursues these aims in partnership with regional and global agencies, the private sector and the international community. A Strategic Plan for Partnership for Integral Development guided OAS actions in area during 2006–13. In June 2012 the 42nd OAS General Assembly adopted a new Social Charter of the Americas. The 43rd General Assembly, held in June 2013, issued the Declaration of Antigua, which urged governments of the region to promote 'public health, education, and social inclusion', and also adopted the Inter-American Convention against All Forms of Discrimination and Intolerance (which by September 2014 had been signed by seven member states), and the Inter-American Convention against Racism, Racial Discrimination and Related Forms of Intolerance (which by that time had been signed by nine member states). In June 2014 the 44th General Assembly approved, unanimously, the Declaration of Asunción: Development with Inclusion, in which member states determined to focus on 'eradicating hunger and poverty, in particular extreme poverty, on combating inequity, inequality, discrimination, and social exclusion, and on increasing equitable access to health services, as well as to quality and inclusive education' in the Americas. The Declaration urged member states to strengthen their capacities to withstand external shocks, and to incorporate, as appropriate, the results of the post-2015 development agenda into programmes and activities. OAS development policies and priorities are determined by the organization's political bodies, including the General Assembly, the Permanent Council and the Inter-American Council for Integral Development (CIDI), with direction from the Summits of the Americas. The OAS Executive Secretariat for Integral Development (SEDI) implements the policies through projects and programmes. Specialized departments within SEDI focus on education, culture, science and technology; sustainable development; trade, tourism and competitiveness; and social development and employment. SEDI also supports the regional ministerial meetings on topics such as culture, education, labour and sustainable development that are held periodically as part of the Summit of the Americas process. These regional meetings foster dialogue and strengthen co-operation in specific sectors and ensure that Summit policies are implemented at the national level. The OAS convenes the ministerial meetings, prepares documents for discussion and tracks the implementation of Summit mandates. In June 2009 the General Assembly adopted a resolution committing members to strengthening co-operation to control the spread of communicable diseases, in particular the outbreak of the swine influenza variant pandemic (H1N1), through greater surveillance and other disease control methods.

In June 2008 a technical secretariat was established in Panama City, Panama, to co-ordinate the implementation of an action plan in support of the Decade of the Americas for the Rights and Dignity of Persons with Disabilities (2006–16). The theme of the Decade, which had been inaugurated in Santo Domingo, Dominican Republic, was 'Equality, Dignity, and Participation'. In July 2008 the first Meeting of Ministers and High Authorities of Social Development, within the framework of CIDI, was convened in Valparaiso, Chile.

The OAS Department of Sustainable Development assists member states with formulating policies and executing projects that are aimed at integrating environmental protection with rural development and poverty alleviation, and that ensure high levels of transparency, public participation and gender equity. In December 2006 regional ministers responsible for the environment met in Santa Cruz de la Sierra, Bolivia, to define strategies and goals related to sustainable development, environmental protection, the management of resources and the mitigation of natural disasters. Water resource management projects include initiatives that support member states in managing transboundary water resources in the major river basins of South and Central America, in partnership with the UN Environment Programme (UNEP), the World Bank and the Global Environment Facility (GEF). The OAS is also active in various international fora that address water-related issues.

Projects focusing on natural disasters and climate adaptation include a new programme, launched in April 2006, which is aimed at assisting member countries to reduce the risk of natural disasters, particularly those related to climatic variations that have been linked to rises in sea levels. The OAS also works with CARICOM on the Mainstreaming Adaptation to Climate Change project. Activities include: incorporating risk reduction into development and economic planning; supporting good governance in such areas as the use of appropriate building codes and standards for public and residential buildings; supporting innovative financial instruments related to risk transfer; and supporting regional collaboration with different agencies and organizations.

The OAS serves as the technical secretariat for the Renewable Energy in the Americas initiative, which offers governments access to information on renewable energy and energy-efficient technologies, and facilitates contacts between the private sector and state energy entities in the Americas. The OAS also provides technical assistance for developing renewable energy projects and facilitating their funding.

The Inter-American Biodiversity Information Network (IABIN), which has been supported since 2004 by the GEF, the World Bank and other sources, is a principal focus of OAS biodiversity efforts. The Department of Sustainable Development also supports the work of national conservation authorities in areas such as migratory species and biodiversity corridors. It co-operates with the private sector to support innovative financing through payment for ecological services, and maintains a unique online portal regarding land tenure and land title, which is used throughout the Americas.

In the areas of environmental law, policy and economics the OAS conducts environmental and sustainability assessments to help member states to identify key environmental issues that impact trade. The OAS works with countries to develop priorities for capacity building in such areas as domestic laws, regulations and standards affecting market access of goods and services. Other initiatives include supporting countries in water and renewable energy legislation; supporting efforts towards the more effective enforcement of domestic laws; and facilitating natural disaster risk reduction and relief.

The OAS supports member states at national, bilateral and multilateral level to cope with trade expansion and economic integration. Through its Department of Trade, Tourism and Competitiveness the OAS General Secretariat provides support in strengthening human and institutional capacities, and in enhancing trade opportunities and competitiveness, particularly for micro, small and medium-sized enterprises. One of the Department's key responsibilities is to help member states (especially smaller economies) to develop the capacity they need to negotiate, implement and administer trade agreements and to take advantage of the benefits offered by free trade and expanded markets. Many member states seek assistance from the OAS to meet successfully the challenges posed by increasing globalization and the need to pursue multiple trade agendas. The OAS also administers an Inter-American Foreign Trade Information System, which acts as a repository for information about trade and trade-related issues in the region, including the texts of trade agreements, information on trade disciplines, data, and national legislation. In October 2008 a meeting of Ministers and High Authorities on Science and Technology, convened in Mexico City, Mexico, declared their commitment to co-ordinating activities to promote and enhance policies relating to science, technology, engineering and innovation as tools of development, increasing productivity, and sustainable natural resource management.

A specialized unit for tourism was established in 1996 in order to strengthen and co-ordinate activities for the sustainable development of the tourism industry in the Americas. The unit supports regional and subregional conferences and workshops, as well as the Inter-American Travel Congress, which serves as a forum to consider and formulate region-wide tourism policies. The unit also undertakes research and analysis of the industry. In September 2011 the 19th Inter-American Travel Congress, convened in San Salvador, El Salvador, adopted, by consensus, the Declaration of San Salvador for Sustainable Tourism Development in the Americas, recognizing the contribution of the tourism sector towards national efforts to reduce poverty and inequality, to advance standards of living in host communities, and to promote sustainable economic development. The Congress approved the establishment of a Hemispheric Tourism Fund, which was to support poor communities in developing their tourism potential. The inaugural meeting of an Inter-American Tourism Commission was held in August 2012. In early 2014 OAS, with other partners including the Central American Integration System, the Caribbean Tourism Organization and Sustainable Travel International, a non-governmental organization, launched the Americas Sustainable Destinations (SDAA) initiative, with the aim of strengthening public-private partnerships to protect, and to improve the lives of local people in, destination areas. In September 2014 seven SDAA destinations in Central America and the Caribbean were announced. During that month the 22nd Inter-American Congress of Ministers and High-Level Authorities of Tourism, held in Bridgetown, Barbados, adopted a Declaration of Bridgetown on Tourism Competitiveness: An Essential Component of Sustainability, which identified relevant challenges and priority areas of focus aimed at advancing regional co-operation.

The OAS assists with the preparation of national and multilateral cultural projects, and co-operates with the private sector to protect and promote cultural assets and events in the region. In July 2002 the first Inter-American meeting of ministers responsible for culture approved the establishment of an Inter-American Committee on Culture, within the framework of CIDI, to co-ordinate high-level dialogue and co-operation on cultural issues. In November 2006 regional ministers responsible for culture met in Montréal, Canada, to address the contribution of the cultural sector towards promoting development and combating poverty. In 2009 the General Assembly declared 2011 as the Inter-American Year of Culture.

The 42nd General Assembly meeting, held in Cochabamba, Bolivia, in June 2012, adopted the Declaration of Cochabamba on Food

Security with Sovereignty in the Americas, committing, *inter alia*, to promote agricultural development, eradicate hunger and malnutrition, and support inter-American and regional efforts to advance a common agenda on food and nutrition security.

In November 2013 a meeting of OAS ministers responsible for labour and of representatives of regional workers and employers, held in Medellín, Colombia, adopted the Medellin Declaration and Plan of Action on 'Fifty Years of Inter-American Dialogue for the Promotion of Social Justice and Decent Work: Progress and Challenges towards Sustainable Development'. The Declaration reaffirmed regional commitment to the articulation of improved economic and labour policies, with a special emphasis on youth access to the employment market, respect for labour rights, and the provision of vocational training initiatives and employment services.

MULTIDIMENSIONAL SECURITY

The promotion of hemispheric security is a fundamental purpose of the OAS. In October 2003, at a Special Conference on Security convened in Mexico City, Mexico, the member states established a 'multidimensional' approach that recognized both traditional security concerns and threats such as international terrorism, drugs-trafficking, money-laundering, illegal arms dealing, trafficking in persons, institutional corruption and organized crime. In some countries problems such as poverty, disease, environmental degradation and natural disasters increase vulnerability and undermine human security. In March 2006 member states determined to enhance co-operation on defence issues by formally designating the Inter-American Defense Board (IADB) as an OAS agency. Under its new mandate the operations and structure of the IADB were to be in keeping with the OAS Charter and the Inter-American Democratic Charter, including 'the principles of civilian oversight and the subordination of military institutions to civilian authority'. The IADB provides technical and educational advice and consultancy services to the OAS and its member states on military and defence matters. The OAS Secretary-General chairs the Inter-American Committee on Natural Disaster Reduction, which was established in 1999 comprising the principal officers of regional and international organizations concerned with the prevention and mitigation of natural disasters. The Committee met in November 2012 to consider the impact of Hurricane Sandy, in particular in the Bahamas, Haiti, Jamaica and the east coast of the USA.

Following the 11 September 2001 terrorist attacks perpetrated against targets in the USA, the OAS member states strengthened their co-operation against the threat of terrorism. The Inter-American Convention against Terrorism, which seeks to prevent the financing of terrorist activities, strengthen border controls and increase co-operation among law enforcement authorities in different countries, was opened for signature in June 2002 and entered into force in July 2003. By 2014 it had been signed by all 34 active member states and ratified or acceded to by 24. The Inter-American Committee against Terrorism (CICTE) offers technical assistance and specialized training in key counter-terrorism areas including port security, airport security, customs and border security, and legislation and legal assistance. Through CICTE member countries have also improved co-operation in improving the quality of identification and travel documents, strengthening cybersecurity and adopting financial controls to prevent money-laundering and the funding of terrorist activities. In October 2008 the first meeting of ministers responsible for public security in the Americas was convened, in Mexico City. In June 2009 the General Assembly, meeting in Honduras, adopted the Declaration of San Pedro Sula, promoting the theme 'Towards a Culture of Non-violence'.

In January 2010 the OAS established an emergency committee to help to co-ordinate relief efforts for Haiti, which had suffered extensive damage and loss of life as a result of a massive earthquake. A joint mission of the OAS and representatives of four inter-American institutions visited Haiti at the end of that month to assess its immediate relief and reconstruction needs. In March the OAS hosted a Haiti Diaspora Meeting, with the collaboration of the Haitian Government, which made recommendations, in particular concerning nation-building, recovery and development, for the forthcoming International Donors' Conference, held in New York, USA, at the end of that month.

The Inter-American Drug Abuse Control Commission (CICAD) seeks to reduce the supply of and demand for illegal drugs, building on the 1996 Anti-Drug Strategy in the Hemisphere. The CICAD Executive Secretariat implements programmes aimed at preventing and treating substance abuse; reducing the supply and availability of illicit drugs; strengthening national drug control institutions; improving practices to control firearms and money-laundering; developing alternate sources of income for growers of coca, poppy and marijuana; and helping member governments to improve the gathering and analysis of data. The Multilateral Evaluation Mechanism (MEM) measures drug control progress in the member states and the hemisphere as a whole, based on a series of objective indicators. Following each evaluation round the MEM process exam-

ines how countries are carrying out the recommendations. In June 2009 the OAS General Assembly agreed to initiate a review of the organization's anti-drugs strategy and its instruments to counter drugs-trafficking and abuse. In June 2013 the Assembly issued the Declaration of Antigua Guatemala for a Comprehensive Policy against the World Drug Problem in the Americas. A special session of the OAS General Assembly was held in mid-September 2014 on the theme 'For a Hemispheric Drug Policy in the Twenty-First Century'.

In 1997 the member states adopted the Inter-American Convention against the Illicit Manufacturing of and Trafficking in Firearms, Ammunition, Explosives, and other Related Materials (known as CIFTA), which, by 2014, had been ratified by 30 member states. These countries have strengthened co-operation and information sharing on CIFTA-related issues. In 2005 the OAS convened the first meeting of national authorities that make operational decisions on granting export, import and transit licenses for firearms, with a view to creating an information exchange network to prevent illegal manufacturing and trafficking. In June 1999 20 member states signed an Inter-American Convention on Transparency in Conventional Weapons Acquisition; it had been ratified by 15 members by 2014.

The OAS co-ordinates a comprehensive international programme to remove many thousands of anti-personnel landmines posing a threat to civilians in countries that have been affected by conflict. The OAS oversees the process of identifying, obtaining and delivering the necessary resources, including funds, equipment and personnel; the IADB co-ordinates technical demining operations, working with field supervisors from various countries; and the actual demining is executed by teams of trained soldiers, security forces or other personnel from the affected country. In addition to supporting landmine clearance the OAS Program for Comprehensive Action against Anti-personnel Mines helps with mine risk education; victim assistance and the socio-economic reintegration of formerly mined zones; the establishment of a mine action database; and support for the global ban on the production, use, sale, transfer and stockpiling of anti-personnel landmines. It has also helped to destroy more than 1m. stockpiled mines in Argentina, Colombia, Chile, Ecuador, Honduras, Nicaragua and Peru. By mid-2009 Costa Rica, El Salvador, Guatemala, Honduras and Suriname had declared their territory to be clear of anti-personnel landmines. Nicaragua was officially declared to be free of landmines in June 2010.

The OAS Trafficking in Persons Section organizes seminars and training workshops for law enforcement officials and others to raise awareness on human trafficking, which includes human exploitation, smuggling and other human rights violations. In March 2006 the Venezuelan Government hosted the first Meeting of National Authorities on Trafficking in Persons in order to study ways to strengthen co-operation and to develop regional policies and strategies to prevent human trafficking. Gang violence is another growing public security concern in the region. A second Meeting was convened in Buenos Aires, Argentina, in March 2009.

The OAS, Inter-American Development Bank and OECD jointly implement the Continuous Reporting System on International Migration in the America (SICREMI), which aims rigorously to monitor international migration movements and key policies and programmes being implemented in the region; the first and second SICREMI reports were released in August 2011 and January 2013, respectively.

In June 2010 the 40th meeting of the OAS General Assembly, meeting in Lima, determined to strengthen a collective commitment to peace, security and co-operation, as the principal means of confronting threats to the region.

In June 2012 the 42nd OAS General Assembly issued a Declaration on the Question of the Status of the Islas Malvinas (Falkland Islands), and determined to examine that issue at subsequent sessions. The 43rd General Assembly, held in June 2013, approved a further Declaration on the Malvinas, proposed by Argentina, which reaffirmed that both Argentina and the United Kingdom should resume as soon as possible negotiations over the disputed sovereignty of the islands. In June 2014 the 44th Assembly adopted a Declaration on the Question of the Malvinas Islands, which similarly emphasized the need for the prompt resumption of bilateral negotiations over the issue.

A Meeting of Consultation of OAS ministers responsible for foreign affairs held in late August 2012 adopted a resolution urging Ecuador and the United Kingdom to resolve, through peaceful dialogue, a diplomatic impasse that had ensued from the granting by Ecuador in that month of political asylum to Julian Assange, the Australian founder of WikiLeaks. Assange had sought sanctuary in Ecuador's London embassy to avoid extradition to Sweden, where he was wanted for questioning over alleged sexual misconduct, for fear that he might eventually be extradited to the USA, whose authorities had been investigating the activities of WikiLeaks.

SUMMITS OF THE AMERICAS

Since December 1994, when the First Summit of the Americas was convened in Miami, USA, the leaders of the region's 34 democracies have met periodically to examine political, economic and social development priorities and to determine common goals and forge a common agenda. This process has increasingly shaped OAS policies and priorities and many OAS achievements, for example the adoption of the Inter-American Democratic Charter and the creation of mechanisms to measure progress against illicit drugs and corruption, have been attained as a result of Summit mandates. The Summits of the Americas have provided direction for the OAS in the areas of human rights, hemispheric security, trade, poverty reduction, gender equity and greater civil society participation. The OAS serves as the institutional memory and technical secretariat to the Summit process. It supports the countries in follow-up and planning, and provides technical, logistical and administrative support. The OAS Summits Secretariat co-ordinates the implementation of mandates assigned to the OAS and chairs the Joint Summit Working Group, which includes the institutions of the inter-American system. The OAS also has responsibility for strengthening outreach to civil society to ensure that NGOs, academic institutions, the private sector and other interests can contribute ideas and help to monitor and implement Summit initiatives.

In December 1994 the First Summit of the Americas was convened in Miami. The meeting endorsed the concept of a Free Trade Area of the Americas, and also approved a Plan of Action to strengthen democracy, eradicate poverty and promote sustainable development throughout the region. The OAS subsequently realigned its priorities in order to respond to the mandates emerging from the Summit and developed a new institutional framework for technical assistance and co-operation, although many activities continued to be undertaken by the specialized or associated organizations of the OAS. In 1998, following the Second Summit, held in Santiago, the OAS established an Office of Summit Follow-Up, in order to strengthen its servicing of the meetings, and to co-ordinate tasks assigned to it. The Third Summit, convened in Québec, Canada, in April 2001, reaffirmed the central role of the OAS in implementing decisions of the summit meetings and instructed the organization to pursue the process of reform in order to enhance its operational capabilities, in particular in the areas of human rights, combating trade in illegal drugs, and enforcement of democratic values. The Summit declaration stated that commitment to democracy was a requirement for a country's participation in the summit process. The Third Summit urged the development of an Inter-American Democratic Charter to reinforce OAS instruments for defending and promoting democracy; the Democratic Charter was adopted in September of that year. The Third Summit also determined that the OAS was to be the technical secretariat for the summit process, assuming many of the responsibilities previously incumbent on the host country. Further to its mandate, the OAS established a Summits of the Americas Secretariat, which assists countries in planning and follow-up and provides technical, logistical and administrative support for the Summit Implementation Review Group and the summit process. An interim Special Summit of the Americas was held in January 2004, in Monterrey, Mexico, to reaffirm commitment to the process. The Fourth Summit of the Americas, convened in Mar del Plata, Argentina, in November 2005, approved a plan of action to achieve employment growth and security. The Fifth Summit was held in Port of Spain, Trinidad and Tobago, in April 2009, focusing on the theme 'Securing our citizens' future by promoting human prosperity, energy security and environmental sustainability'. All governments determined to enhance co-operation to restore global economic growth and to reduce social inequalities. The meeting mandated the OAS to pursue various objectives, including the establishment of an Inter-American Social Protection Network, to facilitate the exchange of information with regard to policies, programmes and best practices; the convening of a Conference on Development; organizing regional consultations on climate change; and strengthening the leadership of the Joint Summit Working Group. A Summit of the Americas follow-up and implementation system was inaugurated in January 2010. The Sixth Summit was held in Cartagena, Colombia, in April 2012, on the theme 'Connecting the Americas: Partners for Prosperity'. The meeting mandated the OAS to review its strategies to counter the trafficking of illegal drugs. However, no unanimity was reached on the admission of Cuba to the next summit, scheduled to be convened in Panama, in 2015.

Finance

The OAS regular budget for 2014, approved by the General Assembly in November 2013, amounted to US $82.98m.

Publications

(in English and Spanish)

Américas (6 a year).
Annual Report.
Numerous cultural, legal and scientific reports and studies.

Specialized Organizations and Associated Agencies

Inter-American Children's Institute (Instituto Americano del Niño, la Niña y Adolescentes—IIN): Avda 8 de Octubre 2904, POB 16212, Montevideo 11600, Uruguay; tel. 2487 2150; fax 2487 3242; e-mail iin@iinoea.org; internet www.iin.oea.org; f. 1927; promotes the regional implementation of the Convention on the Rights of the Child, assists in the development of child-oriented public policies; promotes co-operation between states; and aims to develop awareness of problems affecting children and young people in the region. The Institute organizes workshops, seminars, courses, training programmes and conferences on issues relating to children, including, for example, the rights of children, children with disabilities, and the child welfare system. It also provides advisory services, statistical data and other relevant information to authorities and experts throughout the region. The 20th Pan American Child Congress was convened in Lima, Peru, in September 2009; Dir-Gen. María de los Dolores Aguilar Marmolejo; publ. *iinfancia* (annually).

Inter-American Commission of Women (Comisión Interamericana de Mujeres—CIM): 1889 F St, NW, Suite 350 Washington, DC 20006, USA; tel. (202) 458-6084; fax (202) 458-6094; e-mail cim@oas.org; internet www.oas.org/cim; f. 1928 as the first official intergovernmental agency created expressly to ensure recognition of the civil and political rights of women; the CIM is the principal forum for generating hemispheric policy to advance women's rights and gender equality; comprises 34 principal delegates; the Assembly of Delegates, convened every two years, is the highest authority of the Commission, establishing policies and a plan of action for each biennium and electing the seven-mem. Executive Committee; Pres. Alejandra Mora (Costa Rica); Exec. Sec. Carmen Moreno Toscano (Mexico).

Inter-American Institute for Co-operation on Agriculture (IICA) (Instituto Interamericano de Cooperación para la Agricultura): Apdo Postal 55–2200, San Isidro de Coronado, San José, Costa Rica; tel. (506) 216-0222; fax (506) 216-0233; e-mail iicahq@iica.ac.cr; internet www.iica.int; f. 1942 (as the Inter-American Institute of Agricultural Sciences, present name adopted 1980); supports the efforts of mem. states to improve agricultural development and rural well-being; encourages co-operation between regional orgs, and provides a forum for the exchange of experience; Dir-Gen. Víctor M. Villalobos (Mexico).

Pan American Health Organization (PAHO) (Organización Panamericana de la Salud): 525 23rd St, NW, Washington, DC 20037, USA; tel. (202) 974-3000; fax (202) 974-3663; e-mail webmaster@paho.org; internet www.paho.org; f. 1902; co-ordinates regional efforts to improve health; maintains close relations with national health orgs and serves as the Regional Office for the Americas of the World Health Organization; Dir Dr Carissa Etienne (Dominica).

Pan American Institute of Geography and History (PAIGH) (Instituto Panamericano de Geografía e Historia—IPGH): Ex-Arzobispado 29, 11860 México, DF, Mexico; tel. (55) 5277-5888; fax (55) 5271-6172; e-mail secretariageneral@ipgh.org; internet www.ipgh.org; f. 1928; co-ordinates and promotes the study of cartography, geophysics, geography and history; provides technical assistance, conducts training at research centres, distributes publications, and organizes technical meetings; Pres. Rigoberto Ovidio Magaña Chavarría (El Salvador); Sec.-Gen. Rodrigo Barriga Vargas (Chile); Publs *Revista Cartográfica* (2 a year), *Revista Geográfica* (2 a year), *Revista de Historia de América* (2 a year), *Revista Geofísica* (2 a year), *Revista de Arqueología Americana* (annually), *Folklore Americano* (annually), *Boletín de Antropología Americana* (annually).

SOUTHERN COMMON MARKET—MERCOSUR/ MERCOSUL

(MERCADO COMÚN DEL SUR/MERCADO COMUM DO SUL)

Address: Edif. Mercosur, Luis Piera 1992, 1°, 11200 Montevideo, Uruguay.

Telephone: 2412 9024; **fax:** 2418 0557; **e-mail:** secretaria@ mercosur.org.uy; **internet:** www.mercosur.int.

MERCOSUR (known as MERCOSUL in Portuguese) was established in March 1991 by the heads of state of Argentina, Brazil, Paraguay and Uruguay with the signature of the Treaty of Asunción. The primary objective of the Treaty is to achieve the economic integration of member states by means of a free flow of goods and services, the establishment of a common external tariff, the adoption of common commercial policy, and the co-ordination of macroeconomic and sectoral policies. The Ouro Preto Protocol, which was signed in December 1994, conferred on MERCOSUR the status of an international legal entity with the authority to sign agreements with third countries, groups of countries and international organizations.

MEMBERS

Argentina   Brazil   Paraguay   Uruguay   Venezuela

Note: Bolivia, Chile, Colombia, Ecuador, Guyana, Peru and Suriname are associate members. In December 2012 Bolivia signed the adhesion protocol to become a full member of MERCOSUR. Its admission to the grouping required ratification by each member's legislature.

Organization

(September 2014)

COMMON MARKET COUNCIL

The Common Market Council (Consejo del Mercado Común) is the highest organ of MERCOSUR and is responsible for leading the integration process and for taking decisions in order to achieve the objectives of the Treaty of Asunción. In December 2010 the Council decided to establish the position of High Representative, with a three-year term-in-office, in order to support the integration process, to promote trade and investment and to represent the grouping internationally.

High Representative: IVÁN RAMALHO (Brazil).

COMMON MARKET GROUP

The Common Market Group (Grupo Mercado Común) is the executive body of MERCOSUR and is responsible for implementing concrete measures to further the integration process.

TRADE COMMISSION

The Trade Commission (Comisión de Comercio del MERCOSUR) has competence for the area of joint commercial policy and, in particular, is responsible for monitoring the operation of the common external tariff. The Brasília Protocol may be referred to for the resolution of trade disputes between member states.

CONSULTATIVE ECONOMIC AND SOCIAL FORUM

The Consultative Economic and Social Forum (Foro Consultivo Económico-Social) comprises representatives from the business community and trade unions in the member countries and has a consultative role in relation to MERCOSUR.

WORKING GROUPS

Technical discussions are held by 12 working groups, directed by MERCOSUR's incumbent six-monthly rotational chairmanship (Aug. 2014–Jan. 2015).

PARLIAMENT

Parlamento del MERCOSUR: Pablo de María 827, 11200 Montevideo, Uruguay; tel. 2410 9797; e-mail secadministrativa@ parlamentodelmercosur.org; internet www.parlamentodelmercosur .org; f. 2005, as successor to the Joint Parliamentary Commission (Comisión Parlamentaria Conjunta); inaugural session held in May 2007; aims to facilitate implementation of MERCOSUR decisions and regional co-operation; each mem. holds 18 seats; an agreement concluded October 2010 determined that, with effect from 31 December 2014, seats were to be allocated proportional to each country's

population; concluded in Aug. 2014 a Framework Cooperation Arrangement with the International Criminal Court; special parliamentary session focusing on the Malvinas/Falkland Islands scheduled to be held in Nov. 2014.

SECRETARIAT

Director: JEFERSON MIOLA (Brazil).

Activities

In June 1996 MERCOSUR heads of state, meeting in San Luis de Mendoza, Argentina, endorsed a 'Democratic Guarantee Clause', whereby a country would be prevented from participation in MERCOSUR unless democratic, accountable institutions were in place. In June 2012 Paraguay was suspended from participation in a regular meeting of heads of state, following the impeachment of that country's president, Fernando Lugo, in a process which the remaining members of MERCOSUR condemned as a breach of the democratic order. At the meeting, convened in Mendoza, Argentina, the heads of state of Argentina, Brazil and Uruguay determined to suspend Paraguay's membership of the grouping until democratic presidential elections were conducted. It was agreed not to impose economic measures against the country in the mean time. With the suspension from the grouping of Paraguay, whose congress had vetoed the membership of Venezuela, the heads of state announced that Venezuela would be admitted as a full member of MERCOSUR with effect from 31 July. Following the April 2013 presidential election in Paraguay, MERCOSUR heads of states agreed at a summit convened in early July, in Montevideo, Uruguay, that Paraguay should be permitted to reintegrate into the grouping following the inauguration on 15 August of its then President-elect, Horacio Cartes. In December, following diplomatic negotiations, both houses of the Paraguay legislature approved Venezuela's adhesion protocol, enabling Paraguay to resume active membership of the grouping.

In December 2010 MERCOSUR heads of state, meeting in Foz do Iguaçú, Brazil, concluded further agreements to accelerate regional integration. These included the appointment of a new High Representative, a Customs Union Consolidation Program, a Strategic Social Action Plan, which aimed to support the eradication of poverty and greater social equality, and a roadmap for the formation of a MERCOSUR citizenship statute in order to facilitate the free movement of persons throughout the region. A common MERCOSUR vehicle license plate was endorsed by the summit meeting.

In February 2014, in response to ongoing political unrest in Venezuela, MERCOSUR issued a statement condemning acts of violence and acts aimed at destabilizing the elected Venezuelan government. In late June MERCOSUR heads of state affirmed their solidarity with and support for Argentina with respect to a recent US Supreme Court ruling that Argentina should pay in full debt repayments to US hedge fund investors (representing a minority of holders of its outstanding sovereign debt) who had refused to participate in debt restructuring arrangements agreed for the country in 2005 and 2010—thereby blocking funds allocated towards paying debt interest due to those bondholders that had complied with the restructuring process.

A regular summit meeting of MERCOSUR heads of state that had been scheduled to be held in December 2013 was postponed several times; initially this was attributed to the then poor health of the Argentinian President, while later postponements were reportedly due to difficulties drafting the agenda. The summit was eventually convened in July 2014, in Caracas, Venezuela, although the Chilean President failed to attend. Addressing the summit, the President of Argentina thanked member states for their solidarity with Argentina on the debt restructuring issue.

ECONOMIC INTEGRATION

MERCOSUR's free trade zone entered into effect on 1 January 1995, with tariffs removed from 85% of intra-regional trade. A regime of gradual removal of duties on a list of special products was agreed, while regimes governing trade in the automobile and sugar sectors remained to be negotiated. MERCOSUR's customs union also came into force at the start of 1995, comprising a common external tariff (CET) of 0%–20%. A list of exceptions from the CET was agreed; these products were to lose their special status and were to be subject to the general tariff system concerning foreign goods by 2006. In December 2012 heads of state agreed that Venezuela could implement the CET in four stages from April 2013, to be concluded by 2016.

In June 1995 MERCOSUR ministers responsible for the environment agreed to harmonize environmental legislation and to form a permanent sub-group of MERCOSUR. In December of that year MERCOSUR presidents affirmed the consolidation of free trade as MERCOSUR's 'permanent and most urgent goal'. To this end they agreed to prepare norms of application for MERCOSUR's customs code, accelerate paper procedures and increase the connections between national computerized systems. It was also agreed to increase co-operation in the areas of agriculture, industry, mining, energy, communications, transport and tourism, and finance. At this meeting Argentina and Brazil reached an accord aimed at overcoming their dispute regarding the trade in automobiles between the two countries.

In December 1996 MERCOSUR heads of state, meeting in Fortaleza, Brazil, approved agreements on harmonizing competition practices (by 2001), integrating educational opportunities for postgraduates and human resources training, standardizing trading safeguards applied against third country products (by 2001) and providing for intra-regional cultural exchanges. An Accord on Subregional Air Services was signed at the meeting (including by the heads of state of Bolivia and Chile) to liberalize civil transport throughout the region. In addition, the heads of state endorsed texts on consumer rights. In December 1997 a separate Protocol was signed providing for the liberalization of trade in services and government purchases over a 10-year period. In December 1998 MERCOSUR heads of state agreed on the establishment of an arbitration mechanism for disputes between members, and on measures to standardize human, animal and plant health and safety regulations throughout the grouping.

The summit meeting held in December 2000 approved criteria, formulated by MERCOSUR ministers responsible for finance and central bank governors, determining monetary and fiscal targets which aimed to achieve economic convergence, to promote economic stability throughout the region, and to reduce competitive disparities affecting the unity of the grouping. However, unilateral economic action by member governments, in particular to counter economic instability, and bilateral trade disputes have persistently undermined MERCOSUR's integration objectives. In early 2001 Argentina imposed several emergency measures to strengthen its domestic economy, in contradiction of MERCOSUR's external tariffs. In February 2002, at a third extraordinary meeting of the Common Market Council, held in Buenos Aires, MERCOSUR heads of state expressed their support for Argentina's application to receive international financial assistance, in the wake of that country's economic crisis. Although there were fears that the crisis might curb trade and stall economic growth across the region, Argentina's adoption of a floating currency made the prospect of currency harmonization between MERCOSUR member countries appear more viable. At a summit convened in June 2003, in Asunción, Paraguay, heads of state of the four member countries agreed to strengthen integration of the bloc and to harmonize all import tariffs by 2006, thus creating the basis for a single market. In August 2010 MERCOSUR heads of state, meeting in San Juan, Argentina, endorsed a new common customs code, incorporating agreements on the redistribution of external customs revenue and elimination of the double taxation on goods imported from outside the group.

The July 2004 summit of MERCOSUR heads of state announced that an Asunción-based five-member tribunal (comprising one legal representative from each of MERCOSUR's four member countries, plus one 'consensus' member) responsible for ruling on appeals in cases of disputes between member countries was to become operational in the following month. In September 2006 the tribunal criticized the Argentine Government for allowing blockades of international bridges across the River Uruguay by protesters opposing the construction of two pulp mills on the Uruguayan side of the river. (In April 2010 the International Court of Justice delivered a judgment supporting the ongoing operations of the mills; Argentina and Uruguay subsequently agreed to co-operate in the implementation of environmental protection measures to limit pollution of the River Uruguay.)

In June 2005 MERCOSUR heads of state announced a US $100m. structural convergence fund to support education, job creation and infrastructure projects in the poorest regions, in particular in Paraguay and Uruguay, in order to remove some economic disparities within the grouping. The meeting also endorsed a multilateral energy project to link gasfields in Camisea, Peru, to existing supply pipelines in Argentina, Brazil and Uruguay, via Tocopilla, Chile. In July 2008 MERCOSUR heads of state considered the impact of escalating food costs and the production of biofuels. In December a summit meeting, convened in Bahia, Brazil, agreed to establish a $100m. guarantee fund to facilitate access to credit for small and medium-sized businesses operating in the common market in order to alleviate the impact of the global financial crisis.

EXTERNAL RELATIONS

In June 1996 MERCOSUR heads of state approved the entry into MERCOSUR of Bolivia and Chile as associate members. An Economic Complementation Accord with Bolivia, which includes Bolivia in MERCOSUR's free trade zone, but not in the customs union, was signed in December 1995 and was to come into force on 1 January 1997, later extended until 30 April 1997. Measures of the free trade agreement, which was signed in October 1996, were to be implemented during a transitional period commencing on 28 February 1997 (revised from 1 January). Chile's Economic Complementation Accord with MERCOSUR entered into effect on 1 October 1996, with duties on most products to be removed over a 10-year period (Chile's most sensitive products were given 18 years for complete tariff elimination). Chile was also to remain outside the customs union, but was to be involved in other integration projects, in particular infrastructure projects designed to give MERCOSUR countries access to both the Atlantic and Pacific Oceans (Chile's Pacific coast was regarded as MERCOSUR's potential link to the economies of the Far East). In March 1998 the ministers of the interior of MERCOSUR countries, together with representatives of the Governments of Chile and Bolivia, agreed to implement a joint security arrangement for the border region linking Argentina, Paraguay and Brazil. In particular, the initiative aimed to counter drugs-trafficking, money-laundering and other illegal activities in the area. Procedures to incorporate Chile as a full member of MERCOSUR were suspended in 2000 following an announcement by the Chilean Government that it had initiated bilateral free trade discussions with the USA, which was considered, in particular by the Brazilian authorities, to undermine MERCOSUR's unified position at multilateral free trade negotiations. In July 2008 MERCOSUR and Chile concluded a protocol on trade in services.

In April 1998 MERCOSUR and the Andean Community signed an accord that committed them to the establishment of a free trade area by January 2000. Negotiations in early 1999 failed to conclude an agreement on preferential tariffs between the two blocs, and the existing arrangements were extended on a bilateral basis. In March the Andean Community agreed to initiate free trade negotiations with Brazil; a preferential tariff agreement was concluded in July. In August 2000 a similar agreement between the Community and Argentina entered into force. In September leaders of the two groupings, meeting at a summit of Latin American heads of state, determined to relaunch negotiations. The establishment of a mechanism to support political dialogue and co-ordination between the two groupings, was approved at the first joint meeting of ministers responsible for foreign affairs in July 2001. In April 2004 MERCOSUR and the Andean Community signed a free trade accord, providing for tariffs on 80% of trade between the two groupings to be phased out by 2014, and for tariffs to be removed from the remaining 20% of, initially protected, products by 2019. The entry into force of the accord, scheduled for 1 July 2004, was postponed owing to delays in drafting the tariff reduction schedule. Peru became an associate member of MERCOSUR in December 2003, and Colombia and Ecuador were granted associate membership in December 2004. In July 2004 Mexico was invited to attend all meetings of the organization with a view to future accession to associate membership. In 2005 MERCOSUR and the Andean Community formulated a reciprocal association agreement, to extend associate membership to all member states of both groupings. In February 2010 ministers responsible for foreign affairs agreed to establish an Andean Community-MERCOSUR Mixed Commission to facilitate and strengthen co-operation between member countries of both organizations. In December 2005 Bolivia was invited to join as a full member, while MERCOSUR heads of state agreed to a request by Venezuela (which had been granted associate membership in December 2004) to become a member with full voting rights. The leaders signed a protocol, in July 2006, formally to admit Venezuela to the group. The accord, however, required ratification by each country's legislature, and by mid-2012 the Paraguayan parliament had not endorsed the protocol, as it was blocked by the country's senate. In late June, following the decision to suspend Paraguay's membership of MERCOSUR, heads of state, meeting in Mendoza, Argentina, agreed to admit Venezuela to the grouping at the end of July. Venezuela was welcomed as the fifth full member of MERCOSUR by the heads of state of Argentina, Brazil and Uruguay at an Inclusion Ceremony, held in Brazil on 31 July. In December, at a meeting of heads of state in Brasília, Bolivia signed an adhesion protocol formally admitting it into the grouping as a full member. The protocol required ratification by each country's legislature. Paraguay, at that time still suspended from MERCOSUR, criticized the decision to admit Bolivia without its consent. Guyana and Suriname joined the grouping as associate members in July 2013. By September 2014 the incorporation of Bolivia into the grouping had been ratified by Argentina, Uruguay and Venezuela.

In 2014 the creation of a broad Latin American and Caribbean sustainable economic development zone was under consideration by MERCOSUR, UNASUR, the Bolivarian Alliance for the Peoples of our America, Petrocaribe and the Community of Latin American and Caribbean States.

In December 1995 MERCOSUR and the European Union (EU) signed a framework agreement for commercial and economic co-operation, which provided for co-operation in the economic, trade, industrial, scientific, institutional and cultural fields and the promotion of wider political dialogue on issues of mutual interest. Negotiations between MERCOSUR and the EU on the conclusion of an Interregional Association Agreement commenced in 1999. Specific discussion of tariff reductions and market access commenced at the fifth round of negotiations, held in July 2001, at which the EU proposed a gradual elimination of tariffs on industrial imports over a 10-year period and an extension of access quotas for agricultural products; however, negotiations stalled in 2005 owing to differences regarding farm subsidies. In July 2008 MERCOSUR heads of state condemned a new EU immigration policy that would permit the detention and forcible return of illegal immigrants. Leaders attending a MERCOSUR-EU summit meeting, convened in Madrid, Spain, in May 2010, determined to restart promptly the Association Agreement negotiations. The first discussions took place in Buenos Aires, in July, and subsequently at regular intervals. An announcement made in April 2012 by the Argentine Government that is was to renationalize the petroleum company YPF, of which the Spanish company Repsol had hitherto been the majority shareholder, was expected to impact negatively on the MERCOSUR–EU negotiations process. In May the EU filed a complaint with the World Trade Organization (WTO) contesting restrictions on imports imposed (since 2005) by Argentina. The ninth round of negotiations on an Association Agreement, were held in October 2012, in Brazil. Further discussions were held in January 2013 on the sidelines of the first EU–Community of Latin American and Caribbean States (CELAC) summit meeting, convened in Santiago, Chile. An initial deadline of December 2013 for the exchange of proposals on trade liberalization between MERCOSUR and the EU was postponed, with a view to enabling all participating states to present their individual initiatives. In August 2014 it was reported that an agreement had been concluded between Argentina, Brazil, Paraguay and Uruguay for a trade proposal covering 90% of imports to be presented to the next meeting with EU negotiators.

At a summit of MERCOSUR heads of state convened in July 2013, in Montevideo, Argentina, Brazil, Uruguay and Venezuela

announced the recall of their ambassadors from France, Italy, Portugal and Spain, in protest against the diversion from those countries' airspace of a flight carrying the Bolivian President, Evo Morales, following speculation that Edward Snowden, an information specialist wanted for questioning by the US security services, and who had requested political asylum in several Latin American countries, might be on board the aircraft.

Regional integration and co-operation were the principal focus of the sixth summit of the Americas, held in Cartagena, Colombia, in April 2012, on the theme 'Connecting the Americas: Partners for Prosperity'.

In December 2007 MERCOSUR signed a free trade accord with Israel, which entered into effect in January 2010. At the meeting of heads of state, held in San Miguel de Tucumán, Argentina, in July 2008, a preferential trade agreement was signed with the Southern African Customs Union. Framework agreements on the preparation of free trade accords were also signed with Turkey and Jordan. In June 2009 a preferential trade agreement with India entered into force. A framework agreement on trade with Morocco entered into effect in April 2010. In August MERCOSUR signed a free trade agreement with Egypt, and in December MERCOSUR signed a trade and economic co-operation agreement with the Palestinian National Authority and a framework agreement to establish a free trade agreement with Syria. Agreements to establish mechanisms for political dialogue and co-operation were signed with Cuba and Turkey at that time.

Finance

The annual budget for the Secretariat is contributed by the full member states.

Publication

Boletín Oficial del MERCOSUR (quarterly).

UNION OF SOUTH AMERICAN NATIONS—UNASUR

Address: Avda 6 de Diciembre N24-04 y Presidente Wilson, Quito, Ecuador.
Telephone: (2) 4010400; **e-mail:** secretaria.general@unasursg.org; **internet:** www.unasursg.org.

The establishment of UNASUR as the lead organization for regional integration—superseding the South American Community of Nations, endorsed in 2004—was approved in April 2007 by the heads of state of 12 Latin American countries.

MEMBERS

Argentina	Guyana
Bolivia	Paraguay
Brazil	Peru
Chile	Suriname
Colombia	Uruguay
Ecuador	Venezuela

Organization
(September 2014)

COUNCIL OF HEADS OF STATE

The member countries' heads of state meet once a year in regular session. The seventh regular summit of UNASUR heads of state was convened in August 2013, in Paramaribo, Suriname. An extraordinary summit was held in July of that year, in Cochabamba, Bolivia. The 2014 summit meeting, to be held in Montevideo, Uruguay, was initially scheduled to be convened in August but, owing to scheduling conflicts among member states, was postponed until October.

COUNCIL OF MINISTERS OF FOREIGN AFFAIRS

UNASUR ministers responsible for foreign affairs gather at six-monthly intervals. The Council adopts resolutions to be approved for implementation by the Council of Heads of State.

COUNCIL OF DELEGATES

Comprises one representative from each member state. The Council elaborates decisions, resolutions and regulations to be reviewed by the Council of Ministers of Foreign Affairs. Meetings are usually convened every two months.

SECTORAL MINISTERIAL COUNCILS

There are South American ministerial councils covering citizen security, justice and the fight against transnational organized crime; culture; defence; combating drugs-trafficking; economy and finance; education; elections; energy; health; infrastructure and planning; science, technology and innovation; and social development.

SECRETARIAT

The Secretary-General, who serves a two-year term of office, is elected by UNASUR heads of state.
Secretary-General: Dr ERNESTO SAMPER (Colombia).

The Lima Centre for Communication and Information aims to further regional integration through the use of ICTs.

Activities

In December 2004 leaders from 12 Latin American countries attending a pan-South American summit, convened in Cusco, Peru, approved in principle the creation of a new South American Community of Nations (SACN), to entail the merger of the Andean Community, MERCOSUR and ALADI, with the additional participation of Chile, Guyana and Suriname. The first SACN meeting of heads of state was held in September, in Brasília, Brazil. In April 2007, at the first South American Energy Summit, convened in Margarita Island, Venezuela, heads of state endorsed the establishment of UNASUR to replace SACN as the lead organization for regional integration. UNASUR was to have political decision-making functions and was to co-ordinate with the Andean Community,

MERCOSUR and ALADI on economic and trade matters. The constituent treaty establishing UNASUR was signed by heads of state meeting in Brasília, Brazil, in May 2008, and entered into force in March 2011, having received the required nine ratifications. It was envisaged that eventually a regional UNASUR parliament would be established in Cochabamba, Bolivia. In November 2012 the sixth UNASUR summit of heads of states, convened in Lima, Peru, signed an Additional Protocol on Commitment to Democracy; this entered into force in March 2014, and provided for the exclusion from participation in meetings of the Union of any member state suffering an interruption to its democratic order.

In June 2012 Paraguay was suspended from participation in meetings of the Union by an emergency summit convened in view of the undemocratic impeachment of that country's president, Fernando Lugo. Paraguay was readmitted following the inauguration on 15 August 2013 of Horacio Cartes, elected as the new president in April.

ECONOMICS AND FINANCE

The South American Economy and Finance Council, inaugurated in August 2009, has participation by ministers of economy, ministers of finance and presidents of member states' central banks. It aims to foster inclusive human and social development; economic development and growth aimed at reducing inequalities between states; and regional financial integration. The Council promotes the use of local currencies.

In September 2009 UNASUR heads of state determined to establish a regional bank, Banco del Sur, to promote economic independence from international lending institutions. Banco del Sur commenced preliminary operations in June 2013.

The establishment of a regional forum to settle investment disputes, to supersede, locally, the functions of the International Centre for the Settlement of Investment Disputes (from which Bolivia, Ecuador and Venezuela had decided to withdraw, respectively, in 2007, 2009 and 2012) is under consideration.

In June 2014 the Council of Heads of State issued a statement of solidarity with the Argentinian Government and people, with respect to a recent US Supreme Court ruling that Argentina should pay in full some US $1,300m. to US hedge fund investors (representing a minority of holders of the outstanding sovereign debt) who had refused to participate in debt restructuring arrangements agreed for Argentina in 2005 and 2010—thereby blocking funds allocated towards paying debt interest due to participating bondholders. In July 2014 the Banco del Sur Board of Directors reiterated this position.

In 2014 the creation of a broad Latin American and Caribbean sustainable economic development zone was under consideration by UNASUR, MERCOSUR, the Bolivarian Alliance for the Peoples of our America, Petrocaribe and the Community of Latin American and Caribbean States.

EDUCATION AND CULTURE

The South American Council on Education was established in November 2012. A five-year work plan, covering the period 2013–17, included initiatives on improving quality and equity in education (including through promoting access to the educational use of ICTs, and the development of education policies committed to raising environmental awareness and sustainable development); analysing South American citizenship in education in member states; and a comparative study of educational systems. The South American Council on Culture, also established in November 2012, was in 2013–14 pursuing a work plan covering the following priority areas: cultural industries; inter-cultural activities; protection and preservation of cultural heritage; and communication and culture. The first meeting of ministers of culture, held in June 2013, launched the 'Bank of Audiovisual Content' and 'Southern Express' projects, which aimed to strengthen regional cultural integration. In December 2013 a UNASUR Forum on Science, Technology, Innovation and Industrialization in the South was convened, in Rio de Janeiro, Brazil. A regional ministerial meeting on Education for All in Latin America and the Caribbean, tasked with adopting an agenda to guide regional education policy during 2015–30, was to be held in October 2014, in Lima, Peru.

DEFENCE AND REGIONAL SOLIDARITY

A South American Defence Council (Consejo de Defensa Suramericano—CDS) was inaugurated in Santiago, Chile, in March 2009, to oversee regional military co-ordination. In May a UNASUR centre for strategic defence studies (Centro de Estudios Estratégicos de la Defensa—CEED) was inaugurated in Buenos Aires, Argentina. In February 2014 the CDS endorsed the proposed establishment of a South American Defence College (Escuela Suramericana de Defensa—ESUDE), which was to offer military training to member states' armed forces. In August UNASUR ministers of defence adopted a regulatory framework for ESUDE. A South American

Registry of Defence Expenses is maintained by the CDS. The CDS is developing a series of maps that plot natural disaster risks.

In November 2012 UNASUR heads of states adopted the Declaration of Lima, comprising some 16 actions aimed at promoting regional integration, 'building a South American citizenship', and the development of a regional zone of peace.

In April 2014, in response to the eruption in Venezuela from February of violent protests against prevailing social and economic conditions, UNASUR initiated and mediated a formal dialogue between representatives of the Venezuelan Government and opposition elements; UNASUR was represented at the negotiations by the ministers responsible for foreign affairs of Brazil, Colombia and Ecuador. In late May representatives of the opposition suspended participation in the dialogue process, citing the lack of progress achieved on matters such as the release of detained anti-government protesters, and recent large-scale arrests of demonstrating students.

COMBATING ORGANIZED CRIME

In October 2009 a Council on Combating Drugs Trafficking was established, with participation by regional ministers of the interior and anti-narcotics police chiefs. In October 2010 the Council adopted a joint action plan aimed at addressing drugs-related problems in the region, including consumption and addiction; trafficking; and related organized crime and money laundering. In November 2012 a Council of Citizen Security, Justice and Fight Against Transnational Organized Crime was established. In November 2013 the Council agreed a joint work programme for developing strengthened legislation aimed at combating money laundering in the region. In late 2014 the development of a new 'Corte Penal'—a UNASUR criminal court to be tasked with addressing transnational crime—was under way.

ELECTIONS

UNASUR convenes election observation missions with the aim of promoting regional co-operation and democratic participation. A UNASUR Electoral Council was established in June 2012. The grouping's inaugural election observation mission monitored a general election held in November 2011 in Guyana. UNASUR subsequently dispatched teams of observers to monitor presidential elections held in Venezuela in October 2012 and again in April 2013, and municipal elections held there in December; the presidential election held in Paraguay in April 2013; a presidential election held in Ecuador in February 2013, and local elections held there in February 2014; and legislative and presidential elections held in Colombia in March and May–June, respectively.

INFRASTRUCTURE AND PLANNING

In November 2012 UNASUR heads of state approved a strategic plan, developed by the Council on Infrastructure and Planning, and covering the period 2013–22, which provided for investments totalling US $116,000m. in projects aimed at developing the regional infrastructure, including five schemes for the construction of roads and railways lines linking Brazil, Colombia, Guyana, Suriname and Venezuela. At that time the regional heads of state also affirmed their intention of promoting the intensive use of information technology, universal internet access, and the construction of a regional fibre optic ring.

SOCIAL DEVELOPMENT

In March 2011 UNASUR's Social Council (UNASUR-Social), convened in Guyana, reviewed progress in the implementation of UNASUR's first plan of action on social development; the plan, adopted in 2009, covered the period 2009–11, and set out guidelines for the advancement of common social development policies among the grouping's member states, as well as for the establishment of technical working groups on social development. A meeting of the Council held in November 2012, in Lima, Peru, adopted a second plan of action—Agenda Priority Social Action—to guide the organization's activities relating to social development during 2012–14. The second plan focused on combating inequality and poverty in the region, addressing the alleviation of malnutrition, and the promotion of citizen participation and of a social- and solidarity-based communal economy, providing for the promotion of opportunity and social inclusion. Meeting in August 2014 the Council addressed the development of a new plan, to cover the period 2015–17.

EXTERNAL AFFAIRS

In November 2012 UNASUR heads of state approved Policy Guidelines for Relations with Third Parties, reaffirming regional commitment to the promotion of dialogue and co-operation with other regional groupings, states and entities.

In August 2010, in response to the earthquake that had devastated parts of Haiti in January of that year, UNASUR established the Technical Secretariat of UNASUR-Haiti; by the end of 2012 UNA-

SUR-Haiti had supported the implementation of 144 projects in that country.

An emergency summit of UNASUR ministers responsible for foreign affairs met in mid-August 2012, in Guayaquil, Ecuador, to discuss perceived intimidation from the United Kingdom authorities concerning the territorial integrity of Ecuador's diplomatic mission to London, following Ecuador's granting in that month of political asylum to Julian Assange, the founder of 'WikiLeaks', who had sought sanctuary in its embassy; the summit adopted a resolution reiterating the inviolability of embassies and supporting Ecuador's right to grant asylum to Assange. In July 2013 an emergency meeting of UNASUR heads of state, held in in Cochabamba, Bolivia, condemned the recent refusal of France, Italy, Portugal and Spain to grant a flight from Moscow, Russia, that was carrying the Bolivian President, Evo Morales, access to their airspace, reportedly owing to their belief that Edward Snowden—a former computer analyst at the US National Security Agency who had publicized secret security material—was also on board the aircraft; the leaders demanded an apology from the governments concerned. The seventh UNASUR summit, convened in late August in Paramaribo, Suriname, reiter-ated the condemnation, and strongly rejected the alleged interception of telecommunications and espionage actions in member states by the US National Security Agency or other bodies.

Regular Africa-South America ('ASA') summits are convened by UNASUR and the African Union. The third ASA summit took place in May 2012, in Malabo, Equatorial Guinea, and the fourth was to be held in Ecuador in 2016. Arab-South American ('ASPA') summit meetings are also convened, most recently in October 2013, in Lima, Peru. An Arab-South American Business Forum is organized on the sidelines of the ASPA summits.

Finance

An annual budget of US $9.8m. was approved for 2014. Member states' payments are assessed on a quota basis, with Brazil (39%), Argentina (16%) and Venezuela (12.4%) making the largest contributions.

OTHER REGIONAL ORGANIZATIONS

Agriculture, Food, Forestry and Fisheries

(For organizations concerned with agricultural commodities, see Commodities)

CAB International (CABI): Nosworthy Way, Wallingford, Oxon, OX10 8DE, United Kingdom; tel. (1491) 832111; fax (149) 1833508; e-mail enquiries@cabi.org; internet www.cabi.org; f. 1929 as the Imperial Agricultural Bureaux (later Commonwealth Agricultural Bureaux), current name adopted in 1985; aims to improve human welfare worldwide through the generation, dissemination and application of scientific knowledge in support of sustainable devt; places particular emphasis on sustainable agriculture, forestry, human health and the management of natural resources, with priority given to the needs of developing countries; a separate microbiology centre, in Egham, Surrey (UK), undertakes research, consultancy, training, capacity building and institutional devt measures in sustainable pest management, biosystematics and molecular biology, ecological applications and environmental and industrial microbiology; compiles and publishes extensive information (in a variety of print and electronic forms) on aspects of agriculture, forestry, veterinary medicine, the environment and natural resources, and Third World rural devt; maintains regional centres in the People's Republic of China, India, Kenya, Malaysia, Pakistan, Switzerland, Trinidad and Tobago, and the USA; mems: 45 countries and territories; Chair. JOHN RIPLEY (United Kingdom); CEO Dr TREVOR NICHOLLS (United Kingdom).

Inter-American Tropical Tuna Commission (IATTC): 8901 La Jolla Shores Drive, La Jolla, CA 92037-1509, USA; tel. (858) 546-7100; fax (858) 546-7133; e-mail info@iattc.org; internet www.iattc.org; f. 1950; administers two programmes, the Tuna-Billfish Programme and the Tuna-Dolphin Programme; the principal responsibilities of the Tuna-Billfish Programme are to study the biology of the tunas and related species of the eastern Pacific Ocean to estimate the effects of fishing and natural factors on their abundance; to recommend appropriate conservation measures in order to maintain stocks at levels which will afford maximum sustainable catches; and to collect information on compliance with Commission resolutions; the principal functions of the Tuna-Dolphin Programme are to monitor the abundance of dolphins and their mortality incidental to purse-seine fishing in the eastern Pacific Ocean; to study the causes of mortality of dolphins during fishing operations and to promote the use of fishing techniques and equipment that minimize these mortalities; to study the effects of different fishing methods on the various fish and other animals of the pelagic ecosystem; and to provide a secretariat for the International Dolphin Conservation Programme; mems: Belize, Canada, People's Republic of China, Colombia, Costa Rica, Ecuador, El Salvador, European Union, France, Guatemala, Japan, Kiribati, Republic of Korea, Mexico, Nicaragua, Panama, Peru, Chinese Taipei (Taiwan), USA, Vanuatu, Venezuela; co-operating non-contracting parties: Bolivia, Cook Islands, Honduras, Indonesia; Dir GUILLERMO A. COMPEÁN; publs *Bulletin* (irregular), *Annual Report*, *Fishery Status Report*, *Stock Assessment Report* (annually), *Special Report* (irregular).

International Centre for Tropical Agriculture (Centro Internacional de Agricultura Tropical—CIAT): Apdo Aéreo 6713, Cali, Colombia; tel. (2) 445-0000; fax (2) 445-0073; e-mail ciat@cgiar.org; internet www.ciat.cgiar.org; f. 1967 to contribute to the alleviation of hunger and poverty in tropical developing countries by using new techniques in agriculture research and training; focuses on production problems in field beans, cassava, rice and tropical pastures in the tropics; Dir-Gen. RUBEN G. ECHEVERRÍA; publs *Annual Report*, *Growing Affinities* (2 a year), *Pasturas Tropicales* (3 a year), catalogue of publications.

International Food Policy Research Institute (IFPRI): 2033 K St, NW, Washington, DC 20006, USA; tel. (202) 862-5600; fax (202) 467-4439; e-mail ifpri@cgiar.org; internet www.ifpri.org; f. 1975; co-operates with academic and other institutions in further research; develops policies for cutting hunger and malnutrition; committed to increasing public awareness of food policies; participates in the Agricultural Market Information System (f. 2011); calculates an annual Global Hunger Index, measuring global, regional and national rates of hunger; Dir-Gen. SHENGGEN FAN (People's Republic of China).

South Pacific Regional Fisheries Management Organisation: POB 3797, Wellington 6140, New Zealand; tel. (4) 499-9889; fax (4) 473-9579; e-mail secretariat@southpacificrfmo.org; internet www.southpacificrfmo.org; f. Aug. 2013 with the entry into force of the Convention on the Conservation and Management of High Seas Fishery resources in the South Pacific Ocean (negotiations for which had commenced in 2005); committed to the long-term conservation and sustainable use of the fishery resources of the South Pacific Ocean; Chair. BILL MANSFIELD; Exec. Sec. JOHANNE FISCHER.

Arts and Culture

Caribbean American Cultural Caucus: Caribbean American Cultural Caucus Inc., 122–15 Lakeview Lane, POB 300389, Jamaica, NY 11430, USA; tel. (646) 395-0288; e-mail info@caccus.org; internet www.caccus.org; aims to promote and develop the Caribbean entertainment industry in the region and among diaspora; forms partnerships with global orgs oriented towards promoting Caribbean culture, collaborates with industry experts and hosts educational workshops and conferences; inaugural Caribbean Cultural Conference held in New York in 2009; Chair. JUNIOR FORBES.

International Association of Art (IAA Latin America and the Caribbean): 1 rue Miollis, 75732 Paris; tel. 1-45-68-44-54; e-mail iaa.aiap@gmail.com; internet www.aiap-iaa.org; facilitates regional bodies and asscns; co-ordinates regional events as the representative body of the International Association of Art; Int. Pres. ROSA-MARIA BURRILLO (Mexico); Regional Co-ordinator ULISES ROMAN.

Organization of World Heritage Cities: 835 Ave Wilfrid-Laurier, Québec, QC G1R 2L3, Canada; tel. (418) 692-0000; fax (418) 692-5558; e-mail secretariat@ovpm.org; internet www.ovpm.org; f. 1993 to assist cities inscribed on the UNESCO World Heritage List to implement the Convention concerning the Protection of the World Cultural and Natural Heritage (1972); promotes co-operation between city authorities, in particular in the management and sustainable devt of historic sites; holds a World Congress every two years (2013: Oaxaca, Mexico, in Nov.); mems: 250 cities worldwide; Sec.-Gen. DENIS RICARD; publ. *OWHC Newsletter* (2 a year).

Commodities

Alliance of Cocoa Producing Countries (COPAL): National Assembly Complex, Tafawa Balewa Sq., POB 1718, Lagos, Nigeria; tel. (9) 8141735; fax (9) 8141734; e-mail info@copal-cpa.org; internet www.copal-cpa.org; f. 1962 to exchange technical and scientific information, to discuss problems of mutual concern to producers, to ensure adequate supplies at remunerative prices and to promote consumption; organizes a Research Conference (Oct. 2012: Yaoundé, Cameroon); mems: Brazil, Cameroon, Côte d'Ivoire, Dominican Republic, Gabon, Ghana, Malaysia, Nigeria, São Tomé and Príncipe, Togo; Sec.-Gen. NANGA COULIBALY.

Gas Exporting Countries Forum: POB 23753, Tornado Tower, 47-48th Floors, West Bay, Doha, Qatar; tel. 44048400; fax 44048415; e-mail gecfsg@gmail.com; internet www.gecf.org; f. 2001 to represent and promote the mutual interests of gas exporting countries; aims to increase the level of co-ordination among mem. countries and to promote dialogue between gas producers and consumers; a ministerial meeting is convened annually; the seventh ministerial meeting, convened in Moscow, Russia, in Dec. 2008, agreed on a charter and a permanent structure for the grouping; first meeting of heads of state convened in Doha, in 2011; second summit meeting held in Moscow, in July 2013; mems: Algeria, Bolivia, Egypt, Equatorial Guinea, Iran, Libya, Nigeria, Oman, Qatar, Russia, Trinidad and Tobago, UAE, Venezuela; observers: Iraq, Kazakhstan, Netherlands, Norway; Sec.-Gen. SEYED MOHAMMAD HOSSEIN ADELI.

International Cocoa Organization (ICCO): Westgate House, Ealing, London, W5 1YY, United Kingdom; tel. (20) 8991-6000; fax (20) 8997-4372; e-mail info@icco.org; internet www.icco.org; f. 1973 under the first International Cocoa Agreement, 1972; the ICCO supervises the implementation of the agreements, and provides mem. govts with up-to-date information on the world cocoa economy; the seventh International Cocoa Agreement (2010) entered into force in Oct. 2012; mems: 18 exporting countries and 30 importing countries, plus the European Union; Exec. Dir Dr JEAN-MARC ANGA

(Côte d'Ivoire); publs *Quarterly Bulletin of Cocoa Statistics, Annual Report, World Cocoa Directory,* studies on the world cocoa economy.

International Coffee Organization (ICO): 22 Berners St, London, W1T 3DD, United Kingdom; tel. (20) 7612-0600; fax (20) 7612-0630; e-mail info@ico.org; internet www.ico.org; f. 1963 under the International Coffee Agreement, 1962, which was renegotiated in 1968, 1976, 1983, 1994 (extended in 1999), 2001 and 2007; aims to improve international co-operation and provide a forum for intergovernmental consultations on coffee matters; to facilitate international trade in coffee by the collection, analysis and dissemination of statistics; to act as a centre for the collection, exchange and publication of coffee information; to promote studies in the field of coffee; and to encourage an increase in coffee consumption; mems: 39 exporting countries and 5 importing countries, plus the European Union; Exec. Dir ROBÉRIO OLIVEIRA SILVA (Brazil).

International Energy Forum (IEF): POB 94736, Diplomatic Quarter, Riyadh 11614, Saudi Arabia; tel. (1) 4810022; fax (1) 4810055; e-mail info@ief.org; internet www.ief.org; f. 1991; the IEF is an intergovernmental arrangement aimed at promoting dialogue on global energy matters among its membership; ministers responsible for energy affairs from states accounting for about 90% of global oil and gas supply and demand convene every two years; the gathering in recent years has been preceded by a meeting of the International Business Energy Forum, comprising energy ministers and CEOs of leading energy cos; 14th IEF: May 2014, Moscow, Russia; mems: 89 states, including the mems of OPEC and the International Energy Agency; Sec.-Gen. ALDO FLORES-QUIROGA.

International Rubber Research and Development Board (IRRDB): POB 10150, 50908 Kuala Lumpur, Malaysia; tel. (3) 42521612; fax (3) 42560487; e-mail sec_gen@theirrdb.org; internet www.irrdb.com; f. 1960 following the merger of International Rubber Regulation Committee (f. 1934) and International Rubber Research Board (f. 1937); mems: 19 natural rubber research institutes; Sec. Dr ABDUL AZIZ B. S. A. KADIR (Malaysia).

International Sugar Organization: 1 Canada Sq., Canary Wharf, London, E14 5AA, United Kingdom; tel. (20) 7513-1144; fax (20) 7513-1146; e-mail enquiries@isosugar.org; internet www.isosugar.org; administers the International Sugar Agreement (1992), with the objectives of stimulating co-operation, facilitating trade and encouraging demand; aims to improve conditions in the sugar market through debate, analysis and studies; serves as a forum for discussion; holds annual seminars and workshops; sponsors projects from developing countries; mems: 87 countries producing some 86% of total world sugar; Exec. Dir JOSÉ ORIVE; publs *Sugar Year Book, Statistical Bulletin, Monthly Market Report, Quarterly Market Outlook,* seminar proceedings.

International Tropical Timber Organization (ITTO): International Organizations Center, 5th Floor, Pacifico-Yokohama, 1-1-1, Minato-Mirai, Nishi-ku, Yokohama 220-0012, Japan; tel. (45) 223-1110; fax (45) 223-1111; e-mail itto@itto.int; internet www.itto.int; f. 1985 under the International Tropical Timber Agreement (ITTA, 1983); subsequently, a new treaty, ITTA 1994, came into force in 1997, and this was replaced by ITTA 2006, which entered into force in Dec. 2011; provides a forum for consultation and co-operation between countries that produce and consume tropical timber, and is dedicated to the sustainable devt and conservation of tropical forests; facilitates progress towards 'Objective 2000', which aims to move as rapidly as possible towards achieving exports of tropical timber and timber products from sustainably managed resources; encourages, through policy and project work, forest management, conservation and restoration, the further processing of tropical timber in producing countries, and the gathering and analysis of market intelligence and economic information; mems: 28 producing and 37 consuming countries and the European Union; Exec. Dir EMMANUEL ZE MEKA (Cameroon); publs *Annual Review, Market Information Service* (every 2 weeks), *Tropical Forest Update* (quarterly).

Kimberley Process: e-mail kpcs.chair@dmr.gov.za; internet www.kimberleyprocess.com; launched following a meeting of Southern African diamond-producing states, held in May 2000 in Kimberley, South Africa, to address means of halting the trade in 'conflict diamonds' and of ensuring that revenue derived from diamond sales would henceforth not be used to fund rebel movements aiming to undermine legitimate govts; in Dec. of that year a landmark UN General Assembly resolution was adopted supporting the creation of an international certification scheme for rough diamonds; accordingly, the Kimberley Process Certification Scheme (KPCS), detailing requirements for controlling production of and trade in 'conflict-free' rough diamonds, entered into force on 1 Jan. 2003; it was estimated in 2013 that participating states accounted for 99.8% of global rough diamond production; a review of the core objectives and definitions of the Process was undertaken during 2012–13; participating countries, with industry and civil society observers, meet twice a year; working groups and cttees also convene frequently; implementation of the KPCS is monitored through 'review visits', annual reports, and through ongoing exchange and analysis of statistical data; mems: 54

participants representing 81 countries (the European Union is a single participating mem. representing its 27 mem. states); observers incl. the World Diamond Council; chaired, on a rotating basis, by participating states (2014: China).

Organization of the Petroleum Exporting Countries (OPEC): 1010 Vienna, Helferstorferstr. 17; tel. (1) 211-12-279; fax (1) 214-98-27; e-mail prid@opec.org; internet www.opec.org; f. 1960 to unify and co-ordinate mems' petroleum policies and to safeguard their interests generally; holds regular conferences of mem. countries to set reference prices and production levels; conducts research in energy studies, economics and finance; provides data services and news services covering petroleum and energy issues; mems: Algeria, Angola, Ecuador, Iran, Iraq, Kuwait, Libya, Nigeria, Qatar, Saudi Arabia, United Arab Emirates, Venezuela; Sec.-Gen. ABDULLA SALEM EL-BADRI (Libya); publs *Annual Report, Annual Statistical Bulletin, OPEC Bulletin* (10 year), *Monthly Oil Market Report, World Oil Outlook* (annually).

Petrocaribe: e-mail info@petrocaribe.org; internet www.petrocaribe.org; f. June 2005; an initiative of the Venezuelan Govt to enhance the access of countries in the Caribbean region to petroleum on preferential payment terms; aims to co-ordinate the devt of energy policies and plans regarding natural resources among signatory countries; seventh summit held in Caracas, Venezuela, in May 2013, resolved to establish an economic zone, in collaboration with ALBA-TCP, to promote intra-regional devt projects, trade, food security and tourism; the proposal was reconfirmed by heads of state and govt meeting in Caracas, in Dec., along with plans to elaborate and co-ordinate the economic zone; efforts were to be made to incorporate mems of Mercosur into the new grouping; mems: Antigua and Barbuda, Bahamas, Belize, Cuba, Dominica, Dominican Republic, El Salvador, Grenada, Guyana, Haiti, Honduras, Jamaica, Nicaragua, Saint Christopher and Nevis, Saint Lucia, Saint Vincent and the Grenadines, Suriname, Venezuela.

Regional Association of Oil and Natural Gas Companies in Latin America and the Caribbean (Asociación Regional de Empresas de Petróleo y Gas Natural en Latinoamérica y el Caribe—ARPEL): Javier de Viana 1018, 11200 Montevideo, Uruguay; tel. 2410 6993; fax 2410 9207; e-mail info@arpel.org.uy; internet www.arpel.org; f. 1965 as the Mutual Assistance of the Latin American Oil Companies; aims to initiate and implement activities for the devt of the oil and natural gas industry in Latin America and the Caribbean; promotes the expansion of business opportunities and the improvement of the competitive advantages of its mems; promotes guidelines in support of competition in the sector; and supports the efficient and sustainable exploitation of hydrocarbon resources and the supply of products and services. Works in co-operation with int. orgs, govts, regulatory agencies, technical institutions, univs and non-governmental orgs; mems: 28 state-owned enterprises, representing more than 90% of regional operations, in Argentina, Bolivia, Brazil, Canada, Chile, Colombia, Costa Rica, Cuba, Ecuador, Jamaica, Mexico, Nicaragua, Paraguay, Peru, Suriname, Trinidad and Tobago, Uruguay, Venezuela; Exec. Sec. JORGE CIACCIARELLI; publ. *Boletín Técnico.*

Sugar Association of the Caribbean (Inc.): c/o Caroni, Brechin Castle, Trinidad and Tobago; f. 1942; administers the West Indies Central Sugar Cane Breeding Station (in Barbados) and the West Indies Sugarcane Breeding and Evaluation Network; mems: nat. sugar cos of Barbados, Belize, Guyana, Jamaica and Trinidad and Tobago, and Sugar Asscn of St Kitts–Nevis–Anguilla; publs *SAC Handbook, SAC Annual Report, Proceedings of Meetings of WI Sugar Technologists.*

West Indian Sea Island Cotton Association (Inc.): c/o Barbados Agricultural Development Corporation, Fairy Valley, Christ Church, Barbados; mems: orgs in Antigua and Barbuda, Barbados, Jamaica, Montserrat and Saint Christopher and Nevis.

World Diamond Council: 580 Fifth Ave, 28th Floor, New York, NY 10036, USA; tel. (212) 575-8848; fax (212) 840-0496; e-mail worlddiamondcouncil@gmail.com; internet www.worlddiamondcouncil.com; f. 2000, by a resolution passed at the World Diamond Congress, convened in July by the World Federation of Diamond Bourses, with the aim of promoting responsibility within the diamond industry towards its stakeholders; lobbied for the creation of a certification scheme to prevent trade in 'conflict diamonds', and became an observer of the ensuing Kimberley Process Certification Scheme, launched in Jan. 2003; has participated in review visits to Kimberley Process participating countries; in Oct. 2002 approved—and maintains—a voluntary System of Warranties, enabling dealers, jewellery manufacturers and retailers to pass on assurances that polished diamonds derive from certified 'conflict-free' rough diamonds, with the aim of extending the effectiveness of the Kimberley Process beyond the export and import phase; meets annually; mems: more than 50 diamond and jewellery industry orgs; Pres. EDWARD ASSCHER.

Development and Economic Co-operation

Amazon Co-operation Treaty Organization: SHIS-QI 05, Conjunto 16, casa 21, Lago Sul, Brasília, DF 71615-160, Brazil; tel. (61) 3248-4119; fax (61) 3248-4238; internet www.otca.org.br; f. 1978, permanent secretariat established 1995; aims to promote the co-ordinated and sustainable devt of the Amazonian territories; there are regular meetings of ministers of foreign affairs; there are specialized co-ordinators of environment, health, science technology and education, infrastructure, tourism, transport and communications, and of indigenous affairs; mems: Bolivia, Brazil, Colombia, Ecuador, Guyana, Peru, Suriname, Venezuela; Sec.-Gen. ROBBY DEWNARAIN RAMLAKHAN (Brazil); Exec. Dir MAURICIO DORFLER.

Asia-Pacific Economic Cooperation (APEC): 35 Heng Mui Keng Terrace, Singapore 119616; tel. 68919600; fax 68919690; e-mail info@apec.org; internet www.apec.org; f. 1989 as an informal consultative forum to promote multilateral economic co-operation in the Asia-Pacific region; aims to promote free and open trade and investment, to accelerate regional economic integration, encourage economic and technical co-operation, and to aid in the development of a favourable business environment in the region; an annual meeting of economic leaders is held to uphold the commitments outlined in the group's mandate: the 20th Economic Leaders' Meeting was convened in September 2012, in Vladivostok, Russia; mems: Australia, Brunei, Canada, Chile, People's Republic of China, Hong Kong, Indonesia, Japan, Republic of Korea, Malaysia, Mexico, New Zealand, Papua New Guinea, Peru, Philippines, Russia, Singapore, Taiwan (as Chinese Taipei), Thailand and Viet Nam; Exec. Dir. Dr ALAN BOLLARD (New Zealand).

Association of Caribbean States (ACS): 5–7 Sweet Briar Rd, St Clair, POB 660, Port of Spain, Trinidad and Tobago; tel. 622-9575; fax 622-1653; e-mail mail@acs-aec.org; internet www.acs-aec.org; f. 1994 by the govts of the 13 CARICOM countries and Colombia, Costa Rica, Cuba, Dominican Republic, El Salvador, Guatemala, Haiti, Honduras, Mexico, Nicaragua, Suriname and Venezuela; aims to promote economic integration, sustainable devt and co-operation in the region; to preserve the environmental integrity of the Caribbean Sea which is regarded as the common patrimony of the peoples of the region; to undertake concerted action to protect the environment, particularly the Caribbean Sea; and to co-operate in the areas of trade, transport, sustainable tourism, and natural disasters. Policy is determined by a Ministerial Council and implemented by a Secretariat based in Port of Spain. The fourth ACS summit meeting of heads of state and govt was held in Panama, in July 2005. A final declaration included resolutions to strengthen co-operation mechanisms with the European Union and to promote a strategy for the Caribbean Sea Zone to be recognized as a special area for the purposes of sustainable devt programmes, support for a strengthened social agenda and efforts to achieve the Millennium Development Goals, and calls for mem. states to sign or ratify the following accords: an ACS Agreement for Regional Co-operation in the area of Natural Disasters; a Convention Establishing the Sustainable Tourism Zone of the Caribbean; and an ACS Air Transport Agreement. The fifth summit was held in Haiti, in April 2013; a final Plan of Action incorporated commitments to strengthen co-operation in sustainable tourism, the promotion of trade, transport, disaster risk reduction, and education, culture, science and technology; signed a Memorandum of Understanding with the UN World Tourism Organization in Feb. 2014 to strengthen collaboration in sustainable tourism; the sixth summit meeting was held in Mexico in April; mems: 28 signatory states, 5 assoc. mems, 20 observers, 6 founding observer countries; Sec.-Gen. Dr ALFONSO MUÑERA CAVADÍA (Colombia).

BRICS: informal grouping of large emerging economies, comprising Brazil, Russia, India, the People's Republic of China, and South Africa (which together accounted for some 20% of global gross domestic product in 2011); known as BRIC prior to the accession of South Africa in Dec. 2010; convened an inaugural summit of heads of states and govt in June 2009, in Yekaterinburg, Russia, at which principles for future co-operation and devt were adopted; a second summit was held in April 2010, in Brasília, Brazil; and a third in Sanya, China, in April 2011, which adopted the Sanya Declaration, outlining the future deepening of co-operation in areas including trade, energy, finance and industry; a fourth summit, convened in New Delhi, India, in March 2012, directed mem. state ministers responsible for finance to examine the feasibility of establishing a Development Bank to mobilize resources in support of infrastructure and sustainable development projects in BRICS economies, other emerging economies, and developing countries, with the aim of supplementing the existing efforts of multilateral and regional financial institutions; the creation of the BRICS Development Bank was approved in principle by the fifth summit, held in Durban,

South Africa, in March 2013; and leaders attending the sixth summit, held in Fortaleza, Brazil, in July 2014, concluded an accord establishing the Bank—which was to be headquartered in Shanghai, People's Republic of China, and was initially to have capital of US \$50,000m., to be provided in equal shares by the five member states—and also establishing a \$100,000m. Contingency Reserve Arrangement; meetings of BRICS ministers responsible for foreign affairs are held every Sept. on the sidelines of the UN General Assembly; regular meetings are also convened of ministers responsible for finance and economics, security, agriculture, trade, and health; BRICS business forums, and meetings of officials of national statistics authorities, are held periodically; mems: Brazil, People's Republic of China, India, Russia, South Africa.

Caribbean-Britain Business Council: Temple Chambers, 3-7 Temple Ave, London, EC4Y 0HP, United Kingdom; tel. (20) 7583-8739; e-mail david.jessop@caribbean-council.org; internet www.caribbean-council.org; f. 2001; promotes trade and investment devt between the United Kingdom, the Caribbean and the European Union; Man. Dir DAVID JESSOP; publs *Caribbean Insight* (weekly), *Cuba Briefing* (weekly).

Council of American Development Foundations (Consejo de Fundaciones Americanas de Desarrollo—SOLIDARIOS): Calle 6 No. 10 Paraíso, Apdo Postal 620, Santo Domingo, Dominican Republic; tel. 549-5111; fax 544-0550; e-mail solidarios@claro.net.do; internet www.redsolidarios.org; f. 1972; exchanges information and experience, arranges technical assistance, raises funds to organize training programmes and scholarships; administers devt fund to finance programmes carried out by mems through a loan guarantee programme; provides consultancy services. Mem. foundations provide technical and financial assistance to low-income groups for rural, housing and micro enterprise devt projects; mems: 18 institutional mems in 9 Latin American and Caribbean countries; Pres. MERCEDES CANALDA; Sec.-Gen. ZULEMA BREA DE VILLAMÁN; publs *Solidarios* (quarterly), *Annual Report*.

G-20 (Doha Round negotiating group): e-mail g-20@mre.gov.br; f. 2003 with the aim of defending the interests of developing countries in the negotiations on agriculture under the WTO's Doha Development Round and meets regularly to address WTO-related agricultural trade issues; now comprises 23 developing countries; mems: Argentina, Bolivia, Brazil, Chile, People's Republic of China, Cuba, Ecuador, Egypt, Guatemala, India, Indonesia, Mexico, Nigeria, Pakistan, Paraguay, Peru, Philippines, South Africa, Tanzania, Thailand, Uruguay, Venezuela, Zimbabwe.

Group of Three (G-3): c/o Secretaría de Relaciones Exteriores, 1 Tlatelolco, Del. Cuauhtémoc, 06995 México, DF, Mexico; e-mail gtres@sre.gob.mx; f. 1990 by Colombia, Mexico and Venezuela to remove restrictions on trade between the three countries; in Nov. 2004 Panama joined the Group, which briefly became the Group of Four until Venezuela's withdrawal in Nov. 2006; the trade agreement covers market access, rules of origin, intellectual property, trade in services, and govt purchases, and entered into force in early 1994. Tariffs on trade between mem. states were to be removed on a phased basis. Co-operation was also envisaged in employment creation, the energy sector and the fight against cholera. The secretariat function rotates between the mem. countries on a two-yearly basis; mems: Colombia, Mexico and Panama.

Group of 15 (G15): G15 Technical Support Facility, 1 route des Morillons, CP 2100, 1218 Grand Saconnex, Geneva, Switzerland; tel. 227916701; fax 227916169; e-mail tsf@g15.org; internet www.g15.org; f. 1989 by 15 developing nations during the ninth summit of the Non-Aligned Movement; retains its original name although current membership totals 17; convenes biennial summits to address the global economic and political situation and to promote economic development through South-South co-operation and North-South dialogue; mems: Algeria, Argentina, Brazil, Chile, Egypt, India, Indonesia, Iran, Jamaica, Kenya, Malaysia, Mexico, Nigeria, Senegal, Sri Lanka, Venezuela, Zimbabwe; Head of Office SAURABH BHANDARI.

Group of 77 (G77): c/o UN Headquarters, Rm NL-2077, New York, NY 10017, USA; tel. (212) 963-4777; fax (212) 963-3515; e-mail secretariat@g77.org; internet www.g77.org; f. 1964 by the 77 signatory states of the Joint Declaration of the Seventy-Seven Countries (the G77 retains its original name, owing to its historic significance, although its membership has expanded since inception); first ministerial meeting, held in Algiers, Algeria, in Oct. 1967, adopted the Charter of Algiers as a basis for G77 co-operation; subsequently G77 Chapters were established with liaison offices in Geneva (UNCTAD), Nairobi (UNEP), Paris (UNESCO), Rome (FAO/IFAD), Vienna (UNIDO), and the Group of 24 (G24) in Washington, DC (IMF and World Bank); as the largest intergovernmental org. of developing states in the UN the G77 aims to enable developing nations to articulate and promote their collective economic interests and to improve their negotiating capacity with regard to global economic issues within the UN system; in Sept. 2006 G77 ministers of foreign affairs, and the People's Republic of China, endorsed the establishment of a new Consortium on Science, Technology and Innovation for the South; a chairperson, who also acts as spokesperson, co-ordinates the G77's activities in each Chapter; the chairmanship rotates on a regional basis between Africa, Asia, and Latin America and the Caribbean; the supreme decision-making body of the G77 is the South Summit, convened for the first time in Havana, Cuba, in April 2000, and then in Doha, Qatar, in June 2005; it is envisaged that the third Summit will be held in Africa; an annual meeting of G77 ministers of foreign affairs is convened at the start (in Sept.) of the regular session of the UN General Assembly; an Intergovernmental Follow-up and Coordination Committee on South-South Cooperation meets every two years; periodic sectoral ministerial meetings are organized in preparation for UNCTAD sessions and prior to the UNIDO and UNESCO General Conferences, and with the aim of promoting South-South co-operation; other special ministerial meetings are also convened from time to time; the first G77 Ministerial Forum on Water Resources was convened in Feb. 2009, in Muscat, Oman; mems: 133 countries.

Inter-American Planning Society (Sociedad Interamericana de Planificación—SIAP): c/o Revista Interamericana de Planificación, Casilla 01-05-1978, Cuenca, Ecuador; tel. (7) 823860; fax (7) 823949; e-mail siap1@siap.org.ec; f. 1956 to promote development of comprehensive planning; mems: institutions and individuals in 46 countries; publs *Correo Informativo* (quarterly), *Inter-American Journal of Planning* (quarterly).

Latin American Association of Development Financing Institutions (Asociación Latinoamericana de Instituciones Financieras para el Desarrollo—ALIDE): Apdo Postal 3988, Paseo de la República 3211, Lima 27, Peru; tel. (1) 4422400; fax (1) 4428105; e-mail sg@alide.org.pe; internet www.alide.org.pe; f. 1968 to promote co-operation among regional devt financing bodies; programmes: technical assistance; training; studies and research; technical meetings; information; projects and investment promotion; mems: more than 70 active, 3 assoc. and 5 collaborating (banks and financing institutions and devt orgs in 22 Latin American countries, Canada, Germany and Spain); Pres. MARÍA SOLEDAD; Sec.-Gen. ROMMEL ACEVEDO FERNANDEZ DE PAREDES; publs *ALIDE Bulletin* (6 a year), *ALIDENOTICIAS Newsletter* (monthly), *Annual Report*, *Latin American Directory of Development Financing Institutions*.

Latin American Economic System (Sistema Económico Latinoamericano—SELA): Torre Europa, 4°, Urb. Campo Alegre, Avda Francisco de Miranda, Caracas 1060, Venezuela; Apdo 17035, Caracas 1010-A, Venezuela; tel. (212) 955-7111; fax (212) 951-5292; e-mail fguglielmelli@sela.org; internet www.sela.org; f. 1975 in accordance with the Panama Convention; aims to foster co-operation and integration among the countries of Latin America and the Caribbean, and to provide a permanent system of consultation and co-ordination in economic and social matters; conducts studies and other analysis and research; extends technical assistance to sub-regional and regional co-ordination bodies; provides library, information service and databases on regional co-operation. The Latin American Council, the principal decision-making body of the System, meets annually at ministerial level and high-level regional consultation and co-ordination meetings are held; acts as the Executive Secretariat of the Working Group on Trade and Competition in Latin America and the Caribbean; mems: 28 countries; Perm. Sec. Dr ROBERTO GUARNIERI (Venezuela); publs *Capítulos del SELA* (3 a year), *Bulletin on Latin America and Caribbean Integration* (monthly), *SELA Antenna in the United States* (quarterly).

Mesoamerican Integration and Development Project (Proyecto de Integración y Desarrollo de Mesoamérica): Urbanización Madre Selva 2, Pasaje E Sur, No. 11, Antiguo Cuscatlán, El Salvador; tel. 2246-0816; fax 2246-0820; e-mail c.trinidad@proyectomesoamerica.org; internet www.proyectomesoamerica.org; f. 2001 as the Puebla-Panamá Plan (PPP); relaunched with formal institutionalized structure in 2004; current name and mandate approved in June 2008 by the Tuxtla summit meeting; aims to promote economic devt and reduce poverty in mem. countries; eight key areas of activity: energy, transport, telecommunications, tourism, trade environment and competitiveness, human devt, sustainable devt, prevention and mitigation of natural disasters; administers the Mesoamerica Biological Corridor initiative to enhance the management of the region's biodiversity; mems: Belize, Colombia, Costa Rica, Dominican Republic, El Salvador, Guatemala, Honduras, Mexico, Nicaragua, Panama; Exec. Dir ELAYNE WHYTE GÓMEZ.

OPEC Fund for International Development: Postfach 995, 1010 Vienna, Austria; tel. (1) 515-64-0; fax (1) 513-92-38; e-mail info@ofid.org; internet www.ofid.org; f. 1976 by mem. countries of OPEC, to provide financial co-operation and assistance in support of social and economic development in low-income countries, and to promote co-operation between OPEC countries and other developing states; in 2012 new approvals amounted to US $1,301.9m., of which $558.0m. was for Africa, $438.6m. for Asia, $204.1m. for Europe, and $101.3m. for Latin America and the Caribbean; mems: Algeria, Ecuador,

Gabon, Indonesia, Iran, Iraq, Kuwait, Libya, Nigeria, Qatar, Saudi Arabia, United Arab Emirates, Venezuela; Dir-Gen. SULEIMAN J. AL-HERBISH (Saudi Arabia); publs *Annual Report*, *OPEC Fund Newsletter* (3 a year).

Organization of the Co-operatives of America (Organización de las Cooperativas de América): Apdo Postal 241263, Carrera 11, No 86-32, Of. 101, Bogotá, Colombia; tel. (1) 6103296; fax (1) 6101912; f. 1963 for improving socio-economic, cultural and moral conditions through the use of the co-operatives system; works in every country of the continent; regional offices sponsor plans and activities based on the most pressing needs and special conditions of individual countries; mems: nat. or local orgs in 23 countries and territories; publs *América Cooperativa* (monthly), *OCA News* (monthly).

Pacific Alliance (Alianza del Pacífico): e-mail info@alianzapacifico.net; internet www.alianzapacifico.net; f. June 2012 when Presidents of Chile, Colombia, Mexico and Peru, meeting in Antofagasta, Chile, signed a framework agreement establishing the Alliance; the inaugural meeting of the Alliance determined to finalize the establishment of a pan-Latin American stock exchange; to bring about the elimination of visa restrictions for citizens of mem. countries; to open joint export promotion offices in Asian countries; to establish a joint univ. system; and to seek to eliminate import duties and country-of-origin rules between mem. states; an agreement to eliminate trade tariffs was concluded at the 2013 presidential summit, held in Santiago de Cali, Colombia, in May; the meeting also resolved to establish a Pacific Alliance Partnership Fund; at the eighth summit meeting, held in Cartagena, Colombia, in Feb. 2014, heads of state signed an agreement to eliminate 92% of trade tariffs on goods and services; at the meeting Costa Rica signed a declaration of accession to the Alliance; the ninth meeting of heads of state was convened in Punta Mita, Mexico, in June; mems: Chile, Colombia, Mexico, Peru; 32 observer states.

Pacific Basin Economic Council (PBEC): 2803–04, 28/F, Harbour Centre, 25 Harbour Rd, Wanchai, Hong Kong SAR; tel. 2815-6550; fax 2545-0499; e-mail info@pbec.org; internet www.pbec.org; f. 1967; an asscn of business representatives aiming to promote business opportunities in the region, in order to enhance overall economic devt; advises govts and serves as a liaison between business leaders and govt officials; encourages business relationships and co-operation among mems; holds business symposia; mems: 20 economies (Australia, Canada, Chile, People's Republic of China, Colombia, Ecuador, Hong Kong SAR, Indonesia, Japan, Republic of Korea, Malaysia, Mexico, New Zealand, Peru, Philippines, Russia, Singapore, Taiwan, Thailand, USA); Chair. WILFRED WONG YING-WAI; publs *PBEC Update* (quarterly), *Executive Summary* (annual conf. report).

Trans-Pacific Strategic Economic Partnership Agreement: c/o Coordinator, Trans-Pacific Partnership, Free Trade Agreement Unit, Ministry of Foreign Affairs and Trade, Private Bag 18901, Wellington, New Zealand; tel. (4) 439-8765; e-mail tpp@mfat.govt.nz; f. 2006 upon entry into force of agreement signed by the four founding mems (the P4, i.e. Brunei, Chile, New Zealand, Singapore); eliminated some 90% of tariffs on trade between mems; negotiations on financial services and investment commenced in March 2008 with the participation of the USA; negotiations on an expanded Trans-Pacific Partnership agreement (TPP), to include, additionally, Australia, Malaysia, Peru and Viet Nam, commenced in March 2010; Canada and Mexico were invited to join the TPP negotiations in June 2012, and Japan joined in April 2013, taking part in negotiations for the first time at the 18th round of talks, held in Brunei, in July; TPP negotiating states' heads of state and govt convened on the sidelines of the APEC summit in Oct. to review progress in the negotiations and to reaffirm their commitment to the process; ministerial meetings were convened in Singapore in Dec. and in Feb. 2014.

World Economic Forum: 91–93 route de la Capite, 1223 Cologny/Geneva, Switzerland; tel. 228691212; fax 227862744; e-mail contact@weforum.org; internet www.weforum.org; f. 1971; the Forum comprises commercial interests gathered on a non-partisan basis, under the stewardship of the Swiss Government, with the aim of improving society through economic devt; convenes an annual meeting in Davos, Switzerland; organizes the following programmes: Technology Pioneers; Women Leaders; and Young Global Leaders; and aims to mobilize the resources of the global business community in the implementation of the following initiatives: the Global Health Initiative; the Disaster Relief Network; the West-Islamic World Dialogue; and the G20/International Monetary Reform Project; the Forum is governed by a guiding Foundation Board; an advisory International Business Council; and an administrative Managing Board; regular mems: representatives of 1,000 leading commercial cos in 56 countries worldwide; selected mem. cos taking a leading role in the movement's activities are known as 'partners'; Exec. Chair. KLAUS MARTIN SCHWAB.

Economics and Finance

Banco del Sur (South American Bank): Caracas, Venezuela; f. Dec. 2007; formal agreement establishing the bank signed in Sept. 2009; aims to provide financing for social and investment projects in South America; auth. cap. US $20,000m.; mems: Argentina, Brazil, Bolivia, Ecuador, Paraguay, Uruguay, Venezuela.

Bank for International Settlements (BIS): Centralbahnplatz 2, 4051 Basel, Switzerland; tel. 612808080; fax 612809100; e-mail email@bis.org; internet www.bis.org; f. pursuant to the Hague Agreements of 1930 to promote co-operation among national central banks and to provide additional facilities for international financial operations; provides the secretariat for the Basel Committee on Banking Supervision and the Financial Stability Board; representative offices in Hong Kong SAR, and Mexico; mems: central banks in 60 countries; Chair. CHRISTIAN NOYER (France); Gen. Man. JAIME CARUANA (Spain); publs *Annual Report, Quarterly Review: International Banking and Financial Market Developments, The BIS Consolidated International Banking Statistics* (every 6 months), *Joint BIS-IMF-OECD-World Bank Statistics on External Debt* (quarterly), *Regular OTC Derivatives Market Statistics* (every 6 months), *Central Bank Survey of Foreign Exchange and Derivatives Market Activity* (every 3 years).

Caribbean Financial Action Task Force: Nicholas Tower, Level 21, 63–65 Independence Sq., Port of Spain, Trinidad and Tobago; tel. 623-9667; fax 623-1297; e-mail cfatf@cfatf.org; internet www.cfatf-gafic.org; f. 1992; co-ordinates and supports efforts by mem. states to uphold implementation of the Financial Action Task Force recommendations, as well as of the 19 'Aruba recommendations' approved at a ministerial meeting held in May 1990; in Jan. 2011 signed a Memorandum of Understanding to provide for greater co-operation with the CARICOM Implementation Agency for Crime and Security (IMPACS); mems: 29 countries; Exec. Dir CALVIN WILSON.

Centre for Latin American Monetary Studies (Centro de Estudios Monetarios Latinoamericanos—CEMLA): Durango 54, Col. Roma, Del. Cuauhtémoc, 06700 México, DF, Mexico; tel. (55) 5061-6640; fax (55) 5061-6695; e-mail cemla@cemla.org; internet www.cemla.org; f. 1952; organizes technical training programmes on monetary policy, devt finance, etc; runs applied research programmes on monetary and central banking policies and procedures; holds regional meetings of banking officials; mems: 30 assoc. mems (Central Banks of Latin America and the Caribbean), 23 co-operating mems (supervisory institutions of the region and non-Latin American Central Banks); Dir-Gen. FERNANDO TENJO GALARZA; publs *Bulletin* (every 2 months), *Monetaria* (quarterly), *Money Affairs* (2 a year).

Eastern Caribbean Central Bank (ECCB): POB 89, Basseterre, St Christopher and Nevis; tel. 465-2537; fax 465-9562; e-mail info@eccb-centralbank.org; internet www.eccb-centralbank.org; f. 1983 by OECS govts; maintains regional currency (Eastern Caribbean dollar) and advises on the economic devt of mem. states; mems: Anguilla, Antigua and Barbuda, Dominica, Grenada, Montserrat, Saint Christopher and Nevis, Saint Lucia, Saint Vincent and the Grenadines; Gov. Sir K. DWIGHT VENNER; Man. Dir JENNIFER NERO.

Equator Principles Association: tel. (1621) 853-900; fax (1621) 731-483; e-mail secretariat@equator-principles.com; internet www.equator-principles.com; f. July 2010; aims to administer and develop further the Equator Principles, first adopted in 2003, with the support of the International Finance Corporation, as a set of industry standards for the management of environmental and social risk in project financing; a Strategic Review conf. was convened in Beijing, People's Republic of China, in Dec. 2010; holds an annual meeting and workshop (2013: Tokyo, Japan, in Nov.); 77 signed-up Equator Principles Financial Institutions (EPFIs) and two assoc. mems; Administrators JOANNA CLARK, SAMANTHA HOSKINS.

Financial Action Task Force (FATF) (Groupe d'action financière—GAFI): 2 rue André-Pascal, 75775 Paris Cedex 16, France; tel. 1-45-24-90-90; fax 1-44-30-61-37; e-mail contact@fatf-gafi.org; internet www.fatf-gafi.org; f. 1989, on the recommendation of the Group of Seven (G7) industrialized nations, to develop and promote policies to combat money-laundering and the financing of terrorism; formulated a set of recommendations (40+9) for countries worldwide to implement; these are periodically revised (most recently in 2012); established partnerships with regional task forces in the Caribbean, Asia-Pacific, Central Asia, Europe, East and South Africa, the Middle East and North Africa and South America; mems: 36 state jurisdictions, the European Commission, and the Cooperation Council for the Arab States of the Gulf; there are also 8 regional assoc. mems; Pres. ROGER WILKINS (Australia); Exec. Sec. RICK McDONELL; publs *Annual Report, News Alerts*.

Financial Stability Board: c/o BIS, Centralbahnplatz 2, 4002 Basel, Switzerland; tel. 612808298; fax 612809100; e-mail fsb@bis.org; internet www.financialstabilityboard.org; f. 1999 as the Financial Stability Forum, name changed in April 2009; brings together senior representatives of national financial authorities, international financial institutions, international regulatory and supervisory groupings and cttees of central bank experts and the European Central Bank; aims to promote international financial stability and to strengthen the functioning of the financial markets; in March 2009 agreed to expand its membership to include all Group of 20 (G20) economies, as well as Spain and the European Commission; in April 2009 the meeting of G20 heads of state and govt determined to re-establish the then Forum as the Financial Stability Board, strengthen its institutional structure (to include a plenary body, a steering cttee and three standing cttees concerned with Vulnerabilities Assessment; Supervisory and Regulatory Co-operation; and Standards Implementation) and expand its mandate to enhance its effectiveness as an international mechanism to promote financial stability; the Board was to strengthen its collaboration with the IMF, and conduct joint early warning exercises; in Dec. 2009 the Board initiated a peer review of implementation of the Principles and Standards for Sound Compensation Practices; in Nov. 2010 determined to establish six FSB regional consultative groups; Chair. MARK CARNEY (Canada).

Group of 20 (G20): internet www.g20.org; f. Sept. 1999 as an informal deliberative forum of ministers responsible for finance and central bank governors representing both industrialized and 'systemically important' emerging market nations; aims to strengthen the international financial architecture and to foster sustainable economic growth and devt; in 2004 participating countries adopted the G20 Accord for Sustained Growth and stated a commitment to high standards of transparency and fiscal governance; the IMF Managing Director and IBRD President participate in G20 annual meetings; an extraordinary Summit on Financial Markets and the World Economy was convened in Washington, DC, USA, in Nov. 2008, attended by heads of state or govt of G20 mem. economies; a second summit meeting, held in London, United Kingdom, in April 2009, issued as its final communiqué a *Global Plan for Recovery and Reform* outlining commitments to restore economic confidence, growth and jobs, to strengthen financial supervision and regulation, to reform and strengthen global financial institutions, to promote global trade and investment and to ensure a fair and sustainable economic recovery; detailed declarations were also issued on measures agreed to deliver substantial resources (of some US $850,000m.) through international financial institutions and on reforms to be implemented in order to strengthen the financial system; as a follow-up to the London summit, G20 heads of state met in Pittsburgh, USA, in Sept. 2009; the meeting adopted a *Framework for Strong, Sustainable, and Balanced Growth* and resolved to expand the role of the G20 to be at the centre of future international economic policymaking; summit meetings were held in June 2010, in Canada (at the G8 summit), and in Seoul, Republic of Korea, in Nov. of that year; the sixth G20 summit, held in Cannes, France, in Nov. 2011, concluded an *Action Plan for Growth and Jobs* but was dominated by discussion of measures to secure financial stability in some countries using the euro; the seventh summit, convened in Los Cabos, Baja California Sur, Mexico, in June 2012, further considered means of stabilizing the eurozone, with a particular focus on reducing the borrowing costs of highly indebted mem. countries; the ongoing crisis in Syria was on the agenda of the eighth G20 summit of heads of state, which took place in Sept. 2013 in St Petersburg, Russia; 11 heads of state participating in the summit issued a statement condemning an alleged chemical attack perpetrated against civilians in Ghouta, Syria, on 21 Aug., and urging a strong international response; the heads of state also adopted a new Base Erosion and Profit Shifting Action Plan, developed by OECD with the aim of combating corp. tax avoidance globally; the 2014 summit was to be held in Brisbane, Australia, in November; a parallel Business 20 summit, facilitating dialogue between prominent business asscns, is convened annually; mems: Argentina, Australia, Brazil, Canada, People's Republic of China, France, Germany, India, Indonesia, Italy, Japan, Republic of Korea, Mexico, Russia, Saudi Arabia, South Africa, Turkey, United Kingdom, USA and the European Union; observers: Netherlands, Spain; the presidency rotates among the participating states on an annual basis (2014: Australia).

Intergovernmental Group of 24 (G24) on International Monetary Affairs and Development: 700 19th St, NW, Rm 3-600 Washington, DC 20431, USA; tel. (202) 623-6101; fax (202) 623-6000; e-mail g24@g24.org; internet www.g24.org; f. 1971; aims to co-ordinate the position of developing countries on monetary and devt finance issues; operates at the political level of ministers of finance and governors of central banks, and also at the level of govt officials; mems (Africa): Algeria, Côte d'Ivoire, Democratic Republic of the Congo, Egypt, Ethiopia, Gabon, Ghana, Nigeria, South Africa; (Latin America and the Caribbean): Argentina, Brazil, Colombia, Guatemala, Mexico, Peru, Trinidad and Tobago and Venezuela; (Asia and the Middle East): India, Iran, Lebanon, Pakistan, Philippines, Sri Lanka and Syrian Arab Republic; the People's Republic of China has the status of special invitee at G24 meetings; G77 participant states may attend G24 meetings as observers.

Latin American Banking Federation (Federación Latino-americana de Bancos—FELABAN): Cra 11A No. 93-67 Of. 202 A.A 091959, Bogotá, Colombia; tel. (1) 6215848; fax (1) 6217659; e-mail mangarita@felaban.com; internet www.felaban.com; f. 1965 to co-ordinate efforts towards wide and accelerated economic devt in Latin American countries; mems: 19 Latin American nat. banking asscns, representing more than 500 banks and financial institutions; Pres. JORGE HORACIO BRITO; Sec.-Gen. GIORGIO TRETTENERO CASTRO (Peru).

Education

Association of Caribbean University, Research and Institutional Libraries (ACURIL): POB 21609, San Juan 00931-1906, Puerto Rico; tel. 763-6199; e-mail executivesecretariat@acuril.org; internet www.acuril.uprrp.edu; f. 1968 to foster contact and collaboration between mem. univs and institutes; holds annual confs, meetings and seminars; circulates information through newsletters and bulletins; facilitates co-operation and the pooling of resources in research; encourages exchange of staff and students; mems: 250; Pres. JANE W. SMITH; Exec.-Sec. LUISA VIGO-CEPEDA; publ. *Cybernotes*.

Inter-American Centre for Research and Documentation on Vocational Training (Centro Interamericano de Investigación y Documentación sobre Formación Profesional—CINTERFOR): Avda Uruguay 1238, Casilla de correo 1761, Montevideo, Uruguay; tel. 2902 0557; fax 2902 1305; e-mail oitcinterfor@oitcinterfor.org; internet www.oitcinterfor.org; f. 1964 by the International Labour Organization for mutual help among the Latin American and Caribbean countries in planning vocational training; services are provided in documentation, research, exchange of experience; holds seminars and courses; Dir ENRIQUE DEIBE; publs *Bulletin CINTERFOR / OIT Herramientas para la transformación, Trazos de la formación*, studies, monographs and technical papers.

Inter-American Confederation for Catholic Education (Confederación Interamericana de Educación Católica—CIEC): Carrera 24, No. 34, Bogotá 37 DC, Colombia; tel. (1) 2871036; e-mail asistente@ciec.edu.co; internet www.ciec.edu.co; f. 1945 to defend and extend the principles and rules of Catholic education, freedom of education, and human rights; organizes congress every three years; Sec.-Gen. JOSÉ LEONARDO RINCÓN CONTRERAS (Colombia); publ. *Educación Hoy*.

Inter-American Organization for Higher Education (IOHE): Université de Montréal, 3744, Jean-Brillant, bureau 592, Québec H3T 1P1 6128, Canada; tel. (514) 343-6980; fax ((514) 343-6454; e-mail info@oui-iohe.org; internet www.oui-iohe.org; f. 1980 to promote co-operation among univs of the Americas and the devt of higher education; mems: some 281 institutions and 35 nat. and reg. higher education asscns; Exec. Dir PATRICIA GUDIÑO.

International Council for Adult Education (ICAE): Ave 18 de Julio 2095/301, CP 11200, Montevideo, Uruguay; tel. and fax 2409 7982; e-mail secretariat@icae.org.uy; internet www.icae2.org; f. 1973 as a partnership of adult learners, teachers and orgs; General Assembly meets every four years; mems: 7 reg. orgs and over 700 literacy, adult and lifelong learning asscns in more than 50 countries; Pres. ALAN TUCKETT; Sec.-Gen. KATARINA POPOVIĆ; publs *Convergence, ICAE News*.

International Institute of Iberoamerican Literature (Instituto Internacional de Literatura Iberoamericana): 1312 CL, University of Pittsburgh, PA 15260, USA; tel. (412) 624-3359; fax (412) 624-0829; e-mail iilisus@pitt.edu; internet www.iilionline.org; f. 1938 to advance the study of Iberoamerican literature, and intensify cultural relations among the peoples of the Americas; mems: scholars and artists in 37 countries; publs *Revista Iberoamericana, Memorias*.

Italian-Latin American Institute: Via Giovanni Paisiello 24, 00198 Rome, Italy; tel. (06) 684921; fax (06) 6872834; e-mail info@iila.org; internet www.iila.org; f. 1966; aims to promote Italian culture in Latin America; awarded observer status at the UN General Assembly in 2007; Dir-Gen. SIMONETTA CAVALIERI; Sec.-Gen. GIORGIO MALFATTI DI MONTE TRETTO.

Organization of Ibero-American States for Education, Science and Culture (Organización de Estados Iberoamericanos para la Educación, la Ciencia y la Cultura—OEI): Centro de Recursos Documentales e Informáticos, Calle Bravo Murillo 38, 28015 Madrid, Spain; tel. (91) 5944382; fax (91) 5944622; internet www.oei.es; f. 1949 (as the Ibero-American Bureau of Education); promotes peace and solidarity between mem. countries, through education, science, technology and culture; provides information, encourages exchanges and organizes training courses; the General Assembly (at ministerial level) meets every four years; mems: govts of 20 countries; Sec.-Gen. ÁLVARO MARCHESI ULLASTRES; publ. *Revista Iberoamericana de Educación* (quarterly).

Organization of the Catholic Universities of Latin America (Organización de Universidades Católicas de América Latina—ODUCAL): Av. Libertador Bernardo O'Higgins 340, Of. 242, 2° piso, Santiago, Chile; tel. and fax (2) 354-1866; e-mail oducal@uc.cl; internet www.oducal.uc.cl; f. 1953 to assist the social, economic and cultural devt of Latin America through the promotion of Catholic higher education in the continent; mems: 43 Catholic univs in 15 countries; Pres. Dr PEDRO PABLO ROSSO; Sec.-Gen. ANTONIO DAHER HECHEM; publs *Anuario, Sapientia, Universitas*.

Union of Universities of Latin America and the Caribbean (Unión de Universidades de América Latina y el Caribe—UDUAL): Circuito Norponiente del Estadio Olímpico, Apartado Postal 70-232, Ciudad Universitaria, Del. Coyoacán, 04510 México, DF, Mexico; tel. (55) 5616-2383; fax (55) 5622-0092; e-mail enlace@udual.org; internet www.udual.org; f. 1949 to organize exchanges between professors, students, research fellows and graduates and generally encourage good relations between the Latin American univs; arranges confs; conducts statistical research; maintains centre for univ. documentation; mems: 240 univs and 8 univ. networks; Pres. JOSE TADEU JORGE (Brazil); Sec.-Gen. Dr ROBERTO ESCALANTE SEMERENA (Mexico); publs *Universidades* (2 a year), *Gaceta UDUAL* (quarterly), *Censo* (every 2 years).

Environmental Conservation

Caribbean Conservation Association: Chelford Bush Hill, St Michael, Barbados; tel. 426-5373; fax 429-8483; e-mail admin@caribbeanconservation.org; internet www.caribbeanconservation.org; f. 1967; aims to conserve the environment and cultural heritage of the region through education, legislation, and management of museums and sites; mems: 17 govts, 60 NGOs and 130 associates; Pres. ERMATH NICHOLAS HARRINGTON; publ. *Caribbean Conservation News* (quarterly).

Conservation International: 2011 Crystal Drive, Suite 500, Arlington, VA 22202, USA; tel. (703) 341-2400; e-mail community@conservation.org; internet www.conservation.org; f. 1987; aims to demonstrate to govts, institutions and corporations that sustainable global devt is necessary for human well-being, and provides strategic, technical and financial support to partners at local, national and regional level to facilitate balancing conservation actions with devt objectives and economic interests; focuses on the following priority areas: biodiversity hotspots (34 threatened habitats: 13 in Asia and the Pacific; eight in Africa; five in South America; four in North and Central America and the Caribbean; and four in Europe and Central Asia) that cover just 2.3% of the Earth's surface and yet hold at least 50% of plant species and some 42% of terrestrial vertebrate species); high biodiversity wilderness areas (five areas retaining at least 70% of their original vegetation: Amazonia; the Congo Basin; New Guinea; North American deserts—covering northern parts of Mexico and south-western areas of the USA; and the Miomo-Mopane woodlands and savannas of Southern Africa); and oceans and seascapes; organized Summit for Sustainability in Africa in May 2012, in Gaborone, Botswana; maintains offices in more than 30 countries worldwide; partners: govts, businesses, local communities, non-profit orgs and univs worldwide; Chair. and CEO PETER SELIGMANN.

Global Coral Reef Monitoring Network: c/o IUCN Conservation Centre, 28 rue Mauverney, 1196 Gland, Switzerland; tel. 229990217; fax 229990025; e-mail coordinator@gcrmn.org; internet www.gcrmn.org; f. 1994, as an operating unit of the International Coral Reef Initiative; active in more than 80 countries; aims include improving the management and sustainable conservation of coral reefs, strengthening links between regional organizations and ecological and socio-economic monitoring networks, and disseminating information to assist the formulation of conservation plans; publ. *Status of Coral Reefs of the World*.

International Coral Reef Initiative: c/o Biodiversity Policy Div., Ministry of the Environment, 1-2-2 Kasumigaseki, Chiyoda-ku, 100-8975 Tokyo, Japan; tel. (3) 5521-8274; fax (3) 3591-3228; e-mail icri@env.go.jp; internet www.icriforum.org; f. 1994 at the first Conference of the Parties of the Convention on Biological Diversity; a partnership of govts, international orgs and non-governmental orgs; aims to raise awareness at all levels on the degradation of coral reefs around the world; promotes sustainable management practices and supports the conservation of reefs and related marine ecosystems; the Secretariat is co-chaired by a developed and a developing country, on a rotational basis among mem. states (2014–15, Japan and Thailand); mems: 60 govts, int. and reg. orgs; Co-Chair. REIJI KAMEZAWA (Japan), NIPHON PHONGSUWAN (Thailand).

International Renewable Energy Agency: C67 Office Bldg, Khalidiyah (32nd) St, POB 236, Abu Dhabi, United Arab Emirates; tel. (2) 4179000; internet www.irena.org; f. 2009 at a conf. held in Bonn, Germany; aims to promote the devt and application of renewable sources of energy; to act as a forum for the exchange of information and technology transfer; and to organize training seminars and other educational activities; inaugural Assembly convened in April 2011; mems: 133 mems (incl. the European Union); at Sept. 2014 a further 36 countries had signed but not yet ratified the founding agreement or had applied to become full mems; Dir-Gen. ADNAN Z. AMIN (Kenya).

International Seabed Authority: 14–20 Port Royal St, Kingston, Jamaica; tel. 922-9105; fax 922-0195; e-mail postmaster@isa.org.jm; internet www.isa.org.jm; f. Nov. 1994 upon the entry into force of the 1982 United Nations Convention on the Law of the Sea; the Authority is the institute through which states parties to the Convention organize and control activities in the international seabed area beyond the limits of national jurisdiction, particularly with a view to administering the resources of that area; Sec.-Gen. NII ALLOTEY ODUNTON (Ghana).

IUCN—International Union for Conservation of Nature: 28 rue Mauverney, 1196 Gland, Switzerland; tel. 229990000; fax 229990002; e-mail mail@iucn.org; internet www.iucn.org; f. 1948, as the International Union for Conservation of Nature and Natural Resources; supports partnerships and practical field activities to promote the conservation of natural resources, to secure the conservation of biological diversity as an essential foundation for the future; to ensure the equitable and sustainable use of the Earth's natural resources; and to guide the devt of human communities towards ways of life in enduring harmony with other components of the biosphere, developing programmes to protect and sustain the most important and threatened species and eco-systems and assisting govts to devise and carry out national conservation strategies; incorporates the Species Survival Commission, a science-based network of volunteer experts aiming to ensure conservation of present levels of biodiversity; compiles annually updated Red List of Threatened Species (www.iucnredlist.org); the 2014 list, released in June of that year, comprised some 73,686 species, of which 22,103 were threatened with extinction; maintains a conservation library and documentation centre and units for monitoring traffic in wildlife; mems: more than 1,000 states, govt agencies, non-governmental orgs and affiliates in some 140 countries; Pres. ZHANG XINSHENG (People's Republic of China); Dir-Gen. JULIA MARTON-LEFÈVRE (Switzerland); publs *World Conservation Strategy, Caring for the Earth, Red List of Threatened Plants, Red List of Threatened Species, United Nations List of National Parks and Protected Areas, World Conservation* (quarterly), *IUCN Today*.

Permanent Commission of the South Pacific (Comisión Permanente del Pacífico Sur): Av. Carlos Julio Arosemena, Km 3 Edificio Inmaral, Guayaquil, Ecuador; tel. (4) 222-1202; fax (4) 222-1201; e-mail sgeneral@cpps-int.org; internet www.cpps-int.org; f. 1952 to consolidate the presence of the zonal coastal states; Sec.-Gen. HÉCTOR SOLDI (Peru).

Secretariat of the Antarctic Treaty: Maipú 757, piso 4, Buenos Aires, Argentina; tel. (11) 4320-4250; fax (11) 4320-4253; e-mail ats@ats.aq; internet www.ats.aq; f. 2004 to administer the Antarctic Treaty (signed in 1959); has developed an Electronic Information Exchange System; organizes annual Consultative Meeting; mems: 50 states have ratified the Treaty; Exec. Sec. Dr MANFRED REINKE.

World Rainforest Movement (WRM): Maldonado 1858, Montevideo 11200, Uruguay; tel. 2413 2989; fax 2410 0985; e-mail wrm@wrm.org.uy; internet www.wrm.org.uy; f. 1986; aims to secure the lands and livelihoods of rainforest peoples and supports their efforts to defend rainforests from activities including commercial logging, mining, the construction of dams, the devt of plantations, and shrimp farming; issued the Penang Declaration in 1989 setting out the shared vision of an alternative model of rainforest devt based on securing the lands and livelihoods of forest inhabitants; released in 1998 the Montevideo Declaration, campaigning against large-scale monocrop plantations, for example of pulpwood, oil palm and rubber; and issued the Mount Tamalpais Declaration in 2000, urging govts not to include tree plantations as carbon sinks in international action against climate change; Co-ordinator WINFRIDUS OVERBEEK; publ. *WRM Bulletin* (monthly).

WWF International: 27 ave du Mont-Blanc, 1196 Gland, Switzerland; tel. 223649111; fax 223648836; e-mail info@wwfint.org; internet www.wwf.panda.org; f. 1961 (as World Wildlife Fund), name changed to World Wide Fund for Nature in 1986, current nomenclature adopted 2001; aims to stop the degradation of natural environments, conserve biodiversity, ensure the sustainable use of renewable resources, and promote the reduction of both pollution and wasteful consumption; addresses six priority issues: forests, freshwater, marine, species, climate change, and toxics; has identified, and focuses its activities in, 200 'ecoregions' (the 'Global 200'), believed to contain the best part of the world's remaining biological diversity; global initiatives being implemented in 2014 focused on climate and energy, forest and climate, smart fishing, tigers, and, geographically, on the Amazon, the Arctic, 'China for a Global Shift' (relating to the growing global influence of the People's Republic of

China), Coastal East Africa, the Coral Triangle (a marine area in the Western Pacific), the Green Heart of Africa, the Heart of Borneo, and Living Himalayas; actively supports and operates conservation programmes in more than 90 countries; mems: 54 offices, 5 assoc. orgs, c. 5m. individual mems worldwide; Pres. YOLANDA KAKABADSE (Ecuador); Dir-Gen. MARCO LAMBERTINI (Italy); publs *Annual Report, Living Planet Report*.

Government and Politics

Agency for the Prohibition of Nuclear Weapons in Latin America and the Caribbean (Organismo para la Proscripción de las Armas Nucleares en la América Latina y el Caribe—OPANAL): Schiller 326, 5°, Col. Chapultepec Morales, 11570 México, DF, Mexico; tel. (55) 5255-2914; fax (55) 5255-3748; e-mail info@opanal.org; internet www.opanal.org; f. 1969 to ensure compliance with the Treaty for the Prohibition of Nuclear Weapons in Latin America (Treaty of Tlatelolco), 1967; to ensure the absence of all nuclear weapons in the application zone of the Treaty; to contribute to the movement against proliferation of nuclear weapons; to promote general and complete disarmament; to prohibit all testing, use, manufacture, acquisition, storage, installation and any form of possession, by any means, of nuclear weapons; the organs of the Agency comprise the General Conference, meeting every two years, the Council, meeting every two months, and the secretariat; mems: 33 states that have fully ratified the Treaty; the Treaty has two additional Protocols: the first signed and ratified by France, the Netherlands, the United Kingdom and the USA, the second signed and ratified by the People's Republic of China, the USA, France, the United Kingdom and Russia; Sec.-Gen. LUIZ FILIPE DE MACEDO SOARES GUIMARÃES (Brazil).

Bolivarian Alliance for the Peoples of our America-People's Trade Treaty (Alianza Bolivariana para los Pueblos de Nuestra América-Tratado de Comercio de los Pueblos—ALBA-TCP): Av. Francisco Solano, Esq. Calle San Gerónimo, Edif. Los Llanos, 8° Sabana Grande, Parroquia El Recreo, Caracas, Venezuela; tel. (212) 905-9384; fax (212) 761-1364; e-mail secretaria@alba-tcp.org; internet alba-tcp.org; f. 2002 (as the Bolivarian Alternative for the Americas) by the then President of Venezuela, Hugo Chávez, to promote an alternative model of political, economic and social co-operation and integration between Caribbean and Latin American countries sharing geographic, historical and cultural bonds; aims to reduce disparities in devt between countries in the region and to combat poverty and social exclusion; the so-called People's Trade Treaty (Tratado de Comercio de los Pueblos) was signed in April 2006 to formalize a process of complementarity; in June 2007 ministers of foreign affairs convened for the inaugural meeting of ALBA's Council of Ministers agreed to the establishment of joint enterprises, as an alternative to transnational corporations, a joint bank to finance projects supported by the grouping and to develop bilateral agreements; the establishment of a Bank of ALBA was endorsed at the sixth summit meeting of heads of state, convened in Jan. 2008; the use of a Unified System of Regional Compensation (Sistema Único de Compensación Regional—SUCRE) as a means of currency exchange for commercial transactions between mems was agreed in 2009 and first used in 2010; the agreement establishing SUCRE, signed in Oct. 2009, also envisaged the establishment of a Regional Monetary Council, a Central Clearing House, a regional reserve and emergency fund; in Feb. 2012 the Ecconomic Complementation Council agreed to establish an ALBA-TCP economic space ('ECOALBA'); in Aug. ALBA ministers of foreign affairs reaffirmed support for the sovereign right of the Ecuador Govt to grant asylum to the WikiLeaks founder Julian Assange, who was at that time accommodated in Ecuador's London embassy, and rejected perceived intimidation from the United Kingdom authorities concerning the territorial integrity of the Ecuador mission to London; in May 2013 mems agreed to strengthen co-operation with Petrocaribe through the establishment of a new economic zone to promote regional investment, trade, food security, tourism and devt projects; a second summit meeting between the two orgs, convened in Dec., reaffirmed support for the economic zone and agreed to develop mechanisms to support its establishment; Exec. Sec. BERNARDO ÁLVAREZ; mems: Antigua and Barbuda, Bolivia, Cuba, Dominica, Ecuador, Nicaragua, Saint Lucia, Saint Vincent and the Grenadines, Venezuela.

Alliance of Small Island States (AOSIS): c/o 800 Second Ave, Suite 400K, New York, NY 10017, USA; tel. (212) 599-0301; fax (212) 599-1540; e-mail grenada@un.int; internet www.aosis.info; f. 1990 as an ad hoc intergovernmental grouping to focus on the special problems of small islands and low-lying coastal developing states (SIDs); activities cover three regions (the Caribbean; Africa, Indian Ocean, Mediterranean and South China Sea—'AIMS'; and the Pacific; nominated, in April 2014, representatives of the three SIDS regions to lead a strategy governing the UN-designated International Year of Small Island Developing States, culminating in the

Third International Conference on SIDS, convened by the UN in Apia, Samoa, in early Sept; mems: 44 island nations and observers; Chair. MARLENE MOSES (Nauru); publ. *Small Islands, Big Issues*.

Community of Latin American and Caribbean States (CELAC) (Comunidad de Estados de América Latina y el Caribe): e-mail cumbre.calc@mppre.gob.ve; internet www.celac.gob.ve; f. 2010; heads of state of the Rio Group (f. 1987) and the Latin American and Caribbean Summit on Integration and Development agreed to establish CELAC as a pan-regional body to strengthen co-operation on political, cultural, social and economic issues; inaugural summit held in Dec. 2011; the first Ministerial Meeting on infrastructure for the physical integration of transport, telecommunications and frontiers was convened in Oct. 2012; second summit held in Jan. 2013, in Santiago, Chile, preceded by an inaugural CELAC-EU summit at which a revised Action Plan for bilateral relations was adopted; third summit: Jan. 2014: Havana, Cuba; the first meetings of ministers responsible for education and for culture took place in Feb. and March, respectively; 33 Latin American and Caribbean states; Chair. RAÚL CASTRO (Cuba).

Comunidade dos Países de Língua Portuguesa (CPLP) (Community of Portuguese-Speaking Countries): rua de S. Mamede (ao Caldas) 21, 1100-533 Lisbon, Portugal; tel. (21) 392-8560; fax (21) 392-8588; e-mail comunicacao@cplp.org; internet www.cplp.org; f. 1996; aims to produce close political, economic, diplomatic and cultural links between Portuguese-speaking countries and to strengthen the influence of the Lusophone Commonwealth within the international community; in Nov. 2010 adopted, jointly with ECOWAS, the CPLP-ECOWAS roadmap on reform of the defence and security sector in Guinea-Bissau; mems: Angola, Brazil, Cabo Verde, Guinea-Bissau, Mozambique, Portugal, São Tomé and Príncipe, Timor-Leste; assoc. observers: Equatorial Guinea, Mauritius, Senegal; Exec. Sec. MURADE ISAAC MIGUIGY MURARGY (Mozambique).

Ibero-American General Secretariat (Secretaría General Iberoamericana—SEGIB): Paseo de Recoletos 8, 28001 Madrid, Spain; tel. (91) 5901980; fax (91) 5901984; e-mail info@segib.org; internet www.segib.org; f. 2003; aims to provide institutional and technical support to the annual Ibero-American summit meetings, to monitor programmes agreed at the meetings and to strengthen the Ibero-American community; meetings of Ibero-American heads of state and govt (the first of which was convened in Guadalajara, Mexico in 1991, and the 23rd was held in Oct. 2013, in Panama City, Panama) aim to promote political, economic and cultural co-operation among the 19 Spanish- and Portuguese-speaking Latin American countries and three European countries; Sec.-Gen. REBECA GRYNSPAN (Costa Rica).

International Institute for Democracy and Electoral Assistance (IDEA): Strömsborg, 103 34 Stockholm, Sweden; tel. (8) 698-3700; fax (8) 20-2422; e-mail info@idea.int; internet www.idea.int; f. 1995; aims to promote sustainable democracy in new and established democracies; works with practitioners and institutions promoting democracy in Africa, Asia, Arab states and Latin America; mems: 28 mem. states and 1 observer; Sec.-Gen. YVES LETERME (Belgium).

Inter-Parliamentary Union (IPU): 5 chemin du Pommier, CP 330, 1218 Le Grand-Saconnex/Geneva, Switzerland; tel. 229194150; fax 229194160; e-mail postbox@mail.ipu.org; internet www.ipu.org; f. 1889 to promote peace, co-operation and representative democracy by providing a forum for multilateral political debate between representatives of national parliaments; mems: nat. parliaments of 162 sovereign states; 10 assoc. mems; Pres. ABDELWAHAD RADI (Morocco); Sec.-Gen. MARTIN CHUNGONG (Cameroon); publs *Chronicle of Parliamentary Elections* (annually), *The World of Parliaments* (quarterly), *World Directory of Parliaments* (annually).

Latin American Parliament (Parlamento Latinoamericano): Casilla 1527, Edif. 1111-1113, Apdo 4, Avda Principal de Amador, Panama; tel. 201-9028; e-mail secgeneral@parlatino.org; internet www.parlatino.org; f. 1965; permanent democratic institution, representative of all existing political trends within the national legislative bodies of Latin America; aims to promote the movement towards economic, political and cultural integration of the Latin American republics, and to uphold human rights, peace and security; Pres. ELÍAS ARIEL CASTILLO GONZÁLEZ; Sec.-Gen. BLANCA MARÍA DEL SOCORRO ALCALÁ RUIZ; publs *Acuerdos*, *Resoluciones de las Asambleas Ordinarias* (annually), *Parlamento Latinoamericano–Actividades de los Órganos*, *Revista Patria Grande* (annually), statements and agreements.

Non-aligned Movement (NAM): c/o Imam Khomeini St, Tehran, Iran; tel. (21) 61151; fax (21) 66743149; e-mail matbuat@mfa.gov.ir; internet nam.gov.ir; f. 1961 by a meeting of 25 heads of state, with the aim of linking countries that had refused to adhere to the main East/West military and political blocs; co-ordination bureau established in 1973; works for the establishment of a new international economic order, and especially for better terms for countries producing raw materials; maintains special funds for agricultural devt, improve-

ment of food production and the financing of buffer stocks; South Commission promotes co-operation between developing countries; seeks changes at the UN to give developing countries greater decision-making power; holds summit meeting every three years (17th summit: Caracas, Venezuela, in 2015); a 50th anniversary conf. was convened in Bali, Indonesia, in May 2011; in Sept. 2013 a ministerial meeting on Co-operation for the Rule of Law at the International Level was convened in New York, USA; a ministerial conf. was held in Algiers, Algeria, in May 2014; mems: 120 countries, 17 observer countries and 10 observer orgs.

Organisation of Eastern Caribbean States (OECS): Morne Fortune, POB 179, Castries, Saint Lucia; tel. 455-6327; fax 453-1628; e-mail oecss@oecs.org; internet www.oecs.org; f. 1981 by the seven states which formerly belonged to the West Indies Associated States (f. 1966); aims to promote the harmonized devt of trade and industry in mem. states; single market created on 1 Jan. 1988; principal institutions are the Authority of Heads of Government (the supreme policymaking body), the Foreign Affairs Committee, the Defence and Security Committee, and the Economic Affairs Committee; other functional divisions include an Export Development and Agricultural Diversification Unit (based in Dominica), a Pharmaceutical Procurement Service, a Regional Integration Unit, a Regional E-Government Unit and an HIV/AIDS Project Unit; an OECS Technical Mission to the World Trade Organization in Geneva, Switzerland, was inaugurated in June 2005; in Aug. 2008 heads of govt determined to achieve economic union by 2011 and political union by 2013; an agreement to establish an economic union was signed in Dec. 2009; a Revised Treaty of Basseterre Establishing the OECS Economic Union was signed by heads of govt of six mem. states (Antigua and Barbuda, Grenada, Dominica, Saint Christopher and Nevis, Saint Vincent and the Grenadines, and Saint Lucia) in June 2010; the Treaty envisaged a new governance structure, in which an OECS Commission was to be established as a supranational executive institution; the Revised Treaty entered into force in Feb. 2011, having been ratified by four of the signatory states; the inaugural session of the OECS Assembly was held in Aug. 2012, in Antigua and Barbuda; the inaugural meeting of an OECS Economic Affairs Council (EAC) took place in June 2014; mems: Antigua and Barbuda, Dominica, Grenada, Montserrat, Saint Christopher and Nevis, Saint Lucia, Saint Vincent and the Grenadines; assoc. mems: Anguilla, British Virgin Islands; Dir-Gen. Dr DIDACUS JULES (Saint Lucia).

Organization of Solidarity of the Peoples of Africa, Asia and Latin America (OSPAAAL) (Organización de Solidaridad de los Pueblos de Africa, Asia y América Latina): Calle C No 670 esq. 29, Vedado, Havana 10400, Cuba; tel. (7) 833-4048; fax (7) 830-5520; e-mail secretario.general@tricontinental.cu; internet www.tricontinental.cu; f. 1966 at the first Conference of Solidarity of the Peoples of Africa, Asia and Latin America, to unite, co-ordinate and encourage national liberation movements in the three continents, to oppose foreign intervention in the affairs of sovereign states, colonial and neo-colonial practices, and to fight against racialism and all forms of racial discrimination; favours the establishment of a new international economic order; mems: 76 orgs in 46 countries; Sec.-Gen. LOURDES CERVANTES; publ. *Tricontinental* (quarterly).

Industrial and Professional Relations

Caribbean Congress of Labour: NUPW Bldg, Dalkeith Rd, POB 90B, St Michael, Barbados; tel. 427-5067; fax 427-2496; e-mail cclres@caribsurf.com; f. 1960; fights for the recognition of trade union organizations; to build and strengthen the ties between the free trade unions of the Caribbean and the rest of the world; supports the work of the International Trade Union Confederation; encourages the formation of national groupings and centres; mems: 30 unions in 17 countries; Pres. DAVID MASSIAH (Antigua and Barbuda); Gen.-Sec. CHESTER HUMPHREY (Grenada).

International Trade Union Confederation (ITUC): 5 blvd Roi Albert II, 1210 Brussels, Belgium; tel. (2) 224-02-11; fax (2) 201-58-15; e-mail info@ituc-csi.org; internet www.ituc-csi.org; f. 2006 by the merger of the International Confederation of Free Trade Unions, the World Confederation of Labour and eight national trade union organizations; aims to promote the interests of working people and to secure recognition of workers' orgs as free bargaining agents; mems: 315 affiliated orgs in 156 countries; Pres. JOÃO ANTONIO FELICIO; Gen. Sec. SHARAN BURROW (Australia).

Latin American Federation of Agricultural Workers (Federación Latinoamericana de Trabajadores Agrícolas, Pecuarios y Afines—FELTRA): Antiguo Local Conadi, B° La Granja, Comayaguela, Tegucigalpa, Honduras; tel. 2252526; fax 2252525; e-mail feltra@123.hn; f. 1999 by reorganization of FELTACA (f. 1961) to represent the interests of workers in agricultural and related industries in Latin America; mems: national unions in 28 countries and territories; Sec.-Gen. MARCIAL REYES CABALLERO; publ. *Boletín Luchemos* (quarterly).

Trade Union Confederation of the Americas (TUCA-CSA) (Confederación Sindical de los Trabajadores y Trabajadoras de las Americas): Rua Formosa 367, 4to. Andar, Cjto. 450 Centros, Sao Paulo, Brazil; tel. (11) 21040750; fax (11) 21040751; e-mail sede@csa-csi.org; internet www.csa-csi.org; f. 2008 as successor to the regional organization of the International Confederation of Free Trade Unions (f. 1951); mems: trade unions in 23 countries (including Canada and the USA) with over 50m. individuals; Pres. HASSAN YUSSUFF; Gen. Sec. VICTOR BÁEZ MOSQUEIRA.

Young Americas Business Trust: 1889 F Street, NW, Washington, DC 20006, USA; tel. (202) 370-4723; e-mail info@yabt.net; internet www.yabt.net; f. 1999 to promote social devt among youth by stimulating entrepreneurial initiatives and thereby providing job opportunities for young people; works through leadership and training programmes and allies with international and national bodies for technical assistance and funding; works with the General Secretariat of the Organization of American States; Chair. ROY THOMASSON; CEO LUIS VIGURIA.

Law

Eastern Caribbean Supreme Court: Heraldine Rock Bldg, Block B, Waterfront, POB 1093, Castries; tel. 457-3600; fax 457-3601; e-mail offices@eccourts.org; internet www.eccourts.org; f. 1967 as the West Indies Associated States Supreme Court, in 1974 as the Supreme Court of Grenada and the West Indies Associated States, present name adopted in 1979; composed of the High Court of Justice and the Court of Appeal, High Court is composed of the Chief Justice and 22 High Court Judges. The Court of Appeal is itinerant and presided over by the Chief Justice who is also President of the Court of Appeal, six other Justices of Appeal and three Masters; the Court is a superior court of record and has unlimited jurisdiction in the nine mem. states/territories of the OECS; jurisdiction of the Court extends to fundamental rights and freedoms, membership of the parliaments, and matters concerning the interpretation of constitutions; Chief Justice Dame JANICE MESADIS PEREIRA.

Inter-American Bar Association (IABA): 1211 Connecticut Ave, NW, Suite 202, Washington, DC 20036, USA; tel. (202) 466-5944; fax (202) 466-5946; e-mail iaba@iaba.org; internet www.iaba.org; f. 1940 to promote the rule of law and to establish and maintain relations between asscns and orgs of lawyers in the Americas; mems: 90 asscns and 3,500 individuals in 27 countries; Pres. Dr WILFRIDO FERNANDEZ (Paraguay); Sec.-Gen. HENRY DAHL; publs *Newsletter* (quarterly), *Conference Proceedings*.

International Commission against Impunity in Guatemala (Comisión Internacional contra la Impunidad en Guatemala—CICIG): Apdo Postal 934, 'A' Guatemala, Guatemala; internet cicig .org; f. 2007, following the signing of an agreement between the UN and Government of Guatemala in Dec. 2006; aims to support the office of the public prosecutor, the national civilian police and other state institutions to investigate the existence and activities of illegal security groups; the Commission may help to bring cases to trial in national courts and assist the devt of policies to uphold the rule of law; Commissioner IVÁN VELÁSQUEZ GÓMEZ (Colombia).

International Criminal Police Organization (INTERPOL): 200 quai Charles de Gaulle, 69006 Lyon, France; tel. 4-72-44-70-00; fax 4-72-44-71-63; e-mail website@interpol.int; internet www .interpol.int; f. 1923, reconstituted 1946; aims to promote and ensure mutual assistance between police forces in different countries; co-ordinates activities of police authorities of mem. states in international affairs; works to establish and develop institutions with the aim of preventing transnational crimes; centralizes records and information on international criminals; operates a global police communications network linking all mem. countries; holds General Assembly annually; mems: 190 countries; Pres. MIREILLE BALLESTRAZZI; Sec.-Gen. RONALD K. NOBLE (USA); publ. *Annual Report*.

International Union of Latin Notaries (Union Internationale du Notariat Latin—UINL): Av. Las Heras 1833, 9°, Buenos Aires, Argentina; tel. (11) 4809-7161; fax (11) 4809-6851; e-mail onpiuinl@onpi.org.ar; internet www.uinl.org; f. 1948 to study and standardize notarial legislation and promote the progress, stability and advancement of the Latin notarial system; mems: orgs and individuals in 81 countries; Pres. DANIEL-SÉDAR SENGHOR (Senegal); publs *Revista Internacional del Notariado* (quarterly), *Notarius International*.

Medicine and Health

Global Fund to Fight AIDS, Tuberculosis and Malaria: 8 chemin de Blandonnet, 1214 Vernier-Geneva, Switzerland; tel. 587911700; fax 587911701; e-mail info@theglobalfund.org; internet www.theglobalfund.org; f. 2002; the Fund provides support for countries to implement prevention programmes, as well as for the treatment and care of people affected by the diseases; US $12,000m. was pledged by international donors at a conf. convened in Dec. 2013 to replenish the Fund during 2014–16; Exec. Dir MARK R. DYBUL (USA).

Inter-American Association of Sanitary and Environmental Engineering (Asociación Interamericana de Ingeniería Sanitaria y Ambiental—AIDIS): Av. Angélica 2355, 01227-200 São Paulo, SP, Brazil; tel. (11) 3812-4080; fax (11) 3814-2441; e-mail aidis@aidis.org .br; internet www.aidis.org.br; f. 1948 to assist in the devt of water supply and sanitation; aims to generate awareness on environmental, health and sanitary problems and assist in finding solutions; mems: 32 countries; Pres. JORGE TRIANA (Colombia); Treas. EVERTON DE OLIVEIRA (Brazil); publs *Revista Ingeniería Sanitaria* (2 a year), *Desafío* (quarterly).

Latin American Odontological Federation (Federación Odontológica Latinoamericana): c/o Federación Odontológica Colombiana, Calle 71 No 11-10, Of. 1101, Apdo Aéreo 52925, Bogotá, Colombia; e-mail arn@codetel.net.do; internet www.folaoral.com; f. 1917; linked to FDI World Dental Federation; mems: national orgs in 12 countries; Pres. Dr ADOLFO RODRÍGUEZ.

Pan-American Association of Ophthalmology (PAAO): 1301 South Bowen Rd, Suite 450, Arlington, TX 76013, USA; tel. (817) 275-7553; fax (817) 275-3961; e-mail info@paao.org; internet www.paao .org; f. 1939 to promote friendship within the profession and the dissemination of scientific information; holds Congress every two years (2015: Bogota, Colombia); mems: nat. ophthalmological socs and other bodies in 39 countries; Pres. ANA LUISA HÖFLING-LIMA; Exec. Dir TERESA BRADSHAW; publ. *Vision Panamerica* (quarterly).

Pan-American Medical Association (Asociación Médica Panamericana): c/o Pan-American Medical Association of Central Florida, POB 536488, Orlando, Florida 32853-6488, USA; internet www .pamacfl.org; f. 1925; holds inter-American congresses, conducts seminars and grants post graduate scholarships to Latin American physicians; Pres. Dr ARMANDO REGO; Sec. Dr OSCAR ARNAUD; mems: 6,000 in 30 countries.

Pan Caribbean Partnership against HIV and AIDS: POB 10827, Georgetown, Guyana; tel. 222-0001; fax 222-0203; e-mail pancap@caricom.org; internet www.pancap.org; f. 2001 by heads of state and government of CARICOM; aims to co-ordinate efforts by national, regional and international agencies to counter the spread of HIV/AIDS and mitigate its impact throughout the region; Dir DERECK SPRINGER (Guyana).

World Federation for Ultrasound in Medicine and Biology: 14750 Sweitzer Ln, Suite 100, Laurel, MD 20707-5906, USA; tel. (301) 498-4100; fax (301) 498-4150; e-mail admin@wfumb.org; internet www.wfumb.org; f. 1973; Pres. HASSEN GHARBI; Sec. DIETER NURENBERG; publs *Ultrasound in Medicine and Biology* (monthly), *Echoes* (2 a year).

World Medical Association (WMA): 13 chemin du Levant, CIB-Bâtiment A, 01210 Ferney-Voltaire, France; tel. 4-50-40-75-75; fax 4-50-40-59-37; e-mail wma@wma.net; internet www.wma.net; f. 1947 to achieve the highest international standards in all aspects of medical education and practice, to promote closer ties among doctors and national medical asscns by personal contact and all other means, to study problems confronting the medical profession, and to present its views to appropriate bodies; holds an annual General Assembly; mems: 107 nat. medical asscns; Pres. Dr MARGARET MUNGHERERA (Brazil); Sec.-Gen. Dr OTMAR KLOIBER (Germany); publ. *The World Medical Journal* (quarterly).

Posts and Telecommunications

International Telecommunications Satellite Organization (ITSO): 4400 Jenifer St, NW, Washington, DC 20015, USA; tel. (202) 243-5096; fax (202) 243-5018; internet www.itso.int; f. 1964 to establish a global commercial satellite communications system; Assembly of Parties attended by representatives of mem. govts, meets every two years to consider policy and long-term aims and matters of interest to mems as sovereign states; meeting of Signatories to the Operating Agreement held annually; 24 INTELSAT satellites in geosynchronous orbit provide a global communications service; provides most of the world's overseas traffic; in 1998 INTELSAT agreed to establish a private enterprise, incorporated in the Netherlands, to administer six satellite services; mems: 150 govts; Dir-Gen. JOSÉ TOSCANO (USA).

Internet Corporation for Assigned Names and Numbers (ICANN): 12025 Waterfront Dr., Suite 300, Los Angeles, CA 90094-2536, USA; tel. (310) 301-5800; fax (310) 823-8649; e-mail icann@icann.org; internet www.icann.org; f. 1998; non-profit, private sector body; aims to co-ordinate the technical management and policy devt of the Internet in relation to addresses, domain names and protocol; supported by an At-Large Advisory Committee (representing individual users of the internet), a Country Code Names Supporting Organization, a Governmental Advisory Committee, a Generic Names Supporting Organization, and a Security and Stability Advisory Committee; through its Internet Assigned Numbers Authority department ICANN manages the global co-ordination of domain name system roots and internet protocol addressing; at 30 June 2011 there were 310 top-level domains (TLDs), 30 of which were in non-Latin scripts, and the most common of which were generic TLDs (gTLDs) (such as .org or .com) and country code TLDs (ccTLDs); in June 2011 ICANN adopted an expanded gTLD programme, under which, from 2012, applications were accepted from qualified orgs wishing to register domain names of their choosing; details of the first 1,930 filed applications were published in June 2012 ('app' being the most popular): the ensuing objections process was administered by the International Chamber of Commerce International Centre for Expertise; the expanded programme provides for Internationalized Domain Names (IDNs) incorporating non-Latin character sets (Arabic, Chinese and Cyrillic), with a view to making the internet more globally inclusive; launched in Oct. 2012, jointly with the African Regional Registry for Internet Number Resources, a three-year 'New Approach to Africa' initiative aimed at expanding activities in Africa; Pres. and CEO FADI CHEHADÉ (Lebanon).

Postal Union of the Americas, Spain and Portugal (PUASP) (Unión Postal de las Américas, España y Portugal): Cebollatí 1468/70, 1°, Casilla de Correos 20.042, Montevideo, Uruguay; tel. 2410 0070; fax 2410 5046; e-mail secretaria@upaep.com.uy; internet www.upaep.com.uy; f. 1911 to study, extend and facilitate the postal relationships of mem. countries; mems: 27 countries; Sec.-Gen. ROBERTO CAVANNA.

Press, Radio and Television

Inter-American Press Association (IAPA) (Sociedad Interamericana de Prensa): Jules Dubois Bldg, 1801 SW 3rd Ave, Miami, FL 33129, USA; tel. (305) 634-2465; fax (305) 635-2272; e-mail info@sipiapa.org; internet www.sipiapa.org; f. 1942 to guard the freedom of the press in the Americas; to promote and maintain the dignity, rights and responsibilities of the profession of journalism; to foster a wider knowledge and greater interchange among the peoples of the Americas; mems: 1,400; Exec. Dir JULIO E. MUÑOZ; publ. *IAPA News* (monthly).

International Association of Broadcasting (Asociación Internacional de Radiodifusión—AIR): Carlos Quijano 1264, 1110 Montevideo, Uruguay; tel. 2901 1319; fax 2908 0458; e-mail mail@airiab.com; internet www.airiab.com; f. 1946 (as the Interamerican Association of Broadcasting) to preserve free and private broadcasting; to promote co-operation between the corporations and public authorities; to defend freedom of expression; mems: national asscns of broadcasters; Pres. ALEXANDRE JOBIM (Brazil); Dir-Gen. Dr HÉCTOR OSCAR AMENGUAL; publ. *La Gaceta de AIR* (every 2 months).

International Christian Organisation of the Media (ICOM) (World Forum of Professionals and Institutions in Secular and Religious Journalism): CP 197, 1211 Geneva 20, Switzerland; tel. 227340017; e-mail icom@bluewin.ch; internet www.icomworld.info; f. 2011, as a successor org. to the International Catholic Union of the Press (f. 1927); focuses on inspiring and encouraging all media professionals worldwide, irrespective of differences, and on promoting the rights to information and freedom of opinion, and supports journalistic ethics; World Congress: Sept.–Oct. 2013, in Panama City, Panama; mems: in 172 countries.

World Catholic Association for Communication (SIGNIS): 310 rue Royale, 1210 Brussels, Belgium; tel. (2) 734-97-08; fax (2) 734-70-18; e-mail sg@signis.net; internet www.signis.net; f. 2001; brings together professionals working in radio, television, cinema, video, media education, internet and new technology; Sec.-Gen. ALVITO DE SOUZA.

Religion

Caribbean Conference of Churches: POB 876, Port of Spain, Trinidad and Tobago; tel. 662-3064; fax 662-1303; e-mail trinidad-headoffice@ccc-caribe.org; internet www.ccc-caribe.org; f. 1973; governed by a General Assembly which meets every five years and appoints a 15-mem. Continuation Committee (board of management) to establish policies and direct the work of the org. between Assemblies; maintains two subregional offices in Antigua, Jamaica and Trinidad with responsibility for programme implementation in various territories; mems: 33 churches in 34 territories in the Dutch-, English-, French- and Spanish-speaking territories of the region; Gen. Sec. GERARD GRANADO; publ. *Ecuscope Caribbean*.

Latin American Council of Churches (Consejo Latinoamericano de Iglesias—CLAI): Casilla 17-08-8522, Calle Inglaterra N.32–113 y Mariana de Jesús, Quito, Ecuador; tel. (2) 250-4377; fax (2) 256-8373; e-mail rita@claiweb.org; internet www.claiweb.org; f. 1982; mems: some 150 churches in 21 countries; Pres. Pastor FELIPE ADOLF (Argentina); Gen. Sec. Rev. NILTON GUISE (Brazil); publs *Nuevo Siglo* (monthly, in Spanish), *Latin American Ecumenical News* (quarterly), *Signos de Vida* (quarterly), other newsletters.

Latin American Episcopal Council (Consejo Episcopal Latinoamericano—CELAM): Carrera 5A 118–31, Apartado Aéreo 51086, Bogotá, Colombia; tel. (1) 5879710; fax (1) 5879117; e-mail celam@celam.org; internet www.celam.org; f. 1955 to co-ordinate Church activities in and with the Latin American and the Caribbean Catholic Bishops' Conferences; mems: 22 Episcopal Conferences of Central and South America and the Caribbean; Pres. Archbishop CARLOS AGUIAR RETES (Mexico); publ. *Boletín* (6 a year).

World Council of Churches (WCC): 150 route de Ferney, Postfach 2100, 1211 Geneva 2, Switzerland; tel. 227916111; fax 227910361; e-mail info@wcc-coe.org; internet www.oikoumene.org; f. 1948 to promote co-operation between Christian Churches and to prepare for a clearer manifestation of the unity of the Church; activities are grouped under the following programmes: The WCC and the ecumenical movement in the 21st century; Unity, mission, evangelism and spirituality; Public witness: addressing power, affirming peace; Justice, *diakonia* and responsibility for creation; Education and ecumenical formation; and Inter-religious dialogue and co-operation; mems: 349 Churches in more than 110 countries; Gen. Sec. Dr OLAV FYKSE TVEIT (Norway); publs *Current Dialogue* (2 a year), *Ecumenical News International* (weekly), *Ecumenical Review* (quarterly), *International Review of Mission* (quarterly), *WCC News* (quarterly), *WCC Yearbook*.

World Union of Catholic Women's Organisations: 76 rue des Saints-Pères, 75007 Paris, France; tel. 1-45-44-27-65; e-mail wucwoparis@wanadoo.fr; internet www.wucwo.org; f. 1910 to promote and co-ordinate the contribution of Catholic women in international life, in social, civic, cultural and religious matters; General Assembly held every four or five years (2014: Fátima, Portugal, in Oct.); mems: some 100 orgs representing 5m. women; Pres. MARIA GIOVANNA RUGGIERI (Italy); Sec.-Gen. MARIA LIA ZERVINO; publ. *Women's Voice* (quarterly, in 3 languages).

Science

Association for Tropical Biology and Conservation: e-mail chazdon@uconn.edu; internet www.tropicalbiology.org; f. 1963 as the Association for Tropical Biology (present name adopted in 2002), to promote research and to foster exchange of ideas among biologists working in tropical environments; holds annual Congress (July 2014: Cairns, Australia); Exec. Dir Dr ROBIN L. CHAZDON (USA); publ. *Biotropica* (2 a year).

Interamerican Network of Academies of Sciences: Calle Cipreses s/n, Col. San Andrés Totoltepec, Tlalpan, 14400 Mexico City, DF, Mexico; tel. (55) 5573-6501; fax (55) 5849-5112; e-mail ianas@ianas.org; internet www.ianas.org; f. 2004 as a regional network of the Academies of the Sciences; aims to build and assist national scientific capacities through shared research and technical knowledge; provides a forum for co-operation and decision-making for the scientific communities of the region; mems: 18 nat. and reg. asscns; Co-Chair. JUAN ASENJO, MICHAEL T. CLEGG; publs. scientific research reports.

International Council for Science (ICSU): 5 rue Auguste Vacquerie, 75116 Paris, France; tel. 1-45-25-03-29; fax 1-42-88-94-31; e-mail secretariat@icsu.org; internet www.icsu.org; f. 1919 as International Research Council; present name adopted 1998; revised statutes adopted 2011; incorporates national scientific bodies and International Scientific Unions, as well as 19 Interdisciplinary Bodies (international scientific networks established to address specific areas of investigation); through its global network co-ordinates interdisciplinary research to address major issues of relevance to both science and society; advocates for freedom in the conduct of science, promotes equitable access to scientific data and information, and facilitates science education and capacity building; General Assembly of representatives of national and scientific mems meets every three years to formulate policy. Interdisciplinary Bodies and Joint Initiatives: Future Earth; Urban Health and Well-being;

Committee on Space Research; Scientific Committee on Antarctic Research; Scientific Committee on Oceanic Research; Scientific Committee on Solar-Terrestrial Physics; Integrated Research on Disaster Risk; Programme on Ecosystem Change and Society; DIVERSITAS; International Geosphere-Biosphere Programme; International Human Dimensions Programme on Global Environmental Change; World Climate Research Programme; Global Climate Observing System; Global Ocean Observing System; Global Terrestrial Observing System; Committee on Data for Science and Technology; International Network for the Availability of Scientific Publications; Scientific Committee on Frequency Allocations for Radio Astronomy and Space Science; World Data System; mems: 121 national mems from 141 countries, 31 Int. Scientific Unions; Pres. LEE YUAN-TSEH (Taiwan); publs *Insight* (quarterly), *Annual Report*.

Social Sciences

International Peace Institute: 777 United Nations Plaza, New York, NY 10017-3521, USA; tel. (212) 687-4300; fax (212) 983-8246; e-mail ipi@ipinst.org; internet www.ipinst.org; f. 1970 (as the International Peace Academy) to promote the prevention and settlement of armed conflicts between and within states through policy research and devt; educates govt officials in the procedures needed for conflict resolution, peacekeeping, mediation and negotiation, through international training seminars and publications; off-the-record meetings are also conducted to gain complete understanding of a specific conflict; Chair. RITA E. HAUSER; Pres. TERJE RØD-LARSEN.

Latin American Faculty of Social Sciences (Facultad Latinoamericana de Ciencias Sociales—FLACSO): McDonald's de Curridabat, 300 m sur y 50 m oeste, Apdo 11801, 1000 San José, Costa Rica; tel. 2253-0082; fax 2234-6696; e-mail info@flacso.org; internet www.flacso.org; f. 1957 as a UNESCO initiative conceived at the Latin American Conference of Social Sciences, Rio de Janeiro; aims to develop research and teaching in the field of social sciences in South and Central America and the Caribbean; mems: Argentina, Brazil, Chile, Costa Rica, Cuba, Ecuador, El Salvador, Guatemala, Mexico, and Dominican Republic; Sec-Gen. Dr ADRIÁN BONILLA.

Social Welfare and Human Rights

Co-ordinator of the Indigenous Organizations of the Amazon Basin (COICA): Calle Sevilla 24–358 y Guipuzcoa, La Floresta, Quito, Ecuador; tel. (2) 3226-744; fax (2) 3226-744; e-mail com@coica.org.ec; internet www.coica.org.ec; f. 1984; aims to co-ordinate the activities of national orgs concerned with the indigenous people and environment of the Amazon basin, and promotes respect for human rights and the self-determination of the indigenous populations; mems: 9 orgs; Co-ordinator-Gen. EDWIN VÁSQUEZ CAMPOS; publ. *Nuestra Amazonia* (quarterly, in English, Spanish, French and Portuguese).

Global Migration Group: 4 route des Morillons, 1211, 19 Geneva, Switzerland; tel. 227179111; fax 227986150; e-mail supportteam@globalmigrationgroup.org; internet www.globalmigrationgroup.org; f. 2003, as the Geneva Migration Group; renamed as above in 2006; mems: the ILO, IOM, UNCTAD, UNDP, United Nations Department of Economic and Social Affairs (UNDESA), UNESCO, UNICEF, UNFPA, UNITAR, OHCHR, UNHCR, UNODC, UN Women, the UN Regional Commissions, WHO and the World Bank; holds regular meetings to discuss issues relating to international migration, chaired by mem. orgs on a six-month rotational basis.

Inter-American Conference on Social Security (Conferencia Interamericano de Seguridad Social—CISS): Calle San Ramón s/n Col. San Jeronimo Lidice Del. Magdalena Contreras, CP 10100, México, DF, Mexico; tel. (55) 5377-4700; fax (55) 5377-4716; e-mail ciss@ciss.org.mx; internet www.ciss.org.mx; f. 1942 to contribute to the devt of social security in the countries of the Americas and to co-operate with social security institutions; CISS bodies are: the General Assembly, the Permanent Inter-American Committee on Social Security, the Secretariat General, six American Commissions of Social Security and the Inter-American Center for Social Security Studies; mems: 66 social security institutions in 36 countries; Pres. Dr JOSÉ ANTONIO GONZÁLEZ ANAYA (Mexico); Sec.-Gen. JUAN LOZANO; publs *Social Security Journal / Seguridad Social* (every 2 months), *The Americas Social Security Report* (annually), *Social Security Bulletin* (monthly, online), monographs, study series.

International Federation of Red Cross and Red Crescent Societies (IFRC): 17 chemin des Crêts, Petit-Saconnex, CP 372, 1211 Geneva 19, Switzerland; tel. 227304222; fax 227330395; e-mail secretariat@ifrc.org; internet www.ifrc.org; f. 1919 to prevent and alleviate human suffering and to promote humanitarian activities by national Red Cross and Red Crescent societies; conducts relief operations for refugees and victims of disasters, co-ordinates relief supplies and assists in disaster prevention; Pres. TADATERU KONOÉ (Japan); Sec.-Gen. ELHADJ AMADOU G. SY (Senegal); publs *Annual Report*, *Red Cross Red Crescent* (quarterly), *Weekly News*, *World Disasters Report*, *Emergency Appeal*.

Sport and Recreations

Confederation of North, Central American and Caribbean Association Football: 1000 5th St, Suite 304, Miami Beach, FL 33139, USA; tel. (305) 704-3232; fax (305) 397-8813; e-mail contact@concacaf.org; internet www.concacaf.com; f. 1961 with the merger of the Football Confederation of Central America and the Caribbean (CCCF) and the North American Football Confederation (NAFC); governs football (soccer) in the North and Central America and Caribbean region in association with the FIFA; organizes regional inter-club and international competitions, and qualifying tournaments for the FIFA every four years; mems: 40 nat. asscns (35 full, 5 assoc mems); Pres. JEFFREY WEBB; Gen. Sec. ENRIQUE SANZ; publs *CONCACAF Signals* (weekly), *Newsletter* (online), statutes, regulations.

International Federation of Association Football (Fédération internationale de football association—FIFA): FIFA-Str. 20, POB 8044, Zürich, Switzerland; tel. 432227777; fax 432227878; e-mail media@fifa.org; internet www.fifa.com; f. 1904 to promote the game of association football and foster friendly relations among players and national asscns; to control football and uphold the laws of the game as laid down by the International Football Association Board; to prevent discrimination of any kind between players; and to provide arbitration in disputes between national asscns; organizes World Cup competition every four years (2014: Brazil); the FIFA Executive Committee—comprising the Federation's President, eight vice-presidents and 15 mems—meets at least twice a year; mems: 208 nat. asscns, 6 continental confeds; Pres. JOSEPH (SEPP) BLATTER (Switzerland); Sec.-Gen. JÉRÔME VALCKE (France); publs *FIFA News* (monthly), *FIFA Magazine* (every 2 months) (both in English, French, German and Spanish), *FIFA Directory* (annually), *Laws of the Game* (annually), *Competitions' Regulations* and *Technical Reports* (before and after FIFA competitions).

International Olympic Committee (IOC): Château de Vidy, 1001 Lausanne, Switzerland; tel. 216216111; fax 216216216; internet www.olympic.org; f. 1894 to ensure the regular celebration of the Olympic Games; the IOC is the supreme authority on all questions concerning the Olympic Games and the Olympic movement; established the independent World Anti-Doping Agency in 1999; Olympic Games held every four years (summer games 2016: Rio de Janeiro, Brazil; winter games 2014: Sochi, Russia; youth games 2014: Nanjing, People's Republic of China); mems: 115 representatives; Pres. THOMAS BACH (Germany); publs *Newsletter* (weekly), *Olympic Review* (quarterly).

International Rugby Board: Huguenot House, 35–38 St Stephen's Green, Dublin 2, Ireland; tel. (1) 240-9200; fax (1) 240-9201; e-mail irb@irb.com; internet www.irb.com; f. 1886; serves as the world governing and law-making body for the game of rugby union; supports education and devt of the game and promotes it through regional and world tournaments; since 1987 has organized a Rugby World Cup every four years (2011: New Zealand); holds General Assembly every two years; mems: 97 nat. unions as full mems, 20 assoc. mems and six reg. asscns; Chair. BERNARD LAPASSET; CEO BRETT GOSPER.

International Volleyball Federation (Fédération internationale de volleyball—FIVB): Château Les Tourelles, Edouard-Sandoz 2–4, Lausanne 1, Switzerland; tel. 213453535; fax 213453545; e-mail info@fivb.org; internet www.fivb.org; f. 1947 to encourage, organize and supervise the playing of volleyball, beach volleyball, and park volley; organizes biennial congress; mems: 220 nat. feds; Pres. Dr ARY DA SILVA GRAÇA FILHO (Brazil); publs *VolleyWorld* (every 2 months), *X-Press* (monthly).

Technology

Latin American Association of Pharmaceutical Industries (Asociación Latinoamericana de Industrias Farmaceuticas—ALIFAR): Av. Libertador 602, 6°, 1001 ABT Buenos Aires, Argentina; tel. and fax (11) 4819-9550; e-mail info@alifar.org.ar; f. 1980; mems: about 400 enterprises in 15 countries; Sec.-Gen. RUBÉN ABETE.

Latin-American Energy Organization (Organización Latinoamericana de Energía—OLADE): Avda Mariscal Antonio José de

Sucre, No N58–63 y Fernándes Salvador, Edif. OLADE, Sector San Carlos, POB 17-11-6413 CCI, Quito, Ecuador; tel. (2) 2598-122; fax (2) 2531-691; e-mail oladel@olade.org.ec; internet www.olade.org; f. 1973 to act as an instrument of co-operation in using and conserving the energy resources of the region; mems: 27 Latin-American and Caribbean countries; Exec. Sec. Dr FERNANDO CÉSAR FERREIRA; publ. *Enerlac Magazine*.

Tourism

Caribbean Hotel and Tourism Association: 2655 Le Jeune Rd, Suite 910 Coral Gables, FL 33134, USA; tel. (305) 443-3040; fax (305) 443-3005; internet www.caribbeanhotelandtourism.com; f. 1962 (as the Caribbean Hotel Asscn; name changed July 2008); represents and promotes the hotel and tourism industry in the Caribbean region; jointly owns and operates, with the Caribbean Tourism Organization, the Caribbean Tourism Development Co; mems: 849 hotels in 36 nat. hotel asscns; Chair. RICHARD DOUMENG; Pres. EMIL LEE; publ. *CHA Weekly News*.

Caribbean Tourism Organization: Ground Floor, Baobab Tower, Warrens, St Michael, Barbados; tel. 427-5242; fax 429-3065; e-mail ctobarbados@caribsurf.com; internet www.onecaribbean.org; f. 1989, by merger of the Caribbean Tourism Association (f. 1951) and the Caribbean Tourism Research and Development Centre (f. 1974); aims to encourage tourism in the Caribbean region; organizes annual Caribbean Tourism Conference, Sustainable Tourism Development Conference and Tourism Investment Conference; conducts training and other workshops on request; maintains offices in New York, Canada and London; mems: 32 Caribbean govts, 400 allied mems; Sec.-Gen. HUGH RILEY; publs *Caribbean Tourism Statistical News* (quarterly), *Caribbean Tourism Statistical Report* (annually).

Latin-American Confederation of Tourist Organizations (Confederación de Organizaciones Turísticas de la América Latino—COTAL): Viamonte 640, 3°, 1053 Buenos Aires, Argentina; tel. (11) 4322-4003; fax (11) 5277-4176; e-mail cotal@cotal.org.ar; internet www.cotal.org.ar; f. 1957 to link Latin American national asscns of travel agents and their mems with other tourist bodies around the world; mems: in 21 countries; Pres. LUIS FELIPE AQUINO; Sec. MARIA JOSE MANCHEGO; publ. *Revista COTAL* (every 2 months).

Trade and Industry

Cairns Group: (no permanent secretariat); e-mail agriculture .negotiations@dfat.gov.au; internet www.cairnsgroup.org; f. 1986 by major agricultural exporting countries; aims to bring about reforms in international agricultural trade, including reductions in export subsidies, in barriers to access and in internal support measures; represents mems' interests in WTO negotiations; mems: Argentina, Australia, Bolivia, Brazil, Canada, Chile, Colombia, Costa Rica, Guatemala, Indonesia, Malaysia, New Zealand, Pakistan, Paraguay, Peru, Philippines, South Africa, Thailand, Uruguay.

Caribbean Association of Industry and Commerce (CAIC): 27A Saddle Rd, Ground Floor, Maraval, Trinidad and Tobago; tel. 628-9859; fax 622-7810; e-mail caic.admin@gmail.com; f. 1955; aims to encourage economic devt through the private sector; undertakes research and training and gives assistance to small enterprises; encourages export promotion; mems: Antigua and Barbuda, Bahamas, Barbados, Belize, British Virgin Islands, Cayman Islands, Dominica, Dominican Republic, Grenada, Guyana, Haiti, Jamaica, Saint Christopher and Nevis, Saint Lucia, Saint Vincent and the Grenadines, Suriname, Trinidad and Tobago; Pres. RAMESH DOOKHOO (Guyana); publ. *Caribbean Investor* (quarterly).

CropLife International: 326 ave Louise, POB 35, 1050 Brussels, Belgium; tel. (2) 542-04-10; fax (2) 542-04-19; e-mail croplife@croplife .org; internet www.croplife.org; f. 1960 as European Group of National Asscns of Pesticide Manufacturers, international body since 1967, present name adopted in 2001, evolving from Global Crop Protection Federation; represents the plant science industry, with the aim of promoting sustainable agricultural methods; aims to harmonize national and international regulations concerning crop protection products and agricultural biotechnology; promotes observation of the FAO Code of Conduct on the Distribution and Use of Pesticides; holds an annual General Assembly; mems: 8 cos, reg. bodies and nat. asscns in 91 countries; Pres. and CEO HOWARD MINIGH.

Federación de Cámaras de Comercio del Istmo Centroamericano (Federation of Central American Chambers of Commerce): 9A avda Norte y 5, Calle Poniente 333, San Salvador, El Salvador; tel. 2231-3054; e-mail aechevarria@fecamco.com; internet www.fecamco.com; f. 1961; plans and co-ordinates industrial and commercial exchanges and exhibitions; mems: Chambers of Commerce in 11 countries; Pres. RAUL DELVALLE.

Instituto Centroamericano de Administración de Empresas (INCAE) (Central American Institute for Business Administration): Apdo 960, 4050 Alajuela, Costa Rica; tel. 2443-9908; fax 2433-9983; e-mail costarica@incae.edu; internet www.incae.edu; f. 1964; provides a postgraduate programme in business administration; runs executive training programmes; carries out management research and consulting; maintains a second campus in Nicaragua; libraries of 85,000 vols; Pres. ROBERTO ARTAVIA; publs *Alumni Journal* (in Spanish), *Bulletin* (quarterly), books and case studies.

Latin American Steel Association (Asociación Latinamericana del Acero—Alacero): Benjamín 2944, 5°, Las Condes, Santiago, Chile; tel. (2) 233-0545; fax (2) 233-0768; e-mail alacero@alacero.org; internet www.alacero.org; f. 1959 as the Latin American Iron and Steel Institute to help to achieve the harmonious devt of iron and steel production, manufacture and marketing in Latin America; conducts economic surveys on the steel sector; organizes technical conventions and meetings; disseminates industrial processes suited to regional conditions; prepares and maintains statistics on production, end uses, etc., of raw materials and steel products within this area; mems: 18 hon. mems, 48 active mems, 27 assoc. mems; Chair. MARTÍN BERARDI (Argentina); Sec. ROBERTO DE ANDRACA BARBAS (Chile); publs *Industry Year Book*, *Latin American Steel Directory* (online); also technical books, bulletins and manuals.

Transport

Pan American Railway Congress Association (Asociación del Congreso Panamericano de Ferrocarriles): Av. Dr José María Ramos Mejía 1302, Planta Baja, 1104 Buenos Aires, Argentina; tel. (11) 4315-3445; fax (11) 4312-3834; e-mail acpf@acpf.com.ar; f. 1907, present title adopted 1941; aims to promote the devt and progress of railways in the American continent; holds Congresses every three years; mems: govt representatives, railway enterprises and individuals in 20 countries; Pres. LORENZO PEPE; Gen. Sec. JULIO SOSA; publ. *Boletín ACPF* (5 a year).

Youth and Students

International Law Students Association (ILSA): 701 13th St, NW, 6th Floor Washington, DC 20005 USA; tel. (202) 729-2470; fax (202) 639-9355; e-mail ilsa@ilsa.org; internet www.ilsa.org; f. 1962; aims to educate students and lawyers around the world in the principles and purposes of international law, international orgs and institutions, and comparative legal systems; Exec. Dir LESLEY A. BENN.

Latin American and Caribbean Alliance of Young Men's Christian Associations (La Alianza Latinoamericana y del Caribe de Asociaciones Cristianas de Jóvenes): Rua N Pestana 125, 10° andar, Conj. 103, São Paulo 01303-010, Brazil; tel. (11) 3257-5867; fax (11) 3151-2573; e-mail secretariogeneral@lacaymca.org; internet www.lacaymca.org; f. 1914; aims to encourage the moral, spiritual, intellectual, social and physical devt of young men; to strengthen the work of national asscns and to sponsor the establishment of new asscns; mems: affiliated YMCAs in 94 countries; Pres. MAURO FONTICIELLA (Uruguay); Gen. Sec. MAURICIO DIAZ VANDORSEE (Brazil); publs *Diecisiete/21* (bulletin), *Carta Abierta*, *Brief*, technical articles and other studies.

WFUNA Youth Network: c/o WFUNA, 1 United Nations Plaza, Room DC1-1177, New York, NY 10017, USA; tel. (212) 963-5610; fax (212) 963-0447; e-mail youth@wfuna.org; internet www.wfuna.org/ youth; f. 1946 by the World Federation of United Nations Associations (WFUNA) as the International Youth and Student Movement for the United Nations, independent since 1949; an international non-governmental org. of students and young people dedicated especially to supporting the principles embodied in the United Nations Charter and Universal Declaration of Human Rights; encourages constructive action in building economic, social and cultural equality and in working for national independence, social justice and human rights on a worldwide scale; organizes periodic regional WFUNA International Model United Nations (WIMUN) confs; maintains regional offices in Switzerland and the USA; mems: asscns in over 100 mem. states of the UN.

World Alliance of Young Men's Christian Associations: 12 Clos-Belmont, 1208 Geneva, Switzerland; tel. 228495100; fax 228495110; e-mail office@ymca.int; internet www.ymca.int; f. 1855; organizes World Council every four years (2014: Estes Park, USA, in June–July); mems: YMCAs in 119 countries; Pres. PETER POSNER (United Kingdom) (2014–18); Sec.-Gen. Rev. JOHAN VILHELM ELTVIK (Norway) (2014–18); publ. *YMCA World* (quarterly).

MAJOR COMMODITIES OF LATIN AMERICA

Note: For each of the commodities in this section, there is a statistical table relating to recent levels of production and another table relating to prices on world markets. Each production table shows estimates of output for the world and for Latin America. In addition, the table lists the main Latin American producing countries and, for comparison, the leading producers from outside the region.

ALUMINIUM AND BAUXITE (Aluminium or aluminum, *Al*)

Aluminium (known as aluminum in the USA and, generally, Canada) is the second most abundant metallic element in the earth's crust after silicon, comprising about 8% of the total. However, it is much less widely used than steel, despite having about the same strength and only half the weight. Aluminium has important applications as a metal because of its lightness, ease of fabrication and other desirable properties. Other products of alumina (aluminium oxide trihydrate, into which aluminium ore is refined) are materials in refractories, abrasives, glass manufacture, other ceramic products, catalysts and absorbers. Alumina hydrates are used for the production of aluminium chemicals, fire retardant in carpet-backing, and industrial fillers in plastics and related products. Bauxite is the principal aluminium ore. Nepheline syenite, kaolin, shale, anorthosite and alunite are all potential alternative sources of alumina, but these are not currently economic to process. Of all bauxite mined, approximately 85% is converted to alumina (Al_2O_3) for the production of aluminium metal. The developing countries, in which at least 70% of known bauxite reserves are located, supply some 60% of the ore required. According to the US Geological Survey (USGS), in 2013 32% of potential world bauxite resources were located in Africa, 23% in Oceania, 21% in Latin America and the Caribbean, and 18% in Asia.

The industry is structured in three stages: bauxite mining, alumina refining, and smelting. The alumina is separated from the ore by the Bayer process. After mining, bauxite is fed direct to process if mine-run material is adequate (as in Jamaica), or else it is crushed and beneficiated. Where the ore 'as mined' presents handling problems, or weight reduction is desirable, it may be dried prior to shipment. At the alumina plant the ore is slurried with spent-liquor direct, if the soft Caribbean type is used, or, in the case of other types, it is ball-milled to reduce it to a size that will facilitate the extraction of the alumina. The bauxite slurry is then digested with caustic soda to extract the alumina from the ore while leaving the impurities as an insoluble residue. The digest conditions depend on the aluminium minerals in the ore and the impurities. The liquor, with the dissolved alumina, is then separated from the insoluble impurities by combinations of sedimentation, decantation and filtration, and the residue washed to minimize the soda losses. The clarified liquor is concentrated and the alumina precipitated by seeding with hydrate. The precipitated alumina is then filtered, washed and calcined to produce alumina. The ratio of bauxite to alumina is approximately 1.95:1. The smelting of the aluminium is generally by electrolysis in molten cryolite. Owing to the high consumption of electricity by the smelting process, alumina is usually smelted in areas where low-cost electricity is available. However, most of the electricity now used in primary smelting in the Western world is generated by hydroelectricity—a renewable energy source.

Production of Bauxite
(crude ore, '000 metric tons)

	2010	2011	2012	2013*
World total (excl. USA).	238,000	259,000	258,000	259,000
Latin America and Caribbean . . .	47,255	51,393	41,600	51,850
Latin American and Caribbean producers				
Brazil	32,028	33,695	34,000	34,200
Guyana	1,083	1,818	2,214	2,250
Jamaica†	8,540	10,189	9,339	9,550
Suriname	3,104	3,236	3,400	3,400
Venezuela . . .	2,500	2,455	2,000	2,500
Other leading producers				
Australia	68,414	69,976	76,282	77,000
China, People's Repub. .	44,000	45,000	47,000	47,000
Guinea†	15,300	15,300	17,823	17,000
India	18,000	19,000*	19,000*	19,000

—continued	2010	2011	2012	2013*
Indonesia* . . .	27,000	40,000	29,000	30,000
Kazakhstan . . .	5,310	5,495	5,170	5,100
Russia	5,690	5,943	5,700	5,200

* Estimated production.
† Dried equivalent of crude ore.

Source: US Geological Survey.

The World Market and the Region The high degree of 'vertical integration' (i.e. the control of successive stages of production) in the industry means that a significant proportion of trade in bauxite and alumina is in the form of intra-company transfers. The increasing tendency to site alumina refineries near to bauxite deposits has also resulted in a shrinking bauxite trade, but there is a growing free market in alumina, serving the needs of the increasing number of independent (i.e. non-integrated) smelters. The major markets for aluminium are in transportation, packaging, building and construction, electrical and other machinery and equipment, and consumer durables. Although the production of aluminium is energy-intensive, its light weight results in a net saving, particularly in the transportation industry, where the use of the metal as a substitute for steel, in particular in the manufacture of road motor vehicles and components, is well established. Aluminium is valued by the aerospace industry for its weight-saving characteristics and for its low cost relative to alternative materials. Aluminium-lithium alloys command considerable potential for use in this sector, although the traditional dominance of aluminium in the aerospace industry has been challenged since the 1990s by 'composites' such as carbonepoxy, a fusion of carbon fibres and hardened resins, the lightness and durability of which can exceed that of many aluminium alloys. The recycling of aluminium is economically, as well as environmentally, desirable, as the process uses only 5% of the electricity required to produce a similar quantity of primary aluminium. Recycling is of commercial significance in many countries, but the world leaders are Brazil, Japan and Argentina (2009 figures).

Based on mine output, in 2011 the world's largest aluminium companies were estimated to be United Company RUSAL (Russia), Rio Tinto Group (Australia/United Kingdom), Alcoa (USA) and Aluminium Corporation of China Ltd (Chinalco—especially its listed subsidiary, Chalco). Many of the remaining major companies are located in countries boasting the availability of cheap power: Norsk Hydro of Norway, Dubai Aluminium Co, China Power Investment Co, BHP Billiton (Australia/United Kingdom), Shandong Xinfa Aluminium and Electricity Group (China) and Aluminium Bahrain BSC, or Alba.

In 2013, according to USGS estimates, the People's Republic of China alone provided 45% of world primary aluminium production (21.5m. metric tons of a world total of 47.3m. tons), followed by Russia (8%), Canada (6%), the USA (4%), the United Arab Emirates (4%), Australia (4%), India (4%) and Brazil (3%). China displaced the USA as the most significant country for the international aluminium industry in the 2000s, accounting for about two-fifths of both consumption and production globally by 2013. The USA was for many years the world's principal producing country, but in 2001 US output of primary aluminium was surpassed by that of Russia and of China. From 2002 Canadian production also exceeded that of the USA. In 2013 production of primary aluminium by China was estimated to be 11 times that produced by the USA.

Brazil possesses extensive bauxite reserves in Pará and Minas Gerais states and in the Amazon region. A joint venture, Mineração Rio do Norte SA, accounted for one-half of Brazil's bauxite output in 2011 and was also one of the world's largest bauxite producers and exporters. The country's principal alumina producer in 2011 was Alumínio do Norte do Brasil (Alunorte). Alunorte is the world's largest refinery, helping to make Brazil the world's third largest alumina producer. The largest shareholder in Alunorte is Norsk Hydro, which bought the aluminium and bauxite assets of Companhia Vale do Rio Doce (Vale) in 2010. Primary aluminium production is dominated by Alumínio Brasileiro SA (Albras), Companhia Brasileira de Alumínio (CBA), Alcoa and BHP Billiton. Venezuela's aluminium industry achieved rapid growth in the 1980s, as a result of the availability of raw materials and cheap hydroelectric power. Aluminium production, based on imported alumina, subsequently overtook iron ore to become Venezuela's main export industry after petroleum. The country also has native bauxite resources and now produces some of its own alumina. Primary aluminium is produced at two smelters, in both of which state-controlled Corporación Venezolana de Guayana has a majority share. According to USGS, Venezuela's production of primary aluminium reached a record 634,000 tons in 1997 (which level it approached again in 2004), but subsequently declined, not only because of a less favourable world market, but because of the increasing problem of power shortages in the country. Unwrought aluminium sold abroad earned the country US $437m. in 2010, or 0.7% of total export revenues (compared with 2.4% in 2004). In 2011 bauxite and aluminium exports were estimated to be second only to petroleum in the minerals sector. The only other regional player in the aluminium industry is Argentina, which has a smelter. There have also been intermittent plans for a smelter in Trinidad and Tobago, which is strategically located on the shipping lanes from the bauxite-rich north-eastern coast of South American (see below).

Suriname and Guyana, sharing the north-eastern coast of the continent with Venezuela, also boast significant bauxite reserves. The economy of Suriname relies heavily on the mining and export of bauxite. In 1993 bauxite, alumina and aluminium accounted for 91.5% of Suriname's annual export earnings, whereas in 1978 the corresponding proportion had been 83.8%. The Suriname Aluminium Co, LLC (Suralco)—owned by Alcoa—has an alumina refinery at Paranam (in 2005 exports of alumina alone contributed about 48% of total export revenue). Provisional figures for Suriname from the Bank of Jamaica put exports of alumina and raw bauxite (the latter worth only 9% of alumina exports) up slightly in value in 2008; together, these accounted for 52.9% of general merchandise exports. Guyana's bauxite production industry is a major source of the country's export revenue (excluding revenue from re-exports), providing 11% of export revenues in 2012. Most of the country's production is by the Aroaima Bauxite Co, in which Russia's United Company RUSAL holds a 90% stake (the Government retains the other 10%). The other main company is Omai Bauxite Mines Incorporated (OBMI), which is 70% owned by Bosai Minerals of China. Both RUSAL and Bosai have considered establishing alumina refineries in Guyana, but in 2014 Bosai announced that international market conditions did not favour such a project at that time.

A production levy on the Jamaican bauxite industry provides an important source of government revenue. Production capacity in the Jamaican industry had increased in the second half of the 1980s in order to supply the strategic mineral stockpiles of both the USA and the USSR (sales of aluminium ores and concentrates, including alumina, accounted for 63% of total export earnings in 1990), but, post-Cold War, depressed conditions in the international market affected Jamaican income adversely in the 1990s. The recovering industry suffered again in the global recession that began in 2008, with alumina output badly affected (production facilities suspended operations for a time). By 2011 bauxite exports earnings had recovered steadily to J $12,200m., and alumina exports performed particularly well in that year to reach J $49,200m. Together alumina and bauxite accounted for 48% of domestic exports in 2011. The only other bauxite producer in the Caribbean is the Dominican Republic, which revived exploitation of its reserves in the 2000s, reaching production of some 0.5m. metric tons each year in 2005–07. By 2009 it was clear that any consolidation of production levels, given the global economic situation, was unlikely. In 2010 the USGS withdrew any estimates of bauxite production later than the figure given for 2005, which was 534,555 tons.

Global Forum The IAI, based in London, United Kingdom, is a global forum of producers of aluminium dedicated to the development and wider use of the metal. In 2014 the IAI had 26 member companies, representing every part of the world, including Russia and China, and responsible for more than 70% of global primary aluminium production and a significant proportion of the world's secondary output.

Aluminium Price on the London Metal Exchange
(average settlement price, US $ per metric ton)

	Average	High	Low
2000 .	1,549.14	(January) 1,680.28	(April) 1,457.14
2005 .	1,898.31	(December) 2,247.45	(June) 1,731.30
2010 .	2,173.12	(December) 2,350.67	(June) 1,931.39
2011 .	2,401.39	(April) 2,678.11	(December) 2,022.25
2012 .	2,023.28	(February) 2,207.92	(August) 1,845.38
2013 .	1,846.67	(February) 2,053.60	(December) 1,739.81

Source: World Bank, *Commodity Price Data* (Pink Sheet).

Prices The international benchmark price for aluminium cited here and by the World Bank is the average settlement price (unalloyed primary ingots, high grade—minimum 99.7% purity) traded on the London Metal Exchange (LME). Aluminium prices were particularly impacted upon by the global recession precipitated by the international financial crisis of 2008, with the average price falling to US $1,664.83 per metric ton for 2009, the lowest level since 2003. Recovery was strong, but average annual prices have declined since 2011, although an improvement was noted after February 2014 and had reached a monthly average of US $1,948 per ton by July of that year.

BANANA (*Musa sapientum*)

Although it is often erroneously termed a 'tree', the banana plant is, in fact, a giant herb. It grows to a height of 3–9 m (10–30 ft) and bears leaves that are very long and broad. The stem of the plant is formed by the overlapping bases of the leaves above. Bananas belong to the genus *Musa*, but the cultivated varieties are barren hybrid forms which cannot therefore be assigned specific botanical names. These banana hybrids, producing edible seedless fruits, are now grown throughout the tropics, but originally diversified naturally or were developed by humans in prehistoric times from wild bananas which grow in parts of South-East Asia. The plantain hybrid has grown in Central Africa for thousands of years, and traders and explorers gradually spread this and other varieties to Asia Minor and East Africa. The Spanish and Portuguese introduced them to West Africa and took them across the Atlantic to the Caribbean islands and the American continent. However, the varieties which are now most commonly traded internationally were not introduced to the New World until the 19th century.

The banana is propagated by the planting of suckers or shoots growing from the rhizome, which is left in the ground after the flowering stem, having produced its fruit, has died and been cut down. Less than one year after planting, a flowering stem begins to emerge from the tip of the plant. As it grows, the stem bends and hangs downwards. The barren male flowers which grow at the end of the stem eventually wither and fall off. The seedless banana fruits develop, without fertilization, from the clusters of female flowers further up the stem. Each stem usually bears between nine and 12 'hands' of fruit, each hand comprising 12–16 fruits. Before it is ripe, the skin of the banana fruit is green, turning yellow as it ripens. When ripe, the fruit is most commonly eaten raw, owing to its high sugar content (17%–19%). To obtain edible white flesh, the skin is peeled back. The numerous high-starch varieties with a lower sugar content, which are not eaten in their raw state, are used in cooking, mostly in the producing areas. Such varieties are picked when their flesh is unripe and more readily resistant to damage during transport, although they are occasionally of a type that would become sweet if left to ripen. Cooking bananas, sometimes called 'plantains' (though this term is also applied to types of dessert banana in some countries), form the staple diet of millions of inhabitants of the tropics, in particular in Eastern and Central Africa. Since they produce fruits all year round, bananas, like plantains, are of vital importance to food security in these countries. Bananas can also be used for making beer, and in East Africa special varieties are cultivated for that purpose. Advances in production methods, packaging, storage and transport (containerization) have made bananas available worldwide.

The process of fruiting and propagation can repeat itself indefinitely. In commercial cultivation the productive life of a banana field is usually limited to between five and 20 years before it is replanted, although small producers frequently allow their plants to continue fruiting for up to 60 years. Banana plantations are vulnerable to disease and to severe weather (particularly tropical storms), but the banana plant is fast-growing, and a replanted field can be ready to produce again within a year, albeit at a high cost. Since the 1950s international trade has been almost exclusively based on the Cavendish variety, which gained predominance after the formerly mass-produced Gros Michel variety became virtually extinct as a result of Panama disease—caused by a fungus that attacks the roots of the banana plant. A reinvigorated strain of the disease, known as tropical race 4 (TR4), became prevalent in South-East Asia from the mid-1990s and, ultimately, threatens the viability of the Cavendish variety. By 2010s, however, it was feared that the production of Cavendish bananas in the Americas was more immediately threatened by black sigatoka disease, or black leaf streak, a fungal leaf spot disease first identified in the 1960s, but hitherto held at bay by intensive spraying. Honduras succumbed to the disease in 1972; it reached Cuba in 1992 and all the smaller Caribbean islands by 2012. No alternative cultivar has yet emerged as a suitable replacement for the Cavendish variety, should that become necessary.

Production of Bananas
('000 metric tons, excluding plantains)

	2009	2010	2011	2012
World total . . .	100,224	105,726	106,058	101,993
Latin America and the Caribbean . . .	26,661	27,563	27,814	27,103
Leading Latin American and Caribbean producers				
Brazil	6,783	6,969	7,329	6,902
Colombia . . .	1,994	2,020	2,043	1,983
Costa Rica* . . .	1,795	2,020	2,125	2,136
Dominican Republic . .	590	735	830	872
Ecuador	7,637	7,931	7,428	7,012
Guatemala . . .	2,544	2,637	2,680	2,700†
Honduras . . .	719	751	755†	765†
Mexico . . .	2,232	2,103	2,139	2,204
Panama . . .	321	338	328	335†
Venezuela† . . .	400	413	416	450
Other leading producers				
Angola	1,985	2,048	2,646	2,991
Burundi . . .	1,846	1,913	1,849	1,184
China, People's Repub. .	8,834	9,561	10,400	10,550†
India	26,470	29,780	28,455	24,869
Indonesia . . .	6,374	5,755	6,133	6,189
Philippines . . .	9,013	9,101	9,165	9,226
Tanzania . . .	3,006	3,156	3,144	2,525
Thailand . . .	1,528	1,585	1,600†	1,650†
Viet Nam† . . .	1,428	1,490	1,523	1,560

* Unofficial figures.
† FAO estimate(s).
Source: FAO.

The World Market and the Region Dessert bananas are the leading exported fresh fruit in terms of volume, while their exports rank second in terms of value after those of citrus fruits. Only about one-sixth of banana production is traded internationally. Apart from the trade in fresh, sweet bananas, the fruit has few commercial uses, although there is a small industry in dried bananas and banana flour as well as in fibre production. Although international trade is principally in the sweet dessert fruit, this type comprises less than one-fifth of total annual world banana production. On the basis of gross value of production, bananas are the world's fourth most important food crop, after rice, wheat and maize. In 2011 they were cultivated in more than 130 countries and territories. Many types of sweet banana, unsuitable for export, are consumed locally. Indeed, most types of bananas and the vast majority of bananas grown in the tropics are produced by small-scale farmers either for home consumption or for local markets.

The banana was introduced into Latin America and the Caribbean by the Spanish and the Portuguese during the 16th century. The expansion of the banana industry in the small Latin American (so-called 'green' or 'banana') republics between 1880 and 1910 had a decisive effect in establishing this region as the centre of the world banana trade. Favourable soil and climatic conditions, combined with the ease of access around the Caribbean and to a major market in the USA, were important factors in the initial commercial success of the Latin American banana industry. Although advances in storage and transportation made the US market more accessible to producers in other areas, they also made available an equally important market in Europe (see below). Owing to considerably lower production costs than in other producing areas, bananas from South and Central America and the Caribbean command the major portion of the world export market (by weight, 67% in 2011, according to FAO—by value, 57%). Ecuador, Costa Rica, Colombia and Guatemala were among the five leading banana exporters in 2011, with Ecuador alone providing 31% of global banana exports in that year (one-quarter by value). It is there that the large multinational companies (notably Chiquita Brands International, Fresh Del Monte Produce and Dole Food Co) that dominate the world banana market are established operationally. The fourth global banana company is Ireland-based Fyffes, which in March 2014 agreed a merger with Chiquita, a move that would create the world's largest banana supplier, worth US \$4,600m. in annual revenues; the merger would involve relocating the statutory headquarters from the USA to Ireland, for tax reasons (in August 2014 Chiquita rejected an alternative merger proposal from Brazilian interests). According to FAO, the Philippines was the world's second largest exporter in 2011, at 11% of total global exports, but was closely followed by Costa Rica and Colombia, each on 10%, and Guatemala on 8%.

Bananas are grown in most Latin American countries. The Americas accounted for one-half of world banana production in the 1970s, and Asia for little more than one-third, but by 2012 the respective shares were 27% and 56%, although Latin America remains dominant in the export market. Brazil has traditionally been the leading producer of the Americas, but again the crop is mainly for local consumption and bananas contribute only a small proportion of the country's total export earnings. In Ecuador, however, where production in 1996–2000 and 2009–12 surpassed that of Brazil, bananas are the leading cash crop. Ecuador is the world's leading exporter of bananas, with shipments valued at an estimated US \$2,246.4m. in 2011, or 25% of the total worth of world exports (FAO figures). In 2013 banana exports accounted for 9.3% of the country's total export earnings. One in seven of the population is reportedly dependent on the banana trade in Ecuador. Banana shipments also make a marked contribution to the export receipts of Belize (14.7% in 2013), Honduras (providing 12.8% of the total in 2013), Panama (10.5% in 2012) and Costa Rica (7.1% in 2011), and are a useful source of foreign exchange in Guatemala (6.0% in 2013), the Dominican Republic (3.2% in 2010) and Colombia (2.5% of total export earnings in 2009; in the 2000s cut flowers displaced bananas as the second most important agricultural export in terms of value after coffee). Once important in Nicaragua, bananas provided 3.6% of total export revenue as recently as 2006, but barely 0.1% in 2012. The territories most dependent on bananas for export revenue tend to be the smaller producers, including Dominica (where bananas represented 21.8% of total exports, by value, in 2009—only 9.1% in 2010 owing to hurricane damage), Saint Lucia (13.3% in 2008) and Saint Vincent and the Grenadines (14.2% in 2010—down from 38% of total exports, including re-exports, in 2004). The French overseas departments of Guadeloupe (22% in 1997) and Martinique (40% in 2003) also remained highly dependent on banana exports; in 2012 they produced an estimated 60,000 and 260,000 metric tons of bananas, respectively. Jamaica and Grenada no longer export bananas. Banana exports from the region are frequently adversely affected by tropical storms and hurricanes, which can have a devastating effect on banana harvests.

Regional Associations There is no international agreement governing trade in bananas, but there are various associations—such as the Union of Banana-Exporting Countries (UPEB), comprising Colombia, Costa Rica, Ecuador, Guatemala, Honduras, Nicaragua and Panama; the Caribbean Banana Exporters' Association, comprising Jamaica, Belize, the Windward Islands and Suriname; and WIBDECO, the Windward Islands Banana Development Co—which have been formed by producer countries to protect their commercial interests. Prices have varied greatly, depending on relative wages and yields in the producing countries, freight charges, and various trade agreements negotiated under the Lomé Conventions or the later Cotonou Agreement between the European Community (EC, now the European Union—EU) and 71 African, Caribbean and Pacific (ACP) countries. The Lomé arrangements included a banana protocol, which ensured producers an export market, a fixed quota and certain customs duty concessions. The importance of these arrangements come from the fact that the major producers are not ACP countries, while the EU market is the most valuable in the world—the EU and the USA are the world's largest markets for bananas. There was, therefore, a lot at stake in the negotiations and disputes that evolved into the so-called 'banana wars' (see below).

Banana Prices
(average annual import price, US \$ per kg)

	European Union	USA
2000	0.71	0.42
2005	1.17	0.60
2010	1.00	0.87
2011	1.12	0.97
2012	1.10	0.98
2013	1.02	0.92

Source: World Bank, *Commodity Price Data* (Pink Sheet).

Prices Owing to local factors such as hurricanes or diseases in traditional suppliers, and transport costs, or the more general influence of differing trading regimes, prices in the two main markets could vary considerably and follow separate patterns. The two main benchmark prices are those for the EU market (major-brand bananas from Central and South America, free on truck Southern Europe, including duties) and for the USA (average import prices for major-brand bananas from Central and South America, free on truck US Gulf ports). In the first seven months of 2014, of the two markets, that serving the EU proved the more volatile: it ranged between US 99 cents per kg in January (monthly average) to US \$1.23 per kg in April, then declined to \$1.02 per kg in July. The US price started the year at 93 cents per kg and rose to 96 cents per kg in March, but fell to

91 cents per kg in May; the average monthly price in June and in July was stable again at 93 cents per kg.

The Banana Wars The prospect of the 1993 completion of the EC internal market provoked the trade dispute known as the 'banana wars', because the protection afforded to traditional national suppliers could not survive the removal of trade barriers between the different European nations. Powerful non-traditional suppliers also argued against any continuing distortion of the free market. Under the market arrangements prior to the end of 1992, just over one-half of banana imports were subject to quota controls under the Lomé Convention. Approximately 20% of market supplies were imported, duty-free, from former British, French and Italian colonies. The Windward Islands of Saint Lucia, Dominica and Grenada together accounted for some 90% of banana exports to the EC under the Lomé Convention's banana protocol, Jamaica and Belize also being parties to the Convention. About 70% of bananas from the Windward Islands were exported to the United Kingdom. France maintained similar arrangements with its traditional suppliers (overseas territories such as Guadeloupe and Martinique), as did Italy (Somalia). Another 25% of EC demand was satisfied internally, mainly from Spain (the Canary Islands), with smaller quantities from Portugal (Madeira and the Azores) and Greece (Crete). The remainder of quota imports (representing 10% of overall market demand) were imported, duty-free, into Germany, mainly from Latin and Central American countries. Banana imports into the residual free market originated mainly from the same countries, but attracted a 20% import tariff. This complex market structure strongly favoured the Caribbean islands and was maintained by barriers to internal trade, preventing the re-export of imports into Germany from, for instance, Honduras or Ecuador to the United Kingdom and France. Central and Latin American exporters, enjoying the cost advantages of modern technology and large-scale production (but subject to a 20% import tariff on their EC exports), would otherwise have substantially expanded their market share. The intent to end the tariff-free quota system after 1992 held serious implications for Caribbean producers. They were part of the ACP grouping, which sought to persuade the EC to devise a new preference system to protect their existing market shares and to accord with the obligations of the EC countries in relation to trade with the ACP under the terms of the Lomé Convention. In December 1992 the EC Commission announced that ACP banana producers were to retain their preferential status under the EC's single-market arrangements due to enter into force in July 1993, guaranteeing 30% of the European banana market to ACP producers by way of an annual duty-free quota. Imports of Latin American bananas were to be limited at a tariff of 20%, with any additional shipments to be subject to a tariff rate of 170%. Since tariffs were linked with quotas, the EC argued that it was not in contravention of the General Agreement on Tariffs and Trade (GATT) regulations on the restriction of market access. The arrangements were opposed by Germany, Denmark, Belgium and Luxembourg, as well as by the Latin American banana producers. In early 1993 the German Government unsuccessfully sought a declaration from the Court of Justice of the European Communities that the EC Commission was in violation of GATT free trade regulations. Ecuador, Guatemala, Honduras, Mexico and Panama obtained a GATT panel ruling in their favour in February 1994, provoking a compromise of an increased EC (now EU) quota, which was accepted by Colombia, Costa Rica, Nicaragua and Venezuela, but rejected by Ecuador and other Latin American producers.

The EU banana regime was complicated by the accession of new members in 1995 and 2004 and by the involvement of the US Government (the USA is only a marginal producer of bananas, but US business interests hold substantial investments in the multinational companies operating in Central and South America), which in September 1995 formally instituted a complaint against the EU with the World Trade Organization (WTO), the successor organization to the GATT. Further representations to the WTO by the US Government, supported by the Ecuador, Guatemala, Honduras and Mexico, followed in February 1996. In 2000 the EU, which ultimately favoured a tariff-only banana regime, proposed a licensed tariff quota system, but in response to further objections from Latin America and the USA in 2001 suspended its proposals in favour of consideration of a suggestion from US company Chiquita Brands International, which involved quotas with licenses based on historic market share rather than 'first come, first served'. The interim deal allowed some scope for new entrants to the market, but it was mainly designed to allow time to negotiate a tariff-only system, in which the EU's European Commission still sought some protection for domestic and ACP producers. (In 2001, at a WTO meeting in Doha, Qatar, the EU obtained a waiver allowing it to grant ACP countries a quota for duty-free exports of bananas to its market, although in return the EU assumed obligations that the Latin American producers later alleged it had reneged on.) In January 2006 the EU abandoned its tariff quota banana import regime in favour of a tariff-only system of €176 per metric ton for most favoured nation (MFN) suppliers. The new regime included a duty-free quota of 775,000 tons for ACP suppliers, which was mostly to be allocated on a 'first come, first served' basis.

In November 2006 Ecuador was the first to resume the long-standing dispute at the WTO, on the grounds that its banana exports were still unfairly discriminated against. The other main banana producers followed suit in March 2007, and the USA lodged a separate complaint in July. In February 2008 a WTO panel ruled that the EU's banana import regime, the tariff in particular, violated international trade rules and requested that the EU bring its regime into conformity with its obligations under the GATT. An EU appeal was rejected in November, although time was allowed for negotiations. The EU favoured a compromise that would involve a so-called 'peace clause' to end ongoing WTO banana-dispute procedures. The ACP banana-producing countries favoured a longer period for the introduction of any new regime and more compensatory support for their growers. The Latin American producers urged that the new tariff be lowered still further. Complicated by the wider negotiations around the stalled WTO Doha Round on world trade liberalization, the banana negotiations were broken off in July 2009 by Ecuador, backed by Colombia and Peru. However, in December the 'banana wars' seemed to be over, when the EU agreed to reduce the import tariffs for Latin American bananas from €176 per ton to €114 per ton over a transition period of eight years. The cases before the WTO were suspended, pending European compliance with the agreement concluded with the banana producers and the USA. The European Commission adopted the relevant proposals on 17 January 2010 (as well as proposing the Bananas Accompanying Measures, to assist the disadvantaged ACP suppliers, which were not party to the agreement, with €190m. in 2011–13).

Meanwhile, under the terms of the Cotonou Agreement, the successor convention to the fourth Lomé Convention which covers the period 2000–20, the system of trade preferences hitherto pertaining for the ACP countries was to be gradually replaced by new economic partnerships based on the progressive and reciprocal removal of trade barriers. In a protocol to the Cotonou Agreement (the Second Banana Protocol), the EU agreed to seek to ensure the continued viability of ACP banana export industries, and the continued access of their bananas to the EU market. (Given such provision, the ACP countries complained that they were not involved in the December 2009 agreement with the Latin American banana producers.) In a parallel move, in May 2010, at the EU-Latin American summit in Spain, the EU signed free trade agreements with a number of Central American countries and, separately, with Colombia and Peru, which promised a further reduction in tariffs, from €114 per metric ton to €75 per ton by 2020. Ecuador, however, rejected such an arrangement, arguing that its small economy had little chance against the weight of the European economy if openness was reciprocal. Instead, the country sought an 'accord for development', leaving the country a measure of protection, before tariff reductions for its regional competitors began to take effect. The 'banana' wars were considered formally over when the European Parliament legislated the tariff deal between the EU and the Latin American producers in February 2011; this was, however, strongly condemned by small farmers, in particular in the 10 most affected ACP states.

COCOA (*Theobroma cacao*)

The cacao or cocoa tree, up to 14 m tall, originated in the tropical forests of Central and South America. The first known cocoa plantations were in southern Mexico around AD 600, although the crop may have been cultivated for some centuries earlier. Cocoa first came to Europe in the 16th century, when Spanish explorers found the beans being used in Mexico as a form of primitive currency as well as the basis of a beverage. The Spanish and Portuguese introduced cocoa into West Africa at the beginning of the 19th century. Cultivated cocoa trees may be broadly divided into three groups. Most cocoas belong to the Amazonian Forastero group, which now accounts for more than 80% of world cocoa production. It includes Amelonado varieties, suitable for chocolate manufacturing, and widely cultivated in Brazil and in West Africa. Criollo cocoa is rarely grown and is used only for luxury confectionery. The third group is Trinitario—descending from a cross between the Criollo and Forastero varieties, first grown in Trinidad (Trinidad and Tobago)—which comprises about 15% of world output and is cultivated mainly in Central America and the northern regions of South America.

Cocoa is widely grown in the tropics, usually at altitudes of less than 300 m above sea-level, where it needs a fairly high rainfall and good soil. Cocoa trees can take up to four years from planting before producing enough fruit to merit harvesting. They may live for 80 years or more, although the fully productive period is usually about 20 years. The tree is very vulnerable to pests and diseases, and it is highly sensitive to climatic changes. Its fruit is a large pod, about 15–25 cm (6–10 in) long, which at maturity is yellow in some varieties and red in others. The ripe pods are cut from the tree, on which they grow directly out of the trunk and branches. When opened, cocoa pods disclose a mass of seeds (beans) surrounded by white mucilage. After harvesting, the beans and mucilage are scooped out and fermented.

Fermentation lasts several days, allowing the flavour to develop. The mature fermented beans, dull red in colour, are then dried, ready to be bagged as raw cocoa which may be further processed or exported. Much cocoa-processing takes place in importing countries, notably the USA and the Netherlands. The processes include shelling, roasting and grinding the beans. The primary product of grinding is chocolate liquor, a part of which is sold directly to chocolate-manufacturers; the remainder is then processed further, in order to extract a fat—cocoa butter—and chocolate powder. Almost half of each bean after shelling consists of cocoa butter. Cocoa powder for use as a beverage is largely fat-free. Cocoa is a mildly stimulating drink, because of its caffeine content, and, unlike coffee and tea, is highly nutritious. The most important use of cocoa liquor is in the manufacture of chocolate, of which it is the main ingredient. About 90% of all cocoa liquor produced is used in chocolate-making, for which extra cocoa butter is added, as well as other substances, such as sugar and, in the case of milk chocolate, milk. Cocoa butter is also used in cosmetic products, while the by-products of cocoa beans—the husks and shells—are used to make fertilizers and animal feed.

Production of Cocoa Beans
('000 metric tons)

	2009	2010	2011	2012
World total . . .	4,207	4,339	4,679	5,003
Latin America and the Caribbean . . .	594	627	767	708
Leading Latin American and Caribbean producers				
Brazil	218	235	249	253
Colombia	45	40	44	50
Dominican Republic . .	55	58	54	72
Ecuador	121	132	224	133
Mexico*	60	61	83	83
Peru	37	47	57	39
Other leading producers				
Cameroon	236	264	239†	256†
Côte d'Ivoire . . .	1,223	1,301	1,559	1,650*
Ghana	711	632	700	879
Indonesia	810	845	712	936
Nigeria	364	399	391*	383*
Papua New Guinea† .	59	39	48	39
Togo†	105	102	143	35

* FAO estimate(s).
† Unofficial figure(s).

Source: FAO.

The World Market and the Region In the 2000s mounting concerns about European Union (EU) and US moves to permit chocolate-manufacturers to substitute vegetable fats for some of the cocoa solids and cocoa fats used in the manufacture of chocolate products were alleviated to an extent by consumer demand for high cocoa-content products (driven by perceived health benefits and the promotion of refined flavours) and the growing interest in organic produce. According to the International Cocoa Organization (ICCO), such changes in consumption have mainly benefited the economies of those countries recognized by the International Cocoa Council (ICC) as exporters of premium cocoa (Colombia, Costa Rica, Dominica, the Dominican Republic, Ecuador, Grenada, Indonesia, Jamaica, Madagascar, Papua New Guinea, Peru, Saint Lucia, São Tomé and Príncipe, Trinidad and Tobago, and Venezuela). At the same time as this qualitative shift in consumption, which has expanded existing, saturated markets, increased consumption in emerging and newly industrialized countries, in particular in Russia and in Asia, has sustained demand for bulk cocoa. Another development has been the combination of growing consumer concerns about poverty in less developed countries with a more organized fair-trade movement, which has established steady growth in sales of fair-trade products since the early 1990s, mainly in Europe.

The cocoa production chain is extremely labour-intensive: the International Cocoa Organization (ICCO) estimated that in the 2000s some 3m. smallholders accounted for 90% of global cocoa output. Large-scale plantations are found only in Brazil and Indonesia. The cocoa-processing industry, meanwhile, is highly concentrated. In the 2000s the ICCO reckoned that the three major companies (Archer Daniels Midland—ADM and Cargill of the USA, and Barry Callebaut of Switzerland) processed about 40% of global cocoa production. Into the 2010s further consolidation took place. In July 2013 Barry Callebaut bought the cocoa unit of Petra Foods of Singapore, making the Swiss company the world's largest cocoa processor (alone accounting for 25% of the global market); later

that year Cargill was reported to be negotiating to buy the cocoa business of ADM, which would have created another giant to challenge Barry Callebaut—the two companies would have controlled up to 60% of cocoa processing. ADM resolved to keep its processing interests in April 2014, instead looking to divest simply its chocolate business. Other major cocoa traders include Olam International Ltd (Singapore) and Ecom Agroindustrial Corporation (Switzerland).

In 2012, according to FAO, the most important producing area in the world was Africa, which accounted for 66% of total output, followed by South-East Asia and Oceania, at 20%, and Latin America and the Caribbean, at 14%. In 2011 Africa accounted for 73% of foreign sales of cocoa beans worldwide, by volume, South-East Asia and Oceania only 10% (more usually up to one-fifth) and Latin America and the Caribbean 8% (the balance includes re-exports). According to provisional ICCO figures, the largest single producer of cocoa beans in 2013/14 (the cocoa year runs October–September) was Côte d'Ivoire, with a forecast 1.61m. metric tons, followed by Ghana with 850,000 tons and Indonesia with 425,000 tons; Nigeria produced 230,000 tons and was followed by the largest Latin American producers, Brazil and Ecuador, each harvesting some 210,000 tons, with Cameroon on 205,000 tons. World output of cocoa beans was put at 4.12m. tons (compared with 3.93m. tons in 2012/13 and 4.09m. tons in 2011/12); ICCO figures for production tend to be lower. Only about two-fifths of the processing (grinding) of cocoa beans still takes place in the country of origin (44% in 2013/14, according to the ICCO), but the Netherlands remains the world leader, accounting for an estimated 13% of the expected world total of 4.20m. tons in 2013/14, followed by Côte d'Ivoire (12%—firmly back in second place after its political upheavals) and then the USA and Germany (each on 10%). Overall, Europe accounted for 39% of grindings, Asia and Oceania 21%, the Americas 21% and Africa 19%. Global consumption of chocolate products is dominated by the European Union (EU—more than one-half) and by Northern America (one-quarter).

Brazil is Latin America's largest producer of cocoa beans, but its exports are far exceeded by those of Ecuador and indeed most other major regional producers (notably the Dominican Republic, Peru and Haiti, and to a lesser extent Colombia, Nicaragua and Panama), which have far smaller domestic markets. Furthermore, Brazil has more processing facilities and is the leading regional exporter of cocoa butter and cocoa paste. The crops of the Latin American countries can be affected by weather conditions related to El Niño (an aberrant current which periodically causes the warming of the Pacific coast of South America, disrupting usual weather patterns). Since the devastation caused to Ecuador's cocoa crop as a result of El Niño in 1997–98, and fluctuating fortunes thereafter, the country began to benefit into the 2000s both from its efforts to focus increasingly on the production of high-quality chocolate and from rising world prices for cocoa beans. Export earnings continued to rise after 2009, according to UN figures, reaching $471.7m. in 2011, or 2.1% of total exports. In 2012 the Dominican Republic derived 2.7% of its export earnings from cocoa beans (excluding exports from free trade zones). According to FAO, the third largest regional exporter in 2011 was Peru, with 20,264 tons, compared with 50,994 tons from the Dominican Republic and 157,782 tons from Ecuador (together the three countries accounted for 95% of cocoa bean exports from Latin America and the Caribbean).

International Associations In accordance with the first International Cocoa Agreement (ICCA—see below), the International Cocoa Organization (ICCO) was established in 1973. The ICCO is based in London, United Kingdom. Under the 2001 sixth ICCA, at October 2010 the membership of the Agreement, and hence of the Organization, comprised 44 countries (15 exporting members, 29 importing members), representing about 85% of world cocoa production and some 60% of world cocoa consumption. The European Union (EU) was also an intergovernmental party to the 2001 Agreement, but the USA, a leading importer of cocoa, was not a member, nor was Indonesia. Membership of the 2010 ICCA by March 2014 included Indonesia (by now the third largest producer in the world) among the 18 exporting members; the 29 importing members included all 28 EU members and Switzerland, as before, but not Russia (nor, still, the USA). The governing body of the ICCO is the International Cocoa Council (ICC), established to supervise implementation of the ICCA. The ICC is also based in London (a review of plans to relocate to Abidjan, Côte d'Ivoire, was postponed to 2015, pending security considerations). The Cocoa Producers' Alliance (COPAL), with headquarters in Lagos, Nigeria, had 10 members as of 2014: Brazil, Cameroon, Côte d'Ivoire, the Dominican Republic, Gabon, Ghana, Malaysia, Nigeria, São Tomé and Príncipe, and Togo. The alliance was formed in 1962 with the aim of preventing excessive price fluctuations by regulating the supply of cocoa. Members of COPAL currently account for about three-quarters of world cocoa production. COPAL has acted in concert with successive ICCAs.

ICCO Cocoa Price

(ICCO daily price, selected quotations, US $ per metric ton)

		Average	High	Low
2000	.	910	(July) 970	(February) 860
2005	.	1,540	(March) 1,760	(November) 1,440
2010	.	3,130	(January) 3,530	(September) 2,880
2011	.	2,980	(February) 3,470	(December) 2,200
2012	.	2,390	(November) 2,480	(June) 2,260
2013	.	2,440	(December) 2,820	(March) 2,150

Source: World Bank, *Commodity Price Data* (Pink Sheet).

Prices The principal centres for cocoa-trading in the industrialized countries are the London Cocoa Terminal Market, in the United Kingdom, and the New York Coffee, Sugar and Cocoa Exchange, in the USA. The ICCO daily price is based on the average of the first three positions on the terminal markets of New York and London (nearest three future trading months). Prices were at their highest in the late 1970s, even in nominal terms, when they reached an annual average of US $3.79 per kilogram ($3,790 per metric ton) in 1977 and $3.29 per kg in 1979. Prices only rose above $3.00 per kg again in the 2000s ($3.13 per kg in 2010). Average monthly prices fell as low as $2.02 per kg in February 2013, but recovered thereafter, rising above $3.00 per kg in March 2014 and reaching $3.20 per kg ($3,200 per ton) in July.

The International Cocoa Agreements World prices for cocoa are highly sensitive to changes in supply and demand, making its market position volatile. Negotiations to secure international agreement on stabilizing the cocoa industry began in 1956. Full-scale cocoa conferences, under UN auspices, were held in 1963, 1966 and 1967, but all proved abortive. A major difficulty was the failure to agree on a fixed minimum price. In 1972 the fourth UN Cocoa Conference took place in Geneva, Switzerland, and resulted in the first International Cocoa Agreement (ICCA), adopted by 52 countries, although the USA, the world's principal cocoa importer at that time, did not sign. The ICCA took formal effect in October 1973, bringing into existence the ICCO, based in London. Agreements in that year, in 1979, in 1981 (plus extension) and in 1987 initially operated for three quota years and provided for an export quota system for producing countries, a fixed price range for cocoa beans and a buffer stock to support the agreed prices. The buffer stock (which ceased to operate during 1983–88) and other financial operations under the fourth ICCA contributed to problems in the price stabilization mechanism. The fourth ICCA was extended for a two-year period from October 1990, although the suspension of the economic clauses rendered the agreement ineffective in terms of exerting any influence over cocoa market prices.

A fifth ICCA was delayed by agreement to extend the fourth ICCA for a further year (until October 1993), because consumer members refused to accept producers' proposals for the creation of an export quota system, on the grounds that such arrangements would not impose sufficient limits on total production to restore equilibrium between demand and supply. Additionally, no agreement was reached on the disposition of cocoa buffer stocks. In July 1993 terms were finally agreed for a new ICCA, to take effect from October, subject to its ratification by at least five exporting countries (accounting for at least 80% of total world exports) and by importing countries (representing at least 60% of total imports). Unlike previous commodity agreements sponsored by the UN, the fifth ICCA aimed to achieve stable prices by regulating supplies and promoting consumption, rather than through the operation of buffer stocks and export quotas. The new ICCA took effect in February 1994, to operate until 1998, although it was subsequently extended until September 2001. Stocks reduction and limitation were complemented by a number of other measures to achieve a closer balance of production and consumption. In April 2000 the ICCO agreed to implement measures to remedy low levels of world prices, centring on the elimination of sub-grade cocoa in world trade, which was perceived to be having a damaging effect on prices.

A sixth ICCA was negotiated in February 2001. It aimed not only for stable prices through the regulation of supplies and the promotion of consumption, but for the development of a sustainable cocoa economy. The Agreement took provisional effect on 1 October 2003, for an initial five-year period; it was twice extended for two years, latterly from 1 October 2010. In November 2005, on its ratification by the Dominican Republic, the sixth ICCA entered definitively into force. (This was the first time that an ICCA had ever entered definitively into force.) The Agreement was to remain open to new signatories until 2010, and was extended to when the next Agreement was due to enter into force. A seventh ICCA was signed in Geneva on the last day of the UN Cocoa Conference of 21–25 June 2010. It was opened for signature on 1 October for two years (subsequently extended to 2026). In July 2011 Costa Rica became the third signatory to the document, after Switzerland and the EU. Previous agreements had been for five years, with exten-

sions possible. The new document built on the strengths of the 2001 Agreement, improving product quality and co-operation between exporters and importers, emphasizing improved incomes for farmers and other producer benefits, and aiming for sustainability in the cocoa economies. The 2010 Agreement, unlike the previous five-year accords, was to be in effect for 10 years, provisionally from 1 October 2012, with the possibility of two four-year extensions, recognizing the perceived success of the existing regime.

COFFEE (*Coffea*)

The coffee plant is an evergreen shrub or small tree, generally 5–10 m tall, indigenous to Asia and tropical Africa. Wild trees grow to 10 m, but cultivated shrubs are usually pruned to a maximum of 3 m. The dried seeds (beans) are roasted, ground and brewed in hot water to provide one of the most popular of the world's non-alcoholic beverages. Coffee is drunk in every country in the world, and its consumers comprise an estimated one-third of the world's adult population. Although it has little nutrient value, coffee acts as a mild stimulant, owing to the presence of caffeine, an alkaloid also present in tea and cocoa.

There are about 40 species of *Coffea*, most of which grow wild in the eastern hemisphere. The two species of chief economic importance are *C. arabica* (native to Ethiopia), which in the mid-2000s accounted for about 60%–65% of world production, and *C. canephora* (the source of Robusta coffee), which accounted for almost all of the remainder. Arabica coffee is more aromatic, but Robusta, as the name implies, is a stronger plant. Coffee grows in the tropical belt, between 20°N and 20°S, and from sea-level to as high as 2,000 m above. The optimum growing conditions are found at 1,250–1,500 m above sea-level, with an average temperature of around 17°C and an average annual rainfall of 1,000–1,750 mm. Trees begin bearing fruit three to five years after planting, depending upon the variety, and give their maximum yield (up to 5 kg of fruit per year) from the sixth to the 15th year. Few shrubs remain profitable beyond 30 years.

Arabica coffee trees are grown mostly in the American tropics and supply the largest quantity and the best quality of coffee beans. The yield of Arabica trees has a propensity to follow a biennial cycle, whereby a heavy crop alternates with a light crop. In Africa and Asia Arabica coffee is vulnerable in lowland areas to a serious leaf disease, and consequently cultivation has been concentrated in highland areas. Some highland Arabicas, such as those grown in Kenya, are renowned for their high quality. The Robusta coffee tree, grown mainly in East and West Africa, and in the Far East, has larger leaves than Arabica, but the beans are generally smaller and of lower quality and, consequently, fetch a lower price. However, Robusta coffee has a higher yield than Arabica, as the trees are more resistant to disease. It can also be grown at lower elevations than Arabica, from 500 m to 1,500 m above sea level. Robusta varieties are popular among multinational roasters and soluble ('instant') coffee producers.

Each coffee berry, green at first but red when ripe, usually contains two beans (white in Arabica, light brown in Robusta) which are the commercial product of the plant. To produce the best quality Arabica beans—known in the trade as 'mild' coffee—the berries are opened by a pulping machine and the beans fermented briefly in water before being dried and hulled into green coffee. Much of the crop is exported in green form. Robusta beans are generally prepared by dry-hulling. Roasting and grinding are usually undertaken in the importing countries, for economic reasons, and because roasted beans rapidly lose their freshness when exposed to air. Apart from beans, coffee produces a few minor by-products. When the coffee beans have been removed from the fruit, what remains is a wet mass of pulp and, at a later stage, the dry material of the 'hull' or fibrous sleeve that protects the beans. Coffee pulp is used as cattle feed; the fermented pulp makes a good fertilizer; and coffee bean oil is an ingredient in soaps, paints and polishes.

More than one-half of the world's coffee is produced on smallholdings of less than 5 ha in area. In most producing countries coffee is almost entirely an export crop, for which (with the exception of Brazil, after the USA the world's second largest coffee consumer) there is little domestic demand. Green coffee accounts for some 96% of all the coffee that is exported, with soluble and roasted coffee comprising the balance. Tariffs on green/raw coffee are usually low or non-existent, but those applied to soluble coffee may be as high as 30%. The USA is the largest single importer, although its volume of coffee purchases was overtaken in 1975 by the combined imports of the (then) nine countries of the European Community (EC, now the European Union—EU). By 2012/13 the USA accounted for 24% of world coffee imports, followed by Germany, itself buying 20% (the EU as a whole, 66%).

Production of Green Coffee Beans
('000 bags, each of 60 kg, local coffee years)

	2010/11	2011/12	2012/13	2013/14*
World total . . .	133,065	132,207	145,323	145,194
Latin America and the Caribbean† . . .	80,986	78,583	86,098	82,210
Leading Latin American and Caribbean producers				
Brazil	48,095	43,484	50,826	49,152
Colombia	8,523	7,652	10,415	11,000
Costa Rica . . .	1,392	1,462	1,571	1,437
El Salvador . . .	1,184	1,152	1,360	844
Guatemala . . .	3,950	3,840	3,743	3,130
Honduras . . .	4,331	5,903	4,537	4,200
Mexico	4,001	4,563	4,327	3,900
Nicaragua . . .	1,634	2,193	1,884	1,500
Peru	4,069	5,373	4,453	4,334
Venezuela . . .	1,202	902	952	900
Other leading producers				
Côte d'Ivoire . . .	982	1,886	2,046	2,100
Ethiopia . . .	7,500	6,798	6,233	6,600
India	4,728	5,117	5,303	5,075
Indonesia . . .	9,129	7,288	13,048	11,667
Papua New Guinea . .	870	1,414	717	828
Tanzania . . .	846	544	1,109	791
Uganda . . .	3,203	2,817	3,698	3,600
Viet Nam . . .	19,467	22,289	22,030	27,500

* Estimated figures.

† Excluding Guyana and Trinidad and Tobago, which, with other unlisted non-members of the ICO, are included in the world total.

Source: International Coffee Organization.

The World Market and the Region After petroleum, coffee is the major raw material of world trade, and it is the single most valuable agricultural export of the tropics. In the 2010s about 26m. small producers worldwide depended on coffee. Coffee is the most important cash crop of Latin America, with a number of countries heavily dependent on it as a source of foreign exchange. Of the estimated total world crop of coffee beans in 2013/14, Latin American and Caribbean countries accounted for 57% (Brazil alone contributed 34% of the world total). Africa, which formerly ranked second, was overtaken in 1992/93 by Asian producers; in 2013/14 African producers accounted for 11% of the estimated world coffee crop, compared with 29% for countries in eastern Asia and Oceania—Far East and Australasia. India harvested a further 3.5% of the world coffee crop in the same year; the only other producer in South Asia was Sri Lanka, not a member of the International Coffee Organization—ICO. (The above shares have been calculated on the basis of data released by the ICO. Non-members of the ICO accounted for 6% of the world coffee crop in 2013/14.) The 2013/14 harvest was lower than it would otherwise have been primarily because it was the higher yield year in the biennial Arabica cycle for the important Brazilian crop.

Robusta coffee beans, which are more suitable for the production of instant coffee or coffee for flavouring, etc., are favoured by multinational roasters and instant coffee producers because of the lower cost and less volatile price. Soluble ('instant') coffee accounted for about 12.5% of all coffee exports in 2000–11. In the mid-2000s four main roaster companies (Kraft Foods, Nestlé, Procter & Gamble, and Sarah Lee) purchased more than 50% of global Robusta coffee production. Some predicted a shift towards more mass Arabica purchases from 2014 by the large roasting companies.

Brazil and Colombia together consistently accounted for more than 32% of world trade in green (unroasted) coffee during the 1990s. By 2002 more than 43% of all coffee traded worldwide emanated from Brazil and Colombia. In the ICO year to June 2014 exports by Brazil and Colombia represented about 41% of all coffee exported worldwide. Coffee (roasted, unroasted and decaffeinated) provided 1.9% of Brazil's total merchandise exports in 2013. In terms of volume, Brazilian coffee exports reached a record level of 33.4m. bags (each of 60 kg) in 2013/14. The state of Minas Gerais—which grows mainly Arabica trees—accounted for an average 48% of total Brazilian coffee production and 63.4% of Brazil's Arabica output in 2001/02–2006/07, according to data compiled by the US Department of Agriculture (USDA). Between 70% and 75% of Brazil's harvest (depending on the biennial cycle) comes from Arabica trees, and the country's coffee output (and all the more so that of Minas Gerais) is largely determined by that tree's biennial cycle.

Coffee remains the leading legal cash export crop in Colombia, although its relative importance in the country's economy declined in the 1990s, when it was overtaken by petroleum and its derivatives as the main source of export earnings. Colombia produces only Arabica varieties of coffee. 'Colombian Mild' Arabica coffee beans, to which the country has given its name, are regarded as being of a superior quality to other coffee types and are grown primarily in Colombia, Kenya and Tanzania. (Colombian Milds are one of four internationally designated coffee groups, the others being Other Milds, which are produced primarily in Central America; Brazilian Natural Arabicas, which are produced primarily in Brazil and Ethiopia; and Robustas, of which the main producers are Viet Nam, Indonesia and Brazil.) According to the ICO, Colombian coffee output suffered from 2008, because of the impact of the global economic crisis as well as the besetting problems of pests, disease, climate change and the short-term effect of the tree renovation programme. Shipments of coffee from Colombia accounted for 6%–7% of the country's total export earnings in the mid-2000s, but the proportion declined after 2008 (3.2% in 2013) as production declined, although offset somewhat by increased international prices from 2010. Coffee consumption in Colombia (around 2 kg per caput per year) is far below the consumption levels of neighbouring countries, and Colombia exports 85% of its production. Colombian exports of coffee totalled 10.6m. bags in 2013/14. In response to the mounting competition from Brazilian or Vietnamese producers—who benefit from extremely low labour costs—from the 1990s onward, the Colombian coffee sector focused increasingly on 'gourmet' coffee, which commands a higher profit margin. According to USDA, high-quality 'specialty' coffee exports quadrupled in 2002–08.

Traditionally, Arabica coffee was the principal export crop in El Salvador, Guatemala, Haiti, Mexico, Nicaragua and Peru, and the second most important crop in Costa Rica, the Dominican Republic, Ecuador, Honduras and Puerto Rico. By the second decade of the 21st century Honduras was firmly in the first group. Sales of coffee contributed 38.7% of El Salvador's total export earnings in 1997, but unfavourable weather, disease (rust), civil war and falling coffee prices reduced production thereafter, and from 2001 the contribution of coffee to the country's export revenue was less than 10%. In 2008 exports of coffee (excluding the *maquila* zones), bolstered by high international prices, represented 12.7% of total export earnings, but the share then fell to only 6.3% in 2010 and, despite strengthening international prices pushing the figure to 11.3% in 2011, to 5.4% of the total by 2013. The global economic crisis of 2008 and international prices thereafter had a similar effect in all countries. Coffee provided only 7.1% of Guatemala's total export earnings in 2013, owing to a serious disease infestation (see below). Sales of Nicaraguan coffee, which also exhibit signs of the biennial fluctuation of the Arabica crop, accounted for 18.7% in 2008, but reached 19.5% in 2012, before falling to 14.6% in 2013. In Honduras coffee has displaced bananas as the country's principal agricultural export commodity; it contributed about one-fifth of export revenue (excluding the *maquila* zones and gold exports) in the mid-2000s, but then increased steadily, and record shares for coffee exports were recorded from 2008, reaching 27.1% in 2010 and an overwhelming 36.2% in 2011; exports increased slightly in value in 2012, although the share was 33.2%, but in 2013 exports fell sharply and only contributed 19.6% of exports, owing to the affliction of coffee rust. Honduras was the only producer to experience an expansion in the sector after 2008, because national policies to encourage farmers continued. Honduras surpassed Guatemala as Central America's largest exporter in 2010/11. In Costa Rica coffee ranks second to bananas as the principal export commodity. The country grows only Arabica highland coffee, which commands a premium on the world market, and achieves some of the highest yields in the world. None the less, coffee contributes a diminishing share of the country's export revenue on account of Costa Rica's successful economic diversification away from cash crops since the 1960s. In 2011 coffee accounted for 3.7% of Costa Rica's total export earnings, compared with 10.8% in 1997. Mexico has a large domestic market and is not as important an exporter as Guatemala or Honduras. Moreover, the country's varied economy means that it is not dependent on coffee exports in any way. Panama produces a small amount of coffee for local consumption.

Peru's export volumes went from 3.1m. bags in 2009/10 to 5.1m. bags in 2011/12, to surpass even Honduran sales abroad and to exceed the exports of any country in Latin America and the Caribbean except Brazil and Colombia—indeed, globally, only three other countries outside the region managed more exports. Coffee accounted for 2.2% of Peru's total export earnings in 2012, the low year of the Arabica biennial cycle and when coffee rust began to become a serious problem for the country's crop. Peru accounted for 54% of the coffee produced by non-members of the ICO in 2013. Elsewhere, Jamaica's speciality Blue Mountain coffee, though produced in small amounts, is much sought after, particularly in Japan.

Since the last decades of the 20th century Latin American Arabica production has been inhibited by the coffee berry borer, or broca, beetle, which has been described as the most damaging pest to coffee worldwide. Endemic to Central Africa, the beetle was first detected in Brazil in 1926. Guatemala and Mexico were affected in the 1970s, followed by Colombia in the late 1980s and the Dominican Republic in the 1990s. It was identified in Puerto Rico in August 2007. The beetle has been estimated to cost Latin American producers US $500m. annually in lost production. Infestation has been particularly acute in Colombia, where, at one time the beetle, which cannot be effectively eliminated by pesticides, depredated two-thirds of the total area under coffee. From the late 1990s experimental research aimed at eliminating the beetle through biotechnological methods was proceeding in Ecuador, Guatemala, Honduras, Jamaica, Mexico and India. In 2013, however, another disease emerged to threaten coffee production in Central America in particular; coffee crops were already under threat from a warmer climate in the region, but climate seems to have contributed to an upsurge of a fungal disease known as coffee rust (roya), which attacks Arabica varieties. First reported in Kenya in 1861, the disease devastated coffee production in many places in Africa and Asia in the late 19th and 20th centuries; it first reached the Americas in the 1970s, but emerged as a particular problem in 2013, prompting a 'national emergency' in the Guatemalan coffee industry and continuing problems in Peru, for example.

International Associations The International Coffee Organization (ICO) was established in London, United Kingdom, in 1963 under the first International Coffee Agreement (see below). At July 2014, the ICO consisted of 39 exporting members and six importing members (33 importing nations in all, because one member was the 28-country EU); a further five countries had signed the seventh ICA but had not yet completed all membership procedures, while six more countries had not signed. In addition, there was an Association of Coffee Producing Countries (ACPC), also based in London, but it closed in 2002, although there is still an Inter-African Coffee Organization (IACO), based in Côte d'Ivoire (see below).

ICO Coffee Prices
(ICO average annual indicator, US $ per metric ton)

						Arabicas	Robustas
2000	.	.	.	.	.	1,920	910
2005	.	.	.	.	.	2,530	1,110
2010	.	.	.	.	.	4,320	1,740
2011	.	.	.	.	.	5,980	2,410
2012	.	.	.	.	.	4,110	2,270
2013	.	.	.	.	.	3,080	2,080

Source: World Bank, *Commodity Price Data* (Pink Sheet).

Prices Coffee is traded on a number of exchanges worldwide. The ICO has two main indicator prices, one for Arabica beans (other mild Arabicas, average New York and Bremen/Hamburg markets, ex-dock) and the other for Robusta beans (Robustas, average New York and Le Havre/Marseilles markets, ex-dock). In the 2010s coffee again approached price levels similar to those experienced in the late 1970s, but only at current prices. Moreover, that is mainly true of the Arabica price, because the differential from the Robusta price has become more pronounced, although the indicators to some echo each other's movement on a price graph: the all-time coffee price peak was in April 1977, the average monthly price for Arabicas reaching US $7.00 per kg (the Robusta price peaked at $6.88); the 2011 peak for Arabicas was $6.62 per kg in April (but for Robustas, $2.69 per kg in May); prices fell to a low point in November 2013, $2.69 per kg for Arabicas ($1.76 per kg for Robustas); the monthly price rose to $4.93 per kg in April 2014 ($2.33 per kg) and was $4.34 per kg ($2.24 per kg) in July 2014.

The International Coffee Agreements Effective international attempts to stabilize coffee prices began in 1954, when a number of producing countries made a short-term agreement to fix export quotas. After three such agreements, a five-year International Coffee Agreement (ICA), covering both producers and consumers and introducing a quota system, was signed in 1962. This led to the establishment in 1963 of the ICO. Successive ICAs took effect in 1968, 1976, and 1983. The system of export quotas to stabilize prices was eventually abandoned in July 1989, contributing to a crisis in coffee prices as oversupply undermined market stability. In October 1993 the USA withdrew from the ICO (it did not rejoin it until 2005), which was increasingly perceived at that time to have been eclipsed by the Association of Coffee Producing Countries (ACPC—see below). In 1994 the ICO agreed provisions for a new five-year ICA (later extended), again with primarily consultative and administrative functions, and a successor ICA took effect provisionally in October 2001, and definitively in May 2005. By May 2007 the new ICA had been endorsed by 74 of the 77 members (45 exporting countries, 32 importing countries) of the International Coffee Council (ICC), the highest authority of the ICO. A seventh ICA, agreed between the 77 members of the ICC, was formally adopted in September 2007. The new agreement reiterated the objectives contained in the sixth ICA, emphasizing the need to support the advancement of a sustainable coffee economy to benefit small-scale farmers. It established in particular a Consultative Forum of Coffee Sector Finance that was to facilitate access to financial and market information in the coffee sector, and a Promotion and Market Development Committee that was to co-ordinate information campaigns, research and studies.

The ICAs are concerned with maintaining a stable price environment for the worldwide coffee market, but numerous and various disagreements led to the collapse of the quota system and of the extant ICA's economic provisions. The failure to agree on a new formulation for quotas and the existence of high stock levels combined to keep coffee prices at historic 'lows' in the early 1990s. In September 1993 the Latin American producers announced the formation of an Association of Coffee Producing Countries (ACPC) to implement an export-withholding, or coffee-retention, plan. In the following month the 25-member Inter-African Coffee Organization (IACO) agreed to join the Latin American producers in a new plan to withhold 20% of output whenever market prices fell below an agreed level. With the participation of Asian producers, a 28-member ACPC, with headquarters also in London, was formally established in August (its signatory member countries numbered 28 in 2001, 14 of which had ratified). Production by the 14 ratified members in 1999/2000 accounted for 61.4% of coffee output worldwide. In the meantime the ACPC coffee-retention plan had come into operation in October 1993 and gradually generated improved prices. Ultimately, however, the ACPC was unable—even with the support of non-members—to bring about lasting price stability by pursuing coffee/export-retention strategy. In October 2001 the ACPC announced that it would dissolve itself in January 2002, its relevance compromised by breaches of the retention plan and poor finances. Meanwhile, in May 2001 the collapse in the price of coffee had been described as the most serious crisis in a global commodity market since the 1930s, with prices at their lowest level ever in real terms. The collapse of the market was regarded, fundamentally, as the result of an ongoing increase in world production at twice the rate of growth in consumption, this oversupply having led to an overwhelming accumulation of stocks. (In this connection, some observers highlighted the role of Viet Nam, which had substantially increased its production and exports of coffee in recent years: by mid-2000 Viet Nam had overtaken Indonesia to become the world's leading supplier of Robusta coffee and was rivalling Colombia as the second largest coffee-producing country overall.) In early July 2001 the price of the Robusta coffee contract for September delivery fell below US $540 per metric ton, marking a record 30-year 'low'. At about the same time the ICO recorded its lowest composite price ever. Despite a recovery beginning in October, the average composite price recorded by the ICO for 2001 was 29% lower than the average composite price recorded in 2000. In 2001 coffee prices were at their lowest level since 1973 in nominal terms, and at a record low level in real terms. Although prices began to recover slowly, the low returns for producers in the early 2000s created what was sometimes called the 'coffee crisis'. In its review of the 2004/05 crop year, the ICO noted that the crisis in the coffee economy of exporting countries had abated somewhat, although oversupply of Robustas and increased demand for Arabicas increased the differential between the two prices. Against this background, the seventh ICA sought to protect not only markets, but farmers, in future.

COPPER (*Cu*)

Copper is a reddish-orange metal (copper compounds, by contrast, often give a blue or green colour to minerals) in use even before the 'Bronze Age', the characteristic metal of which was obtained by the addition of tin to copper. The ores containing copper are mainly copper sulphide or copper oxide. They are mined both underground and by open-cast or surface mining. After break-up of the ore body by explosives, the lumps of ore are crushed, ground and mixed with reagents and water, in the case of sulphide ores, and then subjected to a flotation process by which copper-rich minerals are extracted. The resulting concentrate, which contains about 30% copper, is then dried, smelted and cast into anode copper, which is further refined to about 99.98% purity by electrolysis (chemical decomposition by electrical action). The cathodes are then cast into convenient shapes for working or are sold as such. Oxide ores, less important than sulphides, are treated in ways rather similar to the solvent extraction process described below.

Two alternative copper extraction processes were developed in the 20th century. The first of these techniques, and of little importance in the industry, is known as the 'Torco' (treatment of refractory copper ores) segregation process, which can be used for extracting copper from silicate ores that were previously not treatable. A commercial plant was operated in Zambia from the 1960s, until 1983, and another in Mauritania in the 1970s. The second, and relatively low-cost, technique is the solvent extraction process. This is suited to the treatment of very low-grade oxidized ores and is used on both new ores and waste dumps that have accumulated over previous years from conventional copper working. The copper in the ore or waste material is dissolved in acid, and the copper-bearing leach solution is then mixed with a special organic-containing chemical reagent which selectively extracts the copper. After allowing the two layers to separate, the layer containing the copper is separated from the acid leach solution. The copper is extracted from the concentrated leach solution by means of electrolysis to produce refined cathodes.

Production of Copper Ore
(copper content, '000 metric tons)

	2010	2011	2012	2013*
World total . . .	16,100	16,100	16,900	17,900
Latin America . .	7,309	7,083	7,170†	7,480†
Leading Latin American producers				
Chile	5,419	5,263	5,430	5,700
Mexico	270	444	440	480
Peru	1,247	1,235	1,300	1,300
Other leading producers				
Australia	870	958	958	990
Canada	525	566	579	630
China, People's Repub.* .	1,200	1,310	1,630	1,650
Congo, Democratic Repub.*	430	520	600	900
Kazakhstan . . .	427	417	424	440
Poland	425	427	427	430
Russia*	703	713	883	930
USA	1,110	1,110	1,170	1,220
Zambia*	686	668	690	830

* Estimated production.
† Figures represent the sum of output in listed countries.
Source: US Geological Survey.

The World Market and the Region Copper is ductile, resists corrosion, and is an excellent conductor of heat and electricity. Its industrial uses are mainly in the electrical industry (about 60% of copper is made into wire for use in power cables, telecommunications, domestic and industrial wiring) and the building, engineering and chemical industries. Bronzes and brasses are typical copper alloys used for both industrial and decorative purposes. There are, however, substitutes for copper in almost all of its industrial uses, and in recent years aluminium has presented a challenge in the electrical and transport industries. The major copper-importing countries are the People's Republic of China, the member states of the European Union (EU), Japan and the USA. According to the International Copper Study Group (ICSG), worldwide usage of refined copper reached a new record in 2013 of 21.2m. metric tons (provisional figure), with the rising trend continuing into 2014. In 2013 Asia accounted for 65% of refined usage and Europe 20%.

Since 1982, when it overtook the USA, Chile—where, according to the US Geological Service (USGS) in 2013, 28% of world copper reserves are located—has been the world's leading producer of copper. It is also the biggest exporter. The world's two largest copper mines (La Escondida and CODELCO Norte, which includes Chuquicamata—expected to become an underground mine by 2020), as well as the fourth, fifth and seventh (Collahuasi, Los Pelambres and El Teniente) in 2012, are located within the country. (The third largest mine, at 2012, is Grasberg in Indonesia.) Production at the Escondida Norte open pit copper mine, which is adjacent to the original Escondida open pit mine, began in 2005. The Chilean economy relies heavily on the copper industry; in 2011 copper exports accounted for 53% of total merchandise sold abroad. Chile's copper industry benefited from the 2004 conclusion of a free trade agreement with the USA and, later, from high international prices, although the industry has been vulnerable to labour unrest and to geographical and climatic adversities; nevertheless, foreign investment in Chilean mining development has risen. The state-owned copper corporation CODELCO is the world's leading copper mining company. Chile also has significant refinery capacity.

After Chile, the Latin American country to which the copper industry is most important is Peru. For a decade until the mid-1990s, however, the industry was adversely affected by the country's economic instability and by guerrilla attacks on the mines. The restoration of relative internal stability, together with the phased privatization of the state-owned mining corporation, Centromín, stimulated foreign investment in mining exploration ventures. In June 1999 it was announced that financing had been secured for the proposed development of the Antamina copper-zinc mine, which began operations in late 2001, and by April 2002 was already the most productive in Peru. In 2012 Antamina was the sixth largest copper mine in the world. Chinese investment had become increasingly evident in the 2000s. Earnings from foreign sales of copper (including copper and copper alloys and copper ores and concentrates), valued at US $10,542m., accounted for 23% of Peru's total export revenues in 2011. Mexico's two leading mines are the Cananea mine in the state of Sonora, operated by Mexicana de Cananea, and Mexicana de Cobre's La Caridad mine; 80% of Mexico's copper in 2011 came from Sonora. In 2008 copper still accounted for the largest share of the value of Mexican mineral production (21%), but in 2009, with 16.6% of the total, it came after gold (22.9%) and silver (18.3%),

reflecting lower industrial activity in the world and the soaring investment value of the precious metals.

Elsewhere in Latin America, Brazil is hoping that Vale's Salobo project, located at the country's largest copper deposit, will increase production enough to make Brazil self-sufficient in copper supplies by 2015. The development of deposits of copper in Argentina commenced in 1997; almost all the country's output comes from Minera Alumbrera's Bajo de la Alumbrera facility. In 2011 Brazil produced 221,050 metric tons of copper, Argentina 116,829 tons, Colombia some 1,000 tons and the Dominican Republic 300 tons. In Panama, as of 2014, two of the world's largest copper deposits, one in Cerro Colorado district, Chiriqui province, the other in Cerro Petaquilla district, province of Colón, remained undeveloped, although First Quantum of Canada had begun work at the latter.

International Association The International Copper Study Group (ICSG), initially comprising 18 producing and importing countries, was formed in 1992 to compile and publish statistical information and to provide an intergovernmental forum on copper. In 2014 ICSG members and observers totalled 23 countries, plus the European Union (EU), accounting for more than 80% of world trade in copper. The ICSG, which is based in Lisbon, Portugal, does not participate in trade or exercise any form of intervention in the market.

Copper Price on the London Metal Exchange
(average settlement price, US $ per metric ton)

	Average	High	Low
2000 .	1,813.47	(September) 1,960.41	(April) 1,678.75
2005 .	3,678.88	(January) 3,170.00	(December) 4,576.78
2010 .	7,534.78	(December) 9,147.26	(June) 6,499.30
2011 .	8,828.19	(April) 9,867.60	(October) 7,394.19
2012 .	7,962.35	(March) 8,470.78	(June) 7,423.02
2013 .	7,332.10	(February) 8,060.93	(July) 6,906.64

Source: World Bank, *Commodity Price Data* (Pink Sheet).

Prices There is no international agreement between producers and consumers governing the stabilization of supplies and prices. Although most of the world's supply of primary and secondary copper is traded direct between producers and consumers, prices quoted on the London Metal Exchange (LME), the New York Commodity Exchange (COMEX) and the Shanghai Futures Exchange (SHFE) provide the principal price-setting mechanism for world copper trading. The World Bank cites the average settlement price of Grade 'A' copper (minimum purity 99.9935%) traded on the LME.

Along with other commodities, copper experienced exceptionally high prices into the beginning of 2008, until economic recession occasioned by the global financial crisis of that year set in. In real terms at least, the price did not exceed the record levels of early 1974, which had collapsed with the onset of the oil crisis of that year. In nominal terms, the average annual copper price in 1974 was only US $2,58.5 per metric ton (monthly averages peaked in April at $3,031.8 per ton), and compared with, in 2008, $6,955.8 per ton (peaking in April at $8,684.93 per ton). Copper recovered to a new nominal record in 2011, the monthly average peaking at an all-time high, at current prices, of $9,867.6 per ton in February, with the highest daily price reaching over $10,100 per ton. Prices tended downwards thereafter into 2014, reaching as low as $6,650.04 per ton in March 2014, although they recovered to $7,113.38 per ton in July.

IRON ORE (Iron, *Fe*)

Iron is, after aluminium, the second most abundant metallic element in the earth's crust, and its ore volume production is far greater than that of any other metal. Some ores contain 70% iron, while a grade of only 25% is commercially exploitable in certain areas. The main economic iron-ore minerals are magnetite and haematite, which are used almost exclusively to produce pig-iron and direct-reduced iron (DRI—also known as sponge iron). These comprise the principal raw materials for the production of crude steel (which makes up about 95% of global metal production).

Most iron ore is processed after mining to improve its chemical and physical characteristics, and is often agglomerated by pelletizing or sintering. The transformation of the ore into pig-iron is achieved through reduction by coke in blast furnaces; the proportion of ore to pig-iron yielded is usually about 1.5:1 or 1.6:1. Pig-iron is used to make cast iron and wrought iron products, but most of it is converted into steel by removing most of the carbon content. Particular grades of steel (e.g. stainless) are made by the addition of ferro-alloys such as chromium, nickel and manganese. From the 1990s processing technology was being developed in the use of high-grade ore to produce DRI, or sponge iron, which, unlike the iron used for traditional blast furnace operations, requires no melting or refining. The DRI process, which is based on the use of natural gas, expanded rapidly in Venezuela, but, owing to technological limitations, is not expected within the foreseeable future to replace more than a small proportion of the world's traditional blast-furnace output. Venezuela and Mexico were the leading producers of DRI into the beginning of the 21st century, but India became increasingly the world's largest single producer from 2003 (Venezuelan production fell dramatically in the 2010s). The energy-rich Middle East and North Africa was the leading producing region for DRI.

Production of Iron Ore
(iron content, '000 metric tons)

	2008	2009	2010	2011*
World total . . .	1,130,000	1,090,000	1,290,000	1,390,000
Latin America . . .	265,164	226,468	279,306	281,789
Leading Latin American producers				
Brazil	233,514	198,710	247,772	248,000
Chile	5,670	5,006	5,852	7,747
Mexico	7,013	7,007	8,400	7,722
Peru*	5,244	4,490	6,140	7,124
Venezuela* . . .	13,423	11,100	11,100	11,100
Other leading producers				
Australia	209,000	228,000	271,000	277,000
Canada†	20,300	20,000*	23,300*	21,000
China, People's Repub.* .	270,000	280,000	332,000	412,000
India*	138,000	144,000	147,000	154,000
Russia*	57,500	53,200	58,500	60,000
South Africa‡ . . .	30,800	34,800	38,000	38,500
Ukraine*	40,000	36,600	43,000	44,300
USA	33,800	16,600	31,300	34,300

2012 (gross weight, million metric tons): Brazil 398, Venezuela 27; Australia 521, China 1,310, India 144, Russia 105. **2013** (gross weight, million metric tons, estimates): Brazil 398, Venezuela 30; Australia 530, China 1,320, India 150, Russia 102.
* Estimated production.
† Including the metal content of by-product ore.
‡ Including magnesite ore ('000 metric tons): 3,987 in 2008; 4,725 in 2009; 5,474 in 2010; 5,325 in 2011.

Source: US Geological Survey.

The World Market and the Region As the basic feedstock for the production of steel, iron ore is a major raw material in the world economy and in international trade. After petroleum, the iron ore trade is the second largest commodity market by value (but still generally equivalent to less than one-10th of the crude market). Mining the ore usually involves substantial long-term investment, so until about 2010 up to 60% of trade was conducted under long-term contracts, while the mine investments were financed with some participation from consumers. Stability was undermined by the arrival of the People's Republic of China on the international markets; in 2004 China surpassed Japan as the world's leading importer, and its burgeoning internal market ended a system based on steady slow growth in the iron ore mining sector. After the international financial crisis in 2008 particularly, but also given preceding commodity price fluctuations, producers became frustrated with the inflexibility of long-term contracts and began to favour quarterly and then monthly average-based contracts, or 'spot' pricing, thereby fuelling a derivatives market (see below).

The international trade in iron ore expanded for a 12th successive year in 2013. In that year, on the basis of data compiled by the International Steel Statistics Bureau (ISSB), almost one-half of world exports of iron ore were provided by Australia (49%) and a further one-quarter by Brazil (26%), followed by South Africa (5%). India, previously an important exporter, faced problems in dealing with illegal mining from 2010 and exports collapsed. According to data from the UN Conference on Trade and Development (UNCTAD) Trust Fund Project on Iron Ore Information, between 2001 and 2010 four countries—China, Japan, the Republic of Korea (South Korea) and Germany—had consistently accounted for more than two-thirds of all world imports of iron ore; over that period, however, China's share in the world total had gone from 19% to 59%, while Japan's share declined from 26% to 13%, South Korea's from 9% to 5% and Germany's from 8% to 4%. Iron ore exports globally had doubled between 1999 and 2008, mainly owing to increased demand from China. The three largest iron ore companies in the world together accounted for 35.2% of global iron ore production in 2012 (Vale 16.0%, Rio Tinto 9.9% and BHP Billiton 9.3%). The three companies are even more significant in export markets, controlling 57% of the world seaborne trade of iron ore in 2011.

Iron ore is widely distributed throughout Latin America. Brazil is by far the dominant producer in the region, and its ore is of a high quality (67% iron). Brazil's vast open-cast mine in the Serra do Carajás began production in 1986. The project, now the largest iron ore mine in the world, was developed by the Companhia Vale do Rio Doce (CVRD—now known as Vale), which also operates several other mines in the state of Minas Gerais. The Carajás deposit contains 7,200m. metric tons of high-grade proven and probable reserves (67% iron). Vale, which has invested huge amounts in order to protect its leading global position in the iron ore industry, produced about 85% of Brazil's beneficiated iron ore in 2012, which totalled 401m. tons; the other main companies were Minerações Brasileiras Reunidas—MBR SAMARCO Mineração and Companhia Siderúrgica Nacional—CSN. Iron ore is the main export commodity in Brazil, which is the major supplier to the world market after Australia. Sales of iron ore and concentrates provided 13.4% of Brazil's total export earnings in 2013. Brazil also has a major iron and steel industry, producing extra export revenue. Venezuela has proven reserves of more than 4,000m. metric tons of crude ore. About one-half of total proven reserves is classified as high-grade ore. Iron ore vies with aluminium to be the second most important export industry (after petroleum). Ferrominera Orinoco (FO) is the country's sole producer; some disruption to the processing industry occurred in the 2000s owing to nationalization policies, which affected the level of foreign investment. Sales of iron ore and concentrates provided 1.0% of Venezuela's total export earnings in 2010, but sales of iron and steel provided a further 1.6% contribution to the total. Latin America's only other iron ore producers of significance are Mexico, which produces mainly to satisfy the demands of its local steel industry, and Chile.

International Association The Association of Iron Ore Exporting Countries (Association des Pays Exportateurs de Minerai de Fer—APEF) was established in 1975 to promote close co-operation among members, to safeguard their interests as iron ore exporters, to ensure the orderly growth of international trade in iron ore, and to secure 'fair and remunerative' returns from its exploitation, processing and marketing. Since 1975 APEF, which also collects and disseminates information on iron ore from its secretariat in Geneva, Switzerland, has had nine members: Algeria, Australia, Chile, India, Mauritania, Peru, Sierra Leone, Tunisia and Venezuela. UNCTAD compiles statistics on iron ore production and trade, and has established a permanent international forum for discussion of issues affecting the industry.

Iron Ore Price
(unless otherwise indicated, average 'spot' settlement, US $ per metric ton)

	Average	High	Low
2000* .	28.79	—	—
2005* .	65.00	—	—
2010 .	145.86	(April) 172.47	(January) 125.72
2011 .	167.75	(February) 187.18	(November) 135.54
2012 .	128.50	(April) 147.64	(September) 99.47
2013 .	135.36	(February) 154.64	(June) 114.82

* Annual contract price (Brazil to Europe, f.o.b., $ per ton).

Source: World Bank, *Commodity Price Data* (Pink Sheet).

Prices Until 2009 world reference prices for iron ore were decided annually at a series of meetings between producers and purchasers (the steel industry accounts for about 95% of all iron ore consumption), but when China failed to agree prices with major producers, and with 'spot' prices for iron ore soaring in the latter half of that year when miners were still selling at prices agreed in March, the system effectively collapsed in 2010. The USA and the republics of the former USSR, although major steel producers, rely on domestic ore production and had taken little part in the price negotiations. It was generally accepted that, because of its diversity in form and quality, iron ore was ill-suited to price stabilization through an international buffer stock arrangement.

Given the complexity of the old pricing system, a general trend can be indicated from the prices cited by the World Bank—the average 'spot' price per dry metric ton (cost and freight) to China of iron ore (fines, 62% *Fe*) of any origin. By the 2000s Chinese demand was the principal determinant of prices in the international iron ore trade, although fears about prospects for growth in the world economy, in particular because of the European sovereign debt crisis, contributed to price volatility. In the 2010s less clarity on prices and greater volatility were also encouraged by the pressure on supply, expected up to 2015, given the length of time new capacity takes to come into production. From November 2013, however, through to June 2014, the average monthly iron ore price tended downwards, to reach US $92.74 per metric ton in the latter month; the July price was $96.05 per ton.

As previously outlined, the annual series of benchmark negotiations to determine iron ore prices finally ended in early 2010. Even the commercially dominant Chinese steel companies, as well as the Japanese and European steel industry organizations, could not resurrect the process, which was replaced by a general model of quarterly semi-negotiated prices. Criticism of the new system is focused on the inherent uncertainties and lack of transparency, according to the UNCTAD Trust Fund Project on Iron Ore Information: price settlements were no longer announced and the published 'spot' prices remained unreliable.

MAIZE (Indian Corn, Mealies) (*Zea mays*)

Maize is one of the world's three principal cereal crops, with wheat and rice. The main varieties are dent maize (which has large, soft, flat grains) and flint maize (which has round, hard grains). Dent maize is the predominant type worldwide, but flint maize is widely grown in southern Africa and parts of South America. Maize may be white or yellow (there is little nutritional difference) but the former is preferred for human consumption. Native to the Americas, maize was brought to Europe by Christopher Columbus and has since been dispersed to many parts of the world. It is an annual crop, planted from seed, and matures within three to five months. It requires a warm climate and ample water supplies during the growing season. Genetically modified varieties of maize, with improved resistance to pests, are now being cultivated, particularly in the USA, Argentina and the People's Republic of China. However, further development of genetically modified maize may be slowed by consumer resistance in importing countries and doubts about its possible environmental impact.

Maize is an important food source in regions such as sub-Saharan Africa and the tropical zones of Latin America, where the climate precludes the extensive cultivation of other cereals. It is, however, inferior in nutritive value to wheat, being especially deficient in lysine, and tends to be replaced by wheat in diets when the opportunity arises. As food for human consumption, the grain is ground into meal, or it can be made into (unleavened) corn bread and breakfast cereals. In Latin America maize meal is made into cakes, called tortillas. Maize is also the source of an oil used in cooking.

The high starch content of maize makes it highly suitable as a compound feed ingredient, especially for pigs and poultry. Animal feeding is the main use of maize in the USA, Europe and Japan, and large amounts are also used for feed in developing countries in the Far East Asia, Latin America and, to some extent, in North Africa. Maize has a large variety of industrial uses, including the preparation of ethyl alcohol (ethanol), which may be added to petrol to produce a blended motor fuel. Maize is also a source of dextrose and fructose, which can be used as artificial sweeteners, many times sweeter than sugar. The amounts of maize used for these purposes depend, critically, on its price to the users relative to those of petroleum, sugar and other potential raw materials. Maize cobs, previously regarded as a waste product, may be used as feedstock to produce various chemicals (e.g. acetic acid and formic acid).

Production of Maize
('000 metric tons)

	2010	2011	2012	2013
World total	851,271	887,855	872,792	1,016,432
Latin America and the Caribbean . . .	117390	113,479	131,516	155,005
Leading Latin American producers				
Argentina	22,677	23,800	21,197	32,119
Brazil	55,364	55,660	71,073	80,517
Chile	1,358	1,438	1,493	1,519
Colombia	1,422	1,681	1,826	1,779
Ecuador	984	963	1,330	1,543
Guatemala	1,634	1,672	1,724	1,732
Mexico	23,302	17,635	22,069	22,664
Paraguay	3,109	3,346	3,080	4,120
Peru	1,541	1,516	1,674	1,670
Venezuela	1,796	1,817	1,753	2,548*
Other leading producers				
Canada	11,715	10,689	13,060	14,193
China, People's Repub. .	177,541	192,904	205,719	217,830
France	13,975	15,913	15,614	15,053
India	21,726	21,760	22,260	23,290
Indonesia	18,328	17,629	19,387	18,512
Italy	8,496	9,753	8,195	6,503
Nigeria	7,677	9,180	9,410*	10,400*
Romania	9,042	11,718	5,953	11,348
South Africa	12,815	10,360	11,830	12,365*
Ukraine	11,953	22,838	20,961	30,950
USA	316,165	313,949	273,820	353,699

* Unofficial figure.

Source: FAO.

The World Market and the Region The USA is by far the largest producer of maize (in years of drought or excessive heat, US output can fall dramatically) and the People's Republic of China, whose maize output has been expanding rapidly, is the second largest producer—its harvest doubled in 2000–13. China's production, however, is mainly destined for the domestic market, whereas US output makes the country generally the world's largest exporter by far. Figures from the US Department of Agriculture (USDA) for 2012/13 show that US exports collapsed in that year, so a surge in Argentinian and Brazilian sales briefly promoted those two countries to the principal exporters. In 2013/14 US exports recovered, to provide 40% of total world sales abroad, with Brazil accounting for 17%, a resurgent Ukraine for 16% and Argentina (where exports halved) 9%. The world's principal maize importer is Japan. However, the volume of Japanese imports remained stable through the 2000s, as the domestic livestock industry was rationalized to compete with imported meat. Japanese imports of maize totalled about 15.5m. metric tons in 2013/14 and, in that year, were matched by European Union (EU) imports as a whole. Apart from Japan, rapidly growing livestock industries elsewhere in East Asia made the region the major world market for maize, although in terms of individual countries Mexico sometimes challenges the Republic of Korea (South Korea) as the next largest importer (10.7m. tons and 10.0m. tons in 2013/14, respectively). Egypt is by far the largest importer in the African continent, its importing of 8.0m. tons putting it in fifth place among world importers.

Maize is grown widely as a subsistence crop in Central America; the main grower is Guatemala. It is one of the most important foods in El Salvador and Guatemala, where consumption per head is around 100 kg per year, but in South America maize in food use is generally declining, although it remains important in Bolivia, Colombia, Paraguay and Venezuela, in each of which consumption averages 40–50 kg per year. Maize production in Latin America and the Caribbean, however, is dominated by Brazil, Argentina and Mexico (Mexican production is mainly to satisfy its domestic market). Brazil is the largest producer and, in the north and north-east of the country, which account for about 10% of Brazil's production, maize is an important food for human consumption, and is largely grown by subsistence farmers. The droughts to which these regions are prone can occasion considerable hardship. Most of Brazil's maize is grown commercially for use as animal feed in the centre and south of the country. Production there varies according to the amount of government support (mostly in the form of subsidized credit) and the prices of alternative crops, especially oilseeds. Although Brazil's animal feed requirements are growing rapidly, many of the feed mills are located in the far south of the country, where maize supplies may be obtained more cheaply from Argentina than from domestic sources. Brazil is therefore also an important importer.

Argentina was usually Latin America's most substantial maize-exporting country, although from 2012 it slipped behind Brazil. Market liberalization in the early 1990s, particularly the abolition of export taxes, encouraged maize production in Argentina. Farmers were able to plan their activities more rationally, and to make longer-term investments in land improvement and up-to-date equipment. At the same time, privatization of the ports and transport systems resulted in much greater efficiency in grain movement. However, farmers are no longer shielded from international price trends, so many might switch from maize to oilseeds or other more profitable crops from one year to the next. Argentina's maize production (and therefore exports) can fluctuate. Paraguay, too, is an important exporter and ranked sixth in the world in 2013/14. Mexico is now Latin America's third largest maize producer, although much of the Mexican crop consists of white corn rather than the yellow variety. The establishment of CIMMYT (Centro Internacional del Mejoramiento de Maíz y Trigo—the International Wheat and Maize Improvement Centre) at Sonora, in northern Mexico, has made the country the testing-ground for many of the technical advances in the development of different maize varieties since the 1960s. Local production, however, has been hampered by the small size of most agricultural holdings, competition for irrigated land from other crops, and the inability of small producers to afford enough fertilizers. Shortages of irrigation water commonly result in poor crops. Maize in Mexico is mainly used for human consumption, particularly in the form of tortillas. Domestic maize is mostly reserved for this purpose, with animal feed manufacturers traditionally preferring to use sorghum and, increasingly, yellow corn imported from the USA. Policy changes implemented from the 1980s ended crop subsidies and controls on the prices of tortillas, a staple food in Mexico. Annual imports of cheaper, US-produced white maize have increased since the inception of the North American Free Trade Agreement (NAFTA) in 1994, and have made a further contribution towards discouraging local farmers from maize production. While the volume of Mexican maize production remained stable in 1994–2006, imports of maize more than doubled during the same period. As part of the Government's response to the so-called 'tortilla crisis' in early 2007 (when a shortage of maize in the country and a concomitant sharp increase in the price of tortillas provoked mass protests), imports rose by a further 32% in 2006/07 and remained high into the 2010s, as production levels did not generally increase.

Maize (Corn) Price
(US $ per metric ton)

	Average	High	Low
2000 .	88.53	(December) 97.56	(July) 75.27
2005 .	98.67	(July) 107.52	(February) 94.14
2010 .	185.91	(December) 250.38	(June) 152.75
2011 .	291.68	(April) 319.27	(December) 258.65
2012 .	298.42	(July) 333.05	(June) 267.31
2013 .	259.39	(March) 309.04	(December) 197.39

Source: World Bank, *Commodity Price Data* (Pink Sheet).

Prices Export prices of maize are mainly influenced by the level of supplies and demand in the USA, and the intensity of competition between the exporting countries. The price of US No. 2 Yellow Corn (f.o.b. Gulf ports) first rose above US $200 per metric ton in January 2008, but global recession pushed it below that mark again from October until September 2010 (in terms of average monthly prices). Prices then rose sharply for a time, reaching above $300 per ton in April–August 2011 and again in July 2012–March 2013, only to dip below $200 per ton for three months from November to February 2014. Lower prices were expected to stimulate consumption and imports worldwide, but also fuelled a huge increase in stocks. Plantings might decline, however, as average monthly prices for maize in 2014 rose no higher than $222.36 per ton (April) and fell to their lowest point since the beginning of 2011 in July 2014, at $182.73 per ton.

Maize and grain prices were also generally projected to increase in line with the expanding market for ethanol, which is closely linked to the price of petroleum. New energy legislation in 2007, in both the European Union and the USA, stipulated the greater use of biofuels for motor vehicles. According to the World Bank, the share of global maize production used for ethanol increased from 2.5% in 2000 to 11.0% in 2007, and the trend remained evident thereafter. However, maize-based ethanol production was still a heavily subsidized industry in the USA, and it remained a costly and relatively inefficient substitute for its sugar-based equivalent (see below). Critics remained sceptical regarding the long-term prospects for the industry, especially as sugar-based ethanol was already being produced more cheaply in Latin America.

PETROLEUM

Crude oils, from which petroleum is derived, consist essentially of a wide range of hydrocarbon molecules which are separated by distillation in the refining process. Refined oil is treated in different ways to make the different varieties of fuel. More than four-fifths of total world oil supplies are used as fuel for the production of energy in the form of power or heating.

Petroleum, together with its associated mineral fuel, natural gas, is extracted both from onshore and offshore wells in many areas of the world. It is the leading raw material in international trade. Worldwide, demand for this commodity totalled an estimated 91.3m. barrels per day (b/d) in 2013, a rise of 1.4% compared with the previous year. The world's 'published proven' reserves of petroleum and natural gas liquids at 31 December 2013 were estimated to total 238,204m. metric tons, equivalent to 1,667,891m. barrels (1 metric ton is equivalent to approximately 7.3 barrels, each of 42 US gallons or 34.97 imperial gallons, i.e. 159 litres). The dominant producing region is the Middle East, whose proven reserves in December 2013 accounted for 47.9% of known world deposits of crude petroleum, gas condensate and natural gas liquids. The Middle East accounted for 32.2% of world output in 2013. Latin America (including Mexico) held 52,616m. tons of proven reserves (20.2% of the world total) at the end of 2013, and accounted for 12.5% of world production in that year.

From storage tanks at the oilfield wellhead, crude petroleum is conveyed, frequently by pumping for long distances through large pipelines, to coastal depots where it is either treated in a refinery or delivered into bulk storage tanks for subsequent shipment for refining overseas. In addition to pipeline transportation of crude petroleum and refined products, natural (petroleum) gas is, in some areas, also transported through networks of pipelines. The properties of different crude petroleums (e.g. colour, viscosity, etc.) vary considerably, and these variations are a determinant both of price and of end-use after refining.

The most important of the petroleum products is fuel oil, composed of heavy distillates and residues, which is used to produce heating and power for industrial purposes. Products in the kerosene group have a wide number of applications, ranging from heating fuels to the powering of aviation gas turbine engines. Gasoline (petrol) products fuel internal combustion engines (principally in road motor vehicles), and naphtha, a gasoline distillate, is a commercial solvent that can also be processed as a feedstock. Propane and butane, the main

liquefied petroleum gases, have a wide range of industrial applications and are also used for domestic heating and cooking.

Production of Crude Petroleum
('000 metric tons, including natural gas liquids)

	1985	1995	2005	2013
World total	2,796,768	3,286,082	3,947,499	4,132,919
Latin America and the Caribbean . . .	338,442	450,351	561,410	516,276
Leading Latin American and Caribbean producers				
Argentina	24,159	37,457	39,396	30,534
Brazil	29,422	37,567	88,720	109,941
Colombia	9,521	31,016	27,713	52,880
Ecuador	15,223	20,999	28,577	28,243
Mexico	145,854	150,213	186,492	141,846
Peru	9,853	6,407	4,462	4,572
Trinidad and Tobago .	8,636	6,736	8,955	5,868
Venezuela	91,504	155,325	169,700	135,089
Other leading producers				
Algeria	49,997	56,596	86,438	68,862
Angola	11,452	31,173	68,862	87,361
Canada	85,685	111,906	142,281	193,013
China, People's Repub.	124,900	149,020	181,353	208,129
Iran	110,351	185,457	206,381	166,082
Iraq	69,839	26,026	89,934	153,242
Kazakhstan	22,660	20,633	62,614	83,814
Kuwait	55,489	104,889	130,377	151,253
Libya	48,391	67,893	82,176	46,455
Nigeria	73,837	97,495	122,099	111,259
Norway	39,211	138,400	138,730	83,172
Qatar	15,318	21,813	52,602	84,238
Russia	542,306	310,749	474,819	531,434
Saudi Arabia	172,075	437,209	521,276	542,340
United Arab Emirates .	58,326	112,329	135,790	165,674
United Kingdom . .	127,611	129,894	84,721	40,624
USA	498,686	383,572	309,909	446,231

Source: BP, *Statistical Review of World Energy 2014*.

The World Market and the Region Mexico's oil industry was nationalized in 1938, and it remains in the control of a government agency, Petróleos Mexicanos—PEMEX—which is divided into four subsidiaries, with responsibility, respectively, for exploration and production, natural gas and basic petrochemicals, petrochemicals, and refining. In 2008, with the aim of arresting an ongoing decline in national oil production (see below), the Government enacted a number of reforms, including the extension of seats on PEMEX's administrative board to external oil industry specialists, the establishment of an advisory board with long-term strategic functions, and the creation of a regulatory authority for the sector. Other measures granted PEMEX a greater degree of flexibility vis-à-vis procurement and investment. Mexico was the world's leading petroleum producer in 1921, but by 1938 output had fallen dramatically. The discovery of extensive deposits of petroleum in the states of Tabasco and Chiapas, and off shore in the Bay of Campeche, enabled output to increase significantly in the 1970s. However, the country's reserves of petroleum and other hydrocarbons are now in decline. Mexico's proven reserves of petroleum stood at 1,527m. metric tons at the end of 2013. About 75% of Mexico's crude oil is sourced off shore, in the Bay of Campeche. The country's largest oilfield, and one of the largest in the world, is the Cantarell field, but production there is now in steep decline. In 2004, according to the Energy Information Administration (EIA) of the US Department of Energy, Cantarell contributed about 63% of Mexico's total output of crude oil. In 2013 Cantarell was the source of only 17% of total production. Moreover, the combined production of the Litoral Tabasco and Abkatun-Pol-Chuc projects—located in the southwest of the Bay of Campeche—had overtaken that of Cantarell. The former has made up in part for the declining production of Cantarell, its output rising from 200,000 b/d in 2008 to almost 300,000 b/d in 2013. Meanwhile, thanks to a nitrogen re-injection programme, output from the Ku-Maloob-Zaap (KMZ) production centre—itself located in the Bay of Campeche—has also compensated to some extent for that lost from Cantarell. KMZ's output reportedly doubled in 2006–09, but production there, too, is forecast to peak in the near future. In 2011 the Cantarell and KMZ fields produced some 51% of Mexico's total output of crude oil. Output from onshore fields contributes about one-quarter of Mexico's total production of crude petroleum, and it is hoped that this may be boosted by the development of the Chicontepec project, which comprises dozens of small fields located north-east of Mexico City. In 2013, however, output from Chicontepec reportedly amounted to just

66,000 b/d (a decline compared with the previous year), although PEMEX aims to increase this to 300,000 b/d by 2020. In 2008 tenders were invited to drill some 1,000 wells at Chicontepec; this was followed, in 2009, by an invitation for bids to operate more than 150 development wells there. However, Mexico's energy regulator, Comisión Nacional de Hidrocarburos (CNH), has called into question PEMEX's development plan and the project's profitably—given that a large portion of the company's exploration and production budget is allocated to Chicontepec. The heavy crude Maya generally accounts for about 60% of total Mexican production, with the remainder comprising the lighter crudes Isthmus and Olmeca. Mexico was the world's 10th largest producer of petroleum in 2013, with estimated output of 141.8m. tons, a decline of 1.1% compared with 2012. Mexico's foreign sales of petroleum largely comprise heavy crude, with the country retaining the lighter grades produced for domestic consumption. In 2013 crude exports amounted to some 1.19m. b/d, with 71% of Mexico's exports being sold to the USA in that year. Overall, Mexico's oil sector contributed 13% of export revenue in 2013. Mexico is usually one of the USA's three leading suppliers of crude petroleum—the others are Canada and Saudi Arabia. The largest of Mexico's six oil refineries is the Salina Cruz complex, which has a capacity of 330,000 b/d. In 2009 PEMEX announced plans to construct, at a cost of some US $10,000m., a seventh refinery at Tula, in the state of Hidalgo—to be completed in 2016. In February 2012 PEMEX awarded the contract to design the new facility, which was already experiencing development delays later in that year. The Tula plant is to be specially adapted to refine Mexico's heavy crudes, with the aim of reducing the country's continued reliance—despite its high ranking in world terms as a producer of crude oil—on imports of refined petroleum products, of which it remains a net purchaser. Imports totalled about 603,000 b/d in 2013. Gasoline accounted for about 60% of Mexico's total refined imports in the same year. In December 2013 the Government legislated significant oil and gas sector reforms aimed at ending PEMEX's monopoly and opening up the sector to foreign investment. The reforms concern licences, production- and profit-sharing, and service contracts. Moreover, the legislation supports the expansion of regulatory authorities Secretaría de Energía and CNH, and the creation of a new National Agency of Industrial Safety and Environmental Protection.

With 2,266m. metric tons at the end of 2013, Brazil had the second largest national petroleum resource in the region, after that of Venezuela. It is anticipated that Brazilian reserves will continue to rise as Petróleo Brasileiro (Petrobras), the state-owned petroleum company, continues to make substantial investments in exploration—for both petroleum and natural gas. Most of Brazil's oil is produced in the Rio de Janeiro and Espírito Santo states, while some 90% of production is off shore. The offshore (Santos Basin) Tupi oilfield has been described by Petrobras as comparable with the most important fields already in production world-wide, with a recoverable resource of 5,000m.–8,000m. barrels, and potential to increase the country's natural gas reserves by 50%. The Tupi field—and others like it that were discovered subsequently—has further significance for exploration in that, unlike Brazil's older oilfields, it is located in a geological formation referred to as the sub-salt layer and comprises lighter, sweeter crude than has hitherto, for the most part, been located in the country. While they have not accepted Petrobras's assessment of these sub-salt layer resources without reservation, analysts have acknowledged the potential of the Tupi and similar fields to make a huge impact on world markets for oil. In December 2010 Petrobras commenced an extended test at the Tupi and Iracema fields (renamed Lula and Cernambi). The reserve estimate for each was 6,500m. barrels and 1,800m. barrels, respectively. The extended well test represents the first of three phases into which the development of pre-salt resources—both at Tupi and elsewhere—has been divided in Petrobras's strategic plan. These included new production-sharing agreements (PSAs) rather than the concessions that had been employed for existing resources. The creation of a new agency—Petrosal—was also envisaged to manage a Petrobras stake of at least 30% in each PSA. Revenues accruing to the Government from the development of the pre-salt reserves were to be channelled into a development fund. Finally, a new law would permit the Government to capitalize Petrobras by allocating it pre-salt reserves that are unlicensed at present. The Tupi Pilot project began in October 2010. The project has a production capacity of some 100,000 b/d. Petrobras plans to invest US $147,500m. in the sector as part of its 2013–17 business plan. Some $53,000m. had been targeted at pre-salt exploration and production activity in the previous year's plan, but this had increased to 73,000m. for the current plan. Significantly increased production would severely stretch Brazilian infrastructure specifically, and that, if achieved, would have a significant impact on world oil markets. Brazil's current production is already overwhelmingly focused on deep-water fields off shore in the state of Rio de Janeiro. Potential output has been boosted considerably by the completion of production/expansion projects undertaken by Petrobras at the Albacore Leste, Golfinho, Jubarte, Piranema and Espadarte fields. In 2013 Brazil's production of crude petroleum amounted to an estimated 109.9m. metric tons, which represented a decline of 1.7%

compared with 2012. It was the second consecutive year of production decline. Annual output had risen consistently in 1999–2011 (with the exception of 2004, when a small decline was recorded). In 2008 Brazil achieved its aim of becoming a net exporter of petroleum (a position it maintained in 2009–10), but the EIA estimated that the country was a net importer in both 2011 and 2012. Petrobras operates 11 of the country's 13 petroleum refineries. National refining capacity at the end of 2013 was, at some 2.1m. b/d, by far the largest in the region. The largest refinery is the Paulínia facility, operated by Petrobras in São Paulo, which has a daily capacity of 360,000 barrels. To this end, Petrobras began preparatory work for the construction of a new, 230,000-b/d refinery (Abreu e Lima) in the north-eastern state of Pernambuco in 2007. The project, the cost of which had been estimated initially at US $2,300m., was intended to be undertaken as a joint venture with Petróleos de Venezuela SA (PDVSA), which would hold a 40% stake. Some 70% of the refinery had been completed by late 2013, with analysts suggesting it would be finished towards the end of 2014. However, PDVSA had yet to fulfil its financial commitment to the project and in early 2014 it was reported that Petrobras had cancelled the debt. Overall, Brazil has a target of raising national refining capacity to more than 3.2m. b/d by 2020 in order to meet increasing demand from domestic customers, and aims to increase its capacity for refining the predominantly heavy crudes that it produces. Although the country's production of these crudes has risen steadily in recent years, it remains insufficient to meet domestic demand and has to be supplemented by imports of lighter crudes.

Brazil is an exporter of heavy crudes to, for example, the People's Republic of China. Petrobras's monopoly of the Brazilian petroleum sector was ended in 1997 by the adoption of legislation allowing private sector investment in all parts of the industry. At the same time, a National Petroleum Agency (Agência Nacional do Petróleo) was established. These and other reforms of the sector were undertaken as part of Brazil's pursuit of self-sufficiency in petroleum supply. Foreign participation has proceeded slowly, however, and Petrobras remains by far the country's dominant producer. Following the decision by US petroleum exploration company Anadarko not to sell its petroleum assets in mid-2012, analysts suggested the interest in Brazil's petroleum industry among foreign companies was waning. (Between 2007, when most of the important yields were discovered, and mid-2012 no offshore licences were sold.) Indeed, the oil spill in the Campos Basin—and the resulting fine for US multinational company Chevron—appeared to have made Brazil a less attractive proposition for petroleum investment.

The production of petroleum is the dominant economic activity in Venezuela. In 2012, according to the USGS, the value of the country's petroleum exports amounted to US $92,100m., representing about 95% of the total value of the country's export earnings, and petroleum revenues contributed about 12% of gross domestic product (GDP) and some 45% of federal budget revenues. The country is consistently one of the four leading suppliers of petroleum to the USA. In 2013 Venezuela was the USA's fourth largest supplier of crude oil and petroleum products, shipping 0.8m. b/d. Net oil exports amounted to an estimated 1.7m. b/d in 2013, but will continue to decline as production falls and domestic consumption rises. Venezuela supplied 8.3% of the USA's total petroleum imports (including derivatives) in 2011. According to the EIA, the country ranked ninth among the world's leading exporters of petroleum (and first in the western hemisphere) in 2013. In addition to the USA, Venezuela finds markets for its oil elsewhere in South America, in Europe and in the Caribbean. Indeed, Venezuela's exports to the USA have declined in recent years—by some 49% since 2003. None the less, US and European sanctions on Iranian oil have benefited Venezuelan exports, as it has been able to capture markets in Asia in particular. (US sanctions are designed to punish those countries that import Iranian oil.) The People's Republic of China and India have gained rapidly in significance as purchasers of Venezuelan crude in recent years: in 2013, according to the EIA, China's imports of Venezuelan crude oil totalled some 260,000 b/d, while India's imports totalled more than 400,000 b/d. Venezuela also supplies crude petroleum and derivatives on favourable terms (including at discounted prices) to a number of neighbouring, Caribbean and Central American countries. Under another agreement, Venezuela supplies Cuba with some 30m. barrels of crude petroleum and petroleum products annually. In 2013, when Venezuela accounted for 26.2% of Latin American production, it ranked as the world's 11th largest producer. The country's proven reserves were estimated at 46,576m. metric tons at the end of 2013. In 1992, for the first time since the nationalization of PDVSA in 1976, exploration and production were opened up to foreign participation, via PDVSA subsidiary Corporación Venezolana de Petróleo (CVP). Hydrocarbons legislation stipulates, among other provisions, that PDVSA must take a 51% share in all new production and exploration projects; and that in future joint ventures would supersede existing operating service agreements, risk/profit-sharing agreements and strategic associations as the only permitted vehicles for foreign participation. According to the EIA, the conversion of all joint ventures, risk/profit-sharing agreements and strategic associations had been completed by the end of 2007. Investment in the oil sector has subsequently been sought from foreign national oil companies, including those of China and Russia. Petroleum resources estimated to amount to as much as 270,000m. barrels in Venezuela's Orinoco Belt are currently the focus of much development effort, via the so-called 'Magna Reserva' programme, for which PDVSA's partners include the national oil companies of Brazil, Iran, China and India—respectively, Petrobras, Petropars (a wholly owned subsidiary of the National Iranian Oil Co), China National Petroleum Corpn (CNPC), and Oil and Natural Gas Corpn Ltd. It was reported in late 2011 that Russian state-owned Rosneft would pay $1,200m. and loan PDVSA a further $1,000m. for access to the Carabobo 2 block. Industry sources assessed Venezuela's domestic petroleum-refining capacity in 2013 at some 1.4m. b/d. This was supplemented by additional capacity overseas, including in the USA and Europe. PDVSA was collaborating in a joint venture with Petrobras to construct a new refinery in Brazil's north-eastern state of Pernambuco, although by mid-2014 it had yet to fulfil its financial commitments to the project (see above). Following the death of President Hugo Chávez in early 2013, there appeared to be little or no change in the new leadership's petroleum policy, which continued to emphasise the strategic importance of China and Russia over the USA.

Ecuador's petroleum industry has been a significant contributor to the economy since 1972, when petroleum was exported for the first time, after the completion of the 480-km (300-mile) trans-Andean pipeline, linking the oilfields of Oriente Province with the tanker-loading port of Esmeraldas. The country's most important oilfields lie in the north east of the country, and, of these, Shushufindi, operated by state-owned Petroecuador, is the largest, providing about 9% of total output. Petroecuador is the country's most important producer of crude. However, private producers have begun to play a greater part in the sector, and Petroecuador's production has declined in recent years. The most significant private producers are foreign-owned. Spain's Repsol YPF is the largest private foreign oil company active in Ecuador. Highlighting China's growing influence in Ecuador's petroleum industry, in mid-2013 CNPC signed a framework agreement with the Government and Petroecuador to help build the Pacific Refinery—at a cost of some $12,500m. CNPC was expected to provide part of the financing for the project, along with Venezuela's PDVSA. Having declined significantly in 2001–05, Petroecuador's share of national production was boosted in 2006 as a result of the company's takeover of the production assets of Occidental Petroleum. The Government had alleged, prior to the takeover, that Occidental had failed to meet contractual obligations by transferring assets to another oil company. Meanwhile, Chevron's lengthy battle with Ecuadorean indigenous communities over allegations of environmental and social harm resulting from the operations of Texaco (which Chevron had acquired after the operations had been completed), was ongoing. In early 2011 an Ecuadorean court had found in favour of the plaintiffs. This case, together with the appropriation of Occidental's operations, led some analysts to question the viability of the cost and risk associated with investing in Ecuador. Ecuador's output of crude comprises two varieties: Oriente, a medium-heavy, medium-sour grade; and Napo, a heavy, sour crude. As of early 2014 Ecuador's three refineries had a total capacity of some 176,000 b/d. In 2008, as part of its effort to reduce the country's dependence on foreign supplies of refined petroleum products, of which it is a net importer, the Government concluded an agreement with Venezuela and established a joint venture for the construction of a new refinery in Manabi province, with daily capacity of 300,000 barrels. The upgrading of Ecuador's three existing refineries is also pending, most notably that of the largest, the 100,000-b/d facility at Esmeraldas, which South Korea's SK Engineering is contracted to undertake at an estimated cost of $200m. More than 60% of Ecuador's exports of petroleum and petroleum derivatives were destined for the USA, to whom it was the fourth largest Latin American supplier, after Mexico, Venezuela and Colombia, in 2012. In that year it was the USA's 11th largest supplier. Ecuador's proven published reserves of petroleum at the end of 2013 amounted to 1,203m. metric tons, the third largest in South America. Petroleum and petroleum products accounted for about 64% of export revenue in 2008, but the share fell to 55% in 2012 as a result of rising domestic demand. The oil industry generally accounts for about one-third of all tax revenue accruing to the Government. The future growth of Ecuador's oil sector will probably depend on the development of the Ishpingo-Tapococha-Tiputini (ITT) block, which is located in the Amazon region. The Government reportedly intends to offer foreign operators licences to operate in the block, where proven reserves have been assessed at 900m. barrels. However, according to the EIA, the block's reserves mainly consist of a very heavy variety of crude that would require blending before distribution. The development of Amazonian reserves has been impeded in the past by opposition from indigenous groups and environmentalist groups. In 2007 Ecuador's President, Rafael Correa, proposed a measure to protect the environment involving the payment to Ecuador by developed countries of at least one-half of the estimated total revenues that exploitation of some 850m. barrels of heavy crude oil in the Yasuní National Park, located in the Amazon region, would generate. However, in August 2013,

following a lack of funding support, President Correa announced an end to the moratorium, abandoned the conservation plan and announced that exploration would begin immediately.

Other notable Latin American and Caribbean producers of petroleum include Colombia, Argentina, Trinidad and Tobago, and Peru. At December 2013 Colombia had proven reserves of some 343m. metric tons. However, large areas of Colombia remain unexplored for petroleum. In 2013 Colombia ranked as the fourth largest producer of crude petroleum in Latin America, contributing 10.3% of the region's output. According to the EIA, the increases in production recorded in 2006–11 were the result of regulatory changes and greater security, which have encouraged investment in the sector. The improvement in Colombia's petroleum industry in recent years has also been attributed to an influx of Venezuela's PDVSA employees (engineers, geologists and managers), who left that country following strike action in 2006. Although Colombia is a net exporter of petroleum, the country is obliged to import petroleum products as domestic refining capacity is insufficient to meet local demand. Sales of petroleum and its derivatives accounted for 32.5% of export earnings in 2008, and this percentage had increased to 55.2% by 2013, based on exports worth $58,824m. Argentina is South America's largest producer of natural gas, and its proven reserves of crude petroleum totalled 325m. metric tons at December 2013. Production in Argentina increased substantially during the 1990s, allowing the country, the fourth largest consumer of petroleum in Latin America (after Brazil, Mexico and Venezuela), to become a significant regional exporter, shipping mainly to Brazil and Chile. Failure to compensate for declining output at mature fields, however, has led to a steady decline in overall production since 2002. In 2011, according to the USGS, the value of Argentina's exports of crude petroleum (and natural gas) declined by 17.9%, to just $2,300m. At the end of 2013 Trinidad and Tobago's proven reserves of petroleum amounted to 113m. metric tons, while Peru's proven reserves totalled 192m. tons in the same year.

Organization of the Petroleum Exporting Countries (OPEC) International petroleum prices are strongly influenced by the Organization of the Petroleum Exporting Countries (OPEC), founded in 1960 in Baghdad, Iraq. Its purpose is to co-ordinate the production and marketing policies of those countries with substantial net petroleum exports in order to secure stable and fair prices for producing countries, a regular supply of petroleum for consuming countries and a return on capital for countries and corporations that invest in the industry. OPEC came under scrutiny in the 1970s when Arab countries imposed an oil embargo (in 1973), which led to a steep rise in prices on world markets. The embargo—initiated by the Organization of Arab Petroleum Exporting Countries (OAPEC)—was initiated in response to US involvement in the Yom Kippur War. In the meantime, however, the USA had withdrawn from the Bretton Woods Accord, which led to the floating of the US dollar (and other currencies) and an increase in US dollar reserves. The resultant devaluing of that currency meant that petroleum-producing countries were receiving less real income from their exports (since petroleum, at this time, was priced and traded in US dollars). OPEC subsequently released a statement confirming that it would henceforth peg the price of a barrel of oil against the price of gold.

OPEC member countries experienced severe economic setbacks in the mid-1980s as prices dropped substantially (by as much as two-thirds). The overall decline in prices was attributed to an oversupply of petroleum and significantly reduced consumer demand. Prices recovered somewhat in the late 1980s, but only to around one-half of the record levels seen at the start of the decade. Recovery was encouraged by the introduction of a production ceiling and the OPEC reference 'basket' (ORB) for pricing. The 1990s was a comparatively stable decade, although Iraq's invasion of Kuwait and the resultant Gulf War created some volatility in world markets. However, the decade was characterized by general weakness in pricing, with a particularly mild winter in the northern hemisphere countries in the late 1990s causing prices to drop to 1986 levels. None the less, crude prices strengthened and then stabilized in the early 2000s, before reaching record levels later in the decade (see below).

OPEC distinguishes between founder members and full members. In 2014 it had 12 members in total. Venezuela (a founder member) and Ecuador (a full member) are the only Latin American participants. Ecuador, which had withdrawn from OPEC in 1992 owing to disagreements regarding its membership fee and production quota, rejoined the organization in 2007, and is the smallest oil-producing member of OPEC. It was anticipated that the country would align itself with those members, including Venezuela and Iran, seeking to ensure that a greater proportion of oil revenues accrued to national authorities at the expense of that appropriated by international oil companies involved in production activities. Elsewhere in Latin America, Mexico, like some other non-members, has collaborated closely with OPEC in recent years.

Regional Association The Regional Association of Oil and Natural Gas Companies in Latin America and the Caribbean (Asociación Regional de Empresas de Petróleo y Gas Natural en Latinoamérica y el Caribe—ARPEL) exists to promote co-operation in matters of technical and economic development. ARPEL, with headquarters in Montevideo, Uruguay, has 35 members, including companies based outside the region.

Price History of the OPEC 'Basket' of Crude Oils
(US $ per barrel)

	Average	High		Low	
2003	.	28.10	(February) 31.54	(April) 25.34
2004	.	36.05	(October) 45.37	(February) 29.56
2005	.	50.54	(September) 57.88	(January) 40.24
2006	.	61.08	(July) 68.89	(October) 54.97
2007	.	69.08	(November) 88.84	(January) 50.79
2008	.	94.45	(July) 131.22	(December) 38.60
2009	.	61.06	(November) 76.29	(February) 41.41
2010	.	77.45	(December) 88.56	(July) 72.51
2011	.	107.46	(April) 118.09	(January) 92.83
2012	.	109.45	(March) 122.97	(June) 93.98
2013	.	105.87	(February) 117.75	(May) 100.65

Source: OPEC, *Annual Reports* and *Monthly Oil Market Reports*.

Prices Compared to 2002, the average price of the ORB of crude oils increased significantly in 2003, by 15.4%. (The price of Brent crude was a major contributor to this growth, as it rose by over 15%, to US $28.81 per barrel.) Year-on-year growth in demand reached 2.1% in 2003, which aided the overall price growth during the year. Moreover, a particularly cold winter in much of the northern hemisphere, an oil workers' strike in Venezuela in February and the Iraq War, which began in March, also contributed to strong price growth overall. However, OPEC members took the decision to cover the shortfall in Iraqi output (some 2m. b/d in exports), which mitigated, initially, an overall price increase. Indeed, the price declined to a yearly low at the end of April, but had recovered by the end of the year. In 2004 the average price of the ORB increased significantly once more, by 28.0%, compared to the previous year, buoyed by a strong world economy and further growth in demand, particularly in developing countries. The price of Brent crude increased by 32.7% during 2004, averaging $38.23 per barrel for the year. Record prices were attributed to fears of supply shortages as a result of intermittent production in Iraq as a consequence of the ongoing US military intervention and the disruptive effects of Hurricane Ivan in the Gulf of Mexico. The British section of the North Sea also saw a significant decline in output in that year (of some 241,000 b/d). Compared to 2004, the average price of the ORB in 2005 increased by 40.5%, demonstrating a further accelerated rate of growth in spite of OPEC raising the production ceiling for its members. The price of Brent crude rose by 42.4% during the same period, to $54.44 per barrel. Disruptions caused by Hurricanes Katrina and Rita in the Gulf of Mexico in August and September were blamed for the record highs. However, the International Energy Agency brought some calm to the market when it announced it would release strategic reserves to cover any shortfall. Furthermore, OPEC offered its own assurances, namely some 2m. b/d of spare capacity. However, by the end of the year demand began to increase once again, as an early northern hemisphere winter was predicted.

Price volatility characterized 2006–08, partly the result of the financial crisis in the latest year. In 2006, however, global real GDP growth continued to accelerate (5.4% compared to 2005), with developing countries (China and India in particular) driving demand in the petroleum sector. Compared with 2005, the average price of the ORB was 20.6% higher than in 2005. The price of Brent crude rose by 19.7% to average $65.16 per barrel for the year. The price growth over the year was attributed to Middle East tensions, while the all-time weekly high achieved in August—when the average price of the ORB rose to more than US $70 per barrel—was the result of pipeline leaks in Russia and limited supply in the North Sea. The price increases in the first three quarters of the year were in spite of crude oil inventories in the Organisation for Economic Co-ordination and Development (OECD) being at a 20-year high. In 2007 the average price of the ORB rose by 13% compared with the previous year, demonstrating a more moderate growth rate following two years of rapid growth. The price of Brent crude was 11.3% higher than in 2006, averaging $72.55 per barrel. The steady rise coincided with a global petroleum market that was well supplied, but was once again supported by strong global GDP growth (5.2%) with China and India contributing some 43% of world GDP growth in that year. The consequences of refinery disruptions in the USA in the middle of 2007 were offset to some degree by an improvement in Middle East geopolitics. However, by late 2007 and throughout 2008 a weaker US dollar contributed to further volatility in pricing. In 2008 the ORB fluctuated from more than $140 per barrel (in July) to less than $35 per barrel (in December). The average price of the ORB rose by 36.7% in 2008 (compared with the previous year), although this growth belied the true picture of pricing for the year. Following exponential growth in the first six months of 2008—spurred on by the weaker US dollar and port workers' strikes

in France—the financial crisis in the latter stages of the year had a huge negative impact on consumer confidence. The average price of the ORB was just $38.60 per barrel in December of that year. The price of Brent crude was $40.35 per barrel in December, although it averaged $97.35 per barrel for the year—34.2% higher than 2007.

Global demand for petroleum contracted by 1.6% in 2009, with the average price of the ORB declining by 35.4% compared with the previous year. However, December year-on-year prices actually grew by 91.7% between 2008 and 2009. The growth in prices was closely managed and supported by OPEC, which took the decision to cut production among its member countries by 4.2m. b/d, effective from 1 January 2009. Following global GDP growth of 2.9% in 2008—which had been tempered in the second half of the year following the financial collapse—the world economy contracted by 0.9% in 2009. Consequently, world demand for petroleum was more than 1.5m. b/d lower than it was in 2007, although demand from developing countries remained largely unaffected. The ORB price rose steeply towards the end of 2009 as a result of a weaker US dollar before falling in the latter stages of the year. The price of Brent crude averaged US $61.68 per barrel in 2009, which represented a decline of 36.7% compared to the previous year. In 2010 the average price of the ORB continued to recover, rising by 26.8% compared with the previous year. The recovery was buoyed by strong global economic growth (4.7%), although countries with export-driven economies were primarily responsible for this trend, helping to offset ongoing sluggishness among many OECD countries. None the less, growth in that region was 2.8% (following a contraction of 3.5% in 2009), largely a result of stimulus packages in the USA, Japan and elsewhere. Indeed, ongoing government stimulus initiatives continued to bolster demand during the year, which benefited prices. Following concerns about macroeconomic growth midway through the year (especially in the eurozone)—which led to a brief weakening of prices—cold weather in Europe and the USA sent prices in December 2010 to their highest levels since the financial crisis in late 2008. Meanwhile, the price of Brent crude increased by 29.1% in 2010, averaging $79.60 for the year. The growth in petroleum prices continued apace in 2011, with the average price of the ORB rising by 38.7%. The global economy grew by 3.6% in 2011 in spite of fiscal conservatism in many countries. Export-driven countries once again performed well, but OECD countries—especially Japan, which weathered an earthquake and associated tsunami and nuclear disaster in March of that year that pushed the country into recession—again struggled to maintain growth. Overall demand declined during the year, as the financial crisis undermined consumer confidence in OECD and non-OECD countries alike. US demand was especially weak, as high retail prices for gasoline led to lower consumption. The significant increase in prices during the year was attributed mostly to ongoing violence in Libya, which severely disrupted exports. All 'basket' components performed well in 2011, with African crudes performing particularly well. In that year the average price of Brent crude reached $111.36 per barrel, which represented growth of just less than 40% compared with 2010.

There was international concern over the volatility of prices in the first half of 2012, as the ORB moved from US $124 per barrel to less than $90 per barrel, in spite of steady supply levels (including a recovery in Libyan production). The average price of the ORB grew by 1.9% compared with the previous year. Global economic growth decelerated to 3.0%, with China alone contributing around one-third. The moderate growth was attributed to the ending of financial assistance packages in many developed economies, and the resulting decline in petroleum demand among OECD countries. However, demand in non-OECD countries remained robust, growing by 1.2m. b/d. In Japan, however, crude petroleum consumption increased by 36% as nuclear power plants remained closed and the country sought an alternative electricity supply. Price growth over the year was attributed to resurgent turmoil in the Middle East and supply disruptions in the North Sea fields. The price of Brent crude in 2012 was 0.2% higher than in 2011, averaging $111.63 for the year. The world economy demonstrated some growth in the first half of 2013, but gathered momentum in the second half. Global economic growth slowed to 2.9% in the year overall, while the fluctuation in petroleum prices witnessed in 2012—causing a great deal of market volatility—was largely avoided. Overall world demand for crude increased in 2013 (by some 1.3m. b/d), aided in OECD countries by optimism in manufacturing and other industrial sectors. Japanese demand, meanwhile, declined during the year as it relied more heavily on natural gas and coal for its energy needs, although this was partly offset by increased naphtha consumption resulting from growth in the petrochemical industry. In 2013 the average price of the ORB declined by 3.3%. Following strong growth early in the year (supported by healthy demand and ongoing maintenance issues in the North Sea), petroleum prices declined in the third quarter following the publication of poor economic data from the USA and China, the world's two largest consumers. Ongoing economic problems in the eurozone and record inventories in the USA also exerted downward pressure on prices later in the year. The price of Brent crude averaged $108.62 per barrel in 2013, which represented a fall of 2.7% compared with the previous year. The price of the ORB remained steady in the first half of 2014. In June its average price reached $107.89 per barrel, which represented its highest level for the year thus far. Oil markets were adequately supplied, but the price gains in May and June suggested fears over future production and supply routes: ongoing conflicts in Libya and Ukraine, together with a resurgent security crisis in Iraq, threatened to send prices higher. In June 2014 the average price of Brent crude was $111.66 per barrel.

SILVER (*Ag*)

Known since prehistoric times, silver is a white metal which is extremely malleable and ductile. It is the best metallic conductor of heat and electricity, hence its use in electrical contacts and in electroplating, and highly reflective. Silver's most important compounds are the chloride and bromide, which darken on exposure to light and form the basis of photographic emulsions.

Worldwide, 83% of silver production in 2013 was mined, usually being generated as a by-product, or co-product, of gold, copper, lead and zinc, and other mining operations (only 29% of production came from exploitation of primary sources of silver ore). Methods of recovery depend upon the composition of the silver-bearing ore. As an investment metal (much of the world's silver bullion stocks are speculative holdings), silver is highly sensitive to factors other than the comparative levels of supply and demand. Silver, like gold and platinum, is customarily measured in troy weight. The now otherwise obsolete troy pound contains 12 ounces (oz), each of 480 grains. One troy ounce is equal to 31.1 grams (1 kg = 32.15 troy oz), compared with the avoirdupois ounce of 28.3 grams.

Production of Silver Ore
(silver content, metric tons, provisional figures)

	2010	2011	2012	2013
World total	23,345	23,471	24,644	25,494
Latin America . . .	11,650	11,785	12,321	12,748
Leading Latin American producers				
Argentina	721	703	755	768
Bolivia	1,274	1,214	1,235	1,281
Chile	1,276	1,273	1,151	1,218
Guatemala . . .	195	273	205	324
Mexico	4,411	4,778	5,358	5,277
Peru	3,640	3,414	3,481	3,674
Other leading producers				
Australia	1,880	1,725	1,727	1,840
Canada	573	582	663	646
China, People's Repub. .	2,942	3,191	3,516	3,669
Kazakhstan . . .	548	547	545	617
Poland	1,171	1,270	1,284	1,171
Russia	1,145	1,198	1,400	1,412
USA	1,270	1,120	1,060	1,090

Sources: The Silver Institute; Thomson Reuters GFMS.

The World Market and the Region Three different uses for silver exert varying influences on the international market: silver for industrial purposes; silver for investment; and silver for jewellery and decoration. In 2013 the worldwide use of silver in fabricated products accounted for 54% of total physical demand of 1,081.1m. troy ounces (33,624 metric tons); electrical and electronic uses of silver alone accounted for 22% of total demand. A surge in investment interest in 2013 meant that coins and bars accounted for 23% of physical demand for silver, with jewellery at 18% and silverware 5%. Industrial purposes included the manufacture of electronic equipment and batteries in the major industrialized countries, boosted by the uptake of digital equipment in consumer markets, which impacted on the use of silver in the production of photographic material (including X-ray film). Other industrial uses for silver include the production of brazing alloys, mirrors and catalysts, while newer areas of growth, particularly in the 2000s, included electronics (plasma screens), health (antibacterial dressings) and renewable energy (photovoltaic cells). Most silver fabrication takes place in the People's Republic of China (24% of world demand in 2013), followed by the USA (16%) and India (9%); in terms of global regions, Asia as a whole accounts for 50% of use (China, India and Japan alone 41%), followed by the USA and Canada (20%) and Europe (15%, led by Russia, Italy and Germany).

World mine production of silver increased for an 11th successive year in 2013, to reach 819.6m. troy oz (25,294 metric tons). Of this total, Latin America accounted for 50%, Asia 21% (China alone 14%) and Europe 13%. The most significant mining country is Mexico, followed by Peru and China. The world's largest silver mining companies in 2013 were Fresnillo (Mexico), BHP Billiton (Austra-lia/United Kingdom), KGHM Polska Miedź SA (Poland) and Glencore Xstrata (Switzerland/United Kingdom). The largest primary silver mines in the world are the Cannington mine in Australia, the Fresnillo mine in Mexico and the Dukat mine in Russia.

Peru overtook Mexico as the world's leading producer of silver in 2002, retaining the top rank in each year in 2003–09. Peruvian mined output of silver reached peak production of 123.6m. oz in 2009; the fall in production in 2010 and 2011 allowed Mexico's increasing output to displace Peru as the world's main mine producer, while China pushed Peru into third place in 2012. Peru possessed 17% of total reserves of silver worldwide in 2013, according to the US Geological Survey (USGS), just behind Australia and followed by Poland, Chile and China, all ahead of Mexico. Mexico's reserves of silver ore in 2013 were estimated by the USGS to represent 7% of total reserves worldwide. Chile, despite its continuing problems in the silver sector, is reckoned to have the world's fourth largest reserves (15% of total in 2013), but the country's output was exceeded by that of Bolivia in 2012 and 2013. The other main producers of Latin America were Argentina and Guatemala, while there were smaller-scale silver mining industries in the Dominican Republic (2.8m. oz), Honduras, Colombia, Ecuador, Brazil, Nicaragua and Panama.

International Association The Silver Institute is an international association of miners, refiners, fabricators and manufacturers, with its headquarters in Washington, DC, USA, and is the source of many of the figures in this survey; at mid-2014 it had 31 members.

Silver Prices on the New York Commodity Exchange
(average COMEX 'spot' settlement, US $ per troy ounce)

		Average	High	Low
2000	.	4.966	(February) 5.448	(December) 4.570
2005	.	7.322	(December) 9.000	(January) 6.427
2010	.	20.313	(December) 29.394	(February) 15.898
2011	.	35.196	(April) 48.584	(January) 26.811
2012	.	31.091	(February) 37.140	(June) 26.247
2013	.	23.747	(January) 32.409	(June) 18.533

Sources: The Silver Institute; Thomson Reuters GFMS.

Prices Fluctuations in the price of silver bullion traditionally tended to follow trends in prices for gold and other precious metals. However, silver has come to be viewed increasingly as an industrial raw material and hence as likely to decrease in price in times of economic recession. Two of the main centres for trading in silver are the New York Commodity Exchange (COMEX) and the London Bullion Market (LBM). Dealings in silver on the LBM are only on the basis of 'spot' contracts (for prompt delivery), while COMEX contracts are also for silver 'futures' (options to take delivery at specified future dates). In March 1980 the attempt by the two Hunt brothers from Texas, USA, who had attempted to 'corner' the silver market and sent the price soaring by over 700% in 1979, ended in a collapse in the silver price, amid panic on the markets. Although falling back from the peak price of US $48.70 per troy oz, the average price over 1980 was still $20.98 per oz (London price), which was not exceeded even in nominal terms until 2011 ($35.12 per oz). This had resulted from a price rally driven by investment, industrial demand and the gold price rise—illustrating silver's dual nature as both a precious metal ('safe haven') and an industrial commodity (silver is more volatile than gold). By 2013 the average annual price had fallen to $23.79 per oz, which was still nominally higher, but in real 2013 prices the 1980 figure was equivalent to $59.74 per oz. Silver prices in the first half of 2014 remained slightly lower than in the year before, but relatively stable.

SOYBEANS (*Glycine max*)

The soybean plant (*Glycine max*, or its wild ancestor, *G. soja*) is a legume, a member of the pea family (*fabaceae*). Like other legumes it is able to collect its own nitrogen from the air and release it into the soil. The soybean has accordingly played an important role in the maintenance of soil fertility under traditional crop rotation regimes. Owing to the plant's sensitivity to light, it has been possible to optimize cultivation through the selection of varieties adapted, according to the length of their crop durations, to geographical differences in daylight hours. It is the breeding of such varieties that has allowed successful cultivation to extend from northern, temperate zones, where the soybean originated, to, for example, subtropical and tropical regions of the USA and South America. In North America, the main area of cultivation, soybeans are generally planted in the late spring. The plant flowers in the summer, producing 60–80 pods from which two to four pea-sized beans are harvested in the autumn.

Cultivation of the soybean plant is thought to have originated more than 5,000 years ago in northern China, and to have spread southwards from there to Korea, Japan and throughout South-East Asia.

In the regions of its origin and early dissemination the soybean has for centuries been a primary source of protein for human consumption. However, it was not until the mid-20th century that soybeans began to be traded internationally to a significant degree. Up to 19% of the soybean seed is oil, which is extracted by cracking the bean, adjusting for moisture content, rolling into flakes and using a solvent to extract. The oil is refined and blended to varying degrees, dependent on end-use, and sometimes hydrogenated (it is widely used in processed foods or as 'vegetable oil'). The residue is known as soybean meal or cake, which is 50% soy protein content; it is 'toasted' (in actual fact, heated with moist steam) and ground in a hammer mill (it is mainly used for animal feed).

Production of Soybeans
('000 metric tons)

	2010/11	2011/12	2012/13	2013/14
World total	263,888	239,525	267,859	283,946
Latin America*	131,428	110,673	139,502	149,600
Major Latin American producers				
Argentina	49,000	40,100	49,300	54,000
Brazil	75,300	66,500	82,000	87,500
Paraguay	7,128	4,043	8,202	8,100
Other major producers				
Canada	4,445	4,298	5,086	5,200
China, People's Repub.	15,080	14,485	13,050	12,200
India	9,800	11,000	11,500	11,000
USA	90,605	84,192	82,561	89,507

* Figures represent the sum of output in listed countries only.

Source: US Department of Agriculture, *Oilseeds: World Markets and Trade* (August 2014).

The World Market and the Region During the Second World War, and into the 1950s and 1960s, US soybean production was greatly expanded, with the aim of substituting domestically produced soybean oil for imported oils and fats. Thereafter, the protein-rich meal, which is a by-product of crushing for oil, was used to boost livestock production in the USA. Until recently the soybean had for long been the most important source of vegetable oil worldwide. Today, however, the oil palm surpasses it as the most important source, production of palm oil superseding soybean oil definitively in 2004 (FAO figures). Soybean meal, meanwhile, accounts for about 70% of the world's supply of protein-rich animal feedstuffs. The meal is the most valuable product obtained from processing soybeans, generally accounting for 50%–75% of total value, depending on the difference in the prices of meal and oil. Furthermore, in addition to the traditional foods derived from soy for human consumption, the plant's derivatives are widely employed in processed foods marketed in Europe and North America. Among many industrial applications, the soybean also provides a raw material for the manufacture of ink, soap, paint, polymers and a fuel for diesel engines. It remains uncertain, however, the extent to which demand will increase for soybeans as a biofuel feedstock, since, under production and trading regimes at the beginning of the 2010s, especially in the European Union (EU), the economic viability of many other crop-derived feedstocks was superior to that of soybeans. US demand for soybean-derived biofuel continued to encourage the market.

The USA has dominated world production of soybeans since the 1950s, when its output overtook that of the People's Republic of China. The USA's share of world production has been in decline since the 1970s, when the country was regularly the source of more than two-thirds of global output. One of the reasons for that decline has been the substantial increases in the output of Latin America and the Caribbean, which since 2002 (with the exception of 2004, when North America—the USA and Canada—regained primacy) has ranked as the world's largest producer region. Soybeans are by far the most important oilseed in international trade. In 2013/14, according to the US Department of Agriculture (USDA), exports of soybeans, at some 113m. metric tons, were equivalent to about 85% of world exports of oilseeds amounting to 133m. tons (including, additionally, copra, cottonseed, groundnuts, palm kernels, rapeseed and sunflowerseed). Rapeseed, which ranks as the second largest oilseed in international trade, accounted for 11% of all oilseeds exported in 2013/14. China was, overwhelmingly, the principal importer of soybeans in 2013/14, receiving shipments totalling 69m. tons, or about 63% of total world imports, followed by the member states of the EU (12%). The USA is traditionally the leading exporter of soybeans, but it was displaced by Brazil from 2012/13. In 2013/14 Brazil accounted for 41% of world exports totalling 113m. tons, while the USA provided 40%.

Production of Soybean Meal
('000 metric tons)

	2010/11	2011/12	2012/13	2013/14
World total	174,634	180,418	180,949	189,703
Latin America*	60,342	60,365	56,289	60,485
Major Latin American producers				
Argentina	29,312	27,945	26,089	28,825
Brazil	28,160	29,510	27,310	28,500
Mexico	2,870	2,910	2,890	3,160
Other major producers				
China, People's Repub.	43,560	48,288	51,440	54,451
European Union	9,760	9,674	10,194	9,938
India	7,520	7,680	7,800	6,880
USA	35,608	37,217	36,174	37,204

* Figures represent the sum of output in listed countries only.

Source: US Department of Agriculture, *Oilseeds: World Markets and Trade* (August 2014).

The pattern of production of soybean meal is similar to that of unprocessed soybeans, except that the USA, hitherto the dominant world producer, was edged out of the leading position in 2009/10 by China. On a regional basis, however, world output is dominated by Latin America and the Caribbean—the overwhelming majority of the regional total is accounted for by Argentina, Brazil and, to a lesser extent, Mexico. Soybean meal is the leading protein meal in international trade, accounting for 74% of all world exports of protein meal in 2013/14, according to USDA. In comparison, exports of palm kernel meal, usually the second most widely traded protein meal, accounted for almost 8% of total world exports of protein meal in that year. International trade in soybean meal has increased steadily since the 1970s. Latin America is the leading exporting region, Argentina and Brazil between them accounting for about 66% of world exports, which totalled 61m. metric tons in 2013/14, according to USDA. Within the region, Argentina overtook Brazil as the leading exporter in the late 1990s. In 2013/14 Argentina exported 27m. tons and Brazil 14m. tons; the USA ranked as the world's third largest exporter of soybean meal, with foreign sales by weight totalling about 11m. tons—some 17% of total world exports—followed by India (5%) and Paraguay (4%). In 2013/14 the member states of the EU accounted for by far the largest share—32%—of world imports of soybean meal totalling about 58m. tons. South-East and East Asian countries were also important importers.

Production of Soybean Oil
('000 metric tons)

	2010/11	2011/12	2012/13	2013/14
World total	41,285	42,601	42,894	44,955
Latin America*	14,799	14,806	13,777	14,845
Major Latin American producers				
Argentina	7,181	6,839	6,364	7,030
Brazil	6,970	7,310	6,760	7,100
Mexico	648	657	653	715
Other major producers				
China, People's Repub.	9,840	10,914	11,626	12,317
European Union	2,246	2,226	2,317	2,269
India	1,675	1,710	1,740	1,540
USA	8,568	8,954	8,990	9,169

* Figures represent the sum of output in listed countries only.

Source: US Department of Agriculture, *Oilseeds: World Markets and Trade* (August 2014).

As with soybean meal in 2009/10, in 2010/11 China displaced the USA as the world's leading producer of soybean oil, according to USDA figures. Although soybeans dominate international trade in unprocessed oilseeds, and soybean meal dominates world trade in protein meals, trade in vegetable oils is now increasingly dominated by palm oil. In 2013/14, according to USDA, palm oil accounted for about 35% of vegetable oil production (soybean oil for 26%); however, palm oil contributed 62% of world exports of vegetable oils totalling about 69m. metric tons (including, additionally, coconut, cottonseed, olive, palm kernel, groundnut, rapeseed or canola, soybean and sunflowerseed oils). Soybean oil, which costs about one-fifth more than palm oil to produce, ranks second, accounting for 14% of world vegetable oil exports in 2013/14. In that year Argentina ranked as the world's leading exporter of soybean oil, its foreign sales, at more than 4m. metric tons, accounting for 46% of world exports totalling some 10m. tons. The combined exports of Argentina, Brazil, Paraguay and

Bolivia represented 70% of world exports of soybean oil in 2013/14, far greater than those of any other region or trading bloc. China is usually the world's leading importer of soybean oil, and it accounted for 14% of world imports in 2013/14, but in that year India bought 17% of the total of some 9m. tons. According to some forecasts, it is anticipated that demand, supply and trade in vegetable oil might increase substantially. Owing to the complexity of the calculations involved, increasing demand for biofuels has not always been factored into medium-term predictions. Soybean oil has hitherto accounted for only a small proportion—relative to, above all, rape-seed oil and sunflowerseed oil, which have therefore been increasing their presence in international commodity markets—of biodiesel derived from vegetable oil, and, under current production and trading conditions, in terms of economic viability it trails palm oil and rapeseed oil, as well as other crops (e.g. sugar and cassava) that can be used as biodiesel feedstocks.

As there are relatively few major producers of soybeans worldwide, and as soybeans are the most important oilseed in world trade, US policy has influenced not only the world market for soybeans, but also the markets for the eight major competing oilseeds—rapeseed, sunflowerseed, cottonseed, groundnuts, flaxseed, copra, palm and palm kernels. Moreover, with regard to unprocessed soybeans, US influence has been reinforced by the fact that international trade has historically been comparatively free of tariffs and other restrictions on imports. (Tariffs applied to protect the oilseed-processing indus-tries of importing countries, by contrast, have typically been fixed at about twice the rate applied to the unprocessed commodity.) Since the mid-1970s, however, the USA's dominance of the international soybean market has steadily declined, despite growth in both pro-duction and export volume. Above all, this has been due to the rapid expansion in production and exports by Argentina and Brazil, whose individual exports of soybean meal and soybean oil have both over-taken those of the USA. Lower-cost production of soybeans in Argentina and Brazil has given those countries a considerable competitive advantage in international markets.

Soybean Prices
(annual averages, US $ per metric ton)

	Soybeans	Soybean meal	Soybean oil
2000 .	211.83	189.17	338.08
2005 .	274.69	214.38	544.92
2010 .	449.80	378.40	1,004.60
2011 .	540.67	397.98	1,299.33
2012 .	591.42	524.08	1,226.25
2013 .	538.42	545.25	1,056.67

Source: World Bank, *Commodity Price Data* (Pink Sheet).

Prices The leading role of the USA in the production and export of soybeans means that, traditionally, US prices are the most accurate and readily available guide to the international market. The price for US soybeans (c.i.f. Rotterdam) is cited in this survey, using data from the World Bank, which also supplies annual average prices for soybean meal of any origin (45/46% extraction, c.i.f. Rotterdam) and for crude soybean oil of any origin (f.o.b., ex-mill Netherlands). During 2014 all three prices tended to decline, although the price of soybean oil proved most robust, as the tight supply situation of the previous year was easing. In July 2014 soybeans commanded US $480 per metric ton, soybean meal $502 per ton and soybean oil $888 per ton.

SUGAR

Sugar is a sweet crystalline substance which may be derived from the juices of various plants. Chemically, the basis of sugar is sucrose, one of a group of soluble carbohydrates which are important sources of energy in the human diet. It can be obtained from trees, including the maple and certain palms, but virtually all manufactured sugar is derived from two plants, sugar beet (*Beta vulgaris*) and sugar cane, a giant perennial grass of the genus *Saccharum*.

Sugar cane, found in tropical areas, grows to a height of up to 5 m (16 ft). The plant is native to Polynesia, but its distribution is now widespread. It is not necessary to plant cane every season, as if the root of the plant is left in the ground it will grow again in the following year. This practice, known as 'ratooning', may be continued for as long as three years, when yields begin to decline. Cane is ready for cutting 12–24 months after planting, depending on local conditions. More than one-half of the world's sugar cane is still cut by hand, but rising costs are hastening the change to mechanical harvesting. The cane is cut as close as possible to the ground, and the top leaves, which may be used as cattle fodder, are removed.

After cutting, the cane is loaded by hand or by machine into trucks or trailers and transported directly to a factory for processing. Sugar cane rapidly deteriorates after it has been cut and should be pro-cessed as soon as possible. At the factory the cane passes first through shredding knives or crushing rollers, which break up the hard rind

and expose the inner fibre, and then to squeezing rollers, where the crushed cane is subjected to high pressure and sprayed with water. The resulting juice is heated, and lime is added for clarification and the removal of impurities. The clean juice is then concentrated in evaporators. This thickened juice is next boiled in steam-heated vacuum pans until a mixture or 'massecuite' of sugar crystals and 'mother syrup' is produced. The massecuite is then spun in centri-fugal machines to separate the sugar crystals (raw cane sugar) from the residual syrup (cane molasses).

After the milling of sugar, the cane has dry fibrous remnants known as bagasse, which is usually burned as fuel in sugar mills. Bagasse can also be pulped and used for making fibreboard, particle board and most grades of paper. As the costs of imported wood pulp have risen, cane-growing regions have turned increasingly to the manufacture of paper from bagasse. In view of rising energy costs, some countries (such as Cuba) have encouraged the use of bagasse as fuel for electricity production in order to conserve foreign exchange expended on imports of petroleum. Another by-product, cachaza, has been utilized as an animal feed.

The production of beet sugar follows the same process as sugar from sugar cane, except that the juice is extracted by osmotic diffusion. Its manufacture produces white sugar crystals that do not require further refining. In most producing countries, it is consumed domes-tically, but any fall in the production of beet sugar by the European Union (EU) can mean that it becomes a net importer of white refined sugar. Beet sugar accounted for about one-fifth of estimated world sugar production in 2013/14 (19%), according to the US Department of Agriculture (USDA). The production data in the first table, there-fore, is for sugar cane, covering all crops harvested, except crops grown explicitly for feed. The second table covers the production of raw sugar by the centrifugal process (including beet sugar). While global output of non-centrifugal sugar (i.e. produced from sugar cane which has not undergone centrifugation) is not insignificant, it tends to be destined for domestic consumption. The main producer of non-centrifugal sugar is India, where it is known as gur, but countries such as Brazil and Colombia are also significant producers.

Most of the raw cane sugar produced in the world is sent to refineries outside the country of origin, unless the sugar is for local consumption. Cuba, Thailand, Brazil and India are among the few cane-producers that export part of their output as refined sugar. The refining process further purifies the sugar crystals and eventually results in finished products of various grades, such as granulated, icing or castor sugar. The ratio of refined to raw sugar is usually about 0.9:1.

In the closing decades of the 20th century sugar encountered increased competition from other sweeteners, including maize-based products, such as isoglucose (a form of high-fructose corn syrup, or HFCS), and chemical additives, such as saccharine, aspartame (APM) and xylitol. APM was the most widely used high-intensity artificial sweetener in the early 1990s, its market dominance then came under challenge from sucralose, which is about 600 times as sweet as sugar (compared with 200–300 times for other intense sweeteners) and is more resistant to chemical deterioration than APM. In 1998 the US Government approved the domestic marketing of sucralose, the only artificial sweetener made from sugar. Sucralose was stated to avoid many of the taste problems associated with other artificial sweeteners. From the late 1980s research was conducted to formulate means of synthesizing thaumatin, a substance derived from the fruit of the West African katemfe plant, *Thaumatococcus daniellii*, which is about 2,500 times as sweet as sugar. As of 2005, the use of thaumatin had been approved in the EU, Israel and Japan, while in the USA its use as a flavouring agent had been endorsed. By 2011 sugar use was resurgent because of health concerns about other sweeteners—for example, sugar producers attempted to preserve this advantage in the US courts by preventing the Corn Refiners Association from renaming HFCS 'corn sugar'.

Production of Sugar Cane
('000 metric tons)

	2010	2011	2012	2013
World total . . .	1,700,648	1,807,957	1,842,266	2,165,231
Latin America and the Caribbean . . .	932,400	954,582	840,104	970,083
Leading Latin American and Caribbean producers				
Argentina	25,960*	26,960*	23,000†	23,700†
Brazil	717,464	734,006	721,077	739,267
Colombia	33,300*	34,890	33,364	34,876
Cuba	11,500	15,800	14,400	14,400*
Guatemala	22,314	20,586	23,653	26,335
Mexico	50,422	49,735	50,946	61,182
Peru	9,855	9,885	10,369	10,992

—continued	2010	2011	2012	2013
Other leading producers				
Australia	31,457	25,182	25,957	27,136
China, People's Repub. .	111,501	115,124	124,038	126,136†
Egypt	15,709	15,765	15,950*	16,100*
India	292,302	342,382	361,037	341,200
Indonesia†	26,600	24,000	28,700	33,700
Pakistan	49,373	55,309	58,397	63,750
Philippines*	28,000	30,000	32,000	32,000
South Africa . . .	16,016	16,800	17,278	18,000*
Thailand	68,808	95,950	98,400	100,096
USA	24,821	26,656	29,236	27,906
Viet Nam	16,162	17,540	19,017	20,018

* FAO estimate(s).
† Unofficial figure(s).
Source: FAO.

Production of Centrifugal Sugar
(raw value, '000 metric tons, Oct.–Sept. marketing year)

	2010/11	2011/12	2012/13	2013/14*
World total† . .	161,940	172,166	177,486	175,703
Latin America and the Caribbean . . .	51,973	51,024	53,952	53,077
Leading Latin American and Caribbean producers				
Argentina	2,030	2,150	2,300	1,780
Brazil	38,350	36,150	38,600	37,800
Colombia	2,280	2,270	1,950	2,300
Cuba	1,150	1,400	1,510	1,500
Guatemala . . .	2,048	2,499	2,778	2,852
Mexico	5,495	5,351	7,393	6,731
Other leading producers				
Australia	3,700	3,683	4,250	4,300
China, People's Repub. .	11,199	12,341	14,0017	14,346
European Union (EU) .	15,939	18,320	16,655	16,100
India	26,574	28,620	27,337	27,045
Pakistan	3,920	4,520	5,000	5,215
Russia	2,996	5,545	5,000	4,400
Thailand	9,663	10,235	10,024	11,390
USA	7,104	7,700	8,148	7,693

* Advance estimates.

† Including beet sugar production ('000 metric tons): 31,939 in 2010/11 (Chile 330; China, People's Repub. 863; EU 15,664; Pakistan 20; Russia 2,996; USA 4,226); 38,579 in 2011/12 (Chile 325; China, People's Repub. 1,095; EU 18,033; Pakistan 20; Russia 5,545; USA 4,446); 36,675 in 2012/13 (Chile 295; China, People's Repub. 1,179; EU 16,364; Pakistan 20; Russia 5,000; USA 4,605); 33,876 in 2013/14 (Chile 300; China, People's Repub. 811; EU 15,341; Pakistan 40; Russia 4,400; USA 4,355).

Source: US Department of Agriculture (USDA), Foreign Agricultural Service.

The World Market and the Region Production of sugar cane is dominated by Latin America and the Caribbean, which usually grows about one-half of the world total: 45% in 2013, according to FAO (South America 39%, Central America 5% and the Caribbean 1%). Eastern Asia and Oceania—the Far East and Australasia—grew 30% of the world's sugar cane, South Asia 19% and Africa 4% (sub-Saharan Africa 3%). The area under sugar cane cultivation in the whole of Latin America and the Caribbean more than doubled in the 40 years from the late 1960s. The area from which sugar cane was harvested went from 4.6m. ha in 1968 to 13.2m. ha by 2013 (FAO), as part of an attempt to satisfy greater domestic consumption and to diversify from predominant industries (such as coffee and cocoa), but this figure conceals important sub-regional variations. In Central America the area harvested increased by 76% (1968–2010), to 1.2m. ha, meaning that in importance to sugar production it displaced the Caribbean, where the area harvested fell by 59% over the same period (to 0.6m. ha). In South America, however, the area harvested for sugar cane increased more than fourfold between 1968 and 2010, from 2.4m. ha to 10.2m. ha. Moreover, South America enjoyed productive yields, whereas the Caribbean yield was the lowest in the world. According to the US Department of Agriculture (USDA), exports of (centrifugal) sugar from Latin American and Caribbean countries contributed 57% of total world sales abroad in 2013/14, compared with 22% from eastern Asia and Oceania, notably Thailand and Australia (major producers such as China being net importers). South Asia, likewise, is a net importer, despite India being the second largest producer in the world. The main importing region was eastern Asia and Oceania (31% in 2013/14, mainly Indonesia and China) and the Middle East and North Africa (23%), followed by sub-Saharan Africa (13%).

Brazil is firmly established as the world's largest producer of sugar cane and sugar, and as a leading producer of ethanol (its PROAL-COOL programme is the oldest and largest ethanol-based fuel initiative in the world, dating from 1975, the era of the first major petroleum crisis). The central-southern region is the most important producing area (in 2009/10 it accounted for about 90% of national output, while the remaining 10% was produced in the north-east, in particular the states of Pernambuco and Alagoas) and also produces 86% of the country's centrifugal sugar. Owing to the relatively greater economic significance of sugar production to the north-eastern region, the Government has tended to grant it the entire annual US sugar import quota allocation, for which premium prices are obtained. Brazil is one of the world's most efficient sugar producers, and, because it possesses the infrastructure to process cane into either sugar or ethanol, the country is able to respond swiftly to market conditions. As the world's largest producer of sugar cane, Brazil exerts considerable influence on the world market price of sugar, of which the balance in the country between ethanol and raw sugar production is a major determinant. The ratio of ethanol to raw sugar as products of the sugar crop increased in ethanol's favour during the 2000s as a consequence of rising national consumption of ethanol. Domestic demand for ethanol and for sugar itself determine export availability, since Brazil is a leading consumer as well as exporter of each. Reduced direct exports to the USA and India set in from 2011 or so, but US regulations and import quotas were such that a significant amount of Brazilian ethanol went as re-exports through countries of the Caribbean Basin Initiative. Income from exports fluctuated in line with commodity prices, currency values and the amount of sugar cane processed for ethanol, so raw sugar exports earned US $3,650m. in 2008 (1.8% of total exports), but $11,843m. in 2013 (4.9%).

Of Brazil's neighbours to the south and west, Argentina is a major producer of sugar, while Peru is the second largest ethanol producer of the region. Argentina vied with Colombia to hold next place as sugar producers to Brazil in South America, but they are far behind Mexico, while Guatemalan sugar output now exceeds both Argentina and Colombia (Guatemalan exports exceeded Mexico's in 2012/13). Moreover, as exporters on to the international commodity markets, neither Argentina or Colombia are significant, and Mexico is erratic. Peru boasts the highest sugar cane yields in the region (and among the highest in the world), with the intensive use of fertilizers and irrigation compensating for the natural disadvantages of light soil and aridity. In 2007 Peru was the second largest producer of sugar cane ethanol in the region, although it boasts only a fraction of Brazil's output, despite recent investment. As with many sugar industries in the region, the sugar sector in Colombia underwent a major expansion from the 1960s in an attempt to diversify the economy away from coffee. The area planted to sugar cane peaked in 2006 (up 45% on 1961). In the main production zone, the Cauca river valley in south-western Colombia, climatic conditions permit the cultivation of sugar uninterrupted throughout the year, resulting in exceptionally low fixed investment costs per ton of sugar produced. Colombia has also developed considerable capacity in the production of ethanol since it commenced output in 2005. The sugar industry in Guatemala has been expanded rapidly since the late 1960s (output up 10-fold in 40 years). In 2013 sugar exports earned the country 9.4% of total exports. International labour organizations have criticized some aspects of working conditions in the Guatemalan sugar industry. Guatemala is a party to the Dominican Republic-Central American Free Trade Agreement (DR-CAFTA, see below), and one of the principal objections of opponents of that Agreement, both in Guatemala and the USA, has been its scant provision for safeguarding and enforcing national labour legal rights. Mexico was a sugar exporter until 1979, but has been only intermittently since then. Under the North American Free Trade Agreement (NAFTA), which entered into operation in January 1994, Mexico was permitted to increase substantially its sugar exports to the USA and Canada after NAFTA arrangements for the duty-free access of Mexican sugar to the US market took effect in 2001. However, the USA's interpretation of the sugar-related provisions of NAFTA prevented Mexico from obtaining a significant sugar quota for the US market, which was believed to have been a factor motivating a 2002 Mexican tax on sweeteners in soft drinks—the dispute was settled in the USA's favour in 2006 by a ruling of the World Trade Organization (WTO). Mexico reportedly planned to raise its output of bioethanol as part of its efforts to improve the competitiveness of its sugar sector prior to market liberalization under NAFTA in 2008.

The Cuban economy has traditionally relied heavily on sales of sugar and sugar products. Before the revolution of 1959–60, Cuba exported more than 50% of its sugar to the USA, while afterwards it relied on the USSR and other Eastern bloc countries. Those preferential prices ceased after 1991, and Cuba sought new, additional markets in Canada, North Africa, the Middle East and the Far East. However, Cuban sugar production has declined sharply since the early 1990s, owing both to adverse weather conditions, especially drought, and to disruptions in the procurement of fuel, fertilizers, mill equipment and other essential production inputs, as a result of the US embargoes. These factors (which resulted in the 1994/95 harvest declining to the lowest level in 50 years) necessitated over-extended harvests and the use of reserves of cane intended for future crops, so in 1993 sugar exports were temporarily suspended. Various attempts have been made to rationalize and make thing more efficient, but, according to USDA, a large amount of investment would be needed to convert the Cuban sugar industry. There is also, reportedly, high-level political resistance in Cuba to the diversion of much of the country's land resources into large-scale production of ethanol, and Cuba's current access to low-cost petroleum imports from Venezuela may act as a further disincentive. The next largest Caribbean sugar producer and exporter is the Dominican Republic. Sugar cane is the principal commercial crop in the country, but inefficient production techniques, lack of investment and falling international sugar prices depressed the industry at the end of the 20th century. Exports of sugar and sugar confectionary (overwhelmingly, raw sugar) earned US $182.0m. and accounted for an estimated 2.6% of the Dominican Republic's total export revenue in 2012. In some of the smaller American countries and the Caribbean islands, sugar cultivation is the main bulwark of the economy. Sugar is the most important agricultural product of the Caribbean Community and Common Market (CARICOM) economic and political grouping, for instance. In Belize sugar cane plantations occupy about one-half of the total cultivated area, while the sugar industry employs about one-quarter of the labour force. In 2013 sales of sugar contributed 17.1% of total export revenue. In Guyana sugar contributed 8.3% of total export revenue in 2013. In other countries, the tradition of sugar exporting has been all but abandoned: in 2005 it was reported that Barbadian production had declined to the point that the island was unable to meet its EU export quota (in 2003 sugar and molasses had contributed an estimated 9.2% of total export revenue, including re-exports), although domestic consumption and the local rum industry remained important; and in Saint Christopher and Nevis, where 21% of total export revenue was derived from sales of raw sugar in 2001, the Government announced in 2005 that the year's sugar harvest would be the country's last, as rising production costs and a fall in revenues had left the state-owned sugar company heavily in debt. Rising sugar prices in the second half of the decade helped the industry, but it remained in decline in the Caribbean generally.

International Associations and Agreements The first International Sugar Agreement (ISA) was negotiated in 1958, and its economic provisions operated until 1961. A second ISA did not come into operation until 1969. It included quota arrangements and associated provisions for regulating the price of sugar traded on the open market, and established the International Sugar Organization (ISO—see below) to administer the agreement. However, the USA and the six original members of the European Community (EC, now the EU) did not participate in the ISA and, following its expiry in 1974, it was replaced by a purely administrative interim agreement; this remained operational until the finalization of a third ISA, which took effect in 1978. The new agreement's implementation was supervised by an International Sugar Council (ISC), which was empowered to establish price ranges for sugar-trading and to operate a system of quotas and special sugar stocks. Owing to the reluctance of the USA and of EC countries (which were not party to the agreement) to accept export controls, the ISO ultimately lost most of its power to regulate the market, and since 1984 the activities of the organization have been restricted to recording statistics and providing a forum for discussion between producers and consumers. Subsequent ISAs, without effective regulatory powers, have been in operation since 1985. At the end of 1992 the USA withdrew from the ISO, following a disagreement over the formulation of members' financial contributions. Special arrangements for the sugar trade were incorporated into the successive Lomé Conventions that were in operation from 1975 between the EU and a group of African, Caribbean and Pacific (ACP) countries. A special protocol on sugar, forming part of each Convention, required the EU to import specified quantities of raw sugar annually from ACP countries. In June 1998, however, the EU indicated its intention to phase out preferential sugar prices paid to ACP countries within three years. Under the terms of the Cotonou Agreement, a successor to the fourth Lomé Convention covering the period 2000–2020, the protocol on sugar was to be maintained initially, but would become subject to review within the framework of negotiations for new trading arrangements (negotiations for more WTO-compatible Economic Partnership Agreements—EPAs began in 2002). In 2001 the EU Council adopted the EBA (Everything but Arms) regulation, whereby the least developed countries were granted unlimited duty-free access to the EU for all goods except arms and ammunition. EBA was to apply to sugar from

October 2009. Meanwhile, in September 2007 the EU Council of Ministers criticized the protocol on sugar on the grounds that it was not compatible with EU sugar reforms (themselves undertaken in response to upheld complaints before the WTO by Australia, Brazil and Thailand about export subsidies for the ACP countries) and did not take into account the specific needs of different ACP regions. The EU offered duty- and quota-free access to the ACP countries after 2015, in compensation for the loss of subsidies and quotas. A transitional period from October 2009 until September 2015 was to effect the progressive removal of reciprocal trade barriers. However, there was concern that the benefits that ACP countries were intended to derive from unlimited access to the EU market would be undermined by falling sugar prices. It was also uncertain whether some countries that had refused to embrace the EPA arrangements, such as Malawi, would be allowed to continue trading under EBA in order to take advantage of unrestricted access to the EU market sooner (i.e. from 2009 instead of 2015), while sugar prices were still guaranteed to be maintained at a relatively high level. On the basis of data for 2009, the 86 members of the ISO together contributed 83% of world sugar production and 95% of world exports of sugar; ISO members additionally accounted for 69% of global sugar consumption and 47% of world imports. At June 2013 the ISO had 87 members (Indonesia joined in 2011), including both the EU and its (then) 27 member states. The ISO is based in London, United Kingdom. The Group of Latin American and Caribbean Sugar Exporting Countries (GEPLACEA), founded in 1975, which represents 23 Latin American and Caribbean countries and the Philippines, complements the activities of the ISO as a forum for co-operation and research.

Sugar Prices
(annual averages, US $ per metric ton)

	ISA (World)	USA	EU
2000	180	430	560
2005	220	470	670
2010	470	790	440
2011	570	840	450
2012	470	640	420
2013	390	450	430

Source: World Bank, *Commodity Price Data* (Pink Sheet).

Prices In tandem with world output of cane and beet sugars, stock levels (of centrifugal sugar) are an important factor in determining the prices at which sugar is traded internationally. These stocks, which were at relatively low levels in the late 1980s, increased significantly, if not consistently, in the 1990s. Stocks increased fairly steadily after 2000, reaching the high level of almost 46m. metric tons in 2013/14.

The World Bank records three sugar prices, to reflect the major markets. The world price that it quotes is the ISA daily price for raw sugar (f.o.b., stowed at greater Caribbean ports); the US price is for sugar under nearby futures contract (c.i.f.); and the increasingly anachronistic EU-negotiated import price for raw, unpackaged sugar from African, Caribbean and Pacific (ACP) countries under the Lomé Conventions (c.i.f., European ports). In 2014 stagnating production and increasing consumption kept prices stable or, in the USA, rising slightly. In July 2014 the ISA world price stood at US $400 per metric ton, the US price $550 per ton and the EU price $440 per ton.

TIN (*Sn*)

Tin is a silvery malleable metal, long used in alloys, such as pewter or bronze, or to coat other metals to help resist corrosion ('tin cans' are made of tinplate, which is tin-coated steel). Tin must be extracted from ores and cassiterite is the only economically important tin-bearing mineral; it is generally associated with tungsten, silver and tantalum minerals. There is a clear association of cassiterite with igneous rocks of granitic composition (granite), and 'primary' cassiterite deposits occur as disseminations, or in veins and fissures in or around granites. If the primary deposits are eroded, as by rivers, cassiterite may be concentrated and deposited in 'secondary', sedimentary deposits. These secondary or placer deposits form the bulk of the world's tin reserves. The world's known tin reserves, estimated by the US Geological Survey (USGS) to total 4.7m. metric tons in 2013, are located mainly in the equatorial zones of Asia and Africa, in central South America and in Australia.

About 60% of the world's tin mining production is from hard-rock mines, the rest is from alluvial mining. The ore is treated, generally by gravity method or flotation, to produce concentrates prior to smelting or carbothermic reduction. The metal can exist in different forms, or allotropes, the two most common being grey tin (beta or tin), a powdery substance with few uses, and the more usual metallic white tin (alpha or tin). The spontaneous degradation of white tin into grey tin, particularly at low temperatures, is known as tin pest. Tin therefore benefits from the presence of small amounts of impurities. The earliest use of tin was as an alloy, notably pewter and, when added to copper, bronze. Tin's low toxicity and resistance to corrosion resulted in its use to coat other metals, especially steel (tinplate), for food storage; the first 'tin can' was made in London, United Kingdom, in 1812.

Production of Tin Concentrates
(tin content, metric tons)

	2010	2011	2012	2013*
World total (excl. USA)*	247,000	244,000	240,000	230,000
Latin America . . .	64,438	60,255	59,900	63,500
Latin American producers				
Bolivia	20,190	20,373	19,700	18,000
Brazil	10,400	11,000	10,800	11,900
Peru	33,848	28,882	26,100	26,100
Other leading producers				
Australia	6,600	6,500	5,000	5,900
China, People's Repub.* .	115,000	120,000	110,000	100,000
Congo, Democratic Repub.* . . .	6,800	2,900	4,000	4,000
Indonesia	43,258	42,000	41,000	40,000
Malaysia	2,668	3,346	3,000	3,700
Rwanda	1,400	1,400	2,300	1,600
Viet Nam* . . .	5,400	5,400	5,400	5,400

* Estimated production.

Source: US Geological Survey.

The World Market and the Region Tin owes its special place in industry to its unique combination of properties: low melting point, the ability to form alloys with most other metals, resistance to corrosion, non-toxicity and good appearance. Its main uses are in industrial and electronic solders (54% of total consumption in 2010), in other alloys (bronze, brass, pewter, bearing and type metal), in tinplate and in chemical compounds (paints, plastics, medicines, coatings and as fungicides and insecticides). Since the late 1990s a number of possible new applications for tin have been under study, including its use in fire-retardant chemicals and as an environmentally preferable substitute for cadmium in zinc alloy anti-corrosion coatings on steel. According to the USGS, the world's largest tin producers are the People's Republic of China (43% of estimated global production in 2013) and Indonesia (17%), followed by Peru (11%), although Indonesia is the world's largest exporter. Despite China's high production, its strong internal market made the country a net importer of tin from 2008, although there were indications by 2014 that it might again become an exporter. From the second half of 2013, however, the main development on the international tin market was Indonesia's change in export policy, as the country tried to improve domestic value added (Malaysia smelts much Indonesian tin) and raise prices. In August the country's regulations increased the minimum purity standards and required the ingots to be traded on a local exchange before export, also challenging the position of the London Metal Exchange (LME) in setting the benchmark price for the commodity. Hitherto, most of the world's trade has been traded on the LME (from eight countries, using 19 brands in 2014).

In 2010 the world's largest tin-producing companies were Yunnan Tin (China), PT Timah (Indonesia), the Malaysia Smelting Corporation (MSC—Malaysia), Minsur (Peru) and another smelting company, Thaisarco (Thailand). All five were members of the International Tin Research Institute (ITRI), and they accounted for 85% of ITRI production, which was estimated to be two-thirds of total world production of refined tin. The largest non-ITRI company and the world's sixth largest producer was Guangxi China Tin (China). The Chinese companies mainly satisfied domestic demand, since China was by far the world's largest consumer of tin (the decade average for 2000–09 had China accounting for 29% of world refined tin consumption, Europe 22%, the USA 14% and Japan 9%).

According to the USGS, China and India each produced more tin than Latin America until 2007, even though the region includes the world's next three largest producers (closely followed by Myanmar). In that year the three major Latin American producers between them just exceeded Indonesia's mine production (22.2%% of the world total, compared with 22.0%); in 2013 the region accounted for 24.4% of the world total. In 1994 Peru emerged as the region's leading producer of tin and the world's third largest source, a position the country has maintained. Until the 1990s almost all of Peru's tin exports were in the form of ores and concentrates, which provided 1.5% of the country's total export earnings in 1996. However, Peru's first tin smelter, at Pisco, began operating in 1997, with an initial production capacity of 15,000 metric tons of metal per year. Malaysia displaced Peru as the world's third largest producer of primary tin (after China and Indonesia) in 2009, but the country still smelted an

estimated 32,290 tons in 2011—equivalent to almost 10% of total world production—although that was considerably down on the 2004 peak of 67,675 tons. Minsur, Peru's only fully integrated supplier of tin, operates the San Rafael mine in Mariategui (the largest underground tin mine in the world) and the smelter at Pisco; the latter was expected to become more dependent on imports as mine production declined (unless new resources were identified, the mine would cease production before 2020, although treatment of tailings from 2013 was offsetting declining output to some extent). Peruvian tin exports were worth far less to the country than other minerals, but still accounted for 1.2% of total exports in 2011, according to the USGS. In 2002 Bolivian production of tin surpassed that of Brazil, making it the region's second largest producer. Bolivia's largest tin mine is located south-east of La Paz, at Huanuni, where, in 2006, there were disputes between the salaried employees of the state-owned mining company, Corporación Minera de Bolivia (COMIBOL), and independent, co-operatively organized workers. Following violent unrest, 4,000 independent miners formally became COMIBOL employees and the Government took control of the Huanuni mine in October. In February 2007 the Government seized control of Bolivia's principal tin smelter, the Vinto smelter, which had been sold to Glencore International AG of Switzerland in 2005. A legal dispute between Glencore and the Government of Bolivia ensued and, in fact, with the Government refusing to pay compensation and, in May 2010 the Government also nationalized a Glencore subsidiary's antimony smelter. The Government planned to reactivate processing of minerals in the country and, in 2011, it nationalized the still unopened tin mine at Karachipampa, after foreign investors had failed to begin operations. In June 2012, it nationalized a third Glencore operation, the Colquiri tin and zinc mine. Revised mining legislation under the new 2009 Constitution and restructuring of COMIBOL and other state-owned assets was likely to transform the mining sector over the course of the 2010s, but such developments could also hinder investment in the industry. In 2011 tin was the country's third most important non-fuel mineral export.

Brazil possesses the world's largest tin mine, located at Pitinga, in Amazonas state. From 2008 the mine was owned by Minsur of Peru, which anticipated dramatic increases in production as extraction from the main pit recommenced, in contrast with treatment of existing tailings only for the previous few years. Despite the ambitions of the country's leading tin-mining company, Grupo Paranapanema, in 2006 and 2009 mine production of tin had fallen to its lowest level—some 9,500 metric tons—since 1982. Figures indicated an erratic recovery thereafter. Brazil is the world's fifth largest tin producer; it possesses the world's largest tin resources after China and Indonesia, although the metal was not among Brazil's leading mineral ore exports. Elsewhere in Latin America, Canada's Silver Standard Resources Inc. estimated in 2006 that some 25% of future revenues from its Pirquitas silver project in Argentina could derive from tin resources located there. The mine began silver and zinc production at the end of 2009, but tin was still not being exploited by 2014. Mexican tin production, meanwhile, had ceased in 2009 (the country had produced about 25 tons annually in 2006 and 2007, and 15 tons in 2008).

International Associations The International Tin Council (ITC) was dissolved in 1990, but the role of the Association of Tin Producing Countries (ATPC) in restoring orderly conditions to the international tin trade unofficially in effect established it as the successor of the ITC as the international co-ordinating body for tin interests. (The ATPC worked to reduce stockpiles and had a system of voluntary quotas until 1996—for international price mechanisms, see below). The ATPC was founded in 1983 by Malaysia, Indonesia and Thailand and later joined by Bolivia, Nigeria, Australia, Zaire (now the Democratic Republic of the Congo—DRC) and then, finally, China in 1994, when the organization accounted for almost two-thirds of world tin production. Brazil, Peru and Viet Nam were observers. In 1996, with the failure of the quota system, Australia and Thailand withdrew. Malaysia, Australia and Indonesia left the ATPC in 1997, and Brazil became a full member in 1998. In June 1999, when the organization's headquarters were moved from Kuala Lumpur, Malaysia, to Rio de Janeiro, Brazil, the membership comprised Brazil, Bolivia, China, the DRC and Nigeria. Meanwhile, however, the International Tin Study Group (ITSG), comprising 36 producing and consuming countries, was established by the ATPC in 1989 to assume the informational functions of the ITC. In 1991 the secretariat of the United Nations Conference on Trade and Development (UNCTAD) assumed responsibility for the publication of statistical information on the international tin market. ITRI, founded in 1932 and based in London, promotes scientific research and technical development in the production and use of tin.

International Tin Price
(US $ per metric ton)

	Average	High	Low
1970	3,637.45	(April) 3,849.30	(December) 3,496.50
1980	16,774.88	(March) 17,470.30	(December) 14,707.00
1990	6,085.38	(January) 6,592.00	(December) 5,615.20
2000	5,435.71	(January) 5,927.80	(December) 5,233.70
2005	7,379.83	(March) 8,407.39	(November) 6,160.00
2010	20,405.62	(October) 26,342.62	(February) 16,361.75
2011	26,053.68	(April) 32,363.31	(December) 19,375.01
2012	21,125.99	(July) 18,546.09	(February) 24,293.31
2013	22,282.80	(January) 24,545.90	(July) 19,563.83

Source: World Bank, *Commodity Price Data* (Pink Sheet).

Prices During 1956–85 much of the world's tin production and trade was covered by successive international agreements, administered by the ITC, based in London. The regime was built on a unique system of agreements between producer and consumer countries in place since 1921. The aim of each successive International Tin Agreement (ITA), of which there were six (the first in 1956), was to stabilize prices within an agreed range by using a buffer stock to regulate the supply of tin. The buffer stock was financed by producing countries, with voluntary contributions by some consuming countries. 'Floor' and 'ceiling' prices were fixed, and market operations conducted by a buffer stock manager who intervened, as necessary, to maintain prices within these agreed limits. For added protection, the ITA provided for the imposition of export controls if the 'floor' price was being threatened. Tin consumption fell after the 1981–82 world recession, but the ITC attempted to compensate by increased buying for its stocks. The ITA was effectively terminated in October 1985, when the ITC's buffer stock manager informed the LME that he no longer had the funds with which to support the tin market. The factors underlying the collapse of the ITA included its limited membership (Bolivia and the USA, leading producing and consuming countries, were not signatories) and the accumulation of tin stocks, which resulted from the widespread circumvention of producers' quota limits. The LME responded by suspending trading in tin, and the crisis was eventually resolved in March 1990, when a financial settlement was reached between the ITC and its creditors. The ITC was itself dissolved in July of that year. Transactions in tin contracts were resumed on the LME in 1989.

These events lent new significance to the activities of the ATPC, which had been intended to operate as a complement to the ITC and not in competition with it. The ATPC had introduced export quotas for tin for the year from 1 March 1987. Brazil and China agreed to cooperate with the ATPC in implementing these supply restrictions, which, until their suspension in 1996, were renegotiated to cover succeeding years, with the aim of raising prices and reducing the level of surplus stocks. The ATPC membership also took stringent measures to control smuggling. Brazil and China (jointly accounting for more than one-third of world tin production) both initially held observer status at the ATPC and agreed to participate in the export quota arrangements, for which the ATPC had no power of enforcement, and which were undermined by low international prices. The ATPC finally suspended its quota arrangements in May 1996.

Tin had been delisted for about three years from the LME in the late 1980s but, in the more free market environment of the 1990s, the price fell dramatically and only began to recover in the 2000s, especially in 2007 and early 2008 as China moved from being a net exporter to a net importer. The international benchmark price of tin in London (i.e. the average quotation for tin for immediate delivery traded on the LME) rose steeply, from an average of US $16,337 per metric ton in January to $24,214 per ton in May. The average price recorded in May represented an all-time high, and, on a daily basis, the 'spot' price of $25,000 per ton recorded on 15 May was also a record. Prices declined dramatically in the final quarter of 2008, owing to the onset of global recession, but average prices for the year remained higher than in 2007. According to the World Bank (based on the LME settlement price), the average price of refined tin in the final quarter of 2008 was down to $13,100 per ton, restraining the average price for the whole of 2008 to $18,510 per ton. In the first quarter of 2009 the price fell further, to an average of $11,030 per ton, but by the second quarter prices were recovering, following strong demand in China and supply problems in Indonesia. Economic recovery and increased demand contrasted with the weak performance of certain key economies and the European sovereign debt crisis, as well as supply restrictions, to influence prices in the following years. In 2013 new Indonesian export controls required higher purity standards and trading through a local exchange, initially only the Indonesia Commodity and Derivatives Exchange, which established the Indonesia Tin Exchange (INATIN). The immediate impact was to reduce Indonesian exports from September, but, if the bottleneck effect could be overcome and non-domestic trade be encouraged, INATIN could provide a powerful challenge to the LME to set the international benchmark price. The London price of tin was rising in the first two quarters of 2014, but falling through May to July, the average monthly price by then being $22,424 per ton (only January had recorded a lower monthly price in 2014).

ACKNOWLEDGEMENTS

We gratefully acknowledge the assistance of the following organizations in the preparation of this section: the Food and Agriculture Organization of the United Nations (FAO); the International Aluminium Institute; the International Cocoa Organization; the International Coffee Organization; the International Copper Study Group; the International Iron and Steel Institute; the International Monetary Fund; the International Sugar Organization; The Silver Institute; the US Department of Agriculture; the US Department of Energy; the US Geological Survey, US Department of the Interior; and the World Bank.

RESEARCH INSTITUTES

ASSOCIATIONS AND INSTITUTIONS STUDYING LATIN AMERICA AND THE CARIBBEAN

ARGENTINA

Centro Argentino de Datos Oceanográficos (CEADO) (Argentine Centre of Oceanographic Data): Avda Montes de Oca 2124, C1270ABV Buenos Aires; tel. and fax (11) 4303-2240; e-mail ceado@hidro.gov.ar; internet www.hidro.gov.ar/ceado/ceado.asp; f. 1974; stores oceanographic data of national area, provides information to the scientific community, private and public enterprises and other marine users; Dir ARIEL HERNÁN TROISI.

Centro Argentino de Información Científica y Tecnológica (CAICYT) (Argentine Centre for Scientific and Technological Information): Saavedra 15, 1°, C1083ACA Buenos Aires; tel. (11) 4951-6975; fax (11) 4951-7310; e-mail info@caicyt.gov.ar; internet www.caicyt-conicet.gov.ar; f. 1958; attached to Consejo Nacional de Investigaciones y Técnicas; Dir JORGE L. ATRIO.

Consejo Argentino para las Relaciones Internacionales (CARI) (Argentine Council for International Relations): Uruguay 1037, 1°, 1016 Buenos Aires; tel. (11) 4811-0071; fax (11) 4815-4742; e-mail cari@cari.org.ar; internet www.cari.org.ar; f. 1978; Pres. Dr ADALBERTO RODRÍGUEZ GIAVARINI.

Instituto para la Integración de América Latina y el Caribe (Institute for the Integration of Latin America and the Caribbean): Esmeralda 130, 16°, 1035 Buenos Aires; tel. (11) 4223-2350; fax (11) 4323-2365; e-mail intal@iadb.org; internet www.iadb.org/intal; f. 1965 under auspices of Inter-American Devt Bank's Integration and Regional Program Dept; research on all aspects of regional integration and co-operation; activities are channelled through four lines of action: regional and national technical projects on integration; policy forums; integration forums; journals and information; documentation centre includes 100,000 documents, 12,000 books, 400 periodicals; Dir GRACIELA SCHAMIS; publs *Integración y Comercio* (2 a year), *INTAL Carta Mensual* (monthly newsletter), *Serie Informes Subregionales de Integración*.

Instituto Torcuato di Tella (ITDT) (Torcuato di Tella Institute): Miñones 2177, 1428 Buenos Aires; tel. (11) 5169-7000; fax (11) 478-3061; e-mail postmaster@itdtar.edu.ar; internet www.itdt.edu; f. 1960; library of 60,000 vols and 1,400 domestic and foreign periodicals.

AUSTRALIA

Australian Institute of International Affairs: Stephen House, 32 Thesiger Court, Deakin, ACT 2600; tel. (2) 6282-2133; fax (2) 6285-2334; e-mail ceo@aiia.asn.au; internet www.aiia.asn.au; f. 1933; 1,800 mems; brs in all states; Pres. JOHN MCCARTHY; Exec. Dir MELISSA H. CONLEY TYLER; publs *The Australian Journal of International Affairs* (5 a year), *Australia in World Affairs* (series).

AUSTRIA

Österreichische Forschungsstiftung für Entwicklungshilfe (Austrian Foundation for Development Research): 1090 Vienna, Sessengasse 3; tel. and fax (1) 317-40-10; e-mail office@oefse.at; internet www.oefse.at; f. 1967; documentation and information on development aid, developing countries and international development, particularly relating to Austria; library of 40,000 vols, 250 periodicals; Pres. Dr WERNER RAZA; publs *Österreichische Entwicklungspolitik* (annual), *Länder-profile*.

Österreichische Gesellschaft für Aussenpolitik und die Vereinten Nationen (Foreign Policy and United Nations Association of Austria): 1010 Vienna, Hofburg/Stallburg, Reitschulg. 2/2 OG; tel. (1) 535-46-27; e-mail office@oegavn.org; internet www.oegavn.org; f. 1945; lectures, discussions; approx. 600 mems; Pres. WOLFGANG SCHUESSEL; publ. *Österreichisches Jahrbuch für Internationale Politik*, *Global View*, *Society*.

Österreichisches Lateinamerika Institut (Austrian Latin American Institute): 1090 Vienna, Schlickgasse 1; tel. and fax (1) 310-74-65; fax (1) 310-74-65-21; e-mail office@lai.at; internet www.lai.at; f. 1965; Pres. Dr BENITA FERRERO-WALDNER; publs *Atención: Jahrbuch des Österreichischen Lateinamerika Instituts* (annual), *Diálogo Austria-América Latina* (annual).

BARBADOS

Sir Arthur Lewis Institute of Social and Economic Studies: University of the West Indies, Cave Hill Campus, POB 64, Bridgetown; tel. 417-4478; fax 424-7291; e-mail salises@cavehill.uwi.edu; internet www.cavehill.uwi.edu/salises; f. 1948; applied research and graduate teaching programme relating to the Caribbean; Dir DON MARSHALL (acting); publ. *Journal of Eastern Caribbean Studies* (quarterly).

BELGIUM

Académie Royale des Sciences d'Outre-Mer/Koninklijke Academie voor Overzeese Wetenschappen (Royal Academy for Overseas Sciences): Ave Louise 231, 1050 Brussels; tel. (2) 538-02-11; fax (2) 539-23-53; e-mail kaowarsom@skynet.be; internet www.kaowarsom.be; f. 1928 as the Royal Academy of Colonial Sciences, present name adopted 1959; the promotion of scientific knowledge of overseas areas, especially those with particular development problems; 140 mems, 66 assoc. mems, 111 correspondent mems; Pres. MICHÈLE WILMET; Perm. Sec. Prof. PHILIPPE GOYENS; publs *Bulletin des Séances/Mededelingen der Zittingen*, *Mémoires/Verhandelingen*, *Recueils d'Etudes Historiques/Historische bijdragen*, *Biographie belge d'Outre-Mer/Belgische Overzeese Biographie*, *Actes Symposiums/Acta Symposia*.

Le Centre d'Etudes du Développement (DVLP) (The Centre for Development Studies): Université Catholique de Louvain, 1 pl. des Doyens, 1348 Louvain-La-Neuve; tel. (10) 47-94-05; fax (10) 47-28-05; e-mail ephanie.lorent@uclouvain.be; internet www.uclouvain.be/dvlp; f. 1961; incorporates the Groupe de Recherches Interdisciplinaires sur l'Amerique Latine (Interdisciplinary Latin America Research Group); Dir ISABEL YEPEZ DEL CASTILLO.

EGMONT—The Royal Institute for International Relations: 69 rue de Namur, 1000 Brussels; tel. (2) 223-41-14; fax (2) 223-41-16; e-mail info@egmontinstitute.be; internet www.egmontinstitute.be; f. 1947 as Institut Royal des Relations Internationales—Koninklijk Instituut Voor Internationale Betrekkingen; adopted current name in 2007; research in foreign policy, international relations, law, economics, European issues, environment and defence; specialist library of 700 vols and 1,200 periodicals; archives; organizes lectures and conferences; Pres. ETIENNE DAVIGNON; Dir-Gen. M. OTTE; publ. *Studia Diplomatica* (4 a year).

Institute of Development Policy and Management: Prinsstraat 13, 2000 Antwerp; tel. (3) 265-57-70; fax (3) 265-57-71; e-mail iob@uantwerp.be; internet www.uantwerp.be/iob; f. 1965; autonomous institution of the University of Antwerp; courses in development studies; library of 50,000 vols; Dir TOM DE HERDT.

BRAZIL

Instituto Brasileiro de Economia (Brazilian Institute of Economics): Getúlio Vargas Foundation, Praia de Botafogo 190, Botafogo, 22253-900 Rio de Janeiro, RJ; tel. (21) 2559-6087; fax (21) 2553-6372; e-mail conjunturaeconomica@fgv.br; internet portalibre.fgv.br; f. 1951; Dir LUIZ GUILHERME SCHYMURA DE OLIVEIRA; publs *National Accounts* (annual), *Conjuntura Econômica* (monthly), *Agroanalysis* (monthly).

Instituto Brasileiro de Relações Internacionais (Brazilian Institute of International Relations): JCP 4400, 70919-970, Brasília, DF; tel. and fax (61) 2192-9460; internet www.ibri-rbpi.org; f. 1954; 4,100 vols; Dir Prof. JOÃO PONTES NOGUEIRA; publ. *Revista Brasileira de Política Internacional* (quarterly).

Instituto Nacional de Pesquisas Da Amazônia (INPA) (National Institute for Amazonian Research): Avda André Araújo 2936, Aleixo, CEP 69060-001, Manaus, AM; tel. (92) 3643-3377; e-mail ascom@inpa.gov.br; internet www.inpa.gov.br; f. 1952; basic and applied research on Amazonian biodiversity, including botany, entomology, aquatic biology, ecology, earth sciences, human health, agriculture, aquaculture, forestry, forest products, natural products and food technology; postgraduate programme in tropical biology and natural resources; Dir ADALBERTO LUIS VAL; publ. *Revista Ciência Para Todos*.

Instituto de Pesquisa Econômica Aplicada (Institute of Applied Economic Research): Avda Presidente Antônio Carlos 51, 13° andar, CP 2672, 20020-010 Rio de Janeiro, RJ, Brazil; tel. (21) 3315-5334; e-mail ascom@ipea.gov.br; internet www.ipea.gov.br; library of 60,000 vols; Pres. MARCELO CORTES NERI; publs *Jornal* (monthly).

Superintendência de Estudos Econômicos e Sociais da Bahia (SEI) (Bahia Economic and Social Studies Superintendency): Centro Administrativo da Bahia, 4a Avda 435, 41745 002 Salvador, BA; tel. (71) 3115-4704; fax (71) 3116-1781; e-mail diger@sei.ba.gov.br;

internet www.sei.ba.gov.br; f. 1995; statistics, natural resources, economic indicators; library of 25,000 vols; Dir José Geraldo dos Reis Santos; publ. *Bahia Análise e Dados* (every 4 months).

CANADA

Canadian Association for Latin American and Caribbean Studies/Association Canadienne des Etudes Latino-Améri-caines et des Caraïbes (CALACS/ACELAC): York University, 8–17 Kaneff Tower, 4700 Keele St, Toronto, ON M3J 1P3; tel. (416) 736-2100; fax (519) 732-2270; e-mail calacs@yorku.ca; internet www.can-latam.org; f. 1969; Pres. Nathalie Gravel; publ. *Canadian Journal of Latin American and Caribbean Studies* (2 a year).

Canadian Council for International Co-operation/Conseil canadien pour la coopération internationale: 450 Rideau St, Suite 200, Ottawa, ON K1N 5Z4; tel. (613) 241-7007; fax (613) 241-5302; e-mail info@ccic.ca; internet www.ccic.ca; f. 1968 (fmrly Overseas Institute of Canada, f. 1961); co-ordination centre for voluntary agencies working in international development; 100 mems; Chair. Jim Cornelius; publs *Newsletter* (2 a year), *Directory of Canadian NGOs*.

Canadian International Council: 1 Devonshire Pl., Rm 064S, Toronto, ON M5S 3K7; tel. (416) 946-7209; fax (416) 946-7319; e-mail info@opencanada.org; internet www.opencanada.org; f. 2007; Chair. Bill Graham; publs *International Journal* (quarterly), Annual Report.

Centre for Research on Latin America and the Caribbean (CERLAC): York University, Research Tower, 8th Floor, 4700 Keele St, North York, ON M3J 1P3; tel. (416) 736-5237; fax (416) 736-5688; e-mail cerlac@yorku.ca; internet www.yorku.ca/cerlac; f. 1978; interdisciplinary research organization; seeks to build academic and cultural links with the region; research findings made available through publs, lectures, seminars, etc.; Dir Andrea Davis.

Institute of Island Studies: University of Prince Edward Island, 550 University Ave, Charlottetown, PE C1A 4P3; tel. (902) 566-0386; fax (902) 566-0756; e-mail iis@upei.ca; internet www.upei.ca/iis; f. 1985; public policy research and facilitation of public debate; comparative island studies; Dir Irene Novaczek.

International Development Research Centre: POB 8500, Ottawa, ON K1G 3H9; tel. (613) 236-6163; fax (613) 238-7230; e-mail info@idrc.ca; internet www.idrc.ca; f. 1970 by the Government of Canada; est. to support research in developing countries to promote growth and devt; has regional offices incl. Montevideo; Pres. David M. Malone; publs include *IDRC Bulletin* (monthly), online e-books, and the IDRC in_focus collection.

CHILE

Centro de Estudios Públicos: Monseñor Sótero Sanz 162, Santiago, Chile; tel. (2) 3282400; fax (2) 3282400; e-mail biblioteca@cepchile.cl; internet www.cepchile.cl; f. 1980; Pres. Eliodoro Matte L.; publ. *Estudios Públicos* (quarterly).

Centro Latino Americano de Desarrollo Sustentable (CLADES) (Latin American Centre for Sustainable Development): Casilla 97, Correo 9, Santiago; tel. (2) 2341141; fax (2) 2338918; e-mail clades@terra.cl; internet www.clades.cl; f. 1989; aims to prevent the collapse of rural agriculture by the adoption of efficient and sustainable practices; undertakes research, oversees training programmes and facilitates information exchange; Pres. Andrés Yurjevic.

Centro Latinoamericano y Caribeño de Demografía (CELADE): Avda Dag Hammarskjöld 3477, Casilla 179-D, Santiago; tel. (2) 2102002; fax (2) 2080196; e-mail celade@eclac.cl; internet www.eclac.cl/celade; f. 1957; Population Division of the UN Economic Commission for Latin American and the Caribbean (ECLAC); analysis of demographic trends, population and development research, teaching and training, and diverse information on population; Dir Dirk Jaspars-Faijer.

Corporación de Estudios para Latinoamérica (CIEPLAN): Avda Dag Hammarskjöld 3269, 3°, Vitacura, Santiago; tel. (2) 7965660; fax (2) 4269989; e-mail contacto@cieplan.cl; internet www.cieplan.cl; f. 1976; economic research; Pres. Alejandro Foxley.

Facultad Latinoamericana de Ciencias Sociales (FLACSO): Avda Dag Hammarskjöld 3269, Vitacura, Santiago; tel. (2) 2900200; fax (2) 2900263; e-mail docencia@flacso.cl; internet www.flacso.cl; f. 1957; research in sociology, education, political science, international affairs; library of 18,000 vols, 592 periodicals; Dir Angel Flisfisch; publs *Nueva Serie, Serie Libros FLACSO, Fuerzas Armadas y Sociedad* (quarterly).

Instituto Antártico Chileno (INACH): Plaza Muñoz Gamero 1055, Punta Arenas; tel. (61) 298100; fax (61) 298149; e-mail inach@inach.cl; internet www.inach.cl; f. 1964; a centre for technological and scientific development on matters relating to the Antarctic; 43 mems; library of 2,550 vols and 400 periodicals; Dir Retamales Espinoza; publs *Serie Científica* (annual), *Boletín Antártico Chileno* (2 a year).

Instituto de Estudios Internacionales: Universidad de Chile, Avda Condell 249, Suc. 21, Providencia, Casilla 14187, Santiago; tel. (2) 4961200; fax (2) 2740155; e-mail inesint@uchile.cl; internet www.iei.uchile.cl; f. 1966; research and teaching institute for international relations, political science, international law, economics and studies on Pacific Basin; Dir Prof. José Morandé Lavin; publ. *Revista de Estudios Internacionales* (quarterly).

Instituto Latinoamericano y del Caribe de Planificación Económica y Social (ILPES) (Latin American and Caribbean Institute for Economic and Social Planning): Edif. Naciones Unidas, Avda Dag Hammarskjöld 3477, Vitacura, Casilla 179-D, Santiago; tel. (2) 2102507; fax (2) 2066104; e-mail ilpes@cepal.org; internet www.ilpes.cl; f. 1962 by UN Economic Commission for Latin America; provides technical assistance, training for govt officials and research on planning techniques; Dir Jorge Mattar-Marquéz; publs *Cuadernos del ILPES, Boletín* (2 a year).

PEOPLE'S REPUBLIC OF CHINA

Institute of Latin American Studies, Chinese Academy of Social Sciences: 5 Jianguomen Nei Da Jie, Beijing 100732; tel. (10) 64014011; e-mail cssnenglish@yahoo.com.cn; internet www.cssn.cn; f. 1961; 60 mems; library of 40,000 vols; Dir Deng Bingwen; publ. *Latin-American Studies*.

Institute of World Economics and Politics, Chinese Academy of Social Sciences: 5 Jianguomen Nei Da Jie, Beijing 100732; tel. (10)85196063; fax (10) 65126180; e-mail cassrose9@gmail.com; internet en.iwep.org.cn; f. 1980; advises the Govt on economic reform through its 8 areas of research; conducts academic exchanges with foreign institutions; Dir Zhang Yuyan; publs *The Yellow Book of International Economy, The Yellow Book of International Politics*.

COLOMBIA

Centro de Estudios sobre Desarrollo Económico (CEDE) (Centre for Economic Development Studies): Calle 19A, No. 1-37, Este Bloque W, Bogotá, DC; tel. (1) 339-4949; fax (1) 332-4492; e-mail pregecon@uniandes.edu.co; internet economia.uniandes.edu.co; f. 1958; research in all aspects of economic development; 40 research staff; library of 40,000 vols; Dir Ana Maria Ibáñez; publs *Desarrollo y Sociedad* (quarterly), *Cuadernos CEDE*, documents series.

Centro de Información y Documentación Biblioteca José Fernández de Madrid: Universidad de Cartagena, Centro Carrera 6, No 36-100, Cartagena; tel. and fax (95) 660-0682; e-mail biblioteca@unicartagena.edu.co; internet www.unicartagena.edu.co; f. 1827; Rector Germán Arturo Sierra Anaya; publs *Revista Unicarta, Revista Palobra (Palabra que Obra)*.

Centro Latinoamericano (CLAM) (Latin American Centre): Pontifíca Universidad Javeriana, Edif. José Rafael Arboleda, S.J., 4°, Transv. 4, No-42–00, Bogotá, DC; tel. and fax (1) 320-8320; e-mail ena.ortiz@javeriana.edu.co; internet www.javeriana.edu.co/centrolatino; academic unit within the university's School of Communication and Language; concerned with teaching Spanish as a foreign language and increasing knowledge of Latin American and Colombian culture; Chancellor Nancy Agray Vargas.

Centro Regional para el Fomento del Libro en América Latina y el Caribe (CERLALC) (Regional Centre for the Promotion of Books in Latin America and the Caribbean): Calle 70, No 9-52, Apdo Aereo 57348, Bogotá, DC; tel. (1) 540-2071; fax (1) 541-6398; e-mail libro@cerlalc.org; internet www.cerlalc.org; f. 1972 by UNESCO and Colombian Govt; promotes production and circulation of books and development of libraries; provides training; promotes protection of copyright; 21 mem. countries; Dir Fernando Zapata López; publs *El Libro en America Latina y el Caribe* (quarterly), *Boletín Informativo* CERLALC (quarterly).

COSTA RICA

Centro Agronómico Tropical de Investigación y Enseñanza (CATIE) (Tropical Agricultural Research and Higher Education Center): Apdo 19, 7170 Cartago, Turrialba 30501; tel. 2558-2000; fax 2558-2048; e-mail comunica@catie.ac.cr; internet catieeducacion-web.sharepoint.com; f. 1973; applied research, graduate and short-term training; mems: Inter-American Institute for Co-operation on Agriculture—IICA, Belize, Brazil, Colombia, Costa Rica, Dominican Republic, Ecuador, El Salvador, Guatemala, Honduras, Mexico, Nicaragua, Panama, Venezuela; library of 80,000 vols; Dir-Gen. Dr José Joaquín Campos; publs *Boletín de Semillas Forestales, Revista MIP, Revista Forestal Centroamericana, Revista Agroforestería—las Américas, Noticias de Turrialba* (quarterly), *Informe Anual*.

Instituto Centroamericano de Administración Pública (ICAP) (Central American Institute of Public Administration): Apdo 10025-1000, San José; tel. 2234-1011; fax 2225-2049; e-mail info@icap.ac.cr; internet www.icap.ac.cr; f. 1954; technical assistance from UNDP; public administration, economic development, management, social science, international projects, environmental issues and integration; library of 30,800 vols; Dir RETHELNY FIGUEROA DE JAIN; publ. *Revista* (2 a year).

Instituto de Estudios Centroamericanos (Institute of Central American Studies): Apdo 1524, 2050 San Pedro; tel. 2253-3195; fax 2234-7682; e-mail mesoamerica@ice.co.cr; internet www .mesoamericaonline.net; f. 1982; Exec. Dir LINDA J. HOLLAND.

Instituto de Estudios de Desarrollo Centroamericanos (Institute for Central American Development Studies—ICADS): Apdo 300-2050, San Pedro de Montes de Oca; tel. 2225-0508; fax 2234-1337; e-mail info@icads.org; internet www.icads.org; Dir ANTHONY CHAMBERLAIN.

Inter-American Institute for Co-operation on Agriculture: Apdo 55, 2200 San Isidro de Coronado, San José; tel. 2216-0222; fax 2216-0233; e-mail iicahq@iica.ac.cr; internet www.iica.int; f. 1942; agricultural development and rural well-being; mems: 32 countries of the Americas and Caribbean; library of 75,000 vols; Dir-Gen. Dr VICTOR M. VILLALOBOS; publ. *Turrialba* (quarterly).

CUBA

Centro de Información Bancaria y Económica, Banco Central de Cuba (CIBE) (Banking and Economic Information Centre, Central Bank of Cuba): Cuba 410, Municipio Habana Viejo, Havana 10100; tel. (7) 860-4811; fax (7) 863-4061; e-mail webmaster@bc.gob .cu; internet www.bc.gob.cu; f. 1950; library of 57,508 vols; Pres. ERNESTO MEDINA VILLAVEIRÁN; publs *Cuba: Half Yearly Economic Report* (annual), *Journal of the Central Bank of Cuba*.

CZECH REPUBLIC

Ústav mezinárodních vztahů (Institute of International Relations): 118 50 Prague 1, Nerudova 3; tel. 251108111; fax 251108222; e-mail iir@iir.cz; internet www.iir.cz; f. 1957; research on European integration, international relations and foreign and security policy of the Czech Republic, publishing, training, education; Dir PETR KRATOCHVÍL; publs include *International Relations* (quarterly) in Czech, *International Politics* (monthly) in Czech, and *Perspectives* (2 a year) in English.

DENMARK

Institute for International Studies (DIIS): Strandgade 56, 1401 Copenhagen V; tel. 32-69-87-87; fax 32-69-87-00; e-mail diis@diis.dk; internet www.diis.dk; f. 2002 following merger of Centre for Development Research, Danish Institute of International Affairs, Copenhagen Peace Research Institute and Danish Centre for Holocaust and Genocide Studies; forms part of Danish Centre for International Studies and Human Rights; Dir NANNA HVIDT; publs *Den Ny Verden* (quarterly).

Udenrigspolitiske Selskab (Danish Foreign Policy Society): Amaliegade 40A, 1256 Copenhagen K; tel. 33-14-88-86; fax 33-14-85-20; e-mail udenrigs@udenrigs.dk; internet www.udenrigs.dk; f. 1946; studies, debates, courses and conferences on international affairs; library of 150 periodicals and publs from UN, OECD, WTO, EU; Dir MICHAEL EHRENREICH; publs *Udenrigs, Udenrigspolitiske Skrifter-LandeLommofermal*.

DOMINICAN REPUBLIC

Centro de Investigación Económica para el Caribe (CIECA) (Economic Research Centre for the Caribbean): Calle Juan Parada Bonilla 8A, Plaza Winnie, La Arboleda Ans. Naco, Apdo 3117, Santo Domingo, DN; tel. 563-9338; fax 227-2533; e-mail ciecard@verizon .net.do; f. 1987; Pres. PÁVEL ISA CONTRERAS.

ECUADOR

Centro Internacional de Estudios Superiores de Comunicación para América Latina (CIESPAL): Diego de Almagro 2155 y Andrade Marín, Apdo 484, Quito; tel. (2) 2254-8011; fax (2) 2502-487; e-mail info@ciespal.net; internet www.ciespal.net; f. 1959; research in communications and training of communicators; library of 16,500 documents, 2,000 vols; Dir Dr FERNANDO CHECA MONTÚFAR; publ. *Revista Chasqui* (quarterly).

Instituto Latinoamericano de Investigaciones Sociales (ILDIS) (Latin American Social Sciences Research Institute): Avdo República 500 y Diego de Almagro, Edif. Pucará, 4°, Casilla 17 03 367, Quito; tel. (2) 2562-103; fax (2) 2504-337; e-mail info@fes .ec; internet www.fes-ecuador.org; f. 1974; research in economics, sociology, political science and education; library of more than 8,000 vols; Dir ANJA MINNAERT.

FRANCE

Centre de Coopération Internationale en Recherche Agronomique pour le Développement (CIRAD): 42 rue Scheffer, 75116 Paris; tel. 1-53-70-20-00; fax 1-47-55-15-30; e-mail presse-com@cirad.fr; internet www.cirad.fr; f. 1992; scientific and technical research; experimental stations, industrial plantations; researchers based in over 50 countries; Pres. MICHEL EDDI; publ. *Plantations Recherche Développement* (every 2 months).

Centre d'Etudes Prospectives et d'Informations Internationales (CEPII): 113 rue de Grenelle, 75007 Paris; tel. 1-53-68-55-00; fax 1-53-68-55-01; e-mail cepiiweb@cepii.fr; internet www.cepii.fr; f. 1978; study of international economics; affiliated with the Centre d'analyse stratégique; 50 mems; library of 20,000 vols, 400 periodicals; Pres. JEAN LEMIERRE; publs *L'economie mondiale* (annual), *Economie Internationale* (quarterly), *La Lettre du CEPII* (monthly), *CEPII News-letter* (quarterly), books, working papers.

L'École des Hautes Études Internationales et L'École des Hautes Études Politiques (HEI-HEP): 54 av Marceau, 75008 Paris; tel. 1-47-20-57-47; fax 1-47-20-57-30; e-mail contact@hei-hep .com; internet www.hei-hep.com; f. 1889; Chair. ODILE LAUNAY.

Institut Européen-European Institute (IE-EI): 10 ave des Fleurs, 06000 Nice; tel. 4-93-97-93-70; fax 4-93-97-93-71; e-mail ie-ei@cife.eu; internet www.ie-ei.eu; f. 1964; dept of Centre International de Formation Européenne; library of 6,000 vols; Dir-Gen. MATTHIAS WAECHTER.

Institut Français des Relations Internationales (IFRI): 27 rue de la Procession, 75740 Paris Cédex 15; tel. 1-40-61-60-00; fax 1-40-61-60-60; e-mail accueil@ifri.org; internet www.ifri.org; f. 1979; international politics and economy, security issues and regional studies; library of 30,000 vols and 200 periodicals; Pres. THIERRY DE MONTBRIAL; publs *Politique Etrangère* (quarterly), *Notes, Travaux et recherches, Cahiers et Conférences, Rapport Annuel sur le Système Economique et les Stratégies—RAMSES* (annual).

Institut des Hautes Etudes de l'Amérique Latine: 28 rue Saint-Guillaume, 75007 Paris; tel. 1-44-39-86-20; fax 1-45-48-79-58; e-mail iheal@univ-paris3.fr; internet www.iheal.univ-paris3.fr; teaching and research unit of Université de Paris III Sorbonne Nouvelle; shares its library, publications service and website with Centre de recherche et de documentation sur l'Amerique latine—CREDA; Dir SÉBASTIEN VELUT; publs *Cahiers des Amériques latines* (3 a year), *Travaux et Mémoires*.

Institut Pluridisciplinaire d'Etudes sur l'Amérique de Toulouse (IPEAT): Bâtiment de l'Arche, Université de Toulouse Le Mirail, 5 allée Antonio Machado, 31058 Toulouse Cédex; tel. 5-61-50-43-93; fax 5-61-50-36-25; e-mail ipeat@univ-tlse2.fr; internet w3 .ipeat.univ-tlse2.fr; f. 1985; specialized research; economic documentation centre; 31 staff; Dir SONIA V. ROSE; publs *Caravelle, L'Ordinaire latino américain, Les Ateliers de Caravelle*.

Institut de Recherche pour le Développement (IRD): 44 blvd de Dunkerque, 13002 Marseille; tel. 4-91-99-92-00; fax 4-91-99-92-22; e-mail webmaster@ird.fr; internet www.ird.fr; f. 1944; a public corporation mandated to aid developing countries through research, with special application to human environment problems, tropical climate and diseases, water resources, biodiversity and food production; library and documentation centre; Pres. MICHEL LAURENT; publ. *Sciences au Sud* (5 a year).

Laboratoire Interdisciplinaire de Recherche sur Les Amériques (LIRA): Université de Rennes II, Place du Recteur Henri Le Moal, Rennes Cedex; tel. 2-99-14-17-53; e-mail jean-pierre.sanchez@ uhb.fr; f. 1966; general and musical studies on region; Dir JEAN-PIERRE SÁNCHEZ; publ. *Amerika*.

Musée de l'Homme: 17 pl. du Trocadéro, 75116 Paris; tel. 1-44-05-72-72; fax 1-44-05-72-91; e-mail contact@museedelhomme.fr; internet www.museedelhomme.fr; f. 1878; library of 250,000 vols, 5,000 periodicals; ethnography, anthropology, pre-history; attached to the Muséum National d'Histoire Naturelle; research and education centre; Dir ANDRÉ LANGANEY; publ. *Objets et mondes* (quarterly).

Société des Américanistes: Musée du quai Branly, 222 rue de l'Université, 75343 Paris; e-mail societedesamericanistes@yahoo.fr; f. 1896; 500 mems; Pres. PHILIPPE DESCOLA; Gen. Sec. VALENTINA VAPNARSKY; publ. *Journal*.

GERMANY

Deutsche Gesellschaft für Auswärtige Politik eV (DGAP) (German Council on Foreign Relations): 10787 Berlin, Rauchstr. 17–18; tel. and fax (30) 2542310; fax (30) 25423116; e-mail info@dgap .org; internet www.dgap.org; f. 1955; 2,400 mems; discusses and promotes research on problems of international politics; research library of 75,000 vols and 250 journals; Pres. Dr AREND OETKER; Dir, Research Institute Prof. Dr EBERHARD SANDSCHNEIDER; publs *Die Internationale Politik* (annual), *Internationale Politik: Transatlantic Edition* (quarterly), *Internationale Politik* (6 a year).

Ibero-Amerikanisches Institut Preussischer Kulturbesitz (IAI): 10785 Berlin, Potsdamer Str. 37; tel. (30) 266451500; fax (30) 266351550; e-mail iai@iai.spk-berlin.de; internet www.iai .spk-berlin.de; f. 1930; library, research institute and cultural centre; 1.5m. vols (899,000 monographs); Dir Dr BARBARA GÖBEL; publs *Revista Internacional de Lingüística Iberoamericana, Indiana, Iberoamericana, Bibliotheca Ibero-Americana, Biblioteca Luso-Brasileira, Revista Internacional de Lingüística Iberoamericana, Estudios Indiana, Ibero-Online, Ibero-Bibliographien.*

Institut für Lateinamerika-Studien (ILAS) (Institute for Latin American Studies): 20354 Hamburg 36, Neuer Jungfernstieg 21; tel. (40) 42825561; fax (40) 42825562; e-mail ilas@giga-hamburg.de; internet www.giga-hamburg.de/ilas; f. 1962; part of the German Institute of Global and Area Studies (GIGA); Dir Dr BERT HOFFMANN (acting); publs *Journal of Politics in Latin America, GIGA Focus Lateinamerika, Lateinamerika Analysen.*

Stiftung Wissenschaft und Politik (SWP): Deutsches Institut für Internationale Politik und Sicherheit (German Institute for International and Security Affairs), 10719 Berlin, Ludwigkirchpl. 3–4; tel. (30) 880070; fax (30) 88007100; e-mail swp@swp-berlin.org; internet www.swp-berlin.org; f. 1962; Dir Prof. Dr VOLKER PERTHES.

ZI Lateinamerika-Institut der Freien Universität Berlin (Institute for Latin American Studies): 14197 Berlin, Rüdesheimer Str. 54–56; tel. (30) 83853072; fax (30) 83855464; e-mail lai@zedat .fu-berlin.de; internet www.lai.fu-berlin.de; f. 1970; teaching and research; part of the Freie Universität Berlin; Chair. SUSANNE KLENGEL.

GUATEMALA

Instituto de Nutrición de Centroamérica y Panamá (INCAP) (Institute of Nutrition of Central America and Panama): Calzada Roosevelt 6–25, Zona 11, Apdo 1188, 01001 Guatemala City; tel. 2472-3762; fax 2473-6529; e-mail info.incap@sica.int; internet www .sica.int/incap; f. 1949; represents the following countries: Belize, Costa Rica, El Salvador, Guatemala, Honduras, Nicaragua, Panama; administered by Pan American Health Organization (PAHO)/World Health Organization (WHO); programmes to promote food and nutrition security among Central American countries through: technical co-operation; human resources; development research; dissemination of information and resources mobilization; main areas of interest are: Food Protection; Nutritionally Improved Foods; Food Nutrition and Security in Disaster Areas; Health and Nutrition of Vulnerable Groups; library of 70,500 vols; Dir MIRTA ROSES; publs various documents.

Instituto de Relaciones Internacionales y de Investigaciones para la Paz (IRIPAZ) (International Relations and Peace Research Institute): 1A Calle 9-52, Zona 1, 01001 Guatemala City; tel. 2232-8260; fax 2253-1532; e-mail iripaz@iripaz.org; internet www.iripaz .org; f. 1989; research, training and lobbying in international relations, social and peace studies; Dir-Gen. DIEGO PADILLA VASSAUX.

INDIA

Indian Council of World Affairs: Sapru House, Barakhamba Rd, New Delhi 110 001; tel. (11) 23319055; fax (11) 23311208; e-mail dg@ icwa.in; internet www.icwa.in; f. 1943; non-governmental institution for the study of Indian and international questions; 2,625 mems; library of more than 125,000 vols; Dir-Gen. RAJIV K. BHATIA; publs *India Quarterly, Foreign Affairs Reports* (monthly).

ISRAEL

The Harry S Truman Research Institute for the Advancement of Peace: Hebrew University, Mount Scopus, Jerusalem 91905; tel. (2) 5882300; fax (2) 5828076; e-mail truman@savion.huji.ac.il; internet truman.huji.ac.il; f. 1965; fosters peace and advances co-operation in the Middle East and the peoples of the world through research; library of more than 1,500 periodicals; Exec. Dir NAAMA SHPETER; publs works on Latin America.

ITALY

Istituto Affari Internazionali (IAI): Palazzo Rondinini, Via Angelo Brunetti 9, 00186 Roma; tel. (06) 3224360; fax (06) 3224363; e-mail iai@iai.it; internet www.iai.it; f. 1965; research on European integration, the international political economy, the Mediterranean and the Middle East; defence and security; transatlantic relations; library of 25,000 vols and 270 periodicals; Pres. FERDINANDO NELLI FEROCI; Dir ETTORE GRECO; publs *The International Spectator* (quarterly, in English), *L'Italia e la politica internazionale* (annual, in Italian), *IAI Quaderni* (monograph series, in Italian and English), *Documenti IAI* (working papers, in Italian and English), *Affarinternazionali* (online, in Italian).

Istituto Italo-Latino Americano: Via Giovanni Paisiello 24, 00198 Roma; tel. (06) 684921; fax (06) 6872834; e-mail info@iila

.org; internet www.iila.org; f. 1966 by 20 Latin American states and Italy; cultural activities, commercial exchanges, economic and sociological, scientific and technical research, etc.; awards student grants; library of 90,000 vols; Dir-Gen. SIMONETTA CAVALIERI.

Istituto per le relazioni tra l'Italia e i paesi dell'Africa, America Latina e Medio Oriente (IPALMO) (Institute for Relations between Italy and the Countries of Africa, Latin America and the Middle East): Via Ennio Quirino Visconti 8, 00193 Roma; tel. (06) 32699701; fax (06) 32699750; e-mail ipalmo@ipalmo.com; internet www.ipalmo.com; f. 1971; library and archive of over 20,000 vols; Pres. GIANNI DE MICHELIS; publ. *Politica Internazionale* (every 2 months).

Istituto per gli Studi di Politica Internazionale (ISPI): Palazzo Clerici, Via Clerici 5, 20121 Milano; tel. (02) 8633131; fax (02) 8692055; e-mail ispi.segreteria@ispionline.it; internet www .ispionline.it; f. 1933 for the promotion of the study and knowledge of all problems concerning international relations; operates under supervision of foreign affairs ministry; seminars at postgraduate level; library of 100,000 vols; Exec. Vice- Pres. PAOLO MAGRI; publs *Relazioni Internazionali* (quarterly), *Working Papers, Policy Brief.*

JAMAICA

Asociación de Universidades e Institutos de Investigación del Caribe (UNICA) (Association of Caribbean Universities and Research Institutes): c/o Office of Administration and Special Initiatives, University of the West Indies, Kingston 7; tel. 977-6065; fax 977-7525; e-mail unica@uwimona.edu.jm; internet www.unica .uprm.edu; f. 1968 to foster contact and collaboration between member universities and institutes; conferences, meetings, seminars, etc.; circulation of information; facilitates co-operation and the pooling of resources in research; encourages exchanges of staff and students; mems: 50 institutions; Pres. Prof E. NIGEL HARRIS; publ. *Caribbean Educational Bulletin* (quarterly).

Caribbean Food and Nutrition Institute: University of the West Indies, POB 140, Mona, Kingston 7; tel. 927-1540; fax 927-2657; e-mail e-mail@cfni.paho.org; internet www.new.paho.org/cfni; f. 1967; specialized centre of the Pan American Health Organization (PAHO); research and field investigations, training in nutrition, dissemination of information, advisory services, production of educational material; mems: all English-speaking Caribbean territories, Belize, Guyana and Suriname; library of 4,500 vols; Dir Dr CARISSA F. ETIENNE; publs *Cajanus* (quarterly), *Nyam News Nutrient-Cost Tables* (quarterly).

JAPAN

Ajia Keizai Kenkyujo (IDE-JETRO) (Institute of Developing Economies): Wakaba 3-2-2, Mihamaku, Chiba 261-8545; tel. (4) 3299-9500; fax (4) 3299-9724; e-mail info@ide.go.jp; internet www .ide.go.jp; f. 1960; merged with Japan External Trade Org. in 1998; researches industrial devt and political change in Latin America; library of 590,000 vols; Pres. TAKASHI SHIRAISHI; publ. *Developing Economies* (quarterly), *Latin America Report* (2 a year).

Centre for Latin American Studies: Nanzan University, 18 Yamazato-cho, Showa-ku, Nagoya 466; tel. (52) 832-3111; fax (52) -833-6985; e-mail centro-latino@ic.nanzan-u.ac.jp; internet www .nanzan-u.ac.jp/LATIN; f. 1983; an institute specializing in the study of contemporary Latin America (social sciences); Dir TAKAHIRO KATO.

Tokyo University of Foreign Studies: 3-11-1, Asahi-cho, Fuchushi, Tokyo 183; tel. (42) 330-5126; fax (42) 330-5599; e-mail ml-zenhp@tufs.ac.jp; internet www.tufs.ac.jp; f. 1899; programmes of study into world languages, cultures and international relations; Pres. HIROTAKA TATEISHI.

MEXICO

Centro de Cooperación Regional para la Educación de Adultos en América Latina y el Caribe (CREFAL) (Regional Co-operation Centre for Adult Education in Latin America and the Caribbean): Avda Lázaro Cardenas 525, Col. Revolución, 61609 Pátzcuaro, Mich.; tel. (434) 342-8200; fax (434) 342-8151; e-mail crefal@crefal.edu.mx; internet www.crefal.edu.mx; f. 1951 by UNESCO and OAS; admin. by Board of Directors from mem. countries; regional technical assistance, specialist training in literary and adult education, research; library of 42,799 vols; Dir MERCEDES CALDERÓN GARCÍA; publ. *Revista Interamericana de Educación de Adultos* (quarterly).

Centro de Estudios Educativos, AC (Education Studies Centre): Avda Revolución 1291, Col. Campestre, 01040 México, DF; tel. (55) 5593-5719; fax (55) 5651-6374; e-mail cee@cee.edu.mx; internet www .cee.edu.mx; f. 1963; scientific research into the problems of education in Mexico and Latin America; 64 researchers; library of 60,862 (reference) vols and 10,671 periodicals; Dir-Gen. FERNANDO MEJÍA BOTERO; publ. *Revista Latinoamericana de Estudios Educativos* (quarterly).

Centro de Estudios Históricos (Historical Studies Centre): Colegio de México, AC, Camino al Ajusco 20, Col. Pedregal de Santa Teresa, 10740 México, DF; tel. (55) 5449-3000; fax (55) 5645-0464; e-mail hsoto@colmex.mx; internet www.colmex.mx/centros/ceh; f. 1941; Dir Dr ARIEL RODRÍGUEZ KURI.

Centro de Estudios Internacionales (Centre for International Studies): Colegio de México, Camino al Ajusco 20, Col. Pedregal de Santa Teresa, 10740 México, DF; tel. (55) 5449-3000; fax (55) 5645-0464; e-mail psoto@colmex.mx; internet cei.colmex.mx; f. 1960; research and teaching in international relations and public administration; Dir ANNA COVARRUBIAS; publ. *Foro Internacional* (quarterly).

Centro de Estudios Monetarios Latinoamericanos (Centre for Latin American Monetary Studies): Durango 54, Col. Roma, Del. Cuauhtémoc, 06700 México, DF; tel. (55) 5061-6640; fax (55) 5525-6695; e-mail cemla@cemla.org; internet www.cemla.org; f. 1952; organizes technical training programmes on monetary policy, development finance, etc.; applied research programmes, regional meetings of banking officials; 50 mems; Dir-Gen. JAVIER GUZMÁN CALAFELL; publs *Boletín* (every 2 months), *Monetaria* (quarterly), *Money Affairs* (2 a year).

Centro de Investigaciones sobre América Latina y el Caribe (CIALC): Torre II de Humanidades 8°, Ciudad Universitaria, 04510 México, DF; tel. (55) 5623-0211; fax (55) 5623-0219; e-mail asantana@servidor.unam.mx; internet www.ccydel.unam.mx; f. 1978; fmrly Centro Coordinador y Difusor Estudios Latinoamericanos; attached to Universidad Nacional de México; study of Latin America and the Caribbean in all disciplines (history, literature, philosophy, etc.); library of over 22,000 vols; Dir Dr ADALBERTO SANTANA HERNÁNDEZ; publ. *Latinoamérica: Revista de estudios latinoamericanos* (3 a year).

Centro de Relaciones Internacionales (CRI) (Centre for International Relations): Ciudad Universitaria, FCPM, 04510 México, DF; tel. (55) 5622-9412; e-mail cri.coordinacion@mail.politicas.unam.mx; internet www.politicas.unam.mx/carreras/ri; f. 1970; attached to the Faculty of Political and Social Sciences of the Universidad Nacional Autónoma de México; co-ordinates and promotes research in all aspects of international relations and Mexico's foreign policy, as well as the training of researchers in different fields: disciplinary construction problems, co-operation and international law, developing nations, current problems in world society, Africa, Asia, peace research; 30 full mems; library of 16,000 vols; Dir FERNANDO CASTAÑEDA SABIDO; publs *Relaciones Internacionales* (quarterly), *Cuadernos, Boletín Informativo del CRI*.

Pan American Institute of Geography and History: Ex-Arzobispado 29, Col. Observatorio, 11860 México, DF; tel. (55) 5277-5888; fax (55) 5271-6172; e-mail secretariageneral@ipgh.org; internet www.ipgh.org; f. 1928; promotes, co-ordinates, and publicizes studies in cartography, geography, geophysics, history, anthropology and archaeology in the Americas; mems: nations of the Organization of American States; library of 228,285 vols; Pres. HÉCTOR O. J. PENA; Sec.-Gen. SANTIAGO BORRERO; publs *Revista Cartográfica, Revista Geográfica, Revista de Historia de América, Revista Geofísica, Boletín de Antropología Americana, Revista de Arqueología Americana*, more than 500 books and monographs.

THE NETHERLANDS

Institute of Social Studies: Kortenaerkade 12, 2518 AX The Hague; tel. (70) 4260460; fax (70) 4260799; e-mail info@iss.nl; internet www.iss.nl; f. 1952; university institute of Erasmus University Rotterdam; postgraduate courses, research and consultancy in development studies; Rector Prof. LEO DE HAAN; publs *Development and Change* (5 a year), *Development Issues* (3 a year), *Working Papers*.

NICARAGUA

Coordinadora Regional de Investigaciones Económicas y Sociales (CRIES) (Regional Co-ordinating Committee of Economic and Social Research): De Iglesia El Carmen 1c. al Largo, Apdo 3516, Managua; tel. 22-5137; fax 22-6180; e-mail info@cries.org; internet www.cries.org; research into economic development and other socio-economic and socio-political issues in Central America and the Caribbean; Pres. Dr ANDRÉS SERBÍN; publs *Cuadernos de Pensamiento Propio, Revista Pensamiento Propio* (monthly), *Servicios Especiales* (2 a month).

Instituto Histórico Centroamericano (IHCA) (Central American Historical Institute): Universidad Centroamericana, Apdo A-194, Managua; tel. (2) 278-2557; fax (2) 278-1402; e-mail info@envio.org.ni; internet www.envio.org.ni; f. 1981; Dir JUAN RAMIRO MARTÍNEZ; publ. *Envío* (monthly).

PAKISTAN

Area Study Centre for Africa, North and South America: Quaid-i-Azam University, Islamabad; tel. (51) 2896006; fax (51) 2896007; f. 1978; teaching and research; library of 11,915 vols, microfilm/microfiche collection; Dir Dr RUKHSANA QAMBER; publ. *Pakistan Journal of American Studies* (2 a year).

PANAMA

Centro de Estudios Latinoamericanos 'Justo Arosemena' (CELA) (Centre for Latin American Studies 'Justo Arosemena'): Calle 55, No 23, Apto 1, Bella Vista, El Cangrejo, Apdo 0823-01959, Panamá; tel. 223-0028; fax 269-2032; e-mail cela@salacela.net; internet www.salacela.net; f. 1976 for the analysis and dissemination of international agreements and intervention and other foreign affairs issues; Pres. CARMEN A. MIRÓ G.

Instituto Interamericano de Estadística (Inter-American Statistical Institute—IASI): INEC, Apdo 0816-01521, Panamá; tel. 223-1931; fax 510-4890; e-mail fabpan@cwpanama.net; internet www.contraloria.gob.pa/inec/iasi; f. 1940; research, seminars, technical meetings; consultative status with the UN Economic and Social Council; affiliated to the International Statistical Institute; Pres. JUAN CARLOS ABRIL; Exec. Dir EVELIO O. FABBRONI; publs *Estadística* (2 a year), *Newsletter* (4 a year).

PERU

Centro Peruano de Estudios Internacionales (CEPEI) (Peruvian Centre for International Studies): San Ignacio de Loyola 554, Miraflores 8, Lima 18; tel. (1) 4457225; fax (1) 4451094; internet www.cepei.org.pe; f. 1983; external relations, incl. Peru's border relations; Exec. Pres. Dr EDUARDO FERRERO COSTA; publ. *Cronología de Las Relaciones Internacionales del Peru* (quarterly).

Instituto de Economía de Libre Mercado (IELM) (Institute of Free Market Economics): Avda Santa Cruz 398, San Isidro, Lima 27; fax (1) 4216242; f. 1993; studies economic, political and social history of the area; Exec. Pres. CARLOS BOLOÑA BEHR.

POLAND

Centrum Studiów Latynoamerykańskich (Centre for Latin American Studies): University of Warsaw, ul. Smyczkowa 14, 02-678 Warsaw; tel. (22) 5534209; fax (22) 5534210; e-mail cesla@uw.edu.pl; internet www.cesla.uw.edu.pl; f. 1988; documentation, publications and library service; Sec. ELŻBIETA DOBKOWSKA-VELASCO; publs *CESLA 'Estudios y Memorias' Series, Documentos de Trabajo, Revista de CESLA*.

Polski Instytut Spraw Międzynarodowych (Polish Institute for International Affairs): 00-950 Warsaw, Warecka 1A; tel. (22) 5568000; fax (22) 5568099; e-mail pism@pism.pl; internet www.pism.pl; f. 1999; international relations; library of 155,000 vols; Dir Dr MARCIN ZABOROWSKI; publs *Polski Przeglad Dyplomatyczny* (6 a year), *Polish Foreign Affairs Digest* (quarterly, in English), *Europa* (quarterly, in Russian).

PUERTO RICO

Institute of Caribbean Studies: POB 23361, University Station, Río Piedras, PR 00931; tel. (787) 764-0000; fax (787) 764-3099; e-mail iec@uprrp.edu; internet iec-ics.uprrp.edu; f. 1959; research and publishing; 10 mems; library of 150 vols; Dir Dr HUMBERTO GARCÍA MUÑIZ; publ. *Caribbean Studies*.

RUSSIA

Institute of Latin America of the Russian Academy of Sciences: 113035 Moscow, B. Ordynka 21; tel. (495) 951-53-23; fax (495) 953-40-70; e-mail ilac-ran@mtu-net.ru; internet www.ilaran.ru; f. 1960; concerned with the economic, social, political and cultural development of Latin American countries; Dir Dr VLADIMIR M. DAVYDOV; publ. *Latinskaya Amerika* (monthly).

Institute of World Economics and International Relations: 117859 Moscow, Profsoyuznaya 23; tel. (499) 120-52-36; fax (499) 120-65-75; e-mail imemoran@imemo.ru; internet www.imemo.ru; f. 1956; attached to the Russian Academy of Sciences; Dir ALEXANDER A. DYNKIN.

SERBIA

Institute of International Politics and Economics: 11000 Belgrade, POB 750, Makedonska 25; tel. (11) 3373633; fax (11) 3373835; e-mail iipe@diplomacy.bg.ac.rs; internet .www.diplomacy.bg.ac.rs; f. 1947; international relations, world economy, international law, social, economic and political development in all countries; library of more than 150,000 vols; Dir Dr DUŠKO DIMITRIJEVIĆ; publs *International Problems* (annual), *Review of International Affairs* (quarterly).

SPAIN

Agencia Española de Cooperación Internacional (AECID) (Spanish Agency for International Co-operation): Avda de los Reyes Católicos 4, Ciudad Universitaria, 28040 Madrid; tel. (91) 5838100; fax (91) 5838310; e-mail centro.informacion@aecid.es; internet www.aecid.es; f. 1988; promotes cultural understanding and promotes international co-operation by organizing conferences, exhibitions and exchanges, scholarships; finances programmes of cultural, scientific, economic and technical co-operation; information department; library of more than 600,000 vols; Pres. JESÚS MANUEL GARCÍA ALDAZ; Dir-Gen. for Co-operation with Latin America JUAN LÓPEZ-DÓRIGA; numerous publs on international development and co-operation.

Escuela de Estudios Hispanoamericanos: Alfonso XII 16, 41002 Seville; tel. (95) 4501120; fax (95) 4500954; e-mail bibescu@cica.es; internet www.eeha.csic.es; f. 1943; studies history of the Americas; Dir SALVADOR BERNABÉU ALBERT.

Instituto de Cuestiones Internacionales y Política Exterior (INCIPE) (Institute of International Affairs and Foreign Policy): Alberto Aguilera 7, 6°, 28015 Madrid; tel. (91) 4455847; fax (91) 4457489; e-mail info@incipe.org; internet www.incipe.org; f. 1988; Pres. JOSÉ LLADÓ FERNÁNDEZ-URRUTÍA; Dir VICENTE GARRIDO REBOLLEDO; publs *Ensayos, Informes*.

Real Academia Hispano-Americana (Royal Spanish-American Academy): Paseo Carlos III 1A, 9°, 11003 Cádiz; tel. (956) 221680; fax (956) 222124; e-mail raha@raha.es; internet www.raha.es; f. 1910; 29 mems; Dir CARMEN CÓZAR NAVARRO; publs *Anuario, Boletín*.

Real Instituto Elcano: Príncipe de Vergara 51, 28006 Madrid; tel. (91) 7816770; fax (91) 4262157; e-mail info@rielcano.org; internet www.realinstitutoelcano.org; f. 2001; independent body for the study of international affairs; Pres. EMILIO LAMO DE ESPINOSA; Dir CHARLES POWELL; publs *Analysis of the Real Instituto Elcano (ARI)*, *Barometer of the Real Instituto Elcano* (3 a year), *ARI Magazine* (monthly).

SWEDEN

Latin American Studies at the School of Global Studies: University of Göteburg, Konstepidemins väg 2, Övre Husargatan 36, POB 700, 405 30 Göteburg; tel. (31) 786-00-00; internet www.globalstudies.gu.se/english/iberoamericanstudies; f. 1939; information, research, courses; library of 50,000 vols; Co-ordinator ISABELL SCHIERENBECK; publs *Anales*(annual), *Serie Haina*.

Latinamerika-Institutet i Stockholm (Institute of Latin American Studies, Stockholm University): Universitetsvägen 10B, 106 91 Stockholm; tel. (8) 16-34-36; fax (8) 15-65-82; e-mail secretaria@lai.su.se; internet www.lai.su.se; f. 1951; research on economic, political and social development in the region; library of 50,000 vols; Dir MONA ROSENDAHL; publ. *Iberoamericana: Nordic Journal of Latin American and Caribbean Studies* (2 a year).

SWITZERLAND

Institut de Hautes Etudes Internationales et du Développement (Graduate Institute of International and Development Studies): 132 rue de Lausanne, CP 136, 1211 Geneva 21; tel. 229085700; fax 229085710; e-mail info@graduateinstitute.ch; internet graduateinstitute.ch; f. 2008 by merger of Institut Universitaire de Hautes Etudes Internationales (f. 1927) and Institut Universitaire d'Etudes du Développement (f. 1961); African history, Middle Eastern and Latin American studies, international relations, Switzerland–Developing World economic relations; Dir PHILIPPE BURRIN.

Schweizerisches Institut für Auslandforschung (Swiss Institute of International Studies): Augustinergasse 15, 8001 Zürich; tel. 2121313; fax 2127854; e-mail info@siaf.ch; internet www.siaf.ch; f. 1943; Man. Dir Dr MARTIN MEYER.

Zentrum für Vergleichende und Internationale Studien (Centre for Comparative and International Studies): Affolternstr. 56, 8050 Zürich; tel. 6327968; fax 6321942; e-mail cispostmaster@sipo.gess.ethz.ch; internet www.cis.ethz.ch; f. 1997; international relations, comparative politics, security studies and conflict research; Dir Prof. KATHARINA MICHAELOWA.

TRINIDAD AND TOBAGO

Caribbean Agricultural Research and Development Institute (CARDI): University of the West Indies, St Augustine Campus, St Augustine; tel. 645-1205; fax 645-1208; e-mail infocentre@cardi.org; internet www.cardi.org; f. 1975; mems: CARICOM countries (see Regional Organizations); provides technical assistance, technology devt and transfer in agriculture and animal sciences; library of 3,000 vols; Exec. Dir Dr ARLINGTON CHESNEY; publs *CARDI Weekly*, *CARDI Review*, technical bulletins and papers.

Caribbean Association of Industry and Commerce (CAIC): 27a Saddle Rd, Ground Floor, Maraval; tel. 628-9859; fax 625-8766; e-mail caic.admin@gmail.com; policy advocacy to improve trading conditions for regional private sector; CEO CAROL AYOUNG; publ. *CAIC Newsletter* (monthly).

Institute of International Relations: University of the West Indies, St Augustine Campus, St Augustine; tel. 662-2002; e-mail iirt@sta.uwi.edu; internet sta.uwi.edu/iir; f. 1966; diplomatic training and postgraduate teaching and research; library of some 20,000 vols; Dir Prof. W. ANDY KNIGHT.

UNITED KINGDOM

Centre of Latin American Studies: University of Cambridge, Alison Richard Bldg, 7 West Rd, Cambridge, CB3 9DT; tel. (1223) 335390; fax (1223) 335397; e-mail webmaster@latin-american.cam.ac.uk; internet www.latin-american.cam.ac.uk; f. 1969; research and graduate teaching, mainly in comparative history and anthropology, and in Latin American culture, sociology, politics and economics; Dir Dr CHARLES JONES; publs *Cambridge Latin American Miniatures*, *Working Paper Series*.

Hispanic and Luso-Brazilian Council: Canning House, 14/15 Belgrave Sq., London, SW1X 8PJ; tel. (20) 7811-5600; fax (20) 7811-5623; e-mail enquiries@canninghouse.org; internet www.canninghouse.org; f. 1943; cultural, educational, corporate and economic links with Latin America, Spain and Portugal; 130 corporate mems; library of 60,000 vols; CEO ROBERT CAPURRO; publ. *British Bulletin of Publications on Latin America, the Caribbean, Portugal and Spain* (2 a year).

Institute of Commonwealth Studies: Senate House, 2nd Floor, South Block, Malet St, London, WC1E 7HU; tel. (20) 7862-8844; fax (20) 7862-8813; e-mail ics@sas.ac.uk; internet www.commonwealth.sas.ac.uk; f. 1949; attached to University of London; for postgraduate research in social sciences, recent history and advance study relating to the Commonwealth; lead institution of CASBAH project (Caribbean Studies Black and Asian History); library of 200,000 vols, includes library of West India Committee; Dir Prof. PHILIP MURPHY.

Institute of Development Studies: Library Rd, Brighton, BN1 9RE; tel. (1273) 606261; fax (1273) 621202; e-mail ids@ids.ac.uk; internet www.ids.ac.uk; f. 1966 as an independent institute attached to the University of Sussex; research, training, post-graduate teaching, advisory work, information services; Dir Prof. LAWRENCE HADDAD; publs *IDS Bulletin* (quarterly), research reports, working papers development bibliographies, discussion papers, policy briefings, annual report, publications catalogue.

Institute of Latin American Studies: Senate House, 2nd Floor, South Block, Malet St, London, WC1E 7HU; tel. (20) 7862-8844; fax (20) 7862-8886; e-mail ilas@sas.ac.uk; internet ilas.sas.ac.uk; f. 2004; graduate study centre within the School of Advanced Study of the University of London; co-ordinates national information on Latin America and the Caribbean in the United Kingdom; postgraduate courses on politics, economics, history, sociology, globalization and development of Latin America and the Caribbean; library of bibliographies, guides and research aids; wide range of seminars, workshops and conferences on Latin America and the Caribbean; Dir Prof. LINDA NEWSON; publs monographs, research papers and miscellaneous documents.

Latin American Centre: St Antony's College, Oxford, OX2 6JF; tel. (1865) 274486; fax (1865) 274489; e-mail enquiries@lac.ox.ac.uk; internet www.lac.ox.ac.uk; f. 1964; promotes research on Latin America, particularly with regard to the post-Independence period and in the fields of history, the social sciences, literature and geography; organizes seminars; library of 12,000 vols; Dir LEIGH A. PAYNE.

Overseas Development Institute: Overseas Development Institute, 203 Blackfriars Rd, London, SE1 8NJ; tel. (20) 7922-0300; fax (20) 7922-0399; e-mail odi@odi.org.uk; internet www.odi.org.uk; f. 1960 to act as a research and information centre on overseas development issues and problems; library of 16,000 vols; Exec. Dir KEVIN WATKINS; publs *Development Policy Review* (quarterly), *Disasters: the Journal of Disaster Studies, Policy and Management* (quarterly), books, pamphlets, briefing papers.

Progressio: Units 9–12, The Stableyard, Broomgrove Rd, London, SW9 9TL; tel. (20) 7733-1195; e-mail enquiries@progressio.org.uk; internet www.progressio.org.uk; f. 1940; known as the Catholic Institute for International Relations (CIIR) until 2006; information and analysis of socio-economic, political, church and human rights issues in the developing countries, incl. the Dominican Repub., Ecuador, El Salvador, Haiti, Honduras, Nicaragua and Peru; Exec. Dir MARK LISTER; publs include specialized studies on EU development policy.

Research Institute of Latin American Studies: Dept of Cultures, Languages and Area Studies, University of Liverpool, Cypress Bldg, Chatham St, Liverpool, L69 72R; tel. (151) 794-2000; fax (1517) 94-3080; e-mail sml@liv.ac.uk; internet www.liv.ac.uk/cultures-languages-and-area-studies/iberian-and-latin-american--studies/; f. 2006; specialist centre for the development of teaching and research on Latin America; library of 50,000 vols; publs *Bulletin of Latin American Research*, monographs, research papers.

Royal Commonwealth Society: 25 Northumberland Ave, London, WC2N 5AP; tel. (20) 7766-9200; fax (20) 7930 9705; e-mail info@ thercs.org; internet www.thercs.org; f. 1868; int. educational charity; Chair. PETER KELLMAN; Dir MIKE LAKE (acting); publs *Annual Review*, *The View* (e-newsletter, monthly), *RCS Exchange* (3 a year).

Royal Institute of International Affairs (Chatham House): 10 St James's Sq., London, SW1Y 4LE; tel. (20) 7957-5700; fax (20) 7957-5710; e-mail contact@chathamhouse.org.uk; internet www .chathamhouse.org.uk; f. 1920; an independent body that aims to promote the study and understanding of international affairs; over 300 corporate mems and many individual mems; library of 160,000 vols, 650 periodicals; Chair. STUART POPHAM; Dir Dr ROBIN NIBLETT; publs *The World Today* (6 a year), *International Affairs* (6 a year).

UCL Institute of the Americas: 51 Gordon Sq., London, WC1H 0PN; tel. (20) 7679-9746; internet www.ucl.ac.uk/americas; part of University College London; research into 19th and 20th century history and social sciences; Man. ABI ESPIE; Dir IWAN MORGAN (acting); edits *Palgrave Macmillan Series Studies of the Americas*.

Yesu Persaud Centre for Caribbean Studies: University of Warwick, Coventry, CV4 7AL; tel. (24) 7652-3523; fax (24) 7652-1606; e-mail caribbeanstudies@warwick.ac.uk; internet www2 .warwick.ac.uk/fac/arts/ccs; f. 1984 as the Centre for Caribbean Studies; renamed 2010; MA and PhD programme, conferences and symposia, lectures, publishing; Dir Dr DAVID LAMBERT; publ. *Warwick/Macmillan Caribbean Series*.

USA

Brookings Institution: 1775 Massachusetts Ave, NW, Washington, DC 20036; tel. (202) 797-6000; fax (202) 797-6004; e-mail communications@brookings.edu; internet www.brookings.edu; f. 1916; research, education and publishing in the fields of economics, government and foreign policy; library of 80,000 vols; Pres. STROBE TALBOTT; Man. Dir WILLIAM ANTHOLIS.

Center for International Policy (CIP): 1717 Massachusetts Ave NW, Suite 801, Washington, DC 20036; tel. (202) 232-3317; fax (202) 232-3440; e-mail cip@ciponline.org; internet www.ciponline.org; f. 1975; promotes international co-operation and demilitarization; Chair. CYNTHIA MCCLINTOCK; publ. *International Policy Reports*.

Center for International Studies: Massachusetts Institute of Technology, Bldg E40, 1 Amherst St, Cambridge, MA 02139; tel. (617) 253-8093; fax (617) 253-9330; e-mail cis-info@mit.edu; internet web.mit.edu/cis; f. 1952; development, migration, defence and arms control studies, environment, trade, political economy; Dir RICHARD SAMUELS.

Center for Latin American Studies: University of Florida, 319 Grinter Hall, POB 115530, Gainesville, FL 32611-5530; tel. (352) 392-0375; fax (352) 392-7682; e-mail info@latam.ufl.edu; internet www.latam.ufl.edu; f. 1931; graduate teaching and research; tropical conservation and development, business, crime, Haitian Creole and Portuguese language programmes; extensive Latin American collection in library; Dir PHILIP J. WILLIAMS; publ. *The Latinamericanist* (2 a year).

Council on Foreign Relations, Inc: The Harold Pratt House, 58 East 68th St, New York, NY 10065; tel. (212) 434-9400; fax (212) 434-9800; e-mail communications@cfr.org; internet www.cfr.org; f. 1921; 4,000 mems; Foreign Relations Library of 5,000 vols, 300 periodicals; Pres. RICHARD N. HAASS; publs *Foreign Affairs* (6 a year) and books on major issues of US foreign policy.

Council on Hemispheric Affairs: 1250 Connecticut Ave, NW, Suite 1C, Washington, DC 20036; tel. (202) 223-4975; fax (202) 223-4979; e-mail coha@coha.org; internet www.coha.org; f. 1975; conducts research into relations between North and South America; Dir LARRY BIRNS; publ. *News and Analysis* (2 a week).

Hispanic Society of America: 613 West 155th St, New York, NY 10032; tel. (212) 926-2234; fax (212) 690-0743; e-mail info@ hispanicsociety.org; internet www.hispanicsociety.org; f. 1904; maintains a public museum, rare book room, research staff, publishing section; 400 hon. mems; library of 250,000 vols and 15,000 rare books; Dir MITCHELL A. CODDING.

Institute of Latin American Studies: Rm 830, 420 West 118th St, Columbia University, New York, NY 10027; tel. (212) 854-4643; fax (212) 854-4607; e-mail ilas-info@columbia.edu; internet www .columbia.edu/cu/ilas; f. 1961; co-ordinates events, lectures and seminars on subjects relating to Latin America and Spain; Dir JOSÉ MOYA; publs *Newsletter* (3 a year), working paper series.

Inter-American Dialogue: 1211 Connecticut Ave, Suite 510, Washington, DC 20036; tel. (202) 822-9002; fax (202) 822-9553; e-mail michael@thedialogue.org; internet www.thedialogue.org; f. 1982; centre for policy analysis, communication and exchange on Western affairs; 100 mems; Pres. MICHAEL SHIFTER; publs *Dialogue* (2 a year), *Latin America Advisor* (newsletter).

Kellogg Institute for International Studies: University of Notre Dame, 130 Hesburgh Center for International Studies, Notre Dame, IN 46556-5677; tel. (574) 631-6580; fax (574) 631-6717; e-mail kellogg@nd.edu; internet kellogg.nd.edu; f. 1982; international research, particularly focused upon Latin America; Dir PAOLO CAROZZA; publs *Working Papers*, *Newsletter* (2 a year), monograph series.

Latin American and Caribbean Center: DM 353, 11200 SW Eighth St, Miami, FL 33199; tel. (305) 348-2894; fax (305) 348-3593; e-mail lacc@fiu.edu; internet lacc.fiu.edu; f. 1979; university research institute; Dir FRANK O. MORA; publ. *Hemisphere* (2 a year), *Journal of Latin American Anthropology*.

Latin American and Iberian Institute: University of New Mexico, 801 Yale NE, MSC02 1690, Albuquerque, NM 87131-0001; tel. (505) 277-2961; fax (505) 277-5989; e-mail laii@unm .edu; internet www.laii.unm.edu; Dir Dr SUSAN B. TIANO; publ. research papers.

Latin American Institute: University of California, Los Angeles (UCLA), 10343 Bunche Hall, Hilgard Ave, POB 951447, Los Angeles, CA 90095-1447; tel. (310) 825-4571; fax (310) 206-6859; e-mail latinamctr@international.ucla.edu; internet www.international .ucla.edu/lai; Dir KEVIN TERRACIANO.

Latin American Studies Association: 416 Bellefield Hall, University of Pittsburgh Pittsburgh, PA 15260; tel. (412) 648-7929; fax (412) 624-7145; e-mail lasa@pitt.edu; internet lasa.international.pitt .edu; Exec. Dir MILAGROS PEREYRA-ROJAS; publs *Latin American Research Review* (3 a year), *LASA Forum* (4 a year).

Middle American Research Institute: Tulane University, New Orleans, LA 70118; tel. (504) 865-5110; fax (504) 862-8778; e-mail mari@tulane.edu; internet www.tulane.edu/~mari; f. 1924; publs on archaeology in Mesoamerica and related subjects; Dir MARCELLO A. CANUTO; publs books, miscellaneous papers.

Pre-Columbian Studies, Dumbarton Oaks: 1703 32nd St, NW, Washington, DC 20007; tel. (202) 339-6440; fax (202) 625-0284; e-mail pre-columbian@doaks.org; internet www.doaks.org/ research/pre-columbian; f. 1962; residential fellowships, annual symposia, seminars, etc.; Pre-Columbian art collection; library of 26,000 vols on Pre-Columbian history; Dir JAN M. ZIOLKOWSKI; publs annual symposia vols and occasional monographs.

Princeton Institute for International and Regional Studies (PIIRS): Aaron Burr Hall, Princeton University, Princeton, NJ 08544; tel. (609) 258-7497; fax (609) 258-3988; e-mail piirs@ princeton.edu; internet www.princeton.edu/~piirs/index.html; f. 2003; an academic institute of Princeton University; international relations; 65 faculty associates; Dir MARK R. BEISSINGER; publs *World Politics* (quarterly), monographs, occasional papers.

School of Advanced International Studies (SAIS): Johns Hopkins University, Nitze Bldg, 1740 Massachusetts Ave, NW, Washington, DC 20036; tel. (202) 663-5600; fax (202) 663-5656; e-mail fdimarco@jhu.edu; internet www.sais-jhu.edu; Dir RIORDAN ROETT.

School of International and Public Affairs (SIPA): Columbia University, 420 West 118th St, Rm 1414, New York, NY 10027; tel. (212) 854-3213; fax (212) 864-8660; internet www.sipa.columbia.edu; Dean MERIT E. JANOW; publ. *Journal of International Affairs* (2 a year).

Teresa Lozano Long Institute of Latin American Studies (LLILAS): University of Texas, Austin, TX 78712; tel. (512) 471-5551; fax (512) 471-3090; e-mail hgatlin@austin.utexas.edu; internet www.utexas.edu/cola/insts/llilas; f. 1940; Dir CHARLES R. HALE.

Washington Office on Latin America (WOLA): Suite 400, 1666 Connecticut Ave, NW, Washington, DC, USA; tel. (202) 797-2171; fax (202) 797-2172; e-mail wola@wola.org; internet www.wola.org; f. 1974; resource and interlocutor for Latin American non-governmental organizations working for human rights and social justice; Exec. Dir JOY OLSON.

Woodrow Wilson Center—Latin American Program: 1 Woodrow Wilson Plaza, 1300 Pennsylvania Ave, NW, Washington, DC 20004; tel. (202) 691-4170; fax (202) 691-4001; e-mail cynthia .arnson@wilsoncenter.org; internet www.wilsoncenter.org/ program/latin-american-program; f. 1977; residential fellowship programme; inter-American dialogue, inter-American economic issues, conferences, history and culture of Latin America, administration of social policy and governance, resolution of civil conflict; Dir CYNTHIA J. ARNSON; publs *Centerpoint* (monthly newsletter), *The Wilson Quarterly*, *Working Paper Series*.

URUGUAY

Centro de Estadísticas Nacionales y Comercio Internacional del Uruguay (CENCI Uruguay) (Centre for National Statistics and International Trade): Juncal 1327 D, 16°, Of. 1603, Montevideo; tel. 2915-2930; fax 2915-4578; e-mail cenci@cenci.com.uy; internet www.cenci.com.uy; f. 1955; economic and statistical information on all Latin American countries, import tariffs on commodities; mem. of ALADI and CEPAL; library of 900 vols; publs *Anuario Estadístico sobre el intercambio comercial* (annual), *Boletines: Noticias Latinoamericanas, Dictámenes de Clasificación Arancelaria—MERCOSUR, Estudios del Mercado, Industrias por sectores de actividad, Manual Práctico del Importador* (monthly), *Manual Práctico del Exportador* (monthly), *Manual Práctico Aduanero* (monthly), *Manual Práctico del Contribuyente* (monthly), *Régimen de Origen—ALADI y MERCOSUR.*

Centro Latinoamericano de Economía Humana (CLAEH) (Latin American Centre for Human Economy): Zelmar Michelini 1220, POB 5021, 11100 Montevideo; tel. 2900-7194; e-mail info@claeh.org.uy; internet www.claeh.org.uy; f. 1958 to conduct research into economics and other social sciences; Dir NÉSTOR DA COSTA; publ. *Cuadernos del CLAEH* (3 a year).

VENEZUELA

Centro de Estudios del Desarrollo (CENDES) (Centre for Development Studies): Universidad Central de Venezuela, Ciudad Universitaria, Los Chaguaramos, Caracas 1050; tel. (212) 753-3475; fax (212) 751-2691; internet www.ucv.ve/cendes; f. 1961; centre for research and graduate studies on all aspects of development in Venezuela and Latin America; library of 30,000 vols; Dir CARLOS WALTER; publs *Anuario de Estudios del Desarrollo, CENDES Newsletter* (3 a year), *Cuadernos del CENDES* (3 a year).

Centro Experimental de Estudios Latinoamericanos (CEELA) (Experimental Centre for Latin American Studies): Universidad del Zulia, Maracaibo 4011, Zulia; tel. (261) 759-8144; internet www.ceela.luz.edu.ve; research in socio-economic development, especially the Andean Pact model, inflation and crises in Latin America; conferences and seminars; Dir Dr ÉDGAR ÁVILA; publ. *Cuadernos Latinoamericanos.*

Instituto de Altos Estudios de América Latina (IAEAL) (Institute for Advanced Latin American Studies): Universidad Simón Bolívar, Biblioteca Central, Entrada Nivel Jardín, Caracas 1010; tel. (212) 906-3116; fax (212) 906-3117; e-mail iaeal@usb.ve; internet www.iaeal.usb.ve; f. 1975; research, seminars, publs on Latin America; attached to the Universidad Simón Bolívar; library of 3,000 vols; Dir Prof. HÉCTOR MALDONADO LIRA; publs *Mundo Nuevo: Revista de Estudios Latinoamericanos* (quarterly), working papers, books.

Instituto de Investigaciones Económicas y Sociales (IIES) (Institute of Economic and Social Research): Edif. Cincuentenario, 5°, Universidad Católica Andrés Bello, Urb. Montalbán, La Vega, Caracas 1020; tel. (212) 407-4173; fax (212) 407-4174; e-mail iies@ucab.edu.ve; internet www.ucab.edu.ve; studies labour and demographic economics; Dir LUIS PEDRO ESPAÑA.

SELECT BIBLIOGRAPHY (BOOKS)

South America

Adams, F. *The United Nations in Latin America: Aiding Development*. Abingdon, Routledge, 2009.

Alcántara Sáez, M. (Ed.). *Politicians and Politics in Latin America*. Boulder, CO, Lynne Rienner Publrs, 2007.

Albert, B. *South America and the First World War*. Cambridge, Cambridge University Press, 2002.

Allison, G. T. *Essence of Decision: Explaining the Cuban Missile Crisis*. Boston, MA, Little Brown, 1971.

Almond, G. A., and Verba, S. *The Civic Culture: Political Attitudes and Democracy in Five Nations*, 2nd edn. Newbury Park, CA, Sage Publications, 1989.

Andolina, R., Laurie, N., and Radcliffe, S. A. *Indigenous Development in the Andes: Culture, Power and Transnationalism*. Durham, NC, Duke University Press, 2010.

Angeles Castro, G., Perrotini-Hernández, I., and Rios-Bolivar, H. *Market Liberalism, Growth and Development in Latin America*. Abingdon, Routledge, 2011.

Angell, A. *et al. Decentralizing Development: The Political Economy of Institutional Change in Colombia and Chile*. Oxford, Oxford University Press, 2001.

 Democracy after Pinochet: Politics, Parties and Elections in Chile. London, Institute for the Study of the Americas, 2007.

Aravena, F. R. *América Latina y el Caribe: Multilateralismo vs. Soberanía: La Construcción de la Comunidad de Estados Latinoamericanos y Caribeños*. Buenos Aires, Editorial Teseo, 2011

Arceneaux, C. L. *Bounded Missions: Military Regimes and Democratization in the Southern Cone and Brazil*. Pennsylvania, PA, Penn State University Press, 2001.

Arias, E. D., Goldstein, D. (Eds). *Violent Democracies in Latin America: The Cultures and Practice of Violence*. Durham, NC, Duke University Press, 2010.

Aviel, J. F. 'Political Participation of Women in Latin America', in *Western Political Quarterly*, Vol. 34. 1981.

Bebbington, A. (Ed.). *Social Conflict, Economic Development and Extractive Industry: Evidence from South America*. Abingdon, Routledge, 2011.

Bernardi, L., Barreix, A., Marenzi, A., and Profeta, P. *Tax Systems and Tax Reforms in Latin America*. Abingdon, Routledge, 2011.

Bethell, L., and Roxborough, I. (Eds). *Latin America between the Second World War and the Cold War, 1944–1948*. Cambridge, Cambridge University Press, 1993.

Biswas, A. (Ed.). *Managing Transboundary Waters of Latin America*. Abingdon, Routledge, 2012.

Boville, B. *The Cocaine War: Drugs, Politics, and the Environment*. New York, Algora Publishing, 2004.

Bowman, K. S. *Militarization, Democracy and Development: The Perils of Praetorianism in Latin America*. Pennsylvania, PA, Penn State University Press, 2004.

Brands, H. *Latin America's Cold War*. Cambridge, MA, Harvard University Press, 2010.

Brannstrom, C. (Ed.). *Territories, Commodities and Knowledges: Latin American Environmental Histories in the Nineteenth and Twentieth Centuries*. London, Institute for the Study of the Americas, 2005.

Brass, T. *Latin American Peasants*. London, Frank Cass, 2003.

Bruneau, T. C. *The Political Transformation of the Brazilian Catholic Church*. Cambridge, Cambridge University Press, 1974.

Bulmer-Thomas, V. *The Economic History of Latin America Since Independence*. Cambridge, Cambridge University Press, 1994.

 The New Economic Model in Latin America and its Impact on Income Distribution and Poverty. Basingstoke, Macmillan, 1996.

 Britain and Latin America: A Changing Relationship. Cambridge, Cambridge University Press, 2008.

Calleros-Alarcón, J. C. *The Unfinished Transition to Democracy in Latin America*. Abingdon, Routledge, 2008.

Calvert, P. *A Study of Revolution*. Oxford, Clarendon Press, 1970.

 'Latin America: Laboratory of Revolution', in O'Sullivan, N. (Ed.), *Revolutionary Theory and Political Reality*. Brighton, Harvester Press, 1983.

 (Ed.). *Political and Economic Encyclopedia of South America and the Caribbean*. Harlow, Essex, Longman, 1991.

 The International Politics of Latin America. Manchester, Manchester University Press, 1994.

 A Political and Economic Dictionary of Latin America. London, Europa Publications, 2004.

Calvert, P., and Calvert, S. *Latin America in the Twentieth Century*, 2nd edn. Basingstoke, Macmillan, 1993.

Cameron, M. A., and Hershberg, E. (Eds). *Latin America's Left Turns: Politics, Policies, and Trajectories of Change*. Boulder, CO, Lynne Rienner Publrs, 2010.

Camp, R. A. *Democracy in Latin America: Patterns and Cycles*. Wilmington, DE, SR Books, 1996.

Carruthers, D. V. (Ed.). *Environmental Justice in Latin America: Problems, Promise, and Practice*. Cambridge, MA, MIT Press, 2008.

Cason, Jeffrey, W. *The Political Economy of Integration: The Experience of Mercosur*. Abingdon, Routledge, 2010.

Castañeda, J. G. *Utopia Unarmed: The Latin American Left after the Cold War*. New York, Vintage Books, 1994.

Castro, D. (Ed.). *Revolution and Revolutionaries, Guerrilla Movements in Latin America*. Scholarly Review Books, 1999.

Chávez, D., and Goldfrank, B. (Eds). *The Left in the City: Participatory Local Governments in Latin America*. London, Latin America Bureau, 2004.

Clawson, P., and Lee, R. *The Andean Cocaine Industry*. Basingstoke, Palgrave Macmillan, 1999.

Clissold, S. *Soviet Relations with Latin America, 1918–1968: A Documentary Survey*. London, Oxford University Press for Royal Institute of International Affairs, 1969.

Cohen, M. *The Global Economic Crisis in Latin America: Impacts and Responses*. Abingdon, Routledge, 2012.

Collinson, H. (Ed.). *Green Guerrillas: Environmental Conflicts and Initiatives in Latin America*. London, Latin America Bureau, 1996.

Cooper, A. F., and Heine, J. (Eds). *Which Way Latin America?: Hemispheric Politics Meets Globalization*. Tokyo, United Nations University, 2009.

Couso, J., Huneeus, A., Sieder, R. (Eds). *Cultures of Legality: Judicialization and Political Activism in Latin America*. Cambridge, Cambridge University Press, 2010.

Cubitt, T. *Latin American Society*, 2nd edn. Harlow, Longman, 1995.

Dabène, O. *The Politics of Regional Integration in Latin America*. Basingstoke, Palgrave Macmillan, 2009.

Dammert, L. *Fear and Crime in Latin America: Redefining State-Society Relations*. Abingdon, Routledge, 2012.

Dávila, J. *Dictatorship in South America*. Oxford, Wiley-Blackwell, 2013.

De Janvry, A. *The Agrarian Question and Reformism in Latin America*. Baltimore, MD, Johns Hopkins University Press, 1981.

DeHart, M. C. *Ethnic Entrepreneurs: Identity and Development Politics in Latin America*. Palo Alto, CA, Stanford University Press, 2010.

Deutsch, S. M. *Las Derechas: The Extreme Right in Argentina, Brazil and Chile, 1890–1939*. Stanford, CA, Stanford University Press, 1999.

Devereux, S., and Justino, P., (Eds). *Overcoming Inequality in Latin America: Issues and Challenges for the 21st Century*. Abingdon, Routledge, 2005.

Di Tella, T. S. *Latin American Politics: A Theoretical Framework*. Austin, TX, University of Texas Press, 1990.

Domingues, J. M. *Latin America and Contemporary Modernity: A Sociological Interpretation*. Abingdon, Routledge, 2011.

Domínguez, F. (Ed.). *Identity and Discursive Practices: Spain and Latin America*. Bern, Peter Lang AG, 2000.

Domínguez, F., and Guedes de Oliveira, M. (Eds). *Mercosur: Between Integration and Democracy*. New York, Peter Lang Publrs, Inc, 2004.

Domínguez, J. I. *Parties, Elections, and Political Participation in Latin America*. Abingdon, Routledge, 2013.

Domínguez, J. I., and Fernández de Castro, R. (Eds). *Contemporary US–Latin American Relations: Cooperation or Conflict in the 21st Century?* Abingdon, Routledge, 2010.

Domínguez, J., and Shifter, M. (Eds). *Constructing Democratic Governance in Latin America*. Baltimore, MD, Johns Hopkins University Press, 2003.

Dunkerley, J. *Bolivia: Revolution and the Power of History in the Present*. London, Institute for the Study of the Americas, 2007.

Edwards, S. *Left Behind: Latin America and the False Promise of Populism*. Chicago, IL, Chicago University Press, 2010.

Farcau, B. W. *The Ten Cents War: Chile, Peru, and Bolivia in the War of the Pacific, 1879–1884*. Westport, CT, Praeger Publrs, 2000.

Ferrell, R. H. *Latin American Diplomacy: The Twentieth Century*. New York, W. W. Norton, 1988.

Fisher, J. *Out of the Shadows: Women, Resistance and Politics in South America*. London, Latin America Bureau, 1993.

Foders, F., and Feldsieper, M. *The Transformation of Latin America: Economic Development in the Early 1990s*. Northampton, MA, Edward Elgar Publishing, 2000.

Foweraker, J. *Theorizing Social Movements*. London, Pluto Press, 1995.

Fowler, W. *Ideologues and Ideologies in Latin America*. Westport, CT, Greenwood Press, 1997.

Frieden, J. A. *Debt, Development and Democracy: Modern Political Economy and Latin America, 1965–1985*. Princeton, NJ, Princeton University Press, 1992.

Frieden, J. A., Pastor, M., and Tomz, M. *Modern Political Economy and Latin America: Theory and Policy*. Boulder, CO, Westview Press, 2000.

Fung, K. C., and Garcia Herrero, A. *Sino-Latin American Economic Relations*. Abingdon, Routledge, 2011.

Gardini, G. L. *The Origins of Mercosur: Democracy and Regionalization in South America*. Basingstoke, Palgrave Macmillan, 2010.

Latin America in the 21st Century: Nations, Regionalism, Globalization. London, Zed Books, 2012

Gilbert, A. *Latin America*. London, Routledge, 1990.

Gill, L. *School of the Americas: Military Training and Political Violence in the Americas (American Encounters/Global Interactions)*. Durham, NC, Duke University Press, 2004.

The Latin American City, revised edn. London, Latin America Bureau, 1998.

Gledhill, J., and Schell, P. A. (Eds). *New Approaches to Resistance in Brazil and Mexico*. Durham, NC, Duke University Press, 2012.

Gonzalez, F. E. *Dual Transitions From Authoritarian Rule: Institutionalized Regimes in Chile and Mexico, 1970–2000*. Washington, DC, Johns Hopkins University Press, 2008.

Creative Destruction? Economic Crises and Democracy in Latin America. Washington, DC, Johns Hopkins University Press, 2012.

Grandin, G., and Joseph, G. M. (Eds). *A Century of Revolution: Insurgent and Counterinsurgent Violence during Latin America's Long Cold War*. Durham, NC, Duke University Press, 2010.

Green, D. *Faces of Latin America*. London, Latin America Bureau, 1997.

Silent Revolution: The Rise of Market Economics in Latin America. 2nd edn, London, Cassell/Latin America Bureau, 2003.

Grosse, R. *Government Responses to the Latin American Debt Problem*. Boulder, CO, Lynne Rienner Publrs, 1996.

Grugel, J., and Riggirozzi, P. (Eds). *Governance after Neoliberalism in Latin America*. Basingstoke, Palgrave Macmillan, 2009.

Guillermoprieto, A. *Looking for History: Dispatches from Latin America*. New York, Pantheon Books, 2001.

Gwynne, R. N., and Kay, C. (Eds). *Latin America Transformed: Globalization and Modernity*. London, Arnold, 1999.

Hall, A. (Ed.). *Global Impact, Local Action: New Environmental Policy in Latin America*. London, Institute for the Study of the Americas, 2005.

Hall, A., and Patrinos, H. A. (Eds). *Indigenous Peoples, Poverty and Human Development in Latin America: 1994–2004*. Basingstoke, Palgrave Macmillan, 2005.

Hammergren, L. A. *Envisioning Reform: Improving Judicial Performance in Latin America*. University Park, PA, Penn State University Press, 2007.

Heinz, W. S., and Fruhling, H. *Determinants of Gross Human Rights Violations by State and State-sponsored Actors in Brazil, Uruguay, Chile and Argentina*. Leiden, Martinus Nijhoff Publrs, 1999.

Hellin, J., and Higman, S. *Feeding the Market: South American Farmers, Trade and Globalization*. ITDG Publrs, Colchester, 2003.

Hellinger, D. C. *Comparative Politics of Latin America: Democracy at Last?*. Abingdon, Routledge, 2011.

Jones, G. A., and Varley, A. 'The Contest for the City Centre: Street Traders versus Buildings', in *Bulletin of Latin American Research*, Vol. 13, No. 1 (Jan.). 1994.

Kalman, J., and Street, B. V. *Literacy and Numeracy in Latin America: Local Perspectives and Beyond*. Abingdon. Routledge, 2012.

Kennedy, J. J. *Catholicism, Nationalism and Democracy in Argentina*. South Bend, IN, University of Notre Dame Press, 1958.

Kilty, K. M., and Segal, E. (Eds). *Poverty and Inequality in the Latin American-U.S. Borderlands: Implications of U.S. Interventions*. Binghamton, NY, Haworth Press, Inc, 2005.

Kingstone, P. *The Political Economy of Latin America: Reflections on Neoliberalism and Development*. Abingdon, Routledge, 2010.

Kingstone, P., and Yashar, D. J. *Routledge Handbook of Latin American Politics*. Abingdon, Routledge, 2012.

Kirk, J. 'John Paul II and the Exorcism of Liberation Theology...', in *Bulletin of Latin American Research*, Vol. 4, No. 1. 1985.

Koonings, K., and Kruijt, D. *Fractured Cities: Social Exclusion, Urban Violence and Contested Spaces in Latin America*. London, Zed Books, 2007.

Kozloff, N. *Revolution!: South America and the Rise of the New Left*. Basingstoke, Palgrave Macmillan, 2008.

Larson, B. *Trials of Nation Making: Liberalism, Race and Ethnicity in the Andes, 1810–1910*. Cambridge, Cambridge University Press, 2004.

Lehmann, D. *Democracy and Development in Latin America*. Cambridge, Polity Press, 1990.

LeoGrande, W. 'Enemies Evermore: US Policy Towards Cuba After Helms-Burton', in *Journal of Latin American Studies*, Vol. 29, 1997.

Levine, D. H. (Ed.). *Churches and Politics in Latin America*. Beverley Hills, CA, Sage Publications, 1979.

Lievesley, G., and Ludlam, S. (Eds). *Reclaiming Latin America: Experiments in Radical Social Democracy*. London, Zed Books, 2009.

Lockhart, J., and Schwartz, S. B. *Early Latin America: A History of Colonial Spanish America and Brazil*. New York, Cambridge University Press, 1983.

Lopez-Calva, L. F., and Lustig, N. C. (Eds). *Declining Inequality in Latin America: A Decade of Progress?* Washington, DC, Brookings Institution, 2010.

Lora E. (Ed.) *The State of State Reforms in Latin America*. Washington, DC, World Bank Publications, 2006.

Loveman, B., and Davies, T. M. (Eds). *The Politics of Antipolitics: The Military in Latin America*. Lincoln, NE, University of Nebraska Press, 1978.

Loveman, B. *The Constitution of Tyranny: Regimes of Exception in Latin America*. Pittsburgh, PA, University of Pittsburgh Press, 1994.

Lowenthal, A. F. (Ed.). *Armies and Politics in Latin America*. New York, Holmes and Meier, 1976.

MacDonald, S. B., and Fauriol, G. A. *Fast Forward: Latin America on the Edge of the 21st Century*. Piscataway, NJ, and London, Transaction Publrs, 1997.

Mace, G., Cooper, A. F., and Shaw, T. M. (Eds). *Inter-American Cooperation at a Crossroads*. Basingstoke, Palgrave Macmillan, 2010.

Mahoney, J. *Colonialism and Postcolonial Development: Spanish America in Comparative Perspective*. Cambridge, Cambridge University Press, 2010.

Mainwaring, S., O'Donnell, G., and Valenzuela, J. S. (Eds). *Issues in Democratic Consolidation: The New South American Democracies in Comparative Perspective*. South Bend, IN, University of Notre Dame Press, 1992.

Mainwaring, S., and Scully, T. R. (Eds). *Democratic Governance in Latin America*. Palo Alto, CA, Stanford University Press, 2009.

Malloy, J. M., and Seligson, M. A. (Eds). *Authoritarians and Democrats: Regime Transition in Latin America*. Pittsburgh, PA, University of Pittsburgh Press, 1987.

Martz, J. D. (Ed.). *United States Policy in Latin America: A Quarter Century of Crisis and Challenge, 1961–1986*. Lincoln, NE, University of Nebraska Press, 1988.

McKinney, J. A., and Gardner, H. S. (Eds). *Economic Integration in the Americas*. Abingdon, Routledge, 2009.

Meade, T. A. *A History of Modern Latin America: 1800 to the Present*. Hobeken, NJ, Wiley-Blackwell, 2009.

Meso-Lago, C. *Market, Socialist, and Mixed Economies: Comparative Policy and Performance in Chile, Cuba, and Costa Rica*. Baltimore, MD, Johns Hopkins University Press, 2000.

Middlebrook, K. J. *Conservative Parties, the Right and Democracy in Latin America*. Baltimore, MD, Johns Hopkins University Press, 2000.

Millett, R. L., Holmes J. S., and Pérez, O. J. *Latin American Democracy: Emerging Reality or Endangered Species?* Abingdon, Routledge, 2008.

Morgenstern, S., and Nacif, B. *Legislative Politics in Latin America.* Cambridge, Cambridge University Press, 2002.

Munck, R. *Contemporary Latin America.* Basingstoke, Palgrave Macmillan, 2007.

Murillo, M. V. *Labour Unions, Partisan Coalitions and Market Reforms in Latin America.* Cambridge, Cambridge University Press, 2001.

Nunn, F. M. *The Time of the Generals: Latin American Professional Militarism in World Perspective.* Lincoln, NE, University of Nebraska Press, 1992.

O'Donnell, G. *Delegative Democracy.* South Bend, IN, University of Notre Dame Press, 1992.

Counterpoints: Selected Essays on Authoritarianism and Democratization. Notre Dame, IN, University of Notre Dame, 2000.

Organisation for Economic Co-operation and Development (OECD). *Challenges to Fiscal Adjustment in Latin America: The Cases of Argentina, Brazil, Chile and Mexico.* Paris, OECD Publishing, 2007.

Oxhorn, P., and Starr, P. *Markets and Democracy in Latin America: Conflict or Convergence?* Boulder, CO, Lynne Rienner Publrs, 1998.

Painter, M., and Durham, W. H. *The Social Causes of Environmental Destruction in Latin America.* Ann Arbor, MI, University of Michigan Press, 1995.

Pang, E. *The International Political Economy of Transformation in Argentina, Brazil and Chile since 1960.* Basingstoke, Palgrave Macmillan, 2002.

Panizza, F. *Contemporary Latin America: Development and Democracy beyond the Washington Consensus—The Rise of the Left.* London, Zed Books, 2009.

Parkinson, F. *Latin America, the Cold War and the World Powers, 1945–1973.* Beverley Hills, CA, Sage Publications, 1974.

Pastor, R. A. *Condemned to Repetition: The United States and Nicaragua.* Princeton, NJ, Princeton University Press, 1987.

Petras, J., and Morley, M. *Latin America in the Time of Cholera: Electoral Politics, Market Economy, and Permanent Crisis.* New York, Routledge, 1992.

Philip, G. *Oil and Politics in Latin America: Nationalist Movements and State Companies.* Cambridge, Cambridge University Press, 1982.

The Military and South American Politics. London, Croom Helm, 1985.

Phillips, N. *The United States and Latin America: Myths and Stereotypes of Civilization and Nature.* Austin, TX, University of Texas Press, 1992.

The Southern Cone Model: The Political Economy of Regional Capitalist Development in Latin America. London, Routledge, 2004.

Posada-Carbó, E., and Malamud, C. (Eds). *The Financing of Politics: Latin American and European Perspectives.* London, Institute for the Study of the Americas, 2005.

Pribble, J. *Welfare and Party Politics in Latin America.* Cambridge, Cambridge University Press, 2013.

Rakowski, C. A. (Ed.). *Contrapunto: The Informal Sector Debate in Latin America.* Albany, NY, State University of New York Press, 1994.

Randall, L. 'Lies, Damn Lies and Argentine GDP', in *Latin American Research Review*, Vol. 11. 1974.

Reid, M. *Forgotten Continent: The Battle for Latin America's Soul.* New Haven, CT, Yale University Press, 2007.

Reyes, J. A., and Sawyer, W. C. *Latin American Economic Development.* Abingdon, Routledge, 2011.

Roberts, B. R. *The Making of Citizens: Cities of Peasants Revisited.* London, Arnold, 1995.

Roberts, K. M. *Deepening Democracy? The Modern Left and Social Movements in Chile and Peru.* Stanford, CA, Stanford University Press, 2000.

Santiso, J. *Latin America's Political Economy of the Possible: Beyond Good Revolutionaries and Free Marketeers.* Cambridge, MA, MIT Press, 2006.

Schwindt-Bayer, L. A. *Political Power and Women's Representation in Latin America.* New York, Oxford University Press USA, 2010.

Segura-Ubierga, A. *The Political Economy of the Welfare State in Latin America: Globalization, Democracy, and Development*, Cambridge, Cambridge University Press, 2007.

Shafer, D. M. *Deadly Paradigms: The Failure of US Counterinsurgency Policy.* Princeton, NJ, Princeton University Press, 1988.

Sherman, J. W. *Latin America in Crisis.* Boulder, CO, Westview Press, 2000.

Sieder, R., Schjolden, L., and Angell, A. (Eds). *The Judicialization of Politics in Latin America.* London, Institute for the Study of the Americas, 2005.

Silva, E. *Challenging Neoliberalism in Latin America.* Cambridge, Cambridge University Press, 2009.

Silvert, K. H. *The Conflict Society: Reaction and Revolution in Latin America.* New York, American Universities Field Staff Inc, 1966.

Skidmore, T. E., and Smith, P. H. *Modern Latin America.* Oxford, Oxford University Press, 2000.

Smith, B. *The Church and Politics in Chile: Challenges to Modern Catholicism.* Princeton, NJ, Princeton University Press, 1982.

Spalding, H. A. *Organised Labor in Latin America: Historical Case Studies of Urban Workers in Dependent Societies.* New York, Harper and Row, 1977.

Stein, E., and Tommasi, M. (Eds). *Policymaking in Latin America: How Politics Shapes Policies.* Cambridge, MA, Harvard University Press, 2008.

Tamarin, D. *The Argentine Labor Movement, 1930–1945: A Study in the Origins of Peronism.* Albuquerque, NM, University of New Mexico Press, 1985.

Teichman, J. A. *The Politics of Freeing Markets in Latin America: Chile, Argentina and Mexico.* Chapel Hill, NC, University of North Carolina Press, 2001.

Thomas, J. R. *Bibliographical Dictionary of Latin American Historians and Historiography.* Westport, CT, Greenwood Press, 1984.

Thorp, R. (Ed.). *Latin America in the 1930s: The Role of the Periphery in World Crisis.* Basingstoke, Macmillan, 1984.

Thorp, R., and Whitehead, L. (Eds). *Latin American Debt and the Adjustment Crisis.* Basingstoke, Macmillan, 1987.

Timerman, J. *Prisoner without a Name, Cell without a Number.* Harmondsworth, Penguin, 1982.

Tokman, V. E., and Klein, E. *Regulation and the Informal Economy: Microenterprises in Chile, Ecuador and Jamaica.* Boulder, CO, Lynne Rienner Publrs, 1995.

Trubowitz, P. *Defining the National Interest: Conflict and Change in American Foreign Policy.* Chicago, IL, University of Chicago Press, 1998.

Tulchin, J. S., and Garland, A. M. (Eds). *Social Development in Latin America.* Boulder, CO, Lynne Rienner Publrs, 2000.

Tulchin, J. S., and Espach, R. H. *Latin America in the New International System.* Boulder, CO, Lynne Rienner Publrs, 2000.

Turner, B. (Ed.). *Latin America Profiled: Essential Facts on Society, Business and Politics in Latin America* (Syb Factbook). New York, St Martin's Press, 2000.

Ungar, M. *Policing Democracy: Overcoming Obstacles to Citizen Security in Latin America.* Baltimore, MD, Johns Hopkins University Press, 2010.

Vadjunec, J., and Schmink, M. (Eds). *Amazonian Geographies: Emerging Identities and Landscapes.* Abingdon, Routledge, 2012.

Van Cott, D. L. *The Friendly Liquidation of the Past: The Politics of Diversity in Latin America* (Pitt Latin American Series). Pittsburgh, PA, University of Pittsburgh Press, 2000.

From Movements to Political Parties in Latin America: The Evolution of Ethnic Politics. Cambridge, Cambridge University Press, 2005.

Weyland, K. G. *The Politics of Market Reform in Fragile Democracies: Argentina, Brazil, Peru and Venezuela.* Princeton, NJ, Princeton University Press, 2002.

Wilgus, A. C. (Ed.). *South American Dictators During the First Century of Independence.* New York, Russell and Russell, 1963.

Wilkie, J. W., and Perkal, A. (Eds). *Statistical Abstract of Latin America.* Los Angeles, CA, University of California (Los Angeles) Latin American Center, annual.

Williams, M. E. *Understanding US—Latin America Relations: Theory and History.* Abingdon, Routledge, 2011.

Youngers, C., and Rosin, E. *Drugs and Democracy in Latin America: The Impact of US Policy.* London, Lynne Rienner Publrs, 2004.

Central America

Aguilera, G. *El Fusil y el Olivo: La Cuestión Militar en Centroamérica.* USA, FLACSO/DEI, 1988.

Anderson, T. P. *Politics in Central America: Guatemala, El Salvador, Honduras and Nicaragua.* New York, Praeger Publrs, 1988.

Arashiro, Z. *Negotiating the Free Trade Area of the Americas*. London, Institute for the Study of the Americas/Palgrave Macmillan, 2011.

Barry, T. *Roots of Rebellion: Land and Hunger in Central America*. Cambridge, MA, South End Press, 1987.

Bendaña, A. *Demobilization and Reintegration in Central America: Peace Building Challenges and Responses*. Managua, Centro de Estudios Internacionales, 1999.

Binational Study: The State of Migration Flows Between Costa Rica and Nicaragua—An Analysis of Economic and Social Implications for Both Countries. Geneva, Intergovernmental Committee for Migration, 2003.

Booth, J. A. *Understanding Central America: Global Forces, Rebellion and Change*, 5th edn. Boulder, CO, Westview Press, 2010.

Booth, J., and Seligson, M. *Elections and Democracy in Central America, Revisited*. Chapel Hill, NC, University of North Carolina Press, 1995.

Booth, J. A., and Walker, T. W. *Understanding Central America*, 3rd edn. Boulder, CO, Westview Press, 1999.

Brockett, C. D., et al. (Eds). *Political Movements and Violence in Central America*. Cambridge, Cambridge University Press, 2005.

Bulmer-Thomas, V. *Studies in the Economics of Central America*. London, Macmillan, 1989.

Bunker, R. (Ed.). *Criminal Insurgencies in Mexico and the Americas: The Gangs and Cartels Wage War*. Abingdon, Routledge, 2012.

Calvert, P. (Ed.). *The Central American Security System: North-South or East-West?* Cambridge, Cambridge University Press, 2008.

Chomsky, A., and Lauria-Santiago, A. (Eds). *Identity and Struggle at the Margins of the Nation-State: The Laboring Peoples of Central America and the Hispanic Caribbean*. Durham, NC, Duke University Press, 1998.

Colburn, F. D., and Cruz S., A. J. *Varieties of Liberalism in Central America: Nation-States as Works in Progress*. Austin, TX, University of Texas, 2007.

Desruelle, D. and Schipke, A. *Central America: Economic Progress and Reforms*. Washington, DC, International Monetary Fund, 2008.

Domínguez, J., and Fernández de Castro, R. *United States and Mexico*. Abingdon, Routledge, 2009.

Dunkerley, J. *Power in the Isthmus: A Political History of Modern Central America*. London, Verso, 1988.

   The Pacification of Central America. London and New York, Verso, 1994.

Domínguez, J., and Lindenberg, M. (Eds). *Democratic Transitions in Central America*. Gainesville, FL, University Press of Florida, 1997.

Goodman, L. W., Leogrande, W. M., and Mendelson Forman, J. (Eds). *Political Parties and Democracy in Central America*. Boulder, CO, Westview Press, 1992.

Greentree, T. R. *Crossroads of Intervention: Insurgency and Counterinsurgency Lessons from Central America*. Santa Barbara, CA, Praeger Security International, 2008.

Holden, R. H. *Armies Without Nations: Public Violence and State Formation in Central America, 1821–1960*. Oxford, Oxford University Press, 2006.

Horton, L. R. *Grassroots Struggles for Sustainability in Central America*. Boulder, CO, University Press of Colorado, 2007.

Karnes, T. L. *The Failure of Union in Central America, 1824–1960*. Chapel Hill, NC, University of North Carolina Press, 2012.

Keeley, J. *Containing the Communists: America's Foreign Policy Entanglements*. San Diego, CA, Lucent Books, 2003.

Krenn, M. L. *The Chains of Interdependence: US Policy toward Central America, 1945–1954*. Armonk, NY, M. E. Sharpe, 1996.

Krujit, D. *Guerrillas: War and Peace in Central America*. London, Zed Books, 2008.

Landau, S. *The Guerrilla Wars of Central America: Nicaragua, El Salvador, and Guatemala*. London, Weidenfeld & Nicolson, 1993.

Lehoucq, F. *The Politics of Modern Central America: Civil War, Democratization, and Underdevelopment*. Cambridge, Cambridge University Press, 2012.

Mahoney, J. *The Legacies of Liberalism: Path Dependence and Political Regimes in Central America*. Baltimore, MD, Johns Hopkins University Press, 2002.

Meara, W. R. *Contra Cross: Insurgency and Tyranny in Central America, 1979-1989*. Annapolis, MD, Naval Institute Press, 2006.

Paige, J. M. *Coffee and Power: Revolution and the Rise of Democracy in Central America*. Cambridge, MA, Harvard University Press, 1998.

Pearce, J. *The Report of the President's National Bipartisan Commission on Central America*. London, Collier Macmillan, 1984.

Pérez-Brignoli, H. *A Brief History of Central America*. Berkeley, CA, University of California Press, 1989.

Putnam, L. *The Company They Kept: Migrants and the Politics of Gender in Caribbean Costa Rica, 1870–1960*. Chapel Hill, NC, University of North Carolina Press, 2002.

Rockwell, R. J., and Janus, N. *Media Power in Central America*. Champaign, IL, University of Illinois Press, 2003.

Roniger, L. *Transnational Politics in Central America*. Gainesville, FL, University Press of Florida, 2013.

Rosenberg, M. B., and Solís-Rivera, L. G. *United States and Central America: Geopolitical Realities and Regional Fragility*. Abingdon, Routledge, 2007.

Saint-Germain, M. A., and Chávez Metoyer, C. *Women Legislators in Central America: Politics, Democracy, and Policy*. Austin, TX, University of Texas Press, 2008.

Sánchez Sánchez, R. *The Politics of Central American Integration*. Abingdon, Routledge, 2012.

Sandoval-García, C. *Threatening Others: Nicaraguans and the Formation of National Identities in Costa Rica*. Columbus, OH, Ohio University Press, 2004.

Scranton, M. E. *The Noriega Years: US-Panamanian Relations, 1981–1990*. Boulder, CO, Lynne Rienner Publrs, 1991.

Sieder, R. (Ed.). *Central America: Fragile Transition*. London and Basingstoke, Macmillan with Institute of Latin American Studies Series, 1996.

Torres-Rivas, E. *Repression and Resistance: The Struggle for Democracy in Central America*. Boulder, CO, Westview Press, 1989.

Tulchin, J. S., and Garland, A. M. (Eds). *Social Development in Latin America: The Politics of Reform*. Boulder, CO, Lynne Rienner Publrs, 2000.

Vilas, C. *Between Earthquakes and Volcanoes, Market, State, and the Revolutions in Central America*. New York, Monthly Review Press, 1995.

Wearne, P., and Menchu, R. *Return of the Indian: Conquest and Revival in the Americas*. Philadelphia, PA, Temple University Press, 1996.

Wiarda, H. J. (Ed.). *US Policy in Central America: Consultant Papers for the Kissinger Commission*. Washington, DC, American Enterprise Institute for Public Policy Research, 1984.

The Caribbean

Adler-Nissen, R., and Gad, U. (Eds). *European Integration and Post-Colonial Sovereignty Games*. Abingdon, Routledge, 2012.

Ahmed, B., and Afroz, S. *The Political Economy of Food and Agriculture in the Caribbean*. Kingston, Ian Randle Publrs, 1996.

Ayala, C. J. *American Sugar Kingdom: The Plantation Economy of the Spanish Caribbean 1898–1934*. Chapel Hill, NC, University of North Carolina Press, 1999.

Baker, G. (Ed.). *No Island is an Island: The Impact of Globalization on the Commonwealth Caribbean*. London, Chatham House, 2007.

Baldacchino, G. *Island Enclaves: Offshoring Strategies, Creative Governance, and Subnational Island Jurisdictions*. Montreal, QC, McGill-Queen's University Press, 2010.

Barnes, N. *Cultural Conundrums: Gender, Race, Nation, and the Making of Caribbean Cultural Politics*. Ann Arbor, MI, University of Michigan Press, 2006.

Besson, J., and Momsen, J. (Eds). *Caribbean Land and Development Revisited*. Basingstoke, Palgrave Macmillan, 2007.

Braveboy-Wagner, J. A. *Small States in Global Affairs: The Foreign Policies of the Caribbean Community (CARICOM)*. Basingstoke, Palgrave Macmillan, 2008.

Bulmer-Thomas, V. *The Economic History of the Caribbean since the Napoleonic Wars*. Cambridge, Cambridge University Press, 2012.

Burton, R. D. E., and Reno, F. (Eds). *French and West Indian: Martinique, Guadeloupe, and French Guiana Today*. Charlottesville, VA, University of Virginia Press, 2006.

Chamberlain, M. (Ed.). *Caribbean Migration: Globalised Identities*. London, Routledge, 1998.

Clegg, P. (Ed.). *Governance in the Non-independent Caribbean: Challenges and Opportunities in the Twenty-first Century*. Kingston, Ian Randle Publrs, 2009.

Clegg, P., and Killingray, D. (Eds). *The Non-Independent Territories of the Caribbean and Pacific: Continuity and Change*. London, Institute of Commonwealth Studies, 2012.

Craton, M. and the Cayman Islands New History Committee. *A History of the Cayman Islands and Their Peoples*. Kingston, Ian Randle Publrs, 2004.

Desch, M. C., Domínguez, J. I., Serbin, A. (Eds). *From Pirates to Druglords, the Post-Cold War Caribbean Security Environment*. Oxford, Heinemann, 1998.

Domínguez, J. I. *Democratic Politics in Latin America and the Caribbean*. Baltimore, MD, Johns Hopkins University Press, 1998.

Dubois, L. *A Colony of Citizens: Revolution and Slave Emancipation in the French Caribbean, 1787–1804*. Chapel Hill, NC, University of North Carolina Press, 2004.

Dunn, H. S. (Ed.). *Globalization, Communications and Caribbean Identity*. Kingston, Ian Randle Publrs, 1995.

Flint, A. *Trade, Poverty and The Environment: The EU, Cotonou and the African-Caribbean-Pacific Bloc*. Basingstoke, Palgrave Macmillan, 2008.

Forte, M. C. *Indigenous Resurgence in the Contemporary Caribbean: Amerindian Survival and Revival*. New York, Peter Lang Publishing, 2006.

Frazier, E. F., and Williams, E. *The Economic Future of the Caribbean*. Dover, MA, Majority Press, 2004.

Gaspar, D. B., and Geggus, D. P. (Eds). *A Turbulent Time: The French Revolution and the Greater Caribbean*. Bloomington, IN, Indiana University Press, 1997.

Gibson, C. *Empire's Crossroads: A History of the Caribbean from Columbus to the Present Day*. Basingstoke, Macmillan, 2014.

Gleijeses, P. *The Dominican Crisis: The 1965 Constitutional Revolt and American Intervention*. Baltimore, MD, Johns Hopkins University Press, 1979.

Griffith, I. L., and Sedoc-Dahlberg, B. N. (Eds). *Democracy and Human Rights in the Caribbean*. Boulder, CO, Westview Press, 1997.

Grossman, L. S. *The Political Ecology of Bananas, Contract Farming, Peasants and Agrarian Change in the Eastern Caribbean*. Chapel Hill, NC, University of North Carolina Press, 1998.

Gruegel, J. *Politics and Development in the Caribbean Basin: Central America and the Caribbean in the New World Order*. Basingstoke, Palgrave Macmillan, 1995.

Hall, K., and Benn, D. (Eds). *Contending with Destiny: The Caribbean in the 21st Century*. Kingston, Ian Randle Publrs, 2000.

Hallward, P. *Damming the Flood: Haiti, Aristide, and the Politics of Containment*. London, Verso, 2008.

Harrison, M. *King Sugar: Jamaica, the Caribbean and the World Sugar Industry*. New York, New York University Press, 2001.

Hendry, I., and Dickson, S. *British Overseas Territories Law*. Oxford, Hart Publishing, 2011.

Hennessy, A. (Ed.). *Intellectuals in the Twentieth Century Caribbean—Unity in Variety*, Vol. II: *The Hispanic and Francophone Caribbean*. Basingstoke, Macmillan, 1992.

Hepburn, E., and Baldacchino, G. (Eds). *Independence Movements in Subnational Island Jurisdictions*. Abingdon, Routledge, 2013.

Heron, T. *The New Political Economy of United States-Caribbean Relations: The Apparel Industry and the Politics of Nafta Parity*. Aldershot, Ashgate Publishing, 2004.

Hodge, A. *The Caribbean*. Hove, East Sussex, Macdonald Young, 1998.

Holme, P. *Colonial Encounters: Europe and the Native Caribbean 1492–1797*. London, Methuen, 1986.

Jayawardena, C. (Ed.). *Caribbean Tourism: More Than Sun, Sand and Sea*. Kingston, Ian Randle Publrs, 2006.

Klak, T. *Globalization and Neoliberalism: The Caribbean Context*. Lanham, MD, Rowman & Littlefield Publrs, 1998.

Klein, A., Harriott, A., and Day, M. (Eds). *Caribbean Drugs: From Criminalization to Harm Reduction*. London, Zed Books, 2004.

Klein, H. S. *African Slavery in Latin America and the Caribbean*. New York, Oxford University Press, 1986.

Lewis, G. K., and Maingot, A. P. *Main Currents in Caribbean Thought: The Historical Evolution of Caribbean Society in its Ideo-logical Aspects, 1492–1900*. Lincoln, NE, University of Nebraska Press, 2004.

Mandle, J. R. *Persistent Underdevelopment: Change and Economic Modernization in the West Indies*. Newark, NJ, Gordon & Breach, 1996.

Mars, P., and Young, A. H. *Caribbean Labor and Politics: Legacies of Cheddi Jagan and Michael Manley*. Detroit, MI, Wayne State University Press, 2004.

Marshall, D. D. *Caribbean Political Economy at the Crossroads: NAFTA and Regional Developmentalism*. Basingstoke, Macmillan, 1998.

Martínez-Fernández, L. *Protestantism and Political Conflict in the Nineteenth-Century Hispanic Caribbean*. Piscataway, NJ, Rutgers University Press, 2002.

Moberg, M. *Slipping Away: Banana Politics and Fair Trade in the Eastern Caribbean*. Oxford, Berghahn Books, 2010.

Mora, F. O., and Hey, J. A. K. (Eds). *Latin America and Caribbean Foreign Policy*. Lanham, MD, Rowman and Littlefield Publrs, 2003.

Olwig, K. F. (Ed.). *Small Islands, Large Questions: Society, Culture and Resistance in the Post-Emancipation Caribbean*. London, Frank Cass, 1995.

Oostindie, G., and Klinkers, I. *Decolonising the Caribbean. Dutch Policies in a Comparative Perspective*. Amsterdam, Amsterdam University Press, revised edn, 2014.

Palmer, C. A. *Eric Williams and the Making of the Modern Caribbean*. Chapel Hill, NC, University of North Carolina Press, 2006.

Palmer, R. W. (Ed.). *US-Caribbean Relations, Their Impact on Peoples and Culture*. Westport, CT, Greenwood Press, 1998.

Pattullo, P. *Last Resorts*. London, Cassell, 1996.

Fire from the Mountain: The Story of the Montserrat Volcano. London, Constable and Co Ltd, 2000.

Payne, A., and Sutton, P. (Eds). *Modern Caribbean Politics*. Baltimore, MD, Johns Hopkins University Press, 1993.

Potter, R. B. *The Contemporary Caribbean*. Harlow, Prentice Hall, 2004.

Puri, S. (Ed.). *The Legacies of Caribbean Radical Politics*. Abingdon, Routledge, 2010.

Randall, S. J., and Mount, G. S. *The Caribbean Basin: An International History*. London, Routledge, 1998.

Reinhart, C. *Claims to Memory: Beyond Slavery and Emancipation in the French Caribbean*. Oxford, Berghahn, 2008.

Richardson, B. C. *The Caribbean in the Wider World, 1492–1992: A Regional Geography*. Cambridge, Cambridge University Press, 1992.

Economy and Environment in the Caribbean. Jamaica, University of the West Indies Press, 1997.

Ritter, A. R. M., and Kirk, J. M. *Cuba in the International System: Normalization and Integration*. London, Macmillan, 1995.

Sanders, R. *Crumbled Small: The Commonwealth Caribbean in World Politics*. London, Hansib Publishing (Caribbean) Ltd, 2005.

Sutton, P. *Dual Legacies in the Contemporary Caribbean: Continuing Aspects of British and French Domination*. London, Frank Cass, 1986.

Thomas-Hope, E. M. (Ed.). *Explanation in Caribbean Migration, Perception and the Image: Jamaica, Barbados, Saint Vincent*. London, Macmillan, 1992.

Thompson, A. O. *The Haunting Past: Politics, Economics and Race in Caribbean Life*. Oxford, James Curry Publrs, 1997.

Williams, E. E. *From Columbus to Castro: The History of the Caribbean 1492-1969*. London, André Deutsch, 1970.

Wright, T. C. *Latin America in the Era of the Cuban Revolution*. New York, Praeger Publrs, 2000.

Wucker, M. *Why the Cocks Fight: Dominicans, Haitians, and the Struggle for Hispaniola*. New York, Hill & Wang Publishing, 2000.

SELECT BIBLIOGRAPHY (PERIODICALS)

AméricaEconomía: Santiago, Chile; tel. (2) 290-9400; internet www .americaeconomia.com; f. 1986; Latin American business, economics and finance; Spanish; monthly; Editorial Dir FELIPE ALDUNATE.

Américas Magazine: Organization of American States, Suite 300, 1889 F St, NW, Washington, DC 20006, USA; tel. (202) 458-3000; fax (202) 458-6217; e-mail americasmagazine@oas.org; internet www .oas.org/americas; f. 1949; culture, history, literature, travel, art, music, book reviews, Inter-American System; English and Spanish edns; Man. Editor CHRIS SHELL; 6 a year.

Anuario de Estudios Americanos: Escuela de Estudios Hispano-Americanos, Alfonso XII, 16, 41002 Seville, Spain; tel. (95) 4501120; fax (95) 4224331; e-mail anuario@eehaa.csic.es; internet www.estudiosamericanos.revistas.csic.es/index.php/estudiosameri-canos; f. 1944; humanities and social sciences of the Americas; Spanish, Portuguese, English and French; Editor-in-Chief CONSUELA VARELA; 2 a year.

Anuario de Estudios Centroamericanos: Editorial de la Universidad de Costa Rica, Apdo 75, 2060 Ciudad Unversitaria Rodrigo Facio, San José, Costa Rica; tel. 2207-3505; e-mail oscarf@cariari.ucr.ac.cr; internet cariari.ucr.ac.cr/~anuario/index.html; f. 1974; published by the Social Sciences Research Institute of the University of Costa Rica; history, society, politics and economics relating to Central America; Spanish; Dir EUGENIA IBARRA; Editor RONALD SOLANO; 2 a year.

Anuario Indigenista: Nubes 232, Col. Pedregal de San Angel, México, DF, Mexico; tel. (55) 5568-0819; fax (55) 5652-1274; f. 1962; Indians of the Americas, policies, anthropology, government, minorities; Spanish, Portuguese; Dir JOSÉ MATOS MAR (Instituto Indigenista Inter-americano); annual.

Apuntes del CENES: Centro de Estudios Económicos—CENES, Universidad Pedagógica y Tecnológica de Colombia, Apdo Aéreo 1234, Carretera Central del Norte, Tunja, Boyacá, Colombia; tel. and fax (87) 44-1550; e-mail luvallejo1@hotmail.com; internet www .apuntesdelcenes.org; f. 1981; national economic and development studies, politics and culture; Spanish; Editor LUIS EUDORO VALLEJO ZAMUDIO; 2 a year.

Archivo Ibero Americano: Joaquín Costa 36, 28002 Madrid, Spain; tel. (91) 5619900; f. 1914; history of Spain and Hispanic America, mainly relating to the Franciscan Order; quarterly.

¡Basta!: Chicago Religious Task Force on Central America, Suite 1400, 59 East Van Buren, Chicago, IL 60605, USA; tel. (312) 663-4398; fax (312) 427-4171; f. 1984; analysis of social and political events in Central America: theological debate, news and information; English; 3 a year.

Boletín de la Academia Nacional de la Historia: Avda Universidad, Bolsa a San Francisco, Caracas, Venezuela; tel. (212) 482-2706; fax (212) 482-6720; e-mail admite@an-historia.org.ar; f. 1924; history of the Americas, functions principally as review of activities of the Academia Nacional de la Historia; Spanish; annual.

Boletín Americanista: Universitat de Barcelona, Facultat de Geografia i Història, Departament d'Anthropologia Social i d'Historia d'Amèrica i d'Africa, Montagegre 6, 08001 Barcelona, Spain; tel. (93) 4037767; fax (93) 4037774; e-mail pgarciajordan@ub.edu; internet www.raco.cat/index.php/BoletinAmericanista; f. 1959; anthropology, economics, geography, history of America; Spanish, English and French; Editor PILAR GARCÍA JORDÁN; 2 a year.

Brazil: Brasília, DF, Brazil; tel. (61) 223-5180; deals with trade and industry of Brazil and is published by Fundação Visconde de Cabo Frio under the auspices of the Trade Promotion Department of the Ministry of Foreign Affairs and of the Vice-Presidency of Resources and Operations of the Banco do Brasil; Editor FERNANDO LUZ; Portuguese, German and French edns (quarterly), English and Spanish edns (monthly).

Bulletin of Hispanic Studies: Liverpool University Press, 4 Cambridge St, Liverpool, L69 7ZU, United Kingdom; tel. and fax (151) 794-3135; fax (151) 794-2235; e-mail clare.hooper@liv.ac.uk; internet www.liverpooluniversitypress.co.uk; f. 1923; language, literature and civilization of Spain, Portugal and Latin America; mainly English and Spanish, occasionally Portuguese, Catalan and French; Gen. Editor Dr CLAIRE TAYLOR; quarterly.

Bulletin de l'Institut Français d'Etudes Andines: IFEA, Ave Arequipa 4500, Lima 18, Peru; tel. (1) 4476070; fax (1) 4457650; e-mail secretariat@ifea.org.pe; internet www.ifeanet.org; f. 1972; human and social sciences in the Andes; French, Spanish and English; Editor ANNE-MARIE BROUGÈRE; 3 a year.

Bulletin of Latin American Research: Wiley-Blackwell Publishing, 9600 Garsington Rd, Oxford, OX4 2DQ, United Kingdom; tel. (1865) 776868; fax (1865) 714591; internet www.blackwellpublishing.com/ blar; on behalf of The Society for Latin American Studies; current interest research in social sciences and humanities; English; Editors DAVID HOWARD, GEOFFREY KANTARIS, TONY KAPCIA, JASMINE GIDEON, LUCY TAYLOR; quarterly.

Bulletin of Spanish Studies: Hispanic Studies and Researches on Spain, Portugal and Latin America: Routledge, Taylor & Francis, 4 Park Sq., Milton Park, Abingdon, Oxon, OX14 4RN, United Kingdom; tel. (20) 7017-6000; fax (20) 7017-6336; e-mail authorqueries@ tandf.co.uk; internet www.tandf.co.uk/journals/cbhs; f. 1923; fmrly Bulletin of Hispanic Studies; publ. by University of Glasgow; language, literature, history and civilization of Spain, Portugal and Latin America; mainly English and Spanish, occasionally Portuguese, Catalan and French; Gen. Editors Prof. ANN L. MACKENZIE, JAMES WHISTON, JULIA BIGGANE, ISABEL TORRES; 8 a year.

Cahiers des Amériques Latines: Institut des Hautes Etudes de l'Amérique Latine, 28 rue Saint-Guillaume, 75007 Paris, France; tel. 1-44-39-86-60; fax 1-45-48-79-58; e-mail iheal@univ-paris3.fr; f. 1968; political science, economy, urbanism, geography, history, sociology, ethnology, etc; mainly French, but also Spanish and English; 3 a year.

Canadian Journal of Latin American and Caribbean Studies (CJLACS): University of Guelph, College of Arts, MacKinnon, 279 Ontario, N1G 2W1, Canada; tel. (514) 343-6569; fax (514) 343-7716; e-mail rogomez@uoguelph.ca; internet www.can-latam.org; f. 1976; political, economic, cultural, etc; English, French, Portuguese and Spanish; Editor CATHERINE KRULL; 2 a year.

Caribbean Affairs: 93 Frederick St, Port of Spain, Trinidad and Tobago; tel. 624-2477; fax 627-3013; f. 1988; business, political and social affairs of the Caribbean; English; Editor OWEN BAPTISTE; quarterly.

Caribbean Business: Casiano Communications, 1700 Fernández Juncos Ave, San Juan, PR 00909, Puerto Rico; tel. 728-3000; fax 268-1001; internet www.casiano.com/html/cb.html; f. 1975; business and finance; English; Man. Editor MANUEL A. CASIANO, Jr; weekly.

Caribbean Handbook: FT Caribbean (BVI) Ltd, 19 Mercers Rd, London, N19 4PH, United Kingdom; tel. (20) 7281-5746; fax (20) 7281-7157; e-mail ftcaribbean@btinternet.com; internet www .candoo.com/ftcarribean; f. 1983; business, economic and political information on the Caribbean region, including country profiles; English; Editor LINDSAY MAXWELL; annual.

Caribbean Insight: c/o Caribbean Council, Temple Chambers, 3–7 Temple Ave, London, EC4Y 0HP, United Kingdom; tel. (20) 7283-8739; fax (20) 7583-9552; e-mail insight@caribbean-council.org; internet www.caribbean-council.org; f. 1978; business, political and social; English; Publr DAVID JESSOP; Assoc. Editor DEBBIE RANSOME; weekly.

Caribbean Investor and the CAIC Times: Caribbean Asscn of Industry and Commerce, 27A Saddle Rd, Maraval, Trinidad & Tobago; tel. 628-9859; fax 622-7810; e-mail caic.admin@gmail.com; internet www.caic.org.tt; finance and trading; Pres. CAROL EVELYN; quarterly.

Caribbean Quarterly: University of the West Indies, POB 130, Kingston 7, Jamaica; tel. 970-3261; fax 970-3261; e-mail cquarterlyedit@gmail.com; internet www.uwi.edu/cq; f. 1949; general; English; Editor KIM ROBINSON-WALCOTT; quarterly.

Caribbean Review: 9700 SW 67th Ave, Miami, FL 33156-3272, USA; tel. (305) 284-8466; fax (305) 284-1019; f. 1969; all subjects relating to the Caribbean, Latin America and their emigrant groups; quarterly; Editor BARRY B. LEVINE.

Caribbean Studies: Institute of Caribbean Studies, POB 23345, University Station, Río Piedras, PR 00931, Puerto Rico; tel. (787) 764-0000; fax (787) 764-3099; e-mail viiglesias@rrpac.upr.clu.edu; Caribbean affairs; English; Editor OSCAR MENDOZA RIOLLANO; 2 a year.

Caribbean Update: 116 Myrtle Ave, Millburn, NJ 07041, USA; tel. (973) 376-2314; e-mail kalwagenheim@cs.com; internet www .caribbeanupdate.org; f. 1985; business and economic news and opportunities in the Caribbean and Central America; English; Editor and Publr KAL WAGENHEIM; monthly.

Carta Internacional: Programa de Pesquisa de Relações Internacionais, Universidade de São Paulo, Rua do Anfiteatro 181, Colméia, Cidade Universitária, 05508-900 São Paulo, SP, Brazil; tel. (11) 3091-3046; fax (11) 3091-3044; e-mail nupri@edu.usp.br; internet www .usp.br/cartainternacional; Brazilian foreign and economic policy, regional integration, NAFTA and Mercosur; English, Portuguese and Spanish; Dir Prof. Dr JOSÉ AUGUSTO GUILHON ALBUQUERQUE; monthly.

Central America Report: Inforpress Centroamericana, Calle Mariscal o Diagonal 21 6-58 Zona 11, Guatemala City, Guatemala; tel. 2473-7001; fax 2473-2231; e-mail inforpre@inforpressca.com; internet www.inforpressca.com/CAR; f. 1972; review of economics and politics of Central America; English; Dir MATTHEW CREELMAN; weekly.

CEPAL Review/Revista de la CEPAL: Casilla 179-D, Santiago, Chile; tel. (2) 2102000; fax (2) 2080252; e-mail revista@eclac.cl; internet www.cepal.org; f. 1976; a publication of the UN Economic Commission for Latin America and the Caribbean dealing with socio-economic topics; English and Spanish; Chair. of Editorial Council OSVALDO SUNKEL; Dir ANDRÉ A. HOFMAN; 3 a year.

Colombia Internacional: Centro de Estudios Internacionales, Universidad de los Andes, Calle 19, No 1–46, Apdo 4976, Bogotá, Colombia; tel. (1) 286-7504; fax (1) 284-1890; e-mail edrodrig@uniandes.edu.co; internet colombiainternacional.uniandes.edu.co; f. 1988; international co-operation, Latin American integration, drugs-trafficking controls; Spanish; Editors LAURA WILLS, MIGUEL GARCÍA; quarterly.

Colonial Latin American Review: Routledge, Taylor & Francis, 4 Park Sq., Milton Park, Abingdon, Oxon, OX14 4RN, United Kingdom; tel. (20) 7017-6000; fax (20) 7017-6336; e-mail authorqueries@tandf.co.uk; internet www.tandf.co.uk/journals/ccla; f. 1992; colonial period in Latin America; English, with articles in Portuguese and Spanish; Gen. Editor KRIS LANE; 3 a year.

Comercio Exterior: Banco Nacional de Comercio Exterior, Periférico Sur 4333, Col. Jardines en la Montaña, 14210 México, DF, Mexico; tel. (55) 5449-9000; e-mail revcomer@bancomext.gob.mx; internet www.bancomext.com; f. 1951; international trade, analysis of Latin America's economics, general economics; Spanish with English abstracts; monthly.

Contexto Internacional: Instituto de Relações Internacionais, Pontifíca Universidade Católica de Rio de Janeiro, Rua Marquês de São Vicente 225, Gávea, 22453-900 Rio de Janeiro, RJ, Brazil; tel. and fax (21) 3527-1557; e-mail revistasonline@puc-rio.br; internet contextointernacional.iri.puc-rio.br; international relations, Brazilian foreign policy, Latin American and European integration, US-Latin American relations; Portuguese; Editor MÔNICA HERZ; 2 a year.

Cronología de las Relaciones Internacionales del Peru: Peruvian Centre for International Studies, San Ignacio de Loyola 554, Miraflores 8, Lima 18, Peru; tel. (1) 4457225; fax (1) 4451094; economic and political international relations of Peru; Spanish; quarterly.

Cuadernos de Economía (Latin American Journal of Economics): Instituto de Economía, Pontificia Universidad Católica de Chile, Avda Vicuña Mackenna 4860, Macul, Santiago, Chile; tel. (2) 3544303; fax (2) 5536472; e-mail cuadecon@faceapuc.cl; internet www.cuadernosdeeconomia.cl; f. 1963; applied economics as contribution to economic policy, with special emphasis in Latin America; Spanish, with English abstracts; Editors RAIMUNDO SOTO, FELIPE ZURITA; 2 a year.

Cuadernos Hispanoamericanos: Avda de los Reyes Católicos 4, 28040 Madrid, Spain; tel. (91) 5838399; e-mail cuadernos@hispanoamericanosaeci.es; f. 1948; humanities, particularly relating to Hispanic America; Spanish; Dir BENJAMÍN PRADO; monthly.

Cuba Update: Center for Cuban Studies, 124 West 23rd St, New York, NY 10011, USA; tel. (212) 242-0559; fax (212) 242-1937; e-mail cubanctr@igc.org; internet www.cubaupdate.org; f. 1977; Cuban foreign affairs, culture and development; English; Editor SANDRA LEVINSON; quarterly.

The Developing Economies: Nihon Boeki Shinkokiko Ajia Keizai Kenkyusho (Institute of Developing Economies, Japan External Trade Organization—JETRO), 3-2-2 Wakaba, Mihama-ku, Chiba-shi, Chiba 261-8545, Japan; tel. (43) 299-9500; fax (43) 299-9726; internet www.ide.go.jp; f. 1962; quarterly; Editor SHUJIRO URATA.

Development Policy Review: Overseas Development Institute, 111 Westminster Bridge Rd, London, SE1 7JD, United Kingdom; tel. (20) 7922-0300; fax (20) 7922-0399; e-mail publications@odi.org.uk; internet www.odi.org.uk; f. 1982; Editor PILAR DOMINGO; 6 a year.

Economia Brasileira e Suas Perspectivas: Associação Promotora de Estudos de Economia, Rua Sorocaya 295, Botafogo, Rio de Janeiro, RJ, Brazil; fax (21) 266-3597; f. 1962; Brazilian economic issues, published by the Assen for the Promotion of Economic Studies; Portuguese and English; annual.

Economía Mexicana Nueva Época: Centro de Investigación y Docencia Económicas—CIDE, Carretera México-Toluca 3655 (km 16.5), Col. Lomas de Santa Fe, Del. Alvaro Obregón, 01210 México, DF, Mexico; tel. (55) 5727-9800; fax (55) 5727-9878; e-mail ecomex@cide .edu; internet www.economiamexicana.cide.edu; f. 1992; economic problems in Mexico and Latin America; Spanish and English; Editor JUAN ROSELLÓN; 2 a year.

Economic Development and Cultural Change: University of Chicago Press, 1427 East 60th St, Chicago, IL 60637, USA; tel. (213) 702-7700; fax (213) 753-9756; e-mail edcc@press.uchicago.edu; internet www.journals.uchicago.edu/EDCC; f. 1952; multidisciplinary journal of development economics; English; Editor JOHN STRAUSS; quarterly.

Estudios de Cultura Maya: Centro de Estudios Mayas, Instituto de Investigaciones Filológicas, Circuito Mario de la Cueva, Ciudad Universitaria, 04510 México, DF, Mexico; tel. and fax (55) 5622-7490; e-mail cem@servidor.uma.mx; internet filologicas.unam.mx/indices/estculmay_col.htm; f. 1961; anthropology, archaeology, history, epigraphy and linguistics of the Mayan groups; Spanish, English and French; Editor MARICELA AYALA; 2 a year.

Estudios Económicos: Universidad Nacional del Sur, Departamento de Economía, 12 de Octubre y San Juan, B8000CTB Bahía Blanca, Argentina; tel. and fax (91) 25432; e-mail estudioseconomicos@uns .edu.ar; internet bibliotecadigital.uns.edu.ar/revistas/ee; f. 1962; Spanish; Editor ELENA O. DE GUEVARA; annual.

Estudios de Historia Moderna y Contemporánea de México: Instituto de Investigaciones Históricas, Circuito Metropolitano Mario de la Cueva, Del. Coyoacán, Ciudad Universitaria, 04510 México, DF, Mexico; tel. (55) 5622-7521; fax (55) 5622-7536; e-mail moderna@unam.mx; internet www.iih.unam.mx/moderna/index.html; f. 1967; history of Mexico from independence war (1810) to present; Spanish; Editor FELIPE ARTURO ÁVILA; 2 a year.

Estudios Internacionales: International Relations and Peace Research Institute, 1a Calle 9-52, Zona 1, 01001 Guatemala City, Guatemala; tel. 2232-8260; fax 2253-1532; e-mail iripaz@iripaz.org; internet www.iripaz.org; international relations; Spanish; 2 a year.

Estudios Internacionales: Institute of International Studies, University of Chile, Avda Condell 249, Casilla 14187, Santiago 9, Chile; tel. (2) 4961200; fax (2) 2740155; e-mail inesint@uchile.cl; internet www.iei.uchile.cl; f. 1966; contemporary international relations, particularly concerning Latin America; Spanish; Editor ROSE CAVE S.; quarterly.

Estudios Latinamericanos: Centro de Estudios Latinoamericanos, Facultad de Ciencias Políticas y Sociales, Universidad Nacional Autónoma de México, 04510 México, DF, Mexico; tel. (55) 5622-9417; fax (55) 5622-9427; e-mail gserrato@servidor.unam.mx; internet www.catalogoderevistas.unam.mx; f. 1985; contemporary international relations, primarily concerning Latin America; Spanish; Dir JOSÉ MIGUEL CANDIA; 2 a year.

Estudios Políticos: Facultad de Ciencias Políticas y Sociales, Universidad Nacional Autónoma de México, Ciudad Universitaria, Apdo 70-266, 04510 México, DF, Mexico; tel. (55) 5622-9419; e-mail revistaestudiospoliticos@yahoo.com.mx; internet www.journals .unam.mx; f. 1975; political philosophy, social sciences, political science; Spanish; Editor JUAN PABLO ROMERO ROISIN; Dir MARÍA MARCELA AHUJA RUIZ; quarterly.

Estudios Públicos: Centro de Estudios Públicos, Monseñor Sótero Sanz 162, Santiago, Chile; tel. (2) 3282441; fax (2) 3282440; e-mail biblioteca@cepchile.cl; internet www.cepchile.cl; f. 1980; forum of ideas and commentary on diverse issues in Latin America, incl. philosophy and literature, economics, politics and sociology; English, Spanish; Dir ARTURO FONTAINE; quarterly.

Estudios Sociales: Almirante Pastene 7, Depto 51, Providencia, Santiago, Chile; tel. (2) 2369329; fax (2) 2369008; e-mail cpu@cpu .cl; internet www.cpu.cl; f. 1973; sociology, history, anthropology, economics, political science, education, philosophy, social psychology, law; Spanish; Editor RAÚL ATRIA; 2 a year.

EURE Revista Latinoamericana de Estudios Urbanos y Regionales: Instituto de Estudios Urbanos, Universidad Católica de Chile, Casilla 16002, Correo 9, Santiago, Chile; tel. (2) 365511; fax (2) 2328805; e-mail eure@eure.cl; internet www.eure.cl; f. 1970; urban and regional development in Latin America; Spanish, with English abstracts; Dir PEDRO BANNEN; quarterly.

European Review of Latin American and Caribbean Studies/Revista Europea de Estudios Latinoamericanos y del Caribe: Centre for Latin American Research and Documentation (CEDLA), Keizersgracht 395-397, 1016 EK Amsterdam, Netherlands; tel. (20) 525-34-98; fax (20) 625-51-27; e-mail nalacs@cedla.nl; internet www.cedla.uva.nl; f. 1989; social scientific and historical research on Latin America and the Caribbean (anthropology, economics, geography, history, politics, sociology, etc.); English and Spanish; Man. Editor Prof. Dr MICHIEL BAUD; 2 a year.

FIDE, Coyuntura y Desarrollo: Development Research Foundation—FIDE, Avda 538, C1032ABS Buenos Aires, Argentina; tel. and fax (11) 4964-3331; e-mail info@fide.com.ar; internet www.fide .com.ar; national and international socio-economic analysis and economic theory; Spanish; Dir MERCEDES MARCÓ DEL PONT; monthly.

Foro Internacional: Colegio de México, Camino al Ajusco 20, Col. Pedregal de Santa Teresa, 10740 México, DF, Mexico; tel. (5) 5449-3013; fax (5) 5645-0464; e-mail revfi@colmex.mx; internet revistas .colmex.mx; f. 1960; international relations, Latin American politics, comparative politics; Mexican politics, public administration and public policy; Spanish, with English abstracts; Dir REYNALDO YUNUEN ORTEGA ORTIZ; quarterly.

Fuerzas Armadas y Sociedad: Latin American Faculty of Social Sciences—FLACSO Chile, Avda Dag Hammarskjöld 3269, Vitacura, Santiago; tel. 2900200; fax 2900270; e-mail flacso@flacso.cl; internet www.fasoc.cl/php/fasoc.php; military affairs and international relations; Spanish; quarterly.

GIGA Focus Lateinamerika: GIGA—German Institute of Global and Area Studies, 20354 Hamburg, 21 Neuer Jungfernstieg, Germany; tel. (40) 42825561; fax (40) 42825562; e-mail giga-focus@giga-hamburg.de; internet www.giga-hamburg.de/giga-focus/lateinamerika; f. 1962; political, economic and social development; German; Editor SABINE KURTENBACH; monthly.

Global Studies: Latin America: McGraw Hill Higher Education, 2 Penn Plaza, New York, NY 10121, USA; tel. (212) 904-2000; e-mail nichole_altman@mcgraw-hill.com; internet www.dushkin.com; f. 1991; articles on Mexico, Central America, South America and the Caribbean; English; Editor PAUL GOODWIN; every 2 years.

Handbook of Latin American Studies: University of Texas Press, POB 7819, Austin, TX 78713-7819; tel. (512) 471-7233; fax (512) 232-7178; e-mail utpress@uts.cc.utexas.edu; internet www.utexas.edu/utpress; f. 1936; edited by the Hispanic Division of the US Library of Congress; bibliography of Latin American articles and publications; Editor (Humanities) KATHERINE D. McCANN; Editor (Social Sciences) TRACY NORTH; annual, alternating between humanities and social science topics, online edn published weekly.

Hemisphere: Latin American and Caribbean Center, Florida International University, Modesto A. Maidique Campus, Miami, FL 11200, USA; tel. (305) 348-2894; fax (305) 348-3593; e-mail lacc@fiu.edu; internet lacc.fiu.edu; f. 1988; Latin American and Caribbean Affairs; English; Editor CRISTINA EGUIZÁBAL; 2 a year.

Hispanic American Historical Review (HAHR): Duke University, Dept of History, Carr Bldg 226, POB 90719, Durham, NC 27708, USA; tel. (919) 684-2103; e-mail hahr@duke.edu; internet www.dukeupress.edu; f. 1918; published in co-operation with the American Historial Asscn; Editors JOHN D. FRENCH, JOCELYN H. OLCOTT, PETER H. SIGAL; quarterly.

Historia: Casilla 6277, Santiago 22, Chile; tel. (2) 23547836; e-mail revhist@uc.cl; internet www.revistahistoria.uc.cl; f. 1961; publ. by the Pontífica Universidad Católica de Chile; history of Chile and related subjects; mainly Spanish; Editor JAIME VALENZUELA MÁRQUEZ; 2 a year.

Historia Mexicana: Colegio de México, Camino al Ajusco 20, Pedregal de Santa Teresa, 01000 México, DF, Mexico; tel. (55) 5449-3067; fax (55) 5645-0464; internet historiamexicana.colmex.mx; f. 1951; history of Mexico; Spanish; Editor OSCAR MAZÍN; quarterly.

Iberoamericana: 60594 Frankfurt am Main, Elisabethenstr. 3–9, Verlag Klaus Dieter Vervuert, Germany; tel. (69) 5974617; fax (69) 5978743; e-mail iberoamericana@iai.spk-berlin.de; internet www.iberoamericanalibros.com; f. 2001; comprises fmrly separate journals *Iberoamericana, Ibero-Amerikanisches Archiv* and *Notas*; Latin American literature, history and social sciences; Spanish, Portuguese, English and German; quarterly.

Iberoamericana: Nordic Journal of Latin American and Caribbean Studies: Institute of Latin American Studies, Stockholm University, Universitetsvägen 10B, 106 91 Stockholm, Sweden; tel. (8) 16-28-86; fax (8) 15-65-82; e-mail lai@lai.su.se; internet www.lai.su.se; f. 1960; articles on economic, political and local developments in Latin America and the Caribbean; English, Portuguese, Spanish; Chief Editor Prof. MONA ROSENDAHL; 2 a year.

Indicadores Económicos: Contraloría-General de la República, Avda Cuba y Ecuador, Calle 33A, Panamá, Panama; tel. 207-3400; fax 207-3422; e-mail comsocial@cwpanama.net; internet www.panacamara.com; f. 1996; economic indicators for Panama; Spanish; annual.

Industria: Sindicato de Industriales de Panamá, Apdo 6-4798, El Dorado, Panamá, Panama; tel. 230-0169; fax 230-0805; e-mail sip@cableonda.net; internet www.industriales.org; f. 1953; economics and industry in Panama; Spanish; Editor FLOR ORTEGA; quarterly.

Información Sistemática: Valencia 84, Insurgentes Mixcoac, Del. Benito Juárez, 03920 México, DF, Mexico; tel. (55) 5598-6043; e-mail bac@infosis21.com.mx; f. 1976; clippings archive since 1976; electronic database since 1988; research on media impact on public opinion and the correlation between media statistics and public opinion polls; daily summary and statistics of 11 newspapers; Spanish; Dirs BERNARDO AVALOS, LUPITA FLORES; customized frequency.

Information Services Latin America: POB 6103, Albany, CA 94706, USA; tel. (510) 526-4870; e-mail isla@lmi.net; internet www.igc.org/isla; f. 1970; selected articles from major daily news sources in the USA and the United Kingdom; English; online edn; Dir KAREN CRUMP; monthly.

Integración y Comercio (INTAL): Institute for the Integration of Latin America and the Caribbean, Esmeralda 130, 16°, CADB1035 Buenos Aires, Argentina; tel. (11) 4320-1850; fax (11) 4320-1865; e-mail intal@iadb.org; internet www.iabd.org/intal; f. 1965; Latin American integration; Spanish and English; Dir RICARDO CARCIOFI; 2 a year.

Integración Financiera—pasado, presente y futuro de las finanzas en Colombia y el mundo: Medios and Medios Publicidad Cía Ltda, No 11–45, Of. 802, Calle 63, Apdo 036943, Bogotá, DC, Colombia; tel. (1) 255-0992; fax (1) 249-4696; f. 1984; financial sector development in Colombia and the rest of Latin America; Spanish; Editor RAÚL RODRÍGUEZ PUERTO; 6 a year.

Investigaciones y Ensayos: Balcarce 139, C1064AAC Buenos Aires, Argentina; tel. and fax (11) 4343-4416; e-mail publicaciones@an-historia.org.ar; internet www.an-historia.org.ar; f. 1966; history of Argentina and the Americas; Spanish; published by the Academia Nacional de la Historia; Editorial Co-ordinator MARÍA SOL RUBIO GARCÍA; 2 a year.

Jahrbuch für Geschichte Lateinamerikas: 20146 Hamburg, Von-Melle-Park 6, Universität Hamburg Historisches Seminar, Germany; tel. (40) 428384839; fax (40) 428382371; e-mail ulrich.muecke@uni-hamburg.de; internet www-gewi.uni-graz.at/jbla; published by Böhlau-Verlag, Cologne and Vienna; f. 1964; political, economic, social and cultural history of Latin America from colonial period to present; articles in Spanish, English, French, German and Portuguese; Chief Editor Prof. Dr ULRICH MÜCKE; annual.

Journal of Development Studies: Routledge, Taylor & Francis, 4 Park Sq., Milton Park, Abingdon, Oxon, OX14 4RN, United Kingdom; tel. (20) 7017-6000; fax (20) 7017-6336; internet www.tandf.co.uk/journals; f. 1964; Editors OLIVER MORRISSEY, Dr RICHARD PALMER-JONES, KEN SHADLEN, HOWARD WHITE; monthly.

Journal of Iberian and Latin American Research: Routledge, Taylor & Francis, 4 Park Sq., Milton Park, Abingdon, Oxon, OX14 4RN, United Kingdom; tel. (20) 7017-6000; fax (20) 7017-6336; e-mail tf.enquiries@tandf.co.uk; internet www.tandfonline.com/rjil; f. 2010; research on the histories, political economies, sociologies, literatures, and cultures of Latin America and the Iberian peninsula; Man. Editors DAVID CAHILL, VEK LEWIS; 2 a year.

Journal of Iberian and Latin American Studies: Routledge, Taylor & Francis, 4 Park Sq., Milton Park, Abingdon, Oxon, OX14 4RN, United Kingdom; tel. (20) 7017-6000; fax (20) 7017-6336; e-mail tf.enquiries@tandf.co.uk; internet www.tandfonline.com/cjil; fmrly *Tesserae*; language, literature, history and culture of Latin America and Iberian peninsula; English, with articles in Catalan and Spanish; Editors JORDI LARIOS, MONTSERRAT LUNATI; 3 a year.

Journal of Latin American Cultural Studies (Travesia): Routledge, Taylor & Francis, 4 Park Sq., Milton Park, Abingdon, Oxon, OX14 4RN, United Kingdom; tel. (20) 7017-6000; fax (20) 7017-6336; e-mail authorqueries@tandf.co.uk; internet www.tandf.co.uk/journals/cjla; f. 1992; history and analysis of Latin American culture; English; Editors JENS ANDERMANN, BEN BOLLIG, PHILLIP DERBYSHIRE, LORRAINE LEU, DANIEL MOSQUERA, RORY O'BRYEN, DAVID WOOD; 4 a year.

Journal of Latin American Studies: Cambridge University Press, The Edinburgh Bldg, Shaftesbury Rd, Cambridge, CB2 8RU, United Kingdom; tel. (1223) 326070; fax (1223) 325150; e-mail journals@cambridge.org; internet www.journals.cambridge.org/jid_LAS; Editors Dr GARETH JONES, Dr RORY MILLER, FIONA MACAULAY; 4 a year.

Journal of Politics in Latin America: GIGA—German Institute of Global and Area Studies, 20354 Hamburg, Neuer Jungfernstieg 21, Germany; tel. (40) 42825593; fax (40) 42825547; e-mail jpla@giga-hamburg.de; internet hup.sub.uni-hamburg.de/giga/jpla; f. 2009; fmrly Lateinamerika: Analysen; comparative politics and international relations of Latin America; English; Exec. Editor JORGE P. GORDIN; 3 a year.

Journal de la Société des Américanistes: Maison René-Ginouvès (Archéologie et Ethnologie), 21 allée de l'université, 92023 Nanterre, France; tel. 1-46-69-26-34; fax 1-46-69-25-08; e-mail jsa@mae.u-paris10.fr; internet jsa.revues.org; f. 1896; archaeology, ethnology, ethnohistory and linguistics of the American continent; French, Spanish, English and Portuguese; Editor DOMINIQUE MICHELET; annual.

Kañina: Revista de Artes y Letras: Facultad de Letras, Ciudad Universitaria Rodrigo Facio, Universidad de Costa Rica, San Pedro, San José, Costa Rica; tel. 2511-8402; e-mail kanina@ucr.ac.cr; internet www.latindex.ucr.ac.cr; f. 1977; arts and literature; mainly Spanish, but also French, English and Italian; Editor VICTOR SÁNCHEZ CORRALES; 2 a year.

Lateinamerika Anders: Informationsgruppe Lateinamerika, Währingerstrasse 59, 1090 Vienna, Austria; e-mail igla@aon.at; internet www.lateinamerika-anders.org; f. 1976; news and analysis of Latin American affairs; German; Editors LEO GABRIEL, RALF LEONHARD, ROBERT LESSMANN; 2 a year.

Latin American Business Review: Routledge, Taylor & Francis, 4 Park Sq., Milton Park, Abingdon, Oxon, OX14 4RN, United Kingdom; tel. (20) 7017-6000; fax (20) 7017-6336; e-mail tf.enquiries@

tandf.co.uk; internet www.tandf.co.uk/journals; f. 2008; Editor CARLOS HEITOR CAMPANI; 4 a year.

Latin America and Caribbean Contemporary Record: Holmes and Meier Publishers Inc, POB 943, Teaneck, NJ 07666, USA; tel. (201) 833-2270; fax (201) 833-2272; e-mail info@holmesandmeier.com; internet www.holmesandmeier.com; f. 1981; analysis of events and trends in Latin America and the Caribbean; English; Editors JAMES MALLOY, EDUARDO GAMARRA; annual.

Latin American and Caribbean Ethnic Studies: Routledge, Taylor & Francis, 4 Park Sq., Milton Park, Abingdon, Oxon, OX14 4RN, United Kingdom; tel. (20) 7017-6000; fax (20) 7017-6336; e-mail authorqueries@tandf.co.uk; internet www.tandf.co.uk/journals/rlac; f. 2006; ethnicity, race relations and indigenous peoples in Latin America and the Caribbean; Editor-in-Chief LEON ZAMOSC; 3 a year.

Latin American Economy and Business: Latin American Newsletters, 61 Old St, London, EC1V 9HW, United Kingdom; tel. (20) 7251-0012; fax (20) 7253-8193; e-mail subs@latinnews.com; internet www.latinnews.com; economic data and indicators; English; monthly.

Latin American Monitor: Business Monitor International, Senator House, 85 Queen Victoria St, London, EC4V 4AB, United Kingdom; tel. (20) 7248-0468; fax (20) 7248-0467; e-mail enquiries@latinamericamonitor.com; internet www.latinamericamonitor.com; publishes 6 regional reports covering Mexico, Brazil, Central America, Andean Group, Southern Cone and Caribbean; English; monthly.

Latin American Perspectives: University of California, POB 5703, Riverside, CA 92517-5703, USA; tel. (951) 827-1571; fax (951) 827-5685; e-mail laps@ucr.edu; internet www.latinamericanperspectives.com; economics, political science, international relations, philosophy, history, sociology, geography, anthropology and literature; English; Man. Editor RONALD H. CHILCOTE; 6 a year.

Latin American Politics and Society: Center for Latin American Studies, University of Miami, POB 248123, Coral Gables, FL 33124C, USA; tel. (305) 284-5554; fax (305) 284-2796; e-mail laps.sis@miami.edu; internet www.wiley.com/bw/journal.asp?ref=1531-426X; f. 1959; fmrly Journal of Interamerican Studies and World Affairs; Latin American comparative politics, democratization, Latin American-US relations; English; Editor WILLIAM C. SMITH; quarterly.

Latin American Regional Reports: Latin American Newsletters, 61 Old St, London, EC1V 9HW, United Kingdom; tel. (20) 7251-0012; fax (20) 7253-8193; e-mail subs@latinnews.com; internet www.latinnews.com; 4 regional reports covering Andean Group, Mexico and Nafta, Brazil and Southern Cone, and Caribbean and Central America; English; Publr JOE DE COURCY; monthly.

Latin American Research Review (LARR): Latin American Studies Asscn, 416 Bellefield Hall, University of Pittsburgh, Pittsburgh, PA 15260, USA; tel. (412) 648-7929; fax (514) 624-7145; e-mail lasa@pitt.edu; internet lasa.international.pitt.edu/eng/larr/index.asp; f. 1965; articles, research notes and essays dealing with contemporary issues; English, Spanish and Portuguese; Editor-in-Chief Dr PHILIP OXHORN; 3 a year.

Latin American Special Reports: Latin American Newsletters, 61 Old St, London, EC1V 9HW, United Kingdom; tel. (20) 7251-0012; fax (20) 7253-8193; e-mail subs@latinnews.com; internet www.latinnews.com; each edn provides detailed information on and analysis of one specific subject; English and Spanish; Editors EDUARDO CRAWLEY, JON FARMER, EILEEN GAVIN, SARAH SHELDON; 6 a year.

Latin American Weekly Report/Informe Latinoamericano: Latin American Newsletters, 61 Old St, London, EC1V 9HW, United Kingdom; tel. (20) 7251-0012; fax (20) 7253-8193; e-mail info@latinnews.com; internet www.latinnews.com; political, economic and general news; English and Spanish edns; Editor JON FARMER; weekly.

Lecturas de Economía: Centro de Investigaciones y Consultorías, Universidad de Antioquia, Calle 67, No 53–108, Bloque 13, Of. 121, Ciudad Universitaria, Medellín, Antioquia, Colombia; tel. (4) 219-5840; fax (4) 233-1249; e-mail lecturas@economicas.udea.edu.co; internet economicas.udea.edu.co/lecturas/rev_lectecono/rev_lectecono.html; f. 1980; economic issues; Spanish; Editor CATALINA GRANDA CARVAJAL; 2 a year.

Luso-Brazilian Review: University of Wisconsin Press, Journals Division, 1930 Monroe St, Madison, WI 53711, USA; tel. (608) 263-0668; fax (608) 263-1173; e-mail jlusobraz@mailplus.wisc.edu; internet uwpress.wisc.edu/journals/journals/lbr.html; f. 1964; history, social sciences and literature; English and Portuguese; Editors PETER M. BEATTIE, ELLEN W. SAPEGA, SEVERINO J. ALBUQUERQUE; 2 a year.

Memoria Anual de Fondo Latinamericano de Reservas (FLAR): Fondo Latinamericano de Reservas—FLAR, Bogotá, DC, Colombia; tel. (1) 285-8511; fax (1) 288-1117; internet www.flar.net; f. 1979;

economic summary of Bolivia, Colombia, Ecuador, Peru and Venezuela; Spanish and English; annual.

Mesoamérica: Tulane Univ., Dept of History, 6823 St Charles Ave, New Orleans, LA 70118, USA; tel. (504) 862-8630; fax (504) 862-8739; e-mail editors@mesoamericarevista.org; internet www.mesoamericarevista.org; f. 1980; Plumsock Mesoamerican Studies; anthropology, history, linguistics and social sciences of southern Mexico and Central America; Spanish; Editors JUSTIN WOLFE, AARON SCHNEIDER; annual.

Mexico Watch: Americas News Intel Publishing LLC, 2520 Coral Way, Miami, FL 33145, USA; e-mail jwright@latinintel.com; internet www.latinintel.com; politics, economics and business of Mexico; suspended in 2009, exists in archived form; English; Editor JEFFREY WRIGHT; monthly.

MicAméricas: 1300 New York Ave, NW, Washington, DC 20577, USA; tel. (202) 623-2791; e-mail micamericas@iadb.com; internet www.iadb.org/micamericas; research on the economic development of Latin America; supported by the Fondo Multilateral de Inversiones (FOMIN); Spanish; Editors-in-Chief SERGIO NAVAJAS, LENE MIKKELSEN.

Mundo Nuevo. Revista de Estudios Latínoamericanos: Universidad Simón Bolivar, Caracas 1080, Venezuela; tel. (212) 906-3809; internet www.iaeal.usb.ve; f. 1975; international relations, politics, economy of Latin America; Spanish, but some articles are published in their original languages, English, French and Portuguese; published by the Instituto de Altos Estudios de América Latina, Universidad Simón Bolívar; Dir Dr HÉCTOR MALDONADO LIRA; quarterly.

Mundus: Wissenschaftliche Verlagsgesellschaft GmbH, Birkenwaldstr. 44, 70191 Stuttgart, Germany; tel. (711) 25820; fax (711) 2582290; f. 1965; review of German research on Latin America, Asia and Africa; English; Editor JÜRGEN HOHNHOLZ (Institute for Scientific Co-operation); quarterly.

NACLA Report on the Americas: North American Congress on Latin America, 38 Greene St, 4th Floor, New York, NY 10013, USA; tel. (646) 613-1440; fax (646) 613-1443; e-mail mfox@nacla.org; internet www.nacla.org; f. 1967; publication of North American Congress on Latin America covering US foreign policy towards Latin America and the Caribbean, and domestic developments in the region; English; Editor MICHAEL FOX; 6 a year.

Negobancos—Negocios y Bancos: Insurgentes Sur N° 1442, Col. Actipan. Delegación Benito Juárez. CP 03230 México, DF, Mexico; tel. (55) 5524-0871; fax (55) 5534-9469; f. 1951; business and economics; Spanish; Dir ALFREDO FARRUGIA REED; fortnightly.

NotiCen: University of New Mexico, Latin American and Iberian Institute, Latin American Data Base, 801 Yale NE, Albuquerque, NM 87131, USA; tel. (505) 277-6839; fax (505) 277-5989; e-mail info@ladb.unm.edu; internet ladb.unm.edu/noticen; online news digest; sustainable development, economic and political affairs in Central America and the Caribbean; Editor CARLOS M. NAVARRO; weekly.

NotiSur: University of New Mexico, Latin American and Iberian Institute, Latin America Data Base, 801 Yale, NE, Albuquerque, NM 87131, USA; tel. (505) 277-6389; fax (505) 277-5989; e-mail info@ladb.unm.edu; internet ladb.unm.edu/notisur; online news digest; provides alternative viewpoints on political and economic affairs in South America, particularly on human rights and peace issues and sustainable development; English; Editor CARLOS M. NAVARRO; weekly.

Opciones: Territorial, esq. Gen Suárez, Plaza de la Revolución, Havana, Cuba; tel. (7) 881-8934; e-mail chabela@opciones.cu; internet www.opciones.cu; f. 1994; economics and politics; Spanish; weekly; Dir PELAYO TERRY.

Panorama Económico: Bancomer, SA, Grupo Investigaciones Económicas, Centro Bancomer, Avda Universidad 1200, 03339 México, DF, Mexico; tel. (55) 5534-0034; fax (55) 5621-3230; f. 1966; Mexican economy, in particular the automobile and textiles industries; Spanish and English; Editor EDUARDO MILLAN LOZANO; 6 a year.

Panorama Económico Latinoamericano (PEL): Ediciones Cubanas, Obispo 527, Apdo 605, Havana, Cuba; tel. (7) 63-1981; fax (7) 33-8943; e-mail difusion@prensa-latina.cu; f. 1960; book reviews and statistics; available on micro-film; Spanish; Editor JOSÉ BODES GÓMEZ; 2 a month.

Pesquisa e Planejamento Econômico: Institute of Applied Economic Research, Avda Antônio Carlos 51, 16° andar, CP 2672, 20.020-010 Rio de Janeiro, RJ, Brazil; tel. (21) 3804-8118; fax (21) 2220-5533; e-mail editrj@ipea.gov.br; internet ppe.ipea.gov.br; f. 1970; economics and planning; Portuguese and English; Editor MARCO ANTONIO CAVALCANTI; quarterly.

Problemas del Desarrollo—Revista latinoamericana de economía: Instituto de Investigaciones Económicas de la Universidad Nacional Autónoma de México, Ciudad Universitaria, Del. Coyoacán, 04510, México, DF, Mexico; tel. (55) 5623-0105; fax (55) 5623-0097; e-mail revprode@servidor.unam.mx; internet www.probdes.iiec.unam.mx; f. 1969; economic, political and social affairs of Mexico, Latin America and the developing world; Spanish, with English and French abstracts; Dir ALICIA GIRÓN; quarterly.

Puerto Rico Business Review / Puerto Rico Economic Indicators: Government Development Bank for Puerto Rico, POB 42001, San Juan, PR 00940-2001, Puerto Rico; tel. 722-2525; fax 268-5496; e-mail gdbpr@bgf.gobierno.pr; internet www.gdb-pur.com/economy/latest-information-monthly-indicators_pub.htm; f. 1976; English; quarterly.

Quarterly Economic Review: Central Bank of the Bahamas, Research Dept, Frederick St, POB N-4868, Nassau, Bahamas; tel. 302-2600; fax 322-4321; e-mail cbobadministration@centralbankbahamas .com; internet www.centralbankbahamas.com; review of Bahamian economy; English; quarterly.

Quehacer: Centro de Estudios y Promoción del Desarrollo—DESCO, León de la Fuente 110, Magdalena del Mar, Lima 17, Peru; tel. (1) 6138300; fax (1) 6138308; e-mail postmaster@desco.org.pe; internet www.desco.org.pe; f. 1979; business development and research; Spanish; Dir MOLVINA ZEBALLOS; quarterly.

Relaciones Internacionales: Facultad de Ciencias Políticas y Sociales, Universidad Nacional Autónoma de México, México, DF, Mexico; tel. (55) 5622-9412; f. 1973; international relations; Spanish; Editor ROBERTO DOMÍNGUEZ; Dir CONSUELO DÁVILA; 3 a year.

Review: Literature and Arts of the Americas: Routledge, Taylor & Francis, 4 Park Sq., Milton Park, Abingdon, Oxon, OX14 4RN, United Kingdom; tel. (20) 7017-6000; fax (20) 7017-6336; e-mail authorqueries@tandf.co.uk; internet www.tandf.co.uk/journals/rrev; f. 1967; Latin American literature in translation, articles on visual arts, theatre, music, cinema, book reviews; English, but poetry is, in addition, published in the vernacular; Man. Editor DANIEL SHAPIRO; 2 a year.

Revista Argentina de Estudios Estratégicos: Argentine Centre of Strategic Studies, Viamonte 494, 3°, Of. 11, C1053ABJ Buenos Aires, Argentina; tel. (11) 4312-1605; fax (11) 4312-5802; the armed forces; Spanish; quarterly.

Revista de Biología Tropical: Universidad de Costa Rica, Ciudad Universitaria Rodrigo Facio, San José, Costa Rica; tel. and fax 2207-5550; e-mail rbt@cariari.ucr.ac.cr; f. 1953; biology, ecology, taxonomy, etc., of Neotropics and African tropics; Spanish and English; Man. Editor DAISY ARROYO MORA; Dir JULIÁN MONGE-NÁJERA; quarterly, with supplements, and online edn.

Revista Brasileira de Economia: Escola de Pós-Graduaçao em Economia, Praia de Botafogo 190, Of. 1100, 22.253-900 Rio de Janeiro, RJ, Brazil; tel. (21) 3779-5831; e-mail ricardo.cavalcanti@fgv.br; internet bibliotecadigital.fgv.br/ojs/index.php/rbe; f. 1947; economic theory, economic policy and econometrics; Portuguese and English; Editor RICARDO CAVALCANTI; quarterly.

Revista Brasileira de Estatística: Fundação Instituto Brasileiro de Geografia e Estatística, Avda Chile 500, 10° andar, 20.031-170 Rio de Janeiro, RJ, Brazil; tel. (21) 2142-4551; fax (21) 2142-4548; e-mail ibge@ibge.gov.br; f. 1940; statistical subjects by means of articles, analysis, etc; Portuguese; Editor FRANCISCO LOUZADA NETO; 2 a year.

Revista Brasileira de Estudos Políticos: Faculdade de Direito da UFMG, Av. João Pinheiro, 30130 180 Belo Horizonte, MG, Brazil; tel. (31) 3409-8641; fax (31) 3224-5856; e-mail rbep@direito.ufmg.br; internet www.pos.direito.ufmg.br/rbep; f. 1956; public law, political science, economics, history; Portuguese; published by Universidade Federal de Minas Gerais; Dir MARIA ELIZABETH DE OLIVEIRA COSTA; 2 a year.

Revista Brasileira de Geografia: Fundação Instituto Brasileiro de Geografia e Estatística, Directoria de Geociências, Av. Brasil 15.671, Parada de Lucas, 21.241-051 Rio de Janeiro, RJ, Brazil; tel. (21) 2142-4990; fax (21) 2142-4910; internet www.ibge.gov.br; f. 1936; advanced geographic, socio-economic and scientific articles, also news and translations; Portuguese, with English summaries; Dir of Geosciences WADIH JOÃO SCANDAR NETO; 2 a year.

Revista Centroamericana de Ciencias Sociales: Latin American Faculty of Social Sciences, Costa Rica—FLACSO, General Secretariat, Apdo 5429, 1000 San José, Costa Rica; e-mail eazofeifa@flacso.or .cr; internet www.flacso.or.cr; social sciences in Central America; Spanish.

Revista Chilena de Historia y Geografía: Sociedad Chilena de Historia y Geografía, Londres 65, Casilla 1386, Santiago, Chile; tel. (2) 6382497; f. 1911; history, geography, anthropology, archaeology, genealogy, numismatics; Spanish; Pres. SERGIO MARTÍNEZ BAEZA; annual.

Revista de Ciencias Sociales de la Universidad de Costa Rica: Vicerectoría de Investigación, Apdo 49-2060, Montes de Oca 2050, Costa Rica; tel. 2511-8703; fax 2511-6112; e-mail revista.cs@ucr.ac .cr; internet revistacienciassociales.ucr.ac.cr; f. 1956; sociology, anthropology, geography, history, etc., with special reference to

Costa Rica and Central America; Spanish; Editor MARIA FERNANDA ARGUEDAS; Dir DANIEL CAMACHO; quarterly.

Revista Econômica do Nordeste: Banco do Nordeste do Brasil, Escritório Técnico de Estudos Econômicos do Nordeste, Praça Murilo Borges, No 1, CP 628, Fortaleza, CE, Brazil; tel. (85) 3299-3000; f. 1969; Brazilian economy, regional development; Portuguese; 4 a year.

Revista Ecuador Debate: Apdo 17 15 1738, Quito, Ecuador; tel. (2) 252-2763; fax (2) 256-8452; e-mail caaporg.ecuio@satnet.net; internet www.ecuadordebate.com; f. 1983; economic conditions and agriculture; Spanish; Editor HERNÁN IBARRA CRESPO; Dir FRANCISCO RHON DÁVILA; 3 a year.

Revista Educación: Facultad de Educación, Universidad de Costa Rica, 2060 San Pedro, Montes de Oca, San José, Costa Rica; tel. 2511-8868; fax 2225-3749; e-mail revedu@gmail.com; internet www .revista-educacion.ucr.ac.cr; f. 1977; education; Spanish; Editor KAROL RÍOS CORTÉS; Dir LASTENIA MARÍA BONILLA SANDOVAL; 2 a year.

Revista Geológica de América Central: Escuela Centroamericana de Geología, Apdo 214-2060 Universidad de Costa Rica, San José, Costa Rica; tel. 2207-4042; fax 2207-5311; e-mail pdenyer@geologia.ucr.ac .cr; internet www.geologia.ucr.ac.cr; f. 1983; geology and geophysics of Central America; Spanish, with abstracts in English, and English, with abstracts in Spanish; Editor WALTER MONTERO; Dir PERCY DENYER; 2 a year.

Revista Homines: Recinto Metropolitano, Universidad Interamericana de Puerto Rico, Apdo 191293, San Juan, PR 00919, Puerto Rico; internet www.revistahomines.com; f. 1957; sociology, anthropology, history, economics, geography, political sciences, psychology; Spanish; Editor and Dir ALINE FRAMBES BUXEDA DE ALZÉRRECA; 2 a year.

Revista do Instituto Histórico e Geográfico Brasileiro: Av. Augusto Severo 8, 10° andar, 20.021-040 Rio de Janeiro, RJ, Brazil; tel. (21) 232-1312; fax (21) 252-4430; e-mail revista@ihgb.org.br; internet www.ihgb.org.br/rihgb.php; f. 1838; history and geography; Portuguese; Editorial Dir LUCIA MARIA PASCHOAL GUIMARÃES; quarterly.

Revista do Mercado Comum do Sul—Mercosul / Revista del Mercado Común del Sur—Mercosur: Rua Teófilo Ontoni 123, 3° andar, 20090-3001 Rio de Janeiro, Brazil; tel. (21) 2223-1180; fax (21) 2223-3001; e-mail revistadomercosul@etm.com.br; internet www.uol.com.br/revistadomercosul; f. 1992; Latin American integration; Portuguese and Spanish; Editor ANTÔNIO CARLOS DA CUNHA; monthly.

Revista Mexicana de Ciencias Políticas y Sociales: Facultad de Ciencias Políticas y Sociales, Universidad Autónoma de México, 04510 México, DF, Mexico; tel. (55) 5622-9433; fax (55) 5665-1786; e-mail bokser@mail.politicas.unam.mx; f. 1955; political and social sciences; Spanish; Dir JUDIT BOKSER MISSES; quarterly.

Revista Mexicana de Política Exterior: Matias Romero Institute for Diplomatic Studies, Calle República de El Salvador 43-47, Col. Centro Histórico, Del. Cuauhtémoc, 06080 México, DF, Mexico; tel. (55) 3686-5160; fax (55) 5709-6314; e-mail imrinfo@sre.gob.mx; internet www.sre.gob.mx/imr; Spanish; Dir-Gen. ALFONSO CAMPOS CASTELLÓ; quarterly.

Revista Repertorio Americano: Instituto de Estudios Latino-americanos, Universidad Nacional, Apdo 86-3000, Heredia, Costa Rica; tel. and fax 2562-4241; e-mail isotomarybel@yahoo.com.mx; internet www.una.ac.cr; f. 1919; Latin American and Spanish culture; Spanish; Co-ordinator MARYBEL SOTO RAMIREZ; 2 a year.

Revista Venezolana de Análisis de Coyuntura: Research Institute of the Faculty of Economic and Social Sciences, Universidad Central de Venezuela, Of. de Publicaciones, Apdo 54057, Caracas 1051-A, Venezuela; tel. and fax (212) 605-2523; e-mail coyuntura@cantv .net; f. 1980 as Boletín de Indicadores Socio-económicos; adopted existing name in 1995; socio-economic issues; Spanish; 2 a year.

Revista Venezolana de Economía y Ciencias Sociales: Research Institute of the Faculty of Economic and Social Sciences, Universidad Central de Venezuela, Of. de Publicaciones, Apdo 54057, Caracas 1051-A, Venezuela; tel. and fax (212) 605-2523; f. 1958 as Economía y Ciencias Sociales; changed name as above in 1995; Spanish; Editor LUIS E. LANDER; 3 a year.

Semana Económica: Avda 28 de Julio 1370, Miraflores,, Lima 18, Peru; tel. (1) 2130600; fax (1) 4445240; e-mail redaccion@semanaeconomica.com; internet www.semanaeconomica.com; f. 1985; economic affairs; Spanish; Dir GONZALO ZEGARRA MULANO-VICH; weekly.

Sourcemex: University of New Mexico, Latin American and Iberian Institute, Latin America Data Base, 801 Yale, NE, Albuquerque, NM 87131, USA; tel. (505) 277-6839; fax (505) 277-5989; e-mail info@ladb .unm.net; internet ladb.unm.edu/sourcemex; online news digest; political and economic news and analysis in Mexico; Editor CARLOS M. NAVARRO; weekly.

Suplemento Antropológico: Centro de Estudios Antropológicos de la Universidad Católica, Casilla 1718, Asunción, Paraguay; tel. (21) 446252; fax (21) 445245; e-mail ceaduc@uca.edu.py; internet www .ceaduc.uca.edu.py; f. 1965; practical and theoretical problems of the indigenous peoples of the River Plate basin (Bolivia, Brazil, Uruguay, Argentina and Paraguay); Spanish; Dir JOSÉ ZANARDINI; 2 a year.

Third World Quarterly: Dept of Geography, Royal Holloway, University of London, Egham, Surrey, TW20 0EX, United Kingdom; e-mail editor@thirdworldquarterly.com; internet www.tandf.co.uk/journals; f. 1979; Editor SHAHID QADIR; 12 a year.

Tricontinental: Organization of Solidarity of the Peoples of Asia, Africa and Latin America, Calle C, No 668, esq. 29, Vedado, Apdo 4224, Havana, Cuba; tel. (7) 30-4941; fax (7) 33-3985; f. 1967; analysis of cultural, political and social developments in Cuba and other developing countries; Spanish, French and English; Dir ÁNGEL PINO; quarterly.

El Trimestre Económico: Fondo de Cultura Económica, Carretera Picacho Ajusco 227, Col. Bosques del Pedregal, Del. Tlaplan, 14200 México, DF, Mexico; tel. (55) 5227-4671; fax (55) 5227-4640; e-mail trimestre@fondodeculturaeconomica.com; internet www.fondodeculturaeconomica.com/trimestre.asp; f. 1934; theoretical or empirical investigation with special interest in economies of Latin America and Spain; economic development and economic theory, employment and investment policy; Spanish; Editor FAUSTO HERNÁNDEZ TRILLO; quarterly.

Visión (La Revista Latinoamericana Visión): Arguímedes 199, 6° y 7°, Col. Polanco, 11570 México, DF, Mexico; tel. (5) 530-3800; e-mail info@revistavisiondigital.com; internet www.larevistavision.com; f. 1950; news and analysis of Latin America; 2 a month.

INDEX OF REGIONAL ORGANIZATIONS

(Main reference only)